C000172473

A Gaelic Dictionary, in Two Parts

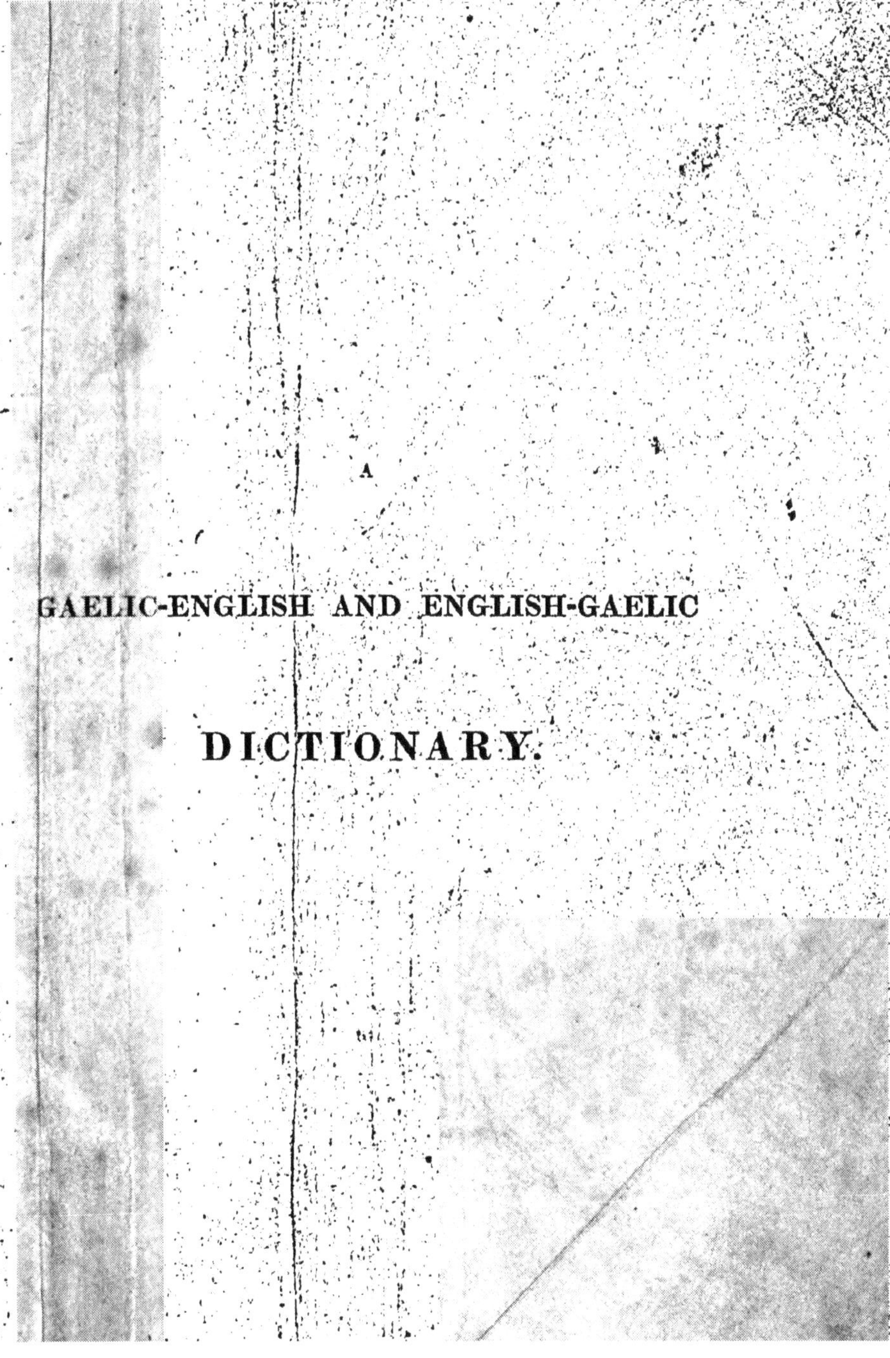

A

GAELIC-ENGLISH AND ENGLISH-GAELIC

DICTIONARY.

LONDON:
Printed at the Temple Printing Office,
BY J. MOYES, BOUVERIE STREET.

GAELIC DICTIONARY,

IN TWO PARTS:

I. GAELIC AND ENGLISH.—II. ENGLISH AND GAELIC;

IN WHICH

THE WORDS, IN THEIR DIFFERENT ACCEPTATIONS,

ARE ILLUSTRATED BY QUOTATIONS FROM THE BEST GAELIC WRITERS,

AND

THEIR AFFINITIES TRACED

IN MOST OF THE LANGUAGES OF ANCIENT AND MODERN TIMES;

WITH A SHORT

Historical Appendix of Ancient Names,

DEDUCED FROM THE AUTHORITY OF OSSIAN AND OTHER POETS.

TO WHICH IS PREFIXED,

A NEW GAELIC GRAMMAR.

By R. A. ARMSTRONG, A.M.

LONDON:

PRINTED FOR JAMES DUNCAN, 37, PATERNOSTER ROW;

HOWELL AND STEWART, 295, HOLBORN; BELL AND BRADFUTE, W. LAING, W. BLACKWOOD, OLIVER AND BOYD, AND WAUGH AND INNES, EDINBURGH; M. OGLE, GLASGOW; AND R. M TIMS, DUBLIN.

M.DCCC.XXV.

Presented to
Robt Cameron, Killin,
by
Captn. John Macgregor,
4th Royal Vet Bn
Perth.

CHUM A

MHORALACHD RIOGHAIL

SEORUS IV.

RIGH BHREATUIN AGUS ERIN, FEAR-DION A ' CHREIDIMH.

GU MA TOIL LE DO MHORALACHD RIOGHAIL!

Tha 'm barrachd so agad os-cionn na h-uile neach fuidh sgeith am b' urrainn mi mo Leabhar a chur a mach do 'n t-saoghal,—na 'm bu dàna leam ionnsuidh a thoirt air do mholadh, (a dh'aindeoin na dh'fhaotainn a radh air mhath mu 'd thimchioll) nach cuireadh duine beò miodal beoil as mo leth; agus, an àite sin, gu 'n aidicheadh na h-uile, gun d'thàinig mi fada gearr air an fhìrinn.—Ach tha thu fada nan càan an neor-eisiomail mo mholaidh.

Thog dealradh do Phearsa, agus òirdheirceas do bhuadhannan nàdurra—thog buan-shloinneadh urramach do Shinnsearachd Rioghail, agus mòr-fharsuingeachd do Thighearnais an ceithir chearnaibh na Cruinne—thog gliocas do Chomhairlean, agus Greadhnachas do Riaghlaidh, maille ri buaidh anabarrach d'Fheachd air muir is air tìr,—do chliù co ard agus nach ruig mise, no duin' eil' a choidhche air a mhullach, le streap cainnte.

Ach am feadh a tha do Chliù thar chàch uile air sgaoileadh anns gach dùthaich mu 'n iadh grian, measaidh Tu féin mar d'onoir a 's mò, Thu bhi riaghladh ann an cridhibh slòigh shaorsail, shona agus dhìlis. An sin " O a Righ mair beò gu bràth!" Agus am feadh a bhios buan-chaithream buaidh do bhearta ionmholta ag éiridh am binn-chéilleiribh gach Cànmhuin 'san Roinn Eorp; gu robh e mar shochair shònruicht' aig mo Leabhar-sa so, bhith 'g innseadh do 'd Ghaidheilibh féin, gu 'n do cheaduich Thu dha dol a mach, fuidh fhasgadh d' Ainm mhòir, airson sior-chumail suas eòlais an Gailige graidh.

Is mise, gu ma toil le do Mhòralachd Rioghail,

d' Iochdaran ro-ùmhal,

Agus do Sheirbheiseach ro-dhìleas,

RAIBEART GILLEASBUIG ARMSTRONG.

PREFACE.

Many of those who cultivate literature will acknowledge, that their exertions are oftener the result of accident, or of precipitate resolution, than of long cherished design, or mature reflection;—that their most laborious enterprises are, sometimes, undertaken without due regard to the difficulties which stand in the way of their completion; and that although the possibility or likelihood of ultimate success be at intervals contemplated, the ardour of the pursuit is kept up by causes independent of such considerations.

Firmness of purpose is peculiarly requisite in the Lexicographer who has had no precursor in his particular walk of compilation; who has had to encounter, at every step, the ruggedness and perplexities of an untrodden path; to contend with difficulties at every turn; to find barrenness where he hoped for fertility, obscurity where he looked for light, and misapprehension and error, where he expected certainty and truth. His difficulties are, without question, of a disheartening character: this I may be allowed to say from my own experience; yet I should be unwilling to utter an expression of dissatisfaction or regret: for I might be told that my labour was voluntary; that he who throws himself into trouble has nothing to blame but his own rashness; and that he who challenges difficulties or misfortune, deserves only ridicule for his complaints.

In undertaking the present task, I did not, perhaps, sufficiently consider the disadvantages under which I laboured, nor the odds against which I had to contend; but I knew that formidable obstacles have often yielded to steady resolution, and unremitting diligence.

It is not easy, in speaking of one's own labours, to avoid the imputation of egotism; I shall, therefore, leave it to others to form their own estimate of the present publication. I can only say that, though my task has been severe, it has not been without advantage; and that though it should never be crowned with great public approbation, it has not been altogether without its reward. It has pointed my way to various sources of learning which otherwise I should not have approached; it has led me to consult authors whom otherwise I should not have known; it has procured for me patronage which cannot be exalted by my praise, and friendship which I shall ever be proud to cherish.

The first remark which may occur in opening these sheets is, that I have been too lavish of quotations in some instances, and too sparing in others. On this subject I shall only observe, that I considered myself as engaged in the double task of instructing the ignorant, and of assisting the well-informed; that a Lexicographer ought not to take for granted the knowledge of those who consult him; and that I had, moreover, the design of throwing every facility in the way of future compilers. To the charge of being too sparing, I have to answer, that the list of authors in our language is so small, that, for a vast variety of words, I could not find, nor does there, I believe, exist, any written authority.

In the Gaelic-English Dictionary, the different acceptations of the Gaelic words might have been arranged with the same precision, and after the same method, as in some other dictionaries, but that the size and price of the work would be thereby nearly doubled.

In translating the Gaelic language, the inflections of nouns and verbs are apt to embarrass the young student. On that account I deemed it expedient, in a great variety of instances, to insert, as separate articles, the nominatives and datives plural of nouns, and such tenses of the verbs as are in most frequent use, and, at the same time, bear the least resemblance to the root; such are the preterite active, the future affirmative active and passive, and the past participle. I have also arranged many of the aspirate forms of words, as separate articles, and have referred for explanation to the simple form. This will, it is hoped, be found useful. Few students would conjecture that they must turn up *cluas* for *cluasaibh; tigh* for *thigh; òl* for *dh'òl; dìrich* for *dhìrich; buail* for *buailidh; beir* for *rug; cluinn* for *chual; thoir*, or *thabhair*, for *bheirinn*. If, in this, I should be considered diffuse by those who already know the language, I feel assured that I shall have the acknowledgment of those who know it not, and are desirous to acquire it.

It will be seen that, in many words, especially in those which I considered primitive, I have traced affinities to a considerable extent. In doing so, my object was to leave grounds for inferring the common origin of all languages, and to establish the antiquity of the Celtic. For, if nations far remote and unconnected, dissimilar in manners and customs, shall have preserved the same terms for all such objects as are most familiar to the observation of a people in a state of nature, the obvious inference is, that these terms must have been derived from a common origin;—from the language of the earliest inhabitants of the earth. Again, if the Celtic should be found to contain all such terms as are common to all languages, it is evident that it must have derived them from man's primeval tongue.

It is true that almost every language of antiquity has asserted its title to be considered the most ancient; and men whose erudition cannot be disputed, have supported their respective claims. Of these, the Celtic has found an able advocate in Pezron, and other philologists; the Hebrew, in Leibnitz; the Phœnician, in Bochart; and the Dutch, in Gor. Becanus.

The diversity of opinions entertained on this subject, may, perhaps, be accounted for. All the languages of antiquity, which are, in truth, but so many dialects of the primeval speech, have nearly an equal number of primitives; and each of them, therefore, in as far as roots are concerned, seems to carry, on the face of it, an argument for the earliest existence. There is little wonder, then, if a scholar should decide in favour of that with which he is most familiar, and that a great question in philology should be affected by that prejudice which intrudes itself into every department of human inquiry.

With all my admiration of the Celtic, I cannot join with those who ascribe to it an antiquity beyond that of many other languages; for I have not been able to discover, that it can be said, with truth, of any language, that it is the most ancient.

I do not propose to meddle, in this place, with the keenly contested point, whether the Gaelic of the Highlands be the parent of the speech of Ireland. However, I may be permitted to observe, that the Scotch Gaelic bears a closer resemblance to the parent Celtic, and has fewer inflections than the Welsh, Manks, or Irish dialects. It has this circumstance, too, in common with the Hebrew, and other oriental languages, that it wants the simple present tense; a peculiarity which strongly supports the opinion, that the Gaelic of Scotland is the more ancient dialect. This question has been long discussed with eagerness and ability. The one party draws its opinions partly from history, partly from acute hypothetical reasoning, and from the natural westward progress of early migration; the other argues from legends for which credulity itself is at a loss to discover a foundation.

Throughout this work, I have followed the orthography of two writers, who are relied on as guides by their countrymen;—the one, Dr. Stewart of Luss, the translator of the Holy Scriptures into Gaelic; the other, Dr. Smith of Campbelton, the author of a Gaelic metrical version of the Psalms, and other creditable works. These writers spent much of their time in settling the orthography of our language; and, as they have a just and acknowledged claim to be considered authorities, it is much to be desired that they should, henceforth, be regarded in that light. Fluctuations in the Gaelic language are perilous at this stage of its existence; for, if it be not transmitted to posterity in a regular, settled form, it is to be feared, that it must soon share the fate of the forgotten Cornish.

The rule *caol ri caol agus leathan ri leathan*, has been carefully observed by the writers already mentioned, especially by Dr. Stewart. It directs that two vowels, contributing to form two different syllables, should be both of the same class or denomination of vowels,—either both broad, or both small. Agreeably to this rule, we ought to write *deanaibh*, not *deanibh; fòidean*, not *fòidan; bioran*, not *biran;* and so on, with other words. This mode of spelling is a modern invention. It was first introduced by the Irish, and adopted by the Gael, with, I confess, more precipitation than propriety. It has its advantages and its disadvantages. It mars the primitive simplicity and purity of the language; but it removes from it that appearance of harshness which arises from too great a proportion of consonants. It not unfrequently, darkens somewhat the ground on which we trace the affinities of Gaelic words with those of the sister dialects, and of other languages; yet it has infused into our speech a variety of liquid and mellow sounds which were unknown, or at least not so perceptible before. It may be asked, why I have adhered to a rule of which I did not altogether approve? I reply, that any attempt at innovation—even at restoring the language to its primitive purity, might introduce more inconveniencies and evils than can result from the present settled system of orthography.

I have bestowed pains on referring derivative words to their primitives—in resolving compound words to their component parts—in affixing to substantives their genitive singular and gender—and to verbs their signification, whether active or neuter. The quotations from Gaelic writers are translated into English as literally as the idioms of these languages will allow.

The edition of Stewart's Gaelic Bible, of which I made use, was that printed at Edinburgh in 1807, for the Society in Scotland for Propagating Christian Knowledge. The particular book of the sacred volumes from which I take a quotation is almost always mentioned. Occasionally, however, *O. T.* or *N. T.* will be met with, where I could not remember the precise part of the Old or New Testament which contained my authority. *G. B.* occur where I could not remember nor ascertain from which of the Testaments the quotation was taken. These abbreviations are, I believe, of rare occurrence; and I have here adverted to them, in order to explain what, otherwise, might appear a want of precision.

The Gaelic, like all the languages of early times, does not abound in terms of science or art. It will be seen, therefore, in the English-Gaelic Dictionary, that terms in mathematics, metaphysics, and other sciences, I have been compelled to express by ambiology, and often by definition.

If it be found that, of names of instruments, as in agriculture and mechanics, some are rendered, perhaps, imperfectly, and others overlooked, let it be remembered, that no compilation ever yet recorded every vocable which floated in a spoken language; and that I could not, when an uncertainty occurred, transport myself to the proper sources of information, to make up for the scarcity of books and the defects of memory.

The Gaelic vocabularies of Shaw, Macfarlane, and Macdonald, and the Irish dictionaries of O'Brien and O'Reilly, were of considerable service to me. The mere collecting of words, however, was but a small part of my labour, compared with the wearisome and almost endless pursuit of authorities for different acceptations of the same word.

In tracing affinities, I derived great benefit from the works of Suidas, Cambry, Court de Gebelin, Menage, Rostrenen, Bullet, Pezron, Spellman, Lye, and Edward Lhuyd, among philologists; and, in matters of antiquity, from Strabo, Diodorus Siculus, Solinus, Tacitus, Ammianus, Usher, Toland, Huddleston, Keating, Malcolm, Dr. John Macpherson, Pennant, Smith, and a forgotten multitude of other erudite and ingenious writers.

In the English-Gaelic Dictionary, I have followed the orthography and arrangement of Perry.

It was once my design to prefix to this work a dissertation on the mechanism and philosophy of the Gaelic language; but, on reflection, I substituted a compendious view of its structure, as being more suitable to such a performance, and more likely to be of service. In this department of my compilation, I am indebted to the works of Shaw, O'Reilly, and O'Connor.

A circumstance not unworthy of notice concerning this Dictionary is, that a great part of it was printed while it was generally thought to be only in preparation. Hence it happened that, during the progress of these sheets through the press, I was, not unfrequently, favoured with communications from most respectable quarters, conveying encouragement which excited my gratitude, and offers of assistance which were, I lament, too late to be rendered available. No doubt, it would have been useful to my work, if I had obligations, on this account, to acknowledge. Be that as it may, I consider it due to myself to state, that neither in compiling this Dictionary, nor even in transcribing the mass of manuscript for publication, nor in superintending the press, have I received the least assistance whatever. For patronage, however, I am deeply beholden to several whom my commendations cannot affect, but whom gratitude compels me to mention.

The early and effective patron of this work, I am proud to make known, was Lord Strathavon; a young nobleman who, to many other acquirements, has added a most accurate knowledge of the Gaelic language. I have not vanity enough to attribute to the humble merits of my performance his Lordship's powerful support, to which I owe almost all the more splendid names on my list of subscribers; but rather to that liberal and active spirit with which he lends his aid to every cause which concerns the literature of the Scottish Gael, and the honour of their country.

To his Grace the Duke of Hamilton I feel greatly indebted for attention and encouragement; as also to Lord Archibald Hamilton, and to Lord Glenorchy,

Sir Charles Forbes, Bart., of Edinglassie, whose patriotic character is well known, laid me under early and great obligations. I value the kindness of this gentleman the more, because it procured for me the acquaintance of General Gordon of Balbithan, a very superior Celtic scholar and philologist, from whose conversation and suggestions I derived essential benefit.

I am gratified to rank, among my most zealous patrons, Dr. Mackinnon of Adelphi, and the Rev. Dr. Ross of Lochbroom; gentlemen whose knowledge of every branch of the Celtic language is the least of their acquirements.

Mr. Simon Mac Gillivray of Suffolk Lane has done this Dictionary a service, which I can never forget nor sufficiently acknowledge.

Mr. Robert Kennedy of Grenada will, I hope, accept of this expression of my gratitude for his most active support, to which I owe a great proportion of my West India subscribers.

My sense of the friendly and successful efforts of the late Dr. Charles Kennedy of St. Vincent, my schoolfellow and college companion, is equalled only by my regret for his untimely death, and my respect for his memory.

I have also my thanks to offer to the following gentlemen, who, though mentioned the last in order, are not the least in my esteem:—Capt Duncan Mac Dougall of the 79th Regt. of Foot; the Rev. Daniel Mac Naughton of Glenco and Appin, the Rev. Alexander Anderson of Strontian; and the Rev. Alexander Kennedy of Mull.

It would be most ungrateful in me not to take this opportunity of mentioning, that, notwithstanding all the patronage with which I have been favoured, it is questionable whether I could ever have offered these sheets to the public, but for the disinterested spirit of my publisher, Mr. Duncan.

To my Subscribers, in general, I return my sincerest acknowledgments. They may be assured that very strenuous exertions have been made to fulfil the promises held out in the Prospectus; and I trust that I shall be considered as having redeemed my pledge.

To hope that this Dictionary is free from imperfections, even after all the pains I have bestowed on it, would be presumptuous; and to expect that any circumstance shall cause those to be overlooked or forgiven, would be to hope for a favour which has been withheld from far higher claims and deserts than mine;—for the merits of one's cause are not always a protection from hostility and censure; and diligence, however laborious and sincere, is not always requited with approbation.

I forbear to mention the time which this work has occupied, and the labour which it has required. I might be discredited by some, and considered by others as indulging my vanity;—especially when I should add, that I had in the meanwhile to provide for my own subsistence, and that the compilation which I now send forth to the world, is, in truth, the production of such hours as I could spare from harassing occupations, or snatch from the proper seasons of repose.

Having stated this much, I must guard against misconstruction. I have no desire to conciliate hostility, nor to soften criticism. My cause is good. I have, under all disadvantages, done it the best service in my power; and I now, without presumption, yet without undue anxiety, submit my work to a public intelligent enough to know the value of every man's labour, and sufficiently generous to assign to all the degree of honour which they may deserve.

SUBSCRIBERS.

Asterisks (*) precede the names of those Subscribers who are now no more.

HIS MOST EXCELLENT MAJESTY KING GEORGE IV.—FIVE COPIES.

HIS ROYAL HIGHNESS THE DUKE OF YORK

HIS ROYAL HIGHNESS THE DUKE OF CLARENCE.

A.

Argyll, His Grace the Duke of

Aboyne, the Right Honourable the Earl of.

Aberdeen, the Right Honourable the Earl of.

Allan, Grant, Esq. Gower Street.

Anderson, the Rev. Alexander, Strontian.

Andrew, James, LL D. Sutton.

Armstrong, Alexander, Esq Grenada.

Armstrong, Simon, Esq St Vincent

Atcheson, Robert Shank, Esq. Duke Street, Westminster.

B

Breadalbane, the Right Honourable the Earl of.

Beresford, Lord John, M.P.

Brisbane, Governor Sir Charles, K.C.B St' Vincent, 2 *copies.*

Brougham, Henry, Esq. M P.

Boucher, James, Esq. Grenada.

Britton, John, Esq. F S.A. Burton Street, Burton Crescent

Brown, Fielding, Esq. Grenada

C

Canning, the Right Honourable George, M P.

Calder, Hector, Esq. St Vincent

Campbell, Walter Frederick, Esq. of Shawfield and Isla, 2 *copies.*

Campbell, Colonel, Balveolan.

Campbell, the Rev. Alexander, Strathtay

Campbell, James, Esq. St. Vincent

Carmichael, John, Esq. St Vincent

Clark, John, Esq St Vincent

Collins, John, Esq Bath

Cruickshank, Alexander, Esq St Vincent.

Cumming, Alexander, Esq St. Vincent.

Cochran, Mr. 108, Strand, 2 *copies*.

D

Davidson, H Esq of Tulloch

Davidson, Duncan, younger, Esq. of Tulloch.

Downie, Robert, Esq of Appin, M P.

Dear, William, Esq. St Vincent.

Denton, John, Esq St. Vincent.

Dickie, John, Esq St. Vincent

Dickson, Thomas, Esq St Vincent

Donald, Alexander, Esq St Vincent

Duff, James Gordon, Esq Gloucester Place

F

Fife, the Right Honourable the Earl of

Fergusson, General Sir Ronald, M P

Forbes, Sir Charles, Bart of Edinglassie, M P. Fitzroy Square, 5 *copies*

Forbes, John, Esq Fitzroy Square.

Forbes, Charles, Esq Fitzroy Square

Forbes, Miss Katherine Stewart, Fitzroy Square

Forbes, George, Esq. Fitzroy Square.

Forbes, Master James Stewart, Fitzroy Square

Forbes, Lieutenant Colonel David, 78th Regt. ..

Frazer, Archibald, Esq. Grenada

Frazer, Malcolm, Esq Grenada

G

Gordon, his Grace the Duke of.

Gwydyr, the Right Honourable Lady, 2 *copies*

Glenorchy, the Right Honourable Lord, M P 3 *copies*

Grant, the Right Honourable Sir William, Lincoln's-Inn-Fields.

Grant, the Honourable Charles, M.P

Grant, Sir Alexander, Albany

Gordon, Major-General Benjamin

Gaskill, Robert, Esq. St. Vincent

Glen, William, Esq Grenada.

Gordon, the Rev. Donald, Ederachilis

Grant, Patrick, Esq of Redcastle

Grant, John, Esq St. Vincent

Guthrie, ——, Esq of Craigie

H

Hamilton and Brandon, his Grace the Duke of.

Hamilton, the Right Honourable Lord Archibald, M.P

Huntingdon, the Right Honourable the Countess of, 3 *copies*.

Haddington, the Right Honourable the Earl of

Hutton, Lieutenant-General

Hindley, ——, Esq. Doughty Street.

Hutchinson, ——, Esq Wellington Place, Commercial Road

Harding and Co Messrs. 4 *copies*.

K

Keith, Dr. Ronald, Grenada.

Kennedy, the Rev. Alexander, Isle of Mull.

Kennedy, Robert, Esq Grenada, 3 *copies*

Kennedy, Evan, Esq Grenada

• Kennedy, John H Esq Surgeon, Grenada

• Kennedy, Charles N. Esq. Surgeon, St. Vincent, 3 *copies*.

L.

* Londonderry, the Most Honourable the Marquess of
Lyndoch, Lord.
Lumsden, Lieutenant Colonel D.
Livingston, Dugald, Esq Grenada.

M

Montrose, his Grace the Duke of
Moray, the Right Honourable the Earl of
Menzies, Lady, of Menzies, Castle-Menzies.
* Murray, Sir John Mac Gregor, Bart
Mac Gregor, Lieutenant Colonel Sir Evan, Bart.
Mackintosh, Sir James, M P.
Mac Donell, Colonel Alexander Ronaldson, of Glengarry and Clanranald.
Mac Kinnon, Donald, M D. and F R.S. Adelphi
Mac Gillivray, Simon, Esq. of Beinn' Ghaidheal
Mac Gregor, P. Esq. Surgeon, Golden Square
Mac Arthur, the Rev Donald, Isle of Mull
Mac Arthur, Duncan, Esq. St Vincent
Mac Barnet, Alexander, Esq. St. Vincent
Mac Coll, the Rev. Alexander, Lismore.
Mac Dougall, Captain Duncan, 79th Regt.
Mac Dougall, Patrick, Esq. Grenada.
Mac Dowall, Allan, Esq. St. Vincent, 2 *copies*
Mac Ewan, Dr. George, Grenada.
Mac Ewan, Dr. James, Grenada.
Mac Fee, John, Esq St. Vincent
Mac Gregor, Alexander, Esq. Grenada.
Mac Gregor, William, Esq Grenada.
Mac Innes, John, Esq Grenada
Mac Ivor, Mr Farquhar, Preacher of the Gospel, Lochbroom.
Macintyre, Captain John, Kenmore.
Macintyre, Archibald, Esq. St. Vincent.
Mac Kenzie, the Rev. Dr. Hugh, Assynt
Mac Kenzie, Roderick, Esq St. Vincent
Mac Kenzie, Colin, Esq.
Mac Kinnon, Charles, Esq. Cambden Hill.
Mac Kinnon, William Alexander, Esq Portswood House, near Southampton
Mac Lean, the Rev. J Argyllshire.
Mac Lean, George, Esq Grenada.
Mac Lean, John, Esq Grenada
Mac Leod, Alexander, Esq. St. Vincent, 2 *copies*
Mac Leod, James, Esq. St Vincent.
Mac Naughton, the Rev Daniel, Appin.
Mac Naughton, the Rev. Allen, Campbelton
Mac Naughton, Alexander, Esq. Surgeon, R.N.
Mac Naughton, Dr James, United States.
Mac Pherson, D Esq. Chandos Street, Covent Garden
* Mac Vean, Archibald, Esq. Grenada.
Malcolm, William, Esq. St. Vincent.
Menzies, Stewart, Esq. of Culdares.
Menzies, H. Esq Mary Street, Fitzroy Square.
Miller, James, Esq. St Vincent
Munro, George Gun, Esq Grenada.
Murray, Patrick, Esq St Vincent

N.

Nott, the Rev Dr Winchester.

O

O'Neil, John, Esq Grenada.

P

Paris, Royal Institute of
Petit, Louis Hayes, Esq Lincoln's Inn
Prescod, W. H. Esq. St. Vincent, 2 *copies*

R.

Roseberry, the Right Honourable the Earl of

Ramsay, the Honourable Colonel John, Kelly House, near Arbroath.

Richardson, Clement Thomas, Esq. Grenada

Robertson, Divie, Esq Bedford Square.

Robertson, E. Esq Beverley, Yorkshire

Robertson, Colin, Esq Russell Square.

Robertson, Andrew, Esq. Gerrard Street, Soho.

Robertson, Alexander, Esq St Vincent.

* Robertson, the Rev. Dr. Ebury Street, Chelsea

Ross, the Rev. Dr. Lochbroom, Rosshire.

Ross, the Rev. Alexander, Ullapool

Rivington, Messrs. Strand, 6 *copies*

S.

Stafford, the Most Honourable the Marchioness of

Strathavon, the Right Honourable Lord, M. P. 4 *copies*

Salton and Abernethy, the Right Honourable Lord

Stewart, the Honourable John

Stewart, Major General, of Garth.

Shaw, Major General John

Stewart, the Rev. James, Ardgower

Salami, A. Esq

Stewart, J., M. D. Appin.

Stewart, James Fleming, Esq. Grenada.

Stewart, William, Esq. Piccadilly.

Shand, Alexander, Esq St. Vincent

Smith, John, Esq. St. Vincent

Symon, James, Esq. St Vincent.

T.

Tennant, R. J. W. Esq Belfast

Todd, James Ruddell, Esq. of Balintagart, Adelphi.

Treasurer, Kennet, Esq Edinburgh

Thomson, William, Esq St Vincent

U

Upham, ——, Esq. Bath

Urquhart, ——, Esq. St. Vincent

W.

Wemyss and March, the Right Honourable the Earl of.

Whitely, ——, Esq. Halifax.

Wilkinson, Thomas, Esq. St. Vincent.

A GRAMMAR

OF THE

GAELIC LANGUAGE.

GRAMMAR, or the art of speaking and writing a language according to certain established rules, is divided into four parts, viz. Orthography, Etymology, Syntax, and Prosody.

ORTHOGRAPHY, or right spelling, teaches the true arrangement of letters in words, the correct utterance of which is called ORTHOEPY

ETYMOLOGY teaches how to derive a word from its root or primitive,—the parts of speech,—the inflection of nouns and verbs,—and the modifications by which the sense of a word is diversified

SYNTAX teaches how to arrange words into sentences.

PROSODY teaches the accent and quantity of syllables, and the measure of verse

---

OF ORTHOGRAPHY, OR RIGHT SPELLING.

The old Gaelic, commonly called the Irish, alphabet, consists of eighteen letters, which are divided into vowels and consonants

THE ALPHABET.

Roman Characters		Old Gaelic, or Irish.		Ancient Gaelic Name	Translation.
A	a	A	a	Ailm.	*Elm.*
B	b	B	b	Beithe.	*Birch.*
C	c	C	c	Coll.	*Hazel.*
D	d	D	d	Duir.	*Oak.*
E	e	E	e	Eagh	*Aspen.*
F	f	F	f	Fearn	*Alder.*
G	g	G	g	Goibh, *or* gath	*A spear.*
H	h	H	h	Huath.	
I	i	I	i	Iogh.	*Yew.*
L	l	L	l	Luis.	*The quicken tree.*
M	m	M	m	Muir.	*Vine.*
N	n	N	n	Nuin.	*Ash*
O	o	O	o	Ogh.	*The spindle tree*
P	p	P	p	Peith bhog	
R	r	R	r	Ruis.	*Elder.*
S	s	S	s	Suil.	
T	t	T	t	Tin	
U	u	U	u r	Uir, *or* iuthar.	*Yew*

OF VOWELS, AND VOWEL SOUNDS

Of these, *a, e, i, o, u,* are vowels, which Irish grammarians have divided into broad and small · *a, o, u,* are broad, *e, i,* small.

A

A represents three different sounds; in the first two of which it is both long and short *A* long, sounds like the English *a* in *bar*, or the Italian *a* in *amo*, as, *àl*, broad; *sàr*, excellent. and short, like *a* in *cat*, as, *cas*, a foot; *falt*, hair.

A, immediately preceding *dh* and *gh*, has a long and a short diphthongal sound, to which there is none correspondent in English. In this situation it much resembles the sound of the French diphthong *eu*, long, as, *ladhar*, a hoof; *aghmhor*, fortunate: short, as *a* in *lagh*, law; *tagh*, choose.

A sounds short and obtuse, like *e* in *open*, in the three forms of the article *a*, *an*, *am*, and in the plural terminations *a* and *an*, as, *laghanna*, laws; *beanntan*, mountains.

E

E represents three different sounds.

E, with the grave accent (*è*), sounds long, like the Greek η, as pronounced in Scotland and on the Continent, or like *e* in *where*, as, *è*, he; *rè*, during the time of and short, like *e* in *wet*; as, *teth*, hot; in which state it is never accented.

E, with the acute accent (*é*), sounds like the Greek η, as, pronounced in England; as, *té*, a female.

E final has an obtuse sound, like *e* in *open*, as, *beannuichte*, blessed; *buailte*, struck;—there being no silent final vowels in Gaelic.

I.

I sounds like *ee* in English, but sometimes long and sometimes short; long, as, *sìn*, stretch; *sìth*, peace: short, like *ee* in *feet*, as, *bith*, existence.

O.

O represents three different sounds, in each of which it is both long and short.

O long, sounds sometimes like *o* in *lord*; as, *òl*, drink; *ròmach*, hairy: and sometimes like *o* in *fold*; as, *còt*, a coat; *tom*, a hillock.

O short, sounds sometimes like *o* in *pot*, as, *brod*, a lid; *grod*, rotten; *borb*, fierce: and sometimes like *o* in *rope*; as, *slob*, a puddle

O, before *gh*, has a long and a short diphthongal sound. long, as, *sogh*, luxury; short, as, *roghainn*, choice.

U

U sounds like *u* in French and Italian, or like the English *oo* in *moon*, but sometimes long and sometimes short: long, as, *fudar*, powder; short, as, *furan*, a welcome.

OF THE DIPHTHONGS.

A diphthong is the meeting of two vowels in one syllable. In Gaelic there are thirteen diphthongs, and they are derived from the vowels in the following manner:

From *a* { *ae*, *ai*, *ao* } From *e* { *ea*, *ei*, *eo*, *eu* } From *i* { *ia*, *io*, *iu* } From *o*, *oi* From *u* { *ua*, *ui* }

Of these, *ao*, *eu*, are improper diphthongs, the rest are proper

PROPER DIPHTHONGS.

Ae

Ae occurs but in a few words, as, *Gael*,* a Highlander.

Ai.

Ai sounds like *ai* in the French *canaille*, as, *caill*, lose; *saill*, salt; *pailteas*, plenty. Very frequently *i* is but faintly sounded, as in *àite*, a place, *fàilte*, welcome

Ea

Ea sounds like *ea* in the English noun *bear*, as, *each*, a horse, *fear*, a man; but before a palatal, *c*, *g*; or a lingual, *l*, *n*, *r*, or a dental, *d*, *s*, *t*, not silent, the prepositive is often either quiescent, or but faintly sounded; as, *cealg*, deceit; *geall*, a wager.

Ei

Ei sometimes gives the sound of both vowels; as, *feidh*, deer; and sometimes that of *e* alone; as, *réidh*, a plain. Before the palatals, *c*, *g*, the linguals, *l*, *n*, *r*, or the dentals, *d*, *s*, *t*, not silent, *i* is but faintly heard; as, *reic*, sell; *leig*, let; *féin*, self and often confers on a following palatal, a double palatal sound; as, *thig*, (pronounce *heek*), shall come, and on a dental, a double dental sound, as, *theid*, shall go (pron. *héich*, articulating *ch* as in *church*).

Eo.

Eo sounds somewhat like *aw* in *yawl*; as, *ceòl*, music; *ceò*, mist

Ia

Ia has both vowels heard, as, *fiar*, crooked; *iall*, a thong; *ciar*, dusky; but in *cia*? what? and *iad*, they, *ia* often sounds like *e* in *where*

* Gael and Gaelach are more commonly written Gaidheal and Gaidhealach, to preserve the rule, *caol ri caol, is leathan ri leathan.*

Io.

Io sounds both long and short: long, as, *ea* in *fear*; as, *sior*, ever; *fior*, true: and short, not unlike the French *eu*, as, *fiodh*, timber. Before a palatal, lingual, or dental, *o* is not always, or but faintly, heard; as, *pioc*, pick; *ciod*, what; *sgiol*, skill; *bior*, a thorn; *fios*, knowledge.

Iu.

Iu sounds both its vowels; as, *fiù*, (pron. *few*), worthy; except before *c*, *g*, or *d*, *l*, *n*, *r*, *s*, *t*, where it is not sounded; as, *tiugh*, thick, (pron. *chiŭ*); *diùlt*, deny, (pron. *chùlt*).

Oi

Oi sounds both its vowels: long, as, *doigh*, manner; *sloigh*, host. short, as, *troidh*, a foot; *bloidh*, a piece Except before *c*, *g*, *l*, *n*, *r*, *s*, *t*, not silent, *i* is quiescent, and affects the sound of the consonant which it precedes; as, *toic*, substance, (pron. τοιχκ); *foid*, a turf, (pron. *fòch*, *ch* sounding as in *chair*), *coise*, gen of *cas*, foot, (pron. *coish*).

Ua

Ua sounds both its vowels; as, *tuar*, colour; *fuar*, cold. Except before *ch*, *dh*, *gh*, *th*, the *a* of *ua* commonly sounds like *e* in *her*; as, *bruach*, a bank; *tuadh*, a hatchet, *sluagh*, people; *luath*, swift.

Ui.

Ui sounds both its vowels; as, *buidhinn*, gain; *luidh*, lie. Except before *c*, *g*, *l*, *n*, *r*, *s*, *t*, the *i* of *ui* is not heard; but it affects the sound of the consonant following, as, *luis*, (pron. *luish*), *tuit*, fall, (pron. *tuich*, *ch* as in *church*), *sluig*, swallow, (pron. *slluk*,—*k* as in *key*).

IMPROPER DIPHTHONGS.

Ao.

Ao has a peculiar sound, not attainable by the ear, much resembling that of *eu* in the French *heure*, as, *laogh*, a calf, and a nasal sound, as, *maoth*, soft.

*Eu.**

Eu sounds like *ei* in *feign*, *beum*, a blow; *feum*, need.

OF THE TRIPHTHONGS.

The triphthongs are these five: *aoi*, *eoi*, *iai*, *iui*, *uai*. They are pronounced respectively, like the diphthongs, *ao*, *eo*, *ia*, *iu*, *ua*, with the addition of a short *i*, which serves to liquefy the sound of the following consonant. They are all long, and never occur but in monosyllables, or in the first syllable of polysyllables.

OF THE CONSONANTS.

There are twelve consonants, *b*, *c*, *d*, *f*, *g*, *l*, *m*, *n*, *p*, *r*, *s*, *t*, *h* is rather a mark of aspiration than a radical letter.

The consonants in Gaelic may be conveniently brought into the following arrangement Labials, Palatals, Dentals, and Linguals.

Labials	Palatals	Dentals	Linguals
b.	*c.*	*d.*	*l.*
f.	*g.*	*t.*	*n*
m.		*s.*	*r.*
p.			

Of these, *b*, *c*, *d*, *f*, *g*, *m*, *p*, *s*, *t*, are mutable, or capable of aspiration, by having *h* subjoined; in which state their *simple* sound is either altered or lost. The immutables are *l*, *n*, *r*.

Labials.

B.

B simple sounds somewhat harder than *b*, and softer than *p*, in English; as, *buail*, strike; *bean*, touch. *Bh* sound like *v* in English, French, and Italian; as, *bhean*, touched; *bhac*, hindered. *Bh*, at the end of a word or syllable, either sound like *u*, or stand for a gentle aspiration; as, *searbh*, bitter; *fiabhras*, a fever. Sometimes *bh*, in the middle of a word, are silent; as, *soirbheas*, prosperity; *doirbheas*, adversity.

F.

F simple is pronounced as in most other languages; *fh* are silent; as, *fhad*, long; *an Fhraing*, France. In a very few words, as, *mi fhèin*, myself, *fh* sound like *h* in English.

M.

M simple, the same as in English; as, *mòr*, great; *caman*, a club; *lom*, bare *Mh* sound like *v* in English, as, *amhàin*, only; *a mhusgaid*, the musket. Frequently, though never at the *beginning* of a word, *mh* sound like a nasal *oo*, or stand for a gentle aspiration; as, *ramh*, an oar; and sometimes they are altogether quiescent, as, *comhnard*, level, *dhomh*, to me

* In the West and Northern Highlands, this diphthong is often pronounced like *ia*, as, *miad*, size, for *meud*, *ian*, bird, for *eun*.

P.

P simple sounds as in English and other languages; as, *pronn*, bruise; *peasg*, a gash; *ph* like *f* in English, as, *phronn*, bruised.

Palatals.

C.

C simple has two sounds· (1.) Like c in *cub*, as, *cù*, a dog; *crath*, shake (2.) When preceded in the same syllable by a small vowel, it has, in most parts of the Highlands, a sound to which that of *χκ* is pretty similar; as, *airc*, distress, (pron. *αιρχκ*) In some parts it sounds like *k*.

Ch sound like the *Gr.* *χ* in *χορδη*, or like the Irish *gh* in *lough*, or the vulgar Scotch *ch* in *loch*, as, *moch*, early; and, when followed by a small vowel, like *χ* in *χιμὼν*; as, *chì*, shall see.

G.

G simple sounds, at the beginning of a word, nearly as in English; at the end of a word, its sound more nearly resembles that of the English *k* in *rock*, as, *rug*, bore, *thug*, gave

G aspirated, or *gh*, followed by *a*, *o*, or *u*, sounds somewhat softer than the Greek *χ*, as, *ghàir*, laughed; excepting at the end of a syllable, and then it is silent, as, *tigh*, a house; *rioghachd*, a kingdom.

Gh, followed by *e* or *i*, sounds like *y* in *ye*, as, *ghios*, (pron yeess), towards

Dentals.

D.

D simple is more a dental than in English, and sounds somewhat like the French and Italian *d*, as, *dàn*, a song; *duine*, a man; *dlagh*, a handful, *madadh*, a mastiff, *rud*, a thing. *Except* when it is followed by *e* or *i*, or is preceded in the same syllable by *i*, for then it sounds like *ch* in *child*, as, *clogaid*, a helmet, *càirdeas*, friendship.

D, preceded by *dh*, sounds like *χκ*, as, *lochd*, harm, (pron. llo*χκ*)

Dh, at the beginning of a word, has a somewhat softer sound than the Greek *χ*; as, *dha*, to him; but if followed by *e* or *i*, it sounds like *y* in English, as, *dheth*, of him; *dh'i*, of her, (*pron.* yeă, yĕ).

Dh, at the end, or in the middle of a word, is most frequently quiescent; as, *chaidh*, went, *faidheadaireachd*, prophecy.

T

T simple, immediately followed by *a*, *o*, or *u*, or a consonant, sounds like the French *t* in *tems*, or the Italian *t* in *tempo;* as, *tamh*, rest; *taom*, pour, *tlà*, smooth

T simple, preceded in the syllable by *u*, or immediately followed by *e* or *i*, sounds like *ch* in *child;* as, *tein*, fire, (pron. *chein*), *fàilte*, welcome, (pron *failch*, *ch* sounding as in *church*)

T aspirated, or *th*, like *h* in *home*, as, *thoir*, give; but in the middle, or at the end of a word, it is silent; as, *fitheach*, a raven, *bith*, existence

S.

S simple, preceded or followed by *a*, *e*, or *i*, sounds like *sh* in English, as, *sion*, (pron. *shion*), a blast, *gnuis*, (pron. *gnŭish*), a visage. Except *is*, (pron *iss*), am.

S simple, preceded or followed by *a*, *o*, or *u*, sounds like *s* in English; as, *sabh*, a salve; *sogh*, luxury; *mios*, a mouth

S simple, followed by *d*, *t*, *l*, or *n*, and a short vowel, sounds like *sh* in English; as, *sdiùir*, or *stiùir*, steer; *slios*, a side, *sniomh*, spin

S, before any other consonant, even though followed by a short vowel, sounds like *s* in English; as, *smig*, (pron *smik*), a chin, *sméid*, (pron *smēich*), a nod.

S aspirated, or *sh*, is silent, as, *sheòl*, directed, (pron. *heōl*); excepting when followed by *l* or *n*, and then there is no aspiration, as, *shnàmh*, (pron *nāv*), swam; *shlànuich*, (pron *lāni*χ), healed

Linguals.

The lingual consonants, as has been said, are incapable of aspiration; but they have often a double lingual sound, to which there is none similar in English.

L

L simple, like *l* in *large*, as, *las*, flamed. It has this sound when it begins the preterites of verbs and the feminine form of adjectives.

L has its *double* lingual sound when followed by *e* or *i*, and then it is articulated like *ll* in million, or like the Italian *gl*, or the Portuguese *lh*, as, *linn*, an age; *léin*, a shirt Yet, with regard to nouns beginning with *l*, if the *masc poss. pron* goes before, *l* sounds as in English, as, *a litir*, his *letter*, where *l* differs materially in sound from *l* in *a litir*, her *letter*.

L has another *double* lingual sound, generally, when it is preceded by itself, or when it is followed by *a*, *o*, or *u*, in verbs and in adjectives masculine, as, *fallain*, healthy, *làn*, full, *lom*, bare; *lus*, an herb.

ll, preceded or followed by a short vowel, also sounds as the Italian *gl*

ll, preceded or followed by *a*, *o*, or *u*, has the same double lingual sound as in *làn*, masculine, but has no sound similar to it in English

N

N simple sounds like *n* in English in the beginning of preterites, and whenever it is preceded by *a, o,* or *u*, as, *nigh*, washed; *làn*, full; *lon*, a thrush; *rùn*, affection; and in the middle of words, as, *sìnidh*, shall stretch.

N has its *double* sound in the beginning of a verb in the imperative mood, and followed by *a, o,* or *u*, as, *nochd*, shew; or at the beginning of a masculine adjective, and followed by a broad vowel, as, *naomh*, holy, *nuadh*, new In this situation it has no similar sound in English, but is the same with the first *n* in the French *non*.

The same observations apply to the reduplicated *nn*

N has another *double* sound, when immediately preceded by *i*, or when *i* is the last vowel of the same syllable; as, *linn*, an age; *càirn*, cairns; *uinneag*, a window; and at the beginning of imperatives, and certain other tenses, when followed by a small vowel; as, *nigh*, wash In this situation it sounds exactly like *gn*, in the French *guigne*, or the Italian *regno*.

N, preceded by *m* or *c*, is in some words pronounced like *r*, as, *cnaimh* (*craimh*), a bone; *cnò* (*crò*), a nut.

Lastly, *an* and *nan*, when the next word begins with *c* or *g*, sound like *ng* and *nung*, as, *an cù*, the dog; *an gial*, the cheek; *nan cealgair*, of the deceivers

R

R simple sounds like *r* in English; as, *rath*, (pron *ra*), luck; *righ*, a king. *Righ*, in the vocative, has no sound similar to it in English, but it is exactly that of *ri* in the French *infériorité*

R, if preceded by *i*, or if followed by *i*, and forming a syllable, sounds as above, like *ri* in the French *infériorité*, as, *rithe*, with her; *mairbh*, dead; *còir*, right

---

OF ETYMOLOGY.

Etymology is that part of grammar which teaches how to derive a word from its primitive,—shews the parts of speech, the inflections of nouns, and the modifications by which the sense of a word is diversified

OF THE PARTS OF SPEECH.

In Gaelic there are nine parts of speech, viz. Article, Noun, Pronoun, Verb, Participle, Adverb, Preposition, Interjection, Conjunction. These are divided into *declinable* and *indeclinable*.

The *declinable* parts of speech are,—the Article, Noun, Pronoun, Verb, Participle.

The *indeclinable* are,—the Adverb, Preposition, Interjection, Conjunction

OF THE ARTICLE

There is no indefinite article in Gaelic. *An*, the, is the definite article, and is declined by genders, cases, and numbers

	Singular.		Plural
	Mas.	*Fem*	*Mas* and *Fem*
Nom	An, am.	An, a'.	Na.
Gen.	An, a'.	Na	Nan, nam
Dat.	An,* a'.	An, a'.	Na

The form *am* of the article is used before a *simple* (not aspirated) labial; as, *am buille*, the blow, *am fear*, the man. before any aspirated consonant (except *fh*) the article is written *a'*.

A substantive noun, beginning with *s*, followed by a liquid or by a vowel, requires the insertion of *t* between it and the article, in the *gen* and *dat. sing. mas.* of nouns, and in the *nom.* and *dat.* of feminine nouns

A *sub. mas.* beginning with a vowel has *t* between it and the article in the *nom. sing.*

A *sub. fem.* has *h* in the same situation in the *gen sing.*

Nouns which are either *mas.* or *fem.* have *h* in the *nom.* and *dat. plural.*

Nan, of the *gen. pl*, is always used, except before words beginning with *b, f, p.* *Nan*, before *c* or *g*, sounds *nung*

OF GENDER.

The genders are two, masculine and feminine

The Gaelic language is very anomalous in its distinction of nouns by gender; and perhaps no set of rules can be devised to ascertain the gender of every noun in the language. It personifies every object, whether animate or inanimate The gender is not determined by termination, or any circumstance, but by immediate distinction of sex, and by custom

Masculines.

Nouns signifying males, are masculine; as, *duine*, a man; *laoch*, a hero; *each*, a horse

Note —That *leòmhann*, lion; *laogh*, calf; *uan*, lamb; and several other names for the young of animals, are masculine, though the objects be feminine.

Nouns in *o*, or having *o* in the last syllable, are commonly masculine; as, *ceò*, mist; *roth*, a wheel; *corp*, a body.

Polysyllables in *a, o,* or *u*, are commonly masculine.

Diminutives in *an* are masculine; as, *caman*, a club, *fuaran*, a well, *barran*, a thorn-fence.

* *An*, after a vowel, is written *'n*.

Derivatives in *ach*, *iche*, *as*, *air*, *ear*, are for the most part masculine, as, *marcach*, a rider; *maraiche*, a seaman; *piobair*, a piper; *muillear*, a miller; *càirdeas*, friendship.

Names of trees are commonly masculine.

Feminines.

Nouns signifying females are feminine; as, *màthair*, a mother.

Aggregate names of trees are feminine; as, *darach*, oak-wood.

Names of countries, especially those ending in *achd*, or which have a short vowel in the last syllable, as, *Gaidhealtachd*, the Highlands; *Eirin*, Ireland. The names of districts have their gender commonly regulated by their termination

Names of musical instruments; as, *piob*, a pipe; *cruit*, a harp.

Names of diseases; as, *buinneach*, a diarrhœa.

Polysyllables (except agents in *air* and *iche*) whose least vowel is *e*, or *i*, are commonly feminine, as, *neasgaid*, a boil; *doirlinn*, an isthmus.

Diminutives in *ag*; as, *sradag*, a spark.

Derivatives in *achd*, as, *maiseachd*, comeliness; *rioghachd*, a kingdom.

Comparatives used substantively, are feminine; as, *maoile*, baldness; *gile*, whiteness.

Nouns in *ua*, and *ui*, a diphthong, the subjunctive of which is a slender or small vowel, are commonly feminine; as, *cuach*, a cup; *compailt*, company.

OF NUMBER.

A noun has two numbers, singular and plural.

The cases are four, viz. Nominative, Genitive, Dative, Vocative.

A noun is either simple or aspirated, e. g. *mòr*, *mhòr*, where *mòr* is the simple form, and *mhòr* the aspirated

Nouns in a definite sense are declined with the article.

The flection of a Gaelic noun is carried on not so much by a change of the termination, as of the last vowel, or of the diphthong of the nominative, and by aspirating the initial consonant.

The Gael have only two declensions. Nouns whose last vowel is *a*, *o*, or *u*, are of the first, nouns whose last vowel is *e*, or *i*, are of the second

FIRST DECLENSION.

Example of a Noun Masculine, indefinite.

Fear, a man; *mas.*

	Sing.		*Pl.*
Nom	Fear, *a man.*	*Nom.*	Fir, *or* feara, *men.*
Gen	Fir, *of a man*	*Gen.*	Fear, *or* feara, *of men*
Dat	Fear, *to a man*	*Dat.*	Fearaibh,* *to men.*
Voc	Fhir, *O man*	*Voc.*	Fheara, *O men.*

The same Noun declined with the Article.

	Sing.		*Pl.*
Nom	Am fear, *the man*	*Nom*	Na fir, *the men.*
Gen.	An fhir, *of the man*	*Gen.*	Nam fear, *of the men.*
Dat	An 'n fhear, *to the man*	*Dat.*	Na fearaibh, *to the men.*

Example of a Noun Feminine, indefinite, beginning with a Palatal Consonant.

Cuach, a cup; *fem.*

	Sing.		*Pl.*
Nom.	Cuach, *a cup.*	*Nom.*	Cuachan, *cups.*
Gen	Cuaiche, *of a cup.*	*Gen.*	Cuach, *of cups.*
Dat	Cuaich, *to a cup.*	*Dat.*	Cuachaibh, *to cups.*
Voc	Chuach, *O cup*	*Voc.*	Chuacha, *O cups.*

The same Noun declined with the Article.

	Sing		*Pl.*
Nom.	A' chuach, *the cup.*	*Nom.*	Na cuachan, *the cups.*
Gen.	Na cuaiche, *of the cup.*	*Gen.*	Nan cuach, *of the cups.*
Dat.	An, 'n chuaich, *to the cup*	*Dat*	Na cuachaibh, *to the cups.*

Example of a Noun Masculine, indefinite, beginning with a Dental.

Dorus, a door; *mas.*

	Sing.		*Pl.*
Nom.	Dorus, *a door.*	*Nom.*	Dorsan, *doors*
Gen.	Doruis, *of a door.*	*Gen.*	Dorsa, *of doors.*
Dat	Dorus, *to a door.*	*Dat.*	Dorsaibh, *to doors.*
Voc.	Dhoruis, *O door.*	*Voc*	Dhorsa, *O doors.*

* The nominative and dative plural of surnames are alike.

The same Noun declined with the Article.

	Sing.		*Pl.*
Nom.	An dorus, *the door.*	*Nom.*	Na dorsan, *the doors.*
Gen.	An doruis, *of the door.*	*Gen.*	Nan dorsa, *of the doors*
Dat.	An, 'n dorus, *to the door*	*Dat.*	Na dorsaibh, *to the doors*

Example of a Feminine Noun, indefinite, beginning with a Dental.

Teasach, a fever; *fem.*

	Sing.		*Pl*
Nom.	Teasach, *a fever.*	*Nom*	Teasaichean, *fevers*
Gen.	Teasaiche, *of a fever.*	*Gen*	Teasach, *of fevers.*
Dat.	Teasach, *to a fever.*	*Dat*	Teasaichibh, *to fevers.*
Voc.	Theasach, *O fever.*	*Voc.*	Theasaiche, *O fevers.*

The same Noun declined with the Article.

	Sing.		*Pl*
Nom.	An teasach, *the fever.*	*Nom.*	Na teasaichean, *the fevers*
Gen.	Na teasaiche, *of the fever.*	*Gen*	Nan teasach, *of the fevers.*
Dat	An, 'n teasach, *to the fever.*	*Dat.*	Na teasaichibh, *to the fevers*

Note.—I. That nouns, definite, beginning with *s*, and followed by a lingual, insert *t* between the article, and the *gen* and *dat. singular.*

II. That nouns *masc.* beginning with a vowel, insert *t* in the *nom. sing*, and nouns *fem.* insert *h* in the *gen sing*, and also in the *nom* and *dat. pl.*

Example of a Noun Masculine, indefinite, beginning with s, *and followed by a Vowel.*

Soc, a socket; *mas.*

	Sing.		*Pl*
Nom.	Soc, *a socket.*	*Nom.*	Suic, *sockets.*
Gen	Suic, *of a socket*	*Gen.*	Soc, *of sockets.*
Dat	Soc, *to a socket.*	*Dat.*	Socaibh, *to sockets.*
Voc.	Shoc, *O socket.*	*Voc.*	Shuic, *O sockets.*

The same Noun declined with the Article

	Sing.		*Pl.*
Nom.	An soc, *the socket*	*Nom.*	Na suic, *the sockets*
Gen.	An t-suic, *of the socket.*	*Gen*	Nan soc, *of the sockets.*
Dat.	An, 'n t-soc, *to the socket.*	*Dat.*	Na socaibh, *to the sockets*

Example of a Noun Masculine, indefinite, beginning with s, *and followed by a Lingual.*

Sluagh, people; *mas.*

	Sing.		*Pl.*
Nom.	Sluagh, *a host.*	*Nom.*	Slòigh, *hosts.*
Gen.	Sluaigh, *of a host.*	*Gen*	Slogh, *of hosts*
Dat	Sluagh, *to a host.*	*Dat*	Slòigh, *to hosts.*
Voc.	Shluagh, *O host.*	*Voc.*	Shlòigh, *O hosts.*

The same Noun declined with the Article.

	Sing.		*Pl*
Nom.	An sluagh, *the host.*	*Nom*	Na sloigh, *the hosts*
Gen.	An t-sluaigh, *of the host.*	*Gen.*	Nan slogh, *of the hosts.*
Dat	An, 'n t-sluaigh, *to the host.*	*Dat*	Na sloigh, *to the hosts*

Note.—That nouns *masculine*, definite, beginning with a vowel, insert *t* between the article and the *nom sing*, and *h* between the article and the *nom.* and *dat. pl.*

Example of a Noun Masculine, definite, beginning with a Vowel.

Iasg, a fish; *mas*

	Sing.		*Pl.*
Nom	An t-iasg, *the fish*	*Nom.*	Na h-iasgan, *the fishes.*
Gen.	An éisg, *of the fish.*	*Gen.*	Nan iasg, *of the fishes*
Dat	An, 'n iasg, *to the fish*	*Dat*	Na h-iasgaibh, *to the fishes.*

Note.—That feminine nouns, definite, beginning with a vowel, insert *h* between the article and the *gen. sing* and the *nom.* and *dat. plural.*

Example of a Noun Feminine, definite, beginning with a Vowel.

Osag, a breeze; *fem.*

	Sing.		*Pl.*
Nom.	An osag, *the breeze.*	*Nom.*	Na h-osagan, *the breezes.*
Gen	Na h-osaig, *of the breeze*	*Gen.*	Nan osag, *of the breezes.*
Dat	An, 'n osaig, *to the breeze.*	*Dat.*	Na h-osagaibh, *to the breezes.*

Bean, a woman, *is declined irregularly; thus,*

	Sing.		*Pl.*
Nom.	Bean, *a woman*	*Nom.*	Mnai, *or* mnathan, *women*
Gen.	Mna, *of a woman.*	*Gen.*	Ban, *of women.*
Dat	Mnaoi, *to a woman.*	*Dat.*	Mnathaibh, *to women.*
Voc	Bhean, *O woman.*	*Voc.*	Mhnathan, *O women*

Bean, *declined with the Article.*

	Sing.		*Pl.*
Nom	A bhean, *the woman*	*Nom.*	Na mnathan, *the women.*
Gen	Na mna, *of the woman.*	*Gen.*	Nam ban, *of the women.*
Dat	An, 'n mhnaoi, *to the woman.*	*Dat.*	Na mnathaibh, *to the women.*

OF THE FLECTIONS OF THE FIRST DECLENSION.

SINGULAR NUMBER.

General Rule—The genitive is formed by inserting *i* after the last vowel of the nominative, as, *slat*, fem., gen *slait*, a rod, *cluaran*, masc, gen *cluarain*, a thistle. Feminines of one syllable also insert *i* after the last vowel of the noun, and often add *e* to the last letter; as, *lamh*, *laimhe*, a hand

Special Rules.

Nouns ending in *a*,* *o*, or *u*, have their *nom* and *gen.* alike, *là*, mas. gen. *là*, a day; *cnò*, mas. gen. *cno*, a nut; *cliù*, fame, except *bò*, *cù*, *brù*, which have respectively, *boin*, *coin*, *bronn*, and *broinn*.

Nouns in *achd*, *eachd*, *iochd*, *rr*, have their *nom.* and *gen.* alike *Slochd* has *sluichd* in the genitive singular.

Nouns in *adh*, of more than one syllable, form their *gen. sing.* in *aidh*; as, *mortadh*, mas. murder, gen. *mortaidh*; *naomhachadh*, mas sanctifying, *naomhachaidh*.

Monosyllables in *gh* and *th* form their gender from the *nom.* by adding *a*, except *agh*, mas *joy*, gen. *aigh*.

Monosyllables change *ea* into *ei*, as,

Nom.	*Gen.*
Beann,	Beinne, *f. a hill.*
Ceard,	Ceaird *and* ceird, *m. a tinker.*
Each,	Eich, *m. a horse.*
Feall,	Feill, *m. deceit.*
Fearg,	Feirg, *f. wrath.*
Learg,	Leirg, *f. sea.*

Some change *ea* into *i*, as,

Nom	*Gen.*
Breac,	Bric, *m. a trout*
Ceann,	Cinn, *m. a head.*
Ceap,	Cip, *m. a last*
Dreas,	Dris, *m. a thorn-bush.*
Fear,	Fir, *m. a man*
Meall,	Mill, *m. a lump*
Preas,	Pris, *m a bush*

Some also add *e*, as,

Nom.	*Gen.*
Breac,	Brice, *f small-pox.*
Cearc,	Circe, *f. a hen.*
Gleann,	Glinne, *m. a valley*
Leac,	Lice, *f. a flag.*

Dissyllables in *each* and *eann* change *ea* into *i*, as,

Nom.	*Gen.*
Aigeach,	Àigich, *m. a stallion*
Cinneach,	Cinnich, *m a nation.*
Buidheann,	Buidhinn, *contr* buidhne, *f a company.*
Sitheann,	Sithinn, *contra* sithne, *f. venison.*

Dissyllables in *ean* change *ean* into *ein*, as,

Nom.	*Gen.*
Binnean,	Binnein, *m. a pinnacle*
Cuilean,	Cuilein, *m a whelp.*
Ceisdean,	Ceisdein, *m. a sweetheart.*
Guirean,	Guirein, *m a pimple.*
Isean,	Isein, *m a gosling.*

Monosyllables change *ia* into *ei*, as,

Nom.	*Gen.*
Biadh,	Beidh, *or* bidh, *m food.*
Ciall,	Céill, *f. judgment.*
Ciar,	Céir *and* ciair, *m. darkness*
Cliabh,	Cleibh, *f. a hamper.*
Cliath,	Cleith, *f. a harrow.*
Fiadh,	Feidh, *m. a deer.*
Grian,	Gréin *and* Gréine, *f sun*

* Dissyllables in *a* (now written *adh*) have their genitive singular in *ai*, like the ancient Latin Talla, *gen* tallai, *a hall*, *Lat.* aula, *gen* aulai cala, *a harbour*, *gen* calai, &c.

Nom.	Gen.
Iall,	Éill, *f. a thong.*
Iasg,	Eisg, *m. fish.*
Liadh,	Leidh, *f. a ladle.*
Sgian,	Sgeine, *or* sgine, *f. a knife.*
Sgiath,	Sgeith, *f. a shield.*
Sliabh,	Sleibh, *m. a mountain.*

Dia, has Dia *and* Dè in the genitive singular.

Monosyllables in *eu* change *eu* into *eoi*; as,

Nom.	Gen.
Beul,	Beoil, *or* béil, *m. a mouth.*
Deur,	Deòir, *m. a drop.*
Eun,	Eoin, *m. a bird.*
Feur,	Feòir, *m. grass.*
Leus,	Leòis, *m. a flame.*
Meur,	Meòir, *m. a finger.*
Neul,	Neoil, *m. a cloud.*
Sgeul,	Sgeoil, *or* sgéil, *f. a tale.*

Eug, *m. ghost*, has Éig in the singular.

Some nouns in *eu* merely add to the *nom.*; as,

Nom.	Gen.
Beum,	Beuma, *m. a blow.*
Ceum,	Ceuma *and* céim, *m. a step.*
Feum,	Feuma *and* féim, *m. need.*
Treud,	Treuda, *m. a flock.*

Some characterized by *eu* have the *nom.* and *gen. sing.* alike; as,

Nom.	Gen.
Beuc,	Beuc, *m. a rod.*
Freumh,	Freumh *and* freimh, *f. a root.*
Leud,	Leud *and* leòid, *m. breadth.*
Seud,	Seud, *m. a jewel.*

Some nouns change *a* into *oi*; as,

Nom.	Gen.
Cas,	Cois, *or* coise, *f. a foot.*
Clach,	Cloich, *f. a stone.*
Cràg,	Cràig, *or* cròig, *f. a paw.*
Smàg,	Smàig, *or* smòig, *a pan.*

But, Mac, *a son*, has Mic.

Some nouns in *ann* have a double gender; as,

Nom.	Gen.
Clann,	Clainne, *or* cloinne, *f. children.*
Crann,	Crainn, *or* croinn, *m. a tree.*
Lann,	Lainne, *or* loinne, *f. a sword.*

Aghann, *f. a pan*, has Aighne.

Monosyllables characterized by *a*, *o*, or *u*, often change *a*, *o*, *u*, into *ui*; as,

a into *ui*.

Nom.	Gen.
Alld,	Uilld, *m. a streamlet.*
Allt,	Uillt, *m. a streamlet.*
Balg,	Builg, *m. a bag.*
Ball,	Buill, *m. a member.*
Calg,	Cuilg, *m. awn.*
Car,	Cuir, *m. a turn,* or *twist.*
Carn,	Cuirn, *m. a cairn.*
Clag,	Cluig, *m. a bell.*
Falt,	Fuilt, *m. hair.*

o into *ui*.

Nom.	Gen.
Bolg,	Builg, *m. a bag.*
Bonn,	Buinn, *m. a coin.*
Colg,	Cuilg, *m. awn.*
Cord,	Cuird, *m. a rope.*
Folt,	Fuilt, *m. hair.*
Gob,	Guib, *m. a bird's bill.*
Long,	Luing, *f. a ship.*
Lorg,	Luirg, *f. a staff.*
Moll,	Muill, *m. chaff.*
Ord,	Ùird, *m. a hammer.*
Poll,	Puill, *m. mire.*
Sonn,	Suinn, *m. a hero.*

u into *ùi*.

Nom.	Gen.
Cùl,	Cùil, *m. a corner.*
Lùs,	Lùis, *m. pith.*
Lus,	Luis, *m. an herb.*
Mult,	Muilt, *m. a wether.*
Tùr,	Tùir, *m. a tower.*

Nouns in *eòl* change *eòl* into *iùil*; as,

Nom.	Gen.
Ceòl,	Ciùil, *m. music.*
Seòl,	Siùil, *m. a sail.*

Nouns in *eag* change *eag* into *eig*; as,

Nom.	Gen.
Caileag,	Caileig, *f. a young girl.*
Duilleag,	Duilleig, *f. a leaf.*
Fàireag,	Fàireig, *f. a gland.*
Filleag,	Filleig, *f. a fold.*
Piseag,	Piseig, *f. a kitten.*

Nouns in *òg* and *òn* follow the general rule; as,

Nom.	Gen.
Bròg,	Bròig, *f. a shoe.*
Cròg,	Cròig, *f. a paw.*
Smòg,	Smòig, *f. a paw.*
Bròn,	Bròin, *m. food.*
Lòn,	Lòin, *m. food.*

Some nouns in *ua* change *ua* into *uai*; as,

Nom.	Gen.
Bruach,	Bruaich, *f. an ascent.*
Cuach,	Cuaich, *f. a cup.*
Luadh,	Luaidh, *m. praise.*
Sluagh,	Sluaigh, *m. people.*

Others add *a* to the nominative; as,

Nom.	Gen.
Fuath,	Fuatha, *m. hatred.*

Some nouns in *io* lose *o* in the genitive; as,

Nom.	Gen.
Cioch,	Cìche, *f. a pass.*
Crioch,	Crìche, *f. an end.*
Lion,	Lìn, *m. flax.*
Siol,	Sìl, *m. seed.*
Sion,	Sìne, *m. a blast.*

Some nouns in *io* only add *a* to the *nom.*; as,

Nom.	Gen.
Bior,	Biora, *m. spit.*
Crios,	Criosa, *m. a belt.*
Fion,	Fiona, *m. wine.*
Fios,	Fiosa, *or* fios, *m. notice.*
Lios,	Liosa, *m. a garden.*

Criosd, *Christ*, is undeclinable.

The following nouns form their genitive irregularly.

Nom.	Gen.
Ceathramh,	Ceithreimh, *m. a quarter.*
Leabaidh,	Leapa, *or* leapach, *f. a bed.*
Leanabh,	Leinibh, *m. a child.*
Piuthair,	Peathar, *f. a sister.*
Talamh,	Talmhainn, *f. land.*

DATIVE.

General Rule.—Nouns masculine have their *dat.* and *nom. sing.* alike; nouns feminine have their *dat.* like the *gen.*

NOUNS MAS.		NOUNS FEM.		
Nom.	*Dat.*	*Nom.*	*Gen.*	*Dat.*
Cabar,	Cabar, *a deer's horn.*	Teasach,	Teasaich,	Teasaich, *a fever.*
Dorus,	Dorus, *a door.*	Misneach,	Misnich,	Misnich, *courage.*
Tobar,	Tobar, *a well.*	Osag,	Osaig,	Osaig, *a blast of wind.*

Special Rules for the Dative case of Nouns Feminine.—When the genitive is formed by contraction, the *dat.* is like the *nom.*

Nom.	*Gen.*	*Dat.*
Sitheann,	Sithne,	Sitheann, *f. venison.*
Piuthair,	Peathar,	Piuthair, *f. sister.*

Monosyllables drop *e* from the genitive.

Nom.	*Gen.*	*Dat.*
Cluas,	Cluaise,	Cluais, *f. an ear.*
Lamh,	Laimhe,	Laimh, *f. a hand.*

In Gaelic there is no Accusative differing from the Nominative.

VOCATIVE.

The vocative singular of masculine monosyllables is the genitive *aspirated.*

Nom.	*Gen.*	*Voc.*
Cù,	Coin,	Choin, *m. a dog.*
Bard,	Baird,	Bhaird, *m. a bard.*
Bròn,	Bròin,	Bhròin, *m. grief.*
Fleasgach,	Fleasgaich,	Fhleasgaich, *a youth.*

Nouns masculine beginning with a vowel have their vocative and genitive alike.

Nom.	*Gen.*	*Voc.*
Ord,	Ùird,	Ùird, *m. a hammer.*
Amadan,	Amadain,	Amadain, *m. a fool.*
Oglach,	Oglaich,	Òglaich, *m. a youth.*

Feminine nouns form their vocative by aspirating the nominative; as,

Nom.	*Voc.*
Cluas,	Chluas, *f. ear.*
Gealach,	Ghealach, *f. nurse.*
Grian,	Ghrian, *f. sun.*

PLURAL NUMBER.

NOMINATIVE.

General Rule for the Nominative.—The nominative plural is formed from the nominative singular, by adding *an*;* as, sliseag, *f. a slice, n. pl.* sliseagan; srad, *f. a spark, n. pl.* sradan; spiorad, *m. a spirit, n. pl.* spioradan; rioghachd, *f. a kingdom, n. pl.* rioghachdan; geug, *f. a branch, n. pl.* geugan.

Special Rules.—Many dissyllables in *ach* add *ean*† to the *gen. sing.*; as,

Nom. sing.	*Gen. sing.*	*Nom. pl.*
Clàrsach, *f. a harp,*	Clarsaich,	Clarsaichean.
Cullach, *m. a boar,*	Cullaich,	Cullaichean.
Deudach, *f. a jaw,*	Deudaich,	Deudaichean,
Mullach, *m. a top,*	Mullaich,	Mullaichean.

Some masculines in *ach* have their *nom. pl.* like the *gen. sing.*; as,

Nom. sing.	*Gen. sing.*	*Nom. pl.*
Oglach, *a youth,*	Oglaich,	Oglaich.
Fear, *m. a man,*	Fir,	Fir.

Nouns in *ar* sometimes transpose the final letter and add *iche*, or *ichean*; as,

Nom. sing.	*Nom. pl.*
Tobar, *m. a well,*	Tobraichean.
Leabhar, *m. a book,*	Leabhraichean.

Nom. sing.	*Nom. pl.*
Bata, *m. a staff,* has	Batachan *and* bataichean.
Là, *m. a day,*	Làithe, làithean, *and* lathachan.
Leabaidh, *f. a bed,*	Leapaichean.
Piuthair, *f. a sister,*	Peathraichean.
Lann, *f. enclosure,*	Lanndaichean.

Masculine monosyllables in *ea*, which change *ea* into *i*, in the *gen. sing.* have their *gen. sing.* and *nom. pl.* alike; as,

Nom.	*Gen. sing.*	*Nom. pl.*
Fear, *a man,*	Fir,	Fir.
Meall, *a lump,*	Mill,	Mill.
Ceann, *m. head.*	Cinn,	Cinn.

Some nouns in *l* and *nn* have their *nom.* in *tan*; *on* and *oin* have *tean*; as,

Nom. sing.	*Nom. pl.*
Reul, *m. a star,*	Reultan.
Seul, *m. a seal,*	Seultan.

* In forming the nominative plural of these and other words, some writers only add *a* to the nominative singular; and several nouns are made to end in *idh*, in the nominative plural; as, *beann, beanntaidh; bile, bilidh; coille, coilltidh.*

† Some writers only add *e*.

Nom. sing	Nom. pl
Beann, *f. a hill,*	Beanntan *and* beanntaidh.
Gleann, *m a valley,*	Gleanntan, glinn, *and* gleanntaidh
Lionn, *m. beer,*	Lionntan
Lòn, *m. a meadow,*	Lointean.
Mòin, *f. peat,*	Mòintean
Sliabh, *a mountain,* has	Sléibhte, *or* sléibhtean.
Sabhul, *m. a barn,*	Saibhlean

Nom. sing.	Nom. pl.
But, Dia, *a god,* has	Dée *and* diathan.
Sluagh, *m. people,*	Sloigh
Sgian, *f. a knife,*	Sginichean *and* sgeinichean.
Bo, *f. a cow,*	Ba
Gniomh, *m. work,*	Gniomharan
Lion, *m. flax,* has	Liontan *and* liontaichean
Linn, *m. a pool,* has	Linnte, linntean, linnichean, *and* linntichean

GENITIVE

Monosyllables have their *gen. pl.* like the *nom sing.*; as,

Nom sing	Gen. pl.
Bard, *m a poet,*	Bard.
Breug, *m. a lie,*	Breug
Cat, *m. a cat,*	Cat
Ceard, *m a tinker,*	Ceard
Feart, *m a quality,*	Feart.
Sloc, *m a pit,*	Sloc.

Some trisyllables have the *gen. pl.* like the *nom sing*, as,

Nom. sing	Gen. pl
Freiceadan, *m a guard,*	Freiceadan.
Teampullach, *m. a churchman,*	Teampullach

Dissyllables having *ean* in the *nom. pl* have *ean* also in the *gen. pl*, as,

Nom. sing	Nom. and gen pl.
Leabaidh, *f. a bed,*	Leapaichean.
Leabhar, *m a book,*	Leabhraichean.
Tobar, *m a well,*	Tobraichean.

A few nouns form their genitives irregularly, as,

Nom sing.	Gen pl.
Bean, *f a woman,*	Ban.
Caor, *f. a sheep,*	Caorach
Cu, *m a dog,*	Con.
Sluagh, *m. people,*	Slogh *and* sluagh

DATIVE.

The dative plural ends in *aibh*, or *ibh*, and is formed from the nominative singular, or plural: thus,

Monosyllables commonly add *aibh* to the *nom. sing.*; as,

Nom. sing	Dat. pl.
Bard, *m. a bard,*	Bardaibh
Crann, *m. a tree,*	Crannaibh.
Cruach, *f. a heap,*	Cruachaibh
Feart, *m. a virtue.*	Feartaibh.
Mac, *m. a son,*	Macaibh.
Ord, *m. a hammer,*	Ordaibh.

If the *nom. pl* end in *ta* or *tan*, these are changed into *aibh*, as,

Nom sing.	Nom. pl.	Dat. pl.
Beann, *f hill,*	Beanntan,	Beanntaibh
Cuan, *m sea,*	Cuanta, *or* -an,	Cuantaibh

If the *nom pl* end in *e* or *ean*, these terminations are changed into *ibh*, as,

Nom. sing.	Nom. pl.	Dat. pl.
Mullach, *m. a top,*	Mullaichean,	Mullaichibh
Sliabh, *m. a hill,*	Sleibhte, *or* -ean,	Sleibhtibh
Teasach, *f. a fever,*	Teasaichean,	Teasaichibh

Trisyllables in *ch* have their *dat.* and *nom. pl* alike, as,

Nom sing.	Nom. and Dat pl
Comhairleach, *m a counsellor,*	Comhairlich

Monosyllables in *eadh*, *iadh*, and *eagh*, add *aibh* to the *nom. sing.*, but,

Nom. sing	Dat. pl.
Fiadh, *m deer,* has	Feidh.
Sluagh, *m. people,* has	Sloigh

Monosyllables in *amh* and *ath* form their *dat pl.* in *aibh*, as,

Nom sing	Dat pl.
Lamh, *f. a hand,*	Lamhaibh.
Ramh, *m an oar,*	Ramhaibh
Flath, *m a prince,*	Flathaibh.
Sgiath, *f. a wing,*	Sgiathaibh.
But, Damh, *m an ox,* has	Daimh.
Bean, *f. a woman,* has	Mnathaibh.

VOCATIVE.

The vocative plural is commonly the aspirated form of the nominative plural, as,

Nom. plur.	Voc plur
Beannta, beanntan, *hills,*	Bheannta, *or* bheanntan.
Dorsa, dorsan, *doors,*	Dhorsa, *or* dhorsan.

Monosyllables often add *a* to the aspirated form of the nominative singular; as,

Nom sing	Asp form.	Voc plur.
Bard, *m. a poet,*	Bhard,	Bharda
Cluas, *f. an ear,*	Chluas,	Chluasa.

Bean has *mhnathan* in the vocative plural, as, damh, *an ox*, dhaimh, sluagh, *people*, shloigh, and shluagh.

SECOND DECLENSION.

Under this declension may be classed all those nouns whose characteristic or last vowel is *i*.

Example of a Noun Masculine, indefinite, beginning with cl.

Cladhair, *a coward.*

	Sing		*Pl*
Nom	Cladhair, *a coward.*	*Nom*	Cladhairean, *cowards*
Gen	Cladhair, *of a coward,*	*Gen.*	Cladhair, *of cowards.*
Dat.	Cladhair, *to a coward.*	*Dat.*	Cladhairibh, *to cowards.*
Voc.	Chladhair, *O coward.*	*Voc.*	Chladhaire, *O cowards.*

The same Noun declined with the Article.

	Sing		*Pl.*
Nom.	An cladhair, *the coward.*	*Nom*	Na cladhairean, *the cowards.*
Gen	A' chladhair, *of the coward.*	*Gen*	Nan cladhair, *of the cowards.*
Dat.	An, 'n chladhair, *to the coward.*	*Dat.*	Na cladhairibh, *to the cowards.*

Example of a Feminine Monosyllable, indefinite, beginning with a Vowel.

Airc, *fem. an ark.*

	Sing		*Pl.*
Nom	Airc, *an ark*	*Nom.*	Aircean, *arks.*
Gen	Airce, *of an ark.*	*Gen.*	Airc, *of arks.*
Dat	Airc, *to an ark.*	*Dat.*	Aircibh, *to arks.*
Voc	Airc, *O ark.*	*Voc.*	Airce, *O arks.*

The same Noun declined with the Article.

	Sing		*Pl*
Nom	An airc, *the ark.*	*Nom.*	Na h-aircean, *the arks.*
Gen	Na h-airce, *of the ark.*	*Gen*	Nan airc, *of the arks*
Dat.	An, 'n airc, *to the ark*	*Dat*	Na h-aircibh, *to the arks.*

Example of a Noun Feminine, indefinite, beginning with s, *followed by a Vowel*

Sùil, *fem. an eye.*

	Sing		*Pl*
Nom	Sùil, *an eye*	*Nom.*	Sùilean, *eyes.*
Gen.	Sùl *and* sùla, *of an eye.*	*Gen.*	Sùl, *of eyes.*
Dat	Sùil, *to an eye*	*Dat.*	Suilibh, *to eyes.*
Voc	Shùil, *O eye.*	*Voc.*	Shùil, *O eyes.*

The same Noun declined with the Article.

	Sing		*Pl.*
Nom	An t-sùil, *the eye.*	*Nom*	Na sùilean, *the eyes*
Gen	Na sùl, *of the eye*	*Gen.*	Nan sùl, *of the eyes.*
Dat	An, 'n t-sùil, *to the eye*	*Dat.*	Na sùilibh, *to the eyes.*

FLECTIONS OF THE SECOND DECLENSION.

SINGULAR NUMBER

GENITIVE

General Rules.—I Dissyllables and trisyllables form their *gen* like the *nom*, as,

Nom sing	*Gen sing*
Aimsir, *f weather,*	Aimsir
Cealgair, *m. a deceiver,*	Cealgair.
Cladhair, *m a coward,*	Cladhair
Gealtair, *m. a coward,*	Gealtair
Breabadair, *m a weaver,*	Breabadair.

II. Monosyllables add *e* to the nominative, as,

Nom. sing	*Gen sing.*
Ainm, *m. a name,*	Ainme
Airc, *m. an ark,*	Airce.
Clais, *f. a furrow,*	Claise
Tuil, *f. a flood,*	Tuile

Special Rules for the Genitive.—I. Some nouns in *ail* change *ail* into *alach*, as,

Nom.	*Gen.*
Dăil, *f a meadow,*	Dălach
Săil, *f a beam,*	Sălach
Làir, *f a mare,*	Làrach.
But, Dàil, *f. delay,* has	Dàile
Sàil, *m brine,*	Sàile.

Some monosyllables in *ui* have their *gen* and *nom.* alike; as,

	Nom.		Gen.
	Cruit, *f. a harp,*		Cruit
	Smuid, *m. smoke,*		Smùid
	Truid, *a starling,*		Truid.
	Cuid, *f. part,*		Cuid *and* codach
But,	Muir, *f. sea,*	has	Mara.
	Fuil, *f. blood,*		Fala *and* Fola
	Druim, *f ridge,*		Droma.
	Sùil, *f. an eye,*		Sùla.

Feminines in *oi* drop the subjunctive, and add *a*, as,

Nom. sing.	Gen. sing.
Feòil, *flesh,*	Feòla.
Sroin, *f a nose,*	Sròna, *or* sròine.
Tòin, *f bottom,*	Tòna

Feminine dissyllables in *air* change *air* into *rach*, as,

	Nom.		Gen.
	Cathair, *f. a city,*		Cathrach.
	Lasair, *f. a flame,*		Lasrach.
	Machair, *f. a plain,*		Machrach.
	Nathair *f. a serpent,*		Nathrach.
So also,	Staidhir, *f. a stair,*	has	Staidhreach.
	Faighir, *f. a fair,*	has	Faighreach

Some dissyllables, characterized by the diphthong *ai*, lose the subjunctive in the genitive; as,

Nom		Gen.
Athair, *m a father,*		Athar
Bràthair, *m. brother,*		Bràthar.
Màthair, *m mother,*		Màthar.
Piuthair, *f. sister,*	has	Peathar *and* piuthair

Feminine dissyllables in *eir* sometimes form their genitive by adding *e* to the nominative, and sometimes by changing *eir* of the nominative in *earach*, as,

Nom. sing.	Gen sing.
Dinneir, *f. dinner,*	Dinneire, *or* dinnearach.
Inneir, *f dung,*	Inneire, *or* innearach.
Suipeir, *f. supper,*	Suipeire, *or* suipearach.

Ni, righ, brìgh, sìth, ré, té, have their genitive and nominative alike

The following nouns form their genitives irregularly :—

Nom sing.	Gen. sing.
Abhainn, *f a river,*	Aibhne.
Aghann, *f. a pan,*	Aighne.
Banais, *f a wedding,*	Bainnse.
Colunn, *f a body,*	Colla, colna.
Dùthaich, *f a country,*	Dùthcha *and* dùcha
Fiacail, *f a tooth,*	Fiacla *and* fiacail.
Gamhuinn, *m a steer,*	Gamhna.
Gualainn, *f shoulder,*	Guaille *and* guailne
Madainn, *f. morning,*	Maidne.
Obair, *f. work,*	Oibre
Uilinn, *f. elbow,*	Uille *and* uilne.

DATIVE

The dative singular is like the nominative.

VOCATIVE.

The vocative singular is the nominative aspirated; and in nouns beginning with a vowel it is the same as the nominative

PLURAL NUMBER.

NOMINATIVE.

General Rule.—The nominative plural is formed from the nominative singular by adding *ean*, as, *cealgair, m* a deceiver, *nom. pl. cealgairean*, *clàrsair, m.* a harper, *nom. pl clarsairean*

Special Rules —Some nouns, which form their *gen. sing* by contraction, retain the contraction in the *nom. pl.*; as,

Nom. sing.	Gen. sing.	Nom. pl.
Abhainn, *f.*	Aibhne,	Aibhnichean *and* aibhnean
Aghann, *f*	Aighne,	Aighnichean
Banais, *f.*	Bainse,	Bainsean
Duthaich, *f.*	Duthcha,	Duchan *and* duchannan
Fiacail, *f.*	Fiacla,	Fiaclan.
Gamhuinn, *m.*	Gamhna,	Gamhnan
Gualainn, *f.*	Guaille,	Guaillean.
Madainn, *f.*	Maidne,	Maidnean
Namhaid, *m*	Naimhde,	Naimhdean.
Uilinn, *f*	Uille *and* uillne,	Uillean *and* uilnean.

Feminine nouns in *air* change *ach* of the *gen sing* into *aich*, and add *ean*; as,

Nom. sing.	Gen sing	Nom. pl.
Cathair, *f. seat,*	Càthrach,	Cathraichean.
Lasair, *f. flame,*	Lasrach,	Lasraichean
Measair, *f. tub,*	Measrach,	Measraichean
Nathair, *f serpent,*	Nathrach,	Nathraichean
Athair, *m father,*	has	Aithrichean.
Mathair, *f. mother,*		Maithrichean
Uisge, *m water,*		Uisgeachan.

Nom. sing	Nom. pl.
Cridhe, *m heart,*	Cridheachan.
Cuid, *f. part,*	Codaichean.

Nouns in *eile* and *ein* often add *tean*, as,

Nom sing.	Nom pl.
Féil, *f a kilt,*	Féiltean.
Léin, *f a shirt,*	Léintean

Monosyllables in *ail* and *aile* add *ean* to the *nom. sing*, as,

Nom. sing.		Nom pl
Fàil, *f. a ring,*		Fàilean.
Dàil, *f. delay,*		Dàilean.
Caile, *f. a girl,*		Cailean.
Sàil, *f a heel,*	has	Sàiltean.
Săil, *f a beam,*	has	Sailthean.
Dăil, *f a meadow,*	has	Dailthean *and* dailean

Some nouns in *aile, ain,* and others, add *tean* to the *nom. sing.*, as,

Nom. sing.	Nom. pl.
Bail, *m a town,*	Bailtean
Smuain, *m a thought,*	Smuaintean
Smaoin, *m. a thought,*	Smaointean.
Aithne, *f. a precept,*	Aithntean.
Coille, *f. a wood,*	Coilltean.

Some nouns in *ùil* and *uille* add *ean* to the *nom. sing*; as,

Nom. sing.		*Nom. pl.*
Sùil, *f. an eye,*		Sùilean.
Buille, *a blow,*	has	Buillean, builleachan, *and* builleannan

The following nouns in *uil* add *tean* for the *nom. pl.* irregularly; as,

Nom sing	*Nom. pl.*
Cùil, *m a corner,*	Cùiltean.
Dùil, *f. element,*	Duiltean.
Tuil, *f. a flood,*	Tuiltean.

The following nouns form their *nom. pl.* irregularly; as,

Nom. sing.	*Nom pl.*
Cliamhuinn, *m. a son-in-law,*	Cleamhna *and* cliamhnan.
Duine, *m. a man,*	Daoine.
Fear, *m. a man,*	Fir *and* feara.
Ni, *m a thing,*	Nithe *and* nitheannan
Righ, *m a king,*	Righre *and* righrean.

GENITIVE.

Many words of one or more syllables have their genitive plural like the *nom. sing.* and *pl.*, as,

Nom. sing	*Nom pl*	*Gen. pl.*
Ni, *m a thing,*	Nithe, Nitheannan	Ni, Nithe, Nitheannan
Righ, *m a king,*	Righre, Righrean	Righ, Righre, Righrean
Cladhair, *m a coward,*	Cladhaire, Cladhairean.	Cladhair, Cladhaire, Cladhairean

Feminine polysyllables have commonly their *nom.* and *gen. pl.* alike; as,

Nom. pl.		*Gen. pl.*
Cridheachan,	*hearts,*	Cridheachan
Linntean, Linntichean,	*pools,*	Linntean, Linntichean.
Aibhnean, Aibhnichean,	*rivers,*	Aibhnean, Aibhnichean.
Duil, *f. an element,*	has	Dul.
Sùil, *an eye,*	has	Sùl

DATIVE.

The dative plural is formed from the nominative plural by changing the last vowel or syllable into *ibh*, as,

Nom pl.	*Dat. pl.*
Bailtean, *towns,*	Bailtibh.
Cùiltean, *corners,*	Cùiltibh.
Féiltean, *kilts,*	Féiltibh.
Righre, *kings,*	Righribh
Fiaclan, *teeth,*	Fiaclaibh.

VOCATIVE

The vocative plural is the aspirated form of the nominative plural; as,

Nom pl.	*Voc. pl.*
Coillte, *or* Coilltean,	Choillte, *or* Choilltean
Cealgaire, *or* Cealgairean,	Chealgaire, *or* Chealgairean.

METHODS OF DISTINGUISHING SEX.

The Gaelic Language has three Methods of Distinguishing the Sex; viz.

I. By different Words.

Male.	*Female*
Fleasgach,	Nighean no maighdeann,
Righ,	Banrigh.
Balaoch,	Caile
Balachan,	Caileag
Boc,	Eilid.
Oid,	Muim.
Coileach,	Cearc.
Athair,	Mathair.
Dràc,	Tunnag
Sgalag,	Searbhanta.
Aonaranach,	Bantrach.
Fear,	Bean.
Duine,	Té.
Oganach,	Oigh.
Tarbh,	Bò
Cù,	Galla.
Brathair bochd,	Cailleach dubh.
Crochair,	Baobh.
Each,	Capull.
Cullach,	Muc.
Brathair,	Piuthair.
Reithe,	Caor
Mac,	Nighean.
Gannra,	Geadh
Brathair athar,	Piuthair athar.
Fear bainnse,	Bean bainnse.
Brathair màthar,	Piuthair màthar
Firionnach,	Boirionnach.

II By prefixing *ban* or *bain* to nouns feminine; as,

Male	*Female*
Tighearn,	Bain-tighearn
Aba,	Ban-aba
Sealgair,	Ban-sealgair.
Morair,	Ban-mhorair.
Maighistir,	Ban-mhaighistir.
Tàillear,	Ban-fhualaiche.
Prionnsa,	Ban-phrionnsa
Diùc,	Ban-diùc

III. By putting an adjective after the substantive; as,

Leomhann firionn,	Leomhann boirionn.
Uan firionn,	Uan boirionn

OF ADJECTIVES.

An adjective is a word which denotes some quality belonging to the substantive; as, *duine math*, a good man, *tigh mòr*, a large house.

In Gaelic, the adjective is varied on account of gender, number, and case.

The changes which an adjective undergoes in the course of flection are twofold first, by aspirating the initial consonant; and, secondly, by changing the termination.

Adjectives, like substantives, are either of the first or second declension

Adjectives which are characterized by *a*, *o*, or *u*, are of the first declension

Adjectives characterized by *i*, are of the second.

ADJECTIVES OF THE FIRST DECLENSION

Marbh, dead.

	SINGULAR		PLURAL.
	Masc.	*Fem.*	*Masc* and *Fem*
Nom.	Marbh,	Mharbh,	Marbha.
Gen.	Mhairbh,	Mairbhe,	Marbha.
Dat.	Marbh,	Mhairbh,	Marbha
Voc.	Mhairbh	Mharbh,	Marbha.

RULES FOR THE INFLECTION OF ADJECTIVES OF THE FIRST DECLENSION

SINGULAR NUMBER

NOMINATIVE

The initial consonant, when it admits of aspiration, is aspirated for the feminine gender, and terminates like the masculine, as, *mòr, m mhòr, fem* great; *fann, m. fhann, fem* weak; *ceart, m. cheart, fem.* right

OBLIQUE CASES.

The oblique cases of each gender are formed like those nouns of the first declension, and follow the same rules

GENITIVE.

In general, the genitive singular feminine is formed from the genitive singular masculine by throwing aside the aspirate of the initial consonant; and monosyllables, after this change, commonly add *e*

If the noun masculine ends in *e*, that vowel is retained throughout.

The learner may derive some help from the following table.—

Nom sing. mas	*Nom sing. fem.*	*Gen. sing mas*	*Gen. sing. fem*
Bàn, *pale*,	Bhàn,	Bhàin,	Bàine.
Bochd, *poor*,	Bhochd,	Bhochd,	Bochd.
Briagh, *fine*,	Bhriagh,	Bhriagha,	Briagh.
Buan, *lasting*,	Bhuan,	Bhuaine,	Buaine
Cam, *crooked*,	Cham,	Chaim,	Caime.
Caomh, *mild*,	Chaomh,	Chaoimh,	Caoimhe
Ceart, *right*,	Cheart,	Cheairt, cheirt,	Cearte *and* ceirte.
Crion, *little*,	Chrion,	Chrìn,	Crìne
Daor, *dear*,	Dhaor,	Dhaoir,	Daoire
Dubh, *black*,	Dhubh,	Dhuibh,	Duibhe.
Fann, *weak*,	Fhann,	Fhainn,	Fainne
Gann, *scanty*,	Ghann,	Ghainn,	Gainne.
Gearr, *short*,	Ghearr,	Ghearr,	Gearr.
Goirt, *sour*,	Ghoirt,	Ghoirt,	Goirt.
Marbh, *dead*,	Mharbh,	Mhairbh,	Mairbhe.
Mòr, *great*,	Mhòr,	Mhòir,	Mòire
Pronn, *pulverised*,	Phronn,	Phroinn,	Proinne.
Saor, *free*,	Shaor,	Shaoir,	Saoire.

Monosyllables in *all* change *a* into *oi* in the genitive masculine and feminine.

Nom. sing. mas.	*Nom. sing. fem.*	*Gen. sing. mas.*	*Gen. sing fem.*
Dall, *blind*,	Dhall,	Dhoill,	Doille.
Mall, *slow*,	Mhall,	Mhoill,	Moille.

Monosyllables in *om, onn, orb, orm,* change *o* into *ui*, as,

Nom. sing. mas.	*Nom. sing fem.*	*Gen. sing. mas.*	*Gen. sing fem.*
Crom, *crooked,*	Chrom,	Chruim,	Cruime.
Lom, *bare,*	Lom,	Luim,	Luime.
Trom, *heavy,*	Throm,	Thruim,	Truime.
Borb, *fierce,*	Bhorb,	Bhuirb,	Buirbe.
Gorm, *blue,*	Ghorm,	Ghuirm,	Guirme.

Monosyllables in *ea, eu, ia,* change these diphthongs into *ei* in the genitive singular; as,

Nom. sing. mas.	*Nom. sing. fem.*	*Gen sing mas.*	*Gen sing. fem.*
Dearg, *red,*	Dhearg,	Dheirg,	Deirge.
Deas, *ready,*	Dheas,	Dheis,	Deise.
Geur, *sharp,*	Gheur,	Ghéir,	Géire.
Liath, *grey-haired,*	Liath,	Leith,	Leithe.

Some change *ea* into *i*, as,

Breac, *spotted,*	Bhreac,	Bhric,	Brice.
Geal, *white,*	Gheal,	Ghil,	Gile.

Adjectives beginning with a vowel have no *initial* change; as,

Nom sing. mas.	*Nom sing. fem.*	*Gen. sing. mas*	*Gen. sing fem.*
Ait, *joyful,*	Ait,	Ait,	Aite.
Aosda, *old,*	Aosda,	Aosda,	Aosda.
Ùr, *fresh,*	Ur,	Uir,	Ùire.

Adjectives ending with a diphthong have no change in the termination; as,

Beo, *alive,*	Bheo,	Bheo,	Beo.

Adjectives of two syllables, or more than two, do not commonly add to the genitive singular masculine; as,

Nom. sing. mas.	*Nom sing. fem*	*Gen sing. mas*	*Gen. sing. fem.*
Cinnteach, *sure,*	Chinnteach,	Chinntich,	Cinntich.
Eagallach, *fearful,*	Eagallach,	Eagallaich,	Eagallaich
Maiseach, *handsome,*	Mhaiseach,	Mhaisich,	Maisich.
Bodhar, *deaf,* has	Bhodhar,	Bhuidhir,	Buidhir.
Odhar, *sallow,* has	Odhar,	Uidhir,	Uidhir.

DATIVE

General Rule—The dative singular masculine, without the article, as that of substantives, is like the nominative singular; and the dative singular feminine is like the genitive masculine, as,

Nom sing mas.	*Gen sing fem.*	*Dat. sing mas.*	*Dat. sing. fem.*
Bodhar, *deaf,*	Bhuidhir,	Bodhar,	Bhuidhir.
Caol, *small,*	Chaoil,	Caol,	Chaoil.
Donn, *brown,*	Dhuinn,	Donn,	Dhuinn.
Geal, *white,*	Ghil,	Geal,	Ghile
Trom, *heavy,*	Thruim,	Trom,	Thruim
Uasal, *noble,*	Uasail,	Uasal,	Uasail.

VOCATIVE.

The vocative singular masculine of adjectives, as that of substantives, is like the genitive singular masculine; and the vocative singular feminine is like the nominative singular feminine; as,

Nom sing fem	*Gen sing mas*	*Voc sing. mas*	*Voc sing. fem.*
Bhàn, *pale,*	Bhàin,	Bhàin,	Bhàn.
Bheag, *little,*	Bhig,	Bhig,	Bheag.
Bhodhar, *deaf,*	Bhuidhir,	Bhuidhir,	Bhodhar.
Dhall, *blind,*	Dhoill,	Dhoill,	Dhall.
Gheal, *white,*	Ghil,	Ghil,	Gheal.
Throm, *heavy,*	Thruim,	Thruim,	Throm.
Truagh, *wretched,*	Thruaigh,	Thruaigh,	Thruagh.

PLURAL NUMBER.

A monosyllabic adjective adds *a* to the nominative singular masculine; as, *nom. sing. mas.* mòr, *great, pl.* mòra.

Adjectives of more than one syllable have their plural cases like the nominative singular; as, *nom sing.* brònach, *sorrowful, pl.* brònach; cinnteach, *sure, pl.* cinnteach

ADJECTIVES OF THE SECOND DECLENSION.

These adjectives are characterized by i, and they form their cases like substantives of the second declension.

Some adjectives of two syllables, of both declensions, are contracted in the plural; as, reamhara, *contr.* reamhra, *fat*, milise, *contr* milse, *sweet*.

The initial form of the adjective depends, (1) on the gender of its noun, (2) on its termination, (3) on its sense being definite or indefinite.*

Example of an Adjective with a Masculine Substantive, indefinite, of the First Declension.

Fear marbh.

	Sing.		*Pl.*
Nom.	Fear marbh, *a dead man*,	*Nom*	Fir mharbha, *dead men*.
Gen.	Fir mhairbh, *of a dead man*,	*Gen*	Fheara marbha, *of dead men*.
Dat.	Fear marbh, *to a dead man*.	*Dat.*	Fhearaibh marbha, *to dead men*.
Voc.	Fhir mhairbh, *O dead man*.	*Voc.*	Fheara marbha, *O dead men*.

The same Words declined with the Article.

	Sing.		*Pl*
Nom.	Am fear marbh, *the dead man*,	*Nom.*	Na fhir mharbha, *the dead men*.
Gen	An fhir mhairbh, *of the dead man*,	*Gen*	Nam fear marbha, *of the dead men*.
Dat.	An, 'n fhear mharbh, *to the dead man*,	*Dat.*	Na fearaibh marbha, *to the dead men*.

Example of a Noun Feminine and Adjective of the First Declension, indefinite.

Beann mhòr.

	Sing		*Pl*
Nom.	Beann mhor, *a high hill*,	*Nom.*	Beanntan mora, *high hills*
Gen.	Beinne moire, *of a high hill*,	*Gen*	Beann mora, *of high hills*.
Dat.	Beinn mhoire, *to a high hill*,	*Dat*	Beanntaibh mora, *to high hills*
Voc.	Bheann mhòr, *O high hill*,	*Voc.*	Bheannta mora, *O high hills*

The same Words declined with the Article.

	Sing.		*Pl.*
Nom	A bheann mhor, *the high hill*,	*Nom.*	Na beanntan mora, *the high hills*.
Gen.	Na beinne mòire, *of the high hill*,	*Gen.*	Nam beann mora, *of the high hills*.
Dat.	An, 'n bheinn mhoir, *to the high hill*,	*Dat.*	Na beanntaibh mora, *to the high hills*.

Rule—A substantive preceded by its adjective, is aspirated, and both are declined as one word; as,

Sgòr-bheann, *s f a rocky hill.*

INDEFINITE.

	Sing.		*Pl*
Nom.	Sgòr-bheann,	*Nom.*	Sgòr-bheanntan.
Gen.	Sgòr-bheinn,	*Gen*	Sgòr-bheann
Dat.	Sgòr-bheinn,	*Dat.*	Sgòr-bheanntaibh
Voc.	Sgòr-bheann,	*Voc.*	Sgòr-bheannta

The same Noun with the Article.

	Sing.		*Pl.*
Nom.	An sgòr-bheann,	*Nom.*	Na sgòr-bheantan.
Gen.	Na sgòr-bheinne,	*Gen*	Nan sgòr-bheann.
Dat.	An, 'an sgòr-bheinn,	*Dat.*	Na sgòr-bheanntaibh

OF THE COMPARISON OF ADJECTIVES.

In Gaelic there are three degrees or states of comparison; the *Positive*, *Comparative*, and *Superlative*.

The *Positive* merely expresses the quality; as, tha 'n dath so dearg, *this colour is red*

The *Comparative* enlarges or diminishes the quality; as, is e so dath is deirge, *this is the redder colour*.

The *Superlative* expresses the quality of an object in the highest degree; as, is e so an dath is deirge dhiubh uile, *this is the reddest colour of them all*.

* If a substantive feminine ends in *n*, and its adjective begins with *d*, there is no initial change in the adjective; as, *cailinn dubh*, *ailinn donn*.

OF THE FORMATION OF THE DEGREES OF COMPARISON.

The comparative of monosyllables is commonly like the genitive singular feminine, and is generally followed by *na.**

Positive	*Gen. sing fem*	*Comp.*	*Positive.*	*Gen. sing. fem.*	*Comp*
Bàn, *fair*,	Bàine,	Bàine.	Donn, *brown*,	Duinne,	Duinne.
Borb, *fierce*,	Buirbe,	Buirbe.	Dubh, *black*,	Duibhe,	Duibhe.
Buan, *lasting*,	Buaine,	Buaine.	Fann, *weak*,	Fainne,	Fainne.
Cam, *crooked*,	Caime,	Caime	Geal, *white*,	Gile,	Gile.
Caomh, *mild*,	Caoimhe,	Caoimhe	Gorm, *blue*,	Guirme.	Guirme.
Ceart, *right*,	Ceirte,	Ceirte.	Lag, *weak*,	Laige,	Laige
Crion, *little*,	Crîne,	Crîne.	Leath, *grey*,	Leithe,	Leithe.
Crom, *crooked*,	Cruime,	Cruime.	Lom, *bare*,	Luime,	Luime.
Daor, *dear*,	Daoire,	Daoire	Mall, *slow*,	Maille,	Maille.
Dearg, *red*,	Deirge,	Deirge.	Marbh, *dead*,	Mairbhe,	Mairbhe.
Deas, *ready*,	Deise,	Deise	Trom, *heavy*,	Truime,	Truime

If the positive end in *ach* or *each*, the comparative is formed by adding *e* to the genitive singular feminine; as,

Positive.	*Gen. sing. fem.*	*Comp*	*Positive.*	*Gen. sing fem.*	*Comp*
Cealgach, *deceitful*,	Cealgaich,	Cealgaiche	Ciontach, *guilty*,	Ciontaich,	Ciontaiche.
Cinnteach, *sure*,	Cinntich,	Cinntiche.	Maiseach, *handsome*,	Maisich,	Maisiche.

The following adjectives are contracted in the comparative; as,

Pos	*Comp.*	*Pos*	*Comp.*
Bodhar, *deaf*,	Buirdhe	Bòidheach, *pretty*,	Bòidhche
Domhainn, *deep*,	Doimhne	Odhar, *sallow*,	Uidhre.

If the positive be characterized by *i*, the comparative is formed by adding *e*; as,

Pos	*Comp*	*Pos*	*Comp*
Banail, *modest*,	Banaile.	Caoimhneil, *kind*,	Caoimhneile.
Caomhail, *kind*,	Caomhaile	Làidir, *strong*,	Làidire.

If the positive end in *o* or *uidhe*, the positive and comparative are alike; as, beo, *lively*, *comp* beo; buidhe, *yellow*, *comp.* buidhe

THE SUPERLATIVE DEGREE.

The superlative is like the comparative, and is followed by the preposition *do* or *dhe*, either simple, or compounded with a pronoun.

Ro, *fior*, and *sàr*, put before an adjective, answer respectively to the English *very*, *truly*, *exceedingly* They always throw the adjective into the aspirated form, as, ro mhath, *very good*, fior mhath, *truly good*; sàr mhath, *exceeding good.*

Comparatives and superlatives undergo no change in the termination

IRREGULAR COMPARISONS.

Pos	*Comp*	*Sup.*
Beag,	Lugha,	Lugha, *little*, *less*, *least.*
Cairdeach,	Càra, cairdiche,	Càra, cairdiche, *akin*, *more akin*, *most akin.*
Duilich	Dorra,	Dorra, *difficult*, *more difficult*, *most difficult.*
Fagus,	Fhaisge, fhaigse,	Fhaisge, fhaigse, *near*, *nearer*, *nearest.*
Fogus,	Fhoisge, fhoigse,	Fhoisge, fhoigse, *near*, *nearer*, *nearest.*
Furas,	Fhasa,	Fhasa, *easy*, *easier*, *easiest.*
Gearr, goirrid,	Giorra,	Giorra, *short*, *shorter*, *shortest*
Ionmhuinn,	Annsa, ionnsa,	Annsa, ionnsa, *dear*, *dearer*, *dearest.*
Leathan,	Leatha, Leithne, Lithne,	Leatha, Leithne, Lithne, } *broad*, *broader*, *broadest.*
Math, maith,	Fearr, fhearr,	Fearr, fhearr, *good*, *better*, *best.*
Mòr,	Mò,	Mò, *great*, *greater*, *greatest.*
Olc,	Miosa,	Miosa, *bad*, *worse*, *worst.*
Teth,	Teoithe,	Teoithe, *hot*, *hotter*, *hottest.*
Toigh,	Docha,	Docha, *dear*, *dearer*, *dearest.*

* There is a *double* comparative, having the nature of both a substantive and adjective it is formed from the comparative by changing *e* into *id*, as, *teoithe*, hotter, *teothid* Every adjective does not admit of this form of comparison

OF PRONOUNS.

A Pronoun is a word put instead of a noun, to prevent the too frequent repetition thereof; as, tha Dia mòr; tha *e* sona; tha *e* gràsmhor; tha *e* naomh.

There are six kinds of pronouns; viz. the *Personal*, the *Relative*, the *Adjective*, the *Interrogative*, the *Indefinite*, and the *Compound* pronouns.

PERSONAL PRONOUNS.

There are four personal pronouns; they admit of Person, Gender, Number, and of a Simple and Emphatic form. A personal pronoun is thrown into an emphatic form by the addition of *sa*, or *san*, *se*, *ne*, to the simple form.

SIMPLE FORM.

Mi, mhi, *I*, the first person,	*Singular.*	Sinn, *we*, the first person,	*Plural*
Tu,* thu, *thou*, the second person,		Sibh,† *you*, the second person,	
E, se, *he*, / I, si, *she*, — the third person,		Iad, siad, *they*, the third person,	

EMPHATIC FORM.

Mise, mhise, *I*, the first person,	*Singular.*	Sinne, *we*, the first person,	*Plural.*
Tusa, thusa, *thou*, the second person,		Sibhse, *you*, the second person,	
Esa, esan, *he*, / Ise, — *she*, — the third person,		Iadsa, iadsan, *they*, the third person,	

The forms of the personal pronoun governed by a transitive verb are,

Simple form.	*Emph. form.*		*Simple form*	*Emph. form.*	
Mi,	Mise, *me*,	*Singular.*	Sinn,	Sinne, *us*,	*Plural*
Thu,	Thusa, *thee*,		Sibh,	Sibhse, *you*,	
E,	Esan, *him*,		Iad,	Iadsan, *them*,	
I,	Ise, her,				

Note.—That *féin* when added to a personal pronoun, is equivalent to the Latin syllabic adjection *met*, English *self*, or *selves*, mi féin, *or* mi fhéin, *myself*; mise fein, *my own self*

Thu féin, *or* thu fhéin, *thyself*; thusa féin, *thy own self*

E féin, *or* e fhéin, *himself*, esan féin, *his own self.*

I féin, *or* i fhéin, *herself*, ise féin, *her own self.*

Sinn féin, *or* sinn fhéin, *ourselves*, sinne féin, *our own selves*

Sibh féin, *or* sibh fhéin, *yourselves*, sibhse féin, *your own selves.*

Iad féin, *or* iad fhéin, *themselves*, iadsa féin, *themselves.*

Gender has respect only to the third person singular of the pronouns, *e*, *i* *E* is masculine, *i* is feminine There is no neuter gender in Gaelic, as has been already observed

RELATIVE PRONOUNS

There are three relative pronouns, *nom.* a, *who, which*; *gen.* and *dat* an, nach, *who not, which not, that not*; na, *that which.*

ADJECTIVE PRONOUNS.

The adjective pronouns may be subdivided into the *Possessive*, the *Demonstrative*, and the *Distributive.*

I. The *Possessive Pronouns* are,

Mo, *my*,	*Singular.*	Ar, *our*,	*Plural.*
Do, *thy*,		Bhur, *or* ur, *you*,	
A, *her*,		An, *or* am, *their*,	

These pronouns never have the emphatic syllable subjoined, like the personal pronouns, but when they agree with a substantive, the emphatic form is expressed as follows:

Simple form	*Emph. form*		*Simple form.*	*Emph form.*	
Mo cheann,	Mo cheann-sa,	*Singular.*	Ar ceann,	Ar ceann-ne,	*Plural*
Do cheann,	Do cheann-sa,		Bhur, *or* ur ceann,	Bhur, *or* ur ceann-sa.	
A cheann,	A cheann-san,		An‡ ceann,	An ceann-san.	

* The personal pronoun *tu, thu*, or *thusa*, is used in addressing our equals and our inferiors, and, what is remarkable, in our addresses to the Supreme Being

† *Sibh*, or *sibhse*, is commonly used when we address our superiors in age or in rank, yet the second personal pronoun is beautifully applied to majesty, and to people of very high rank.

‡ *Am* is used before words beginning with a labial not aspirated, *an* is used before all other consonants, and before words beginning with a vowel

If the substantive be followed by an adjective, the emphatic adjection is put after the adjective only; and if it be followed by more adjectives than one, the adjection is put after the last; as,

Do ghnùis bhòidheach-sa, *thy pretty face.*
Do lamh bhòidheach gheal-sa, *thy pretty white hand.*
Do phiuthair gaoil-sa, *thy beloved sister.*

Before a vowel or *f* aspirated, *mo* and *do* are written with an apostrophe; as, m' athair, *my father;* d' ainm, *thy name.*

II The *Demonstrative Pronouns* are three, so, sin, sud *or* ud, so, *this*, sin, *that*, sud* *or* ud, *yon, yonder.*

III. The *Distributive Pronouns* are, gach, *each, every*, gach uile, contracted chuile, *or* h-uile, *every;* a chéile, *each other.*

INTERROGATIVE PRONOUNS.

The interrogative pronouns are, co? *who?* cia? *which?* ciod? *what?* and *nach*, which is used when a question is put in a negative form.

INDEFINITE PRONOUNS.

The indefinite pronouns express their subjects in a general manner; the following are of this description:

Càch, *the rest,*
Cuid, *some,*
Cuid eile, *some others,*
Eigin, *some,*
Eile, *other.*
Cia b' e, *whoever.*
Cia b' e air bith, *whoever.*
Co air bith, *whoever.*
Ciod air bith, *whatever*

COMPOUND PRONOUNS

The personal pronouns in Gaelic are often found combined with prepositions, which generally govern different cases, and, in that state, they form a part of speech which may be termed Compound Pronouns. The prepositions which are capable of being thus united, are the following: aig *or* ag, *at;* air, *on*, ann, *in*, as, *out of;* de, *off*, do, *to*, eadar, *between*, fo, fodha, *or* fuidh, *under*, gu, *till*, le, *with*, mu, *about*, o or ua, *from*, ri, *to*, roimh, *before*, thar, *over*, troimh, *through* The syllabic adjections, as has been said, throw the pronouns into the emphatic form.

AG, *or* AIG, AT.

	Singular	*Plural*
1st *pers*	Agam-sa, *at me,*	Againn-ne, *at us.*
2d *pers.*	Agad-sa, *at thee,*	Agaibh-se, *at you*
3d *pers*	Aige-se, *at him,* Aice-se, *at her*	Aca-sa, *at them*

AIR, ON.

	Singular.	*Plural.*
1st *pers.*	Orm-sa, *on me,*	Oirnn-ne, *on us.*
2d *pers.*	Ort-sa, *on thee,*	Oirbh-se, *on you.*
3d *pers.*	Air-san, *on him,* Oirre-se, *on her,* Orra-sa, *on her.*	Orra-san, *on them.*

ANN, IN.

	Singular	*Plural*
1st	Annam-sa, *in me,*	Annainn-ne, *in us.*
2d	Annad-sa, *in thee,*	Annaibh-se, *in you.*
3d	Ann-sa, *in him,* Innte-se, *in her*	Annta-sa, *in them.*

AS, OUT OF

	Singular.	*Plural.*
1st.	Asam-sa, *out of me,*	Asainn-ne, *out of us.*
2d	Asad-sa, *out of thee,*	Asaibh-se, *out of you.*
3d	As-san, *out of him,* Aisde-se, *out of her*	Asda-san, *out of them.*

DE, OF, or OFF.

	Singular.	*Plural.*
1st	Dhiom-sa, *off me,*	Dhinn-ne, *off us.*
2d.	Dhiot-sa, *off thee,*	Dhibh-se, *off you.*
3d	Dheth-se, *off him,* Dhi-se, *off her*	Dhiubh-san, *off them.*

DO, TO.

	Singular.	*Plural*
1st.	Dhomh-sa, *to me,*	Dhuinn-ne, *to us.*
2d.	Dhuit-se, *to thee,*	Dhuibh-se, *to you.*
3d.	Dha-san, *to him,* Dhi-se, *to her.*	Dhoibh-san, *to them.*

EADAR, BETWEEN.

No Singular.

	Plural
1st	Eadarainn-ne, *between us*
2d	Edaraibh-se, *between you*
3d	Eatorra-san, *between them.*

FO, FODHA, *or* FUIDH, UNDER

	Singular.	*Plural.*
1st.	Fodham-sa, *under me,*	Fodhainn-ne, *under us*
2d	Fodhad-sa, *under thee,*	Fodhaibh-se, *under you*
3d.	Fodha-sa, *under him,* Fuidhpe-se, *under her.*	Fodhpa-san, *under them*

GU, TO

	Singular	*Plural.*
1st.	H-ugam-sa, *to me,*	H-ugainn-ne, *to us.*
2d	H-ugad-sa,† *to thee,*	H-ugaibh-se, *to you.*
3d.	H-uige-san, *to him,* H-uice-sa, *to her.*	H-uca-san, *to them.*

LE, WITH.

	Singular.	*Plural.*
1st	Leam-sa, *with me,*	Leinn-ne, *with us.*
2d	Leat-sa, *with thee,*	Leibh-se, *with you*
3d.	Leis-san, *with him,* Leatha-sa, *with her*	Leo-san, *with them*

* *Sud* is perhaps a contracted form of *is ud*, yonder *is*, or are.

† *H-ugad*, and *h-ugaibh* are often used in the sense of *here is at you, beware, take care.*

MU, *about.*

	Singular.	*Plural.*
1st.	Umam-sa, *about me,*	Umainn-ne, *about us*
2d.	Umad-sa, *about thee,*	Umaibh-se, *about you.*
3d.	Uime-se, *about him,* Uimpe-se, *about her.*	Umpa-san, *about them.*

O, *or* U, *from.*

	Singular	*Plural*
1st.	Uam-sa, *from me,*	Uainn-ne, *from us*
2d.	Uait-se, *from thee,*	Uaibh-se, *from you.*
3d.	Uaith-se, *from him,* Uaipe-se, *from her.*	Uapa-sa, *from them.*

RI, *to.*

	Singular.	*Plural.*
1st.	Rium-sa, *to me,*	Ruinn-ne, *to us.*
2d.	Riut-sa, *to thee,*	Ribh-se, *to you.*
3d.	Ris-san, *to him,* Ria-sa, } *to her.* Rithe, }	Riu-san, *to them.*

ROIMH, *before*

	Singular.	*Plural.*
1st.	Romham-sa, *before me,*	Romhainn-ne, *before us*
2d.	Romhad-sa, *before thee,*	Romhaibh-se, *before you.*
3d.	Roimhe-se, *before him,* Roimpe-se, *before her*	Rompa-sa, *before them*

THAR, *over*

	Singular.	*Plural.*
1st.	Tharam-sa, *over me,*	Tharrainn-ne, *over us.*
2d.	Tharad-sa, *over thee,*	Tharraibh-se, *over you.*
3d.	Thairte, *over her,*	Tharta, *over them.*

TROIMH, *through.*

	Singular	*Plural.*
1st.	Tromham-sa, *through me,*	Tromhainn-ne, *through us*
2d.	Tromhad-sa, *through thee,*	Tromhaibh-se, *through you*
3d.	Troimhe-se, *through him,* Troimpe-se, *through her*	Trompa-san, *through them.*

CARDINAL NUMBERS.

1 Aon, a h-aon.	15 Cuig deug, còig deug.	28 Ochd ar fhichead.	300 Tri ceud.
2. Dhà, a dhà.	16 Se deug, sia deug.	29. Naoi 'r fhichead.	400 Ceithir cheud
3. Tri.	17. Seachd deug	30. Deich ar fhichead	500. Cuig ceud.
4 Ceithir	18. Ochd deug.	31. Aon deug 'ar fhichead	1,000. Mìle.
5 Cuig, còig.	19 Naoi deug.	32. Dha dheug ar fhichead	2,000 Da mhile
6. Sè, sia.	20 Fichead.	40. Da fhichead	3,000 Tri mile.
7. Seachd.	21 Aon thar fhichead	50 Da fhichead is deich	4,000. Ceithir mìle
8. Ochd.	22. Dha 'r fhichead	60. Tri fichead.	5,000 Cùig mìle
9 Naoi, naoth.	23. Tri 'ar fhichead	70. Tri fichead is deich.	10,000 Deich mile
10. Deich.	24. Ceithir 'ar fhichead.	80. Ceithir fichead.	20,000. Fichead mìle
11. Aon deug.	25. Cuig 'ar fhichead.	90. Ceithir fichead is deich.	100,000 Ceud mìle
12. Dhà dheug.	26. Sè ar fhichead.	100. Ceud, ciad.	200,000 Dà cheud mìle
13. Tri deug.	27. Seachd ar fhichead	200. Dà cheud.	1,000,000. Muillion, deich ceud mile
14. Ceithir deug.			

Cardinals joined to a Noun Masculine.	*Cardinals joined to a Noun Feminine*
1 Aon fhear, *one man.*	Aon chloch, *one stone.*
2. Dà fhear.	Dà chloich
3 Tri fir.	Tri clachan
4 Ceithir fir.	Ceithir clachan.
5 Cuig fir.	Cuig clachan.
6 Sè fir.	Sè clachan
7 Seachd fir.	Seachd clachan
8. Ochd fir.	Ochd clachan.
9. Naoi fir	Naoi clachan.
10 Deich fir.	Deich clachan
11. Aon fhear deug.	Aon chlach dheug.
12. Da fhear dheug.	Da chloich dheug
13. Tri fir dheug.	Tri clachan deug
14. Ceithir fir dheug.	Ceithir clachan deug.
15. Cuig fir dheug.	Cuig clachan deug.
16. Sè fir dheug.	Sè clachan deug.
17. Seachd fir dheug.	Seachd clachan deug.
18. Ochd fir dheug.	Ochd clachan deug.
19 Naoi fir dheug.	Naoi clachan deug.
20 Fichead fear.	Fichead clach
21 Aon fhear 'ar fhichead.	Aon chlach 'ar fhichead.
22. Da fhear 'ar fhichead	Da chloich 'ar fhichead.
23 Tri fir 'ar fhichead	Tri clacha fichead.
24 Ceithir fir fhichead.	Ceithir clacha fichead.
30 Deich fir fhichead.	Deich clachan fichead
31. Aon fhear deug 'ar fhichead.	Aon chlach dheug 'ar fhichead.
32. Da fhear dheug 'ar fhichead.	Da chloich dheug 'ar fhichead.
35. Cuig fir dheug 'ar fhichead.	Cuig clachan deug 'ar fhichead
40. Da fhichead fear.	Da fhichead clach.

Cardinals joined to a Noun Masculine.		*Cardinals joined to a Noun Feminine.*
41.	Fear is da fhichead.*	Clach 's da fhichead †
42.	Da fhear is da fhichead.	Da chloich 's da fhichead.
50	Deich fir is da fhichead ‡	Deich clachan 's da fhichead
60.	Tri fichead fear	Tri fichead clach.
61.	Tri fichead fear is h-aon.	Tri fichead clach is h-aon.
70.	Tri fichead fear is deich.	Tri fichead clach is deich.
80	Ceithir fichead fear.	Ceithir fichead clach.
100	Ceud fear.	Ceud clach.
101	Ceud fear is h-aon.	Ceud clach is h-aon
102.	Ceud fear is dhà.	Ceud clach is dha.
200.	Dà cheud fear	Da cheud clach.
300	Tri cheud fear.	Tri cheud clach.
400	Ceithir cheud fear	Ceithir cheud clach.
500.	Cuig ceud fear.	Cuig ceud clach
600.	Sè ceud fear.	Sè ceud clach
700	Seachd ceud fear.	Seachd ceud clach.
800	Ochd ceud fear	Ochd ceud clach
900	Naoi ceud fear	Naoi ceud clach.
1,000	Mile fear	Mile clach
1,001	Mile fear is h-aon.	Mile clach is h-aon.
1,020	Mile fear fhichead	Mile clacha fichead
1,021	Mile fear fhichead is h-aon.	Mile clacha fichead is h-aon.
1,030	Mile fear fhichead is deich.	Mile clacha fichead is deich.
2,000.	Da mhile fear	Da mhile clach.
3,000	Tri mile fear.	Tri mile clach.
4,000	Ceithir mile fear.	Ceithir mile clach
5,000	Cuig mile fear.	Cuig mile clach
10,000.	Deich mile fear.	Deich mile clach
10,020	Deich mile fhichead fear.	Deich mile fichead clach
20,000	Fichead mile fear.	Fichead mile clach
100,000.	Muillion fear.	Muillion clach.

ORDINALS

1. An ceud.
2. An dara.
3. An treas.
4. An ceathramh
5 An cuigeamh
6. An seathamh.
7. An seachdamh.
8 An t-ochdamh.
9. An naothamh.
10 An deicheamh.
11 An t-aon deug
12. An dara deug
13. { An treas / An triamh } deug.
14. An ceathramh deug
15. An cuigeamh deug.
16 An seathamh deug.
17 An seachdamh deug.
18. An t-ochdamh deug
19. An naothamh deug.
20. Am ficheadamh.
21 An t-aon 'ar fhichead
22 An dar' 'ar fhichead
23. An treas 'ar fhichead.
24. An ceathramh 'ar fhichead.
25. An cuigeamh 'ar fhichead.
26. An seathamh fhichead.
27. An seachdamh 'ar fhichead.
28. An t-ochdamh 'ar fhichead.
29 An naothamh 'ar fhichead
30 An deicheamh 'ar fhichead.
31. An t-aon deug 'ar fhichead
32. An dara deug 'ar fhichead.
33 An treas deug 'ar fhichead
34 An ceathramh deug 'ar fhichead
35 An cuigeamh deug 'ar fhichead.
36. An seathamh deug 'ar fhichead.
37. An seachdamh deug 'ar fhichead.
38 An t-ochdamh deug 'ar fhichead.
39 An naothamh deug 'ar fhichead
40. An da fhicheadamh.
41 An t-aon 'ar da fhichead.
50 { An deicheamh 'ar da fhichead. / An leth-cheudamh }
51 An t-aon deug 'ar da fhichead.
60. An tri ficheadamh.
70 An deicheamh 'ar tri fichead
80 An ceithir ficheadamh.
90 An deicheamh 'ar ceithir fichead.
100. An ceadamh
110. An deicheamh 'ar ceud.
120. An seathamh fichead.
130. An deicheamh 'ar sè fichead.
140. An seachdamh fichead.
150 An deichamh 'ar seachd fichead.
160. An t-ochdamh fichead.
170. An deicheamh 'ar ochd fichead.
180. An naothamh fichead
190. An deichamh 'ar naoi fichead.
1,000. Am mileamh.
2,000. An da mhìleamh.
3,000. An tri mileamh.
4,000 An ceithir mileamh
5,000 An cuig mileamh.
6,000. An sia mileamh
10,000. An deich mileamh.

* We also say, *da fhichead fear 's a h-aon, da fhichead fear 's a dha*, &c

† We also say, *da fhichead clach 's a h-aon, da fhichead clach 's a dhà*, &c

‡ Also, *leth cheud fear*

Ordinals joined to a Noun Masculine.	*Ordinals joined to a Noun Feminine.*
1. An ceud fhear, *the first man.*	A cheud chlach, *the first stone*
2. An dara fear	An dara clach.
3. An treas fear, an triamh fear	An treas clach
4. An ceathramh fear.	An ceathramh clach
5. An cuigeamh fear.	An cuigeamh clach
6. An seathamh fear	An seathamh clach
7. An seachdamh fear.	An seachdamh clach
8. An t-ochdamh fear.	An t-ochdamh clach
9. An naothamh fear.	An naothamh clach.
10. An deicheamh fear	An deicheamh clach
11. An t-aon fhear deug	An t-aon chlach deug
12. An dara fear deug	An dara clach deug.
13. An treas fear deug.	An treas clach deug
14. An ceathramh fear deug.	An ceathramh clach deug
15 An cuigeamh fear deug.	An cuigeamh clach deug.
16. An seathamh fear deug	An seathamh clach deug.
17. An seachdamh fear deug.	An seachdamh clach deug.
20 Am ficheadamh fear.	Am ficheadamh clach.
21. An t-aon fhear fichead.*	An t-aon chlach fichead †
22. An dara fear fhichead.	An dara clach fichead
31. An t-aon fhear deug 'ar fhichead.	An t-aon chlach deug 'ar fhichead
32 An dara fear deug 'ar fhichead.	An dara clach deug 'ar fhichead
40. An dà fhicheadamh fear	An da fhicheadamh clach
70. An deichamh fear 'ar tri fichead.	An deicheamh clach 'ar tri fichead.
100. An ceudamh fear	An ceudamh clach
101. An t-aon fhear thar cheud.	An t-aon chlach thar cheud.
102. An dara fear thar cheud.	An dara clach thar cheud.
200. An da cheudamh fear	An da cheudamh clach.
230. An deicheamh fear fhichead thar da cheud	An deichamh clach fhichead thar dà cheud.
300. An tri cheudamh fear.	An tri cheudamh clach.
500. An cuig ceadamh fear.	An cùig ceudamh clach.
1000. Am mileamh fear.	Am mileamh clach
10,000. An deich mileamh fear	An deich mileamh clach.

The following Numerals are applied only to Persons; thus,

2. Dithis mhac, *two sons*
3. Triùir mhac, *three sons*
4. Ceathrar mhac, *four sons.*
5. Cuignear mhac, *five sons*
6. Sèanar mhac, *six sons.*
7. Seachdnar mhac, *seven sons.*
8. Ochdnar mhac, *eight sons*
9. Naothnar mhac, *nine sons.*
10. Deichnar mhac, *ten sons.*

OF THE VERB.

A Verb expresses action, being, or suffering

In Gaelic there are two conjugations The first comprehends all those verbs which begin with any consonant, except *f*, as, paisg, *wrap*. Under the second are arranged those which begin with a vowel or with *f*, as, òb, *refuse*, fill, *fold*.

The Gaelic verb is declined by Voices, Moods, Tenses, Numbers, and Persons.

There are two Voices; Active and Passive.

The different particles of conjunction and adverb in Gaelic might give rise to a variety of moods, but they may be reduced into the five following:—The Affirmative, or Indicative, the Negative, or Interrogative, the Subjunctive, or Optative, the Imperative, and the Infinitive.

There are three times or tenses; the Present, Preterite, and Future.

There are two numbers, Singular and Plural

There are three persons, First, Second, and Third.

Verbs, like nouns, are inflected by aspirating the initial consonant, and by an occasional change of termination.

* We also say, *An t-aon fear 'ar fhichead, an dara fear 'ar fhichead, an treas fear 'ar fhichead*, &c.

† We also say, *An t-aon chlach 'ar fhicheud, an dara clach 'ar fhichead, an treas clach 'ar fhichead*, &c.

THE FIRST CONJUGATION.

PAISG, wrap.

ACTIVE VOICE.

AFFIRMATIVE, or INDICATIVE MOOD.

	Preterite		*Future.*
Sing	Phaisg mi, *I wrapped* Phaisg thu, *thou wrappedst*, or *didst wrap*. Phaisg e, *he wrapped*.	*Sing.*	Paisgidh mi, *I shall* or *will* Paisgidh tu, *thou shalt* or *wilt* Paisgidh se *or* e, *he shall* or *will* } *wrap*.
Plur	Phaisg sinn, *we* Phaisg sibh, *ye* or *you* Phaisg iad, *they* } *wrapped*.	*Plur.*	Paisgidh sinn, *we shall* or *will* Paisgidh sibh, *ye* or *you shall* or *will* Paigidh siad *or* iad, *they shall* or *will* } *wrap*.

NEGATIVE, or INTERROGATIVE MOOD.

	Preterite.		*Future.*
Sing Cha	Do phaisg mi, *I wrapped not*, or *did not wrap* Do phaisg thu, *thou didst not wrap*. Do phaisg e, *he did not wrap*	*Sing.* Cha	Phaisg mi, *I shall* or *will not* Phaisg thu, *thou shalt* or *wilt not* Phaisg e, *he shall* or *will not* } *wrap*.
Plur. Cha	Do phaisg sinn, *we did not* Do phaisg sibh, *ye* or *you did not* Do phaisg iad, *they did not* } *wrap*.	*Plur* Cha	Phaisg sinn, *we shall* or *will not* Phaisg sibh, *ye* or *you shall* or *will not* Phaisg iad, *they shall* or *will not* } *wrap*.
Sing Nach	Do phaisg mi, *did I not* Do phaisg thu, *did thou not* Do phaisg e, *did he not* } *wrap?*	*Sing.* Nach	Paisg mi, *shall I not* Paisg thu, *shalt thou not* Paisg e, *shall he not* } *wrap?*
Plur. Nach	Do phaisg sinn, *did we not* Do phaisg sibh, *did ye* or *you not* Do phaisg iad, *did they not* } *wrap?*	*Plur.* Nach	Paisg sinn, *shall we not* Paisg sibh, *shall ye* or *you not* Paisg iad, *shall they not* } *wrap?*
Sing Mur	Do phaisg mi, *if I did not* Do phaisg thu, *if thou didst not* Do phaisg e, *if he did not* } *wrap*.	*Sing.* Mur	Paisg mi, *if I shall* or *will not* Paisg thu, *if thou shalt* or *wilt not* Paisg e, *if he shall* or *will not*. } *wrap*.
Plur. Mur	Do phaisg sinn, *if we did not* Do phaisg sibh, *if ye* or *you did not* Do phaisg iad, *if they did not* } *wrap*.	*Plur.* Mur	Paisg sinn, *if we shall* or *will not* Paisg sibh, *if you shall* or *will not* Paisg iad, *if they shall* or *will not* } *wrap*.

SUBJUNCTIVE MOOD.

	Preterite		*Future.*
Sing	Phaisginn, *I might, could*, or *would* Phaisgeadh tu, *thou mightst, couldst*, or *wouldst* Phaisgeadh e, *he might, could*, or *would* } *wrap*.	*Sing.* Ma	Phaisgeas mi, *if I shall* or *will* Phaisgeas tu, *if thou shalt* or *wilt* Phaisgeas e, *if he shall* or *will* } *wrap*.
Plur.	Phaisgeadh sinn, *or* phaisgeamaid, *we might, could*, or *would* Phaisgeadh sibh, *ye* or *you might, could*, or *would* Phaisgeadh iad, *they might, could*, or *would* } *wrap*.	*Plur* Ma	Phaisgeas sinn, *if we shall* or *will* Phaisgeas sibh, *if you shall* or *will* Phaisgeas iad, *if they shall* or *will* } *wrap*.

Sing Nam	Paisginn, *if I might* or *were to* Paisgeadh tu, *if thou mightst* or *wert to* Paisgeadh e, *if he might* or *were to* } *wrap*
Plur. Nàm	Paisgeadh sinn, *if we might* or *were to* Paisgeadh sibh, *if ye* or *you might* or *were to* Paisgeadh iad, *if they might* or *were to* } *wrap*.

IMPERATIVE MOOD.

Sing.	Paisgeam, *let me wrap*. Paisg, *wrap thou*. Paisgeadh e, *let him wrap*
Plur.	Paisgeamaid, *let us wrap* Paisgibh, *wrap ye* or *you* Paisgeadh iad, *let them wrap*

INFINITIVE MOOD.

A phasgadh,
Do phasgadh, } *to wrap*.

PARTICIPLE.

A pasgadh,
Ag pasgadh, } *wrapping*.

PASSIVE VOICE.

AFFIRMATIVE, or INDICATIVE MOOD.

Preterite.	*Future.*
Sing. Phaisgeadh { mi, *I was*; thu, *thou wast*; e, *he was* } *wrapped.*	*Sing* Paisgear { mi, *I shall* or *will be*; thu, *thou shalt* or *wilt be*; e, *he shall* or *will be* } *wrapped.*
Plur. Phaisgeadh { sinn, *we were*; sibh, *ye* or *you were*; iad, *they were* } *wrapped.*	*Plur.* Paisgear { sinn, *we shall* or *will be*; sibh, *ye* or *you shall* or *will be*; iad, *they shall* or *will be* } *wrapped*

NEGATIVE, or INTERROGATIVE MOOD.

Preterite.	*Future.*
Sing. An do phaisgeadh { mi, *was I*; thu, *wert thou*; e, *was he* } *wrapped?*	*Sing* Am paisgear { mi, *shall I be*; thu, *shalt thou be*; e, *shall he be* } *wrapped?*
Plur An do phaisgeadh { sinn, *were we*; sibh, *were ye* or *you*; iad, *were they* } *wrapped?*	*Plur* Am paisgear { sinn, *shall we be*; sibh, *shalt ye be*; iad, *shall they be* } *wrapped?*
Sing. Cha do phaisgeadh { mi, *I was not*; thu, *thou wert not*; e, *he was not* } *wrapped*	*Sing.* Cha phaisgear { mi, *I shall not be*; thu, *thou shalt not be*; e, *he shall not be* } *wrapped.*
Plur. Cha do phaisgeadh { sinn, *we were not*; sibh, *ye* or *you were not*; iad, *they were not* } *wrapped*	*Plur* Cha phaisgear { sinn, *we shall not be*; sibh, *ye* or *you shall not be*; iad, *they shall not be* } *wrapped*
Sing. Nach do phaisgeadh { mi, *was I not*; thu, *wert thou not*; e, *was he not* } *wrapped?*	*Sing.* Nach paisgear { mi *shall I not be*; thu, *shalt thou not be*; e, *shall he not be* } *wrapped?*
Plur. Nach do phaisgeadh { sinn, *were we not*; sibh, *were ye not*; iad, *were they not* } *wrapped?*	*Plur.* Nach paisgear { sinn, *shall we not be*; sibh, *shall ye* or *you not be*; iad, *shall they not be* } *wrapped?*
Sing. Mur do phaisgeadh { mi, *if I was not*; thu, *if thou wert not*; e, *if he was not* } *wrapped.*	*Sing.* Mur paisgear { mi, *if I shall not be*; thu, *if thou shalt not be*; e, *if he shall not be* } *wrapped*
Plur. Mur do phaisgeadh { sinn, *if we were not*; sibh, *if ye were not*; iad, *if they were not* } *wrapped.*	*Plur.* Mur paisgear { sinn, *if we shall not be*; sibh, *if you shall not be*; iad, *if they shall not be* } *wrapped*

Sing. Nam paisgeadh { mi, *if I were*; thu, *if thou wert*; e, *if he were* } *wrapped*

Plur. Nam paisgeudh { sinn, *if we were*; sibh, *if you were*; iad, *if they were* } *wrapped*

SUBJUNCTIVE MOOD.

Preterite.	*Future.*
Sing. Phaisgteadh { mi, *I could* or *would be*; thu, *thou couldst* or *wouldst be*; e, *he could* or *would be* } *wrapped.*	*Sing.* Ma phaisgear { mi, *if I shall be*; thu, *if thou shalt be*; e, *if he shall be* } *wrapped*
Plur. Phaisgteadh { sinn, *we could* or *would be*; sibh, *ye could* or *would be*; iad, *they could* or *would be* } *wrapped*	*Plur.* Ma phaisgear { sinn, *if we shall be*; sibh, *if you shall be*; iad, *if they shall be* } *wrapped*

IMPERATIVE MOOD.	PARTICIPLE.
Sing Paisgtear { mi, *let me be*; thu, *be thou*; e, *let him be* } *wrapped.*	Paisgte, Air pasgadh, } *wrapped.*
Plur. Paisgtear { sinn, *let us be*; sibh, *be ye*; iad, *let them be* } *wrapped*	

PAISG, DECLINED WITH THE AUXILIARY VERB *BI* AND THE PRESENT PARTICIPLE.

ACTIVE VOICE

AFFIRMATIVE MOOD.

Present

Sing	Tha mi	'pasgadh,	*I am*	*wrapping.*
	Tha thu		*thou art*	
	Tha e		*he is*	
Plur.	Tha sinn	a pasgadh,	*we are*	*wrapping*
	Tha sibh		*ye are*	
	Tha iad		*they are*	

Preterite.

Sing	Bha mi	'pasgadh,	*I was*	*wrapping.*
	Bha thu		*thou wert*	
	Bha e		*he was*	
Plur.	Bha sinn	a pasgadh,	*we were*	*wrapping.*
	Bha sibh		*ye were*	
	Bha iad		*they were*	

Future.

Sing.	Bithidh mi	'pasgadh,	*I shall be*	*wrapping.*
	Bithidh tu		*thou shalt be*	
	Bithidh se		*he shall be*	

Future.

Plur	Bithidh sinn	a pasgadh	*we shall be*	*wrapping.*
	Bithidh sibh		*you shall be*	
	Bithidh siad		*they shall be*	

NEGATIVE, OR INTERROGATIVE MOOD.

Present

Sing	Am bheil mi	'pasgadh,	*am I*	*wrapping?*
	Am bheil thu		*art thou*	
	Am bheil e		*is he*	
Plur	Am bheil sinn	a pasgadh,	*are we*	*wrapping?*
	Am bheil sibh		*are ye*	
	Am bheil iad		*are they*	

Preterite.

Sing	An robh mi	'pasgadh,	*was I*	*wrapping?*
	An robh thu		*wert thou*	
	An robh e		*was he*	
Plur.	An robh sinn	a pasgadh,	*were we*	*wrapping?*
	An robh sibh		*were ye*	
	An robh iad		*were they*	

Future.

Sing.	Am bi mi	'pasgadh,	*shall I be*	*wrapping?*
	Am bi thu		*shalt thou be*	
	Am bi e		*shall he be*	
Sing	Cha 'n 'eil mi	'pasgadh,	*I am not*	*wrapping.*
	Cha 'n 'eil thu		*thou art not*	
	Cha 'n 'eil e		*he is not*	
Plur	Cha 'n 'eil sinn	a pasgadh,	*we are not*	*wrapping.*
	Cha 'n 'eil sibh		*you are not*	
	Cha 'n 'eil iad		*they are not*	
Sing	Cha bhi mi	'pasgadh,	*I shall not*	*be wrapping.*
	Cha bhi thu		*thou shalt not*	
	Cha bhi e		*he shall not*	

Future.

Plur.	Am bi sinn	a pasgadh,	*shall we be*	*wrapping?*
	Am bi sibh		*shall ye be*	
	Am bi iad		*shall they be*	
Sing.	Cha robh mi	'pasgadh,	*I was not*	*wrapping.*
	Cha robh thu		*thou wert not*	
	Cha robh e		*he was not*	
Plur.	Cha robh sinn	a pasgadh,	*we were not*	*wrapping.*
	Cha robh sibh		*ye were not*	
	Cha robh iad		*they were not*	
Plur	Cha bhi sinn	a pasgadh,	*we shall not*	*be wrapping.*
	Cha bhi sibh		*you shall not*	
	Cha bhi iad		*they shall not*	

Present

Sing	Nach 'eil mi	'pasgadh,	*am I not*	*wrapping?*
	Nach 'eil thu		*art thou not*	
	Nach 'eil e		*is he not*	
Plur	Nach 'eil sinn	a pasgadh,	*are we not*	*wrapping?*
	Nach 'eil sibh		*are ye not*	
	Nach 'eil iad		*are they not*	

Preterite

Sing.	Nach robh mi	'pasgadh,	*was I not*	*wrapping?*
	Nach robh thu		*wert thou not*	
	Nach robh e		*was he not*	
Plur	Nach robh sinn	a pasgadh,	*were we not*	*wrapping?*
	Nach robh sibh		*were ye not*	
	Nach robh iad		*were they not*	

Future

Sing.	Nach bi mi	'pasgadh,	*shall I not*	*be wrapping?*
	Nach bi thu		*shalt thou not*	
	Nach bi e		*shall he not*	

Future

Plur	Nach bi sinn	a pasgadh,	*shall we not*	*be wrapping?*
	Nach bi sibh		*shall ye not*	
	Nach bi iad		*shall they not*	

Present.

Sing	Mur 'eil mi	'pasgadh,	*if I am not*	*wrapping.*
	Mur 'eil thu		*if thou art not*	
	Mur 'eil e		*if he is not*	
Plur	Mur 'eil sinn	a pasgadh,	*if we are not*	*wrapping.*
	Mur 'eil sibh		*if ye are not*	
	Mur 'eil iad		*if they are not*	

Preterite.

Sing.	Mur robh mi	'pasgadh,	*if I was not*	*wrapping.*
	Mur robh thu		*if thou wert not*	
	Mur robh e		*if he was not*	
Plur	Mur robh sinn	a pasgadh,	*if we were not*	*wrapping.*
	Mur robh sibh		*if ye were not*	
	Mur robh iad		*if they were not*	

Future

Sing.	Mur bi mi	'pasgadh,	*if I shall not*	*be wrapping.*
	Mur bi thu		*if thou shalt not*	
	Mur bi e		*if he shall not*	

Future.

Plur	Mur bi sinn	a pasgadh,	*if we shall not*	*be wrapping.*
	Mur bi sibh		*if ye shall not*	
	Mur bi iad		*if they shall not*	

SUBJUNCTIVE MOOD.

Preterite.

Sing.	Bhithinn	'pasgadh,	*I would be*	*wrapping*
	Bhitheadh tu		*thou wouldst be*	
	Bhitheadh e		*he would be*	
Plur	Bhitheamaid	a pasgadh,	*we would be*	*wrapping*
	Bhitheadh sibh		*ye would be*	
	Bhitheadh iad		*they would be*	

Future.

Sing	Ma bhitheas mi	'pasgadh,	*if I shall be*	*wrapping*
	Ma bhitheas tu		*if thou shalt be*	
	Ma bhitheas e		*if he shall be*	
Plur.	Ma bhitheas sinn	a pasgadh,	*if we shall be*	*wrapping*
	Ma bhitheas sibh		*if you shall be*	
	Ma bhitheas iad		*if they shall be*	

THE PRETERITE DECLINED WITH CHA.

Sing.	Am bithinn	'pasgadh,	*would I be*	*wrapping?*
	Am bitheadh tu		*wouldst thou be*	
	Am bitheadh e		*would he be*	
Plur	Am bitheamaid	a pasgadh,	*would we be*	*wrapping?*
	Am bitheadh sibh		*would ye be*	
	Am bitheadh iad		*would they be*	
Sing.	Cha bhithinn	'pasgadh,	*I would not be*	*wrapping*
	Cha bhitheadh tu		*thou wouldst not be*	
	Cha bhitheadh e		*he would not be*	
Plur.	Cha bhitheadh sinn	a pasgadh,	*we would not be*	*wrapping.*
	Cha bhitheadh sibh		*ye would not be*	
	Cha bhitheadh iad		*they would not be*	
Sing.	Mur bithinn	'pasgadh,	*if I would not be*	*wrapping.*
	Mur bitheadh tu		*if thou wouldst not be*	
	Mur bitheadh e		*if he would not be*	
Plur.	Mur bitheamaid, *or*	a pasgadh,	*if we would not be*	*wrapping.*
	Mur bitheadh sinn		*if ye would not be*	
	Mur bitheadh sibh		*if they would not be*	
	Mur bitheadh iad			

IMPERATIVE MOOD,

Sing.	Bitheam	'pasgadh,	*let me be*	*wrapping.*
	Bi, bi thusa		*be thou*	
	Bitheadh e		*let him be*	
Plur.	Bitheamaid	a pasgadh,	*let us be*	*wrapping*
	Bithibh		*be ye*	
	Bitheadh iad		*let them be*	

INFINITIVE MOOD.

Bhith, *or* a bhith pasgadh, } *to be wrapping*
Do bhith pasgadh,

PASSIVE VOICE.

AFFIRMATIVE.*

Present.

Sing.	Tha mi	paisgte,	*I am*	*wrapped*
	Tha thu		*thou art*	
	Tha e		*he is*	
Plur	Tha sinn	paisgte,	*we are*	*wrapped.*
	Tha sibh		*ye are*	
	Tha iad		*they are*	

Preterite.

Sing.	Bha mi	paisgte,	*I was*	*wrapped.*
	Bha thu		*thou wert*	
	Bha e		*he was*	
Plur.	Bha sinn	paisgte,	*we were*	*wrapped*
	Bha sibh		*ye were*	
	Bha iad		*they were*	

Future

Sing.	Bithidh mi	paisgte,	*I shall be*	*wrapped.*
	Bithidh tu		*thou shalt be*	
	Bithidh se		*he shall be*	
Plur.	Bithidh sinn	paisgte,	*we shall be*	*wrapped.*
	Bithidh sibh		*ye shall be*	
	Bithidh siad		*they shall be*	

* Another form of the present, preterite, and future affirmative is, *Tha mi air mo phasgadh, &c.*, *Bha mi air mo phasgadh, &c.*, *Bithidh mi air mo phasgadh, &c.*

NEGATIVE, OR INTERROGATIVE MOOD.

Present.

Sing. Am	bheil mi	paisgte,	*am I*	*wrapping?*
	bheil thu		*art thou*	
	bheil e		*is he*	
Plur. Am	bheil sinn	paisgte,	*are we*	*wrapping?*
	bheil sibh		*are ye*	
	bheil iad		*are they*	

Preterite

Sing. An	robh mi	paisgte,	*was I*	*wrapped?*
	robh thu		*wert thou*	
	robh e		*was he*	
Plur. An	robh sinn	paisgte,	*were we*	*wrapped?*
	robh sibh		*were ye*	
	robh iad		*were they*	

Future.

Sing. Am	bi mi	paisgte,	*shall I be*	*wrapped?*
	bi thu		*shalt thou be*	
	bi e		*shall he be*	
Plur. Am	bi sinn	paisgte,	*shall we be*	*wrapped?*
	bi sibh		*shall ye be*	
	bi iad		*shall they be*	

Present.

Sing Nach	'eil mi	paisgte,	*am I not*	*wrapped?*
	'eil thu		*art thou not*	
	'eil e		*is he not*	
Plur Nach	'eil sinn	paisgte,	*are we not*	*wrapped?*
	'eil sibh		*are ye not*	
	'eil iad		*are they not*	

Preterite.

Sing Nach	robh mi	paisgte,	*was I not*	*wrapped?*
	robh thu		*wert thou not*	
	robh e		*was he not*	
Plur Nach	robh sinn	paisgte,	*were we not*	*wrapped?*
	robh sibh		*were ye not*	
	robh iad		*were they not*	

Future.

Sing. Nach	bi mi	paisgte,	*shall I not be*	*wrapped?*
	bi thu		*shalt thou not be*	
	bi e		*shall he not be*	
Plur. Nach	bi sinn	paisgte,	*shall we not be*	*wrapped?*
	bi sibh		*shall ye not be*	
	bi iad		*shall they not be*	

Present

Sing Cha 'n	'eil mi	paisgte,	*I am not*	*wrapped.*
	'eil thu		*thou art not*	
	'eil e		*he is not*	
Plur. Cha 'n	'eil sinn	paisgte,	*we are not*	*wrapped.*
	'eil sibh		*ye are not*	
	'eil iad		*they are not*	

Preterite.

Sing. Cha	robh mi	paisgte,	*I was not*	*wrapped.*
	robh thu		*thou wert not*	
	robh e		*he was not*	
Plur. Cha	robh sinn	paisgte,	*we were not*	*wrapped.*
	robh sibh		*ye were not*	
	robh iad,		*they were not*	

Future

Sing Cha	bhi mi	paisgte,	*I shall not be*	*wrapped.*
	bhi thu		*thou shalt not be*	
	bhi e		*he shall not be*	
Plur Cha	bhi sinn	paisgte,	*we shall not be*	*wrapped.*
	bhi sibh		*ye shall not be*	
	bhi iad		*they shall not be*	

SUBJUNCTIVE MOOD.

Preterite.

Sing.	Bhithinn	paisgte,*	*I would be*	*wrapped*
	Bhitheadh tu		*thou wouldst be*	
	Bhitheadh e		*he would be*	
Plur.	Bhitheamaid, *or*	paisgte,	*we would be*	*wrapped*
	Bhitheadh sinn			
	Bhitheadh sibh		*ye would be*	
	Bhitheadh iad		*they would be*	

Future

Sing. Ma bhitheas	mi	paisgte,	*if I shall be*	*wrapped*
	tu		*if thou shalt be*	
	e		*if he shall be*	
Plur. Ma bhitheas	sinn	paisgte,	*if we shall be*	*wrapped.*
	sibh		*if ye shall be*	
	iad		*if they shall be*	

IMPERATIVE MOOD.

Sing	Bitheam	paisgte,	*let me be*	*wrapped.*
	Bi, bi thusa		*be thou*	
	Bitheadh e		*let him be*	
Plur.	Bitheamaid	paisgte,	*let us be*	*wrapped.*
	Bithibh, bithibhse		*be ye*	
	Bitheadh iad		*let them be*	

INFINITIVE MOOD.

A bhith paisgte,
Do bhith paisgte, } *to be wrapped*

PARTICIPLE.

Air bhith paisgte, *having been wrapped*

* Another form of the preterite and future subjunctive is, *Bhithinn air mo phasgadh, &c* , *Ma bhitheas mi air mo phasgadh, &c*

THE SECOND CONJUGATION.*

ÒL, drink

ACTIVE VOICE

INDICATIVE, OR AFFIRMATIVE MOOD.

	Preterite			Future.	
Sing. Dh' òl	mi, *I drank* thu, *thou drankest.* e, *he drank.*		*Sing* Òlaidh	mi, *I shall* or *will* tu, *thou shalt* or *wilt* se, *he shall* or *will*	*drink*
Plur Dh' òl	sinn, *we drank* sibh, *ye drank.* iad, *they drank*		*Plur.* Òlaidh	sinn, *we shall* or *will* sibh, *ye shall* or *will* siad, *they shall* or *will*	*drink*

NEGATIVE, OR INTERROGATIVE MOOD

	Preterite			Future	
Sing. An d' òl	mi, *did I drink*, or *have I* thu, *didst thou drink*, or *hast thou* e, *did he drink*, or *has he*	*drunk?*	*Sing* An òl	mi, *shall* or *will I* thu, *shalt* or *wilt thou* e, *shall* or *will he*	*drink?*
Plur. An d' òl	sinn, *did we drink*, or *have we* sibh, *did ye drink*, or *have ye* iad, *did they drink*, or *have they*	*drunk?*	*Plur* An òl	sinn, *shall* or *will we* sibh, *shall* or *will ye* iad, *shall* or *will they*	*drink?*
Sing. Cha d' òl	mi, *I did not drink*, or *have not* thu, *thou didst not drink*, or *hast not* e, *he did not drink*, or *has not*	*drunk*	*Sing* Cha 'n ol	mi, *I shall* or *will not* thu, *thou shalt* or *wilt not* e, *he shall* or *will not*	*drink*
Plur. Cha d' òl	sinn, *we did not drink*, or *have not* sibh, *ye did not drink*, or *have not* iad, *they did not drink*, or *have not*	*drunk*	*Plur* Cha 'n òl	sinn, *we shall* or *will not* sibh, *ye shall* or *will not* iad, *they shall* or *will not*	*drink*
Sing. Nach d' òl	mi, *did I not drink*, or *have I not* thu, *didst thou not drink*, or *hast thou not* e, *did he not drink*, or *has he not*	*drunk?*	*Sing.* Nach òl	mi, *shall* or *will not I* thu, *shalt* or *wilt not thou* e, *shall* or *will not he*	*drink?*
Plur. Nach d' òl	sinn, *did we not drink*, or *have we not* sibh, *did ye not drink*, or *have ye not* iad, *did they not drink*, or *have they not*	*drunk?*	*Plur* Nach òl	sinn, *shall* or *will not we* sibh, *shall* or *will not ye* iad, *shall* or *will not they*	*drink?*

SUBJUNCTIVE MOOD

	Preterite			Future.	
Sing	Dh' òlainn, *I would* or *could* Dh' òladh tu, *thou wouldst* or *couldst* Dh' òladh e, *he would* or *could*	*drink.*	*Sing* Ma dh' òlas	mi *if I shall* or *will* tu, *if thou shalt* or *wilt* e, *if he shall* or *will*	*drink*
Plur	Dh' òlamaid, *or* dh' òladh sinn, *we would* or *could* Dh' òladh sibh, *ye would* or *could* Dh' òladh iad, *they would* or *could*	*drink.*	*Plur.* Ma dh' òlas†	sinn, *if we shall* or *will* sibh, *if ye shall* or *will* iad, *if they shall* or *will*	*drink*

IMPERATIVE MOOD.

Sing.
- Òlam, *let me drink*
- Òl, ol thusa, *drink thou*
- Òladh e, *let him drink*

Plur
- Òlamaid, *let us drink*
- Òlaibh, *drink ye.*
- Òladh iad, *let them drink*

INFINITIVE MOOD

A dh' òl, *to drink*

PARTICIPLE

Ag òl, *drinking*

* The second conjugation, as has been said, comprehends all those verbs which begin with a vowel or with the letter *f*

† It does not appear necessary to exemplify, any further, the preterite subjunctive inflected with the various particles of conjunction. The young student cannot be at any loss if he but turn back to the preceding verbs

PASSIVE VOICE.

This verb is not often used in the passive voice, excepting in the third person singular and plural.

AFFIRMATIVE, OR INDICATIVE MOOD.

Preterite.	*Future.*
Sing. Dh' òladh e, *it was drunk.*	*Sing.* Òlar e, *it shall be drunk.*

NEGATIVE, OR INTERROGATIVE MOOD.

Preterite.	*Future.*
Sing Cha d' òladh e, *it was not drunk.*	*Sing* Cha 'n òlar e, *it shall not be drunk*
Plur Cha d' òladh iad, *they were not drunk.*	*Plur.* Cha 'n òlar iad, *they shall not be drunk*
Sing. Nach d' òladh e, *was it not drunk?*	*Sing.* Nach òlar e, *shall it not be drunk?*
Plur Nach d' òlar iad, *were they not drunk?*	*Plur.* Nach òlar iad, *shall they not be drunk?*

SUBJUNCTIVE MOOD

Preterite.	*Future.*
Sing Dh' òltadh e, *it would be drunk*	*Sing.* Ma dh' òlar e, *if it shall be drunk.*
Plur Dh' òltadh iad, *they would be drunk.*	*Plur.* Ma dh' òlar iad, *if they shall be drunk*

IMPERATIVE MOOD.	PARTICIPLE
Sing Òltar e, *let it be drunk.*	Olta, òilte, } *drunk.*
Plur Òltar iad, *let them be drunk*	Air òl, } *drunk.*

ORDUICH, *order.*

ACTIVE VOICE.

AFFIRMATIVE, OR INDICATIVE MOOD.

Preterite.	*Future*
Sing. Dh' orduich { mi, *I* / thu, *thou* / e, *he* } *ordered.*	*Sing.* Orduichidh { mi, *I shall* or *will* / tu, *thou shalt* or *wilt* / e, *he shall* or *will* } *order*
Plur Dh' orduich { sinn, *we* / sibh, *ye* / iad, *they* } *ordered.*	*Plur.* Orduichidh { sinn, *we shall* or *will* / sibh, *ye shall* or *will* / iad, *they shall* or *will* } *order.*

NEGATIVE, OR INTERROGATIVE MOOD.

Preterite	*Future.*
Sing. An d' orduich { mi, *did I order*, or *have I* / thu, *didst thou order*, or *hast thou* / e, *did he order*, or *has he* } *ordered?*	*Sing* An orduich { mi, *shall* or *will I* / thu, *shalt* or *wilt thou* / e, *shall* or *will he* } *order?*
Plur An d' orduich { sinn, *did we order*, or *have we* / sibh, *did ye order*, or *have ye* / iad, *did they order*, or *have they* } *ordered?*	*Plur* An orduich { sinn, *shall* or *will we* / sibh, *shall* or *will ye* / iad, *shall* or *will they* } *order?*
Sing Nach d' orduich { mi, *did I not*, or *have I not* / thu, *didst thou not*, or *hast thou not* / e, *did he not*, or *has he not* } *ordered?*	*Sing.* Nach orduich { mi, *shall* or *will I not* / thu, *shalt* or *wilt thou not* / e, *shall* or *will he not* } *order?*
Plur. Nach d' orduich { sinn, *did we not*, or *have we not* / sibh, *did ye not*, or *have ye not* / iad, *did they not*, or *have they not* } *ordered?*	*Plur* Nach orduich { sinn, *shall* or *will we not* / sibh, *shalt* or *wilt thou not* / iad, *shall* or *will they not* } *order?*

SUBJUNCTIVE MOOD.

Preterite.	*Future.*
Sing. { Dh' orduichinn, *I would* / Dh' orduicheadh tu, *thou wouldst* / Dh' orduicheadh e, *he would* } *order.*	*Sing.* Ma dh' orduicheas { mi, *if I shall* or *will* / tu, *if thou shalt* or *wilt* / e, *if he shall* or *will* } *order*
Plur. { Dh' orduicheamaid, *or* dh' orduicheadh sinn, *we would* / Dh' orduicheadh sibh, *ye would* / Dh' orduicheadh iad, *they would* } *order.*	*Plur.* Ma dh' orduicheas { sinn, *if we shall* or *will* / sibh, *if ye shall* or *will* / iad, *if they shall* or *will* } *order.*

IMPERATIVE MOOD.

Sing. { Orduicheam, *let me order.* / Orduich, *order thou.* / Orduicheadh e, *let him order.* }

Plur. { Orduicheamaid, *let us order.* / Orduichibh, *order ye.* / Orduicheadh iad, *let them order.* }

INFINITIVE MOOD.

Dh' orduchadh, / A dh' orduchadh, } *to order.*

PARTICIPLE.

Ag orduchadh, *ordering.*

PASSIVE VOICE.

AFFIRMATIVE, OR INDICATIVE MOOD.

Preterite.

Sing. Dh' orduicheadh { mi, *I was* / thu, *thou wast* / e, *he was* } *ordered.*

Sing. Dh' orduicheadh { sinn, *we were* / sibh, *ye were* / iad, *they were* } *ordered.*

Future.

Sing. Orduichear { mi, *I shall* or *will be* / thu, *thou shalt* or *wilt be* / e, *he shall* or *will be* } *ordered.*

Plur. Orduichear { sinn, *we shall* or *will be* / sibh, *ye shall* or *will be* / iad, *they shall* or *will be* } *ordered.*

NEGATIVE, OR INTERROGATIVE MOOD.

Preterite.

Sing. An d' orduicheadh { mi, *was I* / thu, *wert thou* / e, *was he* } *ordered?*

Plur. An d' orduicheadh { sinn, *were we* / sibh, *were ye* / iad, *were they* } *ordered?*

Sing. Nach d' orduicheadh { mi, *was I not* / thu, *wert thou not* / e, *was he not* } *ordered?*

Sing. Nach d' orduicheadh { sinn, *were we not* / sibh, *were ye not* / iad, *were they not* } *ordered?*

Future.

Sing. An orduichear { mi, *shall I be* / thu, *shalt thou be* / e, *shall he be* } *ordered?*

Plur. An orduichear { sinn, *shall we be* / sibh, *shall ye be* / iad, *shall they be* } *ordered?*

Sing. Nach orduichear { mi, *shall* or *will I not be* / thu, *shalt* or *wilt thou not be* / e, *shall or will he not be* } *ordered?*

Plur. Nach orduichear { sinn, *shall* or *will we not be* / sibh, *shall* or *will ye not be* / iad, *shall* or *will they not be* } *ordered?*

SUBJUNCTIVE MOOD.

Preterite.

Sing. Dh' orduichteadh { mi, *I would* or *could be* / thu, *thou wouldst* or *couldst be* / e, *he would* or *could be* } *ordered.*

Plur. Dh' orduichteadh { sinn, *we would* or *could be* / sibh, *ye would* or *could be* / iad, *they would* or *could be* } *ordered.*

Future.

Sing. Ma dh' orduichear { mi, *if I shall* or *will be* / thu, *if thou shalt* or *wilt be* / e, *if he shall* or *will be* } *ordered.*

Plur. Ma dh' orduichear { sinn, *if we shall* or *will be* / sibh, *if ye shall* or *will be* / iad, *if they shall* or *will be* } *ordered.*

IMPERATIVE MOOD.

Sing. Orduichtear { mi, *let me be* / thu, *be thou* / e, *let him be* } *ordered.*

Plur. Orduichtear { sinn, *let us be* / sibh, *be ye* / iad, *let them be* } *ordered.*

PARTICIPLE.

Orduichte, / Air orduchadh, } *ordered.*

FILL, fold.

ACTIVE VOICE.

AFFIRMATIVE, OR INDICATIVE MOOD.

Preterite.

Sing. Dh' fhill { mi, *I* / thu, *thou* / e, *he* } *folded.*

Plur. Dh' fhill { sinn, *we* / sibh, *ye* / iad, *they* } *folded.*

Future.

Sing. Fillidh { mi, *I shall* or *will* / tu, *thou shalt* or *wilt* / se, *he shall* or *will* } *fold.*

Plur. Fillidh { sinn, *we shall* or *will* / sibh, *ye shall* or *will* / siad, *they shall* or *will* } *fold.*

NEGATIVE, OR INTERROGATIVE MOOD.

Preterite.

Sing. An d' fhill — mi, *did I fold*, or *have I*; thu, *didst thou fold*, or *hast thou*; e, *did he fold*, or *has he* — *folded?*

Plur. An d' fhill — sinn, *did we fold*, or *have we*; sibh, *did ye fold*, or *have ye*; iad, *did they fold*, or *have they* — *folded?*

Future.

Sing. Am fill — mi, *shall* or *will I*; thu, *shalt* or *wilt thou*; e, *shall* or *will he* — *fold?*

Plur. Am fill — sinn, *shall* or *will we*; sibh, *shall* or *will ye*; iad, *shall* or *will they* — *fold?*

SUBJUNCTIVE MOOD.

Preterite

Sing. Dh' fhillinn, *I would* or *could*; Dh' fhilleadh tu, *thou wouldst* or *couldst*; Dh' fhilleadh e, *he would* or *could* — *fold*

Plur. Dh' fhilleamaid, or Dh' fhilleadh sinn, *we would* or *could*; Dh' fhilleadh sibh, *ye would* or *could*; Dh' fhilleadh iad, *they would* or *could* — *fold*

Future.

Sing. Ma dh' fhilleas — mi, *if I shall* or *will*; tu, *if thou shalt* or *wilt*; e, *if he shall* or *will* — *fold.*

Plur. Ma dh' fhilleas — sinn, *if we shall* or *will*; sibh, *if ye shall* or *will*; iad, *if they shall* or *will* — *fold*

IMPERATIVE MOOD

Sing. Filleam, *let me fold*; Fill, *fold thou*; Filleadh e, *let him fold*.

Plur. Filleamaid, *let us fold*; Fillibh, *fold ye*; Filleadh iad, *let them fold*.

INFINITIVE MOOD.

Dh' fhilleadh, A dh' fhilleadh, — *to fold*

PARTICIPLE.

A filleadh, Ag filleadh, — *folding*

PASSIVE VOICE.

AFFIRMATIVE, OR INDICATIVE MOOD.

Preterite.

Sing. Dh' fhilleadh — mi, *I was*; thu, *thou wast*; e, *he was* — *folded.*

Plur. Dh' fhilleadh — sinn, *we were*; sibh, *ye were*; iad, *they were* — *folded*

Future.

Sing. Fillear — mi, *I shall* or *will be*; thu, *thou shalt* or *wilt be*; e, *he shall* or *will be* — *folded.*

Plur. Fillear — sinn, *we shall* or *will be*; sibh, *ye shall* or *will be*; iad, *they shall* or *will be* — *folded.*

NEGATIVE, OR INTERROGATIVE MOOD.

Preterite

Sing. An d' fhilleadh — mi, *was I*; thu, *wert thou*; e, *was he* — *folded?*

Plur. An d' fhilleadh — sinn, *were we*; sibh, *were ye*; iad, *were they* — *folded?*

Sing. Nach d' fhillear — mi, *was I not*; thu, *wert thou not*; e, *was he not* — *folded?*

Plur. Nach d' fhillear — sinn, *were we not*; sibh, *were ye not*; iad, *were they not* — *folded?*

Future.

Sing. Am fillear — mi, *shall* or *will I be*; thu, *shalt* or *wilt thou be*; e, *shall* or *will he be* — *folded?*

Plur. Am fillear — sinn, *shall* or *will we be*; sibh, *shall* or *will ye be*; iad, *shall* or *will they be* — *folded?*

Sing. Cha 'n fhillear — mi, *I shall* or *will not be*; thu, *thou shalt* or *wilt not be*; e, *he shall* or *will not be* — *folded.*

Plur. Cha 'n fhillear — sinn, *we shall* or *will not be*; sibh, *ye shall* or *will not be*; iad, *they shall* or *will not be* — *folded*

SUBJUNCTIVE MOOD

Preterite.

Sing. Dh' fhillteadh — mi, *I would* or *could be*; thu, *thou wouldst* or *couldst be*; e, *he would* or *could be* — *folded*

Plur. Dh' fhillteadh — sinn, *we would* or *could be*; sibh, *ye would* or *could be*; iad, *they would* or *could be* — *folded.*

Future.

Sing. Ma dh' fhillear — mi, *if I shall* or *will be*; thu, *if thou shalt* or *wilt be*; e, *if he shall* or *will be* — *folded*

Plur. Ma dh' fhillear — sinn, *if we shall* or *will be*; sibh, *if ye shall* or *will be*; iad, *if they shall* or *will be* — *folded.*

IMPERATIVE MOOD.

Sing. Filltear { mi, *let me be* / thu, *be thou* / e, *let him be* } *folded*

Plur. Filltear { sinn, *let us be* / sibh, *be ye* / iad, *let them be* } *folded.*

PARTICIPLE.

Fillte, / Air fhilleadh, } *folded*

The learner, having come thus far, can have no difficulty, it is presumed, in declining the *compound* tenses of any verb, as they are, both in the active and passive voices, similar to those of the first conjugation, to which I refer him

---

A TABLE OF VERBS,

REGULAR AND IRREGULAR,

ALPHABETICALLY ARRANGED, EACH WITH ITS PRETERITE, PAST AND PRESENT PARTICIPLE

Imperative.	*Preterite.*	*Past Participle.*	*Present Participle.*
Abair, *say*,	Thubhairt,	Air radh,	Ag radh.
Adhlaic, *bury*,	Dh' adhlaic,	Adhlaicte,	Ag adhlac, *or* -adh
Amais, *find*,	Dh' amais,	Amaiste,	Ag amas.
Ainmich, *name*,	Dh' ainmich,	Ainmichte,	Ag ainmeachadh
Aisig, *restore*,	Dh' aisig,	Aisigte,	Ag aiseag.
Aithn, *command*,	Dh' àithn,	Àithnte,	Ag àithneadh.
Aithnich, *know*,	Dh' aithnich,	Aithnichte,	Ag aithneachadh.
Amail, *hinder*,	Dh' amail,	Amailte,	Ag amal.
Arduich, *exalt*,	Dh' arduich,	Arduichte,	Ag arduch, *or* -adh.
Bac, *hinder*,	Bhac,	Baçta, bacte,	A bacadh.
Bean, *touch*,	Bhean,		A beanachd, a beantuinn
Bearr, *crop*,	Bhearr,	Bearrta, bearrte,	A bearradh
Blais, *taste*,	Bhlais,	Blaiste,	A blasdachd
Biath, *feed*,	Bhiath,	Biathta, biathte,	A biathadh
Bogaich, *soften*,	Bhogaich,	Bogaichte,	A bogachadh.
Bris, *break*,	Bhris,	Briste,	A briseadh
Bruadair, *dream*,	Bhruadair,	Bruadairte,	A bruadaradh
Buail, *strike*,	Bhuail,	Buailte,	A bualadh
Buain, *cut down*,	Bhuain,	Buainte,	A buaineadh.
Buair, *tempt*,	Bhuair,	Buairte,	A buaireadh
Buidhinn, *win*,	Bhuidhinn,	Buidhinte,	A buidhneadh
Buin, *deal with*,	Bhuin,	Buinte,	A buntuinn
Caill, *lose*,	Chaill,	Caillte,	A call
Caith, *spend*,	Chaith,	Caithte,	A caitheamh
Ciallaich, *mean*,	Chiallaich,	Ciallaichte,	A ciallachadh
Cinn, *grow*,	Chinn,		A cinntinn
Caomhain, *spare*,	Chaomhain,	Caomhainte,	A caomhnadh
Ceangail, *bind*,	Cheangail,	Ceangailte,	A ceangladh.
Céil, *conceal*,	Chéil,	Céilte,	A céiltinn
Céill, *declare*,	Chéill,	Céillte,	A céillinn
Ceannuich, *buy*,	Cheannuich,	Ceannuichte,	A ceannuchadh
Cluinn, *hear*,	Chual,		A cluintinn
Codail, *sleep*,	Chodail,		A codal.
Coghain, *aid*,	Choghain,	Coghainte,	A còghnadh
Coinnich, *meet*,	Choinnich,	Coinnichte,	A coinneach, *or* -adh.
Coirich, *blame*,	Choirich,	Coirichte,	A coireachadh
Coisg, *extinguish*,	Choisg,	Coisgte,	A cosgadh.
Coisich, *travel*,	Choisich,	Coisichte,	A coiseachd
Comhdaich, *cover*,	Chomhdaich,	Comhdaichte,	A comhdachadh.
Creach, *spoil*,	Chreach,	Creachta, creachte,	A creachadh
Crath, *shake*,	Chrath,	Crathta,	A crath
Crioslaich, *gird*,	Chrioslaich,	Crioslaichte,	A crioslachadh
Croch, *hang*,	Chroch,	Crochta,	A crochadh
Ciùrr, *hurt*,	Chiùrr,	Ciurrta,	A ciurradh
Crup, *shrink*,	Chrup,	Crupta,	A crupadh
Cuimsich, *hit*,	Chuimsich,	Cuimsichte,	A cuimseachadh.
Cuir, *put*,	Chuir,	Air chur,	A cur.

Imperative	*Preterite.*	*Past Participle.*	*Present Participle.*
Cum, *hold,*	Chum,		A cumail.
Cuitich, *quit,*	Chuitich,	Cuitichte,	A cuiteachadh.
Daighnich, *strengthen,*	Dhaighnich,	Daighnichte,	A daighneachadh.
Dealbh, *form,*	Dhealbh,	Dealbhta,	A dealbhadh.
Dean, *do,*	Rinn,	Deanta, deante,	A deanamh.
Diobair, *forsake,*	Dhiobair,	Diobairte,	A diobradh.
Diol, *pay,*	Dhiol,	Diolta, diolte,	A dioladh.
Dion, *protect,*	Dhion,	Dionta, dionte,	A dionadh.
Dòirt, *spill,*	Dhòirt,	Dòirte,	A dòrtadh.
Dùin, *shut,*	Dhùin,	Dùinte,	A dùnadh.
Dùisg, *waken,*	Dhuisg,	Duisgte,	A dùsgadh.
Dùraig, *dare,*	Dhuraig,		A dùrachdainn.
Eid, *clothe,*	Dh' eid,	Eidte,	Ag eideadh.
Eigh, *shout,*	Dh' eigh,		Ag eigh.
Eirich, *rise,*	Dheirich,		Ag eiridh.
Faic, *see,*	Chunnaic, chunna,		A faicinn, a faicsinn.
Faigh, *get,*	Fhuair,		A faotainn, a faghail.
Fainich, *feel,*	Dh' fhainich,	Fainichte,	A faineachadh.
Fan, *wait,*	Dh' fhan,		A fanachd, a fanticinn.
Falbh, *go,*	Dh' fhalbh,	Air dol,	A falbh
Fàs, *grow,*	Dh' fhas,	Air fàs,	A fas.
Feith, *wait,*	Dh' fheith,		A feitheamh.
Feuch, *shew,*	Dh' fheuch,		A feuchainn.
Fàisg, *squeeze,*	Dh' fhaisg,	Faisgte,	A fàsgadh
Figh, *weave,*	Dh' fhigh,	Fighte,	A figheadh.
Fill, *fold,*	Dh' fhill,	Fillte,	A filleadh.
Fliuch, *wet,*	Fhliuch,	Fliuchta,	A fliuchadh.
Folaich, *hide,*	Dh' fholaich,	Folaichte,	A folachadh.
Fosgail, *open,*	Dh' fhosgail,	Fosgailte,	A fosgladh.
Fuin, *bake,*	Dh' fhuin,	Fuinte,	A fuineadh.
Fuirich, *wait,*	Dh' fhuirich,		A fuireach
Fuaigh, *sew,*	Dh' fhuaigh,	Fuaighte,	A fuaghal.
Fulaing, *suffer,*	Dh' fhulaing,	Fulaingte,	A fulang.
Gabh, *take,*	Ghabh,	Gabhta,	A gabhail.
Gàir, *laugh,*	Ghàir,		A gàireachdaich.
Gairm, *proclaim,*	Ghairm,	Gairmte,	A gairmeadh.
Geall, *promise,*	Gheall,	Gealltuinte,	A gealltuinn.
Gearr, *cut,*	Ghearr,	Gearrta, gearrte,	A gearradh.
Geum, *low,*	Gheum,		A geumnaich.
Gin, gion, *produce,*	Ghin, Ghion,	Ginte, gionta,	A gintinn, a giontuinn, a ginmhuinn
Glac, *catch,*	Ghlac,	Glacta,	A glacadh
Gleidh, *keep,*	Ghleidh,	Gleidhte,	A gleidheadh.
Gluais, *move,*	Ghluais,	Gluaiste,	A gluasad.
Gnathaich, *use,*	Ghnathaich,	Gnathaichte,	A ghnathachadh
Goil, *boil,*	Ghoil,		A goileadh
Goir, *crow,*	Ghoir,		A goirsinn.
Grab, *catch,*	Ghrab,	Grabta,	A grabadh.
Grabh, *engrave,*	Ghrabh,	Ghrabhta,	A grabhadh.
Greas, *hasten,*	Ghreas,	Greasta,	A greasdachd.
Iarr, *request,*	Dh' iarr,		Ag iarruidh.
Iomain, *drive,*	Dh' iomain,	Iomainte,	Ag ioman
Ith, *eat,*	Dh' ith,	Ithte,	Ag itheadh.
Labhair, *speak,*	Labhair,		A labhradh.
Las, *kindle,*	Las,	Lasta,	A lasadh.
Leagh, *melt,*	Leagh,	Leaghta, leaghte,	A leaghadh.
Lean, *follow,*	Lean,		A leantuinn, a leanachd, a leanmhuinn.
Leig, *let,*	Leig,	Leigte,	A leigeil,
Leighis, *cure,*	Leighis,	Leighiste,	A leigheas.
Léir, *torment,*	Léir,	Léirte,	A leireadh
Lùb, *bend,*	Lùb,	Lùbta, lùbte,	A lùbadh.
Leugh, *read,*	Leugh,	Leughta, leughte,	A leughadh.
Lion, *fill,*	Lion,	Lionta,	A lionadh.
Loisg, *burn,*	Loisg,	Loisgte,	A losgadh.
Lomair, *shear,*	Lomair,	Lomairte,	A lomairt
Luchdaich, *burden,*	Luchdaich,	Luchdaichte,	A luchdachadh
Luidh, *lie,*	Luidh,	Air luidhe,	A luidhe.
Mair, *last,*	Mhair,		A marsuinn, a mairsinn.
Marbh, *kill,*	Mharbh,		A marbhadh.
Marcaich, *ride,*	Mharcaich,		A marcachd.

Imperative.	*Preterite.*	*Past Participle.*	*Present Participle.*
Meal, *enjoy,*	Mheal,		A mealtuinn.
Meall, *cheat,*	Mheall,	Meallta,	A mealladh
Meas, *estimate,*	Mheas,	Measta,	A measadh.
Mèil, *grind,*	Mheil,	Meilte,	A méilleadh.
Mill, *spoil,*	Mhill,	Millte,	A milleadh.
Minich, *explain,*	Mhìnich,	Mìnichte,	A mìneachadh.
Mionnuich, *swear,*	Mhionnuich,	Mionnuichte,	A mionnuichte.
Mosgail, *waken,*	Mhosgail,	Mosgailte,	A mosgladh
Mùth, *change,*	Mhuth,	Muthta,	A muthadh.
Nàraich, *shame,*	Nàraich,	Nàraichte,	A nàrachadh.
Naisg, *bind,*	Naisg,	Naisgte,	A nasgadh.
Nigh, *wash,*	Nigh,	Nighte,	A nigheadh.
Òb, *refuse,*	Dh' òb,	Obta,	Ag obadh.
Oibrich, *work,*	Dh' oibrich,	Oibrichte,	Ag oibreachadh.
Ol, *drink,*	Dh' òl,	Olta, oilte,	Ag òl
Orduich, *order,*	Dh' orduich,	Orduichte,	Ag orduchadh.
Pàigh, *pay,*	Phàigh,	Pàighte,	A pàigh
Paisg, *wrap,*	Phàisg,	Pàisgte,	A pasgadh.
Pian, *pain,*	Phian,	Pianta,	A pianadh
Pill, *return,*	Phill,	Air pilltinn,	A pilltinn.
Put, *push,*	Phut,		A putadh.
Reic, *sell,*	Reic,	Reicte,	A reiceadh.
Reub, *tear,*	Reub,	Reubta,	A reubadh
Ruathar, *dig,*	Ruathar,	Ruathairte,	A ruathradh
Ruig, *reach,*	Ràinig,		A ruigheachd, a ruigsinn.
Ruith, *run,*	Ruith,		A ruith.
Sàbh, *saw,*	Shàbh,	Sàbhta, sàibhte,	A sàbhadh.
Salaich, *soil,*	Shalaich,	Salaichte,	A salachadh.
Saltair, *tread,*	Shaltair,		A saltairt.
Saoil, *think,*	Shaoil,		A saoilsinn.
Sàth, *thrust,*	Shàth,	Sàthta, saithte,	A sàthadh.
Sdiùir, *steer,*	Sdiuir,	Sdiùrta,	A stiùradh
Seachain, *shun,*	Sheachain,	Seachainte,	A seachnadh.
Seall, *look,*	Sheall,		A sealltuinn.
Searg, *wither,*	Shearg,	Seargta, seargte,	A seargadh.
Seas, *stand,*	Sheas,		A seasamh.
Séid, *blow,*	Shéid,	Séidte,	A séideadh, a séidil.
Sgàin, *burst,*	Sgàin,	Sgàinte,	A sgàineadh
Sgaoil, *spread;*	Sgaoil,	Sgaoilte,	A sgaoileadh.
Sgap, *scatter,*	Sgap,	Sgapta, Sgapte,	A sgapadh
Sgar, *separate,*	Sgar,	Sgarta,	A sgaradh, a sgarachduinn.
Sgath, *prune,*	Sgath,	Sgathta, sgathte,	A sgathadh.
Sgeaduich, *adorn,*	Sgeaduich,	Sgeaduichte,	A sgeaduchadh.
Sgoilt, *split,*	Sgoilt,	Sgoilte,	A sgoltadh.
Sgriob, *scratch,*	Sgriob,	Sgriobta,	A sgriobadh.
Sgriobh, *write,*	Sgriobh,	Sgriobhta, sgriobhte	A sgriobhadh
Sguab, *sweep,*	Sguab,	Sguabta,	A sguabadh.
Sguir, *stop,*	Sguir,		A sgurachd, a sgur.
Smuainich, *think,*	Smuainich,	Smuainichte,	A smuaineachadh.
Snaidh, *hew,*	Shnaidh,	Snaidhte,	A snaidheadh.
Snàig, *creep,*	Shnàig,		A snàgadh.
Snaim, *knot,*	Shnaim,	Snaimte,	A snaimeadh
Snamh, *swim,*	Shnamh,	Snamhta, snaimhte,	A snamhadh.
Sniomh, *spin,*	Shniomh,	Sniomhte,	A sniomh
Spoth, *geld,*	Spoth,	Spothta, spothte,	A spothadh.
Srachd, *tear,*	Shrachd,	Srachta,	A srachdadh.
Tachair, *meet,*	Thachair,		A tachairt
Tachrais, *wind,*	Thachrais,	Tachraiste,	A tachras.
Tagh, *choose,*	Thagh,	Taghta, taghte,	A taghadh.
Taisg, *lay up,*	Thaisg,	Taisgte,	A tasgadh
Taom, *pour,*	Thaom,	Taomta,	A taomadh.
Tarruing, *draw,*	Tharruing,	Tarruingte,	A tarruing.
Teagaisg, *teach,*	Theagaisg,	Teagaiste,	A teagasg
Teanail, *gather,*	Theanail,	Teanailte,	A teanaladh.
Teasairg, *save,*	Theasairg,	Teasàirgte,	A teasairginn.
Teich, *fly,*	Theich,		A teicheachd.
Teirig, *wear out,*	Theirig,		A teireachduinn
Thig, *come,*	Thàinig,	Air teachd,	A teachd, a tighinn.
Thoir, thabhair, *give,*	Thug,		A toirt, a tabhairt.

Imperative	*Preterite.*	*Past Participle.*	*Present Participle*
Tilg, *throw*,	Thilg,	Tilgte,	A tilgeadh, a tilgeil.
Tionndaidh, *turn*,	Thionndadh,	Tionndaidhte,	A tionndadh.
Tionsgail, *contrive*,	Thionsgail,	Tionsgailte,	A tionsgladh
Tionsgain, *begin*,	Thionsgain,	Tionsgainte,	A tionsgnadh
Tiormaich, *dry*,	Thiormaich,	Tiormaichte,	A tiormachadh.
Tochail, *dig*,	Thochail,	Tochailte,	A tochladh
Tog, *lift*,	Thog,	Togta, togte,	A togail.
Togair, *desire*,	Thogair,		A togradh.
Toinn, *twist*,	Thoinn,	Toinnte,	A toinneamh.
Tòisich, *begin*,	Thòisich,	Tòisichte,	A tòiseachadh.
Trèig, *forsake*,	Thrèig,	Trèigte,	A trèigsinn
Treoruich, *lead*,	Threoruich,	Treoruichte,	A treoruchadh.
Tuig, *understand*,	Thuig,		A tuigsinn
Tuirling, *descend*,	Thuirling,	Tuirlingte,	A tuirling.
Tuislich, *fall*,	Thuislich,	Tuislichte,	A tuisleachadh.
Tuit, *fall*,	Thuit,	Air tuiteam,	A tuiteam
Uigheamaich, *dress*,	Dh' uigheamaich,	Uigheamaichte,	Ag uigheamachadh
Ùraich, *renew*,	Dh' ùraich,	Uraichte,	Ag ùrachadh.

THE AUXILIARY VERB BI, BE*

AFFIRMATIVE, OR INDICATIVE MOOD.

Present	*Preterite.*	*Future.*
Sing Ta *or* tha: mi, *I am.* thu, *thou art* e, *he is.*	*Sing.* Bha: mi, *I was* thu, *thou wert* e, *he is*	*Sing.* Bithidh: mi, *I shall* or *will* tu, *thou shalt* se, *he shall* — *be*
Plur. Ta *or* tha: sinn, *we are* sibh, *ye are.* iad, *they are*	*Plur.* Bha: sinn, *we are* sibh, *ye are* iad, *they are*	*Plur.* Bithidh: sinn, *we shall* or *will* sibh, *ye shall* iad, *they shall* — *be*

NEGATIVE, OR INTERROGATIVE MOOD.

Present	*Preterite*	*Future*
Sing †Am bheil: mi, *am I?* thu, *art thou?* e, *is he?*	*Sing* An robh: mi, *was I?* thu, *wert thou?* e, *was he?*	*Sing* Am bi: mi, *shall* or *will I* thu, *shalt thou* e, *shall he* — *be?*
Plur Am bheil: sinn, *are we?* sibh, *are you?* iad, *are they?*	*Plur* An robh: sinn, *were we?* sibh, *were you?* iad, *were they?*	*Plur* Am bi: sinn, *shall* or *will we* sibh, *shall you* iad, *shall they* — *be?*
Sing ‡Cha 'n 'eil: mi, *I am not* thu, *thou art not* e, *he is not*	*Sing* Cha robh: mi, *I was not.* thu, *thou wert not.* e, *he was not*	*Sing.* Cha bhi: mi, *I shall* or *will not* thu, *thou shalt not* e, *he shall not* — *be.*
Plur. Cha 'n 'eil: sinn, *we are not* sibh, *you are not.* iad, *they are not*	*Sing* Cha robh: sinn, *we were not* sibh, *you were not* iad, *they were not*	*Plur* Cha bhi: sinn, *we shall* or *will not* sibh, *you shall not* iad, *they shall* — *be.*
Sing Nach 'eil: mi, *am I not?* thu, *art thou not?* e, *is he not?*	*Sing.* Nach robh: mi, *were I not?* thu, *wert thou not?* e, *was he not?*	*Sing* Nach bi: mi, *shall* or *will I not* thu, *shalt thou not* e, *shall he not* — *be?*
Plur Nach 'eil: sinn, *are we not?* sibh, *are you not?* iad, *are they not?*	*Plur.* Nach robh: sinn, *were we not?* sibh, *were you not?* iad, *were they not?*	*Plur* Nach bi: sinn, *shall* or *will we not* sibh, *shall you not* iad, *shall they not* — *be?*

* Dean, *do*, or *make*, and rach, *go*, are often used as auxiliary verbs, as, dean luidhe, *lie down*, dean seasamh, *stand*, literally, *make a lie down*, *make a stand*, chaidh mo chreachadh, *I was plundered*, i e *my plundering is gone* or *past*, rachadh mo bhualadh, *I would be struck*, i e *the striking of me would have passed* or *happened*. These auxiliaries are declinable with all the conjunctive and adverbial particles

† *Am bheil* is, almost always, pronounced *'m bheil* or *bheil*, in some districts of the Highlands, as in Badenoch, they say *am beil*

‡ *'Eil* for *bheil* After the conjunctive particles *cha*, *nach*, *mur*, bheil is written *'eil*, and in order to separate the two vowels, and also to prevent an *hiatus*, we insert the letter *n*, and write *cha 'n 'eil*, rather than *cha 'eil*

SUBJUNCTIVE MOOD.

Preterite.

Sing. { Bhithinn, *I would* / Bhitheadh tu, *thou wouldst* / Bhitheadh e, *he would* } *be*

Plur. { Bhitheamaid, *or* Bhitheadh sinn, *we would* / Bhitheadh sibh, *you would* / Bhitheadh iad, *they would* } *be*

Sing. Am* { Bithinn, *would I* / Bitheadh tu, *wouldst thou* / Bitheadh e, *would he* } *be.*

Plur. Am { Bitheamaid, *or* Bitheadh sinn, *would we* / Bitheadh sibh, *would you* / Bitheadh iad, *would they* } *be*

Sing. Nam { Bithinn, *if I would* / Bitheadh tu, *if thou wouldst* / Bitheadh e, *if he would* } *be.*

Plur. Nam { Bitheamaid, *or* Bitheadh sinn, *if we would* / Bitheadh sibh, *if you would* / Bitheadh iad, *if they would* } *be*

Future.

Sing. Ma bhitheas† { mi, *if I shall* or *will* / tu, *if thou shalt* or *wilt* / e, *if he shall* or *will* } *be*

Plur. Ma bhitheas { sinn, *if we shall* or *will* / sibh, *if you shall* or *will* / iad, *if they shall* or *will* } *be*

Sing. Cha { Bhithinn, *I would not,* / Bhitheadh tu, *thou wouldst not* / Bhitheadh e, *he would not* } *be*

Plur. Cha { Bhitheamaid, *or* Bhitheadh sinn, *we would not* / Bhitheadh sibh, *you would not* / Bhitheadh iad, *they would not* } *be*

Sing. Nach { Bithinn, *would I not* / Bitheadh tu, *wouldst thou not* / Bitheadh e, *would he not* } *be?*

Plur. Nach { Bitheamaid, *or* Bitheadh sinn, *would we not* / Bitheadh sibh, *would you not* / Bitheadh iad, *would they not* } *be?*

IMPERATIVE MOOD

Sing. { Bitheam, *let me be.* / Bi, bi-sa, bi thusa, *be thou.* / Bitheadh e, *let them be* }

Plur. { Bitheamaid, *let us be.* / Bithibh, *be you.* / Bitheadh iad, *let them be.* }

INFINITIVE MOOD

A bhith, do bhith, *to be.*

PARTICIPLE.

Perf. Air bhith, *having been*

Fut. Gu bhith, ri bhith, *to be*, or *about to be*

IS, am

AFFIRMATIVE, OR INDICATIVE MOOD.

Present.

Sing. Is { mi, *or* mise, *it is I* / tu, tusa, *it is thou.* / e, esan, *it is he.* }

Plur. Is { sinn, sinne, *it is we.* / sibh, sibhse, *it is you.* / iad, iadsan, *it is they.* }

Preterite

Sing { Bu mhi, *or* mhise, *it was I* / Bu tu, tusa, *it was thou* / B' e, esan, *it was he* }

Plur { Bu sinn, sinne, *it was we* / Bu sibh, sibhse, *it was you* / B' iad, iadsan, *it was they* }

INTERROGATIVE, OR NEGATIVE MOOD

Present

Sing. { Am mi, *or* mise, *is it I?* / An tu, tusa, *is it thou?* / an e, esan, *is it he?* }

Plur. { An sinn, sinne, *is it we?* / An sibh, sibhse, *is it you?* / An iad, iadsan, *is it they?* }

Sing. Nach { mi, *or* mise, *is it not I?* / tu, tusa, *is it not thou?* / e, esan, *is it not he?* }

Plur. Nach { sinn, sinne, *is it not we?* / sibh, sibhse, *is it not you?* / iad, iadsan, *is it not they?* }

Sing. Cha { mhi, *or* mhise, *it is not I* / tu, tusa, *it is not thou.* / 'n e, esan, *it is not he.* }

Plur. Cha { sinn, sinne, *it is not we* / sibh, sibhse, *it is not you* / 'n iad, iadsan, *it is not they* }

Preterite

Sing Am { bu mhi, *or* mhise, *was it I?* / bu tu, tusa, *was it thou?* / b' e, esan, *was it he?* }

Plur. Am { bu sinn, sinne, *was it we?* / bu sibh, sibhse, *was it you?* / b' iad, iadsan, *was it they?* }

Sing Nach { bu mhi, *or* mhise, *was it not I?* / bu tu, tusa, *was it not thou?* / b' e, esan, *was it not he?* }

Plur Nach { bu sinn, sinne, *was it not we?* / bu sibh, sibhse, *was it not you?* / b' iad, iadsan, *was it not they?* }

Sing. Cha { bu mhi, *or* mhise, *it was not I.* / bu tu, tusa, *it was not thou* / b' e, esan, *it was not he.* }

Plur Cha { bu sinn, sinne, *it was not we* / bu sibh, sibhse, *it was not you* / b' iad, iadsan, *it was not they* }

* *Bitheadh* is often contracted *biodh*

† *Bhitheas* is often written *bhios*, both in prose and in verse

SUBJUNCTIVE MOOD.

Present.		*Preterite.*	
Sing. Ma's	mi, *or* mise, *if it be I*	*Sing* Nam	bu mhi, *or* mhise, *if it were I.*
	tu, tusa, *if it be thou.*		bu tu, tusa, *if it were thou.*
	e, esan, *if it be he.*		b' e, esan, *if it were he.*
Plur. Ma's	sinn, sinne, *if it be we*	*Plur* Nam	bu sinn, sinne, *if it were we*
	sibh, sibhse, *if it be you.*		bu sibh, sibhse, *if it were you*
	iad, iadsan, *if it be they.*		b' iad, iadsan, *if it were they.*

IMPERSONAL VERBS.

The Preterite Affirmative of Neuter Verbs, and the Future of the Negative or Interrogative Mood of Active Verbs, are often used impersonally, as, *ghuileadh, buailear, gluaisear, faicear, faighear.* Any verb used in this way may be declined with the compound pronoun *leam,* through all its persons; yet it is not accounted so elegant to express the pronoun, as to leave it to be supplied according to the sense of the context. The impersonal verbs are used after this manner

Sing Buailear	leam, *I* / leat, *thou* / leis, *he*	*struck.*	*Plur.* Buailear	leibh, *we* / leinn, *ye* / leo, *they*	*struck.*

OF IRREGULAR VERBS

The Irregular Verbs are reckoned ten; seven of the first conjugation, *viz dean, cluinn, beir, rach, ruig, thig, thoir,* or *thabhair,* and three of the second, *viz. faic, faigh, abair.*

THE FIRST CONJUGATION.

DEAN, make

ACTIVE VOICE.

AFFIRMATIVE, or INDICATIVE MOOD

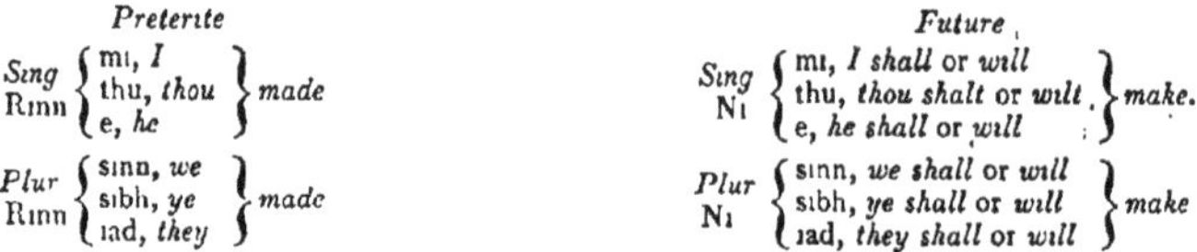

Preterite			*Future*		
Sing Rinn	mi, *I* / thu, *thou* / e, *he*	*made*	*Sing* Ni	mi, *I shall* or *will* / thu, *thou shalt* or *wilt* / e, *he shall* or *will*	*make.*
Plur Rinn	sinn, *we* / sibh, *ye* / iad, *they*	*made*	*Plur* Ni	sinn, *we shall* or *will* / sibh, *ye shall* or *will* / iad, *they shall* or *will*	*make*

NEGATIVE, or INTERROGATIVE MOOD.

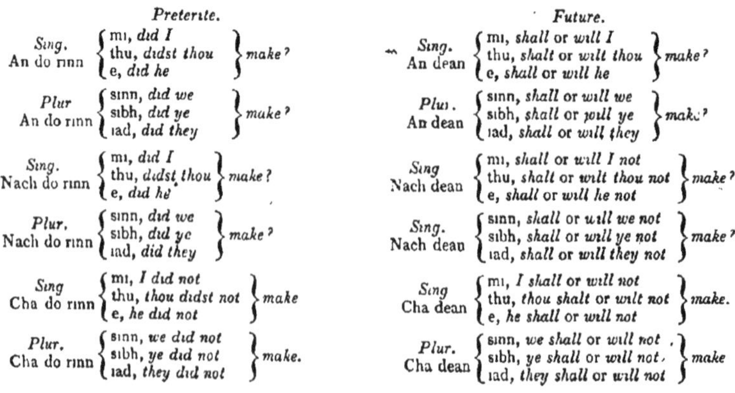

Preterite.			*Future.*		
Sing. An do rinn	mi, *did I* / thu, *didst thou* / e, *did he*	*make?*	*Sing.* An dean	mi, *shall* or *will I* / thu, *shalt* or *wilt thou* / e, *shall* or *will he*	*make?*
Plur An do rinn	sinn, *did we* / sibh, *did ye* / iad, *did they*	*make?*	*Plur.* An dean	sinn, *shall* or *will we* / sibh, *shall* or *will ye* / iad, *shall* or *will they*	*make?*
Sing. Nach do rinn	mi, *did I* / thu, *didst thou* / e, *did he*	*make?*	*Sing* Nach dean	mi, *shall* or *will I not* / thu, *shalt* or *wilt thou not* / e, *shall* or *will he not*	*make?*
Plur. Nach do rinn	sinn, *did we* / sibh, *did ye* / iad, *did they*	*make?*	*Sing.* Nach dean	sinn, *shall* or *will we not* / sibh, *shall* or *will ye not* / iad, *shall* or *will they not*	*make?*
Sing Cha do rinn	mi, *I did not* / thu, *thou didst not* / e, *he did not*	*make*	*Sing* Cha dean	mi, *I shall* or *will not* / thu, *thou shalt* or *wilt not* / e, *he shall* or *will not*	*make.*
Plur. Cha do rinn	sinn, *we did not* / sibh, *ye did not* / iad, *they did not*	*make.*	*Plur.* Cha dean	sinn, *we shall* or *will not* / sibh, *ye shall* or *will not* / iad, *they shall* or *will not*	*make*

SUBJUNCTIVE MOOD.

Preterite.		Future.	
Sing.	Dheanainn, *I would* or *could* Dheanadh tu, *thou would* or *couldst* Dheanadh e, *he would* or *could* } *make*	*Sing.* Ma ni	mi, *if I shall* or *will* thu, *if thou shalt* or *wilt* e, *if he shall* or *will* } *make*
Plur.	Dheanamaid, *we would* or *could* Dheanadh sibh, *ye would* or *could* Dheanadh iad, *they would* or *could* } *make.*	*Plur.* Ma ni	sinn, *if we shall* or *will* sibh, *if ye shall* or *will* iad, *if they shall* or *will* } *make.*
Sing. Nan	deanainn, *if I would* or *could* deanadh tu, *if thou wouldst* or *couldst* deanadh e, *if he would* or *could* } *make*	*Sing.* Mur dean	mi, *if I shall* or *will not* thu, *if thou shalt* or *wilt not* e, *if he shall* or *will not* } *make*
Plur. Nan	deanamaid, *if we would* or *could* deanadh sibh, *if ye would* or *could* deanadh iad, *if they would* or *could* } *make.*	*Plur.* Mur dean	sinn, *if we shall* or *will not* sibh, *if ye shall* or *will not* iad, *if they shall* or *will not* } *make*

IMPERATIVE MOOD.

Sing. Deanam, *let me make.* / Dean, *make thou* / Deanadh e, *let him make.*

Plur. Deanamaid, *let us make.* / Deanaibh, *make ye.* / Deanadh iad, *let them make*

INFINITIVE MOOD

A dheanamh, *to do,* or *make*

PARTICIPLE.

A, *or* ag deanamh, *doing* or *making.*

PASSIVE VOICE.

AFFIRMATIVE, OR INDICATIVE MOOD.

Preterite.		Future.	
Sing. Rinneadh	mi, *I was* thu, *thou wert* e, *he was* } *made*	*Sing.* Nithear	mi, *I shall* or *will be* thu, *thou shalt* or *wilt be* e, *he shall* or *will be* } *made.*
Plur. Rinneadh	sinn, *we were* sibh, *ye were* iad, *they were* } *made.*	*Plur.* Nithear	sinn, *we shall* or *will be* sibh, *ye shall* or *will be* iad, *they shall* or *will be* } *made*

INTERROGATIVE, OR NEGATIVE MOOD.

Preterite.		Future.	
Sing. An do rinneadh	mi, *was I* thu, *wert thou* e, *was he* } *made?*	*Sing.* An deanar	mi, *shall* or *will I be* thu, *shalt* or *wilt thou be* e, *shall* or *will he be* } *made?*
Plur. An do rinneadh	sinn, *were we* sibh, *were ye* iad, *were they* } *made?*	*Plur* An deanar	sinn, *shall* or *will we be* sibh, *shall* or *will ye be* iad, *shall* or *will they be* } *made?*
Sing Nach do rinneadh	mi, *was I not* thu, *wert thou not* e, *was he not* } *made?*	*Sing.* Nach deanar	mi, *shall* or *will I not be* thu, *shalt* or *wilt thou not be* e, *shall* or *will he not be* } *made?*
Plur Nach do rinneadh	sinn, *were we not* sibh, *were ye not* iad, *were they not* } *made?*	*Plur* Nach deanar	sinn, *shall* or *will we not be* sibh, *shall* or *will ye not be* iad, *shall* or *will they not be* } *made?*
Sing. Cha do rinneadh	mi, *I was not* thu, *thou wert not* e, *he was not* } *made.*	*Sing* Cha deanar	mi, *I shall* or *will not be* thu, *thou shalt* or *wilt not be* e, *he shall* or *will not be* } *made*
Plur. Cha do rinneadh	sinn, *we were not* sibh, *ye were not* iad, *they were not* } *made.*	*Plur.* Cha deanar	sinn, *we shall* or *will not be* sibh, *ye shall* or *will not be* iad, *they shall* or *will not be* } *made*

SUBJUNCTIVE MOOD

Preterite.		Future.	
Sing. Dheantadh	mi, *I would* or *could be* thu, *thou wouldst* or *couldst be* e, *he would* or *could be* } *made*	*Sing* Ma nithear	mi, *if I shall* or *will be* thu, *if thou shalt* or *wilt be* e, *if he shall* or *will be* } *made*
Plur. Dheantadh	sinn, *we would* or *could be* sibh, *ye would* or *could be* iad, *they would* or *could be* } *made.*	*Plur.* Ma nithear	sinn *if we shall* or *will be* sibh, *if ye shall* or *will be* iad, *if they shall* or *will be*

Preterite

Sing Nan deantadh { mi, *if I would* or *could be* / thu, *if thou wouldst* or *couldst be* / e, *if he would* or *could be* } *made*

Plur. Nan deantadh { sinn, *if we would* or *could be* / sibh, *if ye would* or *could be* / iad, *if they would* or *could be* } *made.*

Future.

Sing. Nan deanar { mi, *if I shall* or *will be* / thu, *if thou shalt* or *wilt be* / e, *if he shall* or *will be* } *made.*

Plur Nan deanar { sinn, *if we shall* or *will be* / sibh, *if ye shall* or *will be* / iad, *if they shall* or *will be* } *made.*

IMPERATIVE MOOD.

Sing Deantar { mi, *let me be* / thu, *be thou* / e, *let him be* } *made.*

Plur Deantar { sinn, *let us be* / sibh, *be ye* / iad, *let them be* } *made*

PARTICIPLE

Deanta, deante, *done.*

CLUINN, hear.

ACTIVE VOICE

AFFIRMATIVE, OR INDICATIVE MOOD.

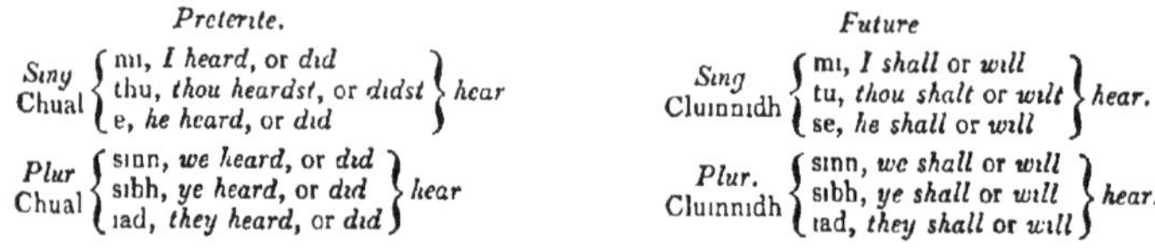

Preterite.

Sing Chual { mi, *I heard*, or *did* / thu, *thou heardst*, or *didst* / e, *he heard*, or *did* } *hear*

Plur Chual { sinn, *we heard*, or *did* / sibh, *ye heard*, or *did* / iad, *they heard*, or *did* } *hear*

Future

Sing Cluinnidh { mi, *I shall* or *will* / tu, *thou shalt* or *wilt* / se, *he shall* or *will* } *hear.*

Plur. Cluinnidh { sinn, *we shall* or *will* / sibh, *ye shall* or *will* / iad, *they shall* or *will* } *hear.*

NEGATIVE, OR INTERROGATIVE MOOD

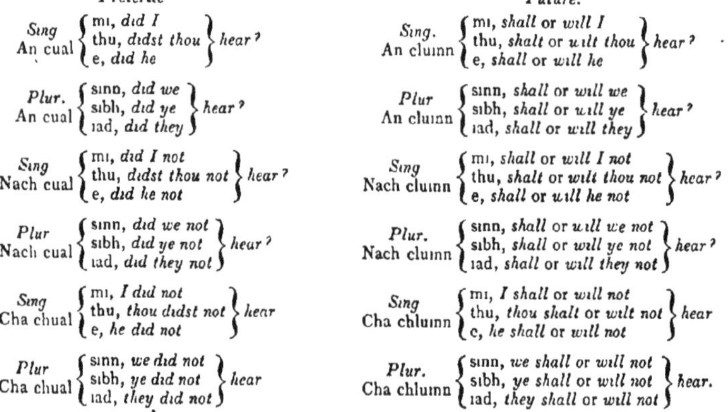

Preterite

Sing An cual { mi, *did I* / thu, *didst thou* / e, *did he* } *hear?*

Plur. An cual { sinn, *did we* / sibh, *did ye* / iad, *did they* } *hear?*

Sing Nach cual { mi, *did I not* / thu, *didst thou not* / e, *did he not* } *hear?*

Plur Nach cual { sinn, *did we not* / sibh, *did ye not* / iad, *did they not* } *hear?*

Sing Cha chual { mi, *I did not* / thu, *thou didst not* / e, *he did not* } *hear*

Plur Cha chual { sinn, *we did not* / sibh, *ye did not* / iad, *they did not* } *hear*

Future.

Sing. An cluinn { mi, *shall* or *will I* / thu, *shalt* or *wilt thou* / e, *shall* or *will he* } *hear?*

Plur An cluinn { sinn, *shall* or *will we* / sibh, *shall* or *will ye* / iad, *shall* or *will they* } *hear?*

Sing Nach cluinn { mi, *shall* or *will I not* / thu, *shalt* or *wilt thou not* / e, *shall* or *will he not* } *hear?*

Plur. Nach cluinn { sinn, *shall* or *will we not* / sibh, *shall* or *will ye not* / iad, *shall* or *will they not* } *hear?*

Sing Cha chluinn { mi, *I shall* or *will not* / thu, *thou shalt* or *wilt not* / e, *he shall* or *will not* } *hear*

Plur. Cha chluinn { sinn, *we shall* or *will not* / sibh, *ye shall* or *will not* / iad, *they shall* or *will not* } *hear.*

SUBJUNCTIVE MOOD.

Preterite

Sing. { Chluinninn, *I could* or *would* / Chluinneadh tu, *thou couldst* or *wouldst* / Chluinneadh e, *he could* or *would* } *hear.*

Plur { Chlúinneamaid, *we could* or *would* / Chluinneadh sibh, *ye could* or *would* / Chluinneadh iad, *they could* or *would* } *hear*

Future

Sing Ma chluinneas { mi, *if I shall* or *will* / tu, *if thou shalt* or *wilt* / e, *if he shall* or *will* } *hear*

Plur. Ma chluinneas { sinn, *if we shall* or *will* / sibh, *if you shall* or *will* / iad, *if they shall* or *will* } *hear*

IMPERATIVE MOOD.

Sing.
Cluinneam, *let me hear.*
Cluinn, *hear thou,* or *do thou hear.*
Cluinneadh e, *let him hear.*

Plur.
Cluinneamaid, *let us hear.*
Cluinnibh, *hear ye.*
Cluinneadh iad, *let them hear.*

INFINITIVE MOOD.

A chluinntinn, *to hear.*

PARTICIPLE.

A cluinntinn, *hearing*

PASSIVE VOICE.

Preterite.

Sing Chualadh	mi, *I was* thu, *thou wert* e, *he was*	*heard*
Plur. Chualadh	sinn, *we were* sibh, *ye were* iad, *they were*	*heard*

Future.

Sing Cluinnear	mi, *I shall* or *will be* thu, *thou shalt* or *wilt be* e, *he shall* or *will be*	*heard*
Plur. Cluinnear	sinn, *we shall* or *will be* sibh, *ye shall* or *will be* iad, *they shall* or *will be*	*heard*

NEGATIVE, OR INTERROGATIVE MOOD.

Preterite.

Sing An cualadh	mi, *was I* thu, *wert thou* e, *was he*	*heard?*
Plur. An cualadh	sinn, *were we* sibh, *were ye* iad, *were they*	*heard?*
Sing. Nach cualadh	mi, *was I not* thu, *wert thou not* e, *was he not*	*heard?*
Plur. Nach cualadh	sinn, *were we not* sibh, *were ye not* iad, *were they not*	*heard?*

Future.

Sing. An cluinnear	mi, *shall* or *will I be* thu, *shalt* or *wilt thou be* e, *shall* or *will he be*	*heard?*
Plur. An cluinnear	sinn, *shall* or *will we be* sibh, *shall* or *will ye be* iad, *shall* or *will they be*	*heard?*
Sing. Nach cluinnear	mi, *shall* or *will I not be* thu, *shalt thou not be* e, *shall* or *will he not be*	*heard?*
Plur. Nach cluinnear	sinn, *shall* or *will we not be* sibh, *shall* or *will ye not* iad, *shall* or *will they not be*	*heard?*

SUBJUNCTIVE MOOD

Preterite

Sing. Chluinnteadh	mi, *I could* or *would be* thu, *thou couldst* or *wouldst be* e, *he could* or *would be*	*heard.*
Plur Chluinnteadh	sinn, *we could* or *would be* sibh, *ye could* or *would be* iad, *they could* or *would be*	*heard*

Future

Sing Mu chluinnear	mi, *if I shall* or *will be* thu, *if thou shalt* or *wilt be* e, *if he shall* or *will be*	*heard*
Plur. Mu chluinnear	sinn, *if we shall* or *will be* sibh, *if ye shall* or *will be* iad, *if they shall* or *will be*	*heard*

IMPERATIVE MOOD

Sing Cluinntear	mi, *let me be* thu, *be thou* e, *let him be*	*heard.*
Plur Cluinntear	sinn, *let us be* sibh, *be ye* iad, *let them be*	*heard*

THIG, come.

ACTIVE VOICE.

AFFIRMATIVE, OR INDICATIVE MOOD

Preterite.

Sing. Thainig	mi, *I came,* or *did* thu, *thou camest* or *didst* e, *he came* or *did*	*come*
Plur. Thainig	sinn, *we came,* or *did* sibh, *ye came,* or *did* iad, *they came,* or *did*	*come*

Future.

Sing Thig	mi, *I shall* or *will* thu, *thou shalt* or *wilt* e, *he shall* or *will*	*come.*
Plur Thig	sinn, *we shall* or *will* sibh, *ye shall* or *will* iad, *they shall* or *will*	*come*

INTERROGATIVE, OR NEGATIVE MOOD.

Preterite.

Sing. An d' thainig { mi, *did I* / thu, *didst thou* / e, *did he* } *come?*

Plur. An d' thainig { sinn, *did we* / sibh, *did ye* / iad, *did they* } *come?*

Future.

Sing. An tig { mi, *shall* or *will I* / thu, *shalt* or *wilt thou* / e, *shall* or *will he* } *come?*

Plur. An tig { sinn, *shall* or *will we* / sibh, *shall* or *will ye* / iad, *shall* or *will they* } *come?*

Preterite.

Sing. Nach d'thainig { mi, *did I not* / thu, *didst thou not* / e, *did he not* } *come?*

Plur. Nach d'thainig { sinn, *did we not* / sibh, *did ye not* / iad, *did they not* } *come?*

Future.

Sing. Nach tig { mi, *shall* or *will I not* / thu, *shalt* or *wilt thou not* / e, *shall* or *will he not* } *come?*

Plur. Nach tig { sinn, *shall* or *will we not* / sibh, *shall* or *will ye not* / iad, *shall* or *will they not* } *come?*

Preterite.

Sing. Cha d' thainig { mi, *I came not*, or *did not* / thu, *thou camest not*, or *didst not* / e, *he came not*, or *did not* } *come*

Plur. Cha d' thainig { sinn, *we came not*, or *did not* / sibh, *ye came not*, or *did not* / iad, *they came not*, or *did not* } *come*

Future.

Sing. Cha tig { mi, *I shall* or *will not* / thu, *thou shalt* or *wilt not* / e, *he shall* or *will not* } *come.*

Plur. Cha tig { sinn, *we shall* or *will not* / sibh, *ye shall* or *will not* / iad, *they shall* or *will not* } *come*

SUBJUNCTIVE MOOD.

Preterite

Sing. { Thiginn, *I would* / Thigeadh tu, *thou wouldst* / Thigeadh e, *he would* } *come.*

Plur { Thigeamaid, *we would* / Thigeabh sibh, *ye would* / Thigeadh iad, *they would* } *come*

Sing Nan { Tiginn, *if I had* or *would* / Tigeadh thu, *if thou hadst* or *wouldst* / Tigeadh e, *if he had* or *would* } *come*

Plur Nan { Tigeamaid, *if we had* or *would* / Tigeadh sibh, *if ye had* or *would* / Tigeadh iad, *if they had* or *would* } *come*

Future.

Sing. Ma thig { mi, *if I shall* or *will* / thu, *if thou shalt* or *wilt* / e, *if he shall* or *will* } *come.*

Plur. Ma thig { sinn, *if we shall* or *will* / sibh, *if ye shall* or *will* / iad, *if they shall* or *will* } *come*

Sing Mar { Tiginn, *if I had* or *would not* / Tigeadh thu, *if thou hadst* or *wouldst not* / Tigeadh e, *if he had* or *would not* } *come*

Plur Mar { Tigeamaid, *or* Tigeadh sinn, *if we had* or *would not* / Tigeadh sibh, *if ye had* or *would not* / Tigeadh iad, *if they had* or *would not* } *come.*

IMPERATIVE MOOD.

Sing { Thigeam, *let me come* / Thig, *come thou* / Thigeadh e, *let him come.* }

Plur. { Thigeamaid, *let us come.* / Thigibh, *come ye.* / Thigeadh iad, *let them come* }

INFINITIVE MOOD.

A thighinnn, / A theachd, } *to come.*

PARTICIPLE.

A tighinn, / A teachd, } *coming.*

BEIR, bear.

ACTIVE VOICE.

AFFIRMATIVE, OR INDICATIVE MOOD.

Preterite

Sing. Rug { mi, *I bore.* / thu, *thou borest* / i, *she bore.* }

Plur. Rug { sinn, *we bore.* / sibh, *ye bore* / iad, *they bore.* }

Future.

Sing Beiridh { mi, *I shall* or *will bear.* / thu, *thou shalt* or *wilt bear.* / si, *she shall* or *will bear.* }

Plur. Beiridh { sinn, *we shall* or *will bear.* / sibh, *ye shall* or *will bear.* / iad, *they shall* or *will bear.* }

NEGATIVE, OR INTERROGATIVE MOOD.

Preterite.	*Future.*
Sing. An do rug { mi, *did I bear?* / thu, *didst thou bear?* / i, *did she bear?* }	*Sing.* Am beir { mi, *shall I bear?* / thu, *shalt thou bear?* / i, *shall she bear?* }
Plur. An do rug { sinn, *did we bear?* / sibh, *did ye bear?* / iad, *did they bear?* }	*Plur.* Am beir { sinn, *shall we bear?* / sibh, *shall ye bear?* / iad, *shall they bear?* }
Sing. Cha do rug { mi, *I bore not*, or *did not* / thu, *thou borest not*, or *didst not* / i, *she bore not*, or *did not* } *bear*	*Sing.* Cha bheir { mi, *I shall* or *will not* / thu, *thou shalt* or *wilt not* / i, *she shall* or *will not* } *bear*
Plur. Cha do rug { sinn, *we bore not*, or *did not* / sibh, *ye bore not*, or *did not* / iad, *they bore not*, or *did not* } *bear.*	*Plur* Cha bheir { sinn, *we shall* or *will not* / sibh, *ye shall* or *will not* / iad, *they shall* or *will not* } *bear.*
Sing. Nach do rug { mi, *did I not* / thu, *didst thou not* / i, *did she not* } *bear?*	*Sing* Nach beir { mi, *shall I not* / thu, *shalt thou not* / i, *shall she not* } *bear?*
Plur. Nach do rug { sinn, *did we not* / sibh, *did ye not* / iad, *did they not* } *bear?*	*Plur* Nach beir { sinn, *shall we not* / sibh, *shall ye not* / iad, *shall they not* } *bear?*

SUBJUNCTIVE MOOD.

Preterite.	*Future.*
Sing. { Bheirinn, *I could* or *would* / Beireadh tu, *thou couldst* or *wouldst* / Bheireadh i, *she could* or *would* } *bear.*	*Sing.* Ma bheireas { mi, *if I shall* or *will* / tu, *if thou shalt* or *wilt* / i, *if she shall* or *will* } *bear.*
Plur. { Bheireadhmaid, *we could* or *would* / Bheireadh sibh, *ye could* or *would* / Bheireadh iad, *they could* or *would* } *bear.*	*Plur.* Ma bheireas { sinn, *if we shall* or *will* / sibh, *if ye shall* or *will* / iad, *if they shall* or *will* } *bear*

IMPERATIVE MOOD.

Sing. { Beiream, *let me bear.* / Beir, *bear thou* / Beireadh i, *let her bear.* }

Plur. { Beireamaid, *let us bear.* / Beiribh, *bear ye* / Beireadh iad, *let them bear.* }

INFINITIVE MOOD.

A bheirsinn, / A bhreith, } *to bear.*

PARTICIPLE.

A beirsinn, / A breith, } *bearing.*

PASSIVE VOICE

AFFIRMATIVE, OR INDICATIVE MOOD.

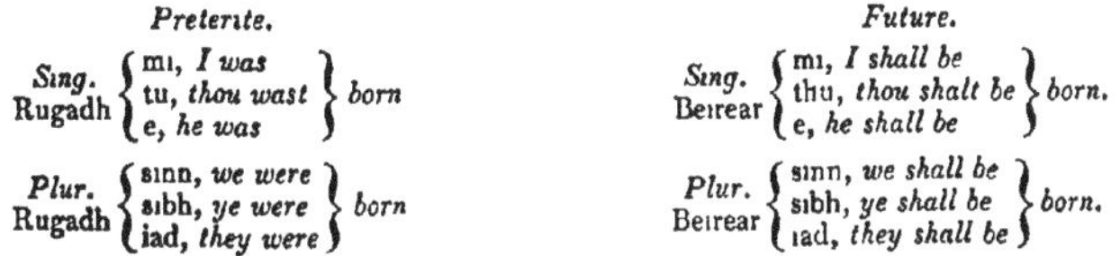

Preterite.	*Future.*
Sing. Rugadh { mi, *I was* / tu, *thou wast* / e, *he was* } *born*	*Sing.* Beirear { mi, *I shall be* / thu, *thou shalt be* / e, *he shall be* } *born.*
Plur. Rugadh { sinn, *we were* / sibh, *ye were* / iad, *they were* } *born*	*Plur.* Beirear { sinn, *we shall be* / sibh, *ye shall be* / iad, *they shall be* } *born.*

NEGATIVE, OR INTERROGATIVE MOOD.

Preterite.	*Preterite.*
Sing. An do rugadh { mi, *was I* / thu, *wert thou* / e, *was he* } *born?*	*Sing* Cha do rugadh { mi, *I was not* / thu, *thou wert not* / e, *he was not* } *born.*
Plur. An do rugadh { sinn, *were we* / sibh, *were ye* / iad, *were they* } *born?*	*Plur.* Cha do rugadh { sinn, *we were not* / sibh, *ye were not* / iad, *they were not* } *born*

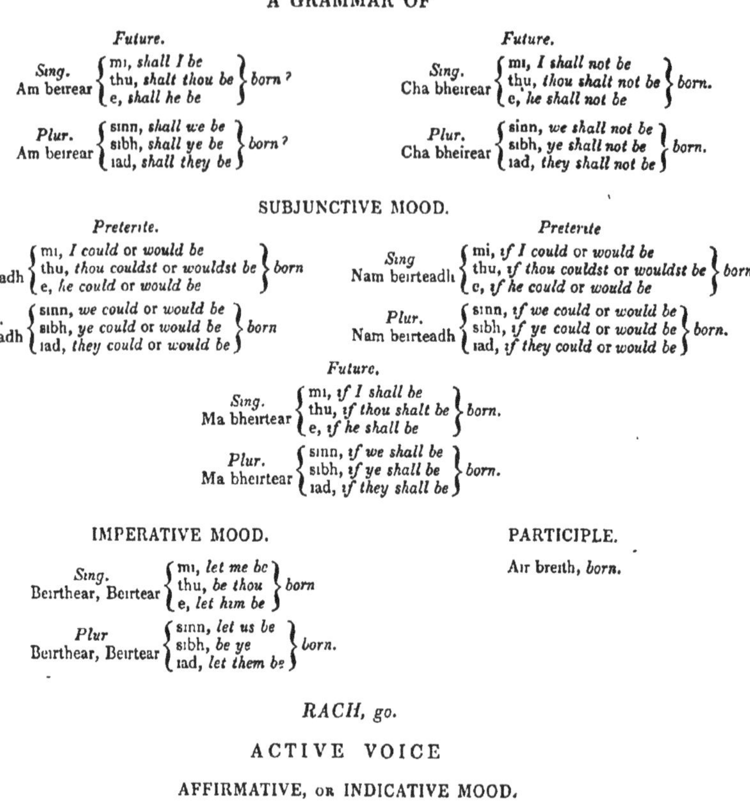

Future.

Sing. Am beirear { mi, *shall I be* / thu, *shalt thou be* / e, *shall he be* } *born?*

Plur. Am beirear { sinn, *shall we be* / sibh, *shall ye be* / iad, *shall they be* } *born?*

Future.

Sing. Cha bheirear { mi, *I shall not be* / thu, *thou shalt not be* / e, *he shall not be* } *born.*

Plur. Cha bheirear { sinn, *we shall not be* / sibh, *ye shall not be* / iad, *they shall not be* } *born.*

SUBJUNCTIVE MOOD.

Preterite.

Sing Bheirteadh { mi, *I could* or *would be* / thu, *thou couldst* or *wouldst be* / e, *he could* or *would be* } *born*

Plur. Bheirteadh { sinn, *we could* or *would be* / sibh, *ye could* or *would be* / iad, *they could* or *would be* } *born*

Preterite

Sing Nam beirteadh { mi, *if I could* or *would be* / thu, *if thou couldst* or *wouldst be* / e, *if he could* or *would be* } *born*

Plur. Nam beirteadh { sinn, *if we could* or *would be* / sibh, *if ye could* or *would be* / iad, *if they could* or *would be* } *born.*

Future.

Sing. Ma bheirtear { mi, *if I shall be* / thu, *if thou shalt be* / e, *if he shall be* } *born.*

Plur. Ma bheirtear { sinn, *if we shall be* / sibh, *if ye shall be* / iad, *if they shall be* } *born.*

IMPERATIVE MOOD.

Sing. Beirthear, Beirtear { mi, *let me be* / thu, *be thou* / e, *let him be* } *born*

Plur Beirthear, Beirtear { sinn, *let us be* / sibh, *be ye* / iad, *let them be* } *born.*

PARTICIPLE.

Air breith, *born.*

RACH, go.

ACTIVE VOICE

AFFIRMATIVE, OR INDICATIVE MOOD.

Preterite

Sing. Chaidh { mi, *I went,* or *did* / thu, *thou wentest,* or *didst* / e, *he went,* or *did* } *go.*

Plur. Chaidh { sinn, *we went,* or *did* / sibh, *ye went,* or *did* / iad, *they went,* or *did* } *go.*

Future.

Sing Théid { mi, *I shall* / thu, *thou shalt* / e, *he shall* } *go.*

Plur. Théid { sinn, *we shall* / sibh, *ye shall* / iad, *they shall* } *go.*

NEGATIVE, OR INTERROGATIVE MOOD

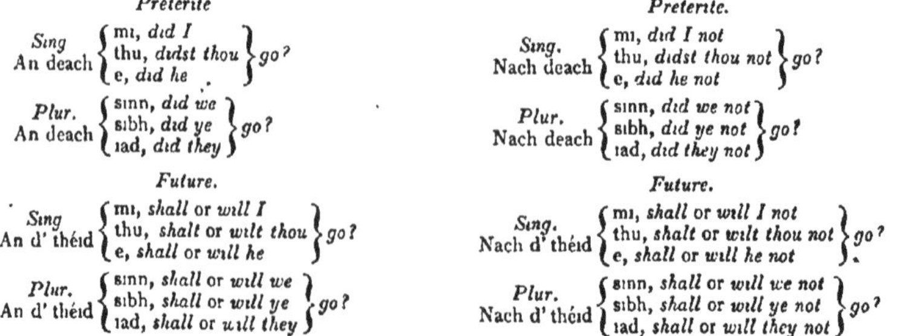

Preterite

Sing An deach { mi, *did I* / thu, *didst thou* / e, *did he* } *go?*

Plur. An deach { sinn, *did we* / sibh, *did ye* / iad, *did they* } *go?*

Preterite.

Sing. Nach deach { mi, *did I not* / thu, *didst thou not* / e, *did he not* } *go?*

Plur. Nach deach { sinn, *did we not* / sibh, *did ye not* / iad, *did they not* } *go?*

Future.

Sing An d' théid { mi, *shall* or *will I* / thu, *shalt* or *wilt thou* / e, *shall* or *will he* } *go?*

Plur. An d' théid { sinn, *shall* or *will we* / sibh, *shall* or *will ye* / iad, *shall* or *will they* } *go?*

Future.

Sing. Nach d' théid { mi, *shall* or *will I not* / thu, *shalt* or *wilt thou not* / e, *shall* or *will he not* } *go?*

Plur. Nach d' théid { sinn, *shall* or *will we not* / sibh, *shall* or *will ye not* / iad, *shall* or *will they not* } *go?*

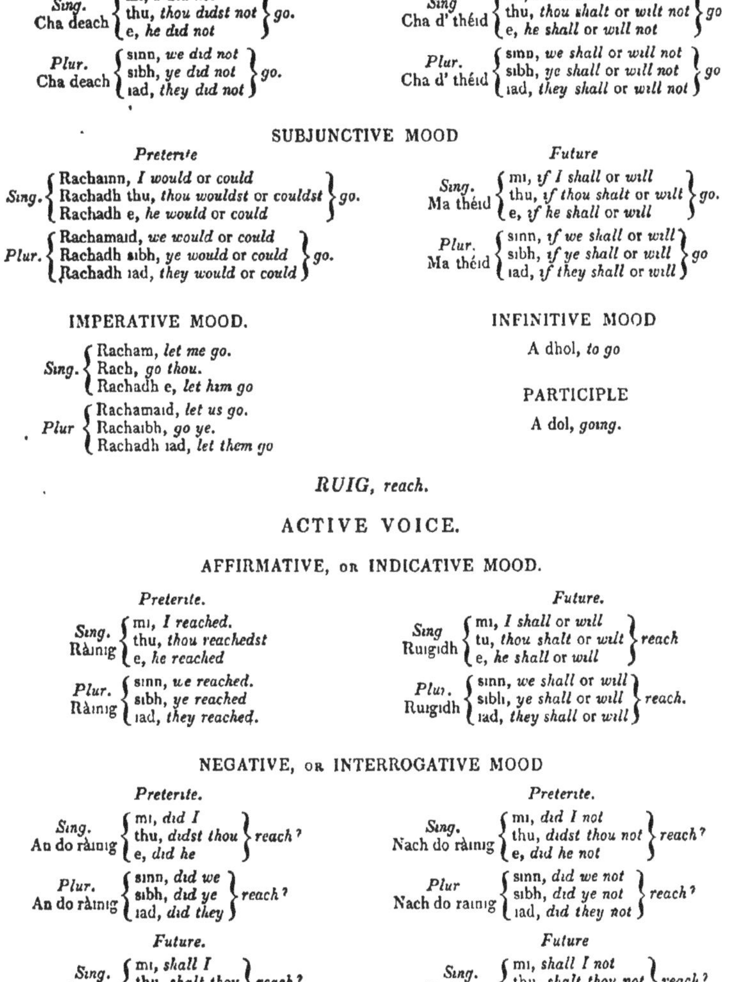

Preterite.		Future	
Sing. Cha deach	mi, *I did not* / thu, *thou didst not* / e, *he did not* } *go.*	*Sing* Cha d' théid	mi, *I shall* or *will not* / thu, *thou shalt* or *wilt not* / e, *he shall* or *will not* } *go*
Plur. Cha deach	sinn, *we did not* / sibh, *ye did not* / iad, *they did not* } *go.*	*Plur.* Cha d' théid	sinn, *we shall* or *will not* / sibh, *ye shall* or *will not* / iad, *they shall* or *will not* } *go*

SUBJUNCTIVE MOOD

Preterite	Future
Sing. Rachainn, *I would* or *could* / Rachadh thu, *thou wouldst* or *couldst* / Rachadh e, *he would* or *could* } *go.*	*Sing.* Ma théid mi, *if I shall* or *will* / thu, *if thou shalt* or *wilt* / e, *if he shall* or *will* } *go.*
Plur. Rachamaid, *we would* or *could* / Rachadh sibh, *ye would* or *could* / Rachadh iad, *they would* or *could* } *go.*	*Plur.* Ma théid sinn, *if we shall* or *will* / sibh, *if ye shall* or *will* / iad, *if they shall* or *will* } *go*

IMPERATIVE MOOD.

Sing. Racham, *let me go.* / Rach, *go thou.* / Rachadh e, *let him go*

Plur Rachamaid, *let us go.* / Rachaibh, *go ye.* / Rachadh iad, *let them go*

INFINITIVE MOOD

A dhol, *to go*

PARTICIPLE

A dol, *going.*

RUIG, reach.

ACTIVE VOICE.

AFFIRMATIVE, or INDICATIVE MOOD.

Preterite.		Future.	
Sing. Ràinig	mi, *I reached.* / thu, *thou reachedst* / e, *he reached*	*Sing* Ruigidh	mi, *I shall* or *will* / tu, *thou shalt* or *wilt* / e, *he shall* or *will* } *reach*
Plur. Ràinig	sinn, *we reached.* / sibh, *ye reached* / iad, *they reached.*	*Plur.* Ruigidh	sinn, *we shall* or *will* / sibh, *ye shall* or *will* / iad, *they shall* or *will* } *reach.*

NEGATIVE, or INTERROGATIVE MOOD

Preterite.		Preterite.	
Sing. An do ràinig	mi, *did I* / thu, *didst thou* / e, *did he* } *reach?*	*Sing.* Nach do ràinig	mi, *did I not* / thu, *didst thou not* / e, *did he not* } *reach?*
Plur. An do ràinig	sinn, *did we* / sibh, *did ye* / iad, *did they* } *reach?*	*Plur* Nach do rainig	sinn, *did we not* / sibh, *did ye not* / iad, *did they not* } *reach?*
Future.		**Future**	
Sing. An ruig	mi, *shall I* / thu, *shalt thou* / e, *shall he* } *reach?*	*Sing.* Nach ruig	mi, *shall I not* / thu, *shalt thou not* / e, *shall he not* } *reach?*
Plur. An ruig	sinn, *shall we* / sibh, *shall ye* / iad, *shall they* } *reach?*	*Plur* Nach ruig	sinn, *shall we not* / sibh, *shall ye not* / iad, *shall they not* } *reach?*
Preterite.		**Future.**	
Sing Cha do ràinig	mi, *I reached not*, or *did not* / thu, *thou reachedst not*, or *didst not* / e, *he reached not*, or *did not* } *reach*	*Sing* Cha ruig	mi, *I shall* or *will not* / thu, *thou shalt* or *wilt not* / e, *he shall* or *will not* } *reach*
Plur. Cha do ràinig	sinn, *we reached not*, or *did not* / sibh, *ye reached not*, or *did not* / iad, *they reached not*, or *did not* } *reach*	*Plur.* Cha ruig	sinn, *we shall* or *will not* / sibh, *ye shall* or *will not* / iad, *they shall* or *will not* } *reach*

SUBJUNCTIVE MOOD.

Preterite.

Sing. { Ruiginn, *I would* / Ruigeadh tu, *thou wouldst* / Ruigeadh e, *he would* } *reach*

Plur. { Ruigeamaid, *we would* / Ruigibh, *ye would* / Ruigeadh iad, *they would* } *reach.*

Future.

Sing. Ma ruigeas { mi, *if I shall* or *will* / tu, *if thou shalt* or *wilt* / e, *if he shall* or *will* } *reach.*

Plur Ma ruigeas { sinn, *if we shall* or *will* / sibh, *if ye shall* or *will* / iad, *if they shall* or *will* } *reach.*

IMPERATIVE MOOD.

Sing. { Ruigeam, *let me reach* / Ruig, *reach thou.* / Ruigeadh e, *let him reach* }

Plur. { Ruigeamaid, *let us reach* / Ruigibh, *reach ye* / Ruigeadh iad, *let them reach* }

INFINITIVE MOOD.

A ruigsinn, / A ruigheachd, } *to reach.*

PARTICIPLE

A ruigsinn, / A ruigheachd, } *reaching.*

*THOIR, or THABHAIR,** *give.*

AFFIRMATIVE, OR INDICATIVE MOOD.

Preterite

Sing Thug { mi, *I gave*, or *did* / thu, *thou gavest*, or *didst* / e, *he gave*, or *did* } *give.*

Plur. Thug { sinn, *we gave*, or *did* / sibh, *ye gave*, or *did* / iad, *they gave*, or *did* } *give.*

Future.

Sing. Bheir { mi, *I shall* or *will* / thu, *thou shalt* or *wilt* / e, *he shall* or *will* } *give.*

Plur Bheir { sinn, *we shall* or *will* / sibh, *ye shall* or *will* / iad, *they shall* or *will* } *give.*

NEGATIVE, OR INTERROGATIVE MOOD.

Preterite

Sing. An tug† { mi, *did I* / thu, *didst thou* / e, *did he* } *give?*

Plur An tug { sinn, *did we* / sibh, *did ye* / iad, *did they* } *give?*

Preterite.

Sing. Nach tug { mi, *did I not* / thu, *didst thou not* / e, *did he not* } *give?*

Plur Nach tug { sinn, *did we not* / sibh, *did ye not* / iad, *did they not* } *give?*

Future

Sing. Bheir { mi, *I shall* or *will* / thu, *thou shalt* or *wilt* / e, *he shall* or *will* } *give*

Plur. Bheir { sinn, *we shall* or *will* / sibh, *ye shall* or *will* / iad, *they shall* or *will* } *give.*

Future,

Sing. An toir { mi, *shall* or *will I* / thu, *shalt* or *wilt thou* / e, *shall* or *will he* } *give?*

Plur. An toir { sinn, *shall* or *will we* / sibh, *shall* or *will ye* / iad, *shall* or *will they* } *give?*

Preterite

Sing Nach tug { mi, *did I not* / thu, *didst thou not* / e, *did he not* } *give?*

Plur Nach tug { sinn, *did we not* / sibh, *did ye not* / iad, *did they not* } *give?*

Sing. Cha tug { mi, *I did not* / thu, *thou didst not* / e, *he did not* } *give*

Plur Cha tug { sinn, *we did not* / sibh, *ye did not* / iad, *they did not* } *give.*

Future.

Sing. Nach toir { mi, *shall* or *will I not* / thu, *shalt* or *wilt thou not* / e, *shall* or *will he not* } *give?*

Plur Nach toir { sinn, *shall* or *will we not* / sibh, *shall* or *will ye not* / iad, *shall* or *will they not* } *give?*

Sing. Cha toir { mi, *I shall* or *will not* / thu, *thou shalt* or *wilt not* / e, *he shall* or *will not* } *give*

Plur. Cha toir { sinn, *we shall* or *will not* / sibh, *ye shall* or *will not* / iad, *they shall* or *will not* } *give*

* *Thabhair* is also written *tabhair*

† *Tug* is also written *d' thug* by some of our best writers.

SUBJUNCTIVE MOOD

Preterite.

Sing. Bheirinn, *I could* or *would* / Bheireadh tu, *thou couldst* or *wouldst* / Bheireadh e, *he could* or *would give* — *give.*

Plur. Bheireamaid, *we could* or *would* / Bheireadh sibh, *ye could* or *would* / Bheireadh iad, *they could* or *would* — *give.*

Preterite

Sing. Cha tugainn, *I would not* / tugadh tu, *thou wouldst not* / tugadh e, *he would not* — *give*

Plur. Cha tugamaid, *we would not* / tugadh sibh, *ye would not* / tugadh iad, *they would not* — *give.*

Future.

Sing. Ma bheir mi, *if I shall* or *will* / thu, *if thou shalt* or *wilt* / e, *if he shall* or *will* — *give.*

Plur. Ma bheir sinn, *if we shall* or *will* / sibh, *if ye shall* or *will* / iad, *if they shall* or *will* — *give*

Preterite.

Sing. Cha toirinn, *I would not* / toireadh tu, *thou wouldst not* / toireadh e, *he would not* — *give*

Plur. Cha toireamaid, *we would not* / toireadh sibh, *ye would not* / toireadh iad, *they would not* — *give*

IMPERATIVE MOOD.

Sing. Thoiream, thugam, *let me give* / Thoir, thug, *give thou.* / Thoireadh e, thugadh e, *let him give.*

Plur. Thoireamaid, thugamaid, *let us give* / Thoiribh, thugaibh, *give ye.* / Thoireadh iad, thugadh iad, *let them give.*

INFINITIVE MOOD.

A thoirt, / A thabhairt, — *to give.*

PARTICIPLE.

A toirt, / A tabhairt, — *giving.*

PASSIVE VOICE.

AFFIRMATIVE, OR INDICATIVE MOOD.

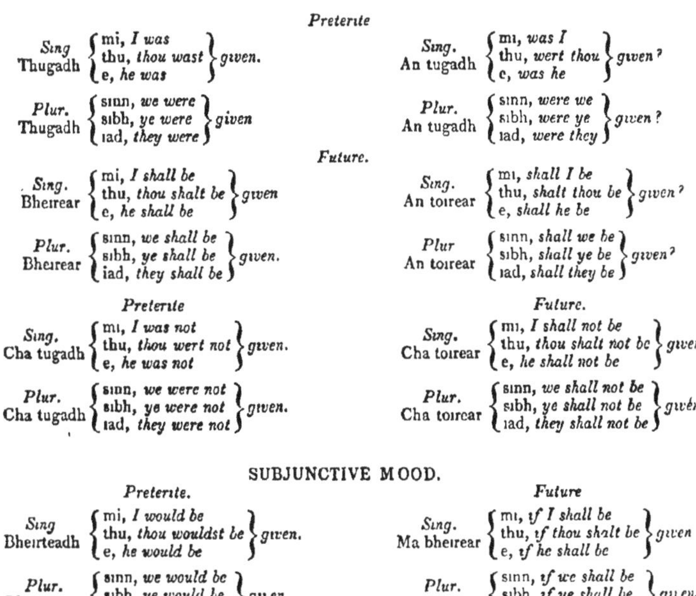

Preterite

Sing. Thugadh mi, *I was* / thu, *thou wast* / e, *he was* — *given.*

Sing. An tugadh mi, *was I* / thu, *wert thou* / e, *was he* — *given?*

Plur. Thugadh sinn, *we were* / sibh, *ye were* / iad, *they were* — *given*

Plur. An tugadh sinn, *were we* / sibh, *were ye* / iad, *were they* — *given?*

Future.

Sing. Bheirear mi, *I shall be* / thu, *thou shalt be* / e, *he shall be* — *given*

Sing. An toirear mi, *shall I be* / thu, *shalt thou be* / e, *shall he be* — *given?*

Plur. Bheirear sinn, *we shall be* / sibh, *ye shall be* / iad, *they shall be* — *given.*

Plur. An toirear sinn, *shall we be* / sibh, *shall ye be* / iad, *shall they be* — *given?*

Preterite

Sing. Cha tugadh mi, *I was not* / thu, *thou wert not* / e, *he was not* — *given.*

Plur. Cha tugadh sinn, *we were not* / sibh, *ye were not* / iad, *they were not* — *given.*

Future.

Sing. Cha toirear mi, *I shall not be* / thu, *thou shalt not be* / e, *he shall not be* — *given*

Plur. Cha toirear sinn, *we shall not be* / sibh, *ye shall not be* / iad, *they shall not be* — *given*

SUBJUNCTIVE MOOD.

Preterite.

Sing. Bheirteadh mi, *I would be* / thu, *thou wouldst be* / e, *he would be* — *given.*

Plur. Bheirteadh sinn, *we would be* / sibh, *ye would be* / iad, *they would be* — *given.*

Future

Sing. Ma bheirear mi, *if I shall be* / thu, *if thou shalt be* / e, *if he shall be* — *given*

Plur. Ma bheirear sinn, *if we shall be* / sibh, *if ye shall be* / iad, *if they shall be* — *given.*

Preterite.

Sing. Cha tugtadh	mi, *I would not be* / thu, *thou wouldst not be* / e, *he would not be*	*given.*

Preterite.

Plur. Cha tugtadh	sinn, *we would not be* / sibh, *ye would not be* / iad, *they would not be*	*given.*

IMPERATIVE MOOD.

Sing. Thugthar	mi, *let me be* / thu, *be thou* / e, *let him be*	*given.*
Plur. Thugthar	**sinn, *let us be* / sibh, *be ye* / iad, *let them be***	***given.***

FAIC, see

ACTIVE VOICE.

AFFIRMATIVE, OR NEGATIVE MOOD.

Preterite.

Sing Chunna, *or* Chunnaic	mi, *I saw*, or *did* / thu, *thou sawest*, or *didst* / e, *he saw*, or *did*	*see.*
Plur Chunna, *or* Chunnaic	sinn, *we saw*, or *did* / sibh, *ye saw*, or *did* / iad, *they saw*, or *did*	*see*

Future.

Sing. Chi	mi, *I shall* or *will* / thu, *thou shalt* or *wilt* / e, *he shall* or *will*	*see.*
Plur. Chi	sinn, *we shall* or *will* / sibh, *ye shall* or *will* / iad, *they shall* or *will*	*see.*

NEGATIVE, OR INTERROGATIVE MOOD.

Preterite

Sing Am fac	mi, *did I* / thu, *didst thou* / e, *did he*	*see?*
Plur Am fac	sinn, *did we* / sibh, *did ye* / iad, *did they*	*see?*

Preterite

Sing Nach fhac	mi, *did I not* / thu *didst thou not* / e, *did he not*	*see?*
Plur. Nach fhac	sinn, *did we not* / sibh, *did ye not* / iad, *did they not*	*see?*

Future.

Sing. Am faic	mi, *shall I* / thu, *shalt thou* / e, *shall he*	*see?*
Plur Am faic	sinn, *shall we* / sibh, *shall ye* / iad, *shall they*	*see?*

Future.

Sing. Nach fhaic	mi, *shall I not* / thu, *shalt thou not* / e, *shall he not*	*see?*
Plur. Nach fhaic	sinn, *shall we not* / sibh, *shall ye not* / iad, *shall they not*	*see?*

Preterite.

Sing Cha 'n fhac mi, *I did not see.*
Plur Cha 'n fhac sinn, *we did not see.*

Future.

Sing Cha 'n fhaic mi, *I shall not see.*
Plur. Cha 'n fhaic sinn, *we shall not see.*

SUBJUNCTIVE MOOD.

Preterite

Sing.	Chithinn, *I would* / Chitheadh thu, *thou wouldst* / Chitheadh e, *he would*	*see?*
Plur	Chitheamaid, *we would* / Chitheadh sibh, *ye would* / Chitheadh iad, *they would*	*see.*

Future

Sing Ma chi	mi, *if I shall* / thu, *if thou shalt* / e, *if he shall*	*see.*
Plur. Ma chi	sinn *if we shall* / sibh, *if ye shall* / iad, *if they shall*	*see*

Sing Nam	faicinn, *if I would* or *could* / faiceadh thu, *if thou wouldst* or *couldst* / faiceadh e, *if he would* or *could*	*see*
Plur Nam	faiceamaid, *or* faiceadh sinn, *if we would* or *could* / faiceadh sibh, *if ye would* or *could* / faiceadh iad, *if they would* or *could*	*see.*

IMPERATIVE MOOD.

Sing.	Faiceam, *let me see.* / Faic, *see thou.* / Faiceadh e, *let him see*
Plur.	Faiceamaid, *let us see* / Faicibh, *see ye.* / Faiceadh iad, *let them see*

INFINITIVE MOOD.

A dh' fhaicinn, / Dh' fhaicsinn, } *to see*

PARTICIPLE

A faicinn, / A faicsinn, } *seeing.*

PASSIVE VOICE.

AFFIRMATIVE, OR INDICATIVE MOOD.

Preterite.

Sing. Chunnacadh*	mi, *I was* thu, *thou wert* e, *he was*	*seen.*
Plur. Chunnacadh	sinn, *we were* sibh, *ye were* iad, *they were*	*seen.*

Future

Sing. Chithear	mi, *I shall be* thu, *thou shalt be* e, *he shall be*	*seen.*
Plur. Chithear	sinn, *we shall be* sibh, *ye shall be* iad, *they shall be*	*seen*

NEGATIVE, OR INTERROGATIVE MOOD.

Preterite.

Sing Am facadh	mi, *was I* thu, *wert thou* e, *was he*	*seen?*
Plur. Am facadh	sinn, *were we* sibh, *were ye* iad, *were they*	*seen?*

Sing. Nach fhacadh mi, *was I not seen?*
Plur. Nach fhacadh sinn, *were we not seen?*

Sing. Cha 'n fhacadh mi, *I was not seen.*
Plur. Cha 'n fhacadh sinn, *we were not seen*

Future

Sing Am faicear	mi, *shall I be* thu, *shalt thou be* e, *shall he be*	*seen?*
Plur Am faicear	sinn, *shall we be* sibh, *shall ye be* iad, *shall they be*	*seen?*

Sing Nach fhaicear mi, *shall I not be seen?*
Plur. Nach fhaicear sinn, *shall we not be seen?*

Sing. Cha 'n fhaicear mi, *I shall not be seen*
Plur. Cha 'n fhaicear sinn, *we shall not be seen*

SUBJUNCTIVE MOOD.

Preterite.

Sing. Chiteadh	mi, *I would be* thu, *thou wouldst be* e, *he would be*	*seen.*
Plur. Chiteadh	sinn, *we would be* sibh, *ye would be* iad, *they would be*	*seen.*

Preterite

Sing Nam faicteadh	mi, *if I would be* thu, *if thou wouldst be* e, *if he would be*	*seen*
Plur. Nam faicteadh	sinn, *if we would be* sibh, *if ye would be* iad, *if they would be*	*seen*

Future.

Sing. Ma chithear	mi, *if I shall be* thu, *if thou shalt be* e, *if he shall be*	*seen.*
Plur Ma chithear	sinn, *if we shall be* sibh, *if ye shall be* iad, *if they shall be*	*seen*

IMPERATIVE MOOD.

Faicthear, faicear e, } *let it be seen.*

INFINITIVE MOOD

Dh' fhaicinn, Dh' fhaicsinn, } *to see*

FAIGH, get.

ACTIVE VOICE.

AFFIRMATIVE, OR INDICATIVE MOOD.

Preterite

Sing. Fhuair mi, *I got*, or *did get*
Plur. Fhuair sinn, *we got*, or *did get.*

Future.

Sing. Gheibh mi, *I shall* or *will get*
Plur Gheibh sinn, *we shall* or *will get*

NEGATIVE, OR INTERROGATIVE MOOD

Preterite.

Sing. An d' fhuair mi, *did I get?*
Plur. An d' fhuair sinn, *did we get?*

Sing. Nach d' fhuair mi, *did I not get?*
Plur. Nach d' fhuair sinn, *did we not get?*

Sing. Cha d' fhuair mi, *I shall not get*
Plur. Cha d' fhuair sinn, *we shall not get.*

Future.

Sing. Am faigh mi, *shall I get?*
Plur. Nach faigh sinn, *shall we get?*

Sing. Nach faigh mi, *shall I not get?*
Plur Nach faigh sinn, *shalt we not get?*

Sing. Cha 'n fhaigh mi, *I shall not get*
Plur. Cha 'n fhaigh sinn, *we shall not get*

* Also written *Chunnacas*

SUBJUNCTIVE MOOD

Preterite.

Sing { Gheibhinn, *I would* or *could* / Gheibheadh tu, *thou wouldst* or *couldst* / Gheibheadh e, *he would* or *could* } *get*

Plur { Gheibheamaidh, *or* gheibheadh sinn, *we would* or *could* / Gheibheadh sibh, *ye would* or *could* / Gheibheadh iad, *they would* or *could* } *get*

Sing Nam { faighinn, *if I would* or *could* / faigheadh tu, *if thou wouldst* or *couldst* / faigheadh e, *if he would* or *could* } *get.*

Plur Nam { faigheamaid, *or* faigheadh sinn, *if we would* or *could* / faigheadh sibh, *if ye would* or *could* / faigheadh iad, *if they would* or *could* } *get*

Future.

Sing Ma gheibh { mi, *if I shall* / thu, *if thou shalt* / e, *if he shall* } *get.*

Plur. Ma gheibh { sinn, *if we shall* / sibh, *if ye shall* / iad, *if they shall* } *get.*

IMPERATIVE MOOD.

Sing { Faigheam, *let me get.* / Faigh, *get thou.* / Faigheadh e, *let him get* }

Plur. { Faigheamaid, *let us get* / Faighibh, *get ye.* / Faigheadh iad, *let them get.* }

INFINITIVE MOOD

A dh' fhaotuinn, / A dh' fhaghail, } *to get*

PARTICIPLE.

A faotainn, / A faghail, } *getting*

PASSIVE VOICE.

AFFIRMATIVE, OR INDICATIVE MOOD

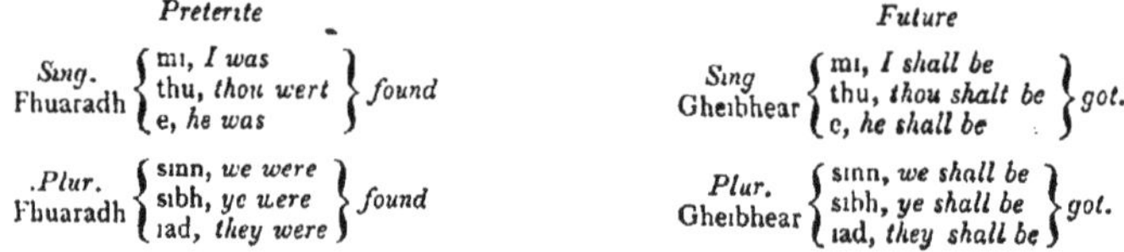

Preterite

Sing. Fhuaradh { mi, *I was* / thu, *thou wert* / e, *he was* } *found*

Plur. Fhuaradh { sinn, *we were* / sibh, *ye were* / iad, *they were* } *found*

Future

Sing Gheibhear { mi, *I shall be* / thu, *thou shalt be* / e, *he shall be* } *got.*

Plur. Gheibhear { sinn, *we shall be* / sibh, *ye shall be* / iad, *they shall be* } *got.*

NEGATIVE, OR INTERROGATIVE MOOD.

Preterite

Sing. An d' fhuaradh { mi, *was I* / thu, *wert thou* / e, *was he* } *found?*

Plur An d' fhuaradh { sinn, *were we* / sibh, *were ye* / iad, *were they* } *found?*

Sing Nach d' fhuaradh mi, *was I not got?*
Plur Nach d' fhuaradh sinn, *were we not got?*

Future.

Sing Am faighear { mi, *shall I be* / thu, *shalt thou be* / e, *shall he be* } *got?*

Plur Am faighear { sinn, *shall we be* / sibh, *shall ye be* / iad, *shall they be* } *got?*

Sing. Nach faighear mi, *shall I not be got?*
Plur Nach faighear sinn, *shall we not be got?*

SUBJUNCTIVE MOOD

Preterite.

Sing Gheibhteadh { mi, *I was* / thu, *thou wert* / e, *he was* } *got*

Plur. Gheibhteadh { sinn, *we were* / sibh, *ye were* / iad, *they were* } *got.*

Sing Nam faighteadh mi, *if I would be got.*
Plur. Nam faighteadh sinn, *if we would be got.*

Future.

Sing. Ma gheibhear { mi, *if I shall be* / thu, *if thou shalt be* / e, *if he shall be* } *got*

Plur. Ma gheibhear { sinn, *if we shall be* / sibh, *if ye shall be* / iad, *if they shall be* } *got.*

IMPERATIVE MOOD.

Faightear, faighear e, *let it be got*

ABAIR, *say*.

ACTIVE VOICE.

AFFIRMATIVE, OR INDICATIVE MOOD.

Preterite.

Sing. Thubhairt
mi, *I said*, or *did*
thu, *thou saidst*, or *didst*
e, *he said*, or *did*
say

Plur. Thubhairt
sinn, *we said*, or *did*
sibh, *ye said*, or *did*
iad, *they said*, or *did*
say

Future

Sing. Their
mi, *I shall* or *will*
thu, *thou shalt* or *wilt*
e, *he shall* or *will*
say

Plur. Their
sinn, *we shall* or *will*
sibh, *ye shall* or *will*
iad, *they shall* or *will*
say

NEGATIVE, OR INTERROGATIVE MOOD.

Preterite

Sing. An dubhairt
mi, *did I*
thu, *didst thou*
e, *did he*
say?

Plur. An dubhairt
sinn, *did we*
sibh, *did ye*
iad, *did they*
say?

Preterite

Sing. Nach dubhairt
mi, *did I not*
thu, *didst thou not*
e, *did he not*
say?

Plur. Nach dubhairt
sinn, *did we not*
sibh, *did ye not*
iad, *did they not*
say?

Future.

Sing. An abair
mi, *shall* or *will I*
thu, *shalt* or *wilt thou*
e, *shall* or *will he*
say?

Plur. An abair
sinn, *shall* or *will we*
sibh, *shall* or *will ye*
iad, *shall* or *will they*
say?

Future

Sing. Nach abair
mi, *shall* or *will I not*
thu, *shalt* or *wilt thou not*
e, *shall* or *will he not*
say?

Plur. Nach abair
sinn, *shall* or *will we not*
sibh, *shall* or *will ye not*
iad, *shall* or *will they not*
say?

Preterite.

Sing. Cha dubhairt
mi, *I said not*, or *did not*
thu, *thou saidst not*, or *didst not*
e, *he said not*, or *did not*
say

Plur. Cha dubhairt
sinn, *we said not*, or *did not*
sibh, *ye said not*, or *did not*
iad, *they said not*, or *did not*
say

Future

Sing. Cha 'n abair
mi, *I shall* or *will not*
thu, *thou shalt* or *wilt not*
e, *he shall* or *will not*
say

Plur. Cha 'n abair
sinn, *we shall* or *will not*
sibh, *ye shall* or *will not*
iad, *they shall* or *will not*
say

SUBJUNCTIVE MOOD

Preterite

Sing.
Theirinn, *I would*
Theireadh tu, *thou wouldst*
Theireadh e, *he would*
say

Plur.
Theireamaid, *we would*
Theireadh sibh, *ye would*
Theireadh iad, *they would*
say

Sing. Nach
abairinn, abrainn, *would I not*
abaireadh, abradh tu, *wouldst thou not*
abaireadh, abradh e, *would he not*
say?

Plur. Nach
abaireamaid, abramaid, *would we not*
abaireadh, abradh sibh, *would ye not*
abaireadh, abradh iad, *would they not*
say?

Preterite

Sing. Nan
abairinn, abrainn, *if I would*
abaireadh, abradh tu, *if thou wouldst*
abaireadh, abradh e, *if he would*
say

Plur. Nan
abaireamaid, abramaid, *if we would*
abaireadh, abradh sibh, *if ye would*
abaireadh, abradh iad, *if they would*
say

Future

Sing. Ma their
mi, *if I shall* or *will*
tu, *if thou shalt* or *wilt*
e, *if he shall* or *will*
say

Plur. Ma their
sinn, *if we shall* or *will*
sibh, *if ye shall* or *will*
iad, *if they shall* or *will*
say

IMPERATIVE MOOD.

Sing.
Abaiream, abram, *let me say*
Abair, *say thou.*
Abaireadh, abradh, e, *let him say*

Plur.
Abaireamaid, abramaid, *let us say*
Abairibh, abraibh, *say ye.*
Abaireadh, abradh iad, *let them say*

INFINITIVE MOOD

A radh, *to say*

PARTICIPLE

Ag radh, *saying*

PASSIVE VOICE.

AFFIRMATIVE, or INDICATIVE MOOD.

Preterite.	*Future.*
Sing. *Thubhradh e, *it was said.*	*Sing.* Theirear e, *it shall be said.*

NEGATIVE, or INTERROGATIVE MOOD.

Preterite.	*Future.*
An dubhradh e, *was it said?*	An abairear, abrar e, *shall it be said?*
Nach dubhradh e, *was it not said?*	Nach abairear, abrar e, *shall it not be said?*
Cha dubhradh e, *it was not said.*	Cha 'n abairear, abrar e, *it shall not be said.*

SUBJUNCTIVE MOOD.

Preterite.	*Future.*
Theirteadh e, *it would be said.*	Ma theirear e, *if it shall be said.*
Nan abairteadh e, *if it would be said.*	

IMPERATIVE MOOD.

Abairear, abrar e, *let it be said.*

DEFECTIVE VERBS.

The defective Verbs are, *Arsa, Ol, Feudaidh, Theab, Tiucainn.*

ARSA, says, said.

Arsa, *says, said,* always precedes its verb, as, arsa Seumas, *said James.* When it is declined with the personal pronouns, it throws them into the emphatic form; as,

	Singular		Plural
Sing. Arsa	mise, *said I*	*Plur* Arsa	sinne, *said we.*
	thusa, *saidst thou*		sibhse, *said ye*
	esan, *or* ise, *said he* or *she.*		iadsan, *said they.*

FEUDAIDH,† *may.*

AFFIRMATIVE, or INDICATIVE MOOD.

Preterite.		*Future.*	
Sing Dh'fheud	mi, *I was able.*	*Sing.* Feudaidh	mi, *I may*
	thu, *thou wert able*		thu, *thou mayest.*
	e, *he was able.*		e, *he may.*
Plur Dh'fheud	sinn, *we were able*	*Plur.* Feudaidh	sinn, *we may.*
	sibh, *ye were able.*		sibh, *ye may.*
	iad, *they were able*		iad, *they may.*

INTERROGATIVE, or NEGATIVE MOOD.

Future.		*Future.*	
Sing Am feud	mi, *may I?*	*Sing.* Cha 'n fheud	mi, *I may* or *must not.*
	thu, *mayst thou?*		thu, *thou mayst* or *must not.*
	e, *may he?*		e, *he may* or *must not.*
Plur Am feud	sinn, *may we?*	*Plur.* Cha 'n fheud	sinn, *we may* or *must not.*
	sibh, *may ye?*		sibh, *ye may* or *must not.*
	iad, *may they?*		iad, *they may* or *must not.*

SUBJUNCTIVE MOOD.

Preterite		*Preterite*	
Sing	Dh' fheudainn, *I might.*	*Sing* Ma dh' fheudas	mi, *if I may.*
	Dh' fheudadh tu, *thou mightst.*		thu, *if thou mayst*
	Dh' fheudadh, *he might.*		e, *if he may*
Plur.	Dh' fheudamaid, *we might.*	*Plur.* Ma d' fheudas	sinn, *if we may.*
	Dh' fheudadh sibh, *ye might.*		sibh, *if ye may.*
	Dh' fheudadh iad, *they might.*		iad, *if they may.*

* Some write *dubhradh,* which rather belongs to the Irish dialect

† *Feudaidh* and *feud* are often written *faodaidh* and *faod*

Feudaidh is often and elegantly used *impersonally*, either with or without the compound pronoun.

Sing. Is fheudar	dhomh, *I must.* dhuit, *thou must.* dha, *he must.*	*Plur.* Is fheudar	dhuinn, *we must.* dhuibh, *ye must.* dhoibh, *they must.*

TIUCAINN, come along.

IMPERATIVE MOOD.

Sing. Tiucainn, *come along* *Plur.* Tiucainnibh, *come ye along.*

THEAB, had almost.

AFFIRMATIVE, OR INDICATIVE MOOD.

Sing Theab	mi, *I had almost.* thu, *thou hadst almost* e, *he had almost.*	*Plur* Theab	sinn, *we had almost.* sibh, *ye had almost.* iad, *they had almost.*

NEGATIVE, OR INTERROGATIVE MOOD.

Sing An do theab	mi, *had I almost?* thu, *hadst thou almost?* e, *had he almost?*	*Sing.* Nach do theab	mi, *had I not almost?* thu, *hadst thou not almost?* e, *had he not almost?*
Plur. An do theab	sinn, *had we almost?* sibh, *had ye almost?* iad, *had they almost?*	*Plur* Nach do theab	sinn, *had we not almost?* sibh, *had ye not almost?* iad, *had they not almost?*
Sing Cha do theab	mi, *I had not almost.* thu, *thou hadst not almost.* e, *he had almost.*	*Sing* Mur do theab	mi, *if I had not almost.* thu, *if thou hadst not almost.* e, *if he had not almost.*
Plur Cha do theab	sinn, *we had almost.* sibh, *ye had almost.* iad, *they had almost*	*Plur.* Mur do theab	sinn, *if we had not almost.* sibh, *if ye had not almost.* iad, *if they had not almost.*

OF THE ADVERB.

THE ADVERB, in Gaelic, expresses Place, Time, and Manner or Quality. *Gu*, before any adjective, imparts to it an adverbial meaning.

Adverbs of Place, are such as signify,

1. *Motion or rest in a place.*

A bhàn, bhàn, *down, downwards.*
A bhàn is a 'n airde, *up and down, upwards and downwards*
A bhos, bhos, *on this side.*
A mach, mach, *out, without*
Air astar, *afar.*
Air deireadh, Air dheireadh, *last, hindermost.*
Air thoiseach, Air toiseach, *first, foremost.*
Air tùs, *first, foremost.*
Am fad, *afar.*
Am fagus, *near, at hand.*
An céin, *afar.*
An cois, *near.*
An gàr, *near.*
An laimh, *in custody, in hands*
An sin, *there.*
An so, *here.*
An sud, *yonder.*
An taic, *close, adjoining*
A steach, steach, *within*
A stigh, stigh, *within.*
A thaobh, *sideways*
Bhàn, *down, downwards.*
Bhos, *on this side*
C'àite, *where.*
Deas, *south*
Ear, *east.*
Fas as, Fad air falbh, Fad air astar, *far away.*
Fagus, Fogus, *near*
Far, *where, in which*
Iar, *west.*
Iolar, Ioras, *below there*
Mach, Muigh, *without*
Oir, *east.*
Ris, *exposed, bare.*
Shios, *east, below there,* or *yonder.*
Shuas, *west, up there,* or *yonder*
Tarsuing, *across.*
Thall, *on the other side*
Thar, Thair, Thairis, *over*
Tuath, *north.*
Uthard, *up*

2 *Motion to, or towards a place.*

A leth-taobh, *aside, to a side*
A 'n airde, *upwards, up*
A nall, *to this side.*
A null, } *to the other side, over*
A nunn, }
Air ais, *backwards.*
Air adhairt, } *forward, onward*
Air aghaidh, }
A sios, *eastwards, downwards.*
A suas, *upwards, westwards.*
Cia 'n car? } *whither? in what direction?*
Cia 'n taobh? }
C' ionadh? *whither? to what place?*
Gu deas, } *to the south, southward*
Gus an airde deas, }
Gus an airde an ear, *to the east, eastward*
Gu tuath, } *to the north, northward*
Gus an airde tuath, }

H-uig agus uaithe, *to and fro.*
Le leathad, *down hill.*
Leis, *with,* or *down, the stream.*
Mu 'n cuairt, *round.*
Nall, *hitherwards.*
Nùll, } *to the other side.*
Nunn, }
Ri bruthach, *upwards*
Ri leathad, *downwards*
Sios, *east, eastwards.*
Suas, *west, westwards.*

3. *Motion from a place.*

A deas, *from the south*
A nuas, nuas, *down, from above*
A tuath, *from the north*
O 'n ear, *from the east.*
O 'n iar, *from the west.*

Adverbs of Time are twofold, namely, such as signify,

1 *Some specific period, either past, present, future, or indefinite.*

A cheana, cheana, *already*
A chianamh, chianamh, *a little while ago*
A chlisge, chlisge, *soon, quickly.*
A choidhch, choidhch, } *for ever*
A chaoidh, chaoidh, }
A ghnàth, *always, usually*
A nis, } *now*
A nise, }
Air ball, *immediately.*
Air bhò 'n de, *yesterday.*
Air bhò 'n raoir, *the night before last*
Air bhò 'n uiridh, *the year before last*
Air deireadh, } *last, hindermost*
Air dheireadh, }
Air a mhionaid, *immediately, this moment.*
Air an uair, *presently*
Air thoiseach, } *first, foremost*
Air toiseach, }
Air thùs, } *at first, foremost*
Air tùs, }
Air uairibh, *at times, occasionally*
A là, *by day*
Am bliadhna, *this year*
Am fad agus, *whilst.*
Am feadh, } *whilst*
An fheadh, }
Am feasd, *for ever, never in future*
Am màireach, *to-morrow*
An ceart 'air, } *immediately, just now*
An ceart uair, }
An dé, *yesterday*
An deaias, *since, seeing that*
An deigh laimh, *afterwards*
An diugh, *to-day*
An dràsda [an tràth so], *at this time*
An ear-thràth, } *the day after to-morrow.*
An iar-thràth, }
An la roimh, *the other day*
An nochd, *to-night*
An raoir, } *last night.*
An reidhir, }
An sin, *then, thereupon.*
An so, *then, hereupon.*
An tràth, *when.*

An tràths', } *now, at this time*
An tràth-so, }
An uair, *when.*
An uiridh [an uair ruith], *last year*
Aon uair, *once*
A so suas, *henceforward.*
As ùr, *a-new*
C' uine, *when.*
Do là, do làth, *by day.*
Dh' oidhche, *by night.*
Dh' oidhche is do là, *by night and by day.*
Fathast, fhathast, *yet, still.*
Fòs, *yet, still*
Idir, *at all*
Mar tha, *as it is.*
Mu dheireadh, *at last, at length.*
Ni 's mò, *any more.*
Nur [an uair], *when, whilst.*
O cheann fad, *long ago.*
O cheann ghoirrid, *lately.*
O chian, *of old*
Riamh, *ever,* (*in reference to the past*)
Roimh laimh, *beforehand.*
Seach, seachad, *past*
Uair, *once, once on a time*
Uair gin, } *sometime.*
Uair eigin, }

2 *Continuance, vicissitude, or repetition of time.*

A ghnàth, } *always*
Do ghnàth, }
Ainmig, *seldom.*
Air uairibh, *at times, sometimes.*
Am bidheantas, } *continually*
An comhnuidh, }
An cumaint, *commonly*
Cia fhad? *how long?*
Cia minic? } *how often?*
Cia tric? }
Fad, *long.*
Fhadsa, *as long as, so long*
Gu bràth, } *for ever*
Gu là bhràth, }
Gu dilinn, *to the end,* or *failing of time.*
Gu minig, *often*
Gu sior, } *for evermore*
Gu siorruidh, }

Gu siorruith,
Gu suthainn,
Gu suthainn siorruidh, } *for evermore.*
Gu tric, *frequently, often.*
O so suas, *henceforward.*

Ma seach,
Mu seach,
Mu 'n seach, } *alternately, by turns.*
Re seal,
Re sealladh, } *for a time.*

Adverbs of Manner and Quality.

Ach beag, *almost.*
Ach gann, *nearly.*
Air achd,
Air mhodh,
Air sheòl, } *in a manner*
Air athais, *leisurely*
Air a chuthach,
Air bhoil, } *mad.*
Air chall, *lost.*
Air charn, *outlawed*
Air choir, *aright*
Air chor, *in a manner*
Air chor eigin,
Air chor no chor eigin, } *somehow or other.*
Air chuairt, *sojourning*
Air chuimhne, *in mind, by heart*
Air chuthach, *mad.*
A dh' aon obair,
A dh' aon ghnothuch, } *purposely.*
A dheòin, *spontaneously.*
A dh' aindeoin, *in spite of*
Air éigin, *with much ado.*
Air fògradh,
Am fògradh, } *in exile.*
Air ghleus, *in trim, tuned, ready for action*
Air iomadan, *adrift*
Air iomroll, *astray.*
Air ionndrainn, *amissing.*
Air lagh, *ready for action*
Air mhodh, *in a manner*
Air seachran, *astray.*
Air sgeul, *found, not lost*
Am bidhcantas, *habitually*
Am feabhas, *convalescent*
Amhain, *only.*
Amhuil,
Amhluidh, } *like, as*
An coinnimh chinn,
An comhair chinn, } *headlong*
An coinnimh chùil,
An comhair chùil, } *backwards*
A dhith, *wanting, without*
An deidh,
An geall, } *desirous, in love*
An nasgaidh, *gratis.*
An tòir, *in pursuit, after*
Araon, *together, both.*
As an aghaidh, *outright*
As a chéile, *asunder, loosened.*
Car air char, *rolling.*
Cia mar? *how?*
C' arson? *why?*
C' ionnas? *how?*
Cha, *not.*
Comhladh,
Comhluath, } *together.*

Cuideachd, *together, in company*
Cuige? *why? wherefore?*
C' uime? *why? for what? about what?*
Dh' aindeoin, *in spite of*
Dh' aon ghnothuch,
Dh' aon obair, } *purposely.*
Do dheòin, *spontaneously*
Do dhìth, *a wanting*
Do rìreadh, *really, actually, indeed.*
Fa leth, *severally, individually*
Far nasgaidh, *gratis.*
Gle, *very*
Gu beachd, *clearly*
Gu baileach,
Gu buileach, } *thoroughly, wholly.*
Gu dearbh, *truly, certainly.*
Gu deimhin, *truly, verily*
Gu fior, *truly, in truth.*
Gu léir, *altogether, wholly*
Gu leoir, *enough.*
Gu taobh, *aside*
Gun amharus, *doubtless*
Gun chàird, *incessantly*
Idir, *at all*
Leth mar leth, *half and half.*
Le cheile, *together.*
Maraon, *together, as one, in a body.*
Mar an ceudna, *also.*
Mar chomhladh,
Mar chomhluath, } *together.*
Mar gu, *as if*
Mar sin, *so, in that manner.*
Mar so, *thus*
Mar sud, *in yon manner, so*
Ma seach,
Mu seach,
Mun seach, } *alternately.*
Na,
Nar, } *not, let not*
Nach, *not*
Nasgaidh, *gratis*
Ni, *not.*
Ni h-eadh, *no, not so, it is not so*
Os àird, *openly.*
Os iosal, *privately, secretly*
Rìreadh,
Riteamh, } *truly, really*
Ro, *very.*
Roimh chéile, *prematurely, hurriedly*
Seadh, *yes, it is so, really!*
Thar a chéile, *disordered*
Theagamh, *perhaps.*
Troimh chéile, *in confusion, stirred about*
Tuille fos, *moreover.*
Uidh air an uidh, *by degrees*

OF PREPOSITION.

Prepositions, in Gaelic, are either simple or compounded.

SIMPLE PREPOSITIONS.

A, *as, of, out of.*
Ag, aig, *at.*
Air, *on, after*
An, ann, *in.*
Bhàrr, *off*
Car, *during*
Do, *of, to.*
Eadar, *between*
Fa, *upon*
Fo, fodha, fu', fuidh, *beneath*
Gu, gus, *to, until.*
Le, leis, *with, by, along.*
Mar, *like to, as*
Mu, *about.*
O, *from*
Os, *above*
Ré, *during*
Re, ri, ris, *to*
Ro, roimh, *before*
Seach, *past, in comparison with*
Tar, thar, thair, thairis, *over, across*
Thun, *to.*
Tre, troimh, throimh, *through*
Trid, *through; by means of.*
Ua, *from.*

COMPOUND PREPOSITIONS.

The Compound Prepositions are, for the most part, made up of a Simple Preposition and a Noun. They commonly govern the Noun in the *genitive* case

A chois, *near to*
Air beulaobh, *before, in front of.*
Air cheann, *at the end, against*
Air culaobh, *behind.*
Air fad, *throughout, during.*
Air feadh, *throughout, during*
Air muin, *on the back, on the top*
Air sgàth, *for the sake*
Air son, *for, on account.*
Air tòir, *in pursuit*
Am fianuis, } *in presence*
Am fochair, }
Am measg, *among, amidst.*
An aghaidh, *against*
An ceann, *in the end.*
An codhail, } *to meet*
An coinneamh, }
An cois, *near to*
An dàil, *to meet hostilely, towards.*
An deaghaidh, } *after.*
An deigh, }
An déis, }
An éiric, *in recompense.*
An làthair, *in presence*
An lorg, } *in consequence.*
An tòir, }
As easbhuidh, } *without.*
As eugmhais, }
As leth, *in behalf*
A bhrìgh, *because.*
A chòir, *near.*
A chum, *to, towards.*
A dhìth, *for want, without*
A réir, *according to*
A thaobh, *concerning.*
Do bhrìgh, *because.*
Do chòir, *near*
Do chum, *to, toward*
Do dhìth, *for want, without.*
Dh' easbhuidh, } *for want*
Dh' uireasbhuidh, }
Dh' fhios, } *to, towards*
Dh' ionnsuidh, }
Do réir, *according, in proportion to*
Do thaobh, *concerning, with respect.*
Fa chomhair, } *opposite, against.*
Fa chomhar, }
Fa chùis, *because, by reason.*
Ghios, (*contr* for dh' ionnsuidh), *to, towards*
Mu choinneamh, *opposite.*
Mi thimchioll, *around, about.*
O bhàrr, *from the top.*
Os ceann, *above*
Ré, *during*
Tareis, *after.*

INSEPARABLE PREPOSITIONS.

There are various syllables, viz. *an, ain, ana, aim, aimh, ao, ea, eu; eas, ais, ath, bith, co, com, comh, con; di, do, im, iom, in, ion, mi, mio, neo,* and *so,* which may be called Inseparable Prepositions, being found only in composition with other words, the signification of which they change or modify.

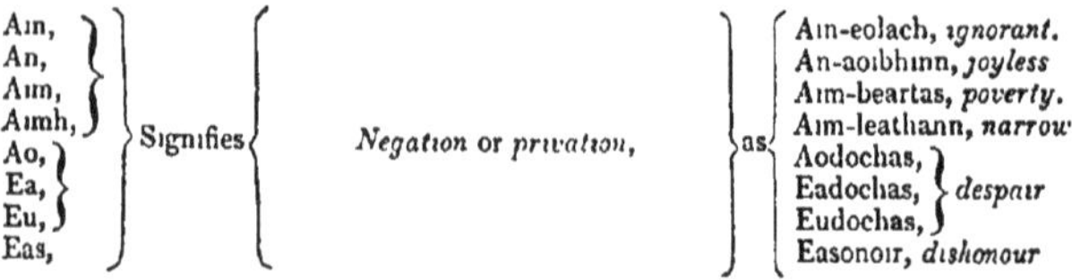

Ain, An, Aim, Aimh, Ao, Ea, Eu, Eas, } Signifies { *Negation or privation,* } as { Ain-eolach, *ignorant.* An-aoibhinn, *joyless* Aim-beartas, *poverty.* Aim-leathann, *narrow* Aodochas, Eadochas, Eudochas, } *despair* Easonoir, *dishonour*

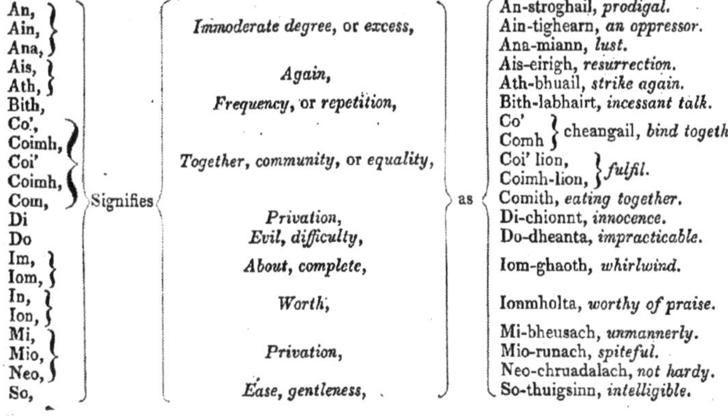

Prefix	Signifies	as
An, Ain, Ana,	*Immoderate degree*, or *excess*,	An-stroghail, *prodigal.* Ain-tighearn, *an oppressor.* Ana-miann, *lust.*
Ais, Ath,	*Again*,	Ais-eirigh, *resurrection.* Ath-bhuail, *strike again.*
Bith,	*Frequency*, or *repetition*,	Bith-labhairt, *incessant talk.*
Co', Coimh, Coi', Coimh, Com,	*Together*, *community*, or *equality*,	Co' / Comh cheangail, *bind together.* Coi' lion, Coimh-lion, *fulfil.* Comith, *eating together.*
Di	*Privation*,	Di-chionnt, *innocence.*
Do	*Evil, difficulty*,	Do-dheanta, *impracticable.*
Im, Iom,	*About, complete*,	Iom-ghaoth, *whirlwind.*
In, Ion,	*Worth*,	Ionmholta, *worthy of praise.*
Mi, Mio, Neo,	*Privation*,	Mi-bheusach, *unmannerly.* Mio-runach, *spiteful.* Neo-chruadalach, *not hardy.*
So,	*Ease, gentleness*,	So-thuigsinn, *intelligible.*

OF INTERJECTIONS.

An Interjection is an indeclinable part of speech, and expresses some sudden emotion of the mind.

Grief; as, och! ochain! ochòin! och nan ochain; och is ochain nan och eire! mo chreachadh! mo nuar! mo leòn! mo thruaighe! mo thruaighe léireadh! mo sgaradh!

Wonder; aobh, aobh! obh, obh! O!

Aversion; tut! ab, ab! fuigh!

Disgust; ach! ach!

Shame; mo nàire! mo mhasladh!

Laughter; ha, ha! ah!

Demonstration; feuch! faic! scall!

Calling; h-aoibh! h-oilò.

Terror; h-ugad! h-ugaibh.

OF CONJUNCTIONS.

A Conjunction is an indeclinable part of speech, and serves to join words and sentences together.

Ach, *but.*
A chionn, *because.*
Agus, *as, and.*
Co, Cho, *as.*
Cuideachd, *likewise.*
Fòs, *yet.*
Ga, *though.*
Ged, giodh, *though.*
Gidheadh, *yet.*
Gu, gur, *that.*
Is, *and.*
Ma, *if.*
Mar, *as, like as.*
Mur, *if not.*

Mu'n, Mus, Mus an, *before, ere.*
Na, *than.*
Nach, *that not.*
Nam, nan, *if.*
No, *or.*
O, on, *since.*
Oir, *before.*
Os-barr, *moreover.*
'S (*for* agus), *and.*
Sol, suil, *before that.*
Tuille eile, tuille fòs, *further.*
Uime sin, *therefore.*

There are also several phrases which have a conjunctive force; as,

Chum as gu, *or* a chum as gu,
Chum is gu, *or* a chum is gu,
Chum agus gu, *or* a chum agus gu, } *so as that, in order that.*
Chum is nach, *or* a chum is nach, *so as that not.*
Air chor is gu, *so that.*
Air chor is nach, *so that not.*
Air eagal gu, *lest, for fear that.*

Air son gu, *by reason that.*
D' eagal gu, *lest, for fear that.*
D' eagal nach, *lest not.*
Do bhrigh gu, *by reason that.*
Do bhrigh nach, *by reason that not*
Bheil fhios, } *is it known, I wonder.*
'L fhios, }

Ged tha, *notwithstanding.*
Gun fhios, *not knowing, in case.*
Ionnas gu, *so that.*
Mar sud agus, *so also*
Ma seadh, ma ta, *if so, then*
Mur bhiodh, *were it not*
Mur bhiodh gu, *were it not that.*

OF THE FORMATION OF THE PARTS OF SPEECH.

GENTILE, or PATRONYMIC NOUNS, end in *ach*, and are derived from other proper substantives, as names of natives; Albannach, *a Scot*, Sasunnach, *an Englishman*, Suaineach, *a Swede*, Lochlinneach, *a Dane*, so also, an individual of a clan, as, from Stiùbhart, Stiùbhartach, *a Stewart*, from Grannd, Granndach, *a Grant.*

DIMINUTIVE NOUNS in *an* and *ag* are formed most commonly from substantives; as, leabhar, *a book*; leabhran, *a little book*, caile, *a girl*, caileag, *a little girl*, sguab, *a sheaf*, sguabag, *a little sheaf*, leanabh, leanaban, *a little child*

COLLECTIVE NOUNS are not confined to any particular termination; of these some are primitives, as, clann, *a clan*; sluagh, *people* and some derivatives, as, òigridh, *a band of youth*, laochraidh, *a band of warriors.* Some collectives end in *ach*, as, duilleach, *foliage*, from duille, *a leaf.*

Nouns, denoting *AGENTS*, in *air*, *ear*, *oir*, *ach*, *iche*, are derived from other substantives; as, sgriobhair, *a writer*, from sgriobh, sgriosadair, *a destroyer*, from sgrios, sloightear, *a knave*, from sloighte, *knavery*, ciontach, *a culprit*, from ciont, *guilt*, oibriche, *a workman*, from obair, *work.*

ABSTRACTS.

Comparatives are often used as abstract nouns; as, doille, *blindness*, truime, *heaviness*, gile, *whiteness.*

Abstracts in *ad* are formed from the comparative, as, bàinead, *fairness*, from bàine; lughad, *littleness*, from lugha, *less*, teircead, *fewness*, from teirce, *more few*

Some substantives in *as* are formed from substantives, and some from adjectives; as, ùghdarras, *authority*, from ùghdar; luathas, *swiftness*, from luath; cruadhas, *hardness*, from cruaidh.

Some substantives in *achd* are formed from substantives, and some from adjectives; as, iasgaireachd, *fishery*, from iasgair; caonntachd, *parsimony*, from caonntach, *saving*

OF ADJECTIVES.

Adjectives in *ach* are formed commonly from substantives; as, ballach, *spotted*, from ball, *a spot*, grianach, *sunny*, from grian, *sun*, peasgach, *gashed*, from peasg, *a gash*

Adjectives in *agach*, *anach*, from diminutives in *ag* and *an*, as, bachlagach, *curled*, from bachlag, *a curl*, badanach, *tufty*, from badan, *a tuft.*

Adjectives in *mhor*, or in its contractions, *ar* and *or*, are derived from substantives; as, from sluagh, *people*, sluagh-mhor, sluaghar, *populous*: and from adjectives; as, treunmhor, *strong*, from treun

Adjectives in *ail* and *eil*, are derived from substantives, as, feumail, *needful*, from feum, *need*, lathail, *daily*, from lath, *day*, duineil, *manly*, from duine, *man*, gaisgeil, *brave*, from gaisge, *bravery* The terminations *ail* and *eil* are contractions of *amhuil*, like, and have a strong affinity with the English termination *ly*, as, friend*ly*, i e friend*like*, man*ly*, man*like*, gentleman*ly*, gentleman*like*

Adjectives in *da* or *ta* are derived from substantives, as, macanta, *gentle*, from mac, cailleachanta, *cowardly*, from cailleach, *an old woman*

Adjectives denoting *practicability* or *facility* commonly have *so* prefixed; as, so-thuigsinn, *intelligible*, so-dheanamh, *easily done.*

Adjectives denoting *impossibility* or *difficulty* commonly have *do* prefixed; as, do-thuigsinn, *unintelligible*, do-dheanamh, *not easily done*

OF VERBS.

Verbs in *aich* are formed from adjectives or substantives characterised by *a*, *o*, or *u*, as, teannaich, *tighten*, from teann, *tight*, cronaich, *blame*, from cron, *ill.*

Verbs in *ich* are formed from adjectives characterised by *i*, as, cruinnich, *gather*, from cruinn, *round*, minich, *smooth*, from min, *smooth*

OF THE COMPOSITION OF THE PARTS OF SPEECH.

Composition is effected in Gaelic by prefixing to substantives, adjectives, participles, and verbs a substantive, adjective, verb, adverb, or preposition.

A Substantive with a Substantive.

Grian-chrios, *the zodiac*; grian-chearcall, *a solar halo*; marc-shluagh, *cavalry*, cuach-fhalt, *curled hair*

Adjectives with the Substantives prefixed

Taobh tuath, *north country*, bru-dhearg, *a redbreast*; ceann-lom, *bare-headed*.

Substantives with the Adjectives prefixed

Droch-bheart, *mischief*, treun-laoch, *a warrior*, fuar-bheann, *a cold hill*, dubh-fhocal, *a dark saying*.

Adjectives with Adjectives.

Gorm-eutrom, *light blue*, dubh-dhonn, *livid*, liath-ghlas, *greyish*; gorm-bhreachd, *blue spotted*, uile-chumhachdach, *almighty*.

Verbs with Substantives.

Cuairt-imich, *walk around*, cridh-bhris, *heart-break*, corp-shnàs, *anatomise*.

Verbs with Adjectives.

Geur-lean, *persecute*, cruaidh-ruith, *run speedily*, beo-sgar, *divorce*, min-phronn, *pulverise*.

Verbs with Prepositions.

Eadar-dhealaich, *separate*, as-tharruing, *extract*, roimh-òrduich, *fore-ordain*

Substantives with Prepositions

Eadar-sgaradh, *separation*, timchioll-ghearradh, *circumcision*, fo-bhuille, *an under-stroke*

Adverbs with Substantives.

Ro-dhuine, *an excellent man*, ro-fheum, *much need*, mach-bhailtean, *suburbs*.

SYNTAX, OR CONSTRUCTION

Syntax is the right arrangement of the words of a language into sentences or phrases. Its parts are two, viz. *Concord*, and *Government* or *Regimen*.

OF CONCORD.

Concord is the agreement which one word has with another, in Gender, Number, Case, or Person.

RULE I.

The article is placed immediately before its substantive, and agrees with it in gender, number, and case; as,

Am bord.	*The table.*
A bhean.	*The woman*
An fhoid	*The turf*
Na sluic.	*The pits*

RULE II.

Sometimes an adjective comes between the article and its noun; as,

Is tu an droch leanabh,	*Thou art a bad child*
Is e am fior laoch,	*He is a real hero*

RULE III.

An adjective agrees with its substantive in gender, number, and case; as,

Duine saibhir	*A rich man*
Bean ghasd.	*A chaste wife*
Tighean mora	*Large houses*

RULE IV.

The possessive pronouns *mo* (my), *do* (thy), *a* (his), precede the substantive, and throw it into the aspirated form, as,

Mo dhorn.	*My fist*
Do chas	*Thy foot*
A chlaidheamh	*His sword*

RULE V

The substantive most commonly precedes its adjective, as,

Lann geur.	*A sharp blade*
Duine glic.	*A wise man*

RULE VI.

Some monosyllabic adjectives precede their substantives, and then the substantives assume the aspirated form; as,

Droch dhuine.	*A bad man*
Og-bhean.	*A young wife.*
Garbh chuan	*A rough sea.*

RULE VII.

If *is* be the verb of a sentence, the adjective comes before the noun; as,

Is domhainn do chreuchd —*Oss*	*Deep is thy wound*

RULE VIII.

Two or more substantives in apposition, or signifying the same thing, ought to agree in case; as,

[a]Oscar [a]mac [b]Oisein [b]mhic [b]Fhionnghail mhic Chumhail	*Oscar the son of Ossian, the son of Fingal, the son of Cumhal.*

RULE IX.

Numerals precede their nouns, as,

Tri lathan	*Three days*
Seach fir.	*Seven men.*

Such instances as the following are excepted

Righ Seoras a ceithir	*King George the Fourth*
Righ Uilliam a h-aon	*King William the First.*

RULE X

When the possessive pronoun *a* (her) precedes a substantive beginning with a vowel, *h-* is inserted between them, as,

A h-aire	*Her attention*
A h-oillt.	*Her terror.*

RULE XI.

When the possessive pronouns *ar* (our), *bhur* or *ur* (your), precede a noun beginning with a vowel, *n-* is inserted between them; as,

Bhur n-aithrichean.	*Your fathers.*

RULE XII

Possessive pronouns are of the same number with their antecedents; as,

Aig a dhorus	*At his door.*
Folt a cinn	*The hair of her head.*

RULE XIII

If a sentence or a clause be an antecedent, the pronoun is put in the 3d singular masculine, as,

Ged bha mi sgith, cha d' aithnich mi orm e.	*Though I was tired, I felt it not.*

RULE XIV.

The nominative is commonly placed after the verb; as,

Tha iad.	*They are*
Theasd iad.	*They died*
Ghabh e	*He took.*

RULE XV.

The nominative to the verb is often understood with the poets, as,

Ghabh [e] tùinidh.	*He dwelt —Oss Lod*
Bhuail [e] craobh Loduinn.	*He struck the tree of Lodin —Oss. Lod*

RULE XVI.

The relative pronouns *a*, *nach*, *na*, come before the verb; as,

An oigh a sheinn	*The maid who sang.*
Cridhe nach bris	*A heart that will not break.*
Gleidh na fhuair thu	*Keep what you got.*

OF GOVERNMENT.

Government is that power which one part of speech has over another, in determining its Form, Mood, Tense, or Case

THE GOVERNMENT OF SUBSTANTIVES.

RULE I

One substantive governs another in the genitive when it signifies a different thing; as,

Inneal ciùil	*An instrument of music*
Lòd dhaoine	*A crowd of men*

RULE II.

If a second genitive follows, the former substantive is governed in the nominative; as,

Tigh *fear* na bainnse	*The bridegroom's house*
Ainm *mac* an Righ	*The name of the king's son*

RULE III

When a substantive governs another definitely in the genitive, the article is placed before the latter only; as,

Tigh an Righ.	*The king's house.*
Solus na greine	*The light of the sun.*
Airde nam beann.	*The height of the hills.*

RULE IV.

A noun governed without the article is commonly in the aspirated form, as,

Claidheamh Shumais	*James's sword.*
Tigh Dhomhnuill	*Donald's house*

THE GOVERNMENT OF ADJECTIVES.

RULE I

Adjectives of plenty, fulness, satiety, govern the genitive, and are followed by the preposition *de*, either simple or compounded, as,

Lan arbhair	*Full of corn.*
Buidheach bidh	*Filled with food.*
Sgith dheth	*Tired of him* or *it.*

RULE II.

Adjectives signifying merit or demerit; knowledge, remembrance, and some other affections of the mind, are commonly followed by the preposition *air*, either simple or compounded; as,

Airidh air peanas.	*Worthy of punishment.*
Eòlach air Seumas.	*Acquainted with James.*
Cuimhneachail orm.	*Mindful of me.*
Deidheil air fion.	*Fond of wine.*

RULE III.

Adjectives signifying likeness or unlikeness, compassion or friendship, generally require the preposition *ri*, either simple or compounded; as,

Cosmhal ri d' athair.	*Like your father.*
Trucanta rithe.	*Compassionate to her.*
Cairdeil ris.	*Friendly to him*

RULE IV

Adjectives signifying profit or disprofit, nearness,* and relationship, commonly require the preposition *do*, either simple or compounded; as,

Maith do gach neach	*Good to all.*
Feumail dhuit.	*Useful to thee.*
Fagus do Lunnuinn.	*Near to London.*
Cairdeach dhomh.	*Related to me*

RULE V

Adjectives followed by a noun of measure take the preposition *air*, as,

Seachd troidhean air airde.	*Seven feet high.*
Tri mile air fad.	*Three miles long*
Da shlat air leud	*Two yards in breadth.*

RULE VI

The comparative degree,† when preceded by *ni 's*, requires the particle *na*, as,

Ni 's luaithe na 'ghaoth	*Swifter than the wind*
Ni 's milse na mil	*Sweeter than honey*
Ni 's fhearr na 'n t-or.	*Better than gold*

RULE VII.

Superlatives require the preposition *do* or *dhe*, either simple or compounded; as,

An té 's grinn dhiubh uile	*The finest woman of them all*
Am fear is airde do 'n triùir	*The tallest man of the three*

THE GOVERNMENT OF VERBS.

RULE I.

An active verb governs its object in the nominative case, which is sometimes put after the verb, and sometimes before it; as,

Buail an sgiath.	*Strike the shield —Oss*
Caomhain do sholus.	*Spare thy light —Id*
Mo lann do neach cha gheill.	*My sword to none shall yield.—Id.*

RULE II.

Some active verbs require between them and their objects a preposition, either simple or compounded; as,

Leig leis.	*Let him alone.*
Iarr air.	*Desire him*
Labhair ri Seumas.	*Speak to James*

RULE III.

Verbs in the passive voice have after their nominative the preposition *le*, simple or compounded, expressive of the agent or the instrument, either expressed or understood; as,

Leònadh e le claidheamh.	*He* or *it was wounded with a sword.*
Mharbhadh e leatsa.	*He* or *it was slain by thee.*

RULE IV.

Verbs used impersonally commonly require after them the preposition *le*, compounded with a personal pronoun, either expressed or understood, as,

Dìrear (leinn) an tulach.	*We ascended the hill.*
Seallar (leinn) mu 'n cuairt.	*We looked around.*

RULE V.

Bu, was, aspirates the word which follows it; as,

Bu chruaidh do chàs.	*Hard was the case.*
B' fhuar do chridhe.	*Cold was thy heart*
Bu mhise a rinn e.	*It was I who did it.*

RULE VI.

The dentals *d* and *t* are sometimes aspirated, and sometimes not, as,

Bu dorch a laithe	*Dark were his days — Oss. Fing.*
Bu thaitneach do shluagh a thir.	*Pleasant to his countrymen —Id*
Bu taitneach dha	*Pleasant to him was.—Id.*

RULE VII.

The infinitive of active verbs governs the genitive; as,

A chosgadh feirg.	*To appease wrath.*
A thogail creich.	*To gather booty*

* Adjectives of nearness have also the preposition *air*, either simple or compounded, as, fagus orm, *near me*.

† There is a form of comparison, already mentioned, among the Gael, which has sometimes the meaning of a substantive, and sometimes of an adjective; as, *feairrd, meisd, moid, lughaid, giorraid, teothad* Is feairrd mi so, *I am the better for this*, a dol am feairrd, *growing better*, literally, *advancing in betterness*. The rest are construed after the same manner

THE GOVERNMENT OF PARTICIPLES.

RULE I.

Participles of the present time govern the genitive; as,

Ag iarruidh comhraig.	*Wishing for battle.—Oss.*
A siubhal an fhraoich.	*Traversing the heath.—Id*
Ag ath-cheannuchadh na h-aimsir	*Redeeming the time.—Stew.*

RULE II.

Participles of the past time are followed by the preposition *le*, signifying the agent or the instrument, either simple or compounded; as,

Buailte le claidheamh.	*Struck with a sword.*
Leònta le Seumas.	*Wounded by James.*

THE GOVERNMENT OF ADVERBS.

RULE I

Ro, gle, as also *fior, sàr,* used adverbially, aspirate the noun to which they are prefixed; as,

Ro-mhath	*Very good*
Ro-dhuine	*An excellent man.*
Gle ghrinn	*Fine enough.*
Fior-mhaiseach	*Truly handsome*
Sàr-Ghaisge.	*Heroism*

RULE II

The negative *cha* aspirates the following verb, if it begins with a labial or a palatal, as,

Cha mhair e.	*He, or it will not last*
Cha chluinn mi	*I shall not hear.*
Cha phòs iad	*They will not marry.*
Cha ghuil i	*She will not weep.*

Cha sometimes aspirates a dental, and sometimes not; as,

Cha dean e feum,	*It will do no good*
Cha sir mi ni	*I will seek nothing.*
Cha tuit iad	*They shall not fall.*

Cha inserts *n* before a vowel or *f* aspirated; as,

Cha n-ann leis fein bha'n laoch —Oss.	*The hero was not alone*
Cha n-fhiach e.	*It is of no value.*

The negative *ni* inserts *h* before an initial vowel; as,

Ni h-eadh	*Not so.*
Ni h-e	*He is not.*

THE GOVERNMENT OF PREPOSITIONS.

RULE I

The prepositions, *aig, air, an,* &c govern the dative, and sometimes the nominative, and are always placed before; as,

Aig a chluais.	*At his ear.*
Tonn air tràigh.	*A wave on the shore —Oss.*
Na 'shoillse	*In his sight —Id*
Air clann nan seòd	*On the sons of the brave --Id*

Air sometimes governs the dative in the aspirated form, as,

Air bharraibh nan tonn.	*On the tops of the waves —Oss*

RULE II

The preposition *gun* governs the aspirated nominative and dative, but oftener the dative; as,

Gun cheann	*Without head.*
Gun chloinn.	*Without children.*

RULE III.

The prepositions *gu,* or *gus,* and *mar* govern a definite noun in the nominative; as,

Gus an solus.	*To the light.*
Mar a chraobh.	*Like the tree*

RULE IV.

But if the article be not prefixed to a noun, *gu* or *gus* commonly governs the dative, and *mar* either the nominative or dative; as,

Gu crich na cruinne.	*To the world's end.*
Mar sholus corr	*As a bright light*

RULE V.

The prepositions *de, do, fo,* or *fuidh, fa, gun, mar, mu, o, tre,* or *troimh,* are commonly followed by an aspirated nominative; as,

Do dhuine	*To a man.*
Fo bhròn.	*Under grief.*
Gun mheirg.	*Without rest.*
Mar thonn.	*As a wave.*
Mu cheann na h-oigh	*About the maiden's head*
Troimh chruadal.	*Through hardship.*

RULE VI

Eadar governs sometimes the nominative in the simple and sometimes in the aspirated form; as,

Eadar talamh is athar	*Betwixt earth and air.*
Eadar bheag is mhòr	*Both great and small*

COMPOUND PREPOSITIONS.

Compound prepositions govern the genitive, as,

Air feadh na tire.	*Throughout the land*
Air deireadh na feachd	*In the rear of the army*
A dh' ionnsuidh na h-aimhne	*Towards the river.*

INTERJECTIONS

Some interjections are followed by the preposition *do,* either simple or compounded; as,

Is an-aoibhinn duit.	*Woe unto thee.*

Mo naire! is followed by the preposition *air,* either simple or compounded, expressed or understood, as,

Mo naire! [ort]	*Shame! [upon thee]*
Mo naire! [oirbh]	*Shame! [upon you]*

Mo thruaighe is often followed by the nominative case; as,

Mo thruaighe mi!	*Woe's me!*
Mo thruaighe e!	*Woe be to him!*

CONJUNCTIONS.

RULE I.

The conjunctions *agus*, *as*, or is, and *no* or *na*, couple like cases and moods; as,

A sguabadh chlod 's chlach	*Sweeping turf and stones* — *Ullin*.
Cha mheal e sith no sòlas.	*He shall not enjoy peace nor comfort.*
Thig no cha tig e.	*He shall come*, or *shall not*.

RULE II.

Co, or *cho*, as, may have after it an adjective in the aspirate or initial form; as,

Cho *or* co chinnteach Cho cinnteach	ris a bhàs	*As sure as death.*
Cho glan Cho ghlan	ris an òr.	*As bright as gold.*

RULE III.

Mur, *gur*, and *gu*, *gum*, or *gun*, precede the interrogative mood; as,

Mur tig e.	*If he shall not come.*
Gu bheil sinn.	*That we are*
Gum faic sinn.	*That we shall see.*
Gun toir e.	*That he will give*

RULE IV

Nam or *nan*, has after it the preterite substantive; as,

Nam faighinn	*If I got*
Nan tuitinn.	*If I fell*

Ged may precede any mood except the future indicative

PROSODY.

The great excellence of any language consists in the power which its sounds possess, of communicating certain impressions or meanings.

The Gaelic, being a branch of the primeval tongue, has this quality in a far superior degree to any language, the structure of which is concocted or complex. It is a language of nature; and its sounds may be truly said to be echoes to the sense. Hence arises its success in descriptive poetry, and in all its addresses to the passions When the nature of the object described is harsh and hard, sounds of a similar kind are employed, which impel their meaning to the mind, by noisy, hard-sounding consonants: whereas, in subjects of tenderness, solemnity, or of mournful interest, scarcely is any sound perceived, but the music of mellow vowels and diphthongs

Mr. Shaw, to whose ill-requited labour the Gaelic owes a great deal, observes correctly, that the combinations *ai*, *ei*, are cheerful and soft; and *ao*, solemn. He might have added that *oi*, *ao*, *aoi*, are significant of softness and affection, and *ui*, *ua*, *uai*, of sadness. Among the consonants, *ll* is soft and mild, so is the gentle aspiration *mh*, as in *caomh*, mild, *seimh*, quiet; *cr*, *dr*, and *tr*, are hard, loud, and violent

VERSIFICATION.

The Gaelic Bards had peculiar facilities in composing; as they were not restrained by any fixed law of verse A termination of lines by similar letters was never deemed requisite; for, if the closing syllable, or the penult of corresponding lines, were somewhat similar in sound, it was reckoned sufficient for the purposes of rhyme, and was all that they usually aimed at.

The following Verses exemplify this Remark.

Thug an deise do Ainnir *gaol*,
Ach air Goll bha 'gorm-shùil *chaoin*,
B' e cùis a h-aisling anns an *oidhche*,
'S cùis a caoidh mu 'n chaochan *choillteach* —
Cha b' ionnan is Garna na *gruamaich*,
Mar lasair 's an tòit ag a cuartach '—*Oss Cathluno.*

Another method of rhyme consisted in a conformity of sound between the last word, or part of the last word, of a foregoing verse, and some word, or part of a word, about the *middle* of the following

Ciod am fà bhi 'g udal *cuain*,
Is eilean *fuar* na geotha crom,
A sgaoileadh a sgiath na 'r *coinneamh*.
Gu 'r dion o *dhoinionn* na h-oidhche —*Ullin*

Mar dha bheuin sleibh o 'n *fhireach*
Le chéile a *sireadh* gu gleanntai. - *Oss*

Sometimes there is a conformity of sound between the last word of a foregoing verse, and a word in the beginning of the following.

Cha do thuit e gun chliù san *àraich*,
Bu *ghàbhaidh* le moran 'imeachd;
Mar thorunn ro' choillte, no mar *dhealan*,
'G a *falach* an deigh an leir-sgrios.—*Ardar.*

In some stanzas of four lines, there is sometimes observed a double conformity; that is, in the concluding words of each couplet, and in other words throughout the preceding line of every couplet. This kind of verse possesses great beauty.

Shéid gaoth dhileas air BEANN
'S cha b' FHANN air buillean 'g a *còghnadh*;
Sinn a bualadh mhullach nan TONN,
'Sgach SONN is a shùil ri *comhraig*.—*Ullin.*

MEASURE.

The poetry of the ancient Gael, as it has come down to us, resembles that of the present day, in its setting every law of scanning at defiance Ossian, and the poets of his time, adapted their compositions to the song, in other words, they set them to music. and there seem to be but two suppositions on which we can account for the irregularity of their verses. Either the music itself must have been very anomalous, or, the strains having been forgotten, and thus the guides to uniformity lost, the poems must have suffered from the liberties which had been taken with them, by the rehearsers of succeeding ages. I am inclined to think, however, that the music was simple and uniform, and that the poetry was correctly adapted thereto However irregular the music may be imagined to have been; as the bards must have accurately set their verses to it, there would be observable in their poems a regular recurrence of similar irregularities. This is not the case The anomaly of their verses must, therefore, be owing to the reciting Bards, who, in some parts, suffered words and turns of expression to fall into oblivion through their indolence; and introduced, in others, expressions which their own conceit informed them were superior to the original; for there never yet was a poet so transcendently good, that a worse did not suppose himself in many respects better.

Add to this, that the language was pronounced differently in different districts, and at different periods of time, yet in these abused fragments of ancient poetry—these remains of Ossian's ruins, we have numberless displays of the might and magnificence of his genius.

Notwithstanding the freedoms which have been taken with the works of the Fingalian poet, they afford numberless examples of correct and measured rhymes, and this circumstance affords a strong presumption that the rhyme, or at least the measure of the poetry, was uniform and regular throughout.

The verses of the Fingalian poets seldom exceed eight syllables, and most frequently the second foot and the third are dactyles, with a short syllable at the beginning of the verse, and a long syllable, or a trochee at the end

COUPLETS.

The Measure.

˘ | ¯ ˘ ˘ | ¯ ˘ ˘ | ¯ |
Thă | 'Ceūmánnă | flāthăıl ăır | lom,
Nur | thōg ĭad rĭ | āghaĭdh năn | tom;
Is | b' ēagăl dĭ | seāllădh ăn | rıgh
A | dh' fhāg ĭ ăm | Āthă năm | frıth —*Temora.*

ALTERNATE RHYMES.

˘ | ¯ ˘ ˘ | ¯ ˘ ˘ | ¯
Cuır | Ōscaĭr cŭır | mīsĕ săn | uaıgh.
Cha | ghēıll mĭ ăn | crūăs dŏ | threun
'S mı 'n | tōıseăch nă | strīghĕ fō | chruaıdh,
Gabh | eōlŭs năm | būădh uăm | féın —*Fıngal.*

The ancient poems published by Dr Smith of Campbelton, are still more irregular in their measure than those collected by Macpherson, it being seldom that the same measure applies to four successive lines. They cannot be scanned, therefore, by any set of rules I can devise. In one of these poems, entitled Conn, there is preserved a wild effusion—an incantation of the Scandinavian priests It consists of five stanzas of four lines each. The last line of each staff has six syllables, consisting of a short syllable, a dactyle, and a trochee; the rest four, consisting of a trochee and a pyrrhic.

The Measure.

˘ ˘ | ˘ ˘
˘ | ¯ ˘ ˘ | ¯ ˘ | *fourth line*

• • •

Cheo na | Lanna
Aom nan | cara;
'S buair an | codal,
Chruth | Lodda nan | léir-chreach.
Sgap do | dhealan;
Luaisg an | talamh;
Buail an | anam;
'S na | maireadh ni | beo dhiubh.

The modern Gaelic poems are more regular and measured, as they are almost all composed to some known air

Iambics of four feet.

˘ ¯ | ˘ ¯ | ˘ ¯ | ˘ ¯ |

O cair | ibh mi | ri taobh | nan allt,
A shiubh | las shuas | le ceum | aibh ciùin;
Fo sgàil | a bharr | aich leig | mo cheann,
'S bi thus, | a ghrian | ro chàird | eil rium —*The Bard's Wish.*

Macintyre, our Burns, an uninstructed shepherd, and a man of extraordinary talents for poetry, wrote pieces which may stand comparison with the pastoral and descriptive poetry of any land or age As the structure of some of them is peculiar, a view of their measure may not here be unacceptable, or misplaced. His best poems are *Coire Cheathaich, Beinn Dobhrain*, and *Mairi Bhàn òg*. The first of these is divided into strophes of eight verses each; but they might have been more judiciously arranged in stanzas of four lines The measure repeats at every second line. There is, moreover, in every first line, a conformity of sound between the first syllable of the second and third foot, and in the second line, between the first syllable of the second, and the middle of the third, foot. This poem may be scanned by an amphybrach and trochee alternately on the first line; the second line is the same, excepting that it terminates with a long syllable

˘ ˘ ˘ | ¯ ˘ | ˘ ˘ ˘ | ¯ ˘
˘ ˘ ˘ | ¯ ˘ | ˘ ˘ ˘ | ¯

'S ă' mhādămn | chiūin gheăl, | ănn ām dhŏmh | *dūs*gădh
Aĭg būn nă | stūicĕ | b' ē 'n *sūg*rădh | leam;
Ă cheārc lĕ | sgiūcăn | ă gābhaĭl | *tūch*ăin,
'Săn cōileăch | *cūirt*eĭl | ăg *dūr*dăil | trom.
Ăn drēathăn | *sūr*dăil, | 's ă rībhĭd | chiū*il* aĭge
Ă cūr năn | smū*id* dhēth | gŭ *lū*thăr | binn
Ăn trūid săm | brū dheărg | lĕ mōrăn | ūnaĭch
Rē cēilĕir | sūnntăch | bŭ shiūbhlăch | rann

Or, thus:

Three first, | ¯ ˘ ˘ | ¯ ˘
Last, ¯ ˘ ˘ | ¯

'Sa mhadainn | chiuin gheal
Ann am dhomh | dùsgadh,
Aig bun na | stùice,
B' e 'n sùgradh | leam;
A chearc le | sgiùcan,
A gabhail | tùchain
'S an coileach | cùirteil
A dùrdail | trom, &c.

Beinn Dobhrain is similar in measure to a much older poem, entitled, *Moladh Mhòraig*. It contains three distinct measures: first, the *urlar*; secondly, *siubhal*, quicker than the *urlar*; and thirdly, *crùn-luath*, the most rapid of the three These terms are taken from corresponding strains in *piobaireachd*. The first stanza, *urlar*, consists of spondees and dactyles.

B' ĭ sīn | ă mhaōis | leăch luāineach
Feadh | ōgănăn;
Bīolăicheăn | năm brūach
'S aite | cōmhnŭidh dhĭ
Dūilleăgăn | năn craōbh,
Crīomăgăn | a gaoil.
Chă b' ē 'm | fōtărăs.
Ă h-aīgn | ĕ eū | trŏm suāirc;
Gŭ Āo | bhăch ăit | gŭn ghrūaim
Ă' ceānn | bŭ bhrăis | ĕ ghuăn | aiche,
Ghŏrăichĕ
Ă chrē | bŭ cheān | ălt stūaim.
Chălăich | ī gŭ | buan;
Aīm gleānn | ă bhārr | ăich uāine.
Bu | nōsaīrĕ.

The Second Part, or *Siubhal,*

May be scanned thus; the first, third, fifth, sixth, and seventh lines, a short syllable, a dactyle, a pyrrhic; for the second, fourth, and last, a short syllable, a dactyle, and a trochee

'S ĭ 'n | ēilīd bhēag | bhīnnĕach,
Bŭ | ghūnăichĕ | sraōnădh,
Lĕ | cūinnĕan geūr | bīorăch,
Ăg | sīrĕadh nă | gaoithe;
Gŭ | gāsgănăch | spēirĕach,
Feadh | chrēachăn nă | bēinnĕ,
Lĕ | eāgăl rŏ | thĕinĕ,
Cha | tēirīnn ĭ | aōnăch.

The Third Part, or *Crun-luath,*

Consists of a short syllable, a dactyle repeated, for the first, third, fifth, sixth, and seventh lines; and for the second, fourth, and last, a short syllable, a dactyle, and a spondee, or a trochee.

Chă | b' āithnĕ dhŏmh | co | leānădh ĭ,
Dŏ | fheāră nă | rŏinn Eōrpa;
Mūr | fāicĕadh ĕ | deāgh | gheān ŏrră,
'S tighinn | fārăsdă | nă | cō-dhăil;
Gu | fāiteăch bhīth | 'n a | h-eārălăs,
Tighinn | 'm fāigsĕ dh' ĭ | m' an | cārrăich ĭ,
Gu | fāicĕalăch | gle | eārălăch,
Mu 'm | fāirīch ĭ | na | cōir ĕ

The beautiful love song, entitled, *Marai bhàn òg*, so often imitated, but never equalled, may be scanned thus: a short syllable, three trochees, and a pyrrhic, for the first line; and, for the second, a short syllable, a trochee, a dactyle, and a long syllable.

˘ | ¯ ˘ | ¯ ˘ | ¯ ˘ | ˘ ˘ |
¯ ˘ ˘ |
˘ | ¯ ˘ | ¯ ˘ ˘ | ¯

Do | chuach-fhalt | bàn air | fàs cho | barrail,
'Sa | bhàrr lan | chamag is | dhual;
T' aghaidh ghlan | mhalta, | nàrach, | bhanail:
Do | dhà chaol- | mhala gun | ghruaim.
Sùil ghorm, | liontach, | mhln-rosg | mheallach,
Gun dlth | cur fal' ann | do ghruaidh;
Deud gheal | iobhrai | dhionach | dhaingean,
Beul | bith nach | cànadh ach | stuaim

I shall conclude this exemplification of Gaelic verse with one of those famous songs of incitement to battle, called, *Brosnachadh catha*. These songs were not all precisely in the same measure; but they were all quick, rapid, and animating, descriptive of hurried movements, activity, and exertion. The whole song measures like the first staff.

˘ ˉ | ˘ ˉ
˘ ˉ | ˉ ˘
˘ ˉ | ˘ ˉ | ˘ ˉ

Ă mhāc | aĭn cheānn,
Năn cūr | săn strānn
Ărd leūm | năch rīgh | năn sleăgh,

Lamh threun | 's gach cas,
Cridhe ard | gun sgath.
Ceànn airm | nan roinn geur goirt,

Gearr sios gu bàs,
Gun bharc-sheol bàn,
Bhi snamh mu dhubh Innistore

Mar thairnich bhaoil,
Do bhuill' a laoich,
Do shùil mar chaoir ad cheann,

Mar charaig chruinn,
Do chridhe gun roinn,
Mar lasan oidhche do lann.

Cum fuar do sgiath,
Is craobh-bhuidh nial,
Mar chith o reul a bhàis.

A mhacain cheann,
Nan cùrsan strann,
Sgrios nàimhde sios gu làr.

FOCLAIR

GAILIG AGUS BEURLA.

A.

A, *a.* (ailm, the elm.) The first letter of the Gaelic alphabet. It has three sounds: (1.) both long and short. Long, like *a* in *bar*, *car;* as àl, *brood*, àr, *slaughter*. Short, like *a* in *fat*, *cat;* as falt, *hair*, cas, *foot*. (2.) Both long and short, when immediately preceding *dh*, and *gh;* in which state it has no corresponding sound in English. Long, as adhradh, *worship;* aghmhor, *fortunate*. Short, as lagh, *law;* tagh, *choose;* adharc, *horn*. (3.) Short and obscure, like *e* in *hinder;* as an, am, a, *the;* ma, nam, nan, *if;* and the plural terminations *a*, or *an*, as laghanna, *laws*, beanntan, *mountains*. In the interrogative pronouns *an* and *am*, *a* is scarcely ever pronounced.

A, *article*. The. Used before words beginning with aspiration; as, a chraobh, *the tree;* a bheinn, *the hill*, or *mountain*.

A, *rel. pron.* Who, which, whom, what, that. An duine a bhuail mi, *the man whom I struck;* mar aisling chaoin a chaidh seach, *like a pleasant dream that has passed.—Ull.* B'esan a rinn so, *it was he who did this.*

A, *pos. pron.* His, her, hers, its. Caireadh gach aon air a léis a lann, *let every one gird his sword on his thigh.—Ull.* Grad theichidh a geillt 's a bruadar, *speedily her terror and her dream shall vanish.—Oss. Taura.* Where the succeeding word begins with a vowel, this pronoun is ellipsed; as, thuit e bharr' each, *he fell from his horse:* in speaking of a female, however, the pronoun is used, and, to prevent an *hiatus*, *h*, with a hyphen (h-), precedes the noun; as, thuit i bhàrr a h-each, *she fell from her horse;* but the pronoun is omitted if the *preceding* word *end* with a vowel; as, a dùsgadh le h-osnaich, *awakening with her sobs.—Oss. Taura.* *Syr.* ha, ah. *Heb.* a. *Chald.* eh. *Arab.* ha. *Pers.* ou. *Gr.* ἀυ. *Ir.* a. *Manx.* e. *Corn.* e, i.

A', (*for* ag), the sign of the present participle. If the participle begin with a vowel, *ag*, or 'g, is most frequently used, and *a'*, if it begin with a consonant. A gaol 'g a caoidh is ise ag acain, *her beloved deploring her, and she wailing bitterly.—Oss. Taura.* Le h-osnaich o cadal a dùsgadh, *with her own sobs awakening from her sleep.—Id.* Ta h-anam ag imeachd gu neoil, *her spirit is travelling to its clouds.—Id.* It may be said, that in general this particle is used, though with infinitely more elegance and propriety, in the same sense as the English use *a*, when they say, *he is a walking*, *he is a fishing*, tha e ag imeachd, tha e ag iasgachadh.

A, the sign of the infinitive, *To.*

A, the sign of the vocative. O. (*Corn.* a.) Caomhain do sholus, a ghrian, *spare thy light, O sun.—Oss. Trathal.* A Sheallama, theach mo ghaoil! *O Selma, thou home of my heart!—Oss. Gaul.*

A, (*for* ann), *prep.* In, into, within, on. Ciod chuir sin a d'cheann, *what put that into your head?* A d'chridhe, *in your heart.*

A, sometimes a sign of the preterite tense. Nuair a thuirt e rium, *when he said to me.—Sm.*

A, *obj. pron.* Him, her, it. Cha n'urrainn iad a thogail no'fhagail, *they could neither lift nor leave him. Oss. Derm.* Theab iad a marbhadh, *they had almost killed her.*

A, *pers. pron.* [for e.] Him, he, it. *A* is never *written* for e, but, in many districts of the Highlands, e, *he* or *him*, is pronounced a; as, Bhuail iad a, *they struck him;* thainig a, *he came.*

A, *prep. and used before a consonant.* Out, out of, from; also in. Na h-earb a foirneart, *trust not in oppression. Stew. O. T.*, a so, *from this time. Arm.*, a so.

A is often used before many adverbs, prepositions, and conjunctions, and some numerals: a bhàrr, *besides*, a bhos, *here*, *on this side*, a choidhch, *for ever.* A cheana, *already;* a chéile, *each other*, a chianamh, *a little ago.* A cheann, *because;* a chlisgeadh, *in a start*, *soon.* A chum, *in order to;* a dhà, *two;* a dhà dheug, *twelve.* A ghnàth, *always;* a h-aon, *one;* a h-aon deug, *eleven;* a latha 's a dh'oidhche, *day and night;* a lathair, *present.* A leth-taobh, *aside;* a mach, *out;* a mhain, *only;* a muigh, *without;* a nall, *hither;* a nios, *up.* A nis, a nise, *now;* a nuas, *down hither;* a null, a nunn, *thither*, *across;* a réir, *according to.* A ris, *again.* A sios, *downwards;* a suas, *upwards.*

† A, *s.* A chariot, car, waggon.—*Glossary of Colum Cille.*

† A, *s.* An ascent, hill, promontory.

† Ab, *negative particle;* as ablach, *i. e.* ab-laoch, a brat.

Ab, *g.* aba, *s. f.* An ape; a spell, *anciently* any little creature. *Dan.* abe. *Du.* aap. *Swed.* apa. *W.* epa. *Sclav.* apinia. *Finland.* apini, an ape.

† Ab, aba, *s. m.* A father, a lord, an abbot; *n. pl.* aban, or abannan, abbots. *Heb.* ab, or abh. *Chald.* ab. *Turk.* aba. Greek, αππα. *Dor. D.* απφυς. *Lat.* abbas. *Span.* abad. *Calmuc Tartars*, abagài. *Hung.* apa. *Grisons*, bab. *Syracusan and Bithynian*, pappas. *Syr.* abba. *W.* abad. *Arm. and Corn.* abatæ, abad. *It.* papa. *Hottentots*, bo. *Antilles*, baba. Herodotus tells us, that the Scythians called father Jove papæus; a modern author says that the Scythian term for father was pappas.

† **Ab**, aba, *s. m.* Water. *Pers.* ab, *river. Turk.* ab. *Mogul*, ab, *river. Heb.* saab, *carry water;* from sa, *carry*, and ab, *water. Ethiop.* abbi, *wave. Armen.* ahp, *pool. Pers.* ab, ap, av, *water. Jap.* abi, *wash with water.*

This word is found in Martin's description of the Hebrides, and in Irvine's nomenclature on the word *Avus*, which is the name of a lake and river in Argyllshire (Awe); so Ab-us is a name given to the Humber. Wytfleet, in his Supplement to Ptolemy's Geography, calls the place where Columbus first landed in America, Cuanabi, or Guanahani. Both these words have the same signification, meaning a bay, harbour, or sea of water. *Cuan* is a harbour, and *ab* is water, and *i* seems to be an Indian termination. Guanahani: *Guan* is the same as *cuan; g* and *c*, being palatals, are easily changed the one into the other, and *an* [see *an*] or *han* is water: the *i*, as in the former instance, is an Indian adjection.

Aba, *gen. sing.* of ab; of an ape; of an abbot.

Aba, *s. m.* A cause, affair, matter, circumstance, business. *Syr. and Chald.* aba.

Abab! *interj.* Tush! fie! oh! for shame! nonsense! pshaw!

† Abac, aic, *s. m.* See Abhag.

† Abach, aich, *s. m.* Entrails of a beast; pluck; also proclamation. *Ir.* abhach.

Abachadh, aidh, *s. m.* A ripening, the circumstance of ripening; a growing to maturity.

Abachadh (ag), *pr. part.* of abaich. Ripening. Tha 'n t-arbhar ag abachadh, *the corn is ripening.*

† Abachd, *s. f.* Exploits; gain, lucre.

Abachd, *s. f.* Ripeness, maturity. *Contr.* for abaicheachd, the regularly formed, though not used, derivative, of abaich.

† Abact, *s. f.* Irony, jesting.—*Glossary of Colum Cille.* Now written *abhachd.*

† Abadh, aidh, *s. m.* A lampoon, a satirical poem; *n. pl.* abaidhean.

Abaich, *a.* Ripe, mature, at full growth; ready, prepared, expert. *Com. and sup.* abaiche, *more or most ripe. Ir.* abaidh. *Manx.* appee. *W.* adhved.

Abaich, *v.* Ripen; bring or grow to maturity. *Pret. a.* dh' abaich, *ripened; fut. aff. a.* abaichidh, *shall or will ripen; fut. pass.* abaichear, *shall be ripened.*

Abaichead, eid, *s. m.* and *f.* Ripeness, maturity; increase in ripeness, advancement in ripeness. Air abaichead 's gum bi e, *however ripe it shall be.* Tha e dol an abaichead, *it is growing more and more ripe.*

Abaichear, *fut. pass.* of abaich; shall be ripened.

Abaichidh, *fut. aff. a.* of abaich; shall or will ripen.

Abaid, aide, *s. f.* (*i. e.* ab-aite, the place of an abbot), an abbey; also an abbot. *Pers.* abad, *a booth; plur.* abadan. *Dan.* abbedie. *Span.* abbadia. *N. pl.* abaide, or abaidean, *abbeys.* Lios an abaid, *the abbot's court. Arm.* les an abad.

Abaide, *gen. sing.* of abaid.

Abaideachd, *s. f.* (*from* abaid), an abbacy.

Abaidh, *gen. sing.* of abadh.

† Abaidh, *s. f.* A bud, blossom. *Heb. and Chald.* abi, *green fruits.*

† Abail, *s. f.* Death. *Arab.* Hebil.

Abailt, *s. f.* An abbey; more frequently abaid; which see.

† Abailt, *s. f.* Death. *Arab.* Hebil.

Abair, *v. irr.* Say, speak, utter, pronounce. *Pret. a.* thubhairt, said; *fut. aff. a.* their, shall or will say; *fut. neg.* dubhairt. Abair ri, ris, riu, *say to her, him, them;* na h-abair sin, *or*, na abair sin, *do not say that. W.* ebru. *Ir.* abair. *Eng.* jabber. *Du.* jabberen. *Heb.* dabar.

Abaiream, *first sing. imper. a.* of abair. Let me say, speak, utter, or pronounce.

Abairear, *fut. and imper. pass.* Shall be said, let be said; abairear e, *let it be said.* It is often contracted abrar.—*Stew. Luke, ref.*

Abairt, *s. f.* (*from* abair.) Education; politeness, breeding; speech, articulation. *Ir.* abairt.

† Abairt, *s. f.* Custom, use, habit, usage. See Abhairt.

Abait, aite, *s. f.* (ab-àite). An abbey.

† Abaoi, *s. f.* Sunset, descent. *Eng.* eve.

† Abar, air, *s. m.* Speech.

Abar, air, *s. m.* A marsh, bog, fen; marshy ground. *Arab.* ybr, *margin of a river*, and abar, *wells. Heb. by met.* baar. *Ir.* abar.

Abarach, *a.* (*from* abar.) Fenny, boggy, marshy; of or pertaining to a marsh; likewise of or pertaining to Lochaber; a Lochaber-man; also bold, daring. Gu h-aghmhor abarach, *in a brave and bold manner.—Old Song. Com. and sup.* abaraiche, *bolder, boldest.*

Abarachd, *s. f.* Marshiness, bogginess.

Abardair, *s. m.* (*from* abair.) A dictionary.

Abardairiche, *s. m.* (*from* abardair.) A lexicographer.

Abartach, *a.* (*from* abair.) Bold, daring, forward, impudent, talkative. *Com. and sup.* abartaiche, *more or most bold.*

Abartachd, *s. f.* (*from* abair.) A mode of speech; an idiom; talkativeness.

Abartair (*from* abair), *s.* A dictionary.

Abartairiche, *s. m.* (*from* abartair.) A lexicographer.

Aber, *s. m.* (*Corn.* aber. *Heb.* habar, *to join together;* haber, *a companion;* heber, *a junction; Chald. Syr. Ethiop.* habar, *to unite.*) A place where two or more streams meet, a confluence, a conflux, as Aberfeldy; a place where a river falls into the sea, as Aberdeen, in Scotland; Aberistwyth, in Cardiganshire. "Seu mari," says Boxhorn, "seu duo fluvii junctis aquis consociantur, locus in quo fit hæc conjunctio Britannicè vocatur *aber.*" The place where a river falls into the sea, or where two rivers join, is, in the old British tongue, called *aber.* Boxhorn seems to think that *aber* is a Phenician word. In some districts of the Highlands, as Breadalbane and Strathtay, this word is improperly pronounced *obair.*

Abh, *s. m.* A landing net; a sack net; an instrument.

† Abh, *s. m.* Water. *Tonq.* hài, *sea. Shans.* ab, *and* aw, *water. Arab.* ahba, *pool. Pers.* awe. *Gr. Æol.* ἄφ-ᾶ. *Lat.* a-qua. *Dan.* aae. *W.* aw. *Fr.* eau. *Gothic*, a. *Isl.* aa. *Low Germ.* aa. *Swed.* a, *a river. Old Sax.* a, ea, eha. See also Ab.

Abh, in its original acceptation, is a *fluid*, and from this root are derived all words that imply fluidity, or the action or motion of fluids, as well as many words which imply motion. Hence also *amnis*, a river, and *abhuinn*, a river; properly *abh-an*, the flowing element. See also *amh.*

Abhac, aic, (more properly abhag.) A terrier; a dwarf, a sprite; also, in derision, a petulant person. *N. pl.* abhaic, *or* abhacan.

Abh-ciùil, *s. f.* A musical instrument.

Abhacan, *n. pl.* of abhac. Terriers.

Abhacas, *s. m.* and *f.* Diversion, sport, ridicule, merriment; boisterous day. Ball abhacais, *a laughing stock.—Stew. Jer.* Fear na h-abhacais, *a merry fellow, a man for merriment.*

† Abhach, *a.* Joyful, glad, humorous; sportful, merry. *Comp.* and *sup.* abhaiche, *more or most joyful;* now written aobhach; which see.

Abhaiche, *com.* and *sup.* of abhach, *more or most joyful.*

Abhachd, *s. f.* (*from* abhach.) Joy, humour, hilarity; gibe; irony; jesting; also capability. Ri h-abhachd, *merry making.—Macint.* A togail abhachd, *raising joy.—Old Song.*

Abhachdach, *a.* Humorous, merry, joyous, joyful; jolly, corpulent; inclined to gibe, jesting, or raillery. Gu h-abhachdach, *joyfully.—Macint. Com.* and *sup.* abhachdaiche, *more or most humorous.*

Abhachdaiche, *s. m.* (*from* abhach.) An humorous person; one who is fond of jesting or raillery, a railer.

Abhachdaiche, *com.* and *sup.* of abhachdach. More or most humorous, joyful or jocose.

Abhachdail, *a.* (*from* abhach.) Joyful, humorous, jocose. The terminations *ail* and *eil* of adjectives are but smoothings and contractions of amhuil, *like*; abhachdail, therefore, is abhachd-amhuil. The case is the same in English: as, gentlemanly, *i. e.* gentlemanlike; cowardly, cowardlike.

Abhachdas, ais, *s. m.* (*from* abhach.) Merriment, ridicule, sport; clamorous joy.

Abhadh, aidh, *s. m.* An instrument; abhadh-ciùil, a musical instrument.—*Stew. Eccles.*

Abhadh, aidh, *s. m.* A landing-net, a sack-net; a fold; a hollow.

Abhadh, aidh, *s. m.* A flying camp. *Ir. id.*

Abhadh-ciùil, *s. m.* A musical instrument.—*Stew. Ecc.*

Abhag, aig, *s. m.* A terrier; a contemptuous name for a petulant person; *rarely* a dwarf; a spectre. An abhag bh' aig Fionn, *the terrier which Fingal had.—Fingalian Poem.* Neas-abhaig, *a ferret. Heb.* abhak, *dust.*

Abhagach, *a.* (*from* abhag.) Like a terrier; of or relating to a terrier; petulant, snappish, waspish.

Abhagail, *i. e.* abhag-amhuil, *a.* (*from* abhag.) Like a terrier; waspish, snappish.

Abhagan, *n. pl.* of abhag. Terriers.

Abhagas, ais, *s. m.* A report, a rumour, a surmise.

Abhaic, *gen. sing.* and *n. pl.* of abhac.

Abhaig, *gen. sing.* and *n. pl.* of abhag.

Abhail, *gen. sing.* of abhal.

† **Abhail**, *s. m.* Death. *Ir. Bisc.* Hivil.

Abhaill, *gen. sing.* of abhall.

Abhainn, (*i. e.* abh-an, *the flowing element*; *see* abh *and* an), *s. f. gen.* abhann, *or* aibhne. A river, a stream. Bruach na h-aibhne, *the bank of the river*; *n. pl.* aibhnean *and* aibhnichean, ruithidh na h-aibhnean, *the rivers flow.—Stew. Pro.* Written also *amhainn* and *abhuinn*. *Lat.* amnis. *W.* afon, or avon. *English*, † afene. *Swed.* aen, *or* an. *Arm.* afon. *Ir.* abhan. *Corn.* auan. *Manx.* aon. *Germ.* am.

One may venture to assert that all over the globe, more especially in Europe and Asia, the names of rivers ending in an, ane, en, eine, ein, in, on, onne, &c. are derived from the old Celtic root, *an*, signifying an element, water; see *an*. The Seine is a contraction of seimh-an, *the smooth water*; and a more descriptive name of that majestic river could not be given. Rhen-us, *the Rhine*, is reidh-an, *the placid water*; a name which well accords with the general appearance of that river. Garumn-us, Garonne, *is* garbh-an, *the rough water*. Marne, marbhan, *the dead water*. So also Pad-an-us, *the Po*; and the Asiatic rivers, Arn-on, Jord-an, Gib-on, Jih-on, &c. I have been agreeably surprised to find that in some of these remarks I had been anticipated by a few learned and ingenious etymologists.

Abhainneach, *a.* (*from* abhainn.) Fluvial; abounding in rivers; of, or pertaining to, a river.

Abhair, *gen. sing.* of abhar.

† **Abhais**, *s. f.* A bird. *Arm.* afais. *Lat.* avis.

Abhaist, aiste, *s. f.* (*Heb.* davash.) Custom, habit, usage, manner, consuetude; also adjectively, usual, wont. A leanachd an abhaist a b' aoibhinn, *following the habits that once were pleasant.—Oss. Gaul.* Cha b' e sud abhaist Theadhaich, *that was not the manner or custom of Tedaco.—Old Legend.* Tha thusa an sin, a chnoc an easain, ann ad sheasamh mara b' àbhaist, *hillock of the dark torrent, thou art there standing as usual.—Macint.* *N. pl.* abhaiste *and* abhaistean.

Abhaisteach, *a.* (*from* abhaist.) Customary, usual, habitual, adhering to custom; according to use, custom, or habit. *Comp.* and *sup.* abhaistiche, *more or most customary.*

Abhaistiche, *comp.* and *sup.* of abhaisteach. More or most customary.

Abhal, ail, *s. m. n. pl.* abhlan. An apple; an apple-tree. Abhal fiadhain, *a crab-apple*; crann abhail, *an apple-tree.—Stew. G. B.* Ruaidhe nan abhal, *the ruddiness of apples.—Old Song. W.* aval. *Dan.* aeble. *Ir.* abhall. *Arm.* afall *and* aval. *Corn.* aval *and* avel. *Old Germ.* effel. *Mod. Germ.* apfel. *Lith.* apfal. *Old Pruss.* wabelko. and *Procopius*, in *Cherson Taur.* apel. *Servia*, iablo. *Turk.* and *Hung.* alma, by transposition for amal. The right orthography of this word is *abhall*, being derived from the pure Celtic term *ball*, any round body; in *Stiria* and *Carinthia* they say iablan; in *Bohemia*, gablon; *Isl.* eple; *Runic*, eple; *Little Tartary*, apel.

Abhal ghort, *or*, abhall-ghort, *gen.* abhall-ghoir, *s. m.* An orchard. Sometimes written all-ghart. *Dan.* aeblegaart. *W.* afallach. *Ir.* abhal-ghort.

Abhall, aill, *s. m.* An apple; an apple-tree. Ar n' abhall 's ar ùbhlan, *our apple-trees and apples.—Old Song.* Written also *abhal.*

Abhall-ghortach, *a.* Abounding in orchards; of or pertaining to an orchard.

A bhàn, *adv.* Down, downwards. See **Bhàn**.

Abhar, air, *s. m.* A reason, cause, motive. *Chald.* abhor; more frequently written aobhar, which see; *n. pl.* àbhair *and* àbharan.

† **Abharach**, aich, *s. m.* A youth under age, who acts as a man. *Gr.* ἁβρὰ, *a delicate female.*

Abhlain, *gen. sing.* and *n. pl.* of abhlan, which see.

† **Abhlabhra**, *a.* Dumb, mute, speechless.

Abhlan, *n. pl.* of abhal and abhall.

Abhlan, ain, *s. m.* (*Dan.* ablad. *Ir.* abhlan.) A wafer; a round cake; whatever is taken with bread in the way of sauce, or condiment, vulgarly called kitchen.—*Shaw.* A bhlas mar abhlain, *its taste like wafers.—Stew. Exod.* *N. pl.* abhlain *and* abhlana. Abhlan, signifying *kitchen*, is more frequently written and pronounced *annlan*, which see. Abhlan coisrichte, *a holy wafer.*

Abhlanach, *a.* Like a wafer, wafery.

Abhlan-coisrigte, *s. m.* A holy wafer, such as is used by the Roman Catholics in the sacrament of the Lord's Supper.

Abh-mhathair, mhathar, *s. f.* A mother abbess.

† **Abhra**, *a.* Dark.—*Shaw.*

Abhra, abhradh, *s. m.* The eye-brow. *Gr.* ὀφρὺς. *Arm.* abrant. *Ir.* abhra.

Abhrais, *gen. sing.* of abhras.

† **Abhran**, ain, *s. m.* A song.—*Shaw.*

Abhran, *s. pl.* Eye-lids. *W.* amrant. *Corn.* abrans.

Abhras, ais, *s. m.* Yarn; flax and wool, stuff for spinning; also a ready answer. Ag abhras, *spinning.* *Ir.* abhras.

Abhrasach, *a.* (*from* abhras.) Of or belonging to yarn.

† **Abhsan**, ain, *s. m.* A hollow; a furrow.

Abhuinn, aibhne, *s. f.* A river. See **Abhainn**.

Abhuinneach, *a.* (*from* abhuinn.) See **Abhainneach**.

Abhuist, *s. f.* See **Abhaist**.

† **Abhus**, uis, *s. m.* Any wild beast; also a stall for cattle.

Ablach, aich, *s. m.* A mangled carcass; carrion; the remains of a creature destroyed by any ravenous beast; a term of personal contempt, a brat. Ablach gun deo, *a breathless carcass.* *N. pl.* ablaich *and* ablaichean. In the sense of a *brat*, ablach ought perhaps to be written ablaoch.

Ablaich, *gen.* and *voc. sing.* and *n. pl.* of ablach. Ablaich tha thu ann! *you brat, that you are!*

Ablaichean, *n. pl.* of ablach. Carcases.

Ablaoch, laoich, *s. m.* (ab *neg.* and laoch.) A brat; a pithless person. Ablaoich tha thu ann! *You brat, that you are!*

Ablaoich, *gen. sing.* of ablaoch.

† Abrad, *a.* Exalted; far removed. *Arm.* brat, sovereign.

Abram. Contracted for abaiream, which see.

† Abrann, *s. m.* Bad news.

† Abrann, *a.* Lustful, lecherous, lascivious.

Abraon, aoin, *s. m.* April. *Ir.* abran.

Abrar, for abairear, *fut.* and *imper. pass.* of abair. Shall or will be spoken.

Abstoil, *gen. sing.* of abstal.

Abstol, oil, *s. m.* An apostle. *Gr.* ἀποστολ-ος. *Lat.* apostolus. *Ir.* absdol. *Fr.* † apostre. *Arm.* apstol. *Corn.* abestel. *The letter of the apostle*, litir an abstoil; *the letters of the apostles*, litrichean nan abstol. *N. pl.* abstoil and abstolan.

Abstolach, *a.* (*from* abstol.) Apostolical; of or belonging to an apostle.

Abstolachd, *s. f.* (*from* abstol) Apostleship. Gràs agus abstolachd, *grace and apostleship.—Stew. Rom.*

Abu! *interj.* The war cry of the ancient Irish

Abuchadh, aidh, *s. m.* The process of ripening, the circumstance of ripening, a ripening, progress toward maturity. Written also *abachadh.*

Abuchadh, (ag) *pr. part.* of abuich. Ripening, mellowing, maturating.

Abuich, *v.* Ripen, mellow, maturate. *Pret. a.* dh' abuich, *ripened; fut. aff. a.* abuichidh, *shall or will ripen; fut. pass.* abuichear, *shall or will be ripened.*

Abuich, *a.* Ripe, mellow, mature. M' arbhar abuich, *my ripe corn.—Stew. O. T. Ir.* abuidh *and* abuigh.

Abuichead, eid, *s.* Ripeness, advancement in ripeness. Tha 'n t-arbhar dol an abuichead, *the corn is growing riper.*

Abuichear, *fut. pass.* of abuich. Shall or will be ripened.

Abuicheas, *fut. sub. a.* of abuich. Used with the conjunction *ma*, if, *nur*, when; ma dh' abuicheas e, *if it shall ripen.*

† Abulta, *a.* Strong, able, capable. Gaisgich abulta, *able warriors.—Old Poem. Ir.* abulta.

† Abultachd, *s. f.* (*from* abulta.) Strength, ability, capability. Abultachd ur feachd, *the strength of your army.—Old Poem.*

† Ac, aca, *s. m.* A denial, a refusal; also a son. Hence, mac, *a son.*

† Ac, aca, *s. m.* Speech; tongue.

Aca and ac', *comp. pron.* (*Corn.* aga, *theirs.*) Of them, with them, on their side, at them, on them, in their possession; *also* their. Tha mòran ac' ag radh, *many of them say.—Smith.* Tha e aca na sheirbheiseach, *he is with them as a servant;* aca sud, *in the possession of those people.—Smith.* An tigh aca, *their house; i. e.* an tigh th' aca, literally, *the house which is to them;* chaidh ac' air, *they conquered him;* theid ac' orm, *they shall conquer, or get the better of, me.*

† Acadamh, daimh, *s. m.* (ac, *speech*, and † damh, *learning.*) An academy. *Gr.* ἀκαδημία. *Lat.* academia. *Ir.* acadamh.

Acaid, *s. f.* (*Ir.* aicid.) Pain; hurt; a transient lancinating pain. Is trom an acaid tha 'm lot, *intense is the pain in my wound.—Macint.*

Acaideach, *a.* (*from* acaid.) Painful, uneasy; also groaning. *Comp.* and *sup.* acaidiche, *more or most painful.*

† Acaideadh, idh, *s. m.* An inhabitant, tenant.

Acaidiche, *comp.* and *sup.* of acaideach. More or most painful.

Acain, *s. f.* (*perhaps* ath-chaoin.) *W.* açwyn *and* oçain. A moan, a sob, plaintive voice; wailing, weeping, murmur; rarely a tool, tackle, furniture. Acain 'g a taomadh an comhnuidh, *his plaintive voice pouring forth incessantly.—Oss. Fin.* and *Lor.* Acain air acain, *moan upon moan.—Oss. Dargo.* When *acain* is preceded by 'g or *ag*, it is, as are most substantives in a similar situation, rendered as the present participle. Crathaidh e a cheann 's e 'g acain, *he shall shake his head, moaning;* literally, *and he moaning.*

Acaineach, *a.* (*from* acain.) *W.* açwynawl, *a.* Plaintive; distressful; causing sorrow or wailing; sobbing. Guth acaineach, *a sobbing voice; comp.* and *sup.* acainiche, *more or most plaintive.*

Acainear, ir, *s. m.* (acain, *and* fear.) A complainer, mourner, weeper, wailer; one who ails. *W.* açwynwr.

Acainiche, *s. m.* (*from* acain.) A wailer, a mourner, a sobber, weeper, complainer.

Acainiche, *comp.* and *sup.* of acaineach. More or most plaintive.

Acair, *s. f.* A ship's anchor; *n. pl.* acraichean, *anchors;* acair an anama, *the anchor of the soul.—Stew. Heb.* Ceithir acraichean, *four anchors.—Stew. Acts. Ir.* accair.

Acair, *s. f.* An acre of ground; *n. pl.* acraichean, *acres. Pers.* akar. *Gr.* ἀγρος. *Lat.* ager. *Maeso-Goth.* akrs. *Isl.* akur, akker, *and* akkeri. *Swedo-Goth.* aker *and* akrs. *Swed.* acker. *Dan.* ager. *Anglo-Sax.* acere. *Ir.* acra. *Arm.* acre. *Germ.* akar, akare, achre, acker. *High Germ.* acker. *Low Germ.* akker. *Heb.* ickar, *a ploughman. Syr.* akoro. *Arab.* akkoro. This is one of the few words which have come down to us from the original language of man.

Acair-pholl, phuill, *s. m.* (acair *and* poll.) An anchorage, a harbour, a road for ships; *n. pl.* acair-phuill. *Ir.* id.

Acairseid, (*from* acair,) *s. f.* A port, harbour, haven; anchorage; a road for ships; *n. pl.* acairseidean, *harbours. Ir.* id.

† Acais, *s. f.* Poison. *Ir.* id.

† Acalla, *s.* Conversation.

Acanaich, *s. f.* (*from* acain.) Wailing, moaning, sobbing, weeping; grief. Iadsan a b' aille m' acanaich, *they who would desire to partake of my grief.—Old Song.*

† Acar, *a.* (*Lat.* acer. *Fr.* aigre.) Sharp, sour, bitter.

Acarach, *a.* Gentle, obliging, mild, moderate, kind, compassionate, merciful; respectful. *Comp.* and *sup.* acaraiche.

Acarachd, *s. f.* (*from* acarach.) Gentleness, kindness, mildness, moderateness, compassionateness, mercifulness; respectfulness. Gun acarachd, *without mercy.—Smith.* Ghlac e sinn le h-acarachd, *he grasped us (our hands) with kindness.—Old Song.*

† Acaradh, aidh, *s. m.* Profit; the loan of any thing; usury. See Ocar.

Acaraiche, *comp.* and *sup.* of acarach. More or most gentle, kind, respectful, mild, or compassionate.

† Acaran, ain, *s. m.* Lumber.

† Acartha, *a.* See Acarach.

Acasa, acasan. Emphatic form of the *comp. pron.* aca, which see.

Acasdair, *s. m.* An axle-tree. *N. pl.* acasdairean. *Ir.* acastair.

Acasdairean, *n. pl.* of acasdair.

Acastair, *s. m.* An axle-tree. *N. pl.* acastairean, *axle-trees.*

Acastairean, *n. pl.* of acastair.

Acastarain, *gen. sing.* of acastaran.

† Acastaran, ain, *s. m.* An axle-tree. *N. pl.* acastarain, *or* acastarana.

Acduinn, *s. f.* Tools, instrument, utensil, tackle, tackling; furniture; equipage, harness; also a salve.—*Macfar.* Acduinn gunna, *the lock of a gun;* acduinn eich, *horse harness;* written also *acfuinn, acfhuinn,* and *achduinn; n. pl.* acduinnean.

Acduinneach, *a.* Of or pertaining to tools, tackling, harness; equipped, harnessed; expert, able, sufficient, active. *Com.* and *sup.* acduiniche, written also *acfuinneach, acfhuinneach*, and *achduinneach.*

ACDUINNEAN, *n. pl.* of acduinn.

ACDUINNICHE, *comp.* and *sup.* of acduinneach.

ACFUINN, *s. f.* Tools; instrument, utensil, tackling, tackle, harness, equipage, furniture; also a salve.—*Macfar.* Acfuinn gunna, *the lock of a gun;* acfuinn is inneal ciùil, *instruments of death.—Smith.* Acfuinn sgriobhaidh, *writing utensils.—Stew. Ezek.* Acfuinn na luinge, *the tackling of a ship.—Stew. Acts. N. pl.* acfuinnean; written also *acduinn, acfhuinn*, and *achduinn.*

ACFUINNEACH, *a.* (*from* acfuinn.) Of or pertaining to tools, tackling, harness, or furniture; equipped, harnessed; expert, able, sufficient, active. *Comp.* and *sup.* acfuinniche, *more or most expert. Ir.* acfuinneach.

ACFUINNEAN, *n. pl.* of acfuinn.

ACFHUINN, *s. f.* See ACFUINN or ACDUINN.

ACFHUINNEACH, *a.* (*from* acfhuinn.) See ACDUINNEACH, or ACFUINNEACH.

ACFHUINNEAN, *n. pl.* of acfhuinn. See ACDUINN, or ACFUINN.

ACH, *conj.* (*Goth.* ak. *Ir.* ach. *Lat.* ac. *Germ.* auch.) But, except, besides. Cha do rinn neach ach thusa e, *none but you did it;* ach co sud air a charraig mar cheò, *but who is yonder on the hill like a mist.—Oss.* Dh' fhalbh iad uile ach h-aon, *they all departed but one;* ach beag, *almost.*

ACH! ach! An interjection expressive of disgust.

† ACH, acha, *s. f.* A skirmish.

ACH, *s. m.* A field. See ACHADH.

† ACHA, ai, *s. f.* A mound or bank.—*Bisc.* Acha, *a rock.*

ACHADH, aidh, *s. m.* (*Sax.* haga. *Scotch*, haugh.) A field, a plain, a meadow; a corn field. An t-achadh a cheannaich Abraham, *the field that Abraham bought.—Stew. Gen.* A ceangal sguab san achadh, *binding sheaves in the corn field.—Id. N. pl.* achanna.

ACHAIDH, *gen. sing.* of achadh.

† ACHAIDH, *s. f.* An abode, a home. This vocable is seldom or never used by itself; but it is very common to say, dachaidh *and* dh'achaidh, *home or homewards; n. pl.* achaidhean.

ACHAIN, *s. f.* A prayer, entreaty, supplication; a wailing voice; petition. B' amhluidh sin achain nan slogh, *such were the prayers of the people.—Mac Lach.* The proper orthography of this word would seem to be *athchuinge*, which see.

ACHAINEACH, *a.* (*from* achain.) Supplicatory; perhaps *ath-chuingeach.*

ACHAINICHE, *s. m.* A petitioner; perhaps *ath-chuingiche.*

† ACHAMAIR, *a.* Soon, timely, short, abridged; perhaps *ath-chuimir.*

† ACHAMAIREACHD, *s. f.* Abridging, abridgment; perhaps *ath-chuimireachd.*

† ACHAR, air, *s. m.* A distance.

† ACHARADH, aidh, *s. m.* A sprite; a diminutive person.

ACH-BEAG, *adv.* Almost, well nigh. *Ir.* acth beag.

ACHD, *s. f.* (*Dan.* act. *Swed.* ackt, *purpose. Germ.* echt, *a law.*) An act, statute, decree; deed; case; account; state, condition; way, manner, method. Air an achd so, *in this way;* air aon achd, *on any account, in any case.—Smith.* Achd parlamaid, *an act of parliament.*

† ACHD, *s. f.* A body; peril; a nail; a claw.

ACHDAIR, *s. f.* An acre. See ACAIR.

ACHDAIR, *s. f.* A ship's anchor; *n. pl.* achdraichean, ar n-achdair, ar siùil 's ar be airtean, *our anchor, our sails, and tackling.—Macfar.* Written also *acair*, which see.

ACHDAIRPHOLL, phuill, *s. m.* A road for ships; written also *acairpholl.*

ACHDAIRSEID, *s. f.* An anchorage, a harbour, port; a road for ships. See ACAIRSEID.

† ACHDRA, ai, *s. f.* A naval expedition.

† ACHDRAN, ain, *s. m.* An adventurer, a foreigner. *Ir. id.*

† ACHDRANACH, aich, *s. m.* A foreigner, an adventurer.

† ACHDRANACH, *a.* Foreign; adventurous.

ACHDUINN, *s. f.* Instrument, tools, tackle, harness, equipage, furniture; also a salve. Grinn achduinn na h-eachraidh, *the beautiful harness of the stud.—Old Poem. N. pl.* achduinnean, written also *acduinn* and *acfuinn.*

ACHDUINNEACH, *a.* Of or relating to tools, harness, or furniture; also equipped; expert, able, sufficient. *Comp.* and *sup.* achduinniche.

† ACHIAR, *a.* (*Ir. id. Lat.* acer. *Fr.* aigre.) Sharp, sour, bitter.

† ACLADH, aidh, *s. m.* A fishery.

† ACLAIDH, *a.* Smooth, fine, soft.

ACHLAIS, aise, *s. f.* The arm, armpit; bosom, breast. Lag na h-achlais, *the armpit. N. pl.* achlaisean. Raimh ann achlaisean ard-thonn, *oars in the bosoms of lofty surges.—Macfar. Ir.* achlais.

ACHLAIS, *gen. sing.* of achlas.

ACHLAISE, *gen. sing.* of achlais.

ACHLAS, ais, *s. f.* A bundle; a little truss; also the armpit, the arm.

† ACHMHAING, *a.* Powerful.

ACHMHASAIN, *gen. sing.* and *n. pl.* of achmhasan.

ACHMHASAN, ain, *s. m.*; *n. pl.* achmhasain. (*Corn.* acheson, *guilt.*) A reproof, reprimand, scold, reproach. Thug athair achmhasan da, *his father rebuked him.—Stew. Gen.* Achmhasain teagaisg, *the reproofs of instruction.—Stew. Pro.* Fuath no eud no achmhasan, *nor hate, nor jealousy, nor reproach.—Old Poem.*

ACHMHASANACH, *a.* Causing a rebuke; liable to rebuke; of or pertaining to a rebuke; prone to rebuke; reprehensive. *Comp.* and *sup.* achmhasanaiche, *more or most prone to rebuke.*

ACHMHASANAICH, *v.* Rebuke, reprove, chide, censure; *pret. a.* dh'achmhasanaich, *rebuked; fut. aff. a.* achmhasanaichidh, *shall or will rebuke.*

ACHMHASANAICHE, *s. m.* One who rebukes or censures.

ACHMHASANAICHE, *comp.* and *sup.* of achmhasanach.

ACHMHASANAICHIDH, *fut. aff. a.* of achmhasanaich. Shall or will rebuke.

† ACHRAN, ain, *s. m.* Intricacy, entanglement, perplexity.

† ACHRANACH, *a.* Intricate, entangled, perplexed.

ACHUINGE, *s. f.* (*for* ath-chuinge.) A supplication, prayer, petition, request. See ATH-CHUINGE.

ACHUINGEACH, *a.* (*from* achuinge.) Petitionary; prone to supplicate or pray; of or pertaining to a petition or prayer.

† ACOMAIL, *v.* Heap together; increase; congregate.

† ACOMAIL, *s. f.* An assembly, a meeting, a gathering.

† ACON, ain. A refusal, denial.

† ACOR, oir, *s. f.* Avarice, penury, covetousness; written now *ocar.*

ACRACH, *a.* (*W.* açrev. *Gr.* ἀκρος, *faint.*) Hungry; also an hungry person. Ant-anam acrach, *the hungry soul.—Stew. Pro. ref.* Biadh do 'n acrach, *food to the hungry.—Smith. Comp.* and *sup.* acraiche, *more or most hungry;* written also *ocrach*, which see.

ACRAICHE, *comp.* and *sup.* of acrach.

ACRAICHEAN, *n. pl.* of acair. See ACAIR.

Acrais, *gen. sing.* of acras.

† Acrann, ainn, *s m.* A knot; perplexity, entanglement.

† Acrannach, *a.* Knotty, knotted; perplexed, entangled

Acras, ais, *s. m.* (*Gr.* ακρασια, *hunger;* and ακρος, *faint. Ir.* acras.) Hunger; famine. Tha acras orm, *I am hungry;* tha mi air acras, *I am hungry;* bheil acras ort, oirre, air, oirbh, orra, *art thou, is she, he, are you, they, hungry?* mar mhiol-choin air acras, *like hungry dogs.—Roy Stewart.*

Acsa, acsan; emphatic form of *aca*, which see.

† Acuil, *s. f.* An eagle. *Lat.* aquila. *Ir.* acuil.

Acuinn, *s. f.* A tool, tackle, tackling, equipment See Acfuinn.

Acuinneach, *a.* (*from* acuinn) Provided with tools, tackling, harness; equipped, harnessed; of or pertaining to a tool or harness.

† Ad, *s. m.* Water. *Ir.* id.

Ad, aid, *s. f.* A hat. Ad a bhile òir, *the gold-laced hat.—Macint.* Bile na h-aid, *the rim of the hat.*

Ad, *provincial for* iad.

Ad, *a pron.* (*for* do) Thy, thine. Ann ad ghialaibh, *in thy jaws.—Stew. Ezek.* 'N ad chluais, *in thine ear.—Oss. Fing.*

A' d', ad, (*for* ann ad, *or,* ann do) In thy, as a. Na bi a'd'uamhas domh, *be not a* (as a) *terror to me.—Stew. Jer.*

† Ada, adai, *s. f.* Victory.

Adag, aig, *s. f.* (*Ir.* adag.) A shock of corn, consisting of twelve sheaves; by the Lowlanders called *stouk*, also a haddock. *N pl.* adagan, an da chuid na h-adagan agus an t-arbhar, *both the shocks and the standing corn.—Stew. Judg.*

Adagach, *a.* (*from* adag.) Abounding in shocks of corn; of or pertaining to a shock of corn.

Adagachadh, aidh, *s. m.* The employment of making shocks of corn. *Scotch,* stooking.

Adagachadh, (ag), *pr. part.* of adagaich Gathering corn into shocks

Adagaich, *v.* Gather corn into shocks. *Pret. a.* dh'adagaich; *fut aff. a.* adagaichidh, *shall or will gather corn into shocks.*

Adagaichte, *p. part.* of adagaich. Gathered into shocks.

Adagan, *n. pl.* of adag, which see.

† Adamhair, *s. f.* Play, sport, diversion

† Adamhair, *v.* Play, divert, sport.

† Adamhradh, aidh, *s. m.* (*Lat.* admiratio) Admiration; wonder.

† Adh, adha, *s m.* A law

Adh, adha, *s m.* Prosperity, good luck, happiness, joy; also an heifer; a hind; but in these two last senses it is oftener written *agh*, which see. Is mòr an adh, *great is the joy.—Macint.*

† Adhach, *a.* (*from* adh.) Prosperous, lucky; happy, joyful *Comp.* and *sup* adhaiche, *more or most prosperous.*

Adhachd, *s. f.* Prosperousness, luckiness, happiness, joyfulness.

Adhail, *gen. sing.* of adhal.

† Adhailg, *s. f.* Desire, will, inclination

Adhainn, *gen. sing.* of adhann; written more frequently *aghann*, which see

Adhairc, *gen. sing* of adharc.

Adhairceach, *a.* (*from* adharc.) Horned; having large horns. Bo adhairceach, *a horned cow. Ir.* adharcach.

Adhaircean, *n. pl.* of adharc. Horns.

Adhaircean, ein, *s. m.* A lapwing; written also *adharcan*

Adhairt, *gen.* of adhart.

Adhairt, *s.* Forwardness, front; van. *Ir.* adhairt. See Aghairt.

Adhal, ail, *s. m.* A flesh-hook.—*Shaw.*

Adhalach, *a.* (*from* adhal.) Like a flesh-hook; of or pertaining to a flesh-hook.

† Adhall, *a.* Deaf; dull, stupid, senseless.

† Adhall, aill, *s. m.* Sin, corruption. *Ir. id.*

† Adhallach, *a.* Sinful, corrupt, perverse. *Comp.* and *sup.* adhallaiche.

† Adhaltan, ain, *s. m.* A simpleton; a dull stupid fellow.

Adhaltranach, aich, *s. m.* An adulterer; *n. pl.* adhaltranaichean.

Adhaltranach, *a* Adulterous. Ginealach adhaltranach, *an adulterous generation.—Stew. Mat.* Leanabh adhaltrannach, *an adulterous child;* urr adhaltrannach, *an adulterous child.*

Adhaltranachd, *s. f.* The practice of adultery.

Adhaltranaich, *gen. sing.* of adhaltranach

Adhaltranaichean, *n. pl.* of adhaltranach. Adulterers.

Adhaltranais, *gen. sing.* of adhaltranas. Fear adhaltranais, *an adulterer.*

Adhaltranas, ais, *s. m.* Adultery. A dianamh adhaltranais, *committing adultery.—Stew. Jer.* Làn do adhaltranais, *full of adultery.—Stew. O. T.*

Adhaltras, ais, *s. m.* Adultery. Urr adhaltrais, *an adulterous child;* written also *adhaltrus.*

Adhaltrasach, *a* (*from* adhaltras.) Adulterous.

Adhaltrasachd, *s. f.* The practice of adultery.

Adhaltrus, uis, *s. m.* Adultery. Luchd adhaltruis, *adulterers.—Stew. O. T.*

Adhaltrusach, *a.* Adulterous; guilty of adultery.

Adhaltrusachd, *s. f* The practice of adultery.

Adhamh, *s. m.* Adam; *from* adh, *bless;* and literally meaning *the blessed person.*

Adhann, *gen;* adhainn *and* aidhne, *s. f.* A pan; a goblet; more commonly *aghann;* also coltsfoot. *Ir.* adhann.

Adhannta, *a.* Kindled; exasperated, inflamed.

† Adhanntach, *a.* Bashful, modest.

† Adhanntachd, *s. f.* A blush, bashfulness.

Adharadh, aidh, *s m.* and *f.* Worship, adoration; more frequently written *aoradh.*

Adhar, *gen.* adhair *and* adheir, *s. m.* (*Heb.* aver. *Syr.* air. *Gr.* αηρ. *Croatian,* aier. *Dal.* aer. *Brazilian,* arre. *Lat.* aer. *Span* ayre. *It.* aria. *Corn.* and *W.* awyr. *Ir.* aedhar.) The atmosphere, the air, firmament, sky, cloud. Tha 'n fhardoch gun druim ach adhar, *the dwelling has no roof but the sky.—Oss. Gaul.* Boisge teine o 'n adhar bholgdhubh, *flashes of flame from the dark bellying cloud. Id.*

Adharach, *a.* (*from* adhar.) Aerial, atmospheric; airy; glorious.

Adharail, *a.* (*i. e.* adhar-amhuil), *from* adhar. Aerial, atmospheric *W* awrawl

Adharc, airc, *s. f.* A horn; a sounding horn. *Bisc.* adurra. *Ir.* adharc.

Adharcach, *a.* Horny; also horned.

Adharcan, ain, *s. m.* A lapwing. Adharcan luachrach, *a lapwing.—Stew. Lev.*

Adharc-fhùdair, *s. f.* A powder-horn.

Adharcan-luachrach, *s. m.* A lapwing.—*Stew Lev.*

Adhart, airt, *s m* (*Ir* adhart.) Linen; bed-linen; pillow; bolster. B'i m'adhart a chreug, *the rock was my pillow.—Oss. Conn.*

Adhart, airt, *s. m.* Forwardness; seldom used but in connexion with the *prep.* air, *as,* thig air d' adhart, *come forward, advance;* air d' aghart, *come on, go on;* tha i teachd air a h-adhart, *she is very forward, she is coming on.*

Adhartach, *a.* (*from* adhart.) Like linen, of or belonging to linen.

ADHARTACH, a. Forwards; having a wish or a tendency to be onwards or forwards; progressive; diligent, assiduous.

ADHARTAN, s. pl. of adhart. A pillow, a bolster; linens, bed-linens.

† ADHARTAR, air, s. m. A dreamer.

† ADHAS, a. Good; proper.

ADHASTAR, air, s. m. A halter; properly *aghastar*, which see.

† ADHBHA, ai, s. m. An instrument; a musical instrument. See also ABHADH.

† ADHBHADH, aidh, s. m. A house, palace, garrison.

† ADHBHAGHAN, ain, s. m. (*dim.* of adhbha.) A musical instrument.

ADHBHAR, air, s. m. Cause, reason. Air an adhbhar sin, *therefore.*—*Stew. Gen. ref.* Adhbhar mulaid, *a cause of grief.*—*Macint.* Written also *aobhar.*

† ADHBHARAS, ais, s. m. Carded wool; also yarn. See ABHARAS.

† ADHBHARSACH, aich, s. m. A comber or carder of wool.

† ADHBHUIDH, s. f. Joy, merriment.

ADHLAC, aic, s. f. A burial, interment, funeral. Aite-adhlaic, *burying ground.*

ADHLACADH, aidh, s. m. The ceremony of interring. Aite adhlacaidh, *a burying ground.* *Ir.* adhlacadh.

ADHLACADH (ag), *pr. part.* of adhlaich. Burying, interring.

ADHLACAIR, s. m. (adhlac-fhear.) A burier, an undertaker.

ADHLAIC, v. Bury, inter. M' anam adhlac' an sceò, *to bury my spirit in the mist.*—*Oss. Carthon.* *Pret. a.* dh'adhlaic, *buried; fut. aff. a.* adhlaicidh, *shall or will bury; p. part.* adhlaicte, *buried.*

† ADHLAIC, s. f. A longing desire for what is good.

ADHLAICEAR, *fut. pass.* of adhlaic. Shall or will be buried.

ADHLAICIDH, *fut. aff. a.* of adhlaic. Shall or will bury.

ADHLAICTE, *p. part.* of adhlaic. Buried, interred. *Ir.* adhlaicthe.

† ADHLAN, ain, s. m. A hero, champion.—*Ir.*

ADHMHOIRE, *comp.* and *sup.* of adhmhor.

ADHMHOL, v. Praise, extol. *Pret. a.* dh' adh-mhol, *praised; fut. aff. a.* adhmholaidh, *shall or will praise.*

ADH-MHOLADH, aidh, s. m. Praise.

ADHMHOR, a. (*from* adh.) Prosperous, fortunate, lucky, joyous, happy; *comp.* and *sup.* adhmhoire. *Ir.* adhmhor.

ADHNADH, aidh, s. m. A kindling of fire.

ADH'OR. See ADHMHOR.

ADHRACH, a. (*from* adhradh.) Devout, religious; written also *aorach.*

ADHRACHAIL, a. (*i. e.* adhrach-amhuil), *from* adhradh. Devotional. Dleasnasan adhrachail, *devotional duties.*

ADHRADH, aidh, s. m. (*Ir.* adhradh. *Dan.* aere, *honour.*) Worship, adoration, devotion. Thoir adhradh, *worship;* bheir mi adhradh, *I will worship;* written also *aoradh,* which see.

ADH-UAMHARRA, a. Abominable.

ADH-UAMHARRACHD, s. Abomination, abominableness.

AD-OLAINN, s. f. Felt.

† ADUADH, aidh, s. m. Horror, detestation.

† ADUARRA, a. (*i. e.* ad-uamharra.) Horrid, detestable.

AFRAIGHE, s. f. A rising or preparing for battle.—*Ir.*

AG, (perhaps another form of *aig*), *prep.* At. It is the sign of the present participle. Ag iarruidh, ag iasgachadh, ag acain, *asking, fishing, wailing;* literally *at asking, at fishing, at wailing.* It is prefixed to words beginning with a vowel, though sometimes it is seen before words beginning with a consonant; as, ag ruidh a réis, *running a race;* ag dol a mach, *going forth.*—*Smith.*

AG, aig, s. m. (*Swed.* agg, *grudge.*) Doubt, scruple, hesitation, contradiction; a hesitation, or lisp in speech.

AG, v. Doubt; hesitate; refuse, contradict. *Pret. a.* dh'ag, *doubted; fut. aff. a.* agaidh, *shall or will doubt.*

† AGA, s. f. The bottom of any depth.

AGACH, a. Inclined to doubt or refuse; scrupulous; sceptical; stammering, lisping.

AGAD, *comp. pron.* (aig *and* tu.) At thee, on thee, with thee; in thy possession. *Agad* is also used in the sense of a possessive pronoun; as, an tigh agad, a bhean agad, *thy house, thy wife.* This use of *agad* is not often met with in our classical writers; but in common language it is very frequent. Tha, *is* or *are,* is understood, as, a bhean th'agad, *your wife; uxor quæ est tibi.* The same remark is applicable to all the pronouns compounded of *aig,* as, *agam, aige, aice, againn, agaibh, aca.*

AGADH, aidh, s. m. Doubt, hesitation, contradiction. Gun agadh sam be, *without any contradiction.*—*Stew. Heb. ref.* *Ir.* agamh.

AGADSA, agadse. Emphatic form of agad, which see.

† AGAG, aig, s. f. An habitation or settlement.

AGAIBH, *comp. pron.* made up of *aig* and *sibh.* At you, on you, with you; in your possession; of you; from among you. Co agaibh do 'n iarrar i? *whom of you is she sought for?*—*Fingalian Poem.* Chaidh agaibh orra, *you got the better of them.* It is also used as a possessive pronoun, *your;* as, an tigh agaibh, *your house;* in which sense it seems to be contracted for *a th' agaibh;* as, an tigh th' agaibh, *your house;* literally, *the house which is to you;* which, though bad English, is as correct in Gaelic as it is in Latin.

AGAIBHSE. Emphatic form of agaibh, which see.

AGAIDH, *gen. sing.* of agadh.

AGAIL, (*i. e.* ag-amhuil), a. Doubtful; in jeopardy; sceptical: suspicious; lisping.

AGAILEACHD, s. f. (*from* ag.) Doubtfulness, suspiciousness; scepticism; a tendency to lisp, a habit of lisping.

AGAINN, *comp. pron.* (*Corn.* agan, *ours,*) made up of *aig* and *sinn.* At us, of or from amongst us, with us, or in our possession. Gràs do gach aon againn, *grace to every one of us.*—*Stew. Eph.* It is also, like all the pronouns compounded of *aig,* used as a possessive pronoun, *our;* as, an crodh againn, *our cattle;* in which sense it is contracted for a th' againn, *which is or are to us.*

AGAINN-NE. Emphatic form of againn, which see.

AGAIR, v. Plead, plea, accuse, charge, lay to one's charge, crave; require, demand. *Pret. a.* dh' agair, pled; *fut. aff. a.* agairidh, *or,* agraidh. Cha d' agair mi cruaidh e, *I did not plead hard with him.*—*Old Song.* Na agrar orra e, *let it not be laid to their charge;* agraidh se, *he will demand.*—*Stew.* 2 *Chron.*

AGAIRG, s. f. (agaricus.) A species of mushroom.—*Ir. id.*

AGAIRIDH, *fut. aff. a.* of agair.

AGAIRT, s. f. Pleading, plea, accusing; craving. Ann an agairt a chùise, *in the pleading of his cause.*—*Stew. Pro.*

AGAIT, s. f. An agate.—*Macd.*

AGAITEACH, a. Like an agate, of or pertaining to an agate, full of agates.

AGALL, ail, s. m. Speech; dialogue. *Ir.*

AGALL-ACH, a. Conversational; of or pertaining to a speech or dialect. *Com.* and *sup.* agallaiche.

AGAM, *comp. pron.* (*Ir.* agam), made up of *aig* and *mi.* At me, with me, on me, or in my possession. Cha 'n eil mo ghunn agam, *I have not my gun;* chaidh agam air, *I got the better of him.*—*Smith.* *Agam,* like all the pronouns compounded of *aig,* is used also as a possessive pronoun, *my, mine;* as, an claidheamh agam, *my sword;* which expression seems to be a contraction of an claidheamh a th' agam, (gladius qui est mihi), *the sword which is to me,* consequently *my sword;* againn fhéin, *at or with ourselves.* *Corn.* agan honan.

† AGAN, *a.* Precious, dear.

AGARACH, aich, *s. m.* (*from* agradh.) A claimer, a pretender. *Ir. id.*

AGARACH, *a.* (*from* agradh.) Prone to plead, plea, or crave, or accuse; litigious; vindictive. *Comp.* and *sup.* agaraiche, *more or most prone to plea.*

AGARTACH, *a.* (*from* agairt.) Inclined to accuse, plead, or plea; accusatory; litigious; quarrelsome. *Com.* and *sup.* agartaiche. *Ir. id.*

AGARTACHD, *s. f.* (*from* agairt.) Quarrelsomeness; litigiousness.

AGARTAICHE, *com.* and *sup.* of agartach. More or most quarrelsome.

AGARTÀS, ais, *s. m.* A plea, a suit at law; prosecution, accusation. Agartas coguis, *remorse;* féin-agartas, *self-reproach, compunction;* inntinn saor o fhéin-agartas, *a mind free from self-reproach.—Macfar.* *Ir. id.*

AGH, aighe, *s.* A heifer, a young cow; a fawn; rarely an ox, bull, or cow. Agh thri bliadhna dh' aois, *an heifer three years old.—Stew. Gen.* Reamhar mar agh, *fat as a heifer.—Stew. Jer.* Air tòir nan agha ciar, *in pursuit of the dusky fawns.—Oss.* Luaithre aighe, *the ashes of an heifer.* *—Stew. Heb.*

AGH, aigh, *s. m.* Joy, happiness; success, prosperity; also joyful, happy. Choinnich sinn Lochlinn 's cha b' agh dhuinn, *we met Lochlin, and it was not a gay meeting.—Ull.* Bidh agh aig na naoimh, *the holy shall have joy.—Smith.* A thréin a b' fhearr agh, *thou hero who excelledst in success.* *Old Song.* Written also *adh.*

AGH, aigh, *s. m.* Fear, astonishment, awe. *Gr.* αγη, *veneration.*

† AGH, aigh, *s. m.* Battle, conflict.

AGHACH, *a.* (*from* agh.) Warlike, brave, prosperous, successful, conquering; joyous, happy. *Com.* and *sup.* aghaiche, *more or most warlike.*

AGHAIDH, *s. f.* Face, visage, countenance; brow; surface. Aghaidh na talmhainn, *the face of the earth.—Stew. O. T.* Thoir aghaidh dha, *oppose him;* gabh air d' aghaidh, *pass on, go on, go forwards.—Stew. Pro.* Cuir an aghaidh is fhearr dh' fheudas tu air, *put the best face on it you can;* an aghaidh, *the face,* also *against;* cuir an aghaidh, *oppose, contradict, thwart;* cuir na aghaidh, *oppose him, thwart him.—Stew. Exod.* Cuir na h-aghaidh, *oppose her;* cuir nan aghaidh, *oppose them;* as an aghaidh, *outright.*

AGHAIDH, (an), *prep.* governing the genitive. Against, in opposition. An aghaidh na gaoithe, *against the wind;* an aghaidh mic an righ, *against the king's son.—Stew.* 1 *Chron.*

AGHAIDHICHTE, *a.* (*from* aghaidh.) Opposed, opposing; fronting, facing; confronted.

AGHAIS, *s. f.* Ease, leisure. See ATHAIS.

AGHAISEACH, *a.* (*from* aghais.) Easy; slow; at leisure. ATHAISEACH.

† AGHANAICH, *s. m.* An advocate, a pleader.

AGHART, airt, *s. m.* (*from* aghaidh.) Advance; forwardness. Air d' aghairt is buail, *forward and strike.—Oss. Tem.* Rach air d' aghairt, *go on.*

AGHANN, *gen.* aghainn, *and* aighne, *s. f.* A pan; a goblet.

AGHASTAR, air, *s. m.* (aghaidh-stiùir.) A horse's halter.

AGHMHOR, *and* AGH'OR, *a.* (*from* agh.) Pleasant, joyful, prosperous, happy; bold, brave. Gu h agmhor, abarach, *in a bold and brave manner.—Old Song.* Mun do bhoisg an solus gu agh'or, *ere the light shone joyfully.— Oss.* *Ir.* aghmhar.

AGRACH, *a.* (*from* agradh.) Accusatory; pleading, craving; inclined to accuse, plead, or crave.

AGRADH, 3 *sing.* and *pl. imper.* of agair, which see.

AGRADH, aidh, *s. m.* An accusation; craving, pleading.

AGRAIDH, *gen. sing.* of agradh.

AGRAIDH, (*for* agairidh), *fut. aff. a.* of agair, which see.

AGRAR, *fut. pass.* of agair. Shall or will be accused. See AGAIR.

† AGSAL, *a.* Generous, noble. *Ir.*

AGUS, *conj.* (*Dan.* og. *Corn.* ag. *Lat.* ac.) And; as. Thusa agus mise, *thou and I;* tha e ceart cho mhath agus a bha e, *it is just as good as it was.* The contracted form [*is* or *'s*] of *agus* is used both in prose, poetry, and common language. See IS, and 'S.

† AI, *s.* A controversy; a cause; a region, territory; inheritance of land, possession.

† AI, *s.* A herd; a sheep; a cow; also a swan. *Ir. id.*

† AIBH, *s. f.* Likeness, similitude, resemblance. *Ir. id.*

AIBHE! *interj.* (*Lat.* ave. *Ir.* aibhe.) Hail! all hail!

AIBHEIS, *s. f.* The sea, ocean; a gulf; boasting; emptiness. Ri aodann aibheis, *on the surface of the sea.—Macdon.* *Ir. id.*

AIBHEISEAR, ir, *s. m.* The adversary, the devil.

AIBHGHITIR, *s. f.* Alphabet. *Lat.* abgetorium.

AIBHIDEACH, *a.* Great, monstrous, enormous.

AIBHIRSEAR, ir, *s. m.* The devil. *Ir.* See AIBHISTEAR.

AIBHIST, *s. f.* Ruin, destruction; an old ruin. Ged tha e 'n diugh na aibhist fhuar, *though it be to-day a cold ruin.—Oss. Conn.*

AIBHISTEACH, *a.* (*from* aibhist.) Full of ruins; like a ruin.

AIBHISTEAR, ir, *s. m.* The devil; a destroyer. This is the old Celtic term for the devil. *Diabhol* (whence διαβολος, diabolus, diavolo, diable) is much more modern. It literally means, *a man of ruin.*

AIBHISTEARACHD, *s. f.* Demonism, the conduct of a devil, of a destroyer; destructiveness.

AIBHLE, *s. f.* Fire, spark; more frequently written *eibhle.* *Ir. id.*

AIBHLEAG, *s. f.* (dim. *of* aibhle.) A burning coal; a little fire; rarely a flake of snow. See EIBHLEAG.

AIBHLITIR, *s. f.* Alphabet. *N. pl.* aibhlitirean.

AIBHLITIREACH, *a.* Alphabetical. Ordugh aibhlitireach, *alphabetical order.*

AIBHNE, *gen. sing.* of abhainn, which see.

AIBHNEACH, *a.* (*from* abhainn.) Fluvial; abounding in ruins.

AIBHNICHEAN, *n. pl.* of abhainn. Rivers, streams. Ri taobh nan aibhnichean, *beside the streams.—Smith.*

AIBHSE, *s. m.* A spectre; sprite; a diminutive creature. *Ir. id.* Hence *taibhse.*

AIBHSEACH, *a.* (*from* aibhse.) Like a spectre or sprite; enormous.

† AIBID, *s. f.* Habit. *Ir. id.* *Lat.* habit-us.

AIBIDEAL, eil, *s. f.* Alphabet. *N. pl.* aibidealan, *alphabets.*

AIBIDEALACH, *a.* Alphabetical. Ordugh aibidealach, *alphabetical order.*

† AIC, aice, *s. f.* A tribe, family; a nourishing; a desire; a prop. *Ir.*

AICE, *comp. pron.* At her, with her, on her, in her possession; in her remembrance. Tha duslach òir aice, *it hath gold dust.—Stew. Job.* *Aice,* like all the other compounds of *aig,* is often used as a possessive pronoun; as, an tigh aice, *her house,* which may be considered an abbreviated form of *an tigh a th' aice.*

† **Aice**, *adv.* Near, close, at hand.

Aicear, *a.* Angry, severe, cruel. *Lat.* acer.

Aichbheil, *s. f.* Revenge, vengeance. Thoir dhomh aichbheil, *revenge me.—Stew. G. B.* Written also *aichmheil.*

Aichbheileach, *a.* (*from* aichbheil.) Revengeful, vindictive, full of vengeance. *Com.* and *sup.* aichbeiliche, *more or most revengeful.*

Aichbheileachd, *s. f.* (*from* aichbheil.) Revengefulness, vindictiveness.

Aicheadh, *s. m.* Refusal, denial, disavowal, recantation. Cuir as aicheadh, *deny, disavow;* thug e dhomh an aicheadh, *he gave me the refusal.*

Aicheadh, *v. a.* Deny, refuse, disavow, recant, renounce. *Pret. a.* dh'aicheadh, *refused; fut. aff. a.* aicheadhaidh, *shall refuse;* aicheadhaidh mise esan, *I will deny him.—Stew. Mat.*

Aicheadhaidh, *fut. aff. a.* of aicheadh. Shall or will deny.

Aicheun, *v. a.* Deny, refuse, disavow, recant, renounce. *Pret. a.* dh'aichean, *denied; fut. aff. a.* aicheunaidh, *shall deny.*

† **Aichill**, *a.* Able, powerful; dexterous, handy. *Ir.*

† **Aichilleachd**, *s. f.* Strength; dexterity. *Ir.*

† **Aicid**, *s. f.* A disease, sickness; accident; a stitch; a sudden pain.

Aichmheil, *s. f.* Vengeance, revenge; written also *aichbheil.*

Aichmheileach, *a.* Revengeful, vengeful; written also *aichbheileach.*

† **Aid**, *s. m.* A piece, portion, morsel.

Aideachadh, aidh, *s. m.* Confession, acknowledgment.

Aideachaidh, *gen. sing.* of aideachadh.

Aideachail, (*i. e.* aideach-amhuil), *a.* Affirmatory; confessing, acknowledging.

† **Aidhbhean**, *s. m.* A stranger, foreigner. *Ir.*

† **Aidhbheil**, *s.* A wonder; a boasting.

† **Aidbheil**, *s.* Huge, enormous, vast.

† **Aidhbhsean**, ein, *s. m.* A spectre, a phantom, sprite.

† **Aidheach**, ich, *s. f.* A milch cow.—*Shaw.*

Aidhear, ir, *s. m.* Joy, gladness; firmament. Dhuisg an aidhear, *their joy broke forth.—Oss. Trath.* Rinn e an t-aidhear, *he made the firmament.—Stew. Gen. ref.* Written also, except in the last sense, *aighear*, which see.

Aidhearach, *a.* Joyful, glad.

Aidhle, *s. f.* A cooper's adze.

† **Aidhme**, *s. f.* Dress, decoration. See **Aigheam**.

† **Aidhne**, *s. f.* Age.

Aidich, *v. a.* Confess, own, acknowledge; affirm, avow, avouch. *Pret. a.* dh'aidich, *confessed; fut. aff. a.* aidichidh, *shall or will acknowledge; fut. neg.* aidich, cha n àidich mi, *I will not confess.*

Aidicheam, (*for* aidichidh mi), 1 *sing. fut. aff. a.* of aidich. I will confess. Aideacheam thu, *I will confess thee.—Stew. Rom.*

Aidicheam, 1 *sing. imp. a.* of aidich. Let me confess, own, or acknowledge.

Aidichear, *fut. pass.* of aidich. Shall be confessed, owned, or affirmed.

Aidichte, *p. part.* of aidich. Confessed, owned, acknowledged, affirmed.

Aidmheil, *s. f.* Confession, profession, declaration, acknowledgment. A reir bhur n-aidmheil, *according to your profession.—Stew.* 2 *Cor.* Aidmheil na firinn, *the acknowledgment of the truth.—Stew.* 2 *Tim.*

Aidmheileach, *a.* (*from* aidmheil.) Of or belonging to a confession; declaratory.

Aidmheilear, ir, *s. m.* (aidmheil-fhear.) A confessor, a professor; a declarer.

Aidmheint, *s. f.* (*Lat.* adventus.) The advent.—*Shaw.*

Aidmhich, *v. a.* Confess, own, acknowledge. *Pret. a.* dh' aidmhich, *confessed; fut. aff. a.* aidmhichidh, *shall or will confess.*

Aidmhichte, *p. part.* of aidmhich. See **Aidich**.

† **Aifir**, *s. f.* Blame, fault.

Aifrionn, inn, *s. m.* The Romish mass. *Ir.* aifrionn.

Aig, *prep.* At, on, or in possession. Tha claidheamh aig an duine so, *this man has a sword. Aig* often imparts to the noun it governs, the signification of a genitive case, and then it may be considered as an abbreviated form of th'aig; as, an stoc aig Fionnghal, *Fingal's horn;* (*i. e.* an stoc a tha aig Fionnghal.)—*Oss. Fing.*

† **Aig**, *s. f.* This ancient vocable is now gone into disuse; but it is seen in composition with other words; as, *aigeal, aigean.* It means the source of all substances; also a sea, a shoal. The word *aigo*, in Languedoc and in Cantabria, has the same signification.

Aige, *comp. pron.* At him, with him, on him, in his possession; at it, with it; also his; its. *Ir. id.*

† **Aigbheil**, *s. f.* Terror; now written *cagal.*

† **Aigbheileach**, *a.* Terrific, terrible, fearful; now written *eagalach.*

Aigeach, ich, *s. m.* (aigh, *mettlesome*, and each, *horse.*) A stallion.

Aigeal, eil, *s. m.* (*from* † aig.) The deep; an abyss; pool; sea; bottom of an abyss. Do bhreacan air uachdar aigeil, *thy plaid [floats] on the surface of the pool.—Old Song.* Iuchair an t-sluichd gun aigeal, *the key of the bottomless pit.—Stew. Rev. ref. N. pl.* aigealan. *Ir.* aigiol, *the bottom of a valley;* written also *aigean*, which see.

Aigealach, *a.* (*from* aigeal.) Of or pertaining to an abyss; full of abysses.

Aigealan, *n. pl.* of aigeal. Abysses, seas, pools.

Aigeallach, *a.* Puffed up, elate; spirited, mettlesome, gallant. *Com.* and *sup.* aigeallaiche, *more or most spirited.*

Aigealladh, aidh, *s. m.* Speech, conversation, language; a dialogue. Ag èisdeachd aigeallaidh do bheòil, *listening to thy speech.—Old Song.*

Aigeallaiche, *com.* and *sup.* of aigeallach. More or most spirited. Is e 's aigeallaiche na thusa, *he is more spirited than thou art;* is tu 's aigeallaiche dhe 'n triùir, *thou art the most spirited of the three.*

Aigeallan, *s. m.* A breast-pin; a jewel; ear-ring; tassel; toy. *Ir.* aigilin.

Aigean, ein, *s. m.* (*from* † aig.) *Gr.* ωκεαν-ος, *ocean. W.* eigiawn. *Ir.* aigean. An abyss; deep; pool; sea; the bottom of an abyss. Aghaidh an aigein, *the surface of the deep.—Stew. Gen.* Written also *aigeal.*

Aigeanach, *a.* (*from* aigean.) Of or belonging to an abyss; full of abysses.

Aigeannach, *a.* (*from* aigne.) Spirited, mettlesome; magnanimous; cheerful.

Aigeannachd, *s.* (*from* aigne.) Mettlesomeness; sprightliness; magnanimity; cheerfulness.

Aigeantach, *a.* (*from* aigne.) Spirited; sprightly; mettlesome; cheerful; magnanimous; written also *aigeannach.*

Aigeantachd, *s. f.* (*from* aigne.) Spiritedness, sprightliness; cheerfulness; magnanimity; written also *aigeannachd.*

Aigeich, *gen. sing.* of àigeach, which see.

Aigeil, *gen. sing.* of aigeal. Of an abyss; of a pool.

Aigein, *gen. sing.* of aigean.

Aigh, *a.* Happy, prosperous; liberal; auspicious; proud; mettlesome; glorious. An reul aigh Iulorno, *the glorious star Iulorno.—Oss. Dargo.*

Aigh, *s. m.* Happiness; prosperity; joy; mettlesomeness;

liberality; gloriousness, glory; auspiciousness; also deer. An do threig thu mi sholuis m' aigh? *hast thou left me, thou light (beam) of my joy?—Oss. Dargo.* Meirg righ Lochlinn an aigh, *the standard of the king of Lochlinn the glorious;* aigh do choillte fein, *the deer of thine own woods. Oss. Cathula.* D'aighean ciar, *thy dusky deer. Id.*

Aighe, *gen. sing.* of aighe. Of a heifer.—*Stew. Heb.*

Aigheach, *a.* (*from* aigh.) Happy, joyous. *Ir. id.*

Aighean, *n. pl.* of aigh. Deer. Aighean siùbhlach, *the wandering deer.—Macint.*

Aigheanach, aich, *s. m.* A thistle; a place where thistles grow.

Aigheannaich, *gen. sing.* of aigheanach.

Aigheann, aighne, *s. f.* A pan; a goblet; a skillet; a small kettle or boiler. *N. pl.* aigheannan; aigheannan a ghabhail luaithre, *pans to contain ashes.—Stew. O. T.* Written also *adhann* and *oigheann.*

Aighear, eir, *s.* Gladness, mirth, joy, gaiety, festivity. Tha aighear a bruchdadh na shùil, *gladness bursts from his eyes.—Ull.* Ceòl is aighear, *music is mirth.—Oss. Derm.* Aighear d' òige, *the joy of thy youth.—Smith.* Written also *aidhear.*

Aighearach, *a.* (*from* aighear.) Glad, mirthful, joyous, gay, festive.

Aighearachd, *s. f.* (*from* aighear.) Gladness, mirthfulness, joyousness, festivity.

Aighne, *gen. sing.* of aghann and of aigheann, which see.

† Aighneach, *a.* Liberal. *Comp.* and *sup.* aigniche, *more or most liberal.*

Aiglean, ein, *s. m.* An ear-ring, a tassel, a toy.

Aigleanach, *a.* Hung with tassels; gaudy, beauish.

Aigne, *s. f.* Mind, temper, disposition; spirit, affection, thought. Is cianail m' aigne, *sad is my mind.—Ardar.* Written also *aigneadh. Ir.* aicne.

Aigneach, *a.* (*from* aigne.) Spirited; affectioned; of or belonging to mind, temper, affection, or thought.

Aigneadh, idh, *s. m.* Mind, temper, disposition; spirit, affection, thought. Fionn an aignidh chianail, *Fingal whose mind is sad.—Death of Carril.* Lean mi le h-aigneadh neo-ghlic, *I followed with unwise affection.—Mac Lach.* Written also *aigne.*

Aignidh, *gen. sing.* of aigneadh.

Ail, *gen. sing.* of àl, which see.

Ail, *s. m.* A mark, impression, trace. Ail do chois, *the trace of thy foot.*

† Ail, *s. m.* A mouth; a rebuke; a stone; a request; weapons.

Ailbhe, *s. f.* A flint; a stone; a rock. *N. pl.* ailbhean.

Ailbheach, *a.* (*from* ailbhe.) Flinty, stony, rocky. *Com.* and *sup.* ailbhiche, *more or most rocky.*

Ailbheag, eig, *s. f.* A ring; a ring of any coarse metal. *N. pl.* ailbheagan. Ailbheagan airgiod, *silver rings.—Mac Lach.* Ailbheag cluais, *an ear-ring.*

Ailbheagach, *a.* (*from* ailbheag.) Full of rings; like a ring; of or belonging to a ring.

Ailbheinn, *s. f.* (ail *and* beinn.) A flint; a rock; a mountain rock; written also *ailbhinn.*

Ailbhinn, *s. f.* (ail-bheinn.) A rock; a flint; a flinty rock; a mountain rock. Ag imeachd air an ailbhinn oillteil, *walking on the dreadful precipice.—Oss. Dargo.* Do sgiath mar ailbhinn, *thy shield like a rock.—Oss.*

† Aile, *s. f.* A stone; also behaviour, manners.

† Ailcne, *s. pl.* Paving stones.

† Ailcneach, ich, *s. m.* (*from* aile.) A pavier.

Aile, *s.* (*Gr.* Αιολ-ος. *Lat.* Æol-us, *wind;* also hal-o, *breathe;* and perhaps αελλα. *Corn.* aual. *Ir.* aile, *smell.*) The atmosphere, air, breath; smell, savour; the sense of smell. Tra chaidleas sa ghleann an t-àile, *when the air sleeps [is still] in the valley.—Oss. Duthona.*

Aile, *a.* Handsome; more properly *aille;* which see.

Ailebeart, beairt, *s. f.* A halbert. *N. pl.* ailebeartan.

Ail-each, eich, *s. m.* († ail, *stone,* and each, *horse.*) A stone-horse, a stallion.

Aileach, *a.* (*from* àile.) Atmospheric, aerial; savoury; of or belonging to the atmosphere, air, breath, or smell. Iongantas àileach, *an atmospheric phenomenon;* iongantas-an àileach, *atmospheric phenomena.*

Aileach, *a.* (*from* àile.) Causing marks or impressions.

Aileadh, aidh, *s. m.* A smell, odour; the sense of smell; air, atmosphere. Aileadh deadh bholaidh, *an odour of sweet smell.—Stew. Eph.* Sròine gun àileadh, *noses without the sense of smell.—Smith.* Written also *àile.*

Aileag, eig, *s. f.* Hiccup.—*Macint. Ir. id.*

Aileagach, *a.* (*from* aileag.) Causing the hiccup, hiccupy, relating to the hiccup.

Ailean, *n. pl.* of ail. Marks, impressions, traces.

Ailean, ein, *s. m.* A meadow, a plain. Cath air an ailean rèith, *a battle on the level plain.—Mac Lach.*

† Aileanta, *a.* (*from* aile.) Atmospheric, aerial.

Ailear, eir, *s. m.* A porch.—*Stew. Acts, ref. Ir. id.*

Ai'leathan, *a.* (*for* aimh-leathan.) Narrow; strait; light.

Aile-bheathail, *a.* Vital air, oxygen.

Aile-mheidh, *s.* (àile *and* meidh.) An anemometer. *N. pl.* ailemheidhean.

Ailghios, *s. f.* (*perhaps* àill-fhios.) Will, pleasure, longing, desire, pride. Nach lùb air ailghios na garbh ghaoith, *that will not bend at the pleasure of the [rough wind] storm. —Ull.* Ailghios dhaoine, *the pride of men.—Smith.* Fearann gu 'r n ailghios, *land to your will.—Mac Co. Ir.* ailgheas.

Ailghiosach, *a.* (*from* ailghios.) Wilful, headstrong, proud. *Com.* and *sup.* ailghiosaiche, *more or most wilful.*

Ailghiosachd, *s. f.* (*from* ailghios.) Wilfulness, pride.

Ailghiosaiche, *comp.* and *sup.* of ailghiosach.

Ail-innisean, ein, *s. m.* (*from* àile, *atmosphere,* and innis, *tell.*) An anemoscope.

† Aill, *s. f.* A rugged bank; a rough steep; a steep river-bank; a bridle, course, place, stead.

† Aill, *s. f.* Praise.

Aill, *s. f.* Desire, will, pleasure. Na 's àill le chridh, *what his heart desires.—Smith.* Literally, *that which is a pleasure to his heart;* an ni nach b' àille, *the thing I would not.—Stew. Rom.* Ciod a b' àill leat? *what wouldst thou have?* ma 's àille leibh cliù dhuibh fèin, *if you desire fame for yourselves.—Old Song.* Is àill leam so na sin, *I prefer this to that.*

Aillbhil. A bridle-bit. *Ir.*

Aill-bhruach, aich, *s. f.* A steep; a rugged bank; a rocky steep.

Aill-bhruachach, *a.* Steep, rugged, rocky.

Aille, *a.* (*Corn.* ailla.) Handsome, fair, comely. B' aille Cridhmhor, *handsome was Crimora.—Oss. Fing.* B' aille na sùil-sa bha Ossian, *fairer in her eyes was Ossian.—Id.* Thuit a cheann aille air an t-sliabh, *his comely head fell on the hill.—Id.*

Aille, *s. f.* Beauty, handsomeness, comeliness. Thainig i na h-àille, *she came in her beauty.—Oss. Fing.* Aille talmhaidh, *earthly beauty.—Smith. Ir.* aille.

Ailleach, *a.* (*from* aille.) Beautiful, handsome, comely.

Ailleachd, *s. f.* (*from* aille.) Beauty, beautifulness, handsomeness, comeliness. Ailleachd Eibhir-chaomha, *the beauty of Evircoma.—Oss. Gaul.* Bha h-ailleachd gun choimeas, *her handsomeness was unequalled.—Oss. Derm.* A h-ailleachd, *her beauty.*

Ailleag, eig, *s. f.* (*from* aille.) A jewel; a gewgaw; a pretty young maid. Nach cuimhne leat an ailleag? *dost thou not remember the beauteous maid?—Oss. Taura.*

Ailleagan, ain, *s. m.* (*from* aille.) A little jewel; a term of affection for a young person; a pretty maid. Soraidh slainnte do 'n ailleagan, *health to the pretty maid.—Old Song. N. pl.* ailleagain *and* ailleagana.

Ailleagan, *n. pl.* of ailleag. Gewgaws, ornaments, jewels; pretty girls.

Ailleagana, *n. pl.* of ailleagan.

Aillean, ein, *s. m.* (*from* ail.) A causeway.

Aillean, ein, *s. m.* Elecampane; a young beau; a minion. —*Macd. Ir.* ailean.

Ailleanta, *a.* (*from* aille.) Beautiful, handsome, comely, delicate, bashful; having an imposing appearance.

Ailleantachd, *s. f.* (*from* ailleanta.) Personal beauty; delicacy, bashfulness, modest reserve. Is i ailleantachd maise nam ban, *delicacy is the ornament of females.*

Ailleig, *gen. sing.* of ailleag, which see.

Aillein, *gen. sing.* of aillean.

Aillidh, *a.* Bright, resplendent, beauteous, fair. Lasair nan lochran aillidh, *the flame of the resplendent lamps.—Oss. Gaul.* Og-mhnaoi a b' aillidh leac, *a virgin of the fairest cheeks.—Oss.*

† Aillin, *a.* Another. *Lat.* alien-us.

Aillse, *s. f.* A fairy; a ghost; a diminutive creature; rarely a cancer; delay. *Ir.* aillse. In some parts of the Highlands this word is pronounced *taillse.*

Aillseach, *a.* (*from* aillse.) Like a fairy, of or pertaining to a fairy; spectral.

Ailm, *s. f.* A helm, stern. An ailm na asgaill, *the helm in his arm.—Macfar.*

Ailm, *s. f.* The first letter of the Gaelic alphabet; also, though rarely, the elm-tree. (*Ir.* ailm. *Dan.* alm, *an elm. Swed.* alm. *Lat.* ulm-us.) *N. pl.* ailmean.

† Ailmeadh, eidh, *s. m.* A prayer.

Ailmeag, eig, *s. f.* (*dim. of* ailm.) A little elm, a young elm. *N. pl.* ailmeagan.

Ailmeagan, *n. pl.* of ailmeag.

Ailmean, *n. pl.* of ailm. Elms.

Ailmeig, *gen. sing.* of ailmeag.

Ailmse, *s. m.* A spectre; a spectral-looking person; a mistake.

Ailmseach, *a.* (*from* ailmse.) Spectral; ghastly.

Ailne, *s. f.* (*Corn.* ailne.) Beauty, comeliness.

† Ailp, *s. m.* A protuberance; any gross lump; a mountain. *Lat.* Alp-es, *the Alps.*

† Ailp, *a.* White. *Gr.* αλφος and αλπος. *Lat.* albus. Hence too, perhaps, and not from *ailp*, a mountain, may be derived *Alpes*, Alps, as being always white with snow.

† Ailt, *s. f.* A house. *Lat.* alt-us, *high.*

Ailt, *a.* Stately; beautiful, comely. (*Lat.* alt-us.) Aghaidh is ailte lith, *a face of the most beautiful colour.—Fingalian Poem. Com.* and *sup.* ailte, *more or most beautiful.*

Ailte, *com.* and *sup.* of ailt.

Ailteachd, *s. f.* (*from* ailt.) Stateliness; comeliness, beauty, handsomeness. Barrachd air d' ailteachd, *superiority over thy handsomeness.—Macint.*

Aimbeairt, *gen. sing.* of aimbeart, which see.

Aimbeart, beairt, *s. f.* Poverty, want, indigence; calamity, mischief. Cridh fial an aimbeart, *a generous heart in poverty.—Old Song.*

Aimbeartach, *a.* (ain, *priv. and* beartach.) Poor, needy, indigent, necessitous; also mischievous; calamitous. Tha mi aim-beartach, *I am indigent.—Sm.*

Aimbeartas, ais, *s. m.* (aim, *priv. and* beartas.) Poverty, indigence; calamity, mischief.

† Aimhean, *a.* Pleasant, agreeable, smooth.

Aimhleas, eis, *s. m.* (aimh. *priv. and* leas. *Ir.* aimhleas.) Hurt, harm, mischief; ruin, misfortune; perverseness, folly. Luchd aimhleis, *unfortunate people;* ag iarruidh m' aimhleis, *desiring my harm.—Stew. O. T.* Aimhleas air a chlaigionn, *mischief on his head.—Sm.* A labhairt aimhleas, *uttering perverseness.—Stew. G. B.* Ni thu d' aimhleas, *thou wilt harm thyself.—Fingalian Poem.*

Aimhleasach, *a.* (*from* aimhleas.) Unfortunate; mischievous; ruinous; foolish, imprudent. *Comp.* and *sup.* aimhleasaiche, *more or most unfortunate;* nithe aimhleasach, *mischievous things.—Smith.*

Aimhleasachd, *s. f.* (*from* aimhleas.) The condition or state of being unfortunate; mischievousness; ruinousness, imprudence, foolishness.

Aimhleasaiche, *com.* and *sup.* of aimhleasach. More or most unfortunate.

Aimhleasg, *a.* (aimh. *intens. and* leasg.) Lazy, indolent, inactive, drowsy, sluggish. *Ir. id.*

Aimhleathan, *a.* (aimh. *priv. and* leathan.) Narrow, strait, tight. Is aimhleathan an t-slighe, *narrow is the way.—Stew. Mat.*

Aimhleathanachd, *s. f.* (*from* aimhleathan.) Narrowness, straitness, tightness.

Aimhleisge, *s. f.* (aimh. *intens. and* leisge.) Laziness, indolence, inactivity, drowsiness, sluggishness.

Aimhneart, neirt, *s. m.* (aimh. *intens. and* neart.) *Ir.* aimhneart. Force, violence, oppression; more frequently written *ainneart;* which see.

Aimhneartach, *a.* (*from* aimhneart.) Violent, oppressive; more frequently written *ainneartach. Comp.* and *sup.* aimhneartaiche, *more or most violent.*

Aimhneartaiche, *com.* and *sup.* of aimhneartach.

Aimhneirt, *gen. sing.* of aimhneart.

Aimhreadh, aimhreidh, *s.* (aimh. *priv. and* reidh.) Disturbance, disagreement, confusion; also, adjectively, wrong, disturbed, disagreeing. Tha so air aimhreadh, *this is wrong;* tha thu 'g am chur air aimhreadh, *thou art putting me wrong;* cuireamaid an cainnte air aimhreidh, *let us confound their language.—Stew. Gen. ref. Ir.* aimhreidh.

† Aimhreidhe, *s. pl.* Defiles, passes, forests, fastnesses.

† Aimhreis, *a.* Difficult, arduous.

Aimhreit, reite, *s. f.* (aimh. *priv. and* réite.) Discord, disagreement, contention, disturbance.

Aimhreiteach, *a.* (*from* aimhreite.) *Ir.* aimhreighteach. Quarrelsome, litigious, contentious; of or belonging to a quarrel or disturbance. *Com.* and *sup.* aimhreitiche, *more or most quarrelsome;* maille ri mnaoi aimhreitich, *with a quarrelsome woman.—Stew. Pro.*

† Aimhriar, *s. m.* Mismanagement.

Aimhriochd, *s.* (aimh. *priv. and* riochd.)

† Aiminn, *a.* (*Lat.* amœn-us.) Pleasant, agreeable, smooth.

Aimisichte, *a.* Bold, daring, resolute; written also *aimsichte.*

Aimlisg, *s. f.* Confusion, disorder. Is aimlisg e, *it is confusion.—Stew. Lev. ref.*

Aimlisgeach, *a.* Confused, causing confusion, of or pertaining to confusion.

Aimrid, aimrit, *a.* Barren, unproductive. Macfarlane has properly introduced this word as Gaelic into his Vocabulary; yet Stewart, the translator of the Bible, says it is Irish. See *Gen.* xi. 31, *ref.*

Aimsgith, *a.* Profane, impious, mischievous, impure.

AIMSGITHEACHD, *s. f.* Profanity, impiousness, michievousness, impurity. Le tuairisgeul 's le aimsgitheachd, *with slander and impurity.—Old Song.*

AIMSICHTE, *a.* Bold, daring, resolute; written also *aimisichte.*

AIMSIR, *s. f.* (*from* am.) *Arm.* and *Corn.* amser. *Ir. aimsir.* Weather, time, season. Aimsir ghaillionach, *stormy weather*; an aimsir a dh' fhalbh, *the time that has gone by.—Ull.* An t-sean aimsir, *the olden time.—Stew. Ecc.* Aimsir bhriagh, *fine weather.—Arm.* amser vrao. Aimsir a gheamhraidh, *the winter season*; aimsir an earraich, *the spring season*; aimsir an t-samhraidh, *the summer season*; aimsir an fhogharaidh, *the harvest season*; aimsir fogharaidh, *harvest weather*; an aimsir so, *this weather. Arm.* en amzer ze, *in this weather.*

AIMSIREIL, *a.* (*i. e.* aimsir-amhuil,) *from* aimsir. Temporal, worldly; that lasts but a season. Tha na nithe a chithear aimsireil, *the things which are seen are temporal.—Stew. Cor.*

AIN; an intensive and privative particle. It is only used in composition with another word, as, ain-tighearnas, *tyranny.*

AIN, *a.* Honourable, praiseworthy, respectful. D' uirghiol àin, *thy respectful speech.—Old Song.*

† AIN, *s. f.* Water. Hence amhainn, *or,* abhainn, *a river.* See ABH. *Ain* is also the *gen. sing.* of † *an,* which see.

AIN-BHEACH, *s.* A drone bee; also much rain.

† AINBHEACH, *a.* Manifold.

AINBHEART, bheirt, *s. f.* (ain, *priv.* and beart.) A misdeed. *Ir. id.*

AINBHEIL, *s. f.* (ain, *intens.* and bheul.) Impertinent language.

† AINBHIDH, *s. f.* Rainy weather.

AIN-BHITH, (ain, *intens.* and bith.) A ferocious animal.

AIN-CHEARD, cheirde, *s. m.* A buffoon; also buffoonery, low jesting; an ingenious thief. *Ir. id. N. pl.* ain-cheirde.

AINCHEARDACH, *a.* Like a buffoon; of or belonging to a buffoon, or to buffoonery.

AINCHEARDACHD, *s. f.* (*from* aincheard.) The behaviour of a buffoon; ingeniousness.

AIN-CHEIRDE, *gen. sing.* of aincheard.

AINCHEART, *a.* (ain, *priv.* and ceart.) Unjust, iniquitous.

AINCHEART, cheirt, *s. m.* A prank, or trick; injustice. *Ir. id.*

AINCHEIST, *s. f.* (ain, *intens.* and ceist.) Danger, jeopardy, dilemma; doubt, perplexity; puzzle, a riddle.

AINCHEISTEACH, *a.* (aincheist.) Doubtful, puzzling; of or pertaining to doubt or perplexity; in jeopardy, doubt, or danger.

AINCHIALL, chéil, *s. f.* Peevishness; forwardness; testiness; madness.

AINCHIALLACH, *a.* Peevish; forward; testy; mad.

AINCHRIONNAILT, *s. f.* Acuteness, discernment, sagacity.

AINGHRIONNA, *a.* Acute, sagacious.

† AINDEAR, *s. f.* A maid fit for marriage. See AINNIR.

AINDEAS, *a.* (ain, *priv.* and deas.) Awkward, not clever, not ready-handed.

AINDEISE, *s. f.* Affliction, calamity; awkwardness.

AINDEOIN, *s. f.* (ain, *priv.* and deoin, *will.*) *Ir.* aindeoin. Reluctance, compulsion, force. Co dhiùbh is deòin leat no 's aindeoin, *whether it be thy will or not.—Macint.* Dh' aindeoin ort, *in spite of thee.*

AINDEONACH, *a.* (ain, *priv.* and deonach.) Reluctant, unwilling. Chaidh e dhachaidh gu h-aindeonach, *he went home unwillingly. Ir.* aindeonach.

AINDEONACHD, *s. f.* (ain, *priv.* and deonach.) Unwillingness, reluctance, obstinacy, compulsion.

† AINDHIARRIDH, *a.* Angry. *Ir.*

AIN-DIADHACHD, *s. f.* (*i. e.* ain-diadhuidheachd.) Ungodliness, profaneness, iniquity, impiety.—*Stew. Jer. Ir.* aindiadhacht.

AIN-DIADHAIDH, *a.* (ain, *priv.* and diadhaidh.) Profane, wicked, ungodly, impious, irreligious. Tha 'm faidh 's an sagairt ain-diadhaidh, *the prophet and the priest are profane.—Stew. Jer.*

AINDIADHUIDHEACHD, *s. f.* (ain, *priv.* and diadhuidheachd.) See AINDIADHACHD.

AIN-DILEAS, *a.* (ain, *priv.* and dileas.) Faithless.

AINDILSEACHD, *s. f.* Faithlessness.

AINDITH, *s. f.* (ain, *intens.* and dith, *want.*) Extreme poverty. *Gr.* ἐνδεια.

AINDLIGHE, *s. f.* (ain, *priv.* and dlighe.) Injustice, unlawfulness, usury. *Ir. id.*

AINDLIGHEACH, *a.* (ain, *priv.* and dligheach.) Unjust, unlawful; also, substantively, a transgressor. *Ir. id.*

AINDLIGHEACHD, *s. f.* Unlawfulness, the practice of injustice.

AIN-DREANNACH, *a.* Fretful, peevish. *Com.* and *sup.* aindreannaiche.

AINDREANNACHD, *s. f.* Fretfulness, peevishness.

AINE, *s. f.* Delight, joy, pleasure; music, harmony. Aine an lath, *broad day-light.*

† AINE, *s. f.* Experience; agility, expedition; also a platter.

AINEAL, eil, *s. m.* (*more properly* aineol.) A stranger, a foreigner, a guest. Cha n' fheoraich an t-aineal co mac Morna, *the stranger shall not ask who is the son of Morna.—Oss. Gaul.*

AINEAL, *a.* Strange, foreign; ignorant.

AINEALACH, *a.* (*properly* aineolach.) Ignorant; strange, foreign, unknown. *Com.* and *sup.* ainealaiche, *more or most ignorant*; duine ainealach, *an ignorant man.*

AINEAMH, eimh, *s. m.* (*W.* and *Corn.* anav. *Ir.* aineamh.) A fault, blemish, flaw, defect, injury. Dà reithe gun aineamh, *two rams without blemish.—Stew. Exod.*

AINEAMHACH, *a.* (*from* aineamh.) Faulty, blemished, maimed; having defects, or an injury; causing defects or blemishes. *Com.* and *sup.* aineamhaiche, *more or most faulty. Ir.* aineamhach.

AINEAMHAG, aig, *s. f.* A phœnix.

AINEAMHAIG, *gen. sing.* of aineamhag.

AINEAN, *s. pl.* Liver. Os cionn nan ainean, *above the liver.—Stew. Exod.*

AINEAS, eis, *s. m.* Joy, passion; cruelty; frenzy; bravery. Duthaich gain àineas, *a friendly country.—Mac Co.*

AINEASACH, *a.* (*from* aineas.) Furious, passionate, enraged, raging, frantic; cruel; also brave, hardy. Mar stuadhan aineasach, *like furious billows.—Old Poem. Comp.* and *sup.* aineasaiche, *more or most furious.*

AINEASACHD, *s. f.* Furiousness, passionateness, frenzy, fury.

† AINEASGAIR, *a.* Rude, uncouth, unpolished.

AINEIL, *gen. sing.* of aineal.

AINEIMH, *gen. sing.* of aineamh.

AINEIS, *gen. sing.* of aineas.

AINEOL, *s.* and *a.* A stranger, a foreigner; a guest; also strange, foreign. A dol air aineol, *wandering abroad.—Stew. G. B.* See also AINEAL.

AINEOLACH, *a.* (ain. *priv.* and eolach.) Ignorant, unintelligent, rude, unlearned. Aineolach air so, *ignorant of this.—Stew. 2 Pet. Com.* and *sup.* aineolaiche, *more or most ignorant. Ir. id.*

AINEOLAICHE, *com.* and *sup.* of aineolach. More or most ignorant.

Aineolas, *s. m.* (ain, *priv. and* eolas.) Ignorance, want of knowledge; nescience, illiterateness. Am bhur aineolais, *the time of your ignorance.—Stew. Pet. Ir.* aineolas.

† **Ainer**, *a.* Proud; great; cruel.

Ainfheoil, fheola, *s. f.* Proud flesh, corrupt flesh.

Ainfheola, *gen. sing.* of ainfheoil.

Ainfhiach, fhéich, *s.* (ain, *priv. and* fiach.) Debt. *Ir.* ainbhfhiach *and* ainfhiach. *N. pl.* ainfhiachan.

Ainfheich, *gen. sing.* of ainfhiach.

Ainfhios, *s.* (ain, *priv. and* fios.) Ignorance.—*Stew. Rom. Ir.* ainbhfhios.

Ainfhiosach, *a.* Ignorant; illiterate. *Ir.* ainbhfhiosach.

Ainfhiosrach, *a.* (ain, *priv. and* fiosrach.) Ignorant, unintelligent, illiterate. *Com.* and *sup.* ainfhiosraiche, *more or most ignorant.*

Ainfhiasrachd, *s. f.* Ignorance; illiterateness.

Aingeal, eil, *s. m.* An angel; a messenger; also fire, light, sunshine. *Gr.* αγγελος. *Lat.* angelus. *Swed.* angel. *Dan.* angle. *Goth.* angelus. *Belg.* engelen. *Anglo-Sax.* engelas. *W.* angel. *It.* angelo. *Fr.* ange, *angel. W.* engyl. *Corn.* engil, *fire. Ir.* aingeal.

Aingealach, *a.* (*from* aingeal.) Angelic; of or pertaining to an angel; of or pertaining to fire.

Angealag, eig, *s. f.* Angelica. *Ir. id.*

Aingealta, *a.* (*from* aingidh.) Perverse, wicked, headstrong, froward.

Aingealtachd, *s. f.* Perverseness, wickedness, frowardness. A gabhail tlachd ann aingealtachd, *taking pleasure in wickedness.—Stew. Prov.* Aingealtachd na chridhe, *frowardness in his heart.—Id.*

Aingheán, *s. m.* (ain, *intens. and* gean.) Excessive love; excessive greed or avarice.

Ainghéanach, *a.* (ain, *intens. and* geanach.) Exceedingly attached; excessively greedy or avaricious.

Ainghniomh, *s. m.* (ain, *intens. and* gniomh.) A bad deed.

Ainghniomhach, *a.* Facinorous; wicked.

Aingidh, *a.* Wicked, vicious, bad; perverse, mischievous; cross, ill-natured. *Comp.* and *sup.* aingidh. *Ir.* aingidhe.

Aingidheachd, *s. f.* (*from* aingidh.) Wickedness, viciousness; perverseness, iniquity, evil. Aingidheachd a bhaile, *the iniquity of the city.—Stew. Gen.* Aingidheachd ur deanadais, *the evil of your doings.—Stew. Jer. Ir.* aingidheacht.

Ainglidh, *a.* (*from* aingeal.) Angelic. *Ir. id.*

Ainiochd, *s. f.* (ain, *priv. and* iochd.) Cruelty; oppression. Le h-ain-iochd, *with cruelty.—Stew. Ezek.* Luchd ainiochd, *oppressors. Ir.* ainiocht.

Ain-iochdmhoireachd, *s. f.* (*from* ain-iochdmhor.) Oppressiveness; unfeelingness; cruelty.

Ain-iochdmhor, *a.* (ain, *priv. and* iochdmhor.) Oppressive, unfeeling, cruel. *Com.* and *sup.* ain-iochdmhoire.

Ainiosal, *a.* Haughty. *Arm.* and *Corn.* ainisle.

Ainise, *s. f.* Anise.—*Macd. Ir. id.*

† **Ainle**, *a.* Fair, comely, well-featured.

† **Ainleachd**, *s. f.* (*from* ainle.) Comeliness.

† **Ainleag**, eig, *s. f.* A snare; a sting.

Ainleag, eig, *s. f.* A swallow.—*Macd. Ir.* ainle.

Ainleag-mhara, *s. f.* A black martin.—*Macd.*

Ainlean, *v. a.* (ain, *intens. and* lean.) Pursue, persecute. *Pret. a.* dh' ainlean, *pursued; fut. aff. a.* ainleanaidh, *shall or will pursue.*

Ain-leanmhuin, *s. f.* Persecution.

Ain-leas, *s. m.* Difference, mischief, theft. *Ir.* ainleas.

Ainm, ainme, *s. m.* A name; a substantive noun. C' ainm th' ort? *what is your name?* Ciod is ainm do so, *or* c' ainm th' air so? *what is the name of this?* Duine do 'm b' ainm Aonghas, *a man named Angus.* Thug iad Seumas mar ainm air (*or* dha), *they named him James.* C' ainm è? *what is his name? what is its name?* Maighistir-c'ainm è? *Mr.—what's his name?*

Pers. nam. *Shans.* naman. *Gr.* ονομα. *Lat.* nomen. *Maeso-Gothic*, namo. *Swed.* namn. *Dan.* navn. *Anglo-Sax.* nama, *and* noma. *Germ.* name, *and* naam. *Fr.* nom. *It.* nome. *Box. Lex.* enw. *Ir.* ainim. *Arm.* hanv.

Ainmchlàr, chlàir, *s.* A catalogue; an index. *N. pl.* ainmchlaran.

Ainmeachadh, aidh, *s. m.* The act or circumstance of naming, mentioning, or appointing; a naming, nominating; nomination.

Ainmeachadh (ag), *pr. part.* of ainmich. Naming, appointing; mentioning, nominating.

Ainmeanach, aich, *s. m.* (*from* ainm.) Nominative; a nominator.

Ain-measarrach, Ainmeasarradh, *a.* Intemperate, immoderate; vast, huge.

Ain-measarrachd, *s. f.* (ain, *priv. and* measarrachd.) Intemperance, immoderateness, vastness.

Ainmeil, *a.* (*i. e.* ainm-amhuil.) Namely; renowned, famed, famous. Gu h-ainmeil, *especially, famously.*

Ainmeileachd, *s. f.* (*from* ainmeil.) Nameliness; renown.

Ainmheas, *s. m.* Reward, recompense.

Ainmheid, *s. f.* (*from* ainneamh.) A wonder, a rarity.

Ain-mhiann, *s.* (ain, *intens. and* miann.) Lust. See **Anamhiann**. *Ir.* ainmhiann.

Ain-mhiannach, *a.* See **Anamhiannach**. *Ir.* ainmhiannach.

Ainmhidh, *s. m.* (*Ir.* and *Corn.* ainmhidh.) Animal, brute, beast. *N. pl.* ainmhidhean, *beasts;* an ainmhidhean uile, *all their beasts.—Stew. Gen.*

Ainmhidheach, *a.* Brutal, brutish; of or belonging to a brute.

Ainmhidheachd, *s. f.* (*from* ainmhidh.) Brutishness.

Ainmich, *v. a.* (*from* ainm.) Name, appoint, mention, fix upon, nominate. *Pret. a.* dh' ainmich, *named; fut. aff. a.* ainmichidh, *shall or will name.* Ainmich do thuarasdal, *appoint your wages.—Stew. Gen.* Ainmich co e sud, *mention who yonder man is.—Mac Lach.*

Ainmig, **Ainmic**, *a.* Seldom, rare, scarce. Is ainmig thig e, *he seldom comes;* b' ainmig a leithid, *his like (equal) was rare.—Macint.* B' ainmic bha mo bhuilean fann, *seldom were my blows weak.—Fingalian Poem.*

Ainmigead, eid, *s. m.* (*from* ainmig.) Rareness, scarceness; increase in scarceness. A dol an ainmigead, *growing more and more scarce.*

Ainm-lite, *s. f.* A catalogue; an index.

† **Ainn**, ainne, *s.* A circle; a ring. *Lat.* annus, *a year.* Hence also fainne, *a ring.*

† **Ainneadh**, eidh, *s. m.* Patience.

Ainneamh, *a.* Rare, scarce, curious; curiously formed; valuable. Crios ainneamh, *a curious girdle.—Stew. Exod.*

Ainneart, neirt, *s. f.* (ain, *intens. and* neart.) Oppression, violence. Ainneart air a choigreach, *violence on the stranger.—Stew. Jer.* Luchd ainneirt, *oppressors. Ir.* aineart.

Ainneartach, *a.* Oppressive, violent, tyrannical, overbearing.

Ainneartachd, *s. f.* The practice of oppression.

Ainnichte, *a.* Tamed; made patient.

Ainnir, *s. f.* A marriageable woman; a virgin, a maid, a young woman. Ainnir fo bròn, *a maiden mourning.—Oss. Cathloda.* Ainnir a cheud ghraidh, *the maid of his first love.—Oss. Fing.*

AINNIS, Ainniseach, *a.* Poor, destitute, needy, abject. Tha mi ainnis lom, *I am poor and naked.—Smith.* A slugadh an ainnis, *swallowing up the needy.—Stew. Amos.* *Ir. id.*

AINNIS, Ainniseachd, *s.f.* Poverty; abjectness.

AINREITE, *s.f.* (ain, *priv.* and réite.) Strife, quarrel, confusion; more frequently written *aimhreite;* which see.

AINRIOCHD, *s.* A miserable plight; a woful condition; a frightful bodily appearance. *Ir. id.*

AINSGEUN, Ainsgiàn, *s.* Fury; fright, terror. Bhaidh an t-each air ainsgeun, *the horse ran off in a fright.* *Ir.* ainsgian.

AINSGEUNACH, Ainsgianach, *a.* Furious, wild; apt to take fright; as a wild horse. *Ir.* ainsgianach.

AIN-SHEIRC, *s.f.* (ain, *priv.* and seirc.) Hatred; excessive hatred; cruelty.

AIN-SHEIRCEIL, *a.* (*i. e.* ain-sheirc-amhuil.) Hating; abominating; cruel.

AIN-SRIANTA, *a.* Unbridled, uncurbed; obstinate, untamed; debauched. *Ir.* ainshrianta.

AIN-SRIANTACH, aich, *s. m.* A libertine; a debauchee.

AIN-SRIANTAS, ais, *s. m.* Libertinism; the condition of being untamed, as a horse.

† AINTEACH, *a.* Boastful; vain-glorious.

AIN-TEAS, *s. m.* (ain, *intens.* and teas.) Extreme heat; fervour; a violent inflammation.—*Stew. Deut.* Also ardour, enthusiasm, fervent zeal. *Ir.* ainteas.

AIN-TEASACHD, *s.f.* (*from* ainteas.) Feverishness.

AINTEIST, *s. m.* (ain, *priv.* and teist.) A false witness. *N. pl.* ainteistean.

AIN-TEISTEANEAS, eis, *s. m.* (ain, *priv.* and teisteanas.) A false testimonial; a false certificate; an unjust certificate.

AIN-TEISTEAS, eis, *s. m.* (ain, *priv.* and teisteas.) False evidence; false testimony.

AIN-TETH, *a.* (ain, *intens.* and teth.) Ardent; exceeding hot; vehement; eager. Ainteth chum àir, *ardent for battle.—Mac Lach.*

AIN-TIGHEARN, *s. m.* (ain, *intens.* and tighearna.) An oppressor, a tyrant; an overbearing master or ruler. See also ANTIGHEARN. *Ir.* aintighearn.

AIN-TIGHEARNAS, ais, *s. m.* Oppression; tyranny; domineering. *Ir. id.*

AIN-TREUN, *a.* (ain, *intens.* and treun.) Very strong. *Com.* and *sup.* ain-tréine.

AINTREUNAS, ais, *s. m.* Great strength.

AIPOL, *s. m.* Apollo.

AIR, *prep.* (*governing the dative.*) *Corn.* ar. *Ir.* air. On, upon; for, about, of, concerning. Iomradh air do ghliocas, *the fame of thy wisdom.—Stew.* 1 *K.* Air mo shonsa, *for me; on my account.* Air mo shonsa dheth, *as for me; for my part of it.—Stew. Gen.* *Air* sometimes takes after it a noun in the aspirate form, as in the following example: Air bharraibh nan tonn, *on the tops of the waves.—Oss.* Air eigin, *with much ado;* air leth, *apart, aside, by itself.* Air choir, *so that, in a manner; nobly, properly; as usual.* Air lamh, *on hand; by the hand.* Air mo lamh, *on hand; on my hand.* Air h-aon, *for one.* Thuit tri le Bràn air h-aon, *Bran, for one, killed three.—Oss. Fing.* Air choir eigin, *contracted* Air choir 'gin, *some way or other.* Air bheag, *almost.* Air so, *on this, upon this, then.* Chaidh am bàt air, *the boat went aground.* Air ais, *backwards;* air aghaidh, *forwards;* air adhairt, *forwards, onwards;* air seachran, *astray;* air iomrol, *astray;* air chuthach, *mad;* air neo, *else, or else,* in some districts, air dheo. Air muin, *on, upon, above.* Chaidh e air a muin, *he had carnal connexion with her;* bithidh sin air bhuil, *that will come to pass.—Stew. Is.*

AIR, *comp. pron.* On him or it; upon him or it; in his possession; on him as a duty. Tha 'eudach air, *his clothes are on him;* cha d' fhuair mi ni air, *I got nothing in her possession;* tha e air pàigh, *he is bound to pay;* chaidh agam air, *I got the better of him,* or *it;* ciod tha cur air, *what ails him?*

AIR, *gen. sing.* of àr; which see.

AIR, *v.* Plough, till, cultivate. *Lat.* aro. *Pret. a.* dh' air, *ploughed; fut. aff. a.* airidh, *shall or will plough.* Iadsan a dh' aireas euceart, *they who plow iniquity.—Stew. Job, ref.*

† AIRBHE, *s.f.* A story; ribs.—*Ir.*

† AIRBHEART, bheirt, *s.* Meaning.

† AIRBHEARTACH, *a.* Sagacious.

AIRBHRE, *s.f.* A multitude; an host; an army; a legion.

AIRC, airce, *s.f.* An ark; a large chest; a granary. Stad an airc, *the ark rested.—Stew. Gen.* *Heb.* argads. *Lat.* arca. *Span.* arca. *Arm.* arch. *Gr.* airc. *Old Sax.* erk, *and* eark.

AIRC, *s.f.* Trouble, distress, affliction, difficulty, hardship, strait. Saoi na airc, *a hero in distress.—Oss. Manos.* Aran na h-airce, *the bread of affliction;* tha mi am airc, *I am in a strait.*

† AIRC, airce, *s. f.* A cork tree; a sow; a lizard. Airc luachrach, *a lizard.*

† AIRCEACH, *a.* Ingenious; shifty.

† AIRCEADH, eidh, *s. m.* An earnest penny.

AIRCEANN, *a.* Certain, positive. *Ir.* aircheann.

AIRCEANNAS, ais, *s. m.* Certainty, positiveness.

AIRCEAS, eis, *s. m.* (*from* airc.) Sorrow, trouble, distress, pain, difficulty, restraint, straitness. Gun airceas mealaidh sibh, *ye shall enjoy without restraint,* or, *without trouble.—Smith.*

AIRCEASACH, *a.* Sorrowful; troublous; causing sorrow, or pain.

AIRCHILL, *s.f.* A keeping.—*Ir.*

AIRCHIS, *s.f.* A complaint.

AIRD, *gen. sing.* of ard; which see.

AIRD, airde, *s.f.* An earth, or point of the compass; a quarter, a cardinal point. Thionail an Fhiann as gach aird, *the Fingalians assembled from every quarter.—Old Poem.* *Arab.* ardhi. *Pers.* ard, *earth.* *Maeso-Goth.* airtha. *Isl.* jord. *Swed.* jord. *Germ.* aerd *and* erd. *Scotch,* airt, art, airth.

AIRD, *s.f.* Preparation, improvement, order, state; happiness. Dheanadh e aird, *he would make preparation.—Macint.*

AIRD, airde, [an] *or* 'n aird, *adv.* Up, upwards, upward; from below. Gun eiridh 'n aird a choidh, *never more to rise.—Sm.* Dh éirich e le buaidh an airde, *he rose up with triumph.—Id.* O 'n airde, *from above; from on high.*

AIRD-DEAS, *gen.* airde-deas, *s. f.* The south; the south point. Gaoth na h-airde deas, *the south wind;* dh' ionnsuidh na h-airde deas, *to the south.—Stew. Gen.*

AIRD-AN-EAR, *gen.* airde-an-ear, *s.f.* The east point; the east. Gaoth na h-airde an ear, *the east wind;* dh' ionnsuidh na h-airde an ear, *to the east.—Stew. Gen.*

AIRD-AN-IAR, *gen.* airde an iar, *s. f.* AIRD 'N-IAR, *gen.* airde 'n iar, *s.f.* The west point; the west. Dh' ionnsuidh na h-airde an iar, *to the west.—Stew. Gen.*

ÀIRD-TUATH, *gen.* airde tuath, *s.f.* The north point; the north. Dh' ionnsuidh na h-airde tuath.—*Stew. Gen.*

AIRDE, *s.f.* Height, quality, condition; a rising ground, a high place; altitude, excellency, highness. Bha t-airde mar dharraig sa ghleann, *thy height was like an oak of the valley.—Ull.* Bha ghrian na h-airde, *the sun was at its height; the sun was (on the meridian) at its height.—Oss. Duthona.* An airde mhòir, *in high condition.—Stew. Ecc.* Ged éirich 'airde, *though his excellency should mount.—Stew. Job.* Airde na craoibh, *the height of the tree.*

AIRDE, *com.* and *sup.* of ard. Higher, highest.

AIRDEACHD, *s. f.* (*from* airde.) Highness; greatness, quality, excellency.

AIRDEANNA, *s. pl.* (*from* ard.) Constellations.

AIRDHE, *s. f.* A wave; also a sign.

AIRDLEAG, eig, *s. f.* A jerk; a sudden pull; more properly *airleag*; which see.

† AIRDREACHD, *s. f.* A synod.

† AIRE, *s. f.* A judge; a servant; also a name given to different orders of Irish nobility.

AIRE, *s. f.* (*Ir.* aire.) Notice, regard, attention; thoughts, observation, watching. Thug iad aire dhomh, *they gave me attention.* Aire leagte air saoghail dhorcha, *his thoughts fixed on worlds unknown.—Oss. Conn.* Fo aire, *under observation; in custody.—Oss. Fing.* An ti a bheir an aire, *he who regards or attends.—Stew. Pro.* Gun aire dhomh, *unknown to me; without my notice.* Thoir an aire, *take care.* Ait aire, *an observatory;* tigh aire, *an observatory; also a house where there is a corpse; a house where vigils are held over a corpse;* Scotch, *late-wake.* Thoir an aire dhomh, *attend to me.*

AIREACH, ich, *s. m.* (*from* aire.) A grazier; a keeper of cattle; a shepherd; a watchman. *N. pl.* airichean.

AIREACH, *a.* (*from* aire.) Watchful, attentive, observant; sober; *rarely* hostile, violent. *Comp.* and *sup.* airiche, *more or most watchful.—Stew. Tit.*

AIREACHAIL, *a.* (*i.e.* aireach-amhuil.) Attentive, watchful, observant, circumspect.

AIREACHAS, ais, *s. m.* A pastoral life; tending cattle; the occupation of a shepherd; watchfulness.

AIREAMH, eimh, *s. m.* (*W.* eiriv.) Number, quantity; numbering, numeration. Gann an aireamh, *few in number.—Stew. Gen.*

AIREAMH, *v.* Number, count, compute. *Pret. a.* dh' aireamh, *counted; fut. aff. a.* aireamhaidh, *contr.* airmhidh, *shall or will count; fut. pass.* aireamhar, *shall be counted.* Airmhidh tu iad, *thou shalt number them.—Stew. Num.*

AIREAMHACH, aich, *s. m.* (*from* aireamh.) An accountant; a numerator.

AIREAMHACHD, *s. f.* Numeration, computation, numbering.

AIREAMHAR, *fut. pass.* of aireamh.

AIREAMH'EAR, ir, AIREAMHFHEAR, fhir, *s. m.* An accountant.

AIREAN, ein, *s. m.* A goadsman.

† AIREANNACH, aich, *s. m.* A beginning.—*Shaw.*

† AIREAR, ir, *s. m.* Food; satisfaction, choice; a harbour, bay.

† AIREARRA, *a.* Pleasant, satisfactory.

AIREASG, eisg, *s. f.* The apple of the eye; vision, sight. *Ir. id.*

AIR FAD, *prep.* Throughout, during.

AIR FEADH, *prep.* Throughout, among, during.

AIRFIDEACH, *a.* Musical, harmonious, melodious.

AIRFIDEADH, idh, *s. m.* Harmony, melody, music.

† AIRG, *s. m.* A prince.

AIRGHEAN, ein, *s. m.* A bridle rein; a symptom. Airgheanna bhais, *the symptoms of death.—Old Poem.*

AIRGIOD, 'eid, *s. m.* (*anciently* airgent *and* argant; *hence* argentum.) Silver, money, riches. Uireadair airgeid, *a silver watch;* cha robh mi gun airgiod, *I was not without money.—Macint.* Airgiod ullamh, *ready cash;* airgiod beò, or beò-airgiod, *quicksilver;* airgiod cagailte, *hearth money;* airgiod cinn, *poll money;* airgiod reidh, *interest of money;* airgiod ullamh, *ready money.*

AIRGIODACH, *a.* (*from* airgiod.) Abounding in silver or money; silvery; of or pertaining to silver; having silver or money; rich.

AIRGIOD-BEO, *s. m.* Quicksilver, mercury; literally live silver; so the French say *vif-argent* and *argent-vif,* and the Italians *argento vivo.*

AIRGIOD-CAGAILTE, *s. m.* Hearth money.

AIRGIOD-CINN, *s. m.* Poll money.

AIRGIOD-REIDH, *s. m.* Interest of money.

† AIRGNE, or AIRGNEADH, *s. m.* A robbery; pillage, plunder.—*Ir.*

AIRID, *a.* Particular, special. Gu h-airid, *especially.*

AIRIDH, *s. m.* Worth, merit, desert. Is math an airidh, *it is well or deservedly done;* is ole an airidh e, *it is a pity.*

AIRIDH, *a.* Worthy, excellent, fit, meet, suitable. Is airidh thu air peanas, *thou art worthy of punishment;* is ro airidh thu air moladh, *very worthy art thou of praise;* airidh air aithreachas, *meet for repentance.—Stew. Acts, ref.*

AIRIDH, *s. m.* A green grove; a place where osiers grow. Thig taibhse gu dian an àiridh, *ghosts shall issue wildly from the osier meadow.—Oss. Temo.*

AIRIDH, and AIRIGH, *s. m.* (*perhaps* aire-thigh.) A shealing; hill pasture; a mountain booth or hut; a shepherd's cottage. Thig do 'n airidh mo chailinn, *come to the shealing, my maid.—Old Song.* Bothan àiridh am braighe Raineach, *a mountain hut in the braes of Rannoch;—the name of one of the finest Highland melodies;* àiridh dhamh, *pasture for oxen.—Stew. Is.*

† AIRIGH, *s. m.* A ruler, a prince.—*Ir.*

† AIRILLEAN, ein, *s. m.* A party, a faction.

AIRE-IONAD, *s. m.* An observatory.

† AIRIS, *s. f.* A firebrand, charcoal; also knowledge. (*Ir.* airis.) A history. In this last sense *airis* is now written *aithris;* which see.

AIRISEACH, *a.* See AITHRISEACH.

† AIRISEAN, ein, *s. m.* An appointment, an order.

† AIRLE, *s. f.* An advice. Though this vocable be gone into disuse, we have *comh-airle,* a counsel, advice.

† AIRLEAC, *v.* Borrow; lend.

AIRLEACACH, *a.* Ready or willing to lend; ready to borrow; of or pertaining to a loan.

† AIRLEACADH, aidh, *s. m.* A borrowing; a lending.

† AIRLEACH, ich, *s. m.* A skirmish; a rencontre.

AIRLEAG, eig, *s. f.* A jerk, a sudden pull; a shove, a toss, a fling, jostle.—*Ir.* airleag.

AIRM, *n. pl.* of arm. (*Ir.* airm.) Arms, weapons; armour. *Gen. pl.* arm. Fuaim nan arm, *the noise of the arms.—Oss.* Airm àluinn, *beauteous armour.—Oss. Fin. and Lor.* Na h-airm a bhuin e bho aineal, *the armour he took from foreigners.—Id.* Ball airm, *a weapon;* airm theine, *fire arms;* airm thilgidh, *missile weapons;* airm-mhuir, *naval arms, a navy.* Armoric, arm vor, *a navy.*

† AIRM, *s. m.* A place.—*Ir.*

AIRM-CHRIOS, *s.* A shoulder belt.—*Ir. id.*

AIRM-CHEARD, cheairde, *s. m.* An armourer.

AIRM-CHEARDACH, aich, *s. m.* An armourer's forge.

† AIRMEART, eirt, *s. m.* An order; custom.—*Ir.*

AIRMHEADH, (3 *sing. and pl. imper. a.* of aireamh.)

AIRMHEAR, *fut. pass.* of aireamh. Shall be counted. See AIREAMH.

AIRMHIDH, *fut. aff. a.* of aireamh. Shall or will count.

† AIRMHIDH, *s. m.* A vow, a promise.—*Ir. id.*

† AIRMID, *s. f.* Honour, worship, reverence; a custom; a swan.—*Ir.*

AIRMIS, *v.* Find; find by searching. *Pr. a.* dh' airmis, *found; fut. aff. a.* airmisidh, *shall or will find;* dh' airmis mi air, *I found it,* or *him.*

AIRMISEACH, and AIRMSEACH, *a.* Exploratory; good at finding or at searching.

AIRMISEACHD, and AIRMSEACHD, *s. f.* (*from* airmis.) Finding after a search.

AIRM-LANN, lainn, *s. m.* An armoury; a depot; a magazine.

Air muin, *comp. prep.* On, upon, above; on the back; on the top, or summit. Air mhuin, *on his back, upon him;* air a muin, *on her;* chaidh e air a muin, *he had carnal connexion with her.*

Airm-theine, *s. pl.* Fire-arms.

Airne, *s. f.* (*Ir.* airne.) A sloe; a wild plumb; a damascene; also a kidney, kidneys, reins. Tha m' airne ga m' theagasg, *my reins teach me.—Smith.*

† **Airneach**, eich, *s. m.* The seed of shrub trees.

Airneach, eich, *s. m.* The murrain in cattle.

Airneag, eig, *s. f.* (*dim.* of airne.) A sloe; a wild plumb. *N. pl.* airneagan; *d. pl.* airneagaibh. Preas airneag, *a sloe bush.*

Airneagach, *a.* (*from* airneag.) Abounding in sloes; like a sloe; of, or belonging to, a sloe. Preas airneagach, *a bush loaded with sloes; also a sloe bush.*

Airneagaibh, *dat. pl.* of airneag.

Airneagan, *n. pl.* of airneag. Sloes; wild plums.

† **Airneamh**, eimh, *s. m.* A grinding stone; a hone.

Airnean, *s. pl.* Kidneys; reins. (*It.* arnione.) A chith na h-airnean, *who seeth the reins.—Stew. Jer. Dat. pl.* airnibh. Maille ris na h-airnibh, *along with the kidneys.—Stew. Lev.*

Airneig, *gen. sing.* of airneag. Of a sloe.

Airneis, *s.* Household furniture; household stuff; cattle, stock, chattels, moveables. Am measg an airneis fein, *in the midst of their own stuff.—Stew. Jos.* Airneis tighe, *household furniture.—Stew. Gen. Arm.* harnes. *English, harness.*

Airnibh, *dat. pl.* of airne, or airnean. See **Airne**, or **Airnean**.

Airsan. Emphatic form of the *comp. pron.* air; which see.

Airse, *s. f.* An arch, a vault. *Lat.* arcus.

† **Airsge**, *s. f.* Contemplation, musing.—*Ir.*

Airsideach, *a.* Unanimous, harmonious; agreeing. *Com. and sup.* airsidiche.

Airsideachd, *s. f.* Unanimity; harmony, agreement, concord.

Airsneag, eig, *s. f.* Arsenic.

Airsneal, eil, *s. m.* (*Ir.* airsneal.) Sadness, heaviness, distress, sorrow, strait, difficulty, weariness, fatigue, trouble. Co dh' innseas airsneal na Feinne, *who can tell the sorrows of the Fingalians!—Oss. Gaul.* Spiorad airsneil, *the spirit of heaviness.—Stew. O. T.*

Airsnealach, *a.* Sad, sorrowful, weary, troubled; causing sadness; vexing. Tir airsnealach, *a weary land.—Stew. Is.*

Air son, *prep.* For, on account of; by reason of; instead of. Air son an fhuachda, *by reason of the cold.—Stew. Pro.* Air a son, *for her;* air an son, *for them.*

Airt, *gen. sing.* of art; which see.

Airteagal, ail, *s. m.* An article.—*Macd. Ir. id.*

Airtean, ein, *s. m.* (*dim.* of art.) A little stone; a pebble; a flint stone. *N. pl.* airteana. *Ir.* airtin.

Airtein, (*gen. sing.* of airtean.) Of a pebble; of a stone.

Airtneul, neil, *s. m.* See **Airsneal**.

Airtneulach, *a.* See **Airsnealach**.

† **Ais**, *s. m.* (*Ir.* ais.) A hill, a strong hold, a covert; shingles to cover houses; dependence; a loan; a cart, or waggon.

† **Ais**, *s. m.* Money. *Lat.* æs.

† **Ais**, *s. m.* Back. This word is seldom or never used but in composition with some other word, as the *prep.* air; and then it signifies *backwards*, or *back;* like the Latin *re.*

Ais, [air], *adv.* Back; backwards. Thig air ais, *come back, return;* cum air t-ais, *keep back;* cum air t-ais, a ghaoth, *keep back, O wind.—Oss. Fin. and Lorm.* Bheir mi iad air an ais, *I will bring them back.—Stew. Zech.* Thig i air a h-ais, *she will return.*

† **Aisc**, aisce, *s. f.* A request, petition; damage; trespass; reproach.—*Ir.*

Aisde, *comp. pron.* (*Ir.* aiste.) Out of her; out of it. Aisde thugadh thu, *out of her* (*the earth*) *wast thou brought.—Stew. Gen.* Earbaidh e aisde, *he will trust in her.—Stew. Pro.*

† **Aisde**, *s. f.* A poem; ingenuity.

Aisdeach, ich, *s. m.* A gay, diverting fellow.

Aisdeachan, *s. pl.* Sports, diversions, pastimes.

Aisdridh, *s. f.* A translation.

Aisead, eid, *s. f.* Delivery, as in childbed. Tha i air a h-aisead, *she is delivered.—Stew. Gen.*

Aisead, eid, *s. f.* A platter; a large plate. *Fr.* aisiette. *Arm.* aczyed.

Aisead, *v.* Disburden or deliver a woman of a child. *Pret. a.* dh' aisead; *fut. aff.* aiseadaidh, *shall deliver.—Stew.* 1 *K.*

Aiseag, ig, *s. f.* (*i. e.* ais-thig.) *Ir.* aisioc. A ferry; deliverance; a return; a vomit. Fear aisig, *a ferryman;* fear na h-aisig, *the ferryman;* bat-aisig, *a ferryboat.—Stew.* 2 *Sam. N. pl.* aiseagan.

Aiseal, eil, *s. m.* Jollity, fun, merriment. Ri h-aiseal, *merry-making.*

Aisealach, *a.* Funny, merry, jolly; of or pertaining to fun.

Aisean, aisne, *s. f.* (*Corn. and Arm.* asen.) A rib. *N. pl.* aisnean, *and* aisnichean, *ribs. W.* eisen. *Corn.* azan. An aisean a thug e o 'n duine, *the rib he took from the man.—Stew. Gen. Dat. pl.* aisnibh. Aon d' a aisnibh, *one of his ribs.—Stew. Gen.*

Aiseil, *gen. sing.* of aiseal.

Ais-eirich, *v.* Rise again, as in the resurrection. *Pret. a.* dh'ais-éirich, *rose again; fut. aff. a.* ais-éirichidh, *shall rise again.*

Ais-eirigh, *s. f.* Resurrection; a second rising. Ais-eirigh nam marbh, *the resurrection of the dead.—Stew.* 1 *Cor.* La na h-ais-eirigh, *the day of resurrection.*

† **Aisge**, and **Aisgidh**, *s. f.* A gift; a donation.

Aisig, *s. f.* A ferry. See **Aiseag**.

Aisig, *v.* Restore, deliver, give back; ferry over. *Pret. a.* dh'aisig, *ferried; fut. aff. a.* aisigidh, *shall or will ferry;* aisigidh e, *he will restore.—Stew. Prov. Fut. pass.* aisigear, *shall be ferried.*

Aisigear, *fut. pass.* of aisig.

Aisigidh, *fut. aff. a.* of aisig. Shall or will ferry.

Aisigte, *p. part.* of aisig. Restored, delivered; ferried over.

Aisil, *s. f.* An axletree. *N. pl.* aisilean, *axletrees.* Aisil na carbaid, *the axletree of the chariot;* aisilean nan roth, *the axletrees of the wheels.—Stew.* 1 *K.*

Ais-innis, *v.* Rehearse, narrate; say or tell over again; repeat. *Pret. a.* dh' ais-innis, *repeated; fut. aff. a.* aisinnsidh, *shall or will repeat; fut. pass.* ais-innsear, *shall be repeated.*

Ais-innleachd, *s. f.* A mischievous contrivance, or invention.—*Stew. Ecc. ref. N. pl.* ais-innleachdan; *dat. pl.* aisinnleachdaibh.

Ais-innleachdach, *a.* Plotting, mischievous, crafty, scheming. Ann an comhairlibh ais-innleachdach, *in crafty counsels.—Stew. G. B. Com. and sup.* ais-innleachdaiche, *more or most crafty.*

Ais-innsear, *fut. pass.* of ais-innis. Shall or will be rehearsed.

Ais-innsidh, *fut. aff. a.* of ais-innis. Shall or will rehearse.

† **Aision**, *s. m.* A relic; a diadem.

† **Aisith**, *s. f.* Strife, disturbance, discord.

Aislear, eir, *s. m.* (ais *and* lear.) A spring-tide.—*Ir.*

Aisleine, *s. f.* A death-shroud. *N. pl.* aisleintean.

Aisleir, *gen. sing.* of aislear.

Aisling, *s. f.* (*Ir.* aisling.) A dream, a reverie, a vision. Eirich an aisling mo chadail, *rise in the dream of my sleep.—Oss. Fin. Lor.* Mhosgail e o aisling an laoch, *he awoke the hero from his dream;* chunnaic e aisling, *he saw a vision;* aisling chonain, *a lascivious dream.* *N. pl.* aislinge, *and* aislingean. Aislinge faoin, *empty dreams.—Stew. Zech.* *Dat. pl.* aislingibh.

Aislingeach, *a.* Dreamy, dreaming, visionary; of, or relating to, a dream.

Aislingean, *n. pl.* of aisling; which see.

Aislingiche, *s. m.* (*from* aisling.) A dreamer. Tha an t-aislingiche so a teachd, *this dreamer is coming.—Stew. Gen.* *Ir.* aislingtheach.

Aisling chonain, *s. m.* A lascivious dream.

Aisne, *gen. sing.* of aisean; which see.

Aisneach, *a.* Ribbed; having strong ribs, having large ribs; of, or belonging to, a rib.

Aisneis, *s. f.* A rehearsing. See Ais-innseadh.

Ais-innseadh, idh, *s. m.* A telling, a rehearsing, a repeating.

Aisre, and **Aisridh**, *s.* An abode; a receptacle; a hill; a path. Aisridh nam ban, *the abode of women; a seraglio.—Fingalian Poem.* An ruath aisridh, *the red path.—Macint.*

Ais-sith, *s. f.* (*perhaps* ais-shith.) Discord, strife, wrangling, disturbance. Siol-chuiridh e ais-sith, *he will sow discord.—Stew. Prov. ref.*

Aisteidh, *s.* The hatches of a ship.

Ait, *a.* Glad, joyful, cheerful. *Ir.* ait. *Old French,* haitè.

Ait, àite, *s. m.* (*Gr.* αἰδ-ια. *Lat.* aed-es, *a house.* *Ir.* àit.) A place; part; spot, region. *N. pl.* aitean, *and* aiteachan, *places.* C' àit, *where?*

Ait-aire, *s. m.* An observatory.

† **Ait-cheas**, *s. f.* A warrior's concubine.

Ait-chiomach, aich, *s. m.* A petitioner. *N. pl.* aitchiomaichean.

Ait-comhnuidh, *s. m.* A dwelling place; a dwelling, or abode. Thog sinn ait-comhnuidh do 'n mhnaoi, *we built a dwelling for the dame.—Ull.*

Aiteach, eich, *s. m.* (*from* àit.) Habitation; dwelling. Bheil an aiteach fuar? *is their dwelling cold?—Oss. Tem.* *N. pl.* aiteacha, *and* aiteachan, *dwellings;* aiteacha comhnuidh, *habitation.—Stew. Exod.*

† **Aiteach**, *a.* Anxious; careful.

Aiteachadh, aidh, *s. m.* (*Ir.* aitiughadh.) The circumstance of inhabiting; a placing. Luchd-aiteachaidh, *inhabitants.*

Aiteachadh (ag), *pr. part.* of àitich. Inhabiting, dwelling. Ag àiteachadh an domhain, *inhabiting the earth.*

Aiteachas, ais, *s. m.* A colony; an inhabiting.

Aiteag, eig, *s. f.* A shy girl; a coquette. *N. pl.* aiteagan.

Aiteagach, *a.* Coquettish; shy, indifferent, scornful. Ainnir aiteagach, *a shy maid.*

Aiteal, eil, *s. m.* Juniper. Freumhan an aiteil, *juniper roots.—Stew. Job.* Fuidh chraoibh aiteil, *beneath a juniper tree.—Stew.* 1 *K.*

Aiteal, eil, *s. m.* (*W.* adyl.) A blast, a breeze, a breath of wind; light; music. Aiteal an earraich, *the breeze of spring.—Oss. Fing.* Gun aiteal bho reul air sàil, *on the deep without starlight.—Oss. Gaul.*

Aitealach, *a.* Abounding in juniper; of or pertaining to juniper.

Aitealach, *a.* Breezy; bright; shining, luminous.

Aiteam, eim, *s. m.* and *f.* A people, a tribe; folk, persons. Aiteam chathach, *a warlike people.—Old Poem.* Is beannaichte an aiteam, *blessed are the people.—Smith.*

† **Aiteamh**, eimh, *s. m.* A convincing proof; an argument, demonstration.

Aiteamh, eimh, *s. m.* A thaw; fresh weather. Tha 'n làth ris an aiteamh, *the day thaws.*

Aiteann, inn, *s. m.* (*Ir.* aiteann.) Juniper; also furze. Dearcan aitinn, *juniper berries;* preas aitinn, *a juniper bush.*

Aiteannach, *a.* Abounding in junipers, or in furze; like juniper, or furze; of, or pertaining to, juniper, or to furze.

Aiteannach, aich. *s.* A place where junipers grow; a quantity of juniper bushes.

Aiteas, eis, *s. m.* (*from* ait.) *Old French,* haitè, *joyous.* Gladness, joy; laughter, fun. Aiteas an sùil Ghormaluinn, *gladness in the eye of Gormallin.—Oss. Oimara.* Aiteas air na sleibhte uaine, *joy on the green mountains.—Oss. Duthona.* Cuirm chum aiteis, *a feast for laughter.—Stew. Ecc.*

Aiteig, *gen. sing.* of aiteag.

Aiteil, *gen. sing.* of aiteal.

† **Aith**, *s. m.* A hill; a skirmish.

† **Aith**, *a.* Keen; sharp; anxious.

Aith, *an iterative particle;* more commonly written *ath.*

Aith-cheas, chise, *s. f.* A whore, a bawd.

Aithchuimir, *a.* Compendious; brief; abridged.

† **Aithe**, *s. f.* Revenge.—*Ir.*

† **Aithe**, *a.* Keen.

† **Aitheach**, ich, *s. m.* A giant; a clown; a sow. *Ir. id.*

Aitheach, *a.* Gigantic; clownish; swinish.

Aitheadh, idh, *s. m.* An elf shot.

Aitheamh, eimh, *s. m.* A fathom. Fichead aitheamh, *twenty fathoms.—Stew. Acts.* *N. pl.* aitheamhan; *contr.* *aithean.*

Aithean, *s. pl.* The liver.—*Macd.*

Aitheas, eis, *s. m.* A reproach; a blemish.

† **Aitheasg**, eisg, *s. f.* An admonition, advice.

Aith-ghearr, aith-ghearradh, *s. m.* An abbreviation; a contraction; a short way; a short time. Gu h-aith-ghearr, *shortly, soon.*

Aith-ghearr, *a.* (*W.* ehegyr.) Short; quick, brief; soon, instantaneous. Sgaoil sinn cho aithghearr, *we dispersed so soon.—Roy Stewart.* Gu h-aithghearr, *shortly, quickly, soon.*

Aith-ghearr, *v.* Cut again; subdivide; shorten, curtail. More frequently written *ath-ghearr;* which see.

Aitheimh, *gen. sing.* of aitheamh.

† **Aithid**, *s. m.* A viper; a snake.

† **Aithidean**, ein, (*dim.* of aithid), *s. m.* Any venomous reptile; a little beast.

Aithinne, *s. m.* (*Ir.* aithinne.) A firebrand. Mar aithinne as an losgadh, *like a firebrand from the burning.—Stew. Amos.*

Aithir, *s. f.* A serpent.—*Stew. G. B.* More frequently written *nathair.*

Aithir-lus, luis, *s. m.* Ground-ivy.

† **Aithis**, *v.* Reproach, rebuke, abuse, affront. *Pret. a.* dh' aithis, *rebuked; fut. aff. a.* aithisidh, *shall rebuke.*

Aithis, *s. f.* A reproach, rebuke, affront, scandal; a check, abuse; ease, leisure. Gun tuit e ann an aithis, *that he may fall into reproach.—Stew. Tim.* Bheil thu air d' aithis, *are you at leisure?*

Aithiseach, *a.* Reproachful, abusive, scandalous; slow; leisurely, tardy, dilatory.

Aithiseach, ich, *s. m.* (*from* aithis.) An abusive person; a dilatory person.

Aithiseachadh, aidh, *s. m.* Defamation; abuse.

Aithmheal, eil, *s. m.* Repentance, compunction, fear. Lan aithmheil, *a man full of compunction.—Old Song.*

† **Aithmheas**, *s. m.* The ebbing of the sea.

Aithmheileach, *a.* Repentant.

Aithn, *v.* Command, order, bid, direct, enjoin. *Pret. a.* dh' àithn, *command; fut. aff. a.* àithnidh, *shall or will command; fut. neg.* àithn; as, cha n' àithniad, *they shall not order.*

Aithne, *s. f.* A command, commandment, order, injunction, mandate, direction; a charge; *rarely* a store. *N. pl.* àitheantean; *dat. pl.* àitheantibh. Lagh nan àitheanta, *the law of the commandments.—Stew. Eph.* Thug mi àithne dhuit, *I ordered you.*

Aithne, *s. f.* Knowledge, discernment, acquaintance. (*Swed.* ana, *to foreknow.*) Cha n eil aithne agaim air, *I have no knowledge of him;* cuir aithne air, *get acquainted with him, make yourself known to him.*

Aithne-an-làtha, *s. f.* Broad day-light; the height of day.

Aithneachadh, aidh, *s. m.* A recognising, knowing, discerning.

Aithneachadh, (ag), *pr. part.* of aithnich. Knowing, recognising.

Aithneadail, *a.* (*from* aithne.) Familiar, knowing.

Aithneadair, *s. m.* (*from* aithne.) A man of general knowledge; a learned man.

Aithneadh, eidh, *s. m.* The act of commanding; a commanding, ordering.

Aithneadh, (ag), *pr. part.* of àithn. Commanding, ordering, charging, enjoining.

Aithnich, *v.* (*from* aithne.) Know, recognise, feel; have sexual intercourse. *Pret. a.* dh' aithnich, *knew; fut. aff. a.* aithnichidh, *shall know; fut. neg. and interrog.* aithnich; *fut. pass.* aithnichear, *shall be known.* Cha d' aithnich mi orm e, *I did not feel it;* cha n' aithnichteadh orra e, *it would not be known on them.*

Aithnichean, ein, *s. m.* A stranger, visitor, acquaintance. —*Stew. Lev. ref.*

Aithnichear, *fut. pass.* of aithnich. Shall be known.

Aithnichidh, *fut. aff. a.* of aithnich. Shall or will be known.

Aithnichte, *p. part.* of aithnich. Known, recognised. Dean aithnichte, *make known.—Stew. Rom. Arm.* anzad, *known. Swed.* ainsichte, *a face.*

Aithre, *s. c.* A bull, a cow, ox. *N. pl.* aithrean.

Aithreach, *a.* Wonderful, curious, strange, droll; sorry, penitent. Dh' eisd sinn is b' aithreach leinn, *we listened, and surprised we were.—Ull.* Nior aithreach leis, *nor does he repent.—Sm.* Is aithreach leinn do bhuaidh, *we are amazed at thy prowess.—Fingalian Poem.* Is aithreach an t-oglach thu, *you are a droll fellow.*

Aithreachail, *a.* (aithreach-amhuil.) Penitent, repenting, repentant.

Aithreachais, *gen. sing.* of aithreachas.

Aithreachas, ais, *s. m.* Repentance, penitence, regret. Dean aithreachas, gabh aithreachas, *repent;* ni mi aithreachas, *or* gabhaidh mi aithreachas, *I will repent;* gun aithreachas cha bhi maitheanas, *without repentance there shall not be forgiveness.—Stew. N. T.*

Aithreachag, aig, *s. f.* A female penitent. *N. pl.* aithreachagan.

Aithreachan, ain, *s. m.* A penitent.

Aithreachd, *s. f.* (*from* athair.) Ancestry, ancestors. A chaoidh cumaibh an cuimhne ur n-aithreachd, *ever keep your ancestry in mind.—Old Song.*

Aithriche, and **Aithrichean**, *n. pl.* of athair. Fathers, ancestors. See **Athair**.

Aithrichibh, *dat. pl.* of athair.

† **Aithridhe**, *s. f.* Repentance, sadness, tears, sorrow.

Aithridheach, *a.* (*from* aithridhe.) Repentant, sad, sorrowful.

† **Aithrine**, *s. m.* A calf.—*Ir.*

Aithris, *s. f.* (*Ir.* aithris.) Report, repetition, rehearsal, recital, narration; imitation; tradition, tale. Aithris anraidh, *a tale of distress.—Oss. Cathula. N. pl.* aithrisean.

Aithris, *v.* Rehearse, report, narrate, relate, tell, repeat. *Pret. a.* dh' aithris, *told; fut. aff. a.* aithrisidh, *shall tell.* Aithrisibh am measg an t-sluaigh, *tell among the people.—Smith.* Aithrisibhse agus aithrisidh sinne, *report you, and we will report.—Stew. G. B.* Sgeul ri aithris, *a tale to be told.—Oss. Lodin.*

Aithriseach, *a.* (*from* aithris.) Tautological, repeating, traditionary.

Aithriseachd, *s. f.* (*from* aithris.) Frequent repetition, tautology.

Aithriseadh, eidh, *s. m.* The act of repeating; a repetition.

Aithrisiche, *s. m.* A tautologist; a tale-bearer; a reciter; a narrator; an imitator.

Aitich, *v. a.* (*from* àit.) Inhabit, cultivate, settle; place; give place to. *Pret. a.* dh' àitich, *inhabited; fut. aff. a.* àitichidh, *inhabited.*

Aitichte, *p. part.* of aitich. Inhabited; settled; placed. Gu tìr àitichte, *to an inhabited land.—Stew. Exod.*

Aitidh, *a.* Wet, damp, moist. Tha t-aodach àitidh, *your clothes are damp.*

Aitidheachd, *s. f.* (*from* aitidh.) Dampness, wetness, moistness.

Aitreabh, eibh, *s.* (*perhaps* àite-threabh.) An abode, dwelling; a building; a *steading.* Theid an aitreabh sios, *their building will decay.—Stew. Ecc. W.* athrev, *a house,* and adrev, *home. N. pl.* aitreabhan. Written also *aitreamh.*

Aitreabhach, *a.* (*from* aitreabh.) Of, or pertaining to, an abode, or building; domestic.

Aitreabhach, aich, *s. m.* (*from* aitreabh.) An inhabitant; a lodger; a tenant; a farmer. *N. pl.* aitreabhàiche.

Aitreabhan, *n. pl.* of aitreabh.

Aitreach, eich, *s. m.* *Contr.* for aitreabhach; which see.

Aitreamh, eimh, *s. m.* An abode; dwelling-house. Written also *aitreabh;* which see.

Aitreamhach, eich, *s. m.* (*from* aitreamh.) See **Aitreabhach**.

† **Al**, *v.* Nurse; praise. (*Lat.* alo.) *Pret. a.* dh' àl, *nursed; fut. aff. a.* àlaidh, *shall nurse.*

Al, àil, *s. m.* (*Ir.* àl.) A brood; litter, offspring; the young of a bird; a generation. A solar dhearc dha h-àl beag, *gathering berries for its callow young.—Oss. Gaul.* Al stiallach, *speckled offspring.—Stew. Gen.* Trom le h-al, *heavy with young.—Id.* Iad fein 's an cuid àil, *themselves and their young.—Old Song.* An t-àl a tha ri teachd, *the generation to come.—Sm. Lat.* al-o, *to rear. W.* al.

† **Al**, ail, *s. m.* A rock, a stone; fear; a horse. For this last sense, see **All**.

Al, àil, *s. m.* Nurture; food.—*Ir.*

† **Ala**, ai, *s. m.* A trout; a wound.—*Ir.*

Alach, aich, *s. m.* (*from* àl.) Brood, the young of a bird, a litter; tribe, crew, generation. Mar iolair Laoir, air a h-alach, *like an eagle of Lora over her young.—Oss.* Tra thig un sealgair gun fhios air alach, *when the hunter comes unexpectedly on a brood.—Orr.*

Alach, aich, *s. m.* The nails in a boat; a new set; activity, alacrity; also a request.—*Macdon.* Alach-ramh, *a bank of oars.—Macfar.*

Alach, *a.* Of, or belonging to, a brood; prolific.

Alach-ramh, raimh, *s. m.* A bank of oars.

Alachag, aig, *s. m.* A hook; a crook; a peg, a pin. *N. pl.* alachagan.

Alachagach, *a.* Full of hooks, or crooks; full of pegs; like a crook, peg, or pin.

† **Aladh**, aidh, *s. m.* Wisdom, skill; also malice, a lie.

Aladh, aidh, *s. m.* (*from* àl.) A nursing.

Alain, *a.* White; bright, clear. *Ir.* alain.

Alaineachd, *s. f.* (*from* alain.) Beauty; whiteness; brightness, clearness.

A LATHAIR, adv. Present, at hand; in existence, in life. See also LATHAIR.

† ALB, a. (Lat. alb-us.) White. Greek, according to Heyschius, αλφος. Chald. alban, to be white. Syr. alben, to whiten. Teut. alp, a swan.

† ALB, ailb, s. m. An eminence; a height.

ALBA, Albainn, and Albuinn, s. f. (Corn. Alban.) Scotland. Eididh na h-Alba, the costume of Scotland; tha mi dol dh' Albuinn, I am going to Scotland; Albainn bheadrach, beloved Scotland; a chlann Alba nam buadh, ye sons of victorious Albion.—Fingalian Poem.

The oldest name of Britain is allowed to have been Albion. This is the name given to Scotland by the Scotch Celts: and they do not know it by any other appellation. "Sed hoc nomen," says Buchanan, "magis e libris eruitur, quam in communi sermone usurpatur, nisi præsertim apud Scotos, qui se Albinich, regionem suam, Albin adhuc vocant."

ALBANNACH, a. Scotch, Scottish; of or belonging to Scotland. Eorp ag amharc Ghaidheal Albannach, Europe beholding the Scotch Gael.—Old Song.

ALBANNACH, aich, s. m. A Scot, a Scotsman. Is Albannach an duine so, this man is a Scot; is fior Albannach e, he is a true Scotchman. N. pl. Albannaich, Scotchmen.

ALBANNAICH, gen. sing. and n. pl. of Albannach.

ALD, uild, s. m. A rivulet; a mountain stream. Ag aomadh thar an uild, bending over the stream. N. pl. uild. Old British, aled, a flowing stream.

ALDAN, ain, s. m. (dim. of ald.) A rivulet; a streamlet.—Oss. Tem.

ALDANACH, a. Abounding in rivulets; of or belonging to a rivulet.

† ALFAD, aid, s. m. Cause, reason.

† ALGA, a. Noble, great.—Ir.

† ALGACHD, s. f. Nobleness, greatness, nobility.

† ALL, aill, s. m. A horse.

This is an ancient Celtic vocable, long gone into disuse among the Gael; but we have it in composition with cab, or cap: as caball, or capall, a horse or mare; literally a tamed horse, or a horse accustomed to the bridle; from cab, mouth, and all, horse.

† ALL, Aill, s. m. (Corn. als. Ir. all.) A rock, a cliff; a great hall; a generation; race.

Arab. hhal, high. Chald. hhali, high. Syr. hholi, height. Chald. hhalas, height. Heb. hal, above. Teut. hel, high. Pers. and Arab. al, high. In some parts of Africa, alle, high. Ethiop. alal, to elevate. Turk. al and ali, high. Mantcheou Tartars, al-in, a hill. Alin, a mountain, in Mogul. Malacca, ala, surpass. Dan. holl, a hill. Sax. hull. English, hill. Etrurian, alse. It. alzare, to elevate. Turk. allah, God, or the High Being. Jap. ala, God. Armen. ael, God. Pun. ille. Syr. eloha, God.

† ALL, a. (Ir. all. Gr. αλλ-ος, other. Arm. all. Arab. hhal, high. Chald. hhali.) Foreign; great, prodigious. Seldom used but in composition with some other word, as allmharach.

† ALL, a. White.

This word has long been obsolete; but we see it in the name of a stream that runs into the Tweed, namely, Allan; i. e. All-an, or All-amhainn, the white or foaming stream. Anciently Alwen.

† ALLA, s. m. The Most High.

ALLABAN, ain, s. m. Wandering, deviation, aberration.

† ALLABHAIR, s. m. (All, cliff, and labhair.) An echo.—Ir.

ALLADH, aidh, s. m. Fame, report, greatness. Alladh Dhaibhidh, the fame of David.—Stew. 1 Chron. ref. Deagh alladh, a good report; droch alladh, a bad report.

ALLAIDH, a. (from all.) Corn. alta. Wild, ferocious, savage, terrible; boisterous; also beauteous. See ALLUIDH. Beathaiche allaidh, wild beasts. Corn. beathuige alta.

ALLAIL, a. (from alladh.) Noble, illustrious, excellent, glorious. Daoine allail, illustrious men.—Stew. 1 Chron. Written also alloil; which see.

ALLA-MHADADH, aidh, s. m. A wolf. Chual an t-allamhadadh an fhuaim, the wolf heard the sound.—Oss. Conn.

† ALLBHUADHACH, aich, s. m. A prince's hall.

ALLBHUADHACH, a. (from † all, great, and buadhach.) Triumphant, victorious, conquering.

† ALLCHUR, s. m. Transposition.

ALLGHLOIR, s. f. Gibberish, jargon, vainglory, gasconading.

ALL-GHLÒRACH, a. Inclined to utter jargon; vainglorious, boastful.

ALLGHORT, ghoirt, s. m. An orchard. Contracted for abhall ghort; which see.

ALLMHADADH, aidh, s. m. A wolf. Written also allamhadadh.

ALLMHAIDH, a. Fierce, terrible, wild, boisterous. Armailt allmhaidh, a terrible army.—Old Poem. Written oftener, allaidh and alluidh.

ALLMHARA, Allmharach, a. Foreign, strange, transmarine, exotic; wild, ferocious, untameable. W. allmyr, a place beyond the sea.

ALLMHARACH, aich, s. m. A stranger, a foreigner, an alien, a barbarian; one from beyond the seas; a foreign foe; a transmarine foe. Iarmad nan allmharach, the remnant of the strangers.—Sm. Luingeas nan allmharach, the ship of the sea-borne foe.—Old Poem. Ir. id.

ALLMHARACHD, s. f. Barbarity, cruelty; the state of being foreign.

† ALLOD, adv. Formerly, of old.—Ir.

ALLOIL, a. Noble, excellent, illustrious, glorious, renowned. Daoine alloil, men of renown.—Stew. Num. ref. Is alloil thusa, thou art glorious.—Stew. G. B. Written also allail.

ALLOILEACHD, s. f. Nobleness, excellentness, illustriousness, gloriousness, renown.

ALLONTA, a. Brave, noble; excellent, of good reputation.

ALLONTACHD, s. f. Bravery; good fame.

† ALLRAON, raoin, s. m. A foreign expedition; a journey to a foreign land.

ALLSACHAIL, a. Prone to respite; worthy of respite.

ALLSACHD, s. f. Respite; reprieve; suspension.

ALLSAICH, v. a. Respite; reprieve; suspend. Pret. a. dh' allsaich, respited; fut. aff. a. allsaichidh, shall respite; fut. pass. allsaichear, shall be respited.

ALLSMUAINN, s. f. A great buoy; a float.

ALLT, uillt, s. m. A mountain stream; a rill, a brook. N. pl. alltan and uillt. Bruach an uillt, the bank of the brook; thréig torman nan allt, the murmur of the brooks has subsided.—Oss. Diarm. Lat. alt-us, deep. Old British, aled, a running stream. Written also alld.

ALLTA, and ALLTADH, a. (Ir. allta.) Fierce, wild, foreign; strange. Beathaich allta na machrach, the wild beasts of the field.—Sm. Mar leomhann allta, like a fierce lion.—Id. W. allda, a stranger.

ALLTAN, n. pl. of allt; which see.

ALLTAN, ain, s. m. (dim. of allt.) A brook; a little mountain stream; a streamlet. Drochait air gach alltan, a bridge over every streamlet.—Macint.

ALLUIDH, a. (Ir. alluigh.) Wild, ferocious, fierce, savage, boisterous, terrible; also beauteous. Stoirm alluidh, terrible storms.—Oss. Trath. B' alluidh do shuil, fierce was thine eye.—Oss. Temo. Dh' aom e air a sgéith umha alluidh, he bowed over his beauteous shield of brass.—Oss. Gaul.

ALLUIGH, a. See ALLUIDH.

† ALLUIN, a. Fair, handsome. Now written àluinn.

† Almachadh, a. Charitable.

† Alp, ailp, s. m. A mountain.

Alt, uilt, s. m. (Ir. alt.) A joint; a joining; a condition, state, order, method. N. pl. altan; dat. pl. altaibh; as an alt, *out of joint.*—*Stew. Gen.* Eadar altaibh na luirich, *between the joints of the harness.*—*Stew.* 1 *K.*

† Alt, uilt, s. m. (Ir. alt.) A nursing, rearing, feeding. *Lat.* alt-um, *to nourish.*

† Alt, s. m. A section of a book; time.

† Alt, s. m. A high place, a hill, eminence; exaltation; a leap; a valley. *Lat.* alt-us, *high. W.* alht. *Corn.* als, *a hill*, or *a cliff.*

Altach, aich, s. m. A grace at meat. *N. pl.* altaichean; *d. pl.* altaichibh.

Altachadh, aidh, s. m. The act of saluting, or of thanking; a saluting; a salute; a bracing, as of the joints; moving, budging.

Altachadh, (ag), pr. part. of altaich. Saluting, thanking; bracing, as of the joints; moving, budging.

Altachadh-beatha, s. m. A salutation; a greeting; a welcome.

Altaich, v. a. Salute; thank; inquire after one's welfare; relax the joints; also brace, move, budge. *Pret. a.* dh' altaich, *saluted; fut. aff. a.* altaichidh, *shall salute; fut. pass.* altaichear, *shall be saluted.* Dh' altaich iad beath a cheile, *they asked for each other's welfare.*—*Stew. Exod.*

Altaich, gen. sing. of altach.

Altaichean, n. pl. of altach.

Altaichear, fut. pass. of altaich; which see.

Altaichidh, fut. aff. a. of altaich. Shall or will brace.

Altail, a. (alt-amhuil.) Arthritic.

Altair, gen. altair, and altarach, s. f. (Ir. altoir.) An altar. Adhaircean na h-altair, *the horns of the altar.*—*Sm.* Fa chomhair na h-altarach, *opposite to the altar.*—*Stew. Zech.* *N. pl.* altraichean, or altraiche.

Altan, ain, s. m. Dim. of alt; which see.

Altan, n. pl. of alt; which see.

Alt-cheangal, ail, s. m. Articulation, or the juncture of bones.

Altrach, aich, s. m. One who fosters; a nurse. *Lat.* altrix. *N. pl.* altraichean.

Altradh, aidh, s. m. A man who fosters. Ban-altradh, *a nurse.*

Altraiche, s. m. One who fosters. *N. pl.* altraichean, *one who prospers.*

Altram, v. a. See Altruim.

Altranas, s. m. A fostering; a nursing. *Ir.* altrannas.

Altruim, v. a. Nurse, nourish, maintain, educate, foster, cherish. *Pret. a.* dh' altruim, *nursed; fut. aff. a.* altrumaidh, *shall nurse;* altrumaidh mise, *I will nourish.*—*Stew. Gen.*

Altrumach, a. Fostering, rearing, educating.

Altrumachadh, aidh, s. m. The act of fostering; a nursing, rearing, educating.

Altrumachadh, (ag), pr. part. of altruimich.

Altrumadh, aidh, s. m. A fostering, nursing, rearing, educating.

Altrumaich, v. Foster, rear, nourish, educate. *Pret. a.* dh' altrumaich, *fostered; fut. aff. a.* altrumaichidh, *shall foster.*

Altrumaidh, fut. aff. a. of altruim.

Altruman, ain, s. m. A chief. Seachd altrumain aig loch Làin, *seven chiefs at the lake of Lanno.*—*Fingalian Poem.* *N. pl.* altrumain.

Altrumain, gen. sing. and n. pl. of altruman.

Altuchadh, aidh, s. m. See Altachadh. *Ir.* altughadh.

Altuich, v. a. Written also *altaich*; which see.

† Alughain, s. f. Potter's clay.

Aluinn, a. Beautiful, fair, handsome, elegant, goodly. Meas chraobh aluinn, *the fruit of goodly trees.*—*Stew. Lev.* *Ir.* aluin.

Am, def. art. before words beginning with *b, f, m,* or *p*, when not aspirated; as am baile, *the town;* am fear, *the man;* am mor'ear, *the grandee;* am pàisd, *the child.*

Am, interrog. particle; used before verbs beginning with *b, f, m,* or *p.* Am buail thu? *will you strike?* Am fàg thu mi am aonar? *wilt thou leave me alone?*—*Oss. Fing.* Am maith thu dha? *wilt thou forgive him?* Am pàigh thu mi? *wilt thou pay me?*

'Am, a colloquial abbreviation of *agam*; used in the following phrases: Cha n-'eil fhios 'am, *I do not know (non est notitia mihi);* cha-n'eil fhios 'am fhein, *I do not know;* cha n-'eil fhios am fhéin gu dearbh, *I do not know, I am sure; I really do not know.*

Am, [*for* mo], poss. pron. My. Ann am lagh, *in my law.*—*Stew. Exod.* *Corn.* am, *my.*

Am, [*contr. for* ann mo.] In my. Ghlac mi am shuain mo shleagh, *I grasped in my dream my spear.*—*Oss. Dargo.*

Am, [*for* anns am.] Lagain am bi na neòinein, *dells where daisies grow.*—*Macint.*

Am, [*for* ann am.] In the. Tha anam am mòrchuis, *his soul is in (actuated by) pride.*—*Oss. Tem.* Am bùthaibh, *in tents.*—*Stew. Gen.* Am faoghaid fàsaich, *in the forest chase.*—*Oss. Comala.*

A'm, s. m. (Ir. am.) Time, season, convenience. *N. pl.* àmanna, *times; dat. pl.* àmannaibh, *to times;* na h-àmanna so, *these times;* âm o aois, *olden times.*—*Oss. Lodin.* Ann àm na h-oidhche, *in the night time.*—*Oss. Fing.* San àm, *at the time, in the time, in the meantime.*—*Oss. Temo.* Sna h-àmannaibh chaidh seachad, *in times past.*—*Stew. Eph.* Ann an àm is ann an an-am, *in season and out of season.*—*Stew.* 2 *Tim.* Am a gheamhraidh, *the winter season;* àm an earraich, *the spring time;* àm an t-samhraidh, *summer time;* àm an fhogharaidh, *harvest time.*

† Am, a. Soft, moist, damp. *Siamese,* am, *water. Canadian,* am, *water. Bisc.* ama, *sea.*

† Ama, ai, s. m. A horse's collar.

A mach, adv. Out; without; out of. Tha e a mach, *he is without;* thig a mach, *come out.* *Ir. id.*

Amach, aich, s. m. A vulture; any ravenous bird. *N. pl.* amaichean.

Amad, aid, s. m. A fool.—*Ir.*

Amadain, gen. sing. and n. pl. of amadan.

Amadan, ain, s. m. (dim. of amad.) *Ir.* amadan. A fool. Bithidh e na amadan, *he will be a fool.*—*Stew. Jer.* Ni e amadain, *he will make fools.*—*Stew. Job.* *N. pl.* amadain. Amadan-mòintich, *a dotterel.*—*Ir. id.*

Amadanach, a. Foolish; like a fool.

Amadanachd, s. f. Foolishness; the conduct of a fool.

Amadan-mòintich, s. m. A dotterel. *N. pl.* amadain-mòintich, *dotterels.*

Amadanta, a. (*from* amadan.) Foolish. *Ir. id.*

Amaid, a. Foolish, silly; also (substantively) folly, silliness; a foolish woman.

Amaideach, a. Foolish. Nithe amaideach, *foolish things.*—*Stew. Pro.* Gu h-amaideach, *foolishly.*

Amaideachd, s. f. Foolishness; folly; silliness. Ann am faidhean amaideachd, *foolishness in prophets.*—*Stew. Jer.*

Amail, a. (am-amhuil), *from* àm. Seasonable, timely; in time; temporal.

Amail, v. Hinder, prevent, stop, interrupt, debar, impede. *Pret. a.* dh' amail, *hindered; fut. aff. a.* amailidh, *shall or will hinder.*

† AMAIL, *adv.* Now written *amhuil;* which see.

AMAILIDH, *fut. aff. a.* of amail. Shall or will hinder.

AMAILL, *s. f.* Hinderance, impediment, interruption. A cur amaill orm, *hindering me.*

AMAILL, *gen. sing.* of amall.

AMAIR, *gen. sing.* of amar; which see.

AMAIS, *v.* Hit, mark, aim; find. *Pret. a.* dh' amais, *found; fut. aff. a.* amaisidh, *shall or will find; fut. pass.* amaisear, *shall be found.*

AMAISCEACH, *a.* Wanton, lewd, lustful. Gu h-amaisceach, *wantonly.*

AMAISCEACHD, *s. f.* Wantonness, lewdness.—*Stew. Mark, ref*

AMAISIDH, *fut. aff. a.* Shall or will find.

AMALADH, aidh, *s. m.* The act or circumstance of hindering; stoppage, impediment, interruption.

AMALADH, (ag), *pr. part.* Hindering, impeding, stopping. Tha thu 'g am amaladh, *you are hindering me.*

AMALL, aill, *s. m.* A swingle-tree.

† AMAN, ain, *s. f.* Now written *amhainn;* which see.

AMAR, air, *s. m.* (*Gr.* ἀμάρα, *a drain.*) A trough; a narrow rocky channel. Dh' fhalmhuich i a soitheach san amar, *she emptied her vessel into the trough.*—*Stew. O. T.* Amar brùthaidh, *a wine-press, a press vat.*—*Stew. Hag.* Amar mùin, *a vessel for holding urine, a water-pot, or chamber-pot;* amar fuail, *a water pot, a vessel for holding urine,* amar fuinidh, *a baking trough;* amar baistidh, *a font.*

† AMAR, air, *s. m.* A chain; a cable *Gr.* ἅμμα. Hence also the French sea-term *amarer,* to bind or fasten.

AMARAICH, *s. f.* Scurvy-grass.—*Macd.*

AMAR-BAISTIDH, *s. m.* A baptismal font

AMAR-BRUTHAIDH, *s. m.* A wine-press; a pressing vat.—*Stew. Hag.*

AMARCACH, *a.* Fond of —*Ir. id.*

AMAR-FUAIL, *s. m.* A vessel for holding urine; a urinal; a chamber-pot.

AMAR-FUINIDH, *s. m* A baking trough.—*Stew. Exod.*

AMAS, ais, *s. m.* A hitting, aiming, marking; finding; a finding after a search.

AMAS, (ag), *pr. part* of amais. Hitting, marking, aiming; finding; finding after a search. Is tearc iadsan tha ag amas oirre, *few there be that find it.*—*Stew. N. T.*

AMASADH, aidh, *s. m.* A hitting, marking, aiming; finding; a finding after a search.

AMASADH, (ag), *pr. part. a* of amais Hitting, marking, finding.

† AMASGAIDH, *a.* Profane; helter skelter.

AMASGAIDHEACHD, *s. f.* Profaneness.

A MEASG, *prep.* Among, amongst.

AMH, *s. m.* A fool, a simpleton; a dwarf.

AMH, *a.* (*Ir.* amh.) Raw, crude; unsodden, unboiled, unroasted; naughty. Feoil amh, *raw flesh* —*Stew. Sam.* Na ithibh dheth amh, *eat not of it (unroasted) raw.*—*Stew. Exod.*

† AMH, *s. m.* Water; ocean.

Gr. Æol. ἀφ-ὰ, *water. Lat.* a-qua. *Shans* ab *and* aw. *Pers* awe. 'Aa, *a river in Courland.*' *Dan.* aae. *Fr.* eau *Goth.* a. *Isl.* aa. *Low Germ.* aa., *Swed* a, *a river;* and perhaps *Gr* αὐὴ, *a blast. Chin.* ho, *river. Tart.* ou, *water.* See also ABH.

† AMH, *adv.* Even, so, as, like. Hence *amhuil.*

† AMH, *s.* A denial.

AMHACH, *a.* Like a dwarf; like a fool.

AMHACH, aich, *s m.* (*Gr.* αὐχὴ) Neck. Brisidh tu' amhach, *thou shalt break its neck.*—*Stew Exod.* G' ar n-amhach, *up to our necks.*—*Macint* *N. pl.* amhaichean.

AMHACHD, *s f.* (*from* amh.) Conduct of a fool, or simpleton.

AMHACHD, *s. f.* Rawness, crudeness.

AMHAIL, *adv.* (*from* †amh) Like to, such as, as. See AMHUIL.

A MHAIN, *adv* Only, alone. *Ir. id*

AMHAINN, *s. f.* A river. (*Comp. of* amh *and* ain) See also ABHAINN.

W. afon *and* avon. *English,* † afene. *Swed.* aen, *or* an *Arm* afon *Corn* auan. *Manx* aon. *Germ.* am *Lat.* † amanis, *contr.* amnis, and in the old dialect of the *Scoto-Brigantes,* amon *and* aman *Ir.* amhan *Moorish,* aman, *water. Copt.* pi-aimen, *a lake Brazilian,* amen, *rain.* 'Men, *or* min, *a river in China* 'In *Huron,* aoucn is *water; Chinese,* yven, *source of a river.* In *Franche Comté,* an osier is called *avan,* as it grows beside waters. *Mar-an-on,* the American name for the river Amazon, seems to be *Mor-an,* a great flowing stream, with *on,* an Indian adjection

AMHAIRC, *v.* Look, see, behold, observe, regard *Pret a.* dh' amhairc, *looked, fut. aff. a* amhaircidh, *shall or will look,* amhairc thairis, *overlook, take no notice of.*—*Stew. Pro.* Amhaircidh mi oirbh, *I will regard you, or have respect unto you.*

† AMHANTAS, ais, *s. m.* Royal privilege; good luck.

† AMHAON, *s.* Twins; plurality.

† AMHAR, air, *s. m* A vessel for holding malt; music.

AMHARAG, *s. f* Mustard; also sweet marjoram *Lat.* amar-us, *bitter, and* amaracus, *sweet marjoram.*

† AMHARC, airc, *s m* A fault.

AMHARC, airc, *s m* A look; a looking, viewing, observing, inspecting; a look, a view; sight, observation, beholding, inspection.

AMHARC, (ag), *pr. part* of amhairc. Looking, viewing, observing, inspecting, beholding.

AMHARCHOLL, *s* Apthongs —*Shaw.*

AMHARTAN, ain, *s. m.* Fortune, luck, prosperity; also a lucky person.

AMHARTANACH, *a* Fortunate, lucky, prosperous. *Com.* and *sup.* amhartanaiche, *more, or, most fortunate.*—*Stew. Deut*

AMHARTANACHD, *s. f.* (*from* amhartan.) Good fortune; a course of good fortune, prosperity.

AMHARUS, uis, *s. m.* (*Ir.* amharus.) Doubt, suspicion, distrust. Fuidh amharus, *in doubt, suspected,* fuidh amharus umaibh, *in doubt about you.*—*Stew Gal.* Gun amharus, *without doubt, indeed;* am bi thusa gun amharus a' d' righ? *wilt thou be indeed a king?*—*Stew. Gen.*

AMHARUSACH, *a.* Distrustful, suspicious, doubtful; ambiguous. Deasboireachd amharusach, *doubtful disputation.*—*Stew Rom* *Com* and *sup.* amharusaiche, *more or most suspicious. Ir. id.*

AMHARUSACHADH, aidh, *s. m.* A mistrusting, a doubting.

AMHARUSACHD, *s. f.* (*from* amharus.) Distrustfulness, suspiciousness, doubtfulness.

AMHARUSAICH, *v.* Mistrust, suspect, doubt. *Pret. a.* dh' amharusaich; *fut. aff. a.* amharusaichidh.

AMHAS, ais, *s. m* (*Ir* amhas, *wild*) A madman; a wild ungovernable man; also a dull, stupid person. *N. pl.* amhasan.

AMHASACH, *a.* (*from* amhas.) Wild, ungovernable; like a madman; also dull, stupid. *Com.* and *sup.* amhasaiche, *more or most wild.*

AMHASAG, aig, *s. m* A foolish female. *N. pl.* amhasagan. *Ir.* amhasag.

† AMHASAN, ain, *s m.* A sentry.

AMHASAN, *n pl* of amhas

AMHGHAIR, *gen. sing.* of amhghar; which see.

AMHGHAR, air, *s. m* (*Lat* angor. *W.* avar. *Ir.* amhgar.) Affliction, anguish, trouble, sorrow, distress, adversity, calamity. Dh' amhairc e air m' amhghar, *he looked on my affliction.—Stew. Gen.* Am tharruingeas ar n-amhghar gu ceann, *a time which shall draw our troubles to a close.—Mac Lach.*

AMHGHARACH, *a.* (*from* amhghar.) Distressed, distressful, troublous; calamitous. *Com.* and *sup.* amhgharaiche, *more or most distressful.*

AMHGHARAICHE, *s. m.* A distressed person; one who has long been in distress.

AMHGHARAICHE, *a.; com.* and *sup.* of amhgharach.

† AMHLABHAIR, *a.* Mute, dumb, speechless. *Corn.* anlavar.

AMHLADH, aidh, *s. m.* A duplicate; a copy; a transcript.

AMHLAIR, *s. m.* A fool, an idiot; a brutish man; a boor. Sparradh tu céill san amhlair, *thou wouldst drive wisdom into a fool.—R. N. pl.* amhlairean.

AMHLAIREACH, *a.* Foolish; brutal; like an idiot; boorish. *Com.* and *sup.* amhlairiche.

AMHLAIREACHD, *s. f.* (*from* amhlair.) Foolishness; brutality; boorishness.

AMHLAISG, *s. f.* Bad beer; taplash.

AMHLAISGEACH, ich, *s. m.* A brewer of bad beer; also, adjectively, insipid or weak as bad beer.

AMHLUADH, aidh, *s. m.* Confusion; trouble; astonishment. Amhluadh air na sagairtibh, *astonishment on the priests.—Stew. O. T.* Is amhluadh e, *it is confusion.—Stew. Lev.* Air an amhluadh cheudna, *in like manner.—Stew. Is.*

AMHLUAIDH, *gen. sing.* of amhluadh.

AMHLUIDH, and AMHLUI', *adv.* As, like as, in like manner, resembling, so. Amhlui' mar shruth a ruitheas bras, *like as a stream that runs amain.—Sm.* Ni h-amhluidh sin a bhios na daoine peacach, *not so shall be the wicked men.—Id.*

AMHNARACH, *a.* Shameless, impudent.

† AMHNAS, ais, *s. m.* Impudence, shamelessness.

† AMHRA, ai, *s. m.* A dream; a poem; a sword-hilt.—*Ir.*

† AMHRA, *a.* Great, noble, good; dark.

† AMHRADH, aidh, *s. m.* Mourning, wailing, lamentation.

† AMHRAN, ain, *s. m.* A song.

AMHRAN, *s. pl.* Eyelids. *W.* amrant. Written also *abhran*, and *fabhran*.

AMHUIL, *adv.* (*W.* evel. *Corn.* avel. *Arm.* hanvel, evel, *and* eval.) Like, resembling, as, in like manner, so, such as. Amhuil ceòl tannais ag éiridh air cuile na Léig mall, *like the strain of a ghost rising amid the reeds of slumbering Lego.—Ull.* Amhuil sin, *so, in like manner.—Stew. Rom.* Amhuil tonn air tràigh, *like a wave on the shore.—Ull.* Amhuil mar so, *even as this, just like this. Armoric,* evel ma so. Amhuil mar an duine so, *just like this man. Armoric,* evel ma zeo den.

† AMHUIL, *v.* Spoil, plunder.

AMHUINN, *s. f.* An oven; a furnace. Amhuinn dheataich, *a furnace of smoke.—Stew. O. T. Germ.* offen. *Goth.* auhn.

AMLACH, *a.* Curled; having ringlets; flowing as hair; tressy. Falt amlach or-bhuidh, *curled yellow locks.—Fingalian Poem. Com.* and *sup.* amlaiche.

AMLADH, aidh, *s. m.* A stop, hinderance, impediment, interruption.

AMLAG, aig, *s. f.* A curl, a ringlet. *N. pl.* amlagan.

AMLAGACH, *a.* Curled; tressy; full of ringlets. Amlagach, cleachdach, *curled and tressy.—Macint.*

AMRAIDH, *s. f.* A cupboard. *Ir.* amri. *Fr.* armoirie. *Lat.* armarium.

AMUIGH, *adv.* Out, without. An taobh amuigh, *the outside.*

† AMUS, uis, *s. m.* An ambush, surprise; sudden onset; also leisure.—*Ir.*

AMUSACH, aich, *s. m.* One who is punctual to an appointment. *N. pl.* amusaich.

† AMUSACH, *a.* (*from* àmus.) Of or pertaining to an ambush.

AN, *def. art.* (*Corn.* an. *Ir.* an.) The. An oidhche dhubhradh, *the gloomy night.—Oss. Com.* An steud each san t-sliabh, *the war-horse in the hill.—Id. An* is also written *'n*, as, 'n t-àl a tha ri teachd, *the generation to come;* an t-eun, *the bird;* the other *def. art.* is *am*, which is used before words beginning with *b, p, f, m*, not aspirated; in other instances *an* is used.

AN, *prep. for* ann. In. Mar dharraig an gleann, *like an oak in a valley.—Oss. Fing.*

AN, *priv. particle.* Not; equivalent to the English *un.* As, an-aoibhinn, *joyless.* In the Coptic tongue, *an* means *not. Arm.* an, *a priv. particle. Gr.* αν, and ανυ, *without. Old Fr.* ana, *without. Old Sax.* and *Old Germ.* an, *a priv. particle. Eng.* un, *a priv. particle.*

AN, *an intensative particle,* as, antighearnas, *tyranny.*

AN, *interrog. particle.* An d' thig iad? *will they come?* An d' fhuair thu i, mar eal' air chuantai? *found you her like a swan on the deep?—Oss. Conn. An* is often written *'n*, as, 'n d' thig thu? *wilt thou come?*

† AN, *s. m.* (*W.* and *Ir.* an. *Old Swedish,* ana, *water.*) An element; a principle; water.

From *An* are derived the names of a great variety of rivers throughout Europe; as, *Anio*, in Italy; *Anemo*, near Ravenna; *Anapus*, in Sicily, in Illyria, and in Chaonia; *Anaurus* in Thessaly; and many others.

A great antiquary observes, that there is a striking resemblance between many words in the Celtic and Darien languages which might give rise to very useful disquisition. *Antilles*, is a general name for those islands which lie beyond Bermudas, towards the gulph of Mexico, including the Lucayan, Bahama, and Caribbees; "and it signifies," says he, "*water lands*, from † an, *water*, and tealla, *land.*" There is certainly much acuteness, and seemingly much truth, in this observation; for it will be found that, in many languages, the word which signifies *island*, means also *water land*: what is *insula*, for example, but *unda-solum?* undergoing, in the course of time, the following changes:—*undasol, unasol*, by transposition, *unsola*, and lastly *insula*, an island.

AN, *priv. and intens. particle.*

† AN, *a.* Still; pleasant; pure; noble; true; swift. *Ir.*

† AN, ain, *s. m.* A falsehood; also a planet. Hence comes luan, [which, by metathesis, is the Latin luna] *moon*; being compounded of luath, *swift*, and an, *planet*.

AN, *poss. pron.* Their. Na dichuimhnich an ùir, *forget not their dust.—Oss. Temo.*

† ANA, *s.* Riches; fair weather; a silver cup.

ANA, *priv.* and *intens. particle;* sometimes used for *an*, as, anameasarach, *immoderate*.

ANABAICH, *a.* See ANABUICH.

ANABAISTEACH, ich, *s. m.* (*from* an, *intens. and* baisteach.) An anabaptist. *N. pl.* anabaistiche.

ANABAN, *s.* Excess, superfluity, too much, redundance; rioting; written also *anabhar;* which see.

ANABARRACH, *a.* Excessive, superfluous, exceeding; shocking, terrible. Meudaichidh mi thu ga h-anabarrach, *I will increase you exceedingly.—Stew. Gen. Com.* and *sup.* anabarraiche, *more or most excessive;* ni 's ro anabarraiche, *much more exceeding.*

ANABAS, ais, *s. m.* Refuse, dregs, offscouring.

ANABASACH, *a.* Full of dregs; muddy. *Com.* and *sup.* anabasaiche.

ANABASACHD, *s. f.* The state of being full of dregs; muddiness.

ANABEACHD, *s. f.* (ana, *intens. and* beachd.) A strange fancy; a wild idea; ambition.

ANABEACHDAIL, *a.* Fanciful; wild; chimerical; haughty; ambitious.

ANABEACHDALACHD, *s. f.* Fancifulness; wildness; haughtiness; ambitiousness.

Anabharr, *s.* Excess, superfluity, too much, redundance; rioting. Ri h-anabharr, *going to excess.*

Ana-bhiorach, aich, *s. m.* (*from* ana, *intens. and* biorach, *sharp.*) A small venomous insect.

Ana-bhiorach, *a.* (*from* ana, *intens. and* biorach, *sharp.*) Very sharp, very pointed.

Anablas, ais, *s. m.* (ana, *priv. and* blas.) Tastelessness, insipidity. Anablas t-uirghioll, *the insipidity of thy eloquence.*—*Old Song.*

Anablasda, *a.* Insipid, tasteless. Deoch anablasta, *an insipid drink.*

Ana-blasdachd, *s. f.* Insipidness, tastelessness.

Anabrais, *s. f.* Lust.—*Macd.*

Anabuich, *a.* (an, *priv. and* abuich.) Unripe, raw; premature; abortive. Fion-dhearcan anabuich, *unripe grapes.*—*Stew. Job.* Torrachas anabuich, *a fœtus, an untimely birth, an embryo.*—*Stew. Job.* and *Eccles.*

Anabuidh. See **Anabuich.**

Anabuidheachd, *s. f.* (an, *priv. and* abuidheachd.) Unripeness, crudity, immaturity, abortiveness.

† **Anac**, aic, *s. m.* A wound.

Anacail, *s. f.* Quietness, tranquillity, repose; preservation, safety. *Ir.*

Anacail, *v.* Preserve, deliver, save, protect, secure. *Pret. a.* dh' anacail, *delivered; fut. aff. a.* anacailidh.

Anacainnt, *s. f.* (ana, *intens. and* cainnt.) Abusive language; ribaldry; blasphemy.—*Stew. Eph. ref.*

Anacainnteach, *a.* Abusive in speech; prone to ribaldry; blasphemous. Gu h-anacainnteach, *abusively.*

Anacair, *s. f.*; more properly *anshocair;* which see.

Anacaithteach, *a.* Extravagant, wasteful, prodigal. *Com.* and *sup.* anacaithtiche.

Anacaithtiche, *s. m.* A spendthrift, a prodigal.

Anacaitheadh, eidh, **Anacaitheamh**, eimh, *s. m.* and *f.* Extravagance, prodigality, profusion, waste; riot. Fear na h-anacaitheadh, *the waster.*—*Stew. Pro.* Thaobh anacaitheimh, *on account of riot.*—*Stew. Tit.*

† **Anacal**, ail, *s. m.* A quiet person.—*Shaw.*

Anacaladh, **Anacladh**, aidh, *s. m.* A preserving; a delivering; preservation; deliverance.

Anacaladh, **Anacladh**, (ag), *pr. part.* of anacail. Preserving, saving, securing, protecting.

Anaceart, *a.* (ana, *priv. and* ceart.) Unjust, impartial, iniquitous, unfair. Gniomh anaceart, *an unjust deed.*

Anaceartas, ais, *s. m.* (ana, *priv. and* ceartas. Injustice, iniquity, oppression, unfairness, partiality.

Anaceist, *s. f.* A puzzle, a riddle; a difficulty, dilemma.

† **Anach**, aich, *s. m.* A path; also a washing, a cleansing.

† **Anachain**, *s. f.* Danger, peril, hazard, misfortune, crisis.

† **Anachan**, ain, *s. m.* One who keeps in the way; an intruder.

† **Anachrach**, *a.* Full of pity, compassionate.

† **Anachradh**, aidh, *s. m.* A wretch, an object of pity.

† **Anachras**, ais, *s. m.* Pity, compassion.

Anachaoin, *v.* Lament, deplore to excess. *Pret. a.* dh' anachaoin.

Anachaoineadh, idh, *s. f.* Excessive weeping, wailing.

Anachinnteach, *a.* Uncertain, unsure.

Anachruas, ais, *s. m.* Avarice, extreme avarice.

Anachuram, aim, *s. m.* Care, anxiety.

Anachùramach, *a.* (ana, *intens. and* curamach.) Anxious, solicitous, over-anxious. Gu h-anachuramach, *over-anxiously.*

Ana-cinnte, *s. f.* (ana, *priv. and* cinnte.) Uncertainty.

Anachleachd, *s. m.* Inexperience. Is mor d' anachleachd, *great is thy inexperience.*

Anacneasda, **Anacneasta**, *a.* (ana, *priv. and* cneasta.) Inhuman, cruel, unjust, perverse. Le beul anacneasta, *with a perverse mouth.*—*Stew. Pro.*

Anacneasdachd, **Anacneastachd**, *s. f.* Inhumanity, cruelty, perverseness.—*Stew. Pro. ref.*

Anacothrom, oim, *s. f.* Injustice, violence, oppression, unfairness, disadvantage. Luchd-anacothrom, *oppressors.*—*Stew. Cor. ref.*

Anacothromach, *a.* (ana, *priv. and* cothromach.) Unjust, violent, oppressive, unfair. Gu h-anacothromach, *oppressively.*

Anacreideach, ich, *s. m.* (*for* anacreidimheach.) A sceptic, infidel, unbeliever. An lathair nan anacreideach, *before the unbelievers.*—*Stew.* 1 *Cor.*

Anacreideach, *a.* (an, *priv. and* creidimheach.) Sceptical, unbelieving. Bean anacreideach, *an unbelieving wife.*—*Stew.* 1 *Cor.*

Anacreidimh, *s. f.* (ana, *priv. and* creidimh.) Infidelity, unbelief, scepticism. *Ir.* aincreideamh.

Anacriosd, *s.* Antichrist. Thig an t-anacriosd, *Antichrist shall come.*—*Stew.* 1 *John.*

Anacriosdachd, *s. f.* (*contr. for* anacriosduigheachd.) Paganism, heathenism, infidelity, irreligion.

Anacriosduidh, *s. m.* A heathen, pagan, infidel.

Anacriosduigheachd, *s. f.* ana, *priv. and* criosduidheachd. See **Anacriosdachd.**

Anacuimse, *s. f.* (ana, *priv. and* cuimse.) Vastness, immensity; immoderateness, intemperateness. Fear na h-ana-cuimse, *an intemperate man.*

Anacuimseach, *a.* (ana, *priv. and* cuimseach.) Vast, immense; immoderate, intemperate. Gu h-anacuimseach, *immoderately.*

Anacuimseachd, *s. f.* (ana, *priv. and* cuimseachd.) Immenseness; immoderateness, intemperateness.

Ana-cul, *s. f.* (ana, *priv. and* cul.) A lean condition of body. Is baileach a chaith gu h-anacul, *how very lean you have become!*

Anaculach, *a.* Lean, thin, slender. *Comp.* and *sup.* anaculaiche, *more or most lean.*

Anaghlais, *s. f.* Hog-wash.—*Shaw.*

Anaghnàth, *s. m.* (ana, *priv. and* ghnàth.) Bad custom; irregular habit; innovation. *N. pl.* anaghnathana.

Anagnàthach, *a.* (ana, *priv. and* gnàthach.) Unusual, not customary, irregular. *Com.* and *sup.* anagnathaiche, *more or most unusual.*

Anagnàthana, *n. pl.* of anagnàth. Bad customs. *D. pl.* anagnathanaibh.

Anagoireas, eis, *s. m.* (ana, *priv. and* goireas.) Excess, want of moderation; inconvenience. Chaidh e gu h-anagoireas, *he went to excess.*

Anagoireasach, *a.* Excessive, immoderate; inconvenient. *Com.* and *sup.* anagoireasaiche, *more or most excessive.*

Anagoireasachd, *s. f.* Excessiveness, immoderateness.

Anail, *gen.* anaile *and* analach, *s. f.* (*Ir.* anal.) Breath, breeze, air. A caoidh air anail na gaoithe, *her moan on the breath of the winds.*—*Oss. Derm.* Anail nan speur, *the breath of the skies,* i. e. *wind.*—*Oss. Fin. and Lor.* Anail a shròin, *the breath of his nostrils.*—*Stew. Job.* Blas a h-analach, *the smell of her breath;* leig t-anail, *draw your breath, take rest;* leigibh ur n-anail, *rest yourselves.*—*Stew. Gen.* Gabh t-anail, *take rest.* *Corn.* anal *and* anadl. *W.* anadyl, *breath of life.* *Swed.* andhal, *a breathing hole.*

Anaim, *gen.* and *voc. sing.* of anam. Anaim chrin air d' ais, *back, thou little soul.*—*Oss. Fin. and Lor.*

AN-AIMSIR, *s. f.* (an, *priv. and* aimsir.) Unfavourable weather; tempest; improper time. *W.* anamser.

ANAIMSIREIL, *a.* (an, *priv. and* aimsireil. Unseasonable, ill-timed. *W.* anamserawl.

† ANAITHNE, *s. m.* (an, *priv. and* aithne.) A private man, an obscure man.

† ANAITHNICHTE, *a.* Unknown, obscure, unnoticed.

A NALL, *adv.* Hither, to this side; over, from the other side. *Ir.* an'all.

AN-AM, *s. m.* (an. *priv. and* am.) Unseasonable time, unseasonableness.

ANAM, aim, *s. m.* (*Gr.* ανεμ-ος. *Lat.* anim-us. *Fr.* âme. *Ir.* anam.) The soul; life; spirit; love. Is aoibhinn d' anam a'd neòil, *joyous is thy soul in thy clouds.—Oss. Trath.* Teich airson t-anam, *escape for thy life.—Stew. Gen.* Anam fàis, *a vegetative soul;* anam fàsmhor, *a vegetative soul.—Macd.* Anam reusonta, *a reasonable soul;* anam mothachail, *a sensitive soul.* Air m' anam, *on my soul.*

AN-AMACH, *a.* Late; unseasonable. *Com.* and *sup.* anamaiche. Gu h-anamach, *unseasonably.*

ANAMADACH, *a.* (*from* anam.) Lively, sprightly; having soul, life, or animal spirits.

ANAMADAIL, *a.* (*from* anam.) Lively, sprightly; having soul, or life, or spirits.—*Macint.*

ANAMAIN, *gen.* and *voc. sing.* of anaman.

ANAMAN, ain, *s. m.* (*dim. of* anam.) A little soul. Anamain chrìne nan gniomh neoghlic, *thou little soul of deeds unwise.—Mac Lach.* An t-anaman truagh, *the poor soul;* anaman dé, *a butterfly.*

ANAMAN-DÉ, *s. m.* A butterfly. Na h-anamain de, *the butterflies.*

ANAMANTA, *a.* (*from* anaman.) Full of soul, of life, or animal spirits.

ANAM-CHARA, *s. m.* A bosom friend.

ANAM-CHARAID, *s. m.* A bosom friend. *N. pl.* anamchairdean.

† ANAM-CHAIDH, *a.* Brave.

ANAMEASARRA, ANAMEASARACH, *a.* Intemperate, immoderate, vast, licentious. Caitheamh anameasarach, *immoderate expense or extravagance.*

ANAMEASARRACHD, *s. f.* Intemperateness, immoderateness, vastness, licentiousness, excess.

ANAMÉINEACH, *a.* Perverse, stubborn, malicious. *Com.* and *sup.* anaméiniche.

ANAMEINEACHD, *s. f.* Perverseness, stubbornness, maliciousness.—*Stew. Rom. ref.*

† ANAMHACH, *a.* Lively, sprightly.

† ANAMHAIN, *s. m.* A panegyrist.

ANAMHARUS, uis, *s. m.* Extreme distrust or suspicion. Buailteach dh' anamharus, *liable to extreme distrust.—Macfar.*

ANAMHARUSACH, *a.* (an, *intens. and* amharusach.) Suspicious, jealous, extremely suspicious, extremely jealous. *Com.* and *sup.* anamharusaiche, *more or most jealous.*

ANAMHIANN, *s.* (ana, *intens. and* miann.) *N. pl.* anamhiannan; *dat. pl.* anamhiannaibh. Sensuality, lust. Fear anamhiann, *a sensualist;* luchd anamhiann, *sensualists;* anamhiann na feòla, *the lusts of the flesh.—Stew. N. T.*

ANAMHIANNACH, *a.* (ana, *intens. and* miannach.) *Ir.* anbhianach. Sensual, lustful, carnal. Fonn anamhiannach, *sensual desire, lust of concupiscence.—Stew.* 1 *Thess. Com.* and *sup.* anamhiannaiche, *more or most sensual.*

ANAMHRUS, uis, *s. m.* See ANAMHARUS.

ANAMHRUSACH, *a.* See ANAMHARUSACH.

ANAMOCH, *a.* Late, unseasonable; also the evening. Tha e anamoch, *it is late, he is late;* is binn guth Laoire san anamoch, *sweet at evening is the voice of Lora.—Oss. Taura.*

ANAMIANN, *s. m.* (an, *intens. and* miann.) Sensuality, lust; written also *anamhiann.*

ANAMIANNACH, *a.* (an, *intens. and* miannach.) Sensual, lustful, carnal; written also *anamhiannach.*

ANAOBHACH, *a.* (an, *priv. and* aobhach.) Cheerless, joyless, gloomy. Anaobhach gun solus do chiùilsa, *joyless, without the light of thy song.—Oss. Taura. Com.* and *sup.* anaobhaiche, *more or most joyless.*

ANAOIBHINN, *s.* (an, *priv. and* aoibhinn.) Woe, grief. Is anaoibhinn dhasan, *woe unto him.—Stew. Jer.* Is anaoibhinn duit, *woe unto thee.—Stew. Matt. Ir. id.*

ANAOIBHINN, ANAOIBHNEACH, *a.* Joyless, mournful, unhappy. Anaoibhinn airson mhic Dhuibhne, *mournful for the son of Duno.—Oss. Derm.*

ANAOIS, *s. f.* (an, *priv. and* aois.) Non-age, minority.

ANART, airt, *s. m.* Linen. Anart grinn, *fine linen;* anart bùird, *table linen;* anart gealaichte, *bleached linen;* anart glas, *dowlass;* anart canaich, *fustian.*

† ANASDA, *a.* Stormy.—*Shaw.*

† ANASGAR, *a.* Restless; irksome.

† ANASGARACHD, *s. f.* Restlessness; irksomeness.

A NASGUIDH, *a.* Gratis; for nothing; as a present; more frequently 'nasguidh; which see.

ANÀTHACH, *a.* Fierce; fearless. Gu h-aigeantach anathach, *in a joyous and fearless manner.—Old Song.*

ANBARRACH, *a.* Exceeding, excessive, overmuch; awful, terrible. Le ball-chrith anbarraich, *with exceeding [dismay] trembling.—Stew. Gen.* Written also *anbharrach.*

† ANBHAIL, *a.* Shameless, haughty,

† ANBHAL, *a.* Prodigious.—*Shaw.*

ANBHANN, *a.;* more properly *anfhann;* which see.

ANBHARRACH, *a.* (an, *intens. and* barrach, *topped.*) Exceeding, excessive, overmuch; awful, terrible. Anbharrach fireanta, *overmuch righteous.—Stew. Ecc. Com.* and *sup.* anbharraiche, *more or most excessive;* ni 's ro anbharraiche, *much more excessive.*

ANBHARRAICHE, *a.; com.* and *sup.* of anbharrach.

ANBHÀS, ais, *s. m.* (an, *intens. and* bhàs.) A sudden death; a shocking death; a catastrophe.

ANBHÀTHADH, aidh, *s. m.* A deluge, inundation; a melancholy drowning.

ANBHLAS, ais, *s. m.* (an, *priv. and* blas.) A bad taste, an insipid taste. *W.* anmlas.

ANBHOCHD, *a.* (an, *intens. and* bochd, *poor.*) Extremely poor.

ANBHOCHDUINN, *s. m.* (an, *intens. and* bochduinn.) Extreme poverty; extreme misfortune.

† ANBHROD, oid, *s. m.* A tyrant.

† ANDACH, aich, *s. m.* Wrath, anger; evil.

ANDÀN, *a.* (an, *intens. and* dàn.) Impudent; presumptuous. *Com.* and *sup.* àndaine.

ANDÀNADAS, ais, *s. m.* (an, *intens. and* dànadas.) Impudence, presumption.

† ANDADH, *a.* Just.

AN DÉ, *adv.* Yesterday. Air bhò 'n dé, *the day before yesterday;* an diugh san dé, *to-day, and yesterday.*

AN DEIDH, *adv.* In love; fond; desirous. Tha e 'n deidh oirre, *he is fond of her;* an deidh air an òl, *fond of drinking;* written *'n deidh,* when a vowel precedes.

AN DEIGH, *adv.* After; behind. An deigh an duine sin, *behind that man;* 'mo dheigh, *behind me;* 'na dheigh, *behind him;* n'a deigh, *behind her;* nan deigh, *behind them;* written *'ndeigh,* when a vowel precedes.

AN DEIGH-LAIMH, *a.* Afterwards; after-hand; behind-hand. Written *'n deigh laimh,* when a vowel precedes.

An-deurach, *a.* Mournful; tearful; weeping excessively; causing excessive grief.

Andeistinn, *s. f.* Squeamishness; loathsomeness.

An-deistinneach, *a.* Squeamish; loathsome.

Andiadh'achd, *s. f.; contr. for* andiadhaidheachd.

Andiadhaidh, Andiadhuigh, *a.* (an, *priv. and* diadhaidh.) Ungodly, impious, profane.

Andiadhaidheachd, Andiadhuidheachd, *s. f.* Ungodliness, impiousness, profanity, irreligion.

An diugh, *adv.* To-day. Written also *'n diugh*, when preceded by a vowel, as, thig e 'n diugh, *he will come to-day.*

Andochas, ais, *s. m.* (an, *intens. and* dòchas.) Presumption; sanguine expectation. *Ir.* andothchas.

Andochasach, *a.* (an, *intens. and* dochasach.) Presumptuous; sanguine.—*Macd. Ir.* andothchasach.

Andlighe, *s.* Illegality; injustice. Fear andlighe, *an unjust man.*

Andligheach, *a.* Illegal, unjust; also a transgressor.

Andoigh, *s. m.* (an, *priv. and* doigh.) Bad condition; bad state.

Andolas, ais, *s. m.* (an, *intens. and* dolas.) Sadness; privation of comfort.

Andolasach, *a.* (an, *intens. and* dolasach.) Sad; comfortless; sorrowful; irksome. *Com.* and *sup.* andolasaiche, *more or most sad.*

† **Andras**, ais, *s. m.* A fury; an infernal divinity.

An dràsd, *adv.* Now, at present. An dràsd 's a ris, *now and then;* more properly *an tràths.*

Andrasdaich, *adv. provincial.* Now, at present.

† **Androbhlasach**, aich, *s. m.* A spendthrift.

† **Androbhlasachd**, *s. f.* Extravagantness, prodigality.

† **Andualarasc**, *s. m.* (*Ir. id.*) The figure in rhetoric called *catachresis.*—*Shaw.*

Anduine, *s. m.* (an, *priv. and* duine.) A wicked man.—*Ir.*

† **Andul**, uil, *s. m.* Avidity.

Aneadargnaidh, *s. m.* A stranger.

Aneagal, ail, *s. m.* (an, *intens. and* eagal.) Astonishment, extreme terror.

Aneagalach, *a.* Timid; also formidable, or causing terror.

Anearb, *v.* (an, *priv. and* earb.) Distrust; suspect. *Pret. a.* dh' anearb, *distrusted.*

Anearbsa, Anearbsadh, aidh, *s. m.* Distrust, suspicion, jealousy; non-reliance.

Anearbsach, *a.* (an, *priv. and* earbsach.) Distrustful, suspicious, jealous; also causing suspicion or distrust.

Anearbsachd, *s. f.* (an, *priv. and* earbsachd.) Distrustfulness, suspiciousness.

Anfadh, aidh, *s. m.* A storm, a tempest. Anfadh cuain, *a storm at sea;* written also *anfadh.*—*Ir. id.*

Anfadhach, *a.* Stormy, tempestuous. Cuan anfadhach, *a stormy sea.*

† **Anfas**, ais, *s. m.* Fear, terror.

Anfhainne, *com.* and *sup.* of anfhann.) More or most weak. Iadsan a b' anfhainne, *those who were weaker.*—*Stew. Gen.*

Anfhainneachd, *s. f.* (an, *intens. and* fann.) Weakness, debility, infirmity.

Anfhann, *a.* (an, *intens. and* fann.) *Corn.* anvan. *W.* anfan. Weak, feeble, infirm; tender. Suilean anfhann, *tender eyes.*—*Stew. Gen. Com.* and *sup.* anfhainne.

Anfhannachadh, aidh, *s. m.* The circumstance of enfeebling, or making less strong; a weakening, a debilitating.

Anfhannachadh (ag), *pr. part.* of anfhannaich. Weakening, enfeebling, debilitating.

Anfhannachd, (an, *intens. and* fannachd.) Weakness, infirmity, debility.

Anfhannaich, *v. a.* (an, *intens.* and fannaich.) Weaken, debilitate, make infirm. *Pret. a.* dh' anfhannaich, *weakened; fut. aff. a.* anfhannaichidh, *shall weaken; fut. pass.* anfhannaichear, *shall be weakened.*

Anfhannaichidh, *fut. aff. a.* of anfhannaich. Shall or will weaken.

An-fharsuing, *a.* (an, *priv. and* farsuing.) Narrow, strait, tight.

An-fharsuingeachd, *s. f.* (an, *priv. and* farsuingeachd.) Narrowness, straitness, tightness.

Anfheillidh, *a.* (an, *priv. and* feillidh.) Loud, boisterous, rough, unhospitable, wild. Le toirm anfheillidh, *with a boisterous noise.*—*Oss. Conn.*

Anfhios, *s. m.* (an, *priv. and* fios.) Ignorance. Luchd anfhios, *ignorant people.*

Anfhiosach, *a.* (an, *priv. and* fios.) Ignorant, untaught, unlearned, illiterate. *Com.* and *sup.* anfhiosaiche.

Anfhiosrach, *a.* (an, *priv. and* fiosrach.) Ignorant; unapprized, not aware.—*Stew. Lev.*

Anfhiosrachd, *s. f.* Ignorance; the state of not being aware or apprized.

Anfhocail, *gen. sing.* of anfhocal.

† **Anfhocain**, *s. f.* Danger, hazard.

Anfhocal, ail, *s. m.* (an, *intens. and* focal.) A bad word; an improper expression; a taunt; a reproach.

Anfhoighideann, inn, *s. m.* (an, *priv. and* foighideann.) Impatience, restlessness.

Anfhoighidinneach, *a.* (an, *priv. and* foighidinneach.) Impatient, restless.

† **Anfhoralamh**, aimh, *s. m.* Constraint; danger.

† **Anfhorlan**, ain, *s. m.* Power; plundering; oppression. —*Ir.*

Anfhuras, *a.* (an, *priv. and* furas.) Not easy, difficult.

† **Ang**, aing, *s. m.* Renown; rank; a string; a twist.

† **Angach**, *a.* Full of nails.

Angadh, aidh, *s. m.* The gusset of a shirt.

Anganach, aich, *s. m.* A snare.

Angar, air, *s. m.* A stall for cattle; anger.

Angathlannach, *a.* Glittering, bright, burnished.

An-ghlaodh, *s. m.* (an, *intens. and* glaodh.) A loud shout; a piercing cry.—*Ir. id.*

Anghlaodhaich, *s.* A loud shouting, a continued loud shouting.

Anglonn, *a.* Very powerful; very strong; brave.

Anglonn, oinn, *s. m.* Adversity; danger; strength.—*Ir.*

Anglonnach, *a.* Very powerful; very strong; brave; also adverse; dangerous.

Angnath, *s. m.* See **Anaghnath**.

Angnathach, *a.* See **Anaghnathach**.

Anghradh, aidh, *s. m.* (an, *intens. and* gradh.) Great attachment, ardent love, doting fondness.

Anghradhach, *a.* Very fond, dotingly fond, ardently fond; ardently loved.

Anghradhaiche, *s. m.* A dotard; one who loves to excess.

Angrach, *a.* Angry, *provincial.*

† **Angraidh**, *s. m.* (*from* ang.) A man of rank; a ruler; nobility.

† **Angrais**, *s. m.* An engine; a machine.

Aniartas, ais, *s. m.* (an, *intens. and* iartas.) An unreasonable demand; a mandate.

An-iochd, *s. f.* (an, *priv. and* iochd.) Cruelty; want of feeling; rigour; oppression. Le h-an-iochd, *with rigour.* —*Stew. Lev.*

Aniochdar, *a.;* more properly *aniochdmhor.*

Aniochdmhoire, *com.* and *sup.* of aniochdmhor. More or most cruel.

Aniochdmhor, *a.* (an, *priv. and* iochdmhor.) Cruel, unfeeling, merciless, uncompassionate, imperious. Bha i an iochdmhor, *it was cruel.—Stew. Gen.* Creachadairean aniochdmhor, *merciless plunderers.—Macfar.*

A nios, *or,* 'nios, *adv.* Up, from below; from the east. Thig 'nios an so, *come up here.*

A nis, *or,* 'nis, *adv.* Now; at this time. Dean a nis e, *do it at this time;* a nis mata, *now then.*

† Aniudadh, *a.* Depraved.—*Shaw.*

† Aniuid, *s. f.* Error; depravity.

Anlaoch, aoich, *s. m.* (an, *intens. and* laoch.) A bloody warrior. Fo chasaibh nan anlaoch, *under the feet of the bloody warriors.—Oss. Trath.*

Anlaoich, *gen.* and *voc. sing.* and *n. pl.* of anlaoch.

Anluchd, *s. m.* A grievous weight; an oppressive burden; overweight. Fo anluchd, *oppressed.*

Anluchdaich, *v.* Overload; surcharge. *Pret. a.* dh' anluchdaich, *overloaded.*

Anmhaoin, *s.* Strife; great riches.

Anmhiann, *s.* See Anamhiann.

Anmhiannach, *a.* See Anamhiannach.

Anmhodh, *s. m.* (an, *priv. and* modh.) Disrespect; bad breeding; a bad habit.

Anmhodhail, *a.* (an, *priv. and* modhail.) Disrespectful; ill bred.

Anmhor, *a.* (an, *intens. and* mòr.) Exceeding, excessive, very great, exorbitant. Sonas anmhor, *exceeding joy.—Smith. Ir. id. Com.* and *sup.* anmhoire.

Anmhuinne, *com.* and *sup.* of anmhunn. More or most weak.

Anmhuinneachd, *s.* (*from* anmhunn.) Weakness, debility, infirmity, decrepitude, unhealthiness. Anmhuinneachd na feòla, *the weakness of the flesh.—Stew. Gal.*

Anmhunn, *a.* Weak, feeble; slender; decrepit; sickly; pliant; not stiff. Chum nan ceud thoiseach anmhunn, *to the weak elements.—Stew. Gal.*

Anmhunnachadh, aidh, *s. m.* (anmhunn.) A weakening, enfeebling.

Anmhunnachd, *s. f.* (*from* anmhunn.) Weakness, feebleness, decrepitude, unhealthiness.

Anmhunnaich, *v.* Weaken, enfeeble, enervate, make faint. *Pret. a.* dh' anmhunnaich; *fut. aff. a.* anmhunnaichidh, *shall weaken;* anmhunnaichidh e neart nan treuna, *he will weaken the strength of the strong.—Stew. Job.*

The last six words are spelt according to Dr. Stewart's orthography. See his Translation of the Scriptures, *Mat.* xxvi. 41; *Job,* xii. 21; 1 *Cor.* i. 25, &c. &c. Macfarlane's spelling is preferable; as, *anfhann,* &c.; the words being considered, as they clearly are, compounds of *fann.*

Anmoch, *a.* (an, *priv. and* moch, *early.*) Late. Bithidh tu anmoch, *you will be late. Com.* and *sup.* anmoiche.

Ammoch, oich, *s. m.* Evening; night. Madadh alluidh an anmoich, *the evening wolves.—Stew. Zeph.*

† Ann, *s. m.* A circle; a revolution. *Lat.* ann-us, *a revolution of the earth, or year;* hence also, reann (*i. e.* rè and ann) *a star,* and its diminutive reannag.

Ann, *prep.* (*Ir.* ann.) In, therein; in existence, alive. Ann fein, *in himself, with himself.—Stew. Jon.* An linn a bha ann o shean, *the race that existed of old.—Oss. Fing.* Cha 'n ann, *not, no, it is not;* bheil thu ann? *art thou there?* an d' thu th' ann? *is it you? is it you that are? are you there? is it you I see?* Is mise th' ann. A chrochair tha thu ann, *you rascal, that you are!*

Gr. εν. *Lat.* in. *Arm.* en. *Goth.* and, *and* ana. *Ir.* ann. *Teut.* an. *Bisc.* an. *Span.* en.

Ann, *comp. pron.* In him, in it. Cha 'neil ann ach an crochair, *he is but a rascal.*

† Annach, *a.* Clean.

Annad, (*for* ann tu.) In thee. *Ir.* ionnad.

† Annadh, aidh, *s. m.* Delay.

Annag, aig, *s. m.* Evil, anger, displeasure.

Annaibh, *comp. pron.* (*for* ann sibh.) In you, within you. Cha 'n eil ciall annaibh, *you have no judgment.*

Annaibhse, emphatic form of *annaibh;* which see.

Annainn, *comp. pron.* (*for* ann sin.) In us, within us; in our power. Annainn fèin, *in ourselves.*

Annam, *comp. pron.* (*for* ann mi.) In me, within me; in my power. *Ir.* ionnam.

Annamh, *a.* Few, rare, scarce, seldom; curious. See Ainneamh.

Annas, ais, *s. m.* Rarity; change for the better; perhaps *annos,* from an, *priv. and* nos, *custom.*

Annasach, *a.* (*from* annas.) Rare, unusual, strange; dainty; desirable. Nithe anasach, *dainties, rarities.—Stew. Pro. ref. Com.* and *sup.* annasaiche, *more or most rare.*

Annlan, ain, *s. m.* What the Lowland Scots call *kitchen;* that is, whatever food, as, butchers' meat, butter, cheese, eggs, &c. is taken at dinner, after broth, which forms the first course of a Scotch dinner. It expresses all the more substantial eatables, *ab ovo usque ad mala.*

An nochd, *or,* 'nochd, *adv.* To-night, this night. An nochd is an reidhir, *this night and the last.*

A nois, *or,* nois, *adv.* Now, at present, at this time. In the southern districts of the Highlands they say *a nis,* and *nis.*

Annrach, aich, *s. m.* A stranger. See Anrach.

Annrachd, *s. f.* The highest degree in poetry next the ollamh.

† Anradh, *v.* Grieve; afflict; harass.

Annradh, aidh, *s. m.* A storm, a storm at sea; also a poet next in degree to an ollamh; a boon. See Anradh.

Annsa, *and* Ansadh, *a.* (*Ir.* annsa. *Swed.* annse, *to respect.*) Dear; desirable, wished for; attached; beloved; acceptable; glad; also a love; a person beloved. Ged nach b' annsa dhi an t-òg, *though the youth was not dear to her;* b' annsa thu na dearrsa grein, *more acceptable wert thou than a sun-beam.—Oss. Derm.* Fo bhròn mu m' annsa, *mourning for my beloved.—Id.* An caladh aigh annsadh, *the joyous wished for harbour.—Old Song.* B' annsa leo sgur, *they were glad to desist.—Old Poem.*

Annsachd, *s. f.* (*from* annsa.) A person beloved. Tha m' annsachd mar-bhogha san speur, *my beloved is like a cloud in the skies.—Oss. Cathluno.* Annsachd Dhe, *the beloved one of God.—Sm. Ir.* annsacht.

Anra, ai, *s. m.* A storm, a tempest; misfortune, trouble, disaster, calamity. Anra cuain, *a storm at sea.—Oss. Gaul.* T-anra san speur, *thy trouble in the sky.—Oss. Trath.* Written also *anradh.*

Annsadh, *a.* See Annsa.

Anns, *prep.* In, within; used before the definite article. Anns an t-saoghal, *in the world.*

Annsan, *comp. pron.* (*for* ann esan.) In him.

Anrach, aich, *s. m.* (*from* anradh.) A stranger; a distressed person. Tha dorus Fhinn do 'n anrach fial, *Fingal's door is open to the stranger.—Oss.* Is i do ghnùis do 'n anrach a ghrian, *thy countenance is to the forlorn a sun.—Old Poem.*

Anrach, *a.* (*for* anradhach.) Stormy; distressed; floating; streaming, as hair in the wind. Air a chuan anrach, *on the stormy sea.—Oss. Gaul.* D' fhalt anrach, *thy streaming hair.—Ull.*

Anradh, aidh, *s. m.* (perhaps *an-thrath.*) A storm, tempest; distress, misfortune, trouble, disaster. Mac Morna 's e 'm meadhon anraidh, *the son of Morni in the midst of a tempest.—Oss. Gaul.* Theirgeadh mo dheòir nan teirgeadh gach anradh, *my tears would cease if every trouble were to vanish.—Id. N. pl.* anradhan; written also *anrath.*

Anradhach, *a.* (*from* anradh.) Stormy; distressed; also floating, streaming, as ringlets in the wind. *Com.* and *sup.* anradhaiche.

Anraidh, *gen. sing.* of anradh.

Anraidh, *a.* Distressful, sorrowful, sad. Aithris anraidh mo chreach, *the sad tale of my bereavement.—Oss. Cathula.*

Anrath, aith, *s. m.* (*perhaps* an-thrath, *from* an, *priv. and* trath, *season.*) A storm, a tempest; misfortune, calamity.

Anrathach, *a.* (*from* anrath.) Stormy; distressed; also, substantively, a distressed person.

An reidhir, *or*, **'nreidhir**, *adv.* Yesternight, last night, last evening.

Anriadh, reidh, *s. m.* (an, *intens. and* riadh.) Usury, extortion, exorbitant interest.

Anriaghailt, *s. f.* (an, *priv. and* riaghailt.) Disorder, confusion, tumult, uproar, riot; misrule, mismanagement.

Anriaghailteach, *a.* (an, *priv. and* riaghailteach.) Confusing, disordering, disordered, riotous. *Com.* and *sup.* an-riaghailtiche.

† **Anrodhach**, *a.* See **Anradhach**.

† **Anrodhaidh**, *s. m.* (*Ir. id.*) Affliction, trouble; more properly *anradh*; which see

An roir, **'nroir**, *adv.* Last night, last evening.

An-sgaineadh, eidh, *s. m.* A violent bursting; a chasm.

An-sgainteach, *a.* Apt to burst; apt to open into chasms; causing chasms. Talamh an-sgainteach, *chasing ground.*

† **Ansgairt**, *v.* Shriek aloud, cry.—*Ir. id.*

Ansgairt, *s. f.* (an, *intens. and* sgairt.) A loud shout; a piercing shriek or cry. Phill sibh le 'r n-ansgairt, *you returned with your piercing shrieks.—Oss. Gaul.* Also a thicket of brambles.

Ansgairteach, *a.* (an, *intens. and* sgairteach.) Uttering a loud shriek; shouting, shrieking; loud, piercing.

An-shamhlachd, *s. f.* (an, *priv. and* samhlachd.) Incomparability.

An-shamhluichte, *part.* Incomparable; unmatched.

Anshannt, *s. m.* (an, *intens. and* sannt.) Greed, covetousness; extreme avarice.

Anshanntach, *a.* (an, *priv. and* sanntach.) Greedy, covetous, immoderately greedy. *Com.* and *sup.* anshanntaiche, *greedier, greediest.*

Anshanntach, aich, *s. m.* (*from* anshannt.) A greedy person; a greedy gut.

Anshaoghalta, *a.* (an, *intens. and* saoghalta.) Worldly, immoderately fond of the world, worldly-minded.

Anshaoghaltachd, *s. f.* (an, *intens. and* saoghaltachd.) Worldliness, immoderate regard for the world.

Anshocair, *s. f.* (an, *priv. and* socair.) *Ir.* anacar. Distress; disease; bodily or mental trouble; restlessness; disquiet. Droch anshocair, *an evil spirit; a bad disease.—Stew. Ecc.*

Anshocrach, *a.* (an, *priv. and* socrach.) Troubled in mind or body, distressed, afflicted, restless. Sluagh anshocrach, *an afflicted people.—Stew. Zeph. Com.* and *sup.* anshocraiche, *more or most afflicted.*

Anshocraiche, *com.* and *sup.* of anshocrach; which see.

Anshogh, *s. m.* (an, *priv. and* sogh.) Misery, adversity, mischance.—*Ir. id.*

Anshoghail, *a.* Miserable, adverse, unfortunate.

Anstrogh, trogha, *s. f.* (an, *intens. and* strogh.) Prodigality, waste, extravagance; written also *anstruidhe.*

Anstroghail, *a.* Prodigal, wasteful, extravagant. Duine anstroghail, *a prodigal.*

Anstruidhe, **Anstruighe**, *s. f.* Prodigality, wastefulness, extravagance. Luchd anstruidhe, *prodigal people.*

Anstruidheachd, *s. f.* Prodigality, wastefulness, extravagance.

Anstruidheachadh, aidh, *s. m.* The act of wasting or spending extravagantly.

Anstruidheasach, **Anstruigheasach**, *a.* (an, *intens. and* struidheasach.) Profuse, prodigal, wasteful, extravagant. *Com.* and *sup.* anstruidheasaiche, *more or most profuse.*

Anstruidheasachd, *s. f.* Profuseness, prodigality, wastefulness, extravagantness.

An-tighearna, *s. m.* (an, *intens. and* tighearna,) A tyrant, a despot. A brosnuchadh nan an-tighearnan, *stirring up the tyrants.—Macfar.*

Antighearnach, *a.* Oppressive in governing, tyrannical, despotic.

Antighearnas, ais, *s. m.* (an, *intens. and* tighearnas.) Despotism, oppression, tyranny. Am fuath th' againn air antighearnas, *the hatred we have of despotism.—Macfar.*

Antogar, air, *s. m.* (an, *intens. and* togar.) An inordinate wish; ambition; an unreasonable desire.

Antogarach, **Antograch**, *a.* (an, *intens. and* togarach.) Lustful; covetous; immoderately desirous.

Antogradh, aidh, *s. m.* Lust; concupiscence; covetousness; immoderate desire.—*Stew. N. T.*

Antlachd, *s.* (an, *priv. and* tlachd.) Dislike, displeasure, disgust, dissatisfaction, discontent. Saor o bhraid 's o antlachd, *free from theft and discontent.—Macdon.*

Antlachdmhoire, *com.* and *sup.* of antlachdmhor.

Antlachdmhoireachd, *s. f.* (an, *priv. and* tlachdmhoireachd.) Disgustfulness; unpleasantness.

Antlachdmhor, *a.* Disgustful; unpleasant; causing discontent. *Com.* and *sup.* antlachdmhoire.

Antlas, ais, *s. m.* A ludicrous trick, a frolic: also a cattle fair.

Antlasach, *a.* (*from* antlas.) Frolicsome; also a frolicsome fellow.

Antoile, *s. f.* (an, *intens. and* toile.) Lust, inordinate desire; ambition. Fear na h-antoile, *the ambitious man;* ioma gné do antoilibh, *many sorts of lusts.—Stew. Tit. Ir. id.*

Antoileach, *a.* (an, *intens. and* toileach.) Lustful; ambitious; inordinately desirous. *Com.* and *sup.* antoiliche.

Antoileil, *i. e.* antoil-amhuil, *a.* (an, *intens. and* toileil.) Wilful, obstinate, perverse. Gu h-antoileil, *perversely.*

† **Antomhail**, *s. f.* Gluttony.—*Shaw.*

† **Antomhailtear**, ir, *s. m.* A glutton. *N. pl.* antomhailtearan.

Antràth, *s.* (an, *priv. and* trath.) Unfavourable weather; stormy weather; a storm. This perhaps is the proper orthography, and not *anfadh, onfadh*, and *anradh.*

Antrathach, *a.* (*from* antrath.) Unseasonable, untimely, abortive.

Antrocair, *s. f.* (an, *priv. and* trocair.) Mercilessness, cruelty, want of compassion. Fear antrocair, *a merciless man.*

Antrocaireach, *a.* (an, *priv. and* trocaireach.) Merciless, cruel. *Com.* and *sup.* antrocairiche.

Antrom, *a.* (an, *intens. and* trom.) Grievous to be borne, intolerable; oppressive; atrocious. *Com.* and *sup.* antruime.

Antromachadh, aidh, *s. m.* The act or circumstance of aggrieving, aggravating, making heavy or burdensome.

Antromachadh (ag), *pr. part.* of antromaich; which see.

ANTROMAICH, *v.* Oppress; aggrieve, aggravate; overload; make insufferably heavy. *Pret. a.* dh' antromaich, *oppressed; fut. aff. a.* antromaichidh, *shall make heavy;* dh' antromaich e ar cuinge, *he made our yoke heavy.—Stew.* 1 *K.*

ANTROMAICHEAR, *fut. pass.* of antromaich. Shall be made heavy.

ANTROMAICHIDH, *fut. aff. a.* of antromaich; which see.

ANTRUACANTA, *a.* (an, *priv. and* truacanta.) Pitiless, merciless.

ANTRUACANTA, *a.* (an, *intens. and* truacanta.) Compassionate, merciful.

ANTRUAS, ais, *s. m.* (an, *priv. and* truas.) Want of pity, or of mercy.

ANTRUAS, ais, *s. m.* (an, *intens. and* truas.) Great pity, sympathy.

ANTRUIME, *com.* and *sup.* of antrom.

ANTRUIME, *s. f.* (an, *intens. and* truime.) Oppression; burdensomeness. Luchd na h-antruime, *oppressors.*

ANUAIBHIR, *s. f.* Excessive pride. Luchd na h-anuaibhir, *the excessively proud.*

ANUAIBHREACH, *a.* (an, *priv. and* uaibhreach.) Not proud, humble, lowly. *Com.* and *sup.* anuaibhriche.

ANUAIBHREACH, *a.* (an, *intens. and* uaibhreach.) Proud, haughty; proud to excess. *Com.* and *sup.* an-uaibhriche.

ANUAILLE, *s. f.* (an, *priv. and* uaille.) Want of pride, humility, affability.

ANUAILLE, *s. f.* (an, *intens. and* uaille.) Extreme pride. Air mhor anuaille 's air bheag céill, *proud and silly.—Old Song.*

ANUAIR, *s. f.* (an, *intens. and* uair.) A storm; unfavourable weather; mischief.

AN UAIR, *adv.* When; often written and almost always pronounced *'nuair,* and *nur.—Ir. id.*

† ANUAIS, *a.* Fierce, barbarous.—*Shaw.*

ANUALLACH, *a.* (an, *priv. and* uallach.) Not haughty; humble-minded.

ANUALLACH, *a.* (an, *intens. and* uallach.) Haughty, proud; airy, supercilious.

ANUALLACH, aich, *s. f.* (an, *intens. and* uallach, *burden.*) An oppressive burden; oppression; hardship.

A NUAS, *adv.* Down, from above, from the west. Thig a nuas an so, *come down here.—Ir. id.*

ANUASAL, *a.* (an, *priv. and* uasal.) Mean, ignoble; not proud. *Ir.* anuasal.

ANUINN, *s.* The eaves of a house.

AN UIRIDH, *adv.* An uair a ruith, *last year.* Written also *'nuiridh.* See UIRIDH.

ANUR, *s. m.* (an, *priv. and* ur.) *W.* anwr. A mean, sorry person; a wretch, miscreant.

† AOBH, aoibh, *s. m.* Similitude.

AOBHACH, *a.* Joyous, glad, cheerful; also beautiful. Ceud ogan aobhach, *a hundred joyous youths.—Orr.* B' aobhach mise, *glad was I.—Macint. Com.* and *sup.* aobhaiche, *more or most joyous.*

AOBHACHD, *s. f.* Joyfulness; also beauty.

AOBHAICHE, *com.* and *sup.* of aobhach. More or most glad.

AOBHAIR, *gen. sing.* of aobhar.

AOBHAR, air, *s. m.* (*Corn.* ara.) Cause, subject, reason, matter. C' àit am bheil aobhar uaill? *where is there cause for pride?—Orr.* Thuit iad an deagh aobhar, *they fell in a good cause.—Old Poem.* An t-aobhar mu 'n d' thainig sinn, *the reason why we came.—Old Poem.* Air an aobhar sin, *therefore, for that reason;* aobhar ghàir, *laughing-stock;* aobhar bhròin, *cause for sorrow;* aobhar ghuil, *cause for weeping;* bheir mise aobhar ghuil dhuit, *I will give you reason to cry;* aobhar eagail, *a cause of terror;* aobhar ghearain, *a cause of complaint.*

AOBRAINN, *gen. sing.* of aobrann.

AOBRAINNEAN, *n. pl.* of aobrann.

AOBRANN, ainn, AOBRUNN, uinn, *s. m.* The ancle, the ancle-bone, the ancle-joint. Gu ruig na h-aobranna, *to the ancles;* as, an aobrann, *out of the ancle-joint.—Stew. Ezek. N. pl.* aobrainnean, aobranna, *and* aobrunnan, *ancles.—Stew. Acts.*

AOBRANNA, AOBRUNNAN, *n. pl.* of aobrann, *and* aobrunn.

AO-COLTACH, *a.* (ao, *priv. and* coltach.) Unlike, dissimilar; improbable, unlikely. See EU-COLTACH. *Com.* and *sup.* ao-coltach.

AO-COLTACHD, *s. f.* Unlikeness, dissimilarity; unlikeliness, improbability. See EUCOLTACHD.

AODACH, aich, *s. m.* Cloth, clothes, dress. Aodach leapach, *bed clothes;* aodach canaich, *cotton cloth, calico;* aodach olladh, *woollen cloth;* aodach sassunnach, *English cloth;* aodach lìn, *linen cloth;* written also *eudach.*

AODACHADH, aidh, *s. m.* A clothing, a dressing, a covering.

AODAICH, *gen. sing.* of aodach.

AODAICH, *v.* Clothe, dress, cover. *Pret. a.* dh' aodaich, *clothed; fut. aff. a.* aodaichidh, *shall or will clothe.*

AODAICHEAR, *fut. pass.* of aodaich. Shall or will be clothed.

AODAICHIDH, *fut. aff. a.* of aodaich. Shall or will clothe.

AODAICHTE, *p. part.* of aodaich. Clothed, clad, covered, dressed.

AODAINN, *gen. sing.* of aodann.

AODANN, ainn, *s. f.* (*Arm.* adyn.) Face, forehead, front, visage; surface. Re aodann sleibhe a leumnaich, *bounding on the face of the hill.—Oss. Trath.* As an aodann, *to the face;* clàr an aodainn, *the brow. N. pl.* aodainnean, *faces.* Written also *eudan;* which see.

AODANNACH SRÉINE, *s. m.* The front-stall of a bridle.

AODARMAN, ain, *s. m.* A bladder; properly *eutroman.*

† AODH, *s. m.* A sheep.

Though this word be seldom used separately, it is seen in composition, as in the following vocable.

AODHAIR, *s. m.* (aodh-fhear.) *Ir.* aodhaire. A shepherd; a pastor; a protector. *N. pl.* aodhairean. Tri aodhairean, *three shepherds.—Stew. Zech.* Bheir mi dhuibh aodhairean, *I will give you pastors.—Stew. G. B.* Contracted *aoir;* which see.

† AODHAIR, *s. m.* A conflagration; a fiery desolation.

AODHAIREACHD, *s. f.* The occupation of a shepherd; herding.

AODHAIREAN, *n. pl.* of aodhair. Herds; shepherds; protectors; pastors.

AODHAR, air, *s. m.* (*Lat.* ador-o.) Worship, religious reverence. Bheir sinn aodhar dha, *we will worship him.*

AODHNAIR, *s. m.* An owner; an author. *N. pl.* aodhnairean, *owners.*

AODHNAIREACHD, *s. f.* Ownership; authorship.

AO-DIONACH, *a.* (ao, *priv. and* dionach.) Leaky; not water-proof; not air-proof; not affording shelter.

AO-DIONACHD, *s. f.* Leakiness; the state of being not water-proof; the state of being not air-proof.

AO-DOCHAS, ais, *s. m.* (ao, *priv. and* dochas.) Despair, despondency.

AO-DOCHASACH, *a.* (ao, *priv. and* dochasach.) Hopeless, despairing, despondent; causing despair. *Com.* and *sup.* aodochasaiche, *more or most desperate.*

AO-DOCHASACHD, *s. f.* Despondency, melancholy, tendency to melancholy.

AODRAMAIN, *gen. sing.* and *n. pl.* of aodraman.

AODRAMAN, ain, *s. m.* A bladder; better *aotroman,* or *eutroman.*

AOG, aoig, *s. m.* Death; a ghost, spectre, skeleton. Dol aog, *dying;* neul an aoig, *the colour of death;* written also *eug:* which see.

Aogaidh, *a.* (*from* aog.) Ghastly, ghostly, spectral, death-like.

Aogail, *a.* (*i. e.* aog-amhuil.) Ghastly, ghostly, spectral, death-like.

Aogaileachd, *s. f.* (*i. e.* aog amhuileachd.) Ghastliness, ghostliness.

Aogas, ais, *s. m.* (*Gr.* εικος.) Likeness, resemblance; appearance; image, form, countenance. Aogas do bharca, *the likeness of thy bark.—Oss. Gaul.* Is cosmhuil aogas ri Dearmad, *his form is like to Dermed.—Oss. Derm.* D' aogas maiseach, *thy lovely countenance.—Stew. Song. Sol.* Written also *aogasg.*

Aogasach, *a.* (*from* aogas.) Seemly, decent, becoming; pretty, comely; of a good appearance. *Com.* and *sup.* aogasaiche, *more or most seemly.*

Aogasachd, *s. f.* (*from* aogas.) Seemliness, comeliness, decentness.

Aogasaiche, *a.*; *com.* and *sup.* of aogasach. Seemlier, seemliest.

Aogasail, *a.* (*i. e.* aogas-amhuil.) Seemly, comely, becoming; of an imposing exterior.

Aogasg, aisg, *s. m.* Appearance; resemblance. See Aogas.

† **Aogh**, *s. m.* The name Hugh.

Aognaich, *v.* (*from* aog.) Make pale or ghastly, grow pale or ghastly; disfigure. *Pret. a.* dh' aognaich, *grew pale; fut. aff. a.* aognaichidh, *shall grow pale;* aognaichidh aogas nan aonach, *the face of the hills shall grow pale.—Macfar.*

† **Aoi**, *s.* (*Ir.* aoi.) A swan; a compact; a guest or stranger; knowledge; honour; an island; a trade; a hill; a possession.

Aoibh, *s. m.* A civil look; a patrimony.

Aoibh, *a.* Pleasant, comely, joyous, courteous, cheerful. —*Ir.*

Aoibheal, eil, *s. f.* A fire; merriment, rejoicing.—*Ir.* Written more frequently *eibhle.*

Aoibhinn, *a.* Joyful, glad, cheerful, pleasant. Is aoibhinn d' anam a' d neoil, *joyous is thy soul in thy clouds.—Oss. Trath.* Oigr h aoibhinn, *ye cheerful youth.—Oss. Fin. and Lor.*

† **Aoibhle**, *s. f.* A sign, mark, omen, token.

† **Aoibhlich**, *v.* Explain an omen.

Aoibhneach, *a.* (*i. e.* aoibhinneach.) Joyful, glad, agreeable, pleasant. *Com.* and *sup.* aoibhneiche, *more or most joyful;* a toirt sgéil aoibhneich, *giving glad tidings.—Stew. Rom.*

Aoibhneas, eis, *s. m.* Joy, gladness, pleasure. Aoibhneas a shlighe, *the joy of his way.—Stew. Job.* Dean aoibhneas, *be glad;* ni t-athair aoibhneas, *thy father will be glad.—Stew. Pro.*

Aoibhneasach, *a.* (*from* aoibhneas.) Joyful, glad, causing joy. *Com.* and *sup.* aoibhneasaiche, *more or most joyful.*

Aoibhneich, *gen. sing.* of aoibhneach; which see.

Aoibhneiche, *com.* and *sup.* of aoibhneach. More or most glad.

† **Aoide**, *s. f.* A web; also a youth.—*Ir.*

Aoideach, *a.* Youthful. *Com.* and *sup.* aoidiche.

Aoideag, eig, *s. f.* A hair lace; fillet.—*Ir. id.*

† **Aoidean**, ein, *s. m.* A leak.

† **Aoideanach**, *a.* Leaky; also youthful.

Aoidhe, *s. m.* A guest, a stranger, a traveller; a skilful person. *N. pl.* aoidhean, *guests.—Ir. id.*

Aoidheach, *a.* (*from* aoidhe.) Hospitable; also a guest, a stranger; a hospitable person.

Aoidheachd, *s. f.* (*from* aoidh.) Hospitality, bounty; lodging; entertainment. Air aoidheachd, *enjoying hospitality.—Stew.* 1 *K.* Thug iad aoidheachd dhuinn, *they lodged us, they entertained us.*

Aoidhealachd, *s. f.* Hospitableness, bountifulness. Bu mhòr d' aoidhealachd, *great was thy hospitality.—Old Song.*

Aoidhean, **Aoidheanna**, *n. pl.* of aoidhe. Guests. Na h-aoidhean, *the guests.—Stew. K.*

Aoidheil, *a.* (aoidh-amhuil.) Kind, hospitable. An gasan aoidheil, *the hospitable stripling.—Old Song.*

Aoig, *gen. sing.* of aog; which see.

† **Aoigh**, *s. m.* A hero. *N. pl.* aoighean.

Aoil, *gen. sing.* of aol; which see.

† **Aoil**, *s. f.* The mouth.—*Ir. id. Bisc.* ahol.

† **Aoilbhinn**, *s. f.* A small flock.

† **Aoilbhreo**, *s. m.* Lime kiln.—*Ir.*

† **Aoileach**, eich, *s. m.* A gazing-stock; dung: for this latter sense, see Aolach.

Aoileann, *a.* Fine, excellent, charming.

Aoileann, inn, *s. m.* A sea maw, a gull. *N. pl.* aoilinnean. Corp is gile thu na aoilinnean, *a fairer body thou art than the sea maw.—Old Poem.*

Aoileannachd, *s. f.* (*from* aoileann.) Beauty, beautifulness.

Aoileanta, *a.* Beautiful, charming. Oigh aoibhinn aoileanta, *a cheerful beauteous maid.—Old Poem. Ir.* aoileanda.

Aoilinn, *gen. sing.*

Aoilinneach, *a.* (*from* aoileann.) Abounding in sea maws; like a sea maw; of, or belonging to, a sea maw.

Aoilseag, eig, *s. f.* A caterpillar. *N. pl.* aoilseagan, *caterpillars.*

Aoilseagach, *a.* Abounding in caterpillars; like a caterpillar.

† **Aoin**, *s. m.* A rush; honour; a fast.—*Ir.*

Aoin, *gen. sing.* of aon. Lamh gach aoin, *the hand of every one.—Stew. Exod.*

† **Aoine**, *s. f.* Skill.

† **Aoine**, *s.* Friday. Di h-aoine, *Friday.*

Aoineagan, ain, *s. m.* Wallowing; weltering; rolling on the ground. 'G a aoineagan fèin, *wallowing himself.—Stew. Mark, ref.* Written also *aoirneagan;* which see.

Aoir, *s.* Satire, lampoon, ribaldry; raillery; a curse.

Aoir, *v.* Satirize, lampoon. *Pret. a.* dh' aoir, *satirized; fut. aff. a.* aoiridh, *shall or will satirize.*

Aoir, *s. m.* a contraction of aodhair. A keeper of cattle.

Aoireachd, *s. f.* (*from* aoir.) The vice of lampooning; the habit of satirizing.

Aoireadh, eidh, *s. m.* A satirizing; a lampooning.

Aoireannan, *n. pl.* of aoir. Herds, or keepers of cattle.

The *aoireannan* of the Hebrides, according to Pennant, are farm-servants who have the charge of cultivating a certain portion of land, and of overseeing the cattle it supports. These have grass for two milch cows and six sheep, and also the tenth sheaf of the produce of the said ground, and as many potatoes as they choose to plant.

Aoirneagan, *v.* See Aoirnagain.

Aoirneagan, ain, *s. m.* A wallowing, a weltering, a rolling on the ground. Chum a h-aoirneagan san làthaich, *to her wallowing in the mire.—Stew.* 2 *Pet.*

Aois, aoise, *s. f.* (*Gr.* Ἔτος. *Lat.* aetas. *Corn.* huis, *and* oys. *Ir.* aes, *and* aos.) Age, old age, antiquity. Bloidh sgeith air a caithe' le h aois, *the half of a shield worn with age.—Oss. Gaul.* Iarguinn na h-aoise, *the troubles of age.—Oss. Conn.* Tha m' aois fo dhoruinn, *my old age is sorrowful.—Oss. Fing.* Ann an làn aois, *in full age.—Stew. Job.* Thainig e gu h aois, *he has come to age.*

Aois-dana, *s. pl.* (aois, *age, and* dàn, *song.*) Bards, poets; rehearsers of ancient poetry; a genealogist; soothsayers.

The *aoisdana* were in high esteem throughout the Highlands. So late as the end of the seventeenth century they sat in the *sreath*, or circle, among the nobles and the chiefs of families.

They took precedence of the *ollamh*, or the doctor in medicine. After the extinction of the Druids, they were brought in to preserve the genealogy of families, and to repeat genealogical traditions at the succession of every chieftain. They had great influence over all the powerful men of their time. Their persons, their houses, their villages, were sacred. Whatever they asked was given them; not always, however, out of respect, but from fear of their satire, which frequently followed a denial of their requests. They lost by degrees, through their own insolence and importunacy, all the respect which their order had so long enjoyed, and consequently all their wonted profits and privileges. Martin thus describes their mode of studying and courting the muse. "They shut their doors and windows for a day's time, and lay on their backs in darkness with a stone upon their belly, and plaids about their heads and eyes, and thus they pumped their brains for rhetorical encomiums."

AOISDANACHD, *s. f.* The employment of rehearsing ancient poetry; bardism; genealogical tradition.

AOL, *v. a.* Lime; plaster with lime; manure land with lime. *Pret. a.* dh' aol, *limed; fut. aff. a.* aolaidh.

AÒL, aòil, *s. m.* Lime. Ath-aòil, *a lime-kiln. Ir. id.*

AOLACH, aich, *s. m.* Manure, dung, mire; dross, rubbish. Bithidh iad nan aolach, *they shall be as dung.—Stew. Jer.*

AOLACHADH, aidh, *s. m.* The process of manuring with lime.

AOLACHADH, (ag), *pr. part.* of aolaich. Manuring with lime; liming.

AOLADAIR, *s. m.* (aol. *and* fear.) One who works among lime; a plasterer. *N. pl.* aoladairean.

AOLADAIREACHD, *s. f.* The occupation of a plasterer; plastering; working among lime.

AOLADH, aidh, *s. m.* A liming, a plastering.

AOLAICH, *v. a.* (*from* aòl.) Lime; cover with lime; manure with lime. *Pret. a.* dh' aolaich, *limed; fut. aff. a.* aolaichidh, *shall or will lime.*

AOLAISDEACH, *a.* Slothful, indolent, sluggish.

AOLAR, [*i. e.* aol-mhor.] Abounding in lime; limy. Talamh aolar, *limy ground.*

AOL-UISGE, *s. m.* Lime water.

AOM, *v. a.* and *n.* Bow, bend, droop, incline; yield; lean; persuade; dispose; fall; belly, bulge; descend, pass by; decay. *Pret. a.* dh' aom, *leaned; fut. aff. a.* aomaidh, *shall lean.* Dh' aom e air sgiath Threinmhòir, *he leaned on the shield of Trenmor.—Oss. Fing.* Com 'nach d' aom thu gu m' aisling? *why didst thou not descend to my dream?—Oss. Gaul.* Aomaibh in cluas, *incline your ear.—Stew. G. B.* Dh' aom e a thriall, *he bent his way. Oss. Fing.* An t-am a dh' aom, *the time that has passed by*, literally *gone down*, according to the poetical fancy of time flowing in a stream. —*Oss. Fing.* Na làì a dh' aom a shean, *the days that have long gone by.—Oss. Fing.* Aomaidh an aitreabh, *their building shall decay.—Stew. Ecc.*

AOMADH, 3 *sing. and pl. imper.* of aom. Aomadh e, *let him lean;* aomadh iad, *let them lean.*

AOMADH, aidh, *s. m.* A bending, a leaning; drooping, yielding, inclining; inclination; a persuading, a disposing, a descending, a passing by: also a descent, a slope; a fall, a downfal; a bellying out from a line; the surface of the sea. A cheann air aomadh, *his head drooping.—Ull.* Dubhach air aomadh chreag, *sorrowful on the mountain side, on the slope of the rock.—Oss. Gaul.* Air a ghlùn ag aomadh, *bending on his knee.—Orr.* An t-aomadh, *the downfal.—Stew. Is.*

AOMADH, (ag), *pr. part.* of aom. Bowing, bending, drooping, yielding, leaning, persuading, disposing; falling.

AOMAIDH, *gen.* of aomadh.

AOMAIDH, *fut. aff. a.* of aom. Shall or will lean. See AOM.

AOMAR, *fut. pass.* of aom; which see.

† AON, aoin, *s. m.* A country.

† AON, *a.* Excellent; noble; illustrious. *Bisc.* on. *Ir.* aon.

AON, *gen.* aoin, *a.* (*Ir.* aon.) One; alone. Thoir dhomh h-aon, *give me one;* aon air bith, *any one;* aon eile, *one other, another;* aon làtha, *one day, some day or other.* Bithidh sibhse mar mise aon latha, *you shall be like me (one day) some day or other.—Oss. Fin. and Lor.* Aon seach aon, *one from another.—Sm.* Latha 'gin, là h-eigin, *one day, some day.* Ann an aon luing ri allmharaich, *in the same ship with a transmarine foe.—Old Poem.* Lamh gach aòin, *the hand of every one.—Stew. Judg.* Is tu fein an t-aon duine, *you are the only man, you are a proper fellow.* Aon eile, *one another. Arm.* un eil. Tri laithe bha e na aon, *three days he was alone.—Oss. Carricth.*

Gr. εν. *Lat.* un-us. *Dan.* een. *Swed.* en. *Fr.* un *and* une. *Sax.* an. *Scotch*, ane. *Germ.* ain *and* ein. *Span. and It.* un-o. *Corn.* uynyn. *Arm.* yunan *and* un. *Teut.* een *and* eyn. *Du.* een *and* eene. *Chald.* hena. *Malabar*, onnou, *one.*

AONACH, aich, *s. m.* A hill, height, heath, desert place; *rarely* a fir. Ceum do theachd air an aonachd, *thy coming on the heath:* literally *the step of thine approach.—Oss. Trathal.* A siubhal nan aonach ciar, *travelling the dusky deserts.—Oss. Comala.* A direadh nan aonach àrd, *climbing the heights sublime.—Oss.*

AONACHADH, aidh, *s. m.* A uniting, reconciling; a reconciliation; an assenting; an assent.

AONACHADH, aidh, *s. m.* Galloping; a hand gallop; swift running.

AONACHADH, (ag), *pr. part.* of aonaich.

AONACHD, *s. f.* (*Ir.* eaondachd.) Sameness; unanimity, harmony; unity, agreement, one mind. In the sense of unanimity, perhaps *aonachd* is but a contraction of *aon-bheachd*, one mind or opinion. Aonachd an Spioraid, *the unity of the Spirit.—Stew. Eph.*

AON-ADHARCACH, *a.* Unicorned, having but one horn.

AONADHARCACH, aich, *s. m.* A unicorn. Neart an aonadharcaich, *the strength of the unicorn.—Stew. O. T.*

AONAGRAICH, *v.* Wallow, welter. *Pret.* dh' aonagraich; *fut. aff.* aonagraichidh.

AONAICH, *v. a.* Unite, reconcile, join into one; assent; side with. *Pret. a.* dh' aonaich, *united; fut. aff. a.* aonaichidh, *shall unite; fut. pass.* aonaichear, *shall be united.*

AONAICHEAR, *fut. pass.* of aonaich. Shall be united.

AONAICHIDH, *fut. aff. a.* of aonaich. Shall unite.

AONAICHTE, *p. part.* of aonaich. United, reconciled. Gaidheal aonaichte cruadhaichte, *united, hardy Highlandmen.—Old Song.*

AONAIRT, *s. f.* Wallowing, weltering, a rolling on the ground.

AONAIRT, *v.* Wallow, welter, roll on the ground. 'G a aonairt fein, *wallowing on the ground.—Stew. Mark, ref.*

AONAR, *a.* (*from* aon.) Alone, solitary, singular. Tha mise ri faireadh am aonar, *I am watching alone.—Oss. Gaul.* Rinn e so na aonar, *he did this alone.*

AONARACHD, *s. f.* Solitariness, singularity.

AONARAN, ain, *s. m.* (*from* aonar.) A recluse, a hermit, a solitary person. Aonaran liath nan creag, *the grey-headed hermit of the rock.—Oss. Conn.*

AONARANACH, *a.* (*from* aonar.) Solitary; desolate; forsaken. Aitean aonaranach, *desolate places.—Stew. Job.* Clann na mna aonaranaiche, *the children of the desolate women.—Stew. Gal.*

AONARANACHD, *s. f.* Solitariness, desolateness; the state of being forsaken, deserted, or forlorn.

† AONARDHA, *a.* See AONAR.

AON-BHEACHD, *s. f.* Unanimity. Often written, in a contracted form, *aonachd.*

AON-BHEANNACH, *a.* Unicorned, having but one horn.

AON-BHEANNACH, aich, *s. m.* A unicorn.

AON-BHITH, *s. m.* Co-essentiality; co-substantiality.

Aon-chathaireach, *a.* Of, or from, the same city; having one city.

Aon-chridhe, *s.* Unanimity.

Aon-chridheach, *a.* Unanimous; having one heart. Gu h-aonghuthach, aonchridheach, *with one voice and one heart —Old Song.*

Aonda, *a.* Singular, particular.

Aonda, Aondadh, *s. m* A lease, a license, consent Written also *aonta.*

Aondachd, *s. f.* Acquiescence; the state of being particular or singular.

Aondathach, *a.* (aon, *one, and* dath, *colour.*) Of the same colour.

Aon-dealbhach, *a.* (aon, *and* dealbh) Uniform; similar

Aon-deug, *a.* (*Gr* ἕνδεκα) Eleven. Bha aon deug ann, *there were eleven;* aon fhear deug, *eleven men,* aon chlach dheug, *eleven stones.*

Aon'eachd, **Aonfheachd**, *adv.* Together, at once. Perhaps *aon-bheachd.*

Aon-fhillte, *a.* (aon, *and* filleadh.) Single; simple, foolish, sincere, innocent. A deanamh an duine aon-fhillte glic, *making the simple (foolish) man wise.—Stew. Ps.* Na daoine aon-fhillte, *the simple,* i e. *the innocent.—Id.*

Aon-fhillteachd, *s f* (*Dan.* eenfoldighed.) Singleness of mind; simplicity, sincerity, foolishness. Le aon fhillteachd, *with simplicity —Stew. Rom. ref.*

Aonfhlaith, *gen. sing* of aonfhlath.

Aonfhlaitheach, *a.* Monarchic; of, or pertaining to, a monarch.

Aonfhlaitheachd, *s. m.* (*from* aonfhlath) Monarchy

Aonfhlaitheachdail, *a.* Monarchical.

Aon-fhlath, aith, *s. m.* A monarch. *N. pl.* aon-fhlaithean

Aon-fhuirm, *s.* Uniformity

Aon-ghin, *s. m.* (*Ir.* ein-ghin) An only-begotten. Mar aon-ghin mic, *like an only-begotten son —Stew. Pro.* M' aon-ghin cloinne, *my only child.*

Aon-ghnetheach, *a* (aon, *and* gnéth) Homogeneous; of one kind.

Aon-ghnetheachd, *s f.* (aon, *and* gneth.) Homogeneousness.

Aon-ghuthach, *a.* Having one voice, or vote; consonous Gu h aon-ghuthach aon-chridheach, *with one voice and heart.—Old Song.*

Aon-inntinn, *s f* One mind, one accord, unanimity Le h-aon inntinn, *with one accord.*

Aon-inntinneach, *a.* (aon intinn.) One-minded, unanimous, consentient. Gu h-aon-inntinneach, *unanimously.*

Aon-inntinneachd, *s. f.* Unanimousness.

Aon-mhac, mhic, *s. m.* An only son. Thuit e air aodainn aon-mhic, *he fell on the face of his only son.—Oss. Cath.*

Aonracain, *gen. sing.* and *n. pl.* of aonracan.

Aonracan, ain, *s. m.* (*from* aonar.) A solitary person; a recluse; a widower, a widow, an orphan; a deserted person. *N. pl.* aonracain.

Aonracanach, *a.* (*from* aonracan.) Solitary, like a recluse; of, or belonging to, a recluse.

Aonracanachd, *s. f.* Solitariness; the condition of a recluse, or of a deserted person.

† **Aonsuirt**, *s f.* Wallowing, weltering.

Aonta, Aontadh, aidh, *s. m.* A lease, license, consent; a bachelor.

Aontach, *a.* Accessory, acceding to, conniving at; ready to yield, ready to assent

Aontachadh, aidh, *s. m.* A consenting, a yielding, acceding, abetting, abetment.

Aontachadh, (ag), *pr. part.* of aontaich. Consenting, acceding, abetting. Ag aontachadh leis an lagh, *consenting to the law.—Stew Rom*

Aontachd, *s. f* Consent, unanimity, agreement, connivance.

Aontadh, aidh, *s. m.* A lease, license, consent.

Aontaich, *v.* Consent, agree, accede, yield to importunity, abet, take part, or side with. Aontaich leis, *take his part,* aontaicheamaid leo, *let us consent to them —Stew. Gen* Thug i air aontachadh, *she made him yield —Stew Pro. Pret a.* dh' aontaich, *consented, fut. aff. a.* aontaichidh, *shall consent*

Aontaiche, *s. m.* An abettor; a conniver. *N. pl* aontaichean.

Aontigheachd, *s f.* Cohabitation; a living under one roof.

Aon-tlachd, *s m.* Sole source of joy; only beloved M' aon-tlachd 's mo sholus thu, *thou art my light and my only source of joy —Old Song.*

Aor, *v* (by met *Lat.* ora, *entreat*) Worship, adore, also join, adhere *Pret a* dh' aor, *fut. aff. a* aoraidh. Aoraibhse gu ceart, *worship in sincerity.—Sm.* Aoram dhuit, *I will worship thee —Id*

Aoradh, aidh, *s m* Worship, adoration; also joining, adhering. A deanamh aoraidh, *worshipping.—Stew. N. T.* Aoradh fein-thoileil, *will worship.—Stew. Col.*

Aoradh, (ag), *pr part* of aor. Worshipping, adoring; also joining, adhering.

Aoraidh, *gen sing.* of aoradh.

Aoram, (*contr. for* aoraidh mi) I will worship. Aoram dhuit, *I will worship thee.—Sm*

Aornagain, *v. a.* Wallow. Aornagain thu fein, *wallow thyself.—Stew. G. B.* Aornagaimbh sibh fein, *wallow yourselves.—Stew. Jer. Pret a* dh' aornagain, *wallowed, fut aff. a.* aornagaimidh, *shall or will wallow.*

Aornagan, ain, *s. m.* A wallowing, a weltering. Aornagan muic, *the wallowing of a sow.*

† **Aos**, *s.* A community, a set of people.—*Ir.*

Aosar, *a.* (*for* aosmhor.) Aged; old, antiquated.

Aos-chiabh, *a.* Aged locks, hoary hair. Com' am bheil d' aos-chiabh snitheach? *why are thine aged locks moist?—Ull.* M' aos-chiabh air sgei' na gaoithe, *my aged hair on the wings of the wind.—Oss Conn. N. pl.* aos-chiabhan.

Aos-chrann, chrainn, *s.* An aged tree, a trunk. Aos-chrann briste, *an aged broken trunk.—Oss. Trathal*

Aoschrith, *s* The tremor of age. Aos-chrith air mo cheann, *the tremor of age on my head —Old Poem.*

Aos-chritheach, *a* Trembling with age —*Orr*

Aosda, *a.* (*from* aois.) Old, aged, ancient. A bhaird aosda nan linn a thréig, *ye ancient bards of bygone ages.—Oss. Fin and Lor.* Anns na h-aosda tha ghliocas, *in the aged is wisdom.—Stew. Job*

Aosdachd, *s f* (*from* aois.) Agedness, antiquity

Aosdana, *s. m* A poet, soothsayer, genealogist; a rehearser of ancient poetry.—*Oss Cathula,* and *Macfar.* See **Aos-dana**.

Aoslarach, aich, *s* An aged site; an aged ruin. 'N e 'n torr so d' aos làrach? *is this hillock thine aged seat?—Oss. Gaul.*

Aos-lia, Aos-liath, *a.* Grey-haired; old. Aos-lia, lag, *aged and weak.—Oss Trathal*

Aosmhoire, *com* and *sup* of aosmhor.

Aosmhoireachd, *s f* Great age, antiquity, agedness.

Aosmhor, *a.* Aged, old, ancient. Tuigse nan aosmhor, *the understanding of the aged.—Stew Job. Com. and sup.* aosmhoire.

† **Aoth**, *s. m* A bell, a crown. *Ir id.*

† **Aothachd**, *s. f.* (*from* aoth.) A ringing of bells, a chime of bells. *Ir. id.*

Aotrom, a. (ao, priv. and trom.) Light; not heavy; giddy. Written also eutrom; which see. Com. and sup. aotruime, lighter, lightest.

Aotromaich, v. a. (aotrom.) Ease, lighten, alleviate; make less heavy. Pret. a. dh' aotramaich, lightened; fut. aff. a. aotromaichidh, shall or will lighten; fut. pass. aotromaichear, shall be lightened.

Aotromaichidh, fut. aff. a. of aotromaich.

Aotromain, n. pl. of aotroman. Bladders.

Aotroman, ain, s. m. (aotrom.) A bladder. N. pl. aotromain, bladders.

Aotruime, com. and sup. of aotrom. Lighter, lightest.

Aotruimid, s. Lightness; also adjectively, lighter. Is aotruimid thu e, thou art the lighter for it.

† Ap. Fit, proper, ripe. Lat. ap-tus.

† Ap, gen. apa, s. m. Any little creature. Hence the Welch ap, signifying a son, and perhaps n-ep-os, a grandson.

Ap, apa, s. m. An ape, a mimic. A giùlan apa, carrying apes.—Stew. 1 K.

Dan. abe. Du. aap. W. epa. Swed. apa. Germ. affe. Ir. apa. Finland. apini. Sclavonic, affinia.

Apach, a. Like an ape; abounding in apes.

Aparan, Apran, ain, s. m. An apron. N. pl. aparain. Corn. appran. Ir. aprun.

Ar, poss. pron. Our. (Bisc. ure. Ir. ar.) Ar comhstri ri daimh, our battle with strangers.—Oss. Comala.

† Ar, s. m. A bond, a tie; a guiding, conducting.

† Ar. Slow. Hence Arar, a river in Provence, meaning a slow-flowing river. Claudianus says, " Lentus Arar, Rhodanusque celer," the tardy Arar and the rapid Rhone. " Arar dubitans quò suos cursus agat," the Arar doubting which way to flow.—Seneca, in Apoth. The Arar is now called Soane, which is sogh-an, the placid water.

Ar, s. m. (Ir. ar.) Ploughing, tillage, agriculture. Arm. and W. ar, plough-land. Tha e ris ar, he is ploughing.

Ar, v. a. Plough, till, cultivate. Pret. a. dh' ar, ploughed; fut. aff. a. araidh, shall or will plough.

Gr. αρ-οω, to till, and ἄρουρα, (a Gael would say ar-uire), arable ground. Lat. aro. Teut. aeren, to till. Arm. arar, a plough. Etrurian, arfer, and ar, ploughing. Bisc. ara, plough. Isl. aria. Heb. Chald. and Ethiop. haras, to plough. Syr. and Arab. harath, ploughman.

A'r, àir, s. m. Battle, slaughter; field of battle. Dàn an àir, the song of battle; an heroic poem.—Oss. Cathula. Tuath chum àir, a battle-axe.—Oss. Manos. Dithis nan codal san àr so, two asleep in this field of battle.—Oss. Gaul.

Gr. αρης, Mars. Cantabrian, hara. Dan. ar, a wound. W. aer. Corn. ar.

† Ar, s. Land, earth. An ancient Celtic word.

Bisc. ar, land. Etrurian, ar and arv, a field. Lat. arvum, a field. Chald. area and areka, field. Arab. ardhi. Du. aert. Old French, artos, a country.

† Ara, ai, s. m. A conference; a bier.—Ir.

Ara, s. A kidney. N. pl. airnean. An da àra, the two kidneys.—Stew. Exod. Ir. id.

† Arach, aich, s. m. A tie, a bond, or collar on a beast; also restraint; authority; strength; fishing ware.—Ir.

† Arach, aich, s. m. (from ar.) A ploughshare.—Ir.

Arachair, s. m. An insurer.

Arachas, ais, s. m. Insurance. Fear arachais, an insurer; buth arachais, an insurance office; tigh fo' arachas, a house insured.

Arachd, s. m. A dwarf. See Arrachd.

Arachdach, a. Dwarfish; also manly, powerful. Written also arrochdach.

† Arad, a. Strong, brave.—Ir.

† Arad, aid, s. m. A ladder.—Ir. See Aradh.

† Aradain, s. m. A desk, a pulpit.

Aradair, s. m. (ar, plough, and fear, man.) An agriculturist; a ploughman; a tiller.

Lat. aratr-um, a plough. Corn. ardar. Arm. arar. Span. har. Bisc. uoro. Corn. aradernr.

Aradh, aidh, s. m. (Ir. arad.) The reins, loins; also a ladder. In this last sense aradh is written also fàradh; which see.

Aragaradh, aidh, s. m. Abandonment; prescience, secret anticipation.

Araich, v. Rear, bring up, educate. Pret. a. dh' araich, reared; fut. aff. a. araichidh, shall or will rear. Ged àraich iad an clann, though they bring up their children.—Stew. Hos.

Araich, s. f. (perhaps àr-fhaiche.) A field of battle; a plain; a plain field; a meadow. Do mhac a teicheadh o'n arach, thy son flying from the battle field.—Oss. Mar dhoinionn a dortadh do 'n araich, like a flood pouring to the plain.—Oss. Dargo.

Araid, a. Particular, certain, special, peculiar. Duine araid, a certain man; gu h-àraid, especially. Written also araidh.

Araideach, a. Joyous, glad, elated, elevated. Com. and sup. araidiche, more or most joyous.

Araidh, a. (Gr. ἀραιός, scarce.) Particular, peculiar, special, certain. Duine àraidh, a certain man; gu h-àraidh, in particular, especially.

† Araigh, s. pl. The reins of a bridle.

Arain, gen. sing. of aran; which see.

Arainn, s. A kidney. N. pl. arainnean, contracted airnean; which see.

Arair, s. m. (àr and fear.) W. aerwr. A slaughterer; a warrior.

Ar-amach, s. m. A rebellion, insurrection, mutiny, treason. Rinn iad ar-amach, they have rebelled.—Stew. Gen. ref.

A'ran, n. pl. of ara. Kidneys; also ladders.

Aran, ain, s. m. (Ir. aran.) Bread, a loaf; livelihood, sustenance. Aran coirce, oat bread; aran eorna, barley bread; aran cruineachd, wheat bread; aran seogail, rye bread; aran donn, brown bread; aran milis, ginger bread, sweet bread. Greim arain, a morsel of bread.—Stew. Gen. N. pl. arain, loaves; cuig arain, five loaves.—Stew. Mat.

† Aran, ain, s. m. A conversation, or discourse; dialogue.

Aranach, aich, s. m. (from aran, bread.) A pantry. Ir. arancha.

Aranailt, s. f. A bread-basket, a pannier.

Arannach-sréine, s. m. A bridle rein.—Macd.

† Aroid, s. f. A cover, a table cloth.

Araon, conj. (Ir. araon.) Together; both; as one. A Chonail 's a Charruil araon! Conal and Carruil, both of you!

Ar'ar, contr. for arbhar; which see.

Ar'arach, a. contr. for arbharach. Abounding in crops; of, or belonging to, a crop; fertile. Gu h-ar'arach pòrach, full of crops and grain.—Old Song.

Aras, ais, s. m. A house, abode, dwelling; lodging; apartment; settlement. Ir. id.

Arasach, a. Having many houses, having many apartments.

Arbhach, a. Destructive, slaughtering.—Ir.

Arbhadh, aidh, s. m. Destruction, slaughtering.

Arbhar, air, s. m. (i. e. ar-bhàr, the ploughing crop.) Corn, corn crop, standing corn; rarely a host, an army. Deasaichidh tu arbhar, thou wilt prepare corn.—Stew. O. T. Pailteas arbhair, plenty of corn.—Stew. Gen. Na h-adagan is an t-arbhar, the shocks and the standing corn.—Stew. O. T. Ir. arbhar.

Arbharach, a. Abounding in corn crops; fertile; of, or belonging to, corn crops.

Arbharachd, s. f. Embattling as an army; forming into line.

Arbhraigneach, ich, *s. m.* A snare.

† **Arc**, airc, *s. m.* (*W.* arç. *Swed.* ark. *Lat.* arc-a.) An ark. Now written *airc;* which see.

† **Arc**, airc, *s. m.* A sucking pig; a bee; a wasp, lizard; a dwarf; a body; impost, tax.

Arcain, *gen. sing.* and *n. pl.* of arcan.

Arcan, ain, *s. m.* A cork, a stopple. Arcan buideil, *a bottle cork,* or *stopple;* àrcan bairill, *a bung;* crann-arcain, *a cork tree.* *N. pl.* arcain, *corks.*

Arcan-luachrach, aich, *s. m.* A lizard; an adder. *N. pl.* arcain-luachrach.

† **Archu**, *gen.* archoin, *s. m.* A chained dog, a mastiff, a fierce dog.—*Ir.*

† **Archuisg**, *s. f.* An experiment.

Arc-luachrach, aich, *s. m.* A lizard; an adder.—*Ir. id.*

† **Ard**, aird, *s. m.* God, or the High Being. Written also *Art;* hence *sag-art,* a priest.

Ard, *a.* (*Lat.* ard-uus. *Ir.* and *Corn.* ard. *Old Persic,* ard *and* art, *high,* and arta, *a hero.* *Armen.* ardyan, *a summit.* Hence too the name Arthur. In *Calmuc Tartary* and *Mogul,* artaga, *I put higher;* *Gaelic,* ard-thog, *raise aloft.*) High, lofty, exalted, loud; noble, eminent, excellent; proud; also an eminent person, a chief. B' ard air carraig a sgread, *loud on a rock was her scream.*—*Oss. Trathal.* Fuil ard nan saoi, *the noble blood of heroes.*—*Oss. Fing.* Sealladh ard, *a proud look.*—*Stew. Pro.* Fear a b' airde guth, *a man of the loudest voice.*—*Oss. Comala.* Uaigh an aird, *the grave of the chief.*—*Oss. Temo.* *Com.* and *sup.* airde; *n. pl.* arda. *Ard* is derived from the Celtic primitive *ar,* signifying a rock, a mountain; also high: hence many words in other tongues signifying elevation; as, *Bisc.* arre, *a rock;* *Malay.* arang; *Arab.* and *Ethiop.* hhar, *hill;* *Armen.* ar, *elevated;* *Malabar,* aria, *mountain,* and are, *elephant;* *Heb.* ar, *a rock, or mountain.*

Ard, aird, *s. m.* (*Ir.* ard.) A height, an eminence, a hill, a high land, an upland; heaven. O 'n ard, *from the height.*—*Oss. Temo.* *N. pl.* arda, *or* ardan; *dat. pl.* ardaibh. A ruith an aon slugan o ardaibh, *rushing in one channel from the heights.*—*Oss.* Na h-arda ciar, *the dusky eminences.*—*Oss. Temo.* Anns na h-ardaibh, *in heaven, on high.*—*Stew. Pro.* Ard a chuain, *the high seas.*

Arda, *n. pl.* of ard, *adj.* and *sub.* Cho' fhreagair na creagan arda, *the lofty rocks re-echoed.*—*Fingalian Poem.*

Ardachadh, aidh, *s. m.* (*Ir. id.*) The act of raising, exalting, or heightening; advancement, promotion, exaltation, honour, preferment. Ardachadh nan amadan, *the promotion of fools.*—*Stew. Pro.* Written also *arduchadh.*

Ardachadh, (ag), *pr. part.* of ardaich. Raising, exalting, extolling, elevating. 'G a ardachadh fein, *exalting himself.*—*Stew. Thess.*

Ardachaidh, *gen. sing.* of ardachadh.

Ardaich, *v. a.* (*from* ard.) Exalt, extol, elevate, raise aloft, heighten. *Pret. a.* dh' ardaich, *exalted;* *fut. aff. a.* ardaichidh, *shall or will exalt;* *fut. pass.* ardaichear, *shall be exalted.* Ardaich i, *exalt her.*—*Stew. Pro.* Written also *arduich.*

Ardaichear, *fut. pass.* of ardaich. Shall be elevated.

Ardaichidh, *fut. aff. a.* of ardaich. Shall or will elevate.

Ardain, *gen. sing.* of ardan.

Ard-aingeal, eil, *s. m.* An archangel. Le guth 'n ard aingeil, *with the voice of the archangel.*—*Stew. Thess.*

Ard-aithrichean, *n. pl.* of ard-athair. Patriarchs.

Ardan, *n. pl.* of ard.

Ardan, ain, *s. m.* (*from* ard.) Pride; proud wrath; childish haughtiness; spurting, arrogancy; also a little eminence; a knoll, a hillock. An droch dhuine na ardan borb, *the wicked man in his fierce pride.*—*Sm.* Ardan gruaidh, *pride of face.*—*Id.* Tha m' ardan na'd chliù, *my pride is in thy fame.*—*Oss. Fing.* Dh' at ardan na chridhe, *proud wrath swelled in his heart.*—*Id.* Uabhar is ardan, *pride and arrogancy.*—*Stew. Pro.* Gach aon ardan, *every one knoll; each knoll.*—*Old Song.*

Ardanach, *a.* (*from* ardan.) Proud, haughty; prone to take offence; arrogant; elate. Spiorad ardanach, *a haughty spirit.*—*Stew. Pro.* *Com.* and *sup.* ardanaiche, *more or most haughty.* *Ir.* ardanach.

Ardanachd, *s. f.* (*from* ardan.) Haughtiness, proudness; arrogancy. Uaille is ardanachd, *pride and haughtiness.*—*Old Song.*

† **Ardarc**, airc, *s. m.* A blazon; armorial bearings.

Ard-athair, *s. m.* A patriarch.—*Stew. Heb. ref.* *N. pl.* ard-aithrichean, *patriarchs.*

Ard-bhaile, *s. m.* A city, metropolis; a great city. Esan a ghabhas ard-bhaile, *he who takes a city.*—*Stew. Pro.* *N. pl.* ard-bhailtean, *cities;* *dat. pl.* ard-bhailtibh.

Ard-bhailtean, *n. pl.* of ard-bhaile, *cities;* *dat. pl.* àrd-bhailtibh.

Ard-bhandiùchd, *s. f.* An archduchess.

Ard-bheann, bheinn, *s. f.* A pinnacle; a mountain. Ait mar iolair nan ard-bheann, *joyous as the mountain eagle.*—*Oss.* *N. pl.* ard-bheanntan; *dat. pl.* ard-bheanntaibh.

Ard-bheinn, *s. f.* The name of a hill in the Highlands. Also *gen. sing.* of ard-bheann.

Ard-bhlath, *s.* Height of flourish, full flower; flower; prime. Tha i 'n ard-bhlàth a h-aimsir, *she is in the flower of her life.*

Ard-bhreitheamh, eimh, *s. m.* A chief justice. Ard-bhreitheamh cùirt na Righ-Bheinc, *chief justice of the King's Bench.*

Ard-bhreitheimh, *gen. sing.* of ard-bhreitheamh.

Ard-chantair, *s. m.* An arch-chanter. *N. pl.* ard-chantairean.

Ard-chath, *s. m.* A general engagement, a pitched battle; the thick of battle. Gaoir an ard-chath, *the din of the pitched battle.*—*Old Poem.*

Ard-chathair, chathrach, *s. f.* A chief city, a metropolis. *N. pl.* ard-chathraichean; *dat. pl.* ard-chathraichibh.

Ard-cheann, chinn, *s. m.* (ard *and* ceann.) A superior, ruler, lord; head. Ard-cheann na h-eaglais, *the head of the church.*

Ardcheannas, ais, *s. m.* Superiority, dominion, command, pre-eminence. Ard-cheannas anns gach uile, *pre-eminence in all things.*—*Stew. Col.* *Ir. id.*

Ard-cheum, chèim, *s. m.* A strut; a bound; lofty gait; a prancing.

Ard-cheumnachadh, aidh, *s. m.* A strutting, a bounding, a walking proudly, a prancing.

Ard-cheumnaich, *v.* Strut; bound; walk proudly; prance.

Ard-chlachair, *s. m.* An architect; a master mason. *N. pl.* ard-chlachairean.

Ard-chlachaireachd, *s. f.* The business of an architect, or of a master mason; architecture.

Ard-chnoc-faire, *s. m.* A great beacon; a sconce.

Ard-chomas, ais, *s. m.* Discretionary power; despotic power. Thug e ard-chomas dhomh, *he gave me a discretionary power.*

Ard-chomasach, *a.* Having discretionary power; despotic.

Ard-chomhairle, *s. f.* Parliament; supreme council; a synod. Ball na h-ardchomhairle, *a member of parliament;* ard-chomhairle Bhreatuinn, *the British parliament.*

Ard-chuan, chuain, *s. m.* The high sea. Na h-ard-chuantan, *the high seas.*

ARD-CHUMHACHD, *s. f.* Supreme power, chief power, high power; state office; authority. *N. pl.* ard-chumhachdan; *dat. pl.* ard-chumhachdaibh, *to the high powers.—Stew. Rom.*

AR-DHAMH, dhaimh, *s. m.* A plough-ox.—*Ir.*

ARD-DHRUIDH, *s. m.* An arch-druid.

He was chosen by a plurality of voices from the worthiest and most learned of the order. He was deemed infallible. He was referred to in all cases of controversy, and from his judgment there was no appeal. He was president of the general assemblies of the Druids, and had the casting vote. He was likewise named *Coibhi-Druidh*. His aid and friendship were much valued and confided in, as may be learned from the very ancient saying—*Ged is fagus clach do 'n làr, is faigse na sin cobhair Choibhi;* Though a stone be near to the ground, nearer still is Coibhi's aid.

ARD-DORUS, uis, *s. m.* A lintel. *N. pl.* ard-dorsan, *lintels.*

ARD-EASPUIDHEACHD, *s. f.* An archbishoprick.

ARD-EASPUIG, *s. f.* An archbishop. *N. pl.* ard-easpuigean, *archbishops.*

ARD-EASPUIGEACH, *a.* Archiepiscopal; of, or pertaining to, an archbishop; like an archbishop.

ARD-EASPUIGEACHD, *s. f.* An archbishoprick.

ARD-FHEAMANACH, aich, *s. m.* A high steward.

ARDFHÉILL, *s. f.* A great solemnity; a great festival.—*Stew. Ezek.* Ard-fhéill na h-Eadailt, *the carnival.*

ARD-FHUAIM, *s. f.* Bombilation; a loud noise, a murmur.

ARD-FHUAIMNEACH, *a.* Sounding, murmuring; making a loud noise.

ARD-FHUAIMNICH, *s. f.* Any loud noise; a continued loud noise.

ARD-GHAIRM, ghairme, *s. f.* A loud shout; high calling. Duais na h-ard-ghairm, *the reward of the high calling.—Stew. Phil.*

† **ARD-GHAOIS**, *s. f.* A liberal art.

† **ARD-GHAOISEAR**, ir, *s. m.* A master of arts.

ARD-GHAOTH, ghaoithe, *s. f.* A high wind.

ARD-GHAOTHACH, *a.* Windy, stormy, blowing loudly. A bhuilg shéididh, ard-ghaothach, *his loudly blowing bellows.—Old Song.*

ARD-GHLEADHRAICH, *s. f.* Bombilation; any loud noise, a rattling noise.

ARD-GHLÒR, glòir, *s. m.* Bombast, loud speaking; altiloquence; a boasting; vainglory.

ARDGHLORACH, *a.* Bombast; inclined to speak loud; boasting; vainglorious.

ARD-GHNIOMH, *s. m.* A feat, exploit; an achievement. Ard ghniomh an righ, *the exploit of the king.—Oss. Fing.* *N. pl.* ard-ghniombara, *or* -an.

ARD-GHNIOMHARAN, *n. pl.* of ardghniomh. Feats, exploits.

ARD-GHUL, ghuil, *s. m.* Loud weeping, howling.—*Stew. Mic.* Tha e ri ard-ghul, *he is weeping aloud.*

ARD-GHUTH, *s. m.* A loud voice, a loud cry, a shout.

ARD-GHUTHACH, *a.* Clamorous; loud, shouting loudly.—*Stew.* 1 *Chron.*

ARD-INBHE, *s. f.* High rank, dignity, eminence. Oirdheirceas ard-inbhe, *excellence of dignity.—Stew. Gen.*

ARD-INBHEACH, *a.* Eminent, of high rank, high in office.

ARD-INBHEACHD, *s. f.* Eminence, high rank, dignity, station.

ARD-INNTINN, *s. f.* Haughtiness, high-mindedness; a high spirit.

ARD-INNTINNEACH, *a.* High-minded, haughty, conceited, vain. Na bi ard-inntinneach, *be not high-minded.—Stew. Rom.*

ARD-INNTINNEACHD, *s. f.* High-mindedness, pride, conceitedness, vanity, haughtiness. Ard-inntinneachd 'nar measg, *pride amongst you.—Stew.* 2 *Cor. ref.*

ARD-IOLACH, aich, *s. m.* A loud shout. Le h-ard-iolaich, *with loud shout.—Stew. Thess.*

ARD-LOSGADH, aidh, *s. m.* Extreme burning, extreme heat, or inflammation. Le h-ard-losgadh, *with extreme burning.—Stew. Deut.*

ARD-MHARAICHE, *s. m.* An admiral. Priomh ard-mharaiche, *lord high admiral.*

ARDOLLADH, aidh, *s. m.* A chief professor; primarius professor; a principal of an university; an historiographer royal.

ARDORUS, uis, *s. m.* A lintel of a door. *N. pl.* ardorsan.

ARD-REACHDAS, ais, *s. m.* A general assembly; a convention.

ARD-RIGH, *s. m.* A monarch, emperor. *N. pl.* ard-righrean.

ARD-SGEIMHLEIR, *s. m.* A curious person. *N. pl.* ard-sgeimhleirean.

ARD-SGOIL, *s. f.* (*Ir. id.*) An academy, college, high school. Ard-sgoil Dhunéidinn, *the high school of Edinburgh.*

ARD-SGOILEAR, ir, *s. m.* A student at an university; a student at an academy; a high school boy. *N. pl.* ard-sgoilearean.

ARD-SGOIL-MHAIGHISTIR, *s. m.* A master at an academy; a professor; a high school master. *N. pl.* ard-sgoil-mhaighistirean.

ARD-SHAGART, airt, *s. m.* An high priest. *N. pl.* ard-shagairtean, *high priests.*

ARDSHAGARTACHD, *s. f.* An high priesthood.

ARD-SHEANADH, aidh, *s. m.* A general assembly, supreme council, parliament. Ard-sheanadh na h-Alba, *the general assembly of the kirk.*

ARD-SHEANAIR, *s. m.* A member of a general assembly; a member of a senate; a member of any supreme council. *N. pl.* ard-sheanairean.

ARD-SHONA, *a.* (ard *and* sona.) Supremely blessed; supremely happy.

ARD-SHONAS, ais, *s. m.* Supreme bliss; perfect happiness. Ard-shonas mo chridhe, *the supreme bliss of my soul.—Old Poem.*

ARDSHUIDHEAR, ir, *s. m.* A president. *N. pl.* ard-shuidhearan.

ARD-THIGHEARNA, *s. m.* A supreme lord. *N. pl.* ard-thighearnan.

ARDTHIGHEARNAS, ais, *s. m.* Supreme rule, supreme power.

ARD-THREITH, *gen. sing.* and *n. pl.* of ard-thriath.

ARD-THRIATH, threith, *s. m.* Supreme chief, supreme ruler. Ard-thriath a chruinne-ché, *supreme ruler of the universe.—Smith.* *N. pl.* ard-threith.

ARD-UACHDARAN, ain, *s. m.* (ard *and* uachdar.) A chief ruler, a sovereign. *N. pl.* ard-uachdarain.

ARD-UAILLSEAN, ARD-UAISLEAN, *s. pl.* Nobles; princes; nobility. *D. pl.* ard-uaillsibh *and* ard-uaislibh, *to princes.* Tàir air ard uaislibh, *contempt on princes.—Stew. Job.*

ARDUCHADH, aidh, *s. m.* A raising, exalting, extolling, exaltation, preferment. Written also *ardachadh*; which see.

ARDUCHADH, (ag). *pr. part.* of arduich.

ARD-UGHDARRAS, ais, *s. m.* Supreme, or sovereign authority; full authority. Fhuair mi ard-ughdarras, *I got full authority.*

ARDUICH, *v.* Heighten, raise aloft, exalt, prefer, promote, elevate, dignify, extol. *Pret. a.* dh' arduich, *exalted; fut. aff. a.* arduichidh, *shall elevate; fut. pass.* arduichear, *shall be elevated.* Arduichear iad, *they shall be exalted.—Stew. Job.* Written also *ardaich.*

ARDUICHEAR, *fut. pass.* of arduich. Shall be raised.

ARDUICHIDH, *fut. aff. a.* of arduich. Shall or will raise.

ARDUICHTE, *p. part.* of arduich. Raised, elevated.

AR-EAR, ir, *s. m.* (ar, *ploughing, and* fear.) A ploughman, a tiller, a peasant. *Arm.* arer.

AR-EAR, ir, *s. m.* (àr, *slaughter, and* fear.) A hero. *W.* arwr.

ARFUNTACHADH, aidh, *s. m.* A disinheriting; a forfeiting.

Arfuntaich, *v.* Disinherit; forfeit. *Pret. a.* dh' arfuntaich, *disinherited; fut. aff. a.* arfuntaichidh, *shall forfeit.*

Arfuntaichte, *p. part.* of arfuntaich. Disinherited, forfeited. Na h-oighreachdan arfuntaichte, *the forfeited estates.*

† **Arg**, *a.* White. *Gr.* ἀργος. *Ir.* arg.

† **Arg**, airg, *s. m.* A champion *Dan.* arg, *angry.* *Ir.* arg.

† **Argnach**, aich, *s. m.* A robber, a plunderer.

Argnadh, aidh, *s. m.* A robbery, pillage, plunder.—*Ir.*

Argair, *s. m.* A plunderer; a destroyer.

Arguinn, *v.* (*Lat.* arguo.) Argue, dispute, contest, wrangle *Pret. a.* dh' arguinn, *argued, fut. aff. a.* arguinnidh, *shall or will argue.*

Arguinn, *s. f.* An argument. *Lat* arguens. *Ir.* arguin.

Argumaid, *s. f.* An argument. *N. pl.* argumaidean; *dat pl.* argumaidibh. Le h-argumaidibh, *with arguments.*—*Stew. Job.*

Argumaideach, *a.* Argumentative; fond of argument; of, or pertaining to, argument.

† **Arigh**, *s. pl.* Chiefs.

† **Arinn**, *s. f.* Friendship

A ris, *adv.* Again; a second time; another time.

A rithist, *adv.* Again; a second time. In some districts of the Southern Highlands they say *a rithistich.*

Arlas, ais, *s. m.* Earnest money; a pledge. Written also *earlas.*

† **Arleag**, eig, *s. f.* A high flight; a project; a fancy, a whim.—*Ir.* airleog.

Arleagach, *a.* Flighty; fanciful, whimsical *Ir.* airleogach.

Arlogh, oigh, *s. m.* Carting corn. Feisd an arloigh, *the harvest feast, the harvest home* *Ir.* arloigh.

Arm, *v.* Arm; provide with arms; put on arms. *Pret a.* dh' arm, *armed, fut. aff. a.* armaidh, *shall arm*

Arm, *gen. sing.* airm. (*Arm* and *Ir.* arm. *Lat.* and *Span* arma); *n. pl.* airm. Arms, weapon, armour; also an army Tha e san arm, *he is in the army;* sgian, arm bu mhiann leis, *a knife, a weapon he was fond of*—*Old Poem. Dat. pl.* armaibh, fuidh armaibh, *armed, under arms.*—*Stew. Pro.*

Armach, *a.* (*from* arm) Armed; warlike; covered with armour, mailed; also an armed person, a warrior. Mar ghaisgeach armach, *like an armed hero.*—*Sm.* Labhair an dubh armach, *the dark warrior spoke.*—*Old Poem.*

Armachd, *s. f.* (*from* arm.) Armour; arms; feats of arms Nigh iad armachd, *they washed his armour.*—*Stew.* 1 *K* Armachd an t-soluis, *the armour of light*—*Stew. Rom.*

Armaich, *v. a.* Arm, gird on arms, clothe with armour *Pret. a.* dh' armaich, *armed; fut. aff. a.* armaichidh, *shall or will arm.* Armaichibh sibh fein, *arm yourselves.*—*Stew. Pet.*

Armaichidh, *fut. aff. a.* of armaich. Shall or will arm

Armaichte, *p. part.* of armaich. Armed, clothed in armour.

Armailt, ailte, *s. m.* An army. Ann an armailt, *in an army.*—*Stew. Job.* An toiseach na h-armailte, *in the front of the army;* armailt nam Breacan, *the Highland army.*—*Roy Stewart.*

Armailteach, *a.* Of, or belonging to, an army; having great armies.

† **Armaire**, *s. f.* A cupboard; a bread closet. *Fr.* armoire.

Armaradh, aidh, *s. m.* A reproof, a scold, a check.

Armeinneach, *a.* (àr, *slaughter, and* miannach.) Warlike, sanguinary, bloody.

† **Armhaigh**, *s. m.* A buzzard.

† **Ar-mhiannach**, *a.* Bloody, sanguinary, warlike, bloody-minded.

† **Armhind**, *a.* Respect, reverence.

Arm-lann, lainn, *s. m.* An armoury, a magazine, a military depot. *N. pl.* airm-lainn, *magazines.*

Arm-oilean, ein, *s. m.* Military discipline, drilling.

Arm-thaisg, *s. m.* A military magazine; an armoury.

Armuinn, *gen. sing.* of armunn, which see.

† **Armuinn**, *v. a.* Bless, revere.—*Shaw.*

Armuinte, *p part.* of armuinn. Blessed.

Armunn, uinn, *s. m.* (*from* àr) A hero, warrior; a chief. Air slios an armuinn, *on the warrior's side.*—*Old Poem.* Suil mheallach an armuinn, *the winning eye of the hero.*—*Macfar.*

† **Arn**, airn, *s. m.* A judge.

† **Arnaidh**, *s. m.* A surety, a bond.—*Ir.*

† **Aroch**, oich, *s. m.* A little village, a hamlet.—*Shaw.*

† **Aroch**, *a.* Straight; upright *Lat* arrect-us.

Arois, *gen sing* of aros.

† **Aroll**, oill, *s. m.* Great slaughter; a great many; a great deal—*Shaw.*

Aros, ois, *s. m.* A house, abode, residence. Aros nan long, *the abode of ships*—*Oss. Fing.* An loisgear aros nam Fiann? *shall the abode of the Fingalians be burnt?*—*Oss Taur.*

Arosach, *a* (*from* aros.) Habitable, having or containing houses; of, or belonging to, a house.

Arosach, aich, *s. m.* (*from* aros.) An inhabitant; a lodger, a resident householder. *N pl.* arosaichean, *householders.*

Arpag, aig, *s. f.* An harpy; any ravenous creature.—*Macd.* *N. pl* arpagan.

Arpagach, *a.* (*from* arpag.) Ravenous, grasping. *Lat.* harpago, *a grappling hook.*

† **Arr**, *s. m.* A stag, a hind.

Arra, ai, *s. m.* Treachery; also a pledge

Arra-bhalaoch, laoich, *s. m.* A traitor; a treacherous fellow. Arrabhalaoch garg, *a fierce traitor*—*Old Song.*

Arrach, aich, *s. m.* A pigmy, a dwarf; a spectre, an apparition; a centaur. Uaill san arrachd, *pride in the dwarf.*—*Ross.*

Arrachar, air, *s m.* A rowing, steering; also the name of a place in Argyllshire.

Arrachd, aichd, *s. m.* See **Arrach**

Arrachdach, *a.* (*from* arrachd.) Dwarfish, diminutive; spectral; also manly, able. Written also *arraiceach.*

Arrachdas, ais, *s. m.* (*from* arrachd.) Power, strength, manliness.

Arrachogaidh, *s m.* The hound that first winds, or comes up with the deer—*Shaw.*

† **Arradh**, aidh, *s. m.* An armament—*Ir.*

Arraghaideach, *a.* Negligent, idle, careless.—*Shaw.*

Arraghloir, *s. f.* Prattle, garrulity, idle talk.

Arraghloireach, *a.* Garrulous, given to prattle.

Arraiceach, *a.* Large; able-bodied, effective; manly. Each arraiceach treasdach, *a large thorough-pacing horse.*—*Old Poem* *Com.* and *sup.* arraiciche

Arraichdean, *s pl.* Jewels; precious things.

Arraid, *s. f.* Vice. Fear làn arraid, *a man full of vice*—*Old Song.*

Arraid, *v. a.* Corrupt, deprave, make vicious

† **Arraidh**, *s. pl.* Misdeeds; evil deeds; misconduct.

Arraidh, *a* Generous, liberal; hospitable.

Arraing, *s. f.* A stitch, convulsion. *N. pl.* arraingean

† **Arrais**, *v n.* Arrive at, reach.

Arronnach, *a.* Becoming, fit, suitable, decent. *Com.* and *sup.* arronnaiche, *more or most becoming.*

Arronnachd, *s. f.* Fitness, suitableness; decentness.

† Arronnaich, v. a. Fit, suit. *Pret. a.* dh' arronnaich, *fitted; fut. aff. a.* arronnaichidh, *shall or will fit.*

Arronnaiche, *com.* and *sup.* of arronnach. More or most becoming.

Arronta, *a.* Bold, daring, brave; confident. Fior-dheas arronta, *truly active and bold.—Macdon.*

Arrontachd, *s. f.* Boldness, bravery; confidence.

Ars', Arsa, *v. def.* Said. This verb is never used with propriety, excepting in corresponding expressions, with *said I, said he,* &c. In the order of syntax, the nominative case never precedes this verb, not even by a poetical license; and this forms the distinction between it and the corresponding preterite *thubhairt,* said. The Gael say, *Duine a thubhairt gu,* but not *duine arsa gu,* a man who said that. Ars' an ceannaiche, *said the buyer.—Stew. Pro.* Ars' oighe nan aodann gradhach, *said the maids of the lovely visages.—Old Poem.*

Arsachd, *s. f.* (*for* arsaidheachd.) Antiquity; antiquarianism; the pursuits of an antiquary.

Arsadh, aidh, *s. m.* Antiquity; age.

Arsaidh, *a.* Old, superannuated; old-fashioned, ancient, antique. A Bhla-bheinn arsaidh, *thou ancient Bla-bheinn.—Old Song.* Bla-bheinn is a mountain in Skye.

Arsaidheachd, *s. f.* Antiquity; antiquarianism.

Arsaidh'ear, ir, *s. m.* An antiquary. *N. pl.* arsaidh'earan.

Arsaidh'earachd, *s. f.* Antiquity; antiquarianism.

Arsair, *s. m.* (*for* arsaidh'ear.) An antiquary.

Arsaireachd, *s. f.* (*from* arsair.) Antiquarianism; the pursuits of an antiquary.

Arsantach, *a.* Old, antique, ancient, old-fashioned; fond of the study of antiquity.

Arsneal, eil, *s. m.* Sadness. More commonly written *airsneal;* which see.

Arsnealach, *a.* Sad. See Airsnealach.

Arson, *prep.* For. See Air-son.

† Art, Airt, *s. m.* God. Hence *sagart,* a priest.

† Art, airt, *s. m.* A bear. *Gr.* αρκτος. *W.* aerth. *Corn.* arth *and* orth. *Ir.* art.

† Art, airt, *s. m.* (*Lat.* art-us.) A limb, a joint; flesh.

Art, airt, *s. m.* (*Ir.* art) A stone; also a house. (*Dan.* aerts, *a mineral.* Hence also *Eng.* hard, and *Germ.* hart, *hard.*) Tarruing art, *a loadstone;* gach réile-art, *every shining pebble.—Old Poem. N. pl.* artan.

Artach, *a.* (*from* art.) Stony; also a quarry; stony ground.

Artan, ain, *s. m.* (*dim. of* art.) A little stone, a pebble.

Artarach, aich, *s. m.* A ship-boat.

Art-theine, *s. m.* A flint; literally a fire stone.

† Arthrach, aich, *s. m.* A wherry, a boat; a ship.

† Arthraich, *v.* Navigate; also enlarge.—*Shaw.*

Aruinn, *s.* A kidney. See Arainn.

† Arusg, uisg, *s. m.* The neck.—*Ir.*

† As, ais, *s. m.* Milk, beer, ale.

As, *prep.* (*Arm.* eus.) Out of, from out. As a mhuir, *out of the sea;* as an Eadail, *from Italy;* as an taobh eile, *from the other side. Arm.* eus an tu all.

† As, *v. a.* Kindle, as a fire; also do, make. *Pret. a.* dh' as, *kindled; fut. aff. a.* asaidh, *shall kindle.*

As, *comp. pron.* Out of him, out of it; from him, from it.

A 's, [a, *is.*] Who is, who are, who art; who has, who hast, who have. Oigh a 's gile lamh, *a maid* [*who is*] *of the fairest hands.—Oss. Comala.* Fear is liathe colg, *a man of* [*who has*] *the greyest hair.—Id.*

As, *conj.* (*for* agus.) And.

† Asach, aich, *s. m.* A shoemaker.

† Asach, *a.* (*from* as.) Milky, watery; like milk, beer, or ale.

Asad, *comp. pron.* [as tu.] Out of thee, from thee, in thee, on thee.

Asada, *emph. form. of* asad. Out of thee, from thee, in thee, on thee. Asada rinn ar sinnsir bun, *in thee our fathers trusted.—Sm.*

† Asadh, aidh, *s. m.* Anchoring, resting, settling.

Asaichte, *a.* Shod.

Asaid, *s. f.* Delivery, as in childbed.

Asaid, *v. a.* Deliver, as a female in childbed. *Pret.* dh' asaid; *fut. aff. a.* asaididh. Dh' asaideadh mise, *I was delivered.—Stew.* 1 *K. ref.*

Asaidh, *gen. sing.* of asadh.

† Asaidh, *s. f.* A resting, a settling; reposing, anchoring.

Asaibh, *com. pron.* [as sibh.] Out of you, from you, in you. Tha mi 'cur earbsa asaibh, *I trust in you. Ir.* aseabh.

Asaibhse, *emph. form of* asaibh.

† Asaidh, *v. n.* Rebel, revolt.

Asal, *gen. sing.* of asal.

Asainn, *comp. pron.* [as sinn.] Out of us, from us, from amongst us.

Asainne, *emph. form of* asainn.

Asair, *s. m.* The herb called *asarabacca.—Macd.*

Asair, *s. m.* A shoemaker. *N. pl.* asairean.

† Asaitich, *v.* Abandon, quit, evacuate; put out of place; eject. *Pret. a.* dh' asaitich, *evacuated.*

Asal, ail, *s. f.* An ass. Marcachd air asail, *riding on an ass.—Stew. Zech.* Mac na h-asail, *a colt.—Id.*

Dan. aesel. *Croat.* ossal. *Dal.* oszal. *Pol.* osiel. *Boh.* wosel *and* ossel. *Lus.* wosel. *Germ.* esel. *Belgic,* esal. *Anglo-Sax.* asal. *Manx.* assyl. *Lat.* asinus. *It.* asino. *Fr.* †asne. *Corn. and Arm.* asen. *Ir.* asal. *Span.* asno. This is one of the few vocables which may be considered antediluvian.

Asam, *comp. pron.* [as mi.] Out of me, from me; on me, in me. *Ir.* aseim.

† Asantadh, aidh, *s. m.* Mutiny, sedition, rebellion.

† Asard, aird, *s. m.* A debate, dispute; assertion.

† Asardach, *a.* Litigious; quarrelsome; contentious.

† Asardair, (*from* asard.) A litigious person; a wrangler; a disputant. *Lat.* assertor.

Asarlaigheachd, *s. f.* Conjuration, magic; intoxication.

Asbhuain, *s. f.* (as *and* buain.) Stubble. Asbhuain an àite conlaich, *stubble instead of straw.—Stew. Gen.*

† Asc, *s.* A snake, an adder.

† Ascach, aich, *s. m.* An escape.

† Ascaich, *v.* Escape.

Ascain, *v. n.* Ascend, mount, climb. *Pret. a.* dh' ascain, *ascended; fut. aff. a.* ascainidh, *shall climb.*

Ascaill, *gen. sing.* of ascall.

Ascaird, *gen. sing.* of ascard.

Ascairt, *s. f.* A budding, sprouting.

Ascall, aill, *s. m.* An onset; a conference; a flowing of the tide; a mangling, a mangled carcass, carrion; a term of much personal contempt; a miscreant. An t-ascall a rinn tàir oirnn, *the miscreant who has reviled us.—Old Song. Ir.* ascall.

Ascaoin, *a.* Harsh; inclement; unkind.

Ascaoin, *s. f.* A curse; excommunication; hardness; inclemency; also *adjectively,* harsh, inclement. Tionndadh ascaoin na sine gu tlàths, *turn to mildness the inclemency of the blast.—Macfar.*

Ascaoin, *v. a.* Curse, excommunicate. *Pret. a.* dh' ascaoin, *cursed; fut. aff. a.* ascaoinidh, *shall or will curse.*

Ascaoineach, *a.* (*from* ascaoin.) Of, or belonging to, a curse; harsh, inclement.

Ascaoineadh, idh, *s. m.* The act of cursing, or excommunicating; a cursing, an excommunicating.

Ascaoin-eaglais, *s. f.* Excommunication; a curse; a commination.

Ascard, aird, *s. m.* Tow, hards. Snathainn asgaird, *a thread of tow.—Stew. Jud.*

† **Ascath**, *s. m.* (*from* cath.) A soldier; a combatant.

† **Aschu**, choin, *s. m.* A water dog; an eel; a conger eel.

Ascnadh, aidh, *s. m.* An ascending, climbing, mounting.

Ascnadh, (ag), *pr. part.* of ascain; which see.

Ascull, *s. m.* See **Ascall.**

Asda, *comp. pron.* [as iad.] Out of them, from them, in them, on them, from amongst them.

Asdar, air, *s. m.* See **Astar.**

Asgach, aich, *s. m.* A winnower. *N. pl.* asgaichean.

Asgaidh, *s. f.* A boon, a present; also free, gratis.

Asgaill, *gen. sing.* of asgall.

Asgailt, *s. f.* A bosom, breast, armpit. Asgailt dhorch na h-iargaill, *the dark bosom of the storm.—Oss. Gaul.*

Asgall, aill, *s. m.* A bosom, a breast, an armpit; a sheltered place; a covert. Thug mi do d' asgaill, *I gave to thy bosom.—Stew. Gen. ref.*

Gr. μ-ασχαλ-η. *Lat.* axill-a. *Heb.* azzel. *It.* ascella. *Swed.* by met. axsel. *Goth.* ocksel. *Germ.* achsel. *Anglo-Sax.* ehsle, eaxle, *and* exla. *Arm.* asell. *Corn.* ascle.

Asgan, ain, *s. m.* A grig; a merry creature; any thing below the natural size.

Asgnail, *s. f.* The bosom; armpit; covering. See **Asgall.**

Asgnag, aig, *s. f.* A fan for hand-winnowing.

† **Asion**, *s. f.* A crown, or coronet.—*Ir.*

Aslachadh, aidh, *s. m.* A supplicating, entreating; a requesting; an entreaty or request.

Aslachadh, (ag), *pr. part.* of aslaich. Supplicating, begging, requesting.

Asladh, aidh, *s. m.* A supplication; an entreaty.

Aslaich, *s. f.* A bosom; armpit; breast. Sgian aslaich, *a dirk;* na aslaich, *in his bosom.—Stew. Pro. ref.*

Aslaich, *v.* Supplicate, beg, beseech, request. *Pret. a.* dh' aslaich, *entreated; fut. aff. a.* aslaichidh, *shall entreat.* Nan aslaicheadh tu, *if thou wouldst entreat.—Stew. Job.*

Aslonach, *a.* Prone to tell; tattling.

Aslonadh, aidh, *s. m.* A discovery, a telling.

Asluchadh, aidh, *s. m.* A supplicating, an entreating; a supplication, an entreaty. Le gach uile asluchaidh, *with all supplication.—Stew. Eph.*

Asluchadh, (ag), *pr. part.* of asluich.

Asluich, *v.* Supplicate, entreat, beg, request. Written also *aslaich.*

Asnag, aig, *s. f.* A hand-winnow. *N. pl.* asnagan.

Asnagach, *a.* (*from* asnag.) Of, or belonging to, a hand-winnow; like a hand-winnow.

Astar, air, *s. m.* (*Gr.* αστηρ. *Lat.* astrum, *a wandering star. Ir.* aisdear.) A journey; a space; distance; a way, a path. *N. pl.* astara *and* astaran. Air astar gu dian, *journeying with speed.—Oss. Fing.* Astar nam faobh, *the path of spoils or conquest.—Id.* Fad air astar, *far away;* an earb air astar, *the roe afar off.—Oss. Conn.* A gearradh a h-astar feadh thonn, *cutting her way among the waves.—Oss. Lodin.* Astar sheachd laithean, *seven days' journey.—Stew. Gen.* Chluinnte an saltraich astar cian, *their tread was heard at a great distance.—Old Poem.* Ag astar o 'n ear, *travelling from the east.—Fingalian Poem.*

Astaraich, *v.* (*from* astar.) Travel, journey. *Pret. a.* dh' astaraich, *travelled; fut. aff. a.* astraichidh, *shall or will travel.*

Astaraiche, *s. m.* (*from* astar.) A pedestrian, a traveller. *N. pl.* astraichean.

Astarair, *s. m.* A porter.—*Ir.*

Astaran, *n. pl.* of astar.

Astaranaiche, *s.* A traveller, a pedestrian.

† **Astas**, ais, *s. m.* A spear, or javelin; a missile weapon. *Lat.* hasta. *Acc. pl.* hastas.

A steach, or **'s teach**, *adv.* [san teach.] In, within; in the house. *Ir. id.*

As-tharruing, *s. f.* An extract; an abstract. *Ir.* astarraing.

As-tharruing, *v. a.* Extract; abstract.

As-tharruingeadh, idh, *s. m.* The process of abstracting or of extracting; an abstracting, an extracting.

A stigh, or **'stigh**, *adv.* [*i. e.* san tigh.] In, within; in the house. Cuir 'stigh e, *put it in;* bheil t-athair a stigh? *is your father in the house?*

Astrachadh, aidh, *s. m.* A travelling, a journeying.

Astrachadh, (ag), *pr. part.* of astaraich.

Astraichean, *n. pl.* of astaraiche. Travellers.

Astranach, aich, *s. m.* (*from* astar.) A traveller.

At, *v.* Swell, puff up, become tumid. *Pret. a.* dh' at, *swelled; fut. aff. a.* ataidh, *shall swell.* Ataidh an t-eolas, *knowledge puffeth up.—Stew.* 1 *Cor.* Tha m' eudann air a h-atadh, *my face is swelled.—Stew. Job.*

At, *s. m.* A swelling; a tumour. At bàn, *a white swelling.—Ir. id.*

Ata, *sub. verb.* Am, art, is, are.

Atach, aich, *s. m.* A request; a fermentation.—*Ir.*

Ata'd, (*for* ata iad.) They are. Ni 's millse na 'mhil ata'd, *sweeter they are than honey.—Sm.*

Atadh, aidh, *s. m.* A swelling, a tumour. Atadh bàn, a *white swelling.*

Atadh, (ag), *pr. part.* of at.

† **Atail**, *a.* Deaf.

Ataim, (*for* ata mi.) I am. Lag ataim gun cheist, *weak I am, without doubt.—Sm.*

Ataimse, [ata mise], *emphatic form of* ataim. I am. Ataims' a labhairt, *I am speaking.—Stew. Mat.*

Ataireachd, *s. f.* (*from* at), *contraction for* atmhoireachd. Swelling, raging, blustering; a fermentation. Ataireachd Iordain, *the swelling of Jordan.—Stew. Jer.*

† **Atais**, *s. f.* Woe, grief, lamentation.

Atan, ain, *s. m.* A cap; a garland.—*Shaw.*

At-chuisle, *s.* Aneurism.

Ath, *a.* Next; again. Air an ath làth, *on the next day.—Stew. John.* An ath-bliadhna, *next year;* an ath-sheachduin, *the next week.*

Ath, in composition, denotes repetition, and may be compounded with every active verb. It is equivalent to the Latin *re*, again.

Ath, *s. m.* A ford; any shallow part of a river reaching from side to side. Ath na sùl, *the corner of the eye.—Macd.*

Ath, *s. m.* A kiln. Nur bha sinn san àth le chéile, *when we were in the kiln together.—Old Song.* Ath-chruachaidh, *a drying kiln, a corn kiln;* ath-bhrachaidh, *a malt kiln;* ath-chriadh chlach, *a brick kiln;* ath-aòil, *a lime kiln;* ath chlacha creadha, *a brick kiln.* Tre ath nan clacha creadha, *through the brick kiln.—Stew. Sam.*

† **Athach**, aich, *s. m.* A space; also waves; a blast. Athach gaòithe, *a blast of wind.—Ir. id.*

Athach, aich, *s. m.* (*from* athadh, *fear.*) A giant, a champion, a monster. *N. pl.* athaich, *giants.* Cath ris an athach mhòr, *fight with the mighty champion.—Oss. Cathula.* Chunnaic sinn athaich, *we saw giants.—Stew. Numb. ref.*

Athach, *a.* (*from* athadh.) Timid, modest, bashful; also monstrous, huge, fearful. Oganach athach, *a bashful youth.*

—*Oss. Taura.* B' athach an torc a mhill e, *monstrous was the boar that destroyed him.—Oss. Derm.*

ATHADH, aidh, *s. m.* Fear, cowardice, timidity.—*Old Song.* Also a gust or blast of wind.

ATHAICH, *gen. sing.* and *n. pl.* of athach.

ATHAILE, *s. f.* Inattention, neglect.

ATHAILT, *s. f.* A mark, scar, impression; vestige; trace.

ATHAILTEACH, *a.* (*from* athailt.) Full of scars or marks; causing a scar or mark; of, or pertaining to, a scar; like a scar.

ATHAIN, *gen. sing.* of athan; which see.

ATHAINNE, *s. f.* A firebrand.

ATHAIR, *gen. sing.* of athar.

ATHAIR, *gen.* athar, *s. m.* A father; an ancestor. *Gr.* πατηρ. *Lat.* pater. *It.* padre. *Swed. and Dan.* fadder. *Eng.* father. *Pers.* phader. *Fr.* † pêtre; now written *père*. *Goth.* atta. *Germ.* tad.

Athair céile, *a father-in-law;* literally *a spouse's father.* Athair baistidh, athair faosaid, *a father confessor.* *N. pl.* aithriche *and* aithrichean, *fathers.* Aithriche Ardair stiùiribh ur mac, *ye fathers of Ardar, guide your son.—Ardar.*

Athair is derived from the old Celtic *at*, father; whence are derived the *Tartar* and *Turkish* ata, *father.* *Tobolsk*, atai. *Calm. Tart.* atey. *Phrygian* and *Thessalian*, atta. *Hung.* atya. Αττα was a Greek term of respect to an aged man; *at* signifies parent in *atavus*, great-grandfather. *Carinth.* atci. *Mogul Tartars*, atzia. *Bisc.* aita, *father.*

† ATHAIREAG, eig, *s. f.* (athair.) An aunt by the father's side. *N. pl.* athaireagan.

ATHAIREIL, *a.* (athair-amhuil.) Fatherly, fatherlike, paternal.

ATHAIREILEACHD, *s. f.* (athair.) Fatherliness.

ATHAIRICH, *v.* Adopt; father. *Pret. a.* dh' athairich, *adopted; fut. aff. a.* athairichidh, *shall adopt.*

ATHAIR-LUS, *s. m.* Ground ivy. *Ir. id.*

ATHAIR-MHAOIN, *s. m.* Patrimony. Sgap thu d' athair-mhaoin, *you have squandered your patrimony.*

ATHAIR-MHORT, ATHAIR MHORTADH, aidh, *s. m.* Parricide. *Dan.* f-adder mort.

ATHAIR-MHORTAIR, *s. m.* A parricide.

ATHAIR-THALMHAINN, *s. m.* Yarrow, milfoil.

ATHAIS, *s. f.* (*Ir.* athais.) Leisure; ease: also reproach, rebuke. *Gr.* ησυχια. *Fr.* aise. *English*, ease. *Corn.* aise, *gentle.* Bheil thu air d' athais? *are you at leisure?* Thig air d' athais, *come at leisure.* Athais namhaid, *the reproach of an enemy.—Old Poem.* Gun dad athais, *without any leisure, without delay.—Old Song.*

† ATHAIS, *v.* Rebuke, revile, reproach. *Pret. a.* dh' athais, *rebuked; fut. aff. a.* athaisidh, *shall rebuke.*

ATHAISEACH, *a.* Slow, tardy, lazy, leisurely; rebuking, reviling. *Com.* and *sup.* athaisiche, *more or most slow.* *Ir.* aghaiseach *and* athaiseach.

ATHAISEACHD, *s. f.* (*from* athais.) Slowness, laziness, tardiness.

ATHAL, ail, *s. m.* A flesh hook.

ATHAN, ain, *s. m.* A ford, a shallow; a shallow part of a river, reaching from bank to bank. *N. pl.* athanna. Aig beul an àthain bhàthadh an gaisgeach, *at the mouth of the ford the hero was drowned.—Old Song.* Athanna Iordain, *the fords of Jordan.—Stew. Judg.*

ATHANNA, *n. pl.* of athan. Fords.

ATHAR, air, *s. m.* Sky, firmament; air, atmosphere. *Gr.* ἀιθηρ. *Lat.* æther.

The Gael do not pronounce *th* in athar. The Latins made a similar omission, and wrote *aer*.

ATHAR, *gen. sing.* of athair.

ATHARAIL, *a.* Ethereal, atmospheric.

† ATHARAIS, *s. f.* Mimicry, mocking; ludicrous gesticulation.

ATHAR-AMHARC, *s. m.* Aeroscopy.

ATHAR-EOLAS, ais, *s. m.* Aeromancy.

† ATHARGADH, aidh, *s. m.* A sharp engagement.

ATHAR-IÙL, *s.* Aerology.

ATHARLA, *s.* A quey, a heifer. *N. pl.* atharlan.

ATHAR-MHEIDH, *s. m.* A barometer. *N. pl.* athar-mheidhean.

† ATHARRACH, *a.* Strange, curious, droll.

ATHARRACH, aich, *s. m.* A change, an alteration, a removal.

ATHARRACHADH, aidh, *s. m.* A changing, a flitting, altering, removing; a change, alteration, removal; a version. Atharrachadh gullain, *a changing of conduct.—Stew. Pro.* Atharrachadh inntinn, *a change of mind, repentance.—Stew. Cor. ref.* Cha robh thu riamh air atharrachadh, *you were never otherwise.*

ATHARRACHADH, (ag), *pres. part.* of atharraich.

ATHARRACHAIL, *a.* Changeable; changing; alterative.

ATHARRAICH, ATHARRUICH, *v. a.* Change, alter; remove; turn; budge; translate; flit. *Pret. a.* dh' atharraich, *changed; fut. aff. a.* atharraichidh, *shall change.* Dh' atharraich e iad, *he removed them.—Stew. Gen.* Dh' atharruich e cuibhrionn mo shluaigh, *he hath changed the portion of my people.—Stew. Mic.* A shaor agus a dh' atharraich sinn, *who delivered and translated us.—Stew. Col.*

ATHBHACH, aich, *s. m.* Strength.

ATH-BHARR, *s. m.* A second crop; an after crop.

ATHBHÀS, ais, *s. m.* A second death.

ATHBHEACHD, *s. f.* (ath, *again, and* beachd.) A retrospect; a second thought, an after thought, consideration, reconsideration.

ATH-BHEOTHACHADH, aidh, *s. m.* A reviving, a rekindling, a refreshing, reanimating. Rinn do bhriathran m' ath-bheothachadh, *thy words have revived me.—Sm.*

ATH-BHEOTHACHADH, (ag), *pr. part.* of ath bheothaich. Reviving, rekindling, refreshing, reanimating.

ATH-BHEOTHACHAIL, *a.* (*W.* advywiawl.) Causing to revive, refresh, or rekindle.

ATH-BHEOTHAICH, *v.* (ath, *and* beothaich.) *W.* advywiaw, advywiocaw. Revive, refresh, rekindle, reanimate, quicken. *Pret. a.* dh' ath-bheothaich, *revived; fut. aff. a.* ath-bheothaichidh, *shall revive.* Ath-bheothaich t-obair, *revive thy work.—Stew. Heb.* Dh' ath-bheothaicheadh e, *he revived, became reanimated.—Stew. K.* Ath-bheothaichidh e, *he will refresh.—Stew. Pro.* Ath-bheothaich mi, *quicken me.—Smith.* Ath-bheothaich an teine, *rekindle the fire.*

ATH-BHEOTHAICHIDH, *fut. aff. a.* of ath-bheothaich.

ATH-BHEOTHAICHTE, *p. part.* of ath-bheothaich. Revived, refreshed, reanimated, rekindled, quickened.

ATH-BHLIADHNA, *s. f.* Next year; a second year. Anns an ath-bhliadhna, *in the next year.—Stew. Gen.* Mu 'n tràth so 'n ath-bhliadhna, *about this time next year.*

ATH-BHREITH, *s.* An after birth, a second birth; regeneration.

ATH-BHRIATHAR, air, *s. m.* Tautology; repetition; a second-hand saying.

ATH-BHRIATHRACH, *a.* Tautological.

ATH-BHRIATARACHAS, ais, *s. m.* Tautology, repetition.

ATH-BHRIATHRAICHE, *s. m.* A tautologist; also one who uses second-hand expressions.

† ATH-BHROD, *v.* Resuscitate, reawaken. *Pret. a.* dh' ath-bhrod.

ATH-BHROSNACHADH, aidh, *s. m.* A rallying, a resuming of courage; a reinspiring with courage.

ATH-BHROSNACHADH, (ag), *pr. part.* of ath-bhrosnaich. Rallying; resuming courage; reinspiring with courage. Ag ar n-ath-bhrosnachadh, *rallying us.*

Ath-bhrosnaich, Ath-bhrosnuich, *v. a.* Rally; re-encourage; resume courage. *Pret. a.* dh' ath-bhrosnaich, *rallied;* dh' ath-bhrosnaich iad, *they rallied; fut. aff. a.* ath-bhrosnaichidh, *shall or will rally.*

Ath-bhrosnaichte, *p. part.* of ath-bhrosnaich. Rallied; re-encouraged.

Ath-bhuail, *v.* Strike again; beat again. *Pret. a.* dh' ath-bhuail, *struck again; fut. aff. a.* ath-bhuailidh, *shall strike again.* Com' nach d' ath-bhuail thu do shleagh? *why didst thou not again strike thy shield?—Oss. Gaul.*

Ath-bhuailidh, *fut. aff. a.* of ath-bhuail.

Ath-bhuailte, *p. part.* of ath-bhuail. Struck again, beaten again, reconquered, or a second time conquered. Gu bràth na pillibh ath-bhuailte, *never come back reconquered.—Oss. Oi'mara.* Sgrios ath-bhuailte, *double destruction.—Stew. Jer.*

Ath-bhuain, *v.* Cut down, or shear again.

Ath-bhualadh, aidh, *s. m.* A second striking; a reconquering; repercussion.

Ath-bhuanaich, *v. a.* Regain, recover, gain a second time. *Pret. a.* dh' ath-bhuanaich, *regained; fut. aff. a.* ath-bhuanaichidh, *shall or will regain.*

Ath-bhuanaichte, *pret. a.* of ath-bhuanaich. Regained, recovered.

Ath-bhuidhinn, *v.* Regain, recover, repossess.

Ath-bhuidhinneadh, idh, *s. m.* A regaining, a recovering, a repossessing.

Ath-chagain, *v. a.* Chew again; ruminate; chew the cud.

Ath-chagnach, *a.* That chews the cud; ruminating. Ainmhidh ath-chagnach, *an animal that chews the cud.*

Ath-chagnadh, aidh, *s. m.* A chewing of the cud; ruminating.

Ath-chairich, *v. a.* Repair, mend again.

Ath-chairt, *s. f.* A granting a charter; renewal of a lease. *Lat.* adcartatio.

Ath-charamh, *s.* A repairing, a mending a second time.

Ath-chas, *v. a.* Retwist.

Ath-chasaid, *s. f.* Second charge; a second complaint.

Ath-chasta, *a.* Retwisted; strongly twisted.

Ath-cheannachadh, aidh, *s. m.* The act of redeeming, a redeeming; repurchasing.

Ath-cheannachadh (ag), *pr. part.* of ath-cheannaich. Redeeming; repurchasing. Ag ath-cheannachadh na h-aimsir, *redeeming the time.—Stew. Col.*

Ath-cheannaich, *v.* Redeem; repurchase. *Pret. a.* dh' ath-cheannaich, *repurchased; fut. aff. a.* ath-cheannaichidh, *shall repurchase; fut. pass.* ath-cheannaichear, *shall be repurchased.*

Ath-cheannaichte, *p. part.* of ath-cheannaich. Redeemed; repurchased.

Ath-cheasnachadh, aidh, *s. m.* A re-examination.

Ath-cheasnaich, *v. a.* Re-examine.

Ath-cheumnachadh, aidh, *s. m.* A repacing; a recapitulating.

Ath-cheumnaich, *v.* Repace, pace over again; remeasure by pacing; recapitulate.

Ath-chleamhnas, ais, *s. m.* A connexion by a second marriage. Is fuar comain an h-ath-chleamhnais, *bold is the connexion with a first alliance after a second is formed.—G. P.*

Ath-chneadh, *s. m.* A second wound. Is leigh fear ath-chneadh, *a man is a surgeon for his second wound.—G. P.*

Ath-choisich, *v.* Repass; travel again. *Pret. a.* dh' ath-choisich; *fut aff. a.* ath-choisichidh, *shall or will repass.*

Ath-choisichte, *p. part.* of ath-choisichte. Repassed, retravelled.

Ath-choimhearan, ain, *s. m.* A register.

Ath-choimhre, *s. f.* An abridgment.

Ath-chomain, *s. f.* A requital, recompense; retaliation.

† **Ath-chomhairc,** *v.* Shout again.

Ath-chomhairleachadh, aidh, *s. m.* A readvising, a readmonishing.

Ath-chomhairleachadh (ag), *pr. part.* of ath-chomhairlich. Readvising, readmonishing.

Athchomhairlich, *v. a.* Readvise, readmonish. *Pret. a.* dh' ath-chomhairlich, *readvised; fut. aff. a.* ath-chomhairlichidh, *shall readvise.*

Ath-chomhairlichte, *p. part.* of ath-chomhairlich. Readvised; readmonished.

Ath-chostas, ais, *s. m.* An after-cost.

Ath-chre, Ath-chriadh, *s. m.* A brick-kiln.—*Stew. Nah.*

Ath-chruinneachadh, aidh, *s. m.* A regathering; a reuniting; a rallying.

Ath-chruinneachadh (ag), *pr. part.* of ath-chruinnich. Regathering; rallying; reuniting.

Ath-chruinnich, *v.* Regather; reunite; rally. *Pret. a.* dh' ath-chruinnich, *regathered; fut. aff. a.* ath-chruinnichidh, *shall regather.*

Ath-chruinnichear, *fut. pass.* of ath-chruinnich. Shall be gathered again.

Ath-chruinnichte, *p. part.* of ath-chruinnich. Gathered again; reunited; rallied.

Ath-chruthachadh, aidh, *s. m.* A recreating; a regenerating, regeneration, a reformation. Anns an ath-chruthachadh, *in the regeneration.—Stew. Mat. ref.*

Ath-chruthachadh (ag), *pr. part.* of ath-chruthaich. Recreating, regenerating.

Ath-chruthaich, *v. a.* Create again; regenerate, reform; reconstruct. *Pret. a.* dh' ath-chruthaich, *regenerated; fut. aff. a.* ath-chruthaichidh, *shall regenerate.*

Ath-chruthaichear, *fut. pass.* of ath-chruthaich. Shall be regenerated.

Ath-chruthaichte, *p. pass.* of ath-chruthaich. Regenerated, reformed; reconstructed.

Ath-chuimhne, *s. f.* Recollection, remembrance.

Ath-chuimhneachadh, aidh, *s. m.* A recollecting, a remembering.

Ath-chuimhneachadh (ag), *pr. part.* of ath-chuimhnich. Recollecting, remembering.

Ath-chuimhnich, *v.* Recollect, remember, bring to mind again, put in mind a second time.

† **Ath-chuimirc,** *s. f.* A rehearsal of a cause.—*Shaw.*

Ath-chuinge, *s. f.* (*Ir. id.*) A prayer, petition, request, supplication. Ag iarruidh athchuinge bige, *asking a small petition.—Stew.* 1 *K.* Written also *achuinge.* The proper othography is perhaps *ath-chuimhne; i. e.* a second putting in mind; so the corresponding term in English, *request,* from the *Lat. requiro,* strictly, means a second asking.

Ath-chuingeach, *a.* Supplicatory, petitionary, entreating; supplicant; like a prayer or petition; of, or belonging to, a petition.

Ath-chuingean, *n. pl.* of ath-chuinge.

Ath-chuingiche, *s. m.* A petitioner, a supplicant.

† **Ath-chuir,** *v. a.* Banish; surrender.—*Ir.*

† **Ath-chumain,** *v.* Deform, transform.

† **Ath-chur,** *s.* Banishment, exile.—*Ir.*

Ath-dhàn, dhàin, *s. m.* A byeword, byename, nickname. Bithidh tu a d' ath-dhàn, *thou shalt be a byeword.—Stew. Deut. ref.*

Ath-dhiol, *v.* Repay, requite, recompense, refund. *Pret. a.* dh' ath-dhiol, *repaid; fut. aff. a.* ath-dhiolaidh, *shall repay.* ath-dhiolaidh mise, *I will repay.—Stew. O. T.*

Ath-dhiol, Ath-dhioladh, aidh, *s. m.* A restitution, a requital, a repayment, a requiting, a recompensing, refunding; retaliation. Mar ath-dhiol air caoimhneas, *as a requital of kindness.—Mac Lach.*

ATH-DHIOLADH (ag), *pr. part.* of athdhiol. Requiting, repaying, refunding, recompensing.

ATH-DHIOLTA, *a.* Requited, repaid, recompensed, refunded.

ATH-DHRUID, *v.* Shut again, close again. *Pret. a.* dh' athdhruid, *shut again; fut. aff. a.* ath-dhruididh, *shall shut again.*

ATH-DHRUIDTE, *p. part.* of ath-dhruid. Shut or closed again.

ATH-DHÙBLACHADH, aidh, *s. m.* A redoubling, a reduplication.

ATH-DHUBLACHADH, (ag), *pr. part.* of ath-dhublaich. Redoubling.

ATH-DHUBHLAICH, *v.* (ath, *again*, and dublaich.) Redouble. *Pret. a.* dh' ath-dhublaich, *redoubled; fut. aff. a.* athdhublaichidh, *shall or will redouble; fut. pass.* ath-dhublaichear, *shall be redoubled.*

ATH-DHUBLAICHTE, *p. part.* of ath-dhublaich.

ATH FHÀS, *s. m.* After-growth, second growth, second crop.

ATH-FHEAR, fhir, *s. m.* A second man, a second thing. An t-ath-fhear, *the next man, or second man; the next or second object or thing.—Stew.* 1 *Chron. ref.*

ATH-FHUARACHADH, aidh, *s. m.* A recooling, the act of cooling again, or a second time.

ATH-FHUARACHADH, (ag), *pr. part.* of ath-fhuaraich. Recooling.

ATH-FHUARAICH, *v.* Recool; cool again. *Pret. a.* dh' athfhuaraich, *recooled; fut. aff. a.* ath-fhuaraichidh, *shall or will recool.*

ATH-FHUARAICHTE, *p. part.* of ath-fhuaraich. Recooled.

ATH-GHABH, *v.* Retake, recover, regain, resume. *Pret. a.* dh' ath-ghabh, *regained; fut. aff. a.* ath-ghabhaidh, *shall or will retake; fut. pass.* ath-ghabhar, *shall be retaken.*

ATH-GHABHTE, *p. part.* of ath-ghabh. Retaken, recovered, regained, resumed.

ATH-GHEARR, *a.* Short, brief, quick. Gu h-aith-ghearr, *shortly, briefly, quickly.*

ATH-GHEARR, *v.* Abridge, shorten, cut again. *Pret. a.* dh' ath-ghearr, *abridged; fut. aff. a.* dh' ath-ghearr.

ATH-GHEARRACHADH, aidh, *s. m.* The act of abridging, an abbreviating, an abbreviation, an abridgment.

ATH-GHEARRACHADH, (ag), *pr. part.* Abridging, abbreviating.

ATH-GHEARRAD, aid, *s. m.* Shortness, briefness.

ATH-GHEARRADH, aidh, *s. m.* An abbreviation, a shortening; a second cutting.

ATH-GHEARRADH, (ag), *pr. part.* of ath-ghearr.

ATH-GHEARRAICH, *v.* Abridge, abbreviate. *Pret. a.* dh' ath-ghearraich, *abridged; fut. aff. a.* ath-ghearraichidh, *shall abridge.*

ATH-GHEARRAICHTE, *p. part.* of ath-ghearraichte. Abridged, abbreviated.

ATH-GHIN, *v.* Regenerate, renew, produce a second time; recreate, renovate. *Pret. a.* dh' ath-ghin, *regenerated; fut. aff. a.* ath-ghiridh, *shall regenerate.*

ATH-GHINEAMHUINN, *s. f.* Regeneration; reproduction. Anns an ath-ghineamhuinn, *in the regeneration.—Stew. Mat.* Written also *ath-ghinmhuinn* and *ath-ghiontuinn.*

ATH-GHINMHUINN, *s. f.* A regeneration; reproduction.

ATH-GHINTE, *p. part.* of ath-ghin. Regenerated; reproduced.

ATH-GHIONTUINN, *s. f.* A regeneration; a reproduction.

ATH-GHLAC, *v. a.* Retake, resume, catch again, apprehend a second time. *Pret. a.* dh' ath-ghlac, *retook; fut. aff. a.* ath-ghlacaidh, *shall or will retake; fut. pass.* ath-ghlacar, *shall be retaken.—Ir. id.*

ATH-GHLACTE, *p. part.* of athlac. Retaken, recaught, reapprehended.

ATH-GHLAN, *v. a.* Repolish, refine, recleanse. *Pret. a.* dh' ath-ghlan, *repolished; fut. aff. a.* ath-ghlanaidh, *shall repolish; fut. aff. a.* ath-ghlanar.

ATH-GHLÀN, *v. a.* Recleanse, repolish, refine, furbish, scour. *Pret. a.* dh' ath-ghlan, *recleansed; fut. aff. a.* ath-ghlanaidh, *shall or will recleanse.*

ATH-GHLANADH, aidh, *s. m.* A recleansing; the act or the process of recleansing.

ATH-GHLANADH, (ag), *pr. part.* of ath-ghlan. Repolishing, recleansing, or furbishing.

ATH-GHLANTA, *p. part.* of ath-ghlan. Recleansed, repolished, furbished, scoured, burnished.—*Ir. id.*

ATH-GHOIRRID, *s.* A short time, a moment.

ATH-IARR, *v. a.* Seek again; request. *Pret. a.* dh' ath-iarr, *sought again.*

ATH-IARRTAS, ais, *s. m.* A request; a second asking or seeking; a second order; repetitions as in prayer. *N. pl.* ath-iarrtais, *repetitions.* Ah-iarrtais dhiomhain, *vain repetitions.—Stew. Mat.*

ATH-IARRAIDH, (ag), *pr. part.* Requesting; seeking again.

ATH-LAMH, *a.* Ready, expert, ready-handed.

ATH-LÀN, *s. m.* A refilling.

ATH-LÀNH MARA, *s.* Next tide, reflux of the sea.

ATH-LATH, *s. m.* Next day.

ATH-LATHACHADH, aidh, *s. m.* A procrastinating, procrastination.

ATH-LATHAICH, *v.* Procrastinate, delay. *Pret. a.* dh' athlathaich, *procrastinated; fut. aff. a.* ath-lathaichidh, *shall or will procrastinate.*

ATH-LEASACHADH, aidh, *s. m.* A reforming, amending, reformation, amendment, correction, an amelioration, improvement. Ath-leasachaidh obair, *amendments [additions] of work.—Stew.* 1 *K.*

ATH-LEASACHADH, (ag), *pr. part.* of ath-leasaich. Reforming, amending, ameliorating, correcting.

ATH-LEASACHAIR, *s. m.* A reformer, a corrector. *N. pl.* ath-leasachairean.

ATH-LEASAICH, *v. a.* Reform, amend, ameliorate, correct, improve. *Pret. a.* dh' ath-leasaich, *reformed; fut. aff. a.* ath-leasaichidh. Ath-leasaich do chombradh agus do bheusan, *amend thy conversation and manners.—Old Poem.*

ATH-LEASAICHTE, *p. part.* of ath-leasaich. Reformed, amended, ameliorated, corrected, improved.

ATH-LEUM, *v. n.* Rebound; spring or jump again. Dh' ath-leum, *rebounded.*

ATH-LEUMARTAICH, *s. f.* A rebounding; a continued jumping or bounding.

ATH-LION, *v. a.* Refill, recruit, replenish, reflow. *Pret. a.* dh' ath lion, *refilled; fut. aff. a.* ath-lionaidh, *shall or will refill.*

ATH-LIONADH, aidh, *s. m.* A refilling, a replenishing, recruiting, reflowing. Ath-lionadh feachd, *a recruiting of the army;* ath-lionadh na mara, *a reflowing of the sea.*

ATH-LIONADH, (ag), *pr. part.* of ath-lion. Refilling, replenishing, recruiting.

ATH-MHALAIRT, *s. f.* A re-exchange; a second bargain.

ATH-MHALAIRTICH, *v. a.* Re-exchange; make a second bargain.

ATH-MHALAIRTICHTE, *p. part.* of ath-mhalairtichte.

ATH-MHEAL, *v. a.* Re-enjoy. *Pret. a.* dh' ath-mheal, *reenjoyed; fut. aff. a.* ath-mhealaidh.

ATH-MHEALTUINN, *s. f.* A re-enjoying, re enjoyment.

ATH-MHEALTUINN, (ag), *pr. part.* of ath-mheal. Re-enjoying.

ATH-NEARTACHADH, aidh, *s. m.* A restrengthening, a recruiting, a reinforcing, a reinforcement.

ATH-NEARTACHADH, (ag), *pr. part.* of ath-neartaich. Restrengthening, reinforcing.

ATH-NEARTACHAIL, *a.* Strengthening. Leigheas athneartachail, *a strengthening medicine.*

Ath-neartaich, *v. a.* (ath, *again, and* neart.) Reinforce, recruit, restrengthen, refresh, renew. *Pret. a.* dh' ath-neartaich, *recruited*, *fut. aff. a.* ath-neartaichidh, *shall recruit.*

Ath-nuadhachadh, aidh, *s. m.* A renewing; a renovating, renewal, renovation, redintegration. Ath-nuadhachadh bhur n-inntinn, *the renewal of your minds.—Stew. N. T.*

Ath-nuadhachadh, (ag), *pr. part.* of ath-nuadhaich.

Ath-nuadhaich, *v.* Renew, renovate, redintegrate. *Pret. a.* dh' ath-nuadhaich, *renewed*, *fut. aff. a.* ath-nuadhaichidh, *shall or will renew; fut. pass.* ath-nuadhaichear, *shall be renewed;* ath-nuadhaichear a bhliadhna, *the year shall be renewed.—Macfar.*

Ath-nuadhaichte, *p. part.* of ath-nuadhaich. Renewed, renovated. Tha gach ni ath-nuadhaichte, *every thing is renewed.—Sm.*

Ath-phill, *v. a.* Return, turn again. *Pret. a.* dh' ath-phill, *returned; fut. aff a.* ath-phillidh, *shall or will return;* ath-phillidh a ghaoth, *the wind shall return.—Stew. Pro.*

Ath-philleadh, idh, *s. m.* A returning, a return, a coming back. Bhiodh ath-philleadh mar ghrian, *his return would be like the sun.—Ardar.*

Ath-philleadh, (ag), *pr. part.* of ath-phill. Returning. Tha sibh ag ath-philleadh, *you are returning again.—Stew. Gal.*

Ath-philltinn, *s. f.* A returning.

Ath-réiteachail, *a.* Reconciliatory, pacificatory.

Ath-réiteachadh, aidh, *s. m.* A reconciliation, a reconciling, reconcilement; atonement, expiation; a second disentangling; a second clearing or arranging

Ath-réiteachadh, (ag), *pr. part.* of ath-reitich. Reconciling, pacifying; re-expiating, re-atoning; disentangling again; clearing anew.

Ath-réitich, *v. a.* Reconcile; re-expiate, re-atone; disentangle again; clear again; re-arrange. *Pret. a.* dh' ath-reitich, *reconciled; fut. aff a.* ath-reitichidh.

Ath-réitichte, *p. part.* of ath-reitich. Disentangled again; cleared again

Ath-roinn, *s. f.* A subdivision; a second division.

Ath-roinn, *v. a.* Subdivide; divide again. *Pret. a.* dh' ath-roinn, *subdivided; fut. aff. a.* ath-roinnidh, *shall divide.*

Ath-roinnte, *p. part.* of ath-roinn. Subdivided.

Ath-ruadhar, *v.* Dig or delve again. *Pret. a.* dh' ath-ruadhar, *dug again.*

Ath-ruadhradh, aidh, *s m.* A second digging or delving.

Ath-ruadhradh, (ag), *pr. part.* of ath-ruadhar. Digging or delving again

Ath-sdiùir, *v. a.* Steer again; reconduct. *Pret. a.* dh' ath-sdiùir.

Ath-sgal, *s. m.* A second squall; an echo; the echo of a bag-pipe, or of any loud and shrill sound.

Ath-sgath, *v. a.* Reprune, lop again, cut down again *Pret. a.* dh' ath-sgath, *repruned; fut. aff. a.* ath-sgathaidh, *shall reprune.*

Ath-sgeul, *gen.* ath sgeòil, *or* ath-sgéil. A tale at second-hand.

Ath-sgriobh, *v. a.* Write again; transcribe. *Pret a.* dh' ath-sgriobh, *transcribed; fut. aff. a.* ath-sgriobhaidh, *shall transcribe.*

Ath-sgriobhadh, (ag), *pr. part.* of ath-sgriobh. Transcribing.

Ath-sgriobhadh, aidh, *s. m.* A transcribing, a transcript.

Ath-sgriobhair, *s. m.* A transcriber. *N. pl.* ath-sgriobhairean.

Ath-sgriobhar, *fut. pass.* of ath-sgriobh. Shall be transcribed.

Ath-sgriobhte, *p. part.* of ath-sgriobh. Re-written, transcribed.

Ath-shaor, *v. a.* Re-deliver. *Pret. a.* dh' ath-shaor, *re-delivered; fut. aff. a.* ath shaoraidh, *shall re-deliver.*

Ath-shaoradh, aidh, *s. m* A re-delivering, re-deliverance

Ath-shaoradh, (ag), *pr. part.* of ath-shaor. Re-delivering

Ath-shaorta, *p. part.* of ath-shaor. Re-delivered

Ath-shaothrachail, *a.* Painstaking, assiduous.

Ath-shealbhachadh, aidh, *s m.* A repossessing, re-inheriting; reversion; re-investment

Ath-shealbhachadh, (ag), *pr part* of ath-shealbhaich. Re-possessing, re-inheriting.

Ath-shealbhaich, *v. a* Re-possess, re-inherit. *Pret. a* dh' ath-shealbhaich, *re-possessed; fut. aff. a.* ath-shealbhaichidh, *shall repossess.*

Ath-shealbhaichte, *p. part* of ath-shealbhaich Re-possessed, re-inherited.

Ath-sheall, *v. n* Look again *Pret a.* dh' ath-sheall, *looked again, fut. aff. a.* ath-sheallaidh, *shall look again*

Ath-shealladh, aidh, *s m.* A second look; retrospect, a second sight, a second view

Ath-shealltuinn, *s. f* A second looking, a second viewing

Ath-shealltuinn, (ag), *pr. part.* of ath-sheall Looking or viewing again.

Ath-smuaine, *s. f* A second thought, an after-thought. *N. pl* ath-smuaintean, *after-thoughts.*

Ath-smuainteachadh, aidh, *s. m* A re-considering, pondering, reflecting.

Ath-smuainteachadh, (ag), *pr. part* of ath-smuaintich. Reconsidering, pondering, reflecting.

Ath-smuainteachail, *a* Apt to reflect, considerate

Ath-smuaintean, *n. pl.* of ath smuaine. Second thoughts, after-thoughts.

Ath-smuaintich, *v. a.* Re-consider, ponder, meditate, reflect. *Pr a.* dh' ath-smuaintich, *re-considered.*

Ath-shnamh, *v a* Re-swim, swim over again *Pret a* dh'ath-shnamh, *re-swam; fut aff. a.* ath-shnamhaidh, *shall re-swim.*

Ath-shnamhadh, aidh, *s m* A re-swimming, a swimming a second time, a swimming back again.

Ath-shnamhadh, (ag), *pr part* of ath-shnamh. Re-swimming, swimming back again.

Ath-shnamhta, *p. part.* of ath-shnamh Swum over a second time

Ath-thagh, *v. a.* Reflect; re-choose, make another choice *Pret. a.* dh' ath-thagh, *re-elected; fut. aff. a.* ath thaghaidh, *shall or will re-elect.*

Ath-thaghadh, aidh, *s m* A re-election, a re-choosing.

Ath-thaghta, *p. part* of ath-thagh. Re-electing, re-choosing.

Ath-theachd, *s* A second coming, next arrival.

Ath-theògh, *v a.* Warm again. *Pret. a* dh' ath-theogh, *warmed again; fut aff. a* ath-theoghaidh, *shall or will warm again.*

Ath-theòghadh, aidh, *s. m* Warming a second time

Ath-theòghadh, (ag), *pr. part.* of ath-theògh, *re-warming.*

Ath-thighinn, *s.* A second coming; next arrival Ath-thighinn an teachdair, *the next arrival of the messenger.*

Ath-thionndadh, *v.* Return a second time. *Pret. a* dh' ath-thionndadh; *fut. aff. a.* ath-thionndaidh.

Ath-thionndadh, aidh, *s. m.* A second return; a causing to turn a second time, an eddy Gaoth air luing, gaoth tre tholl, is gaoth ath-thionndadh: bad winds, wind in a ship, wind through a hole, and an eddy-wind.—*G P.*

Ath-thionnsgain, *v.* Re-commence, resume, re-devise. *Pret. a.* dh' ath-thionnsgain, *re-commenced.*

Ath-thionnsgnadh, aidh, *s m* A re-commencing, a re-commencement, a resuming, a re-devising *N. pl.* ath-thionnsgnaidh.

Ath-thog, *v. a.* Rebuild, rear again, lift or rise again. *Pret. a.* dh' ath-thog, *rebuilt; fut. aff. a* ath-thogaidh, *shall or will rebuild; fut. pass.* ath-thogar.

Ath-thogail, thogalach, *s. f.* A rebuilding, a second rearing, raising, or lifting.

Ath-thogta, *pr. part.* of ath-thog. Rebuilt.

Ath-thòiseachadh, aidh, *s. m.* A re-commencing, a resuming, a re-commencement.

Ath-thòisich, *v.* Re-commence, resume. *Pret. a.* dh' ath-thoisich, *re-commenced; fut. aff. a.* ath-thoisichidh, *shall or will re-commence.*

Ath-threorachadh, aidh, *s.m.* A re-conducting, re-guiding.

Ath-threorachadh (ag), *pr. part.* of ath-threoraich. Re-conducting, re-guiding.

Ath-threòraich, *v. a.* Re-conduct, re-guide. *Pret. a.* dh' ath-threòraich, *re-conducted; fut. aff. a.* ath-threòraichidh, *shall re-conduct; fut. pass.* ath-threoraichear, *shall be re-conducted.* Written sometimes *ath-threoruich.*

Ath-threòraichte, *p. part.* of ath-threoraich.

Ath-thuisle, *s. f.* A second fall, a second stumble.

Ath-thuisleachadh, aidh, *s. m.* A second falling; a second slipping or stumbling; a relapse. Ath-thuisleachadh tinneis, *a relapse into sickness.*

Ath-thuisleachadh, (ag, *pr. part.* of ath-thuislich. Relapsing; falling again; slipping or stumbling a second time.

Ath-thuislich, *v.* Fall or stumble again; relapse. *Pret. a.* dh' ath-thuislich, *relapsed; fut. aff. a.* ath-thuislichidh, *shall relapse.*

Ath-thuit, *v. n.* Fall again, or a second time. *Pret. a.* dh' ath-thuit, *fell again; fut. aff. a.* ath-thuitidh, *shall fall again.*

Ath-thuiteam, eim, *s. m.* A second fall; a relapse.

Ath-thuth, *s.* A second thatching; a second cover. *W.* attuth.

Ath-thuth, *v. a.* Thatch again. *Pret. a.* dh' ath-thuth, *re-thatched; fut. aff.* ath-thuthaidh, *shall or will re-thatch.*

Ath-thuthte, *p. part.* of ath-thuth. Thatched again.

Ath-uair, *s.* Next time; second time. An ath-uair a thig e, *the next time he comes.*

Ath-uamharra, **Ath-uamharrach**, *a.* Abominable, odious, execrable, detestable, horrid, terrible.—*Ir. id.*

Ath-uamharrachd, *s. f.* Abomination, detestation; hatefulness, atrociousness, abominableness.

Ath-ùrachadh, aidh, *s. m.* A renewing, reviving, refreshing, a reanimating; a regenerating; a renewal, renovation, a revival, reanimation; regeneration. Anns an ath-ùrachadh, *in the regeneration.—Stew. Mat. ref.* Tha e air ath-ùrachadh, *he is revived.*

Ath-ùrachadh, (ag), *pr. part.* of ath-ùraich. Renewing, reviving, refreshing, reanimating, regenerating.

Athùraich, *v. a.* Revive, refresh, renew, renovate; reanimate; regenerate. *Pret. a.* dh' ath-ùraich, *revived; fut. aff. a.* ath-uraichidh, *shall renew;* dh' ath-ùraich an cath, *the battle renewed.—Old Poem.*

Ath-uraichte, *p. part.* of ath-uraich. Revived, refreshed, renewed, renovated; re-animated; regenerated.

Atmhoire, *com.* and *sup.* of atmhor. More or most swelling or turgid.

Atmhoireachd, *s. f.* A tendency to swell, turgidness; pride, vanity; bombast, boisterousness; the state of being swelled, or puffed up. Atmhoireachd nar measg, *swellings (of pride) amongst you.—Stew.* 2 *Cor.*

Atmhor, *a.* (at *and* mòr.) Swelling; raging; turgid; boisterous; bombast. Briathran atmhor, *swelling words.—Stew.* 2 *Pet.* Na aonar sa chuan atmhor, *alone on the raging ocean.—Oss. Gaul. Com.* and *sup.* atmhoire, *more or most boisterous.*

Athte, *a.* and *p. part.* of at. Swelled, swollen, puffed up, in a rage.

† **Aur**, *s. m.* Gold. This is an ancient Celtic word, now in disuse among the Gael, but often heard among their brother Celts in Brittany. Hence *Gr.* αυρον, *gold;* αυρος, *rich;* and θησαυρος, *treasury. Lat.* aur-um, *gold;* thes-aurus, *a treasury. Aur* is now written òr; which see.

B

B, b, (beith, *birch.*) The second letter of the Gaelic alphabet. It sounds somewhat harder than *b*, and softer than *p*, in English. When immediately followed by *h*, it has an aspirated sound like *v* in English. As, bhuail, *struck;* bhac, *hindered.* At the end of a word, however, or of a syllable, the aspiration is so feeble as not always to be perceived; passing into the sound of the vowel *u;* as, searbh, *bitter;* fiabhras, *fever;* dabhach, *vat.*

'B, (*for* a bu.) Who was, who wert, who were? which was, which wast, which were.

B' (*for* bu.) Was, wert, were. Co b' urradh comhrag ri Dearg? *who was able to contend with Dargo?—Oss. Dargo.* B' iomad oigh san làth sin dubhach, *many were the maidens on that day sorrowful.—Ull.*

Ba, *s. f.* (*Ir.* bath.) Cow, cows. An aite gu mànaich bithidh geum ba, *instead of the voice of a monk, there shall be the lowing of cows.—St. Columba.* Seachd ba, *seven cows.—Stew. Gen.* Written more frequently *bò.*

† **Ba**, *s.* Immersion; hence baist, *baptize. Ba* is now written *bàth.*

† **Ba**, *a.* Good, honest; simple-minded.—*Ir.*

† **Ba**, *s. m.* Death.

Bàb, *s. m.* (*Ir. id.*) A babe.—*Shaw.*

Babag, aig, *s. f.* A tassel; a fringe; a cluster; short pieces of yarn. An lili na bhabagan cruinn, *the lily in round clusters.—Macdon. N. pl.* babagan.

Babagach, *a.* Having tassels or fringes; like a tassel, fringe, or cluster; of, or belonging to, tassels, fringes, or clusters. *Com.* and *sup.* babagaiche, *more or most fringed or tasselled.*

Babaig, *gen. sing.* of babag.

Baban, ain, *s. m.* A tassel; a fringe; short pieces of thread. *N. pl.* babana.

Babanach, *a.* (*from* baban.) Having tassels or fringes; of, or belonging to, tassels or fringes. *Com.* and *sup.* babanaiche.

† **Babhachd**, *s. f.* Innocence, harmlessness, simplicity, sweetness of temper.

Babhaid, *s. f.* A tassel. *N. pl.* babhaidean.

Babhaideach, *a.* Hung with tassels; like a tassel.

Babhuinn, *gen. sing.* and *n. pl.* of babhunn.

Babhuinneach, *a.* (*from* babhunn.) Having bulwarks; like a bulwark; of, or pertaining to, a bulwark.

Babhunn, uinn, *s.* A bulwark, rampart; tower; enclosure; a place for milking cattle. *N. pl.* babhuinn, *and* babhuinnean. Brisidh iad a babhuinn, *they shall break her bulwarks.—Stew. Ezek.*

† **Bac**, *s. m.* A boat. *Ir.* bac. *Gr.* βάκη. Hence also the *German* back, meaning a vessel in general. *Fr.* bacette. *English*, bucket. *Scotch*, backet.

Bac, *s. m.* (*Portug.* baque, *a fall.*) A hinderance, interruption, impediment, delay; a hollow; a thowl, or the fulcrum of an oar; the notch of a spindle, a crook; a hook; the hinge of a door. Cuir bac air, *hinder him.* Cogull ramh air na bacaibh, *the friction of oars on the thowls.—Macfar.* Bac na h-achlais, *the armpit;* bac na ruighe, *the armpit;* bac na h-iosgaid, *the hough;* bac na cruachainn, *the haunch.* *N. pl.* bacan; *dat. pl.* bacaibh.

Bac, *v. a.* Interrupt, hinder, obstruct, oppose, stop, prevent; lame. *Pret. a.* bhac, *prevented; fut. aff. a. shall prevent;* bac an aoibhneas, *interrupt their joy.—Oss.*

Bacach, *a.* (*Ir.* bacach. *Swed.* backug.) Lame, cripple, halt; causing hinderance, obstruction, or delay; hilly; of uneven surface, rugged; also, *substantively,* a lame person. Duine bacach, *a lame man or cripple.—Stew. Lev.* Bacach air aon chois, *lame on one leg;* bacach air a' dha chois, *lame on both his legs.—Stew.* 2 *K.* Aite bacach, *a rugged place;* na bacaich, *the lame.—Stew. Mat.*

Bacadh, aidh, *s. m.* The act or circumstance of hindering, preventing, or obstructing; an opposing, a hinderance, obstruction, delay.

Bacadh, (a), *pres. part.* of bac. Preventing, hindering, obstructing, stopping.

Bacag, aig, *s. f.* (*dim. of* bac.) A little hollow; also a trip, a stumble, a fall. *N. pl.* bacagan.

Bacaich, *v. a.* Lame; stop, obstruct, oppose. *Pret. a.* bhacaich, *lamed; fut. aff. a.* bacaichidh, *shall lame.*

Bacaiche, *s. f.* Lameness. *Ir.* bacuidhe.

Bacaiche, *com.* and *sup.* of bacach. More or most lame or cripple.

Bacaichead, eid, *s.* Lameness, increase in lameness. Tha e dol am bacaichead, *he is growing more and more lame.*

Bacaichidh, *fut. aff. a.* of bacaich. Shall or will make lame.

Bacaid, *s. f.* A bucket. *Scotch,* backet. *N. pl.* bacaidean.

Bacaidh, *fut. aff. a.* of bac. Shall or will hinder. See Bac.

Bacaiseach, *a.* (*from* bac.) Obstructive, hindering.

Bacal, ail, *s. m.* (*from* bac.) An obstacle, hinderance, interruption, a stop; a thowl, or fulcrum of an oar; *rarely* a slave; a prisoner. *N. pl.* bacalan; *dat. pl.* bacalaibh.

Bacaladh, aidh, *s. m.* An oven; a bakehouse. *Ir.* bacala.

† Bacalta, *a.* (*Ir. id.*) Baked.—*Shaw.*

Bacan, ain, *s. m.* A tether stake; a palisade; a hook; a crook; a door hinge; a stake of any kind; a knoll. An smeòrach air bacan, *the mavis perched upon a stake.—Macdon.*

Bacanach, *a.* (*from* bacan.) Like a palisade, like a stake, full of palisades; knolly.

Bacar, *fut. pass.* of bac. Shall or will be hindered.

Bach, *gen.* bacha, *s. m.* Drunkenness, revelling, rioting. (*Ir.* bach. *Lat.* Bacch-us, *the god of wine and of revels.*) Bach-thinneas, *sickness occasioned by excess in drinking; a surfeit.—Macd.* Bach-thoirm, *the noise of revelry.—Old Song.*

† Bach, *s. m.* A breach; a violent attack; a surprise; also loving. *Ir.* bach.

† Bachaid, *s. f.* The boss of a shield. *Ir.* bachoide.

Bachaill, *v. a.* Clip round, trim. *Pret. a.* bhachaill; *fut. aff a.* bachaillidh.

Bachair, *s. m.* (*from* bach.) A drunkard, a tippler; a reveller, a riotous man.

Bachaireachd, *s. f.* (*from* bachair.) Continued drinking; the practice or habit of drinking to excess, drunkenness; riotousness, revelling.

Bachall, aill, *s.* See Bachull.

Bachanta, *a.* Clamorous; garrulous. *It.* baccano, *a voice.*

Bachantachd, *s. f.* Clamorousness; garrulousness.

Bachar, air, *s. m.* The herb lady's glove. *Ir.* bachar. *Lat.* baccar.

Bachd. See Bac.

Bachdach, *a.* See Bacach.

Bachdaiche, *s. f.* See Bacaiche.

Bàchdanach, *a.* Noisy, tumultuous, contentious.

† Bachladh, aidh, *s. m.* (*Ir.* bachla.) An armful; a cup, a chalice.

Bachlach, *a.* Curled. *Ir.* bachlach.

Bachlag, aig, *s. f.* A ringlet, a small curl in the hair; a lisp, or halt in speech.

Bachlagach, *a.* (*from* bachlag.) Curled; having curls or ringlets; full of curls or ringlets; like a curl or ringlet; bushy as hair. Falt bachlagach dualach, *curled luxuriant hair.—Macint.* A chiabha bachlagach, *his bushy locks.—Stew. Song. Sol.* *Com.* and *sup.* bachlagaiche, *more or most curled.*

Bac-lamh, *s. m.* A manacle, a handcuff.

Bac-lamhach, *a.* Disabled in hand or arm; preventing the free use of one's hand or arm.

Bach-thinneas, eis, *s. m.* Sickness occasioned by excessive drinking; a surfeit.—*Macd.*

Bach-thoirm, *s.* The noise of revelling.—*Old Song.*

Bach-thorman, ain, *s. m.* The noise of revelling.

Bachull, uill, *s. m.* (*Lat.* bacul-um. *Span.* baculo. *It.* bacchio. *Ir.* bachol. *Corn.* and *Arm.* bagl.) A staff; a shepherd's crook; a crosier; the rim of a cart.

The pastoral staff among the primitive Christians of Britain was called *bahul* and *bachul,* from the Latin baculus, which, like the lituus of the augurs, was, according to Cicero, crooked. Romuli lituus, id est, incurvum, et leviter à summo inflexum bacillum. From the circumstance of its being crooked, it was also called *cam-bhatta,* or *cam-bhat,* i. e. a crooked staff. The crosier of Columbarius, we are told, who, in the early part of the seventeenth century, founded the monastery of Bobio in Italy, was called *cambhatto,* or *cambutta.*—See *Theodor. Monach. de Vita Sancti Mag.* tom. i. It may here be observed, that, by virtue of an ancient grant from an Earl of Argyll, a piece of land in the island of Lismore is held on condition that the holder do keep and take care of the *baculus* of Maluag, from whom its church is named. Hence the holder is called Baran a Bhachuill, or the Landholder of the Baculus.

Bachullach, *a.* Like a staff, crook, or crosier; relating to a staff, crook, or crosier; provided with a rim as a cart; curled as hair; having ringlets. D' fhalt bachullach, *thy curled hair.—Macint.*

Bacrach, aich, *s. m.* The name of a certain British Druid, of whom it is said that he apprized his prince of our Saviour's passion, at the very time when it happened, by means of a solar eclipse.

B'ad, (*for* b' iad, *i. e.* bu iad.) It was they.

Bàd, baid, *s. m.* (*W.* bâd. *Swed.* bat. *Ir.* bàd. *Fr.* bâteau.) A boat. *N. pl.* bàdaichean. More frequently written *bàt;* which see.

Bad, baid, *s. m.; n. pl.* badan. A tuft; a bunch, cluster; a wisp; thicket, clump, copse, grove. Morbheinn nam bad, *woody Morven.—Oss. Gaul.* Gabhaidh sibh bad, *you shall take a bunch.—Stew. Exod.* Balbh mar bhadan na h'oidhche, *quiet as the grove of evening mild.—Oss. Fing.* Badmullaich, *a top tuft or cluster; the hair on the top of the head.*

Bàdan, *n. pl.* of bad; which see.

Badan, ain, *s. m.* (*dim.* of bad); *n. pl.* badain. A little tuft; a tuft or clump of trees; a thicket; a grove; a tuft of hair. Badan coille, *a tuft of wood; a clump or grove.—Stew. Ex.* Ghearr e na badain, *he cut down the thickets.—Oss. Comal.*

Badanach, *a.* (*from* badan.) Tufty, bushy, bunchy; clustered, in tufts, in bushes, bunches, or clusters; abounding in thickets, groves, or clumps; like a thicket, grove, or clump; of, or belonging to, a thicket, grove, or clump. An sobhrach a chinneas badanach, *the primrose that grows in tufts.—Macdon.* Bàrr an fhraoich bhadanaich, *the top of the bunchy heath.—Old Song.* *Com.* and *sup.* badanaiche, *more or most tufty.*

BADH, *s.* (*Ir.* badh.) Friendship, affection, love; also a promise, a bond.

BADH, baidh, *s.* A harbour, a bay, a creek, an estuary. Sronbhàidh, *or* Stronbhàidh, *Stornoway*, literally *the nose of the bay.*

BADHACH, *a.* (*from* badh.) Loving, kind, affectionate, friendly; also beloved. Freasdal badhach, *affectionate Freasdal.—Fingalian Poem.* A laoich mheidhich bhadhaich, *thou mild and friendly hero.—Death of Carril.* *Com.* and *sup.* badhaiche, *more or most kind.*

BADHACH, *a.* (*from* badh, *harbour.*) Abounding in bays or harbours, creeks or estuaries; like a bay or harbour; of, or belonging to, a bay or harbour, creek, or estuary.

BADHACHD, *s.f.* (*from* badh.) Kindness, affectionateness, friendliness; the state of being beloved.

BADHAN, ain, *s. m.* (*dim.* *of* badh.) A little harbour, a creek, a narrow estuary, a road for ships; *rarely* a bulwark.

BADSADH, aidh, *s. m.* Provision for a journey, *viaticum.—Macd.* Perhaps biatsadh.*

BAG, baig, *s. m.* A bag, a pock; a stomach, a belly. Bag pioba, *the bag of a pipe.* *N. pl.* bagaichean.

BAGACH, *a.* (*from* bag.) *Ir.* bagach. Corpulent, bellying; also warlike. *Com.* and *sup.* bagaiche, *more or most corpulent.*

BAGAICH, *v. a.* and *n.* Make bellied or corpulent, grow corpulent; belly, bulge. *Pret. a.* bhagaich; *fut. aff. a.* bagaichidh.

BAGAICHE, *com.* and *sup.* of bagach. More or most corpulent.

BAGAICHEAN, *n. pl.* of bag. Bags.

BAGAID, *s.f.* A cluster, a bunch. Bagaidean searbh, *sour clusters.—Stew. Deut.* Bagaidean abuich, *ripe clusters.—Stew. Gen.* Bagaid fhion-dhearcan, *a cluster of grapes.* *N. pl.* bagaidean.

BAGAIDEACH, *a.* (*from* bagaid.) Full of clusters, clustered, in bunches.

BAGAIDEAN, *n. pl.* of bagaid; which see.

BAGAILT, *s.f.* A cluster, a bunch. Bagailt chno bu taine plaosg, *a cluster of thin-shelled nuts.—Macint.* *N. pl.* bagailtean.

BAGAILTEACH, *a.* (*from* bagailt.) In clusters or bunches, as nuts.

BAGAIR, *s. m.* (*from* bag.) A glutton, epicure. *N. pl.* bagairean.

BAGAIR, *v.* (*Ir.* bagair.) Threaten, denounce evil, terrify. *Prèt. a.* bhagair; *fut. aff. a.* bagairidh, *shall or will terrify.* This verb is commonly followed by the preposition *air*, either simple or compounded. Bagramaid orra, *let us threaten them.—Stew. Acts.*

BAGAIREACHD, *s.* (*from* bagàir.) Gluttony; threatening.

BAGAIRT, *s. f.* (*Ir.* bagairt.) A threat, a threatening, a denouncing. Cha d' theid plàst air bagairt, *no plaster is applied to a threat.—G. P.*

BAGAIRT, *a.*; *pres. part.* of bagàir. Threatening, denouncing. A bagairt oirnne, *threatening us.*

BAGAIST, *s. f.* A cluster, a bunch, as of nuts; baggage. *N. pl.* bagaistean. Written also *bagaid.*

BAGAISTEACH, *a.* Clustered, in bunches, as nuts; having baggage.

BAGANNTA, *a.* Warlike; also plump, corpulent, tight. An dreathan bagannta, *the plump wren.—Macfar.*

BAGAR, air, *s. m.* A threat. *N. pl.* bagaran, *threats*; *d. pl.* bagaraibh.

BAGARACH, *a.* (*from* bagar.) Threatening, minacious, prone to threat. *Asp. form*, bhagarach. Is i 'n Aoine bhagarach ni 'n Sathairn deurach, *the gloomy Friday makes the rainy Saturday.—G. P.*

BAGARACHD, *s.f.* A threatening, a habit of threatening.

BAGARADH, aidh, *s. m.* A threatening, a denouncing, a threat.

† BAGH, *s.* (*Ir.* bagh.) Kindness, friendship; a bond, a tie. Written also *badh.*

BAGHACH, *a.* Kind, friendly, loving; binding, obligatory.

BAGHACHD, *s.f.* Kindness, friendliness; obligatoriness.

† BAGHADH, aidh, *s. m.* Fighting, quarrelling.

BAGHLACH, *a.* Dangerous, hazardous.

BAGHLACHD, *s.f.* Danger, hazard.

BAGRADH, aidh, *s. m.* A threat, denunciation; the act or circumstance of threatening.

BAGRADH, (a), *pres. part.* of bagair. Threatening, denouncing. Tha e a bagradh orm, *he is threatening me*; more frequently written *bagairt.*

BAGUID, *s.f.* A cluster, a bunch. Written also *bagaid*; which see.

BAGUIDEACH, *a.* In clusters, in bunches. See also BAGAIDEACH.

† BAIC, *gen.* baice, *s.f.* A turn or twist.—*Shaw.*

† BAICEACH, *a.* Having twists or turns.

BÀICH, *s.* (*i. e.* ba-theach.) A cow-house; a cattle-house. *N. pl.* bàichean; *d. pl.* baichibh.

† BAICH, *v.* (*Ir. id.*) Strike; touch.—*Shaw.*

BAIDEAL, eil, *s. m.* A pillar; fortress, tower. Baideal neòil, *a pillar of cloud.—Stew. Ps.* Mo bhaideal àrd, *my high tower.—Sm.* *N. pl.* baidealan, *pillars.*

BAIDEALACH, *a.* (*from* baideal.) Like a pillar, tower, or fortress; of, or belonging to, a pillar, tower, or fortress; abounding in pillars, towers, or fortresses.

BAIDEAN, ein, *s. m.* (*dim. of* bàd.) A little boat, a yawl, a pinnace.

BAIDEANACH, *s.* Badenoch in the Highlands of Scotland; the Βαναγία of Ptolemy.

BAIDEIL, *gen. sing.* of baideal.

† BAIDH, *s.f.* (*Ir. id.*) A wave.—*Shaw.*

BAIDH, *s.f.* (*Ir.* baidhe.) Compassion. See BAIGH.

† BAIDHEACH, ich, *s. m.* A coadjutor; a champion.

BAIDHEACH, *a.* (*from* baidh.) See BAIGHEACH.

† BAIDHEAL, eil, *s. m.* A cow-stall. *Ir.* baidheal.

BAIGEAN, ein, *s. m.* (*dim. of* bag.) A little bag; a little glutton; a little corpulent person. Baigean lèasaiche, *a rennet bag.*

BAIGEANACH, *a.* (*from* baigean.) Bagged, bellied, corpulent.

BAIGEIR, *s. m.* and *f.* A beggar, a mendicant; a covetous or greedy person. Peilear nam baigearean, *a pebble*; literally, *the beggar's bullet.*

BAIGEIREACH, *a.* (*Swed.* begarig.) Inclined to beg; needy; covetous.

BAIGEIREACHD, *s.f.* Beggary. Air bhaigeireachd, *begging.*

† BAIGH, *v. a.* Endear. *Pret. a.* bhaigh, *endeared*; *fut. aff. a.* baighidh, *shall endear.*

BAIGH, *s. f.* (*Ir.* baidhe.) Kindness, benignity, humanity, mercy, friendship, fondness; hospitality. Dh' fheoraich i le baigh, *she asked with benignity.—Oss Lod.* Is mòr a bhaigh ris, *great is his fondness for him.—Ull.* Shèid osnadh gun bhaigh, *a wind blew without mercy*; ceann-uighe nam mile baigh, *the mansion of boundless hospitality; literally, the stage of a thousand welcomes.—Ull.*

Baigheach, ich, *s. m.* (*from* baigh.) *Ir.* baidheach. A companion, a coadjutor.

Baigheach, *a.* (*from* baigh.) Friendly, kind, merciful, humane, hospitable, noble.

Baigheachas, ais, *s. m.* Grace, favour, friendship.

Baigheachd, *s. f.* (*from* baigh.) *Ir.* baidheachd. Friendliness, kindness, mercifulness; hospitableness; companionship, coadjutorship.

Baighealachd, *s. f.* (*from* baigheil.) Friendliness, kindness, humanity.

Baigheil, *a.* (*i. e.* baigh-amhuil, *from* baigh.) Humane, merciful; favourable, kind. Cha bhi thu baigheil, *thou shalt not* [*countenance*] *be favourable.—Stew. Exod.*

† **Baighin**, *s. f.* A chariot; a waggon or wain; a dray. *Ir. id.*

Bail, *s. f.* Economy; the allowance of a mill to the poor; also prosperity, good luck. Dean bail, *spare, save, or economize.* Cha bhi bail air aran fuinte, *baked bread is not spared.—G. P.*

Bailbh, *gen. sing.* of balbh. Mute. Aspirated form, *bhailbh.* Teangadh an duine bhailbh, *the tongue of the dumb man.*

Bailbhe, *s. f.* Dumbness, muteness. *Ir.* bailbhe.

Bailc, *s. f.* A balk, or ridge of earth between two furrows. —*Macd.* A flood; a mountain-torrent; in the Scotch Lowlands called a *speat;* a loud noise; also a ligature. Bailc nan sgiath, *the noise of the shields.—Fingalian Poem.*

† **Bailc**, *a.* Strong, bold, daring.

Bailceach, *a.* Balked; like a balk; abounding in balks; of, or belonging to, a balk.

Bailceach, *a.* Rainy, inundating, causing a flood; of rain, of a flood; like a flood. A bhealtuinn bhailceach, *rainy May.—Macfar.*

Bailceach, ich, *s. m.* A strong robust man; a stout straight-bodied man.

† **Baile**, *s. m.* A clan; a tube.—*Shaw.*

Baile, *s. m.* A city, town, village. *N. pl.* bailte, *or* bailtean. Am fear a bhios carrach sa bhaile so bithidh e carrach 'sa bhaile ud thall, *he who is mangy here will be mangy every where.—G. P.* Hence the Latin † *billa*, a country-seat, now *villa; b* and *v*, being palatals, are easily changed the one into the other. I think it is O'Reilly who observes, that the Celtic word *bàile*, a town, and the Latin *vallis*, a valley, were originally the same; as the ancients built their dwellings in low sheltered places, near rivers and rivulets.

Baileach, *a.* (*from* baile.) Careful, economical, frugal; thorough, complete; quite. Gu baileach, *wholly, completely, quite, thoroughly.* Glanaidh e gu ro bhaileach, *he will purge thoroughly.—Stew. Mat. Com.* and *sup.* bailiche.

Baile-dhuthaich, *s.* Tain in Scotland; literally, the village of St. Duthac, the tutelary saint of the place.

Baile-geamhraidh, *s. m.* An infield; ground always ploughed.

Baile-margaidh, *s. m.* A market-town, a burgh.—*Macint.*

Baile-mhòid, *s.* Rothesay; *literally*, the town where the court of justice is held.

Baile-mor, *s. m.* A large town, a city, a metropolis; a large village. *N. pl.* bailteam-mòra.

Baile-puirt, *s. m.* A sea-port town. *N. pl.* bailtean puirt.

Bailgeann, Bailg-fhionn, *a.* (balg, *belly*, and fionn, *white.*) Spotted, speckled, pie-bald; white-bellied. Laogh bailgeann, *a white-bellied calf.—Macfar.* Na gabhair bhailg-fhionn, *the spotted goats.—R.*

Bailisdear, ir, *s. m.* A vain-glorious fellow; a man who talks idly; a blusterer.

Bailisdearach, *a.* Vaunting; inclined to talk idly; blustering.

Bailisdearachd, *s. f.* The habit of talking idly or blusteringly.

B'àill, (*for* bu àill.) Would. B' aill leam, leat, leis, leatha, *I, thou, he, she would;* b' aill leinn, leibh, leo, *we, you, they would;* am b' àill leat mo mharbhadh? *wouldst thou kill me?* ciod a b' àill leat? *what would you have? what would you like? what is your pleasure?*

Bailleag, eig, *s. f.* A twig, a sprout; a sucker.

Bailleagach, *a.* Full of twigs, sprouts, or suckers; like a sprig or sucker; slender, pliable.

† **Baillean**, ein, *s. m.* A boss; a stud; any thing round.—*Shaw.*

Bailleanach, *a.* Bossy; studded.

Baillidh, *s. m.* A bailiff; a baillie, *Scotch;* an underling officer of the peace. *Fr.* baillie. *It.* balio, *a bailiff.*

Baillidheachd, *s.* A bailiwick; a province, a district.—*Shaw.*

Bailm, *s. f.* (*Ir.* bailme.) Balm, balsam.—*Macd.*

Bailmeach, *a.* Balmy, abounding in balm, made of balm.

Bailmeanta, *a.* Balmy, balsamic.

Bailte, *n. pl.* of baile. Towns, cities, villages. Leig thusa bailte treun, *thou hast thrown down mighty cities.—Sm.*

Bailteach, *a.* (*from* baile.) Abounding in towns or in villages; of, or belonging to, a town or village; civic.

Bailteachas, ais, *s. m.* (*from* baile.) Planting or founding towns, colonizing.

Bailtean, *n. pl.* of baile. Towns, cities, villages. *D. pl.* bailtibh.

Bàin, *gen. sing.* of bàn; which see.

Bainbh, *s. f.* A young pig. *Ir.* banabh *and* banbh. *W.* banw, *swine. Arm.* vano. *Corn.* banv.

Bainbheachd, *s. f.* See Bainbhidheachd.

Bainbhidheachd, *contr.* bainbheachd, *s. f.* (*from* bainbh.) Pigging; furrowing; piggishness, swinishness. Tha mhuc a teannadh ri bainbhidheachd, *the sow is about pigging.*

Bainbhinn, *s. f.* A suckling pig.

Bainchead, *a.* Authority, license.

Bain-cheadaichte, *part.* Authorized, licensed.

Baindeachd, *s. f.* (*contr. for* baindidheachd.) Female modesty, bashfulness; effeminacy, reserve. Ge mor am baindeachd, *though great be their modesty.—Old Song.*

Baindidh, *a.* (*from* ban.) *Ir.* banda, *a female.* Modest, feminine, female, effeminate; unassuming. Gu baindidh, *modestly.*

Baindidheachd, *s. f.* (*from* baindidh.) Female modesty, bashfulness, reserve; effeminacy, delicacy. Cha n fhaic mi leithid air baindidheachd, *I shall not see her equal for modesty.*

Bàine, *s. f.* Paleness, whiteness, fairness. *Aspirated form,* bhàine. A sioladh a bhàine, *concealing his paleness.—Oss. Tem.*

Bàine, *com.* and *sup.* of bàn. More or most pale. *Ir.* bàine.

Baineasg, isg, *s. m.* A ferret.—*Ir. id.*

Baineasgach, *a.* Like a ferret; abounding in ferrets; of, or pertaining to, a ferret.

Bainidh, *s. f.* Fury, madness, rage. *Ir.* bainidhe. *Corn.* buanegez.

Bainisg, *s. f.* A little old woman. *N. pl.* bainisgean.

Bainisgeag, eig, *s. f.* (*dim.* of bainisg.) A little old woman. *N. pl.* bainisgeagan.

Bainisgeil, *a.* (bainisg-amhuil.) Like an old woman.

Bainionn, **Bainnionn**, *a.* (*Ir.* bainion.) Female, feminine; she. Firionn agus bainionn, *male and female.—Stew. G. B.* Na gabhair bhainionn, *the she-goats.—Stew. Gen.* Written also *boirionn.*

Bainionnach, **Bainnionnach**, aich, *s. f.* A female. Written also *boirionnach.*

Bainionnach, *a.* Female, feminine, effeminate. Firionnach agus bainionnach, *male and female.—Stew. Gen.*

Bainionnachd, *s. f.* (*from* bainionn.) Effeminacy.

Bainionnas, ais, *s. m.* Muliebrity.—*Shaw.*

† **Bainne**, *s. f.* A drop of any liquid. Now written *boinne;* which see.

Bainne, *s. m.* (*Ir.* bainne.) Milk, milky juice. A sruthadh le bainne agus mil, *flowing with milk and honey;* bo-bhainne, *a milch cow;* cro-bhainne, *milch cattle;* camhail bhainne, *milch camels.—Stew. Gen.* Bainne na cìpe, *the milky juice of the mountain-herb.—Macint.* Bainne blàth, *fresh milk;* bainne ùr, *fresh milk;* bainne milis, *sweet or fresh milk;* bainne lom, *skimmed milk;* bainne chaorach, *sheep's milk;* bainne ghabhar, *goat's milk;* bainne chapull, *mare's milk;* bainne asal, *asses' milk;* bainne nòis, *biestings;* bainne binntichte, *curdled milk;* bainne goirt, *sour milk;* bainne na cìche, *the milk of the breast;* bainne-ghamhnach, *honeysuckle.*

Bainneach, *a.* Milky, lacteal, like milk, abounding in milk; milk-producing. A Bhealtuinn bhainneach, *milk-producing May.—Macfar.*

† **Bainnealach**, aich, *s. m.* A dropping of rain.

Bainnear, *a.* Milky, abounding in milk.—*Macint.*

Bainn-fhreagradh, aidh, *s. m.* A bond; a stipulation. —*Shaw.*

Bainnse, *gen. sing.* of banais. Of a wedding.—*Ir. id.* See **Banais.**

† **Bainnseach**, ich, *s. m.* A plain, a field; sheep-walk; a solitary place.—*Shaw.*

Bainnseachd, *s. f.* Feasting, banquetting.—*Shaw.*

Bainnsean, *n. pl.* of banais. Weddings.

Bain-spireag, eig, *s. f.* A sparrow-hawk.—*Shaw.* The falco nisus of Linnæus. *N. pl.* bain-spireagan.

Bain-spireagach, *a.* Like a sparrow-hawk, of a sparrow-hawk.

Bain-tighearna, *s. f.* A lady; the lady of a baronet, or of a knight; a name for ladies in general; a gentlewoman. *N. pl.* bain-tighearnan, *ladies;* guidheam ort a bhain-tighearna, *I beseech thee, lady.—Stew. N. T.*

Bain-tighearnas, ais, *s. m.* The rule or sway of a lady. Tha e fu' bhain-tighearnas, *he is under petticoat government.*

Bain-tighearnachd, *s. f.* Ladyship. Do bhain-tighearneachd, *your ladyship.*

Bain-treabhach, *contr.* baintreach, iche, *s. f.* A widow.

Bain-treabhachas, *contr.* baintreachas, ais, *s. m.* Widowhood.

Baintreach, ich, *s. f.* A widow. *N. pl.* baintrichean, *widows.* Written also *bantrach.*

Baintreachas, ais, *s. m.* Widowhood. Written also *bantrachas.*

Bàir, bàire, *s. f.* A battle; a strife; a game; also a road, a path.—*Macd.* Air magh na bàire, *on the plain of battle. —Fingalian Poem.*

Bairceàn, ein, *s. m.* A ferret.—*Shaw.*

† **Bairche**, *a.* Strong; brave.—*Ir. id.*

† **Bairche**, *s. f.* A battle.—*Ir.*

Baircinn, *s. pl.* Cross sticks, or side timbers for a house.

Baird, *gen. sing.* and *n. pl.* of bard.

† **Bairdheis**, *s. f.* The point, tip, or end, of any sharp instrument.

Bairead, eid, *s. m.* (barr, *top*, and eididh, *dress.*) A bonnet, cap, hat, helmet.
Ir. bairead. *Vulgar Gr.* βιρετα. *Lat.* biretum. *Germ.* baret. *Sclav.* baretta. *It.* baireat.

Bair-eatrom, *a.* Light-headed; nimble, swift.

Bairgeanta, *a.* Strong, stout, sturdy; swift.

† **Bairghean**, ein, *s. m.* A cake; a floor; a plot of ground. —*Shaw.*

Bairghin, *s. m.* A begotten son.—*Shaw.*

Bair-ghinteach, *a.* Begetting sons; also, *substantively,* a woman who bears sons.—*Shaw.*

† **Bairicean**, ein, *s. m.* A ferret.

Bàirich, *v. n.* Low, bellow, roar. *Pret. a.* bhàirich, *roared; fut. aff. a.* bàirichidh, *shall roar.*

Bairich, *s. f.* A lowing, a bellow, a roar. A leum ri bàirich nam bò, *jumping at the lowing of the cows.—Macdon.* Ciod a bhàirich th'ort? *what are you bellowing at?*

Bàiricheadh, idh, *s. m.* A lowing, a bellowing; a continued lowing or bellowing.

Bàirichidh, *fut. aff. a.* of bàirich. Shall or will low.

Bairig, *v.* (*Du.* bereik, *reach.*) Bestow, confer, grant, present. *Pret. a.* bhairig, *bestowed; fut. aff. a.* bairigidh, *shall or will present.*

Bairill, *s. f.* A barrel of any description. See **Baraill.**

Bairin, *s. f.* A small cake. *Heb.* baroth; *and* barah, *take refreshment.—Buxtorf. Lex. Gr.* βορα, *meat. W. bara.*

† **Bairinn**, *s. f.* A firebrand. *Ir. id.*

Bàirlinn, *s. f.* A rolling wave, or sea; a high sea; also a warning or summons of removal. Gaoir na bairlinn, *the noise of the rolling sea.—Macfar. N. pl.* bair-linntichean, or bair-linntean. Am fear a thug dhomh a bhairlinn, *he who gave me the warning.—Old Song.*

Bairlinneach, *a.* Rolling, as a high sea; billowy; summoning, or warning, to quit one's residence.

Bairneach, ich, *s. m.* A limpet.—*Macd.*

† **Bairneach**, *a.* Perverse, obstinate, fretful; also filial.

† **Bairnich**, *v. a.* Fret; judge. *Pret. a.* bhairnich, *fretted; fut. aff. a.* bàirnichidh, *shall or will fret.*

Bairneachd, *s. f.* A judging; a judgment, a decision at law; also perverseness, obstinacy, fretfulness.

Bairseach, ich, *s. f.* A scold, a shrew. *Ir. id.*

Bairseachd, *s. f.* A scolding, raillery; satire. *Ir.* bairseachd.

Bairseag, eig, *s. f.* A young scold; a young shrew. *N. pl.* bairseagan.

Bairseag, eig, *s. f.* The top of the windpipe.—*Shaw.*

Bairsich, *v. a.* (*Ir.* bairsigh.) Scold, rail; satirize, lampoon. *Pret. a.* bhàirsich, *scolded; fut. aff.* bàirsichidh, *shall scold.*

† **Bais**, *s. f.* Water. *Ir. id.*

Bàis, *gen.* of bàs; which see.

Bais, *gen.* of bas; more commonly written *bos;* which see.

† **Baisc**, *a.* Round. *Ir. id.*

Baischailce, *s. f.* Ruddle.—*Shaw.*

Baisceall, ill, *s. m.* A wild, ungovernable person; a mad person. *Ir. id.*

Baisceanta, *a.* See **Basganta.**

Baiseach, *a.* Having a large palm; flat, smooth.

Baiseachd, *s. f.* (*from* bas.) Palmistry. More frequently written *boiseachd,* from *bos.*

† **Baiseal**, eil, *s. m.* Pride; arrogance. *Ir. id.*

Baisealach, *a.* (*from* baiseal.) Proud, arrogant. *Com.* and *sup.* baisealaiche, *more or most proud.*

† **Baisleach**, ich, *s. m.* An ox; also a handful of water or any thing.—*Shaw.*

Baist, *v. a.* Baptize; perform the ceremony of baptism. *Pret. a.* bhaist, *baptized; fut. aff. a.* baistidh, *shall baptize.*

Nach do bhaist mi h-aon agaibh, *that I have not baptized any of you.—Stew.* 1 *Cor.*

Baiste, *p. part.* of baist. Baptize.

Baisteadh, idh, *s. m.* A baptism; a baptizing. Aon bhaisteadh, *one baptism.—Stew. Eph.* Tha e air a bhaisteadh, *he is baptized;* tha i air a baisteadh, *she is baptized.*

Baistidh, *fut. aff. a.* of baist. Shall or will baptize.

Baistidh, *a.* Baptismal. Amar baistidh, *a baptismal font.*

† **Baistidhe**, *s.* Drops from a house.—*Shaw.*

Bàitē, (*for* bathte), *p. part.* of bath. Drowned. *Asp. form,* bhàite. A bhileag bhaite, *a green weed that is observed on the surface of pools or standing water; a water lily.*

Baiteal, eil, *s. m.* A battle. Chuir iad baiteal, *they had a pitched battle.*

W. batel. *Fr.* bataille. *Span.* batella. *Swed.* batalje. *Bisc.* batalla. *Old Burgundian,* batalia. *Portug.* batalha.

Baithis, *s. f.* A forehead, a brow. Do bhaithis bhog bhàn, *thy soft and fair forehead.—Old Song.*

Bàl, bàil, *s. m.* A ball or dance.

Old Celtic, bàll. *Eng.* ball. *It.* ballo. *Span.* bayle. *Fr.* bâl. *Gr.* βαλλισμος.

Balach, aich, *s. m.* (*contr. for* balaoch, *i. e.* ba-laoch.) A lad, a young man, a clown, a fellow, a sturdy fellow. *Ir.* bathlach. *N. pl.* balaiche, *lads.* Balach na h-aimhreite, *a name given to a quarrelsome disorderly fellow.*

Balachail, (*i. e.* balach-amhuil), *a.* Clownish; boyish, puerile.

Balachan, ain, *s. m.* (*dim.* of balach.) A little boy; a boy. Nuair bha thu do bhalachan faoin, *when thou wert a helpless boy.—Oss. Tem.* Maide balachain, *a boy's stick.—Id.*

Balachain, *gen. sing.* of balach; which see.

Balagam, aim, *s. m.* A mouthful; a sip; a gulp. Balagam bainne, *a mouthful of milk;* gabh balagam, *take a mouthful.*

† **Balaighe**, *s. f.* Advantage, profit, benefit.—*Ir. id.*

Balaist, *s. f.* Ballast.—*Macd.*

Balaoch, laoich, *s. m.* (*i. e.* ba-laoch, *a cowherd.*) A boy, lad; clown; a fellow. *N. pl.* balaoich. Chuireadh tu uaill anns a bhalaoch, *thou wouldst put pride into the clown.—R.*

Balbh, *a.* (*Ir.* balbh.) Mute, dumb, silent, quiet, at peace. Mar uisge balbh a glinn, *like the silent water of the valley.—Oss. Fin. and Lor.* Mar bhalbh dhriuchd, *like the silent dew.—Oss. Fing. Gen. sing.* bailbh; *aspirated form,* bhailbh. Airson an duine bhailbh, *for the dumb man.—Stew. Pro. Com.* and *sup.* bailbhe.

Balbhachd, *s. f.* (*from* balbh.) Dumbness, muteness; silence, quietness. Marbh bhalbhachd na h-oidhche, *the dead silence of night.—Old Poem.*

Balbhan, ain, *s. m.* (*Ir.* balbhan.) A dumb person. Labhair am balbhan, *the dumb spoke.—Stew. Mat. N. pl.* balbhain.

Balbhanachd, *s. f.* (*from* balbhan.) Dumbness, muteness; dumb show.

Balc, bailc, *s.* A balk; a boundary; a ridge of earth between two furrows: also the crusty surface of the earth occasioned by long heat. *W.* balc. *Swed.* balk, *a partition.*

† **Balc**, *a.* Strong, stout; lusty, sturdy.—*Ir. id.*

Balcanta, *a.* Stout, firm, strong. Gu balcanta, *firmly, stoutly.—Macfar.*

Balg, *s. m.* A man of learning.—*Ir. id.*

Balg, builg, *s. m.* A leather bag, a budget, a wallet, a pock, a scrip, a satchel; a belly, womb; a blister. Balg-saighead, *a quiver;* balg-losgainn, *a mushroom;* balg séid, *a pair of bellows.*

Gr. Æol. βολγος. *Lat.* † bulga. *Belg.* balg. *Hind.* baelg, *a sack. Sax.* belge. *Germ.* balg.

Balg is an ancient Celtic vocable, and in every language where it is seen, it has the same signification as in Gaelic. The ancient Gauls and Britons, the Goths, Saxons, and Franks, used it to denote a wallet, and often a quiver. " Bulgas Galli saccos scorteos appellant."—Festus. And Boxthorn, in *Lex. Ant. Brit.* has *balgan* and *bolgan,* meaning a quiver. From *balg* comes the word Belgae itself, which means quiver-bearers; for these people were always armed with bows and arrows. *Balg* is often written *bolg;* which see.

Balgach, *a.* Like a bag, like a wallet; bagged, bellied, blistered.

Balgaich, *v. a.* and *n.* Belly out, as a sail; blister; stow in a bag or satchel.

Balgair, *s. m.* A fox; a dog: also, *in contempt,* a cunning fellow. *N. pl.* balgairean. A bhalgair òglaich, *thou fox of a fellow;* a bhalgair tha thu an, *thou fox that thou art;* buail am balach air a charbad, is buail am balgair air an t-sròin, *strike the clown on the cheek and the dog on the nose.—G. P.*

Balgaireachd, *s. f.* Slyness, cunning, craftiness.

Balgairean, *n. pl.* of balgair. Foxes.

Balgan, ain, *s. m.* (*dim.* of balg.) A little bag, a satchel, a wallet; a little pock, a little sack; a little blister; a belly. *N. pl.* balgain. Balgan-uisge, *a water bubble.*

Balgan seididh, *s. m.* A little pair of bellows; also a fuzz-ball.

Balgan-suain, *s. m.* A sleepy bag. Chuir iad am balgan suain fo 'n ceann, *they have put the sleepy bag under their heads.—G. P.*

According to Mackintosh, this proverb, said of a person who indulges in sleep, alludes to the dormant state of the caterpillar when it is enclosed in something like a bag, here called the sleepy bag.

Balgan-uisge, *s. m.* A water bubble; also a blister full of watery humour.

Balg-bhronnach, *a.* Swag-bellied. Badach beag balg-bhronnach, *a little swag-bellied churl.—Old Song.*

Balg-chosach, *a.* Bow-legged.

Balg-losgainn, *s. m.* A mushroom; toad-stool; paddock-stool.

Balg-saighead, *s. m.* A quiver. Bha bhalg saighead ri thaobh, *his quiver was at his side.—Oss. Cathluno.*

Balg-seididh, *s. m.* A pair of bellows.

Balg-shùil, *s. f.* A large prominent eye.

Balg-shuileach, *a.* Having prominent eyes.

† **Ball**, *s. m.* (*Bisc.* bull.) A skull.

Ball, *gen.* buill, *s. m.* A member, a limb; a member of a society; the male instrument of generation; an instrument, tool, or implement; a ball, a foot-ball, a globular body; a boss; a spot, a plat of ground, a place; rarely a cable. *N. pl.* buill. Do 'n bhacach lùgh nam ball, *strength of limbs to the lame.—Smith.* Dh' uireasbhuidh na bhallaibh, *lacking in his parts.—Stew. Lev.* Buill shoilleir, *bright spots.—Id.* Buill a Chomuinn Ghaidhealaich, *the members of the Highland Society.* A bhall so, *this plat.—Stew. Heb. ref.* Ball oibre, *a tool to work with;* ball airm, *a weapon;* ball acfhuinn, *a tool;* ball amhairc, *a spectacle;* ball sampuill, *a specimen;* ball seirc, *a beauty spot;* ball-dobhrain, *a mole;* ball faobhrach, *a sharp instrument;* ball-fearais, *the male instrument of generation;* ball àbhachd, ball àbhachais, *a gazing stock;* ball sgòid, *a sheet rope;* ball tàmailt, *an object of disgrace;* ball-magaidh, *an object of derision;* ball sgòd, *a blemish;* ball otraiche, *a puddle.*

This old Celtic word is to be met with in many tongues, signifying a globular body. *Gr.* πάλλα, *apud Heyschium. Gr.* βαλλω, *throw. Germ.* ball, *a globe. Belg.* bal. *Fr.* balle. *Du.* bal. *Span.* bala, *a bullet. Ir.* ball. *English,* ball. *Pol.* piela.

Ball [air], *adv.* Immediately; on the spot. *Ir.* ar bal.

Balla, ai, *s. m.* See **Balladh**.

Ball-àbhachais, *s. m.* A gazing stock; a laughing stock. Ball àbhachais bi-bhuan, *a perpetual laughing stock.—Stew. Jer.* and *Heb. ref. N. pl.* buill àbhachais.

BALL-ÀBHACHD, *s. f.* A laughing stock; an object of mockery; a gazing stock. Ball abhachd do na bheil mun cuairt, *a laughing stock to all around.—Smith.*

BALLACH, *a.* (*from* ball.) *Gr.* βαλιος, *maculosus.* Spotted; striped; tartan; bossy; walled; having lofty walls. Breac agus ballach, *speckled and spotted.—Stew. Gen.* An sgiath bhallach, *the bossy shield.—Oss. Fing.* Sgiath bhallach nam beum, *the spotted shield of blows.—Oss. Tem.* Bonaid bhallach, *a spotted or tartan bonnet.—Macfar. Com.* and *sup.* ballaiche.

BALL', *for* balladh.

BALL-ACFHUINN, *s. m.* A tool; instrument; tackling.

BALLADH, aidh, BALLA, ai, *s. m.* (*Lat.* vall-um. *Swed.* vall. *Ir.* balla.) A wall, a rampart; also the boss of a shield. Balladh a bhaile, *the wall of the town.—Stew. Jos.* Baile nam balla cam, *the town of the winding walls.—Oss. Tem.* Meirg air a balla, *rust on its boss.—Oss. Cath. and Col.* Balladh dealachaidh, *a partition-wall.—Stew.* 1 *K. N. pl.* ballachan.

BALLAG, aig, *s. f.* An egg-shell; also a skull. *Ir.* ballog, *a skull.*

BALLAG-LOSGAINN, *s. f.* A toad-stool; a mushroom.

BALL-AIRM, *s. m.* A weapon. Thilg gach ball-àirm, *every weapon was thrown aside.—Oss. Fing.*

BALLAIRT, *gen. sing.* of ballart.

BALLAN, ain, *s. m.* (*Ir.* ballan. *Scotch,* balden.) A tub; a bucket; a churn; a shell; a covering; a broom; a teat or udder. Ballan binntiche, *a cheese-press;* ballan losgainn, *a toad-stool;* ballan bainne, *a milk-tub;* ballan nigheachain, *a washing-tub;* ballan seilcheig, ballan stiallach, *a kind of pillory.*

BALLAN-BINNTICHE, *s. m.* A cheese vat or press.

BALLAN-LOSGAINN, *s. m.* A toad-stool; a mushroom.

BALLAN-NIGHEACHAIN, BALLAN-NIGHEADAIREACHD, *s. m.* A washing-tub.

BALLAN-SEILCHEIG, *s. m.* A snail-shell.

BALLAN-STIALLACH, *s. m.* A pillory. Air ballan stiallach 'g ad sparradh, *fastening thee to the pillory.—Old Poem.*

The *ballan-stiallach* was a kind of pillory, used of old in the Highlands, for punishing liars and petty offenders. It was a sort of frame erected on a pillar, to which the culprit was tightly bound with a rope about the shoulders, by which he hung, exposed to the ridicule and maltreatment of passengers.

BALLARD, BALLART, airt, *s. m.* Loud noise, clamour, turbulence. Gun bhallart, gun mhòrchuis, *without noise or boasting.—Moladh mhoraig.*

BALLARDACH, BALLARTACH, *a.* Noisy, turbulent, clamorous, troublesome. *Com.* and *sup.* ballardaiche or ballartaiche, *more or most noisy.*

BALLARDACHADH, BALLARTACHADH, aidh, *s. m.* A proclamation; the act of proclaiming, bawling, or making a noise.

BALLARDACHD, BALLARTACHD, *s. f.* A proclamation; noise; clamour.

BALLARDADH, BALLARTADH, aidh, *s. m.* A proclamation.

BALLARDAICH, BALLARTAICH, *s. f.* A loud noise; a howling; a shouting, hooting. Ciod a bhallartaich th' art? *what are you howling at?*

BALLARDAICH, BALLARTAICH, *v. n.* Proclaim; howl, shout, hoot. *Pret. a.* bhallardaich, *shouted; fut. aff. a.* ballardaichidh, *shall shout.*

BALL-BHREAC, BALL-BHREACHD, *a.* Variegated, chequered, spotted, grisled. A bheath bhall-bhreachd, *variegated life.—Oss. Conn.* Mar neulaibh ball-bhreac, *like spotted clouds, i. e.* like that modification of cloud which metereologians term *cirro-cumulus.*

BALL-CHRITH, *s.* Trembling; terror; tremor; a trembling with terror. An darach air ball-chrith, *the oak trembling.—Orran.* Fo bhall-chrith mar dhuilleach, *trembling like leaves.—Oss. Duthona.* Ball-chrith air righrean an domhain, *terror on the kings of the earth.—Stew. O. T.* Le ball-chrith deanaibh gairdeachas, *rejoice with trembling.—Sm.*

BALL-CLUAISE, *s. m.* The sheet rope of a vessel.

BALL-COISE, *s. m.* A foot-ball.

BALL-DEISE, *s. m.* An instrument to which two persons have a right; a tool; any useful instrument or weapon.

BALL-DHEARG, *a.* Grisled; bay-coloured. Eich bhall-dhearg, *bay horses.—Stew. Zech.*

BALL-DIOMHAIR, *s. m.* A secret member: *membrum pudendum.* Buill dhiomhair, *secret members.*

BALL-DOBHRAIN, *s. m.* A mole.

BALL-DUBH, *s. m.* A blot, a blemish.—*Macd.*

BALL-FANAID, *s. m.* A laughing stock; an object of mockery.

BALL-FAOBHRACH, aich, *s. m.* A sharp-edged instrument.

BALL-FEARAIS, *s. m.* *Membrum virile.*

BALL-FOCHAID, *s. m.* A laughing stock; an object of derision.—*Stew. Job.*

BALL-GHALAR, air, *s. m.* A plague; a gonorrhœa.

BALL-IOMCHAIR, *s. m.* A support, a prop; an undersetter.—*Stew.* 1 *K. ref.*

BALL-MAGAIDH, *s. m.* A laughing stock; an object of derision.—*Stew. Job.*

BALL-MOSGLAIDH, *s. m.* An instrument for sounding an alarm.—*Oss. Tem.*

BALL-OIBRE, *s. m.* A tool, an instrument. *N. pl.* buill oibre.

BALL-ÒTRAICHE, *s. m.* A puddle or slough; a miry place.

BALL-SAMPUILL, *s. m.* An example; a sample, a specimen. Rinn e ball sampuill dhiubh, *he made an example of them.—Stew. Col.*

BALL-SEIRCE, *s. m.* A beauty-spot.—*Macd.*

BALL-SGEIG, *s. m.* A laughing stock, a mocking stock, an object of derision. Ni mi a chathair na ball-sgeig, *I will make the city a (hissing) laughing stock.—Stew. G. B.*

BALL-SGEIMHE, *s. m.* A beauty-spot.—*Macd.*

BALL-SGIATH, -sgeithe, *s. f.* A bossy shield. Fionnghal nam ball-sgiath, *Fingal with the bossy shield.—Oss. Fing.*

BALL-SGIORRADH, aidh, *s. m.* A deed done unexpectedly; a feat.

BALL-SGIORRAIL, *a.* Performing unexpected deeds.

BALL-SGÒID, *s. m.* A sheet rope; a spot, a blemish.—*Macd.* A blister.—*Shaw.*

BALL-TAMAILT, *s. m.* An object of disgrace, or of reproach. Tha thu do bhall tàmailt, *thou art an object of disgrace.—Mac Lach.*

BALL-TOIRMISG, *s. m.* A forbidden tool; a forbidden weapon.

BALT, bailt, *s. m.* (*Ir.* balta.) A welt; a belt, a border. *N. pl.* baltan.

BALTACH, *a.* Welted, belted, bordered.

BALTAICH, *v. a.* Welt, belt, border. *Pret. a.* bhaltaich; *fut. aff. a.* baltaichidh.

BÀN, bàin, *s. m.* The matrix of a cow.

† BAN, bain, *s. m.* Copper; a copper mine.—*Ir. id.*

BAN, *s. f.* (*Pers.* bann, *a dame. Ir.* ban.) A female; a woman, wife, a dame. *Asp. form,* bhan. Beul bhan coimheach, *the mouth of strange women.—Stew. Pro.* Am measg bhan òg, *among young females.—Old Song.*

BÀN, *a.* White, pale, fair, fair-haired; also vacant, waste. Nighean bhroillich bhàin, *white-bosomed maid.—Oss. Fing.* Siùil bhàn, *white sails.—Oss. Carricth.* Fhir bhàin, *thou fair-haired man;* talamh bàn, *waste ground;* eich bhàn, *white horses.—Stew. Zech. Com.* and *sup.* bàine.

Ir. bàn. *Manx,* bàn. *Heb.* and *Chald.* la-ban, *white. Syr.* labano, *white. Samaritan,* laban, *white. Arab.* labana, *a white poplar.*

Ban-aba, *s. f.* An abbess. *Ir.* banab.

Bànachadh, aidh, *s. m.* A whitening, a bleaching; growing pale or white; a laying waste.

Bànachadh, (a), *pr. part.* of banaich. Whitening; growing pale, laying waste.

Bana-chàra, **Bana-charaid**, *s. f.* A female relative, a kinswoman.—*Stew. Song of Sol*

Ban-adhaltranach, aiche, *s. f.* An adulteress —*Stew. Pro.* Goirear ban-adhaltranach dhith, *she shall be called an adulteress.*—*Stew Rom.*

Bànag, aig, *s. f.* (*dim. from* bàn.) Any thing white; a white-faced girl; a grilse; a cant term for a shilling.

Banag, aig, *s. f.* (*from* ban.) A smart little woman. *N. pl.* banagan.

Banaich, *v. a.* and *n.* Whiten, bleach, make pale, lay waste, make waste or vacant; grow white, pale, or bleached. *Pret. a.* bhànaich, *whitened*, *fut. aff. a.* bànaichidh, shall or will whiten. *Ir.* banaigh.

Banail, *a.* (*i. e.* ban-amhuil) *W.* benywawl *Ir.* banamhail Modest, womanly, womanish, feminine; comely. A bhean bhanail, *his modest wife.*—*Oss. Lodin.* Giùlan banail, *womanly deportment.*—*Old Song.* Lic bhanail, *comely cheeks. Oss. Carth.*

† **Banailt**, *s. f.* A nurse. *Ir.* banailt. *Bisc.* banlitu.

Banais, *gen.* bainnse. (*Ir.* banais) A wedding; *perhaps* ban-fhéis, *a female feast.* Fear na bainnse, *the bridegroom;* bean na bainnse, *the bride*, culaidh bainnse, *a wedding dress.*—*Macdon.* *N. pl.* bainnsean, *weddings.*

† **Banaiteach**, *a.* Serious, grave, sedate.

Banaltrachd, *s. f.* Nursing; the business of a nurse. Mach air bhanaltrachd, *out at nursing.*

Banaltradh, aidh, *s. f.* A nurse. *Ir.* banaltra.

Banaltrum, uim, *s f.* A nurse. Fhuair i banaltrum, *she got a nurse.*—*Stew. Gen.*

Banaltrumachd, *s. f.* Nursing. Commonly pronounced *banaltrachd.*

Banamhalta, *a.* Shamefaced, modest, bashful. *Ir.* banamhalta.

Banamhaltachd, *s. f.* Shamefacedness, modesty, bashfulness. *Ir. id*

Banarach, aich, *s. f* A dairy-maid, a milk-maid. Teann air a bhanarach, *close to the dairy-maid* —*Macint*

Ban-bharan, ain, *s. f.* A baroness.

Ban-bhard, -bhaird, *s f* A poetess.

Ban-bhardachd, *s. f.* The verses of a poetess.

Ban-bhiicas, ais, *s. f.* A viscountess.—*Macd*

Bàn-bhroilleach, *a.* White-bosomed. Comhnuidh nam bàn-bhroilleach oigh, *the dwelling of the white-bosomed maids* —*Oss. Temo.*

Ban-bhuachaill, *s. f.* A shepherdess. *N pl.* ban-bhuachaillean.

Ban-bhuachailleachd, *s. f.* The business of a shepherdess, the condition of a shepherdess.

Ban-bhuidseach, ich, *s. f.* A witch, a sorceress —*Stew Exod.* *N. pl* ban-bhuidsichean.

Ban-bhùsdraich, *s. f.* A witch, a sorceress —*Stew Exod.*

Banc, bainc, *s. m.* A balk; a limit. *N. pl.* bancan. *Eng* bank. *Swed.* bank. *It.* banca.

Bancach, *a.* Having a balk; like a balk; of, or belonging to, a balk or limit.

Bancait, *s. f.* A banquet. *N. pl.* bancaitean.

Bancaiteach, *a.* Banqueting, fond of banqueting

Bancaiteachd, *s. f.* Continued or frequent banqueting

Ban-charaid, *s. f.* A female relative, a kinswoman. Do ban-charaid, *thy kinswoman.*—*Stew. Pro.* Written also *bana-charaid;* which see.

Ban-cheard, *s f.* A female gipsy, a female tinker; often applied in contempt to a mannerless female.

Ban-chéile, *s. f.* A wife; *literally*, a female spouse.

Ban-cheileadair, *s. m.* An executrix. *N. pl.* ban-cheileadairean.

Ban-chleamhuinn, *s f* A daughter-in-law. Nochd do bhan-chleamhna, *the nakedness of the daughter-in-law.*—*Stew Exod.* Maille ri a ban-chleamhuinn, *with her daughter-in-law.*—*Stew. O T.*

Ban-chocair, *s f.* A female cook, a woman cook —*Stew Sam.* *N. pl.* ban-chocairean.

Ban-chocaireachd, *s. f.* The business of a female cook, the handiwork of a female cook. Tha i 'g ionnsachadh na ban-chocaireachd, *she is learning the business of cookery.*

Ban-choigle, *s. f.* A female gossip; a female companion. *Ir.* ban-choigle

Ban-chomh-dhalta, *s. f.* A foster-sister. *N. pl.* ban-chomh-dhaltan.

Ban-chompanach, aich, *s. f.* A female companion.—*Stew Judg.* *N. pl* ban-chompanaich.

Ban-chompanas, ais, *s. m.* Female companionship. Na dean ban-chompanas ri, *keep not company with her*

Ban-chruitear, ir, *s. f.* (*Ir* ban-chruitire) A female harper *N pl* ban-chruitearan.

Ban-chuisleanaiche, *s f.* A female who plays on a wind instrument. *Ir.* ban-chuisleanaich.

Bandachd, *s. f.* Contracted for *bandaidheachd;* which see.

Bandaidh, *a* (*from* ban) *Ir.* bandha. Modest, delicate, effeminate, womanish. Bean bhandaidh, *a modest woman.*

Bandaidheachd, *s. f.* Delicacy, modesty, effeminacy, womanishness

Bandalta, **Bandhalta**, *s f* A foster-daughter.

Bandhalta-baistidh, *s. f.* A god-daughter.

Ban-dia, *gen* ban-dé, *s. f.* (*Ir. id*) A goddess. A bhan-dia a ni am bogh frois, *the goddess who forms the rainbow.*—*Mac Lach.*

Ban-druidh, *s. f.* An enchantress, a sorceress. *Ir.* ban-druadh.

Ban-eigneachadh, idh, *s m.* A rape

Ban-fhaidh, *s f.* A prophetess. *N. pl.* ban-fhaighean, *prophetesses.*

Ban-fheadanach, aiche, *s. f.* A female piper; a female who plays on any wind instrument. *Ir.* ban-fheadanach.

Ban-fhigheach, iche, *s m* A female weaver; a female who knits.

Ban-fhigheadaireachd, *s. f.* The work of a female weaver.

Ban-fhiosaiche, *s. f* A fortune-teller; a prophetess. *N. pl* ban-fhiosaichean.

Ban-fhlath, *s. f* A lady; a heroine. *N. pl* ban-fhlaitheau, *ladies*

Ban-fhluasgach, *a* Menstrual.

Ban-fhluasgadh, aidh, *s m* Menstrual courses.

Ban-fhuaidhealachd, *s. f.* (*pronounced* banalachd) Sewing, seaming; the business of a sempstress, or of a milliner; millinery; mantua-making.

Ban fhuaidhealaiche, **Ban-fhualaiche**, *s. f.* (*pronounced* banalaiche.) A sempstress, a milliner, a mantua-maker. *N. pl.* ban-fhualaichean.

Ban-fhuineadair, *s. f* A woman who bakes bread; a female cook.—*Stew. Sam*

† **Bang**, baing, *s m.* (*Ir. id*) A nut; a touch; a hinderance.

Bangait, *s. f.* A feast. *Teut* bancket *Eng.* banquet. Written also *bancait.*

Ban-ghrùdair, *s. f.* The landlady of an alehouse, or of an inn; a female brewer. *N. pl.* ban-ghrudairean. Cagar na ban-ghrudair, *the ale-wife's whisper soon turns loud.*—*G. P.*

BAN-IARLA, *s. f.* A countess. *N. pl.* ban-iarlan.

BAN-LAOCH, laoich, *s. f.* A heroine; Amazon; a virago. *N. pl.* ban-laoich.

BAN-LEIGH, *s. f.* A female skilled in medicine. *N. pl.* ban-leighean.

BAN-MHAIGHISTIR, *s. f.* A mistress; a schoolmistress. Ban-mhaighistir nan druidheachdan, *the mistress of the witchcrafts.—Stew. Nah. N. pl.* ban-mhaighistirean.

BAN-MHAIGHISTIREAS, eis, *s. m.* The rule or sway of a mistress, or of a schoolmistress.

BAN-MHARCAICHE, BAN-MHARCAIR, *s. f.* A female rider.

BAN-MHARCAIS, *s. f.* A marchioness. *N. pl.* ban-mharcaisean.

BAN-MHORAIR, BAN-MHOR'EAR, ir, *s. f.* A countess. *N. pl.* ban-mhorairean.

BANN, *a.* High. *Box. Lex.* bann. *Gr.* βουνος. Hence also the English, *banner.*

BANN, bainn, *s. m.* A band; a bond, bill; a tie; a hinge; a chain; a fetter; a band, as of a shirt, or any piece of clothing; a girth, a belt, a sash; a bann, a proclamation. *N. pl.* bannan *and* banntan, *bonds; d. pl.* bannaibh *or* banntaibh. Bannan bhur cuinge, *the bonds of your yoke.—Stew. Lev.* Le banntaibh daingean, *with firm bands.—Macint.* A fuaidheal bhann, *sowing bands.—Id.* A ceangal bhann mu sguaban, *binding sheaves.—Macfar.*

Germ. bann *and* band, *a bond. Teut.* bandi. *Franc.* bant. *Belg.* band. *Span.* banda, *a sash. Ir.* bann. *Pers.* bend. *Arm.* banden, *a fillet. Eng. and Runic,* band. *Old Sax.* bend. *Fr.* bande. Also *Eng. and Dan.* bind. *Cimbric,* binda, *to tie. Swed.* bundin, *tied. Tonquinese,* bun, *join. Portug.* bando, *a bann.*

† BANNACH, *a.* (*Ir.* bannach.) Active, expert; crafty.—*Shaw.*

† BANNACH, aich, *s. m.* A fox; *in ridicule,* a crafty person. *Ir.* bannach.

† BANNACHD, *s. f.* Craftiness, deceit. *Ir.* bannachd.

BANNAG, aig, *s. f.* A new-year's gift; a treat given to one on his first visit on new-year's day. Is mairg a rachadh air a bhannaig is a theanna aig fein, *it is woful to take from others when one has enough of his own.—G. P.*

BANNAL, ail, *s. m.* A company; a troop; band; a covey; a gathering, a collection, a crowd. Am bannal uchd-ruadh, *the red-breasted covey.—Macdon. Arm.* bannal, *in company, or in common.*

BANNALACH, *a.* In companies, in troops, in crowds.

BAN-NAOMH, naoimh, *s. f.* A female saint; a nun; a sainted female. *Ir. id. N. pl.* ban-naoimh, *nuns.*

BANN-BHRAGHAD, aid, *s. m.* A neckcloth, a cravat.

BANN-CHEANGAIL, *v. a.* Bind by bond. *Pret. a.* bhann-cheangail, *bound by bond; fut. aff. a.* bann-cheanglaidh; *fut. pass.* bann-cheanglar.

BANN-CHEANGAIL, *s. m.* An obligatory bond. *N. pl.* bannan-cheangail, *obligatory bonds.*

BANNDAIR, *s. m.* (*from* bann.) A covenanter; a drawer up of bonds or bills. *N. pl.* banndairean, *covenanters.*

BANNDAIREACHD, *s. f.* Covenant-making; a confederacy.

BANN-DUIRN, *s. m.* A wristband. Bann-dùirn léine, *the wristband of a shirt.*

BANN-LAMH, laimh, *s. m.* (*Ir. id.*) A cubit; also handcuffs. Aon bhann-lamh, *one cubit.—Stew. Mark, ref.*

† BANNSACH, aich, *s. m.* An arrow; any sharp-pointed missile weapon. *N. pl.* bannsaichean, *arrows.*

BANN-SHAOR, *a.* Free by law, licensed, authorized. *Ir.* bannshaoirseach.

BANN-SHAORSACHD, *s. f.* The condition of being free by law or bond.

BANN-SHAORSADH, aidh, *s. m.* A freedom or liberty sanctioned by law or by a bond.

BANN-SHAORSAICH, *v. a.* License. *Pret. a.* bhann-shaorsaich, *licensed; fut. aff. a.* bhann-shaorsaichidh, *shall license.*

BANN-SHORN, shoirn, *s. m.* A kind of girdle or bake-stove.—*Shaw.*

BANN-TAISBEANAIDH, BANN-TAISBEIN, *s. m.* A bond of appearance.

BAN-OGHA, *s. f.* A granddaughter. Ban-ogha an fhir ogha, *the grandson's granddaughter;* ban-ogha 'n fhir fhiar ogha, *the great-grandson's granddaughter.—Macd.*

BAN-ÒGLACH, aich, *s. f.* A female slave; a maid-servant; a handmaid; a maiden. *N. pl.* ban-òglaichean *and* banòglaich. Do bhan-oglaich, *thy maidens.—Stew. Pro, ref.*

BAN-OIGHRE, *s. f.* An heiress. *N. pl.* ban-oighrean.

BAN-OIGHREACHD, *s. f.* An estate that goes to heirs-female.

† BANRACH, aich, *s. m.* A fold for sheep, a pen; a cattle-house.—*Ir. id. N. pl.* banraichean.

BAN-RIDIR, *s. f.* A baroness, a baronet's lady. *N. pl.* bann-ridirean.

BAN-RIGH, *s. f.* A queen. Mairi, Ban-righ na h-Alba, *Mary, Queen of Scotland;* Ban-righ Bhreatuinn, *Queen of Britain.*

BAN-RIGHDIRE, *s. f.* See BAN-RIDIR.

BAN-RIGHINN, *s. f.* A queen. O bhi na ban-righinn, *from being a queen.—Stew.* 1 *K. N. pl.* ban-righinnean, *queens.* Iomarach na Ban-righinn, *the Queensferry in the Firth of Forth.*

BAN-SEALGAIR, *s. f.* A huntress. Ban sealgair Ardbheinn, *the huntress of Ardven.—Oss. Comal.* Bhan-shealgair nam fuar bheann faoin, *thou huntress of the cold desert hills.—Id. N. pl.* ban-sealgairean.

BANSGAL, ail, *s. f.* A woman; an aged female. This word is often applied to a female as a term of reproach. *N. pl.* bansgalan.

BAN-SHEARACH, aich, *s. f.* A mare-colt. *Ir. id. N. pl.* ban-shearaich.

BAN-SITH, *s. f.* A female fairy.

The Highlanders were wont to say that the wailings of this being were frequently heard before the death of a chieftain. She was seldom visible; but when she did make her appearance, it was in a blue mantle, and with dishevelled hair.

BAN-SNIOMHAICHE, *s. f.* A female spinner. *N. pl.* ban-sniomhaichean.

BAN-SOLARAICHE, *s. f.* A cateress. *N. pl.* ban-solaraichean.

† BAN-SPIORAG, aig, *s. f.* A sparrow-hawk. *N. pl.* ban-spioragan.

BAN-STIUBHART, airt, *s. f.* A housekeeper, a stewardess. *N. pl.* ban-stiùbhartan, *stewardesses.*

BAN-STIÙBHARTACH, *s. f.* A female surnamed Stewart.

BAN-TIGHEARNA, *s. m.* A baronet's lady; a lady. *N. pl.* ban-tighearnan, *ladies.*

BAN-TIGHEARNAIL, (*i. e.* ban-tighearnail.) Lady-like.

BANTRACH, aich, *s. f.* Fingal's seraglio.—*Shaw.*

BANTRÀCH, aich, *s. f.* (ban-treabhach.) A widow. *Aspirated form,* bhantrach. Do bhantrach mar eun tiamhaidh, *thy widow like a lonely bird.—Macfar. N. pl.* bantraichean, *widows.* Is olc a bhantrach a phiob, *the bagpipe is a sorry widow.—G. P.*

BANTRACHAS, ais, *s. m.* (*i. e.* ban-treabhachas.) Widowhood.

BAN-TRAILLE, *s. f.* A female slave, a bond-maid; a maid-servant. Ceud-ghin na ban-tràille, *the first-born of the maid-servant.—Stew. Exod. N. pl.* bantràillean, *female slaves;* do bhan-traillean, *thy bond-maids.—Stew. Lev.*

BAN-TREABHACH, aiche, *s. f.* A widow. Biodh bhean na ban-treabhach, *let his wife be a widow.—Smith. N. pl.* ban-treabhaichean; *contracted* bantrach; which see.

BAN-TUATHANACH, aich, *s. f.* A female who farms; a farmer's wife, a peasant's wife. *N. pl.* ban-tuathnaichean.

Ban-tuathanachas, ais, *s. m.* Agriculture done under the direction of a female.

Ban-tuathanaich, *gen. sing.* of ban-tuathanach.

Ban-tuathanaichean, *n. pl.* of ban-tuathanach.

Bao', *a.* Contracted for *baodh*, or *baoth*.

Baobh, *gen.* baoibh, *s. f.* A wizard; a wicked person, a mischievous female, a foolish woman. *W.* baw, *dirty*.

Baobhachd, *s. f.* (*from* baobh.) The conduct of a mischievous woman; also the croaking of a raven. *Ir.* badhbhachd.

Baobhai, Baobhaidh, *a.* (*W.* bawai, *dirty.*) Mad, wild, foolish, fearful, destructive. Dearg nam feachd baobhai, *Dargo of destructive hosts.—Oss. Conn.*

Baobhail, *a.* Mad, wild, foolish, fearful, destructive. Buillean trom baobhail, *heavy, fearful blows.—Oss. Derm.*

Baobhaileachd, *s. f.* Madness, wildness, fearfulness, destructiveness.

Baodh, *a.* Vain, giddy, foolish, soft, simple. Le sòlas baodh, *with giddy joy.—Smith.* Written also *baoth.*

Baoghal, ail, *s. m.* (*Ir.* baoghal.) Peril, danger; crisis; an important matter. Uisge beatha baoghal, *whiskey four times distilled, so powerful as to affect all the senses.* Fear an t-saoghail fhada cha bhi baoghal h-uig, *nothing will cut short the life of a long-liver.—G. P.*

Baoghalach, *a.* Wild, furious; destructive, perilous, dangerous. Roimh na gaothaibh baoghlach, *before the wild winds.—Old Poem.* Lag ri uair bhaoghlach, *weak in the hour of danger.—Oss. Duthona.* Is baoghalach am buille, *perilous is the blow.—Death of Carril.* *Com.* and *sup.* baoghalaiche.

Baoghalta, *a.* Foolish, credulous, silly, simple, idiotical. Creididh an duine baoghalta, *the simple man shall believe.—Stew. Pro.*

Baoghaltachd, *s. f.* Foolishness, credulousness, silliness, simpleness, idiocy. Cia fhad a ghradhaicheas sibh baoghaltachd? *how long will ye love simplicity?—Stew. Pro.*

Baoghan, ain, *s. m.* A calf; any thing jolly. Baoghan an cois gach bò, *each cow followed by its calf.—Old Song.*

Baoghanach, *a.* (*from* baoghan.) Like a calf; of, or belonging to, a calf.

Baoghlan, ain, *s. m.* (*from* baogh.) A foolish fellow. *N. pl.* baoghlain.

Baoghlanachd, *s. f.* (*from* baoghlan.) Foolishness; the behaviour of a foolish fellow.

Baois, *s. f.* Concupiscence, lust, levity; idle talk, madness. *Ir.* baois.

Baoiseach, *a.* (*from* baois.) Lewd, lascivious; giddy; lustful. *Com.* and *sup.* baoisiche, *more or most lewd.*

Baoiseachd, *s. f.* (*from* baois.) Concupiscence, lust, lasciviousness. Luchd baoiseachd, *lewd people.*

Baoisg, *v. n.* Shine forth, gleam, beam, radiate; peep, look. *Pret. a.* bhaoisg, *shone*; *fut. aff. a.* baoisgidh, *shall shine.* Nur bhaoisgeadh a gnuis, *when its face would shine forth.—Macdon.*

Baoisge, *s. f.* A flash of light, a gleam, a coruscation, a peep.

Baoisgeach, *a.* Gleaming; sparkling; emitting flashes of light; peeping.

Baoisgealachd, *s. f.* Refulgence, brightness.

Baoisgeil, (*i. e.* baoisg-amhuil), *a.* Shining, gleaming, bright, refulgent, radiant. A gnùis bhaoisgeil, *her gleaming countenance.—Macint.*

Baoisleach, ich, *s. m.* A brothel, a house of revelry or riot; also a frequenter of brothels. *Ir.* baoisteach.

Baoisleachd, *s. f.* (*from* baois.) Lewdness, lust; revelry. Luchd baoisleachd, *lewd people.*

Baoith, *a.* Airy, giddy, light, youthful. *Ir. id.* Mo bheanag bhuidhe bhaoith, *my yellow-haired, airy damsel.—Old Song.*

Baoithe, *s. f.* Airiness, giddiness, lightness, or levity; youthfulness.

Baoithe, *com.* and *sup.* of baoth; which see.

Baolach, *a.* *Contr. for* baoghalach; which see.

† **Baos**, *a.* Capricious, giddy. *Ir. id.*

Baosrach, aich, *s. m.* (*from* baos.) Madness, frenzy; also mad, frantic.

Baoth, *a.* (*Ir.* baoth.) Profane; wild, fierce, dreadful, horrid; vast; stupid, simple; soft; useless; deaf. Slighe nam peacach baoth, *the way of profane sinners.—Sm.* Fuathasach is baoth, *terrible and fierce.—Oss. Temo.* Fuaim bhaoth, *a horrid sound.—Oss. Fing.* Cho baoth ri d' airm, *as useless as thine arms.—Oss. Carricth.* Ann cunnart baoth, *in dreadful danger;* tional baoth an t-sluaigh, *the vast concourse of the people.—Id.* *Com.* and *sup.* baoithe, *more or most profane.*

Baothair, *i. e.* baoth-fhear, *s. m.* (*Germ.* bauer, *a rustic.*) A foolish fellow, a simpleton, an idiot. Is tu am baothair! *what a fool you are!* *N. pl.* baothairean.

Baothaireachd, *s. f.* (*from* baothair.) Stupidity; the talk or conduct of a fool.

Baothairean, *n. pl.* of baothair. Fools.

Baothan, ain, *s. m.* (*from* baoth.) A young fool, a blockhead. *N. pl.* baothair.

Baothanach, *a.* Foolish, simple, silly. Gu baothanach, *foolishly.*

Baothanachd, *s. f.* Foolishness, simpleness, silliness.

Baoth-bheus, *s. m.* Immorality; dishonest conduct. Comar nam baoth-bheus, *immoral Comar.—Orran.* *N. pl.* baoth-bheusan.

Baoth-bheusach, *a.* Immoral; dishonest. Gu baoth-bheusach, *immorally.*

Baoth-bheusan, *n. pl.* of baoth-bheus.

Baoth-cheideamh, imh, *s. m.* A wild creed.

Baoth-chreideamhach, *a.* Credulous; professing a wild creed.

Baoth-chreidmheach, *a.* *Contr. for* baoth-chreideamhach.

Baoth-chreidmhiche, *s. m.* One who professes an extravagant creed.

Baoth-leum, *s. m.* A fearful or dangerous leap; a bound; a prancing, a vaulting.

Baoth-leumnach, *a.* Wildly leaping; proudly prancing. Each baoth-leumnach, *a proudly prancing horse.—Old Poem.*

Baoth-radh, *s. m.* A profane expression; an idiotism.

Baoth-radhach, *a.* Profane, impious, blasphemous; talking idly or foolishly. An teangadh bhaoth-radhach, *the profane tongue.—Old didactic Poem.*

Baoth-shugrach, *a.* Inclined to profane jesting; of, or pertaining to, a profane jest.

Baoth-shugradh, aidh, *s. m.* Profane jesting.—*Stew. Eph.*

† **Bar**, *s. m.* A son.

Ir. bar. *Heb.* bar; as bar-Ionah, *the son of Jonah.* *Chald.* and *Syr.* bar. *Crim. Tartars,* baar, *child.* *Goth.* *Teut. Swed. Dan.* barn. *Scotch,* bairn. *Old Sax.* bearn. From *bar* comes the Latin *par-io,* to beget.

† **Bàr**, bàir, *s. m.* A learned man; a man; also a dart; bread.

W. bara, *bread.* From *bar*, a man, comes, *Eng.* baron; *Old Sax.* beorn, *a man;* and *Old Dan.* biorn.

Bàr, bàir, *s. m.* (*Ir. Corn. id.*) A top or summit. Written also *bàrr;* which see.

Barach, aich, *s. m.* See **Barrach**.

Bàrach, *a.* (*from* bàr.) High-topped, beetling, pinnacled. Mar chraig bhàrach, *like a beetling rock.—Oss. Cathula.*

Barag, aig, *s. f.* See **Barrag**.

Baragan, ain, *s. m.* A bargain. *Fr.* barguigner, *to haggle or bargain.* *N. pl.* baragain.

Baraig, *v. a.* Restore, give away, grant. *Pret. a.* bharaig, *bestowed; fut. aff. a.* baraigidh, *shall or will bestow.*

Barail, *s. f.* (*Ir.* barmhail.) Opinion; a conceit; a guess or conjecture; supposition, expectation. Am barail leat? *is it your opinion?—Oss. Tem.* Is faoin do bharail, *vain is thy expectation.—Old Poem.* Glic na 'r barail fein, *wise in your own conceits.—Stew. Rom.* Thoir barail, *guess;* ciod i do bharail? *what is your opinion?*

Baraill, *s. f.* *N. pl.* baraillean. A barrel or cask; the barrel of a gun. Min ann am baraill, *meal in a barrel.—Stew.* 1 *K.*

It. barile. *W.* baril. *Arm.* barilh. *Span.* barral, *a twenty-five pint bottle.* *Sclav.* bargella, *a barrel.*

Baralach, *a.* (*from* barail.) Conjectural; hypothetical.

Baralachadh, aidh, *s. m.* The circumstance of conjecturing; a guessing or conjecturing.

Baralachadh, (a), *pr. part.* of baralaich. Conjecturing, guessing, supposing, opining.

Baralaich, *v. a.* Guess, conjecture, suppose. *Pret. a.* bharalaich, *guessed; fut. aff. a.* baralaichidh, *shall or will guess.*

Baran, ain, *s. m.* A baron. *N. pl.* barain, *barons.*

Baranachd, *s. f.* A barony.

Barandach, **Barantach**, *a.* Warranting; also warranted, sure, certain.

Barandachadh, **Barantachadh**, aidh, *s. m.* A warranting; a warrant.

Barandachadh, **Barantachadh**, (a), *pr. part.* of barandaich. Warranting.

Barandaich, **Barantaich**, *v.* Warrant; assure; make certain; give authority or privilege. *Pret. a.* bharantaich, *warranted; fut. aff. a.* barantaichidh, *shall or will warrant.*

Barandail, **Barantail**, *a.* (*i. e.* barantamhuil.) Warrantable.

Barandas, **Barantas**, ais, *s. m.* A commission; warrant; also a pledge, a pawn.

Barbair, *s. m.* A barber or hairdresser. *N. pl.* barbairean, *barbers.* *Span.* barbero. *Corn.* barbeir. *Swed.* barber. *Arm.* barber.

Barbaireachd, *s. f.* (*from* barbair.) The business of a hairdresser. Ag ionnsachadh na barbaireachd, *learning the business of a barber.*

Barbarra, *a.* Barbarous, wild, fierce, cruel.—*Stew. Col. ref.* Gu barbarra, *barbarously.*

Lat. and *Span.* barbara. *It.* burbero. *Swed.* barbar.

Barbhas, ais, *s. m.* A village in the Isle of Lewis.

The inhabitants of this village retain the very ancient Highland custom of sending a man early in the morning of the first of May to cross the river Barbhas, in order to prevent a female crossing it first; for in that case the people believe that the salmon would not enter the river on that year, at least in desirable numbers. Throughout all the Highlands the fisher regards it unlucky to meet a female on his way to the scene of his sports.

Bar-bhrigein, *s. m.* Silver weed.

Barbrag, aig, *s. f.* A barberry bush; a barberry.

Barc, bairc, *s.* A boat, a ship, a skiff. Ruitheadh ur barc thar chuanta, *let your vessel bound speedily over the seas.—Ull.* Barc breid-gheal, *a white-sailed boat.—Old Poem.*

Germ. bark. *Swed.* bark. *Dan.* barke. *It.* barca. *Fr.* barque. *Span.* barca. *Arm.* barcq. *Eng.* bark. *Du.* boork. *Basque*, barca. *Turk.* barce, *a little ship.*

This is one of the many Celtic words which straggled into the English tongue from some one of the dialects of the Celtic, probably that which is spoken in Bretagne, commonly called the Armoric. Pelletier is not correct when he states that this word is peculiar to the Armoric dialect.

Barc, *s. m.* A book. *Ir. id.*

Barc, *v. n.* (*from* barc.) Embark; also rush, burst forth. *Pret. a.* bharc, *rushed; fut. aff. a.* barcaidh, *shall rush.*

Barcachd, *s. f.* (*from* barc.) Embarkation.

Barc-lann, -lainn, *s. m.* A library.

† **Bard**, baird, *s. m.* A corporation. *N. pl.* baird *and* bardan.

Bard, baird, *s. m.* A bard, a poet, a rhymer. *N. pl.* baird *and* barda. *W.* barth. *Ir.* bard. *Arm.* barth. *Gr.* βαρδος. *Lat.* bardus. Thigeadh barda le toirm, *let poets come with music.—Oss. Tem.* Thaom na baird am fonn, *the bards poured forth their strains.—Id.*

The Celtic bards were known to the writers of antiquity under the name *βαρδοι* and *bardi.* Εισι δε παρ' αυτοις και ποιηται μελων ους βαρδους ονομαζουσιν.—*Diod. Siculus.* There are also among them versifiers, whom they call *bards.* Βαρδοι μεν υμνηται και ποιηται.—*Strabo*, b. iv. They were not only poets, but musicians. Respecting the etymon of this term, Bochart, liv. i. *Des Colonies des Phœniciens*, chap. 42, observes, that it is of Hebrew origin, being derived from the word *parat*, to modulate or tune; and this he endeavours to confirm by a quotation from Tacitus *de Mor. Germ.* "Ituri in prælia canunt; sunt et illis hæc quoque carmina, quorum relatu, quem *baritum* vocant, accendunt animos," &c. Dr. John Macpherson, who, himself a Celt, might have known better, asserts that it is idle to attempt tracing its etymon, and that, as it is a *monosyllable*, it *cannot* be traced to any root. In opposition to these opinions, it may be stated that *bard* is of Celtic origin; and that it properly means one who extols; being resolvable into *b-ard.* And, by the way, I may remark, that *ard* itself, a three-lettered *monosyllable*, is not a radical word, but is derived from the primeval root, *ar*, high, which is seen in every language on earth, [see *Ard* and *Barr*], and, though now gone into disuse among the Gael, is still retained by the Celts of Bretagne in their dialect called the Armoric. That *bard* is derived from *ard*, is the more likely, to say the least of it, since the northern word *scald*, or *poet*, whose pursuits were similar to the bard's, means also an extoller, being derived from *alt*, *allt*, or *ald*, forms of the same word, which is common to the Celtic and Gothic languages, and signifying *high.* *Bard* and *scald*, therefore, are synonymous terms.

Poetry being, in the opinion of the warlike Celts, the likeliest method of eternizing their bravery, the bards were held by them in the highest veneration. Princes and warriors did not disdain to claim affinity with that order. The Celts, being passionately fond of poetry, would listen to no instruction, whether from priest or philosopher, excepting it was conveyed in rhymes. Hence the word *bard* meant also a priest, philosopher, or teacher of any kind. Thus we find a bard often entrusted with the education of a prince; and about two centuries ago, a Highland chieftain had seldom any other instructor. Such was the respect paid to the ancient bards, that, according to Diodorus the Sicilian, already quoted, they could put a stop to armies in the heat of battle. After any bloody engagement they raised the song over the deceased, and extolled the heroes who survived.

"Vos quoque qui fortes animas, belloque peremptas
Laudibus in longum vates dimittitis ævum,
Plurima securi fudistis carmina bardi."

When a bard appeared in an army, it was either as a herald or ambassador; hence his person and property were sacred in the midst of his enemies and amid their wildest ravages. In earlier times he never bore arms; and Owen asserts that it was unlawful to unsheathe a weapon in his presence. Among the ancient British there were, according to Jones, three orders of bards; the Privardd, or chief bard, whom the Gael would call Priomh-bhard; the Poswardd, who taught what was set forth by the Privardd; and the Arwyddward, *i. e.* the ensign bard, or herald-at-arms, who employed himself in genealogy, and in blazoning the arms of princes and nobles, as well as altering them according to their dignity or deserts. Owen observes that their dress was sky-blue, an emblem of peace.

Among the Irish Celts the bards enjoyed many extraordinary privileges. The chief bard was called Fileadh, or Ollamh ri dàn, a graduate or doctor in poetry, and had thirty inferior bards as attendants, whilst a bard of the second-rate or order had fifteen. The ancient Gael were not behind any of their brother Celts in this absurd veneration. A bard had lands bestowed on him, which became hereditary in his family. A Highland chieftain retained two bards, who, like those of the Irish, had their retinue of disciples; and though the office did by no means procure the same deep respect as in times of old, yet, like every department, secular or otherwise, that permits laziness and procures lucre, it was filled to the uttermost man. Its avarice and its insolence, together with other causes, contributed to the decline of the order. Its indiscriminate satire and ungrateful abuse brought it finally into contempt; and the Gaelic bard of the present day is but a homeless, sarcastic mendicant, who will sing a song of his own composing for a morsel of bread.

Another Gaelic term for bard is *aoisdana*; which see.

Barda, *n. pl.* of bard.

Bardachd, *s. f.* (*from* bard.) *Ir. id.* Poetry, rhyming; satire, lampooning; a sarcasm; *rarely* a corporation town. Ged theirinn e cha bhardachd, *though I were to say it, it would be no satire.—Old Poem.*

† **Bardag**, aig, *s. f.* A box, a pannier, a hamper.—*Ir. id. N. pl.* bardagan.

Bardail, *a.* (i. e. bard-amhuil.) Satirical, poetical. *Ir.* bard-amhuil.

Bardainn, *s. f.* A summons of removal, a warning. Fhuair mi bardainn, *I got a summons of removal.*

† **Bardal**, ail, *s. m.* A drake. *Ir.* bardal.

Bardas, ais, *s. m.* A satyr, a lampoon. *Ir.* bardas.

Bard-cluiche, *s. m.* A dramatist. *N. pl.* baird-cluiche, *dramatists.*

Bard-dealbh-cluiche, *s. m.* A dramatist.

Bard-dhàn, -dhàin, *s. m.* (*W.* barth-gan.) Poetry, rhyme.

† **Barg**, *a.* Red-hot.—*Ir. id.*

Bàr-gheal, *a.* White-topped.

Baris, *s. m.* The ancient Gaulic name of Paris, still retained in the Armoric dialect of the Celtic.

† **Barn**, bairn, *s. m.* A nobleman; a judge; a battle.

Ir. barn, *a judge. W. Corn.* barn, *judgment.*

Barnaig, *v. a.* Summon, warn; give summons of removal. —*Ir. Pret. a.* bharnaig, *summoned; fut. aff. a.* barnaigidh, *shall or will summon.*

Barnaigeadh, idh, *s. m.* A summons of removal.

Bàrr, *s. m.* A crop, as of corn or grass; also bread, food. Bàrr bhuntàit, *potatoe crops.*

Arm. bara. *Basque,* bar, *nourishment. Heb.* bar, *corn. Goth.* bari. *Old Sax.* bere. *Scotch,* bear, *barley. Gr. Ion.* βαρ, *food;* also *English,* barn. *Runic,* bar, *foliage.*

Bàrr, *s. m.* from the primeval root *ar.* (*Ir.* bar *and* barr. *W.* bar. *Corn.* bar. *Arm.* bar. *Cantabrian,* barna. Hence also *It.* barruca; *Fr.* perruque.) *D. pl.* barraibh. A point, as of a weapon; acme; a top, summit; a crop; a branch; a height or hill; a heap; scum; a head, a helmet; superiority; *rarely* a son. For this last acceptation see *bàr.* Bàrr mo shleagh, *the point of my spear.—Oss. Gaul.* Mar cheo air bharraibh nam beann, *like a mist on the tops of the hills.—Oss. Duthona.* Buntàta ag a chrathadh o'n bhàrr, *potatoes a-shaking from the crops.—Macfar.* Cha 'n fhàg e bun no bàrr, *he will leave neither root nor branch. —Stew. Mal.* A ruith fhiadh air bhàrraibh, *chasing deer on the heights.—Fingalian Poem.* Bàrr maise, *superiority in beauty.—Macdon.*

It is worthy of observation, that in all the Eastern languages, and indeed in every language in the world, the word *bàrr* is found either simple or in composition, and signifying *height* of some description or other. *Heb.* and *Syr.* bar, *great. Heb.* barhh, *high. Old Pers.* bar, *above. Chald.* bar, *above,* and baratz, *heap up. Heb.* cabar, *to increase. Syr.* cabar, *increased. Ethiop.* cabar, *renowned. Arab.* cabar, *elevated. Malay,* bara, *lifted up. Gr.* βαρος, high. *Canaries,* bara, *great. Du.* baar, *a lofty surge. Sclav.* and *Dal.* bardo, *a hill. Pol.* barzo, *vastly. Moscovite,* boyar, *noble. Arab.* pharahh, *to be elevated. Pers.* phar, *high. Old Egyptian,* Pharaoh, *a king. Armen.* partr, *mountain. Alban,* pari or pare, *an elevated man. Bohem.* pharbek, hill. *Madagascar,* barou, *a great deal.*

Barra, *s. m.* A court; a spike; a bar. *Ir. id.*

Barrabhailc, *s. m.* A cornice; entablature; a constellation.—*Macd. Ir. id. N. pl.* barrabhailcean; *d. pl.* barrabhailcibh.

Barrabhall and **Barrabhalladh**, aidh, *s. m.* Parapet, battlements, embrazures, bartizans.—*Macd.*

Barra-bhard, aird, *s. m.* A chief poet, a poet-laureate; a graduate in poetry: called also *filidh.* He was entitled to an escort of thirty inferior poets. See Bard.

Barra-bhardachd, *s. f.* The condition of a poet-laureate; the verses of a poet-laureate.

Barrabhuidhe, *a.* (*Ir.* barrabhuidhe.) Yellow-topped; yellow-tipped; having yellow hair.

Barrabròg, bròig, *s. f.* A barberry; a barberry tree. *Ir.* barbrog.

Barracaideach, *a.* Proud, saucy. Gu barracaideach, *proudly. Com.* and *sup.* barracaidche.

Barracaideachd, *s. f.* Pride, sauciness.

Bàrrach, *a.* (*from* bàrr.) High-topped, beetling, pinnacled.

Barrach, *a.* (*from* bàrr.) Topped; heaped up as a loaded cart; heaped up over the rim of a vessel. Cairt bharrach, *a cart loaded over its rim.*

Barrach, aiche, *s. m.* (*from* bàrr.) *Ir.* barrach. Branches of trees; brushwood; also fine tow. Feadh rainich is barraich, *among ferns and brushwood.—Macint.* Snathainn barraiche, *a thread of tow.—Stew. Jud. ref.* Fo sgaile a bharraich, *beneath the shady branches.—Miann a Bhaird.*

† **Barrachad**, aid, *s. m.* A cottage, a hut or booth.—*Ir. id.*

Barrachaol, *a.* Pyramidical; conical, tapering; also (substantively) a pyramid.

Barrachaoin, *a.* Very mild or gentle. Triùir bhraithre bharrachaoin, *three gentle brothers.—Old Poem.*

† **Barrachas**, ais, *s. m.* Curled hair; waving locks.—*Ir. id.*

Barrachd, *s. f.* Superiority, pre-eminence; advantage, overplus; more, besides. Tha barrachd nan dàn duit, *thou hast the superiority in song.—Oss. Fing.* Thoir barrachd, *excel;* cha d' thoir thu barrachd, *thou shalt not excel;* a toirt barrachd, *excelling.—Stew. Ezek.* A bharrachd air sin, *besides that, over and above that, moreover;* a bharrachd air a cheud ghorta, *besides the first famine.—Stew. Gen.* Chì dithis barrachd air aon fhear, *two will see better than one.—G. P.*

Barr', *contr.* for barradh; which see.

† **Barradh**, aidh, *s. m.* A hinderance, an obstacle. *Portug.* bàrra, *a bar at the mouth of a river.*

Barradh, aidh, *s. m.* A barrow; a bier. Cuidhle-barr', *a wheel-barrow;* barradh-ròtha, *a wheel-barrow;* barradh-bocsa, *a box-barrow,* barr' laimh, *a hand-barrow.*

Gr. φερειν, *to carry. It.* bara, *a coffin. Germ.* bar. *Eng.* bier. *Fr.* biere. *Swed.* bera *and* baera, *a bier. Servian,* bera. *Teut.* bar *and* bara. *Turk.* bar, *a burden.* According to Herodotus, the bier of the ancient Egyptians was called *bar.*

Barradh-dhias, -dhéis, *s. m.* The point of a sword; the top of an ear of corn.

Barradhriopair, *s. m.* A butler. *N. pl.* barradhriopairean.

Barradhriopaireachd, *s. f.* The employment of a butler.

† **Barrag**, aig, *s. f.* (*Ir. id.*) Posset; scum, cream; a sudden pain; a grappling, wrestling; a girl. Cha chinn barrag air cuid cait, *there is no cream on cat's milk.—G. P.*

† **Barrag**, aig, *s. f.* Weeds that float on the water; a switch, a rod.—*Ir. id.*

Barraghlach, aich, *s. m.* Tops or branches of trees; brushwood.

Bàrraibh, *d. pl.* of bàrr.

Barraich, *a.* (*from* bàrr.) Matchless; surpassing, pre-eminent, transcendent.

BARRAICH, *v.* Top; heap up as a measure of grain; excel, surpass. *Pret. a.* bharraich, *surpassed; fut. aff. a.* barraichidh, *shall surpass.*

BARRAICHTE, *a.* and *p. part.* of barraich. Tipped, topped; excelled, surpassed; also excellent, exceeding. Barraichte mar na seudair, *excellent as the cedars.—Stew. Song Sol.*

BÁRRAIG, *v. a.* Bestow, grant, present. *Pret. a.* bharraig; *fut. aff. a.* barraigidh, *shall give.*

BARRAIL, *a.* Gay, sprightly, transcendent, genteel. *Ir.* barramhuil. A mhaighdean bharrail, *the sprightly maiden.—Old Song.*

BARRAIN, *gen. sing.* of barran; which see.

BARRAIST, *s. f.* The herb called borage; green kail.—*Ir. id.*

BARRAISTEACH, *a.* Full of borage; like borage; of borage.

BARRAMHAIS, *s. f.* A cornice.—*Macd. N. pl.* barramhaisean.

BARRAMHAISEACH, *a.* Having cornices.

BARRAN, ain, *s. m.* (*from* bàrr.) Edder; any kind of fence, as thorns, glass, &c. on the top of a wall; a tip; a crest; also a fence, a hedge; the top of a rock or mountain. *N. pl.* barrain; *d. pl.* barranaibh. Anns na barranaibh, *in the fences.—Stew. Nah.* Fraoch sléibhe mar bharran air, *tipped with mountain heath.—Old Song.*

BARRANDACH, *a.* Sure, certain, warrantable. Written also *barrantach.*

BARRANDADH, aidh, *s. m.* A warrant. Written also *barrantadh.*

BARRANDAS, ais, *s. m.* A commission, a warrant; a pledge, a pawn.—*Macint. Ir.* barantas. Written also *barrantas.*

BARRANTACH, *a.* Sure, certain, warrantable. Gu barrantach, *warrantably.*

BARRANTADH, aidh, *s. m.* A warrant, a commission.

BARRANTAS, ais, *s. m.* A warrant, a commission; a pledge, a pawn. *Ir.* barantas. *N. pl.* barrantais *or* barrantasan.

BARRA-ROCHD, *s. f.* Sea-weed, tangles.

BARRAS, ais, *s. m.* (*from* bàrr.) Superiority; residue, surplus. A bharras air sin, *over and above that; moreover.*

BARRASACH, *a.* Lofty; superior; ambitious; residual.

BARRA-THONN, -thuinn, *s. m.* A high surge; the top of a wave; the surface of the deep. A siubhal nam barra-thonn, *bounding over the surges.—Ullin.*

BÀRR-BHUIDHE, *a.* Yellow-topped; yellow-haired. Mo mhaighdean bharr-bhuidhe, *my yellow-haired maid.*

BARR-FHIONN, *a.* White-topped, white-headed. Canach barr-fhionn, *white-topped cotton.—Macdon.*

BARR-GHNIOMH, *s. m.* A work of supererogation; a transcendent exploit.

BARR-GUCHD, *s. f.* Bloom, blossom; most frequently applied to the bloom of leguminous vegetables, as pease. Barr-guchd air a mheuraibh, *a bloom on its branches.—Macint.*

BARR-IALL, -éill, *s. m.* A shoe-tie, a latchet, a thong. *Ir.* barial.

BAS, bais, *s. f.* (*Ir.* bas.) The palm of the hand. *N. pl.* basan, *palms; d. pl.* basaibh, *palms.* Bas réidh, *a smooth palm;* leòis air basaibh, *blisters on her hands.—Old Song.* Written also *bos.*

BÀS, bàis, *s. m.* (*Heb.* baas, *putrefied.*) Death, destruction; also a dead body. Guin bàis, *the agony of death.—Ull.* Dealan bàis, *the lightning of death.—Oss. Gaul.* Faigh bàs, *die;* gheibh gach ni bàs, *every thing shall die.—Stew. Gen.* Ma shaltraicheas slugh air mo bhàs, *if people tread on my dead body.—Oss. Tem.* Droch bhàs ort! *a bad death to you!* a common imprecation among the Gael.

BÀSACHADH, aidh, *s. m.* Dying, expiring; perishing, withering. Tha e air basachachadh, *it has died or withered.*

BÀSACHADH, (a), *pr. part.* of bàsaich. Dying, expiring; starving, withering. A basachadh leis an fhuachd, *starving with cold; dying or withering with cold.*

BASADH, aidh, *s. m.* A term applied to the rubbing of the thread ends of tape-work, to prevent their running into threads.

BASAICH, *v. n.* Die, expire, perish, starve; wither as a plant; grow vapid, as beer. *Pret. a.* bhàsaich, *died; fut. aff. a.* basaichidh, *shall or will die.*

BÀSAIL, *a.* (*i. e.* bas-amhuil.) Deadly; deathlike; mortal, fatal, destructive.

BASAL, ail, *s. m.* Judgment; also pride, arrogance.—*Ir. id.*

BÀSALACHD, *s. f.* (*from* bas.) Mortality; deadliness.

BAS-AIRM, *gen.* bàs-arm, *s. pl.* Deadly weapons. Fhir nam bas-arm geur, *thou hero of deadly weapons.—Oss. Lodin.*

BASART, airt, *s. m.* A bastard. *N. pl.* basartan.

BASBAIR, *s. m. N. pl.* basbairean. A fencer or swordsman. Bha thu na do bhasbair còrr, *thou wert a noble swordsman.—Gael. Song. Ir. id.*

BASBAIREACHD, *s. f.* Swordmanship, fencing.

BASBAIREAN, *n. pl.* of basbair; which see.

BAS-BHUALADH, aidh, *s. m.* A clapping of hands; a rubbing of hands, whether from grief or joy.—*Stew. Luke, ref.*

BÀS-BHUILLE, *s. m.* A death-blow. Fhuair e' bhàs-bhuille, *he received his death-blow.*

BASBRUIDHEACH, *a.* Lecherous.

BASBRUIDHEACHD, *s. f.* Lecherousness.

† BASC, *a.* (*Ir. id.*) Red; round.—*Shaw.*

BASCACH, aich, *s. m.* A catch-pole, a bailiff. *N. pl.* bascaichean, *catchpoles.*

BASCAID, (*perhaps* bascaite), *s. from* basc. A basket. *Box. Lex. Ant. Brit.* basgawd *and* basged. *Old French,* bascod. *N. pl.* basgaide *and* basgaidean. Tri bascaide geala, *three white baskets.—Stew. Gen.* Martial writes,

> "Barbara de pictis venit BASCAUDA Britannis,
> Sed me jam vult dicere Roma suam."

† BASC-AIRM, *s. m.* A circle.—*Ir. id.*

BASCALL, aill, *s. m.* A wild man; a savage. *N. pl.* bascaill.

BASCARNACH, aich, *s. m.* Lamentation.

BASCART, airt, *s. m.* Cinnabar.

BASC-CHRIADH, *s. m.* Ruddle.—*Shaw.*

BASDALACH, *a.* Showy, gay, flashy. Og basdalach, *a gay youth.—Macint.* A ribhinn bhuidhe bhasdalaiche, *thou yellow-haired showy maiden.—Moladh Mhoraig. Com.* and *sup.* basdalaiche, *more or most showy.*

BASDALACHD, *s. f.* Showiness, gayness. Cha n fhac mi a leithid air basdalachd, *I have not seen his equal for showiness.*

BASDARD, aird, *s. m.* A bastard. *Box. Lex.* bastardd, *spurious. Ir.* basdard. *Span.* and *Portug.* bastardo. *Du.* bastaard.

Basdard is probably derived from *baos,* fornication.

† BASG, *v. a.* Stop, stay. *Pret. a.* bhasg, *stopped; fut. aff. a.* basgaidh, *shall or will stop.*

BASGAIREACH, *a.* Clapping the hands in the agitation of grief.

BASGAIREACHD, *s. f.* A mournful clapping of hands. *Ir.* basgaire.

BASGANTA, *a.* Warbling, melodious.—*Macdon.*

BASLACH, aich, *s. m.* A palmful.

BASG-LUAIDH, *s. m.* Vermillion.—*Macd.*

BÀSMHOIRE, *com.* and *sup.* of basmhor; which see.

BASMHOIREACHD, *s. f.* Mortality, deadliness.

BÀSMHÒR, *a.* Deadly, mortal, liable to death. An corp basmhor, *the mortal body.—Stew.* 1 *Cor. Com.* and *sup.* basmhoire, *more or most deadly.*

BASMHORACH, *a.* Mortal, liable to death. Tha gach crè basmhorach, *every body is liable to death.—Old Song.*

BASRAICH, *s. f.* A shouting, roaring, calling aloud, wailing aloud. Ri basraich, *shouting aloud.—Oss. Tem.*

BAS-SHLEAGH, *s.* A deadly spear. Bàs-shleagh nan triath, *the deadly spear of the chiefs.—Oss. Tem.*

Bastalach, *a.* See **Basdalach.**

Bat, *s. m.* A bath. Bat fiona, *a wine-bath.* Bat olaidh, *an oil-bath.—Stew. Ezra.*
Du. bad. *Dan.* bad. *Swed.* bad. *W.* bath. *Ir.* bath.

Bat, *s. m.* A stick, a staff, a baton, a cudgel, a bludgeon. *Asp. form*, bhat. Gabh mo bhat, *take my stick.* *N. pl.* bataichean. Ni thu bataichean, *thou shalt make staves.—Stew.* 2 *K.*
Germ. batt. *Anglo-Sax.* bat. *Eng.* bat. *Ir.* bat. *Fr.* baton.

Bàt, *s. m.* A boat, pinnace, barge; any sailing vessel of inferior size. *N. pl.* bataichean. Bat aigheir, *a pleasure-boat;* bat da chroinn, *a wherry;* bat aiseig, *a ferry-boat.—Stew. O. T.* Bàt iasgaich, *a fishing-boat.* Chuir e bhàt air acair, *he brought his boat to anchor.—G. P.*
Dan. baad. *Fr.* bat-eau. *Old Sax.* bat. *Old Swed.* baat, *secundùm Rudbeck.* *Runic*, baatus. *Isl.* baatur. *Du.* boot. *Span.* bat-el. *It.* bat-ello.

Bàtaichean, *n. pl.* of bàt. Boats.

Bataichean, *n. pl.* of bat. Staves.

Batail, *s. f.* A fight, a skirmish. *Fr.* bataille.

Batair, *s. m.* (*from* bat.) A cudgeller; a lounger, an idler; a noisy fellow. *Fr.* batteur, *a striker.* *Portug.* batedor, *one who beats.* *N. pl.* batairean.

Bataireachd, *s. f.* (*from* bat.) Cudgelling; lounging; making a rattling noise. Is ann ort tha bhataireachd! *what a noise you make!*

† **Bath**, *s.* (*Ir. id.*) The sea; also slaughter, massacre, murder; death; thirst.—*Shaw.*

Bàth, *a.* Simple, foolish; more frequently written *baoth*; which see.

Bàthachd, *s. f.* Simpleness, foolishness; a massacre. Thig bathachd ort, *foolishness shall come upon thee.—Mac Co.*

Bàth, *v. a.* Drown; quench, slake; smother, as a flame; *rarely* faint. *Pret. a.* bhàth, *drowned; fut. aff. a.* bàthaidh, *shall or will drown.* Cha bhàth na tuiltean e, *the floods shall not drown him.—Stew. Song. Sol.* Bathadhmaid gach smàlan, *let us drown all care.—Old Song.* Bath an teine, *quench the fire.* *P. part.* bathte, *drowned.*

Bàthadh, aidh, *s. m.* A drowning, a quenching, a slaking, a smothering. Bathadh mòr aig oir-thir, *wrecks are most frequent on the shore.—G. P.*

Bàthadh, *a.; pr. part.* of bàth. Drowning.

Bathaich, *s. m.* A cow-house. *Bathaich* is a corruption of *ba-theach.* *N. pl.* bathaichean.

Bathais, *s. f.* A forehead, front, crown of the head. Na bhathais mhaoil, *in his bald forehead.—Stew. Lev.* *N. pl.* bathaisean.

Bathalaich, *s. m.* A vagabond.

Bàthar, air, *s. m.* Crop; wares, goods. Am bàthar a bha san luinge, *the wares that were in the ship.—Stew. Don.*

Ba-thigh, *s. m.* A cow-house.—*Macint.*

† **Bathlan**, ain, *s. m.* († bath *and* lan.) The flux of the sea, a tide; a calm.

Bath-laodh, *s. m.* (*Ir. id.*) A helmet.—*Shaw.*

† **Bathroid**, *s. f.* A token. *N. pl.* bathroidean.

Bath-shruth, *s. m.* A calm smooth stream. *Ir.* bath-shruth.

† **Bath-throid**, *s. f.* A helmet or headpiece.—*Ir. id.*

† **Batros**, *s. m.* Rosemary.—*Shaw.*

B'e, (*for* bu e.) It was he or it.

Bè, *s.* (*Ir. id.*) Night; also a woman, a female.—*Shaw.*

† **Beabh**, *s. m.* A tomb, a grave.

† **Beacan**, ain, *s. m.* A mushroom.

† **Beacanach**, *a.* Abounding in mushrooms; like a mushroom; of mushrooms.

Beach, *s. m.* A bee; a wasp; a beast; a bird. (*Bisc.* bechon. *Ir.* beach, *a bee.*) *N. pl.* beachan; *d. pl.* beachaibh. Dranndan bheachan an aonaich, *the murmur of the mountain-bees.—Oss. Dargo.* Mar bheachaibh, *like bees.—Sm.*

Beachach, *a.* Full of bees or wasps; like a bee or wasp, waspish; of, or belonging to, a bee or wasp. Mios beachach seilleanach, *the month that produces wasps and bees.—Macfar.*

Beachan, (*dim.* of beach.) A little bee. Beachan chapull, *a wasp.*

Beachanta, *a.* Waspish, cross. Gu beachanta, *waspishly.*

Beacharn, airn, *s. f.* A prostitute. *N. pl.* beachairnean.

† **Beachd**, *s. m.* A covenant, surety; a multitude; a ring, a circle. *Ir.* beacht.

Beachd, *s. m.* Opinion, memory, perception; conception, feeling, idea; aim, thought, attention, notice, observation; vision, eyesight; intention. A reir mo bheachd, *according to my opinion.* An do chaill thu mar mise do bheachd? *hast thou, like me, lost thy memory?—Oss. Conn.* Tharruing i 'n t-sreang le rogha a beachd, *she pulled the string with her best aim.—Ull.* Chuir baird am beachd air triath, *the bards fixed their notice on the chiefs.—Oss. Fing.* Ma 's comhrag do bheachd, *if battle be thy intention.—Old Poem.* O bheachd, *out of sight.—Oss. Fing.* Na bheachd féin; *in his own opinion or conceit.—Stew. Pro.* Gabh beachd, *observe, watch, make an observation.* Ghabh e beachd air an treun, *he observed the hero.—Mac Lach.* Gu beachd, *perfectly, clearly.*

† **Beachd**, *v. a.* (*Ir.* beacht.) Meditate, consider, observe, attend, view, watch; embrace, compass; criticise. *Pret. a.* bheachd, *viewed; fut. aff. a.* beachdaidh, *shall view.*

Beachdachadh, aidh, *s. m.* A considering, viewing, meditating, watching; consideration, meditation.

Beachdachadh, *a.; pr. part.* of beachdaich. Considering, viewing, meditating.

Beachdaich, *v. a.* Consider, meditate, perceive, observe, attend, watch, eye. *Pret. a.* bheachdaich, *observed; fut. aff. a.* beachdaichidh, *shall or will observe;* cha bheachdaich sùil a h-aite, *no eye shall observe her place.—Oss. Duthona.* Bheachdaich mi gu dùr, *I observed attentively.—Mac Lach.* Bheachdaich iad am fear mòr, *they eyed the mighty man.—Id.*

Beachdaichte, *p. part.* of beachd. Considered, observed, watched.

Beachdaidh, *a.* Sure, certain; observant, watchful, considerate. Gu beachdaidh, *considerately.*

Beachdail, *a.* (*from* beachd.) Observant, watchful, meditative, considerate; *rarely* circular.

Beachdair, *s. m.* An observer, a spy, an informer, a scout; a critic, a reviewer. *N. pl.* beachdairean.

Beachdaireachd, *s. f.* Spying, informing; the occupation of a critic or reviewer; espionage.

Beachd-àite, *s. m.* An observatory; a watch-tower. *N. pl.* beachd-àitean *or* beachd-àiteachan.

Beachd-ionad, aid, *s. m.* An observatory; a watch-tower. *N. pl.* beachd-ionadan.

Beachd-sgeul, *gen.* beachd-sgeòil *or* beachd-sgéil, *s. m.* Information.

Beachd-smuaineach, **Beachd-smuainteach**, *a.* Meditating.

Beachd-smuaineachadh, **Beachd-smuainteachadh**, aidh, *s. m.* Meditation, contemplation; the act of meditating or contemplating.

Beachd-smuaineachadh, **Beachd-smuainteachadh**, (a), *pr. part.* of beachd-smuainich *or* beachd-smuaintich. Meditating, contemplating; talking. Tha e a beachd-smuainteachadh, *he is talking.—Stew.* 1 *K.*

Beachd-smuaineachail, **Beachd-smuainteachad**, *a.* Contemplative, meditative.

Beachd-smuainich, **Beachd-smuaintich**, *v. n.* Muse, meditate, contemplate; talk. *Pret. a.* bheachd-smuainich, *mused; fut. aff. a.* beachd-smuainichidh, *shall muse;* a bheachd-smuaineachadh san fhàiche, *to meditate in the field.—Stew. Gen.*

Beach-lann, lainn, *s. m.* A bee-hive.

† **Beachran**, ain, *s. m.* Wandering, straying.—*Shaw.*

Bead, *s. m.* Flattery; cunning, a trick.

Beadach, *a.* (*from* bead.) Forward, impudent; prone to flatter. *Com.* and *sup.* beadaiche, *more or most forward.*

Beadachd, *s. f.* (*from* bead.) Forwardness, impudence; flattery.

Beadag, aig, *s. f.* (*from* bead.) A lying, enticing young female; a gossip. *N. pl.* beadagan.

Beadagach, *a.* (*from* beadag.) Like a lying female; like a gossip.

Beadagan, *n. pl.* of beadag.

Beadagan, ain, *s. m.* A petulant fellow; a tale-telling fellow. *N. pl.* beadagan.

Beadaiche, *com.* and *sup.* of beadach. More or most forward.

Beadaiche, *s. m.* A flatterer, a cajoler; an enticing fellow. *N. pl.* beadaichean.

Beadaidh, *a.* Forward, pert, petulant; mannerless; nice, fond of delicacies, luxurious; sweet-mouthed; flattering. Cho beadaidh, *so forward.—Macint.* Beadaidh ri linn socair, *luxurious in time of peace.—Smith.* Oran na circe beadaidh, *a song from the pert hen.—G. P.*

Beadaidheachd, *s. f.* Forwardness; petulance; flattery; luxuriousness.

Beadan, ain, *s. m.* Calumny; also a forward petulant person.

Beadanach, *a.* (*from* beadan.) Calumnious; forward; petulant. Gu beadanach, *calumniously. Com.* and *sup.* beadanaiche.

Beadanachd, *s. f.* The habit of calumniating; forwardness, pertness.

Beadarach, *a.* (*Swed.* bedraga, *to deceive.*) Beloved, lovely; flattering, cajoling; pampered; delicate; indulged. Is beadarach an ni 'n onoir, *honour is delicate.—G. P. Com.* and *sup.* beadaraiche, *more or most flattering.*

Beadaradh, aidh, *s. m.* Fondness, endearment; fondling, flirting, toying; flattering. Beadaradh gu leòir, *enough of flirting.—Macint.* Chuireadh tu bodaich gu beadaradh, *thou wouldst set old men a fondling.—R.*

Beag, *a.* (*Ir.* beag.) Little; young; small; light, trifling, insignificant; few. *Asp. form,* bheag. Leanabh beag, *a babe;* na sionnaich bheag, *the young foxes.—Stew. Song. Sol.* Air bheag do lathaibh, *in a few days.—Stew. Acts.* A bheag, *a little, the least;* a bheag a dh' aon ni 's leatsa, *any* [*the least*] *particle of what is thine.—Stew. Gen.* Cha 'n fhaigh a bheag bàs, *nothing shall die.—Stew. Exod.* Beag is beag, *little and little, by degrees.—Id.* Is beag so, *this is a* [*trifling*] *light thing.—Stew.* 2 *K.* Air bheag, *almost;* air bheag nithe, *almost.—Stew. Acts, ref.* Is beag orm e, *I dislike him;* iadsan air am beagsibh, *they who hate you.—Stew. Lev.* Ach beag, *almost;* beag nach, *almost.* Na big agus na mòir, *the small and the great.—Stew. Ps.* An rud chi na big, ni na big, *what the young see they do.—G. P.* An ni chluinneas na big 's e chànas na big, *what the young hear they repeat; as the old cock crows, the young cock learns.—G. P. Com.* and *sup.* lugha, *less, least.*

Beagachadh, aidh, *s. m.* A lessening, a diminishing, diminution.

Beagachadh, *a.; pres. part.* of beagaich. Lessening, diminishing.

Beagaich, *v. a.* Lessen, diminish, abate. *Pret. a.* bheagaich, *lessened; fut. aff. a.* beagaichidh, *shall or will diminish;* cha bheagaich sibh, *ye shall not diminish.*

Beagaiche, *s. m.* (*from* beag.) An abater, a diminisher.

Beagaichear, *fut. pass.* of beagaich. Shall be lessened or diminished.

Beagaichidh, *fut. aff. a.* of beagaich. Shall or will diminish.

Beagaichte, *p. part.* of beagaich. Lessened, diminished.

Beagan, *s.* and *a.* A little, a few, a small number, a small quantity or portion. Air bheagan céille, *with little wisdom, witless.—Sm.* Beagan uisge, *a little water.—Stew. Gen.* Fuireach beagan, *stop a little;* beagan ni's fhaide, *a little longer;* beagan crion, *a very little;* bheagan a bheagan, *by little and little, by degrees;* a dol am beaganaibh, *growing into small portions, crumbling.*

Ir. beagan. *W.* bechan. *Arm.* bihan. *Corn.* bian and vichan. In old French books we see *bechan,* little. In Franche Comté they say *pechon.*

Beagchionta, *s.* A petty crime; a foible. *N. pl.* beag chiontan.

Beag-eagallach, *a.* Bold, fearless.—*Ir. id.*

Beag-luach, *a.* Valueless, useless.

Beag-narach, *a.* Shameless, impudent. Gu beag-narach, *shamelessly, impudently.—Stew. Hos.*

Beagnarachd, *s. f.* Shamelessness, impudence.

Beairt, *s. f.* A loom; engine, machine; harness; tackling of a ship; exploit; a scabbard; a truss. Fhuair e i aig a beairt, *he found her at her loom.—Mac Lach.* Da steud fo bheairt, *two studs in harness.—Id.* Beairt thuairnear, *a turning loom. N. pl.* beairtean.

Beairtich, *v. a.* Yoke, as a chariot; provide with tackling; enrich. *Pret. a.* bheairtich, *yoked; fut. aff. a.* beairtichidh, *shall or will yoke;* written also *beartaich;* which see.

Beal, **Beil**, *s. m.* A mouth; *provincial* for beul.

Beal, **Beil**, *s. m.* The god Belus. Written also *Beul;* which see.

Bealach, aich, *s. m.; n. pl.* bealaichean. (*Ir.* bealach.) A defile, a narrow passage, the pass or gorge of a mountain, a glen, a gap, a way. *Asp. form,* bhealach. Mar eibhle sa bhealach, *like a fire in the mountain gorge.—Oss. Fing.* Ciod am bealach am buail sinn? *through what pass shall we strike our way.—Old Legend.* Air bealach ceairt, *on a right way.—Sm.* Druid am bealach, *shut the way.—Id.*

Bealaidh, **Bealuidh**, *s. m.* Broom. Buidheag bhealaidh, *a yellow-hammer.*

Bealbhan-ruadh, *s. m.* A sort of hawk.—*Shaw.*

† **Bealtaine**, *s. f.* An agreement, a compact, a bargain.—*Ir. id.*

Beatlainn, **Bealtuinn**, *s. f.* May-day; Whitsuntide; the month of May. La buidhe bealtuinn, *a common name for May-day.*

On the first of May was held a great Druidical festival in honour of the Asiatic god, Belus, whom the Druids worshipped. On this day fires were kindled on the mountain tops for the purposes of sacrifice; and through these fires, according to Keating, the Druids ordered the cattle of the country to be driven, with the design of preserving them from contagion till next May-day. On this day too it was usual to extinguish all the hearth fires, in order that they should be kindled from this purifying flame. Hence it would seem that the right orthography of *Bealtuinn* is *Bèil-teine,* Belus's fire. *La Bealtuinn,* therefore, signifies the day of Belus's fire. In some parts of the Highlands, the young folks of a hamlet meet in the moors on the first of May. They cut a table in the green sod, of a round figure, by cutting a trench in the ground of such circumference as to hold the whole company. They then kindle a fire, and dress a repast of eggs and milk in the consistence of a custard. They knead a cake of oatmeal, which is toasted at the embers against a stone. After the custard is eaten up, they divide the cake into so many portions, as similar as possible to one another in size and shape, as there are persons in the company. They daub one of these portions with charcoal until it is perfectly black. They then put all the bits of the cake into a bonnet, and every one, blindfold, draws out a portion. The bonnet-holder is entitled to the last bit. Whoever draws the black bit is the devoted person who is to be sacrificed to Baal, whose favour they mean to implore in rendering the year productive. The devoted person is compelled to leap three times over the flames.—*Statistics. Callender.*

Bealuidh, *s. m.* Broom. Goisean bealuidh, *a tuft of broom;* written also *bealaidh.*

Bean, *v.* Touch, handle, meddle. *Pret. a.* bhean, *touched; fut. aff. a.* beanaidh, *shall or will touch;* an ti a bheanas ribh, *he who touches you.*—*Stew. Zech.*

Bean, *gen. mna.* (*Corn.* benen.) A wife, a woman, a female. Bean a ghaòil, *the wife of his affections.*—*Orr.* Goirear bean dith, *she shall be called woman.*—*Stew. Gen.* Bean nan deagh bheus, *a virtuous female.* A Gael, in speaking to his mother, says, a bhean! *woman!* and not a mhathair! *mother!* Bean-ghlùin, *a midwife;* bean-shiubhlaidh, *a woman in childbed;* bean-tighe, *a housewife; d. sing.* mnaoi. Air do bhreth le mnaoi, *born of a woman.*—*Smith.* Mar mhnaoi, *as a wife, to wife.*—*Stew. Gen. N. pl.* mnai *and* mnathan, *wives, women; d. pl.* mnathaibh.

† **Beanadh**, aidh, *s. m.* Dulness, bluntness.

Beanag, aig, *s. f.* (*dim.* of bean.) *W.* benan. *Corn.* benen. A little wife, a little woman: a term of endearment for a wife, or for any female. Mo bheanag ghaolach, *my dear little wife.*—*Macint.*

Beanail, *a.* (*from* bean.) *W.* benywawl. *Ir.* beanamhail. Womanly, womanlike, effeminate, feminine, modest, delicate.

Bean-baile, *s. f.* The lady or proprietress of a village.

Bean-bainnse, *s. f.* A bride; *literally,* the woman of the wedding.

Bean-bharain, *s. f.* A baron's lady.

Bean-bhochd, *s. f.* A female mendicant, a poor woman. Mnathan bochd, *poor women.*

Bean bhrathar-athar, *s. f.* An uncle's wife, the wife of a father's brother.

Bean bhrathar-màthar, *s. f.* An uncle's wife, the wife of a mother's brother.

Bean bhrathar-sean-athar, *s. f.* A grand-uncle's wife, the wife of a grandfather's brother.

Bean-charaid, *s. f.* A female friend; a kinswoman.

Bean-chéile, *s. f.* A spouse, a wife.

Bean-chìche, *s. f.* A wet-nurse. *N. pl.* mnathan ciche, *wet-nurses.*

Bean-chinnidh, *s. f.* A kinswoman; female; a namesake.

Bean-chliamhuinn, *s. f.* A daughter-in-law; a sister-in-law.

Bean-choimheadachd, *s. f.* A waiting-maid; a bridemaid.—*Shaw.*

Bean-chomharbadh, *s. f.* A dowager.

Bean-dalta, *s. f.* A foster-daughter.

Bean-eigneachadh, aidh, *s. m.* A rape.

Beangan, ain, *s. m.* A branch, a bough. *N. pl.* beangain, *branches.* See also **Meangan**.

Bean-ghluine, *s. f.* (bean, *woman,* and glùn, *offspring.*) A midwife. Thuirt a bhean-ghlùine ria, *the midwife said to her.*—*Stew. Gen.*

Bean-leigh, *s. f.* A female physician. *N. pl.* mnathan-leigh.

Bean-nigheachain, *s. f.* A washerwoman, a laundry-maid. *N. pl.* mnathan-nigheachain.

Bean-osda, *s. f.* A hostess. *N. pl.* mnathan-osda.

Bean-righdir, *s. f.* A baronet's lady. Mnathan righi-direan.

Bean-shiùbhlaidh, *s. f.* A woman in childbed. *N. pl.* mnathan-shiùbhlaidh.

Bean-striopachais, *s. f.* An adulteress, a faithless wife. —*Stew. Hos.*

Bean-tighe, *s. f.* A housewife; a housekeeper; landlady, mistress.

Bean-uasal, *gen.* mna uasail, *s. f.* A lady, a gentlewoman. *N. pl.* mnathan-uasal.

Beann, **Beinn**, *s. f.* A degree; a step; a horn; a skirt; a drinking-cup; a beam; a corner. A bheann iùbhraidh, *its beam of yew.*—*Fingalian Poem.* Fiadhachd bheann, *the hunting of mountain-deer.*—*Old Song.*

Beann, **Beinne**, *s. f.* A hill, a mountain, a summit. Aghaidh na beinne, *the brow of the mountain.*—*Oss. Fing. Ir.* beann. *W.* bann *and* pen. *Pers.* avien. *Gr.* βουνος. *Germ.* bann, *high.* Hence also, *Eng.* banner. *Germ.* pinn, *a summit. Lat.* pinnæ, pinnacula, *summits or pinnacles.* Hence *Apenninus;* hence also *Deus Penninus,* (Dia nam beann, *the god of the hills*), worshipped, as mentioned by Livy, book xxxi., on the top of the Alps. Cluverius thinks that this was the Celtic deity whom the old Germans called *Pinn.*

Beannach, *a.* (*from* beann.) Horned; cornerways; skirted; chequered; mosaic. *Com.* and *sup.* beannaiche, *more or most horned.*

Beannachadh, aidh, *s. m.* The act or circumstance of blessing; a blessing. Thug e leis mo bheannachadh, *he took with him my blessing.*—*Stew. Gen.* Sruth-bheannachadh nan ceatharn, *the smooth address of the robber.*—*G. P.*

Beannachadh, *a.; pr. part.* of beannaich. Blessing.

Beannachd, *s. f.* (*Ir.* beannacht. *Corn.* banneth.) A blessing; salutation, compliment; a farewell expression; as, beannachd leat, *farewell;* i. e. *a blessing go with you.* Beiribh beannachd, *be ye blessed.*—*Fingalian Poem.* Beannachd le cleachda na h-òige, *farewell to the pursuits of youth.*—*Ardar.* Beannachd do t-anam is buaidh, *blessing to thy soul and victory.*—*Ull.* Cuir mo bheannachd, *send my compliments;* thoir mo bheannachd, *give my compliments. N. pl.* beannachdan.

Beannachd a bhàird, *s.* The poet's congratulation.

Among the ancient Gael, if at any jovial meeting, any man retired, for however short a time, he was obliged, before he was permitted to resume his seat, to make an apology for his absence in rhyme.* If he had no talent for poetry, or if, from humour, he did not choose to comply, which was seldom the case, he was obliged to pay such a proportion of the reckoning as the company thought proper to propose; and this, according to Martin, was *beannachd-a-bhàird.*

Beannachdach, *a.* Prone to bless; prone to salute.

Beannaich, *v. a.* (*Ir.* beannaigh.) Bless, salute, hail; invoke a blessing. *Pret. a.* bheannaich, *blessed; fut. aff. a.* beannaichidh, *shall or will bless.* Na beannaich dha, *do not salute him.*—*Stew.* 2 *K.* Dhia beannaich sinn! *God bless us! Fut. sub.* bheannaicheas; *fut. pass.* beannaichear, *shall be blessed.*

Beannaichidh, *fut. aff. a.* of beannaich. Shall or will bless.

Beannaichte, *p. part.* Blessed; saluted. *Asp. form,* bheannaichte. Barr beannaichte, *a blessed crop. Arm.* bara benniguet, *blessed bread. Runic,* benediged. *Corn.* benigaz. *Ir.* beannuighte. *Arm.* beneguet.

Beannag, aig, *s. f.* A coif; a linen cap. *Ir. id. N. pl.* beannagan.

Beannagach, *a.* Having a coif, like a coif.

Beannan, ain, *s. m.* (*dim.* of beann.) A little hill. *N. pl.* beannain.

Beannta, Beanntan, *n. pl.* of beann. Hills, mountains.

Beanntach, *a.* Hilly, mountainous, rocky, pinnacled. Dùthaich bheanntach, *a hilly country.*

Beanntachd, *s. f.* Hilliness, mountainousness.

Bean-nuadh-phosda, *s. f.* A young wife, a newly married wife.

Beannuchadh, aidh, *s. m.* (*Ir.* beannughadh.) The act of blessing; a blessing. Written also *beannaich.*

Beannuich, *v. a.* Bless; invoke a blessing; salute. *Pret. a.* bheannuich; *fut. af. a.* beannuichidh, *shall or will bless.* Written also *beannaich;* which see.

† **Bear, Bir,** *s. m.* A spit. See **Bior.**

† **Bear,** *s. m.* A bear. See **Beithir.**

Bearachd, *s. f.* Judgment.

† **Bearan,** ain, *s. m.* A young man; also pen; a little spit. *N. pl.* bearain.

† **Bearg,** *s. m.* Anger; also a champion.

† **Beargachd,** *s. f.* Diligence.—*Shaw.*

Beargnadh, aidh, *s. m.* The vernacular language of a country.

Bearla, *s. f.* The language of the Scotch Lowlanders.

Bearn, Beairn, and **Beirn,** *s. f.* (*Ir.* bearn.) *N. pl.* bearnan; *dat. pl.* bearnaibh. A breach; a gap, an aperture; a separation; a fissure. *Asp. form,* bhearn. Ro bhearna nan neul, *through the fissure of the clouds.*—*Oss. Lodin.* Le bearnaibh, *with breaches.*—*Stew. Amos.*

Bearn, *v. a.* Notch; hack; make a breach or gap. *Pret. a.* bhearn, *notched; fut. aff. a.* bearnaidh, *shall or will notch.*

Bearnach, *a.* (*from* bearn.) Chopped; having breaches or gaps; notched, hacked; fractured; having fissures, apertures, or clefts; causing gaps, notches, fractures, or clefts. An sgiath mheallach bhearnach, *the bossy fractured shield.*—*Oss. Derm.*

Bearnan, *n. pl.* of beairn; which see.

Bearnan, ain, *s. m.* (*dim.* of bearn.) A little breach; a little notch. *N. pl.* bearnain.

Bearnan brìde, *s. m.* The flower called dandelion. Am bearnan brìde is a pheighinn rioghail, *the dandelion and the pennyroyal.*—*Macint.* *N. pl.* bearnain brìde.

Bearn-mhiol, *s. m.* A hare-lip.—*Shaw.*

† **Bearr,** *a.* Short, brief.

Bearr, *v. a.* Shave; shear, clip; crop, curtail, lop, prune. *Pret. a.* bhearr, *shaved; fut. aff. a.* bearraidh, *shall or will shave.* Bhearr se e fein, *he shaved himself.*—*Stew. Gen.*

Bearra, ai, *s. m.* A spear, a dart; any sharp-pointed instrument; also short hair; a cut, a slice, shred, or fragment; a segment.—*Shaw.*

Bearradair, *s. m.* (*from* bearr.) A barber, a hairdresser; a critic; one who carps, clips, or crops. Ealtain bearradair, *the razor of a barber.*—*Stew. Ezek.* *N. pl.* bearradairean.

Bearradaireachd, *s. f.* (*from* bearr. The occupation of a barber; a clipping, a cropping; a carping, criticising.

Bearradairean, *s.; n. pl.* of bearradair.

Bearradh, aidh, *s. m.* (*from* bearr.) A cutting, as of hair, or any other crop; a shearing, clipping, shaving; a lopping, a pruning; a spear; short hair; a cut, a slice, a shred; a segment. Dean do bhearradh, *shave thyself, make thyself bald.*—*Stew. Mic.*

Bearradh, aidh, *s. m.* The top of a mountain; a mountain cliff or pinnacle. *N. pl.* bearraidhean.

Bearrag, aig, *s. f.* (*from* bearn.) *Ir.* bearog. A razor.—*Macd.* *N. pl.* bearragan, *razors.*

Bearraiche, *s. m.* (*from* bearr.) *Ir.* bearrthach. A barber, a hairdresser. *N. pl.* bearraichean.

Bearraideach, *a.* (*from* bearr.) Light, nimble, active. Gu bearraideach, *lightly.*

Bearra-sgian, sgein, *s. m.* A razor; a pruning-hook.—*Macd.* *N. pl.* bearra-sgeinichean, *razors.*

Bearrta, Bearrte, *p. part.* of bearr. Shaven, cropped, clipped, pruned, shorn.—*Stew. Jer.* An treud bhearrta, *the shorn flock.*—*Stew. Song. Sol.*

Bearrtach, *a.* Shaving, cropping, clipping, pruning; carping; fond of cropping, clipping, or pruning.

† **Beart, Beairt,** *s. f.* A judgment; a covenant, or compact; a game at tables.—*Shaw.* *N. pl.* beairtean.

Beart, Beairt, *s. f.* (*Ir.* beart.) An engine, a machine; a loom, a frame; a deed, work, or exploit; a harness, a yoke; a burden; shrouds; tackling, as of a ship; a sheath or scabbard; a bundle or truss; clothes. *N. pl.* bearta, beairt, beartan. A bhearta iongantach, *his wonderful works.*—*Stew. Ps.* Bearta treubhantais, *feats of valour.*—*Sm.* Cuig barcai fo 'm beairt, *five ships in full equipment.*—*Oss. Conn.* A lann fo bheart, *his sword in the scabbard.*—*Oss. Tem.* Ar siùil 's ar beartan, *our sails and our shrouds.*—*Macfar.* Beart-thuairnein, *a turner's loom;* beart-fhigheadair, *a weaver's loom;* beart-treabhaidh, *a plough;* beart-uchd, *a poitrel.*

Beartach, *a.* Rich, wealthy; of, or belonging to, a machine; like a sheath or scabbard, sheathed. Cha bhi e beartach, *he shall not be rich.*—*Stew. Job.* *Com.* and *sup.* beartaiche, *more or most rich.*

Beartaich, *v. a.* (*from* beart.) Yoke, as a chariot; prepare, make ready; begin; enrich; brandish, flourish; also meditate.—*Shaw.* *Pret. a.* bheartaich, *yoked; fut. aff. a.* beartaichidh, *shall or will yoke.* Bheartaich e a charbad, *he yoked his chariot.*—*Stew. Gen.* *Fut. pass.* beartaichear.

Beartair, *s. m.* A brandisher.—*Shaw.*

Beartas, ais, *s. m.* Riches; honour. Beartas agus urram, *riches and honour.*—*Stew. Pro.*

† **Beartha,** *a.* Clean, fine, spruce, genteel.—*Shaw.*

Beas, *s.* See **Beus.**

Beasan, ain, *s. m.* (*Fr.* bassin. *Ir.* baisin.) A basin. *N. pl.* beasanan.

† **Beasg,** *s. f.* A prostitute.—*Shaw.*

† **Beasgnadh,** aidh, *s. m.* A speech, a dialect; peace.

Beath, *s. f.* Birch-wood, a birch-tree. Written also *beithe;* which see.

Beath, *s. f.* (*Ir.* beatha. *Gr.* βιωτη. *Dor.* βιωτα. *Lat.* vita.) Life; food; livelihood; welcome; salutation. Is amhuil aisling ar beath, *our life is like a dream.*—*Oss. Taura.* Is i do bheath 'n so, *you are welcome here.* Bhur beath-sa, ghaisgich! *you are welcome, O heroes!*—*Oss. Fing.* Bheir duine beath air éigin, ach cha toir e rath air éigin, *a man may force a livelihood, but cannot force good luck.*—*G. P.*

Beathach, aich, *s. m.* (*from* beath.) *Ir.* beathach. A beast, animal, creature; strictly speaking, it has the same comprehensive meaning with the *Gr.* ζωον, and the *Lat.* animal *or* animans, *any living thing;* yet it is never applied, but by way of reproach or pity, to a human being. *N. pl.* beathaichean. *Beathach* is also written *beothach,* from *beo.* Beathach fiadhaich, *a wild beast;* beathach oibre, *a beast of burden;* am beathach mosach, *the nasty beast;* a bheathaich thruaighe! *poor creature! poor thing!*

Beathachadh, aidh, *s. m.* A feeding; a nourishing; also food, sustenance, nourishment; a living, a benefice; maintenance. Arson beathachadh, *for food.*—*Stew. Gen.* Chum beathachaidh, *for maintenance.*—*Stew. Pro.* *Ir.* beathaghadh.

Beathachadh, *a.; pr. part.* of beathaich. Feeding, nourishing, maintaining.

Beathadach, aich, *s. m.* A beaver. *Ir.* beathodach. *N. pl.* beathadaiche.

Beathag, aig, *s. m.* A bee; a beech-tree.—*Shaw.* Also the name Sophia.

Beathaich, *v. a.* (*Ir.* beathaigh.) Feed, nourish, maintain, support; welcome, salute. *Pret. a.* bheathaich, *fed; fut. aff. a.* beathaichidh, *shall or will feed.* Bheathaich e chuid eile, *he fed the rest.*—*Stew. Gen.* Bheathaich e athair, *he maintained his father.*—*Id. Fut. pass.* beathaichear. Beathaich thusa mise an diugh, is beathaichidh mise thusa am maireach, *feed me to-day, and I will feed you to-morrow.*—*G. P.*

Beathaichidh, *fut. aff. a.* of beathaich; which see.

Beathaichte, *p. part.* of beathaich. Fed, nourished, maintained, supported; welcomed.

Beathail, *a.* (*i. e.* beath-amhuil.) Vital; pertaining to life. Aile bheathail, *vital air, or oxygen.*

Beath-àile, *s. f.* Vital air, oxygen.

Beathalach, *a.* (*from* beath.) Lively, sprightly. Gu beathalach, *lively.*

Beathalachd, *s. f.* Liveliness, sprightliness.

Beathanan, *s. sing.* and *pl.* Food, victuals.—*Macd.*

Beath-eachdraidh, *s. f.* A biography.

† **Beathra**, ai, *s. m.* (*th* silent.) Water.
Old Celtic, ber. *Turk.* bar *and* behr, *sea. Pers.* baran, *rain. Phen.* bir, *wells. Arab.* bir, *wells. Ir.* bir, *a well.* In *Madagascar*, bihar means *sea.*

Beic, *s. f.* A courtesy. Dean beic, *courtesy.*

Béic, *s. f.* A cry, shout, roar; an outcry, an uproar. More commonly written *beuc;* which see.

Beic, *s. f.* A point, a nib, the bill of a bird. Hence *Fr.* bec. *It.* becco. *Eng.* beak *and* peak.

Beiceasach, *a.* (*from* beic.) Bobbing; courtesying; skipping; hopping.—*Macint.*

Beiceil, *a.* (*from* beic.) Courtesying, bobbing.

Beiceil, *s. f.* A courtesying, bobbing, frequent bobbing. A beiceil gu foirmeil, *courtesying formally.*—*Macfar.* Ciod a bheiceil th' ort? *why do you bob so?*

Beiceil, (a), *pr. part.* of beic. Courtesying, bobbing.

Beic-leumnach, *a.* Prancing, skipping, bobbing, hopping, dancing.

Beigneid, *s. f.* A bayonet. *N. pl.* beigneidean.

Béil, *gen. sing.* of beul.

Be'il, (*i. e.* beath-uile, *the life of all.*) Bel, the name under which the British Druids adored the Divinity. *Bel*, in Welch, means war or havoc. Owen observes, that Mars was called *Bel* by the Britons; and he grounds his opinion on the following inscription upon a British Roman altar, which was found in the north of England, "Bel y dw Cadyr;" *Bel, the god of war.*

† **Beil**, *gen.* beile, *s. f.* A meal of meat, a diet.—*Ir. id.*

Beilbheag, aig, *s. f.* A corn-poppy; wild poppy. *N. pl.* beilbheagan.

Beilbheagach, *a.* Abounding in wild poppies; like a wild poppy.

Beilean, ein, *s. m.* (*from* beul.) A mouth, a prattling mouth; prattling; a prattling person. *Asp. form*, bheilean. Ciod a bheilean th' ort? *why do you prattle so?*

Beileanach, *a.* (*from* beul.) Garrulous; prating. Beul beileanach, *a prating mouth;* gu beileanach, *garrulously. Com.* and *sup.* beileanaiche.

Beileanachd, *s. f.* (*from* beul.) Garrulousness; prating. Is ann ort tha bheileanachd, *how you do prate.*

† **Beille**, *s. f.* (*Ir. id.*) A kettle, a caldron. *N. pl.* beilleachan.

Beilleach, *a.* Blubber-lipped.

Beilleachd, *s. f.* The deformity of blubber-lips.

Beilleachas, ais, *s. m.* The deformity of a blubber-lip.

† **Beilt, Beilte**, *s. f.* A belt, girth, cingle.—*Ir. id.*

Béim, *gen. sing.* of beum; which see.

† **Beim**, *s. f.* A tribe, a generation; also a help; a piece of timber. *Ir.* beim. *Eng.* beam.

Béin, *gen. sing.* of bian. Of a skin or hide. Clogaid béin an ruadh-bhuic, *a helmet of the skin of the roe.*—*Oss. Cathula.*

Beinc, *s. f.* A bench, a form, a table.
Swed. bank, *a shelf. Teut.* bancke *and* panch, *a bench. Dan.* benc. *Span.* banca. *It.* banco. *Basque*, banco. *Du.* bank. *Old Sax.* benc. *W.* and *Corn.* benk. *Ir.* beinc. *N. pl.* beincean.

† **Beinc**, *s. f.* (*Ir. id.*) A separation, partition, disjunction. —*Shaw.*

† **Beine**, *s. m.* A champion; also evening.—*Ir. id.*

Beinean, ein, *s. f.* A little woman. *Ir.* beinin. *Corn.* banen.

Beinn, *gen.* beinne, *s. f.* A mountain; hill; pinnacle; a bin. *W.* pen. *Box. Lex.* bann. *Gr.* βουνος; hence also Πηνικος. The *pen* of the Cimbrians and Sabines also meant a summit; hence Apennines, mountains in Italy. See also Beann.

Beinne, *gen. sing.* of beann *and* beinn.

Beinnean, ein, *s. m.* (*dim.* of beinn.) A little hill, a pinnacle.

Beir, *v.* Take hold; bear, carry; bring forth; give; overtake. *Pret. a.* bheir, *bare; fut. aff. a.* beiridh, *shall bear.* Bheir i mac, *she bore a son.* Beiridh tu mac, *thou shalt bear a son.*—*Stew. Gen.* Beir uam fuaim d' òran, *take from me the noise of thy song.*—*Stew. Am.* Beiribh beannachd, beiribh buaidh, *be ye blest, be ye victorious.*—*Fingalian Poem. Beir*, with the preposition *air*, means *overtake, take hold;* beir air, *take hold of him, overtake him;* Beiridh mi orra, *I will overtake them.* Nur chi thu bean oileanach beir oirre, mar beir thusa oirre beiridh fear eile oirre, *when you find an accomplished woman, take her; if you will not, another will.*—*G. P.*
Gr. φερι. *Lat.* fer. *Dan.* baere. *Maeso-Gothic*, bairan. *Swedo-Gothic*, baera. *Swed.* bara. *Isl.* bera. *Franconian*, bera. *Germ.* baeren, *bear a child. Anglo-Sax.* bearan. *Ir.* beir. *Eng.* bear. *Ber*, in the end of compounded German words, means *bearing;* as, beigam-ber, *a prophet, or bringer of good news.*

† **Beirbheis**, *s. f.* Anniversary, feast, vigil.—*Ir. id.*

Beirm, *s. m.* Barm, yeast. *Germ.* berm. *Anglo-Sax.* beorm. *Dan.* baermes. Aran gun bheirm, *unfermented bread.*—*Stew. Gen. ref.*

Beirn. See Bearn.

Beirneach, *a.* See Bearnach.

† **Beirt**, *s.* A burden; a help; also two persons.—*Ir. id.*

Beirte, *p. part.* of beir. Born. *Ir.* beirthe; hence *Eng.* birth.

† **Beirtean**, ein, *s. m.* A little burden.

Béist, Béiste, *s. f.* A beast, a monster, a beast of prey; a wretch. Tuiteam an stri na beiste, *falling in contest with the monster.*—*Oss. Derm.* Chuir droch bheist as da, *an evil beast has devoured him.*—*Stew. Gen.* Beistean doirbh, *oppressive wretches.*—*Old Song. Lat.* bestia. *Dan.* baest. *Swed.* best. *Du.* beest. *Port.* besta. *Fr.* † bêste, now written *bête. N. pl.* beistean.

Beistean, ein, *s. m.* (*dim.* of béist.) A little beast. *Ir.* beistin.

Béistean, *n. pl.* of béist.

Beitean, ein, *s. m.* The scorched or frost-bitten grass of the hills.

Beith, *s. f.* The second letter (B) of the Gaelic alphabet.

Beith, Beithe, *s. f.* (*W.* bedu. *Ir.* beithe.) Birch. Sa bheith chubhraidh, *in the fragrant birch.—Oss. Derm.*

Beithir, *s. m.* (*th* silent.) A bear; any wild beast.

Heb. behir, *a beast of burden*, and pere, *a wild ass. Chald.* beira, *an elephant. Arab.* phor, *a heifer. Gr.* βειρος, *rough*, and φηρ, *a wild beast. Lat.* fera. *Sabine* and *Lat.* barrus. Hence also verres, *a boar pig*; a-per, *a boar*; and vervex. *Germ.* baer. *Ir.* bear. *Eng.* bear *and* boar. *Anglo-Sax.* bera. *Belg.* beer. *Dan.* biorn. *Hung.* barom, *a beast of burden. Bohem.* beran, *a lamb. Bisc.* abere, *a beast of burden.*

Beithir, *a.* Wild, destructive, savage. *Gr.* βειρος.

Beitir, *a.* Neat, clean, tidy.

Bel. See **Beil**.

† **Ben**, *s. f.* An old Celtic term signifying a wain or chariot. *Lat.* benna.

I have somewhere seen the following remark on *benna*:—"Benna linguâ Gallicâ genus vehiculi appellatur, unde vocantur *combennones* in eâdem bennâ sedentes." *Benna*, in the language of Gaul, is a kind of vehicle; hence they who ride in the same chariot are called *combennones*.

From *combennones* evidently comes, through the medium of the French *compagnon*, the English *companion*.

Beo, *a.* (*W.* byw. *Arm.* and *Corn.* bew. *Ir.* beo.) Alive, living; sprightly, lively; also, *substantively*, a living person. Am beo e? *is he alive?* Am beo i? *is she alive?* Tir nam beò, *the land of the living.* Am beo dhuit a Dheirg? *art thou alive, O Dargo?—Ull.* B' aluinn thu ri d' bheo, *thou wert handsome when alive.—Oss. Carricth.* Ri d' bheo, *as long as you live.—Macint.* Thoir beo, *bring alive.* Cho beo ri breac, *as surely as a trout.* Gu ma fad beo an righ! *long live the king!—Stew. Sam.* Mar is beo mi, *as I live*; cho chinnte 's a tha thu beo, *as sure as you are alive.*

Beo-airgiod, *s.* Quicksilver; *literally*, live silver. So the French *vif-argent*, and the Italian *argento-vivo*.

Beochan, ain, *s. m.* A small fire. Beochan teine, *a little flickering fire.*

Beochanta, *a.* (*from* beo.) Vigorous; lively, sprightly.

Beochantachd, *s. f.* (*from* beo.) Vigorousness; liveliness, sprightliness.

Beo-eachdaireachd, *s. f.* The occupation of a biographer.

Beo-eachdraidh, *s. f.* A biography.

Beo-eachdraidhiche, Beo-eachdraiche, *s. m.* A biographer. *N. pl.* beo-eachdraidhchean *or* beo-eachdraichean.

Beo-fhàl, fhàil, *s. m.* An enclosure.

Beo-ghaineamh, eimh, *s.* Quicksand. Gun tuiteadh iad sa bheò-ghaineamh, *that they would fall into the quicksand.—Stew. Acts.*

Beo-ghlac, *v. a.* Take alive; take prisoner alive. *Pret. a.* bheo-ghlac, *took alive.*

Beo-ghriosach, aich, *s. f.* Hot embers.

Beòil, *gen. sing.* of beul. Of a mouth. Làn beòil bhiadh is lan bail nàire, *a mouthful of meat, and a townful of shame.—G. P.* See **Beul**.

† **Beoill**, *s. f.* Fatness.

Beo-iobairt, *s. f.* A living sacrifice. Bhur cuirp nam beo iobairt, *your bodies as a living sacrifice.—Stew. Rom. N. pl.* beo-iobairtean.

Beòir, *gen. sing.* beòir *and* beorach, *s. f.* Beer. (*Run.* bior.) Gloine beòrach, *a glass of beer.—Old Song.* Beòir laidir, *strong beer*; beòir chaol, *small beer.*

† **Beol, Beoil**, *s. m.* A robber.

Beolach, *a.* Talkative.

Beolaiche, *s. m.* A chronicler; a talkative person.

Beo-laoch, laoich, *s. m.* A lively fellow, a lively lad. *N. pl.* beo-laoich.

Beo-luath, luaith, *s. f.* Hot ashes or embers. *N. pl.* beo-luaithre.

Beo-radharc, *s. m.* Quick sight; clear sight; a lively view.—*Ir. id.*

Beo-radharcach, *a.* Quick-sighted, clear-sighted.—*Ir. id.*

† **Beosach**, *a.* Bright, glittering; brisk; trim, spruce; dapper.

† **Beosaich**, *v. a.* Beautify, adorn, make spruce or tidy. *Pret. a.* bheòsaich.

Beo-sgar, *v. a.* Divorce. *Pret. a.* bheo-sgar, *divorced*; *fut. aff. a.* beo-sgaraidh, *shall or will divorce.*

Beo-sgaradh, aidh, *s. m.* A divorce, a separation during life.

Beo-shlainnte, *s. f.* A life-rent. Tuarasdal re d' bheòshlainnte, *a salary during thy life, or as a life-rent.—Old Song.* Ridir beo-shlainnte, *a knight bachelor.*

Beo-shlainnteach, *a.* Of, or pertaining to, a life-rent.

Beothach, aich, *s. m.* (*from* beo.) A beast; properly any living creature. *Arm.* bieuch. *Portug.* becho, *a worm. N. pl.* beothaichean. *Beothach* is also written *beathach*; which see.

Beothachadh, aidh, *s. m.* A re-animating, quickening; a kindling.

Beothachadh, *a.*; *pr. part.* of beothaich. Reanimating, quickening, kindling, reviving.

Beothachail, (*i. e.* beothach-amhuil.) Having a reanimating or quickening influence.

Beothachair, *s. m.* A reviver. *W.* bywiocawr.

Beothaich, *gen. sing.* beothach.

Beothaich, *v. a.* Kindle, light; reanimate, revive, quicken. *Pret. a.* beothaich, *revived*; *fut. aff. a.* beothaichidh, *shall revive.* Réir t-fhocail beothaich mi, *according to thy word, quicken me.—Sm.* Beothaich a choinneal, *light the candle. Fut. pass.* beothaichear. Is tric bheothaich srad bheag teine mòr, *often has a spark kindled a conflagration.—G. P.*

Beothaichidh, *fut. aff. a.* of beothaich.

Beothaichte, *p. part.* of beothaich. Quickened, animated, kindled, lit.

Beothail, *a.* (*i. e.* beo-amhuil, *from* beo.) *W.* bywawl. Lively, brisk, smart, vigorous, diligent, active; fervent, zealous. Tha iad beothail, *they are lively.—Stew. Exod.* Beothail na 'r spioraid, *fervent in your spirit.—Stew. Rom. ref.*

Beothalachd, *s. f.* (*from* beo.) Liveliness, smartness, agility.

Beo-thorrach, *a.* Quick with child; also ready to conceive. *Com.* and *sup.* beo-thorraiche.

† **Betarlagh**, *s. m.* An ancient law. *Ir.* beterlach.

Beth, *s. f.* The second letter of the Gaelic alphabet. Written also **Beith**.

Beubanachadh, aidh, *s. m.* A mangling, a bruising, a maltreating. Fhuair e a bheubanachadh, *he got himself bruised or maltreated.*

Beubanachadh, (a), *pr. part.* of beubanaich.

Beubanachd, *s. f.* Mangling, bruising, maltreatment, tearing.

Beubanaich, *v. a.* Mangle, bruise, maltreat, tear. *Pret. a.* bheubanaich, *mangled*; *fut. aff. a.* beubanaichidh, *shall or will tear or mangle.*

Beubanaichte, *p. part.* of beubanaich. Torn, mangled, bruised, maltreated.

Beuc, *s. m.* (*Heb.* bechi *and* becheh.) A roar, a bellow, an outcry, a noise, clamour.

Beuc, *v. n.* (*Heb.* bachah *and* bechah, *wept.*) Roar, bellow, make a noise as the sea. *Pret. a.* bheuc, *roared; fut. aff. a.* beucaidh, *shall or will roar.*

Beucach, *a.* Roaring, noisy, clamorous; apt to roar or bellow. Beucach dubhlaidh, *roaring and dark.—Oss. Fing.* Muir bheucach fo ghaoith a' stri, *the roaring main contending with the winds.—Oss. Lodin.*

Beucaich, *s. f.* A roaring, a loud noise, a roar. Beucaich do thonn, *the roaring of thy waves.—Oss. Duthona.* Ciod bheucaich th' ort? *what are you roaring for?*

Beucaidh, *fut. aff. a.* of beuc. Shall or will roar.

Beucair, *s. m.* (*from* beuc.) A roarer. *N. pl.* beucairean.

Beuc-shruth, *s. m.* A roaring stream, a cataract. Turthor nam beuc-shruth, *Turthor of roaring streams.—Oss. Lod.*

Beud, *s. m.* Loss, pity, harm, injury; a defect or blemish; distress; fate; a blow, an action, an evil deed; vice; gloom. Cha d' fhuiling e beud, *he suffered no harm.—Oss. Derm.* Thill e fo bheud, *he returned with loss.—Oss. Lodin.* Duan gun bheud, *a poem without defect.—Id.* Fina gun bheud, *unblemished Fina.—Id.* Faiceam mo bheud, *let me see my fate.—Oss. Fing.* 'Eudan fo bheud, *his visage under a gloom.—Oss. Tem.* From *beud* comes the English *beat.*

Beudach, *a.* (*from* beud.) Hurtful, iniquitous, blemished, guilty; fatal, gloomy. Is beudach borb am buille, *fatal and fierce is the blow.—Death of Carril.* Am fear a bhios beudach cha sguir e dh' èigneach chàich, *he who is guilty tries to involve others.—G. P. Com.* and *sup.* beudaiche, *more or most hurtful.*

Beudag, aig, *s. f.* A trifling little woman; a gossip; a lying female. *N. pl.* beudagan.

Beudagach, *a.* Like a gossip.

Beudagan, *n. pl.* of beudag.

Beud-fhocal, ail, *s. m.* A taunting word or expression. *N. pl.* beud-fhocail, *taunting words.*

Beud-fhoclach, *a.* Foul-mouthed, opprobrious, taunting.

Beul, Beil, *s. m.* The Celtic god, Belus or Bel. See **Beil.**

Beul, *gen.* bèil *and* beòil, *s. m.* (*Ir.* beul. *Gr.* βηλ-ος, *a threshold.*) A mouth, opening, aperture. Beul nach cànadh ach stuaim, *a mouth that would not utter but modest words.—Macint.* Cluinnear nuallan do bheoil, *the murmur of thy mouth shall be heard.—Ull.* An taobh beòil, *the forepart.—Stew.* 1 K. Beul ri, *about, or near about.* Beul ri tri miosa, *about three mouths.—Stew. Gen.*

Beulach, *a.* (*from* beul.) Fair-spoken; plausible; prating; flattering; large-mouthed; mouthed.

Beulais, *s. f.* Prating, babbling.

Beul-aithris, *s. f.* Tradition, oral tradition. Beul-aithris dhaoine, *the tradition of men.—Stew. Col.*

Beulan, ain, *s. m.* (*dim.* of beul.) A little mouth; an orifice.

Beulanach, *a.* (*from* beul.) Fair-spoken, smooth-worded, inclined to flatter.—*Macint.* Also the bit of a bridle.

Beulaobh, *s.* (*i. e.* beul-thaobh.) A foreside; a front. Air a beulaobh, *before her, or in front of her.* Air a bheulaobh, *before him, before his face.—Stew. Gen.*

Beul-bhach, aich, *s. m.* A bridle bit.—*Ir. id.*

Beul-bhochd, *s. m.* A pleading of poverty.—*Shaw.*

Beul-chainnteach, *a.* Garrulous, prating.

Beulchar, (*from* beul.) Fair-spoken, flattering, smooth-worded.

Beul-chrabhach, *a.* Lip-religious, hypocritical, canting.

Beul-chrabhadh, aidh, *s. m.* Lip-religion, cant, hypocrisy.

Beul-dhruid, *v. a.* Silence. *Pret. a.* beul-dhruid, *silenced; fut. aff. a.* beul-dhruididh, *shall silence.*

Beulgradh, aidh, *s. m.* Flattery, dissimulation.

Beul-maothain, *s. m.* The sloat of the throat.

Beul-mòr, *s. m.* A bung-hole; a wide mouth.

Beul-oideas, eis, *s. m.* Tradition, oral tradition.—*Shaw.*

Beul-oilean, ein, *s. m.* Tradition, oral tradition.—*Macd.*

Beul-phurgaid, *s. f.* A gargle. *N. pl.* beul-phurgaidean.

Beul-phurgaideach, *a.* Gargling; of, or belonging to, a gargle.

Beul-phurgaideachd, *s. f.* Gargarization.

Beul-radh, *s. m.* A phrase, a proverb, a bye-word.

Beum, *v. a.* Smite, strike, cleave; strike, as a bell, toll; cut, or make a cutting remark; utter a sarcasm or criticism. *Pret. a.* bheum, *smote; fut. aff. a. shall or will smite.* An dubh-bhàs 'g am beumadh nan ruaig, *gloomy death smiting them in their flight.—Oss. Tem.* Teine athair a beumadh nan nial, *lightning cleaving the clouds.—Id.* On bheum na cluig, *since the bells have tolled.—Old Song.*

Beum, *gen.* bèim *and* beuma, *s. m.* A blow, a stroke; a cut; a taunt or sarcasm; a gap; a stream, a torrent; a knell; a misfortune. Gach cath 's na bhuail mi beum, *every battle where I struck a blow.—Fingalian Poem.* Mo chuis lean mar bheum, *my veins like a torrent.* Bhrùchd iad a dh' aon bheum, *they poured forward in one body.—Mac Lach.* Beum-cheap, *a whipping-post;* beum-grèine, *a coup-de-soleil;* beum-sgeithe, *an alarm;* beum sleibhe, *a torrent;* beum-soluis, *a sun-beam;* beum sùla, *the blasting influence of an evil eye.*

Beumach, *a.* (*from* beum.) Full of gaps; destructive; taunting, bitter, sarcastic. Mar theine beumach, *like a destructive fire.—Oss. Trathal.* Aineolach, beumach, *ignorant and bitter.—Macint.*

Beum-cheap, -chip, *s.* A whipping-stock.

Beum-cluige, *s. m.* A knell.

Beumnach, *a.* (*from* beum.) Destructive; causing breaches, taunting; reproachful, depraved. Buillean cothromach beumnach, *heavy, destructive blows.—Oss. Cathula.* Bilean beumnach, *reproachful or depraved lips.—Stew. Pro.*

Beum-sgeithe, *s. m.* A striking the shield; the usual mode of giving a challenge, or of sounding an alarm, among the old Caledonians. Le beum-sgeithe ghlaodh iad comhrag, *with a blow on the shield they called to battle.—Oss. Dargo.* Bhuail Treunmor beum-sgeithe, *Treunmor sounded an alarm.—Ull.*

Beum-sleibhe, *s. m.* A mountain torrent, especially that which is caused by the bursting of a thunder-cloud. Mar dhà bheum-sleibhe o 'n fhireach, *like two torrents from the height.—Oss. Dargo.*

Beum-sùl, *s. m.* A blasting of the eye; the supposed influence of a malignant eye; an optical delusion; a *coup-d'œil.*

Beum-soluis, *s. m.* A sun-beam; a beam of light. Feuch am beum-soluis caol, *behold yon small beam of light.—Oss. Manos.*

Beur, *s. m.* A point; a pinnacle. Beur ard, *a lofty pinnacle.—Oss. Lodin.* Ro bhearna beur nan neul, *through the fissures of the castled clouds.—Id.*

Beurla, *s. f.* The English tongue; the language of the Scotch Lowlanders.

Beurlach, *a.* Relating to the English tongue, or to that of the Scotch Lowlanders.

Beurra, beurtha, *a.* (*W.* berth.) Genteel, clean, well-spoken; sharp. Fir bheurra, *genteel men.—Macdon.*

Beus, beusa, *s. f.* A bass-viol.

Beus, *s.* Moral quality, virtue; behaviour, conduct; deeds; custom; a quality, whether good or bad. Bean nan deadh bheus, *a virtuous woman.—Stew. Pro. ref.* Aithnichear leanabh le bheus, *a child is known by his doings.—Stew. Pro.* Beus na dh' fhalbh, *the deeds (conduct) of the departed.—Orr.* Fo bheus, *quiet, on one's good behaviour;* tonnan fo bheus, *waves at peace.—Oss.* *N. pl.* beusan. Beus na tuath air am bithear, is e 'nithear, *the way of the folk you live with is what you must follow.—G. P.*

BEUSACH, *a.* (*from* beus.) Well-behaved, modest, well-bred, gentle. Mar aiteal beusach, *like a gentle breeze.—Oss. Tem. Com.* and *sup.* beusaiche.

BEUTAIL, *s. f.* Cattle; a cow. *Fr.* bataille.

B'FHEARR, (*for* bu fhearr.) Were better, was better, wert better. See FEARR.

BH', (*for* bha), *v.* Was, wert, were.

BHA, (*pret. of aux. verb* be.) Was, wert, were. Bha samhladh na bha a boillsgeadh, *the spectres of those who* [*were*] *once existed were shining.—Oss. Comala.* Bha ghealach air eudan nan carn, *the moon was on the face of the rocks.—Oss. Lodin.*

BHAC, *pret. a.* of bac. Hindered, interrupted, forbade. See BAC.

BHAGAIR, *pret. a.* of bagair. Threatened.

BHAIGH, *asp. form* of baigh; which see.

BHÀIN. See BÀN.

BHAIRD, *voc. sing.* and *gen. sing. asp.* of bard. See BARD.

BHÀIS, *asp. form* of bàis, *gen. sing.* of bàs; which see.

BHALBH, *asp. form* of balbh. See BALBH.

BHALLACH, *asp. form* of ballach; which see.

BHALLAIBH, *dat. pl. asp. form* of balla.

BHALLAIBH, *dat. pl. asp. form* of ball; which see.

BHÀN, *a.*, *asp. form* of bàn. White, fair, pale. *Arm.* venn. See BÁN.

BHÀN, a bhàn, *adv.* (*Swed.* afan, *from above.*) Down, downwards. Gun suidheadh e bhàn gu fonn, *that he would sit down to sing.—Oss. Tem.* Cuir a bhan e, *put him or it down.*

BHAOBH, *voc.* of baobh. O wicked woman! Also the *asp. form* of baobh. Mad, foolish, wicked.

BHAOTH, *asp. form* of baoth; which see.

BHARD, *asp. form* of bard; which see.

BHÀRR, *s.*, *asp. form* of bàrr. See BÀRR.

BHÀRR, [o bhàrr], *prep.* From, from off, down from. Bhàrr aghaidh na talmhainn, *from the surface of the earth.—G. B.* Theiring i bhàrr a chamhuil, *she alighted from the camel.—Stew. Gen.* Bharr do chos, *from off thy feet.—Stew. Ex.* A bharr air sin, *over and above that, besides that;* bhàrr an rathaid, *off the way;* bhàrr an fheòir, *off the grass, off the pasture.—Stew.* 1 *K.* Bhàrr a leapach, *from his bed, off his bed.—Stew.* 2 *Sam.* Bhàrr na ciche, *weaned.*

BHARRACHD, (a), *prep.* Besides; over and above. A bharrachd air a cheud ghorta, *besides the first famine.—Stew. Gen.*

BHÀS, *asp. form* of bas; which see.

BHAT, *asp. form* of bat. A staff. Mo bhat, *my stick.* See BAT.

BHÀT, *asp. form* of bàt. A boat. A bhàt, *his boat.* See BAT.

BHEACH, *s.*, *asp. form* of beach.

BHEACHD, *asp. form* of beachd, *s. f.* Opinion. A réir mo bheachd, *in my opinion.*

BHEACHDAICH, *pret. a.* of beachdaich. Viewed, reviewed.

BHEAG, *asp. form* of beag. Little. Cha d' fhuair iad a bheag, *they got not the least.*

BHEAIRT, *asp. form* of beairt.

BHEAN, *pret. a.* of bean. Touched, handled. See BEAN.

BHEAN, *asp. form* of bean. Wife, woman. A bhean, *his wife.* Also *voc. sing.*

BHEANNAICH, *pret. a.* of beannaich. Blessed.

BHEANNAICHTE, *asp. form* of beannaichte; which see.

BHEIL, *pres. neg.* and *inter.* of bi. Am, art, are.

BHEILEAM, (*for* bheil mi.) Am I. Am bheileam féin am aonar? *am I left alone?—Oss. Gaul.*

BHEART, *asp. form* of beart.

BHEIR, *fut. aff. a.* of tabhair. Shall or will give. Co e a bheir comhrag? *who is he that will give battle?—Oss. Lod.* Bheir mise ort gum fainich thu e, *I will make you feel it, or smart for it;* bheir me ort a dheanamh, *I will make you do it.*

BHEIR, *pret.* of beir. Caught; overtook; bore, or bare, as a child. See BEIR.

BHEIREAR, *fut. pass.* of tabhair. Shall be given.

BHEIRINN, 1 *sing. pret. sub.* of tabhair, and also of beir. I would give; I would bear.

BHEIRTEADH, 1 *sing. pret. sub. pass.* of tabhair. Should or would be given.—*Stew. Pro.*

BHEO, *asp. form* of beo.

BHEÒIL, *asp. form* of beòil; also *voc. pl.* of beul. A bheoil nan dàn, *ye mouths of the song, ye bards.—Oss.*

BHEOTHAICH, *pret. a.* of beothaich; which see.

BHEUC, *pret. a.* of beuc. Roared, bellowed, shouted, hallowed. See BEUC.

BHEUCACH, *asp. form* of beucach; which see.

BHEUL, *asp. form* of beul; which see.

BHEUM, *pret. a.* of beum. Smote. See BEUM.

BHEUM, *asp. form* of beum.

BHIADH, *asp. form* of biadh. Meat. *Arm.* vyou. See BIADH.

BHIADH, *pret. a.* of biadh. Fed. See BIADH.

BHINN, *asp. form* of binn, *a.* See BINN.

BHITH, *s.*, *asp. form* of bith; which see.

BHITH, (a), *infin.* of bi. To be.

BHITHEADH, *imperf. sub.* of bi. Would be.

BHITHEAS, *fut. sub.* of bi. Shall or will be.

BHITHINN, 1 *sing. imp. sub.* of bi. I would be.

BHLAIS, *pret. a.* of blais. Tasted. See BLAIS.

BHLÀR, *asp. form* of blàr; which see.

BHÒ, *asp. form* of bò. A cow.

BHO, *prep.* and *adv.* From; of or belonging to; since; since the time at which. Iosa bho Nazaret, *Jesus of* (i. e. *from*) *Nazareth.—Stew. Mat. ref.* Bho chunnas thu se ladh nan nial, *since I saw thee sailing in the clouds.—Ull.*

BHOBH! *interj.* O dear! strange!

BHOCHD, *asp. form* of bochd. See BOCHD.

BHOG, (peith-bhog). The fourteenth letter (P) of the Gaelic alphabet.

BHOG, *pret. a.* of bog. Dipped.

BHOG, *asp. form* of bog, *a.* Soft.

BHOGAICH, *pret. a.* of bogaich. Softened. See BOGAICH.

BHOGHA, *asp. form* of bogha; which see.

BHOIDHEACH, *a.* See BÒIDHEACH.

BHOIDHICHE, *asp. form* of boidhiche.

BHOIL, *asp. form* of boil.

BHOIRIONN, *asp. form* of boirionn; which see.

BHÒISG, *pret. a.* of boisg. Shone, gleamed. See BOISG.

BHOLGACH, aich, *s. f.* The venereal.

BHOLGACH, *a.*, *asp. form* of bolgach. Bossy.

BHÒ 'N DÉ, *s.* The day before yesterday. An dé no air bho 'n dé, *yesterday or the day before.—Stew. Deut. ref.*

BHONN, *asp. form* of bonn.

BHOS, *prep.* On this side; here. An taobh bhos, *this side.*

BHOTHAN, *asp. form* of bothan.

BHRAT, *asp. form* of brat; which see.

BHRATH, *asp. form* of brath. Air brath, *found; to be found.* Cha bhi 'm bard air bhrath, *the bard shall be no more.—Bard's Wish.*

Bhrathair, *voc. sing.* of brathair. O brother! Also *asp. form* of brathair. A bhrathair, *his brother.*

Bhreab, *pret. a.* of breab. Kicked. See Breab.

Bhréid, *s.* See Bréid.

Bhrè. See Brè.

Bhriachaill Bhrochaill, *s. f.* The banner of Gaul, the son of Morni. His motto was, Toiseach teachd is deireadh falbh, *first to come, and last to go.*

Bhrigh, *conj.* Because. A bhrigh, *because;* do bhrigh, *because.*

Bhris, *pret. a.* of bris. Broke, splintered; failed, became bankrupt. See Bris.

Bhriseas, *fut. sub.* of bris; which see.

Bhriste, *asp. form* of briste; *p. part.* of bris; which see.

Bhròn, *asp. form* of bròn; which see.

Bhruach, *asp. form* of bruach; which see.

Bhruan, *pret. a.* of bruan. Broke, splintered.

Bhruth, *pret. a.* of bruth. Bruised. See Bruth.

Bhuaidh, *asp. form* of buaidh.

Bhuail, *pret. a.* of buail. Struck, smote.

Bhuain, *pret. a.* of buain. Reaped. See Buain.

Bhuair, *pret.* of buair. Tempted, vexed, disturbed, distracted.

Bhuaireas, *fut. sub.* of buair; which see.

Bhuaireas, *asp. form* of buaireas.

Bhuaithe, *provincial* for uaith; which see.

Bhuanaich, *pret.* of buanaich. Continued. See Buanaich.

Bhuapa, *provincial* for uapa; which see.

Bhuig, *gen. m. voc.* of bog. Soft, moist, effeminate. Fhir bhoidhich bhuig, *thou handsome effeminate man.—Mac Lach.*

Bhuige, *asp. form* of buige; *com.* and *sup.* of bog.

Bhuill, *voc. pl.* of ball.

Bhuin, *pret. a.* of buin; which see.

Bhuineadh, *pret. pass.* of buin; which see.

Bhuinnte, *asp. form* of buinnte; *past part.* of buin.

Bhur, *poss. pron.* Your. Spiorad bhur n-inntinn, *the spirit of your minds.* *Bhur* is often written *ur.*

Bhus, *asp. form* of bus; which see.

Bi, *aux. v.* Be. *Pr. aff.* ta or tha, *am, art, is, are; pret.* bha, *was, wert, were; fut. aff.* bithidh, *shall be; pret. inter.* and *neg.* robh, *was;* an robh e, *was he;* nach robh e, *was he not; pret. sub.* bhithinn, *I would be.* Bi falbh, *begone;* bi sambach, *be quiet.*

B' i, (*for* bu i.) It was she; she.

Biachar, (*from* biadh.) *Contr.* for biadhchar; which see.

Biadh, *v. a.* Feed, nourish, maintain. *Pret. a.* bhiadh, *fed; fut. aff. a.* biadhaidh, *shall or will feed.* Biadhaidh se iad, *he will feed them.—Stew. Hos.*

Biadh, *gen.* beidh *and* bidh, *s. m.* Meat, food, victuals, diet; fodder, provender. Chum bidh, *for food.—Stew. G. B.* Biadh-briste, *fragments;* biadh-eoinein, *wood-sorrel;* biadh-nòin, *lunch;* biadh-madainn, *breakfast.*

W. bwyd. *Ir.* biadh. *Corn.* boet. *Arm.* vyou. *Manx.* bi. *It.* biada. *Bisc.* viauda.

Biadhadh, aidh, *s. m.* A feeding, a nourishing; a feed; meat, victuals, provender. Is fearr a bhiadhadh no ionnsachadh, *he is better fed than taught.—G. P.*

Biadhadh, (a), *pr. part.* of biadh. Feeding, nourishing.

Biadh-briste, *s.* Fragments; crumbled food.

Biadh-eoinein, *s. m.* Wood-sorrel. Mu 'm biodh am biadh eoinean a fàs, *about which the wood-sorrel grows.—Macdon.*

Biadh-eunain, *s. m.* Wood-sorrel. Written also *biadh-eoinein.*

Biadh-feasgair, *s. m.* An evening meal, supper.

Biadh-madainn, *s. m.* Breakfast.

Biadhchar, *a.* Fruitful, substantial; affording substance; esculent. Arbhar biadhchar, *substantial crops.—Macint.* Tha thu biadhchar pailt, *thou art substantial and prolific.—Macdon.*

Biadh-chluan, ain, *s. m.* A kitchen.—*Shaw.*

Biadh-lann, lainn, *s. m.* A pantry.

Biadh-luibh, *s.* Salad. *W.* bwydlyss. *N. pl.* biadh-luibhean.

Biadh-lus, -luis, *s. m.* Salad. *W.* bwydlys. *N. pl.* biadh-lusan.

Biadh-noin, *s. m.* A luncheon, a mid-day meal.—*Stew. Pro.*

Biadhta, biadhte, *p. part.* of biadh. Fed, nourished. Damh biadhta, *a stalled or fed ox.—Stew. Pro.*

Biadhtach, aich, *s. m.* (*from* biadh.) A hospitable farmer; a certain order of Irish tenants, who procured provisions for the nobles.—*Shaw.*

Biadh-thigh, *s. m.* An eating-house. *W.* bwythy. *N. pl.* biadh-thighean.

† **Biail**, *s. f.* An axe or hatchet.—*Ir. id.*

† **Bial**, biail, *s. m.* Water.—*Ir. id.*

Bian, béine, *s. m.* (*Ir.* bian.) A skin or hide; a pelt; abode. Bian an tuirc, *the boar's hide.—Ull.* Bu ghile a bian na canach sleibhe, *whiter was her skin than mountain cotton.—Oss.*

Bian-dhubh, *a.* Swarthy; black-skinned.

Bian-gheal, *a.* White-skinned, fair-skinned. Nan gnuis bhian ghil, *in their white-skinned faces.—Old Song.*

Bian-leasaiche, *s. m.* A currier, a tanner. *N. pl.* bian-leasaichean.

Biast, béist, *s. m.* (*Ir.* biast. *Lat.* bestia. *Fr.* † beste.) A beast; a reptile; in contempt, an insignificant person. Biast-donn, *an otter;* biast-dubh, *an otter.*

Biastail, *a.* (biastamhail.) Beastly, beastlike, impish; niggardly. Gu biastail, *impishly.*

Biastalachd, *s. f.* (*from* biast.) Beastliness, impishness, niggardliness.

Biast-donn, *s. m.* An otter.—*Shaw.*

Biast-dubh, *s. m.* An otter.—*Macdon.*

Biatach, aich, *s. m.* A hospitable man; a provider; a procurer of provision; a raven.—*Ir. id.* *N. pl.* biataichean.

Biatas, ais, *s. m.* The herb *betony.*

Biatsadh, aidh, *s. m.* Provision for a journey; viaticum.—*Macd.*

Bibh, (*for* bithibh) Be ye or you. Bibh tric an tigh a bhròin, *be often in the house of mourning;* bibh coimeas do cheud, *be a match for a hundred.—Oss. Fing.*

Bicas, ais, *s. m.* A viscount.

Bicear, eir, *s. m.* A cup; a bottle; a little ansated wooden dish. *W.* bicre, *a bottle.* *Scotch,* bicker.

† **Bi-chearb**, -chirb, *s.* Mercury, quicksilver.—*Ir. id.*

† **Bi-cheardach**, aich, *s. m.* A victualling-house, a tavern.—*Ir. id.* *N. pl.* bi-cheardaich.

Bi-chiontas, ais, *s. m.* The state of being common.

Bi-chionnta, *a.* Common, general, frequent.

Bi-churam, aim, *s. m.* Continual care, continual solicitude, anxiety.—*Macd.*

† **Bid**, *s.* A hedge.—*Ir. id.*

Bìd, *s.* The chirping of birds, or any shrill sound that resembles chirping.

Bideag, eig, *s. f.* A little bit, a morsel. Bideag chrion, *a little bit.* *N. pl.* bideagan.

Bidag, aig, *s. f.* (more correctly *biodag.*) A dirk, or Highland dagger; a stiletto. *N. pl.* bidagan, *dirks.* *W.* bidawg. Fhir na féile-bhig 's na bidaig, *thou man with the kilt and dirk.—Old Song.* See Biodag.

Bidean, ein, *s. m.* A hedge or fence.

Bideil, *s. f.* A continued chirping.—*Stew Is.* A shrill sound, a squeak.

Bidh, *gen. sing.* of biadh; which see.

Bidh, *a* Quiet, peaceable. Bi bìdh, *be quiet; hold your peace.* Cho bìdh ri luchag, *as quiet as a mouse.*

Bidh, (*for* bithidh.) Shall or will be Bidh ar leaba sa bhàs co-ionann, *our bed in death shall be the same.—Oss Gaul.*

Bidheantas, ais, *s. m.* Frequency. Am bidheantas, *frequently, perpetually.*

Bidhis, *s. f* A screw. *N. pl.* bidhisean.

Bidhiseach, *a.* Like a screw, spiral.

Bidse, *s. f.* (*Germ.* baetse.) A whore; a bitch.

Bidseachd, *s f* Whoremongering; the conduct of a prostitute

Big, *gen. sing.* of beag; which see.

Big, *a*, *n pl.* of beag. Little, small, young Na big agus na mòir, *the small and the great.—Stew. Ps.* An rud chi na big ni na big, *the young will do as they see done.—Old Prov.* Na cloinne bige, *of the little children.—Stew Jos.* See **Beag**.

Bigh, *s f* Glue; birdlime. Bigh chraobh, *the gum of trees,* bigh-eòin, *birdlime.*

† **Bil**, bile, *s. m.* A beard; a mouth; a bird's bill, a blossom —*Ir. id.*

Bil, bile, *s. m.* (*W* byl) A lip, a border, a welt, a lid; a rim; a brim, the margin of any thing. Air a bhil uachdaraich, *on his upper lip —Stew. Lev* Ag imeachd air bil na tràigh, *walking on the sea-shore —Oss. Trath* *N. pl.* bilean *and* bilidh A bilidh cur faillte ort, *her lips saluting thee*

Bilbheag, eig, *s. f.* Corn-poppy; papaver agrestis.—*Macd.* *N. pl.* bilbheagan.

Bileach, *a* (*from* bil) Lipped; bladed as grass; having a border or welt; billed as a bird.

Bileach, ich, *s m.* The leaf of a tree or herb, a quantity of leaves; also a young leafy tree *N pl* bilichean Barr nam bilichean blàthmhor, *the tops of the flourishing green trees.—Macfar.*

Bileag, eig, *s. f.* (*Ir.* billeog.) A little bag; a blade; the leaf of a tree or herb. *N. pl.* bileagan. Bileagan nan eun, *a species of wood-sorrel,* bileag chàile, *a blade of colewort.*

Bileag-bhàite, *s. f* A water-lily or flower.

Bileil, (*i. e.* bil-amhuil), *a.* Labial; talkative.

Bil-fhocalach, *a.* Labial.

Bilidh, *s pl.* Lips. See **Bil**.

† **Bille**, *s. f* A rag. *Ir* bille, *mean*

Billeachd, *s f* (*from* bille) Poverty, raggedness.

Bi'm, (*for* biom, bitheam, *or* bithidh mi.) I shall be.

Binealta, *a.* Fine, handsome, elegant.—*Ir id* Written more frequently *finealta*

Binid, *s. f.* Runnet. *Ir* binid

Binideach, *a.* Like runnet; of, or belonging to, runnet.

Binn, *a.* (*Ir id*) Melodious, musical, shrill, harmonious, sweetly sounding. Is balbh do bheul a bha binn, *mute is thy mouth that was musical.—Ull.* Is binn leam do cheum, *sweet to me is the sound of thy footstep.—Oss Taura.*

Binn, *s. f.* The hopper of a mill.—*Shaw.*

Binn, binne, *s f* Sentence, judgment, fate; melody. Binn an aghaidh dhroch obair, *sentence against an evil work.—Stew. Ecc.* Ceart am binn, *just in judgment.—Smith.* Thoir binn, *judge, pronounce sentence;* faigh binn, *receive sentence.*

Binndeach, *a* Coagulative; apt to coagulate.

Binndean, ein, *s. m.* Runnet. *Ir.* bindean.

Binne, *com.* and *sup.* of binn. More or most sweet or musical Carruill bu bhinne fonn, *Carril of the sweetest strains;* is binne do chombradh nan smeòrach, *sweeter is thy voice than the mavis.—Macfar.*

Binneach, *a.* Hilly, pinnacled; horned; light, light-headed.—*Macint.* Eilid bhinneach, *the horned deer.—Old Song.*

Binnead, eid, *s. m.* (*from* binn) Melodiousness, melody. Is fhearr leam do chombradh na 'n smeorach air a binnead, *I rather thy conversation than the mavis when most melodious. —Old Song.*

Binnealach, aich, *s. f.* The chirping of birds.—*Shaw.*

Binnealta, **Binnealtach**, *a.* Pretty, handsome; fair, comely. Written more frequently *finealta.*

Binnear, eir, *s. m.* A hill, a pinnacle; a pin, a bodkin, a hair-pin.

Binneas, eis, *s. m.* (*from* binn.) Melody, music, harmony. A togail a guth le binneas, *raising her voice melodiously.—Oss. Lod.*

Binnein, *s. f.* A pinnacle; a high conical hill; also a bell. Binnein na carraig, *the pinnacle of the rock —Oss. Gaul.*

Binn-fhocalach, *a.* (*Lat.* bene-vocalis.) Melodious; having a sweet-toned voice. Eunlaith binn-fhocalach, *melodious birds —Oss. Conn.* Gach eun binn-fhoclach, *every melodious bird.—Macfar.*

Binn-ghuth, *s.* A melodious voice; a sweet tone or note. Marr bhinn-ghuth ealaidh, *like the sweet note of a dying swan.—Ull.*

Binnse, *s f.* A bench. *N. pl.* binnseachan.

Binnseach, *a.* Having benches; like a bench.

Binnteach, *a.* (*i. e.* binnideach.) Coagulative; curdling.

Binnteachadh, aidh, *s m.* A curdling, a coagulating, coagulation. Ballan binnteachaidh, *a cheese-vat.*

Binnteachadh, (a), *pr. part.* of binntich. Curdling, coagulating.

Binntean, ein, *s. m.* Runnet.

Binnteanach, *a.* Like runnet; of, or pertaining to, runnet.

Binntich, *v. a.* Curdle or coagulate. (*Ir.* binntigh.) *Pr. a.* bhinntich, *curdled, fut. aff. a.* binntichidh, *shall or will curdle.*

Binntichte, *p. part.* of binntich. Curdled, coagulated. Bainne binntichte, *curdled milk.*

Biodag, aig, *s. f.* *N. pl* biodagan. A dirk, a dagger; more frequently applied to the dagger of a Scotch Celt. Cha mhios a thig dhuit am biodag, *no worse does the dirk become thee.—Macint.*

The *biodag* is a very old Caledonian weapon Dio observes, that the Caledonians, against whom Severus fought, were armed with this weapon

Biodagach, *a.* Like a dirk or dagger, having a dirk or dagger

Biodagan, *n. pl.* of biodag.

Biodailt, *s f.* Food; victuals —*Macd.*

Biodanach, *a.* Tattling, prating.—*Shaw.*

† **Biodh**, *s m.* The world.

Biodh, 3 *sing. and pl. imper.* of bi. Let be; be. Biodh t-aisling aoibhinn, Aoibhir-Chaomha! *pleasant be thy dreams, Evircoma!—Oss Gaul.* *Biodh* is contracted for *bitheadh.*

† **Biodhanas**, ais, *s. m.* Discord.—*Shaw.*

Biog, *s. f.* A chirp, as of a young chicken.—*Stew. Is.*

Biog, *s. f.* A start.

Biogach, *a.* Apt to start; causing to start.

Biogadh, aidh, *s m.* A starting, a palpitation.

Biogail, *s. f.* Chirping; continued chirping, as of chickens.

Biogail, *a.* Lively; active; frisky; apt to start.

† **Biol**, *s. m.* A musical instrument.

Biolag, aig, *s. f.* A little musical instrument; *in derision,* a person who is fond of singing or whistling.

Biolagach, *a.* Musical; melodious; fond of singing or whistling. *Com.* and *sup.* biolagaiche, *more or most melodious.*

Biolar, air, *s. m.* Cresses, water-cresses. Am biolar uaine, *the green water-cresses.—Macint.* Biolar an fhuarain, *the fountain-cresses.—Old Song. Ir.* biolar. *N. pl.* biolaire, *or* biolairean.

† **Biolar**, *a.* Dainty, fine, neat, spruce.

Biolarach, *a.* (*from* biolar.) Abounding in cresses; of, or belonging to, cresses. Glacag bhiolarach, *a dell abounding in cresses.—Macdon.*

Biolasg, aisg, *s. m.* Prattle, gabble, loquacity.

Biolasgach, *a.* Loquacious, prating, gabbling.

Biom, (*for* bithidh mi, *or for* bitheam.) I shall be, let me be. Biom ait air marcachd na sìne, *I shall be joyous in riding the blast.—Ardar.*

† **Bion**, *adv.* Readily, easily, usually.

† **Bior**, *s.* Water; a well, a fountain.

Ir. bior. *Arab.* bir, *wells. Pers.* bar-an, *rain. Turk.* bar *and* behr, *sea. Heb.* and *Phen.* baran, *wells. Madag.* bihar, *sea. Arm.* ber, *sea.*

Bior, *s. m.* A thorn; any sharp-pointed thing; a spit; a bodkin; a pin; a goad. *N. pl.* bioran; *gen. pl.* bior; *dat. pl.* bioraibh. A geurachadh nam bior, *sharpening the goads.—Stew. Sam.* Nam bioraibh nar sùilibh, *as thorns in your eyes.—Stew. Jos.* Bior nam bride, *dandelion;* bior ann iasgair, *the bird called a kingsfisher;* bior ann do dhearn na faisg, *squeeze not a thorn in thy fist.—G. P.*

Arab. habar, *a lance. Lat.* as-per, *rough or prickly;* and veru, *a spit. Span.* ber, *a point. Ir.* bior, *a pin. W.* and *Corn.* ber, *a lance. Arm.* bir *and* ber.

Bior, *v. a.* Prick; gall; sting; goad; spur on. *Pret. a.* bhior, *pricked; fut. aff. a.* bioraidh, *shall or will prick.*

Biorach, aich, *s. f.* A cow-calf, a two-year-old heifer. *N. pl.* bioraichean.

† **Biorach**, aich, *s. m.* A boat. See **Bior-linn**.

Biorach, *a.* (*from* bior.) Sharp-pointed, mucronated, piercing; sharp-sighted; horned, having branching horns; also watery. A ghreidh bhiorach na dheigh, *the branching-horned herd behind him.—Oss. Carricth.* A d' lannaibh biorach, *with thy pointed swords.—Macint.* Sùil bhiorach, *a quick or sharp eye.*

Bioradh, aidh, *s. m.* A stinging, a pricking, a piercing.

Bioradh, (a), *pr. part.* of bior. Pricking, stinging, piercing.

Biorag, aig, *s. f.* The foretooth of brutes.

Biorag-lodain, *s. f.* The fish called a bandstickle.—*Macd.*

Bioraich, *v.* Sharpen at the point. *Pret. a.* bhioraich, *sharpened; fut. aff. a.* bioraichidh.

Bioraiche, *com.* and *sup.* of biorach. Sharper, sharpest.

Bioraiche, *s. f.* A colt; a foal; a filly. Bioraiche, mac na h-asail, *a colt, the son of an ass.—Stew. Mat. ref. N. pl.* bioraichean.

Bioraide, *s. f.* A helmet or headpiece; a hat; an osier; *rarely*, strife. Bioraid bu loinntreach snàs, *a burnished helmet.—Mac Lach.* Written also *bàiread;* which see. *N. pl.* bioraidean.

Bioraideach, *a.* High-headed; conical.

† **Bioraidh**, *s. m.* A bullock. *N. pl.* bioraidhean.—*Ir.*

Biorain, *gen. sing.* of bioran.

Bioran, ain, *s. m.* (*Ir.* bioran.) A stick; a staff; a little stake; a sharp-pointed thing; also strife, anguish, vexation. *Asp. form*, bhioran. Bhioran ri thaobh, *his spear like a staff at his side.—Oss. Fing.* Bioran na laimh, *a stick in his hand.—Oss. Carricth.*

Bioranach, *a.* (*from* bioran.) Like a stick; abounding in sticks: also, *substantively*, a contentious person; a pincushion.

Bioranachan, ain, *s. m.* A pinmaker.

Bioranaich, *v. a.* Vex. *Pret. a.* bhioranaich; *fut. aff. a.* bioranaichidh.

Bioranaiche, *s. m.* A pinmaker. *N. pl.* bioranaichean.

Bioranaichte, *p. part.* Vexed.

Biorar, air, *s. m.* Water-cresses.—*Shaw.*

Bioras, ais, *s. m.* A water-lily; *perhaps* bior-ròs. *N. pl.* biorasan.

† **Bior-bhogha**, *s. m.* A rainbow.

† **Bior-bhuasach**, aich, *s. m.* A water-serpent, a conger-eel.

Bior-chluaiseanach, *a.* Having pointed ears; sharp-eared.—*Macint.*

Bior-chluas, -chluais, *s. f.* A sharp-pointed ear. *N. pl.* bior-chluasan.

Bior-chluasach, *a.* Having sharp or pointed ears; sharp-eared; quick of hearing.

Bior-chomhladh, aidh, *s. m.* A flood-gate, a sluice.

Bior-dhorus, -dhoruis, *s. m.* (*Ir. id.*) A flood-gate, a sluice. *N. pl.* bior-dhorsan.

Bior-dhruidheachd, *s. f.* A mode of divining by means of water.

Bior-dhubh-luinge, *s. m.* A ship's stern.—*Macd.*

Bior-eidhe, *s.* An icicle.

Bior-fheadan, ain, *s. m.* A water-pipe.

Bior-fhiacall, aill, *s. m.* A toothpick.

Bior-fuinn, *s. m.* A landmark, a beacon. Bheirinn bior-fuinn a mach, *I would descry the landmark.—Old Song.*

Biorganta, *a.* Perplexing; hampering; vexatious.

Biorgantachd, *s. f.* Perplexity.

Bior-greasaidh, *s. m.* A goad; an ox-goad.—*Stew. Jud. ref.*

Bior-linn, *s. m.* A boat.

This is a very ancient word, as its composition *bior-linn (pool-log)* may show. It was formed in the earliest periods of society, and in the infancy of navigation, before the ingenuity of man contrived any other vehicle for sailing than the hollowed trunk of a tree, or a piece of wood, in which he might venture across the smooth pool of his river. This kind of boat was also called *amar* by the Gael, in allusion to its resemblance to a large trough. Virgil had in his mind, or had seen, such canoes, when he wrote, in Georg. I. "Tunc alnos primum fluvii sensêre cavatas."

Bior-shruth, *s. m.* The old bed of a river.

Bior-shùil, *s. f.* A sharp eye, a quick-sighted eye. *N. pl.* bior-shuilean.

Bior-shuileach, *a.* Sharp-eyed, quick-sighted. *Com.* and *sup.* bior-shuiliche. Gabhair bhior-shuileach, *sharp-sighted goats.—Ross.*

Biosa, *v.* (*for* bi thusa.) Be thou. Sior bheannaichte biosa, *be thou ever blessed.—Smith.*

† **Bireid**, *s. f.* A breeding cow.—*Shaw.*

† **Biosar**, air, *s. m.* Silk.

Biosgair, *s. m.* A scrub. *N. pl.* biosgairean.

Biosgaireachd, *s. f.* Scrubbishness, meanness.

† **Birt**, *s. f.* A hilt; a handle, a haft.

† **Bis**, *s. f.* A buffet, a box, a slap.

B'ise, (*i. e.* bu ise.) It was she.

Biseach, eich, *s. f.* Prosperity. *Ir.* biseach. See **Piseach**.

Biseachd, *s. f.* Prosperity. More frequently *piseachd.*

Biteag, eig, *s. f.* A morsel; a fragment, a bit, a little bit. *N. pl.* biteagan. Chaidh e na bhiteagean, *it went into bits.*

Biteig, *gen. sing.* of biteag.

Bith, *s.* (*Gr.* βίος.) Life, existence, being; living; the world. Aon air bith, *any one;* ciod air bith, *whatever;* ni air bi, *any thing;* ni sam bi, *any thing;* cia b' e air bith ni, *what thing soever.*

† **Bith**, *s.* Custom, habit; a blow, a wound; contest. Hence *Baile-bhithan*, a place in Aberdeen, meaning *the place of wounds, or of contest.* In affinity to *bith* are the English *beat*, and the French *battre.*

Bìth, *a.* Quiet, tranquil, peaceable. Bi bìth, *be quiet;* cho bìth ri luch, *as quiet as a mouse.*

Bith. (*W.* byth.) A prepositive particle, signifying *ever*, *always*; as, bith-bhuan, *everlasting*; bith-dheanamh, *always doing*.

Bith-bheo, *a*. Everliving; perennial; evergreen; everlasting.

Bith-bhriathrach, *a*. Talkative, garrulous.—*Stew. Pro.*

Bith-bhrigh, *s*. Essence, life-blood.

Bith-bhuan, *a*. Everlasting, eternal; perpetual. Eisd Athair Bhith-bhuan! *Hear, O Everlasting Father!*—*Mac Lach.*

Bith-bhuantachd, *s. f.* Eternity; perpetuity. O bhith-bhuantachd, gu bith-bhuantachd, *from everlasting to everlasting*.—*Stew. Ps.*

Bith-churam, aim, *s. m.* Anxiety; continual care.

Bith-churamach, *a*. Extremely careful.

Bith-chraoibh, *s*. Gum; the sap or substance of a tree.

Bith-dheanamh, *s*. A continual acting.

Bith-dheanta, *a*. Frequent, continual.

Bith-dheantas, ais, *s. m.* Frequency, commonness; common occurrence. Am bith-dheantas, *frequently, continually*.

† **Bithe**, *a*. Female; of, or belonging to, the female sex.

Bitheadh, *s.*, *sing. and pl. imper.* of bi. Let be. Bitheadh e, *let him be*.

Bithidh, *fut. aff. a.* of bi. Shall or will be.

Bith-labhairt, *s. f.* Talkativeness; continued talking, garrulity.

Bithre, *s. f.* Lifetime.

Bith-shior, *a*. Everlasting, eternal.

† **Biùidh**, *s. m.* A hero; a champion.

Biuthas, ais, *s. m.* A good or bad report; reputation, fame.—*Stew. Is. ref.*

† **Blà**, *s. m.* A town, a village; also piety, devotion; a green field; a cry, a shout; the fruit of the womb; praise.

† **Blà**, *a*. Yellow; health; safe; well; warm.

† **Blachd**, *s. f.* Word.

Blad, blaid, *s. m.* A mouth; a dirty mouth; a foul or abusive mouth.

Bladach, *a*. (*from* blad.) Garrulous; abusive, foul-mouthed. *Com.* and *sup.* bladaiche.

Bladair, *s. m.* (*from* blad.) *Ir.* bladaire. *Lat.* blatero. A flatterer, a sycophant; also one of the followers of a Highland chieftain. *N. pl.* bladairean.

Bladaireachd, *s. f.* Flattery, sycophancy.—*Ir. id.*

† **Bladh**, *a*. Smooth; soft.—*Shaw.*

Bladh, *s*. A blossom, a flower; a garland, foliage; renown, fame; meaning; essence. Chaochail do shnuadh mar bhlàdh, *thy beauty has vanished like a flower.*—*Death of Carril.* Am bladh buidhe, *the yellow flower.*—*Old Poem.* Daraig is guirme blàdh, *an oak of the greenest foliage*.
Ir. bladh. *Dan.* blad, *a leaf*. *Germ.* blat, *a leaf*. *W.* blaw.

Bladhach, *a*. Blossomy, flowery; like a garland.

Blàdhach, aich, *s. m.* (*Scotch*, bladach.) Buttermilk. Deoch bhlàdhaich, *a draught of buttermilk*.

† **Bladhachd**, *s. f.* A smashing, a crumbling or breaking to pieces.—*Ir. id.*

Bladh-leabhair, *s. m.* The contents of a book.—*Shaw.*

Bladh-leasgaidh, *s. m.* A garland, or wreath of flowers. Written also *bladh-fleasgaidh*.

Bladh-shugh, *s. m.* Elixir.

Blad-shronach. Flat-nosed; *Com.* and *sup.* blad-shrònaiche.

Blad-spagach, *a*. Flat-soled.

Blàghach, aich, *s. m.* Buttermilk. Written also *blàdhach*.

Blàghach, *a*. Effectual; famous, renowned. *Com.* and *sup.* blaghaiche.

† **Blagh**, *v. n.* (*gh* silent.) Puff, blow. Hence *Eng.* blow, and *Scotch*, blaw.

Blaghair, *s. m.* A blast; a blustering wind; a blusterer, a boaster. *N. pl.* blaghairean.

Blaghaireachd, *s. f.* Blustering; boasting; bravado.

Blaghantach, *a*. Boastful; blustering. *Com.* and *sup.* blaghantaiche, *more or most boastful*.

Blaghmhanach, aich, *s. m.* A blustering fellow.

† **Blai**, *s. f.* The womb.—*Ir. id.*

Blaidh. See **Bloidh**.

Blais, *v. a.* (*Ir.* blais.) Taste; sip; relish; try by experience. *Pret.* bhlais, *tasted*; *fut. aff. a.* blaisidh, *shall or will taste*.

Blaisidh, *fut. aff. a.* of blais. Shall or will taste.

Blàiteachadh, aidh, *s. m.* A warming, a hatching.

Blàiteachadh, (a), *pr. part.* of blaitich. Warming, hatching. A blàiteachadh nan ubha bhreachda, *hatching the spotted eggs*.—*Macfar.*

† **Blaith**, *v. a.* Smooth, polish, level. *Pret.* bhlaith.

Blaithe, *com.* and *sup.* of blàth. Warmer, softer, smoother; warmest, softest, smoothest. Nighean bu bhlàithe sùil, *a maid of softest eye*.—*Old Legend.*

Blaithean, ein, *s. m.* (*dim.* of blàth.) A little blossom.

Blaith-fhleasgaidh, *s. m.* A garland or wreath of flowers.

Blaith-leac, lic, *s. f.* A polished flag, a smooth stone.

Blàitich, *v. a.* Warm, foment, hatch, cherish. *Pret. a.* bhlàitich; *fut. aff. a.* blàitichidh.

Blanag, aig, *s. f.* Fat, tallow. More frequently written *blonag*.

Blanagach, *a*. See **Blonagach**.

† **Blanda**, *a*. Gentle, mild, flattering. *Lat.* blanda. *Ir.* blanda.

Blandar, air, *s. m.* Flattery, cajoling; *blarney*.

† **Blaoc**, blaoic, *s. m.* A whale.

† **Blaodh**, blaoidh, *s. m.* A shout, a loud calling; a breath.—*Shaw.*

Blaodhag, aig, *s. f.* A noisy female.

Blaodh-eun, *s. m.* A bird-call.—*Shaw.*

† **Blaodhrach**, *a*. (*Ir. id.*) Clamorous, noisy.—*Shaw.*

† **Blaor**, blaoir, *s. m.* A cry, a shout.—*Ir. id.*

Blàr, blàir, *s. m.* A plain, a field, a plain field; ground; floor; spot; a green. As plain fields were chosen for engagements, *blàr* came to signify a battle, a field of battle. *N. pl.* blàran *and* blair, *plains*; *dat. pl.* blàraibh, *plains*. Sgeudaichear na blàir, *the plains shall be adorned*.—*Macfar.* Rèith a bhlair, *the plain of battle*.—*Mac Lach.* Fraoch nam blàr, *the rage of battle*.—*Oss. Cathula.* Cuir blàr, *fight*; air a bhlàr, *on the floor*.—*Stew. Gen.* On bhlàr gu 'bhàrr, *from the ground to its top*.

Blàr, *a*. White-faced; having a white forehead; more frequently applied to black cattle and horses with white foreheads. Each blàr, *a white-faced horse*. *Arm.* blawr, *white*. *Corn.* blawr.

Blarag, aig, *s. f.* (*dim.* of blar.) A white spot on the face of cattle; also a white-faced cow. An gobhal na blàraig, *between the legs of the white-faced cow*.—*Old Song.* *N. pl.* blaragan.

Blàran, (*dim.* of blàr.) Which.

Blàran, (*dim.* of blàr.) A little plain, a little green; a small spot.

Blas, blais, *s. m.* (*Ir. W. Corn.* and *Arm.* blas.) Taste; savour; flavour; experience. Blas na meal air do phogan, *the taste of honey on thy kisses*.—*Mac Co.* Air bhlas nam fioguis, *tasted like figs*.—*Old Song.*

Blàs, blais, *s. m.* *Contr.* of blàthas. Warmth. See **Blàthas**.

Blasachd, *s. f.* (*from* blas.) A tasting.

Blasad, (a), *pr. part.* of blas. Tasting. Gun am blasad, *without tasting them*.—*Oss. Gaul.*

Blas-bheum, *gen.* -bhéim, *s. m.* Blasphemy.—*Macd.*

Blas-bheumach, *a*. Blasphemous; prone to blaspheme.

Blasda, *a.* (*Ir.* blasda. *Arm.* blashaat, *taste.*) Savoury; sweet, tasteful; seasoned. Biadh blasda, *savoury meat.—Stew. Gen.* Blasda le salann, *seasoned with salt.*

Blasdachd, *s. f.* (*from* blas.) Sweetness, savouriness; tastefulness.

Blasmhoire, *com.* and *sup.* of blasmhor. More or most sweet.

Blasmhoireachd, *s. f.* Savouriness, sweetness, tastefulness.

Blasmhoiread, eid, *s. m.* Increase in savouriness or sweetness. A dol am blasmhoiread, *growing more and more savoury.*

Blasmhor, *a.* Savoury, tasty; sweet; tasteful. *Com.* and *sup.* blasmhoire, *more or most savoury.*

Blas-phog, -phòig, *s. f.* A sweet kiss.

Blàth, blaith, *s.* (*W.* blaw. *Ir.* bladh. *Eng.* blow. *Germ.* blat, *a leaf. Dan.* blad.) A blossom, a flower; bloom, blow; fruit, effects, consequence; *rarely*, a form or manner, praise. Fuidh làn bhlàth, *in full blossom.—Stew. Gen.* Thig e mach mar bhlàth, *he comes forth like a flower.—Stew. Job.*

Blàth, *a.* Warm; warm-hearted; tender, pleasant; *rarely*, white, clean. Smuainte blàth a steach, *warm (tender or pleasant) thoughts within.—Oss. Cathula.* Cha n'eil neach blàth, *no one is warm.—Stew. Hag.* Gu bog blàth, *snug and warm;* is blath anail na màthar, *warm is the mother's breath.—G. P.*

Blàthach, aich, *s. m.* (*Ir. id. Scotch*, bladach.) Butter-milk. Deoch bhlathaich, *a drink of buttermilk.*

Blàthachadh, aidh, *s. m.* A warming, a fomenting, cherishing; a hatching.

Blàthachadh, (a), *pr. part.* of blathaich.

Blathaich, *v. a.* Warm, foment, cherish; hatch; flower as a plant; polish, smooth. *Pr. act.* bhlàthaich; *fut. aff. a.* blathaichidh, *shall warm.* Bhlàthaich a chridhe, *his heart warmed.—Oss. Cathula.* Mur do bhlathaicheadh e, *if he was not warmed.—Stew. Job.*

Blathaichte, *p. part.* of blàthaich. Warmed, fomented, cherished; hatched.

Blàthas, ais, *s. m.* Warmth, heat; kindness. Thig tìus is blàthas, *mildness and warmth shall come.—Macint.* Blàthas na gréine, *the heat of the sun.—Ull.*

Blàth-chridheach, *a.* Tender-hearted, affectionate.

Blàth-fhleasgaidh, *s.* A garland or wreath of flowers.—*Stew. Acts.*

† **Blàth-leig**, *s. f.* A pumice-stone.—*Ir. id.*

Blàth-obair, -oibre, *s.* Embroidered work.

† **Bleachd**, *s. f.* Milk; kine.—*Ir. id. Corn.* and *W.* blith. Written also *bliochd.*

Bleachdair, *s. m.* A soothing, flattering fellow. *N. pl.* bleachdairean.

Bleachdaireachd, *s. f.* Flattery, soothing, cajoling.

Bleaghainn, *v. a.* See **Bleoghainn**.

† **Bleasghanach**, *a.* Emulgent.—*Shaw.*

Bleath, *v. a.* Grind, make meal, pulverize. *Pret. a.* bhleath, *ground; fut. aff. a.* bleathaidh, *shall grind.* Written also *bleth;* which see.

Bleath, Bleathadh, aidh, *s. m.* Grinding; pulverizing. Luchd bleath, *grinders, millers.—Stew. Ecc.*

Bleathach, *a.* Grinding, that grindeth.

Bleath-ghlunach, *a.* In-kneed, knock-kneed.

† **Bleathmhor**, *a.* Fruitful.—*Shaw. Com.* and *sup.* bleathmhoire.

Bleid, *s. f.* Larceny; cajoling, wheedling; solicitation, impertinence, envy, spite. *Ir.* bleid.

Bleid'ear, ir, *s. m.* See **Bleideire**.

Bleideil, *a.* (*from* bleid.) Impertinent, teazing, troublesome; pilfering, thievish; invidious, spiteful. Fear dubh dàn, fear bàn bleideil, *a black man is bold, a fair man impertinent.—G. P.*

Bleideire, *s. m.* A pilferer; a beggar; a teazing petitioner; an impertinent fellow. *N. pl.* bleideirean. Urram a bhleidire do 'n stràcair, *the compliments of the impertinent and the troublesome;—said of those who scold each other scurrilously.—G. P.*

Bleideireachd, *s. f.* Begging; beggary, solicitation; thievishness. Bleideireachd mholaidh, *the beggary of praise.—Old Poem.*

† **Bleidh**, *s. f.* A cup, a goblet.—*Ir. id.*

† **Blein**, *s. f.* A harbour for boats.—*Shaw.*

Bleoghainn, Bleothainn, *v. a.* Milk. *Pret. a.* bhleoghainn *or* bhleothainn; *fut. aff. a.* bleoghainnidh *or* bleothainnidh, *shall milk.*

Bleoghann, Bleothann, ainn, *s.* A milking. Aig a bleoghann, *at the milking;* stò bleothainn, *a milk pail.*

Bleoghann, Bleothann, (a), *pr. part.* of bleoghainn. Milking. A bleoghann a chruidh, *milking the cows.*

Bleth, *s.* A grinding, making of meal, pulverizing.

Bleth, *v. a.* (*Ir.* bleith, *grind. Fr.* blé, *corn.*) Grind; pulverize; powder; make meal. *Pret. a.* bhleth, *ground; fut. aff. a.* blethidh, *shall grind.* Bha e a bleth, *he was grinding.—Stew. Jud.*

Bleth-ghlunach, *a.* Knock-kneed. Balaoch blethghlunach, *a knock-kneed fellow.*

Blethte, *p. part.* of bleth. Ground. Gràn blethte, *ground corn.—Stew. Sam. ref.*

Bliadhna, *s. f.* A year; the space of a year. (*Corn.* blidhan. *Manx.* blien. *Arm.* blizenu. *Ir.* bliaghain.) *N. pl.* bliadhnaichean *and* bliadhnan. Bliadhna leum, *leap year;* an ceann bliadhna, *in a year's time; at the end of a year.—Stew. K. ref.* Eadar so is ceann bliadhna, *within a year;* o bhliadhna na tiom so, *this time last year;* a bhliadhn' ùr, *the new year.* **Bliadhn' a Phrionnsa**, *the common name among the Gael for the year* 1745; *literally*, **the Prince's Year**. Bliadhna Chuilodair, *the year of Culloden, or* 1746. Am bliadhna, *this year.*

I believe it is O'Brien who will have it that *bliadhna* is a corruption of *Beil-an*, meaning a circle of Bel or of the sun; an opinion which explains the composition of the word in a very simple and ingenious manner.

Bliadhna, (am), *adv.* This year.

Bliadhnach, aich, *s. m.* A yearling. Leanaidh bliadhnach ris na sràbhan, *lean flesh cleaves to straw.—G. P.*—applied to worthless people who adhere to one another. *N. pl.* bliadnaichean.

Bliadhnail, *a.* (bliadhna-amhuil.) Yearly, annual. *Ir.* bliaghan-amhail.

Bliadhna-chàin, *s. f.* An annuity.

Blian, blein, *s. m.* (*Ir.* bleun.) The flank, the groin. Laimh ris a bhlian, *near the flank.—Stew. Lev.*

† **Blimh, Blinn**, *s. f.* Spittle; the froth of a dead body.—*Shaw.*

Blincean, ein, *s. m.* A torch; a blink.

Bliochan, ain, *s. m.* Yellow marsh anthericum.—*Shaw.*

Bliochd, *s. f.* (*Corn.* and *W.* blith. *Ir.* bleachd.) Milk; milkiness; the profit arising from selling milk.

Bliochdach, *a.* (*from* bliochd.) Milky; lacteal; milk-producing, giving plenty of milk. Chiun an spreidh gu bliochdach, *the cattle became teeming with milk.—Macint.* An coire bliochdach, *the milk-producing dell.—Macdon.*

Bliochdar, Bliochdmhor, *a.* Milky, teeming with milk.

Blionach, aich, *s. m.* Lean flesh.—*Macint.* Also a slow inactive person. *N. pl.* blionaichean.

† **Bliosan**, ain, *s. m.* An artichoke. *N. pl.* bliosain.

† **Blob**, *a.* Thick-lipped; blubber-lipped.

Blobach, *s. f.* The deformity of blubber lips.

† **Blobaran**, ain, *s. m.* A stutterer; a blubber-lipped person.

† Bloc, *a.* Round, orbicular. *Eng.* block.

† Bloc, Bluic, *s. m.* A block. More frequently written *ploc;* which see.

Blocan, ain, *s. m.* (*dim.* of bloc.) A little block.

Bloide, Bloidean, *s. pl.; d.* bloidibh. Splinters, shivers, fragments, halves. A shleagh na bloidibh, *his spear in shivers.—Oss. Derm.* Nam bloidibh beaga pronnar iad, *they shall be bruised into small pieces.—Smith.*

Bloidh, *s.* The half of any thing; a share, part, portion, splinter. *N. pl.* bloidhean *and* bloidhdean, *halves. Ir.* blodh.

Bloidhdeag, eig, *s. f.* A fragment, a splinter. *N. pl.* bloidhdeagan.

Bloidhdean, *n. pl.* of bloidh. Fragments, splinters.

Bloidhdear, ir, *s. m.* A battery; a place from which an attack is made.

Bloinigean-gàraidh, *s. m.* Spinage.

† Blomas, ais, *s. m.* Ostentation.

† Blomasach, *a.* Ostentatious.

Blonag, aig, *s. f.* Fat, suet, lard, swine's-grease. *W.* bloneg. *Corn.* and *Arm.* bloanek. *Ir.* blunag *and* blanag.

Blonagach, *a.* (*from* blonag.) Abounding in fat; fat, greasy.

† Blor, Bloir, *s. m.* A voice; a noise, a loud noise, clamour.—*Ir. id.*

Blorach, *a.* Clamorous, noisy; also a clamorous, noisy fellow.

Bloracan, ain, *s. m.* A noisy fellow.

† Blos, *a.* Open, manifest, plain.

† Blosgadh, aidh, *s. m.* A congregation; a sound; a report.

Blosgach, aich, *s. m.* A clown, a rustic.—*Ir. id.*

Blosgair, *s. m.* A collector. *N. pl.* blosgairean.

† Blosg-mhaor, -mhaoir, *s.* A crier at court.

† Blot, *s. m.* A cave, a den or cavern.—*Ir. id.*

† Blotach, aich, *s. m.* One who dwells in a cave.—*Shaw.*

† Blotach, *a.* Full of dens or caverns; like a den or cavern.—*Shaw.*

† Blotach, aich, *s. m.* A cave or den. *N. pl.* blotaichean. —*Ir. id.*

Bluirc, *s.* A fragment; a crumb; also *plural,* fragments, crumbs.

† Blusar, air, *s. m.* Noise, outcry, tumult.—*Ir. id.*

Bo! An interjection to excite terror in children.

Bò, Boin, *s. f.* (*N. pl.* bà.) A cow; *rarely* a fawn. Bò bhainne, *a milch cow;* bo sheasg, *a barren cow;* bo gheamhraidh, *a cow slain for winter food;* bo laoidh, *a cow that has a calf;* bo mhaol, *a cow without horns;* bo bhreac, *a spotted cow;* bo riabhach, *a brindled cow;* bo cheann-fhionn, *a white-faced cow;* bò dhruim-fhionn, *a white-backed cow;* bo liath, *a grey cow;* bò chas-fhionn, *a white-footed cow;* bo-alluidh, *a buffalo.*

From *bò* come the *Gr.* βοος, *an ox,* and βοω, *to roar;* and also βου, which means any thing that is terrible. *Lat.* bos, *an ox. It.* bue, *ox. Ir.* bo, *a cow. W.* buw. *Corn.* buih *and* bu. *Arm.* bu. *Manx,* bua. *Bisc.* beya. *Portug.* boy, *ox. Span.* buey. *Turk.* bugha, *an ox. Tonq.* bo. *Jap.* arbo, *ox. Hottentots,* boa *and* bubaa.

Bo! bo! *interj.* Strange! *Gr.* βα βαι! *Lat.* papae!

† Boag, aig, *s. f.* A sea-lark.—*Shaw. N. pl.* boagan.

Bò-alluidh, *s. f.* A buffalo.

Boban, ain, *s. m.* A term of affection for a boy; also papa. *Gr.* βουπαις, *a very young child. Germ.* bub. *Arm.* boubon, *a child.*

Boc, *s. m.* Deceit; fraud; a blow, a box.—*Shaw.*

Boc, Buic, *s. m.* (*N. pl.* buic.) A buck; a roe, a roe-buck; a he-goat; a term of ridicule for a fop. Boc-earb, *a roebuck;* fichead boc, *twenty he-goats.—Stew. Gen. Arm.* buch. *Corn.* byk *and* bouch. *W.* bwch. *Ir.* boc. *Swed.* and *Germ.* bock. *Fr.* buc. *Eng.* buck. *It.* becco. *Belg.* boecke. *Anglo-Sax.* bucca.

Boc, *v. n.* See Bochd.

Bocach, *a.* (*asp. form,* bhocach.) Like a roe-buck; abounding in roes; of, or pertaining to, a roe-ruck. A Bhealtainn bhocach, *roe-producing May.—Macfar.*

Bocaide, Bocaidean, *n. pl.* Studs or bosses.

Bòcan, ain, *s. m.* A hobgoblin, a sprite or spectre.

Bocan, ain, *s. m.* A covering, a cottage; a hook, a crook; a mushroom.

Bocanach, *a.* (*from* bocan.) Hooked, bent. *Asp. form,* bhocanach.

Bocan-bearrach, aich, *s. m.* A mushroom.—*Shaw.*

Boc-earba, *s. m.* A roe. *N. pl.* buic-earba. Co luath ri boc-earba, *as swift as a roe.—Stew.* 2 *Sam.*

Boc-gaibhre, *s. m.* A he-goat. Boc-gaibhre on aird an iar, *a he-goat from the west.—Stew. Dan. N. pl.* buic-ghaibhre.

Bochail, *a.* Lively; animated.—*Shaw.*

Bochan, ain, *s. m.* A cottage, a hut or hovel. More frequently *bothan.*

Bochd, *a.* Poor; needy; wretched; a poor person. (*Ir.* bochd *and* bocht.) Treabhadh nam bochd, *the tillage of the poor.—Stew. Pro.* Leaghaidh bròn am bochd anam, *sorrow* [*dissolves*] *melts the wretched soul.—Oss. Croma.* Is fearr bhi bochd na bhi breughach, *better be poor than false.—G. P.*

Bòchd, *v.* (*Ir.* boc.) Swell; puff; grow turgid. *Pret. a.* bhochd; *fut. aff. a.* bochdaidh, *shall or will swell.*

Bochdadh, aidh, *s. m.* A swelling; the act of swelling.

Bochdainn, Bochduinn, *s. f.* (*Ir.* bochdaine.) Poverty; trouble; mischief; mishap, bad luck. Gu bochdainn, *to poverty.—Stew. Gen.* Ann am bochduinn, *in trouble.—Stew. Chr. ref.* Gun gabh' a bhochdainn thu! *plague take you!* tha bhochdainn ort, *bad luck attends you; the devil is in you;* mar bha bhochdainn ann, *as bad luck would have it.*

Bochdainneach, Bochduinneach, *a.* Causing trouble, poverty, or misery.

Bochdan, *n. pl.* of bochd, *s.* The poor. *D. pl.* bochdaibh; *v. pl.* bhochdan. A bhochdan nan treud, *ye poor of the flock.—Stew. Zech.* Truas do na bochdaibh, *pity to the poor.*

Bòchdan, ain, *s. m.* (*W.* bwgan.) A hobgoblin; a bugbear. Written also *bòcan.*

Bochdan, ain, *s. m.* A covering; a cottage; a hook; a crook; also a mushroom.

Bochdan-bearrach, -aich, *s. m.* A mushroom.

Bochdan-beucach, aich, *s. m.* A mushroom.

Bochdas, ais, *s. m.* Poverty; indigence. Bochdas agus beartas, *poverty and riches.—Old Song.*

† Bochdnadh, aidh, *s. m.* The sea, a narrow sea, a strait, the mouth of a river.

Bochd-thonn, -thuinn, *s. f.* A surge or billow; *literally,* a swelling wave. *N. pl.* bochd-thonnan. Written also *boch-thonn.*

Bochduinn, *s. f.* See Bochdainn.

Boch-thonn, -thuinn, *s. f.* A surge or billow; a swelling wave. Boch-thuinn thonnach, *a raging billow.—Macfar. N. pl.* boch-thonnan.

Boch-thonnan, *n. pl.* of boch-thonn.

Boch-thuinn, *gen. sing.* of boch-thonn.

Bocsa, *s. m.* Boxwood.

Bocsa, *s.* A box, a coffer; a trunk or little chest.—*Stew. Mat. N. pl.* bocsaichean. Barradh bocsa, *a rimmed barrow.*

Bocsaichean, *n. pl.* of bocsa. Boxes, coffers, trunks, or little chests.

Bod, buid, *s. m.* (*Ir.* bod.) *Membrum virile;* also a tail. *N. pl.* buid.

Bodach, aich, *s. m.* An old man; a rustic; a sorry fellow; a churl; a *mutchkin*, a Scotch liquid measure of four gills, somewhat less than an English pint. *N. pl.* bodaich, *old men.* Chuireadh tu bodaich gu beadradh, *thou wouldst set old men a fondling.—R.* Bodach ruadh, *a cod;* bodach nam briogan, *a piobrachd, called Breadalbane's March;* trudar bodaich, *an ugly fellow.—Old Song.* Sliob bodach is sgròbaidh e thu, buail bodach is thig e gu d' laimh, *stroke a sorry fellow and he will scratch you; strike him, and he will come to your hand.—G. P.*

Bodachail, *a.* (bodach-amhuil.) Clownish, boorish, churlish; like an old man.

Bodachan, ain, *s. m.* (*dim.* of bodach.) A little old man; a squat young fellow; *in derision,* iomad bodachan gnòdh, *many a surly old man.—Old Song.*

Bodach-ruadh, *s. m.* A codfish. *N. pl.* bodaich-ruadh.

Bodag, aig, *s. f.* (*Ir.* bodog.) Rage, anger; a short fit of passion; a yearling calf, a heifer; a bawd.—*Shaw.* *N. pl.* bodagan.

Bodagach, *a.* Apt to fly into a passion; like a heifer; like a bawd; wanton.

† **Bodagachd**, *s. f.* Rage, anger; rage for copulation; *furor interinus;* also a heifer that wants bulling.—*Shaw.*

Bodaireachd, *s. f.* (*from* bod.) *Scortatio.*

Bodan, ain, *s. m.* (*dim.* of bod.) *Membrulum puerile.*

† **Bodar**, *a.* Deaf. See **Bodhar**.

Bod-chrann, -chrainn, *s. f.* A kind of crupper.

Bodhag, aig, *s. f.* The human body; the skin of the human body. Oigh is gloine bodhaig, *a maid of the fairest skin.—Old Song.*

Bodhair, *v. a.* Deafen; stun with noise. *Pret. a.* bhodhair, *deafened; fut. aff. a.* bodhraidh, *shall or will deafen.*

Bòdhar, air, *s. m.* Murrain in cattle.

Bodhar, *a.* (*Ir.* bodhar. *W.* bydhar. *Corn.* bothur.) Deaf; also a deaf man. Co rinn am bodhar? *who made the deaf?—Stew. Exod. Com.* and *sup.* buidhre, *more or most deaf.*

Bodhrach, *a.* Infected with the murrain. Cò bhodhrach, *a diseased cow.*

Bodhradh, aidh, *s. m.* A deafening, a stunning with noise. Tha mi air mo bhodhradh leat, *I am stunned with the noise you make.*

Bodhradh, (a), *pr. part.* Deafening, stunning with noise. Ag am bhodhradh, *deafening me;* 'g a bodhradh, *deafening her;* 'g am bodhradh, *deafening them.*

Bog, **Buig**, *s. m.* A marsh, a fen, swampy ground.—*Macd.*

Bog, *a.* (*Ir.* bog. *Corn.* and *Arm.* boucq.) Soft; penetrable; tender; damp, moist; mellow; sweet or soft sounding; timid, feminine, effeminate. A ciabh bhog, *her soft hair.—Oss. Temo.* Le ribheid bhuig, *with his softly-sounding reed.—Macfar.* A Bhealtainn bhog, *moist* [*showery*] *May.—Id.* Fhir bhuig! *thou effeminate man!—Mac Lach.* Gu bog blàth, *snug and warm;* cridhe bog, *a tender heart. Com.* and *sup.* buige. Brisidh an teangaidh bhog an cneadh, *the smooth tongue softens anger.—G. P.*

Bog, *v. a.* and *n.* Dip; steep; bob; wag. *Pret. a.* bhog, *dipped; fut. aff. a.* bogaidh, *shall dip;* 1 *sing. imp. sub.* bhogainn, *I would dip.* Bhogainn anns an allt e, *I would dip him in the stream.—Old Song.*

Bogach, aich, *s. m.* A swamp, a quagmire. *N. pl.* bogaichean.

Bogachadh, aidh, *s. m.* The act of softening, making tender, or mellow or effeminate; a softening into tears.

Bogachadh, (a), *pr. part.* of bogaich. Softening; making mellow; making timid.

Bogadach, aich, *s. m.* Gesture; a bobbing gesture.

Bogadaich, *s. f.* A continued or frequent bobbing. Anns a bhogadaich, *bobbing.*

Bogadan, ain, *s. m.* A shaking, a bobbing, a wagging.—*Macint.* A fellow who walks with a mincing pace or a foppish gait, *in derision.*

Bogadanaich, *s. f.* A continued shaking, a wagging or bobbing. 'Sa bhogadanaich, *bobbing.*

Bogadh, aidh, *s. m.* The act of steeping or dipping; a steeping, a dipping; a bobbing; softness, tenderness, mellowness.

Bogaich, *v. a.* and *n.* Soften; make mellow; make effeminate; soften or melt into tears. *Pret. a.* bhogaich, *softened; fut. aff. a.* bogaichidh, *shall soften; fut. pass.* bogaichear, *shall be softened; p. part.* bogaichte, *softened.*

Bogaichear, *fut. pass.* of bogaich. Shall be softened.

Bogaichidh, *fut. aff. a.* of bogaich. Shall or will soften.

Bogaichte, *p. part.* of bogaichte. Softened.

Bogan, ain, *s. m.* An egg in embryo; *rarely,* bacon.—*Shaw.*

Boganach, aich, *s. m.* (*from* bog.) A soft fellow; a bumpkin, a booby. *N. pl.* boganaich.

Boganachd, *s. f.* Softness; the behaviour of a bumpkin.

Bogbhuine, *s. f.* A bulrush. *N. pl.* bog-bhuinnean.

Bogh, *v. a.* Bend, like a bow; bow. *Pret. a.* bhogh; *fut. aff. a.* boghaidh.

Bogh, **Bogha**, *s. m.* An archer's bow; a bow or bend; a vault, an arch. Bogh-saighead, *an archer's bow;* bogh-catha, *a battle-bow;* bogh-cogaidh, *a battle-bow;* mar bhogha air ghleus, *like a bow on the stretch;* bogh-fìdhle, *a fiddle-bow;* fear-bogha, *an archer;* fir bhogha, *archers.—Stew. Gen.* Bogha air a gheug, *a bend in the branch.—Macdon.* Bogha-frois, *a rainbow.*

W. bwa *and* bw, *a bow. Swed.* bogd, *bowed. Germ.* bogen, *a bow. Anglo-Sax.* boga. *Island.* bog. *Gr.* βιος. *Lat. barb.* bauga. *Scotch,* boo. *Eng.* bow. *Dan.* bue, *arch. Tonq.* bo, *vault.*

Boghadair, *s. m.* (*from* bogha.) An archer, a bowman. *Ir.* boghadoir.

Boghadaireachd, *s. f.* Archery.

Boghar, *a.* See **Bodhar**.

Bogh-braoin, *s. m.* A rainbow. Bogh-braoin a soillseadh, *a rainbow shining.—Oss. Com.*

Bogh-cath, *s. m.* A battle-bow. *N. pl.* boghan-cath.

Bogh-cogaidh, *s. m.* A battle-bow.

Bogha-fìdhle, *s.* A fiddle-bow.

Bogh-frais, **Bogh-frois**, *s. m.* A rainbow. A dhreach mar bhogh na frois, *his form like a rainbow.—Oss. Gaul.*

Bog-ghiogan, ain, *s. m.* The plant called sowthistle.

Boghsdair, *s. m.* A bolster. *N. pl.* boghsdairean.

Bogh-uisge, *s. m.* A rainbow.

Boghun, uin, *s. m.* (*perhaps* bo-dhùn.) An enclosure for cattle, intended as a security against cattle-lifters.

Boglach, aich, *s. m.* A bog, a slough, a morass. *N. pl.* boglaichean.

Bog-luachair, *gen.* bog-luachrach, *s. f.* A bulrush.

Bogluibh, *s. m.* The herb ox-tongue. *N. pl.* bogluibhean.

Bog-lus, *s. m.* The herb ox-tongue. *Ir.* boglus. *N. pl.* boglusan.

Boiceanach, aich, *s. m.* A boy fourteen years of age.—*Shaw.*

Boiceann, inn, *s. m.* A hide; a skin; a goat's-skin. *N. pl.* boiceannan.

Boicneachadh, aidh, *s. m.* A skinning, a belabouring, thumping, or beating a person; a thrashing. Fhuair e a bhoicneachadh, *he got his thrashing.*

Boicnich, *v. a.* Skin, belabour, thump, thrash. *Pret. a.* bhoicnich, *thrashed; fut. aff. a.* boicnichidh, *shall or will thrash.*

Bòid, **Boide**, *s. f.* A vow, an oath, a solemn promise; also the surname Boyd; the Isle of Bute. *N. pl.* boidean, *vows.* Bhòidich thu bòid, *thou vowedst a vow.—Stew. Gen.* Naisg am bòidean, *bind their oaths.—Mac Lach.* Boid a chiaraig ris na fearaibh, is boid nam feara uile ri ciaraig, *like the swarthy maid who foreswore the men, as she had been foresworn by them.—G. P.*

Bòideach, *a.* Pertaining to a vow; like a vow; tolerable, well.—*Shaw.* Also one surnamed Boyd.

Bòideachan, ainn, *s. m.* A bodkin.

Bòidean, *n. pl.* of bòid.

† **Boidh**, *a.* Neat, tidy, trim, spruce.—*Shaw.*

† **Boidhe**, *a.* Yellow. Now written *buidhe;* which see.

Bòidheach, (*from* boidh. *Asp. form,* bhòidheach.) Pretty, beautiful, fair, handsome, comely. Is bòidheach am fàs, *beauteous is their growth.—Ull.* Oigheana bòidheach, slan leibh, *ye pretty maidens, farewell.—Old Song.* Cha dean a ghlòir bhòidheach an t-amadan sàthach, *fine words fill not a fool's belly.—G. P.*

Bòidhiche, *s. f.* Beauty, prettiness, comeliness, handsomeness. Mar Ailltheas na bhòidhiche, *like Ailltheas in his beauty.—Oss. Fin. and Lor.*

Bòidhiche, *com.* and *sup.* of bòidheach. More or most pretty. *Asp. form,* bhòidhiche. Is i bu bhòidiche leam, *I deemed [her] it the prettiest.—Macint.*

Bòidhichead, eid, *s. m.* Beauty, increase in beauty. Bòidhichead mios Mhaigh, *the beauty of the month of May. —Macdon.* A dol am bòidhichead, *growing more and more beautiful.*

Bòidhicheas, eis, *s. m.* Beauty, comeliness. Cha 'n e 'mheud a bhoidhicheas, *bulk is not beauty.—G. P.*

Bòidich, *v.* Promise solemnly, vow, swear. *Pret. a.* bhòidich, *vowed; fut. aff. a.* boidichidh, *shall vow.*

Boige, *com.* and *sup.* of bog. More or most effeminate. Written also *buige.* See **Bog.**

Boige, *s. f.* Softness, effeminacy.

† **Boigh**, *s. f.* A teat or udder.—*Ir. id. N. pl.* boighean.

Bòigheach, *a.* See **Bòidheach.**

† **Boigrean**, ein, *s. m.* A bulrush; also flummery; any thing flabby.

Boigreanach, *a.* Abounding in bulrushes; like a bulrush; also a place where bulrushes grow; like flummery; flabby.

Boile, *s. f.* Issue, result, consequence, success. Written more frequently *buile.*

Boile, *s. f.* Madness, rage, passion, fury. (*Ir.* buile. *Lat.* bilis.) Boile nan cath, *the rage of battles.—Oss. Gaul.* Fear na boile, *the passionate man.—Stew. Pro. ref.* Air bhoile, *mad.* Boile chath, *rage for battle;* tha 'm boile ort, *you are mad.*

Boile, (air), *adv.* Mad, raging, distracted.

Boileach, *a.* (*from* boile.) Apt to fly into a rage, furious; also altogether, complete.

Boilg, (*oftener* builg), *gen. sing.* of bolg.

Bòilich, *s. f.* Idle talk; vain boasting, blustering. Is beag orm do bhòilich, *I heed not your idle talk.—Old Song.* Cha mhaithinn duit do bhoilich, *I would not pardon thy blustering.—Id.*

† **Boillrinn**, *s. f.* A ring, a circle.—*Ir. id.*

Boillsge, *s.* A gleam; a glare, flash, effulgence, glitter. Boillsge faoin a mhàile, *the languid gleam of his helmet.—Oss. Com.* Fo bhoillsge an lath, *in the effulgence of day. —Oss. Tem.*

Boillsg, **Boilsg**, *v.* Gleam, shine, flash, glitter. *Pret. a.* bhoillsg, *shone.*

Boillsgeach, *a.* Glittering, gleaming, shining.

Boillsgeadh, (a), *pr. part.* of boillsg. Shining, gleaming, glittering. A boillsgeadh air sliabh, *shining on the mountain. —Oss. Fing.* Mala nan scorr a boillsgeadh, *the brow of the rocks glittering.—Oss. Temo.*

† **Boilsgean**, ein, *s. m.* The middle, midst; also a mountain.—*Shaw.*

† **Boilsgean**, *v. a.* Make round and bulging.—*Shaw.*

Boin, *gen.* of bò; which see.

† **Boinneadh**, idh, *s. m.* A running issue, a scrofulous sore; a sprouting or budding.

Boineanta, *a.* Mild, gentle; handsome.—*Macint.* Also stout, firm, of good bottom.

Boineantachd, *s. f.* Mildness, gentleness; also stoutness, firmness; handsomeness.

Boineid, *s. f.* (*i. e.* beann-eididh.) *Ir.* boneid. A bonnet. *N. pl.* boineidean. Ni thu boineidean, *thou shalt make bonnets.—Stew. Exod.* Boineid an losgainn, *paddock-stool.*

Boineid-an-losgainn, *s. f.* A paddock-stool; brown boletus.

Boinne, *s. f.* A drop of any liquid. Boinne fala, *a drop of blood.—Macfar.* Boinne uisge, *a drop of water.*

Boinneag, eig, *s. f.* A cake. (*Ir.* boineog. *Scotch,* bannock.) *N. pl.* boinneagan, *cakes.*

Boinnealach, aich, *s. m.* (*from* boinne.) A dropping of rain.

† **Boir**, *s. m.* An elephant.

Boirbe. See **Buirbe.**

Boirbeachd, *s. f.* (*from* borb.) Written also *buirbeachd;* which see.

Boirche, *s. f.* An elk; a buffalo.—*Ir. id.*

† **Boirchriadh**, *s. f.* A kind of fat clay.—*Ir. id.*

† **Boire**, *s. f.* A hole. *Scotch,* boir.

Boireal, eil, *s. f.* (*from* boir.) A small auger, a wimble. *N. pl.* boirealan. Toll boireil, *an auger-hole.*

Boireann, **Boirionn**, *a.* Female, feminine. Leomhan boirionn, *a lioness.* Cha 'n eil firionn na boirionn ann, *there is neither male nor female.—Stew. Gal.* Urr firionn boirionn, *an hermaphrodite.*

Boireannach, **Boirionnach**, aich, *s. f.* A female. Boirionnach eireachdail, *a handsome female.* Hence *Gr.* πόρις *for* παῖς, and *Lat.* purus.

Bois, *gen. sing.* of bos.

Boisceal, ill, *s. m.* A savage man or woman.

Boisceil, *a.* Wild, savage, untamed. Thog thu oirnne gu bheil sinn boisceil, *thou hast reported of us that we are savage.—Old Poem.*

Boiseachd, *s. f.* (*from* bos) Palmistry.

Boiseag, eig, *s. f.* A box or spank in the ear; a slap with the palm of the hand; also a little palm.

† **Boiseid**, *s. f.* A belt, a girdle. *N. pl.* boiseidean.

Boisg, *v. n.* Shine, gleam, flash, dart. *Pret. a.* bhoisg, *shone; fut. aff. a.* boisgidh, *shall or will gleam.* Air anam bhoisg platha, *a ray shone on his soul.—Oss. Derm.*

Boisge, *s. f.* A beam of light, a gleam; a flash, a flame. Mar bhoisge fuaimneach droighinn, *like the noisy flame of thorns.—Sm.* Boisge dealanaich, *a flash of lightning.*

Boisgeach, *a.* (*from* boisge.) Gleaming; flashing, flaming; radiant, luminous.

Boisgealachd, *s. f.* Radiance; a gleaming; a flashing.

Boisgeanta, *a.* (*from* boisge.) Shining, radiant, luminous; dazzling, flashing, brilliant.

Boisgeil, *a.* (boisg-amhuil.) Shining, luminous, radiant, dazzling, flashing. Co boisgeil ri òr, *shining like gold.—Oss. Croma.*

Bòit, *s. f.* The Isle of Bute.

Boiteach, *a.* Of Bute; also a native or an inhabitant of the Isle of Bute.

Boiteal, eil, *s. m.* A wisp, or bundle of straw or hay; *rarely*, arrogance, presumption. Boideal fodair, *a bundle or bottle of straw.* *N. pl.* of boitealan.

† **Boitealach**, *a.* Arrogant, presumptuous.

Boitealaich, *v. a.* Tie up, as straw, in bundles. *Pret. a.* bhoitealaich.

Boitean, ein, *s. m.* A wisp, or bundle of hay or straw.

Boiteanach, *a.* In bundles, as straw or hay.

† **Bol**, *s. m.* A bard; art, skill; also a cow.—*Shaw.*

Ból, **Bóil**, *s. m.* A bowl or cup. *Corn.* bolla, *a drinking-cup.* *N. pl.* bólan.

Boladh, aidh, *s. m.* A smell, a stink; savour. Boladh graincil, *an abominable smell.—Stew. Exod.* Boladh breun, *a stinking savour.—Stew. Ecc.* *Ir.* boladh.

Bo-lann, -lainn, *s. m.* A cow-house; a fold.

Bolanta, *a.* Exquisite; fine. Gu balanta, *exquisitely.*

Bolantachd, *s. f.* Exquisiteness.

Bolb, **Builb**, *s. m.* (*Ir. id.*) A species of caterpillar.—*Shaw.*

Bolg, *v.* Swell, puff, blow, blister. *Pret. a.* bholg; *fut. aff. a.* bolgaidh.

Bolg, *s. m.* One of the Belgæ.—*Oss.*

Bolg, **Builg**, *s. f.* A pair of bellows; a budget, a wallet, a bag, a sack, a pock; a pimple, a blain, a blister; a belly, the womb; the boss of a shield. *N. pl.* bolgan; *dat. pl.* bolgaibh. A briseadh mach na bholgaibh, *breaking out in blains.—Stew. Exod.* O bholg na maidne, *from the womb of morn.—Sm.* Do bholg mar dhùn cruithneachd, *thy belly like a heap of wheat.—Stew. Song. Sol.* Sgiath nam bolg *the bossy shield.—Oss.* Bolg saighead, *a quiver*; bolg an t-sollair, *a magazine.*

Gr. Æol. βολγος. *Lat.* † bulga. *Belg.* balg, *a sack.* *Sax.* belge. *Eng.* bilge. Hence too the *Lat.* Belgæ, *i. e.* the quiver-bearing people, so named from their being always armed with bows and arrows.

Bolgach, *a.* (*from* bolg.) Like a budget or wallet; blistering; bellying, bilging, bagged; bossy. Thar a sgeith bholgaich, *over his bossy shield.—Oss.*

Bolgam, aim, *s. m.* A sip; a mouthful; a gulp; a dram.

Bolgan, ain, *s. m.* (*dim.* of bolg.) A little budget or bag; a little pimple; a little blister; a little boss; a quiver.

Bolgan-beiceach, ich, *s. m.* A fuzz-ball.

Bolg-saighead, *s. f.* A quiver. Bha bholg-saighead ri thaobh, *his quiver was at his side.—Oss. Cathluno.*

Bolg-séid, **Bolg-seididh**, *s. f.* A pair of bellows. *N. pl.* builg-séid *or* builg-séididh. Sguiridh na builg-seididh, *the bellows shall cease.—Macfar.* *Ir. id.*

† **Boll**, *s. m.* The boss of a bridle or gorget.

Bolladh, aidh, *s. m.* A boll, or sixteen pecks; *rarely*, a bowl, a goblet. *N. pl.* bollaichean.

Bolladh, aidh, *s. m.* A bladder upon nets. Bolladh stiuraidh, *a buoy.*

† **Bollag**, aig, *s. f.* A shell, a skull; top of the head; also heifer; hence bullock.

Bollsgair, *s. m.* (*Ir. id.*) An antiquary; a herald; a crier at court; a bawler; a boaster. *N. pl.* bollsgairean.

Bollsgair-buird, *s. m.* (*Ir. id.*) A grand carver.—*Shaw.*

Boltadh, aidh, *s. m.* A bolt or bar.

Boltanas, ais, *s. m.* (*from* boladh.) Smell, perfume.

Boltrach, aich, *s. m.* A smell, odour, scent, perfume. Bhuir boltrach cubhraidh, *your sweet odours.—Stew. O. T.* Oladh agus boltrach, *oil and perfume.—Stew. Pro.*

Boltrachan, ain, *s. m.* A perfume; also a perfumer. Ni thu boltrachan, *thou shalt make a perfume.—Stew. Exod.*

Boltrachas, ais, *s. m.* (*from* bol.) Perfumery.

Boltraich, **Boltruich**, *v. n.* Smell, scent, perfume. *Pret. a.* bholtruich, *perfumed*; *fut. aff. a.* boltraichidh, *shall perfume.* Bholtruich e boladh, *he smelt a smell.—Stew. O. T.*

Bomanach, *a.* Boasting, vaunting, blustering; also a boasting or blustering fellow.

† **Bomanachd**, *s. f.* A habit of boasting, vaunting, blustering.

Bonaid, *s. f.* A bonnet. (*Arm.* boned. *Fr.* bonnet. *Teut.* bonet.) Bonaid ghorm, *a blue bonnet.—Macint.* Bonaid bhallach, *a tartan bonnet.—Macfar.* Bonaid chath-dath, *a tartan bonnet.* *N. pl.* bonaidean; *d. pl.* bonaidibh. Bonaid losgainn, *a paddock stool*; written also *boineid.*

Boncait, *s. m.* A balk.—*Macd.* *N. pl.* boncaitean.

† **Bonn**, *a.* Good. *Lat.* bonus. *Ir.* bonn.

Bonn, **Buinn**, *s. m.* (*Ir.* bon.) A heel; a sole; a socket; a piece of money, a coin; a base or bottom, pedestal. A chu ri bhonn, *his dog at his heels.—Oss. Cathluno.* Fo bhonnaibh ur cos, *under the soles of your feet.—Stew. Mal.* Fichead bonn, *twenty sockets.—Stew. Exod.* Rothan aig gach bonn, *wheels at every base.—Stew.* 1 *K.* Bonn h-ochd, *a piece of eight*; bonn leth-chruin, *a half-crown piece.* Air chuig bonnaibh airgid, *for five pieces of silver.—Stew.* 2 *K.* Thug e na buinn as, *he took to his heels.* Bonn ri bonn, *heel to heel; foot to foot.* Tuiteam fo 'r bonn, *falling under our feet.—Fingalian Poem.*

Bonnach, aich, *s. m.* A barley-scon; by the Scots called a bannock. Mar is miannaich brù bruichear bonnach, *as the stomach craves, the scon is toasted.—G. P.*

Bonnag, aig, *s. f.* (*from* bonn.) A leap, a spring; the sole of a shoe; a new year's gift. *N. pl.* bonnagan.

Bonnagach, *a.* Leaping, springing, bounding.

† **Bonnan**, ain, *s. m.* (*from* bonn.) A footman, a lacquey; also a bittern.—*Shaw.*

Bonnanta, *a.* (*from* bonn.) Well set; stout; having a good bottom or foundation.

Bonn-chumadair, *s. m.* A shoe-last. *N. pl.* bonn-chumadairean.

Bonn-h-ochd, *s. m.* A piece of eight.

Bonnsachd, *s. f.* A leaping, a springing, a vaulting.

Bonnsaich, *v. n.* Bounce, dart, spring. *Pret. a.* bhonn-saich, *bounced*; *fut. aff. a.* bonnsaichidh.

Bonnsè, **Bonnsia**, *s. m.* A halfpenny.

Bonn-shuidheachadh, aidh, *s. m.* An establishing or founding; a getting a firm footing.

Bonn-shuidhich, *v. a.* Found, establish; get or give a firm bottom. *Pret. a.* bhonn-shuidhich.

† **Bor**, *a.* High, proud, noble. *Germ.* por. *Ir.* borr.

Boraisd, *s. f.* Borage.—*Macd.*

† **Borb**, **Buirb**, *s. m.* A tyrant, an oppressor.

Borb, *a.* (*Ir. id.*) Fierce, cruel, barbarous, raging, haughty; rude, ignorant. Tha 'n t-amadan borb, *the fool rages.—Stew. Pro.* Namhaid borb, *a fierce foe.—Oss. Lodin.* *Com.* and *sup.* buirbe.

Borbachd, *s. f.* (*from* borb.) Barbarity, fierceness.

Borbadh, aidh, *s. m.* (*from* borb.) Fierceness; pride, haughtiness.

Borbarra, *a.* Barbarous, wild, fierce, uncivilized, untamed, Buidhne borbarra, *fierce bands.—Old Poem.*

Lat. barbarus. *Ir.* barbaro. *It.* burbero. *Swed.* barbar.

Borb-bhriathrach, *a.* Speaking fiercely, boisterous in language.

Borbhan, ain, *s. m.* A murmur; a low sound; the gurgling of a stream; a humming; any continued low sound; a grumbling. Is binn, a shruthain, do bhorbhan, *sweet is thy murmur, O stream!—Oss.*

Borbhanaich, *s. f.* A murmuring, grumbling, muttering;

gurgling. Ciod a bhorbhanaich th'ort? *what are you grumbling about?*

BORC, *v. n.* Spring, sprout, bud; swell. *Pret. a.* bhorc; *fut. aff. a.* borcaidh, *shall spring.*

BÒRCACH, *a.* Swelling; budding, sprouting, springing; tall. Do luachar bhorcach, *thy springing rushes.—Old Song.*

BORCADH, aidh, *s. m.* A swelling; a springing or sprouting.

BORCADH, (a), *pr. part.* of borc. Swelling; springing, sprouting. A borcadh suas mu d' chòir, *springing forth near thee.—Macdon.*

BORD, bùird, *s. m.* (*n. pl.* buird.) A table; a plank, a deal, a board; also boarding. Da bhòrd, *two tables.* Ochd buird, *eight tables.—Stew. Exod.* Air bhord, *boarded, as a boarder;* air bord, *on board;* bord beulaobh, *the starboard side of a ship;* bord culaobh, *the larboard side of a ship.* Bord mòr, *the board of green cloth;* cuir air bhord, *board.* *Swed.* bord. *Goth.* baurd. *Ir.* bord. *Run.* bord. *Corn.* bord. *Eng.* board.

BORD-BEULAOBH, *s. m.* The starboard side of a ship. Bord beulaobh 's bord culaobh, *starboard and larboard.*

BORD-CULAOBH, *s. m.* The larboard of a ship.

BORD-LUING, *s. m.* The deck of a ship.

BORD-MÒR, *s. m.* The table of green cloth.—*Shaw.*

BORD-NA-CÌSE, *s. m.* The board of customs; the board of excise.—*Stew. Matth.*

BORD-ÙIRCHRAINN, *s. m.* The earth-board of a plough.

† BORG, *s. m.* A tower; a village; a house. *Gr.* πύργος, *a tower.* *It.* borgo, *a village.* *Sax.* burg. *Dan.* borg. See also BURG.

BORR, *s. m.* A knob.

† BORR, *v.* Swell, grow big, grow proud; bully; swagger; parch.—*Shaw.*

† BORR, *a.* Great, noble; haughty; splendid.

† BORRACH, aich, *s. m.* A haughty man; a great man.—*Shaw.*

† BORRACHAS, ais, *s. m.* Bravado.

† BORRADH, aidh, *s. m.* A swelling; a bravading; parching.

BORRAIDH, *s. f.* Borrage.

BORRAL, *a.* Proud, swaggering, boastful.

BORRAN, ain, *s. m.* A haunch, a buttock.

BORRFHUAIM, *s. m.* A loud noise; a murmur.

BORR-SHÙIL, shùl, *s. f.* A full round eye.

BORR-SHUILEACH, *a.* Full-eyed, large-eyed.

BORRUNN, uinn, *s. m.* The haunch, buttock.

† BORSA, *s.* A purse. *Germ.* bursa. *Belg.* beurs. *W.* pwrs. *Lat.* barbar, bursa; hence also *Eng.* burse, bursar, bursary.

† BÒRSAIR, *s. m.* A burser. *N. pl.* borsairean.

BOS, BOISE, *s.* (*Ir.* and *Corn.* bos.) The palm of the hand; the hand. A bois fa ceann, *her palm under her head.—Oss. Dargo.* Leud boise, *a hand-breadth.—Stew. Exod.* and *Smith.*

† BOS, *a.* Abject, mean, low, vile; of humble origin.—*Shaw.*

† BOSARGAINN, *s. f.* Destruction.

BOS-BHUAIL, *v.* Extol, by clapping of hands; clap the hands.

BOS-BHUALAIDH, aidh, *s. m.* A clapping of hands.

BÒSD, *v. n.* Boast, vaunt. *Pret. a.* bhòsd, *boasted; fut. aff. a.* bòsdaidh, *shall boast.*

BÒSD, *s. m.* (*W.* bôst.) A boast or vaunt, boasting language. Bha chualas a bosd.—*Old Song.* Am bòsd gun fheum, *the useless boast.—Mac Lach.*

BÒSDAIL, *a.* (bòsd-amhuil.) Inclined to boast, vaunting. Luchd bòsdail, *boasters.—Stew. Rom. ref.*

BOSDAN, ain, *s. m.* A basket.

BOS-GHÀIRE, *s. f.* Applause by clapping of hands.

BOS-LUADH, luaidh, *s. m.* Applause by clapping of hands. —*Ir. id.*

BOS-LUATH, *a.* Nimble-handed; ready-handed.

BOSRAICH, *s. f.* A shouting, a roaring; a squall, a high wind. Mar bhosraich geamhraidh, *like the loud winter gale.* —*Old Poem.*

BÒST, *s. m.* (*W.* bôst.) A boast, a vaunt.

BÒSTAIL, *a.* (bost-amhuil.) Vaunting, boastful; *better* bòsdail.

BOS-UAILL, *v. a.* Extol by clapping of hands.—*Shaw.*

BÒT, BÒIT, *s.* (*Corn.* bottas. *Portug.* bota.) A boot. *N. pl.* bòtan, *boots.—Macint.*

BÒTACH, *a.* Wearing boots, booted. Gu bòtach sporach, *booted and spurred.*

BÒTAICH, *v. a.* Boot. *Pret. a.* bhòtaich, *booted; fut. aff. a.* bòtaichidh, *shall or will boot.*

BÒTAIR, *s. m.* A bootmaker. *N. pl.* bòtairean.

BOTAL, ail, *s. m.* A bottle. *N. pl.* botalan. Botal fion, *a bottle of wine.*

BOTALAICH, *v. a.* Bottle. *Pret. a.* bhotalaich; *fut. aff. a.* botalaichidh, *shall bottle.*

BOTALAICHTE, *p. part.* of botalaich. Bottled.

† BOTH, *s.* A cottage, hut, tent, bower; now written *buth.* *Teut.* bod, *house.* *Old Swed.* according to Rudbeck, buda, *a village.* *Goth.* bouden, *temple.* *Swed.* boo, *a dwelling.* *Thibet,* bo, *to hide.* *Carib.* boa, *a house.* *Old Sax.* boed. *Eng.* abode *and* booth. *Span.* bodega, *cellar.* *Fr.* boutique, *shop.* *Germ.* bude, *house.* *Pol.* bauda *and* budo, *a house.* *Georgian,* budo, *a nest.*

BOTHACH, aich, *s. f.* A marsh; a quagmire.

BOTHAG, aig, (*dim.* of both.) A hut, booth, or tent. *N. pl.* bothagan; *dat. pl.* bothagaibh, *to tents.* Ann am bothagaibh, *in tents.—Stew. Gen. ref.*

BOTHAN, ain, *s. m.* (*dim.* of both.) A hut, cottage, tent, booth, bower; a cottage. *N. pl.* bothain. Bothan am fasgadh nam fuar bheann, *a hut in the shelter of the bleak mountains.—Oss. Cathula.* Rinn e bothain d'a spreidh, *he made booths for his cattle.—Stew. Gen. ref.*

BOTHAR, air, *s. m.* A lane, a road, a street.

BOTHAR, *a.* Deaf. *Com.* and *sup.* buithre, *deafer, deafest.* *Corn.* bothur.

BOTH-THIGH, *s. m.* An ox-stall; a cow-house.

BOTRUMAID, *s. f.* A slattern; a drab. *N. pl.* botrumaidean.

BOTRUMAIDEACH, *a.* Drabbish. Gu botrumaideach, *drabbishly.*

BRÀ, *s. m.* A quern, a handmill. Muileann brà, *a handmill.* *Fr.* moulin a bràs. See MUILEANN-BRÀ.

† BRÀ, *s. m.* A brow.—*Shaw.*

BRABHDADH, aidh, *s. m.* Idle talk; bravado.

BRABHDAIR, *s. m.* (*Dan.* brauter.) A noisy, talkative fellow; a swaggerer, a blusterer, a braggadocio, an idle talker.

BRABHDAIREACHD, *s. f.* Loud talk, blustering language; a habit of talking loudly; a swaggering, a bravado.

† BRAC, BRAIC, *s. m.* An arm. *Gr.* βραχίων. *Lat.* brachium.

† BRAC, *v. a.* Break down as earth with a harrow; embrace. *Pret. a.* bhrac.

BRACACH, *a.* Greyish.

BRACAILLE, *s. f.* A bracelet; a sleeve. *N. pl.* bracaillean.

BRACAN, ain, *s. m.* Broth.—*Ir.*

† BRACH, BRAICH, *s. m.* A pimple.—*Ir. id.*

BRÀCH, (gu), *a.* For ever; a corruption of *gu bràth.* See BRÀTH.

Brachadair, *s. m.* (*from* braich.) A maltman. *N. pl.* brachadairean.

Brachadh, aidh, *s. m.* A fermenting, a fermentation; malting; rotting.—*Macint.* Ath-bhrachaidh, *a malt-kiln.*

Brachag, aig, *s. f.* A pimple, a stye; ophthalmia.—*Ir. id.*

Brachagach, *a.* Pimply; ophthalmic.

Brachan, ain, *s. m.* Any thing fermented; leaven; fermented liquor.

Brachd, *s. f.* Hatred; sap, juice; increase of wealth; reaping, mowing.—*Ir. id.*

Bra-cheò, *s.* (*perhaps* breith-cheo.) Bewilderment. Chaidh e na bra-cheò, *he has gone stupid,* or *his judgment has dispersed in mist.*

Brach-shuileach, *a.* Blear-eyed.—*Ir.*

Bradach, *a.* (*from* braid.) *W.* bradawg, *treacherous.* Thievish; stolen. Measar e mar ni bradach, *it shall be counted stolen goods.* Tha thu cho bhreugach 's a tha 'n luch cho bhradach, *you lie as the mouse pilfers.*—*G. P.*

Bradag, aig, (*from* braid.) A thievish female; a sly young girl. *N. pl.* bradagan. Ceist bradaig air breugaig, *ask the thief if I be a liar.*—*G. P.*

Bradaiche, *s. m.* A thief, a robber. *N. pl.* bradaichean. Saoilidh bradaiche gur goidichean uile càch, *a thief suspects an honest man.*—*G. P.*

Bradalach, *a.* Haughty. Gu bradalach, *haughtily.*

Bradalachd, *s. f.* Haughtiness.

Bradan, ain, *s. m.* (*Ir. id.*) A salmon. Bradan an fhior uisge, *the salmon of the running stream.*—*Old Song. N. pl.* bradain.

Bràdh, *s. f.* A quern, a handmill.—*Macd.* Muileann bràdh, *a handmill.* *Fr.* moulin a bràs. Is feaird bràdh a breachdadh, gun a briseadh, *pick a quern, but break it not.*—*G. P.* See **Muileann-bràdh**.

Bradhadair, *s. m.* Kindling; fuel.

Brag, *s. m.* A boast or brag. Thoir brag, *give a brag.*

Bragàd, aid, *s. m.* A brigade.—*Macd.* *N. pl.* bragadan.

Bragàdach, *a.* In brigades.

Bragainn, *s. f.* A bragging, boasting, vaunting. Thòisich e air bragainn, *he began to vaunt.*

Bragainn, *v. n.* Brag, boast. *Pret.* bhragainn; *fut. aff. a.* bragainnidh, *shall brag.*

Bragair, *s. m.* A braggadocio; also the broad leaves that grow on the top of the alga marina.

Bragaireachd, *s. f.* A vaunting, a boasting. Ri bragaireachd, *vaunting.*

Braghad, aid, *s. m.* (*Ir. id.*) The neck, throat, windpipe; a back. A braghad gu seimh a soillseadh, *her neck softly shining.*—*Oss. Derm.* Ruisgidh bru braghad, *the belly will strip the back.*—*G. P.* Losg bhràghaid, *the heartburn.*

Braghadach, *a.* (*from* braghad.) Jugular; of, or belonging to, a neck or throat; having a long neck.

Bragsaidh, *s. f.* A disease among sheep, which is found to arise from eating withered grass, and from want of water.

† **Braiceam**, eim, *s. m.* A pack-saddle; also a horse-collar. *Scotch,* braicheam.

† **Braich**, *s. m.* A stag, a buffalo.

Braich, *gen.* bracha, *s. f.* Malt; *literally,* fermented grain. (*Corn.* and *W.* brag. *Ir.* braich.) Ath-bracha, *a malt-kiln;* muileann bracha, *a malt-mill.*

The Old Gauls, according to Pliny, prepared a sort of fine grain, of which they made beer; and this grain they called *brace.* "Genus farris quod illi vocant bracem."

† **Braicne**, *s.* A cat.—*Ir. id.*

Bràid, *s. f.* (i. e. braghaid.) A horse-collar; an upper part. Braid chluaisein, *hames, or the crooked piece of wood by which a horse draws a cart;* bràid phaib, *a horse-collar made of coarse flax.*

Braid, *s. f.* Theft. Luchd braid, *thieves.* Saor o bhraid 's o antlachd, *free from theft and discontent.*—*Macdon.*

Bràidean, ein, *s. m.* (*dim.* of bràid.) A little horse-collar; a calf's-collar. *Contr.* for braghaidean.

Bràidh. See **Bràigh**.

Braigh, *s.* A hostage. *N. pl.* braighdean *and* braighde.

Braigh, *s. f.* A loud report; a loud crack or clap; a heavy stroke; a monosyllable. Leig an gunn braigh as, *the gun made a loud report.*

Bràigh, *s. m.* The upper part of any thing or place; a neck, a throat; the top of a mountain; an upland country; high lands, high grounds; the upper or higher part of any country; as, Braigh Raineach, *the high grounds of Rannoch, the head of Rannoch.* Braigh Bhealaich, *the high grounds or braes of Taymouth in Perthshire.* Do bhraigh bàn, *thy fair neck.*—*Oss. Fing.*

W. brâi, *breast.* *Arm.* breich. *Lat.* brachium, *arm.* *Scotch,* brae. *W.* bre, *hill.*

Braighde, Braighdean, *n. pl.* of braigh. (*Ir. id.*) Hostages, captives. Iadham ur braighde, *I will compass your captives.*—*Fingalian Poem.* Braighdean gill, *hostages.*—*Stew.* 2 *K.*

Braighdeanas, ais, *s. m.* Bondage, captivity. Am braighdeanas, *in captivity.* Bruid am braighdeanas, *captivity captive.*—*Stew. Eph.*

Braighe, *gen. sing.* of braigh.

Bràigheach, *a.* Having a long neck; having a handsome neck; of, or belonging to, the neck; also uplandish.

Bràigheach, *a.* Giving a loud report; explosive.

Bràigheach, ich, *s. m.* A Highlander; the inhabitant of an upland country.

Braigheachd, *s. f.* Imprisonment, constraint, confinement.

Braighead, eid, *s.* A neck, throat, breast. Lann ro m' braighead, *a sword through my breast.*—*Oss.*

† **Braile**, *s. f.* Heavy rain.—*Ir. id.*

Braileis, *s. f.* Wort.

† **Bràin**, *s. f.* A quern.—*Ir. id.*

† **Brain, Braineach**, ich, *s. m.* A chief.

Brainn, (*for* broinn.) An inflection of *brù;* which see.

Brais, *a.* Rash; bold; impetuous; sudden; *rarely,* fabulous, inventive. *Com.* and *sup.* braise.

Bràisd, *s. f.* A brooch, a bracelet. Written also *bràist;* which see.

Braise, *s. f.* Rashness; boldness; impetuosity; suddenness; a paroxysm; wantonness.—*Macd.*

Braise, *com.* and *sup.* of brais. More or most rash.

Braisead, eid, *s. m.* Rashness, forwardness, impetuousness; increase in rashness or forwardness. A dol am braisead, *growing more and more rash.*

Brais-sgeul, sgeòil, *s.* A fabulous history, a romance.

Bràist, *s. f.* A brooch, a bracelet. *N. pl.* bràistean. Thug iad leo bràistean, *they took with them bracelets.*—*Stew. Exod.*

Braith-lin, *s. f.* A sheet; *perhaps* brat-lin. *Ir.* braithlin.

Bram, *s.* A flatus. Mar bha gille mòr nam bram, cha 'n fhuirich e thall 's cha 'n fhuirich e bhos, *like the never-do-well, he will stay nowhere.*—*G. P.*

Corn. W. Arm. and *Ir.* bram, *a flatus.* *Gr.* βρεμω, *to make a noise;* and βρομος, *noise.*

Bramach, aich, *s. m.* A colt.—*Ir. id.* *N. pl.* bramaiche, *colts.*

Bramair, *s. m.* One addicted to f—ting; a flatulent person; an unpolished fellow; a noisy fellow; a boor. *Ir.* bramair. *W.* bramiwr. *Span.* bramador, *a crier.*

Braman, ain, *s. m.* A crupper.

Bramanach, aich, *s. m.* A noisy fellow; a boorish fellow. *N. pl.* bramanaiche.

Bramanachd, *s. f.* Noisiness, boorishness, sulkiness.

Bramanta, *a.* Boorish, sulky, unpolished.

Bramartaich, *s. f.* A frequent blowing of wind backwards; a habit of blowing wind backwards.

Bramsag, aig, *s. f.* Flatulence.

† **Bran**, *a.* Poor; black; also, *substantively*, a raven, a rook. *Sclav.* bran, *black.* *Dalmat.* gravran. *Bohem.* hawran. *Croat.* chafran.

Bràn, **Bràin**, *s. m.* (*contr.* for bràigh-an.) A mountain-stream: the name of several streams in the Highlands of Scotland.

Bràn, **Bràin**, *s. m.* Husks of corn, bran. *W.* bran.

Brandair, *s. m.* A gridiron.—*Macd.*

Brandal, ail, *s. m.* A gridiron.—*Macd.* *N. pl.* brandalan.

Brangach, *a.* Snarling.

Brangas, ais, *s. m.* An instrument once in the Highlands for the punishment of pilfering vagrants.

† **Brann**, **Brainn**, *s. m.* A burning coal; a woman. *Ir.* brann. *Eng.* brand.

Brannamh, aimh, *s. m.* A coat of mail.

Branndaidh, *s. f.* Brandy. (*Fr.* brandi.) Is meirg a dh' oladh branndaidh! *what folly it is to drink brandy!*—*Old Song.*

† **Brannrach**, aich, *s. m.* The border or boundaries of a country.

† **Braoi**, *s. pl.* Eyebrows.—*Ir. id.*

Braoileadh, eidh, *s. m.* A great noise, a bounce. *Ir.* braoileadh.

Braoileag, eig, *s. f.* A whortle-berry. Braoileag nan con, *a dog-berry, a bear-berry.* *N. pl.* braoileagan.

Braoileagach, *a.* Abounding in whortle-berries. Do leacan braoileagach, *thy rocks abounding in whortle-berries.*—*Macint.*

Braoileagan, *n. pl.* of braoileag.

Braoilich, *s. f.* A loud noise; a rattling sound. Ri braoilich, *making a loud rattling noise.* *Asp. form*, bhraoilich. Ciod bhraoilich th'ort? *why do you make such noise?*

Braoisg, *s. f.* A grin; a yawn; a gaping; a distortion of the mouth. Chuir e braoisg air, *he began to grin.*

Braoisgeach, *a.* Grinning; gaping; having a distorted mouth. Fear braoisgeach, *a man with a distorted mouth.* A bhodaich bhraoisgich! *thou grinning old man!* *Com.* and *sup.* braoisgiche, *more or most grinning.*

Braoisgean, ein, *s. m.* (*from* braoisg.) A person who grins; one with a distorted mouth.

Braoisgeanachd, *s. f.* The habit of grinning.

Braon, braoin, *s. m.* Dew; a drop; drizzle; rain; a shower. (*Ir.* braon.) *N. pl.* braoin; *d. pl.* braonaibh. Mar bhogha Lena nam braon mall, *like the rainbow of drizzling Lena.*—*Oss.* Braon nan sian, *the drizzling of the blast.*—*Oss. Fing.* Le braonaibh na h-oidhche, *with the drops of night.*—*Stew. Song. Sol.*

Braonach, *a.* (*from* braon.) Showery, drizzly, rainy, dewy. Sa mhadainn bhraonach, *in the dewy morn.*—*Oss.*

Braonachd, *s. f.* Continual drizzling; a continual dropping.

Braonan, ain, *s. m.* An earthen nut; the bud of a brier.—*Macint.* Braonan bachlaig, *an earthen nut.*—*Macd.*

Braon-dhealt, *s.* Heavy dew. Braon-dhealt na madainn, *the heavy dew of morn.*—*Oss. Cathula.*

Braos, **Braois**, *s.* See **Braoisg**.

Braosach, *a.* See **Braoisgeach**.

Bras, *a.* (*Ir.* bras.) Rash, impetuous; bold, intrepid; sudden; active, brisk, lively. Bras le d' bheul, *rash with thy mouth.*—*Stew. Ecc.* Mar steud-shruth bras, *like an impetuous torrent.*—*Oss. Gaul.* Ag radh ri mhic bhras, *saying to his intrepid sons.*—*Id.*

† **Brasailte**, *s. f.* A panegyric.

† **Brasair-buird**, *s. m.* A sycophant, one who subsists by flattering his patron.

Bras-bhuinne, *s. f.* A torrent; also a stormy sea. A seòladh air bras bhuinne, *sailing on a stormy sea.*—*Oss. Conn.*

Bras-chomhrag, aig, *s. f.* A tilt or tournament.

Brasgalladh, aidh, *s. m.* A declamation.—*Ir. id.*

Brasluidhe, *s. f.* Perjury. Luchd brasluidhe, *perjured people.*

Bras-sgeul, -sgeòil, *s.* A romance, a fable.—*Ir. id.*

Brat, brait, *s. m.* *Anglo-Sax.* bratt. (*Ir.* brat, *mantle.* *W.* brat, *a rag.* *Scotch*, brat, *clothing.* In *Lincolnshire* brat *is an apron.*) A mantle, a cloak, a covering, a veil, coverlet, blanket, curtain. Brat na h-oidhche, *the mantle of night.*—*Oss. Dargo.* Crochaidh tu am brat, *thou shalt hang the veil.*—*Stew. Exod.* Brat-leapach, *a coverlet, a quilt;* brat-roinn, *a partition veil;* brat-spèillidh, *swaddling-cloth;* brat-urlair, *a carpet;* brat-broin, *mort-cloth;* brat-folaich, *a cloak.*

† **Brat**, *s.* Judgment.

Bratach, aich, *s. f.* (*Ir.* bratach.) *N. pl.* brataichean. Banners, flags, colours, an ensign. Bratach aluinn righ nam magh, *the beauteous banner of the king of the plains.*—*Oss. Cathula.* A bhratach dhaithte uaine, *his green-coloured flag.*—*Oss. Dargo.*

Bratag, aig, *s. f.* A worm, a caterpillar; also a rag; an impudent girl; a pilfering female.

Brat-bròin, *s. m.* A mort-cloth.

Bràt-chosach, *a.* Bow-legged.

Brat-folaich, *s. m.* A cloak; a blind man. Mar bhrat-folaich do 'n dall, *as a cloak for the blind.*—*Stew. Pet.*

Brath, *v. a.* (*Ir.* brath.) Betray; spy; guess, suppose; design; entertain an opinion. *Pret. a.* bhrath, *betrayed;* *fut. aff. a.* brathaidh, *shall betray.* Esan a bhrath e, *he who betrayed him.*—*Stew. N. T.*

Brath, *s.* Guess, opinion, idea, expectation, design, judgment; a spying, an informing, treachery, betraying; a mass, a lump. Bheil brath agad? *have you any idea? do you know?* Gun bhrath furtachd, *without expectation of relief.*—*Macint.* Air bhrath, *found.* Cha bhi am bard air a bhrath, *the bard shall not be found.*—*Old Song.* From *brath* very probably comes the *Hindoo* brachman; *literally, the man of judgment.*

Bràth, *s.* A conflagration; destruction. La bhràth, *the last day, the day of the conflagration.* Gu la bhràth, *never;* gu bràth, *for ever.* Gu la bhràth cha n' eirich Oscar, *Oscar shall never rise.*—*Oss. Temo.* Cliù gach linn gu bràth, *the praise of every age for ever.*—*Old Song.*

† **Brathach**, *a.* Continual, constant.

Brathadair, *s. m.* (*from* brath.) An informer, a spy, a betrayer, a traitor; also a kindling; fuel. *N. pl.* brathadairean. *W.* bradwr, *a traitor.*

Brathadh, aidh, *s. m.* A betraying, a spying, an informing; treachery. Luchd brathaidh, *spies;* fear brathaidh, *a spy or informer.* Luchd brathaidh an siothchainnt, *spies in peace.*—*Stew. Heb.*

Brathadh, (a), *pr. part.* of brath.

Brathaidh, *fut. aff. a.* of brath. Shall or will betray.

Bràthair, *gen.* bràthar, *s. m.* (*i. e.* bru-ath-urr, *a second person of the same womb.*) A brother. Ardan do bhràthar, *the proud anger of thy brother.*—*Oss. Lod.* Brathair màthar, *an uncle by the mother's side;* brathair-athar, *an uncle by the father's side;* brathair sean-athair, *a granduncle, a grandfather's brother;* brathair sean-mhathair, *a grand-mother's brother;* brathair-céile, *a brother-in-law;* literally, *a spouse's brother;* brathair bochd, *a friar;* brathair-mbort, *fratricide.* Is lag gualainn gun bhrathair, *feeble is the arm of him who has no brother.*—*G. P.*

Gr. Æol. φρατωρ *and* φρατηρ. *Lat.* frater. *Fr.* † frêtre, *now* frère. *Dan.* broder. *Swed.* broder *and* bror. *Isl.* brodur. *Anglo-Sax.* brather. *Eng.* brother. *Germ.* bruother. *Belgic,* braeder. *Pol.* brât. *Lus.* bradt. *Russ.* bräte. *Sclav.* brat. *Bohem.* brat *and* brodr. *Teut.* broeder *and* bruder. *Ir.* brathair. *W.* brawd *and* brawdair. *Corn.* brawd, breur, *and* bredar. *Arm.* breuzr (z *silent*). *Cimb.* brodir. *Tar.* bruder. *Pers.* berader, burader, *and* braeder. *Hindost.* brooder. Every language in Europe, and almost all the languages in Asia, have nearly the same term to express *brother:* hence we may conclude that the root is antediluvian.

Brathair-athar, *s. m.* An uncle, a father's brother. Brathair m' athar, *my uncle.*

Brathair-bochd, *s. m.* A friar; a lay-capuchin; a poor brother.

Brathair-céile, *s. f.* A brother-in-law; *literally,* the brother of a spouse.

Brathaireachas, ais, *s. m.* Brotherhood; partnership. Gum brisinn am brathaireachas, *that I might break their brotherhood.*—*Stew. Zech.* Cha bhi brathaireachas gu mnaoi na gu fearann, *there is no partnership in women or land.*—*G. P.*

† **Brathaireag**, eig, *s. f.* An aunt by the father's side.

Brathairean, *n. pl.* of brathair; which see.

Brathaireil, *a.* (*i. e.* brathair-amhuil.) Brotherly; *literally,* brotherlike. Gradh brathaireil, *brotherly love.*—*Stew. Rom.*

Brathaireileachd, *s. f.* Brotherliness; unanimity.

Brathair-mathar, *s. m.* An uncle by the mother's side. Brathair mo mhathair, *my uncle.*

Brathair-mhort, *s. m.* Fratricide. *Swed.* broder-mort.

Brat-leapach, *s. m.* A bed-cover or quilt.

Brat-lìn, *s. m.* A linen cloth; a sheet.

Brat-spéillidh, *s. m.* Swaddling-cloth. Phaisg i e am brat-spéillidh, *she wrapped him in swaddling-clothes.*

Brat-urlair, *s.* A carpet.

Breab, *s. m.* A kick; a prance; a spurn. Thug e breab dha, *he gave him a kick.*

Breab, *v. a.* Kick; prance; spurn; stamp with the foot. *Pret. a.* bhreab, *kicked; fut. aff. a.* breabaidh, *shall kick.*

Breabach, *a.* (*from* breab.) Apt to kick or to prance. Each breabach brògach, *a prancing strong-hoofed horse.*

Breabadair, *s. m.* (*from* breab.) A weaver; one who kicks. *N. pl.* breabadairean.

Breabadaireachd, *s. f.* The business of a weaver; the habit of kicking or of stamping.

Breabadairean, *n. pl.* of breabadair.

Breabadh, aidh, *s. m.* A kicking; a prancing; a spurning; a stamping; a kick; a prance; a stamp of the foot.

Breabadh, (a), *pr. part.* of breab. Kicking; prancing; spurning; stamping.

Breabail, *s. f.* A kicking; prancing; spurning; stamping; also a gurgling noise. Tha na sruthain ri breabail, *the streamlets are gurgling.*—*Oss. Dargo.*

Breabain, *gen. sing.* of breaban.

Breaban, ain, *s. m.* A patch on the tip of a shoe.

Breabanaiche, *s. m.* A shoemaker; a cobbler.—*Macd.*

Breabartaich, *s. f.* (*from* breab.) A yerking, kicking, prancing, or spurning.

Breac, bric, *s. m.* A trout, the *salmo fario* of Linnæus; a salmon; *rarely,* a wolf; a brock or badger. *N. pl.* bric; *d. pl.* breacaibh.

Breac, bric, *s. f.* (*W.* brech. *Ir.* breac.) A pox; most commonly applied to the small-pox; any spotted appearance. Breac-otraiche, *chicken pox;* breac-seunain, breachd-sheunain, *freckles;* breac-fhrangach, *the venereal;* each breac, *a piebald horse;* breac mhuilinn, that modification of cloud called *cirro-cumulus.* It is called *breac mhuilinn* by the Gael, probably from the resemblance which a *cirro-cumulus* sky bears to a picked or punctured millstone.

Breac, Breachd, *a.* (*W.* and *Arm.* brech. *Ir.* breac.) Spotted, marked with the small-pox, speckled, particoloured, chequered, piebald. A blàiteachadh nan ubha breachd, *hatching the spotted eggs.*—*Macfar.* Gach spreidh tha breachd, *all the cattle that is speckled.*—*Stew. Gen.* Eich bhreac, *speckled* [*piebald*] *horses.*—*Stew. Zech.* Breac le feireagaibh, *chequered with cloud-berries.*—*Macint.*

Breac, Breachd, *v. a.* Chequer, spot, speckle; embroider; carve; mix; pick a millstone. *Pret. a.* bhreac, *chequered; fut. aff. a.* breacaidh, *shall or will chequer.*

Breacadh, Breachdadh, aidh, *s. m.* A chequering, spotting; embroidering; picking a millstone.

Breacag, Breachdag, aig, *s. f.* A cake, a scon; a pancake. *N. pl.* breacagan, *cakes.* Breacagan neo-ghoirtichte, *unleavened cakes.*—*Stew. Lev.*

Breacain, *gen. sing.* and *n. pl.* of breacan.

Breacaich, Breachdaich, *v. a.* Spot, chequer. *Pret. a.* bhreacaich, *spotted; fut. aff. a.* breacaichidh, *shall chequer.*

Breacaichte, Breachdaichte, *p. part.* of breacaich *or* breachdaich, *spotted, chequered.*

Breacair, *s. m.* A graving tool, a graver. *N. pl.* breacairean.

Breacaireachd, *s. f.* The employment of a graver; chequering; chequer-work.

Breacan, ain, *s. m.* (*Ir. id.* *W.* brychan, *a tartan covering.*) A Highland plaid, a tartan.

Particoloured habiliments were used by the Celts from the earliest times; but the variety of colours in the *breacan* was greater or less according to the rank of the wearer. The *breacan* of the Celtic king had seven different colours; the Druidical tunic had six; and that of the nobles four.

Breacanach, *a.* Tartan; plaided. Aodach breacanach, *tartan clothes.* Na gaisgich bhreacanach bhuadhach, *the plaided, victorious warriors.*—*Old Song.*

Breac-an-t sìl, *s. m.* The bird called a wagtail; the *motacilla alba* of Linnæus.

Breac-beididh, *s. m.* A loach.—*Macd.*

† **Breachd**, *s. f.* A doubt.—*Ir. id.*

† **Breachdan**, ain, *s. m.* (*Ir. id.*) Wheat; custard; fresh meat; a plaid: for this last sense, see **Breacan.**

Breac-iteach, *a.* Having speckled feathers. Glacagan nan eun bhreac-iteach, *the dells of the speckled birds.*—*R.*

Breac-iteag, -eig, *s. f.* A spotted or speckled feather.

Breac-liath, *a.* Greyish.

Breac-lion, lin, *s. m.* A trout-net; a drag-net; a landing-net. Breac-lionntaichean, *drag-nets.*

Breacnachadh, aidh, *s. m.* A chequering, spotting; embroidering.

Breacnaich, *v. a.* Chequer, make spotted or particoloured; embroider. *Ir.* breacnuigh. *Pret. a.* bhreacnaich; *fut. aff. a.* breacnaichidh.

Breacnaichte, *p. part.* of breacnaichte. Chequered, made spotted or particoloured; embroidered.

Breac-shoillsich, *v. n.* Glimmer as the twilight. *Pret. a.*

bhreac-shoillsich, *glimmered; fut. aff. a.* breac-shoillsichidh, *shall glimmer.*

BREAC-SHOLUS, -sholuis, *s. m.* Twilight.

BREACTA, BREACTE, *p. part.* of breac. Spotted, chequered; embroidered; carved.—*Stew.* 1 *K. ref.*

BREAD, BREID, *s. m.* A breach.

BREADH, *a.* See BREAGH.

BREADHACHD, *s. f.* See BREAGHACHD.

BREAG, BRÉIG, *s. f.* A lie. More frequently written *breug;* which see.

BREAGACH, *a.* False. See BREUGACH.

BREAGAIR, *s. m.* A liar. See BREUGAIR.

BREAGH, *a.* (*Arm.* brao. *Scotch,* braw. *Ir.* breo *and* breagh. *W.* briaw, *dignity.*) Fine, well-dressed, splendid; fair, specious, showy, pleasant. Cia breagh a snuadh! *how splendid her appearance!—Sm.* Nur labhras e gu breagh, *when he speaks fair.—Stew. Pro.* Is breagh an dealradh ni grian, *splendid is the sun's shining.—Old Poem.*

BREAGHACHD, *s. f.* (*from* breagh.) Finery, ornaments, showiness; speciousness. A bhreaghachd, *his ornaments.*

BREAGHAD, aid, *s. m.* Attire, ornament, finery, showiness. —*Stew. Is.*

BREAGHAS, ais, *s. m.* (*from* breagh.) Finery, ornaments.

BREAGHASLACH, aich, *s. m.* A dream; a delirium. More commonly written *breisleach.*

BREAGHNA, *s.* The river Boyne in Ireland.

BREALL, breill, *s. m.* An uncovering of the glans penis; a phymosis.

BREALLACH, *a.* (*from* breall.) Having a phymosis; of, or relating to, a phymosis.

BREAMAIN, *gen. sing.* and *n. pl.* of breaman; which see.

BREAMAN,* ain, *s. m.* A tail. Bàrr a breamain, *the tip of her tail.—Macint. N. pl.* breamain, *tails.*

BREAMANACH, *a.* (*from* breaman.) Tailed; like a tail; of, or belonging to, a tail.

BREAMAS, ais, *s. m.* Mischief; mishap, mischance; fatality. Ri breamas, *at mischief.—Old Song.* Tha 'm breamas ort, *the devil is in you.*

BREAMASACH, *a.* Fatal; causing mischance; unlucky. *Com.* and *sup.* breamasaiche, *more or most fatal.*

BREAMASACHD, *s. f.* (*from* breamas.) Fatality; a continuation of mischances; a liability to mischance.

BREAN, bréin, *s. m.* A stink. See BREUN.

BREANACH, *a.* See BREUNACH.

BREANAN, ain, *s. m.* A dunghill. More frequently written *breunan.*

BREANTAG, aig, *s. f.* See BREUNTAG.

BREANTAS, ais, *s. m.* (*from* brean.) See BREUNTAS.

† BREAS, *s. m.* A prince, a potentate; a voice; a sound.

† BREAS-CHATHAIR, *gen.* breas-chathrach. A throne.—*Macd. N. pl.* breas-chathraichean.

† BREAS-CHOLBH, *s. m.* A sceptre.—*Ir. id. N. pl.* breas-cholbhan.

† BREASDA, *a.* Principal; lively; active.—*Ir. id.*

† BREAS-LANN, lainn, *s. m.* A place; a court of justice.—*Ir. id.*

† BREAS-OIRCHISTE, *s. f.* A royal treasure.—*Ir. id.*

† BREATH, *a.* Clean, pure, bright, innocent.

BREATH, *s. f.* A row, a rank. *N. pl.* breathan. Tri breathan, *three rows.—Stew.* 1 *K.* Written also *breith.*

BREATH, BREITH, *s. f.* A judgment; opinion; censure; confidence. Written also *breith;* which see.

BREATHACH, *a.* In ranks, in rows; also judicial, critical.

BREATHAL, ail, *s. m.* Confusion of mind; terror; flurry.—*Stew. Acts, ref.*

BREATHALACH, *a.* Causing confusion of mind, terror, or flurry; apt to be confused.

BREATHALAICH, *s. f.* Confusion of mind, flurry.

BREATHAMH, *s. m.* A judge. See BREITHEAMH.

BREATHAMHNAS, ais, *s. m.* Judgment, decision. See BREITHEANAS.

BREATHAS, ais, *s. m.* Frenzy; extreme fury; flaming wrath. Tha e air bhreathas, *he is frantic;* tha breathas a chuthaich air, *he is in a frenzy.*

Breathas is either *breath-theas,* i. e. judgment on fire, or *bràth-theas,* a flame of anger, like to a conflagration; *bràth* signifying the last conflagration.

BREATHNACH, aich, *s. m.* A Welchman. *N. pl.* Breathnaich.

BREATHNAICH, *v.* Perceive, judge, opine. *Pret. a.* bhreathnaich, *judged.*

† BREATHNAS, ais, *s. m.* A skewer, a clasp, a bodkin; the tongue of a buckle.—*Ir. id.*

BREATUNN, tuinn, *s. m.* Britain.

Of all the attempts that have been made to decompose this word, the most ingenious and the most successful is that of Mr. Clarke, in his Caledonian Bards, mentioned by Dr. MacArthur in his Supplementary Observations on the Authenticity of Ossian's Poems. *Bràith-tonn,* the top of the wave, is, according to him, the meaning of *Breatunn.* To perceive the force of this account, one has merely to imagine himself viewing Britain across the Channel from the north coast of France, from whence came our Celtic ancestors. Our island, from that quarter, seems a low dark line, lying along the surface of the deep; and no term could have been found more descriptive of that appearance than *Bràith-tonn* or *Bràith-tuinn,* (pronounced *Braitonn* or *Braituinn,*) the land on the top of the waves? Others will have it that *Breatunn* is a corruption of *Bretinn,* a high island, compounded of the old Celtic term *bret,* high, and *inn,* island.

BREATUNNACH, aich, *s. m.* A Briton. *N. pl.* Breatunnaich.

BREICE, *s. f.* (*from* breac.) Spots, spottedness, maculation. An liopard a bhreic, *the leopard his spots.—Stew. O. T.*

BRÉID, *s. f.* (*Ir. id.*) A kerchief, a napkin; a sail; a woman's head-dress, consisting of a square of fine linen, which is pinned neatly round the head, with part of it hanging down behind, not unlike the head-dress of the women in some parts of Normandy and Bretagne. Bréid-uchd, *a stomacher;* bréid-bronn, *an apron;* bréid-shoitheachan, *a dish-clout.*

BRÉIDEACH, *a.* Like a kerchief; like a woman's head-dress; white-spreading. Ar siùil bhréideach, *our white-spreading sails.—Oss. Manos.*

BRÉIDEACH, eich, *s. f.* A married woman. Bha mi am bhréidich, mo ghruagaich 's mo bhantraich san aon am, *I was a married woman, a virgin, and a widow at the same time.—Old Song.*

BRÉIDEADH, idh, *s. m.* A dressing of the head; a clothing or attiring; patching.

BREIDEAN, ein, *s. m.* (*dim.* of bréid.) A coif; a little rag; a web of frieze.

BREIDEAN, *n. pl.* of bréid; which see.

BREID-GHEAL, *a.* White-sailed; with a white napkin, with a white head-dress. Boirrionnach bréid-gheal, *a female with a white head-dress;* luingeas breid-gheal crannach, *a white-sailed high-masted ship.—Ull.*

† BREIG, *s. m.* A rustic, a boor.—*Ir. id.*

BRÉIG, *v. a.* Soothe, cajole, flatter. Written also *breug;* which see.

BREIGE, *gen. sing.* of breug. Of a lie. Beul na brèige, *a lying mouth.* See BREUG.

BRÉIGE, *s. f.* A falsehood. *Ir.* bréig.

† BRÉIG-FHIOS, *s.* Enthusiasm.—*Ir. id.*

† BRÉIG-FHIOSACH, *a.* Enthusiastic.—*Ir. id.*

BREILL, *gen. sing.* of breall.

Breilleis, *s. f.* Delirium; raving. Tha e na bhreilleis, *he is raving.*

Breilleiseach, *a.* Delirious; causing delirium.

Breilleiseachd, *s. f.* Liableness to delirium; deliriousness.

Breim, *s.* A *flatus.* Breim an diabhoil duibh, *nigri diaboli flatus.*—*Macvurich.*

Corn. W. and *Arm.* bram. *Ir.* breim. *Gr.* βρέμω, *to make a noise.* *Lat.* fremo.

Brein, *gen. sing.* of breun.

Breine, *com. and sup.* of breun.

Breine, *s. f.* A stink. Thig a bhreine nios, *his stink shall ascend.*—*Stew. Job.*

Breineag, eig, *s. f.* (*from* breine.) A dirty young female, a slattern or drab. *N. pl.* breineagan.

Breinean-brothach, *s.* The great daisy.

Breinid, *s. f.* Stink; a putrid smell.

† **Breis**, *s. f.* A tear.

Breis, *v. a.* Break. See **Bris**.

Breisg, *a.* Brisk. See **Brisg**.

Breisleach, ich, *s. m.* A dream, delirium, raving. Tha e na bhreisleach, *he is raving.*

Breith, *s.* Judgment, sentence, decision; a row or rank; a layer; also birth, descent; a bearing, a carrying; penance. Breith air a phobull bheir thu, *thou shalt judge the people.*—*Smith.* Na h-aingidh anns a bhreith, *the wicked in the judgment.*—*Smith.* Thoir breith, *judge;* breith-air-eiginn, *rapine, deforcement.*—*Macd.* Breith-buidheachais, *thanksgiving;* breith-dhitidh, *sentence of condemnation.*

Breith, *v. a.* Judge, sentence; bear, bring forth, produce. Sguir i bhreith cloinne, *she left off bearing children.*—*Stew. Gen.* *Pret. a.* bhreith; *fut. aff. a.* breithidh.

Breitheach, *a.* (*from* breith.) Judicial, critical. *Ir.* breitheach.

Breitheal, eil, *s. m.* Confusion; turmoil; astonishment.

Breitheamh, imh, *s. m.* A judge; an umpire; judgment, decision, sentence. *Ir.* breitheamh.

Breitheamhnas, ais, *s. m.* See **Breitheanas**.

Breitheanas, ais, *s. m.* (*from* breith.) *Ir.* breitheamnas. A judgment; a decision; a sudden calamity. La bhreitheanais, *the day of judgment;* thainig breitheanas ort, *a judgment came upon you.*

Breitheanas is evidently a contraction of *breith a nuas*, a judgment from above. It is well known that the sentences passed by the Druids on criminals were often rigorous in the extreme. When they found it expedient to doom a culprit to a severe punishment, or to an awful death, they alleged that they acted by the compulsion of Heaven, which directed all their judgments, and of course approved of all their decisions. Hence their sentence, from the word *breith*, meaning any ordinary decision, was called *breitheanuas*, or *breitheamhnuas*, now contracted *breitheanas;* meaning a judgment from God, or any rigorous decision. This word is still the term among the Gael to express the decision of a judge, or any sudden calamity.

Breith-air-eiginn, *s.* Deforcement, rapine.—*Macd.*

Breith-buidheachais, *s. m.* Thanksgiving. Gu ma fearr leibh breith-buidheachais, *may you rather thanksgiving.*—*Stew. Eph.*

Breith-dhitidh, *s.* Sentence of condemnation.

Breitheadaireachd, *s. f.* Interpretation, as of dreams.

Breitheantach, *a.* Judicial; judicious.—*Shaw.*

Breithneach, *a.* Imaginative.

Breithneachadh, aidh, *s. m.* An apprehension; a way of thinking; a conceiving; imagination. Uile bhreithneachadh a smuaintean, *all the imaginations of his thoughts.*—*Stew. Gen.* A dh' aon bhreithneachadh, *of one mind or way of thinking.*—*Stew. Phil.*

Breithnich, *v.* Conceive, imagine, apprehend. *Pret. a.* bhreithnich, *imagined;* *fut. aff. a.* breithnichidh, *shall imagine.*

† **Brenn**, *a.* An ancient Celtic term, long gone into disuse among the Gael, but retained in the Armoric dialect. Hence *Brennus*, the name of the Gaulish king who took Rome, and of the prince who attempted to plunder the temple at Delphi.

Breo, *s.* A fire, a flame. Breo-clach, *a flint;* breo-choire, *a warming-pan;* breo-chual, *a bonfire, a funeral pile.*

† **Breoch**, *s. m.* A brim, a brink.—*Ir. id.*

Breo-chlach, -chloich, *s. f.* A flint. *N. pl.* breo-chlachan.

Breo-choire, *s. f.* A warming-pan.—*Shaw.*

Breo-chual, -chuail, *s. f.* A funeral pile, a bonfire.—*Shaw.* *N. pl.* breo-chualan.

Breo-dhruidheachd, *s. f.* Pyromancy.

Breog, **Breoig**, *s. f.* A leveret.—*Ir. id.*

† **Breog**, *a.* Feeble; sickly.

† **Breogach**, aich, *s. m.* A baker.—*Ir. id.* *N. pl.* breogaichean.

Breoillean, ein, *s. m.* A darnel.

Breoilleanach, *a.* Abounding in darnel; like darnel.

Breòite, *a.* Infirm, frail, weak, sickly; slender; bruised; tender. Ged tha mi crionaidh breòite, *withered and bruised though I be.*—*Old Song.*

Breòiteachd, *s. f.* Infirmity, frailty; weakness, sickliness; slenderness.

† **Breon**, **Breoin**, *s. m.* A blemish, blur, or spot.—*Ir. id.*

Breoth, *v. a.* Bruise, crush, maim. *Pret. a.* bhreoth, *bruise;* *fut. aff. a.* breòthaidh, *shall or will bruise.*

Breothadh, aidh, *s. m.* A wounding, crushing, bruising; a maiming; a decay or consumption; a wound; a crush or bruise.

Breòthadh, (a), *pr. part.* of breoth. Wounding, crushing, bruising, maiming.

† **Breothan**, ain, *s. m.* Wheat.—*Ir. id.*

† **Bret**, *a.* High. Hence, according to some, the name *Breatunn;* which see.

Breth. See **Breith**.

Breug, **Breig**, *s. f.* A lie, a falsehood. *N. pl.* breugan; *gen. pl.* breug; *d. pl.* breugaibh. Bilean nam breug, *lips of falsehood.*—*Stew. Pro.*

Breug, *v. a.* Soothe; flatter; cajole; entice. *Pret. a.* bhreug, *soothed;* *fut. aff. a.* breugaidh, *shall soothe;* *fut. sub.* bhreugas. Mu bhreugas peacaich thu, *if sinners entice thee.*—*Stew. Pro.*

Breugach, *a.* Lying, false, deceitful; flattering, cajoling, soothing; deceived. Diomhanasa breugach, *lying vanities.*—*Stew. Jonah.* Fianuis bhreugach, *false witness;* is breugach thu an diu, *thou art deceived to-day.*—*Old Poem.* Tha thu cho bhreugach 's a tha 'n luch cho bhradach, *you lie as much as the mouse pilfers.*—*G. P.* *Com.* and *sup.* breugaiche, *more or most false.*

Breugadh, aidh, *s. m.* A cajoling, flattering, or soothing.

Breugag, aig, *s. f.* A lying female. *N. pl.* breugagan. Ceist bradaig air breugaig, *ask the thief if I be a liar.*—*G. P.*

Breugaich, *v. a.* (*from* breug.) Belie, falsify, give the lie; disprove; gainsay. *Pret. a.* bhreugaich, *belied;* *fut. aff. a.* breugaichidh, *shall or will belie;* *fut. pass.* breugaichear. Ged dh' eignichear an sean fhocal cha bhreugaichear e, *though the proverb be gainsaid, it cannot be disproved.*—*G. P.*

Breugaiche, *s. m.* A liar. Is feaird breugaiche fianuis, *a liar requires a voucher.*—*G. P.*

Breugair, *s. m.* A liar. Eisdidh am breugair, *the liar shall listen.*—*Stew. Pro.* *N. pl.* breugairean.

Breugaireachd, *s. f.* A habit of lying; the vice of lying.

Breugan, *n. pl.* of breug. Lies.

Breug-chrabhach, *a.* Hypocritical.

Breug-chrabhadh, aidh, *s. m.* Hypocrisy.

Breuglachadh, aidh, *s. m.* A forswearing, perjuring; gainsaying, falsifying.

Breuglaich, *v. a.* Forswear, perjure, belie, gainsay. *Pret. a.* bhreuglaich; *fut. aff. a.* breuglaichidh, *shall forswear; p. part.* breuglaichte.

Breuglaichte, *p. part.* of breuglaich. Forsworn; gainsaid.

Breugnachadh, aidh, *s. m.* A falsifying, belying, contradicting, gainsaying.

Breugnachair, *s. m.* A gainsayer. *N. pl.* breugnachairean.

Breugnaich, *v. a.* Belie, falsify, contradict. *Pret. a.* breugnaich, *belied; fut. aff. a.* breugnaichidh, *shall or will belie; p. part.* breugnaichte, *falsified; fut. pass.* breugnaichear.

Breugnaichidh, *fut. aff. a.* Shall or will falsify.

Breugnaichte, *p. part.* of breugnaich. Belied, falsified, contradicted.

Breug-riochd, *s. f.* A disguise.

Breun, *a.* Stinking, putrid, loathsome, nasty; clumsy; also a stink, a smell. O'n otrach bhreun, *from the putrid dunghill.—Smith.* Tha e breun, *it is loathsome.—Stew. Job.* Boladh breun, *a stinking savour.—Stew. Ecc.*

W. braen. *Arm.* bren. *Teut.* bren *and* bern. *Ir.* breun.

Breunach, *a.* Stinking; nasty; surly. *Com.* and *sup.* breunaiche.

Breunag, aig, *s. f.* A dirty female, a slattern or drab. *N. pl.* breunagan.

Breunan, ain, *s. m.* A dunghill; any stinking thing.

Breunan-brothach, aich, *s. m.* The great daisy.

Breun-ladhrach, *a.* Rotten-toed.

Breuntag, aig, *s. f.* A filthy drab. *N. pl.* breuntagan.

Breuntas, ais, *s. m.* (*Ir.* breantas.) A putrid smell, any loathsome smell.

† **Bri**, *s. f.* Anger; a word; a rising ground; an effort; essence. For the last sense, see **Brigh**.

† **Bria**, *s. m.* A town.

This vocable has gone into disuse among the Scottish and Irish Celts, but is preserved by their brethren of Bretagne. *Bria* meant a town, in the ancient Thracian language; and it is found in the names of many towns in France, Spain, and Britain. Ancient geographers, as Strabo, Ptolemy, and Pliny, write this word respectively *briga*, *brica*, and *briva*; not because the meaning was different, for it was the same, but because *bria* was pronounced differently by different nations.

† **Briagh**, *s.* A wound, a mortal wound.

Briagh, *a.* (*Arm.* brao. *Scotch*, braw. *Ir.* breo *and* breagh. *W.* briaw, *dignify. Swed.* braf, *good.*) Fine; well-dressed; showy; elegant; well. La briagh, *a fine day;* boirionnach bbriagh, *a showy female;* tha mi gu briagh, *I am quite well.*

Briaghachd, *s. f.* Finery; showiness; gaudiness.

Briaghas, ais, *s. m.* Finery; showiness; gaudiness.

† **Brian**, **Brein**, *s. m.* A word; composition; a warrant; an author.—*Ir. id.*

† **Brianach**, *a.* (*from* brian.) Full of fair speeches; specious; prosing.

† **Briar**, *s.* Briar; a thorn; a pin; a prickle.

Bri'ar, *a.* See **Brighmhor**.

Briarach, *a.* Thorny, prickly.

Briathar, *s.* (*Ir. id.*) A word; a saying; an assertion; an oath; a verb; *rarely* a victory or conquest. Air mo bhriathar, *upon my word.*

Briatharach, **Briathrach**, *a.* Wordy; verbal; verbose; talkative. Ni thu 'm fear tosdach briathrach, *thou makest the silent man talkative.—R.*

Briatharachas, **Briathrachas**, ais, *s. m.* Eloquence; elocution; verbosity.

Briathraich, *v. a.* Affirm, assert, dictate, swear to. *Pret. a.* briathraich, *affirmed; fut. aff. a.* briathraichidh, *shall or will affirm.*

Briathrail, *a.* (briathar-amhuil.) Verbal. Eadar-theangachadh briathrail, *a verbal translation.*

Brib, **Bribe**, *s. f.* A bribe. *N. pl.* bribeachean.

Bric, *n. pl.* of breac. Trouts.

Brice, *com.* and *sup.* of breac. More or most spotted.

Brice, *s. f.* (*from* breac.) Spottedness.

Brice, *s. f.* A brick.—*Macd.*

Bricean, ein, *s. m.* A sprat; a small trout.

Bric-shoirn, *s. f.* A brick-kiln.

† **Brìd**, *gen.* bride. *s. f.* A bridle. *Gr.* βρυτης. *Fr.* bride.

Brìde, *s. f.* A pimple. Written more frequently *fride.*

Brideach, ich, *s. m.* and *f.* (*Ir. id.*) A dwarf; a bride, a virgin. *N. pl.* bridichean. Cha bhrideach air an fhaich e, *he is not a dwarf in the field of battle.—Old Song.*

Brideachail, *a.* (brideach-amhuil.) Dwarfish; like a virgin, like a bride; bridal.

Brideag, eig, *s. f.* Part of the jaw.—*Shaw.*

Brigan. See **Briogan**.

Brigh, *s. f.* (*Scotch*, bree.) Sap, juice; essence; elixir; relish; vigour, pith, strength; capacity; substance, wealth; meaning, interpretation; virtue, valour; effect, avail, benefit; price; *rarely*, a tomb, a miracle. Craobh gun bhrigh, *a sapless tree;* briathran gun bhrigh, *words without pith, or without meaning;* innis da ar brigh, *tell him of our strength.—Oss. Carth.* Ged gheibhinn brigh Eirinn, *though I were to get the wealth of Ireland.—Fingalian Poem.* B'i so bu bhrigh d' an dàn, *this was the substance of their song.—Smith.* Is deacair brigh do sgeoil, *sad is the substance* [*subject*] *of thy tale.—Oss. Derm.* Ullin na brigh, *valiant Ullin.—Oss. Carth.* Caithidh cumha gun bhrigh, *weeping consumes without avail.—Oss. Croma.*

Brigh'ar, *a.* See **Brighmhor**.

† **Brighide**, *s. c.* A hostage.—*Shaw.*

Brighmhoire, *a.; com.* and *sup.* of brighmhoire.

Brighmhoireachd, *s. f.* Substantialness; juiciness; vigorousness.

Brighmhor, *a.* Substantial; juicy; vigorous; effectual. *Com.* and *sup.* brioghmhoire.

Brigh'or, *a.* See **Brighmhor**.

Brigis, *s. pl.* Breeches. See **Briogais**.

Brillean, ein, *s. m.* The clitoris.

Brilleanach, *a.* Lewd.

† **Brin**, *s. f.* A dream, a reverie.

† **Brin-dealan**, ain, *s. m.* A frontlet.—*Shaw.*

Brinneach, ich, *s. f.* An old woman; a hag; a mother.

Brinnichte, *a.* (*Ir. id.*) Hag-ridden.—*Shaw.*

† **Briochd**, *s. f.* (*Ir. id.*) A wound; an art, a trade; a beauty.—*Shaw.*

Briodal, ail, *s. m.* Chit-chat; flattery; caressing. Do bhriodal cùil, *the secret flattery.—Mac Lach.* Written also *briotal.*

Briodal, *v. a.* Caress, cajole, flatter, tattle; small talk. *Pret. a.* bhriodal, *caressed.*

Briodalach, *a.* Flattering; inclined to flatter or cajole; tattling. Is tu am fear briodalach, *a flattering fellow thou art.—R.* *Com.* and *sup.* briodalaiche, *more or most cajoling.*

Briodalachd, *s. f.* Tattling; a propensity to flatter.

Briodaladh, aidh, *s. m.* A caressing, a cajoling, a flattering, a tattling.

Briodaladh, (a), *pr. part.* of briodal. Caressing, cajoling, flattering, tattling. Ag am briodaladh, *caressing them.—Macint.*

Briodalaiche, *s. m.* A flatterer, a cajoler, a tattler; also the *com.* and *sup.* of briodalach.

† **Briog**, *s. f.* Confinement, restraint.

Briogaid, *s. f.* An elderly woman; a morose old female. Esan a phòsas briogaid, *he who marries a morose old woman.*—*Old Song.*

Briogais, *s. pl.* Breeches; trowsers. Briogais anairt, *linen breeches.*—*Stew. Lev.*

Lat. braccæ, a name given by the Romans to the covering for the thighs used by the Persians, Scythians, and Gauls. The word *braccæ* is used by Diodorus the Sicilian, St. Jerome, and Lucan; but the *laxæ braccæ* of the last seem to be the loose hose once used by mariners. *Swed.* bracka. *Teut.* bracca. *Arm.* brag. *Belg.* broeck. *Germ.* brechen. *It.* braga. *Syr.* brace. *Vulgar Gr.* βρακι. *Corn.* bryccan. *Sclav.* bregesche. In old French writers we find *bragues* and *bragis*, which were once pronounced as they spell. In Languedoc and in Gascony they still say *bragues.*

Briogan, ain, *s. m.* Breeches; trowsers. *Germ.* brechen. *Corn.* bryccan. *N. pl.* briogain.

Brioganach, *a.* (*from* briogan.) Having breeches or trowsers.

Briogh, *s.* See **Brigh**.

Brioghach, *a.* (*from* brìogh.) Juicy, substantial; efficacious.

Briollag, aig, *s. f.* An illusion. *Ir.* briollog.

Briollagach, *a.* Illusory; deceitful.

Briollair, *s. m.* A whoremonger; a lecherous fellow; one who is afflicted with incontinence of urine.

Briollan, ain, *s. m.* A chamber-pot; a urinal; an ignorant spiritless fellow.

Briollanach, *a.* Stupid; boorish; ignorant.

Briollanachd, *s. f.* Stupidity; boorishness; ignorance.

† **Brion**, *s. m.* A fiction, a lie; a drop.

† **Brionach**, aich, *s. m.* A liar.

Brionglaid, *s. f.* Confusion; a dream; a reverie.

Brionglaideach, *a.* Causing confusion; dreaming.

Brionnach, *a.* Pretty; fair; comely.—*Macint.* Also flattering, lying.

Brionnachd, *s. f.* Prettiness; comeliness; falsehood.

Brionnal, ail, *s. m.* Flattery; fawning, sycophancy; a caressing, a toying, flirting. Ni e brionnal, *he will flatter.*—*Sm.* Ri brionnal, *flirting.*

Brionnalach, *a.* Flattering, fawning, sycophantic; toying, flirting. *Com.* and *sup.* brionnalaiche, *more or most.*

Brionnalachd, *s. f.* A habit of flattering or fawning; sycophancy.

Brionndal, ail, *s. m.* See **Brionnal**.

Brionndalach, *a.* See **Brionnalach**.

Briosaid, *s. f.* A belt, a girdle. *N. pl.* briosaidean.

Briosaideach, *a.* Belted, girdled; like a belt or girdle.

Briosg, *s. f.* A start, a sudden movement through fear or joy; a very short space of time, an instant; a brisk movement.

Briosg, *v.* Start; move suddenly. *Pret. a.* bhriosg, *started*; *fut. aff. a.* briosgaidh, *shall or will start.* Briosgadh fiadh air Cromla, *let the deer start away from Cromla.*—*Oss. Fing.*

Briosgadh, (a), *pr. part.* of briosg.

Briosgadh, aidh, *s. m.* A starting, a sudden motion, a springing; briskness. Gun bhriosgadh, *without briskness.*—*Macint.*

Briosgaid, *s. f.* A biscuit. *N. pl.* briosgaidean.

† **Briot**, *a.* Speckled, spotted, piebald.

Briot, *s. f.* Chit-chat, tattle, small-talk, flattery.

Briotach, *a.* Chattering; prone to tattle; prattling.

Briotachan, ain, *s. m.* A prater; a tattling fellow.

Briotal, ail, *s. m.* Chit-chat, tattle, small-talk, flattery, caressing. Briotal a bheir gàir air gruagaichean, *chit-chat that makes maidens laugh.*—*Macfar.* See also **Briodal**.

Bris, *v. a.* Break, fracture, splinter, burst; break forth, exclaim; become insolvent. *Pret. a.* bhris; *fut. aff. a.* brisidh, *shall or will break.* Bhris fàire air monadh nan sruth, *dawn broke on the mountain of streams.*—*Oss.* Bhris e a shleagh, *he broke his spear.*—*Oss. Fing.* Gus am bris an là, *till break of dawn.*—*Stew. O. T.* Bhris le guth a graidh an oigh, *the maid exclaimed with her voice of love.*—*Oss.* Bhris e, *he failed*; brisidh an aimsir, *the weather will draw to rain.*

Lat. † briso. *Eng.* bruise. *Swed.* brista. *Old Sax.* brysan, *break.* *Teut.* brusan.

Brisdeach, *a.* Breaking, splintering; brittle. Written also *bristeach.*

Brisdeadh, idh, *s. m.* A breaking, a splintering, a bursting; a breach; a fissure. Luchd-bristidh mhionn, *the breaker of oaths.*—*Mac Lach.* Written also *bristeadh.*

Briseadh, 3 *sing. and pl. imperat.* of bris. Briseadh e, *let him break*; briseadh iad, *let them break.*

Briseadh, idh, *s. m.* (*Ir. id.*) A breaking, a bursting, a splintering; a breach, a break, a failure or insolvency. Gu briseadh na fàire, *till daybreak.*—*Stew. Gen.* Am briseadh so, *this breach.*—*Id.* Briseadh air bhriseadh, *breach upon breach.*—*Stew. Job.* Briseadh air son brisidh, *breach for breach.*—*Stew. Lev.* Briseadh-cridhe, *heart-break*; briseadh-céille, *derangement*; briseadh-mach, *an out-breaking of any kind, an eruption on the skin.*

Briseadh, (a), *pr. part.* of bris; which see.

Briseadh-céille, *s. m.* Derangement of mind.—*Oss. Tem.*

Briseadh-cridhe, *s. m.* A heart-breaking; dejection of mind; discouragement.—*Stew. Job.*

Briseadh-mach, *s. m.* An eruption, an out-breaking of any kind.

Brisg, *a.* Brittle; quick in motion, lively, active, hasty.

W. brysg, *brittle.* *Arm.* bresg. *Ir.* briosg. *Fr.* brusque, *lively.*

Brisg, *v. n.* See **Briosg**.

Brisg-bhuille, *s. m.* A smart blow, a sudden blow, a jerk.

Brisgean, ein, *s. m.* A gristle or cartilage; also wild skerret. Brisgean milis, *the sweet-bread of any creature.*

The brisgean, or wild skerret, is a succulent root not unfrequently used by the poorer people in some parts of the Highlands for bread or potatoes.

Brisgeanach, aich, *s. f.* Crackling, or the rind of roasted pork.

Brisgeanach, *a.* Abounding in gristle, gristly; like gristle.

Brisg-gheal, *a.* Limpid, clear.

Brisg-ghlòir, *s. f.* Loquacity; prattle.

Bris-ghloireach, *a.* Loquacious, prating.

Brisleach, ich, *s. f.* A breach; the dispersement or derout of an army.

Brislean, ein, *s. m.* White tansy.

Brisleanach, *a.* Like white tansy; abounding in white tansy; of, or belonging to, white tansy.

Briste', *for* bristeadh; which see.

Briste, *p. part.* of bris. Broken, bruised, wounded; splintered; insolvent. A ghairdean air clarsaich bhriste, *leaning on a broken harp.*—*Oss. Duthona.* Tha mo chridhe briste, *my heart is broken.*—*Stew. Jer.* Spiorad briste, *a bruised spirit.*—*Stew. Pro.* Fear briste, *a bankrupt.*

Bristeach, *a.* (*from* bris.) Brittle; inarticulate; broken, glimmering; splintering. Solus bristeach nan reultan, *the broken light of the stars.*—*Ull.* Fhuaim bhristeach d'ainme, *the inarticulate sound of thy name.*—*Oss. Gaul.*

Bristeadh, idh, *s. m.* A breaking, a bursting; a fissure, a crack; an opening; a break, a breach. Ro bhristeadh nan neul, *through the opening of the clouds.—Oss. Cathula.* Mar bhristeadh builgein, *like the bursting of bubbles.—Oss.*

BRIS-THROISG, *s. f.* A breakfast.

† BRO, *a.* Old, antique.—*Ir. id. Shaw.*

† BRO, *a.* Champion; a grinding-stone; a quern or hand-mill.

† BROC, *a.* Grey, dark-grey.

BROC, bruic, *s. m.* A badger, a brock. *N. pl.* bruic. Croicinne bhroc, *badgers' skins.—Stew. Exod. Arm.* and *Corn.* broch. *Ir.* broc.

BROCACH, *a.* Greyish; like a badger; speckled on the face, freckled, spotted.

BROCAIR, *s. m.* (*from* broc.) A badger-hunter; a fox-hunter. *N. pl.* brocairean.

BROCAIREACHD, *s. f.* Badger-hunting, fox-hunting.

BROCANTA, *a.* Shy, like a badger.

BROCHAILL, *s. f.* The name of the banner of Gaul, the son of Morni.

BROCHAN, ain, *s. m.* (*Ir.* brocan. *W.* brwchan.) Porridge, pottage. Brochan do ghall-pheasair, *pottage of lentiles.—Stew. Gen.* A phoit bhrochain, *the pottage (porridge) pot.—Stew.* 1 *K.*

BROCHD, *s. m.* (*Corn.* broch.) A badger. See BROC.

BROCHDACH, *a.* Variegated, greyish, spotted; coloured like a badger.

BROCLACH, aich, *s. f.* A warren. *N. pl.* broclaich.

BROC-LANN, -luinn, *s. m.* A badger's den; a cavern, the hole or hiding-place of any wild beast. Ceum an sealgair 'n caradh a bhroc-luinn, *the huntsman steps towards his den.—Oss. Conn.*

BROC-LUIDH, *s. m.* A badger's den; a den or cavern, the hole or hiding-place of any wild beast. Broc-luidh aig na sionnaich, *foxes have holes.—Stew. Mark, ref.*

BROD, broid, *s.* (*Ir.* brod. *Dan.* brod. *Scotch,* brod.) A goad, a prickle, a sting. *N. pl.* brodan.

BROD, broid, *s.* (*Scotch,* brod.) A lid; a small board; the best of grain, or of any other substance.

BROD, *v. a.* Stimulate, goad. *Pret. a.* bhròd, *stimulated; fut. aff. a.* bròdaidh, *shall stimulate.*

BRÒD, bròid, *s. m.* A crowd, a swarm; pride, arrogance; chastisement. Féin spéis agus bròd, *self-conceit and arrogance.—Old Song.*

† BROD, bròid, *s. m.* A blemish, a spot. *It.* broda, *dirt.*

BRÒDACH, *a.* In crowds, in swarms; arrogant.

BRODACH, *a.* Goading, stimulative, prickling; stirring up.

BRODADH, aidh, *s. m.* A goading or spurring; a winnowing; a stirring up.

BRODAIL, *a.* Proud, arrogant.

BROD-GHAINEAMH, imh, *s. f.* Gravel.—*Macd. and Shaw.*

† BRODH, *s. m.* A straw, a stem.—*Shaw.*

BROD-IASG, -eisg, *s. m.* A needle-fish.

BRÒG, BRÒIG, *s. f.* Sorrow; a house, a village. *Bròg,* in the last two senses, is also written *borg* and *burg;* which see. Bhuail an t-earrach bròg orm, *the spring has smitten me with grief.—Macfar.*

BRÒG, BRÒIG, *s. f.* (*Ir.* brog. *Scotch,* brogue.) A sandal, a shoe; *by a figure of speech,* a foot. *N. pl.* bròga *and* brògan. Cuir dhiot do bhròga, *put off thy shoes.—Stew. Exod.* O mhullach gu bròig, *from head to foot.—Macint.* Bròg na cuthaig, *butterwort.*

The Highland *bròg* was made of a piece of raw hide, with the hair turned inwards, and tied before and behind with a thong.

BROG, *v. a.* (*Scotch,* brog.) Spur, stimulate, goad. *Pret.* bhrog, *spurred; fut. aff.* brogaidh, *shall spur.*

BROGACH, *a.* Sturdy; also lewd, filthy, nasty.

BROGACH, aich, *s. m.* A sturdy little fellow. *N. pl.* brogaich.

BROGACH, *a.* Spurring, goading, stimulating.

BRÒGACH, *a.* (*from* brog.) Shod; having large shoes; like a shoe; of, or belonging to, a shoe: also strong-hoofed, in which sense it is applied to one of Cuchullin's horses.—*Oss. Fing.* Bi curraiceach brògach brochanach, *be ye well-hooded, well-shod, and well-fed.—G. P.*

BROGAIDH, *s.* A name given to a cow that puts with her horns; a squat sturdy fellow, *in derision.*

BROGAIL, *a.* Sturdy, lively, active; hale. Bodach brogail, *a lively old man.*

BRÒGAIR, *s. m.* (*from* brog.) A shoemaker, a cobbler. *N. pl.* brogairean.

BRÒGAIREACHD, *s. f.* Shoemaking, cobbling.

BROGALACHD, *s. f.* Sturdiness, activity.

BROGANACH, aich, *s. m.* A lively, sturdy fellow. *N. pl.* broganaiche.

BROGANACH, *a.* Lively, sturdy, jocose. Bodach broganach, *a sturdy old man.*

BROGANTA, *a.* Lively, sturdy, active. Bodach broganta, *a sturdy old man;* cailleach bhroganta, *a lively old woman.*

† BROGH, *s. m.* Filthiness, dirt.—*Ir. id. Shaw.*

† BROGHACH, *a.* Filthy, dirty; also excessive, superfluous. *Ir.* broghdha.

† BROGHAIN, *s. f.* Excess, superfluity.—*Shaw.*

BROG-NA-CUTHAIG, *s. f.* The flower called butterwort.

BROICE, *s. f.* A mole, a freckle.

BROICEAN, ein, *s. m.* (*Ir.* broicne.) A freckle, a mole.

BROICNEACH, *a.* (*from* broicean.) Freckled. Aghaidh bhroicneach, *a freckled face.*

† BROIDINNEAL, eil, *s. m.* A richly-embroidered garb.—*Ir. id.*

BROID-INEALTA, *a.* Embroidered.

BROIGHEAL, il, *s. m.* A cormorant, a sea-raven.

BROIGHLEAG, eig, *s. f.* A whortle-berry, *vitis Idæa* of naturalists. Written also *braoileag.*

BROIGHLEAGACH, *a.* Abounding in whortle-berries.

BRAOILEACH, *a.* Bustling, noisy, tumultuous.

BROILEADH, idh, *s. m.* Bustle, confusion, turmoil; loud noise.

BROILICH, *s. f.* Noise, bawling, confusion, tumult; continued noise. Written *braoilich.*

BROILLEACH, ich, *s. f.* A breast, a bosom. A broilleach mar chobhar nan stuadh, *her breast like the foam of the waves.—Oss. Carthon.* 'Na bhroilleach, *in his bosom.—Stew. Exod.* Written also *brollach.*

† BROIMEIS, *s. f.* Anger; boldness.—*Shaw.*

BRÒIN, *gen. sing.* of bròn.

BRÒIN, *v. a.* Mourn, lament, deplore. *Pret. a.* bhròin, *mourned; fut. aff. a.* bròinidh, *shall or will mourn.*

† BROIN, *s. f.* A height; a large company.—*Ir. id. Shaw.*

BRÒINEAG, eig, *s. f.* (*from* bròn.) A disconsolate female; a querulous female.

BROINEAG, eig, *s. f.* A little rag. *N. pl.* broineagan, *rags; asp. form,* bhroineagan. Seann bhroineagan, *old rags.—Stew. Jer.*

BROINEAGACH, *a.* Ragged; full of rags.

BROINEAN, ein, *s. m.* (*from* bròn.) A sickly person; a querulous, complaining person.

BROINN, *gen. sing.* of brù. *Ir.* broinne. See BRÙ.

BROINN-DEARG, -deirg, *s. m.* The robin-redbreast.

BROISDE, *s. f.* A brooch.

BROISG, *v. a.* Excite, incite, stir up, provoke. *Pret. a.* bhroisg; *fut. aff. a.* broisgidh, *shall provoke.*

† BROISNEAN, ein, *s. m.* A small faggot.

† BROITH, *s.* Carnation colour.—*Ir. id.*

BROLASGACH, *a.* Talkative.

Brolasgadh, aidh, *s. m.* Loquacity.

Brollach, aich, *s. m.* (*Ir. id.*) A breast; a bosom; brisket; a preface. A' bhrollach leònta, *his wounded breast.—Oss. Dargo.* Am brollach a bhàis, *in the bosom of death.—Oss. Tem.* Written also *broilleach.*

† **Brollachan**, ain, *s. m.* A ragged person.

† **Bromach**, *s. m.* A colt.—*Ir. id. Shaw. N. pl.* bromaiche.

Broman, ain, *s. m.* A rustic; a rude person, a booby.—*Ir. id.*

Bromanach, *a.* Rustic, rude, boorish.—*Ir. id.*

† **Bron**, *a.* Perpetual. *Shaw.*

Bròn, broin, *s. m.* (*W.* brwyn. *Ir.* brón.) Grief; sorrow; mourning; wailing, weeping. Fà mo bhròin, *the cause of my mourning.—Oss. Taura.* Eiridh bròin, *the rising of grief.—Oss. Conn.* Ainnir ri bron na h-aonar, *a maiden wailing in solitude.—Oss.* Mo bhròn! *alas! woe's me!*

Brònach, *a.* (*from* bròn.) *Ir. id.* Sorrowful; sad; mournful; mourning. Le cumha brònach, *with sad lamentation.—Stew. Mic.* Guth nan oighean bronach, *the voice of the mourning maidens.—Orran. Com.* and *sup.* bronaiche.

† **Bronadh**, aidh, *s. m.* Destruction.

Brònadh, (a), *p. part.* of bròin. Deploring. Fionn 'g ad bhrònadh, *Fingal deploring thee.—Death of Carril.*

Bròn-bhrat, -bhrait, *s. m.* A mortcloth or pall.

Bròn-chuimhne, *s. f.* A sad remembrance. Bhur bròn-chuimhne, *the sad remembrance of you.—Oss. Taura.*

† **Bronn**, *v. a.* Distribute, divide.

Bronn, *gen. sing.* of bru. Of a belly. *Ir.* brun *and* bronn. *Arm.* brun.

† **Bronn**, broinn, *s. f.* A breast; a favour; a track, a mark. *Ir. id.*

Bronnach, *a.* Swag-bellied, gluttonous; bagged, bellied; well-fed. Caoraich bhronnach, *well-fed sheep.—Macfar.*

Bronnach, aich, *s. m.* A girth or belly-band.

† **Bronnadh**, aidh, *s. m.* A distributing, a bestowing; generosity.—*Ir. id. Shaw.*

Bronnag, aig, *s. f.* A gudgeon; a little bulky female.—*N. pl.* bronnagan.

Bronn-ghabh, *v.* Conceive, as a female.

Bronn-ghabhail, *s. f.* (*Ir. id.*) A conception; the act of conceiving, as a female does.

Bronn-sgaoileadh, idh, *s. m.* A flux or dysentery.

Bronn-sgaoilteach, *a.* Causing a flux or dysentery.

† **Bronnta**, *a.* Bestowed; given away, distributed.—*Ir. id. Shaw.*

† **Bronntas**, ais, *s. m.* A gift; a favour; a track.—*Ir. id.*

Bronnthach, aich, *s. m.* A girth; a belt, a belly-band. Written also *bronnach.*

Brosduich, *v. a.* See **Brosnuich**.

Brosgadh, aidh, *s. m.* An exhortation; an incitement.

Brosgul, uil, *s. m.* Flattery; lively talk.

Brosglach, *a.* (*for* brosgulach.) Lively; active, brisk, prompt, clever; flattering, loquacious. *Com.* and *sup.* brosgulaiche, *more or most flattering.*

Brosglachadh, **Brosgluchadh**, aidh, *s. m.* The act of flattering; a cheering up, briskening.

Brosglachadh, (a), *pr. part.* of brosglaich.

Brosglaich, **Brosgluich**, *v. a.* Cheer up; flatter. *Pret. a.* bhrosglaich; *fut. aff. a.* brosglaichidh, *shall cheer up.* Bhrosglaich e ri faicinn an righ, *he cheered up on seeing the king.—Oss. Conn.*

† **Brosna**, ai, *s. m.* A faggot.—*Ir. id.*

Brosnachadh, **Brosnuchadh**, aidh, *s. m.* An incitement, a provocation, a spurring on. *Ir.* brosdachadh. Mar anns a bhrosnuchadh, *as in the provocation.—Stew. Heb.* Brosnuchadh cath, *a battle song, an incitement to battle.*

Brosnachadh, **Brosnuchadh**, (a), *pr. part.* of brosnaich or brosnuich; which see.

Brosnachail, *a.* Instigating.

Brosnaich, **Brosnuich**, *v. a.* Provoke, incite, spur on; actuate. *Pret. a.* bhrosnaich, *provoked; fut. aff. a.* brosnaichidh, *shall provoke.* Bhrosnaich thu mi, *thou hast provoked me.—Stew. O. T.*

Brosnaichte, **Brosnuichte**, *part.* Provoked, incited, actuated.

Brosnuchadh, aidh, *s. m.* see **Brosnachadh**.

Brot, *s. m.* Broth. *It.* broda. *Ir.* broth.

Brotachadh, aidh, *s. m.* Improving; improving in personal appearance; thriving; fattening.

Brotachadh, (a), *pr. part.* of brotaich.

Brotaich, *v. a. & n.* Improve in appearance; improve in bodily appearance; fatten, grow fat. *Pret. a.* bhrotaich, *grew fat; fut. aff. a.* brotaichidh, *shall or will grow fat.*

† **Broth**, *s. m.* A mole, a ditch; a straw; flesh, fire.—*Ir. id.*

Broth, *s. m.* A cutaneous eruption; a bruise. In this last sense the orthography is more frequently *bruth* and *bruthadh*; which see.

Brothach, *a.* Scabbed, mangy. Cu brothach, *a mangy dog;* caor bhrothach, *a scabbed sheep.*

Brothag, aig, *s. f.* A bosom; a little ditch; a little hollow. *N. pl.* brothagan.

Brothair, *s. m.* A bruiser; also a butcher; a caldron.

Brothaireachd, *s. f.* Bruising, mauling, maiming; butchering.

Brothas, ais, *s. m.* Farrago, brewis.

Brothlach, aich, *s. m.* A place for dressing meat.

Brothlain, *s. m.* A part of the internals of a sheep called the king's-hood.

Brothluinn, *s. f.* Agitation, confusion, struggle; the struggle betwixt wind and tide.

Broth-luinneach, *a.* Agitative, causing commotion; disturbed.

Broth-thigh, *s. m.* A slaughter-house, shambles. *N. pl.* broth-thighean.

Bru, *gen.* broinn *or* bronn, *s. f.* (*W.* and *Corn.* bru *and* bry. *Ir.* bru. *Arm.* brun, *belly.*) A belly, a womb. A bru torrach, *her womb pregnant.—Stew. Jer.* Torradh na bronn, *the fruit of the womb.—Stew. Gen.* Air do bhroinn, *on thy belly.—Id.* Bru-ghoirt, *a belly-ache;* làn-bronn, *a bellyful;* cha lion beannachd brù, *blessings do not fill a belly.—G. P.* Is mo do shuilean na do bhrù, *your eyes are bigger than your belly.—Id.*

† **Bru**, *s. f.* A hind; a country, a bank.—*Shaw.*

Bruach, bruaiche, *s. f.* (*It.* bracca. *Ir.* bruach. *Scotch,* brae.) A bank; a steep, a precipice; an edge, brim, brink, border; a short ascent. *N. pl.* bruachan; *dat. pl.* bruachaibh. A dìreadh na bruaiche thall, *climbing the further bank.—Oss. Conn.* Mar chrith reo air bruachaibh na Leig, *like a hoar-frost on the banks of Lego.—Oss.* Mar bhruaiche san duibhre, *like a precipice in the dark.—Oss. Comala.* Mu bhruaichaibh do leapach, *about thy bed-sides.—Old Song.*

Bruachag, aig, *s. f.* (*dim.* of bruach.) A little bank; a little precipice. *N. pl.* bruachagan.—*Macint.* A shobhrach nam bruachag, *thou primrose of the banks.—Macdon.*

Bruachair, *s. m.* (*from* bruach.) A lounger; a hoverer.

Bruachaireachd, *s. f.* Hovering about, lounging.

Bruachan, ain, *s. m.* A short ascent, a little bank; *rarely* a fawn.

† **Bruachdach**, *a.* Magnificent.

Bruadair, *gen. sing.* of bruadar. Of a dream.

Bruadair, *v. a.* Dream. *Pret. a.* bhruadair, *dreamed;*

fut. aff. a. bruadairidh, *shall or will dream.* Bhruadair mi bruadar, *I dreamed a dream.—Stew. O. T.*

Bruadar, air, *s. m.* (*Ir. id.*) A dream, a reverie. *N. pl.* bruadaran. Tra dh' aomas bruadar mar cheò, *when a dream descends like a mist.—Oss. Derm.*

Bruadaradh, aidh, *s. m.* A dreaming; the act of dreaming.

Bruadaradh, (a), *pr. part.* of bruadair. Dreaming.

Bruadaraiche, *s. m.* A dreamer.

† Bruaidh, *s. m.* A peasant. *N. pl.* bruaidhean.—*Ir. id.*

Bruaidlean, ein, *s. m.* Grief, melancholy. A cheann fo bhruaidlein, *his head dropping under grief.—Oss. Gaul.*

Bruaidleaneach, *a.* Grieved, vexed; causing grief or vexation; disturbed. Is bruaidleanach m' aigne, *my thoughts are disturbed.—Old Song.*

Bruaidleaneachd, *s. f.* Grief; melancholy; the state of being grieved or vexed; disturbance.

Bruaillean, ein, *s. m.* Murmur, confusion; stir; tumult; noise; annoyance; trouble. Loch gun bhruaillein, *a quiet lake.—Oss. Fing.* Chuir mi bruaillean air an oigh, *I have troubled the maid.—Oss.*

Bruan, *v. a.* Break in bits; crumble, pound, pulverize; smash. *Pret. a.* bhruan, *smashed; fut. aff. a.* bruanaidh, *shall or will smash.*

Bruan, bruain, *s. m.* A morsel; a fragment, a bit, a splinter; a crumb. Chaidh iad nam bruan, *they went to splinters.—Macfar.*

Bruanach, *a.* Causing to crumble, pound, or break; crumbled, pounded.

Bruanachd, *s. f.* Continued or frequent smashing; the state of being in smashes or crumbled.

Bruanadh, aidh, *s. m.* A breaking, a crumbling, a smashing; a crashing noise. Bruanabh o na cnocaibh, *crashing from the hills.—Stew. Zeph.*

Bruanadh, (a), *pr. part.* of bruan.

Bruanag, aig, *s. f.* (*dim.* of bruan.) A morsel, a crumb, a piece. *N. pl.* bruanagan.

Bruanagach, *a.* Full of crumbs; apt to fall into crumbs.

Bruanan, ain, *s. m.* (*dim.* of bruan.) A morsel, a crumb, a piece, a fragment. *N. pl.* bruanain. *Corn.* breuyonen *and* bruenen. *Arm.* bruhunen *and* bryenen.

Bruansgail, *s. f.* A deep crashing noise, a grating noise, a clashing noise. Mar eith na Lèig a bruansgail, *deeply crashing like the ice of Lego.—Oss. Duthona.* Written also *bruasgail.*

Bruasgail, *s. f.* A deep crashing noise, a grating noise; a clashing. Feadh bhruasgail lann is chrann is chnamhan, *amid the crashing of swords and spears and bones.—Oss. Dargo.* Written also *bruansgail.*

Bruanspealt, *v. a.* Splinter, smash; hack down, hew. *Pret. a.* bhruanspealt, *splintered; fut. aff. a.* bruanspealtaidh, *shall splinter.*

Bruanspealtach, *a.* Splintering, smashing, crashing.

Bruanspealtadh, aidh, *s. m.* A splintering, a crashing, a smashing; a hewing down.

Bruanspealtadh, (a), *pr. part.* of bruanspealt. Splintering, crashing, hewing down, smashing. A bruanspealtadh chraobh, *hewing down trees.—Mac Lach.*

Brucach, *a.* Spotted, especially in the face; freckled, speckled, pimpled. Caitean brucach, *spotted shag.—Macdon.*

Brucainneach, *a.* Spotted, freckled, speckled, pimpled. Eudan brucainneach, *a pimpled face.—Macint.*

Brucainneachd, *s. f.* Spottedness; freckledness.

Bruchag, aig, *s. f.* A chink; an eyelet; a leaky vessel, a leaky boat. Cha bu bhruchag air meirg i, *she was not a leaky vessel.—Old Song.*

Brùchd, *s. m.* A belch, a rift; a bilge; a sally; a rushing forth.

Brùchd, *v. n.* Belch, rift; bilge; sally; rush out; burst; pour. *Pret. a.* bhrùchd, *rushed out; fut. aff. a.* brùchdaidh, *shall or will rush out.* Bhrùchd iad gu 'r còghnadh, *they rushed to our aid.—Ull.* Brùchdaidh a dheoir, *his tears shall burst forth.—Oss. Trathal.* Bhrùchd an tuil o'n aonach, *the flood poured from the hill.—Oss. Fin. and Lorm.*

Brùchdach, *a.* Causing a rift, or belch, or sally; of, or pertaining to, a rift, belch, or sally.

Brùchdadh, aidh, *s. m.* A sallying, belching; a rushing out; a pouring.

Bruchdail, *s. f.* A rifting; a rushing; a bilging; a belching.

Bruchlas, ais, *s. m.* The fluttering of fowls going to rest or to roost.

† Brudan, ain, *s. m.* A simmering noise; also a salmon. In the latter sense it is almost always written *bradan.*

Brudhainn, *s. f.* Warmth, sultriness.

Brudhainneach, *a.* Warm, sultry.

Brudhainneachd, *s. f.* A continuance of warmth; sultriness.

Brudhaiteach, ich, *s. m.* A threadbare coat.

Bru-dhearg, -dheirg, *s. m.* A robin-redbreast.

† Brug, Brugh, *s.* (*Ir. id.*) A large house; a village; a hillock, the residence of fairies; a tower; a fortified town.

Germ. bruiga. *Franc.* briga. *Span.* braga. *Eng.* burgh. Hence the Latin termination in *briga* of the names of certain places, as Latobriga, Samobriga, and the Greek termination in *bria,* as Mesambria. Hence also the name Phryges, a people who were formerly called Bryges, or Bruges, according to Strabo, lib. xvii.

Brug seems to be but another form of *borg* or *burg;* which see.

Brughach, aich, *s. m.* A steep ascent, an acclivity. Written also *bruthach;* which see. *N. pl.* brughaichean.

Brughaiche, *s. m.* A burgher; a farmer.—*Shaw.*

Bruich, *v. a.* Boil, seethe, simmer. *Pret. a.* bhruich, *boiled; fut. aff. a.* bruichidh, *shall or will boil.* Cha bhruich e meann, *he shall not seethe a kid.—Stew. Exod.* 2 *pl. imperat.* bruichibh, *boil ye.* Bruichibh an fheòil, *boil the flesh.* Bruicheadh e, *let him boil.—Id.* Written also *bruith.*

Bruich, *a.* (*Ir.* bruithe.) Boiled; seethed; sultry. *Asp. form,* bhruich. La bruich, *a sultry day;* feòil bhruich, *boiled flesh.*

Bruicheadh, 3 *sing. and pl. imperat.* of bruich; which see.

Bruicheadh, idh, *s. m.* A boiling; a decoction; a seething.

Bruicheadh, (a), *pr. part.* of Bruich. Boiling, seething.

Bruicheil, *a.* (bruich-amhuil.) Sultry; somewhat sultry.

Bruichidh, *fut. aff. a.* of bruich. Shall or will boil.

Bruichte, *p. part.* of bruich. Boiled, seethed.

Bruid, *v. a.* Torture, oppress, enslave. *Pret. a.* bhruid; *fut. aff.* bruididh.—*Shaw.*

Bruid, *s. f.* (*Ir.* bruid.) Captivity; a stab, a thrust. Bheir mi air a h-ais am bruid, *I will cause their captivity to return.—Stew. Jer.*

Brùid, *s. m.* A brute, a beast; a brutal person. *N. pl.* brùidean, *brutes. Lat.* brut-us.

Brùidean, *n. pl.* of brùid.

Brùideil, *a.* (*from* brùid.) Brutal, beastly. *Ir.* bruidamhail.

Brùideileachd, *s. f.* (brùid-amhuileachd.) Brutality, beastliness. *Ir.* bruidamhlacht.

† Bruidhe, *s. f.* A farm.—*Ir. id.* Written also *bruighe.*

Bruidheachd, *s. f.* A colony.—*Ir. id.*

Bruidheann, inn, *s. f.* Written also *bruidhinn;* which see.

Bruidhinn, bruidhne, *s. f.* Talk, speech, conversation; a quarrel; a report. Tha e ri bruidhinn, *he is talking.—Stew. 1 K. ref.* Fear na mòr bhruidhne, *the talkative man.—Stew. Job.*

Bruidhneach, *a.* (*contr. for* bruidheannach.) Talkative;

querulous, loud. Tha i bruidhneach, *she is [loud] talkative.—Stew. Pro. ref.*

Bruidleachadh, aidh, *s. m.* A stirring up of the surface, a digging.

Bruidleachadh, (a), *pr. part.* of bruidlich. Digging, stirring up of the surface.

Bruidlich, *v. a.* Stir up, dig. *Pret. a.* bhruidlich, *stirred up; fut. aff. a.* bruidlichidh, *shall or will stir up.*

Bruigheann, inn, *s. m.* A palace.

† **Bruim-fheur**, -fheòir, *s.* Switch-grass.—*Shaw.*

Bruin, *s. f.* A caldron; a kettle; a belly.

Brùin, *v. n.* Make a rattling noise. *Pret. a.* bhrùin; *fut. aff. a.* brùinidh.

Bruine, Bruinne, *s. f.* A waist; a chest. Bruinne seang, *a slender waist.—Old Song.*

Bruinard, *a.* Having a high breast or chest; high-bosomed. An ainnir bhruinard, *the high-bosomed maid.—Old Poem.* Anacreon makes mention of deep-bosomed maids.

Brùinidh, *s.m.* A spectral being called *brownie.* See **Uruisg.**

† **Bruinneach**, *s. c.* A nurse; a mother; a glutton.

Bruinneadach, aich, *s. m.* An apron.—*Shaw.*

Bruinnean, ein, *s. m.* The knap of cloth.

Bruinneanach, *a.* (*from* bruinnean.) Knappy, as cloth.

Brùis, *s. pl.* Shivers, splinters, fragments.

Bruis, *s. f.* A brush. *N. pl.* bruisean *and* bruiseachan.

Bruisinn, *s. f.* A brushing. *Asp. form,* bhruisinn.

Bruisinn, *v. a.* Brush. *Pret. a.* bhruisinn, *brushed, fut. aff. a.* bruisinnidh, *shall brush.*

Brùite, *p. part.* of brùth. (*Dan.* brudt.) Bruised, broken, crushed, oppressed. Daoine brùite truagh, *poor oppressed men.—Smith.* Tha m' anam brùite, *my soul is bruised.—Id.* Osnadh bhrùite a' d' chliabh, *a broken sigh within thy breast.—Old Poem.* Fùil bhrùite, *extravasated blood.—Old Poem.*

Bruith, *v. a.* Boil, seethe, simmer. *Pret. a.* bhruith; *fut. aff. a.* bruithidh, *shall boil.*

Bruitheadh, idh, *s. m.* A boiling, seething, or simmering.

Bruitheadh, (a), *pr. part.* of bruith.

Bruitheadh, 3 *sing. and pl. imper.* of bruith.

† **Bruithneach**, *a.* Glowing; red hot. *Com.* and *sup.* bruithniche.

Brùliontach, *a.* Satiating, cloying.

Brulionta, *a.* Satiated, cloyed. *Ir.* bruidhlionta.

Brumair, *s. m.* A pedant.—*Shaw.* *N. pl.* brumairean.

Brumaireachd, *s. f.* Pedantry.

† **Brun**, bruin, *s.* A firebrand.

Brus, *v. n.* Browse. *Pret. a.* bhrus; *fut. aff. a.* brusaidh, *shall browse.*

† **Bruscar**, air, *s. m.* Broken ware; baggage.

Bruth, *s. f.* (*Ir. id.*) A cave; the dwelling of fairies; dew; a bruise; *rarely* the hair of the head; heat; any thing red hot. Am mairiche ag eisdeachd o bhruth, *the mariner listening from his cave.—Ull.*

Brùth, *v. a.* (*Ir.* bruth. *Dan.* brud. *Swed.* brod. *Arm.* bruvo.) Bruise; pound; crush, squeeze, compress. *Pret. a.* bhruth, *bruised; fut. aff. a.* bruthaidh.

Bruthach, aich, *s. m.* and *f.* An ascent; a steep; a hill side; a precipice. Ri bruthach, *upwards, hillwards;* le bruthach, *downwards.* Fo chraig na bruthaich, *under the rock of the steep.—Oss. Tem.* Ruithidh an taigeis féin ri bruthach, *the haggis itself will run down hill.—G. P.*

Bruthadair, *s.m.* (*from* bruth.) A pestle; a pounder; a bruiser. *N.pl.* bruthadairean. Le bruthadair, *with a pestle.*

Bruthadaireachd, *s. f.* (*from* bruth.) A pounding, a bruising, a crushing; pugilism.

Bruthadh, aidh, *s. m.* A bruising; a pounding, as with a pestle; a crushing; a bruise, a crush. *Germ.* bruch, *a fracture.*

Bruthadh, (a), *pr. part.* of bruth. Bruising; pounding; crushing; squeezing.

Bruthaidh, 3 *sing. and pl.* of bruth. Shall or will bruise.

Bruthaidh, *fut. aff. a.* of bruth. Shall or will bruise.

Bruthainneach, *a.* Hot, sultry. Aimsir bhruthainneach, *sultry weather.*

Bruthaiste, *s. f.* (*Anglo-Sax.* briwas.) A mess composed of oatmeal on which boiling water has been poured, and which is then stirred about; by the Lowland Scots called *brose.* Bruthaiste is mairt-fheoil, *brose and beef.—Macd.*

Bu ! A sound to excite terror.

Bu, *preterite of the def. verb* Is. (*W.* bu. *Ir.* bu.) Was, wert, were. Bu dorcha a mhala, *dark was his brow.—Oss. Lod.* Taibhse bu ghlaise snuadh, *a spectre of the palest visage.—Id.*

Bu, before a vowel or *f* aspirated, is written *b'*; as, b'aille leam, *I would like;* b' fhearr leam, *I had rather.*

Buabhall, aill, *s. m.* A cornet, a trumpet; an unicorn, a buffalo. See **Buabhull.**

Buabhallach, *a.* Like a trumpet, unicorn, or buffalo; of, or pertaining to, a trumpet, unicorn, or buffalo.

Buabhallaiche, *s. m.* A trumpeter.

Buabhall-chorn, *s.* (*W.* bual-gorn.) A bugle-horn.

Buabhull, uill, *s. m.* A cornet; a trumpet; an unicorn, a buffalo. Fuaim a bhuabhuill, *the sound of the cornet.—Stew. O. T.* O adhaircibh nam buabhull, *from the horns of the unicorn.—Smith.*

Corn. buaval, *a trumpet.* *Ir.* buabhal. *Arm.* bual, *a buffalo.*

In *buabhull* we may see the *Gr.* βουβαλος. *Lat.* bubulus. *Fr.* bufle.

Buabhullaiche, *s. m.* A trumpeter.

Buabhull-chorn, *s.* (*W.* bual-gorn.) A bugle-horn.

† **Buacachan**, ain, *s. m.* A bleacher.

† **Buacais**, *s. f.* The wick of a candle.

† **Buach**, buaich, *s.* (*Ir. id.*) Buck-yarn, cloth; bleaching; the brow of a hill; a vault; a cap.—*Shaw.*

† **Buachach**, *a.* Fine, beauish.

Buachaill, *s. m.* A cowherd; a shepherd, a herd; protector; also a youth.—*Macd.* *N. pl.* buachaillean. Is buachaillean na daoine, *the men are shepherds.—Stew. Gen.* Am buachaill da 'n còir, *the herd near them.—Macdon.*

Arm. bugall, *a boy.* *W.* bygel, *a cowherd.* *Corn.* begel *and* bugel. *Ir.* buachail. *Box. Lex.* bugiul. *Gr.* βουκόλος.

Buachailleach, *a.* Pastoral; of, or belonging to, a shepherd or cowherd.

Buachailleachd, *s. f.* The occupation of herding. Ris a bhuachailleachd, *herding;* ri buachailleachd, *herding.*

Buachaill-seomair, *s. m.* A valet-de-chambre.

Buachar, air, *s. m.* Cow's dung; the dung of cattle in general; a dunghill; a stall. Buachar bhò, *cow-dung.—Stew. Ezek.* Dubh-chail a bhuachair, *a dunghill trollop.—Old Song.* *Heb.* bakar, *ox or cow.* *Chald.* bakar.

Buadh, buaidh, *s. m.* and *f.* Sustenance; food; also *gen. pl.* of buaidh; which see.

Buadhach, *a.* (*from* buadh.) *Ir.* buadha. Victorious; also having virtues. Connal buadhach, *victorious Connal.—Oss. Cathula.*

Buadhach, aich, *s. m.* (*from* buaidh.) A champion; a conqueror; a tribute. Gheibh am buadhach, *the conqueror shall receive.—Mac Lach.*

Buadhachadh, aidh, *s. m.* The act of conquering; a conquest.

Buadhachadh, (a), *pr. part.* of buadhaich. Conquering.

Buadhaich, *v.* Conquer, overthrow; prevail, subject. *Pret. a.* bhuadhaich, *conquered; fut. aff. a.* buadhaichidh, *shall* *conquer.* Bhuadhaich fheachd, *his army conquered.—Oss. Duthona.* Bhuadhaich tonn is gaoth, *the east winds and its waves prevailed.—Oss. Carthon.*

Buadhair, *s. m.* A conqueror; a champion. *N. pl.* buadh-airean.

† Buadhal, *a.* Victorious.—*Ir. id.*

Buadhalachd, *s. f.* Prosperity; conquest; a flourishing condition. Am buadhalachd, *in prosperity.—Macint.*

Buadhar, *a.* See Buadhmhor.

Buadhas, ais, *s. m.* Victory, conquest; a succession of victories.

Buadhdharg, airg, *s. m.* A victorious champion.—*Shaw.*

Buadh-ghallan, ain, *s. m.* Rag-weed.

Buadh-ghuth, *s. m.* A triumphant shouting; clamour.

Buadhlan-buidhe, *s. m.* Ragwort.—*Macd.*

Buadhmhoire, *com.* and *sup.* of buadhmhor.

Buadh-mhor, *a.* (*Ir.* buadh-mhar.) Victorious, triumphant. Breatunnaich nan arm buadh-mhor, *Britons of victorious arms.—Death of Carril.* *Com.* and *sup.* buadhmhoire.

† Buaf, *s. m.* A toad; any ugly venomous creature.—*Ir. id.*

† Buafach, *a.* Venomous.—*Ir. id.*

† Buafair, *s. m.* An adder.—*Shaw.*

Buag, buaig, *s. m.* A spigot, a plug. *N. pl.* buagan.

Buagair, *s. m.* A faucet, or pipe inserted into a vessel to give vent to the liquor, and stopped up by a peg or spigot. —*Shaw.*

† Buagair, *v. a.* Tap, as a hogshead.—*Shaw.*

Buaghar, air, *s. m.* (*Lat.* boarius, *relating to oxen.*) A herd; a shepherd; a cow-herd. Thachair orra buaghar bhò, *a cow-herd met them.—Fingalian Legend.*

Buagharra, *a.* Grieved, vexed; also vexatious, oppressive. Mios bhuagharra, *an oppressive month.—Macfar.*

Buaic, Buaichd, *s. f.* (*Ir.* buaic.) The wick of a candle, lamp, or torch; *rarely* a wave.

Buaiceach, *a.* Giddy, light-headed, thoughtless; of, or belonging to, a wick; having a wick.

Buaicean, *n. pl.* of Buaic.

Buicean, ein, *s. m.* A veil; a lappet; a little wick.

Buaiceis, *s. f.* A small wick.—*Shaw.*

Buaidh, *v.* Conquer; overcome. This verb takes after it the preposition *air*, simple or compounded; as, buaidh orra, *conquer them;* bhuaidh e orm, *he conquered me.*

Buaidh, *s. f.* (*Ir.* buaidh. *Corn.* budh.) *N. pl.* buaidhean, *and sometimes* buadhannan. Victory, conquest, success, palm; qualification, accomplishment mental or bodily; virtue, excellence, attribute; gem. Buaidh sa chomhstri, *victory in the strife.—Oss. Comala.* Buaidh leat, *success to you;* beannachd is buaidh leat, *blessing and success go with you.* Malmhin nam buadh, *virtuous or accomplished Malvina.—Oss. Carricth.* Thoir buaidh, *conquer;* thug coigrich buaidh, *strangers conquered.* Deadh bhuadhannan naduir, *excellent natural accomplishments.—Old Song.*

Buaidh-chaithream, eim, *s. m.* A triumphant shout, a song of triumph, a triumph. A deanamh buaidh-chaithreim, *triumphing.—Stew. Col.*

Buaidh-chaithreamach, *a.* Triumphant; uttering a triumphant shout.

† Buaidheart, eirt, *s. m.* A tumult, confusion.

Buaidh-fhear, -fhir, *s. m.* A conqueror. *N. pl.* buaidh-fhir; *voc. pl.* a bhuaidh-fheara, *ye conquerors.*

Buaidh-fhocal, ail, *s. m.* An adjective; a qualifying term; an epithet.

Buaidh-ghair, *s. f.* A shout of victory, a shout of triumph.

Buaidh-ghaireach, *a.* Like a shout of triumph; triumphant.

Buaidh-ghaireachdaich, *s. f.* A continued shout of triumph.

Buaidh-ghuth, *s. m.* A shout of triumph; the voice of victory.

Buaidh-larach, aich, *s. m.* A decisive victory; victory, conquest.—*Macint.* Buaidh-larach 's gach stri, *victory in every battle.—Old Song.*

† Buaifeach, *a.* Angry, fretting.—*Shaw.*

† Buaific, *s. f.* An antidote.

Buail, *v. a.* Strike, smite, beat, thrash; thrust; touch or land at; strike up as a tune: used also to describe rapid motion, rush, move, proceed. *Pret. a.* bhuail; *fut. aff. a.* buailidh, *shall or will strike; fut. pass.* buailear, *shall be struck.* Bhuail mi beum, *I struck a blow.—Fingalian Poem.* Buail as, *thrash off.—Stew. Ruth.* Bhuail chuige Dearg, *Dargo moved* [*rushed*] *towards him.—Oss. Dargo.* Ciod am bealach am buail sinn? *through what pass shall we strike our way?—Fingalian Legend.* Bhuail sinne comhrag, *we sounded the signal of battle, we engaged in battle.—Oss. Tem.* Bhuail e chruaidh na taobh, *he thrust his steel into her side. —Oss. Fing.* Buailibh clarsach, *strike up the harp.—Oss. Com.* A cheud fhear a bhuail an tìr, *the first man who landed.—Oss. Tem.*

† Buail, *s. f.* A step, a degree.—*Ir. id.*

Buaile, *s. f.* (*Gr.* βουκόλιον. *Lat.* bovile. *Ir.* buaile.) A fold for sheep or for black cattle; a stall; a dairy; also cattle, herds. *N. pl.* buailtean, *folds.* Buailtean spreidhe, *herds of cattle.—Stew. Joel.* *Dat. pl.* buailtibh. Buar air na buailtibh, *a herd in the fold.—Stew. Hab.* A bhò is miosa tha sa bhuaile 's i is aird geum, *the sorry cow has the loudest low. —G. P.*

Buaileach, ich, *s. m.* An ox-stall; a stall; a fold. *N. pl.* buailichean.

Buailear, *fut. pass.* of buail. Shall be struck. *Buailear* is also used as an impersonal verb; as, buailear suas leam, *I struck or proceeded upwards.*

Buailidh, *s. f.* A dairy or milk-house; a stall; a fold. Steach do 'n bhuailidh, *into the milking-house.—Macfar.*

Buailsa, Buailse, (*for* buail thusa.) Strike thou.

† Built, *s. f.* A locker; a niche.—*Shaw.*

Buailte, *p. part.* of buail. Struck, beaten, thrashed. Cha bhi bail air fodar buailte, *thrashed corn is not spared.— G. P.*

Buailteach, *a.* Liable, subject; obnoxious; apt to strike or to thrash. Buailteach do chìs, *liable to tax.* Gun bhi buailteach, *without being given to strike.—Stew. Tim.* *Com.* and *sup.* buailtiche, *more or most liable.*

† Buailteachan, ain, *s. m.* A flying camp.

Buailtean, *n. pl.* of buaile. Sheep-folds; cattle-houses.

Buailtean, ein, *s. m.* (*from* buail.) A flail, that part of a flail which thrashes the sheaf. *Ir.* buailtean.

Buailtear, ir, *s. m.* A thrasher.

† Buain, *s. f.* Equality; deprivation.—*Ir. id.*

Buain, *s. f.* (*Ir.* buain.) A reaping; a cutting down as of corn. Buain lorna, *barley harvest.—Stew. Ruth.* Am fear nach dean cur ri là fuar, cha dean e buain ri la teth, *he who will not sow on a cold day shall not reap on a warm. —G. P.*

Buain, *v. a.* Reap, cut down, shear; tear by the root; engap. *Pret. a.* bhuain, *reaped; fut. aff. a.* buainidh, *shall reap.* A buain na h-araich, *cutting down the* [*files of*] *battle.—Oss. Cathula.* Craobh bhuain a ghaoth, *a tree torn up by the wind.—Oss. Carricth.* Buainidh sinn, *we shall reap.—Stew. Gal.*

Buaine, *s. f.* Perpetuity, duration; hardiness, durableness.—*Ir. id.*

Buaine, *com.* and *sup.* of buan. (*Ir. id.*) More or most

lasting or hardy. Darraig is buaine dreach, *an oak of the hardest form.—Oss.* Is buaine na gach ni an nàire, *more lasting is shame than any thing else.—G. P.*

Buainead, eid, *s. m.* Hardiness, durableness.

Buaineadh, eidh, *s. m.* A reaping, cutting down; enjoying, as the fruits of one's labour. Muinntir a' bhuainidh, *the reapers.—Stew. Jam.*

Buaineadh, 3 *sing.* and *pl. imperat.* of buain. Buaineadh e, *let him reap;* buaineadh iad, *let them reap.*

Buaineadh, (a), *pr. part.* of buain; which see.

Buainear, *fut. pass.* of buain. Shall or will be shorn.

Buainiche, *s. m.* and *f.* A shearer or reaper. *N.* and *gen. pl.* buainichean, *shearers.* Ri taobh nam buainichean, *beside the reapers.—Stew. Ruth.*

Buainte, *p. part.* of buain. Reaped, shorn; torn up by the root; hewn down.

Buainteair, ir, *s. m.* (*from* buain.) A reaper, shearer, or mower. *N. pl.* buaintearan.

Buair, *v. a.* Tempt; vex, disturb, annoy, distract, madden. *Pret. a.* bhuair, *tempted; fut. aff. a.* buairidh. Cha bhuair thu, *thou shalt not tempt.—Stew. Mat.* Air a bhuaireadh, *tempted.—Stew. Mat.* Air a bhuaireadh, *troubled.—Stew. Dan.* Fear air bhuaireadh, *a man distracted.* Chum a buaireadh, *to vex her.—Stew. G. B.*

Buaire', *contracted* for buaireadh; which see.

Buaireadair, *s. m.* A tempter; a disturber; one who vexes or troubles. *N. pl.* buaireadairean. Air teachd don bhuaireadair, *when the tempter came.—Stew. Mat.*

Buaireadh, idh, *s. m.* Temptation; trouble; disturbance, annoyance; severe trial; a tempting; a maddening; distraction. Bha a spiorad air a bhuaireadh, *his spirit was troubled.—Stew. Gen.* Buaireadh, *a severe trial.—Stew. Cor. ref.* Tuinn gun bhuaireadh, *untroubled waves.—Oss. Derm.* A feartan buairidh, *her tempting qualities.—Mac Lach.*

Buaireas, eis, *s. m.* Confusion, trouble, ferment, tumult. Buaireas mòr, *a great tumult.—Stew. Zech.* Fo bhuaireas, *troubled.—Stew. 1 K.*

Buaireasach, *a.* Turbulent, raging, stormy, tumultuous. Geamhradh buaireasach, *a stormy winter.—Macfar.* Is buaireasach deoch laidir, *strong drink is raging.—Stew. Pro.*

Buaireasachd, *s. f.* Turbulence, storminess, tumultuousness.

Buaireasaiche, *com.* and *sup.* of buaireasach.

Buairte, *p. part.* of buair. Distracted, enraged; tempted; stormy. *Asp. form,* bhuairte. Sìth air a mhuir bhuairte, *peace on the stormy sea.—Oss. Duthona.*

Buait, buaite, *s. f.* A lantern. *N. pl.* buaitean.

† **Bual**, buail, *s. m.* Remedy; physic; water.—*Ir. id.*

Bual, buail, *s. m.* (*contr.* for buabhall.) A buffalo; any wild horned creature. Perhaps the *bual* of the Gael and of the Armoric Celts is *bu-nll,* a wild ox.

Bualachd, *s. f.* A drove of cattle. *Ir.* buallachd.

† **Baladh**, aidh, *s. m.* A remedy; physic.—*Shaw.*

Bualadh, aidh, *s. m.* A striking; a thrashing; a battle. Bhur bualadh, *your threshing.—Stew. Lev.* Bualadh arbhair, *thrashing of corn.—Stew. Jud.* Bualadh nan laoch, *the battle of heroes.—Oss. Tem.*

Bual-chrannach, aich, *s. m.* A float, a raft.—*Shaw.*

Bualohas, ais, *s. m.* A mill-pond.

Bualtrach, aich, *s. m.* Cow-dung.

Buamsdair, *s. m.* One who talks boisterously; a vain boaster; a dolt, a looby. *N. pl.* buamsdairean.

Buamsdaireachd, *s. f.* Boisterous talking; vain boasting. Ri buamsdaireachd; *talking boisterously.*

† **Buan**, *a.* Good; harmonious. *Lat.* bonus. *Fr.* bon. *Ir.* buan.

† **Buan**, buain, *s. f.* A nurse.—*Shaw.*

Buan, *a.* (*Ir.* buan.) Lasting, durable; long, tedious; hardy, tough. Cead buan, *a long farewell.—Old Song.* Ge buan an t-slighe, *though tedious be the way.—Macint.* Bodach buan, *a tough or hardy old man.*

Buanachadh, aidh, *s. m.* A continuing, persevering, obtaining; continuance, perseverance.

Buanachadh, (a), *pr. part.* of buanaich; which see.

Buanachd, *s. f.* (*Ir. id.*) Continuance, tediousness, duration; durableness, hardiness; acquirement, gain, profit; an oppressive quartering of soldiers. Buanachd na slighe, *the tediousness of the way.* Ni gun bhuanachd, *a profitless thing.—Stew. Hos.* Ciod a bhuanachd dhuinn? *what profit have we?—Stew. Mal.*

Buanaich, *v. a.* & *n.* Last, abide; persevere; obtain, win, or acquire. *Pret. a.* bhuanaich, *lasted; fut. aff. a.* buanaichidh, *shall last.* Bhuanaich iad cliù, *they won renown.—Old Poem.*

Buanaiche, *s. m.* and *f.* A shearer, a reaper; one who enjoys; a winner. *N. pl.* buanaichean. Written also *buainaiche.*

Buanaichidh, *fut. aff. a.* of buanaich. Shall last. See Buanaich.

Buanaichte, *p. part.* of buanaich. Acquired, obtained, won.

Buanas, ais, *s. m.* Perpetuity, durability.

Buan-chuimhne, *s. f.* A memorial, a chronicle; a retentive memory.

Buan-chuimhneachail, *a.* Having a retentive memory.

Buan-mhair, *v. n.* Last long, endure.

Buan-mhaireachduinn, *s. f.* Perseverance, continuance, perpetuity.

Buan-mhaireannach, *a.* Everlasting, durable, perpetual, perennial.

Buan-mhaireannachd, *s. f.* Perpetuity, eternity.

† **Buanna**, *s. m.* A billetted soldier.—*Shaw.*

Buannachail, *a.* Profitable, useful, emolumentary.

Buannachd, *s. f.* Profit, gain; also a billetting or quartering of soldiers.—*Shaw.* Sanntach air buannachd, *greedy of gain.—Stew. Pro.*

Buan-sheasamhach, *a.* Firmly footed; lasting, perennial, perpetual, stable.

Buan-sheasamhachd, *s. f.* Continuance; firmness, stability, durability.

Buar, buair, *s. m.* (*Ir.* buar. *W.* buarth, *a cow-yard.*) Cattle; a herd of cattle; oxen. Buar air na buailtibh, *a herd in the stalls.—Stew. Hab.* Ard bhàirich bhuar, *the loud lowing of cattle.—Macdon.*

Buarach, aich, *s. m.* A cow-spaniel; a milking-fetter.—*Macint.* Buarach na laimh, *a milking-fetter in her hand.—Old Poem.*

Buarach-na-baòidh, *s. m.* A lamprey.

† **Buas**, buais, *s. m.* (*Ir. id. It.* buzzo, *the belly.*) A belly; a breach; a rout; a trade, art.—*Shaw.*

Buath, buaith, *s. f.* Rage, madness, frenzy, fury; a mad frolic. Ghlac e le buath, *he seized in a rage.—Mac Lach.* Tha buath air, *he is in a rage;* tha buath chuthaich air, *he is raging mad.*

Buathach, *a.* (*from* buath.) Subject to fits of madness; apt to fly into a rage.

Buathadh, aidh, *s. m.* A mad fit, a wild ramble; a mad frolic.

Bùb, *v. n.* Bellow, roar. *Pret. a.* bhùb; *fut. aff. a.* bubaidh.

Bùb, bùba, *s. m.* A roar, a bellow, a yell. Leig e bùb as, *he uttered a roar.*

Bùbail, *s. f.* A bellow, a roar; a continued bellowing, a loud lament. Bùbail tairbh, *the roaring of a bull;* ri bùbail, *roaring or bellowing;* ciod a bhùbail th'ort? *what are you bellowing for?*

Buban, ain, *s. m.* A coxcomb.

Bubanach, *a.* Like a coxcomb; of, or belonging to, a coxcomb.

Bubanachd, *s. f.* The behaviour of a coxcomb.

Buc, *s. m.* Size, bulk; the cover of a book. Hence perhaps the *English* book; *Scotch*, beuk.

Bucaid, *s. f.* A pimple; a bucket.—*Macd.* (*Ir.* boicoid.) *N. pl.* bucaidean.

Bucaideach, *a.* (*from* bucaid.) Pimply, full of pimples, causing pimples; like a bucket.

Bucail, *a.* (buc-amhuil.) Bulky, sizeable.

Bucaill, *gen. sing.* and *n. pl.* of bucall.

Bucall, aill, *s. m.* (*Arm.* bucel. *Fr.* boucle. *Span.* boucle. *Lat.* buculà.) A buckle. *N. pl.* bucaill *and* bucallan, *buckles.* Bucaill airgid, *silver buckles.—Old Song.* Bucallan, *buckles.—Macint.*

Bucallach, *a.* Buckled. Brògan bucallach, *buckled shoes;* gu bucallach brogach, *with buckled shoes.*

Buchuinn, **Buchthuinn**, *a.* Melodious, warbling. Eoin bhuchuinn, *melodious birds.—Macdon.*

Buclaich, *v. a.* Buckle. *Pret. a.* bhuclaich, *buckled; fut. aff. a.* buclaichidh, *shall buckle.* Buclaich ort d' airm, *buckle on your armour.*

Buclaichte, *p. part.* of buclaich. Buckled.

† **Budh**, *s. m.* The world; a breach; a rout.—*Shaw.*

Bugan, ain, *s. m.* An unlaid egg.

Bugh, *s. m.* Fear; a leek.—*Shaw.*

Bugsa, *s. m.* The box-tree; a box. Written also *bocsa.*

Buic, *gen. sing.* and *n. pl.* of boc, *s.;* which see.

† **Buicead**, eid, *s. m.* A mouthful.

Buicean, ein, *s. m.* (*dim.* of boc.) A young roe, a little roe; also a pimple. *N. pl.* buicein, *young roes.* Buicein binneach, *the high-headed young roes.—Macdon.*

Buiceanach, *a.* Like a young roe; of, or belonging to, a young roe; pimply.

† **Buich**, *s. f.* A breach.—*Shaw.*

† **Buichiù**, *s. m.* A young roe. Thionnadh am buichiù, *the young roe turned.—Old Song.*

Buid, *gen. sing.* and *n. pl.* of bod.

Buideal, eil, *s. m.* (*Fr.* bouteille, *bottle.* *Ir.* buideal. *Swed.* buteli, *to bottle.* *It.* bottiglia.) A bottle; anker. Clàr buideil, *a bottle-rack.—Macdon.* *N. pl.* buidealan.

Buidealair, *s. m.* (*from* buideal.) A butler. Buidealair an righ, *the king's butler.—Stew. Gen.* *N. pl.* buidealairean.

Buidealaireachd, *s. f.* (*from* buidealair.) The business of a butler, butlership. *Asp. form,* bhuidlearachd. Chum a bhuidealaireachd, *to his butlership.—Stew. Gen.*

† **Buidh**, *s. pl.* Thanks.—*Shaw.* Hence *buidheach* and *buidheachas.*

Buidhe, *a.* Yellow, like gold. Grian bhuidhe, *the golden sun.—Oss. Tem.* Falt buidhe, *yellow hair.* Buidhe nan ningean, *spurge.—Shaw.*

Buidheach, ich, *s. f.* The jaundice. A bhuidheach, *the jaundice.*

Buidheach, *a.* (*from* † buidh.) Thankful, pleased, satisfied; sated, content.—*Ir. id.* Buidheach bidh, *satisfied with meat;* tha mi buidheach air son sin, *I am pleased at that.* Is buidheach Dia do 'n fhìrinn, *the truth is pleasing to God.—G. P.*

Buidheachas, ais, *s. m.* (*from* † buidh.) *Ir. id.* Thanks, thanksgiving. Guth buidheachais, *the voice of thanksgiving;* thoir buidheachas, *give thanks;* breith buidheachais, *thanksgiving;* buidheachas do Dhia, *thank God;* taing is buidheachas, *many thanks.*

Buidhead, eid, *s. m.* Yellowness; increase in yellowness A fàs am buidhead, *growing more and more yellow.*

Buidheag, eig, *s. f.* (*from* buidhe.) A goldfinch; any little yellow bird; a daisy; a lily; any yellow flower; also a cow of a yellowish colour. Gheibh sinn a bhuidheag san lòin, *we shall find the daisy in the meadow.—Old Song.* *N. pl.* buidheagan.

Buidheagan, ain, *s. m.* (*from* buidhe.) The yolk of an egg.—*Ir. id.*

Buidheagan, *n. pl.* of buidheag. Daisies, lilies.

Buidheag-bhealuidh, *s. f.* A yellow-hammer. A bhuidheag bhealuidh, *the yellow-hammer.—Macd.* Nead na buidheig-bhealuidh, *the yellow-hammer's nest.*

Buidheag-bhuchair, *s. f.* A yellow-hammer.—*Shaw.*

Buidheann, buidhne, *s. m.* A company, a troop, a band; rulers. Bheir buidheann buaidh air, *troops shall conquer him.—Stew. O. T.* Tha mi a faicinn buidhne, *I see a company.—Stew. 2 K.* *N. pl.* buidhnean.

Buidhinn, *s. f.* Gain, profit. Is beag do bhuidhinn deth, *your profit of it is little.*

Buidhinn, *v. a.* Gain, profit, win, acquire. *Pret. a.* bhuidhinn, *won; fut. aff. a.* buidhnidh, *shall win; imp. sub.* bhuidhneadh, *would win.* Bhuidhneadh tu gach rèis, *thou wouldst gain every race.—Macint.* Buidhnibh saorsa, *gain liberty.—Old Poem.*

Buidh-mhios, *s. m.* The month of July. *Ir.* boidh-mhios.

Buidhne, *gen. sing.* of buidheann; which see.

Buidhneach, *a.* Victorious; in bands or companies; successful; acquiring, gainful, profitable. Laoich buidhneach, *victorious heroes.—Macint.*

Buidhneach, ich, *s. f.* A band, a company; a troop. *N. pl.* buidhnicheare, *bands.* Uile bhuidhnichean, *all his bands.—Stew. Ezek.*

Buidhneachd, *s. f.* Victoriousness, successfulness.

Buidhnich, *v. a.* (*from* buidheann.) Arrange into companies. *Pret. a.* bhuidnich.

Buidhnichte, *p. part.* of buidhnich. Arranged or drawn in companies.

Buidhre, *s. f.* Deafness.

Buidhre, *com.* and *sup.* of bodhar. More or most deaf. Cluinnidh tu air a chluais is buidhre e, *you will hear it in the deafest ear.—G. P.*

Buidhe-ruadh, *a.* Of a bay colour; auburn. Falt buidhe ruadh, *auburn hair.*

Buidseach, ich, *s. f.* A witch. *N. pl.* buidsichean.

Buidseachd, *s. f.* Witchcraft, sorcery. Tha buidseachd ort, *you are bewitched.*

Buige, *com.* and *sup.* of bog. Softer, softest; smoother, smoothest. *Asp. form,* bhuige. Bu bhuige a bhriathran, *his words were softer.—Stew. Ps.*

Buige, *s. f.* Softness, effeminacy.

Buigeachas, ais, *s. m.* Tenderness, softness, pity, compassionateness. Gun ath-thruas gun bhuigeachas, *without compassion or pity.—Old Song.*

Buigean, ein, *s. m.* A soft unmanly fellow.

Buig-bhuinne, *s. f.* A bulrush.

Buigleach, ich, *s. f.* A soft place; a bog, a quagmire. *N. pl.* buiglich.

Buigleag, eig, *s. f.* A bog or quagmire.—*Macd.*

Buigneach, ich, *s. f.* A bog, a quagmire; also bulrushes.

Buil, *s. f.* Completion, perfection; issue; consequence, effect; success. A thoirt gu buil fhocail, *to complete his words.—Stew. Joel.* Buil gach aon taisbein, *the effect of every vision.—Stew. Ezek.* Bheir thu a bhuil, *you will reap the consequence;* bithidh sin air bhuil, *that will come to pass.*

Buileach, *a.* Complete, whole. This word is most commonly used *adverbially;* as, gu buileach, *completely, wholly, utterly, altogether.* Na treig mi gu buileach, *do not forsake* *me utterly.—Sm.* Cha bhuain thu gu buileach, *thou shalt not wholly reap.—Stew. Lev.* Gu bileach buileach, *pick and crumb.*

Buileachadh, aidh, *s. m.* A bestowing, giving; improving.

Buileachadh, (a), *pr. part.* of builich. Bestowing; improving.

Buileann, inn, *s. m.* A loaf. Written also *builionn*; which see.

Builg, *gen. sing.* of bolg.

Builg, *n. pl.* of bolg. Bellows; also seeds of herbs.

Builg, *s. f.* A distemper among cattle, proceeding from want of water or from heat.

Builgeann, *s. m.* (*dim.* of bolg.) *Sax.* biligan, *a bladder.* A blister; pimple; bubble or bell; bellows; a little bag, a bladder. Mar bhristeadh builgein, *like the breaking of a bubble.—Macfar.*

Builgeasach, *a.* Spotted.—*Shaw.*

Builich, *v. a.* Grant, bestow, present; improve. *Pret. a.* bhuilich, *granted; fut. aff. a.* builichidh, *shall or will grant.*

Builionn, inn, *s. m.* A loaf. *N. pl.* builinnean, *loaves.* Aon bhuilionn, *one loaf.—Stew. Exod.*

Buill-bheirt, *s. m. pl.* Tackling; instruments.

Buille, *s. m.* A blow, a stroke, a stripe. (*Germ.* beul. *Gr.* βολη, *a throw.*) *N. pl.* buillean, and sometimes builleannan, *blows.* Buille air son buille, *blow for blow, stripe for stripe.—Stew. Exod.* Fead am builleannan, *the noise of their blows.—Macdon.*

Builleach, *a.* (*from* buille.) That gives blows.

Builleachas, ais, *s. m.* A striking, a boxing, a bruising.

Builleanach, *a.* Striking, giving blows. Sàthach builleanach, *giving thrusts and blows.—Old Song.*

Buillsgean, Builsgean, ein, *s. m.* The middle, the centre. Builsgean amhuinn, *the centre of a furnace.—Stew. Dan.*

† Buime, *s. f.* A nurse; a mother.—*Ir. id.*

Buin, *v.* Belong; touch, meddle; deal or treat; take away. *Pret. a.* bhuin, *belonged; fut. aff. a.* buinidh, *shall belong.* Is ann da bhuineas slainnte, *to him belongs health.—Stew. Jon.* Buinibh gu caoineil ri mo ghaol, *deal kindly with my beloved.—Oss.* Buin uam m' anam, *take my life from me.—Stew. Jon.* Cha bhuinnte bho gaol i, *she could not be taken from her love.—Oss. Fut. sub.* bhuineas. Co dha 'bhuineas so? *whom does this belong to?* An rud nach buin duit na buin da, *what belongs not to you meddle not with.—G. P.*

Buinidh, *fut. aff. a.* of buin. Shall belong.

Buinig, *v. a.* Conquer, obtain by conquest. *Pret. a.* bhuinig; *fut. pass.* buinigear. Buinigear buaidh le foighidinn, *victory is got by patience.—G. P.*

Buinig, *s. f.* Superiority.

Buinne, *s. f.* A stream; a torrent; a spout or cataract; a billow; a spigot; *rarely* a sprout or twig; an ulcer. Air buinne reidh, *on a smooth stream.—Macint. N. pl.* buinnean arda, *lofty billows.—Old Poem.*

Buinneach, ich, *s. m.* A diarrhœa; flux. *Ir.* buinneach.

Buinneag, eig, *s. f.* A twig; a germ; a lovely young maid; the sole of a shoe. A bhuinneag Mhoiùra! *thou lovely maid Moiura!—Oss. Conn.* Cha chuir e buinneag air a bhrògan, *it will not sole his shoe.—G. P. N. pl.* buinneagan.

Buinneamh, imh, *s. m.* An effusion.—*Shaw.*

Buinnean-leana, *s. m.* A bittern.—*Shaw.*

Buinnir, *s. m.* A footman. Written also *bonnair.*

Buinne-shruth, *s. f.* A precipitous stream; a cascade. Mar bhuinne-shruth reamhairt, *like a spring-tide stream.—Old Song.*

Buinnteach, *a.* Causing looseness of the bowels.

Buinnteach, ich, *s. m.* One troubled with a flux; one who is habitually loose in his bowels.

Buinnteachd, *s. f.* A flux; a dysentery; habitual looseness of the bowels.

Buintear, ir, *s. m.* A dunce. *N. pl.* buintirean.

Bùir, *v. n.* Roar, bellow. *Pret. a.* bhùir; *fut. aff. a.* bùiridh, *shall roar.*

Buirbe, *s. f.* Fierceness, savageness, boisterousness, wrath, rage; cruelty. Gun gheilt no buirbe, *without fear or wrath.—Sm.* Mharbh sibh iad le buirbe, *you killed them in a rage.—Stew. Chron.*

Buirbe, *com.* and *sup.* of borb. (*Ir.* boirbe *and* buirbe.) More or most fierce.

Buirbeachd, *s. f.* Barbarity, fierceness.

Buirdeasach, aich, *s. m.* A citizen, an inhabitant, a burgess. *N. pl.* bùirdeasaich, *citizens.* Bùirdeasaich sgiathach nan speur, *the winged inhabitants of heaven.—Macdon.*

Bùire, Bùireadh, *s. m.* (*Ir.* bùireadh.) Wailing, loud weeping; a burst of grief; roaring, bellowing; a rutting. Bhrist uaith bùire, *he broke into a loud burst of grief.—Oss. Duthona.* Mo bhùireadh, *my roaring.—Stew. Job.* Poll-bùiridh, *the rutting-place of a deer.*

† Buireadh, idh, *s. m.* Gore, pus.—*Ir. id. Shaw.*

Buireadh, 3 *sing.* and *pl. imperat.* of bùir. Na buireadh am boc, *let not the roe bellow.—Oss. Fin. and Lor.*

Buirean, ein, *s. m.* A roar, a bellow as of a deer; a loud noise. An fhairg a teachd le bùirean, *the sea coming with a noise.—Macfar.*

Bùireanach, *a.* Roaring, bellowing, noisy.

Bùirich, *v. a.* (*from* ùir.) Dig, delve. *Pret. a.* bhùirich *dug; fut. aff. a.* bùirichidh, *shall or will dig; fut. pass.* bùirichear; *p. part.* bùirichte, *dug.*

Bùirich, *v. n.* Howl, roar; make a loud lament. *Pret. a.* bhùirich, *roared; fut. aff.* bùirichidh, *shall roar.*

Bùirich, *s. f.* A loud lament, a burst of grief; a low murmur; a bellowing, a hollow roar as of a bull; a growling.

Bùiriche, *s. m.* A mattock; a hoe, a little spade; a dibble; also one who digs or delves.

Bùirichidh, *fut. aff. a.* of bùirich. Shall or will dig.

Bùiridh, *gen. sing.* of bùireadh.

Buirling, *s. f.* See Biorlinn.

Bùirte, *s. f.* A gibe, a taunt, a sarcasm; a repartee, a witticism.

† Buiscean, ein, *s. m.* A thigh, a haunch; thigh armour. Hence perhaps *buskin.*

Buisdreach, ich, *s. m.* A witch, a wizzard, a sorcerer.

Buisdreachd, *s. f.* Witchcraft, sorcery.

Bùiste, *s. f.* A pouch or pocket, a scrip.—*Shaw. N. pl.* bùistean *and* buisteachan.

Buite, *s. f.* A firebrand.

† Buitealach, aich, *s. m.* A great fire.—*Ir. id.*

Buitse, *s. f.* An icicle.—*Macd.*

Buitseach, ich, *s. m.* and *f.* A witch, a wizzard. *N. pl.* buitsichean, *witches.* Written also *buidseach.*

Buitseachas, ais, *s. m.* Witchcraft, sorcery.—*Stew. Gal. ref.* Written also *buidseachas.*

Buitseachd, *s. f.* Witchcraft, sorcery, enchantment. Written also *buidseachd.*

Buitsear, ir, *s. m.* A butcher; also the butcher's bird.—*Macd.*

Buitsearachd, *s. f.* The business of a butcher; a butchery. Ag ionnsachadh na buitsearachd, *learning the business of a butcher.*

Buithre, *com.* and *sup.* of bothar. Deafer, deafest. Written also *buidhre*, from *bodhar.*

BUITHRE, *s. f.* Deafness. Written also *buidhre*, from *bodhar*.

† BUL, *s. m.* A manner, mode, fashion.

BULAISTEAR, ir, *s. m.* *Ir. id.* A bullace, a sloe.—*Shaw*.

BÙLAS, ais, *s. m.* A pot-hook; a prune. *N. pl.* bùlasan.

BULG, builg, *s. m.* A belly; any thing that is prominent or bellying; a bubble; a lump, a knob, a mass. Written also *bolg*; which see.

BULGACH, *a.* (*from* bolg.) Bellying, prominent; knobby, massy. Ceud srian bulgach, *a hundred massy bridles.*—*Oss. Taura.*

BULLA, ai, *s. m.* A bowl; a ball; a bubble. *Ir.* bulla. *Lat.* bulla, *a bubble.* Hence also bullire, *to boil.*

BULLACH, *a.* Globular; like a bowl, ball, or bubble; also the fish called *connor.*—*Shaw.*

BUN, buin, *s. m.* (*Pers.* bun, *bottom.* *Ir.* bun. *Dan.* bund.) Bottom, base, foundation; foot; a root, a stump; stock; origin; a squat little person; trust, confidence. Bun a mhonaidh, *the bottom or foot of the hill;* bun an uchdain, *the bottom of the ascent.* Bun an earbuill, *the rump.*—*Stew. Exod.* Bun na h-altarach, *the foot of the altar.*—*Stew. Lev.* Cha n' fhàg e bun no bàrr, *he will leave neither root nor branch.*—*Stew. Mal.* Bun craoibh, *the stump of a tree.*—*Stew. Is.* As a bhun, *from the root.* Bun os-cionn, *upside down.*—*Stew. Job.* Asadsa rinn ar sinnsir bun, *in thee our fathers trusted.*—*Sm.* Bun na cìob, *the root of the mountain-grass.*—*Macint.* Bun balaoich, *a stump of a fellow, a stout squat fellow.*

BUNABHAS, ais, *s. m.* An element.

BUNABHASACH, *a.* Elemental.

BUNACH, aich, *s. m.* Coarse tow; the tare of flax; a sturdy little person.

BUNACH, *a.* Squat; short, stumpish; sturdy; clumsy.

BUNACHADH, aidh, *s. m.* A founding, establishing; a taking root.

BUNACHAR, air, *s. m.* A foundation, base, bottom; radix; etymology. O bhunachar luaisgidh an talamh, *the earth shall quake from its foundation.*—*Sm.* Perhaps the proper orthography is *bunachur.*

BUNACHAS, ais, *s. m.* *Ir.* bunadhas. Etymology; authenticity; authority.

BUNACHASACH, *a.* (*from* bunachas.) Authentic; well-founded; etymological; radical.

BUNADAS, ais, *s. m.* Origin, stock, root, foundation.

BUNAICH, *v. a.* Found, establish, make firm, take root. *Pret. a.* bhunaich, *fut. aff.* bunaichidh.

BUNAILT, *s. f.* Steadiness; constancy; a sure foundation; inflexibility.

BUNAILTEACH, *a.* (*from* bunailt.) Steady, firm, constant, stable, fixed; authentic; firmly seated or founded. Bha d' inntinn bunailteach, *thy mind was constant.*—*Macint.*

BUNAILTEACHD, *s. f.* Steadiness; firmness; constancy; firmness of foundation.

BUNAIT, *s. m.* (*i. e.* bun-àit.) *Ir.* bunait. *N. pl.* bunaitean. A foundation. Bunaitean an domhain, *the foundations of the earth.*—*Stew. Gal.*

BUNAITEACH, *a.* (*from* bunait.) Steady, grounded, fixed, stable, stedfast, immoveable. Bunaiteach agus daingeann, *grounded and settled.*—*Stew. Col.*

BUNAITEACHADH, aidh, *s. m.* (*from* bunait.) A founding, an establishing.

BUNAITEACHD, *s. f.* Written also *bunailteachd;* which see.

BUNAITICH, *v. a.* Found, establish; inherit, possess.

BUNAMAS, ais, *s. m.* Deep discernment; quickness of comprehension.

BUNANTA, *a.* Firm, well built, well set, sturdy; having a good bottom or foundation.

BUNANTACHD, *s. f.* Firmness, sturdiness.

BUN-BHEAN, -mhna, *s. f.* A female of discreet years. *N. pl.* bun-mnathan.

BUN-CHIALL, -chéill, *s. f.* A moral; having a concealed meaning.

BUN-CHIALLACH, *a.* Containing a moral, as a fable.

BUN-CHÌS, *s. f.* A pension; chief rent.

BUNDUNACH, *a.* Ungainly.—*Shaw.*

BUN-GLAS, ais, *s. m.* Purple melie-grass.—*Macd.*

BUN-LUCHD, *s. pl.* Aborigines.

BUN-MHÀS, mhàis, *s. f.* A buttock.

BUN-MHÀSACH, *a.* Having large buttocks; of, or belonging to, the buttocks.

BUNNAN, ain, *s. m.* A bittern.—*Shaw.*

BUN-NÒS, -nòis, *s. m.* An old custom.—*Shaw.*

BUNSACH, aich, *s.* (*Ir.* bunnsach.) A rod; an osier; a place where osiers grow. *N. pl.* bunsaichean, *twigs.*

BUNSAG, aig, *s. f.* A twig, a soft osier.—*Macd.* *Ir.* bunsagan.

BUNSAIDH, *a.* (*from* bun.) Firm, solid, strong; having a good bottom. Perhaps *bunsuidh.*

BUN-TAGHTA, *s. m.* A potato; *literally*, a choice root.

For this ingenious rendering of the word *potato*, the Gaelic language is indebted to the late Sir John Mac Gregor Murray, Bart.

BUNTAIS, *s. pl.* (*from* buin.) Perquisites.—*Shaw.*

BUNTAMAS, ais, *s. m.* See BUNAMAS.

BUN-TÀT, àit, *s. m.* A potato. *N. pl.* buntàit. See BUN-TAGHTA.

BUNTUINN, (a), *pr. part.* of buin. Belonging to; meddling, treating, touching, taking away. A buntuinn gu naimhdeil, *persecuting.*—*Stew. N. T.*

BÙR, bùir, *s. m.* A boor, a clown; a boorish person.

† BURACH, aich, *s. m.* An exploit; a file of soldiers; a swelling, an imposthume.

BÙRACHADH, aidh, *s. m.* A digging, a delving.

BÙRACHADH, (a), *pr. part.* of bùraich. Digging, delving. Ag a bùrachadh le rùdan, *digging it with his knuckles.*—*Macint.*

BÙRAICH, *v. a.* Dig, delve. *Pret. a.* bhuraich, *dug; fut. aff. a.* buraichidh, *shall dig.* Written also *bùirich.*

BÙRAICHE, *s. m.* A pickaxe; a delver; one who digs.

BÙRAICHTE, *p. part.* of bùraich. Dug, delved.

BURAIDH, *s. m.* (*from* bur.) A clown, a boor, a foolish fellow, a blockhead, a looby. *N. pl.* buraidhean. A bhur-aidh tha thu ann! *fool that thou art!* *Span.* burro, *stupid.*

BUR-BHUACHAILL, *s. m.* The bird called northern diver. The colymbus glacialis of *Linnæus*, and the speckled diver of *Pennant.* Of this bird it is remarked, that it makes a great noise previous to a storm.

BÙRDAN, ain, *s. m.* A gibe; a sing-song.—*Macd.* Also the surname Burdon.

BURDANACH, *a.* Gibing; also one of the name Burdon.

† BURG, *s. m.* A town; a tower; a fortress; a village.

Gr. πυργος, *a tower.* *Pers.* Burj, *a town.* *Arab.* borg *and* borch. *Syr.* bor, *a village.* *Chald.* borgan, *a town.* *Isl.* borg *and* biorg, *a village.* *Swed.* † berga *and* borga. *Arm.* bourch *and* burg. *Germ.* berg, burg, *and* purg. *Dan.* borg. *Du.* burg. *Sax.* burug, burgh, *and* beorg. *Run.* borg. *Belg.* borg, borcht, *and* burcht. *Eng.* burgh. *Bisc.* burgua.

BURGAIR, *s. m.* A burgess, a citizen. *N. pl.* burgairean, *burgesses.*

BURMAID, *s. f.* Wormwood. Mar a bhurmaid, *as the wormwood.*—*Stew. Pro.*

BÙRN, bùirn, *s. m.* (*Scotch*, burn.) Water; fresh water. Sàil is bùrn, *salt water and fresh.*—*Macd.* Cho saor ri bùrn, *as cheap as water.* *Asp. form*, bhùrn. Chitheam am fuil do bhùrn, *I see thy water in blood.*—*Oss. Com.*

Ni bùrn salach lamhan glan, *foul water will make clean hands.—G. P.*

Bùrnach, *a.* (*from* bùrn.) Watery.

† Burr, *a.* Great. Written also *borr.*

Burrais, *s. m.* A caterpillar. Written also *burruis.*

Burral, ail, *s. m.* A howl, a burst of grief; clamorous grief; weeping. Chual le glinn a bhurral, *the glens heard his howl.—Oss. Manos.*

Burralach, *a.* Crying; sulky; apt to howl; howling.

Burralaich, *s. f.* Loud lamentation; a howling. Thòisich e air burralaich, *he began to howl.*

Burruis, *s. m.* A caterpillar. Ma bhios burruis ann, *so there be caterpillars.—Stew.* 1 *K.*

Bururus, uis, *s. m.* A warbling; a purling noise; a gurgling. Ri bururus seimh, *warbling softly.—Macdon.*

Bus, buis, *s. m.* A mouth; lip; snout; a ludicrous term for the human mouth; a kiss; a cat.

Ir. bus. *W.* bus, *lip. Eng.* buss. *Span.* buz, *a kiss. Germ.* buss. *Pers.* buz, *lip. Lat.* bas-ium, *a kiss. Fr.* bàser, *to kiss.*

Busach, *a.* (*from* bus.) Snouty; having a large mouth; blubber-lipped; pouting. *Com.* and *sup.* busaiche.

Busag, aig, *s. f.* A young girl with thick lips.

Busaidh. A word by which a cat is called.

Bus-dubh, *s. m.* A name for a dog and a democrat.

Busg, *v. a.* Dress, adorn; hinder. *Pret. a.* bhusg, *dressed. fut. aff.* busgaidh, *shall dress.*

Busgadh, aidh, *s. m.* A dressing, an adorning. A coiffure, *a head-dress.*

Busgainn, *s. f.* A dressing, adorning. Busgainn dubhain, *the dressing of a fishing-hook.*

Busgainn, *v. a.* Dress, decorate; dress a hook. *Pret. a.* bhusgainn, *dressed; fut. aff.* busgainnidh, *shall dress.*

Busiall, éill, *s. f.* A muzzle.

Butag, aig, *s. f.* An oar-pin. More properly *putag.*

Butagochd, *s. m.* A snipe. Gob a bhutagochd, *the bill of the snipe.*

Buth, bùtha, *s.* A shop; a tent; pavilion; a booth; a cot. *N. pl.* bùthan; *d. pl.* bùthaibh; *asp. form,* bhùthaibh. Shuidhich e a bhùth, *he pitched his tent.—Stew. Gen.* Do d' bhuthaibh, *to your tents.—Stew.* 1 *K.* Sròl o'n bhùth, *a riband from the shop.—Old Song.*

Turk. and *Arab.* beit *and* beith, *a house. Chald.* betha *and* bith. *Syr.* baitho *and* bitho. *Phen.* bith *and* beth. *Pers.* bat *and* abad. *Ethiop.* beti, *a house. Mogul Tartars,* po, *a house. Germ.* buen, bude, *and* bau. *Eng.* booth. *Polon.* budo. *Span.* buhyo, *cot. Swed.* bod *and* bu. *Eng.* abode. *Darien,* bo *and* bu. *W.* buth, both, *and* bot, *house. Dan.* boe, *to dwell. Isl.* bua *and* byad, *house. Bohem.* obit, *a house. Bisc.* bit. *Arm.* bod. *Corn.* buyth, *a house. Du.* boede. *Teut.* boed. *Old Sax.* boede *and* bode. *Serv.* and *Lus.* buda, *house. Scotch,* byde, *wait.*

Bùthal, ail, *s. m.* A pot-hook. Bùthal raimh, *the fulcrum of an oar.*

Bùthan, ain, *s. m.* (*dim.* of buth.) *Germ.* buen. A little booth; a bothy; a pavilion; a tent.

Bùthan, *n. pl.* of bùth. Booths; pavilions; cots; tents. See Buth.

Bùthlas, ais, *s. m.* A poot-hook. *N. pl.* bùthlasan; *d. pl.* buthlasaibh.

Buthlasan, *n. pl.* of bùthlas. Pot-hooks.

C

C, (coll, *hazel.*) The third letter of the Gaelic alphabet. When the names of letters began with suitable initials, the Gael named them after natural objects, as trees. *C,* when not aspirated, sounds broad, like *c* in *cub,* as *cù,* a dog, *crath,* shake; or small, like *c* in *cane,* as *faic,* see; *tric,* often. When aspirated, it sounds like the Greek χ in χόρδη, as *moch,* early; or small, like χιμών, as *chi,* shall see.

† Ca, *s. m.* A house.—*Ir. id.*

Cà, *adv.* (c'àite.) Where. Cà nis am bheil do ghath! *where now is thy sting!—Sm.*

Cab, *v. a.* Indent, notch as the edge of a bladed weapon; break land. *Pret. a.* chab, *notched; fut. aff. a.* cabaidh, *shall notch.*

Cab, caib, *s. m.* A mouth, a mouth ill set with teeth; a head; a gap; also a Hebrew measure equal to nearly three English pints and a half, or two Scotch pints.—*Stew. K.*

Gr. καβη, *food. Ir.* cab, *mouth. Lat.* cap-ut, *head. Heb.* cabah, *hat. Pol.* kapua, *head. Boh.* kape, *head. Germ.* kappen, *hat. Sclav.* kappa, *cowl. Eng.* cap. *It.* capo, *head. Corn.* kappa, *hat. Bisc.* cab, *head. Span.* cab, *head. Hottentot,* cabba, *hat.* Hence also *Fr.* capitaine, and *Eng.* captain; *i. e.* cap-†den, *head man. Pers.* † caf, *a hill.*

Cabach, *a.* (*from* cab.) *Ir.* cabach. Long-toothed; ugly-mouthed; notched, indented; full of gaps; toothless; babbling; garrulous. *Com.* and *sup.* cabaiche.

Cabachadh, aidh, *s. m.* An indenting, a notching; a growing indented or notched; indentation.

Cabachadh, (a), *pr. part.* of cabaich; which see.

† Cabad, aid, *s. m.* (*from* † cab.) A head. *Lat.* caput. See Cab.

Cabadh, aidh, *s. m.* A notching, an indenting; a breaking of land.

Cabadh, (a), *pr. part.* of cab; which see.

Cabag, aig, *s. f.* A cheese. (*Ir.* cabag. *Scotch,* kebbuck.) *N. pl.* cabagan.

Cabag, aig, *s. f.* (*from* cab.) A toothless female; a loquacious female; *rarely,* a strumpet. *N. pl.* cabagan. *Ir.* cabag.

Cabaich, *v. a.* (*from* cab.) Notch, indent, make blunt. *Pret. a.* chabaich, *notched; fut. aff. a.* cabaichidh, *shall notch.*

† Cabaig, *s. f.* A pillory.—*Ir. id.*

Cabail, *s. f.* A fleet, a navy.—*Ir. id.*

Cabair, *gen. sing.* and *n. pl.* of cabar.

Cabaire, *s. m.* (*from* cab.) A tattler, a gabbler; a toothless fellow. *N. pl.* cabairean.

Cabaireachd, *s. f.* The habit of tattling or prating.

Cabais, Cabaiseachd, *s. f.* Tattling, prating.

Cabaisd, *s. f.* Cabbage. Càl agus cabaisd, *colewort and cabbage.—Old Song.*

Cabaisdeach, *a.* Abounding in cabbage; like cabbage; of, or belonging to, cabbage.—*Macdon.*

† Cabal, ail, *s. m.* A cable. *Du.* cabel. *Teut.* kabel. *Ir.* cabla.

Caball, aill, *s. f.* A mare; *of old,* a horse; also a young dromedary. *N. pl.* cabaill.

Gr. καβαλλης, *a work-house. Lat.* cavallus, according to Isodorus and Papias. *It.* cavallo. *Span.* caballo. *Fr.* cavale, *a mare.* *Pol.* kobela. *Boh.* kobyla. *Hung.* kabalalo. The *Old Celtic* for horse is *all;* and *cab* is *mouth;* so *caball* means a horse broken to the bridle. See also CAPULL.

CABAIN, *gen. sing.* and *n. pl.* of caban.

† CABAN, ain, *s. m.* (*dim.* of cab.) A cottage, a tent, a booth; also a cottager.

Pers. kabah, *a cot.* *Sam.* cab, *tent.* *Bisc.* cabia, *cage.* *It.* gabbia. *Arab* kaban, *tent.* *Turk.* ciobani. *Gr.* καβαιη. *Span.* cabana. *Lat.* caupona, *an inn.* *Fr.* cabane. *Corn.* *Arm.* *W.* and *Eng.* cabin.

CÀBAN, ain, *s. m.* (*Lat* capo) A capon.

CABAR, air, *s m.* (*Arm.* ceibr, *rafter.* *Corn.* keber.) A deer's horn, an antler; a deer; a stake; a rung; lath; *rarely,* a joint, a confederacy. Cabar fèidh, *a deer's antler.* Mu chabar bha dealan, *lightning was about his horns.*—*Oss. Com.*

CABARACH, *a* (*from* cabar) Branchy, branching; having branching horns or antlers; like a rung or stake; full of rungs. Gu cabarach, *with antlers*—*Macint.* *Com.* and *sup.* cabaraiche.

CABARACH, aich *s.* A deer; a thicket, a copse. An deigh chabrach, *in pursuit of deer.*—*Oss. Fing.* Mar astar dall an cabarach, *as a blind man's progress through a thicket.*—*G. P*

† CABASDAN, ain, *s m.* A sort of curb; a bit, a bridle Written also *cabstar,* which see

CABHAG, aig, *s. f.* Hurry, haste, dispatch, speed. Dean cabhag, *make haste*—*Stew. Gen.* Cabhag ghaoth agus chuan, *the speed of winds and waves.*—*Fingalian Poem.* Tha thu ad chabhaig, *you are in a hurry.*

CABHAGACH, *a* (*from* cabhag) Hasty, impatient, abrupt, hurrying; causing haste or hurry, requiring haste. Gach neach cabhagach, *every hasty* [*impatient*] *person*—*Stew. Pro.* Gnothach cabhagach, *business requiring haste.*—*Stew. Sam.*

CABHAIG, *gen. sing.* of cabhag.

CABHAIR, *s f.* Help, assistance, relief, deliverance. (*Ir.* cabhair) *Asp form,* chabhair. Mo chabhair, *my help*—*Stew Job* Dean cabhair, *help* Is fad cabhair o Chruachan, *help is far from Cruachan,* an old adage expressive of the remoteness and inaccessible situation of that mountain. Written also *cobhair.*

CABHAIR, *v.* Assist, help, relieve, deliver. *Pret. art.* chabhair, *assisted; fut. aff. a.* cabhairidh. Cabhair orm, *help me.*—*Stew. Sam.* Written also *cobhair.*

CABHAIREACH, *a* Ready to help; auxiliatory, helpful.

† CABHAN, ain, *s. m.* A field, a plain.—*Ir. id.*

CABHANACH, aich, *s m.* Dawn. See CÀMHANACH.

† CABHAR, air, *s m* Any aged bird.

CABHLACH, aich, *s. f* (*Ir. id*) A fleet. Na chabhlach dorcha, *in his dark fleet.*—*Oss Cathula* *N. pl.* cabhlaichean.

CABHLACHAN, ain, *s m* A mariner.

CABHLACHDACH, *a.* Of, or pertaining to, a fleet; having a large fleet.

CABHLAICH, *gen.* of cabhlach

CABHRUICH, *s. f.* (càth-bhruich) Flummery; a mess made of the boiled filtered juice of corn seeds, and called by the Lowland Scots *sowens*

CABHSAIR, *s. f.* A causeway, a pavement. *N. pl.* cabhsairean.

CABHSAIREACH, *a.* Having a causeway or pavement; causewayed, paved

CABHSAIREACHD, *s. f.* The business of paving; pavier's work.

CABHSAIRICHE, *s. f.* A pavier. *N. pl.* cabhsairichean.

CABHSANTA, *a.* Dry; snug.—*Shaw.*

CABRACH, *a.* Contracted for *cabarach;* which see.

CABRACH, aich, *s. m.* A deer; a copse, a thicket; timbermoss; also the parish of Cabrach in Banff, where timbermoss abounds.

CABSTAR, air, *s. m.* A curb; the bit of a bridle. Cruaidh chabstar shoilleir, *hard polished bits.*—*Oss. Carricth.* *N. pl* cabstaran.

CABSTARACH, *a.* Having a curb; having a bit; like a curb or bit.

CAC, *s m* Excrement, dung, dirt, mire, filth. *Asp. form,* chac.

W. and *Arm.* cach. *Du.* kak. *Ir.* cac. *Span.* and *Port.* caca. *Lat.* caco. Aristophanes, in his comedy of the Clouds, has κακκη.

CAC, *v. n.* Go to stool; shite. *Pret. a.* chac; *fut. aff. a.* cacaidh.

CAC, *a.* Dirty, filthy, besmeared with dirt, nasty. Biast cac, *a nasty beast.*

CACACH, *a.* (*from* cac.) Filthy, dirty, miry, nasty, besmeared with dirt, excrementitious

CACADH, aidh, *s. m.* A voiding of excrement.

CACADH, (a), *pr part.* of cac.

CACAIDH, *fut. aff. a.* of cac.

CÀCH, *pron* (*Ir. id*) The rest. Ard ro chàch, *high above the rest.*—*Oss Dargo.* Air thus chàich, *in front of the rest.*—*Mac Lach.*

† CACHAN, ain, *s. m.* Profit, use; also a gate.—*Ir. id.*

† CACHD, *s.* A maid-servant; also a confinement; a fasting; clamour.

CACHLIADH, *s. f.* A rustic gate; a temporary breach made in a park wall as a thoroughfare for carts or cattle.

CAC-RADH, *s. m.* Cacophony.

† CAD, caid, *s. m.* A friend; also high; holy.—*Ir. id.*

† CADACH, aich, *s. m.* Friendship.—*Ir. id.*

CADACHAS, ais, *s m.* Atonement.—*Shaw.*

† CADAD, aid, *s. m.* An eclipse.—*Ir. id.*

CADAIL, *gen. sing.* of cadal.

CADAIL, *v. n.* Sleep, slumber; delay. *Pret. a.* chadail, *slept; fut aff. a.* cadailidh, *shall sleep.* Na cadail ach eutrom, *let thy sleep be light.*—*Old Song.*

CADAL, ail, *s. m.* Sleep, slumber; delay. Cha robh cadal mu 'n righ, *the king was sleepless*—*Oss. Carricth.* Dean cadal, *sleep;* drùb chadail, *a wink of sleep;* tha e na chadal, *he is asleep;* tha i na cadal, *she is asleep.* Written also *codal.*

CADALACH, *a.* Sleepy, drowsy, lethargic; causing sleep; narcotic; dilatory Galar cadalach, *lethargy.*

† CADAM, aim, *s. m.* (*Lat.* cado, *to fall.*) A fall, ruin, destruction.

† CADAMACH, *a.* Ruinous, destructive.—*Ir. id.*

CADAN, ain, *s. m.* Cotton; a pledget.—*Ir. id.*

CADAS, ais, *s. m* A pledget; caddice; cotton; *rarely,* friendship. *Ir* cadas. *W.* cadas, *a kind of stuff.*

CADATH, *s.* Tartan plaid. Eididh chadath, *a tartan dress.* *Cadath* is probably *cath dath, i. e.* battle-colour.

CADHAG, aig, *s f.* (*Ir* cag.) A jackdaw; the *corvus monedula* of Linnæus. *N. pl.* cadhagan.

CADHAL, ail, *s. m.* A bason; a hide, a skin.

† CADHAL, *a.* (*Gr.* καλος.) Fair, handsome, beautiful.—*Ir. id.*

CÀDHAL, ail, *s. m.* Colewort; kail; also broth of which colewort or kail is an ingredient. See CÀL.

CADHAN, ain, *s m.* A wild goose; a barnacle.—*Shaw.*

CADHAS, ais, *s. m.* (*Ir. id.*) Friendship; honour.—*Shaw.*

† **Cadhasach**, *a.* (*Ir. id.*) Respectful, friendly, honourable.—*Shaw.*

† **Cadhasachd**, *s. f.* Respectfulness, friendliness, honourableness.

† **Cadhla**, ai, *s. m.* A goat.—*Ir. id. Shaw.*

† **Cadhlach**, aich, *s. m.* A goatherd. *N. pl.* cadhlaichean.

Cad-luibh, *s. f.* Cudwort.

Cadluibheach, *a.* Abounding in cudwort; like cudwort; of cudwort.

Cadran, ain, *s. m.* Contention, broil, quarrel.

† **Cadranta**, *a.* Contentious, obstinate, stubborn. *Bisc.* cadarn, *brave*. *Turk.* kadyr. *Arab.* kadar.

† **Caec**, *a.* Blind.—*Ir. id. Lat.* cœcus. *Corn.* caic.

† **Cagaidh**, *s. f.* Strangeness.—*Ir. id.*

Cagail, *v. a.* (*Ir. id.*) Spare, save, economize. *Pret. a.* chagail, *spared.* Written also *coigil;* which see.

Cagailt, *s. f.* A hearth; also parsimony, frugality, economy. Corra-chagailt, *the sulphureous hue seen in hot embers on a frosty night.*

Cagainn, *v. a.* (*Ir. id.*) Chew, gnaw, champ. *Pret. a.* chagainn, *chewed; fut. aff. a.* cagnaidh, *shall chew or champ.* Cha chagainnin cùl mo chompanaich, *I would not backbite my comrade.—G. P.*

Cagair, *v. n.* Whisper; listen to a whisper. *Pret. a.* chagair, *whispered.* Cagair rium, *whisper to me.*

Cagall, aill, *s. m.* The herb-cockle. Written also *cogall. Ir.* cagal.

Cagallach, *a.* Parsimonious; miserly, sparing; economical; also, *substantively*, a penurious person; an economical person.

Cagallachd, *s. f.* Parsimoniousness; penury.

Cagar, air, *s.* A whisper; a buzzing sound; a hum; a secret. Dean cagar, *whisper.* Cagar beach na bruaich, *the hum of the mountain-bee.—Oss. Fin. and Lor.* Written also *cogar;* which see.

Cagaraich, **Cagarsaich**, *s. f.* A whispering, a continued whispering. Tha thu ri cagarsaich, *thou art whispering. Asp. form.* chagarsaich. Ciod a chagarsaich th'ort? *what are you whispering at?*

Cagnadh, aidh, *s. m.* A chewing, a gnawing, a champing, mastication.

Cagnadh, (a), *pr. part.* of cagainn. 'G a chagnadh na 'm beul, *chewing it in their mouths.—Sm.*

Cagnaidh, *fut. aff. a.* Shall chew, champ, or gnaw.

Cagnar, *fut. pass.* of cagainn. Shall be chewed.

† **Cai**, *s. f.* A road; a house; a titling.—*Ir. id.*

Caib, caibe, *s. m.* (*W.* caib.) A spade, a mattock. A gheurachadh a chaibe, *to sharpen his spade.—Stew. Sam. N. pl.* caibeachan. Iasad a chaibe gun a chur fuidh thalamh, *the loan of a spade that is not put in the ground.—G. P.*

Caibeal, eil, *s. m.* A chapel; a family burying-place. *N. pl* caibealan.

Caibeineachd, *s. f.* Gabbling, prating.

Caibhne, *s. f.* Friendship.—*Shaw.*

Caibideal, eil, *s. f.* A chapter. *Ir.* caibidil. *Corn.* cabydul, *a chapter. Lat.* capitellum, *a little head.*

† **Caibne**, *s. f.* The mouth.

† **Caideal**, eil, *s. m.* A pump. *N. pl.* caidealan.

† **Caidh**, *a.* Chaste, immaculate; also, *substantively*, order, manner, method.

† **Caidhe**, *s. f.* Dirt, blemish.—*Shaw.*

† **Caidheach**, *a.* Dirty, blemished, polluted.

† **Caidheachd**, *s. f.* Chastity.—*Shaw.*

Caidhean, ein, *s. m.* The leader of a flock of goats; a turtle dove.—*Shaw.*

† **Caidheil**, *a.* (caidh-amhuil.) Chaste, decent.

Caidil, *v. n.* Sleep, slumber, repose. *Pret. a.* chaidil, *slept; fut. aff. a.* caidilidh, *shall sleep.* Written also *cadail.*

Caidir, *v. a.* Permit, connive at; also converse; fondle. *Pret. a.* chaidir; *fut. aff. a.* caidiridh, *shall permit.* Olc ni 'n caidir thu, *thou shalt not permit wickedness.—Sm.*

Caidreach, *a.* Friendly, kind, familiar, conversant, fond; also an acquaintance; a partner.

Caidreamh, eimh, *s.* (*perhaps* comh-aitreamh.) Fellowship, partnership, familiarity, acquaintance; discourse; commerce; assemblage.—*Macint. Ir.* caidreadh. *W.* caidreav, *a joint dwelling.*

Caidreamhach, aich, *s. m.* (comh-aitreamhach.) An acquaintance, a companion; a room-companion, a fellow-lodger. Làimh ri treudaibh do chaidreamhach, *near the flocks of thy companion.—Stew. Song. Sol. ref.*

Caidreamhach, *a.* (*from* caidreamh.) Familiar, conversant, fond, social, companionable. Gu caidreamhach, *familiarly. Com.* and *sup.* caidreamhaiche.

Caidreamhas, ais, *s. m.* (*W.* cyddras.) Consanguinity; familiarity, intimacy, fondness.

Caigeann, *a.* Couple together, link together. *Pret. a.* chaigeann; *fut. aff. a.* caigeannaidh, *shall couple.*

Caigeann, inn, *s. m.* Two linked or coupled together.

Caigne, *s. f.* A fan to winnow with.—*Shaw.*

Càil, càile, *s. f.* (*Ir.* cail.) Disposition, temper; quality, condition; life; strength; sense; constitution; voice; appetite; look or appearance. Gum fainich naimhde a càil, *that enemies may feel its temper.—Oss.* San tigh chaol gun chàil, *in the narrow house without life.—Oss. Derm.* Mo chàil a treigsinn, *my strength failing.—Id.* Chaill iad càil an claisteachd, *they lost their sense of hearing.—Macdon.*

† **Cail**, caile, *s. f.* A spear; a shield.—*Shaw.*

† **Cailbhe**, *s. f.* A mouth, an orifice.—*Ir. id.*

Cailbheach, *a.* Wide-mouthed; yawning.

† **Cailbheachd**, *s. f.* Continued or frequent yawning.

† **Caile**, *s. f.* A shield, a buckler.—*Shaw.*

Cailc, cailce, *s. f.* (*Corn.* caleh.) Chalk. D' aodainn mar chailc, *the face like chalk.—Old Song.*

Cailceach, *a.* Chalky, like chalk.

Cailceanta, *a.* Hard.—*Ir. id.*

Cailceil, *a.* (cailc-amhuil.) Chalky, like chalk.

Caile, *s. f.* *Ir. id.* (*Arm.* calch.) A girl; a vulgar girl, a hussy; a quean; a strumpet. *N. pl.* cailean, *girls.* Caile-bhalaoch, *a romp.*

Caile-bhalaoch, *s. f.* A romp.

Càileach, *a.* (*from* càil.) Of, or belonging to, disposition; having a good disposition or quality; tempered.

Càileachd, *s. f.* (*Ir.* càilidheachd.) Natural endowments, accomplishments, genius; constitution, temper, nature. Aois a leaghadh do chàileachd, *age dissolving thy constitution.—Old Song.* Gun chron càileachd, *without blemish of temper.—Old Song.*

Caileachdach, *a.* Having natural endowments; accomplished; having genius.

Càileachdan, *n. pl.* of càileachd. Accomplishments, dispositions, passions or affections of the mind.

Caileadair, *s. m.* A calendar.—*Macd. N. pl.* caileadairean.

Caileag, eig, *s. f.* A girl, a young girl. *N. pl.* caileagan.

Caileagan, *n. pl.* of caileag. Girls.

Càileanach, aich, *s. m.* A breeze.

Caileanta, *a.* (*from* caile.) Girlish; also fond of girls.

Caileas, eis, *s. m.* Lethargy.—*Shaw.*

Cail-eigin, *a.* and *adv.* Some, somewhat, a little, something, in some degree, in some measure. Labhram caileigin, *I will speak something.*

† CAILG, cailge, *s. f.* A sting; resentment.—*Shaw.*

† CAILG, *v. n.* Sting, prick, pierce. *Pret. a.* chailg.

† CAILIDEAR, eir, *s. m.* Rheum, phlegm, snot.

CAILINN, *s. f.* (*Ir.* cailin.) A girl, a damsel, a maiden; a company of young women. *Asp. form,* chailinn. Bha chailinn ro mhaiseach, *the maiden was very fair.*—*Stew. O. T.* Chum beathachaidh do chailinn, *for the maintenance of thy maidens.*—*Stew. Pro.*

CAILL, *v. a.* Lose, win not, suffer loss. *Pret. a.* chaill, *lost; fut. aff. a.* caillidh. Mun caill iad an treòir, *ere they lose their strength.*—*Ardar.*

† CAILL, *s. m.* (*Arm.* caill.) A testicle. Hence caillteanach, *an eunuch.*

CAILLE, *s. f.* A veil, a hood. (*Ir.* caille. *Eng.* cowl.) Hence cailleach, *an old woman.*

CAILLEACH, ich, *s. f.* (*from* caille.) An old woman, an old wife; *in derision,* a coward. *N. pl.* cailleachan. Ma 's cailleach gun bhrigh thu, *if thou beest a sapless old woman.*—*Old Song.* Cailleach-chòsach, *a cheslip;* cailleach cheann-dubh, *a titmouse;* cailleach oidhche, *an owl.*

CAILLEACH, *s.* Husks of corn.

CAILLEACHAG, eig, *s. f.* (*dim.* of cailleach.) A little old woman. *N. pl.* cailleachagan.

CAILLEACHAIL, *a.* (cailleach-amhuil.) Like an old woman; also cowardly.

CAILLEACHANTA, *a.* Cowardly; soft; unmanly.

CAILLEACHAS, ais, *s. m.* The conduct of an old woman; dotage; cowardice.

CAILLEACHCHEANN-DUBH, *s. f.* A titmouse; a colemouse; the *parus ater* of Linnæus.

CAILLEACH-CHÒSACH, aich, *s. f.* A cheslip; a milleped.—*Shaw.*

CAILLEACH-DHUBH, *s. f.* A nun. Cailleachan dubh, *nuns.*

CAILLEACH-OIDHCHE, *s. f.* An owl; the *strix ulula* of Linnæus. Cumha na caillich-oidhche, *the owl's lament.*—*Stew. Mic.* Written more correctly *coileach-oidhche.* Cailleach-oidhche gheal, *a white owl; the strix flammea of Linnæus.*

† CAILLEADH, idh, *s. m.* (*from* caille.) The process of castration; castration.

CAILLEAG, eig, *s. f.* A loss; a detriment. *N. pl.* cailleagan.

CAILLEAN, ein, *s. m.* (*from* càth.) A seed; a husk of grain. Caillean ann am fhiacaill, *a seed between my teeth.*—*Macfar.* *N. pl.* càilleanan. Ni caillean am fiacail inntinn loisnich, *a seed in the gums disturbs the mind.*—*G. P.*

CAILLEANACH, *a.* Full of seeds or husks of grain.

CAILLEANACH, aich, *s. m.* (*from* caill.) One who loses, one who is apt to lose or drop any thing, one who suffers a loss.

† CAILLEASG, eisg, *s. m.* A horse or mare.—*Shaw.* *N. pl.* cailleasgan.

CAILLTE, *p. part.* of caill. (*Arm.* collet.) Lost, ruined, damned. Caillte is fadheoidh air sgeul, *lost and found again.*—*Sm.* An ni nach caillte gheibhear e, *what is not lost will be found.*—*G. B.*

CAILLTEACH, *a.* Ruinous, causing loss; losing, apt to lose. Brù chailltleach, *a miscarrying womb.*—*Stew. Hos.*

CAILLTEANACH, aich, *s. m.* (*from* † caille.) An eunuch.—*Stew. G. B.* *N. pl.* caillteanaich.

CAILTEARNACH, aich, *s. m.* A shrubby place, a shrubbery.

CAIM, *s. f.* A stain, a blot, a fault.—*Ir. id.*

CAIME, *s. f.* Crookedness.

CAIME, *com.* and *sup.* of cam. More or most crooked.

CAIMEAN, ein, *s. m.* A mote.—*Stew. Mat. ref.* A little blot, a little stain.

CAIMEANACH, *a.* Full of motes; like a mote.

CAIMHDEAN, ein, *s. m.* A multitude.

CAIMHEACH, ich, *s. m.* A protector.—*Shaw.*

† CAIMIS, caimse, *s. f.* A shirt; a shift.—*Ir. id.* *It.* camiscia. *Fr.* chemise.

† CAIMLEAR, eir, *s. m.* A bent stick used by butchers.—*Shaw.* *N. pl.* caimlearan.

† CAIMNEACH, *a.* (*Ir. id.*) Chaste.—*Shaw.*

CAIMPEAR, ir, *s. m.* (fear-caimp.) A champion; a warrior. *N. pl.* caimfearan.

† CAIN, *a.* Chaste; beloved.—*Ir. id.*

CÀIN, *s. f.* Tribute, tax; rent; a fine; also slander. Nach ioc iad càin? *will they not pay tribute?*—*G. B.*

CAIN, *v. a.* (*Ir. id.*) Slander; revile; scold; dispraise *Pret. a.* chàin; *fut. aff. a.* càinidh, *shall slander; fut. pass.* càinear.

† CAINDEAL, eil, *s. f.* A candle. Now written *coinneal;* which see.

CAINEAB, eib *and* cainbe, *s. f.* (*from* can, *white.*) A canvas; also hemp. Is fearr crathadh na cainbe no crathadh na cirbe, *the shaking of a canvas sheet is better than the dusting of a bag.*—*G. P.*

Gr. κανναβις. *Lat.* cannabis. *Anglo-Sax.* hoenep. *Arm.* canab. *Du.* kennip. *Teut.* kenneb. *Pers.* cannab.

CAINEAB-AODACH, aich, *s. m.* Canvas.

CÀINEACH, *a.* (*from* càin.) Tributary; like a tribute or fine; prone to slander.

CAINEACHD, *s. f.* Taxation, taxing; the habit of slander.

CÀINEADH, idh, *s. m.* (*Ir. id.*) A reviling, a traducing; slander. An càineadh, *their reviling.*—*Stew. Is.* Fear càinidh, *a traducer;* luchd-càinidh, *traducers.*

† CAINEAG, eig, *s. f.* A mote; a farthing; barley, oats. *N. pl.* caineagan.

CAINEAL, eil, *s. m.* Cinnamon. *W.* kanuylk. *Span.* and *Port.* canela.

CAINGEAL, eil, *s. m.* A hurdle; a reason.—*Shaw.*

† CAINGEAN, ein, *s. m.* A prayer; also an agreement or compact; a rule; a cause.

CÀINICH, *v. a.* (*from* cain.) *Ir. id.* Fine, amerce, tax. *Pret. a.* chàinich, *taxed; fut. aff. a.* càinichidh, *shall fine.*

CAINIDH, *fut. aff. a.* Shall traduce.

CAINNEAL, eil, *s. f.* A channel, a canal.—*Macd.*

CAINNEAL, *s. f.* A candle. More frequently written *coinneal;* which see.

CAINNT, càinnte, *s. f.* (*Ir. id.*) Language, speech; discourse, conversation; a language or tongue. Cainnt bhallsgach, *burlesque.* Cha robh cainnt ann, *he had not the power of speech.*—*Stew. K.* *N. pl.* cainntean.

CAINNTEACH, (*from* cainnt.) Talkative; peevish, cross, malicious. Gu cainnteach, *peevishly.* *Com.* and *sup.* cainntiche, *more or most talkative.*

CAINNTEACHD, *s. f.* Pronunciation; talkativeness; peevishness.

CAINNTEAG, eig, *s. f.* A peevish cross young female; a canticle.—*Ir. id.*

† CAINNTEAL, eil, *s. m.* A press; a lump.—*Shaw.*

CAINNTEAN, ein, *s. m.* A peevish person, a cross person.

CAINNTEAR, eir, *s. m.* An orator, a linguist; a babbler. *Ir.* cainnteoir.

CÀIR, *s. f.* (*Ir. id.*) A gum. See CAIREAN.

CÀIR, *v. a.* Dig; raise; prepare; gird on; bury; repair, mend; lay up; send away; assert; persuade, make to believe. *Pret. a.* chàir; *fut. aff. a.* cairidh, *shall dig.* Caireadh iad m' uaigh, *let them raise my tomb.*—*Oss. Gaul.* Cairibh mise le m' ghaol, *bury me with my beloved.*—*Oss. Derm.* Caireadh gach aon a lann, *let every one gird on his sword.*—*Ull.* Cairidh mi a balla, *I will repair her walls.—Smith.* Chàireadh e orm, *he would assert to me, he would make me believe.*

CAIRB, *s. f.* A fusee; a chariot; a ship; a plank.

CAIRBEAN, ein, *s. m.* A species of basking shark, by sailors called a sailfish. It is found on the western coasts of the northern seas; according to Linnæus, in the Arctic circle. They have been caught, however, among the Orkneys and Hebrides, in Ballishannon Bay in Ireland, and in Wales. They measure in length from thirty-six to forty feet. Pennant mentions one which he saw caught in Arran.

CAIRBEIL, *s. f.* A large eel.

CAIRBH, *v. a.* Man a fleet; shake, quiver. *Pret. a.* cairbh; *fut. aff. a.* cairbhidh.

CAIRBHE, *s. f.* A dead body; a carcass; a corpse. *N. pl.* cairbhean; *d. pl.* cairbhibh. Air na cairbhibh, *on the carcasses.—Stew. G. B.*

W. cwrv, *a corpse. Heb.* careb, *a dead body embalmed.*

CAIRBHEAN, *n. pl.* of cairbh. Carcasses; corpses.

CAIRBHINN, *s. f.* (*Eng.* carrion.) A carcass, a corpse; lean meat; carrion. *N. pl.* cairbhinnean; *d. pl.* cairbhinnibh. Cairbhinnean an righrean, *the carcasses of their kings.—Stew. Ezek.* Cha 'n eil crioch air an cairbhinnibh, *there is no end to their corpses.—Stew. Nah.*

CAIRBHINNEACH, *a.* Full of carcasses; of, or pertaining to, a corpse or carcass; like a corpse or carcass; cadaverous.

CAIRBHINNEACHD, *s. f.* A slaughtering, a massacring; cadaverousness.

CAIRBINN, *s. f.* A carabine. *N. pl.* cairbinnean.

CAIRBINNEACH, ich, *s. m.* A toothless person; also, *adjectively,* toothless.

† CAIRC, cairce, *s. f.* Hair; fur; eagerness.

† CAIRCEACH, *a.* Hairy; eager. Gu cairceach, *eagerly.*

CAIRCHEAS, ais, *s. m.* A little vessel; a twist.

CAIRD, cairde, *s. f.* (*Ir. id. Corn.* herd, *affection.*) Friendship; a bosom friend; delay, respite, rest; scruple. Fasgadh is caird, *shelter and rest.—Fingalian Poem.* Gun chaird, *incessantly; without scruple.*

CAIRDE, *n. pl.* (*Ir. id.*) Friends; relations. *Asp. form,* chairde. Mo chairde san fhrith, *my friends in the forest.—Oss. Fing.* Cairde gaoil, *kinsfolk.*

CAIRDEACH, *a.* (*from* caird.) (*W.* caredig. *Ir.* cairdeoch, *related. Corn.* caradow.) Related; connected by birth or by marriage; friendly. Do na h-uaislean tha thu cairdeach, *thou art related to the gentry.—Old Song. Com.* and *sup.* cairdiche.

CAIRDEALACHD, *s. f.* (caird-amhuileachd.) Friendliness.

CAIRDEALAS, ais, *s. m.* Friendliness.

CAIRDEAN, *n. pl.* of caird, (or contracted for *caraidean.*) Friends, relations, cousins. Cha bu cheo mo chairdean, *my friends were not as mist.—Oss. Manos.* Cairdean, nigheanan an dà bhràthar, *cousins, the daughters of two brothers;* cairdean, mic an dà bhràthar, *cousins, the sons of two brothers;* cairdean, mic an dà pheathar, *cousins, the sons of two sisters;* cairdean, nigheanan an dà pheathar, *cousins, the daughters of two sisters.—Macd.*

CAIRDEAS, eis, *s. m.* Relationship, friendship, fellowship. Cairdeas no comunn, *nor friendship nor fellowship;* cairdeas fola, *blood relationship;* cairdeas marraiste, *affinity;* comhaltas gu ceud, is cairdeas gu fichead, *the relation of fostering connects by hundreds, the relation of blood only by twenties.—G. P.*

CAIRDEIL, *a.* (caird-amhuil.) Friendly; *literally,* friendlike.

CAIR-DHEARG, *s. f.* A blush.—*Shaw.*

CAIREACHAN, ain, *s. m.* A big-mouthed person.

CAIREAG, eig, *s. f.* A prating young girl. *N. pl.* caireagan.

CAIREAGACH, *a.* Prating; applied to a garrulous young female.

CÀIREAN, ein, *s. m.* The gum of the mouth; a palate; the taste of the mouth; a grin; a beloved person; a darling. *N. pl.* càireanan *and* càirein. Do m' chairein, *to my* [*gums*] *taste.—Stew. Song Sol. ref.* Do chairean, *thy palate.—Stew. O. T.*

CÀIREANACH, *a.* Having gums; of gums.

CAIR-FHIADH, -fheidh, *s. m.* A hart, a stag. *N. pl.* cair-fheidh.—*Ir. id. Arm.* karo.

CAIRICH, *v. a.* (*Ir.* cairrigh.) Repair, mend; inter, bury; raise a monumental mound; accuse, lay to one's charge. *Pret. a.* chàirich, *mended; fut. aff. a.* càirichidh. Chàirich e 'n altair, *he repaired the altar.—Stew. K.* Na càirich am peacadh oirnne, *lay not the sin* [*to our charge*] *on us.—Stew. Numb.*

CAIRID, *s. m.; provincial for* caraid; which see.

CAIRINN, *s. c.* A darling. *Lat.* car-us, *dear.*

† CAIRLEUM, *v. a.* and *n.* Tumble about; beat or toss about.—*Shaw.*

CAIRMEAL, eil, *s. m.* Wild pease, heath pease; the *crobus tuberosus* of Linnæus.

The ancient Caledonians are said to have made much use of this root as an article of food. The Hebridians, according to Pennant, chew this root like tobacco, and also make a fermented liquor from it. They say that it is a good medicine; that it promotes expectoration, and is very serviceable in pulmonary complaints. It grows in heaths and birchwoods to the size of a filbert: sometimes four or five roots are joined by fibres. The stalk of it is green, and bears a red flower. When the root is pounded and infused, with yeast superadded, as is done by many of the Hebrideans, a palatable and wholesome liquor is produced. Some have supposed that this is the *chara* which the soldiers of Valerius found, as is mentioned by Cæsar *de Bello Civ.* lib. iii.

CAIRN, *gen. sing.* of carn. Of a cairn.

CAIRNEACH, ich, *s. m.* A kingsfisher, an osprey; also, in allusion to his dwelling-place, a druid.

CAIRNEACH, *a.* (*from* carn.) Rocky, stony, shelvy. Iasgair cairneach, *a kingsfisher, an osprey.*

CAIRNEAN, ein, *s. m.* An egg-shell. Cairnean uibh, *an egg-shell.*

CAIRREALL, eill, *s. m.* A noise; the sound of distant music; harmony, melody, caroling.

CAIRREALLACH, *a.* Harmonious, caroling.

CÀIRT, *s. f.* (*Lat.* quart-us.) A quarter of a yard; a fourth part of a yard. Slat agus càirt, *a yard and a quarter.* Leth-chrun an càirt, *half-a-crown a quarter.*

CAIRT, cartach, *s. f.* A cart; bark of a tree or rhind; a card; a chart, a charter; a deed or bond; *rarely* a stone, a rock. *N. pl.* cairtean. Cairt nomha, *a new cart.—Stew. Sam.* Fuidh 'n chairt, *under the bark.—Macint.* A cluich' air chairtean, *playing at cards;* cuidhle na cartach, *the cart-wheel.*

Span. carreta, *a cart. Ir.* cairt. *W.* cart. *Lat.* charta, *paper,* and cortex, *bark. Swed.* kort, *a cord.*

CAIRT, *v. a.* (*Ir. id.*) Cleanse, as a stable; strip off the bark; tan as leather. *Pret. a.* chairt, *cleansed; fut. aff. a.* cairtidh, *shall cleanse.*

CAIRT-CHEAP, -chip, *s.* The name of a cart-wheel.—*Ir. id.*

CAIRTEAG, eig, *s. f.* (*dim.* of cairt.) A little cart; a tumbrel. *N. pl.* cairteagan.

CAIRTEAL, eil, *s. m.* (*Span.* cartel.) A quarter of any thing, a gill; a lodging; a chartulary; a challenge; an edict. *N. pl.* cairtealan.

CAIRTEALAN, *n. pl.* of cairteal. Quarters, lodgings; also a chartulary, a challenge. Air chairtealan, *on quarters; quartered, lodged.—Old Song.* Nan cairtealaibh geamhraidh, *in their winter quarters.—Macdon.*

CAIRTEAR, eir, *s. m.* A carter, a carman, a waggoner. *Ir.* cairteoir.

CAIRT-IÙIL, *s. f.* A mariner's compass.—*Macint.* Also a sea-chart. Air cairt-iùil air falbh uainn, *our sea-chart away from us.—Old Song.*

Cairtlan, ain, *s. m.* A chartulary. *N. pl.* cartlain.

† **Cais**, *a.* Spruce, trim.—*Shaw.*

† **Cais**, *s. f.* Regard, love, esteem; also hatred. *Ir.* cais. *W.* cas.

Cais-bheart, *s.* Shoes and stockings; greaves. Written more frequently *coisbheart.*

Cais-chiabh, *s. m.* A curl or ringlet. *N. pl.* cais-chiabhan, *curls.*

Cais-chiabhach, *a.* Curly; having ringlets or tresses.

Caisd, *v. n.* Listen, hearken, be quiet; silence! *Pret.* chaisd, *became quiet; fut. aff.* caisdidh, *shall become quiet;* chaisd i ri caithream na seilg, *she listened to the noise of the chase.—Oss. Gaul.* Nach caisd thu? *wilt thou not be quiet?* caisd a sin thu, *be quiet.*

Caisdeachd, *s. f.* (*Ir.* coisteachd.) A listening; a silencing. With *a* it forms the *pres. part.* of caisd. Ceòl air tuinn is ròin a caisdeachd, *music on the waters and seals listening.—Oss. Derm.* Cluas ri caisteachd, *a personage in Highland mythology.*

Caisdeal, eil, *s. m.* A castle; a fort, a garrison; a turretted house. Caisdeal Bhealaich, *Taymouth Castle;* Caisdeal Ionmhar-lòchaidh, *Fort-William, in the West Highlands;* caisdeal a chuirp, *the trunk.*

Lat. castellum. *W.* castell. *Arm.* castel. *Du.* kasteal.

Caisdealach, *a.* Castelled, turretted; full of forts, castles, or garrisons; of, or pertaining to, a fort or castle; like a fort or castle. Carraig chaisdealach, *a castled rock.*

Càise, *s. f.* Cheese. Mulachag chàise, *a cheese;* càise cruidh, *cow's-milk cheese.—Stew. Sam.*

Lat. caseus. *It.* caccia. *W.* caws. *Ir.* càise. *Du.* caas. *Corn.* kez *and* caus. *Arm.* caus. *Teut.* kaese *and* kase. *Germ.* caes. *Span.* queso.

Caise, *com.* and *sup.* of cas. More or most steep.

Caise, *s. f.* A wrinkle; a fold; passion; steepness; a stream; *rarely* a mushroom, discord. Aghaidh gun sgraing gun chaise, *a face without frown or wrinkle.—Old Song.*

Caiseach, *a.* Wrinkled; passionate; impetuous.

Càiseach, *a.* Abounding in cheese; like cheese; of, or belonging to, cheese. Aranach càiseach, *abounding in bread and cheese.—Macd.*

Caisead, eid, *s. m.* Steepness; suddenness; rapidity; impetuosity.—*Macint.* Increase in steepness, or in rapidity. A dol an caisead, *growing more and more steep.*

Caiseag, eig, *s. f.* The stem of a weed.—*Shaw.*

† **Caiseal**, eil, *s. m.* A bulwark, a wall; a castle, a garrison. *N. pl.* caisealan.

Caisealach, *a.* Having bulwarks; walled; castelled; like a bulwark, wall, or garrison.

Càisear, ir, *s. m.* (càis-fhear.) A cheesemonger. *W.* cawswr.

Càisearachd, *s. f.* The business of a cheesemonger; cheesemongery.

Caisearbhan, ain, *s. m.* A dandelion.

Cais-fhionn, *a.* White-footed; also a name given to a white-legged cow.

Càisg, *s. f.* (*Ir. id.*) The passover; Easter. Di-dòmhnuich càisg, *Easter Sunday.* Earrach fad an deigh Chàisg, *Spring long after Easter is a bad sign of the season.—G. P.*

Perhaps *caisg* should have been *paisg*, agreeably to the analogy of other languages. *Gr.* πασχα. *Lat.* pascha. *Heb.* pasadh, *pass over;* the angel having passed over the Israelitic habitations which had their doors sprinkled with the blood of the lamb.

Caisg, *v. a.* and *n.* Restrain, check, stop, still, calm, quell, subside, put an end to. *Pret. a.* chaisg; *fut. aff. a.* caisgidh, *shall or will restrain.* Caisgidh mi an sruth, *I will stop the stream.—Oss. Tem.* Caisgidh mi shiubhal, *I will check his progress.—Id.* Chaisg an onfha, *the storm subsided.—Oss. Trath.* A chaisgeas fuaimneach mara is tuinn, *who stills the roar of sea and surge.—Sm. Fut. pass.* caisgear.

Caisgear, *fut. pass.* of caisg. Shall be checked or quelled.

Caisgidh, *fut. aff. a.* Shall restrain, check, or stop.

† **Caisil-chro**, *s. f.* A bier. An caisil-chro tha 'n laoch, *the hero is on his bier.—Oss. Conn.*

This bier was made of wicker, and used by the ancient Gael. The Roman bier, or *feretrum*, was seemingly of the same structure, according to Ruæus, in Æn. vi. 221. "Feretrum e ligno et vimine contextum," *a bier made of deal and woven twigs.*"

Caisleach, ich, *s. f.* A ford; a footpath; a smooth place, a smooth path. Caisleach spuinc, *touchwood.*

Caisleach-spuing, *s. f.* Touchwood, spunk.

† **Caislear**, ir, *s. m.* A projector. *N. pl.* caislearan.

Caislichte, *a.* Polished, smoothed, burnished.

Caismeachd, *s. f.* (*i. e.* cas-imeachd, *hurried movement.*) An alarm; a warning; a hint; a Highland march, a war-song. Caismeachd na maduinn, *the warning of morn.—Oss.* Caismeachd nan sonn, *the alarm of heroes.—Oss. Lodin.*

Caismeachdach, *a.* Warning; giving an alarm or warning; alarming.

Caismeart, eirt, *s. m.* (cas-iomairt.) The heat of battle; armour; a band of combatants.

Caisreabhachd, *s. f.* Legerdemain, juggling.—*Ir. id.*

Caisreabhaiche, *s. m.* A juggler, a conjurer.

Caisreag, eig, *s. f.* A wrinkle; a curl; a ringlet. *N. pl.* caisreagan; *gen. pl.* caisreag; *asp. form,* chaisreag, *full of ringlets, tressy.—Macint.*

Caisreagach, *a.* (*from* caisreag.) Curled; bushy, as hair; wrinkled. A chiabha caisreagach, *his bushy locks.—Stew. Song Sol. Com.* and *sup.* caisreagaiche, *more or most curled.*

Caisteal, eil, *s. m.* A castle, a fort, a garrison; a turretted mansion. Bu chaisteal dhomh thu, *thou wert a garrison to me.—Sm.* Caisteal a chuirp, *the trunk of the body.*

Lat. castellum. *W.* castell. *Arm.* castel *and* gastell. *Du.* kasteal.

C'ait, *adv.* (cia àit.) *Ir. id.* Where, in what place; whither. C'ait as, *whence.* C'àit tha thu dol? *whither art thou going?—Stew. Gen.* C'ait am bheil e? *where is he?*

Caiteach, ich, *s. f.* Chaff; husks, as of seed; also, *adjectively,* full of chaff, full of husks.

Caiteach, *a.* Extravagant. More correctly *caithteach.*

Caiteachas, ais, *s. m.* Extravagance. See **Caithteachas.**

Caiteag, eig, *s. f.* A pot, a butter-pot. *Ir.* caiteog. *N. pl.* caiteagan.

Caitean, ein, *s. m.* The knap of cloth, shag; rough hairy surface; what is rubbed from off a soft surface; the blossom of osier. Caitean brucach nan craobh, *the shaggy speckled moss of trees.—Macdon. Ir.* caitin.

† **Caitean**, ein, *s. m.* A chain. *Lat.* catena. *Teut.* keten.

Caiteanach, *a.* Rough, shaggy; knappy, as cloth; rough-skinned; curled: also, *substantively,* a hairdresser; a cloth-dresser.

Caiteas, eis, *s. m.* Caddis; the scrapings of linen.

Caith, *v. a.* Spend, waste, squander, pass, consume, exhaust, wear. *Pret. a.* chaith, *spent; fut. aff. a.* caithidh, *shall spend.* Na caith do lochrain, *waste not thy flames.—Oss. Gaul.* Caitheadhmaid an oidhche, *let us pass [spend] the night.—Ull.* Caithidh an t-amadan, *the fool will squander.—Stew. Pro.* Caith do shaothair, *bestow thy labour in vain.* Gu 'm meall is gun caith thu e, *may you enjoy and wear it.—Old Saying.*

† **Caith**, *a.* Chaste, mild.—*Ir. id.*

Caith' aimsir, *s. m.* Pastime; a waste of time.

Caith-beatha, *s. m.* Behaviour, conduct, conversation. Air caith-beatha roimh so, *our conversation [conduct] in former times.—Stew. Eph.*

Caitheach, ich, *s. m.* A spendthrift; also, *adjectively*, profuse, extravagant.

Caitheadh, idh, *s. m.* A spending; extravagance. More frequently written *caitheamh*.

Caitheamh, eimh, *s. m.* and *f.* The act of spending, the act of consuming; a wearing, a decaying; extravagance, waste; consumption, decay. Gu caitheamh ullamh, *ready to consume.—Sm.* Caitheamh agus fiabhrus, *decay and fever.—Id.* Caitheamh-aimsir, *pastime.* Bithidh sonas an lorg na caitheimh, *happiness follows the generous.—G. P.* Tinneas caitheimh, *a consumption.*

Caithear, *fut. pass.* of caith. Shall be spent or consumed.

Caithleach, *s.* (*from* càth.) Husks of corn; seeds; chaff. Diasan arbhair nan càithleach, *ears of corn in their husks.—Stew. K.*

Caithlean, ein, *s. m.* (*from* càth.) A husk, as of corn. *D. pl.* caithleinibh. Le 'n càithleinibh, *with their husks.—Stew. K. ref.*

Caithleanach, *a.* Husky as corn, seedy.

Caithream, eim, *s. m.* (*Ir. id. Gr.* χαρμα, *mirth.*) A shout of triumph or of joy; a loud shout; symphony; triumph; information; notice. Do 'n chaithream aoibhinn, *to the joyful shout.—Smith.* Mar chaithream chlàr, *like the symphony of harps.—Oss. Derm.*

Caithream seems to be made up of *cath*, battle, and † *reim*, power; or perhaps it is *cath-thoirm*.

Caithreamach, *a.* Triumphant, victorious; making a loud shout. *Ir.* cathreimach.

Caithris, *s. f.* A watching; circumspection, attention; a watch by night.—*Macd.*

Caithriseach, *a.* Watchful, attentive, circumspect. Gu caithriseach, *watchfully.* *Com.* and *sup.* caithrisiche.

Caithriseachd, *s. f.* Continued or frequent watching, watchfulness, attentiveness, circumspection.

Caithte, *p. part.* of caith. Spent, wasted, squandered.

Caithteach, *a.* (*from* caith.) Lavish; consuming, wasting, wearing. Tinneas caithteach, *a wasting disease.* *Com.* and *sup.* caithtiche.

Caithteachas, ais, *s. m.* (*from* caith.) Lavishness, profusion, a wasting.

Caithtiche, *s. m.* (*from* caith.) A spendthrift, a waster.

† **Cal**, cail, *s. m.* Sleep.—*Ir. id.*

Càl, càil, *s. m.* Kail, colewort; a name for all sorts of cabbage; Scotch broth, of which kail is a principal ingredient; a dinner; *rarely*, a joke. Càl cearslach, *cabbage;* càl-gruidheam, *cauliflower;* càl colag, *cauliflower.—Macd.* An d' fhuair do chàl? *have you got your* [*dinner*] *kail?* Garadh càil, *a kitchen-garden.*

Gr. καυλος. *Lat.* caulis. *Teut.* koolc. *Belg.* koole. *Germ.* kohl. *Swed.* kol. *Sax.* cawl. *Eng.* cole *and* kail. *Arm.* caulen. *W.* and *Corn.* cowl. *Ir.* càl.

Cal, Caladh, aidh, *s. m.* Condition of body; grief, despondency; darkness. Is math a chal, *he is in good condition of body;* mu 'm fàs air d-inntinn cal, *before grief falls on thy soul.—Smith.*

† **Cal**, *v. n.* Enter a port or harbour.—*Ir. id. Shaw.*

Càla, ai, **Càladh**, aidh, *s. m.* A harbour, a port; a shore; a ferry. Fhuair sinn an càla, *we gained the harbour.—Orr.* An càladh ait, *the joyful shore.—Smith.*

Lat. † cala. *It.* cala, *a lee-shore, a bay.* *Fr.* cale. *Span.* cala, *bay.* *Teut.* kille *and* kielle.

From *càla* come the names of all sea-port towns and of countries noted for good harbours, ending in *cal*, *gal*, or *cala;* as Burdicala, or Burdigula, on the Garonne; Portucal, or Portugal. Hence also Cala-is (Caletum), a sea-port in France.

Calaich, *v. a.* (*from* cala.) Bring into harbour; harbour; reside; continue. *Pret. a.* chalaich, *resided; fut. aff. a.* calaichidh.

† **Calair**, *s. m.* A crier.

† **Calaireachd**, *s. f.* Proclamation; shouting; burying.

† **Calaiseachd**, *s. f.* A juggler.

† **Calaist**, *s. f.* A college.—*Ir. id.*

Calaman, ain, *s.* A dove. *Provincial for* columan.

Calba, *s. m.* A leg; the brown of the leg. More frequently written *calpa;* which see.

† **Calbh**, *a.* Bald.

Ir. calbh. *Lat.* calvus. *Chald.* chalaph, *strip of bark.* *Heb.* chalal, *smooth.*

† **Calbhach**, *a.* Causing baldness.

Calbhachd, *s. f.* Baldness.

Calc, *v. a.* (*Lat.* calco, *to tramp.*) Caulk, drive, beat, ram, cram; push violently forward; beat a bullet into a gun with a ramrod. *Pret. a.* chalc, *crammed; fut. aff. a.* calcaidh.

† **Calc**, cailc, *s. f.* Chalk, lime.

Lat. calx. *W.* calch. *Swed.* kalk. *Du.* kalk. *Teut.* calk.

Calcadh, aidh, *s. m.* The act of caulking, beating, or driving by percussion; driving with a rammer; oakum. Luchd-calcaidh, *caulkers.—Stew. Ezek.* Air a chalcadh, *crammed.—Macint.*

Calcadh, (a), *pr. part.* of calc. Caulking, driving by percussion, ramming, cramming.

Calcaich, *v. a.* Cram, caulk; harden by tramping; grow obdurate. *Pret. a.* chalcaich, *hardened.*

Calcaichte, *p. part.* of calcaich. Caulked, hardened; obdurate.

Calcaidh, *fut. aff. a.* Shall or will caulk or cram.

Calcair, *s. m.* A caulker, a rammer. *N. pl.* calcairean.

Calcaireachd, *s. f.* A caulking, a ramming; the business of a caulker.

Caldach, aich, *s. m.* Loss; mischief. Written also *calldach.*

Caldrait, *s.* Callender, in Stirlingshire; perhaps the κολανια of Ptolemy.

Calg, cuilg, *s.* (*Ir.* calg.) Awn; a prickle, a spear, a sword; any sharp-pointed thing; wrath; ardour; hair, as of a quadruped; the grain. Calg an tuirc, *the boar's bristle.—Oss. Derm.* An aghaidh a chuilg, *against the bristle.—Id.* An aghaidh a chuilg, *against the grain, invitâ Minervâ;* an cluaran a call a chalg, *the thistle losing its prickle.—Oss.* Iomairt nan calg, *the contest of spears.—Fingalian Poem.*

Calgach, *a.* (*from* calg.) *Ir. id.* Bristly, prickly, sharp-pointed, piercing; sprightly; passionate; ardent; having awn, as ears of barley; shaggy, as a quadruped. Le slataibh calgach, *with piercing lashes.—Stew. K.* Armach, calgach, ullamh, *armed, ardent, and ready.—Old Song.*

Calg-dhìreach, *a.* Direct, contrary; against, against the grain. Calg-dhìreach am aghaidh, *directly against me.*

Call, *s. m.* (*Corn. W. Arm.* coll. *Ir.* caill. *Heb.* acholl, *to lose.*) Loss, damage, detriment, calamity; privation, destitution. Call ùine, *loss of time.—Stew. Exod.* Cha bu shuarach an call e, *it was no small loss.—Macfar.* Air chall, *lost, amissing, wanting.—Stew.* 2 *K.* Call an aimsir, *losing time.* *Arm.* coll an amser.

Call, (a), *pr. part.* of caill. Losing, dropping.

Callaid, *s. f.* A fence, a partition, a hedge; a lurking place; a cap, a leather cap; a wig; a wrangling noise; a funeral cry; an elegy. *N. pl.* callaidean. A callaid bhriseadh leat, *thou hast broken down her fences.—Sm.* Callaid dhroighinn, *a hedge of thorns.—Stew. Pro. ref.* Chlisg eilde o 'n challaid chòsaich, *a deer started from its lurking place.*

Callaideach, *a.* Fenced, hedged, partitioned; like a fence, hedge, or partition; of, or belonging to, a fence, hedge, or partition.

† **Callaidh**, *a.* Active, nimble, agile, clever.—*Shaw.*

† **Callaidheachd**, *s. f.* Activity, nimbleness, agility, cleverness.

Call-aimsir, s. m. Loss of time. W. and Arm. coll-amser.

† Callair, s. m. (Ir. id. W. calwr.) A crier. N. pl. callairean.

Callais, s. f. Buffoonery.—*Shaw.*

† Callan, ain, s. m. Noise, clamour, shouting.—*Shaw.*

Calldach, aich, s. m. (*from* call.) Loss, detriment, damage, calamity; a succession of losses. Ni e suas an calldach, *he will make up the loss.—Stew. Exod.*

Calldainn, Callduinn, s. f. (*Corn.* colwiden.) Hazle; a hazle copse. Slatan do 'n challdainn, *hazle rods.—Stew. Gen.* Preas challdainn, *a hazle bush;* cnò challdainn, *a hazle nut;* nathair challdainn, *a species of snake.*

Calm, Calma, a. (*Ir. id.*) Stout, strong; personable; also a stout man, a champion. An anama calma, *their stout souls.—Oss. Cathluno.* Luchd a chridhe chalm, *the stout-hearted.—Sm.* Do radh an calma, *the champion replied.—Fingalian Poem.*

Calmachd, s. f. (*from* calm.) Stoutness, strength, personableness, bravery.

Calmadas, ais, s. m. (*from* calm.) Stoutness, strength, courage.

Calmai, s. pl. Heroes, champions; stout-hearted men. *D. pl.* calmaibh. Fionn le chalmaibh, *Fingal with his heroes.—Fingalian Poem.*

Calman, ain, s. m. A dove. *Provincial for* columan.

Calm-lann, -lainn, s. m. A dovecot.

Calpa, s. m. A leg; the brawn of the leg. *N. pl.* calpan *and* calpanna. Garbh chalpan an righ, *the brawny legs of the king.—Oss. Fing.*

Teut. kalf, *a stout man.* Hence also *Galba*, the name of a Roman emperor, so called from his corpulence.

Càl-phleadhag, aig, s. m. A gardener's dibble.—*Macd.*

Calunn, uinn, s. m. Callosity.

Cam, a. Crooked, bent, distorted, awry; curved; deceitful; blind of an eye. A bhile cam a crith, *his distorted lips quivering.—Oss. Tem.* An ni ata cam, *that which is crooked.—Stew. Ecc.* Duine cam, *a man blind of an eye.*

Gr. καμπ-τω, *to bend. Pers.* cumu, *bending. Chald.* kamar, *to make a vaulted roof. Barbarous Lat.* camus *and* camurus. *Teut.* cam, *bent. Old Eng.* kam. *W. Corn. Arm.* and *Ir.* cam.

Cam, v. a. Bend, distort, curve. *Pret. a.* cham; *fut. aff. a.* camaidh, *shall bend.*

Camacag, aig, s. f. (cam-bhacag.) A trip, a sudden tripping of the heels. Leig e mi le camacag, *he tripped him down;* cuir camacag, *trip. N. pl.* camacagan.

Camadh, aidh, s. m. A bending, a distorting, a curving.

Camag, aig, s. f. (*from* cam.) A curl, a ringlet, a crook, a clasp; the side of the head, the temple; a quibble, a quirk; a small bay. *Asp. form*, chamag. Lan chamag, *full of curls, tressy.—Macint.* Do chamaga am meadhon do chiabh, *the temples in the midst of thy locks.—Stew. Song Sol.*

Camagach, a. (*from* camag.) Curled, as hair; having ringlets; winding; crooked. Do chùl donn camagach, *thy brown curled hair.—Macfar.*

Caman, ain, s. m. (*from* cam.) *W.* camen, *a bend.* A club, a hurling club. *N. pl.* camain, *clubs.* A cluich air a chaman, *playing at shinty, playing at golf.*

Camanachd, s. f. (*from* caman.) A game at *shinty*, a game at golf.

Camas, ais, s. m. A bay, a creek, a harbour; a crooked rivulet; the perineum. An camas dh' aitich an long, *the vessel anchored in the bay.—Oss. Tem.*

Camasach, a. Abounding in bays; of, or pertaining to, a bay.

Cam-bheulach, a. Wry-mouthed.

Cam-bhileach, a. Wry-lipped.

Cam-bhuidh, a. Yellow-waving; yellow-curled. D' fhalt cam-bhuidh, *they curled yellow hair.—Old Song.*

Cam-chosach, a. Bow-legged. *W.* kamgoes. *Span.* cancaiso. *Ir.* cam-chosach.

Cam-dhan, -dhàin, s. m. Iambic verse.

Ca meud, (*for* cia meud.) How many?

Cam-ghlas, ais, s. m. The bird called a red-shank.—*Macd.* and *Shaw.*

Camh, caimh, s. Power, might; also a cave.—*Macint.*

Camhal, ail, s. (*Ir.* camal.) A camel. Uisge airson do chamhal, *water for thy camels.—Stew. Gen. N. pl.* camhail. Deich cambail, *ten camels.—Id.*

Camhan, ain, s. m. (*dim.* of camh.) A little cave; a cove. *N. pl.* camhanan. Feadh nan lùb 's nan camhanan, *among the bays and coves.—Old Song.*

Camhanaich, s. f. The dawn of day, early morn. 'Sa chamhanaich ag éiridh, *rising at dawn.—Macfar.*

Camh-fhàir, s. f. Dawn or daybreak. *Ir.* camhaoir.

Cam-lorg, luirg, s. f. A crooked staff; a crooked or meandering path; a circuitous road. Am fear nach gabh comhairle, gabhaidh e cam-lorg, *he who takes not advice will go astray.—G. P.*

Cam-luirgneach, a. Bow-legged. *Ir.* camloirgneach.

Cam-mhuineal, eil, s. m. A wry neck; the bird called wry-neck.

Cam-mhuinealach, a. Wry-necked.

Camp, caimp, s. m. A camp. *N. pl.* campan.—*Stew. Numb. Ir.* campa. Am meadhon a chaimp, *in the middle of the camp.—Stew. O. T.*

Campachadh, aidh, s. m. An encamping; an encampment.

Campaich, v. n. Encamp. *Pret. a.* champaich; *fut. aff. a.* campaichidh, *shall encamp.* Champaich iad, *they encamped.—Stew. Exod.*

Campar, air, s. m. Anger, grief, vexation, fret; also camphire. Na biodh campar ort, *do not fret.—Stew. Pro.* Fu champar, *grieved.—Macfar.*

Camparach, a. Angry, vexed; fretting; vexatious, troublesome, troubled.

Cam-shronach, a. Hook-nosed; crook-nosed.

Cam-shuileach, a. Squint-eyed. Cailleach chrosda chamshuileach, *a cross-grained squinted beldame.—Old Song.*

Camus, uis, s. m. A bay, a creek, a harbour; the perineum. Thug iad aire do chamus, *they observed a bay.—Stew. Acts.* Written also *camas.*

Camusach, a. Abounding in bays, creeks, or harbours; like a bay or creek; of, or belonging to, a bay or creek.

† Can, a. White.

This word is now obsolete; but we see it in *canaib* or *caineab*, canvas, and *canach*, moss-cotton. *Chin.* can, *a bright object. Tonq.* canh, *white. Mogul* and *Calmuc Tartars*, zagan, *white. Lat.* canus, *grey*, and candidus, *white. Corn. W. Ir.* and *Arm.* can, *white.*

Càn, v. n. (*Lat.* can-o. *Arm.* cana *and* kan. *W.* kan. *Corn.* kana.) Sing, rehearse, say, name, call. *Pret. a.* chàn; *fut. aff. a.* cànaidh, *shall sing.* Càn oran, *sing a song.—Stew. Jud. Fut. pass.* canar. Prionnsa na siothchaint cànar ris, *he shall be named the prince.—Smith.*

Cànach, aich, s. Cotton; mountain-down or moss-cotton; standing water; a cat's tail; deceit. Bu ghile na 'n canach a cruth, *whiter was her form than mountain-down.—Oss. Lod.*

Canach, a. Soft, kind, mild, pretty. Written also *cannach.*

Cànach, aich, s. f. A tribute, impost; also a porpoise; bombast.—*Shaw.*

Cànachd, s. f. (*from* càin.) Taxing. Fu chanachd, *under tribute, taxed.*

Canaib, s. f. Canvas, white cloth; hemp. *Arm.* and *W.* canab. *Lat.* cannabis.

Cànaichte, part. Taxed.

Cànaidh, *fut. aff. a.* of càn. Shall or will sing.

Cànain, *s. f.* See Canmhain.

Cànal, ail, *s. m.* (*Arm.* canel.) Cinnamon. Cànal cubhraidh, *sweet cinnamon.—Stew. Exod.*

Canamhuinn, *s. f.* See Canmhain.

Cànar, *fut. pass.* of càn. Shall be sung.

Can-fhonn, -fhuinn, *s. m.* (*W.* canon.) A song; a precept; *also*, a canon; for, in the times of bardism, all maxims, whether political, moral, or religious, were delivered and promulgated in verse.

Canmhain, **Canmhuin**, *s. f.* Language, tongue; pronunciation, accent.
Lat. † canmen, *old form of carmen.* *W.* cynan. *Arm.* kanaven, *a song.*

Canmhainiche, *s. m.* A linguist.

† **Cann**, cainn, *s. m.* A reservoir; a vessel.
Syr. canir, *vase.* *Gr.* κανθαρος. *Hung.* kanna. *Germ.* kan. *Span.* cana. Juvenal has *canna*, a can.

Cannach, *a.* Pretty, comely, beautiful; mild, soft. Grisdhearg, cannach, *ruddy and comely.—Macint.* *Com.* and *sup.* cannaiche.

Cannach, aich, *s. m.* Sweet willow; myrtle; any fragrant shrub.

Cannran, **Cànran**, ain, *s. m.* Contention; a grumbling, a murmuring, a muttering; a grumble, a murmur, a mutter; a purring; a cackling; a chattering, as a bird. Luchd cànrain, *mutterers.—Stew. Jud.* Rinn mi cànran, *I chattered.—Stew. Is.*

Cannranach, **Cànranach**, *a.* Grumbling, murmuring, muttering. Mar ghaoth channranach, *like the murmuring wind.—Fingalian Poem.* *Com.* and *sup.* canranaiche.

Cannranaich, **Cànranaich**, *s. f.* A continued grumbling or murmuring.

† **Cantach**, *a.* Dirty, puddly, miry. *Com.* and *sup.* canntaiche.

† **Cantaig**, *s. f.* (*Lat.* cantic-um.) A canticle, a song. *N. pl.* cantaigean.

Càntair, *s. m.* A singer. *N. pl.* cantairean.
Lat. cantor. *W.* cantur. *Span.* cantor.

Càntaireachd, *s. f.* (*Ir. id.*) Singing, singing by note; vocal music; warbling; melodiousness—(*Macint.*); songsinging, merriment. Rinn iad cantaireachd, *they made merry.—Stew. Jud.*

Càntal, ail, *s. m.* Grief, weeping.

Càntuinn, *s. f.* The act of singing; singing, speaking.

Càntuinn, (a), *pr. part.* of càn. Singing.

Cànuin, *s. f.* (*for* canmhuin.) Language; pronunciation; accent. *N. pl.* canuinean; *d. pl.* canuinibh. Uile chànuinean nan cinneach, *all the languages of the nations.—Stew. Zech.* Written also *canmhuin.*

Caob, *v. a.* Clod; strike with clods. *Pret. a.* chaob, *clodded; fut. aff. a.* caobaidh, *shall clod.*

Caob, *s. f.* (*Ir. id.*) A clod, a sod, a piece of turf. Caobshneachdaidh, *a snowball.*

Caobach, *a.* Like a clod or sod; full of clods.

† **Caobhan**, ain, *s. m.* A prison.—*Shaw.*

† **Caoch**, *a.* (*Ir. id.* *Lat.* cæcus, *blind.*) Blind; empty; blasting.

Caoch-nan-cearc, *s.* Henbane.

Caochag, aig, *s. f.* A nut without a kernel; a turned shell; a mushroom; a puff-ball; blind-man's-buff. *N. pl.* caochagan. Na caochagan eutrom, *the light hollow nuts.—Macint.*

Caochagach, *a.* Full of nuts without kernels; full of turned shells; full of mushrooms or of puff-balls; like a hollow nut, like a turned shell, like a mushroom or a puff-ball.

Caochail, *v. a.* and *n.* Change; alter; pass away; travel; expire. *Pret. a.* chaochail, *changed; fut. aff. a.* caochlaidh, *shall change.* Caochlaidh a ghlòir, *his glory shall change.—Sm.* Chaochail e, *he expired.—Stew. Gen.*

Caochailear, *fut. pass.* of caochail. Shall be changed. Caochailear e, *he shall be changed.*

Caochan, ain, *s. m.* A rivulet; whisky in its first process of distillation; an eddy of air; an eddy on the surface of any fluid; a mole; the fundament. Caochan nan sliabh, *the mountain rivulet.—Ull.*

Caochla, **Caochladh**, aidh, *s. m.* (*Ir.* caochladh.) A change, an alteration; death; dying; passing away. Caochladh an t-soluis, *the change of the moon;* caochladh na beatha 's na bliadhna, *the changes of life and of time.—Oss.* Air chaochladh dreach, *in a different form.—Oss. Derm.* Bu ghrad do chaochladh, *sudden was thy death.—Fingalian Poem.*

Caochlaideach, *a.* Changeable, variable, inconstant, fickle. Caraid caochlaideach, *a fickle friend.*

Caochlaideachd, *s. f.* Changeableness, inconstancy, fickleness.

Caochlaidh, *fut. aff. a.* of caochail. Shall change.

Caochlan, ain, *s. m.* A rivulet. *N. pl.* caochlain.

† **Caod**, *s. m.* St. John's wort. Caod Choluim-chill, *St. John's wort.*

† **Caodh**, caoidh, *s. m.* (*Ir. id.*) Good order, good condition; a tear.

† **Caodhan**, ain, *s. m.* A person in good condition.—*Shaw.*

Caog, *v. a.* and *n.* Wink; connive; take aim by shutting the eye. *Pret. a.* chaog, *winked; fut. aff. a.* caogaidh, *shall wink.* Caogaidh e le shùil, *he winks with his eye.—Stew. Pro.* Ge b' e ball air an caog iad, *at whatever they shut their eye, or aim at.—Old Song.* Caog ris, *wink at him.*

Caogach, *a.* Winking; squint-eyed; blinking; twinkling.

Caogad, *a.* Fifty. Caogad claidheamh, *fifty swords.—Oss. Trath.* Phill iad nan caogadaibh, *they returned in fifties.—Fingalian Poem.*

Caogadh, aidh, *s. m.* A winking, a conniving; a wink, a connivance. Caogadh sùl, *a winking of the eye.—Sm.*

Caogadh, 3 *sing.* and *pl. imper.* of caog. Caogadh e, *let him wink;* caogadh iad, *let them wink.*

Caogadh, (a), *pr. part.* of caogh; which see.

Caog-shuil, -shùl, *s. f.* An eye that winks; a squint-eye.

Caog-shùileach, *a.* Squint-eyed; winking, blinking.

† **Caoich**, *a.* (*Ir. id.* *Lat.* cæcus.) Blind of an eye.—*Macd.*

† **Caoiche**, *s. f.* (*Ir. id.*) Blindness.

Caoidh, *v.* Lament, mourn, moan; weep, wail. *Pret. a.* chaoidh, *lamented; fut. aff. a.* caoidhidh, *shall* or *will lament.* Cha chaoidh am priosunach, *the prisoner shall not mourn.—Sm.*

Caoidh, *s. f.* (*Ir.* caoi.) Lamentation, wailing, weeping, mourning; a lament, a wail, a moan. Mo chaoidh cha do sguir, *my moan did not cease.—Ull.* Ri caoidh, *weeping, wailing.*

Caoidheadh, idh, *s. m.* A lamenting, a wailing, a weeping, a deploring.

Caoidheadh, (a), *pr. part.* of caoidh. Weeping, bewailing. Turlach a caoidheadh a chlainne, *Turlach weeping for his children.—Oss. Fin. and Lor.*

Caoidh-chòradh, aidh, *s. m.* A wailing voice; mournful expressions. Dh' fhailnich a caoidh-chòradh, *her wailing voice ceased.—Ull.*

Caoidh-ghuth, *s. m.* A plaintive voice.—*Oss. Fin. and Lor.*

Caoidhrean, ein, *s. m.* A wailing; a mournful voice; a low murmuring sound, as of a brook. Written also *caoirean.*

CAOIL, *gen. sing.* of caol; which see.

CAOILE, *s. f.* (*Ir.* caoil.) Leanness; smallness; attenuation; narrowness, as of a stream; trouble; destruction; the waist; a distemper among sheep and goats. Caoile air m' anam, *trouble on my soul.—Stew. Ps.*

CAOILE, *com.* and *sup.* of caol. More or most lean.

CAOILEAD, eid, *s. m.* Leanness; smallness; progression in leanness. A dol an caoilead, *growing more and more lean.*

CAOILTEAN, *n. pl.* of caol. Straits.

CAOIMH, *gen. sing.* of caomh; which see.

CAOIMH, *a.* (*Ir.* caoimh.) Gentle, kind, affable, affectionate; beloved; hospitable. See CAOMH.

CAOIMHE, *com.* and *sup.* of caomh. More or most gentle.

CAOIMHEACH, ich, *s. m.* (*Ir.* caoimhtheach.) A stranger; a bedfellow. *N. pl.* caoimhich.

CAOIMHEACHAN, ain, *s. m.* (*from* caoimh.) An entertainer; an hospitable person; a beloved person. *N. pl.* caoimheachain.

CAOIMHEACHAS, ais, *s. m.* Society; social love; hospitality.

CAOIMHNE, *s. f.* (*from* caomh.) Kindness, gentleness, affability. Caoimhne ort, *be gentle, be affable.*

CAOIMHNEALACHD, *s. f.* Kindness, gentleness, affability.

CAOIMHNEALAS, ais, *s. m.* Kindness, gentleness, affableness.

CAOIMHNEAS, eis, *s. m.* Kindness, mildness, affability. Dean caoimhneas domh, *shew kindness to me.—Stew. Gen.*

CAOIMHNEIL, *a.* (caoimhne-amhuil.) Kind, mild, affable; lenient; genial; of pleasing manners.—*Stew. N. T. ref.* An samhradh caoimhneil, *the genial summer.—Old Song.* Gu caoimhneil, *kindly.*

CAOIN, *v. n.* and *a.* Weep, wail, lament, deplore. *Pret. a.* chaòin, *wailed; fut. aff. a.* caoinidh, *shall wail.* Cha chaoin oigh, *virgins shall not weep.—Oss. Lodin.*
Ir. caoin. *Germ.* quinen, *mourn. Corn.* cwyna.

CAOIN, *a.* (*Ir. id.*) Kind, mild, pleasant, gentle; dry; smooth; soft, mellow; smoothly polished; lowly. *Asp. form,* chaoin. Mar aisling chaoin, *like a pleasant dream.—Oss. Dargo.* Og-bhean chaoin, *thou gentle bride.—Ull.* A lamh caoin, *her soft hand.—Oss.* Caoin mar bhalbh-dhriùchd, *mild as the silent dew.—Oss. Fing.* A chaòin-ghaoith, *thou gentle wind.—Oss. Com.* A taghadh a chlocha caoin, *picking smooth stones.—Id.* Sa chaoin-fhuaim, *in the mellow sound.—Id.* Caoin-chnaimh, *a polished bone;* caoin-shian, *a gentle shower;* caoin-shuarach, *indifferent.*

CAOINE, *com.* and *sup.* of caoin.

† CAOINEACH, ich, *s. m.* Stubble; moss.—*Shaw.*

CAOINEACHADH, aidh, *s. m.* A drying, as of hay; an exposing to the sun's heat for the purpose of drying.

CAOINEACHADH, (a), *pr. part.* of caoinich. Drying. A caoineachadh na saidh, *drying the hay.*

CAOINEADH, idh, *s. m.* (*Ir.* caoine. *W.* kuyn.) Weeping; wailing; howling; Irish lamentation over the dead.

† CAOINEASGAR, air, *s. m.* A garrison.

CAOIN-GHEAL, *a.* White and soft. Do chanach caoin-gheal, *thy soft, white mountain-down.—Old Song.*

CAOINICH, *v.* Dry; expose any thing to dry. *Pret. a.* chaoinich, *dried; fut. aff.* caoinichidh, *shall dry.*

CAOIN-SHUARACH, *a.* Indifferent, careless.—*Shaw.*

CAOINTEACH, *a.* Sad, sorrowful; mournful, plaintive, whining. Caointeach fad na h-oidhche, *mournful the whole of the night.—Orr. Com.* and *sup.* caointiche.

CAOINTEACHAN, ain, *s. m.* A person who mourns or whines.

CAOIR, *s. pl.* Sparks; gleams; flames; flashes. *D. pl.* caoiribh. A choille na caoiribh, *the wood in flames.—Oss.* Caoir dhealan, *gleams of lightning.—Oss. Fing.* Caoir-theine, *a fire-brand;* caoir-lasair, *a flaming coal.*

CAOIR-DHREAS, -dhris, *s. m.* A thicket, a bush of thorns; brambles.—*Stew. Gen. ref.*

CAOIREACH, *a.* (*from* caoir.) Sparkling, gleaming, flashing, flaming; fiery; impetuous.

CAOIREAG, eig, *s. f.* A small dry *peat;* a small piece of coal; a small peat, or coal on fire. *N. pl.* caoireagan. Cha tuit caoireag a cliabh falamh, *nothing will fall from an empty basket.—G. P.*

CAOIREAGACH, *a.* Full of small dry peats; crumbled like peat or coal.

CAÒIREAN, ein, *s. m.* A plaintive song; a murmur; a moan; the cooing of a dove; a plaintive sound; a purling sound. Caoirean na coille, *the murmur of the woods.—Ull.* Ni e caoirean, *he will mourn.—Stew. Ezek.* Ri sior-chaoirean, *making a continued plaintive sound; wailing.—Stew. Is.*

CAOIREANACH, *a.* Moaning, murmuring; gurgling, purling.

CAOIREANACHD, *s. f.* Frequent or continued moaning; a continued murmur; a purling noise.

CAOIR-GHEAL, *a.* Red hot; heated to incandescence.

CAOIRIBH, *d. pl.* of caoir; which see.

CAOIRICH, *n. pl.* of caor. Sheep.

CAOIR-LASAIR, -lasrach, *s. f.* A flaming coal; a sparkling flame.

† CAOIRLE, *s. f.* (*Ir. id.*) A club.

† CAOIRLEACHD, *s. f.* A tossing or driving with clubs.

CAOIR-SHOLUS, uis, *s. m.* A gleaming light; effulgence.

CAOIRTHEACH, *a.* Fiery; sparkling, gleaming; impetuous. Sruth caoirtheach, *an impetuous stream.—Oss. Fing.*

† CAOIS, *s. f.* A furrow; a young pig.

† CAOISEACHAN, ain, *s. m.* A swine-herd. *N. pl.* caoiseachain.

CAOL, caoil, *s. m.* A frith, a strait; the narrow part of a river. Caol na droma, *the small of the back;* caol an dùirn, *the wrist;* caol a chalpa, *the small of the leg.*

CAOL, *a.* Small, thin, lean, slender, attenuated; narrow; shrill, high-toned. Caol nam feòil, *lean in their flesh.—Stew. Gen.* Toinntean caol, *an attenuated thread;* da chaol-chù, *two slender-footed dogs.—Oss. Com.* Ceòl caol, *shrill, high-toned music.—Oss. Tem.* Caol direach, *straight, straight on.*

CAOL RI CAOL. A rule observed by the most approved writers in Gaelic or Irish. It prescribes that two vowels contributing to form two different syllables should both be of the class of small vowels; as, buailteach, *liable,* not buailtach; oillteil, *shocking;* not oilltail. Leathan ri leathan is caol ri caol, leughar na sgriobhar gach focal san t-saoghal, *broad to broad, and small* (vowel) *to small, you may read or write every word in the world.—G. P.*

† CAOLACH, aich, *s. m.* The plant fairy-flax.—*Shaw.*

CAOLACHADH, aidh, *s. m.* A making small, thin, or slender.

CAOLAICH, *v. a.* and *n.* Make small or slender; grow small or slender. *Pret. a.* chaolaich, *grow slender; fut. aff. a.* caolaichidh, *shall grow slender.* Caolaichidh tu a chasan, *thou wilt make his legs slender.—Old Song.*

CAOLAICHTE, *p. part.* of caolaich. Made slender.

CAOL-AMHAINN, *s. f.* A narrow river; hence *Culleh,* the name of a place in the north of Scotland; probably the κέλλιου ποτάμοῦ ἔκβολαι of Ptolemy.

CAOLAN, ain, *s. m.* A small gut; a tripe. *N. pl.* caolain, *guts.* Caolan cait, *cat-gut.*

CAOLANACH, *a.* Like guts; of, or belonging to, a gut; made of guts.

CAOLAS, ais, *s. m.* A frith; a strait; a ferry. Snamhaiche a chaolais, *the swimmer of the frith.—Old Song. N. pl.* caolasan.

CAOL-CHASACH, *a.* Having small legs, slender-legged, slim-footed.

CAOL-CHOMHNUIDH, *s. m.* A narrow bed, a narrow abode, a grave. A chaol-chomhnuidh, *his grave.—Fingalian Poem.* Written also *caol-chonuidh.*

Caol-chònuidh, *s.m.* A narrow bed, a narrow abode, a grave.

Caol-chosach, *a.* Having small legs; slender-legged; slim-footed; shanky. Each caol-chosach, *a slender-legged horse.—Old Poem.*

Caol-chroma, ai, *s. m.* A narrow curve. Caol-chroma na gealaich, *the narrow curve of the moon.—Oss. Cathula.*

Caol-fairge, *s. m.* A strait; a frith.

Caol-ghealach, aich, *s. f.* The new moon. A chaol-ghealach tro' neul, *the new moon* [*seen*] *through a cloud.—Oss. Gaul.*

Caol-ghleann, -ghlinn, *s. m.* A narrow valley, a glen. Air astar an caol-ghleann, *travelling in the narrow valley.—Oss. Lodin.*

Caol-ghlorach, *a.* Shrill.

Caol-ghruagach, *a.* Having a thin mane. Each caol-ghruagach, *a thin-maned horse.—Fingalian Poem.*

Caol-ghuth, *s. m.* A shrill voice.

Caol-ghuthach, *a.* Having a shrill voice.

Caol-mhalach, *a.* Having narrow eyebrows.

Caol-mhaladh, aidh, *s. m.* A narrow eyebrow; also the name of one of Ossian's Poems.

Caol-mhiosachan, ain, *s. m.* Purging flax.—*Shaw.*

Caol-shrath, *s. m.* A narrow strath; a narrow valley. Caol-shrath nan alld, *the narrow valley of streams.—Oss. Temo.*

Caomh, *v. a.* Protect, spare. *Pret.* chaomh, *spared; fut. aff.* caomhaidh, *shall spare.*

Caomh, *a.* Gentle, mild, tender; *also, substantively,* a friend, a beloved object; *rarely,* a feast. Is caomh thu, a thannais! *mild art thou, O ghost!—Oss. Duthona.* A chaoimh mo ghaoil-sa! *thou gentle object of my love.—Oss. Conn.* Gun chaomh am fogus, *without a friend at hand.—Oss. Cathluno.* *Com.* and *sup.* caoimh.

Caomhach, aich, *s. m.* A friend, a bosom friend; a companion, a chum. Gun mhac gun chaomhach, *without son or friend.—Old Poem.* *N. pl.* caomhaich.

Caomhag, aig, *s. f.* A mildly-tempered female; an affectionate girl. *N. pl.* caomhagan.

Caomhail, *a.* (caomh-amhuil.) Gentle, mild, kind, affectionate; favourable. Caomhail ri 'n cairdean, *kind to their friends.—Old Poem.*

Caomhain, *v. a.* Spare, save, reserve, economize. *Pret. a.* chaomhain, *spared; fut. aff. a.* caomhnaidh, *shall spare.* Caomhain do sholus, *spare thy light.—Oss. Gaul.* Cha chaomhain e smugaid thilg orm, *he will not spare to spit on me.—Stew. Job.*

Caomhalach, *a.* Kindly, disposed to be mild. Gu caomhalach, *kindly.* *Com.* and *sup.* caomhalàiche.

Caomhalachd, *s. f.* Kindness; affability. Lagh na caomhalachd, *the law of kindness.—Stew. Pro. ref.*

Caomhan, ain, *s. m.* A noble person; an affable person—(*Shaw*); a beloved person. A chaomhain! *my dear sir!*

Caomhantach, *a.* Frugal, fond of saving, economical; protecting.

Caomhantachd, *s. f.* Frugality, economy.

Caomh-chridhe, *a.* A tender or compassionate heart, an affectionate heart. *N. pl.* caomh-chridheachan.

Caomh-chridheach, *a.* Tender-hearted, kind. Athair chaomh-chridhich! *thou tender-hearted father!—MacLach.*

Caomh-chruth, *s. m.* A slender form or person, as of a female.

Caomh-ghradh, -ghraidh, *s. m.* Tender mercy; tender love.—*Stew. Hos.*

Caomh-leus, **Caomh-loise**, *s. f.* A pleasant blaze.

Caomhnach, aich, *s. m.* A friend; a feeder.—*Shaw.*

Caomhnach, *a.* Sparing; frugal, economical.

Caomhnadh, aidh, *s. m.* A saving, sparing, an economizing; economy; *rarely,* protection. Dean caomhnadh, *spare.*

Caomhnadh, (a), *pr. part.* of caomhain. Sparing, saving, economizing.

† **Caon**, caoin, *s. m.* A resemblance.—*Shaw.*

† **Caonaran**, ain, *s. m.* A solitary person, a recluse. *N. pl.* caonarain.

Caonnag, aig, *s. f.* A fight, a skirmish, fray, squabble; a boxing-match; a nest of wild bees. *N. pl.* caonnagan; *d. pl.* caonnagaibh. Daoine nach do rinn caonnag, *men who fought not.—Macint.* Dheanadh tu caonnag ri do dha lurgainn, *you would quarrel with your own shins.—G. P.*

Caonnagach, *a.* Fond of fighting or boxing; riotous, quarrelsome.

Caonntach, *a.* (*for* caomhantach.) Saving, frugal, economical. *Com.* and *sup.* caonntaiche.

Caonntachd, *s. f.* (*for* caomhantachd.) A saving disposition; frugality, economy.

† **Caonta**, *a.* Private.—*Shaw.*

Caor, caoir, *s. f.* A berry; a firebrand; a thunderbolt. *N. pl.* caoran, *berries; wild ash-berries.*

Caor, caoir *or* caorach, *s. f.* A sheep; *in derision,* a sheepish person. O chrò nan caorach, *from the sheepfold.—Sm.* *N. pl.* caoraich, *sheep.*

In Grelman's collection of gipsey words *baukero* means a sheep. On the west coast of Africa there are several languages in which *baukero* has the same signification.

Caorachd, *s. f.* (*from* caor.) A stock of sheep; sheep; cattle; sheepishness.

Caoraich, *n. pl.* of caor; which see.

Caorag, aig, *s. f.* A small dry peat; a dry clod or turf. *N. pl.* caoragan.

Caoran, *s. pl.* The berries of the mountain-ash or service; the wood of the mountain-ash. Bu deirge a ghruaigh na caoran, *ruddier was his cheek than the wild ashberry.—Oss. Derm.*

Caoran, ain, *s. m.* A small dry peat.

Caor-bheirteach, *a.* Producing berries; bacciferous.

Caor-dromain, *s. m.* The alder-berry.

Caor-gheal, *a.* Incandescent; red hot; emitting sparks.

Caor-lann, -lainn, *s. m.* (*Corn.* corlan.) A sheepfold.

Caor-teinntidh, *s. m.* A thunderbolt.—*Shaw.*

Caor-theine, *s. m.* A firebrand.

Cap, capa, *s. m.* A cup; *rarely,* an old person; a cart; a tumbrel.

† **Capat**, ait, *s. m.* (*Ir. id. Lat.* caput.) A head.

† **Cap-fhlath**, -fhlaith, *s. m.* (*Ir. id.*) A commander-in-chief.

Capull, uill, *s. f.* A mare. *N. pl.* capuill.

Gr. καβαλλης, *a work-horse. Lat.* caballus, *a horse. It.* cavalla. *Fr.* cavale, *a mare. Pol.* kobela. *Boh.* kobyla. *Hung.* kabalalo.

Capull-coille, *s. f.* A capercailzie; a mountain-cock; a kind of moor-fowl, once very abundant in the Highlands. The species is now nearly extinct. The capercailzie is considerably larger than the black-cock, and is seen only on remote and unfrequented mountains.

Car, cuir, *s. m.* A twist, a bend, a turn, a winding, as of a stream; a trick; way, course; a bar of music; care. Lubar nan car, *winding Lubar.—Oss. Duthona.* Cuir car dhiot, *be clever.* Thoir car mu 'n cuairt, *take a turn round.* Car oidhche, *during one night.—Stew. Jer.* Car bliadhna, *for a year.* Thoir an car as, *cheat him.* Car air char, *tumbling.—Stew. Jud.* Theid sinn an car so, *we shall go this way.* An car a bhios san t-sean mhaide, is duilich a thoirt as, *the bend of the old tree cannot be removed; what is bred in the bone is ill to take out of the flesh.—G. P.* Car neamhuinn, *a string of pearls.—Shaw.*

Car, *prep.* (*W.* car.) During; for; near about, in reference to time. Car uair, *near an hour;* car tiota, *for a moment;*

car greis, *for a while.—Macdon.* Car tamuil bhig, *for a short time.—Stew. N. T. ref.*

CÀR, *a.* (*Ir. id. Lat.* carus.) Related; also contracted for *cairdeach;* which see.

CAR, *a.* Bending, twisting, tortuous, winding, undulating.

CÀR, *s. m.* (*Old Swed.* kaerre, *a cart. Chald.* carron, *a chariot.*) Scab, mange, itch; a chariot. Written also *càrr.*

CARA', CARADH, aidh, *s. m.* A way, a direction, a course; a turn, a winding, a twist. Aom nan cara', *bend in their way* [*towards their course.*]—*Oss. Conn.* An caradh a bhrocluinn, *in the direction of its den.—Id.*

CÀRA'. See CÀRAMH.

CARA', CARADH, aidh, *s. m.* A friend, relation, kinsman; an ally. Gun cluinn mi mo chara, *that I may hear my friend.—Oss. Tem.* Bi d' chara dha 'n righ, *be an ally to the king.—Oss. Fing.*

Chald. and *Arab.* karis, *parent. Du.* kaar, *friend. Sp.* caro. *Teut.* kare. *Corn. W.* and *Arm.* car.

CARACH, *a.* (*from* car.) Deceitful; whirling, circling, winding, turning; scabbed; changeable, unstable. Saoghal carach, *a deceitful world.* Measg osna charach, *amid the circling breezes.—Fingalian Poem.*

CARACH', *for* CARACHADH.

CARACHADH, aidh, *s. m.* A moving, a stirring. Carachadh céille, *insanity.*

CARACHADH, (a), *pr. part.* of caraich. Moving, stirring. Oiteag a carach' an duillich, *a breeze stirring the leaves.*

CÀRACHADH, aidh, *s. m.* The act of burying.

CARACHD, *s. f.* A motion, a movement.

CARACHDACH, *a.* Athletic, wrestling.

CARACHDAICH, *s. f.* Wrestling.—*Shaw.*

CÀRADH, (a), *pr. part.* of càir; which see.

CARAICEACH, *a.* Hairy; eager; keen. *Com.* and *sup.* caraiciche.

CARAICEAG, eig, *s. f.* A sort of pancake. *N. pl.* caraiceagan.

CARAICH, *v. a.* and *n.* Remove, move, stir, turn. *Pret. a.* charaich; *fut. aff. a.* caraichidh. Mar charaicheas iolar a nead, *as an eagle stirreth up her nest.—Stew. Deut.* Nach caraich thu? *wilt thou not move?* Cha charaich e ceum, *he will not move a step.*

CARAICHE, *s. m.* A wrestler; a pugilist. *N. pl.* caraichean.

CARAICHTE, *p. part.* of caraich. Moved, stirred, turned.

CARAID, *s. f.* (*Ir. id.*) A pair, a couple, a brace, twins, twain; *also,* defence. Caraid-rann, *a couplet;* caraid na maoislich, *roes that are twins.—Stew. Song. Sol. N. pl.* caraidean; *d. pl.* caraidibh. Nan caraidibh, *two by two.—Stew. G. B.*

CARAID, *s. m.* and *f.* (*Arm.* caret.) A friend, a relation. Caraid chìsmhaor, *the friend of publicans.—Stew. Mat.* Mo dheagh charaid, *my good friend;* caraid, mac peathar athar, *a cousin, the son of a father's sister;* caraid nighean peathar athar, *a cousin, the daughter of a father's sister;* caraid, mac brathar mathar, *a cousin, the son of a mother's brother;* caraid mac brathar athar, *a cousin, the son of a father's sister.—Macdon.*

CARAIDEACH, *a.* In pairs, in couples or braces.

CÀR-AINGEAL, il, *s. m.* A guardian angel. *N. pl.* carain-gealan.

CARAINNEAN, *s. pl.* The refuse of threshed barley.

CARAISTE, *s. f.* A carrying, a conveying; carriage, conveyance; a beating, a thrashing. Fhuair a dheadh charaiste, *he got a proper thrashing.*

CARAISTEACH, ich, *s. m.* A carrier.

CARAMASG, aisg, *s. f.* A contest, a confusion.

CÀRAMH, aimh, *s. m.* A repairing, a mending; treatment; abuse. Fear càramh a bheum, *repairer of the breach.—Stew. G. B.* Is duileach leam an caramh, *I regret the abuse.—Macint.* Fhuair e a droch caramh, *he was maltreated.*

† CARAN, ain, *s. m.* (*W.* caran. *Lat.* corona. *Ir.* caran.) The crown of the head.

CARAN-CREIGE, *s. m.* A sea-eel; a conger-eel.

CARANTACH, *a.* (*from* càradh.) Kind, charitable, affectionate. *Com.* and *sup.* carantaiche. Written also *carthannach.*

CARANTACHD, *s. f.* (*from* càradh.) Kindness, friendliness, friendship, charity. Blàs is carantachd, *warmth and friendliness.—Old Song.* Written also *carthannachd.*

CARANTAS, ais, *s. m.* Kindness, friendliness; friendship, charity. Carantas fuar, *cold friendship.—Old Song.*

† CARAS, ais, *s. m.* A first-rate ship.—*Shaw.*

† CARB, cairb, *s. m.* (*Lat.* corbis.) A basket; a chariot; a plank; a ship. *N. pl.* carban.

CARBAD, aid, *s. m.* (*Box. Lex.* cerbyd.) A chariot, a war-chariot; a waggon; a coach; a litter; a bier; any pleasure vehicle; a jaw. Carbad do ghaothaibh, *a chariot of the winds.—Sm.* Carbad cogaidh, *a war-chariot.—Id.* Fiacal carbad, *a jaw-tooth, a cheek-tooth.—Stew. Joel.* Buail am balaoch air a charbad, is buail am balgair air an t-sròin, *strike the clown on the ear, and the dog on the nose.—G. P.*

CARBADAIR, *s. m.* A charioteer, a coachman, a driver. *N. pl.* carbadairean.

CARBADAIREACHD, *s. f.* The business of a charioteer or coachman.

CARBAL, ail, *s. m.* The roof of the mouth.

CARBAN, ain, *s. m.* An unlucky person. *N. pl.* carbain.

† CARBH, cairbh, *s. f.* A ship.

CARBHAIDH, *s. f.* (*Sp.* carvi.) Carraway.

CARBHAIREACHD, *s. f.* Mangling; massacring.

CARBHAN, ain, *s. m.* (*dim.* of carbh.) A little ship; a carp. *N. pl.* carbhain.

CARBHANACH, aich, *s. m.* (*from* carbh.) A ship-master; a carp. *N. pl.* carbhanaich.

CARBHANACH UISGE, *s. m.* A carp.

CAR-BHODACH, aich, *s. m.* A clown; a sailor.—*Shaw. N. pl.* car-bhodaich.

CHARBHAS, ais, *s. m.* Intemperance; *also,* Lent; quadragesimal. Ann an deireadh a charbhais, *at the end of Lent.—Macvuirich.*

CARC, cairc, *s. m.* (*W.* carch. *Eng.* † cark.) Care, anxiety.

CARCAR, air, *s. m.* A prison.

Lat. carcer. *W.* carchar. *Teut.* karch[illegible] *Germ.* kirker. *Ir.* carcar. *Corn.* carchar. *Arm.* carchar.

† CARCHAILL, *v. a.* Destroy, abuse.—*Shaw. Pret. a.* charchaill; *fut. aff. a.* carchaillidh, *shall destroy.*

CARD, caird, *s. m.* (*Span.* carda.) A card for teazing wool. *N. pl.* cardan.

CARD, *v. a.* Card or comb wool. *Pret. a.* chard; *fut. aff. a.* cardaidh, *shall or will comb.*

CARDADH, aidh, *s. m.* The process of carding wool; a carding.

CARDAIR, *s. m.* (*Sp.* cardador.) A comber or teazer of wool.

CARDAIREACHD, *s. f.* The employment of a wool-comber; the trade of wool-combing. Ris a chardaireachd, *at the wool-combing trade.*

CAR-FHOCAL, ail, *s. m.* A quibble, a prevarication, a double-entendre; antiphrasis; a pun. *N. pl.* car-fhocail.

CAR-FHOCLACH, *a.* Quibbling, prevaricating; antiphrastic; disposed to quibble, prevaricate, or pun.

CAR-FHOCLAICHE, *s. m.* A quibbler, a prevaricator; a punster.

Carghas, ais, *s. m.* (*Ir.* carghios.) Lent.

† Carla, ai, *s. m.* A wool-card. *N. pl.* carlan.

† Carlach, aich, *s. m.* A cart-load.

† Carlachan, ain, *s. m.* A carder or comber of wool. *N. pl.* carlachain.

Carlag, aig, *s. f.* A tuft of wool. *N. pl.* carlagan.

Carlagach, *a.* Like a tuft of wool; full of tufts of wool.

† Carlair, *s. m.* A carder of wool.—*Shaw. N. pl.* carlairean.

Carmhanach, aich, *s. m.* A carp. *N. pl.* carmhanaich. See also Carbhanach. Carmhanach uisge, *a carp.*

Car-mhogal, ail, *s. m.* A carbuncle.—*Shaw.*

† Carn, cairn, *s.* A quern or handmill for grinding corn.

Germ. quern. *Goth.* quairn. *Swed.* quarn. *Isl.* kuern. *Pezron's Glossary,* quirn. *Anglo-Sax.* cweorn *and* cwyrn.

† Carn, carna, *s. m.* (*Lat.* caro; *gen.* carnis. *Ir.* carn.) Flesh; a booty.

Carn, cairn, cuirn, *s. m.* (*Corn. W.* and *Ir.* carn.) A heap of stones loosely thrown together; a *cairn;* a monumental heap of stones; a barrow; a rock; a sledge; a province. *N. pl.* cuirn. O iomall nan carn, *from the edge of the rocks.—Oss.* Carn-cuimhne, *a monument;* carn-aolaich, *a dunghill.*

Cairns or *barrows* are very numerous in the Highlands of Scotland, in Ireland, and in Wales. They are also to be seen in Sweden, in Norway, and in other parts of the Continent, as also in America. They were intended for monuments; and the probability is, that they were used as such from the earliest ages by every people who could associate their ideas of duration with the properties of stone and rock.

These *cairns* often measure three hundred feet in circumference at the base, and twenty feet in height. They consist of stone, and the whole pile is shaped like a cone. Several opinions have been formed concerning the intention of them. In several instances they have been explored, and found to contain sepulchral urns; a circumstance which seems to be decisive in favour of the opinion that they are monuments of the dead. Many of these piles consist wholly of earth; and this gave rise to an opinion that the coped heaps of stone were intended for malefactors, and those of earth for the virtuous and the brave. I never could ascertain to what extent this distinction was observed. From ancient authors we learn that malefactors were buried under heaps of stone, and we know that it was a common practice among the Druids to erect *cairns* on the spot where a criminal had been burnt. Hence *fear air charn* means an outlaw among the Gael. Tha e air a charn, *he is an outlaw.* 'Is oil leam nach robh do luath fo charn', *I wish your ashes were under a cairn.* 'B' fhearr leam bhi fo charn chlach', *I would rather be under a cairn,* i. e. *punished as an outlaw.* Though the ceremony of *cairn-raising* be still prevalent in the Highlands, the meaning of it is changed: for on whatever spot a person is found dead, a few stones are immediately huddled together, and every passenger pays his tribute of a stone; the larger it is, the greater is the respect shewn to the deceased: hence a common saying among the Gael,—'Cuiridh mi clach ad charn, *I will add to thy cairn,* betokens a friendly intention, and means, *I will keep the remembrance of thee alive.* The ghost of the deceased is supposed to haunt his cairn; and there are few Highlanders who would pass the spot for the first time without adding to the heap, and thus keeping on good terms with the spectre. At no remote time the compiler of this work used to discharge this debt with devout punctuality, and, if alone and in the dark, would take the best aim in his power, and fling his contribution from a prudent distance.

Carn, *v. a.* Heap, pile, accumulate, throw together. *Pret. a.* charn; *fut aff. a.* carnaidh. Carnaibh connadh, *heap on wood.—Stew. Ezek.* Ged charn e airgiod, *though he accumulate silver.—Stew. Job.*

Carnach, *a.* Rocky; abounding in cairns; like a cairn; *substantively,* a heathenish priest.

Carnadh, aidh, *s. m.* A heaping or piling; an accumulating; a riddance.—*Shaw.*

Carnadh, (a), *pr. part.* of carn. Heaping, piling, accumulating.

Carnaid, *s. f.* Carnation or flesh colour.

Carnal, ail, *s. m.* A small heap of stones.—*Shaw.*

Carnan, ain, *s. m.* (*dim.* of carn. *W.* carnen.) A little cairn; a little heap.

Carnanaich, *s. pl.* Scotch Highlanders; the Καρνονακαι of Ptolemy.

Carn-cuimhne, *s. m.* A monument.

Car-neamhnuid, *s. m.* A string of pearl.—*Shaw.*

Carnta, Carnte, *p. part.* of carn. Heaped or piled up, accumulated.

Càrr, *s. m.* A rock. O chàrr monaidh, *from a mountain-rock.—Oss. Duthona.*

Arab. càrr, *rock. Armen.* carr, *stone. Dan.* and *O. Sax.* carr, *rock. Pers.* char, *a stone. Turk.* caria, *marble.*

Carr is seen in the following names of rocks and rocky places:—*Car-pathus,* mountains in Hungary; *I-car-ia,* the isle of rocks in the Egean sea; *Icarus,* in Attica; *Carina,* a mountain in Crete; *Corasius,* near Antioch; *Corasiæ,* rocks in the Egean sea.

Càrr, càirr, *s. m.* (*Teut.* karr, *chariot. Corn.* and *Arm.* carr.) A bog, a fen or morass; moss; a dray; a waggon; a spear. Mar chanach càirr, *like the moss cotton.—Old Song.*

Carr, carra, *s. f.* (*Old Swed.* kaerre.) Scab, mange, itch; scurvy; a scall or dry leprosy; a crust; a chariot; bran. Càrr thioram, *a dry scald.—Stew. Lev.* Plaigh na carra, *the plague of the scall.—Id.* Duine aig am bheil càrr, *a man who has the* [*itch*] *scurvy.—Id.*

Carrach, *a.* (*from* carr.) Scabbed, itched, mangy, scorbutic; rocky; having an uneven surface; having a cross temper. Am fear a bhios carrach sa bhaile so, bithidh e carrach 's a bhaile ud thall, *he who is mangy here will be mangy every where; the manners which a man has at home, he carries abroad.—G. P. Com.* and *sup.* carraiche.

Carradh, aidh, *s. f.* A rock; a pillar; an erect stone; a monument. Carradh nan tonn, *the rock of the ocean.—Oss. Fing.* Carradh salainn, *a pillar of salt.—Stew. G. B. N. pl.* carraidhean. Written also *carragh.*

Carragh, aigh, *s. f.* A rock, a pillar, an erect stone, a monument. Thannais nan carragh geur, *spectre of the flinty rocks.—Oss. Fing.* Far an d' ung thu an carragh, *where thou didst anoint the pillar.—Stew. Gen. N. pl.* carraighean.

Carraid, *s. f.* Conflict; distress, vexation, trouble. Carraid nan sian, *the conflict of winds, whirlwinds.—Oss. Fing.* Le carraid ghéir, *with sharp trouble.—Sm.*

Carraideach, *a.* Distressed, vexed; causing trouble or vexation; grievous; conflicting. *Com.* and *sup.* carraidiche.

Carraig, *s. f.* (*dim.* of carr.) A rock, a cliff; a pinnacle. Carraig mo neart, *the rock of my strength.—Sm. Asp. form,* charraig. Mar thuinn mu charraig, *like waves round a rock.—Oss. Duthona.*

Corn. and *W.* careg. *Arm.* carric. *Scotch,* craig.

Carraigeach, *a.* (*from* carraig.) Rocky, like a rock; of, or belonging to, a rock; rugged.

Carraigeag, eig, *s. f.* A sort of pancake.

Carraighin, *s.* The thick part of butter-milk.

Carran, ain, *s. m.* A weed growing amidst corn; a shrimp, a prawn—(*Macd.*); *rarely,* a sickle.

Carran-creig, *s. m.* A conger eel; a shrimp, a prawn.—*Macd.*

Carrasan, ain, *s. m.* Hoarseness; a wheezing of the throat; catarrh. Casd is carrasan, *a cough and hoarseness.*

Carrasanach, *a.* Hoarse; wheezing.

Carrasanaich, *s. f.* A continued wheezing of the throat; a catarrh.

Carr-fhiadh, -fheidh, *s. m.* A hart. *N. pl.* carr-fheidh.

Carr-fhiodh, *s. m.* A knot in timber.—*Shaw.*

Carroid, *s. f.* See Carraid.

CARRUICH, *v. a.* (*Ir.* corruigh.) Remove, move, stir; turn. *Pret. a.* charruich, *moved; fut. aff. a.* carruichidh, *shall or will move.* Carruich do chos, *remove thy foot.—Stew. Pro.* Written also *carraich.*

CARS, *s. f.* This word, meaning a level fertile tract of country, is used in many districts of the Southern Highlands, into which it seems to have straggled from the speech of the Lowland Scots. There is, however, in the Armoric dialect of the Celtic, a word *ceirs* or *ceyrs*, which has the same meaning with *cars.*

C'ARSON, *adv.* (co airson.) Why? for what? C'arson so? *why so?*

CAR-SHÙIL, -shùl, *s. f.* A rolling eye. *N. pl.* car-shuilean.

CAR-SHUILEACH, *a.* Having rolling eyes.

CÀRT, càirt, *s. f.* A fourth; a quart; a quarter of a yard.

CARTACH, *gen. sing.* of cairt; which see.

CARTADH, aidh, *s. m.* The act of cleansing any place of mire, as a stable or stie; tanning of leather; stripping a tree of its bark. Cartadh an daraich, *stripping the oak of its bark.*

CARTHAN, ain, *s. m.* Charity, friendship, affection. Luchd carthain, *charitable people.*

CARTHANNACH, *a.* (*Ir. id.*) Charitable, friendly, affectionate, loving. Do ghràs carthannach, *thy loving grace.—Sm. Com.* and *sup.* carthannaiche.

CARTHANNACHD, *s. f.* (*Ir. id.*) Charity, friendship, kindness; the practice of charity.

CAR-THUINNICH, *v. a.* Separate, part, put asunder. *Pret. a.* charthuinnich; *fut. aff. a.* carthuinnichidh, *shall separate.*

CART-IÙIL, *s. m.* A mariner's compass.

CAR-TUAL, *s. m.* (car-tuath-iùil.) Unprosperous or fatal course; a moving contrary to the sun's course.

This term has its origin in a Druidical superstition. The Druids, on certain occasions, moved three times round their stony circles or temples. In performing this ceremony (*car-deise*) they kept the circle on the right, and consequently moved from east to west. This was called the prosperous course; but the *car-tual*, or moving with the circle on the left, was deemed fatal or unprosperous, as being contrary to the course of the sun. See DEISIUIL.

CARUCHADH, aidh, *s. m.* See CARACHADH.

CARUILL, *v. n.* (*W.* carawl. *Corn.* karol, *a choir.*) Carol, sing, warble. *Pret. a.* charuill, *caroled; fut. aff.* caruillidh, *shall carol.*

CAS, *v. a.* Gape; gnash; brandish; turn against; be angry with; wreathe; twist; bend; curl; climb. *Pret. a.* chas; *fut. aff. a.* casaidh. Chas iad am beul, *they gaped with their mouth.—Stew. Job.* Chas e fhiaclan, *he gnashed with his teeth.—Id.* Chas e a shleagh, *he brandished his spear.—Oss. Tem.*

CAS, *a.* (*Ir. id.*) Steep; abrupt; headlong; hasty, passionate; eager, quick, forward; twisted, curled, wreathed. Sruthan cas, *headlong streams.—Oss. Lodin.* Cas gu comhrag, *eager for battle.—Oss.* Gu cas, *quickly.—Sm.* Caireal cas, *passionate Carril.—Old Poem.* Cas-fhalt, *curled locks.—Old Song.*

CÀS, *s. m.* (*Fr.* càs, *incident. Lat.* casus.) A difficulty, emergency, anxiety, distress; plague; case; respect; *rarely*, fear; pity. Anns gach càs, *in every emergency.—Sm.* An càs, *eager;* an càs air, *eager for him* or *it. Asp. form,* chas. Sa chàs so, *in this case.—Stew. Cor.* Tha e na chàs, *he is eager for it.*

CAS, coise, *s. f.* (*W.* coes.) A foot; a leg; a shaft; the handle of any bladed instrument; money; a wrinkle. *N. pl.* casan; *d. pl.* casaibh. Fo chasaibh nan an-laoch, *under the feet of ruthless warriors.—Oss. Trath.* Cas sgeine, *the handle of a knife;* cas tuaidh, *the handle of a hatchet;* casan corrach, *stilts.* Written also *cos.*

CASACH, *a.* (*W.* coesawg.) Footed, many-footed; of, or belonging to, feet. Gu casach lamhach, *exerting legs and hands.*

CASACHDAICH, *s. f.* Coughing; continued coughing.

CASADH, aidh, *s. m.* A climbing; gnashing; a gaping; a brandishing; turning against; a wreathing, a twisting, a curling; a wrinkle. Le casadh an gruaige, *with curling [broidering] their hair.—Stew. Tim.* Lan chasadh, *full of wrinkles.—Stew. Job. ref.*

CASADH, (a), *pr. part.* of cas. Gnashing; gaping; climbing; brandishing; turning against; wreathing, twisting, curling. An torc a casadh ri Diarmad, *the boar turning impetuously on Dermid.—Oss. Derm.* Sleagh a casadh na laimh, *a spear brandishing in his hand.—Oss. Tem.*

CASAG, aig, *s. f.* A long coat; opposite in meaning to a short coat or jacket. *N. pl.* casagan.

CASAGACH, *a.* Long-coated; wearing a long coat; like a long coat.—*Macdon.*

CASAGAICHE, *s. m.* A man with a long or skirted coat.

CASAID, *s. f.* (*Ir. id.*) A complaint, an accusation. Dean casaid, *complain; make a complaint.* Na gabh casaid, *receive not an accusation.—Stew. Tim. N. pl.* casaidean.

CASAIDEACH, *a.* Complaining, accusing; prone to complain or to accuse; like a complaint or accusation.

CASAIDEACHD, *s. f.* A complaining; readiness to make a complaint.

CASAIDICHE, *s. m.* A complainer, a complainant, an accuser.

CASAIN-UCHD, *s. m.* A bit cut off a sheep from the lip along the belly to the tail, three inches broad.—*Shaw. Also*, a bosom.

CASAIR, *s. f.* A faint phosphoric light proceeding from old wood in the dark.

CASAIR, casrach, *s. f.* A thorn; a buckle; a clasp; a shower; hail; massacre, slaughter.

CASAN, ain, *s. m.* A foot-path; also a name given to the parallel roads of Glenroy. *N. pl.* casain.

CASANACH, *a.* Having foot-paths; like a foot-path.

CAS-AODAINNEACH, *a.* Having a wrinkled face. A shene chas-aodainneach, *wrinkle-faced age.—Old Song.*

CASAR, air, *s. m.* A little hammer; a foot-path.

† CASARNACH, aich, *s. m.* Lightning.

CASBANACH, *a.* Parallel, side by side.

CAS-BHAIRNEACH, ich, *s. m.* A limpet, a cunner.—*Shaw.*

CAS-BHARD, -bhaird, *s. m.* A satirist.

CAS-BHARDACHD, *s. f.* Satire; lampooning; invective.

CAS-BHARDAIL, *a.* (cas-bhardamhuil.) Satirical.

CAS-BHEART, eirt, *s. f.* (cas *and* beairt.) Shoes and stockings, armour for the legs.

CAS-BHRIATHAR, air, *s. m.* A hasty expression; intemperate language.

CAS-BHRIATHRACH, *a.* Hasty or intemperate in speech.

CAS-BHUIDH, *a.* Yellow and curled, as hair. Cuach fhalt cas-bhuidh, *curled yellow hair.—Macint.*

† CASCAR, air, *s. m.* A cup.—*Shaw.*

CAS-CHEUM, *s. m.* A foot-path; a stride; a long pace; a steep or difficult way. Cas-cheum nach gann, *a great stride.—Old Poem.*

CAS-CHEUMACH, *a.* Steep; difficult to pace; striding; having a foot-path.

CAS-CHIABH, *a.* A curled lock, a ringlet. *N. pl.* cas-chiabhan.

CAS-CHIABHACH, *a.* Tressy; having ringlets or curled hair.

CAS-CHREAG, *s. f.* A steep rock. *N. pl.* cas-chreagan.

CAS-CHREAGACH, *a.* Full of steep rocks.

Cas-crom, *s. f.* A little spade, crooked at the lower end, formed in such a way as to turn over the soil in furrows.

This primitive kind of plough is still used in the Hebrides. It is, of course, very unexpeditious, eight men being necessary to dig as much in one day as a horse would plough in the same time. Where traces are wanting, the harrow is tied to the horse's tail; but in wet grounds the glebe is broken by means of a heavy-toothed instrument, called *racan*, which men, women, and children, drag along the surface of the ground. The following minute description of the *cas-crom* is taken from *Sinclair's Statistics, Edderrachylis*:—"This instrument, chiefly used for tillage, consists of a crooked piece of wood; the lower end somewhat thick, about two feet and a half in length, pretty straight, and armed at the end with iron, made thin and square, to cut the earth. The upper end of this instrument is called the shaft; whereas the lower is termed the head. The shaft above the crook is pretty straight, being six feet long, and tapering upwards to the end, which is slender. Just below the crook or angle, which is an obtuse one, there must be a hole, wherein a strong peg must be fixed for the workman's right foot, in order to push the instrument into the earth; while in the meantime standing on his left foot, and holding the shaft firm with both hands, when he has in this manner driven the head far enough into the earth, with one bend of his body, he raises the clod by the iron-headed part of his instrument, making use of the heel or hind part of the head as a fulcrum; in so doing, he turns it over always towards the left hand, and then proceeds to push for another clod in the same form. To see six or eight men all at work with this instrument, as is often to be seen, standing all upon one leg, and pushing with the other, would be a pretty curious sight to a stranger.

"With all its disadvantages, the *cas-crom* is, of all instruments, the fittest for turning up the ground in the country; for among so many rocks a plough can do little or nothing; and where no rocks are, the earth is commonly so marshy that cattle are not able to pass over it without sinking deep. Therefore it is of pretty general use in the Highlands, and is of great antiquity. One man can turn over more ground with it in a day than four are able to do with a common spade. For a single man to delve as much ground as will require two pecks of bear-seed in a day is nothing uncommon; nay, some have sown four in a day's work. There are many instances of single men who, in good seasons, have reared as much corn as, with the help of potatoes, has subsisted the families of six or seven persons plentifully by the *cas-crom*."

Cas-chorrach, aich, *s. f.* A stilt. *N. pl.* casan-corrach, *stilts.*

Cas-cùirn, *s. f.* A draught-tree.—*Shaw.*

Casd, *s. m.* A cough. An triugh-chasd, *the whooping cough.*

Casd, *v. n.* Make a cough; cough. *Pret. a.* chasd, *coughed; fut. aff. a.* casdaidh, *shall* or *will cough.*

Casdach, *a.* (*from* casd.) Coughing; causing a cough or cold. Am mios casdach, *the cough-producing month.*—*Macdon.*

Casdadh, aidh, *s. m.* A coughing, the act of coughing; a cough.

Casdaich, *s. f.* A coughing, a continued coughing. Làn casdaich, *full of coughing.*—*Macint. Asp. form*, chasdaich. Ciod a chasdaich th'ort? *why do you cough so?*

Casdaich, (a), *pr. part.* of casd. Coughing.

Cas-dìreach, *s.* A straight delving-spade, used in the Hebrides.

Cas-fhionn, *a.* White-footed. Bha i cas-fhionn, *she was white-footed.*—*Macint.*

Casg, *v. a.* Restrain, stop, staunch, quell, curb, appease. *Pret. a.* chasg; *fut. aff. a.* casgaidh. A casgadh a chreuchdan, *staunching his wounds.*—*Oss. Trath.* Written also *cosg.*

Casgach, *a.* Apt to staunch; apt to quell, curb, or appease; apt to restrain; having the quality of staunching.

Casgadh, aidh, *s. m.* A quenching, stopping, staunching, curbing, appeasing, a restraining; the act of quenching or of staunching. Cuir casg' air, *staunch it.*

Casgadh, (a), *pr. part.* of casg. Quenching, stopping, staunching, appeasing. An fhuil a ruith gun luibh ga casgadh, *the blood flowing without herb to staunch it.*—*Oss. Derm.*

Casgaidh, *fut. aff. a.* of casg. Shall or will quench, staunch, or appease.

Casgair, *v. a.* Kill, slaughter, massacre, mangle, butcher. *Pret. a.* chasgair; *fut. aff. a.* casgraidh, *shall massacre; fut. pass.* casgrar. An lamh le 'n casgrar e, *the hand by which it shall be slaughtered.*—*Sm.* Co chasgras an torc, *who will slay the boar.*—*Oss. Derm.*

Casgairt, *s. f.* A slaughtering, a massacring, a butchering; a slaughter, a massacre. Written also *cosgairt.*

Casgrach, *a.* Slaughtering, massacring; of, or belonging to, a slaughter or massacre; like a slaughter; mangling.

Casgradh, aidh, *s. m.* A slaughter, a massacre, a mangling, a butchering. Mar uan thun a chasgraidh, *like a lamb to the slaughter.*—*Stew. G. B.*

Casgradh, (a), *pr. part.* of casgair. Slaughtering, mangling.

Caslach, aich, *s. m.* Children; a tube; a clan.

Casladh, aidh, *s. m.* Frizzled wool.—*Shaw.*

Cas-lom, *a.* Barefoot, barefooted; barelegged. Cas-lom, ceann-lom, *barefoot and bareheaded.*

Cas-maidhiche, *s. f.* The herb haresfoot.—*Shaw.*

Casnaid, *s. f.* Split wood, chips.

Casrach, aich, *s. f.* A slaughter, massacre.—*Shaw.*

Cas-ruisgte, *a.* Barefoot, barefooted; barelegged. Lomnochd agus cas-ruisgte, *naked and barefoot.*—*Stew. Is.*

† **Cast**, *a.* (*Gr.* καστος, *adorned. Lat.* castus.) Pure, undefiled, chaste.

Castearbhan, ain, *s. m.* Succory. Castearbhan nam muc, *dandelion.*—*Shaw.*

Castreaghainn, *s. f.* Straw on which grain is laid during the process of kiln-drying.

Cas-urla, *s. m.* A curled lock, a ringlet.

Cas-urlach, *a.* Having curls, ringlets, or tresses. D' òr chùl na shlamagan casurlach, *thy yellow hair in curled tresses.*—*Moladh Mhoraig.*

Cat, cait, *s. m.* A cat. Cat fiadhaich, *a wild cat;* cat-luch, *a mouse;* is tu an cat, *you are a cat.* Faodaidh cat sealtuinn air an righ, *a cat may look at a king.*—*G. P.*

Barbarous Gr. καττος, κάττης, *and* κατα. *Lat.* catus. *Fr.* chat. *Arm.* and *Ir.* cat. *Isl.* katt. *Swed.* katt. *Da.* kat. *Anglo-Sax.* cat. *Germ.* katze. *W.* and *Corn.* cat. *It.* gatta. *Span.* gato. *Russ.* kotte. *Pol.* kotka. *Turk.* keti. *Teut.* katt. *Pers.* kitt. *Javanese*, cota. *Georgian*, kata.

† **Cata**, ai, *s. m.* A sheep-cote.

Càtachadh, aidh, *s. m.* A taming, a soothing, a domesticating.

Càtadh, aidh, *s. m.* A taming, a soothing, a domesticating.

Càtaich, *v. a.* Tame, soothe, domesticate; honour, reverence. *Pret. a.* chàtaich, *tamed; fut. aff. a.* càtaichidh, *shall tame; p. part.* càtaichte.

† **Cataidh**, *s. f.* Generosity, nobility; *also*, generous, noble.

Catanach, *a.* Hairy, rough, shaggy, freezy; one of the clan Cattan. *Com.* and *sup.* catanaiche.

Catas, ais, *s. m.* Caddice.

Cat-fiadhaich, *s. m.* A wild cat; the *catus silvestris* of naturalists.

Cath, *s. m.* A battle, a skirmish, a contest, a struggle; a company of soldiers. Cuir cath, *engage.* Chuir iad cath air, *they strove against him.*—*Sm. N. pl.* cathan. 'G ar feitheamh le seachd cathan, *waiting us with seven companies.*—*Fingalian Poem.*

W. and *Corn.* cad. *Germ.* cat. *Ir.* cath; *hence* caterva, *a fighting band. Bisc.* cuda, *battle. Arab.* cahad. *Eth. Arab.* cathal, *to fight. Chald.* katat. *Gr.* κατα, *against.*

Cath, *v.* Fight, fight a battle; carry on war; contend, strive. *Pret. a.* chath, *fought; fut. aff. a.* cathaidh, *shall fight.*

Càth, *v. a.* Fan, winnow. *Pret.* chath; *fut. aff.* cathaidh.

Càth, *s.* Seeds; husks of corn; pollards. Càth làgain, *corn seeds*, of the juice of which the Scotch Gael make exquisite flummery. Cath-bhruich, *a kind of flummery.*

Cathach, aich, *s. m.* (*from* cath.) A warrior, a fighting man, a champion. *N. pl.* cathaich. Seachd cathaich diongmhalta, *seven able-bodied warriors.—Old Poem.*

Cathachadh, aidh, *s. m.* A striving; a fighting; a battling; a struggling; a tempting; a provoking strife; struggle; temptation; provocation. A chur cathachaidh, *to provoke.* —*Stew. Is.*

Cathachadh, (a), *pr. part.* of cathaich. Striving, struggling, fighting, battling; trying; tempting.

Cathadh, aidh, *s. m.* A drift. Thig ioma-chath, *a whirling drift shall come.*—*Macfar.* Cathadh mara, *spoondrift;* cathadh cuir, *falling snow.*

Cathag, aig, *s. f.* A daw, a jackdaw; a jay; the *corvus monedula* of Linnæus. *N. pl.* cathagan.

Cathagach, *a.* Abounding in jackdaws; like a jackdaw; of jackdaws.

Cathaich, (*from* cath.) Fight, contend; fight a battle; engage; carry on war; try, tempt. *Pret. a.* chathaich, *fought; fut. aff. a.* cathaichidh, *shall fight.* Cathaich nan aghaidh, *fight against them.*

Cathair, cathrach, *s. f.* A town, a city, a fortified city; a chair, a seat, a bench; a bed of any garden-stuff; a stock of colewort or of cabbage; a plot; a marsh, a bog; a sentinel. *N. pl.* cathraichean. Do 'n chathair dhaingean, *to the fortified city.—Sm.* Gu gleann cathair, *to a marshy vale.—Oss. Lod.* Air cathair, *on a seat.—Stew. Pro.* An creamh na chathraichean, *gentian in beds or plots.—Macint.* *Pers.* car, *town.* *Phen.* kartha. *Pun.* karta, cartha, *and* cirtha, *a town.* *Chin.* cara, *dwell.* *Jap.* kar, *a house.* *Syr.* karac, *enclosure, and* kerac, *a fortress.* *Chald.* and *Syr.* kartha, *town.* *Arab.* carac, *a fortress.* *Bisc.* caria. *W.* and *Corn.* cadair *and* caer. *Arm.* cador *and* codoer, *a chair;* kaer, *a city.*

Usherus, bishop of Armagh, in his book on the Origin of British Churches, has the following observations on the word *cathair*, chap. v. p. 65. " Johannes Caius ex Gervasio Tilberiense *cair* linguâ Trojanâ civitatem addit, et Cambris murum significat, ut quemadmodum Hebræi קיר (Kyr) murum, et קריה (Kyria) urbem vocant. Ita Britannis vox non absimilis *cair*, et mœnia et urbem mœnibus cinctam denotat. Sed et apud Scythas *car* est urbs."

Cathair-beinn-thorraiche, *s. f.* Caerlavrock. The καεβαντοειγον of Ptolemy.

Cathair-breatheamhnais, *s. f.* A judgment-seat. Air a chathair bhreatheamhnais, *on the judgment-seat.—Stew. Acts.*

Cathairiche, *s. m.* A citizen. *N. pl.* cathairichean.

Cathair-righ, *s. f.* A throne. Chi gach sùil a chathair righ, *every eye shall see his throne.—Sm.*

Cathair-rioghail, *s. f.* A throne.

Cathair-thalmhainn, *s. f.* Milfoil or yarrow.—*Macd.*

Cathaiseach, *a.* Brave, stout, warlike; quick. Gu cathaiseach, *bravely.* *Com.* and *sup.* cathaisiche.

Cathamh, *s.* The drift of snow. Tha cur is cathamh ann, *it snows and drifts;* cathamh fairge, *spoon-drift;* dorus cathamh, *the middle door of a kitchen-passage.*

Cathamhach, *a.* (*from* cathamh.) Drifty; like drift; of, or belonging to, drift.

Cathan, ain, *s. m.* A species of wild goose with a black bill.—*Shaw.* Cathan aodaich, *a web.*

Cathan, *n. pl.* (*from* cath.) Warriors, champions. Còdhail nan cathan, *the meeting of warriors.—Oss. Dargo.*

Cathan aodaich, *s. m.* A web.—*Shaw.*

Cathar, air, *s. m.* Soft, boggy ground; a marsh. O chathar 's o chruaich, *from marsh and from mountain.—Oss. Fing.*

Càthar, *a.* (càth-mhor.) Husky, seedy; full of seeds or husks.

Cath-bhàrr, *s. m.* A helmet, a headpiece. Bhris e an cath-bharr, *he broke the helmet.—Death of Oscar.*

Càth-bhruich, *s. f.* Flummery; *sowens.*

Cath-fhear, -fhir, *s. m.* A warrior, a hero, a champion. *N. pl.* cath-fhir.

Cath-labhradh, aidh, *s. m.* The speech of a general before or after battle.

Cathlun, uin, *s. m.* A corn.—*Shaw.*

Cath-mhilidh, *s. m.* A commander, a colonel, a chief officer; a field officer.

Cathraichean, *n. pl.* of cathair; *dat. pl.* cathraichibh. Cities, towns. See **Cathair.**

Cat-luibh, *s. f.* Cudwort.—*Shaw.*

Cé, *s.* (*Gr.* γη. *Ir.* cé.) The earth, the world; night; a spouse; *also*, a pier.—*Macd.* An cruinne cé, *the globe of the earth, orbis terrarum.*

C' è, (co è.) Who is he? who is it? what is he? what is it? where is he? where is it? C' è tha dorch air an t-sliabh, *who is he that is dark on the hill?—Oss. Fing.*

† **Ceach**, *a.* Each, every one. More frequently written *gach;* which see.

Ceachail, *v. a.* Dig; hackle; destroy. *Pret. a.* cheachail, *dug; fut. aff. a.* ceachlaidh, *shall dig.*

Ceachair, ceachrach, *s. f.* Dirt, filth; penury.

† **Ceachdlach**, aich, *s. m.* Coal-black.

Ceachrach, *a.* Dirty, filthy; penurious, stingy. *Com.* and *sup.* ceachraiche.

Ceachrachd, *s. f.* Dirtiness, filthiness; penuriousness, stinginess.

Cead, *s. m.* Leave, permission, liberty, license; farewell, adieu. Thoir cead dhomh, *give me leave;* gabhaidh mi mo chead dhiot, *I will take my leave of thee.—Old Song.* Cead buan, *a long adieu;* leig cead duit! *enough of thee!*

Cead, *a.* Hundred. See **Ceud.**

Ceadach, *a.* Talkative; cloth.

Ceadachadh, aidh, *s. m.* A granting, a permitting; a permission; liberty; a dismissing.

Ceadachadh, (a), *pr. part.* of ceadaich. Granting, permitting.

Ceadachail, *a.* Lawful, allowable, permissible.

Ceadaich, *v.* (*from* cead.) Permit, suffer, let, allow. This verb has the *prep.* do, simple or compounded, construed with it. *Pret. a.* cheadaich, *permitted; fut. aff. a.* ceadaichidh, *shall permit.* Ceadaich do t-oglach, *permit thy servant.—Sm.* *Fut. pass.* ceadaichear.

Ceadaich is sometimes written *ceaduich.*

Ceadaichidh, *fut. aff. a.* of ceadaich; which see.

Ceadaichte, *p. part.* of ceadaich. Permitted; suffered; lawful. Bheil e ceadaichte? *is it lawful?—Stew. Mat.* Sometimes written *ceaduichte?*

† **Ceadal**, ail, *s. m.* A story; a narrative; a malicious report.

Ceadalach, *a.* Malicious, as a story.

Ceadalaiche, *s. m.* He who raises malicious stories.

Ceadhal, ail, *a.* Blistered; full of sores.

Ceaird, *gen. sing.* and *n. pl.* of ceard.

Ceairde, ceirde, *s. f.* A trade; an occupation. Ciod is ceairde duibh? *what is your occupation?—Stew. Gen.* Cha 'n uailse duine no 'cheirde, *a man is not higher than his trade.—G. P.* Fear-ceirde, *a tradesman;* luchd-ceirde, *trades-people.*

† **Ceal**, *s.* (*Lat.* cœlum. *Ir.* ceal. *Fr.* ciel.) Heaven.

† **Ceal**, ceala, *s. m.* A joint; forgetfulness; stupidity; fine flour.

Ceal, *v. a.* Eat. *Pret. a.* cheal, *ate*; *fut. aff. a.* cealaidh, *shall eat.*

Cealachadh, aidh, *s. m.* The act of concealing; a concealing, hiding; concealment; eating.

Cealachadh, (a), *pr. part.* of cealaich.

Cealadh, aidh, *s. m.* Eating.

Cealaich, *v. a.* Conceal; hide; deny; eat. *Pret. a.* chealaich; *fut. aff. a.* cealaichidh, *shall conceal.* A chealaich m' aran, *who ate my bread.—Smith.* Cha chealaich mi ort e, *I will not conceal it from you.*

Cealaichte, *p. part.* of cealaich. Eaten; concealed.

Ceal-chobhair, *s. f.* A sanctuary, a place of safe concealment.

Ceal-fhuath, -fhuaith, *s. m.* A private grudge.

Cealg, ceilg, *s.* (*Ir.* cealg. *W.* celc.) Deceit, wile, treachery; hypocrisy; malice. Spiorad ceilg, *the spirit of deceit.—Stew. Mic.* Ulluichidh iad cealg, *they shall prepare treachery.—Stew. Job.*

Cealg, *v. a.* Beguile, deceive. *Pret. a.* chealg; *fut. aff. a.* cealgaidh.

Cealgach, *a.* (*from* cealg.) Crafty, deceitful, wily, hypocritical; malicious; false. Tha 'n cridhe cealgach, *the heart is deceitful.—Stew. Jer.* Fianuis cealgach, *a false witness.—Stew. Pro.* *Com.* and *sup.* cealgaiche.

Cealgair, *s. m.* (*W.* celgawr, *apt to hide.*) A deceitful man, a hypocrite, a traitor. *N. pl.* cealgairean.

Cealgaireachd, *s. f.* Deceitfulness, hypocrisy, treachery. —*Smith.* Ri cealgaireachd, *practising deceit.*

Cealg-chordadh, aidh, *s. m.* Collusion; private understanding.

† **Ceall**, cealla, *s. m.* A cell; a church. *Lat.* cella. Hence ceall-shlad, *sacrilege.*

Ceallach, aich, *s. f.* A peat cart; a *rung* cart, employed in carrying peats from the moss; also a *creel*, formed like a cone, with the base upwards, placed upon a sledge, and used to carry out manure. In the Southern Highlands these creels have given place to more convenient vehicles.

Cealladh, aidh, *s. m.* Custody.

Ceallair, *s. m.* The superior of a monastery.

Ceall-ghoid, *s.* Sacrilege.

Ceall-shlad, -shloid, *s. f.* Sacrilege.

Ceall-stòl, -stoil, *s. m.* A close stool.

† **Cealt**, *s. m.* Apparel, clothes, garments, dress.—*Ir. id.*

Cealtach, aich, *s. m.* A Celt, a Gaul.

† **Cealltair**, *s. m.* A spear; a cause; a castle.—*Ir. id.*

Cean, *s. m.* Love, favour, fondness; desire; elegance; a fault, a crime. Tha mo chean air an og mhnaoi, *my love is on the virgin.—Old Song.*

Ceanail, *a.* (cean-amhuil.) Kind, mild, loving; fond; elegant; faulty. Thuit Carruill ceanail, *the elegant Carril fell.—Death of Carril.*

Ceanail, *s. f.* Kindness, mildness, fondness. Beul a cheanail, *the mouth of mildness.—Old Song.*

Ceanalta, *a.* Handsome; clean; seemly; mild, kind. Gille ceanalta, *a handsome lad;* oigh cheanalta, *a handsome maid.*

Ceanaltachd, *s. f.* Handsomeness, cleanness, seemliness; mildness, kindness.—*Macint.*

Ceanaltas, ais, *s. m.* Handsomeness, cleanness, seemliness, mildness, kindness.

Ceanan, *a.* A corruption of *ceann-fhionn;* which see.

Ceangail, *v. a.* Tie, bind, fasten, fetter; tighten; oblige; compel; restrain. *Pret. a.* cheangail; *fut. aff. a.* ceanglaidh, *shall bind.* Ceanglaibh le cordaibh, *bind with ropes.—Sm.* Ceangail teann, is faigh tearuinte, *fast bind, fast find.—Old Proverb.* Am fear a cheanglas 's e shiubhaileas, *he who ties his bundle fast walks on without stop.—G. P.*

Ceangailte, *p. part.* of ceangail. Bound, tied, fastened; obliged; restrained; compelled; under obligation.

Ceangal, ail, *s. m.* (*Ir.* ceangail. *Lat.* cingul-um.) A tie, a bond, a restraint, a fetter or chain; an obligation; a ligature; a knot, a fastening, a bandage. *N. pl.* ceanglaichean. Ceanglaichean posaidh, *marriage-bonds.—Stew. Gen.* Ceangal iall a sgeith, *the knot of the thongs of his shield.—Oss. Fing.* Ceangal nam mionn, *the obligation of the oaths.—Mac Lach.* Ceangal pòsaidh, *betrothment;* ni thu ciangal pòsaidh, *thou shalt betroth a wife.—Stew. Deut.*

Ceangalach, *a.* Binding; obliging; obligatory.

Ceanglachan, ain, *s. m.* A truss; a bundle. Ceanglachan airgid, *a bundle of silver.—Stew. Gen.* *N. pl.* ceanglachain.

Ceangladh, aidh, *s. m.* A binding, a tying, a fastening; a betrothing; a tie, a fetter, a fastening; a betrothment.

Ceangladh, (a), *pr. part.* of ceangail. Binding, tying, fastening; betrothing; obliging.

Ceanglaiche, **Ceanglaichean**, *n. pl.* of ceangal. Ties, bonds, obligations; ligatures, bandages; fetters, chains, fastenings; knots.

Ceanglaidh, *fut. aff. a.* of ceangail.

Ceanglar, *fut.* of ceangail. Shall be bound or fastened; shall be restrained; shall be obliged.

Ceann, cinn, *s. m.* (*Ir.* ceann. *W.* cwn *and* cyn. *Corn.* kyn.) A head; a point; a hilt; a top; an end; a chief, a commander; a high headland, a promontory. *N. pl.* cinn. Thog tuinn an cinn, *waves reared their heads.—Ull.* Dh' fhill i a ceann an ceo, *she wrapped her head* [*top*] *in mist.—Oss. Cathluno.* Ceann gach lainn, *the hilt of every sword.—Oss. Lod.* Sleagh is geire ceann, *a spear of the sharpest point.—Oss. Croma.* Ceann nan laoch, *the chief of heroes.—Mac Lach.* Ceann deireadh, *the hinder end, the latter end;* ceann toiseach, *the beginning.* A chuir ceann air strì, *to put an end to the strife.—Oss. Lod.* An ceann lai araidh, *at the end of certain days, in process of time.—Stew. Gen.* Mu cheannaibh nan crann; *about the tops of the trees.—Oss. Tem.* Eadar so 's ceann bliadhna, *before a year expire;* an ceann a chéile, *assembled together;* o cheann gu ceann, *from end to end.—Stew. 2 K.* Air ar ceann, *on our part.—Old Poem.* Am a tharruingeas ar n-amhghar gu ceann, *a time that shall draw our troubles to a close.—Mac Lach.* An ceann ghrathuinn, *in a while;* o cheann ghrathuinn, *a while ago;* an ceann tacain, *in a little while;* o cheann tacain, *a while ago;* cinn agus cinn-bheairt, *heads and helmets.—Orr.* Ceann na ciche, *a nipple.—Macd.* Fear togalach mo chinn, *the uplifter of my* [*spirits*] *head;* o cheann fada, *long ago, long since.—Stew.* 1 *Chron.*

It is observable that *ceann*, promontory, is seen in the ancient names of many capes and promontories throughout Europe; as *Ceneum*, a cape on the north-west of Eubœa; *Cenchreæ*, a cape on the Isthmus of Corinth; *Canastræum*, a cape in Macedonia; *Candaria*, a cape in Cos; and many others.

Ceannach, aich, *s. m.* Hire; price; wages; a purchase; a reward; a covenant.—*Stew. Deut. ref.* *N. pl.* ceannaichean. Bu cheannach leam t-ubh air do ghloç, *dear-bought egg with so much cackling.—G. P.*

Ceannachachd, *s. f.* Buying, bartering, commerce, trucking.

Ceannachadh, aidh, *s. m.* A buying; the act of buying; a purchase.

Ceannachadh, (a), *pr. part.* of ceannaich. Buying; purchasing.

Ceannachd, *s. f.* (*Ir.* ceannaidheachd.) Buying; merchandise; a purchase. Is fearr a ceannachd, *her merchandise is better.—Stew. Pro.*

Ceannachdrach, aich, *s. m.* The upper part of the throat. —*Shaw.*

Ceann-adhart, airt, *s. m.* A pillow; a bed-head. Ceann-adhairt na leapach, *the bed's head.—Stew. Gen.*

Ceann-aghaidh, *s. m.* A forehead.

Ceannaich, aiche, *s. f.* Strife; contention for supremacy or superiority.

Ceannaich, *v. a.* (*Ir.* ceannaigh.) Buy, purchase. *Pret. a.* cheannaich, *bought; fut. aff. a.* ceannaichidh, *shall buy; fut. pass.* ceannaichear. Ceannaich le duais, *buy with a price.* Ceannaich mar d' fheum is creic mar d' ailghios, *buy as you need, and sell what you please.*—*G. P.*

Ceannaich, aiche, *s. m* (*Ir.* ceannaidhe.) A buyer, a purchaser; a shopkeeper; a merchant. Ars' an ceannaich, *said the buyer.*—*Stew Pro.* Written also *ceannuich. N. pl.* ceannaichean.

Ceannaichte, *p. part.* of ceannaichte. Bought.

† **Ceannaide**, *s. m* A shopkeeper; a merchant. *N. pl.* ceannaidean.

Ceann-aimsir, *s. f.* A date, an epoch, an era. *N. pl.* cinn-aimsir, *dates*

Ceannair, *s m* A driver, a goadsman. *N. pl.* ceannairean

Ceannairc, *v. n* Rebel, mutiny. *Pret.* cheannairc, *rebelled, fut. aff. a.* ceannaircidh, *shall rebel.*

Ceannairc, *s f.* (*from* ceann) Rebellion, insurrection, mutiny, conspiracy; perverseness; insubordination. Làn ceannairc, *full of rebellion*—*Smith.* Dean ceannairc, *rebel,* rinn iad ceannairc, *they rebelled.*—*Stew. Gen.* Luchd ceannairc, *rebellious people.*

Ceannairceach, *a.* (*from* ceannairc.) Rebellious, mutinous; perverse, insubordinate. Daoine dall is ceannairceach, *blind and rebellious men.*—*Smith. Com.* and *sup.* ceannairciche, *more or most mutinous*

Ceannairceas, eis, *s. m* A proneness to rebel; insubordinateness.

Ceannaird, *gen. sing.* of ceannard

Ceann-aobhar, air, *s. m.* A prime cause, a first cause. Ceann aobhair ar bròn, *the first cause of our woe.*—*MacLach.*

Ceannard, aird, *s. m.* (ceann-ard) A chief, a chieftain; a commander; a commander-in-chief. Ceannard nam frith 's nan gleann, *the chieftain of forests and glens.*—*Oss. Fing.*

Ceannardach, *a.* Arrogant, proud, ambitious. *Com.* and *sup.* ceannardaiche.

Ceannardachd, *s f* Arrogance, pride, ambition.

Ceannas, ais, *s. m.* (*from* ceann.) Superiority; chieftainry; ambition; the upper hand Is ann doibh a ghéilleadh gach ceannas, *to them would all superiority yield.*—*Old Song.*

Ceannasach, *a.* (*Ir.* id.) Superior; ambitious, aspiring, commanding; haughty, headstrong. *Com.* and *sup.* ceannasaiche.

Ceannasachd, *s. f.* A wishing to be superior; superiority; ambition; haughtiness.

† **Ceannasg**, aisg, *s f.* A forehead —*Shaw.*

Ceann-bhàrr, -bhàirr, *s. m.* A hat, a bonnet; any male head-dress.

Ceann-bheart, -bheairt, *s. m* A helmet, a headpiece. *N. pl.* cinnbheairt *Ir.* ceinbheart.

Ceann-bheartach, *a.* Wearing a helmet or headpiece.

Ceann-bhrat, -bhrait, *s. m.* A canopy.

Ceann-bhriathar, *s. m.* An adverb.

Ceann-biorach, aich, *s. m.* The bow of a ship.—*Shaw.*

Ceann-caol, -caoil, *s. m* The bow of a ship.—*Shaw.*

Ceann-chlaon, *a.* Steep; headlong —*Shaw.*

Ceann-cinnidh, *s. m.* A chief, a chieftain; the head of a clan, the chief of a tribe; as, Ceann-cinnidh nan Dònullach, *Glengarry.*

Ceann-dàn, *a.* Pertinacious, stubborn, headstrong.

Ceann-danadàs, *s. m.* Pertinacity, stubbornness.

Ceann-dearg, -deirg, *s. m.* The redstart; called also *ceann-deargan;* which see.

Ceann-deargan, ain, *s. m.* The bird called a redstart.—*Macd.* The *motacilla phœnicurus* of Linnæus. Nead a chinn-deargain, *the redstart's nest.*—*Old Song.*

Ceann-eideadh, idh, *s. m.* A head-dress; a mitre; a turban. Le ceann-eideadh daithte, *with a dyed head-dress.*—*Stew. Ezek.*

Ceann-eudach, aich, *s. m.* A head-dress; a mitre; a turban. Ceann-eudach, *a mitre.*—*Stew. Zech.*

Ceann-feadhna, *s. m.* A chief, a chieftain; a leader, a commander. Tra chunn e gun deo cheann-feadhna, *when he saw his chieftain breathless.*—*Ull. N. pl.* cinnfeadhna.

Ceann-feadhnais, *s. m.* A chieftain, a leader.—*Oss. Conn.*

Ceann-feodhna, *s. m.* See **Ceann-feadhna**.

Ceann-fhionn, *a.* White-headed, as a cow or sheep.—*Macint.* and *Macdon.* Also a name given to a white-headed or a white-faced cow.

Ceann-fhocal, ail, *s. m.* An adverb.

Ceann-fineadh, *s. m.* (*Ir.* cean-fine.) The head of a tribe or clan, a chieftain; a chief. Chaill iad ceann-fineadh no dhà, *they lost a chieftain or two.*—*Old Song.*

Ceann-fineacha, *s. m.* The head of a clan or tribe; the head of a nation.—*Oss. Temo.*

Ceann-fiodha, *s. m.* The end of a ship-timber.

Ceann-ghalar, air, *s. f.* Dandriff; scales in the head; a headach

Ceann-ghalarach, *a.* Subject to dandriff; like a disease in the head; of, or pertaining to, a disease in the head.

Ceann-ghiumhasaich, *s m.* Kingussie, in Scotland; *literally,* the head of the fir-wood.

Ceann-ghrabh, aibh, *s. m.* A motto; a superscription; a title.

Ceann-iùil, *s. m* A leader; a guide; a chieftain; a leader of the way. *N. pl.* cinn-iùil. Cinn-iùil nan dall, *leaders of the blind.*—*Stew. Mat.*

Ceann-laidir, *a.* Headstrong, stubborn; opinionative. Tha i ceann-laidir, *she is stubborn*—*Stew. Pro.*

Ceann-laidireachd, *s. f.* Stubbornness; stiffness; obstinacy; opinionativeness.

Ceann-liath, *a.* Grey-headed. Tha mi aosmhor ceann-liath, *I am aged and grey-headed.*—*Stew. Sam.*

Ceann-lom, *a* Bareheaded. Mo nighean mhiog-shuileach cheann-lom, *my smirking bareheaded maid.*—*Old Song.*

Ceann-maide, *s. m.* A block; a blockhead.

Ceann-mhor, -mhoir, *s. m.* (*properly* ceann-mòr.) Kenmore, (*literally,* a high promontory,) a village romantically situated on the eastern shore of Loch Tay, in Scotland.

Ceann-phuroaid, *s f.* A gargle *N. pl* cinn-phurgaidean.

Ceann-pluic, *s. m.* A block, a blockhead.

Ceann-puist, *s. m.* A chapiter.—*Stew. O. T.*

Ceannrach, aich, *s. m.* (*from* ceann.) A halter; a horse-collar, a tether.—*Macd.*

Ceann-ruadh, -ruaidh, *s. m.* Celendine.

Ceannsa, Ceannsach, *a.* Continent, temperate; bashful, mild, gentle; subordinate; under authority. *Com.* and *sup.* ceannsaiche, *more or most continent.*

Ceannsachadh, aidh, *s. m.* A subduing; a commanding, a keeping under authority; a subjugation, a reducing.

Ceannsachadh, (a), *pr. part.* of ceannsaich. Subduing, commanding, keeping under authority.

Ceannsachd, *s. f.* Authority; the condition of being kept under; government; subordination; continence, docility, meekness. Le ceannsachd, *with meekness.*—*Stew. Jam.*

Ceannsaich, *v. a.* (*from* ceann.) Subdue, conquer; tame, bring under, suppress; train; discipline; keep under. *Pret. a.* cheannsaich; *fut. aff. a.* ceannsaichidh. A cheannsaich, rioghachdan, *who subdued kingdoms.*—*Stew. Heb.* *Fut. pass.* ceannsaichear, *shall be subdued.*

CEANNSAICHEAR, *fut. pass.* of ceannsaich. Shall be subdued.

CEANNSAICHIDH, *fut. aff. a.* of ceannsaich. Shall subdue or tame. See CEANNSAICH.

CEANNSAICHTE, *p. part.* of ceannsaich. Subdued, conquered, tamed, trained. *Asp. form,* cheannsaichte.

CEANNSAL, ail, *s. m.* Rule, authority, government, sway. Do m' cheannsal géillibh, *yield to my authority.*—*Smith.* Fo cheannsal, *subjected.*

CEANNSALACH, *a.* Authoritative, supreme; prone to lord or govern; swaying. *Com.* and *sup.* ceannsalaiche.

CEANNSALACHD, *s. f.* Rule, government; supremacy; authoritativeness; tyranny.

CEANNSALAICHE, *s. m.* A subduer, a conqueror; an overbearing man.

CEANN-SGAL, ail, *s. m.* Command, authority, sway. Ri ceannsgal, *commanding.* Ri ceannsgal o shlogh gu slogh, *commanding from host to host.*—*Mac Lach.*

CEANNSGALACH, *a.* Commanding, swaying; imperious, authoritative; active.—*Macdon.* Ceannard ceannsgalach, *a commanding chief.*—*Old Song.* *Com.* and *sup.* ceannsgalaiche.

CEANNSGALACH, aich, *s. m.* An active leader, a commander. An ceannsgalach mileanta, *the brave commander.*—*Mac-Vuirich.*

CEANNSGRIOBH, *s. m.* A title, a motto. *N. pl.* ceannsgriobhaichean.

CEANNSGUR, *s. m.* A full stop, a full pause in reading, a period.—*Macd.*

CEANN-SIMID, *s. m.* A tadpole.

CEANN-STUAIGH, *s. m.* An arch.—*Shaw.*

CEANNSUICH, *v. a.* See CEANNSAICH.

CEANN-TAIL, *s.* Cintail, a parish in Scotland; more correctly, *ceann an t-sàil,* the boundary of the sea.

CEANN-TALA, *s. m.* (*Lat.* cantela.) A bard.—*Oss. Tem.*

CEANNTIGHE, *s. m.* The head of a branch of a family; the master of a house or household. *N. pl.* cinntighe.—*Stew. 1 Chron.*

CEANN-TIRE, *s. m.* (*Ir.* cean-tire.) A peninsula, a promontory, a headland; land's end; also Kyntire, in Argyllshire.

CEANN-TOBAIR, *s. m.* A well-cover; a mother-spring.

CEANNTROM, *a.* Heavy-headed; dull, drowsy.—*Ir. id.*

CEANN-UIDHE; CEANN-UIGHE, *s. m.* A stage; a journey's end; a dwelling-place; a chieftain. Ceann-uidhe na baigh, *the dwelling-place of mercy.*—*Old Poem.* Ceann-uighe na fëile, *the chief of the generous.*—*Oss. Fing.* *N. pl.* cinnuighe.

CEAP, cip, *s. f.* (*Ir. id.*) A block; a shoemaker's last; stocks; a cap; (*Box. Lex.* cap, *a bonnet*); the top, as of a hill; a head; a stock; a sign set up in time of battle. Peanas a chip, *the punishment of the stocks.*—*Stew. Pro.* Ceap nam mor chruach, *the tops of the lofty hills.*—*Macfar.* Ceap-tuislidh, *a stumbling-block;* ceap-cartach, *the nave of a cart-wheel.*

CEAP, *v. a.* Catch, hold, stop, keep, intercept. *Pret. a.* cheap; *fut. aff. a.* ceapaidh, *shall or will catch.*

CEAPACH, aich, *s. f.* A decayed wood; also a place in Lochaber.

CEAPADH, aidh, *s. m.* A catching, a holding, a stopping, intercepting.

CEAPADH, (a), *pr. part.* of ceap. Catching, holding, stopping. A ceapadh chuileag, *catching flies.*—*Macdon.*

CEAPAINN, *v. a.* Catch, snatch, hold, intercept. *Pret. a.* cheapainn; *fut. aff.* ceapainnidh.

CEAPAIRE, *s. m.* A piece of bread with butter spread on it.—*Macint.* *N. pl.* ceapairean.

CEAPAN, ain, *s. m.* A stump; a pin. *N. pl.* ceapain.

CEAPANTA, *a.* Niggardly, stiff.—*Shaw.* Gu ceapanta, *in a niggardly manner.*

CEAP-SGAOIL, *v. a.* Propagate.—*Shaw.*

CEAP-TUISLIDH, *s. m.* A stumbling-block. Ceap-tuislidh roimh an dall, *a stumbling-block before the blind.*—*Stew. Lev.*

† CEAR, *s. m.* (*Ir. id.*) Progeny, race.—*Shaw.*

† CEAR, *s. m.* Blood.—*Ir. id.* *W.* guyar. *Eng.* gore.

† CEARACHADH, aidh, *s. m.* A wandering, a straying.

† CEARACHAR, air, *s. m.* (*Ir. id.*) A grave.

CEARB, cirb, *s. f.* (*Ir. id.*) A rag, a tatter; a lappet; a piece of cloth; a skirt; *rarely,* money. Cearb nan nial, *the skirt of the clouds.*—*Oss. Tem.* Faigh cearb, *cavil, rail, slander;* a faghail cearb orra, *railing at them.*—*Old Song.*

CEARBACH, *a.* (*Ir. id.*) Ragged; untidy; awkward in dress. *Com.* and *sup.* cearbaiche.

CEARBAN FEÒIR, *s. m.* A healing herb.

† CEARBHAL, ail, *s. m.* A massacre, a carnage.—*Shaw.*

CEARC, circe, *s. f.* (*Gr.* κίρκος, *a kind of hawk.* *Ir.* cearc, *hen.*) A hen. *N. pl.* cearcan, *hens.* Ceann circe, *a witless head.*—*Macint.* Cearc-fhraoich, *a moor-hen;* cearc-fhrangach, *turkey hen;* cearc-thomain, *a partridge;* cearc-Innseanach, *an Indian hen;* cearc-ghlopach, *a hen whose head is covered with down;* cearc-thopach, *a topped hen;* cearc-choille, *a partridge.* Cridhe circe an gob na h-airc, *a hen's heart in the mouth of poverty.*—*G. P.*

CEARCACH, *a.* Full of hens; like a hen; of, or belonging to, a hen.

CEARCALL, aill, *s. m.* (*Ir. id.* *Lat.* circulus. *Swed.* cirkel. *Span.* cerco, *a hoop,* and circulo, *a circle.*) A hoop, a circle, a circumference; a ring. *Asp. form,* chearcall. Mar chearcall fuileach ré 's i làn, *like the bloody circumference of the full moon.*—*Oss. Tem.*

CEARCALLACH, *a.* (*from* cearcall.) Circular, orbicular; like a hoop, rounded. A braighe cearcallach bàn, *her rounded fair neck.*—*Oss. Taura.*

† CEARCHALL, aill, *s. m.* A pillow, a bolster.—*Ir. id.*

CEARC-CHOILLE, *s. f.* A partridge.—*Stew. Sam.*

CEARC-LANN, -lainn, *s. m.* A poultry yard; a hen court.

CEARC-LOBHTA, *s. m.* A henroost.

CEARC-MHANRACH, aich, *s. m.* A hencoop.—*Shaw.*

CEARC-THOMAIN, *s. f.* A partridge; the *tetrao perdrix* of Linnæus.

CEARD, ceaird, *s. m.* (*Gr.* κέρδος, *gain.* *Ir.* ceard. *Corn.* ceard *and* keard, *artificer.*) A tinker; a smith; a tradesman. *Ceard* is seldom used in the last sense except in composition; as, fear-ceaird, *a tradesman.* *N. pl.* ceaird, ciùird, *tinkers.* Ceard airgiod, *a silversmith;* ceard òir, *a goldsmith;* ceard staoin, *a tinsmith;* ceard umha, *a coppersmith.*

CEARDACHD, *s. f.* The business of a tinker; forging.

CEARDAICH, aiche, *s. f.* A forge, a smithy, a smith's shop. O'n cheardaiche, *from the smithy.*—*Macint.* *N. pl.* ceardaichean.

CEARDAIL, *a.* (ceard-amhuil.) Like a tinker; artificial; well-wrought.

CEARDALACHD, *s. f.* Artificialness; handicraft; ingenuity.

† CEARLA, ai, *s. m.* A clew. *N. pl.* cearlan.

† CEARLACH, *a.* (*from* cearla.) Round, globular; like a clew.

CEARMANTA, *a.* Tidy, spruce, trim; succinct.

CEARMANTAS, ais, *s. m.* Tidiness, trimness; succinctness.

† CEARN, *s.* A victory; a man.—*Ir. id.* Cearn duais, *athletic laurel.*—*Shaw.*

CEARN, *s. m.* (*Ir. id.*) A corner; a quarter; a kitchen. *N. pl.* cearnan; *d. pl.* cearnaibh. Anns na cearnaibh iomallach, *in the utmost corners.—Stew. Jer.* Sluagh o gach cearn, *people from every quarter.—Stew. Gen.*

CEARNABHAN, ain, *s. m.* A corner; a hornet. *N. pl.* cearnabhain. Cuiridh mi cearnabhain, *I will send hornets.—Stew. Exod.*

† CEARNACH, *a.* (*from* † cearn.) Victorious.—*Shaw.* Perhaps *ceatharnach.*

CEARNACH, *a.* (*from* cearn.) Angular, rectangular, square; of, or belonging to, a kitchen. Ceithir-chearnach, *quadrangular.—Stew. Exod.*

CEARNADH, aidh, *s. m.* A kitchen, a quarter.

CEARNAG, aig, *s. f.* A little square; a little kitchen. Cearnag ghloine, *a square of glass.*

CEARN-LUACH, *s. m.* A prize.

CEARR, *a.* Wrong; awkward; left; left-handed. Tha so cearr, *this is wrong*; an lamh chearr, *the left hand;* deilg nan guaillibh chearr, *pins in their left shoulders.—Old Song.* A bheirt sin nach faighear ach cearr, is foighidinn is fear a dheanamh ris, *what cannot be helped ought to be borne.—G. P.*

CEARRAICHE, *s. m.* (*Ir.* cearbhach.) A gamester or gambler; a master of his profession or art. Cha cheilich cearraiche a dhìstean, *a gamester will not conceal his dice.—G. P.*

CEARR-LAMHACH, *a.* Left-handed, awkward. Fearr cearrlamhach, *a left-handed man.—Stew. Jud.*

CEART, *a.* (*Ir. id.*) Right; just; honest, upright; proper; certain. Ceart anns gach gniomh, *right in every action.—Smith.* Ceart mar sin, *just so;* ceart mar nach tugadh Dia fanear, *just as if God did not observe.—Id.* Le dlighe cheairt, *with just right.—Id.* Is ceart gun cuimhnichear thu, *it is proper that thou shouldst be remembered.—Oss. Carricth.* Is ceart gun tuit Silric, *it is certain that Silric shall fall.—Id.* Ceart cho maith riutsa, *just as good as you, just as well as you;* is ceart cho maith leam so ri sin, *I like this just as well as that.*

CEART, ceairt, ceirt, *s. m.* Justice; righteousness; redress; propriety. Bhrigh ceirt, *for justice.—Smith.* Coir is ceart, *right and justice.—Id.* Ceart na cleir ri chéil, *the redress that clergymen give to each other.—G. P.*

CEARTACH, aich, *s. m.* An adjustment; a trimming; a setting in order; a little domestic job. *N. pl.* ceartaichean.

CEARTACHADH, aidh, *s. m.* An adjusting; a mending; a trimming; a setting in order; an adjustment, an amendment; a paring, a pruning, a dressing.

CEARTACHADH, (a), *pr. part.* of ceartaich. Adjusting, mending, trimming; pruning, dressing.

CEARTACHAIL, *a.* (ceartach-amhuil.) Rectifiable; ready to rectify, or to adjust.

CEARTACHAIR, *s. m.* An adjuster; a rectifier; a regulator. Ceartachair uaireadair, *a watch regulator.* *N. pl.* ceartachairean.

CEARTAICH, *v. a.* Adjust; amend, set to rights, rectify; cut, prune, trim. *Pret. a.* cheartaich; *fut. aff. a.* ceartaichidh, *shall adjust.*

CEARTAIS, *gen. sing.* of ceartas.

CEARTAS, ais, *s. m.* Equity, justice. Le ceartas riaghlaidh e, *he will rule with justice.—Smith.* *Asp. form,* cheartas. Tha do cheartas ard, *thy justice is lofty.—Id.*

CEART-BHREATHAMH, eimh, *s. m.* A just judge. *N. pl.* ceart-bhreathamhna, *judges.*

CEART-BHREITH, *s. f.* A just decision or judgment; a birthright.

CEART-BHREITHEACH, *a.* Just in judging.

CEART-CHOIMEAS, eis, *s. m.* A just resemblance, a just comparison. Ceart-choimeas combrag nam fear, *a just comparison to the strife of heroes.—Oss.*

CEART-CHREIDIMH, *s. f.* Orthodoxy; sound belief.

CEART-CHREIDIMHICH, *s. m.* An orthodox person; one of sound faith.

CEART-CHREIDMHEACH, *a.* Orthodox; of sound faith.

CEARTLA, *s. f.* A clew. *N. pl.* ceartlan.

CEARTLAICH, *v. a.* Conglomerate, conglobate, wind up as a clew. *Pret. a.* cheartlaich; *fut. aff. a.* ceartlaichidh, *shall wind up; p. part.* ceartlaichte.

CEARTLAICHTE, *p. part.* of ceartlaich.

CEART-LANN, lainn, *s. m.* A house of correction.—*Ir. id.*

CEART-LUIGHEACHD, *s. f.* A just recompense; a just reward. Ceart-luigheachd agus duais, *just recompense and reward.—Smith.*

CEART-SGRIOBHADH, aidh, *s. m.* Orthography.

CEART-SGRIOBHAICHE, *s. m.* An orthographer.

CEARTUICH, *v. a.* See CEARTAICH.

† CEAS, ceasa, *s. m.* Obscurity, sadness; irksomeness.—*Ir. id.*

† CEASAD, aid, *s. m.* A grumbling, a complaining; a complaint; an accusation. More frequently written *casaid.*

CEASADACH, *a.* Inclined to grumble or complain; like a complaint; of, or belonging to, a complaint or accusation.

CEASADAIR, *s. m.* A grumbler; a complainer; a tormentor. *N. pl.* ceasadairean.

CEASADH, aidh, *s. m.* Vexation; punishment.—*Shaw.*

CEASLACH, aich, *s. m.* Fine wool; also coarse wool on the legs.—*Shaw.*

CEASLAID, *s. f.* Sacrilege.—*Shaw.*

CEASNACHADH, aidh, *s. m.* An examination; a scrutiny; a search; a questioning. *Ir.* ceistniughadh.

CEASNACHADH, (a), *pr. part.* of ceasnaich. Examining; questioning.

CEASNAICH, *v. a.* Examine, catechize, question, search. *Pret. a.* cheasnaich; *fut. aff. a.* ceasnaichidh. Written also *ceasnuich.*

CEASNAICHTE, *p. part.* of ceasnaich. Examined, catechized, questioned, searched.

CEASNUICH, *v. a.* Examine, catechize, question, search. *Pret. a.* cheasnaich; *fut. aff. a.* ceasnuichidh, *shall examine.* Ceasnuichibh sibh fein, *examine yourselves.—Stew. Cor.*

CEASNUICHTE, *p. part.* of ceasnuich. Examined, catechized, searched.

† CEAST, *s. m.* (*Arm.* cest. *Gr.* κεστος. *Ir.* ceast.) A girdle.

CEATACH, *a.* See CIATACH.

CEATAIN, *s. f.* See CÉITUIN.

CEATFADH, aidh, *s. m.* A conjecture, a guess; judiciousness.

CEATH, ceatha, *s. m.* A quay; cream; a shower; *rarely,* a sheep.—*Ir. id.*

CEATH, *v. a.* Skim, as milk. *Pret. a.* cheath, *skimmed; fut. aff.* ceathaidh, *shall skim.*

CEATHACH, aich, *s. m.* (*Ir.* ciach.) Mist, fog, vapour. An ceathach a seòladh, *the mist sailing.—Ull.* *Asp. form,* cheathach. Mar cheathach air bheanntaibh, *like mist on the mountains.—Oss. Duthona.*

CEATHACHAIL, *a.* (ceathach-amhuil.) Misty, smoky, vapoury, foggy.

CEATHAIRNE, *n. pl.* of ceatharn. Bands of robbers. Ceathairne choille, *freebooters; underhiding.*

CEATHARN, airn, *s. m.* (*Box. Lex.* cadarn, *brave.*) A troop; a banditti; a guard; a fighting band; a troop of Caledonian freebooters. *N. pl.* ceathairne. Mar dh' fheitheas ceathairne, *as bands of robbers wait.—Stew. Hos.*

They were commonly armed with a *scian* or dirk. Hence the *Eng.* kern. *Scotch,* kaitrine. *Lat.* caterva. The κεςωνι of Ptolemy (*cearns*) were in the North Highlands, on the coast of Caithness.

CEATHARNACH, aich, *s. m.* One of a banditti; a freebooter;

a soldier; a guardsman; a hero; a boor, a sturdy fellow. Is olc cuid a cheatharnaich a thasgadh, *the freebooter's share is ill laid up.*—*G. P.* *N. pl.* ceatharnaich.

Ceatharnachd, *s. f.* Valour, heroism; freebooting; peasantry, yeomanry.

Ceathramh, eimh, *s. m.* (*Ir.* ceathramh.) A fourth part; a quarter; a bushel; a firlot; a stanza; a lodging; also, *adjectively*, the fourth. Air a cheathramh là, *on the fourth day.*—*Ull.* Ceathramh eorna, *a bushel [firlot] of barley.*

Ceathramhan, ain, *s. m.* A cube; a quadrant. *N. pl.* ceathramhain.

Ceathramhanach, *a.* Cubical; like a quadrant.

Ceathrar, *a.* (*Ir. id.*) Four persons; four in number. Ceathrar ag eiridh mu' ramhan, *four men rising at his oars.*—*Oss. Trath.*

† **Ceide**, *s. f.* A market, a fair; a green; a hillock.

Ceigeach, *a.* Squat; shapeless; inactive.

Ceigean, ein, *s. m.* A turd; *in contempt*, a diminutive person.—*Macint.* An affected person.

Ceigeanach, *a.* Squat; diminutive in person; affected; like a turd.

Ceigeanachd, *s.* Squatness; diminutiveness; affectation; stoutness.

Ceil, *v. a.* (*Ir.* ceil. *W.* cèl. *Heb.* cili, *one who conceals his goods.*) Conceal, hide, shelter, screen, deny. *Pret. a.* cheil; *fut. aff. a.* ceilidh; *p. part.* ceilte, *concealed.* Ceilibh a cheuma, *hide his steps.*—*Oss. Com.* Cha cheil sinn e air ar cloinn, *we shall not conceal it from our children.*—*Sm.*

Ceil is commonly construed with the *prep.* air, either simple, as in the preceding example, or compounded, as in the following, Na ceil orm d' aitheanta, *hide not from me thy laws.*—*Sm.*

Ceile, *s. c.* (*Ir. id.*) A spouse; a husband; a wife; a servant. Céile a h-oige, *the husband of her youth.*—*Stew. Joel.* Athair céile, *a father-in-law;* mathair céile, *a mother-in-law;* brathair céile, *a brother-in-law;* piuthar céile, *a sister-in-law.* *Asp. form,* chéile.

Céileachadh, aidh, *s. m.* A concealing, hiding; covering, sheltering, screening; denying; a concealment, a hiding-place; a purloining.

Céileachadh, (a), *pr. part.* of céilich.

Céilear, eir, *s. m.* A warbling, a chirping, as of birds; a sonnet; melody. Cluinnidh Goll an céilear, *Gaul shall hear the warbling.*—*Oss. Gaul.*

Ceilear, ir, *s. m.* A concealer; a coverer, a screener, a shelterer. *W.* celawr.

Céilear, *fut. pass.* of céil.

Ceilearach, *a.* (*from* ceilear.) Musical; warbling, melodious; also warbling, melody. Bu lionmhor céilearach eoin, *numerous and warbling were the birds.*—*Old Song.*

Ceileiriche, *s. pl.* Warblers; songsters.

Ceilg, *gen. sing.* of cealg.

Céil-gheall, *v. a.* Betroth.—*Shaw.*

Céilich, *v. a.* Conceal, hide, screen; cover; deny; purloin. *Pret. a.* chéilich, *concealed; fut. a.* ceilichidh, *shall conceal.* Ceilichidh seirc aineamh, *charity conceals faults.*—*G. P.*

Ceilidh, *s. f.* A gossiping, a visit. Air cheilidh, *on a visit, gossiping;* earrag chéilidh, *the gossiping stroke;*—said of a person who is hurt at a visit.

Ceilinn, 1 *sing. fut. sub.* of ceil. Would conceal.

Ceilinn, *s. m.* A large codling.—*Macd.*

Céill, céille, *s. f.* Sense, judgment, reason. See **Ciall**.

Céille, *gen. sing.* of ciall.

Céillidh, *a.* Prudent, sober, discreet, wise. B' fhearr dhuit chi céillidh, *it were better for thee to be prudent.*—*Old Song.* Gu céillidh, *soberly.*

Céilt, *s. f.* Concealment, secrecy; any thing concealed or hidden. An céilt, *concealed, hidden.*—*Stew. N. T.* Céilt-inntinn, *equivocation.*

Ceilte, *p. part.* of céil. Concealed, hidden, secret. A ghaisgich ceilte, *his heroes concealed.*—*Oss. Fing.*

Ceiltinn, *s. f.* A concealing, a hiding, a covering; a concealment.

Ceiltinn, (a), *pr. part.* of céil. Concealing, hiding, covering.

Céilt-inntinn, *s. f.* Equivocation.

Céim, *gen. sing.* of ceum.

Ceimhleag, eig, *s. f.* A fillet. *N. pl.* ceimhleagan.

Ceimhleagach, *a.* Like a fillet; abounding in fillets.

Céin, *a.* (*Ir. id.*) Far; foreign, distant, remote. Dùthaich chéin, *a foreign country;* an aimsir chéin, *bygone time, remote time.*—*Smith.*

Céin, (an), *adv.* Far off; long since; far away; afar; from afar. An céin tha madainn na h-uaigh, *far off is the morning of the grave.*—*Oss. Derm.*

Céin-thir, *s. f.* A distant land. Tra tharlas dhoibh an céin-thir, *when they meet in a distant land.*—*Ull.*

Céir, *s. f.* Wax. Ceir bheach, *bees'-wax, honeycomb;* céir cluaise, *ear-wax;* mar leaghar teine céir, *as fire melts wax.*—*Smith.* Coinneal chéir, *a wax candle;* coinnlean céir, *wax candles.*

Lat. cera. *Gr.* κηρὸς. *W.* cwyr. *Arm. Corn.* coar, coir. *Ir.* ceir. *Span.* cera.

Céir, *v. a.* Cover with wax, seal with wax. *Pret. a.* chéir, *waxed.*

Ceir-bheach, *s. f.* Bees'-wax; honeycomb. Ceir-bheach na chnuachdaibh, *honeycomb in heaps.*—*Macint.*

† **Ceirbheadh**, idh, *s. m.* A carving.

Ceirde, *s. f.* A trade. See **Ceairde**.

Ceirdeach, *a.* Having a trade; expert, dexterous, ingenious. Is an-uasal mac an usail mar bi e ceirdeach, *without parts the son of a noble is mean.*—*G. P.*

Céireach, *a.* Waxen, waxy; like wax; of, or belonging to, wax.

Céire, *s. f.* A buttock; a haunch; a breech. Am broc 's a shròin na chéire, *the badger smelling his buttocks.*—*Old Song.*

Ceirsleadh, eidh, *s. m.* A clew of yarn. *Ir.* ceirtle.

Ceirtle, *s. f.* A clew or bottom of yarn. *N. pl.* ceirtlean.

† **Ceirt**, *s. f.* A rag. *N. pl.* ceirtean.

Ceirt, *gen. sing.* of ceart; which see.

Céirte, *a.* (*Lat.* cerata.) Waxed; covered with wax; sealed with wax. Eudach ceirte, *wax-cloth;* litir chéirte, *a sealed letter.*

Ceirte, *com.* and *sup.* of ceart. More or most just or righteous. Ni bu cheirte na mise, *more righteous than me.*—*Stew. Gen.*

† **Ceirteach**, *a.* Tawdry, ragged. Gu ceirteach, *raggedly.*

† **Ceirteachd**, *s. f.* Tawdriness, raggedness.

Ceirteag, eig, *s. f.* A tawdry girl. *N. pl.* ceirteagan.

Ceirtle, *s. f.* A clew of yarn. *N. pl.* ceirtean.

Ceirtleach, *a.* Like a clew.

Ceirtlich, *v. a.* Form into a clew, wind up into a clew. *Pret.* cheirtlich; *fut. aff.* ceirtlichidh.

† **Ceis**, *s. f.* A furrow; a sow, a pig.—*Ir. id.* *N. pl.* ceisean.

Céis, *s. f.* A spear, a lance. See **Gais**.

† **Ceisd**, *a.* Dear. Hence *ceisdean*, a sweetheart, and *other words.*

Ceisd, *s. f.* (*Ir.* ceist.) A question; a problem; a puzzle; a dispute; a controversy. *N. pl.* ceisdean; *d. pl.* ceisdibh. Cuir ceisd, *ask a question, put a question;* aobhar do cheisdibh, *occasion to questions.*—*Stew. Tim.*

Ceisdeachadh, aidh, *s. m.* A questioning; an examination.

Chàr, Chàra, *asp. form* of càr *or* càradh. A friend. Mo chàr, *my friend; my relative.*

Char, *asp. form* of car. A turn, a twist. Car air char, *rolling.*

Charn, *asp. form* of carn; which see.

Charn, *pret. a.* of carn. Heaped up. See **Carn**.

Charraid, *asp. form* of carraid; also *voc. sing.* of carraid; which see.

Charraig, *asp. form* of carraig. A rock. Mo charraig, *my rock;* also *voc. sing.* of carraig.

Chas, *s. f.; asp. form* of cas, *a foot.* See **Cas**.

Chas, *pret. a.* of cas. Gape; set the teeth. Chas iad am fiacal, *they set their teeth.—Stew.* 2 *K.*

Chasaibh, *d. pl. asp. form* of cas; which see.

Chathair, *asp. form* of cathair. A seat or chair; a city. Mo chathair, *my seat;* also *voc. sing.* of cathair.

Chead, *asp. form* of cead. Leave, liberty, permission. Thoir chead da, *give him his leave;* leig chead da, *let him alone; let him go;* le do chead, *with your leave.*

Cheadaich, *pret. a.* of ceadaich. Permitted, granted. See ceadaich.

Cheana, Cheanadh, *adv.* Already; before now. Is ard ar n-inbhe cheana, *high is the rank we already possess.—Sm.* An do rinn thu cheanadh e? *have you done it already?*

Cheangail, *pret. a.* of ceangail. Bound, fettered.

Cheangladh, *pret. pass.* and *pret. sub.* of ceangail. Was bound, would bind. Cheangladh e ri darraig, *he was bound to an oak.—Oss. Lod.*

Cheangladh, (a), *inf.* of ceangail. To bind, to fetter. See **Ceangail**.

Cheann, *asp. form* of ceann; which see.

Cheannachadh, (a), *inf.* of ceannaich. To buy. See **Ceannaich**.

Cheannaich, *pret. a.* of ceannaich. Bought. See **Ceannaich**.

Cheannsaich, *pret. a.* of ceannsaich. Subdued, tamed, managed. See **Ceannsaich**.

Cheannsaicheadh, *pret. sub.* of ceannsaich. Would tame or subdue; also *pret. pass.* was tamed.

Chearb, *asp. form* of cearb.

Cheart, *asp. form* of ceart. Real, just, true, honest, right, upright. A cheart duine sin, *that very man;* a cheart là sin, *that very day;* ro cheart, *very right;* a cheart rireadh, *in real earnest.*

Chéil, *pret. a.* of céil. Concealed, hid, denied. See **Céil**.

Chéile, *a. pron.* Each other, one another. Dlù ri chéile, *close on each other; close in succession.* Beuma beucach dlù ri chéile, *loud sounding blows in close succession.—Oss. Lod.* Thair chéile, *in confusion; in disorder.* Ri chéile, *together, joined.* Ra chéile, *together, joined.* Fanaibh ré cheile, *wait for one another.—Stew.* 1 *Cor.* Le cheile, *together; tête-a-tête;* a réir a chéile, *one with another; at an average; on good terms.*

Chéile, (le), *adv.* Together, both together; tête-a-tête; *solus cum sola.*

Chéile, (o), *adv.* Asunder, from each other.

Chéile, *s. c.; asp. form* of céile. A spouse. Mo chéile, *my spouse.* See **Céile**.

Chéin, *asp. form* of céin. Distant, foreign. Ann an tìr chéin, *in a distant land;* o chéin, *from afar;* an céin, *afar.*

Chéin, (o), *adv.* From afar; of old.

Chéir, *pret. a.* of céir. Waxed, covered with wax, sealed with wax.

Cheir, *asp. form* of céir; which see.

Cheirte, *asp. form* of ceirte; which see.

Cheo, *asp. form* of ceo. Mist. Chaidh e na cheò, *he became bewildered; it has gone to smoke.* See **Ceo**.

Cheum, *s. m.; asp. form* of ceum; which see.

Cheum, *pret. a.* of ceum. Marched, paced, strutted. See **Ceum**.

Chi, *fut. aff. a.* of *v. irr.* faic. Shall see; shall look; shall observe.

Chiabh, *s. m.; asp. form* of ciabh. A lock of hair, a ringlet; a side look. See **Ciabh**.

Chiabhag, aig, *s. f.; asp. form* of ciabhag. A ringlet. See **Ciabhag**.

Chiall, *asp. form* of ciall. Wit. A chiall, *his wit.* See **Ciall**.

Chianamh, *adv.* A little while ago. Thainig e chianamh, *he came a little while ago.* Am fear a mharbh a mhathair a chianamh, bheireadh e beo nios i, *he who killed his mother a little ago would now bring her alive.—G. P.* Said when fine weather succeeds a storm.

Chiar, *asp. form* of ciar; which see.

Chiar, *pret. a.* of ciar. Grow dusky. Nuair chiar am feasgair, *when the evening grew dusky.—Old Song.*

Chinn, *asp. form* of cinn; *gen. sing.* of ceann; which see.

Chinn, *pret. a.* of cinn. Grew, increased; become. See **Cinn**.

Chinnte, *asp. form* of cinnte. Sure, certain. A cheart co chinnte is am bàs, *just as sure as death.—Old Song.*

Chinnte, *s. f.; asp. form* of cinnte. Certainty. Air chinnte, *certainly, to be sure.* See **Cinnte**.

Chinnteach, *asp. form* of cinnteach. Sure, certain; steady, secure. Ro chinnteach, *very sure.*

Chion, (a), *prep.* Without; for want of. A chionn tearmuinn, *for want of protection.—Stew. Job. ref.*

Chionn, *conj.* (*Goth.* chan.) Because; as; for the reason that; since. Chionn nach do chreid iad, *as they did not believe.—Sm.* Chionn gu, *because that.* D'a chionn, *thereby.* Gheibh e bàs d'a chionn, *he shall die thereby.—Stew. Ezek.*

Chionta, *asp. form* of cionta; which see.

Chìr, *pret. a.* of cìar. See **Cìr**.

Chir, *asp. form* of cir.

Chìr, *inflection* of cair; which see.

Chite, Chiteadh, *sub. pass.* of *v. irr.* faic. Would or might be seen.

Chitear, *fut. pass.* of faic. Shall or will be seen.

Chitheam, (*for* chì me.) I shall see; I do see.

Chithear, *fut. pass.* of *v. irr.* faic. Shall be seen. Chithear le sùilibh dhaoine, *shall be seen by human eyes.—Sm.*

Chithinn, I *sing. sub. act.* of *v. irr.* faic. I might, could, or would see.

Chiùin, *asp. form* of ciùin.

Chladhaich, *pret. a.* cladhaich. Dug, delved.

Chlàr, *asp. form* of clàr; which see.

Chlàrsach, *asp. form* of clarsach. A harp.

Chleachd, *pret. a.* of cleachd. Accustomed, habituated.

Chleibh, *asp. form* of cleibh; *gen. sing.* of cliabh.

Chliabh, *asp. form* of cliabh.

Chlisg, *pret. a.* of clisg. Started; startled. See **Clisg**.

Chlisgeadh, (a), *adv.* Soon; in a short while; in a start; instantly. Thig e a chlisgeadh, *he will come instantly, he will come soon.*

Chliù, *asp. form* of cliù. Fame, reputation, renown, character. Gun chliù, *infamous; without fame; obscure.*

Chloch, *pret. a.* of cloch; which see.

Chloch, *asp. form* of cloch. A stone. See **Cloch**.

Chlogaid, *s. f.; asp. form* of clogaid.

CHLUAIN, *asp. form* of cluain; which see.

CHLUAS, *asp. form* of cluas.

CHLUINNEAR, *asp. form* of cluinnear; *fut. pass.* of cluinn. Shall or will be heard; might or would be heard. Cha chluinnear mo dhàn, *my song shall not be heard.—Oss. Duthona.*

CHLUINNEAS, *asp. form* of cluinn. Shall hear, shall have heard.

CHLUINNINN, *pret. sub.* of cluinn. Would hear.

CHLUINNT', *for* chluinnte.

CHLUINNTE, CHLUINNTEADH. Was heard; would be heard. Chluinnteadh guth briste, *a tremulous voice was heard.—Oss. Lodin.*

CHLUINNTINN, (a), *pr. inf.* of cluinn. To hear, to listen.

CHNEAS, *asp. form* of cneas; which see.

CHOBHAIR. See COBHAIR.

CHÒDHAIL, *asp form* of còdhail. Chaidh mi na chòdhail, *I went to meet him* See CODHAIL.

CHOG, *pret. a.* of cog. Fought, strove, contended, warred.

CHOIDH, CHOIDHCHE, *adv.* Ever, always, for ever, incessantly. A so suas a choidhche, *henceforward, for ever.*

CHOIGREACH, *asp. form* of coigreach. A stranger. See COIGREACH.

CHOIGILL, *pret. a* of coigill. Spared, pitied, showed mercy to.

CHOIMEAS, *pret. a.* of coimeas. Compared.

CHOIMEAS, *asp form* of coimeas, which see.

CHOIMHEAD, *pret a.* of coimhead. Kept; looked, watched, preserved.

CHÒINEACH, *asp form* of coineach; which see.

CHOINNICH, *pret. a* of coinnich. Met; opposed. See COINNICH.

CHÒIR, *s.; asp form* of còir. Right, justice. Tha chòir aige, *he has the right.* See CÒIR.

CHÒIR, (a), *prep.* To the presence; near; *implying motion*

CHÒIR, *a.; asp form* of coir. Good, kind; proper. Bu chòir dhuit, *you ought.* Bu chòir dhomh, dha, *I, he ought.*

CHÒIR, (do), *prep.* To the presence; near; *implying motion.*

CHOISE, *asp. form* of coise; *gen. sing.* of cas; which see.

CHOIS, (a), *prep.* Near to, hard by.

CHOISINN, *pret* of coisinn. Gained, won; also *fut. neg.* of coisinn. Cha choisinn amadan oighreachd, *a fool will not win a property —G. P.*

CHOIRBTE, *asp. form* of coirbte; which see.

CHOMHLA, (air *or* mu.) Together, in a body; at the same time. Dh' fhalbh iad mu chomhla, *they went off together* Taomadh an rann air chomhla, *pouring their strains in a body.—Oss. Lodin.*

Chomhla is also written *chomhlath,* i e *chomh-luath.*

CHOMHLATH, (mu *or* air.) Together, in a body; at the same time. Da chùraidh air chomhlath, *two champions together. —Oss. Fing*

Mu chomhlath, together, is properly *mu chomh-luath.*

CHOMRAICH, *asp. form* of comraich. Protection. Mo chomraich ort, *I claim thy protection; I throw myself on thy protection.* See COMRAICH.

† CHONNAIRC, *v.* Saw, observed, beheld. Chonnairc mi 'n lasadh ann ad ghruaigh, *I saw the flush in thy cheek — Old Song.*

CHÒP, *asp. form* of còp; which see.

CHÒPANACH, *a.; asp. form* of còpanach.

CHOR, *asp. form* of cor; which see.

CHORR, *a.; asp. form* of corr; which see.

CHOS, *s. f.; asp. form* of cos; which see.

CHÒS, *asp. form* of còs. See CÒS.

CHOSG, *pret. a.* of cosg.

CHOSGRADH, (a), *inf.* of cosgair. To slaughter, or massacre. A chosgradh mo naimh, *to slaughter my enemies.*

CHOSMHUIL, *asp form* of cosmhuil; which see.

CHRANN, *asp. form* of crann; which see.

CHRAOBH, *asp. form* of craobh, which see

CHRAOS, *s.; asp. form* of craos; which see.

CHRAOSNACH, *s; asp form* of craosnach.

CHRATH, *pret a* of crath Shook, trembled. See CRATH

CHRÈ, *s, asp form* of crè, which see.

CHREACH, *pret a.* of creach. Plundered, robbed. See CREACH.

CHREACH, *asp form* of creach; which see.

CHREAG, *s., asp form* of creag, which see.

CHREID, *pret a.* of creid. Believed See CREID.

CHREIDIMH, *asp form* of creidimh

CHREIDINN, 1 *sing. perf sub* of creid. I would believe Nior chreidinn, *I would not believe* In Bretagne they say, Ne 'r chredan, *I do not believe*

CHREIDSINN, (a), *pr. inf.* of creid To believe

CHRIADH, *asp. form* of criadh; which see

CHRIDHE, *asp form* of cridhe. A heart Mo chridhe, *my heart, my dear,* mo chridhe geal, *my dear love,* laoigh mo chridhe, *my darling,* a ghille mo chridhe, *my dear fellow*

CHRÌN, *asp form* of crìn, *from* crion; which see.

CHRIOS, *asp form* of crios; which see.

CHRITH, *pret a* of crith Shook, trembled

CHRITH, *s, asp. form* of crith; which see.

CHROCH, *pret. a.* of croch. Hung, suspended

CHROCHAIR, (a), *v. s.* of crochair. Thou scape-gallows

CHROM, *pret. a.* of crom Bent, curved; stooped.

CHROM, *asp. form* of crom; which see.

CHRUACHANN, *asp. form* of cruachann; which see.

CHRUADAL, *s m., asp. form* of cruadal. Hardship See CRUADAL.

CHRUADHAICH, *pret. a.* of cruadhaich. Hardened

CHRUAIDH, *a, asp. form* of cruaidh; which see

CHRUAIDH-CHÀS, *s. m, asp form* of cruaidh-chàs, Hardship Troimh chruaidh-chàs, *through hardship.*

CHRUINN, *asp form* of cruinn Round See CRUINN

CHRUINNE, *s f, asp form* of cruinne, which see.

CHRUINNICH, *pret a* of cruinnich. Gathered, met, assembled. See CRUINNICH.

CHRUIT, *asp form* of cruit. See CRUIT

CHRUTH, *asp. form* of cruth; which see.

CHUACH See CUACH.

CHUAIN. See CUAN.

CHUAIRT, *asp. form* of cuairt.

CHUAL, *pret. a.* of cluinn Heard Chual mi, *I heard.*

CHUALADH, *pret pass* of cluinn Was heard. See CLUINN

CHUALAM, (*for* chual mi) I heard. Chualam guth am' aisling féin, *I heard a voice in my dream —Oss. Croma.*

CHUALAS, *pret pass* of cluinn. Was heard Chualas a chomhachag a creig, *the owl was heard from its rock.—Ull*

CHUAN, *asp* of cuan. A sea

CHUANTA, CHUANTAN, *asp. form* of cuanta *and* cuantan *N. pl* of cuan. Seas See CUAN.

CHUCA, *comp pron.* To them *—Stew. Acts.* Properly *h-uga*

CHUGAD, *comp. pron.* To thee; towards thee. Chugad thig gach ni, *to thee every thing shall come.—Sm* More properly *h-ugad*

CHUGAIBH, *comp. pron.* To you, towards you, in your

direction A gabhail chugaibh céill, *getting for yourselves wisdom.—Sm.* More properly *h-ugaibh.*

CHUID, *asp. form* of cuid. Part. Chuid a chuid, *by degrees, by little and little —Stew. Ex.* More properly *chuid is a chuid*

CHUIDEACHD, *s f., asp form* of cuideachd A company. Chuideachd a chridhe, *beloved people, good folk, good people.*

CHUIGE, *comp pron.* To him, towards him; to it Gabhaidh e mi chuige fein, *he will take me to himself.—Sm.* A dol chuige is uaith, *going hither and thither, rocking to and fro.—Sm* More properly *h-uige*

CHUILC, *asp form* of cuilc

CHUILE, *a* All, a provincial corruption of *h-uile.* Chuile duine, *every man*

CHUILM, *asp form* of cuilm

CHUIM, *asp form* of cuim; *gen sing* of com. Of the belly See COM

CHUIMHNE, *asp form* of cuimhne Memory, remembrance Air chuimhne, *in remembrance, by heart*

CHUIMHNICH, *pret. a* of cuimhnich. Remembered.

CHUIR, *pret a* of cuir Put; sent, invited, laid, placed

CHUIRM, *asp form* of cuirm

CHUISEAG, *s f., asp* of cuiseag, which see

CHUISLE, *asp. form* of cuisle.

CHÙL, *asp form* of cùl Air chùl, *behind* Mu theid mi air chùl, *if I shall be vanquished —Oss Fing* Theich e air chùl a shluaigh, *he fled behind his people.—Mac Lach* See CÙL.

CHÙLAOBH, *i e* chul-thaobh. See CÙLAOBH

CHUM, *pret. a.* of cum Held, kept, detained; shaped, formed, contained. Ciod so a chum thu? *what is this that has detained thee?—Oss Gaul*

CHUM, *prep* To, towards, in order to. In many places this word is pronounced as if it were written *h-un* or *thun*

CHUM, *conj* In order to; to Chum agus gu, *in order that,* chum agus gum, *in order that,* chum agus gun, *in order that, so as that,* chum as nach, *that not, in order that not,* chum agus nach, *in order that not.*

CHUM, (a), *prep.* See CHUM

CHUM, (do), *prep.* See CHUM.

CHUMHACHD, *asp. form* of cumhachd

CHUNN, CHUNNAIC, *pret. a* of faic. Saw.

CHUNNACADH, *pret pass* of faic Was seen

CHUNNACAS, *pret pass* of faic. Was seen or observed. Chunnacas leamsa fiadh, *a deer was seen by me —Oss. Com*

CHUNNADH See CHUNN.

CHUNNAIC, *pret a* of faic Saw, observed, beheld. Chunnaic Innisfàil sinn, *Innisfail saw us —Ull* Am fac thu e? chunnaic, *did you see him? yes*

CHUNNAM, (chunn mi) I saw, I observed. Chunnam na h-oig-fhir shuas, *I saw the youth aloft —Oss Carricth*

CHUNNAS, *for* chunnacas; *pret. pass* of faic. Was seen

CHUNNCADAR See CHUNNACAS.

CHUR, (a), *inf* of cuir. To send; to put, to place; to sow.

CHÙRAIDH, *asp. form* of cùraidh

CHÙRAM, *asp. form* of cùram

† CI, *v n.* Lament, wail, weep. *Pret.* chi

CIA, *s m* A spouse, a husband; a man

CIA, *adv* Where, how. Cia meud? *how much?* cia fhad? *how long?* cia lion? *how many?* cia mar? *how? in what way? in what manner? in what condition?* cia mar tha thu? *how are you?* cia meud thug thu air? *how much did you give for it?* cia meud bliadhna tha thu? *how old are you?* cia dha? *to whom?*

CIA, AS, *adv* Whence; from whence; from what place Cia as thainig thu? *whence came you?—Stew. Gen.*

CIA AS AIR BITH, *adv.* Whencesoever; from whatever place.

CIAB, *s m.* A lock of hair, a ringlet, a side lock. *N. pl.* ciaban

CIABAN, ain, *s. m.* A gizzard. Ciaban coilich, *a cock's gizzard*

CIABH, *s. m.* (*Ir id*) A lock of hair, a ringlet. An osnaich a seideadh an ciabh, *their sighs wafting their locks.—Ull.* A ciabha clearc, *her radiant locks.—Id.* Ciabh-chasda, *a curled lock,* ciabh bhachlach, *curled hair or locks.*

CIABHACH, *a.* Hairy, bushy; having long hair, having ringlets *Com.* and *sup* ciabhaiche.

CIABHAG, aig, (*dim.* of ciabh) A ringlet, a lock of hair. *N. pl* ciabhagan.

CIABHAG-CHOILLE, *s f.* A woodlark.—*Shaw.*

CIABH-BHACHLACH, *a.* Having curled locks, tressy. Mo chaileag chiabh-bhachlach, *my tressy girl.—Old Song.*

CIABH-CHUCANN-DUBH, *s. m.* Deer's hair.

† CIACH, *s m* Mist, fog; sorrow, concern. Now written *ceathach*

CIAD, *a.* A hundred More frequently written *ceud.*

CIADACH, *a.* See CIATACH.

CIADAN, ain, *s. m.* A moor, a height.

CIADNA, *a* Same, similar. San iùl chiadna, *in the same direction —Old Poem.* Written more frequently *ceudna.*

CIADNAICH, *s.* Wednesday. Nur is Ciadnaich an t-samhainn, *when Hallowday falls on Wednesday —G P.*

CIAL, *s* (*Gr* χειλος) A jaw More commonly written *gial*; which see

CIALL, ceill, *s. f* (*Ir* ciall) Sense; meaning; discretion, reason, *rarely,* death Ciod is ciall do so? *what is the meaning of this?* Ciod is ciall duit? *what do you mean?* Ciod is ciall duit leis an iomain so? *what meanest thou by this drove?—Stew Gen.* Coimhead ciall, *regard discretion. —Stew Pro.* Tha e dhìth céill, *he lacks understanding.—Stew Pro* Gun chéill, *witless,* air bheag céill, *witless.* As a chéill, *out of his wits, doting.—Stew. Tim.* As a céill, *out of her wits.* Is i chiall a cheannaich is fearr, *bought wisdom is best.—G. P.*

CIALLACH, *a.* (*from* ciall) Intelligent, prudent, rational, discreet, significant Duine ciallach, *a prudent man.—Stew Pro* Gu ciallach, *rationally. Com.* and *sup.* cial-laiche

CIALLACHADH, aidh, *s. m.* A meaning, a signifying; a signification, interpretation.

CIALLACHADH, (a), *pr. part* of ciallaich Meaning. Ciod tha thu a ciallachadh? *what do you mean?*

CIALLACHAIL, *a.* Emblematical; rational; significant.

CIALLAICH, *v. n.* Signify, mean, allude, interpret. *Pret. a.* chiallaich, *meant, fut aff a* ciallaichidh, *shall mean.*

CIALLAIDHEACH, *a.* Significant.

CIALL-CHOGAR, air, *s m* A watch-word —*Shaw.*

CIALLRADH, *s m* (ciall *and* radh) A sentence, a full or complete sentence —*Macd.*

CIA MAR, *adv.* How? in what way? in what condition, state, or manner? Cia mar thuit an crann? *how did the tree fall?—Oss Tem* Cia mar tha thu? *how art thou?*

CIA MEUD, *adv* How much? how many? Cia meud thug thu air? *how much gave you for it?* Cia meud bliadhna tha thu? *how old art thou?* literally, *how many years art thou?*

CIAMHAIR, *a* Sad, weary, lonely Gu ciamhair, *sadly.*

CIAMHAIREACHD, *s f.* Sadness, weariness, loneliness.

CIAN, *a* (*Ir. id.*) Long, tedious, lasting; distant, far, remote, foreign; causing regret or pain. Is cian an oidhche, *tedious is the night.—Orr.* Bu trom a tuirse is bu chian, *heavy was her grief and lasting.—Oss.* Is cian mo leannan, *my love is far away.—Orr.* Bu chian leinn gaire am buillean, *the sound of their blows caused us pain.—Death of Carril.* Gu cian nan cian, *for ever.—Stew. Is.* An cian, *long since; long ago.* Sgeul cho binn cha chual sinn o chian, *a sweeter tale we have not heard this long while.—Macfar.*

CIAN, (an), *adv.* Long since; long ago. See CIAN.

CIANAIL, *a.* Solitary, lonely; sad, lamentable, mournful; weary; *also,* mild, loving. *Asp. form,* chianail. Taibhse cianail nan glas eide, *the grey-shrouded lonely ghost.—Oss. Trathal.* Da chraoibh chianail, *two solitary trees.—Oss. Fin. and Lor.* Is cianail m' aigne, *my thoughts are sad.—Ardar.*

CIANALACH, *a.* Solitary, lonely, sad, lamentable, mournful; fatigued, fatiguing. *Com.* and *sup.* cianalaiche, *more or most solitary.*

CIANALAS, ais, *s. m.* Loneliness, sadness, mournfulness, sorrow, wearisomeness; mildness of manner. Thainig smàl oirnne le cianalas, *we are darkened with sadness.—Old Song.*

CIAN-FHULANG, aing, *s. m.* Long-sufferance; perseverance; longanimity.

CIAN-FHULANGACH, *a.* Long-suffering; persevering.

CIAN-MHAIREANNACH, *a.* Lasting, durable, perennial.

† CIAP, *v. a.* (*Ir. id.*) Vex, torment.

CIAPALL, aill, *s. m.* Vexation, strife, contention, quarrelling, quarrelsome.

CIAPALLACH, *a.* Vexatious, tormenting, contentious.—*Shaw.*

CIAPALLAICHE, *s. m.* A vexatious or troublesome fellow, a quarrelsome fellow.

CIAR, *a.* (*Ir. id.*) Dark, dusky; dark brown, gloomy; stern. Sleibhte nan earba ciar, *the hills of the dusky roes.—Orr.* Carraig chiar nan laoch, *the dark brown rock of heroes.—Oss. Carricth.* Fonn ciar a bhròinn, *the gloomy strain of grief.—Oss.* A ghaisgich chiar, *thou stern hero.—Oss. Fing.* Ciar-imeachd an aineil, *the dark path of the stranger.—Oss. Taura.*

CIAR, ciair, *s. m.* Darkness, duskiness, gloom, evening. Fear astair fo chiar, *the traveller benighted.—Oss. Tem.* Ciar nan carn, *the gloom of the rocks.—Id.* Roi a chiàr, *through the dusk.—Id.*

CIAR, *v. n.* Grow dark, grow dusky, grow brown. *Pret. a.* chiar, *grew dark; fut. aff.* ciaraidh.

CIARACH, aich, *s. m.* A swarthy person. *N. pl.* ciaraichean.

CIARACHADH, aidh, *s. m.* A growing dark or dusky; a making dark or dusky; dusk. Aig ciarachadh an fheasgair, *at the dusk of evening.—Old Song.*

CIARADH, aidh, *s. m.* A darkening, growing dusky, gloom. Ciaradh nan speur, *the darkening of the heavens.—Oss. Tem.*

CIARAG, aig, *s. f.*; *dim.* of ciar. (*Ir.* ciarog.) Any little dark-coloured creature; a dark-brown-haired girl; a swarthy maid; a chafer. *N. pl.* ciaragan. Bòid a chiaraig ris na fearaibh, is bòid nam fear ris a chiaraig, *the swarthy maid forswore marriage, as men would not have her.—G. P.*

CIARAICH, *v. a.* and *n.* Grow dusky, make brown or dusky. *Pret. a.* chiaraich; *fut. aff. a.* ciaraichidh. Chiaraich am feasgar, *the evening grew dusky.*

† CIARAIL, *s. f.* A quarrel, contention, a brawl, a fray.

CIARALACH, *a.* Quarrelsome, contentious, perverse. *Com.* and *sup.* ciaralaiche.

CIARALACHD, *s. f.* Quarrelsomeness, contentiousness, perverseness.

CIAR-CHEO. A dark mist, a dusky mist. Ciar-cheo na h-oidhche, *the dusky mist of night.—Orr.*

CIARSAN, ain, *s. m.* A kerchief.

CIAR-SHUIL, -shùl, *s. m.* A dark eye; a scowling eye.

CIAR-SHUILEACH, *a.* Having a dark eye, dark-eyed; having a scowling eye. B' fhada spairn nan ciar-shuileach, *long was the struggle of the dark-eyed* [*chiefs*].—*Oss. Lodin.*

† CIASAIL, *s. f.* A dispute, a quarrel, a brawl. *N. pl.* ciasailean.

CIASALACH, *a.* Quarrelsome, brawling.

CIAT, ciata, *s. f.* Pleasure; satisfaction; opinion. Ciat mhor, *much pleasure.—Sm.* Ciod do chiat deth? *what think you of him?* Cha 'n 'eil ciat air an t-saoghal agam dheth, *I have no opinion in the world of him.*

CIATACH, *a.* (*from* ciat.) Handsome, goodly, graceful, becoming, seemly; esteemed; conceited. Luach ciatach, *a goodly price.—Stew. Zech.* A Chonail chiataich, *graceful Connal.—Old Poem.* Tha e ciatach as fein, *he is conceited.*

CIATACHAS, ais, *s. m.* Handsomeness, seemliness, gracefulness; estimation.

CIATADH, aidh, *s. m.* Pleasure; satisfaction; opinion.

CIATAICHEAD, id, *s. f.* Gracefulness; improvement in gracefulness; comeliness, seemliness; improvement in comeliness or external appearance.—*Macint.* A dol an ciataichead, *growing more and more graceful.*

Ciataichead, like many other nouns in Gaelic, is used as a kind of second comparative. Is ciataichid i an eide sin, *that dress renders her more comely.*

CIATFACH, *a.* Becoming, handsome, goodly, graceful. Ciatfach do 'n amadan, *becoming a fool.—Stew. Pro.* More properly *ciatach.*

CIATFADH, *s. m.* See CIAT and CIATADH.

CÌB, *s. f.* A species of mountain-grass; coarse tow. See CIOB.

CIBHEARG, eirg, *s. m.* A rag; a little ragged woman.

CIBHEARGACH, *a.* Ragged; tawdry.

CIBHEARGAN, ain, *s. m.* A little rag; a little ragged wight.

CÌCHE, *gen. sing.* of cioch. Of a pap; of a breast. See CIOCH.

CÌCHEAN, *n. pl.* of cioch. Breasts, paps. Cìchean liontach, *full breasts.—Old Song.* See CIOCH.

† CIDH, *s. f.* (*Ir. id.*) A fight; a view.

CIDHIS, *s. f.* A mask, a disguise; a vizor.

CÌDHISEAR, ir, *s. m.* One in mask; a guiser. *N. pl.* cìdhisearan.

CÌDHISEARACHD, *s. f.* (*from* cidhis.) A masquerade; a masking.

CIGEALL, ill, *s. m.* A tickling; a tickling sensation. Bheil cigeall annad? *can you be tickled?*

CIGEALLACH, *a.* Tickling; easily tickled; difficult.

CIGEALLADH, aidh, *s. m.* The act of tickling; a tickling sensation.

CIGILL, *v. a.* Tickle. *Pret. a.* chigill, *tickled; fut. aff. a.* cigillidh, *shall or will tickle.*

CILL, *s. f.* (*Lat.* cella. *Corn.* cil *and* cel. *Ir.* cill. *Heb.* cela, *a place enclosed.*) A burying-ground; a cemetery; a churchyard; a cell; a chapel; a grave; ruddle. (*Scotch*, keel, *ruddle.*) Thug am bàs an corpaibh do 'n chill, *death has given their bodies to the cemetery.—Old Song.* Cill-bhruic, Rothesay, *i. e. the church of St. Broke, the tutelary saint of the parish.* The Swiss say *cilch*, a church.

† CILL, *s. f.* Partiality; prejudice.

CILLEAN, ein, *s. m.* A repository; any thing laid up or concealed from observation.

CILL-MHÀNACH, *s. m.* An abbey, a monastery.

† CIM, *v. a.* Captivate, capture, enslave. *Pret. a.* chim.

CIMEACH, ich, *s. m.* A captive, a prisoner, a slave. *N. pl.* cimichean, *captives; d. pl.* cimichibh, *to captives.* Written also *ciomach.*

CIMEACHAS, ais, *s. m.* Captivity, imprisonment, bondage, slavery.

CIN, *adv.* (*Bisc.* kein, *how*) Where? whither? to what place? Cin chaidh e? *whither did he go?*

CINE, *s m* (*Gr.* γενος. *Goth.* kun. *Lat.* genus. *Ir.* cine *Eng* kind) A race, a tribe, a clan, a family, kindred, progeny, offspring. An cine maiseach treubhach, *the handsome powerful clan*—*Macdon*

CINEADACH, *a.* (*from* cine) Clannish; in clans. Gu cineadach, *clannishly.*

CINEADAIL, *a.* Clannish; fond of one's name or family.

CINEADAS, ais, *s. m* Kindred, relationship; clannishness. Do chineadas còrr, *thy noble kindred.*—*Old Song*

CINEADH, idh, *s. m.* An offspring, a progeny; a tribe, a clan, a family.

CINEAL, eil, *s m* (*W.* cenel. *Ir.* cineal) A kind, a sort, a race, a progeny, an extraction; a nation, a tribe, a clan.

CINEALACH, *a.* In tribes or clans; national; clannish; populous.

CINEALTA, *a* (*Ir.* cinealta.) Kind, gentle; clannish.

CINEALTACHD, *s f* Kindness, gentleness; clannishness. Aghaidh làn do chinealtachd, *a face full of gentleness*—*R*

CINEALTAS, ais, *s. m* (*Ir.* cinealtas.) Fondness, affection, clannishness.

CINEAMHUINN, *s. f.* See CINNEAMHUINN.

CINGEACH, *a* (*Ir. id*) Brave; strong, impetuous.

† CINGEACHD, *s f.* Bravery; strength; impetuousness.

CINN, *gen sing.* and *n pl* of ceann; which see

CINN, *v. n.* Grow, vegetate, become, wax, grow in number or in bulk, multiply, increase; happen; agree to. *Pret. a.* chinn, *fut aff. a.* cinnidh.

CINNEACH, ich, *s. m.* A nation; a heathen; a gentile; a surname; a cognation Air feadh nan cinneach sin, *among these nations.*—*Stew* 1 *K.*

CINNEACHADH, aidh, *s. m.* A growing, a budding, a vegetating.

CINNEACHDACH, *a.* Vegetative *Com.* and *sup.* cinneachdaiche.

CINNEACHDAINN, *s f* Increase, growth

CINNEADAIL, *a* (*W.* cenedawl, *kindred*) Clannish; fond of one's name; fond of a namesake Cinneadail còir, *clannish and hospitable*—*Macint.*

CINNEADAS, ais, *s m* Kindred—*Macd*

CINNEADH, idh, *s. m.* (*Sax* cynne. *Eng.* kin) A clan, a tribe, relation, kin, kindred. Cinneadh mòr gun bhòsd, *a powerful and peaceful clan.*—*Old Song* Fear cinnidh, *one of the same clan, a namesake* Ceann cinnidh, *a chieftain.*

CINNEAMHNACH, *a* Fatal, accidental

CINNEAMHUIN, *s. f.* Chance, fortune, fate Am agus cinneamhuin, *time and chance.*—*Stew. Ecc* Clach na cinneamhuinn, *the fatal stone*,—the stone on which the ancient Caledonian kings were inaugurated See LIA FÀIL.

CINNEALTAS, ais, *s. m.* Fondness, affection, clannishness.

CINNEAS, eis, *s m.* Growth, produce, crop, increase A chinneas agus fhochann, *its produce and brier.*—*Sm.*

CINNEASACH, *a.* Fruitful, vegetative; inclined to grow; germinative.

CINNEASACHD, *s f* Fruitfulness, vegetativeness.

CINNFEADHNA, *n. pl.* of ceannfeadhna Chieftains.

CINNICH, *gen. sing.* and *n pl* of cinneach.

CINNICH, *v a.* and *n.* Grow, make to grow, rear; increase, abound; make to vegetate. *Pret. a* chinnich; *fut. aff. a.* cinnichidh Cha chinnich craobh ni 's aillidh, *a fairer tree shall never grow.*—*Macfar.*

CINNMHIRE, *s. f.* Frenzy, delirium.—*Shaw.*

CINNSEACH, ich, *s. m.* Want; need.

CINNSEAL, eil, *s m.* Want; necessity, hardship; desire; search.

CINNTE, *s. f.* Certainty; truth; reliance, assurance, confidence. Cha 'n 'eil cinnte nam beul, *there is no certainty in their mouth.*—*Sm.* Air chinnte, *certainly, for certain, to be sure.*

CINNTE, CINNTEACH, *a.* (*Ir. id*) Certain, sure; unerring, plain, evident; assured; confident; positive. Saighde co cinnteach 's am bàs, *arrows as certain as death.*—*Oss. Fin. and Lor.* Is cinnte do lamh, *thy hand is unerring.*—*Old Poem.* Tha mi cinnteach as, *I am certain of it*, làn chinnteach, *full certain.*

CINNTEACHD, *s. f.* (*Ir.* cinteacht.) Certainty, assurance, positiveness, confidence; clearness, unquestionableness, evidence.

CINNTEADAIR, *s. m.* An insurer. *N. pl* cinnteadairean.

CINNTEAGAN, ain, *s. m.* A coarse cloak—*Shaw.*

CINNTEALAS, ais, *s m.* Certainty, assurance. Bheil cinntealas agad air? *are you certain of it?*

† CINNTICH, *v. a.* Appoint, determine. *Pret.* chinntich, *appointed, fut. aff.* cinntichidh, *shall appoint.*

CINNTINN, *s. f.* Growth; growing, a vegetating; a becoming.

CINNTINN, (a), *p part.* of cinn. Growing, vegetating; becoming

CIOB, *s f.* (*Gr.* κιβος, *food*) A species of mountain-grass; tow, coarsely-dressed flax. Ciob nan ciar-bheann, *the grass of the dusky hills.*—*Oss Duthona.* Bun na ciob, *the root of the mountain-grass.*—*Macint.*

CIOB, *v* Bite, wound, maim *Pret a.* chiob; *fut. aff. a.* ciobaidh

CIOBHAL, ail, *s m.* A jaw; the jaw-bone. More commonly written *gial*, which see.

CIOCAR, air, *s. m.* A hungry creature, a ravenous creature. *N pl.* ciocaran.

CIOCARACH, *a.* Hungry, ravenous. Gu ciocarach, *ravenously.* *Com.* and *sup* ciocaraiche.

CIOCH, ciocha, *and* ciche, *s. f.* (*Ir. id. Pol.* cyc *and* cycek.) A pap; a breast, the nave of a wheel. Leanabh ciche, *a babe* Bainne mo chiocha, *the milk of my breasts.*—*Oss. Gaul.* An crochadh ris a chiche, *hanging to the breast*—*Sm* Cioch a mhuineil, *the uvula*, cioch-shlugain, *the uvula;* cioch-chinn, *the uvula.*

CIOCHAN, ain, *s m.* A titmouse.—*Shaw* and *Macd.*

CIOCHRAN, ain, *s. m* (*from* cioch.) An infant on the breast; a suckling. Beul nan ciochran, *the mouths of sucklings.*—*Sm* *N pl.* ciochrain.

CIOCHRANACHD, *s f.* The condition of a babe; suckling.

CIOCH-SHLUGAIN, *s. f.* The uvula.

CIOCHT, *s.* (*Ir. id*) Children, a carver; an engraver.

CIOCRACH, *a.* (*Ir.* ciocarach.) Hungry, ravenous, greedy, avaricious An t-anam ciocrach lionaidh e, *he will fill the hungry soul*—*Sm.* Roimhich chiocrach, *avaricious Romans*—*Macfar.*

CIOCRAS, ais, *s. m.* (*Ir. id.*) Hunger, ravenousness, greediness, avariciousness, a false appetite; earnest desire. Air chiocras fola, *through thirst of blood*—*Old Poem.*

CIOCRASACH, *a.* Hungry, ravenous, greedy, avaricious. Gu ciocrasach, *ravenously.*

CIOCRASAN, ain, *s. m.* (*Ir.* ciocarasan.) A hungry fellow; a greedy fellow.

CIOD, *interrog. pron.* What. Ciod tha thu ag radh? *what do you say?* Ciod so? *what is this?* Ciod sud? *what is that?* Ciod so a chi sibh? *what is this you see?*—*Oss. Fin. and Lor.* Ciod gus an d' thig e, *what it shall come to.*—*Stew. Acts.* Ciod ged tha, *what though there be.* Ciod ged bhiodh, *what though there were.* Ciod mu dheimhinn, *what about it.*

Ir. cad. *Gr.* κοτα, *how many? Lat* quot, *how many?* quod, quid, *what.*

† **Ciol**, cil, *s. m.* Death; inclination, prosperity.

Ciolag, aig, *s. f.* A hedge-sparrow.—*Shaw.*

Ciolam, aim, *s. m.* (*Ir. id*) A vessel.

† **Ciolrath**, *v. n.* Chatter; twitter.—*Shaw.*

Ciom, *s. m.* A comb; a wool-card. *N. pl.* ciomaichean.

Ciom, *v. a.* (*Lat.* como. *Scotch,* kame.) Comb, card wool, teaze wool. *Pret.* chiom.

Ciomach, aich, *s. m.* A prisoner, a slave, a captive. *N. pl.* ciomaich. Ceud-ghin a chiomaich, *the first-born of the captive.*—*Stew. Exod.*

Ciomachas, ais, *s. m.* Captivity, slavery, bondage, imprisonment. Thug d' aghaidh gach aon an ciomachas, *thy face has brought every one into captivity.*—*R.*

Ciomadh, aidh, *s. m.* A fault.

Cioman, ain, *s. m.* (*dim.* of ciom.) A comb or card for teazing wool; a combing, a teazing.

Ciombal, ail, *s. m.* A bell; a cymbal. *N. pl* ciombalan.

Ciombalair, *s m.* One who plays on cymbals. *N. pl.* ciombalairean.

Cion, *s. m.* Love, desire, fondness; fault; a cause. An cion air a leannain, *fond of her lovers*—*Stew. Jer.* Ormsa tha 'chion, *his desire is on me*—*Stew. Song. Sol.* Mo chion ort, *I love thee.*—*Sm.* Cion-fath, *a reason or ground.*

† **Cionag**, aig, *s f.* A kernel. *N. pl.* cionagan.

Cionail, *a* (cionamhuil.) In love; desirous, fond; faulty, guilty. Cionail air moran fiona, *fond of much wine.*—*Stew. Tim. ref*

Cion-aire, *s. f.* Inattention.

Cion-aireachail, *a.* Inattentive.

Cionar, air, *s. m.* (*Ir.* cionthar.) Music, melody, song. Ri cionar, *singing.*—*Macfar.*

Cion-chorran, ain, *s. m.* A hook.—*Shaw* *N. pl.* cion-chorrain.

Cion-eolach, *a.* Ignorant.

Cion-eolas, ais, *s. m.* Ignorance; lack of knowledge.

Cion-fath, *s. m.* Occasion, cause, reason, or ground, quarrel. Cion-fàth na 'r n-aghaidh, *occasion against us.*—*Stew. Gen* Written also *cionnfath.*

Cion-fhaobhair, *s m* Bluntness.

Cion-fhoighidinn, *s. m.* Impatience.

Cion-leirsinn, *s m.* Blindness; shortness of sight.

Cion-mhothuchadh, aidh, *s. m.* Apathy; insensibility; privation of sense or feeling.

Cionn, *s* A reason or ground; occasion, cause. A chionn gu, *because that.*

Cionnas, *adv.* (*Ir.* cionnus) How, in what way or manner. Cionnas thainig orra claoidh? *how has trouble come upon them?*—*Sm.* Cionnas tha thu? *how do you do?*

Cionnfa', **Cionnfàth**, *s. m.* Reason, cause, excuse, occasion; quarrel. Gun chionnfa', *without reason*—*Sm.* Cionnfath air bi, *any occasion whatever.* See also **Cion-fàth.**

Ciont, ciònta, *s. m.* and *f.* (*Ir.* cionnt.) Guilt, fault, blame, crime, sin. Làn cionta, *full of guilt*—*Sm.* Gun chionta, *blameless.*—*Id.* Na maith an cionta, *pardon not their sin.*—*Stew Jer.* Dean ciont, *sin, offend.*

Ciontach, *a.* (*Ir. id*) Guilty, faulty, criminal, sinful, iniquitous, chargeable Ciontach do pheacadh, *guilty of sin.* *Com.* and *sup.* ciontaiche

Ciontachadh, aidh, *s. m.* (*Ir.* ciontaghadh) Trespassing, sinning, blaming. Le ciontachadh am aghaidh, *with trespassing against me.*—*Stew Jer.*

Ciontaich, *v. a.* Sin, trespass, blame. *Pret. a.* chiontaich; *fut. aff. a.* ciontaichidh. Cha chiontaich sibh, *ye shall not sin.*—*Stew. 2 Chr.*

† **Cion-tìre**, *s f.* Tax, tribute.—*Shaw.*

Ciopair, *s. m.* A shepherd, a herd; a keeper. Fead ciopair an aonaich, *the whistle of the mountain-shepherd*—*Mac Co.* *N. pl.* ciopairean. This seems to be a corrupt use of the English word *keeper.*

Ciopaireachd, *s. f* The occupation of a shepherd. Ris a chiopaireachd, *herding sheep.*

Ciorb, *v. a.* and *m.* Mangle; mortify; become black. *Pret. a.* chiorb; *fut. aff.* ciorbaidh.

† **Ciorghal**, *a.* Brave, fearless, strong Bi ciorghal treubhanta, *be fearless and strong*—*Old Song*

Ciorramach, *a.* (*Ir.* ciorrthamach.) Maimed, lamed, lame, hurt, blemished; causing a flaw or blemish; hurtful; mean. *Com.* and *sup.* ciorramaiche

Ciorramachd, *s. f.* Lameness, the state of being maimed.

Ciorusgrach, *a.* Clearing, or driving aside with the hands.

Cios, *s f* Tax See Cìs.

† **Ciosach**, *a.* Importunate; sluggish, slovenly—*Shaw.* Gu ciosach, *importunately.* *Com.* and *sup.* ciosaiche.

Ciosachadh, aidh, *s. m* An appeasing, a calming, a restraining, subduing, quieting.

Ciosachadh, (a), *pr. part.* of ciosaich. Appeasing, calming, subduing, quieting, restraining.

Ciosachdach, *a.* Importunate; sluggish, slovenly.—*Shaw.*

Ciosaich, *v. a.* Appease, calm, restrain, assuage, subdue. *Pret. a.* chiosaich, *subdued*, *fut. aff a.* ciosaichidh, *shall subdue.*

Ciosaiche, *s m* An appeaser, a subduer.

Ciosaichte, *p. part.* of ciosaich. Subdued, appeased.

Ciosal, ail, *s. m.* The wages of a nurse.—*Shaw.*

Ciosnachadh, aidh, *s. m.* The act of appeasing, a subduing, a calming Tha 'n tir air a ciosnachadh, *the land is subdued*—*Stew. Chron*

Ciosnachadh, (a). Subduing, appeasing, calming.

Ciosnachail, *a* Placable, tranquillizing

Ciosnaich, *v. a.* Subdue, calm, pacify. *Pret. a.* chiosnaich, *tranquillize.*

Ciotach, *a.* Left-handed; awkward. Duine ciotach, *a left-handed man*—*Stew Jud.*

Ciotachd, *s. f.* Left-handedness, the habit of using the left hand more than the right; awkwardness.

Ciotag, aig, *s. f.* (*Ir id.*) The left hand, a little plaid, a scarf. *N pl* ciotagan.

Cìp, *gen sing.* and *n. pl.* of ceap; which see.

Cìr, *gen. sing* of ciar. See **Ciar**

Cìr, *v. a.* (*Gr.* κειρω, *shear*) Comb; curry-comb; hackle as wool. *Pret. a.* chìr, *combed*, *fut. aff. a.* cìridh, *shall comb.* Cìr d' fhalt, *comb your hair.*

Cìr, *s. f.* (*Gr.* κειρια, *a tuft.* *Ir.* cior *and* cìr.) A comb; the crest of a cock; the cud; a jaw; a key. Eun cìr-dhearg an aonaich, *the red-crested fowl of the heath*—*Orr* Gach aon a chnamhas a chìr, *every one that chews the cud.*—*Stew. Lev*

† **Cirb**, *a.* Swift, fleet.—*Shaw*

Cirb, *gen. sing.* of cearb; which see.

Circ-fheòil, *s. f.* The flesh of a hen or chicken.

Cìreach, *a.* (*from* cìr) Crested, like a crest; of, or belonging to, a crest; inclined to comb; combing. Cha mhinnean gorm no coileach cìreach, *it is neither a grey kid nor a crested cock.*—*Orr.*

Cìreachan, ain, *s. m.* A comb-case.

Cìreadh, idh, *s. m.* A combing; a teazing

Cìreadh, (a), *pr. part* of cìr. Combing; teazing as wool.

Cìrean, ein, *s. m* (*dim.* of cìr.) A cock's crest; a little comb

Cireanach, *a.* Crested; like a crest; of, or pertaining to, a crest.

Cir-mheala. *s. f.* A honey-comb. Mar chir mheala, *as an honey-comb.—Stew. Pro.*

Cìs, *s. f.* (*Ir.* clos.) Tax, tribute, impost; reverence; subjection. Seirbheiseach do chìs, *a servant to tribute.—Stew. Gen.* Fuidh chìs, *under tribute, under subjection.—Stew. Jud.* Chaidh Suaran fo chis, *Suaran went under subjection.—Oss. Fing.*

Cìs-bhuailteach, *a.* Taxable, liable to tax.

Cìs-chàin, *s. f.* Tribute, tax; poll-tax.—*Shaw. Ir.* cios-chain.

Cisde, *s. f.* A chest or box. See Ciste.

Cisdeag, eig, *s. f.* (*dim.* of cisde.) A little chest. See Cist.

† **Ciseal**, eil, *s. m.* A nurse's wages.—*Shaw.*

Cisear, eir, *s. m.* (cis-fhear.) An exciseman; a taxgatherer. *N. pl.* cìsearan.

Cìsearachd, *s. f.* The business of an exciseman, the business of a taxgatherer.

Cìs-leagadh, aidh, *s. m.* Assessment; an assessing.

Cìs-leagair, *s. m.* An assessor. *N. pl.* cis-leagairean.

Cìs-mhaor, aoir, *s. m.* A taxgatherer, a publican. Caraid chis-mhaor, *the friend of publicans.—Stew. Mat. N. pl.* cis-mhaoir.

Ciste, *s. f.* A chest, a box, a trunk, a treasure; a coffer; a coffin; *rarely*, a cake.. *N. pl.* cisteachan. Ghabh e ciste, *he took a chest.—Stew.* 2 *K.*
Heb. Arab. Chald. cis, *a purse. Pers.* kiste, *a vessel. Gr.* κιστη. *Lat.* cista. *Corn. W.* cist. *Arm. Ir.* ciste. *Swed.* kista. *Isl.* kista. *Du.* kist. *Da.* kiste.

Cisteachan, *n. pl.* of ciste.

Cisteag, eig, *s. m.* (*dim.* of ciste.) A little chest, a little box.

Cistean, ein, *s. m.* (*dim.* of ciste.) *W.* cistan. *Du.* cisjen. A chest, a little trunk.

Cisteil, *a.* (ciste-amhuil.) Capsular.

Ciste-mhairbhe, *s. f.* A coffin. Chuireadh ann an ciste-mhairbhe e, *he was put into a coffin.—Stew. Gen.*

Cistinn, *s. f.* A kitchen. *N. pl.* cistinnean.

Cistinneach, *a.* Culinary.

Cistinneadh, idh, *s. m.* A rioting.

Citag, aig, *s. f.* A little plaid; a scarf; the left hand. *N. pl.* citagan. More properly *ciotag;* which see.

Cith, *s. f.* Ardour; havoc; also a shower, a mist, a peal. Cith-chath na shùil, *the ardour of battle in his eye.—Oss.* Cith fola, *a shower of blood.—Fingalian Poem.* Cathamh na fhuar chithibh, *drift in cold showers.—Macfar.*

Cith-chath, *s. f.* Ardour for battle. Cith-chath na shuilibh lasrach, *ardour for battle in his gleaming eyes.—Oss.*

Citheach, *a.* Showery; destructive; keen. Fo laimh chithich Dhorlai, *under the destructive hand of Dorla.—Oss. Duthona.*

Citsinn, *s. f.* More properly *cistinn;* which see.

Ciubhrach, aich, *s. m.* A drizzling shower. Frasan thig nan ciubhraich, *showers that come in drizzles.—Macfar.*

Ciuch, *s. m.* A pass.

Ciuchair, *a.* Beautiful, dimpling.—*Shaw.*

Ciùil, *gen. sing.* of ceòl.

Ciùin, *a.* Calm, gentle, meek, mild; smooth, unruffled; peaceful, quiet, composed. Is ciùin mo chomhnuidh anns na neoil, *calm is my dwelling in the clouds.—Oss. Carricth.* Cha chiùin e, *he is not mild.—Oss. Tem. Com.* and *sup.* ciùine.

Ciùine, *s. f.* Calmness; a calm; gentleness, meekness; mildness, smoothness; peacefulness, quietness, repose; a gentle gale. Ciùine mhor, *a great calm.*

Ciùine, *com.* and *sup.* of ciùin. More or most calm.

Ciùineachadh, aidh, *s. m.* The act of pacifying; a calming or quieting.

Ciùineachadh, (a), *pr. part.* of ciùinich. Pacifying, calming, quieting.

Ciùinead, eid, *s. m.* Calmness; increase in calmness. A dol an ciùinead, *growing more and more calm.*

Ciùineas, eis, *s. m.* Quietness, mildness, meekness; calmness; smoothness; composure.

Ciùinich, *v. a.* Pacify, appease, assuage, make mild or calm. *Pret. a.* chiùinich, *pacified; fut. aff. a.* ciùinichidh, *shall or will pacify.* Ciùinichidh tiodhlacadh, *a gift will pacify.—Stew. Pro.*

Ciùinichte, *p. part.* of ciùinich. Pacified, appeased, calmed.

Ciumhas, ais, *s. m.* A selvage, a border. *N. pl.* ciumhasan.

Ciumhasach, *a.* Having a selvage or border.

Ciùr, *v. a.* (*Corn.* curo, *to beat.*) Hurt, harm, injure, blemish, put to pain, smart. *Pret. a.* chiùr, *hurt; fut. aff. a.* ciuraidh, *shall hurt; fut. pass.* ciurrar, *shall be hurt, shall smart.—Stew. Pro.*

Ciurrach, *a.* Hurtful, injurious, harmless; destructive.

Ciurradh, aidh, *s. m.* An hurt; blemish, injury. Chum mo chiurraidh, *to my harm.—Stew. G. B.* Fhuair e chiurradh, *he got himself hurt.*

Ciurraidh, *a.* Hurtful, destructive. A ghaillion chiurraidh, *the destructive storm.—Macfar.*

Ciurrail, *a.* Hurtful, destructive, injurious. Anamhiann ciurrail, *hurtful lust.—Stew. Tim.*

Ciurramach, *a.* Hurtful; maimed, lamed; lame; maiming; a lame person.—*Stew. Lev.* An t-sleagh chiurramach, *the destructive spear.—Mac Lach. Com.* and *sup.* ciurramaiche.

Ciurta, *p. part.* of ciùr. Hurt, harmed, maimed, blemished; sore; bruised. Is ciurta tha mo chridhe, *bruised is my heart.—Old Song.*

Clab, *s. m.* A wide mouth, a gaping mouth, a thick-lipped mouth; a lip; a garrulous mouth. When pronounced with a peculiar aspiration, it means a gonorrhœa, or any venereal affection.

Clabach, *a.* Thick-lipped; garrulous; open-mouthed, wide-mouthed.

Clabag, aig, *s. f.* A garrulous female; a thick-lipped female; a scoff. *N. pl.* clabagan.

Clabair, *s. m.* A garrulous fellow, a prater: also *gen. sing.* of clabar.

Clabaireachd, *s. f.* Babbling, tattling; the habit or vice of tattling.

Clabar, air, *s. m.* A mill-clapper; clack.

Clàbar, air, *s. m.* Filth, dirt, nastiness, mire; kennel; clay. Clabar creadh, *miry clay.—Smith.* Clabair an t-sraid, *the kennel.—Id.*

Clabarach, *a.* Miry, dirty, filthy, nasty.

Clabarachd, *s. f.* Miriness, dirtiness, filthiness, nastiness.

Clabhair, *s. f.* Mead.—*Shaw.*

† **Clabsal**, ail, *s. m.* The column of a book.

Clach, cloich, *s. f.* A stone; a pebble; a rock; a stone-weight; a monument; a testicle. *N. pl.* clachan; *d. pl.* clachaibh. Clach olainn, *a stone-weight of wood;* clachan an cliù, *the monuments of their fame.—Oss. Fing.* Clach na sùl, *the apple of the eye;* clach-bhalg, *a rattle;* clach-buaidh, *a gem;* clach-bràth, *a rocking-stone;* clach-cheangail, *a key-stone;* clach-chinn, *a top-stone;* clach-chreadh, *a brick;* clach-chriche, *a bound-stone, a landmark;* clach-chuimhneachain, *a monument;* clach-chrotaidh, *a mortar-stone;* clach-fhaobhair, *a hone;* clach-fhuail, *gravel;* clach-ghaireil, *freestone;* clach-ghuail, *sea-coal;* clach-iùil, *load-*

stone; clach-liobhair, *a grinding-stone;* clach-niaraidh, *a grinding-stone;* clach-mhealhain, *hail;* clach-mhìle, *a mill-stone;* clach-mhuilinn, *a mill-stone;* clach-mhullaich, *a top-stone;* clach-neart, *a putting-stone;* clach-oisinn, *a corner-stone.*

Clach, *v. a.* Stone, strike with stones; kill by stoning. *Pret. a.* chlach, *stoned; fut. aff. a.* clachaidh, *shall stone; fut. pass.* clachar, *shall be stoned.*

Clachach, *a.* Stony, rocky, pebbly.

Clachaidh, *fut. aff.* of clach. Shall or will stone.

Clachair, *s. m.* A mason, a stone-builder. *N. pl.* clachairean. A chlach a dhiùlt na clachairean, *the stones which the masons refused.—Smith.*

Clachaireachd, *s.* Masonry, the trade of a mason; stone-building. Ris a chlachaireachd, *at the business of a mason.*

Clachan, *n. pl.* of clach; which see.

Clachan, ain, *s. m.* A burying-ground; a parish village; a church; a Druidical place of worship, composed of a circle of stones raised on end; hence the name. Didòmhnuich dol do 'n chlachan, *on Sunday going to church.—Macfar.* Baile chlachain, *a name commonly given to a parish village, as it contains a church.*

The Druidical circles, or places of worship, so often to be seen throughout Britain, differ considerably in form and in extent; a circumstance which has given rise to the opinion (see Huddlestone's Notes to Toland), that some of a particular form were intended for judicial, and others for religious assemblies. These are to be found from twelve feet to twenty yards in diameter; and there is much diversity in regard to the number, magnitude, and arrangement of the stones. Near the more spacious circles, in which the Druids held their larger meetings or general assemblies, there was another lesser circle or square, where the arch-druid, or president, sat. These circles did not always consist of the same number of obelisks; some consisting of seven, some of twelve, some of nineteen; some, as Stonehenge, of 140, and others, as the splendid temple which existed a few years ago at Avebury, Wilts, of 652;—numbers which probably conveyed some emblematical meaning or reference, which cannot now be ascertained. The circle at Avebury enclosed many acres. The obelisks are commonly erect, and are often of vast dimensions; some have measured from fifteen to twenty feet in height, and ten or twelve in circumference.—See *Keysler. Antiq. Septent.* In the centre there was commonly a stone still larger, which served as an altar; and when a mass of sufficient magnitude could not be found, they substituted an oblong flag, supported by columnar pieces of rock. This altar, the size of which was prodigious, was called *cromleac*, or *clach sleuchd*, the stone of bending, or the worship-stone. The very small circles, of twelve feet in diameter, Borlase supposes to have been burial-grounds. Such of those monuments of ancient times as remain among the Gael, are regarded by them with ignorant veneration, amounting almost to terror. They are often commanded to lay hands on them when considered as a deformity to a landlord's grounds; but threats of ejectment and imperious remonstrance do not always dispose them to obey. A belief that these circles are haunted by supernatural beings strengthens this feeling of veneration; and thus they, for the most part, abide undisturbed on their site of ages.

Clachar, *fut. pass.* of clach. Shall or will be stoned.

Clach-bholg, -bhuilg, *s. m.* A bag with stones in it to scare off birds by rattling; hence it has become an arbitrary term for a rattle of any description.

Clach-brath, *s. f.* A rocking-stone; a judgment-stone; an immense spherical mass of rock, so situated that the least touch can rock it in one certain direction, but which cannot be made to move in any other, by all the force that can be applied to it.

Such stones were once frequent in Britain. There is one in the grounds of Balfracks, in Perthshire; another near Pitcaithlie, in the same county. Mention is made of these stones by the writers of antiquity. Pliny says of a rocking-stone which was near Harpasa, a town in Asia: "Cautes horrenda, uno digito mobilis, eadem si toto corpore impellatur, resistens."—Pliny, lib. ii. c. 69. There are also stones in the far-famed isle of Iona, which are called *clachan-bràth;* they are within the precincts of the burial-ground, and are placed on the pedestals of a cross, and have been, according to Pennant, the supports of a tomb. They derive their name from the belief that the *bràth*, or *world's end*, will not come until the stone on which they stand is worn through.

Clach-buaidh, *s. f.* A pebble, a gem, a precious stone.—*Stew. Zech.* and *Oss. Fing.*

Clach-cheangail, *s. f.* A key-stone.

Clach-chinn, *s. f.* A top-stone; a head-stone; an upright tomb-stone. Clach chinn na h-oisinn, *the head corner-stone.—Smith.*

Clach-chreadh, *s. f.* A brick. Deanamaid clacha creadha, *let us make bricks.—Stew. G. B.*

Clach-chriche, *s. f.* A landmark.

Clach-chrotainn, *s. f.* A mortar-stone; a hollowed cylindrical stone, not unlike an apothecary's mortar, where moistened barley is put and pounded with a mallet till it be completely unhusked; the grain is then washed, and forms a principal ingredient of Highland broth.

Clach-chrùbain, *s. f.* An Hebridian amulet for curing rheumatisms and all pains in the joints. It is a species of gryphites.

Clach-chuimhneachan, ain, *s. f.* A monument.—*Stew. Sam.*

Clach-fhaobhair, *s. f.* A hone, a whetstone.

Clach-fhuail, *s. f.* The gravel. *N. pl.* clachan fuail, *stones ejected with urine.*

Clach-ghaireil, *s. f.* Freestone. *N. pl.* clachan gaireil.

Clach-gheurachaidh, *s. f.* A hone, a whetstone.

Clach-ghuail, *s. f.* Sea-coal.—*Macd.*

Clach-glùin a choilich, *s. f.* The cock-knee-stone, an Hebridian amulet for curing sundry distempers. It is so called from the notion that it is obtained from the knee of a cock; but is, in truth, a common pebble.

Clach-iùil, *s. f.* A loadstone.

Clach-liobhair, *s. f.* A grinding-stone, a smoothing-stone, a polishing-stone.

Clach-mheallain, *s. f.* Hail, hailstone.—*Stew. Exod. N. pl.* clachan meallain.

Clach-mhìle, *s. f.* A mile-stone.

Clach-mhineachadh, aidh, *s. m.* Smoothing or polishing of stones.

Clach-mhineachair, *s. m.* A lapidary, a stone-polisher.

Clach-mhuilinn, *s. f.* A mill-stone.

Clach-mhullaich, *s. f.* A top-stone; abacus.

Clach na cineamhuinn, *s. f.* The fatal stone; the stone of fortune, on which the ancient Caledonian kings were inaugurated in the times of old. It was so called from a belief, that wherever the stone remained, some one of the race would reign. See also Lia fail.

Clach-na-sùl, *s. f.* The apple of the eye.—*Stew. Ezek.*

Clach-neart, *s. f.* A putting-stone; *literally*, a stone of strength.

Clach-oisinn, *s. f.* A corner-stone.

Clachran, ain, *s. m.* A pier; a landing-place; stepping-stones in water, or on watery ground.

Clach-shloc, -shluic, *s. m.* A stone quarry. O na clach-shlocaibh, *from the stone quarries.—Stew. Judg.*

Clach-shneachd, Clach-shneachdaidh, *s. f.* Hail, hailstones. Le cloich shneachd chruaidh, *with hard hail.—Sm.*

Clach-tabhuill, *s. f.* A sling-stone.—*Stew. Zech.*

Clach-theine, *s. f.* Flint. *N. pl.* clachan-teine, *flints.*

Clach-thuislidh, *gen.* cloich-thuislidh, *s. f.* A stumbling-stone, a rock of offence.—*Stew. Rom.*

Clach-tomhais, *s. f.* A weight. Clachan-tomhais ceart, *just weights.—Stew. Lev.*

Cladach, aich, *s. m.* A shore, a beach, a coast; a sandy plain; clay. Cladach gun chaochan, *a streamless beach.—Oss. Gaul.* Ad chladach mìltean èisg, *a thousand fish on thy shores*—*Macdon.* Cha suaicheantas corr air cladach, *a heron on the shore is no wonder.—G. P.* *N. pl* cladaich.

Clàdan, ain, *s. m.* A bur; a flake of snow.—*Shaw* and *Macd.*

Cladh, claidh, *s. m.* A burying-ground, a churchyard; a bank, a mound, a dike, a trench; *rarely*, a wool-comb

Box. Lex. cladd, *ditch.* *Corn* kledh, *a trench.* *W.* clag, *a trench.* *Corn.* claddu, *make a ditch.*

Cladhach, *a.* Digging, delving; poking.

Cladhachadh, aidh, *s m.* A digging, a burying. Air cladhachadh dhuinn leapa an laòich, *on our digging—Oss Trath.*

Cladhachadh, (a), *pr part.* of cladhaich. Digging An tulach uaine ag a cladhachadh, *the green mound is a-digging—Oss. Taura.*

Cladhaich, *v a.* Dig, delve. *Pret. a.* chladhaich, *dug, fut aff. a.* cladhaichidh, *shall dig.*

Cladhair, *s. m* A coward; a rogue. Cha teich ach cladhair, 's cha 'n fhuirich ach seapair, *none will fly but a coward, nor stay but a sneaking fellow.—G P.* *N. pl.* cladhairean, *cowards*

Cladhaireach, *a* Cowardly, roguish

Cladhaireachd, *s f.* Cowardice, cowardliness, roguery.

† **Cladhe**, *s. f* (*Gr.* κλαδων, *a branch*) Genealogy—*Ir id*

Cladh-naire, *s. m.* Modesty, bashfulness—*Macd.*

Clag, cluig, *s m.* (*Corn W.* cloch. *Du* klok) A bell, a mill-clapper; loud talk. Clag-laimh, *a hand-bell.* *N pl.* cluig, *bells.* Cluig nan each, *the bells of the horses*—*Stew. Zech.*

Clag-aite, *s m.* A belfry; a steeple.

Clagan, ain, *s m* (*dim.* of clag) A little bell, a hand-bell. *Ir* clogan

Clagarnach, aich, *s. m.* A loud noise.

Clagharra, *a.* Sluggish, slovenly. Gu clagharra, *sluggishly.*

Claghartas, ais, *s. m* Sluggishness; slovenliness.

Clag-lann, -lainn, *s. m.* A steeple; a belfry.

Clagunn, uinn, *s. m.* A flagon; a lid

Claidheamh, eimh, *s m.* (*W.* glaiv. *Corn* clethe. *Fr* glaive *Arm* cleze *and* glaif) A sword; one of the upright spars of a spinning-wheel *N pl* cloidhean. Nach soillsich tuille do chlaidheamh? *shall thy sword never gleam again?—Oss Gaul.* *Asp form,* chlaidheamh. Claidheamh cùil, *a back-sword*, claidheamh caol, *a small sword*, claidheamh leathann, *a broad-sword*, claidheamh mòr, *a broad-sword*, claidheamh dà làimh, *a two-handed sword*, perhaps the *ingens gladius* of the Caledonians. Cha 'n eil fhios ciod an claidheamh bhios san truaill gus an tairnear e, *it is not known what sword is in the sheath, until it be drawn.—G. P.* Seasamh 'chlaidheimh, *standing on one's head* A reir Rostrenein, Frangach foghluimte, tha mìle ainm aig na h-Arabaich airson claidheamh

Claidheamhail, *a* (slaidheamh-amhuil) Ensiform; like a sword

Claidheamhair, *s f.* A swordsman, a fencer.

Claidheamhaireachd, *s. f.* Swordsmanship, fencing.

Claidheil, *a* (*for* claidheamhail) Ensiform.

Claigeach, ich, *s m* (*from* clag) A steeple—*Shaw.*

† **Claigeag**, eig, *s. f* Deceit—*Shaw.*

Claigeann, inn, *s. m.* (*Ir* cloigionn) A skull. Bhris e 'chlaigeann, *he broke his skull*

Claigeannach, aich, *s m.* The headstall of a halter or bridle Claigeannach srèine, *the headstall of a bridle.*

Claigeannach, *a* Of, or belonging to, the skull

Claigeannachd, *s f* Craniology.

Claigeannaiche, *s. f.* A craniologist.

Clàir, *gen. sing.* and *n. pl.* of clàr; which see.

Clais, *s. f.* (*Arm.* cleug. *W.* clais.) A furrow, a trench, a ditch; a pit; a gutter; a hollow, a groove; a streak; a stripe. *N. pl.* claisean; *d. pl* claisibh. Gach clais na ghnùis, *every furrow in his face.—Oss. Gaul.* Anns na claisibh, *in the gutters.—Stew. Gen.* Rinn e clais, *he made a trench.—Stew. K.* Làn do chlaisibh, *full of ditches.—Stew. 2 K.* Clais bhlàir, *a trench;* sruth-chlais, *a channel*—*Stew. 2 K.*

Clais-bhlàir, *s. f.* A trench—*Stew. Sam.*

Claisdeachd, *s. f.* See **Claisteachd.**

Clais-dhionaidh, *s. f.* A trench.—*Stew. Sam. ref*

Claisdinn, *s f.* See **Claistinn.**

Claiseach, *a.* Furrowed, trenched; full of ditches, pits, or hollows; grooved, fluted; streaked, striped.

† **Claiseach**, ich, *s. m.* A sword.—*Shaw.*

Claisich, *v. a.* Furrow; dig; trench; flute. *Pret. a.* chlaisich; *fut. aff. a.* claisichidh, *shall furrow.*

Claisichte, *p. part.* of claisich. Furrowed; trenched.

Claisteachd, *s. f.* Hearing; the sense of hearing; listening, hearkening. Cha robh claisteachd aige, *he had no hearing*—*Stew 2 K.*

Claistinn, (a), *pr. part* Listening, hearkening. A claistinn farum do cheum, *listening to the sound of the footsteps.—Oss. Manos.*

† **Claithe**, *s f* A jest; ridicule, game, sport; a genealogical table.—*Shaw*

Clambar, air, *s. m.* A wrestle, a struggle, a scramble; a scuffle, a wrestling, a struggling, a scrambling. Ri clambar, *struggling or wrestling.*

Clamh, *s. m.* Mange, itch; itchiness

Clamhainn, *s. m* Sleet. Sneachd is clamhainn air gach tom, *snow and sleet on every hillock.—Old Song* Ris a chlamhuinn, *showering sleet*

Clamhuinneach, *a.* Sleety

Clamhan, ain, *s. m.* A buzzard, a kite. Am fang agus an clamhan, *the vulture and the kite.—Stew. Lev.* Cha d' thainig eun glan riamh a nead a chlamhain, *a clean bird comes not from a kite's nest*—*G. P.* *N. pl.* clamhain.

The *clamhan*, or common buzzard, is the *falco buteo* of Linnæus

Clamhan gobhlach, *s. m.* A kite, a glead; the *falco milvus* of Linnæus. *N. pl.* clamhain gobhlach.

Clamhar, *v a* Scratch by shrugging *Pret. a* chlamhar; *fut. aff.* clambraidh.

Clamharach, *a.* Shrugging; prone to shrug; litigious; wrangling.

Clamhradh, aidh, *s m.* A shrugging; a scratching by shrugging.

Clamhsadh, aidh, *s. m.* A court or close.

Clamras, ais, *s m* (*Eng.* clamorous.) Brawling, chiding, scolding; a brawl, a scold.

Clann, clainne, cloinne, *s f* Children, descendants; a clan, a tribe. A chlann nan sonn, *ye descendants of heroes.—Oss. Lod* Clann diolain, *bastard children.—Stew. Zech.* Clann cloinne, *children's children*—*Stew. Pro.*

Teut clein, *children.* *Germ* klein, *little* In the *Patois* of Besançon, *quelin* is a name for young children.

Clann an oistir, *s.* Ostuarii, or doorkeepers to the monastery of Iona. The first of the family came over from Ireland with Columbus; but, falling under the displeasure of that saint, he invoked a curse on him, by which it was decreed that never more than five of his clan should exist at the same time. Accordingly, when a sixth was born, one of the five was to look for death, which always happened until the race was extinguished. A female, who died about the middle of the last century in Iona, was the last person who could trace a lineage to the doorkeepers of this monastery.

Clannach, *a.* Prolific, fruitful; hanging in locks, bushy, luxuriant. Falt clannach dualach, *luxuriant waving hair.—Old Song.*

Clannar, *a.* Prolific, fruitful; sleek, shining; bushy; hanging in locks or in clusters.

Clannmhor, *a.* Prolific, fruitful, having issue.

Claoidh, *s. f.* (*Ir.* claoidheadh.) Sorrow, pain, affliction; vexation; anguish; defeat; torments. Gu bràth cha n' fhaicear claoidh, *sorrow shall never be seen.—Smith.* Rinn thu claoidh, *thou didst affect.—Id.*

Claoidh, *v. a.* Vex, annoy, afflict, trouble, torment; harass; wound; consume; dazzle; defeat, overthrow; mortify. *Pret. a.* chlaoidh, *vexed; fut. aff. a.* claoidhidh. Claoidhidh mi iadsan a chlaoidheas tu, *I will afflict them who afflict thee.—Stew. Exod.* Mar chlaoidheas teine coillteach, *as fire consumes wood.—Smith.* A claoidh fradhairc, *dazzling the sight.—Old Song.* Claoidhibh bhur buill, *mortify your members.—Stew. Col.*

Claoidheach, *a.* Vexing, annoying, afflictive, troublesome, harassing; defeating, overthrowing.

Claoidheachd, *s. f.* (*from* claoidh.) Distress, vexation, annoyance, mortification; continued or frequent distress, continued vexation or annoyance.

Claoidheadh, idh, *s. m.* An oppressing; an overthrow; a harassing.

Claoidhte, *p. part.* of claoidh. (*Ir. id.*) Afflicted, distressed, tormented, harassed, conquered, defeated. An laoch claoidhte, *the distressed* [*conquered*] *hero.—Oss. Dargo.*

Claon, *v. a.* and *n.* (*Gr.* κλινω. *Lat.* clino.) Incline; turn aside; pervert; meander; move aslant or oblique; decline; squint; make awry. *Pret. a.* chlaon; *fut. aff. a.* claonaidh. Chlaon iad, *they turned aside.—Stew. Exod.*

Claon, *a.* (*Ir. id.*) Partial; inclining; oblique; meandering; winding; squint, squint-eyed; perverse; moving obliquely or aslant. Mar ghrèin tha claon sa ghleann, *like the sun that moves aslant in the valley.—Oss. Tem.* Linne tha claon sa ghleann, *a deep stream meandering in the valley.—Oss. Lod.* Nithe claon, *perverse things.—Stew. Pro.* Sùil chlaon, *a squint eye.*

Claonad, aid, *s. m.* A proclivity.—*Shaw.*

Claonadh, aidh, *s. m.* A bending, an inclining, a moving aslant or obliquely; a turning aside; a bend, an inclination; oblique motion, as of the descending sun; declining, squinting.

Claonadh, (a), *pr. part.* of claon. Bending, turning aside, declining, starting, squinting. Mar sgàile a claonadh sios, *declining as a shadow.—Smith.*

Claonard, aird, *s. m.* An inclining steep.—*Shaw.*

Claon-bhaigh, *s. f.* Partiality.—*Stew. Heb.*

Claon-bhaigheil, *a.* Partial.

Claon-bhord, -bhuird, *s. m.* A sloping table; a desk.

Claon-bhreathamh, *s. m.* An unjust judge.

Claon-bhreith, *s. f.* Partiality; an unfair decision, an unjust judgment.

Claon-chomhnard, aird, *s. m.* An inclined plane.

Clàr, clàir, *s. m.* (*Ir. id.*) A table or plate; a board, a plank; a trough; the stave of a cask; a lid; a harp. *N. pl.* clàir *and* clàran; *d. pl.* claraibh. Clàir cloich, *tables of stone.—Stew. Exod.* Le clàraibh giuthais, *with planks of fir.—Stew.* 1 *K.* Clàir umha, *plates of brass.—Id.* Clàr beoil, *a lid.—Stew.* 2 *K.* Mar chlàr taibhse, *like the harp of a ghost.—Oss.* Clàr aodainn, *the brow.*

Clàrach, *a.* (*from* clàr.) Full of tables or plats; like a board or plank; in staves; also bare, bald.

Clarag, aig, *s. f.* A fore-tooth; also wattled work, as on a sledge. *N. pl.* clàragan, *fore-teeth.*

Claraidh, *s. f.* A partition; also, *adjectively,* dividing; of deal or plank; floating. Urlar chlaraidh, *a deal floor;* leabaidh chlàraidh, *a deal bed, a bed having a bottom of deal.*

Claraineach, *a.* Flat-nosed. Perhaps *clàr-shroineach.*

Clar-ainmich, *s. m.* A title-page; an index.

Clàran, *n. pl.* of clàr; which see.

Clàran, ain, *s. m.* (*dim.* of clàr.) A little table; a little plate; a little stave; a little trough; a little deal or plank. *N. pl.* clarain.

Clàr aodainn, *s. m.* A front; a visage or forehead.

Clàr-aodainneach, *a.* Broad-browed; broad-visaged.

Clàr beòil, *s. m.* A lid.

Clàr buideil, *s. m.* A bottle rack. Cho tiorram ri clàr buideil, *as dry as a bottle rack.—Macdon.*

Clàr-chos, -chois, *s. f.* A splay foot. *N. pl.* clàr-chosan.

Clàr-chosach, *a.* Splay-footed, crump-footed.

Clàr-fhiacal, ail, *s. m.* A fore-tooth.

Clàr-fuinidh, *s. m.* A kneading trough.

Clàr-innsidh, *s. m.* An index; a title-page.

Clàrsach, aich, *s. m.* A harp. Cho caoin ri clàrsach, *as melodious as the harp.—Oss. Fing.* *N. pl.* clàrsaichean. See Cruit.

Clàrsaich, *gen. sing.* of clarsach.

Clàrsair, *s. m.* A harper, a minstrel. *N. pl.* clarsairean.

Clàrsaireachd, *s. f.* Harping, playing on the harp; the employment or occupation of a harper.

Clàr-sgithe, *s. m.* A name for the Isle of Skye.—*Macmhuirich.*

† **Clas**, clais, *s. m.* A play, craft; a furrow, a pit; melody, harmony.—*Shaw.*

† **Clasach**, *a.* Crafty, playful; melodious.

† **Clasachd**, *s.* Craftiness, subtlety.

Clasb, clasba, *s. m.* (*Ir. id.*) A clasp. *N. pl.* clasban.

Clasb, *v. a.* Clasp, button, tie. *Pret.* chlasb, *clasped; fut. aff.* clasbaidh, *shall clasp.*

† **Cle**, *a.* Partial, prejudiced; left-handed.

Cleachd, *v. a.* and *n.* (*Ir. id.*) Accustom, habituate, inure; acquaint; plait. *Pret. a.* chleachd, *accustomed; fut. aff. a.* cleachdaidh, *shall accustom.* Chleachd mi mòran deth fhaotainn, *I was accustomed to receive much of it.—Macfar.* Cleachd thu fein ris, *inure yourself to it.*

Cleachd, *s. m.* (*Ir. id.*) Custom, practice, usage; exercise; a ringlet; a plait. B'e so do chleachd fèin, *this was thine own practice.—Oss. Fing.* Cha bu chleachd dhuit bhi mall, *it was not thy custom to be slow.—Id.* *N. pl.* cleachda *and* cleachdan, *usages.* Cleachda na Morbheinn, *the usages of Morven.—Oss. Manos.* Helen nan or-chleachda, *Helen with the golden locks.—Mac Lach.* Cleachd a ni teòmadh, *practice makes perfect.—G. P.*

Cleachdach, *a.* Full of ringlets or tresses; waving, flowing, as hair; plaited; customary; habitual; accustomed. Fhalt cleachdach, *his waving hair.—Oss. Trath.*

Cleachdadh, aidh, *s. m.* An accustoming, an inuring; habit, custom, usage.

Cleachdag, aig, *s. f.* (*dim.* of cleachd.) A ringlet or tress. *N. pl.* cleachdagan.

Cleachdagach, *a.* (*from* cleachdag.) Full of ringlets; curled. D' òr-chul chleachdagach, *thy curled golden locks.—Moladh Mhòraig.*

Cleachdainn, *s. f.* Custom, habit, practice; use and wont; also, *adjectively,* accustomed, customary. Written also *cleachduinn.*

Cleachdan, *n. pl.* of cleachd. Customs, practices, usages; tresses, ringlets; flowing or waving locks; plaits. Do chleachdan, *thy golden locks.—Oss. Trath.*

Cleachdna. See **Cleachdan.**

Cleachdta, Cleachdte, *p. part.* of cleachd. Accustomed, habituated, inured; trained; expert; plaited. Cleachta ri olc, *accustomed to evil.—Stew. O. T.* Cleachta an cogadh, *expert in war.—Stew. Song Sol.*

Cleachduin, *s. f.* Custom, habit, practice; use and wont: also, *adjectively*, accustoming, customary.

Cleamhnas, ais, *s. m.* Affinity; copulation. Dean cleamhnas, *become connected by marriage;* cleamhnas am fogus, is goisdeachd am fad, *marriage near, and gossiping afar.—G. P.*

† **Clearadh**, aidh, *s. m.* (*Ir. id.*) Familiarity.—*Shaw.*

Clearc, *a.* Bright, radiant; of a bright yellow; shining. A ciabha clearc sileadh dheur, *her radiant locks dreeping.—Ull.*

Cleas, *s. m.* (*Ir. id.*) A play, a trick; a feat; a gambol; deeds, movements; a feat in legerdemain; a warlike exercise. *N. pl.* cleasan. Cuchullin nan cleas, *Cuchullin of warlike deeds.—Fingalian Poem.*

Cleasach, *a.* (*from* cleas.) *Ir. id.* Playful; sportive; crafty; full of schemes or tricks; juggling. *Com.* and *sup.* cleasaiche, *more or most playful.*

Cleasachd, *s. f.* Playing, diverting; play, pastime, gamboling; legerdemain, slight of hand; strife. Dh' eirich iad gu cleasachd, *they rose to play.—Stew. Exod. ref.* Cleasachd nan saoi, *the strife of heroes.—Oss. Fing.* Cleasachd dhaoine, *the sleight of men.—Stew. Eph.*

Cleasadh, aidh, *s. m.* A bounding, leaping, sporting, gamboling. Miolchoin a cleasadh ard, *greyhounds bounding high.—Oss. Fing.*

Cleasaich, *v. n.* Perform feats; gambol; vault, tumble as a rope-dancer. *Pret. a.* chleasaich; *fut. aff.* cleasaichidh.

Cleasaiche, *s. m.* (*Ir.* cleasaidhe.) A juggler, a conjuror; a buffoon; a cunning fellow.

Cleasanta, *a.* (*from* cleas.) Frolicsome, playful, frisky, brisk, active, agile. Gu cleasanta, *playfully.*

Cleasantachd, *s. f.* Frolicsomeness, playfulness, friskiness, activity.

Cleath, *s. m.* (*Ir. id.*) Wattled work; the body of any thing; an oar, a stake; a goad; a rib. Cleathan righinn, *tough oars.—Macfar.*

† **Cleathaireachd**, *s. f.* Rusticity; boldness.

† **Cleathramh**, aimh, *s. m.* Partiality, prejudice.—*Shaw.*

Cleibh, *gen. sing.* of cliabh.

Cléir, *s. f.* Clergy. (*W.* clêr. *Arm.* cloer. *Span.* clero. *Gr.* κληρος, *destiny.*)

An ingenious antiquary observes, that the learned men of the Druidical order, who, under the primitive bardic system, were employed in going periodical circuits to instruct the people, answered the purpose of a priesthood; but in later times the name implied a society of wanderers, or those bards who strolled about like English harpers. These wandering classes originated when the priesthood was a distinct branch from the bardic system; for the latter then ceased to have sufficient means to support its own members. As a compensation, a law was made, that such as were of this description should have regular periodical circuits, and receive fees according to the quality of those they visited. This ended at last in mendicancy.

Cléireach, ich, *s. m.* (*Ir. id. Corn.* kloirec. *Lat.* clericus.) A clerk; a writer; a precentor; a clergyman. *N. pl.* cléirich. Cha n'eil cléireach na pearsa eaglais, *there is neither clerk nor churchman.—R.*

Cléireachd, *s. f.* The condition of a churchman; clerkship; a body of churchmen.

Cléireanach, aich, *s. m.* A sword; *provincial.*

Cléirsinneachd, *s. f.* Clerkship; writing. Ris a chléirsinneachd, *clerking.*

Cléit, *s. f.* (*Ir.* cleite.) A quill; a feather; a flake, as of snow; down; a penthouse; the eaves of a roof. Cléit sgriobhaidh, *a pen.—Stew. Jer.*

Cléiteach, *a.* Feathery, flaky; rocky.

Cléiteadh, idh, *s. m.* A ridge of rocks in the sea.

Cléiteag, *s. f.* (*dim.* of cléit.) A flake of snow; down; a little quill; a little feather. *N. pl.* cléiteagan, *flakes.* Cho pailt ri cléiteagan sneachd, *as plentiful as flakes of snow.—Mac Lach.*

Cléiteagach, *a.* Flaky, feathery, downy. Sneachd cléiteagach, *flaky snow.—Macfar.*

Cleith, *gen. sing.* of cliath.

Cleith, *v. a.* Conceal, hide, keep secret. *Pret. a.* chleith; *fut. aff. a.* cleithidh.

Cleith, *s. f.* A stake, a goad, a post; a residence; concealment, secrecy. Cha n' eil cleith air an olc ach gun a dheanamh, *the best way to conceal evil is not to commit it.—G. P.* An cleith, *in concealment, secret.—Stew. Mat.*

Cleitheach, *a.* Concealing, skulking, clandestine, private; feathery.—*Shaw.* Gu cleitheach, *clandestinely.*

Cleitheachd, *s. f.* Lurking, skulking, concealment, secrecy.

Cleòc, *s. m.* A cloak, a mantle. Cleòc nam meanbh bhall ruadh, *a cloak with small red spots.—Macfar.*

Cleòc, *v. a.* Cloak, cover with a cloak or mantle. *Pret. a.* chleòc, *cloaked; fut. aff. a.* cleòcaidh, *shall cloak.*

Cleòcan, ain, *s. m.* (*dim.* of cleòc.) A little cloak; a scarf; a mantle.

Clì, Clìth, *s. m.* Pith, vigour, strength, force; the power of motion; *rarely*, the body, the ribs. Gun chlì ad chois, *without pith in thy foot.—Ull.* Chunnaic e ghaoth gun chlìth, *he saw the wind was without force.—Oss.* Daoine gun chlì, *vigourless men.—Oss. Fing.*

Clì, Clìth, *a.* (*Ir. id. Arm.* cley.) Left-handed; left; awkward, slow; feeble; humble; also strong. Dh' ionnsuidh na laimh clìthe, *to the left hand.—Stew.* 1 *K.* Air a thaobh clì, *on his left side.—Stew. Zech.* Clì sa chomhrag, *feeble in battle.—Oss. Fing.* Labhair clìth, *speak humbly.—Oss. Tem.* An taobh chlì, *the left side; Arm.* an tu cley. An troidh chlì, *the left foot; Arm.* an troad cley.

Cliabh, cleibh, *s. f.* (*Ir. id.*) The chest; the breast; a basket; an osier basket; a hamper. A taomadh mu chliabh, *pouring about his breast.—Oss. Tem.* Acain a chleibh, *the sigh of his breast.—Oss. Fin. and Lor.* Cliabh gùin, *the boddice of a gown.*

Cliabhach, *a.* Chested; having a large chest; of, or belonging to, the chest; like a basket.

† **Cliabhach**, aich, *s. m.* A wolf.—*Shaw.*

Cliabhan, ain, *s. m.* (*dim.* of cliabh.) A small basket; a cage.—*Ir. id.*

Cliabhrach, aich, *s. m.* The side or trunk of the body.—*Shaw.*

Cliadan, ain, *s. m.* A bur. *N. pl.* cliadain.

Cliadanach, *a.* Abounding in burs; of burs; like a bur.

Cliamhnas, ais, *s. m.* See **Cleamhnas.**

Cliamhuinn, *s. m.* (*Ir. id.*) A son-in-law. Do chleimhuinn, *your son-in-law.—Stew. Gen.*

Cliamhuinn is perhaps *cliabh-dhuine*, a man that is dear to one as his heart.

Cliar, cliair, *s. m.* (*Gr.* † κλειρος. *Lat.* clarus.) A poet; a brave man; also, *adjectively*, brave, renowned. Fuil nan cliar, *the blood of the brave.—Oss. Manos.* Cliar-shean-chain, *the songsters of the ancient tax;*—a name given to those bards who, according to Keating, were entitled by law to live half a year, from All-Hallow till May, at the expense of the people.

Cliarach, *a.* Like a poet; like a brave man; brave.

Cliarachd, *s. f.* Bardism; versification; heroism; fighting. Ri cliarachd ré fad an la, *fighting all day.—Death of Carril.*

Cliaraiche, *s. m.* A songster, a bard, a minstrel. *Ir.* cliaraich.

Cliaranach, aich, *s. m.* A bard, a songster, a harper; a sword.

Cliath, cleith, *s. f.* (*Ir. id.*) A harrow; a hurdle; a grate; a lattice, a casement; a breast; a chest; a running or darning of stockings. *N. pl.* cleith *and* cliathan; *d. pl.* cliathaibh. Le cliathaibh, *with harrows.—Stew. Chron.* Cliatha chliata, *a harrow.—Shaw.* Troimh mo chleith, *through my casement.—Stew. Pro.* Cuid an t-searraich do 'n chliath, *the foal's share of the harrow;* meaning *idleness*, as the foal only follows its mother while at work.

Cliath, *v. a.* Harrow; copulate as fowls; run a stocking. *Pret. a.* chliath, *harrowed; fut. aff. a.* cliathaidh, *shall harrow.*

Cliathach, aich, *s.* The side of the human body; the flank of a quadruped; the slope of a hill, the ridge of a hill; a conflict. Minnean bu luime cliathach, *a bare-flanked fawn.—Macint.* Cliathach a mhonaidh, *the ridge of the hill.*

Cliathadh, aidh, *s. m.* A harrowing; treading, as the males of poultry.

Cliathadh, (a), *pr. part.* of cliath. Harrowing; treading, as poultry.

Cliathag, aig, *s. f.* The chine; a hurdle.—*Shaw.*

Cliathaich. See **Cliathach**.

Cliathaidh, *fut. aff. a.* of cliath. Shall or will harrow.

Cliathan, ain, *s. m.* The breast.

Cliath-iarruinn, *s. m.* A trivet.—*Shaw.*

Cliath-laimh, *s. m.* A hand-harrow.

Cliathrach, *a.* Breast-high.—*Shaw.*

Cliath-sheanchaidh, *s. m.* A genealogical table.

Cliath-sheanchais, *s. m.* A genealogical table.—*Macint.*

Cliath-uinneig, *s. m.* A lattice. Troimh chliath-uinneig, *through a lattice.—Stew.* 2 *K.*

Cliathrach, *a.* Breast-high.—*Shaw.*

Clibeach, *a.* Rough, hairy. *Ir.* cliobach.

Clibeadh, eidh, *s. m.* The act of stumbling or slipping; a stumble, a slip; a tearing in pieces.

Clibeag, eig, *s. f.* A filly. *N. pl.* clibeagan.

Clibean, ein, *s. m.* A dewlap; any flabby thing.

† **Clibhiseachd**, *s. f.* Peevishness.—*Shaw.*

Clic, *v. a.* Hook, catch with a hook. *Pret.* chlic, *hooked; fut. aff.* clicidh, *shall hook.*

Clic, *s. f.* A hook, a crook.

Cli-lamhach, *a.* Left-handed, awkward. Duine cli-lamhach, *a left-handed man.—Stew. Jud. ref.*

Cliogarach, *a.* Croaking.

Cliotach, *a.* Left-handed.

Clip, *v. a.* Hook, catch with a hook. *Pret. a.* chlip, *hooked; fut. aff.* clipidh, *shall hook.*

† **Clip**, clipe, *s. f.* A hook to catch fish; fraud, deceit, cunning.—*Shaw.*

† **Clipeach**, *a.* Deceitful, cunning; hooked.

Clipse, *s. f.* An eclipse. *Scotch*, clipps.

Clis, *a.* Active, agile, keenly, nimble, speedy. Gu clis na chéile shàs iad, *they seized each other keenly.—Oss. Cathluno.* Bradan grad-chlis, *a nimble young salmon.—Macfar.* Na fir chlis, *the phenomenon observed in the northern skies on winter evenings, vulgarly called the merry-dancers.*

Clisbeach, *a.* Cripple, lame.

Clisbeachd, *s. f.* Lameness.

Clisg, *v. a.* and *n.* Start, startle. *Pret.* chlisg, *started; fut. aff. a.* clisgidh, *shall start.* Chlisg na sleibhte, *the hills started.—Oss. Duthona.*

Clisg, *s. f.* A start; a brisk movement.

Clisgeach, *a.* Apt to start; skittish; causing to start; skipping; starting.

Clisgeadh, idh, *s. m.* The act of starting; a skipping.

Clisgeadh, (a), *pr. part.* of clisg. Starting. An earbag a clisgeadh, *the young roe starting.—Oss. Gaul.*

Clisneach, ich, *s. m.* The human body; a carcass; the outward appearance.

Clist, *a.* Active, nimble, swift, dexterous. Gu clist, *nimbly.*

Clisteachd, *s. f.* Activity, nimbleness, swiftness, dexterity.

Clith, *a.* See **Cli**.

Cliù, *s. m.* (*Ir.* clu. *Gr.* κλεος.) Fame, renown; character, reputation. *Asp. form*, chliù. Cha n'eireadh mo chliù na bhàs, *my fame would not rise by his death.—Oss. Dargo.*

Cliùar, *a.* See **Cliùmhor**.

Cliudan, ain, *s. m.* A slap on the face, a slight stroke with the fingers; a fillip.

Cliudanachd, *s. f.* A continued or frequent slapping on the face; a fillipping.

Cliùmhor, *a.* Renowned, famous, noted. *Com.* and *sup.* cliùmhoire.

Cliùiteach, *a.* (*from* cliù.) (*Gr.* † κλυτος. *Lat.* † clutos, inclytus.) Famous, renowned, noted, celebrated. Fionnghal cliùiteach, *renowned Fingal.—Oss. Temo.* *Com.* and *sup.* cliùitiche. Is cliùitiche an onoir nan t-òr, *honesty is better than gold.—G. P.*

Cliùthachadh, aidh, *s. m.* The act of praising; an extolling.

Cliùthaich, *v. a.* Praise; make famous; extol. *Pret. a.* chliùthaich, *praised; fut. aff. a.* cliùthaichidh, *shall praise.* Chliùthaich mi, *I praised.—Stew. Dan.*

Clò, *s. m.* Slumber; rest; a nail, a pin, a peg. Clò do 'n t-sùil, *slumber to the eye.—Sm.* Bròn gun chlò, *sorrow without rest.—Id.* Clò codail, *slumber.—Stew. Ps.*

Cló, *s. m.* Raw cloth, coarse home-made cloth.

Clobh, clobha, *s.* A pair of tongs. *N. pl.* clobhachan. A chlobhachan, *its tongs.—Stew. Exod.*

Clobhsa, ai, *s. m.* A little court or area; a close; an entry; a passage. *Scotch*, close. *Belg.* kluyse.

Cloch, cloich, *s. f.* (*Ir. id.*) A stone; a pebble; a rock; a stone-weight; a testicle; a monument; *rarely*, henbane. *N. pl.* clochan; *more frequently*, clachan. Clochan bruite, *bruised* [*testicles*] *stones.—Stew. Lev.* Cloch-bholg, *a rattle;* cloch-bhrath, *a rocking-stone;* cloch-buaidh, *a gem;* cloch-chinn, *a tomb-stone, an upright tomb-stone;* cloch-chreadh, *a brick;* cloch-chriche, *a landmark;* cloch-chrotaidh, *a mortar-stone;* cloch-dhealbh, *an image-stone;* cloch-fhaobhair, *a hone;* cloch-fhuail, *the gravel;* cloch-ghaireil, *freestone;* cloch-gheurachaidh, *a whetstone;* cloch-iùil, *a loadstone;* cloch-liobhair, *a smoothing-stone;* cloch-mheallain, *a hailstone;* cloch-mhile, *a mile-stone;* cloch-mhineachair, *a lapidary;* cloch-mhullaich, *a top-stone;* cloch na cineamhuinn, *the fatal stone;* cloch na sùl, *the apple of the eye;* cloch-oisinn, *a corner-stone;* cloch-shnaigheadair, *an engraver;* cloch-shneachd, *hailstone;* cloch-shreathal, *freestone;* cloch-theine, *a flint or freestone.*

Clochach, *a.* (*from* cloch.) *Ir. id.* Stony, pebbly, flinty, rocky. Air aitibh clochach, *on stony ground.—Stew. N. T.*

Clochair, *s. m.* A mason. See **Clachair**.

Clochaireachd, *s. f.* See **Clachaireachd**.

Clochan, ain, *s. m.* A pavement, a causeway; stepping-stones in water.

Clochar, air, *s. m.* (*Scotch*, clochar.) A wheezing in the throat; an assembly; a convent.

Clochara, *a.* Set with stones; wheezing in the throat. A cheann-bheart clochara neamhain, *his head-piece set with stones and pearls.—Fingalian Poem.*

Cloch-bholg, -bhuilg, *s. f.* See Clach-bholg.

Cloch-bhrath, *s. f.* See Clach-bhrath.

Cloch-buaidh, *s. f.* A gem, a precious stone.

Cloch-chinn, *s. f.* A tomb-stone; an upright tomb-stone.

Clo-chodal, ail, *s. m.* Slumber, dozing, lethargy. Clo-chodal do d'rosgaibh, *slumber to thine eyelids.—Stew. Pro.* Clo-chodal na h-aois, *the lethargy of age.—Oss. Taura.*

Cloch-chreadh, *s. f.* A brick. *N. pl.* clochan-creadha.

Cloch-chriche, *s. f.* A bound-stone; a land-mark. *N. pl.* clachan-criche.

Cloch-chrotainn, *s. f.* A mortar-stone. See Clach-chrotainn.

Cloch-dhealbh, *s. f.* An image of stone. Cloch-dhealbh na 'r fearann, *an image of stone in your land.—Stew. Lev.*

Clach-fhaobhair, *s. f.* A hone, a whetstone.

Cloch-fhuail, *s. f.* The gravel. *N. pl.* clochan-fuail, *stones ejected with urine.*

Cloch-ghaireil, *s. f.* Freestone.

Cloch-gheurachaidh, *s. f.* A hone, a whetstone; a grinding-stone. *N. pl.* clochan-geurachaidh.

Cloch-iùil, *s. f.* A loadstone, a magnet.

Clochlain, *s. f.* The bird called a stone-chatter. More commonly, *cloichrean;* which see.

Clo-chlàr, -chlàir, *s. m.* A copperplate.

Cloch-liobhair, *s. f.* A grinding-stone; a smoothing-stone.

Cloch-mheallain, *s. f.* A hailstone. *N. pl.* clochan-meallain, *hailstones.* Cloch-mheallain a breabadh, *hailstones bounding.—Oss. Fing.*

Cloch-mhìle, *s. f.* A mile-stone. *N. pl.* clochan-mìle, *mile-stones.*

Cloch-mhineachair, *s. m.* A stone-polisher; a lapidary.

Cloch-mhuilinn, *s. f.* A mill-stone. Mir do cloich mhuilinn, *a piece of mill-stone.—Stew. Judg.*

Cloch-mhullaich, *s. f.* A top-stone; abacus.

Cloch-neart, -neirt, *s. f.* A putting-stone. A tilg na cloich-neirt, *throwing the putting-stone.*

Cloch na cineamhuinn, *s. f.* The stone of fate. See Clach na cineamhuinn.

Cloch na sùl, *s. f.* The apple of the eye.

Cloch-oisinne, *s. f.* A corner-stone.

Clochran, ain, *s. m.* A landing-place; stepping-stones in water or in watery ground. *N. pl.* clochrain.

Cloch-shnaigheadair, *s. m.* An engraver.

Cloch-shreathal, *s. f.* Freestone.—*Shaw.*

Cloch-theine, *s. f.* A flint. *N. pl.* clochan-teine.

Clod, cloid, *s.* (*Du.* klot *and* kluit.) A clod, a turf, a sod; *in derision,* a sluggish person. A sguabadh chlod 's a chlach, *sweeping clods and stones.—Oss. Dargo.*

Clod, *v. a.* Clod; strike with clods; cover with clods or turf. *Pret. a.* chlod, *clodded; fut. aff. a.* clodaidh, *shall clod.*

Clodach, aich, *s.* See Cladach.

Clodach, *a.* Abounding in clods or turf; like a clod or turf. *Ir.* clodach, *dirt.*

Clodaireachd, *s. f.* Clodding; a throwing of clods; a striking with clods.

Clodan, *n. pl.* of clod. Clods, turfs, sods.

Clodan, ain, *s. m.* (*dim.* of clod.) A little clod.

Clòdh, clodha, *s. m.* Coarse home-made cloth.

Clodh, cluidh, *s. m.* A printing-press; a print; an impression; variety.

Clodhachadh, aidh, *s. m.* Drawing close together.

Clodhaich, *v. a.* Draw close together; approach. *Pret.* chlodhaich.

Clodhair, *s. m.* A printer. *N. pl.* clodhairean.

Clodhaireachd, *s. f.* The business of a printer; the process of printing; typography.

Clodh-bhuail, *v. a.* Print; exercise the art of typography. *Pret. a.* chlodh-bhuail, *printed; fut. aff. a.* clodh-bhuailidh, *shall print.*

Clodh-bhuailte, *p. part.* of clodh-bhuail. Printed.

Clodh-bhualadair, *s. m.* A printer.

Clodh-bhualadh, aidh, *s. m.* The act of printing; typography.

Clodh-fhear, fhir, *s. m.* A printer; a compositor. Contracted *clodhair.*

Clodh-ghalar, air, *s. m.* A vertigo.—*Shaw.*

Clog, cluig, *s. m.* A bell, a clock. Beum cluig, *a knell.* (*Ir.* clog. *Du.* klok. *Corn. W.* clock. *Germ.* klocke. *Arm.* cloch.)

Clogaid, *s. f.* A helmet or headpiece; a cone, a pyramid. *N. pl.* clogaidean. Clogaid is ceannbheart, *helmet and headpiece.—Oss. Dargo.*

Clogaideach, *a.* Like a helmet or headpiece; of, or belonging to, a helmet or headpiece; armed with a helmet.

Clogan, ain, *s. m.* (*dim.* of clog.) A little bell.

Clogarnach, *a.* Tinkling.

Clog-mheur, *s. m.* The hour-hand of a dial-plate or clock.

Clog-shnathad, aid, *s. f.* The gnomon of a dial, the hand of a clock.

Cloich, *gen. sing.* of cloch.

Cloichreach, ich, *s. m.* A stony place.—*Shaw.*

Cloichrean, ein, *s. m.* The bird called a stone-chatter; the *rubicula* of Linnæus.

Some say that the toad covers the egg of this bird during its absence from the nest, and others, that the egg is hatched by the toad. These assertions are monstrous and absurd. The stone-chatter nestles on the ground; its nest is, on that account, in the way of frogs, toads, and other creeping reptiles, which, in the absence of the bird, find an easy access thereto. If toads, therefore, be occasionally observed in possession of the nest, it is accidental, and not from any design or purpose of nature.

Cloidheag, eig, *s. f.* A shrimp, a prawn.—*Macd.* and *Shaw.*

Cloidhean, ein, *s. m.* The pith of the box-tree; the pith of any shrub-tree.

Cloidhean, *n. pl.* of claidheamh. Swords, small swords, scimetars; knives. *D. pl.* cloidhibh.

Cloidhibh, *d. pl.* of claidheamh. Le cloidhibh, *with knives.—Stew.* 1 *K.*

Cloimh, *s. f.* The itch; a distemper now chiefly confined to dogs and English sheep. Carr no cloimh, *scurvy hor itch.—Stew. Lev.*

Clòimh, *s. m.* (*Ir.* clumh.) Down, feathers, plumage. Leabadh chlòimh, *a feather-bed; a down-bed.* A gheuban maille ri chloimh, *its crop along with its feathers.—Stew. Lev.* Air a thughadh le clòimh, *thatched with down.—Old Poem.*

Cloimheach, *a.* (*from* cloimh.) Downy, feathery. *Ir.* clumhach.

Cloimhneag, eig, *s. f.* A small feather, a flake of snow. *N. pl.* cloimhneagan.

Cloimhneagach, *a.* Feathery, downy, flaky.

Cloinne, *gen. sing.* of clann; which see.

Clomhach, *a.* Scabbed, affected with itch, mangy.

Clo-mheas, *s. m.* Cloves.—*Macd.*

Clomhsadh, aidh, *s. m.* A court; a yard; a back-court; a close; an entrance; a narrow passage. The *mh* and *dh* of this word are silent.

W. claws. *Germ.* klause, *a shut-up place.* *Lat.* clausus. *Eng.* close.

CLOS, *s. m.* Rest, repose, quietness, peace; quiet, silence; report; hearing. Gu talamh nan neul 's gu clos, *to the land of clouds and to rest.—Orr.* Clos na min lear uaine, *the repose of the calm green sea.—Oss.* A plosgail gun chlos, *panting incessantly.—Oss. Gaul.* Gabh gu clos, *be silent; be at rest.*

CLOS, *v. n.* Rest, repose; grow calm or quiet. *Pret. a.* chlos, *reposed; fut. sub.* chlosas. Nur chlosas caoin-shith air an raoin, *when gentle peace reposes on the plain.—Oss. Tem.*

CLOS, *s. m.* A close. *W.* claws. *Germ.* klause, *a shut-up place. Lat.* clausus. See also CLOMHSADH.

CLOSACH, aich, *s. f.* A carcass; a dead body, a corpse. Closach fiadh bheathach, *of a wild beast.—Stew. Lev.*

CLÒSAID, *s. f.* A closet, a study. *N. pl.* clòsaidean.

CLO-SUAINE, *s. f.* A slumber. Ag aomadh gu clo-suaine, *drooping in slumber.—Oss. Derm.*

† CLOTH, *a.* Noble, generous.—*Shaw.*

† CLOTHACH, *a.* Famous, illustrious.

CLOTHADH, aidh, *s. m.* (*from* clò, *rest.*) The act of mitigating; a calming.

CLUAIN, *s. f.* (*Ir. id.*) A pasture, a meadow, a green field, a lawn; a bower; a burying-ground; intrigue; deceit, dissimulation, ambush, flattery. Cluain nan speur, *the green fields of the sky.—Oss. Duthona.* Air cluainibh an fhasaich, *on the pastures of the desert.—Sm.* Le 'n cluain, *with their dissimulation.—Stew. Gal. N. pl.* cluaintean.

CLUAINEACH, *a.* Meadowy, abounding in meadows.—*Macint.* Deceitful, dissembling, flattering.

CLUAINEAN, ein, *s. m.* (*dim.* of cluain.) A little pasture, a little meadow, a little lawn; pasture-ground. Fo chluainein an fheidh, *beneath the deer's pasture-ground.—Ull.*

CLUAINEAR, ir, *s. m.* (*Ir.* cluainire.) A cunning fellow; a hypocrite, a flatterer, a seducer. *N. pl.* cluainearan.

CLUAINEAS, eis, *s. f.* Gamboling, frisking. Ri cluaineas mhear, *frisking merrily.—Macfar.*

CLUAINIDH, *s. f.* (*from* cluain.) A parish in Perthshire, called Cluny.

CLUAINTEAN, *n. pl.* of cluain; which see.

CLUAINTEARACHD, *s. f.* Deceit, flattery, deception; the practice of deceit.

CLUAIS, *gen. sing.* of cluas.

CLUAISEAN, ein, *s. m.* (*Ir. id.*) A blow on the ear; a pillow; a porringer; an ansated dish. Pinne cluaisein, *the tram-pin of a cart.*

CLUANAG, aig, *s. f.* A little meadow, a lawn.—*Macint.* Rarely, joy.

CLUANAGACH, *a.* Abounding in little meadows.

CLUANAISEACH, *a.* Sauntering, lounging alone.

CLUARAN, ain, *s. m.* A thistle; a sort of daisy; a sponge. *N. pl.* cluarain. A lubadh cluarain, *bending the thistle.—Oss. Lodin.* Droighionn agus cluarain, *thorns and thistles. Stew. Gen.*

CLUARANACH, aich, *s. m.* A thistle.—*Shaw.*

CLUARANACH, *a.* Abounding in thistles, thistly; also a thistle; a crop of thistles.

CLUAS, cluais, *s. f.* (*Ir. id. Manx.* cluss.) The ear; the handle of a dish. Tha chluas 'g cromadh, *his ear inclines.—Sm.* Cluas ri caisdeachd, *a character in Highland romance; one who is apt to listen.* Chailleadh tu do chluasan mar biodh iad ceangailte riut, *you would lose both your ears if they were not fixed to you.—Old saying.*

CLUASACH, *a.* (*from* cluas.) *Ir. id.* Having ears or handles; ansated; having large ears. Meadar cluasach, *an ansated wooden dish.* An sobhrach cluasach, *the round-leaved primrose.—Macdon.*

CLUASAG, aig, *s. f.* A pillow; a pincushion. Cluasag do fhionnadh ghabhar, *a pillow of goat's-hair.—Stew. Sam. N. pl.* cluasagan.

CLUASAGACH, *a.* Pillowed; like a pillow; of, or relating to, a pillow.

CLUASAG-GHLÙIN, *s. f.* A hassock, a cushion.

CLUAS AN FHEIDH, *s. f.* Melancholy thistle.

CLUAS-BHIORACH, *a.* Sharp-eared; having pointed ears.

CLUAS-CHROCHAG, aig, *s. f.* An ear-ring; an ear-pendant. *N. pl.* cluas-chrochagan.

CLUAS-FHÀIL, *s. f.* An ear-ring. *N. pl.* cluas-fhàilean. Na cluas-fhàilean, *the ear-rings.—Stew. Exod.*

CLUAS-FHAINNE, *s. f.* An ear-ring. Cluas-fhainne òir, *a gold ear-ring.—Stew. Gen.*

CLUAS-LIATH, *s. f.* The herb called *coltsfoot.*

CLUAS RI CAISDEACHD, *s. m.* One who is curious to overhear conversation; a character in Gaelic mythology.

CLÙBADH, aidh, *s. m.* A winding bay.

CLÙD, clùid, *s. m.* (*W.* clwt. *Corn.* klut.) A clout, a rag, a patch. *N. pl.* clùdan. Clùd soithichean, *a dish-cloth.*

CLÙD, *v. a.* Patch, clout; cover up warm; cherish. *Pret. a.* chlud, *clouted; fut. aff. a.* cludaidh, *shall clout.*

CLÙDACH, *a.* Patched, clouted, ragged.

CLUDADH, aidh, *s. m.* The act of clouting, botching, or patching; cobbling.

CLÙDAIR, *s. m.* (*from* clùd.) A patcher, a botcher, a cobbler. *N. pl.* clùdairean.

CLÙDAIREACHD, *s. f.* A patching, a clouting, a cobbling.

CLÙDAIR, *n. pl.* of clùd. Clouts, rags, patches.

CLÙDAN, ain, *s. m.* (*dim.* of clùd.) A little clout, a little rag. *W.* clwtyn.

CLUICH, *v. n.* Play, sport, game; finger a musical instrument; represent a character. *Pret. a.* chluich; *fut. aff. a.* chluichidh.

CLUICH, cluiche, *s. f.* (*It.* cluithe.) Sport, play, pastime, game; gaming; flirting; a theatrical performance. Fuain an cluich, *the noise of their sport.—Oss. Derm.* Dh' éirich iad gu cluich, *they rose to play.—Stew. Exod. ref.* Tigh cluiche, *a theatre.* Cluiche cloinne, *children's play.*

CLUICHEACH, *a.* Playful, sportive, frolicsome.

CLUICHEADAIR, *s. m.* A player. *N. pl.* cluicheadairean.

CLUICHEADH, idh, *s. m.* (*Ir.* cluitheadh.) A playing, a sporting; a playing on a musical instrument.

CLUICHEADH, (a), *pr. part.* of cluich. Playing, sporting; performing, as on the stage, or on an instrument of music. Am fear ciùil a cluicheadh, *the musician playing.—Stew.* 2 *K.*

CLUICHEAG, eig, *s. f.* Children's play; pastime. Ri cluicheag, *playing.*

CLUID, *s. f.* A rag; a nook.

CLÙID, *gen. sing.* of clùd.

CLUIG, *gen. sing.* and *n. pl.* of clag or clog; which see.

CLUIGEAN, ein, *s. m.* (*Ir.* cloigean.) A pendant; an ear-pendant; a little bell; a cluster; a bubble. Cluigean cluais, *an ear-pendant.*

CLUIGEANACH, *a.* Belled; clustered, clustering. Barr-chluigeanach, *bell-topped.—Macint.*

CLÙIMH, *s. f.* Down, plumage, feathers; written also *clòimh.*

CLUIN, *s. f.* Fraud; enclosure.

CLUINN, *v. irr.* (*Gr.* κλυω.) Hear, hark, listen. *Pret. a.* chual, *heard; fut. aff.* cluinnidh, *shall hear.* Cluinn a h-osnaidh, *hear her sobs.—Ardar.* Cluinn! armailt neamh! *hark! the hosts of heaven!—Sm.* Cluinneam ri luaidh do dhàn, *I will listen to the praises of thy tale.—Oss. Fing. Fut. sub.* chluinneas. An ni chluinneas na big 's e chànas na big, *what the young hear they repeat; as the old cock crows the young cock learns.—O. P.*

CLUINNEAM, 1 *sing. imper.* of cluinn. Let me hear. And with the poets, 1 *sing. ind. act.* cluin ream fuain, *I hear a sound.—Oss. Tem.*

CLUINNEAM, (*for* cluinnidh mi.) I will hear or listen.

CLUINNEAR, *fut. pass.* of cluinn. Shall be heard. Cluinnear nuallan do bheòil, *thy whisper shall be heard.—Ull.*

CLUINNTINN, *s. f.* A hearing, a listening; hearsay.

CLUINNTINN, (a), *pr. part.* of cluinn. Hearing; listening.

CLÙMHACH, aich, *s.* Down, feathers, plumage. Làn do chlùmhach, *full of feathers.—Stew. Ezek.*

CLÙMHACH, *a.* Downy, feathered, plumy.

CLÙMHAR, *a.* (*Corn. Arm.* and *W.* clauar.) Warm, sheltered, snug. Na leabaidh chlùmhair, *in his sheltered bed.—Oss. Duthona.*

CLU-NEAD, -nid, *s. m.* A sheltered nest.—*Oss. Gaul.*

CLÙT, clùit, *s. m.* A clout. See CLÙD.

CLUTACH, *a.* Clouted. See CLÙDACH.

CLUTH, *v. a.* Clothe. *Pret.* chluth, *clad; fut. aff.* cluthaidh, *shall clothe.*

CLÙTHAICH, *v. a.* Clothe. *Pret. a.* clùthaich, *clothed; fut. aff.* clùthaichidh, *shall clothe.*

CLÙTHAR, *a.* See CLUMHAIR.

CLÙTH-EUDAICH, *v. a.* Clothe, clothe warmly. *Pret. a.* chluth-eudaich. Is eigin duinn bhi air ar clùth-eudachadh, *we must be clothed.—Stew. 2 Cor.*

† CNA, *a.* Good, gracious, bountiful.

CNABAR, eir, *s. m.* Drowsiness, heaviness.

CNAC, cnaic, *s. f.* (*Swed.* knak, *a loud report.*) A crack; a fissure; a breach; the crack of a whip; any loud report. Bheirinn cnac anns na h-aitheantibh, *I would make a breach in the commandments.—Mac Co.* Ann an cnac, *in a crack; in an instant.* Leig e cnac as, *it gave a crack.*

CNAC, *v. a.* and *n.* (*Swed.* knaka, *to crack.*) Crack; break; crash; split; splinter. *Pret.* chnac; *fut.* cnacaidh.

CNACAIR, CNACHDAIR, *s. m.* A cracker; the cracker of a whip.

CNADAIR, *s. m.* A prater, a jester. *N. pl.* cnadairean.

† CNADAN, ain, *s. m.* A frog. *N. pl.* cnadain.

CNAG, cnaig, *s.* (*Ir. id. Da.* knag, *a wart.*) A pin; a knob; a peg; a knock; a wrinkle; a crack or noise. An gabhar cnag dheth, *shall a pin of it be taken.—Stew. Ezek.*

CNAGACH, *a.* Knobby; full of pegs or pins; like a peg or pin.

CNAGACHD, *s. f.* Knobbiness; knottiness; *rarely*, sternness.

CNAGADH, aidh, *s. m.* A knocking down; the act of driving; a making knobby.

CNAGAID, *s. f.* A rap. *N. pl.* cnagaidean.

CNAGAIDH, *a.* Bunchy.

CNAID, *s. f.* A scoff, a jeer, derision. Na dean cnaid air an duin bhochd, *do not jeer a poor man.—Old Didactic Poem.*

CNAIMH, *s.* (*Ir. id.*) A bone. *N. pl.* cnaimhean; *d. pl.* cnaimhibh. Cnaimh do m' chnaimhibh, *bone of my bones.—Stew. Gen.* Cnaimh deud, *ivory.* Cnaimh gobhail, *the share-bone.* Cnaimh mor do dhuine gionach, *the great bone to the greedy man.—G. P.*

CNAIMH-BRISTEACH, *s. m.* Ossifrage. An cnaimh-bristeach, *the ossifrage.—Stew. Lev.*

CNAIMH-DEUD, *s. m.* Ivory.—*Stew. Ezek.*

CNAIMHEACH, *a.* Bony, having large bones.

CNAIMH-FHITHEACH, *s. m.* A rook.

CNAIMH-GHEADH, gheoidh, *s. m.* A bird between a goose and a duck.

CNAIMH-GOBHAIL, *s. m.* The share-bone.

CNAIMH-NIGHIDH, *s.* A beetle; an instrument for beating clothes in the washing.

CNAIMHTEACH, *a.* Consuming without flame; corrosive; gnawing, chewing.

CNÀMH, *v. a.* (*Gr.* χναω. *W.* cnoi. *Ir.* cnaoi.) Chew; digest; waste; consume without flame. *Pret. a.* chnàmh; *fut. aff. a.* chnàmhaidh. Chionn gun cnamh e chir, *because it chews the cud.—Stew. Lev.* Bròn ga m' chnamh, *grief consuming me.—Mac Lach.*

CNÀMHACH, *a.* Wasting slowly; deleterious; corroding.

CNAMHACH, *a.* Bony; having large bones; full of bones.

CNÀMHACHD, *s. f.* Deleteriousness; corrosiveness; a wasting or consuming.

CNAMHADH, aidh, *s. m.* (*W.* cnova.) A chewing, a masticating; a digesting; a wasting; a consuming.

CNAMHAN, *n. pl.* of cnaimh.

CNÀMHAN, ain, *s. m.* Continued talking.

CNAMHANACH, *a.* Fretting as a sore; corroding; consuming gradually. Luibhre cnamhanach, *a fretting leprosy.—Stew. Lev.*

CNAMH-CNUIMH, *s. m.* A cankerworm. Mar a chnamh-chnuimh, *like a cankerworm.—Stew. Nah.*

CNAMHTACH, *a.* Wasting without flame; consuming; corrosive; chewing.

CNAP, cnaip, *s. m.* A button; a knob; a knot; a lump; a boss; a stud; a little blow; a little hill; a stout boy. Cnap agus blath, *a knob and a flower.—Stew. Exod.* Cnapsaic, *a knapsack.*
W. Arm. and *Ir.* cnap. *Old Eng.* cnaep. *Dan.* cnap. *Swed.* knap.

CNAPACH, *a.* Knobby; hilly; lumpy; bossy; stout.—*Ir. id.*

CNAPAN, *n. pl.* of cnap.

CNAPAN, ain, *s. m.* (*dim.* of cnap.) *Ir. id.* A little lump; a little knob; a little boss.

CNAPARRA, *a.* Stout, bulky, sturdy. Gu cnaparra, *stoutly.*

CNAP-SAIC, *s. m.* A knapsack. *N. pl.* cnapanna-saic, *knapsacks.*

CNAP-STARRADH, aidh, *s. m.* An obstruction; also a brass ball which the ancient Caledonian fastened to the lower end of his spear to terrify his antagonist, or to distract his attention with the noise it made when shaken.—*See Dion. Cassius apud Xiph.* lib. lxiii. A dearg-shruthadh mu chnap-starradh, *pouring red about his brazen ball.—Oss. Gaul.*

† CNARRA, *s. m.* A ship.—*Ir. id.*

CNATAN, ain, *s. m.* A cold; an obstruction of perspiration. Le tùchan 's le cnatan, *with hoarseness and cold.*

CNATANACH, *a.* Causing cold or cough; pertaining to a cold. Mios cnatanach, *the cold-causing month.—Macdon.*

CNEAD, *v. n.* Groan, sigh; scoff. *Pret. a.* chnead, *groaned; fut. aff. a.* cneadaidh, *shall groan.*

CNEAD, *s. f.* (*Ir. id.*) A sigh, a groan; a scoff. Gun ochain gun chnead, *without sob or sigh.—Old Song.* Cha 'n oil leam cnead mo leas-mhathar, *I pity not the sigh of my stepmother.—G. P.*

CNEADACH, *a.* Sobbing, sighing, groaning; puny; asthmatic.

CNEADACH, aich, *s. m.* A puny person; one who sobs or sighs; an asthmatic person. Is tric à chinn an cneadach is a dh' fhalbh an sodach, *often the puny thrives when the vigorous drop.—G. P.*

CNEADAIL, *s. f.* A continued sobbing or sighing.

CNEADH, cneidh, *s. f.* (*Ir. id.*) A wound, a bruise; a disaster. Guirme cneidhe, *the blueness of a wound.—Stew. Pro.* Coidlidh duine air gach cneadh ach a chneadh fein, *a man will sleep over every wound [disaster] but his own.—G. P.*

CNEADHACH, *a.* (*from* cneadh.) Wounded; full of wounds; causing wounds.

CNEADHALACH, aich, *s. m.* One who is wounded; a sufferer. Co air bi is coireach is mise an cneadhalach, *whoever is to blame, I am the sufferer.—G. P.*

Cneadh-shliochd, *s. m.* A scar.

Cneamhair, *s. m.* An artful fellow. *N. pl.* cneamhairean.

Cneas, cneis, *s. m.* (*Ir.* cneas.) The form; the waist; skin; the breast; the body; the neck. Cneas mo ghraidh, *the form of my love.—Ull.* Cobhar o 'n cneasa geal, *foam from their white breasts.—Death of Carril.* Is lionmhor cneas san do chuir e lann, *many were the breasts he stabbed.—Fingalian Poem.*

Cneasaich, *v. a.* Cure, heal, remedy; shape; make slender, as the waist. *Pret. a.* chneasaich; *fut.* cneasaichidh.

Cneasda, *a.* Humane, temperate, moderate; modest, meek; ominous. Gu cneasda, *temperately.*

Cneasdach, *a.* Humane, temperate, moderate; modest, meek, mild.

Cneasdachd, *s. f.* Humanity, temperance, moderation; modesty, meekness, mildness. Gun chneasdachd, *intemperate.—Macint.*

Cneasgheal, *a.* Fair-skinned; white-bosomed; white-bodied.

Cneasmhoireachd, *s. f.* Shapeliness; handsomeness; humaneness; mildness.

Cneasmhor, *a.* Shapely, handsome, well-formed; humane; modest, meek, mild. *Com.* and *sup.* cneasmhoire.

Cneas-mhuir, *s. m.* The strait of a sea.

Cneath. See **Cneadh**.

Cneasnachadh, aidh, *s. m.* A squeezing; a tightening. Is feairrd gach cneadh a cneasnachadh, *every wound is the better for being squeezed.—G. P.*

Cneasnaich, *v. a.* Squeeze tighter; straiten; press. *Pret.* chneasnaich, *squeezed; fut. aff.* cneasnaichidh, *shall squeeze.*

Cneidh, *gen. sing.* of cneadh; which see.

Cneidh-shliochd, *s. f.* A scar.

Cneidh-shliochdach, *a.* Full of scars.

Cneim, *v. a.* and *n.* Nibble; erode; bite; become scabbed. *Pret. a.* chneim, *nibbled; fut. aff. a.* cneimidh, *shall nibble.*

Cneim, *s. f.* A bite; a nibble; erosion; a scab.

Cniocht, *s. m.* (*Sax.* cniht.) A knight.—*Ir.*

Cniopair, *s. m.* A poor rogue. *N. pl.* cniopairean.

Cniopaireachd, *s. f.* Roguery.

Cnò, *s. m.* A nut, a filbert. *N. pl.* cnothan, *nuts.* Lios nan cnò, *the nut-garden.—Stew. Song Sol.* Cnò dharaig, cnò dharaich, *an acorn;* cnò-chomhlaich, *a double nut;* coille chnò, *a hazel-wood;* cnothan-spuinc, *Molucca nuts.*

Cnò, *a.* Famous; excellent; gruff.

Cnoc, cnoic, *s. m.* A hillock, a little hill, a knoll, an eminence, a hill. *N. pl.* cnuic. Daimh chabrach nan cnoc, *the branchy-horned deer of the hills.—Ull.* Cnoc seallaidh, *a hill of observation, an observatory.* Cnoc seallta, *a hill of observation.—Oss. Duthona.* The *cnocs* were the ancient scenes of religious ceremonies, and, in process of time, of festivity, among the Gael. Hence *cnocaireachd* signifies *merry-making.*

Cnocach, *a.* (*from* cnoc.) Hilly, full of hills; rugged. *Com.* and *sup.* cnocaiche, *more or most hilly.*

Cnocan, ain, *s. m.* (*dim.* of cnoc.) *Ir. id.* A little hill, a little knoll, a hillock, a mound, a little heap.

Cnocanach, *a.* Abounding in knolls or hillocks; rugged.

Cnocaireachd, *s. f.* (*from* cnoc.) Sauntering; walking abroad; merry-making.

Cnòd, cnòid, *s. m.* A patch; a piece on a shoe; a piece joined to strengthen another; a knot. *Lat.* nod-us. *Sax.* cnotta. *Eng.* knot. *Da.* cnutte. *Swed.* knut.

Cnòdach, *a.* (*from* cnòd.) Patched; scraping together; gaining.

Cnoic, *gen. sing.* and *n. pl.* of cnoc. Hills. Cnoic is uisge is Ailpeinich, *hills, waters, and Mac Alpins.* An adage meaning that the Mac Gregors, called also Mac Alpins, from king Alpin, their ancestor, are as old as hills or waters.

Cnòd, *s. m.* See **Cnòd**.

Cnoidh, cnoidhe, *s. m.* A severe pain; a throbbing pain; the tooth-ache.

Cnoidheach, *a.* Painful; giving pain. Gu cnoidheach lotach, *causing pain and wounds.—Old Song.*

Cnòth, *s. m.* A nut. *N. pl.* cnothan, *nuts.* (*Corn.* cnauen.) See **Cnò**. Written also *cnù.*

Cnothach, *a.* (*from* cnò.), Abounding in nuts. Coille chnòthach, *a wood abounding in nuts.—Macdon.*

Cnothair, *s. m.* A nut-cracker. *N. pl.* cnothairean.

Cnothan, *n. pl.* of cnòth *or* cnò. Nuts.

Cnù, *s. m.* (*Ir. id.*) A nut. *N. pl.* cnuthan, *nuts.—Stew. Gen. ref.* More frequently written *cnò;* which see.

Cnuachd, **Cnuaichd**, *s. f.* The brow; the forehead. A sgoltadh chnuachd, *splitting brows.—Old Song.*

Cnuachdach, *a.* Large-browed; little-browed. Maolchmachdach, *having a bald forehead.*

Cnuaiste, *p. part.* Gnashed; chewed; scraped together; collected; gathered.

Cnuas, *v. a.* (*Ir. id.*) Gnash; chew voraciously; scrape together; collect; gather carefully; assemble. *Pret. a.* chnuas, *collected; fut. aff. a.* cnuasaidh, *shall collect.*

Cnuas, cnuais, *s. m.* A gnashing; a chewing voraciously; a scraping; a collecting; a collection; an acquisition. An cnuas is fearr, *the best collection.—Macdon.*

Cnuasach, aich, *s. f.* A pondering, a ruminating; a scraping together, a hoarding. See also **Cnuasachd**.

Cnuasachadh, aidh, *s. m.* A gathering; a scraping together; a pondering, a ruminating.

Cnusachadh, (a), *pr. part.* of cnuasaich. Gathering; scraping together; ruminating; gnashing; chewing; pondering; reviewing; reflecting.

Cnuasachd, *s. f.* Pondering, ruminating; a recollection; a scraping together; a hoarding; a collection of any sort of matter. Cnuasachd le 'n lùbadh slait, *a collection beneath which the bough bends.—Macdon.* Cnuasachd na gràinig, *the store of the hedgehog; useless labour.* Dean cnuasachd san t-samhradh ni 'n geamhradh chur seachad, *make up a store in summer that will make the winter to pass.—G. P.*

Cnuasadh, aidh, *s. m.* A gnashing; a voracious chewing.

Cnuasaich, *v. a.* Ponder, ruminate, reflect; review; gather; scrape together; collect. *Pret. a.* chnuasaich, *pondered; fut. aff. a.* cnuasaichidh. Far an cnuasaich sibh barrachd, *where you will gather abundance.—Mac Co.*

Cnuasaichte, *p. part.* of cnuasaich. (*Ir.* cnuasaighte.) Pondered, ruminated; gathered or scraped together; chewed.

Cnuasair, *s. m.* A gatherer; a scraper; a hoarder; one who ponders or ruminates.

Cnuidh. See **Cnuimh**.

Cnuimh, *s. f.* A worm, a maggot; the tooth-ache; pain, suffering. Dh' ullaich e cnuimh, *he prepared a worm.—Stew. Dan. N. pl.* cnuimhean. Ghin e cnuimhean, *it bred worms.—Stew. Exod.* Bithidh chnuimh dheireannach craiteach, *the last pains will be sorrowful.—G. P.*

Cnuimheach, *a.* (*from* cnuimh.) Wormy; vermicular; abounding in worms; of, or relating to, a worm; painful.

Cnuimheag, eig, *s. f.* (*dim.* of cnuimh.) A worm, a little worm; a maggot. *N. pl.* cnuimheagan.

Cnuimheagach, *a.* Full of worms or maggots; vermicular.

Cnuimheagan, *n. pl.* of cnuimheag.

Cnuimhean, *n. pl.* of cnuimh. Worms.

Cnuimh-itheach, *a.* Insectivorous.

† Cnùs-mhor, *a.* Fruitful, prolific. *Com.* and *sup.* cnuismhoire.

Co, *interrog. pron.* Who, which. Co sud air a chraig mar cheo? *who is that on the hill like a mist?—Oss. Gaul.* Co sam bi, *whoever;* co air bi, *whoever;* co dhiubh, *which of them? whether; at any rate;* co aca, *whether.—Stew. Exod.* Co eile, *who else;* tha mi comadh co dhiùbh, *I care not whether; I care not which;* cha dean mi e co dhiùbh, *I will not do it at any rate;* cho dhiùbh thig thu no nach tig, *whether you come or not.*

Co, *conj.* As. This word is placed before an adjective, and requires the initial consonant of that adjective to be aspirated, as, *co mhor,* as great; *co mhaith,* as good. In some good Gaelic authors, however, we find this aspiration dispensed with. Sometimes the aspiration is transferred to the conjunction, as, *cho treun,* as strong; and it is often seen in both, as, *cho ghrinn,* as fine.

Còail, (*for* codhail.) A meeting. An coail a ghaoil, *to meet his love.—Ull.*

Co'ainm, Comhainm, *s. f.* A surname.

Co air bi, *comp. rel.* Whoever, whosoever.

Co'aiteachadh, Comh-aiteachadh, aidh, *s. m.* A dwelling together; co-inhabiting.

Co'àitich, Comhàitich, *v. n.* Dwell together, co-inhabit. *Pret. a.* chomh-aitich; *fut. aff.* comh-àitichidh.

Co'aois, Comhaois, *s. a.* Equal age; a cotemporary; contemporary; of equal age. Mòran do m' chomhaoisibh, *many of my cotemporaries.—Stew. Gal. N. pl.* comhaoisean.

Co'aontachadh, Comh-aontachadh, aidh, *s. m.* An agreeing, a consenting; an agreement, a consent; a collusion.

Co'aontachd, Comh-aontachd, *s. f.* Unanimity, agreement, unity, consent.

Co'aontaich, Comh-aontaich, *v. a.* Agree, consent, yield, admit; grant as a point in an agreement. *Pret. a.* chomh-aontaich, *consented; fut. aff. a.* comh-aontaichidh.

Co'arguinn, Comh-arguinn, *s. f.* A syllogism.

Co'astaraich, Comh-astaraich, *s. m.* A fellow-traveller.

Cob, còib. (*Lat.* copia. *Ir.* cob.) Plenty, abundance.

† Cobh, *s. m.* A victory, triumph, conquest.—*Ir. id.*

Cobhach, aich, *s. m.* A tribute.—*Shaw.*

Cobhach, *a.* Stout, brave, victorious.—*Shaw.*

Co'bhaigh, Comhbhaigh. Sympathy, fellow-feeling.

Co'bhaigheach, Combhaigheach, *a.* Feeling, sympathetic.

† Co'bhail, Combhail, *s. f.* An enclosure.

Cobhair, *s. f.* (*Ir. id.*) Aid, relief. Bheir e cobhair dhuinne, *he will aid us.—Sm.* Da 'r cobhair, *to our relief.—Fingalian Poem.* Fear cobhair, *a saviour.* M' fhear cobhair, *my saviour.—Sm.*

Còbhair, *s. m.* A dry-stone-mason; a dyke or dry-stone-wall builder.

Còbhaireachd, *s. f.* The business of a dry-stone-builder; dry-stone-building.

Cobhair, *v. a.* Aid, assist, relieve. *Pret. a.* chobhair. Chobhair mi na baird, *I aided the bards.—Oss. Fing. Cobhair* is elegantly followed by the *prep.* air, either simple or compounded. Cobhair oirnne, *save us.* An luibh nach fhaigh cha 'n i chobhaireas, *the herb that cannot be found will heal no wound.—G. P.*

Cobhaltach, *a.* (*from* cobh.) Victorious, triumphant. Gu cobhaltach, *successfully.*

Cobhan, ain, *s. m.* (*Gr.* κόφινος. *Lat.* covinus. *Chald.* gosphan, *a chariot.*) A coffer, a little box; a car, a chariot; an ark; a coffin. This last rendering is evidently derived from *cobhan.*—The ancient Gaelic poets often use *cobhan* in the sense of a bier or coffin; as in the following examples, Cobhan an laoich, *the hero's bier.—Oss. Trathal.* Cobhan na gaoithe, *the chariot of the wind.—Oss. Gaul.* Cobhan cuilce, *an ark of bulrushes.—Stew. Gen.* Cobhan, as it frequently means a chariot, may be a contraction of *co-bhuain,* i. e. a heaving down on all sides, in allusion to the ancient British method of fastening scythes to their war-chariots; or it may be derived from *cobh,* victory. That cobhan was an old British term for a chariot, is evident from *Mela.* Dimicant bigis et curribus, Gallice armati, *covinos* vocant.—*Mela de Britannis,* lib. iii.

Co'bhann, Comh-bhann, -bhoinn, *s. m.* A confederacy, a league; a bond, a compact, a contract. Comh-bhann na sith, *the bond of peace.—Stew. Eph. ref.*

Co'bhan-oighre, Comh-bhan-oighre, *s. f.* A coheiress.

Cobhar, air, *s. m.* (*Ir.* cubhar.) Foam, froth; sillabub. Mar chobhar thonn, *like the foam of waves.—Oss. Cathluno.*

Cobharach, *a.* Foaming; aiding, relieving; ready to relieve. Mar steuda cobbarach, *like foaming steeds.—Oss. Cathula.* Fear cobharach an righ, *the auxiliary of the king.—Oss. Tem.*

Cobhartach, aich, (*from* cobh.) Prey, plunder, booty. Le cobhartach ro mhòr, *with very great prey.—Sm.*

Co'bheothaich, Comh-bheothaich, *v. a.* Quicken together; revive together.

Co'bhithbhuan, Comh-bhithbhuan, *a.* Co-eternal.

Co'bhithbhuantachd, Comh-bhithbhuantachd, *s. f.* Co-eternity.

Co'bhitheach, Comh-bhitheach, *a.* Co-existent.

Co'bhoinn, Comh-bhoinn, *s.* Confederacy; a compact, a copartnership.

Cobhra, *s. m.* A shield; a target.—*Shaw.*

Cobhrach, *a.* Foamy; prone to aid.

Cobhragach, aich, *s. m.* Foam; sillabub.

Co'bhrathair, Comh-bhrathair, *s. m.* A fellow; a chum.

Co'bhrathaireachas, Comh-bhrathaireachas, ais, *s. m.* Fellowship; consanguinity.

Co'bhrigheach, Comh-bhrigheach, *a.* Consubstantial.

Co'bhrigheachadh, Comh-bhrigheachadh, aidh, *s. m.* Cosubstantiation.

Co'bhrigheachd, Comh-bhrigheachd, *s. f.* Consubstantiality.

Co'bhrigheil, Comh-bhrigheil, *a.* Consubstantial.

† Cobhsach, *a.* (*from* cobh.) Victorious, triumphant.

† Coc, *a.* Manifest, plain, intelligible.

Coc, *v. a.* Cock as a Highland bonnet. *Pret.* choc, *cocked; fut. aff. a.* cocaidh, *shall cock.*

Coc, coca, *s. m.* The cocking or stiffening of a Highland bonnet.

Còc, *s.* Cooking. *Lat.* coquo, *cook. Swed.* koka, *boil food.*

† Coca, *s. m.* A cook. *Lat.* coquus. *Arm.* coq.

Cocainn, *s. f.* A cocking or dressing of a bonnet. Tha 'bhoneid air a cocainn, *his bonnet is cocked.*

Còcair, *s. m.* (còc-fhear.) A cook. Is math an còcair an t-acras, *hunger is a good cook.—G. P.*
Ir. id. Lat. coquo. *It.* cocere. *Span.* cozer. *Du.* and *Germ.* kocken. *It.* cuoco. *Lat.* coquus. *Dalm.* kuchats. In Congo, cocais, *to roast.*

Còcaireachd, *s. m.* (*Ir.* cocaireacht.) Cooking; the business of a cook. Ris a chòcaireachd, *cooking.*

Co'chaidreamh, Comh-chaidreamh, eimh, *s. m.* A comate, a companion, a chum.

Co'cheannachd, Comh-cheannachd, *s. f.* Commerce.

Cochall, aill. See Cochull.

Cochallach, *a.* Capsular; husked; coated. See also Cochullach.

Co'cheangal, Comh-cheangal, ail, *s. m.* A covenant, a compact, a bond.

Co'chearraiche, Comh-chearraiche, *s. m.* A fellow-player.

Co'cheart, Comh-cheart, *a.* Fashioned; formed round about; proportioned.

Co'cheartaich, Comh-cheartaich, *v. a.* Fashion round about; proportion; adjust.

Co'cheilidh, Comh-cheilidh, *s. c.* A paramour; a fellow-visitor. *N. pl.* co'chéilidhean. A co'cheilidhean, *her paramours.—Stew. Ezek.*

Co'chiallach, Comh-chiallach, *a.* Synonymous.

Co'chliamhuinn, Comh-chliamhuinn, *s. m.* A brother-in-law. *N. pl.* co'chliamhuinnean.

Co'chogadh, Comh-chogadh, aidh, *s. m.* Opposition. Comh-chogadh eòlais, *opposition of [knowledge] science.—Stew. Tim.*

Co'chòir, Comh-chòir, *s. f.* An equal right; an equal title; an equal claim.

Co'choisiche, Comh-choisiche, *s. m.* A fellow-traveller.

Co'chomunn, Comh-chomunn, uinn, *s. m.* Partnership, fellowship, communion.

Co'chòrdachd, Comh-chòrdachd, *s. f.* Unanimity, agreement, concord; mutual understanding.

Co'chordadh, Comh-chordadh, aidh, *s. m.* Unanimity, concord.

Co'chorp, Comh-chorp, -chuirp, *s. m.* A corporation.

Co'chorpaich, Comh-chorpaich, *v. a.* Incorporate, embody. *Pret. a.* chomh-chorpaich, *incorporated.*

Co-chorpachadh, Comh-chorpachadh, aidh, *s. m.* Incorporating, incorporation.

Co'choslachd, Comh-choslachd, *s. f.* Conformity; equality.

Co'chosmhal, Comh-chosmhal, *a.* Conformable, like.

Co'chothrom, Comh-chothrom, oim, *s. m.* Counterpoise.

Co'-chothromaich, Comh-chothromaich, *v. a.* Counterpoise, counterbalance. *Pret. a.* cho'chothromaich.

Co'chreutair, Comh-chreutair, *s. m.* A fellow-creature. *N. pl.* comh-chreutairean.

Co'chruinneachadh, Comh-chruinneachadh, aidh, *s. m.* A gathering, a congregation.

Co'chruinnich, Comh-chruinnich, *v. a.* Gather, assemble, congregate. *Pret.* chomh-chruinnich, *assembled; fut. aff.* comh-chruinnichidh, *shall assemble.*

Co'chruth, Comh-chruth, *s. m.* Resemblance, sameness of form, equiformation, conformation.

Co'chudthrom, Comh-chudthrom, uim, *s. m.* Equilibrium.

Co'chuideachd, Comh-chuideachd, *s. m.* A company; partnership; association; a junto.

Co-chuir, Comh-chuir, *v. a.* Apply, dispose; put together; compose as a discourse.

Cochull, uill, *s. m.* (*Gr.* κοχλια. *Lat.* cochlea.) A husk; the shell of a nut or of grain; a capsule; a mantle; a cockle.

Cochullach, *a.* Husky, shelled; capsular; coated with a shell or husk.

Co'chum, Comh-chum, *v. a.* Conform; proportion. *Pret. a.* chomh-chum; *fut. aff. a.* comh-chumaidh.

Co'chur, Comh-chur, *s. m.* An application; composition; arrangement; adjustment.

† **Cod**, *s. m.* Victory.

Còdach, aich, *s. m.* (comh-eudach.) Clothing; a covering; a cover; a proof. *N. pl.* codaichean.

† **Codach**, aich, *s. m.* Invention; friendship.

Codach, aich, *s. m.* A share, a part, a portion; also *gen. sing.* of cuid; which see.

Còdachadh, aidh, *s. m.* A clothing, a covering; a proving.

Còdachadh, (a), *pr. part.* of còdaich. Clothing, covering; proving. Dubh-neul 'g a còdachadh, *dark clouds covering her.—Oss.*

Còdaich, *v. a.* (comh-eudaich.) Clothe, cover; prove. *Pret. a.* chòdaich, *covered; fut. aff. a.* còdaichidh, *shall cover; fut. pass.* codaichear, *shall be covered.*

Codaichean, *n. pl.* of cuid; which see.

Còdaichte, *p. part.* of còdaich. Covered, clothed, clad; proved.

Codail, *v. n.* Sleep, slumber, doze. *Pret. a.* chodail, *slept; fut. aff.* codailidh, *shall sleep.* Written also *cadail.*

Codal, ail, *s. m.* Sleep, slumber. Beagan codail, *a little sleep.—Stew. Pro.* Dean codal, *sleep;* tha e na chodal, *he is asleep;* tha i na codal, *she is asleep;* tha iad nan codal, *they are asleep.* An neach nach cinn na chodal, cha chinn e na fhaireach, *he who grows not in his sleep, will not grow when awake.—G. P.*

Codalach, *a.* Sleepy, drowsy; like sleep; of, or belonging to, sleep. *Com.* and *sup.* codalaiche.

Codalachd, *s. f.* Sleepiness, drowsiness.—*Stew. Pro. ref.*

Codaleun, eoin, *s. m.* A mandrake.—*Macd. N. pl.* codaleòin.

Codaltach, *a.* Sleepy, drowsy; like sleep; *substantively*, a drowsy person.

Codaltachd, *s. f.* Sleepiness, drowsiness.

Còdhail, *s. f.* A meeting; apposition; a convention; an assembly. Ghluais e na chòdhail, *he went to meet him.—Oss. Tem.* Thoir còdhail dha, *give him a meeting.*

Co'dhaingneachadh, Comh-dhaingneachadh, aidh, *s. m.* A strengthening; a conferring strength; confirming; a confirmation.

Co'dhaingnich, Comh-dhaingnich, *v. a.* Strengthen; confirm. *Pret. a.* chomh-dhaingnich, *confirmed.*

Co'dhalta, Comh-dhalta, *s. m.* (*Ir. id.*) A foster-brother. Perhaps *comhalta.*

Co'dhas, Comh-dhas, ais, *s. m.* An equal right or privilege.

Co'dhe, Comh-dhé, *s. m.* The Trinity.—*Macd.*

Co'dhealbh, Comh-dhealbh, *v. a.* Form; constitute; make up, as a constitution. *Pret. a.* chomh-dhealbh, *formed; fut. aff. a.* comh-dhealbhaidh, *shall form.*

Co'dhealbhadh, Comh-dhealbhadh, aidh, *s. m.* A constitution. Gu mair ar reachd 's ar comh-dhealbhadh, *may our laws and our constitution stand.—Old Song.*

Co'dheuchainn, Comh-dheuchainn, *s. f.* A competition; a trial; a rivalry. *N. pl.* co'dheuchainnean.

Co'dheuchainniche, Comh-dheuchainniche, *s. m.* A candidate; a competitor; a rival.

Co'dhiol, Comh-dhiol, *v. a.* Compensate; retaliate; remunerate, make amends for. *Pret. a.* chomh-dhiol; *fut. aff. a.* comh-dhiolaidh, *shall or will compensate.*

Co'dhioladh, Comh-dhioladh, aidh, *s. m.* The act or circumstance of compensation; a compensation, retaliation, remuneration.

Co'dhoilghios, Comh-dhoilghios, *s.* Condolence. Dean comh-dhoilghios, *condole.*

Co'dhùin, Comh-dhùin, *v. a.* Conclude, bring to an end. *Pret. a.* chomh-dhùin; *fut. aff. a.* comh-dhùinidh, *shall conclude.*

Co'dhùnadh, Comh-dhùnadh, aidh, *s. m.* A concluding; a conclusion.

Co'dhùthchasach, Comh-dhùthchasach, *a.* Of the same county.

Co'DUCHADH, aidh, *s. m.* See CÒDACHADH.

CÒDUICH, *v. a.* See CÒDAICH.

Co'ÉIGNICH, COMH-ÉIGNICH, *v. a.* Constrain, compel, force; ravish. *Pret. a.* chomh-éignich, *constrained.* Chomh-éignich i e, *she forced him.—Stew. Pro.*

Co'EÒLAS, COMH-EÒLAS, ais, *s. m.* Interknowledge, reciprocal knowledge; mutual acquaintance.

Co'EUD, COMH-EUD, *s. m.* Rivalry, mutual jealousy or suspicion.

Co'EUDMHOR, COMH-EUDMHOR, *a.* Mutually jealous or suspicious.

Co'FHAD, COMH-FHAD, *a.* (*W.* cyhyd.) Equally long; even, in a line, lineal.

Co'FHAD-THRATH, COMH-FHAD-THRATH, *s. m.* The equinox.

Co'FHAILTEACH, COMH-FHAILTEACH, *a.* Congratulatory.

Co'FHAILTEACHD, COMH-FHAILTEACHD, *s. f.* Congratulation.

Co'FHAILTICH, COMH-FHAILTICH, *v. n.* Congratulate. *Pret. a.* chomh-fhailtich; *fut. aff. a.* comh-fhailtichidh, *shall congratulate.* Chomh-fhailtich iad a chéile, *they congratulate each other.*

Co-FHÀIR, COMH-FHÀIR, *s. f.* Twilight; dawn.

Co'FHARPUIS, COMH-FHARPUIS, *s. f.* Emulation, rivalry. Connsachadh, comh-fharpuis, *variance and emulation.*

Co'FHÀS, COMH-FHÀS, *s. m.* A concretion; a growing together.

Co'FHIÒS, COMH-FHIOS, *s.* Conscience.

Co'FHLAITHEACH, COMH-FHLAITHEACH, *a.* Aristocratical, democratical, republican.

Co'FHLAITHEACHD, COMH-FHLAITHEACHD, *s. f.* Aristocracy, democracy, a commonwealth, republicanism. Comh-fhlaitheachd Israel, *the commonwealth of Israel.—Stew. Eph.*

Co'FHOGHAIR, COMH-FHOGHAIR, *s. m.* A consonant; a chime, as of bells.

Co'FHREAGAIR, COMH-FHREAGAIR, *v. a.* Echo, resound; agree, suit, correspond. *Pret. a.* chomh-fhreagair, *resounded; fut. aff. a.* comh-fhreagairidh, *shall resound.* Chomh-fhreagair creagan arda, *lofty rocks resounded.—Fingalian Poem.*

Co'FHREAGARACH, COMH-FHREAGARACH, *a.* (*Ir.* comh-fhreagarthach.) Answerable; fitted to each other, suitable; conformable, consonant; corresponding.

Co'FHREAGARACHD, COMH-FHREAGARACHD, *s. f.* Answerableness, congruence, conformity, correspondence, symmetry.

Co'FHREAGARADH, COMH-FHREAGARADH, aidh, *s. m.* (*Ir.* coimh-fhreagradh.) Agreement, conformity, correspondence.

Co'FHREAGARTAS, ais, *s. m.* Conformity, correspondence, symmetry.

Co'FHUAIM, COMH-FHUAIM, *s. m.* Musical concordance, harmony; equitone.

Co'FHUIL, COMH-FHUIL, -fhola, *s. f.* (*Ir. id.*) Consanguinity, relationship.

Co'FHULANGAIR, COMH-FHULANGAIR, *s. m.* A fellow-sufferer.

Co'FHULANGAS, COMH-FHULANGAS, ais, *s. m.* Fellow-feeling, sympathy. Tha co'fhulangas aige, *he has a fellow-feeling.—Sm.*

Co'FHURTACHAIL, COMH-FHURTACHAIL, *a.* Consolatory, comfortable.

Co'FHURTACHD, COMH-FHURTACHD, *s. f.* (*Ir. id.*) Comfort, consolation. Gach co'fhurtachd, *every comfort.—Sm.*

Co'FHURTAIR, COMH-FHURTAIR, *s. m.* A comforter. *N. pl.* comh-fhurtaireachd.

† COFRA, ai, *s. m.* (*Ir. id. Arm.* couffr.) A coffer, a box, a chest.

COG, *v. n.* Fight, war, carry on war. *Pret. a.* chog, *fought; fut. aff. a.* cogaidh, *shall fight.* Co chogas riut? *who will fight against thee?—Sm.*

COGACH, *a.* (*from* cog.) *Ir.* cogthach. Belligerent; warlike; of, or pertaining to, war. Na fir ghasda chogach, *the active warlike men.—Old Song.*

COGADH, aidh, *s. m.* War, warfare, fighting. Deanta ri cogadh, *trained to war.—Stew.* 1 *K.* Cogadh choilleach, *cock-fighting.* Luingeas chogaidh, *a ship of war;* cogadh no sìth, *peace or war; the name of a Gaelic air.*

COGADH, (a), *pr. part.* of cog. Fighting, carrying on war.

COGAIDH, *fut. aff. a.* of cog. Shall or will fight.

COGAIDH, *gen. sing.* of cogadh.

COGAIL, *a.* (cog-amhuil.) *Ir. id.* Warlike; belligerent.

COGAIR, *v. n.* Whisper; listen to a whisper. Cogair rium, *listen to my whisper; whisper to me. Pret. a.* chogair, *whispered; fut. aff.* cogairidh.

COGAIR, *gen. sing.* of cogar.

COGALL, aill, *s. m.* (*Ir. id.*) Tares, husks; the herb cockle; the beard of an ear of barley; a rubbing, a chafing; friction. Diasan arbhair le 'n cogall, *ears of corn with their husks.—Stew.* 2 *K. ref.*

COGALLACH, *a.* Husky; full of tares; bearded like ears of barley.

COGAR, air, *s. m.* A whisper; a suggestion. Dean cogar, *whisper;* also, *listen to a whisper;* dean cogar rium, *whisper to me; listen to my whisper;* cogar na ban-ghrùdair, *the ale-wife's whisper soon turns loud.—G. P.*

COGARAICH, *s. f.* Whispering. Ciod chogaraich th'ort? *what are you whispering at?* Ri cogaraich, *whispering.*

COGARAICH, *v.* Whisper. *Pret. a.* chogaraich, *whispered.*

COGARAS, ais, *s. m.* (*Ir. id.*) Peace, amity.

COGARSAICH, *s. f.* Whispering; a suggestion. Fear na cogarsaich, *a whisperer.—Stew. Pro.* Luchd cogarsaich, *whisperers.—Stew. Rom.*

COGARSAICH, *v.* Whisper. *Pret. a.* chogarsaich, *whispered.*

COGARSAICH, (a), *pr. part.* Whispering. Sior chogarsaich an cluas a chéile, *ever whispering to each other.—Sm.*

COGARSNACH, aich, *s. m.* A whispering.

Co'GHAIR, COMH-GHAIR, *s. f.* (*Ir. id.*) A conclamation; a simultaneous shout; simultaneous laughter; a congratulation.

Co'GHAIRDEACHAS, COMH-GHAIRDEACHAS, ais, *s. m.* Congratulation; mutual solace. Deanamaid comh-ghairdeachas, *let us solace ourselves.—Stew. Pro.*

Co'GHAIRM, COMH-GHAIRM, *s. f.* (*Ir. id.*) A general shout; a convocation. Comh-ghairm naomh, *a holy convocation.—Stew. Exod.* and *Lev.*

Co'GHAOIR, COMH-GHAOIR, *s. f.* A tumultuous noise—(*Stew. Amos*); a simultaneous shout.

Co'GHAOL, COMH-GHAOL, aoil, *s. m.* Mutual love.

Co'GHEARRADH, COMH-GHEARRADH, aidh, *s. m.* Concision.

Co'GHLEACHD, COMH-GHLEACHD, *s. f.* (*Ir.* coimghleic.) A conflict, a combat, wrestling.

Co'GHLÒIR, COMH-GHLÒIR, *s. f.* Equal glory, consonance.

Co'GHNATH, COMH-GHNATH, *s. m.* (*Ir.* congnamh.) Assistance and relief. Guidhidh sinn a chòghnath, *we will beg his aid.—Sm.* Dean còghnath, *assist.* A ghaoil, dean mo chòghnath, *assist me, my love.—Ull.*

Co'GHNATHACH, COMH-GNATHACH, *a.* Ready to aid or help; auxiliatory.

Co'GHREIMICH, COMH-GHREIMICH, *v. a.* (*Ir. id.*) Grasp; adhere to. Co'ghreimich ris, *adhere to him.*

Co'GHUIL, COMH-GHUIL, *v. n.* Condole. *Pret.* chomh-ghuil, *condoled; fut. aff.* comh-ghuilidh.

Coguis, *s. f.* (*Ir.* cogus.) Conscience. Agartas coguis, *remorse of conscience*; coguis mhaith, *a good conscience.*—*Stew. Tim.*

Coguiseach, *a.* Conscientious.

Cogull, uill, *s. m.* A rubbing, a chafing, friction; tares; cockle; the beard of barley. Cogull ramh, *the friction of oars on the fulcrum.*—*Macfar.*

Cogullach, aich, *s. m.* Filings.

† **Coib**, *s. f.* (*Ir. id.*) A copy; a troop; a company.

Coibhdean, ein, *s. m.* A troop.

Coibhi, *s. m.* (*perhaps* comh-bhaigh.) A name given by the British Celts to an Archdruid.

The benevolence of this person, who was always chosen from the worthiest of his order, is recorded in the following verse, as mentioned by Dr. Smith: Ged is fagus clach do 'n làr, is faigse na sin cobhair Choibhi, *Near though a stone be to the ground, nearer still is Coibhi's aid.*

† **Coic**, *s. f.* (*Ir. id. Lat.* cœcus.) A secret, a mystery; *also*, blind.

Coi'cheangail, **Coimh-cheangail**, *v. a.* Tie together; bind; make a compact; couple. *Pret. a.* choimh-cheangail; *fut. aff. a.* coimh-cheanglaidh.

Coi'cheangal, **Coimh-cheangal**, ail, *s. m.* A covenant, a bond, a mutual obligation, a compact; a coupling. Coi'cheangal an dara h-aon, *the coupling of the one.*—*Stew. Exod.*

Coi'chruinneachadh, **Coimh-chruinneachadh**, aidh, *s. m.* A meeting, an assembly.

Coi'chruinnich, **Coimh-chruinnich**, *v. a.* and *n.* Assemble, gather together.

† **Coid**, *s. pl.* Sticks; firewood; brushwoods.

† **Coidhean**, ein, *s. m.* A barnacle.

Coidheis, *a.* Indifferent. Tha mi coidheis mu dhéimhinn, *I am indifferent about him* or *it.*

Coi'fhearsnach, **Coimh-fhearsnach**, aich, *s. m.* A neighbour. *N. pl.* coi'fhearsnaich, *neighbours.*

Coi'fhearsnachd, **Coimh-fhearsnachd**, *s. f.* Neighbourhood. Droch choimh-fhearsnachd, *a bad neighbourhood.*

Còig, *a.* (*Ir.* coige.) Five.—*Stew. Gen. ref.* Written also *cùig.*

Coigeart, eirt, *s. m.* Judgment; a question.

Coigill, *v. a.* (*Ir. id.*) Spare; preserve; keep alive; cover a fire to keep it alive. *Pret. a.* choigill, *spared*; *fut. aff. a.* coiglidh, *shall spare.* Coiglidh mi mar choigleas duine, *I will spare as a man spares.*—*Stew. Mal.* Coigill an teine, *cover the fire.*

Coigill, *s. f.* A thought, a secret.

Coigle, *s. m.* A companion; a secret.

Coigleachd, *s. f.* A train, a retinue.

Coiglich, *v. a.* Attend; accompany. *Pret. a.* choiglich, *attended.*

† **Coigne**, *s. f.* A spear, a dart.—*Shaw.*

Còignear, *a.* Five persons; five in number. Còignear dhaoine, *five men.* Written also *cuignear.*

Coigreach, *a.* Strange, foreign. Fearann coigreach céin, *a foreign distant land.*—*Sm.* Dia coigreach, *a strange god.*—*Id.*

Coigreach, ich, *s. m.* A stranger, a foreigner. Na d' thigeadh an coigreach, *let not the stranger come.*—*Stew. G. B.*

Coigreachail, *a.* (coigreach-amhuil.) Like a stranger.

Coigridh, *s. f.* Strangers, a company of strangers. Guilibh, a choigridh, an laoch, *ye strangers, weep for the hero.*—*Orr.*

Còigroinn, *s.* Five parts or divisions.

Coig-shliosnach, *a.* Pentagonal; pentelateral.

Coig-shliosnag, aig, *s. f.* A pentagon.

† **Còil**, *s. f.* A corner. Now written *cùil*; which see.

Còil, *s. f.* A coil; a cock of hay.

Còil, *v. a.* Coil or gather hay into cocks. *Pret.* chòil, *coiled*; *fut.* còilidh, *shall coil.*

Coilbhinn, *s. f.* A small shaft.

Coi'leabach, **Coimh-leabach**, aich, *s. c.* A bed-fellow; a concubine.—*Stew. Gen. N. pl.* coi'leabaich, *bed-fellows.*

Coileach, ich, *s. m.* A cock.—*Stew. Matt.* Coileach gaoithe, *a vane, a weather-cock*; coileach dubh, *a black cock, a mountain bird of a deep glossy black, and somewhat larger than a pheasant*; coileach spoghta, *a capon*; coileach dùnain, *a dunghill cock, a game cock*; coileach ruadh, *a heath cock*; coileach Francach, *a Turkey cock*; coileach coille, *a woodcock*; coileach dùitseach, *a curtailed cock*; coileach-oidhche, *an owl.*

Bisc. oillaoc, *a hen. W.* ceiliawg, *a cock. Corn.* kuileog, cheilioc, *and* olyek. *Arm.* quillocq. *Arab.* gheles. *Pers.* kelash.

Coileachach, *a.* Like a cock; of, or belonging to, a cock; abounding in cocks.—*Macdon.*

Coileachail, *a.* (coileach-amhuil.) Like a cock.

Coileachanta, *a.* Like a cock.

Coileach ruadh, aidh, *s. m.* Grouse; the *lagopus altera* of Pliny.

Coileach coille, *s. m.* A woodcock, the *scolopax rusticola* of Linnæus.

Coileach-dubh, *s. m.* A black cock; a mountain bird of a deep glossy black, and somewhat larger than a pheasant; the *tetrao tetrix* of Linnæus.

Coileir, *s. f.* A collar; a neck; *rarely*, a mine, a quarry. *Box. Lex.* coler. *Arm.* collyer. *Fr.* collier.

Coiligeann, inn, *s.* (*Ir.* coilice.) A colic. Coiligeann adhairceach, *a ludicrous name for pregnancy, or for the pains of childbed.*

Coi'lion, **Coimh-lion**, *v. a.* Fulfil, complete, perform, accomplish. *Pret. a.* choi'lion, *fulfilled*; *fut. aff. a.* coi'lionaidh.

Coi'lionadh, **Coimh-lionadh**, aidh, *s. m.* The act of fulfilling; fulfilment, completion; complement; full quantity. Le 'choi'lionadh bogha, *with his complement of bows.*—*Oss. Fin. and Lorm.* Coi'lionadh na h-aimsir, *the fulfilment of time.*—*Stew. Eph.*

Coi'lionta, **Coimh-lionta**, *p. part.* Perfect, perfected; complete, completed, fulfilled; upright. Bha Iacob na dhuine coi'lionta, *Jacob was a [plain] upright man.*—*Stew. Gen.*

Coille, *s. f.* (*Arm.* call. *Corn.* kelli. *Ir.* coill.) A wood, a grove, a forest. Caoirean na coille, *the murmur of the wood.*—*Ull. N. pl.* coiltean. Coille dharaich, *an oakwood*; coille ghiuthais, *a fir-wood*; coille chaltuinn, *a hazel-copse*; coille chnò, *a nuttery*; coille dhearcag, *a wood where blackberries grow.* Fasgadh choilltean, *the shelter of woods.*—*Oss. Cathula.* Cearc choille, *a partridge.*—*Stew. Sam.* Maor coille, *a wood-keeper.*

Coille, *s.* New year's time. Oidche coille, *the first night of January.*

On this night the Gael were wont to observe with great attention the disposition of the atmosphere. According as it is found calm or boisterous, as the wind blows from east, west, south, or north, they prognosticate the nature of the weather till the year's end. The first night of the new year, when the wind blows from the west, they call Dàir na coille, *the night of the fecundation of trees.*—*Statistics, Par. Kirkmichael.*

Coilleag, eig, *s. f.* A cockle—(*Macd.*); *also*, a rural song. Nur sheinneadh tu coilleag, *when thou wouldst sing a song.*—*Macdon.*

Coillearnach, aich, *s. m.* A wooded place.

Coillinn, coinnle, *s. f.* A candle. *Coillinn* seems to be *coille-theine*, the flame of a wooden torch or fir candle;

splinters of fir are at this day used as candles in many parts of the Highlands. *Coillinn* is also written *coinneal.*

Coill-mhias, -mhéis, *s. m.* A wooden dish.

Coillte, *n. pl.* of coille. (*Ir.* coillte.) Woods, forests.

Coillte, *a.* Gelded.

Coillteach, *a.* Woody, wooded, sylvan, woodland. Chlisg na sleibhte coillteach, *the wooded hills startled.—Oss. Duthona.* Coire coillteach, *a wooded dell.—Macdon.*

Coillteach, ich, *s. m.* A wood, a forest; a Celt. Mar chlaoidheas teine coillteach, *as fire consumes a wood.—Sm.* An doimhneachd choillteach, *in the depth of forests.—Mac Lach.*

Coilltean, *n. pl.* of coille. Woods, forests. See Coille.

Coilltear, ir, *s. m.* (*from* coille.) An absconder, a fugitive. *N. pl.* coilltearan.

Coilltearachd, *s. f.* The condition of a fugitive; an absconder.

Coillteil, *a.* (*Ir.* coilltamhail.) Savage, untamed; sylvan, wild, woodland.

Co'imeachd, *s. f.* Attendance; company; train. Na co'-imeachd, *in her attendance, in her train.—Stew. Nah.*

Coimeas, *s. n.* (*Ir. id.*) Comparison, likeness, resemblance; equality; mate; *also*, equal; like. Dithis da 'm b' ionann coimeas, *two who were in all respects equal.—Fingalian Poem.* Thusa is coimeas ri craig, *thou who art like a rock.—Oss. Fing.* Gun do choimeas ri taobh do shoillse, *without thy mate near thy effulgent light.—Oss. Cathula.*

Coimeas, *v. a.* Compare, liken, equal. *Pret. a.* choimeas, *compared; fut. aff. a.* coimeasaidh, *shall compare.*

Coimeasg, *v. a.* (*Corn. Arm.* quemesq. *Lat.* commisceo.) Commingle; mix; compound; amalgamate. *Pret. a.* choimeasg, *mixed: fut. aff. a.* coimeasgaidh, *shall mix.*

Coimeasg, *s. m.* Mixture; a composition; a compound.

Coimeasgadh, aidh, *s. m.* The act of mixing or compounding; a compound; a mixture.

Coimeasgadh, (a), *pr. part.* of coimeasg. Mixing.

Coimeasgta, Coimeasgte, *p. part.* of coimeasg. Mixed, compounded, adulterated.

Coimeasta, *p. part.* of coimeas. Likened, compared, of equal worth or value.

Coimh-chealg, -cheilg, *s. f.* Rebellion; conspiracy.—*Stew. 2 K. ref.*

Coimh-cheangail, *v. a.* (*Ir. id.*) Tie together, unite, couple, bind by compact; league. *Pret. a.* choimh-cheangail.

Coimh-cheangal, ail, *s. m.* (*Ir. id.*) Covenant, agreement, compact, stipulation, league; conspiracy. Luchd brisidh choimh-cheangail, *covenant-breakers.—Stew. Rom.*

Coimh-cheangladh, aidh, *s. m.* A covenanting, a stipulating, a leaguing; a covenant; a stipulation; a compact; a league; a conspiracy.

Coimh-cheumnaich, *v. a.* Accompany; walk together with; keep the same step or pace with another.

Coimh-chliamhuinn, *s. m.* A son-in-law.

Coimh-chothrom, oim, *s. m.* Equilibrium; counterbalance; equipoise.

Coimh-chothromaich, *v.* Counterpoise; counterbalance.

Coimh-dhreachta, *a.* Conformed; proportioned.

Coimheach, *a.* Strange, foreign; shy; sharp; bitter; careless; *also*, a stranger. Do dhia coimheach, *to a strange god.—Sm.* Shéid osnadh choimheach, *a sharp wind blew.—Ull.* Coimhich do 'n chomhfhlaitheachd, *strangers to the commonwealth.—Stew. Eph.* Bò mhaol am buaile choimhich, *a hornless cow in a strange fold.—G. P.*

Coimheachas, ais, *s. m.* (*Ir. id.*) Estrangement; strangeness; shyness; sharpness, as of wind. Coimheachas an teangaidh, *the strangeness of their tongue.—Sm.*

Coimhead, *v. a.* and *n.* (*Ir.* coimead.) Keep, preserve; reserve; look, observe, watch. *Pret. a.* choimhead. Dha coimheadam gràs, *I will keep grace for him.—Sm.* Is e choimheadas daoine simplidh, *it is he who preserves upright men.—Id.* Tannas a coimhead gu h-ard, *a spectre looking loftily.—Oss. Lodin.* Coimhead ri, *look for, expect;* a coimhead ri bàs, *expecting death.—Oss.* Coimhead orm, *look on me.*

Coimhead, id, *s. m.* A looking; a watching, observing; inspection; a watch; observation; a keeping; a reserving. Fear coimhid, *an inspector, a watch, a scout;* luchd-coimhid, *watchmen, inspectors, scouts.*

Coimheadachd, *s. f.* A convoy; an inspecting; a watching; observation. Thoir coimheadachd, *convoy;* a thoirt coimheadachd, *to convoy.*

Coimheadaiche, *s. m.* A keeper—(*Stew. Ecc.*); an inspector; a scout; a spy. *N. pl.* coimheadaichean.—*Stew. Ecc. ref.*

Coimhearsnach, aich, *s. m.* (coimh-fhearsnach.) A neighbour. *N. pl.* coimhearsnaich.

Coimhearsnachd, *s. f.* Neighbourhood, vicinity. Anns a choimhearsnachd, *in the neighbourhood;* air fad na coimhearsnachd, *throughout the neighbourhood.*

Coimheas, *a.* (*Ir. id.*) Equal; indifferent; alike. Is coimheas leam bhi beo no marbh, *life and death are alike to me.—Old Poem.*

Coimheasail, *a.* Equally respectable; of equal worth.

Coimheasda, *a.* Of equal worth; comparable.

† Coimheasgar, air, *s. m.* A conflict.—*Shaw.*

Coimh-éigneachadh, aidh, *s. m.* A constraining; a forcing, urging, compelling; constrainment, compulsion.

Coimh-éignich, *v. a.* (*Ir. id.*) Constrain, force, urge, compel. *Pret. a.* choimh-éignich, *constrained.* Choimh-éignich i e, *she constrained him.—Stew. 2 K. ref.*

Coimh-fhearsnach, aich, *s. m.* A neighbour. *N. pl.* coimh-fhearsnaich.

Coimh-fhearsnachd, *s. f.* A neighbourhood. Anns a choimh-fhearsnachd, *in the neighbourhood.*

Coimh-fhios, *s. f.* Conscience. An inntinn agus an coimh-fhios, *their minds and their consciences.—Stew. Tit.*

Coimh-fhiosach, *a.* Conscientious. Gu coimh-fhiosach, *conscientiously.*

Coimh-fhiosrach, *a.* Conscious.

Coimh-fhiosrachd, *s. f.* Consciousness.

Coimh-fhreagair, *v. a.* Suit; correspond. *Pret.* choimh-fhreagair.

Coimh-fhreagarach, *a.* Suitable; corresponding; fit; proper.

Coimh-ghleac, *s. m.* A wrestle; a struggle; a conflict; a competition.

Coimh-ghreimich, *v.* Fasten to, cling to, adhere to. *Pret.* choimh-greimich.

Coimh-ionann, *a.* Alike, equal. Written also *comh-ionann.*

Coimh-ionannas, ais, *s. m.* Equality; similarity.

Coimh-leabach, aich, *s. m.* A bed-fellow; a concubine.—*Stew. Song Sol. ref. N. pl.* coimh-leabaichean.

Coimh-leasaich, *v. a.* Restore, requite. *Pret. a.* choimh-leasaich; *fut. aff.* coimh-leasaichidh.

Coimh-lion, *v. a.* Fulfil, accomplish, perform, complete. *Pret. a.* choimh-lion, *fulfilled; fut. aff. a.* coimh-lionaidh.

Coimh-lionadh, aidh, *s. m.* A fulfilling; an accomplishing; a fulfilment.

Coimh-liong, *s. m.* A race; a running together. Ruitheamaid a choiliong, *let us run the race.—Stew. Heb.*

Coimh-lionta, *p. part.* of coimh-lion. Fulfilled, accomplished, perfected; perfect; upright.

Coimh-liontachd, *s. f.* Completion, fulfilment; completeness, perfectness.

Coimhmeas, *s. m.* See Coimeas.

Coimh-neartachadh, aidh, *s. m.* A confirming; a strengthening; a confirmation.

Coimh-neartaich, *v. a.* Confirm; strengthen. *Pret. a.* choimh-neartaich, *strengthened.*

Coimh-neartaichte, *p. part.* Strengthened, confirmed.

† **Coimhreach**, ich, *s. m.* An assistant.—*Shaw.*

Coimh-reir, *s. f.* Syntax, construction.—*Shaw.*

Coimh-reite, *s. f.* Agreement, reconciliation.—*Stew.* 2 *Cor.*

Coimh-reult, *s.* A constellation. *N. pl.* coimh-reultan.

Coimh-riachdantas, ais, *s. m.* Distress; great want.

Coimhsich, *v. a.* Perceive. *Pret.* choimhsich, *perceived; fut. aff.* coimhsichidh, *shall perceive.*

Coimh-theach, *s. m.* A house where several families dwell.

Coimh-theachaiche, *s. m.* One who lives in the same house with another.

Coimh-theachas, ais, *s. m.* (*Ir. id.*) Cohabitation; a living together.

Coimh-thigheas, eis, *s. m.* Cohabitation; a living together.

Coimh-thionail, *v. a.* Assemble, gather together. *Pret. a.* choimh-thionail.

Coimh-thional, ail, *s. m.* An assembly, a congregation. *N. pl.* coimh-thionalan.

Coimin, *s. f.* (co'iomain.) *Ir. id.* A common; suburbs.

Coimirc, *s. f.* A brief; an extract; an abridgment.

Coimisdear, ir, *s. m.* A commissary.

Coimisdearachd, *s. f.* The office or business of a commissary; a commissariat.

Coimpire, *s. m.* A match, an equal; one who is of the same mind with another. Fear bu choimpire dhomh féin, *a man who was my equal.*—*Stew. Ps.*

Coimpreadh, idh, *s. m.* A conception.

Coimseach, *a.* Indifferent, careless; deliberate.—*Shaw.*

Coin, *gen. sing.* and *n. pl.* of cu. (*Arm.* qon, *dogs. Lat.* can-is.) Of a dog; dogs.

† **Coinbhearsaid**, *s. f.* Conversation.

† **Coin-bheath**, *s. f.* A feast, an entertainment.

Coin-bheathaiche, *s. m.* A guest at an entertainment.

Coin-bhile, *s. f.* The dog-berry tree.

† **Coin-bhliochd**, *s. f.* (*Lat.* conflictus.) A conflict, a battle.

Coin-bhraghad, aid, *s. m.* A disease in the throat.—*Shaw.*

Coin-chriche, *s. pl.* Gag-teeth.

† **Coindealg**, eilg, *s. m.* (*Ir. id.*) Counsel; comparison; similitude; criticism.—*Shaw.*

Coindean, ein, *s. m.* A kit.

Coindris, *s.* Dog-brier.

Còineach, ich, *s. m.* Moss. *N. pl.* coinich. Clachan le 'n còinich, *stones with their grey moss.*—*Oss. Cathluno.* Air lic chòinich, *on mossy stones.*—*Orr.*

Coineadh, idh, *s. m.* A reproof.

Coineall, eill, *s. m.* A loan. See Coingheall.

Coineallach, *a.* See Coingheallach.

Coinean, ein, *s. m.* A rabbit, a coney. Tha 'n coinean neo-ghlan, *the rabbit is unclean.*—*Stew. Lev. N. pl.* coineana *and* coineanan, *rabbits.*—*Stew. Pro.*

Da. cainin. *Du.* conyn. *Ir.* coinin. *Corn.* couniel *and* kynin. *Fr.* † conin: in the *Patois* of Franche Comté, *queni.* *Vulgar Gr.* κουνετι. *Lat.* cuniculus.

Coineanach, *a.* Abounding in rabbits; like a rabbit; of, or belonging to, a rabbit.

Coin-fheasgar, air, *s. m.* Evening.

Coin-fheasgarach, *a.* Late.

Coin-fhiacall, aill, *s. m.* Dog-teeth; canine madness.—*Shaw.*

† **Coin-fliochd**, *s. f.* (*Ir. id. Lat.* conflictus.) A battle, a conflict.

Coingheall, *s. m.* A loan; a condition. *N. pl.* coingheallan. Thoir coingheall, *lend;* thoir an coingheall, *lend;* gabh coingheall, *borrow;* thug iad an coingheall, *they lent.*—*Stew. Exod.*

Coingheallach, *a.* Ready to lend; like a loan; of, or pertaining to, a loan; conditional. Duine a bhios coingheallach, *a man who is ready to lend.*—*Stew. Ps.*

Coinicear, eir, *s. m.* A rabbit warren.

Coinlin, *s. f.* A stalk, a bud. Air aon choinlin, *on one stalk.*—*Stew. Gen.*

Coinlion, lin, *s. m.* A nostril. *N. pl.* coinliona, *nostrils.*

Coinne, *s. m.* (*for* coinneamh.) *Ir. id.* A meeting, a gathering, a congregation. Sa choinne mhòir, *in the great congregation.*—*Sm.*

† **Coinne**, *s. f.* A woman.

Gr. γυνη *and* γυναικος, *woman. Pruss.* and *Lith.* ganna. *Hung.* kone, *a new-married woman. Goth.* quino. *Lat. by synecd.* cunnus, *a woman:* cunnus fuit causa teterrima belli.—*Hor. Isl.* kona, kuenna. *Swed.* qwina. *Anglo-Sax.* cwen. *Eng.* queen *and* quean. *Old Eng.* gouine, *a prostitute:* hence the expression, *son of a gun,* i. e. *gouine.*

Coinneachadh, aidh, *s. m.* The act or circumstance of meeting; a meeting; an assembly.

Coinneal, coinnle, *s. f.* A candle; a torch. *N. pl.* coinnlean; *d. pl.* coinnlibh, *to candles.* Cha d' theid a coinneal as, *her candle goes not out.*—*Stew. G. B.* Rannsuichidh mise le coinnlibh, *I will search with candles.*—*Stew. Zeph.* Las a choinneal, *light the candle;* cuir as a choinneal, *put out the candle;* coinneal chéire, *a wax-candle;* coinneal ghiumhais, *a fir-candle.*

Arm. cantal. *Gr.* κανδηλα. *Lat.* candela. *Turk.* kaendyl. *Fr.* chandelle.

Coinnealach, *a.* Abounding in candles; like a candle.

Coinnealair, *s. m.* A tallow-chandler, a candle-maker.

Coinnealdair, *s. m.* (*from* coinneal.) A candle-maker, a tallow-chandler.

Coinneamh, eimh, *s. f.* (*Ir.* coinne, *meeting. W.* cyvnod, *conjunctive.*) A meeting; a facing or opposing; an assembly; a convention; interview; opposite. Coinneamh nan cairdean, *the meeting of friends.*—*Ull.* Nar coinneamh, *to meet us.*—*Id.* Rach an coinneamh, *go to meet.* Chaidh i na choinneamh, *she went to meet him.*—*Stew. Gen.* Thoir coinneamh, *give a meeting, give an interview;* cum coinneamh, *hold a meeting; face; keep an assignation;* mu 'choinneamh, *opposite; opposite him* or *it;* mu 'coinneamh, *opposite her;* mu 'n coinneamh, *opposite to them.*

† **Coinneas**, eis, *s. m.* A ferret.—*Shaw. N. pl.* coinneasan.

Coinneasach, *a.* Abounding in ferrets; like a ferret.

Coinnich, *v. a.* Meet, face, oppose, encounter; stop the progress of a person or thing. *Pret. a.* choinnich, *met; fut. aff. a.* coinnichidh.

Coinnichte, *p. part.* of coinnich. Met, opposed, encountered, faced. *Asp. form.* choinnichte.

Coinnle, *gen. sing.* of coinneal.

Coinnlean, *n. pl.* of coinneal. Candles.

Coinnlearachd, *s. f.* Candle-making.

Coinnleir, *s. m.* (*Ir.* coinloir.) A candlestick. *N. pl.* coinnleirean. Ann an coinnleir, *in a candlestick.*—*Stew. Mat.*

Coinnseas, eis, *s. m.* Conscience. More properly *coimhfhios.*

† **Coint**, *s. f.* A woman.

Runic, quind, *a wife. Da.* quinde, *woman.* Chaucer has *queint, pars nefanda mulieris.*

† COINTEAN, ein, *s. m.* (*Ir.* comtin.) A contentious man, a wrangler; a controversy. Perhaps *cainntean.*

COINTEANACH, *a.* Contentious.—*Shaw.* Gu cointeanach, *contentiously.*

COINTEANACHD, *s. f.* Contentiousness, quarrelsomeness.

CO'IONANN, *a.* (*Gr.* κοινωνος, *of the same condition. Ir.* coimhionann) Alike, similar, equal. Co'ionann riumsa, *equal to me.*

CO'IONANNACHD, *s. f.* Similarity, equality.

† COIP, *s. f.* (*Lat* copia, *forces. Ir.* coip.) A troop; a tribe; a copy.

CÒIP, *gen. sing* of còp; which see

COIP-GHEAL, *a.* Foamy; white with foam. Mhuir choip-gheal, *the foamy sea.*—*Old Song.*

CÒIR, *gen* coire, còrach, *s. f.* (*Gr* χωρος, *land Arm.* guyr *and* guir) Right, justice; possession; property; business; presence, vicinity, nearness; custom, usage. Càis na còrach, *the cause of justice.*—*Old Song.* Cum còir, *support right*, cumaibh còir riu, *support their right.*—*Sm* Tog romham air chòir an sgiath, *carry the shield as usual before me.*—*Oss. Fing.* Thuille na còrach, *more than the just quantity, over and above what is right;* gach fear thachair nan còir, *every man who came near them.*—*Old Legend.*

CÒIR, *a* (*W.* cywir. *Ir.* coir.) Good, just, kind; civil; proper; near. Gairdeachas air daoine còir, *joy on good men.*—*Sm* Is còir dhomh, *I ought*, bu chòir dha am maille treun, *he ought* [*would require*] *to be in strong armour.*—*Oss. Fing.* An duine còir! *the worthy man!*

COIR, *v.*, *provincial* for cuir; which see.

CÒIR, (an) Near; in the way. Nam chòir, *near me, in my way*, thig am chòir, *come near me.*—*Oss. Com*

CÒIR-BHREITH, *s* Birthright. Mo chòir-bhreith, *my birthright.*—*Stew. Gen.*

COIRBTE, *a* Corrupt; cross; perverse; hostile. An triath bu choirbte colg, *the chief of the most hostile wrath.*—*Oss Fing. Lat* corruptus. *Ir.* coiripthe.

COIRBTEACHD, *s f.* (*Ir* coiriptheachd) Corruptness; crossness; perverseness; hostility.—*Stew. Pro. ref*

COIRC, coirce, *s m* (*W* ceirch. *Arm.* qerch) Oats. Aran coirce, *oat bread*, coirc nan speur, [*celestial corn*] *manna.*—*Sm* Am cur a choirce, *oat-sowing time.*—*Old Song.*

COIRCEACH, *a* Abounding in oats; made of oats; of, or belonging to, oats

COIRCEAG, eig, *s m.* A bee-hive. *N. pl.* coirceagan

CÒIRD, *v* Agree; reconcile *Pret a* choird, *agreed*, *fut aff* coirdidh, *shall agree.* Coirdibh, *agree, be reconciled.*

COIRDEAN, ein, *s. m* A small rope; a string.

COIRDEAS, eis, *s. m.* Agreement, reconciliation.

COIRE, *s. m* (*Ir. id*) A caldron, a kettle; a mountain dell. Cuir air coire, *put on a caldron.*—*Stew. Ez.* Gach coire 's gach cas, *each dell and waterfal.*—*Ull.* Coire togalach, *a brewer's caldron. N. pl.* coireachan. As a choire anns an teine, *out of the kettle into the fire.*—*G. P.*

COIRE, *s. f* (*Ir. id*) Harm; wrong, crime; offence; damage; trespass; defect; charge; complaint. *N. pl.* coireannan. Dean coire, *offend, do wrong*, ma ni anam coire, *if a soul trespass.*—*Stew. Lev.* Gach gnè coire, *every kind of damage.*—*Stew Exod.* Coire bàis, *a capital crime.*—*Stew Acts.* Coireannan lionmhor, *various charges or complaints.*—*Id.*

COIREACH, *a* Faulty; guilty, criminal; in fault. Is tusa 's coireach, *it is you who are to blame.*

COIREACHADH, aidh, *s. m.* The act of blaming or of accusing; an accusation.

COIREACHAN, *n. pl.* of coire. Kettles, caldrons.

CÒIREAD, eid, *s. m.* Probity, goodness, kindness. Cha n' fhac mi a leithid air chòiread, *I saw not his equal for kindness.*

COIREADH, idh, *s. m.* A caldron. See COIRE.

COIREAL, eil, *s. m.* Coral.—*Stew. Job.*

COIREALACH, *a.* Like coral; abounding in coral; of coral.

COIREAMAN, ain, *s m.* Coriander.

COIREAMANACH, *a.* Abounding in coriander; like coriander.

COIREAN, ein, (*dim.* of coire) A little caldron; a little dell. Gach allt 's gach caol-choirean, *every brook and narrow dell.*—*Old Legend. N. pl.* coireinean; *d. pl.* coireinibh.

COIREANACH, *a.* Abounding in little dells.

COIREISEACH, *a.* Important; with an air of importance.

COIRIB, *v. a.* Corrupt. *Pret.* choirib; *fut. aff.* coiribidh.

COIRICH, *v a.* (*Ir.* coirigh) Blame, find fault with; charge, accuse; reprove. *Pret. a.* choirich, *blamed; fut. aff.* coirichidh, *shall blame.*

COIRICHEAN, *s. pl.* Records; title-deeds.

COIRICHTE, *p. part.* of coirich. Blamed, accused, charged, reproved.

† COIRIOLL, *s. f.* Noise; *also*, symphony, music. More frequently written *caireall.*

COIRRIOLLACH, *a.* Noisy; *also*, harmonious.

COIRM, *s. f.* A kind of beer or ale used by the old Irish; a pot companion. See CUIRM.

COIRMEAG, eig, *s. f.* A female gossip.

COIRNEACH, ich, *s. m.* The kingsfisher. Written also *cairneach.*

COIRNEALAIR, *s. m.* A colonel. On chaidh an coirnealair fu thalamh, *since the colonel was buried.*—*Old Song.*

COIRNEAN, ein, *s. m.* A curl.

COIRNEANANACH, *a.* Frizzled, curled.—*Shaw.*

COIRT, *s. f.* (*Lat.* cortex, *bark.*) Bark; a cart. See CAIRT.

COIRTEAR, eir, *s. m.* See CAIRTEAR.

CÒIS, *gen. sing.* of còs; which see.

COIS, (an), *adv* and *prep.* Near, beside, by, close by. An cois na mara, *near the sea.*—*Oss.* An cois nan aibhnichean, *close by the rivers.*—*Sm.* Na chois, *near him* or *it;* nan cois, *near them*, nam chois, *near me.*

COIS, (ri), *adv.* and *prep.* Near, beside, by, close by. Ri cois na Mara Ruaidh, *near the Red Sea.*—*Sm.*

COIS-BHEAIRT, *s pl* Shoes and stockings; boots; greaves. Cois-bheairt umha, *greaves of brass.*—*Stew Sam.* Cuir ort do chois-bheairt, *put on your shoes and stockings.*

COIS-CHEUM, *s m* (*Ir. id.*) A step, a pace; a stride

COIS-CHEUMNACH, *a.* Stepping; pacing.

COIS-CHEUMNAICH, *v. n.* and *a.* Step; pace; measure by pacing.

† COISDE, *s f* (*Ir id.*) A coach; *also*, a jury.

COISDEAR, eir, *s. m* A coachman *N. pl.* coisdearan.

COISE, *gen sing.* of cas *or* cos Of a foot. Do bhonn a choise, *to the sole of his foot.*—*Stew. Gen.* Saighdear coise, *a foot-soldier.*

COISE, *s. f* (*provincial.*) *Scotch*, coshe. A coach.

COISEACHADH, aidh, *s. m* (*from* cos.) The act of walking; pedestrianism

COISEACHADH, (a), *pr. part.* of coisich Walking.

COISEACHD, *s. f.* (*from* cos) Walking, pedestrianism; the habit of walking. A coiseachd, *walking*, bi coiseachd, *be going, be off*

CÒISEAGACH, *a.* Snug, warm, sheltered.

† COISEAMHAN, ain, *s. m.* A shoemaker.—*Shaw. N. pl.* coiseamhain

COISEAN, ein, *s. m.* A stalk, a stem.

COISEANACH, *a.* Having a stalk or stem; having a long stalk or stem.

† **Coiseanaich**, *v.* Conjure; bless one's self.—*Shaw.*

Coisg, *v. a.* (*Ir. id.*) Quench, extinguish; silence; quell; quiet; wean; restrain; staunch, as blood. *Pret. a.* choisg; *fut. aff. a.* coisgidh. Coisg do phathadh, *quench thy thirst.* Choisgeadh an teine, *the fire was quenched.*—*Stew. Numb.* Choisgeadh an t-uisge, *the water was restrained.*—*Stew. O. T.*

Coisgeach, *a.* Quenching, quelling; restraining; staunching.

Coisgeadh, idh, *s. m.* A quenching; a quelling; a restraining; a staunching.

Coisgear, *fut. pass.* of coisg. Shall be quenched.

† **Coisgidh**, *fut. aff. a.* of coisg. Shall or will quench.

† **Coisglidh**, *a.* Still, quiet; diligent.—*Shaw.*

Coisgte, *p. part.* of coisg. Quenched; extinguished; calmed; appeased; settled; tranquillized.

Coisich, *v. n.* Walk; travel; move off; depart. *Pret. a.* choisich, *walked*; *fut. aff. a.* coisichidh, *shall walk.*

Coisiche, *s. m.* (*Ir.* coisidhe.) A pedestrian; a footman; a traveller. Se ceud mile coisiche, *six hundred thousand footmen*; a choisiche na beinne, *thou traveller of the hill.*—*Old Song.* Saighdear coisiche, *a foot-soldier.*

Coisinn, *s. f.* Gain, advantage, profit; earning.

Coisinn, *v. a.* Gain, win; obtain; earn. *Pret. a.* choisinn, *gained*; *fut. aff. a.* coisinnidh *and* coisnidh, *shall gain*; *fut. sub.* choisneas. An laoch a choisneas buaidh, *the hero who gains victory.*—*Mac Lach.* Tha i 'g a coisinn, *she is out at service.*

Coisinnte, *p. part.* of coisinn. Gained, won, obtained; earned. Anns gach ceaird tha thu coisinnte, *in every trade you are an adept.*—*Old Song.*

† **Coisir**, *s. f.* A company; a feast.

Coisneadh, idh, *s. m.* A gaining or winning; profit, gain; service. Mach air choisneadh, *out at service.*

Coisneadh, (a), *pr. part.* of coisinn. Gaining, winning.

Coisreagan, ain, *s. m.* A consecration.

Coisridh, *s. f.* A jovial club; infantry; a company on foot; an entertainment; a concert of birds.

Coisrig, *v. a.* Consecrate; make sacred; sanctify; bless. *Pret. a.* choisrig, *consecrated*; *fut. aff. a.* coisrigidh, *shall consecrate.*

Coisrigeach, *a.* Consecrative.

Coisrigeadh, idh, *s. m.* The act or ceremony of consecrating; a consecration; a sanctifying.

Coisrigidh, *fut. aff. a.* of coisrig.

Coisrigte, *p. part.* of coisrig. Consecrated.

† **Coist**, *v.* See **Caisd**.

Coistear, eir, *s. m.* A coachman. *N. pl.* coistearan.

Coistearachd, *s. f.* Coach-driving; the business of a coachman.

Coit, *s. f.* A small boat, a coracle; a canoe; a quoit. *N. pl.* coitean.

Coit-cheann, *a.* (*Ir. id.*) Common, public, general. Gu coit-cheann, *publicly, commonly.*

Coit-cheannachd, *s. f.* Community; commonness; generalness.

Coit-cheannas, ais, *s. m.* Community; the state of having things in common; copartnership.

Coit-cheanta, *a.* Common, public, general. Gu coit-cheanta, *commonly.*

Coit-chionn, *a.* Common, public, general. Gu coit-chionn, *commonly*; air aithris gu coit-chionn, *commonly reported. Stew. N. T.*

Coit-chionnas, ais, *s. m.* Community; partnership.

Coit-chionnta, *a.* Common, public, general. Gu coit-chionnta, *commonly.*

Coitear, eir, *s. m.* A cottager. *N. pl.* coitearan.

Col, *s. m.* (*Ir. id.* G. κωλυω, *prevent.*) Incest; impediment, obstacle, prohibition.

Còla, **Còladh**, aidh, *s. m.* A bar; an obstacle; a door. Bha dhorus gun chòla fial, *his door without bar was open.*—*Oss. Fin. and Lor.* Da chòladh, *two doors.*—*Stew.* 1 *K.* See also **Comhladh**.

Còlach, *a.* (*Ir. id.*) Wicked, impious, incestuous.

Còlach, aich, *s. m.* A door. *N. pl.* còlaichean, *doors.* Colaichean do 'n òr bhuidhe, *doors of yellow gold.*—*Old Poem.*

Còlachadh, **Comhlachadh**, aidh, *s. m.* A meeting, an encounter, an intercepting.

Colagag, aig, *s. f.* The forefinger.

† **Colagan**, ain, *s. m.* A salmon. *N. pl.* colagain.

Còlaich, **Comhlaich**, *v. a.* Meet; oppose; interpret; stop the progress of a person or thing. *Pret. a.* chòlaich, *met.* Chòlaich sinn am farum ar stailinn, *we met in the noise of our steel.*—*Oss. Duthona.* *Fut. pass.* còlaichear.

Còlaichidh, **Comhlaichidh**, *fut. aff. a.* of còlaich *or* comhlaich, *shall meet.*

Colaidh, *a.* Incestuous, lewd, carnal, venereal.

Colaidheachd, *s. f.* The practice of incest; lewdness, carnality, venery.

† **Colais**, *s. f.* Cabbage.

Colaisde, *s. f.* (*Ir. id.*) A college or university.

Colaisdeach, *a.* Belonging to a college; *also, substantively,* a collegiate.

Colaman, ain, *s. m.* (*Lat.* columba. *Corn.* golom.) A dove, a pigeon. Colaman fiadhaich, *a wild dove.*

Còlan, ain, *s. m.* (*perhaps* comh-lann.) A companion, a companion in arms. Sgiath chòlain mo dheagh Oscair, *the shield of my beloved Oscar's companion.*—*Oss. Gaul.* Righdir còlain, *a knight companion.*

Colann, ainn, *s. f.* (*Ir.* colan.) A body; a carcass; flesh, See **Coluinn**.

Co'lannachd, **Comh-lannachd**, *s. f.* Duelling; fighting with swords or spears.

Co'lannaireachd, **Comh-lannaireachd**, *s. f.* Sword-exercise.

Colbain, *s. m.* The rope of a ship.—*Macd.*

Colbh, *s. m.* (*Ir. id.*) A sceptre; a reed; the stalk of a plant; a pillar, a post, a bed-post. Colbh nam buadh, *the sceptre of victory.*—*Mac. Lach.* Neoil mar cholbh, *clouds like pillars.*—*Old Poem.*

† **Colbh**, *s. m.* Love, esteem, friendship.—*Shaw.*

Colbhairt, *s. f.* Colewort.

† **Colbhtach**, aich, *s. m.* A cow-calf.

Colach, aich, *s. m.* A flock-bed.—*Shaw.*

Co'leagh, **Comh-leagh**, *v. a.* Melt together, amalgamate.

Colg, cuilg, *s. m.* (*Ir. id.*) A prickle; awn; any sharp-pointed thing; a sword, a spear; a fierce look; rage; ardour; hair; the point of a weapon. Colg eorna, *the awn of barley*; am measg nan ceud colg, *amid the hundred swords.*—*Oss. Gaul.* Laoich fo cholg, *heroes in a wrath.*—*Sm.* Is liath colg, *of the greyest hair.*—*Oss. Com.* A tilgeadh a chuilg, *casting the hair.*—*Macint.* An aghaidh a chuilg, *against the grain.*—*Oss. Derm.*

Colgach, *a.* (*Ir. id.*) Prickly; bearded; awny; hairy; scaly; fierce, furious, wrathful, fretful. A shùil colgach, *his fierce eye.*—*Oss. Cathluno.* Mar thannas nan leum colgach, *like a furiously bounding spectre.*—*Oss. Tem.*

Colgan, ain, *s. m.* A salmon. *N. pl.* colgain.

Colganta, *a.* (colg.) Brisk; lively; martial; smart; bitter; freezing; prickly. Fir cholganta, *smart-looking men.*—*Macint.* Gu colganta, *martially.*

Colgantas, ais, *s. m.* Briskness; liveliness; smartness; bitterness.

Colgaradh, *a.* Brisk; lively; smart; bitter; biting, as frost; freezing. Mios colgaradh, *a freezing month.*—*Macfar.*

Colg-bhruidhinn, *s. m.* Butcher's broom.

Colgrasach, *a.* Prickly.

Coll, *s. m.* (*Ir. id.*) Destruction; hazel; the name of the letter C.

Colla, *gen. sing.* of coluinn; which see.

Collach, aich, *s. m.* A fat heifer; a boar. In this latter sense it is more frequently written *cullach*; which see.

† **Colladh**, aidh, *s. m.* Sleep, rest.—*Shaw.*

Collaid, *s. f.* (*Ir. id.*) A two-years-old heifer.

Collaidh, *a.* Incestuous; carnal, lewd, venereal. Gu collaidh, *carnally.*—*Stew. Lev.*

Collaidheachd, *s. f.* Incestuousness; carnality; lewdness; venery.

Coll-leabaidh, *s. f.* A bedstead.

† **Coll-chno**, *s. f.* A filbert.—*Shaw.*

† **Coll-choille**, *s. f.* A hazel-wood.

Colltach, aich, *s. f.* A fleet, a navy.

Colm, *s. m.* A dove, a pigeon.
Lat. columba. *Corn.* goulm *and* coulm. *Arm.* coulm *and* kulm. *Ir.* colm.

Colmach, aich, *s. m.* A dove-cote, a pigeon-house.

Colman, ain, *s. m.* (*dim.* of colm.) A dove, a pigeon. Colman coille, *a ring-dove*; colman cathaich, *a whoop.*—*Shaw.* Written also *columan*; which see.

Colmhuinn, *s. f.* A pillar, a post.
Lat. columna. *Gr.* κολωνα. *W.* colovn. *Span.* coluna.

Colmhuinneach, *a.* Columnar; full of pillars; like a pillar.

Colm-lann, -lainn, *s. n.* (*Ir. id.*) A dovecote.

Colna, *gen. sing.* of coluinn; which see.

Colog, aig, *s. f.* (*Ir. id.*) A collop, a steak.

Colpa, ai, *s. m.* A single cow or horse.—*Shaw.*

Colpach, aich, *s. m.* (*Ir. id.*) A heifer; a cow; a steer; a colt. *N. pl.* colpaich. Bheirear colpaich dhuit, *heifers shall be offered to thee.*—*Sm.*

† **Colt**, colta, *s. m.* Meat, victuals.

Coltach, *a.* Like, similar; likely.

Coltachd, *s. f.* Likeliness; similarity, resemblance; likelihood; appearance.

Coltar, air, *s. m.* A coulter or ploughshare. Gu speal is coltar, *to pruning-hook and ploughshare.*—*Sm. N. pl.* coltair.
Lat. culter. *W.* cwlltyr. *Arm.* coultr. *Ir.* coltar. *Corn.* colter.

Coltas, ais, *s. m.* Likeness; appearance; likeliness; resemblance; likelihood. A réir coltais, *in all likelihood; according to appearance.* Mar sin bha 'choltas, *such was his appearance.*—*Oss. Tem.* Fear do choltais, *a man of thy appearance; a man like thee.*—*Old Song.*

† **Coltra**, *a.* Dark, gloomy.

Coltraiche, *s. m.* A razor-bill.

Co'luadar, **Comhluadar**, air, *s. m.* A company. Cum comhluadar, *keep company.*

† **Coluinn**, *s. f.* A collection of dressed victuals made all over the country by the poor on New Year's day.

Coluinn, *gen.* colla *and* colna, (*for* coluinne.) *Gr.* κωλον, *a limb.* A body, a carcass. Gniomhara na colla, *the deeds of the body.*—*Stew. Rom. N. pl.* coluinnean.

Colum, uim, *s. m.* A dove, a pigeon. Mar cholum air carraig na h-Ullach, *like a dove on the rock of Ullach.*—*Oss. Gaul.*
Ir. colom. *Corn.* golom *and* kolom. *Arm.* kulm, coulm, *and* kulym. *Lat.* columb-a.

Columan, ain, *s. m.* (*dim.* of colum.) A dove, a pigeon; a young dove or pigeon. Chuir e mach columan, *he sent out a dove.*—*Stew. Gen.* Columan coille, *a ring-dove*; columan fiadhaich, *a wild pigeon.*

Columhan, ain, *s. m.* (*Ir.* colamhuin.) A prop, a post, a pillar. See **Colmhuinn**.

Còm, cuim, *s. m.* (*Ir. id.*) The body, breast, bosom, waist; belly, bowels; womb; protection, guard. Corruich a chuim, *the rage of his breast.*—*Mac Lach.* Chlisg a chridhe na com, *her heart started in her bosom.*—*Old Legend.* M'anam am chom, *my soul in my body.*—*Oss. Gaul.* Ulluichidh an com cealg, *their bellies shall conceive deceit.*—*Stew. Job.* Iochdar a chuim, *the abdomen.*—*Stew. Pro.* Tinneas cuim, *a bloody flux; any disorder of the intestines.*

Com, *adv.* Why. Mhic Arair com ad thosd? *son of Arar, why art thou silent?*—*Orr.* Written also *c'uime.*

Com, **Comadh**, *a.* Indifferent; careless. Tha mi comadh, *I care not*; is comadh leam iad, *I care not for them.*—*Old Song.* Is comadh leam cogadh na sith, *I care not for peace or war*; tha mi com ort, *I care not for you*; is comadh co dhiùbh, *it is indifferent which*; comadh leat e, *never heed him* or *it.*

† **Comach**, aich, *s. m.* A breach; a defeat, a disaster.—*Shaw.*

Comadair, *s. m.* A romancer; a story-teller. *N. pl.* comadairean.—*Shaw.*

Comadaireachd, *s. f.* Romancing; the habit of feigning stories.

Comaidh, *s. f.* (*more properly* comith, *i. e.* comh-ith.) A share of one's food; eating of the same food. Thoir dhomh comaidh, *give me a share of your food*; gabh comaidh ris, *take out of the same dish with him*; is sona gach cuid an comaidh, *pleasant is every morsel that is shared.*—*G. P.*

Comain, *s. f.* Obligation; recompence; gratuity; favour; a thing agreeable. Tha mi ad chomain, *I am obliged to you*; cha n'eil mi ad chomain, *I am not in your reverence*; comain an uile a ni, *the recompence of evil that shall be done.*—*Sm.* Cha sheall cù air comain, *a dog forgets a favour.*—*G. P.*

Comanach, aich, *s. m.* (*Ir.* cumaineach.) The communion. Làth 'chomanaich, *the communion-day*; làth comanaich, *a communion-day*; luchd comanaich, *communicants.*

Comairce, *s. f.* Written also *comaraich*: which see.

† **Comaoine**, *s. f.* A benefit.

Comar, air, *s. m.* (*for* comh-amar.) A confluence; a way; a meeting; help; a nose.—*Shaw.*

Comarach, *a.* Confluent; auxiliatory; helpful.

Comaradh, aidh, *s. m.* Help, assistance. Thoir comaradh, *give help.*

Comarc, airc, *s. m.* A part; a share. *N. pl.* comaircean.

Comaraich, *v. a.* (*Ir.* comairc.) Protect. *Pret.* chomaraich; *fut.* comaraichidh.

Comaraich, *s. f.* (*Ir.* comairce.) Protection; obligation; favour. Mo chomaraich ort, Oisein, mhic Fhinn, *I ask thy protection, Ossian, son of Fingal.*—*Oss.* Tha mi 'dol a chur comaraich ort, *I have a favour to ask of thee.* Written also *comraich.*

Comas, ais, *s. m.* (*Ir.* cumas.) Power, ability; liberty, permission; the pulse. Gun chomas ruith, *without power of running.*—*Sm.* Thoir comas dha, *give him liberty*; cha 'n eil comas caruch' aig, *he has no power to stir, he has no room to stir.*

Comasach, *a.* (*Ir.* cumasach.) Powerful; able; capable; active; effective. Daoine comasach, *effective men.*—*Stew. Gen.* Comasach air a dheanamh, *capable of doing it. Com.* and *sup.* comasaiche, *more* or *most able.*

Comasaiche, *com.* and *sup.* of comasach.

Comasdair, *s. m.* A commissary. *N. pl.* comasdairean.

Comasdaireachd, *s. f.* A commissariat; the business of a commissary.

Comasg, aisg, *s. m.* A mixture; a composition; a fight.

Comasgachd, *s. f.* A composition; a mixture.—*Shaw.*

Combach, aich, *s. m.* A companion; a mate; a breach; a defeat. Ceud combach do mhnaoi, *the first companion [husband] of thy wife.*—*Mac Lach.* *N. pl.* combaich.

Combaiche, *s. f.* Friendship; companionship.

Combaisd, *s. f.* A compass, a mariner's compass. Dh' fhalbh a chombaisd is na siùil, *the compass and the sails are gone.*—*Macfar.*

Combeirce, *s. f.* Dedication.—*Shaw.*

Comh, *insep. prep.*, equal to the Latin *con* in composition; as, comh-chruinnich, *congregate.* *Comh* is also written *co'* and *coimh.*

Comhachag, aig, *s. f.* An owl or owlet. Chualas a chomhachag a creig, *the owl was heard from its rock.*—*Ull.* This bird is the *strix ulula* of Linnœus.

† **Comhachd**, *s. f.* Now written *cumhachd.*

Comhachdach, *a.* Now written *cumhachdach.*

Comhad, *a.* (*i. e.* comh-fhad.) Equal, even, lineal; like. See **Comhfad**.

Comhad, aid, *s. m.* A parable, a resemblance, a comparison; the two last quartans of a verse. *N. pl.* comhadan; *d. pl.* comhadaibh. Ann an comhadaibh, *in parables.*

Comhadh, aidh, *s. m.* Preservation; a groan; a bribe. More commonly written *cumhadh.*

† **Comhagal**, ail, *s. m.* A conference.—*Shaw.*

Comhaich, *v. a.* Collect, gather.—*Stew. G. B.* *Pret. a.* chomhaich, *collected; fut. aff. a.* comhaichidh, *shall collect.*

Comhaidh, *s. m.* A keeper; a reward.—*Shaw.*

Comh-aigne, *s. f.* A similar passion or affection; a similar feeling; a fellow-feeling. Duine aig an robh comh-aigne ruinne, *a man who had like passions with ourselves.*—*Stew. Pet.*

Comh-aigneach, *a.* Having similar passions or affections.

Còmhail, *s.* See **Comhdhail**.

Comh-aimsireach, ich, *s. m.* (*Ir. id.*) A cotemporary.

Comh-aimsireach, *a.* Cotemporary, coeval.

Comh-ainm, *s. m.* A surname; a namesake.

Còmhair, *s. m.* A dry-stone-builder. *N. pl.* còmhairean.

Còmhaireachd, *s. f.* Dry-stone-building.

Comhair, (an), *adv.* and *prep.* (*Ir. id.*) Opposite, against, over-against. Chaidh mi an comhair mo chùil, *I went backwards;* chaidh iad an comhair an cùil, *they went backwards.*—*Stew. Gen.* Chaidh e an comhair a chinn, *he fell headlong;* dh' eirich Fionn na comhair, *Fingal rose to meet her.*—*Old Poem.*

Comhairce, *s. f.* Mercy, quarter; protection. See **Comraich** and **Comaraich**.

Co-mhaireann, *a.* Equally lasting. Co-mhaireann ris a ghrèin, *as lasting as the sun.*—*Sm.*

Comhairle, *s. f.* An advice; a council; a convocation; a synod. Bheir mi comhairle ort, *I will give thee an advice.*—*Stew. Exod.* Gabh comhairle, *take advice, be advised;* cuir comhairle, *confer, consult, ask advice;* chuir e chomhairle ri daoinibh òg, *he consulted young men.*—*Stew.* 1 *K.* Luchd comhairle, *counsellors;* luchd comhairle an righ, *the king's counsellors.*—*Mac Lach.* Ball na comhairle diomhair, *a member of the privy council;* comhairle carraid gun a h-iarruidh, cha d' fhuair i riamh am meas bu chòir dhi, *a friend's advice unasked, is never appreciated.*—*G. P.*

Comhairle seems to be *comh-thuirle*, a sitting down together; so *consilium* (from *con-salio*) *quasi in sententiam unam consiliens.*

Comhairle-dhiomhair, *s. f.* Private advice; privy council. Ball na comhairle diomhair, *a member of the privy council.*

Comhairleach, ich, *s. m.* A counsellor. *N. pl.* comhairliche. Comhairleach diomhair, *a privy counsellor;* cò bu chomhairleach dha? *who was his adviser?*—*Stew. Rom.*

Comhairleachadh, aidh, *s. m.* An advising; an admonition. Cha ghabh e comhairleachadh, *he cannot be advised.*

Comhairleachadh, (a), *pr. part.* of comhairlich. Advising, counselling. Ciod tha sibh a comhairleachadh? *what do you advise?*—*Stew.* 1 *K.*

Comhairlich, *v. a.* (*Ir.* comhairligh.) Advise, admonish. *Pret.* chomhairlich, *advised; fut. aff. a.* comhairlichidh.

Comh-airp, *s. f.* Strife; emulation; rivalry. Perhaps *comh-oidhrip.*

Comh-airpeach, *a.* Striving; emulous.

Comh-àiteachadh, aidh, *s. m.* A dwelling together, a co-inhabiting.

Comh-àiteachas, ais, *s. m.* A neighbourhood.

Comh-àitich, *v. a.* Co-inhabit, dwell or reside together. *Pret. a.* chomh-àitich.

Comh-àitiche, *s. m.* A neighbour; a townsman. *N. pl.* comh-àitichean.

Comhal, *a.* (*Ir. id.*) Brave, courageous.

† **Comhal**, ail, *s. m.* The performance or execution of any thing.

† **Comhal**, *v. a.* Heap together; join together.—*Shaw.*

Comh-alt, *s. m.* (*Lat.* co-altus.) A foster-brother.—*Macint.* Is caomh le duine a charaid, ach 's e smior a chridhe a chomh-alt, *a man respects his friend, but he loves his foster-brother.*—*G. P.*

Highland chieftains were wont to foster their heirs with such of their poor vassals as had a promising family of sons; in order that mutual attachment might ensure fidelity and friendship in future life.

Comh-altaich, *v. a.* Join together, rear together; congratulate. *Pret. a.* chomh-altaich; *fut. aff.* comh-altaichidh.

Comhaltas, ais, *s. m.* A fostering; a relation of fostering. Comhaltas gu ceud, is cairdeas gu fichead, *fostering connects a hundred, relationship only twenty.*—*G. P.*

Comhan, ain, *s. m.* A shrine.

Comh-aois, *s. m.* A cotemporary; one's equal in age. *N. pl.* comh-aoisean. Moran do m' chomh-aoisibh, *many of my equals.*—*Stew. Gal.*

Comh-aolachd, *s. f.* A college.—*Shaw.*

Comh-aontachadh, aidh, *s. m.* Agreement, collusion, a consenting.

Comh-aontachadh, (a), *pr. part.* of comh-aontaich. Agreeing, consenting.

Comh-aontachd, *s. f.* (*Ir. id.*) Unanimity, agreement; unity, consent.

Comh-aontaich, *a.* Agree, consent; yield; admit; grant, as a point in an argument. *Pret. a.* chomh-aontaich, *consented; fut. aff. a.* comh-aontaichidh, *shall consent.*

Comh-aosda, *a.* (*Ir. id.*) Of equal age; cotemporary, coeval.

Comhar, air, *s. m.* A mark; a print; a vestige; a sign; a token; a proof. *N. pl.* comharan. Mar chomhar air am buaidh, *as a sign of their victory.*—*Sm.* Comharan beud, *marks of mischief.*—*Oss. Carricth.* Is olc an comhar e, *it is a bad sign;* comhar crìche, *a landmark.*—*Stew. Pro.* Mu chomhar, *opposite;* droch chomhar, *a bad sign;* deagh chomhar, *a good sign;* comhar cluais, *an ear-mark.*

Comhar, (mu), *prep.* Opposite; opposite him or it. Mu comhar, *opposite her;* mu 'n comhar, *opposite them.*

Comharaich, *v. a.* Mark; observe; descry. *Pret. a.* chomharaich, *marked; fut. aff. a.* comharaichidh, *shall mark.* Chomharaich mi dealra an t-soluis, *I observed the gleam of the light.*—*Oss. Tem.* Comharaichibh iadsan, *mark them.*—*Stew. Rom.* *P. part.* comharaichte.

Comharaichte, *p. part.* of comharaich. Marked, observed, noted; notable; notorious; distinguished; goodly. Duine comharaichte, *a goodly man.*—*Stew. Sam.*

† Comharba, *s. m.* A partner in church lands; a vicar; a successor; protection.—*Shaw.*

† Comharbachd, *s. f.* (*Ir. id.*) A vicarage.

Comh-arguinn, *s. f.* A syllogism.

Comh-arguinneach, *a.* Syllogistical.

† Comharsan, ain, *s. m.* (*Ir. id.*) A neighbour.

† Comhartha, *s. m.* (*Ir. id.*) A sign; a mark; a print; a vestige; a token; a proof. Comhartha suidhichte, *an appointed sign.*—*Stew. Jud.* More frequently written *comhar.*

Comharthan, *n. pl.* of comhartha. Marks, signs.—*Stew. Gen. ref.* More frequently *comharan.*

Comh-astaraiche, *s. m.* A fellow-traveller.

Comh-bhagair, *v.* Comminate.—*Shaw.*

Comh-bhagradh, aidh, *s. m.* A commination.

Comh-bhaigh, *s. f.* Sympathy; fellow-feeling. Tha comh-bhaigh agam ris, *I have a fellow-feeling for him.*

Comh-bhaigheach, *a.* Sympathetic, compassionate, tender-hearted.

Comh-bhann, *s. m.* A confederacy, a league, a bond, a compact, a contract. Comh-bhann na sìth, *the bands of peace.*—*Stew. Eph. ref.*

Comh-bhan-oighre, *s. f.* A co-heiress.

Comh-bheothachadh, aidh, *s. m.* A quickening together; a maintaining or feeding together.

Comh-bheothaich, *v. a.* Quicken together; revive together; maintain together. *Pret. a.* chomh-bheothaich, *revived.* Chomh-bheothaich e sinn, *he quickened us together.*—*Stew. Eph.*

Comh-bhith, *s. f.* Co-existence.

Comh-bhibhuan, Comh-bhithbhuan, *a.* Co-eternal.

Comh-bhibhuantachd, Comh-bhithbhuantachd, *s. f.* Co-eternity.

Comh-bhitheach, *a.* Co-existent.—*Shaw.*

Comh-bhoinn, *s. f.* A confederacy; a conspiracy. Ann an comh-bhoinn, *in a conspiracy.*—*Stew. Sam.*

Comh-bhrathair, -bhrathar, *s. m.* A fellow, a chum.

Comh-bhrathaireachas, ais, *s. m.* Fellowship, consanguinity.

Comh-bhrigheach, *a.* Consubstantial.

Comh-bhrigheachadh, aidh, *s. m.* Consubstantiation.

Comh-bhrigheachd, *s. f.* Consubstantiality.

Comh-bhrigheil, *a.* Consubstantial.

Comh-bhruach, aich, *s. f.* The marches of a country; the hills or eminences which separate countries from one another. *N. pl.* comh-bhruachan.

Comh-bruachach, *a.* Bordering on; bounding with each other, as countries.

Comh-bhruth, *v. a.* Oppress. *Pret. a.* chomh-bhruth, *oppressed; fut. aff. a.* comh-bhruthaidh, *shall oppress.*

Comh-bhuail, *v. a.* Strike; come in contact; strike mutually.

Comh-bhuair, *v. a.* Raise a tumult, tempt.

Comh-bhuaireadh, idh, *s. m.* A tumult, uproar.

Comh-bhualadh, aidh, *s. m.* A mutual striking; contact.

Comh-chaidreach, *a.* Corresponding; trafficking; companionable.

Comh-chaidreachd, *s. f.* Correspondence, traffic, commerce; companionship.

Comh-chaidreamh, cimh, *s. m.* A co-mate, a companion; a chum.

Comh-chainnt, *s. f.* A conference; a dialogue. Cum comh-chainnt, *hold a conference.*

Comh-chaochladh, aidh, *s. m.* Exchange; commutation.

Comh-chaochlaideach, *a.* Commutable; exchangeable; equally subject to change.

Comh-chaochlaideachd, *s. f.* Commutability.

Comh-chaoidh, *v. n.* Condole, sympathise. *Pret.* chomh-chaoidh, *condoled; fut. aff.* comh-chaoidhidh, *shall condole.*

Comh-charnta, *a.* Heaped together; accumulated.

Comh-charraideachd, *s. f.* A mutual struggle; violent competition.

Comh-chealg, -cheilg, *s. f.* Conspiracy; rebellion. Luchd comh-cheilg, *conspirators.*

Comh-cheangal, ail, *s. m.* A covenant; a confederacy; a compact; a bond; a league.

Comh-cheangail, *v. a.* Bind together; bind mutually; bind by covenant or bond. *Pret. a.* chomh-cheangail; *fut.* comh-cheangalaidh, *shall bind.*

Comh-cheannachd, *s. f.* Traffic, commerce.

Comh-cheannaich, *v. a.* Traffic.

Comh-chearraiche, *s. m.* A fellow-player, a fellow-gambler. *N. pl.* comh-chearraichean.

Comh-cheart, *a.* Formed or fashioned round about; proportioned; adjusted.

Comh-cheartaich, *v.* Fashion or form round about; proportion, adjust. *Pret. a.* chomh-cheartaich, *adjusted; fut. aff. a.* comh-cheartaichidh, *shall adjust.*

Comh-chéilidh, *s. m.* A paramour. *N. pl.* comh-chéilidhean, *paramours.* A comh-chéilidhean, *her paramours.*—*Stew. Ezek.*

Comh-chiallach, *a.* Synonymous. Briathran comh-chiallach, *synonymous words.*

Comh-chliamhuinn, *s. m.* A brother-in-law. *N. pl.* comh-chliamhuinnean.

Comh-chnuasachd, *s. f.* A collection.

Comh-chnuasaich, *v. a.* Collect together, gather together. *Pret.* chomh-chnuasaich.

Comh-chogadh, aidh, *s. m.* Opposition; mutual contention. Comh-chogadh eòlais, *the oppositions of science.*—*Stew. Tim.*

Comh-chòir, *s. f.* An equal right; equal title; equal claim.

Comh-choisiche, *s. m.* A fellow-traveller.

Comh-chomunn, uinn, *s. m.* Fellowship, communion, partnership.—*Stew.* 1 *Cor.*

Comh-chordachd, *s. f.* Congruence, agreement; mutual understanding.

Comh-chordadh, aidh, *s. m.* Unanimity, concord, agreement.

Comh-chorp, -chuirp, *s. m.* A corporation.

Comh-chorpaich, *v.* Incorporate. *Pret. a.* chomh-chorpaich, *incorporated; fut. aff.* comh-chorpaichidh, *shall incorporate.*

Comh-choslach, *a.* Conformable; like; equal; bearing a mutual resemblance.

Comh-choslachd, *s. f.* Conformity; equality; likeness.

Comh-chosmhal, *a.* Conformable; like; equal; bearing mutual resemblance.

Comh-chothrom, uim, *s. m.* Counterpoise; balance; an equivalent.

Comh-chothromaich, *v. a.* Counterpoise, counterbalance.

Comh-chraithte, *a.* Conquassated, shaken together.

Comh-chras, *s. m.* Good-fellowship, mutual agreement or understanding.

Comh-chreutair, *s. m.* A fellow-creature. *N. pl.* comh-chreutairean.

Comh-chruinneachadh, aidh, *s. m.* A congregation, a gathering.

Comh-chruinnich, *v. a.* Gather together, assemble, collect. *Pret. a.* chomh-chruinnich, *gathered.*

Comh-chruinnichte, *p. part.* of comh-chruinnich. Assembled, collected.

Comh-chruth, *s.* Resemblance, sameness of form; conformation; equiformation.

Comh-chudthrom, uim, *s. m.* Equilibrium, equipoise, counterbalance.

Comh-chudthromaich, *v.* Poise; equalize in weight; weigh together.

Comh-chuibhreachadh, aidh, *s. m.* A concatenation, a chaining together.

Comh-chuibhrich, *v. a.* Concatenate; chain together.

Comh-chuideachd, *s. f.* A company; partnership.

Comh-chuir, *v. a.* Apply; dispose; set in order; arrange; compose, as a poem. *Pret. a.* chomh-chuir, *composed.*

Comh-chum, *v. a.* Conform; proportion. *Pret.* chomh-chum, *proportioned; fut. aff.* comh-chumaidh.

Comh-chur, *s.* Application; composition; arrangement; a setting in order.

Comhdach, aich, *s. m.* (*Ir.* cumhdach.) A covering; a shelter; a proof; a quotation. Gorm-chomhdach nam mòr-chrann, *the green covering of the lofty trees.—Macfar.*

Comhdachadh, aidh, *s. m.* The act of covering or sheltering; a proving, quoting; a cover, a covering, a shelter; a proof, a quotation.

Comhdachadh, (a), *pr. part.* of comhdaich. Covering, sheltering; proving; quoting.

Còmhdaich, *v. a.* (comh-eudaich.) Cover, shelter, protect, screen; prove; quote. *Pret. a.* chomhdaich, *covered; fut. aff. a.* comhdaichidh. Chomhdaich an doimhne mi, *the deep covered me.—Stew. Jon.*

Còmhdaichte, *p. part.* of comhdaich. Covered, sheltered; proved. Comhdaichte le braonaibh na h-oidhche, *covered with the drops of night.—Stew. Song. Sol.*

Còmh-dhail, *s. f.* (*Ir.* comhdail *and* comhdhail.) A meeting, an interview; assembly; opposition. Rach na chomhdhail, *go to meet him; give him a meeting.* Bhrùchd iad na chomh-dhail, *they burst forth to meet him.—Mac Lach.*

Còmh-dhail, (an), *prep.* To meet; in opposition; *in meeting.*

Comh-dhaingneachadh, aidh, *s. m.* (*Ir. id.*) A strengthening, a confirming, a confirmation.

Comh-dhaingnich, *v. a.* (*Ir. id.*) Confirm, strengthen. *Pret.* chomh-dhaingnich; *fut. aff.* comh-dhaignichidh.

Comh-dhalta, *s. m.* (*Ir. id.*) A foster-brother.

Comh-dhaltas, ais, *s. m.* Fosterage; the relation subsisting by fosterage.

Comh-dhas, ais, *s. m.* (*Ir. id.*) An equal right.

Comh-dhé, *s. m.* The Trinity.—*Macd.*

Comh-dhealbh, *v.* Configure, construct, delineate. *Pret. a.* chomh-dhealbh; *fut. aff.* comh-dhealbhaidh, *shall configure.*

Comh-dhealbhadh, aidh, *s. m.* A constitution; a configuration. Gu mair ar reachd 's ar comh-dhealbhadh, *may our laws and constitution last.—Old Song.*

Comh-dhealradh, aidh, *s. m.* A corradiation.—*Shaw.*

Comh-dheuchainn, *s. f.* A competition, a trial, a rivalry. *N. pl.* comh-dheuchainnean.

Comh-dheuchainniche, *s. m.* A competitor.

Comh-dhiol, *v.* Compensate; retaliate; remunerate; make amends for. *Pret. a.* chomh-dhiol, *compensated; fut. aff.* comh-dhiolaidh.

Comh-dhioladh, aidh, *s. m.* The act of compensating; a compensation.

Comh-dhoilghios, *s.* Condolence. Dean comh-dhoilghios, *condole.*

Comh-dhùin, *v. a.* Conclude; bring to an end. *Pret. a.* chomh-dhùin, *concluded; fut. aff. a.* comh-dhùinidh, *shall conclude.*

Comh-dhùnadh, aidh, *s. m.* The act of concluding; a conclusion.

Comh-dhùthchas, ais, *s. m.* The circumstance of belonging to the same country; the relation that subsists from belonging to the same country.

Comh-dhuthchasach, *a.* Of the same country; *also, substantively,* one of the same country.

Comh-éignich, *v. a.* Constrain, compel, force. *Pret. a.* chomh-éignich, *constrained; fut. aff. a.* comh-éignichidh, *shall constrain.* Chomh-éignich i e, *she forced him.—Stew. Pro.*

Comh-eòlach, *a.* Mutually acquainting; equally knowing.

Comh-eòlas, ais, *s. m.* Interknowledge; mutual acquaintance.

Comh-eud, *s. f.* Mutual jealousy or suspicion; rivalry.

Comh-eudmhor, *a.* Mutually jealous.

Comh-fhad, *a.* (*W.* cyhyd.) Equal, even, lineal; equally long; like.

Comh-fhad-thràth, *s. m.* The equinox. Comh-fhad-thràth an earraich, *the vernal equinox;* comh-fhad-thràth an fhogharaidh, *the autumnal equinox.*

Comh-fhad-thràthach, *a.* Equinoctial.

Comh-fhailteachd, *s. f.* Congratulation; mutual salutation.

Comh-fhailtich, *v.* Congratulate, salute. *Pret. a.* chomh-fhailtich, *saluted; fut. aff.* comh-fhailtichidh, *shall salute.*

Comh-fhair, *s. f.* Twilight.

Comh-fharpuis, *s. f.* Emulation, rivalry. Connsachadh, comh-fharpuis, *variance, emulation.—Stew. Gal.*

Comh-fharpuiseach, *a.* Emulative.

Comh-fharpuiseachd, *s. f.* Emulativeness; frequent or continued emulation.

Comh-fhàs, -fhais, *s. m.* A concretion; a growing together.

Comh-fhàs, *v. n.* Grow together. *Pret. a.* chomh-fhas, *grew together; fut. aff.* comh-fhàsaidh, *shall grow together.*

Comh-fhios, *s.* Conscience.

Comh-fhiosach, *a.* Conscientious. Gu comh-fhiosach, *conscientiously.*

Comh-fhiosrach, *a.* Conscious.

Comh-fhiosrachd, *s. f.* Consciousness.

Comh-fhlaitheach, *a.* Democratical; aristocratical; republican.

Comh-fhlaitheachd, *s. f.* Republic; commonwealth; republicanism; aristocracy; democracy. Comh-fhlaitheachd Israel, *the commonwealth of Israel.—Stew. Eph.*

Comh-fhoghair, *s. f.* A consonant; consonance; a chime, as of bells.

Comh-fhoghaireach, *a.* Consonant; chiming.

Comh-fhogus, *a.* Equally near. Tha e comh-fhogus dhuitse agus dhomsa, *it is equally near you and me.*

Comh-fhreagair, *v. a.* and *n.* Suit, correspond, agree, fit; resound, echo. *Pret. a.* chomh-fhreagair, *resounded; fut. aff. a.* comh-fhreagairidh, *shall resound.* Chomh-fhreagair creagan àrda, *lofty rocks resounded.—Fingalian Poem.*

Comh-fhreagarach, *a.* Suitable; corresponding; fit; answerable; fitted to each other; responsive.

Comh-fhreagarachd, *s. f.* Suitableness; correspondence; fitness; responsiveness; congruence; conformity.

Comh-fhreagaradh, aidh, *s. m.* (*Ir.* coimh-fhreagradh.) A suiting; a fitting; a conforming; a corresponding; agreement; conformity.

Comh-fhreagartas, ais, *s. m.* Correspondence; fitness; symmetry.

Comh-fhuaim, *s. m.* Musical concordance, equitone, harmony; consonance.

Comh-fhuil, -fhola, *s. f.* (*Ir. id.*) Consanguinity, relationship.

Comh-fhulangach, *a.* Tender-hearted, feeling.

COMH-FHULANGAICHE, *s. m.* A fellow-sufferer.

COMH-FHULANGAIR, *s. m.* A fellow-sufferer.

COMH-FHULANGAS, ais, *s. m.* Sympathy, fellow-feeling. Tha comh-fhulangas aige, *he has a fellow-feeling.—Sm.*

COMH-FHURTACHAIL, *a.* Consolatory, comfortable.

COMH-FHURTACHD, *s. f.* (*Ir. id.*) Consolation, comfort. Gach comh-fhurtachd, *every comfort.—Sm.*

COMH-FHURTAICH, *v. a.* Console, comfort. *Pret. a.* chomh-fhurtaich, *comforted.*

COMH-FHURTAIR, *s. m.* A comforter. An Comh-fhurtair, *the Comforter.*

COMH-GHAIR, *s. f.* (*Ir. id.*) Conclamation; a simultaneous shout; congratulation. Rinn iad comh-ghair, *they shouted together.*

COMH-GHAIRDEACHAS, ais, *s. m.* Congratulation, mutual joy, mutual solace. Deanamaid comh-ghairdeachas, *let us solace ourselves.—Stew. Pro.*

COMH-GHAIRDICH, *v. a.* Congratulate, wish joy. *Pret. a.* chomh-ghairdich.

COMH-GHAIRM, *s. f.* (*Ir. id.*) A general shout; a convocation. Comh-ghairm naomh, *a holy convocation.—Stew. Ex. and Lev.*

COMH-GHAOL, aoil, *s. m.* Mutual love; consanguinity.

COMH-GHEARRADH, aidh, *s. m.* Concision.

COMH-GHLEACHD, *s. f.* (*Ir.* coimhghleic.) A conflict; a combat; a wrestling.

COMH-GHIOL, *s. m.* A condition.

COMH-GHLÒIR, *s. f.* Equal glory; *also,* consonance.

COMH-GHLUASACHD, *s. f.* Simultaneous movement; fermentation.—*Shaw.*

COMH-GHNA, COMH-GHNATH, *s. m.* Assistance. A ghaoil dean mo chomh-ghnath, *my love, assist me.—Ull.*

COMH-GHREIMICH, *v.* (*Ir. id.*) Grasp; cohere; grasp mutually. *Pret. a.* chomh-ghreimich; *fut. aff.* comh-ghreimichidh.

COMH-GHUIL, *v. n.* Condole, weep together. *Pret. a.* chomh-ghuil, *condoled; fut. aff.* comh-ghuilidh.

COMH-IONANN, *a.* (*Ir. id.*) Equal, alike.

COMH-IONANNACHD, *s. f.* Equality, likeness, co-equality.

COMH-ITH, *v. n.* Eat together, partake of food. *Pret. a.* chomh-ith, *ate together; fut. aff.* comh-ithidh.

COMH-ITHEADH, idh, *s. m.* An eating together, messing together. Tigh comh-ithidh, *an eating-house.*

COMH-ITH-THIGH, *s. m.* An eating-house.

COMH-LABHAIR, *v. n.* Converse, confer. *Pret. a.* chomh-labhair.

COMH-LABHAIRT, *s. f.* (*Ir. id.*) A speaking together; a dialogue; a conference.

CÒMHLACH, aich, *s. m.* A door, a gate; a comrade. Dà chomhlach, *two doors.—Stew.* 1 *K. N. pl.* còmhlaichean.

CÒMHLACHADH, aidh, *s. m.* A meeting, opposing, or intercepting.

CÒMHLADH, aidh, *s. m.* A door, a gate; a two-leaved door or gate; a sluice; a barrier; an obstacle. Bu chòmhladh phrais ar sgiath, *our shields were barriers of brass.—Orr.* A dh' fhosgladh nan còmhladh, *to open the two-leaved gates.—Stew. Is.*

CÒMHLAICH, *v. a.* Meet; intercept; stop the progress of any object. *Pret. a.* chòmhlaich, *met; fut. aff. a.* còmhlaichidh, *shall meet.*

CÒMHLAN, ain, *s. m.* A complement of men. Do loingeas agus a còmhlan, *the vessel and its complement.—Mac Lach. N. pl.* còmhlain.

CÒMHLANN, ainn, *s. m.* A young hero; a companion; a companion in arms; a duel. Righdir comhlainn, *a knight's companion.*

COMH-LANNACHD, *s. f.* Duelling; fighting with swords or spears.

COMH-LANNAIR, *s. m.* A sword-fighter; a prize-fighter. *N. pl.* comh-lannairean.

COMH-LANNAIREACHD, *s. m.* Sword-fighting; sword-exercise; fighting with spears.

COMH-LAOCH, -laoich, *s. m.* A fellow-soldier, a fellow-warrior.

COMHLATH, COMHLUATH, *adv.* and *prep.* Together; at the same time. Mu chomhlath, *at the same time;* comhlath riutsa, *together with thee.*

COMH-LEAGH, *v. a.* Colliquefy; amalgamate. *Pret.* chomh-leagh, *amalgamated; fut. aff.* comh-leaghaidh, *shall amalgamate.*

COMHLEAGHADH, aidh, *s. m.* Colliquefaction; amalgamation.

COMHLEAGHAN, ain, *s. m.* An amalgam.

COMHLION, *v. a.* Fulfil. See COIMHLION.

COMHLORG, -luirg, *s. f.* Consequence, result. An comhlorg sin, *in consequence of that.—Macfar.*

COMH-LOSGADH, aidh, *s. m.* A conflagration.

COMH-LUADAR, air, *s. m.* (*Ir. id.*) A company, a party; communication, conversation. Comh-luadar mòr, *a great company.* Truaillidh droch chomhluadar, *evil communication corrupts.—Stew.* 1 *Cor.*

COMH-LUCHD, *s. pl.* Partners, associates, allies. Comh-luchd oibre, *fellow-labourers, fellow-workers.—Stew.* 1 *Cor.*

COMH-LUIDHE, *s. f.* Partnership, association, alliance; a lying together.

COMH-MHALAIRT, *s. f.* Counterchange; barter. Dean comh-mhalairt, *make an exchange.*

COMH-MHARBH, *v. a.* Massacre, kill together. *Pret. a.* chomh-mharbh, *massacred; fut. aff.* comh-mharbhaidh.

COMH-MHARBHADH, aidh, *s. m.* (*W.* cyvarv, *a combat.*) A massacre; mutual bloodshed; a battle.

COMH-MHEASG, *v. a.* Commix. *Pret. a.* chomh-mheasg, *commixed; fut. aff.* comh-mheasgaidh, *shall commix.*

COMH-MHEASGADH, aidh, *s. m.* A mixing, a commixing, a mixture, a composition.

COMH-MHEASGTA, *p. part.* Mixed, commixed, commingled.

COMH-MHIONNACHADH, aidh, *s. m.* A conspiring; a conspiracy.

COMH-MHIONNAICH, *v. n.* Conspire. *Pret. a.* chomh-mhionnaich, *conspired; fut. aff.* comh-mhionnaichidh, *shall conspire.*

COMH-MHIRE, *s. f.* Mutual flirting.—*R.* Tha iad ri comh-mhire, *they are flirting with each other.*

COMH-MHOL, *v. a.* (*W.* cyvawl.) Praise together. *Pret.* chomh-mhol; *fut. aff.* comh-mholaidh.

COMH-MHOTHUCHADH, aidh, *s. m.* A sympathizing, a fellow-feeling; sympathy, compassion. Comh-mhothuchadh le 'r n' uile chradh, *a fellow-feeling for all our pains.—Sm.*

COMH-MHOTHUCHAIL, *a.* Compassionate.

COMHNADH, aidh, *s. m.* (*properly* comh-ghnath.) Assistance, help, relief.

COMHNARD, *a.* Plain, level, even, equal, smooth. Seoil chomhnard, *equal sails.—Oss. Oinam.* Rathad comhnard, *a plain road.—Stew. Jud.*

COMHNARD, aird, *s. m.* A plain, a field, level ground. Comhnard Mhamre, *the plain of Mamre.—Stew. O. T.*

COMH-NEARTACHADH, aidh, *s. m.* A confirming, a corroborating, confirmation.

COMH-NEARTAICH, *v. a.* Confirm, corroborate. *Pret. a.* chomh-neartaich.

COMHNUICH, *v. n.* (*Ir.* comhnaigh.) Dwell, inhabit, reside, abide, continue, stand still. *Pret. a.* chomhnuich, *dwelt; fut. aff. a.* comhnuichidh. Co chomhnuicheas, *who shall dwell.—Stew. Ps.*

Còmhnuidh, *s. f.* A house, a dwelling, an abode. Is dubhach do chomhnuidh, *sad is thy dwelling.—Ull.*

Còmhnuidh, (an), *adv.* Always, ever, continually. An cumaint 's an còmhnuidh, *continually.*

Comh-ogha, *s. m.* and *f.* A cousin-german.—*Shaw.*

Comh-oglach, aich, *s. m.* (*Ir. id.*) A male fellow-servant. *N. pl.* comh-oglaich.

Comh-oibreach, *a.* Co-efficient; working together; co-operating.

Comh-oibreachadh, aidh. A working together; a co-operating; co-operation.

Comh-oibreachail, *a.* Co-operative.

Comh-oibrich, *v. n.* Co-operate; assist; work together. *Pret. a.* chomh-oibrich, *co-operated.* Gun comh-oibrich na h-uile nithe, *that all things shall work together.—Stew. Pro. Fut. aff.* comh-oibrichidh, *shall co-operate.*

Comh-oibriche, *s. m.* A fellow-labourer; a coadjutor; a co-operator.—*Stew. Rom.*

Comh-oighre, *s. m.* (*Ir. id.*) A coheir. *N. pl.* comh-oighreachan, *coheirs.—Stew. Rom.*

Comh-pairt, *s. f.* A partnership, a share, participation. Luchd comh-pairt, *partakers.*

Comh-pairteach, *a.* Portionable, divisible; communicable; willing to share or to communicate.—*Stew. Tim.*

Comh-pairtich, *v. a.* Communicate; share, divide.

Comh-phriosunach, aich, *s. m.* A fellow-prisoner. *N. pl.* comh-phriosunaich.—*Stew. Rom.*

Comhra, Comhradh, aidh, *s. m.* (comh-radh.) Conversation, dialogue, speech, language. Chluinnte a chomhra ri laoich, *his converse with heroes was heard.—Oss. Lodin.*

Comhrachadh, aidh, *s. m.* The act of marking; a spying, a descrying.

Comhradh. See **Comhra.**

Comhrag, aig, *s. f.* (*Ir.* comhrac.) A fight, a combat, battle, struggle, strife. Dealan na comhraig, *the lightning of battle.—Oss. Com.*

Comhragach, *a.* Warlike. Sluagh garg comhragach, *a fierce warlike people.—Old Song.*

Comhragair, *s. m.* A fighting man; a warrior; an encounterer.—*Shaw.*

Comhraich, *v. a.* Mark, spy, observe, descry. *Pret.* chomhraich, *marked; fut. aff.* comhraichidh, *shall mark.* Written also *comharaich.*

Còmhraichte, *p. part.* of comhraich. Marked, spied, observed, descried.

Comhraig, *gen. sing.* of comhrag.

Comhraig, *v. n.* Fight, contest, strive. *Pret. a.* comhraig, *fought; fut. aff. a.* comhraigidh, *shall fight.* Chomhraig mi deadh chomhrag, *I fought a good fight.—Stew.* 1 *Tim.*

Comhraiteach, *a.; from* comhradh. (*Ir. id.*) Talkative, conversible.

Comh-roghainn, *s. f.* An election, a choice; a general election, an unanimous election.

Comh-roghnaich, *v. a.* Elect unanimously. *Pret. a.* chomh-roghnaich; *fut. aff.* comh-roghnaichidh; *fut. pass.* comh-roghnaichear.

Comh-roghnaichte, *p. part.* of comh-roinn. Elect unanimously.

Comh-roinn, *s. f.* (*Ir. id.*) A share, a division; participation, partnership. Comhroinn do 'n toradh, *a share of the fruits.—Stew. Tim.*

Comh-roinn, *v. a.* Share, divide, distribute; participate. *Pret. a.* chomh-roinn, *shared; fut. aff. a.* comh-roinnidh, *shall* or *will share.* A comh-roinn ri uireasbhuidh nan naomh, *distributing to the necessities of the saints.—Stew. Rom.*

Comh-ruith, *s. m.* A race, a running together.—*Stew. Ecc.* Ri comh-ruith timchioll nan raon, *running together around the upland fields.—Macfar.*

Comh-ruith, *v. n.* (*W.* cyred.) Run together; run at the same time; concur. *Pret. a.* chomh-ruith, *ran together; fut. aff.* comh-ruithidh, *shall run together.*

Comh-rùnachadh, aidh, *s. m.* (*Ir. id.*) A communication; a conspiring; a conspiracy.

Comh-rùnaich, *v. n.* Conspire; communicate; concur. *Pret. a.* chomh-rùnaich, *conspired; fut. aff.* comh-rùnaichidh, *shall conspire.* Chomh-rùnaich mi leis, *I conspired with him; I concurred with him.*

† **Comhsanach**, *a.* Perpetual, everlasting.—*Shaw.*

Comh-sgoilear, eir, *s. m.* (*Ir. id.*) A schoolfellow. *N. pl.* comh-sgoileirean.

Comh-shaighdear, eir, *s. m.* A fellow-soldier. *N. pl.* comh-shaighdearan, *fellow-soldiers.* Mo chomh-shaighdeara, *my fellow-soldiers.—Macfar.*

Comh-shamhlach, *a.* Comparative.

Comh-shamhlachadh, aidh, *s. m.* A comparing, a comparison.

Comh-shamhlaich, *v. a.* Compare. *Pret. a.* chomh-shamhlaich, *compared.*

Comh-shéid, *v. n.* Conflate; blow together. *Pret. a.* chomh-sheid.

Comh-shéideadh, eidh, *s. m.* A conflation.

Comh-sheirbheiseach, ich, *s. m.* A fellow-servant. *N. pl.* comh-sheirbheisich, *fellow-servants.*

Comh-sheirbheiseachd, *s. f.* Fellow-service.

Comh-sheirm, *s. f.* Harmony, symphony, concert. Cànaibh comh-sheirm chiùil, *sing in concert.—Sm.* Ni iad comh-sheirm, *they will produce harmony.—Macfar.*

Comh-sheirmeach, *a.* Harmonious, in concert.

Comh-sheòd, -sheòid, *s. m.* A brother-champion; a brother-hero. Innsidh e 'n sgeul do chomh-sheòid, *he will tell the tale to his brother-heroes.—Oss. Derm.*

Comh-sheomaraiche, *s. m.* A room-companion; a chum.

Comh-shion, *s. f.* Calm weather.—*Shaw.*

Comh-shiorruidh, *a.* Co-eternal. Comh-shiorruidh, comh-stuthail, *co-eternal and consubstantial.*

Comh-shiorruidheachd, *s. f.* Co-eternity.

Comh-shliosnach, *a.* Equilateral

Comh-shoillse, *s. f.* A constellation. *N. pl.* comh-shoillsean.

Comh-sholus, uis, *s. m.* A constellation.

Comh-shruth, *v. n.* Flow together or in one stream; converge.

Comh-shruth, *s. m.* A confluence of streams.

Comh-shuain, *v. n.* Sleep together. *Pret. a.* chomh-shuain; *fut. aff.* comh-shuainidh.

Comh-shugradh, aidh, *s. m.* Playing together; a play; a pastime. Tha iad ri comh-shugradh, *they are playing together.*

Comh-shugraiche, *s. m.* A playfellow.

Comh-shuiriche, *s. m.* A rival in courtship. *N. pl.* comh-shuirichean.

Comh-spairn, *s. f.* Emulation, rivalry; a wrestle, a mutual struggle.

Comh-spairneach, *a.* Emulous; wrestling, struggling. Gu comh-spairneach, *emulously.*

Comh-spairneachd, *s. f.* Emulousness; frequent or continued rivalry; frequent wrestling or struggling.

Comh-stri, Comh-strigh, *s. f.* A contest; rivalry; strife, struggle; battle. Buaidh sa comh-stri, *victory in battle.—Oss. Com.*

Comh-strigheach, *a.* Emulous; rivalling; causing rivalry.

Comh-stuthachadh, aidh, *s. m.* Consubstantiation.

Comh-stuthachd, *s. f.* Consubstantiality.

Comh-stuthail, *a.* Consubstantial.

Comh-thach, aich, *s. m.* A companion, a chum. *N. pl.* comh-thaich.

Comh-tharruing, *v. a.* Contract; draw together; pull at the same time. *Pret. a.* chomh-tharruing, *contracted; fut. aff.* comh-tharruingidh, *shall contract.*

Comh-tharruingeach, *a.* Contractive; having the power of contracting.

Comh-tharruinn. See **Comh-tharruing.**

Comh-thath, *v. a.* Join; articulate; solder. *Pret. a.* chomh-thath.

Comh-thathadh, aidh, *s. m.* A joining together; a cementing, a soldering, a joining; a joint; articulation; syntax.

Comh-thàthte, *p. part.* of comh-thàth. Joined; articulated; soldered.

Comh-thionail, *v. a.* Assemble, gather together, convoke. *Pret.* chomh-thionail, *assembled; fut. aff.* comh-thionailidh, *shall assemble.*

Comh-thional, ail, *s. m.* (*Ir. id.*) An assembly, a congregation.

Comh-thog, *v. a.* Raise together; construct; rear together; educate or bring up together. *Pret. a.* chomh-thog, *raised together.* Chomh-thog e sinn, *he raised us up together.—Stew. Eph.*

Comh-thogail, *s. f.* A raising together, a rearing together; a bringing up or educating together; a construction.

Comh-thomhaiseach, *a.* Commensurable.

Comh-thomhaiseachd, *s. f.* Commensurableness

Comh-thras, *s. m.* A sweet smell.—*Shaw.*

Comh-throm, *a.* Equally heavy; even, equal.

Comh-throm, *s.* See **Cothrom.**

Comh-thruacanta, *a.* Compassionate.

Comh-thruacantas, ais, *s. m.* Compassionateness.

Comh-thruaighe, *s. f.* Compassion, sympathy, fellow-feeling.

Comh-thruas, ais, *s. m.* Compassion, sympathy.

Comh-thrus, *v. a.* Truss up together. *Pret.* chomh-thrus; *fut. aff.* comh-thrusaidh.

Comh-uchdach, *a.* Having breast to breast.

Comith, *s. f.* A portion of one's food; participation of one's food; eating of the same food. Thoir dhomh comith, *give me a share of your food; let me take out of the same dish with you.—G. P.*

Comortas, ais, *s. m.* Rivalry, emulation.—*Stew. Gal. ref.*

Compach, aich, *s. m.* A companion, a chum. *N. pl.* compaich.

Compailt, *s. f.* A company.—*Shaw.*

Companach, aich, *s. m.* (*Da.* kompan. *Ir.* companach.) A companion, an associate, a chum. Companach 'nan amadan, *the companion of fools.—Stew. Pro. N. pl.* companaich.

Companas, ais, *s. m.* Companionship, fellowship, society. Ann an companas, *in fellowship.—Stew. Lev.*

Compantas, ais, *s. m.* Written also *companas;* which see.

† **Compas**, ais, *s. m.* A compass; a ring, a circle.—*Shaw.*

† **Compraid**, *s. f.* (*Ir. id.*) A comparison.—*Shaw.*

Comraich, *s. f.* Protection; favour; obligation. Mo chomraich ort, Oisein, mhic Fhinn, *oblige me, Ossian, thou son of Fingal.—Oss. Dargo.* Mo chomraich ort on is tu Fionn, *I ask thy protection, as thou art Fingal.—Old Poem.* Chuir i comraich air Fionn, *she placed her protection on Fingal.—Old Poem.*

Comunach, aich, *s. m.* Communion. See **Comanach.**

Comunn, uinn, *s. m.* (*W.* cymun. *Ir.* comunn.) A society, a company, a club; a confederacy; a meeting; fellowship, intercourse. Uile dhaoine do chomuinn, *all the men of thy confederacy.—Stew. Obad.* Comunn liath nan sean-fhear, *the grey meeting of aged men.—Mac Lach.* Cairdeas no comunn, *nor friendship nor fellowship.—Sm.* Is coma leam comunn an òil, *I dislike the friendship that is formed in liquor.—G. P.*

† **Con**, *s. m.* Sense, meaning; appetite.

Con, *gen. pl.* of cù. Of dogs, to dogs. Chum nan con, *to the dogs.—Stew. Exod.*

Cona, *s.* Cat's-tail or moss-crops.—*Shaw.*

Conablach, aich, *s. m.* (*Ir. id.*) A mangled carcass; a carcass. *N. pl.* conablaich; *d. pl.* conablaichibh. Le conablaichibh, *with carcasses.—Stew. Ezek.*

† **Conach**, aich, *s. m.* (*Ir. id.*) Prosperity, affluence; murrain; a shirt.—*Shaw.*

Conachlon, oin, *s. m.* (*Ir. id.*) An equal, a companion; a kind of Irish verse.—*Shaw.*

Conachuileag, eig, *s. f.* A fly; a murrain of flies.—*Stew. Ps. ref.*

Cònadh. See **Comhgnath.**

Conadh, aidh, *s. m.* Sense; appetite; a greedy appetite—(*Macdon.*); *also,* prosperity.—*Shaw.*

Conaghair, *s. f.* Tumult, uproar, confusion. More properly written *conghair.*

Conail, *s. f.* A plague that once raged in Ireland.—*Shaw.*

† **Conailbhe**, *s. f.* Friendship.

† **Conailbheach**, *a.* Friendly; upholding..

† **Conair**, *s. f.* (*Ir. id.*) A way, a path.—*Shaw.*

Conairt, *s. f.* (*Ir. id.*) Hunting with dogs; a rout of wolves.

Conairt, *v.* Hunt with dogs.—*Shaw.*

† **Conaisleach**, *a.* (*Ir. id.*) Busy.

Conalach, *a.* Brandishing.

† **Conall**, aill, *s. m.* Friendship, regard, love.—*Shaw.*

Conaltrach, *a.* Social; fond of company; of, or relating to, company. Do chuilm chonaltrach, *thy social feast.—Macfar.*

Conaltradh, aidh, *s. m.* Company; conversation. Cum conaltradh, *keep company, associate;* na chonaltradh, *in his company;* na conaltradh, *in her company;* nan conaltradh, *in their company.*

Cònas, ais, *s. m.* (*Ir. id.*) War; a battle; a dispute; a carcass. Cònas na Cluaithe, *the war of Clutha.—Oss. Fin. and Lor.* A cònas ri cheile, *opposing each other.—Macdon.*

Conasg, aisg, *s. m.* Furze. Làn conaisg is phreasaibh, *full of furze and thickets.—Old Song.*

Conasgach, *a.* Abounding in furze; like furze; of, or belonging to, furze.

Conbhallach, *a.* Having buttresses; like a buttress.

Conbhalladh, aidh, *s. m.* A buttress; a battlement.

† **Conbhallas**, ais, *s. m.* A support, a prop, a buttress.—*Shaw.*

Conbharsaid, *s. f.* Conversation; conduct, demeanour.—*Stew. Phil. ref.*

Conbhliochd, *s. f.* (*Ir. id.*) A conflict, a battle.—*Shaw.* Written also *confhliochd.*

† **Condaghais**, *s. f.* (*Ir. id.*) A countess.—*Shaw.*

Condasach, *a.* Furious, enraged. Gu condasach, *furiously.*

Condasachd, *s. f.* Fury, rage.

Confadh, **Confhadh**, aidh, *s. m.* Rage, fury, boisterousness; a roaring, a howling. Confadh ro dhian, *impetuous fury.—Old Song.*

Conphadhach, *a.* Enraged, raging, furious.

† **Congasach**, aich, *s. m.* (*Ir. id.*) A kinsman.—*Shaw.*

Conghail, *s. f.* Gallantry, bravery.

Conghair, *s. f.* Uproar, clamour; a shout, a conclamation; confusion; tumult; a faction. Fuaim na conghair, *the noise of the tumult.—Stew. Sam.*

Conghaireach, *a.* Clamorous, tumultuous, factious.

Conghaireachd, *s. f.* Clamorousness, tumultuousness, factiousness.

† **Conghaidhe**, *s. f.* (*Ir. id.*) Relationship.

Congnadh, *s. m.* See Còghnath.

Congraim, *s. f.* Cunning, craft; clothing, apparel.

Conlàn, *a.* (*Ir. id.*) Healthy.

Conn, *s.* Pleasantry; meaning, sense, reason; the frame, the body. Oinid gun chonn, *senseless ideot.—Mac Lach.*

Connadh, aidh, *s. m.* (*Ir. id.*) Fuel; wood. Mar chonnadh, *for fuel.—Stew. Ezek.* Am measg connaidh, *in the midst of wood.—Stew. Zech.*

Connail, *a.* (conn-amhuil.) Pleasant; intelligent, reasonable, rational.

† **Connairc**, *v. n.* See, behold. *Pret.* chonnairc, *saw.* Chonnairc mi an lasadh bha d' ghruaidh, *I saw the flush in thy cheek.—Old Song.*

Connar, *a.* See Connmhor.

Connlach, aich, *s. f.* Straw; fodder. Tha againne connlach, *we have straw.—Stew. Gen.*

Connlann, lainn, *s. m.* A hero; a companion in arms. *N. pl.* connlainn.

Connmhor, *a.* (*from* conn.) Cheerful, pleasant; intelligent. Is connmhor fonnmhor thu, *thou art pleasant and sprightly.—Old Song.* Gu connmhor, *cheerfully. Com.* and *sup.* connmhoire.

Connmhorachd, *s. f.* Cheerfulness, pleasantness; intelligence.

Connsachadh, aidh, *s. m.* The circumstance of disputing; the act of disputing; a quarrelling; a quarrel; a dispute, dissension, a contention. Rinn iad connsachadh, *they strove.—Stew. Gen.* Briathar-chonnsachadh, *a war of words.—Stew. Tim.*

Connsachadh, (a), *pr. part.* of connsaich.

Connsachail, *a.* (connsach-amhuil.) Controversial; quarrelsome.

Connsachair, *s. m.* A disputant; a quarrelsome person; a wrangler. *N. pl.* connsachairean.

Connsaich, *v. n.* Dispute; wrangle; quarrel; strive. *Pret. a.* chonnsaich, *disputed; fut. aff. a.* connsaichidh, *shall dispute.* Chonnsaich iad, *they quarrelled.*

Connspaid, *s. f.* A dispute, strife, controversy, a row. Written also *connspoid.*

Connspaideach, *a.* Quarrelsome; contentious; litigious; of, or pertaining to, a quarrel. Written also *connspoideach.*

Connspaidiche, *s. m.* A wrangler; a contentious person. Written also *connspoidiche.*

Connspair, *s. m.* A wrangler; a reasoner; a contentious person; one who is fond of argument or disputation.

Connspairn, *s. f.* Rivalry, emulation; mutual struggle.

Connspeach, *s. m.* A hornet. *N. pl.* connspeachan.

Connspoid, *v. n.* Dispute, argue, wrangle, quarrel.

Connspoid, *s. f.* (*Ir. id.*) A dispute, strife, controversy, a row, wrangling. Le connspoid is le h-an-iochd, *with strife and cruelty.—Sm.*

Connspoideach, *a.* Quarrelsome, contentious, litigious; wrangling. Dhoibhsan a tha connspoideach, *to them who are contentious.—Stew. Rom.*

Connspuid, *s. f.* See Connspoid.

Connspullach, *a.* Heroic; warlike. Do shiol na fola connspullaiche, *of the race of the warlike blood.—Old Song. Com.* and *sup.* connspullaiche.

Connspullachd, *s. f.* Heroism, bravery.

Conradh. See Cunradh.

Constabullach, aich, *s. m.* (*Ir. id.*) A constable.

† **Constal**, ail, *s. m.* Advice, counsel.
Arm. consailh. *Fr.* conseil. *Lat.* consilium.

Contabhairt, *s. f.* (*Ir. id.*) Chance, peril, hazard, a venture. See the contracted form Cunnart.

Contabhairteach, *a.* Dangerous, hazardous, venturous. See Cunnartach.

Contagair, *v.* Affirm, allege.—*Shaw. Pret.* chontagair, *alleged.*

Contagairt, *s. f.* An affirmation; an allegation; an affirming; an alleging.

† **Contar**, air, *s. m.* (*Ir. id.*) A doubt.

Contrachd, *s. f.* An imprecation, a curse; misfortune, calamity. Is e miann an duine lochdaich càch uile a bhi contrachd, *the wicked man wishes all to be on a level with himself.—G. P.*

Contraigh, *s. f.* Neap tide.

Contruagh, *a.* Lean, poor, slender; emaciated.—*Shaw.*

Cònuich, *s. f.* A hornet. *N. pl.* cònuichean, *hornets.* Cuiridh mi conuichean, *I will send hornets.—Stew. Exod. ref.*

Cònuidh, *s. f.* (*contracted for* comhnuidh.) A dwelling, a house. Cònuidh nan droch dhaoine, *the abode of wicked men.—Sm.*
Ethiop. kòn, *a house. Pers.* con. *Tonq.* chon. *Chin.* quon, *a palace. Jap.* kuni, *a house. Turk.* and *Sclav.* konac, *a lodging.*

Cònuidh, (an), *adv.* Always, incessantly, ever. Mo dheòir a sruthadh an cònuidh, *my tears ever falling.—Ull.* See Comhnuidh, (an).

Co'oibriche, Comh-oibriche, *s. m.* A fellow-labourer, a fellow-worker, a coadjutor.

Co'oighre, *s. m.* A co-heir.

Co'oighreachd, *s. m.* Co-heirship.

Cop, copa, *s. m.* A cup, a bowl.
Gr. κύβϐα, κύπελλον, *a drinking-cup,* and κυπη, *a little boat. Da.* kop, *a cup. Germ.* kopf. *Swed.* kopp. *Fr.* coupe. *Sp.* copa.

Còp, coip, *s.* Foam. A chraos fo chòip, *his mouth foaming.—Oss. Derm.*

Còp, coip, *s. m.* The boss of a shield. Sgiatha bu dubh-ghorm còp, *shields of dark-blue bosses.—Oss. Fing.*

Copach, *a.* Like a cup; campanulated; belled. Plùran copach, *a campanulated flower.*

Còpach, *a.* Foaming; bossy. Gheibh e sgiath chòpach, *he shall receive a bossy shield.—Oss. Derm.* Bu chòpach an sruth, *foaming was the stream.—Oss. Tem. Com.* and *sup.* còpaiche.

Copag, aig, *s. f.* A dock, a dock-leaf.

Copagach, aich, *s. f.* A place where docks grow; a crop of docks.

Copagach, *a.* Abounding in docks or dockens; of, or pertaining to, docks.

Copaibh, *d. pl.* of cop.

Copain, *gen. sing.* and *n. pl.* of copan.

Copair, *s. m.* (*Du.* kooper.) A buyer and seller, especially of horses; a dealer; a truckster.

Copaireachd, *s. f.* Dealing, as in horses; trucking.

Copan, ain, *s. m.* (*dim.* of cop. *Span.* copon.) A little cup, a cup; a bowl, a flagon. Copan fiona, *a flagon of wine.—Stew. 1 Chr.*

Còpan, ain, *s. m.* (*dim.* of còp.) The boss of a shield; a little boss. Bàrr mo shleagh bhuail a còpan, *the point of my spear struck its boss.—Oss. Fing.* Còpan sreine, *the boss of a bridle.*

Copanach, *a.* Like a cup; of, or pertaining to, a cup.

Còpanach, *a.* Bossy. Sgiath chopanach, *a bossy shield.—Oss. Tem.*

Copar, air, *s. m.* Copper; copperas.
Ir. copar. *Corn.* kober. *Span.* cobre.

Cor, *s. m.* (*Ir. id.*) A condition, state, situation; method, manner; custom, usage; account; a surety. Bu neo-amhluidh do chor, *unlike was thy condition.—Orr.* Doc-rach biodh ar cor, *let our case be hopeless.—Sm.* Cor na talmhainn, *the custom of the land.—Stew. Gen. ref.* Air aon chor, *on any account;* air chor sam bi, *on any account.* Na guilibh air aon chor, *weep not on any account.—Stew. Mic.* Air na h-uile cor, *by all means.* Air chor 's gu, *so as that.* Air chor 's nach, *so that not.—Stew. 2 K.*

Cor, (*for* car.) A twist, a turn; a trick; a cast, a throw; a circular motion. Cor-shioman, *a bent stick for twisting straw.* Na siomain chor, *the twisted ropes of straw.—Macfar.*

Còr, còir, *s. m.* (*Ir. id.*) Music; a choir.—*Shaw.*

Còrach, *gen. sing.* of còir. Of right, of justice. Airson na còrach, *for the sake of righteousness.—Stew. Mat.* Thuille na còrach, *over and above enough.*

Còradh. See Comhradh.

Corag, aig, *s. f.* A finger; the fore-finger. *N. pl.* coragan. Corag a chroinn, *a plough-handle.—Macd.* Cha dean corag mhilis im, *a sweet finger will never make butter.—G. P.*

Còrag, aig, *s. f.* See Comhrag.

Coragach, aich, *s. m.* Foam; sea-foam.—*Macd.*

Coragach, *a.* (*from* corag.) Having fingers; digital; of, or relating to, a finger.

Corag a chroinn, *s. f.* A ploughtail or handle.—*Macd.*

Coragadh, aidh, *s. m.* Neatness, trimness.—*Shaw.*

Coraid, *s. f.* (*Ir. id.*) Runnet; a pair. In this latter sense *coraid* is oftener written *caraid.*

† Coraidh, *s. m.* A hero, a champion. Now written *curaidh;* which see.

Coraidheachd, *s. f.* Heroism; *also,* recognizance.—*Shaw.*

Coraig, *gen. sing.* of corag.

† Coraise, *s. f.* A curtain.—*Shaw.* *N. pl.* coraisean.

Còraiteach, *a.* See Comhraiteach.

Coranach, aich, *s.* (*Scotch,* cronach.) A mournful ejaculation; a howl or conclamation over the grave of a newly-buried person; a singing at funerals; bagpipe music when used at funerals or on mournful occasions.

> The loud *corrinoch* then did me exile
> Throw Lorn, Argile, Menteith, and Breadalbane.
> *Duncan Laider. MS. Warton. Hist. E. P. quoted by Dr. Jamieson.*

The Highland *coronach,* like the Irish, was a panegyric on the deceased, with a recital of the bravery or worth of his ancestors. O'Brien derives this word from *cora,* a quoir, and from the Latin *chorus.*

† Corb, cuirb, *s. f.* A waggon; a chariot.

† Corbadh, aidh, *s. m.* Lewdness; a cast, a throw.—*Shaw.*

Corbaidh, *s. f.* The cramp.

Corbair, *s. m.* A charioteer, a coachman; a waggoner; a cartwright. *N. pl.* corbairean.

Corc, cuirc, *s. f.* (*Ir.* cuirc.) A knife; *rarely,* a caldron, a pot. Corc an ionad cuinnseir, *a knife in place of a sword.—Old Saying.*

Còrcach, aich, *s. m.* Hemp. Buill do 'n chaol-chòrcach, *tackling of hempen ropes.—Macdon.*

† Corcach, aich, *s. m.* A moor; a marsh.—*Shaw.*

Corcag, aig, *s. f.* A bee-hive. *N. pl.* corcagan.

Corcair, *v. a.* Make red, make crimson, make purple, make bloody. *Pret. a.* chorcair; *fut. aff. a.* corcraidh; *pret. pass.* chorcradh. Is ioma sleagh a chorcradh leis, *many a spear was made bloody by him.—Fingalian Poem.*

Corcan, ain, *s. m.* (*Ir. id.*) A pot.

Corcan-coille, *s. m.* A little red woodland flower; a bull-finch—(*Macd.*); the *loxia pyrrhula* of Linnæus.

Corcuir, *gen. sing.* of corcur.

Corcuir, *a.* Red, purple, bloody. An sgiath chorcuir so, *this bloody spear.—Fingalian Poem.*

Corcur, uir, *s. m.* Purple, crimson; a purple or crimson dye. Dearg mar chorcur, *red as crimson.—Sm.* Gorm agus corcur, *blue and purple.—Stew. Exod.*

What the Highlanders call *corcur* is a white mossy scurf adhering to large stones, and with which they make a pretty crimson dye. It is first well dried in the sun, then pulverized and steeped, commonly, in urine, and the vessel made air-tight. In this state it is suffered to remain for three weeks, when it is fit to be boiled in the yarn which it is to colour.

Corcurach, *a.* Purple, crimson; purpled, crimsoned; of, or belonging to, purple; abounding in purple.

Corcurachd, *s. f.* A purple colour.

Cord, cùird, *s. m.* (*W.* cord, cort. *Ir.* corda. *Sp.* cuerda.) A cord, a rope, or cable; a line, a string. *N. pl.* cuird. Cuird air ar ceann, *ropes on our heads.—Stew. 1 K.* Cord sgéinnidh, *a string of twine.*

Cord, *v. a.* Rope; bind; fasten or secure with ropes; agree. *Pret. a.* chord; *fut. aff. a.* cordaidh, *shall bind; fut. pass.* cordar.

Cordadh, aidh, *s. m.* An agreement, a contract, a good understanding; the act of roping or fastening with ropes. Droch cordadh, *a dispute, disagreement.*

Cordadh, (a), *pr. part.* of cord. Roping; fastening with ropes; agreeing.

Cordaidh, *gen. sing.* of cordadh.

Cordaidh, *s. pl.* Spasms.—*Shaw.*

Cordail, *s. f.* Lace; cordage. Le cordail, *with lace.—Stew. Exod.*

Corn, *s.* A kind of sweet bulbous root.

Corn, cuirn, *s. m.* A drinking-horn, a drinking-cup; a flagon; a cruise; a sounding-horn, a trumpet; a convex surface. Talla nan corn, *the hall of* [*cups*] *revelry.—Oss. Tem.* Neart nan corn, *the strength of the drinking-horns,* i. e. *strong drink.—Oss. Fing.* Corn caismeachd an righ, *the king's sounding-horn.—Oss. Tem.* Oladh ann an corn, *oil in a cruise.* Sithe nan cop corn-dubh, *the shock of black convex bosses.—Fingalian Poem. D. pl.* cornaibh. Le cornaibh, *with flagons.—Stew. Song. Sol.*

Heb. kern *and* keren, *a horn.* *Eth.* karan *and* karn, *a trumpet.* *Syr.* karen, karn, *a horn.* *Gr.* κερων, *a sounding-horn.* *Sp.* cuerno. *Lat.* cornu. *W.* corn. *Ir.* corn. *Arm.* corn *and* gorn. *Fr.* corne.

All the northern nations formerly drank out of horns, which were most commonly those of the Urus or European buffalo, which bred in the Hercynian or Bohemian forest. "Urorum cornibus barbari septentrionales potant."—*Pliny,* b. ii. ch. 37. Cæsar observes that these horns were carefully dressed up, and their edges lipped all round with silver. "Haec (cornua) studiosè conquisita, ab labris argento circumcludunt, et in amplissimis epulis pro poculis utuntur." —*Cæs. Bell. Gall.* vi. 26. One of these immense horns, at least an ox-horn of prodigious size, is still preserved in the castle of Dunvegan, Isle of Sky. It was produced only before guests; and, in using it, the drinker twisted his arm round its spires, and turning his mouth towards the right shoulder, drank it off.

Corn, *v. a.* Plait; fold; curl. *Pret. a.* chorn, *plaited; fut. aff. a.* cornaidh, *shall plait.*

Cornach, *a.* Curled, as hair; waving; like a drinking-horn; of a drinking-horn; full of drinking-horns; festive; like a sounding-horn; of a sounding-horn. D' òr-chul casurlach cornach, *thy waving curled yellow locks.—Old Song.*

Cornadh, aidh, *s. m.* A folding, a plaiting, a rolling; a corner; a skirt; a fold; a plait; a curl.

Corn-chlar, -chlàir, *s. m.* A cupboard.

Cornta, *p. part.* of corn. (*Ir. id.*) Folded; plaited; twisted; curled.

Coron, oin, *s. m.* A crown, a coronet, a chaplet. Coron òir, *a crown of gold.—Stew. Ex.* (*Arm.* curun aour, *a crown of gold.*) Coron Mhuire, *a rosary of beads;* literally, *St. Mary's coronet.*

Lat. corona. *Dan.* crone. *W.* coron. *Swed.* krona. *Arm.* curun. *Du.* kroon. *Scotch,* croun.

Coronach, *a.* Like a crown or chaplet; having a crown or chaplet.

Corp, cuirp, *s. m.* A corpse, a carcass; body, in contradistinction to soul. *N. pl.* cuirp; *d. pl.* corpaibh. Do chorp do uaigh t-athar, *thy corpse to the father's sepulchre.—Stew.* 1 *K.* Le corpaibh marbh, *with dead bodies.—Sm.* Cho chinnte 's a tha 'n t-anam ad chorp, *as sure as the soul is in your body.* In Vannes they say *corf marv*, dead body, and in the northern districts of Brittany, *corf maro.* Corp-léin, *a winding-sheet.* Corp-Chriosd, *the eucharist.*

Lat. corpus. *It.* corpo. *Fr.* corps. *Span.* cuerpo. *Da.* krop. *Bisc.* corp-utza. *Ir.* and *Manks,* corp. *Corn.* and *Arm.* corf.

Corpag, aig, *s. f.* Tiptoe. Tha e ag imeachd air a chorpagan, *he is walking on his tiptoes.*

Corpanta, *a.* Bulky, corpulent, solid.

Corpantachd, *s. f.* Bulkiness, corpulence.

Corporra, Corporradh, *a.* (*Ir.* corpordha.) Bodily, corporeal. Gu corporra, *bodily.—Stew. Col.*

Corp-chriosd, *s. m.* The eucharist; *literally,* Christ's body.

Corp-léin, *s. f.* A winding-sheet or shroud. *N. pl.* léintean.

Corp-shnasach, *a.* Anatomical.

Corp-shnasachd, *s. f.* Anatomy, dissection.

Corp-shnasadair, *s. m.* An anatomist, a dissector.

Corr, Corra, *s. f.* (*Ir. id.*) A heron, a crane, a stork; *rarely,* a water-pit; a snout; a bill; a corner. A chorra ri caoirean, *the crane lamenting.—Oss. Gaul.* Corr-riobhach, *or* corr-riabhach, *a heron;* corr-bhan, *a stork;* corr-mhonaidh, *a crane;* corr-ghlas, *a stork;* corr-chòsag, *a cheslip;* corr-ghribheach, *a crane.*

Còrr, *a.* (*Ir. id.*) Odd, not even; remaining, remainder, upwards of, more than; excellent, chief, renowned; stately, lofty, beauteous, vast; stormy. Uimhir chorr, *an odd number.* Còrr is mìle fear, *upwards of a thousand men;* fichead fear is còrr, *twenty men and upwards.* Mac Stairn bu chòrr, *the renowned son of Starno.—Oss. Fing.* Bha rùn do ainnir 's bu chorr i, *he loved the maid, and beauteous she was.—Id.* An giuthasach chòrr, *the stately fir.—Id.* Cho dorcha, cho còrr, *so dark and so vast.—Id.* Corr-ghaoithe nan speur, *the stormy winds of heaven.—Oss. Tem.* Air chorr, *especially, particularly.—Oss. Lodin.*

Corra-bhàn, ain, *s. f.* A stork, a crane.—*Macd.* Is aithne do 'n chorra-bhàn, *the stork knoweth.—Stew. G. B.*

Corra-cagailt, *s. f.* A fluctuating sulphureous hue observed among hot embers in a frosty night.

† **Corrach**, aich, *s. m.* (*Ir. id.*) A marsh; a fetter; a shackle.—*Shaw.*

Corrach, *a.* Steep, precipitous; erect; wavering, inconsistent; rolling, as the eye. In this last sense *corrach* is the same with *carrach.* Thar bruaich chorrach, *over a steep precipice.—Stew. Mic.* Air chreagaibh corrach, *on steep rocks.—Oss. Dargo.* Os cionn nan ceannbheart corrach, *above the erect helmets.—Fingalian Poem.* Sùil chorrach, *a rolling eye.—Macfar.*

Corra-cheann, -chinn, *s. m.* A dunderhead.

Corra-chòsach, aich, *s. f.* A cheslip.

Corra-chòsag, aig, *s. f.* A cheslip. *N. pl.* corra-chòsagan.

Corraghlas, ais, *s. f.* (*Ir. id.*) A heron, a crane, a stork, or bittern. Sgiathan na corra-ghlàise, *the wings of the stork.—Stew. Zech.*

Corra-ghrian, -ghréin, *s. f.* (*Ir. id.*) A bittern; a crane.

Corra-ghribheach, ich, *s. f.* A crane, a stork, a heron.

Corra-mhonaidh, *s. f.* A stork, a crane, a heron. Is aithne do'n chorra-mhonaidh, *the crane knoweth.—Stew. G. B.*

Corran, ain, *s. m.* (*Ir. id.*) A hook or sickle; a prickle, a sharp-edged weapon; the point of a weapon; a pointed weapon; a spear; an arrow. Gach té le corran cam, *every woman with her crooked sickle.—Macfar.* Ceud corran na thaobh an sàs, *a hundred weapons fixed in his side.—Oss. Gaul.* Corran saighde, *the point of an arrow.—Orr.* Corran sgathaidh, *a pruning-hook;* corran bearraidh, *a pruning-hook.*

Corranach, *a.* (*Ir. id.*) Like a sickle; sharp, destructive, deadly; barbed, prickly. Do shaighde corranach, *thy deadly* [*barbed*] *arrows.—Sm.* and *Macint.*

Corra-riabhach, aich, *s.* A heron; the *ardea major* of Linnæus.

Corran-sgathaidh, *s. m.* A pruning-hook.

Corr-ghleus, *s. m.* Good condition. Fir air chor-ghleus, *men in good condition.—Old Song.*

Corr-ghleusach, *a.* Well prepared, in good condition; preparing, putting in good condition.

Corr-mheur, -mheòir, *s. m.* An odd finger. Cha chuir mi mo chorr-mheur air, *I will not touch it.*

Corr-riabhach, aich, *s. f.* A heron or bittern; the *ardea major* of Linnæus. Written also *corra-riathach.*

Corr-sgreachag, aig, *s. f.* An owl.

Corruich, *s. f.* Wrath, anger. Na chorruich ghéir, *in his fierce anger.—Sm.*

Corruich, *v. a.* Move, stir. More commonly written *carruich;* which see.

Còrsa, Còrsadh, aidh, *s. m.* A coast, a shore; a district. Ann ar corsaibh, *on our coasts.—Old Poem.*

Còrsachadh, aidh, *s. m.* A coasting, a cruising.

Còrsaich, *v. n.* Cruise, coast. *Pret. a.* chòrsaich, *cruised; fut. aff.* còrsaichidh, *shall cruise.*

Còrsair, *s. m.* (*from* corsa.) A cruiser, a coaster; a pirate or corsair.

Còrsaireachd, *s. f.* Cruising, coasting; piracy.

Cor-shioman, ain, *s. m.* A bended stick used for making ropes of straw.

† **Cortas**, ais, *s. m.* (*Ir. id.*) A debt.

† **Corughadh**, aidh, *s. m.* An armament; armour.

Cos, coise, *s. f.* (*W.* coes. *Ir.* cos.) A foot; a leg; a shaft; a handle. Cos airson cois, *foot for foot.—Stew. Exod.* Cos na sgein, *the handle of the knife.* Air leth choise, *on one foot; having but one foot.*

Còs, còis, *s. m.* (*Ir.* cuas.) A cavern, a cave; a crevice, a hole. Còs mo shuain, *the cavern of my rest.—Oss. Fing.* *N. pl.* còsan; *d. pl.* còsaibh. A leum on còsaibh, *bounding from holes.—Oss. Derm.*

Cosach, *a.* (*from* cos. *W.* coesawg.) Many-footed; footed; having large feet or legs; having the use of one's feet or legs. Gu cosach lamhach, *the legs and hands in full exertion.*

Còsach, *a.* (*from* còs. *Ir.* cuasach.) Cavernous; full of holes or crevices.

Cosag, aig, *s. f.* A long coat. Luchd nan cosag, *Scotch Lowlanders.* *N. pl.* cosagan.

Còsag, aig, *s. f.* (*dim.* of còs.) A little crevice; a little cave.

Còsagach, *a.* Having or wearing a long coat.

Còsagach, *a.* Full of holes or crevices; snug, warm, sheltered.

Cosail, *a.* See Comhuil.

† **Cosain**, *v. a.* (*Ir. id.*) Defend, keep off; preserve; avouch, maintain.—*Shaw.*

Cosaint, *s. f.* A reply; a defence; averment.

Cosair, *s. m.* (*Ir. id.*) A feast; a bed.—*Shaw.*

Cosalachd, *s. f.* See Cosamhlachd.

Co sam bi, *comp. rel.* Whoever, whosoever.

Co'samhlach, *a.* Comparative; like.

Co'samhlachd, *s. f.* (*Ir. id.*) A parable; a comparison, similitude, resemblance. Co'samhlachd, *parable.*—*Stew. N. T.*

Cosan, ain, *s. m.* (*Ir. id.*) A foot-path.

Cosan, *n. pl.* of còs. Feet; shafts; handles.

Còsan, *n. pl.* of còs. Crevices, holes, coves. *Gen. pl.* còs; *d. pl.* cosaibh.

Cosanta, *a.* (*Ir. id.*) Defended; perplexed, entangled.—*Shaw.*

Cosantach, aich, *s. m.* The defender in a process.—*Shaw.*

Cosarach, *s. pl.* Fetters.

Cosbair. More frequently written *cuspair.*

Cos-bheairt, *s. pl.* Shoes and stockings; armour for the legs.

Cos-cheum, -chéim, *s. m.* A foot-path; a step. Cos-cheuma dìreach, *a straight foot-path.*—*Stew. Heb.*

Cosd, *s. m.* Cost, expense, expenditure, extravagance. *Bisc.* costua. *Arm.* coust. *Eng.* cost. *Germ.* and *Du.* kost. *It.* costo. *Sp.* costa.

Cosd, *v. a.* (*W.* costiaw. *Swed.* kosta. *Arm.* cousta.) Spend, waste; cost; squander. *Pret. a.* chosd, *cost.* Cia meud a chosd e? *how much cost it?* Na cosd t-airgiod, *do not spend your money.* *Fut. aff.* cosdaidh, *shall spend.*

Cosdail, *a.* (cosd-amhuil.) Costly, expensive, extravagant. *W.* costiawl, *bearing expense.*

Cosdas, ais, *s. m.* Expensive cost, expenditure; extravagance. Fear cosdais, *an extravagant man.*

Cosdasach, *a.* Expensive, costly, extravagant; precious; valuable. Gu cosdasach, *expensively.* *Com.* and *sup.* cosdasaiche.

Cosdasachd, *s. f.* Expensiveness, costliness; preciousness, valuableness.

Cosg, *v. a.* Spend, waste; cease, stop; calm; staunch. *Pret. a.* chosg; *fut. aff. a.* cosgaidh. Cosg, *to staunch,* is more frequently written *casg.*

Cosgach, *a.* Having the power of staunching; expensive, wasteful.

Cosgadh, aidh, *s. m.* (*Ir. id.*) A spending; a staunching; ceasing; the act of staunching.

Cosgadh, (a), *pr. part.* of cosg. Spending; ceasing; staunching.

Cosgail, *a.* Expensive, costly.

Cosgair, *v. a.* Slaughter, butcher, massacre; cut, hew, hash, mangle, as a body. *Pret. a.* chosgair, *massacred; fut. aff. a.* cosgraidh, *shall massacre.*

Cosgairt, *s. f.* Slaughter, massacre, havoc; dressing food. See Casgairt.

Cosgar, air, *s. m.* Triumph, rejoicing—(*Shaw*); massacre, butchering.

Cosgarach, *a.* (*Ir. id.*) Bloody, sanguinary—(*Macint.*); triumphant. Gu cosgarach, *bloodily.* *Com.* and *sup.* cosgaraiche.

Cosgaraiche, *s. m.* A sanguinary person.

Cosgas, ais, *s. m.* Expense; waste, profusion.—*Stew. Acts, ref.*

Cosgradh, aidh, *s. m.* (*Ir. id.*) Slaughter, havoc; triumph. Damh chum a chosgraidh, *an ox to the slaughter.*—*Stew. Pro.* Sleagh chosgraidh, *the shield of slaughter.*—*Mac Lach.*

Co'shamhlach, *a.* See Comh-shamhlach.

Co'shamhlaich, *v.* See Comh-shamhlaich.

Co'sheirm, *s. f.* (comh-sheirm.) Harmony; a concert. See Comh-sheirm.

Co'sheirmeil, *a.* Harmonious.

Co'sheomaraiche, *s. m.* (comh-sheomaraiche.) A room-companion, a fellow-lodger. See also Comh-sheomaraiche.

Co'shìnnte, **Co'shìnte**, *part.* Stretched together, laid together at full length. Co'shinnte san uaigh le chéile, *stretched together in the grave.*—*Sm.*

Co'shion, -shìn, *s. f.* Calm weather. Contracted for *comh-shion;* which see.

Co'shoillse, *s. f.* Contracted for *comh-shoillse;* which see.

Coslach, *a.* (comh-samhlach.) Like, similar; likely, probably. Coslach ruit, *like thee;* cha n' eil sin coslach, *that is not likely.*

Coslas, ais, *s. m.* (comh-samhlas.) Resemblance, likeness; appearance; likelihood, probability. Mar choslas each, *as the appearance of horses.*—*Stew. Joel.* A reir coslais, *according to appearance; in all likelihood.* Is fearr e na choslas, *he is better than he appears to be.*—*G. P.*

Cos-leathann, *a.* Broad-footed, web-footed.

Coslom, *a.* (cos *and* lom.) Bare-footed; bare-legged. Written also *caslom.*

Cos-luath, *a.* Swift-footed.—*Shaw.*

Cosmhal, *a.* Like, similar, resembling.

Cosmhalachd, *s. f.* (co-samhnileachd.) Resemblance; appearance; likelihood; a parable. Cosmhalachd 'n ur n-aghaidh, *a parable against you.*—*Stew. N. T.*

Cosmhalas, ais, *s. m.* Resemblance, likeness; appearance, likelihood. Written also *caslas.*

Cosmhuil, *a.* (comh-samhuil.) *Ir.* cosamhuil. Like, similar.

Cosmhuileachd, *s. f.* Similitude, resemblance; comparison; probability, likelihood; imitation; a parable.

Cosnadh, aidh, *s. m.* A gaining, a getting, a winning; gain; earning; *also,* defence; preservation. Spreidh a chosnaidh, *the cattle of his getting.*—*Stew. Gen.*

Cosnadh, (a), *pr. part.* of coisinn; which see.

Cosrach, aich, *s. m.* Slaughter, havoc. A deanamh cosraich, *slaughtering.*

Cosruisgte, *a.* Barefoot, barefooted; barelegged.—*Stew.* 2 *Sam.*

Cost, *s. m.* See Cosd.

Costag a bhaile gheamhruidh, *s. f.* Wild chevril.

Costail, *a.* Costly, expensive, dear. See Cosdail.

Costadhach, *a.* Friendly.

Costas, ais, *s. m.* Expense, expenditure. See also Cosdas.

Cos-stòl, -stòil, *s. m.* A footstool.

Co'stri, **Co'strigh**, *s. f.* Strife. See Comh-strigh.

Co'strigheach, *a.* Striving, emulous. See Comh-strigheach.

Costus, uis, *s. m.* Expense, waste, cost.—*Stew. Acts.* Written also *cosdas.*

Co'stuthach, *a.* Consubstantial. See Comh-stuthach.

Co'stuthachadh, aidh, *s. m.* See Comh-stuthachadh.

Co'stuthachd, *s. f.* See Comh-stuthachd.

Co'stuthail, *a.* See Comh-stuthail.

Cos-uisge, *s. f.* Wild chevril.—*Shaw.*

† **Cot**, *s. m.* Share, portion, part; *rarely,* a cottage. Hence *cotach,* more commonly written *codach;* which see.

Còta, *s. m.* (*Ir. id.*) A coat; a petticoat; a covering. Còta mo mhic, *my son's coat.—Stew. Gen.* Còta gearr, *a short coat, a jacket.—Mac Co.* Còta goirrid, *a short coat or jacket;* còta iochdair, *a female's under-petticoat;* còta-bàn, *a female's flannel petticoat;* còta cadath, *a tartan coat;* còta mòr, *a great coat;* còta nodha, *a new coat. N. pl.* còtaichean. Còtaichean croicinn, *coats of skins.—Stew. Gen.* Cha d' thig còta glas do na h-uile fear, *a grey coat does not become every one.—G. P. N. pl.* còtaichean.

Cotaich, *v. a.* (*from* còta.) Coat; provide with a coat; cover. *Pret. a.* chòtaich, *coated; fut. aff. a.* còtaichidh, *shall coat.*

Còtaichean, *n. pl.* of còta. Coats. See **Còta**.

† **Cotaig**, *s. f.* Harmony; a good understanding.

Còtan, ain, *s. m.* (*dim.* of còta.) A little coat; a little petticoat; a little pile; a part or portion.—*Shaw.*

Cota preasach, *s. m.* The herb Ladies'-mantle.

† **Coth**, *s. m.* Meat, victuals.

Cothachadh, aidh, *s. m.* Earning; support; a contention, a struggle; a battle. For the two last senses see **Cathachadh**.

Cothadh, aidh, *s. m.* (*Ir. id.*) A supporting, a protecting; a support, a protection.

Co'thaghadh, aidh, *s. m.* Syntax.

Cothaich, *v.* Earn, gain, win; debate; contend, struggle, fight. *Pret. a.* chothaich; *fut. aff. a.* cothaichidh. In these last senses *cothaich* is more frequently written *cathaich;* which see.

Cothan, ain, *s. m.* A cough; anhelation; asthma; froth.

Cothanach, *a.* Frothy; asthmatic.

Cothanachd, *s. f.* Frothiness; anhelation.

Co'thional, ail, *s. m.* A congregation, an assembly, a gathering. Co'thional nan tuath, *the gathering of heroes.—Oss. Lodin.* Written also *coimh-thional.*

Co'thlàm, *v. a.* Mix.

Co'thlamadh, aidh, *s. m.* A mixing.

Cothrom, uim, *s. m.* (*Ir.* comh-throm.) Weight; support; justice; mercy; opportunity; fair play. Ar n-airgiod na làn chothrom, *our silver in full weight.—Stew. Gen.* Cum cothrom rium, *support me.—Sm.* Cothrom agus ceart, *justice and equity.—Id.* Cothrom Feinne, *equal combat.* Cha robh cothrom agaibh, *ye had no opportunity.—Stew. Phil.*

Cothromach, *a.* Just, equitable; equal; weighty; firm; firmly situated. Meighean cothromach, *just weights.—Stew. Ezek.* Cha n' eil an slighe cothromach, *their way is not equal.—Id.* Duine cothromach, *a just man;* also, *a man in comfortable circumstances.* Calpa cruinn cothromach, *brawns, well rounded and firm.—Macint.*

Cothromachadh, aidh, *s. m.* A weighing, a poising, a pondering; an establishing, a placing on a firm foundation.

Cothromachadh, (a), *pr. part.* of cothromaich.

Cothromaich, *v. a.* Weigh, measure by weight, poise; ponder, consider; establish. *Pret. a.* chothromaich; *fut. aff. a.* cothromaichidh.

Cothromaichte, *p. part.* of cothromaich. Weighed, poised, measured. An talamh cothromaichte, *the poised earth.—Sm.*

Cràbhach, aich, *s. m.* A devout person; a hypocrite. Cràbhach, teallsanach, no sagairt, *neither devotee, philosopher, nor priest.—R.*

Cràbhach, *a.* Devout, religious; hypocritical. Lè anamaibh cràbhach, *with souls devout.—Sm.*

Cràbhachd, *s. f.* Devotion, religion; hypocrisy.

Cràbhadh, aidh, *s. m.* (*Ir. id.*) Devotion, religion; hypocrisy.

Crac, Crachd, *v. a.* and *n.* (*Corn.* crakye. *Germ.* crachen.) Crack, break by cracking, split; make a cracking noise. *Pret. a.* chrac; *also* crachd.

Crac, Crachd, *s. m.* A crack; a fissure; a breach; a crack, as of a whip. Leig e crachd as, *it gave a crack.* Written also *cnac.*

Cracail, *s. f.* A cracking; a crackling; a cracking or splitting.

Cracair, *s. m.* A cracker; the cracker of a whip; a talker. Cracair neòil, *a rocket.*

Cracaireachd, *s. f.* Conversation, chat. Tha iad a cracaireachd, *they are conversing* or *chatting.*

Cracaireachd, *s. f.* Cracking. Thoiseach e air cracaireachd, *he began to crack.*

The two last words are similar in spelling; but the first syllable of the latter is pronounced nasally.

Cracan, ain, *s. m.* A hill-side; a crackling noise.—*Shaw.*

Crachann, ainn, *s. m.* See **Creachan**.

Crachd, *s. m.* A crack; a fissure or split; a crack, as of a whip; a smart explosion. Leig e crachd as, *it made a crack.*

Crachd, *v. a.* Crack, split; make a cracking noise. *Pret. a.* chrachd. Crachd do chuip, *crack your whip.*

Crachdadh, aidh, *s. m.* A cracking; a crack, a fissure or split.

Crachdail, *s. f.* A cracking noise; a continued cracking; a splitting.

Cradh, craidh, *s. m.* (*Ir. id.*) Pain, anguish, torment, a pang. Cùis mo chraidh, *the cause of my anguish.—Oss. Derm.* Moran craidh, *much pain.—Stew. Nah.* Cradh cridhe, *mental anguish.—Stew. Pro.*

Cradh, *v. a.* Torment, pain, vex, harass. *Pret. a.* chradh, *pained; fut. aff. a.* cradhaidh, *shall pain.*

Cradhadh, aidh, *s. m.* The act of tormenting, vexing, or harassing; vexation.

Cradhaich, *v. a.* Pain, torment, vex, harass. *Pret. a.* chradhaich, *pained; fut. aff. a.* cradhaichidh, *shall torment.*

Cradhaichte, *p. part.* of cradhaich. Pained, tormented, vexed, harassed.

Cradhar, *fut. pass.* of cradh. Shall be tormented. Cradhar an daoi, *the wicked shall be tormented.—Sm.*

Cradh-lot, *s. m.* A grievous wound; mental anguish. Cuis mo chradh-lot, *the cause of my distress.—Mac Lach.*

Cradh-lot, *v. a.* Inflict a grievous wound. *Pret. a.* chradhlot; *fut. aff.* chradh-lotaidh.

Cràg, cràig, *s.* A paw; a broad palm of the hand; a splay foot. Written also *cròg.*

Crag, *gen. pl.* of craig; which see.

Cràgach, *a.* (*from* cràg.) Having paws; in-footed; like a paw. *Com.* and *sup.* cràgaiche.

Cragach, *a.* (*from* craig.) Rocky.

Cràgaireachd, *s. f.* Pawing, handling.—*Shaw.*

Cràgairt, *s. f.* A pawing; a handling awkwardly.

Cràgan, *n. pl.* of cràg.

Cragan, ain, *s. m.* A little rock. Cragan dubh ruadh, *a dark brown* [*dusky*] *rock.—Oss. Tem.*

Craganach, *a.* Abounding in little rocks; rocky.

Cràganach, aich, *s. m.* An in-footed person; a splay-footed person. Is tu an cràganach! *what a splay-footed being you are!*

Cràg-chasach, *a.* Splay-footed, in-footed.

Cràideach, *a.* More properly *craiteach;* which see.

Craidh, *gen. sing.* of cradh.

Cràidh, *v. a.* Pain, torment, harass, oppress, gall, grieve. *Pret. a.* chraidh; *fut. aff. a.* craidhidh, *shall pain.* Chum nach cràidh e mi, *that he may not grieve me.—Stew. Chron.*

Craidhte, *p. part.* of craidh. (*Ir. id.*) Tormented, pained, galled.

CRAIG, *s. f.* A rock, a cliff
W. careg. *Scotch*, craig *Ir.* craig. *Dal.* kruug. In many eastern tongues *crac* means *a rock.*
Brochardus,* in his "Description of the Holy Land," has the following words "Transibis terram Moab usque ad petram deserti quæ *crac* nunc dicitur," *you will pass over the land of Moab as far as the rock in the desert now called* crac In Cilicia, also, there is a rock called *cragus*

CRAIGEACH, *a.* Rocky, cliffy, stony

CRÀIGEAN, ein, *s. m* A splay-footed person.

CRÀIGEANACHD, *s f.* The gait of a splay-footed person; the infirmity of being splay-footed or in-footed

CRAIG-EILEACHAIDH, *s. f.* A rock in Strathspey; also the war-cry of the Grants

CRAIGHEACH, *a.* Splay-footed, in-footed; *also*, a splay-footed person —*Macint.*

CRAIGHTE, *s f* A little farm, a little patch of arable ground, a croft.

CRAIGHTEAR, ir, *s. m* A crofter, a peasant.

CRAIMB-IASG, -eisg, *s m* (*Ir. id.*) The cramp-fish, the torpedo —*Shaw*

CRAIMH See CNAIMH.

CRAIMHEACH, ich, *s m.* A rook

CRÀIN, *s f.* A sow off pigs

CRAINN, *gen sing* and *n pl* of crann See CRANN.

CRAINNSEAG, eig, *s. f* A crackling. *N. pl.* crainnseagan

CRAINNSEILE, *s f.* Tough phlegm.

CRÀITLACH, *a* (*for* craidhteach) Sore, painful; tormenting, sorrowful, troubled; vexatious; oppressive. Bithidh chnuimh dheireannach cràiteach, *the last pains will be sorrowful* —*G. P*

CRAMB, craimb, *s f* A cramp, a holdfast, a knot; a clincher; a cramp-iron; a quarrel.

CRAMBACH, *a.* Clenching, griping; quarrelsome

CRAMBADH, aidh, *s m* A quarrel, a holdfast, a knotting, a clenching

CRAMBAID, *s f* (*i e* cramb-ait) A chape; a ferril; a buckle; a hook or catch, by which any thing, as a buckle, is held in its place; a silver or brass top at the end of a sword. Gun chrios gun chrambaid, *without belt or buckle* —*Macint.* *N pl* crambaidean.

CRÀMH, *v a* Chew See CNAMH

CRAMHAG, aig, *s f.* Caput mortuum—(*Shaw*), dead embers, cinders; standing corn spoilt by cattle

CRÀMHAN, ain, *s. m* A scolding, a rebuking, a scold

CRAMPADH, *s m* See CRAMBADH

CRAMPAID, *s f.* See CRAMBAID.

† CRANAICHE, *s. m.* (*Ir* cranaidhe) A decrepit old man.

CRANN, *v. a* Bar, bolt, as a door; plough. *Pret a.* chrann, *barred*, *fut aff a* crannaidh, *shall bolt* Crann an dorus, *bolt the door.*

CRANN, crainn, *and* croinn, *s. m.* (*Ir* crann) *N. pl.* crainn *and* croinn A plough, a bar, a bolt, a tree; a branch, a mast; a lot Ris a chrann, *at the plough, ploughing*; cuir an crann air an dorus, *bolt the door*, ard mar chrann giuthais, *lofty as a fir-tree.*—*Oss Duthona.* Lebanon nan crann, *woody Lebanon* —*Sm.* Ghairm e ghaoth gu' chrann, *he invited a breeze to his mast* —*Oss Lodin.* An crann meadhonach, *the middle bar* —*Stew Exod* Cùig croinn, *five bars* —*Id* Thilg iad crainn, *they cast lots.*—*Mac Lach* Cuir fu chrann, *put under the yoke.*—*Old Song* Crann-airneag, *a sloe-tree*; crann-arbhair, *a plough*, crann-arain, *a thin piece of wood for turning bread on a gridiron, a baker's bread-shovel, the Pleiades*, crann-arcain, *a cork-tree*, crann-caltuin, *a hazel-tree*, crann-canaich, *a cotton-tree*, crann-ceusaidh, *a cross, a crucifix*, crann-criothann, *an aspen, a poplar*, crann-cuinnse, *a quince*, crann-cuilinn, *the holly-tree*; crann-faibhile, *a beech*, crann-fige, *a fig-tree*, crann-fiona, *a vine*, crann-fearna, *alder*; crann-gallchno, *a walnut-tree*; crann-giuthais, *a fir-tree*, crann-iuthair, *a yew-tree*, crann-leamhain, *an elm*; crann-laibhreal, *a laurel*; crann-maol-dhearc, *a mulberry-tree*; crann-meas, *a fruit-tree*, crann-meidil, *a medlar-tree*; crann-neochdair, *a nectarine-tree*; crann-olaidh, *an olive-tree*, crann-pailme, *a palm-tree*, crann-siris, *a cherry*; crann-seudair, *a cedar-tree*; crann-seilich, *a willow-tree*; crann-sice, *a sycamore-tree*, crann-tèile, *a lime-tree*, crann-tuilm, *the holm-oak*, crann-tùise, *a frankincense-tree*; crann-uinnsinn, *an ash.*

CRANNAG, aig, *s f.* A pulpit, a hamper; a round top; a boat Crannag air a stiùradh le gaoithe, *a boat steered by the winds* —*Old Song*

CRANNAICH, *v. a.* Fit with masts; bolt. *Pret a.* chrannaich; *fut aff. a* crannaichidh, *shall fit with masts.*

CRANNAICHTE, *p part* Fitted with masts

CRANN-AIRNEAG, *s. m.* A sloe-tree

CRANN-ARAIN, *s. m* A thin piece of wood for turning bread on a gridiron; a baker's bread-shovel, also a name given to the Pleïades.

CRANN-ARBHAIR, *s m* A plough *N pl* crainn-arbhair.

CRANN-ARCAIN, *s m* A cork-tree *N. pl* crainn-àrcain, *or* croinn-àrcain.

CRANN-BEITH, *s. m* A birch-tree.

CRANN-BOCSA, *s m* A box-tree.

CRANN-CALTUINN, *s m* A hazel-tree. *N pl* crainn-caltuinn.

CRANN-CANAICH, *s m* A cotton-tree. *N pl.* crainn-canaich.

CRANN-CAORAN, *s. m.* A wild ash-tree, a service-tree

CRANN-CEUSAIDH, *s. m.* A cross, a crucifix.

CRANN-CHU, -choin, *s. m* A lap-dog *N. pl* crann-choin.

CRANNCHUR, uir, *s m.* (*Ir. id*) A lot, a portion, a share; fortune. Gach tuiteamas thig na chrannchur, *every occurrence that may fall to his lot.*—*Sm's Address to a Highland Regiment*

CRANN-COIRNEIL, *s m.* A cornel-tree

CRANN-COSGAIR, *s. m* A laurel.

CRANN-CRIOTHAINN, *s m.* An aspen-tree, a poplar.

CRANN-CUILINN, *s. m* A holly-tree

CRANN-CUINNSE, *s. m* A quince

CRANNDA, *a.* Decrepit, frail.—*Shaw*

CRANN-DARAICH, *s. m.* An oak-tree

CRANN-DEIRIDH, *s. m* A mizen-mast

CRANN-DROMAIN, *s. m* A bore-tree

CRANN-DURDAIN, *s. m* (*Ir. id*) A kind of music made by putting the hand to the mouth —*Shaw*

CRANN-EBOIN, *s. m.* An ebony-tree —*Shaw.*

CRANN-FAIBHILE, *s m* A beech-tree.—*Shaw*

CRANN-FEARNA, *s m* An elder-tree *N pl* crainn-fearna.

CRANN-FIGE, CRANN-FIGIS, *s m.* A fig-tree Ged nach tior an cran-fige blàth, *though the fig-tree should not blossom.*—*Sm.* An crann-figis ard, *the lofty fig-tree.*—*Id.*

CRANN-FIONA, *s m* A vine *N. pl* croinn-fiona.

CRANN-GAFAINN, *s. m.* Henbane.

CRANN-GALLCHNO, *s m* A walnut-tree

CRANN-GIUTHAIS, *s. m.* A fir-tree, a pine.

CRANN-GRÀIN-UBHALL, aill, *s. m* A pomegranate.

CRANN-IUTHAIR, *s. m* A yew-tree

CRANNLACH, *s. pl* Boughs, branches; brushwood.—*Shaw.*

CRANN-LACHADH, aidh, *s. m* A teal, the *anas crecca* of Linnæus *N pl.* crann-lachaidh, *teals*

CRANN-LAIBHREAL, *s m.* A laurel or bay-tree.

CRANN-LEAMHAIN, *s. m.* An elm. *N. pl* crainn-leamhain.

CRANN-LINOIN, *s m* A lemon-tree

Crann-lithe, *s. m.* A carpenter.—*Macd.*

Crann-lochan, ain, *s. m.* A churn.—*Shaw.*

Crann-mailp, *s. m.* A maple-tree.

Crann-maol-dhearc, *s. m.* A mulberry-tree.

Crann-meadhon, *s. m.* A main-mast.

Crann-meas, *s. m.* A fruit-tree. Liosan chrann-meas, *orchards.*—*Stew. Ecc.*

Crann-meidil, *s. m.* A medlar-tree.

Crann-mòr, -mòir, *s. m.* A main-mast. Thuit mo chrann-mòr, *my main-mast fell.*—*Old Song.*

Crann-neochdair, *s. m.* A nectarine-tree.—*Macd.*

Crann-ola, **Crann-oladh**, *gen.* crainn-ola *or* crainn-oladh. An olive-tree. Saothair a chrainn-ola, *the labour of the olive.*—*Sm.*

Crann-pailme, *s. m.* A palm-tree.—*Stew. Exod.*

Crann-riaslaidh, *s. m.* A sort of plough.—*Shaw.*

Crann-seilg, *s. m.* An arrow; a hunting spear.

Crann-seilich, *s. m.* A willow-tree, a sallow-tree.

Crann-seudair, *s. m.* A cedar-tree.

Crann-sgòid, *s. m.* A boom.—*Shaw.*

Crann-shaor, ir, *s. m.* A ploughwright.—*Shaw.*

Crann-siris, *s. m.* A cherry-tree.

Crann-sitroin, *s. m.* A citron-tree.

Crann-siùil, *s. m.* A mast. Air bàrr croinn siùil, *on the top of a mast.*—*Stew. Pro.*

Crann-sleagh, *s. m.* A pikestaff.—*Shaw.*

Crann-spreòid, *s. m.* A bowsprit.

Crann-tabhuil, *s. m.* A sling. Clach ann an crann-tabhuil, *a stone in a sling.*—*Stew. Pro.* Luchd nan crann-tabhuil, *the slingers.*—*Stew. K.*

Crann-tachrais, *s. m.* A winding-wheel.

Crann-tàir, **Crann-tàraidh**, *s. m.* A fire-cross, or beam of gathering; a piece of half-burnt wood dipped in blood, and used as a signal of distress, or to spread an alarm. *Crann-taraidh* is often used as an arbitrary term for any flame that is kindled for the purpose of spreading an alarm, or for signifying distress. Ciod so an solus ann Innisfàil o chrann-tàraidh an fhuathais? *what light is this from Innisfail from the terrible alarm-fire?*—*Ull.* See also *Oss. Carricth.*

When one Highland chieftain received any provocation or slight from another, or when he had reason to apprehend an invasion of his territories, he straightway formed a cross of light wood, seared its extremities in the fire, and extinguished it in the blood of some animal (commonly a goat) slain for the purpose. He next gave it to some messenger in whose fidelity and expedition he could confide, who immediately ran with it to the nearest hamlet, and delivered it into the hands of the first active brother vassal he met; mentioning merely the name of the place of gathering, which he had previously learned from his chief. This second person, who well understood the purport of the message, proceeded to the next village with the same expedition and with the same words as his precursor. And thus, from place to place, was this instrument conveyed through extensive districts, with a celerity that can scarcely be credited. Degradation or death fell upon all who refused the summons of this mute messenger of bloodshed. In 1745, the *crann-tàir*, or *crois-tàir*, traversed the wide district of Breadalbane, upwards of thirty miles, in three hours. The *crann-tàir* was also in use among the Scandinavian nations.

Crann-tarruing, *s. m.* (*Ir. id.*) A wooden pin, a peg; a linch-pin; *also*, a drawing of lots. Cha robh crann-tarruing gun tarruing, *there was not a wooden pin undrawn.*—*Macdon.*

Crann-tarsuing, *s. m.* A cross-bar, a diameter.—*Shaw.*

Crann-teach, *s. m.* An arbour.—*Shaw.*

Crann-teannta, *s. m.* A printing-press; a bookbinder's press; a rackpin.

Crann-teile, *s. m.* A lime-tree.

Crann-togalach, *s. m.* A crane, a lever or crow.

Crann-toisich, *s. m.* A foremast.

Crann-tuilm, *s. m.* The holm oak.—*Shaw.*

Crann-tùise, *s. m.* The frankincense-tree.—*Macd.*

Crann-uinsinn, *s. m.* An ash.—*Stew. Is.* *N. pl.* crainn-uinsinn.

Crann-uisge, *s. m.* A bowsprit. *N. pl.* crainn-uisge.

Craobh, craoibh, *s. f.* (*Ir. id.*) A tree; a bush; foam, froth. Ged sheargas craobh, *though a tree should wither.*—*Sm.* Meas craoibh, *the fruit of a tree.*—*Stew. Gen.*

Craobh, *v. n.* Branch out, sprout, bud. *Pret. a.* chraobh, *branched; fut. aff. a.* craobhaidh.

Craobhach, *a.* Woody; wooded, like a tree; having tall trees; branchy; foaming; flowing in a branching or forked stream. Mo dhùn craobhach, *my wooded hill.*—*Oss. Duthona.* 'Sa choille chraobhaiche, *in the woody forest.*—*O'Neil's Elegy.* 'Fhuil craobhach, *his blood flowing in a branching stream.*—*Sm.* An t-sleagh chraobhach, *the tree-like spear.*—*Oss. Fin. and Lor.*

Craobh-airneag, *s. f.* A sloe-tree.

Craobh-bheithe, *s. f.* A birch-tree.

Craobh-challtuinn, *s. f.* A hazel-tree.

Craobh-chanaich, *s. f.* A cotton-tree.

Craobh-chaoran, *s. f.* A wild-ash-tree; a service-tree.

Craobh-choirneil, *s. f.* A cornel-tree.

Craobh-chasgair, *s. f.* A laurel-tree; a trophy.

Craobh-chriothainn, *s. f.* An aspen, a poplar.

Craobh-chuilinn, *s. f.* A holly-tree.

Craobh-chuinnse, *s. f.* A quince.

Craobh-dharaich, *s. f.* An oak.

Craobh-fhaibhile, *s. f.* A beech-tree.

Craobh-fhearna, *s. f.* An elder-tree.

Craobh-fhigis, *s. f.* A fig-tree.

Craobh-fhioghag, *s. f.* A hardberry-tree.

Craobh-fhiona, *s. f.* A vine.

Craobh-ghallchno, *s. f.* A walnut-tree.

Craobh-ghiuthais, *s. f.* A fir-tree, a pine-tree.

Craobh-ghràin-ubhall, *s. f.* A pomegranate.

Craobh-iuthair, *s. f.* A yew-tree.

Craobh-laibhreil, **Craobh-laibhreis**, *s. f.* A laurel or bay-tree.

Craobh-leamhain, *s. f.* An elm-tree.

Craobh-limoin, *s. f.* A lemon-tree.

Craobh-mhailp, *s. f.* A maple-tree.

Craobh-mhaol-dhearc, *s. f.* A mulberry-tree.

Craobh-mheas, *s. f.* A fruit-tree. Craobh-mheas a bheir mach meas, *a fruit-tree that beareth fruit.*—*Sm.*

Craobh-mheidil, *s. f.* A medlar-tree.

Craobh-neochdair, *s. f.* A nectarine-tree.—*Macd.*

Craobh-phailm, *s. f.* A palm-tree.

Craobh-sgaoil, *v. a.* (*Ir. id.*) Propagate, spread, publish; sprout, branch. *Pret. a.* chraobh-sgaoil.

Craobh-sgaoileadh, idh, *s. m.* A propagating, a publishing; a branching, a sprouting.

Craobh-sgaoileadh, (a), *pr. part.* Propagating, publishing, branching. A craobh-sgaoileadh shith, *publishing peace.*—*Stew. Nah.*

Craobh-sgaoilteach, *a.* Propagative; publishing.

Craobh-sheilich, *s. f.* A willow-tree; a sallow-tree.

Craobh-sheudair, *s. f.* A cedar-tree.

Craobh-shiris, *s. f.* A cherry-tree.

Craobh-shitroin, *s. f.* A citron-tree.

Craobh-théile, *s. f.* A lime-tree.

Craobh-thuilm, *s. f.* A holm oak.

CRAOBH-THÙISE, s. f. A frankincense-tree.

CRAOBH-ÙBHLAN, s. f. An apple-tree. *N. pl.* craobhan-ubhlan.

CRAOBH-UINSINN, s. f. An ash-tree.

CRAOIM, s. f. A morsel; a bite; a nibble; a mouthful, as of bread; a scab.

CRAOIM, v. n. Nibble; crop grass, as cattle. *Pret. a.* chraoim; *fut. aff. a.* craoimidh, *shall* or *will nibble; fut. sub.* chraoimeas.—*Macint.* Written also *creim.*

CRAOIS, *gen. sing.* of craos.

CRAOS, craois, *s. m.* (*Ir. id.*) A wide mouth; a ludicrous term for the human mouth; the mouth of a quadruped, particularly of a voracious quadruped; gluttony; appetite; excess; revelry. A chraos fo chòip, *its mouth covered with foam.—Oss. Derm.* Air a thabhairt do chraos, *given to gluttony or appetite.—Stew. Pro.* Meisg is craos, *drunkenness and revelry.—Stew. Gal. ref.* Luchd craois, *gluttons.—Stew. Pro.*

From *craos* are evidently derived the English word *carouse*, and the French, *carousser.*

CRAOSACH, *a.* (*from* craos.) Wide-mouthed; gluttonous; voracious. *Com.* and *sup.* craosaiche, *more* or *most gluttonous.*

CRAOSACHD, *s. f.* Gluttony, greediness, voracity.

CRAOSAIL, *s. f.* (*Eng.* carousal.) Gluttony.

CRAOSAIR, *s. m.* (*Ir.* craosoir.) A glutton; an epicure; a blubber-lipped fellow; a wide-mouthed fellow; a gaper. *N. pl.* craosairean.

CRAOSAIREACHD, *s. f.* The practice of gluttony; gaping.

CRAOSAL, ail, *s. m.* (*Eng.* carousal.) Drunkenness, revelry; excess in eating or drinking; carousal.

CRAOSAN, ain, *n. pl.* of craos.

CRAOSAN, ain, *s. m.* (*dim.* of craos.) A glutton.—*Shaw.*

CRAOS-GHLAN, *v. a.* Gargle.—*Shaw.*

CRAOSNACH, aich, *s. m.* A spear, a dart. Crath do chraosnach, *shake thy spear.—Ull.* Craosnach dearg, *a fiery dart.* See GATH TETH.

CRAP, *s.* Written more frequently *cnap;* which see.

CRAPADH, aidh, *s. m.* A shrinking, a crushing, a contracting.—*Shaw.*

CRAPARRA, *a.* Strong, stout, lusty. Fear craparra, *a lusty man.—Macfar.*

† CRAS, crais, *s. m.* The body.

† CRASAN, ain, *s. m.* (*dim.* of † cras.) The body; a little body.

† CRASACH, *a.* Corpulent, bulky.

CRASACHD, *s. f.* Corpulence; bulkiness.

CRASGADH, aidh, *s. m.* (*Ir. id.*) A box, a coffer.

CRATAN, ain, *s. m.* A cold, a cough; a cold in the head. Gu h-olc leis a chratan, *badly with a cold.*

CRATANACH, *a.* Causing a cold or cough; coughing; liable to catch cold.

CRATH, *v. a.* and *n.* Shake; tremble; quiver; wave; brandish; sprinkle; churn. *Pret. a.* chrath; *fut. aff. a.* crathaidh, *shall shake.* Chrath e ruighe, *he shook his arm.—Oss. Tem.* Mar chrathas na beanntann an cranna, *as the hills shake their woods.—Id.* Chrath e an t-sleagh, *he brandished the spear.—Oss. Fing.*

CRATHADH, aidh, *s. m.* (*Ir. id.*) A shaking; a brandishing; a sprinkling; a waving, as of trees; a churning. Reultan a crathadh a cheò dhiubh, *stars shaking the mist from them.—Oss. Cathula.* Crathadh bainne, *churning.—Stew. Pro.*

CRATHADH, (a), *pr. part.* of crath. Shaking, brandishing; sprinkling; churning.

CRATHAIDH, *fut. aff. a.* of crath. Shall or will shake.

CRATHAR, *fut. pass.* of crath. Shall be shaken.

CRATH-GHLAN, *v. a.* Clean by shaking, sifting, or sprinkling. *Pret. a.* chrath-ghlan; *fut. aff. a.* crath-ghlanaidh.

CRÀTHRACH, *s. f.* (*Ir. id.*) A boggy place or marsh.

CRÈ, *s.* Clay; dust; the body; breast; being; *rarely,* a creed. Fois air an leabadh chreadh, *rest on the beds of clay.—Orr.* Is beath ur cliù do m' chrè, *your fame is health to my body.—Old Song.* Fhuair iuthaidh a chrè, *an arrow found [hit] his breast.—Oss. Fing.*

CREABALL, aill, *s. m.* A garter. *N. pl.* creabaill, *garters.*

CREABALLACH, *a.* Having or wearing garters; gartered.

CREABALLAICH, *v. a.* Fasten with a garter; provide with garters.

CREABALLAICHTE, *p. part.* of creaballaich.

CREABAN, ain, *s. m.* A four-legged stool. *N. pl.* creabain.

† CREABH, *v. a.* Dun; crave. *Pret. a.* chreabh, *craved; fut. aff.* creabhaidh, *shall crave.*

CREABHACH, aich, *s. m.* Brushwood; dry brushwood; *also, adjectively,* full of brushwood, dry as brushwood.

CREABHAG, aig, *s. f.* The body, the human constitution; a twig; a young woman.

† CREACH, creich, *s. m.* A rock. Now written *creag* or *creig.*

† CREACH, *a.* Blind; grey.—*Shaw.*

CREACH, creich, *s. m.* (*Ir. id.*) Plunder; booty; Highland freebooting; spoil; ruin; *rarely,* a wave. Creach nan ruadh-bhoc, *the spoils of the roes.—Oss. Derm.* Mo chreach! *my ruin!*

CREACH, *v. a.* Plunder; spoil; lay waste; ruin. *Pret. a.* chreach, *ruined; fut. aff. a.* creachaidh, *shall plunder.* Chreach iad am baile, *they plundered the town.—Stew. Gen.* Tha sinn air ar creachadh, *we are spoiled* (or) *plundered.—Stew. Mic.*

† CREACH, creich, *s. f.* A scollop-shell; a cup.—*Shaw.*

CREACHACH, *a.* (*from* creach.) Plundering, rapacious; abounding in shells or in cups.

CREACHADAIR, *s. m.* A plunderer, a robber, a spoiler, a freebooter. *N. pl.* creachadairean. Ithidh an creachadair, *the robber shall devour.—Stew. Job.* Creachadairean an-iochdmhor, *merciless plunderers.—Macfar.*

CREACHADAIREACHD, *s. f.* The practice of plunder or of robbery.

CREACHADH, aidh, *s. m.* A plundering; a spoiling; free-booting; a ruining; plunder, spoil, ruin. Theab 'e mo chreachadh, *he had almost ruined me.*

CREACHADH, (a), *pr. part.* of creach. Plundering, robbing, spoiling.

CREACHAIDH, *fut. aff. a.* of creach. Shall or will plunder.

CRÈACHAN, ain, *s. m.* A kind of pudding made of a calf's entrails.

CREACHAN, ain, CREACHANN, ainn, *s. m.* A rock; the summit of a rock; a mountain; a hard rocky surface; a scollop-shell; a cup. Guilidh creachan nam beann, *the mountain rock shall weep.—Macdon.* Is ard ceann an fheidh 'sa chreachan, *the deer carries its head high on the mountain.—G. P.*

† CREACHAR, air, *s. m.* A vestry.

CREACHAR, *fut. pass.* of creach. Shall or will be ruined.

CREACHD, *s.*; more frequently written *creuchd;* which see.

CREACHTA, *p. part.* of creach. Plundered, spoiled, ruined, robbed. An creachta an aghaidh an treun, *the spoiled against the strong.—Stew. Amos.*

CREADH, creadha, *s.* (*Arm.* creiz.) Clay; the human body; the grave. Mar chuirp creadha, *like bodies of clay;* uidhe gach aon chreadha, *the goal of every human body,* i. e. *the grave.—Stew. Job.* Written also *criadh;* which see.

CREADH-CHUMADAIR, *s. m.* A potter. *N. pl.* creadh-chumadairean.

Creag, creig, *s. f.* A rock, cliff, a hill. Garna air sgeilp creig, *Garno on a splintered cliff.—Oss. Cathluno.* *N. pl.* creagan. Fhreagair na creagan, *the rocks resounded.—Oss. Manos.* *Asp. form*, chreag. Bhuail e 'chreag, *he smote the rock.—Sm.* See Craig.

Creagach, *a.* (*Ir. id.* *W.* kreigiog.) Rocky, cliffy, stony. Chlisg na sleibhte creagach, *the rocky hills started.—Oss. Duthona.* Air aitibh creagach, *on stony ground.—Stew. Mat.*

Creagag, aig, *s. f.* The fish called a perch—(*Shaw*); *also* a conger.

Creagag uisge, *s. f.* A perch.

Creagan, *n. pl.* of creag. Rocks. See Creag.

Creagan, ain, *s. m.* (*dim.* of creag.) A little rock; a rocky or stony place.

Creag-shalann, ainn, *s. f.* Saltpetre, nitre. Air chreag shalann, *on nitre.—Stew. Pro.*

Ceam, *v.* See Creim.

Creamadair, *s. m.* A carper; a verbal critic.

Creamadaireachd, *s. f.* The habit of carping; nibbling.

Creamh, *s. m.* (*W.* krâv.) Gentian. An creamh na chathraichibh, *gentian in beds or plots.—Macint.* Garlic.—*Stew. Num.* Wild garlic.—*Shaw.* Creamh-garaidh, *leeks.*

Creamhach, *a.* Abounding in gentian or in wild garlic; of, or belonging to, gentian or garlic.

Creamhachdan, ain, *s. m.* A root of a tree, a stump, a block of wood.

Creamh-garaidh, *s. m.* A leek.

Creamh-mac fiadh, *s. m.* Hartstongue; asparagus.

Creamh-nuall, aill, *s. m.* (*Ir. id.*) The noise of revelry.

† **Crean**, crein, *s. m.* A purchase; a market-place.

Crean, *v. n.* Consume; remove.—*Shaw.* Smart for, suffer. *Pret. a.* chrean; *fut. aff. a.* creanaidh, *shall suffer.* Creanaidh tu air, *thou shalt suffer for it.*

Creanair, *s. f.* Sedition; tumult.

† **Creanait**, *s. m.* A market-place. *N. pl.* creanaitchean.

Creanas, ais, *s. m.* A whetting, a hacking of sticks; *also, adjectively*, neat-handed.

† **Creapail**, *v. a.* Stop, hinder, stay.—*Shaw.*

Creapan, ain, *s. m.* (*Sax.* crypan, *crawl.*) A stool, a low stool.

Creapull, uill, *s. m.* A garter.

Creas, *s.*; more frequently written *crios.*

† **Creas**, *a.* Narrow, strait.—*Shaw.*

Creas-mara, *s. m.* A strait of the sea. Written also *cneas-mara.*

Creat, *s.* A groan. See Cnead.

† **Creat**, *s. m.* (*Ir. id.*) The form or figure of one's complexion.—*Shaw.*

Creatach, *a.* See Cneadach.

Creatach, aich, *s. m.* A hurdle.—*Shaw.*

Creatachan, ain, *s. m.* A churning-stick.—*Shaw.*

Creathach, aich, *s. m.* Brushwood.—*Macd.*

Creathail, *gen.* creathlach, *s. f.* A cradle; *also*, a horse-fly. Luaisg a chreathail, *rock the cradle;* a luasgadh na creathlach, *rocking the cradle.* *N. pl.* creathlaichean.

Creathair, *s. f.* A sieve. See Criathar.

Creathlach, *gen. sing.* of creathail.

Creathlaichean, *n. pl.* of creathail.

Creic, *v. a.* Sell, barter, exchange. *Pret. a.* chreic, *sold; fut. aff. a.* creicidh, *shall sell; fut. sub.* chreiceas. Ma chreiceas duine a nighean, *if a man sell his daughter.—Stew. Exod. ref.*

Creich, creiche, *s. f.* Plunder, spoil, prey. Lionaidh sinn le creich, *we shall fill with plunder.—Stew. G. B.*

Creid, *v. a.* (*Arm.* credu. *Ir.* creid. *Lat.* crede.) Believe, credit; confide or trust. *Pret. a.* chreid; *fut. aff. a.* creididh, *shall believe; fut. pass.* creidear, *shall be believed.*

Creideach, ich, *s. m.* (*for* creideamhach.) A believer. Creideach no ban-chreideach, *a man or woman who believes.—Stew. Tim.*

Creideach, *a.* (*for* creideamhach.) Believing, faithful. Maighstirean creideach, *believing masters.—Stew. Tim.*

Creideamh, imh, *s. m.* and *f.* Belief; faith; confidence; trust; credit. Le creideamh beó, *with a lively faith.—Sm.* *Arm.* creiden. *Corn.* crêd. *Ir.* creideamh *or* creidiomh.

Creideamhach, aich, *s. m.* A believer. *N. pl.* creideamhaich.

Creideamhach, *a.* Believing, faithful. Tha thu creideamhach, diaduidh, *thou art believing and pious.—Old Song.*

Creideas, eis, *s. m.* (*Gr. by met.* κερδος. *Arm.* cred.) Credit; trust; belief; confidence. Gheibh sinn creideas, *we shall obtain credit.—Old Song.* Tha creideas agad as, *you have credit of him;* thar creideas, *incredible.*

Creideasach, *a.* Creditable, reputable; credible. *Com.* and *sup.* creideasaiche, *more* or *most creditable.*

Creideasachd, *s. f.* Creditableness, reputableness; credibleness.

Creidimh, *gen. sing.* of creideamh.

Creidsinn, *s. f.* The circumstance of believing; belief.

Creidsinn, (a), *pr. part.* of creid. Believing; trusting; confiding.

Creidte, *pr. part.* of creid. Believe.

Creig, *gen. sing.* of creag; which see.

Creigeag, eig, *s. f.* A conger.—*Shaw.*

Creim, *v. a.* Gnaw, chew, nibble. *Pret. a.* chreim, *chewed; fut. aff. a.* creimidh, *shall chew.* Is lom an leac air nach creim thu, *it is a bare stone from which you will pick nothing.—G. P.*

Creim, *s. m.* A scab; a scar; a nibble.

Creimeach, *a.* (*Ir.* creidhmeach.) Scabbed; mangy; full of sores; nibbling.

Creimeadair, *s. m.* A carper; a carping fellow; a verbal critic. *N. pl.* creimeadairean.

Creimeadaireachd, *s. f.* Carping; captious criticism.

Créis, *s. f.* Grease, tallow.

Creisidh, *a.* Greasy.

† **Creithir**, *s. f.* (*Ir. id.* *Lat.* crater *and* cratera.) A cup.

† **Creon**, *v.* See Crion.

Creóp, *v. a.* (*Ir. id.*) Seduce. *Pret. a.* chreóp, *seduced; fut.* creópaidh, *shall seduce.*

Creubh, creubha, *s. m.* The body; a corpse; clay. Is fuar do chreubh, *cold is thy body.—Old Song.*

Creubhag, aig, *s. m.* (*dim.* of creubh.) The body. Written also *créabhag;* which see.

Creuch, créich, *s.* Clay; mortar—(*Stew. Lev.*); a corpse.

Creuchach, *a.* Clayey. Talamh creuchach, *clayey soil.*

Creuchd, *s. f.* (*Ir.* creachd.) A wound; a sore; a scar. A chreuchd tha na chliabh, *the wound in his breast.—Ull.* Creuchd shilteach, *a running issue.—Stew. Lev. ref.*

Creuchdach, *a.* Full of wounds, sores, or scabs; causing wounds; destructive, bloody. Comhrag creuchdach, *a battle full of wounds.—Old Poem.* An leomhann creuchdach, *the bloody lion.—Macdon.*

Creud, creuda, *s.* A creed; a belief.

Creud, *interrog. pron.* (*Ir.* cread.) What. Creud fàth? *wherefore? what cause?* More properly *ciod;* which see.

Creúdag, aig, *s. f.* A wooden football; a cricket-ball. A cluich' air a chreudaig, *playing at cricket; playing at shinty.*

CREUG, creig, *s.* A rock. More frequently written *craig* and *creag*, which see.

CREUGAN, ain, *s m* (*dim* of creug.) A little rock; a rocky place.

CREUGACH, *a.* Rocky, stony.

CREUMHACH, aich, *s m.* A rook; the *frugilegus* of Linnæus

† CREUN, *s. m.* (*Arm.* cren. *Gr* κρανιον) The body; *also*, the skull, as being rotund, from *cruinn*, round.

CREUPAN, ain, *s. m* (*Scotch*, creepie) A low stool.

CREUTAIR, *s. m.* A creature; a body; a being; a person An creutair truagh, *the poor body, the poor soul.* *N pl* creutairean
Arm. crouedur, credur, *and* croedur *Ir.* cretur

CREUTAIREAN, *n pl.* of creatair. (*Arm.* crouaduryen *and* creduryen) Creatures.

CRIABHAR, air, *s m.* (*Lat* cribrum.) A sieve Written also *criabhar*, which see

CRIADH, *s m* (*Ir. id*) Clay, earth. Clabar criadh, *miry clay*—*Sm* Cumhachd air a chriadh, *power over the clay*—*Stew Rom*

CRIADHACH, *a* Clayey, clayish; made of earth or clay; like earth or clay.

CRIADHADAIR, *s m* (*from* criadh.) A potter Tigh a criadhadair, *the potter's house.*—*Stew G B* *N pl* criadhadairean, *potters* Na criadhadairean —*Stew* 1 *Chr.*

CRIADHADAIREACHD, *s f* (*from* criadh) The occupation or trade of a potter; a pottery

CRIADHCHEANGAIL, *v. a* Lute, cement *Pret a.* chriadhcheangail, *cemented.*

CRIADH-FHEAR, -fhir, *s. m* A potter. Tha cumhachd aig a chriadh-fhear, *the potter has power* —*Stew N. T.*

CRIADH-LUCHAG, aig, *s f* A mole *N. pl* criadh-luchaidh *or* criadh-luchagan

CRIADHAOL, aoil, *s. m.* Mortar.

CRIADH-THIGH, *s m.* A house of earth or clay; the grave. Sìth an do chriadh-thigh caol, *peace in thy [cold dwelling of clay] grave.*—*Oss Derm*

CRIAN, *a* See CRION.

CRIANTA, *a* Written also *crionta*, which see

CRIAPACH, *a* Rough —*Shaw*

CRIATACH, *a* Prone to caress, caressing, patting, smoothing, stroking

CRIATACHADH, aidh, *s m* A caressing, patting, smoothing, stroking. Triùir nach fhuilinn criatachadh, sean bhean, cearc is caor, *three that will not bear caressing, an old woman, a hen, and a ewe* —*G P.*

CRIATAG, aig, *s f* A wooden football, a cricket-ball. *N. pl.* criatagan.

CRIATAICH, *v a.* Caress, smooth, pat, stroke *Pret a* chriataich; *fut. aff. a.* criataichidh, *shall stroke*, *p part* criataichte.

CRIATAIR, *s. m* A caresser, a cajoler; a fondler

CRIATHAR, air, *s f* A sieve; a riddle, a cribble. (*Arm.* crouzer *Corn* krodar *and* cruder.) Criathar glanaidh, *a husbandman's riddle*; criathar meala, *a honeycomb* *N. pl.* criathan.

CRIATHAR, *v a.* Sift; filter, examine minutely. *Pret a* chriathar, *sifted*, *fut. aff. a.* criathraidh, *shall sift.*

CRIATHRACH, aich, *s m* (*Ir. id.*) A wilderness; marshy ground, a swamp.

CRIATHRACH, aich, *a.* Like a sieve or riddle.

CRIATHRACHADH, aidh, *s. m.* A sifting, a filtering; a minute examination Fhuair e a chriathrachadh, *he was properly sifted.*

CRIATHRADH, aidh, *s. m* The process of sifting.

CRIATHRAICH, *v. a* Sift, filter; examine minutely. *Pret. a* chriathraich, *sifted*, *fut.* criathraichidh, *shall sift*

CRIATHRAICHTE, *p. part.* of criathraich.

CRIATHRAN, ain, *s. m.* (*dim.* of criathar.) A little sieve, a little riddle.

CRIATHRAN, *n. pl.* of criathar.

† CRIB, *s. f.* Swiftness, haste, speed.—*Shaw.*

CRICHE, *gen. sing.* of crioch.

CRIDHE, *s. m* (*Ir.* cri) A heart; understanding; courage. Is aon an cridhe, *their hearts are one.*—*Sm.* Gun chridhe, *without understanding.*—*Stew. Pro. ref.* Fhir mo chridhe, *my dear fellow*, laogh mo chridhe, *my darling*; cha 'n 'eil chridhe agad, *you have not the heart, you dare not*, cha 'n' eil chridhe no dh' anam agad, *you dare not*; cha dean cridhe misgeach breug, *the drunken soul tells no lies.*—*G. P.* *N. pl* cridheachan, *hearts.*

CRIDHEACH, ich, *s. m.* Hearts at cards. Eus a chridhich, *the ace of hearts.*

CRIDHEAG, eig, *s. f.* (*Ir.* croidheag.) A mistress; a female favourite. *N. pl.* cridheagan.

CRIDHEALAS, ais, *s. m.* Merriness, animal spirits, cheerfulness, mirth.

CRIDHEAN, ein, *s. m.* (*Ir.* croidhean) A gallant; a favourite.

CRIDHE-CHRIONACHD, *s f.* Systole or contraction of the heart.

CRIDHEIL, *a* (cridhe-amhuil) Merry, hearty, cheerful. Bha iad cridheil maille ris, *they were merry with him.*—*Stew. Gen.*

CRILIN, *s. f.* (*Ir. id.*) A box, a small coffer.

CRIMAG, aig, *s f.* A bit, a morsel, a small piece of any thing More properly *criomag*; agreeably to the rule, *leathann ri leathann.* See CRIOMAG.

CRIMAN, ain, *s. m.* (*Arm.* crevenn.) A bit, a morsel; a small piece of any thing, a crust. See CRIOMAN.

CRINDREAS, dris, *s. m.* A bramble —*Shaw.*

CRÌNE, *com.* and *sup.* of crion. Less, least; smaller, smallest.

CRÌNE, *s. f.*, *from* crion. (*Ir id.*) A withered state, rottenness; littleness of size or of heart; meanness. Crine agus dolum, *littleness and moroseness* —*Old Song.*

CRÌNEACHD, *s. f.* Rottenness; diminutiveness, littleness; meanness, pusillanimity.

† CRINEAMH, eimh, *s. m.* The fatal or coronation stone of the Scottish kings, taken by stealth from the palace of Scone, in Perthshire, to Westminster Abbey, where it still remains It is also called *lia fail* and *clach na cineamhuinn.*

CRIN-MHIAL, *s. f.* A wood-louse. *N. pl.* crin-mhiolan, *wood-lice.*

CRIOBH, *s* (*Ir. id*) A jest, a trifle.

CRION-MHIOLACH, *a.* Abounding in wood-lice.

CRIOBH, criobha, *s. m.* A jest, a trifle

CRIOCH, criche, *s. f.* (*Ir. id*) An end; a conclusion or close, a boundary or frontier, a border; a country; *rarely*, a brief; preferment Gu criche ar seachrain sgìth, *to the end of our weary wanderings.*—*Sm.* An la' dlùthachadh r'a chriche, *the day drawing to its close* —*Stew. Judg.* Criocha cian, *distant countries* —*Sm* *N. pl.* criochan.

CRIOCHAN, *n. pl* of crioch. Boundaries, limits, bounds. Na garbh-chriochan, *the rough bounds.*

CRIOCH-CLUICHE, *s f* An epilogue; the end of a play.

CRIOCHDAIR, *s. m* A borderer; a finisher; a gag-tooth. *N. pl.* criochdairean, *gag-teeth* —*Macd.*

CRIOCHNACHADH, aidh, *s. m.* The act of completing; a finishing, a completion. Fear criochnachaidh, *a finisher.* —*Stew Heb.*

CRIOCHNACHADH, (a), *pr. part.* of criochnaich. Finishing.

CRIOCHNAICH, *v. a.* (*from* crioch) Finish, make an end; complete; accomplish; fulfil. *Pret. a.* chriochnaich; *fut. aff. a* chriochnaichidh, *shall finish.* Chriochnaich mi mo thùrus, *I have finished my course* —*Stew. Tim.*

Criochnaichte, *p. part.* of criochnaich. Finished, completed, fulfilled. Tha e criochnaichte, *it is finished.—Stew. N. T.*

Criochnaidheach, *a.* Finite.

Criochnaidheachd, *s. f.* Finitude, finiteness.

Criochnuchadh, aidh, *s. m.* See **Criochnachadh**.

Criochnuich, *v. a.* See **Criochnaich**.

Crioch-sgeòil, *s. f.* An epilogue; the end of a tale.—*Shaw.*

Criomadan, *s. pl.* Bits; splinters; fragments.

Criomag, aig, *s. m.* A morsel, a bit; a tit-bit; a mouthful; a splinter or piece of any thing. *N. pl.* criomagan. Criomagan a gaoil, *its delicious morsels.—Macint.*

Crioman, ain, *s. m.* A morsel; a bit; a mouthful; a splinter or piece of any thing.—*Macint.* Crioman arain, *a bit of bread;* crioman càise, *a bit of cheese;* crioman crion, *a little bit.*

Crion, *v. a.* and *n.* Wither; decay; blast; depress; prevent growth. *Pret. a.* chrion; *fut. aff. a.* crionaidh, *shall wither.* Marrainich làir crionaidh Daorla, *like the fern of the field, Dorla shall decay.— Oss. Duthona.* Ged chrionas lus, *though an herb should wither.—Sm.*

Crion, *a.* (*Ir.* crion. *Corn. Arm.* crin, *dry.*) Little, diminutive; pusillanimous, mean, niggardly; withered, shrunk, decayed; dry, parched. Conan crion, *pusillanimous Conan.—Oss. Derm.* Coillteach chrion, *a decayed wood.—Sm.*

Crion, criona, *s. m.* (*Gr.* κρινω.) A slit in wood produced by heat.

Crionach, *a.* Withered; rotten; like brushwood. Cha chuirinn mo thuadh bheirneach ann do choille chrionaich, *I would not put my chipped axe in thy rotten wood.—G. P.*

Crionach, aich, *s. m.* Dry brushwood; decayed wood; withered leaves; littleness of mind; a pusillanimous person; a term of extreme personal contempt. A crionach aosda air feadh a ghlinne, *her aged leaves throughout the valley.—Oss.* A chrionaich nam Fiann! *thou disgrace of the Fingalians!—Oss. Manos.*

Crionachadh, aidh, *s. m.* A withering, a decaying; a blasting, or scorching with heat.

Crionadh, aidh, *s. m.* A withering, a decaying; a blasting; a scorching up. Air crionadh, *withered.—Macint.*

Crionadh, 3 *sing.* and *pl. imper.* of crion. Crionadh e, *let it wither.*

Crionaich, *v. n.* and *a.* Wither, decay, scorch. *Pret. a.* chrionaich, *withered.*

Crionaidh, *gen. sing.* of crionadh.

Crionaidh, *fut. aff. a.* of crion. Shall *or* will wither.

Crionaidh, *a.* Withered, decayed, scorched; little, pusillanimous. Ged tha mi crionaidh breoite, *though I be withered and bruised.—Old Song.*

Crion-ald, -uild, *s. m.* A stream dried up with the sun's heat; a stream which dries by the summer heat. *N. pl.* crion-uild.

Crioncan, ain, *s. m.* Strife; a quarrel.

Crioncanach, *a.* Quarrelsome; relating to a quarrel.

Crioncanachd, *s. f.* Quarrelsomeness; wrangling; continued quarrelling.

Crion-dhuilleach, ich, *s. m.* and *f.* Withered foliage. Crion-dhuilleach an daraich, *the withered foliage of the oak.—Ull.*

Crion-dhuilleag, eig, *s. f.* A faded or withered leaf. Thuit e mar chrion-dhuilleig, *he fell like a faded leaf.—Old Song.*

Crionlach, aich, *s.* Brushwood; touchwood.

Crion-lus, luis, *s. m.* A withered herb.

Crionna, *a.* (*Ir. id.*) Wise, prudent; cautious; discreet; ancient; antiquated; old-fashioned; advisable. Gu crionna glic, *cautious and wise.—Sm.*

Crionnachd, *s. f.* (*Ir. id.*) Prudence, wisdom; caution; discretion; wit; antiquatedness. Coimhead crionnachd, *regard discretion.—Stew. Pro.* Eolas is crionnachd, *knowledge and wisdom.—Old Song.*

Crion-shearg, *v. a.* and *n.* Wither, fade, scorch.—*Sm. Pret. a.* chrion-shearg.

Crion-sgolt. See **Crion-sgoltadh**.

Crion-sgoltach, *a.* Splitting, causing fissures and cracks, as in wood.

Crion-sgoltadh, aidh, *s. m.* A fissure in wood caused by heat or age; a crack in any surface caused by heat.

Criontach, *a.* Saving; parsimonious; niggardly.

Criontachd, *s. f.* Parsimony; a saving spirit. Cinnidh a chriontachd, ach theid an ro-chriontachd a dholaidh, *the saving will increase his store, the too saving will destroy it.—G. P.*

Criontag, aig, *s. f.* A sorry or parsimonious female. *N. pl.* criontagan. Caitheadh criontaig air a cualaig, *the sorry female spends her means without satisfaction.—G. P.*

Criopag, aig, *s. f.* A wrinkle. *N. pl.* criopagan, *wrinkles.*

Criopagaich, *v. a.* Wrinkle. *Pret. a.* chriopagaich.

Crioplach, aich, *s. m.* and *f.* A cripple; one who has not the use of his legs.—*Stew. Acts, ref. N. pl.* crioplaichean.

Crioplachadh, aidh, *s. m.* A crippling or laming.

Crioplachd, *s. f.* Lameness; extreme decrepitude.

Crioplaich, *v. a.* Lame; cripple. *Pret. a.* chrioplaich, *lamed; fut. aff.* crioplaichidh, *shall lame.*

Crioplaichte, *p. part.* Lamed; crippled.

Crios, *v. a.* (*W.* crys.) Gird, border, belt; envelop; bend round. *Pret. a.* chrios; *fut. aff. a.* criosaidh, *shall gird.*

Crios, *s. m.* (*Ir.* crios. *W.* creas. *Arm.* guris.) A belt; a band; a girdle. A cheann fo m' chrios, *his head under my belt.—Orr.* Crioslaichidh e crios, *he girdeth a girdle.—Stew. Job.* Crios-guaille, crios-guailne, *a shoulder-belt.—Macint.* Crios-muineal, *a necklace.—Stew. Exod.* Crios-pasgaidh, *a swaddling-band;* crios-spéillidh, *a swaddling-band;* cha 'n 'eil mo theangaidh fo do chrios, *my tongue is not under your girdle.—G. P.*

Criosach, *a.* Girdled, belted; striped; like a girdle or belt; tight.

Criosadair, *s. m.* (*from* crios.) A belt-maker.—*Macd. N. pl.* criosadairean.

Criosadaireachd, *s. f.* The employment of belt-making; the occupation of a belt-maker.

Criosaich, *v. a.* Belt; tighten. *Pret. a.* chriosaich, *belted; fut. aff.* criosaichidh; *p. part.* criosaichte.

† **Criosd**, *a.* (*Ir. id.*) Swift; active; clever; smart.—*Shaw.*

Criosd. (*Ir.* Criosd. *Corn.* Grest. *Gr.* Χριστος.) **Christ.**

Criosdachd, *s. f.* Christendom.

Criosd-athair, -athar, *s. m.* A god-father.—*Shaw. N. pl.* criosd-aithrichean.

Criosduigh, *s. m.* A Christian. *N. pl.* Criosduighean. *Arm.* Cristenes.

Criosduigh, *a.* Christian.

Criosduigheachd, *s. f.* Christianity.

Crios-guaille, *s. m.* A shoulder-belt.

Crios-guailne, *s. m.* A shoulder-belt.—*Macint.*

Crioslach, aich, *s. m.* (*Ir. id.*) A bosom; a belt; a girdle; a border; a girding of the loins.—*Shaw.*

Crioslachadh, aidh, *s. m.* The act of girding, belting, or bordering.

Crioslachadh, (a), *pres. part.* of crioslaich. Girding, belting, bordering. 'G a chrioslachadh féin le dealan, *girding himself with lightning.—Oss. Cathluno.*

Crioslaich, *v. a.* (*Ir. id.*) Gird, belt, border. *Pret. a.*

chrioslaich; *fut. aff. a.* crioslaichidh, *shall or will gird.* Crioslaichidh e crios, *he girdeth a girdle.—Stew. Job. Fut. pass.* crioslaichear, *shall be girded.*

CRIOSLAICHTE, *p. part.* of crioslaich. Girded, belted, bordered, begirt.

CRIOS-MUINEAL, eil, *s. m.* A necklace.—*Stew. Exod.*

CRIOS-PASGAIDH, *s. m.* A swaddling-band.

CRIOS-SPÉILLIDH, *s. m.* A swaddling-band.

CRIOSRACHADH, aidh, *s. m.* A girding, a belting, a bordering.

CRIOSRAICH, *v. a.* Gird, belt, surround with a border. *Pret. a.* chriosraich; *fut. aff. a.* criosraichidh. Criosraichidh tu e, *thou wilt gird him.—Stew. Exod.*

CRIOSRAICHTE, *p. part.* of criosraich. Girt, belted, bordered.

CRIOSTAL, ail, *s. m.* (*Ir. id. Gr.* κρυσταλλος.) Crystal. Air dhreach criostail, *having the appearance of crystal.—Old Song.* Sruthan criostail, *crystal streamlets.—Macdon.*

CRIOSTALACH, *a.* Crystalline; like crystal; transparent.

CRIOTACH, *a.* See CRIATACH.

CRIOTHNACH, *a.* Shaking; apt to shake; tremulous; causing to shake.

CRIOTHNACHADH, aidh, *s. m.* (*Ir.* criothnughadh.) A shaking, a trembling.

CRIOTHNAICH, *v. a.* and *n.* (*Ir.* criothnuigh.) Shake, tremble. *Pret. a.* chriothnaich; *fut. aff. a.* criothnaichidh, *shall shake.* Chriothnaich am fonn, *the earth trembled.—Sm.*

CRITH, *s.* (*Ir.* crith. *Box. Lex.* cryd.) A trembling, a shaking, a tremor; a fit of the ague. Air chrith, *trembling.* An talamh air chrith, *the earth trembling.—Sm.* Crith-ghalar, *a palsy;* crith-chath, *a panic;* crith-thalmhainn, *an earthquake;* crith-reothadh, *hoar-frost, weak ice;* cuir air chrith, *shake, cause to shake;* crith-òillt, *a shudder;* geilt-chrith, *a trembling from terror.—Stew. Is.*

CRITH, *v. n.* Shake, tremble, quiver. *Pret. a.* chrith; *fut. aff. a.* crithidh, *shall shake.* Crithidh am fear-siubhail, *the traveller shall tremble.—Oss. Lodin.*

CRITH-CHATH, *s. m.* A panic.

CRITH-CHEÒL, -chiùil, *s. m.* A warbling, a quavering.

CRITH-CHREIDEACH, ich, *s. m.* A quaker. *N. pl.* crith-chreidich.

CRITHEACH, *a.* (*Ir. id.*) Trembling; quavering.

CRITHEACH, iche, *s. m.* (*Ir. id.*) A poplar; an aspen; *populus tremula.* Mar chritheach san t-sìne, *like an aspen in the blast.—Ull.* Slatan do 'n chritheach, *rods of the poplar.—Stew. Gen.* Written also *critheann.*

CRITH-EAGAL, ail, *s. m.* (*Ir. id.*) Astonishment; extreme terror.

CRITH-EAGALACH, *a.* Astonished; exceedingly terrified; also causing extreme terror.

CRITHEANN, inn, *s. m.* A poplar; the *populus tremula,* or aspen.

This tree is often mentioned by Ossian and his brother bards; and Laing, in combating the authenticity of Ossian's Poems, asserts that it is not a native plant of Scotland, and consequently that it could not have existed in Caledonia in the time of Ossian. Observation, however, contradicts this assertion; for in every glen of the Highlands this tree is to be seen. It grows and flourishes where the foot of man never trod—in the inaccessible clefts of lofty rocks; thus presenting an unquestionable appearance of its being an indigenous plant.

CRITHEACHADH, aidh, *s. m.* A trembling, a tremor.

CRITHEACHADH, (a), *pr. part.* of crithich. Shaking, trembling, starting.

CRITH-GHALAR, air, *s. m.* (*Ir. id.*) A palsy—(*Stew. Acts, ref.*); an ague.

CRITHICH, *v. a.* Tremble; shake; start. *Pret. a.* chrithich, *trembled; fut. aff. a.* crithichidh, *shall tremble.* Chrithich, theich, is thuit an namh, *the enemy trembled, fled, and fell.—Ardar.*

CRITHIDH, *fut. aff. a.* of crith. Shall or will shake.

† CRITHNEAL, eil, *s. m.* A shower.

† CRITHRE, *s. pl.* Small sparks from the collision of arms; small particles of any thing.

CRITH-REO, CRITH-REOTH, *s.* Hoar-frost; mildew; a blasting mist; *also,* weak ice, frost. Mar dhuilleach 's a chrith-reo, *like leaves in hoar-frost.—Oss. Duthona.* Ma bhios crith-reoth ann, *if there be a mildew.—Stew.* 1 *K. ref.*

CRITH-SHUILEACH, *a.* Dim-sighted; blear-eyed.—*Stew. Is. ref.*

CRITH-THALMHAINN, *s. f.* An earthquake. *N. pl.* crith-thalmhainnean.

CRITH-THEAS, *s. m.* The tremulous exhalation observed near the surface of the ground on a very warm day.

CRIUDARNACH, aich, *s. m.* The hiccup.

† CRIUN, *s. m.* (*Ir. id.*) A wolf.

CRÓ, *s.* (*Arm.* craou.) A nut; the name of a wheel. *N. pl.* crothan, *nuts.* Cró chòrnaich, *a cluster of cohering nuts;* cró dharaich, *an acorn;* crothan spuing, *Molucca nuts,* or *beans.*

The nuts called *Molucca nuts,* or *Molucca beans,* are found on the shores of the Western Isles, where the kernels of them are used as a cure for diarrhœa and dysentery. In what way Molucca nuts should be cast ashore among the Hebrides, has been explained in the following manner:—These nuts, or beans, are the seeds of the *Dolichos urens Guilandia Bonduc. G. Bonducetta,* and *Mimosa Scandens* of Linnæus, natives of Jamaica. They grow in vast quantities along the rivers of that island, and are generally supposed to be dropped into the water, and carried into the sea; from thence, by tides and currents, and the predominancy of the east wind, to be forced through the Gulf of Florida into the North American ocean; in the same manner as the *Sargasso,* a plant growing among rocks in the seas around Jamaica. When arrived in that part of the Atlantic, they fall in with the westerly winds, which blow two-thirds of the year in that tract, and which may help to waft them to the shores of the Hebrides.

Cró is also written *cnó.*

CRÒ, *s. m.* A fold for sheep; a cattle-house; a stall; a stable; a crop; the eye of a needle; a high wattled cart-rim; *rarely,* children. O chrò nan caorach, *from the sheep-fold.—Sm.* Crò chamhal, *a stable for camels.—Stew. G. B.* Crò snathaid, *the eye of a needle.—Stew. N. T.* Crò na mòin, *the peat-cart.*

CRO, *s.* Cattle; cows; blood-money; a dowry, a portion.

Cro is the name of a fine imposed by the ancient Scots on one who was guilty of murder. The *cro* of every man differed according to the dignity which the person held. The *cro* of a king was one thousand cows; of an earl, one hundred and forty; of a thane or earl's son, one hundred cows; of a villain or plebeian, sixteen cows.—*Scot. Stat. Reg. Maj.* lib. iv. ch. 24.

This law was old even in the time of William the Conqueror. A clause of an act passed in his reign runs thus: "Give anie slaies anie man, he shall give twentie nine kye and one young kow, and make peace with the friends of the defunct, *according to the law of the countrie.*"—*Skene's Statutes of King W.* ch. vi.

Cro, in the sense of cattle, is also written *crodh;* which see.

CRÒBH, crobha, *s. m.* A claw; a paw; a hoof; a clumsy hand. *N. pl.* cròbhan. Cròbh priachian, *the herb crane's-bill.*

CROBHAN, ain, *s. m.* (*dim.* of cròbh.) A claw; a paw; a hoof; a little paw, a little claw. *N. pl.* crobhain. Reubaidh e an crobhain, *he will tear their claws.—Stew. Zech.*

CROBHANACH, *a.* Having hoofs or claws; like a hoof, like a claw; having large hoofs or claws. Tarbh crobhanach, *a bull that has hoofs.—Stew. Ps.*

CROBH-PRIACHAIN, *s. m.* The herb crane's-bill.—*Shaw.*

CROC, croic, *s. m.* (*Corn.* kryk.) A hillock, a hill. *N. pl.* croic. Written also *cnoc;* which see.

Cròc, croic, *s. m.* A deer's horn; an earthen vessel. M' iuthar cam is croc an fheidh, *my bended yew and the deer's horn.—Oss. Fing.*

† **Croc**, *v. a.* Beat, pound. *Pret. a.* chroc, *pounded; fut. aff. a.* crocaidh.

Cròcach, *a.* (*from* cròc.) Horny, horned; having large horns.—*Macint.*

Crocach, *a.* (*from* croc.) Hilly, knolly. Written also *cnocach;* which see.

Crocaid, *s. f.* A cockernony. *N. pl.* crocaidean.

Crocaireachd. See **Cnocaireachd**.

Croc-cheannach, *a.* Horned; having branchy horns; antlered. Eilidean croc-cheannach, *the antlered deer.—Old Song.*

Cròch, cròich, *s. m.* (*Lat.* crocus. *Ir.* croch.) Saffron; a red colour. Spiocnard is cròch, *spikenard and saffron.—Stew. Song. Sol.* Léin cròich, *an ancient Highland mantle.* See **Léin-croich**.

Cròch, *a.* Saffron, red.—*Shaw.*

Croch, *v. a.* Hang, suspend; punish by hanging; depend; linger, hover. *Pret. a.* chroch, *hanged.—Stew. Mat. Fut. aff. a.* crochaidh, *shall hang; fut. pass.* crochar, *shall be hung.* Chaidh 'chrochadh, *he was hanged.*

Crochadair, *s. m.* A hangman. (*Ir.* crochdoir.) *N. pl.* crochadairean, *hangmen.* A chrochadair tha thu ann! *you hangman that you are!*

Crochadaireachd, *s. f.* The business of a hangman; hovering about.

Crochadan, ain, *s. m.* A pendulum; a pendant; a tassel. *N. pl.* crochadain.

Crochadh, aidh, *s. m.* (*Ir. id. Arm.* crok.) A hanging; suspending; suffocation; a depending; a hovering; grief.

Crochadh, (a), *pr. part.* of croich. Hanging; suspending; depending; lingering; hovering.

Crochag, aig, *s. f.* An ear-pendant; a pendulum. *N. pl.* crochagan.

Crochair, *s. m.* (*from* croich.) A rascal; a villain; a scape-gallows; an idle fellow; a hangman. A chrochair! *thou villain! N. pl.* crochairean.

Crochaireachd, *s. f.* Villainy; idleness; lounging.

Croch-aodach, aich, *s. m.* Hangings.—*Shaw.*

† **Crochar**, air, *s. m.* (*Ir. id.*) A body; a bier.

† **Crocharsach**, aich, *s. m.* (*Ir. id.*) A sheepfold.—*Shaw.*

Croch-bhrat, -bhrait, *s. m.* A curtain—(*Stew. Song. Sol.*); a screen; a blind; a drop-scene.

Crochd, *s.* More frequently written *cnoc;* which see.

Crochdach, *a.* More properly *cnocach;* which see.

Crochta, Crochte, *p. part.* of croch. Hung; hanged; suspended. Crochte re géig, *suspended to a branch.—Oss. Fin. and Lor.*

Crodal, ail, *s. m.* A species of moss adhering to large stones, wherewith a coarse red dye is made. The colour which it produces is not so fine as that of the *corcur.* It only dyes a filemot. Written also *crotal.*

Cròdh. See **Crò**.

Cròdh, cròdha, *s. m.* A claw; a paw; the palm of the hand; a large hand.

Crodh, cruidh, *s. m.* (*Ir. id.*) Cows; black cattle; herds; *rarely,* a portion, a dowry. Caoraich agus crodh, *flocks [of sheep] and herds of [black] cattle.—Stew. Gen.* Caise cruidh, *cow's milk-cheese.—Stew. Sam.* Also written *cro.*

Cròdh, *v. a.* Fold; enclose in a fold; hem in together. *Pret. a.* chròdh, *folded; fut. aff. a.* cròdhaidh, *shall fold.* Cròdhaidh am fuarachd iad, *the cold shall hem them in.—Macdon.*

Crodha, *a.* Brave; hardy; active; clever. Fir chrodha, *active men.—Mac Co.* Ri faicinn Ghuill chrodha, *on seeing the brave Gaul.—Fingalian Poem.*

Crodhachd, *s. f.* Bravery; prowess; activity; cleverness; hardihood.

Cròdhadh, aidh, *s. m.* A gathering into a fold; a gathering-in of corn. Féisd a chròdhaidh, *the feast of the in-gathering.—Stew. Ex. ref.*

Crodhall, aill, *s. m.* See **Croghall**.

Cròdhan, ain, *s. m.* (*dim.* of cròdh.) A hoof; a claw; the palm of the hand; the hoof of a cow or sheep. An cròdhan mo laimh, *in the palm of my hand.—Oss. Carricth.*

Crodh-dhearg, -dheirg, *s. m.* Saffron; *also, adjectively,* red as saffron; red-footed.

Crodh-fhionn, *a.* White-hoofed; white-footed.—*Macint.*

Cròg, cròig, *s. m.* The palm of the hand; a fist; a clumsy palm; a clutch; a claw; a paw. *N. pl.* crògan.—*Macint.* Lan cròig, *a fist-full;* làn mo chròig do 'n òr bhuidhe, *my fist-full of the yellow gold.—Old Song.*

Crògach, *a.* Having large palms; having large fists; having paws; like a paw.

Crògairt, *s. f.* (*from* cròg.) A pawing; a handling.

Crogan, ain, *s. m.* A pitcher. *N. pl.* crogain.

Crògarsaich, *s. f.* A pawing; an awkward handling; a fingering.

Croghall aill, *s. m.* (*Ir. id.*) A crocodile, an alligator. Croghall mòr, *an alligator.*

Croghall-mòr, *s. m.* An alligator. *N. pl.* croghaill-mhòr.

Croibheall, bhil, *s. m.* Coral.—*Shaw.*

Croic, *s. f.* (*Gr.* χροος.) The skin; a hide; *rarely,* difficulty; a venison feast.

Croic, *gen. sing.* and *n. pl.* of croc. See **Croc**.

Croiceach, *a.* Meadowy.

Croich, *s. f.* (*Ir.* croch. *Arm.* crouq.) A gallows or gibbet; a cross. Gabh thun na croich, *go to the gallows;* am fear da 'n dàn a chroich, cha d' théid gu bràth a bhàthadh, *he who is born to be hanged shall never be drowned.—G. P.*

Croicionn, croicinn, *s. m.* (*W.* kroen. *Arm.* krochen. *Corn.* krohan *and* croine. *Ir.* croicionn.) The skin of the human body. Croicionn airson croicionn, *skin for skin.—Stew. Job.* *N. pl.* croicnean *and* croicne, *skins.* Croicne reitheachan, *rams'-skins.—Stew. Ex.* Croicionn beothaich, *a beast's skin.* (*Arm.* krochen bioc'h, *a cow's hide.*) Croicionn laoigh, *a calf's skin.* (*Arm.* krochen lue.) Croicionn uain, *a lamb's skin.* (*Arm.* krochen oan.) Croicionn tairbh, *a bull's hide.* (*Arm.* krochen tarf.) Dh' aindeoin do chroicinn, *in spite of your skin.*

Croicionn is also written and pronounced *craiceann.*

Croicionnach, *a.* Skinny.

Croidh-chosach, *a.* Crump-footed.—*Macd.*

Croidhe. More frequently written *cridhe;* which see.

Croidheachd, *s. f.* (*from* crodh.) A portion, dowry.

Criodh-fhionn, *a.* White-hoofed.—*Shaw.*

Croidheag, eig, *s. f.* A sweetheart; a mistress.—*Shaw.*

Croidhean, ein, *s. m.* A gallant, a lover.

Croidhle, *s. f.* (*Scotch,* creel.) A basket; a hamper.

Croidhleag, eig, *s. f.* (*dim.* of croidhle.) A small basket. *N. pl.* croidhleagan.

Cròilean, ein, *s. m.* A little fold; a group.

† **Croinic**, *s. f., from* † cron. (*Gr.* χρονικος. *Ir.* croinic.) A chronicle; an annal.

Croinn, *gen. sing.* and *n. pl.* of crann; which see.

Crois, *s. f.* A cross; a reel, or yarn windlass; a market-place. Crois-bhogha, *a cross-bow;* crois-shlighe, *a bye-way; a cross road.*

Lat. crux. *Span.* cruz. *Ir.* crois. *W.* kroes. *Corn.* crois *and* krouz. *Eng.* cross.

CROIS-BHOGHA, *s. m.* A cross-bow.—*Macd.*

CROISEID, *s. f.* A rail; a barrier. *N. pl.* croiseidean.

CROISLIN, *s. f.* A diameter.—*Shaw.*

CROIS-SHLIGHE, *s. f.* (*Ir.* crois-slighe.) A bye-path; a cross road.

CROIS-TÀRADH, aidh, *s. f.* A signal for arming; an alarm; a fire-cross.—*Macint.* See CRANNTÀIR.

CROIS-THACHRAIS, *s. f.* A reel, or yarn-windlass.

CROIT, *s. f.* A hump on the back; a ludicrous term for the back; a little eminence; a *croft*; a little farm. Croit ministeir, *a glebe.* *N. pl.* croiteachan.

CROITEAR, ir, *s. m.* A crofter. *N. pl.* croitearan.

† CROLOC, *s. m.* (*Ir. id.*) A place where malefactors are executed.—*Shaw.*

CRO-LOT, *v. a.* Wound dangerously. *Pret.* chro-lot, *wounded dangerously.*

CROM, *a.* Crooked, bent; bending; winding; eddying; having crooked horns, as a sheep. Crom mar bhogha, *bent like a bow.*—*Ull.* Croit chrom, *a crooked back.* Crom osag nan stuadh, *the eddying wind of the waves.*—*Oss. Fing.*

Dan. krum. *Teut.* kroome. *Belg.* krom. *Germ.* krumb. *W.* krum. *Ir.* crom. *Corn.* and *Arm.* croum *and* crom, *bent.* *Eng.* crump.

CROM, *v. a.* and *n.* Bend, incline, stoop, bow; descend; make crooked. *Pret. a.* chrom, *bended; fut. aff. a.* cromaidh, *shall bend.* Chrom e a cheann, *he bent his head.*—*Stew. Ex.* Cromaibh ur cluas, *incline your ears.*—*Sm.* Cromaibh a dh' iarruidh 'ur Deirg, *descend in quest of Dargo.*—*Ull.*

CROM, Cruim, *s. m.* A bending, a curvature; a bend, a curve; a concave, a circle. Crom nan speur, *the concavity of the heavens.*—*Oss. Tem.* An cuireadh tu mi o m' chrom? *wouldst thou send me from my circle?*—*Oss. Carricth.*

CROMADH, aidh, *s. m.* (*Ir. id.*) A bending, a stooping, a bowing, a kneeling; an inclination; a bend, a curve, a curvature, a turn or winding; a concavity. Cromadh a chuain, *the bending of the sea; a bay, a headland.*—*Oss. Fing.* Deanar cromadh leinn, *let us kneel.*—*Sm.*

CROMADH, (a), *pr. part.* of crom. Bending, stooping, inclining, kneeling, bowing, drooping, making crooked. Tha 'chluas 'g a cromadh, *his ear is inclining.*—*Sm.* A cromadh fo dhrùchd na maidne, *bending under the dew of morn.*—*Oss. Fin. and Lor.*

CROMAG, aig, *s. f.* A hook; a crook; a catch; a clasp; a tache; a gallows. Cromag òir, *a tache of gold.*—*Stew. Ex.* *N. pl.* cromagan.

CROMAN, ain, *s. m.* (*Ir. id.*) A kite; a large hawk; the hip-bone, the hip.

CROMAN COILTEACH, *s. m.* A woodcock; the *scolopax rusticola* of Linnæus.

CROMAN LOCHAIDH, *s. m.* A kite; the *falco milvus* of Linnæus.

CROMAN LÒIN, *s. m.* The common snipe; the *gallinula* of Linnæus.

CROMAN LUATHA, *s. m.* A wooden instrument for raking ashes; a wooden fire-shovel.

CROMCHRUACH, aich, *s. f.* An Irish idol.

CROMGHOBACH, *a.* Having a hooked bill; *also,* a bird with a hooked bill.

CROMLEAC, lice, *s. f.* (*Ir. id.*) A druidical altar; a druidical chapel.

Cromleac, literally, means the stone of bending, or of worship. Keysler, in his "Northern Antiquities," mentions one in the confines of Alsace, which measured thirty-six feet round, and twelve feet broad, and more than four feet in thickness, raised on other stones several feet from the ground. Toland, in his "Miscellany," makes mention of one in Pembrokeshire, twenty-eight feet high, and twenty feet in circumference: and Cherveau, in his work on "Druidical Monuments," writes of a mass of rock in Poictiers, sixty feet in circumference, and placed on five large stones.

CROMLUS, luis, *s. m.* A poppy. *N. pl.* cromlusan.

CROM NAN DUILLEAG, *s. f.* A woodcock.

CROM NAN GAD, *s. m.* A kind of plough used in the Western Isles or Hebrides.

CROM-SGIATH, -sgeithe, *s. f.* A sort of crooked target.

CROM-SHLIA, CROM-SHLIABH, eibh, *s. f.* A druidical chapel; *literally,* the hill of [worship] bending. This chapel was supposed to be guarded by spectres. Hence Ossian calls it *Crom-shlia nan taibhse,* spectry Cromla.—*Gaul.*

CROM-SHLINNEANACH, *a.* Round-shouldered; hump-backed.

CROM-SHRONACH, *a.* Hook-nosed; aquiline; *also, substantively,* a person with a hooked or aquiline nose.

† CRON, *s. m.* (*Ir. id. Gr.* χρόνος.) Time.

† CRON, *a.* (*Ir. id.*) Brown, dun-coloured, swarthy.—*Shaw.*

CRON, *v. a.* Blame, find fault with, reprove; bewitch; blush with shame.—*Shaw.* *Pret. a.* chron; *fut. aff.* cronaidh.

CRON, croin, *s. m.* (*Ir. id.*) A fault; blame; mischief; harm, hurt; *rarely,* a sign, a mark. A faotainn croin, *finding fault.*—*Stew. Heb.* Gun chron, *harmless, faultless.*

CRONACH, aich, *s. m.* (*Scotch,* cronach.) A mournful cry uttered at Irish and Highland funerals. See CORONACH.

CRONACHADH, aidh, *s. m.* A blaming, a reproving, a chastening; blame, reproof, harm, hurt.

CRONACHADH, (a), *pr. part.* of cronaich. Blaming, reproving.

CRONAICH, *v. a.* (*from* cron.) Blame, rebuke, reprove, find fault with; hurt. *Pret. a.* chronaich, *blamed; fut. aff. a.* cronaichidh, *shall blame.* Cronaich an duine glic, *reprove the wise man.*—*Stew. Prov.*

CRONAICHTE, *p. part.* of cronaich. Blamed, reproved; harmed.

CRONAIL, *a.* (cron-amhuil.) Harmful, hurtful, pernicious.

CRÒNAN, ain, *s. m.* (*Ir. id. Scotch,* croyn, crone, croon. *Belg.* kronen.) Any low murmuring sound; a lulling voice; the buzzing of a fly; the humming of a bee; the purring of a cat; the bellowing of a deer; bass in music; the noise of a bagpipe drone; the purling sound of a brook; a dirge; a pathetic ode. A crònan na chluais, *her lulling voice in his ear.*—*Oss. Gaul.* Crònan an uilt, *the murmur of the mountain-stream.*—*Oss. Duthona.* Seillean le crònan, *the bee with a humming sound.*—*Macdon.*

CRÒNANACH, *a.* (*from* crònan.) Murmuring; lulling; gurgling; purring; bellowing, as a deer. Damh crònanach dearg, *a bellowing red deer.*—*Old Song.*

CRÒNANAICH, *s. f.* A continued low murmur; a continued humming, buzzing, or purling; a purring; the bellowing of a deer.—*Macint.*

CRONNAG, aig, *s. f.* A kind of basket or hamper. Written also *crannag.*

CRON-SEANACHAIS, *s. m.* An anachronism.—*Shaw.*

† CROS, crois, *s. m.* (*Ir. id.*) A hindrance; a cross.

† CROS, *v. a.* (*Ir. id.*) Stop, obstruct, hinder; cross.—*Shaw.*

CROSACH, *a.* Streaked, striped.

CROSAN, ain, *s. m.* A cross-grained person.

CROSANACH, *a.* Perverse, obstinate, cross. Gu crosanach, *perversely.* *Com.* and *sup.* crosanaiche.

CROSANACHD, *s. f.* Perverseness, crossness; *also,* a species of verse.

CROSANTA, *a.* (*Ir. id.*) Perverse, cross-grained, obstinate. Gu crosanta, *perversely.*

CROSANTACHD, *s. f.* Perverseness, obstinacy.

† **Crosra**, ai, *s. m.* (*Ir. id.*) A cross road; a bye-path.

Crosda, *a.* Cross, perverse, froward, peevish. Fear crosda, *a cross man*; tè chrosda, *a cross female*. Dhoibhsan a tha crosda, *to them who are perverse.—Stew. Phil.* Written also *crosta.*

Crosdachd, *s. f.* Fretfulness, perverseness, peevishness. Crosdachd a dhroch cridhe, *the peevishness of his evil heart.—Stew. Jer.*

Croso, croisg, *s.* A cross.

Crosgach, *a.* Transverse; cross; diagonal; awry.

Crosta, *a.* Fretful, cross, perverse, froward. A mhic na mna crosta, *thou son of the perverse woman.—Stew. Sam.* Written also *crosda.*

Crostachd, *s. f.* Fretfulness, perverseness, crossness, frowardness.

Cròt, cròit, *s. f.* A knot. Written also *cnòt.*

Crotach, *a.* (*Ir. id.*) Hump-backed; crook-backed. Duine crotach, *a crook-backed man.—Stew. Lev. Com.* and *sup.* crotaiche.

Cròtach, *a.* Knotty. Written also *cnòtach.*

Crotach, aich, *s. m.* A hump-backed man.

Crotach-mara, *s. m.* A curlew.—*Shaw.*

Crotag, aig, *s. f.* A sort of plover.

Crotaiche, *s. f.* The deformity of hunch-back.

Crotainn, *s.* Barley hulled by pounding; also broth, in which barley so hulled is a principal ingredient.

Crotair, *s. m.* A hump-backed man. *N. pl.* crotairean.

Crotaireachd, *s. f.* The infirmity of a hump-back. Ug imeachd sa chrotaireachd, *walking like a hump-backed person.—Old Song.*

Crotal, ail, *s. m.* A species of moss adhering to stones, which dyes a filemot or feuille-morte; an awn; a husk; a cod; the rind of a kernel. *Crotal*, signifying *moss*, is also written *crodal.*

Crotalach, *a.* Dyed filemot; like filemot.

Cròth, *s. f.* A nut. See Cno.

Croth, crotha, *s. m.* A shape or form. More frequently written *cruth*; which see.

Crothaid, *s.* A gravel.—*Shaw.*

Crothan, *n. pl.* of cròth, (*th* silent.) Nuts. *Arm.* croan, *nuts. Gr.* καρυον, *a nut.*

† **Cru**, *s. m.* Gore, blood.
Lat. cruor. *It.* cru. *W.* kray. *Pol. Bohem.* krew. *Sclav.* kry.

Cruabair, *s. m.* A cruncher; one who chews awkwardly.

Cruabaireachd, *s. f.* A crunching; a chewing.

Cruac, cruaic, *s. m.* The forehead.

Cruacach, *a.* (*from* cruac.) Occipital; having a large forehead; of, or pertaining to, the forehead; having a bald forehead; steady; shrewd.

Cruach, cruaich, *s. f.* (*Ir. id.*) A heap; a pile; a hill, a mountain, a pinnacle; a high rick or stack of corn or hay. Gu cruaich fhichead tomhais, *to a heap of twenty measures.—Stew. Hag.* Cruach is carn air gach taobh, *hill and rock on every side.—Oss. Lod.* Air cruaich nam beann, *on the pinnacle of the mountain.—Oss. Fing. N. pl.* crauachan, *heaps.* Cruachan arbhair, *stacks of corn.—Stew. Ex.* Cruach phadruig, *the herb plantain.* Ithear a chruach na breacagan, *a stack may be eaten in cakes.—G. P.*

Cruach, *v. a.* Heap up, accumulate; gather into a heap; stack, as hay or corn. *Pret. a.* chruach; *fut. aff. a.* cruachaidh.

Cruachach, *a.* Hilly, lofty; full of heaps; like a hill, like a heap. Sliabh cruachach, *a lofty mountain.—Stew. Is.*

Cruachadh, aidh, *s. m.* The act of heaping or gathering into a heap; stacking.

Cruachadh, (a), *pr. part.* of cruach. Heaping or piling up; stacking. A cruachadh na saidh, *heaping or stacking the hay.*

Cruachainn, *gen. sing.* of cruachann.

Cruachainneach, *a.* Having large thighs or hips; of, or pertaining to, a thigh or hip.

Cruachan, *n. pl.* of cruach. Heaps; stacks; hills.

Cruachan, ain, *s. m., dim.* of cruach. (*Ir. id.*) A little hill, a mount, a mound.—*Oss. Tem.* A little rick, a little stack; a cock, as of hay. *N. pl.* cruachanan, *cocks.* A cruinneachadh saoidh an cruachanan, *gathering hay in cocks.—Macfar.*

Cruachann, ainn, *s. f.* The haunch, the thigh, the hip; the side of the human body. Tharruing e 'lann o' chruachann, *he drew his sword from his side.—Oss. Tem. N. pl.* cruachainnean.

Cruachd, cruaichd, *s. f.* The brow, the forehead. Written also *cnuachd.*

Cruach-phadruig, *s. f.* (*Ir. id.*) The herb plantain. Written also *cuach phadruig.*

Cruadail, *gen. sing.* of cruadal.

Cruadal, ail, *s. m.* (*from* cruaidh.) Courage, bravery; virtue; danger; hardihood; trial; hardship; adversity; stinginess. Ròs is fearr cruadal, *a flower* (youth) *of the greatest hardihood.—Macdon.* Iadsan a chleachd cruadal, *they who were inured to trial.—Old Song.*

Cruadalach, *a.* Courageous; hardy; desperate; adverse, trying, calamitous; hard-hearted, ruthless; bloody; narrow-hearted. Is cruadalach an ni e, *it is a calamitous circumstance.* Laoich is cruadalaich beum, *heroes of desperate strokes.—Oss. Fing.* Fear bu chruadalach sleagh, *a man of the most ruthless spear.—Id. Com.* and *sup.* cruadalaiche.

Cruadalaich, *v. a.* Inure, harden, habituate. *Pret. a.* chruadalaich.

Cruadhach, *a.* Of steel; *also, substantively*, steel.—*Stew. Ps. ref.*

Cruadhachadh, aidh, *s. m.* A hardening; a drying, as of grain in a kiln. Ath-chruadhachaidh, *a drying kiln.* Cha 'n e cruathach' na h àtha sealltuinn fuidh, *what dries corn in a kiln is not looking under it.—G. P.*

Cruadhachadh, (a), *pr. part.* of cruadhaich. Hardening; drying, as on a kiln.

Cruadhachas, ais, *s. m.* Rigour, hardness, hardship, trial.

Cruadhag, aig, *s. m.* Distress, difficulty. An t-anfhann na chruadhaig, *the weak in his distress.—Old Song.*

Cruadhaich, *v. a.* Harden; dry, as grain in a kiln; make hardy; make insensible or unfeeling. *Pret. a.* chruadhaich, *hardened.* Chruadhaich e a chridhe, *he hardened his heart.—Stew. Ex.*

Cruadhalach, *a.* Hard; niggard; poor.

Cruadhaichte, *p. part.* of cruadhaich. (*Ir.* cruaidhte.) Hardened; made insensible; made hardy; dried, as in a kiln. Gràn cruadhaichte, *dried corn.—Stew. Sam.*

Cruadhas, ais, *s. m.* Hardness; rigour.

Cruaic, *s. f.* A brow, a forehead, face, front; a pate.

Cruaich, *gen. sing.* of cruach.

Cruaidh, *a.* (*Arm.* crou. *Ir.* cruadh, *hard. Gr.* κρυος, *ice.*) Hard; narrow-hearted, niggardly; severe, strict; stiff, stubborn; difficult; calamitous; irksome; made of metal. Cho cruaidh ri craig, *as hard as a rock.* Ni 's cruaidhe ri chosnadh, *more difficult to be won.—Stew. Pro.* Muineal cruaidh, *a stubborn neck.—Sm.* Màile chruaidh, *a helmet of metal.—Oss.* Is cruaidh leam do chor, *I think thy condition is hard*; is cruaidh an gnothuch e, *it is a hard case*; cruaidh ruithe, *full speed.*

Cruaidh, cruaidhe, *s. f.* A spear; a sword; arms; steel;

metal; armour. Farum nan cruaidh, *with the clangour of arms.—Oss Fing.* A chruaidh mar lasair, *his armour like a flame.—Id.* O chruaidh nan lann, *from the hard metal of the sword.—Id.*

CRUAIDH-BHEUM, -bhéim, *s. m* A hard blow, a heavy or severe blow; a disaster

CRUAIDH-BHEUMNACH, *a.* Giving hard or heavy blows; wounding; felling; satirical. Aig na treunaibh cruaidh-bheumnach, *with the felling heroes.—Old Song.*

CRUAIDH-CHAS, -chais, *s m.* Difficulty, distress, trouble, hardship, adversity. La mo chruaidh-chais, *the day of my distress —Stew Gen.* Fulaing cruaidh-chas, *suffer hardship —Stew. Tim.*

CRUAIDH-CHEANGAIL, *v a* Bind fast. *Pret.* chruaidh-cheangail

CRUAIDH-CHEISD, *s. f.* A hard question; a riddle. *N pl.* cruaidh-cheisdean

CRUAIDH-CHOMHRAG, aig, *s. f.* A hard contest; the hottest part of battle. Anns a chruaidh-chomhrag, *in the hard contest.—Death of Carril.*

CRUAIDH-CHRIDHEACH, *a* Hard-hearted, unfeeling; niggardly Clann chruaidh-chridheach, *hard-hearted children —Stew. Ezek*

CRUAIDH-CHUING, *s f* Hard slavery, rigorous service; a heavy or oppressive yoke.

CRUAIDH-CHUIS, *s f.* A hard case, a hardship; a trial. Là na cruaidh-chuis, *the day of hardship.—Old Song.*

CRUAIDH-CHUISEACH, *a.* Difficult; calamitous.

CRUAIDH-FHORTAN, ain, *s. m.* Hard fortune.—*Turn*

CRUAIDH-FHORTANACH, *a.* Unfortunate.

CRUAIDHLINN, *a* Mountainous; rocky. A thriath Chramo chruaidhlinn, *chief of rocky Cramo —Oss Lodin.*

CRUAIDH-LUS, luis, *s. m.* Sneeze-wort —*Shaw.*

CRUAIDH-MHUINEAL, eil, *s. m.* A hard neck; a stiff or stubborn neck.

CRUAIDH-MHUINEALACH, *a* Hard-necked; stiff-necked; stubborn *Ir.* cruadh-mhuinealach

CRUAIDH-RATHAD, aid, *s. m.* A causeway Cruaidh-rathad an uchdaich, *the causeway of the ascent —Stew* 1 *Ch.*

CRUAIDH-RUITH, *v n* Run hard, run at full speed; pursue at full speed. Gaothair 'g an cruaidh-ruith, *hounds pursuing them at full speed —Oss. Cathluno.*

CRUAIDH-RUITHE, *s m* Hard running, full speed. Each na chruaidh-ruithe, *a horse at full speed*

CRUAIDH-SHION, -shìne, *s m* and *f* Dry wind or weather The word of opposite signification is *feur-shion*, commonly written *feur-thuinn*

CRUAIDH-THEUD, *s m* A wire. *N pl* cruaidh-theudan.

† CRUAN, *a from* † cru. (*Ir id*) Red, blood-colour.

CRUAS, ais, (*contr* for cruadhas) Hardness; hardihood; niggardliness; strength Cruas a lamh, *the strength of his arm.—Old Poem* Cruas do chridhe, *the hardness of thy heart* A réir do chruais, *after thy hardness —Stew. Rom.*

CRUASACHD See CNUASACHD.

CRUASD, *v. n* Crunch.

CRUATHAS, ais, *s. m.* Hardness, hardihood; rigour. Le cruathas, *with rigour —Stew Gen* See CRUADHAS, which is the more proper orthography.

† CRUB, *s m.* (*Ir id*) A horse's hoof; a claw; a fang; the nave of a wheel —*Shaw*

CRÙB, *v n* Creep; crouch; couch, stoop *Pret. a.* chrùb; *fut. aff. a.* crùbaidh Crùbaidh am minnean, *the kid shall creep.—Oss Gaul* Crùbaidh e gu làr, *he shall crouch to the ground.—Sm.* Chrùb e mar leòmhann, *he couched like a lion —Stew. Gen.* Chrùb iad, *they crouched.—Stew Is*

CRÙBACH, *a.* Lame; hirpling; *rarely*, difficult. *Com.* and *sup.* crubaiche, *more or most lame.*

CRÙBACH, aich, *s. m.* A cripple, a lame person. An dall air muin a chrùbaich, *the blind on the lame.—G. P.*

CRÙBAG, aig, *s. f.* (*Ir. id.*) A thrum; a knot in a thread in weaving.

CRÙBAIDH, *fut. aff. a.* of crùb.

CRÙBAIN NA SAONA, *s. f* Dwarf mountain-bramble.

CRÙBAIN, *v. n.* Creep, cringe, crouch; contract or shrug the shoulders, as in cold. *Pret. a.* chrùbain; *fut. aff. a.* crùbainidh.

CRÙBAN, ain, *s. m.* A disease which attacks cows about the latter end of summer and during autumn. It is supposed to be produced by hard grass, scanty pasture, and severe sucking of calves. The cows become lean and weak, with their hind-legs contracted towards the fore-feet, as if pulled by a rope.

CRÙBAN, ain, *s* m. (*Ir. id*) A crouching attitude; a creeping, also a crab fish; any crooked creature. Dean crùban, *crouch down.* Crùban na saona, *dwarf mountain-bramble.*

CRUBÀNACH, *a.* Crouching, creeping; fond of crouching or creeping.

CRÙBANACHD, *s. f* Crouching, creeping

CRÙBANADH, aidh, *s. m.* The act of creeping, a cringing, a crouching, a couching

CRUBH, cruibh, *s. m.* (*Ir. id.*) A horse's shoe Written also *crudh.*

CRUBHACH, *a.* Having shoes, as a horse, shod; well shod. Each crubhach, *a well-shod horse —Old Poem*

CRUBH-SITHNE, *s. m.* A haunch of venison.—*Macd.*

† CRUC, *s. m.* (*Ir id*) A crook; a hook.

CRUDH, cruidh, *s. m*, A horse's shoe. *N. pl.* crudhean.

CRUDH, *v a* Shoe, as a horse. *Pret a.* chrudh, *shod, fut. aff a.* crudhaidh, *shall shoe.*

CRUDHACH, CRUIDHEACH, *a* Shod, as a horse; well shod. Each cruidheach nach pilleadh, *well-shod horses that were to return no more —Old Song.*

CRUGH, crugha, *s. m.* Curds. Written also *gruth.*

CRUGHALACH, *a* Hard, difficult.

CRUIDHEAN, ein, *s. m.* A paw; as much of any pulverised substance as can be lifted by the five fingers.

CRUIDHEARG, *a.* Of a scarlet colour.

CRUIM-SHLINNEIN, *s m.* A hunch on the back —*Shaw.*

CRUIN, *gen. sing.* and *n. pl.* of crùn.

CRUINEACHD, *s f.* Flour; wheat Smior cruineachd, *the best part of wheat —Sm.*

CRUINN, *a* (*W.* crun *Arm.* cren.) Round, circular, rotund; succinct; well rounded; assembled together; sound or sane. Calpa cruinn, *well-rounded legs —Macint.* An t-àit san robh iad cruinn, *the place where they were assembled.—Stew. Acts* Gu cruinn, *succinctly;* innsidh mi gu cruinn mo sgeul, *I will tell succinctly my tale.*

CRUINNE, *s. m.* and *f* (*Ir. id.*) Roundness; circularity; succinctness; the globe of the earth; the universe. This word is commonly masculine in the nominative case, and feminine in the genitive; as, an cruinne cé, *the globe of the earth.* Gu crich na cruinne, *to the extremity of the globe. Sm.*

CRUINNE, *com.* and *sup.* of cruinn. Rounder, roundest.

CRUINNE CÉ, *s. m* The globe, the world, the earth. Gach ni sa chruinne cé, *every thing in the world —Sm*

CRUINNEACHADH, aidh, *s. m.* (*Ir.* cruinniughadh) The act of gathering, a gathering, a meeting or assembly. Trid cruinneachaidh nan uisgeacha, *through the gathering of the waters —Stew. Hab.*

CRUINNEACHADH, (a), *p. part.* of cruinnich.

CRUINNEACHD, *s. f.* See CRUINEACHD.

Cruinnead, eid, *s. m.* Circularity; increase in roundness. A dol an cruinnead, *growing more and more round.*

Cruinneag, eig, *s. f.* A neat tidy girl; a little plump young female; a young woman. Mac samhailt na cruinneig, *the maiden's equal.—Moladh Mhòraig. N. pl.* cruinneagan.

Cruinneagach, *a.* Fond of young women; of, or relating to, young women.

Cruinn-eolach, *a.* Having a knowledge of geography.

Cruinn-eolas, ais, *s. m.* Geography; *also* address.—*Shaw.*

Cruinne-thomhas, ais, *s. m.* Geometry.

Cruinne-thomhasach, *a.* Geometrical.

Cruinne-thomhasair, *s. m.* A geometrician.

Cruinnich, *v. a.* (*from* cruinn.) Gather, assemble, convene; accumulate, sweep together. *Pret. a.* chruinnich, *gather; fut. aff. a.* cruinnichidh, *shall gather.*

Cruinnichte, *p. part.* of cruinnich. Assembled, gathered, convened; accumulated.

Cruinn-leum, leuma, *s. m.* A leap without a race; a bound. Thoir cruinn-leum, *leap without a race.*

Crùinte, *part.* Crowned.

Crùintean, *n. pl.* of crùn. Crowns.

Cruipean, ein, *s. m.* A crupper.

Crùisgean, ein, *s. m.* (*Ir.* cruisgin.) A cruse; a lamp. Oladh ann an cruisgein, *oil in a cruse.—Stew.* 1 *K. ref.*

Cruit, *s. f.* (*Ir. id. W.* crwdd. *Lat.* crotta.) A hump on the back; a ridge; a harp; a fiddle. Meoir a sguabadh na cruit, *fingers sweeping along the harp.—Oss. Trathal.* Cruit an aonaich, *the ridge of the hill.—Macint.*

The *cruit* was a six-stringed instrument used of old in Scotland and Ireland. It is now confined to the mountains of North Wales. The *cruit* of the Gael, and the *crwdd* of the Welch, were the same instrument.

> " Romanusque *lyra* plaudat tibi, Barbarus harpa,
> Græcus Achilliaca, Crotta Britannia canet."
> *Venantius, lib.* 7. *Carm.* 8.

From these lines, which were written in the sixth century by Venantius Fortunatus, some have imagined the *harpa* or *clarsach*, and the *crotta* or *cruit*, to have been different kinds of instruments; and yet a Bishop of Lyons, who wrote a century earlier, makes mention of a barbarian Cythara, shaped triangularly like the Greek Δ, not unlike the Irish harp, which seems to favour the opinion that the cruit and the clarsach were but different names for the same instrument. The probability is, that the cruit and the clarsach differed only in this, that the strings of the former were sinews or cat-gut, and those of the latter were brass wire.

The Rev. Mr. Evans, in describing the Welch *crwdd*, has the following expressions: " Ex sex chordis felinis constat, nec eodem modo quo violinum modulatur, quamvis à figura haud multum abludat."

Cruit-chiùil, *s. f.* A harp, a lyre; a fiddle. Ghlac e chruit-chiùil, *he grasped his lyre.—Ull.*

Cruiteag, eig, *s. f.* A female crowder or performer on the harp; a hump-backed female. *N. pl.* cruiteagan.

Cruiteal, *a.* (*Ir. id.*) Lively, pleasant, sprightly.

Cruitean, ein, *s. m.* A hump-backed person; a little hump; a little ridge; the bird called a kingsfisher.

Cruiteanach, *a.* Hump-backed.

Cruitear, ir, *s. m.* (*Ir.* cruitire. *W.* crwder.) A harper; a musician; a hump-backed person. *N. pl.* cruitearan. Na cruitearan binn, *the melodious harpers.—Old Song.*

Cruitearachd, *s. f.* Harping or playing on the harp; the occupation of a harper.

Crùith, *a.* (*Ir. id.*) Lively; ingenious, expert; prudent. —*Shaw.*

Crùithe, *s. f.* (*Ir. id.*) Prudence; liveliness.

Crùitheachd, *s. f.* (*Ir. id.*) Prudence; liveliness; expertness.

Cruitheachd, *s. f.* The universe, the creation. Air fad na cruitheachd, *throughout the universe.*

Cruith-fhear, **Cruith'ear**, ir, *s. m.* A creator. An Cruith-fhear, *the Creator. Arm.* crouer. *Box. Lex.* crythor.

Cruithneach, ich, *s. m.* A Pict. *N. pl.* Cruithnich, *Picts.*

Cruithneachd, *s. f.* Wheat. Do phlùr a chruithneachd, *of the flour of wheat.—Stew. Ex.* See also **Cruineachd.**

† **Crum**, *v.* See **Crom.**

Crumag, aig, *s. f.* (*Ir. id.*) A skerret.—*Macd.*

Cruman, ain, *s. m.* The hip-bone; a bended instrument used by surgeons.

† **Crumhor**, *a.* (*from* † cru.) Bloody, gory.—*Shaw.*

Crum-shuileach, *a.* Frowning.

Crum-shuileachd, *s. f.* Sourness of look.

Crùn, *v. a.* Crown. *Pret. a.* chrùn, *crowned; fut. aff. a.* crunaidh, *shall crown; fut. pass.* crùnar, *shall be crowned. —Stew. Pro.*

Crùn, crùin, *s. m.* (*Ir.* coron. *Arm.* curun. *Fr.* couronne. *Lat.* corona.) A crown or diadem; a coronet; a crown piece; the crown of the head. Crùn nan daoine glic, *the crown of wise men.—Stew. Pro.* Dolair is crùin, *dollars and crowns. Macint.* Gu seirbheis a chrùin, *to the service of the crown.—Old Song.* Crùn mo chinn, *the crown of my head;* crùn na h-airte, *ornaments in the description of a shield;* crùn sagairt, *a mitre;* bonn crùin, *a crown piece. N. pl.* crùintean.

Crùnadh, aidh, *s. m.* The act of crowning.

Crùnluath, *s. m.* A quick measure in Highland music.

Crùn-sagairt, *s. m.* A mitre.

Crùnta, **Crùnte**, *a. p. part.* of crùn. Crowned.

Crup, *s. m.* The croup; a contraction; a wrinkle.

Crup, *v. a.* Contract, shrink, shrivel. *Pret. a.* chrup; *fut. aff. a.* crupaidh.

Crupach, *a.* Contractive, shrinking, shrivelling.

Crùpach, *a.* Lame. *Germ.* krupel. *Eng.* cripple.

Crupadh, aidh, *s. m.* A contracting, a shrinking, a shrivelling; a contraction, a shrivel; the croup.

Crupag, aig, *s. f.* (*from* crup.) A wrinkle; a fold or plait. *N. pl.* crupagan.

Crupagach, *a.* Wrinkled; plaited; causing wrinkles; like a wrinkle.

Crup-phutag, aig, *s. f.* A blood-pudding.—*Shaw. N. pl.* crup-phutagan.

Crupta, **Crupte**, *p. part.* of crup. Contracted, shrunk, shrivelled.

Cru-sgaoileadh, idh, *s. m.* A bloody flux.—*Shaw.*

Crutair, *a.* (*W.* crwdder.) A harper; a crowder; a musician. *N. pl.* crutairean.

Crutaireachd, *s. f.* The occupation of a harper; minstrelsy.

Cruth, *s. m.* (*Ir. id.*) A form, a shape, a figure; a person; personal appearance; a phantom; a countenance. Cruth mo ghaoil, *the form of my love.—Ull.* Crutha aillidh, *beauteous phantoms.—Oss. Tem.* Co thug dhi a cruth? *who gave her her shape?—Sm.*

Cruthach, *a.* (*from* cruth.) Having shape or figure; resembling.

Cruthachadh, aidh, *s. m.* The act of creating; an asserting; a proving; a creation; a created being; a creature; a proof; an assertion. O chruthachadh an t-saoghail, *from the creation of the world.* An cruthachadh féin, *the creature himself. Stew. Rom.*

Cruthachadh, (a), *p. part.* of cruthaich. Creating.

CRUTHAICH, *v. a.* (*from* cruth.) *Ir. id.* Create, make, form; figure; assert. *Pret. a.* chruthaich, *formed; fut. aff. a.* chruthaichidh, *shall form.* An duine chruthaich thu, *thou madest man.—Sm.*

CRUTHAICHTE, *p. part.* of cruthaich. (*Ir.* cruthaighte.) Created.

CRUTHAIDHEACHD, *s. f.* The creation. Air fad na cruthaidheachd, *throughout the creation.*

CRUTHAIDH-FHEAR, CRUTHAI'EAR, ir, *s. m.* The Creator.

CRUTH-ATHARRACHADH, aidh, *s. m.* A transfiguring, a transfiguration, a metamorphosis, a transformation.

CRUTH-ATHARRACHAIL, *a.* Transformative, transfigurative.

CRUTH-ATHARRAICH, *v. a.* Transfigure, transform, metamorphose. *Pret. a.* chruth-atharraich, *transfigured.* Bithibh air bhur cruth-atharrachadh, *be ye transformed.—Stew. Rom.*

CRUTH-CHAOCHLADH, aidh, *s. m.* A transformation, a metamorphosis.

CRUTH-CHAOCHLAIDEACH, *a.* Transforming, metamorphosing; causing a transformation; of, or pertaining to, a transformation.

CRUTH-LACHD, *s. f.* A belt; a sword-girdle.—*Shaw.*

Cù, coin, *s. m.* A dog. Da chaol-chu, *two gaunt dogs;* cu eunaich, *a pointer;* cù feoladair, *a bull-dog;* cù luirg, *a blood-hound, a gaze-hound, a beagle;* cù uisge, *a water-dog;* cù cuthaich, *a mad dog;* cù-allaidh, *a wolf. N. pl.* coin, *dogs; gen. pl.* con; *asp. form,* chon. Tigh chon, *a kennel;* tigh nan con, *the kennel.* Is feairrd cù, cù a chrochadh, *a dog is the better of a dog's being hanged.—G. P.* Cù sassunnach, *an English dog. Arm.* cy sass. *Gr.* κυ-ων, *a dog. Lat.* canis. *Chin.* keu. *Tart.* chi. *Ir.* cu. *Arm.* ky, cun *and* ki. *Corn.* kei. *W.* ki.

† CUA, *s. m.* Flesh.

CUACH, aich, *s. f.* (*Ir.* cuach. *W.* cwch. *Scotch,* quaich, *cup.*) A bowl, a cup, a goblet; a drinking-cup; a cuckoo; a nest; a curl in the hair, a ringlet. *N. pl.* cuachan. Na cuachan fa chomhair na h-altarach, *the bowls before the altar.—Stew. Zech.* Ma dhiùltas iad a chuach, *if they refuse the cup.—Stew. Jer.* Mar chuaich chruinn, *like a round goblet.—Stew. Song Sol.* A chuach, *the cuckoo.—Stew. Lev.* Measg a cuach-chiabh, *amongst her ringlets.—Oss. Tem.* Cuach phadraig, *the herb plantain;* cuach bhleothainn, *a milking-pail.* The whiskey *cuach* is a shallow ansated cup of wood or of silver, somewhat less than a common saucer.

CUACH, *v. a.* Fold; plait; curl. *Pret.* chuach; *fut. aff.* cuachaidh.

CUACHACH, *a.* (*Ir. id.*) Poculated; like a cup or goblet; hollowed, as a cup; curled; frizzled; of, or belonging to, a cup; full of cups or goblets; like a cuckoo; of, or belonging to, a cuckoo. Buidheann chuachach neoinein, *a group of poculated daisies.—Macfar.* An clre cuachach, *their curled crests.—Oss. Cathula.*

CUACHAG, aig, *s. f.* (*dim.* of cuach.) A little cup; a curl, a ringlet; a young cuckoo; a female with curled hair.—*Macdon.*

CUACHAN, ain, *s. m.* A little cup or goblet; a ringlet or curl; a bird's nest.

CUACHANACH, *a.* Cupped or poculated; having curled hair; also a name given to an inhabitant of Glenquaich in Perthshire.

CUACH-BHLEOTHAINN, *s. f.* A milk-pail.

CUACH-CHLÀR, air, *s. m.* A cupboard. *N. pl.* cuach-chlàran.

CUACH-FHALT, -fhuilt, *s.* Curled hair; waving locks. Do chuach-fhalt bàn, *thy fair-waving hair.—Macint.*

CUACH-PHADRAIG, *s. f.* The herb plantain.

† CUA-CHROMAG, aig, *s. f.* (*Ir. id.*) A flesh-hook. *N. pl.* cua-chromagan.

CUACH-SHRANN, ainn, *s. m.* A violent snorting.—*Shaw.*

CUAG, cuaig, *s. f.* (*W.* kòg.) A cuckoo; the *cuculus canorus* of Linnæus. A chuag is an smeòrach, *the cuckoo and the mavis.—Macint. In derision,* a person affected with itch. Cuir a ruith na cuaig, *send on a fool's errand, make an April fool of one.* Cuag ghliogarach, *a snipe. N. pl.* cuagan.

CUAGACH, *a.* Crump-footed.—*Macd.* Like a cuckoo; abounding in cuckoos.

CUAGAN, ain, *s. m.* The hinder part of the head.—*Shaw.*

CUAICHEANACH, *a.* (*i. e.* cuach-cheannach, *from* cuach *and* ceann.) Curly-headed.

CUAIL, *s. f.* An impediment to marriage.—*Shaw.*

CUAIL, *gen. sing.* of cual. Of a burden.

CUAILEAN, ein, *s. m.* The hair; a wreath; a lock or curl; a small stick used by Highland women for adjusting the *bréid* or head-dress. Mar chuailein a bhaird, *like the hair of the poet.—Oss. Conn.* Cuailean amlach, *curled locks.—Old Song.*

CUAILLE, *s. f.* A pole, a stake. (*Ir.* cuaille.) *N. pl.* cuaillean, *stakes.—Stew. Is. D. pl.* cuaillibh. Cha ghluaisear aon d'a chuaillibh, *not one of its stakes shall be moved.—Id.*

CUAIN, *gen. sing.* of cuan.

CUAIN, *s. f.* A litter; a corner; an angle.—*Shaw.*

† CUAINTE, *a.* (*Ir. id.*) Able.

CUAIREALTA, *a.* Curious.

CUAIREAN, *n. pl.* Rullions.—*Macd.*

CUAIRSG, *v. a.* Roll, wrap up. *Pret. a.* chuairsg; *fut. aff.* cuairsgidh, *shall roll.*

CUAIRSGEACH, *a.* In rolls or volumes; circuitous; twisted; wreathed.

CUAIRSGEADH, eidh, *s. m.* A volume; a roll; a wreath; a circuit.

CUAIRSGEAN, ein, *s. m.* (*Ir. id.*) A wrapper, the felloe of a wheel; the heart.

CUAIRSGTE, *part.* Rolled, wrapped up.

CUAIRT, *s. f.* (*Ir. id.*) A round, a circuit; a journey, pilgrimage, sojourning; a circle, cycle, zone, a circumference; a whirl, an eddy; a circulation; a compass; a visit; a tour; a general gathering of sheep; a circumlocution. An dara cuairt, *the second* [*round*] *time.—Oss. Tem.* Luchd-faire air an cuairtibh, *watchmen on their rounds.—Stew. Song Sol.* Fear cuairt, *a sojourner.* Luchd-cuairt, *sojourners.—Stew. Heb.* Mo chuairt, *my pilgrimage.—Stew. Gen.* Air chuairt, *sojourning*—(*Stew. O. T.*); also, *on a round of visits; at a general sheep-gathering; on a tour.* Cuairt na gaoithe, *the eddy of the wind.—Oss.* Mu 'm chuairt, *about me.—Oss. Carricth.* Tri chuairt, *thrice.—Oss. Fing.* Cainnt gun chuairt, *language without circumlocution.—Mac Lach.* Cuairt na fola, *the circulation of the blood;* cuairt-ghaoth, *a whirlwind;* cuairt-linn, cuairt-shruth, *a whirlpool;* cuairt-radh, *a circumlocution.*

CUAIRT, (mu'n), *adv.* Around, round about; about. Chaidh 'n t-slige mu'n cuairt, *the shell went round.—Oss.* Mu 'n cuairt do dheich bliadhna, *about ten years.*

CUAIRTEACH, *a.* (*from* cuairt.) Circuitous; circumambient.

CUAIRTEACHADH, aidh, *s. m.* The act of surrounding; encircling; a whirling; circulation; a compass; a visiting; a tour; a circuit; a circumlocution. Cuairteachadh chaorach, *a general gathering of sheep into a fold.*

CUAIRTEACHADH, (a), *pr. part.* of cuairtich. Surrounding, encircling, whirling, compassing.

CUAIRTEACHAS, ais, *s. m.* A tour, a round of visits; a gossipping; a visiting.

Cuairteag, eig, *s. f.* A round hollow; a nest; a circle; a fillet; a wheel; an eddy. Eun an fhraoich na chuairteag, *the heath-fowl in its nest.—Oss. Cathluno.* Cuairteag dh' airgiod, *a fillet of silver.—Stew. Exod.* Cuairteag shluganach, *a whirlpool. N. pl.* cuairteagan.

Cuairteagach, *a.* Round, globular, circular; eddying. Aitreabh cuairteagach, *a circular dwelling; a nest.—Macfar.*

Cuairteag-shluganach, *s. f.* A little whirlpool.

Cuairtean, *n. pl.* of cuairt.

Cuairtean, ein, *s. m.* (*from* cuairt.) A little circle; a little circuit; a maze, a labyrinth.

Cuairteanach, *a.* Full of circles; mazy.

Cuairtear, ir, *s. m.* (cuairt-fhear.) A visitor; a sojourner; a tourist. *N. pl.* cuairtearan.

Cuairt-ghaoth, -ghaoithe, *s. f.* A whirlwind. Sa chath mar chuairt-ghaoth, *in battle like a whirlwind.—Orr.*

Cuairtich, *v. a.* Surround, encircle; enclose. *Pret. a.* chuairtich; *fut. aff. a.* cuairtichidh, *shall enclose.* Chuairtich iad mi, *they surrounded me.—Sm. Fut. pass.* cuairtichear.

Cuairtichte, *p. part.* of cuairtich. Surrounded. Cuairtichte le neòil, *surrounded with clouds.—Sm.*

Cuairt-linn, *s. f.* A whirlpool. *N. pl.* cuairt-linntean.

Cuairt-radh, *s. m.* A circumlocution.

Cuairt-shlugan, ain, *s. m.* A whirlpool, an eddy in a stream. *N. pl.* cuairt-shlugain.

Cuairt-shluganach, *a.* Abounding in whirlpools.

Cuairt-shruth, *s. f.* A whirlpool; an eddy in a stream.

Cual, cuail, *s. m.* (*Ir. id.*) A burden, a back-burden, a back-load; a faggot. *N. pl.* cualan. Cleas gille nan cual, cual bheag is tighinn tric, *the carrier's motto, "little at a time and often."—G. P.*

Cual, *pret. neg.* and *interr.* of cluinn. Heard. Nach cual thu? *have you not heard?*

Cualag, aig, *s. f.* (*dim.* of cual.) A bundle; a little burden.

Cualan, ain, *s. m.* (*dim.* of cual.) A little burden; a faggot.

Cualas, *pret. pass.* of cluinn. Was heard. Innis gù 'n cualas mu 'bhuaidh, *till we have heard of his victory.—Oss. Tem.* See **Cluinn**.

Cuallach, aich, *s. m.* (*Ir. id.*) A keeper of cattle.

Cuallachadh, aidh, *s. m.* A tending of cattle; herding.

Cuallachadh, (a), *pr. part.* of cuallaich. Tending cattle, herding. A cuallachadh spréidhe, *tending cattle.—Macfar.*

Cuallachd, *s. f.* The occupation of herding; a number of followers or dependents; *rarely*, a colony.

Cuallaich, *v. a.* Tend cattle, herd. *Pret. a.* chuallaich; *fut. aff. a.* cuallaichidh, *shall herd.*

Cuallaiche, *s. m.* A keeper of cattle; society.

† **Cuallas**, ais, *s. m.* (*Ir. id.*) An assembly.

† **Cua-mhargadh**, aidh, *s. m.* (*Ir. id.*) A flesh-market; shambles.

† **Cuamhor**, *a.* (*Ir. id.*) Fat, corpulent.

Cuan, cuain, *s. m.* (*Ir. id.*) A sea, an ocean, the deep; a large lake; *rarely*, a harbour or haven, a bay. Cuan dobhaidh nan tonn, *the stormy sea of waves.—Ull.* Mar eala air cuan na Lanna, *like a swan on the lake of Lanno.* An iar-chuan, *the western ocean.—Oss. Lodin.* Cuan na mheadhon-thìr, *the Mediterranean sea*; an ard-chuan, *the high sea*; air ard a chuain, *on the high seas.*

Cuanar, *a.* (*Ir. id.*) Soft; calm.—*Shaw.*

Cuanna, *a.* (*Arm.* coanta.) Handsome, neat, fine, showy, engaging. Bean bu chuanna càil, *a woman of the most engaging temper.—Old Poem.* Written also *cuanta.*

Cuanta, **Cuantan**, *n. pl.* Seas, oceans; *rarely*, lakes. Thar chuanta, *over the seas.—Ull.*

Cuanta, *a.* (*Ir.* cuanna. *Arm. Corn.* coanta.) Handsome, neat; tidy, trim; fine, showy; engaging. Urar, sliochdmhor, cuanta, *fresh, numerous, and handsome.—Macdon.*

Cuantachd, *s. f.* Handsomeness, fineness, neatness, tidiness; showiness.

Cuantaibh, *d. pl.* of cuan; which see.

† **Cuar**, *a.* (*Lat.* curvus. *W.* guyr. *Ir.* cuar.) Crooked; perverse.—*Shaw.*

Cuarag, aig, *s. f.* A sock; a shoe made of untanned leather with the hair on. *N. pl.* cuaragan.

Cuaran, ain, *s. m.* (*Lat.* cothurn-us. *Ir.* cuaran. *Box. Lex.* cuaran.) A sock; a bandage; a kind of shoe made of untanned leather; any part of a shoe; buskin. *N. pl.* cuarain. Cuarain air an cosaibh, *shoes on their feet.—Stew. Mark, ref.*

Cuaranach, *a.* Like a sock or shoe; of, or belonging to, a sock, shoe, or buskin.

Cuarsgach, *a.* Twisted, twirled.

Cuartachadh, aidh, *s. m.* A surrounding, enclosing; investing; enclosure; a siege. Written more properly *cuairteachadh*; which see.

Cuartachadh, (a), *pr. part.* of cuartaich. Surrounding, enclosing; investing; besieging. A cuartach' Innisfàil le 'm feachd, *investing Inisfail with their host.—Ull.*

Cuartaich, *v. a.* Surround. More properly *cuairtich*; which see.

Cuartaich, (fear.) A farm-servant among the Hebrideans, whose sole business is to preserve the grass and corn of his employer. His wages are, grass for four cows, and as much arable land as one horse can plough and harrow.

Cuas, cuais, *s. m.* A cave, a cavity; the hollow of a tree. Bu chuas e, *it was a cave.—Stew. John, ref.* More commonly *còs*; which see.

Cuasach, *a.* Cavernous; full of hollows or holes; concave.—*Shaw.*

Cuasachd, *s. f.* Hollowness; subterraneousness; concavity.

Cuasag, aig, *s. f.* A little cave; honeycomb in hollow trees.

Cuasan, ain, *s. m.* (*dim.* of cuas.) A hole; a cavity.

Cuasan, *n. pl.* of cuas. Caves; holes; hollows.

Cùb, cuba, *s. m.* A tumbril; a rimmed cart; a coop.

Gr. κυφος and κυβος, *a little boat. Span.* cuba, *a cask. Eng.* coop.

Cùb, *v. n.* and *a.* (*Lat.* cubo.) Stoop; bend; yield; lie down.—*Shaw.*

Cùbadh, aidh, *s. m.* Stooping; yielding.

Cùbaid, *s. f.* (*Span.* cubeta, *a cask.*) A pulpit. *N. pl.* cùbaidean, *pulpits.*

Cùbair, *s. m.* (*Span.* cubero.) A cooper. *N. pl.* cùbairean.

Cùbaireachd, *s. f.* The occupation of a cooper. Ris a chùbaireachd, *working as a cooper.*

Cubait, *s. f.* A cubit.—*Macd. N. pl.* cubaitean.

Cubhag, aig, *s. f.* A snipe.—*Shaw.*

Cubhaidh, *a.* Seemly, becoming, decent, fit. Mar is cubhaidh dhoibh, *as becomes them.—Stew. N. T.*

† **Cubhais**, *s. f.* (*Ir. id.*) An oath.

Cubhaidheachd, *s. f.* (*Ir.* cuidbheachd.) Seemliness, decentness, fitness, decency.

† **Cubhal**, ail, *s. m.* (*Ir. id.*) A religious habit.

Cubhar, air, *s. m.* A corner; foam, froth.

Cubhas, ais, *s. m.* (*Ir. id.*) A word, a promise; a tree, a block.

Cubhraidh, *a.* Fragrant, redolent, sweet to smell, perfumed. Sa bheithe chubhraidh, *in the fragrant birch.—Oss. Derm.* Fàil cubhraidh, *a sweet smell.—Stew. Gen.*

Rinn mi mo leabadh cubhraidh, *I have perfumed my bed.* —*Stew. Pro.*

CUBHRAIDHEACHD, *s. f.* Fragrance, perfume. Cubhraidheachd t-eudainn, *the fragrance of thy face.*—*Stew. Song Sol.*

CUBHRAIG, *s. f.* A coverlet; a cover.

CUBHRAINN, *s. f.* A coverlet. *N. pl.* cubhrainnean.

CUCHAILTE, *s. m.* A seat or residence.

CUCHAIR, *s. m.* A hunter.

CUDAM, aim, *s. m.* A scar on the head; a fault in the hair of the head.

CUDAMACH, *a.* Frail, fallible, corruptible.—*Shaw.*

CUDAMACHD, *s. f.* Frailty, fallibility, corruptibleness.

CUDAN, ain, *s. m.* The fish called a cuddy.

CUDROM, oim, *s. m.* A weight, a burden, a load. Cudrom do gach aon, *a burden to every one.*—*Stew. Jer.* More properly *cudthrom.*

CUDROMACH, *a.* Weighty, burdensome; important; grave, sedate; just. More properly *cudthromach.*

CUDROMACHD, *s. f.* Weightiness, burdensomeness; importance; gravity, sedateness; justness.—*Stew.* 1 *Tim. ref.*

CUDTHROM, oim, *s. m.* A weight, a burden or load; importance. Leig cudthrom, *lean.*—*Stew. Heb.* Leig do chudthrom orm, *lean upon me.*

CUDTHROMACH, *a.* Weighty, burdensome—(*Stew. Jer.* and *Zech.*); important; just; sedate, grave. *Com.* and *sup.* cudthromaiche, *more* or *most weighty.*

CUGANN, ainn, *s. m.* Rich standing milk; milk set for cream.

CUGHAINNEACH, ich, *s. m.* A mixing together, as of wool.

CUGHAINNICH, *v. a.* Mix together, as wool; tighten.

CUGHANN, *a.* (*Ir.* cumhang. *W.* cywng.) Narrow, strait, close, tight. Druidibh a chònuidh chughann, *close his narrow bed.*—*Oss. Taura.* *Com.* and *sup.* cuinge *and* cughainne. More frequently written *cumhann;* which see.

CUIBEANACH, *a.* Ill-favoured.

† CUIBH, *s. m.* A dog; a greyhound.

CUIBHE, *a.* Fit, becoming, seemly, decent, proper, consistent.

CUIBHEACHD, *s. f.* Fitness, seemliness, decency, consistency, propriety. Contracted for *cubhaidheachd.*

CUBHEIS, *s. m.* Sufficiency, moderation. Fhuair mi mo chuibheis, *I have got enough;* cha 'n 'eil thu ad chuibheis, *you have no moderation.* Perhaps *cuibheis* is *cuimheas,* i. e. *cubhaidh-mheas.*

CUIBHLE, *s. f.* See CUIDHIL.

CUIBHLE, *v. a.* Roll, whirl, wheel. *Pret. a.* chuibhle.

CUIBHLEAN, ein, *s. m.* (*dim.* of cuibhle.) A little wheel.

CUIBHNE, *s. f.* The horn of a deer; a dart.—*Ull.*

CUIBHREACH, *s. pl.* (*Ir. id.*) Bonds; chains; slavery; a cover. An cuibhreach cruaidh, *in hard chains.* Cuibhreach righre, *the bond of kings.*—*Stew. Job.*

CUIBHREACHADH, aidh, *s. m.* A covering, a clothing; a fettering; bondage.

CUIBHREACHADH, (a), *pr. part.* of cuibhrich.

CUIBHRICH, *v. a.* (*Ir. id.*) Bind with chains or ropes; cover. *Pret. a.* chuibhrich, *covered;* *fut. pass.* cuibhrichear, *shall be covered.*

CUIBHRICHTE, *p. part.* of cuibhrich. (*Ir. id.*) Bound with chains or ropes; covered.

CUIBHRIG, *v. a.* Cover, conceal, hide.—*Stew. Lev. ref.* *Pret. a.* chuibhrig, *covered;* *fut. aff.* cuibhrigidh, *shall cover.*

CUIBHRIGTE, *p. part.* of cuibhrig. Covered, concealed, hidden.

CUIBHRINN, *s. f.* A cover; a coverlet.

CUIBHRIONN, inn, *s. m.* (*Ir.* cuimhrean. *W.* cyrran. *Arm.* gevrenn.) A part, a share or participation; an allowance. Cuibhrionn mo shluaigh, *the portion of my people.*—*Stew. Mic.* *N. pl.* cuibhrinnean, *parts.* An cuibhrinnean, *in parts, in shares.* *Cuibhrionn* is perhaps *cuibhe roinn.*

CUIBHSEACH, ich, *s. m.* Enough, sufficiency.

CUID, *gen.* cuid *and* codach, *s. f.* (*Ir. id.*) *N. pl.* codaichean. A part, portion, or share; some; a meal or diet; property, means, substance; also a name for the privy parts. Feòil na cuid a tha reamhar, *the flesh of the part which is fat.*—*Stew. Zech.* Dh' fhag soillse cuid dhiubh, *the light has left some of them.*—*Oss. Fing.* Aon chuid, *either.*—*Stew. Ex.* An dara cuid, *either;* an dà chuid, *both.* An dà chuid na h-adagan 's an t-arbhar, *both the shocks and the standing corn.*—*Stew. Judg.* Cuid ri, *together with, along with, in company with.*—*Macint.* Cuid an tràth, *a meal or diet;* cuid àlaich, *litter;* cuid oidhche, *night's lodgings;* a gharbh chuid, *the rough part; the greatest part.* Is sona 'm fear a thig an ceann a chodach, *lucky is the man who comes in time for his food.*—*G. P.*

Cuid seems to be another form of *coed* or *cued,* from *co,* together, and † *ed* or † *eid,* food. See EID.

CUIDEACHADH, aidh, *s. m.* An assisting, a helping, a help. An t-ainnis gun chuideachadh, *the poor man without help.*—*Sm.* Chum mo chuideachaidh, *to my relief.*—*Id.*

CUIDEACHADH, (a), *pr. part.* of cuidich.

CUIDEACHAIL, *a.* (cuideach amhuil.) Assisting, helpful, prone to help.

CUIDEACHD, *s. f.* (*Ir. id.*) A company, a troop; a throng; a private company. Cuideachd naomh, *a holy* [*celestial*] *company.*—*Sm.* A chuideachd a chridhe, *my dear people.* *N. pl.* cuideachdan.

CUIDEACHD, *conj.* Also, likewise; together, in company; close together, in contact. Chluinnte taibhse cuideachd, *ghosts were also heard.*—*Orr.* Chomhnuidh a ghabhail cuideachd, *to dwell together.*—*Stew. Gen.* Theann i an lomairt cuideachd, *she pressed the fleece together.*—*Id.* Cuir cuideachd, *join, put together.*

CUIDEAL, eil, *s. m.* Pride.

CUIDEALACH, *a.* Proud, haughty.

CUIDEALACHD, *s. f.* Pride.

CUIDHIL, cuidhle, *s. f.* (*W.* çwil.) A wheel; a spinning-wheel; a reel, or yarn-windlass; a whirling, a reeling, a whirl; a cock of hay. Cuir cuidhil dhiot, *wheel about.* *N. pl.* cuidhleachan, *wheels;* saor chuidhleachan, *a wheel-wright.*

CUIDHIL, *v. a.* Roll; wheel; whirl; twirl; hurl; coil; gather into cocks, as hay. *Pret. a.* chuidhil, *rolled;* *fut. aff. a.* cuidhlidh, *shall roll.* Cuidhil an saoidh, *coil the hay.*

CUIDHLEACHAN, *n. pl.* of cuidhil. Wheels.

CUIDHLEAG, eig, *s. f.* (*dim.* of cuidhil.) A cock of hay. *N. pl.* cuighleadan.

CUIDHLEAN, ein, *s. m.* (*dim.* of cuidhle.) A little wheel.

CUIDHLEARACHD, *s. f.* Wheeling, rolling; hurling; spinning on a wheel.

CUIDHLIDH, *fut. aff. a.* of cuidhil.

CUIDHTICH, *v. a.* Restore, requite; quit. *Pret. a.* chuidhtich, *restored.*

CUIDICH, *v. a.* (*Ir. id.*) Help, relieve; countenance, favour. *Pret. a.* chuidich; *fut. aff. a.* cuidichidh. Ad thròcair cuidich mi, *in thy mercy help me.*—*Sm.* *Cuidich* has often the preposition *le,* simple or compounded, put after it, as, Cuidich le Seumas, *help James;* cuideach leam, *help me.* Cuidich leat fein, is cuidichidh Dia leat, *do your best, and God will help.*—*G. P.*

Cuidichidh, *fut. aff. a.* Shall or will help.

Cuidichte, *p. part.* of cuidich. Helped, relieved.

Cuid' ri, *prep.* With, together with. Cuid rium, *with me;* cuid riu, *with them.*

Cuidrigh, *a.* Common.

Cuifean, ein, *s. m.* The wadding of a gun.

Cùig-bhile, *s.* A quinque-foil.

Cùig-bhileach, *a.* Quinquefoliated.

Cùig, *a.* (*Ir. id.*) Five. Cùig 'ar fhichead, *five-and-twenty;* literally, *five over twenty.* Cùig ceud, *five hundred.*

Cùig deug, *a.* Fifteen. The substantive agreeing with *cùig deug* is commonly put in the middle, as, cùig *fear* deug, *fifteen men.*

Cùigeadh, **Cùigeamh**, *a.* Fifth. An cùigeadh cuid, *the fifth part.—Stew. Lev.*

Cuigeil, *gen.* cuigealach, *s. f.* A distaff; the flax put on a distaff. Greim do 'n chuigeil, *a hold of the distaff.—Stew. Pro.*

Arm. cogail *and* qeiguel. *W.* kogel. *Corn.* kigal. *Ir.* coigeal. *Germ.* kunckel.

Cuigealach, *a.* Of, or belonging to, a distaff.

Cuigealach, aich, *s. f.* A stack of flax or lint; the flax or lint of a distaff; *also*, the *gen. sing.* of cuigeil.

Cùigear, **Cùignear**, *a.* Five. Cùigear ghruagach, *five damsels.—Stew. Sam.* Cùignear do bhrathraibh, *five of his brothers.—Stew. Gen.*

Cuil, *s. f.* A fly. Hence *cuileag.*

Cùil, *s. f.* A corner; a niche; a closet; secrecy; an angle. *N. pl.* cùilteau. Meall thu le d' bhriodal cùil, *thou didst deceive with thy secret flattery.—Mac Lach.* Seomar cùil, *a back-room; an inner chamber.—Stew.* 1 *K.*

Cuilbhear, eir, *s.* (*Fr.* calibre.) A gun, a fowling-piece; the calibre or bore of a gun. *N. pl.* cuilbheirean; *d. pl.* cuilbheiribh. Le 'n cuilbheiribh gleusta na 'n lamh, *with their cocked guns in their hands.—Old Song.*

Cuilbheart, -bheairt, *s. f.* (cùil *and* beart; *literally*, a deed done in a corner.). Cunning, craft, wile, a trick. *N. pl.* cuilbheartan.

Cuilbheartach, *a.* Cunning, crafty, wily, full of tricks. Innleachdan nan cuilbheartach, *the designs of the crafty.—Stew. Job. Com.* and *sup.* cuil-bheartaiche, *more* or *most cunning.*

Cuilbheartachd, *s. f.* Craftiness, wiliness, trickery. Nan cuilbheartachd féin, *in their own craftiness.—Stew. Job.*

Cuilc, cuilce, *s. f.* (*Ir. id.*) Reeds; bulrushes. Cuilc na Léig, *the reeds of Lego.—Ull.* Cobhan cuilce, *an ark of bulrushes.—Stew. Gen.* Cuilc-chrann, *cane.*

Cuilceach, ich, *s. m.* A place where reeds grow; a crop or growth of reeds—(*Stew. Jer.*); a veil; a hood; a steeple.

Cuilceach, *a.* Abounding in reeds or bulrushes; like a reed or bulrush; of reed. Raon cuilceach, *a plain where reeds grow.—Oss. Tem.*

† **Cuilcheannag**, aig, *s. f.* (*Ir. id.*) A bribe.—*Shaw.*

Cuilcearnach, aich, *s. f.* A place where reeds grow.

Cuilc-lorg, -luirg, *s. f.* A cane.

Cùileachan, ain, *s. m.* A deep wicker-basket.

Cuileag, eig, *s. f.* (*Lat.* culex. *Arm.* qelguen. *Ir.* cuileog.) A fly; a gnat. *N. pl.* cuileagan; *d. pl.* cuileagaibh. Ioma gnè do chuileagaibh, *many kinds of flies.—Sm.* Sgaoth chuileag, *a* [*swarm*] *murrain of flies.—Stew. Ex.* Cuileag Spainnteach, *a Spanish fly;* cuileag shionnachain, *a glow-worm.*

Cuileagach, *a.* Full of flies; like a fly; lively, frisky. *Com.* and *sup.* cuileagaiche.

Cuilean, ein, *s. m.* (*Corn.* coloin *and* coilean. *Arm.* qolen. *Ir.* cuilean.) A whelp, a puppy, a cub. Cuilean leomhain, *a lion's whelp.—Stew. Gen.* Cuilean coin, *a puppy.* (*Arm.* qolen cy.) Cuilean maighich, *a leveret.* *N. pl.* cuileanan. Cuileanan mathghamhuinn, *the cubs of a bear.—Stew. Hos.* Cluich a chuilein ris a mhial-chu, *the puppy's play with the greyhound.—G. P.*

Cuileann, inn, *s. m.* Holly; elm. Fo chrannaibh chuilinn, *under elms.—Old Poem.*

Arm. gelen. *Corn.* kelinen. *W.* kelyn. *Ir.* cuileann.

Cuileannach, aich, *s. f.* A place where holly grows.

Cuileannach, *a.* Abounding in elms; like an elm; of, or belonging to, an elm.

Cuileasg, eisg, *s. m.* A jade; a horse.—*Shaw.*

Cuilg, *gen. sing.* of calg *and* colg.

Cuilgeara, *a.* Sharp-pointed, prickly; keen; spirited. Carruill cuilgeara, *spirited Carril.—Death of Carril.*

Cuiliobhair, *s.* A fowling-piece, a musket.—*Turn.*

Cuilionn. See **Cuileann**.

Cuilleasg, *s. pl.* Hazel-rods or twigs.

Cuilm, *s. f.* A feast; an entertainment. A greadh na cuilm, *preparing the feast.—Oss. Derm.* Written also *cuirm.*

Cuilmhionnachadh, aidh, *s. m.* An abjuration.

Cùil-mhionnan, *s. pl.* An oath of abjuration. Thug e chùil-mhionnan, *he gave his oath of abjuration.*

Cùil-sheomar, air, *s. m.* A back-room; a bed-chamber. *N. pl.* cùil-sheomraichean.

Cuilt, *s. f.* A quilt, a bed-tick.—*Shaw.*

Cùilteach, *a.* (*from* cùil.) Having corners; angular; skulking.

Cùilteach, *s.* Corners; a place full of corners; *rarely*, a bakehouse.—*Shaw.*

Cùiltean, *n. pl.* of cùil. Corners.

Cùiltear, eir, *s. m.* A skulking fellow. *N. pl.* cuiltearan.

Cùiltearachd, *s. f.* Skulking; low cunning.

† **Cùim**, *s. f.* (*Ir. id.*) A shirt; a feast; mercy; protection.

Cuim, *gen. sing.* of com; which see.

Cuimbrìgh, *s. f.* (*W.* Cymra.) Wales.

C'uime, (cia uime), *adv.* Wherefore? why? concerning what? concerning whom? about what? about whom? of what? of whom? C' uime a thréig thu ma chluas? *why hast thou left mine ear? why do I not hear thee?—Oss. Lodin.* C' uime tha thu 'labhairt? *of whom are you talking?*

Cuimear, ir, *s. m.* (*W.* Cymro.) A Cambrian or Welchman.

Cymry is the name which the Welch give to themselves, and to all other people of the same race.

Cuimein, *s. f.* Cummin.

Cuimeir, *a.* (*W.* comer.) Neat, trim, succint—(*Macint.*); elegant, proportioned, well-formed. Carbad cuimeir Chuchullin, *the well-formed chariot of Cuchullin.—Oss. Fing.*

Cuimeis, *s. f.* (*perhaps* comh-amais.) Contracted *cuimse;* which see.

Cuimheas, *a.* (cubhaidh-mheas.) Moderation; a sufficiency; temperance. Fhuair mi cuimheas, *I got a sufficiency*, or *moderate quantity.* Cha 'n 'eil thu ad chuimheas, *you have no moderation.*

Cuimheasach, *a.* Moderate; temperate; enough; *substantively*, sufficiency. Cha 'n 'eil thu cuimhseach, *you have lost all moderation.* Fhuair mi cuimheasach, *I have got enough.*

Cuimhne, *s. f.* (*Ir. id. Arm.* côun.) The memory; recollection, remembrance; a record, a memorial. Cuimhne nan gaisgeach a thriall, *the memory of departed heroes.—Fingalian Poem.* Cum an cuimhne, *remember.* An gleidh thu mo chuimne, a leac? *wilt thou, O flag, preserve my memory?*—*Oss Duthona* Cuimhne mhath, *a good memory* Is cuimhne leam an oigh, *I remember the maid* —*Oss Lod* Leabhar cuimhne, *a note-book, a book of remembrance, a record.*—*Stew Mal* Cuir na 'chuimhne, *put him in mind*, cha 'n 'eil cuimhne agam, *I do not remember*, cha chuimhne leam e, *I do not remember him* or *it*, cha 'n 'eil cuimhne agam air, *I do not remember him* or *it*.

CUIMHNEACH, *a* Mindful —*Shaw*

CUIMHNEACHADH, aidh, *s m* (*Ir id*) Remembering, a calling to memory, a keeping in remembrance; commemoration

CUIMHNEACHADH, (a), *pr. part* of cuimhnich

CUIMHNEACHAIL, *a*. Mindful, heedful, attentive. Cuimhneachail air an dùthaich sin, *mindful of that country* —*Stew Heb.* Gu cuimhneachail, *mindfully*

CUIMHNEACHAIR, *s m*. A remembrancer, a recorder.

CUIMHNEACHAN, ain, *s m* (*from* cuimhne.) A keepsake; a memorial, a remembrance, a memorandum Cuimhneachan shéideadh thrompaidean, *a memorial for blowing trumpets* —*Stew Lev*. Mar chuimhneachan ormsa, *in remembrance of me* —*Stew Cor*

CUIMHNICH, *v a* (*Ir id*) Remember, recollect *Pret a*. chuimhnich, *recollected*, *fut aff a* cuimhnichidh, *shall recollect* Cuimhnich orm, *remember me*, cuimhnich ort fein, *recollect yourself*

CUIMHNICHEAR, *fut pass* of cuimhnich Shall be remembered

CUIMSE, *s f* (*W*. cymmes, *mediocrity*) An aim, aiming, exactness of aim, a mark; a hit, moderation, mediocrity, a moderate portion, or share. Cha 'n 'eil cuimse ort, *you have no moderation*, fhuair mi cuimse, *I got a moderate portion*, gabh cuimse, *take an aim*

CUIMSEACH, *a* (*W* cymmesawl) Moderate; in a state of mediocrity, sure of aim, unerring; indifferent, adjusted Bogh bu chuimseach beachd, *a bow of sure aim*.—*Sin* Sealgair cuimseach, *a good hunter, a good shot* —*Old Song* Cho chuimseach lamh ri Conloch, *as unerring as the hand of Conloch* —*Old saying*.

CUIMSEACHADH, aidh, *s m* The act of aiming; a hitting, an aim

CUIMSEACHADH, (a), *pr part* of cuimsich

CUIMSICH, *v. a*. Hit, as a mark; aim, take aim. *Pret. a* chuimsich, *fut aff. a*. cuimsichidh, *shall hit*. Chuimsich na fir bhogha e, *the archers hit him*.—*Stew* 1 *Chr* Chuimsich e 's a thilg, *he took his aim and threw* —*Mac Lach*

CUIMSICHTE, *p. part* Hit after being aimed at

CÙIN, *s f* A coin Cùin òir, *a gold coin* *N. pl*. cùintean

CÙIN, *v a* Coin. *Pret a* chùin, *coined*, *fut aff a*. cùinidh

C'UIN, C'UINE, *adv* (Cia uine) (*Goth* quan. *Lat* quando *Ir. id*) When? at what time or period? C'uin dhùisgeas esan o shuain? *when shall he awake from his slumber?*—*Ull*

CÙINEADH, idh, *s m*. (*Scotch*, cuinyie) Coinage, the process of coining, a coin

CUINEAG, eig, *s f*. A copy

CUING, cuinge, *s. f* (*Ir. id*) A yoke, slavery, a bond, a duty, an obligation. Mo chuing-sa, *my yoke* —*Sm* Ar cuing-ne, *our yoke*.—*Stew K*. Cuing dhamh, *a yoke of oxen* —*Stew. Sam*

CUING-ANALACH, *s. f*. Asthma —*Shaw*.

CUINGE, *s f* A channel, a narrow strait, narrowness, straitness, difficulty, *rarely*, a solicitation, an entreaty Cuinge garbhalaich, *a stony narrow channel* —*Oss. Gaul* Cuinge-aualach, *asthma*

CUINGE, *com*. and *sup*. of cughann. More or most straitened. —*Stew. Ezek*.

CUINGEACHADH, aidh, *s m*. The act of lessening, abridging, or straitening; an abridgment.

CUINGEIS, *s f* Whitsuntide; Pentecost. Fanaidh mi gu Cuingeis, *I will stay till Whitsunday* —*Stew* 1 *Cor*. La Cuingeis, *Whitsunday*

CUINGICH, *v a*. Put in smaller bulk, abridge, lessen; make narrow, straiten *Pret. a* chuingich; *fut. aff. a*. cuingichidh, *shall straiten*

CUINGICHTE, *p part*. of cuingich. Abridged, straitened.

CUINGREACH, ich, *s. f* A kind of waggon.—*Shaw*.

CUINNE, *s f*. A nostril —*Shaw*

† CUINNE, *s f* A corner, an angle. *Lat*. cuneus. *Fr*. coin. *Gr* γωνια.

CUINNEAG, eig, *s f*. (*Ir*. cuinneog *W*. kynnog) A pail, a bucket, a narrow deep wooden vessel for carrying water; a stoup; a barrel, a cask Cuinneag bhùirn, *a water-pail*, cuinneag bhleothainn, *a wooden milk-pail*, min ann an cuinneig, *meal in a barrel* —*Stew*. 1 *K* *N. pl*. cuinneagan

CUINNEAGAN, *n. pl*. of cuinneag.

CUINNEAN, ein, *s m* (*dim*. of cuinne) A nostril *N pl*. cuinneanan; *d pl* cuinneinibh. Ann an cuinneinibh a shròine, *in his nostrils* —*Stew Gen*.

CUINNEANACH, *a* Having nostrils, having large nostrils.

CUINNSE, *s f* A quince *N pl* cuinnsean.

CUINSEAL, *s m* A face, remembrance.—*Shaw*

CUIPE, *s f*. A whip, a lash —*Stew John, ref* *N. pl*. cuipeachan.

CUIP, *s. f* Foam, froth; also the *gen sing*. of cop.

CUIPEACHAN, *n. pl* of cuip Whips, lashes.

CUINNSEAR, eir, *s m*. A sword

CUIP-GHEAL, *a* Foaming, white with foam Muir chuip-gheal, *a foaming sea* —*Old Song*

CUIPINN, *s. f*. A lashing, a whipping Fhuair e 'chuipinn, *he got a lashing*, thoill e a dheagh chuipinn, *he deserves to be well whipped*

CUIPINN, *v a*. Whip, lash *Pret a* chuipinn, *lash; fut. aff a* cuipinnidh, *shall lash*

CUIPINNTE, *p part*. of cuipinn Lashed, whipped.

CUIR, *v a* (*Ir id*) Put, place; lay; send, invite; sow. *Pret a* chuir, *put*, *fut aff a* cuiridh, *shall put*. Cuir cabar nan ruadh rium fhéin, *place the deer's branchy horn by my side* —*Oss Tem* Chuir sinn 'san uaigh na mairbh, *we laid the dead in the grave* —*Oss Lod* 'G a chuireadh gu cuirm an tràigh, *to invite him to a feast on the shore*.—*Oss. Fing* Cuir do shiol, *sow thy seed* —*Old Poem*. Cuir as, *extinguish, destroy, devour*, cuir as a choinneal, *extinguish the candle*, cuir as da, *destroy him* Chuir droch bhéist as da, *an evil beast has devoured him* —*Stew. Gen*. Cuir o, *send away, put away* An cuireadh tu mi o m' chrom? *wouldst thou send me from my circle?*—*Oss. Carricth*. Cuir ort, *put on thee*, ciod thà 'cur ort? *what ails thee?* Cuir as leth, *impute*, cuir car dhiot, *bestir yourself, be clever*, cuir cuidhil dhiot, *wheel about*, cuir suarach, *set at nought, despise* —*Stew Heb* Cuir beannachd, *send compliments*, cuir cath, *fight*, cuir deagh chath, *fight a good battle* —*Stew* 1 *Tim* Cuir air theicheadh, *put to flight* —*Stew Heb* Cuir ri, *add*, cuir ris, *study*, *apply to it*, *add to it or him*, *work on*, cuir gu taic, *trim, manage, give a dressing to*, cuir air mhire, *transport with joy*, cuir foghad, *put under thee*, *weather*, cuir an gniomh, *work, do, perform*, cuir dheth, *put off, delay*, cuir dhiot, *put off thee; deliver, as a speech*, cuir an aghaidh, *oppose;* cuir an céill, *describe*, cuir air falbh, *discharge, send off*, cuir an seilbh, *install;* cuir geall, *bet or wager*, cuir an geall, *bet; mortgage*, cuir h-uige, *exert, put to the push; prosecute*, cuir comhairle, *confer, consult* —*Stew*. 1 *K*.

Cuir comhairle ris, *consult with him;* cuiribh bhur cinn ri chéile, *consult with one another;* cuir air chùl, *put behind; forget; leave, abandon;* cuir cùl ri, *leave, abandon;* cuir fàilte, *salute;* cuir deathach, *emit smoke;* cuir smùid, *emit smoke;* cuir thairis, *put over, overflow; pass, as time;* chuir sinn an oidhche tharruinn, *we passed the night.—Old Legend.* Cuir gu bàs, *kill;* cuir aithne, *get acquainted, renew acquaintance;* cuir aithne air, *get acquainted with him, renew acquaintance with him;* cuir dragh, *trouble, annoy;* cuir mach, *put out; publish; extinguish; precent; disagree;* chuir e mach sailm, *he precented;* cuir mach air, *quarrel with him;* cuir faire, *place a watch, observe;* cuir faire air coigrich a chuain, *place a watch on the strangers of the sea.—Oss.* Cuir ruith na cuaig, *send on a fool's errand;* cuir air dìoghladh, *wean;* cuir air adhairt, *forward;* cuir eatorra, *separate them, part them, put them asunder;* cuir roimhe, *prompt him, dictate to him;* cuir sùrd, *prepare;* cuir ar lagh, *prepare; adjust, as a bow; cock, as a gun;* cuir a shean, *spend extravagantly;* cuir ghal, *set a-crying;* cuir am farsuingeachd, *enlarge, extend.—Stew.* 1 *Chr.* Cuir air chrith, *cause to shake;* cuir mu 'n seach, *lay by, accumulate;* cuir leam, *favour me, aid me;* cuir ceart, *put to rights;* cuir dholaidh, *spoil, abuse;* cuir ghlan dholaidh, *spoil completely;* cuir air aimhreidh, *put wrong;* cuir as leth, *impute;* cuir air thiormachadh, *put out to dry;* cuir gu fulang, *put to trial.—Mac Co.*

Cuir, *gen. sing.* and *n. pl.* of car. Turns, twists, windings; tricks.

Cuirc, *gen. sing.* and *n. pl.* of corc.

† Cuirc, *s. f.* (*Ir. id.*) A multitude.

Cùird, *gen. sing.* and *n. pl.* of cord.

Cuireadach, *a.* Sly, wily, cunning; inviting. Gu cuireadach, *slyly.*

Cuireadh, idh, *s. m.* An inviting; a placing, a laying; a sending; an invitation; a deputation. Chuir iad cuireadh gu rìgh nan lann, *they sent a* [*deputation*] *invitation to the kings of swords.—Oss. Tem.* Là chuiridh, *the invitation-day; the day on which a bride and bridegroom take their rounds, inviting their acquaintance to the wedding;* thug e cuireadh, *he invited.—Stew. Sam.*

Cuirm, *s. f.* (*Ir. id.*) An entertainment, a feast or a banquet; a kind of beer or ale once used by the Gaelic and Irish Celts. Cuirm an tràigh, *the feast of the shore.—Oss. Fing.* Rinn e cuirm, *he made a feast.—Stew. Gen.*

The *courmi,* which Dioscorides says the old Britons drank, is the same with the *cuirm* of the Gael and Irish. It was a powerful intoxicating liquor made of barley, and used, of course, at all their banquets; hence *cuirm,* in Gaelic and Irish, signifies a feast. Some have asserted that this liquor was the same as the modern *uisge beatha;* but the idea of distillation not being so obvious, nor the process so intelligible, as that of brewing, it is very probable that the liquor was obtained by the latter method.

Cùirn, *gen. sing.* and *n. pl.* of carn; which see.

Cùirnean, ein, *s. m.* The head of a pin or any such thing; a brooch; a ringlet; a knoll. Mar chùirnean daimein, *like a diamond brooch.—Macfar. N. pl.* cùirnein.

Cùirneanach, *a.* Full of ringlets.—*Macint.* Like a ringlet; like a brooch; wearing a brooch; also knolly.—*Macdon.*

Cuirp, *gen. sing.* and *n. pl.* of corp.

† Cuirpeachd, *s. f.* Wickedness, corruption.—*Shaw.*

Cuirpean, ein, *s. m.* A crupper.

Cuirpidh, *a.* Wicked, impious, corrupt. Gu cuirpidh, *wickedly.*

Cuir-sa, (cuir-thusa.) Send thou. Cuir-sa bard 'g a ghairm, *send a bard to call him.—Oss. Carricth.*

† Cuirt, *s. f.* (*Ir. id.*) An apple-tree; a wilding.—*Shaw.*

Cùirt, cùirte, *s. f.* A court; a palace; an area; a yard. Puist na cùirt, *the pillars of the court.—Stew. Num.*

Gr. χοςτος. *Span. It.* corte. *Fr.* cour. *Eng.* court. *Ir.* cuirt. *Turk.* kurta, *a palace. Teut.* gurth, *a house. Germ.* koert, *a barn. N. pl.* cùirtean.

Cùirt seems to be derived from the ancient Celtic word *cort,* an enclosure.

† Cuirteag, eig, *s. f.; dim.* of cuirt. (*Ir. id.*) A wild apple-tree; a kind of cup.—*Shaw.*

Cùirtealachd, *s. f.* Courtliness; gallantry.

Cùirtean, *n. pl.* of cùirt; which see.

Cùirtean, ein, *s. f.* A curtain. Cùirtean ceutach nan speur, *the beauteous curtain of the skies.—Macfar. Asp. form,* chùirtean. Mar chùirtein, *like a curtain.*

Cùirtear, ir, *s. m.* A courtier. *N. pl.* cuirtearan.

Cùirteas, eis, *s. m.* Courtesy; courtliness; ceremony.

Cùirteasach, *a.* Courteous; courtly; ceremonious. Gu cùirteasach, *courteously.*

Cùirteasachd, *s. f.* Courtesy; the practice of courtesy; courtliness.

Cùis, *s. f.* A case, affair, matter, circumstance; a subject; a cause. Anns a chùis so, *in this case;* cùis na còrach, *the cause of right.—Old Song.* Cuis-ghearain, *a cause of complaint;* cùis chasaid, *a ground of accusation.—Stew. Luke, ref.* Cùis dhitidh, *a ground of accusation.—Stew. Luke.* Cuis-mhagaidh, *a laughing-stock.—Stew. G. B.* Cùis a h-aisling, *the subject of her dream.—Oss. Cathluno. N. pl.* cùisean. Cùisean cruaidh, *hard causes.—Stew. Exod.* Is e sin a chùis, *that is the business; that is the point; there is the difficulty.*

Span. caso. *Lat.* casus, causa. *Fr.* cas. *Corn.* cus. *W.* açws. *Ir.* cùis.

Cuisdeag, eig, *s. f.* The little finger.—*Shaw.*

Cuiseag, eig, *s. f.* A straw, a reed; a rash; a bulrush; a stalk. A chuiseag dhìreach, *the straight rash.—Macint. N. pl.* cuiseagan; *d. pl.* cuiseagaibh. Le cuiseagaibh an lìn, *with the stalks of flax.—Stew. Jos.* An cuiseig nan gleanntaidh, *among the reeds of the valley.—Ull.*

Cuiseagach, *a.* Abounding in reeds or rashes; like a reed or rash. Gleannan cuiseagach mo ghraidh, *my beloved reedy glen.—Old Song.*

Cuis-eagail, *s. f.* An object of terror; a bugbear.

Cuisean, ein, *s. m.* A crime.

Cuis-ghearain, *s. f.* A subject of complaint; a cause of complaint.

Cùis-lagha, *s. f.* A law-process, a law-suit. Comhstri no cùis-lagha, *a quarrel or law-suit.—Stew. Sam.*

Cuisle, *s. f.* (*Ir. id.*) A vein, an artery; a pipe. *N. pl.* cuislean; *d. pl.* cuislibh. Air mo chuislibh, *on my veins.—Macint.* Troimh cham-chuislibh bhad-chrann, *through the crooked veins of tufted trees.—Macfar.*

Cuisleach, *a.* (*from* cuisle.) Veinous; arterial; veined; having veins or arteries; like a vein or artery; blustering; freezing.

Cuisleag, eig, *s. f.* (*dim.* of cuisle.) A lancet. *N. pl.* cuisleagan.

Cuislean, ein, *s. m.* (*dim.* of cuisle.) A little vein, a little artery; a chanter; a little pipe; *rarely,* a castle.

Cuislean, *n. pl.* of cuisle; which see.

Cuisleanach, aich, *s. m.* (*from* cuislean.) A piper, a chanter, one who plays on an oaten reed.

Cuisle-mhòr, òir, *s. f.* An artery, a great artery. A chuisle-mhòr, *the great artery, the aorta.*

† Cuislin, *s. f.* (*Ir. id.*) A pole.—*Shaw.*

Cuis-mhagaidh, *s. f.* A laughing-stock. Tha mi am chuis-mhagaidh, *I am mocked.—Stew. G. B.*

Cuisneach, *a.* Freezing, congealing, frosty.

Cuisnich, *v. a.* and *n.* Freeze, congeal. *Pret. a.* chuisnich; *fut. aff.* cuisnichidh.

Cuisnichte, *p. part.* of cuisnich. Frozen, congealed

Cuiste, *s f.* A couch.—*Shaw.*

† **Cuite**, *s. f.* (*Ir id*) The head

Cuite, *a.* Quit, freed. Tha mi cuite dheth, *I am quit of him.*
Arm. quyt. *Germ* quitt *Belg* quyt. *Fr.* quite. *Eng.* quit

Cuiteach, ich, *s m.* A denial; a revenging.

Cuiteachadh, aidh, *s m* A leaving, a forsaking, an abandoning; a recompensing, a requiting.

Cuiteachadh, (a), *pr. part.* of cuitich. Leaving, forsaking, recompense

Cuitheach, ich, *s. f.* Foam, froth; rage, fury; also, *adjectively*, *contr.* for cuitheamhach, *having wreaths of snow*

Cuitheamh, imh, *s m.* A wreath of snow. Dh' aom i mar chuitheamh, *she fell like a wreath of snow* —*Oss Fing*

Cuitich, *v. a* Quit, forsake; recompense, requite *Pret a.* chuitich; *fut. aff. a.* cuitichidh, *shall quit* Chuitich Dia mi, *God rewarded me* —*Sm* *Fut. pass.* cuitichear, *shall be forsaken.*

Cuitichear, *fut. pass* of cuitich Shall be forsaken

Cuitichte, *p part* of cuitich Quitted, forsaken, forlorn, requited.

† **Cul**, cuil, *s m* (*Ir. id*) Custody; defence, a chariot; a waggon.

† **Cul**, *v a* (*Ir id*) Push, shove, thrust *Pret.* chul, *pushed*, *fut* culaidh, *shall push.*

Cùl, (air), *adv.* Behind; rejected; forgotten; absent; superseded, put aside or behind Cuim bhiodh Connal air chùl? *why should Connal be absent?*—*Oss Tem*

Cùl, cùil, *s m* (*Ir. id.* *W* cwl, *head*) The back of any thing, the hinder part; the back of the head, the hair of the head. Thionndadh i cùl, *she turned her back* —*Oss Lodin.* Cul dubh-ghorm nan stuadh, *the back of the azure waves* —*Oss. Fing* Eiric a chùl-duinn, *brown-haired Eiric* —*Oss* Cuir cùl, *forsake* A tùnaidh air chùl, *dwelling behind* —*Oss Fing.* Chaidh esan bha treun air chùl, *he who was strong has perished* Air cul lainn, *handling a weapon, grasping a weapon* Cùl an dùirn, *the back of the hand* Chaidh iad an comhar an cùil, *they went backward* —*Stew Gen* Cum cùl, *support, countenance* Cùl-taic, *a support, a prop* Air chùl, *absent*

Cùl, (gu). Completely, perfectly; to the back. Chunnaic mi 'anam gu chùl, *I saw his soul perfectly* —*Oss Lodin.* Staillinn gu chùl, *steel to the back*, *steel every inch of it.*

Cùlachadh, aidh, *s m.* A forsaking, a renouncing, abandonment.

Cùladh, aidh, *s f.* (*Ir* cubhal) A suit of clothes; garments; vestments

Cùlag, aig, *s m.* Dried turf used as fuel, the cheek-tooth.

Culag, aig, *s. f.* A collop; a piece of flesh

Cùlagach, *a* Abounding in turf, made of turf

Cùlagan, *n pl* The grinders; back teeth

Cùlaich, *v a* (*from* cùl) Forsake, renounce, put behind, turn the back upon. *Pret a* chùlaich, *forsook*, *fut aff. a.* cùlaichidh

Culaidh, *s f* A suit of clothes, attire, dress, garments, robes; an instrument, a tool, a boat; a kept miss A culaidh bhanntraich, *her widow's garments* —*Stew. Gen* Culaidh eudaich, *a suit of clothes; robes.*—*Sm* Goll na chulaidh chruaidh, *Gaul in his suit of steel.*—*Old Poem* Culaidh a dhusgadh nan deomhan, *an instrument to rouse the devils.*—*Mac Mhuirich* Culaidh-shiùil, *canvass*, culaidh bainnse, *a wedding-suit*

Cùlan, ain, *s m* Hair, tresses.

Culantas, ais, *s m* Bashfulness.

Cùlaobh, *s.* (cul-thaobh, *the backside.*) (*Span.* culo.) The back part of any thing, behind. Ag aomadh ri craoibh o chùlaobh, *leaning on a tree from behind.*—*Oss. Tem.* Air mo chùlaobh, *behind me* Sheas e air an cùlaobh, *it stood behind them* —*Stew. Ex.* Air cùlaobh chàich, *behind the rest.*—*Old Song* Mo chùlaobh, *my back parts.*—*Id.*

Cularan, ain, *s. m* (*Ir. id.*) A cucumber. *N. pl.* cu-larain.

Cul-bhoc, -bhuic, *s. m.* A wether-goat; a buck. *N. pl* culbhuic.—*Shaw.*

Cùlchàin, *v* (cùl, *the back*, càin, *slander.*) (*Ir. id.*) Backbite, slander *Pret* chùl-chàin; *fut. aff. a.* culchàinidh.

Cùl-chàineadh, idh, *s m.* Backbiting, slander Luchd cùl-chàineadh, *backbiters.*—*Stew. Rom. ref.*

Cùl-chainnt, *s. f.* (*Ir. id.*) Calumny, slander.

Cùl-chainnteach, *a.* Calumnious; tattling; inclined to slander Cailleach cabach, cùl-chainnteach, *a toothless, tattling old woman.*—*Old Song.*

Cùl-chainntear, ir, *s. m.* A backbiter or slanderer; a tattler

Cùl-cheum, -chéim, *s. m.* A back-step.

Cùl-cheumnachadh, aidh, *s m.* Tergiversation.—*Shaw.*

Cùl-choimhead, id, *s m* A rear-guard; a looking behind; retrospection

Cùl-earalais, *s m.* A body of reserve.—*Shaw.*

Cùl-fhradharc, *s m* Retrospection; a looking behind.

Cùl-fhradharcach, *a* Retrospective; circumspect; looking behind.

Cùl-ghairm, *s f.* A recalling, a calling from behind

Cùl-ghairm, *v a* Recall; call from behind. *Pret.* chùl-ghairm

Cùl-ith, *s f.* Slander, backbiting.

Cullach, aich, *s. m.* A boar. *N. pl* cullaich.

Culladh, aidh, *s m.* A cowl, a hood *N. pl.* cullaidhean.

Cullaid, *s f.* (*Ir.* culloid.) Noise, tumult; uproar, a brawl

Cullaideach, *a* (*Ir.* culloideach) Noisy, tumultuous; quarrelsome *Com.* and *sup.* cullaidiche, *more or most noisy*

Cull-bhoc, -bhuic, *s. m.* A buck; a wether goat.

Cùl-mhionnachadh, aidh, *s. m.* Abjuration

Cùl-mhionnaich, *v. a.* Abjure

Cùl-mhutair, *s m* A mutineer, a smuggler. *N. pl.* cùl-mhutairean.

Cùl-mhutaireachd, *s f* Sedition; mutiny, smuggling.

Cùl-radharc, *s m* Retrospection; a looking behind; circumspection

Cùl-radharcach, *a.* Retrospective; circumspect.

Cùl-sleamhnach, *a* Backsliding; prone to backslide.

Cùl-sleamhnachadh, aidh *s* m. A backsliding. *N. pl* cul-sleamhnachaidh Leighisidh mi bhur cul-sleamhnachaidh, *I will heal your backsliding* —*Stew. G. B.*

Cùl-sleamhnachair, *s m.* A backslider. *N pl.* cul-sleamhnachairean.

Cùl-sleamhnaich, *v. n* Backslide

Cùl-taic, *s f* A support, a prop; a defence; a supporter; an abettor. Rinn thu dhoibh cul-taic, *thou hast supported them* —*Sm*

† **Culthaideach**, *a.* (*Ir id.*) Preposterous.—*Sh.*

Cùl-tharruing, *v. a.* Retract *Pret. a* chul-tharruing, *retracted*, *fut. aff.* cùl-tharruingidh, *shall retract*

Cum, *s m* Shape; form See Cumadh.

† **Cum**, cuma, *s. m.* (*Ir. id.*) A battle; a fight; a duel.

Cum, *v. a.* (*Ir. id.*) Shape, form, fashion. *Pret. a.* chum, *shaped; fut. aff. a.* cumaidh. Air a dheagh chumadh, *well-shaped.*

Cum, *v. a.* (*Ir. id.*) Hold; keep; keep hold; contain; comprise; preserve; uphold; maintain; detain. *Pret. a.* chum; *fut. aff. a.* cumaidh. Cum greim dheth, *keep hold of him;* chum mi gun doghruinn thu, *I kept thee without harm.—Oss. Fing.* Chum thu d'onoir, *thou hast preserved thy honour.—Old Poem.* Chumadh gach soitheach, *each vessel would contain.—Stew.* 1 *K.* Cum ri, *support, supply;* cum codhail, *keep an appointment;* cum mach, *maintain, hold out, assert;* cum suas, *support, maintain;* cum roimh, *prop, hold against;* cum ort, *forbear, contain thyself; keep on thee;* cum air d'aghaidh, *hold on; go forward;* cum air d'ais, *hold back, keep back;* cum air falbh, *keep off;* cum air do laimh, *stay thy hand.—Stew. K.* Cum do theangadh, *be quiet;* am fear aig am bheil, cumadh e, *he who has, let him keep.—G. P.*

Cumach, aich, *s. m.* (*Ir. id.*) A breach; a derout.—*Shaw.*

Cumachd, *s. f.* A shape, form, fashion; proportion. Cumachd do mhin-chalpanna, *the shape of the smooth legs.—Old Song.*

Cumachdail, *a.* (cumachd-amhuil.) Shapely, well-made, proportioned. Garbh, cumachdail, *thick and shapely.—Macint.*

Cumadail, *a.* Shapely, well-formed; proportioned. Do chalpannan cumadail, *thy shapely legs.—Macfar.* Sgiath chumadail, *a well-formed shield.—Mac Lach.*

Cumadair, *s. m.* A framer, a former; one who shapes. *N. pl.* cumadairean.

Cumadaireachd, *s. f.* The occupation of shaping; also a device, invention.—*Shaw.*

Cumadh, aidh, *s. m.* (*Ir.* cum.) A shape, form, or fashion; the trunk of the body. Cumadh na h-altarach, *the fashion of the altar.—Stew.* 2 *K.* Gun chumadh, *shapeless.*

Cumaidh, *fut. aff. a.* of cum. Shall hold, keep, or contain.

Cumail, *s. f.* A holding; a keeping; a comprising; a detaining; detention; a maintaining or supporting. Mo chumail suas, *my support* (or) *sustenance.—Macfar.*

Cumail, *v. a.* (*Ir. id.*) Touch; wipe; rub off.

Cumail, (a), *pr. part.* of cum. Holding; keeping; comprising; detaining. Ciod tha 'g adchumail? *what is keeping you?* 'Ga m'chumail suas, *supporting me.—Sm.* Nur nach b' urradh sin cumail oirnn, *when we could not forbear.—Stew. Thess.*

Cumailteach, *a.* Tenacious; adhesive.

Cumailteachd, *s. f.* Tenaciousness: adhesiveness.

Cumaint, *a.* Common; general; usual. *Provincial for* cumannta.

Cumaint, (an), *adv.* Commonly; generally; usually; continually.

Cumait, *a.* Neat; well-made; handsome. Bu chumait do chalpana, *well-made were thy legs.—Old Song.*

Cuman, ain, *s. m.* A pail; a small wooden dish without a handle, *Scotch,* a cogue.—*Macint.* A skimmer. A cuman eadar dà ghlùn, *her pail between her knees.—Old Poem. N. pl.* cumanan. Le 'n cumanan làn, *with their pails full.—Old Song.*

Cumannta, *a.* (*Ir.* cumann. *Arm.* coumun.) Common; general; usual; ordinary. Aon do 'n phobull chumannta, *one of the common people.—Stew. Lev. ref.* Gu cumannta, *commonly;* an cumannta, *commonly.*

Cumanntas, ais, *s. m.* Usualness. An cumanntas, *generally, usually.*

Cumar, air, *s. m.;* properly *comar;* which see.

Cumas, ais, *s. m.;* more frequently written *comas;* which see.

Cumasach, *a.;* more frequently written *comasach.*

Cumasg, aisg, *s. f.* (*Ir. id.*) A mixture; an amalgam; a medley; a confusion; a battle. Cumasg sluaigh, *a mixture of people.—Stew. Ex. ref. N. pl.* cumasgan. Teas nan cumasgan, *the heat of battles.—Macfar.*

Cumasgach, *a.* Confused; mixed; disordered; causing confusion or disorder. Anns na ruagaibh cumasgach, *in the disordered routs.—Macfar.*

Cumasgadh, aidh, *s. m.* A mixing; a confusing; a mixture, a confusion; a medley; an amalgam.

Cumasgta, *a.* Mixed; confused; in a medley.

Cumha, **Cumhadh**, aidh, *s. m.* (*Ir.* cumha.) A lamentation; sorrow; a doleful voice; a reward; a bribe; a condition; a covenant. Cumha ro gheur, *very bitter lamentations.—Stew. G. B.* Cumha na caillich oidhche, *the doleful voice of the owl.—Stew. Mic.* Thairg Fionn dhoibh cumha, *Fingal offered them a reward.—Fingalian Poem.* Air a chumha so, *on this covenant.*

Cumhach, *a.* Sad; disconsolate; wailing; bribing. Cumhach air lag-mhànra, *disconsolate with a low stifled voice.—Death of Carril.*

Cumhachag, aig, *s. f.* An owl. More properly written *comhachag;* which see.

Cumhachd, *s. f.* (*Ir. id.*) Power; might; authority; strength; ability. Gach uile chumhachd, *all power.—Sm.* Gùth cumhachd o Sheallama, *a voice of authority from Selma.—Oss. Lodin.* Toil nan cumhachd air neamh, *the will of the powers in heaven.—Mac Lach.*

Cumhachdach, *a.* Powerful, mighty, strong; having great authority. Mo ghairdean cumhachdach, *my powerful arm.—Sm.* Na cumhachdaich, *the mighty.—Stew. Job.* Gu cumhachdach, *powerfully. Com.* and *sup.* cumhachdaiche.

Cumhachdaiche, *com.* and *sup.* of cumhachdach. More or most mighty. Is cumhachdaiche e na mi, *he is mightier than me.—Stew. Mat.*

Cumhadh, aidh, *s. m.* A lamenting, a mourning; a lamentation. See **Cumha**.

Cumhaing, *v. a.* Straiten, tighten, narrow. *Pret. a.* chumhaing, *straitened.*

Cumhainge, *s. f.* A strait; distress; difficulty; straitness, narrowness, tightness.—*Stew. Deut.*

Cumhainge, *com.* and *sup.* of cumhang.

Cumhais, *s. f.* A selvage.

† **Cumhal**, ail, *s. f.* (*Ir. id.*) A maid-servant; a bondmaid; subjection; obedience.

† **Cumhang**, aing, *s. f.* (*Ir. id.*) Power; strength.—*Shaw.*

Cumhang, *a.* (*Ir.* cumhang. *W.* cywng.) Narrow, strait, tight, close. Written also *cumhann.*

Cumhangachadh, aidh, *s. m.* A making narrow, a tightening.

Cumhangachd, *s. f.* Narrowness, straitness, tightness, closeness; difficulty. Ann an cumhangachd, *straitened.—Stew.* 2 *Cor.*

Cumhangaich, *v. a.* Make narrow, straiten.—*Stew. Job. Pret. a.* chumhangaich; *fut. aff. a.* cumhangaichidh, *shall* or *will straiten.*

Cumhann, ainn, *s. m.* Power; strength; a strait: *adjectively,* strong. Fear cumhann a bhlàir, *the strong man of battle.—Oss.*

Cumhann, *a.* Narrow, tight, strait; powerful. An leabadh chumhann, *the narrow bed, the grave.—Oss. Dargo.* Is goirt 's is cumhann a bualadh, *sore and powerful is its blow.—Old Song.*

Cumhannaich, *v. a.* Make narrow, straiten, tighten. *Pret. a.* chumhannaich, *make narrow.*

Cumhannaichte, *p. part.* of cumhannaich.

Cumhdach, aich, *s. m.* (*Ir. id.*) An arch; a covering. See Comhdach.

Cumdaich, *v a.* (*Ir. id*) See Comhdaich.

Cùmhnadh, more properly *caomhnadh*

Cùmhnant, aint, *s f* A covenant, agreement, compact; stipulation, condition Seul cùmhnaint nan gràs, *the seal of the covenant of grace.—Sm.* Air a' chùmhnant so, *on this condition*

Cùmhnantach, *a* Federal, relating to a covenant or bargain

Cùmhnantaich, *v n* Make a covenant; bargain. *Pret. a* chùmhnantaich, *bargained*

Cumhrachadh, aidh, *s m* An encumbrance

Cùmhrachd, *s f* Fragrance More properly *cubhraidheachd*

Cumhrag, aig, *s f* A sweet-apple-tree *N. pl* cumhragan See Cubhrag

Cumraich, *v a* Encumber *Pret* chumraich, *encumbered*, *fut aff a* cumraichidh

Cumhraidh, *a* Fragrant See Cubhraidh

Cumta, *p. part* of cum. Shaped, fitted; set as a task Bhur 'n obair chumta, *your set tasks —Stew Ex* Cumta ris an obair, *fitted to the work —Stew* 1 *K.*

Cumtadh, *pret sub pass* of cum. Would *or* could be held *Stew. Acts* Would *or* could be shaped.

Cunablach, aich, *s* See Conablach.

Cunbhailteach, *a* Firm; durable Gu cunbhailteach, *firmly*

Cun-bhailteachd, *s f* Firmness, durableness

Cungaidh, *s f* Tools, utensils, instruments—(*Stew Ezek*), a name for the privy parts Cungaidh leigheis, *a medicine, a salve*

Cungarach, *a* Exigent.—*Shaw*

Cunnhalach. See Cunnbhalach

Cungarachd, *s f* Exigence

Cungantach, *a* Helpful, ready to help —*Shaw Com* and *sup* cungantaiche

Cunglach aich, *s. f* A cleft, a pass or mountain gorge Ann an cunglach Atha, *in the pass of Atha.—Orr* *N pl* cunglaichean, *straits*

Cunglaichean, *n pl* of cunglach

Cunnarach, aich, *s f* A purchase, a pennyworth, a cheap bargain Is geal gach cunnarach a thig am fad, *sweet is the pennyworth that comes afar —G P*

Cunnart, airt, *s m* Danger; jeopardy; *rarely*, doubt Am a chunnairt, *the time of danger —Oss Lod* *N pl* cunnartan

Cunnartach, *a.* Dangerous, hazardous, *rarely*, doubtful.

† **Cunnbhail**, *v a* (*Ir id*) Grasp hard, keep a firm hold

† **Cunnbhalach**, *a* (*Ir id*) Firm, strong, sturdy, having a firm grasp Fir chunnbhalach, *strong men —Old Poem.*

† **Cunnla**, *a* (*Ir id*) Modest, bashful —*Shaw*

Cùnnt, *v a* (*Arm.* counta) Count, reckon, or tell, calculate, compute *Pret a* chùnnt, *counted*, *fut aff. a* cunntaidh Am fear nach cunnt rium cha chunntainn ris, *him who keeps no account of his good actions to me, I will repay without measure —G P* This was said by Henry Wynd, at the conflict betwixt the Mac Phersons and Davidsons on the North Inch of Perth

Cunntair, *s m* An accountant, a reckoner; an arithmetician *N pl* cunntairean

Swed contor, *a counting-house. Arm* contouer, *a counter*

Cunntaireachd, *s. f* The business of an accountant.

Cunntart, airt, *s. m.* See Cunnart.

Cunntas, ais, *s. m.* (*Ir. id*) An account or sum; arithmetic; a number; an account, detail, narration. Ris a chunntas, *at arithmetic*, triath gun chunntas, *chiefs beyond number.—Oss Tem* Cunntas cheann, *capitulation*, cùnntasan, *accounts.*

Cunntasach, *a.* Calculating; keen, sharp; narrow.

Cunntasan, *n pl.* of cunntas Accounts or sums; details, narratives

Cunnuil, *s f.* (*Ir id*) An objection —*Shaw.*

Cunnuileach, *a* Objecting, inclined to object, objectionable; wrangling.

Cunnuilich, *v* Object; dispute, wrangle.

Cùnradh, aidh, *s. m* A covenant, agreement, compact; condition, stipulation.

Cùnradhach, *a* Federal; of, or belonging to, an agreement or compact.

Cunthart, airt, *s m.* See Cunnart.

Cùp, cùpa, *s. m.* A rimmed cart; a coop. Written also *cùb*, which see

Cup, cupa, *s m* A cup Cup an laimh an Tighearna, *a cup in the Lord's hand.—Sm* *N. pl* cupaichean.

Gr according to Heyschius, κυβα and κυπελλον, *a drinking cup Chald* cuba *Syr* cubo. *Arab* cab *Turk.* copa. *Sclav Dal Hung* kuppa, *a cup. Styr* and *Carn.* kupa, *a cup Polonese*, kubeck *Croatian*, kupis, *a cup Armen.* koup, *an egg-shell. Bisc.* copa, *a cup Arm.* coup *and* cop. *Fr* coupe *Ir.* cup *W* cwb *Germ* kopfe.

Cupaichean, *n pl* of cup. Cups *D. pl.* cupaichibh

Cupair, *s m* (cup-fhear) A cup-bearer.

Cupall, aill, *s m.* (*Arm.* coubl) A couple or pair; a couple or rafter *N pl* cupaill

Cupall, *v. a* (*Arm* coubla) Couple, pair. *Pret. a.* chupall, *coupled*, *fut. aff* cupallaidh, *shall couple*

Cupan, ain, *s m* (*dim* of cup) A little cup; a cup Cupan na slainnte, *the cup of salvation.—Sm.* *N. pl.* cupain, *cup.* In Vannes, in Britanny, *coupan* is a common term for *cup.*

† **Cupar**, air, *s m* (*Ir. id*) Conception.—*Shaw*

Cuphair, *s f.* The cypress tree —*Shaw*

Cur, *s m* (*Ir id*) Power; virility

Hence are derived the words, curaidh, *a hero*, the *Armoric*, couraich, *boldness*; the *English*, courage, *Fr.* courage, *It.* corragio

Cur, *v* Sow; scatter, pour. *Pret. a* chur, *sowed*, *fut. aff a* curaidh, *shall sow*

Cur, (a), *pr part* of cuir. Sending, putting, placing; laying, sowing, pouring A cur an fhionn, *casting the hair*, a cur sneachdaidh, *snowing*, a cur sil, *sowing seed*; a cur chlach, *throwing stones*, a cur as leth, *imputing*, a cur as, *extinguishing.* See Cuir.

Cur, *s m* A sowing, a raining, a snowing; a pouring; a throwing Am cur a choirce, *oat-sowing season.* Ged bhiodh cur is cathamh ann, *though it were snowing and drifting —Turn*

Curach, aich, *s f* A marsh or fen

Curach, aich, *s. m* (*Ir id Span* curo, *a small boat used on the Garonne*) A boat, a skiff; a small boat of wicker, and covered with hides. Le curach faoin, *with her light skiff.* —*Ull*

The *curach*, or boat of leather and wicker, may appear to the moderns a very unsafe vehicle to trust to in tempestuous seas; yet our forefathers fearlessly committed themselves, in these slight pinnaces, to the mercy of the most violent weather They were much in use in the Western Isles, even long after the art of building boats of wood was introduced into those parts by the Norwegians. The size of these pinnaces must have been considerable; for Marianus Scotus makes mention of three Irishmen who came in a *curach* without sails or oars, and landed in Cornwall, after a voyage of seven days. Sidonius Apollinaris, *Carm.* vii., observes, that the Saxon pirates of his time frequently crossed the British seas in such boats.

A ruder and more ancient vessel was the *biorlinn* or *birlinn*, compounded of the Celtic *bir* or *bior* and *linn*. Pennant deviates from his usual accuracy when he derives *birlinn* from the Norwegian *byrdinga*.

Curachan, ain, *s. m., dim.* of curach. (*Ir. id.*) A little boat or coracle; a little skiff; a canoe. Curachan òir, *a gilded coracle.—Old Song.*

Curachd, aichd, *s. f.* A hood, a woman's hood or bonnet; a cap; seed. *N. pl.* curaichdean, *hoods.* Curaichdean lin, *linen bonnets.—Stew. Ezek.* A reir a churachd, *according to its seed.—Stew. Lev. ref.* Curachd oidhche, *a night-cap;* curachd shìde, *the bird called blue-bonnet;* curachd na cuthaig, *the flower blue-bottle.*

Curachdag, aig, *s. f.* A hood; a woman's cap; a rick. Curachdag shaoidh, *a rick of hay.—Macd.*

Curachd na cuthaig, *s. f.* The flower blue-bottle; small-leafed bell-flower.

Curachd-oidhche, *s. f.* A night-cap. *N. pl.* curaichdean-oidhche, *night-caps.*

Curachd-shìde, *s. f.* The bird called blue-bonnet.

Curadh, aidh, *s. m.* The act of sowing. See Cur.

Cùradh, aidh, *s. m.* Severe distress; affliction; an obstacle, hindrance, difficulty. Gu bròn is cùradh geur, *sorrow and bitter distress.—Sm.*

Curadh, (a), *pr. part.* Sowing; pouring; raining. Neoil a curadh gu dùbhlaidh, *clouds pouring darkly.—Oss. Fing.*

Curaichdeach, *a.* Hooded, bonneted; like a hood or bonnet.—*Macdon.* Mulain curaichdeach, *hooded ricks.—Macfar.*

Cùraideach, *a.* Frisky; cunning.—*Shaw.*

Curaideachd, *s. f.* Friskiness; cunning.

Cùraidh, *s. m., from* teur. (*Ir.* curadh. *Arm.* couraich, *courage.*) A hero; a champion; a warrior; a giant. Ard-churaidh nan ciar-bheann, *high chief of the dusky hills.—Oss. Fing. N. pl.* cùraidhean, *champions, giants.—Stew. Gen. ref.* Cùraidhe na craoibh ruaidhe, *the warriors of the red branch;*—a band of ancient warriors in Ulster, so called.

Curaidh, *s. f.* (*Eng.* cower, curry.) A squatting, a cowering. Dean curaidh, *sit squat.*

Cùraidh, *a., for* cubhraidh; which see.

Curaisd, *s. f.* Courage.

Curaisdeach, *a.* Courageous, bold, brave.—*Macint.*

Curaisdeachd, *s. f.* Courageousness, boldness, bravery.

Cùram, aim, *s. m.* (*Ir. id. Lat.* cura. *Swed.* cur.) Care; anxiety; solicitude; a charge. Gabh cùram, *take care, take charge;* gun chùram, *without care;* air an cùram-san, *under their charge.—Stew. Num.*

Cùramach, *a.* (*Ir. id.*) Careful; anxious; solicitous. Gu cùramach, *carefully. Com.* and *sup.* cùramaiche.

Curamas, ais, *s. m.* Care; diligence.—*Shaw.*

Curan, ain, *s. m.* A brave man.—*Turn.*

Curannta, *a.* (*from* curaidh.) Bold, brave. Gu cruaidh curannta, *hardily and bravely.—Old Song.*

Curanntachd, *s. f.* Boldness, bravery, intrepidity.

Curasan, ain, *s. m.* A milk-pail; a firkin for butter. Cuach is curasan, *a cup and milk-pail.—Macdon.*

Curcag, aig, *s. f.* A cock of hay; the bird called sand-piper; a lapwing, the *tringa vanellus* of Linnæus.

Curcais, *s. f.* (*Ir. id.*) Hair; a bulrush.

† **Curr**, *s. m.* (*Ir. id.*) A corner; a pit.—*Shaw.*

Currach, aich, *s. m.* A burying-place; a fen where shrubs grow.

Currachd, aichd, *s. f.* A cap, a woman's head-dress. See also *curachd.*

Currachdag, aig, *s. f.* A lapwing; a sand-piper; a rick of hay.

Curraichdeach, *a.* Hooded; capped; bonneted, as a female; of, or belonging to, a hood or bonnet; like a woman's hood.

Curran, ain, *s. m.* Flannel.

Curran, ain, *s. m.* A carrot; a radish; a root of the carrot or radish kind, *daucus.* Curran geal, *a parsnip;* curran buidhe, *a carrot.—Macd.* Curran dearg, *a radish.—Shaw.*

Curranach, *a.* Abounding in carrots or radishes; like a carrot or radish.

† **Currghalan**, ain, *s. m.* (*Ir. id.*) A bucket; a didapper.—*Shaw.*

Cursa, *a.* (*prov.*) Coarse.

Cùrsa, *s. m.* A course, a direction; order; rank; row; manner; coursing. Oirleach d' a cheart chùrsa, *an inch of the straight course.—Macfar.*

Lat. cursus. *Du.* koers. *Ir.* cursa. *Span.* corso *and* cursa.

Cùrsach, *a.* Winding, folding, meandering; coursing; in ranks or rows. Brat cùrsach, *a flowing robe.—Shaw.*

Cùrsachadh, aidh, *s. m.* (*prov.*) A curse.—*Shaw.*

Cùrsachd, *s. f.* Coursing; traversing; travelling; meandering.

Cùrsadh, aidh, *s. m.* A coursing; a traversing; a meandering; a direction, a course; order; manner; a row or rank.

Cùrsaich, *v. a.* Course, traverse; put in ranks or rows. *Pret. a.* chùrsaich, *coursed; fut. aff. a.* cùrsaichidh, *shall course.*

Cùrsair, *s. m.* (*Lat.* cursor. *Ir.* cursuir.) A courser; a messenger. *N. pl.* cursairean.

Cùrsaireachd, *s. f.* A coursing, a traversing.

Curta, *a.* Bad, sad, shocking, excessive; wearied; overcome. Is curta am balaoch thu, *you are a sad fellow.*

† **Curunn**, uinn, *s. m.* (*Ir. id. Arm.* curunn. *Gr.* κεραυνος.) Thunder.

Curusan, ain, *s. m.* A milk-pail. See Curasan.

Cus, cuis, *s. m.* (*Ir. id.*) A quantity; sufficiency; enough.—*Shaw. Cus* seems to be a corruption of *cuimheas.*

Cus, cusa, *s. m.* (*Ir. id.*) A tax, a subsidy.

Cusag, aig, *s. f.* Wild mustard.

Cusagach, *a.* Abounding in wild mustard.

† **Cusal**, ail, *s. m.* (*Ir. id.*) Courage; boldness.—*Shaw.*

† **Cusalach**, *a.* (*Ir. id.*) Courageous. *Com.* and *sup.* cusalaiche.

Cusb, cusba, *s.* A kibe.

Cusbach, *a.* Having kibes.—*Macint.*

Cusbair, *s. m.* (cusboir.) A mark to shoot at; a marksman; an object, a subject. Cusbair graidh, *an object of love;* cusbair deuchainn, *a criterion;* cusbair chlach, *a slinger. N. pl.* cusbairean. Written also *cuspair.*

Cusbair-deuchainn, *s. m.* A criterion; a subject of experiment.

Cusbaireachd, *s. f.* Shooting or throwing at a mark; aiming; argumentation. Ri cusbaireachd, *throwing or firing at a mark.*

Cùsbairiche, *s. m.* (*Ir.* cusboiridhe.) An opponent; a marksman.

CUSMUNN, uinn, *s. m.* (*Ir. id.*) Impost, tax.—*Shaw* and *Macd.*

CUSPAIR, *s. m.* A mark to shoot at; a marksman; an object, a subject *N. pl.* cuspairean. Cuspairean aoraidh faoin, *objects of idolatrous worship.—Stew. Lev. ref.* Written also *cusbair*, which see.

CUSPAIREACHD, *s f.* See CUSBAIREACHD.

† CUST, *s m* (*Ir. id.*) Skin. *Lat* cutes. *Ir.* cust.

† CUSTAIR, *s. m.* (*Ir. id*) A tanner.—*Shaw* *N pl.* custairean

CUTACH, *a* (*Ir. id.*) Short, diminutive; bobtailed, curtailed, docked. *Com* and *sup.* cutaiche, *shorter, shortest.*

CUTACHADH, aidh, *s m* An elision; a curtailing; curtailment.

CUTACHADH, (a), *pr part.* of cutaich.

CUTAG, aig, *s f* A diminutive female; a short horn spoon *N pl* cutagan.

CUTAICH, *v a.* Shorten; curtail *Pret a* chutaich, *curtailed, fut aff a.* cutaichidh, *shall curtail.*

† CUTALAICHE, *s. m.* (*Ir* cutallaidhe.) A companion, a partner

† CUTH, *s m.* (*Ir. id*) The head.

CUTHACH, aich, *s. m.* (*Ir. id*) Madness; rage, insanity. Buailidh mi le cuthach, *I will strike with madness.—Stew. Zech.* Is e 'n t-eud cuthach, *jealousy is rage.—Stew Pro.* Air chuthach, *insane, beside oneself.—Stew. Acts, ref.* Air a chuthach, *mad.—Stew. Ec.*

CUTHAG, aig, *s. f* (*Corn. gog. Scotch*, gowk) A cuckoo.—*Stew Lev. ref.* *N. pl* cuthagan, *cuckoos.* Cho clomhach ris a chuthag, *all over with itch.*

CUTHAICH, *gen sing.* of cuthach.

CUTHAICH, *a.* Mad; frantic, insane. Cù cuthaich, *a mad dog.*

† CUTHAILEACH, *a.* (*Ir. id*) Bashful; modest; timid.

CUTHAILEACHD, *s f.* Bashfulness; modesty; timidity.

CUTHANN, *a.* See CUMHANN.

† CUTHARLAN, ain, *s. m.* (*Ir. id.*) An onion, an earth nut. *N. pl.* cutharlain.

† CUTHARLANACH, *a.* (*Ir. id*) Abounding in onions; like an onion.

† CUTHBHÀR, air, *s. m.* († cuth *and* bàrr.) (*Ir. id.*) A helmet or head-piece.

† CUTHDARUN, uin, *s. m* (*Ir id*) A sort of cap; a montero cap —*Shaw*

† CUTT, *a.* (*Ir. id*) Short. Hence *cutach*, short; and the English, *cut*

D.

D, d, (duir) The fourth letter of the Gaelic alphabet It has various sounds (1) Broad, more dental than the English *d*, or approaching nearly to the French *d*, as in *dàn*, a song, *duine*, man, *dlagh*, a handful (2) Small, like *g* in genius, when immediately preceded or followed by one of the small vowels, *e*, *i*, or if *e* or *i* be the last vowel in the preceding syllable, as, *faide*, length; *ceaird*, a trade (3) *D*, after *ch*, sounds like *ck* in English; as, *slochd*, a ditch; *sochd*, a sock, pronounced σλοχκ, σοχκ. *D*, followed by *h*, (*dh*), has an aspirated sound, which varies according to the letter that follows *Dh*, followed by *l* or *r*, have no sound similar to them in English, being articulated somewhat softer than the Greek χ, as, *a dhlighe*, his right, *dhrùidh*, penetrated. *Dh*, followed by a small vowel, sound like *y* in English; as, *dheth*, of him; *dhi*, to her; pronounced *yea, ye* Sometimes *dh* are quiescent, as, *buailidh*, shall strike; *fàidh*, a prophet.

'D, (*for* iad.) They, them Ni 'd gairdeachas, *they shall rejoice —Sm.*

D', (*for* do), *poss pron.*, used before words beginning with a vowel and *f* aspirated. D'athair, *thy father*, d' fhearann, *thy farm.*

DA, *a.* Two. Da chaol chu, *two gaunt hounds —Oss. Com Shans* dwau. *Gr.* δυω. *Lat.* duo *Modern Pers.* du *Mol.* dua. *Tart.* tua. *Arab* tu *Malay.* dua *Dalmat.* dua *Pol. Swed.* and *Dan.* dwa *Bohem. Anglo-Sax* and *Scotch*, twa. *Eng* two. *Ir.* da. *W* daw *Arm* daou. *Corn* deau *and* deu. Da dhuine, *two men*, in *Armoric*, it is daou deen; *Cornish*, deu dhean. Da mhìl, *two thousand*, in *Armoric*, daou vil.

D'A, (*for* do a) Of his, to his; of its, to its Chaidh e d'a chois, *he went on foot*

D'A, (*for* do a.) Of her, to her. D'a h-inghean, *to her daughter.*

D'A, (*for* do a, *i. e.* gu a) To him, for him; to his, for his; to it, for it. D'a shaoradh, *to deliver him.—Stew Jon*

DA, *pers. pron.* To him, to it. Bu phubull da, *his pavilion was, i e a pavilion was to him —Sm.* Da 'fheabhas, *however good it be.*

DA ADHARCACH, *a.* Bicornous.

DABH, *comp pron* To them *Provincial* for doibh.

DABHACH, aich, *s m.* (*Ir. id.*) A masking vat, a large vat; a large tub. *N. pl.* dabhaich *and* dabhacha, *vats.* Cuiridh na dabhacha thairis, *the vats shall overflow.—Stew. Joel.* Dabhach-fhiona, *a wine-press.* *Dabhach* is also written *damhach*

DABHAN, ain, *s. m.* A pitcher, a bucket. *N. pl.* dabhain

DABHAR, air, *s m* (*Ir id*) A water-bucket, a pitcher.

DA-BHEATHACH, *a* Amphibious; also, *substantively*, an amphibious animal.

DÀ-BHLIADHNA, DÀ-BHLIADHNACH, aich, *s m* A two-years-old beast; *also*, two years of age

DÀCHA, *comp. a.* (*Ir.* docha) Likely, probable, more likely, more probably. Is dàcha leam, *I presume*, or *it is probable to me*, is e 's dàcha, *the likelihood is.*

† DÀCHADH, aidh, *s. m.* An opinion, conjecture, likelihood.

DACHAIDH, *adv.* Home, homewards. Sheòl sinn dachaidh, *we steered homewards.* *Asp form*, dhacaidh *Dachaidh* is probably a corruption of *da-thigh*

DACHAIDH, *s. f.* (*Germ* dach) A home, a dwelling-place. *Asp. form*, dhachaidh. Cha 'n 'eil dachaidh aige, *he has no home*, na toir droch sgeul dachaidh ort fèin, *take not home a bad report of yourself.—G. P.*

DA-CHEANNACH, *a* Bicipitous; two-topped. Beannan da-cheannach, *a two-topped hill*

DA-CHORPACH, *a* Bicorporal —*Shaw.*

DA-CHOSACH, *a.* Bipedal, also a biped. Beothach da-chosach, *a biped.*

DA-CHRUTHACH, *a.* Biformed.

DAD, *s* and *a.* Ought; any thing; a whit; a trifle; a jot. Cha bheagaich sibh dad, *you shall not diminish ought —Stew. Exod* Cha 'n abair mi dad, *I will say nothing.* Fear gun aon dad, *a poor man*, literally, *a man without any thing.* —*Old Song.*

DADAM. See DADUM

Dadhas, ais, *s. m.* A fallow-deer; the buck of the fallow-deer. *N. pl.* dadhais; *d. pl.* dadhasaibh.

Da-dhuilleach, *a.* Bifoliated; two-folded, as a door; also, *substantively*, a bifoliated herb.

Dadmun, uin, *s. m.* (*Ir. id.*) A mote.

Dadmunach, aich, *s. m.* An atomist; a follower of Des Cartes's opinions concerning the formation of our globe.

Dadum, *s.* A mote; a whit; a jot; any thing; some little thing.

Da-fhaobhrach, *a.* Two-edged. Claidheamh da-fhaobhrach, *a two-edged sword.*

Da-fhiaclach, *a.* Bidental.

Da-fhillte, *a.* Twofold; double.

Da-fhoghair, *s.* A diphthong; two vowels.

Dag, daig, *s. f.* A pistol. *N. pl.* dagachan *and* dagaichean, *pistols.—Macint.* Paidhir dhag, *a pair of pistols.—Id.* Dag-diollaid, *a holster.*

Dagach, *a.* (*from* dag.) Armed with a pistol; like a pistol; of, or belonging to, a pistol. Gu gunnach dagach, *armed with guns and pistols.—Old Song.*

Dagachan, **Dagaichean**, *n. pl.* of dag. Pistols.

Dagh, *a.* (*Ir. id.*) Good.—*Shaw.*

Daghadh, aidh, *s. m.* An empyreuma.

Daibhidh, *s. m.* The name David.

Ir. Daibhi. *Arm.* Devi *and* Deouy. *Scotch*, Davie.

Daibhir, *a.* (*Ir.* daidhbir.) Poor; destitute; needy; *also*, a poor person. The word of opposite meaning is *saibhir.* Saibhir agus daibhir, *rich and poor.*

Daibhireach, *a.* (*contracted* daibhreach.) Poor; destitute; needy.

Daibhireachd, *s. f.* (*from* daibhir.) Poverty; necessity; want.

† **Daibhleag**, eig, *s. m.* (*Ir. id.*) A place of worship. *N. pl.* daibhleagan.

Daibhreas, eis, *s. m.* (*from* daibhir.) Poverty; want. The word of opposite signification is *saibhreas.* Saibhreas is daibhreas, *riches and poverty.*

Dàich, dàiche, *s. f.* Beauty, comeliness, handsomeness.

Dàichealachd, *s. f.* Beauty, comeliness, handsomeness.

Dàicheil, *a.* (*i. e.* daich-amhuil.) Comely, handsome; well-looked; stately. Le ceum dàicheil, *with a stately step.—Oss. Cathluno.*

Daidhbhir, *a.* (*Ir. id.*) See **Daibhir**.

† **Daif**, *s. f.* (*Ir. id.*) Drink.

† **Daigh**, *s. f.* (*Ir. id.*) Pain; fire; roguery; mischief.

Daigh, *s. f.* (*Ir. id.*) Hope, confidence. Now written *doigh*; which see.

† **Daigh**, *v. a.* (*Ir. id.*) Give, grant. *Lat.* da.

† **Daigh-bhiorasg**, aisg, *s. m.* (*Ir. id.*) Fuel.—*Shaw.*

† **Daigheadh**, idh, *s. m.*, *from* daigh. (*Ir. id.*) A giving, a granting, bestowing; *also*, great odds.

Daigheann, *a.* Firm, fortified, tightly bound; strong, tight. Written also *daingeann*; which see.

Daighear, ir, (daigh-fhear.) A rogue.

Daighneach, ich, *s. m.* A fort; a fortress; a garrison; a fortified city; a compact; an assurance. Mo charraig 's mo dhaighneach, *my rock and my fortress.—Sm.* Written also *daingneach.*

Daighneachadh, aidh, *s. m.* A fortifying; a binding, a fastening; the act of establishing a ratification; a fortification; constipation. Daighneachadh cuim, *constipation of the bowels.* Written also *daingneachadh.*

Daighneachadh, (a), *pr. part.* of daighnich. Fortifying; binding, fastening; confirming, establishing, or founding; rati, sanctioning; obliging or compelling; constringing, constipating.

Daighnich, *v. a.* Fortify; bind, fasten, tighten; make firm; confirm, ratify, sanction; found or establish; oblige, constrain; constringe, constipate. *Pret. a.* dhaighnich, *bound*; *fut. aff. a.* daighnichidh, *shall* or *will bind*; *fut. pass.* daighnichear, *shall be bound.* Dhaighnich e am feasd, *he established for ever.—Sm.* *P. part.* daighnichte, *bound.* Written also *daingnich.*

Daighnichidh, *fut. aff. a.* of daighnich. Shall *or* will bind.

Daighnichte, *p. part.* of daighnich.

Dail, dalach, *s. f.* A dale, a field; a meadow; a plain. Dail fhearainn, *a level field; a parcel of ground.—Stew.* 1 *Chr.* *N. pl.* dailean.

Swed. and *Dan.* dal. *Teut.* dal, thal, *and* tal. *Du.* dal. *Goth.* dal *and* dallei. *Runic, Dal. Isl.* doele. *Germ.* tal. *Arm.* dol. *Ir.* dail. *W.* and *Corn.* dol. *Eng.* dale.

Dàil, *s. f.* (*Ir. id. Arm.* dale, *to tarry.*) Delay; a decree; a meeting; nearness, neighbourhood; space betwixt two *couples* in a cottage; a separate tribe; desire, willingness. Onoir diolamaid gun dàil, *let us pay honour without delay.—Sm.* *Dail*, in government with the prep. *an*, commonly means hostile opposition. Chaidh sinn an dàil a cheile, *we rushed towards* [*went in opposition to*] *each other.—Oss. Dargo.* It is also used in the sense of *meeting*, or of *proximity.* Le 'curach chaidh i na dhàil, *in her skiff she went to meet him.—Ull.* Ghabh e Sniobhan na dhàil, *he took Sniobhan near him.—Oss.*

† **Dail**, *s. f.* (from the Celtic primitive, *dal.*) *Goth.* dail. A share, a portion.

† **Dail**, *v. a.* (*Ir. id.*) Give, deliver. Hence the English word, deal, *distribute.*

Dail-chath, *s.* If *dail* be accented, this compounded word means a pitched battle; if *cath* be accented, it means a plain of battle. This remark, *mutatis mutandis*, is applicable to all such compounded words in Gaelic.

Dail-chuach, -chuaich, *s. m.* A kind of poculated meadow-flower.

Dàileach, *a.* (*from* dàil.) Dilatory; tardy; procrastinating.

Dàileachadh, (a), *pr. part.* of dàilich.

Daileadh, idh, *s. m.* Tradition; affiance.—*Shaw.*

Daileag, eig, *s. f.* A date tree; a little dale, a meadow. *N. pl.* daileagan.

† **Dailean**, ein, *s. m.* (*Ir. id.*) A scoff.—*Shaw.*

Dàilich, *v. a.* Delay, procrastinate; prorogue; linger. *Pret. a.* dhàilich, *delayed*; *fut. aff. a.* dàilichidh, *shall* or *will delay.*

Daille, *s. f.* (*from* dall.) Blindness; darkness. More frequently written *doille*; which see.

Daille, *com.* and *sup.* of dall. More *or* most blind. See **Doille**.

Dailte, *a.* Dealt; parted; distributed.

Dailtean, ein, *s. m.* A stripling; a jackanapes; a coxcomb; a puppy; a rascal.—*Shaw.*

Dailteanach, *a.* Like a coxcomb.

Dailteanas, ais, *s. m.* (*from* dailtean.) Scurrility; impertinence; foppery.

Daimh, *s. m.* (*Ir. id.*) Connexion; consanguinity; kindred; friendship; kindness; a friend; a stranger; assent; free will; a poet; a learned man. Co ris do dhaimh? *with whom is thy connexion?—Oss. Duthona.* Dlù an daimh, *near a-kin.—Stew. Lev.* Mar ni athair daimh, *as a father befriends.—Sm.* An comhstri ri daimh, *in contest with strangers*; fear daimh, *a kinsman.—Stew. Ruth.*

† **Daimh**, *s. f.* (*Ir. id.*) A house.

† **Daimh**, *a* (*Ir. id.*) Troublesome.

Daimh, *gen. sing* and *n. pl.* of damh

Daimhheach, ich, *s. m.* (*from* daimh) *Ir.* daimheach. A relation; a companion; a guest *N. pl.* daimhich.

Daimheil, *a.* (daimh-amhail) Friendly, kind, affectionate, related Gu daimheil, *in a friendly manner*

Daimh-fheoil, *s. f.* Beef

† **Daimhliag**, eig, *s. f* (*Ir. id*) A place of worship — *Shaw.*

Daimsean, ein, *s. m* A damson plum. *N pl.* daimseanan

Daimseanach, *a.* Abounding in damsons; of damsons; like a damson

Dàin, *gen. sing.* and *n pl* of dàn; which see

Daindeoin. See Dh'aindeoin.

Dàine, *com.* and *sup.* of dàn Bolder, boldest.

Daingeann, *a* Firm; fortified; tightly bound; strong Gu daingeann laidir, *firmly and strongly.—Ull* Do 'n chathair dhaingeann, *to the fortified city.—Sm. Com* and *sup.* daingne *or* daingínne.

Daingneach, ich, *s m* A fort or fortress; a garrison or castle; a fortified city or place, a bulwark; an assurance, a compact; a contract; a ratification. *N pl.* daingnichean Mar chrannaibh daingnich, *like the bars of a castle —Stew Pro ref* Daingnichean mòr, *great bulwarks.—Stew. Ecc.* Written also *daighneach*

Daingneachadh, aidh, *s. m* A fortifying, a bending, tightening, confirming, ratifying, establishing; a fortification; a ratification; a compact, constipation

Daingneachadh, (a), *pr part.* of daingnich.

Daingneachd, *s f* A fortification, a bulwark, a compact, a ratification.

Daingnich, *v. a* Fortify; bind; fasten, tighten, confirm; ratify, found, establish; oblige, constrain, constringe, constipate *Pret a.* dhaingnich, *bound*, *fut. aff. a.* daingnichidh, *shall* or *will bind* Dhaingnich se e fèin, *he fortified himself—Stew 2 Chr* Daingnich obair ar lamh, *establish the work of our hands—Stew Ps Fut. pass* daingnichear; *p. part.* daingnichte. Written also *daighnich.*

Daingnichidh, *fut aff. a* of daingnich.

Daingnichte, *p. part* of daingnich. Fortified; bound; fastened, tightened, confirmed; founded; obliged, constrained. Baile daingnichte, *a fortified town.*

† **Dainoide**, *s m.* (*Ir id.*) A schoolmaster

† **Dair**, daire, *s. f.* Oak (*Ir.* dair. *Box. Lex* dar.) Hence the modern Gaelic, *darach*

Dàir, *v a.* Bull; copulate, as cattle; take the bull *Pret a* dhàir, *bulled, fut aff a* dàiridh

Dàir, Daireadh, idh, *s m.* A bulling, copulation, as of cattle Bò air dàireadh, *a cow that is a-bulling*

Dàir na coille, *s* The first night of the new year, when the wind blows from the west, some of the Gael call *Dàir na coille*, or *the night of the fecundation of the woods — Statistics, P Kirkmichael.* Perhaps *dàir na coille* is *tarbh coille*, which see.

Dairbh, *s m* A species of worm, a little slender person —*Shaw.*

Dairbhre, *s. f* An oak, a nursery or grove of oaks.

Dairearach, ich, *s. m.* A loud report, a rattling noise; a smart blow

Dairghe, *s. f.* A oak-apple

Dairt, dairte, *s. f* (*Ir. id*) A clod; a heifer.

Dairteach, *a.* (*Ir. id*) Full of clods; of clods —*Shaw*

Dais, dàise, *s. f.* A mow; corn or fodder. *N. pl* daisean and daiseachan

Daiseachan, ain, *s. m.* An insipid rhymer; a low-witted poet.

Daisgean, ein, *s. m.* A writing-desk.

Dait, *s. m.* A father; a child's name for a father. *Arm* tat. *Corn.* tad *and* taz. *Ir.* daid.

Daitean, ein, *s. m* (*dim.* of dait.) A foster-father; a child's name for its father.

† **Daith**, *a* (*Ir. id.*) Quick, nimble, active, supple.—*Shaw.*

† **Daithe**, *s f.* (*Ir. id.*) Revenge.

Daithealachd, *s f* See Daichealachd.

Daithear, ir, *s m.* An avenger, a revengeful man.

† **Daitheasg**, eisg, *s. f.* Eloquence, speech, remonstrance.

Daitheil, *a.* See Daicheil.

Daithte, *p. part.* of dath Coloured; stained. *Asp. form*, dhaithte. A bhratach dhaithte uaine, *his green-coloured banner —Oss Dargo.*

Daitidh, *s. m* A child's name for a father *Ir.* daid. *W* and *Eng* dad. *Arm.* tad. *Corn.* tad.

† **Dal**, dail, *s. m.* An assembly; a convention; a tribe; a dale. In this last sense it is written *dail* by the Gael

† **Dala**, ai, *s m* News; an oath; espousals; a meeting.

Dalach, *gen. sing.* of dail. Of a meadow. Iochdar na dalach, *the lower part of the meadow*

† **Dalba**, *a* (*Ir. id*) Impudent, forward —*Shaw.*

Dalbachd, *s. f.* Impudence, pertness, forwardness.

Dalbh, dailbh, *s. m.* A lie, a contrivance.—*Shaw*

Dalbhadh, aidh, *s. m* Sorcery —*Shaw*

Dall, *a* (*Corn* and *Arm.* dall.) Blind; dark; obscure; ignorant, misled; puzzled; a blind person. Fradharc iùil do 'n dall, *vision to the blind —Sm* San oidhche dhoirche dhaill, *in the pitchy dark night —Fingalian Poem.* An dall air muin a chrùbaich, *the blind mounted on the lame —Old Saying.*

Dall, *v. a* (*Ir. id.*) Make blind, blind; blindfold; mislead; puzzle *Pret. a* dhall, *blinded, fut. aff. a.* dallaidh, *shall* or *will blind* Dallaidh tiodhlac, *a gift blindeth.— Stew Exod.*

Dalladh, aidh, *s. m.* A blinding, a darkening; a misleading, blindness. Dalladh na h-inntinn, *a blinding of the mind.*

Dalladh, (a), *pr part.* of dall. Blinding or darkening; misleading A dalladh a léirsinn, *darkening his vision — Oss. Duthona.*

Dalladh-eun, *s m* Purblindness.

Dallag, aig, *s. f.* (*Ir. id*) A dormouse; a fetid shrewmouse; a mole; a leech; any little blind creature; a buffet. *N pl* dallagan Dallag fheoir, *a dormouse, a mole*, dallag an fhraoich, *a shrew or shrew-mouse.—Shaw.* The *dallag*, or fetid shrew-mouse, is the *sorex araneus* of naturalists

Dallagach, *a.* Like a dormouse, abounding in dormice; like a mole or leech, abounding in moles or in leeches; buffeting.

Dallaig, *gen. sing* of dallag.

Dallan, ain, *s m*, *from* dall (*W.* dallan.) A blind person; a short-sighted person, an improvident person; a blindfolded person, also a fan to winnow with. *N pl.* dallain.

Dallanach, aich, *s. m.* A large fan for winnowing.

Dallanachd, *s.* Winnowing with a large fan.

Dallan-dàit, *s.* The pastime called Blind Harry, or Blindman's-buff, the person who is blindfolded in the play called Blind Harry.

Dall-bhrat, -bhrat, *s. m.* A dark covering or mantle. Dall-bhrat na h-oidhche, *the dark mantle of night —Ull*

Dall-cheo, *s. m.* A dark mist. Thuirlinn dall-cheo, *a dark mist descended.—Ull.*

Dall-cheothar, *a.* Very misty.

Dall-oidhche, *s. f.* The darkest time of night; a dark night. O 'n òg mhaduinn gu dall-oidhche, *from early morn until night—Ull.*

Dall-shùil, *s. f.* A dim eye; a sightless eye. Meallaidh gach neul a dhall-shùil, *each cloud deceives his dim eye.—Ull.*

Dalma, *a.* (*Gr.* τολμα, *audacia.*) Bold, stout; forward; haughty; impudent. Bha 'ur briathran dalma, *your words were bold.—Stew. Mal.* Gu dalma, *stoutly, haughtily.*

Dalmachd, *s f.* Boldness; stoutness; forwardness; impudence; haughtiness; pride. Do dhalmachd, *thy pride—Stew. Is.*

Dalta, Daltadh, aidh, *s. m* (*Ir id.*) A foster-child. *N. pl.* daltaichean, *foster-children.* Mar dhaltaichean, *like foster-children.—Old Song*

Daltach, *a.* Betrothed; like a foster-child

Dalta-baistidh, *s. m.* A god-son.

Daltan, ain, *s. m.* A foster-son; a disciple. *N. pl.* daltana

† **Dam**, *s. m.* (*Ir id*) A dam, a reservoir—*Shaw.*

Damàist, *s. f.* (*Ir. id.*) Damage, harm.

Damanta, *a.* (*Ir. id. Lat.* damnatus) Condemned; damned. —*Shaw.*

† **Damh**, *v. a* (*Ir. id. Lat* da) Give; grant; permit—*Shaw.*

Damh, daimh, *s m.* An ox; a hart; a buck; *rarely*, learning. Damh airson daimh, *ox for ox—Stew. Exod. N. pl* daimh. Damh-feidh, *a buck* or *red deer*, thuit an damh, *the buck has fallen—The Bard's Wish.*
Ir. id. Lat. dama, *a buck. Fr.* daim *Eng.* doe

Damhach, *a.* (*from* damh) Full of oxen or harts, of, or belonging to, an ox or hart. Damhach, aghach, laoghach, *full of oxen, steers, and calves—Old Song*

Damhach, aich, *s. m* A vat, a vine-press. Damhach fhiona, *a vine-press.—Stew Hos.* Written also *dabhach*

† **Damhadh**, aidh, *s m.* (*Ir. id.*) A giving, a granting, a permission.

Damhaich, *gen sing* and *n. pl.* of damhach.

† **Damhail**, *s. m.* (*from* damh, *learning.*) A student *N. pl.* damhailean

Damhair, *a* Earnest; keen; eager; zealous.

Damhair, *s. m.* Rutting time; rutting; a noise. Bhuail chuca an damhair, *the noise came suddenly upon them.—Old Poem.*

Damhaireach, *a.* Keen, eager, industrious, diligent; endeavouring; noisy. *Com.* and *sup.* damhairiche, *keener, keenest.*

Damhaireachd, *s. f.* Keenness, eagerness; diligence, industry; noisiness

Damhan, ain, *s. m.* A spider. *N pl.* damhain.

Damhan-alluidh, *s m.* A spider. Lion an damhain-alluidh, *the spider's web.*

Damhas, *s.*, more frequently written *dannsa*; which see.

Damh-feidh, *s. m.* A hart, a stag, a buck. *Asp. form*, dhamh.

Damh-lann, -lainn, *s m.* (*Ir.* damhlan.) An ox-stall

Damhnadh, aidh, *s. m.* A band, a tie.—*Shaw* The matter out of which any thing is formed

Damh-oide, *s. m.* A doctor, a teacher; a schoolmaster.

Damhs, *v. n.* Dance, hop, skip. *Pret. a* dhamhs, *danced, fut. aff. a.* damhsaidh, *shall* or *will dance* Written also *danns;* which see.

Damhsa, ai; **Damhsadh**, aidh, *s m.* Dancing, hopping, skipping; a dance, a reel. Ri damhsadh, *dancing.* Mo bhròn gu damhsa chaochail thu, *thou hast changed my sorrow to dancing.—Sm.* Damhsadh-deis, *a strathspey*, maighistir damhsaidh, *a dancing-master.* Written also *dannsadh*, which see.

Damhsadh, (a), *pr. part.* of damhs. Dancing.

Damhsadh-deise, *s m.* A strathspey.

Damhsail, *a* Fond of dancing—*Turn.*

Damhsair, *s. m.* A dancer *N pl.* damhsairean Damhsair dubh an uisge, *a water-spider.—Macdon*
Ir. damhsoir. *Swed* dansare. *Arm* dançzer. *Fr.* danseur

Damhsaireachd, *s f* Dancing. Le ceòl is damhsaireachd, *with music and dancing—Turn.*

Damnach, *a* Condemnatory.

Damnachadh, aidh, *s m.* (*Ir.* damnughadh.) A condemning, a condemnation, a doom

Damnachadh, (a), *pr part.* of damnaich.

Damnadh, aidh, *s. m.* (*Lat.* damnatio) A condemning, a condemnation, a doom, a judgment; a punishment—*Stew Mar ref*

Damnaich, *v a* (*Ir.* damnuigh) Condemn, doom, judge, punish *Pret. a* dhamnaich, *condemned, fut. aff a* damnaichidh, *shall condemn.*

Damnaichte, *p. part.* of damnaich. Condemned, doomed, judged, punished *Asp. form*, dhamnaichte.

Dàn, dàin, *s. m.* (*Ir. id Pers. Arab.* dana, *a poet.*) A poem, a song, verse; fate, destiny. *Asp. form*, dhàn. *N pl* dàin, *songs* Iomradh nan treun am dhàn, *the fame of the valiant in my song.—Oss Fin. and Lor.* Bha so an dàn duit, *this was destined for thee*, mo leigheas cha 'n 'eil an dàn, *my remedy is not [in fate] destined—Death of Oscar.* Am fear do 'n dàn an donas's ann da bheanas, *it is he that will suffer, to whom evil is destined—G. P*

Dàn, Dana, *a.* Bold, daring, intrepid, resolute; forward, impudent, confident. Dàna mar leomhann, *bold as a lion—Stew. Pro* Tha 'n t-amadan dàna, *the fool is confident.—Id* *Com.* and *sup.* dàine, *more or most bold*

Dànach, aich, *s m* A fatalist.

Dànach, *a.* (*from* dàn) Poetical, metrical; of, or relating to, a poem or song Aithris dhuinn, Ossein dhànaich, *relate to us, Ossian of songs—Fingalian Poem.*

Dànachd, *s f* (*from* dàn) Boldness, presumption, confidence; also poetry, poesy, fatalism. Le dànachd naomh, *with holy confidence.—Sm. Ir.* dànachd.

Dànadail, *a* (*from* dàn) Fated, destined.

Dànadas, ais, *s. m.* Boldness, presumption *Asp. form*, dhànadas Peacadh dànadais, *presumptuous sins.—Sm* Bheil dhànadas agad mo bhualadh? *have you the boldness to strike me?*

Dànaich, *v a.* (*from* dàn.) Defy, challenge, dare; adventure. *Pret a* dhànaich, *defied, fut. aff. a.* dànaichidh, *shall defy.*

† **Danair**, *s m* (*Ir id.*) A stranger; a foreigner, a guest

† **Danaireachd**, *s f* (*Ir. id*) The state of being strange or foreign.

Danara, *a.* Stubborn, stedfast, opinionative; impudent, forward

Danarachd, *s f.* Stubbornness, stedfastness, opinionativeness; impudence, forwardness

Dànaradh, *a.* Stubborn, opinionative, stedfast; impudent, forward.

Danardha, Danargha, *a* See **Danaradh**

Danardhachd, Dànarghachd, *s. f.* See **Dànarachd**

Danns, *v. n.* Dance, hop, skip. *Pret. a* dhanns, *danced, fut. aff. a.* dannsaidh, *shall dance.* Dhanns e, *he danced.—Stew. Sam.*

Dannsa, Dannsadh, aidh, *s. m.* Dancing, a dance, a ball Chunnaic e 'n dannsa, *he saw the dancing.—Stew. Exod.* Le dannsa, *with dances.—Id.* Maighstir dannsaidh, *a dancing-master*, seomar dannsaich, *a ball-room.*

Teut dannsen. *Arab.* tanza *Corn* dawns. *Bisc.* dantza, *a dance* *Fr.* danse *It.* danza. *Span* dança. *Germ.* tantz *Du* dans. *Styr.* and *Car.* tancj

Dannsaidh, *gen sing* of dannsadh. Of dancing. Maighstir dannsaidh, *a dancing-master.*

Dannsaidh, *fut. aff a* of danns.

Dannsair, *s m* A dancer. Deagh dhannsair, *a good dancer.* (*Swed.* dansare. *Arm.* dançzer. *Fr.* danseur.) *N. pl* dannsairean, *dancers* *Arm.* dançeryen, *dancers.*

† **Dant**, daint, *s m* A morsel, a mouthful, a share or portion.

W. dant, *a tooth* *Arm* dant *Swed.* and *Dan* tand. *Isl* tan *Fr* dent. *Lat* dens, dentis.

Dànachd, *s f* (*from* dàn) Fatalism; *also*, poetry.

Daoch, daoich, *s. m.* A periwinkle, a sea-snail

Daochag, aig, *s. f.* (*dim* of daoch.) A small periwinkle or sea-snail *N. pl.* daochagan

Daochal, ail, *s. m* (*Ir. id*) A morsel, a bit —*Shaw*

Daochan, ain, *s. m.* Anger, vexation, a fit of passion

Daochanach, *a* Angry; passionate. Gu daochanach, *passionately.*

Daoi, Daoidh, *a* Wicked, foolish, worthless, *substantively*, a wicked man; a foolish man; a vain man Cuideachd dhaoine daoi, *the company of foolish men —Sm* Comhairle nan daoi, *the council of the wicked —Id* Rug e air an daoi, *he seized the vain man —Fingalian Poem*

Daoidheachd, *s f.* Wickedness, foolishness, worthlessness Moladh na daoidheachd, *praise from the worthless.—O P*

Daoil, *s f.* A leech. *N pl* daoilean

Daoil, *gen sing.* of daol.

Daoileach, *a.* Like a leech; of a leech, full of leeches

Daoimean, ein, *s m.* Diamond —*Stew Exod.*

Daoimeanach, *a* Of diamond, like diamond.

Daoin, *s* Thursday Air la Daoin, *on a Thursday*

Daoine, *n pl* of duin Men.

Daoineach, *a*, *from* daoine (*Ir id*) Populous, numerous

Daoire, *com* and *sup* of daor. Dearer, dearest See **Daor.**

Daoire, *s. f* Dearth, dearness

Daoiread, eid, *s m* Dearth, increase in dearth A dol an daoiread, *growing more and more dear*, also, comparatively, *dearer.* Is daoiread e sin, *it is dearer on that account.*

Daoir-fhine, *s f* A subjected or enslaved people

Daoirich, *s* Tipsiness, drunkenness Air an daoirich, *tipsy*

Daoir-mhaighstir, *s.* A task-master, an oppressor.

Daoirse, *s f* Dearth, scarcity, captivity, slavery.

Daoirseach, *a* Afflicted with dearth or famine, in captivity or slavery, *substantively*, a captive, a slave

Daoirsinn, *s f.* Captivity, bondage, slavery, dearth.

Daol, daoil, *s m.* (*Ir id.*) A worm, a caterpillar, a black beetle, a chafer, a bug Bheir an daol buaidh air, *the worm shall triumph over him —Oss. Gaul.* An daol a réir a ghné, *the beetle after his kind —Stew. Lev* Daol dubh, *a beetle*

Daolag, aig, *s f.* (*dim.* of daol) A worm, a caterpillar, a beetle; *in derision*, a lazy young female; a miserly person. *N. pl* daolagan. Gun bhi ro chaithteach no m' dhaolag, *without being a spendthrift or a miser.—Old Song.* Daolag-bhreac, *a lady-cow.—Macdon*

Daolagach, *a.* (*from* daol) Abounding in worms, beetles, or caterpillars, vermicular.

Daolag-bhreac, -bhric, *s f.* A lady-cow.—*Macd.* and *Shaw.*

Daolair, *s. m.* (*from* daol.) A lazy, inactive fellow.—*Shaw. N. pl* daolairean.

Daolaireach, *a* (*from* daolair.) Lazy, lounging.

Daolaireachd, *s.* Laziness; frequent or continued lounging.

Daomhais, *v. a.* (*Ir. id*) Ruin, demolish.—*Shaw. Pret.* dhaomhais, *ruined.*

† **Daon**, *v. n.* (*Ir id.*) Ruin, demolish.—*Shaw* *Pret. a.* dhaon, *fut. aff. a.* daonaidh

Daonachd, *s f.* See **Daonnachd**

Daonalt, *adv*, *provincial* for daonann

Daonann, *adv* Always; perpetually, incessantly —*Stew. Lev. ref*

Daon-fhuil, *a.* Akin, allied, related.

Daonna, Daonnach, *a.*, *from* duine. (*Ir. id*) Hospitable, liberal, humane, civil Gu daonnach, *humanely.*

Daonnachd, *s f* (*Ir. id*) Hospitality; liberality; humanity, civility. An daonnachd, *in liberality.—Stew. Cor. ref.* Daonnachd ghabh air fein, *he took humanity upon himself. —Sm.*

Daonnachdadh, *a* (*Ir. id*) Hospitable; liberal, bountiful, civil. Bhur tabhartais dhaonnachdaich, *your liberal offerings.—Stew. Cor.* *Com.* and *sup* daonnachdaiche, *more* or *most liberal.*

Daonnachdail, *a.* (daonnachd-amhuil.) Hospitable, liberal, bountiful, civil, humane. Gu bheil am miodhair daonnachdail, *that the churl is hospitable —Stew. Is.*

Daontach, Daontachail, *a.* See **Daonnachdail.**

† **Daor**, *s. m.* Earth, land

Lat terra *Arm* douar *and* daouar. *Corn* dor, daor, *and* doer *Box Lex.* daear

Daor, *a.* (*Swed* dyr. *Du.* duur. *Ir.* daor) Dear in price; precious; enslaved, bound firmly; imprisoned; guilty, condemned; *substantively*, a slave Mar dhaoine daor, *like bondmen —Stew. Gen.* Bean dhaor, *a bondwoman*, daorbhean, *a bondwoman*, daor-oglach, *a bondman.* Chuir e ceangal gu daor air an righ, *he bound the king firmly*, or *in subjection.—Oss. Cathula* Gu daor, *dearly*, is daor leam e, *I think it dear*, is tuille is daor leam e, *I think it too dear.*

Daor, *v. a* (*Ir. id*) Sentence, doom, condemn.—*Shaw. Pret. a* dhaor, *condemned.*

Daorach, aich, *s. m.* Drunkenness, tipsiness. Air an daorach, *drunk, tipsy*

Daorachadh, aidh, *s. m* A rising in price or value; a raising in price.

Daorachadh, (a), *pr part* of daoraich. Raising in price.

Daorad, aid, *s. m* Dearness; increase in price A dol an daorad, *rising in price.*

Daoradh, aidh, *s. m* A condemning; a condemnation; slavery

Daoraich, *s* See **Daoirich.**

Daoraich, *v. a.* Raise in price, make dear. *Pret a* dhaoraich, *fut aff a* daoraichidh

Daorair, *s m.* (*from* daor) A slave, a bondman; a captive; an oppressed man; *also*, an oppressor. *N. pl* daorairean.

Daoranach, aich, *s m* (*from* daor) A slave, a bondman; a captive.

Daor-bhalaoch, oich, *s m.* A man-slave, a male captive. *N pl.* daor-bhaloich.

Daor-bhodach, aich, *s m.* A man-slave. *N. pl* daorbhodaich

Daor-ghille, *s. m.* A man-slave. *N. pl.* daor-ghillean.

Daorman, Daormun, uin, *s. m.* A miser; a curmudgeon 'Daormun a thaisgeas na buinn, *a miser who hoards his coin.—Old Song.*

Daor-oglach, aich, *s. m.* (*Ir. id.*) A male captive; a bondman. *N. pl.* daor-oglaich.

Daorsa, Daorsadh, aidh, *s. f.* Bondage; captivity; famine; dearth. Tigh na daorsa, *the house of bondage.—Stew. Deut.*

Daorsainn, *s. f* Famine; dearth; captivity, slavery. Fo dhaorsainn, *in bondage*

Daorta, *p. part.* of daor. Condemned, convicted.

Daor-thigh, *s. m.* (*W.* daeardy) A prison; a house of bondage. *N. pl* daor-thighean.

Daosgar-sluaigh, *s. m* A mob; populace.

Daothain, *s. f.* Sufficiency, enough Dh' ith e a dhaothain, *he ate enough.*

Da'r, *for* da ar. (*Ir. id*) To our, of our; from off your. An Fhiann a teachd da'r cobhair, *the Fingalians coming to our aid.—Fingalian Poem.*

Da'r, (*for* da bhur) To your

D'ar, (*for* do ar.) Of our

Dara, *a* (*Ir id.*) Second. An dara àite, *the second place, secondly;* an dara mhaireach, *the second morning —Oss. Gaul.*

Dar-abhall, aill, *s. m.* (*Ir* dar-abhall. *W.* dar-abhal.) An oak-apple, a gall-nut.

Darach, aich, *s. m.* (*Corn.* dar *W.* deru *Arm.* daro. *Ir.* darach) Oak, an oak-tree; an oak-wood; *by met.* a ship Craobh dharaich, *an oak-tree,* sròn daraich, *a ship.—Bard's Wish.*

Dàradh, aidh, *s. m.* Rutting; bulling Am dàraidh, *rutting time.—Macint.* Air dàradh, *in want of a bull,* (as a cow), *bulled*

Darag, aig, *s. f.* and *m.* (*Corn.* dar. *W* deru *Arm.* daro. *Ir.* darach, *oak*) An oak-tree, oak; an oak-wood; *by met.* a ship; *also,* a small stone *N pl.* daraga Am fasgadh na daraig, *in the shelter of the oak —Ull.* Daraga leathan, *broad-spreading oaks.—Oss. Tem*

Darag-thalmhainn, *s. f.* A germander; the name of a bird.—*Macfar. Voc. Shaw* and *Macd.*

Dararaich, *s f.* A loud rattling noise; slap-dash, a smart blow. Written also *dairearaich.*

† **Daras**, ais, *s. m.*, *from* àras *or* aros. (*Ir. id*) A home, a dwelling.

Darb, *s.* (*Ir. id.*) A worm, a reptile.

† **Darbh**, dairbh, *s. m* (*Ir. id*) A car, a chariot

Darcain, *gen. sing.* and *n pl* of darcan.

Darcan, ain, *s. m.* A teal or coot—(*Macd*); an acorn; the hollow of the hand.—*Shaw.*

Darcanach, *a* Abounding in teals or in acorns; of acorns.

† **Dardal**, ail, *s m* (*Ir id.*) Bad weather; a severe season. —*Shaw.*

† **Darn**, dairn, *s. m.* (*Ir. id.*) A school.

Darna, *a.* Second; the one or the other. An darna la, *the second day.—Stew Gen ref* An darna fear dhiubh, *one or other of them; one of the two.* An ni ni subhach an darna h-ab, ni e dubhach an t-ab eile, *what gladdens one abbot will grieve another —G. P.*

† **Darsa**. See **Daras.**

† **Dart**, dairt, *s. m.* A dart.
Ir. id. Span dardo. *Dalm* and *Hung.* darda. *Bisc.* dard-ara. *Eng.* dart.

† **Dart**, *v. a.* (*Ir. id.*) Bull a cow. *Pret* dhart, *bulled; fut. aff.* dartaidh.

Dartan, ain, *s. m.* A herd; a drove. *N. pl* dartain.—*Shaw*

Dar-ubhall, aill, *s m.* An oak-apple, a gall-nut. *N pl.* dar-ùbhlan.

† **Das**, dais, *s. m.* (*Ir id*) A desk. *N. pl.* dasan

† **Dasachd**, *s. f.* (*Ir. id*) Fierceness, furiousness, frenzy, impertinence.

† **Dasachdach**, *a* (*Ir. id*) Fierce, furious, frantic; impertinent, assuming

Dàsa, Dàsan, *emphat pron.* To him.

† **Dasan**, *a.* Binocular.—*Shaw*

Dàsan, ain, *s m* Fury, frenzy

Dàsanach, *a* Furious, fierce, frantic. *Com* and *sup.* dasanaiche

Dasanachd, *s f* Furiousness, fierceness, frenzy

Dasg, daisg, *s m* and *f* A desk —*Macd. N pl* dasgan

Da-sgiathach, *a* Bipennated, two-winged.

Da-shealladh, aidh, *s. m* Second sight. See **Sealladh**

Da-shuileach, *a* Binocular; having two loops.

† **Data**, *a* (*Ir. id*) Pleasant, handsome; agreeable

Datan, ain, *s. m.* A foster-father See **Daitean.**

Dath, *s. m* (*Ir. id*) A colour, a dye, a stain, a tincture, colouring, appearance. *N. pl.* dathan, *colours; d. pl.* dathaibh. Làn dathaibh àillidh, *full of beauteous colours.—Macfar.* Do ghruaidh air dhath na céire, *thy cheek coloured like red wax.—Id* Dath breige, *a false dye,* dathan eag-samhuil, *various colours.*

Dath, *v. a* (*Ir. id*) Dye, colour, stain, tinge *Pret a* dhath, *coloured, fut. aff. a* dathaidh, *shall colour.*

Dathach, *a.* Coloured, colouring, imparting colour, apt to tinge.

Dathachadh, aidh, *s m.* (*Ir.* dathughadh.) A colouring, dying, staining.

Dathadair, *s. m.* (*Ir.* dathadoir) A dyer. *N. pl* dathadairean.

Dathadaireachd, *s. f.* The employment of dying; the trade of a dyer. Ri dathadaireachd, *dying,* ris an dathadaireachd, *at the trade of a dyer.*

Dathadh, aidh, *s m.* A dying, a tincturing; a dye, colour, or tincture.

Dathadh, (a), *pr part.* of dath Dying, tincturing, colouring

Dathag, aig, *s f* A worm in the human body *N. pl.* dathagan.

Dathagach, *a* Abounding in worms, as a body, like a worm

Dathaich, *v a.* (*from* dath) Colour, dye, tincture, stain. *Pret a.* dhathaich, *coloured, fut aff a* dathaichidh, *shall or will colour, p. part.* dathaichte, *coloured*

Dathaichte, *p part.* of dathaich. Coloured

Dathaidh, *fut. aff. a* of dath Shall or will colour

† **Dathail**, *a.* (*Ir.* dath-amhail) Pleasant, comely, decent; coloured.

Dathaileachd, *s f* Pleasantness, comeliness, decentness

Dathan, *n. pl.* Colours, paints, tinctures.

Dathas, ais, *s m* A fallow-deer —*Stew K. N. pl.* dathais

Dath-chlodhach, *a* Parti-coloured —*Shaw*

Dathigh, *adv* Home, homewards. See **Dachaidh**

† **Dathnaid**, *s f* (*Ir id*) A foster-mother. *N. pl* dathnaidean —*Shaw*

Dathta, Dathte, *p part.* of dath. Coloured, dyed, tinctured, tinged.

Dé, *s. f.* The river Dee, in Aberdeen The ancient name was *dubh-abh,* or *dubh-abhainn,* black water This is probably the Δηοῦα ποταμοῦ ἐκβολαὶ of Ptolemy

Dé, *gen. sing.* of Dia. Of God.

De, *com pron* Of him More correctly written *deth;* which see

De, *prep.* (*Lat.* de) Of; from; off Truscan de cheo, *a shroud of mist.—Oss. Tem.* This preposition, when it precedes a vowel, loses *e*, and is aspirated, as, armailt de dhaoinibh, agus dh' eachaibh, *an army of men and horses*, feachd dh' Albannaich, *a regiment of Scotsmen.*

Dé, (an), *adv.* (*Arm.* dech *Corn* dé. *Pers.* dee.) Yesterday. An dé agus an diugh, *yesterday and to-day.—Stew. Exod* An la roimh an dé, *the day before yesterday*, mu 'n tràth so an dé, *this time yesterday*, air bho'n dé, *the day before yesterday* An Dé, *the river Dee*

Dé, *s. m* (*Corn* de) A day

Deabh, *v. a* and *n* (*Ir. id*) Hasten, encounter; battle, drain or dry up *Pret a* dheabh, *fut aff. a.* deabhaidh. Thun air fuil a dheabhadh, *almost drying up our blood —Old Song.*

Deabhach, *a* Contentious, litigious; causing haste, apt to dry up.

Deabhadh, aidh, *s. m* (*Ir. id*) A hasty encounter, a skirmish, battle; a wrangling; haste, despatch, hurry, a draining or drying up; evaporation; a shrinking, as of the staves of a vessel.

Deabhaidh, *gen sing.* of deabhadh.

Deabhaidh, *fut aff. a.* of deabh, which see.

Deabhlach, *a* (*Ir. id.*) Contentious, litigious, wrangling —*Shaw*

Deacair, *a.* (*Ir. id*) Difficult, hard, abstruse; wonderful; powerful, terrible, sad, grievous. Bu deacair co bu treine innseadh, *it was difficult to tell who was the stronger.— Oss Manos* Dearg deacair sin, *that terrible Dargo.— Oss Dargo* Is deacair bri do sgeòil, *sad is the substance of the tale —Oss Derm* Is deacair leinn achmhasan, *grievous to us are his reproofs. Com* and *sup* deacaire *and* deacra

Deacaireachd, *s. f.* Difficulty; wonderfulness, grievousness; terribleness

Deacait, *s. f* A waistcoat or vest. *N pl.* deacaitean

Deacaiteach, *a* Having a waistcoat

Deach, **Deachaidh**, *pret* of *v. irr* rach Went or did go. An deach e dhachaidh? *did he go home?* Gun deachaidh na daoine mach, *that the men went out.—Stew. Josh* Mun deachaidh na sloigh an dlùthas, *before the hosts approached each other.—Fingalian Poem*

Deachainn. See **Deuchainn**.

† **Deachair**, *s f.* (*Ir. id*) A separating, a separation, a following; brightness —*Shaw.*

† **Deachair**, *v. a* (*Ir. id*) Follow —*Shaw*

Deachamh, aimh, *s.* (*Ir.* deachmadh) A tithe, a tenth part. Thugaibh 'ur deachamh, *give your tithe.—Stew Amos* Bheir mi an deachamh dhuit, *I will give you the tenth part.—Stew. Gen*

Deachamhaich, *v a.* Tithe. *Pret a* dheachamhaich, *tithed*

Deachd, *v a* (*Ir.* deachte) Indite, inspire, dictate, interpret; debate; teach. *Pret. a* dheachd, *indited*, *fut. aff. a* deachdaidh, *shall indite.*

Deachd, *s. f* (*Ir.* deacht.) A dictate, a word (hence *Lat* dict-um), also, *contracted* for Diadhachd, *Godhead, Divinity* *N pl* deachda *and* deachdan, *dictates*, *doctrine*

Deachdachadh, aidh, *s m* Inditing, dictating

Deachdadair, *s. m* A dictator *N pl.* deachdadairean

Deachdadaireach, *a.* Dictatorial.

Deachdadaireachd, *s f.* Dictatorship.

Deachdadh, aidh, *s. m.* A dictating; an inditing; an inspiring, a law

Deachdadh, (a), *pr. part* of deachd. Dictating, inditing, inspiring. Ag deachdadh ta mo chridhe, *my heart is inditing.—Sm.*

Deachdaich, *v. a.* (*from* deachd) Dictate; indite. *Pret. a.* dheachdaich, *dictated*, *fut. aff. a.* deachdaichidh, *shall dictate.*

Deachdaichte, *p part.* of deachdaich. Dictated.

Deachdainnear, ir, *s. m.* (*from* † deachd, *a word.*) A dictionary.

Deachdainneareachd, *s. f* Lexicography

Deachdair, *s. m.* (*Ir.* deachtoir. *Lat.* † dictor *and* doctor.) A dictator; a teacher; a doctor, one who dictates. *N. pl.* deachdairean

Deachdaireachd, *s. f.* Dictatorship; teaching

Deachdlach, *a.* Hard, difficult

Deachmhoradh, idh, *s m.* Courtesy, affability

† **Deachradh**, idh, *s. m.* (*Ir. id*) Indignation, anger.—*Shaw*

Deacra, *com* and *sup.* of deacair; which see

† **Dead**, *a.* (*Ir. id*) Meet, proper, decent, becoming—(*Shaw*), *also*, hereditary. Bu dead dhuit a bhi fial, *generosity is hereditary to thee.—Old Song.*

Dead, déid, *s m* A tooth See **Dead**.

Deadach, *a.* Toothed. See **Deudach**.

Deadh, *a.* Good. See **Deagh**.

Deadhachd, *s f.* See **Diadhachd**.

Deadhail, *s. f* (*Ir.* deadhoil.) The separation of night and day, the dawn of day; twilight; a releasing; a weariness. Deadhail na maidne, *morning dawn*

Deadhair, *a.* Swift.—*Shaw*

Deadhan, ain, *s. m.* A dean —*Shaw.*

Deadhanachd, *s. f* Deanery.

Deadh-bheachd, *s.* A civility.

Deadh-ith, *s. f.* A toothach.

Deadla, *a* (*Ir. id*) Bold, confident —*Shaw.*

Deadlas, ais, *s. m* (*Ir id*) Confidence, boldness, assurance —*Shaw.*

Deagailt, *s. f.* (*Ir id.*) A separation, a divorce.

D'eagal, *adv.* For fear; in case; lest D'eagal gu, *for fear that*, d'eagal nach, *for fear that not.*

Deaganach, aich, *s m.* A deacon.—*Shaw.*

Deagh, *a* Good, excellent, worthy *Asp form*, dheagh. Da dheagh mheann, *two good kids —Stew. Gen.* Deagh dhuine, *a good man*, deagh la, *a good day*, deagh-ghean, *favour, good will*, deagh-thoil, *good will*, deagh-bheus, *good conduct*

Deagh-ainm, *s m* A good name; *also*, the name Euphemia.

Deaghair, *a* (*Ir. id.*) Swift, nimble.

Deagh-bheus, *s* (*Ir* deagh-bheas) Good conduct; good morals; virtue; virtuous habits, morality. Mac Ardain nan deagh-bheus, *son of virtuous Ardan.— Oss. Cathluno* *N pl* deagh-bheusan

Deagh-bheusach, *a* Moral, virtuous, well-bred.

Deagh-bhlas, *s. m* A sweet or pleasant taste; a relish.

Deagh-bhlasda, *a.* Tasteful, dainty, well relished.

Deagh-bholadh, aidh, *s m* A pleasant or sweet smell; fragrance. Aileadh deagh-bholaidh, *an odour of sweet smell —Stew Phil.*

Deagh-bholtan, ain, *s m.* A sweet smell, fragrancy, odour.

Deagh-bholtanas, ais, *s m.* A sweet smell or odour, fragrancy

Deagh-bholtrach, *a* Aromatic, perfumed, fragrant.

Deagh-bholtraich, *v a.* Perfume, cense, aromatize. *Pret. a* dheagh-bholtraich, *perfumed.*

Deagh-bhuil, *s. f.* Good use; *also*, well disposed. Cuir gu deagh-bhuil, *set to a good use*

Deagh-bhuileachadh, aidh, *s. m.* (*Ir. id.*) Frugality; setting to a good use.

Deagh-bhuileachas, ais, *s. m.* Economy, proper management; good usage.

Deagh-chruth, *s.* A handsome form or shape.

Deagh-chruthach, *a.* Handsome, shapely, well-formed

Deagh-fhoclach, *a.* (*Ir. id.*) Well-spoken, fair-spoken

Deagh-fhuin, *s. f.* Good-will —*Shaw.*

Deagh-ghean, *s. m.* Good-will; favour; benevolence; grace. Deagh-ghean dligheach, *due benevolence.—Stew. Cor.* Deagh-ghean a' d' shùilibh, *favour in thine eyes.—Stew. Jud.*

Deagh-ghnuis, *s. f.* Pleasant countenance; a good face. —*Sm.*

Deagh-ghradh, -ghraidh, *s. m.* Sincere or true attachment, ardent love

Deagh-ghradhaich, *v. a.* Love sincerely.

Deagh-ghuth, *s. m.* A good word, a good voice; euphony.

Deagh-iomchar, air, *s. m.* Good conduct, good behaviour or bearing

Deagh-labhrach, *a.* Well-spoken, eloquent; also, *substantively*, an orator

Deagh-labhairt, *s. f.* Elocution, good utterance, eloquence.

Deagh-laoch, oich, *s. m.* A good soldier.

Deagh-mhaise, *s. f.* Handsomeness, excellence, comeliness.

Deagh-mhaiseach, *a.* Handsome, comely, excellent, of a fair exterior, decent, becoming. Deanar na h-uile nì gu deagh-mhaiseach, *let every thing be done decently.—Stew. Cor.*

Deagh-mhaiseachadh, aidh, *s. m.* An adorning, a decorating; an ornament.

Deagh-mhaisich, *v. a.* Adorn, decorate. *Pret. a* dheagh-mhaisich, *adorned*, *fut. aff. a.* deagh-mhaisichidh, *shall adorn*

Deagh-mhisneach, ich, *s. f.* Good courage; confidence.

Deagh-mhisneachail, *a.* Confident, bold.

Deagh-mhuinte, *a.* Well-bred.

Deagh-obair, -oibre, *s.* A good work; a good deed.

Deagh-oideas, eis, *s. m.* Good education.

Deagh-oideasach, *a.* (*Ir. id.*) Well-educated; discreet —*Shaw.*

Deagh-orduich, *v. a.* Methodise, arrange *Pret. a* dheagh-orduich, *arranged*, *fut. aff. a* deagh-orduichidh, *shall arrange; p part.* deagh-orduichte, *arranged.*

Deagh-orduichte, *p. part.* of deagh-orduich Methodised, arranged, well-arranged; *also*, prudent, provident —*Shaw.*

Deagh-theis, *s. f* A good report; a good testimony.

Deagh-theisdeas, eis, *s. m.* A good testimony, a favourable evidence.

Deagh-thoil, -thoile, *s. f* (*Ir. id*) Benevolence; good-will, good pleasure; a gratuity. Dh' fhalbh e le deagh-thoil, *he went away with good-will*

Deagh-thoileach, *a* Willing, voluntary, gratuitous; benevolent, favourable, friendly. Gu deagh-thoileach, *willingly.*

Deagh-thoill, *v. a* Deserve well; richly deserve. *Pret. a* dheagh-thoill. Dheagh-thoill e peanas, *he richly deserved punishment.*

Deagh-thriall, *s. m.* A good gait; portliness.

Deagh-uair, *s. f.* A good season; a good opportunity.

Deaguil, *s. f.* (*Ir. id.*) Twilight.

Deaith, *s.* Wind.

Deaitheach, *a.* Windy.

Deala, ai, *s. m.* (*Ir. id.*) A leech; friendship, kindred; refusal or denial—(*Shaw*), a nipple; a cow's udder —*Macd.* Dealan, *leeches*, dealan nan each, *horse-leeches*

Dealach'. See **Dealachadh**.

Dealachadh, aidh, *s. m* A separating; a separation, a divorce; a farewell; a difference. Beannachd dealachaidh, *a parting blessing.—Sm.* Am a dealachaidh, *the time of her separation.—Stew. Lev* Cuir dealachadh eatorra, *separate them*, balladh dealachaidh, *a partition-wall.—Stew 1 K* Cuir dealach' eatorra, *part them, separate them*, dealachadh dà rathad, *a place where two roads diverge.*

Dealachadh, (a), *pr part* of dealaich Separating, parting, divorcing. 'G an dealachadh, *separating them.*

Dealachail, *a.* Separable; causing separation.

Dealachd, *s f.* A separation, a divorce.

Dealag, aig, *s m.* A pin; a skewer; a thorn or prickle *N pl* dealagan.

Dealagach, *a.* Like a pin or skewer; of, or belonging to, a pin or skewer; thorny, prickly. *Com.* and *sup.* dealgaiche.

Dealagain, *gen sing* and *n. pl.* of dealagan

Dealagan, ain, *s. m.* (*dim* of dealag) A little pin; a skewer; a spindle; a thorn, a prickle; a needle; *also, n pl.* of dealagan.

Dealaich, *v. a.* (*Ir.* dealuigh) Separate, part, divorce, make a difference. *Pret. a* dhealaich, *parted*, *fut aff a* dealaichidh, *shall separate.* Cha dhealaich sinn ni 's mò, *we shall part no more.—Sm* Dealaich ri, *part with*, dealaich ris, *part with him* or *it*, *bid him farewell.*

Dealaichear, *fut. pass* of dealaich. Shall be separated

Dealaichte, *p. part.* of dealaich. Separated, parted, divorced.

Dealaidh, *a.* Keen, zealous, affectionate.

Dealaidheachd, *s. f.* Keenness; zealousness; affectionateness.

Dealan, ain, *s. m.* A coal; a flaming coal. Dealan doruis, *a latch*, dealan dé, *a butterfly*

Dealan, ain, *s. m* (*i e* Dia-lan, *God's flash*) (*Gr* δαλον.) Lightning. Dealan bàis, *the lightning of death —Oss. Com.*

Dealanach, *a.* (*from* dealan) Like lightning; flashing.

Dealanach, aich, *s m* Lightning. Mar cheumaibh dealanaich, *like the speed of lightning —Sm.*

Dealanaich, *gen. sing* of dealanach.

Dealanaich, *v n.* (*from* dealan.) Lighten, flash, as lightning. *Pret. a.* dhealanaich, *lightened*, *fut. aff.* dealanaichidh, *shall lighten*

Dealan-dé, *s m* A butterfly Perhaps, *dealbh an dé*

Dealan-doruis, *s m.* A latch.—*Shaw.*

Dealas, ais, *s m.* Zeal, quickness, hurry, speed, eagerness.

Dealasach, *a* (*from* dealas.) Zealous, quick, speedy, eager, keen. Gu dealasach, *zealously.* *Com.* and *sup.* dealasaiche.

Dealasachd, *s f.* Zealousness, quickness, speediness, eagerness, keenness

Dealasaiche, *com* and *sup.* of dealasach. More or most eager.

Deala-thoill, *s m* A lamprey, the *lampetra* of naturalists.

Dealbh, deilbh, *s. m.* (*Corn.* and *W.* delw. *Ir* dealbh.) A picture, an image, a statue, a figure, a form, shape, or person, a frame; a face; a spectre, a spectre-looking person. Na 'r dealbh féin; *in our own image.—Stew. Gen.* Maiseach na dealbh, *comely in her person*, gun dealbh, *shapeless, without form.—Id.*

Dealbh, *v. a.* Frame, form, make, contrive, devise, invent; feign; delineate. *Pret. a.* dhealbh, *framed; fut. aff. a.* dealbhaidh, *shall* or *will frame.* Tra dhealbh e neóil, *when he formed the clouds.—Sm.* A dealbh' aingidheachd, *devising wickedness.—Stew. Mic.*

† **Dealbh**, *a.* (*Ir. id.*) Poor, miserable; spectral.—*Shaw.*

Dealbhach, *a.* (*from* dealbh.) Handsome, shapely; like a picture; specious; inventive; sagacious; resembling. An gasan dealbhach, *the handsome stripling.—Old Song.*

Dealbhachadh, aidh, *s. m.* A forming, a framing, a shaping, a picturing.

Dealbhachadh, (a), *pr. part.* of dealbhaich. Forming, framing.

Dealbhadair, *s. m.* A painter; a framer; a statuary; a contriver. *N. pl.* dealbhadairean.

Dealbhadaireachd, *s. f.* The employment of a painter, of a framer, or of a statuary; painting, frame-work; statuary.

Dealbhadan, ain, *s. m.* A mould.

Dealbhadh, aidh, *s. m.* A framing, a forming; a contriving, a devising; a feigning; imagining; imagination. Uile dhealbhadh nan smuain, *all the imaginations of the thoughts.—Stew.* 1 *Chr.*

Dealbhadh, (a), *pr. part.* of dealbh. Framing.

Dealbhaich, *v. a.* (*from* dealbh.) Form, frame, shape; picture. *Pret. a.* dhealbhaich, *framed; fut. aff. a.* dealbhaichidh, *shall frame.*

Dealbhaiche, *com.* and *sup.* of dealbhach.

Dealbhail, *a.* (dealbh-amhuil. *W.* delwawl.) Shapely; spectral; ghost-like; like an image.

Dealbhair, *s. m.* (*from* dealbh.) A painter; a statuary. *N. pl.* dealbhairean.

Dealbhaireachd, *s. f.* Painting; statuary; delineation.

Dealbhan, ain, *s. m.* (*dim.* of dealbh.) A little picture; a little image.

Dealbhan, *n. pl.* of dealbh. Pictures. See **Dealbh**.

Dealbhan-dé, *s. m.* (*perhaps*, dealbh an dé.) A butterfly. *N. pl.* dealbhain-dé, *butterflies.*

Dealbhas, ais, *s. m.* (*Ir. id.*) Poverty, misery. Cha 'n 'eil ac' ach an dealbhas, *they have nothing but misery.*

Dealbhasach, *a.* In poverty, miserable; causing poverty.

Dealbh-chluich, *s. f.* A play on the stage.

Dealg, deilg, *s. f.* (*Ir. id.*) A pin; a prickle, a thorn; a skewer; a wire; a needle; a bodkin. *N. pl.* deilg *and* dealgan. Deilg nan guaillibh chearr, *pins in their left shoulders.—Old Song.*

Dealgach, *a.* (*Ir. id.*) Prickly, thorny, stinging; like a pin, prickle, or thorn. *Asp. form*, dhealgach. Dreas dhealgach, *a thorny brier.—Stew. Exod.*

Dealgan, ain, *s. m.* (*dim.* of dealg.) A little pin; a spindle; a skewer. Air an dealgan, *on the spindle.—Stew. Pro.*

Dealgan, *n. pl.* of dealg. Pins; prickles; skewers. See **Dealg**.

Dealganach, *a.* Like a pin, spindle, or skewer; full of pins.

Dealg-chluais, *s. f.* An ear-picker.

Dealg-fhiacall, aill, *s. f.* A tooth-pick.

Dealg-fuilt, *s. f.* A hair-pin.

† **Dealgnaiche**, *a.* (*Ir.* dealgnaidhe.) Unjust, unlawful; also, *substantively*, an outlaw; a rebel.

Dealman dé, *s.* More properly *dealbhan dé;* which see.

Dealrach, *a.* (*i. e.* dealradhach.) Bright, beaming, shining, gleaming, clear, resplendent. Cia dealrach glòir a mhathshluaigh ud! *how bright the glory of those saints!—Sm.* Bu dealan na lanna dealrach, *the gleaming swords were lightning.—Oss.* Solus dealrach, *resplendent light.—Sm.*

Dealrachadh, aidh, *s. m.* A shining, a gleaming; resplendence.

Dealrachadh, (a), *pr. part.* of dealraich. Shining, gleaming.

Dealradh, aidh, *s. m.* (*Ir. id.*) Brightness, radiance, effulgence, shining, light. Dealradh glan do ghnùis, *the clear light of thy countenance.—Sm.*

Dealraich, *v. a.* and *n.* (*Ir.* dealraigh.) Shine, brighten; gleam; beam; radiate; glitter. *Pret. a.* dhealraich, *shone; fut. aff. a.* dealraichidh, *shall shine.* Cha dealraich a mhadainn, *the morning shall not shine.—Oss. Derm.* Dhealraich dùil ri sìth gach cridhe, *the hope of peace brightened every heart.—Mac Lach.*

Dealraichead, eid, *s. m.* Increase in brightness. A dol an dealraichead, *growing more and more bright.*

Dealraichidh, *fut. aff.* of dealraich.

Dealruich, *v. n.* See **Dealraich**.

Dealt, dealta, *s. m.* (*Arm.* delt, *moist. Corn. id.*) A dew; a drizzling rain. *Asp. form*, dhealt. Mar dhealt a thig a nuas, *like descending dew.—Sm.* Dealt na madninn, *the morning dew;* dealt-uisge, *a sprinkling of rain, a drizzling rain.*

Dealtach, *a.* (*from* dealt.) Dewy; drizzling; rainy.

Dealuich, *v. a.* See **Dealaich**.

Dealuichte, *p. part.* of dealuich. (*Ir.* dealuighte.) See **Dealaichte**.

† **Deamal**, ail, *s. m.* (*Ir. id.*) A demon.

† **Deamh**, *s.* (*Ir. id.*) Want, deficiency.

Deamh, *a.* Wicked.

Deamhais, *gen. sing.* of deamhas.

Deamhan, ain, *s. m., from* † deamh. (*Gr.* δαιμων. *Lat.* dæmon. *Ir.* deamon *and* deamhon.) A devil, an evil spirit. *N. pl.* deamhain. A tha deamhan aige, *he hath a devil.—Stew. Matt. D. pl.* deamhnaibh, *to devils; asp. form*, dheamhnaibh. Do dheamhnaibh is dhealbhaidh bréige, *to devils and false images.—Sm.* An deamhan ceum, *devil a step.*

Deamhanaidh, *a.* (*from* deamhan.) Devilish, diabolical.

† **Deamharun**, -ruin, *s. m.* (*Ir. id.*) A mystery. *N. pl.* deamhrùintean.

Deamhas, ais, *s. m.* Scissors, sheers; a shepherd's sheers. *N. pl.* deamhaisean.

† **Dean**, *s. m.* (*Ir. id.*) Colour.

Dean, *v. a. irr.* Do, make, perform, act, work. *Pret. a.* rinn, *did; fut. aff. a.* ni, *shall do.* Dean dicheall, *endeavour.—Sm.* Dean suas, *make up.* Dean suas cairdeas, *make up friendship.—Stew. Pro.* Dean comhnuidh, *dwell, take up thine abode.—Macfar.* Dean foighidinn, *have patience;* dean truas, *show pity;* deantar truas rium, *let pity be shown to me.—Mac Lach.* Dean éigin, *compel;* dean suidhe, *sit down;* dean luidhe, *lie down;* dean cabhag, *make haste;* dean ceannairc, *rebel;* dean urnuigh, *pray;* dean dàil, *delay;* dean d' anail, *rest yourself, draw your breath;* dean breug, *tell a lie;* dean do chrochadh, *hang thyself;* dean coghnadh, *assist;* dean coghnadh leinn, *assist us;* dean air do shocair, *at leisure;* dean air d' athais, *at leisure.*

Deanachdach, *a.* Vehement; keen; furious; grievous; bitter. *Com.* and *sup.* deanachdaiche, *more* or *most vehement.* Gu deanachdach, *keenly.*

Deanachdas, ais, *s. m.* (*Ir. id.*) Vehemence; keenness; furiousness; bitterness.

Deanadach, *a.* (*from* dean.) Industrious, laborious, active, busy. Oganach deanadach, *an industrious youth.—Stew.* 1 *K. Com.* and *sup.* deanadaiche, *more* or *most industrious.*

Deanadas, ais, *s. m.* (*from* dean.) Conduct, behaviour, doings; industry. Do dhroch dheanadas, *thy bad doings.—Stew. Jer.* Aingidheachd ur deanadais, *the evil of your doings.—Id.*

Deanamaid, 1 *pl. pr. imper.* of dean. Let us do. See **Dean**.

Deanamh, (a), *pr. part.* of dean. Doing, acting, performing. A bi-dheanamh uile, *always doing what is bad;* bi 'deanamh, *be doing.*

Deanamaich, *s. f.* Doing; behaviour.

Deanannas, ais, *s. m.* Doings.

Deanas, ais, *s. m.* (*Ir. id.*) A space, a while, interval.—(*Shaw*); work. Deanas a meoir, *the work of her fingers.*—*Turn.*

Dean-chlodhach, *a.* (*Ir. id.*) Of changeable colours.—*Shaw.*

Dean-choire, *s. f.* A caldron.—*Shaw.*

Deangan, ain, *s. m.* An ant. See **Seangan**.

Deanmhas, ais, *s. m.* (*Ir. id.*) An effect, a consequence.—*Shaw.*

Deanmhasach, *a.* (*Ir. id.*) Prim, spruce; coy.

Deanmasachd, *s. f.* Primness; coyness.

Deann, *s. m.* (*Ir. id.*) Impetuosity, speed, haste, rapid motion, impetus; noise; colour; figure; a little quantity of any comminuted matter; a pinch, as of snuff. A leum thar sàile na deann, *bounding speedily over the deep.*—*Oss. Gaul. Asp. form*, dheann. A ruith na dheann, *running impetuously.*—*Oss. Cathula.* Mar dheann a bheir dà ord, *like the noise of two hammers.*—*Old Poem.*

Deannach, aich, *s. m.* Dust.—*Macd.* Sguab deannaich, *a whisk.*—*Id.*

Deannag, aig, *s. f.* A little quantity of any comminuted matter; a pinch, as of snuff. *N. pl.* deannagan. Na dheannagan, *in small quantities.*

Deannagach, *a.* In small quantities; in pinches, as snuff, or any pulverised substance.

Deannal, ail, *s. m.* (*Ir. id.*) A conflict; onset; haste; hurly; a flash; a shot. Anns gach ruaig agus deannal, *in every pursuit and conflict.*—*Mac Co.* Thug sinn deannal cruaidh, *we made a furious onset.*—*Fingalian Poem.*

Deannalach, *a. from* deann. (*Ir. id.*) Impetuous, vehement, hasty. Gu deannalach, *impetuously.*

Deannalachd, *s.* Impetuousness, vehemence, hastiness.

Deanntag, aig, *s. f.* A nettle.—*Shaw.* More frequently written *ionntag;* which see. *N. pl.* deanntagan.

Deanntagach, aich, *s. f.* A place where nettles grow; a tuft of nettles.

Deanntagach, *a.* Abounding in nettles; like a nettle; of nettles.

Deanta, **Deante**, *p. part.* Finished, done, performed; trained, habituated. Deanta ri cogadh, *trained to war.*—*Stew. K.* Duine deante, *a grown-up man.*

Deantach, *a.* (*from* dean.) Practical; possible.—*Shaw.*

Deantag. See **Eantag.**

Deantanas, ais, *s. m.* (*Ir. id.*) Doings, conduct.—*Shaw.*

Deantas, ais, *s. m.* Conduct; doings; work; rhyming; poetry.

Deantasach, *a.* Active, industrious, busy. Contracted for *deanadas.*

Deaobachan, ain, *s. m.* Pain occasioned by cold in one's finger ends.

Dear, *s. f.* (*Ir. id.*) A refusal, a denial; a daughter.—*Shaw.*

Dear, *a.* Great, large, prodigious.

The River Darien, or the Gulf of Uraba, as Wytfleet and Borland call it in their maps, signifies, according to Malcolm, a great river; from *dear, great*, and *inn* or *an*, river or water. Uraba itself is synonymous with Darien, *ur*, a Teutonic word meaning great, and *ab* or *aba* [see **Ab**], river. The Derwent, in Cumberland, is but a contraction of *dear-amhainn*, a great river, being the greatest in the north of England.

Dear, *s. m.* A drop. See **Deur.**

Dearail, *a.* (*Ir.* dearoil.) Poor, miserable, wretched.

Dearbadan, ain, *s. m.* A butterfly.—*Macd.* *N. pl.* dearbadain.

Dearbh, *s. m.* A proof, a demonstration; experiment, test, trial; a churn, a milk-pail. *N. pl.* dearbhan. Cuir gu dearbh, *put to the test.*

Dearbh, *a.* Sure, certain; true, genuine; fixed; peculiar, particular. Is dearbh nach tusa ar n-aobhar bròin, *certain it is that thou art not the cause of our grief.*—*Mac Lach.* Gu dearbh, *for certain, of a truth, really, indeed;* gu dearbh fhéin, *really, truly.*

Dearbh, *v. a.* Prove; try; certify; experience; demonstrate; ascertain; affirm; confirm; attest; tempt; put to the test. *Pret. a.* dhearbh, *proved; fut. aff. a.* dearbhaidh, *shall prove.* Mo dhillseachd dhearbh mi, *I have proved my faith.*—*Sm.* Na dearbhmaid Criosd, *let us not tempt Christ.*—*Stew. Cor.*

Dearbhach, *a.* Demonstrative; capable of proof; sure of.

Dearbhachadh, aidh, *s. m.* A proving, a confirming, an attesting; protesting, swearing; an allegation.

Dearbhachadh, (a), *pr. part.* of dearbhaich. Proving, confirming, attesting.

Dearbhachd, *s. f.* Experience; proof; experiment; assurance.

Dearbhadair, *s. m.* An affirmer.

Dearbhadh, aidh, *s. m.* A proof, a demonstration, a confirmation; an experiment, a test, a trial; certainty; a proving, a demonstrating, a confirming. Cuir gu dearbhadh, *put to the test.* Cha 'n 'eil dearbhadh gun fheuchainn, *there is no certainty without trial.*—*G. P.*

Dearbhadh, (a), *pr. part.* of dearbh. Proving, demonstrating, confirming.

Dearbhag, aig, *s. f.* A touchstone.—*Macd.* *N. pl.* dearbhaghan.

Dearbhaich, *v. a.* (*Ir. id.*) Confirm, protest, attest, swear. *Pret. a.* dhearbhaich, *confirmed; fut. aff. a.* dearbhaichidh, *shall confirm.*

Dearbhann, ainn, *s. m.* (*Ir. id.*) An axiom; a truism.

Dearbh-art, -airt, *s. m.* (*Ir. id.*) A touchstone.

Dearbh-bheachd, *s. f.* Assurance, certainty, full assurance, confidence; a confident hope; a full view. Lan dearbhbheachd, *full assurance.*

Dearbh-bhrathair, *s. m.* A full brother. *N. pl.* dearbhbhrathairean, *full brothers.* Dearbh-brathair athar, *a full uncle by the father's side;* dearbh-bhrathair màthar, *a full uncle by the mother's side.*

Dearbh-bhrathair athar, *s. m.* A full uncle by the father's side.

Dearbh-bhrathaireachd, *s. f.* Brotherhood; society.

Dearbh-bhrathair màthar, *s. m.* A full uncle by the mother's side.

Dearbh-bhriathar, *s. m.* An axiom, a truism, a dogma, a true saying. *N. pl.* dearbh-bhriathran.

Dearbh-bhriathrach, *a.* Dogmatical; axiomatic.

Dearbh-chlach, -chloich, *s. f.* A touchstone. *N. pl.* dearbh-chlachan, *touchstones.*

Dearbh-chliamhuinn, *s. m.* A son-in-law. *N. pl.* dearbh-chliamhuinnean.

Dearbh-fhios, *s. m.* An assurance; certain knowledge; correct knowledge; certain news.

Dearbh-fhiosrach, *a.* Fully certain, well assured, convinced. Air an do rinneadh thu dearbh-fhiosrach, *of which thou hast been well assured.*—*Stew. Tim.*

Dearbhta, **Dearbhte**, *p. part.* of dearbh. (*Ir.* dearbtha.) Proved, tried, confirmed, demonstrated, ascertained, affirmed, attested; approved; tempted.

Dearbhtach, *a.* Capable of proof or of demonstration. *Com.* and *sup.* dearbhtaiche.

Dearbh-theachdair, *s. m.* A true messenger. Dearbh-theachdair a bhàis, *the true messenger of death.—Oss. Fing.*

Dearc, *s. f.* (*Ir. id.*) A berry; a lizard; an eye; a cave; grave; grotto.—*Shaw. N. pl.* dearcan; *asp. form*, dhearc. A solar dhearca da h-àl, *in quest of berries for its young.—Oss. Gaul.* Dearc-fhrangach, *a currant;* dearc-roide, *a bilberry;* dearc-aitinn, *a juniper-berry:* dearc-luachrach, *a lizard.*

Dearc, *v. n.* (*Gr.* δερκω.) Behold, look, observe, watch, examine, inspect. *Pret. a.* dhearc; *fut. aff. a.* dearcaidh, *shall* or *will look.* Dhearc me le sòlas, *I looked with delight.—Sm.* Dhearc an dream bha dlù do 'n bhàs, *the dying beheld.—Id.*

Dearc-abhall, aill, *s. m.* (*Ir. id.*) An oak-apple.

Dearcach, *a.* Abounding in berries; bearing berries; like a berry; relating to a berry.—*Macint.* and *Macfar. Also*, watchful, observant.

Dearcadh, aidh, *s. m.* A looking, an inspecting, an examining; a look, inspection, examination.

Dearcadh, (a), *pr. part.* of dearc. Looking, beholding, examining, inspecting. Sealgair a dearcadh o bhothan, *a huntsman looking from his cot.—Oss. Cathula.*

Dearcag, aig, *s. f.* (*dim.* of dearc.) A little berry. Perhaps *deargag. N. pl.* dearcagan. Dearcag-fhiadhaich, *a heath-berry;* dearcag fhrangach, *a currant;* dearcag fhraoich, *a crow-berry* or *blue-berry;* dearcag aitinn, *a juniper-berry.*

Dearcam, 1 *sing. imper.* of dearc. Let me look.

Dearcam, (*for* dearcaidh mi.) I shall or will look. Dearcam air do ghnùis, *I will look on thy face.—Sm.*

Dearcan, *n. pl.* of dearc. Berries. Dearcan-aitil, *juniper-berries;* dearcan-aitinn, *juniper-berries;* dearcan-eidhinn, *juniper-berries;* dearcan-fithich, *heath-berries;* dearcan-fraoich, *heath-berries;* dearcan-luachrach, *lizards.*

Dearcan-allt, Dearcan-alltaidh, *s. m.* The bird called a kestril.—*Shaw.*

Dearc-bhallach, aich, *s.* A speckled serpent.—*Shaw.*

Dearc-luachrach, *s. f.* A lizard; a scaly lizard; the *lacerta agilis* of Linnæus.

Dearcnach, *a.* (*Ir. id.*) Goodly; handsome, likely. *Com.* and *sup.* dearcnaiche.

Dear-dhun, uin, *s. m.* (*Ir. id.*) A penitentiary, oratory.

Dearg, *a.* Red, crimson, ruddy, flaming, red-hot. (*Ir. id.*) A ghealach dearg san ear, *the moon ruddy in the east.—Oss. Carricth.* A dhearg-shùil, *his flaming eye;* teth dearg, *red-hot.* Iarunn dearg, *red-hot iron.—Stew. Tim.* Feoil dhearg, *raw flesh;* talamh dearg, *turned* or *ploughed land; red soil.*

Dearg is often prefixed to a noun, when we wish to express an extraordinary degree of guilt. Tha 'n dearg-chiontach saor, *the glaringly guilty is free.—Mac Lach.*

Dearg, deirg, *s. m.* A deer, red deer, mountain-deer; a roe. Aonach nan dearg, *the hill of deer.—Oss. Fing.* Sruth an deirg, *the stream of deer.—Id.*

Dearg, *v. a.* and *n.* Make red, redden, crimson; blush; kindle, burn; *rarely*, prepare; plough. *Pret. a.* dhearg; *fut. aff. a.* deargaidh, *shall redden.* Dhearg a fuil an tonn, *her blood reddened the wave.—Oss. Fin. and Lor.*

Deargadh, aidh, *s. m.* (*Ir. id.*) A reddening, a blushing; a kindling, a ploughing.

Deargadh, (a), *pr. part.* of dearg.

Deargain, *gen. sing.* and *n. pl.* of deargan.

Deargainn, *gen. sing.* of deargann.

Deargan, ain, *s. m.* (*Ir. id.*) The fish called a bream; *also*, crimson, purple, rouge.

Deargananach, aich, *s. m.* A name given, by the followers of the enterprising Prince Charles Edward Lewis Cassimir Steuart, to any soldier of the house of Hanover; a red-coated soldier; a whig soldier. An aimsir a dhearbhar na deargânaich, *the time which has declared the whig soldiers—Old Song.*

Deargan-aitinn, *s. m.* A Lewis bird, which has a great affection for its mate. When the cock or hen dies, the surviving bird is heard to make a plaintive noise for two or three weeks thereafter.

Deargan-allt, -uillt, *s. m.* The bird called a redstart; a kestril.—*Shaw.*

Deargan-alltaidh, *s. m.* A redstart; a kestril.

Deargan-fraòich, *s. m.* A bullfinch.—*Macd.* A goldfinch.—*Shaw.*

Deargann, ainn, *s. m.* (*Ir.* deargan.) A flea. *N. pl.* deargannan. An deigh deargainn, *after a flea.—Stew.* 1 *Sam.*

Deargannach, *a.* Full of fleas.

Deargant, aint, *s. f.* A flea.—*Shaw. N. pl.* deargantan.

Dearg-chneadh, -chneidh, *s. m.* and *f.* A bloody wound; a severe wound.

Dearg-chneadhach, *a.* Causing bloody wounds; full of deep wounds.—*Old Song.*

Dearg-chriadh, *s. f.* Ruddle; *literally*, red clay; ochre.

Dearg-lasadh, *a.* Red-hot, flaming.

Dearg-leigh, *s. m.* A surgeon.—*Macd.*

Deargnaidh, *a.* (*Ir. id.*) Unlearned.

Dearg-shùil, *s. f.* A red eye, a bloodshot eye, a flaming eye. A dhearg-shùil, fo dheòir, *his red eyes in tears.—Oss. Comala.*

Dearg-shuileach, *a.* Having red eyes; having bloodshot eyes.

Dearlaic, *s. f.* (*Ir. id.*) A gift.

Dearmad, aid, *s. m.* (*Ir. id.*) Neglect, slight, disregard; forgetfulness, inattention. Cuir air dearmad, *neglect, forget.* Ge dàil do fhear an uilc cha dearmad, *delay to the wicked is not a pardon.—G. P.*

Dearmadach, *a.* (*Ir. id.*) Forgetful, unmindful, neglectful, inattentive. Dearmadach air Dia, *forgetful of God.—Stew. Deut. Com.* and *sup.* dearmadaiche, *more* or *most forgetful.*

Dearmadachd, *s. f.* (*Ir. id.*) Forgetfulness, negligence, inattentiveness.

Dearmaid, *v. a.* Forget, neglect, overlook, slight, disregard. *Pret. a.* dhearmaid, *forgot; fut. aff. a.* dearmaididh, *shall forget.* Na dearmaid na deòraidh, *forget not the afflicted.—Sm.*

Dearmail, *s. f.* (*Ir. id.*) Anxiety, solicitude.—*Macd.* and *Shaw.*

Dearmalach, *a.* Anxious, solicitous.—*Mac Co. Com.* and *sup.* dearmalaiche.

† **Dearmhail**, *a.* (*Ir. id.*) Huge, very great.—*Shaw.*

† **Dearmhair**, *a.* (*Ir. id.*) Huge, very great; excessive, violent, vehement.

† **Dearmharadh**, aidh, *s. m.* (*Ir. id.*) A wonder.

Dearn, *v. a.* Do, act, accomplish. *Pret. a.* dhearn; *fut. aff. a.* dearnaidh.

Dearn, dearna, *s. m.* The palm of the hand; the fill of the palm of the hand. *N. pl.* dearnan; *d. pl.* dearnaibh. Air dearnaibh mo dha laimh, *on the palms of my hands.—Sm.* and *Stew. Is.*

Dearnad, aid, *s. f.* (*Ir. id.*) A flea.

Dearnadair, *s. m.* (*from* dearn.) A palmister. *N. pl.* dearnadairean.

Dearnadaireachd, *s. f.* Palmistry, chiromancy, or the pretended art of telling one's fortune, by examining the lines on the palms of the hands.

Dearnadh, aidh, *s. m.* See **Dearna.**

Dearral, *a.* Beggarly, poor, wretched.

Dearralachd, *s.* Want; wretchedness; defeat.

Dearnag, aig, *s. f.* A cake; a wafer; a little hand. *N. pl.* dearnagan. Dearnagan neo-ghoirtichte, *unleavened cakes.—Stew. Lev.*

† **Dearrach**, aich, *s. m.* The apartment in a monastery consecrated for prayers.—*Shaw.*

Dearras, (an), *adv.* After; since; seeing that. An dearras duit sin a dheanamh, *since you have done that.*

Dearrasain, *gen. sing.* and *n. pl.* of dearrasan.

Dearrasan, ain, *s. m.* A buzzing, a rustling noise; a snarling; hurry; a balm cricket. *N. pl.* dearrasain.

Dearr-làn, *a.* Completely full, brimful. Copan dearr-làn, *a brimful cup, a bumper.—Old Song.*

Deàrs, *v. n.* Shine, beam, radiate, gleam. *Pret. a.* dhears, *shone; fut. aff. a.* dearsaidh, *shall shine.*

Deàrsa, ai, *s. m.* See Deàrsadh.

Deàrsach, *a.* Shining, beaming, gleaming, effulgent, resplendent, glittering. *Com.* and *sup.* dearsaiche, *more* or *most shining.*

Deàrsachd, *s. f.* A shining, a gleaming; *also*, vigilance.

Deàrsadh, aidh, *s. m.* A sunbeam or ray; a gleaming, a beaming, a glittering; splendour, effulgence. Deàrsadh na madainn, *the morning ray.—Oss.* Deàrsadh grèine, *a sunbeam.*

Deàrsaich, *v. n.* Shine; beam, gleam, glitter; *also*, watch, observe, be vigilant. *Pret. a.* dheàrsaich, *shone; fut. aff. a.* deàrsaichidh, *shall* or *will shine.*

Deàrsaidheachd, *s. f.* Brightness; vigilance, watchfulness.

Dearsg, *v. a.* Polish, burnish; file; command; surpass. *Pret. a.* dhearsg, *polished; fut. aff. a.* dearsgaidh, *shall polish.*

Dearsgach, *a.* Polished; burnished; filed

Dearsgnach, *a.* Polite; polished; excellent; complete; accomplished; *substantively*, a polished or accomplished man.

Dearsgnachd, *s. f.* Politeness; excellence; accomplishment.

Dearsgnaiche, *s.* A polisher; a polished person; an accomplished person.

Dearsgnaidh, *a.* Polished, burnished; polite; bright; of good parts; accomplished; *substantively*, science.

Dearsgta, *p. part.* of dearsg. (*Ir.* dearsguithe.) Polished, burnished; filed.—*Shaw.*

Dear-theach, *s. m.* An apartment in a monastery appropriated for prayers and acts of penitence.

Deas, *a.* South, southern; *rarely*, order, rule, method. (*W.* dês, *rule.*) In some parts *deas* means a *pew.* An taobh deas, *the south. Asp. form*, dheas. An tìr fa dheas, *south country.* A ghaoth dheas, *the south wind.—Sm.*

Deas, *a.* (*Ir.* deas. *Gr.* δεξια. *Lat.* dextera, *right hand.*) Right; ready, prepared; in order; trim; active; dexterous; clever; pretty; elegant; portly; proper. *Asp. form*, dheas. A dheas-lamh an scleò, *his right hand in mist.—Oss. Lod.* Bheil thu deas? *are you ready?* Fhreagair e mi gu deas, *he answered me readily.—Sm.* Ioma maighdean deas òg, *many a portly active young maid.—Macfar.* Scriobhuiche deas, *a ready* or *expert writer.—Stew. Ez.*

Deas, *v. n.* (*Ir. id.*) Remain, abide, stay.—*Shaw. Pret.* dheas; *fut. aff.* deasaidh.

Deasachadh, aidh, *s. m.* (*Ir. id.*) A preparing, a dressing, an adorning; a preparation. *Asp. form*, dheasachadh an fhuineadair, *of the baker's dressing; of baked meats.—Stew. Gen.* Rinn e deasachadh, *he made preparation.—Stew.* 2 *K.* Dean do dheasachadh fèin, *get yourself in readiness.*

Deasachadh, (a), *pr. part.* of deasaich; which see.

Deasachd, *s. f.* (*Ir. id.*) Qualification, quality.

Deasad, aid, *s. m.* (*Ir. id.*) Appositeness; prettines.

Deasadan, ain, *s. m.* (*Ir. id.*) A repository; a commonplace book; a book of reference.

Deasaich, *v. a.*, *from* deas. (*Ir. id.*) Prepare; make ready; adjust; adorn; dress; mend; correct; bake. *Pret. a.* dheasaich, *prepared; fut. aff. a.* deasaichidh, *shall* or *will prepare.* Dheasaich Cathull a chuilm, *Cathul prepared a feast.—Oss. Cathula. Fut. pass.* deasaichear, *shall be prepared.*

Deasaichte, *p. part.* of deasaich. Prepared; made ready; adjusted; amended; corrected. *Asp. form*, dheasaichte.

Deasail, *s. f.* Turning with the sun. See Deisiùil.

Deasalan, ain, *s. m.* A buffet.—*Shaw.*

Deasboireachd, *s. f.* Disputation, pleading, reasoning, argumentation, wrangling. Deasboireachd mo bhilean, *the pleading of my lips;* mòr dheasboireachd, *much reasoning.—Stew. Acts, ref.*

Deasboirich, *v. n.* Dispute, plead, argue, wrangle. *Pret. a.* dheasboirich.

Deasboiriche, *s. m.* A disputant; a wrangler; a pleader.

Deascadh, aidh, *s. m.* Lees, dregs, yeast. Deascadh fìona, *lees of wine.* More frequently *deasgainn.*

Deas-cheumach, *a.* Having a stately gait; having an easy gait.

Deas-fhocal, ail, *s. m.* A ready word; a quick or smart reply.

Deas-fhoclach, *a.* Ready-worded; ready-witted; loquacious.

Deasgadh, aidh, *s. m.* Lees, dregs, yeast.—*Stew. Ps. ref.* Deasgadh an t-sluagh, *the rabble, the mob.*

Deasgainn, *s. f.* Dregs, lees. Written also *deasguinn;* which see.

† **Deasgair**, *v. a.* Pluck off the ears.—*Shaw.*

Deasghabhail, *s. f.* Ascension-day.

Deas-ghnath, *s.* (*Ir.* deasgnath.) A ceremony, usage, custom. Lagh nan deas-ghnath, *the ceremonial law.*

Deas-ghnathach, *a.* Ceremonial; ceremonious; customary.

Deas-ghnath-torraidh, *s. m.* Obsequies; funeral rites or ceremonies.

Deasguinn, *s. f.* (*Ir.* deasguin.) Dregs, lees, refuse; yeast. *Asp. form*, dheasguinn. A dheasguinn fàisgidh daoine daoi, *wicked men shall wring its dregs.—Sm.* Air an deasguinnibh, *on their lees.—Stew. Zeph.*

Deasguinneach, *a.* (*Ir. id.*) Full of dregs or lees, yeasty.

Deas-iùil, *s.* See Deis-iùil.

Deas-labhairt, *s. f.* (*Ir. id.*) Eloquence; flow of speech.

Deas-labhrach, *a.* Eloquent; having words at command.

Deas-labhradh, aidh, *s. m.* Elocution; eloquence; address.

Deas-lamh, -laimh, *s. f.* (*Ir. id.*) A right hand. *Asp. form*, dheas-lamh. A dheas-lamh an cleò, *his right hand in a cloud.—Oss. Lodin.*

Deas-lamhach, *a.* (*Ir. id.*) Dexterous; ambidexterous; neat-handed; right-handed; of, or pertaining to, a right hand. *Com.* and *sup.* deas-lamhaiche.

Deas-lamhachd, *s. f.* Dexterity; ambidexterity.

Deasoireach, *a.* (*Ir. id.*) Spicy.—*Shaw.*

Deasoireachd, *s. f.* Spiciness.

Deaspoireachd, *s. f.* Disputation, wrangling, argumentation. Written also *deasboireachd;* which see.

Deaspoirich, *v. n.* Dispute, argue, wrangle. See Deasboirich.

Deasuchadh, aidh, *s. m.* See Deasachadh.

Deasuich, *v. a.* See Deasaich.

Deatach, aich, *s. m.* and *f.* (*Ir. id.*) Smoke, vapour, mist, exhalation, fume. *Asp. form*, dheatach. Mar dheatach air ioma-ghaoith, *like smoke in a whirlwind.—Oss.* Written more frequently *deathach;* which see.

Deatachail, *a.* (deatach-amhuil.) *Ir.* deatamhail. Smoky; misty, full of vapour or exhalations Written more frequently *deathachail.*

Deatach-thalmhainn, *s m.* The herb fumitory.—*Shaw.*

Deataich, *gen. sing.* of deatach

Deathach, aich, *s. m.* and *f.* Smoke, vapour, mist, steam, exhalation. Leth-dheante do dheathach 's do cheò, *half formed of smoke and mist*—*Oss Lod.* Cuir deathach, *smoke, emit smoke*, a cur an deathaich, *emitting smoke.* Fhuair e car troimh dheathaich, *he got a toss in the smoke.* —*G P.*

Deathachail, *a.* (i. e. deatachail.) Smoky; full of smoke; like smoke.

Deathach-thalmhainn, *s m.* The herb fumitory.

Decreut, *s. m.* A decree.

Deé, *n pl* of dia Gods *N pl* déibh; *d pl* dhéibh Ainm an deé, *the name of their gods*—*Stew. G. B.* See Dia.

Déibh, *d. pl* of dia. To gods. Gu déibh eile, *to other gods*—*Stew O. T.*

Deibheach, *a* (*Ir. id*) Hasty, hurried, flurried; contentious, passionate

Deibheachd, *s f.* (*Ir. id*) Hastiness; hurriedness, contentiousness; passionateness.

Deibheadh, eidh, *s m* (*Ir id*) Haste, speed, a battle, a skirmish

Deibhidhe, *s f* A sort of verse or *dàn direach*, which requires that the first quartan shall end with a minor termination, and the second with a major termination, with several other rules to be observed

Deibhleach, *a* Diminutive

Deich, *a* Ten Deich fir, *ten men*, deich clachan, *twelve stones*
Gr δέκα. *Lat.* decem *Pers* deh *Chald* deka *Arm* decq. *Corn* deq *Ir.* deich

Deich-bhrigh, *s* (*Ir. id*) The decalogue

Deicheach, *a.* Tenfold, decuple.

Deicheamh, eimh, *s m* (*Corn.* and *Arm* deaug.) A tenth part, a tithe Deicheamh do'n chreich, *a tenth of the spoil*—*Stew Heb*

Deicheamh, *a* Tenth. An deicheamh fear, *the tenth man.*

Deicheamhaich, *v a.* Tithe or decimate *Contr.* deichmhich.

Deichmhich, *v. a* Tithe, decimate; divide into ten parts *Pret a.* dheichmhich

Deich-mhios, *s. m.* December.

Deichnear, *a.* Ten persons; ten men, ten women; a decade *Asp form*, dheichnear. Air sgàth dheichnear, *for the sake of ten persons.*—*Stew Gen.* Ni deichnear greim, *ten men shall take hold*

Deich-shliosnach, *a.* Having ten sides

Deich-shliosnag, eig, *s m* A decagon *N pl* deich-shliosneagan

Deicir, *a.* See Deacair.

Déid (*for* téid) *Q B*—*Gen ref*

Déide, *s f* (*Ir. id*) The toothach; *rarely*, submission, obedience

Déideag, eig, *s f* A bauble or gewgaw *N. pl* déigeagan Déideagan measg feòir, *gewgaws among the grass*—*Macdon.*

Deidh, *s f* (*Ir. id*) Desire, longing, fondness, love, *rarely*, a protector, a defender. Tha e an deigh oirre, *he is fond of her.*

Deidh-bhodach, aich, *s. m* An old lecher, a dotard *N. pl.* deigh-bhodaich

Deidh, (an), *adv* After. See Deigh, (an)

Deidhe, *s. f.* A pair.

Deidheanach, *a.* Fond, loving; pretty. *Com.* and *sup.* deidheanaiche

Deidheil, *a.* (deidh-amhuil.) Fond, amorous; desirous; addicted to. Ro dheidheil oirbh, *very fond of you; affectionately desirous of you*—*Stew. Thess.* Deidheil air an òl, *fond of tippling.*

Deifir, *s f.* (*Ir. id. W* dyvrys.) Speed, haste, hurry, despatch. Thuirt mi 'm dheifir, *I said in my haste.*—*Sm.* Dean deifir, *be quick, make haste.*

Deifireach, *a* (*Ir. id*) Hasty, speedy, expeditious; causing hurry or despatch; requiring despatch. Fhreagair mi gu deifireach, *I answered speedily*—*Sm.* *Com.* and *sup* deifiriche, *more* or *most hasty*

Deifireadh, idh, *s. m* A difference; haste

Deifirich, *v. a* and *n* Hasten, hurry, speed, bestir; make haste. (*Ir.* deifirich.) *Pret. a* dheifirich, *hastened; fut. aff. a.* deifirichidh, *shall* or *will hasten.* More commonly written *deifrich.*

Deifreach, *a* (*contr.* for deifireach) Hasty, expeditious, speedy; causing hurry or despatch.

Deifreachadh, aidh, *s. m.* A hastening, a hurrying, a bestirring; haste, expedition.

Deifreachadh, (a), *pr. part.* of deifrich. A deifreachadh gu mòr, *hastening greatly.*—*Stew Zeph*

Deifreadh, idh, *s m* A difference

Deifrich, *v a.* and *n* (*Ir id*) Hasten, hurry, speed; make haste. *Pret. a* dheifrich, *hastened, fut. aff a* deifrichidh, *shall* or *will hasten.* Deifrich ort, *make haste.*—*Sm.* Deifrichidh mi m' fhocal, *I will hasten my word.*—*Stew. Is.*

Deigh, *s. f.* Ice.—*Macdon.* More commonly written *eidhe* or *eithe.*

Déigh, *s* (*Ir. id*) Desire, longing, fondness; love; a fire, a flame. Written also *deidh*

Deigh, (an), *adv.* and *prep.* After; behind. 'Mo dheigh, *after me*, 'd dheigh, *after thee* Chuir mise nan deigh mo ghlaoth, *I called after them*, literally, *I sent my call after them.*—*Ull.* 'Na deigh, *after her*

Deigheanach, *a* (*Ir.* deighionach.) Late, last, hindermost; dilatory

Deigheil, *a* (deigh-amhuil) Fond; amorous; desirous; addicted to See also Deidheil.

Deigh-laimh, (an), *adv.* Afterhand, afterwards, behind, remaining, in arrears.

Deighlean, ein, *s. m.* (*Ir. id.*) A quire of paper.—*Shaw.*

Deil, *v. a* (*Ir id*) Turn with a lath *Pret. a.* dheil; *fut aff. a* deilidh, *shall* or *will turn.*

Deil, deile, *s. f* (*Ir.* deil) An axletree, a twig; a rod; a turner's lath; a plank, a deal; a cow's udder. Fo' dheile san ùir, *under a deal in the dust*—*Old Song.* *N. pl.* deileachan.

† Deilbh, *a* (*Ir. id.*) Fine, fair, sprightly; brave, sightly. *Formed from* dealbh; *gen.* deilbh.

Deilbh, *gen. sing.* of dealbh

Deilbh, *s. f.* A weaving, a warping, the figure or face of a person or thing Muileann deilbh, *a warping-mill.*

Deilbh, *v a* Weave; warp; form, build; construct. *Pret a.* dheilbh, *wove*, *fut aff. a* deilbhidh, *shall weave.* Dheilbh i a h-eachdraidh, *she wove her history*—*Mac Lach.* Curach a dheilbh m'athair, *a boat constructed by my father.* —*Oss Gaul* Deilbh ceò-eide Chrimine, *weave the misty shroud of Crimina*—*Ull*

Deilbheag, eig, *s f.* (*Ir id.*) A picture, a miniature, a statue.

Deilbhealach, aich, *s. m.* (*Ir. id.*) The meeting of two roads.—*Shaw.*

Deilbhean, ein, *s m.* A little image; a small picture.

Deilbhte, *p part.* of deilbh. Woven; warped, formed; built, constructed.

Deilchead, -a. Ill, sad, bad.—*Shaw*.

Deil-cheannach, *a.* (*Ir. id.*) Two-topped.

Deile, *gen. sing* of deil.

Deileachan, *n. pl.* of deil. Deals, planks. Deileachan tiugha, *thick planks*.—*Stew. Ezek.*

Deileadair, *s. m.* (*Ir. id.*) A turner. *N. pl.* deileadairean.

Deileadaireachd, *s* The business of a turner.

Deileag, eig, *s. f.* A little deal, a board, a rod; lath.

Deilean, ein, *s. m.* (*dim.* of deil) A turner's lath.

† **Deileang**, eing, *s. m.* (*Ir. id.*) A pig; a young sow; a two-year-old sow.

Deileas, eis, *s. m.* (*Ir. id*) Grudging through avarice.

Deile-oidhche, *s. f.* (*Ir. id.*) The space of two nights

Deile-thorc, -thuirc, *s m* A hog of two years.

Deile-eudannach, *a.* Double-faced —*Shaw*.

† **Deilf**, *s.* (*Ir. id*) A dolphin.

Deilg, *gen. sing.* of dealg; which see.

† **Deilgionnadh**, aidh, *s m* (*Ir. id*) Waste; havoc.—*Shaw*.

Deilgne, *n. pl.* (*Ir. id.*) Thorns, prickle.

Deilgneach, *a.* (*Ir. id.*) Thorny, prickly; *also*, spear's-thistle.

Deilgréine, *s. f.* The name of one of Fingal's standards.

Deilich, *v.* Forego, part with. *Pret. a.* dheilich; *fut aff. a.* deilichidh. This verb takes after it the preposition *ri* or *ris*, either simple or compounded. Deilich ri d' airgiod, *part with thy money*; deilich riu, *part with them.*

† **Deill**, *v. n.* (*Ir. id.*) Lean upon.—*Shaw*

Deillseag, eig, *s. f* A box on the ear or cheek; a slap on the breech. *N. pl* deillseagan.

† **Deilm**, *s. f.* A noise, a rumbling, a trembling.—*Shaw*.

Deil-tharruing, *s. f* A trigger or iron nail

Deilt, *s. f.* (*Ir. id*) Separation.

† **Deiltre**, *s. pl.* (*Ir. id*) Druidical idols.

Deiltreadh, idh, *s m.* A gilding.

† **Deim**, *s. f.* (*Ir. id*) Lack, want; failing, deficiency *Lat.* dem-o, *take away*.

† **Deimhe**, *s. f.* (*Ir. id.*) Darkness; protection.—*Shaw*

Deimheas, eis, *s. m.* and *f.* (*Ir. id*) A pair of shears *N. pl.* deimheasan.

Deimhin, *a.* (*Ir. id.*) Certain, true, sure. Gu deimhin, *certainly, verily*, deimhin-sgeul, *a true story, a true account.*

Deimhin, (gu), *adv.* Certainly, truly, surely; of a truth.

Deimhne, *s. f.* (*Ir. id.*) Assurance, certainty; truth

Deimhneach, *a.* (*Ir. id.*) Affirmative

Deimhnich, *v a.* (*Ir.* deimhnigh) Affirm, ascertain, prove, certify, verify, demonstrate; assure. *Pret. a.* dheimhnich, *affirmed*, *fut. aff a.* deimhnichidh, *shall affirm.*

† **Dein**, *a.* (*Ir. id.*) Neat, clean.

Déine, *com.* and *sup.* of dian. More or most vehement or hot. Mu choinneamh a chath is déine, *opposite to the hottest battle* —*Stew. Sam*

Déine, *s. f.* Vehemence, ardour, violence, impetuosity; neatness, cleanness

Déineachd, *s. f.* Keenness, violence, vehemence.

Déineachdach, *a.*, *from* déine. (*Ir. id*) Keen, fierce, vehement, urgent, violent, rude. *Com.* and *sup.* deineachdaiche.

Déineas, eis, *s m.* (*Ir. id.*) Fierceness, impetuousness, violence.

Déineasach, *a.* (*Ir. id*) Fierce, impetuous, violent; keen, ardent; quick, nimble. *Com.* and *sup.* déineasaiche, *more* or *most fierce.*

Déineasachd, *s* Fierceness, impetuousness; keenness; ardour.

Deinmheach, *a* Vain; void; frivolous *Com.* and *sup* deinmhiche.

Deinmheachair, *s. m.* A toyman, a pedlar, a trifler; a vain fellow

Deinmheas, *s m.* (*Ir. id.*) Vanity; frivolousness

Déinmheasair, *s. m.* (*Ir id*) A vain frivolous fellow.

Deinmhich, *v n* (*Ir id*) Vanish. *Pret a* dheinmhich, *vanished*, *fut. aff.* deinmhichidh.

Deinmhin, *s m* (*Ir. id.*) A vain fellow, a trifler —*Shaw*

Deir, *v. irr. fut.* Shall or will say. Deir mi, *I shall say* Deiream ribh, *I say unto you*, deirim, *I say*.—*Stew. N. T.* This word is borrowed from the Irish The Gaelic verb is *their*, which see

Deir, *s. f.* (*Ir id*) The shingles; St Anthony's fire

† **Deirbh**, *s f* (*Ir. id.*) A churn

Déirc, deirce, *s f.* (*Ir. id.*) Alms Thoir deirc, *give alms*, ag iarruidh deirce, *asking alms*, naomh-dhéirc, *alms collected at church*

Déirceach, *a.* Charitable, ready to give alms; seeking alms; like alms —*Macint* *Also*, penurious, poor.

Déirceach, ich, *s m.* (*from* déirc) A beggar; an object of charity. *N pl.* déirciche; *gen. pl* déirceach. Bu tu fuasgladh nan déirceach, *thou wert the beggar's aid.*—*Mac Co*

Déirceag, eig, *s f.* A narrow, penurious female; *also*, a female mendicant.

† **Deire**, *s f* (*Ir. id*) The deep; an abyss, a pool.—*Shaw*.

Deire, **Deireadh**, eidh, *s. m.* (*Ir id.*) An end, conclusion; rear, stern, extremity. Deireadh na bliadhna, *the year's end*, ceann deiridh, *a hinder part*, *a stern*, *posteriors*, air deireadh, *behind, last;* air dheireadh, *behind, last* Air toiseach sa choille 's air deireadh san fhéith, *foremost in the wood and last in the fen* —*G. P.* Toiseach teachd is deireadh falbh, *first to come and last to go*;—the motto of Gaul the son of Morni. Deireadh luinge, *a stern*, deireadh feachd, *the rear of an army*

Deireadh-feachd, *s. m* The rear of an army

Deireadh-luinge, *s m* A stern.

Deiream, (deir mi) I say, I speak; I shall say, I shall speak. Deiream ribh, *I say unto you.*—*Stew. N. T.*

Deireanach, *a* (*from* deireadh) Slow, tardy; dilatory.

Deireannach, *a.* (*from* deireadh) Last, hindermost, latter; behind; dilatory. Anns na laithaibh deireannach, *in the latter days* —*Stew Deut.* An neach deireannach, *the last being.*—*Sm.* Tha thu deireannach, *you are last, you are dilatory. Com.* and *sup.* deireannaiche.

Deireannan, ain, *s. m.* (*Ir. id.*) A dessert.—*Shaw*.

Deireas, eis, *s. m.* (*probably* deir-fhàs) Injury, harm, loss, calamity Cha 'n 'eil deireas ann, *there is no harm done;* tha mi gun deireas, *I am quite well.*

Deireasach, *a* Injurious, hurtful, calamitous *Com.* and *sup.* deireasaiche, *more* or *most injurious.*

Deireasachd, *s. f* Injuriousness, hurtfulness, calamitousness.

Deir-fhiachan, *s. pl* Arrears.

Deirg, *gen.* of dearg; which see

Deirge, *s f* Redness, red, vermilion; ruddiness. Deirge shùl, *redness of eyes.*—*Stew Pro.* Deirge is gile na gnùis, *red and white in her visage* —*R*

Deirge, *com.* and *sup* of dearg More or most red Fion is deirge dreach, *wine of the reddest hue*

Deirgead, eid, *s. m.* Redness; increase in redness. A dol an deirgead, *growing more or most red.*

Deiroid, *a.* (*from* dearg.) This is a species of double comparative, and, like all other words of a similar kind, is thus construed. Is deirgid e so, *it is the redder for this;* cha deirgid e sin, *it is not the redder for that.*

† **Deirginnleadh**, idh, *s. m.* (*Ir. id.*) Red cattle.—*Shaw.*

Deiridh, *s. f.* (*Ir. id.*) A mystery; a secret.—*Shaw.*

Deirideach, *a.* Secret, hidden, private.

Deiridh, *gen. sing.* of deireadh; which see.

Deirim, (*for* deir mi.) I say, I will say.

This word is borrowed from the Irish; the proper Gaelic verb being *their.*

Deirionnach, *a.* More frequently written *deireannach;* which see.

† **Deirlidh**, *s. f.* (*Ir. id.*) A gift, a reward.—*Shaw.*

Deirmid, *s. f.* (*Ir. id.*) Dishonour.

Deirrideach, *a.* Secret, hidden, private.—*Shaw.*

Deirse, *s. f.* (*Ir. id.*) A goal, a gate. *N. pl.* deirsean.

† **Deirte**, *p. part.* Was said.

Deir-thunnan, ain, *s. m.* A dessert, a collation.

Deis, *gen. sing.* of deas.

Déis, *gen. sing.* of dias.

Deis, (an), *adv.* After. An deis do shaothair, *after your pains.*

Deisboireachd, *s. f.* See **Deaspoireachd**.

Deisceart, *s. m.* The southern point, the south quarter.

Deisciobul, uil, *s. m.* A disciple. *N. pl.* deisciobuil.

Lat. discipulus. *Ir.* deisciobal, *a scholar. Arm.* descabl, *docile. Corn.* deisgibl, *scholar.*

Deiscir, *a.* (*Gr. poet.* δεξιτερός.) Active, nimble; quick, fierce, sudden.

† **Deiscréide**, *s. f.* (*Ir. id. Lat.* discretio.) Discretion.

Shaw observes that this word is not Gaelic.

Deiscréideach, *a.* Discreet, prudent; grave, sober.

Deisdinn, *s. f.* (*Ir.* deisdean.) See **Deistinn**.

Deisdinneach, *a.* See **Deistinneach**.

Deise, *com.* and *sup.* of deas. (*Ir. id.*) More or most neat, ready, or handsome. See **Deas**.

Deise, *s. f.* A couple or pair; two persons.

Deise, *s. f.* A suit of clothes; full dress; *also,* a right hand, right side. *Asp. form,* dheise. (*Ir. id.*) *N. pl.* deiseachan. Tha i na deise, *she is in full dress;* deiseachan scarlaid, *suits of scarlet.—Mac Co.* Deise mharcachd, *a riding-habit;* deise-mharcachd gun an t-each, *a riding-habit without a horse.—Macfar.* Bidh Sàtan aig a dheis, *let Satan be at his right hand.—Sm.*

Deise, *s. f.* Handsomeness of person, elegance, beauty.

Deise, *gen. sing. fem.* of deas. Right. Dh' ionnsuidh na laimh deise, *to the right hand.—Stew.* 1 *K. Asp. form,* dheise.

Deiseach, *a.* (*from* deas.) Southern, southerly, towards the south.

Deiseachadh, aidh, *s. m.* A dressing, a going in full dress; decoration, ornament.

Deiseachan, *n. pl.* of deise. Clothes, suits of clothes; full dresses. See **Deise**.

Deiseachd, *s. f.* (*from* deas.) Neatness, handsomeness; ornament; dress; convenience. Deiseachd munaidh, *the ornament of learning.—Old Song.*

Deisead, eid, *s. m.* Neatness; cleanness; elegance of person. Cha 'n fhac mi a leithid air dheisead, *I never saw his match for elegance.*

Deisealan, ain, *s. m.* A blow, a slap.—*Macd.*

Deisearach, *a.* (*Ir. id.*) Sunny; having a southern aspect.—*Macint.* Taobh deisearach, *a country side which has a southern exposure;*—as that part of Breadalbane, in the county of Perth, which lies on the north side of Loch Tay. *Deisearach* is perhaps *deis-thireach.*

Deiseil. A colloquial corruption of *deis-iùil;* which see.

Deiseir, *s. f.* (*perhaps* deis-thir.) A country side having a southern exposure; the north side of a vale; a name given to the northern side of the vale of Breadalbane which lies on the north of Loch Tay. Fonn gun deiseir gréine, *a land without a southern exposure.—Old Song.*

Deisgeadh, eidh, *s. m.* A chink; a crack or fissure.—*Macd.*

Deisgeanan, *s. pl.* Lees, dregs.—*Stew. Is.*

† **Deisibh**, *s. pl.* Lands.—*Shaw.*

Deisich, *v. a.* (*from* deise.) Dress, adorn; go in full dress. *Pret. a.* dheisich, *dressed; fut. aff. a.* deisichidh, *shall dress.*

Déisinn. See **Deistinn**.

Déisinneach, *a.* See **Deistinneach**.

Deis-iùil, *s. f.* A prosperous course; a turning from east to west in the direction of the sun. Deis-iùil air gach nì, *the right course in every thing.—Old Saying.*

This is a Druidical term, and is descriptive of the ceremony observed by the Druids, of walking round their temples, by the south, in the course of their divinations; keeping the temple always on the right. This course was deemed prosperous; the contrary (*tual,* i. e. *tuath-iùil,*) fatal, or at least unpropitious. From this ancient superstition are derived several customs which are still retained amongst us; such as drinking over the left thumb, as Toland expresses it, or according to the course of the sun.

"Some of the poorer sort of people in the Western Isles," Martin says, "retain the custom of performing these circles sunways about the persons of their benefactors three times, when they bless them, and wish good success to all their enterprises. Some are very careful, when they set out to sea, that the boat be first rowed about sunways; and if this be neglected, they are afraid their voyage may prove unfortunate. I had this ceremony paid me," continues the tourist, "when in the isle of Isla, by a poor woman, after I had given her an alms. I desired her to let alone that compliment, for that I did not care for it; but she insisted to make these three ordinary turns, and then prayed that God, and Mac Charmaig, the patron saint of that island, might bless and prosper me in all my affairs."

When a Highlander goes to drink out of a consecrated fountain, he approaches it by going round the place from east to west; and at funerals, the procession observes the same direction in drawing near to the grave. Hence also is derived the old custom of describing, sunways, a circle with a burning brand about houses, cattle, corn, and corn-fields, to prevent their being burnt, or in any way injured by evil spirits, or by witchcraft. This fiery circle was also made around women as soon as possible after parturition, and also around newly-born babes. These circles were in later times described by midwives, and were deemed effectual against the intrusion of the *daoine-sìth* or *sìthichean* (fairies), who were particularly on the alert in times of childbed, and not unfrequently carried infants away (according to vulgar legends), and restored them afterwards, but sadly altered in features and in personal appearance.

Infants stolen by fairies, Martin remarks, are said to have voracious appetites, constantly craving food. In this case it was usual for those who believed that their children were taken away, to dig a grave in the fields on quarter day, and there to lay the fairy skeleton till next morning, at which time the parents went to the place, where they doubted not to find their own child instead of the skeleton.

Deisleann, ein, *s. m.* (*Ir. id.*) A beam or ray of light proceeding from any luminous body.

† **Deismich**, *v. a.* (*Ir. id.*) Dress, adorn. *Pret.* dheismich; *fut. aff.* deismichidh.

† **Deismireach**, *a.* (*Ir. id.*) Curious.

† **Deismireachd**, *s. f.* Curiosity; superstition; a quibble; a quotation; a cunning way of talking.

Déistinn, *s. f.* (*Ir.* deistean.) Disgust, abomination; fright;

sorrow; sadness; squeamishness; numbness. Shil mo dheòir le déistinn, *my tears dropped with sorrow.—Oss. Duthona.* Tha déistinn air d' fhiaclaibh, *thy teeth are numbed, thy teeth are on edge.*

Deistinn, *v. a.* Hate, abhor, detest.

Deistinneach, *a.* Disgustful, abominable; frightful, terrible, ugly; sorrowful, sad, squeamish. Gu tuirseach déistinneach, *heavenly and sad.—Oss. Duthona.* *Com.* and *sup.* deistinniche.

Deistinneachd, *s. f.* Disgustfulness, abominableness; frightfulness, ugliness; sorrowfulness; squeamishness.

† **Deithide**, *s. f.* (*Ir. id.*) Separation; care, diligence.

Déithneas, eis, *s.* See **Déineas**.

Déithneasach, *a.* See **Déineasach**.

Deò, *s.* Breath; air; life, vision; a ray of light; the place where a stream falls into the sea. Gun deò, *lifeless, breathless;* gun deò mar chre, *breathless as the clay.—Oss. Conn.* Glacaibh mo dheò, *catch my [dying] breath.—Ull.* Gun deò leirsinn, *without a ray of vision; stone-blind.—Orr.* Deò gaoithe, *a breath of wind;* gu deò, *for ever.*

Deobhail, *v. a.* Suck, as the young of human beings or of quadrupeds. *Pret. a.* dheobhail, *sucked.* Written also *deoghail* and *deothail.*

Deobhalach, *a.* Sucking.

Deobhaladh, aidh, *s. m.* A sucking of the teat or pap.

Deobhaladh, (a), *pr. part.* of deobhail. Sucking.

Deoch, dibhe, *s. m.* (*Ir.* deoch. *Scotch,* deuch *and* teuch.) A drink, a potion, a draught. *Asp. form,* dheoch. Thoir dhomh deoch, *give me a drink.—Stew. Gen.* Airson dibhe làidire, *for strong drink.—Stew. Mic.* Deoch-eiridinn, *a potion;* deoch-slainnte, *a health* or *toast;* deoch an doruis, *a stirrup-cup.* *N. pl.* deochan *and* deochannan.

† **Deoch**, *v. a.* (*Ir. id.*) Embrace tenderly.—*Shaw. Pret. a.* dheoch, *embraced; fut. aff. a.* deochaidh, *shall embrace.*

Deochair, *s. f.* A difference, a distinction.

Deochal, ail, *s. m.* A grudging.—*Shaw.*

Deoch-an-doruis, *s. f.* A stirrup-cup, a parting dram, a *bon-aller; literally,* the door-drink. In the Manx dialect it is *deouch-a-dorus. Deoch-an-doruis* is also called *deoch Chloinn Donnachaidh,* the drink of the Robertsons, or the children of Duncan; so called from Donnach Crosd, a son of Mac Donald of the Isles.

Deoch-eiridin, *s. f.* A potion; a potation or draught.

Deoch-slainnte, *s. f.* A health or toast; *literally,* a health-drink. Ghabh e mo dheoch-slainnte, *he drank my health;* dh'òl e mo dheoch-slainnte, *he drank my health.*

Deoghail, *v. a.* Suck, as infants; imbibe. *Pret. a.* dheoghail, *sucked; fut. aff. a.* deoghailidh, *shall suck.* See also **Deothail**.

Deoghalach, *a.* Sucking, suckling; apt to suck or suckle.

Deoghaladh, aidh, *s. m.* A sucking, an imbibing; suction.

Deoghalag, aig, *s. f.* Honeysuckle. *N. pl.* deolagan.

Deoghalagach, *a.* Like honeysuckle, full of honeysuckle.

Deoghladair, *s. m.* A sucker. *N. pl.* deoghladairean.

Deo-gréine, *s. f.* A ray, a sunbeam; *also,* one of the names of Fingal's banner. Deo-gréine air aghaidh aosda, *a sunbeam on his ancient visage.—Ull.* Deo-gréine Mhic-Cumhail, *Fingal's banner.—Old Poem.*

Deòin, *s. f.* (*Ir. id.*) Assent, will, accord, purpose. Le m' dheòin, *with my will.* Nach seachnadh le d' dheòin an àrach, *that would not willingly shun the field.—Ull.* Dh' ain-deòin, *involuntarily;* a dheòin Dia, *God willing.*

† **Deòir**, *s. f.* Will, pleasure, inclination, purpose.

Deòir, *gen. sing.* and *n. pl.* of deur; which see.

† **Deòirseach**, ich, *s. m.* (*Ir. id.*) A slave; a porter or doorkeeper.—*Shaw.*

† **Deolaidh**, *s. f.* (*Ir. id.*) Aid, help, succour; a dowry or portion.—*Shaw.*

Deolchadh, aidh, *s. m.* A sotting, drinking copiously.

† **Deolchar**, air, *s. m.* A present.—*Shaw.*

Deònach, *a.* (*Ir. id.*) Willing; agreeable; ready to grant. Gu deònach, *willingly;* gu deònach cromaibh, *willingly incline.—Sm.* An deònach leat? *art thou willing?* *Com.* and *sup.* deònaiche.

Deònachadh, aidh, *s. m.* A granting; a grant; a bestowal.

Deònachadh, (a), *pr. part.* of deònaich. Granting; bestowing.

† **Deònachd**, *s. f.* (*Ir. id.*) Pudendum.—*Shaw.*

Deònaich, *v. a., from* deòin. (*Ir.* deònaigh.) Grant, bestow, impart; vouchsafe, allow, permit; approve, consent. *Pret. a.* dheònaich, *granted; fut. aff. a.* deònaichidh. Deònaich neart, *give strength;* gu 'n deònaicheadh Dia, *God grant.* Written also *deònuich.*

Deòntach, *a.* (*Ir. id.*) Willing, voluntary. Gu deòntach, *voluntarily.*

Deòntas, ais, *s. m.* (*Ir. id.*) Willingness.

Deòr, deòir, *s. m.* A tear. More frequently written *deur.*

Deòra, ai, *s. m.* See **Deòradh**.

Deòrachadh, aidh, *s. m.* A banishing; banishment, exile. Fhuair e 'dheòrachadh, *he got himself banished.*

Deòrachd, *s. f.* Banishment, exile. Contracted for *deoraidheachd.* Air deòrachd, *in banishment.*

Deòradh, aidh, *s. m.* (*Ir.* deòraidhe.) An exile; a fugitive; an outlaw; a stranger, an alien; an afflicted person. *N. pl.* deòraidh. Com' a dheòradh? *why, O stranger?—Ull.* Na deòraidh bhochd, *the poor afflicted ones.—Sm.* Deòradh, *an outlaw, a fugitive.—Shaw.*

Deòraich, *v. a.* Banish; expel. *Pret. a.* dheòraich, *banished; fut. aff. a.* deòraichidh, *shall* or *will expel.*

Deòraidh, *gen. sing.* and *n. pl.* of deòradh.

† **Deoraidh**, *s. f.* Disobedience; a surety who withdraws himself; a stranger; a guest; an exile; a vagabond.

† **Deoraidh**, *a.* (*Ir. id.*) Strong, stout, robust.—*Shaw.*

Deoraidheachd, *s. f.* (*Ir. id.*) Banishment, exile; the condition of an outlaw or of a vagabond.

Deorail, *a.* In tears; wretched.

Deoranta, *a.* (*Ir. id.*) Banished; expelled; cashiered; strange.—*Shaw.*

Deoth, *a.* Active, clever; manly.

Deòthadh, aidh, *s. m.* The herb henbane; *also,* a drying up, as of water; evaporation. Theid an amhainn an deòthadh, *the river shall be dried up.—Stew. Is.*

Deothail, *v. a.* Suck, as an infant or any young creature; imbibe. *Pret. a.* dheothail, *sucked; fut. aff. a.* deothailidh, *shall suck.* Mil a dheothal as a charraig, *to suck honey from the rock.—Stew. Deut.*

Deothas, ais, *s. m.* Desire; fervour; great affection.

Deothasach, *a.* Desirous; fervent; amorous; desirable; causing desire. *Asp. form,* dheothasach. Ro dheothasach umaibh, *affectionately desirous of you.—Stew. Thess.* *Com.* and *sup.* deothasaiche.

Deothasaiche, *s. m.* An amorous fellow; a lecher.

Deothasaiche, *com.* and *sup.* of deothasaiche.

Deothlagan, ain, *s. m.* Honeysuckle.

Deth, *comp. pron.* Of him, of it; from him, from it. *Asp. form,* dheth. Thig dheth, *come off him* or *it;* air mo shonsa dheth, *for my part of it;* air mo shon féin deth, *as for my own part;* tha e gu math dheth, *he is well off;* thoir dheth e, *take him off, deride him;* tha mo thoil agam dheth, *I have enough of him* or *of it;* tha e dheth, *he is gone; he is past recovery; he is past redemption.*

DETIACH, *s f.* The gullet, the wesand or windpipe.

DEUCHAINN, *s f* A trial, an attempt; endeavour; probation, proof Deuchainn nan neo-chiontach, *the trial of the innocent—Stew. Job* Thoir deuchainn, *give a trial, make trial, attempt*, dean deuchainn, *make trial.* Ni iad deuchainn air réith na comhraig, *they shall make trial on the plain of battle—Mac Lach* Fhuair e deuchainn ghoirt, *he got a severe trial. N. pl* deuchainnean.

DEUCHAINNICHE, *s m* One taken on trials, as a candidate for orders in the kirk; a probationer; a candidate; a competitor.

DEUD, déid, *s m.* and *f.* A tooth. *Asp. form*, dheud. Do dheud, *thy teeth.—Stew. Song Sol.* Do chnamha deud, *of ivory.—Stew. Ezek*

DEUDACH, *a* (*from* deudach.) Dental; dentated; of ivory; having teeth, large-toothed; of, or belonging to, a tooth, like a tooth.

DEUDACH, aich, *s f* Teeth; a set of teeth; a jaw. A chagnadh fo d' dheudaich, *to chew it under thy teeth.—Fingalian Poem* Mar comas duit teum, na rùisg do dheudach, *if you cannot bite, show not thy teeth.—G P.*

DEUDADH, aidh, *s. m* (*from* deud) A toothach.

DEUD-CHEARTACHADH, aidh, *s m.* A sorting of the teeth.

DEUD-CHEARTACHD, *s f.* The business of a dentist

DEUD-CHEARTAICH, *v a.* Sort the teeth, as a dentist

DEUD-CHEARTAICHE, *s m* A dentist *N. pl.* deud-cheartaichean

DEUD-CHNAIMH, *s* Ivory. Adharca deud-chnaimh, *horns of ivory—Stew. Ezek*

† DEUNACH, *a.* (*Ir. id*) Sad; heavy; melancholy—*Shaw.*

† DEUNACHAS, ais, *s. m.* (*Ir. id*) Sadness; heaviness; melancholy

DEUR, deòir, *s. m N pl* deòir, *d pl* deuraibh *and* deòiribh A tear; a drop of any liquid. *Asp form*, dheur. Ur deòir a sruthadh, *your tears falling—Ull* A sileadh dheur, *shedding tears—Id.* Fo dheoir, *in tears—Oss Com.* Is truagh leam iad bhi nan deòiribh, *I regret their being in tears—Old Song.*

Ir dear *and* deor *Eng* tear. *Gr* δακρυς, *a tear. Box Lex.* daigr. *Arm* deur, dour, *and* daour, *water. Gr.* διερος, *any thing watered*

DEURACH, *a.* (*from* deur) Tearful; weeping; mournful, sad, dropping Oigh mhìn gu deurach, *a soft maiden weeping.—Oss. Fing.* Gu deurach, *tearfully Com* and *sup* deuraiche.

DEURAN, ain, *s. m, dim* of deur. (*Corn* dewerryan) A little drop; a little quantity of any liquid.

DEUR-SHÙIL, *s. f.* A tearful eye Fhliuch a dheur-shùil an leac, *his tearful eye wet the stone—Ull*

DEUR-SHUILEACH, *a* Having tearful eyes Gu deur-shuileach, *tearfully.*

DHÀ, *a, asp. form* of dà. Two Dà allt o dhà ghleann, *two streams* [*pouring*] *from two valleys—Oss Lodin* Lion am buideal, lion a dhà dhiubh, *fill the bottle, fill them twain—Old Song* Làth no dhà, *a day or two*

DHA, *comp pron.* To him, to it' Thoir dha, *give to him*

DHA, *prep.* To Dha d' fhocal, *to thy mandate.—Oss Fing.* Dha' mac, *to her son—Id*

DHABH, *asp. form* of dabh. To them *Provincial for* dhoibh, which see.

DHACHAIDH, *s* and *adv* Home; homewards Fàd o 'dhachaidh, *far from his home—Ull* Phill e dhachaidh, *he returned homewards—Id. Dhachaidh* is perhaps *dhathigh.*

DH'ADHLACADH, (a), *infin* of adhlaic. To bury

DH'ADHLAIC, *pret. a.* of adhlaic. Buried See ADHLAIC

DH'AIDICH, *pret. aff* of aidich. Confessed. See AIDICH

DHAIGHNEACHADH, (a), *infin.* of daighnich. To bind; to fortify. See DAIGHNICH

DHAIGHNICH, *pret. aff.* of daighnich; which see.

DHÀIL, *asp. form* of dàil; which see

DHAIMH, *asp form* of daimh; which see

DH'AINDEOIN, *adv.* In spite; by force. A dh'aindeoin ort, *in spite of you;* gabhaidh mi a dh'aindeoin, *I will take by force*, a dheòin no dh'aindeoin, *nolens, volens.*

DH'AINMICH, *pret. aff.* of ainmich. Named; called; mentioned. See AINMICHTE.

DH'AIRMEIS, *pret. aff.* of airmeis. Found; found after a search See AIRMEIS.

DH'AISEAD, *pret* of aisead. Delivered, as a woman of a child.—*Stew. Sam.*

DHAITHTE, *asp. form* of daithte, *p. part.* of dath. Coloured; stained. See DATH.

DHALL, *pret.* of dall. Blinded; puzzled

DHALL, *a., asp form* of dall.

DH'AMAIS, *pret.* of amais Hit; found out, aimed Dh' amais mi air, *I found him out.* See AMAIS

DH'AMHAIRC, *pret* of amhairc. Looked, saw, observed. See AMHAIRC.

DHÀN, *asp form* of dàn; which see.

DHÀNADAS, ais, *s. m, asp. form* of dànadas. Boldness. Bheil a dhànadas agad? *have you the boldness?* See DÀNADAS

DHANNSADH, *pret. sub.* of danns. Would dance Dhannsadh e, *he would dance*

DHANNSADH, (a), *inf.* of danns; which see

DH'AODAICH, *pret. aff.* of aodaich. Clad, clothed See AODAICH

DHAOI, *asp form* of daoi, which see.

DHAOINE, *v. pl.* and *gen pl asp* of duine; which see

DHAOL, *asp. form* of daol; which see

DHAOR, *a, asp form* of daor, which see

DHAORSA, *asp. form* of daorsa; which see

DH'FHAOIDTE, *adv.* Perhaps Dh' fhaoidte gun d' thig e, *perhaps he shall come*, maith dh' fhaoidte, *perhaps.*

DH'AR, *pret.* of ar Ploughed. See AR.

DHARACH, *asp. form* of darach; which see.

DHARAG, aig, *asp. form* of darag; which see

DH'ARMAICH, *pret* of armaich Armed; clothed with armour. Dh' armaich se e féin, *he armed himself.*

DH'ASAID, *pret a.* of asaid. Delivered, as a female. Dh' asaideadh mise, *I was delivered.—Stew Sam*

DH'AT, *pret. aff.* of at. Swelled. See AT

DHATH, *pret. aff.* of dath Coloured See DATH

DH'ATH-BHEOTHAICH, *pret. aff.* of ath-bheothaich Revived. See ATH-BHEOTHAICH.

DH'ATH-BHUAIL, *pret aff* of ath-bhuail. Struck again. See ATH-BHUAIL.

DH'ATH-DHIOL, *pret. aff* of ath-dhiol Requited, recompensed, repaid See ATH-DHIOL.

DH'ATH-GHIN, *pret aff.* of ath-ghin Regenerated, reproduced, renewed. See ATH-GHIN.

DH'ATH-LEASACHADH, (a), *infin* of ath-leasaich. To reform. See ATH-LEASAICH.

DH'ATH-LEASAICH, *pret. aff.* of ath-leasaich. Reformed

DH'ATH-ROINN, *pret. aff* of ath-roinn Subdivided See ATH-ROINN.

DH'ATH-ÙRAICH, *pret. aff.* of ath-uraich Renewed, refreshed. See ATH-ÙRAICH.

DHÉ, *gen. sing, asp. form* of Dia. Tigh Dhé, *the house of God Also*, the *voc. sing.* A Dhé ghràsmhoir, *gracious God.*

DHE, *prep* (*for* do) From, of; from off; from amongst.

Dhe 'n linn o shean, *from the time of old.*—*Oss. Fing.* Dhe m' shinnseara, *from among my ancestors.*—*Id.* The superlative is often followed by *dhe;* as, am fear is airde dhe 'n triùir, *the tallest of* [*from amongst*] *the three.*

Dh'eadar-ghuidh, *pret. aff.* of eadar-ghuidh. Interceded. See Eadar-ghuidh.

Dh'eadar-mhìnich, *pret. aff.* of eadar-mhìnich. Interpreted, expounded. See Eadar-mhìnich.

Dheagh, *a.*, *asp. form* of deagh; which see.

Dhealachadh, (a), *infin.* of dealaich. To separate. See Dealaich.

Dhealaich, *pret. aff.* of dealaich. Separated, parted. See Dealaich.

Dh'ealaidh, *pret. aff.* of ealaidh. Crept; watched with jealousy. See Ealaidh.

Dhealain, *asp. form* of dealain; also, *voc. sing.* of dealan; which see.

Dhealbh, *pret. aff.* of dealbh. Formed. See Dealbh.

Dhealbh, *asp. form* of dealbh; which see.

Dhealraich, *pret. aff.* of dealraich. Shone, beamed. See Dealraich.

Dheanadas, ais, *asp. form* of deanadais. Doings. A dheanadas, *his doings.* See Deanadas.

Dheanadh, *imp. sub.* of dean. Would do. Dheanadh e, *he would do.* See Dean.

Dheanamh, (a), *infin.* of dean. To do. See Dean.

Dh'earail, *pret. aff.* of earail. Exhorted. Dh' earail mi air, *I exhorted him.*

Dh'earalachadh, (a), *infin.* of earalaich. To exhort. See Earalaich.

Dh'earb, *pret. aff.* of earb. Intrusted. Dh' earb mi ris, *I trusted to him.* See Earb.

Dhearbh, *pret. aff.* of dearbh. Proved; affirmed. See Dearbh.

Dhearbhadh, *imp. sub.* of dearbh. Would prove. Dhearbhadh e, *he would prove;* also, *pret. pass.* dhearbhadh e, *he was proved.*

Dhearbhadh, (a), *infin.* of dearbh. To prove; to certify; to demonstrate.

Dhearbhta, Dhearbhte, *asp. form* of dearbhte, *p. part.* of dearbh; which see.

Dhearc, *pret. aff.* of dearc. Beheld, saw. See Dearc.

Dhearg, *asp. form* of dearg; which see.

Dheas, *asp. form* of deas; which see.

Dheasaich, *pret. aff.* of deasaich. Prepared; made ready. See Deasaich.

Dheasaichte, *asp. form* of deasaichte.

Dh'easbhuidh, *prep.* For want of; without. Dh' easbhuidh eòlais, *for want of knowledge.*

Dhée, *asp. form* of Dée, *n. pl.* of Dia. Gods. See Dia.

Dheifrich, *pret. aff.* of deifrich. Hastened. Deifrich e, *he hastened.*

Dh'éigh, *pret. aff.* of éigh. Cried, shrieked. See Eigh.

Dheilbh, *pret. aff.* of deilbh; which see.

Dheilbhte, *asp. form* of deilbhte, *past part.* of deilbh.

Dheireadh, *asp. form* of deireadh. Mu dheireadh, *at last.* See Deireadh.

Dheise, *asp. form* of deise; which see.

Dheistinneach, *asp. form* of deistinneach; which see.

Dheo, (air), *adv.* Else; or else; otherwise. Teich air dheo buailidh mi thu, *be off, else I will strike.* It is also written *air neo.*

Dheò, *asp. form* of deò; which see.

Dheoch, *asp. form* of deoch. Drink. Mo dheoch, *my drink.* See Deoch.

Dheoghail, *pret. aff. a.* of deoghail. Sucked. See Deoghail.

Dheoghaladh, (a), *infin.* of deoghail. To suckle.

Dheòin, *asp. form* of deòin; which see.

Dheòir, *asp. form* of deòir.

Dheònaich, *pret. aff. a.* of deonaich. Granted, bestowed. See Deònaich.

Dheòradh, *asp. form* of deoradh; which see.

Dheth, *prep.*, *asp. form* of deth. Of him, of it; off; of; from amongst. Thig dheth, *come off him* or *it.* Is measa a tha thu dheth, *worse art thou off.*—*Death of Oscar.* Is olc a tha mi dheth, *I am ill off;* is maith tha e dheth, *he is well off.* Air mo shon-sa dheth, *as for me, for my part.*—*Stew. Gen.* Agus rud eile dheth, *and more than that; moreover.* Chuir e dheth, *he put off him; he scolded; he speechified.* Tha e dheth, *it is off him; he is gone, dead,* or *past redemption.*

Dheur, *asp. form* of deur; which see.

Dh'fhàg, *pret. a.* of fàg. Left, abandoned, deserted. See Fàg.

Dh'fhàgail, (a), *infin.* of fàg. To leave, to abandon. See Fàg.

Dh'fhaicinn, (a), *infin.* of faic. To see.

Dh'fhàilinn, *pret. aff. a.* of failinn. Failed. See Failinn.

Dh'fhairich, *pret. aff. a.* of fairich. Awoke. See Fairich.

Dh'fhairtlich, *pret. aff. a.* of fairtlich. Worsted, overcame. See Fairtlich.

Dh'fhalbh, *pret. aff.* of falbh. Went, departed. See Falbh.

Dh'fhan, *pret. aff.* of fan. Stayed, waited. See Fan.

Dh'fhannaich, *pret. aff. a.* of fannaich.

Dh'fhaobhachadh, (a), *infin.* of faobhaich. To spoil or strip.—*Stew.* 1 *Sam.*

Dh'fhaodadh, *imp. sup.* of the *def. v.* faodaidh. Might, could.

Dh'fhaoidte, *adv.* Perhaps. Dh' fhaoidte gun tig e, *perhaps he may come;* maith-dh' fhaoidte, *perhaps.*

Dh'fhaoineachd, *pret. aff.* of faoineachd. Inquired. Dh' fhaoineachd e dheth, *he inquired of him.*

Dh'fhaotainn, (a), *infin.* of faotaidh; which see.

Dh'fharraid, *pret. a.* of farraid. Inquired, asked. Dh' fharraid mi dhi, *I asked of her.*—*Stew. Gen. ref.*

Dh'fhàs, *pret. a.* of fàs. Grew; became. See Fàs.

Dh'fheith, *pret. aff.* of feith. Waited. See Feith.

Dh'fheitheamh, (a), *infin.* of feith. To wait. See Feith.

Dh'fheòraich, *pret. aff.* of feòraich. Asked. See Feòraich.

Dh'fheuch, *pret. aff.* of feuch. Showed; tried. Dh' fheuch e dhomh, *he showed me;* dh' fheuch mi ris, *I tried it, I gave it a trial;* dh' fheuch e rium, *he tried me,* or *put me to the push* or *trial.*

Dh'fheuchainn, (a), *infin.* of feuch. To show; to try; to taste; to see. A dh' fheuchainn an robh tuigse aig neach, *to see if any had understanding.*—*Sm.*

Dh'fheud, *pret. aff.* of feud. Might; could; was permitted.

Dh'fheudadh, *pret. sub.* of feud. Might; could; was permitted.

Dh'fheudainn, 1 *sing. per. sub.* of feud. I might or could.

Dh'fheum, *pret.* of *def. v.* feumaidh. Was obliged. Dh' fheum mi, *I was obliged.*

Dh'fhidireas, *fut. sub.* of fidir; which see.

Dh'fhill, *pret. a.* of fill. Folded; plaited. See Fill.

Dh'fhios, *adv.* and *prep.* To; to the knowledge.

Dh'fhiosrachadh, (a), *infin.* of fiosraich. To inquire or examine.

Dh'fhiosraich, *pret. a.* of fiosraich. Asked, inquired, examined. Dh' fhiosraich mi dhithe, *I inquired of her.*—*Stew. Gen.*

DH'FHÌREANNACHADH, (a), *infin.* of fìreannaich. To justify. See FIREANNAICH.

DH'FHOCHAID, *pret. aff.* of fochaid. Mocked, derided. Dh' fhochaid mi air, *I derided him.* See FOCHAID.

DH'FHOILLSICH, *pret. a.* of foillsich. Revealed, discovered. See FOILLSICH.

DH'FHOLAICH, *pret.* of folaich. Hid, concealed. See FOLAICH.

DH'FHOSGAIL, *pret. a.* of fosgail. Opened. See FOSGAIL.

DH'FHOSGLADH, *pret. pass.* of fosgail. Was opened.

DH'FHUAIGH, *pret. aff.* of fuaigh. Sewed.

DH'FHUILING, *pret. aff.* of fuiling. Suffered. See FUILING.

DH'FHUIN, *pret. aff. a.* of fuin. Baked.

DH'FHUIRICH, *pret. aff.* of fuirich. Waited. Dh' fhuirich mi ris, *I waited for him;* dh' fhuirich mi air, *I waited on him as an attendant.*

DH'I, *comp. pron.* (*from* de.) Of her, of it; off her, off it.

DHI, *comp. pron.* (*from* do.) Of her, of it; to her, to it; off her, off it. Dhi féin, *to herself.*

DHIA, *asp. form* of Dia; which see.

DHIABHOIL, *voc. sing.* of diabhol; which see.

DH'IADH, *pret. a.* of iadh. Surrounded. See IADH.

DH'IARR, *pret. a.* of iarr. Sought, desired, inquired. Dh' iarr mi air, *I desired him;* dh' iarr mi e, *I sought for him.*

DH'IARRUIDH, (a), *infin.* of iarr; which see.

DHIBH, *comp. pron.* Off you; of you; from you.

DH'ÌBIR, *pret. a.* of dìbir. Forsook, neglected. See DÌBIR.

DHI-CHUIMHNICH, *pret. a.* of di-chuimhnich. Forgot.

DHÌDEIN, *asp. form* of dìdein; which see.

DHILLSEACHD, *asp. form* of dillseachd.

DH'IMEACHD, *infin.* of imich. To go; to walk; to depart. See IMICH.

DH'IMICH, *pret. aff.* of imich. Went, walked, departed.

DHINN, *comp. pron.* Of us, concerning us; off us, from us, from amongst us.

DH'INNIS, *pret. aff.* of innis. Told, informed. See INNIS.

DHIOBHAIL, (a), *prep.* Without. Dhiobhail céill, *without knowledge, foolish.—Stew. Is.* See DIOBHAIL.

DHIOGHLUIM, *pret. a.* of dioghluim. Gleaned. See DIOGHLUIM.

DHIOL, *pret. aff. a.* of diol. Paid; restored; avenged. See DIOL.

DHIOLADH, (a), *infin.* of diol. To pay, to restore.

DHIOM, *comp. pron.* Off me; from me.

DHION, *pret. aff. a.* of dion. Protected, defended. See DION.

DHIONADH, *pret. sub. a.* of dion. Would defend. Dhionadh e mi, *he would defend me.* Also, *pret. pass.* was defended. See DION.

DH'IONNSUIDH, *prep.* To; towards; unto. Dh' ionnsuidh na h-aimhne, *to the river.*

DHIOT, *asp. form* of diot. Of thee; from thee. Cuir dhiot do chòta, *put off thy coat;* leig dhiot, *give over.*

DHI-SA, DHI-SE, *emphatic form* of dhi. To her; of her; off her.

DHÌT, *pret. aff. a.* of dìt. Condemned. See DÌT.

DHÌTEADH, *pret. sub. a.* of dìt. Would condemn. Dhìteadh e mi, *he would condemn me.* Also, *pret. ind. pass.* was condemned.

DHÌTH, *asp. form* of dìth; which see.

DHÌTH, (a), *adv.* Without; for want of. A dhìth tròcair, *for want of mercy;* bi as a dhìth, *be without it;* bi da dhìth, *be without it.*

DH'ITH, *pret. aff. a.* of ith. See ITH.

DHIÙ. See DHIÙBH.

DHIUBH, *asp. form* of the *comp. pron.* diubh. Off them; of them. Co dhiùbh? *which of them?* co dhiùbh, *whether;* co dhiùbh is tarbh na caor e, *whether he be a bull or a sheep.—Stew. O. T.* See also DIUBH.

DHIÙLT, *pret. aff. a.* of diùlt. Refused. See DIÙLT.

DHLIGHE, *asp. form* of dlighe; which see.

DHLIGHEACH, *asp. form* of dligheach; which see.

DHLÙTHAICH, *pret. aff. a.* of dlùthaich; which see.

DH'ÒB, *pret. aff. a.* of òb. Refused. See OB.

DHOBHAIDH, *asp. form* of dobhaidh; which see.

DHOCHAINN, *pret. aff. a.* of dochainn. Harmed. See DOCHAINN.

DHOCHANN, ainn, *s. m.*, *asp. form* of dochann; which see.

DHOIBH, *asp. form* of doibh. To them. Thoir dhoibh e, *give it to them.*

DH'OIBRICH, *pret. aff. a.* of oibrich; which see.

DH'OIDHCHE, *adv.* By night. Dh'oidhche is a la, *by night and by day.*

DHOILGHEAS, *asp. form* of doilgheas; which see.

DHOILLEIR, *a.*, *asp. form* of doilleir; which see.

DHOININN, *asp. form* of doininn; which see.

DHOINIONN, *asp. form* of doinionn; which see.

DHOIRCHE, *asp. form* of doirche. Dark, gloomy. San oidhche dhoirche, *in the dark night.—Stew. Pro.* See DORCHA.

DHÒIRT, *pret. aff. a.* of dòirt. Poured; spilled. See DÒIRT.

DH'ÒL, *pret. aff. a.* of òl. Drank. See ÒL.

DH'ÒLADH, *pret. sub. a.* of òl. Would drink. Dh' òladh e, *he would drink.* Also, *pret. pass.* of òl, *was drank.*

DHOLAIDH, *asp. form* of dolaidh. Harm; abuse. Chaidh e dholaidh, *he* (or *it*) *has gone useless;* cuir dholaidh, *abuse, spoil.* See also DOLAIDH.

DHOMH, *asp. form* of domh. To me; for me. Thoir eisdeachd dhomh, *listen to me.—Sm.*

DHOMH-SA, *asp. form* of domhsa. To me; for me. Snaigh dhomhsa bogha, *cut a bow for me.—Ull.*

DHONA, *asp. form* of dona; which see.

DHORCH, *asp. form* of dorch. Dark; mysterious. Oidhche dhorch, *a dark night.* See DORCH.

DHORCHAICH, *pret. aff. a.* of dorchaich. Darkened; grew dark. See DORCHAICH.

DHORN, *asp. form* of dorn. Fist. A dhorn, *his fist.*

DHREACH, *asp. form* of dreach; which see.

DHÙCHA, *asp. form* of dùcha. See DÙTHAICH.

DHUIBH, *asp. form* of duibh, *comp. pron.* To you; for you. Is maith thig e dhuibh, *it well becomes you.*

DHUIBH, *a.*, *asp. form* of duibh. Black. San oidhche dhuibh, *in the dark night.—Stew. Pro.*

DHÙIN, *pret. aff. a.* of dùin. Shut; closed. See DÙIN.

DHUINE, *asp. form* of duine, and *voc. sing.* O man! Da dhuine, *two men. Corn.* deu dhen. *Arm.* daou den, *two men.*

DHUINN, *asp. form* of duinn. To us; for us. Thoir dhuinn, *give us;* thig e dhuinn, *it becomes us; it will become us.*

DHÙISG, *pret. aff. a.* of dùisg. Awakened, roused. See DÙISG.

DHUIT, *asp. form* of duit. To thee; for thee. Bheir e dhuit, *he will give thee;* thig e dhuit, *it will become thee.*

DI, *s.* Day. *Di,* in the sense of day, is used among the Gael only as a prefix to the name of a week-day, and then it may be considered a corruption of †dia, *day;* which see. Di-dòmhnuich, *Sabbath;* di-luain, *Monday;* di-màirt, *Tuesday;* di-ciadain, *Wednesday;* di-r-daoine, di-daoirne, *Thursday;* di-h-aoine, *Friday;* di-sathairn, *Saturday.*

It. di. *Pers.* di. *Corn.* and *Arm.* de *and* di. *Span.* dia. *Shans.* divos. *Lat.* dies.

D'I, *comp. pron.* To her, to it; off her, of it; from her, from it. Ni slainnte tearmunn di, *salvation shall be a bulwark to her.—Sm*

DI, DITH, *s. m.* Want; failure; deficiency. *Asp. form*, dhi. Theid na bunaite air dhi, *the foundations shall fail.—Sm* Ribeachan gun di, *snares in abundance.—Id.* Cha 'n 'eil da 'n di ach comhrag, *they want nothing but battle.—Old Poem.* Bi as a di, *be without her, want her*, bi as a dhith, *be without him* or *it, want him* or *it*, di airm, *want of arms. Arm.* diarm, *unarmed.* Di fabht, *want of blame. Arm.* difaut, *blameless.*

DI. A particle used only in composition, and prefixed to nouns and verbs to alter or modify their meaning.

† **DIA**, *s.* A day; (*from* Dia, *God*) So dies, *a day*, (*from* dius, *now* deus)

Shans. divos; dia, *among the old Cretans. Pers.* di. *Arm.* and *Corn.* de, di.

DIA, dé, *s. m.* (*perhaps from* di, *i. e.* ti) God; a god, a divinity. *Asp form*, dhia. *N. pl* diathan *and* dée. A gluasadh mar dhia, *moving like a god.—Mac Lach. Voc.* A Dhia. A Dhia seall oirnne! *God help us!* Dhia gleidh sinn! *God preserve us!*

Gr. Διος, and the oblique cases of Ζευς, Διος, Δια. *Lat.* dius, *now* deus *and* divus, with the digamma Æolicum. *Persic*, dio *and* diu. *Shans.* deva. *Span.* dios. *It.* dio. *Fr.* dieu. *W.* dew, dyw *Corn.* dew. *Arm.* dez, di, *and* due. *Ir.* dia.

DIA-AICHEADH, *s.* Atheism.

DIA-AICHEANAICHE, *s. m* An atheist.

DIA-BHEUM, -bhéim, *s m.* Blasphemy.

DIABHLAIDH, DIABHLUIDH, *a.* (*from* diabhol) Devilish; demoniac; hellish. Diabhluidh olc, *hellishly bad.*

DIABHLUIDHEACHD, *s. f.* Demonism; the conduct of a devil; extreme iniquity.

DIABHOL, oil, *s. m. N. pl.* diabhoil. A devil. An diabhol leis thu, *devil take you*, an diabhol thu, *devil take you*; an diabhol mir dhiot, *devil an inch of you*; an diabhol toirt, *the devil may care.*

Gr. Διαβολος. *Lat.* diabolus *It.* diavolo. *Span* diavlo *and* diablo. *Fr.* diable. *Belg* duyvel. *Polish*, diabel-sto *Dan.* diaevel *and* dieffuel. *Ir* diabhal *Corn.* dzhiaul. *Arm.* diaoul. *W.* diavol *and* diavyl.

A much more ancient name for devil is *aibhisear*, ruiner. See **AIBHISEAR.**

† **DIABLADH**, aidh, *s. m.* (*Ir. id.*) Twice as much, double.—*Shaw.*

† **DIACHAIR**, *s. f.* (*Ir. id*) Sorrow, grief, weeping.—*Shaw*

† **DIACHARACH**, *a.* (*Ir. id.*) Sorrowful, sad, grievous, vexatious. Gu diacharach, *sorrowfully.*

DIADHACHADH, aidh, *s. m.* A deifying.

DIACON, oin, *s. m.* A deacon. *Corn.* diagon.

DIADHACHD, *s. f.* (*from* Dia) Divinity; Godhead, godliness; theology. Iomlaine na Diadhachd, *the fulness of the Godhead.—Stew Col.* Anns an uile dhiadhachd, *in all godliness.—Stew. Tim.*

DIADHAIDH, *a.* Pious, godly, divine, godlike Nan giùlan diadhaidh, *godly in their conduct.—Sm.* Gu diadhaidh, *piously.*

DIADHAIDH, (gu), *adv.* Piously; righteously A ghluais gu diadhaidh, *who walked righteously.—Sm.*

DIADHAIDHEACHD, *s. f* Piety, godliness Written also *diadhuidheachd.*

DIADHAIR, *s. m.* A divine, a theologian. *N. pl* diadhairean.

DIADHAIREACHD, *s. f.* Divinity, theology.

DIADHEAN, *v. a.* Deify.

DIA-DHEANAMH, *s. m.* A deifying; apotheosis

DIADHUIDH, *a.* Pious, godly. Written also *diadhaidh*; which see Perhaps *diadhuidh* is *dia-ghuidh.*

DIADHUIDHEACHD, *s. f.* Piety, godliness. Perhaps *dia-ghuidheachd.*

DIAIGH, (an), *adv.* (*Ir. id*) After; behind Written also *deigh.*

† **DIAIL**, *a* Quick, immoderate, soon.

DI-AIRMHE, DI-AIRMHEADH, *a* Innumerable, that cannot be counted

DIAL, *v a* Wean. *Pret. a.* dhial, *weaned, fut. aff. a.* dialaidh, *shall* or *will wean.*

DIALADH, aidh, *s m.* A weaning Cuir air dhialadh, *wean.*

DIALL, *s f.* Submission; *also*, the breech: *hence*, diollaid, *i e* diall-àite, *a saddle.*

DIALLAO, aig, *s f* A bat

† **DIALON**, oin, *s m* (*Ir. id*) A diary.

DIALTAG, aig, *s f* A bat or rearmouse; the *vespertinus murinus* of Linnæus; *also*, a species of bonnet-grass *N. pl* dialtagan Dialtag anamoch, *a bat*

† **DIAMANN**, ainn, *s. m.* Food, sustenance.

DIAMHAIN, *a* (*Ir. id*) Idle, lazy, useless, vain Iasgair diamhain, *an unsuccessful fisher*, *a species of water-bird* Is diamhain do shaothair, *thy labour is vain*, gu diamhain, *vainly*

DIAMHAIR, *a.* Dark, hidden, secret, mysterious; solitary, lonely Gleannan diamhair, *a solitary glen.—Oss. Trathal* Rùn diamhair, *a mystery*, *a secret purpose* Written also *diomhair*; which see.

DIAMHAIREACHD, *s. f.* A secret, a mystery; secretness, mysteriousness, solitariness, loneliness; a lonely place.

DIAMHANACH, *a.* Idle; vain; lazy. *Com* and *sup.* diamhanaiche.

DIAMHANAS, ais, *s m.* Idleness; vanity; laziness.

DIA-MHAOIN, *s f.* The plate belonging to a church, the charity given at church; a deodand.

DIAMHAR, *a* Huge, enormous; dark, secret, hidden.

DIA-MHASLACH, *a.* Blasphemous.

DIA-MHASLACHADH, aidh, *s. m.* Blasphemy; a blaspheming.

DIA-MHASLACHAIR, *s. m* A blasphemer *N. pl.* dia-mhaslachairean

DIA-MHASLADH, aidh, *s. m* Blasphemy; a ridiculing of religion.

DIA-MHASLAICH, *v a* Blaspheme. *Pret a.* dhi-mhaslaich, *blasphemed*, *fut aff.* dia-maslaichidh, *shall blaspheme*

DIAMHLACHADH, aidh, *s m.* A darkening; a growing dark or coloured.

† **DIAMHLADH**, aidh, *s. m* (*Ir id*) A retreat, a place of refuge.

† **DIAMHLAICH**, *v. a* (*Ir. id*) Make dark *Pret.* dhiamhlaich.

DIAN, *a.* (*Gr* Δεινος.) Vehement, violent; eager, hasty; nimble; brisk; strong; sad, precipitant; headlong Osag dhian, *a violent blast.—Old Song* Tòrachd dhian, *eager pursuit.—Sm* Gach neach dian, *every hasty person.—Stew. Pro ref* *Com* and *sup* déine

DIAN-AIRM, *s. m* A place of refuge, a sanctuary; a depôt

DIANAS, ais, *s m.* (*from* dian.) Vehemence, violence

DIAN-ATHCHUINGE, *s. f* An importunate request; a sincere prayer. *N. pl* dian-athchuingean

DIAN-ATHCHUINGEACH, *a.* Importunate; fervent in prayer

DIAN-CHOMHLADH, aidh, *s. m.* An aid-de-camp; an officer of the life-guards *N. pl* dian-chomhlaichean.

DIAN-CHORRUICH, *s* Fierce wrath.—*Stew. Jonah.*

DIAN-DHEOTHAS, ais, *s. m.* Fervent zeal; bigotry.

Dian-dheothasach, *a.* Fervent; bigoted; zealous. Gu dian-dheothasach, *fervently.*

Dian-fhearg, -fheirg, *s. f.* Great indignation; fiery wrath. Gu crìch na dian-fheirg, *to the end of the indignation.—Stew. Dan.*

Dian-fheargach, *a.* Wrathful; in a great rage; causing great wrath.

Dian-ghluasad, aid, *s. m.* Violent motion; great agitation.

Dian-iarrtachd, *s. f.* Importunity.—*Stew. Luke, ref.*

Dian-liosdach, *a.* Importunate. Gu dian-liosdach, *importunately.*

Dian-liosdachd, *s. f.* Importunacy.

Dian-lorgaich, *v. a.* Pursue hotly; persecute. *Pret. a.* dhian-lorgaich, *pursued hotly; fut. aff.* dian-lorgaichidh, *shall pursue.*

Dian-lorgair, *s. m.* A persecutor; a pursuer.

Dian-lorgaireachd, *s. f.* Hot pursuit, a chase; a persecution; indagation.

Dian-ruith, *v. n.* Run impetuously.

Dian-ruith, *s. m.* Eager running; a rushing; impetuous motion. Tha e na dhian-ruith, *he is running impetuously.*

Dian-shruth, *s. m.* A rapid stream, a torrent.

Dian-sparradh, aidh, *s. m.* An urgent demand, an injunction, a pressing order.—*Stew. Exod.*

Dian-theas, *s. m.* Fervent heat; intense heat; fervent zeal. Na chaoiribh le dian-theas, *sparkling with intense heat.—Sm.*

Dian-theth, *a.* Intensely hot.

Dian-thograch, *a.* Ambitious; extremely covetous; keen.

Dian-thogradh, aidh, *s. m.* Ambition; extreme covetousness; keenness.

Diardan, ain, *s. m.* Anger, surliness, snarling.—*Shaw.*

Diardanach, *a.* Angry, surly, snarling. Gu diardanach, *in a surly manner. Com.* and *sup.* diardanaiche.

Diardanachd, *s. f.* Angriness, surliness, churlishness.

Diarmad, aid, *s. m.* Neglect; neglectfulness. Cuir air diarmad, *neglect.*

Diarmad, aid, *s. m.* The name Dermid; *also,* one of Ossian's heroes, from whom the Campbells derive their origin: hence modern bards call them *sliochd Dhiarmaid an tuirc,* the race of Diarmid who slew the boar.

Dias, déis, *s. f.* (*Ir. id.*) An ear of corn; *also,* corn; the blade of a sword. *N. pl.* diasan *and* diasa. Fàs déis, *the growth of corn.—Sm.* Seachd diasa, *seven ears.—Stew. Gen.* Fa dheis, *in ear;* fo dhéis, *in ear;* eorna fa dheis, *barley in ear.—Stew. Exod.*

† Dias, *a.* Two; a pair. Now written *dithis;* which see.

Diasach, *a.* (*from* dias.) Full of ears of corn; like an ear of corn; of, or belonging to, an ear of corn; bladed, as corn. Coirc diasach, *bladed corn.—Macfar. Com.* and *sup.* diasaiche.

Diasad, aid, *s. f.* An ear of corn, a blade of corn.

Diasag, aig, *s. f., dim.* of dias. A little ear of corn; a little blade. *N. pl.* diasagan.

Diasair, *v. a.* Glean, as a corn field. *Pret. a.* dhiasair, *gleaned; fut. aff. a.* diasairidh, *shall glean.*

Diasan, *n. pl.* of dias; which see.

Diasdach, *a.* Having ears of corn; bladed.

Diasradh, aidh, *s. m.* (*from* dias.) A gleaning.

Diathan, *n. pl.* of Dia. Gods. See Dia.

Dibeadach, *a.* Negative.

Dìbearach, aich, *s. m.* (*Ir.* dibearach.) A fugitive, an exile. Written also *diobarach.*

Dìbearach, *a.* (*Ir.* dibeartha.) Banished; needy; that banishes.

Dibearachd, *s. f.* Banishment; exile; want.

Dìbearaiche, *s. m.* A needy person; an exile.

Di-beoil, *a.* (*Ir. id.*) Mute; dumb.

Dibh, *comp. pron.* Of you; from you; off you. *Asp. form,* dhibh.

Dibhe, *gen. sing.* of deoch. Of drink. Tabhartas-dibhe, *a drink-offering.—Stew. Deut.*

† Dibheach, *s.* (*Ir. id.*) An ant.

† Dibheal, *a.* (*Ir. id. Lat.* debilis, *weak.*) Weak; old.

Dibhealaich, *a.* Without way or passage; pathless; impassable.

† Dibhearadh, aidh, *s. m.* (*Ir. id.*) A consoling; consolation.

Dibheargach, ich, *s. m.* A robber.

Dibheargach, *a.* Vindictive; wrathful.

Dibh-fhearg, -fheirg, *s. f.* Wrath, rage, vengeance.—*Macd.*

Dibhlachadh, aidh, *s. m.* An abrogating; abrogation; repeal.

Dibhladhaich, *v. a.* Repeal, abrogate. *Pret. a.* dhibhladhaich, *repealed.* See Di-laghaich.

† Dibhirce, *s. f.* (*Ir. id.*) An endeavour.

† Dibhirceach, *a.* (*Ir. id.*) Diligent; fierce, violent, unruly.—*Shaw.*

Dibhlasda, *a.* Insipid, tasteless. *Arm.* divlas.

Dibhrigh, *s. f.* Contempt, neglect.

† Dibineachd, *s. f.* (*Ir. id.*) Extremity.—*Shaw.*

Dibir, *v. a.* and *n.* (*Ir. id.*) Forsake, abandon; quit; neglect; forget; depart; put away in anger; expel; banish. *Pret. a.* dhibir, *banished; fut. aff. a.* dibiridh, *shall banish.* Cha dìbir e thu, *he will not forsake thee.—Stew. Deut.* Na dìbir a bhi mar iadsan, *forget not to be like them.—Old Poem.* Na flathan a dhìbir, *the heroes who have departed.—Oss. Duthona.* Na dìbir d'oglach, *put not away thy servant.—Sm.*

Dibir, *s. f.* (*Ir. id.*) Abandonment; neglect; forgetfulness.

Dìbleachd, *s. f.* for *diblidheachd;* which see.

Dìbli, *a.* See Dìblidh.

Diblich, *v. a.* Make vile; become vile or wretched; demean; become drooping. *Pret. a.* dhìblich, *demeaned; fut. aff. a.* diblichidh, *shall* or *will demean.*

Dìblidh, *a.* (*Ir.* dibligh.) Mean, abject, destitute; wretched, poor; vulgar, worthless. Do 'n anrach dhìblidh, *to the destitute wanderer.—Sm. Asp. form,* dhìblidh.

Dìblidheachd, *s. f.* Meanness; wretchedness; destituteness; poverty.

Di-ceadoine, *s. f.* Wednesday. See Di-ciaduin.

Di-chairt, *v. a.* (di, *priv. and* cairt.) Peel, take off the bark, decorticate. *Pret.* dhi-chairt; *fut. aff. a.* di-chairtidh.

Di-cheall, ill, *s. f.* (*Ir. id.*) Diligence, care; application; attention; endeavour, attempt. Le di-cheall, *with diligence.—Sm.* Dean dìcheall, *endeavour;* dean do dhìcheall, *do your diligence.*

Dìcheallach, *a.* Diligent, careful; industrious, busy, persevering; assiduous. Gu dìcheallach, *diligently.—Sm.* An seillean dìcheallach, *the busy bee.—Macfar.* Written also *dichiollach.*

Dìcheallachd, *s. f.* The practice of diligence; industriousness, perseverance; carefulness.

† Dichealtair, *s. m.* (*Ir. id.*) A deer-park; *also,* the shaft of a spear.—*Shaw.*

Dicheann, *v. a.,* di, *priv. and* ceann. (*Ir. id.*) Behead. *Pret.* dhi-cheann, *beheaded.*

Dìcheannachadh, aidh, *s. m.* A beheading.

Dicheannachd, *s. f.* Decapitation.

Dicheannadh, aidh, *s. m.* A beheading.

Dicheannaich, *v. a.* Behead *Pret. a.* dhìcheannaich, *beheaded; fut. aff.* dì-cheannaichidh

Dicheannaichte, *p part* of dìcheannaich. Beheaded.

Di-cheannta, *p. part* of dìcheann. Beheaded Fear dì-cheannta, *an executioner*, or *one who beheads.*

Dìchioll, ill, *s. f.* Diligence; perseverance. Le mòran dìchill, *with much diligence.* Written also dìcheall.

Dìchiollach, *a.* Diligent; persevering; careful. Lamh nan dìchiollach, *the hand of the diligent.—Stew. Pro.* Written also *dìcheallach.*

Dìchrannachadh, aidh, *s. m.* A dismasting.

Di-chrannaich, *v. a.* Dismast *Pret. aff a.* dhì-chrannaich, *dismasted; fut. aff. a* dì-chrannaichidh, *shall dismast.*

Di-chrannaichte, *p. part.* of dìchrannaich Dismasted.

Di-chreid, *v. a.* Disbelieve. *Arm* discridi; in and about Vannes, they say *discreidein*

Di-chreideamh, imh, *s f.* (*Ir id*) Unbelief, disbelief, infidelity, scepticism.

Dìchreideamhach, Dìchreidmheich, ich, *s. m.* An unbeliever, an infidel, an incredulous person

Dìchreideamhach, *a* Incredulous, sceptical *Arm.* dis-crediq, *suspicious*

Dìchuimhne, *s. f.* Oblivion, forgetfulness; neglectfulness Tir na dìchuimhne, *the land of forgetfulness.—Sm.* Air dìchuimhne, *forgotten*, air dhìchuimhne, *forgotten* Leig air dìchuimhne, *forget, allow to fall into oblivion*

Dìchuimhneach, *a.* Forgetful, heedless, oblivious.

Di-chuimhneachadh, aidh, *s m* A forgetting, forgetfulness.

Di-chuimhnich, *v. a* (di, *priv. and* cuimhnich.) Forget; neglect. *Pret. a.* dhì-chuimhnich, *forgot, fut. aff. a.* dì-chuimhnichidh, *shall* or *will forget.*

Di-ciadain, *s. f* Wednesday Di-ciadain na luaithre, *Ash-Wednesday*; dì-ciadain so chaidh, *last Wednesday*, dì-ciadain so 'tighinn, *next Wednesday*, air la ciadain, *on a Wednesday.*

† **Did**, *s. f.* (*Ir. id*) A pap; a diddy.—*Shaw*

Dìdeag, eig, *s. f.* A peep, a sly look; a small candle. Dìdeag ort, *I am peeping at you*

Dìdeagaich, *s. f.* A peeping Ciod an dìdeagaich th'ort? *what are you peeping at?*

Dìdean, ein, *s. m.* Protection, defence, safety, refuge, preservation; a sanctuary, a fort. Baile dìdein, *a city of refuge.—Stew. 1 K.* Fo dhìdein, *in safety —Sm* Is dìdean gliocas, *wisdom is a defence.—Stew Ecc.* A guidh an dìdein, *begging their protection —Old Song.*

Dìdeanach, *a.* (*from* dìdean.) Protection; affording protection or shelter, ready to shelter or protect.

Dìdeanachadh, aidh, *s m.* A protecting; a protection; a fortifying.

Dìdeanaich, *v. a.* (*Ir.* dideannaigh.) Protect, shelter, fortify. *Pret. a.* dhìdeanaich, *protected*

Dìdeanair, *s. m* A defender; a fortifier. *Ir.* didionair.

Dìdein, *gen sing.* of dìdean

Di-dhaoineachadh, aidh, *s. m.* Depopulation; the act of depopulating.

Di-dhaoinich, *v. a.* Depopulate, lay waste; extirpate *P. part.* dì-dhaoinichte.

Di-dhuilleach, *a.* Without leaves or foliage.

Didil, *s. f.* (*Ir. id*) Great love, kindness

Di-domhnuich, *s. f.* Sunday (*Lat* dies Dominica) Di-domhnuich càisg, *Easter Sunday*; dì-dòmhnuich so chaidh, *last Sunday*, dì-domhnuich so 'tighinn, *next Sunday*, la-domhnuich, *a Sunday*, an domhnach, *the Sabbath*

Difir, *s f* (*Ir. id Lat.* differentia) Difference Now written *diubhair.*

Di-fhulang, *a* Intolerable

Dìg, dìge, *s f* A dike; a ditch; a stone wall. *N. pl* dìgeachan, *dikes.* Thuit san dìg a rinn, *he who made the ditch fell into it —Sm.*

Swed and *Scot.* dike. *Du.* dyk. *Fr.* and *Span* digue. *Teut.* dyck *Heb.* daek.

Dìgeach, *a.* Abounding in dikes or in ditches; like a dike or ditch.

Dighe, (*for* dibhe), *gen.* of deoch.

† **Dighe**, *s f.* (*Ir. id*) Succour; help; satisfaction.—*Shaw*

† **Dighe**, *a* (*Ir. id*) Condign; adequate.

† **Dighin**, *v. a* (*Ir id*) Suck. *Pret* dhighin, *sucked, fut. aff.* dighinidh

† **Dighiona**, *a* (*Ir id.*) Morose, surly. Perhaps *di-ghean*

Dighreannt, *a* (*Ir id.*) Bald —*Shaw.*

Di-ghreannachd, *s. f* Baldness.

Di-h-aoine, *s f.* Friday. Di-h-aoine so 'chaidh, *last Friday*, dì-h-aoine so 'tighinn, *Friday next.*

Di-lachdach, aich, *s m* (*from* dì, *want, and* lachd, *milk*) An orphan, a motherless child, who consequently wants suck or milk

Di-lathairreachd, *s. f.* Absence

Dile, *s f* (*Ir id*) Love, affection, friendship —*Shaw*

Dile, *s f* The flower called dill.—*Macd.*

Dile, *s. f.* (*Ir. id.*) *Asp. form*, dhìle. A flood, inundation, heavy rain; a blast; the earth. An dìle ruadh, *the general deluge*, ged thigeadh dìle, *though rains were to come.—Macint.* An searbh-dhìle, *the bitter blast.—Old Song.*

Dìleab, eib, *s. f.* A legacy. *Asp. form*, dhìleab Mar dhìleab, *as a legacy.*

Dìleabach, *a.* Of, or belonging to, a legacy.

Dìleabaiche, *s. m.* A legatee. Cha d'eug duine riomh gun dìleabaiche, *a man never died without an heir —G. P* *N pl.* dìleabaichean

Dìleach, *a* Beloved; affectionate

Dìleag, eig, *s f* A drop, or small quantity of any fluid

Dìleaman, ain, *s m* Love; affection; kindness.

Dìleagh, *v a.* Digest food *Pret* dhìleagh, *digested*

Dìleaghadh, aidh, *s. m.* (*Ir id*) Digestion

Dìleanta, *a.* Inundating; rainy. Mios dìleanta, *a rainy month.—Macfar.*

Dìleas, *a* (*Ir. id*) Faithful; trusty, friendly, related, beloved; favourable *Asp form*, dhìleas. Tearmunn dìleas, *a trusty refuge.—Sm.* Gaoth dhìleas, *a favourable wind —Ull.* Ainm dìleas, *a proper name.*

Dìlghfann, inn, *s. m* (*Ir. id*) Destruction, plundering, pillaging.

† **Dìlgionadh**, aidh, *s m.* An emptying

Dìlich, *v a* Digest, as food *Pret a* dhìlich, *digested, fut. aff. a.* dìlichidh, *shall digest, p part.* dìlichte, *digested*

Dìlichte, *p part* of dìlich.

Dìlinn, *a.* Endless, never, *also*, a flood, the flood of time (*W.* dylan, *ocean*) Gu dìlinn, *never.* Gu dìlinn cha dùisg thu, *thou shalt never awaken —Oss. Cathula* Gus an caillear ann dìlinn aois, *till age is lost in the flood of time.—Oss. Gaul*

Dìlinneach, *a* Diluvian, inundating

Dìlleachd, *s m.* An orphan Do 'n dìlleachd acrach, *to the hungry orphan.—Sm*

Dìlleachdan, ain, *s m.* (*from* dìlleachd.) A little orphan

Ain-neart air an dilleachdan, *oppression on the orphan.*—*Stew Jer.*

Dillse, *com.* and *sup.* of dìleas. More or most faithful; *also,* kindred, relations. Ni 's dìllse na thusa, *more friendly than you,* nuair thig thu chum mo dhìllse, *when you come to my kindred.*—*Stew. Gen.* *N. pl.* dìllsean.

Dillseachd, *s. f.* (*from* dìllse.) Friendship, relationship; relations, kindred; faithfulness, lovingness; love, affection. Mo dhìllseachd, *my relations* or *kindred,* do dhìllseachd chuir mi 'n céill, *I have shown thy faithfulness* —*Sm.*

Dillsean, *n pl* of dìllse. Relations, friends, kindred, connexions. *Asp form,* dhìllsean Dh' imich do dhìllsean, *thy kindred has travelled.*—*Oss Manos.*

Dilmain, *a* Meet, proper, fit, becoming —*Shaw.*

Di-luain, *s f.* Monday. Diluain so 'tighinn, *Monday next,* Di-luain so 'chaidh, *Monday last*
Lat di-es lunæ. *Arm* di lun. *Corn.* delin. *Fr.* lun-di So Monday for Moonday.

† **Dilte,** *s f* (*Ir id*) Nutriment —*Shaw.*

Dimairt, *s f* Tuesday Dimàirt innid, *the Carnival*
Lat dies Martis *Fr* Mardi *Arm* di-Meurs. *Corn* Demer.

Dimbrigh, *s f* Contempt —*Shaw.* Probably *diom-breath*

Dimbrighlach, *a* Contemptuous —*Shaw* Probably *diom-breathach.*

Dimbuaidh, *s f* Unsuccessfulness, bad luck, defeat; mishap, a crime Written also *diom-buaidh,* which see

Dimbuaidheach, *a.* Unsuccessful, luckless, unfortunate. Written also *diombuaidheach*

Dimeas, *s m* (di, *priv.* and meas) Contempt, disrespect, disesteem, a bad name, a bad character *Asp form,* dhìmeas Fo dhìmeas dhaoine, *despised by men.*—*Sm* Written also *dimheas*

Dìmeas, *v. a* Despise, slight, undervalue *Pret a* dhìmeas, *slighted.*

Dìmeasach, *a* Disrespectful, contemptuous Written also *dimheasach*

Dìmeasail, *a* Disrespectful, contemptuous Written also *dìmheasail*

Dìmeasda, *a* Despised, slighted, undervalued.

Dìmeasdachd, *s.* Disrespect —*Shaw.*

† **Dimhe,** *s f.* (*Ir id*) Protection, shelter —*Shaw*

Dìmheas, *s m* (*Ir* dimheas) Disrespect, disesteem, contempt, a bad name Dean dìmheas, *despise,* cuir air dìmheas, *slight, despise,* fu dhìmeas, *despised*

Dìmheas, *v a.* Despise, slight, undervalue *Pret a.* dhìmheas, *despised, fut aff a* dìmheasaidh

Dìmheasail, *a.* Disrespectful; contemptuous Gu dìmheasail, *disrespectfully*

Dìmheasda, *a.* Despised, disrespected, of bad repute

Dìmheasdachd, *a* Disrespect, disrespectfulness, disrepute.

Di-mhill, *v a.* Destroy; abuse *Pret a* dhi-mhill, *destroyed, fut aff a* di-mhillidh, *shall destroy, p part.* di-mhillte, *destroyed*

Di-mhilltear, *fut pass.* of di-mhill Shall be destroyed Di-mhilltear gu grad, *shall be quickly destroyed* —*Sm*

Dimhinich, *v* See **Deimhinich**

Di-mhol, *v. a.* Dispraise, disparage, slander *Pret a* dhi-mhol, *dispraised, fut aff.* di-mholaidh, *shall dispraise*

Di-mholadair, *s m* A slanderer; a disparager *N. pl* di-mholadairean

† **Dimnidheach,** *a* (*Ir. id*) Sad, sorrowful.—*Shaw* Gu dimnidheach, *sadly.*

Dimnidheachd, *s. f.* Sadness, sorrowfulness

Dinneas, eis, *s m.* Necessity; want.—*Shaw.*

† **Din,** *a.* (*Ir. id.*) Pleasant, delightful, agreeable; sucking. —*Shaw.*

Dinait, *v. a.* Desolate.—*Shaw.*

Dinasgadh, aidh, *s. m.* An untying.

† **Dine,** *s f.* (*Ir. id*) A generation, age; a beginning.—*Shaw*

Dineart, eirt, *s m.,* di, *priv. and* neart. (*Ir. id.*) Infirmity, imbecility; *also, for* Dia-neart, *the power of God.*

Dineartuich, *v. a.* (*Ir.* dineartaigh.) Enfeeble; weaken; flank —*Shaw.*

† **Ding,** *v. a.* (*Ir. id.*) Thrust, push, urge, wedge.—*Shaw.*

† **Ding,** *s. f.* (*Ir. id*) A wedge.—*Shaw*

Dingir, *s. f.* Custody; a place of confinement; incarceration.

† **Dinib,** *s. f.* (*Ir. id.*) Drinking.—*Shaw.*

Dinn, *com. pron.* Of us; off us; from us; from amongst us. *Asp form,* dhinn. Gabhaidh e truas dinn, *he will pity us* —*Stew. Mic.*

† **Dinn,** *s. f.* (*W.* din. *Ir.* dinn.) A hill, a fortified hill. Hence the Roman *dinum, dinium,* and *dunum,* terminations of the names of towns in Old Gaul; and in Britain, now *don, ton, town,* &c. See **Dùn.**

Dinneir, dinnearach, *s f.* (*Ir.* dinneir.) Dinner. Dinneir luibhean, *a dinner of herbs.*—*Stew Pro ref.* An deigh thràth dinnearach, *after dinner-time.*

† **Dinnis,** *s f.* (*Ir. id.*) An oath; contempt.

Dinnseir, *s. f.* A wedge; *also,* ginger.—*Shaw.* *N. pl.* dinnseirean, *wedges.*

† **Diobadh,** aidh, *s m* (*Ir. id*) A point; an edge; a prick, a thorn

Diobair, *v. a* Banish; expel; forsake; abandon; forget; circumvent. *Pret. a* dhiobair, *forget; fut. aff. a* diobraidh, *shall forget* An diobair mathair a ciochran? *can a mother forget her suckling?*—*Sm.*

Diobairte, *p. part* of diobair.

Diobanach, *a* (*Ir. id.*) Lawless; *substantively,* an outlaw.

Diobar, air, *s. m.* (*Ir. id.*) Disrespect; contempt.

Diobarach, aich, *s m* An exile or outcast *N. pl.* diobaraich, *outcasts.* Diobaraich Israel, *the outcasts of Israel.*—*Stew G B.*

Diobarachan. See **Diobrachan.**

Diobarachd, *s. f.* Banishment, exile; the circumstance of banishing Fhuair e 'dhiobarachd, *he was banished.* Air dhiobarachd, *banished.*

† **Diobhadh,** aidh, *s. m.* (*Ir. id.*) Destruction, death; inheritance; a portion or dowry, any transitory or worldly inheritance.

Diobhaidh, *a* Impious; destructive; ruinous.—*Shaw.*

† **Diobhaidh,** *v. a* (*Ir. id*) Destroy, ruin —*Shaw*

Diobhail, *s f.* (*Ir id*) Loss, damage, injury, robbery; pity, lack, want; destruction; defeat; profusion. Le diobhail misnich, *with lack of courage* —*Sm.* *Asp. form,* dhiobhail. A dhiobhail laimh, *without his hand, with the loss of his hand* —*Oss Dargo.* Thainig an diobhail, *their destruction came.*—*Old Poem.*

Diobhaileach, *a.* Robbed, spoiled, stripped, damaged; destructive, profuse; extravagant.

Diobhaileachd, *s f* Privation; robbery; damage; destruction.

Diobhall, *a.* (*Ir. id.*) Old, ancient.

Diobhanach, *a.* (*Ir. id.*) Lawless, unruly. *Com.* and *sup.* diobhanaiche.—*Shaw* *Substantively,* an outlaw.

Diobhanachd, *s f.* Lawlessness, unruliness.

Diobhargach, *a.* Keen, fierce. Gu diobhargach, *keenly.* *Com.* and *sup.* diobhargaiche.

Diobhargadh, aidh, *s. m.* Captivity an enslaving; a persecution.

† **Diobhrath**, *v. a.* Discover.

Dio-bhuidheach, *a* (*Ir* diobhuidhe.) Ungrateful—(*Shaw*); thankless. Gu dio-bhuidheach, *ungratefully.*

Diobhuidheachas, ais, *s m.* Ingratitude.

Diobrach. See **Diobarach.**

Diobrachan, ain, *s. m.* A wanderer, an outcast, an exile; a destitute person, an orphan *N. pl.* diobrachain.

Diobradh, aidh, *s. m.* A forsaking, a failing; a banishing; a banishment. *Corn* difraedd.

Diochioll, *s.* See **Dicheall**

Diochairt, *v.* See **Dichairt.**

† **Diochuidh**, *a* Small.—*Shaw*

Diochuimhne, *s. f.* See **Dichuimhne**

Diod, *s. m.* (*Fr.* jet) A drop.

Diodag, aig, *s f.* (*dim.* of diod.) A drop of water. *N. pl.* diodagan. A tuiteam na dhiodagan, *falling in drops.*

† **Diodhailin**, *s* (*Ir. id*) A mote, an atom —*Shaw.*

Diofhlainn, *a.* Pale, bloodless.

Diog, *s.* See **Dioe.**

Diog, *s. m.* A word, a voice. Na h-abair diog, *say not a word*

Diogail, *v. a.* Suck closely; tickle *Pret a* dhiogail, *sucked, fut. aff. a.* diogailidh, *shall suck*

Diogalach, *a* Sucking closely.

Diogaladh, aidh, *s. m.* A sucking closely

Diogan, ain, *s. m* (*Ir. id*) Revenge, spite; severity, cruelty.

Dioganach, *a.* (*Ir.* diogandha.) Revengeful, spiteful; severe, cruel. Gu dioganach, *revengeful. Com.* and *sup.* dioganaiche.

Dioganachd, *s. f.* Revenge, spite, cruelty; revengefulness, spitefulness.

Dioganta, *a.*, *from* diogan. (*Ir. id*) Revengeful, spiteful; severe, cruel.—*Shaw*

Diogantachd, *s. f.* (*Ir.* diogantachd) Revengefulness, spitefulness; severity, cruelty, fierceness.—*Shaw.*

Dioghail, *v. a* Revenge, repay, requite. *Pret. a.* dhioghail, *revenged, fut. aff. a* dioghailidh, *shall revenge*

Dioghailt, *s. f.* (*Ir.* dioghalt) Revenge, vengeance Air ioma-chrith chum dioghailt, *trembling for revenge* —*Mac Lach.*

Dioghailte, *p. part.* of dioghail.

† **Dioghais**, *a.* (*Ir. id*) High, tall, stately.

Dioghaltach, *a* Revengeful, vindictive; fond. Dioghaltach air branndi, *fond of brandy.*—*Old Song. Com* and *sup.* dioghaltaiche.

Dioghaltach, aich, *s m.* An avenger; a revengeful person. An dioghaltach mi-cheart, *the unjust avenger* —*Sm.*

Dioghaltair, *s. m* (dioghalt fhear.) An avenger; a revengeful man. *N. pl.* dioghaltairean —*Stew. Rom*

Dioghaltas, ais, *s m.* (*Ir.* dioghaltus) Revenge; vengeance. Dhomhsa buinidh dioghaltas, *to me belongeth vengeance.*—*Stew Deut.* Dean dioghaltas, *avenge, revenge;* cha dean thu dioghaltas, *thou shalt not avenge* —*Stew. Lev.*

Dioghaltasach, *a* (*Ir.* dioghaltusach.) Revengeful, vindictive. *Com.* and *sup.* dioghaltasaiche, *more* or *most vindictive.*

† **Dioghann**, *a.* (*Ir. id.*) Plentiful, not scanty.—*Shaw.*

Dioghbhail, *s. m.* and *f.* (*Ir id.*) Damage; detriment, destruction.

Dioghbhalach, *a.* See **Diughbhalach.**

Dioghladair, *s. m* An avenger; a revengeful man. Didean o 'n dioghladair, *defence from the avenger.*—*Stew. Num N. pl* dioghladairean.

Dioghladaireachd, *s f.* Revenge; revengefulness

Dioghladh, aidh, *s. m.* An avenging, a revenging; a repaying, revenge; requital, injustice.

Dioghladh, (a), *pr. part.* of dioghail. Avenging, revenging, repaying

Dioghluim, *v. a* (*Ir. id.*) Glean, lease, weed *Pret a* dhioghluim, *gleaned, fut. aff. a* dioghluimidh, *shall* or *will glean.* A dioghluim an arbhair, *gleaning the corn*

Dioghluim, uim, *s. f.* A gleaning or leasing, gleanings Fear dioghluim, *a gleaner*, luchd dio-ghluim, *gleaners* —*Stew Mic.* Dioghluim t-fhogharaidh, *the gleanings of thy harvest* —*Stew Lev.*

Dioghlumair, *s m.* A gleaner, a weeder *N. pl* dioghlumairean

Dioghnadh, aidh, *s. m.* Contempt.

† **Dioghnas**, *a.* Rare —*Shaw*

Dioghradh, aidh, *s. m* (*Ir id*) Moroseness; rudeness

Dioghradhach, *a* Morose, rude, unlovely.

† **Dioghrais**, *adv* (*Ir id*) Constantly, frequently.

Dioghraiseach, *a* Beloved.

† **Dioghrog**, *v* Belch —*Shaw.*

Diogladh, aidh, *s m* A sucking closely, a tickling.

Diogladh, (a), *pr part* of diogail Sucking, tickling. Seillean a diogladh cluarain, *a bee sucking the thistle flower* —*Macdon*

Diograis, *s f.* (*Ir id*) Diligence; a secret —*Shaw.*

Diogras, ais, *s. m.* (*Ir. id*) Honesty, integrity, uprightness; *also*, zeal, ardent zeal

† **Diol**, *a.* (*Ir id*) Worthy; sufficient.

Diol, *s m* (*Ir id*) An object, end; use; a selling; sufficiency; satisfaction.—*Shaw*

Diol, *s. m.* (*Corn.* dyal. *W* dial. *Ir* diol) Restitution, recompense, requital; pay, satisfaction, ransom; a weaning Diol-deirc, *an object of charity* —*Shaw.* Bu dubh a dhiol, *black was his fate.*—*G. P.*

Diol, *v. a.* Restore, recompense, requite, pay; satisfy, empty; change, renew, wean *Pret. a* dhiol, *requited, fut aff. a* diolaidh, *shall requite.* Diol t-fhiacha, *pay thy debts* —*Stew 2 K* Diolamaid do 'n iompachan, *let us pay to the penitent* —*Sm* Diol dhomh, *pay me*, diol riu droch ghniomh an lamh, *requite them their bad deeds* —*Id.* Diolaibh a ghloine gu bonn, *empty the glass to the bottom.*—*Old Song. Fut pass* diolar, *shall be requited*

Diolachd, *s f*, *from* diol (*Ir id*) Requital; restoration; recompense, satisfaction, payment, an orphan.

Dioladair, *s. m* An avenger, a revengeful man

Dioladaireachd, *s f.* The conduct of an avenger; recompense

Dioladh, aidh, *s m* A requiting, a restoring, a recompensing; restitution; requital, recompense, satisfaction, payment. Dioladh iomlan, *full restitution* —*Stew. Exod* Ni e dioladh, *he will make good* —*Stew. Lev*

Diolaidh, *fut aff. a.* of diol. Shall or will requite See **Diol.**

Diolaidh, *gen sing* of dioladh, which see

Diolaidheachd, *s f.* Requital, restoration, recompense, payment.

Diolain, *a* Illegitimate, as a child, bastard Leanabh diolain, *an illegitimate child*, is clann diolain sibh, *you are bastards* —*Stew Heb.* Urr dhiolain, *a bastard.*

Diolain. See **Dioghluim.**

Diolair, *s. m.* (diol-fhear.) An avenger; a restorer, rewarder, requiter. *N. pl.* diolairean.

Diolaireachd, *s. f.* The conduct of an avenger; requital; revengefulness.

Diolam, aim, *s. m.* Gleanings, leasings; a gleaning. See Dioghlum.

Diolamair, *s. m.* A gleaner. Contracted for *dioghlumair*.

Diolanas, ais, *s. m.* (*Ir. id.*) Illegitimacy, bastardy; fornication. Fhuair i urr an diolanas, *she got a child by fornication.*

Diolanta, *a.* (*Ir.* diolunta.) Brave, manly, stout; generous, hospitable.

Diolantas, ais, *s. m.* (*Ir.* dioluntas.) Manhood, bravery; generosity, hospitality.

Diolar, *fut. pass.* of diol; which see.

Diolarachadh, aidh, *s. m.* A depopulating; depopulation; laying waste; pillage.

Diolarachd, *s. f.* Depopulation; laying waste.

Diolaraich, *v. a.* Depopulate, lay waste, pillage. *Pret. a.* dhiolaraich, *pillaged; fut. aff. a.* diolaraichidh, *shall* or *will pillage.*

† **Diolbhrugh**, *s. m.* A shop.

Diol-chuan, ain, *s. m.* A shop.—*Shaw.*

Diol-déirc, *s. m.* An object of charity; *also*, a giving of charity.

† **Diolg**, *v. a.* Dismiss; forgive. *Pret. a.* dhiolg, *dismissed.*

† **Diolgadh**, aidh, *s. m.* Dismissal; forgiveness; a dismissing, a forgiving.

Diollad, aid, *s. f.; properly*, diolaid; which see. (*Ir.* diallaid.) A saddle. Cuiribh diollad air an asail, *saddle the ass.—Stew.* 1 *K.* *N. pl.* diolladan.

Diolladachadh, aidh, *s. m.* A saddling. Dà asail air an diolladachadh, *two asses saddled.—Stew.* 1 *K.*

Diolladair, *s. m.* A saddle-maker. *N. pl.* diolladairean.

Diolladaireachd, *s. f.* Saddle-making. Ris an diolladaireachd, *at saddle-making.*

Diollaidich, *v. a.* Saddle. *Pret. a.* dhiollaidich, *saddled; fut. aff. a.* diollaidichidh, *shall saddle.*

Diolmhanach, aich, *s. m.* (*from* diol, *pay*, and the Germano-Celtic, manach, *man.*) A hired soldier; a mercenary, a hireling; a hero; a stout man; a handsome man. *N. pl.* diol-mhanaich.

In the last two meanings, *diolmhanach* is commonly pronounced and written *diùlnach*. O'Brien observes, that the contracted form of this word, *diùlnach*, is particularly used in the Irish Celtic to signify a soldier, which word properly means a hireling. *Lat.* soldurii, qui salario conducuntur. *Vid. Littlet. Dict.* Hence it signifies a brave, lusty, stout man; also a generous man; one different from the plebeian class. The French call a soldier *soldat*, from *solde*, hire, *or* payment; and the English word *soldier*, it may here be observed, is formed on *soldurius*, a Latinized form of *soldurr*, a Gaulic term, meaning a hired person.

Diolta, *p. part.* of diol. Revenged, avenged; paid, requited. Gum bi mi diolta, *that I be revenged.—Stew. Jud.*

Diol-thuarasdal, ail, *s. m.* Reward, recompense, wages. Diol-thuarasdal dligheach, *a just recompense.—Stew. Heb.*

Dioluim, *v. a.* Glean, weed. *Pret. a.* dhioluim, *gleaned; fut. aff. a.* diolumaidh, *shall glean.* Diolumaidh mi iad gu buileach, *I shall glean them thoroughly.—Stew. G. B.* Written also *dioghluim.*

Diolunta, *a.* (*Ir. id.*) Brave, stout, generous.—*Shaw.*

Dioluntas, ais, *s. m.* (*Ir. id.*) Bravery, stoutness, generosity.

Diom, *comp. pron.* Off me; of me; from off me; on me. *Asp. form*, dhiom. Ghabh e truas diom, *he took pity on me.—Orr.* Cha 'n 'eil ball diom a ghluaiseas, *not a limb of me shall move.—Old Song.*

Diom, *s.* See Diomb.

Diomach, *a.* See Diombach.

Diomadh, aidh, *s. m.* Grief, trouble; displeasure, indignation. Mòran diomaidh, *much trouble.—Stew. Ecc.*

Diomaltair, *s. m.* A glutton.—*Shaw.*

Diomas, ais, *s. m.* Pride, arrogance; defiance.

Diomasach, *a.* Bold, haughty, defying; disrespectful. Ghluais Goll gu diomasach, *Gaul moved on haughtily.—Fingalian Poem.*

Diomb, *s. m.* Displeasure, discontent, dissatisfaction. *Asp. form*, dhiomb. Thoill mi do dhiomb, *I have deserved thy displeasure.—Mac Lach.*

Diombach, *a.* (*from* diomb.) Displeased, dissatisfied, discontented; sorrowful, mournful. Diombach ri m' mhathair, *displeased with my mother.—Old Song. Com.* and *sup.* diombaiche.

Diombadh, aidh, *s. m.* (*Ir. id.*) Grief, sorrow, displeasure, indignation.

Diombaiche, *com.* and *sup.* of diombach.

Diombuaidh, *s. f.* Bad luck, mishap, misfortune, defeat. Fhir bhuig nan diombuaidh, *effeminate man of defeats.—Mac Lach.*

Diombuan, *a.* (*Ir. id.*) Transient, not durable. Diombuan, gearr, *transient and short.—Sm.* Is diombuan gach cois air thir gun eòlas, *they make small progress who travel in a strange land.—G. P. Com.* and *sup.* diombuaine.

Diombuidheach, *a.* Dissatisfied, discontented, displeased.

Diombuile, *s. f.* Waste; extravagance; prodigality; abuse.

Diombuileach, *a.* Wasting; extravagant; prodigal; giving without discretion.

Diombuilich, *v. a.* Put to a bad use; waste; give without discretion.

Diomhagad, *s.* (*Ir. id.*) Enfranchisement; liberty; freedom.

Diomhain, *a.* Vain, useless, to no purpose, unavailable; lazy; frivolous. *Asp. form*, dhiomhain. Is diomhain d' fhuran, *vain is thy joy.—Oss. Gaul.* Beairt dhiomhain, *vain doings.—Sm.* Iasgair diomhain, *the bird called King's-fisher. Com.* and *sup.* diomhaine.

Diomhair, *a.* Secret, hidden, concealed, mysterious, dark, lonely; unintelligible. *Asp. form*, dhiomhair. O chomhairle dhiomhair, *from dark counsels.—Sm.* Ionad diomhair tairneanaich, *the secret place of thunder.—Id.* Thog e gu diomhair a shleagh, *he lifted his spear by stealth.—Oss. Tem.*

Diomhaireach, *a.* Secret, hidden, concealed; mysterious, dark, unintelligible; disposed to be dark, mysterious, or unintelligible; mystic.

Diomhaireachd, *s. f.* Secretness, mysteriousness; mystery; a secret; a secret place; loneliness; solitude; privacy; concealment; obscurity; darkness. Diomhaireachd mhòr, *great mystery.—Stew. Eph.* An diomhaireachd, *their secrets.—Stew. Gen.* Ann an diomhaireachd, *in secret;* diomhaireachd nam bailte beag, *the solitude of villages.—Sm.*

Diomhaltas, ais, *s. m.* (*Ir. id.*) Caution; notice.

Diomhanach, *a.* (*perhaps* diomhaoineach.) Idle; lazy; trifling; frivolous; vain; nugatory. Cainnt dhiomhanach, *vain language, idle talk.—Sm.* Breuga diomhanach, *vain lies*, or *lying vanities.—Id. Com.* and *sup.* diomhanaiche.

Diomhanas, ais, *s. m.* Vanity; idleness; laziness. *Asp. form*, dhiomhanas. Tùis do dhiomhanas, *incense to vanity.—Stew. Jer.* Ann an diomhanas, *in vain. N. pl.* diomhanasa, *or* -an. Diomhanasa breugach, *lying vanities.—Stew. Jon.*

DIOMHAR, *a.* (*Ir. id.*) Dark, mystical; secret; lonely; private. Written also *diomhair*.

DIOMHARACHD, *s.f.* (*Ir. id.*) Darkness; mystery; a secret; secrecy; loneliness; privateness. See also DIOMHAIREACHD.

DIOMHARAN, ain, *s. m.* (*from* diomhair.) A hermit's cell; a mystery; a hermit.

DI-MOLADAIR, *s. m.* A slanderer; one who dispraises or disparages.

DI-MOLADH, aidh, *s. m.* (*Ir. id.*) A dispraising, a disparaging; dispraise, disparagement, slander.

DI-MOLTA, *a.* Dispraised, blamed, censured, disparaged, slandered.

DIOMRAC, aic, *s. m.* (*Ir. id.*) A temple.

DION, *s.* (*Ir. id.*) Shelter, protection, defence, refuge; a covert, a fence. Dion is targaid, *a shelter and a shield.*—*Sm.* Dh' fhalbh an dion, *their defence is gone.*—*Stew. Numb.* Cum dion, *shelter, protect. Asp. form*, dhion. Fu dhion, *sheltered.*

DION, *s. m.* (*Ir. id.*) The second semimetre or *leth-rann* of a verse, consisting of two quartans; it is more commonly called *comhad.*

DION, *v. a.* (*Ir. id.*) Shelter, protect, guard, cover. Dion mi le d' sgeith, *protect me with thy wing.*—*Sm. Pret. a.* dhion, *sheltered; fut. aff. a.* dionaidh, *shall shelter;* dionaidh e le ghràs, *he will protect with his grace.*—*Sm.* Dion am fuar, *cover the cold.*—*Id.*

DIONACH, *a.* (*from* dion.) Secure, sheltered; affording shelter; water-proof, water-tight; closely joined; firmly built, as a vessel. Aite dionach, *a sheltered place, a sheltering place;* leis is dionaiche long, *whose ships are the firmest built.*—*Oss. Lodin.*

DIONACHADH, aidh, *s. m.* A securing, a defending; a making water-tight or water-proof; a sheltering; security.

DIONACHD, *s. f.* Security, shelter; the state of being water-proof.

DIONADAIR, *s. m.* A defender, a protector; a fender. *N. pl.* dionadairean.

DIONADH, aidh, *s. m.* A defending, a protecting, a sheltering; a defence, a shelter, security. Sruthan dionaidh, *streams of defence.*—*Stew. Is.*

DIONADH, (a), *pr. part.* of dion; which see.

DIONAG, aig, *s. f.* A hoggerel. *N. pl.* dionagan.

DIONAICH, *v. a.* Secure; join closely, as a vessel; make water-tight or water-proof; shelter. *Pret. a.* dhionaich; *fut. aff. a.* dionaichidh, *shall make secure.*

DIONAICHE, *com.* and *sup.* of dionach. More or most water-tight. See DIONACH.

DIONAIRM, *s. m.* Refuge.—*Shaw.*

† DIONAISG, *v. a.* Disjoin, loosen, undo.

DION-AITE, *s. m.* A refuge, a place of shelter, a sanctuary. *N. pl.* dion-aiteachan.

DIONASGACH, *a.* (*Ir.* dionasgtha.) Dissolute.

DIONASGADH, aidh, *s. m.* A disjoining, an unloosening.

DION-BHREID, *s. f.* An apron.—*Shaw.*

DION-CHAINNT, *s. f.* A speech in defence of any person.—*Shaw.*

DION-FHEACHD, *s. f.* Fencibles.

DIONG, *v. a.* and *n.* Make a tinkling noise. *Pret. a.* dhiong; *fut. aff.* diongaidh.

DIONG, *v. a.* (*Lat.* jungo.) Join; match, equal; overcome, conquer. *Pret. a.* dhiong, *joined; fut. aff. a.* diongaidh, *shall join.* Diongam-sa righ Inniscon, *let me match the king of Inniscon.*—*Oss. Fing.* Is ioma ceud a dhiong thu, *many a hundred hast thou conquered.*—*Death of Carril.*

DIONG, dionga, *s. m.* A tinkling noise; the chime of a bell.

† DIONG, *a.* (*Lat.* dignus.) Worthy. *Pl.* dionga.

DIONGACH, *a.* Able to overcome; matching; suitable; proper, meet, worthy. *Com.* and *sup.* diongaiche.

DIONGAIL, *a.* (dion-gabhail.) Worthy; fit, proper, suitable; fit to bear.

DIONGAIL, *s. f.* A continued tinkling.

DIONGALTA, *a.* (*perhaps* diongbhuailte. *Ir.* diongmhalta. Firmly joined; fastened; fast; fixed; sufficient; firm, tight; strong, effective, able-bodied; meet, proper, suitable. Seachd cathaich diongmhalta, *seven able-bodied warriors.*—*Old Poem.*

DIONGALTACHD, *s. f.* Firmness; tightness; the state of being fast, fixed, or firmly bound.

DIONGMHALTA, *a.* (*Ir. id.*) See DIONGALTA.

DION-LONG-PHORT, -phuirt, *s. m.* A garrison.—*Shaw.*

† DIONN, *s.* (*Ir. id.*) A hillock, a hill. See Dinn.

DIONNAL, ail, *s. m.* A shot. More frequently written *deannal.*

DIONNAN, ain, *s. m., dim.* of dionn. (*Ir. id.*) A little hill.

DIONTA, dionte, *p. part.* of dion. Defended, protected.

† DIOR, *a.* (*Ir. id.*) Meet, proper, decent.—*Shaw.*

† DIORANG, *v. n.* (*Ir. id.*) Belch.

† DIOR, *s. m.* (*Ir. id. Lat.* jur-is.) A law.

† DIORACH, *a.* (*from* dior.) Lawful. See DÌREACH.

† DIORGAS, ais, *s. m.* (*Ir. id.*) Uprightness, integrity.—*Shaw.*

† DIORACHRACH, *a.* (*Ir. id.*) Lawless.

† DIORMA, *s. m.* A troop; a crowd; a company. *Lat.* turma *and* turba. *Ir.* diorma. *W.* tyrva.

DIORMACH, *a.* In troops; in companies; crowded; numerous; infinite.

† DIORNA, ai, *s. m.* (*Ir. id.*) A quantity.

DIORRÀSACH, *a.* Irascible, hasty in temper; rash, forward, fierce. Farpuis diorrasach, *rash rivalry.*—*Macfar. Com.* and *sup.* diorrasaiche.

DIORRASACHD, *s. f.* Irascibility, hastiness, rashness, forwardness, fierceness.

DIORRASAN, ain, *s. m.* A fretful person; a grasshopper; a snarl.

DIORRASANACH, *a.* Irascible; fretful; snarling.

DIORRASANAICH, *s. f.* Irascibility; snarling.

DIORRASG, aisg, *s. f.* Hastiness of temper, rashness, forwardness, fierceness.

DIORRASGACH, *a.* Irascible, rash, forward, fierce.

† DIORSAN, ain, *s. m.* (*Ir. id.*) Bad news.

DIOSG, *a.* (*Ir.* deasc.) Dry, barren; an epithet applied to a cow that yields no milk. Bo dhiosg, *a cow that yields no milk.*

† DIOSG, *s. m.* (*Ir. id. Lat.* discus.) A plate or platter; a dish. Is brathair do 'n diosgan tuairnear, *the turner is brother to the dish.*—*G. P.*

DIOSGADH, aidh, *s. m.* Dryness, barrenness; the state of a cow when she yields no milk; a grating, a squeaking noise. Tha bhò dol an diosgadh, *the cow begins to grow dry.*

DIOSGAN, ain, *s. m.* A grating of the teeth; a gnashing, a crashing. Diosgan air gach maide, *every timber cracking.*—*Macdon.*

DIOSGAR, air, *s. m.* A mob, a rabble.

DIOSGARNACH, aich, *s. m.* A mob, a rabble; one of a mob.

† DIOSMUIG, *v.* (*Ir. id.*) Snuff a candle.

DIOSNAIDHM, *a.* Smooth, without knots, even.

DIOT, *com. pron.* Of thee, from thee; off thee. *Asp. form*, dhiot. *Ir.* diot.

DIOT, *gen.* diota *and* diotach. A breakfast, a meal of meat.

(*Eng* diet. *Gr.* δίαιτα. *Span.* dieta) Diot-mhòr, *dinner;* an deigh thràth diotach, *after breakfast*, nan itheadh na coin do dhiot, *if the dogs had eaten your breakfast* —*G. P.*

DIOT, *s m.* (*Fr.* jet.) A drop, as of water. Cha 'n 'eil diot ann, *there is not a drop.* More properly *diod.*

DIOTAG, aig, *s f* (*dim* of diot) A little drop, a drop Diotag uisge, *a drop of water, a drop of rain* *N. pl* diotagan, *drops.* Uisge a tuiteam na dhiotagan, *rain falling in drops* Diotag is more properly written *diodag.*

† DIOTH, *v. n* Die, decay Hence *Eng.* die, *and* death.

DIOTH, *s*, written more frequently *dìth*, which see.

DIOTHACHADH, aidh, *s m* A destroying; destruction Diothachadh a shluaigh, *the destruction of his people.*—*Fingalian Poem*

DIOTHADH, aidh, *s m* A decaying, dying, decay, death.

DIOTHADH, (a), *pr part* of dioth Decaying, dying, withering. Mar rainich a searga' 's a diothadh, *like fens withering and dying* —*Oss. Fin and Lor*

DIOTHAICH, *v. a* and *n* Destroy, lay waste, die, wither *Pret a* dhiothaich, *destroyed*, *fut. aff a* diothaichidh, *shall* or *will destroy*

DIOTHREAMH, eimh, *s m* A wilderness, a desert, a hermitage More properly, *dìthreabh;* which see

DIOTHRUAILL, *v a* (*Ir id*) Unsheathe.—*Shaw* *Pret a.* dhiothruaill, *unsheathed*

DIPINN, *s f* A net

† DIPLINN, *s f* April

DÌR, *v.* Climb, ascend, mount *Pret. a.* dhìr, *mounted*, *fut aff a* dìridh, *shall* or *will mount* Dìribh air aghaidh nam beann, *ascend the brow of the hills* —*Oss. Fing*

† DIRE, *s f* (*Ir id*) A tax or tribute —*Shaw*

DIREACH, *a* (*Ir* direach. *Lat.* directus) Straight, even; perpendicular, upright, just, honest, right; direct, frugal Air ceumaibh dìreach rèidh, *on a straight plain path.*—*Sm* Is dìreach Dia, *God is upright* —*Id* Tha dheanadas dìreach, *his work is right* —*Stew Pro.* Caol dìreach, *straightway, straightforward*, dìreach glan, *exactly so*, dìreach nur thàinig e, *just as he came;* dìreach air adhairt, *straightforward* Dìreach nasheasamh, *standing upright*, dan dìreach, *verse, metre* *Com.* and *sup* dìriche

DÌREACHADH, aidh, *s. m.* A making straight, even, or perpendicular, a becoming straight

DÌREACHAN, ain, *s m* (*from* dìreach) A perpendicular —*Shaw*

DÌREACHAS, ais, *s m.* Uprightness; straightness, honesty, perpendicularity.

DÌREACHD, *v. a.* Geld —*Shaw.*

DÌREADH, idh, *s. m* (*W* dirch) A climbing, a mounting, ascending; ascension, a direction

DIREADH, idh, *s m* (*Ir. id*) A panegyric —*Shaw*

DÌREADH, (a), *pr part* of dìr Climbing, ascending, mounting; a panegyric Ceo a dìreadh aonaich, *mist ascending a hill.*—*Oss Trath.*

† DIREAGADH, aidh, *s m* (*Ir id*) A direction

DÌRICH, *v a.* (*Lat.* dirigo *Ir* dirigh) Make straight, even, or perpendicular, direct; mount, ascend, climb *Pret a.* dhìrich; *fut aff. a* dìrichidh, *shall* or *will make straight.* Fear nach dìrich a dhruim, *one who will not straighten his back* —*Macdon.* Cha dìrich thu 'n fireach, *thou shalt not climb the steep* —*Orr* Dhìrich e 'n carbad, *he mounted the chariot.*—*Mac Lach.* *Fut pass* dìrichear.

DÌRICHE, *com* and *sup* of dìreach; which see.

DÌRICHEAR, *fut. pass.* of dìrich This tense is also used impersonally, as, dìrichear [leinn] am monadh, *we climbed the hill.*

† DIRIM, *a.* (*Ir. id*) Numerous, plentiful, great

DIS, *a.* Two. *Span.* dos. See DITHIS.

DIS, *a.* Chill, poor, miserable.

DI-SATHAIRN, *s.* Saturday. Di-sathairn so chaidh, *last Saturday;* di-Sathairn so tighinn, *next Saturday;* an dara di-Sathairn, *the second Saturday.*—*Macdon.* La Sathairn, *a Saturday;* thainig e air la Sathairn, *he came on a Saturday* *Lat.* dies Saturni *Arm* di-Satorn.

DI-SA, *emphatic form of* di. To her, of her; off her; to it, of it; off it. *Asp form*, dhi-sa.

DISBEIRT, *a.* (*Ir. id.*) Twofold, double

DISCIR, *a* (*Ir. id.*) Sudden, quick, active; fierce.

† DISCRÉIDE, *a* (*Ir. id*) Discretion.

DISD, dìsde, *s. f* A mow, a rick; a layer of stalked peats or turf, a die, dice. *N. pl* disdean

DISE, *s f* (*Corn* dise) A mow, a rick.

DI-SE, *emphatic form of* di. Of her; to her; off her.

DISEART, *s.* A corruption of *ti 's airde*, as, Clach an Diseart, *i. e.* clach an Ti 's airde, in Glenorchy

† DISGIR, *a.* (*Ir. id*) Sudden; quick; active, fierce.

DÌSLE, *com.* and *sup.* of dìleas. More or most related.

DÌSLE, *s f.* Love, esteem, friendship; fidelity, loyalty; subjection; subordination; *also*, property; dice *N. pl.* dìslean. Ag iomairt dhìslean, *playing at dice*

DISLEACHD, *s. f.* Faithfulness, relation, connexion, propriety

DISLEAN, *n. pl* of dìsle. Relatives; dice

DISLEAN, ein, *s. m* A dice-box.

DISLEANAICHE, *s. m.* A player at dice, a gambler.

DI-SLIGHEACH, *a*, di, *priv. and* slighe (*Ir id*) Devious, straggling, impervious, immethodical, uncouth.—*Macdon.*

DISNE, *s f* A die or dice. *N. pl.* disnean. A cluich air dhisnean, *playing at dice*

DÌSNEAN, *n pl.* of dìsne. Dice. *D pl.* dìsnibh; *asp. form*, deud shnaithte mar dhìsnibh, *teeth polished like dice.*—*Old Song.* A cluich air dhisnean, *playing at dice.*

DÌSNEAR, air, *s. m* A dice-player

DÌSREAD, id, *s. m* (*Ir. id*) The aspergillum used at mass to sprinkle holy water on the people

DÌST, *s. f* (*W.* dist, *joist*) A joist; *also*, a mow, a rick, a die or dice.

DÌT, *v. a.* Condemn; sentence; reproach; surrender, (*Lat.* ded-o) *Pret. a* dhìt, *fut aff. a.* dìtidh, *shall condemn* Na dit an t-òg, *reproach not the youth* —*Oss Duth.* Co dhìteas iad? *who shall condemn them?*—*Sm. Fut. pass* ditear.

DÌTEADH, idh, *s. m* (*Gr.* δίαιτα, *a judgment*) A condemning, a reproaching, a condemnation, a judgment; a sentence, a reproach, a surrender Ag iarruidh dìtidh, *asking judgment* —*Stew. Acts*

DÌTEAG, eig, *s f* A peep Diteag ort, *a peep at you*, *I peep at you.*

DÌTEAGAICH, *s f.* A peeping; frequent peeping; continued peeping Ri diteagaich, *peeping*

DÌTEAM, 1 *sing pres ind a* of dit. I sentence. *Also, for* dìtidh mi, *I will sentence*

DÌTH, *s. f* (*Ir id*) Want, defect, failure, deficiency; destruction. Dìth bidh, *want of food*, cha robh aon dìth air, *he had no want* *Asp form*, dhìth Air dhìth céill, *void of understanding.*—*Stew Pro. ref.* Thìd iad gu dìth, *they shall go to destruction* —*Oss Tem* A dhìth fasgaidh, *for want of shelter.*—*Stew Job.* Ciod tha dhìth ort? *what do you want?* Written also *dì*

DÌTH, *comp. pron* See D'I.

DÌTHCHEALTAIR, *s. m* A necromantic veil that renders things invisible.

Dìtheach, *a.* (*from* dìth.) Indigent, poor; *also*, an indigent person; a beggar.—*Shaw.*

Dìtheachadh, aidh, *s. m.* A causing to cease; a failing.

Dìtheadh, idh, *s. m.* A hoarding up, a concealing; destruction.

Dìthean, ein, *s. m.* Darnel; corn-marigold, tare; an herb; any flower. *N. pl.* dìthein. Dìthein nan gleann, *the flowers of the valley.*—*Oss.*

Dìtheanach, *a.* (*from* dìthean.) Abounding in darnels; full of wild flowers or of herbs.—*Macint.* and *Macfar.*

Dìthich, *v. a.* and *n.* (*from* dìth.) Cause to cease or fail, fail. *Pret. a.* dhìthich; *fut. aff. a.* dìthichidh. Dìthichidh mi iomhaighean, *I will cause images to cease.*—*Stew. Ezek.* Dhìthich mo chairdean, *my friends have failed.*—*Oss. Conn.*

Dìthis, *a.* Two; twice. *Asp. form*, dhìthis. A dìthis mhac, *her two sons.*—*Stew. Exod.* A dhìthis mhac, *his two sons.* Dìthis deich geamhra, *twice ten summers.*—*Ull.*

Gr. δὶς. *Ir.* dis. *Dan.* twees. *Eng.* twice. *Span.* dos.

Dithist, *a.* Two. Nar dithist, *we two together.*—*Macint.*

† **Dìthleach**, *a.* (*Ir. id.*) Forgetful, neglectful.

Dithreabh, eibh, *s.*, di, *priv. and* treabh. (*Ir. id. W.* didreuvar.) A desert, a wilderness, an uncultivated place; a hermitage; a hermit. A dithreabh, *her desert.*—*Stew. Is.*

Dithreabhach, *a.* (*Ir. id.*) Desert; uncultivated; solitary.

Dithreabhach, aich, *s. m.* A hermit; an anchoret; a man who has no society nor common habitation with others; one living separate from his tribe.

Dith-reachdach, *a.* Lawless, insubordinate. Gu dìthreachdach, *insubordinately.*

Ditidh, *fut. aff. a.* of dit; which see.

† **Diu**, *adv.* (*Ir. id.*) Long since; a long time.

Diu, *s.* Refuse; the worst part of any thing; *also*, abject, worthless; *rarely*, a long time.

Diu, (an), *adv.* (*Lat.* diu.) To-day. Written also *diugh;* which see.

Diu. See **Diugh.**

Diubh, *comp. pron.* Of them; off them; from amongst them. *Asp. form*, dhiubh. Aon diubh, *one of them;* fear diubh, *one of them;* co dhiùbh? *which of them?* co dhiùbh is maith no olc leat e, *whether you take it well or ill;* tha mi coma co dhiùbh, *I care not; I care not which of them.*

Diubhaidh, *a.* Low, abject.

Diùbhail, *s. m.* and *f.* Mischief, harm. Written also *diobhail;* which see.

Diùbhalach, *a.* Mischievous, hurtful, calamitous, noxious. *Asp.* dhiùbhalach. Ro dhiùbhalach, *very destructive.*—*Stew. Exod.* *Com.* and *sup.* diùbhalaiche.

Diubhar, air, *s. m.* (*Lat.* differ. *Ir.* difir.) Difference. Cha dean e diubhar sam bi, *it will make no difference.*

Diubh-sa, Diubh-se, *emphatic form* of diubh.

Diùc, *s. f.* The pip, a disease among fowls.

Diùc, *v. n.* Cry out, exclaim; approach, present one's self. *Pret. a.* dhiùc, *exclaimed.*

† **Diùcair**, *s. f.* A bladder for holding up fishing-nets.—*Shaw.*

Diuchair, *v. a.* Drive away; keep off.

Diùchd, *s. m.* A duke.

Lat. dux *and* duc-o. *Corn.* dug. *leader. Arm.* dug *and* doug. *Fr.* duc. *It.* duce *and* doge. *Span.* duque, *duke. Chald.* ducos, *general. Heb.* duk, *take charge of. Syr.* dok, *take charge of.*

Diudan, ain, *s. m.* Giddiness, thoughtlessness; a thoughtless person.

Diudanach, *a.* Giddy, thoughtless.

Diudhal, ail, *s. m.* Mischief, harm, mischance, calamity.

Diug, *v. n.* (*Ir. id.*) Cluck; cackle.—*Shaw.*

Diug, *s.* A word by which poultry are called, perhaps a corruption of *chuck.* Na abair diug ris an eun gus an tig e as an ubh, *say not chuck to a bird till it comes from the egg.*—*G. P.*

Diugh, (an), *adv.* (*Lat.* diu.) To-day, this day. An diugh air aon raon, *to-day on the field.*—*Oss. Conn.* An diugh fhèin, *on this very day.*—*Oss. Fing.*

Diùide, *a.* (*Ir. id.*) Shy, timid, bashful; tender-hearted; flexible. Gach creutair diùide, *every timid creature.*—*Macfar.*

Diùideach, *a.* Shy, timid, bashful; tender-hearted; flexible.

Diùireas, eis, *s. m.* Any worthless thing; the worst part of any thing. Gach diùireas gu deireadh, *the worst is always reserved to the last.*—*G. P.*

Diùideachd, *s. f.* Shyness, timidity, bashfulness.

Diul, *v. a.* Suck. See **Deoghail.**

Diùl. See **Diol.**

Diùlanta, *a.* (*Ir. id.*) Heroic, brave; stout, lusty; generous, hospitable.

Diùlnach, aich, *s. m.* A youth, a young hero; a handsome youth; a stout man; a hireling. A liuthad diùlnach ainnis, *the many a poor youth.*—*Macfar.*

Diùlnach is more properly written *diùnlaoch;* which see.

Diùlt, *v. a.* (*Ir. id.*) Refuse, deny, reject, disown. *Pret. a.* dhiùlt, *denied; fut. aff. a.* diùltaidh. Toil-inntinn dhiùlt, *refused consolation.*—*Sm.* Nach diùltadh stri, *who would not refuse battle.*—*Macfar.*

Diùlantas, ais, *s. m.* (*Ir. id.*) Heroism, bravery; stoutness; generosity, hospitality.

Diùlt, *s. m.* (*Ir. id.*) A refusal, a denial, a negative. Fhuair e 'n diùlt, *he got a refusal.*

Diùltadh, aidh, *s. m.* A refusing, a denying, a rejecting; a refusal, a denial; a negative. Fhuair mi an diùltadh, *I got a refusal.*

Diùltadh, (a), *pr. part.* of diùlt. Refusing, denying, rejecting.

† **Diùn**, *a.* (*Fr.* jeune. *Ir.* diùn.) Young.

Diùnach, *a.* More frequently written *deonach.*

Diùnlaoch, -laoich, *s. m.* († diùn, *young, and* laoch, *a hero.*) A youth, a young hero; a handsome youth. Ceum air aghairt aig gach diùnlaoch, *each young hero marching forward.*—*Old Poem.*

† **Diùr**, *a.* Bad; difficult; hard; dire. Bu diùr an gabhadh, *it was a dire necessity.*

Arab. dar, *bad. Lat.* dur-us *and* dir-us. *Ir.* diùr. *Eng.* dire.

Diùnach, *a.* Now written *deònach;* which see.

Diurasan, ain, *s. m.* A grasshopper. *N. pl.* diurasain. See **Diorrasan.**

† **Diùrn**, *v. a.* (*Ir. id.*) Drink greedily; gulp, swallow.—*Shaw.*

† **Diùs**, *s. m.* (*Ir. id.*) Protection.

Dlagh, dlaigh, *s. m.* A handful of corn or grass; a lock of hair. *D. pl.* dlaghaibh. Cuid do na dlaghaibh, *some of the handfuls.*—*Stew. Ruth.* Dlaigh gruaige, *a lock of hair.*

Dlaigh. More frequently written *dlagh;* which see.

Dlaimh, *s. f.* Darkness.—*Shaw.*

Dlaogh, *s. m.* (*Stew. Jer.*) More properly *dlagh;* which see.

Dleachd, *s. f.* (*Ir. id.*) A law, statute, ordinance.

Dleas, *v. a.* Procure; merit. *Pret. a.* dhleas, *procured; fut. aff.* dleasaidh, *shall procure.* Dleasaidh arm urram, *arms procure respect.*—*G. P.*

Dleasdanach, *a.* Dutiful; rightful. *Com.* and *sup.* dleasdanaiche.

Dleasdanas, ais, *s. m.* A duty, a right. A reir mo dhleasdanais, *according to my duty.*

Dleasnach, *a.* Contracted for *dleasdanach.*

Dleasnas, ais, *s. m.* Contracted for *dleasdanas.*

Dligead, eid, *s. m.* A separation.—*Shaw.*

Dlighe, *s. f.* (*Corn.* and *Arm.* dle. *Ir.* dlighe.) Right: law; ordinance; due; perquisite; property. Le dlighe cheairt, *with just right.*—*Sm.* Is e so do dhlighe, *this is thy due.*—*Stew. Lev.* Written also *dlithe.*

Dligheach, *a.* (*from* dlighe.) Rightful, lawful; right, due; dutiful. Oighre dligheach, *a rightful heir;* clann dhligheach, *lawful children.*—*Stew. Heb.* An ni a tha dligheach, *that which is right.* Written also *dlitheach.*

Dlighear, *a.* Lawful, due, just, rightful. Thoir moladh dhasan do 'n dlighear e, *give praise to him to whom it is due.*

Dlighear, ir, *s. m.* (*Ir.* dlighthoir.) A lawyer, a magistrate, a justice of the peace.

Dligheil, *a.* (dligh-amhuil), *from* dlighe. Rightful, lawful, just, due; skilled in law; litigious. Duine dligheil, *a litigious person.*

Dlisteanach, *a.* (*Ir. id.*) Lawful, just, rightful; legitimate. Neo-dhlisteanach, *unlawful.*

Dlithe, *s. f.* See **Dlighe.**

Dlitheach, *a.* (*from* dlithe.) Lawful, right, due. An ni sin a tha dlitheach, *that which is lawful.*—*Stew. Ezek.* See also **Dligheach.**

Dlithear, *a.* See **Dlighear.**

Dlochair, *v. a.* Strain, press, squeeze.

Dlochd, *s. m.* A strainer.—*Shaw.*

Dlodan, ain, *s. m.* A strainer.—*Shaw.* *N. pl.* dlodain.

† **Dlomh**, *v.* (*Ir. id.*) Tell, refuse, deny; make plain or evident.

Dlomhadh, aidh, *s. m.* (*Ir. id.*) A refusal, a denial.

† **Dlomhaisinn**, *s. f.* (*Ir. id.*) Destruction.

Dlù, Dlùth, *a.* (*Ir.* dluth.) Thick, dense; close, near; nimble; close in succession; incessant; tight, confined. Neòil a tha dlù mu 'n cuairt, *clouds that are thick around.*—*Oss. Com.* *Asp. form,* dhlù *and* dhlùth. A choille thiugh dhlù, *the thick close wood.*—*Old Song.* Uisge trom dlùth, *heavy incessant rain.*—*Old Song.* Dlù an daimh, *near akin;* gu dlù, *closely, nimbly.* *Dlù* and *dlùth* in government have after them the prepositions *air, do,* or *ri,* either simple or compounded. Is dlù aoibhneas do bhròn, *joy is close upon grief.*—*Ull.* Dlùth ri chéile, *close on each other.*—*Oss. Tem.* Dlù orm, *near me.* Dlùth an daimh, *nearly related.*—*Stew. Ruth.* *Com.* and *sup.* dluithe.

Dlù, Dlùth, *adv.* and *prep.* Near, at hand, close by, close on, bordering on. Mhalmhine, bi dlù, *Malvina, be at hand.*—*Oss. Gaul.* Tha 'chobhair dlù, *his aid is at hand.*—*Sm.*

Dlù-bhailtean, *s. pl.* Suburbs.—*Shaw.*

Dlù-eolach, *a.* Intimate, acquainted, familiar.

Dlù-eolas, ais, *s. m.* Intimacy, familiarity.

Dluigh, *a.* (*Ir. id.*) Active, nimble; prepared.—*Shaw.* Gu dluigh, *actively, nimbly.*

Dluigheachd, *s. f.* Activity, nimbleness.

Dluigheil, *a.* Active, nimble, prepared; tidy, trim, neat, careful.

Dluimh, *s. f.* (*Ir. id.*) A cloud, darkness; a blaze of fire.

Dlùithe, *com.* and *sup.* of dlùth. Near, nearest. See **Dlù.**

Dluithean, *s. m.* (*Ir.* dluithin.) A closet, a little study.

Dlu-lean, *v. a.* Adhere, cleave to, follow closely, pursue. *Pret.* dhlù-lean; *fut. aff.* dlù-leanaidh.

Dlumh, *s.* (*Ir. id.*) Much, plenty.

Dlu-phreas, -phris, *s. m.* A thicket; a thick bush. *N. pl.* dlu-phris *and* dlu-phreasan.

Dlu-phreasach, *a.* Full of thickets or of thick bushes.

Dlùs, *s. m.* Contracted for *dlùthas;* which see.

Dlu-stòl, -stòil, *s. m.* (*Ir. id.*) A close-stool.

Dlùth, *a.* See **Dlù.**

Dlùth, *s. m.* (*Ir. id.*) An enclosure, a fence, a cloister.

Dlùth, *s. m.* The warp of a web. San dlùth no san inneach, *in the harp or woof.*—*Stew. Lev.*

Dlùth, *v. a.* and *n.* Warp; make close; enclose; shut in; pack; compress; join; glue; shrink; approach, draw near. *Pret. a.* dhlùth; *fut. aff. a.* dluthaichidh, *shall warp.*

Dlùthachadh, aidh, *s. m.* A warping; a crowding, a contracting; an approaching; an approach; a contraction.

Dlùthachadh, (a), *pr. part.* of dlùthaich. Approaching, drawing near; crowding, contracting; warping. Do laithean a dlùthachadh, *thy days drawing near.*—*Stew. Deut.* 'G a dlùthachadh fo eigh, *contracting it under the ice.*—*Oss. Tem.*

Dlùthadh, aidh, *s. m.* A joining, glueing; a warping; a crowding; an approaching; a packing close together; a drawing together; a knitting.

Dlùthadh, (a), *pr. part.* of dlùth. Joining, glueing, warping; approaching; packing close; pressing close; knitting; drawing together.

Dlùthaich, *v. a.* and *n.* Join, glue; warp; press together, pack together; approach, draw near. *Pret. a.* dhlùthaich; *fut. aff. a.* dluthaichidh. Dlùthaich ri, *approach;* dluthaichidh e ribh, *he will draw near to you.*—*Stew. Heb.*

Dluthaichear, *fut. pass.* of dlùthaich.

Dluthaichidh, *fut. aff. a.* of dlùthaich. Shall *or* will join. See **Dlùthaich.**

Dluthaichte, *p. part.* of dluthaich. (*Ir.* dluthaighte.) Joined, glued; pressed together, drawn together; compressed; compact, close; knit. Bha an sgiathan dluthaichte, *their wings were joined.*—*Stew. Ezek.*

Dlùthas, ais, *s. m.* Nearness, propinquity, neighbourhood. Mun deachaidh na sloigh an dlùthas, *before the hosts approached each other.*—*Fingalian Poem.*

Dlùth-bhailtean, *n. pl.* Suburbs.

Dlùth-charcair, *s. f.* A labyrinth.

Dlùth-cheangail, *v. a.* Bind firmly.

Dluth-cheangladh, aidh, *s. m.* A binding firmly.

Dlùth-eolach, *a.* Intimate, acquainted, familiar.

Dlùth-eolas, ais, *s. m.* Intimacy, acquaintance, familiarity.

Dluth-lean, *v. a.* Adhere, cleave to, follow closely, pursue. *Pret. a.* dhluth-lean, *pursued; fut. aff. a.* dluth-leanaidh, *shall pursue.* Dluth-leanaibh ris an Tighearna, *adhere to the Lord.*—*Stew. Jos.*

Dlùth-phreas, -phris, *s. m.* A thicket; a thick bush. *N. pl.* dlùth-phreasan. Slios nan dlùth-phreas, *the side of the thickets.*—*Macfar.*

Dlùth-stòl, -stòil, *s. m.* A close-stool.

Dlùth-thairneach, *a.* Attractive.

Dlùth-tharruing, *v. a.* Attract. *Pret. a.* dhluth-tharruing, *attracted.*

Dlùth-tharruingeach, *a.* Attractive, magnetical.

Dluth-tharruingeachd, *s. f.* Magnetism, attraction.

Dluth-tharruingeadh, *s. m.* Attraction.

Dluth-theann, *v. n.* Approach in crowds; crowd together.—*Oss. Fing.* *Pret. a.* dhluth-theann.

Do, *a verbal particle prefixed to the preterite.* Do thubhairt mi, *I said.—Oss. Tem.* Do lub e na neamha, *he bowed the heavens.—Sm.*

This particle is never used affirmatively in the inward Highlands, where the language is spoken in its greatest purity. It is used, however, in the aspirated form, as *dh' èirich*, for *do eirich.*

Do, *prep.* (*Ir.* do.) To, towards, of. When preceding a word beginning with a vowel, *do* very frequently is aspirated; as, dh'Albainn, *to Scotland;* dh' Eirin, *to Ireland;* dh'oidhche is do làth, *by night and by day.*

Do, *pron.* Thy, thine. Do bhean, *thy wife;* d' each, *thy horse.* (*Ir.* do. *Corn.* and *W.* dy. *Arm.* da *and* ta.) Do thigh, *thy house;* in Armoric it is *da tigh.*

Do, *a prepositive particle of negation,* and implies sometimes *difficulty,* and sometimes *impossibility;* as, do-thuigsinn, *unintelligible,* or *difficult to be understood;* do-àireamh, *numberless,* or *difficult to be counted;* do-labhairt, *unspeakable.*

† **Dò**, *a.* (*Ir. id. Lat.* duo.) Two. Now written *dà;* which see.

Doacal, ail, *s. m.* Affliction.

Do'ail, *a.* (*for* domhail.) Crowded; bulky; corpulent; vast.

Do-aireamh, *a.* Numberless, not easily counted.

Do-ainmeachadh, *a.* That cannot be named.

Do-aithneachadh, *a.* Not easily known.

Do-aithriseadh, *a.* Not easily repeated.

Do-aomadh, *a.* Immovable, inflexible, inexorable.

† **Dob**, doib, *s. m.* (*Ir. id.*) A stream, a river.—*Shaw.*

† **Dòb**, *s. m.* (*Ir. id.*) A plaster; a gutter.

† **Dòb**, *v. a.* (*Ir. id.*) Plaster, bedaub, cement. *Pret. a.* dhòb. Hence *Eng.* daub.

Dòbadh, aidh, *s. m.* A plastering, a bedaubing, a besmearing.

Dòbail, *s. f.* A plastering, a daubing over.

Dòbair, *s. m.* (*Ir. id.*) A plasterer. *N. pl.* dobairean.

Dobh, *a.* More frequently written *dobhaidh;* which see.

Dobhaidh, *a.* (*Ir. id.*) Boisterous, stormy; raging, swelling, destructive; felling. Cuan dobhaidh, *a stormy sea.—Ull.* Taibhse dobhaidh na h-oidhche, *the raging spirit of the night.—Oss. Cathula.* Buillean trom dobhaidh, *heavy, felling blows.—Old Poem.*

† **Dobhar**, air, *s. m.* (*Ir. id.*) The border of a country; a territory; water. See **Dur.**

† **Dobhar**, *a.* (*Ir. id.*) Dark, obscure.

Dobhar-chu, -choin, *s. m.* (dobhar *and* cu.) An otter; the king of the otters; *literally,* a water-dog; the *mustela lutra* of Linnæus; *also,* an otter-hound. Iasg a teich' o'n dobhar chu, *fish darting from the otter.—Old Song.*

Dobhar-lus, -luis, *s. m.* Water-cresses; a water plant.

Dobhar-shoitheach, -shoithche, *s. m.* A bucket, a pail, a pitcher.

Do-bheachdachaidh, *a.* Unimaginable, not easily conceived.

Do-bheart, -bheirt, *s. m.* (*Ir.* dobhart.) An evil deed; iniquity; mischief, a prank. Le do-bheart, *with iniquity.—Stew. Mic.* Fear do-bheirt, *an evil doer.—Stew. Is.* Luchd do-bheirt, *transgressors.—Stew. Pro.* Leth do dho-bheirt, *the half of thy vice.—Old Song.*

Do-bhliadhnach, *a corrupted form of* da-bhliadhnach; which see.

Do-bholadh, aidh, *s. m.* A stench.

Dobhran, ain, *s. m.* (*from* dobhar.) An otter; the *mustela lutra* of Linnæus; *also,* a common name given to a dog. *N. pl.* dobhrain.

Do-bhranach, *a.* (*from* dobhran.) Abounding in otters; like an otter; of, or belonging to, an otter.

Dobhran-leaslan, ain, *s. m.* An otter.

Do-bhrìgh, *adv.* Because; as; for the reason that.

Do-bhròn, -bròin, *s. m.;* do, *intens. and* bròn. (*Ir. id.*) Sorrow, sadness, melancholy. Ann an do-bròin, *in sorrow.—Stew. Job.* Moran do-bròin, *much sadness.—Stew. Ecc. ref.*

Do-bhrònach, *a.* (*Ir. id.*) Sorrowful, sad, melancholy, dejected. Gu do-brònach, *sorrowfully.*

† **Docail**, *s. f.* (*Ir.* docamhail.) A hardship, a difficulty.

Docaileach, *a.* (*Ir.* docamhlach.) Hard, difficult.

Docaileachd, *s. f.* (*Ir.* docamhlachd.) Difficulty, hardship.

Docair, *s. f.* (do-shocair.) *Gr. by met.* δάκρυ. Trouble, affliction, agitation of mind, uneasiness, restlessness. Le docair chruaidh, *with hard affliction.—Sm.*

Docair, *a.* Uneasy, troubled, agitated, difficult, painful. A cheuma docair eugsamhluidh, *his peace agitated and mournful.—Oss. Fin. and Lor.*

Docalachd, *s. f.* See **Docaileachd.**

Dòcha, *a.* Likely, probable; more likely; *also,* a likelihood, probability. Written also *dàcha.*

Dòcha, *com.* and *sup.* of toigh. More dear, more beloved. Is e is docha leam, *he is the dearest to me.*

Dochainn, *gen. sing.* of dochann.

Dochainn, *v. a.* Harm, hurt, wound, bruise, injure. *Pret. a.* dhochainn, *harmed; fut. aff. a.* dochainnidh. Cha dochainn smachd an droch righ, *the tyrant's oppression shall not harm.—Sm.* Chaith chliabh a dhochann', *his breast has been wounded.—Oss. Manos.*

Dochair, docharach, *s. f.* (*perhaps* dochoir.) Hurt, wrong, injury, damage, sorrow, pain, wound. *Asp. form,* dhochair. Chum mo dhochair, *to my hurt.—Stew. Gen.* Air dhochair, *wrong.* Dochair geur a bhàis, *the sharp pains of death.—Sm.*

Dochaireas, eis, *s. m.* Hurt, wrong, injury, damage, sorrow, pain.

Dochann, ainn, *s. m.* Hurt, harm, damage, pain, agony, mischief, mishap, calamity. O dhochainn bàis, *from the pains of death.—Sm.* Le dochann, *with damage.—Stew. Acts.* Thaobh mo dhochainn, *for my hurt.—Stew. Jer.*

Dochannach, *a.* Hurtful, mischievous, injurious, prejudicial; causing pain or damage. Gu dochannach, *hurtful. Com.* and *sup.* dochannaiche.

Dochannachd, *s. f.* Hurtfulness, mischievousness, injuriousness.

Dochannaich, *v. a.* Hurt, harm, injure. *Pret. a.* dhochannaich, *harmed; fut. aff. a.* dochannaichidh, *shall harm.*

Docharach, *a., from* dochair. (*Ir. id.*) Wrong; wrongful, hurtful, injurious, grievous. Tha thu 'g a chur docharach, *you are putting it wrong.* Is e an suidhe docharach 's tigh-osda is fearr, *the uneasiest seat in the alehouse is the best.—G. P. Com.* and *sup.* docharaiche.

Docharaich, *v. a.* Wrong, injure, hurt; put wrong. *Pret. a.* dhocharaich.

Docharaiche, *com.* and *sup.* of docharach.

Do-charrachadh, *a.* Immovable, not easily moved.

Dòchas, ais, *s. m.* (*Ir. id.*) Hope, expectation, confidence; conceit; notion. Creideamh 's dòchas, *faith and hope.—Sm.* An dòchas do theachd, *expecting thy coming.—Ull.* Beò-dhochas, *a lively hope.—Sm.* Tha mi 'n dòchas, *I hope. N. pl.* dochasan.

Dòchasach, *a.* (*from* dòchas.) Hopeful, vain, confident, conceited. Tha thu dòchasach, *thou art confident.—Stew. Rom. Com.* and *sup.* dòchasaiche.

Dòchasachd, *s. f.* (*from* dòchas.) Hopefulness, confidence, conceitedness.

Do-chasgaidh, *a.* Unruly, unquenchable; difficult to be quenched or extinguished.

Do-CHEANGAL, *a.* That cannot be bound; not easily bound.

Do-CHEANNSACH, *a.* Unmanageable, unruly.

Do-CHEANNSAICHTE, *part.* Unruly, forward, unmanageable, unappeasable.

Do-CHLAOIDH, *a.* Invulnerable; not easily wounded; invincible.

Do-CHLAOIDHEACHD, *s. f.* Invincibility.

Do-CHLAOIDHTE, *a.* Indefatigable; not easily hurt or wounded; invincible.

† DOCHMA, *a.* (*Ir. id.*) Weak, incapable.—*Shaw.*

Do-CHOIR, *s. f.* (do, *intens. and* coir.) Harm, injury, loss, damage, wrong. See also DOCHAIR.

Do-CHOIREACH, *a.* Injurious, wrong; causing loss or damage.

Do-CHOMHAIRLE, *s. f.* A bad advice. *N. pl.* do-chomhairlean.

Do-CHOMHAIRLEACH, *a.* Incorrigible; that will not be advised.

Do-CHOMHAIRLEACHD, *s. f.* Incorrigibleness.

† DOCHRAIDH, *s. f.* (*Ir. id.*) Lust.

Do-CHREIDSINN, *a.* (*Ir. id.*) Incredible, improbable. Mar ni dochreidsinn, *as an incredible thing.—Stew. Acts.*

† DOCHD, *a.* (*Ir. id.*) Strait, narrow, close.

† DOCHTA, *a.* Learned, instructed. *Lat.* doctus.

DOCHTAIR, *s. m.* (*from* dochta.) A doctor. *N. pl.* dochtairean.

DOCHTRAIL, *s. f.* Luxury.

DOCHUINN, *v. a.* See DOCHAINN.

Do-CHUM, *prep.* To, towards; in order to; to the end that.

DOCRACH, *a.* (do-shocrach.) Uneasy, troubled, agitated, vexed; *also,* noxious.—*Shaw.*

DOCRAN, ain, *s. m.* Anguish, sorrow, vexation, distress; a fit of anger.

DOCRANACH, *a.* Troubled, vexed, distressed; troublesome; causing sorrow or vexation. *Com.* and *sup.* docranaiche, *more* or *most troublesome.*

DOD, doid, *s. f.* (*Scotch,* dod.) A pet or fit of peevishness. Gabh an dod, *take the pet.*

Do'D, (*for* do do.) To thy, to thine; of thy *or* thine.

DODACH, *a.* Pettish, peevish. *Com.* and *sup.* dodaiche, *more* or *most pettish.*

† DODHAIL, *s.* Bad news.—*Shaw.*

Do-DHEALACHAIDH, *a.* Inseparable; not easily separated; indissoluble.

Do-DHEALAICHTE, *a.* Inseparable; not easily separated; indissoluble.

Do-DHEALBHACH, *a.* Unlikely; not easily painted or delineated.

Do-DHEANAMH, *a.* Difficult to be done; impracticable; difficult.

Do-DHEANTA, *a.* Impracticable; difficult; not easily done.

Do-FHAGHAIL, *a.* Not easily found; not to be found; rare.

Do-FHAICSINN, *a.* Not easily seen; invisible.

Do-FHAICSINNEACH, *a.* (*Ir.* do-fhaicseach.) Invisible; not easily seen.

Do-FHAICSINNEACHD, *s. f.* Invisibility.

Do-FHUASGLADH, *a.* Inextricable, insoluble.

Do-FHULANG, *a.* Intolerable; not easily borne.

† DOGALADH, aidh, *s. m.* A revenging; revenge.—*Shaw.*

† DOGALTACH, *a.* (*Ir. id.*) Revengeful.—*Shaw. Com.* and *sup.* dogaltaiche.

DOGANTA, *a.* Revengeful, fierce. Gu doganta, *revengefully.*

DOGANTACHD, *s. f.* Revengefulness, fierceness.

DOGH, *v. a.* Singe, scorch. *Pret. a.* dhogh, *singed; fut. aff. a.* doghaidh, *shall singe.*

DOGHADH, aidh, *s. m.* A scorching, a singeing.

Do-GHIÙLAN, *a.* Unsupportable; not easily borne or carried; unsufferable, intolerable.

Do-GHLACAIDH, *a.* Not easily taken; impregnable.

Do-GHLUASAD, *a.* Immovable; not easily moved.

DOGHRADH, aidh, *s. m.* (*Ir. id.*) Sorrow, sadness, dullness, stupidity.

DOGHRUINN, *s. f.* (*Ir.* doghrann.) Grief, anguish, tribulation, sadness, perplexity, danger. Doghruinn is dorran a chléibh, *the anguish and trouble of his breast.—Oss. Tem.*

DOGHRUINNEACH, *a.* Grieved, troubled; causing grief or vexation; dangerous. *Com.* and *sup.* doghruinniche.

DOIB, *s. f.* (*Ir. id.*) A plaster, a daub.

DOIBEALACH, *a. Ir. id.*) Plastering, daubing.

DOIBEALADH, aidh, *s. m.* (*Ir. id.*) A daubing.

DOIBH, *comp. pron.* To them; them. *Asp. form,* dhoibh. An oidhche mu 'n cuairt doibh, *the night around them.—Ull.* Thoir dhoibh e, *give it them.*

DOIBHEAR, *a.* Rude, uncivil, sulky, boorish. *Com.* and *sup.* doibhre.

DOIBHEART. See DO-BHEART.

DOIBHEAS, eis, *s. m.* Vice.—*Shaw.* Perhaps *do-bheus.*

† DOIBHRE, *s. f.* (*Ir. id.*) Sacrifice.

† DOICH, *a.* (*Ir. id.*) Swift, quick; early. *Com.* and *sup.* doiche.

† DOICH, *v.* (*Ir. id.*) Hasten.

† DOICHE, *s. f.* Hope, confidence.

DOICHEALL, ill, *s. m.* Niggardliness, churlishness, boorishness.—*Shaw.*

DOICHEALLACH, *a.* Niggardly, churlish, boorish.—*Shaw.*

DOID, *s. f.* (*Ir.* doid. *Fr.* doigt, *finger.*) A hand; a little farm; a farthing. Doid gheal, *a fair hand;* also, *fair-handed.*

DOIDEACH, *a.* Strong, muscular; fond of dress. Le 'n gairdeanaibh doideach, *with their muscular arms.—Macfar.*

D'OIDHCHE, *adv.* By night. More frequently *dh'oidhche.*

DOIDHREAN, ein, *s. m.* (*Ir. id.*) A duel.

DOIF, *s. f.* (*Ir. id.*) A potion.—*Shaw.*

DOIGH, *s.* (*Ir.* doigh.) Manner, way, means; case; trim; condition; state, order; *also,* confidence, trust, hope; fire; a guess; opinion; supposition; testimony. Air an doigh so labraidh sibh, *in this manner shall ye speak.—Stew. Gen.* Co-ionann air gach doigh, *in every way equal.* Ciod an doigh th'ort? *how are you?* Ma 's olc no maith mo dhoigh, *whether my condition be good or bad.—Macfar.*

† DOIGH, *a.* (*Ir. id.*) Sure, certain, of direct aim. Gu doigh, *certainly.*

DOIGH-BHIATHAR, air, *s.* A phrase, an idiom; a by-word, proverb.

DOIGH-BHRIATHRACH, *a.* Proverbial.

DOIGHEADH, idh, *s. m.* A hoping; an adjusting.

DOIGHEAR, ir, *s. m.* (*Ir. id.*) A spear.

DOIGHEIL, *a.* (*from* doigh.) In case or trim; in good condition; confident, hopeful, well appointed.

DOI-GHNIOMH, *s. m.* Injury. Perhaps *do-ghniomh.*

DOIGHLEUG, léig, *s. m.* (*Ir.* doigh-liag.) A touchstone.

DOILBH, *a.* (*Ir. id.*) Dark, gloomy, obscure, dusky; sorrowful, sad.—*Shaw.*

DOILBHE, *s. f.* Darkness, obscurity, duskiness.

DOILBHEAS, eis, *s.* See DOILGHIOS.

DOILEAN, ein, *s. m.* An eddying wind, a circling breeze.

Doileanach, *a.* Eddying, circling, as wind.

† **Doilghe**, *a.* (*Ir. id.*) Sore, troublesome, hard. Now written *doilich* and *duilich*; which see.

Doilgheas, eis, *s. m.* (*Ir. id.*) See Doilghios.

Doilgheasach, *a.* See Doilghiosach.

Doilghios, *s. m.* (*Ir.* doilgheas.) Sorrow, trouble, affliction, mourning. Fògraidh e doilghios, *he will banish sorrow.—Sm.* Na biodh doilghios oirbh, *be not grieved.—Stew. Gen.*

Doilghiosach, *a.* (*Ir.* doilgheasach.) Sorrowful, grieved, troubled; causing sorrow or trouble.

Doiliag, eig, *s. f.* (*perhaps* doighleug.) A touchstone.

Doilich, *a.* (*Ir.* doiligh.) Difficult; grieved, sorry, sorrowful. Cia doilich? *how difficult?—Stew. Mark, ref.* Bha na daoine doilich, *the men were sorry.—Stew. Gen.* Is doilich leam d' fhàgail, *I am sorry to leave you; I think it hard to leave you.*

Doill, *n. pl.* of dall. (*Ir. id.*) Blind. Na doill, *the blind.—Stew. N. T.*

Doille, *s. f.* (*Ir. id.*) Blindness; darkness. Bhuail iad le doille, *the struck with blindness.—Stew. Gen.* Doille na h-oidhche, *the darkness of night.—Oss. Conn.*

Doille, *com.* and *sup.* of dall.

Doilleir, *a.*, *from* doille. (*Ir. id.*) Dark, obscure, scarcely visible; indistinctly seen; shaded; shady; mysterious, mystical. Bha 'n oidhche doilleir, *the night was dark.—Oss. Gaul.* Is aoibhinn ge doilleir, an cuimhne, *pleasant though indistinct is the remembrance of them.—Oss. Conn. Asp. form*, dhoilleir.

Doilleireachadh, aidh, *s. m.* A darkening, a shading.

Doilleireachd, *s. f.* Darkness, obscurity; shade; mysteriousness, cloudiness.

Doilleirich, *v. a.* Darken, obscure, shade; cloud; perplex, foul, soil. *Pret. a.* dhoilleirich, *darkened; fut. aff. a.* doilleirichidh, *shall* or *will darken.*

Doilleirichte, *p. part.* Darkened, obscured, shaded, clouded, perplexed, fouled.

Doimeag, eig, *s. f.* A slattern, a slut.—*Turn. N. pl.* doimeagan.

Doimh, *a.* Poor, in want; cumbersome.—*Shaw.* Gu domhail doimh, mar mhathair fir an tighe, *gross and cumbersome, like the goodman's mother.—G. P.*

Doimheal, *a.* (*Ir. id.*) Stormy.—*Shaw.*

Doimhne, *s. f.* (*Corn.* dyfyn.) Depth; the deep; a sea. Gnùis na doimhne, *the face of the deep.—Ull.* Doimhne air dhoimhne a gairm, *deep calling unto deep.—Sm.*

Doimhne, *com.* and *sup.* of domhainn. Deeper, deepest. See Domhainn.

Doimhneachadh, aidh, *s. m.* A deepening, a fathoming.

Doimhneachd, *s. f.* (*from* domhainn.) Depth, deep. *Asp. form*, dhoimhneachd. A doimhneachd mhòir, *from a great deep.—Sm. N. pl.* doimhneachdan, *depths.* Doimhneachdan na fairge, *the depths of the sea.—Stew. Mic.*

Doimhnich, *v. a.* Deepen, fathom. *Pret. a.* dhoimhnich, *deepened; fut. aff. a.* doimhnichidh, *shall* or *will deepen.*

Doindearg, *a.* Auburn.

Doineach, *a.* Sorrowful, sad, mourning, baneful. Tha 'n dùthaich uile doineach, *the whole country is sorrowful.—Mack.*

Doineachas, ais, *s. m.* Sorrow, mourning.

Doineanta, *a.* Stormy, boisterous.

Doinionn, inn, *s. f.* (don-shion.) A storm; stormy weather; a severe blast. *Asp. form*, dhoinionn. Gach doinionn 'g ar leireadh, *every storm distressing us.—Ull.*
The word of opposite meaning is *soinionn.*

Doinionnach, *a.* (*from* doinionn.) Stormy, tempestuous, blustering. Gu doinionnach, *tempestuously.—Sm.*

Doinne, *s. f.* Brown colour.

Doinne, *com.* and *sup.* of donn. Browner, brownest. See also *duinne.*

Do-innseadh, *a.* Inexpressible; unaccountable.

Dointe, *a.* Unintelligible.

Dointe, *s. f.* (*Ir. id.*) A small black insect.—*Shaw.*

Do-iompachaidh, *a.* Inconvertible; difficult to be converted; perverse.

Doirb, *s. f.* A minnow; a worm; a reptile; *in derision*, a pithless person, a diminutive person; an attempt. *N. pl.* doirbean.

Doirbeag, eig, *s. f.* (*dim.* of doirb.) A minnow; a worm; a reptile; *in derision*, a diminutive pithless person. *N. pl.* doirbeagan.

Doirbh, *a.* (*Ir. id.*) Peevish, ill-natured; oppressive, grievous; bitter, sour; quarrelsome; dissatisfied; hard; difficult. Cha 'n 'eil i dàn no doirbh, *she is not forward nor peevish.—Old Song.* Mo reachd cha 'n 'eil doirbh, *my law is not grievous.—Sw. Com.* and *sup.* doirbhe.

Doirbhe, *s. f.* Peevishness, oppressiveness, sourness, quarrelsomeness.

Doirbheachd, *s. f.* Peevishness, quarrelsomeness, sourness, grievousness, dissatisfaction.

Doirbheas, eis, *s. m.* (*Ir. id.*) Adversity, mischance, mischief; grief, anguish. La 'n doirbheis, *the day of adversity.—Stew. Ecc.* Ciod e an doirbheas! *what the d—l!*

Doirbheasach, *a.* Adverse, calamitous.

Doirch, *gen. sing.* of dorch; which see.

Doirche, *com.* and *sup.* of dorch. More or most dark. See Dorch.

Doire, *s. f.* A grove, a thicket, a wood, a clump or tuft of trees, *properly*, of oaks. Gach coille is gach doire, *each wood and grove. N. pl.* doireachan. Doireachan uaine, *green groves.*
Arm. deru. *Ir.* doire, *a grove. Teut.* der, *a tree. Arm.* dar, *a tree, and* andar, *a forest. Turk.* dervent, *a hill covered with trees.* Hence, also, *by transposition, Eng.* tree; *Goth.* triu; *Dan.* trae.

Doireach, *a.* (*from* doire.) Woody; abounding in woods, groves, or thickets; of, or belonging to, a wood, grove, or thicket. Coireach, doireach, *abounding in dells and groves.—Macdon.*

Doireachan, *n. pl.* of doire; which see.

Doireanta, *a.* Sullen.

Doi-riarach, *a.* Difficult, ungovernable.

Doirionn, inn, *s. f.* (doirbh-shion.) A storm; stormy weather; a blast. Written also *doinionn.*

Doirionnach, *a.* Stormy; blustering. More frequently *doinionnach.*

Doirlinn, *s. f.* An isthmus, a peninsula, a promontory; a beach. Bha doirlinn mhòr eadaruinn, *there was a great isthmus betwixt us.—Fingalian Poem.*

Doirlinneach, *a.* Like an isthmus, like a promontory; abounding in promontories; peninsular.

Doirneag, eig, *s. f.* (*from* dorn.) A stone that can be flung with the hand; a large pebble; a round pebble; the handle of an oar. Fras nan doirneag, *the shower of stones.—Mac Lach. N. pl.* doirneagan.

Doirneagach, *a.* (*from* doirneag.) Full of pebbles; pebbled; like a pebble; calculous, gravelly.

Doirse, *gen. sing.* of dorus. Of a door. For *doruis* or *dorsa.*

Dòirt, *v. a.* Spill, pour, shed, stream, rush forth. *Pret. a.* dhòirt, *poured; fut. aff. a.* dòirtidh, *shall* or *will pour.* Dhòirt e 'fhuil airson Thearlaich, *he spilt his blood for Charles.—Old Song.* Dhòirt sinn gu sruthaibh an laoich, *we rushed to the streams of the hero.—Orr.* A dortadh a leon, *pouring out his wounds.—Ull.*

Dòirteach, *a.* Pouring; leaky; spilling; shedding; *also,* one who sheds or spills. Dòirteach fola, *a spiller of blood.*

Dòirteal, eil, *s. m., from* dòirt. (*Ir. id.*) A sink or drain. *N. pl.* dòirtealan.

Dòirtear, *fut. pass.* of dòirt. Shall be spilt. See Doirt.

Doirtheas, *s.* See Doirbheas.

Dòirtidh, *fut. aff. a.* of dòirt; which see.

Dòite, *a.* and *part.* (*Ir. id.*) Singed, scorched, burnt. Is dòite cinn gach fireach, *scorched are the tops of every hill.—Macdon.*

Doithcheall, *s. m.* Niggardliness, illiberality, grudging; churlishness.

Doithcheallach, *a.* Niggardly, illiberal, churlish.

Doithir, *a.* (*Ir. id.*) Dark, gloomy, obscure; ill-featured; ugly, deformed; dull; unpleasant; ill-humoured.

† Doithir, *s. f.* (*Ir. id.*) A contract, a covenant.

† Dol, *s. m.* Cunning; a trap; a kind of fishing-net. *Lat.* dol-us, *guile. Ir. Arm.* dol.

Dol, *s. m.* (*Ir.* dul.) A going, a travelling; proceeding; ways; walking; a space, a distance. Seallaibh air dol an t-saaoghail, *observe the ways of the world.—Old Song.* Dol as, *escape;* cha 'n 'eil dol as aige, *he has no way of escaping.*

Dol, (a), *pr. part.* of rach, *irr. v.* A dol as, *extinguishing* or *dying away, as a flower; escaping.*

Dolach, *a.* Each; individual; single. Gach dolach là, *every single day.*

Do-labhairt, *a.* Unspeakable, inexpressible. A thiodhlacan do-labhairt, *his unspeakable gifts.—Stew. Cor.*

Dolaidh, *s. f.* (*Ir. id. Lat.* dolo, *to hurt.*) Harm; loss; injury; defect; damage. Cha 'n 'eil dolaidh ann, *there is no harm done;* cuir dholaidh, *abuse, destroy;* is lionmhor fear a chuir e dholaidh, *many a man it has injured.—Old Song.* Chaidh e dholaidh, *he* [or *it*] *has gone wrong,* or *useless;* air dholaidh, *damaged, useless.*

Dolaidh, *a.* (*Ir. id.*) Impatient, restless, intolerable.—*Shaw.*

Dolar, air, *s. m.* A dollar. Dolar Spàinnteach, *a Spanish dollar.*

Dòlas, ais, *s. m.* (do, *priv. and* sòlas.) *Eng.* dole. *Ir.* dolas. Grief, woe, trouble; mourning, desolation; abhorrence, disdain, loathing. Fògraidh e gach dòlas, *he will drive away all grief.—Sm.*

Dol as, *s.* An escape. Cha 'n 'eil dol as aig, *he has no escape.*

Dòlasach, *a., from* dolas. (*Ir. id.*) Sad, grieved, melancholy, mournful, grievous, sick.—*Stew. Exod. ref.* Com. and *sup.* dòlasaiche. Gu dòlasach, *sadly.*

Dòlasachd, *s.* Sadness, melancholy, mournfulness.

Do-lasda, *a.* Not inflammable; not easily blown to a flame.

† Dolbh, *a.* (*Ir. id.*) Sorcery, witchcraft.

† Dolbhad, aid, *s. m.* (*Ir. id.*) Fiction.

Do-leaghada, *a.* Not easily melted.

Do-leanachd, *a.* Inimitable; that cannot be followed; difficult to be followed.

Do-leanmhuinn, *a.* Inimitable; that cannot be followed; difficult to be followed.

Do-leanmhuinneachd, *s. f.* Inimitableness.

Do-leasachadh, *a.* Irreparable, incurable, that cannot be helped.

Do-leigheas, *a.* Incurable; not easily healed. Creuchd do leigheas, *an incurable wound.*

Do-leigheasachd, *s. f.* Incurableness.

Do-léirsinn, *a.* Dark, invisible, hidden; inexplicable. Ioma slochd do-léirsinn, *many a hidden gulf.—Sm.*

Do-léirsinneachd, *s. f.* Invisibleness.

Do-leughadh, *a.* Illegible.

Dol mach. A going out; conduct, behaviour. Is olc an dol mach th' agad, *your behaviour is bad.*

Do-lorgachaidh, *a.* Difficult to be traced, impossible to be traced. Cia do-lorgachaich a shlighean! *how hard to be traced are his ways!—Stew. Rom.*

Do-luaidh, *a.* Unspeakable; unutterable.

Do-lùbachd, *s. f.* Inflexibility, stiffness, stubbornness; inexorableness.

Do-lubaidh, *a.* Inflexible, stiff, stubborn.

Doltrum, uim, *s. m.* Grief, anguish, vexation.

Doltrumach, *a.* Grievous, vexatious.

Dolum, *a.* (*Ir. id.*) Surly, morose, peevish, mean. On bha thusa dolum, *as thou wert surly.—Old Song.*

† Dom, *s. m.* A house.

Heb. dom, *to abide. Arab.* dam, *to abide. Syr.* doma, *a house. Turk.* dam. *Scyth.* dum. *Sclav.* dom. *Styr.* and *Carinth.* dom. *Boh.* dum. *Pol.* domu. *Lus.* dom. *Gr.* δωμα, according to Heyschius. *Lat.* domus. *It.* domo. *Eng.* dome, *Ir.* dom, *house. Georgian,* doma, *a garret.*

Do'm, (*for* do am.) To their; of their. Do 'm bailtean, *to their towns.*

Do m', (*for* do mo.) To my; of my. Do m' athair, *to my father;* do m' dheòin, *of my own accord.*

† Domain, *a.* (*Ir. id.*) Transitory.—*Shaw.*

Domairm, *s. f.* (dom, *house, and* airm.) An armoury, a depôt; a magazine; *rarely,* speech.

Domblas, ais, *s. m.* (do *and* blas.) *Ir. id.* Gall, bile, choler, anger.

Domblasda, Domblasta, *a.* Sour, like gall; unsavoury, biliary, choleric; disgustful. Uisge domblasda, *water of gall.—Stew. G. B.*

Dombuidheach, *a.* Unthankful, ungrateful; dissatisfied. Gu dombuidheach, *unthankful.*

† Domh, *s. m.* (*Ir. id. Lat.* domus.) A house.

Domh, *comp. pron.* To me. Cha'n fhios domh, *I know not.—Stew. Jos. Asp. form,* dhomh.

Domhail, *a.* (*perhaps* do-dhail.) Crowded; throng; dense; thick, clumsy, large, bulky in person. Tigh domhail, *a crowded house. Asp. form,* dhomhail. Cuideachd domhail, *a crowded company;* dubh dhomhail, *dark and dense.—Oss. Tem.* Gun bhi meanbh no domhail, *without being puny nor bulky.—Old Song.*

Domhain, *gen. sing.* of domhan.

Domhainn, *a.* Deep; profound; deep or insidious; double-minded; hollow. Is domhainn a chreuchd, *deep is his wound.—Ull.*

The Celtic root is *don. Heb.* adon, *a bottom. Arab.* douna, *under. Gr.* δυω, *sink. Box. Lex.* divin. *W.* duvun. *Corn.* and *Arm.* doun. *Ir.* doimhin. Hence *Eng.* down; *Scotch,* doun. Toll domhainn, *a deep hole;* in the Armoric dialect of the Celtic it is *toul doun.*

Domhainneachd, *s. f.* Contracted *doimhneachd;* which see.

Domhain-sgriobhadh, *s. m.* (*Ir. id.*) Cosmography.

Domhalachd, *s. f.* (*from* domhail.) Crowdedness, bulkiness.

Domhalas, ais, *s. m.* A crowd; a crowded condition; a throng.

Domhan, ain, *s. m.* (*Ir. id.*) The world. Chroch e 'n domhan mòr, *he hung the spacious world.—Sm.* Righ an domhain, *King of the world.—Oss. Com.* Domhain-sgriobhadh, *cosmography.*

Domhar, air, *s. m.* Water. (*Ir. id. Arm.* dour *and* doura.) See Dur and Dobhar.

Do-mharbhadh, *a.* Immortal; difficult to be killed.

† Domhghnas, ais, *s. m.* (*Ir. id.*) Inheritance, patrimony. *Shaw. Also,* hereditary.

DOMHLACHADH, aidh, *s. m.* A crowding.

DOMHLADAS, ais, *s. m.* (*from* domhail.) Crowdedness, bulkiness, weight.

DOMHLAICH, *v. a.* Crowd, assemble, gather in crowds. *Pret. a.* dhòmhlaich, *crowded; fut. aff. a.* domhlaichidh, *shall* or *will crowd.* Dhomhlaich mu Chairbre a shloigh, *his host crowded around Cairbar.—Oss. Tem.*

DOMHLAS, ais, *s. m.* A crowd, a throng. Contracted for *domhalas.*

DOMH-LIOS, *s.* (*Ir. id.*) A house surrounded by a moat or watered trench for a fortification.—*O'Brien.*

DÒMHNACH, *a.* (*Ir. id.*) Sabbatical; *also,* lamentable.

DÒMHNACH, aich, *s. f.* (*Ir. id.*) Sunday, Sabbath; *rarely,* a church, a great house. An domhnach, *the Sabbath;* di-domhnaich, *Sunday.* Air an domhnach, *on the Sabbath;* domhnach cuingeis, *Whitsunday.*

DOMHNACH, a. Lamentable; sad.—*Shaw.*

DOMHNAICH, (di.) *s.* Sunday. Di domhnuich so chaidh, *last Sunday;* di-domhnaich so tighinn, *next Sunday;* di-domhnaich càsg, *Easter Sunday;* di-domhnaich inid, *Shrove Sunday.*

DO-MHOTHACHAIDH, *a.* Imperceptible; callous; unfeeling.

DO-MHÙCHADH, *a.* Inextinguishable; not easily extinguished; not easily smothered.

DO-MHUINTE, *a.* Untractable, indocile, perverse.—*Shaw.*

DON, DONA, *a.* Bad, wicked; sad; dangerous; awkward; worse; contemptible; mean; pusillanimous; unlucky, unfortunate. An dubhra dona, *the sad darkness.—Oss. Lod.* Na daoine dona, *the wicked men.—Sm.*

DO'N, (*for* do an.) To the, of the; to their, of their.

DONA, *a.* See DON.

† DON, *s.* Water.

This ancient Celtic vocable has long been in disuse among the Gaelic Celts, but is still retained in the Armoric dialect. Hence *tonn,* a wave; hence, also, the name of the rivers Don in Britain and in Russia; hence, too, the Celtic name for the Danube, *Donau* or *Dona,* Latinised *Danubius. Donau,* however, may be *don-aw,* the deep water, *comp.* of the Armoric *don* (written *domhainn* by the Gael), and † *au,* † *amh,* or † *abh,* water;—*mh* and *bh* are silent in these words.

DONADH, aidh, *s. m.* Mischief, evil; *also,* bad.

DONAICH, *v. a.* (*from* don.) Deteriorate; hurt, damage; make bad or worse; depreciate; destroy. *Pret. a.* dhonaich; *fut. aff.* a. donaichidh, *shall deteriorate. Ir.* donaigh.

DONAMHARC, *s.* Naughtiness.—*Shaw.*

DONAS, ais, *s. m.* (*from* don.) *Ir. id.* Harm, mischief, evil; bad luck, mishap; a sorry fellow; a devil. Tha donas fo 'theangaidh, *there is mischief under his tongue.—Sm.* Tha 'n donas ort, *the devil is in you;* dhonais chrìne, *thou little devil;* thoir an donas ort, *go to the devil;* am fear gu 'n dàn an donas 's an da 'bheanas, *it is he for whom evil is destined that will suffer.—G. P.* Cha bhi donas toirteach, *a sorry fellow is not ready to give.—Id.* Thig an donas le 'iomradh, *speak of the devil and he will appear.—G. P.* An donas bonn a bhiodh agam, *d—l a coin I would have. —Turn.*

DONN, *a.* Dun, brown, dusky; brown-haired; *rarely,* pregnant. *Asp. form,* dhonn. *Gen. sing.* duinn; *asp. form,* dhuinn. Each donn, *a brown* or *dun horse;* le sgiath dhuinn na doininn, *with the dusky wing of the storm.—Oss. Fin. and Lor.* Nighean donn an t-sugraidh, *the brown-haired flirting maid.—Old Song. Com.* and *sup.* duinne.

DONN, *v. a.* and *n.* Make brown, grow brown.—*Shaw.*

DONNACHADH, aidh, *s. m.* Embrowning; a growing brown or dun.

DONNAG, aig, *s. f.* A kind of fish; a name for a brown cow; a drab or slut. Is mòr le donnag a cuid abhrais, *spinning troubles a drab.—G. P.*

DONNAICH, *v. a.* Make brown, dun, or dusky; grow brown, dun, or dusky. *Pret. a.* dhonnaich, *grew brown; fut. aff. a.* donnaichidh, *shall grow brown.*

DONNAL, ail, *s. m.* A howl, as of a dog; a loud wail. Donnal a leòin, *the wail of his agonised breast.—Oss. Fin. and Lor.*

DONNALACH, *a.* Apt to howl; howling, as a dog.

DONNALADH, aidh, *s. m.* A howling, a yelling; a loud wailing; a burst of lamentation.

DONNALAICH, *v. n.* Howl, as a dog; yell. *Pret.* dhonnalaich.

DONNALAICH, *s. f.* A howl; a continued howling; a yelling; a loud wail. A donnalaich ri thaobh, *howling by his side.—Oss. Tem.* Ciod an donnalaich th'ort? *what are you howling for?*

DONN-CHLEACHDA, *s. m.* Brown hair. Donn-chleachda Dhiarmaid, *Dermid's brown hair.—Oss. Derm.*

DONN-CHLEACHDACH, *a.* Brown-haired.

DONN-SHUILEACH, *a.* Brown-eyed.—*Oss. Trathal.*

DORA. See DORRA.

† DORADH, aidh, *s. m.* (*Ir. id.*) A line, a rule.

DORAIDH, *s. f.* (*Ir. id.*) Strife, dispute, controversy, wrangling, intricate.

DORAINGEACHD, *s. f.* Frowardness.

DÒRAINN, *s. m.* and *f.* See DÒRUINN.

DÒRAINNEACH, *a.* See also DÒRUINNEACH.

† DORAR, air, *s. m.* (*Ir. id.*) A battle, a strife.

DO-RANNSACHAIDH, *a.* Unsearchable, unscrutable. Cia do-rannsachaidh a bhreitheanais! *how unsearchable are his judgments!—Stew. Rom.*

† DORAR, air, *s. m.* (*Ir. id.*) A conflict, a scuffle.

DORAS, ais, *s. m.* See DORUS.

DORCH, DORCHA, *a.* (*Ir. id. Sax.* deorc. *Eng.* dark.) Dark, obscure; dusky; black; proud; gloomy; stern. *Asp. form,* dhorcha; *com.* and *sup.* duirche. Dorch do mhala 's duirche do ghne, *dark is thy brow, and darker thy temper.—Oss. Fing.* Asgailt dhorcha na h-iargail, *the black bosom of the storm.—Oss.* Dorcha air an t-sliabh, *stern on the mountain's side.—Oss. Fing.* Oidhche dhubh dhorch, *a pitchy dark night.*

DORCHADAS, ais, *s. m.* (*Ir. id.*) Darkness, obscurity, duskiness, gloominess. La dorchadais, *a day of darkness. Asp. form,* dhorchadas. Tiugh dhorchadas, *thick darkness.—Stew. Exod.*

DORCHADH, aidh, *s. m.* A darkening, obscuration, shade, gloom, eclipse; darkness. Dorchadh nam blàr, *the darkening of battle.—Oss. Tem.* Chaidh thu fa dhorchadh, *thou hast gone to darkness.—Id.* An deigh' dhorch' oidhche, *after nightfall.*

DORCHAICH, *v. a.* and *n.* Darken, shade, obscure, cloud, sully; grow dark. *Pret. a.* dhorchaich, *darkened; fut. aff. a.* dorchaichidh, *shall darken.* Com' an dorchaich thu làithe na h-aois? *why wilt thou darken the days of age?—Oss. Cathula.*

DORCHAICHTE, *p. part.* of dorchaich. Darkened, shaded; sullied.

DORCH-CHAINNTE, *s. f.* Ambiguity in speech, ambilogy.

DORCH-CHAINNTEACH, *a.* Ambilogous.

DÒRD, *s.* A humming; a muttering. See DÙRD.

DÒRD, *v. n.* Hum, like a bee. See DÙRD.

DÒRDAIL, *s. f.* A humming noise, a buzzing, a murmur. See also DÙRDAIL.

DÒRDAN, ain, *s. m.* A humming noise, as of bees; a murmur, a muttering. Written also DÙRDAN.

DOR-DHUILLE, *s. m.* A folding door; *also*, the leaf of a door.

DO-REIR, *prep.* According to. Written also *réir* and *a réir.*

DO-RÉITEACHAIDH, *a.* Implacable, irreconcilable.—*Stew. Rom.* Not easily disentangled or unloosed; not easily made clear, smooth, or level.

† DORGA, *a.* (*Ir. id.*) Despicable; crusty.

DOROADH, aidh, *s. m.* (*Ir. id.*) A fishing-net.—*Shaw.* A fishing-line.

DORGANTA, *a.* Discourteous; surly.

DO-RIAGHLACHADH, *a.* Unmanageable, ungovernable.

DO-RIARACH, *a.* Insatiable; difficult to be served or satisfied; discontented; ungovernable.

DO-RIATHARACHADH, *a.* Difficult to be served or satisfied; insatiate; surly; peevish, discontented.

DO-RIATHARACHD, *s. f.* Insatiateness, peevishness, discontentedness.

DORLACH, aich, *s. m.* (dorn-luach.) A handful, a fistful; a bundle; a number; a good deal; a quiver. Dorlach sluaigh, *a number of people*; dorlach airgid, *a handful of money*; m'iughar 's mo dhorlach, *my yew* [*bow*] *and my quiver.*—*Oss. Derm.* Dorlach sìl, *a handful of corn.*—*Stew. Ps.* Nan dorlaichean, *in numbers.*—*Macint.*

The *dorlach* was also a kind of truss or wallet, worn of old by Highland soldiers instead of a knapsack. " Those of the English who visited our camp did gaze with admiration upon those supple fellows the Highlanders, with their plaids, targets, and *dorlachs.*" —*An Author quoted by Dr. Jamieson.*

DORN, *v. a.* Box, bruise with the fist, strike with the fist. *Pret. a.* dhorn; *fut. aff. a.* dornaidh, *shall* or *will bruise. Arm.* dourna. *W.* durn. In Vannes, they say *dournein.*

DORN, dùirn, *s. m.* (*Ir.* dorn. *Arm.* dorn. *W.* and *Corn.* durn *and* dorn.) *N. pl.* dùirn; *d. pl.* dornaibh. A fist; a box or blow with the fist; a hilt; a haft, a handle. Le sleaghaibh nan dorn, *with spears in their fists*; lan a dhùirn, *his fistful* or *handful,*—*Stew. Lev.* Lan dùirn, *a fistful*; na dhornaibh, *in his fists.*—*Stew. Pro.* Thug e dorn da, *he gave him a box*; an dorn cli, *the left fist. Arm.* dorn cley, *left hand.*

DORNACHADH, aidh, *s. m.* A boxing; a bruising with the fist.

DORNADH, aidh, *s. m.* A boxing; a thumping with the fist.

DORNAG, aig, *s. f.* (*from* dorn.) A pebble; a stone that one can easily fling with the hand,

DORNAIDH, *s. f.* A narrow channel of the sea where it flows and ebbs, and where, at full sea, a vessel can be towed to either side of the harbour.

DORNAIR, *s. m.* A pugilist. *N. pl.* dornairean, *pugilists. Arm.* dourner, *one who strikes with the fist.*

DORNAIREACHD, *s. f.* Pugilism; bruising with the fist.

DORNAN, ain, *s. m.* (*dim.* of dorn) A little fist; a small bundle; a handful of any thing.—*Stew. Jer. ref.*

DORN-CHUL, -chuil, *s. m.* The hilt of a sword; the haft or handle of any bladed weapon.

DORN-CHUR, -chuir, *s. m.* (*Ir. id.*) The hilt of a sword; the haft or handle of any bladed weapon. An dorn-chur an deigh na loinne, *the haft after the blade.*—*Stew. Judg.*

DORN-CHURAIDH, *s. m.* A pugilist; a pugilistic champion.

DO-ROINNEADH, *a.* Indivisible; not easily divided.

† DORR, *s. m.* (*Ir. id.*) Anger, displeasure; a fit of passion.

DORR, *a.* (*Ir. id.*) Rough; rugged; angry; uncivil; harsh.

DORRA, *com.* and *sup.* of duilich. More or most difficult.

DORRACH, *a.*, *from* dorr. (*Ir. id.*) Harsh; austere; rough; surly, uncivil; cruel. *Com.* and *sup.* dorraiche, *more* or *most uncivil.*

DORRACHD, *s. f.* Harshness of temper; surliness, austerity, ruggedness, cruelty.

DORRAD, aid, *s. m.* Badness; difficulty. A dol an dorrad, *growing more* or *most difficult.*

DORRAN, ain, *s. m.* (*from* dorr.) Anger, vexation; anguish; mental heaviness. Doghruinn is dorran a chleibh, *the grief and vexation of his soul.*—*Oss. Tem.* Dorran air m'anam, *heaviness on my soul.*—*Oss. Asp. form*, dhorran. Trom-dhorran nan laoch, *the deep wrath of the heroes.*—*Oss. Fing.*

DORRANACH, *a. from* dorran. (*Ir. id.*) Angry, vexed; vexatious.

DORRDA, DORTHA, *a.* (*Ir. id.*) Surly, harsh, churlish, austere.—*Shaw.*

DORSA, *n. pl.* of dorus, (*for* dorusan.) Doors, gates. Dorsa prais, *brazen doors.*—*Sm. Asp. form*, dhorsa. A dhorsa siorruidh, *ye everlasting doors.*—*Id.*

DORSAIR, *s. m.*, *from* dorus. (*Ir.* doirseoir.) A doorkeeper, a porter. *N. pl.* dorsairean.

DORSAIREACHD, *s. f.* (*Ir.* doirseoireachd.) Door-keeping. B' fhearr leam bhi ri dorsaireachd, *I would rather be a doorkeeper.*—*Sm.*

DORSAN, (*for* dorusan), *n. pl.* of dorus. Doors. See DORUS.

† DORSAN, ain, *s. m.* A grasshopper. More frequently written *diurrasan.*

DÒRTACH, *a.* Spilling, shedding, dropping; not water-tight. Brù dhòrtach, *a barren womb.*

DÒRTADH, aidh, *s. m.* A spilling, a shedding, a pouring; a rushing forth. Dòrtadh fola, *bloodshed; an issue of blood.*

DÒRTADH, (a), *pr. part.* of doirt. Pouring; spilling, shedding; rushing forth. A dòrtadh do 'n àraich, *pouring to the plain.*—*Oss. Dargo.*

DO-RUIGHEACHD, *a.* Unattainable; that cannot be reached at; difficult to be reached; difficult of access.

DO-RUIGSINN, *a.* Unattainable; that cannot be reached at; difficult of access.

DORUINN, *s. m.* Anguish, torment, pain; danger, perplexity; vexation. Written also *do-ghruinn.*

DORUINNEACH, ich, *s. f.* Calamity; wretchedness.

DORUINNEACH, *a.* (*i. e.* doghruinneach.) Tormented, pained; causing torment or pain; dangerous; perplexed; perplexing, vexatious; wretched. Gu bheil thu doruinneach, *that thou art wretched.*—*Stew. Rev.*

DORUS, uis, *s. m.* A door, a gate, a wicket. *N. pl.* dorsa *and* dorsan; *contracted for* dorusan. Dùin an dorus, *shut the door*; dorus mòr, *a front door*; dorus beòil, *a front door*; dorus cùil, *a back door*; dorus cathamh, *a middle door, a door between the front door and that of the kitchen.* Deoch an doruis, *a stirrup-cup, a parting dram. Manx.* deouch a dorus.

Pers. dor *and* der, *a door. Shans.* dwara. *Teut.* dore, dur, *and* dure. *Goth.* daur. *Old Sax.* durei. *Hind.* doras. *Swed.* and *Dan.* dor. *Cimbric*, dur. *Sclav.* dauri. *Alban.* dera. *Carinth.* duri. *Lus.* duira. *Germ.* thor. *Gr.* θύρα. *Ir.* dorus *and* duras. *Corn.* daras. *Manx.* dorus. *Arm.* dor. *Isl.* dur. *Eng.* door.

DOS, dois, *s. m.* (*Ir. id.*) A bush; a copse, a thicket; a tuft; a plume, a cockade; a tassel; a mane; a forelock; a bramble; froth, scum; *figuratively*, a thick body of men. *N. pl.* dosan; *d. pl.* dosaibh. Dosan nan ruadhag, *the thickets of roes.*—*Oss. Fing.* Dosan nan carn, *the bushes of the rocks.*—*Oss. Carricth.* Dos na ceann-bheairt, *the plume of the helmet.*—*Mac Lach.* Dos do 'n t-sìoda, *a tassel of silk.*—*Macfar.* A sgaoileadh 'dhosan, *spreading his forelocks.*—*Oss. Fing.*

DOSACH, *a.* (*from* dos.) Bushy, tufty, plumy; having tassels; having a flowing mane; full of thickets. *Com.* and *sup.* dosaiche, *more* or *most bushy.*

† DOSAL, ail, *s. m.* (*Ir. id.*) Slumber, sleep.

DOSAN, *n. pl.* of dos.

Dosan, ain, *s. m.*; *dim.* of dos. (*Ir. id.*) A little tuft, as of hair or heath; a little bush, a little thicket, a little plume; a mane.

Dosanach, *a.* Full of little tufts; full of thickets; bushy.

Do-sdiùraidh, *a.* Intractable; not easily steered.

Dosgach, *a.* Sad; mournful; deplorable; morose. Is dosgach eug a ghaisgich, *sad is the death of the hero.—Death of Carril.*

Dosgach, aich, *s. m.* Trouble; evil; mischief. Nach lionmhor dosgaich? *are not troubles numerous?—Oss. Cathula.* Gun éirich dosgaich, *that mischief may arise.—Stew. Gen. ref.*

Do-sgaidheachd, *s. f.* Moroseness; mischief; troublesomeness; sadness; extravagantness.

Do-sgaraidh, *a.* Inseparable; not easily separated.

Do-sgeul, -sgeòil, *s. m.* (*Ir. id.*) A fictitious tale, a romance, a novel.

Do-sgrudach, **Do-sgrudadh**, *a.* Unsearchable, unscrutable.

Dosguinn, *s. f.* Mishap, misfortune. Dosguinn is gniomh nàr, *mishap and shameful deeds.—Mac Lach.*

Do-sguinneach, *a.* (*from* dosguinn.) Unfortunate; calamitous; hurtful. Anamhiann dosguinneach, *hurtful lusts.—Stew. Tim. ref.*

Do-sharta, *a.* Troublesome, difficult.—*Shaw.*

Do-shasachaidh, *a.* Insatiable.

Do-sheachanta, *a.* Inevitable, unavoidable, not easily shunned.

Do-sheachnadh, *a.* Inevitable, unavoidable, not easily avoided.

Do-shior, *adv.* Continually, for ever.

Do-shiubhal, *a.* Impassable, not easily travelled.

Do-smachdachaidh, *a.* Incorrigible, obstinate, stubborn, unmanageable.

Do-smuainteachaidh, *a.* Inconceivable, incomprehensible; not easily conceived or understood.

Do-spionnta, *a.* Unsearchable.—*O'Reilly.*

Do-sprìochta, *a.* Stubborn, untractable.—*Shaw.*

Dosrach, *a.* (*Ir. id.*) Bushy, tufty, thick with foliage, plumy; branchy; flourishing, as a tree. Gu dosrach ùr, *flourishing and fresh.—Sm.* Ite dhosrach an fhìrein, *the eagle's plumy feather.—Old Song.*

Dosraich, *s. f.* Buffeting, as of water; floundering. Dosraich thonn, *the buffeting of waves.—Fingalian Poem.*

Dot. See **Dod.**

Doth, *v. a.* Singe, scorch, burn. *Pret. a.* dhoth, *singed; fut. aff. a.* dothaidh, *shall singe.*

Dothadh, aidh, *s. m.* (*Ir. id.*) A singeing, a scorching, a burning. Air a dhothadh, *scorched.—Stew. Mat.*

Dothag, aig, *s. f.* A slight singeing, a slight scorching.

Dothan, ain, *s. m.* (*Gr.* Φθων.) The earth; land. Written more frequently *domhan.*

† **Dothar**, air, *s. m.* (*Ir. id.*) Water. See **Dur** *and* **Dour.**

† **Dothar-chlais**, *s. m.* A conduit, a water-pipe, a channel.

Do-theagasg, *a.* Unteachable, indocile, untractable.

Do-thogail, *a.* Difficult to be lifted; difficult to be reared.

Do-thomhas, *a.* Immeasurable; immensurable; not easily measured.

Dothte, *p. part.* of doth. Singed, scorched, burned.

Do-thuigsinn, *a.* Unintelligible; not easily understood; hard to be understood. Cuid do nithibh do thuigsinn, *some unintelligible things.—Stew. Pet.*

Do-uair, *s. f.* Unfavourable weather, blasting weather, stormy weather; a blight. Is caoin do bhlàth, ach 's fagus do-uair, *sweet is thy blossom, but the blight is near.—Oss. Cathula.*

† **Dour**, *s.* Water. This vocable has gone into disuse among the Gael, but we have it in the word *douran*, an otter or beaver; more properly, *dobhran*, from *dobhar;* which see.

Douran, ain, *s. m.* (*from* dour.) An otter, a beaver. More properly written *dobhran.*

† **Drab**, *s. m.* (*Ir. id.*) A spot, a stain, a blemish.

Drabag, aig, *s. f.* A dirty female, a slut, a slattern. *N. pl.* drabagan.

Drabair, *s. m.* A dirty fellow, a sloven. *N. pl.* drabairean.

Drabaireachd, *s. f.* Slovenliness.

Drabasda, *a.* Indelicate in speech, smutty; uncouth.

Drabasdachd, *s. f.* Indelicacy of speech, smuttiness; uncouthness.

Drabh, *s.* (*Ir.* drabh. *Eng.* draff. *Swed.* draf.) Grains, draff, malt after its juice is extracted; *rarely*, a cart. Nur bhios a mhuc sàthach, cinnidh an drabh goirt, *when the sow is sated, the chaff grows sour.—G. P.*

Drabhadh, aidh, *s. m.* A separating; a separation.

Drabhag, aig, *s. f.* Lees, dregs, sediment.

Drabhagach, *a.* Full of lees or sediment; like lees or sediment.

Drabhas, ais, *s. m.* Filthiness of speech, obscenity, smut.

Drabhasach, *a.* Filthy, indelicate in speech, obscene.

Drabhasachd, *s. f.* Filthiness of speech, obscenity.

Drabhasda, *a.* Filthy in speech, obscene, smutty; uncouth. Written also *drabasda.*

Drabhluinneachd, *s. f.* Drollery, a ludicrous exhibition, a farce.

Dràc, dràic, *s. m.* A drake. *N. pl.* dràcan.

Dràcach, *a.* (*from* dràc.) Abounding in drakes, like a drake, drakish An coire dràcach, *the dell abounding in drakes.—Macdon.*

Drag, draig, *s. f.* (*Ir. id.*) Fire; a meteor; a thunderbolt; anger. Cruas na craige is luathas na draig, *the hardness of the rock and the speed of the meteor.—Macdon.* See **Dreug.**

† **Drag-aigheann**, -aighne, *s. f.* (*Ir. id.*) A fire-shovel.

Dragart, airt, *s. m.* (drag *and* art.) A flint; *literally*, a fire-stone.

† **Drag-bhod**, -bhuid, *s. m.* (*Ir. id.*) The Lesser Bear; *literally*, a fiery tail.

Dragh, *s. m.* Trouble, vexation, annoyance. Ged éirich dragh, *though trouble should arise.—Sm.* Cuir dragh, *trouble.* Iadsan a chuireas dragh ort, *they who shall annoy thee.—Stew. Hab.* Cha bhith mi aig an dragh, *I won't be at the trouble;* cha ruig thu leas bhith aig an dragh, *you need not be at the trouble;* cha bhi uaill gun dragh, 's cha bhi sinn a dragh ris, *pride has its trouble, and we will not be troubled with it.—G. P.*

Dragh, *v. a.* Pull, tug; pluck; part, separate. Hence *Eng.* draw *and* drag.

Draghadh, aidh, *s. m.* A pulling, a tugging; a plucking; a parting, a separating.

Draghail, *a.* (dragh-amhuil.) Troublesome, teasing, annoying, vexatious.

Draghair, (dragh-fhearr), *s. m.* A dragger, a puller; a troublesome, teasing fellow. *N. pl.* draghairean.

Draghaireachd, *s. f.* (*from* dragh.) A pulling, teasing, tugging; a continued pulling or tugging; teasing behaviour.

Draghalachd, *s. f.* Troublesomeness; a teasing, annoying.

Dràgon, oin, *s. m.* A dragon.—*Stew. Jer.*

† **Draic**, *s. f.* (*Ir. id.*) A dragon.—*Shaw.*

DRÀICHD, s. f. A slattern, a slut, an unthrifty person. *N pl.* draichdean.

DRÀICHDEACH, a. Sluttish, drabbish.

DRÀICHDEALACHD, s f Sluttishness, drabbishness.

DRÀICHDEIL, a. (dràichd-amhuil) Sluttish, drabbish.

DRAIG, s. m. A spendthrift; an unthrifty person Bhiodh sonas aig draig nam faigheadh e mar dhòrtadh e, *the spendthrift would be happy if he got as he squandered.—G. P.*

† DRAIGH-BHIORASG, aisg, s m (Ir id) Fuel —*Shaw*

DRAIGHEANN, s. f. (*Ir.* draigheann *and* draoighion.) See DROIGHIONN.

DRAIGHNEACH, s Thorns See DROIGHIONACH.

DRAIGHNEACH, ich, s f A loud rumbling noise, as of thunder —*Shaw. Also,* black thorn; a place where black thorns grow.

DRAILLSEANACH, a Twinkling, sparkling.

DRÀIN, s. f A grin, grinning

DRAING, s f A snarl, snarling, peevishness Rinn e draing rium, *he snarled at me.*

DRAINGEANTA, a Snarling, cross, peevish

DRAINGEANTACHD, s f. Peevishness; a snarling, a cross peevish temper

DRAINN, s f (*Ir.* id) A hunch on the back

DRAINT, s f A snarl; peevishness.

DRAIP, s. f Vexation, calamity, a slut.

DRAIS, s pl Drawers or under breeches.—*Macdon*

DRAM, drama, s. m. A dram of spirits. Dram mar linig cleibh, *a dram to line the chest —Macdon.*

DRAMAIG, s f (*Scotch,* drammock) A dram of spirits, a dirty mixture; *Scotch,* crowdie.

† DRÀN, dràin, s m. (*Ir.* id) Rhyme, metre, verse —*Shaw.*

† DRÀNAG, aig, s f (*Ir* id) Rhyme, metre, verse.

† DRAND, draind, s m A small quantity; the least bit; a hum, a murmur; (*Scotch,* drant, *a drawling enunciation,*) a snarl

DRANDAN, DRANNDAN, ain, s. m. (*Ir.* dranntan) A humming noise, a buzzing, as of a bee, a hum; a snarl; a grumbling; a growl; a low murmur; the whistling of the wind; a gurgling noise; a complaint Dranndan bheachan an aonaich, *the hum of the mountain bees —Oss. Daryo* Rir dranndan, *humming* Cha bhi aire air dranndan, *he will not think of grumbling —R.*

DRANDANACH, DRANNDANACH. (*Ir* dranntanach) Humming; buzzing; murmuring; grumbling; snarling; growling; complaining, querulous, envious, inclined to murmur, grumble, snarl, or growl; gurgling Am beach dranndanach, *the buzzing bee*; alltan dranndanach, *a gurgling brook —Old Song* Com and *sup.* dranndanaiche

DRANDANACHD, DRANNDANACHD, s f Continued humming, a buzzing, a murmuring; a grumbling, growling, snarling, querulousness

DRANDANAICH, DRANNDANAICH, s f. A humming, a buzzing; a grumbling, a growling, querulousness; a continued gurgling noise, as of a brook.

DRANNDEUN, còin, s. m A humming-bird. *N pl* dranndeoin.

DRAOCH, s. m Hair standing on end, a fretful look

DRAOI, DRAOIDH, s. m A druid; a magician; an augur See DRUIDH.

DRAOIDHEACH, a. Druidical, magical Written also *druidheach.*

DRAOIDHEACH, s. f (*Ir* draoitheachd) Druidism; magic; sorcery; enchantment; conjuring. Written also *druidheachd*

† DRAOILINN, s. f. (*Ir.* id.) Tediousness, delay; inactivity. —*Shaw.*

DRAOIN, s. f. A grin —*Macfar. Voc.*

DRAOS, draois, s. m Trash, filth; obscenity, ribaldry.

DRAOSDA, a. Obscene, smutty, lewd.

DRAOSDACHD, s f. Obscenity, ribaldry, filthiness, smuttiness, lewdness. Draosdachd no comhradh amaideach, *filthiness nor foolish talking —Stew. Eph.*

DRÀS, (an), adv. Now, at present; *properly,* an trath-so, *at this time.*

DRÀSDA, (an), adv. Now, at present; *properly,* an trath-so, *at this time.*

DRÀSDAICH, (an), adv. Now, at present; a provincial expression for *an traths',* that is, *an tràth so.*

† DRE, s. m. (*Ir.* id.) A sledge. Hence *Eng.* dray.

DREACH, s. (*W.* drych. *Arm.* drych *Ir.* dreach) Form, figure, shape; image; statue; vision; fashion; colour; aspect, appearance, seemliness. Air chaochla dreach, *in a different form or shape.—Ull.* Shiubhail an dreach aillidh, *the beauteous vision vanished.—Oss Gaul.* Or is deirge dreach, *the purest coloured gold —Sm* Deud air dhreach caile, *teeth white as chalk.—Old Poem.* Air dhreach an fhithich, *having the appearance of a raven, black as a raven.—Macfar.*

DREACH, v a Dress, adorn, figure; polish. *Pret a.* dhreach *dressed, fut aff a* dreachaidh, *shall dress*

DREACHACH, a. That dresses or polishes; polishing, figuring, delineating, adorning; ornamental; drawn, figured, delineated; fair, handsome, of good appearance.

DREACHADAIR, s m (*from* dreach.) A painter; a dresser; a polisher; a statuary. *N pl.* dreachadàirean.

DREACHADAIREACHD, s f The occupation of a painter or statuary; a polishing, a dressing, ornamenting.

DREACHADAN, ain, s. m. A mould. *N. pl.* dreachadain.

DREACHADH, aidh, s. m. A dressing, an adorning, a figuring, a polishing

DREACHAIL, a. (dreach-amhuil) Comely, handsome, personable, having a good appearance, showy.

DREACHALACHD, s. f. Comeliness, handsomeness, personableness.

DREACHAR, a. See DREACHMHOR.

† DREACHD, s f. (*Ir.* id) A troop.—*Shaw.*

DREACHD, s. Office. See DREUCHD.

DREACHMHOR, a. (*from* dreach.) Shapely, handsome, comely, specious, showy —*Macint. Com.* and *sup.* dreachmhoire, *more* or *most shapely.*

† DREAG, v. n (*Ir.* id.) Fight, dispute, wrangle; signify; or give notice.—*Shaw.*

DREAG, dreig, s f. A meteor See DREUG.

† DREAGADH, aidh, s. m. Advertisement.

DREAGANTA, a. Captious, wrangling, peevish.

DREAGANTACHD, s. f. Captiousness, wrangling, peevishness

DREAGHANN, ainn, s m. A wren. An dreaghann donn, *the wren.* Written also *dreathann.*

DREAM, s. f (*Ir* id) A tribe, a people; a family; folk; company; a band; a handful. Gluaiseadh gach dream, *let every tribe advance —Oss. Fing.* An dream bha dlù do'n bhàs, *the people who were near to death.—Sm.* Chi mi mo dhream, *I see my band —Oss. Lodin*

DREAMACH, a. Morose, peevish, surly; boorish. Dh' fhàgadh tu suairc fear dreamach, *thou wouldst render a surly man mild.—R*

DREAMACHD, s f. Moroseness, peevishness, boorishness.

DREAMAG, aig, s. f A handful, as of hay, or the like; *also,* a peevish female —*Shaw.*

DREAMAN, ain, s m A handful, as of hay, or the like;

also, madness, fury; a fit of madness, a fit of passion; fanaticism; a climax.

† DREAMANACH, *a.* Mad, frantic, furious, fanatical. *Com.* and *sup.* dreamanaiche.

† DREAMHNACH, aich, *s. m.* (*Ir. id.*) A fop, a coxcomb; *also, adjectively*, perverse, foolish.

† DREAN, drein, *s. m.* Strife, debate, wrangling; *also*, bad.

DREAN, *s. m.* A wren. See DREATHAN.

† DREANN, *a.* (*Ir. id.*) Good.

† DREANN, *s. f.* Contention; grief; pain; a skirmish, a scuffle.

† DREANNACH, *a.* Repugnant, opposite; contrary; perverse; contentious.

DREANNAD, aid, *s. m.* (*Ir. id.*) Rashness.

DREAP, *v. n.* (*Ir. id.*) Climb, clamber, scramble, creep. More commonly written *streap.*

DREAPAIR, *s. m.* A climber, a clamberer, a scrambler.

DREAPAIREACHD, *s. f.* Climbing, clambering, scrambling.

DREAS, *v. a.* Decorate, dress. *Pret. a.* dhreas; *fut. aff. a.* dreasaidh. Air an dreasadh suas, *dressed up.—Macint.*

DREAS, dris, *s. m.* (*Ir. id.*) A brier, a thorn, a bramble; a thorn-bush; a place, a stead. An dreas a fas gu h-ùrar, *the brier freshly growing.—Oss. Fin. and Lor. Asp. form,* dhreas. An àite dhroighionn agus dhreas, *instead of thorns and briers.—Sm.* Mar theine dhreas, *as a fire of thorns.—Sm.* Dreas nan smeur, *a bramble-bush. N. pl.* dreasan, *briers.—Stew. Ezek.*

DREASADH, aidh, *s. m.* Dressing, decorating.

DREASAG, aig, *s. m.* A little brier, a little bramble. *N. pl.* dreasagan.

DREASAIL, (dreas-amhuil), *a.* Prickly; full of briers, thorny.

DREASARNACH, aich, *s. m.* A place where brambles grow, a thicket of brambles.

DREAS-CHOILLE, *s. f.* A thicket of briers. *N. pl.* dreaschoilltean.

DREATHAN, ain, *s. m.* A wren, the *motacilla troglodytes* of Linnæus. Dreathan donn, *a wren;* an dreathan talcarra, *the plump wren.—Macfar.* Written also *dreaghan.*

DREIBHSE, *s. f.* (*Ir. id.*) A space, distance; a while. More frequently written *treise.*

DREIGE, *gen. sing.* of dreag or dreug. See DREUG.

† DREIGEASACH, *a.* (*Ir. id.*) Peevish.

† DREIM, *v. n.* (*Ir. id.*) Climb, clamber, scramble. *Pret. a.* dhreim; *fut. aff. a.* dreimidh, *shall climb.*

DREIM, *s. f.* An endeavour, an attempt.—*Shaw.*

DREIMHNE, *s. f.* Warfare.

† DREIMIRE, *s. m.* A ladder, a stair; a scrambler, a climber.

DREISD, *a.* Dressed. Anartan dreisde, *dressed linen.—Turn.*

† DREOGH, *v. a.* and *n.* (*Ir. id.*) Rot; wear out. *Pret. a.* dhreogh; *fut. aff. a.* dreoghaidh, *shall* or *will not.*

† DREÒIGHTE, *p. part.* of dreogh. Rotten.

DREOLLAN, ain, *s. m.* (*Ir. id.*) A wren; *also*, a silly person, a ninny. Dreollan teasbhuidh, *a grasshopper.*

DREOLLANACH, *a.* Silly; like a wren; of, or belonging to, a wren.

DREOLLANACHD, *s. f.* Silliness.

DREOLLAN-TEASBHUIDH, *s. m.* (*Ir. id.*) A grasshopper.

DREUCHD, *s. m.* (*Ir.* dreachd. *Sax.* dreccan, *labour in low offices.*) An office. Dreuchd an t-sagairt, *the office of a priest.—Stew. Exod.* Luchd dreuchd, *office-bearers, officers.—Stew. Sam.*

DREUCHDACH, *a.* (*from* dreuchd.) Official; fond of office; of, or belonging to, office.

DREUCHDAIL, *a.* (dreuchd-amhuil.) Official.

DREUG, dreige, *s.* (druidh-eug.) A meteor; a falling star; a fire-ball.

Among the ancient Britons, a meteor was supposed to be a vehicle for carrying to paradise the soul of some departed Druid. This superstition, like many others, had its origin in Druidical artifice. The priests of that order, to strengthen their influence, took occasion from every aërial phenomenon to blind and overawe the ignorant; and as they laid claim to extraordinary sanctity, they naturally went to the broad fields of the sky for strengtheners to their illusions. So well did they engraft their absurd opinions, that, even at this distant day, the appearance of a ball of fire creates, among the more ignorant Gael, a belief that some illustrious spirit has taken its flight to eternity. From this circumstance we may infer, with Dr. Smith, that *Dreug* is a contraction of *Druidh-eug*, a Druid's death. This ingenious antiquarian thinks, that the Druidical fantasy, just mentioned, must have had its origin in a tradition of Enoch's fiery chariot.

DRIACHADACH, *a.* Stiff; inflexible; obstinate.

DRIACHADAICH, *s. f.* Stiffness; inflexibility; obstinacy.

DRIACHAIREACH, *a.* Stiff, inflexible, obstinate.

DRIACHAIREACHD, *s. f.* Stiffness, inflexibility, obstinacy.—*Shaw.*

DRIACHANACH, *a.* Sickly, fretful.

DRIACHANACHD, *s. f.* Sickness, fretfulness.

DRIAMLACH, aich, *s. m.* A fishing-line. *N. pl.* driamlaichean.

† DRIC, *s. f.* A dragon.

DRILL, *s. f.* A drop.—*Macdon.*

DRILL, *v. n.* Drop, drizzle. *Pret. a.* dhrill, *drizzled; fut. aff. a.* drillidh.

DRILLINN, *s. f.* See DRUILINN.

DRILLINNEACH, *a.* Flashing, flaming, glittering, gleaming. Fo sgàil dhrillinneach mo lainn, *under the shade* [*protection*] *of my glittering sword.—Old Poem.*

DRILLSEACH, *a.* Drizzly, dropping, rainy, dewy.

DRIM, *s. f.* See DRUIM.

DRIOBHUNN. See DROIGHIONN.

DRIODAR, air, *s. m.* Dregs, lees; gore; corrupt matter.

DRIODARACH, *a.* Dreggy; full of lees; gory.

DRIOG, *v. n.* (*Ir. id.*) Drop, distil. *Pret. a.* dhriog; *fut. aff. a.* driogaidh.

DRIOP, *v. a.* (*Ir. id.*) Climb.

DRIP, *s. f.* (*Ir. id.*) Affliction; snare; perplexity; hurry. Tra thuiteas daoi san drip, *when the wicked fell into the snare.—Sm.* Taim fo dhrip, *I am in affliction.—Id.* Daoine faoine an drip, *silly men in perplexity.—Old Song.* Cha 'n fhacas riamh muc gun drip oirre, *you never see a sow that is not in a hurry.—G. P.*

DRIS, *s. f.* (*Corn.* dreizon.) *N. pl.* drisean. A brier, a bramble, a thorn bush. *Asp. form,* dhris. Mar dhris, *like a brier.—Stew. Mic.* Droighionn is drisean, *thorns and briers.—Stew. Heb.* Am fear theid san droighionn domh, theid mi san dris da, *if one pass through thorns for me, I will pass through briers for him.—G. P.*

DRISEACH, *a.* (*from* dris.) Brambly, thorny; cross, fretful.

DRISEAG, eig, *s. f.* (*dim.* of dris.) A little bramble, a little brier; a little fretful female. *N. pl.* driseagan.

DRISEAN, *n. pl.* of dris.

DRISEANTA, *a.* Fretful; thorny, brambly. Gu driseanta, *fretfully.*

DRISLEACH, ich, *s. f.* A bramble; a thicket of thorns; a place where brambles or briers grow.

DRITHLEAN, -lein, *s. m.* A rivet.

DRITHLEAN, inn, *s. m.* A sparkle, a flash. See DRUILINN.

DRITHLEANNACH, *a.* Sparkling, gleamy, flashy.

DRITHLICH, *v. n.* (*Ir.* drithligh.) Sparkle, flash, gleam, shine. *Pret. a.* dhrithlich, *sparkled.*

DRITHLINN, *s. f.* A sparkle. See DRUILINN.

Drithlinneach, *a.* Glittering, glistening; sparkling, flashing, gleaming. *Asp. form*, dhrithlinneach. Fo sgàile dhrithlinneach mo lainne, *under the shade* [*protection*] *of my gleaming sword.—Fingalian Poem.*

Driuch, *s. m.* A beak, a snout; peevishness, fretfulness; a fretful look; hair standing on end.

Driuch, *v. n.* Stand on end, as the hair of the head.—*Shaw.*

† **Driuchal**, ail, *s. m.* Anger; *also, adjectively*, angry.

Driuchadh, aidh, *s. m.* A standing on end, as the hair of the head.—*Shaw.*

Driuchalach, *a.* Angry, fretful, peevish.

Driuchalachd, *s. f.* Angriness, fretfulness, peevishness.

Driùchd, *s. f.* Dew; drizzling rain; hair standing on end.

Driùchdach, *a.* Dewy, drizzly, rainy Duilleach driùchdach, *dewy foliage.—Macfar.*

Driùchdail, *a.* (driùchd-amhuil.) Dewy, like dew; drizzly, rainy.

† **Dro**, *s. m.* A mason's line, a fisher's line.

Dròbh, *s. m.* A drove of cattle, a number of càttle; a cavalcade. Thig dròbh nam mart, *droves of cattle shall come.—Macfar.* *N. pl.* dròbhan.

Germ. drot, *multitude. Eng.* drove. *Scotch*, drave. *Ang.-Sax.* draf. *Isl.* dreig. *Teut.* drifte. *Old Swed.* drift, *drive cattle.*

Dròbhair, *s. m.* (*from* dròbh.) A cattle-driver, a cattle-dealer or drover. *N. pl.* dròbhairean, *drovers.*

Dròbhaireachd, *s. f.* The occupation of cattle-dealing or droving.

Drobhlasach, *a.* (*Ir. id.*) Miserable; pitiable.

Droch, *a.* (*Ir.* droch. *Arm.* drouc. *Teut.* druck. *Box. Lex.* drwg.) Bad, evil, wicked; mischievous, sad, calamitous. Droch rùn, *a wicked intention.—Stew. Pro.* Droch-bheart, *mischief;* droch làth, *a bad day. Droch* is much used as a prepositive word. Droch-fhocal, *a bad word; a bad character given of one; a malediction.*

† **Droch**, *a.* Right, straight, even, direct; *also, substantively*, a coach-wheel; death.

Droch-àbhaist, *s. f.* A bad custom, a bad habit. *N. pl.* droch-àbhaistean.

Droch-àbhaisteach, *a.* Idle, mischievous; having bad tricks.

Drochaid, *s. f.* (*Ir.* drochad.) A bridge. *N. pl.* drochaidean, *bridges.* Bogh drochaid, *the arch of a bridge;* drochaid thogalach, *a draw-bridge;* balladh drochaid, *the parapet of a bridge;* drochaid fhiodh, *a wooden bridge.*

Drochaid-fhiodh, *s. f.* A wooden bridge.

Drochaid-thogalach, *s. f.* A draw-bridge.

Droch-àisteach, *a.* Wicked, mischievous.

Droch-àistean, *s. pl.* Idle, naughty tricks.—*Shaw.* Perhaps *droch-àbhaistean.*

Drochait, *s. f.* A bridge. *N. pl.* drochaitean, *bridges.* Drochait-fhiodh, *a wooden bridge;* drochait-thogalach, *a draw-bridge.*

Droch-bharail, *s. f.* A bad guess; a bad opinion; prejudice. Tha droch-bharail agam dheth, *I have a bad opinion of him.*

Droch-bheairt, *s. f.* Wickedness, mischief. Ri drochbheairt chuir sinn cùl, *we have forsaken wickedness.—Sm.*

Droch-bheairteach, *a.* Vicious, mischievous.

Droch-bheus, *s. m.* Bad morals, misconduct; bad breeding. *N. pl.* droch-bheusan.

Droch-bheusach, *a.* Immoral, ill-bred.

Droch-bhlas, *s. m.* A bad taste.

Droch-bholadh, aidh, *s. m.* A disagreeable smell, a stench.

Droch-bhriathar, air, *s. m.* A bad word; an evil expression. *N. pl.* droch-bhriathran.

Droch-chleachdas, ais, *s. m.* (*Ir. id.*) A malpractice.

Droch-chomhairle, *s. f.* A bad advice. *N. pl.* drochchomhairlean, *bad advices.*

Droch-chomhairlich, *v. a.* Misadvise. *Pret. a.* drochchomhairlich.

Droch-chomhar, air, *s. m.* A bad sign; a bad mark, as from a blow.

Drochd, *a.* Black, obscure.

Droch-fhaistinn, *s. f.* A bad report, misinformation; a false prophecy; a gloomy prophecy.

Droch-fhocal, ail, *s. m.* A bad word or expression; a bad account or character of one.

Droch-ghean, *s. m.* Bad humour.

Droch-ghniomh, *s. m.* (*Ir. id.*) A bad action, a misdeed, a crime. *N. pl.* droch-ghniomharan.

Droch-ghuidhe, *s. m.* (*Ir. id.*) An evil wish; an imprecation; a malediction.

Droch-iomchar, air, *s. m.* Bad conduct, misconduct, misdoings.

Droch-iomradh, aidh, *s. m.* An evil report; bad fame.

Droch-mharbhadh, aidh, *s. m.* (*Ir. id.*) Murder; treacherous homicide.

Droch-mhéin, *s. f.* (*Ir. id.*) A grudge; ill-will.

Droch-mhéineach, *a.* Envious; grudging; *also*, sinful.

Droch-mhisneach, ich, *s.* Pusillanimity; cowardice; low spirits.

Droch-mhisneachail, *a.* Pusillanimous; low-spirited.

Droch-mhuinte, *a.* Ill-bred, forward, saucy, insolent; sinful, wicked. Air daoinibh droch-mhuinte, *on wicked men.—Sm.*

Droch-mhunadh, aidh, *s. m.* Bad breeding, insolence.

Droch-obair, *s.* (*Corn.* drog-ober, *a crime.*) A bad work; a crime.

Droch-rùn, -rùin, *s. m.* Malice; a bad intention; a grudge. *N. pl.* droch-rùintean.

Droch-rùnach, *a.* Malicious, envious, grudging; *substantively*, a malicious person.

Droch-rùnachd, *s. f.* Maliciousness.

Droch-shùil, *s. f.* An evil eye, a blasting eye. *N. pl.* droch-shùilean.

Droch-spiorad, aid, *s. m.* (*Arm.* drouc spered.) An evil spirit, a demon; bad temper.

Droch-thoillteanas, ais, *s. m.* Demerit.

Droch-thuairisgeul, -sgeòil, *s. m.* (*Ir. id.*) An ill report; bad fame; misinformation.

Droch-thuar, -thuair, *s. m.* (*Ir. id.*) A bad omen; a bad look; a bad sign.

† **Drog**, *s. m.* The agitation or motion of the sea.

Drògaid, Drògait, *s. f.* (*Ir. id.*) The cloth called drugget

Drogh, drogha, *s. m.* A fishing-line.—*Macd.*

Drògh, drògha, *s. m.* A drove of cattle; a cavalcade. Written also *drobh;* which see.

Droibheil, *a.* (*Ir. id. Du.* droef, *sorrow.*) Hard; difficult; grievous.

† **Droich**, *v. n.* Do wrong; do evil; abuse.—*Shaw.*

Droich, *s. m.* A hunch-backed person; a dwarf. Written also *troich;* which see.

Droicheil, *a.* (droich-amhuil.) Dwarfish; hump-backed.

Droicheanta, *a.* (*from* droich.) Dwarfish; hump-backed.

† **Droicheoin**, *s. pl.* Deep waters; the deep; depth.—*Shaw.*

† **Droigheil**, *a.* Active, nimble; affecting.—*Shaw.*

† **Droighean**, in, *s.* (*Ir. id.*) The deep; depth.—*Shaw.*

Droigheann. See **Droighionn**.

Droighionn, droighne, *s. m.* Thorns, brambles; the black thorn; a sloe bush. Droighionn is cluarain, *thorns and thistles.—Stew. G. B.* An àite droighne, *in the place of thorns.—Id.* Pairc an droighne, *the bramble field.* In *Cornish* it is *parc an dren.*
Germ. dorn. *Teut.* and *Eng.* thorn. *Goth.* thaurn. *Old Sax.* thyrn. *Du.* doren *and* doernen. *W.* draen. *Corn.* dren.

Droighneach, *a.* (*W.* draenawg.) Thorny, brambly.

Droighneach, ich, *s. m.* A thicket of thorns or brambles; the black thorn. Fuaim droighniche, *the sound of thorns.—Stew. Ecc.* Croinn droighnich o'n ear 's o'n iar, *thorn-trees on either side.—Old Poem.*

Dròilean, ein, *s. m.* A slow, unhandy person.

Droineap, ip, *s. m.* Tackle, tackling. Gach droineap a chrochas ri 'r crannaibh, *every tackle that hangs to our mast.—Macdon.*

Droing, *s. f. pl.* People, persons. An droing a tha do 'n chreidimh, *they* [*the people*] *who are of the faith.—Stew. Gal.*

† **Dròl**, droil, *s. m.* (*Ir. id.*) A bay; a plait, a loop; a trick, a stratagem.

Droll, droill, *s. m.* An idle, inactive person; a clumsy staff. Cho chorrach ri ubh air droll, *a tottering, as an egg on a staff.—G. P.*

Dròlla, *s. m.* (*Ir.* droltha.) A pair of pot-hooks; the handle of a pot or pan.

Drollach, aich, *s. m.* A pair of pot-hooks.

Drollag, aig, *s. f.* A swing.

Droma, *gen. sing.* of druim; which see.

Dromach, aich, *s. f.* The back-band of a horse.

Dromach, *a.* Ridged, ridgy, hilly.

Dromadair, *s. m.* A dromedary; a drummer. *N. pl.* dromadairean.

Droman, ain, *s. m.* (*Ir. id.*) The bore-tree, elder-tree; a dromedary; a ridge; a back. *N. pl.* dromain.

Dromanach, aich, *s. m.* A place where elders grow.

Dromanach, *a.* Made of elder-wood; of, or pertaining to, elder; abounding in elder; like a dromedary; ridged.

Dromanta, *a.* Hunched, or humped; ridged.

† **Dron**, *a.* (*Ir. id.*) Right, straight; sure, stedfast.—*Shaw.*

† **Dron**, *v. a.* (*Ir. id.*) Affirm, assert. *Pret.* dhron, *affirmed.*

† **Dronadh**, aidh, *s. m.* (*Ir. id.*) Direction.—*Shaw.*

† **Dron-dunadh**, aidh, *s. m.* (*Ir. id.*) A shutting, a stopping.—*Shaw.*

Drong, droing, *s. m.* A troop, a company; *also*, a chest or box.—*Macd.* and *Shaw.*

Dronn, droinn, *s. m.* A hunch; a ridge; *also*, the name of a parish in Scotland.

Dronnach, *a.* (*from* dronn.) White-backed; ridgy; *also*, a name given to a white-backed cow.

Dronnag, aig, *s. f.* (*Ir.* dronnog. *Arm.* druyn *and* dryn.) A back; a hump; the highest part of the back of a quadruped; a ridge, the highest part of a ridge; a summit; a burden; a cow having a hunch-back. *N. pl.* dronnagan. Cuan meamnach nan dronnag, *the proud ridgy ocean.—Old Song.*

Dronnagach, *a.* Ridgy; humped. *Com.* and *sup.* dronnagaiche.

Dronnain, *gen. sing.* and *n. pl.* of dronnan.

Dronnan, ain, *s. m.* (*Ir. id.*) A back; a ridge; the back or ridge of a hill; a hump on the back. *N. pl.* dronnain.

Dronn-chuairteach, *a.* Convex.

† **Dron-uileann**, inn, *s. f.* A right angle.—*Shaw.*

† **Dron-uileannach**, *a.* Rectangular.—*Shaw.*

† **Dron-uileannag**, aig, *s. f.* A rectangle.

Drothan, ain, *s. m.* A breeze; a gentle breeze.

Drothlair, *s. m.* A carpenter; a waggon-maker; a waggoner.

Drothlaireachd, *s. f.* The occupation of a carpenter or of a waggoner.

Drothta, ai, *s. m.* (*Ir. id.*) A rafter; a wain-beam.—*Shaw.*

† **Dru**, *s. m.* An oak. Hence *Druidh*, a Druid.

Druaip, *s.* Sediment, dregs; slops, a sloppy potion; tippling. Druaip na Fraine, *the sloppy potions of France.—R.*

Druaipeach, *a.* Having sediment; sloppy.

Druaipear, ir, *s. m.* A tippler. *N. pl.* druaipearan.

Druaipearachd, *s. f.* The habit of tippling.

† **Druath**, druaith, *s. m.* Fornication.

Drùb, drùba, *s. m.* A wink. Cha d' fhuair mi drùb chodail, *I got not a wink of sleep.*

Drùbanta, *a.* Slumbering, sleepy, drowsy.

Drùb-shuileach, *a.* Drowsy, sleepy. Commonly pronounced *drùbleach.*

† **Drubh**, druibh, *s. m.* (*Ir. id.*) A house; a chariot.—*Shaw.*

† **Drubhair**, *s. m.* A charioteer; a cartwright, a coachmaker.—*Shaw.*

Drubhaireachd, *s. f.* The employment of a charioteer; the occupation of a cartwright or of a coachmaker.

† **Druchd**, *s. m.* and *f.* (*Ir. id.*) A heaving; a rising up.

Drùchd, *s. m.* and *f.* A dew; a tear; sweat. San drùchd ri gàire, *smiling in the dew.—Ull.* Drùchd gean, *a tear of joy.—Oss. Cathula.* Drùchd na muine, *an herb used for dying hair.—Shaw.*

Drùchdach, *a.* Dewy; oozing; tearful.

† **Druchdan**, ain, *s. m.* (*Ir. id.*) Whey; a drop.—*Shaw.*

Druchdan-mònaidh, *s. m.* An herb used for dying hair.—*Shaw.*

Drud, druid, *s. m.* An enclosure.

Drug, *s.* A fit of sickness.

Drugair, *s. m.* (*Ir. id.*) A slave, a drudge.—*Shaw.* *N. pl.* drugairean.

Drugaireachd, *s. f.* Slavery, drudgery.

Drughadh, aidh, *s. m.* Ascendancy, superiority.

Druibheal, eil, *s. m.* (*Ir. id.*) A dark place, a recess.

Druid, *s. f.* (*Ir.* druid. *Arm.* dret. *W.* dridu.) A stare, a thrush. Thig druid is bru-dhearg, *the thrush and redbreast shall come.—Macfar.*

Druid, *v. a.* and *n.* (*Ir. id.*) Shut, close; enclose, surround; hasten, approach, or draw near. *Pret. a.* dhruid, *shut; fut. aff. a.* druididh, *shall shut.* Na druid do chridhe, *shut not thine heart.—Sm.* Dhruid a sùil, *her eye closed.—Oss.* Druid-sa gu m' laimh, *hasten to my hand.—Oss. Lodin.* Naimhde a druideadh oirnne, *foes approaching us.—Oss. Tem.*

Druideadh, idh, *s. m.* The act of shutting or of closing; an approaching. Am druididh a gheataidh, *the time of shutting the gate.—Stew. Jos.*

Druideag, eig, *s. f.* (*dim.* of druid.) A young thrush, a little thrush. *N. pl.* druideagan.

Druidear, *fut. pass.* of druidear. Shall be shut. Druidear gach beul, *every mouth shall be shut.—Sm.* *Druidear* is also used impersonally, the preposition *le*, simple or compound, being expressed or understood; as, Druidear [leam] an dorus, *I shut the door.*

Druidh, *v.* Pour out, distil, ooze, drop; operate upon; affect. See **Drùigh**.

Druidh, *s. m.*, *from* † dru, *oak.* (*Arm.* druh. *Corn.* druw. *Ir.* druagh.) A Druid; a magician; a conjurer; a Celtic philosopher. *N. pl.* Druidhean, *Druids.* Dearg nan

Druidhean, *Dargo of the Druids*, i. e. *Dargo the Druid.—Oss. Dargo.* Do na druidhean, *to the magicians.—Stew. Gen.*

Some writers, as Pliny, derive *Druidh* from the Greek δρυς, an oak; but the proper etymon is the ancient Celtic vocable *dru*, from which δρυς is taken. The Druids had their name before the Greek language was in existence; and it is well known that the Greek itself was partly taken from the Celtic.

The Druidh was a priest or philosopher among the Celts; but, among the Gael, the word Druidh commonly signifies a magician, one skilled in occult sciences. Dion Chrysostom observes, that the Celtic kings could not so much as design any public measure without the Druids, who were adepts in divination and philosophy; insomuch that these priests exercised regal authority, and that the kings, who had but the semblance of power, were in truth their servants.

The Druids bore none of the burdens of government. They chose officers for the state and for the army; and, without their consent, even the kings could not declare war. In all respects they affected a distinction from the laity. Their tunics reached to their heels, while those of others only reached the knee. They suffered their beards to grow, whilst others (according to Toland) shaved all theirs but the upper lip. Their hair was cropped, whilst that of others was long. The Druids were entrusted with, or rather, they procured for themselves the trust of, the education of youth. The children of the nobility crowded about them for education; and with them they retired into their solitudes (according to Pomponius Mela), and kept their pupils for twenty years under discipline. That they were learned, is not to be questioned; for they possessed all the learning of their times. They believed and taught the immortality of the soul. *Ενισχύει γαρ παρ' αυτοις ὁ Πυθαγόρου λογος, ὁτι τας ψυχὰς τῶν ἀνθρώπων ἀθανάτους ειναι συμβεβηκε.—Diodorus Siculus*, lib. v. Immortales autem dicunt hi animos esse.—*Strabo*, lib. iv. Imprimis hoc volunt persuadere, non interire animas.—*Cæsar.* lib. iv.

That the British Druids made great progress in astronomy seems evident from *Plutarch, de Facie in Orbe Lunæ*, who says that they observed a feast in honour of Saturn every *thirtieth* year, the time which the planet Saturn takes to complete its course round the sun; and that the feast took place on its entrance into the second sign (Taurus) of the Zodiac. Diodorus the Sicilian, already quoted, makes mention of a certain Hyperborean island (Britain), less than Sicily, opposite to Celtiberia, where the Boreadae (Bards or Druids) could bring the moon near them, so as to see its opacity, its convexity, its mountains, and other phenomena on its surface. Some have, with reason, understood this passage to allude to telescopic observations.

Cæsar, in writing of them in the sixth book of his Commentaries, has " multa præterea de sideribus, atque eorum motu, de mundi ac terrarum magnitudine, de natura rerum . . . . disputant;" and Mela writes,—" Hi terræ mundique magnitudinem et formam, motus cœli ac siderum . . . . scire profitentur."

That they were proficients in mechanical philosophy, the obelisks of Stonehenge and of other places are so many *standing* proofs. Cæsar observes, that the British Druids worshipped a divinity named Taranis or Taran, which in Welch means thunder, as does the Gaelic *torunn*. In the latter times of the Druidical order, all the principal families in the Hebrides had their Druidh, who foretold future events, and decided all causes, civil and ecclesiastical. The British Druids, according to Dr. Smith, owed their decline to the following circumstance:—Trathal, the grandfather of Fingal, being chosen by them generalissimo (vergobretus) of the Caledonian army sent against the Romans, did not feel disposed, on his return, to resign his authority, even at the command of the Druids. Hence arose a civil war, in which the army of the church was defeated in several battles. These overthrows were fatal to the Druids; they made several attempts to regain their dominion, but all were ineffectual. They retired to I-thonn, *the Isle of Waves*, or Iona, where, it is said, their order was not quite extinct on the arrival of St. Columbus in the sixth century.

DRUIDHEACHD, *s. f.* Druidism; magic; enchantment; witchcraft; a charm. *N. pl.* druidheachdan; *d. pl.* druidheachdaibh. Ban-mhaighistir nan druidheachdan, *the mistress of witchcrafts.—Stew. Nah.* Co chuir druidheachd oirbh? *who has bewitched you?—Stew. Gal.*

DRUIDHEAN, *n. pl.* of druidh; which see.

DRUIDHEANN, inn, *s. m.* More properly *droighionn*; which see.

DRUIDHNEACH, *s.* Druids.

DRUIDIDH, *fut. aff. a.* of druid.

DRUIDTE, *p. part.* of druid; which see.

DRÙIGH, *v. a.* Penetrate; affect, operate on; ooze, drop, distil; pour out. *Pret. a.* dhrùigh; *fut. aff. a.* drùighidh, *shall penetrate.* Cha drùigh thu air, *you cannot penetrate it; you cannot affect him.*

DRÙIGHEADH, idh, *s. m.* A penetrating; an oozing, a distilling; an operating, as on the feelings.

DRUIGHEADH, (a), *pr. part.* of drùigh.

DRUIGHIL, *v. a.* Troll, hurl or roll together, or mix by rolling together. *W.* trwyll, *that turns round.*

DRUIGHLEADH, idh, *s. m.* A trolling, a hurling or rolling together.

DRUIGHLEAGAN, ain, *s. m.* Meal and water mixed, hens' food.

DRÙIGHTEACH, *a.* Penetrating; oozing, distilling, dropping; enticing; attractive. Uisge drùighteach, *penetrating rain.* Le briathraibh drùighteach, *with enticing words.—Stew. Col.*

DRUIL, *v. a.* Troll, twirl; roll together, or mix by rolling together. *Pret. a.* dhruil; *fut. aff. a.* druilidh.

DRUILINN, *s. f.* A sudden flash, especially that of iron heated to incandescence, when it is first struck on coming from the forge.

Druilinn (*druidh-lann*) properly signifies the flame of the Druids, and alludes to that instantaneous gleam of light produced in some Druidical ceremonies, by means, as some imagine, of gunpowder. Of the same nature, according to Dr. Smith, was the stratagem of the priests at Delphi, by which Xerxes, and even the bloody Brennus, were driven away with terror, though they approached with the intention of pillaging it.

DRUIM, droma, *s. f.* (*Gr.* δρομος. *Ir.* druim. *W.* trwm.) The back of the human body; the back of a quadruped; the top of a hill; the top of a house; a roof, a ridge; a surface. *Asp. form*, dhruim. Do dhruim nan amadan, *for the back of fools.—Stew. Pro.* Gun druim ach athar, *without roof but the sky.—Oss. Gaul.* Air druim a chuain, *on the surface of the sea*; druim-chroinn, *the beam of a plough*; druim-luinge, *the keel of a ship*; druim-fhionn, *white-backed*; druim-bhreac, *having a speckled back*; druim uachdair a chàirean, *the palate.*

DRUIM-ALBAINN, *s. f.* Drumalbin; the Καληδόνιος δρυμος of Ptolemy.

DRUIM-BOGHA, *s. f.* A vault.

DRUIM-BHREAC, *a.* Having a spotted or speckled back. Bradan druim-bhreac, *a spotted salmon.—Old Song.*

DRUIM-CHROINN, *s. f.* The beam of a plough.

DRUIMEAN, ein, *s. m.* (*from* druim.) A ridge.

DRUIMEANACH, *a.* White-backed; ridged.

DRUIM-FHIONN, *a.* White-backed.—*Macint.* and *Macfar.*

DRUIMIONN, *a.* Ridgy. *Asp. form*, dhruimionn. Mar stuaidh dhruimionn, *like a ridgy wave.—Oss. Tem.*

DRUIN, druine, *s. f.* Needlework, embroidery.—*Shaw.*

DRUINNEACH, ich, *s. m.* (*Ir. id.*) An artist; a mantua-maker, a milliner, an embroiderer; one who works with a needle.—*Shaw.*

DRUINNEACHAS, ais, *s. m.* Embroidery, tapestry, needlework, tambouring; millinery, mantua-making.

DRUINNSE, *s. f.* A burden. *N. pl.* druinnsean.

DRUINNSEACH, ich, *s. m.* A burden. *N. pl.* druinnsichean.

DRUIPE, *s. f.* A drudge.

DRÙIS, *s. f.* (*Ir. id.*) Lust, lechery; perspiration. *Germ.* druse, *dirt*; *light dew.* *Gr.* δρόσος, *light dew.*

DRÙIS, *v. n.* Play the wanton, prostitute. *Pret. a.* dhrùis. Dhrùis i i fein, *she prostituted herself*; *fut. aff.* drùisidh.

Drùiseach, *a.*, *from* drùis. (*Ir.* druiseach) Lustful, lecherous; dewy.

Drùiseadh, idh, *s. m.* A whoring, a wantoning

Drùiseag, eig, *s. f.* A little prostitute, a young prostitute. *N pl.* druiseagan.

Drùisealachd, *s. f.* Lustfulness, wantonness, lecherousness; *also*, moisture, dewiness, sap —*Macint.*

Drùisear, ir, *s. m* (drùis-fhear) A fornicator, a whoremonger, a lecher.

Drùisearachd, *s f* Whoremongering, lecherousness.

Drùiseil, *a.* (drùis-amhuil) Lustful, lecherous, dewy

Drùisdear, ir, *s. m.* (*from* drùis) A fornicator, a whoremonger, a lecher. *N pl.* druisdearan.

Drùisdearachd, *s f.* Fornication, whoremongering, lechery.

Drùis-lann, -lainn, *s m* (*Ir id*) A brothel.

Drùis-thigh, *s. m.* A brothel *N pl.* druis-thighean

Drùiteach, *a.* See **Drùighdeach**.

Drum, *s f* A drum. *N pl.* drumaichean, *drums.* Chluinntear pìob is drumaichean, *pipes and drums might be heard* —*Old Song.*

Drumain, *gen. sing.* of druman; which see.

Drumair, *s. m* (*from* drum) A drummer *N. pl* drumairean; *d. pl.* drumairibh

Drumaireachd, *s f* (*from* drum.) Drum-beating; any loud battering noise, a battering, a drumming Ri drumaireachd, *beating the drum, making a rattling noise*, ciod an drumaireachd th' ort? *what are you drumming for?*

Druman, ain, *s. m* (*W.* truman, *a ridge*) A ridge; a back, a summit; a bore-tree, the wood of the bore-tree, the back-band of a horse

Drùs, druis, *s. m.* Fornication, lechery *Germ* druse, *dirt* See **Drùis**.

Drusdaireachd, *s. f.* Fornication, lecherousness; dirtiness of habit; filthiness

Drusdar, air, *s. m.* A fornicator; a lewd person, a person of dirty habits. Written also *trusdar*

Drutaireachd, *s f.* Fornication; filthiness; filth.

Drutan, ain, *s.* A drudge

Drutar, air, *s m.* (*Ir* drutoir) A fornicator, a person of dirty habits

Drùth, druthta, *s f.* (*Ir* and *Corn. id*) A harlot, also, *adjectively*, lascivious, foolish

Drùth, *v. n.* Penetrate; enter, ooze, distil; touch, as the feelings; affect. *Pret a* dhruth, *fut aff a* druthaidh, *shall* or *will affect* Druthaidh achmhasan air duine glic, *reproof will affect a wise man.*—*Stew. Pro.*

Drùthach, *a.* Penetrating; oozing, distilling, lecherous

Drùthachdainn, *s f* A penetrating, oozing, or distilling, affecting

Drùthaidh, *fut. aff. a.* of drùth.

Drùthanag, aig, *s f.* A harlot, a bawd *N pl.* druthanagan.

Drùth-bhosgair, *s m.* A pimp, or pander. *N. pl* druthbhosgairean.

Druth-lann, -lainn, *s. m* (*Ir id*) A brothel

Druth-labhair, *v. a* (*Ir. id.*) Blab out.

Druth-mhac, -mhic, *s m* A bastard son —*Shaw.*

Du', *a* Black See **Dubh**.

† **Du**, *s. m.* A land, a country; habitation, a place of abode. Hence *duthaich*, i e. *du-teach*, meaning the land in which one's house is, a native country.

Dù, *a.* (*Fr.* dû. *Eng* due) Fit, proper; due, suitable, just. Gaidheal dan dù buaidh, *Gael whose due is victory.*—*Old Song.*

Duach, aich, *s. m.* (*Ir. id.*) A proper name of Irish princes. —*Shaw.*

Duad, *s.* (*Ir. id*) Labour, hardship, difficulty.

† **Duadh**, duaidh, *s m.* (*Ir. id.*) Labour, hardship; *also*, eating —*Shaw.* Duadh-obair, *handicraft, hard labour.*

† **Duadhal**, *a* (*Ir id*) Hard, difficult; laborious.

† **Duadhalachd**, *s. f.* Hardship, difficulty, laboriousness. *Ir.* duadhamhlachd.

† **Duadhmor**, *a* (*Ir. id*) Hard; difficult; laborious

Duadh-obair, -oibre, *s. f.* Hard labour; a handicraft

Duaichneachd, *s. f.* Deformity, corruption; a mask, disfigurement Gu duaichneachd, *to corruption* —*Stew Dan.*

Duaichnich, *v a* and *n.* Deform, corrupt, mask, disfigure *Pret a* dhuaichnich, *disfigured, fut aff a* duaichnichidh *shall disfigure*

Duaichnidh, *a* Deformed, ugly, dismal, black, masked Is duaichnidh do dhreach, *dismal is thy appearance* —*Ull* Tha iad duaichnidh, *they are black* —*Stew O B*

Duaidh, *s f* (*Ir id*) Mischief, evil, a terrible event, a dreadful scene Anns an duaidh sin, *in that dreadful scene* —*Fingalian Poem* Written also *duaigh*

Duaidheach, *a* Mischievous; calamitous.

Duaigh, *s f* Mischief, evil, a terrible event, a dreadful scene

Duaile, *s f* (*Ir id*) Propriety.

† **Duaillbhearta**, ai, *s. m* (*Ir. id*) A dialect —*Shaw*

Duairc, *a.* (*Ir id*) Surly, stern, unamiable; *also, substantively*, a surly person. The epithet of opposite meaning to *duairc* is *suairc.*

Duairceach, *a*, *from* duairc. (*Ir. id.*) Surly, stern; unamiable. *Com.* and *sup* duairciche

Duairceach, *a* (*Ir id*) Surly, stern, squabbling.

Duaireachadh, aidh, *s m* Slander Sgeul duaireachaidh, *a slanderous tale.*—*Old Song*

Duaireachas, ais, *s. m.* Sternness, *also*, commotion, sedition, a squabble, a fray, slander. A deanamh duaireachais, *raising sedition* —*Stew Ezra*

D'uairibh, *adv.* At times, sometimes

Duairidh, *s f* A dowry Written also *dubhairidh* *Fr.* douaire

Duais, *s f.* A reward, wages, gains A toirt duais seachad, *giving wages* —*Stew Ezek* Duais an uilc, *the gains of sin* —*Sm*

Duais-bhrath, -bhraith, *s f* A bribe, bribery; the gains of treachery, a traitor's hire

Duaiseach, *a* (*from* duais) Relating to wages; ready to pay; giving a reward

Duaisiche, *s m.* A hireling, a hired servant *N pl* duaisichean

Dual, *v. a* Fold, plait, loop, curl, as hair; carve. *Pret a.* dhual, *curled*, *fut aff. a* dualaidh.

Dual, duail, *s m* (*Ir* dual) A loop; a fold or plait of a rope, a lock of hair, a ringlet, *also*, a duty, a law, a due, an office Cord thri dual, *a three-plaited cord.*—*Stew Ecc.* Esan do'n dual am bàs, *he whose due is death* —*Mac Lach.* Ceann maiseach nan dual, *the handsome head of ringlets* —*Old Poem* Bu dual athar dhuit sin, *you inherited that from your father.*

Dual, *a.* Hereditary, usual, natural; due Cha bu dual bhi gun noidheachd, *it was not usual to be without hospitality.*—*Ull* Do'n dual gach cliu, *to whom every praise is due* —*Sm* Mar is dual do'n fheur, *as is natural to the grass* *Id.* Bu dual da sin, *he has it in his kind* —*G. P.*

DUALACH, *a.* (*from* dual.) Plaited, in folds; curled, as hair; bushy, as hair; full of ringlets; tressy; flowing in ringlets; having luxuriant hair; beautiful. Cord dualach, *a plaited rope.* A chiabha dualach, *his bushy locks.—Stew. Song Sol. ref.* Falt dubh dualach, *black and curled hair.—Macfar.*

DUALADAIR, *s. m.* A cordwainer; one who plaits; a carver; an embroiderer. *N. pl.* dualadairean.

DUALADAIREACHD, *s. f.* The business of a cordwainer; a plaiting; a carving; an embroidering; embroidery.

DUALADH, aidh, *s. m.* (*Ir. id.*) A carving; embroidering; a fold; a plait; a ringlet. Na dhualadh liath, *in his grey ringlets.—Oss. Gaul.*

DUALAICH, *gen. fem.* of dualach.

DUALAICH, *v. a.* Plait; fold; weave; carve; engrave. *Pret.* dhualaich, *plaited; fut. aff. a.* dualaichidh, *shall plait.*

DUALAICHE, *s. m.* A sculptor, an engraver.

DUALAICHEAS, *s. m.* (*Ir. id.*) Sculpture, engraving.—*Shaw.*

DUALAN, ain, *s. m.* (*dim.* of dual.) A little lock or ringlet, a tress.

DUALANACH, *a.* Having tresses or ringlets.

DUALCHAS, ais, *s. m.* (*from* dual.) Nature, temper, hereditary disposition; a native place; hire, wages, dues; duty. Is e do dhualchas bhi duineil, *it is thy [hereditary] nature to be manly.—Mac Co.*

DUAM, duaim, *s. m.* (*Ir. id.*) A city.

† DUAN, duain, *s. m.* (*Ir. id.*) A poem, an ode, a song, a ditty, a canto; an harangue. *N. pl.* duain. An cuirinn an duan do chreuchdan? *would I celebrate thy wounds in song?—Oss. Lodin.* Duan mòr, *an epic poem.*

DUANACH, *a.* Melodious, tuneful; poetical.

DUANACHD, *s. f.* (*from* duan.) Versification.

DUANAG, aig, *s. f.* (*dim.* of duan.) An ode, a song, a ditty, a sonnet, a canto. *N. pl.* duanagan. Le duanagan, *with ditties.—Macint.*

DUANAICHE, *s. m.* (*Ir.* duanaighe.) A rhymer, a versifier.

DUANAIR, *s. m.* (*Ir. id.*) A chanter; a rhymer. *N. pl.* duanairean.

DUANAIREACHD, *s. f.* (*from* duan.) A chanting; a rhyming.

† DUANARTACH, aich, *s. m.* (*Ir. id.*) A senator.

† DUAN-CHRUITHEACHD, *s. f.* (*Ir. id.*) Policy.

† DUAN-MÒR, *s. m.* An epic poem; *literally,* a great poem.

DUANTACH, *a.* (*from* duan.) Poetical; in verse; full of poetry.

DUANTACHD, *s. f.* Versification, poetry.

† DUAR, duair, *s. m.* (*Ir. id.*) A word, a saying; a verse, a metre.

DUARMAN, ain, *s. m.* A murmur.

DUARMANACH, *a.* Murmuring.

DUARMANAICH, *s. f.* Frequent murmuring; continued murmuring.

† DUAS, ais, *s. m.* (*Ir. id.*) A poet.

DUASACH, *a.* (*Ir. id.*) Inauspicious.

† DUB, *v. a.* (*Ir. id.*) Dip; dub. *Pret. a.* dhubh; *fut. aff.* dubaidh.

† DUBADH, aidh, *s. m.* (*Ir. id.*) A pond.

DÙBAILT, *a.* Double, twofold; cunning, false. Cridhe dùbailt, *a double heart.—Sm.* Dhiolainn e dùbailt, *I would repay him twofold.*—Uisge-beath dùbailt, *double-distilled whisky. Arm.* doubl, *a copy. Du.* dubbeld, *double. Box. Lex.* dwbl.

DUBAIRT, *s. f.* An earnest prayer.—*Shaw.*

DUBH, *a.* Black; dark-haired; dark; gloomy; sad; wicked; *rarely,* great; *also,* darkness; ink. *Asp. form,* dhubh. Oidhche dhubh, *a dark night;* oidhche dhubh dhorch, *a pitchy dark night;* bu dubh a sgeul, *sad was his tale.—Oss.* Daol dubh, *a beetle.*

Heb. dua, black. *Malay,* du, *bad. Arm.* douh, *smoked,* and touh, *black. Pun.* dua, *black. Arab.* duvia, *ink. Chald.* dutha, *ink. Heb.* diu, *ink. Scotch,* (*surnames*) Duff *and* Dow, originally meaning *black. Arm. Corn. W. Manks,* du *and* diu, *black. Ir.* dubh. *Port.* dò, *mourning.* (Duine dubh, *a black man.*) *Arm.* deen du.

DUBH, *v. a.* Blacken, blot, stain, darken; condemn. *Pret. a.* dhubh; *fut. aff. a.* dubhaidh, *shall blacken.* Dubh mise, *blot me.—Stew. Exod.*

DUBHACH, aich, *s. m.* Ink, a black dye; a tub.

DUBHACH, *a.* (*Ir. id.*) Dark, gloomy, sorrowful, sad, mourning; frowning. Tha mise dubhach, *I am sad.—Ull.* Oighean, dubhach, *mourning maidens.—Oss. Derm.* Aodach dubhach, *mourning clothes.* Gealach dubhach donn, *a dark dusky moon.—Oss. Lod.* A shùil a siubhal gu dubhach, *his eye moving darkly, or frowning.—Fingalian Poem. Com.* and *sup.* dubhaiche.

DUBHACHAIS, *gen. sing.* of dubhachas.

DUBHACHAS, ais, *s. m.* (*Ir. id.*) Sorrow, mourning, heaviness of mind; darkness, duskiness. Dubhachas a mhathar, *the heaviness of his mother.—Stew. Pro.*

DUBHADAN, ain, *s. m., from* dubh. (*Ir. id.*) An ink-holder, a standish; soot; blacking. *N. pl.* dubhadain.

DUBHADANACH, *a.* Black, inky, sooty.

DUBHADH, aidh, *s. m.* (*Ir. id.*) A blackening, a darkening, mourning; obscurity, darkness, blackness. Dubhadh nan speur, *the darkness of the skies.—Oss. Tem.*

DUBHADH, aidh, *s. m.* Ink; any black substance.
Arab. duvia. *Chald.* dutha, *ink. Heb.* diu, *ink.*

DUBHADH, (a), *pr. part.* of dubh. Blackening, darkening; shading; blotting; staining; condemning. A ghealach a dubhadh san, *the moon darkening in the skies.—Oss. Lod.*

DUBHADH, aig, *s. f.* A name given commonly in disrespect to a young female. Theid dubhag ri dualchas, *like mother like daughter.—G. P.*

DUBHAGAN, ain, *s. m.* (*from* dubh.) Ink; blacking; the pupil of the eye.

DUBHAGAN-NA-SUL, *s. m.* The black of the eye; the pupil of the eye.—*Stew. Pro.*

DUBH-AGHAIDH, *s. m.* and *f.* A black or dark visage; a dark aspect; a dark surface. Dubh-aghaidh na h-oidhche, *the dark visage of night.—Oss. Tem.*

DUBHAICHE, *com.* and *sup.* of dubhach; which see.

DUBH-AIGEAN, -ein, *s. m.* The sea, ocean; an abyss; the bottom of an abyss. Dubh-aigean na fairge, *the bottomless depths of the sea.—O'Brien.*

DUBHAILC, ailce, *s. f.* Vice, wickedness. *N. pl.* dubhailcean; *d. pl.* dubhailcibh. Combaraichte ann an dubhailc, *noted for vice.—Macfar.* Dol anns na dubhailcibh, *plunging into vices.—Id.*

DUBHAILCEACH, *a.* Vicious, wicked. *Com.* and *sup.* dubhailciche.

DUBHAILCEACH, ich, *s. m.* A wicked person. *N. pl.* dubhailciche.

DUBHAILT, *s. f.* (*from* dubh.) Darkness, gloom.

DUBHAILTEACH, *a.* Dark, gloomy.—*Oss. Gaol nan daoine.*

DUBHAIN, *gen. sing.* and *n. pl.* of dubhan; which see.

DUBHAIR, *gen. sing.* of dubhar.

DUBHAIR, *v. a.* Darken, shade. *Pret. a.* dhubhair, *darkened.*

DUBHAIRIDH, *s. f.* A dowry, a marriage portion. Air a mheud 's gun dean sibh an dubhairidh, *make their dowry never so much.—Stew. Gen.*

DUBHAIRT, *pret.* of *v. irr.* abair. Said. Dubhairt mi, *I said.* More frequently written *thubhairt.*

† DUBHALLADH, aidh, *s. m.* (*Ir. id.*) Want.—*Shaw.*

DUBHAN, -ain, *s. m.* (*Ir. id.*) A hook; a fishing-hook; a snare; a kidney; darkness; soot. *N. pl.* dubhain, *hooks.* Dubhain ann ad ghialaibh, *hooks in thy jaws.*—*Stew. Ezek.* Dubhan busgainte, *a dressed fishing-hook.* Dubhan cuileig, *a fly-hook.*

DUBHAN-ALLUIDH, *s. m.* A spider. Mar lion dubhan-alluidh, *like a spider's web.*—*Oss. Cathula.* See also DAMHAN-ALLUIDH. Perhaps *damhan-ealaidhean.*

DUBHAN-IASGAICH, *s. m.* A fishing-hook.

DUBHAR, -air, *s. m.* Darkness, dusk, shade, gloom. Dubhar an fheasgair, *the dusk of the evening.*—*Macfar.* Dubhar a cheò, *the darkness of mist.*—*Ull.* Fo dhubhar géige, *under the shade of a branch.*—*Id.*

DUBHARA, DUBHARAN, *n. pl.* of dubhar.

DUBHARACH, *a.* (*Ir. id.*) Shadowy, opaque, dark, dusky, cloudy.

DUBHARACHD, *s. f.* Shadiness, opacity; duskiness, cloudiness.

DUBHARADH, aidh, *s. m.* A shadowing, a darkening; darkness, shade, duskiness; an eclipse. Dubharadh gréine, *a solar eclipse.* Dubharadh gealaich, *a lunar eclipse.*

DUBHARAICH, *v. a.* Shade; darken, eclipse. *Pret. a.* dhubharaich, *shaded, fut. aff. a.* dhubharaichidh, *shall shade, p. part.* dubharaichte.

DUBHARAICHTE, *p. part.* of dubharaich. Shaded, darkened.

DUBHARAN, *n. pl.* of dubhar; which see.

DUBH-BHREAC, -bhric, *s. m.* (*Scotch,* dowbreck.) A smelt; a spirling.—*Macd.*

DUBH-BHRON, -bhròin, *s. m.* Deep grief.

DUBH-BHRÒNACH, *a.* Disconsolate.—*Oss. Trathal.*

DUBH-BHUIDH, *a.* Livid, dark yellow; black and blue. Chinn an speur gu dubh-bhuidh, *the sky appeared of a dark yellow.*—*Macdon.*

DUBH-BHUILLE, *s. m.* A fatal blow. *N. pl.* dubh-bhuillean.

DUBH-CHAILE, *s. f.* A trollop, a female scullion, a scullery girl. *N. pl.* dubh-chailean. Dubh-chaile a bhuaraich, *the dunghill trollop.*—*Old Song.*

DUBH-CHEATHACH, ich, *s. m.* A dark mist; a thick mist. Dubh-cheathach air aros nan long, *a dark mist on the ocean.*—*Oss. Fing.* Written also *du'cheathach.*

DUBH-CHEIST, *s. f.* A puzzle, an enigma; a motto; a superscription. *N. pl.* dubh-cheistean.

DUBH-CHIABHACH, *a.* Black-haired, dark-haired.—*Oss. Tem.*

DUBH-CHIS, *s. f.* A tax or impost; black mail.

DUBH-CHLEAS, *s.* A feat in legerdemain or in black art.

DUBH-CHLEASACHD, *s. f.* Black art.

DUBH-CHLEASAICHE, *s. m.* An adept in black art, a conjurer.

DUBH-CHÒSACH, aich, *s. m.* The herb maidenhair.—*Shaw.*

DUBH-CHOSACH, *a.* Black-footed, black-legged; *also,* the name of a dog; melampus; black foot, *a black foot, a black leg.*

DUBH-CHRAIG, *s. f.* A gloomy rock; a ring ouzel; the *turdus torquatus* of Linnæus.

DUBH-CHUIL, *s. f.* A beetle.—*Shaw.*

DÙBHDACH, aich, *s. f.* A sounding horn. *Germ.* duden.

DUBHDAIR, *s. m.* A trumpeter.

DUBHDAIREACHD, *s. f.* The employment of a trumpeter, trumpeting.

DUBH-DHAOL, dhaoil, *s. m.* A beetle.—*Macd.* Written also *du'dhaol.*

DUBH-DHEARG, *a.* Russet, dark brown, auburn. Written also *du'dhearg.*

DUBH-DHONN, *a.* Dark brown, auburn, russet, dusky. Air sgiathaibh dubh-dhonn, *on dark brown wings.*—*Oss. Lodin.* Falt dubh-dhonn, *auburn hair.*

DUBH-DHORCH, *a.* Pitchy dark. Written also *du'dhorch.*

DUBH-DHORCHADAS, ais, *s. m.* Pitchy darkness.—*Sm.* Written also *du'dhorchadas.*

DUBH-DHRUIM, -dhroma, *s. f.* A dark surface; a dark height; a black back; a black ridge. Dubh-dhruim na mara, *the dark surface of the sea.*—*Oss. Tem.*

DUBH-EIREANNACH, aich, *s. m.* A wild Irishman.

DUBH-FHOCAL, ail, *s. m.* A dark saying; a riddle or puzzle, a parable; a bad expression. Written also *du'-fhocal.*

DUBH-FHOLT, -fhuilt, *s. m.* Dark hair. A dhubh-fholt a taomadh mu 'cheann, *his dark hair floating about his head.*—*Oss. Lodin.* Written also *du'fholt.*

DUBH-GHALL, -ghaill, *s. m.* A Lowland Scot, a real Lowlander; *in contempt,* a sneaking mean-spirited fellow; *also,* an Englishman; a foreigner. Written also *du'ghall.*

DUBH-GHLAS, *a.* Dark grey, *also,* the surname Douglas.

DUBH-GHLEANN, -ghlinn, *s. m.* A gloomy vale.

DUBH-GHORM, *a.* Dark blue; black and blue. Written also *du'ghorm.*

DUBH-GHORMADH, aidh, *s. m.* Making black and blue, making dark blue.

DUBH-GHRÀIN, *s. f.* Extreme disgust, abhorrence.

DUBH-GHRÀINICH, *v. a.* Abhor, detest.

DUBH-GHRUAIM, *s. f.* A dark frown.—*Oss. Tem.*

DUBH-LÀ, *s. m.* A mournful day. Cumaibh an dubh-là air chuimhne, *keep the mournful day in mind.*—*Oss. Cathluno.*

DÙBHLACH, aich, *s. m.* Darkness, dimness, wintry weather; depth of winter.

DÙBHLACHADH, aidh, *s. m.* A copying, a copy.—*Stew. Job.*

DUBH-LACHADH, aidh, *s. m.* A coot.—*Macd.* *N. pl.* dubh-lachaidh, *coots.*

DÙBHLACHD, *s. f.* The depth of winter; winter; wintry weather. Dùbhlachd a gheamhraidh, *the depth of winter.*

DÙBHLAIDH, *a.* Dark, wintry, tempestuous. Beucach dùbhlaidh, *noisy and dark.*—*Oss. Fing.* Gu dùbhlaidh, *darkly.*

DÙBHLAIDHEACHD, *s. f.* Darkness, wintriness, tempestuousness.

DÙBHLAN, ain, *s. m.* A challenge, a defiance. Cuir gu dùbhlan, *set at defiance.* A toirt dùbhlain, *challenging.*—*Stew. Sam.*

DÙBHLANACH, *a.* Challenging, defying, prone to challenge or to defy, of, or belonging to, a challenge or defiance. Written also *dùlan.*

DÙBHLANAICH, *v. a.* Challenge, defy. *Pret. a.* dhùbhlanaich, *challenged, fut. aff.* dùbhlanaichidh, *shall challenge.*

DUBH-LATH, *s. m.* A dismal day, a mournful day. Written also *du'lath.*

DUBH-LIATH, *s. f.* The spleen.

DUBH-LIUNN, *s. m.* Melancholy. Fo dhubh-liunn trom, *under heavy melancholy.*—*Macfar.*

DUBH-LOCHLINNEACH, ich, *s. m.* A Dane. Fionn-Lochlinneach, *a Norwegian.* *N. pl.* Dubh-Lochlinnich, *Danes.*

DUBH-NEUL, *v. a.* Obnubilate, darken. Written also *du'neul.*

DUBH-NEUL, -neòil, *s. m.* A dark cloud.—*Oss. Conn.* A dark colour, a swarthy complexion. *N. pl.* dubh-neoil, *dark clouds.*

DUBH-NIAL, -neòil, *s. m.* A dark cloud. *N. pl.* dubh-neòil.

DUBH-NIMHE, *s. f.* The banner of Caoilte, the son of Ratho.

Dubhra, ai, *s. m.* Darkness, gloom, shade; sternness; a spectre An dubhra dubh, *the pitchy darkness*—*Oss Carricth.* Dubhra m' an gruaidh, *sternness in their visage.*—*Oss. Tem*

Dubhra, *a.* Dark, gloomy. An oidhche dubhra, *the night gloomy*—*Oss Com*

Dubhrach, *a* Dark, shady, gloomy, opaque. Contracted for *dubharach.*

Dubhradar, (an Irish inflection of the irregular verb *abair.*) They said

Dubhradh, aidh, *s. m* (*Ir. id*) A darkening, a shading; darkness, shade, gloom. Contracted for *dubharadh.*

Dubhradh, *pret.* of *v. irr.* abair Was said. See **Abair**

Dubhradh, (a), *pr part* of dubhair. Darkening, shading Bròn a dubhradh mo chleibh, *grief darkening my breast*—*Oss Tem*

Dubhram, (from the *v. irr.* abair.) I said

† **Dubhras**, ais, *s m* (*Ir. id*) A house, a room, a habitation—*Shaw*

Dubh-reotha, *s m* and *f* Black frost, a mole. Smùidrich an dubh-reotha, *the mist of black frost*—*Macfar.*

Dubh-ruadh, *a.* Dark brown, auburn. Ciabh dubh-ruadh, *dark brown locks*—*Oss Tem*

Dubh-sgiathach, *a.* Dark-winged—*Oss. Gaul.*

Dubh-shnamhair, *s m* A diver, the bird called a didapper.

Dubh-shiubhal, ail, *s m* A dark stream—*Shaw* The progress of a dark stream, dark rolling, a dark path Dubh-shiubhal na linn, *the dark rolling of the abyss.*—*Oss Comala.*

Dubhta, **Dubhte**, *p part* of dubh. Cancelled, blotted, blackened

Dùbhtach, aich, *s f* (*Germ.* duden) A sounding horn; a bugle

Dubh-thoill, *s f.* (*Ir. id*) Hemorrhoids—*Shaw*

Dubh-thonn, -thuinn, *s* A gloomy wave Guth dubh-thuinn, *the voice of a gloomy wave.*—*Old Poem.* Written also *du'thonn*

Dubla, ai, *s m* (*Ir id*) A sheath, a case, a scabbard.

Dùbhlachadh, aidh, *s. m* A folding, a doubling; a duplicate.

Dùblachadh, (a), *pr part.* of dùblaich Folding, doubling

Dùbladh, aidh, *s m* A covering; a lining; a sheath, a case; a doubling, double Fhuair e 'dhubladh, *he got double of it.*

Dùblaich, *v. a* Double, fold; distil a second time *Pret a* dhùblaich, *doubled*, *fut aff. a* dublaichidh, *shall double.* Dhùblaich thu m' uile mhaoin, *thou hast doubled all my store*—*Sm*

Dùblaichte, *p part* of dublaich Doubled

Dùblainn, *v. a* Double *Pret a* dhùblainn, *fut aff* dùblainnidh.

Dùblainn, *s* A double quantity, as much again

Dùc, duca, *s. m.* A heap, a hillock *N. pl* dùcan

Dùcait, *s. f.* A ducat—*Macd N pl.* dùcaitean

Ducain, *gen. sing.* and *n pl* of dùcan

Dùcan, ain, *s. m* (*dim.* of dùc) A little heap, a little hillock. *N. pl* dùcain Dùcan faimh, *a mole-hill*, dùcan ùir fhamh, *a mole-hill*

Dùcanach, *a* (*from* ducan) Full of hillocks or heaps

Dùcan-uir-fhamh, *s m.* A mole-hill.

Dùcan-faimh, *s. m* A mole-hill

† **Duchan**, ain, *s m* (*Ir. id.*) War

Dùchas, ais, *s. m* Native country, hereditary right; nativity, hereditary temper; visage; a countenance. Tìr a dhùchas, *the shore of his native country*—*Stew. Jer.* Cha bhi dùchas aig mnai no sagart, *women and priests are natives no where.*—*G. P.* Fearann do dhùchais, *the land of thy nativity.*—*Stew. Ezek.* Written also *dùthchas*; which see.

Dùchasach, *a.* Hereditary; patrial; national; patriotic; fond of one's native land, of one's native country; native. Mo thìr dhùchasach, *my native land.*

Dùd, duda, *s m.* The swell of trumpet; the blast of a sounding horn (*Scotch*, towt) *Also*, a silent flatus.

Dud, *s m.* (*Ir. id.*) A tingling of the ear, proceeding from an obstruction, whereby the air which is shut up being continually moved by the beating of the arteries and the drum of the ear, is lightly reverberated, the ear, a rag—*Shaw. Scotch*, dud, *a rag.*

Dùdach, aich, *s f* (*Germ.* duden) A sounding horn, a bugle

Dudach, *a* Ragged.—*Shaw Com* and *sup* dudaiche.

Dudag, aig, *s m.* (*Scotch*, dud) A rag, a small cup; a measure of liquids containing a dram, commonly made of horn, a slight stroke on the ear, a ragged girl

Dùdag, aig, *s f.* (*Ir. id*) A trumpet, a sounding horn.

Dùdair, *s. m* (*Ir id*) One who blows a sounding horn, a trumpeter

Dùdaireachd, *s. f* Trumpeting, the noise of a hunting-horn

Dùdlach, *a* Stormy, wintry

Dùdlachd, *s f* Tempestuous weather, wintry weather, the depth of winter. Ann an am na dùdlachd, *in the depth of winter*—*Macfar*

Dùgh See **Dù.**

Duibh, *gen. sing.* of dubh.

Duibh, *comp pron* To you, for you *Asp form*, dhuibh. An cadal duibh? *are you asleep?*—*Oss Gaul*

Duibhe, *s f.* (*from* dubh) Blackness, darkness, ink.

Duibhe, *com* and *sup* of dubh (*Ir. id*) Blacker, blackest, darker, darkest, more sad, most sad Is duibhe na nial fo' ghaoth, *darker than the wind-driven clouds.*—*Oss. Cathloda* A thriath is duibhe sgeul! *thou hero of the saddest history!*—*Oss Com*

Duibhead, eid, *s m* (*Corn.* douat) Blackness; increase in blackness A dol an duibhead, *growing more and more black*, air a dhuibhead, *however dark it be.*

Duibheagan, ain, *s m.* An abyss, a dagger, a short sword

† **Duibhearach**, *a.* (*Ir* duibheartha) Vernacular.—*Shaw.*

Duibheid, *s f* (*Scotch*, divet) A flat turf used for covering cottages. *N. pl* duibheidean

Duibheidich, *v.* Cover with turf, as the roof of a cottage

Duibhir, *a.* Melancholy; anxious, gloomy

Duibhre, *s f* Darkness, shade, gloom, melancholy, sadness. An duibhre bàis, *in the darkness of death*—*Sm.* Mar bhruaich san duibhre, *like a precipice in the dark.*—*Oss Com.*

† **Duibhghean**, ein, *s m* (*Ir. id.*) A sword, a dagger.

Duibhreas, eis, *s m.* Darkness, mysteriousness, secrecy, a secret.—*Stew Gen ref*

Duibleid, *s f* A doublet.

† **Duigh**, *v. n* (*Ir. id*) Cluck, as a hen.—*Shaw.*

† **Duil**, *s f* (*Ir. id*) A partition; a distribution—*Shaw.*

Dùil, *s f.* (*Ir id*) Hope, expectation; belief, supposition; desire, delight An dùil ri teachd an triath, *in hope of their prince's coming.*—*Sm* Tha dùil agam, *I expect, I believe, I suppose*, tha mi 'n dùil, *I believe, I think*; tha dùil agam ris, *I expect him.* Is dùil leam nach cian an t-am, *I expect the time is not distant.—Mac Lach.*

DUIL, duile, *s. f.* (*Ir. id.*) An element; a creature; partition. *Asp. form*, dhuil. *N. pl.* duilidh *and* duiltean. Gach duil bheo, *every living creature.—Sm.* Na duilidh leaghaidh, *the elements shall melt.—Id.*

DUILBHEAR, *a.* Sad, anxious, melancholy, cheerless, unpleasant. (*Ir.* duilbhir.) The word of opposite meaning is *suilbhear.*

DUILBHEARACHD, *s. f.* Sadness, anxiety, suspense, melancholy.—*Shaw.* The word of opposite meaning is *suilbhearachd.*

DÙILE, *s. m.* A poor creature.

DUILE, *s. f.* A leaf of any kind. Written also *duille.*

DÙILEACHD, *s. f.* (*from* dùil.) Suspicion; doubt; hopelessness.

DUILEAG, eig, *s. f.* (*dim.* of duil.) A leaf; a fold; a scabbard. *N. pl.* duileagan. Written also *duilleag.*

† DUILEAMH, *s.* (*Ir. id.*) God.

† DUILEIL, *a.* (duile-amhuil.) ' Skilled.

DUILE-TEANNSGNAIDH, *s. m.* (*Ir. id.*) An element. *N. pl.* duilidh-teannsgnaidh, *elements.—Shaw.*

DUILGHEAS, eis, *s. m.* See DOILGHIOS.

† DUILGNE, *s. pl.* Wages, hire.

DUILIASG, eisg, *s. m.* Dilse; tangles; palmated fucus.—*Shaw.*

DUILIASGACH, *a.* Abounding in dilse or tangles; like dilse or tangles.

DUILICH, *a.* Hard, difficult; sorry. Tha so duilich, *this is difficult;* tha mi duilich air do shon, *I am sorry for you.* Is duilich camag thoirt e darach, anns an fhàilein an d' fhàs e, *it is difficult to make straight in the oak, the bend that grew in the twig.—G. P. Com.* and *sup.* dorra.

DUILICHINN, *s. f.* Grief, vexation. Fo' mhòran duilichinn, *under much grief.—Macint.*

DUILINN, *s. pl.* Elements.—*Shaw.* and *Macd.*

DUILINN, inne, *s. f.* Tribute.

DUIL-IOMRAL, ail, *s. m.* Error.—*Shaw.*

DUIL-THAOBH, *s. m.* A page, or side of a leaf.

DUILLE, *s. f.* A scabbard; a fold, as of a door; a leaf of a tree or of any plant; leaves. Gun duille chall no blàth, *without losing leaf or blossom.—Sm.* Cha d' eirich duille uaine, *no green leaves flourished.—Oss. Croma.* Duille sgein, *the blade of a knife;* duille dorais, *the leaf of a door. Ir.* duille. *W.* dail. *Arm.* delyaii.

DUILLEACH, ich, *s. f.* Foliage, leaves; withered leaves. An duilleach òg éiridh, *the fresh foliage appearing.—Oss. Carricth.* Gaoth le 'n tuiteadh duilleach, *wind by which the withered leaves fall.—Ull. W.* deiliach. *Arm.* delyiaich. The people in and about *Vannes*, say *delyaii*, leaves.

DUILLEACH, *a.* Leafy, having foliage.

DUILLEACHADH, aidh, *s. m.* A flourishing, as of a tree; putting forth leaves.

DUILLEACHAN, ain, *s. m.* (*Ir. id.*) A pamphlet, a book.

DUILLEAG, eig, *s. f.*, *dim.* of duille. (*Corn.* delk.) A little leaf; the leaf of a tree; the leaf of a book; the leaf of a door. Duilleag luaineach, *a fluttering leaf.—Oss. Conn.* Duilleag leabhair, *the leaf of a book;* duilleag dorais, *the leaf of a door;* duilleag sgein, *the blade of a knife;* dà dhuilleag aon chomhlaidh, *the two leaves of one door;* duilleag-bhàite, *a white water-lily.*

DUILLEAGACH, *a.* (*Ir. id.*) Leafy; like a leaf; in folds, as a door. *Com.* and *sup.* duilleagaiche, *more* or *most leafy; asp. form*, dhuilleagach. Craobh dhuilleagaich, *a leafy tree;* dorus duilleagach, *a folding door.*

DUILLEAG-BHÀITE, *s. f.* A white water-lily.

DUILLICH, *v. n.* Flourish, as a tree; produce leaves. *Pret. a.* dhuillich, *flourished; fut. aff. a.* duillichidh, *shall flourish.*

DUILL-MHIAL, *s. f.* A caterpillar; a convolvulus.—*Shaw.*

DUIL-THAOBH, *s. m.* A page, the side of a leaf.

† DUIM, *a.* Poor, needy.—*Shaw.*

DÙIN, *v. a.* (*Germ.* dun, *enclosure.*) Shut, close; enclose, surround; lace; button. *Pret. a.* dhùin; *fut. aff. a.* dùinidh, *shall shut.* Dhùin ceo bhliadhna air a dhearsa, *the mist of years has closed on his splendour.—Oss. Duthona.*

DUINE, *s. m.* (*from* dùn; which see.) *N. pl.* daoine. A man; a husband; a person of manly spirit. In this last sense *duine* is applied to a female. The oldest man of a village is, by the Gael, called *an duine*, the man. Ro-dhuine, *an excellent man; a man of rank.* Fiadh-dhuine, *a wild man, a satyr.—Stew. Is.* Duine gaòil, *a male relative;* duine math, *a good man;* in *Armoric*, it is *den mat;* and in *Vannes*, they say *deen mad.* Duine nan clog, *a bellman; Corn.* den an clog. Is fear duine na daoine, *a good man is better than many men.—G. P.*

Heb. Chald. Syr. Arab. Ethiop. Adam. *Pers.* ten, *man. Calmuc* and *Crim Tartar.* Adam. *Tonq.* dan. *Run.* dhegn. *Ir.* duine. *Corn.* dean *and* den. *Arm.* den *and* deen. *W.* dyn, *man. Teut.* daen *and* diener, *a servant. Bisc.* duenean, *a servant.*

DUINEADAS, ais, *s. m.* (*from* duine.) Manliness.

DUINEALAS, ais, *s. m.* (*from* duin.) Manliness.

DUINEAN, ein, *s. m.* (*dim.* of duine.) A manikin.

DÙINEAR, *fut. pass.* of dùin. Shall be closed.

DUINEIL, *a.* (duine-amhuil.) Manly, like a man. Bi duineil, *be manly.*

DUINE-MHARBHADH, aidh, *s. m.* Manslaughter.

DUINE-MHARBHAICHE, *s. m.* One who has committed manslaughter; a murderer.—*Stew. John, ref.*

DÙINIDH, *fut. aff. a.* of dùin; which see.

DUINN, an *inflection* of donn; which see.

DUINN, *comp. pron.* To us, for us. Gu slainnte thabhairt duinn, *to give us strength.—Sm. Asp. form*, dhuinn. Thoir dhuinn, *give to us;* cha d' thig so dhuinn, *this will not become us;* is còir dhuinn, *we ought.*

DUINE-OIRCNEACH, ich, *s. m.* An assassin.

DÙINTE, *past part.* of duin. Shut, closed; not communicative.

DUIR, *s. f.* (*W.* duir, *oak. Ir. id.*) The fourth letter of the Gaelic alphabet. An oak-tree, an oak-wood.

† DUIRC, *a.* (*Ir. id.*) Rough, rugged, surly.

DUIRCE, *s. f.* An acorn.—*Macd.* Duirce daraich, *an acorn.*

DUIRCEAN, ein, *s. m.* A diminutive naughty person.

DUIRCHE, *com.* and *sup.* of dorch. Darker, darkest.

DUIRCHE, *s. f.* Darkness, gloom. Thionail an duirche, *the darkness gathered.—Oss. Fing.*

DUIRE, *s. f.* (*Ir. id.*) A grove; an oak-wood. See DOIRE.

DÙIRE, *com.* and *sup.* of dùr. More obstinate, most obstinate.

DÙIRE, *s. f.* Hardness, obstinacy, stupidity.

DÙIREAD, eid, *s. m.* Hardness, obstinacy, stupidity.—*Stew. Sam. ref.* Increase in hardness or in obstinacy. A dol an dùiread, *growing more and more hard. Dùiread* is also used as a kind of comparative. Is dùireid e sin, *he is the more obstinate for that.*

DÙIRN, *gen. sing.* and *n. pl.* of dorn. Lan dùirn, *a fistful. Ir.* lan dùirn.

DUIS, *s. f.* (*Ir. id.*) A present; a jewel; a crow; gloom, mist.—*Shaw. N. pl.* duiseachan.

† **Duischill**, *s. f.* (*Ir. id.*) A sanctuary.

Duiseal, eil, *s. m.* A cloud; gloom; heaviness; dulness; drowsiness; a spout. Gun duiseal san iarmailt, *without a cloud in the firmament.—Oss. Fin. and Lorm.* Gun duiseal cadail, *without the heaviness of sleep.—R.*

Duisealach, **Duisealtach**, aich, *s. m.* Rain.

Dùisg, *v. a.* Awake, waken, rouse, stir up, excite. *Pret. a.* dhùisg, *wakened; fut. aff. a.* dùisgidh, *shall waken.* Dùisg do chumhachd, *stir up thy strength.—Sm.* C'uine dhùisgeas esan? *when will he awaken?—Ull. Fut. pass.* dùisgear; *p. part.* dùisgte.

Dùisgear, *fut. aff. a.* of duisg. Shall awaken, shall be roused or stirred up. Dùisgear na sloigh, *the people shall awaken.—Sm.*

Dùisgidh, *fut. aff. a.* of dùisg.

Duisgioll, ill, *s. m.* A client.—*Shaw* and *Macd.* Perhaps *duis-ghille.*

Dùisgte, *p. part.* of duisg. Wakened, roused.

† **Dùisich**, *v.* (*Ir. id.*) Awake, arouse. *Pret.* dhùisich. More frequently written *dùisg.*

Duisleag, eig, *s. f.* Dilse. *N. pl.* duisleagan.

Duis-neul, neòil, *s. m.* A dark cloud; a gloomy aspect or visage. *N. pl.* dùis-neòil.

Duis-neulach, *a.* Cloudy, dark, gloomy, frowning. Tha 'aghaidh duis-neulach truaillidh, *his visage is gloomy and troubled.—Oss. Fin. and Lorm.*

Duis-oglach, aich, *s. m.* A client.—*Shaw.*

Duit, *comp. pron.* (*Arm.* dout. *Ir.* duit, *to thee. Swed.* ditt, *thine.*) To thee, for thee, unto thee. Sin duit, *there's for you;* sin duitse, *that is for you, take that.* Dheanainn sin duitse, Fheinn, *I would do that for thee, Fingal.—Fingalian Poem.* Ciod sin duitse? *what is that to you? Asp. form,* dhuit.

Duitse, *emphatic form* of duit; which see.

Dùitseach, *a.* Curtailed; docked, as a fowl. Coileach dùitseach, *a docked cock;* cearc dhuitseach, *a docked hen.*

Dùitseach, ich, *s. m.* A Dutchman. *N. pl.* Dùitsich.

Dùl, *gen. pl.* of dùil; which see.

Dùl, dùil, *s. m.* (*Ir. id.*) The terraqueous globe, the universe.

Dul, duil, *s. f.* (*Ir. id.*) A loop, a loop-hole; a trap, a gin; a fishing with nets; a satirist; a pin, a peg.

Dul, *v. a.* Catch with a loop; loop. *Pret. a.* dhul; *fut. aff. a.* dulaidh.

Dùlach, aich, *s. f.* Darkness, dimness, gloom; tempest; depth of winter, wintry weather. Dùlach bròin, *the dimness of grief.—Oss. Taura.* Written also *dùbhlach.*

Dulach, *a.* (*from* dul.) Full of loops, snares, or gins.

Dulag, aig, *s. f.* (*dim.* of dul.) A little loop; a little snare. *N. pl.* dulagan.

Dulagach, *a.* Full of little loops; full of gins or traps.

Dùlan, ain, *s. m.* A challenge, a defiance. Dùlan do ifrinn féin, *defiance to hell itself.—Sm.* Cuir gu dùlan, *defy;* thoir dùlan, *challenge.* Written also *dùbhlan.*

Dùlanach, *a.* Proud; defying; prone to defy or challenge. Gu dùlanach, *proudly; in defiance.—Sm.*

Dùlanachadh, aidh, *s. m.* A defying, a challenging; a defiance, a challenge.

Dùlanachd, *s. f.* Challenging, frequent challenging.

Dùlanaich, *v. a.* (*from* dùlan.) Defy, challenge. *Pret. a.* dhùlanaich; *fut. aff. a.* dulanaichidh. Dhùlanaich e Ghréig 's a sluagh, *he challenged Greece and her hosts.—Mac Lach.*

Dùlanaichidh, *fut. aff. a.* of dulanaich. Shall or will challenge.

Dùlanaichte, *p. part.* of dùlanaich. Defied, challenged.

Dulbhar, *a.* (*Ir. id.*) Doleful, gloomy, cheerless, unpleasant; sad, anxious. Properly *duilbhear;* which see.

Dulbharachd, *s. f.* Dolefulness, cheerlessness, unpleasantness. Properly, *duilbhearachd.*

Dulchann, ainn, *s. f.* Avarice, miserableness, covetousness. *Asp. form,* dhulchann.

Dulchaoin, *s. f.* Lamentation, wailing.

Dulchaointeach, *a.* Wailing, lamenting.

Dulchuis, *s. f.* Earnestness, diligence, perseverance.

Dul-chuiseach, *a.* Earnest, diligent, persevering. *Com.* and *sup.* dul-chuisiche.

Dulchunn, uinn, *s. m.* (*Ir. id.*) Avarice, covetousness; miserableness. *Asp. form,* dhulchunn. Air dhulchunn, air dhoimhneachd tùir, *for avarice, and for depth of knowledge.—Mac Lach.*

Dulchunnach, *a.* Avaricious, covetous, miserable. *Com.* and *sup.* dulchunnaiche, *more* or *most avaricious.*

Dùldach, *a.* Dark, dismal, gloomy. *Com.* and *sup.* duldaiche. Gu duldach, *gloomily.*

Dùldachd, *s. f.* Darkness, dismalness, gloominess; the depth of winter.

Duldai, **Dùldaidh**, *a.* Dark, dismal. San t-slighe dhuldai dhoirch, *in the dismal dark path.—Sm.*

Dùmhail, *a.* Thick, clumsy, bulky; crowded. Written also *dòmhail.*

Dùmhladas, ais, *s. m.* Thickness, bulkiness, clumsiness; heaviness, weight, magnitude; crowdedness. Dùmhladas dòrainn, *a weight of grief.—Macfar.* A dol an dùmhladas, *growing more and more bulky, clumsy,* or *crowded.*

Dùmhlas, ais, *s. m.* (*Ir. id.*) Thickness, clumsiness, bulkiness; crowdedness.

Dùn, dùin, *s. m.* A fort or fortress; a tower; a fortified hill; a fastness; a hill; a hedge, a heap, a hillock. Thainig e do 'n dùn, *he came to the tower.—Stew. K.* Dùn arbhair, *a heap of corn.—Stew. Ruth.*

It is most worthy of remark, that in all languages *dun* (with, in some instances, the change or addition of a vowel, consonant, or syllable) signifies *height,* either literally, as in the Celtic, or figuratively, as may be seen from the following words:

Heb. and *Chald.* dan, *a chief magistrate. Heb.* din, *a height; and* adon, *a lord. Arab.* tun, *a height; and* doun, don, *high, noble. Old Pers.* doen, *a hill;* dun, *powerful; and* dan, *a chief magistrate. Copt.* ton, *mountain. Syr.* doino, *a man of authority. Tonq.* dung, *high; and* dinh, *a summit; and* dun, *the highest part of a building; and* din, *a palace. Old Indian,* duen, *a king. Malay,* deun, *lord; and* dini, *high. Luzon,* thin, *a mountain.* Gr. θὶν, *a heap. Phrygian,* din, *summit. Jap.* ton, *highest in degree; and* tono, *a king; and* tunde, *a superior. Turk.* dun, *high. Congo.* tunene, *great. St. Domingo,* taino, *noble. It.* duna, *downs, pasturage on a hill. Span.* don, *lord. It.* donna, *a lady. Bisc.* dun, *an eminence,* also, *an elevated person. Old Sax.* dun, *a hill; and* thun-den, *elevated. Low. Sax.* dun, *hill. Van.* dun, *the highest part. Germ.* and *Du.* dunsen, *exalt one's self. Du.* duynes. *Fr.* dunes, *heaps of sand on the shore. Fr.* dune, *downs. Eng.* down. *Friesland,* dunen, *to elevate one's self; and* dun, *a sandbank. Corn.* and *Arm.* dun *and* tun. *Ir.* dùn. *Germ.* dun, *a city. Eng.* town. *Scotch,* toun. *W.* dun, *mountain.*

According to Bede, *dùn* means a height in the ancient British; and according to Clitophon it had the same meaning in the old Gaulish. Δοῦνον καλοῦσι τὸν ἐξέχοντα. They (the Gauls) call an elevated place *dun.* Hence comes the termination *dunum* in the names of many towns in Old Gaul; as, Ebrodunum, *Ambrun;* Vindunum, *Mans;* Noviodunum, *Noyon;* Augustodunum, *Autun;* Andomadunum, *Langres;* Melodunum, *Melun;* Caesarodunum, *Tours;* Lugdunum, *Lyons,* according to Plutarch, *Raven-hill;*

Carrodunum, *Cracow*; all situated on rising grounds; hence, also, the British terminations of names of towns, *don* and *ton*.

Is it not probable, that in this vocable *dun*, and not in δυναμαι, as O'Brien would have it, we are to find the root of the Gaelic duine, *man*, as well as of the corresponding terms in the Persic, (see Duine) Tonquinese, Runic, Irish, Cornish, Armoric, and Welsh languages; signifying, literally, the high being, or the highest of terrestrial creatures?

Dùnach, *a*. Hilly, full of heaps or knolls; full of towers or forts; like a tower or a fort.

Dùnadh, aidh, *s. m*. The act of shutting or of enclosing; lacing, binding; barricading; *rarely*, a camp; a dwelling; a multitude.

Dùnadh, (a), *pres. part*. of dùin. Shutting, closing; enclosing, surrounding; lacing, binding, buttoning.

Dunach, Dunaich, *s. f*. Perplexity; affliction; mischief.

Dunaidh, *s. f*. Perplexity; affliction; mischief. Dunaidh gharbh ort, *severe affliction on thee.—Old Song*.

Dùnan, ain, *s. m., dim*. of dùn. (*Ir. id*.) A little hill, a knoll, a little heap; a little fort. *Arm*. tunyen, *a heap*. *Friesland*, duynen, *elevate one's self*. *Congo*. tunene, *great*.

Dùnan, *n. pl*. of dùn; which see.

Dùnanach, *a*. (*from* dùnan.) Knolly; full of heaps or of little hills; full of little forts.

Dùn-aolaich, *s. m*. A dunghill.

Dùn-aros, ois, *s. m*. (*Ir. id*.) A dwelling-place.

Dun-bhalaoch, oich, *s. m*. A mere fellow.

Dun-bhlath,-bheinn. Dumblane. (Contracted *Dumblathan*.) The Αλαυνα of Ptolemy.

Dun-catha, *s. m*. A bulwark; a sconce.

Dundeagh, (*for* Dun Tath, *or perhaps* Dun-Dia.) Dundee. *Lat*. Tao-dunum.

Dun-eudainn, *s. m*. Edinburgh; *literally*, Edinton.

Dùn-lios, *s. f*. (*Ir. id*.) A palace; a garrison; a garden.

† **Dunn**, duinn, *s. m*. (*Ir. id*.) A teacher; a doctor.—*Shaw*.

Dunt, *s. m*. A blow, as on a table, producing a hollow sound; a thump. *Scotch*, dunt. *Old Swed*. dunt. *Island*. dunda.

Duntail, *s. f*. Frequent or continued striking or thumping.

† **Dur**, duir, *s. m*. Water.

Gr. by transposition υδωρ. *Arm*. dour *and* douar. *Corn*. dour. *Ir*. dur. *Bisc*. ura. Dur domhain, *deep water*. A native of Bretagne would say, *dur don*.

From *dur* comes *durum*, the Latin termination and beginning of the names of many towns situated by the sea-side, or near rivers; as, Batavodurum, *in Holland*; Boidurum and Serviodurum, *on the Danube*; Lactodurum, *Bedford*; Durobrevis, *Rochester*; Durocornovium, *Cirencester*; Dura, *on the Euphrates*; Durocortum, *Rheims*.

The root *dur* is observable, also, in the names of many rivers and lakes, as the Adour, *in France*; Durius *or* Douro *in Spain*; Chidurus, *in Macedon*; Badorus, *in Eubœa*; Dur, *the Dingle river, in Ireland*; Tur, *a river in ancient Persia*; Daria, *a lake in Iroquois*; Dara, *a river in Persia*; Diur, *a river in Mauritania*; Daradus, *a river in Gaetulia*; Chidorus, *a river in Greece*.

Dùr, *a*. (*Ir. id*. *Lat*. durus, *hard*. *Box. Lex*. dur, *steel*.) Dull, stupid, obstinate, hard; attentive. *Com*. and *sup*. dùire. Gu dùr, *attentively*. Bheachdaich mi gu dùr, *I observed attentively*.—*Mac Lach*.

Dur, *adv*. (*provincial for* nur.) When, at the time when.

Dùrachd, *s. f*. (*Ir*. duthrachd.) Desire, inclination, a wish; sincerity; good-will; earnestness; diligence, daring, courage; luck's penny. Gun dùrachd cron, *without inclination to harm*.—*Oss. Duthona*. Le dùrachd cridhe, *with sincerity of heart*.—*Sm*. Maille ri dùrachd, *with diligence*.—*Stew. Rom*. *Asp. form*, dhùrachd. Cha 'n 'eil dhùrachd agam, *I have not the courage*; droch dhùrachd, *a bad wish*.

Dùrachdach, *a*. Diligent, sincere, persevering, industrious, assiduous. *Com*. and *sup*. dùrachdaiche, *more* or *most diligent*. Gu dùrachdach, *diligently*.

Dùrachdaiche, *com*. and *sup*. of dùrachdach.

Dùrachdainn, *s. f*. Daring, courage; a secret wishing; a venturing.

Dùraichd. See Dùraig.

Dùraig, *s. f*. (*Ir. id*.) An attempt.

Dùraig, *v. n*. Venture; adventure; dare; wish. *Pret. a*. dhùraig, *ventured*; *fut. aff. a*. dùraigidh. Cha dùraig i pòg dhomh, *she has not the daring to kiss me*.—*Old Song*. Dhùraiginn marbh thu, *I would wish thee dead*. Dhùraigeadh tu mo luath le tonn, *you could wish my ashes on the waves*.—*Old Poem*.

Dùran, ain, *s. m*. A morose fellow; an obstinate fellow. *N. pl*. dùrain.

Dùranta, *a*. (*Ir. id*.) Morose; churlish; rigid.

Dùrantachd, *s. f*. (*Ir. id*.) Moroseness, churlishness; rigidness.

Duras, ais, *s. m*. A house; room.

† **Durb**, duirb, *s. m*. (*Ir. id*.) A disease, a distemper.

Dur-bhalaoch, laoich, *s. m*. An obstinate fellow, a boorish fellow, a clown, a dunce. *N. pl*. dur-bhalaoich.

Dur-bhodach, aich, *s. m*. A churl; a clown; an obstinate old boor. *N. pl*. dur-bhodaich.

† **Durbhuth**, *s. m*. (*Ir. id*.) A cell.

Durc, durca, *s. m*. A lump or piece of any thing; a clumsy knife, a dirk. Durc arain, *a lump of bread*; durc cloich, *a lump of stone*.

Dùrd, dùird, *s. m*. (*Ir*. dord.) A hum; a muttering; a humming sound; sullenness.

Dùrd, *v. n*. Hum, as a bee; mutter. *Pret*. dhùrd; *fut. aff*. durdaidh.

Dùrdail, *s. f*. Humming, a murmur, a cooing, a buzzing. Ri dùrdail, *cooing*.—*Macint*. An dùrdail mhuirneach, *the pleasant murmur*.—*Macdon*.

Dùrdain, *gen. sing*. of dùrdan.

Dùrdan, ain, *s. m*. (*Ir*. dordan.) A murmur, a cooing, a purring, a humming; a bit of dust; a mote. Dùrdan nan duan, *the humming of songs*.—*Oss. Lodin*. Coileach dubh ri dùrdan, *a black cock making a murmuring noise*.—*Macdon*. Nur bhios ni aig a chat ni e dùrdan, *when the cat has got hold of any thing she purs*.—*G. P*.—Said of those who speak much of their riches.

Dùrdanach, *a*. Cooing, murmuring. An colaman dùrdanach, *the cooing pigeon*.

Dùrdanaich, *s. f*. A continued cooing, a soft murmuring.—*Macint*. A purring. Ri dùrdanaich.

Durganta, *a*. (*Ir. id*.) Surly, morose; grim.

Durgantachd, *s. f*. Surliness, moroseness; grimness.

Durlus, luis, *s. m*., dur, *water*, *and* lus. (*Ir. id*.) Water-cress. *N. pl*. durlusan, *water-cresses*.

† **Dùrn**, dùirn, *s. f*. (*Ir. id*.) A fist. See Dorn.

Durrag, aig, *s. m*. A worm, a maggot. *N. pl*. durragan. Fudar nan durrag, *worm-powders*.

Durragach, *a*. Full of worms or maggots; like a worm or maggot; vermicular.

Durragan, *n. pl*. of durrag. Worms, maggots. *D. pl*. durragaibh.

Dursan, ain, *s. m*. (*Ir. id*.) A crack, a report.

† **Durtheach**, *s. m*. (*Ir. id*.) A foundation; a cell; a hut; a pilgrim.

Durunnta, *a*. (*Ir. id*.) See Durannta.

† Dus, duis, *s. m.* (*Ir. id.*) A fort.

Dùs, duis, *s. m.* Dust. Neula dùis, *clouds of dust.—Orr.* Hence *duslach.*

† Dùsachd, *s. f.* (*Ir.* dusacht.) Watchfulness.—*Shaw.*

Dùsail, *a.* (dus-amhuil.) Dusty, earthy, earthlike.

† Dusair, *s. m.* (*Ir. id.*) A client.—*Shaw.*

Dusait, *s. m.* A sanctuary, or place of refuge, safety. *N. pl.* dusaitean.

Dusaitiche, *s m* One who takes refuge in a sanctuary.

Dusal, ail, *s. m.* Sleep. Rinn iad dùsal, *they slept.—Stew. Matt ref.*

Dusan, ain, *s. m.* A dozen; a certain quantity of yarn. Ad dhà dhusan bliadhna, *in your twenty-fourth year.—Turn.*

Dùsgach, *a* Rousing, wakening, stimulating

Dùsgadh, aidh, *s. m.* The act of wakening, the act of rousing, an awakening; excitement. Ni mi cadal gun dùsgadh, *I will sleep without wakening.—Old Song.*

Dusgadh, (a), *pr part.* of dùisg. Wakening, rousing

Dusgairm, *s. f.* A calling, an appellation —*Shaw.*

Duslach, aich, *s. m* (*Ir id.*) Dust, earth, ground Is duslach thu, *thou art dust —Stew Gen.* Amhghar o'n duslach, *trouble from the ground —Sm Asp. form,* dhuslach. Mar dhuslach, *like the dust.—Stew. Gen.*

Duslachail, *a.* (duslach-amhuil.) Dusty, earthy; like dust or earth.

Duslann, -lainn, *s m.* A gloomy deserted place, a deserted house.

Duslannach, *a.* Gloomy; deserted, as a house.

Dusluinn, *s. f.* Dust, earth.

Dusluinneach, *a* Dusty, earthlike, terrestrial, made of earth, *also,* lonely, deserted.

Dut, *comp pron.* (*provincial for* duit.) To thee, for thee *Asp. form,* dhut.

Dùthaich, dùthcha, *s. f.* A country, land, native land, district, territory. Gach duthaich chéin, *every distant land.—Sm.* Feadh dhuthcha chéin, *among distant lands.—Id.* Duthaich Mhic Caoidh, *Lord Reay's country —Old Song. Duthaich* seems to be compounded of †du, *land, and* teach, *house,* and means the land in which one's house is, or native land.

† Duthan, ain, *s. m.* A nation.—*Shaw.*

Duthcha, *gen. sing* of duthaich.

Duthchail, *a.* (duthcha-amhuil.) National; *also,* of a good family.—*Shaw*

Duthchalachd, *s. f.* Nationalness, or reference to the people in general.

Duthchas, ais, *s. m.* Hereditary right; a prescriptive right by which a farm descended from father to son; a native country; hereditary temper or blood; a birth-place. B'e sud dùthchas mo luaidh, *that was the hereditary right of my beloved —Macfar.* Theid duthchas an aghaidh nan crag, *blood will climb the rocks.—G P.*

Duthchasach, *a.* Hereditary, natal; national; natural to one's family, native; *also, substantively,* a native of the same country.

Duthchasachd, *s f* The circumstance of being hereditary, natality, nationalness, nativity.

Du-thrà, Du-thràth, *s m.* (dubh-thràth) Twilight, fall of eve, evening; night Mar anns an du-thràth, *as in the night.—Stew. G. B.* Reultan a du-thrà, *the stars of its twilight.—Stew. Job.*

Dut-sa, a *provincial form* of duitse, the *emphatic form* of *comp. pron.* duit, *asp form,* dhutsa, *to thee* See Duit.

E.

E, (eabh *and* eagh, *the aspen*) The fifth letter of the Gaelic alphabet, and one of the small vowels It has various sounds. With the grave accent (`) it sounds like *e* in *there,* as, rè, *during,* è, *he,* or *it:* with the acute accent (´) like *ai* in *fail,* as, té, *a female,* cé, *the earth.* At the end of a word it sounds like *e* in *brother,* as, duine, *a man,* roghnaichte, *chosen.*

E! An interjection of surprise.

E, *pers, pron* (*Corn.* ef *Ir* e) He, him, or it E féin, *himself, itself.* E, the nominative case, is written (for the sake of sound) *se,* when it precedes *e,* the objective case; as, marbhaidh se e, *he will kill him.*

Ea, a *priv. particle,* signifying *not,* and has the same effect with the English negative, *un* or *in,* as, eaceart, *unjust,* eaceartas, *injustice, ea* is also written *eu.*

Eaban, ain, *s. m.* See Eabar.

Eabar, *s f.* (*Ir. id.*) Mud, mire, filth, kennel; a confluence of waters. In this last acceptation it is more properly spelt *aber,* which see

Eabarach, *a.* Muddy, miry, filthy, grovelling, wallowing *Com.* and *sup.* eabaraiche.

Eabh, *s. f* The name of the fifth letter of the Gaelic alphabet, the aspen tree.

Eabha, *s. f.* The first woman, Eve.

Eabhrach, aich, *s m.* (*contr.* for Eabhraidheach.) A Hebrew, a Jew *N. pl.* Eabhraich. Na h-Eabhraich, *the Jews;* a chainnt Eabhrach, *the Hebrew tongue.*

Eabhrach, *a.* (*contr.* for Eabhruidheach) Hebrew; Jewish.

Eabhruidheach, *a.* See Eabhrach.

Eabrach, *a.* (*from* eabar.) Wallowing, grovelling; prone to wallow.

Eabradh, aidh, *s. m* A wallowing, a grovelling; a kennel; *rarely,* iron Chum a h-eabradh san làthaich, *to her wallowing in the mire.—Stew. Pro*

† Eabron, oin, *s m* (*Ir id*) A pan; a cauldon.

† Eabur, uir, *s m.* (*Ir. id. Lat.* ebur.) Ivory.—*Shaw* and *O'Reilly.*

Eaceart, *a.* (ea *priv. and* ceart) Unjust, iniquitous See also Euceart.

Eaceart, *s f.* (*Ir.* eacceart) Injustice, unfairness; iniquity. Cha dean esan eaceart, *he will do no iniquity.—Stew. Zeph.* See also Euceart.

Eaceartas, ais, *s f.* and *m* Unjustice, unfairness, iniquity. Luchd ea-ceartais, *unjust people;* luchd na h-eaceartais, *the unjust.* Written also *euceartas*

Eacéillidh, *a* (ea *priv. and* ciall.) Foolish, giddy. Bha sinn ea-ceillidh, *we were foolish —Stew. Tit.*

Each, eich, *s m.* A horse Each meamnach, *a proud spirited horse —Stew Nah. N. pl.* eich, *horses.* Eich gheal, *white horses —Stew. Zech.* Eich reidh, *hired horses, hacks;* each donn, *a brown horse,* each buidh, *a dun horse;* each breac, *a piebald horse,* each sréine, *a bridle horse;* each gorm, *a dapple grey horse;* each bàn, *a cream-coloured horse,* each cartach, *a cart-horse;* air muin eich, *on horseback,* each blàr, *a black horse with a white spot on the forehead.*

Gr. Æol. ἵκκος, according to Scaliger. *Lat.* equus.

Ir. each. *Fr.* †hacque. *Span.* haca. *Hottentot,* hacqua, *a horse.*

EACHACH, *a.* Abounding in horses.—*Shaw.*

EACHAN, ain, *s. m.* (*Ir. id.*) A wheel; an instrument for winding yarn; a blast. Eachan gaoithe, *a blast of wind.*—*Shaw.* Eachan gaoithe, *a' blast of whirlwind.*

EACHANACH, *a.* (*Ir. id.*) Windy, stormy, blasty.

EACHANACHD, *s. f.* Windiness.

EACH-AODACH, aich, *s. m.* Horse-clothing, caparison.

EACH-BHALAOCH, oich, *s. m.* A groom, a jockey, a stable-boy. *N. pl.* each-bhalaoich

EACH-BHALAOCHAN, ain, *s. m.* A horse-boy, a stable-boy

EACH-CHÌR, *s. f.* A horse-comb, a currycomb.

† EACHD, *s. f.* (*Ir. id.*) A condition or state. Though this vocable be now obsolete among the Gael, it is seen incorporated with other words, giving them the same meaning as do the English adjectives *ness* and *ship* to the words to which they are annexed. Another form of *eachd* is *achd.*

EACHDA, *a.* Clean, neat, spruce, trim; pure; comely, decent.—*Shaw.*

EACHDAIL, *a.* (eachd-amhuil) Conditional; *also,* cleanly, neat, comely. Gu h-eachdail, *cleanly.*

EACHDAIR, *s. m.* A historian, a recorder, a chronicler; *also,* a history, a story, a relation. Eachdair ar comhraig, *the story of our battle.*—*Oss. Fing.* *N. pl.* eachdairean.

EACHDAIREACHD, *s. f.* History, historiography.

EACHDRADH, aidh, *s. m.* A poindfold. *N. pl.* eachdraidhean.

EACHDRAIDH, *s. f.* A history, a chronicle, a record, a tale, a narrative. Leabhar nan eachdraidh, *the book of Chronicles.*

EACHDRAIDHEACHD, *s. f.* History, historiography.

EACH-LANN, lainn, *s. m.* (*Ir. id.*) A stable. *N. pl.* each-lainn.

EACHLAOCH, oich, *s. m.* (*Ir.* eachlach.) A groom, a jockey, a postboy.

EACH-LASG, aisg, *s. f.* (each-lnasg.) A lash or whip.

EACHLEIGH, *s. m.* A farrier.

EACHRAIDH, *s. f.* (*Ir.* eachradh.) Cavalry; a stud of horses. Acduinn na h-eachraidh, *the harness of the stud.*—*Fingalian Poem.*

† EACHRAIS, *s. f.* A fair; a method; *also,* rowing.—*Shaw.*

EACH-SHLIGHE, *s. f.* A horse-path, a horse-road

EACH-SRÉINE, *s. m.* A bridle-horse. *N pl.* eich-sréine, *bridle-horses.*

EACH-STEUD, *s. m.* A race-horse. *N. pl.* eich-steud.

† EACHT, *s. f.* A condition. See EACHD

EACHTRADH, aidh, *s m.* (*Ir. id*) An adventure, an enterprise

EACHTRANNACH, aich, *s. m.* An adventurer; a foreigner. *N. pl.* eachtrannaich.

EACHTRANNACH, *a.* Adventurous, enterprising; foreign. Gu h-eachtrannach eadar-bhuaiseach, *adventurous and victorious.*—*Old Song.* *Com* and *sup.* eachtrannaiche

EA-CINNTE, *s f.* Uncertainty. Written also *eu-cinnte*

EA-CINNTEACH, *a.* Uncertain, doubtful, hesitating. Written also *eu-cinnteach.*

EA-CINNTEALAS, ais, *s. m.* Uncertainty.

EACNACH, aich, *s. m.* (*Ir. id.*) Blasphemy.—*Shaw.*

EA-CNEASTA, *a.* (ea *priv. and* cneasta.) Inhuman, cruel; rude, unpolite; intemperate. *Ir.* eig-cneasda.

EA-CNEASTACHD, *s. f.* Inhumanity, cruelty; rudeness, unpoliteness.

EACOIR, *gen.* eacorach, *s. f.* Injustice, injury, guilt, impropriety. See EUCOIR.

EACONNACH, *a.* (*Ir.* eacconnach.) Mad, furious.

EACORACH, *gen. sing.* of eacoir

EACORACH, *a.* Unjust, injurious, unrighteous, unfair. A laimh na muinntir eacoraich, *from the hands of the unjust*—*Sm.* *Com.* and *sup* eacoraiche Gu h-eacorach, *unjustly.*

EA-CORDADH, aidh, *s. m.* A jarring, a disagreement, a quarrel.

EA-COSMHAL, EA-COSMHUIL, *a.* (ea *priv and* cosmhal) Unlike, dissimilar; unequal Gu h-ea-cosmhal, *unlikely*

EA-COSMHALACH, *a.* Dissimilar, unlikely, improbable; unequal *Com* and *sup* ea-cosmhalaiche

EA-COSMHALACHD, *s. f.* Dissimilarity, disparity, unlikeliness, improbability; inequality.

EA-COSMHALAS, ais, *s. m.* Dissimilarity, disparity, want of resemblance, inequality

EA-CRIONNA, *a.* (*Ir* eigcriona.) Imprudent, foolish, intemperate, immoderate. Gu ea-crionna, *imprudently.*

EA-CRIONNACH, *s. f.* (*Ir.* eig-crionachd) Imprudence, intemperance, intemperateness, immoderateness.

EAD. See † EID

EAD. See EUD.

EADACHADH, aid, *s. m.* A jealous watching; a stepping or stealing softly.

EADAICH, *v. a.* Watch jealously; steal softly *Pret. a* dh' eadaich

EADAIL, *s f.* (*Ir. id.*) Profit, advantage, treasure, booty, spoil, cattle.

EADAILEACH, *a.* (*Ir id.*) Profitable, advantageous; having profit or advantage; having treasure, rich.—*Shaw.*

EADAILT, *s. f.* Italy Muinntir na h-Eadailt, *the people of Italy.*—*Stew Heb.*

EADAILTEACH, ich, *s m.* An Italian. *N. pl.* Eadailtich Na h-Eadailtich, *the Italians*

EADAILTEACH, *a.* Italian A chainnt Eadailteach, *the Italian language.*

EA-DAINGEANN, *a.* Weak, defenceless.—*Shaw.*

EA-DAINGNEACHD, *s f* Weakness, defencelessness

EADAR, *prep* (*Ir* eidir.) Between, betwixt; both Eadar bheag is mhòr, *between great and small, both great and small.*—*Sm.* Eadarainn, *between us;* eadaraibh, *between you;* eatorra, *between them,* cuir eatorra, *separate them,* eadar an long nodha is an seann ruthadh, *let the new vessel beware of the old headland.*—*O. P.* Eadar an da chuid, *between the two* Eadar leòr is eatorras, *betwixt the two.*—*G P.* Eadar fhal dha 's rlreamh, *between jest and earnest*

EADARADH, aidh, *s m.* (*Ir id*) A division; interest.—*Shaw.*

EADARIBH, *comp. pron.* (*Ir.* eadaribh) Between you

EADARAINN, *comp. pron* Between us Chaidh eadarainn, *we quarrelled,* cuir eadarainn, *part us,* eadarainn agus sibhse, *between us and you.*

EADAR-BHACAN, ain, *s. m.* The space between the ears.—*Macd.*

EADAR-BHUAIDH, *s f* A defeat, a rout, a victory.

EADAR-BHUAISEACH, *a* Discomfiting, routing, victorious, of, or belonging to, a rout or defeat. Gu h-eachtrannach eadar-bhuaiseach, *adventurous and victorious.*—*Old Song*

EADAR-DHA-LIUNN, *s f.* Between sinking and swimming, floundering.

EADAR-DHEALACHADH, aidh, *s. m.* (*Ir.* eidir-dhealughadh) A separating, a parting, a divorcing, a separation, a divorce, a division; a faction, a difference Cha 'n 'eil eadar-dhealachadh ann, *there is no difference.*—*Stew. Rom.*

EADAR-DHEALACHADH, (ag), *pr. part.* of eadar-dhealaich

EADAR-DHEALACHAIL, *a.* Causing separation, causing divorce; like a separation or divorce.

EADAR-DHEALAICH, *v. a.* and *n.* Separate, part, divorce. *Pret. a.* dh' eadar-dhealaich, *separate;* dh' eadar-dhealaich iad, *they separated.*

EADARGAIN, *s. f.* An interposing, a reconciling, a quieting; a parting or putting asunder; a reconciliation. Fear eadargain, *a reconciler.*

EADARGAINEACH, *a.* Interposing, reconciling; parting; quieting; of, or pertaining to, a reconciliation; like a reconciliation.

EADAR-GHNÀTH, *s. m.* Ingenuity.

EADAR-GHNÀTHACH, *a.* Ingenious. Gu h-eadar-ghnàthach, *ingeniously.*

EADAR-GHUIDH, *s. f.* (*Ir. id.*) Intercession, mediation; a supplication. A dheanamh eadar-ghuidh, *to make intercession.—Stew. Jer.*

EADAR-GHUIDHEACH, *a.* Intercessory, mediatory.

EADAR-GHUIDHEAR, ir, *s. m.* An intercessor, a mediator. An t-Eadar-ghuidhear, *the Intercessor, Christ.*

EADAR-GHUIDHEARACHD, *s. f.* The employment of an intercessor, intercessorship.

EADAR-LAMH, aimh, *s. f.* (*Ir. id.*) Temporary happiness.

EADAR-MHALA, *s. m.* (*Ir. id.*) The distance between the eyebrows.

EADAR-MHEADHONACH, *a.* Intercessory, mediatory, reconciliatory; like a go-between.

EADAR-MHEADHONAIR, *s. m.* (eadar meadhon *and* fear. *Ir.* eadir-mheadhantoir.) A mediator, an intercessor, a reconciler; an interpreter; a go-between. *N. pl.* eadar-mheadhonairean.

EADAR-MHEADHONAIREACHD, *s. f.* Mediation, intercession; continued mediation, the practice of intercession.

EADAR-MHÌNEACHADH, aidh, *s. m.* (*Ir.* eidir-mhinughadh.) An interpreting, a translating; interpretation.

EADAR-MHÌNEACHAIR, *s. m.* An interpreter, a translator. *N. pl.* eadar-mhineachairean.

EADAR-MHÌNICH, *v. a.* Interpret, translate. *Pret. a.* dh' eadar-mhìnich, *interpreted; fut. aff. a.* eadar-mhìnichidh.

EADAR-MHÌNICHTE, *p. part.* of eadar-mhìnich. Interpreted, translated.

EADARNACH, *a.* Fraudulent; malicious. Gu h-eadarnach, *fraudulently.*

EADARNAIDH, *s. f.* (*Ir. id.*) Fraud, double dealing; malice.

EADARSGAIN, *s. f.* Interposition; reconcilement; parting; greeting.—*Shaw.* Fear eadarsgain, *a reconciler.*

EADARSGAR, *v. a.* Separate, divorce, pull asunder. *Pret. a.* dh' eadarsgar, *separated; fut. aff.* eadar-sgaraidh, *shall separate.*

EADAR-SGARACH, *a.* Causing separation; causing divorce; separating, divorcing.

EADAR-SGARACHDUINN, *s. f.* A separation; a divorce.

EADAR-SGARADH, aidh, *s. m.* A separating; a divorcing; a separation; a divorce.

EADAR-SHOILLSE, *s. f.* Twilight, dawn.

EADAR-SHOILLSEACH, *a.* Having a glimmering light, as in twilight.

EADAR-SHOILLSICH, *v. n.* Glimmer, as in twilight; dawn. *Pret. a.* dh' eadar-shoillsich.

EADAR-SHOLUS, uis, *s. m.* (*Ir. id.*) Twilight. 'San eadar-sholus, *in the twilight.—Stew. Pro. ref.*

EADAR-SHOLUSACH, *a.* Having twilight; glimmering, as in twilight.

EADAR-THAMUL, uil, *s. m.* (*Ir. id.*) An interval of time.

EADAR-THEANGACHADH, aidh, *s. m.* A translating, an interpreting; a translation.

EADAR-THEANGACHADH, (ag), *pr. part.* of eadar-theangaich.

EADAR-THEANGACHAIR, *s. m.* A translator, an interpreter. *N. pl.* eadar-theangachairean.

EADAR-THEANGAICH, *v. a.* Interpret, translate. *Pret. a.* dh' eadar-theangaich, *translated.* Mur eadar-theangaich e, *except he translate.—Stew.* 1 *Cor.*

EADAR-THEANGAICHTE, *p. part.* of eadar-theangaich. Interpreted, translated.

EADAR-THEANGAIDH, *s. f.* A translation.

EADAR-THEANGAIR, *s. f.* A translator, an interpreter. *N. pl.* eadar-theangairean.

EADAR-THRATH, *s. m.* (*Ir. id.*) Noon.

Eadar-thrath is perhaps a corruption of †*edrath,* the time of the morning when cattle are brought home from pasture to give milk, literally, meat-time. The Celtic *ed,* or *eid,* is the root of the Greek ἔδω, Lat. *edo,* Eng. *eat.* The Greek ἕδρα, *a seat,* has an evident reference to food; it is compounded of two Celtic words, *ed,* food, and *trà,* time. Ἕδνα, "presents which a bridegroom made to his bride," is *ed-nuadh,* or *ed-nu,* raw food.

EADAR-THRIATH, *s. m.* An inter-reign; a regency; *also,* a regent.

EADARUINN, *comp. pron.* (*Ir.* eadruinn.) Between us, betwixt us. Biodh mionnan eadaruinn, *let there be an oath betwixt us.—Stew. Gen.* Thainig eadaruinn, *we disagreed.*

† EADH, *s.* Time, season, opportunity.—*Shaw.*

EADH, (an). Is it? An eadh nach cronuich e? *is it that he will not chastise?—Sm.*

EADH, (is). Yes; it is. Is eadh gu dearbh, *yes, indeed; really!*

EADHOIN, EADHON, *adv.* (*Corn.* eduyen. *Ir.* eadhon.) Even; namely; to wit.

EADMHOIREACHD, *s. f.* More commonly *eudmhoireachd;* which see.

EADMHOR, *a.* See EUDMHOR.

EA-DÒCHAS, ais, *s. m.* Despair; despondency, melancholy, dejection. Written also *eu-dochas.*

EA-DÒCHASACH, *a.* In despair, despondent or melancholy, without hope. *Com.* and *sup.* ea-dochasaiche, *more* or *most despondent.*

EA-DÒCHASACHD, *s. f.* Hopelessness, despondency, melancholy; a tendency to despond.

EAD-TLAITH, *a.* Courageous, strong, undaunted. Gu h-ead-tlaith, *courageously.*

† EAG, *s. f.* The moon.

EAG, èig, *s. m.* (*Ir. id.*) Death. More properly *aog* or *eug.*

EAGACH, *a.* (*Ir. id.*) Deep. Glacag eagach nan neoinean, *the deep dell of daisies.—Macfar.*

EAGAICHTE, *part.* Dove-tailed.

EAGAIL, *gen. sing.* of eagal; which see.

EAGAIR, *v. a.* Arrange; put in order; put in a row. *Pret. a.* dh' eagair; *fut. aff. a.* eagairidh, *shall put in order.*

EAGAL, ail, *s. m.* (*Ir.* eagla.) Fear, terror, timidity. Uallach an eagail, *the burden of fear.—Sm.* Cha 'n eagal domh, *there is no fear of me.* 'N eagal domhsa do chruth? *am I afraid of thy form?—Oss. Carricth.* Ghabh e eagal, *he took fright, he became afraid;* ghabh e an t-eagal, *he became terrified* or *frightened.*

In Badenoch, and elsewhere, they say *feagal.*

EAGAL, (*for* air eagal.) For fear, lest. Eagal gun d'thig osag, *for fear a blast should come.—Oss. Temo.*

EAGAL, (air), *adv.* For fear, lest. Air eagal nach tig e, *for fear he should not come.*

EAGAL, (an t-), *adv.* For fear, lest. An t-eagal gun tuit e, *for fear he fall.*

Eagalach, Eagallach, *a., from* eagal. (*Ir.* eaglach.) Fearful, terrible, dreadful, frightful; *also*, timid, cowardly, skittish. Tha iad uamhasach agus eagalach, *they are terrible and dreadful.—Stew. Heb.* Is eagallach an ni e, *it is a fearful thing;* duine leth-eagallach, *a half-timid* or *cautious man.—Macdon.*

Eagall. See **Eagal.**

Eagan, ain, *s. m.* (*Ir. id.*) A gizzard; depth; bottom.—*Shaw.*

Eagar, air, *s. m.* (*Ir. id.*) Order, terror; a rank, a row, array; appointment. An cath ann an eagar, *the battle in order.—Stew. Sam. ref.* Eagar cath, *battle order.*

Eagarach, *a.* (*from* eagar.) Well-ordered, arranged; in order, in ranks, in rows or files.

Eagaraich, *v. a.* Draw up in order, or in files, as an army; set in order, arrange. *Pret. a.* dh' eagaraich.

Eag-bhroth, *s.* (*Ir. id.*) Carrion.

Eagh, *s. f.* The fifth letter of the Gaelic alphabet; the aspen-tree.

Eaglais, *s. f.* A church. Eaglais-chathach, *a church militant;* eaglais-neamhaidh, *church triumphant;* ceann eaglais na Roimh, *the Pope.*

Pers. keleesa. *Gr.* εκκλησια. *Fr.* eglise. *W.* eglws. *Corn.* eglez. *Bisc.* eliça. *Span.* yglesia. *Arm.* ilis *and* eglos. *Ir.* eaglais.

Eaglaiseach, *a.* Ecclesiastical; like a church.

Eaglaisear, ir, *s. m.* (*W.* eglwyswr.) A churchman.

Eaglaisiche, *s. m.* A churchman or ecclesiastic.

Eaglan, ain, *s. m.* (*Ir. id.*) A biting.—*Shaw.*

Eagmhais. See **Eugmhais.**

Eagmhaiseach, *a.* Famous, great.—*Shaw.*

Eagnach, *a., contr. for* eagnaidheach. (*Ir.* eagnach.) Prudent; subtle.

Eagnach, aich, *s. f.* (*Ir. id.*) Blasphemy; a complaint; resentment.

Eagnachd, *s. f.* (*contr. for* eagnaidheachd.) Prudence; cunning.

Eagnaidh, Eagnuidh, *s. f.* Prudence; wisdom; caution; subtlety; sharpness.—*Shaw.*

Eagnaidh, Eagnuidh, *s. f.* Prudent, wise; subtle. Comhairle o 'n eagnaidh, *counsel from the wise.—Stew. Jer.*

Eagnaidheach, Eagnuidheach, *a.* Prudent, wise; subtle; sharp. Duine eagnaidheach, *a prudent man.—Stew. Pro.* Gu h-eagnaidheach, *prudently.*

Eagnaidheachd, Eagnuidheachd, *s. f.* Prudence, subtlety, sharpness.—*Stew. Pro. ref.*

† **Eagnairc,** *s. f.* (*Ir. id.*) Love; querulousness; complacency.—*Shaw.*

Eagnuidh, *a.* (*Ir. id.*) Prudent, wise; cunning; subtle. O dhaoinibh eagnuidh, *from wise men.—Stew. Matt.*

Eagnuidheachd, *s. f.* Wisdom, prudence; cunning.

Eag-samhlachadh, aidh, *s. m.* A diversifying, a varying, mixing, chequering; a diversity, variety.

Eag-samhlachd, *s. f.* (*Ir. id.*) Diversity, dissimilarity, variety; strangeness.

Eag-samhluich, *v.* Diversify, vary, chequer. *Pret. a.* dh' eag-samhluich, *diversified.*

Eag-samhluidh, *a.* Different, dissimilar; various, mixed, chequered; singular, strange, matchless. Eag-samhluidh ri càch, *different from the rest.—Stew. Dan.* Le dathaibh eag-samhluidh, *with various colours.—Stew. Ezek.*

Eag-samhuil, *a.* (*Ir. id.*) Different, dissimilar; various, mixed, chequered; singular; strange; matchless. Eag-samhuil aon o 'chéile, *different from one another.—Stew. Dan.*

Eal, (*for* neul), *s.* A swoon or trance.

Eala', *for* èaladh *or* èalaidh; which see.

Eala, ai, *s. f.* (*Ir. id.*) A wild swan; the *anas cygnus ferus* of Linnæus. Loch nan Eala, *Loch Nell. N. pl.* ealan, *swans.*

Ealach, *a.* Abounding in swans; like a swan; of, or belonging to, a swan.

Ealach, aich, *s. m.* (*Ir. id.*) A pin or peg to hang any thing on, as clothes or arms; hence *ealachainn*, an armoury.

Ealachainn, *s. f.* (*from* ealach.) An armoury; a wardroom. Mar sgiath ann ealachainn taibhse, *like a shield in the armoury of a ghost.—Oss. Derm.*

Ealadh, aidh, *s. m.* (*Ir.* eala.) A swan. Binn-ghuth ealaidh, *the melody of a swan.—Ull.*

Èaladh, aidh, *s. m.* A creeping, a stealing on; a desertion.

Ealadh, aidh, *s. m.* (*Ir. id.*) An academy; a school; *also*, learning.

Ealadhan, ain, *s. m.* Learning, art, science. A reir ealadhain an leigh, *according to the art of the apothecary.—Stew. Ex.* Fear ealadhain, *an artist; a mechanic.*

Ealadhanach, *a.* (*from* ealadhan.) Ingenious, expert, clever; quick; scientific; curious, artificial.

Ealadhanachd, *s. f.* Ingenuity, expertness; cleverness; quickness.

Ealadhanta, *a.* (*from* ealadhan.) Artificial, curious, ingenious, alert, expert; clever.

Ealag, aig, *s. f.* A block; a hack-stock. *N. pl.* ealagan.

Ealagach, *a.* Like a block.

Ealaidh, *s. f.* Merriment, mirth, music, art, science. Far an greadhnach luchd ealaidh, *where the sons of mirth are glad.—Old Song.* Ealaidh gun rath, *music without luck.—G. P.*

Èalaidh, *v. n.* Creep, step, steal softly, sneak; watch jealously; steal away; desert. *Pret. a.* dh' ealaidh; *fut. aff. a.* èalaidh, *shall creep.*

Èalaidh, (ag), *pr. part.* of èalaidh. Creeping, stealing softly. Ag èala' air eòin na traigh, *stealing on the birds of the shore.—Ull.*

Ealaidheach, *a.* (*from* ealadh.) Creeping softly; stealing softly; sneaking; jealous; deserting. Gu h-ealaidheach, *jealously.*

Ealaidheachd, *s. f.* A creeping softly, a sneaking; propensity to jealousy.

Ealamh, *a.* Quick; nimble; ready. Lann ealamh na laimh, *a sword ready in his hand.—Oss. Fing.* Gu h-ealamh, *quickly;* faiceam an laoch gu h-ealamh, *let me see the hero quickly.—Oss. Tem.*

Ealamhachd, *s. f.* Quickness, nimbleness. Ann an ealamhachd, *soon, quickly.*

Ealan, ain, *s. m.* (*contr. for* ealadhan.) Learning, skill; art, science. Fear ealain, *an artist;* also, *a carpenter.* Luchd ealain, *carpenters.—Stew. Jer.*

Ealanach, *a.* (*for* ealadhanach.) Ingenious, artificial, curious; expert, clever. Gu eisgearra ealanach, *in a severe and clever manner.—Old Song.*

Ealanachd, *s. f.* (*for* ealadhanachd.) Ingenuity; artificialness; expertness.

† **Ealang,** aing, *s. f.* (*Ir. id.*) A fault or blemish.

Ealanta, *a., for* ealadhanta. (*Ir.* ealdhanta.) Artificial, ingenious; curious; skilled in arts or sciences. Obair ealanta, *ingenious work.—Stew. Ex.*

† **Ealar,** air, *s. m.* (*Ir. id.*) Salt.

† **Ealbha,** *s. m.* (*Ir. id.*) A herd, a drove.

Ealc, *a.* (*Ir. id.*) Malicious, spiteful, envious.

EALCMHOR, *a* (*Ir. id.*) Malicious, spiteful, envious; lazy, sluggish.

† EALG, *a.* (*Ir. id.*) Excellent, noble.

† EALL, *s m.* (*Ir. id.*) A trial; a proof, essay.—*Shaw.*

† EALLABHAIR, *s. f.* (*Ir. id.*) A multitude; a vast number. —*Shaw.*

EALLACH, aich, *s. f* (*Ir. id*) A load, a burden, an armful; a trick; a bracket; cattle; a battle. Eadar dha eallaich, *between two burdens.—Stew. Gen.*

EALLAICHE, *s. f.* (*Ir. id.*) Household stuff, furniture.

EALLAG, aig, *s f.* A log, a block, a bracket. *N. pl.* eallagan

EALLAMH, aimh, *s. m* Cattle given as a portion; wonder, astonishment.

EALLSG, *s. f* (*Ir. id*) A termagant, a scolding wife; a scolding female. *N. pl* eallsgan.

EALLSGAIL, *a* (ealsg-amhuil.) Scolding; inclined to scold.

EALT, *s. m* (*Ir. id*) A covey; a flight of birds; a number of quadrupeds, as a drove of cattle, a trip of goats, a rout of wolves, a pace of asses, a sounder of swine. Ealt eun, *a flight of birds, a covey;* ealt ghabhar, *a trip of goats*, ealt mhadadh allaidh, *a rout of wolves*, ealt asal, *a pace of asses*, ealt mhuc, *a sounder of swine.*

† EALTA, *s m.* (*Ir. id*) Repentance.—*Shaw.*

EALTACH, *a.* (*from* ealt) Gregarious; flighty, like a flight of birds.

EALTAIN, EALTUIN, *s. f* (*Ir* ealtain) A razor; any sharp-edged instrument; a flight of birds; a covey. Mar ealtain ghéir, *like a sharp razor —Sm.* Toirm ealtain eun, *the noise of a flight of birds —Oss.* Ealtuin bearradair, *the razor of a barber.—Stew. Ez.*

EALTUINNEACH, *a.* Like a razor, sharp, in flights, as birds

EALUIDH, *s f* Mirth, merriment; *also*, science, art Seòlta air ealuidh, *understanding science.—Stew Dan*

EAMHANTA, *a.* Double.

EAN, *s. m.* See EUN

EANACH GHÀRAIDH, *s f.* Endive

EANACHAILL, *s f.* More frequently written *eanchainn*

EANCHAINN, *s f.* Brains; genius, capacity. Dh' fhagadh e eanchainn, *he would leave his brains.—Old Poem.*

EANCHAINNEACH, *a.* Ingenious; clear-headed; cerebral Gu h-eanchainneach, *ingeniously*

EANCHAINNEACHD, *s f.* Ingeniousness.

† EANDA, *s. m.* (*Ir. id*) A simple in medicine

EANDAG, aig, *s. f.* (*Ir.* iontag) A nettle. See IONNTAG In some parts of the Highlands they say *feandag*

EANDAGACH, aich, *s f* A crop of nettles; a place where nettles grow. See also IONNTAGACH.

EANG, *s.* (*Ir. id*) A gusset, a headland, a track, a footstep; a nail; *rarely*, a year. *Eang*, in the sense of *nail*, is now written *ionga*, which see.

EANGACH, *a* Having a gusset; having headlands; full of footsteps; talkative

EANGACH, aich, *s m.* (*Ir id.*) A fishing-net, a chain of nets for salmon or herring fishery.—*Shaw.* A drag-net, a snare, a net-bladder. Eangach bàis, *the snare of death. —Sm N. pl* eangaich. Na 'n eangaich, *in their drag-nets —Stew Hab.*

EANGHACH, aich, *s. m.* A bladder —*Shaw*

EANGHLAS, ais, *s m.* (*Ir.* canglais.) Gruel, any weak drink; milk and water. Deoch eanghlais, *a drink of milk and water.*

EANGHNATH, *s m.* Prudence, dexterity, cleverness; generosity.

EAN-GHNATHACH, *a.* Prudent; dexterous, clever; generous Gu h-ean-ghnathach, *prudently. Com.* and *sup.* ean-ghnathaiche.

EANGLA, *s* An anniversary feast.

EANLAIR, *s. m.* A fowler, a gamekeeper.

EANLAIREACHD, *s f.* Fowling

EANLAITH See EUNLAITH.

EANNACH, aich, *s. f.* Innocence; spotlessness; *also, adjectively*, innocent. Tè aig am bi eannach, *a spotless female.—Old Song.*

EANNTAG, aig, *s. f.* (*Ir.* iontag.) A nettle. Written also *ionntag*. In some parts of the Highlands they say *feanntag*.

EANNTAGACH, *a.* Abounding in nettles; like nettles. See also IONNTAGACH.

EANNTAGACH, aich, *s. f.* A place where nettles grow; a crop of nettles —*Stew. Pro.*

EANRAICH, *s f.* A kind of fat broth; gravy Perhaps *eunbhrigh* or *eunbhruich.*

EANRUIC, *a.* More frequently written *ionruic*; which see.

† EANTAR, *prep* (*Ir. id.*) Between. Now written *eadar*. Hence *Lat.* inter. *Fr.* entre.

† EAR, *s m.* (*Ir. id.*) A head

EAR, *s* East, eastward. Gaoith an ear, *the east wind.—Sm.* San airde an ear, *east, eastward.—Stew. Gen.* O'n tìr an ear, *from the east country.—Stew. Zech.* An ear 's an iar, *east and west, on every side.*

EARABHRUICH, *a.* Parboiled; fomented.

EARABHRUICH, *v. a.* Parboil, foment. *Pret. a.* dh'earabhruich, *parboiled; fut aff a.* earabhruichidh, *shall parboil.*

EARABHRUICHTE, *part* Parboiled, fomented.

EARADH, aidh, *s m.* (*Ir. id.*) A refusal, a denial; fear, mistrust —*Shaw.* See also EURADH.

EARADH, aidh, *s m.* A garment; a tail; the hinder parts. Written also *earradh*, which see.

EARADHAIN, *s f.* A bit, a bridle Earadhain srèine, *the reins of a bridle.*

EARAIL, *s f.* Exhortation, importunacy; urging; caution; warning; reproof. An tì a bheir earail, *he who exhorts.—Stew Rom* Rinn e ro-earail, *he urged —Stew. Gen.* Pillibh air m' earail-sc, *turn at my reproof —Stew. Gen.*

EARAIL, *v.* Exhort, urge, press, caution, warn. *Pret. a* dh'earail. Dh'earail e orm, *he urged me; fut. aff.* earailidh, *shall urge*

EARAILEACH, EARAILTEACH, *a.* (*from* earail.) Exhorting, giving caution, warning; importunate, urging; like a caution or warning; of, or belonging to, a caution or warning; provident; foreseeing; cautious; proper; that ought to be advised.

EARAILTEACHD, *s f* (*from* earail) Exhortation, warning, importunacy.

EARAIS, *s f.* (*Ir. id.*) End, conclusion —*Shaw.*

EARALACH, *a.* (*Ir. id*) Cautious, prudent; giving caution or warning; importunate Gu h-earaleach, *importunately. Com.* and *sup* earalaiche.

EARALACHADH, aidh, *s. m.* An exhorting, a warning; importunacy, exhortation.

EARALADH, aidh, *s. m.* A cautioning; importunacy, exhortation

EARALAICH, *v. a.* Exhort, warn, caution; urge, press. *Pret. a.* dh'earalaich. Earalaich air, *warn him, exhort him;* teagasg agus earalaich, *warn and exhort.—Stew. G. B.*

EARALAICHIDH, *fut. aff. a* of earalaich. Shall or will exhort.

EARALAICHTE, *p part.* of earalaich. Exhorted, warned, cautioned.

EARALAS, ais, *s. m* Caution, exhortation; prudence, foresight, sagacity; foresightedness.

Earar, (an), *a corruption of* an ear-thrath. The day after to-morrow.

Earas, ais, *s. m.* End, conclusion; consequence.

Earb, *s. f.* (*Ir. id.*) A roe; the *cervus capreolus* of Linnæus; *rarely*, a command; an offer; employment. Mhosgail an earb, *the roe awake.—Oss. Cathula.* *N. pl.* earbaichean.

Earb, *v.* Trust, rely, confide; *rarely*, tell, relate. *Pret. a.* dh'earb, *trusted; fut. aff. a.* earbaidh, *shall trust.* This verb has after it the preposition *a* or *as*, *ri* or *ris*, either simple or compounded. Earbaidh a Dia, *trust ye in God.—Sm.* Earbaidh as, *trust in him.—Id.* Earbaidh mi riut, *I will trust to you*, or *rely on you.*

Earbach, *a.* Full of roes; like a roe; of, or belonging to, a roe.

Earbag, aig, *s. f.*, *dim.* of earb. (*Ir.* earbog.) A young roe; a little roe. An earbag a clisgeadh a leabaidh, *the roe starting from its bed.—Oss. Gaul.* *N. pl.* earbagan.

Earbaidh, *fut. aff. a.* of earb. Shall or will trust.

Earbail, *s. f.* (*Ir. id.*) A trust.

Earball, aill, *s. f.* (*from* earadh.) A tail. See **Earbull**.

Earbar, *fut. pass.* of earb. Shall be trusted. See **Earb**.

Earbchean, *n. pl.* of earb. Roes. Contracted for *earbaichean.*

Earbsach, *a.* Confident; relying; trusting. Earbsach na casaibh, *trusting to its [swiftness] legs.—Macint.*

Earbsadh, aidh, *s. m.* Confidence, trust, reliance. Neart a h-earbsaidh, *the strength of her confidence.—Stew. Pro.* Na cuir earbsadh ann, *do not trust in him.*

Earbsail, *a.* Trusty, confident.

Earbsalachd, *s. f.* Confidence.—*Turn.*

Earbull, uill, *s. f.* (*Ir.* earball.) A tail. Earball sguabach, *a bushy tail.—Macfar.* Earbull an eich, *paddock-pipe, horse-tail;* bun an earbuill, *the rump.*

Earbullach, *a.* (*from* earbull.) Having a tail; long-tailed; like a tail; of, or belonging to, the tail. *Com.* and *sup.* earbullaiche.

† **Earc**, *s. f.* (*Ir. id.*) A cow; a bee; honey; a salmon; a tax; heaven; *also*, speckled, red.

Earcail, *a.* (*Ir.* earcamhuil.) Pleasant, sweet, agreeable.

† **Earcan**, *s. pl.* Sweets, dainties, delicacies.

Earchaill, *s. f.* (*Ir. id.*) A prop; a post or pillar; a barring, a hindrance.—*Shaw.*

Earchall, aill, *s. m.* (*W.* argoll, *destruction.*) A loss, a calamity, a misfortune.

Earchallach, *a.* Calamitous; unfortunate. *Com.* and *sup.* earchallaiche.

Ear-chaomh, *a.* (*Ir. id.*) Noble.

Earc-dhruchd, *s. f.* Mildew. Ma bhios earc-dhruchd ann, *if there be mildew.—Stew.* 1 *K. ref.*

Earc-luachrach, aich, *s. f.* (*Ir. id.*) A lizard; an emmet.—*Shaw.*

† **Eardach**, aich, *s. f.* (*Ir. id.*) A feast, a solemnity.—*Shaw.*

Eardanal, ail, *s. m.* (*Ir. id.*) A piper, a trumpeter.—*Shaw.*

Ear-fhlaitheachd, *s. f.* Aristocracy.

Ear-fhlath, *s. m.* An aristocrat, a grandee, an earl. See **Iar-fhlath**.

† **Earg**, *v.* (*Gr.* ἐϱγω.) Build, frame, make up.—*Shaw.*

Ear-ghabh, *v. a.* (*Ir. id.*) Arrest, apprehend, make prisoner.

Ear-ghabhail, *s. f.* (*Ir. id.*) A miserable captivity.—*Shaw.*

Earghair, *s. f.* Embargo, prohibition.

Ear-ghair, *v. a.* (*Ir. id.*) Congratulate; forbid, prohibit.—*Shaw.*

Ear-ghalan, ain, *s. m.* A piper.—*Shaw.* *Also*, noisy, clamorous.

Earghnaidh, *a.* (*Ir. id.*) Munificent, worthy, virtuous; *also, substantively*, munificence.

Ear-ghobhlach, *a.* Fork-tailed. Na bric ear-ghobhlach, *the fork-tailed trouts.—Macdon.*

Eargna, ai, *s. m.* (*Ir. id.*) Conception, quickness of apprehension.

Earlaid, *s. f.* Expectation; hope; dependence; confidence. Gun airm, gun earlaid, *without arms or hope.—Turn.*

Earlaideach, *a.* Expectant; dependent; confident.

† **Earlamh**, *a.* (*Ir. id.*) Noble, grand, august.—*Shaw.*

Earlas, ais, *s. m.* (*Scotch*, erles. *W.* arles, *advantage.*) A pledge or earnest.—*Stew. Eph.*

Earnach, aich, *s. f.* A distemper among cattle, caused, as is supposed, by eating a poisonous herb, and against which a laxative potion, given in time, is an effectual antidote.

Earnadh, aidh, *s. m.* Payment; assessment; promulgation.

Earnag, aig, *s. f.* (*Corn.* eirinen.) A sloe. *N. pl.* earnagan, *sloes.* Preas earnag, *a sloe-tree.* Also written *fearnag.*

Earnagach, *a.* Abounding in sloes, of sloes, like a sloe.

Earnail, *s. f.* (*Ir. id.*) A part, a share.

Earnais, *s. f.* Furniture. Dh' fhalbh d'earnais, *thy furniture is gone.—Mac Co.* Written also *airneis;* which see.

Earr, *v. a.* Clothe, array. *Pret. a.* dh'earr, *clothed; fut. aff.* earraidh, *shall clothe.*

Earr, *s. m.* (*Gr.* οὐϱα. *Ir.* earr.) A tail; an end, a conclusion, limit, boundary. Glac air a h-earr i, *catch it by the tail.—Stew. Ex.*

† **Earr**, *s. m.* (*Ir. id.*) A champion; noble, grand.—*Shaw.*

Earrach, *a.* Tailed; having a long tail; limited, bounded. Am bradan earrach, *the long-tailed salmon.—Macfar.*

Earrach, aich, *s. m.* (*Ir. id.* *Gr.* ἐαϱ, *spring.*) Spring; *also*, bottom. An t-earrach cruaidh, *the unseasonable spring.—Sm.* Druchd earraich, *spring-dew.—Oss. Carricth.*

Earradh, aidh, *s. m.* (*Ir. id.*) Clothing, apparel; a garment; armour; a tail; a conclusion; a limit or border; merchandise, wares, commodities; accoutrements. Earradh uaine, *green robes.—Oss. Taura.* Earradh bhreagh, *a goodly garment.—Stew. Jos.* Earradh, *merchandise.—Stew. Rev. ref.*

From *earradh*, clothing, through the medium of the French † *arroye*, comes the English word *array.*

Earradhreas, is, *s. m.* The dog-brier.

Earradhubh, dhuibh, *s. m.* A wane; waning moon; *also, adjectively*, waning. Tha mo sholus mar earradhubh, *my light is like the waning moon.—Oss. Taura.* A ghealach earradhubh, *the waning moon.*

Earrag, aig, *s. f.* A blow or stroke; a blow on the head. Earrag cheilidh, *a gossipping stroke.—Old Saying.*—Said of one who is hurt on a visit.

Earragheal, ghil, *s. m.* The pygarg. Written also *earrgheal.*

Erraghloir, *s. f.* Vain-glory, boasting.—*Stew. Gal. ref.*

† **Earraid**, *s. f.* (*Lat.* erratum. *Ir.* earraid.) A mistake, a fault.

Earrann, ainn, *s. m.* *N. pl.* earrainnean. A share, a part, a portion, a division; a clause; a district; a province. Ceithir earrainnean, *four parts.—Stew. Gen.* Do 'n earrainn, *to the province.*

Earras, ais, *s. m.* Goods, stock, substance, capital, commodities. Helen 's a h-earras theid dachaidh, *Helen and her goods shall go home.—Mac Lach.*

Earrasach, *a.* Having goods or commodities; of, or pertaining to, goods or commodities.

Earrasaid, *s. f.* An ancient Highland garment, or loose wrapper, worn by the women. It covered the whole body, and was used without any under clothing. Written also *fearrasaid;* which see.

EARRDHUBH, uibh, *s. m.* The wane of the moon; the moon in wane.

EARRGHEAL, ghil, *s. m* A pygarg. An t-earrgheal, *the pygarg* —*Stew. Deut.*

EARR-GHOBHLACH, *a.* Fork-tailed. Am bradan earr-ghobhlach, *the fork-tailed salmon* —*Macfar.*

EARRLINN, *s f.* The limit of any thing; an end, a conclusion, a close

EAR-THRATH, (an), *adv.* The day after to-morrow

EAS, *s. f* A weasel. An eas agus an luch, *the weasel and the mouse* —*Stew Lev.*

EAS, *s m* (*Ir.* easar, easard.) A cataract; a cascade; a stream with high precipitous banks *Scotch,* linn. Gach doire is gach eas, *every grove and waterfall.*—*Ull*

EASACH, aich, *s f* (*from* eas) A dark, deep, rocky stream, a cataract or waterfall, *also,* pottage. Easach a leum' thar charraig, *a stream bounding over a rock.*—*Oss. Derm.* Osunn easaich, *the noise of a cataract. N pl* easaichean Mar thoirm easaichean, *like the roar of cataracts* —*Old Poem*

† EASADH, aidh, *s. m* (*Ir. id*) A disease, sickness.—*Shaw.*

EASAG, aig, *s f* A pheasant; a little weasel; a squirrel —*Stew Lev. ref. N. pl* easagan.

EASAICH, *gen. sing* of easach.

EASAICHEAN, *n pl.* of eas *or* easach. Cascades, cataracts

EASAILLE, *s f* (*Ir id*) Dispraise, disparagement

EASAL, ail, *s m.* (*Ir. id.*) A tail —*Shaw.*

EASAN, ain, (*dim.* of eas) A little cataract, a little cascade. Crònan t-easain srùlaich, *the murmur of thy little cataracts* —*Macdon*

EASAONACH, *a* (eas, *priv and* aonach) Disobedient; discordant, rebellious, factious; dissenting Gu h-easaonach, *disobediently*

EASAONACHD, *s f* Disobedience, discordance, disagreement, rebellion, schism. Thaobh ar n-eas-aonachd, *by reason of our discord* —*Macfar.*

EASAONTACH, *a.* (eas, *priv and* aontach) *Ir.* easontach. Disobedient, discordant, insubordinate, rebellious, factious, dissenting, repugnant.

EASONTACHD, *s f.* Disobedience, discordance, disagreement, schism, insubordination, factiousness.

EASAONTAS, ais, *s m.* Transgression or trespass, disobedience, insubordination, discordance, faction. Airson easaontais, *on account of transgression.*—*Stew. Mic.*

EASAR, air, *s. m.* (*Ir id*) See EAS

EASARD, aird, *s. m* (*Ir id.*) A quarrel, a cataract, a foul house.

EASARGUIN, *s. f* (*Ir* easargan) Tumult; quarrel, confusion; a mob

EASARLUIDHEACHD, *s. f* Incantation

EASBAIDH, aidh, *s m.*(*Ir. id.*) Want, defect, scarcity; absence.

EASBAL, ail, *s. m.* An apostle (*Ir id.*)

EASBA-RIGHAD, *s. f* The king's evil, or scrofula.

EASBALOID, *s f* (*Ir id*) Absolution

EASBALOIDEACH, *a.* (*Ir. id.*) Absolution.

EASBARTA, *s pl.* Vespers, evening prayers.

EASBHUIDH, *s* Want, lack, necessity Dh'easbhuidh, *for want,* as easbhuidh, *for want,* airson easbhuidh chùigir, *for lack of five persons.*—*Stew. G. B.* Gun easbhuidh gheibh e, *he will receive without fail.*—*Sm.*

EASBHUIDHEACH, *a* Needy, necessitous; poor, empty; lacking. Duine easbhuidheach, *a needy man.*

EASBUIG, *s. m.* (*Ir.* easbog) *N pl.* easbuigean

EASBUIGHEACH, *a.* Episcopal. An eaglais easbuigheach, *the episcopal church*

EASBUIGHEACHD, *s. f.* (*from* easbuig.) Episcopacy; prelacy; a bishopric

† EASC, *s. f.* (*Ir. id*) Water.

† EASCAICH, *s. f.* (*Ir id.*) A quagmire or fen.

EASCAIN, *s. f.* Cursing, imprecation, blasphemy, envy, slander. Le h-eascain is le malluchadh, *with slander and cursing* —*Sm.*

EASCAIR, *s. f.* A storm, a blustering wind; a surprise; a warning —*Shaw.*

EASCAIRDEACH, *a.* (eas, *priv and* càirdeach) Hostile; inveterate. Gu h-eascairdeach, *hostilely.*

EASCAIRDEAN, *n. pl.* of eascaraid. Enemies.

EASCAIRDEAS, eis, *s. m.* Enmity, hostility. Luchd eascairdeis, *private enemies*

EASCAR, EASCARAID, *s. m.* (*Ir* eascara.) An enemy. Cia an t-eascar? *who is the enemy?*—*Sm* Pòg eascaraid, *the kiss of an enemy.*—*Stew. G. B. N. pl.* eascairdean.

EASCOIN. See EASCAIN.

EASCOINEACH, *a.* Malignant, malicious, envious. Gu h-eascoineach, *malignantly.*

EASCOINEACHD, *s. f.* Malignity, maliciousness, enviousness.—*Stew. Rom. ref.*

† EASCOMAN, *a.* (*Ir. id*) Dirty, nasty, filthy.—*Shaw.*

† EASCONN, oinn, *s m.* (*Ir. id*) An old man; the moon.

† EASCRA, *s. m.* (*Ir. id.*) A cup; a drinking vessel.

† EASCRADH, aidh, *s. m.* (*Ir id.*) Walking, stepping, marching.

EASG, *s f.* (*Ir. id*) An eel; *rarely,* the moon. Easg shùileach, *a conger eel. N pl* easgan; *d pl.* easgaibh.

EASGACH, *a.* Like an eel, abounding in eels; of eels.

EASGAID, *s. f.* The hough, the ham. Written also *iosgaid.*

EASGAIDEACH, *a.* Having large houghs or hams Written also *iosgaideach.*

EASGAIDH, *a* (*perhaps* ea-sgith.) Officious; willing to serve, nimble, active, ready As easgaidh an droch ghille air chuairt, *the lazy servant is active from home.*—*G. P.*

EASGAIDH, *s f* A quagmire.

EASGAIDHEACHD, *s f.* Officiousness; willingness to serve; activity

EASGAINN, *a* Nimble, active; willing to serve.

EASGAIRC, *s f.* A quagmire, bog, or fen.—*Shaw.*

EASGALL, aill, *s. m.* A storm; a blustering wind; a wave; a noise

EASGALLACH, *a.* Stormy, blustering, billowy; noisy.

EASGAN, ain, *s. m* (*Ir id*) The hough or ham; a little eel. —*Shaw.*

EASGAN, *n. pl* of easg. Eels.

EASGANN, ainn, *s m* Mar easgann liath-ghlas, *like a dark-grey eel.*—*Turn.* An eel, the *muræna anguilla* of Linnæus.

† EASGBHAINEACH, *a* (*Ir. id.*) Lunatic.

† EASGRADH, aidh, *s m.* (*Ir* eascra.) A cup; a drinking vessel, a grain of corn; the plague.

EASGUID, *s. f.* The hough, the ham. Written also *iosgaid.*

EASGUIDEACH, *a* Having large houghs or hams. Also written *iosgaideach*

EASGUL, uil, *s m.* A wave; a storm; blustering wind; a noise. Written also *easgall.*

EASGUNN. See EASGANN.

EAS-IONRACAS, ais, *s. m.* (eas, *priv. and* ionracas) Dishonesty; faithlessness; wickedness.

EAS-IONRAIC, *a.* (eas, *priv. and* ionraic) Dishonest; faithless; wicked. Gu h-eas-ionraic, *dishonestly.*

EASITH, *s. f.* (ea, *priv. and* sith.) Mischief, disturbance.

Easlabhra, *s.* Bounty, courtesy, affability.

† **Easlach**, aich, *s. m.* (*Ir. id.*) A pool, a lake.—*Shaw.*

Easlainnte, *s. f.* (ea, *priv. and* slainnte.) Sickness. Luchd easlainnte, *sick people.* See also Eu-slainnte.

Eas-lainnteach, *a.* Infirm, sick, unwholesome. Gu h-ea-slainnteach, *sickly.*

Easlan, *a.* (ea, *priv. and* slàn.) Infirm. See also Euslan.

Easmaidh, *s.* (*Ir. id.*) Lath, a spar.

† **Easmail**, *s. f.* (*Ir. id.*) A reproach, a reproof; dependence.—*Shaw.*

† **Easmailteach**, *a.* Reproachful; *also*, a reproachful person.

Easnadh, aidh, *s. m.* Time; music, melody, song.—*Shaw.*

Easnath, aidh, *s. m.* (*Ir. id.*) Want of web enough for the loom.—*Shaw.*

Easomaid, *s. f.* Disrespect, dishonour.—*Shaw.*

Easomaideach, *a.* Disrespectful, disobedient.—*Shaw.*

Easoman, ain, *s. m.* (*Ir. id.*) A welcome.

Easonoir, *s. m.* (eas, *priv. and* onoir.) *Ir. id.* Dishonour; disgrace; reproach; dishonesty. A toirt easonoir, *dishonouring.*—*Stew. Mic.*

Easonorach, *a.* (eas, *priv. and* onorach.) *Ir.* easonoireach. Dishonourable, disgraceful; causing dishonour; abusive, reproachful; dishonest. Gu h-easonorach, *dishonourably.*

Easonorachadh, aidh, *s. m.* A dishonouring, a disgracing.

Eas-onoraich, *v. a.* Dishonour; disgrace, abuse. *Pret. a.* dh'eas-onoraich, *disgraced.*

Eas-ordach, *a.* (*for* eas-ordughach.) Factious; irregular; unruly.

Eas-orduchadh, aidh, *s. m.* A disordering, a confusing, disarranging; disorder, confusion, disarrangement; anarchy.

Easordugh, *s. m.* (eas, *priv. and* ordugh.) Confusion; irregularity; unruliness. Dh'oibrich iad eas-ordugh, *they have wrought confusion.*—*Stew. Lev.*

Easorduich, *v. a.* Confuse, disarrange. *Pret. a.* dh'eas-orduich, *confused.*

Easorgain, *s. f.* (*Ir. id.*) Contrition.

† **Easorgnadh**, aidh, *s. m.* (*Ir. id.*) A squeezing, a crushing.—*Shaw.*

Easpuig, *s. m.* A bishop. *N. pl.* easpuigean.

Easpuigheach, *a.* Episcopal.

Easpuigheachd, *s. f.* Episcopacy; prelacy; a bishoprick.

Easran, ain, *s. m.* (*Ir. id.*) Dispersion.

Easuain, *v. a.* (*Ir. id.*) Scum, skim.

Eas-umhal, *a.* (eas, *priv. and* umhal.) *Ir. id.* Disobedient; irreverent; insubordinate; rebellious. Eas-umhal do phàrantaibh, *disobedient to parents.*—*Stew. Rom.* Gu h-eas-umhal, *disobediently.*

Eas-umhlachd, *s. f.* (eas, *priv. and* umhlachd.) Disobedience; irreverence; insubordination; insubordinateness, rebelliousness; obstinacy. Air gach uile eas-umhlachd, *on all disobedience.*—*Stew.* 2 *Cor.* Luchd na h-eas-umhlachd, *the insubordinate.*

Eas-urram, aim, *s. m.* (eas, *priv. and* urram.) Disrespect, dishonour, disgrace, reproach. A thoirt eas-urraim, *to cause dishonour.*—*Stew. Rom.* A thaobh eas-urraim, *concerning reproach.*—*Stew. Cor.*

Eas-urramach, *a.*, eas, *priv. and* urramach. (*Ir. id.*) Disrespectful, dishonourable, disgraceful; contemptuous; causing dishonour or disrespect.

Eas-urramachadh, aidh, *s. m.* A treating contemptuously, a degrading, a disgracing.

Eas-urramaich, *v. a.* Dishonour, treat with contempt, degrade; despise. *Pret. a.* dh'eas-urramaich, *dishonoured; fut. aff.* eas-urramaichidh.

† **Eata**, *a.* Old, ancient, antique. *Gr.* ἔτος. *Lat.* ætas, *age. Ir.* eata, *old.*

† **Eatach**, aich, *s. m.* (*Ir. id.*) An elderly person; an elder.—*Shaw.*

† **Eatal**, ail, *s. m.* A flight; the world; pleasure, delight.—*Shaw.*

Eathar, air, *s. m.* (*Ir. id.*) A skiff; a bark or boat; a barge; a vessel; a cup. An t-eathar donn, *the brown-coloured bark.*—*Oss. Lodin.* Eathar iasgaich, *a truss. N. pl.* eathraichean; *d. pl.* eathraichibh.

Eathlamh, *a.* Quick, active, nimble, clever, ready-handed. Eathlamh na ghnothuichibh, *quick in his business.*—*Stew. Pro.* Written more frequently *ealamh.*

Eathraichean, *n. pl.* of eathar; *d. pl.* eathraichibh.

† **Eatla**, ai, *s. m.* (*Ir. id.*) Boldness; sadness.—*Shaw.*

Eatlathach, *a.* (*Ir. id.*) Bold, intrepid; sad. Gu h-eatlathach eugmhaiseach, *in a bold and signal manner.*—*Old Song.*

Eatlathachd, *s. f.* Boldness; intrepidity; sadness.

Eatorra, *com.* and *sup.* (*Ir. id.*) Between them; among them. Eatorra féin, *among themselves.*—*Stew. Job.* Cuir eatorra, *separate them;* thainig eatorra, *they quarrelled.*

Eatorras, ais, *s. m.* (*Ir. id.*) Mediocrity; a middling state or way. Tha mi 'n eatorras, *I am in a middling way.*

Eatreòire, *s. f.* Weakness, incapacity; pithlessness. Written also *eu-treòire.*

Eatreòrach, *a.* Weak, incapable, pithless. Written also *eu-treòrach.*

Eatrocair, *s. f.* (ea, *priv. and* trocair.) *Ir.* eatrocair. Cruelty; inhumanity. Written also *eutrocair;* which see.

Ea-trocaireach, *a.* (ea, *priv. and* trocaireach.) Cruel, inhuman. See also *eutrocaireach.*

Eatrom, *a.*, ea, *priv. and* trom. (*Ir. id.*) Light, giddy; tipsy. Fhaileis eatroim na fàs-ghaoithe, *light shadow of the empty wind.*—*Oss. Fing.* *Com.* and *sup.* eatruime. See also Eutrom.

Eatromachadh, aidh, *s. m.* A making light or less heavy; an alleviating; a lightening; alleviation. See also Eutromachadh.

Eatromachadh, (ag), *pr. part.* of eutromaich. Lightening, assuaging, alleviating.

Eatromaich, *v. a.* Lighten, make less heavy; alleviate, assuage, relieve. *Pret. a.* dh'eatromaich, *lightened; fut. aff. a.* eatromaichidh, *shall lighten; fut. pass.* eatromaichear.

Eatromaichte, *p. part.* of eatromaich. Lightened, alleviated.

Eatroman, ain, *s. m.* (*from* eatrom.) A bladder. (*Ir.* eadtroman *and* eatroman.) *N. pl.* eatromain, *bladders.*

Eatruime, *com.* and *sup.* of eatrom. Lighter, lightest.

Eatruime, *s. f.* Lightness; levity; giddiness. Eatruime ceille, *insanity.*—*Macdon.*

Eatruimead, id, *s. m.* Lightness, levity; increase in lightness. A dol an eatruimead, *growing more and more light.*

† **Ed.** See † **Eid.**

Eibh, *s. f.* A shriek, a cry, a shout. Eibh a bhàis, *the cry of death.*—*Oss. Fing.* Is fad an éibh o Loch Abh, *it is a far cry to Loch Awe.*—*Old Saying.*

Eibhinn, *s. f.* Joy. Eibhinn duit, *joy be with you.*—*Turn.*

Eibhinn, *a.* Joyful, glad. Mo ghàir aoibhinn, *my joyful laugh.*—*Macfar.* More frequently written *aoibhinn;* which see.

Eibhle, *s. f.* A fire; a hearth-fire; a flame; a burning coal. Mar eibhle sa bhealach, *like a fire in the pass.*—*Oss. Fing. N. pl.* eibhlean; *d. pl.* eibhlibh. Le eibhlibh teine, *with coals of fire.*—*Stew. Jer.*

Eibhlead, eid, *s. m.* (*from* éibh.) An interjection.

Eibhleadach, *a.* Interjectional

Eibhleag, eig, *s. f.* (*dim* of eibhle.) *Ir* ebhleog. A burning or live coal; a little fire Eibhleag theine, *a burning coal* *N pl* eibhleagan Mhùch iad m'eibhleag, *they have quenched my fire.—Stew* 2 *Sam*

Eibhleagach, *a.* Like a burning coal, full of burning coals.

Eibhlean, *n. pl.* of eibhle. Fires.

Eibhlich, *v.* Sparkle, kindle, flame. *Pret a.* dh'eibhlich, *kindled*, *fut. aff.* eibhlichidh

Eibhneach, *a* Joyous, glad; delighted —*Macfar.* More frequently written *aoibhneach*, which see

Eibhneas, eis, *s. m* Joy See Aoibhneas.

Eiblit, *s* An interjection

Eich, *gen sing* and *n pl* of each.

Éich See Eigh.

† **Eid, Ed** A word used on discovery of any animal of prey, or game: it is meant to give notice to the hunting companion to be in readiness to seize the animal Hence, perhaps, the ἐδω of the Greeks, the *edo* of the Latins; the *eat* of the English, the *ed* of the Irish, which signifies *cattle* So the Scotch *edal* (eudail) means the offspring of cattle, *coed* or *cued* (now *cuid*), means a share, *literally*, common food *Focd* (now *faghaid*), means hunting or gathering of food, *edra*, the time of the morning when cattle are brought from pasture to give milk, *literally*, meal time With the Celtic *eid*, the Greek εἶδαρ has an evident affinity.

Eid, *v a.* Clothe, cover. *Pret. a* dh'eid, *clothed*, *fut aff a* eididh, *shall clothe*, *fut pass* eidear Ged eid thu thu fein le corcur, *though thou clothe thyself with crimson* —*Stew O. T.*

Eide', **Eideadh**, idh, *s. f* A dress; a vestment, robe, clothing, armour, dressing. Na eideadh soillse, *in his mantle of light —Oss Cathluno* Ar n-eide' cuirp, *our body garments —Sm* Gun eide' gun each, *without horse or armour —Oss. Taura.* Eideadh gairdein, *a bracelet*, eideadh uchd, *a breastplate*, eideadh calpa, *greaves* Nur rachadh tu ad eideadh, *when thou wouldst be in full dress —Turn*

Eideam, 1 *sing. pr. aff* of eid. I clothe Eideam na neamha, *I clothe the heavens.* *Also*, 1 *sing imper. of* eid, *clothe thou*, *also for* eididh mi, *I will clothe*

Eidear See Eadar

Eidhe. See Eigh or Eith.

Eidheachail, *a* Icy, slippery

Eidheann, eidhne, *s. f* (*Ir.* eidheann) Ivy Written also *eigheann.*

Eidhneach, *a* Full of ivy; of, or belonging to, ivy, like ivy —*Shaw.*

Eidhnean, ein, *s. m* A bough or branch of ivy; a young ivy

Eidhre, *s f.* (*Ir. id.* *W* eira, *snow*) Ice, frost, a burden. Written also *eithre*

Eididh, *s f.* A web; a dress, clothing, garment; armour. Eididh anairt, *a web of linen*, eididh thùilinn, *a web of twilled linen* Eididh bròin, *a mourning dress —Sm* Na eididh stailinn, *in his armour of steel —Oss Gaul.* Eididh calpa, *greaves*, eididh droma, *a back clothing, a back-piece*, eididh muineil, *a gorget;* eididh uchd, *a breastplate;* eididh Ghaidhealach, *a Highland dress*

Éidigh, *a* Ugly, dismal; deformed. See Eitidh

† **Eidimhin**, *a*, ea *and* deimhin (*Ir. id*) Uncertain, doubtful; fluctuating, changeable.

Eidir-cheart, eirt, *s m.* (*Ir. id.*) An equal distribution —*Shaw.*

† **Eidir**, *s. m.* (*Ir. id.*) A captive, a prisoner, a hostage. —*Shaw.*

Éifeachd, *s. f.* (*Ir. id.* *Lat.* effectus.) Effect; avail; consequence. Tha iad gun éifeachd, *they are without effect —Stew. Pro.*

Éifeachdach, *a.* (*Ir. id.*) Effectual, efficient, of avail. A ghairm éifeachdachb, *effectual calling;* gu h-éifeachdach, *effectually.*

Eifeachdail, *a.* (eifeachd-amhuil.) Effectual. *Ir.* eifeachdamhail

Eio, *gen. sing.* of eug; which see

Eige, *s f* The Isle of Egg, one of the Hebrides. *Ir.* oghe, *an isle.* *Ang' Sax.* eage *and* ig

Eige, *s. f.* A web. *N. pl.* eigeachan Webs Pinne na gairmain agus an eige, *the pin of the beam and the web.—Stew. Jud.*

Éigean. See Eigin.

Eigean, *a.* (*Ir. id.*) Lawful, rightful, just.

† **Eigeas**, is, *s. m* (*Ir. id*) A learned man —*Shaw.*

Eigh, eighe, *s f* (*Ir.* éigh *Gr.* ηχη *Lat.* echo. *Scotch*, aich) A cry, a shout, shriek, a loud lament Eigh còmhraig, *the shout of battle, a war-cry.—Ull.* Is fad an éigh o Loch Abh, *it is a far cry to Loch Awe*,—an adage expressive of the remoteness of that lake.

Éigh, *v. n* (*Ir* éigh. *Gr.* ιαχω) Cry, exclaim, shout, shriek, roar, sound; proclaim. *Pret. a* dh' éigh; *fut. aff. a.* eighidh, *shall cry* Dh' éigh na sruthaidh, *the streams sounded —Ull* Eighidh mi, *I will cry.—Sm* Eighibh caismeachd, *sound an alarm.—Id.* *Fut. pass.* éighear. Cha 'n éighear cath, *battle shall not roar.—Id.*

Eigh, eighe, *s. f.* (*Ir* aigh *and* eag.) Ice; a file. Dubh le h-eigh, *blackish with ice.—Stew. Job.* Bha eigh aca, *they had a file.—Stew. Sam.*

Eigh còmhraig, *s f* A war-cry See Gaoir chatha.

Eigheach, *a.* (*from* éigh.) Crying, shrieking, shouting; clamorous, noisy.

Éigheach, ich, *s. f.* A crying, a loud wailing; a bawling; a cry, a shout, a call; a proclamation; a loud voice. Eigheach mhòr, *great [crying] wailing.—Stew Ex.* Fuaim éighich, *the noise of a cry.—Stew. Zeph.* Is aithne dhoibh d'éigheach, *they know thy call —Ull.*

Eigheach, (a), *pr part.* of éighich. Calling, shouting; proclaiming Guth dhaoine ag éigheach, *the voice of men shouting.—Stew Ex*

Eigheanaich, *s. m.* An icicle.

Eigheann, *g* eighinn *and* eighne, *s f* Ivy Eigheann nan crag, *the rock-ivy.—Oss. Derm.* Fo 'n chreig eighinn, *at the foot of the ivy-rock.—Id.*

Eigheannach, *a.* Abounding in ivy; of ivy, belonging to ivy; like ivy.

Eighich, *v. n.* Cry, call, shout; shriek, bawl; proclaim. *Pret. a.* dh' éighich, *called*

Éigin, *a* (*Ir.* eigean) Some; certain; necessary. Fear h-eigin, *some man*, rud-eigin, *something;* ni h-eigin, *something*, ni'gin, *something.* Nur is éigin, *when it is necessary.* —*Oss Tem.*

Éigin, *s f.* (*W.* egni. *Ir.* eigean) Difficulty; distress; a strait; necessity; force, violence, rape; oppression. An righ tha na éigin, *the king who is in distress.—Ull.* Air éigin, *with difficulty, with much ado* Thog e air éigin a shùil, *with difficulty he raised his eye.—Ull* Is eigin domh, *I must*, i. e *there is a necessity on me.* Dean éigin, *force, violate, deflower.* Rinn iad éigin air mo choimhleabach, *they forced my concubine.—Stew. Jud.* Eigin fhuail, *a dysury*, beò-air-éigin, *just alive, alive and that's all*, teine éigin, *forced fire.* See Teine éigin.

Éigin, (air), *adv* With difficulty, with much ado.

Éigin-fhuail, *s f.* A dysury.

Éiginneach, *a.* (*Ir.* eigeantach.) Necessary, indisputable, needful; *also*, compulsive; oppressive; ravishing, forcing.

Éiginneas, eis, *s. m.* Force, violence; necessity, need; compulsion; a rape.—*Shaw.*

Éiginteach, *a.* Needful, necessary, indispensable.

Eiglidh, *a.* (*Ir. id.*) Mean, abject, feeble.

Eiglidheachd, *s.* Meanness, abjectness.—*Shaw.*

Eigne, *s.* (*Ir. id.*) A salmon.—*Shaw.*

Eigneachadh, aidh, *s. m.* (*Ir.* éigniughadh.) A forcing, a compelling, a constraining, a ravishing; compulsion, constraint, a rape.

Eigneachadh, (ag), *pr. part.* of éignich.

Eigneachair, *s. m.* A ravisher, a constrainer. *N. pl.* eigneachairean.

Eignich, *v. a.* (*Ir.* eignigh.) Ravish, force, constrain, compel, oppress, take by force. *Pret. a.* dh' éignich; *fut. aff. a.* éignichidh, *shall ravish.* Dh' éignich thu mo chridhe, *thou hast ravished my heart.*—*Stew. Song Sol.* Dh' éignich sibh mi, *you have compelled me.*—*Stew.* 2 *Cor.*

Eignichear, *fut. pass.* of éignich. Shall be ravished. Eignichear na mnathan, *the wives shall be ravished.*—*Stew. Zech.*

Eignichte, *p. part.* of éignich. (*Ir.* éignighte.) Ravished, forced, compelled, constrained.

Eigse, *s. f.* (*Ir. id.*) Art, science, knowledge.—*Macdon.*

Eigseach, ich, *s. f.*, *from* eigse. (*Ir. id.*) A school; study.—*Shaw.*

† **Eil**, *v. a.* (*Ir. id.*) Rob.—*Shaw.*

'Eil, (*for* bheil.) Cha 'n 'eil mi, *I am not.*

Eilde, *gen. sing.* of éilid. Of a roe; also the name of a hill in the West Highlands.—*Oss. Derm.*

Eildeach, *a.* Abounding in roes. Gleann eildeach, *the valley of roes.*—*Orr.*

Eildear, ir, *s. m.* An elder, an officer in the Kirk so called; also the name Elder.

† **Eile**, *s. f.* (*Ir. id.*) A prayer, entreaty; oration.—*Shaw.*

Eile, *a.* Other, else. Aon eile, *one other;* rud eile, *another thing;* agus rud eile dheth, *and moreover, more than that.*
Gr. αλλος. *Lat.* alius. *Germ.* el. *W.* all. *Swed.* all. *Arm.* all *and* eil. *Du.* al. *Ir.* eile. Aon eile, *one other. Ir.* aon eile. *Arm.* un eil.

Eileach, ich, *s. f.* A mill-dam, a mill-channel. *N. pl.* eilichean.

† **Eileachadh**, aidh, *s. m.* An accusing; an accusation.

Eilean, ein, *s. m.* (*Germ.* eyland.) An island, isle, or islet. Eilean araidh, *a certain island.*—*Stew. Acts.* Eilean Bhreatuinn Mhòire, *the island of Great Britain.*—*N. pl.* eileanan, *isles; d. pl.* eileanaibh. Nùll da na h-eileanaibh, *away to the isles.*—*Old Song.* Eilean a Mhòid, *or*, Eilean Bhòid, *the isle of Bute.*

Eileanach, *a.* Insular; abounding in islands; like an island; peninsular; *also*, generous, liberal, munificent.

Eileanach, ich, *s. m.* An Islander; an Hebridean; *also*, a generous man. *N. pl.* eileanaich. Ban Eileanach, *an Hebridean woman.*

Eileanachd, *s. f.* Generosity, liberality, munificence.

Eilear, eir, *s. m.* A deer's walk.

Eilgheadh, idh, *s. m.* A burial, interment.

Eilibear, ir, *s. m.* Hellebore.—*Macdon.*

Eilich, *v. a.* Accuse, charge, call to account. *Pret.* dh' eilich, *accused.*

Eilid, eilde, *s. f.* A hind, a roe. Eilid ag iarruidh a h-annsachd, *a hind in search of its mate.*—*Oss. Fin. and Lor.* Mar chosaibh éilde, *like the feet of a hind.*—*Stew. Hab.* Mac na h-eilde, *a young roe.*—*Ull.*

Eill, *s. f.* (*Ir. id.*) Precipice; advantage; flock.

Eill, *gen. sing.* of iall. Of a thong. *Ir.* éill, *a thong.*

Eilne, *s. f.* (*Ir. id.*) Uncleanness, pollution.—*Shaw.*

Eilnich, *v. a.* Corrupt, spoil, violate.

Eil-thìr, *s. f.* A foreign land, a strange country.

Eil-thireach, *a.* Foreign, strange.

Eilthireach, ich, *s. m.* A foreigner, a pilgrim, an alien. A' m' eilthireach bha mi, *I was an alien.*—*Stew. Job.*

Eimh, *a.* (*Ir. id.*) Quick, active, brisk.

Eimheachd, *s. f.* Obedience, compliance.

Eimhilt, *a.* Slow.

Eimhleag, eig, *s. f.* See **Eibhleag**.

Eineach, ich, *s. m.* (*Ir.* eineach. *Corn.* eineach.) A fine countenance; a face.—*Shaw.* Any body.

Eineagh, ich, *s. m.* (*Ir. id.*) Bounty, goodness, courtesy, affability; a truce; a shirt; a smock.—*Macdon.*

Eineachas, ais, *s. m.* Bounty, goodness, courtesy, affability.

Eineachlan, ain, *s. m.* Protection, defence.—*Shaw.*

Eingeal, eingle, *s. f.* (*Corn.* engil.) A fire. More frequently written *eibhle.*

Eintridh, *s. f.* An entrance, an avenue.—*Macdon.*

Eipistil, *s. f.* A letter or epistle.
Gr. επιστολη. *Lat.* epistola. *Fr.* †epistre. *Ir.* eipistil.

Éir, *v. n.* Rise, mount, ascend. *Pret.* dh' éir, *rose; fut. aff.* éiridh, *shall rise.*

Eirbheach, *s. f.* A wasp.—*Shaw.*

Eirbheirt, *s. f.* A moving, a stirring about, a motion.—*Shaw.*

Eirceach, ich, *s. m.* A heretic. See **Eiriceach**.

Eirceachd, *s. f.* See **Eiriceachd**.

Eire, *s. f.* Snow; ice; a burden. (*Ir. id. Box. Lex.* eiry, *snow.*) Is eire mo sgiath, *my shield is a burden.*—*Ardar.* Ta 'd nan eire thruim, *they are a heavy burden.*—*Sm.*

Eireach, *a.* Burdensome, heavy.

Eireachd, *s. f.* Heresy; *also*, a congregation.—*Shaw.* Beauty.

Eireachdail, *a.* Handsome, comely, seemly; specious. Duine eireachdail, *a handsome man;* gu h-eireachdail, *handsomely.*

Eireachdas, ais, *s. m.* (*Ir. id.*) Handsomeness, beauty, seemliness, comeliness; *also*, a congregation.—*Macfar.* Gleann air an robh eireachdas thar gach gleann, *a glen that was beauteous beyond all others.*—*Old Song.*

Eireadh, idh, *s. f.* See **Eire**.

Eireadh, 3 *sing.* and *pl. imper.* of éirich. Éireadh e, *let him rise;* éireadh iad, *let them rise.*

Eireag, eig, *s. f.* A young hen, a pullet.—*Shaw.* *N. pl.* eireagan.

Eireag, eig, *s. f.* A kind of mountain strawberry. See **Oighreag**. *N. pl.* eireagan.

Eireagach, *a.* Abounding in whortleberries or cloudberries.

Eireannach, aich, *s. m.* An Irishman. *N. pl.* Eireannaich.

Eireannach, *a.* Irish. A chainnte Eireannach, *the Irish language.*

Eireirich, *s. f.* Night waking of the dead; drying corn in a pot, as was once common in the Highlands; the grain and bread so prepared.—*Shaw.*

Eiribh, *dat. pl.* of eire.

Eiribh, 2 *pl. imper. a.* of eirich. Rise ye or you.

Éiric, *s. f.* (*Ir. id.*) Amercement, a fine for bloodshed, a ransom; requital, reparation; return; a mulct or fine. Ann eiric m' anam, *as a ransom for my soul.*—*Sm.* Ann eiric graidh, *in return for love.*—*Stew. G. B.*

Among the ancient Caledonians, the *eiric*, or mulct, paid for the murder of any person, depended on his rank. The *eiric* for an ur-

fhlath (earl) was fourteen cows, one hundred for an earl's son, or thane, and sixteen for a plebeian, or villain.—*Scottish Laws of Regiam Majestam.* The words *cro* (see Crodh) and *galnas*, in the said code, are Gaelic; the former meaning cows, the latter an estimate.

Eiriceach, ich, *s. m.* (*Ir.* éiriceach.) A heretic, an unbeliever; *also, adjectively*, heretical, unbelieving. Duine a ta na eiriceach, *a man who is a heretic.*—*Stew. Tit. ref.*

Eiriceachd, *s. f.* Heresy, unbelief.—*Stew. Gal. ref.*

Éirich, *v. n.* (*Lat.* erigo. *Corn. Arm.* erigeo.) Rise, ascend; befall; happen; rebel. *Pret. a.* dh' éirich, *rose; fut. aff. a.* éirichidh, *shall rise.* Cha 'n éirich e ni 's mò, *he shall rise no more.*—*Sm.* Nur dh' éireas maduinn, *when morning shall rise or dawn.*—*Oss. Fing.* Is bochd mar dh' éirich dhuit, *sad is that which has befallen thee.*—*Macint.* Dh' éirich leis, *he succeeded or prospered;* éirich air, *belaboured him* or *it;* dh' éirich mi air le lorg, *I belaboured him with a stick.*

Eirichidh, *fut. aff. a.* of éirich. Shall or will rise.

Eiridh, *s. f.* Snow; ice.—*Macdon. Ir.* eire. *Box. Lex.* eiry, *snow.*

Éiridh, *s. f.* A rising, a mounting; a rise, an ascension; a mutiny, a rebellion. Am éiridh, *time of rising;* bheil thu air éiridh? *have you arisen* [*out of bed*]? éiridh na greine, *sunrise.* Dean éiridh gu farumach, *rise with a bustling noise.*—*Macdon.*

Eiridh, *fut. aff. a.* of éirich, *more properly* of † éir. Shall or will rise. Eiridh m' osna, *my sigh shall rise.*—*Oss. Croma.*

Eiridh, (ag), *pr. part.* of eirich. Rising, mounting; rebelling.

Eiridinn, *v. a.* Nurse, foster, rear, cherish. *Pret. a.* dh' eiridinn, *cherished.*—*Stew.* 1 *K. Fut. aff. a.* eiridnidh, *shall cherish.* Eiridnidh e i, *he will cherish her.*—*Stew. Eph.*

Eiridinn, *s. f.* A nursing, a fostering, a cherishing; a person who is nursed.

Eirig, *s. f.* A ransom.—*Stew. Ps.* Written also *eiric;* which see.

Eirige, *s. f.* A command or government.

Eirigh, *s. f.* Rising, ascending; ascension; a rise; a rebellion. Written also *éiridh;* which see.

Eirinn, *s. f.* (an Irish corruption of *Iar-fhonn*, the Western Land; or *Iar-inn*, contracted for *Iar-innis*, the Western Isle). Ireland. Irish antiquarians hold out, with more ingenuity than truth, that *Eirinn* is a contraction of *Iiaruinn*, the Iron Island; Ireland having once been remarkable for its mines of iron, as well as of tin and copper.

Eirinneach, ich, *s. m.* An Irishman. See Eireannach.

Eirionnach, aich, *s. m.* (*Ir.* aibhrionnach.) A castrated goat. *N. pl.* eirionnaich.

† Eiris, *s. f.* (*Ir. id.*) An era; a friend; mistrust.—*Shaw.*

† Eirle, *s. f.* (*Ir. id.*) A fragment.—*Shaw.*

Eirlioch, *s. m.* (*Ir. id.*) Destruction.—*Shaw.*

Eirr, *s. f.* A shield; an end.—*Shaw.*

Eirr, *gen. sing.* of earr.

Eirthir, *s. f.* A coast; a border; a foreign country.

Eis, *s. f.* (*Ir. id.*) A band, a troop; a footstep or trace. Hence *tareis*, after. Air eis, *back, backwards;* cha 'n 'eil agam da eis sin, *I have nought in consequence.*—*Mac Co.*

Eis, *v. a.* Hinder, prevent, obstruct; trace, search. *Pret. a.* dh' eis, *hindered; fut. aff.* eisidh, *shall hinder.*

Eisceach, ich, *s. m.* Exception, exclusion.

Éisd, *v. n.* (*Ir. id.*) Hark, harken, listen, hear; hist! be silent, attend. *Pret. a.* dh' éisd, *listened; fut. aff. a.* éisdidh, *shall listen.* Eisdibh is mairibh beò, *and hearken and live.*—*Sm.* Eisdeadh e, *let him hear.*—*Stew. Matt.*

Eisdeachd, *s. f.* (*Ir.* eisdeacht.) A hearing, a hearkening; a listening; an audience; an auditory; attention. An ti a bheir éisdeachd, *he who will hear*, or *give an ear.*

Eisdeachd, (ag), *pr. part.* of éisd. Listening, hearkening. Ag éisdeachd ri caoirean na coille, *listening to the murmur of the wood.*—*Ull.*

Eisdeam, (*from* eisd.) Let me hear or listen; *also*, for éisdidh mi, *I shall hear* or *listen.*

Eisdich, *v. n.* Hark, hearken, listen. *Pret. a.* dh' éisdich, *hearkened; fut. aff.* éisdichidh.

Eiseadh, idh, *s. m.* A seeking, a hunting after, a tracing, a research.

Eisean, more frequently written *esan;* which see.

Eiseimpleir, *s. f.* (*Lat.* exemplar.) An example, a pattern or model, ensample. *N. pl.* eiseimpleirean, *examples; d. pl.* eiseimpleiribh. Gun robh sibh na 'r eiseimpleiribh, *that you were examples.*—*Stew.* 1 *Thess.* Written also *eisiomplair.*

Eiseimpleireach, *a.* Exemplary.

Eiseòlach, *a.* Ignorant, rude.—*Shaw.*

Eiseòlas, ais, *s. m.* Ignorance, rudeness.

Éisg, *gen. sing.* of iasg. Of a fish. Gach seorsa éisg, *every kind of fish.*—*Stew. Matt.*

Eisg, *s. f.* A lampoon; a satire; a satirist.

Eisg, *s. m.* A satirist.

Eisgear, eir, *s. m.* A satirist.

Eisgearra, *a.* (*Ir.* eisgeartha.) Bitter; satirical, scurrilous; unsociable. Gu h-easgearra, *bitterly.*

Eisgearrachd, *s. f.* Bitterness of language, scurrility; satire; lampooning.

Eisgeil, *a.* (*from* eisg.) Satirical.

Eisgir, *s.* (*Ir. id.*) A ridge of mountains.

Éisglinn, *s.* A fish-pond. *N. pl.* eisg-linntichean.

Eisinnil, *a.* Weak, infirm.

Eisiomail, *s. f.* (*Ir. id.*) Reverence; dependence; power; courage. Cha 'n 'eil mi a d' eosiomail, *I am not in your reverence.* Gun eisiomail gun umhlachd, *without reverence or obedience.*—*Old Song.* Thoir eisomail, *shew respect;* neor-eisiomail, *independence.*

Eisiomlair. See Eisiomplair.

Eisiomlaireach, *a.* See Eisiomplaireach.

Eisiomplair, *s. f.* An example, a model, or pattern, a copy; a parable. Ni mi eisiomplair dhiot, *I will make an example of you.* See also Eiseimpleir.

Eisiomplaireach, *a.* Exemplary.

Eisir, *s. f.* (*Ir. id.*) An oyster.—*Shaw.*

Eisirean, ain, *s. m.* Escalop, *a shell-fish.*

Eisith, *s. f.* Debate, disagreement.

Eisleach, ich, *s. m.* A crupper.

Eislean, ein, *s. m.* Affliction, sorrow, infirmity. Fò eislean, *in affliction.*—*Ull.* Làn eislein, *full of sorrow.*—*Oss. Gaul.*

Eisleanach, *a.* Sorrowful, heavy, dull, distressful.

† Eislis, *s. f.* (*Ir. id.*) Neglect; mistake; forgetfulness.—*Shaw.*

Eismeach, *a.* (*Ir. id.*) Lying, false; unready.—*Shaw.*

Eismeil. See Eisiomail.

Eisreachd, *s.* (*Ir. id.*) An orphan.

Éist, *v.* See Éisd.

Eite, *s. f.* (*Ir. id.*) A quill, a feather. See Ite.

Eite, *s. f.* (*Ir. id.*) A piece added to a ploughshare when worn.—*Shaw.*

Eiteach, eich, *s.* The roots of burnt heath.

Eiteach, eich, *s. f.* (*Ir. id.*) The root of burnt heather; a denying, a refusing; a denial, a refusal; a consumption or decay; wings, feathers, plumage; fins.

Eiteachadh, aidh, *s. m.* A refusing, a denying; a refusal, a denial. Eiteachadh o ur bordaibh, *a refusing of, or banishing from, your tables.—Old Song.*

Eiteag, eig, *s. f.* (*dim.* of eite.) A feather. See **Iteag**.

Eitean, ein, *s. m.* A kernel; a grain, as of corn. *N. pl.* eiteanan; *d. pl.* eiteanaibh. O na h-eiteanaibh, *from the kernels.—Stew. Num.* Eitean peasrach, *a grain of peas; a pea.*

Eiteanach, *a.* Having kernels.

Eith, *s. f.* Ice; a file. Mar mheall eith, *like a lump of ice.—Ull.*

† **Eitheach**, ich, *s. m.* (*Ir. id.*) An oak.—*Shaw.*

Eitheach, ich, *s. m.* A falsehood; a mistake.—*Shaw.*

Eitheann, inn, *s. f.* Ivy. Spion an eitheann o craoibh, *tear the ivy from its tree.—Old Poem.* Written also *eigheann.*

Eitheannach, *a.* (*from* eitheann.) Covered with ivy; abounding in ivy; of ivy; like ivy.

Eithear, ir, *s. f.* A boat, a bark, a skiff, a barge; a cup. Bhris an t-eithear, *the skiff broke.—Oss. Cathula.* Eithear iasgaich, *a buss.* See also **Eathar**.

Eithich, *a.* False, perjured, perverse. Mionnan eithich, *a false oath; false oaths.* Luchd eithich, *perjured persons.—Stew. Tim.*

Eithich, *v. n.* Perjure, falsify, abjure, deny.—*Shaw. Pret.* dh' eithich; *fut. aff.* eithichidh.

Eithre, *s. f.* Frost; ice; burden; conclusion. Fo eithre aois, *under the burden of age.—Ull.* Written also *eidhre.*

Eithreach, *a.* Icy.

Eithreach, ich, *s. f.* (*Ir. id.*) A wilderness.

Eithreag, eig, *s. f.* Cloudberry; a mountain strawberry. *N. pl.* eithreagan.

Eithreagach, *a.* Abounding in cloudberries; of, or pertaining to, a cloudberry.

Eiti', a poetical contraction for *éitidh;* which see.

Eitich, *v. a.* Refuse, reject, deny, abjure. *Pret. a.* dh' éitich, *refused; fut. aff. a.* eitichidh, *shall refuse.*

Éitidh, *a.* Dismal, frightful, ugly; stormy. Tannas éitidh, *a frightful spectre.—Ull.*

Eitidheachd, *s. f.* Dismalness, frightfulness, ugliness.

Eitleag, eig, *s. f.* (*Ir.* eitleog.) A bat.—*Shaw.*

† **Eitre**, *s. f.* (*Ir. id.*) A trench or furrow.—*Shaw.*

Eitrich, *s. f.* A blustering noise. Eitrich cuain, *the blustering of the sea.—Oss. Cathula.* Perhaps, *séitrich.*

Eitridh, *s. f.* A ditch.

† **Eo**, *s. m.* (*Ir. id.*) A salmon; a peg; a thorn; a pin; a grave; *also*, good, worthy.

† **Eobhrat**, ait, *s. m.* (*Ir. id.*) A head-dress; a cap; a coif.—*Shaw.*

Eochair, *s. f.* A key. Now written *iuchair;* which see.

Eochair, *s. f.* A brim, brink, edge; a tongue; a young plant, a sprout.—*Shaw.*

Eòin, *gen. sing.* and *n. pl.* of eun; which see.

Eòin, *s. m.* John. The name John is, in Scripture, always translated *Eoin;* but, in common language, the Gael say *Iain.*

Eoin-fhiadhachd, *s. f.* Fowling.

Eoin-shealgair, *s. m.* A fowler, a bird-catcher. *N. pl.* eoin-shealgairean.

Eoin-shealgaireachd, *s. f.* Fowling, bird-catching.

Eòl, *s. m.* (*Ir. id.*) Knowledge, discernment, art, science; a charm; a nostrum. Is eòl dhomh, dhuit, dha, dhi, *I, thou, he, she knows;* literally, *knowledge is to me, thee, him, her.* Is eòl dha gach long-phort, *he knows every harbour.—Macdon.*

Eòlach, *a., from* eòl. (*Ir. id.*) Knowing, intelligent, acquainted; expert, skilful; cunning; of, or pertaining to, knowledge. Duine eòlach, *a knowing or intelligent man.—Stew. Pro.* Eòlach air, *acquainted with him or it. Com.* and *sup.* eòlaiche.

Eòlaiche, *com.* and *sup.* of eòlach. More or most cunning.

Eòlais, *gen. sing.* of eòlas.

Eòlas, ais, *s. m., from* eòl. (*Ir. id.*) Knowledge, skill, art, science, acquaintance. Eòlas nach b' fhaòin, *knowledge that was not vain.—Stew. O. T.* Dh' fhalbh e air eòlas, *he has straggled away,*—this is said of a horse when he strays to a distant pasture. Cuir eòlas air, *get acquainted with him, renew acquaintance with him.*

Eolchaire, *s. f.* (*Ir. id.*) Sorrow, grief, mourning, concern.—*Shaw.*

Eolchaireach, *a.* (*Ir. id.*) Sad, sorrowful.

Eollach, aich, *s. f.* More properly *eallach;* which see.

Eònadan, ain, *s. m.* A cage. More frequently written *eunadan.*

Eòrna, *s. m.* (*Ir.* eorna *and* orna.) Barley. An lion is an t-eòrna, *the flax and the barley.—Stew. Ex.* Eòrna fa dhéis, *barley in ear;* treabhadh eòrna, *barley seed-time.*

Eornach, *a.* Abounding in barley; of barley.—*Mac Co.*

Eòrpa, *s. f.* Europe. An roinn Eòrpa, *Europe.*

Eòsag, aig, *s. f.* A nightingale. *N. pl.* eòsagan.

Es', for **Esa**.

Esa, **Esan**, *emphatic form of the sub. pron.* e. He, him, himself. Ghlac esa bogha, *he seized a bow.—Oss. Tem.*

Eubh, *s.* A cry, a shout, a shriek, a call; a proclamation. Is fad an eubh o Loch-Abh, *it is a far cry to Loch-Awe.—Old Saying.*

Eubh, *v. n.* Cry, shout, shriek, call, proclaim, exclaim. *Pret. a.* dh' eubh, *shouted; fut. aff. a.* eubhaidh. Gus an d' eubh an ceannard, *till the chief shouted.—Mac Lach.*

Eucail, *gen.* eucalach, *s. f.* A disease, a distemper. Neart m' eucalach, *the strength of my disease.—Stew. Is. N. pl.* eucailean; *d. pl.* eucailibh. Aon do na h-eucailibh, *one of the diseases.—Stew. Ex.*

Eucaileach, *a.* Diseased, infectious, unhealthy.

Eucaileachd, *s. f.* Infectiousness, the state of being diseased.

Eucalach, *gen. sing.* of eucail.

Eu-ceart, *a.* Unjust, unfair, iniquitous. Fear eu-ceart, *an unjust man.*

Euceart, eirt, *s. f.* (*Ir.* eigceart.) Injustice, unfairness, iniquity.

Euceartas, ais, *s. m.* Injustice, iniquity, oppression. Luchd euceartais, *unjust people.*

Eu-ceillidh, *a.* Foolish, giddy, thoughtless. Gu h-euceillidh, *foolishly.*

Euchd, *s. m.* (*Lat.* actum.) Exploit, or achievement; a mournful event; valour. Mar chuimhne an euchd, *in memory of the achievement.—Old Song.* Torghail na mòr-euchd, *the strife of mighty feats.—Old Poem.*

Euchdach, *a.* Brave, bold, daring. Dùisg a leomhainn euchdaich! *wake, thou bold lion!—Macdon.* Daoine treubhach euchdach, *strong and daring men.—Old Song. Com.* and *sup.* euchdaiche.

Euchdail, *a.* (euchd-amhuil.) Heroic, brave, daring. Eug a ghaisgich euchdail, *the death of the brave hero.—Death of Carril.*

Euchdalachd, *s. f.* Heroism, bravery; the performance of feats; an achievement.

Eu-ciall, céill, *s. f.* Want of judgment.

Eu-ciallach, *a.* Irrational, foolish, senseless. Gu h-eu-ciallach, *irrationally.*

Eu-cinnte, *s. f.* Uncertainty, doubt, doubtfulness.

Eu-cinnteach, *a.* (eu *priv. and* cinnteach.) Uncertain, doubtful, hesitating.

Eu-cinntealas, ais, *s. m.* Uncertainty, doubtfulness.

Eu-cneasta, *a.* (eu *priv. and* cneasta.) Inhuman, cruel; intemperate; rude, unpolite. Gu h-eu-cneasta, *inhumanly.*

Eu-cneastachd, *s. f.* Inhumanity, cruelty; intemperateness; rudeness, unpoliteness.

Eucoir, eucorach, *s. f.* (eu *priv. and* còir. *Ir.* eugcoir.) Injustice, injury, guilt, impropriety. Ris an eucoir, *acting unjustly.*

Eucorach, *a.* Unjust, unfair, injurious. *Com.* and *sup.* eucoraiche, *more* or *most unjust.* Gu h-eucorach, *unjustly.*

Eu-cordadh, aidh, *s. m.* A jarring, a disagreement, a quarrel.

Eu-cosmhal, **Eu-cosmhuil**, *a.* (eu *priv. and* cosmhal. *Ir.* eaccosmhuil.) Unlike, dissimilar, unequal.

Eu-cosmhalach, *a.* Dissimilar, unlike, unequal; improbable, unlikely.

Eu-cosmhalas, ais, *s. m.* Dissimilarity, inequality; improbability, unlikeliness.

Eu-crionna, *a.* (*Ir.* eigcriona.) Imprudent, thoughtless; intemperate. Gu h-eu-crionna, *imprudently.*

Eu-crionnachd, *s. f.* (*Ir.* eigcrionachd.) Imprudence, thoughtlessness; intemperateness.

Eu-cruaidh, *a.* (*Ir.* eag-cruaidh.) Soft, not hard; effeminate, delicate; a delicate person.

Eu-cruas, ais, *s. m.* Softness, effeminateness, delicateness; sickness, infirmity.

Eud, *s. m.* (*Ir. id.*) Jealousy; zeal; a grudge. Fearg is eud, *wrath and jealousy.—Sm.* Le eud do theach-sa, *with zeal for thine house.—Sm.*

Eudach, *a.* (*from* eud.) Jealous; zealous; *substantively,* a jealous or zealous person. Gu h-eudach, *jealously.*

Eudach, aich, *s. m.* Jealousy. Tabhartas eudaich, *an offering of jealousy.—Stew. Num.*

Eudach, aich, *s. m.* (*Ir. id.*) Clothes, dress, garment, robe, covering. Reub e eudach, *he tore his clothes.—Stew. Gen.* Eudach-saic, *sackcloth.—Id.* Eudach uachdair, *upper clothes.—Id.* Eudach taisgidh, *linen kept for the purpose of being made into a shroud.* See also Aodach.

Eudachadh, aidh, *s. m.* (*from* eud.) A jealous watching.

Eudachadh, (ag), *pr. part.* of eudaich. Watch jealously.

Eudachadh, aidh, *s. m.* (*from* eudach.) A clothing, a dressing; clothes, dress, covering.

Eudaich, *gen. sing.* of eudach.

Eudaich, *v. a.* Clothe, cover; array. *Pret. a.* dh' eudaich, *clothed; fut. aff. a.* eudaichidh, *shall* or *will clothe; fut. pass.* eudaichear, *shall be clothed.*

Eudaich, *v. n.* (*from* eud.) Watch jealously. *Pret. a.* dh' eudaich; *fut. aff. a.* eudaichidh. Dh' eudaich e orra, *he watched her jealously.*

Eudaichte, *p. part.* of eudaich. Clothed, clad, covered. Eudaichte le searlaid, *clothed with scarlet.—Stew. Pro.*

Eudainn, *gen. sing.* of eudann; which see.

Eudainnean, *n. pl.* of eudann. Faces.

† **Eudal**, ail, *s. m.* Riches, treasure; store; cattle.

Eudal, cattle, seems to be † *ed-ol,* the offspring of cattle. See † Eid.

Eudanan, ain, *s. m.* A frontispiece, a frontlet.—*Stew. Ex.* and *Deut.*

Eudann, ainn, *s. f.* (*Ir.* eadan. *Manx.* adyn.) A face, a brow, a forehead, a front. Chithear an eudann, *their face shall be seen.—Oss. Cathula.* Eudann nan sliabh, *the brow of the hills.—Oss. Tem.* An eudann comhraig, *in the front of battle.—Oss. Lodin.* As an eudann, *to the face.—Stew. Job.* *Outright, evidently.* Clàr an eudainn, *the forehead.—Stew. Lev.*

Eudmhoire, *com.* and *sup.* of eudmhor. More or most jealous.

Eudmhoireachd, *s. f.* Jealousy; zealousness.

Eudmhor, *a.* (*Ir.* eadmhar.) Jealous; zealous. Dia eudmhor, *a jealous God.—Stew. Deut.* *Com.* and *sup.* eudmhoire.

Eu-dòchas, ais, *s. m.* (eu, *priv. and* dòchas.) Despair, despondency, melancholy. Ann an eu-dòchas, *in despair.*

Eu-dòchasach, *a.* (eu, *priv. and* dòchasach.) Despondent, melancholy, in despair, desperate, hopeless; *also,* a person in despair. *Com.* and *sup.* eu-dochasaiche. Cainnt an eu-dochasaich, *the speech of a desperate man.—Stew. Job.*

Eu-dòchasachd, *s. f.* Despondency, melancholy, hopelessness, desperateness.

Eug, éig, *s. m.* (*Ir.* eag.) Death; a ghost, a spectre. Suain an éig, *the sleep of death.—Oss. Derm.* A dol eug, *dying.—Ull.*

Eug, *v. n.* (*Ir.* eag.) Die, expire, perish. *Pret. a.* dh' eug, *died; fut. aff. a.* eugaidh, *shall die.* An doigh san d' eug i, *the way in which she died.—Ull.* Eugaidh strigh a chaoidh, *strife shall die away for ever.—Mac Lach.*

Eugach, *a.* Deadly, destructive; like death; ghastly. Beum athach eugach, *a terrible deadly blow.—Old Poem.*

Eugaidh, *a.* (*from* eug.) Ghastly, spectral, like death.

Eugaidh, *fut. aff. a.* of eug. Shall or will die, or perish. Eugaidh an lagh, *the law shall perish.—Stew. Ezek.*

Eugail, *a.* (eug-amhuil.) Deathly, ghastly.

Eugail, *s. f.* A distemper. More properly written *eucail;* which see.

Eugais, *gen. sing.* of eugas.

Eugalachd, *s. f.* Ghastliness.

Eugas, ais, *s. m.* (*Gr.* εικος. *Ir.* eaccosc.) Likeness, resemblance; appearance, form; countenance. D' eugas maiseach, *thy comely countenance.—Stew. Song Sol.*

Eugasach, *a.* Seemly, comely, decent; specious. *Com.* and *sup.* eugasaiche.

Eugasg, aisg, *s. m.* (*Ir.* eaccosg.) Likeness, resemblance; appearance, form; countenance. Sunnailt t' eugaisg, *the likeness of thy form.—Old Song.*

Eug-bhoil, *s. f.* Deadly wrath. Bi treun na t-eug-bhoil, *be strong in thy deadly wrath.—Oss. Fin. and Lorm.*

Eugh, *s. m.* A shout, a cry, a clamour, a noise, a shriek. Eas nan eugha mall, *a softly-sounding waterfall.—Old Poem.* Written also *eigh* and *eubh;* which see.

Eughach, *a.* (*from* eugh.) Noisy, clamorous, shrieking.

Eughach, aich, *s. f.* A crying; a shouting, a loud voice. Written also *eigheach;* which see.

Eug-lios, *s.* A burying-ground, a churchyard, a cemetery. *N. pl.* eugliosan.

Eugmhais, *s. f.* (*Ir.* eagmhais.) Privation; *rarely,* fame. *Eugmhais* is not often used by itself; but it forms, together with the particle *as,* a preposition; as, As eugmhais iomraidh, *without reputation.—Oss. Duthona.* Fu' champar as d' eugmhais, *grieved for the loss of thee.—Macfar.*

Eugmhaiseach, *a.* (*Ir.* eagmaiseach.) Remarkable, illustrious, great.

Eugnachadh, aidh, *s. m.* A making pale or ghastly; a becoming pale or ghastly.

Eugnachadh, (ag), *pr. part.* of eugnaich.

Eugnaich, *v. a.* and *n.* (*from* eug.) Make pale or ghastly; becoming pale or ghastly. *Pret. a.* dh' eugnaich; *fut. aff. a.* eugnaichear.

Eugnaidh, Eagnuidh, *a.* Wise, prudent. Comhairle an eugnuidh, *the counsel of the wise.—Stew. Pro.*

Eug-samhlachadh, aidh, *s. m.* (*Ir.* eag-samhlughadh.) A varying, a changing; a chequering.

Eug-samhlachd, *s. f.* (*Ir.* eag-samhladh.) Variety, diversity, change, changeableness of appearance.

Eug-samhlaich, *v. a.* Vary, spot, chequer. *Pret. a.* dh' eug-samhlaich, *chequered; fut. aff. a.* eug-samhlaichidh.

Eug-samhluidh, Eag-samhuil, *a.* (*Ir.* eag-samhail.) Various, different, diverse; chequered, spotted; matchless, strange; mournful, funereal. Dathan eug-samhluidh, *various colours.—Stew. Ezek.* Ceòl eug-samhuil, *a funereal air.—Ull.*

Euladh, aidh, *s. m.* A sneaking, a deserting, a creeping progress, stepping softly.

Eulag, aig, *s. f.* An escape.

Eun, eòin, *s. m.* A bird, a fowl. *N. pl.* eòin; *d. pl.* eunaibh. Aon do na h-eunaibh, *one of the birds.—Stew. Lev.* Eun ruadh, *grouse;* eun circe, *a pullet;* eun uasal, *a foreign bird;* eun-fiadhaich, *a wild bird;* eun an t-sneachdaidh, *the snow-bunting*, or the *emberiza nivalis* of Linnæus; an t-eun fionn, *the hen-harrier*, or the *falco cyaneus* of Linnæus.

Gr. οἰων-ος and οἰν-ιον. *Corn.* edhen. *Box. Lex.* edn. *Ir.* eun. *Arm.* ezn. In Vannes, they say *een* and *ein*.

Eunach, -aich, *s. m.* (*from* eun.) A hunting; a fowling. Cù eunaich, *a pointer.*

Eunachadh, aidh, *s. m.* The act of hunting or of fowling.

Eunadair, *s. m.*, *from* eun. (*Arm.* eznataer.) A fowler; a gamekeeper; a birdcatcher. *N. pl.* eunadairean, *gamekeepers.* A laimh an eunadair, *from the hands of the fowler.—Stew. Pro.* Eunadair mallaichte, *the devil.—Shaw.*

Eunadaireachd, *s. f.* (*from* eun.) Fowling, bird-catching; the occupation of a fowler.

Eunadan, ain, *s. m.* (*Ir.* eonadan.) A bird-cage; an aviary. Eunadan do gach eun, *a cage for every bird.—Stew. Rev. ref.*

Eunag, aig, *s. f.* (*dim.* of eun.) A young bird.—*Turn.*

Eunan, *gen.* eoinein, (*dim.* of eun.) A little bird. Biadh an eòinein, *wood-sorrel.* *N. pl.* eoineinean, *little birds.* Na h-eòineinean bòidheach, *the pretty little birds.—Macfar.*

Eun-bhiadh, *s. m.* Bird's-seed, bird's-meat.

Eun-bhrigh, *s. f.* Chicken broth; gravy, soup.

Eun-chridhe, *s. m.* A faint heart, a chicken heart.

Eun-chridheach, *a.* Faint-hearted, chicken-hearted.

Eun-druidh, *s. m.* An augur. *N. pl.* eun-druidhean.

Eun-druidheachd, *s. f.* Augury or divination by the flight of birds.

Eunlaireachd, *s. f.* Fowling.

Eunlaith, *s. m. pl.* Birds, fowls. Sgaoth eunlaith, *a flight of birds.—Oss. Gaul.* Eunlaith a réir an gne, *fowls after their kind.—Stew. Gen.*

Eunlion, lìn, *s. f.* A bird's net. *N. pl.* eun-liontan.

Eur, *v. n.* and *a.* Refuse, deny. *Pret. a.* dh'eur, *refused; fut. aff. a.* euraidh. Cha d'eur an righ dha, *the king refused him not.—Orr.*

Euradh, aidh, *s. m.* A refusal, a denial; a refusing, a denying. Nior ghabh i euradh, *she took no refusal.—Oss.* Innis gun euradh, *tell without denial, tell frankly.—Old Poem.*

Eurmaireachd, *s. f.* (*Ir. id.*) Gallopping, riding.—*Shaw.*

Euslainnte, *s. f.* (eu, *priv. and* slainnte. *Ir.* easlainnte.) Sickness; ill health; infirmity. Luchd euslainnte, *infirm people.*

Euslainnteach, *a.* Unhealthy, unwholesome; sickly, infirm. Gu h-euslainnteach, *unhealthily.*

Euslainnteachd, *s. f.* Sickliness, infirmity, unwholesomeness.

Euslainnteil, *a.* (eu, *priv. and* slainnteil.) Unhealthy, infirm.

Euslan, *a.* (eu, *priv. and* slàn. *Ir.* easlan.) Infirm; sick; not well. Bha mi euslan, *I was sick.—Stew. Matt.*

Eusontach, *a.* Guilty; transgressing. Gu h-eusontach, *guiltily.* *Com.* and *sup.* eusontaiche.

Eusontas, ais, *s. m.* Trespass; transgression; guilt. Nach maith thu m' eusontas? *wilt thou not pardon my transgression?—Stew. Job.* Luchd eusontais, *transgressors.—Stew. Pro.*

Eutrocair, *s. f.* (eu, *priv. and* trocair.) Cruelty; mercilessness.

Eutrocaireach, *a.* (eu, *priv. and* trocaireach.) Merciless, cruel, unfeeling. Gu h-eutrocaireach, *cruelly.*

Eutrocaireachd, *s. f.* Unmercifulness, unfeelingness; the practice of cruelty.

Eutrom, *a.* (eu, *priv. and* trom.) Light, not heavy; giddy; airy, gay; of no account; light or trifling. Is eutrom so, *this is a [trifling] light thing.—Stew. 2 K.* Ceann eutrom, *a giddy head;* gorm eutrom, *light blue.* *Com.* and *sup.* eutruime.

Eutromachadh, aidh, *s. m.* A making less heavy, a lightening, an alleviating, an alleviation.

Eutromachadh, (ag), *pr. part.* of eutromaich. Making light or less heavy.

Eutromaich, *v. a.* Make light or less heavy; lighten, alleviate. *Pret. a.* dh'eutromaich, *lightened; fut. aff. a.* eutromaichidh, *shall lighten.* Eutromaich dhuinn i, *make it lighter for us.—Stew. 1 K.*

Eutromaichear, *fut. pass.* of eutromaich. Shall or will be made light.

Eutromaichidh, *fut. aff. a.* of eutromaich. Shall make light.

Eutromaichte, *p. part.* of eutromaich. Lightened; alleviated.

Eutroman, ain, *s. m.* (*from* eutrom.) A bladder. *N. pl.* eutromain, *bladders.*

F.

F, (fearn, *the alder.*) The sixth letter of the Gaelic alphabet. It has the same power and sound as in other languages. *F* aspirated, *i. e.* when immediately followed by the letter *h*, is silent; as, an Fhraing, *France*.

F', *for* fa or fo.

Fa, *prep.* (*for* fo' or fuidh.) Under, below, beneath. Fa 'r cosaibh, *under our feet.*—*Stew. Ps.*

Fa, *prep.* On, upon, above. Fa làr, *on the ground; omitted, neglected.*—*Carswell.* Fa 'n aobhar ud, *on that account.*—*Sm.* Ciod fa 'n abradh iad? *wherefore should they say?* Fa seach, *apart, separately;* fa dheireadh, *at last;* fa cheud, *a hundred times;* fa leth, *severally, individually;* fa chùis, *by reason, because;* fa chùl, *backwards;* fa dhruim, *backwards;* fa chomhar, *opposite;* fa thuaiream, *towards, about;* fa ri chéile, *together.*

Fà, *s. m.* Cause, reason; object, opportunity. Is e sud fà mo dheòir, *that is the cause of my tears.*—*Old Song.* See also Fàth.

† Fabhal, ail, *s. m.* (*Lat.* fabula. *Ir.* fabhal.) A fable or fiction; a romance, a journey.

Fabhaltas, ais, *s. m.* (*Ir. id.*) Gain, profit, benefit, advantage, income.

Fabhar, air, *s. m.* See Fabhor.

Fabhd, *s. m.* (*Corn. Arm.* paut *and* faut. *Scotch*, faut. *Fr.* faute.) A fault; blame. Dìth fabhd, *want of blame* or *fault. Arm.* difaut, *blameless.*

Fàbhor, oir, *s. f.* (*Lat.* favor. *Ir.* fabhar.) Favour, interest, friendship; countenance.

Fàbhorach, *a.* Favourable; favouring; disposed to befriend. *Com.* and *sup.* fabhoraiche, *more* or *most favourable.* Gu fabhorach, *favourably.*

Fabhòrachd, *s. f.* Favourableness; a disposition to befriend.

† Fabhra, *s. m.* February.

Fabhra, ai, *s. m.* (*Ir. id.*) An eyelid; a fringe; a flounce; a veil. *N. pl.* fabhrainnean, *eyelids.*—*Stew. Pro.*

Fabhrach, *a.* (*from* fabhra.) Having eyelids; having large eyelids; of, or belonging to, the eyelid; ciliary.

Fabhradh, aidh, *s. m.* An eyelid, a border, a flounce, a veil. *N. pl.* fabhraidh *and* fabhraidhean. Dean fabhradh, *make a flounce* or *fringe.*—*Stew. Num.* Do d' fhabhraidhibh, *to thine eyelids.*—*Stew. Pro. ref.*

Fabhranta, *a.* Having large eyelashes or eyelids.

Facal, ail, *s. m.* A word. More frequently written *focal;* which see.

Fach, faich, *s. m.* The hole of a lobster.—*Shaw.*

Fachach, aich, *s. m.* A water-fowl, called *puffin*, and by the Scotch *tom noddy;* the *alca aretica* of Linnæus.

† Fachail, *s. f.* (*Ir. id.*) Strife, contention, dispute, struggle.

† Fachaill, *a.* (*Ir. id.*) Full of woods.—*Shaw.*

Fa-chainnte, *s. f.* Ridicule, scoff, derision, sneering language.

Fa-chainnteach, *a.* Derisive, scoffing, apt to sneer.

† Fachd, *s. m.* (*Ir.* facht. *Sax.* and *Scotch*, feicht. *Eng.* fight.) A fight.

Fachoill, *s. f.* A thickwood; also, *adjectively*, full of woods.—*Shaw.*

Fa-chomhair, Fa-chomhar, *prep.* Opposite, before, in front; *also*, opposite, or before him or it.

Fa-chùl, *adv.* and *prep.* Backwards; behind.—*Shaw.* Fa'n cùl, *behind them;* fa m' chùl, *behind me;* fa cùl, *behind her.*

Fa-comhair, *comp. pron.* Opposite her, in front of her.

Faclach, *a.* See Foclach.

Fad, *a.* (*Ir. id.*) Long; distant; far; tall. Cian fad san aon aite, *a long while in the same place.*—*Oss. Derm.* O thìr fad, *from a distant land.*—*Oss. Fing.* Am fad 's am fagus, *far and near.*—*Stew. Jer.* Fad as, *far off;* fad o laimh, *far off;* fad air falbh, *far away; long absent;* o cheann fad, *long since;* am fad, *whilst;* gu ma fad beò an righ, *long live the king.*—*Stew. Sam.*

Fad, faid, *s. m.* (*Ir. id.*) Length; distance; talness. Na fhad 's na leud, *in its length and breadth.*—*Stew. Gen.* Fad an t-saoghail, *over the whole world.*—*Macfar.* A dol am fad, *growing longer* or *taller.*—*Macdon.* Air fad, *in length; altogether.* Cha tig mi gu ceann fad, *I shall not come for a long while.*

Fad, (air), *prep.* and *adv.* Throughout, during; altogether; wholly; longitudinally. Air fad an t-saoghail, *throughout the world;* fior air fad, *just altogether.*—*Sm.*

Fad, (am), *adv.* Whilst; during; afar.

Fadachadh, aidh, *s. m.* (*Ir.* fadaghadh.) A lengthening, a prolonging, a stretching.

Fadachadh, (a), *pr. part.* of fadaich; which see.

Fàdadh, aidh, *s. m.* The act of kindling or lighting; inflaming; a blowing into a flame. Fadadh cluaise, *the priming of a gun, a match.* Fadadh cruaidh, *part of a rainbow seen in blustering weather, by sailors called a dog.* Fadadh spuing, *touchwood, tinder.*

Fàdadh, (a), *pr. part.* of fadaidh. Kindling, lighting, inflaming. A fadadh an teine, *kindling the fire.*—*Oss. Fin. and Lor.* A fadadh bhur anamhiann, *inflaming your lusts.*—*Stew. G. B.*

Fàdaich, *v.* Kindle. See Fadaidh.

Fadaich, *v. a.* (*from* fad.) Lengthen, stretch out, prolong; *also*, grow long. *Pret. a.* dh' fhadaich, *lengthened; fut. aff. a.* fad aichidh, *shall lengthen; p. part.* fadaichte, *lengthened.*

Fadaichear, *fut. pass.* of fadaich. Shall be lengthened.

Fadaichidh, *fut. aff. a.* of fadaich. Shall or will lengthen.

Fadaichte, *p. part.* of fadaich. Lengthened.

Fàdaidh, *v. a.* Kindle, light, inflame; blow into a flame. *Pret. a.* dh' fhadaidh, *kindled; fut. aff. a.* fàdaidh.

Fadail, *s.* See Fadal.

Fadal, ail, *s. m.* (*Ir.* fadail.) Delay; prolixity; longing. A gabhail fadail, *longing;* a gabhail an fhadail, *longing.*

Fadalach, *a.* (*Ir. id.*) Late; slow, tedious, lingering, wearisome. Tha thu fadalach, *you are late;* oidhchean fadalach, *wearisome nights.*—*Stew. Job.* *Com.* and *sup.* fadalaiche.

Fad-cheannach, *a.* Long-headed, sagacious.

Fad-cheum, -cheim, *s. m.* A long pace or step; a stride. A teachd le fad cheumaibh, *coming with long strides.*—*Mac Lach.*

Fad-cheumach, *a.* Taking long steps, striding, bounding.

Fad-chluasach, *a.* (*Ir. id.*) Long-eared.

Fa d'chomhair, *comp. prep.* Opposite thee, in front of thee.

Fad-fhulang, aing, *s.* (*Ir. id.*) Forbearance, long-suffering, longanimity.

Fad-fhulangach, *a.* (*Ir. id.*) Long-suffering, patient.—*Stew. Gen.* *Com.* and *sup.* fad-fhulanguiche. Gu fadfhùlangach, *patiently.*

FAD-FHULANGAS, ais, *s. m* Forbearance, long-suffering, patience, longanimity.

† FADH, *s. m.* A mole.—*Shaw.* See FAMH.

FADHAIRT, *s. f.* The temper of a bladed instrument See also FAOBHAIRT.

FADHAIRTEACH, *a.* Tempered, as the metal of a bladed instrument.

FADHARSACH, *a* Trifling, paltry, mean; of no value. *Com.* and *sup.* fadharsaiche. Gu fadharsach, *in a trifling manner.*

FADHARSACHD, *s f.* Paltriness, meanness.

FA-DHEIREADH, *adv.* At last, at length; at the end.

FA-DHEOIDH, *adv.* At last, at length; at the end. Fadheoidh air sgeul, *found at last.—Stew N. T.*

FAD-GHEUGACH, *a.* Having long branches, branches. Iughar fad-gheugach dlù dha, *a branchy yew near him —Oss. Derm.*

FAD-LAMHACH, *a* Long-handed, prone to pilfer, dishonest. Gu fad-lamhach, *thievishly.*

FAD-SHAOGHALACH, *a.* Long-lived Gu ma fad shaoghalach a robh thu! *long may you live!*

FÀG, *v. a.* (*Ir. id.*) Leave, quit, abandon, forsake; render. *Pret. a.* dh' fhàg, *left. fut. aff. a* fàgaidh, *shall leave* Fàg mise am aonar, *leave me in solitude.—Orr.* Na fàg sinn, *do not forsake us —Stew. G. B* Dh' fhàgadh tu 'm buamsdair treubhach, *thou wouldst render the silly boaster brave.—Old Song.*

FAGAID, *s. f.* A faggot.

FÀGAIDH, *fut. aff a.* of fag. Shall or will leave

FÀGAIL, *s. f.* A leaving, a quitting, forsaking; abandonment.

FÀGAIL, (a), *pr. part.* of fàg Leaving, quitting, abandoning, forsaking.

FÀGAM, 1 *sing. imper.* of fàg. Let me leave; *also for* fàgaidh mi, *I will leave.*

FÀGAR, *fut. pass.* of fàg; which see.

† FAGHA, *s. m.* (*Ir. id.*) A spear; an attempt; an offer.

FAGHAIL, *s. f.* An obtaining, a receiving or getting; winning; gain; power.

FAGHAIL, (a), *pr part.* of faigh (*Ir. id.*) Getting, obtaining, receiving, winning. A faghail cuideachd, *getting help.—Sm.* Faghail a bhàis, *dying*

FAGHALTACH, *a.* (*Ir. id.*) Profitable, gainful, lucrative Gu faghaltach, *profitably.*

FAGHALTAS, ais, *s. m.* (*Ir. id*) Profit, gain, advantage.

FAGHARSACH, *a* Trifling, paltry, mean; of no value; noughty.

FAGHARSACHD, *s f.* Paltriness, meanness, noughtiness.

FÀGMAID, 1 *pl. imper.* of fàg Let us leave.

FAGUS, *a.* (*Ir.* fogus *Corn* agos.) Near. Fagus orm, *near me*; fagus domh, *near me*, am fad 's am fagus, *far and near.—Stew. Jer.* Fagus air bhi deas, *almost ready*, fagus do bhith deas, *almost ready.* In some parts of the Highlands, *fagus* is written *fagusg.*

FAIBHILE, *s. f.* Beech.

FAIC, *s. f.* A sparkle

FAIC, *v. irr.* See, behold, look, observe. *Pret. a* chunnaic, *saw; fut. aff. a.* chi, *shall see*, faiceam, 1 *sing. imper.* let me see. Faiceam a lamh-gheal, *let me see her fair hand —Oss. Comala.* Faic mo dheòir, *behold my tears*, faiceam t-iughar, *let me see* [*shew me*] *thy bow —Oss. Duthona.*

FAIC! See! behold! lo!

† FAICE, *s. f* A stitch.—*Shaw.* A tatter

FAICEALL, ill, *s. m.* Attention, chariness; circumspection; observance; caution; evidence. Trid faicill mhaith, *by means of great attention.—Sm.* Air fhaicill, *on his guard.—Stew. Pro.*

FAICEALLACH, *a.* Circumspect, observant, cautious, attentive, evident. Tha 'n aois faiceallach, *age is circumspect.—Mac Lach* Com and *sup* faiceallaiche.

FAICEALLACHD, *s f.* Circumspection, observance, cautiousness, evidence.

FAICEAM, 1 *sing. imper. a.* of faic, which see.

FAICEAN, *s. m* A swaddling-band

FAICEANAICH, *v. a.* Swaddle *Pret. a* dh'fhaiceanaich, *swaddled.*

FAICEANAICHTE, *p. part.* of faiceanaich Swaddled

FAICEAR, *fut neg* and *imper. pass* of faic. Shall be seen Faicear d'obair, *let thy work be seen —Stew Ps* Cha 'n fhaicear an ceum ni 's mò, *their approach shall be seen no more.—Oss Taura.*

FAICEIL, *a* Momentary, in a trice.

FÀICH, fàiche, *s f* A field, a plain; a meadow, a green, a forest. Feur maoth na fàiche, *the tender grass of the field —Stew. Dan.* Fàich na luachrach, *the rushy plain.—Oss. Gaul.* Saoidh na fàiche, *meadow hay.—Macfar.* Fàich-bhùl, *a bowling-green —Shaw*

FAICHEACHD, *s f* (*from* faich) Traversing the fields, field sports; stately gait

† FAICHEALL, ill, *s m.* (*Ir. id*) Salary, wages; reward.—*Shaw.*

FAICHEALLACH, ich, *s. m* (*Ir. id.*) A lamp, a candle, *also,* luminous

FAICHUACH, *s. f.* A violet; any sweet-smelling poculated flower

FAICIBH, 2 *pl. imper.* of faic. See ye or you

FAICILL, *s f* Watchfulness, caution; guard, watch.

FAICILL, *a* Watchful, observant, circumspect; wary Bithibh faicill, *take heed —Stew. Mal*

FAICILLEACH, *a.* Watchful, observant, circumspect. Bithibh faicilleach, *be ye circumspect —Stew Ex* Gu faicilleach, *circumspectly, warily.—Stew Eph*

FAICILLEACHD, *s. f.* Watchfulness, observance, circumspectness.

FAICINN, *s. f* A seeing, observing, beholding; a sight, observation, view.

FAICINN, (a), *pr. part* of faic. Seeing, observing, beholding.

FAICINNEACH, *a* Visible, watchful, observant, circumspect

FAICSE, (*for* faic thusa) See thou, behold, observe. Faicse righ Mhòrbheinn, *observe the king of Morven —Oss. Fing.*

FAICSINN, *s f.* (*Ir. id*) A seeing or observing, a beholding; an observation, a sight, a view; visibility.

FAICSINN, (a), *pr part* of faic; which see

FAICSINNEACH, *a.* (*Ir.* faicsionnach) Visible, conspicuous; watchful, observant. Faicsinneach agus neo-fhaicsinneach *visible and invisible —Stew Col.*

FAICSINNEACHD, *s. f.* The state of being visible; conspicuousness, visibleness

† FÀID, *s. m* (*Lat* vates) A prophet Now written *fàidh*

FAIDE, *com.* and *sup.* of fad. Longer, longest. *Asp form,* fhaide. Is e 's fhaide a mhaireas, *he will last the longest —Macint*

FAIDE, *s. f.* Length, talness of person

FAIDEAD, eis, *s m.* Longitude.

FAIDEAG, eig, *s f.* Lot, chance.

FÀIDH, *s m.* (*Shans.* vadi, *a prophet Ir id. Lat* vates *Gr* φαω, *speak*) A prophet; a soothsayer. Tha 'm fàidh aindiadhaidh, *the prophet is profane.—Stew Jer* *N pl* fàidhean

FÀIDHEACAHD, *s. f.* (*from* fàidh) A prophecy, divination

FÀIDHEADAIR, *s. m.* A prophet. *N. pl.* faidheadairean

FÀIDHEADAIREACHD, *s f.* Prophecy; prophesying, divination Deanamaid fàidheadaireachd, *let us prophecy*—*Stew. Rom.*

Fàidheil, *a* (faidh-amhuil) Like a prophet; prophetic; apt to criticise; happy in expression; witty.

Faidhir, faidhreach, *s f.* (*Ir id Fr* foire.) A market, a fair, a fairing La na faidhreach, *the market* or *fair day*, faidhir na feòla, *the flesh-market*, faidhir an éisg, *the fish-market*, faidhir nan luideag, *the rag-market* *N. pl.* faidhrichean, *fairs.*

Faidhrean, ein, *s m* A fairing, a present purchased at a fair.

Faidhrichean, *n pl* of faidhir, which see

Fàidse, *s. f* A lump, a budge.

Fàidseach, *a* Lumpish; clumsy—*Shaw.*

Fàidseachd, *s f* Lumpishness

† **Fàig**, *s.* A prophet Now written *fàidh.*

† **Faigean**, ein, *s m* (*Ir id Lat* vagina.) A sheath, a scabbard

Faigh, *s* Begging by license, a thickster

Faigh, *v irr* Find, get, receive, obtain, acquire, reach *Pret a* fhuair, *got*, *fut aff. a* gheibh, *shall get.* Faigheam do lorg, *let me get the staff*—*Oss Gaul* Faigh mach, *find out or discover*, fhuair iad mach thu, *they found you out.*—*Mac Lach* *Pret aff pass* fhuaras, *was found*, fhuaras i 'n aite a fir, *she was found in the palace of her husband.*—*Ull.* *Imper pass* faightear

Faighidinn, *s f* See Foighidinn

Faighidinneach, *a* See Foighidinneach.

Faighir, *gen* faighreach, *s. f.* (*Ir id Fr* foire.) A fair, a market; a fairing, or a present bought at a fair. La na faighreach, *the market-day* *N pl* faighrichean *and* foighrichean.

† **Faighleadh**, idh, *s m* Ivy, conversation—*Shaw*

Faighrean, ein, *s m.* A fairing

Faighrichean, *n pl* of faighir Fairs, markets

Faighteadh, *pret. sub pass* of faigh Would be found

Faightear, *imper pass* of faigh Let be found *Faightear* has also the meaning of the future, as, tha e far am faightear e, *it is where it shall be found*

Faigse, *com* and *sup* of fagus Nearer, rearest

Fàil, *gen sing* of fàl, which see

† **Fàil**, fàile, *s. f.* (*Ir id*) A ring, a wreath, an ouch, a jewel, a smell, *rarely*, company, society *N pl* fàilean Ni thu fàilean, *thou shalt make ouches*—*Stew Ex* Mar fhàil òir, *like a jewel of gold.*—*Stew Pro* Fail cubhraidh, *a sweet smell.*—*Stew. O T.* Fàil-chuach, *a violet*, fàil-mhuc, *a hog-sty*, fail-chon, *a dog-kennel*

† **Fail**, *s f* The hiccup; a sty

† **Fail**, *a* Fatal. Lia fàil, *the fatal stone* See Lia-fail.

Fàil, *v a* and *n* Make bare or bald, putrify *Pret a* dh-fhail, *bared*, *fut aff a* fàilidh, *shall make bare*

Failbhe, *s f* Firmament, *also*, emptiness A snamh san fhailbhe mhòir, *swimming in the great firmament*—*Macfar* Do'n fhailbhe lom lan, *quite full of emptiness*—*Old Song.*

† **Failbhe**, *a* Lively, sprightly—*Shaw*

Failbheadh, idh, *s m* Vegetation

Failbheag, eig, *s. f* A ring of any metal. *N pl* failbheagan, *rings* Ceithir failbheagan oir, *four gold rings*—*Stew. Ex.*

Failbheagach, *a* Full of rings; like a ring.

Failbheas, eis, *s m* Liveliness, sprightliness—*Shaw*

Failbhilig, *gen. sing* of failbheag; which see

† **Failbhich**, *v a* Quicken, enliven *Pret a* dh'fhailbhich, *quickened*, *fut aff. a* failbhichidh

Failc, failce, *s. f.* A gap, an opening; a hairlip; a bath. Failc teth, *a hot-bath*—*Macd.* *N. pl* failcean.

Failc, *v* Bathe. *Pret. a.* dh'fhailc, *bathed; fut. aff. a.* failcidh, *shall bathe.*

Failceach, *a.* Like a bath; having a bath

Failceadh, idh, *s. m.* A bathing.

Failcean, ein, *s m.* The rotula, or whirlbone of the knee; a lid

Fàilchon, *s f.* A dog-kennel.

Failcis, *s. f.* A pit.—*Shaw*

Faileachan, ain, *s m* An ear-ring—*Shaw.* *N. pl.* faileachain.

Fàileadh, idh, *s. m* A putrifying, putrefaction This is said of a creature that lies dead till the hair falls off

Faileag, eig, *s. f* A hiccup; a hump or hillock.—*Shaw.* *Faileag*, in the sense of *hiccup*, is more commonly written and pronounced *aileag.*

Fàilleanta, *a* Sharp-scented. Fàileanta, biorach, *sharp-scented, quick-sighted*—*Old Song.*

Faileas, eis, *s. m.* A shadow; a reflected image; a shade, a spectre or ghost *N. pl.* faileasan. Mar fhaileas teichidh tu, *like a shadow shalt thou fly*—*Sm* Fhaileis eutroim, *thou empty shade*—*Oss. Fing* Faileas an ré, *the reflected image of the moon.*—*Oss Fin. and Lorm* Written also *faileus.*

Faileasach, *a* Shadowy; causing a shadow; polished; spectral Iuthar faileasach, *polished yew*—*Oss. Fing.* Written also *faileusach*

Faileasachd, *s f.* Shadowiness; the state of being polished

Faileus, eis, *s. m.* A shadow. More commonly written *faileas*, which see

Faileusach, *a.* See Faileasach

Failgeach, *a.* (*Ir. id*) Poor, necessitous—*Shaw.*

Fàilig, *v n.* Fail, *provincial for* fàilinn.

Failingeach, *a* Weak, fatigued, faint.—*Stew. Gen. ref.* Subject to decay; fallible

Failingeachd, *s f.* Weakness, faintness; fallibility, a falling off

Fàilingeadh, idh, *s m* A failing, a fainting Gun fhaingeadh, *without fail*—*Stew. Ezra*

Fàilinn, *s f* A failing, a falling off, lack; blemish or flaw, default Thig ort fàilinn tuigse, *a failing of judgment shall come on thee.*—*Mac Co.* Gun fhailinn truacantachd, *without lack of compassion*—*Macfar.* Cha d'aithnich mi fàilinn ort, *I never knew a blemish in thee.*—*Old Song.* Gun fhàilinn, *without failing, without fail*

Fàilinn, *a* Failing, decaying, giving way, default

Fàilinneach, *a* Failing, decaying, languid, falling off—*Macdon* Subject to decay, fallible, *substantively*, defaulter

Fàilinneachd, *s f* Fallibility, faintness, a falling off, a failing, a tendency to decay.

Fàillinniche, *s m* A defaulter.

Faill, *s f* (*Ir. id*) Opportunity, advantage, leisure; a kernel

Faill, *s f.* (*Ir. id*) A precipice More properly, *aill.*

Fàill, *s. f* A branch, a twig, a sprout, a kernel. *N. pl.* failllean; *d. pl.* faillibh

† **Fàille**, *s f.* (*Ir. id*) Danger; decay

Failleach, *a.* Branchy, abounding in twigs; sprouty; like a branch, sprout, or twig.

Failleadh, eidh, *s. m.* Neglect, omission, failure.

Fàillean, ein, *s m* (*dim* of faill) A young branch, a little branch; a twig; a sucker; the root of the ear. A faillean òg, *its tender branch.—Stew Job.* Faillean na cluaise, *the lug.—Macd.*

Failleanach, *a* Branchy; full of twigs; like a branch, like a twig, sprouting Glacag fhailleanach, *a dell abounding in twigs —Macfar.*

Failleanachd, *s. f.* Branchiness; the state of sprouting, a tendency to sprout.

Fàillich, *v. n* Fail, neglect, delay *Pret. a* dh'fhaillich, *fut. aff.* faillichidh

† **Faillidheach**, *a.* Drowsy.—*Shaw.*

Failm, *s f.* The tiller of a ship.

Failmhuc, *s. f.* A hog-sty.

Fàillne, *s. f.* See **Failinn**.

Faillseach, *a.* Sudorific

Faillsich, *v.* Sweat, perspire. *Pret* dh'fhaillsich, *sweated*

Failneachadh, aidh, *s. m* A failing, a falling off, a decaying; a growing weary; decay, languor.

Failneachadh, (a), *pr. part.* of failnich. (*Ir.* faillich) Failing, falling off, decaying, giving way.

Failnich, *v n* Fail, give way, fall off; decay; grow fatigued *Pret. a.* dh'fhailnich, *fut. aff. a* fàilnichidh, *shall fail.* Fàilnichidh na h-uisgeachan, *the waters shall fail.—Stew. Is* Fut *sub.* dh'fhàilnicheas.

Failreag, eig, *s. f.* A lump, a hilloch.

Failte! failte! *interj* Hail! hail!

Fàilte, *s. f.* (*Ir. id.*) A welcome; hail; a salute; a salutation. Fàilte do'n la, *hail to the day.—Sm.* Ceud fàilte, a righ! *a hundred welcomes, O king!—Oss.* Fàilte sìth, *a salutation of peace —Orr.* Cuir fàilte, *salute, welcome, hail*, cuir fàilte air, *salute him.*

Fàilteach, *a*, *from* fàilte (*Ir. id.*) Hospitable, ready to welcome, agreeable.—*Macint.* *Com* and *sup* fàiltiche, *more* or *most hospitable*

Fàilteachadh, aidh, *s. m.* (*Ir.* failtiughadh) A saluting, a welcoming, a hailing, a salute, a welcome.

Fàilteachadh, (a), *pr. part.* of fàiltich.

Fàilteachail, *a* Prone to salute, ready to welcome, hospitable.—*Macint.*

Fàiltich, *v. a* (*Ir* failtigh) Hail, greet or salute, welcome *Pret. a.* dh'fhàiltich, *saluted*, *fut aff a* fàiltichidh, *shall salute.* Le 'r n-ait hosanna fàiltichidh, *with our glad hosannas we shall welcome —Sm*

Faim, faime, *s. f* (i. e fath-fhaim) *Ir* faithim A hem, a border.

Faim, *v. a.* Hem, as a garment, *also*, surround. *Pret a* dh'fhaim, *hemmed*, *fut. aff. a* faimidh, *shall hem*, *fut. pass* faimear, *shall be hemmed.*

Faimeach, *a* Hemmed, as a garment; hemming, surrounding.

Faimear, *fut pass.* of faim. Shall be hemmed

Faineachadh, aidh, *s m.* A recognising; a knowing, a feeling, perception Written also *aithneachadh*

Faineachadh, (a), *pr part.* of fainich.

Faineachas, ais, *s m* Perception

Fainear. See **Fanear**

Faing, *gen. sing.* of fang

Faing, *s. f* A certain Irish coin.

Fainich, *v a* Recognise, know; feel, perceive, smell. *Pret. a* dh'aithnich, *felt*, *fut. aff a.* fainichidh, *shall know* Am fainich thu e? *wilt thou know him?* Bheir mise ort gum fainich thu e, *I will make you feel it*

Fàinne, *s. f.* (*Ir.* fainne) A ring. *N. pl* fainnean *and* fàinneachan, *rings.* Thug iad leo fàinneachan, *they took rings with them.—Stew. Exod.*

Fainne, *s. f* Languishment; weakening; weakness; languor

† **Fainne**, *s f.* Ignorance —*Shaw*

Fàinneach, *a.* Curled, like a ring, full of rings. Do chùl fàinneach, *thy curled locks —Old Song*

Fainneal, eil, *s. m.* Ignorance, the state of being astray; bewilderment Air fainneal, *astray, bewildered*

Fair, *v a* (*Ir. id*) Watch; keep guard, keep awake *Pret a* dh'fhair, *watched*, *fut. aff. a.* fairidh, *shall watch*

Fàir, faire, *s. f.* (*Ir. id*) Dawn or daybreak; a ridge, a hill, a rising ground, sunrise, sunset —*Shaw* Tha 'n fhàir a briseadh, *the dawn is breaking —Stew Gen* Briseadh na fàire, *daybreak* Is luath fe. r air fàire ri la fuar earraich, *swift moves a man over the mountain ridge on a cold spring day —G P.*

Fair, faire, *s f* A watch or sentinel, a watching, watchfulness, circumspection; a watch-hill Fear faire, *a watchman*, luchd faire, *watchmen.* A deanamh faire na h-oidhche, *watching by night —Stew N. T.* Tigh faire, *a watch-house*, tigh fhaire, *a house where a wake is held over a corpse*, suidhich faire, *place a watch*

Fair claidh, *s f* A spectre's watch over a grave.

† **Fairbre**, *s f* (*Ir. id*) A notch, an impression; a fault, a stain —*Shaw*

Fairc, fairce, *s f* (*Ir id.*) A mallet, a rammer; a hammer; a beetle *N pl* fairceau.

† **Fairce**, *s f* Extent —*Shaw*

Fairceall, ill, *s m* (*Ir id*) The lid of a pot or of any other vessel —*Macd* A reward —*Shaw*.

Faircealach, *a* Having a lid

Fairche, *s. f.* A beetle, a rammer, a hammer, a mallet; a see, a diocese; choice Fairche an domhain, *the hammer of the earth —Stew Jer* *N pl* fairchean.

Fairdean, ein, *s m* A farthing Bonn an dà fhairdein, *a halfpenny — Turn*

Fairdhris, *s* Bramble

Faire! *interj.* Lo! behold! ay! ay! fie! shame! Fire faire! *what a pother!* Faire! faire! righ Deorsa! *Shame! O King!—Old Song*

Faireach, *a* (*from* fair) Watchful, circumspect, wakeful

Faireach, **Faireachadh**, aidh, *s m.* An awakening, a rousing from sleep, the state of being awake. Bheil tha d'fhaireachadh? *art thou awake?* Chum thu mo shùil na faireachadh, *thou hast kept my eye awake —Sm* Tha mo chridh na fhaireach, *my heart is awake —Stew Song Sol* Eadar codal is faireachadh, *between sleeping and waking.*

Faireachail, *a* Watchful, observant, attentive. Gu faireachail, *watchfully*

Faireadh, idh, *s m.* A watching, watchfulness, attention, a sentinel Ri faireadh, *keeping watch —Oss Gaul.* Fear-fairidh, *a watchman, a sentinel*

Faireadh, (a), *pr part* of fair Watching A faireadh treud san oidhche, *watching a flock by night —Stew N. T.*

Fàireag, eig, *s f* A gland, a wax kernel; a lump; a hillock.—*Shaw* *N pl.* fàireagan

Fàireagach, *a* Glandular, abounding in glands

Fairg, fairge, *s f.* A sea, an ocean, a wave Fairg nan sion, *the sea of storms —Oss Tem* An fhairg mhòr, *the great ocean —Sm* Anrath fairge, *a storm at sea.* *N pl* fairgeachan

Fairgeachan, *n pl* of fairg. Seas —*Stew Gen*

Faireagan! *an interjection of admiration* Written also *fairigean*, which see.

Fairglar, eir, *s m*, fairg-fhear (*Ir. id.*) A seaman

Fairich, *v a* and *n.* (*from* fair) Awake, arouse, bestir; watch, feel; smell, observe, see, perceive *Pret a.* dh'

fhairich; *fut. aff. a.* fairichidh, *shall awake.* Fairich as do shuain, *rouse from thy slumber.—Sm.* Teich no fairich m' fhearg, *fly, or feel my wrath.—Oss. Carricth.* Dh' fhairich e boladh, *he smelled a smell.—Stew. Gen.* Dh' fhairich mo chridhe, *my heart was seen.—Stew. Ecc. Fut. pass.* fairichear.

FAIRICH, *s. f.* A parish.

FAIRICH, *fut. pass.* of fairich.

FAIRICHIDH, *fut. aff. a.* Shall awaken.

FAIRICHTE, *p. part.* of fairich. Awakened, aroused; smelt.

FAIRIGEAN! *an interj. of admiration.* Fairigean! fairigean! fairigean Mòrag! *I am lost in admiration of Morag.—Old Song.*

FAIRLEAG, eig, *s. f.* (*Ir. id.*) A lapwing; a swallow.—*Shaw.*

FAIRLEAGACH, *a.* (*Ir. id.*) Abounding in lapwings or in swallows; like a lapwing or swallow.

† FAIRNIC, *v. a.* Obtain, get; invent, devise, contrive.

FAIRSBEAG, eig, *s. f.* A large gull. *N. pl.* fairsbeagan.

FAIRSBEAGACH, *a.* Abounding in gulls.

FAIRSING, *v. a.* Widen, enlarge. *Pret.* dh'fhairsing, *enlarged.*

FAIRSINN, *a.* See FARSUING.

† FAIRTHE, *s. f.* (*Ir. id.*) A feast.

FAIRTLEACHADH, aidh, *s. m.* A worsting, a conquering; a conquest.

FAIRTLEACHADH, (a), *pr. part.* of fairtlich. Worsting, overcoming.

FAIRTLICH, *v.* Worst, overcome, get the better of. *Pret. a.* dh'fhairtlich, *worsted; fut. aff. a.* fairtlichidh, *shall overcome.* This verb takes after it the preposition *air*, either simple or compounded. Dh'fhairtlich mi air, *I got the better of him.*

† FAISCRE, *s. f.* Compulsion, violence, force.

FÀISG, *s. f.* (*W.* fasg, *a tie. Ir.* faisg.) A cheese-press; a penfold; a band; a tie.

FÀISG, *v. a.* (*Ir. id.*) Press; wring; compress; squeeze by twisting, as water out of cloth. *Pret. a.* dh'fhaisg, *wrung; fut. aff. a.* fàisgidh, *shall wring.* Fàisgidh iad ola, *they shall* [*press*] *make oil.—Stew. Job.* A dheasgnan fàisgidh daoine daoi, *the wicked shall wring its dregs.—Sm.*

FAISG, *prep.* Near; nigh to. Chunnaic iad i tighinn faisg orra, *they saw her coming near them* [*approaching them*].—*Mac Lach.*

FAISGE, *s. f.* Cheese; pressure; violence; extortion.

FAISGEADH, idh, *s.* A penfold.

FÀISGEADH, idh, *s. m.* A wringing, a compressing, a squeezing; compression; a fold.

FAISGEAN, ein, *s. m.* A cheese-press; a sponge.—*Macd.*

FAISGEANACH, *a.* Spungy, fungous.

FAISGEAR, *fut. pass.* of faisg. Shall be wrung.

FAISGEIL, *a.* Flat, compressed.

FÀISGIDH, *fut. aff. a.* Shall or will wring.

FAISGNEACH, *a.* Cathartic.

FAISGRE, *s.* (*Ir. id.*) Cheese; violence; pressure; extortion.

FÀISGTE, *p. part.* of faisg. (*Ir.* faisgthe.) Pressed, wrung, squeezed.

FÀISNEACH, *a.* Prophetic; divining.

FÀISNEACHADH, aidh, *s. m.* A prophesying, a divining; a prophecy, divination.

FÀISNEACHADH, (a), *pr. part.* of fàisnich. Prophesying, divining. Fàisneachadh aislingean brèige, *prophesying false dreams.—Stew. Jer.*

FÀISNEACHD, *s. f.* A prophecy; a soothsaying. Na dean fàisneachd, *do not prophecy.—Stew. G. B.*

FAISNEAG, eig, *s. f.* A pimple. *N. pl.* faisneagan.

FAISNEAGACH, *a.* Pimply.

FÀISNEAR, ir, *s. m.* A prophet, a soothsayer.

FÀISNEIS, *a.* Speakable, utterable.—*Shaw.*

FÀISNICH, *v. a.* Prophecy; divine; certify; tell; prove; abide. *Pret. a.* dh'fhaisnich; *fut. aff. a.* faisnichidh, *shall prophecy.*

FAISNICHE, *s. m.* A prophet, a soothsayer; a wizard.

FÀISNICHIDH, *fut. aff. a.* of fàisnich. Shall or will prophecy.

FÀISNIS, *s. f.* Intelligence; rehearsal; relation.—*Shaw.*

FÀISTINN, *s. f.* (*Ir.* fàistine.) A prophecy; an omen. Droch fhaistinn, *a bad omen.* The Irish say *droch fhàistine.*

FÀISTINNEACH, *a.* Prophetic, ominous.

FÀISTINNEACH, ich, *s. m.* A prophet; an augur; a soothsayer; a wizard.

FÀISTINNEACHD, *s. f.* Prophecy, divination; ominousness.

FÀITCHEAS, FÀITCHIOS, eis, *s. m.* (*Ir. id.*) Fear, apprehension, dismay; reluctance. Na biodh fàitcheas ort, *be not dismayed.—Stew. Jos.* Na biodh fàitchios ort, *be not afraid.—Sm.*

FAITCHEASACH, *a.* Apprehensive; timid.

FÀITE, *s. f.* Timidity; shyness; a smile.

FÀITEACH, *a.* Timid; shy.—*Shaw.* Smiling. Gu fàiteach, *timidly.*

FAITEAL, eil, *s. m.* (*Lat.* flatus.) A breeze, a breath of wind; light; a gleam of light; music. Faiteal tannais, *a spectre's breath.—Oss. Tem.* Written also *aiteal.*

FAITEALACH, *a.* Breezy; gleaming.

FAITEALACHD, *s. f.* Breeziness.

FAITGHEAS, eis, *s. m.* Fear; dismay; dread of bad consequences. Co chuireas faitgheas fum? *of whom shall I be afraid?—Sm.* Written also *faitcheas;* which see.

† FAITH, *s. f.* (*Ir. id.*) Heat; warmth.

† FAITH, *s. f.* (*Ir. id.*) Apparel, raiment.

FAITHILTEAR, ir, *s. m.* A broker.

† FAITH-LIOS, *s. m.* A wardrobe.—*Shaw.* *N. pl.* faidh-liosan.

† FAITSE, *s. f.* The south, the south point.

FAITSEACH, *a.* Southward, southern.

FAL, *a.* (*Arab.* fal, *omen.*) Ominous.

FÀL, fàil, *s. f.* (*W.* fal. *Ir.* fal, *a fold.*) A circle, a fold, a penfold; a fence, an enclosure; a hedge, a wall; spite; cut turf; a sithe, a spade. Fal mòin, *a peat spade, a paring spade. Lat.* falx, *a sithe. Arm.* fals. *Ir.* fal.

FÀL, fail, *s. m.* (*Ir. id.*) A noble; plenty; malice; a trifle.

FÀL, *v. a.* Enclose, hedge; cover with turf. *Pret. a.* dh'fhàl; *fut. aff. a.* fàlaidh.

FALA, *gen. sing.* of fuil. Written more frequently *fola.*

FALA, ai, *s. m.* See FALADH.

FALACH, aich, *s. m.* A veil, a covering, a hiding; a place of concealment. Falach fead, *hide and seek.* Written also *folach.*

FALACHADH, aidh, *s. m.* A hiding, a concealing, a covering; a cover, a concealment. Written also *folachadh.*

FALACHADH, (a), *pr. part.* of falaich. Hiding, concealing, covering.

FALACHAIR, *s. m.* (*Ir.* falaightheoir.) One who covers or hides.

FALACHAN, ain, *s. m.* A concealment; a hidden treasure; a place where treasure is hidden.

FÀLACHD, *s. f.* (*from* fal.) A grudge; a feud. Gach fàlachd air cul, *each grudge forgotten.—Oss. Dargo.* Fàlachd eadar chàirdean, *feuds among friends.—Oss. Taura.*

FÀLACHDACH, *a.* Feudal; grudging; apt to grudge; causing feud; prone to feud.

Fàladair, *s. m.* A sithe; a mower; orts. Iarunn fàladair, *a sithe.*

Fàladaireachd, *s. f.* Cutting with a sithe, as grass. Ris an fhàladaireachd, [*at the*] *mowing* [*of*] *grass.*

Faladas, ais, *s. m.* Chastisement; grudge, spite

Fàladh, aidh, *s. m.* Hatred; a grudge, a feud.

Falaich, *v. a.* Hide, conceal, cover, veil; keep secret; keep covered. *Pret. a.* dh'fhalaich, *hide; fut. aff. a.* falaichidh, *shall hide.* Written also *folaich*, which see.

Falaid, *s. f.* A gloss, a polish, meal put on a cake to whiten it.

Falain, *s. f.* (*Lat.* balæna. *Ir.* folain) A whale —*Shaw*

Falair, *s. m.* An ambler; a pacing horse; an entertainment; a funeral.

Falaireachd, *s. f.* (*Ir.* falarachd) Ambling; pacing; cantering.

Falaisg, *s. f.* A heath-burning, a moor-burning; a festive fire. Mar fhalaisg air Laoire, *like a flame on the heath of Lora.—Oss. Conn.* A leum o fhalaisg an aonaich, *bounding from the heath-burning* —*Id* Perhaps *falaisg* is *fàl-losg*

Falaman, ain, *s. m* The rotula, or whirlbone of the knee; the knee-pan.

Falamh, *a.* (*Ir. id. Eng.* fallow.) Empty, void; vacant; unoccupied; wanting substance; vain. Fàsach falamh, *an empty wilderness —Stew Deut.* Air ionad falamh, *on a void space.—Sm. Com.* and *sup.* falaimhe. *Falamh* is also written *folamh.*

Falamhachd, *s. f.* Emptiness, voidness, vacancy; a void

Falamhaich, *v. a.* Empty; make void. Pret *a.* dh'fhalamhaich, *emptied, fut aff a.* falamhaichidh.

Falaras, ais, *s. m.* Pacing, ambling; horsemanship

Falbh, *v. n.* Go; begone; depart; retire. *Pret a.* dh' fhalbh, *went; fut. aff. a.* falbhaidh, *shall go.* Na suinn a dh'fhalbh, *the departed heroes.—Oss Com* Falbhaibh fathast, *depart yet.—Stew.* 1 *K.* Air falbh, *gone*, bi falbh, *begone.*

Falbh, *s. m* A going, a retiring; a withdrawing; a departure; motion, gait, air. Falbh nam fear cròdha, *the departure of the brave.—Mac Co* Cia mòrdha a falbh! *how majestic her gait!—Mac Lach.* Air falbh, *gone, decayed in person;* fad air falbh, *far off.*

Falbh, (a), *pr. part.* of falbh. Going, retiring, departing Tonnan a briseadh 's a falbh, *waves breaking and retiring.—Oss. Tem*

Falbhach, *a* (*from* falbh) Moving, walking, travelling Is éigin do 'n fheumach a bhi falbhach, *the needy must keep moving.—G. P.*

Falbhach, aich, *s. m.* One troubled with the hiccup —*Shaw.* A body, a carcass.

Falbhaidh, *fut. aff. a.* of falbh. Shall go.

Falbhan, ain, *s. m.* (*from* falbh.) Motion, agitation, locomotion, creeping. Falbhan a chiabh, *the agitation of his locks —Oss Tem.* Tha e air falbhan, *he is able to go about, he walks about.*

Falbhanach, *a.* Ambulatory, in motion.

Falbhanachd, *s f.* Travelling; motion; ambulatoriness, locomotion; struggling.

† **Falc**, failc, *s f* (*Ir id.*) A flood, a frost; barrenness from drought.

† **Falc**, *a.* (*Ir. id*) Sterile, barren, parched, as ground with heat.

Falcag, aig, *s. f* A species of sea-fowl.

Falcair, *s. m.* A scoffer, a cheat *N. pl.* falcairean

Falcaireachd, *s. f.* Scoffing; the practice of scoffing; cheating.

Falcair, Fiadhain, *s. m.* Male pimpernel, *anagallis arvensis.*

Falcas, ais, *s. m* (*Ir. id*) A shade, a shadow.—*Shaw.*

Faldhà, *s. m* A jest; fun, mirth. Ri faldhà, *jesting*, cho robh mi ach ri faldhà, *I was only in fun*, is tric chaidh faldhà gu fal-rireadh, *often has fun ended in earnest —G. P* Eadar fhaldhà 's rireadh, *between jest and earnest.*

Fal-dos, -dois, *s. m* A thorn-hedge

† **Falladh**, aidh, *s m.* (*Ir* falla) Dominion, power, rule

Fallaid, *s f.* See **Falaid**.

Fallain, *a* (*Ir id*) Healthy; salubrious; wholesome, sound Cridhe fallain, *a sound heart —Stew Pro* Teanga fhallain, *a wholesome tongue.—Id* Gu slàn fallain, *sound and healthy* *Com.* and *sup.* fallaine.

Fallaine, *s f* (*Ir. id.*) Healthiness; wholesomeness, salubriousness.

Fallaineachd, *s. f.* Wholesomeness, healthiness, health, soundness. Fallaineachd, *wholesomeness.—Macint* Fallaineachd am fheòil, *soundness in my bones —Sm.* Fallaineachd inntinn, *soundness of mind.*

† **Fallamhnachd**, *s. f.* (*Ir id*) Rule, dominion.—*Shaw*

† **Fallamhnas**, ais, *s m.* (*Ir id*) A kingdom, dominion

Fallsa, *a* False, deceitful, treacherous. Am measg bhraithre fallsa, *among false brethren —Stew Cor. ref*

Lat falsus *Teut* valsch *and* falsch. *Arm.* fals *Ir* fallsa Fallsa-mhanach, *a deceitful monk.* *Arm* fals vanach

Fallsachd, *s f.* (*Ir. id.*) Falseness, deceitfulness, treacherousness; philosophy.

Fallsair, *s. m* (*Arm.* falser.) A liar, a deceiver, a traitor *N. pl.* fallsairean, *liars.* *Arm.* falseyren

Fallsail, *a.* (fallsa-amhuil) False, deceitful, treacherous Gu fallsail, *falsely.*

Fallsanach, aich, *s. m.* A falsifier.

Fallsanachd, *s. f.* Falsehood, treachery.

Faloisgeach, *a* Combustible

Fal-losgadh, aidh, *s m.* A conflagration; combustion; heath-burning.—*Shaw*

Falluinge, Falluinn, *s. f.* A cloak, a mantle, a garment, a hood. Sliabh na falluinge duirche, *the dark-mantled hill —Oss Taura.* Falluinn an fhir, *the hero's mantle —Oss. Derm.*

W faling *Ir* falainn *Arm* fallaenn. *Lat.* pallium

Falluingeach, Falluinneach, *a.* Robed; clothed with a garment; like a garment.

Falluinn. See **Falluinge**.

Fallus, uis, *s. f.* (*Ir id*) Perspiration, sweat. Fallus do ghnùis, *the sweat of thy brow —Stew Gen* Cuir fallus dhiot, *perspire*, tha mi 'm fhliuch fhallus, *I am perspiring all over.* *N. pl.* fallusan.

Fallusach, *a.* Perspiring; sudorific.

Fallusaich, *v.* Perspire, sweat, cause to perspire. *Pret. a* dh'fhallusaich; *fut. aff. a.* fallusaichidh.

Falma, *s.* Alum

Falmadair, *s. m* A rudder; a tiller. Cha robh falmadair gun sgoltadh, *there was not a rudder unsplit.—Macdon*

Falmhaich, *v. a* Empty, pour out *Pret. a.* dh'fhalmhaich, *emptied.* Dh'fhalmhaich i a soitheach, *she emptied her vessel.—Stew. O. T.* *Fut aff a* falmhaichidh, *shall empty —Stew. Ecc.* *Fut. pass* falmhaichear Falmhaichear e, *he shall be made empty.—Stew. Nch.*

Fàl-ni, *s. m.* A trifle; a trifling matter Air fàl-ni na caith do chuid, *waste not thy substance on trifles —Old Didactic Poem.*

Faloisg, *s. f* (*Ir* faolscadh) A moor-burning, a heath-burning; a fire of joy or of triumph Measg faloisg nan dàn, *during the festive fires and the songs.—Oss Fing*

Fal-rireadh, *s. m* Earnest; any thing but jest

Falt, fuilt, *s. m.* The hair of the head; locks, ringlets

Asp. form, fhalt. Fhalt òr-bhuidh, *his gold-yellow locks.*—*Oss. Fin. and Lor.* Cuach-fhalt, *curled hair.*—*Macint.*

Falt signifies the hair of the head: the hair of any other portion of the body is called *gaoisd* or *ròinne*.

Faltan, ain, *s. m.* A ribband for a female's head, a snood; a welt, a belt. Written more frequently *failtean*.

Faltanas, ais, *s. m.* (*Ir. id.*) An occasion; a pretence; a quarrel, enmity.—*Shaw.*

Faluing. See Falluing.

Fa m', (*for* fa mo.) Under my; *also*, upon my. Fa m' chomhair, *opposite to me.*

Fa m'chomhair, *comp. prep.* Opposite to me, in front of me, before me. Fineamhain fa m'chomhair, *a vine opposite me.*—*Stew. O. T.*

Famh, faimh, *s. m.* A mole; the *talpa Europæus* of Linnæus. *N. pl.* faimh. An t-seilcheag 's am famh, *the snail and the mole.*—*Stew. Lev.*

Famhair, *s. m.* A giant; a mole-catcher. *N. pl.* famhairean, *giants.* Bha famhairean ann, *there were giants.*—*Stew. Gen.*

Perhaps the proper orthography of *famhair*, in the sense of *giant*, is *faobhair*; i. e. *faobh-fhear*, a man of spoils or of conquest.

Famhaireachd, *s. f.* Giganticness; the prowess of a giant.

Famh-thorr, *s. m.* A mole-hill.—*Macd.*

Fa 'n. Under the; *sometimes meaning* upon the. According to some, *fa* and *fo* have opposite meanings, the former signifying *upon*, the latter *beneath*.

† Fan, *a.* Prone; propense; headlong; steep.

† Fan, Fanadh, *s. m.* A declivity, a steep, inclination; a wandering, peregrination.

† Fàn, fain, *s. m.* (*Lat.* fan-um. *Ir.* fan. *Eng.* fane.) A temple, a chapel.

Fan, *v. n.* Stay, stop, wait, tarry, continue, remain, endure. *Pret. a.* dh'fhan, *stayed; fut. aff. a.* fanaidh, *shall stay.* Fan thall, *stay on the other side.*—*Oss. Lodin.* Fanaidh bhur mnaoi, *your wives shall remain.*—*Stew. Jos.* Fanaibh ré na h-oidhche, *remain all night.*—*Stew. Gen.* Fan ris, *wait for him;* fan air, *wait on him, attend him;* fan agad féin, *stay by thyself; come not near me.*—*Stew. Jer.* Fan air falbh, *stay off.*

Fanachd, *s. f.* (*Ir. id.*) A staying, a tarrying, a lingering; enduring; a stay, a delay.

Fanachd, (a), *pr. part.* of fan. Staying, remaining, waiting. A fanachd ris, *waiting for him;* a fanachdair, *waiting on him.*

Fanaid, *s. f.* Mockery, ridicule, derision, scoffing, scorn. Ri fanaid, *mocking;* dean fanaid, *mock.* Written also *fanoid*.

Fanaid, *v.* Mock, ridicule, scoff, scorn. *Pret. a.* dh'fhanaid, *mocked; fut. aff. a.* fanaidîdh, *shall mock.* *Fanaid* requires after it the prep. *air*, either simple or compounded.

Fanaideach, *a.* Mocking, scoffing, ridiculing. Written also *fanoideach*.

Fanaidh, *fut. aff. a.* of fan. Shall or will stay.

Fanam, 1 *sing. imper.* of fan. Let me stay; *also for* fanaidh mi, *I will stay.*

Fànas, ais, *s. m.* (*Lat.* vanus, *empty.*) An empty or void space.

Fa 'n comhair, *comp. prep.* Opposite to them, before them, in front of them. Cuir aran fa 'n comhair, *put bread before them.*—*Stew.* 2 *K.*

Fanear, (*i. e.* fa 'n ear, *on*, or *into, the head.*) Observation, attention, heed, notice. Thugaibh fanear, *attend, take notice.*

Fang, fainge, *s. f.* (*Ir.* faing.) A vulture; a raven; *also*, a poindfold; a place for catching cattle; a pen; an Irish coin; gold or silver leaf. Sùil na fainge, *the vulture's eye.*—*Stew. Job.* Am fang agus an clamhan, *the vulture and the kite.*—*Stew. Lev.*

Fang, *v. a.* (*Swed.* fanga, *to catch.*) Drive into a fold or pen. *Pret. a.* dh' fhang, *penned; fut. aff. a.* fangaidh, *shall pen.*

Fangach, *a.* (*from* fang.) Like a vulture; rapacious, ravenous; full of folds or pens; like a fold or pen; of, or belonging to, a vulture, fold, or pen.

Fangachadh, aidh, *s. m.* A driving into a fold; a penning of cattle.

Fangachadh, (a), *pr. part.* of fangaich.

Fangaich, *v. a.* (*from* fang.) Fold; gather into a fold or pen. *Pret. a.* dh' fhangaich, *folded; fut. aff. a.* fangaichidh, *shall fold; fut. pass.* fangaichear, *shall be penned; p. part.* fangaichte, *penned.*

Fangaichear, *fut. pass.* of fangaich. Shall be folded or penned.

Fangaichte, *p. part.* of fangaich. Penned, folded.

Fanlanta, *a.* Slender; small.—*Macd.* and *Shaw.*

Fan-leac, -lic, *s. f.* An altar of rude stones; a stone in an inclined position.—*Shaw.*

Fann, *a.* (*Ir. id.*) Weak, faint, languid; helpless, infirm, Solus fann, *faint light.*—*Oss. Tem.* Is fann do ghuth; *languid is thy voice.*—*Oss. Carricth.* Cridhe fann is com gun treòir, *a faint heart and a pithless person.*—*Mac Lach.* *Com.* and *sup.* fainne.

Fannachadh, aidh, *s. m.* A growing languid or faint; a giving up through fatigue. Tha e air fannachadh, *he is worn out with fatigue.*

Fannachadh, (a), *pr. part.* of fannaich.

Fannad, aid, *s. m.* Weakness, languor.

Fannadh, aidh, *s. m.* (*from* fann.) A slackening, a relaxing of exertion; a remission; intermission. Cha robh fannadh air a chomhrag, *the battle continued without intermission.*—*Old Poem.*

Fannaich, *v. a.* and *n.* (*from* fann.) Faint, grow weary; fail, give up with fatigue; fatigue. *Pret. a.* dh' fhannaich, *fainted; fut. aff. a.* fannaichidh, *shall faint.* Fannaichidh spiorad na h-Eiphit, *the spirit of Egypt shall fail.*—*Stew. Is.* Mar fannaich sinn, *if we faint not.*—*Stew. Gal.*

Fannaichte, *p. part.* of fannaich. Grown weary, fatigued; done up.

Fannan, ain, *s. m.* A gentle breeze. Fannan do ghaoth 'n car, leannan an t-sealgair, *a breeze from the east is the sportsman's feast.*—*G. P.*

Fannanta, *a.* Weak, faint, infirm.

Fann-ghaoth, -ghaoithe, *s. f.* A soft breeze. Mar fhannghaoth sheimh, *like a soft gentle breeze.*—*Old Poem.*

Fann-gheal, *a.* Pale white. Sobhrach fann-gheal, *a pale white primrose.*—*Macdon.*

Fann-ghuth, *s. m.* A weak voice, a faint note. Fhreagair e le fann-ghuth, *he replied with a faint voice.*—*Oss. Fin. and Lor.*

Fannlag, *a.* Weak, languid; fatigued.—*Shaw.*

Fanntas, ais, *s. m.* (*from* fann.) Weakness, faintness; languishing.

Fanntasach, *a.* Weak; causing weakness.

Fanoid, *s. f.* Mockery, ridicule, derision, scorn. Written also *fanaid.*

Fanoid, *v.* Mock, ridicule, scoff. Written also *fanaid.*

Fanoideach, *a.* Mockery, scoffing, scorning. Gu fanoideach, *scoffingly.*—*Sm.* Written also *fanaideach.*

Fanoidiche, *s. m.* A mocker, a scoffer; a lampooner; a mimic.

Fantalach, *a.* Permanent, stable, lasting; durable.

Fantalachd, *s. f.* Permanence, stability, durableness.

Fantuinn, *s. f.* An abiding, a continuing, a lasting.

Fantuinn, (a), *pr. part.* of fann. Staying; remaining; lasting.

Faob, *s. m.* A lump; any round lumpy substance, as a potato.

Faobach, *a.* Lumpy.—*Macfar.*

Faobh, *v. n.* Shout, cry aloud, proclaim.

Faobh, faoibh, *s. f.* A spoil; booty; conquest; dead men's clothes; a carcass. Mhic Rosa nam faobh, *son of victorious* [*spoil-bearing*] *Rosa.—Oss. Fing.* *N. pl.* faoibh, *spoils.* Triath nam faoibh, *the chieftain of spoils* or *victories.—Oss.* Faoibh nan namhaid, *the carcases of the enemies.—Oss. Lod.*

Faobhach, *a.* (*from* faobh.) Victorious; plundering; spoiling.

Faobhachadh, aidh, *s. m.* A spoiling or plundering; robbery, plunder. Air fhaobhachadh, *plundered.—Stew. Col.*

Faobhachadh, (a), *pr. part.* of faobhaich. Plundering, spoiling, robbing.

Faobhaich, *v. a.* (*from* faobh.) Spoil, plunder; strip by force; lay waste. *Pret. a.* dh' fhaobhaich; *fut. aff. a.* faobhaichidh, *shall plunder.* Dh' fhaobhaich iad e, *they stripped him.—Stew.* 1 *Chr.*

Faobhair, *s. m.* (faobh-fhear.) A giant; a conqueror. *Faobhair* seems to be a more correct rendering of *giant* than *famhair.*

Faobhairt, *s. f.* An edge; the temper of any sharp-bladed instrument.

Faobhairte, *part.* Tempered; sharpened.

Faobhairteach, *a.* (*from* faobhar.) Tempering; well-tempered.

Faobhar, air, *s. m.* (*Ir. id.*) The edge of a weapon; the ridge of a hill; the edge or brink of a precipice; surface. Le faobhar a chlaidheimh, *with the edge of the sword.—Stew. Jos.* Air faobhar bheann, *on a ridge of mountains.—Oss. Lod.* Faobhar a chuain, *the surface of the sea.—Oss. Tem.* Air bheag faobhair, *blunt.—Macint.* Faobhar nan nial, *the edges of the clouds.—Oss. Fing.* Claidheamh dà fhaobhair, *a two-edged sword.—Stew. Ps.*

Faobharach, **Faobhrach**, *a.* (*Ir. id.*) Edged; sharp; keen; satirical, pointed; active, nimble. *Com.* and *sup.* faobharaiche.

Faobharaich, **Faobhraich**, *v. a.* (*from* faobhar.) Sharpen a blade; set, as a razor. *Pret. a.* dh' fhaobhraich, *sharpened; fut. aff.* faobhraichidh, *shall sharpen.*

Faobharaichte, **Faobhraichte**, *p. part.* Sharpened.

Faoch, faoich, *s. m.* A shell-fish; *also*, a field.—*Shaw.* Tràigh nam faoch, *the shore of shell-fish.—Oss. Fing.*

Faochach, *a.* Abounding in shell-fish.

Faochadh, aidh, *s. m.* Crisis in sickness.

Faochag, aig, *s. f.* (*Ir.* faochog.) A periwinkle; any small shell-fish; an eddy or curl on the surface of a running stream; the eye. Faochag chuairtein, *a small whirlpool;* faochag thuaichill, *an eddy, a small whirlpool.*

Faochagach, *a.* Abounding in small shell-fish; full of eddies.

Faod, *v. def.* (*Fr.* faut, *must.*) May, must. *Pret.* dh'fhaod; *fut. aff.* faodaidh. Am faod mi falbh? faodaidh; *may I go? you may.*

Faodaidh, *fut. aff.* of faod.

Faodail, *s. m.* Any thing found. Spoltaidh e an fhaodail le ghial, *he will tear with his claws the booty found.—Mac Lach.*

Faodailich, *s. m.* and *f.* Any thing found; a foundling.

Faodalaich, *s. m.* and *f.* Any thing found; a found treasure; a foundling. Cha 'n e sealbh na faodalaich a faotainn, *the luck of a treasure does not always consist in the getting of it.—G. P.*

† **Faodh**, faoidh, *s. m.* (*Ir. id.*) A voice.

† **Faogh**, faoigh, *s. m.* (*Ir. id.*) Punishment.

Faoghaid, **Faoghailt**, *s. f.* A chase, a hunt; starting of game; men who start game. Faoghaid an rèidh, *the chase of the plain.—Oss. Fing.* Faoghaid fàsaich, *a forest hunt.—Oss. Com.*

Faoghaidiche, *s. pl.* Carnivorous birds.—*Shaw.*

Faoi, *s.* A noisy stream.

Faoibh, *gen. sing.* of faobh; which see.

Faoibh, *n. pl.* of faobh. Spoils; dead men's clothes.

Faoich, *gen. sing.* of faoch.

Faoidh, *s. m.* A messenger, an express; a courser; a departure; a gift; generosity. Faoidh fir gun chaoraich, *the generosity of a man who has nothing to give.—G. P.*

† **Faoidh**, *v. n.* (*Ir. id.*) Sleep; rest; depart.—*Shaw.*

† **Faoighle**, *s. pl.* (*Ir. id.*) Words, expressions.

Faoil, *a.* Mild, kind, affable, generous. Gu faoil, *mildly.*

Faoile, *s. f.* Mildness, kindness; welcome, affability; generosity.

Faoileach, *a.* Glad, joyful, thankful; generous.—*Shaw.* Gu faoileach, *gladly.*

Faoileach, *s. f.* Holydays, feastdays, carnival.

Faoileachd, *s. f.* Gladness, joyfulness, thankfulness, generosity, kindness.

Faoileag, eig, *s. f.* A sea-maw or gull. *N. pl.* faoileagan.

Faoileann, inn, *s. m.* A sea-maw; a gull; the *larus canus* of Linnæus. *N. pl.* faoilinnean.

Faoileannach, *a.* Like a sea-maw; abounding in sea-maws.

Faoile, **Faoilidh**, *a.* Kind, mild, inviting; hospitable.—*Oss. Tem.* Coire faoilidh, *an inviting dell.—Macdon.*

† **Faoilich**, *v. n.* and *a.* (*Ir.* faoiligh.) Rejoice, be merry; entertain.

Faoilidh, *a.* See **Faoile**.

Faoilidheachd, *s. f.* Gladness; thankfulness; hospitality; generousness; mildness; kindness.

Faoilleach, *s.* See **Faoilteach**.

Faoilte, *s. f.* Hospitality; a welcome, a welcoming; invitation to a feast. Cha tairis leam ur faoilte, *I shall not accept your invitation.—Old Poem.* Cuir faoilte, *salute.*

Faoilteach, ich, *s. m.* (*perhaps from* faoil, *wolves.*) The latter half of January and the former of February; the stormy month; depth of winter. Neart na gaoithe tuath san fhaoilteach, *the strength of the north wind in winter.—Old Poem.* Na faoiltich, *the stormy days.*

The original meaning of *faoilteach* was, perhaps, the wolf month, from the circumstance that wolves, with which the Highlands once abounded, became more daring and dangerous in the depth of winter. *Faoilteach* may also be derived from *faoile*, welcome, joy. The Highlanders regard stormy weather, towards the end of January, as prognostic of a fruitful season to follow; and *vice versâ*. *Faoilteach* may, therefore, mean the welcome season. An old soothsaying rhyme runs to this effect:—

> Faoilteach, faoilteach, lamh an crios,
> Faoilte mhòr bu chòr bhi ris;
> Crodh is caoraich ruithe air theas,
> Gul is caoin bu chor bhi ris.

"The dead of winter, cold and stormy, let it be gladly welcomed; but, if warm, there is reason for weeping and wailing."

Faoilteach, *a.* Generous, hospitable, inviting; welcoming. *Com.* and *sup.* faoiltiche. Fhir is fhaoiltiche gun fheall! *thou most generous and guileless of all!—Fingalian Poem.* Gu faoilteach, *generously.*

Faoilteachd, *s. f.* The practice of hospitality; a welcoming; a readiness to welcome Le h-aigheir 's le faoilteachd, *with joy and welcoming.—Mac Co.*

FAOILTEAS, eis, *s. m.* Gladness; a hearty welcome.

FAOIN, *a.* Weak; empty; void, vain; idle; lonely; trifling; useless. Faoin, *sloping.—Shaw.* Aisling fhaoin, *an empty dream.—Oss. Tem.* Ur n-achuinge bidh faoin, *your prayers shall be vain.—Sm.* Air nithe faoin, *on trifles.—Id.* Beanntai faoin a dhùcha, *the lonely hills of his country.—Oss Duthona. Com* and *sup* faoine.
Ir. faon. *Lat.* van-us *Arm.* vean, vaen. *Eng* vain.

FAOIN-BHREAGH, *a* Tawdry; foppish.

FAOIN-BHREAGHAS, ais, *s m* Tawdriness; foppishness.

FAOIN-CHOMHRADH, aidh, *s. m* Vain talk, babbling, tattle A seachnadh faoin-chomhradh, *shunning vain talk.—Stew Tim*

FAOIN-DHREUCHD, *s f.* A sinecure *N. pl* faoin-dhreuchdan.

FAOINE, *s f* Vanity; uselessness; idleness.

FAOINEACHD, *s f* Vanity; silliness, idleness; emptiness, vacuity, toying, trifling Luchd faoineachd, *silly people.—Macint.* Clachan na faoineachd, *the stones of emptiness.—Stew Is*

FAOINEADH, idh, *s m.* An indulging or humouring, indulgence.

FAOINEALACH, *a* Foolish, silly, trifling, vain.—*Shaw.* Gu faoinealach, *sillily.*

FAOINEALACHD, *s f* Foolishness, silliness, trifling, vanity.

FAOINEAS, eis, *s m* Vanity; idleness; silliness; vacuity, emptiness; toying, trifling Ri faoineas riu, *trifling with them.—Old Song.*

FAOIN-GHALAR, air, *s m.* Feigned or imaginary sickness

FAOIN-SMUAIN, *s f* A foolish thought, an idle thought, a delusion; a brown study.

FAOISDINN, *s f.* A confession; confessing

FAOISEADH, idh, *s m* Helping, recovering; recovery from sickness; aid.—*Shaw*

FAOISEID, *s. f.* Confession. Written also *faosaid*, which see

FAOISG, *v a* Hull a filbert *Pret. a.* dh' fhaoisg, *hulled; fut. aff. a* faoisgidh, *shall hull*

FAOISGEAG, eig, *s f* A ripe filbert *N pl.* faoisgeagan, *filberts*

FAOISGEAGACH, *a.* Abounding in filberts.

FAOISGNEACH, *a.* Ripe, as a nut; bursting, as a nut, from the husk

FAOISGNEADH, idh, *s m* A bursting from the husk, as a filbert, hulling nuts

† FAOL, *a.* (*Ir id*) Wild.

† FAOL, faoil, *s. m* (*Ir id*) A wolf, *also*, forbearance.

FAOLACH, aich, *s. m.* A bird of prey

FAOLASG, aisg, *s. m* A moor-burning

FAOLCHON, oin, *s m* (*Lat.* falco) A falcon.—*Shaw.*

FAOL-CHU, -choin, *s m* (faol, *wild, and* cù, *dog.*) A wolf; *literally,* a wild dog. *N. pl* faolchoin

FAOL-FHULANG, aing, *s m* A prop

FAOL-SHNAMH, *s m* Swimming

† FAOMH, faoimh, *s m.* Consent, permission

† FAOMH, *v* Assent, consent, permit, bear with

FAONACH, *a.* Mild, meek

FAONDRACH, FAONTRACH, *a.* Wandering, astray, apt to go astray; straggling

FAONDRADH, FAONTRADH, aidh, *s. m.* A wandering; a straying Air faondradh, *astray;* air fhaondradh, *astray,* mar eun air faontradh, *like a wandering bird.—Stew Pro.*

FAOSADH, aidh, *s m.* Protection, relief.—*Shaw.* Collecting

FAOSAID, *s. f.* A confession; avowal; acknowledgment. Cha 'n aideachadh no faosaid, *it is neither acknowledgment nor avowal.—Old Poem.* Dean d' fhaosaid, *confess thyself.*

FAOSAIDEACH, *a.* Confessional.

FAOSGNACH, *a* Auspicious.

FAOSGNADH, aidh, *s. m.* A dropping from the husk, as a filbert; hulling, as of nuts; emerging, as a heavenly body from under a cloud; appearing in the horizon, as the sun. A ghrian a faosgnadh, *the sun appearing.—Macdon.*

FAOTAINN, *s f.* A getting or obtaining; a finding; a receiving.

FAOTAINN, (a), *pr. part.* of faigh. Receiving, getting. See FAIGH

FAOTHACHADH, aidh, *s. m.* A rest, leisure.

FAOTHAID, *s. f.* More commonly written *faoghaid;* which see.

FAR, *prep.* (*prov.* for mar.) With, along with, in company. Co theid far rium? *who will go along with me?—Old Song.*

FAR, *adv* Where. Far am freagair a choille, *where the wood resounds.—Oss. Tem* Cha bhi loinn ach far am bi thu, *there will be no joy but where thou art.—R.*

FARACHAN, aich, *s. m.* (*Ir.* faracha.) A mallet, rammer, or beetle. *N. pl.* farachain.

FARACHDACH, aich, *s. m.* A mallet, a beetle.—*Shaw. N. pl.* farachdaich.

FÀRADH, aidh, *s m.* A ladder. Fàraidh air a chur suas, *a ladder put up.—Stew. Gen.*

FARADH, aidh, *s. m.* A roost; litter in a boat to receive horses or cattle; a freight. Fàradh luing, *a ship's load.*

FARAGAIR, *v n* Welter; flounder, bathe. *Pret. a.* dh' fharagair, *fut aff a* faragairidh, *shall welter.*

FARAGRACH, *a.* Weltering; floundering.

FARAGRADH, aidh, *s m.* A weltering; a floundering; a bathing, a report.

FARAID, *v.* See FARRAID.

FAR-AINM, *s. m.* A nickname.

FAR-AINMEACH, *a* Nicknaming; apt to nickname.

† FARALL, aill, *s m.* (*Ir. id*) A sample or pattern.—*Shaw.*

FARAM, aim, *s m* More properly *farum*, which see.

FARAMACH, *a.* See FARUMACH

† FARAN, ain, *s m* (*Ir id*) Wild garlic; a turtle.

FARAON, *adv.* (*Ir id*) Also, together; in company with; at once. Written also *maraon*, as, far rium, *with me*, is written *mar rium.*

FARASD, FARASDA, *a* (*Ir. id.*) Solemn, soft; composed; mild; easy, sober, solid Gu farasda fòil, *solemnly and softly.—Ull* A sealladh gu farasd, *looking softly.—Oss. Com.*

FARASDACHD, *s f* (*Ir* id.) Solemnity; softness, composedness, mildness; soberness

FAR-BHALACH, aich, *s m.* A stranger.—*Turn. N. pl.* farbhalaich.

FAR-BHALLACH, *a* Having a buttress; like a buttress; of, or belonging to, a buttress or rampart

FAR-BHALLADH, aidh, *s. m* A buttress; a bulwark. *N. pl.* far-bhallachan

FAR-BHEANN, -bheinn, *s f.* A cliffy mountain, a pinnacle; a mountain ridge *N pl* far-bheanntan.

FAR-BHEANNACH, *a.* Cliffy, rocky, pinnacled.

FAR-BHONN, -bhuinn, *s m* The upper sole of a shoe.

FAR-BHUALADH, aidh, *s m* A striking backwards.

FAR-BHUILLE, *s f* A back blow.

FARCAN, ain, *s. m.* Oak.

FAR-CHROICIONN, inn, *s* The epidermis.—*Shaw.*

FAR-CLUAIS, *s. f* A listening, hearkening, overhearing; eaves-dropping

Far-cluaisich, *v. n.* Overhear, listen; eaves-drop, listen under windows.

Fardach, aich, *s. f.* A house, a dwelling; quarters, lodgings. Theid fhardach bun oscionn, *his dwelling shall be overturned.—Sm.* Taobh cùil na fardaich, *the back part of the house.—Old Song.* Fardach oidhche, *a night's lodging. Asp. form*, fhardach. D' fhardach, *thy dwelling.*

Fardal, ail, *s. m.* Hinderance, delay; longing. Obair gun fhardal, *a work without delay.—Macfar.*

Fardalach, *a.* Slow; late; dilatory; obstructing. Gu fardalach, *dilatorily.*

Fàrdan, ain, *s. m.* A farthing.

Fàr-dhorus, uis, *s. m.* (*Ir. id.*) The lintel of a door. *N. pl.* fàrdhorsan.

Fàrdoch, oich, *s. f.* More properly *fardach;* which see.

Far-fhuadachadh, aidh, *s. m.* A banishing; a displacing; ejectment, displacement.

Far-fhuadachadh, (a), *pr. part.* of far-fhuadaich. Banishing; displacing. 'G a fhar-fhuadach' as àite, *banishing him from his place.—Old Song.* 'G a far-fhuadachadh, *banishing her.*

Far-fhuadaich, *v. a.* Banish, displace, drive away by force. *Pret. a.* dh' fhar-fhuadaich, *banished; fut. aff. a.* far-fhuadaichidh, *shall banish; fut. pass.* far-fhuadaichear, *shall be banished.*

Far-fhuadaiche, *s. m.* An exile. *N. pl.* far-fhuadaichean.

Fargradh, aidh, *s. m.* A surmise, a report. Tha fargradh ann, *there is a report, it is reported.*

Farmad, aid, *s. m.* Envy; a grudge. Bha farmad aca ris, *they envied him.—Stew. Gen.* Cuis farmaid, *an object of envy.—Macfar.* Gabh farmad, *envy.*

Farmadach, *a.* Envious; malicious. *Com.* and *sup.* farmadaiche, *more* or *most malicious.* Gu farmadach, *enviously.*

Far-mhaladh, idh, *s. m.* An eyelid. *N. pl.* far-mhalaidhean.

† **Farrach**, aich, *s. m.* (*Ir. id.*) Force, violence, resistance.—*Shaw.*

† **Farradh**, aidh, *s. m.* (*Ir. id.*) Comparison; force; company.

Farraid, *s. f.* A questioning, inquiring; an inquiry. Cha d' thug e farraid orm, *he made no inquiry of me; he did not meddle with me.*

Farraid, *v.* Inquire, ask, question; ask for or after. *Pret. a.* dh' fharraid; *fut. aff. a.* farraididh, *shall inquire.* Farraid dheth, *ask him, inquire of him.*

Farraid, (a), *pr. part.* of farraid. Inquiring, asking for, asking after. C'arson tha thu a farraid mu m' ainm? *why art thou asking after my name?—Stew. Gen.*

Farraideach, *a.* Inquisitive, curious, prying, meddling. *Com.* and *sup.* farraidiche.

Farraideachd, *s. f.* Inquisitiveness, curiousness, a prying habit.

Farran, ain, *s. m.* (*Ir. id.*) Vexation, chagrin, annoyance; anger; *rarely*, force. Mu 'n d' thig farran air eudann, *ere anger fall on his brow.—Oss. Duthona.*

Farranach, *a.* (*from* farran.) Vexatious, provoking, annoying; meddling; vexed. *Com.* and *sup.* farranaiche.

Farranachadh, aidh, *s. m.* A vexing, a provoking, or teasing; provocation, vexation, annoyance.

Farranachadh, (a), *pr. part.* of farranaich. Teasing, provoking, annoying.

Farranaich, *v. a.* Provoke, tease, annoy, pester, gall, exasperate. *Pret. a.* dh' fharranaich, *provoked; fut. aff. a.* farranaichidh, *shall provoke.*

Farranaiche, *com.* and *sup.* of farranach. More or most vexatious.

Farranta, *a.* (*Ir. id.*) Stout, brave, generous. Perhaps *fearanta*, from *fear.*

Farrantachd, *s. f.* Stoutness, bravery, generousness. Perhaps *fearantachd.*

† **Farrantan**, *s. pl.* Tombs.

Farrantas, ais, *s. m.* (*Ir. id.*) Stoutness, manliness, bravery; power; generosity.—*Shaw.*

Farrbhalladh, aidh, *s. m.* See **Farbhalladh.**

Farr-bheann, -bheinn, *s. f.* A cliff, a mountain ridge, a cliffy mountain. Ghealach air farr-bheann a seòladh, *the moon sailing o'er the mountain ridge.—Oss. Gaul.*

Farrbhonn, *s. m.* See **Farbhonn.**

Far ri, *comp. prep.* With, together, in company with. Far rium, *with me;* far riut, *with you;* far rithe, *with her.*

Farsach, aich, *s. m.* A Persian.

Farsaing, Farsuing, *a.* (*Ir.* fairseang.) Wide, spacious, extensive, roomy; liberal, open. Ann an tigh farsaing, *in a wide house.—Stew. Pro.* Talla fursuing, *a spacious hall.—Oss. Tem.* Cridhe farsuing, *a generous* or *open heart.—Old Song.* Gu fad farsuing, *far and wide.*

Farsaingeachd, *s. f.* See **Farsuingeachd.**

Farsuingeachadh, aidh, *s. m.* A widening, an enlarging, enlargement. Cuir am farsaingeachd, *enlarge.—Stew.* 1 *K.*

Farsuingeachd, *s. f.* Width; space; spaciousness; room. Thug e dhuinn farsuingeachd, *he gave us room.—Stew.* 1 *Chr.*

Farsuingich, *v. a.* and *n.* Widen, extend in diameter, enlarge. *Pret. a.* dh' fharsuingich, *enlarged; fut. aff. a.* farsuingichidh, *shall enlarge.—Stew. Job.*

Faruinn, *s. f.* A pinnacle. Farruinn na beinne, *an opening between mountains.*

Faruinn, *comp. pron.;* a *provincial form* of maille ruinn. With us, together with us.

Faruinneag, eig, *s. f.* A lattice. *N. pl.* faruinneagan.

Faruinneagach, *a.* Having lattices.

Farum, uim, *s. m.* A noise; a sound; rustling; report; clangour; clashing. Farum a stàilinn, *the noise of his steel.—Oss. Cathluno.* Farum an duillich sheargta, *the rustling of the withered foliage.—Orr.* Farum nan cruaid, *the clashing of the swords.—Oss. Fing.*

Farumach, *a.* (*from* farum.) Noisy; loud; sonorous; rattling. Gu farumach, *loudly.* Beucadh an cuan gu farumach, *let the sea loudly roar.—Sm.* *Com.* and *sup.* farumaiche.

Farusg, uisg, *s. f.* The inner rind; lees; dregs; one meanly born.

Farusgag, aig, *s. f.* An artichoke.—*Shaw.* *N. pl.* farusgagan.

Farusgagach, *a.* Abounding in artichokes; of artichokes.

Fàs, fàis, *s. m.* (*Ir. id.*) A growing; a becoming; increase; growth. Teachd an fhàis mo dheireadh, *the shooting of the latter growth.—Stew. Amos.* Fas na h-aon oidhche, *a mushroom.*

Fàs, *a.* Empty, void; hollow; waste, desolate; vacant. Fàs ni thu i, *thou shalt make it hollow.—Stew. Ex.* Dean fàs, *lay waste;* rinn mi fàs an sràidean, *I have laid their streets waste.—Stew. Zeph.* Cuir fàs, *lay waste.—Stew. Mic.*

Fas, *v. n.* (*Ir. id.*) Grow; increase; become; rise. *Pret. a.* dh' fhàs, *grew; fut. aff. a.* fàsaidh, *shall grow.* Dh' fhàs e mòr, *he grew tall;* fasadh eunlaith lionmhor, *let fowls become numerous.—Stew. Gen.* Dh' fhàs sleibhte ceò air an lear, *mountains of mist rose on the sea.—Ull.*

Fàs, (a), *p. part.* of fàs. Growing, increasing, becoming. An fhuaim a fàs nan cluas, *the noise increasing in their ears.—Oss. Cathluno.*

FASACH, aich, *s. m.* Stubble.—*Shaw.*

FÀSACH, aich, *s. m.* and *f.*, *from* fàs. (*Ir. id.*) A wilderness, a forest or fastness; solitude. Fàsach falamh, *an empty wilderness.*—*Stew. Deut.* Luchd còmhnuidh na fàsaich, *the dwellers of the desert.*—*Sm.* Faoghaid fàsaich, *a forest hunt.*—*Oss. Com.* Feidh na fasaich, *the forest-deer.*—*Oss. Fin. and Lor.* Fàsach nam frith, *the solitude of the forests.*—*Oss. Fing.* *N. pl.* fàsaichean.

FÀSACHADH, aidh, *s. m.* (*Ir. id.*) A depopulating or laying waste; depopulation.

FASACHADH, aidh, *s. m.* Encumbrance; an encumbering.

FÀSACHADH, (a), *pr. part.* of fasaich. Laying waste. 'G a fàsachadh gu léir, *laying her wholly waste.*—*Sm.*

FASADH, aidh, *s. m.* A protuberance.

FASAICH, *v. a.* Encumber.—*Shaw.* *Pret. a.* dh' fhasaich, *encumbered*; *fut. aff. a.* fasaichidh.

FÀSAICH, *v. a.* Lay waste, depopulate, desolate, destroy. *Pret. a.* dh' fhàsaich, *laid waste*; *fut. aff. a.* fàsaichidh, *shall lay waste.* Fàsaichidh mi, *I will destroy.*—*Stew. Lev. ref.*

FÀSAICHEAR, *fut. pass.* of fasaich. Shall be laid waste.

FÀSAICHTE, *p. part.* of fàsaich. Laid waste, desolated. Ann am bailtibh fàsaichte, *in desolated cities.*—*Stew. Job.*

FÀSAIL, *a.* (fàs-amhuil.) *Ir.* fasamhail. Deserted, desolate, wild, lonely, growing. Aig sruthan fàsail, *beside the lonely streams.*—*Oss.*

FASAIR, fasrach, *s. f.* Harness, equipage. Is olc an t-each nach giùlan fhasair, *he is a bad horse who will not carry his harness.*—*G. P.*

FÀSALACHD, *s. f.* Wasteness, desolation; emptiness; solitude. La fàsalachd, *a day of wasteness.*—*Stew. Zeph.* Fàsalachd, *emptiness.*—*Stew. Is. ref.*

FÀSAM, (*for* fasaidh mi.) I will grow. Also, 1 *sing. imper.* Let me grow.

FÀSAN, ain, *s. m.* Refuse of grain.

FASAN, ain, *s. m.* A fashion or custom, manner, habit. A réir an fhasain, *according to fashion*; anns an fhasan, *in the fashion*; *à-la-mode.*
Teut. fatsoen. *Arm.* feçon. *Fr.* façon.

FASANACH, *a.* Fond of fashion; fashionable. Gu fasanach, *fashionably.* *Com.* and *sup.* fasanaiche.

FASANTA, *a.* Customary; fashionable; in fashion; habitual. Bain-tighearan fhasanta, *a fashionable lady.*—*R.* and *Macfar.*

FASANTACHD, *s. f.* Fashionableness, adherence to fashion.

FÀS-BHEANN, bheinn, *s. f.* A desert hill. Ciob nam fàs-bheann, *the rank grass of the desert hill.*—*Oss.*

FASBHUAIN, *s. f.* (*Ir.* fasbhuin.) Stubble. Mar fhasbhuain, *like stubble.*

FASBHUAINEACH, *a.* Having stubble; having high stubble.

FÀSBHUAINICHE, *s. m.* A stubbler; a creature that grazes among stubble; *also*, a starveling; *in ridicule*, a probationer in the Kirk.

FÀS-CHEILG, *s. f.* Hollow guile; low cunning. Labhair e gun fhàs-cheilg, *he spake without guile.*—*Old Poem.*

FÀS-CHOILLE, *s. f.* (*Ir. id.*) A young grove; a young wood; a grove or wood in the first few years of its growth: hence the name of the romantic seat of the chief of the Butters, on the banks of the Tumel, in Perthshire. *N. pl.* fàs-choilltean.

FASEACH, *adv.* Individually, by turns, alternately. Ceòl is cuilm fa seach, *music and feasting by turns.*—*Oss. Cathluno.*

FASG, aisg, *s. m.* A prison; a band.

FASGA, FASGADH, aidh, *s. m.* (*Ir. id.*) A shelter, refuge, protection; a shadow; sparks from red-hot iron. Fasga na daraig, *the shelter of the oak.*—*Ull.* A dhith fasgaidh, *for want of shelter.*—*Stew. Job.* Taobh an fhasgaidh, *a lee side.*

FASGACH, *a.* Calm; sheltered; affording shelter; screening. Is fasgach do chùilidh, *calm are thy recesses.*—*Old Song.*

FÀSGADAIR, *s. m.* A cheese-press. Fasgadair càise, *a cheese-press.*

FASGADAIR, *s. m.* A Lewis-bird, about the size of a gull. It flies with great velocity. When it observes the smaller birds with food in their bills, it immediately pursues them so closely as to compel them to drop whatever they have, which it catches easily before it touches the ground.

FASGADAN, ain, *s. m.* (*Ir. id.*) A umbrella; a shade; a parasol. *N. pl.* fasgadain.

FASGADH, aidh, *s. m.* See FASGA.

FÀSGADH, aidh, *s. m.* A wringing; a pressing, a squeezing. Fàsgadh na sròin, *a wringing of the nose.*—*Stew. Pro.* Gu sinneachan fhàsgadh, *to press the teat.*—*Old Song.* An ni nach gabh nigheadh cha ghabh e fàsgadh, *what will not wash will not wring.*—*G. P.*

FASGADH, (a), *pr. part.* of fàisg. Wringing, squeezing, pressing.

FASGADHACH, *a.* Sheltering, protecting. Creug fasgadhach, *a sheltering rock.*—*Old Song.*

FASGAICH, *v. a.* Shelter; embower. *Pret. a.* dh' fhasgaich, *fut. aff.* fasgaichidh.

FASGAIDH, *a.* Sheltered; calm.

FASGAIN, *v. a.* Winnow; sift. *Pret. a.* dh' fhasgain, *winnowed.* A dh' fhasgnadh nan cinneach, *to winnow the nations.*—*Stew. Is.*

FASGAINTE, *p. part.* of fasgain. Winnowed; sifted.

FASGAIR, *s. m.* A jailor.

FASGAN, ain, *s. m.* A winnow; a sieve; a muscle.—*Shaw.* *N. pl.* fasgain. Fasgan an diomhanais, *the sieve of vanity.*—*Stew. Is.*

FÀS-GHLEANN, -ghlinn, *s. f.* A desert valley; a lonely glen. Feidh nam fàs-ghleann, *the deer of the desert hill.*—*Oss. Com.* *N. pl.* fàs-ghleanntan.

FASGNADH, aidh, *s. m.* A winnowing. Inneal fasgnaidh, *a fan*; *a winnow*; *a winnowing machine.*—*Stew. O. T.*

FASGNADH, (a), *pr. part.* of fasgain. Winnowing; sifting. A fasgnadh eorna, *winnowing barley.*—*Stew. O. T.*

FA-SGRIOBHADH, aidh, *s. m.* An appendix.

FASLACH, aich, *s. m.* A void, space, a vacuity, a vacuum; an interstice; instigation. *N. pl.* faslaich, *vacuities.*

† FASLAIRT, *s.* Encampment.—*Shaw.*

FÀS-LOMAIRT, *s. f.* An expeditious method of cooking victuals in the stomach of an animal, once practised by the Gael.

FÀSMHOIRE, *com.* and *sup.* of fàsmhor. More or most desolate.

FÀSMHOR, *a.* Lonely, solitary, desolate, desert, waste; vegetative. *Com.* and *sup.* fàsmhoire. Gu fàsmhor, *desolately.*

FASNAG, aig, *s. f.* A winnow.—*Shaw.* A pimple.

FASRADH, aidh, *s. m.* Harness.

FASTACHADH, aidh, *s. m.* A stopping, a binding, making fast or secure; a seizing or apprehending; a stoppage, a seizure.

FASTADH, aidh, *s. m.* A binding, a seizing, a securing.

FASTAICH, *v. a.* (*Swed.* fasta.) Bind, secure, make fast. *Pret. a.* dh' fhastaich, *bound*; *fut. aff. a.* fastaichidh, *shall bind.*

FASTAICHTE, *p. part.* of fastaich. Bound, secured, made fast.

FASTAIDH, *v. a.* More frequently written *fastaich.*

FÀTH, *s. m.* (*Ir. id.*) A cause, a reason, occasion; opportunity; ambush; *rarely*, skill; a poem; field; heat; breath. Fàth iongantais, *a cause of wonder.*—*Sm.* Fàth airson fala, *opportunity for bloodshed.*—*Stew. Mic.* A feitheamh am fàth, *lying in ambush.*—*Stew. Pro.*

† **Fathach**, aich, *s. m.* Prudence, knowledge.—*Shaw.*

Fathach, aich, *s. m.* A giant. Written more frequently *athach.*

Fathan, ain, *s. m.* A journey.—*Shaw.* Coltsfoot.

Fathàs, ais, *s. m.* Skill; poetry; prudence.

Fathast, *adv.* (*Swed.* fast, *though.*) Yet, still, notwithstanding. Is aoibhinn leam fathast d' fhuaim, *thy sound is still pleasant to me.*—*Oss. Gaul.* Dh' fhan e fathast seachd lathan, *he stayed yet seven days.*—*Stew. Gen.* 'N ann fathast? *do you still persist? still?*

Fath-dhorus, uis, *s. m.* A small door, a wicket.—*Macd.* and *Shaw.* *N. pl.* fath-dhorsan.

Fath-fhaim, *s. f.* The hem of a garment.—*Shaw.* More frequently written *faim.*

Fath-fheith, *v.* Belay, lie in wait, ensnare. *Pret. a.* dh' fhath-fheith.

Fath-fheitheamh, imh, *s. m.* An ambuscade.

Fath-oide, *s.* A schoolmaster, an usher, a teacher.—*Shaw.*

Fath-sgriobh, *v. a.* Subjoin; write, as a postscript or appendix.

Fath-sgriobhadh, aidh, *s. m.* An appendix, a postscript.

Fa thuaiream, *comp. prep.* About; towards.

Fathunn, uinn, *s. m.* A report, news, rumour.

Fathur, uir, *s. m.* A report, a rumour, news.

Fè, *a.* Wild, inconsistent, in a frenzy. When a person acts with unusual wildness or inconsistency, he is said to be *fè*, or under the dominion of fairies. In this meaning, it seems to have been borrowed from the Scotch.

Fè, *s.* A calm tranquillity; a gentle breeze; a quagmire; a vein; a sinew; *rarely*, a measuring-rod; a park; a fold; a hedge. Tha 'n oidhche na fè, *the night is calm.*—*Oss.* Fè na fairge, *the calm surface of the sea.*—*Oss. Taura.* Tra thig am fè, *when the calm shall come.*—*Oss. Gaul.* Fè fairge, *a calm at sea.*

† **Feabh**, *s. f.* (*Ir. id.*) A conflict; a storm; means; power; faculty.

Feabhas, ais, *s. m.* (*Ir. id.*) Improvement, goodness, excellence; *also*, better, best. Feabhas d' ùr-labhraidh, *the excellence of thine eloquence.*—*Old Poem.* A dol am feabhas, *improving.* Feabhas, *decency, beauty, comeliness.*—*Shaw.* Is e sin 'fheabhas, *that is in what it is excellent.* Da 'fheabhas, *however good he be.*—*Stew. Ps.*

Feabhradh, aidh, *s. m.* (*Ir.* feabhra.) February. *Feabhradh* is perhaps *feabh-thrath*, the stormy or windy season.

Feabhsach, *a.* Cunning, skilful.—*Shaw.*

† **Feach**, *s.* (*Ir. id.*) A journey; a spade; the handle of a spade.

Feach, *v.* See **Feuch**.

Feachadh, aidh, *s. m.* A spade; a mattock; a pickaxe.

Feachainn, *s.* See **Feuchainn**.

Feachd, *s. m.* and *f.* (*Sax.* feachtan, *fight. Ir.* feachd.) An army, a host, forces; a curve, a bend; cramp; *rarely*, deeds. Ann lathaibh cath is feachd, *in the days of battle and of armies.*—*Sm.* Feachd nan sonn, *a host of heroes.*—*Oss. Carricth.* Feachd, *danger; journey; alternative.*—*Shaw.* Feach-mharasgal, *a field-marshal.*

Feachd, *v. a.* and *n.* (*Ir. id.*) Bend, bow; yield; swerve. *Pret. a.* dh' fheachd, *bowed; fut. aff. a.* feachdaidh, *shall bow.* Ceannard nach gabhadh feachd, *a chief who could not be made to bend* or *yield.*—*Macint.* Esan a dh' fheachd o'n chòir, *he who swerved from the right.*—*Mac Lach.*

Feachdach, *a.* Crooked, bent; pliable; having armies.

Feachdadh, aidh, *s. m.* (*Ir. id.*) A bending, a bowing; a bend or curve.

Feachdair, *s. m.* (*Scotch*, feachtar.) A warrior. *N. pl.* feachdairean.

Feachd-mharasgal, ail, *s. m.* A field-marshal. *N. pl.* feachd-mharasgalan.

† **Feachdnach**, aich, *s. m.* Prosperity; manhood.

Feachdta, *a.* Crooked, bent.

Fead, *s. f.* (*Ir. id.*) A whistle, a shrill voice; a hiss; a bustle; a blow; *rarely*, a bulrush; a fathom; an island. Fead an aonaich, *the whistle* [*of the wind*] *on the heath.*—*Oss.* Bha fead san t-sìne aig fholt, *his hair whistled in the blast.*—*Oss. Duthona.* Fead san leth-cheann, *a blow on the cheek.* Dean fead, *whistle.* Ni e fead, *he will whistle.*—*Stew. Is.*

† **Fead**, *v. a.* (*Ir. id.*) Tell, relate.—*Shaw.*

Fead, *v. n.* (*Ir. id.*) Whistle; hiss. *Pret. a.* dh' fhead, *whistled; fut. aff. a.* feadaidh, *shall whistle.* Feadaidh e, *he will hiss.*—*Stew.* 1 *K. ref.*

Feada-coille, *s. f.* Wood-sorrel, wild sorrel. Feada-coille nan còs, *the wild sorrel of the caverns.*—*Macdon.* Feada-coille, *bulrushes.*—*Shaw.*

Feadadh, aidh, *s. m.* A whistling; a relation; a rehearsal.—*Shaw.*

Feadag, aig, *s. f.* (*Ir.* fideog.) A fife or flute, a flageolet; a whistle; a plover; the third week of February. *N. pl.* feadagan. Le feadagaibh, *with flutes.*—*Stew. Ex. ref.* Binn fheadag is coileach ruadh, *the shrill plover and grouse cock.*—*Old Song.* Cha tugainn feadag ort, *I do not care a rush for you.*

Feadaidh, *fut. aff. a.* of fead. Shall or will whistle.

Feadail, *s. f.* A whistling; a hissing.

Feadail, (a), *pr. part.* of fead. Whistling; hissing. Ogan a feadail sa mhagh, *a youth whistling on the plain.*—*Oss. Derm.*

Féadail, *s. f.* (*Ir. id.*) Cattle.

Feadailich, *s. f.* Whistling, continued whistling.

Feadain, *gen. sing.* and *n. pl.* of feadan.

Feadain, *v. n.* Pipe, whistle. *Pret. a.* dh' fheadain, *piped.*

Feadaireachd, *s. f.* (*from* fead.) Whistling; the habit of whistling. Thoisich e air feadaireachd, *he began to whistle.*

Feadan, ain, *s. m.* (*Ir. id.*) A flageolet; a reed; an oaten pipe; a flute; the chaunter of a bag-pipe; a pipe; a spout; a hollow place through which the wind eddies; a canal. Ceòl an fheadain tlà, *the music of the soft reed.*—*Old Song.* Seachd feadain, *seven pipes.*—*Stew. Zech.* Feadan uisge, *a water-pipe, a water-spout.*

Feadanach, *a.* Like a flageolet or pipe; like a water-pipe.

Feadanachd, *s. f.* Playing on a flageolet or pipe.

Feadanaiche, *s. m.* (*from* feadan.) *Ir.* feadanach. One who plays on a flute or flageolet; a chaunter, a piper.

Feadan-uisge, *s. m.* A water-spout, a water-pipe, a gutter. Fuaimneach d' fheadain-uisge, *the noise of thy water-spouts.*—*Sm.*

Feadar, air, *s. m.* A pass.

Feadaran, ain, *s. m.* Mirth.

Fead-ghoile, *s.* A noise often heard in the belly of horses when trotting.

Fead-ghuil, *s.* (*Ir. id.*) Lamentation.

Feadh, *s. m.* (*Ir. id.*) Extent.

Feadh, *prep.* Among, amid, during, through. Feadh gach re, *for evermore.*—*Sm.* Feadh gach linn, *through every age.*—*Id.* Feadh ghleanntaidh fàsail, *among desert valleys.*—*Oss. Duthona.*

Feadh, (air), *comp. prep.* Among, amid, during, through, throughout. Air feadh an lagh, *during the day.*—*Sm.* Air feadh gach tìre, *through every country.*—*Stew. Rom.*

Feadh, (am), *adv.* While, whilst, so long as. Am feadh a bha e beo, *whilst he was alive.*—*Sm.* An fheadh 's a mhaireas an ruaig, *so long as chase lasts.*—*Oss. Fing.*

Feadhachan, ain, *s. m.* A gentle breeze, a breath of wind. Written also *feochan*.

Feadhainn, *s. pl.* (*Ir.* feadhan.) People, folk, a company, a band of people, a grop of individual objects of any description. Is truagh nach mair d' fheadhainn! *alas, that thy people are no more!—Old Song.*

Feadhaireachd, *s. f.* A gift, a present.—*Shaw.*

Feadhaireachd, *s. f.* Strolling, sauntering, idling.

Feadhair, *a.* Wild, savage.

Feadhanach, aich, *s. m.* A soft breeze, a breath of wind. Feadhanach gaoithe, *a soft breeze.—Macd.*

Feadhmach, *a.* Powerful.—*Shaw.* Gu feadhmach, *powerfully.*

Feadhmach, aich, *s. m.* (*Ir. id.*) A governor, an overseer; a steward; a bailiff.

Feadhmanta, *a.* (*Ir. id.*) Official.

Feadhmantas, ais, *s. m.* (*Ir. id.*) Superintendence, overseeing, stewardship.

Feadhna, *s. m.* (*Ir. id.*) A commander, a chief, a captain.

Feag, *s. f.* A notch, a slit, a gap; *rarely,* a tooth; offence.

Feagamh, *adv.* Perhaps. More commonly written *theagamh.*

Feagh, feagha, *s. f.* A fathom.

Feairrd, *s. f.* Improvement, growing better. A dol am feairrde, *growing better and better, convalescent. Feairrd* is also used as a comparative, signifying *better.* Is feairrd mi so, *I am the better for this.*

Some have called this word a second comparative; perhaps they would have expressed its nature better had they called it a comparative noun.

Fealan, ain, *s. m.* A flesh-worm; itch; a furuncle, a bile. Duine aig am bheil am fealan, *a man who has the itch.—Stew. Lev. ref.*

Fealanach, *a.* Affected with itch; full of flesh-worms; like a flesh-worm.

Fealcaidh, *a.* (*Ir. id.*) Harsh, austere; knavish, deceitful.—*Shaw.*

Fealcaidheachd, *s. f.* (*Ir. id.*) Harshness, austerity; knavishness, deceitfulness.—*Shaw.*

Fealcaidheas, is, *s. m.* (*Ir. id.*) A debate, a dispute.

Feal-dhà, *s. f.* Fun, sport, jest. Ri feal-dhà, *jesting, in fun.* Written also *fal-dha;* which see.

Feall, feill, *s. m.* (*Ir. id.*) Treason; deceit, guile, falsehood, trickery. Fhir gun fheall! *thou guileless man!—Old Song.* Ri feall, *practising guile.*

Feall, *v. a.* Deceive, impose on. *Pret. a.* dh' fheall; *fut. aff. a.* feallaidh; *fut. pass.* feallar, *shall be deceived.* Dia nach feallar le breige, *a God who cannot be deceived by falsehood.—Mac Lach.*

Feallair, *s. m.* (feall-fhear.) A deceiver, a traitor, a liar. *N. pl.* feallairean.

Feallaireachd, *s. f.* A deceiving, deceitfulness; falsehood.

Feallan, ain, *s. m.* A felon; a nescock.—*Shaw. N. pl.* feallain.

Feall-dhuine, *s. m.* A deceiver, a traitor. *N. pl.* fheall-dhaoine.

Feall-fheitheamh, eimh, *s. m.* A lying in wait; an ambush; an ambuscade. Ri feall-fheitheamh, *lying in wait.*

Feall-fholach, aich, *s. f.* Ambuscade, ambush, lying in wait. Ni sibh feall-fholach, *you shall lie in wait.—Stew. Jos.* Luchd na feall-fholach, *the liers in wait.—Id.*

Feall-fholaich, *v. n.* Lie in wait.

Feall-ghniomh, *s. f.* A treacherous deed, a trick, a swindle. *N. pl.* feall-ghniomharan, *tricks.*

Feall-ghniomhach, *a.* Base in action, swindling, cheating.

Feall-innleachd, *s. f.* Deceit, guile; a snare.—*Turn.*

Feall-mhac, -mhic, *s. m.* A learned man, a scholar.—*Shaw. N. pl.* feall-mhic.

Feall-mhiann, *s. m.* A conspiracy; a deceitful intention.

Feallsadh, aidh, *s. m.* (*Ir.* fealsa.) Philosophy; learning; literature.

Feallsanach, aich, *s. m.* (*Ir.* fealsamhnach.) A philosopher. *N. pl.* feallsanaich.

Feallsanachd, *s. f.* (*Ir.* fealsamhnachd.) Philosophy; learning; literature. Trid fheallsanachd dhiomhain, *through vain philosophy.—Stew. Col.*

Fealltach, *a.* Treasonable, treacherous, deceitful, false. Gu fealltach, *treacherously.—Stew. Hos.* Daoine fealltach, *treacherous men, traitors.—Stew. Zeph. and Tim. Com.* and *sup.* fealltaiche.

Fealltachd, *s. f.* (*from* feall.) Treason, treacherousness, deceitfulness.

Fealltail, *a.* (feallt-amhuill.) *Ir.* fealtamhail. Traiterous, treacherous, deceitful.

Fealltair, *s. m.* (*from* feall.) *Ir.* fealtoir. A traitor; a rogue; a deceiver. *N. pl.* fealtairean, *deceivers.—Stew. Pro.*

Fealltaireachd, *s. f.* The conduct of a traitor; roguery, villainy, deceitfulness.

Feam, feama, *s. m.* A tail; the rump of a bird or beast.—*Macd.*

Feamach, *a.* Gross; dirty; silly; superfluous; having a large rump.—*Shaw.*

Feamachas, ais, *s. m* Grossness; dirtiness; silliness; superfluousness.

Feamain, *gen. sing.* and *n. pl.* of feaman.

Feamain, **Feamainn**, *s. f.* (*Ir.* feamuin.) Sea-weed; kali; bladder-wort. Anns an fheamainn, *in the sea-weed.—Stew. Jon.*

Feamaineach, *a.* Abounding in sea-weed; like sea-weed.

Feaman, ain, *s. m.* (*dim.* of feam.) A tail; a rump.—*Macint.*

Feamanach, *a.* Tailed; having a long tail; having a large rump.

Feamanach, aich, *s. f.* A quantity of sea-weed or dilse; sea-ore.

Feana, **Feanadh**, aidh, *s.* A chariot or car; a cart. Written also *feun.*

Feanachas, ais, *s. f.* Genealogy.

Feann, *s.* The hair of a quadruped. See **Fionn**.

Feann, *v. a.* Flay; skin, as a sheep. *Pret. a.* dh' fheann; *fut. aff. a.* feannaidh. Written also *fionn.*

Feannach, *a.* Rough; hairy, as a quadruped.

Feannadh, aidh, *s. m.* A flaying, a skinning.

Feannadh, (a), *pr. part.* of feann.

Feannag, aig, *s. f.* (*Ir.* feannog.) A rook; a hooded crow; a carrion-crow; a royston-crow; a whiting. Feannag ghlas, *a carrion-crow. N. pl.* feannagan.

Feannaidh, *fut. aff. a.* Shall or will fly.

Feannar, *fut. pass.* of feann. Shall or will be flayed or skinned.

Feannar, *a.* (feann-fhuar.) Cold, cool, chill. Written also *fionnar.*

Feannarachd, *s. f.* Atmospheric coolness; chillness. See also **Fionnarachd**.

FEANNARAICH, *v. a.* Cool. *Pret. a.* dh' fheannaraich, *cooled.* See also FIONNARAICH.

FEANNDAG, aig, *s. f.* A nettle. Feanndag ghreugach, *fenugreek.*—*Shaw.* *Feanndag* is more commonly written *ionndag* or *ionntag.*

FEANNSAIR, *s. m.* A fencer, a sword-player.

FEANNSAIREACHD, *s. f.* Fencing or sword-playing.

FEAR, fir, *s. m.* (*Lat.* vir. *Shans.* vir. *Heb.* fir *and* fear. *Ir.* fear.) *N. pl.* fir. A man; a husband; an individual; one. Am fear mòr, *the great man,*—a name given to Fingall by his contemporary poets. Cath an fhir mhòir, *the hero's battle.*—*Ull.* Fear dhiubh, *one of them.*—*Stew. Lev.* An torc a lot t-fhear, *the boar that wounded thy husband;* fear aiseig, *a ferryman;* fear-bainnse, *a bridegroom;* fear amhairc, *an overseer, a scout;* fear-ain-cheirt, *a buffoon, a droll,* or *puppet;* fear an tighe, *the good man,* or *landlord.*—*Stew. Pro.* Fear astair, *a traveller;* fear-bogha, *an archer;* fear brataich, *a standard-bearer.*—*Shaw.* Fear ceaird, *a tradesman;* fear-cheistean, *a catechist;* fear ciùil, *a musician, a minstrel.*—*Stew.* 2 *K.* Fear cuiridh, *an inviter.*—*Shaw.* Fear cùirn, *an outlaw.*—*Id.* Fear cluig, *a bellman;* fear-cuidich, *a helper;* fear-cuideachd, *a jovial companion;* fear-cul-chainidh, *a slanderer;* fear cumaidh, *a former, a framer;* fear dàin, *a poet;* fear-faire, *a sentinel, a watchman;* fear faire-cluais, *an eaves-dropper.*—*Shaw.* Fear faire na h-aon sùl, *a certain character in Highland tales;* fear feòirne, *a chessman;* fear fuadain, *a straggler;* fear-foirneirt, *an oppressor, a robber.*—*Shaw.* Fear gleidhidh, *a keeper;* fear-iasachd, *a borrower.*—*Id.* Fear iomchair, *a bearer;* fear-innleachd, *an engineer; an ingenious person;* fear-lagha, *a lawyer;* fear-labhairt, *a speaker, a spokesman;* fear nuadh-posda, *a bridegroom;* fear-réite, *a reconciler;* fear-riaghlaidh, *a ruler, governor, overseer;* fear-saoraidh, *a saviour;* am Fear-Saoraidh, *the Redeemer.*—*Stew. Rom.* Fear sùilbheachd, *an overseer.*—*Pro. ref.* Fear siubhail, *a traveller;* fear seòlaidh, *a guide, a director, a steerer.*—*Stew. Pro.* Fear suiridh, *a courter, a wooer.*

FEARACH, *s.* A war-cry among the ancient Irish.

FEARACHAS, ais, *s. m.* Manhood, manliness, courage; a trial of manhood; *membrum virile.* Mar leomhann le fearachas, *like a lion for boldness.*—*Macint.* Fearachas tighe, *husbandry.*—*Shaw.*

FEARACHD, *s.* (*from* fear.) Manliness, manhood, strength, power.

FEARAID, *s. f.* A ferret.—*Macd.* *N. pl.* fearaidean.

FEARAIL, *a.* (fear-amhuil.) *Ir.* fearamhail. Manly, courageous. Gu fearail, *courageously.*

FEAR-AINCHEIRT, *s. m.* A buffoon, a droll, a puppet.

FEARAINN, *gen. sing.* of fearann.

FEARALACHD, *s. f.* (*from* fearail.) *Ir.* fearamhlachd. Manliness.—*Macint.*

FEARALAS, ais, *s. m.* Manliness.

FEAR-AMHAIRC, *s. m.* A scout; an overseer. Fir-amhairc, *overseers.*—*Stew. Pro.*

FEARAN, ain, *s. m.* Cives; wild garlic; a ring-dove.—*Shaw.* Fearan eidheann, *a turtle-dove.*—*Id.*

† **FEARANDA**, *s. m.* (*Ir. id.*) A countryman; a boor; a farmer.—*Shaw.*

FEARANN, ainn, *s. m.* (*Ir. id.*) A farm; land, ground; country; earth; land, in contradistinction to water. Deagh fhearann, *a good farm.* Ann am fearann fàs, *in a desert land.*—*Stew. Deut.* Fearann comhrainn, *suburbs.*—*Stew.* 1 *K.* Fearann aillidh na h-Eirin, *the fair country of Ireland.*—*Old Poem.* Am fearann tioram, *the dry land;* fearann bàn, *lay ground;* fearann treabhaidh, *arable ground.*

Fearann seems to be *fear-fhonn*, i. e. the ground or land assigned to one man for cultivation; in process of time, it came to signify land in general.

FEAR-AN-TIGHE, *s. m.* The landlord; the good man.—*Stew. Pro.* Fear tighe, *a landlord.*

FEARASAIR, *s. m.* (*Ir.* fearasoir.) A mimic, an imitator.

FEARASAIREACHD, *s. f.* Mimicry.

FEARAS-BHOGHA, *s. m.* Archery.

FEARAS-CHUIDHEACHD, *s. f.* Sport, fun, jocality. Ri fearas-chuideachd, *in sport.*—*Stew. Pro.* Rinn e fearas-chuideachd, *he made sport.*—*Stew. Jud.*

FEAR-ASTAIR, *s. m.* A traveller, a pedestrian.

† **FEARB**, *s. f.* A cow; an excrescence; a pimple; goodness.—*Ir.*

† **FEARB**, *s. f.* (*Lat.* verbum. *Ir. id.*) A word.

FEAR-BAINNSE, *s. m.* A bridegroom. Fear na bainnse, *the bridegroom.*

FEARBAN, ain, *s. m.* (*Ir. id.*) The herb crowfoot.

† **FEARBHOLG**, uilg, *s. m.* A scabbard, sheath; a budget; *also,* one of the British Belgæ.

FEAR-BOGHA, *s. m.* A bowman or archer.

FEAR-BRATAICH, *s. m.* A standard-bearer. *N. pl.* fir-brataich.

FEAR-CEAIRD, *s. m.* A tradesman; a mechanic; an artificer.

FEARCHUR, *s. m.* A champion. Perhaps, *fear churaidh.* From *fearchur* comes the Scotch name *Ferchar,* and the surname *Mac Fhearchuir,* i. e. *Mac Kercher.*

FEAR-CHEISTEAN, *s. m.* A catechist. *N. pl.* fir-cheistean, *catechists.*

FEAR-CIÙIL, *s. m.* A musician, a minstrel.—*Stew.* 2 *K.*

FEAR-CLUIG, *s. m.* A bellman.

FEAR-CRIOCHNAICH, *s. m.* A finisher.—*Stew. Heb.*

FEAR-CUIDEACHD, *s. m.* A jovial companion, a bottle companion.

FEAR-CUIDICH, *s. m.* A helper, an assistant.

FEAR-CUIRIDH, *s. m.* An inviter.—*Shaw.*

FEAR-CÙIRN, *s. m.* An outlaw.

For the reason why *fear-cùirn* means an *outlaw,* see CARN.

FEAR-CULCHAINIDH, *s. m.* A slanderer.

FEAR-CUMAIDH, *s. m.* A former, a framer, a shaper.—*Stew. Jer.*

FEAR-DÀIN, *s. m.* A poet; a rehearser of poetry.

FEARDHA, *a., from* fear. (*Ir. id.*) Brave; powerful; manly; male. Clann feardha tapaidh, *a brave and active clan.*—*Macdon.*

FEARDHACHD, *s. f.* Bravery; manliness; manhood.

FEAR-EADRAIGINN, *s. m.* A go-between; a reconciler.—*Stew. Job. ref.*

FEAR-FAIRE, *s. m.* A watchman; a sentinel.

FEAR-FAIRE-CLUAIS, *s. m.* An eaves-dropper.—*Shaw.*

FEAR-FEOIRNE, *s. m.* A chessman.

FEAR-FOIRNEIRT, *s. m.* An oppressor, a violator, a robber.

FEAR-FUADAIN, *s. m.* A straggler; a wanderer; a vagabond; an exile.—*Stew. Gen.*

FEARG, feirg, *s. m.* (*Ir. id.*) Anger, wrath, rage; displeasure; irritation; a champion. Fearg dhoinionnach, *stormy wrath.*—*Sm.* A cur feirg air, *making him angry, irritating him.* Fearg, *a champion, a warrior.*—*Shaw.*

FEARG, *v. a.* Irritate, provoke, incite. *Pret. a.* dh' fhearg, *irritated; fut. aff. a.* feargaidh, *shall irritate.*

FEARGACH, *a., from* fearg. (*Ir. id.*). Angry, passionate, irritated, raging; enraged; causing irritation. Duine feargach, *a passionate man.*—*Stew. Pro.* An da righ feargach, *the two princes in a rage.*—*Oss. Com.* San doininn fheirgich, *in the raging storm.*—*Ull. Com.* and *sup.* feargaiche.

Feargachadh, aidh, *s. m.* An irritating or making angry; an irritating, as of an ulcer; irritation.

Feargachd, *s. f.* Irritableness; tending to irritate; anger, passion, irritation.

Feargaich, *v. a.* (*from* fearg.) Irritate, vex, enrage; fret. *Pret. a.* dh'fheargaich; *fut. aff. a.* feargaichidh, *shall irritate.*

Fear-gleidhidh, *s. m.* A keeper.—*Stew. Gen.*

Fear-iasachd, *s. m.* A borrower.—*Shaw.*

Fear-innleachd, **Fear-inntleachd**, *s. m.* An engineer; an ingenious person.

Fear-iomchair, *s. m.* A bearer; a porter.

Fear-labhairt, *s. m.* A speaker, a spokesman.

Fear-lagha, *s. m.* A lawyer.

Fear-laoidh, *s. m.* A hymnist.

Fearn, *gen.* fearna, *or* feairn, *s. m.* (*Ir. id.*) An elder-tree; elder-wood; a shield; a mast; *Ferns*, a bishop's see in Ireland; *also*, the sixth letter of the Gaelic alphabet. Cabar fearna, *a rung of elder.—Macint.* Leis am bristear gach fearn, *by whom every shield shall be broken.—Fingalian Poem.*

Fearnach, *a.* (*from* fearn.) Abounding in elder; made of elder.

Fearnaidh, *a.* Masculine.—*Shaw.*

Fear-nuadh-posda, *s. m.* A bridegroom, a newly married man.

Fear-pòsda, *a.* A married man, a husband.—*Stew. Exod.*

Fear-ogha, *s. m.* A grandson.

Fear-réite, *s. m.* A reconciler.—*Stew. Job.*

Fearr, *com.* and *sup.* of maith. Better; best; preferable. *Asp. form*, fhearr. Is fhearr dhuit falbh, *you had better be going;* an fhearr dhomh a dheanamh? is fhear, *had I better do it? yes.*

Fearrad, aid, *s. m.*, a *comparative noun.* Improvement; amelioration; convalescence. A dol am fearrad, *growing better and better.*

Fearrasaid, *s. f.* A loose garment or wrapper, once much worn by the Gaelic women; *also*, a spindle; a wallet; a cubit. A fearrasaid 'g a falach, *her garment hiding it.—Oss. Derm.*

Fear-rùin, *s. m.* A confidant.

† **Fearsa**, ai, *s. m.* (*Lat.* versus. *Ir. id.*) Verse.

Fearsaid, *s. f.* A spindle or whirl.—*Macd.* Fearsaid na laimh, *one of the bones of the cubit, by anatomists called* ulna.

† **Fearsan**, ain, *s. m.* (*dim.* of fearsa.) A little verse.

Fear-saoraidh, *s. m.* A saviour, a deliverer. Am Fear Saoraidh, *the Saviour.—Stew. Rom.*

Fear-saruchaidh, *s. m.* An oppressor. A laimh an fhir-shàruchaidh, *from the hands of the oppressor.—Stew. Jer.*

† **Fearsda**, *s. m.* (*Ir. id.*) A pool, standing water.

Fear-seòlaidh, *s. m.* A guide, a director.—*Stew. Pro.* A steersman.

Fear-shionn, *a.;* more properly *feur-shionn;* which see.

Fear-siubhail, *s. m.* A traveller.

Fear-sùilbheachd, *s. m.* An overseer.—*Pro. ref.*

Fear-suiridh, *s. m.* A wooer.

Feart, feirt, *s. m.* (*Ir. id. Lat.* virt-us.) Virtue; quality; attribute; a good act; a miracle; forces; a host; a grave; a tomb; country; land. Le feart do fhrasaibh blath, *by the virtue of thy warm showers.—Macfar. N. pl.* feartan, *virtues.* Feartan buairidh, *tempting qualities.—Mac Lach.* Righ Shelma le feart, *Selma's king with his forces.*—Feart, *virtue*, seems to be derived from *fear*, in the same way as *virtus* is derived from *vir.*

Feartach, *a.* (*from* feart.) Virtuous; valorous; renowned; powerful; substantial; having forces. A righ fheartaich! *thou valorous king!—Old Song.* Toradh feartach, *a substantial crop.—Macfar. Com.* and *sup.* feartaiche.

Feartail, *a.* (feart-amhuil.) Valorous; having virtue; miraculous; wonder-working.

† **Feartaille**, *s. f.* (*Ir. id.*) A funeral oration.—*Shaw.*

Feartan, *n. pl.* of feart; which see.

Feartas, ais, *s. m.* Manly conduct, behaviour which becomes a man.

Feartas is derived from fear, *man;* and the *virtus* of the Latins, from *vir*, is but another form of it.

Fear-togalach, *s. m.* A bearer; an uplifter. Fear togalach mo chinn, *the uplifter of my head.—Sm.*

Feart-mholadh, aidh, *s. m.* A funeral oration; a panegyric.—*Shaw.*

Fear-uighe, *s. m.* A traveller; a pedestrian.

Feasag, aig, *s. f.* See **Feusag**.

Feasd, (am), *adv.* (*Ir. id.*) Ever; for ever; never. An do sguir a ghràs am feasd? *has his grace ceased for ever?—Sm.*

Feasdrach, aich, *s. m.* A muzzle; a bridle-bit.

Feasgal, ail, *s. m.* A Fiscal solicitor. Feasgal an righ, *the king's solicitor.—Macd.*

Feasgalaiche, *s. m.* (*Ir.* feasgalaidhe.) A herald.

Feasgar, air, *s. m.* (*Lat.* vesper. *Ir.* feascor.) Evening. Air feasgar, *on an evening.—Stew. Gen.* Beul an fheasgair, *evening twilight.*

Feasgarach, *a.* (*Ir.* feascrach.) Vespereal; late; nocturnal.

Feasgar-luch, *s. m.* (*Ir. id.*) A dormouse; a field-mouse; a cockchafer; a beetle.

† **Feath**, *s. m.* (*Ir. id.*) Learning, science, knowledge.

Fèath, *s. m.* A calm; tranquillity; a bog; a marsh; a vein; a sinew.—*Shaw.*

Fèathail, *a.* (feath amhuil.) Quiet, calm, tranquil.—*Shaw.*

† **Feathal**, ail, *s. m.* (*Ir. id.*) A face; a countenance; a cup; a bowl.—*Shaw.*

Feathan, ain, *s. m.* Fur; hair.—*Shaw.*

Feathanach, *a.* Having fur; hairy.

† **Feibh**, *s. f.* (*Ir. id.*) Riches; goods; a long life.

Féich, *gen. sing.* and *n. pl.* of fiach. Debts, scores. Cha teid féich air beul dùinte, *a close mouth incurs no scores.—G. P.*

Feich, *s. f.* A debt. More frequently written *fiach.*

Feichnean, *n. pl.* of fiach. Debts.

Feichnibh, *d. pl.* of fiàch; which see.

Feidh, *gen. sing.* and *n. pl.* of fiadh; which see.

Feidil, *a.* (*Ir. id. Lat.* fidelis.) Faithful, true, just, chaste.

† **Feidir**, *a.* (*Ir. id.*) Able, possible; *also*, power, possibility.

Feigh, *s. f.* See **Feith**.

† **Feigh**, *a.* (*Ir. id.*) Bloody; sharp.—*Shaw.*

† **Feighe**, *s. m.* (*Ir. id.*) A warrior; a slaughterer; a champion.—*Shaw.*

† **Feighe**, *s. f.* (*Ir. id.*) The top of a house, rock, mountain.

Feighreag, eig, *s. f.* A cloudberry; a mountain strawberry. See **Oighreag**. *N. pl.* feighreagan. Breac le feighreagaibh, *chequered with cloudberries.—Macint.*

Féile, *s. f.*, *from* fial. (*Ir. id.*) Hospitality; conviviality; generosity. Talla na féile, *the hall of hospitality.—Oss. Fing.* Eirinn na féile, *hospitable Eirin.—Oss.*

Fèile, *s. f.* A Highland kilt. *N. pl.* féilean *and* féilichean, *kilts.* Na feilichean aluinn, *the comely kilts.—Mac Co.*

Feile-bhreacain, *s. f.* The kilted plaid.

This article of dress consisted of twelve yards or more of narrow tartan, which was wrapped round the middle, and hung down to the knees. It was most frequently fastened round the middle by a belt, and then it was called *breacan fèile*, or *feile bhreacain*. The *breacan*, or plaid part of this piece of dress, was, according to occasion, wrapped round the shoulders, or fastened on the left shoulder with a brooch or *braiste* of silver, gold, or steel, resembling the Roman *fibula*. It is not correct to say that the kilt is peculiar to the Gael alone; but the graceful plaid is unquestionably their invention.

Feile-bheag, bhig, *s. f.* A Highland kilt. An fhéile-bheag, *the kilt.*

Feile-bheag seems to be *filleadh bheag*, a little fold or plait. This part of the Gaelic garb is an ingenious substitute for the lower part of the plaid, being found to be less cumbersome, especially in the field, where the Gael were wont to tuck their plaids under their girdles.

† **Feileacan**, ain, *s. m.* (*Ir. id.*) A butterfly.

Féileachd, *s. f.* Banqueting; feasting; hospitality.

Feileag, eig, *s. f.* Honeysuckle.

Feileagan, ain, *s. m.* (*Ir.* feiliocan.) A may-bug; a diminutive person.

Feileas, eis, *s. m.* A trifle; variety. Luchd féileis, *triflers.*

Feileasach, *a.* Frivolous; vain.—*Shaw.* Gu feileasach, *frivolously. Com.* and *sup.* feileasaiche.

Feileasachd, *s. f.* Frivolousness; vanity.

Féill, *s. f.* A holyday; a festival; a feast; vigil of a festival; a fair; a market; a banquet whereat the chief presided; it denotes both the entertainment and the company. Cum an fhéill air an lath, *keep the fair on the proper day.*—*G. P. N. pl.* féillean; *d. pl.* féillibh. Air na feillibh, *in the feasts.*—*Stew. Ezek.* Féill an righ, *Epiphany.* Féill bride, *Candlemas.* La fhéill bride, *Candlemas day.*—*Macdon.* Féill Eòin, *St. John's day, the feast of St. John.* Féill-Martuinn, *Martinmas, the feast of St. Martin.* Féill-Mhicheil, *Michaelmas, the feast of the angel Michael.* Lathachan féill, *holydays;* also, *days of folly.*

Féill an righ, *s. f.* Epiphany.

Féill-bride, *s. f.* Candlemas. La fhéill-bride, *Candlemas day.* Mu éiridh na gréine la Fhéill-bride, *about sunrise on Candlemas day.*—*Old Song.*

Féill-eòin, *s. f.* St. John's day; the feast of St. John.

Féill-martuinn, *s. f.* Martinmas; the feast of St. Martin. Cha bheo mi gu feill Martuinn, *I shall not live till Martinmas.*—*Old Song.*

Féill-micheil, *s. f.* Michaelmas; the feast of the archangel Michael, on the twenty-ninth of September.

Féillteach, *a.* Hospitable, festal; fond of feasting. Gu féillteach, *hospitably.*

Féillteachd, *s. f.* (*Ir. id.*) Hospitableness; festivity; feasting; keeping holyday.

Feilteag, eig, *s. f.* (*Ir.* feilteog.) A cod.

Feim, *s. f.* (*Ir. id. Lat.* fœmina. *Shans.* vamini.) A woman, a female, a wife.

† **Feimean**, ein, *s. m.* (*Ir. id. Lat.* fœmen-inus.) The feminine gender.

Fein, *a.* Self; same; very; itself. Ris fein, *with himself, to himself.* Sud féin e mar iolar, *that same is he, like an eagle.*—*Oss. Lod.* Mar so fhéin, *in this very way.*—*Oss. Tem.* An so fhéin, *in this very place, here itself;* mi féin, *myself;* thu féin, *thyself;* i féin, *herself;* sinn fein, *ourselves, we ourselves;* sibh féin, *yourselves, you yourselves;* iad féin, *themselves, they themselves.*

Fein-agartach, *a.* Compunctious; remorseful.

Féin-agartas, ais, *s. m.* Self-reproach, compunction, remorse. Saor o fhéin-agartas, *free from self-reproach.*—*Macfar.*

† **Feine**, *s. m.* (*Ir. id.*) A boor; a ploughman; a farmer.

Feineachas, ais, *s. m.* History; genealogy.

Féineachd, *s. f.* (*from* féin.) Egotism.

Féinear, ir, *s. m.* Egotist.

Féin-fhios, *s.* Consciousness; experience; knowledge procured by experience.

Féin-fhiosrach, *a.* Conscious; experienced. Tha mi féin-fhiosrach air, *I am conscious of it.*

Féin-fhiosrachd, *s. f.* Experience; consciousness; self-knowledge. M' fhéin-fhiosrachd, *my experience.*

Féin-fhoghainteach, *a.* Self-sufficient, self-confident. Tha thu tuille is féin-fhoghainteach, *you are too self-sufficient.*

Féin-fhoghainteachd, *s. f.* Self-sufficiency, self-confidence.

Féin-fhoghainteas, eis, *s. m.* Self-sufficiency, self-confidence.

Féin-ghluasad, aid, *s. m.* Self-motion.

Féin-ghlusadach, *a.* Automatous.

Féin-ghluasadair, *s. m.* An automaton.

Féin-ghluas-rud, *s. m.* An automaton; a *perpetuum mobile.*

Féin-ghradh, aidh, *s. m.* Self-love; selfishness.

Féin-ghradhach, *a.* Selfish, self-interested. Fear féin-ghradhach, *a self-interested man.*

Féin-iriosal, *a.* Condescending; humble-minded.

Fein-irioslachd, *s. f.* Condescension; humble-mindedness.

† **Feinistear**, eir, *s. m.* A window.

Lat. fenestra. *Fr.* † fenestre. *Arm.* fanest. *Ir.* feinistear.

Fein-mheasail, *a.* Self-conceited, vain. Fear féin-mheasail, *a self-conceited man.*

Fein-mhort, **Féin-mhortadh**, aidh, *s. m.* Self-murder, suicide.

Fein-mhortail, *a.* Suicidal. Gu féin-mhortail, *suicidally.*

Fein-mhortair, *s. m.* A self-murderer. *N. pl.* féin-mhortairean, *self-murderers.*

Feinne, *s. pl.* Fingalians, or the followers of King Fingal; the country of the Fingalians, which comprehended the greater portion of the Highlands of Scotland; *also*, troops, fencibles. The *Arabic* has *fenna*, troops.

Féin-shealbhaich, *v. a.* Possess by prescriptive right.

Féin-speis, *s. f.* Self-love, self-interest, self-conceit.

Fein-spéiseil, *a.* Self-interested, self-conceited, self-opinioned.

Féin-thoil, *s. f.* Self-will; wilfulness. Aoradh féin-thoil, *will-worship.*—*Stew. Col.*

Féin-thoileil, *a.* Self-willed; wilful; opinionative; *also*, spontaneous. Gun bhi féin-thoileil, *without being self-willed.*—*Stew. Tit.*

† **Feir**, *s. f.* A bier.

Ir. id. Lat. feretrum, *a bier. Gr.* φερετρον. *Arm.* feirtr *and* phiertre. Also, *Lat.* fer, *carry.*

Feir-dhris, *s.* Bramble.—*Shaw.*

Feiread, eid, *s. m.* A ferret.

Feirg, *gen. sing.* of fearg.

Feirg, feirge, *s. f.* (*Ir. id.*) Anger, wrath. Treun ann am feirg, *strong in wrath.*—*Ull.*

† **Feirsde**, *s. pl.* (*Ir. id.*) Pits or dibs of water on the sand at low ebb; *hence*, Beul na feirsde, *Belfast.*—*Shaw.*

Feirsidh, *s. f.* Strength; courage.

Feirt, *s.* (*Ir. id.*) A cartrut.

† **Feis**, *s. f.* (*Ir. id.*) A convention, a synod; a convocation; a feast; carnal intercourse.

† **Feis**, *s.* (*Ir. id.*) A pig; swine.—*Shaw.*

Féisd, féisde, *s. f.* A banquet, an entertainment. La féisde,

a feast day, a festival, a holyday. Féisd na càisge, *the feast of the passover.—Stew. Ex.*
Ir. feiste. *Swed.* fest. *Da.* feest. *Teut.* feeste. *Germ.* fest. *Fr.* † feste, *now* fête. *Eng.* feast.

FÉISD, *v. n.* Feast. *Pret. a.* dh'fhéisd, *feasted; fut. aff. a.* feisdidh, *shall feast.*

FÉISDEACHD, *s. f.* (*from* féisd.) Entertainment, feasting, revelling.

FÉISDEAS, eis, *s. m.* Entertainment; accommodation. Feisdeas oidhche, *a night's lodging.—Shaw.*

FÉISDEIL, *a.* Feasting; hospitable.

FEISEAG, eig, *s. f.*; more commonly written *fiseag.*

FEISEAN, ein, *s. m.*; more frequently written *fisean.*

FEIST, *s. f.* See FEISD.

FÉISTEAS, eis, *s. m.* See FÉISDEAS.

FEISTEIL. See FÉISDEIL.

FEITH, *s. f.* (*Ir. id.*) Honeysuckle.

FÉITH, *s. f.* (*Ir. id.*) A calm, tranquillity, silence; a vein; a sinew; a bog; fen; morass. Tha 'n oidhche na fèith, *the night is calm.* An fhèith a chrup, *the sinew which shrank.—Stew. Gen.* Am fear a bhios san fhèith cuiridh h-uile duine a chas air, *every one has a kick at him who sticks in the mud.—G. P.* Air toiseach 'sa choille, 's air dheireadh san fhéith, *foremost in the woods, hindmost in the fens.—G. P.*

FEITH, *v. n.* (*Ir. id.*) Wait, remain, or stay, attend. *Pret. a.* dh' fheith, *waited; fut. aff. a.* feithidh, *shall wait. Feith* requires after it the preposition *air*, or *ri*, either simple or compounded. Feith air, *wait on, attend on him;* feith-se ri Cairbre, *wait thou for Cairbar.—Oss. Tem.* Feith rium, *wait for me.—Ardar.*

FÈITH-CHRUPADH, aidh, *s. m.* A spasm, a convulsion.

FÈITHEACH, *a.* Sinewy, muscular, veinous; having large veins; boggy, marshy.

FEITHEAMH, eimh, *s. m.* (*Ir. id.*) A waiting, expecting, attending; attendance; delay; lingering.

FEITHEAMH, (a), *pr. part.* of feith. Waiting, expecting, attending. A feitheamh ri gaoith, *waiting for a wind.* A feitheamh am fàth, *lying in wait.—Stew. Ex. ref.*

FÈITHEAN, ain, *s. m.* (*from* feith.) A sinew, a tendon.

FÈITHEANACH, *a.* Sinewy, muscular.

FÈITHEIL, *a.* (fèith-amhuil.) Calm, silent. Oidhche fheitheil, *a calm night.*

† FEITHIS, *v. a.* (*Ir. id.*) Gather, assemble; keep, preserve.—*Shaw.*

FEITHLEAG, eig, *s. f.* (*Ir. id.*) The pod of leguminous vegetables.

FÈITH-LUTHAIDH, *s. f.* A sinew. Le fèithibh lùthaidh, *with sinews.—Stew. Job.*

† FEN, *s. m.* (*W.* fen.) Air.

FEOBHAS, ais, *s. m.* Improvement; melioration; excellence. Tha e air taobh an fheobhais, *he* or *it is getting better.* Written also *feabhas.*

FEOCALAN, ain. See FÒCLAN.

FEOCH, *v. n.* (*Ir. id.*) Droop, fade, decay. *Pret. a.* dh'fheoch, *drooped.*

FEOCHADAN, ain, *s. m.* Corn-thistle.

† FEODAIDH, *a.* (*Ir. id.*) Hard.

FEODHAICH, *v. n.* Decay, fade. *Pret. a.* dh'fheodhaich, *decayed.*

FEÒDHAS, ais, *s. m.* Written also *feobhas.*

FEODHAINN, *s. pl.* People, folk. See FEADHAINN.

FEODHRADH, aidh, *s. m.* A manner, fashion.

FEOGACHADH, aidh, *s. m.* Drooping.

FEOIL, feola, *s. f.* Flesh of any kind; flesh, in contradistinction to spirit, in a theological sense. Fuil is feòil, *flesh and blood.* Feòil bhocta, *baked flesh.—Macd.* Feòil fhrigheanaichte, *fried flesh*; mairt-fheoil, *beef*; muilt-fheoil, *mutton*; circe-fheoil, *chicken*; muic-fheoil, *pork.*

FEÒIL-CHNUIMH, *s. f.* A flesh-worm; a maggot.

FEOIL-CHNUIMHEACH, *a.* Having maggots; of maggots.

FEÒIL-CHNUIMHEAG, FEOIL-CHRUIMHEAG, eig, *s. f.* A flesh-worm; a maggot.

FEÒIL-DHATH, *s.* Carnation colour.

FEOIL-GHABHAIL, *s. f.* Incarnation; the act of assuming body. An fheoil-ghabhail, *the incarnation.*

FEÒIL-ITHEACH, *a.* Carnivorous. Eun feoil-itheach, *a carnivorous bird.*

FEÒIR, *gen. sing.* of feur. Of grass. FEUR.

FEÒIRLING, *s. f.* (*Ir.* feòirlinn. *Sax.* feoirthling.) A farthing. Air fheoirlinn, *for a farthing.—Stew. Matt.*

FEÒIRN, *s. f.* (*Ir. id.*) Grass; *also,* chess.—*Shaw.*
From *feòirn*, or perhaps from *fioran*, is derived the agricultural term *feorin*, a species of coarse grass.

FEÒIRNEAN, ein, *s. m.* (*dim.* of feoirn.) (*Ir. id.*) A pile of grass; a cock of hay; a blade of grass; a straw; a buckle. Nach dean feoirnean lubadh, *that will not bend a blade of grass.—Old Song.*

FEÒIRNEANACH, *a.* In heaps or cocks, as grass; strawy; light as a straw; grassy.

† FEÒITE, *a.* (*Ir. id.*) Faded, decayed.—*Shaw.*

FEÒLA, *gen. sing.* of feòil; which see.

FEÒLADAIR, *s. m.*, *from* feòil. (*Ir. id.*) A butcher; a slaughterer of cattle. *N. pl.* feoladairean.

FEÒLADAIREACHD, *s. f.* (*from* feòil.) The occupation or business of a butcher. Ris an fheòladaireachd, *butchering.*

FEÒLAR, *a.*; *contracted for* feolmhar, *or* feolmhor.

FEÒLMHACH, aich, *s. m.* Flesh-meat.

FEÒLMHAR, *a.*; more properly *feolmhor*; which see.

FEOLMHOIRE, *com.* and *sup.* of feolmhor.

FEÒLMHOIREACHD, *s. f.* Fleshliness, carnality, lust.

FEÒLMHOR, *a.* (*Ir.* feolmhor.) Fleshly, carnal, lustful; fleshy, fat. An inntinn fheòlmhor, *the carnal mind.—Stew. Rom. Com.* and *sup.* feòlmhoire, *more* or *most carnal.*

FEÒRACHADH, aidh, *s. m.* An inquiry; questioning, asking.

FEÒRACHADH, (a), *pr. part.* of feoraich. Inquiring, questioning, asking.

FEÒRACHAS, ais, *s. m.* Curiosity, inquisitiveness.

FEÒRAG, aig, *s. f.* (*Ir. id.*) A squirrel. *N. pl.* feoragan, *squirrels.* Cho grad ri feoragan ceitein, *as nimble as squirrels in spring.—Macdon.*

FEÒRAICH, *v.* Ask, inquire, question. *Pret. a.* dh'fheòraich, *asked; fut. aff. a.* feòraichidh, *shall ask.* Dh'fheòraich mi dhithe, *I asked of her.—Stew. Gen. ref.*

FEORAN, ain, *s. m.* (*Ir. id.*) A green; a mountain-valley; land adjoining a brook.—*Shaw.*

FEORLAN, ain, *s. m.* A bushel, four pecks; a firlot.—*Shaw.*

FEÒRNAN, ain, *s. m.* A pile of grass: a cock of hay. *N. pl.* feornain.

FEÒRNANACH, *a.* Grassy; abounding in grass; full of haycocks; gathered into cocks, as hay.—*Mucint.*

FEÒSAG, aig, *s. f.* See FEUSAG.

FEÒSAGACH, *a.* See FEUSAGACH.

† FEOTH, *v. n.* (*Ir. id.*) Wither, fade.

FEOTHAS, ais, *s. m.*; more properly *feabhas* or *feobhas*; which see.

FEUBH, *v.*; *provincial for* feith; which see.

FEUCH! *interj.* (*Ir. id.*) Behold! lo! see! Feuch! taibhse Chrimine! *See! the ghost of Crimina!—Ull.*

Feuch, *v. a.* (*Ir.* feach.) See, or behold; see, or take care; shew; try; taste; give. *Pret. a.* dh'fheuch, *shewed; fut. aff. a.* feuchaidh, *shall shew.* Feuch gum pill thu, *see* [*take care*] *that you return.—Sm.* Feuch dhomh mo threun, *shew me my hero.—Oss. Com.* Feuchaibh an toiseach, *try ye in the first place, previously.—Ull.* Feuch ris, *give it a trial, try it;* feuch greim arain, *give me a piece of bread.*

Feuchadair, *s. m.* (*from* feuch.) A wizzard; a seer.—*Stew.* 1 *Sam. ref. N. pl.* feuchadairean.

Feuchainn, *s. f.* (*Ir. id.*) A shewing; a tasting; a trial; attempt; a disclosing; a disclosure; a look; an aspect. Is e sin feuchainn riut, *that is putting you to the test.*

Feuchainn, (a), *pr. part.* of feuch. Trying; tasting; shewing. See **Feuch**.

Feuchar, *fut. pass.* of feuch. Shall or will be shewn. *Imper. pass.* feuchar, *let be shewn.* Feuchar dhomh an oigh, *let the maid be shewn to me.—Oss. Com. Feuchar* is also used impersonally with the prep. *le*, simple or compounded, either expressed or understood. Feuchar ris [leam] mo dheireadh, *I tried it at last.*

Feud, *v.* (*Fr.* faut, *must.*) May; must; can; ought; behove. *Pret.* dh'fheud, *was allowed; fut.* feudaidh, *may.* Cha'n fheud thu 'dheanamh, *you must not do it; you ought not to do it.* Feudaidh gach neach dol as, *every one may escape.—Sm.* Feudaidh bith, *may-be, perhaps.—Id.* Feudaidh e bhith, *it may be, perhaps.—Stew. Gen. ref.* Is fheudar dhomh falbh, *I must go.* Ma 's fheudar tuiteam, *if we must fall.—Oss. Fing.*

Feudail, feudalach, *s.* (*W.* beudail, *cow-dung.*) Cattle; a herd; a cow. An fheudail san fhraoch, *the herd among the heath.—Oss. Fing.*

Feudar, *inflection* of feud. Shall be able; may; can; ought; must; behoves. *Feudar* is used impersonally; the prep. *do*, simple or compounded, being expressed or understood. Ma 's fheudar [dhomh] tuiteam, *if I must fall.—Oss. Fing.* Is fheudar [dhuinn] a dheanamh, *we must do it.*

† **Feughmhas**, ais, *s. m.* (*Ir. id.*) Absence; want.—*Shaw.*

Feum, feim *or* feuma, *s. m.* (*Ir.* feidhm.) Want, need, necessity; use. Cha 'n 'eil feum agam ort, *I have no need of you.* Slànuich mi am fheum, *heal me in my necessity.—Sm.* Gum fheum, *useless.* Fhir dhona gun fheum, *thou naughty useless man.—Oss. Tem.* Cna 'n 'eil feum annad, *there is no use in you;* cha 'n 'eil feum ort, *there is no occasion for*, or, *need of, you;* dean feum, *be of use, be serviceable;* cha dean e feum, *he* or *it will not do.*

Feumach, *a.* (*from* feum.) Needful, needy, necessitous, in want. Feumach air biadh, *in need of food. Com.* and *sup.* feumaiche, *the needy.—Stew. Job.*

Feumail, *a.* (feum-amhuil.) Needful; useful; necessary. *Asp. form,* fheumail. Ro-fheumail, *very useful.*

Feumanach, **Feumnach**, aich, *s. m.* (*from* feum.) A poor person; a destitute person; a tool. Cuis an fheumanaich, *the cause of the needy.—Stew. Jer.*

Feun, fèin, *and* feuna, *s. m.* (*Ir.* fen. *Eng.* wain.) A cart, a waggon, a wain; a war-chariot. Feun do na ceannardaibh, *a waggon to the princes.—Stew. Numb. N. pl.* feuman.—*Id.*

Feunadh, *s. m.* See **Feun**.

† **Feunaidh**, aidh, *s. m.* A cart-horse.

Feunair, *s. m.* (*Ir.* feneoir. Feun-fhear.) A carter, a waggoner, a carman. *N. pl.* feunairean.

Feunaireachd, *s. f.* The business of a waggoner, waggon-driving.

Feur, feòir, *s. m.* Grass; herbage; fodder. Mar am feur, *as the grass.—Sm.* Oscionn feòir, *over grass.—Stew. Jer.* Air an fheur, *on the grass; on grass; grazing.* Bhàrr an fheòir, *off the grass; off the pasture; from grazing. Ir.* feur. *Da.* foer, *grass. Lat.* ver, *spring, and* foènum, *fodder, r* and *n* being interchangeable.

Feurach, aich, *s. m.* (*from* feur.) A hay-loft; a hay-yard; —*Shaw.* Pasture.

Feurach, *a.* (*from* feur.) Grassy; green; verdant.—*Macint.* Cnocan buidhe feurach, *a yellow verdant knoll.—Old Song.*

Feurachadh, aidh, *s. m.* A feeding on grass, grazing, pasturing. A cur an eich air feurachadh, *putting the horse to pasture.*

Feuraich, *v. a.* Feed with grass; *also,* graze, pasture. *Pret. a.* dh'fheuraich, *grazed; fut. aff. a.* feuraichidh, *shall graze.*

Feuran, ain, *s. m.* (*Ir.* feoran.) Sives; *also,* a green; a grassy field.

Feur-itheach, *a.* (feur-ith.) Graminivorous. Beothach feur-itheach, *a graminivorous creature.*

Feur-lann, ainn, *s. m.* (*Ir.* feur-lan.) A hay-loft.

Feur-loch, *s. m.* A marshy lake; a reedy lake; a swamp.

Feur-lochan, ain, *s. m.* A grassy pool.

Feur-shion, *s. f.* Rain, showers, showery weather.

Feur-thuinn, *s. f.* Rain, showers, rainy or wet weather, wet.—*Stew. Job.*

The proper orthography seems to be *feur-shionn*, i. e. *grassy weather*, or such weather as causes grass to grow; *so*, garbh-shion is *rough weather;* gaillionn, *a storm*, i. e. gall-shion, *as if it blew from a strange country.* The word of opposite meaning to *feur-thiunn* is *cruaidh-shion.*

Feur-thuinneach, *a.* Rainy, showery.

Feusag, aig, *s. f.* (*Ir.* feasog.) A beard. Fheusag aosda mu 'bhroilleach, *his aged beard about his breast.—Orr. N. pl.* feusagan.

Feusagach, *a.* Bearded, having a long beard.

Feusgan, ain, *s. m.* The shell-fish called a muscle.—*Shaw.*

Feusganach, *a.* Abounding in muscles; like a muscle.

Fhabhor, *asp. form* of fabhor; which see.

Fhabhorach, *a., asp. form* of fabhorach. See **Fabhorach**.

Fhabhradh, *asp. form* of fabradh.

Fhad, **Fhada**, *a., asp. form* of fad. Long, tall; *also,* length. Air fhad 's gum bi thu, *however long you be;* cia fhad bhitheas tu? *how long will you be?* air fhad 's air leud, *in its length and breadth.*

Fhadalach, *asp. form* of fadalach. Dilatory; late.

Fhad-fhulangach, *asp. form* of fad-fhulangach.

Fhàgail. See **Fàgail**.

Fhaic. See **Faic**.

Fhaicte, *p. part.* of faic. Seen, observed. Leth fhaicte o Chrona nan nial, *half seen from cloudy Crona.—Oss. Com.*

Fhaide, *asp. form* of faide; which see.

Fhàillinn. See **Failinn**.

Fhalt, fhuilt, *s., asp. form* of falt. Hair. D'fhalt, *thy hair;* spion e' fhalt, *he tore his hair.*

Fhan, *asp. form* of fan. Stay. Cha 'n fhan mi, *I will not stay.* See **Fan**.

Fhaoin, *asp. form* of faoin; which see.

Fhaontradh. See **Faontradh**.

Fharasda, *a., asp. form* of farasda.

Fharmad, aid, *s. m., asp. form* of farmad. Envy, grudge. Gun fharmad, *without envy.* See **Farmad**.

Fhàs, *asp. form* of fàs.

Fhasa, *com.* and *sup.* of furas *or* furasda. Easier, easiest. Is e so is fhasa, *this is easier, this is easiest,* or *the easiest.* Written also *fhusa.*

Fheachd, *s. f., asp. form* of feachd.

Fheadh, (an), *adv.* Whilst, while, so long as. An fheadh 's a mhaireas an ruaig, *so long as the chase lasts.—Oss. Fing.*

Fhear, *asp. form* of fear; which see.

Fhearg, *s. f., asp. form* of fearg. Wrath. Bu fhuathasach' fhearg, *terrible was his wrath.*

Fheidh, Fheigh. See Feidh or Feigh.

Fhéin, *asp. form* of féin. (*W.* ein, *our.*) Self. Mi fhein, *myself.* Ochòin fhein! *Oh me! Woes me!* Gu dearbh fhein, *indeed, really.*

Fheirg, *asp. form* of feirg; which see.

Fheirgich, *gen. sing.* of feargach, *a.* Raging, wrathful. San doimhne fheirgich, *in the raging deep.—Ull.*

Fhéisd, *asp. form* of féisd. A feast. See Féisd.

Fheith, *v., asp. form* of feith. Wait. Cha 'n fheith mi, *I will not wait.*

Fheòil, *asp. form* of feoil. Flesh. Gun fhuil gun fheoil, *without flesh or blood.* See Feòil.

Fheòir, *asp. form* of feoir, *gen. sing.* of feur; which see.

Fheòlmhor, *asp. form* of feolmhor.

Fheuchadh, (*for* dh' fheuchainn.) To see; to try. Fheuch' an cluinn mi ur guth, *to see if I can hear your voices.—Oss. Derm.*

Fheudail, *asp. form* of feudail.

Fheum, *asp. form* of feum. Use. Gun fheum, *useless.* See Feum.

Fheur, *asp. form* of feur; which see.

Fhiach, *asp. form* of fiach. Worth; value; debt. Cha 'n fhiach thu, *you are not worth.*

Fhiaclach, *a., asp. form* of fiaclach. Toothed. See Fiaclach.

Fhiadh, *s., asp. form* of fiadh; which see.

Fhial, *a., asp. form* of fial; which see.

Fhiar. See Fiar.

Fhiata, *asp. form* of fiata; which see.

Fhichead, *asp. form* of fichead. Twenty. Bliadhna air fhichead, *twenty-one years.*

Fhilidh, *asp. form* of filidh. A bard; a minstrel. See Filidh.

Fhillte. See Fillte, *p. part.* of fill; which see.

Fhin. See Fhéin.

Fhiodh, *asp. form* of fiodh.

Fhios, *asp. form* of fios. Knowledge. Gun fhios, *without knowledge, unwitting;* gun fhios domh, *unknown to me, without my knowledge.*

Fhiosrachadh, aidh, *s. m., asp. form* of fiosrachadh.

Fhiosrachadh, (dh), *infin.* of fiosraich. To inquire; to examine. See Fiosraich.

Fhir, *asp. form* of fear, and *voc. sing.* Fhir leith! *thou grey-headed man!—Oss. Com.*

Fhirionn, *a.* See Firionn.

Fhiù, *a., asp. form* of fiù; which see.

Fhiùi, *s. m.* See Fiùi.

Fhiùrain. See Fiùrain.

Fhlath, *a., asp. form* of flath; which see.

Fhlathail, *a., asp. form* of flathail; which see.

Fhleadh, *asp. form* of fleadh.

Fhliuch, *a., asp. form* of fliuch. Wet, moist. See Fliuch.

Fhocal, ail, *asp. form* of focal. Word. A réir d' fhocail, *according to thy word.* See Focal.

Fhochaid, *asp. form* of fochaid; which see.

Fhògair. See Fogair.

Fhoghlum, uim, *s. m., asp. form* of foghlum. Learning, knowledge. Gun fhoghlum, *illiterate.*

Fhoighidinn, *s. f., asp. form* of foighidinn. Patience. Gun fhoighidinn, *impatient.* See Foighidinn.

Fhoill, *s. f., asp. form* of foill. Deceit, cunning. Gun fhoill, *without deceit.*

Fhoillsich, *v.* See Foillsich.

Fhois, *asp. form* of fois. Rest. Gun fhois, *without rest.*

Fhoilt, fhuilt, *s., asp. form* of folt. Hair. D' fholt, *thy hair.* See Folt.

Fhonn, *s. m., asp. form* of fonn; which see.

Fhosgladh, *asp. form* of fosgladh. See Fosgladh.

Fhras. See Fras.

Fhreagair, *pret. a.* of freagair. Answered. See Freagair.

Fhrith, *asp. form* of frith; which see.

Fhuadachadh, *asp. form* of fuadachadh; which see.

Fhuadaich. See Fuadaich.

Fhuaim, *asp. form* of fuaim. Sound, noise. Leis an fhuaim, *with the sound.* See Fuaim.

Fhuair, *pret.* of faigh. Got, found, received, obtained, reached, acquired. Fhuair mi mach thu, *I found you out.—Mac Lach.* Fhuair sinn an càla, *we reached the harbour.—Orr.* See Faigh.

Fhuar, *asp. form* of fuar. Cold.

Fhuaras, *pret. pass.* of faigh. Was found, was got, was obtained.

Fhuasgladh. See Fuasgladh.

Fhuil, *asp. form* of fuil; which see.

Fhuilteach, *asp. form* of fuilteach.

Fhuiltean. See Fuiltean.

Fhuinn. See Fonn.

Fhuirich. See Fuirich.

Fhulangach, *asp. form* of fulangach.

Fhulangas, ais, *asp. form* of fulangas.

Fhuras, Fhurasda, *asp. form* of furas *and* furasda. Easy. See Furas.

Fhusa, Fhusadh, *com.* and *sup.* of furas. Easier, easiest.

Fiabhras, Fiabhrus, uis, *s.* (*perhaps* from féith, *a vein, and* brais, *quick* or *rapid.*) A fever, ague; confusion. Fiabhrus critheanach, *an ague.* Fiabhrus loisgeach, *a burning ague.—Stew. Lev.*

Lat. febris. *Fr.* fièvre. *Germ.* fiebar. *Eng.* fever. *Ir.* fiabhrus.

Fiabhrasach, Fiabhrusach, *a.* Feverish, aguish.

Fiabhrus-chosg, *s. m.* A febrifuge.—*Shaw.*

Fiacal, *gen.* fiacail *or* fiacla, *s. f.* (*Ir. id.*) A tooth; a husk; the jag of a saw or of any dentated instrument. Fiacail airson fiacla, *tooth for tooth.—Stew. O. T.* Fiacal cùil, *a back tooth.—Stew. Prov.* Fiacal carbaid, *a cheek tooth.—Stew. Joel.* Fiacal forais, *late-grown teeth; wisdom-teeth.—Shaw.* Fiacal leomhainn, *dandelion.—Id.*

Fiach, féich, *s. f.* (*Ir. id.*) A debt; value; price; worth; hire. *N. pl.* fiachan. Maith dhuinn ar fiacha, *forgive us our debts.—Sm.* Gun fhiach, *without debt;* also, *worthless.* Reic thu do shluagh gun fhiach, *thou didst sell thy people as worthless.—Sm.* Cuiream mar fhiachan oirbh, *I charge you.—Stew. Song Sol.* Cha b' fhiach leam e, *I would scout it;* cha b' fhiach leat ach ni bha mòr, *thou didst not value but costly things.—Old Song.* Dh' fhiachaibh, *incumbent, obligatory;* tha e dh' fhiachaibh ort, *it is incumbent on thee.*

Fiach, *a.* (*Ir. id.*) Worth, valuable, deserving, worthy. Cha 'n fhiach e, *he is not worth, he is worthless;* is fhiach thu do charaisd, *you are deserving of a beating;* ma 's fhiach an teachdair, is fhiach an gnothuch, *if the bearer be respectable, the message is of import.—G. P.*

Fiachach, *a.* (*from* fiach.) Worthy; worth; valuable; relating to a debt.

Fiachail, *a.* (fiach-amhuil.) Worthy; valuable.

Fiaclach, *a.* (*Ir. id.*) Toothed; dentated; serrated; having large teeth. *Com.* and *sup.* fiaclaiche.

Fiaclachadh, aidh, *s. m.* (*Ir. id.*) A gnashing of the teeth; a grinning; a growing angry; indenting, serrating.

Fiaclaibh, *d. pl.* of fiacal; which see.

Fiaclaich, *v. a.* (*from* fiacal.) Grin; shew the teeth; form with jags or indentures, as the edge of a saw. *Pret. a.* dh' fhiaclaich; *fut. aff. a.* fiaclaichidh.

Fiaclan, *n. pl.* of fiacal. Teeth, fangs, tusks; indentures or jags, as of a saw.

† **Fiadh**, *s. m.* (*Ir. id.*) Land, ground; meat, food, victuals. —*Shaw.*

Fiadh, feidh, *s. m.* (*Ir. id.*) A fallow deer; the *cervus dama* of Linnæus. Mar fhiadh air fireach, *like a deer on a mountain.*—*Sm.* Fireach an fheidh, *the hill of deer.*—*Oss. Fing.* *N. pl.* feidh.

† **Fiadh**, *v. a.* Relate, tell.

Fiadhach, aich, *s. m.* A herd of deer; venison; a lord.

Fiadhach, *a.* Abounding in deer; of deer; wild.

Fiadhachadh, aidh, *s. m.* Deer-hunting; a deer-hunt; a roe-hunt.

Fiadhachadh, (a), *pr. part.* of fiadhaich. Hunting. Là dhuinn a fiadhachadh, *one day as we were hunting deer.*—*Ull.* A fiadhachadh bheann, *hunting in the mountains; scouring over the mountains in the chase.*—*Macint.*

Fiadhachd, *s. f.* (*from* fiadh.) Hunting deer; hunting; a chase.

Fiadhadan, ain, *s. m.* (*Ir. id.*) A witness.—*Shaw.*

Fiadhaich, *a.* (*Ir. id.*) Wild, untamed, savage, uncultivated, in a state of nature. Daoine fiadhaich, *savages*; cat fiadhaich, *a wild cat.*

Fiadhaich, *v.* Hunt deer, hunt, chase.

Fiadhaiche, *com.* and *sup.* of fiadhaich. More or most savage.

Fiadhaidh, *a.* Wild, savage, uncultivated. Gu fiadhaidh, *savagely.*

Fiadhaidheachd, *s.* Wildness, savageness.

Fiadhain, *a.* (*Ir. id.*) Wild, uncultivated. Ubhal fiadhain, *a wild apple; a crab-apple.*

Fiadhair, *s. m.* Lay-land.—*Shaw.* Green sward.

Fiadhanta, *a.* (*Ir. id.*) Wild, savage, shy, uncultivated; fierce, cruel. Gu fiadhanta, *wildly.*

Fiadhantachd, *s. f.* (*Ir. id.*) Wildness, savageness, shyness, fierceness, cruelty.

Fiadh-asal, ail, *s. f.* A wild ass. *Stew. Job.* *N. pl.* fiadh-asalan.

Fiadh-bheathach, aich, *s. m.* A wild beast. Fiadh-bheathach na machrach, *the wild beast of the field.*—*Stew. Hos.* *N. pl.* fiadh-bheathaichean.

Fiadh-bheist, *s.* A wild beast. *N. pl.* fiadh-bheistean.

Fiadh-chat, chait, *s. m.* A wild cat. *N. pl.* fiadh-chait.

Fiadh-chu, -choin, *s. m.* (*Ir. id.*) A wolf; *literally*, a wild dog. *N. pl.* fiadh-choin, *wolves.* Fiadh-choin nan carn, *the wolves of the rocks.*—*Fingalian Poem.*

Fiadh-chullach, aich, *s. m.* (*Ir. id.*) A wild boar. *N. pl.* fiadhchullaich.—*Shaw.*

Fiadh-dhuine, *s. m.* (*Ir. id.*) A wild man, a savage, a satyr. *N. pl.* fiadh-dhaoine, *satyrs.* Glaodhaidh am fiadh-dhuine, *the wild man shall cry.*—*Stew. Is.*

Fiadh-fhàl, ail, *s. m.* A deer-park.—*Macd.*

Fiadh-ghabhar, air, *s. m.* (*Ir. id.*) A wild goat.—*Stew. 1 Sam.* *N. pl.* fiadh-ghabhair.

Fiadh-ghath, *s. m.* (*Ir. id.*) A hunting spear.—*Shaw.*

Fiadh-ghleann, ghlinn, *s. m.* (*Ir. id.*) A wild glen; *also*, a glen or valley where deer herd together.

Fiadh-ghullach, aich, *s. m.* A wild boar. Written also *fiadh-chullach.*

Fiadh-lann, -lainn, *s. m.* (*Ir. id.*) A deer-park.

Fiadh-lorg, -luirg, *s. f.* (*Ir. id.*) A hunting-pole; *also*, the slot or track of a deer.

Fiadh-mhuc, -mhuic, *s. m.* (*Ir. id.*) A wild boar; *literally*, a wild son. *N. pl.* fiadh-mhucan.

Fiadh-roidis, *s. f.* (*Ir. id.*) Wild radish.—*Shaw.*

Fiadhta, *a.*, *from* fiadh. (*Ir. id.*) Wild; shy; surly; fierce; unsocial. More commonly written *fiata;* which see.

Fiadhtachd, *s. f.* (*Ir. id.*) Wildness; shyness; surliness; fierceness. Written more frequently *fiatachd.*

† **Fiafrach**, *a.* (*Ir. id.*) Inquisitive.

† **Fiafraich**, *v.* (*Ir. id.*) Inquire, ask.—*Shaw.*

Fiagh, *s. m.* More frequently written *fiadh;* which see.

Fia-ghàire, *s. m.* A smile. Chi mi Crimin is fia-ghaire orra, *I see Crimina smiling.*—*Ull.* Written also and pronounced *fè-ghaire.*

Fiaile, *s. pl.* Weeds.—*Shaw.*

† **Fial**, fèil, *s. m.* (*Ir. id.*) The veil of a temple; a ferret. —*Shaw.*

Fial, *a.* (*Ir. id.*) Generous, liberal, bountiful, hospitable; *also*, hospitality. D' fhardoch fial gach uair, *thy dwelling ever hospitable.*—*Sm.* An t-anam fial, *the liberal soul.*—*Stew. Pro.* Clàr na fial, *table of hospitality.*—*Oss. Tem.* Bha fleagh, bha fial, bha dàn, *there was feasting, hospitality, and song.*—*Oss. Oinam.*

Fialachd, *s. f.* (*Ir. id.*) Hospitality, liberality, open-heartedness, bountifulness.

Fialaidh, *a.* (*Ir. id.*) Generous, liberal, bountiful, hospitable, open-hearted. Fialaidh mu 'n stòras, *liberal with their store.*—*Macfar.* Gu fialaidh, *hospitably.*

Fialaidh, *s. f.* Relationship, consanguinity, affinity.—*Shaw.*

Fialaidheachd, *s. f.* (*Ir. id.*) Generosity, liberality, bountifulness, hospitality, open-heartedness. Saibhreas am fialaidheachd, *the riches of their liberality.*—*Stew.* 2 *Cor.*

† **Fiallach**, aich, *s. m.* (*Ir. id.*) A hero, a champion, a knight-errant.—*Shaw.* Perhaps *fiallach* is *fiadh-laoch*, one who has bravery without judgment.

Fiallachd, *s. f.* (*Ir. id.*) Heroism, bravery, knight-errantry. —*Shaw.*

Fialmhoire, *s. f.* (*Ir.* fialmhuire.) Bounty, liberality; heroism.

Fialmhor, *a.* (*Ir. id.*) Bountiful, liberal; heroic. *Com.* and *sup.* fialmhoire.

Fialteach, *s. m.* A place where ferrets are bred.—*Shaw.*

† **Fiamh**, *a.* (*Ir. id.*) Ugly, disgusting, horrible.—*Shaw.*

Fiamh, *s. m.* (*Ir. id.*) Reverence; fear, fright; trepidation; appearance; trace; a track; a footstep; colour; a chair. Fo fhiamh naimhde, *under the fear of enemies.*—*Oss. Tem.* Gabhaidh e fiamh, *he shall take fright.*—*Sm.* Air fiamh òir, *of the colour of gold.*—*Macint.* Fiamh-ghàire, *a smile.*

Fiamhach, *a.* Fearful, timid; skittish, modest, shy. Is fiamhach an t-sùil a lotar, *the eye which has been wounded is ever fearful of harm.*—*G. P.*

Fiamhachd, *s. f.* Modesty, timidity, shyness, skittishness. Ann an dreach no fiamhachd, *neither in dress nor modesty.* —*Old Song.*

Fiamhadh, aidh, *s. m.* A tracing; a pursuing; indagation.

Fiamhaidh, *a.* Modest, timid, fearful, shy, skittish.

Fiamhan, ain, *s. m.* A heinous crime; fear.

Fiamharachd, *s. f.* A monstrous deed; monstrousness; a monster.

Fiamh-ghàir, *s. m.* A smile. Fiamh-ghàir air an gruaidh-ean, *a smile on their cheeks.—Old Song.* Often written and pronounced *fè-ghaire.*

Fiamhlochd, s. *m.* A heinous crime; fear.

† **Fian-bhuth**, *s. m.* (*Ir. id.*) A hut, a cottage, a booth.

Fiann, *s. m.* (*Ir. id.*) A Fingalian; a giant; a warrior. Flath nam fiann, *the chief of warriors.—Old Song.* Written also *Fionn.*

Fiannach, *a.* Like a Fingalian; heroic; gigantic; *also*, a Fingalian hero.

Fiannachail, *a.* (fiannach-amhuil.) Gigantic; heroic; august.—*Shaw.*

Fiannag, aig, *s. f.* A species of mountain-berry, crowberry; a mite. *N. pl.* fiannagach.

Fiannagach, *a.* Abounding in crowberries; mity, having mites. Càise fiannagach, *mity cheese.*

Fianntan, *n. pl.* of fiann. Fingalians; champions.

Fianuis, *s. f.* (*Ir.* fiadhnaise.) Witness, testimony, evidence; presence; a witness. Airc na fianuis, *the ark of the testimony.—Stew. Exod.* Mar fhianuis, *as a witness.—Stew. Deut.* As m' fhianuis, òig, *from my presence, youth.—Oss. Com.* Thoir fianuis, *give evidence;* dean fianuis, *give evidence, bear record;* tha mi a deanamh fianuis, *I bear record.—Stew. Rom.*

Fianuiseach, *a.* (*from* fianuis.) Present, witnessing, being an eye-witness. Tha thusa fianuiseach air so, *you are witness to this;* an robh thu fianuiseach? *were you present?*

Fiar, *a.* (*Ir. id.*) Crooked, bent, awry; aslant; inclined; winding; unjust; perverse; froward; wild, fierce. Mar bhogha fiar, *like a bent bow.—Sm.* Steud na fiar-ghaoithe, *the speed of the wild wind.—Oss. Tem.* Daoine fiara, *froward men.—Stew. Job.* Ann gleannaibh fiar, *in winding valleys.—Oss. Tem.* Slighe fhiar, *crooked, perverse ways.—Sm.* *Com.* and *sup.* fiaire.

Fiar, *v. a.* (*Ir. id.*) Bend, twist, make crooked; pervert; wrest; incline; go aside or astray. *Pret. a.* dh' fhiar; *fut. aff. a.* fiaraidh. Cha 'n fhiar thu breith, *thou shalt not pervert* [*wrest*] *judgment.—Stew. Exod.*

Fiar, *s. m.* Grass. More frequently written *feur;* which see.

Fiarachadh, aidh, *s. m.* A slanting; a bending; a perverting; a wresting; a slant; a bend; perversion.

Fiarachadh, (a), *pr. part.* of fiaraich. Bending; slanting; perverting; wresting.

Fiaradh, aidh, *s. m.* The act of bending or twisting; a whirling; perverseness; a bend or turn; a meander; the cadence of a strain. Fiaradh na gaoithe, *the whirling of the wind.—Oss. Tem.* Fiaradh luchd do-bheirt, *the perverseness of transgressors.—Stew. Pro.*

Fiaradh, (a), *pr. part.* of fiar. Bending, twisting, wreathing; making crooked; perverting. Fiaradh ceartais, *perverting justice.—Stew. Mic.*

Fiaraich, *v. a.* Bend, twist, make crooked; pervert. *Pret. a.* dh' fhiaraich *bent; fut. aff. a.* fiaraichidh, *shall bend.*

Fiaras, ais, *s. m.* (*Ir. id.*) Crookedness; perverseness.—*Shaw.*

Fiarasach, *a.* Curved, crooked, bended; curve-necked. Each fiarasach, *a curve-necked horse.—Oss. Fing.* Gu fiarasach, *crookedly.* *Com.* and *sup.* fiarasaiche.

Fiar-ogha, *s. m.* A great-grandchild. Fear-ogha 'n fhiar-ogha, *the grandson's grandson;* fear-ogha 'n fhir fhiar ogha, *the great-grandson's grandson;* fear-ogha fir-ogha 'n fhiar-ogha, *the grandson's grandson's grandson.*

Fiar-shùil, *s. f.* A squint eye.

Fiar-shuileach, *a.* Squint-eyed, looking askance or obliquely.

Fiasag. See **Feusag.**

† **Fiasdar**, air, *s. m.* (*Ir. id.*) Anger.—*Shaw.*

Fiat, Fiata, *a.* Shy; strange; fierce; surly; distant in manner; froward. Gu fiat, *shily.* Sheall Garno gu fiat uaipe, *Garno looked shily away from her.—Oss. Cathluno.* An lamh nam fineach fiat, *in the hands of the strange heathen.—Sm.* Fiat do 'n fhiata, *froward to the forward.—Id.*

Fiatachd, *s. f.* Shiness; surliness; fierceness.

Fiatail, *a.* (*Ir.* fiatghail.) A species of weed; vetches; tares.

Fibhras, ais, *s. m.* See **Fiabhras.**

† **Fich**, *s.* (*Ir. id.*) A country village; a castle.

Fichead, *a.* (*Ir.* fichid. *Arm.* viguent. *Lat.* viginti.) Twenty. Fichead fear, *twenty men.* Aon fhear thar fhichead, *twenty-one men;* tri fir fichead, *twenty-three men;* tri clacha fichead, *twenty-three stones.*

† **Ficheall**, ill, *s. m.* (*Ir. id.*) A buckle.—*Shaw.*

Fideag, eig, *s. f.* A small worm; *also*, a kind of bird.—*Shaw.*

Fideagach, *a.* Like a small worm; full of little worms.

Fidh, *v.* More properly *figh;* which see.

Fidheadair, *s. m.* See **Figheadair.**

Fidheall, fidhle, *s. f.* A violin or fiddle. Bogha fidhle, *a fiddle-bow.*
Swed. fiol. *Du.* fiool. *Fr.* violle. *Ir.* fidil. *It.* viola. *Eng.* viol.

Fidhle, *gen. sing.* of fidheall.

Fidhlear, eir, *s. m.* A performer on the violin, a fiddler. *N. pl.* fidhleirean.

Fidhlearachd, *s. f.* (fidhlear.) The occupation of a fiddler; performing on the violin, fiddling. Ag ionnsachadh na fidhlearachd, *learning to play on the fiddle.*

Fidir, *v. a.* Consider, ponder, weigh, examine, sound or search; prove by trial. *Pret. a.* dh' fhidir, *examined; fut. aff. a.* fidiridh. Fidir is ceasnaich mi, *prove and examine me.—Sm.* An d' fhidir sibh an cabhlach ard? *did you examine the lofty fleet?—Fingalian Poem.* Nur dh' fhidireas mi m' athair, *when I shall have sounded my father.—Stew. Sam.*

Fidir, *s. m.* A teacher. *N. pl.* fidirean.

Fidireach, *a.* Considerate, thoughtful; prying, inquisitive. *Com.* and *sup.* fidiriche.

Fidireachadh, aidh, *s. m.* A considering; a prying; an examining; experience.—*Stew. Rom.*

Fidireachd, *s. f.* Considerateness; minuteness: inquisitiveness.

Fidireadh, aidh, *s. m.* A considering, examining, examination; experience.

Fidirich, *v. a.* Examine, ponder, consider. *Pret. a.* dh' fhidirich, *examined; fut. aff. a.* fidirichidh, *shall examine.*

Fidirichte, *p. part.* of fidirich. Examined.

† **Fig**, fige, *s. f.* A slit.—*Shaw.*

Fige, *s. f.* A fig, a fig-tree.—*Stew. Jer.*
Lat. fic-us. *Germ.* fige. *Ir.* fige. *Fr.* figue.

Figeir, *s. f.* A figure; *provincial.*

Figh, *v. a.* Weave, plait, twine, twist, wreathe. *Pret. a.* dh' fhigh, *weaved; fut. aff. a.* fighidh, *shall weave; p. part.* fighte, *woven.*

Figheachan, ain, *s. m.* A garland, a wreath.

Figheadair, *s. m.* A weaver, a plaiter, a twister. Spàl figheadair, *a weaver's shuttle.—Stew. Job.* *N. pl.* figheadairean.

Figheadaireachd, *s. f.* The occupation or trade of a weaver. Ris an fhigheadaireachd, *at the weaving trade.*

Figheis, *s. f.* (*Ir. id.*) A lance; a spear.—*Shaw.*

Fighil, *s. f.* (*Ir. id.*) A prayer.—*Shaw.*

Fighte, *p. part.* of figh. Woven, twisted, twined, wreathed. Slabhruidhean fighte, *wreathed chains.—Stew. Ex.*

Figis, *s. f.* (*Lat.* ficus.) A fig, a fig-tree. Crann-figis, *a fig-tree.*

Filead, eid, *s. m.* A fillet.—*Shaw.*

Fileadach, *a.* Filleted.

Fileanta, *a.* (*from* filidh.) Melodious, tuneful.—*Macint. Also,* poetical; eloquent.

Fileantachd, *s. f.* Melodiousness, tunefulness; eloquence.

Filear, eir, *s. m.* A spruce fellow; a crafty man.

Fileil, *a.* (filidh-amhuil.) Poetical, poetic, bardic.

Filidh, *s. m.* (*Ir. id.*) A poet or bard; a minstrel; an inferior bard; a warbler; a songster; a philosopher. Filidh nam bliadhna nar deigh, *the bards of after years.—Oss. Duthona.* Filidh bhinn nan coillte, *the melodious warblers of the wood.—Oss. Trath.*

Filidheach, *a.* Poetical; rhyming; tuneful. Gu filidheach, *tunefully.*

Filidheachd, *s. f.* Poetry; rhyming; tunefulness.

Fill, *s. f.* A collop; a steak. *N. pl.* fillean, *steaks.* Fillean saille, *collops of salt.—Stew. Job.*

Fill, *s. f.* A fold, a plait. *N. pl.* filltean. Le filltean teine, *with folds of fire.—Stew. Ezek.*

Fill, *v. a.* Fold, plait, double; imply. *Pret. a.* dh'fhill, *folded; fut. aff. a.* fillidh, *shall* or *will plait.* Fillidh tu iad, *thou shalt fold them.—Stew. Heb.* Air am filleadh anns a chéile, *folded together.—Stew. Nah.*
Goth. fildan. *Ang. Sax.* faldan. *Ir.* fill. *Germ.* fald *and* faltan.

Filleadh, idh, *s. m.* (*Ir. id.*) A folding, a plaiting; a fold, a plait; a cloth. Beagan fillidh, *a little folding.—Stew. Pro.*

Filleadh, (a), *pr. part.* of fill. Folding, plaiting, doubling; implying.

Filleag, eig, *s. f., dim.* of fill. (*Ir. id.*) A little fold or plait; a shawl; a wrapper; a doublet; a scarf; a covering. *N. pl.* filleagan.

Filleagach, *a.* Having folds or plaits.

Fillean, ein, *s. m.* A species of worm that breeds in the head and neck of some of the Hebrideans, frequently causing imposthumous and painful swellings.

Filleadh-bheag. See **Féil-bheag.**

Fillear, *fut.* of fill. Shall be folded.

Fillidh, *gen. sing.* of filleadh. Of a fold or plait.

Fillidh, *fut. aff. a.* of fill. Shall fold or plait.

Fillte, *p. part.* of fill. (*Ir. id.*) Folded, plaited, doubled; implied; deceitful. Tri fillte, *threefold.*

† **Fimh**, *s. f.* (*Ir. id.*) Drink; potion; wine.

Fimeanach, aich, *s. m.* (*Ir.* fimineach.) A hypocrite; *also,* hypocritical.

Fimeanachd, *s. f.* (*Ir.* fimineachd.) Hypocrisy.

† **Fin**, *a.* Fine. *Hence* finealta.
Gr. φαινος *and* φαεινος, *clear. Arm.* fin. *Fr.* fin. *It.* and *Span.* fino. *Eng.* fine. *Germ.* fein, *excellent.*

Fine, *s. f.* (*Ir. id.*) A tribe, a clan, a nation, a family, kindred; a soldier. Gach fine gairmidh e, *he will call every tribe.—Sm.* Gu fhine féin gach treun, *every hero to his own nation.—Oss. Tem.* *N. pl.* fineachan.

Fineach, *a.* In tribes or clans; clannish.

Fineachan, *n. pl.* of fine. Tribes, nations, clans; *also,* heathens, gentiles. A reir am fineacha, *according to their nations.—Stew. Gen.* Thàinig na fineachan, *the heathen came.—Sm.*

Fineachas, ais, *s. m.* (*Ir. id.*) Kindred; inheritance; a nation; law.

Fineadach, *a.* (*Ir. id.*) Wise, prudent, sagacious, cunning; *also,* clannish; *substantively,* a clansman.

Fineadail, *a.* National, clannish.

Fineadalachd, *a.* Nationality, clannishness.

Fineadh, idh, *s. m.* A tribe, a clan, a nation, a family, a kindred. Aon fhineadh, *one tribe.—Stew.* 1 *K. ref.*

Fìneag, eig, *s. f.* (*Ir.* fineog.) A mite; *also,* a crowberry. Lan fhìneag, *full of mites.—Macint.*

Fìneagach, *a.* (*Ir.* fineogach.) Mity; full of mites; full of crowberries.

Fineal, eil, *s. m.* (*Ir. id.*) Fennel. Fineal cùbbraidh, *sweet fennel;* fineal sràide, *sow fennel.—Shaw.*

Finealta, *a. from* fin. (*Ir.* fionnalta, *well washed.*) Tidy; fine; well dressed; elegant; brave. Foinneamh finealta, *portly and well dressed.—Macint.*

Finealtachd, *s. f.* Tidiness; fineness; fondness for dress; elegance; bravery.

Fineamhain, **Fineamhuin**, *s. f.* (*Ir. id.*) A vine; a vineyard; a twig; an osier; any small rod. Fineamhain fa m' chomhair, *a vine opposite to me.—Stew. Gen.*

Fineamhuineach, *a.* (*Ir.* fineamhnach.) Having vines or vineyards; full of vineyards; like a vineyard.

Fineun, eoin, *s. m.* (*Ir.* fineon.) A buzzard.

† **Fineur**, eoir, *s. m.* (*Ir. id.*) A stock, a lineage.

Finichd, *a.* (*Ir. id.*) Jet black.

Finiche, *s. f.* A jet black.—*Shaw.*

Finid, *s. f.* An end, close, or conclusion.
Lat. finis. *Teut.* fiin *and* fine. *Fr.* fin. *Corn.* fin *and* fyn.

Finideach, *a.* Wise, prudent. Gu finideach, *wisely.*

† **Finn**, *a.* (*Ir. id.*) White; milk.—*Shaw.*

Finn-dhiol, *v. a.* Enslave.

Finne, *s. f.* (*Ir. id.*) Attendance; testimony, evidence.—*Shaw.* A beautiful woman; whiteness, fairness.

† **Finneal**, eil, *s. m.* (*Ir. id.*) A shield.

Finneul, eoil, *s. m.* A white cloud.

Finneun, eoin, *s. m.* A buzzard. *N. pl.* finneoin.

Finn-gheall, *v. a.* Profess; promise.—*Shaw.*

Finngheinte, *s. pl.* Norwegians.

† **Finnidheach**, *a.* (*Ir. id.*) Vigilant, prudent, cautious.

Finnidheachd, *s. f.* (*Ir. id.*) Vigilance, prudence, caution.

Finn-reic, *s. f.* Proscription.

Finn-reic, *v. a.* Enslave; proscribe.

Finnsgeul, sgeoil, *s.* A romance, a tale, a fiction.

† **Fioch**, *s. m.* (*Ir. id.*) Land; anger, choler.—*Shaw.*

† **Fiochail**, *a.* (fioch-amhuil.) Angry, fierce, choleric; brindled.

Fiochar, *a.* Angry.

Fiochradh, aidh, *s. m.* (*Ir. id.*) Anger, choler.—*Shaw.*

Fiodadh, aidh, *s. m.* Laughter.

Fiodh, fiodha, *s. m.* (*Ir.* fiodh.) Wood, timber; a tree. Snaidheadh fiodha, *a carving of wood.—Stew. Ex.* An t-sail as an fhiodh, *the beam out of the timber.—Stew. Hab.* Nochd e fiodh dha, *he shewed him a tree.—Stew. Ex.* Fiodh-ghual, *charcoal.*

Fiodhach, aich, *s. m.* (*Ir. id.*) A copse, a shrubbery.—*Shaw*

Fiodhach, *a.*, *from* fiodh. (*Ir. id.*) Woody, copsy; full of woods or copses; wooden.

Fiodhag, aig, *s. f.* A bird-cherry; a hard berry. *N. pl.* fiodhagan. Craobh fhiodhag, *a bird-cherry-tree.*

Fiodhagach, *a.* Abounding in bird-berries or hard berries

† **Fiodhain**, *s m.* (*Ir. id.*) A witness.—*Shaw.*

Fiodhan, ain, *s. m.* (*Ir. id.*) A cheese-press. *N. pl.* fiodhain

Fiodh-chait, *s. m.* A mouse-trap.—*Shaw.*

Fiodh-chonnadh, aidh, *s m.* (*Ir. id*) Cordwood; brush-wood —*Macd.*

Fiodh-ghual, ail, *s m* (*Ir. id.*) Charcoal.—*Macd*

Fiodh-ghualach, *a.* Carbonic; abounding in charcoal.

Fiodhnach, *a* (*Ir id.*) Manifest, plain.

Fiodhrach, aich, *s. m.* (*Ir. id.*) Wood for vessel-building, *also*, increase.

Fiodhradh, aidh, *s. m* (*Ir id.*) Fashion; a written testimony.

† **Fiog**, **Fiogh**, *s f.* (*Ir. id*) A wall; a wreath or braid. —*Shaw*

† **Fiogha**, ai, *s m* (*Ir. id.*) The weather or windward side. —*Shaw*

Fioghair, *v.* Figure.

Fioghair, *s f.* (*Lat* figura. *Ir.* fioghar) A figure, a sign, a mart.

Fioghait, *s f* (*Ir* id.) A quadrangle; a square. *N. pl* fiodh-ghaitean.

Fioghaiteach, *a.* Quadrangular; square

Fioghal, *a* Quadrangular. Feunadh fioghal, *a quadrangular chariot* —*Old Poem.*

Fiolar, air, *s m* (*Ir. id.*) An eagle.

Fiomhalach, aich, *s. m.* A giant; a big fellow.—*Shaw.*

Fion, *s m.* (*Gr. by met* φοιν-ος *Lat.* vin-um *Ir* fion.) Wine, *rarely*, truth Fion teantach, *tent wine* —*Macd.* Fion-geur, *vinegar.* Fion mailmhaiseach, *Malmsey* —*Macd.* Fion dearg, *Port wine*, fion geal, *white wine*, fion fionn, *white wine* —*Shaw.*

† **Fion**, *a* Old, small, few.

Fionail, *s. f.* (*Ir id*) A fine —*Shaw.*

Fionach, *a.* Old, ancient, antique, old-fashioned.—*Shaw*

Fion-abhal, ail, *s* A grape.—*Shaw.*

Fionais, *s* See **Fianuis**.

Fion-amar, air, *s m* A vine-press Mach as an fhion-amar, *out of the vine-press* —*Stew. Rev.*

Fionan, ain, *s. f.* and *m* A vine. Luchd saoithreachaidh na fionain, *the vine-dressers* —*Stew G B* Tir nam fionan trom, *the land of the heavy vines* —*Mac Lach.*

† **Fion-bhuth**, *s m* A tent, a boot —*Shaw.*

Fion-chaor, *s m* A grape. *N. pl* fion-chaoran.

Fion-chrann, oinn, *s* A vine Meas air fion-chrann, *fruit on the vine.*—*Sm.*

Fionda, *a* (*Ir id*) Cerulean.—*Shaw.*

Fion-dearc, *s. m* (*Ir. id.*) A grape Fion-dearcan mar-bhtach, *poisonous* [*bitter*] *grapes.*—*Stew. Deut* Fuil nam fion-dhearc, *the blood of the grapes* —*Stew. Gen.*

Fion-dearcag, aig, *s. f.* A grape.

Fion-dearg, *s. m* Red wine, Port

Fion-dhuille, *s. f.* A vine-leaf.

Fion-dhuilleag, eig, *s. f* A vine-leaf. *N pl.* fion-dhuilleagan.

Fion-fhasgan, ain, *s. m.* A vine-press *N. pl.* fion-fhasgain

Fion-fhogharadh, aidh, *s m.* Vintage. Fion-fhogharadh an aingidh, *the vintage of the wicked.*—*Stew. Job*

Fion-geur, *s.* Vinegar. Mar fhion-geur, *like vinegar.*—*Stew. Pro.*

Fionghal, ail, *s. m* (*Ir. id.*) Murder of a relative; treason.

Fionghalach, *a.* Murderous; bloody; *also*, a murderer, a parricide. Gu fionghalach coirbte, *in a hostile and bloody manner.*—*Old Song.*

Fionghalachd, *s. f.* Murder; bloodiness.

Fiongharadh, aidh, *s. m.* A vineyard. *N. pl.* fion-gharachan, *vineyards.*

Fion-lios, *s m.* A vineyard.—*Stew. N. T.* *N. pl.* fion-liosan.

Fion-liosach, *a* Having vineyards

Fion-mheug, -mheig, *s. f.* Wine-whey

Fion-mhor, *a* (*Ir. id.*) Abounding in wine.

Fionn, *s. m.* Fingal. See **Fionnghal**, among the proper names at the end of the work.

Fionn, *a.* (*Ir.* finn *and* fionn.) White; fair; pale; re-splendent, bright; sincere; prudent; certain, sure; known; little; small Fonnadh fioghal, fionn, *a quadrangular, re-splendent chariot.*—*Fingalian Poem.* Aon ni 's fionn duinn, *any thing we know by experience* or *for certain;* eun fionn, *the bird called hen-harrier;* the *falco cyaneus* of Linnæus.

Fionn, *v. a.* (*Ir id*) Skin, flay; *rarely*, behold, look. *Pret. a.* dh'fhionn, *skinned*, *fut aff. a.* fionnaidh, *shall skin.*

† **Fionn**, *s.* (*Ir. id.*) A cow, milk.

Fionna, *s.* (*Ir. id*) Hair; the hair of a quadruped. Fionna ghabhar, *goat's hair.*—*Stew. Ex.* A cur an fhionn, *shedding the hair;* fionna fad, *the middle finger.*

Fionnach, *a* Old, antique.

Fionnach, *a.* (*Ir.* fionnadhmach.) Hairy, rough, shaggy.

Fionnachas, ais, *s. m.* Bravery.

Fionnachdainn, *s. f.* (*Ir id.*) Experience.—*Macd.* Knowledge

Fionnadh, aidh, *s m* (*Ir id*) A flaying, a' skinning; *also*, the hair of a quadruped; beard, fur. Am fionnadh sa phlaigh, *the hair in the plague.*—*Stew. Lev.*

Fionnadh, (a), *pr. part.* of fionn. Skinning, flaying. A fionnadh dhiubh an craicinn, *flaying off their skins* —*Stew. Lev.*

Fionnag, aig, *s. f.* (*Ir.* fionnog.) A hooded crow; the *corvus cornix* of Linnæus. *N. pl.* fionnagan.

Fionnaidh, *a.* (*Ir id*) Antique.

Fionnaireachd, *s. f.* See **Fionnfhuaireachd**.

Fionnaltachd, *s. f* (*Ir. id*) Fineness.

Fionnan-feòir, *s m.* A grashopper; a balm-cricket. *N pl* fionnain-feòir, *grashoppers.* Mar na fionnain feòir, *like the grashoppers.*—*Stew. Nah.* Torman nam fionnan feòir, *the twittering of the grashoppers.*—*Mac Lach.*

Fionnaobh, *a* (*Ir id.*) Neat, clean, clever.

Fionnaolta, *a* (fionn-aol) White-washed; white-washed with lime.

Fionnar, *a.* (*for* fionnfhuar) Cool, chill, cold; fresh.

Fionnarachadh, aidh, *s m.* A cooling.

Fionnarachd, *s f.* See **Fionn-fhuaireachd**.

Fionnaraich, *v. a.* and *n.* Cool; refrigerate; become cool. *Pret a* dh'fhionnaraich, *cooled; fut aff. a.* fionnaraichidh, *shall cool.*

Fionnasga, *s. pl.* Bands wherewith vines are tied.—*Shaw.*

Fionnchair, *s. f.* Wisdom.

Fionn-chosach, *a.* White-footed; rough-legged; *also*, the name of the banner of Rano, a Fingalian chief.

Fionn-chosmhuil, *a.* (*Ir. id.*) Probable, likely.

Fionn-feòir, *s. m.* A grashopper; a balm-cricket.

Fionn-fhuaire, *com.* and *sup.* of fionn-fhuar. Cooler, coolest.

Fionn-fhuaireachd, *s. f.* Coolness; freshness; cool, atmospheric coolness; a cool breeze. Fionn-fhuaireachd an là, *the cool of the day.—Stew. Gen.*

Fionn-fhuar, *a.* Cool, cold; fresh. Gu fionn-fhuar, *coldly.* *Com.* and *sup.* fionn-fhuaire.

Fionn-fhuarachadh, aidh, *s. m.* A cooling, a refrigerating, a freshening.

Fionn-fhuaraich, *v. a.* and *n.* Cool, refrigerate, make cool.

Fionn-sgeul, -sgeòil, *s.* A fable, a romance, a legend. Chàin thu i mar fhionn-sgeul, *thou hast reviled it as a fable.—Old Song.*

Fionn-sgeulach, *a.* Romantic.

Fionn-sgeulaiche, *s. m.* A romancer.

Fionn-sgiath, sgeith, *s. f.* A white ring; a white shield.

Fionn-sgiathach, *a.* White-winged; white-shielded.

Fionn-sgoth, *s. m.* (*Ir. id.*) A flower.—*Shaw.*

Fionn-sgothach, *a.* Flowery.

Fionnta, *a.* (*from* fionn.) Hairy, rough, shaggy, furred. Leathar fionnta an daimh òig, *the hairy hide of a young bullock.—Mac Lach.*

Fionntach, *a.* (*Ir. id.*) Rough, hairy, shaggy, furred; (*Shaw*) —woolly.

Fion-ubhal, ail. A grape.

† **Fionuir**, *s. f.* (*Ir. id.*) A vine.—*Shaw.*

Fior, *a.*, *asp. form*, fhior, *fh* silent. (*Gr.* ἀληθής. *Lat.* verus. *Ir.* fior.) True, sincere, just; real; perfect; notable; truly; very. Suaimhneas fior, *true peace.—Sm.* Duine fior, *a just man.* Fior-ghrunnd an loch, *the very bottom of the lake.—Macdon.* Fior-bhochd, *truly poor, very poor.—Macint.* Fior mhaith, *very good, perfectly good.* Fior chosmhalach, *probable*; gu fior, *truly, indeed*; fior chrochair, *a real rascal.*

Fior, *v. a.* Verify.

Fioradh, aidh, *s. m.* (*Ir. id.*) A verifying, a certifying.

Fioraich, *v. a.* Justify. *Pret. a.* dh'fhioraich; *fut. aff. a.* fioraichidh, *shall justify.*

Fioraidheach, *a.* (*from* fior.) Veritable, true.

Fioraidheachd, *s. f.* (*from* fior.) Veracity, truth.

Fior-aithris, *s. f.* A true tale.

Fioran, ain, *s. m.* Long coarse grass; a welcome; feorin grass.

Fior-charaid, *s. m.* A true friend.

Fior-chosmhalach, *a.* Probable, likely.

Fior-chosmhalachd, *s. f.* (*Ir. id.*) Probability, likelihood.

Fior-chreidimh, *s. f.* Sound faith; orthodoxy.

Fior-chreidmheach, ich, *s. m.* A true believer; an orthodox divine. *N. pl.* fior-chreidmhich, *true believers.*

Fior-chreidmheach, *a.* Believing; faithful; professing the true faith. Abraham fior-chreidmheach, *faithful Abraham.—Stew. Gal.*

Fiordha, *a.* (*Ir. id.*) Sincere, true, religious.—*Shaw.*

Fioreun, eoin, *s. m.* An eagle. Luath mar fhireun, *swift as an eagle.—Oss. Gaul.* *Voc. sing.* fhirein. Fhirein fhiadhaich nam beann! *thou wild eagle of the mountains!—Oss. Fin. and Lorm.* *N. pl.* fireòin.

Fior-ghlan, *a.* (*Ir. id.*) Pure, clean; bright, transparent; spotless, blameless. Le h-òr fior-ghlan, *with pure gold.—Stew. Exod.* Unga fior-ghlan, *bright brass.—Stew.* 1 *K. ref.* Gu fior-ghlan, *purely.*

Fior-ghloine, *s. f.* (*Ir. id.*) Purity, clearness, brightness, transparentness, spotlessness, blamelessness. Ann am fiorghloine, *in purity.—Stew. Tim.*

Fior-iochdar, *s.* (*Ir. id.*) A bottom or lowest part; a basis.—*Shaw.* Fior iochdar an uchdain, *the very bottom of the ascent.*

Fior-mhaith, **Fior-mhath**, *a.* (*Ir. id.*) Truly good, very good, perfectly good.

Fior-mhaitheas, eis, *s. m.* Real goodness.

Fior-naomh, *a.* Truly holy. Biodh e fir-naomh, *let him be truly holy.—Sm.*

Fior-naomhachd, *s. f.* True holiness.—*Stew. N. T.*

Fior-ordha, *a.* (*Ir. id.*) Truly noble, truly excellent, illustrious.—*Shaw.*

Fiorraideach, *a.* (*Ir. id.*) Frivolous, trifling, contemptible. Gu fiorraideach, *frivolously.*

Fiorraideachd, *s. f.* Frivolousness, insignificance.

† **Fiorsa**, ai, *s. m.* (*Ir. id.*) Necessity.

Fior-than, *s.* (*Ir. id.*) Long coarse grass. More properly *fioran* or *feòirne.*

Fior-thobar, air, *s. m.* (*Ir. id.*) A spring-well; a perennial spring. *N. pl.* fior-thobraichean.

Fior-thobarach, *a.* (*Ir. id.*) Abounding in spring-wells.

Fior-uachdar, air, *s. m.* (*Ir. id.*) A top or summit.

Fior-uasal, *a.* (*Ir. id.*) Truly noble.

Fior-uisge, *s. m.* (*Ir. id.*) Spring-water; a perpetual fountain. *N. pl.* fior-uisgeachan.

Fios, *s. f.* (*Ir. id.*) Notice; intelligence; word; message; knowledge, art, understanding. Iomchair fios do 'n righ, *send notice to the king.—Mac Lach.* Is fios domh, duit, dithe, *I, thou, she knows.* Is fios do 'n bheò, *the living know.—Sm.* Cha 'n fhios domh, *I wot not.—Stew. Jos.* Gun fhios, *without notice; without knowledge; unnoticed; unapprised; lest; for fear.* Gun fhios c'arson, *without knowing why.—Sm.* Gun fhios chaidh e suas, *unnoticed he ascended.—Oss. Com.* G'a fios, *to her knowledge*; g'a fhios, *to his knowledge.—Stew. Lev.* G'am fios, *to their knowledge*; gun fhios domh, *unknown to me, without my knowledge*; tha fhios agam, *I know*; cuir fios, *send word, send information*; fios-freagairt, *an answer to a letter or message*; bheil fhios agad? *do you know?* an fhios, *for* gun fhios, *lest, for fear that.*

Fiosach, *a.*, *from* fios. (*Ir.* fiosach *and* feasach.) Knowing; expert; intelligent.—*Shaw.*

Fiosachd, *s. f.* (*from* fios.) Divination; fortune-telling; the faculty of divining; occult science; sorcery. A deanamh fiosachd, *divining.—Stew. Gen.* Fear fiosachd, *a diviner.*

Fiosaiche, *s. m.* (*from* fios.) A fortune-teller; a soothsayer; a diviner; a sorcerer. *N. pl.* fiosaichean. Chunnaic na fiosaichean breug, *the diviners saw a lie.—Stew. Zech.*

Fiosaidheachd. See **Fiosachd**.

Fiosail, *a.* Knowing; expert.

Fiosrach, *a.* (*Ir. id.*) Knowing; apprised; certain; inquisitive; prying; busy. Cha 'n fhiosrach mi, *I am not aware, I know not.—Stew. Gen.* Tha mi fiosrach air, *I am certain of it.* Gu fiosrach, *knowingly.* *Com.* and *sup.* fiosraiche.

Fiosrachadh, aidh, *s. m.* An inquiring, a questioning, an ascertaining, apprising, knowledge, experience. O m' fhéin-fhiosrachadh, *from my own experience.—Stew. Gen.*

Fiosrachadh, (a), *pr. part.* of fiosraich. Inquiring, examining.

FIOSRAICH, *v.*, *from* fios. (*Ir.* fiosraigh.) Inquire, ask, examine, ask for, inquire after; visit. *Pret. a.* dh'fhiosraich, *asked*; *fut. aff. a.* fiosraichidh, *shall ask.*

FIOTHNAISE, *s. f.* Sorcery; poison.—*Shaw.* Bad news, detestable news.—*O'Reilly.*

FIOTHRAN, ain, *s. m.* Common wheat-grass; the *triticum repens* of naturalists.

FIR, *gen. sing.* and *n. pl.* of fear; which see.

† FIRB, *s.* (*Ir. id.*) Swiftness, rapidity.

FIR-BHOGHA, *s. pl.* Archers.—*Stew. Gen.*

FIR-BHOLG, *s. pl.* The ancient Irish; the British Belgæ.

Keating observes, that there are yet three families in Ireland descended from the *Fir-bholg*, viz. Gabhruighe in Connaught, Fairsigh in Failghe, and the Galliuns of Leinster.

FIR-BHRÉIG, *s. pl.* (*Ir. id.*) Puppets.—*Shaw.*

FIR-CHEART, eirt, *s. m.* (*Ir. id.*) Justice, righteousness.

FIR-CHLIS, *s. pl.* The Aurora Borealis, or northern lights, by the Scotch Lowlanders called *merry dancers.*

FIR-CHRANN, ainn, *s. m.* (*Ir. id.*) The sycamore tree; the *acer pseudo-platanus* of naturalists.

FIR-DHRIS, *s.* (*Ir. id.*) A bramble.

FIRE! faire! *interj.* Ay ay! fie fie! what a pother! Is fhearr fire faire no mo thruaighe! *better it is to be envied than pitied!*—*G. P.*

FIREACH, ich, *s. m.* A hill; a moor; the top of a hill; high barren ground; a plain on the top of a hill. Air firich an fheidh, *on the moor of deers.*—*Oss. Fing.* Gheibheadh tu feannagan firich, *you would get crows from off the rocks.*—*G. P.*—Said of those who boast that they can obtain impossibilities.

FIREACHAIL, *a.* Nimble; active; manly; *also*, barren, moorish; upland. Calma, feardha, fireachail, *stout, manly, and active.*—*Old Song.* Gu fireachail, *nimbly.*

FIREAD, eid, *s. m.* (*Ir. id.*) A ferret. *N. pl.* fireadan.

FIREADACH, *a.* Like a ferret; abounding in ferrets.

FIREADH, idh, *s. m.* A bottom; truth; flower.

FIREAN, ein, *s. m.* (*from* fear.) A manikin; a dwarf.

† FIREANN, einn, *s. m.* (*Ir. id.*) A chain; a garter.

FÌREANN, *a.* (*Ir. id.*) Upright, righteous, just. Aoibhneas air an fhìreann, *joy on the righteous.*—*Sm.*

FIREANN, *a.* See FIRIONN.

FÌREANNACH, *a.* Just, upright, righteous, true, faithful, exact, honest. *Com.* and *sup.* fìreannaiche, *more* or *most just.* Gu fìreannach, *faithfully.* Gu fìreannach thig an Tighearna, *truly the Lord shall come.*—*Stew. Jos.*

FÌREANNACHADH, aidh, *s. m.* Justification; the act of justifying.

FÌREANEACHD, *s. f.* (*Ir. id.*) Truth.

FÌREANNAICH, *v. a.* Justify, make just, verify. *Pret. a.* dh'fhìreannaich, *justified*; *fut. aff. a.* fìreannaichidh, *shall justify.*

FÌREANNAICHTE, *p. part.* Justified; verified.

FÌREANTA, *a.* True, faithful, honest, upright, sincere, loyal. Gu fìreanta, *faithfully.*

FÌREANTACHD, *s. f.* Truth, faithfulness, integrity, honesty, uprightness, sincerity, loyalty. Toradh sìth is fìreantachd, *the fruit of peace and integrity.*—*Sm.*

FÌREUN, eoin, *s. m.* An eagle. Fìreun mòr, *a great eagle.*—*Stew. Ez.* Written also *fioreun.*

FÌRINN, *s. f.* (*from* fior.) Truth, verity, faithfulness, righteousness. Trocair as fìrinn, *mercy and truth.*—*Sm.* Luchd na fìrinn, *the faithful.*

FÌRINNEACH, *a.* (*Ir. id.*) True, faithful, honest, sincere, loyal; *substantively*, a just person. *Com.* and *sup.* fìrinniche. Gu fìrinneach, *faithfully.*

FÌRINNEACHD, *s. f.* Truth, faithfulness, honesty, sincerity, loyalty.

FÌRINNICH, *v. a.* Justify, affirm; corroborate or confirm by testimony; absolve from accusation. *Pret. a.* dh'fhìrinnich, *justified*; *fut aff. a.* fìrinnichidh, *shall justify.*

FÌRINNICHTE, *p. part.* of fìrinnich.

FÌR-IOMALL, aill, *s. m.* (*Ir. id.*) The utmost border, or limit.

FIR-IONADACH, aich, *s. m.* A lieutenant.—*Shaw.*

FIRIONN, *i. e.* fir-ghin, *a.* (*Ir.* fireann.) Male; *also, substantively*, a male. Firionn na threud, *a male in his flock.*—*Stew. Mal.* Firionn boirionn, *hermaphroditical.*

The word of opposite meaning to *firionn* is *boirionn.*

FIRIONNACH, *a.* (*Ir.* fireannach.) Male.

FIRIONNACH, aich, *s. m.* (*i. e.* fir-ghineach.) A male, a man. Firionnach agus bainionnach, *male and female.*—*Stew. Gen.*

FIRIONNACHD, *s. f.* (*Ir.* fireannacht.) Manhood, virility; male species.

FIRLION, *v. a.* (*Ir. id.*) Multiply.

FIR-LIONADH, aidh, *s. m.* (*Ir. id.*) A multiplying.

† FIS, fise, *s. f.* (*Ir. id.*) Colour, tincture; a dream.—*Shaw.*

FISEAG, eig, *s. f.* (*Ir.* fiseog.) A kitten. Written also *piseag.*

† FIT, fite, *s. f.* (*Ir. id.*) A collation, a refreshment; food; life; living.

FITEAG, eig, *s. f.* A species of mountain-grass. An fhiteag cham, *the bended mountain-grass.*—*Macint.*

FITEAN, ein, *s. m.* (*Ir. id.*) A quill.—*Shaw.*

FITH, *s. f.* (*Ir. id.*) Land.

† FITH-CHEALL, ill, *s. m.* (*Ir. id.*) A philosopher.

† FITHCHIL, *s. pl.* Tables; a chess-board.—*Shaw.*

FITHEACH, fithiche, *s. m.* A raven; the *corvus corax* of Linnæus. Chuir e mach fitheach, *he sent out a raven.*—*Stew. Gen.* *N. pl.* fithich, *ravens.* Thug na fithich aran, *the ravens brought bread.*—*Stew. O. T.* Fitheach mara, *a cormorant.*

FITHEAN, ein, *s. m.* (*Ir. id.*) A hog.

† FITHIL, *s. m.* (*Ir. id.*) A poetaster.

FITHREACH, ich, *s. m.* (*Ir. id.*) A species of eatable sea-weed, more commonly called *duilleasg.*

FIÙ, *a.* (*Ir. id.*) Worth; worthy; deserving; like; alike; edible. Duine nach fiù, *a naughty man.*—*Stew. Pro.* Cha 'n fhiù e air, *he is not deserving of it.* Cha b' fhiù e, *it was worth nothing, it was profitable for nothing.*—*Stew. Jer.*

FIÙ, *s. m.* (*Ir. id.*) Worth; value; desert. Is beag d' fhiù, *you are little worth.*

FIÙBHAIDH, *s. f.* An arrow. Fiùbhaidh is bolg, *an arrow and quiver.*—*Mac Lach.*

FIUBHAS, ais, *s. m.* (*Ir. id.*) Dignity, worth.

FIUCH, *v.* Boil; simmer; estuate; spring forth.—*Shaw.*

FIUCHACH, *a.* (*Ir. id.*) That boileth; boiling.—*Shaw.*

FIUCHADH, aidh, *s. m.* (*Ir. id.*) A boiling, a simmering; regurgitating; heat.

FIUCHAIREACHD, *s. f.* (*Ir.* fiuchaireacht.) Boiling rage.

FIÙDHAIL, *a.* Worthy.

FIÙGHAIR, *s. f.* Hope; earnest expectation; longing; memory; regard; respect. Gun fhiùghair ri madainn, *without hope of the morning.*—*Oss. Gaul.* D' fhiughair ri meoghair chon, *thy regard for the sport of hounds.*—*Fingalian Poem.*

FIUGHAIREACH, *a.* Hopeful; expectant; having a good memory. Gu fiughaireach, *hopefully.*

FIUGHAIREACHD, *s. f.* Hopefulness; expectancy; reminiscence.

Fiughan, ain, *s. m.* A cheese-press. Written also *fiodhan.*

Fiughantach, *a.* Generous, benevolent. Cridhe fiughantach, *a generous heart.—Old Song.* *Com.* and *sup.* fiughantaiche. Gu fiughantach, *generously.*

Fiughantachd, *s. f.* Generosity, benevolence; the practice of benevolence.

Fiughantas, ais, *s. m.* Generosity, liberality, benevolence. Threig iad am fiughantas, *they have abandoned their generosity.—Old Song.*

Fiughar, air, *s. m.* Hope, earnest expectation. See Fiùghair.

Fiùi, *s. pl.* (*asp. form,* fhiùi.) A hero; an arrow. Air sgath an fhiùi, *for the hero's sake.—Oss.* Chaill e liath-fhiùi, *he lost his grey arrow.—Oss. Tem.*

Fiull. More properly *feall;* which see.

Fiunas, ais, *s. m., from* fiù. (*Ir.* fiuntas.) Worth; price, value.—*Shaw.*

Fiundach, *a.* Worthy, deserving.

Fiundas, ais, *s. m.* Merit, worth; dignity.

Fiundruin, *a.* Polished; smooth; *also,* polished bone. An roth fiundruin, *the polished wheel.—Old Poem.*

Fiuntach, *a.* See Fiundach.

Fiuradh, aidh, *s. m.* (*Ir. id.*) Satisfaction; comfort; completion; sufficiency.

Fiùran, ain, *s. m.* A twig, a sapling, a tendril; a species of rank weed; a germ or sprout; a stripling. *N. pl.* fiùrain. A cur sùgh 's na fiùrain, *putting sap in the tendrils.—Macfar.* Fiùran seasmhach, *a stout stripling.—Mac Co.* Fiùran aigeantach, *a mettlesome youth.—Macdon.*

Fiùranta, *a.* (*from* fiùran.) Like a sapling or twig; strong; juvenile. Tha 'm fear mòr fiùranta, *the man is great and strong.—Old Poem.*

Fiusach, *a.* (*Ir. id.*) Earnest.—*Shaw.* *Com.* and *sup.* fiusaiche. Gu fiusach, *earnestly.*

Fiùthaidh, *s. f.* Matter, subject; an arrow.

Flaiche, *s. f.* (*Ir. id.*) A sudden gust of wind.

Flaicheach, *a.* (*Ir. id.*) Windy, gusty; blustering.

Flaindearg. See Flanndearg.

Flaith, *gen. sing.* of flath.

† **Flaith**, *s. f.* (*Ir. id.*) Milk.

† **Flaith**, *s. m.* A lord; a hero; a flower; a kind of strong ale.

Flaith-chiste, *s. f.* A royal treasure.

Flaitheachd, *s. f.* (*from* flath.) A government, supremacy.

Flaitheamhnas, ais, *s. m.* Sovereignty; a kingdom; a reign; heaven. For the last sense, see Flath-innis.

Flaitheas, eis, *s. m.* Heaven; the heavens; sovereignty; dominion; kingdom. Os cionn nam flaitheas, *above the heavens.—Sm.* See Flath-innis.

Flaitheasach, *a.* (*Ir. id.*) Heavenly; princely, noble, stately. Talla flaitheasach, *a princely hall.—Macint.* Gu flaitheasach, *in a princely manner.*

Flaitheil, *a.* Princely, generous, noble; showy, pompous; celestial. Gu flaitheil, *nobly.*

Flaitheasach, *a.* Celestial.

Flann, *a.* Red; *also,* blood; the name of some Irish chiefs.

Flann-bhuinneach, ich, *s. m.* and *f.* (*Ir. id.*) A dysentery or bloody flux.

Flann-dearg, *a.* (*Ir. id.*) Red; a staynard colour in heraldry, used to express some disgrace or blemish in a family.

Flann-sgaoileadh, *s.* (*Ir. id.*) A dysentery.

Flann-shuileach, *a.* (*Ir. id.*) Having red eyes.

Flasg, flaisg, *s.* A basket; a vessel made of wicker; a bottle covered with wicker; a powder-horn. *N. pl.* flasgaichean. Luchd nam flasgaichean fùdair, *they with the powder flasks.—Turn.*

Flath, flaith, *s. m.* (*Ir.* flaith.) A lord; a prince; a commander; a hero; a champion. *N. pl.* flathan. Flath do 'n fhine laimh-thréin, *commander of the strong-armed clan.—Old Song.* Gniomh nam flathan, *the deeds of the heroes. Oss. Duthona.*

Flathail, *a.* (flath-amhuil.) Princely; stately; showy; elegant; victorious. Le-armailt fhlathail neamh, *with the victorious hosts of heaven.—Sm.* Ceum flathail, *a stately step.—Oss. Tem.* Gu flathail, *in a princely manner.*

Flathaileachd, *s. f.* Princeliness; stateliness; showiness.

Flathan, *n. pl.* of flath; which see.

Flathasach, *a.* Princely; stately; elegant; victorious; heroic.

Flathasachd, *s. f.* Princeliness; stateliness; elegance; victoriousness; heroism.

Flath-innis, *s. f.* Heaven; *literally,* the isle of the brave, or the hero's isle.

This word is still used in the Gaelic language to signify *heaven,* although the composition of it shews that it originated in the wild ideas which the ancient Gael entertained concerning a future state.

Flath-mhaise, *s. f.* Princeliness; nobleness; stateliness; bravery.

Flath-mhaiseach, *a.* (flath *and* maiseach.) Princely; noble; stately; brave. *Com.* and *sup.* flath-mhaisiche. Gu flath-mhaiseach, *in a princely manner.*

Fleadh, *s. f.* (*Ir. id.*) A feast, an entertainment, a carousal. Fleadh do m' réir, *a feast to my mind.—Oss. Tem.*

Fleadh is often used to express both the feast and the persons entertained. Written also *fleagh.*

Fleadhach, *a.* Feasting, entertaining, carousing, convivial; prone to entertain. Written also *fleaghach.*

Fleadhachas, ais, *s. m.* (*Ir. id.*) Feasting, banqueting, carousal, revelry.

Fleagh, *s. f.* A feast, an entertainment, carousal. Written also *fleadh.*

Fleaghach, *a.* Feasting, entertaining, carousing, convivial. Written also *fleadhach.*

Fleaghachas, ais, *s. m.* Feasting, banqueting, carousing, revelry.

Fleasg, fleisg, *s. m.* (*Ir. id.*) A garland, wreath, or fillet; a crown; a chain; a rod; a wand; a ring; *rarely,* a sheaf; moisture. Fleasg òir, *a crown of gold.—Stew. Ex.*

Gleasgach, aich, *s. m.* A bachelor; a lad; a stripling; a clown; *rarely,* a corn-field; a fiddler.—*Macint.* Nuair bha thu ad fhleasgach òg, *when thou wert a young stripling.—Old Song.* Fleasgach fir na-bainnse, *the bridegroom's man;* fleasgach bean na bainnse, *or,* fleasgach mna na bainnse, *the bride's man.* *N. pl.* fleasgaich.

Fleasgachan, ain, *s. m.* (*Ir. id.*) *dim.* of fleasgach. A rustic; a mean fellow.—*Shaw.*

Fleasgaich, *gen. sing.* and *n. pl.* of fleasgach.

Fleasgan, ain, *s. m.* A treasure.—*Shaw.* Also, *n. pl.* of fleasg.

Fleisd, *v.* Slay, slaughter, butcher. *Pret. a.* fhleisd, *butchered; fut. aff. a.* fleisdidh, *shall butcher.*

Fleisdear, eir, *s. m.* An arrow-maker; a butcher or flesher. *N. pl.* fleisdeirean.

Fleisdearachd, *s. f.* Arrow-making; butchering; the business of an arrow-maker, or of a butcher.

Fleodruinn, *s. f.* (*Ir. id.*) A buoy.—*Shaw.*

Fleogan, ain, *s. m.* (*Sax.* fleogan, *to hang loose.*) An untidy person; a flabby person; *also,* a flat fish; a sole; a *fleuk.* *N. pl.* fleogain.

Fleoganach, *a.* Untidy; tawdry; like a flat fish; abounding in flat fish, as soles.

Fliche, *s. f.* (*Ir. id.*) Phlegm; humours; moisture; water.

Flicheachd, *s. f., from* fliche. (*Ir. id.*) Phlegm; humours; moisture; water; ooziness.

Flicheann, flichne, *s.* Sleet.

Flichneach, *a.* Phlegmy; *for* flicheanach.

Flichneachd, *s. f.* (*perhaps* fluich-shneachd.) Sleet; continued sleet; *also*, ooziness; moisture.

Flige, *s. f.* Chickweed: *alsine.*

Fliochd, *s.* The second dram taken after breakfast; the first is called *sgailc.*

Fliodh, *s. m.* (*Ir. id.*) Chickweed.

Fliodh, *s. f.* An excrescence; a wen; chicken-weed. Duine air am bi fliodh, *a man who has a wen.—Stew. Lev.*

Fliodhan, ain, *s. m., dim.* of fliodh. (*Ir. id.*) A little wen or excrescence. *N. pl.* fliodhain.

Fliodhanach, *a.* (*Ir. id.*) Full of wens; like a wen.

Fliuch, *a.* (*Ir. id.*) Wet, rainy, moist, damp, oozy. Fuar fliuch, gun deo leirsinn, *cold, wet, and stark blind.—Orr.* La fluich, *a wet day. Com.* and *sup.* fliuiche. Am fear is fliuiche rachadh e san ald, *let the wettest go to the well.—G. P.*

Fliuch, *v. a.* (*Ir. id.*) Wet, moisten, water. *Pret. a.* fhluich, *watered; fut. aff. a.* fluichaidh, *shall water.* Fhliuch a dheur-shùil an leac, *his tearful eye wet the flag. Ull.*

Fliuchach, *a.* Wet, rainy, moist, oozy.

Fliuchadh, aidh, *s. m.* (*Ir. id.*) A wetting, a watering, a moistening rain, wet weather.

Flichaidh, *fut aff. a.* of fluich. Shall wet.

Fliuchain, *s. f.* (*Ir. id.*) Juice, moisture, wetness.

Fliuch-bheulach, *a.* (*Ir. id.*) Wet-mouthed; spitting; tippling.

Fliuch-bhileach, *a.* Wet-lipped; fond of drinking or tippling; that ships water.—*Shaw.*

Fliuchlachd, *s. f.* (*Ir. id.*) Wet weather; continued rain; a puddle.

Fliuchras, ais, *s. m.* Moisture.

Fliuch-shneachd, *s. f.* (*Ir. id.*) Sleet. Commonly pronounced and written *flichneachd.*

Fliuch-shuileach, *a.* (*Ir. id.*) Tearful; ophthalmic.

Fliuch-shuileachd, *s. f,* A running of water from the eyes; ophthalmia.—*Shaw.*

Flocas, ais, *s. m.* (*Ir. id. Lat.* floccus.) A lock of wool.

† **Floch**, *a.* (*Span.* floxo. *Lat.* flaccus. *Ir.* floch.) Lax, soft.

Flùr, flùir, *s. m.* (*Ir. id.*) Flour; meal; a flower.—*Turn.*

Flusg, fluisg, *s.* (*Ir. id.*) A flux.

† **Fo**, *s. m.* (*Ir. id.*) A king, a prince, a sovereign; regard.

Fo, *prep.* (*Ir. id.*) Under, beneath, below; at the foot of. Fo 'd, foghad, *beneath thee, under thee;* fodham, *under;* tha tighinn fodham, *I intend, I am resolved;* caidleam fo 'n fheur, *let me sleep beneath the turf.—Oss. Gaul.* Da thoman fo dharaig, *two mounds at the foot of an oak.—Oss. Tem.* Fo leòn, *wounded.—Sm.* Fo bhròn, *sorrowful.* Fo mhìle sleagh, *under* [*armed with*] *a thousand spears.—Oss. Fing.*

† **Fo**, *a.* (*Ir. id.*) Easy, quiet, unconcerned; powerful; *also, substantively,* honour; esteem; decency; a king.

† **Foain**, *s. f.* (*Ir. id.*) A swarm, a crowd.

Fobair, *s. f.* (*Ir. id.*) Advancement; rencontre; undertaking.

Fobha, **Fobhaidh**, *a.* (*Ir. id.*) Swift, rapid, quick, nimble.

Fobhailtean, *s. pl.* Suburbs.

† **Fobhair**, *a.* (*Ir. id.*) Sick, infirm, weak.

Fobhair, *s. f.* (*Ir. id.*) A salve, ointment. Fobhair shùl, *an eye-salve.—Stew. Rev. ref.*

Fo-bhuail, *v.* (*Ir. id.*) Strike gently, pat; strike below.

Fo-bhualadh, aidh, *s. m.* (*Ir. id.*) A stroking; a striking or beating gently.

Fo-bhuidhe, *a.* (*Ir. id.*) Tawny, yellowish.

Fo-bhuille, *s. m.* (*Ir. id.*) A slight blow or stroke; an understroke.

† **Fòc**, *s. m.* (*Ir. id. Shans.* vac. *Lat.* vox *and* voc-o.) A voice.

Focal, ail, *s. m., from* fòc. (*Ir. id. Lat.* vocal-is, *a vowel.*) A word; a mandate; a promise; a vowel; Scripture. Focal na thràth, *a word in season.—Stew. Pro.* Focal magaidh, *a by-word, a scoff, a taunt.* Cho maith ri fhocal, *as good as his word;* air m' fhocal, *upon my word.*

Focalach, *a.* Verbal; verbose; diffuse; vocal.

Focalaiche, *s. m.* A speaker, a spokesman, a man of many words.

Focalair, *s. m.* A dictionary; a vocabulary; a lexicographer. *N. pl.* focalairean.

Focalaireachd, *s. f.* Lexicography; the occupation of a lexicographer.

Fòcalan, ain, *s. m.* A fumart or polecat; the *mustela pulorius* of Linnæus; a sneaking fellow. *N. pl.* focalain.

Focal-fhreumh, -fhreimh, *s.* (*Ir. id.*) Etymon; the root of a word.

Focal-fhreumhach, *a.* (*Ir.* focal-fhreumhach.) Etymological.

Focal-fhreumhachd, *s. f.* (*Ir.* focal-fhreumhachd.) Etymology.

Focal-fhreumhaiche, *s. m.* (*Ir.* focal-fhreumhaighe.) An etymologian.

Fochaid, *s. f.* (*Ir.* fochuid.) Mockery, derision, scorn, ridicule. Fear na fochaid, *the mocker, the scorner.—Stew. Pro.* Fear fochaid, *a scorner.* Dean fochaid, *mock.*

Fochaid, *v.* (*Ir.* fochuid.) Mock, deride, ridicule. *Pret. a.* dh'fhochaid, *mocked; fut. aff. a.* fochaididh, *shall mock.* This verb takes after it the prep. *air,* either simple or compound. Fochaid air, orra, *mock him, them.*

Fochaideach, *a.* Scoffing, jeering, deriding; inclined to scoff or mock.

Fochaidhe, *s.* (*Ir. id.*) A disease, a disorder.—*Shaw.*

Fochaidich, *v. a.* (*from* fochaid.) Mock, scoff, sneer.

† **Fochain**, *s. f.* (*Ir. id.*) A cause, a motive, a reason; disturbance.—*Shaw.*

Fochair, *s.* (*Ir. id.*) Propinquity; neighbourhood; nearness; presence. Am fochair, *near to; before; in presence of.* Am fochair an righ, *in the king's presence.* Am fhochair, *in my presence.* Na 'm fochair, *in their presence.* Na fochair, *in her presence.*

† **Fochall**, aill, *s. m.* (*Ir. id.*) Dirt, filth, corrupt matter. —*Shaw.*

Fochann, ainn, *s. m.* (*Ir.* fochan.) Young corn in the blade; a plant; *also,* food, provender. Reothadh a mhill am fochann, *frost which has spoiled the young corn.—Macfar.* Tha fochann air an eorna, *the barley has bladed.*

† **Fochar**, air, *s, m.* (*Ir. id.*) Wind.

Fochas, ais, *s. m.* (*Ir. id.*) Voraciousness.

† **Fochlach**, aich, *s. m.* (*Ir. id.*) The lowest order or degree of poets or philosophers.

Fochladh, aidh, *s. m.* (*Ir.* fochla.) A den, a cave; a palace; the value or worth of any thing; an offering.—*Shaw.*

Fochlas, ais, *s. m.* A prize; a gift; a reward for valour. Fion is fochlas, is feòil, *wine the reward of valour, and venison.—Fingalian Poem.*

Fochnadh, aidh, *s. m.* (*Ir. id.*) Dry rotten wood.

Fòchradh, aidh, *s. m.* (*Ir. id.*) A banishing, banishment. See Fògradh.

Fochraic, *s. f.* (*Ir. id.*) Happiness, bliss, felicity.

Fochras, ais, *s. m.* (*Ir. id.*) A bosom, a breast.—*Shaw.*

Fochuidhe, *s. f.* A flout, a jeer, derision, scorn.

Fochiun. See Fochain.

Foclach, *a.* See Focalach.

Foclair, *s. m.* (*from* focal.) A dictionary, a vocabulary.

Foclaireachd, *s. f.* Lexicography; the labour of a lexicographer.

Foclairiche, *s. m.* A lexicographer.

Fo 'd, (fodhad.) Under thee, beneath thee.

Fo d', (fo do.) Under thee; under thy; beneath thee; beneath thy. Cuir fo'd chèann, *put beneath your head.*

† **Fod**, *s. m.* (*Ir. id.*) Skill, knowledge, science.

† **Fodach**, *a.* (*Ir. id.*) Skilful; knowing; prudent, discreet.—*Shaw.*

† **Fodachadh**, aidh, *s. m.* Obstruction.

Fodair, *gen. sing.* of fodar.

Fodair, *v. a.* Give food or provender to cattle; fodder. *Pret. a.* dh'fhodair, *foddered; fut. aff.* fodairidh.

Fodar, air, *s. m.* (*Da.* foeder. *Eng.* fodder.) Straw; provender. Eadar am feur is am fòdar, *betwixt the grass and the straw.—G. P.*

Fodarach, *a.* Having much straw.

† **Fòdh**, *s. m.* (*Ir. id.*) Skilfulness; knowledge.—*Shaw.*

Fodha, *prep.* Under, below, beneath; at the foot of. Fodha so tha mo ghaol, *underneath lies my love.—Ull.* Fodha do sgòd, *under thy command.*

Fodha, *comp. prep.* Under him or it; below him or it; under his command.

Fodhad, *comp. prep.* Under thee, below thee, beneath thee. An leabadh a ta fodhad, *the bed which is under thee.—Stew. Pro.*

Fodhaibh, *comp. prep.* Under you, beneath you, below you.

Fodhail, *s. f.* (*Ir. id.*) A division, a dissolving, a releasing.—*Shaw.*

† **Fodhail**, *v. a.* (*Ir. id.*) Loose, release, untie.—*Shaw. Pret. a.* dh'fhodhail, *loosed.*

Fodhainn, *comp. prep.* Beneath us, under us, below us.

Fodhair, *s. f.* (*Ir. id.*) Froth.

Fodham, *comp. prep.* Beneath me, under me; under my command. Thàinig e fodham, *he came under* [*supplanted*] *me.—Stew. Gen.* Tha tighinn fodham, *I am resolved, I intend, I propose.*

Fo-dhord, *s. m.* A loud noise.—*Shaw.* A conspiracy.—*O'Reilly.*

Fo-dhorsach, *a.* Having wickets; of a wicket.

Fo-dhorus, uis, *s. m.* (*Ir. id.*) A wicket, a little gate, a little door. *N. pl.* fo-dhorsan.

Fodhpa, *comp. prep.* Under them, beneath them, below them.

Fo-dhuine, *s. m.* A dwarf; a servant; a plebeian. *N. pl.* fo-dhaoine.

Fo-dhùrdan, ain, *s. m.* A humming, a low murmur; a conspiracy.

Fodrach, *a.* (*from* fodar.) Having much straw; strawy.

Fodradh, aidh, *s. m.* (*Ir. id.*) A hand-feeding of cattle.

† **Foduair**, *s. f.* (*Ir. id.*) Caution; notice.

Fodurluasach, *a.* (*Ir. id.*) Busy.—*Shaw.*

† **Fogail**, *v. a.* (*Ir. id.*) Teach; dictate; loosen; untie. —*Shaw. Pret.* dh'fhogail, *taught; fut. aff.* fogailidh, *shall teach.*

Fogair, *s. f.* (*Ir. id.*) A proclamation, a command.

Fògair, *v. a.* Banish, drive away forcibly, expel; chase, pursue; warn; order; *rarely*, command. *Pret. a.* dh'fhògair, *banished; fut. aff. a.* fògraidh, *shall banish.* Gach eagal fògraibh, *banish every fear.—Sm. Fut. pass.* fògrar.

Fògairt, *s. f.* Banishment, exile, expulsion. Chaidh e am fogairt, *he went into exile;* air fhògairt, *in exile.*

Fògarach, *a.* Expelling, banishing; expulsive; relating to exile.

Fògarach, aich, *s. m.* An outlaw, an exile, a fugitive, an outcast, a vagabond. Mar fhògarach o ghràs, *as an outcast from grace.—Sm.* Bithidh mi m' fhògarch, *I shall be a fugitive.—Stew. Gen.*

Fògaradh, aidh, *s. m.* (*Ir.* fochradh.) A banishing; banishment, expulsion. Tha e air fhògradh, *I am banished; fut aff. a.* fògaraichidh, *shall banish.*

Fogaraichte, *p. part.* of fogaraich. Banished, exiled, expelled; persecuted.

† **Fogartha**, *a.* Gracious.—*Shaw.*

Fogasg, *a.* Near, nigh, at hand. Tighinn fogasg uchd ri h-uchd, *coming near, breast to breast.—Mac Lach.* Am fogasg, *at hand.*

† **Fogh**, *s. m.* (*Ir. id.*) An attack; a rape; hospitality; a pirate.

Fogh, *a.* (*Ir. id.*) Careless, unconcerned, indifferent, easy.

Foghail, *s. f.* Offence, offensiveness; robbery; an inroad into an enemy's country. Gun ardan gun fhoghail, *without pride or offensiveness.—Old Song.*

Foghail, *v. a.* Plunder; spoil; make a hostile incursion.—*Shaw. Pret.* dh' fhoghail, *plundered; fut. aff.* foghailidh, *shall plunder.*

Foghailiche, *s. m.* A plunderer; a spoiler.

Fòghain, *v.* Suffice, be sufficient; do for, *in a bad sense;* avail. *Pret. a.* dh'fhòghain *sufficed; fut. aff. a.* foghnaidh, *shall suffice.* Cha 'n fhoghain so, *this is not sufficient.—Sm.* Foghnaidh sin da, *that will suffice him.—Oss. Gaul.* Foghnaidh mi dhuit, *I will do for you.* Cha 'n fhoghnadh a sgia da a tiughad, *the thickness of his shield could not avail him.—Ull.*

Foghainnteach. Stout, able, brave; sufficient; prosperous. Daoine foghainnteach, *able men.—Stew. Ex.* Biodh a lamhan foghainteach, *let his hands be sufficient.—Stew. G. B. Com.* and *sup.* foghainntiche.

Foghainnteachd, *s. f.* Stoutness; strength; sufficiency; prosperity.—*Shaw.*

Foghair, *v. n.* Make a noise; tingle.—*Shaw.*

Foghair, *s.* See Foghar.

Foghann, ainn, *s. m.* (*Da.* fon, *thistledown. Ir.* fothan.) A thistle; thistledown; thistlebeard.

Foghannan, ain, *s. m.* A thistle; thistlebeard. Shaltair e 'm foghannan, *he trampled the thistle.—Stew.* 2 *K.*

† **Foghanta**, *a.*, *from* † fogh. (*Ir. id.*) Good, generous; prosperous; serviceable; powerful.

Foghantachd, *s. f.* (*Ir. id.*) Goodness, generousness; prosperousness; sufficiency.

Fo-ghaoth, ghaoithe, *s. f.* (*Ir. id.*) A gentle wind.—*Shaw.*

Foghar, air, *s. m.* (*Ir. id.*) A vowel; a tone; accent; voice; noise; sound; favour; froth.—*Shaw.* Da-fhogar, *a diphthong;* tri-fhogar, *a triphthong.*

Foghar, air, (fogh-ar, *literally*, a spoiling the fields of their crops.) Harvest; autumn. Foghar an eorna, *the barley-harvest;* foghar a chruithneachd, *the wheat-harvest.—Stew. Ruth.* Foghar na saidh, *the hay-harvest;* air an fhoghar, *out a harvesting.*

Fogharach, *a.* Autumnal; harvest; loud; noisy; echoing.

Fogharachadh, aidh, *s. m.* Working at harvest, harvesting.

Fogharachd, *s. f.* Autumnal labour.

Fogharadh, aidh, *s. m.* (*Ir.* foghmhar.) Harvest; autumn. Ré an fhogharaidh uile, *all the time of harvest.—Stew. Jos.* Air feadh 'n fhogharaidh, *during harvest;* am an fhogharaidh, *harvest time;* la geal fogharaidh, *a fine harvest day.*

Foghard, aird, *s. m.* A tingling noise.—*Shaw.*

Fogharaich, *v. a.* and *n.* Hire for harvest-work; work at harvest. *Pret.* dh'fhogharaich, *hired for harvest.*

Foghladh, aidh, *s. m.* (*Ir. id.*) Trespass, offence.—*Shaw.* Robbery.

Foghlaich, *v. a.* Rob, pillage, plunder. *Pret. a.* dh' fhoghlaich, *plundered; fut. aff.* foghlaichidh.

Foghlaiche, *s. m.* A robber, a plunderer. *N. pl.* foghlaichean.

Foghlas, *v. n.* (*Ir. id.*) Grow pale.—*Shaw.*

Foghlmuine, *s. m.* A learned person; a teacher.—*Stew. Is.*

Foghluich, *v. a.* (*Ir. id.*) Rob.

Foghluiche, *s. m.* (*Ir. id.*) A spoiler, a robber.

Foghluim, *v. a.* Learn, teach, instruct. *Pret. a.* dh'fhòghluim; *fut. aff. a.* foghluimidh, *shall learn.*

Foghluimte, *p. part.* of foghluim. Learned, instructed, taught, trained, disciplined. Mar agh fhoghluimte, *like a heifer that is taught.—Stew. Hos.*

Foghlum, uim, *s. m.* Learning, instruction; discipline, edification. Aom ri foghlum, *apply to learning.—Stew. Pro.*

Foghlumach, *a.* Edifying, instructive; of, or belonging to, learning.

Foghlumach, aich, *s. m.* A teacher, a scholar; a novice; a man of learning. Cho maith ris an fhoghlumach, *as well as the scholar.—Stew.* 1 *Chr.*

Fogmhair, *s. m.* A pirate.

Foghmhaireachd, *s. f.* (*Ir. id.*) Piracy, plundering. Le foghmhaireachd air tràigh 's air muir, *with plundering by sea and land.—Old Song.*

Foghmhairiche, *s. m.* (fogh *and* mairiche.) A corsair or pirate. *Ir.* foghmhorach.

Fòghnadh, aidh, *s. m.* Sufficiency; improvement; availing; sufficing.

Fòghnadh, 3 *sing. imper.* of fòghain. Foghnadh so, *let this suffice.*

Foghnaidh, *fut. aff. a.* of foghain; which see.

Foghnamh, aimh, *s. m.* (*Ir. id.*) Service, slavery, servitude.—*Shaw.*

Foghnan, ain, *s. m.* (*Da.* fön, *thistledown.*) Thistle; thistledown, thistlebeard. Leanaibh am foghnan, *pursue the thistledown.—Oss. Gaul.*

Fòghnas, ais, *s. m.* (*Ir. id.*) Profit, gain, advantage; sufficiency. Tha m' fhoghnas agam, *I have got enough.*

Foghraidh, *s. f.* A warning, a charge, a caution, a proclamation.

Fògrach, *a.* Banishing, expelling, expulsive; relating to exile. Written also *fogarach.*

Fògrach, *a.* Warning, cautionary, admonitory.

Fògrach, aich, *s. m.* An outlaw, an exile, an outcast, a vagabond. Written also *fogarach;* which see.

Fògradh, aidh, *s. m.* (*Ir. id.*) Banishment, exile, expulsion; pursuit; persecution.

Fògradh, aidh, *s. m.* (*Ir. id.*) A warning, a charge, a proclamation; a decree or ordinance.—*Shaw.*

Fògraibh, 2 *pl. imper.* of fogair. Expel ye.

Fògraidh, *fut. aff. a.* of fogair; which see.

Fògrar, *fut. pass.* of fogair. Shall be banished.

Fogus, *a.* Near, nigh, at hand. Am fogus, *near;* thoir am fogus e, *bring it near;* thig am fogus, *come near.* This adjective takes after it the preposition *do* or *air*, either simple or compounded; as, fogus do 'n bhàs, *near death;* fogus domh, *near me;* thig am fogus orm, *come near me;* ged is fogus duinn, is foigse oirnne, *though near us be nigh, upon us is nigher.—G. P.*

Fogusg, *a.* See Fogus *and* Fagus.

Foicheall, ill, *s. m.* A day's hire, a day's wages; salary.—*Shaw.*

Foi-cheumnadh, aidh, *s. m.* A gradation; a series.

Foichill, *v.* Provide, prepare. *Pret.* dh'fhoichill, *provided; fut. aff.* foichillidh.

Foichleadh, idh, *s. m.* (*Ir. id.*) Wages.

Foichlean, ein, *s. m.* A sprout; young corn; corn appearing above ground.

Fòid, foide, *s. f.* (*Ir. id.*) A clod; a peat; turf; sod; glebe. *N. pl.* foidean; *d. pl.* fòidibh. Tha mo ghaol fo 'n fhoid so, *my love is under this turf.—Ull.* An siol fa' fhoidibh, *the seed beneath its clods.—Stew. Joel.* Foid mhòin, *a peat;* fòid chùlaig, *a fire-turf;* fòid a bhreith 's a bhàis, *the spot where a man is destined to be born or to die.—G. P.*

Foidheach, ich, *s. m.* (*Ir. id.*) A mendicant.—*Shaw. N. pl.* foidhich.

Foidheachas, ais, *s. m.* (*Ir. id.*) Mendicancy.

Foidhhe, *comp. prep.* Under her, beneath her, below her; under her command.

† Foidhreach, ich, *s. m.* (*Ir. id.*) A little image.

Foigh, *v. a., provincial* for faigh; which see.

† Foighean, ein, *s. m.* A green plot, a mead, a lawn.

† Foighid, *v. a.* Bear, suffer, endure, put up with.—*Shaw.*

Foighid. See Foighidinn.

Fòighideach, *a.* See Foighidinneach.

Foighidinn, *s. f.* Patience, forbearance. Cha 'n 'eil foighidinn agad, *you have no patience;* glac foighidinn, *have patience.*

Foighidinneach, *a.* (*Ir. id.*) Patient, long-suffering. Gu foighidinneach, *patiently. Com.* and *sup.* foighidinniche.

Foighidneachail, *a.* Patient, long-suffering, forbearing.

Foighin, *s. f.* (*Ir. id.*) A green plot, a mead.

Foighiontas, ais, *s. m.* (*Ir. id.*) Amplitude.

Foighir. See Faighir.

Foi-ghliocas, ais, *s. m.* (*Ir. id.*) Low cunning; great prudence.

Foighneachd, *v.* Inquire, ask, question. *Pret. a.* dh' fhoighneachd, *asked; fut. aff. a.* foighneachdaidh, *shall ask.* This verb takes after it the prep. *do*, either simple or compound; as, foighneachd do Sheumas, *ask* or *inquire of James;* foighneachd dheth, dhi, dhiom, *ask of him, her, me.*

Foighneachd, *s. f.* An inquiring, asking, questioning; inquisitiveness, curiosity.

Foighneachd, (a), *pr. part.* of foighneachd.

Foighnich, *v.* Inquire, ask, question. *Pret. a.* dh'fhoighnich; *fut. aff. a.* foighnichidh. Written also *foighneachd;* which see.

Foighreag, eig, *s. f.* A cloud-berry.

Foigse, *com.* and *sup.* of fogus. Nearer, nearest. *Asp. form,* fhoigse. Am fear is fhoigse domh, *the man who is nearest to me.*

Foigseachd, *s. f.* Propinquity, proximity.—*Shaw.*

Foil, *s.* A while.—*Shaw.*

Foil, *v. a.* Confine in a sty.

Foil, *a.* (*Gr.* φωλεος, *a hiding-place.*) A hog-sty; a while; a den; a hiding-place. Cumaidh a mhuc foil fèin glan, *the sow will keep its own sty clean.*—*G. P.*

Fòil, *a.* Gentle, mild, soft, slow. Farasd, fòil, *solemn and slow.*—*Ull.* Thuirt e, gu fòil, ri threud, *he said mildly to his followers.*—*Sm.*

Foileabadh, leapach, *s. f.* A truckle bed. *N. pl.* foileapaichean.

Foilead, eid, *s. m.* (*Ir. id.*) A fillet; a coif.—*Shaw.*

Foi-lean, *v. a.* (*Ir. id.*) Follow after; hang after; hanker.

† **Foilearbadh**, aidh, *s. m.* (*Ir. id.*) Death.

† **Fòileasan**, ain, *s. m.* (*Ir. id.*) An asp. *N. pl.* foileasain.

Foileid, *s. f.* A wimple; a muffler.—*Shaw.*

Foilidh, *s. m.* A foal, a filley.

Foill, *s. f.* (*Ir. id.*) Deceit, fraud, trickery, treachery; wrong; *rarely*, leisure. Na deanaibh foill, *do no wrong.*—*Stew. Jer.* Labhair e le foill, *he spoke with deceit.*—*Oss. Fing.* Ri foill, *practising deceit, playing unfair.* Fear na foill an iochdair, *the knave undermost.*—*Old Saying.*

Fòill, *s. f.* (*Ir. id.*) A pursuit, a chase; enmity; enemies. Cha lugha na fòill no na freiceadain, *the enemies are no fewer than the guard.*—*G. P.*

Fòilleachd, *s. f.* (*Ir. id.*) A track, a footstep; a tracing.

Foilleachdach, aich, *s. m.* (*Ir. id.*) A research.

Foillealachd, *s. f.* (*from* foilleil.) Treacherousness, the practice of deceit.

Foillear, eir, *s. m.* (*Ir. id.*) The bud of a flower.—*Shaw.*

Foillear, ir, *s. m.* (foill-fhear.) A deceiver, a knave, a traitor. *N. pl.* foillearan; *d. pl.* foillearaibh. Buaidh air na foillearaibh, *victory over the traitors.*—*Old Song.*

Foilleil, *a.* (foill-amhuil.) Deceitful, unfair, treacherous, fraudulent, wrongful. Tha 'mhic foilleil, *his sons are treacherous.*—*Mac Lach.* Gu foilleil, *treacherously.*

Foill-fholach, aich, *s. m.* An ambush. Ri foill-fholach, *laying in ambush, laying snares.*—*Sm.*

Foill-fholachadh, aidh, *s. m.* A lying in wait or in ambush.

Foill-fholachail, *a.* Treacherous; prone to lie in wait.

Foillidh, *a.* (*Ir.* foilligh.) Hidden, latent; that does not externally appear.—*Shaw.*

Foillidheach, *a.* (*Ir.* foilligh.) Negligent, sluggish.

Foillidheachd, *s. f.* (*Ir.* foillidheacht.) Negligence, sluggishness.

Foillse, *s. f.* Light; manifestation.

Foillseach, *a.* (*Ir. id.*) Declaratory.

Foillseachadh, aidh, *s. m.* (*Ir.* foillsiughadh.) The act of revealing, showing, or manifesting; a revealment, discovery, manifestation; declaration; revelation; the Apocalypse. A reir foillseachaidh, *according to revelation.* Foillseachadh an Tighearna, *the Epiphany*; fear foillseachaidh, *one who reveals*; *a publisher.*

Foillseachadh, (a), *pr. part.* of foillsich. Revealing, manifesting, discovering, disclosing.

Foillseachail, *a.* Apocalyptical, revealing, disclosing; explanatory.

Foillseachas, ais, *s. m.* Revealment, manifestation, disclosure.

Foillsichear, *fut. pass.* of foillsich. Shall be revealed.

Foillsich, *v. a.* (*Ir.* foillsigh.) Reveal, declare, set forth, discover, disclose, lay open, express. *Pret. a.* dh'fhoillsich, *revealed*; *fut. aff. a.* foillsichidh, *shall disclose.* Foillsichidh do mhiorbhuilean, *thy wonders will declare.*—*Sm.*

Foillsichte, *p. part.* of foillsich. (*Ir.* foillsighte.) Declared, discovered, laid open.

† **Foilmean**, ein, *s. m.* (*Ir. id.*) Bad dress.—*Shaw.*

Foiltean, ein, *s. m.* A head-band. Na foilteana, *the head-dress.*—*Stew. Is.* Written also *failtean.*

† **Foimeal**, il, *s. m.* (*Ir. id.*) Consumption.

Foineach, ich, *s. m.* (*Ir. id.*) A demand; a question.

Foineachadh, aidh, *s. m.* Inquiring, asking.

Foineachd, *s. f.* An inquiring, asking, question; *also*, inquisitiveness.—*Oss. Tem.* See also **Foighneachd**.

Foineul, eòil, *s. m.* (*Ir. id.*) A little cloud; a gleam; a trance.—*Shaw.*

Foinich, *v.* Ask, inquire, question. *Pret. a.* dh'fhoinich. Nach foinich e mu 'mhac? *shall he not inquire about his son?*—*Oss. Tem.*

Foinne, *s. f.* A wart.—*Shaw.*

Foinneal, eil, *s. m.* (*Ir. id.*) A fool.

Foinneamh, eimh, *s. f.* and *m.* A wart. *N. pl.* foinneamhan.

Foinneamh, *a.* Genteel, handsome, portly, elegant. Foinneamh finealta, *portly and well dressed.*—*Macint.* Foinneamh mileanta, *handsome and brave.*—*Fingalian Poem.*

Foinneasach, *a.* Slight, genteel, slenderly made. *Com.* and *sup.* foinneasaiche. Gu foinneasach, *slightly.*

Foinnich, *v. a.* (*Ir.* foinnigh.) Temper, as a bladed metal instrument. *Pret. a.* dh'fhoinnich; *fut. aff. a.* foinnichidh, *shall temper.*

Foinnichte, *p. part.* of foinnich. Tempered.

Foinnidh. See **Foineamh**.

† **Foinnse**, *s. f.* (*Ir. id.*) The ash-tree.—*Shaw.*

† **Foinnseag**, eig, *s. f.* (*Ir. id.*) The ash-tree.

† **Foinnsi**, *s. pl.* (*Ir. id.*) Springs, wells, fountains.

Foir, *s. f.* (*Ir. id.*) Help; deliverance; a border; an edge; a rim; a brink. Dean foir, *help.* Furtachd is foir, *help and deliverance.*—*Sm.* Foir na h-aimhne, *the brink of the river.*—*Old Song.*

Foir, foire, *s. f.* (*Ir. id.*) A ship's crew; a crowd of people; people crowded together.

Ir. foire. *Fr.* foire, *a fair.* *Gr.* φοιρος.

Foir, *v.* Help, relieve, deliver, or save; wait on; heal; *also*, bless. *Pret. a.* dh'fhoir, *helped*; *fut. aff. a.* foiridh, *shall help.* Foir le trocair orm, *mercifully save me.*—*Sm.* 3 *sing.* and *pl. imper.* foireadh. Foireadh iad orra, *let them relieve them.*—*Stew. Tim.*

Foir-ailich, *v. a.* Adorn, deck.—*Shaw.*

Foirbh, *v. a.* (*Ir. id.*) Adorn, deck.

Foirbhaillidh, *a.* Acceptable.

Foirbheart, eirt, *s. m.* (*Ir. id.*) Help.

Foir-bhreathnaich, *v. a.* Divine, prophesy, guess.

Foir-bhreith, *s. f.* (*Ir. id.*) A conjecture; a random prophecy.

† **Foir-bhriach**, *s. m.* (*Ir. id.*) Power, authority, strength.

Foir-bhriathar, air, *s. m.* (*Ir. id.*) An adverb; an adjective. *N. pl.* foir-bhriathran.

Foir-bhriathrach, *a.* Adverbial.

Foir-bhruach, aich, *s. f.* (*Ir. id.*) A precipice; a pinnacle; the edge of a precipice.

Foir-cheadal, ail, *s. m.* (*Ir. id.*) A catechism; instruction; exhortation; admonition; warning; caution.—*Shaw.*

Foircean, ein, *s. m.* Embrocation.

Foircheadalair, *s. m.* (*Ir. id.*) A teacher.

Foir-cheann, chinn, *s. m.* (*Ir.* foirceann.) An end, a conclusion; a white head; a white face.

FOIR-CHEANNACH, *a.* White-faced; white-headed.

† FOIR-CHEIMNICH, *v. n.* (*Ir. id.*) Proceed, advance.

FOIR-CHROICEANN, -chroicne, *s. m.* (*Ir. id.*) The fore-skin. *N. pl.* foir-chroicnean.

† FOIRCINN, *s. f.* (*Ir. id.*) An embrocation; a fomentation.

† FOIRCIOBAL, ail, *s. m.* (*Ir. id.*) A reinforcement.—*Shaw.*

FOIRCNICH, *v. a.* (*Ir. id.*) Foment, apply embrocations. *Pret. a.* dh'fhoircnich, *fomented; fut. aff.* foircnichidh, *shall foment.*

FOIRDHEALBH, -dheilbh, *s. m.* (*Ir. id.*) A scheme, a schedule, a drawing, a plan.

FOIR-DHEALBH, *v. a.* (*Ir. id.*) Scheme, plan, draw out a scheme or plan.

FOIR-DHEALBHADAIR, *s. m.* (*Ir. id.*) A schemer, a planner. *N. pl.* foir-dhealbhadairean.

FOIRDHEIRC, *a.*, written more frequently *oirdheirc;* which see.

FOIRDHEIRCEAS, eis, *s. m.* See OIRDHEIRCEAS.

FOIR-DHRIS, *s. f.* (*Ir. id.*) Sweet-brier.

FOIREIL, *a.* (*Ir.* foir-amhuil.) Steep; headlong.

FOIREAR, ir, *s. m.* (foir-fhear.) A watchman.

FOIR-EIGEANTAIR, *s. m.* An obstructor; an oppressor. *N. pl.* foir-eigeantairean.

FÒIREIGIN, *v. a.* (*Ir. id.*) Oppress, harass; compel, constrain. *Pret. a.* dh' fhòireigin, *oppressed; fut. aff. a.* fòireignidh, *shall oppress.*

FÒIREIGIN, *s. f.* (*Ir.* foireigean.) Oppression, violence, force, tyranny, compulsion, constraint. Chunnaic mi am fòireigin, *I have seen the oppression.*—*Stew. Ex.* Fear fòireigin, *an oppressor.* Luchd fòireigin, *oppressors.*—*Stew. Cor.*

FOIREIGNEACH, *a.* Oppressive, tyrannical. Gu foireigneach, *oppressively. Com.* and *sup.* foireigniche.

FOIREIGNEADH, eidh, *s. m.* Oppression, tyranny; the act of oppressing, compelling, or constraining. Tha iad air am fòireigneadh, *they are oppressed.*

FOIREIGNICH, *v. a.* Oppress, harass; compel, constrain, force. *Pret. a.* dh' fhoireignich, *compelled; fut. aff. a.* foireignichidh.

FÒIREIGNICHE, *s. m.* A tyrant, an oppressor.

FÒIREIGNICHTE, *p. part.* of fòireignich. Oppressed, harassed, constrained, forced. *Asp. form,* fhòireignichte.

† FOIREIL, *a.* (*Ir. id.*) Clear, evident.

FOIRFE, *a.* (*Ir. id.*) Perfect, complete; faultless; immaculate; old, ancient. Duine foirfe, *a perfect man.*—*Stew. Job.* Gu foirfe, *perfectly, faultlessly.*

FOIRFEACH, ich, *s. m.* (*Ir. id.*) An elder; a person arrived at maturity. *N. pl.* foirfich.

FOIRFEACHD, *s. f., from* foirfe. (*Ir. id.*) Perfection; completeness; perfectness, maturity, old age; excellence. Coimh-cheangal na foirfeachd, *the bond of perfectness.*—*Stew. Col.* Tha e air teachd gu foirfeachd, *he* or *it is arrived at maturity;* foirfeachd, *old age.*—*Shaw.*

† FOIRFEADH, eidh, *s. m.* (*Ir. id.*) Harrowing.

FOIR-FHIACAL, ail, *s. m.* (*Ir. id.*) A fore-tooth. *N. pl.* foir-fhiaclan, *fore-teeth.*

FOIR-FHIACLACH, *a.* (*Ir. id.*) Having fore-teeth; having large fore-teeth.

FOIRFICH, *v. a.* (*Ir.* foirfigh.) Perform, execute, accomplish.

FOIRFIDH, *a.* (*from* foirge.) Perfect; complete; faultless. Foirfidh glan, *faultless and pure.*—*Smith.*

FOIRFIDHEACHD, *s.* Perfectness, completeness, faultlessness.

† FOIRGEALL, eill, *s. m.* (*Ir. id.*) A truth.

FOIRGHEALL, ghealla, *s. m.* (*Ir. id.*) A pledge for protection, a hostage for safety.

FOIRGHIOLL, ill, *s. m.* (*Ir. id.*) A declaration, a proclamation; assertion; proof, witness; decision, judgment. Foirghioll na firinn, *manifestation of the truth.*—*Shaw.*

FOIRGHIOLL, *a.* (*Ir. id.*) Clear, evident.

FOIRGHIOLL, *v. a.* (*Ir. id.*) Prove; declare.

FOIR-GHLAC, *v. a.* (*Ir. id.*) Occupy, possess. *Pret. a.* Dh' fhoir-ghlac, *occupied; fut. aff.* foir-ghlacaidh, *shall occupy.*

† FOIRGHLIDHE, *s. f.* (*Ir. id.*) Nobility; truth.

FOIRGNEACHADH, aidh, *s. m.* (*Ir.* foirgniughadh.) A building.

FOIRGNEADH, idh, *s. m.* (*Ir.* foirgnamh.) A building.

FOIRGNEADH-FUINN, *s. m.* Wood or timber necessary for the use of a farm.

FOIRGNICH, *v. a.* (*Ir. id.*) Build.

FOIRIARACH, *a.* (*Ir. id.*) Preposterous; eccentric; troublesome; not easy to be served.

FOIRICHINN, *s. f.* (*Ir.* foirigthin.) Help.

FOIRICH, *v. n.* (*Ir.* foirigh.) Stay. See FUIRICH.

FOIRIDINN, *s. f.* (*Ir. id.*) A pursuit.

FOIRINN, *s. f.* Help, aid, supply, strength.

FOIR-INNIS, *v. a.* (*Ir. id.*) Predict.

FOIR-INNSEACH, *a.* (*Ir. id.*) Predictive.

FOIR-IONGANTAS, ais, *s. m.* (*Ir. id.*) A prodigy.

FOIR-IOMALL, aill, *s. m.* (*Ir.* foirimeal.) Territory; boundary, bound; frontier, limit, border; circumference of a circle. Foir-iomall nan sliabh, *the utmost bounds of the hills.*—*Stew. Gen.*

FOIR-IOMALLACH, *a.* (*Ir. id.*) Territorial; extrinsic; on the outside; on the border or frontiers; *also, substantively,* utmost bounds, frontiers.

FOIR-IOMRADH, aidh, *s. m.* (*Ir. id.*) A ceremony.

FOIR-IOMRAITEACH, *a.* (*Ir. id.*) Ceremonious.

FOIR-IONGANTACH, *a.* (*Ir. id.*) Wonderful, strange, prodigious.—*Shaw.*

FOIR-IONGANTAS, ais, *s. m.* (*Ir. id.*) A prodigy; a phenomenon.—*Shaw.*

FOIR-LEATHANN, *a.* (*Ir. id.*) Very broad, spacious, extensive; large, general.

FOIR-LEATHANNACH, *a.* (*Ir. id.*) Periphrastic.

FOIR-LEATHANNACHADH, aidh, *s. m.* Periphrasis.

FOIR-LEUD, *s. m.* (*Ir. id.*) Expanse, extent.

FOIRLION, *a.* (*Ir. id.*) Much, great, plenty.

FOIRLION, *v. a.* (*Ir. id.*) Complete, make perfect; fulfil; supply; fill up.—*Shaw.*

FOIRLIONADH, aidh, *s. m.* (*Ir. id.*) A completing, a perfecting, fulfilling, supplying; a completion, a supplement, an appendix.

FOIRLIONTA, *a.* and *p. part.* of foirlion. (*Ir. id.*) Fulfilled, complete, perfected.

† FOIRM, *a.* (*Ir. id.*) Dark, obscure.

FOIRM, *s. f.* (*Ir. id.*) A form, manner; usage; ceremony, pomp; activity, cleverness; noise. Tionndaidh iad gu mùghadh foirm, *they shall come to a change of form.*—*Macfar.* Thug e cuirm le foirm, *he gave a banquet with pomp.*—*Mac Lach.*

FOIRMEALACHD, *s. f.* (*Ir.* foirmalachd.) Formality, ceremony, pompousness; cleverness; forwardness.

FOIRMEIL, *a.* (foirm-amhuil.) Formal; ceremonious, pompous, clever, active; forward, noisy.—*Shaw.*

FOIRNE, FOIRNIDH, *s. pl.* (*Ir. id.*) Dwellers, inhabitants; a brigade, a troop, a crew. Foirne fearail, *a manly crew.*—*Macfar.*

Foirn, *v. a.* Intrude; be arrogant. *Pret. a.* dh' fhoirn, *intruded.*

Foirneadh, idh, *s. m.* (*Ir. id.*) Inclination; sloping; intrusion, arrogance. Air foirneadh, *downwards, headlong;* 'gad fhoirneadh fein, *intruding thyself.—Old Song.* A foirneadh gu dàna, *intruding boldly.—Stew. Col.*

Foirneal, eil, *s. m.* (*Ir. id.*) Appearance, colour.

Foirneanta, *a.* Stout; firm, steady; forward, arrogant. Gu foirneanta, *stoutly.*

Foirneantachd, *s. f.* Stoutness, firmness; steadiness; forwardness, arrogance.

Fòirneart, eirt, *s. m.* (*Ir. id.*) Oppression, violence, force; fraudulence, fraud. Fòirneart m' eascair, *my enemy's oppression.—Smith.* Cha dean thu fòirneart, *thou shalt do no violence; thou shalt not defraud.—Stew. Lev.*

Fòirneartach, *a.* (*Ir. id.*) Oppressive, violent; fraudulent; overbearing. An-tighearnan fòirneartach, *oppressive tyrants.—Macfar.*

Foirneartachadh, aidh, *s. m.* Oppression, overbearing, defrauding.

Foirneartaich, *v. a.* (*from* foirneart.) Oppress, force; overbear, defraud. *Pret. a.* dh' fhoirneartaich, *oppressed; fut. aff.* foirneartaichidh.

† **Foirreil**, *a.* (*Ir. id.*) Manifest, apparent.

Foirseadh, eidh, *s. m.* Harrowing.

Foirsear, ir, *s. m.* (*Ir.* foirseoir.) A harrower; a rummager, a searcher; a constable.

Foirsearachd, *s. f.* (*Ir.* foirseoireachd.) A rummaging, a searching.

Foir-shiol, *v. a.* Propagate.

Foir-shioladh, aidh, *s. m.* A propagating; a propagation. *Shaw.*

Foirtealachd, *s. f.* See **Foirteileachd**.

Foirteil, *a.* (*Lat.* fortis. *Ir.* foirteil.) Brave, hardy; patient; strong. Gu foirteil, *bravely.*

Foirteileachd, *s. f.* Bravery, hardihood; patience; strength.

Foir-theachdair, *s. m.* An usher; a forerunner.—*Macd. N. pl.* foir-theachdairean.

Foir-theagasg, aisg, *s. m.* Rudiments; introduction.

Foir-thir, *s. f.* (*Ir. id.*) A remote or foreign country; farther, remote; *also*, foreign. Eun foirthir, *a foreign bird. Foir-thir* is also written *oir-thir;* which see.

Fois, *s. f.* (*Ir. id.*) Rest; peace, tranquillity; leisure; a dwelling. Fois do t-anam, *peace to thy soul.—Oss. Derm.* Fois do bhonn a chois, *rest for the sole of its foot.—Stew. Gen.* Aig fois, *at peace;* gabh gu fois, *be quiet, be at peace.*

Foiscionn, *s. m.* (*Ir. id.*) Malice, backbiting.

Foiscionnach, *a.* (*Ir. id.*) Malicious; apt to backbite; *also, substantively*, mălice, a cry.—*Shaw.* Gu foiscionnach, *maliciously. Com.* and *sup.* foiscionnaiche.

Foiscionnachd, *s. f.* Maliciousness; backbiting.

Foisdineach. See **Foisneach**.

Foisead, eid, *s. m.* (*Ir. id.*) A faucet.

Foiseamh, imh, *s. m.* (*Ir. id.*) A recovery.—*Shaw.*

Foisgich, *v. n.* (*Ir.* foisgigh.) Approach, draw near. *Pret. a.* dh' fhoisgich, *approached; fut. aff. a.* foisgichidh, *shall approach.*

Foisneach, **Foistinneach**, *a., from* fois. (*Ir. id.*) Sedate, serious; composed, tranquil, peaceable; arranged, in order. Duine foistinneach, *a sedate man, a man of rest.—Stew. Chr.* Gnùis fhoisneach na doimhne, *the tranquil face of the deep.—Ull.* Foisneach, fàilteach, *peaceable and hospitable.—Macint.* Foisneach, *arranged.—Shaw.*

Foisneachd, **Foistinneachd**, *s. f.* Sedateness; composedness; tranquillity, peaceableness; arrangement.

Foiste, *s. f.* (*Ir. id.*) A resting, a residing.

Foisteachair, *s. m.* (*Ir. id.*) A hireling.

Foisteadh, idh, *s. m.* (*Ir. id.*) Wages; salary; hire.—*Shaw.*

Foisteanach, *a.* (*Ir. id.*) Arranged, in good order.

Foistinneach, *a.* See **Foisneach**.

† **Foitheal**, eil, *s. m.* (*Ir. id.*) Plunder, prey.

Foithre, *s.* (*Ir. id.*) Woods.

Fola, *gen. sing.* of fuil; which see.

Folabhairt, *s.* Speaking under one's voice.

Folabhradh, aidh, *s. m.* (*Ir. id.*) A good speech, pleading, reasoning; *also*, low language.

† **Foladh**, aidh, *s. m.* (*Ir. id.*) A garment, a robe.

Fŏlach, *s. m.* (*Ir. id. Goth.* fuilgin.) Concealment; a disguise, a mask; a covering; a skreen. Am folach uainn, *concealed from us.—Smith.* Folach air a bhil, *a covering on his lip.—Stew. Lev.* Folach fead, *the pastime called 'hide and seek.'*

Fòlach, aich, *s. m.* (*Ir. id.*) Long grass; luxuriant grass.—*Oss. Taura.*

Folachadh, aidh, *s. m.* (*Ir. id.*) A hiding, a concealing; concealment; a skreening, a skreen.

Folachan, ain, *s. m.* (*Ir. id.*) A hidden treasure; a concealment; a place where treasure is hidden; a *pose.*

Fòlachd, *s. f.* (*Ir. id.*) Bloodiness; a feud; a grudge; animosity.—*Shaw.* Is fearr sean fhéich na sean fhòlachd, *better is an old debt, than an old grudge.—G. P.* Written also *falachd.*

Folachdan, ain, *s. m.* (*Ir. id.*) Water-sallad, water-parsnip.

Foladair, *s. m., from* fuil. (*Ir. id.*) One who sheds blood.

Foladas, ais, *s. m.* See **Faladas**.

Foladh, aidh, *s. m.* (*Ir. id.*) A cover, a covering, a skreen. —*Shaw.*

† **Fòladh**, aidh, *s. m.* (*Ir. id.*) Power, strength, ability.

Folaich, *v. a.* (*Ir.* folaigh.) Hide, conceal, screen, cover; keep close. *Pret. a.* dh' fholaich, *hid; fut. aff. a.* folaichidh, *shall hide; fut. pass.* folaichear. Folaichibh sibh féin, *hide yourselves.—Stew. Jos.* Folaich air e, *hide it from him.*

Folaichear, *fut. pass.* of folaich. Shall be hidden.

Folaichte, *p. part.* of folaich. Hidden, covered, concealed. Folaichte san talamh, *hid in the earth.—Stew. Jos.*

Folaid, *s. f.* (*Ir. id.*) A veil.

† **Folair**, *s. m.* (*Ir. id.*) A command.

† **Folair**, *v. a.* (*Ir. id.*) Order, command; offer, proffer.

Folamh, *a.* (*Ir. id.*) Empty; void, vacant. Written also *falamh;* which see.

Folamhaich, *v. a.* (*from* folamh.) Empty, pour out. Written also *falamhaich.*

† **Folaradh**, aidh, *s. m.* (*Ir. id.*) A command, an order. —*Shaw.*

Folarnaidheach, *a.* Equal.

Folarnaidheachd, *s. f.* Equality, parity.

Folartair, *s. m.* (*Ir. id.*) An emperor; a commander.

† **Folas**, ais, *s. m.* (*Ir. id.*) A shoe, a slipper, a sandal. *N. pl.* folasan.

Folbh, *v. n.* Go, depart. See **Falbh**.

Folbhach, *a.* Moving, walking, passing, going.

Folbhair, *s. m.* (*Ir.* folabhair.) A mover, a follower, a creeper.

Folbhan, ain, *s. m.* (*from* folbh.) Motion, agitation, locomotion, creeping, stirring; a going about Air folbhan, *able to walk about.*

FOLC. See FAILC.

FOLCADH, aidh, *s. m.* (*Ir. id.*) A bathing, a bath; a cleansing of the hair by bathing; a lye of potash.

FOLDATH, *a.* (*Ir. id.*) Generous, *also*, the name of one of Ossian's heroes.

FO'LEABADH, -leapach, *s f.* A truckle bed. *N. pl.* fo-leapaichean.

† FOLFAIDH, *a.* (*Ir. id.*) Whole, entire.

† FOLG, *a* (*Ir. id.*) Active, nimble, quick, clever.—*Shaw.*

FOLACH, aich, *s. m.* (*Ir. id.*) A covering, a garment; military colours

FOLLACH, aich, *s. m.* (*Ir. id.*) A kind of water-gruel.

FALLADH, aidh, *s. m.* (*Ir. id.*) Government.—*Shaw.*

FOLLAIS, *a* Clear; conspicuous; evident Dean follais, *publish, proclaim*, gu follais, *conspicuously.*

FOLLAIS, *s f.* Openness; publicity, conspicuousness; evidentness, clearness. Am follais, *manifest, clear*, thoir am follais, *make manifest*, thig e 'm follais, *it will come to light.*

FOLLAISEACH, *a*, *from* follais. (*Ir.* folluiseach) Clear, evident; conspicuous; open, public. Ionad follaiseach, *a public [open] place*—*Stew. Gen. Com.* and *sup.* follaisiche.

FOLLASIEACHD, *s f* (*Ir.* folluiseachd) Clearness; evidentness, conspicuousness; publicity; openness.

FOLLAISICH, *v a.* (*from* follais) Publish, make manifest or evident. *Pret. a* dh'fhollaisich, *published.*

FOLLAMH, aimh, *s m* (*Ir. id.*) Ancestry, ancestors.—*Shaw.*

FOLLAMHAN, ain, *s m* Grace, ornaments.

FOLLAS, *a* (*Ir id*) Manifest, evident. Dean follas, *make public, proclaim, expose to view*

FOLLSGADH, aidh, *s. m.* (*Ir. id.*) A scalding

FOLLUS See FALLUS

FOLMHAISE, *s f.* (*Ir. id.*) Advantage, opportunity.

† FOLMHEIN, *s. f.* (*Lat.* fulmen) A thunderbolt—*Mac Pherson's Introduction*

FOLOSG. See FALOISG.

FOLT, fuilt, *s. m* (*Ir id*) The hair of the head; a tail; wages, deceiving; falling Folt liath, *grey hair*, folt dubh, *black hair*, folt donn, *brown hair*, folt dubh-dhonn, *dark brown hair*, falt bàn, *fair hair*, folt buidhe, *yellow hair*, folt dualach, *flowing or curled hair*, fhir an fhuilt bhàin, *thou fair-haired man.*

FOLRACHD, *s. f.* (*Ir id*) Gore.

† FOLTACH, aich, *s. m* (*Ir id*) A vassal, a hireling.

FOLTAN, ain, *s m.* (*from* folt) A riband for tying up the hair of a female; a *snood* Written also *fuiltean.*

FOLUAIMEAN, ein, *s. m.* (*Ir id*) A giddy motion, running, skipping.

FOLUAIMNEACH, FOLUAINEACH, *a.* (*Ir. id*) Moving, stirring, fickle, active; prancing

FOLUMAN, *s* (*Ir. id.*) Bad clothes—*Shaw.*

† FOLUAR, air, *s. m.* (*Ir. id.*) A footstool

FO-LUAISG, *v. a* Rock gently; dandle *Pret a* dh'fholuaisg, *dandled*

FO-LUASGACH, *a.* Rocking, dandling.

FO-LUASGADH, aidh, *s m.* A rocking, a dandling

FOLUICH, *v a* See FOLAICH

FOLUIDHEACH, *a.* Secret; hidden; skulking. Gu foluidheach, *secretly.*

FOLUIDHEACHD, *s f.* Secrecy; skulking. Am foluidheachd, *in secret.*

FO'M (fodham). Under me, beneath me.

FO M' (fo mo) Under my, beneath my. Fo m' cheann, *under my head.*

FOMAS, ais, *s. m.* (*Ir. id*) Obedience, submission.—*Shaw.*

FOMASACH, *a.* (*Ir. id*) Obedient, submissive. Gu fomasach, *obediently.*

FOMHAOL, aoil, *s. m.* A king's slave.

FOMHAR, air, *s. m.* (*Ir. id.*) Harvest. Now written *foghar*, which see.

FOMHEISG, *s. f.* (*Ir. id.*) Tipsiness.

FO-MHEISGEACH, *a.* (*Ir. id.*) Tipsy; half-seas-over.

FO-MHEISGEAR, eir, *s. m.* (*Ir. id.*) A tippler.

FOMHORACH, aich, *s. m.* (*Ir. id.*) A pirate, a giant.

FÒNADH, aidh, *s. m.*, *for* foghnadh. (*Ir. id*) Sufficiency, enough.

FÒNAICH, *v.* Suffice, be sufficient.

FÒNAIDH, (*for* foghnaidh) *fut. act.* of foghain. Shall suffice. Fònaidh dhomh fàsach nam fridhe, *the solitude of the deserts will suffice me.*—*Oss. Fing*

† FONAL, ail, *s m.* (*Ir. id.*) Cold; rigour.

FONAMHAD, aid, *s m.* (*Ir. id*) Mockery, derision; a sneer.—*Shaw.*

FONAMHADACH, aich, *s. m.* (*Ir. id*) A jeerer, a sneerer. *N. pl* fonamhadaich.

FONAMHADACH, *a* (*Ir. id*) Jeering, sneering. *Com.* and *sup* fonamhadaiche.

FO-NEUL, -neòil, *s. m.* A little cloud; a thin cloud; a trance

FO-NEULACH, *a.* Somewhat cloudy; apt to fall into a trance; like a trance.

FONN, fuinn, *s m* (*Ir. id. Gr.* φωνη.) A strain; air; tune; music; pleasure; delight; desire; longing; carnal inclination, the drone of a bagpipe. Fonn orain, *the strain of a song.*—*Oss. Tem.* Fon clarsaich, *harp music.*—*Orr.* Dh' éirich fonn air, *desire awakened within him*; fonn diadhaidh, *a hymn*, fonn codail, *a lullaby*, fonn duan, *a recitative*

FONN, fuinn, *s m* (*Gr.* φθων. *Ir.* fonn *Lat.* fundus) Land; earth; a plain. Cheum e romh 'n fhonn, *he marched over the plain.*—*Mac Lach.* Chriothnaich am fonn, *the earth trembled.*—*Smith.* Fonn is cuan, *land and sea.*—*Id.* Bior fuinn, *a land-mark.*—*Old Poem.*

FONNADH, aidh, *s m* (*Ir. id*) A war chariot; a journey; proficiency. Fonnadh fioghal, *a quadrangular chariot.*—*Fingalian Poem.*

FONNAR. See FONNMHOR.

FONNMHOIRLACHD, *s. f.* Tunefulness, melodiousness, musicalness, propensity; inclination; gravity. Maille ris an uile fhonnmhoireachd, *together with all gravity.*—*Stew. Tim ref.*

FONNMHOR, *a* (*Ir* fonmhar) Tuneful, melodious, musical; desirous; cheerful, dispassionate, meek. *Com* and *sup.* fonnmhoire.

† FONNSA, ai, *s. m.* (*Ir id*) A troop; a band.

† FONNSAIR, *s m* (*Ir id*) A trooper. *N. pl* fonnsairean.

† FOR, *s m* (*Ir. id.*) Discourse; protection; illumination.

† FORACH, aich, *s m.* (*Ir. id.*) A dispute; a controversy.—*Shaw*

FORACHAIR, *s. m.* A watchman.

FORADH, aidh, *s. m.* A purveying; a forcing; a seat; a bench.

FORAGAN, ain, *s. m.* A rustling noise; keenness; anger.

FORAGANACH, *a.* Causing a rustling noise; keen; angry; passionate.

Foraich, *v.* Wait, watch. *Pret.* dh' fhoraich, *watched; fut. aff.* foraichidh.

Foraidheach, *a.* (*Ir. id.*) Wild, fierce; cruel.

Foraidheachd, *s. f.* (*Ir. id.*) Wildness, fierceness; cruelty.

† **Forail**, *v. a.* (*Ir. id.*) Command.

† **Forail**, *s. f.* (*Ir. id.*) Excess, superfluity.

† **Forail**, *a.* (*Ir. id.*) Imperious.

Foraileachd, *s. f.* Excessiveness; imperiousness.

Foraimh, *s. m.* A journey.

Forainn, *s. m.* (*Ir. id.*) A nickname; an epithet; a surname; a pronoun.

Forair, *s. m.* (*Ir. id.*) A watchman; a guard. *N. pl.* forairean.

Foraire, *s. f.* A watch or guard.—*Shaw. N. pl.* forairean.

Foral, ail, *s. m.* (*Ir. id.*) The head of a spindle, wherein is a groove in which the string or band plays that gives it motion.

Foralamh, ainh, *s. m.* (*Ir. id.*) Anger, wrath, vengeance.

Foran, ain, *s. m.* See **Faran**.

Forann, roinn, *s. f.* (*Ir. id.*) A short verse; a versicle; a stanza.

Foranta, *a.* (*Ir. id.*) Angry; resolute; presumptuous.—*Shaw.*

† **Foraos**, aois, *s. m.* (*Ir. id.*) A forest.—*Shaw.*

Foraosaglach, *a.* Old, ancient; *substantively*, an old man.

Foras, ais, *s. m.* and *f.* (*Ir. id.*) Knowledge; law; increase; the ford of a river.—*Shaw.* Depth, foundation, bottom.

Foras, *a.* Old, antique, ancient.

Forasda, *a.* See **Farasda**.

Forasdachd, *s. f.* (*Ir. id.*) Mildness; suavity; gravity; sobriety.

† **Forb**, fuirb, *s. m.* (*Ir. id.*) A landlord; land; glebe land.

Forbadh, aidh, *s. m.* (*Ir. id.*) A cutting; a slaughtering; flaying.—*Shaw.* Spending; finishing; a tax; land, glebe land.

Forbaidh, *s. m.* (*Ir. id.*) A superior.

† **Forbair**, *v.* (*Ir. id.*) Grow, increase.—*Shaw.*

Forbairt, *s. f.* (*Ir. id.*) Increase, profit; emolument.

Forbais, *s. f.* A conquest.

Forban, ain, *s. m.* (*Ir. id.*) Excess; extravagance.

Forbann, ain, *s. m.* (*Ir. id.*) Marriage banns.

Forbhas, ais, *s. m.* (*Ir. id.*) A snare; an ambush.—*Shaw.*

Forbhasach, *a.* Ensnaring, full of snares; treacherous.

Forbhrat, ait, *s. m.* (*Ir. id.*) An upper garment; a wrapper; a cloak. *N. pl.* forbhratan.

For-bhriathar, air, *s. m.* (*Ir. id.*) An adjective; an adverb. *N. pl.* forbhriathran.

For-bhruach, aich, *s. f.* (*Ir. id*) A pinnacle: a steep ascent; the edge of a precipice. *N. pl.* for-bhruachan.

† **Forc**, *a.* (*Ir. id.*) Stedfast, firm.

Forc, *s. m.* (*Ir. id.*) The top or summit.

Forc, *s. m.* (*W.* forç. *Lat.* furca. *Teut.* vorcke. *Eng.* fork.) A fork; a prong. Forc saidhe, *a hay-fork. N. pl.* forcaichean, *forks.*

Forc, *v. a.* Fork, or pitch with a fork; teach, instruct. *Pret. a.* dh' fhorc, *forked; fut. aff. a.* forcaidh, *shall fork.*

Forcachadh, aidh, *s. m.* Forking.

Forcadh, aidh, *s. m.* Forking, pitching with a fork.

Forcaich, *v. a.* (*from* forc.) Fork, pitch with a fork. *Pret. a.* dh' fhorcaich, *forked; fut. aff. a.* forcaichidh, *shall fork.*

† **Forcaidh**, *s. m.* Superfluity; excess; rising or dawning of day.

Forcail, *a.*, forc-amhuil. (*W.* forçawl.) Forked, forky; pronged, furcated.

Forcar, air, *s. m.* (*Ir. id.*) Violence; a wooden hawk.—*Shaw.*

Forchaoin, *s. f.* (*Ir. id.*) A catch in words, a quibble.

Forchar, air, *s. m.* (*Ir. id.*) Violence; a wooden hook.

For-chinnteachd, *s. f.* (*Ir. id.*) Predestination.

Forchongradh, *s. m.* (*Ir. id.*) Persuasion, advice, indulgence; command.

For-chroiceann, -chroicne, *s. m.* The foreskin; scurf.

Fordal, ail, *s. m.* (*Ir. id.*) Error, mistake, delay, hinderance.

Fordalach, *a.* Erroneous; wandering, astray.

† **For-dharc**, *a.* (*Ir. id.*) Manifest; *substantively*, light.

Fordhroin, *s. f.* (*Ir. id.*) A womb; a loin.—*Shaw.*

For-dhorus, uis, *s. m.* A porch. Tre 'n fhor-dhorus, *through the porch.*—*Stew. Jud.*

Fordhubh, uibh, *s. m.* A lid, a cover. Fordhubha an sùl, *their eyelids.*—*Stew. Pro.*

† **Forf**, *s. m.* (*Ir. id.*) A guard.

† **Forfaire**, *s. m.* (*Ir. id.*) A watch or guard.

Forfaireach, *a.* (*Ir. id.*) Vigilant, observant; *also*, a watchman.

For-fhocal, ail, *s. m.* (*Ir. id.*) A by-word, a proverb. Bithidh tu a d' fhor fhocal, *thou shalt be a by-word.*—*Stew. Deut. ref.*

Forgamh, aimh, *s. m.* (*Ir. id.*) A blow, a thrust, a wound.

Forgan, ain, *s. m.* (*Ir. id.*) A rustling noise; keenness; anger.

Forganach, *a.* (*Ir. id.*) Rustling; keen; angry, passionate.

Forghart, airt, *s. m.* (*Ir. id.*) The forepart of the head.

For-ghuin, *s. f.* (*Ir. id.*) A wound; a sharp pain; a beating pain.

† **Forglac**, *v. a.* (*Ir. id.*) Prevent, hinder; catch.—*Shaw.*

Forlach, aich, *s. m.* (*Ir. id.*) A pass or passport; a furlough.—*Macd.*

Forlaimh, *s. f.* (*Ir. id.*) A leaping; a bounding.

Forlamhas, ais, *s. m.* (*Ir. id.*) Possession.

† **Fòrlan**, ain, *s. m.* (*Ir. id.*) Power, force; pain; superfluity; excess; conquest.—*Shaw.*

Forlonn, ainn, *s. m.* (*Ir. id.*) Deadly hatred.

Formach, aich, *s. m.* (*Ir. id.*) An increase; a swelling.

Formad, aid, *s. m.* More frequently written *farmad;* which see.

Formadach. See **Farmadach**.

Formail, *a.* (*Ir.* formamhuil.) Shapely, sightly, of good form or figure.

Formail, *s. f.* Hire, wages.

Formaise, *s. f.* (*Ir. id.*) Ornament.

† **Formalach**, aich, *s. m.* (*Ir. id.*) A hireling.—*Shaw.*

Forman, ain, *s. m.* A type, a mould. *N. pl.* formain.

† **Forn**, *s. m.* (*Ir. id.*) A furnace; a shipwreck.

† **Fornaidheach**, aih, *s. m.* (*Ir. id.*) A glutton.

Fornair, *s. m.* A command; an offer.

Foroideas, eis, *s. m.* (*Ir. id.*) A rudiment; a tradition.

Foroideasach, *a.* (*Ir. id.*) Elemental, elementary.

† **Forrach**, aich, *s. m.* (*Ir. id.*) An angling rod; pole or perch.—*Shaw.* Oppression; compulsion.—*O'Reilly.*

† **Forraid**, *adv.* (*Ir. id.*) Near, hard by.

Forrumha, s. pl. Fringes.

Forsmaltadh, aidh, s. m. (Ir. id.) Injustice.

Fortail, a. (Ir. id. Lat. fortis) Strong; brave. Gu fortail, *bravely.*

For-shoitheach, s. m. A basin N. pl. for-shoithchean.

For-shuidhear, eir, s. m. A president.

Fortachd, s. f. (Ir id.) Comfort.

Fortalachd, s. f. (Ir id) Strength, bravery, hardihood.

Fortan, ain, s m. Fortune, luck Deagh fhortan, *good fortune,* droch fortan, *bad luck;* mar bha 'm fortan, *as good luck would have it*

Fortanach, a. Fortunate, lucky. Com. and sup. fortanaiche. Gu fortanach, *luckily.*

Fortas, ais, s m (Ir id.) Litter; orts; refuse of fodder

For-theachdair, s. m An usher; a squire.—*Shaw.* N. pl. for-theachdairean

For-theagasg, aisg, s. m. Rudiments

Fortraidh, a. A rising. Fortraidh maidne, *the morning dawn*

Fo-ruadh, a Reddish, brown.

For-uinneag, eig, s. f. A balcony. N. pl. for-uinneagan

For-uinneagach, a Having a balcony, belonging to a balcony

Forum. See Farum.

Forus, uis, s. m. (Ir. id.) A dwelling, an abode.

Fòs, *adv.* (Ir. id) Moreover, also, yet, still Ach fos, *but still, but yet,* fòs tamul beag, *yet a little while* —*Stew. N. T.* Mun do ghineadh fòs na cnuic, *ere yet the hills were formed.—Smith.*

† Fos, fois, s m. (Ir. id W. fos. Ir. fos. Lat. fossa) A ditch, a wall, a buttress.

† Fos, v. a. (Ir id.) Prop, stay, pitch, lead —*Shaw*

Fosadh, aidh, s m (Ir id) Cessation, rest, respite; delaying; staying, an atonement; sloping, a prop, a buttress Cha sluagh gun chruaidh bheireadh fosadh orra, *it would not be unarmed people who could make them cease —Mac Don.* Fosadh còmhraig, *a cessation of arms, armistice, a parley*

† Fosadh, aidh, s m (Ir id) Atonement.—*Shaw*

Fosdadh, aidh, s m. (Ir. id) Steadiness

Fosgadh, aidh, s m More frequently written *fasgadh,* which see

Fosgail, v. a. (Ir. foscail) Open, disclose, unlock Pret. a dh' fhosgail, *opened, fut. aff.* a fosgailidh, *shall open,* dh' fhosgail e a bolg, *he opened her womb.—Stew. Gen* An fear nach fosgail a sporan fosglaidh e 'bheul, *he who opens not his purse, must open his mouth with fair words —G P*

Fosgailte, p part of fosgail Opened, disclosed, open, unlocked, public. *Asp form,* fhosgailte Leth-fhosgailte, *half open —Oss Tem* Leabhran fosgailte, *a little book open.—Stew Rev*

Fosgaireachd, s f. See Fosgarachd

Fosgarach, a. Open-hearted, frank, cheerful Com and sup fosgaraiche, *more or most open-hearted* Gu fosgarach, *frankly*

Fosgarachd, s. f Open-heartedness, frankness

Fosgaradh, a Open-hearted; frank, cheerful Labhair e gu fosgaradh rèidh, *he spoke frankly and calm.—Old Song.*

Fosgladh, aidh, s m The act of opening or unlocking; a breach

Fosgladh, (a.) pr. part of fosgail Opening, unlocking; making a breach

Fo-sgriobhadh, aidh, s m. A postscript; an appendix

† Foslong, s. m. (Ir. id.) A mansion or dwelling-house.

Foslongphort, -phuirt, s. m (Ir id.) A harbour; encampment; a camp N. pl. foslongphuirt.

Foslong-phortach, a. Having harbours.

Fosradh, aidh, s m. (Ir. id) Any thing to lighten a leaky dish; a release; dissolution; a dwelling; a bed.

† Fost, v. a. (Ir. id.) Hire; a prop

† Fot, s. m. (Ir. id) A giant; *also, adjectively,* raging.

Fostadh, aidh, s. m. (Ir. id) A securing; a pacifying

Fothach, aich, s m. (Ir. id.) A lake, a pond; a cough; the glanders; a waste; a wilderness, a giant.

Fothach, a (Ir. id.) Glandered, as a horse.

Fothamas, ais, s. m. (Ir. id) A warning

Fothannan, ain, s. m. (Ir. id) See Foghannan.

Fotharoadh, aidh, s. m. (Ir. id) A bath; a well of purification

† Fothlainteach, ich, s. m. (Ir. id) A novice; an apprentice

Fothrag, aig, s f. (Ir id.) A bath N pl fothragan.

Fothram, aim, s. m. (Ir. id.) Now written *farum.*

Fotrus, uis, s m. (Ir. id) Orts

Fotus, uis, s. m. A flaw or blemish. Dream rioghail gun fhotus, *a royal and spotless clan —Old Song.*

Fotusach, s. f Blemished; causing flaws or blemishes Com. and sup fotusaiche.

Fotusachd, s f. The state of being blemished.

Fo-uachdaran, ain, s m. A viceroy; a deputy governor. N. pl. fo-uachdarain.

Fo-uachdaranachd, s. f. Viceroyalty.

Frac, s. m. (Ir. id.) Bleakness.

† Frach, fràich, s m. (Ir. id.) Bleakness

Frachd, s m A freight.

Fradharc, airc, s m Eyesight, vision; view, sight Am fradhrac eilde is bhoc, *in the sight of hinds and roes —Oss. Tem* Fradhrac do shùl, *the sight of thine eyes —Stew. Jonah*

† Frag, fraig, s f. (Ir. id.) A woman, a wife; hand; shield

Fraidh. See Fraigh.

Fraigealachd, s. f. A show of personal strength

Fraigean, ein, s. m. A little man with an erect martial gait

Fraigeanach, a. Squat and strutting

Fraigeil, a. Ostentatious of personal strength.

† Fraigh, s. f (Ir. id) A bush of hair.—*Shaw.*

Fraigh, s f. (Ir id.) A border, an edge or rim, as of a vessel; the borders of a country, an arch; a skirt; a partition wall, a shelf, arch; *rarely,* sea N pl fraighean. Fraigh shnighe, *moisture oozing through a wall,* cha deanar beanas tighe air na fraighean falamh, *it is hard to keep house with empty cupboards —G P.* Fraighean na Criosdachd, *the borders of Christendom.—Turn*

Fraigheach, a (*from* fraighe) Having borders or rims; bordered, rimmed, skirted.

Fraighean, n pl of fraigh

Fraigh-shnidhe, s f Moisture oozing through the walls or roofs of houses

Fraillach, ich, s. m. and f. (Ir. id) Sea-weed —*Shaw,*

Fraing, s f (Ir. id) France. The Gael almost always put the article before this word, and pronounce it in the aspirated form; as, *an Fhraing,* pron. *an raing.*

Fraingeis, s f. The French language Ag ionnsuchadh na Fraingeis, *learning the French language.*

Fraith, *v. f.* See Fraigh.

Framadh, aidh, *s. m.* (*Ir. id.*) A frame.

Framh. More commonly written *freumh*

Framhach, *a.* See Freumhach.

Frangach, aich, *s. m* A Frenchman, a Frank. *N. pl.* Frangaich, *Frenchmen.*

Frangach, *a.* (*Ir.* franncach.) French. Coileach frangach, *a turkey-cock;* cearc fhrangach, *a turkey-hen;* an galar frangach, *the venereal.*

Frangachail, *a.* (Frangach-amhuil.) Frenchman-like.—*Shaw.*

Frang-lus, -luis, *s. m.* (*Ir.* franc-lus) The weed called *t* tansy. *N. pl.* frang-lusan.

Frang-lusach, *a.* Abounding in tansy; made of tansy, like tansy.

Fraoch, fraoich, *s. m* (*W* froç. *Ir.* fraoch. *Span.* breco.) Heath or heather; ling; a ripple on the surface of water. Fleagh air an fhraoch, *a banquet on the heath.—Oss. Carricth.* Tuile Lora an fhraoich, *the flood of heathy Lora.—Oss. Fing.* Air feadh an fhraoich, *among the heather;* coileach fraoich, *a heath-cock.*

Fraoch, fraoich, *s. m* (*Ir. id.*) Wrath, fury, vexation; hunger. Laoch bu gharg fraoch, *a hero of the fiercest wrath.—Ull.*

Fraoch! The war-cry of that branch of the Mac Donells called Mac Donalds.

Fraochach, *a.* (*from* fraoch.) Heathy, heath-covered; passionate, wrathful, raging, furious, stormy. Beanntan fraochach, *heath-covered mountains.—Oss Duth.*

Fraochag, aig, *s. f.* (*Ir. id.*) A whortleberry. *N. pl* fraochagan.

Fraochagach, *a.* Abounding in whortleberries, of whortleberries

Fraochaidh, *a.* (*from* fraoch) Angry, furious; fretful; stormy. Loch Fraochaidh, *a lake in Glenquaich, Perthshire.*

Fraochail, *a.* (*Ir.* fraoch-amhuil) Angry, furious; fretful; stormy. Gu fraochail, *angrily.*

Fraochan, ain, *s m.* (*Ir. id*) A patch on the point or toe of a shoe, as it were a defence against *heath;* a short fit of passion; some part of a deer

Fraochanach, *a.* (*Ir. id.*) Patched, as a shoe; fretful, in a passion; rippling.

Fraochanachd, *s. f.* (*Ir. id.*) Fretfulness.

Fraoch-chearc, -chirce, *s. f.* (*Ir.* frao-chearc.) A heath hen, a grouse hen.

Fraoch-frangach, *s. m.* A species of fragrant heath.

Fraoghaidh, *s.* A warning.

Fraoidh. See Fraigh.

Fraoileach, *a.* (*Ir. id.*) Tipsy, half drunk.

Fraoileach, ich, *s. m.* See Fraoileadh.

Fraoileadh, idh, *s. m* (*Ir. id.*) Tipsiness, drunkenness. Tha fraoileadh ort, *you are tipsy.*

Fraoineasach, *a.* Waving, flourishing.—*Shaw.* Calm, sheltered.

Fraon, Fraoin, *s. m.* (*Ir. id.*) A place of shelter in rock; a sheltered spot among hills.

Fraonaiseach, *a.* Waving, flourishing; affording shelter; calm.

Fras, *v. n.* (*Ir. id*) Shower, rain. *Pret a.* fhras, *showered; fut. aff. a.* frasaidh, *shall shower.* Frasaidh mi aran, *I will rain bread.—Stew. Ex.*

Fras, frais, *s. m.* (*Ir. id.*) A shower; small shot; seed; any small round grain, flower, or blossom, as of flax. *N. pl.* frasan, *showers.* Mu 'n d'thainig fras, *before a shower fell.—Smith.* Frasan sneachd, *falls of snow —Id.* An lion fa fhras, *the flaxen flower.—Stew. Ex* Fras-corcaich, *hemp-seed,* fras-lin, *lint-seed;* fras luaighe, *small shot,* fras-cainceib, *hemp-seed;* fras caol, *small shot,* bogha frais, *a rainbow.*

† **Fras**, *a.* (*Ir. id.*) Ready, active.—*Shaw.*

Frasach, *a., from* fras. (*Ir. id*) Showery, rainy; like a shower, imbriferous; in flower, as flax; fruitful, prolific.

Frasachd, *s f.* (*from* fras) Showeriness, rain, a shower. Frasachd a cheitein, *the showers of spring —Ardar.* Bheir mi dhuibh frasachd, *I will give you rain —Stew. Lev. ref.*

Frasadh, aidh, *s. m.* A raining, a showering.

Frasadh, (a), *pr part.* of fras. Raining, showering. A frasadh fàla, *showering blood.—Fingalian Poem.*

Frasach, *a, from* fras. (*Ir. id*) Like a shower, showery.

Frasrachd, *s. f.* (*Ir. id.*) Showeriness.

Freacadan, ain, *s. m.* See Freiceadan

† **Freac**, *a.* (*Ir id*) Crooked, bent, bending.—*Shaw*

† **Freacar**, air, *s m.* (*Ir. id*) A witness; testimony, evidence; practice, frequency

† **Freacair**, *s.* (*Ir. id*) Use, practice, attendance

† **Freacaran**, ain, *s. m.* (*Ir. id.*) A wrestling school; a place for exercise.

† **Freacaraich**, *v. a* and *n.* (*Ir. id*) Wrestle, exercise, accustom *Pret. a.* fhreacaraich

Freacaraiche, *s. m.* (*Ir. id.*) A wrestler, an exerciser

Freachnamhach, *a.* Cautious, careful.—*Shaw.* Gu freachnamhach, *cautiously.*

Freachnamh, aimh, *s. m.* (*Ir id*) Labour

Freachnamhachd, *s f.* Cautiousness, carefulness

† **Freacnairc**, *s. f.* (*Ir. id.*) Conversation.

Freacnaireach, *a.* Modern.—*Shaw*

† **Freadh**, *s. m.* (*Ir. id*) Pillaging, plundering; booty.

Freagair, *v. a.* (*Ir. id.*) Answer, suit; fit; correspond *Pret. a.* fhreagair, *answered; fut aff. a* freagairidh, *shall answer*

Freagairt, *s. f.* An answer or reply. Fios freagairt, *an answer to a letter or message,* cha d'thug e freagairt domh, *he gave me no answer*

Freagairt, (a), *pr part* of freagair. Answering, replying, suiting, fitting; corresponding. Guth bròin ag a freagairt, *a voice of grief answering her.—Ull*

Freagarach, *a* (*Ir* freagarthach.) Answerable, suitable, fitting; accountable, responsible

Freagarachd, *s. f.* Answerableness, suitableness; accountableness, responsibility.

Freagar, Freagaradh, aidh, *s. m* A reply, answer, the act of answering; suiting; fitting Written also *freagradh.*

Freagaraich, *v.* Answer; suit, fit; adapt *Pret. a.* fhreagaraich, *suited, fut. aff* freagaraichidh.

Freagaraichte, *p part* of freagaraich Answered, suited, fitted, adapted. *Asp form,* fhreagaraichte

Freagarair, *s. m.* A respondent; a defendant —*Shaw*

Freagnadh, aidh, *s m* (*Ir. id*) Labour, work, employment.

Freagnairc, *s. f* (*Ir. id*) Conversation.

Freagrachd, *s f* See Freagarachd

Freagra, Freagradh, aidh, *s. m.* (*Ir id*) A reply or answer; answering, suiting, fitting.

Freagram, (*for* freagairidh mi.) I will answer; *also,* 1 *sing imper.* let me answer.

Freamh, freimh, *s.* See Freumh.

FREAMHACH, *a.* See FREUMHACH.

FREAMHAICH, *v. n.* See FREUMHAICH.

FREANG, *s. m.* (*Ir. id.*) A hide, a skin.

† FREANG, *v. a.* (*Ir. id.*) Make crooked, bend, twist.—*Shaw.*

FREANGACH, *a.* (*Ir. id.*) Crooked, bent, twisted, winding, turning.

FREAPADH, aidh, *s. m.* (*Ir. id.*) A bouncing, a kicking, a skipping.—*Shaw.*

† FREAPADH, aidh, *s. m.* (*Ir. id.*) Medicine.

FREASDAIL, *v. a.* Provide, prepare, take precaution; wait on, serve, attend. *Pret. a.* fhreasdail, *provided*; *fut. aff. a.* freasdailidh. A fhreasdal gu riar, *to attend at her will.*—*Mac Lach.*

FREASDAL, ail, *s. m.* (*Ir. id.*) Providence; foresight; visitation; charge; lot, fate; serving, attending; attendance; a guardian angel. Choimhead do fhreasdal, *thy visitation has preserved.*—*Stew. Job.* Freasdal Dé, *the charge of God.*—*Stew. Lev.* Is fearr freasdal na gàbhadh, *better is foresight than falling into danger.*—*G. P.*

FREASDALACH, *a.*, *from* freasdal. (*Ir. id.*) Providential, provident; foresighted. *Com.* and *sup.* freasdalaiche, *more* or *most provident.* Gu freasdalach, *providentially.*

FREASDALACHADH, aidh, *s. m.* The act of making provision.

FREASDALADH, aidh, *s. m.* A providing, or making provision.

FREASDALAICH, *v. a.* Provide, make provision; take precaution. *Pret. a.* fhreasdalaich, *fut. aff. a.* freasdalaichidh; *p. part.* freasdalaichte.

† FREASG, *v. a.* (*Ir. id.*) Climb, ascend, mount.

FREASGHABHAIL, *s. f.* (*Ir. id.*) Ascension to heaven.

FREASLACH, ich, *s. m.* (*Ir. id.*) Anger, resentment, displeasure.

FREICEADAN, ain, *s. m.* (*Ir. id.*) A watch, a guard or sentinel; a regiment. Ceannard an fhreiceadain, *the captain of the guard.*—*Stew. N. T.* Am freiceadan dubh, *the Black Watch*,—the name originally given to the 42d regiment of Royal Highlanders. See *Stewart's Hist. of Highland Regiments.*

FREICEADANACH, *a.* (*Ir. id.*) Of, or belonging to, a watch or guard; regimental.

FREICEADANACHD, *s. f.* (*Ir. id.*) Watching, guarding; continued watching.

FREICEADANAICHE, *s. m.* A guard or sentinel.

FREIMH. See FREUMH.

FREISLIDH, *s. f.* (*Ir. id.*) Anger, vexation.

FREITEACH, ich, *s. m.* (*Ir. id.*) A vow, an oath. Thoir freiteach nach dean thu eucoir, *make a vow that thou shalt not do evil.*—*Dugald Mac Pherson.*

FREOTHAL, ail, *s. m.* A whirl, an eddy. Mar fhreothal na mara, *like the eddy of the sea.*—*Fingalian Poem.*

FREOTHALACH, *a.* Whirl; eddying; full of eddies.

FREUMH, freimh, *s. f.* (*Ir. id.*) A root, a stock, lineage; *rarely*, sound sleep. Spionar a fhreumh a bun, *his root shall be torn up.*—*Smith.* *N. pl.* freumhan; *d. pl.* freumhaibh.

FREUMHACH, *a.*, *from* freumh. (*Ir.* fremhach.) Rooted; firmly rooted; having roots, having strong roots; fibrous, fundamental. *Com.* and *sup.* freumhaiche.

FREUMHACH, aich, *s. m.* Root; original; lineage, stock, pedigree. Dìridh snothach o 'n fhreumhach, *sap shall ascend from their roots.*—*Macfar.* A chionn nach robh freumhach aige, *because it had no root.*—*Stew. Mark.*

FREUMHACHADH, aidh, *s. m.* (*Ir.* freamhaghadh.) Taking root, propagating. Air dhuibh bhi air bhur freumhachadh, *on your being rooted.*—*Stew. Eph.*

FREUMHACHAS, ais, *s. m.* Firmness of root; etymology.

FREUMHACHD, *s. f.* (*from* freumh.) Rootedness; an original; etymology.

FREUMHAICH, *v. n.* Take root, radicate. *Pret. a.* fhreumhaich, *took root*; *fut. aff. a.* freumhaichidh, *shall take root.*

FREUMHAICHTE, *p. part.* of freumhaichte. Rooted. Freumhaichte na chridhe, *rooted in his heart.*

FREUMHAIL, *a.* (*from* freumh.) Radical.

FREUMHAIR, *s. m.* (*from* freumh.) An etymologist. *N. pl.* freumhairean.

FREUMHAIREACHD, *s. f.* Etymology.

FREUMH-FHOCAL, ail, *s. m.* A radical term or etymon; an original or primitive word.

FREUMH-FHOCLACH, *a.* Etymological.

FREUMH-FHOCLAIR, *s. m.* An etymologist; an etymological dictionary. *N. pl.* freumh-fhoclairean.

FREUMHUINEAN, ein, *s. m.* A sucker, a sprout.

FREUNAICH, *v. n.* Found; establish. *Pret. a.* fhreunaich, *founded*; *fut. aff. a.* freunaichidh, *shall found.*

† FRIALTA, *a.* (*Ir. id.*) Free, freed.—*Shaw.*

FRÌD, fride, *s. f.* A small pimple; a tetter; a pustule. *N. pl.* frìdean.

FRÌDEACH, *a.* (*Ir. id.*) Pimply; pustulous; like a pimple.

FRÌDEAG, eig, *s. f.* (*dim.* of frìd.) A small pimple, a small pustule. *N. pl.* frìdeagan.

FRÌDEAGACH, *a.* Pimply; full of small pimples.

FRIDH, fridhe, *s. f.* (*W.* frith *and* friç.) A forest; a deer pack, a heath or moor. Am measg chranna na fridhe, *amid the trees of the forest.*—*Stew. Ez.* See also FRITH.

FRIOBHRUTH, *s. m.* A refusal, a denial.

FRIOCHANTAIREACHD, *s. f.* Recantation.

FRIOCHDAN, ain, *s. m.* (*Ir. id.*) A frying-pan. *N. pl.* friochdain.

FRIOCHNACH, *a.* Diligent, careful, circumspect. Gu friochnach, *diligently.*

FRIOCHNADH, aidh, *s. m.* Care; consuming care; diligence. Perhaps *friogh-ghnath.*

FRIOCHOIDHEAS, is, *s. m.* Antipathy.

FRIODHAN, ain. See FRIOGHAN.

FRIODHANACH, *a.* See FRIOGHANACH.

FRIOGH, *a.* Sharp, keen, piercing; bristly. Gu friogh, nàmhach, *sharply and hostilely.*—*Old Song.*

FRIOGHACH, *a.* Sharp, keen, piercing; bristly.

FRIOGHAIL, *a.* (friogh-amhuil.) Sharp, keen, piercing; bristly. Gu frioghail, *sharply*, cho frioghail ris na leòmhainn, *as keen as lions.*—*Mac Co.*

FRIOGHALACHD, *s. f.* Sharpness, keenness, bristliness. Frioghalachd d' inntinn, *the sharpness of thy wit.*

FRIOGHAN, ain, *s. m.* (*from* friogh.) A bristle; a sow's bristle.

FRIOGHANACH, *a.* Bristly, bristling; rough. Gu frioghanach, *bristlingly.*

FRIOGHANACHD, *s. f.* Bristliness.

FRIOLAISG, *s. f.* A small splinter rising on the surface of deal, or on the skin.

FRIOLANNA, *s. pl.* Streamers.

FRIOLUAISG, *v. a.* Turn down and open the mouth of a sack or bag.—*Shaw.* Move up and down.

FRIONAS, ais, *s. m.* (*Ir.* friothnas.) Fretfulness; a fret; vexation, chagrin.

FRIONASACH, *a.* Fretful; peevish; bitter; impatient; vexed. *Com.* and *sup.* frionasaiche. Na bìosa frionasach, *be not* impatient.—*Smith.* Ri là frionasach fuar, *during a bitter cold day.—Turn.* Gu frionasach, *fretfully.*

FRIONASACHD, *s. f.* Fretfulness; peevishness; impatience.

FRIOSG, *v. a.* (*Ir. id.*) Turn down and open the mouth of a sack or bag.

FRIOT, friota, *s. m.* A fret; a fit of fretfulness.

FRIOTACH, *a.* (*Ir. id.*) Ill-natured, hasty; fretful; angry. Gu friotach, *fretfully.*

FRIOTACHAS, ais, *s. m.* Ill-nature, anger.

FRIOTAL, ail, *s. m.* (*Ir. id.*) A word; interpretation; a fret. —*Shaw.*

FRIOTALACH, *a.* (*Ir. id.*) Fretful; angry; hasty. *Com.* and *sup.* friotalaiche. Gu friotalach, *fretfully.*

FRIOTALACHD, *s. f.* (*Ir. id.*) Fretfulness, angriness.

FRIOTHAN. See FRIOGHAN.

† FRISCEART, eirt, *s. m.* (*Ir. id.*) An answer.

FRISGIS, *s. f.* (*Ir. id.*) Hope, expectation.—*Shaw.*

FRITH, frithe, *s. f.* (*W.* frith *and* friç, *forest. Fr.* friche, *wild ground.*) A forest, heath, moor; a deer-park; wrath; a surly look; profit, advantage; fate. Mo chairde san fhridhe, *my friends in the forest.—Oss.* Dh'éirich frith, *wrath arose.—Old Poem.*

FRITH, *s. f.* (*Lat.* fretum. *Scotch,* firth. *Ir.* frith. *Eng.* frith.) The mouth of a river; fate.

FRITH, *s. f.* (*Ir. id.*) Suit, attendance.

FRITH-AGHANN, -aighne, *s. f.* (*Ir. id.*) A warming-pan.

FRITH-AINM, *s. m.* (*Ir. id.*) A nickname. *N. pl.* frith-ainmean.

FRITH-AINMEACH, *a.* Nicknaming, apt to nickname.

FRITH-AINMICH, *v. a.* Nickname.

FRITHAIREACH, *a.* (*Ir. id.*) Hasty, peevish. Gu frithaireach, *fretfully.*

FRITHAIREACHD, *s. f.* Hastiness; peevishness.

FRITH-BHAC, *s. m.* (*Ir. id.*) The barb of a hook, arrow, or anchor.

FRITH-BHAILE, *s.* (*Ir. id.*) A suburb, a hamlet, a village. *N. pl.* frith-bhailtean, *suburbs.* Anns na frith-bhailtean, *in the suburbs.—Stew.* 1 *Chr.*

FRITH-BHAILTEACH, *a.* (*Ir. id.*) Abounding in hamlets; having suburbs; suburbine.

FRITH-BHARAIL, *s. f.* (*Ir. id.*) A paradox.—*Shaw.*

FRITH-BHARAILEACH, *a.* Paradoxical.

† FRITH-BHEART, *v. a.* (*Ir. id.*) Contradict; object.—*Shaw.*

FRITH-BHUAIL, *v. a.* (*Ir. id.*) Palpitate; strike back; strike softly; vibrate. *Pret. a.* frith-bhuail, *palpitated.*

FRITH-BHUAILTEACH, *a.* (*Ir. id.*) Repercussive, vibrative. Leighis frith-bhuailteach, *repercussive medicines.—Shaw.*

FRITH-BHUALADH, aidh, *s. m.* A palpitating, a palpitation; pulsation; a striking softly; repercussion.

FRITH-BHUALADH, (a), *pr. part.* of frith-bhuail. Palpitating, vibrating. Tha mo chridhe a frith-bhualadh, *my heart palpitates.*

FRITH-BHUILLE, *s. m.* (*Ir. id.*) A light stroke; a back stroke; a vibration. *N. pl.* frith-bhuillean.

FRITH-CHANTAIR, *s. m.* (*Ir. id.*) A recanter. *N. pl.* frith-chantairean.

FRITH-CHANTAIREACHD, *s. f.* (*Ir. id.*) Recantation.—*Shaw.*

FRITH-CHOILLE, *s. f.* (*Ir. id.*) An underwood, a copse. *N. pl.* frith-choilltean.

FRITHEACHD, *s. f.* (*Ir. id.*) A coming and going, a returning. Perhaps *frith-theachd.*

FRITH-EAGAL, ail, *s. m.* (*Ir. id.*) Surprise, sudden terror, a panic.

FRITH-EAGALACH, *a.* (*Ir. id.*) Causing a panic; apt to be startled.

FRITHEALACH, *a.* (*Ir. id.*) Waiting, attending; officious, attentive. Gu frithealach, *officiously.*

FRITHEALADH, aidh, *s. m.* (*Ir. id.*) A waiting, an attending, attendance; ministry; dispensation. Fear frithealaidh, *an attendant, a waiter;* fear frithealaidh Mhaois, *Moses' attendant.—Stew. Jos.* Aire do ar frithealadh, *attention to our ministry.—Stew. Rom.*

FRITHEAR, FRITHEARACH, *a.* (*Ir. id.*) Peevish, morose, cross, impatient; fervent.

FRITHEARACHD, *s. f.* (*Ir. id.*) Peevishness, moroseness, crossness, impatience.

FRITHEIL, *v.* Attend, wait on, serve, minister. *Pret. a.* fhritheil, *attended; fut. aff. a.* fritheilidh, *shall attend.*

FRITHEILEACH, *a.* Officious; attending, waiting on, attentive.

FRITHEILEACHD, *s. f.* Officiousness; attendance, attentiveness.

FRITH-EILEAN, ein, *s. m.* (*Ir. id.*) A floating island; a small island. *N. pl.* frith-eileanan, *islands.*

FRITH-EILEANACH, *a.* Having small islands; having floating islands.

FRITH-IASG, -éisg, *s. m.* A bait for fish.

† FRITHING, *s. f.* (*Ir. id.*) A relapse.

FRITHIR, *a.* See FRITHEAR.

FRITH-LEUM, *v. n.* Skip, leap; bound, hop. *Pret. a.* frith-leum, *skipped; fut. aff. a.* frith-leumaidh.

FRITH-LEUM, *s. m.* (*Ir.* frith-léim.) A skip, a leap, a bound.

FRITH-LEUMARTAICH, *s. f.* A skipping, bounding, hopping. Re frith-leumartaich, *skipping.*

FRITH-LEUMNACH, *a.* Skipping, bounding.

FRITH-LEUMNAICH, *s. f.* A skipping, a bounding, a hopping.

FRITHNE, *s. f.* (*Ir. id.*) An uninhabited place; an unfrequented place.

FRITHNEASACH, *a.* See FRIONASACH.

FRITH-RATHAD, aid, *s. m.* A by-road; a short cut; a near way. *N. pl.* frith-rathadan, *by-roads.*

FRITH-ROD, roid, *s. m.* A by-road; a short cut; a near way. *N. pl.* frith-rodan.

FRITH-RODACH, *a.* Having by-roads or short cuts.

FRITH-SHEIRC, *s. f.* A return of love; mutual love.

FRITH-SHEOMAR, air, *s. m.* A side-room, a small apartment. *N. pl.* frith-sheomraichean, *small apartments.—Stew.* 1 *K.*

FROG, frog, *s. m.* (*Ir. id.*) A fen or marsh; a hole; a cleft or cranny; anger. Ann am frogaibh nan toll, *in the clefts of caverns.—Macfar.* As na frogaibh, *from the holes.—Stew. Sam.*

FROGACH, *a., from* frog. (*Ir. id.*) Fenny, marshy; having holes or clefts.

FROGAIL, *a.* (frog-amhuil.) Merry, cheerful; tipsy, maudlin. Ag éiridh gu frogail, *rising merrily.—Old Song.*

FROGALACHD, *s. f.* Merriness, cheerfulness; tipsiness.

FROGAN, ain, *s. m.* Tipsiness; a merry fit.—*Macint.* Anger, a slight fit of anger.

FROGANTA, FROGHANTA, *a.* (*Ir. id.*) Merry; lively; pert; tipsy. Gu froganta, *merrily.*

FROGANTACHD, *s. f.* Merriness, liveliness; pertness; tipsiness.

FROISEADH, idh, *s. m.* Rain, a blast.—*Turn.*

Froinis, *s. f.* (*Ir. id.*) A fringe. *N. pl.* froinseachan.

Froinnse, *s. f.* A fringe.

Froinnseach, *a.* Fringed.

Froithlin, *s. f.* A whirl.—*Shaw.*

† **Fromh**, *v. a.* (*Ir. id.*) Try, taste, inquire, examine.

† **Fromhadh**, aidh, *s. m.* (*Ir. id.*) A trial, a tasting; inquiry.—*Shaw.*

† **Fromhaidh**, *a.* (*Ir. id.*) Hoarse.

Fròn, fròin, *s. m.* (*Ir. id. Gr.* φρονεω, *to be wise.*) A nose. The French say of a prudent man, *il a le bon nez*, the Latins said, *vir emunctis naribus.*

Fronnsa, *s. m.* (*Ir. id.*) A kind of play, or mock-wedding, at wakes.

† **Fros**, *a.* (*Ir. id.*) Dark, obscure.

Fros, frois, *s. m.* A shower, rain. *N. pl.* frois *and* frosan, *showers.* Le frois ni thusa tais, *with showers thou wilt mollify.*—*Smith.* Written also *fras*, which see.

Frosach, *a.* (*from* fros.) Rainy, showery. Written also *frasach*, which see.

Frosachd, *s. f.* (*from* fros.) Rain, showeriness. Written also *frasachd.*

Frothal, ail, *s. m.* (*Ir. id.*) A whirl or whern.—*Shaw.*

Frothalach, *a.* (*from* frothal.) Whirling.

Fu, *prep.* (*Ir. id.*) Beneath. See Fo.

Fuabart, airt, *s. m.* (*Ir. id.*) Spoiling.

† **Fuach**, fuaich, *s. m.* (*Ir. id.*) A word.

Fuachaid, *s. f.* (*Ir. id.*) A jilt, a tricking strumpet.

Fuachaideach, *a.*, *from* fuachaid. (*Ir. id.*) Jilting; like a jilt. Gu fuachaideach, *jiltingly.*

Fuachaideachd, *s. f.* (*Ir. id.*) Jilting.

Fuachas, ais, *s. m.* (*Ir. id.*) A cry, an outcry; cold. *N. pl.* fuachasan.

Fuachasach, *a.* (*from* fuachas.) Making an outcry; tumultuous, cold. Gu fuachasach, *tumultuously.*

Fuachasach, aich, *s. m.* (*Ir. id.*) A den, a cave, a hole. —*Shaw.*

Fuachasach, *a.* Full of caves.

Fuachasachd, *s. f.* An outcry, a tumult; continued tumult; a tendency to tumult.

Fuachd, *s. m.* (*Ir. id.*) Cold, chillness, cold weather. Mar eithe san fhuachd, *like ice in the cold.*—*Ull.* Fuachd is lomnochdaidh, *cold and nakedness.*—*Stew.* 2 *Cor.*

Fuachdan, ain, *s. m.* (*Ir. id.*) Any sore occasioned by cold; a chilblain. *N. pl.* fuachdain.

Fuad, *v.* Elope, run away with; impress. *Pret.* dh'fhuad; *fut. aff.* fuadaidh.

Fuadach, aich, *s. m.* (*Ir. id.*) Elopement, or running away with, driving away by force; a rape, plunder. Dh'fhalbh i 'm fuadach leis, *she eloped with him.*

Fuadachadh, aidh, *s. m.* (*Ir. id.*) An eloping, elopement; a driving away by force; banishment.

Fuadachd, *s. f.* (*Ir. id.*) Elopement; a rape; robbery, depredation.

Fuadaich, *v. a.* and *n.*, *from* fuad. (*Ir.* fuadaigh.) Banish, drive or force away; carry off by force; elope; ravish; impress. *Pret. a.* dh'fhuadaich, *banished*, *fut. aff. a.* fuadaichidh. Gum fuadaich e, *that he will drive out.*—*Stew. Jos.* Fuadaich le fonn a ghruaim, *drive away his frown with a song.*—*Oss. Fing.* A dh'fhuadachadh bhan, *to carry off* [*elope with*] *females.*—*Mac Lach.*

Fuadaichte, *p. part.* of fuadaich. (*Ir.* fuaduighte.) Banished, driven or forced away, carried away, snatched away.

Fuadan, ain, *s. m.* Wandering, straggling, straying; exile, an exile. Air fhuadan, *astray.* Is coma leam fear fuadain 's e luath labhar, *I dislike a strange guest who has a loud tongue.*—*G. P.*

Fuadar, air, *s. m.* (*Ir. id.*) Haste, hurry; preparation to do any thing.

Fuadarach, *a.*, *from* fuadar. (*Ir. id.*) Hasty, in a hurry; requiring haste; active, diligent. *Com.* and *sup.* fuadaraiche. Gu fuadarach, *hastily.*

Fuadradh, aidh, *s. m.* (*Ir. id.*) A bier; a hindering; crossing; forbidding.

Fuadh, *s. m.* (*Ir. id.*) A scarecrow; a bugbear; a bier; a spectre, a demon; a slender, ghastly person; a vain fellow; hatred; a foe. In this last sense it is most commonly written *fuath.*

Fuadhmhor, *a.* (*Ir. id.*) Spectral.

Fuagairt, *s. f.* (*Ir. id.*) Adjuration, warning.

Fuaghail, *v. a.* Sew, stitch. *Pret. a.* dh'fhuaghail; *fut. aff. a.* fuaghlidh, *shall sew*; *p. part.* fuaghailte.

Fuagradh, aidh, *s. m.* (*Ir. id.*) A proclamation or edict.

Fuaid, *s. f.* A remnant.

Fuaideach, *a.* (*from* fuaid.) Having remnants.

Fuaidh, *v. a.* (*Ir.* fuaigh.) Sew, stitch. *Pret. a.* dh'fhuaidh, *sewed*, *fut. aff. a.* fuaidhidh. Written also *fuaigh.*

Fuaidheal, eil, *s. m.* A sewing, a stitching. Deagh fhuaidheal, *good stitching.*

Fuaidhlean, ein, *s. m.* (*Ir. id.*) Anger, fury.

Fuaidhte, **Fuaidhilte**, *p. part.* Sewed, stitched.

Fuaigh, *v. a.* Sew, stitch. *Pret. a.* dh'fhuaigh, *sewed*, *fut. aff. a.* fuaighlidh, *shall* or *will sew*; *p. part.* fuaighte, *sewed.* Fuaighidh tu suas, *thou shalt sew up.*—*Stew. Job.* Am fear leis am fuar fuaigheadh e, *he who feels cold let him clothe.*—*G. P.*

Fuaigheal, eil, *s. m.* Sewing, stitching. Am gu fuaigheal, *a time to sew.*—*Stew. Ecc.*

Fuail, *gen. sing.* of fual.

Fuail-fheadan, ain, *s. m.* The urethra.

Fuaim, *s. f.* (*Ir. id.*) Noise; sound, echo. Fuaim an cliù, *the noise of their fame.*—*Oss.* Ri fuaim, *sounding; making a noise.* Tàifeid san osaig a fuaim, *a bow-string sounding in the wind.*—*Oss. Com.*

Fuaimear, *a.* (fuaim-mhor.) Noisy, sounding, sonorous. Tràigh fhuaimear, *a sounding shore.*—*Oss.* Gu fuaimear, *noisily.*

Fuaimeil, *a.* (fuaim-amhuil.) Noisy, sounding; resounding, echoing.

Fuaimneach, ich, *s. m.* A great sound; continued noise. Fuaimneach sleagh, *the noise of spears.*—*Oss. Cath.* Fuaimneach d' fheadan uisge, *the noise of thy water-spouts.* —*Sm.*

Fuaimneach, *a.* (*from* fuaim.) Noisy, sounding, echoing. Le sgiathaibh fuaimneach, *with sounding wings.*—*Oss. Dargo.* *Com.* and *sup.* fuaimniche. Gu fuaimneach, *noisily.*

Fuaimnich, *v.* Resound, echo. *Pret. a.* dh'fhuaimnich, *resounded*; *fut. aff. a.* fuaimnichidh, *shall resound.*

Fuair, *s. f.* (*Ir. id.*) A sound.

Fuaire, *com.* and *sup.* of fuar. Colder, coldest.

Fuairead, eid, *s. m.* (*from* fuar.) Coldness, increase in coldness. A dol am fuairead, *growing more and more cold.* Air fhuairead 's gum bi an t-earrach, *however cold the spring be.*—*Macint.*

Fuairid, *a.* Colder. Is fhuairid e sin, *it is the colder for that, that has rendered it more cold.*

Fuairsgeul, eil, *s.* A silly story.

Fuais, *gen. sing.* of fuas; which see.

† **Fuait**, *s. f.* (*Ir. id.*) Judgment.

Fual, fual, *s. m.* (*Ir. id.*) Urine.

Fualan, ain, *s. m., from* fual. (*Ir. id.*) A chamber-pot; *also*, a pimp.—*Shaw.*

Fualas, ais, *s. m.* (*Ir. id.*) A tribe, a family.

Fual-bhrosnach, aich, *s. m.* (*Ir.* fual-bhroslach) A diuretic; *also, adjectively*, diuretic.

Fual-fheadan, ain, *s. m.* The urethra.

Fualiosg, *s f.* (*Ir. id*) A strangury.

Fualiosgach, *a.* Causing strangury, strangurial.

Fual-losgach, *a.* Causing heat in urine.

Fual-losgadh, aidh, *s. m.* (*Ir. id*) Heat in urine.

Fual-phoit, *s. f.* A chamber-pot.—*Macd. N pl.* fual-phoiteachan.

Fuaman, ain, *s. m.* (*Ir. id.*) A shadow, a shade; whiteness; a rebound.—*Shaw.*

Fuamhair, *s. m.* A giant. *N. pl.* fuamhairean, *giants.*—*Stew. Gen ref.*

Fuamhaireach, *a.* (*from* fuamhair) Gigantic.

Fuamhaireachd, *s. f.* The prowess or the deeds of a giant.

Fuan, ain, *s. m.* A veil, a cover, a mask; cloth. *N. pl.* fuain.

† **Fuan**, *v. a.* (*Ir. id.*) Veil, cover, mask —*Shaw*

Fuar, *a* (*Ir. id.*) Cold, cool, frigid, chilly Fuar gun deo, *cold and lifeless* —*Oss. Com.* Cho fuar ris an reothadh, *as cold as frost.* Tobar fuar nan carn, *the cool spring of the rock.*—*Oss. Carricth. Com* and *sup.* fuaire.

Fuarachadh, aidh, *s. m.* (*from* fuaraich) A cooling, a growing cold; a making cold or cool; *rarely*, ease, relief Dean do gharadh far an do rinn thu d' fhuarachadh, *warm yourself where you grew cold.*—*G. P.*

Fuarachadh, (a), *pr. part.* of fuaraich; which see.

Fuarachas, ais, *s. m.* (*Ir id*) Coldness

Fuarachd, *s. f.* (*from* fuar) Coldness, cold, chilliness. Crodhaidh fuarachd iad, *the cold shall crowd them together.*—*Macdon.*

Fuarad, aid, *s m.* See **Fuairead.**

Fuaradh, aidh, *s. m.* (*Ir id.*) A breeze, a blast; a cooling; the windward, the weather-side Fuaradh fo 'r srònaibh, *a blast under our noses* —*Mac Co* Sùil ri fuaradh, *an eye to the windward.*—*Macfar.* Fuaradh cluais, *a ship's earring.*—*Shaw.*

Fuarag, aig, *s. f.* (*Ir.* fuarog) A beverage of wrought cream, into which oatmeal is put; by the Lowland Scots called *crowdy*, meal and water mixed

Fuaragan, ain, *s. m.* (*from* fuar.) A fan.—*Macd. N pl* fuaragain.

Fuaraich, *v. a.* and *n.* (*from* fuar) Cool, refrigerate *Pret. a.* dh'fhuaraich, *cooled; fut. aff. a.* fuaraichidh, *shall cool.*

Fuaraichte, *p. part* of fuaraich. Cooled, refrigerated

Fuaraidh, *a.* Cold, chilly. Tha 'n oidhche fuaraidh, *the night is cold.*—*Oss. Fin and Lor.*

Fuaralach, *a.* (*Ir. id.*) Cold, chilly —*Shaw* Gu fuaralach, *coldly. Com.* and *sup.* fuaralaiche.

Fuaralachd, *s. f.* (*Ir id*) Coldness, chilliness —*Macint.*

Fuaran, ain, *s. m., from* fuar (*Ir. id*) A well, a spring, a fountain; a pump-well; a pool for cattle to stand in to cool themselves Fuaran nan carn, *the spring of the rocks.*—*Oss. Carricth. N pl* fuarain, *wells* Greidh air d' fhuarain, *a group of horses on the banks of thy pools.*—*Macdon.*

Fuaranach, *a.* (*Ir. id.*) Abounding in wells —*Macint.*

Fuaranta, *a.* (*Ir. id.*) Chill, cold, grown cold.—*Shaw.* Gu fuaranta, *coldly.*

† **Fuarasdair**, *a.* (*Ir. id.*) Judicious.

Fuar-bheann, -bheinn, *s f.* A cold, bleak mountain. A siubhal fhuar-bheann, *traversing the cold mountains.*—*Old Poem*

† **Fuar-bhodradh**, aidh, *s. m.* (*Ir. id*) A benumbing.

Fuar-bholadh, aidh, *s. m* (*Ir id.*) A bad smell, a stench.

Fuar-chosach, *a.* (*Ir id*) Chilly, frigid

Fuar-chrabhach, *a* (*Ir* fuar-chrabhdha.) Hypocritical Gu fuar-chrabhach, *hypocritically*

Fuar-chràbhadh, aidh, *s m.* Hypocrisy. Luchd fuar-chrabhaidh, *hypocrites* —*Stew N T.*

Fuar-chràbhaiche, *s m* A hypocrite.

Fuar-chrapadh, aidh, *s. m.* (*Ir id.*) A benumbing.—*Shaw.*

Fuar-chridhe, *s m.* A cold heart

Fuar-chridheach, *a* Cold-hearted, unfeeling Gu fuar-chridheach, *unfeelingly.*

Fuar-chrithe, *s f.* A cold shiver. Tha i na fuar-chrithe, *she is in a cold shiver*

Fuar-chrithheach, *a.* Shivering with cold

Fuardachd, *s f.* (*from* fuar) Coldness, chilliness —*Shaw.*

Fuar-dhealt, *s. f.* Mildew; blight; a cold dew. Le fuar-dhealt, *with mildew.*—*Stew. Zeph.*

Fuar-dhealtach, *a.* Mildewy; blighty; blighting

Fuarlanach, *a* Cold; unfeeling, malign; *also, substantively*, malignity, hatred. Gu fuaralnach, *unfeelingly.*

Fuarlanachd, *s f.* Coolness, malignity, hatred. D'fhuarlanachd dh' Albainn, *thy hatred to Scotland.*—*Old Song*

Fuar-lite, *s f* (*Ir id*) A cataplasm —*Shaw.*

Fuarmadh, aidh, *s m.* (*Ir. id*) A form, a seat.

Fuar-mharbh, *a.* (*Ir. id.*) Starved with cold; cold in death

Fuar-mharbh, *v. a.* (*Ir. id*) Starve with cold. *Pret. a.* dh'fhuar-mharbh.

Fuar-mharbhadh, aidh, *s m.* (*Ir id*) Perishing with cold.

Fuar-mharbhtachd, *s f* (*Ir id*) Numbness.

Fuarnach, *a* (*Ir. id*) Controversial; wrangling, quarrelsome. *Com.* and *sup* fuarnaiche.

Fuarnadh, aidh, *s m.* (*Ir. id*) A controversy, an argument, a paper war

Fuarrach, *a.* (*Ir id.*) Helping, assisting

Fuas, fuais, *s m.* (*for* fuathas) Dread, surprise, a spectre Da fhuas sa ghaoith, *two spectres in the wind* —*Oss. Fing. N. pl* fuasan *and* fuais

Fuasach, *a.* (*from* fuas) See **Fuathasach.**

Fuasgail, *v a* Loosen, untie; set at liberty, redeem, absolve, relieve; solve. *Pret a.* fhuasgail, *loosened, fut. aff a.* fuasglaidh, *shall loosen* Fuasglaidh e, *he will redeem.*—*Stew Lev* Daoine a dh'fhuasgladh gach snaim, *men who could solve every difficulty, untie every knot* —*Mac Lach.*

Fuasgailte, *p. part.* of fuasgail (*Ir id*) Untied, loosened, freed, set at liberty; absolved; free-limbed, active. Gach laoch fuasgailte, *each free-limbed hero* —*Macfar.*

Fuasgailteach, *a* (*from* fuasgail.) Loose, licentious, aperient; having the free use of one's limbs, giving or causing freedom —*Macint* Gu fuasgailteach, *loosely*

Fuasgailteachd, *s f.* Looseness, licentiousness; unrestrictedness, freedom; openness; simplicity.

† **Fuasgair**, *v a* Terrify, put to flight; scare off *Pret. a* dh'fhuasgair, *fut. aff a* fuasgraidh, *shall terrify.*

Fuasgaladh, aidh, *s m.* See **Fuasgladh.**

Fuasgaldach, *a.* (*Ir. id.*) Aperient.

Fuasgaldair, s. m. (*from* fuasgail.) A saviour, a deliverer, a redeemer. (*Ir.* fuasgluightheoir.) Fuasgaldair a chinneadh daoine, *the Saviour of the world.* The Irish say *Fuasgluightheoir a chine daona.*

Fuasglach, a. Loosening; absolving; ransoming; delivering.

Fuasgladh, aidh, s. m. (*Ir. id.*) A setting free; a loosening; deliverance; ransoming; a ransom; redemption; looseness of the bowels. Fuasgladh deas, *ready deliverance.—Sm.* Thoir fuasgladh dhomh, *set me free.*

Fuasgladh, (a), *pr. part.* of fuasgail. Loosening, untying; absolving, ransoming.

Fuasglaidh, *fut. aff. a.* of fuasgail. Shall or will unloosen.

Fuasglair, s. m. (fuasgal-fhear.) A redeemer, a ransomer. *N. pl.* fuasglairean.

Fuasgradh, aidh, s. m. (*Ir. id.*) Fright.

Fuaslagadh, aidh, s. m. (*Ir. id.*) An explanation; exposition; a ransom.

Fuaslaig, v. a. (*Ir. id.*) Explain; ransom, redeem.

Fuaslaig, s. f. (*Ir. id.*) An exposition.

Fuasmadh, aidh, s. m. (*Ir. id.*) A blow.

Fuasnach, a. Terrible, frightful; tumultuous.—*Shaw.*

Fuasnadh, aidh, s. m. (*Ir. id.*) An astonishing; astonishment; a driving forward; tumult.

Fuatarach, a. Active, diligent, industrious. Written also *fuadarach.* *Com.* and *sup.* fuataraiche.

Fuatarachd, s. f. Activity, diligence, industriousness. Written also *fuadarachd.*

Fuath, s. m. (*Ir. id.*) Hate, hatred, aversion, spite; a scarecrow, a spectre or apparition, a demon or spirit. Dùisgidh fuath, *hatred shall stir up.—Stew. Pro.* Le m' briathraibh fuath, *with their words of spite.—Sm.* Frith nam fuath, *the forest of spectres.—Oss. Tem.* Fuath mhadaidh, *wolfsbane.* Fuath muic, *harebells.—Shaw.* Fuath radan, *ratsbane.*

Fuathach, a., *from* fuath. (*Ir. id.*) Hateful, abhorrent; spectral, demoniacal. Bhur trosg is fuathach leam, *your fasting is hateful to me.—Sm.*

Fuathachadh, aidh, s. m. A detesting, detestation, abhorrence.

Fuathadh, aidh, s. m. A detesting, a detestation, abhorrence.

Fuathaich, v. a. (*from* fuath.) Hate, detest, abhor. *Pret. a.* dh'fhuathaich, *hated; fut. aff. a.* fuathaichidh, *shall* or *will abhor.* Fuathaichibh olc, *hate* [*ye*] *evil.—Sm. Fut. pass.* fuathaichear, *shall be hated.*

Fuathaichte, *p. part.* Hated, detested.

Fuathail, a. (fuath-amhuil.) Spectral, ghostly, ghastly, frightful; hateful.

Fuathais, *gen. sing.* of fuathas.

† Fuathais, s. f. (*Ir. id.*) A den.—*Shaw.*

Fuathas, ais, s. m. (*from* fuath.) Dread, terror, surprise, horror; a terrific spectre or apparition. Fuathas a bhàis, *the spectre of death.—Oss. Com.* Theich an leanabh le fuathas, *the child fled with terror.—Orr.*

Fuathasach, a., fuathas. (*Ir. id.*) Terrible, formidable, hideous, horrible, dreadful; spectral. Fuathasach anns gach àit, *formidable in every place.—Oss. Fing.* B' fhuathasach combrag an dà righ, *dreadful was the contest of the two kings.—Id. Com.* and *sup.* fuathasaiche.

Fuath-ghorm, s. m. (*Ir. id.*) Bittersweet; woody nightshade, *solanum dulcamara.*

Fuath-mhadaidh, s. m. Wolfsbane.—*Shaw.*

Fuath-mhor, a. Hateful, detestable, odious, disgusting, unclean. Gach eun fuath-mhor, *every unclean bird. Stew. Rev.*

Fuath-muic, s. Harebells.

Fuath-radan, s. m. Ratsbane.

Fuath-thannas, ais, s. m. A hideous spectre. Fuath-thannas nan nial, *the hideous spectre of the clouds.—Oss. Fing.*

Fuath-thoilltinneach, a. Hateful, abominable.—*Stew. Tit.*

Fùc, v. a. Full or mill cloth; push. *Pret. a.* dh'fhùc; *fut. aff. a.* fùcaidh, *shall full.*

Fùcadair, s. m. A fuller of cloth. *N. pl.* fùcadairean.

Fùcadaireachd, s. f. Fulling of cloth; the occupation of a fuller.

Fùcadh, aidh, s. m. The act of fulling; a fulling.—*Macint.*

Fudaidh, a. Mean, contemptible, trifling.

Fùdar, air, s. m. Powder; gunpowder. Mhèile e gu fùdar e, *he ground it to powder.—Stew. Ex. ref.* Fùdar dhurag, *worm-powder.* Fùdar cluaisein, *priming.* Fùdar sròine, *hellebore.—Macd.*

Fufaireachd, s. f. The Irish cry or *conclamatio* at funerals.—*Shaw.*

Fugasg, aisg, s. m. (*Ir. id.*) Patience; persecution; steadiness.

† Fughall, aill, s. m. (*Ir. id.*) Judgment.

Fuich! An exclamation of disgust.

Fuicheachd, s. f. Lust, lechery.

Fuicheall, ill, s. m. A reward, hire, wages.

Fuidh! fuidh! An exclamation of disgust. Fuidh ort! *shame on you!*

Fuidheach, a. (*Ir. id.*) Thankful; joyful.

Fuidheal, eil; s. m. See Fuigheall.

Fuidhir, s. f. Gain; wages; a word; a vassal; a hireling; servitude.—*Shaw.*

Fuidhpe, *comp. prep.* Under her.

Fuidhre, Fuidhreach, s. pl. Attendants; an establishment of servants.

Fuidhreach, a. (*Ir. id.*) Naked; exposed.

Fuidreachd, s. f. (*Ir. id.*) A mixing, a mixture.

Fuidreadh, idh, s. m. (*Ir. id.*) Paste.

Fùidsidh, s. (*provincial.*) A craven; a conquered, despirited cock.

Fuigh, v. a. Get, recover, obtain. See Faigh.

Fuigheag, eig, s. f. A thrum; a loose thread or end in weaving cloth. *N. pl.* fuigheagan.

Fuigheagach, a. Having thrums; like a thrum.

Fuigheall, ill, s. m. Remnant, refuse, relic; *rarely,* judgment; word. Fuigheall an t-sluaigh, *the remnant of the people.—Stew.* 1 *K.* Loisgidh tu am fuigheall, *thou shalt burn the remainder.—Stew. Ex.*

Fuighleach, ich, s. m. Remainder, refuse, leavings. Fuighleach bidh, *refuse of meat.*

Fuil, fola, *and* fala, s. f. (*Ir.* fuil.) Blood, gore; bloodshed. Feadh fala is àir, *amid blood and slaughter.—Sm.* Gu fuil is bàs, *to bloodshed and death.—Id.* Fàth airson fala, *opportunity for bloodshed.—Stew. Mic.* Fuil bhrùite, *extravasated blood.—Macfar.*

Fuil-chiont, s. m. (*Ir. id.*) Blood-guiltiness.

Fuil-chiontach, a. (*Ir. id.*) Bloody; blood-guilty.—*Shaw.*

Fuil-dhòrtadh, aidh, s. m. Bloodshed, blood-spilling.

Fuil-dhòrtair, s. m. A spiller of blood; a sanguinary person.

Fuileach, a., *from* fuil. (*Ir. id.*) Bloody, sanguinary, cruel. Comhrag fuileach, *a bloody battle.—Mac Lach. Com.* and *sup.* fuiliche. A righe is fuiliche lann! *thou king of the bloodiest sword!—Oss. Lodin.*

Fuileachd, *s. f.* (*from* fuil.) Bloodiness, bloodshed.

Fuileachdach, *a.* (*from* fuil.) Bloody, sanguinary, cruel ravenous. An duine fuileachdach, *the bloody man.—Sm.* Do 'n eunlaith fhuileachdach, *to the ravenous bird.—Stew. Ez.* Com. and *sup.* fuileachdaiche.

Fuileadh, idh, *s. m.* (*Ir. id.*) Increase, profit, gain.

† **Fuileasan**, ain, *s. m.* (*Ir. id.*) An asp.—*Shaw.*

Fuiliche, *a.* Blood-red. Also, *com.* and *sup.* of fuileach.

Fuilidh, *a.* (*Ir. id.*) Bloody; blood-red.

Fuilig, *v.* Suffer, bear, permit. *Pret. a.* dh'fhuilig; *fut. aff. a.* fuiligidh, *shall permit.—Stew. Pro. ref.* Tàmailt cha d'fhuilig iad, *disgrace they suffered not.—Old Song.*

Fuiling, *v. a.* Suffer, bear, permit. *Pret. a.* dh'fhuiling, *suffered; fut. aff. a.* fuilingidh, *shall suffer.*

Fuilingeach, *a.* (*Ir. id.*) Patient, enduring; *also*, armed with a spear or shield.

Fuilleadh, idh, *s. m.* (*Ir. id.*) A reward; gain; increase.

Fuilmean, ein, *s. m.* (*Ir. id.*) A toe bleeding by striking it against a stone.—*Shaw.*

Fuil-mios, *s. f.* Menstrual discharge.

Fuilteach, *a.*, *from* fuil. (*Ir. id.*) Bloody, cruel.

Fuiltean, ein, *s. m.* (*from* folt.) The hair of the female head; a snood; a single hair. Tog do bhréit is d'fhuiltean, *lift thy head-dress and snood.—Old Song. N. pl.* fuilteine. Fuilteine bhur cinn, *the hairs of your head.—Stew. N. T.*

Fuin, *v. a.* (*Ir. id.*) Bake, knead. *Pret. a.* dh' fhuin, *baked: fut. aff. a.* fuinidh, *shall bake; fut. pass.* fuinear, *shall be baked.—Stew. Lev.*

† **Fuin**, *s. f.* The end or termination of a thing; will, purpose.—*Shaw.* A veil, a covering.—*O'Reilly.*

Fuine, *s. f.* A batch. Is fhearr fuine thana na bhi falamh, *better is a thin batch than no bread.—G. P.*

Fuineachan, ain, *s. m.* (*Ir. id.*) A kernel.

Fuineadair, *s. m.* (*Ir.* fuinteoir.) A baker. *N. pl.* fuineadairean.

Fuineadaireachd, *s. f.* (*Ir.* fuinteoireachd.) Baking; the business of a baker.

Fuineadh, idh, *s. m.* (*Ir. id.*) The act of baking; a quantity of bread baked at a time; a batch.

Fuineadh, (a), *pr. part.* of fuin. Baking, kneading. Na mnai a fuineadh an taoise, *the women baking the dough.—Stew. Jer.*

Fuineall, ill, *s. m.* (*W.* fynell.) A funnel. *Perhaps* fentholl, *an air-hole*, from the obsolete *fen*, air.

Fuinear, *fut. pass.* of fuin; which see.

† **Fuingeall**, ill, *s. m.* (*Ir. id.*) An idiot, a simpleton.

Fuinidh, *fut. aff. a.* of fuin. Shall or will bake.

† **Fuinn**, *s. f.* Conclusion.—*Shaw.*

Fuinn, *gen. sing.* of fonn; which see.

Fuinneag, eig, *s. f.* A window. *N. pl.* fuinneagan, *windows; d. pl.* fuinneagaibh.—*Stew. Ecc. ref.*

Fuinneag is perhaps *feneag*, from the old Celtic *fen*, *air*, and meaning *an air-hole*; from the same word, *fen*, comes the Latin *fenestra*, a window. *Fuinneag* is also written *uinneag.*

Fuinneagach, *a.* Having windows; like a window.

Fuinnseach, ich, *s.* (*Ir. id.*) Common enchanter's nightshade; the *circæa lutelinia* of botanists.

Fùinnsean, inn, *s. m.* Ash. Written more frequently *uinnsean.*

Fuinseag-choille, *s. f.* The herb called *virgo pastoris.—Shaw. Also*, mountain ash.—*O'Reilly.*

Fuinte, *p. part.* of fuin. (*Ir. id.*) Baked, kneaded.

Fùir, *s.* (*Ir. id.*) A sign, a token.

Fuirbearnach, *a.* Strong, stout; *also*, a strong man.

Fuirbi, Fuirbidh, *s. m.* Strong; *also*, a strong man. *N. pl.* fuirbinnean, *strong men.—Macfar.*

Fuireach', **Fuireachadh**, aidh, *s. m.* Staying; lingering; waiting; delay. Thainig e gun fhuireach', *he came without delay.—Old Poem.* Gu fuireach car oidhche, *to stay for one night.*

Fuireachail, *a.* Attentive, vigilant, on the look out. Gu fuireachail, *attentively.*

Fuireachair, *a.* (*Ir. id.*) Attentive, vigilant, diligent, deliberate. Gu fuireachair, *attentively.*

Fuireachd, *s. f.* (*Ir. id.*) A waiting, a delaying, a lingering, delay.

† **Fuireadh**, idh, *s. m.* (*Ir. id.*) Preparation; a feast.

† **Fuirean**, ein, *s. m.* (*Ir. id.*) A crowd, a multitude; a ship's crew; furniture.

Fuireanal, ail, *s. m.* (*Ir. id.*) A urinal.—*Shaw.*

Fuirearach, *a.* Attentive; vigilant.

Fuireas, eis, *s. m.* (*Ir. id.*) Entertainment; a feast.

Fuirich, **Fuirigh**, *v. n.* Wait, stop, delay, linger; abide; dwell; deliberate. *Pret. a.* dh' fhuirich, *waited; fut. aff. a.* fuirichidh, *shall wait.* Guidheam ort, fuirich, *I pray thee, tarry.—Stew. O. T.* Cha 'n fhuirich mi, *I will not stay;* fuirich orm, fuirich ort, *softly;* fuirich beagan, *stop a little.*

Fuirionn, inn, *s. m.* (*Ir. id.*) Furniture; the crew of a ship; a band of men.—*Shaw.* Land.

Fùirleachadh, idh, *s. m.* Overcoming; a victory.

Fùirlich, *v. a.* Overcome, defeat. *Pret. a.* dh' fhùirlich, *overcame; fut. aff.* fùirlichidh, *shall overcome.*

Fuirm, *s. f.* Form, ceremony; manner, fashion.

Lat. forma, *form. Ir.* fuirm. *Teut.* forme. *Fr.* forme. *Arm.* fuirme.

† **Fuirmeadh**, idh, *s. m.* Humiliation; lessening; travelling.—*Shaw.*

Fuirmheadh, eidh, *s. m.* A seat; a foundation.

† **Fuirmhidh**, *a.* (*Ir. id.*) Hard. *Shaw.*

Fùirneis, *s. f.* A furnace, a stove.—*Stew. Gen. ref.*

Ir. fùirneis. *Gr.* φοῦρνος. *Lat.* furnus *and* fornax. *Fr.* fournaise. *Arm.* forn. *Teut.* forneys.

Fuirneiseach, *a.* Like a furnace or stove; furnished with a stove.

† **Fuis**, *a.* (*Ir. id.*) Active; thrifty.

Fuiseag, eig, *s. f.* A lark. Written also *uiseag;* which see.

† **Fuite**, *s.* (*Ir. id.*) A sound, reiterated noise.

† **Fuith**, *s. f.* (*Ir. id.*) A rag of cloth.—*Shaw.*

Fuithe, *comp. pron.* Under him or it.

† **Fuithir**, *s. f.* (*Ir. id.*) Good land.

Fulachdach, *a.* Patient.

Fulachdas, ais, *s. m.* Patience. See **Fulangas.**

Fulaing, *v. a.* Suffer; endure; permit.

Fulair, *s.* and *a.* Occasion, necessity; obligation; necessary, urgent. Is fhulair dhuit falbh, *you must be going.*

Fulang, aing, *s. m.* (*Ir. id.*) Suffering, patience, forbearance; passion; feeling; foundation; shore; prop; buttress; a stud; a boss.—*Shaw.* Fulanga na h-aigne, *the passions* or *affections of the mind.* Cuir gu fulang, *put to trial.—Mac Co.*

Fulangach, *a.* Patient, able to endure, forbearing, hardy, suffering. Fulangach air fuachd, *able to bear cold.—Macint.* Gu fulangach, *patiently. Com.* and *sup.* fulangaiche.

Fulangaiche, *s. m.* (*Ir.* fullanguighe.) A patient, a sufferer; a person of feeling.—*Shaw.* Also, *com.* and *sup.* of fulangach.

Fulangas, ais, *s. m.* (*from* fulang.) Sufferance, endurance, patience; passion; feeling. Fad-fhulangas, *long-suffering; longanimity.*

† **Fulladh**, aidh, *s. m.* (*Ir. id.*) A lie; leaping, skipping.

Fullan, ain, *s. m.* (*Ir. id.*) An ornament.

FULMAIR, *s. m.* A St. Kilda bird. *N. pl.* fulmairean.

"The *fulmair* is a grey fowl," Martin observes, "about the size of a moor-hen. It has a strong bill, with wide nostrils; as often as it goes to sea, it is a certain sign of a western wind. This fowl, the natives say, sucks its food out of live whales, and eats sorrel; for both these sorts of food are found in its nest. When any one approaches the fulmair, it spouts out of its bill about a quart of pure oil: the natives surprise the fowl, and preserve the oil, and burn it in their lamps. It is good against rheumatic pains and aches in the bones. The inhabitants of the adjacent isles value it as a catholicon for diseases; some take it for a vomit, others for a purge. It has been successfully used against rheumatic pains in Edinburgh and London. In the latter it has been lately used to assuage the swelling of a sprained foot, a cheek swelled with the toothache, and for discussing a hard bile, and proved successful in all the three cases."—*Martin's Description of the Western Isles.*

FULPANACH, aich, *s. m.* (*Ir. id.*) Articulation, or joining of things together.—*Shaw.*

FULSHRUTH, *s. m.* Corruption; gore.

FU'LUAISG, *v.* Rock gently, dandle. *Fut. pass.* fu'luaisgear. —*Stew. Is. ref.* Written also *fo'luasig.*

FULUING. See FULAING.

FUM, *comp. prep. for* fodham. (*Ir. id.*) Beneath me, under me, below me. Saighdearan fum, *soldiers under me.*—*Stew. Matt.* Tha tighinn fum, *I intend, I resolve.*

FUNN, *s.* See FONN.

FUNNTAIL, *a.* Frosty; benumbing. Re làth fuar funntail, *during a cold frosty day.*—*Old Song.*

FUNTAINN, *s. f.* Starving with cold; chilliness; benumbedness. Le funtainn an fhuachd, *with the benumbing power of cold.*—*Macfar.*

FUNTAINNEACH, *a.* Cold, benumbing, chill. Aimsir funtainneach, *benumbing weather.*—*Macdon.*

† FUR, fuir, *s. m.* A thief or robber.
Gr. φωρ. *Lat.* fur. *Ir.* fur.

† FUR, *s. f.* (*Ir. id.*) Preparation.

FURACHAIL, *a.* Attentive, vigilant, on the look out. Gu furachail, *attentively.*

FURACHAIR, *a.* Attentive, watchful, circumspect, on the look out, diligent. Furachair mu m' cheuma, *watchful about my steps.*—*Sm.* Gu furachair, *diligently, watchfully.*

FURACHAR, *a.* Watchful, observant, on the look out, diligent. Gu furachar, *diligently.*—*Stew.* 1 *K.*

FURACHAR MAC AN EALAIDH. A character in Gaelic and Irish tales.

FURACHAS, ais, *s. m.* See FURACHRAS.

FURACHRAS, ais, *s. m.* (*Ir.* furachas.) Expectation; watching; attention; attentiveness. Faiceall is furachras, *circumspection and attention.*—*Sm.*

FURAIL, *v. a.* Offer; command; incite; exhort, persuade, urge.

FURAIL, *s. f.* An offering; command; incitement; exhortation, persuasion. Rinn e ro fhurail air, *he urged him.*—*Q. B. ref.*

FURAILT, *s. f.* Courtesy, hospitality, affability, a welcome.

FURAILTEACH, *a.* Courteous, affable, hospitable, welcoming. Gu furailteach, *courteously.*

FURAILTEACHD, *s. f.* Courteousness, affability, hospitableness.

FURAIN, *s. f.* (*Ir. id.*) Plenty, abundance.—*Shaw.* Also, the *gen. sing.* of furan.

FURAIN, *a.* Welcome, salute, invite. *Pret.* dh' fhurain, *welcomed; fut. aff.* furainidh, *shall welcome.*

FURAN, ain, *s. m.* (*Ir.* furain.) A welcome, a courteous salutation, hospitality; joy; fondling; entertainment. Le furàn mòr, *with much welcome.*—*Sm.* Is furan a thog mo lann, *hospitality has raised my sword.*—*Oss. Oinam.* Is faoin d' fhuran, *vain is thy fondling.*—*Oss. Gaul.* Furan, *entertainment.*—*Shaw.*

FURANACH, *a.* (*Ir. id.*) Courteous, ready to welcome, hospitable; cheerful; civil; saluting. Ged b' fhuranach ar n-oighean, *though cheerful were our virgins.*—*Ull.* Tha thu furanach truacanta, *thou art courteous and compassionate.*—*Mac Co.* *Com.* and *sup.* furanaiche.

FURAS, *a.* Easy, not difficult; *also,* able. Tha eòlas furas, *knowledge is easy.*—*Stew. Prov.* *Asp. form,* fhuras. Cha 'n fhuras gèill thoirt o oigh, *it is difficult to obtain a virgin's assent.*—*Oss. Fing.* Cha 'n fhuras leam d' fhàgail, *I am loathe to leave you;* furas, *able.*—*Shaw.* *Com.* and *sup.* fhasa.

FURASD, FURASDA, *a.* Easy, not difficult. Tha eòlas furasd, *knowledge is easy.*—*Stew. Pro. ref.*

FURASDACHD, *s. f.* Easiness.

FURBAIDH, *s. f.* (*Ir. id.*) Wrath.

FURBAIRNEACH, *a.* Strong, stout; *also,* a strong stout man. Written also *fuirbearnach.*

FURBHAILT, *s. f.* Courtesy, hospitality, a welcome. Le furbhailt is le muirn, *with courtesy and joy.*—*Old Song.* Written also *furailt.*

FURBHAILTEACH, *a.* Courteous, affable, hospitable, welcoming. Written also *furailteach.*

† FURFHOGRADH, aidh, *s. m.* A warning of removal.

FÙRLAICH, *v.* Hate, detest. *Pret.* dh' fhùrlaich, *hated; fut. aff.* fùrlaichidh, *shall detest.* This verb takes after it the prep. *ri* or *ris,* either simple or compound. Dh' fhùrlaich i ris, *she detests him.*

FURMAILTE, *s. f.* Ceremony.

† FURNAIDHE, *s. f.* (*Ir. id.*) A dwelling or residence.

FURNAIS, *s. f.* (*Ir. id.*) A furnace, a forge. Uair mu seach air an fhùrnais, *alternately in the forge.*—*Turn.*

FURSAN, ain, *s. m.* (*Ir. id.*) A flame of fire.

FURTACH, *a.* Ready to assist, aiding, helping, relieving.

FURTACHADH, aidh, *s. m.* A helping or assisting; relief, aid, comfort.

FURTACHADH, (a), *pr. part.* of furtaich. Helping, relieving, comforting.

FURTACHAIL, *a.* Helping, comforting, apt to help.

FURTACHAIR, *s. m.* (*Ir.* furtaighthcoir.) A helper, a reliever, a comforter.

FURTACHD, *s. f.* (*Ir. id.*) Help; deliverance; ease; comfort; release; ease at the crisis of a disorder. Furtachd orduich uait, *order deliverance from thee.*—*Sm.* Furtachd is foir, *help and comfort.*—*Id.* Furtachd do d' òg-mhnàoi, *comfort to thy young wife.*—*Ull.*

FURTAICH, *v.* (*Ir.* furtaigh.) Deliver, release; help; comfort. *Pret. a.* dh' fhurtaich, *helped; fut. aff. a.* furtaichidh, *shall help.* This verb requires after it the prep. *air,* either simple or compound. Furtaich air an duine sin, *deliver that man.* Furtaich oirnne, *deliver us.*—*Sm.*

FURTAICHEAR, *fut. pass.* of furtaich. Shall be helped.

FURTAICHIDH, *fut. aff. a.* of furtaich. Shall or will help.

FURTAICHTE, *p. part.* of furtaich. Delivered, aided, released.

FURTHAIN, *s. f.* Satiety, sufficiency.

FURTHANACH, *a.* Plentiful. Gu furthanach, plentifully.

FUTAIL, *a.* (*Ir.* futamhuil.) Foppish; airy, showy.—*Shaw.* Gu futail, *foppishly.*

FUTALACHD, *s.* Foppery; airiness; showiness.

FÙTAR, air, *s. m.* See FÙDAR.

FUTHA, *com. pron.* Under him or it, beneath him or it. More frequently written *fodha.*

FUTHAD, *comp. pron.* Under or beneath thee. More frequently written *fodhad;* which see.

FUTHPA, *comp. pron.* Under or beneath them. More frequently written *fodhpa;* which see.

G.

G, *g.* (goibh.) The seventh letter of the Gaelic alphabet. When this letter is followed by one or more of the vowels, *a, o, u,* it sounds nearly like *g* in *gap, got, goose;* as, gath, *take;* gort, *famine;* guth, *voice.* *G*, at the end of a word, if preceded by one or more of the vowels, *a, o, u,* or a liquid, sounds most frequently like *k* in *rook, hook;* as, rug, *bore;* thug, *gave.* When it is preceded by *i*, or followed by *e* or *i*, it has a mellow sound not unlike *g* in *girl;* as, gin, *produce;* gêire, *sharpness.* *Gh*, before *a, o,* or *u*, have an aspirated power to which there is no correspondent sound in English; but, when followed by *e* or *i*, they sound like *y* in *ye;* as, ghios, (pronounce ghees), *towards.* *Gh*, at the end of words or syllables, are seldom pronounced; as, righ, *a king;* rioghachd, *a kingdom.*

'G, (*contr.* for ag), *prep.* At. This preposition, when prefixed to an infinitive or to most nouns, gives them the force or meaning of the *pr. part.* 'G is used between two vowels; as, Tha mi 'g òl, *I am* [*at*] *drinking.* Co so 'g aom air luirg? *who is this bending over his staff?—Oss.* When preceded by a consonant or followed by a vowel, it is written entire; as, Manus ag iarruidh comhraig, *Manos wishing for battle.—Oss.* Bha anam ag éiridh gun fhiamh, *his soul was rising fearlessly.—Oss. Tem.* *Ag* is used not unfrequently even though followed by a consonant; as, Gathanna liobhte ag tearnadh, *polished darts descending.—Old Poem.* Between two consonants the *g* is dropped; as, Turlach a' caoidh a chloinne, *Turlach bewailing his children.—Oss.*

'G, (*for* aig), *comp. pron.* At whom or which; to whom or which. 'G am bheil an sealladh ard, *who have a lofty look;* literally, *to whom is the look that is lofty.—Sm.*

G', (*for* gu), *prep.* To. Céilte g' a cheann, *covered up to his head.—Oss. Fing.*

'Ga, (*for* ag a.) At him, at her, at it. 'Ga bhuaireadh, *tempting him;* 'ga bualadh, *striking her;* literally, *at striking her.* Guth bròin 'g a freagairt, *a voice of grief answering her.—Ull.*

Ga, (*for* aig a.) Ga bheil beachd air gach ni, *who knowest every thing.—Turn.*

Ga, G'a, (*for* gu a.) To him or her; to his or her; to it. Ga thigh, *to his house;* ga tigh, *to her house.* G'a sgriobadh fein, *to scratch himself.—Stew. Job.*

Ga, *for* gath, *s.* (*Arm.* gwayw.) A sting, spear, dart, javelin; a ray or beam. Ga nathrach, *an adder's sting;* ga gealaich, *a moonbeam;* ga gréine, *a sunbeam;* also, one of the names of Fingal's banner. Ga gréine mhic Cumhail ri crann, *put the banner of Fingal to its staff.—Old Poem.*

Ga, *conj.* Though. See Ged.

† Ga, *adv.* (*Ir.* ga.) Where? in what place? Now written *ca;* as, cà nis am bheil do ghath? *where now is thy sting?—Sm.*

Gab, gaibh, *s. m.;* more frequently written *gob.* A fowl's bill or beak; a mouth; a tattling mouth.

It. gabbo, *jeering.* *Dan.* gab, *the mouth of a river.* *Eng.* gap *and* gab. *Fr.* †gab, *raillery.* *Arm.* goab. *Scotch*, gab.

Gabach, *a.* (*from* gab.) Having a beak or bill; having a large beak or bill; inclined to tattle; garrulous; unable to keep a secret. *Com.* and *sup.* gabaiche, *more* or *most garrulous.* See also Gobach.

Gabachd, *s. f., from* gab. (*Dan.* gaben, *yawning.*) Talkativeness; incontinence of tongue; inability to keep a secret. Written also *gobachd.*

Gabair, *s. m., from* gab. (*Arm.* gaber, *to banter.* *W.* goaper, *mocker.*) A tattler, a garrulous man.

Gabaireachd, *s. f.* (*Ir. id.* *D.* gabberen, *to prate.*) Garrulity; the habit of prating or tattling; the behaviour of a tattler; jibberish.

† Gabaist, aiste, *s. f.* (*Ir. id.*) Cabbage; cauliflower.

Gabh, *v. a.* (*Ir.* gabh. Hence *Eng.* give.) Take, receive, accept, lay hold of, seize, make prisoner, take possession of, hold or contain; require, engage for service. *Pret. a.* ghabh, *took;* *fut. aff. a.* gabhaidh, *shall* or *will take.* Gabh comhnuidh na do raòin, *take up thy dwelling in thy plain.—Oss. Carricth.* Ghabh iad am baile, *they took possession of the town;* ghabh an càla an long, *the harbour received the ship.—Oss. Carricth.* Gabh a ghaoth, *disappear, vanish into air.—Id.* Ghabh e dha féin a ghaoth, *he vanished into air.—Oss. Fing.* Ghabh e truas, *he pitied.—Orr.* Gabh gu clos, *be at peace* or *quiet;* gabh òran, *sing a song;* gabh fois, *repose thyself.—Orr.* Gabh cothrom, *take advantage* or *opportunity;* gabh fradharc, *take a view, take an observation.—Oss. Fing.* Gabh an t-aonach, *repair to the hill.—Id.* Gabh an rod, *keep* [*walk on*] *the road;* so the Latin phrase *corripe viam;* and the French, *prenez le chemin.* Gabh gnothuch, *meddle, have to do with;* na gabh gnothuch ris, *do not meddle with him* or *it; have nothing to do with him* or *it;* gabh curam, *take care, attend, meditate.—Stew.* 1 *Tim. ref.* Gabh an teich, *take to flight;* gabh do chead, *take leave* or *farewell;* gabh do chead dheth, *bid him farewell;* gabh mo leith-sgeul, *excuse me;* gabh comhairle, *take advice, be advised;* gabh ri, *acknowledge;* gabh ris, rithe, rium, riu, *acknowledge him, her, me, them;* *accept of him, her, me, them;* gabh roimh or ro, *intercept, check;* gabh aige, *secure it, make him* or *it secure;* is math tha e air gabhail aig, *he* or *it is well secured,* or *well seen to;* am fear nach gabh nur gheibh, cha 'n fhaigh nur is àille, *he who will not when he may, when he will shall have nay.—G. P.* Gabh iongantas, *be surprised;* gabh neònachas, *be surprised;* gabh aithreachas, *repent;* gabh ceòl, *sing;* guth dhaoine a gabhail ceol, *the voice of men singing.—Stew. Exod.* Gabh as laimh, *undertake, engage;* gabh do cheum, *go thy way.—Old Song.* Ghabhadh gach soitheach, *each vessel contained.—Stew.* 2 *K. ref.* Gabh air, *strike him;* gabh ort, *take on thee, pretend;* ghabh e air, *he struck him; he pretended;* gabh oram, *strike me;* ghabhadh orm le slataibh, *I was beaten with rods.—Stew.* 2 *Cor.* Ghabh iad orra, *they struck him; they pretended;* ghabhainn a bhi falbh, *I would require to be going.*

Gabh, *v. n.*, bh *often silent.* (*Du.* gaa. *Sax.* go. *Scotch*, gae.) Repair to, resort to, begone; betake; enlist; kindle; be made to, or persuaded to. Gabh gu fleagh na h-oigh, *repair to the virgin's feast.—Oss. Com.* Gabh mu, *endeavour, go about, set about;* gabh e mu 'n ordugh le toirt, *he set himself sorrowfully about obeying the order.—Mac Lach.* Gabh mun cuairt, *go round.—Stew. Jos.* Ghabh iad sa chéille, *they grasped each other.—Oss.* Ceannard nach gabh lùbadh, *a chief who cannot be made to yield.—Macint.* Gabhaidh an teine, *the fire shall kindle;* gabh romhad, *go thy way;* gabh seach (no) seachad, *pass on,* or *by;* gabhaidh iad seachad, *they shall pass by.—Oss. Fing.* Gabh air d' aghaidh, *pass on, go forward.—Stew. Prov.* Ghabh e 's na saighdearan, *he enlisted*, gabh le, *side with;* gabh leis, *side with him*

Gabha-bhéil. See Gabhadh-bhéil.

Gàbhach, aich, *s. f* Danger, emergency Am gabhaich, *time of danger*

Gabhach, *a.* Dangerous, perilous —*Shaw. Contr.* for gabhaidheach.

Gabhadan, ain, *s. m.* (*from* gabh.) A receptacle, a storehouse

Gabhadh, 3 *sing.* and *pl. imp a* of gabh. Gabhadh e, *let him take*, gabhadh iad, *let them take*

Gàbhadh, aidh, *s. f* (*Ir* gabha) Danger, needy; jeopardy, want; surprise, wonder. A charaid ri gàbhaidh, *his friend in danger.—Oss. Derm.* Is gàbhadh leam, *I am surprised.* Ri am gàbhaidh, *in time of need —Old Song* An gàbhadh 's gach uair, *in jeopardy every hour.—Stew.* 1 *Cor*

Gàbhadh, Gàbhaidh, *a* Dangerous, dreadful; wonderful, surprising, frugal Bu ghàbhaidh, iomachd, *dreadful was his conduct.—Ardar* Is gàbhaidh an ni e, *it is a wonderful thing* Bu ghabhaidh an iomairt, *dreadful was their strife.— Ull* Is gabhadh leam thu, *I am surprised at you*

Gàbhadh-bheil, *s f.* A Druidical trial by the ordeal of fire; *literally*, the jeopardy of Bel, the god of the Druids hence it comes to denote any kind of danger, emergency, hazardous situation, hazard of such a nature that one's escape is a miracle.

The Druids used the ordeal of fire in cases where the innocence of an accused person could not be ascertained by evidence. They obliged that person to walk barefooted on the hot ashes and embers of the *Samh-theine*, or fire of peace If they had any ground to believe him innocent, yet, if the multitude were impressed with an opinion of his guilt, they, to make a shew of rigour and impartiality, passed sentence of punishment on him, but, with the craftiness of their character, and the ever-scheming trickery of their profession, they privately provided him with an ointment well known among the ancients, (see Ovid, book ii fable 1, and Servius, on line 78 of the eleventh Æneid.) and among modern jugglers, by an application of which to his feet and hands, he could go through the ordeal uninjured, and thus establish his innocence Dr Smith thinks it probable that Paul the Apostle, who might have seen this trial among the nations which he travelled through, alludes to it in 1 Cor iii 15

Gabha-dubh, *s. m* A balm-cricket —*Macd*

Gabhagan, ain, *s m.* A titling, the small bird that is observed following the cuckoo

Gabhaibh, 2 *pl imp a* of gabh Take ye, receive ye, Na gabhaibh geilt no sgà, *be not terrified nor dismayed.—Sm.*

Gàbhaidh, *gen sing* of gàbhadh

Gabhaidh, *fut aff. a* of gabh Shall or will take. See Gabh. *Gr. Ion* καπίω, *shall take*

Gàbhaidh, *a.* See Gàbhadh

Gabhail, *s f* The act of seizing, catching, receiving, betaking, a lease, spoil, conquest, a seizure, a capture; a taking fire, a kindling, a barn, a yoking, a course or direction, a tenure. Cuir an gabhail, *kindle, set on fire* A chumas a gabhail gun dad luasgain, *who preserves her course without agitation.—Macdon.*

W gavael, *a hold. Corn.* gael *and* gavel, *to bind Ir* gabhail *Germ* gabel, *tribute Anglo-Sax* gafal, *tax Span* gabela From *gabhail* comes, very probably, *kevil*, a lot or portion Neque *lot* neque *kevil.—Statuta Gildæ*, ch xx.

Gabhail, (a), *pr part.* of gabh. Taking catching; accepting, seizing, receiving, kindling, it is also used in the sense of motion; as, am bochd a gabhail seach, *the poor man passing by —Sm* A gabhail gnothuich, *meddling, being a busy body.—Stew. Thess.* Gun ghabhail ri saórsa, *without accepting salvation.—Stew. Heb.* A gabhail na pioba, *smoking a pipe*

Gabhail-cine, *s. f.* Gavelkind, an old statute by which the land belonging to any house was distributed among its members.—*Shaw.*

Gabhail-fearrainn, *s f.* A farm; a lease.

Gabhainn, 1 *sing. pret. sub.* of gabh.

Gabhainn, *g.* gabhna, *contr.* for gabhainne, *s m.* A yearling, a stirk, a steer; *also*, a smith. In this last sense, the general orthography is *gobhadh* or *gobhainn. Gabhainn*, in the sense of a steer, is also written *gamhuinn;* which see.

Gabhal, ail, *s.* (*Ir.* gabhal.) See Gobhal.

Gabhaltach, aich, *s. m* A lessee, or the person to whom a lease is given, in Scotland, called *tacksman.*

Gabhaltach, *a* (*from* gabhail) Ready to grasp or catch; infectious. *Com.* and *sup* gabhaltaich, *more* or *most infectious*

Gabhaltachd, *s f.* A readiness to grasp or catch; infectiousness.

Gabhaltaiche, *s. m* See Gabhaltach, *s.*

Gabhaltaiche, *com* and *sup.* of gabhaltach. More or most infectious.

Gabhaltas, ais, *s m*, *from* gabh (*Ir* gabhaltus) Captured or conquered land; land rented from a proprietor; land in *tack*, land divided amongst a tribe.

Gabham, 1 *sing pr. imp* of gabh. Let me take. Also, 1 *sing fut aff a.* for gabhaidh mi. I shall or will take. See Gabh.

Gabhann, ainn, *s m* (*Ir.* gabhann. *Dan* gaben, *yawning.*) Flattery, sycophancy, prating, tattling; *also*, a gaol or prison. Làn do gabhann, *full of smooth flattery.—Sm.* Is mil o'n bheartach an gabhann, *sweet is the prating of the rich —G P.*

Gabhannach, *a* (*Ir. id*) Prone to flatter; tattling; cajoling, of, or pertaining to, flattery; like a prisoner; of, or belonging to, a prison Mar an ceudna gabhannach, *also given to tattling.—Stew.* 1 *Tim* *Com* and *sup.* gabhannaiche

Gabhannaiche, *com.* and *sup* of gabhannach More or most prone to flatter.

Gabhar, *fut pass* of gabh (*Lat* capiar) Shall or will be taken See Gabh *Gabhar* is often significant of motion, and in this sense it is used impersonally; as, gabhar suas leam, *westwards* or *upwards I proceeded.* Gabhar suas leinn gu mullach an t-sleibh, *we struck up to the top of the mountain —Old Legend*

Gabhar, air, *s. f.* A goal

Gabhar, gaibhre, *s f* A goat Croicne ghabhar, *goat's skins.—Stew. Exod.*

Gr. καπρός. *Lat.* caper *and* capra. Also, *Gr* κείρω, *to browse Arm* gafr, gauvr, *and* gaour, *a goat. Corn.* gavar *Ir* gabhar *Manks* gaowr *W.* gavyr. *Span.* and *It.* cabretto. *Port.* cabra *Fr* chèvre.

Gabhar, air, *s m.* (*Ir id.*) Light, comfort

Gabharach, *a.* (*Ir* gabharach.) Like a goat; of, or relating to, a goat, skipping.

Gabhar-bhreac, *s f.* A buck-snail —*Shaw.*

Gabharlann, lainn, *s f.* (*Ir id*) A goat-pen.

Gabhar-adhair, *s f.* (*Ir. id.*) A snipe

Gabhar-oidhche, *s. f.* (*Ir. id*) A snipe

Gabhdach, *a.* Plausible, sly, cunning, deceitful; greedy *Com.* and *sup.* gabhdaiche, *more* or *most plausible.* Cho gabhdach ri meirleach, *as sly as a thief*

Gabhdachd, *s. f.* (*Dan* gautyv) Plausibleness, sliness,

deceitfulness; the conduct of a plausible, deceitful person; low cunning; greediness.

GABHDADH, aidh, *s. m.* A low, cunning trick. Ri gabhdadh, *doing a low, cunning trick.*

GABHDAICHE, *com.* and *sup.* of gabhdach. More or most deceitful, cunning, or plausible. Fear is gabhdaiche na thusa, *a man who is more cunning than thou art;* fear is gabhdaiche dhe 'n triùir, *the most cunning man of the three.*

GABHDAICHEAD, *s.* Sliness, cunning; increase in cunning. A dol an gabhdaichead, *growing more and more cunning.*

GABHDAIR, *s.* (*Runic*, gabbadur.) A plausible fellow; one who is addicted to low cunning, a deceiver, a cheat.

GABHDAIREACHD, *s. f.* Plausibleness, sliness, deceitfulness, cunningness.

GABHIDH, *a.* Dangerous; strange, wonderful. Written also *gabhadh* and *gabhaidh;* which see.

† GABHLA, *s.* (*Ir. id.*) A spear, javelin, a lance.

GABHLACH, *a.* (*Ir. id. W.* gavlaç, *forked.*) Bow-legged; a straddle; forked, furcated. *Com.* and *sup.* gabhlaiche. Written also *gobhlach;* which see.

GABHLACHAN, ain, *s. m.* A young trout; a swallow; an earwig. *N. pl.* gabhlachain.

GABHLADH, *s.* (*Gr.* κοιλη, *hollow. Swed.* gaffel.) The fork or furcated part of any thing; the perinæum. Written more frequently *gobhal.*

GABHLAG, aig, *s. f., dim.* of gabhal *or* gabhladh. (*W.* gavlaç. *Swed.* gaffel. *Ir.* gabhlog.) Any forked piece of timber; a wooden prong; *in ridicule*, a bow-legged female. Written also *gobhlag.*

GABHLAICH, *v. n.* Propagate, shoot, branch.

GABHLAICHE, *com.* and *sup.* of gabhlach. More or most bow-legged; more or most forked.

GABHLAICHEAD, *s.* Increase in furcation or forkedness. A dol an gabhlaichead, *growing more and more furcated.* Written also *gabhlaichid*, to express comparison; as, is gabhlaichid e am buille sin, *that blow has made it more forked.*

GABHLAN, ain, *s. m.* (*dim.* of gabhal.) A little branch.

GABHLANACH, *a.* (*Ir. id.*) Forked; divided; branching.

GABHLAS, ais, *s. m.* (*Ir. id.*) Hatred, envy, malice. See GAMHLAS.

GABHLASACH, *a.* (*from* gabhlas.) Envious, malicious; *also*, causing or incurring hatred. *Com.* and *sup.* gabhlasaiche, *more* or *most envious.*

GABHNA, *gen. sing.* and *pl.* of gabhainn. Of a yearling, sturk, or steer.

GABHNACH, aich, *s. m.* A steer; a furrow cow.—*Macfar.* A stripper.—*Shaw.*

GABHRACH, aich, *s. m.* A flock of goats.

GABHRAG, aig, *s. f.* A sheaf of corn bound slightly near the top, and left standing in the field to dry.

GABHRAGAN, *n. pl.* of gabhrag.

GABHRAN, ain, *s. m.* (*dim.* of gabhar.) A little goat.

GABHTA, GABHTE, *p. part.* of gabh. (*Ir.* gabhtha.) Taken, captured, seized; engaged. Tha thu gabhte agamsa, *you are engaged with me.*

GABHTACH, *a.* Ready to take or grasp; of a grasping or greedy disposition; *also*, a person in want. Gu gabhtach gionach, *greedy and grasping.*—*Mac Co.*

GABHUIDH, *a.*, written also *gabhaidh;* which see.

GABHUINN, *gen.* gabhna, *s. m.* (*Ir.* gabhuin.) A steer; sturk; a young bullock; a yearling deer. Written more frequently *gamhuinn;* which see.

† GABLA, *s. m.* A rope, a cord, or cable. *Ir. id. Germ.* and *Swed.* kabel. *D.* cabel. *Arab.* chabl. *Heb.* chabal. *Syr.* chabol. *Armen.* and *Arm.* gabyl. *Eng.* cable.

GÀC, *v. n.* Cackle, as a hen.

GÀCAIL, *s. f.* Cackling.

GACH, *indef. pron.* (*Ir.* gach.) Each, every. Gach coille, gach doire, 's gach eas, *each grove, each wood, each torrent.*—*Ull.*

GAD, *v. a.* (*Ir. id.*) Lop; pull; dig.

GAD, gaid, *s. n. pl.* gadan *and* gaid; *d. pl.* gadaibh. (*W.* guden. *Ir.* gad.) A withe; a twisted twig. There is another *nom. pl.* frequently in use, namely, *goid.* Seachd goid, *seven withes.*—*Stew. Judg.* Cha chuirear gad air gealladh, *a promise cannot be handcuffed.*—*G. P.*

GÀD, gàid, *s.* A bar of iron or of any other metal; an ingot. Gàd iaruinn, *an iron bar;* gàd tarruich, *a girth;* gàd uchd, *a breast-thong.*

GAD, *conj.* Though, although; *provincial* for ged; which see.

GA 'D, (*for* ga do.) *Literally*, at thy; at thee. Ga d'fhiosrachadh, ga d'iaruidh, *inquiring for thee, calling for thee.*

GADACHD, *s. f.* Theft, larceny, robbery. Now written *goideachd* or *gaduigheachd;* which see.

GADAICHE, *s. m.* (*Ir.* gadaidhe *and* gaduighe.) A thief, a pilferer, a robber. See GOIDICHE.

GADAN, ain, *s. m., dim.* of gad. (*W.* guden.) A little twig. Also, *n. pl.* of gad.

† GÀDAN, ain, *s. m.* (*Ir.* gadan.) A voice; a continued noise.

† GÀDANACH, *a.* Noisy; causing a continued noise. *Com.* and *sup.* gàdanaiche, *more* or *most noisy.*

† GADH, gaidh, *s. m.* (*Ir. id.*) Danger; emergency; want; a skirmish. Perhaps contracted for *gabhadh.*

GADHAR, air, *s. m.* (*Ir.* gadhar *and* gaighear.) A hound; a greyhound; a mastiff. Gadhair is fiadhchoin nan carn, *the hounds and wolves of the rocks.*—*Old Fingalian Poem.* Written also *gaodhar* and *gaothar;* which see.

† GADLUINE, *s. m.* (*Ir. id.*) A man of a slender person; a salmon after spawning.

GADUICHE, GADUIGHE, *s. m.* (*Ir.* gadaidhe.) A thief, pilferer, robber. Mar ghaduighe, *like a thief. N. pl.* gaduichean. No gaduichean, no daoine sanntach, *nor thieves, nor covetous men.*—*Stew.* 1 *Cor.*

GADUIGHEACHD, *s. f.* Theft, an act of theft, robbery. Airson a ghaduigheachd, *on account of his theft.*—*Stew. Exod.*

GAEL, *s. m.* A Scotch Celt, or Scotch Highlander. More properly *Gaidheal*, according to the rule, *caol ri caol is leathan ri leathan.* See GAIDHEAL.

GAELACH, *a.* Celtic, Gaelic, Highland. More properly, *Gaidhealach.*

GAELIG, *s. f.* The language of the Highlands of Scotland, or Gaelic. More correctly *Gaidheilig.*

GAELTACHD, *s. f.* The country of the Scotch Celts; the Highlands of Scotland. More properly, *Gaidhealtachd.*

† GAFANN, ainn, *s. m.* (*Ir. id.*) The plant called henbane; the *hyoscyamus niger* of botanists.

GAG, *v.* Notch; split; grow into chinks or clefts; spring a leak. *Pret. a.* ghag, *split; fut. aff. a.* gagaidh, *shall* or *will split.*

GÀG, gaig, *s. m.* (*W.* gagau, *holes, and* gag. *Ir.* gag.) A cleft or crevice; a chink; a slit; a knot in timber. *N. pl.* gagan, *chinks.*

GAG, gaig, *s. m.* (*Eng.* gag. *Du.* gagbel, *to gag the mouth.*) A lisp, an impediment or stammer in speech. Gag-beoil, *a lisp.*

GÀGACH, *a.* (*W.* gagenawç. *Ir.* gagach.) Full of chinks or clefts; causing chinks; leaky. *Com.* and *sup.* gàgaiche, *more* or *most leaky.*

GAGACH, *a.* Lisping, stammering in speech.

Găgadh, aidh, *s. m.* (*Ir. id.*) A growing into chinks; splitting; leaking.

Gagaiche, *s. m.* One who lisps or stammers in his speech; one who cannot pronounce certain letters.

Gagaid, *s. f.* An agate.—*Macd.*

Gagaidh, *fut. aff. a.* of gag. Shall or will split.

Gagail, *a.* (gag-amhuil.) Stammering, lisping.

Găgan, ain, *s. m.* (*Ir. id.*) A cackling; noisy speech; a knot in timber; *also*, a cluster. Gaganan, *clusters.*—*Q. B. Gen.*

Gaganach, *a.* Knotted, as timber; noisy, cackling; garrulous. Fhraoich ghaganaich! *thou knotted heath!*—*Old Song.*

Gaganach, aich, *s. m.* Noisy speech; garrulity.

Gaibheach, ich, *s. m.* A needy person; a craver; a complainant.

Gaibhne, *gen. sing.* and *n. pl.* of gabhainn. (*Ir. id.*) Smiths. —*Stew.* 2 *K. ref.*

Gaibhneachd, *s.* (*Ir. id.*) The trade of a blacksmith. See **Goibhneachd**.

Gaibhnean, *n. pl.* of gabhainn.

Gaid, *gen. sing.* and *n. pl.* of gad.

Gàid, *n. pl.* of gàd.

Gaidean, ein, *s. m., dim.* of gad. (*Ir.* gaidin.) A small band of twigs; a small withe.

Gaidheal, eil, *s. m.* (*W.* gwythel.) A Gael or Scotch Celt, commonly called a Scotch Highlander; an Irish Celt. Deoch slainnte nan Gaidheal gasta, *health to the heroic Highlanders.*—*Macint.*

This name, in its most common acceptation, is applicable to those only who inhabit the north and north-western parts of Scotland, including the Hebrides; and to them the following remarks are meant to apply:—

The Gael are confessedly the unmixed and unconquered posterity of the Celts, who first peopled Britain from the opposite shores of Gaul, and who left monuments of their language in the names of streams, rivers, mountains, and districts, all over England. The Caledonians of ancient authors were Gael; but, of old, they occupied a much wider tract of country than in aftertimes. Caledonia, according to Tacitus, Dio, and Solinus, comprehended all that country to the north of the Friths of Forth and Clyde; from the southern parts of which the Gael were compelled to retire, to make room for hoards of ferocious incursors from the south,—the Cimbri first, and latterly the Belgæ. The Lowlands of Scotland are now inhabited by a race of men as distinct from the Gael as a difference of language, ancestry, and manners, can render them. Though every Scottish Gael, therefore, be a Caledonian, every Caledonian is not a Gael.

The testimony of ancient authors, the poetry of the Gael, the remains of their buildings, their traditional records, and, above all, the smoothness and harmony of their language above every other branch of the Celtic tongue, present, when considered in the whole, an incontrovertible argument that they were, once on a time, not merely more cultivated than their neighbours, but that they passed through ages of very high civilization and refinement.

The Gael lived under a regular government, modelled and perfected by their Druids, until the accession of Kenneth Mac Alpin, towards the middle of the ninth century. That monarch, after his conquest of the Picts, transferred his seat of government amongst them; and from that period may be dated the anarchy, the confusion and rapine, which so speedily overspread their country. Adventurous and aspiring individuals began to gather bands of retainers,—chieftainry raised its head, and established its strength on the ruins of legitimate power,—jealousy, feud, and clannish animosity were the consequent and inseparable evils of this altered state; and, in a short time, they wrought a speedy but thorough revolution in their character. The refined feelings, so conspicuous in the poems of Ossian and his contemporary poets, disappeared from amongst them,—methodical warfare and reflecting bravery gave ground,—and headlong daring came instead thereof; and of all the good qualities of their fathers, those only of hospitality, faithfulness, and courage remained, and have continued, amid all the vicissitudes of their history, without change and without blemish.

The Gael continued under a feudal government until the memorable disturbances in the last century, when they were taught, by a dearly bought experience, that their pathless fastnesses could present no hiding-place from insulted royalty, and that there was an arm in the land still stronger than a chieftain's power.

The modern Gael is naturally an indolent and unindustrious being; yet, when there is occasion for activity and exertion, he is not often to be paralleled. He is modest and unassuming. His courtesy and good breeding are unstudied and becoming; and no feeling of inferiority betrays him into distraction or awkwardness of manner. Shrewd, inquisitive, and intelligent, he has his faculties collected and at his command. He is sensible of kindness, and deeply susceptible of gratitude; but, with all, he is superstitious, haughty, passionate, and vindictive.

A person who, in the year 1597, wrote an account of the Gael, describes them as follows:—"They seethe their flesh in tripe, or in the skinne of the beast, filling the same full of water. Now and then, in hunting, they straine out the blood, and eate the flesh rawe: their drink is broth of sodden flesh: they love very well the drink made of whey. * * * *

"They delighte in marled clothes, specially that have long stripes of sundry colours. They love chiefly purple and blue. Their predecessors used short mantles, or playds of divers colours, sundry wayes divided; and, amongst some, the same custom is observed to this day; but, for the most part, now they are brown, near to the colour of the hadder, to the effect, when they lye amongst the hadder, the bright colour of their playdes may not bewray them; with the which, rather coloured than clad, they suffer the most cruel tempests that blowe in the open field, in such sort, that vnder a wrythe of snow they sleep sound. In their houses also they lye upon the ground, laying betwixt them and it brakens and hadder, the rootes thereof down, and the top vp, so prettily layde together, that they are soft as feather beds, and much more wholesome; for the tops are dry of nature, whereby it dries the weake humours, and restores againe the strength of the sinews troubled before; and that so evidently, that they who at evening go to rest sore and weary, rise in the morning whole and able. * * * *

"If they travel to another countrie, they reject feather beds and bedding of their hoste. They wrappe themselves in their own playds, so taking their rest, careful lest that barbarous delicacie (as they tearme it) corrupt their natural hardnesse. * * * *

"They fight with broad swords and axes. In place of a drum they vse a bagpipe. They delight much in musike, but chiefly in harps and clarsichoes of their own fashion. The strings of the clarsichoes are of brasse wire, and the strings of the harps of sinews, which strings they strike either with their nayles growing long, or else with an instrument appointed for that vse. They take great pleasure to decke their harps and clarsichoes with silver and precious stones; and poor ones, that cannot attayne hereunto, decke them with chrystall. THEY SING VERSES PRETTILY COMPOUND, CONTAINING, FOR THE MOST PART, PRAYSES OF VALIANT MEN. There is not almost any other argument whereof their rhymes entreat. They speak the auncient French language (Celtic), altered a little."

Dr. Martin, in describing the dress of the Hebrideans of his time, has the following remarks: "The first habit worn by persons of distinction in the islands, was the *lein-croich*, or saffron shirt. The ordinary number of ells used to make this robe was twenty-four; it was the upper garb, reaching below the knees, and was tied with a belt round the middle; but the Islanders have laid it aside about a hundred years ago.

"They now generally use coat, waist, and breeches, as elsewhere; and on their heads wear bonnets made of thick cloth, some blue, some black, and some grey.

"Many of the people wear *trowis;* some have them very fine, woven of stockings; some are made of cloth; some are coloured, and others striped. The latter are as well shaped as the former, lying close to the body, from the middle downwards, and tied round with a belt above the haunches.

"There is a square piece of cloth which hangs down before. The measure for shaping the *trowis* is a stick of wood, whose length is a cubit, and that divided into the length of a finger and half a finger, so that it requires more skill to make it than the ordinary habit.

"The shoes anciently worn were a piece of the hide of a deer, cow, or horse, with the hair on, being tied behind and before with a piece of leather. The generality now wear shoes having one thin sole only, and shaped after the right and left foot, so that what is for one foot will not serve the other.

"But persons of distinction wear the garb in fashion in the south of Scotland.

"The *plad*, worn only by the men, is made of fine hose, the threads as fine as can be made of the kind; it consists of divers colours, and there is a great deal of ingenuity required in sorting the colours, so as to be agreeable to the nicest fancy. For this reason, the women are at great pains, first to give an exact pattern of the *plad* upon a piece of wood, having the number of every thread of the stripe on it. The length of it is commonly seven double ells. The one end hangs by the middle over the left arm; the other, going round the body, hangs by the end over the left arm also; the right hand above it is to be at liberty to do any thing upon occasion. Every isle differs from each other in the fancy of making *plads*, as to the stripes, in breadth and colours. This humour is different through the main land of the *Highlands*, in so far that they who have seen those places, are able, at the first view of a man's *plad*, to guess the place of his residence.

"When they travel on foot, the *plad* is tied on the breast with a bodkin of bone or wood, (just as the *spina* of the Romans, according to the description of C. Tacitus); the plad is tied round the middle with a leather belt; it is plaited from the belt to the knee very nicely: this dress, for footmen, is found much easier and lighter than *breeches* or *trowis*.

"The ancient dress wore by the women, and which is yet wore by some of the vulgar, called *arisad* (earrasaid,) is a white plad, having a few small stripes of black, blue, and red; it reached from the neck to the heels, and was tied before on the breast with a buckle of silver or brass, according to the quality of the person. I have seen some of the former of an hundred marks value: it was as broad as any ordinary pewter plate; the whole curiously engraven with various animals, &c. There was a lesser buckle, which was wore in the middle of the larger, and above two ounces weight: it had in the centre a large piece of crystal, or some fine stone, and this was set all round with several finer stones of a lesser size.

"The *plad*, being plaited all round, was tied with a belt below the breast; the belt was of leather, and several pieces of silver intermixed with the leather, like a chain. The lower end of the belt was a piece of plate, about eight inches long and three in breadth, curiously engraven, the end of which was curiously adorned with fine stones, or pieces of red coral. They wore sleeves of scarlet cloth, closed at the end as men's vests, with gold lace round 'em, having plate buttons set with fine stones. The head-dress was a fine *kerchief* of linen strait about the head, hanging down the back taper-wise: a large lock of hair hangs down their cheeks above their breast, the lower end tied with a knot of ribands."

As the causes no longer exist which separated the Gael from the observation and fellowship of their neighbours, so their character, as a distinct people, is becoming yearly less and less marked. A chieftain has no longer occasion for crowds of retainers, because he is now safe without the protection of his clan. Oppression, too, tames their spirit; disgust drives them from their homes; enterprise carries them into society, and throughout the world; yet it is questionable, if, in their many multitudes of migrators, there could ever be found one who became so thoroughly deformed by a change of country or of circumstances, as to prefer, in his heart, the fairest climes and the politest people, to the rocky land of his nativity, and the simple society of his early years.

Gaidhealach, *a.* Gaelic, Highland.

Gaidhealtachd, *s. f.* The land of the Scotch Celts, or the Highlands of Scotland. Tha Ghaidhealtachd fathast saor, *the Highlands still are free.—Macfar.*

Gaidheilig, *s. f.* The language of the Gael, Scotch Celts, or Gaelic.

Gàidsear, eir, *s. m.* An exciseman; this word is a corruption of *gauger*.

Gàidsearachd, *s.* The business of an exciseman; gauging.

Gaig, gaige, *s. m.* A fop, a proud coxcomb.—*Shaw.*

Gaige, *s. f.* Lisping, a lisp or stammer in speech.

Gail, *s. f.* (*Ir. id.*) Smoke, fume, vapour.—*Shaw.*

† **Gail**, *s. f.* (*Ir. id.*) Slaughter, bloodshed; bravery.

Gail, *v.* Boil; seethe; evaporate. More commonly written *goil*; which see.

Gailbheach, *a.* Stormy; wrathful; boisterous at sea; ponderous; extraordinary. Ur laimh ri lic ghailbhich, *your hands about the ponderous stone.* Là gailbheach, *a stormy day.* *Com.* and *sup.* gailbhiche.

Gailbheinn, *s. f.* A rocky mountain. *N. pl.* gailbheanntan.

Gailbhiche, *com.* and *sup.* of gailbheach. More or most stormy.

Gailbhichead, id, *s. m.* Storminess; increase in storminess. Tha 'n là dol an gailbhichead, *the day is growing more and more stormy.*

Gailbhinn, *s. m.;* more properly *gaill-shion* or *gaillean;* which see.

† **Gailchin**, *s. f.* (*perhaps* gabhail-chinn *or* geall-chinn.) A fine for manslaughter.

Gaileachd, *s. f.* Flattery; gluttony. See **Goileachd**.

Gaileadh, idh. (*Ir. id.*) Evaporation.

Gailean, ein, *s. m.;* more properly *goilean;* which see.

Gaileiridh, *s. f.* A gallery; a loft.

Gàilig, *s. f.* Gaelic.

Gailineach, *a.* Flattering.—*Shaw.*

Gaill, *s. f.* A sulky look. See **Goill**.

Gaill-chearc, -chirc, *s. f.* (*Ir. id.*) A duke; a drake. *N. pl.* gaill-chearcan.

† **Gàilleach**, ich, *s. f.* (*Ir. id.*) The gums.

Gailleag, eig, *s. f.* (*from* gaill.) A blow or slap on the cheek. *N. pl.* gailleagan.

† **Gaillean**, ein, *s. m.* A strange bird. Perhaps *gaill-eun* or *gall-eun.*

Gailleann, inn, *s. m.* and *f.* (gaill-shion.) A storm or tempest; an impetuous blast. Gaileann nan sliabh, *the mountain-storm.—Oss. Fing.* Mòr-ghaillean nan' stoirm, *the mighty force of storms.—Id.*

Gailleannach, *a.* Stormy, tempestuous. Contracted for *gaill-shionach.*

† **Gaillian**, *s. m.* A dart, an arrow; *also*, Leinster; a tribe of the Firbolg.

Gailliasg, eisg, *s. m.* A pike.—*Shaw.*

Gaillimh, *s. f.* Galway in Ireland.

Gaillseach, ich, *s. f.* An earwig.—*Shaw.*

Gaillseag, eig, *s. f.* An earwig. *N. pl.* gaillseagan.

Gaillseagach, *a.* Full of earwigs; like an earwig.

Gaill-shion, -shine, *s. m.* A storm, a rough blast. Written also *gailleann.*

Gaill-shionach, *a.* Stormy, blustering. *Com.* and *sup.* gaill-shionaiche.

† **Gaimhean**, ein, *s. m.* (*Ir. id.*) A skin, a hide.—*Shaw.*

Gain, *s. f.* (*Ir. id.*) Sand; a clapping of hands; applause.

Gain-cheap, -chip, *s. f.* (*Ir. id.*) A pair of stocks; a pillory.

Gaine, *s. f.* A shaft; a dart; an arrow. Written also *gainne.*

Gaineach, **Gaineamhach**, ich, *s. f.* Sand; gravel. Mar ghaineamhach, *like sand.—Stew. Gen. ref.* Written also *gaineamh.*

Gaineamh, eimh, *s. f.* Sand; sands; gravel. Air gaineamh Mhòra, *on the sand of Mora.—Oss.* Garbh-ghaineamh, *gravel.—Stew. Pro. ref.* Gaineamh-art, *a sandstone;* gaineamh-chlach, *sandstone.*

Gaineamh-art, -airt, *s. m.* A sandstone.

Gaineamh-chlac, -chloich, *s. f.* A sandstone.

Gaineamh-chlachach, *a.* Abounding in sandstone; of sandstone.

Gaineamhuinneach, *a.* Sandy; gravelly; like sand or gravel.

Gainear, eir, *s. m.* (*from* gaine.) An archer.

† **Gaing**, *s. f.* (*Ir. id.*) A jet; an agate.—*Shaw.*

Gainne, *com.* and *sup.* of gann. (*Ir. id.*) More or most scanty.

Gainne, *s. f.* (*Ir. id.*) A reed; an arrow; a shaft; a fine. —*Shaw.* *N. pl.* gainnean.

Gainne, *s. f.* (*from* gann.) Scarcity, famine, want, poverty, fewness. Gainne no gort, *want nor famine.—Sm.*

Gainneach, *a.* (*Ir. id.*) Like a reed, arrow, or shaft; abounding in reeds; shafted; *also, substantively*, a place where reeds grow.

Gainnear, ir, *s. m.* An archer; a spearman.

Gainntir, tire, *s. f.* A prison, a place of confinement. Slochd na gainntire, *the prison dungeon.—Stew. Ex.*

Gainntireach, *a.* Like a prison; full of prisons.

Gainntireachadh, aidh, *s. m.* An incarcerating; incarceration.

Gainntirich, *v. a.* Imprison. *Pret. a.* ghainntirich, *imprisoned; fut. aff. a.* gainntirichidh, *shall imprison.*

Gaintiriche, *s. m.* A prisoner; *also*, a jailor.

Gàir, gàire, *s. f.* (*Ir. id.* *Gr.* γηρυς, *vox.* *W.* gair, *report.*) A laugh, laughter, smile; din; outcry; a shout. Gàir chuain, *the noise of the sea.* Rinn iad gàir, *they shouted.* —*Stew. Ex.* Dean gàir, *laugh; shout.* Mu ghàire, *about laughter.—Stew. Ecc.* Gair-theas, *the glittering reflection of the sun from the surface of water, or of any polished body.* Gair-chreag, *an echo;* gair-fanoid, *a scornful laugh.*

Gàir, *v. n.* Laugh; shout; cry; make a noise; resound. *Pret.* ghàir; *fut. aff. a.* gàiridh, *shall laugh.* Ghàir Gormmheall, *Gormal resounded.—Oss. Fing.* Gàiridh am fitheach air do ghruaidh, *the raven shall croak on thy cheek.— Old Song.*

Ir. id. *Gr.* χαιρω, *rejoice*, and γηρυω. *Lat.* garrio.

Gairbhe, *s. f.* (*Ir. id.*) Roughness; fierceness; harshness; rudeness; coarseness.

Gairbhe, *com.* and *sup.* of garbh. Rougher, roughest. See **Garbh.**

Gairbhead, id, *s. m.* Roughness; thickness; increase in roughness or in thickness. Dol an gairbhead, *growing more and more thick.* This word is also used comparatively, as, is gairbheid e' sin, *it is the thicker for that; that has made it thicker.*

Gairbheal, eil, *s. m.* (*Ir. id.*) Freestone; coarse sand; gravel. Do ghairbheal, *with gravel.—Stew. Pro. ref.*

Gairbhealach, aich, *s. m.* (*Ir. id.*) Stony or rocky ground.

Gairbhealach, *a.* (*Ir. id.*) Stony; rocky; gravelly.

Gairbhealta, *a.* (*Ir. id.*) Gravelly.

Gairbhean-creagach, ich, *s. m.* A small plant growing among rocks on the sea-shore, and esteemed good for healing bruises.

Gairbh-shion, *s.* (*Ir. id.*) Stormy weather, a rough blast.

Gair-chatha, *s. m.* (*Ir. id.*) A battle-shout, a war-cry. See **Gaoir-chatha.**

Gair-chreag, *s. m.* (*Ir. id.*) An echo.

Gaird, *s. f.* (*Gr.* χειρ, *hand.*) An arm; a hand.

Gairde, *s. f.* (*Ir. id.*) Joy, joyfulness, gladness.

Gàirdeachas, ais, *s. m.* (*Ir.* gairdeachas.) Joy, pleasure, gratification. Guth gàirdeachais, *the voice of joy.—Sm.* A deanamh gàirdeachais, *rejoicing;* ri gàirdeachas, *rejoicing.*

Gairdean, sin, *s. m.*, *dim.* of gaird. (*Ir.* gairdian.) An arm; a hand. Gairdean air fhoillseachadh, *the arm revealed.— Stew. Is.* Le d' ghairdean deas, *with thy right hand.— Sm.* *N. pl.* gairdeana, *arms.—Stew. Gen.*

Gairdeanach, *a.* Strong-armed; large-armed; long-armed; brachial.

Gairdeas, eis, *s. m.* (*Ir. id.*) Joy, gladness, gratulation.

Gairdich, *v. a.* and *n.* (*Ir.* gairdigh.) Rejoice, congratulate. *Pret. a.* ghairdich.

Gairdin, *s. m.* (*Ir. id.*) A garden.—*Shaw.*

Gàire, *s. f.* See **Gàir.**

† **Gaire**, *s. f.* (*Ir. id.*) Reparation, amendment; good luck; auspices.—*Shaw.*

Gàireachdaich, *s. f.* Laughing, laughter. Ri gàireachdaich, *laughing.* Ciod a ghàireachdaich th'ort? *what are you laughing at?*

Gaireadh, idh, *s. m.* (*Ir. id.*) A vault.—*Shaw.*

Gaireal, eil, *s. m.* (*Ir. id.*) Gravel; freestone. See **Gairbheal.**

Gairealach, *a.* Gravelly; stony; *also, substantively*, stony ground. Written also *gairbhealach.*

Gàiream, (*for* gàiridh mi.) I will laugh, call, or shout. Gaiream ort, *I will call upon thee.—Sm.* Also, I *sing. imper.* of gair, *let me laugh.*

Gaireas, eis, *s. m.* Furniture, apparatus.—*Shaw.*

Gàir-fanaid, *s.* A scornful laugh.—*Stew. Job.*

Gair-fhitheach, -fhithiche, *s. m.* A raven, a vulture.— *Shaw.*

Gairg, *inflection* of garg; which see.

Gairg, *s. f.* (*Ir. id.*) A cormorant; a diver.—*Shaw.*

Gairge, *s. f.* (*Ir. id.*) Bitterness, sourness, sharpness.

Gairge, *com.* and *sup.* of garg. More or most bitter.

Gairgead, eid, *s. m.* (*from* garg.) Sourness, bitterness; increase in sourness. A dol an gairgead, *growing more and more sour.*

Gairgeann, inn, *s. m.* A diver; a cormorant. *N. pl.* gairgeannan.

Gairgeannach, *a.* Like a cormorant; abounding in cormorants; greedy.

Gairginn, *s. f.* (*Ir. id.*) Dung; ordure; stale urine; a pilgrim's dress.

Gairgre, *s. f.* (*Ir. id.*) A pilgrim's dress.

Gàirich, *s. f.* A loud noise; murmur; shouting; a raging; a roaring, as of the sea. Gàirich a chuain, *the raging of the sea.—Oss. Fing.*

Gàirich, *a.* Shouting; loud; noisy; roaring; raging. Sruth gàirich na h-oidhche, *the roaring torrent of night.— Oss. Tem.*

Gairidean, ein, *s. m.* A periwinkle.

Gair-ingean, ein, *s. f.* (*Ir. id.*) A niece.—*Shaw.*

Gairiseag, eig. *s. f.* A wanton, a prostitute. *N. pl.* gairiseagan.

Gairisinn, *s. f.* Horror, detestation; a shuddering with fear; lewdness; nastiness. Tha thu 'cur gairisinn orm, *you make me shudder.*

Gairisneach, *a.* (*Ir. id.*) Horrible, detestable; lewd; nasty.

Gairisnich, *v. a.* and *n.* Abhor, detest; shudder with fear or horror. *Pret. a.* ghairisnich, *abhorred; fut. aff. a.* gairisnichidh.

Gairleag, eig, *s. f.* (*Ir. id.*) Garlic. Gairleag mhuire, *crow garlic, allium vineale.*

Gairm, *v. a.* (*Ir. id.*) Proclaim; call; summon; bawl; shout; qualify; name. *Pret. a.* ghairm, *called; fut. aff. a.* gairmidh, *shall call.* Gairm gaisgich o bhad is o choille, *summon heroes from thicket and wood.—Oss. Fing.* *Fut. pass.* gairmear. *P. part.* gairmte, *proclaimed.*

Gairm, *v. a.* (*Ir. id.*) A proclamation, an edict; a calling; noise; a shouting; a title, a name; a qualification. Gairm pòsaidh, *a marriage proclamation.* Thugadh gairm, *a proclamation was made.—Stew. Ex.* Gairm choilich, *cock crowing*; gairm challan, *the noise of hounds in the chase.*

Arm. garm. *Ir.* gairm. *W.* garm. Hence the *Latin* carmen, *a song*. Also, χαρμη of the Greeks, meaning both *a battle* and *joy*, from the circumstance of the bards singing a war-song before battle. Tacitus says of the Germans, who resembled the Gael in many respects, Ituri in prælia canunt, *on the eve of fighting they sing.*

Gairman, ain, *s. f.* (*Ir.* garmain.) A weaver's beam. A shleagh mar ghairmain, *his spear like a weaver's beam.*—*Stew. Sam.*

Gairmeadair, *s. m.* (*Ir.* garmadoir.) A crier, a proclaimer.

Gairmear, eir, *s. m.* A crier.

Gairmeanach, ich, *s. m.* (*Ir. id.*) The vocative case.

Gairneal. See Gaoirneal.

Gairneag, eig, *s. f.* A noisy little stream.

Gairnealair, *s. m.* A gardener. *N. pl.* gairnealairean.

Gairnealaireachd, *s. f.* The business or calling of a gardener.

Gair-fhitheach, ich, *s. m.* A vulture, a raven.

Gairrigeach, *a.* Rocky, rough; more properly *carraigeach.*

Gairseach, ich, *s. f.* (*Ir. id.*) A bawd; a woman; a drivelling prostitute.

Gairseachd, *s. f.* Lewdness, bawdiness, debauchery.

Gairsealachd, *s. f.* (*Ir.* gairsamhlachd.) Lewdness, debauchery, bawdiness.

Gairsean, ein, *s.* A scold, a shrew.

Gairseil, *a.* (*Ir.* gairsamhail.) Lewd, whorish; nasty, indecent.

Gairsgeal, eil, *s. m.* A rabble; a band of worthless persons.

Gairsneach, *a.* Lewd, debauched, bawdy; horrible; nasty. Gu gairsneach, *bawdily*. *Com.* and *sup.* gairsniche.

Gairsneachd, *s. f.* Lewdness, bawdiness, bebauchery, nastiness, indecency.

Gairsneag, eig, *s. f.* A lewd female, a bawd. *N. pl.* gairsneagan.

Gairteag, eig, *s. f.* A crab-tree; *pyrus malus.*

Gairte, *s. f.* (*Ir. id.*) A narrow path.—*Shaw.*

Gair-theas, *s. m.* (*Ir. id.*) Scorching heat; reflected heat; the glittering reflection of the sun, as from the surface of water.

† Gais, *s. f.* (*Ir. id.*) A torrent, a stream; a surfeit.

Gais, *s. f.* (*Ir. id.*) Cloyment, satiety; a surfeit.

† Gais, *s. f.* A spear, a weapon. This is an ancient Celtic word, which, though not much in use among the Gael, is found in several derivatives; as, gaisge, *valour*, and gaisgeach, *a hero.*

Gr. γαῖσα *and* γαισος, *a weapon. Arab.* gaish. *Heb.* gish. *Lat.* gæsum, a weapon peculiar to the Gauls, as the *pilum* was to the Romans, and *sarissa* to the Lacedæmonians. See also Geis.

Gaisd, gaisde, *s. f.* (*Ir. id.*) A snare or trap; wile, cunning; a trick.

Gaisde, *a.* (*Ir. id.*) Armed, accoutred.—*Shaw.*

Gaisdean, ein, *s. m.* (*from* gaisd.) A cunning fellow; a deceiver or cheat; a snare.

Gaisdiche, *s. m.* (*Ir. id.*) A deceiver; a painter.

Gaise, *s. f.* A flaw or blemish, injury; boldness, valour; a withering, a blasting.

Gaiseach, *a.* (*from* gaise.) Blemished, injured; blasting, withering.

Gaiseadh, idh, *s. m.* A blemish or flaw, injury; bravery; a blasting or withering. Eutrom gun ghaiseadh, *lively, without blemish.*—*Old Song.* Buailidh se e le gaiseadh, *he will strike him with blasting.*—*Stew. Deut. ref.*

† Gaisean, ein, *s. m.* (*Ir.* gaisin.) A scanty crop.

Gaisg, gaisge, *s. f.* (*Ir. id. from* gais.) Bravery; a feat of arms; might; a slope; a place called *Gask.* Clann na gaisge, *the sons of bravery.*—*Orr.* Do ghaisge, *thy might.*—*Stew.* 2 *K. ref.*

Gaisgeach, ich, *s. m.*, *from* gaisg. (*Ir.* gaisgidheach.) A warrior, hero, champion. Gaisgeach liath, *a hoary warrior.*—*Oss. Croma.* *Voc. sing.* ghaisgich.

Gaisgeachd, *s. f.* (*from* gaisg.) Heroism, bravery; feats in arms.

Gaisgealachd, *s. f.* (*Ir.* gaisgamhaileachd.) Heroism, bravery.

Gaisgeanta, *a.* (*from* gaisg.) Heroic, brave, warlike. Gu gaisgeanta, *bravely.*

Gaisgeil, *a.* (gaisg-amhuil.) Heroic, brave, warlike. Is gaisgeil ur mor-thionail cheud, *brave are your gatherings of hundreds.*—*Old Song.*

Gaisidh, *s. m.* (*Ir. id.*) A stream.

Gaist, *v. a.* Ensnare, trepan, deceive, trick. *Pret. a.* ghaist; *fut. aff.* gaistidh, *shall ensnare.*

Gaiste, *s. f.* (*Ir. id.*) A snare, gin, trap; a trick, a wile.

Gaisteach, *a.* (*from* gaiste.) Full of snares; entrapping; cunning, wily.

Gaisteag, eig, *s. f.* (*dim.* of gaiste.) A snare, a gin, a trap; a trick or wile; a cunning female.—*Shaw.*

Gaisteagach, *a.* Cunning.

Gaistean, ein, *s. m.* A deceiver, a wily fellow.

Gaistean-cloich, *s. m.* A certain little bird of the size of a wren.—*Shaw.*

Gaitean, ein, *s. m.* A brief, an abridgement.

Gaithean, ein, *s. m.* A straight branch; an oar. A gaithean réithe, *her smooth oars.*—*Macfar.*

† Gal, *s. m.* (*Ir. id. Dan.* gal, *raging.*) Warfare; slaughter.

Gal, gail, *s. m.* (*Ir. id.*) Smoke, vapour; a gale, a puff, a blast or flame of straw; kindred.

Gal, *s. f.* (*Ir. id. Box. Lex.* galor, *weeping.*) Weeping, lamentation. Is beag eadar do ghal is do ghàire, *there is but little between your weeping and your mirth.*—*G. P.* Written also *gul.*

Gal, *v. n.* Cry, weep. *Pret.* ghuil, *wept*; *fut. aff. a.* guilidh, *shall weep.*

Galabhas, ais, *s. m.* (*Ir. id.*) A parasite; a glutton; a flatterer.

Galach, aich, *s. m.* (*Ir. id.*) Bravery, courage.—*Shaw.*

† Galach, *a.* Brave, courageous; sorry. *Com.* and *sup.* galaiche.

Galad, aid, *s. f.* A girl, a lass, a young girl. *Voc. sing.* a ghalad, *my girl.*

Galadach, *a.* Girlish, queanish.

Galadachd, *s. f.* Girlishness; queanishness.

Galain, *gen. sing.* and *n. pl. of* galan.

Galan, ain, *s. m.* (*Ir. id.*) A gallon; noise; tumult; an enemy. *N. pl.* galain.

Galanach, *a.* (*Ir. id.*) Noisy, tumultuous.

Galann, ainn, *s. m.* An enemy.—*Shaw.*

Galapainn, *s. f.* Gallopping.

Galapainn, *v. a.* and *n.* Gallop.

Galar, air, *s. m.* (*Ir. id.* *Corn.* galaron, *pangs.*) Disease; malady. Galar francach, *the venereal*; galar fuail, *the gravel*; galar gasda, *a flux*; galar mòr, *a plague*; galar

; plocach, *a quinsy, the mumps;* galar greidh, *the strangles;* galar mialach, *the phthyriasis,* or *lousy disease;* galar dibhe-ruith, *diabetes;* galar miosach, *menstrual courses.* Galar goilleach, *the mort.—Shaw.* Galar teth, *the rot.—Id.* Galar fad is eug na bhun, *a lingering disease, and death at its root.—G. P.*

GALARACH, *a.* (*from* galar.) Distempered, diseased; causing disease. Caor ghalarach, *a diseased sheep.*

GALARACHD, *s. f.* A tendency to disease; the condition of being diseased.

GALARAN, *n. pl.* of galar. (*Corn.* galaron.) Diseases.

GALBA, GALBHA, *a.* Hard, vigorous, stout, brawny; *also,* rigour, hardness.

GALBHAIDH, *s. f.* (*Ir. id.*) Heat, warmth.

GALC, *v. a.* Full clothes.

GALCADH, aidh, *s. m.* A fulling, as of clothes. Muileann galcadh, *a fulling-mill.*

GALG. See GALGADH.

GALGACH, *a.* (*Ir. id.*) Stout; warlike.

GALGADH, aidh, *s. m.* (*Ir. id.*) A champion.

GALL, gaill, *s. m.* A rock, a stone. *N. pl.* gailleachan, *stones.*

† GALL, *s. m.* (*Lat.* gallus, *a cock. Ir.* gall.) A cock; a swan; milk.

GALL, *s. m.* A Scotch Lowlander; a foreigner, a stranger. Buaidh air clannaibh nan Gall, *victory over the sons of strangers.—Old Poem.* Cha robh Gall no Gaidheal, *there was neither Lowlander nor Highlander.—Turn.* Gall mhuilinn, *a mill-wheel.*

GALLADH, aidh, *s. f.* A bitch; *rarely,* beauty; brightness.

GALLAIDH, *a.* (*Ir. id.*) Hot.

GALLAN, ain, *s. m.* (*Ir. id. Dan.* galan, *a stripling. Gr. Æol.* γαλανος, *mast of oak.*) A branch; a stripling; a rock. Tha 'n gallan ag aomadh, *the branch is already giving way.—Orr.* Gallan greannchair, *the herb coltsfoot, tussilago farfara.—Macd.* Gallan mòr, *butterbur; pestilent wort;* the *tussilago petasites* of botanists.

GALLANTACHD, *s. f.* (*Ir. id.*) Gallantry.

GALL-BHOLGACH, *s. m.* The venereal.—*Shaw.* Gu soithich leis a ghall-bholgach, *ill of the venereal.*

GALL-CHNO, *s.* A walnut. Craobh ghall-chnò, *a walnut-tree.*

GALLDA, *a.* Lowland; of, or belonging to, the Scotch Lowlanders; foreign, strange; surly; poor-spirited.—*Shaw.*

GALLDACHD, *s. f.* The Lowlands of Scotland; English connexion; association with the English or the Lowland Scots.

GALL-DRUMA, *s. m.* (*Ir. id.*) A kettle-drum.

GALL-GHIUTHAS, ais, *s. m.* A pine-tree. An gall-ghiuthas, *the pine.—Stew. Is.*

GALL-LUCH, *s. m.* A rat. *N. pl.* gall-luchaidh, *rats.*

GALL-MHUILINN, *s.* A mill-wheel.

GALLOBAN, ain, *s. m.* (*Ir. id.*) A dwarf.

GALL-OGLACH, aich, *s. m.* A cuirassier; an armour-bearer; a servant; *also,* a Highland freebooter, armed with a Lochaber axe or sword. He differed from the Ceatharnach, in that the latter wore a *sgian* or dirk. An armour-bearer who attended the chieftain was also called *gall-oglach.* He was remarkable for boldness and bravery. His business was to prevent his employer from being taken by surprise. He had a double allowance of food; which was called *beath fir,* or a champion's victuals.

GALL-PHEASAIR, -pheasrach, *s. f.* Vetches, lentils. Làn do ghall-pheasair, *full of vetches.—Stew.* 2 *Sam.*

GALLRACH, *a.* Infectious.

GALLRACHADH, GALLRUCHADH, aidh, *s. m.* A crucifying; a tormenting; portending.

GALLRADH, aidh, *s. m.* (*Ir. id.*) Infection; disorder.

GALLRAICH, GALLRUICH, *v. a.* Crucify; torture; portend. *Pret. a.* ghallruich, *crucified.*

GALL-SHEILISDEAR, eir, *s. m.* A flag; a bulrush.—*Stew. Job, ref.*

GALLTACH, aich, *s. m.* A Gaul. *N. pl.* Galltaich.

GALLTANACH, *a.* Envious.

GALLTANACHD, *s. f.* Hatred, envy.

GALLTANAS, ais, *s. m.* Hatred, envy. Luchd galltanais, *envious people.*

GALL-TROMP, -truimp, *s. f.* (*Ir. id.*) A trumpet; a clarion; a cornet. Fuaim na gall-truimp, *the sound of the cornet.—Stew. Job.*

GALLUBH, *s. f.* Caithness, a county in Scotland.

GALLUCH, *s. m.* (*Ir. id.* A rat.

GALLUNACH, aich, *s.* Soap.—*Shaw.*

GALLURAN, ain, *s. m.* Wild Angelica, *Angelica sylvestris.*

GALOBAN, ain, *s. m.* A dwarf.

GALRAICH, *v. a.* Punish; torture; portend.

GALRAIDH, *s. f.* (*Ir. id.*) Bodement.

GAM, (*for* ga mo.) *Literally,* at my; at their. Esan a tha gam sharuchadh, *he who oppresses me.—Sm.* Cnuic gam freagairt, *hills answering to them.—Oss. Cathluno.*

† GAMAINEACH, *a.* Few, scarce.

GÀMAL, ail, *s.* A camel.—*Shaw.*

GAMAL, ail, *s. m.* (*Ir. id.*) A fool, a stupid person.

† GAMBAN, ain, *s. m.* (*It.* gamba. *Ir.* gamban. *Fr.* jambon.) A leg; an arm.

GAMH, gaimh, *s. m.* (*Ir.* gamh. *Corn.* guav.) Winter; *also,* woman.

GAMHANN, ain, *s. m.* (*Ir. id.*) A stitch.

GAMHCHOGUS, uis, *s. m.* A dent, a notch.—*Shaw.*

GAMHLAS, ais, *s. m.* Hatred; envy. Ghluais mo ghamlas, *my hatred has gone.—Oss. Tem.* Luchd gamhlais, *envious people.*

GAMHLASACH, *a.* (*from* gamhlasach.) Envious; hating. *Com.* and *sup.* gamhlasaiche.

GAMHLASACHD, *s. f.* Enviousness.

GAMHNACH, aich, *s. f.* (*Ir. id.*) A stripper; an unbulled cow.

GAMHUINN, gamhna, *s. f.* A six months' old cow; a yearling; a sturk; a steer; a young bullock; a yearling deer. Marbhaidh e an gamhuinn, *he will kill the young bullock.—Stew. Ex.* Gamhuinn ruadh, *a yearling deer;* magh-ghamhuinn, *a bear.*

† GAN, *prep.* See GUN.

'GAN, (*for* aig an.) Duine 'gan robh beartas, *i. e.* aig an robh beartas, *a man who had riches.*

GAN, (*for* ag an.) Gan ruagadh, *pursuing them.*

GANAID, *s. f.* (*Ir. id.*) A railing, a fence; a fold.—*Shaw.*

GANDAL, ail, *s. m.* (*Ir. id.*) A gander.

GANGAID, *s. f.* (*Ir. id.*) Falsehood, deceit, a mean trick; a bustle; a giddy person; a naughty female. *N. pl.* gangaidean.

GANGAIDEACH, *a.* (*Ir. id.*) False, deceitful; mean; giddy. Gu gangaideach, *deceitfully.*

GANGAIDEACHD, *s. f.* (*Ir.* gangaideacht.) Falsehood, deceitfulness, knavery; meanness, narrowness.

† GANN, *s.* (*Ir. id.*) Poverty, scarcity; a jug; a fort.—*O'Reilly.*

GANN, *a.* (*Ir. id.*) Scarce, scanty, few, rare, little, small;

difficult; *rarely*, stout, thick. Sruth gann, *a scanty stream.—Oss. Tem.* Mhic an anma ghainne, *son of the little soul.—Oss. Tem.* Gun iongantas gann, *with no small wonder.—Id.* Is gann dh'fhalbh e nur—, *he was scarcely gone when—*; ach gann, *almost. Com.* and *sup.* gainne.

GANNAIL, *s. pl.* (*Ir. id.*) Lattices.

GANNDAR, *a.* (*from* gann.) Scarce, rare; *also, substantively*, scarcity; hunger.

GANNDAS, ais, *s. m.* A grudge, animosity, malice.

GANNDASACH, *a.* (*from* ganndas.) Having a grudge, malicious, envious.

GÀNNRAICH, GÀNRAICH, *s. f.* Noise, tumult, din, clamour. Mar ghannraich eun, *like the noise of birds.—Oss.*

GANNTAR, air, *s. m.* See GANNDAR.

GANTAIR. See GAINNTIR.

GÀNRA, GÀNRADH, aidh, *s. m.* (*Sax.* ganra. *Ir.* ganra.) A gander. *N. pl.* ganraidhean.

† GAOD, gaoid, *s. f.* (*Ir. id.*) A swan; a leech.

† GAOD, *v. a.* (*Ir. id.*) Wound; blemish.

GAODADH, aidh, *s. m.* A wounding, a blemishing; a wound, a blemish.

GOADHAR, air, *s. m.* A hound; a greyhound. *N. pl.* gaodhair.

GAOG, gaoig, *s. m.* (*Ir. id.*) A defect in a thread; a part of a thread spun finer than another.—*Macint.* Defect of any kind; evaporation; staleness; flatness; a squint of the eye. Air dol ghaog, *dead.—Shaw.* Grown stale.

GAOGACH, *a.* Having defects, as thread or yarn; flat, stale; squint-eyed.

GAOGAN, ain, *s. m., dim.* of gaog. (*Ir. id.*) A part of a thread spun finer than the rest.

† GAOI, *s. f.* (*Bisc.* gue, *a lie.*) Wisdom; *also*, a falsehood.

GAOID, *s. f.* A blemish, flaw, or fault; a stain; disease; *rarely*, wind, blasts, flatulence. Gun ghaoid, *without blemish.—Stew. Ex.*

GAOID'BHEINN, *s.* A mountain in Arran.

GAOIDEANTA, *a.* (*Ir. id.*) Idle, slothful, sluggish; blemished.—*Shaw.*

GAOIDEANTACHD, *s. f.* Idleness, slothfulness, sluggishness.

GAOIDEIL, *a.* (gaoid-amhuil.) Diseased, tabid; blemished.

† GAOIDHEAN, in, *s. m.* (*Ir. id.*) False colour, counterfeit.

GAOIL, *gen. sing.* of gaol. Of love. See GAOL.

† GAOINE, *s. f.* (*Ir. id.*) Goodness, honesty.

GAOIR, *s. f.* (*Gr.* γηρυς, *vox. W.* gair *and* gawr.) Confused noise, din; a cry; the throbbing pain of the toothache. Gaoir eòin na tuinn, *the noise of the sea-fowl.—Oss.* Gaoir sa mhaduinn, *a cry in the morning.—Stew. Jer.* Gaoir na chluais, *a tingling in his ear.—Stew.* 2 *K.*

GAOIRBH, *s. f.* (*Ir. id.*) The paunch of a deer.

GAOIR CHATHA, *s.* A shout set up when on the eve of engaging in battle; a war-cry.

The Gael, in common with all wild and warlike people, were wont to raise a loud and confused cry as they rushed on their enemies in the field. Giraldus Cambrensis, as quoted by Dr. Smith, observes, that the war-cry of the ancient Irish was *Phar-roh*; "In congressu *Phar-roh* quam acerrime clamant." "Barditum illum existimo de quo Ammianus," inquit Camden. Any loud clamour is still compared to *gaoir-chatha*; and nothing is more common than for one who is disturbed with the noise of people's voices to say, Cha chluinnte gaoir-chatha leibh.—*Smith.*

GAOIRNEAL, eil, *s. f.* (*Ir.* geirneal. *Scotch*, girnel.) A granary.

GAOIRNEALAIR, *s. f.* A granary.—*Macd.*

GAOIS, *s. f.* Wisdom, prudence.

GAOISD, *s. f.* Horses' hair; the hair of beasts; the hair of any part of the human body except the head. Gaoisd an eich ghlais, *the grey horses' hair.—Mac Lach.*

GAOISDEACH, *a.* (*from* gaoisd.) Hairy; made of horses' hair; like horses' hair.

GAOISDEAN, ein, *s. m.* A single horse-hair.

GAOISEAN, ein, *s. m.* (*Arm.* guezen, *a tree.*) A bush; a bunch or tuft of heath or broom, or of any low growing tufty plant. Gaoisean iosal, *a low bush.* In *Bretagne*, they say, *guezen isel.*

GAOISEANACH, *n.* (*from* gaoisean.) Tufty, bunchy; in tufts or bunches. Am fraoch gaoiseanach, *the tufty heath.*

GAOISNEACH, *a.* (*Ir. id.*) Hairy, shaggy, rough. Le 'n gairdeinibh gaoisneach, *with their hairy arms.—Macfar.*

GAOISNEAN, ein, *s. m.* A single horse hair. Written also *gaoisdean.*

GAOITH, *a.* (*from* gaoth.) Windy, flighty, giddy.

GAOITHE, *gen. sing.* of gaoth. Wind.

GAOITHEAN, ein, *s. m.* (*from* gaoth.) A fop; a giddy fellow; a small pipe attached to a bagpipe for inflating it.

GAOITHEANACH, *a.* Airy; foppish; giddy. Frangach gaoitheanach, *a foppish Frenchman.—Old Song.*

GAOITHREAG, eig, *s. f.* A blast.

GAOL, gaoil, *s. m.* (*Ir. id.*) Love, fondness; liking; a person beloved; *rarely*, kindred. Theach mo ghaoil! *thou home of my love!—Oss. Taura.* Cha 'n fhaic mi mo ghaol, *I do not see my beloved.—Ardar.* Thoir gaol, *love.* Clann mo mhathar gaoil, *the children of my beloved mother.—Mac Lach.* Ann an gaol, *in love*; air ghaol ni math, *for the love of God.*

GAOLACH, *a.* (*from* gaol.) Dear, beloved; lovely, affectionate, fond. Gaolach am bròn, *lovely in grief.—Oss. Com.* Ardar gaolach, *beloved Ardar.—Ardar. Com.* and *sup.* gaolaiche.

GAOLACH, aich, *s. m.* (*from* gaol.) A beloved person, a darling. A caoidh a gaolaich, *mourning her beloved.—Ardar.* A ghaolaich, *my darling!*

GAOLAICH, *gen. sing.* of gaolach.

GAOLAICHE, *com.* and *sup.* of gaolach; which see.

GAOR, *s.* See GAORR.

GAOR, *v. a.* (*Ir. id.*) Cram, glut. *Pret.* ghaor, *crammed.*

GAORAN, ain, *s. m.* (*from* gaor. *Ir. id.*) A glutton; a little glutton.—*Shaw.*

GAORR, gaoirre, *s. f.* (*Ir. id.*) Dung, dirt; ordure contained in the intestines. A mhionach agus a ghaorr, *his entrails and his dung.—Stew. Lev.*

GAORSACH, aich, *s. f.* (*Ir. id.*) A young wanton. Written also *gairiseach.*

GAORSACHD, *s. f.* (*Ir. id.*) Wantonness, lewdness.

† GAORSTA, *s. f.* (*Ir. id.*) A whirlwind.

GAOS, gaois, *s. m.* (*Ir. id.*) Wisdom, prudence.—*Shaw.*

GAOSMHOR, *a.* (*Ir. id.*) Wise and prudent. *Com.* and *sup.* gaosmhoire.

† GAOTH, *s. f.* (*Ir. id.*) A dart; the sea; theft; *adjectively*, prudent.

GAOTH, gaoithe, *s. f.* (*Ir. id.*) Wind; *also*, a shooting pain; a stitch; airiness; vanity; *rarely*, theft; sea. An ni thig leis a ghaoithe, falbhaidh e leis an uisge, *what comes by wind goes by rain.—G. P.* Cuir ri gaoth, *weather*; sgiobal na gaoithe, *the skirts of the wind.—Oss. Duthona.* Gaoth chuairtein, *a whirlwind*; gaoth 'n ear, *east wind*; gaoth 'n iar, *west wind*; gaoth deas, *south wind*; gaoth tuath, *north wind*; a ghaoth a noir, *the east wind*; a ghaoth a niar, *the west wind*; a ghaoth a deas, *the south wind*; a ghaoth a tuath, *the north wind*; a ghaoth a near-dheas, *the south-east wind*; a ghaoth a niar-dheas, *the south-west wind*; a ghaoth a near-thuath, *the north-east wind*; a ghaoth a niar-thuath, *the north-west wind*; a ruith na gaoithe, *on a vain pursuit*; coileach gaoithe, *a weathercock.*

† GAOTHA, *s.* (*Ir. id.*) Streams left at low water.

GAOTHAICHE, *s. f.* The drone-reed of a Highland bagpipe.

GAOTHAIRE, *s.* A blowing reed.

GAOTHAN, ain, *s. m.* (*from* gaoth.) A fop; a light-headed fellow; a small pipe attached to a bagpipe for inflating it.

GAOTHANACHD, *s. f.* Flatulence; giddiness.

GAOTHAR, *a.* (gaoth-mhor.) Windy; blustering; flatulent; painful. Seachran na h-oidhche ghaothair, *the wanderings of the windy night.*—*Oss. Tem. Ir.* gaothmhor.

GAOTHAR, air, *s. m.* A hound; a greyhound. Fuaim ghaothar, *the noise of hounds.*—*Ull. Dargo.*

GAOTHARACHD, *s. f.* (*from* gaoth.) Windiness; flatulence; storminess; pain; a shooting pain; anguish.

GAOTH-INNISEAN, ein, *s. m.* An anemoscope.—*Shaw.*

GAOTH-MHEIDH, *s. f.* An anemometer. *N. pl.* gaoth-mheidhean.

GAOTHRACHADH, *s. m.* A winnowing.

GAOTHRAICH, *v. a.* Winnow.

GAOTHRAN, ain, *s. m.* (*Ir. id.*) A fan.

GAOTHRUADH, aidh, *s. m.* (*Ir. id.*) A blasting wind; mildew.

GÀPAIDH, *s.* A sort of riddle for winnowing.

GAR, gair, *s. m.* (*Ir. id.*) Accommodation; desert, merit; profit.—*Shaw.*

GĂR, *v. a.* Warm the limbs at a fire; ferment; cherish. *Pret. a.* ghăr, *warmed; fut. aff. a.* găraidh, *shall warm.* Gar do lamhan, *warm your hands.* Garaidh se e féin, *he will warm himself.*—*Stew. Is.*

GAR, *v. a.* Gratify; accommodate. (*Ir. id.*) *Pret. a.* ghar, *gratified; fut. aff. a.* garaidh, *shall gratify.*

GÀR. See GARADH.

GÀR, (an), *adv.* and *prep.* (*W.* ger, *near.*) Nigh, near, at hand, close to. An gàr dhuit, *near you.*—*Stew. Job.*

GAR, *conj.* Though, although. Gar an d' thig e, *though he come not.*

GA 'R, (*for* ag ar.) *Literally*, at us; at our. Gach doinionn ga 'r léireadh, *every storm harassing us.*—*Ull.*

GA 'R, (ag 'ur *or* ga bhur.) *Literally*, at you, at your. Ga 'r bualadh, *striking you.*

GARABAN, ain, *s. m.* A rude fellow, a clown or boor; *also*, brave.

GARABANACH, *a.* Rude, boorish, clownish, raw, unexperienced.

GARABHAN, ain, *s. m.* Bran.

GARACH, ais, *s. m.* (*It.* gara.) A brawl.—*Shaw.*

GARACH, aich, *s. m.* A brat. See GARRACH.

GARACH, *a.* Useful. *Com.* and *sup.* garaiche.

GARACHDAIL, *a.* Huge.—*Shaw.*

GARACHDALACHD, *s. f.* Hugeness.

GÀRADAIR, *s. m.* (*from* garadh.) A gardener. *N. pl.* gàradairean.

GÀRADAIREACHD, *s. f.* Gardening; the business of a gardener.

GARADAN, ain, *s. m.* (*Ir. id.*) A register; a minute-book; a note-book.

GÀRADH, aidh, *s. m.* (*Ir.* garda.) A garden; a hedge, fence, dike; a gratuity. *N. pl.* gàraidhean *and* gàrachan, *gardens.* An gàradh Edein, *in the garden of Eden.*—*Stew. Gen.* Garadh luibhean, *a garden of herbs.*—*Stew. 1 K. ref.* Rinn mi garachan, *I made gardens.*—*Stew. Ecc.* Garadh càil, *a kitchen-garden.* (*Scotch*, a kail-yard.) Garadh, *a gratuity.*—*Shaw.* Garadh dhroighionn, a *hedge of thorns.*—*Stew. Pro.* Garadh criche, a *limit* or *landmark; a barrier.*

GĂRADH, aidh, *s. m.* The act of warming; a warming of the body with fire. Dean do gharadh, *warm thyself.*

GARAG. See GARRAG.

GARAIDH, *s. f.* A den, a cave, hole; a hiding-place for wild beasts. Iochdar na garaidh, *the bottom of the den.*—*Stew. Dan.* Garaidh aig na sionnaich, *foxes have holes.*—*Stew. Mark, ref.*

GARAID, *s. f.* Noise, clamour, confusion.

GARAIL, *a.* (gar-amhuil.) Near; neighbouring; warm; comfortable; snug.—*Shaw.*

GARAIT, *s. m.* A garret; a splutter; a noise. *N. pl.* garaitean.

† GARAN, ain, *s. m.* A crane. *N. pl.* garain. *Gr.* γέρανος *Teut.* kraene. *Ir.* garan. *Eng.* crane.

GARAN, ain, *s. m.* (*Ir. id.*) An underwood; a copse; a thicket; a grove; forest.—*Shaw. N. pl.* garain. Written also *garran.*

GARATHAIR, *s. m.* (*Ir. id.*) A great-grandfather. *N. pl.* garaithrichean, *grandfathers.*

GARBAN, ain, *s. m.* See GARABAN.

GARBANACH, *a.* See GARABANACH.

GARBH, *a.* Thick; huge; rough; grained; rugged; severe; fierce; terrible; coarse; boisterous; turbid. Casan garbh, *thick* or *brawny legs.* Innis gur treun is gur garbh sinn, *tell that we are strong and fierce.*—*Oss. Fing.* Bu gharbh gach buille, *terrible was every blow.*—*Id.* Clachan garbh, *rough stones.*—*Old Poem.* Gu garbh, *roughly, severely, fiercely.* Labhair an righ gu garbh, *the king answered roughly.* A gharbh chuid, *the greatest part; the roughest part.*—*Stew. 1 K. Com.* and *sup.* gairbhe, *rougher.* Ni 's gairbhe na leasraidh, *thicker than the loins.*—*Stew. O. T.*
Lat. by met. gravis. *Corn.* garou. *W.* garw. *Arm.* garv. *Phen.* garvv *and* garaav. *Arab.* garaph.

Bochart, in his book "Des Colonies de Phéniciens," observes, that in the *Phenician* language garvv is *rapid*. The *Old Celtic* garv had the same meaning, which is still retained in the *Armoric* dialect, and in the name of the river Garonne, i. e. garv an *or* garbh amhainn, *the rapid river*. According to Gigeius, *sail garaph*, in the *Arabic*, is *a torrent which sweeps all before it*; in *Gaelic*, it means *a stormy sea.*

GARBH, *s. m.* (*Ir. id. Heb.* garab.) A scab; *also*, warfare.

GARBHACH, aich, *s. m.* (*Ir. id.*) A grandson.—*Shaw. N. pl.* garbhaich.

GARBHACHD, GARBHADH, *s. m.* (*Ir. id.*) Roughness; rockiness; asperity; a rocky place.

GARBHAICH, *v. a.* (*Ir. id.*) Roughen.

GARBHAG, aig, *s. f.* Savoury. Garbhag ghàraidh, *savoury.*

GARBH-AITE, *s. m.* A rough place, a rocky place. *N. pl.* garbh-aiteachan.

GARBHALACH, *a.* Rocky, stony. Anns a choire gharbhalaich, *in the rocky dell.*—*Old Song.*

GARBHALACH, aich, *s. m.* Stony or rocky ground.

GARBHAN, ain, *s. m.* Brawn; grit. Garbhan creagach, *a plant good for bruises, growing among rocks on the sea-shore.*

GARBHANACH, aich, *s. m.* A stout fellow. *N. pl.* garbhanaich.

GARBHANACH, *a.* (*Ir. id.*) Having brawn, like brawn; rude, inexperienced.

Garbh-bhuille, *s. f.* A heavy blow.

Garbh-bhuilleach, *a.* Giving heavy blows.

Garbh-chath, *s. m.* A severe engagement or combat; the heat of battle. Dubhradh nan garbh-chath, *the gloom of battles.—Old Poem.*

Garbh-chlachaireachd, *s. f.* Fretwork.

Garbh-chludach, aich, *s. m.* (*Ir. id.*) A coarse blanket; a coverlet.—*Shaw.*

Garbh-chomhrag, aig, *s. f.* A furious engagement; a fierce struggle or combat; the heat of battle.

Garbh-chreuchd, *s.* A deep wound, a severe bruise. *N. pl.* garbh-chreuchdan.

Garbh-chreuchdach, *a.* Inflicting deep wounds; having deep or dangerous wounds or bruises.

Garbh-chrioch, -chriche, *s. f.* A rough bound; a rough or rocky country; the Highlands of Scotland. In this last sense it is generally used in the plural, and is applied to that mountainous ground which separates the counties of Perth and Inverness; it is also applied to the Highlands in general. Gaisgich nan garbh-chrioch, *the heroes of the Highlands.—Old Song.*

Garbh-chuan, ain, *s. m.* A rough or stormy sea. *N. pl.* garbh-chuantan, *rough seas.* An crann nach lùb an garbh-chuan, *a mast that will stand a storm.—Old Saying.*

Garbh-chulaidh, *s. f.* (*Ir. id.*) A frieze-coat. *N. pl.* garbh-chulaidhean.—*Shaw.*

Garbh-churaidh, *s. m.* A fierce warrior; a strong-bodied warrior. A gharbh-churaidh, èirich! *fierce warrior, arise!—Oss. Fing.*

Garbh-eas, *s. m.* A cascade; a rough torrent; a boisterous abyss or *linn.* *N. pl.* garbh-easaichean.—*Oss. Fing.*

Garbh-fhras, -fhrais, *s. m.* A heavy shower. *N. pl.* garbh-fhrasan.

Garbh-fhrasach, *a.* Very showery, very rainy. Am mios garbh-fhrasach, *the rainy month.—Macdon.*

Garbh-ghaineamh, eimh, *s. f.* (*Ir. id.*) Coarse sand; rough gravel.

Garbh-ghaoth, ghaoithe, *s. f.* A rough blast, a furious wind; a hurricane. Mar gharbh-ghaoth nam beann, *like the furious mountain-wind.—Old Poem.*

Garbh-ghniomh, *s.* A mighty deed or feat. Do gharbh-ghniomh, *thy feats in battle.—Oss. Tem.* *N. pl.* garbh-ghniomharan.

Garbhlach, aich, *s.* The rugged part of a country.

Garbh-laoch, -laoich, *s. m.* A fierce warrior; an impetuous hero. *N. pl.* garbh-laoich. Garbh-laoich a 's cruadalaiche beum, *fierce warriors whose blows are deadly.—Oss. Fing.*

Garh-leac, *s. f.* A rugged part of a country.

Garbhleas, *s. m.* A shout.

Garbh-linn, *s. f.* (*Ir. id.*) A rough sea, pool, or stream.

† **Garbh-loc**, *s.* (*Ir. id.*) A crag; a thicket.

Garbh-lus, *s. m.* Hay-ruff, catch-weed, goose-grass, clivers; *gallium asperine.*

Garbhraitheach, ich, *s. m.* Stinking hedge-mustard; *erysimum alliaria.*

Garbh-sheòd, -sheòid, *s. m.* A fierce warrior. Anam nam garbh-sheòd, *the souls of the warriors fierce.—Oss. Fing.*

Garbh-shion, -shine, *s. f.* A rough blast, a tempest.—*Shaw.*

Garbh-shiontach, *a.* Stormy, blasty. Là garbh-shiontach, *a blasty day.*

Garbh-shleagh, *s. f.* A thick spear. Gach garbh-shleagh is iùthaidh, *each thick spear and arrow.—Oss. Fing.*

Garbh-shlios, *s. f.* A rugged country side. An Slios gharbh, *a name given to the south side of the valley of Rannoch in Perthshire.*

Garbh-thonn, thuinn, *s. f.* A breaker, a rough or boisterous wave. *N. pl.* garbh-thonnan, *breakers.*

Garbh-thonnach, *a.* Billowy; raging, as the sea.

Garbhuaic, *s. f.* (*Ir. id.*) A storm, a tumult.

Garbh-uchd, *s. m.* A fierce [breast] mind; a rough bosom; a turbid bosom. Garbh-uchd nan speur, *the turbid bosom of the sky.—Oss. Tem.*

Garbh-uchdach, *a.* Having a rough breast. An cuan garbh-uchdach, *the rough-breasted sea.—Old Poem.*

† **Gard**, *s. m.* A garden; a fenced place; a guard.

Gard is a very ancient, probably a primeval, term, and is seen in most of the languages of ancient and modern times. *Heb. Chald. Syr.* gert, *to enclose.* *Arab.* and *Old Pers.* gherd, *a town.* *Modern Pers.* gard, *a town.* *Run. Sclav. Old Germ.* gard. *Russ,* gorod, gorad, *and* grod. Hence Constantinople, in the *Old Russ,* is Tsargrad or Tsargorad. *Gard* means a fenced place or an enclosure, in the Phenician, Punic, Parthic, and Samaritan tongues. From signifying an enclosure, it came in course of time to denote a fortified city. It has this meaning in the Old Persic or Pahlavi. From *gard* comes Κέρτα, the name of a city in Armenia, meaning an enclosed or fortified place. Κέρτα πολις υπο Αρμενιων, Kerta, a city of the Armenians.—*Heyschius.* Synonymous with the Celtic *gard* or *gart* was the Syrian *Kerta* or *Karta;* whence the Latin *Carthago,* and, as it is more correctly written, the Punic *Karthada* (gart-àite), the fortified place.—See *Cellarius De Geographia,* lib. iii. cap. 6.

From *gard* or *gart* are derived all the names of towns ending in *certa, cart, gard,* or *grad;* as, Tigranicerta, Carcathiocerta, Artasigarta, in Armenia; Belgrad, Stutgard, Stargard, &c.

From *gard,* a fenced place, come the modern terms for a garden, as well as the word *garden* itself. *Teut.* gaerd. *Germ.* gard. *Fr.* jardin. *Span.* giardin. *It.* giardino. *Dan.* gaart. *W. Arm.* gard. *Ir.* garda. *Scotch,* yard. Hence also the *English* word guard.

Gardraich, *s. pl.* A troop, or company.—*Shaw.*

Garg, *a.* (*Ir. id. Gr.* γοργ-ος.) Sour, bitter; fierce, cruel; harsh, rough, austere; satirical; sore. Bha i garg, *it was fierce.—Stew. Gen.* Briathran garg, *fierce* [*rough*] *swords.—Stew. Pro.* Com. and sup. gairge, *sourer, sourest.*

Gargachd, *s. f.* (*Ir. id.*) Sourness, bitterness; fierceness, cruelty; harshness, roughness, rudeness, austereness; satiricalness.

Garoad, aid, *s. m.* See **Gairgead**.

Gargail, *a.* Fierce; keen. A laoich ghargail, *the fierce warrior.—Turn.*

Gargan, ain, *s. m.* Dung, ordure, manure.

Garg-chronachadh, aidh, *s. m.* The act of rebuking severely; a harsh rebuke or reprimand.

Garg-chronaich, *v. a.* Rebuke severely. *Pret. a.* gharg-chronaich. Na garg-chronaich seanair, *rebuke not an elder.—Stew. Tim.*

Garlach, aich, *s. m.* A corruption of *garlaoch;* which see.

Garlaoch, laoich, *s. m.* A pithless boy; a naked starveling boy; a starveling; a bastard; a ragged child; a term of great personal contempt.

Ir. garlach. *Scotch,* garlach, *a bastard.*

Gàr-luch, **Gar-luchadh**, aidh, *s. m.* and *f.* A mole; a rat. *N. pl.* gar-luchaidh. *Gar-luch* seems to be *gearr-luch* or *gàraidh-luch.*

Gàr-luchag, aig, *s. f.* (*dim.* of gar-luch.) A young mole; a young rat; a little mole or rat.

Gàrluchaidh, *n. pl.* of garluch. Rats; moles.

Gar-mhac, -mhic, *s. m.* A grandson.

Garman, ain, *s. m.* See **Gairman**.

Garman, ain, *s. m.* Gallows.—*Shaw.*

† **Garmathair**, -mhathar, *s. m.* (*Ir. id.*) A great grandmother.—*Shaw.*

Garmunn, uinn, *s. m.* A post, pillar; a beam. Dhealbh e a garmuinne, *he formed its pillars.—Stew. Song Sol.*

Gar-ogha, *s. m.* A great grandchild's grandchild.—*Shaw.*

Garrach, aich. *s. m.* (*Ir.* garrfhiach.) A brat; a glutton; a gorbelly. A gharraich tha thu ann! *thou brat that thou art!* *N. pl.* garraichean, *brats.*

Garrach, *a.* Gorbellied; greedy, voracious.

Garrag, aig, *s. f.* An unfledged bird; a young bird. Is toigh leis an fheannaig a garrag féin, *the crow loves its own young.*—*G. P.* *N. pl.* garragan.

Garraid, *s. f.* Splutter; noise.

Garran, ain, *s. m.* (*Ir. id.*) A den; a thicket; a grove.—*Macd.* A copse, underwood; a glutton, a gorbelly.—*Shaw.* *N. pl.* garrain. Garran gaineimh, *a certain little fish.*

Garranach, *a.* Woody, having groves, thickets, or copses; having dens.

Garran-gainmheich, *s. m.* A certain small fish, the English name of which I have not been able to ascertain.

Garr-bhuaic, *s. f.* (*Ir. id.*) Noise; clamour; an assembly.—*Shaw.*

Garr-bhuaiceach, *a.* (*Ir. id.*) Noisy, clamorous.

Garrthaich, *s. f.* A loud tumultuous shout, clamour, any loud noise, continued din. Fearg agus garrthaich, *wrath and clamour.*—*Stew. Eph.*

† **Garsan**, ain, *s. m.* (*Ir. id.* *Fr.* garçon.) A lad.

Gart, gairt, *s. m.* Standing corn; any standing crop; grass. (*Gr.* χορτος, *grass.*) *Gart*, in these senses, is not much in use, but we have it in *gart-ghlan;* which see.

Gart, gairt, *s. m.* (*Ir. id.*) A garden or enclosure; liberality, bounty; a threatening aspect; a threatening posture. Gart a chuain, *the threatening aspect of the sea.*—*Macfar.* *Also*, a district in the Highlands of Perthshire, so called from the bounty of its original proprietor. Gart, *a garden*, is more frequently written *gort.*

Gartach. See **Gortach.**

Gartain, *gen. sing.* and *n. pl.* of gartan.

Gartan, ain, *s. m.* (*Ir.* gartan, *a bonnet.*) A garter; *rarely*, a bonnet; cap; hat. Rìghdir a ghartain, *a knight of the garter.* *N. pl.* gartain, *garters.* Osain ghoirrid 's gartain, *short hose and garters.*—*Macint.*

Gartanach, *a.* (*from* gartan.) Gartered; having garters; like a garter. Osain ghartanach, *gartered hose.*

Gartanachadh, aidh, *s. m.* A gartering.

Gartanaich, *v. a.* Garter. *Pret. a.* ghartanaich, *gartered.*

Gartanaichte, *p. part.* of gartanaich, *gartered.*

Gartar, *a., for* gartmhor; which see.

Gart-ghlan, *v. a.* (gart, *standing corn, and* glan, *clean.*) Weed; pluck weeds out of standing corn, or any standing crop; examine.

Gart-ghlanadh, aidh, *s. m.* The act of weeding a standing crop; an examining.

Garthaich, *s. f.* See **Garrthaich.**

Garthal, *a.* (*Ir. id.*) Snug, warm, comfortable.—*Shaw.*

Gartlann, ainn, *s. m.*, gart, *corn, and* lann. (*Ir. id.*) A corn-yard.

Gartmhoire, *com.* and *sup.* of gartmhor. More or most liberal.

Gartmhoireachd, *s. f.* Munificence, liberality.

Gartmhor, *a.* Munificent.

Garunnach, *a.* (*Ir. id.*) Dirty; horrible, shocking.

Gas, gais, *s. m.* (*Ir. id.*) A branch, a bough, a tuft, a bunch; a copse; a stripling, a boy; a military servant; the stem of an herb. O charn nan gas, *from the copsy rock.*—*Oss. Lodin.*

† **Gas**, gais, *s. m.* (*Ir. id.*) Strength; wrath. *Lat.* gæsus, *strong.* *Gæsi*, a name given by the Old Gauls to strong men, or those who could wield the *gæsum* with effect. *Germ.* gast, *a soldier.* *Turk.* gazi.

† **Gas**, *adv., conj.*, and *prep.* Now written *gus;* which see.

Gas, *v. n.* Shout; sprout; branch; look. *Pret.* ghas; *fut. aff.* gasaidh, *shall shout.*

Gasach, *a.* (*from* gas.) Branchy, bushy, tufty, bunchy, copsy. *Com.* and *sup.* gasaiche.

Gasachd, *s. f.* Branchiness, bushiness, tuftiness, bunchiness.

Gasan, ain, *s. m.* (*dim.* of gasan.) A little branch or bough, a little tuft, a little copse; a tendril; a stripling. *Fr.* garçon, *a lad.* *Ir.* gasun.

Gasar. See **Gasradh.**

Gasbadan, ain, *s. m.* A wasp or hornet.—*Macfar.* *N. pl.* gasbadain.

Gasbaid, *s.* A hornet; a wasp.

Gasda, *a.* (*Germ.* gast, *a soldier.*) Clever; handsome, beauteous; chaste; gallant, brave; neat; ingenious, skilful; well. A bhean ghasda, *his beauteous wife.*—*Oss. Tem.* An laoch gasda, *the gallant hero.*—*Oss. Derm.* Is gasda am balaoch thu, *you are a famous fellow.* Am bheil thu gu gasda? *are you quite well?*

Gasdachd, *s. f.* (*from* gasda.) Bravery; cleverness, ingenuity; neatness. Bha e mòr na ghasdachd, *he was great in his bravery.*—*Old Song.*

† **Gasg**, gaisg, *s. m.* (*Ir. id.*) A tail.—*Shaw.*

† **Gasgach**, *a.* (*Ir. id.*) Having a tail.

Gasgan, ain, *s. m.* (*Ir. id.*) A petulant fellow, a puppy. *N. pl.* gasgain.

Gasganach, aich, *s. m.* (*Ir. id.*) A conceited fellow, a pert fellow, a puppy. *N. pl.* gasganaich.

Gasganach, *a.* (*Ir. id.*) Pert, petulant, conceited. *Com.* and *sup.* gasganaiche.

Gasgara, *s. pl.* (*Ir. id.*) The posteriors.—*Shaw.*

Gasrach, *a.* Proud; salacious; fiery, hot-tempered. *Com.* and *sup.* gasraiche.

Gasradh, aidh, *s. m.* Low company; a band of mercenary soldiers; a crew; domestic soldiers; salaciousness. A bhar is a gasradh, *the vessel and her crew.*—*Macfar.* Galla air ghasradh, *a hot bitch.*

Gast, *a.* See **Gasda.**

Gast, *s. f.* (*Arm.* gasd, *a whore.* *Ir.* gast.) An old woman; a whore; a snare; a wile; a puff, a blast.

Gastachd, *s. f.* See **Gasdachd.**

Gastag, aig, *s. f., dim.* of gastag. (*Ir.* gastog.) A little slut or whore; a trick; a wile.

Gath, *s. f.* (*Ir.* gath *and* ga. *Swed.* gadd.) A sting; a spear, a dart; a ray, or beam. *N. pl.* gathan *and* gathanna. Gath-gréine, *a sunbeam.*—*Ardar.* Gath-oige dol seachad *the ray of youth passing by.*—*Oss. Lodin.* Gath na gealaich, *the moonbeam.*—*Oss. Com.* Gath tannais, *a spectre's spear.*—*Oss Tem.* Gath builg, *a fiery dart;* gath cuip, *medical tent.*—*Shaw.* Gath dubh, *the beard of oats; a weed.* Gath muinne, *a horse's mane;* gath soluis, *a ray of light;* gath teth, *a fiery dart;* see below. Gath tearradh, *a whitlow;* gath fruighe, *a poisoned dart* or *arrow.*

Gath-builg, *s. f.* A fiery dart. See **Gath-teth.**

Gath-cuip, *s. f.* (*Ir. id.*) A medical tent.

Gath-dubh, *s. f.* (*Ir. id.*) The beard of corn; a weed.

Gath-fruighe, *s. m.* A poisoned arrow.—*Shaw.*

Gath-gealaich, *s. f.* A moonbeam. Mar ghath gealaich, *like a moonbeam.*—*Oss. Fing.*

Gath-gréine, *s. f.* A sunbeam; *also*, a name given to the banner of Fingal, king of the Caledonians. B'ise an gath-gréin a measg mhnai, *a sunbeam was she among* *women.—Oss. Fing.* Gath-grèine mhic Cumhail crann, *[put] the banner of Fingal to its staff.—Old Poem.*

GATH-LINN, *s. m.* The north polar star.

GATH-MUINNE, *s. f.* (*Ir. id.*) A mane.—*Shaw.*

GATH-SOLUIS, *s. f.* A sunbeam; a ray of light; a pencil of rays.

GATH-TETH, *s. m.* A fiery dart.

This word is synonymous with *gath-builg* and *craosach dearg.* Tacitus, *De Mor. Germ.*, observes, that such weapons were used by the Persians, a Belgic nation of German extraction. In one of Ossian's poems (Fingal), Cuchullin is described as having slain his friend Feardath, a young Caledonian warrior, with a spear heated into a flame by the wind, *i. e.* by the armourer's forge. This weapon, according to some, must have been the *jaculum fervefactum* mentioned by Cæsar, and the *catein* [*gath-teth* pronounced *ga-te*] of Virgil:

"Teutonico ritu soliti torquere *cateias.*"

The *clavæ ambustæ* of Ammianus, lib. xxxi., seem to have been the same as the Caledonian *gath-teth*:—"Barbari, ingentes clavas in nostros conjicientes ambustas, cornu perrumpunt." This appears to be a simpler and better illustration of the nature of the *cateia* than that of Aventinus, who asserts that it was an engine for throwing stones. Isodorus comes nearer the truth: he says (without making any mention of its being heated) that it was a weapon which, owing to its weight, could not be thrown to a great distance, but was very destructive.

GATH-TEARRADH, *s. f.* A whitlow or agnail.

GÈ, *s. m.* (*Gr.* γῆ.) The earth. More commonly written cè; which see.

GE, *conj.* (*Ir. id.* more properly *ged.*) Though, although. Ge mòr e, *great though he be.—Oss. Tem.* Ge mòr is ge glic, *however great and wise.—Oss. Fing.* Ge as air bi, *whence so ever; better,* cia as air bi.

GEABHAIR, *s. m.* (*Ir. id.*) A carper.—*Shaw.* *N. pl.* geabhairean.

GEAD. (*Ir. id.*) A patch; a spot on a horse's forehead; a ridge; a spot of ground; the fish called a pike. (*Scotch,* ged.) *Rarely,* a buttock or haunch.

GEADACH, *a.* Patched; spotted; ridgy; like a pike.

GEADAG, aig, *s. m.* (*Ir. id.*) A small patch; a little spot of ground; a little ridge; a young pike.

GEADAGACH, *a.* Spotted, patched.

GEADAS, ais, *s. m.* (*Ir.* geadus.) The fish called a pike. *N. pl.* geadasan.

GEADASG, aisg, *s. m.* (gead-iasg.) The fish called a pike; the *esox lucius* of Linnæus.

GEADH, geòidh, *s. m.* (*Ir. id. W.* gwyz.) A goose; a tailor's iron. Geadh dubh, *a solan goose;* geadh-lann, *a goose-pen.* *N. pl.* geòidh, *geese.*

GEADHA, *s. m.* A boat-hook; a boat-pole.

GEADHACH, *a.* Abounding in geese; *also, substantively,* a goose-quill.

GEAG, geig, *s. m.;* more frequently written *geug;* which see.

GEAGACH, *a.* See GEUGACH.

GEAL, *a.* (*Ir. id.* *Gr.* γαλα, *milk.*) White; fair; bright; clear. A lamh gheal, *her white hand.—Oss.* Là geal, *a bright* or *clear day.* Do gheal chlaidheamh, *thy bright sword.—Oss.* Mo laogh geal! an address of much affection among the Gael, however ludicrous it may appear in the translation, *my white calf!* Mar charraig ghil, *like a white rock.—Oss. Fing.* *Com.* and *sup.* gile, *whiter, whitest.* *N. pl.* geala. Eich gheala, *white horses.—Stew. Zech.*

GEALA. See GEALADH.

GEALACH, aich, *s. f., from* geal. (*Ir. id.*) The moon. Gealach air sleibhte, *the moon on the hills.—Oss. Taura.* Mar ghealaich, *like the moon:—Oss. Fing.* Triall na gealaich, *the moon's path.—Ull.* Gealach ùr, *a new moon;* a ghealach ùr, *the new moon;* gealach bhuidhe na Féill-Mhicheil, *the yellow moon of Michaelmas.* *N. pl.* gealaichean.

GEALACHADH, aidh, *s. m.* A whitening; a bleaching or blanching.

GEALADH, aidh, *s. m.* The act of whitening; whiteness; whiting.

GEALADH, aidh, *s. m.* (*W.* gele *and* gelen, *a horse-leech.*) A leech. *N. pl.* gealan (*for* gealadhan), *leeches.*

GEAL-ADHAIRC, *s. m.* An animal with a white horn; a name given to a white-horned cow.

GEAL-ADHAIRCEACH, *a.* White-horned.

GEALAG, aig, *s. f.* (*Ir.* gealog.) The fish called a gilse, a salmon trout; the *salma trutta* of Linnæus. *N. pl.* gealagan. Gealag-bhuachair, *a bunting;* the *emberiza milaria* of Linnæus.

GEALAGACH, *a.* Abounding in gilse or in young salmon; like a gilse or salmon-trout.

GEALAGAN, ain, *s. m.* (*Ir.* gealacan.) The white of an egg; the white of the eye. Gealagan an uighe, *the white of the egg.—Stew. Job.* Also the *n. pl.* of gealag.

GEALAG-BHUACHAIR, *s. f.* The bird called a bunting.

GEALAICH, *gen. sing.* of gealach.

GEALAICH, *v. a., from* geal. (*Ir.* gealaigh.) Whiten; bleach or blanch. *Pret. a.* ghealaich, *bleached; fut. aff. a.* gealaichidh. Gealaich an t-anart, *bleach the linen.*

GEALAICHEAR, *fut. aff. a.* Shall or will be whitened.

GEALAICHTE, *p. part.* of gealaich. Whitened; bleached. Anart gealaichte, *bleached linen.*

GEALAIN, *gen. sing.* and *n. pl.* of gealan.

† GEALAIRGIDH, *s. f.* A prickle.—*Shaw.*

GEALAN, ain, *s. m.* (*Ir. id.*) The white of an eye; the white of an egg; a sparrow.—*Shaw.* *N. pl.* gealain.

GEALBHAN, ain, *s. m.* See GEALBHONN.

GEALBHAN, ain, *s. m.* (*Ir. id.*) A fire.

GEALBHONN, -bhuinn, *s. m.* A sparrow; the *fringilla domestica* of Linnæus; a common fire. An gealbhonn beag, *the little sparrow.—Sm.* Gealbhonn-lin, *a linnet;* the *linaria* of Gesner. Gealbhonn cuilinn, *a bullfinch.* *Ir.* gealbhan. *Arm.* golven. *Corn.* gilvan *and* golven.

GEALBHONN-LÌN, *s. m.* A linnet or lintwhite.

GEALCADH, aidh, *s. m.* Whiteness.

† GEALC, *v.* Whiten. See GEALAICH.

GEAL-CHLAIDHEAMH, eimh, *s. m.* A bright sword. Do gheal-chlaidheamh, *thy bright sword.—Oss.*

GEAL-GHLAC, -ghlaic, *s. m.* A fair hand. A ribhinn nan geal-ghlac! *thou fair-handed maiden!—Old Poem.*

GEALL, gill, *s. m.* (*Ir. id.*) A promise, a pledge; mortgage; a vow; a bet or wager; fondness. Thoir dhomh geall, *give me a pledge.—Stew. Gen.* Cuir geall, *lay a bet;* tha e an geall oirre, *he is fond of her;* is iomad fear tha 'n geall air drama, *many are they who like their [glass] dram.—R.*

GEALL, *v. a.* Promise, pledge, vow. *Pret. a.* gheall, *promised; fut. aff. a.* geallaidh, *shall promise.* Geallaidh iad gealladh, *they shall vow a vow.—Stew. Is.*

GEALLADH, aidh, *s. m.* (*Ir. id.*) The act of promising; a promise; a wager or bet; a pledge, a vow; a mortgage. Geallaidh iad gealladh, *they shall vow a vow.—Stew. Is.* Bheir mi mo ghealladh dhuit, *I will promise you,* or *give you my promise.* Tìr a gheallaidh, *the land of promise.—Stew. Heb.* Gealladh gun cho-ghealladh, *promise without performance.*

GEALLADH, (a), *pr. part.* of geall. Promising; betting; pledging, vowing.

GEAL-LAMH, -laimh, *s. f.* A fair hand.—*Oss.*

GEALL-BARRANTAIS, *s. m.* A pledge; a mortgage; a bet.

Geall-chinn, Geall-chinne, *s. m* A fine imposed by the ancient Caledonians on one who was guilty of manslaughter; it literally means either a *life-mulct* or money paid to kinspeople.

According to the old Scottish code of *Regiam Majestatem*, it is called *kelchin* The *geall-chinn* of an earl was sixty-six cows and two thirds, of a thane, or earl's son, forty-four cows, twenty pence, and two thirds of an obólus or *bodle*, that of a thane's son was less, by a fourth part, than that of his father, or about eleven cows and five-pence farthing For the fine in cases of murder, see Eiric This mode of retribution was prevalent among the northern nations Tacitus says of the Old Germans, "Luitur homicidium certo armentorum et pecorum numero"

Geall-daighneachaidh, *s. m.* A pledge; earnest, earnest-money

Geall-daighnich, *s m.* A pledge, earnest; earnest money A thug dhuinn geall-daighnich, *who has given us an earnest —Stew. Cor.*

Geall-meas, *s m* An estimate Hence the word *galmes*, used in the ancient Scottish code of *Regiam Majestatem*

Geallmhor, *a.* Fond; desirous *Com* and *sup.* geallmhoire.

Geallmhorachd, *s f.* Desirousness; fondness

Geallmhuin, *s f* A promise, a promising.

Geallta, Gealltie, *pr part* of geall Promised, vowed, pledged, betted.

Gealltuinn, *s f* A promising, a vowing; a pledging

Gealltuinn, (a), *pr part* of geall. Promising, vowing, pledging

Gealltuineas, eis, *s m* A promising.

Geal-sheileach, eich, *s f* The sallow-tree

Geal-shùileach, *a* (*Ir. id*) Moon-eyed —*Shaw.*

Gealt, geilt, *s f* Fear, cowardice, skittishness Hence evidently the English word *guilt.*

Gealta, *part.* (*Ir. id*) Whitened; bleached

Gealtach, *a*, *from* gealt. (*Ir id*) Fearful, timid, skittish; cowardly. Thill e gealtach gu dlùth, *he turned fearful and fast —Oss. Fing* Gu gealtach, *timidly* *Com* and *sup.* gealtaiche.

Gealtachd, *s. f* (*Ir id*) Timidness; cowardliness, skittishness Eadar nàir is gealtachd, *between shame and timidness —Old Song*

Gealtaiche, *s m* A coward; a timid person, *also*, jealousy

Gealtaiche, *com* and *sup* of gealtach

Gealtair, *s. m*, gealt-fhear. (*Ir id*) A coward, a timid fellow. *N. pl* gealtairean Is tric bha claidheamh fad an lamh gealtair, *oft has a long sword been in a coward's hand —G P.*

Gealtaireach, *a* (*Ir. id*) Cowardly, timorous

Gealtaireachd, *s. f.* A tendency to cowardice, cowardliness, timidness.

Gealtholl, oill, *s. m.* (*Ir id.*) A horse-leech

Gealtran, ain, *s m.*, *from* gealt (*Ir. id*) A coward; a timid person. *N. pl* gealtrain

Geaman, ain, *s m* A servant, a useful person

Geamanach, aich, *s. m* (*Ir. id*) A servant, a lacquey; a stout young fellow. Perhaps *ceumanach.*

† **Geamh**, geimh, *s. f.* A branch, a slip —*Shaw*

Geamhar, air, *s. m* A blade of corn; corn in blade

Geamhlach, *a.* Sandblind

Geamhladh, aidh, *s m* A chain or fetter

Geamhlag, eig. *s f.* See Geimhleag.

Geamhloch, *a.* Sandblind —*Shaw.*

Geamhrachadh, aidh, *s. m* A spending the winter, wintering; winter quarters

Geamhrachail, *a.* Wintry, cold; stormy.

Geamhradh, aidh, *s. m.* (*Ir.* geimhre.) Winter. Ro ghaoith' gheamhraidh, *before the winds of winter.—Oss. Gaul* Bo (no) mart geamhraidh, *a winter mart, a heifer slain for winter food.*

Geamhraich, *v. a* and *n.* (*from* geamhradh) Winter, spend the winter. *Pret. a.* gheamhraich, *wintered, fut. aff. a.* geamhraichidh, *shall winter.*

Geamh-shuileach, *a.* (*Ir. id.*) Pink-eyed.—*Shaw.*

Geamnachd, *s. f*, *for* geamnaidheachd.

Geamnaidh, Geamnuidh, *a* (*for* geanmnaidh.) Modest; womanly; continent.

Geamnaidheachd, Geamnuidheachd, *s f.* Modesty; womanliness; continence.

Gean, *s. f* (*Ir.* gean. *It.* gana, *willingly*) Good humour; pleasure; fondness; love; approbation; smile; greed. Gean maith, *good will* Laithean ar gean, *the days of our pleasure.—Oss. Conn.* Droch ghean, *bad humour.*

† **Gean**, gein, *s. f.* A woman.

Gr. γυνη *Teut.* quena, *a wife.* *Island.* cona. *Eng.* quean, *and also* queen, i e. *the woman* *Old Eng.* guine, *a prostitute*, hence, a son of a gun, *i e.* of a *guine* or *whore.* Chaucer has *queint*, signifying, *pars feminæ nefanda*

Geanach, *a.* (*Ir. id.*) Greedy. See Gionach.

Geanach, *a.* (*Ir. id*) Pleasant; of a pleasant humour; fond Biodhmaid maranach geanach, *let us be hospitable and good humoured —Old Song.* *Com.* and *sup* geanaiche, *more* or *most pleasant.*

Geanachd, *s. f.*, *from* gean (*Ir. id*) Chastity, continence, womanliness

Geanaiche, *com.* and *sup.* of geanach.

Geanail, *a* (gean-amhuil) Womanly, modest; comely, graceful; pleasant, in good humour.

Geanalachd, *s f* Womanliness, modesty; comeliness, gracefulness, pleasantness.

† **Geanamh**, aimh, *s m.* (*Ir. id*) A sword.

Geanas, ais, *s m*, *from* gean. (*Ir id*) Chastity; pleasant humour.

Geanasach, *a* (*Ir id*) Chaste, continent; in pleasant humour

Geanasachd, *s f* (*Ir id*) Chasteness, continence, purity, womanliness.

† **Geang**, *v a* (*Ir id*) Strike, beat.

† **Geangach**, *a* (*Ir id*) Crooked; apt to strike.

† **Geangachd**, *s. f.* (*Ir id*) Comeliness; beauty; striking.

Gean-maith, Gean-math, *s.* Good-will; good-pleasure; a gratuity, donation, bounty Mar ghean-maith, *as a matter of bounty —Stew 2 Cor.* Cha 'n 'eil do ghean-maith ort, *you are in good humour.*

Geanm-chnò, Geanm-chnù, *s f.* (*Ir. id*) A chesnut. Do chraoibh nan geanm-chnò, *of the chesnut-tree.—Stew. Gen*

Geanmnachd, *s f.*, *for* geanmnaidheachd

Geanmnaidh, Geanmnuidh, *a.* (*Ir. id.*) Pure, chaste, continent, uncorrupted, modest.

Geanmnaidheachd, Geanmnuidheachd, *s. f.* Purity, chastity, continence, modesty.

Geannair, *s m* See Geinnear.

Gear, *s.* A Hare.

Gear, *a* More frequently written *geur*; which see.

Gearain, *gen. sing.* of gearan.

Gearain, *v. n.* Complain, murmur, make a complaint; accuse. *Pret.* ghearain, *complained*, *fut. aff.* gearainidh, *shall complain.* Gearainidh mi, *I will complain.—Stew. Job.*

† **Gearait**, *s. c.* A virgin; a saint; a warrior; *also*, holy; prudent.

Gearan, ain, *s. m.* (*Ir. id. W.* geran.) A complaint, murmur; wailing; sigh; cry; groan; supplication; accusation. Rinn iad gearain, *they murmured.—Stew. Ex.* Ri gearan, *complaining.—Stew. Pro.* Dean gearan, *make a complaint.*

Gearanach, *a.* (*Ir. id.*) Apt to complain; ailing; sad; accusative, apt to make a complaint.—*Macint.* Sgeul mu 'n gearanach daoine, *a tale about which men are sad.—Macfar. Com.* and *sup.* gearanaiche.

Gearanaich, *v. n.* (*Ir.* gearanaigh.) Complain; condole. *Pret. a.* ghearanaich.

Gearasdan, ain, *s. m.* A fort, a garrison. Gearasdan Ionar lòchaidh, *Fort-William in the West Highlands.*

† **Gearb**, *s.* (*Ir. id.*) A scab, a scar; mange, itch.

† **Gearb**, *v. a.* and *n.* (*Ir. id.*) Grieve; hurt, wound.

Gearbach, *a.* (*Ir. id.*) Scabbed; mangy; itched; rugged.

Gearcaig, *s. f.* (*Ir. id.*) A brood.

Geard, *s. f.* (*Fr.* garde. *Teut.* gærde.) A guard of soldiers; a guard or defence. Bi air do gheard, *be on your guard. N. pl.* geardan *and* geardachan, *guards.* Geardachan an righ, *the king's guards.—Mac K.*

Gearg, geirg, *s. f.* (*Ir. id.*) A botch; a boil; a suppuration.

Geargach, *a.* Like a botch or boil; in a state of suppuration.

Gearr, *v. a.* (*Ir. id.*) Cut; carve; hew; slice; engrave; taunt; bite; gnaw. *Pret. a.* ghearr, *cut; fut. aff. a.* gearraidh, *shall cut.* Gearr goirrid, *cut short;* gearraidh e goirrid i, *he will cut it short.—Stew. Rom.* Gear as, *cut off;* gearr sios, *cut down;* gearr bhàn, *cut down;* gearr sùrdag, *bound;* a gearradh shùrdag, *bounding.—Macdon.*

Gr. κείρω, *cut* or *crop. Heb.* garan. *Arab.* and *Chald.* garaph, *to diminish.*

Gearr, *a.* (*Ir. id. W.* ger.) Short; short in size; transient; laconic; deficient; not reaching the intended part; *also, substantively*, a wear for catching fish. Gearr gu robh 'aois, *short be his life.—Sm.* Is gearr a dhearrsa, *transient is his beam.—Oss. Gaul.* Thainig iad gearr air, *they came short of it.—Stew. N. T.* Cainnt ghearr tharbhach, *laconic and pithy language.—Mac Lach.*

Gearra-bhreac, *a.* Guillemot.—*Shaw.*

Gearrach, aich, *s. m.* (*perhaps* gearr-theachd.) A flux or dysentery. Gearrach fola, *a hæmorrhage* or *bloody flux.* Written also *gearrthach;* which see.

Gearra-choileir, *s. m.* An assassin, a cut-throat.

Gearradair, *s. m., from* gearr. (*Ir.* gearradoir.) A carver; an engraver; a lapidary; a hewer; a cutter. *N. pl.* gearradairean. Gearradairean chlach, *stone-hewers; stone-squarers; lapidaries.—Stew.* 1 *K.*

Gearradaireachd, *s. f.* Carving; the business of a lapidary.

Gearradan, ain, *s. m.* (*Ir. id.*) A note-book; a register.

Gearradh, aidh, *s. m.* (*Ir. id.*) A cutting; a biting, gnawing; hewing; slicing; mowing; carving or graving; a taunt; a cut, a tear or rent; *also*, a toll, tribute, or tax. Nach ioc iad gearradh? *will they not pay toll?—Stew. Ezra. N. pl.* gearraidhean. Air a bheul bha gearraidhean, *on its mouth were gravings.—Stew.* 1 *K.* Gearradh airm, *a crest.*

Gearrag, aig, *s. f.* (*Ir. id.*) A wafer; a thin scon; *also*, fortune, fate, destiny.—*Shaw. N. pl.* gearragan, *wafers.* Gearragan neo-ghoirtichte, *unleavened wafers.—Stew. Ex.*

Gearragan, ain, *s. m.* A wafer. *N. pl.* gearragain.

Gearra-ghath, *s. m.* A javelin.

Gearra-gort, -goirt, *s. m.* A quail. *N. pl.* gearra-goirt, *quails.* Thainig na gearra-goirt, *the quails came.—Stew. Ex.* and *Num.*

Gearraich, *v. a.* (*from* gearr.) Shorten, abridge, curtail. *Pret. a.* ghearraich, *shortened; fut. aff. a.* gearraichidh, *shall shorten.* Gearraichidh tu a shaoghal, *thou shalt shorten his life.—Old Song.*

Gearraichte, *p. part.* of gearraich. Shortened, curtailed.

Gearraidhean, *n. pl.* of gearradh. Cuttings; engravings. Air na h-uile làmhan bidh gearraidhean, *on all the hands there shall be cuttings.—Stew. Jer.*

Gearran, ain, *s. m.* (*Ir. id.*) A little farm-horse; a work-horse, a hack; the latter end of February. Gearran ard, *a hobby.—Shaw.*

Gearr-anail, -analach, *s. f.* Asthma; broken wind.

Gearr-anaileach, *a.* Asthmatic; broken-winded. Each gearr-anaileach, *a broken-winded horse.*

Gearra-dhearc, *s. m.* A bilberry.

Gearra-phochd, *s. m.* A satchel. *N. pl.* gearra-phochdan.

Gearrar, *fut. pass.* of gearr. Shall be cut. Gearrar as e, *he shall be cut off.*

Gearra-sgian, -sgein, *s. f.* (*Ir. id.*) A dirk, a stiletto. *N. pl.* gearra-sgeinichean.

Gearra-sporan, ain, *s. m.* A cutpurse.

Gearr-chosach, *a.* (*Ir. id.*) Short-legged; short-footed.

Gearr-chòt, -chota, *s. m.* A short coat, or jacket.

Gearr-chuisle, *s. f.* Venesection, phlebotomy.

Gearr-dhearc, *s. m.* A bilberry. *N. pl.* gearr-dhearcan.

Gearr-earblach, *a.* (*Ir. id.*) Bobtailed, curtailed, docked.

Gearr-earbull, uill, *s.* (*Ir. id.*) A bobtail.

Gearr-fhiadh, -fheidh, *s. m.* A hare. *N. pl.* gearr-fheidh. Mar ghearr-fhiadh am mullach sleibh, *like a hare on the mountain-tops.—Macdon.* Gearr-fhiadh, *a hare.—Stew. Lev. ref.*

Gearr-fhionn, *s. m.* Short hair, as that of quadrupeds.

Gearr-fhionnach, *a.* Short-haired, as cattle. Laoigh gearr-fhionnach, *short-haired calves.—Macfar.*

Gearr-fhoirm, *s. f.* (*Ir. id.*) An abridgment, an abstract.

Gearr-ghath, *s.* (*Ir. id.*) A javelin, a spear. *N. pl.* gearr-ghathan.

Gearr-ghuin, *s.* (*Ir. id.*) A horse-leech.

Gearr-ghunn, *s. f.* A short gun, a carabine. *N. pl.* gearr-ghunnachan, *carabines.*

Gearr-mhagach, *a.* Satirical, sarcastic, ironical. Té ghobach ghear-magach, *a gabbling sarcastic woman.—Old Song.*

Gearr-mhagadh, aidh, *s. m.* Satire, sarcasm, irony; a bitter jest.

Gearr-sgian, -sgein, *s. f.* A dagger, dirk, or stiletto.

Gearr-shaoghlach, *a.* Short-lived, of a few days.—*Stew. Job.*

Gearr-shaoghlachd, *s. f.* Short-livedness.

Gearr-smachd, *s. f.* (*Ir. id.*) Severity; wrath; overbearance.

Gearrta, **Gearrte**, *p. part.* of gearr. Cut; shorn; mown; graven; carved; sliced. Gearrta air na clàraibh, *graven on the tables.—Stew. Ex.* Le oibribh ghearrte, *with carved works.—Stew. Prov.* Feur gearrta, *mown grass.—Stew. Pro.*

Gearrthach, aich, *s. m.* and *f.* (*perhaps* gearr-theachd.)

A flux or dysentery. Gearrthach fhola, *a bloody-flux* or *hæmorrhage*. Written also *gearrach*.

GEARSOM, oim, *s. m.* Entrance money. Pàighibh an gearsom, *pay the entrance money.—Old Song.*

† GEART, *s. m.* (*Ir. id.*) Milk.—*Shaw.*

GEAS, geis, *s. m.* Incantation; enchantment; a charm; an oath; an engagement; a religious vow; a guess or conjecture. *N. pl.* geasan; *d. pl.* geasaibh. Chuir i mi fo gheasaibh, *she laid me under engagements.—Fingalian Poem.*

GEAS, *v. a.* (*Ir. id.*) Divine; guess.

GEASACH, *a.* (*from* geas.) Enchanting, charming; guessing, conjecturing; like a charm or enchantment.

GEASACHD, *s. f.* Enchantment, a charm, conjuration; a vow; a guess or conjecture. C'àite an robh am fàinne geasachd? *where was the enchanted ring?—Old Poem.*

GEASADAIR, *s. m.* (*Ir. id.*) An enchanter, conjurer, or sorcerer; a wizard. *N. pl.* geasadairean, *wizards.*

GEASADAIREACHD, *s. f.* (*Ir. id.*) Enchantment, sorcery.

GEASADAN, ain, *s. m.* (*Ir. id.*) A shrub; *also*, an arrow; a lance.

GEASAG, aig, *s. f.* (*dim.* of geas.) A charm; sorcery; a superstitious ceremony. See also GISEAG.

GEASAGACH, *a.* Superstitious. See also GISEAGACH.

GEASAN, *n. pl.* of geas; which see.

GEASAN, ain, *s. m.* (*from* geas.) An oath; a charm; sorcery. Nathraichean air nach luidh geasan, *serpents that cannot be charmed.—Stew. Jer.*

GEASRAG, aig, *s. f.* A charm; sorcery; a superstitious ceremony. Written also *giseag.*

GEASRAGACH, *a.* Superstitious; superstitiously; ceremonious.

GEASRAGACHD, *s. f.* Superstitiousness; superstitious ceremonies.

† GEAST, geist, *s. m.* (*Ir. id.*) Barm, yeast.

† GEASTAL, ail, *s. m.* (*Ir. id. Lat.* gestale.) A deed, a fact; *also*, want, necessity.

GEAT, *s. m.* A gate. *N. pl.* geatachan, *gates.* Written also *geatadh;* which see.

GEATACHAN, *n. pl.* of geat. Gates. A gheatachan, *ye gates.—Sm.*

GEATADH, aidh, *s. m.* (*Ir. id.*) A gate. Dhruid iad an geatadh, *they shut the gate.—Stew. Jos. N. pl.* geatachan *and* geataidh, *gates.* Geataidh an ionracais, *the gates of righteousness.—Id.*

GEATAIR, *s. m.* (*Ir. id.*) A small cake.

GEATRACH, *a.* (*Ir. id.*) Fearful, timid.

GED, *conj.* Though, although; but. Ged tha, *though it be; notwithstanding.* Ged nach 'eil, *though there be not.*

GEIBHIONN, *s. sing.* and *pl.* Fetters; prison, imprisonment; any great distress.

GEIBHIS, *s. f.* (*Ir. id.*) A valley.

GEIBHLEACH, *a.* Fettered, imprisoned; oppressive; slavish.

GEIBHLEACHADH, aidh, *s. m.* A fettering; imprisoning; enslavement; imprisonment.

GEIBHLEAN, *s. pl.* Fetters.

GEIBHLICH, *v. a.* (*Ir.* geibhligh.) Fetter; enslave; pledge; mortgage. *Pret. a.* gheibhlich; *fut. aff. a.* geibhlichidh.

† GEIBLEID, *s. f.* A sloven or slattern; a drabbish female. *N. pl.* geibhleidean.

GEIBLEIDEACH, *a.* Slovenly; drabbish. Gu geibleideach, *drabbishly.*

GEIBLEIDEACHD, *s. f.* Slovenliness; drabbishness.—*Shaw.*

† GEIDEAL, il, *s. m.* (*Ir. id.*) A fan.

GÉILE, *gen. sing.* of gial; which see.

GEILIOS, *s.* Traffic.—*Shaw.*

GEILL, *s. f.* Meaning, sense. See CIALL *and* CÉILLE.

GÉILL, *v. n.* Submit, yield, give up, bend, assent, obey, fail, give way, do homage. *Pret.* ghéill; *fut. aff.* géillidh, *shall yield.* Dha 'n géill mòr ghaillshion? *to whom yields the great tempest?—Oss. Fing.*—Ghéill a shùil, *his eye failed.—Oss. Croma.* Iadsan a ghéilleas, *they who* [*bend*] *worship.—Sm.*

GÉILL, géille, *s. f.* (*Ir. id.*) Submission, obedience; assent, homage; the act of yielding or submitting; *also*, the thing yielded or given up. Mar faigheam géill, *I receive not submission.—Old Poem.* Thoir géill, *submit.* Bheir e leis ar géill, *he will take with him our captives.—Old Poem.*

† GEILLE, *s. pl.* Gives; fetters.—*Shaw.* See GEIMHLE.

GEILLEACHDUINN, *s.* (*Ir. id.*) A submitting, a yielding, giving up; an assenting.

GEILLEADH, eidh, *s. m.* Submission, obedience, yielding, assent, homage; the act of submitting, assenting, or yielding. Ciùinichidh géilleadh, *yielding will pacify.—Stew. Ecc.*

GEILLIDH, *fut. aff.* of géill; which see.

GÉILLIOS, *s. f.* (*Ir. id.*) Kindness, friendship.—*Shaw.*

GEILMIN, *s.* (*Ir. id.*) A pilchard.

GEILT, *s. f.* (*Ir. id.*) Terror, fear, skittishness, cowardice; *also*, mad. Criothnaich le géilt, *shake with fear.—Sm.* Na biodh geilt orm, *let me not be afraid.—Stew. Jer.* Geilt-chrith, *quaking with fear; extreme terror; a shudder.—Stew. Is.*

GEILT, *s.* (*Ir. id.*) A wild man or woman; one who dwells in woods or deserts; *also*, mad.

Lat. Celtæ. *Gaulish*, Coilte. *W.* guylht, *a wild woman.*

GÉIM, *v. n.* (*Lat.* gemo.) Low, as a cow; bellow. *Pret.* gheim; *fut. aff. a.* géimidh. See also GEUM.

GEIMHEAN, ein, *s. m.* Restraint, bondage.—*Shaw.*

GEIMHLE, *s. f.* A fetter; a lever; a pair of pincers.

W. gevail. *Ir.* geimhiol *and* geibheal.

GEIMHLEACH, *a.* Fettering; like a fetter; oppressive; enslaving; *substantively*, a slave, a captive.

GEIMHLEACHD, *s. f.* Bondage, slavery; *also*, a chain or fetter. Ann an geimhleachd, *in bondage, in chains.*

GEIMHLEAG, eig, *s. f.* (*Scotch*, gavelock.) A lever; an iron crow. *N. pl.* geimhleagan.

GEIMHLEAGACH, *a.* Like a lever.

GEIMHLEAN, *s. pl.* Chains, fetters, bondage. *D. pl.* geimhlibh. Le geimhlibh umha, *with chains of brass.—Stew.* 2 *K.*

GEIMHLICH, *v. a.* Chain, fetter, enslave. *Pret. a.* gheimhlich, *chained; fut. aff. a.* geimhlichidh, *shall chain.*

GEIMHLICHTE, *p. part.* of geimhlich. Chained, fettered.

GEIMHNEACHD, *s. f.* Chastity, continence.

GÉIMNICH, *s. f.* (*Ir.* geamraich.) Lowing; bellowing.

GEIMNIDH, *a.* Chaste, continent; moderate, temperate.—*Macdon.* Gu geimnidh, *chastely.* Written also *geamnuidh.*

GEIMNIDHEACHD, *s. f.* Chastity, continence.

† GEIN, *s. m.* A sword.

GEIN, *v.* Beget, bring forth, produce. *Pret. a.* ghein; *fut. aff.* geinidh. See GIN.

Gr. γειω. *Lat.* † geno. *Ir.* gein.

GEINEAG, eig, *s. f.* A germ or bud. *N. pl.* geineagan.

GEINEALACH, *s.* See GINEALACH.

GEINEALAICH, *v.* Vegetate, grow, produce, branch out, as a tree or as a family. *Pret. a.* gheinealaich, *vegetated.*

GEINEAMHUINN. See GINEAMHUINN.

GEINEIL, *a.* Prolific, productive, genial, generative; *also*, stout, compact.

Geinearalt, *s. m.* A general.

Geinn, *s. f.* A wedge. *N. pl.* geinneachan, *wedges.* *Ir.* gein. *Lat.* cuneus. *W.* cyn. *Span.* cuno. *Arm.* geun, cuen, *and* cyn. *Fr.* coin. *Gr.* *κειῶν and κῶνος, splitting wood.*

Geinn, *v. a.* Wedge; pin; squeeze, press. *Pret. a.* gheinn, *wedged; fut. aff. a.* geinnidh.

Geinneach, *a.* (*Ir. id.*) Wedged; pinned; cuneiform; like a wedge; firm; compact; stout.

Geinneag, eig, *s. f.* A pundle; a short fat female; a little wedge. *N. pl.* geinneagan.

Geinneagach, *a.* Short, squat; full of little wedges.

Geinneal, il, *s. m.* A cuneiform phalanx; an order of battle in the form of a wedge.

Geinneanta, *a.* Firm; like a wedge.—*Turn.*

Geinnear, eir, *s. m.* A rammer, a mallet, a hammer.

Geinnearachd, *s. f.* Ramming, hammering.

Geinnealachd, *s. f.* Stoutness, firmness, compactness.

Géinneil, *a.* (geinn-amhuil.) Cuneiform; stout, firm, compact.

Geinneireachd, *s. f.* Hammering; wedging; a continued hammering.

Geintear, eir, *s. m.* A sower, a planter.—*Shaw.* *N. pl.* geintearan.

Geintileach, ich, *s. m.* A gentile; a pagan. *N. pl.* geintilich.

Geintileach, *a.* Gentile, pagan, heathen.

Geintileachd, *s. f.* Paganism, heathenism, idolatry.

Geintileas, eis, *s. m.* Paganism, heathenism, idolatry.

Geir, *v. a.* Grease, besmear, or anoint with grease. *Pret. a.* gheir; *fut. aff. a.* geiridh, *shall grease.*

Geir, geire, *s. f.* (*Ir. id.*) Tallow or suet, fat, grease. Geir cartach, *cart-grease.*

Géire, *s. f.* Sharpness, acuteness, subtlety, sourness, smartness, cleverness; *also*, stuff; substance. *Scotch*, gear.

Géire, *com.* and *sup.* of geur. Sharper, sharpest; sourer, sourest. Triath is géire cruaidh, *a chief of the sharpest sword.*—*Oss. Fing.*

Geireach, *a.* (*Ir. id.*) Greasy, tallowy; like grease or suet: full of suet or fat.

Géiread, eid, *s. m.* Sharpness; sourness; pungency; acuteness; smartness; increase in sharpness or in sourness. A dol an géiread, *growing more and more sharp* or *sour.* Is géirid e sin, *it is the sharper for that.*

Géir-innleachd, *s. f.* Ingenuity, invention, contrivance.

Geirnean, ein, *s. m.* A gin, trap, or snare.

Geirneanach, *a.* Full of traps or gins; like a trap; of a trap.

Geirseach, ich, *s. f.* (*Ir. id.*) A young girl.

Geirseag, eig, *s. f.* (*Ir. id.*) A young girl.—*Shaw.*

Geis, *s. f.* A spear, a javelin; a fishing-spear. *Gr.* *γαισὸν and γαισὸς.* *Lat.* gæsum, *a Gallic spear.* The *geis*, latinised *gæsum*, (see *Virg. Æn.* vii. and viii.) was a weapon peculiar to the old Gauls, as was the *pilum* to the Romans, and the *sarissa* to the Macedœmonians.

Geis, *s. f.* (*Ir. id.*) A vow; a prayer; a custom; a swan; a prohibition.—*Shaw.*

† **Geiseadh**, idh, *s. m.* (*Ir. id.*) A vow; a prayer; imposing tribute.—*Shaw.*

Géisg, geisge, *s. f.* (*Ir. id.*) A crash; a creaking noise; a loud crashing noise; *rarely*, a roar. Leig e géisg as, *it crashed.*

Géisg, *v. n.* Crash; creak. *Pret. a.* ghéisg, *crashed; fut. aff.* géisgidh, *shall crash.*

Géisge', *for* geisgeadh; which see.

Géisgeach, *a.* Crashing; causing a creaking or a crashing sound.

Géisgeadh, idh, *s. m.* A crashing; a creaking.

Géisgeadh, (a), *pr. part.* of géisg. Crashing; creaking. Crainn le dealan a geisge', *trees crashing with lightning.*—*Oss. Cathula.*

Géisgeil, *a.* Crashing, creaking; roaring.

Géisgeil, *s. f.* (*from* géisg.) A continued crashing noise; clangor; a creaking sound. Ri géisgeil, *crashing* or *changing.*

Geisneach, *a.* Enchanted; like a charm; enchanting; conjuring.

Geò, *s. m.* See **Geodha** *or* **Geothadh**.

Geoc, **Geochd**, *s. f.* See **Geoic**.

Geòc, *s. f.* Gluttony, revelling, debauchery.

Geocach, *a.* (*Ir. id.*) Wry-necked. Geocach giùgach, *wry-necked and jolt-headed.*—*Macint.* Written also *geochdach.*

Geòcach, *a.* Gluttonous; strolling. Duine geòcach, *a gluttonous man.*—*Stew. Matt.*

Geòcach, aich, *s. m.* (*Ir.* geocach, *a low parasite.*) A glutton; a parasite; a stroller, a vagabond. *N. pl.* geòcaich.

Geòcachd, *s. f.* (*Ir. id.*) Gluttony.

Geòcaich, *v. n.* Gormandise; stroll; devour. *Pret.* gheòcaich; *fut. aff.* geòcaichidh.

Geocail, *a.* (geoc-amhuil.) Gluttonous; parasitical; strolling.

Geòcair, *s. m.* (*Ir.* geocthoir.) A glutton or gormandiser; a reveller; a debauchee. Am misgear agus an geòcair, *the drunkard and the glutton.*—*Stew. Pro.* *N. pl.* geòcairean.

Geòcaireachd, *s. f.* Gluttony, debauchery, revelry, depravity. Misg agus geòcaireachd, *drunkenness and revelry.*—*Stew. Gal.*

Geòchdach, *a.* See **Geòcach**.

Geodh, **Geodha**, *s. m.* A cave; a cove; a bay; a creek. Thug iad an aire do gheodha, *they observed a creek.*—*Stew. Acts, ref.*

Geodh-lann, -lainn, *s. m.* A goose-pen.

Geoic, *s. f.* A wry neck. Fear na geoic, *the wry-necked man.*

Geoidh, *gen. sing.* and *n. pl.* of geadh.

Geoin, *s. f.* A fool, a foolish person; a confused noise.—*Shaw.* Derision; assurance; proof.

Geòl, geoil, *s. f.* A yawl, a small barge. Geol chaol, *a river-cutter.*

Geolach, aich, *s. m.* (*perhaps* guailleach.) A shoulder-band, formerly put on dead persons in the Highlands. Geolach ort, *thy death-belt on thee; I wish thou wert dead;*—a common Highland imprecation.

Geolan, ain, *s. m.* (*Ir. id.*) A fan. *N. pl.* geolain.

Geòl-mhac, *s. m.* (*Ir. id.*) A jowl.

† **Geon**, geoin, *s. m.* (*Ir. id.*) An oath; security; proof.

Geòsach, aich, *s. m.* The perinæum. Written more frequently *ceòsach.*

Geosadan, ain, *s. m.* (*Ir. id.*) A shaft; an arrow; a stalk. *N. pl.* geosadain.

Geòsan, ain, *s. m.* (*Ir. id.*) The belly; *also*, a glutton.

Geotha, **Geothadh**, aidh, *s. m.* (*Ir. id.*) A bay, a creek; a cave; a cove; the sea.

Geuban, ain, *s. m.* (*Sax.* gaepan, *open the mouth wide.* *Eng.* gape. *Scotch*, geubie, *a craw.*) The craw or crop of a bird.—*Stew. Lev.*

Geubanach, *a.* (*from* geuban.) Having a large craw or crop, as a bird.

GEUG, *v. n.* Branch, sprout, propagate. *Pret. a.* gheug, *branched; fut. aff. a.* geugaidh, *shall branch.*

GEUG, geuga, *or* géig, *s. f.* A branch or bough of a tree; a young person, *especially,* a young handsome female; a man's arms. *N. pl.* geugan, *branches.* Fo' dhubhar a geuga, *under the shade of its branch.—Stew. Ezek.* A gheugan aillidh, *its beauteous branches.—Orr.* A gheug aillidh, *the beauteous maid.—Oss. Carricth. D. pl.* geugaibh.

GEUGACH, *a.* Branchy, branching, having long boughs or branches. Air craoibh gheugaich, *on a branching tree.—Oss. Derm. Com.* and *sup.* geugaiche, *more* or *most branchy.*

† GEULRAN, ain, *s. m.* A fan. *N. pl.* geulrain.—*Shaw.*

GEUM, géim, *s. m.* (*Gr.* γεμω, *onustus sum. Lat.* gemo, *to groan. Du.* gemor, *murmur.*) A low, a bellow; a lowing or bellowing; a roar. An dean damh geum? *will the ox bellow?—Stew. Job.* Fann-gheum laogh, *the faint lowing of calves.—Macfar.*

GEUM, *v. n.* Low, bellow, roar. *Pret.* gheum, *lowed; fut. aff. a.* geumaidh, *shall low.*

GEUMNAICH, *s. f.* Continued lowing, bellowing; a roaring. Geumnaich a chruidh, *the lowing of the cattle.—Stew. Sam.*

GEUR, *a.* (*Ir. id. W.* egyr, *sharp. Lat.* garum, *pickle.*) Sharp in edge or point; sour in taste or temper; keen; severe, rigid, strict; clever, quick, sagacious, penetrating; shrill. Ann am briathraibh geur, *in bitter words.—Mac Lach.* An iomguinn ghéir, *in keen affliction.—Ardar.* Sleagh is géire ceann, *a sharp-pointed spear.—Oss. Croma.* Fuaim geur, *a shrill sound.—Oss. Fing.* Gu geur, *sharply, severely, quickly. Com.* and *sup.* géire.

GEURA, GEURADH, aidh, *s. m.* Sharpness; the edge of a bladed weapon; a sharp point. Geura na cruaidh, *the sharp edge of the sword.—Oss. Tem.*

GEURACHADH, aidh, *s. m.* A sharpening; a setting, as of a bladed instrument; a souring; a growing sour or bitter.

GEURACHADH, (a), *pr. part.* of geuraich. Sharpening; a souring.

GEURAD, aid, *s. m., from* geur. (*Ir. id.*) Sharpness; sourness; rigidness, strictness; increase in sharpness or sourness. A dol an geurad, *growing more and more sharp.*

GEURAG-BHILEACH, *s. f.* (*Ir. id.*) The herb agrimony.—*Shaw.*

GEURAICH, *v. a.* (*from* geur.) Sharpen; set; make sour; make rigid; make smart, quick, or clever. *Pret. a.* gheuraich; *fut. aff. a.* gheuraichidh; *fut. pass.* geuraichear, *shall be sharpened.—Stew. Pro.*

GEURAICHTE, *past part.* of geuraich. Sharpened; set; soured.

GEUR-AIRE, *s. f.* Marked attention, particular attention. Thoir geur-aire, *mark well.—Stew. Ezek.*

GEUR-AMHRAIC, *v. n.* Looks harply or minutely; search minutely.

GEUR-AMHARC, airc, *s. m.* A sharp or minute search, a sharp look out.—*Stew. Job.*

GEURANACH, *a.* Sarcastic; witty.

GEURANACHD, *s. f.* (*Ir. id.*) Sarcasm, wit; arguing.

GEUR-BHILE, *s. f.* (*Ir. id.*) A foul or opprobrious mouth; a sour leaf or blade.

GEUR-BHILEACH, *a.* Bitter in speech, acrimonious; having a pointed leaf or blade; having a tart blade or leaf.

GEUR-BHILEACH, *s. f.* (*Ir. id.*) The herb agrimony.—*Shaw.*

GEUR-BHILEAG, eig, *s. f.* A sour leaf or blade. *N. pl.* geur-bhileagan, *sour leaves.*

GEUR-CHLUAS, aise, *s. f.* A sharp ear or hearing; short notice.

GEUR-CHLUASACH, *a.* Sharp-eared, having a quick ear.

GEUR-CHUIS, *s. f.* (*Ir. id.*) Subtlety, cunning. Fear na geur-chuis, *the cunning man.*

GEUR-CHUISEACH, *a.* (*Ir. id.*) Subtle, cunning; ingenious; strict, rigorous.

GEUR-FHIACLACH, *a.* Sharp-toothed; serrated. Corran geur-fhiaclach, *a sharp-toothed sickle.—Macfar.*

GEUR-FHIOS, *s. f.* Intelligence, clear knowledge. Tha geur-fhios agam air, *I have a clear knowledge of it.*

GEUR-FHIOSRACH, *a.* Intelligent, thoroughly intelligent.

GEUR-FHOCAL, ail, *s. m.* (*Ir. id.*) A sharp word, a harsh speech; a repartee, a sarcasm; a gibe, a witticism.

GEUR-FHOCLACH, *a.* (*Ir. id.*) Witty, sharp-worded; satirical, sarcastic.

GEUR-GHAOTH, -ghaoithe, *s. f.* (*Ir. id.*) A sharp or biting wind.

GEUR-GHATH, *s. m.* (*Ir. id.*) A sharp spear; a dart; a sting.

GEUR-GHOIMH, *s. f.* Severe pain; a throb of anguish. Written also *geur-ghoith.*

GEUR-GHOIMHEACH, *a.* In severe pain; throbbing with pain; causing severe pain.

GEUR-GHOITH, *s. f.* Severe pain; a throb of anguish.—*Stew. Joel.*

GEUR-INNLEACHD, *s. f.* (*Ir. id.*) Invention; inventiveness, cleverness; sagacity; subtlety.

GEUR-INNLEACHDACH, *a.* (*Ir. id.*) Inventive, ingenious; sagacious.

GEUR-LANN, -lainn, *s. m.* A sharp sword. Iomairt gheur-lann, *the play of sharp swords.—Fingalian Poem.*

GEUR-LANNACH, *a.* Wearing a sharp sword; armed with a sharp sword.

GEUR-LEAN, *v. a.* (*Ir.* gearlean.) Persecute; pursue hotly. *Pret. a.* gheur-lean, *persecuted; fut. aff. a.* geur-leanaidh, *shall persecute.*

GEUR-LEANACHD, *s. f.* Persecution; a hot pursuit, a warm chase.

GEAR-LEANMHUINN, *s. f.* (*Ir.* gear-leanamhuin.) Persecution; a hot pursuit or chase. Geur-leanmhuinn no gorta, *persecution nor famine.—Stew. Rom.* Dean geur-leanmhuinn, *persecute.*

GEUR-LEANMHUINNEACH, *a.* Persecuting; prone to persecute; causing persecution; like persecution; of, or pertaining to, persecution.

GEUR-LEANMHUINNICHE, *s. m.* A persecutor.

GEUR-MHOTHACHADH, aidh, *s. m.* A clear conviction; a keenness of feeling; a lively perception.

GEUR-MHOTHAICH, *v. n.* Feel smartly or keenly. *Pret. a.* Gheur-mothaich, *felt smartly.*

GEUR-RANNSACHADH, aidh, *s. m.* A thorough searching; strict scrutiny or examination; a diligent searching; the act of searching or examining strictly. Rinn iad geur-rannsachadh, *they made a diligent search.*

GEUR-SHEALLACH, *a.* Sharp-sighted; clear-sighted.

GEUR-SHUILE, *s. f.* A sharp or quick eye, a keen or penetrating eye. *N. pl.* geur-shuilean.

GEUR-SHUILEACH, *a.* Having a quick eye; keen or sharp-sighted.

GHABH, *pret. a.* of gabh. Took. Ghabh iad sa chéile, *they grasped each other.* See GABH.

GHABHADH, *imp. sub.* of gabh. Would take or contain. See GABH.

GHABHAIDH, *asp. form* of gabhaidh; which see.

Ghabhar, *s.*, *asp. form* of gabhar; which see.

Ghabhar, *v.*, *asp. form* of gabhar, *fut. pass.* of gabh; which see.

Ghainne. See Gainne *or* Gann.

Ghàir, *pret.* of gàir; which see.

Ghairbh, *asp. form* of gairbh. See Garbh.

Ghairm, *pret.* of gairm. Called; shouted; proclaimed. See Gairm.

Ghaisge, *s. f.*, *asp. form* of gaisge. Bravery. A ghaisge, *his bravery.* See Gaisge.

Ghaisgeach, *asp. form* of gaisgeach; which see.

Ghallan, ain, *s. m.*, *asp. form* of gallan; which see.

Ghann, *asp. form* of gann; which see.

Ghaoil, *voc. sing.* of gaol.

Ghaol. See Gaol.

Ghaoth, *asp. form* of gaoth; which see.

Gharbh, *asp. form* of garbh; which see.

Gheal, *asp. form* of geal. White. Airde gheal an làtha, *broad daylight.*

Ghealach, *asp. form* of gealach.

Gheall, *pret. a.* of geall. Betted, laid a wager; promised. See Geall.

Gheall, *asp. form* of geall.

Ghean, *asp. form* of gean; which see.

Ghearr. See Gearr.

Gheat, *asp. form* of geat; which see.

Gheibh, *fut. aff. a.* of faigh. Shall get or find. See Faigh.

Gheibheadh, *pret. sub.* of faigh. Would get. Gheibheadh iad fasga, *they would obtain shelter.—Old Poem.*

Gheibhear, *fut. pass.* of faigh. Would or might be got.

Gheibhinn, 1 *sing. pret. sub.* of faigh; which see.

Gheibhteadh, *pret. sub. pass.* of faigh. Might be found. Gheibhte a sheasas cath ri m' lann, *there may be found who can contend with my sword.—Old Poem.*

Ghéill, *pret. a.* of géill. Yielded, submitted. See Geill.

Gheilt, *asp. form* of geilt; which see.

Ghéire, *asp. form* of géire, an *inflection* of geur; which see.

Gheuban. See Geuban.

Gheug, *asp. form* of geug; which see.

Gheum, *pret. a.* of geum. Lowed, bellowed.

Gheur, *a.*, *asp. form* of geur; which see.

Ghil, *asp. form* of gil; *inflection* of geal; which see.

Ghin, *pret. a.* of gin. Produced. See Gin.

Ghiomh, *asp. form* of giomh; which see.

Ghiorraich, *pret. a.* of giorraich. Shortened, abridged.

Ghios, *prep.* To, towards. Ghios na tràigh, *towards the shore.—Oss.*

Ghiùlain, *pret. a.* of giùlain. Carried, bore. See Giùlain.

Ghlac, *pret.* of glac. Caught. See Glac.

Ghlac, *asp. form* of glac; which see.

Ghlaic, *asp. form* of glaic; an *inflection* of glac, *s.*; which see.

Ghlaine, *a.* See Glan.

Ghlais, *pret. a.* of glais. Locked; clasped.

Ghlais, *a.*, *asp. form* of glais; an *inflection* of glas; which see.

Ghlaodh, *pret. a.* of glaodh. Glued; shouted. See Glaodh.

Ghlaodh, *s. m.*, *asp. form* of glaodh; which see.

Ghlas. See Glas.

Ghleann, ghlinne, *asp. form* of gleann; which see.

Ghleidh, *pret. a.* of gleidh.

Ghleus, *pret. a.* of gleus. Tuned; prepared; trimmed. See Gleus.

Ghlic, *asp. form* of glic; which see.

Ghlinne, *asp. form* of glinne; *gen. sing.* of gleann; which see.

Ghliocas, ais, *s.*, *asp. form* of gliocas; which see.

Ghloine. See Gloine.

Ghloine, *a.* See Glan.

Ghlòir, *s. f.*, *asp. form* of glòir; which see.

Ghluais, *pret. a.* of gluais. Moved, stirred. See Gluais.

Ghluaiseadh, *pret. sub. act.* and *pret. pass.* of gluais; which see.

Ghlùn, *asp. form* of glùn, *s.*; which see.

Ghnàth, *asp. form* of gnàth. Usage, custom. Bu ghnàth leam, *I was wont.*

Ghnàth, (a), *adv.* Always, continually, usually, incessantly. Is taitneach a ghnàth do ghuth, *pleasant always is thy voice.—Oss. Tem.*

Ghné, **Ghnéth**, *asp. forms* of gné *and* gnéth; which see.

Ghniomh, *asp. form* of gniomh. Work; deed. A ghniomh, *his work.* See Gniomh.

Ghnùis, *asp. form* of gnùis. Countenance, aspect. Mo ghnùis, *my countenance.*

Ghoid, *pret. a.* of goid. Stole. See Goid.

Ghoideadh, *pret. sub. a.* and *pret. pass.* of goid. Would steal; was stolen. See Goid.

Ghoir, *pret. a.* of goir. Crew. See Goir.

Ghorm, *a.*, *asp. form* of gorm; which see.

Ghrad, *a.*, *asp. form* of grad; which see.

Ghràdh, aidh, *s.*, *asp. form* of gradh. Love. A ghràdh, *his love.* See Gradh.

Ghràdhach, *a.*, *asp. form* of gradhach.

Ghreann, *asp. form* of greann; which see.

Ghreas, *pret. a.* of greas. Hastened. Ghreas e, *he hastened;* ghreas e air, *he hastened.*

Ghréine, *asp. form* of greine; *gen. sing.* of grian.

Ghrian, *s. f.*, *asp. form* of grian.

Ghrinn, *a.*, *asp. form* of grinn. Fine; handsome; elegant. Boirionnach ghrinn, *a handsome woman.* See Grinn.

Ghrod, *pret.* of grod. Rotted. See Grod.

Ghruaidh, *s.*, *asp. form* of gruaidh; which see.

Ghruaim, *s. f.*, *asp. form* of gruaim. A frown. A ghruaim, *his frown.* See Gruaim.

Ghruamach, *a.*, *asp. form* of gruamach.

Ghuidh, *pret.* of guidh. Beseeched. See Guidh.

Ghuidh, *s. f.*, *asp. form* of guidh. Prayer, entreaty. Mo ghuidh, *my prayer.* See Guidh.

Ghuil, *pret. a.* of gul *or* gùl. Wept. See Gul.

Ghuth, *s.*, *asp. form* of guth. Voice; word; report.

Giabhair, *s. f.* A prostitute.—*Shaw.* *N. pl.* giabhairean.

Giabhaireachd, *s. f.* Prostitution.

Gial, géile, *s. f.* A jaw, a cheek; gills, as of a fish. Bhuail thu an gial, *thou hast struck their cheeks.—Sm.* Cnaimh géile, *a jawbone.—Stew. Jud. ref.* *N. pl.* gialan; *d. pl.* gialaibh. Ann ad ghialaibh, *in thy jaws.—Stew. Ezek.* *Fr.* gueule. *Ir.* giall. *W.* kill. *Eng.* gills.

Gialach, *a.* Having jaws, jawed, cheeked, having large jaws or cheeks.

Gial-bhrat, ait, *s. m.* (*Ir. id.*) A neckcloth or cravat.

† **Giall**, *s.* Hostages, a pledge.

Giaman. See Geaman.

Giamh, *s. f.* A defect or fault, a flaw or blemish; fear, trepidation; *rarely*, a lock of hair. *N. pl.* giamhan.

GIAMHACH, *a.* (*Ir. id*) Defective, blemished, faulty, in trepidation. *Com* and *sup* giamhaiche, *more* or *most defective.*

GIANACH, *a* (*Ir. id*) Lazy, inactive —*Shaw.* *Com.* and *sup.* gianaiche.

GIANACHAS, ais, *s m* (*Ir. id*) Laziness, inactivity, indolence.

GIANAIR, *s. m.* (*Ir. id.*) A sluggard. *N. pl.* gianairean

GIANAIREACHD, *s f.* Sluggishness, the conduct of a sluggard.

GIAR, *a.* See GEUR

GIBEACH, *a* Neat, tidy, trim, spruce.—*Macint* *Also,* rough, hairy *Com* and *sup* gibiche.

GIBEACHAS, ais, *s. m.* Neatness, tidiness, spruceness; hairiness, roughness

GIBEACHD, *s f.* Neatness, tidiness, spruceness; hairiness, roughness

GIBEAG, eig, *s f* A little sheaf; a bundle, a handful, particularly of dry unmilled flax; a fringe, a flounce *N pl* gibeagan.

GIBEAGACH, *a.* In little sheaves or bundles; having a fringe or flounce.

GIBEAGACHADH, aidh, *s m* A tying up, as unmilled flax, in small bundles.

GIBEAGAICH, *v. a* Tie in small handfuls, as unmilled flax *Pret a* ghibeagaich

GIBEAGAN, ain, *s m.* A fringe —*Macd* Also, *N pl.* of gibeag

GIBEAL, eil, *s m.* See GIOBAL

GIBEAN, ein, *s m* A kind of fat pudding made in the Hebrides

GIBEAN-SUIRICHE, *s m* A bur.

† GIBHIS, *s f* A valley, a glen.—*Shaw.*

GIBHTE, *s f* A gift. *N pl.* gibhtean Mar ghibhte, *as a gift*

GIBHTEALACHD, *s. f.* The condition of being gifted with good qualities.

GIBHTEAMAS, ais, *s m* A donation, a gift.—*Shaw.*

GIBIDH, *s m* A misnaming of Gileabart, *Gilbert*

GIBLINN, *s f.* April.

GIBNE, *s c* (*Ir. id*) A thread; a greyhound, a cub; a cupping-horn.—*Shaw.*

† GIDH, *conj.* See GIDHEADH

GIDHEADH, *conj* (*Ir id*) Though, although, yet. Gidheadh seallaidh mi, *yet I will look* —*Stew Jon*

GIDHIS, *s f.* (*Teut* ghiise. *Fr* and *Eng* guise) A mask or disguise, a masquerade

GIDHISEAR, eir, *s m* (*Scotch,* gysar.) A man in mask, a guiser. *N pl* gidhisearan

GIDHISEARACHD, *s f.* A masquerade; a masking; a going about in mask

GIGEALL, ill, *s m* A tickle, a tickling sensation. Cha 'n 'eil gigeall annad, *you are insensible to tickling.*

GIGEALLACH, *a* Tickling; easily tickled *Com* and *sup* gigeallaiche.

GIGILL, *v. a.* (*Bisc.* kigli *Ir* gigil) Tickle. *Pret a.* ghigill, *tickled, fut aff. a* gigillidh, *shall tickle.*

† GIL, *s f* (*Ir. id*) Water

GIL, *gen* of geal, which see

GILE, *com* and *sup.* of geal. Whiter, whitest. A's gile laimh, *of the whitest hand* —*Oss Com.*

GILE, *s f.* (*Ir. id*) Whiteness; brightness, a white part. Gach aon air an robh gile, *every one that had white in it* —*Stew Gen.* Deirge agus gile na gnùis, *red and white in her visage.*—*R*

GILEAB, eib, *s. f* A chisel. *N. pl* gileaban.

GILEAD, *s m.* Whiteness; increase in whiteness. A dol an gilead, *growing more and more white.*

GILL See GEALL

GILLE, *s. m* (*Ir* giolla) A lad, a young man, a boy; a man-servant. *N. pl* gillean. Na leig do laimh air a ghille, *lay not thine hand upon the lad.*—*Stew. Gen.* Dh' fhàs na gillean, *the boys grew.*—*Stew Gen* Leanabh gille, *a man-child,* gille-bride, *an oyster-catcher,* gille cas-fhiuch, *one of the attendants of a Highland chieftain;* gille cois, *a footman;* gille-comh-streathainn, *one of the attendants of a Highland chieftain,* gille each, *a groom;* gille graidh, *a secretary, a chief servant,* gille greasaidh, *a postilion,* gille guirmein, *corn-scabious;* gille mirein, *a whirligig,* gille trusarnais, *one of the attendants of a Highland chieftain,* gille ruithe, *a footman,* gille mu leann, *a sea-weed like a rope,* gille copain, gille cupain, *a cup-bearer,* gille sguain, *a train-bearer.* The Gael use *ghille* in addressing a young man or boy, as, cia mar tha thu, ghille? *how do you do, lad?*

GILLEAGAN, ain, *s. m.* A doll. *N. pl* gilleagain

GILLE-BHRÒG, *s m.* A shoeblack.

GILLE-BRIDE, *s. m* The bird pied-catcher; the *hæmatopus ostralegus* of Linnæus.

GILLE-CAS-FLIUCH, *s.* One of the attendants of a Highland chieftain, whose business it was to carry his master across streams and fords. *N. pl.* gille-cas-fliuch.

GILLE-COISE, *s. m.* A footman.

GILLE-COMHSTREATHAINN, *s m.* One of the attendants of a Highland chieftain, whose business it was to take care of his master's horse.

GILLE-COPAIN, *s m* A cup-bearer *N pl.* gillean-copain.

GILLE-EACH, *s m* A groom, a stable-boy.

GILLEACHD, *s. f.* (*Ir.* giollachd) Service; management of an affair, conduct —*Shaw.*

GILLEAN, ein, *s m.* (*Ir.* gillin) An eunuch.

GILLEAN, *n pl.* of gille, which see

GILLEAS, eis, *s. m.* The condition of a man-servant.

GILLE-FIONND, *s. m* That species of shell-fish called *wilk.*

GILLE-GORMAIN, *s. m.* Corn-scabious. More frequently written *gille-guirmein.*

GILLE-GREASAIDH, *s. m* A postilion *N pl.* gillean-greasaidh.

GILLE-GUIRMEIN, *s. m.* Corn-scabious.

GILLE-MIREIN, *s m* A whirligig.

GILLE-MÙCHAIN, *s m* A chimneysweep.

GILLE MU LEANN, *s m* Sea-weed like a rope.—*Shaw.*

GILLE-PHIOBAIR, *s. m.* A bagpiper's attendant, who carried the bagpipes when not played upon He formed one of the train of a Highland chieftain, as the piper thought it degrading to carry the instrument about with him.

GILLE-RUITHE, *s m.* A footman, a runner; a post. Ni bu luaithe na gille-ruithe, *swifter than a post.*—*Stew. Job.*

GILLE-SGUAIN, *s m* A trainbearer.

GILLE-TRUSAIRNEIS, *s m.* One of the attendants of a Highland chieftain, whose business it was to carry the baggage or wallet, a baggage-man.

GILM, *s m.* (*Ir id*) A buzzard.

GILMEAN, ein, *s m* A spruce, trim fellow.

GILMEANACH, *a* Dainty; spruce, trim. Gu gilmeanach, *sprucely.*

GIN, *s* A substance, a being, a person; a production, a thing; a sort, a kind; an individual of any description. Am bheil gin an so? *is there any person here?*

Turk gins, *a race* *Run.* kyn. *Goth.* kun. *Teut.* kunne. *Germ.* kunn. *Old Sax* cynne *Eng.* kin. *Syr.* con, *to*

be made. Eth. con, *id. Arab.* can, *to beget. Arm.* gin, *a wife.*

Gin, *v. a.* Beget, produce, gender. *Pret. a.* ghin; *fut. aff. a.* ginidh, *shall produce.* Ginidh an tarbh, *the bull shall gender.—Stew. Job.* Ginibh mic, *beget sons.—Stew. Jer. Gr.* γινω. *Lat.* † geno. *W.* eigian. *Ir.* gin. *Eth.* con. *Arab.* can.

Gineadan, *s.* (*Ir. id.*) The genitals.

Gineag, eig, *s. f.* A germ, a sprout. *N. pl.* gineagan.

Gineagach, *a.* Having germs or sprouts; like a germ or sprout.

Gineal, eil, *s. m.* (*W.* genill.) A race or offspring, lineage, children; a generation. Dannsaidh an gineal, *their children shall dance.—Stew. Job.*

Ginealach, aich, *s. m.* Genealogy, a race, a pedigree, a family, a generation. Ginealach taghta, *a chosen generation.—Stew.* 1 *Pet. N. pl.* ginealachan; *d. pl.* ginealachaibh. Na'r ginealachaibh, *in your generations.—Stew. Ex. Ir.* ginealach, *a race. Gr.* γενεθλιακος, *pertaining to nativities.*

Ginealaich, *v. n.* Produce, grow, vegetate; branch, as a tree or as a family. *Pret. a.* ghinealaich, *produced; fut. aff. a.* ginealaichidh.

Gineamhuinn, *s. f.* (*Ir. id.*) A bud; a sprout; birth; conception; a producing, a sprouting, a production, a birth. O'n ghineamhuinn, *from the conception.—Stew. Hos.*

Gineamhuinneach, *a.* Buddy, breedy, prolific, genitive.

Gineamhuinneachd, *s. f.* The state of being prolific; productiveness, generativeness, genitiveness.

Gineanta, *a.* (*from* gin.) Easy of growth, apt to grow, prolific.

Gineantachd, *s. f.* The state of being prolific, genitiveness, generativeness.

Gineideach, *a.* (*Gr.* γεννητικος.) Prolific, generative, productive. *Com.* and *sup.* gineidiche.

Gineil, *a.*, gin-amhuil. (*Lat.* genialis. *Arm.* guenuell.) Prolific, productive; genial.

Gingean, ein, *s. m.* A cask, a barrel.—*Shaw.*

Ginidh, *s.* A corruption of *guinea.*

Ginntealach, ich, *s. m.* A Gentile, a pagan. *N. pl.* gintealaiche.

Gintealach, *a.* Gentile, pagan.

Ginntealas, ais, *s. m.* Gentilism, paganism.

Gintear, ir, *s. m.* (*Lat.* genitor.) A father, a parent. Umhal do 'd ghinteiribh talmhaidh, *obedient to thy earthly parents.—Old Poem.*

Gintinn, (a), *part.* of gin. Begetting, producing.

Giob, *v. a.* (*Ir. id.*) Pull, pluck.

Giob, gioba, *s. m.* (*Ir. id.*) A tail; any thing hairy or rough; a rug.

Giobach, *a.* Hairy; rough; *also*, neat, trim, tidy. An fhairge ghiobach, *the rough sea.—Macfar. Com.* and *sup.* giobaiche.

Giobachas, ais, *s. m.* Hairiness; roughness; neatness, trimness, tidiness.

Giobadh, aidh, *s. m.* (*Ir. id.*) A pull, a tug.

Giobag, aig, *s. f.* (*Ir. id.*) A fringe; a rag; a little sheaf; a handful, or little sheaf, of unmilled flax; a largesse; a boon. *N. pl.* giobagan.

Giobagach, *a.* Fringed; ragged; in little sheaves. *Com.* and *sup.* giobagaiche.

Giobagachadh, aidh, *s. m.* A fringing; a tying up in small leaves.

Giobagaich, *v. a.* (*from* giobag.) Fringe; tie in small sheaves, as unmilled flax. *Pret. a.* ghiobagaich; *fut. aff.* giobagaichidh.

Giobagan, ain, *s. m.* A fringe.

Giobagan, *n. pl.* of giobag.

Giobaiche, *com.* and *sup.* of giobach; which see.

Giobaichead, eid, *s. m.* Hairiness; roughness; increase in hairiness. A dol an giobaichead, *growing more and more rough.*

Giobal, ail, *s. m.* (*Ir. id.*) A rag or clout; cast clothes; a garment; a covering; a canvass; hair; fur; a term of personal disrespect. Mar ghiobhal sean, *like an old garment.—Sm.*

Giobalach, *a.* (*Ir. id.*) Ragged; hairy; rough. *Com.* and *sup.* giobalaiche.

Giobalach, aich, *s. m.* A ragged person; a rough or hairy man. *N. pl.* giobalaich.

Giobalachd, *s. f.* Raggedness; hairiness; roughness.

Giodal, ail, *s. m.* (*Ir. id.*) Flattery, fawning language. Fear giodail, *a flatterer.*

Giodalach, *a.* (*Ir. id.*) Flattering, fawning; *also*, a flatterer. Gu giodalach, *flatteringly. Com.* and *sup.* giodalaiche.

Giodalachd, *s. f.* The habit or the practice of flattery.

Giodalaiche, *s. m.* A fawning fellow, a flatterer.

† **Giodar**, air, *s. m.* (*Ir. id.*) Dung, ordure.

Giodh, *conj.*, *for* gidheadh. (*Ir.* gidh *and* giodh.) Though, although, yet.

Giodhran, ain, *s. m.* (*Ir. id.*) A barnacle.—*Shaw.*

† **Giofach**, *a.* (*Ir. id.*) Dutiful; officious; attentive.

† **Giofachd**, *s. f.* (*Ir. id.*) Dutifulness; officiousness; attentiveness.—*Shaw.*

† **Giofag**, aig, *s. f.* (*Ir. id.*) A female client; a gipsey. *N. pl.* giofagan.

† **Giofair**, *s. m.* (*Ir. id.*) A client. *N. pl.* giofairean.

Giog, *v. n.* (*Ir. id.*) Cringe, fawn, flatter. *Pret. a.* ghiog, *cringed; fut. aff. a.* giogaidh, *shall cringe.*

Giogach, *a.* (*Ir. id.*) Prone to flatter; fawning, cringing.

† **Giogach**, aich, *s. m.* (*Ir. id.*) A budget; a bag.

Giogadh, aidh, *s. m.* (*Ir. id.*) A cringing or fawning; flattery.

Giogal, ail, *s. m.* A tickle; a pursuit.

Giogaladh, aidh, *s. m.* A tickling; a pursuing.

Giogail, *v. a.* Tickle; follow, pursue. *Pret.* ghiogail, *tickled; fut. aff.* gioglaidh. Written also *gigill*, in the sense of *to tickle.*

Giogan, ain, *s. m.* Flattery.

Giogan, ain, *s. m.* (*Ir.* giogun.) A thistle. *N. pl.* giogain.

Gioganach, *a.* Abounding in thistles; like a thistle; *also*, flattering.

Gioladh, aidh, *s. m.* (*Ir. id.*) A leaping nimbly.

Giolaid, *s. f.* (*Ir. id.*) An inlet, a little creek.

Giolam, aim, *s. m.* (*Ir. id.*) Tattle, idle talk, gabble. Giolam-goileam, *tittle-tattle.*

Giolamach, *a.* (*Ir. id.*) Tattling, prating; apt to prate or tattle; gabbling.

Giolaman, ain, *s. m.* (*Ir. id.*) A tattler, a prater. *N. pl.* giolamain.

Giolamanachd, *s. f.* (*Ir. id.*) Tattling, prating, the habit of prating.

Giolbheist, *s. f.* (*Ir. id.*) A naiad.—*Shaw.*

Giolc, *v. n.* Move nimbly; make a sudden darting movement forward. *Pret.* ghiolc; *fut. aff.* giolcaidh.

Giolc, *s. f.* (*Ir. id.*) A broom; a reed, a cane.

Giolcach, aich, *s.* (*Ir. id.*) A reed; a place where reeds grow.

Giolcadh, aidh, *s. m.* A nimble motion; a bolting forward; flippancy.

Giolcail, *a.* Broomy, reedy.

Giolcair, *s. m.* A flippant fellow; an intruder. *N. pl.* giolcairean.

Giolcanach, *a.* Flippant.

Giolcanachd, *s. f.* Flippancy.—*Shaw.*

Giolag, aig, *s. f.* A reed.

Giolla, *s. m.* More commonly written *gille;* which see.

Giollachd. See Giullachd.

Giollan, ain, *s. m.* See Giullan.

Giollaich. See Giallaich.

Giolman, ain, *s. m.* A tattler.

Giolmanach, *a.* A Tattling.

Giolmanachd, *s. f.* (*Ir. id.*) Tattling.

Giomach, aich, *s. m.* A lobster. *N. pl.* giomaich.

Giomaich, *gen. sing.* and *n. pl.* of giomach.

Giomanach, aich, *s. m.* A huntsman; a sportsman. *N. pl.* giomanaich.—*Macint.* An giomanach ullamh, *the ready sportsman.*—*Old Song.*

Giomh, *s. f.* (*Ir. id.*) A defect, fault; fear, trepidation; *rarely,* a lock or ringlet. A righ gun ghiomh! *thou dauntless king! Oss. Lodin.*

Giomhach, *a.* (*from* giomh.) Faulty, defective; timid. *Com.* and *sup.* giomhaiche, *more* or *most faulty.*

Giomhachd, *s. f.* Faultiness, defectiveness; timidity.

Giomhas, ais, *s. m.* (*Ir. id.*) A fringe.

Giomlaid, *s. f.* A gimlet. *N. pl.* giomlaidean.

Gion, *s.* (*Ir. id.*) Greed; desire; will; ambition; *rarely,* the mouth. Written also *gean.*

Gionach, *a., from* gion. (*Ir. id.*) Greedy, gluttonous, voracious, ravenous, hungry; ambitious. Mar leomhann gionach, *like a greedy lion.*—*Sm. Com.* and *sup.* gionaiche.

Gionachd, *s. f.* (*Ir. id.*) Greediness, voracity, hunger.

Gionaiche, *com.* and *sup.* of gionach. Greedier; greediest.

Gionaiche, *s. f.* Greed; avarice; ambition. Beag airson an gionaiche, *little for their avarice.*—*Mac Lach.*

Gionair, *s. m.*, gion-fhear. (*Ir. id.*) A glutton, a greedy-gut.

Gion-bhair, *s. m.* (*Ir. id.*) January.—*Shaw.*

Giontuinn, *s. f.* A producing, a generating, a breeding.

Gioradan, ain, *s. m.* A periwinkle.

Giorag, aig, *s. f.* (*Ir.* gioraic.) Timidity, fear, dread; cause of dread or fear; noise, tattle. Namhaid gun ghiorraig, *a fearless enemy.*—*Oss. Carricth.* Fo ghiorraig, *troubled; afraid.*—*Stew.* 1 *Thess. ref.*

Gioragach, *a.* Timid, skittish; causing fear; noisy; tattling. Gioragach roimh lotaibh, *afraid of wounds.*—*Old Song. Com.* and *sup.* gioragaiche.

Giorragan, ain, *s. m.* (*Ir. id.*) A babbler.

Gioraman, ain, *s. m.* (*Ir. id.*) A hungry fellow, a greedy-gut. *N. pl.* gioramain.

Gioramhach, *a.* Greedy, gluttonous, insatiate, covetous.

Gioramhachd, *s. f.* Greediness, gluttony, covetousness.

Giorr, *v. a.* (*Ir. id.*) Glut, sate. *Pret. a.* ghiorr; *fut. aff.* giorraidh.

Giorra, *com.* and *sup.* of goirrid. Shorter; shortest. Ni 's giorra na thusa, *shorter than thou art;* is e 's giorra do 'n triùir, *he is the shortest of the three.*

Giorrach, aich, *s. m.* Short dry heath; short hair; stubble.

Giorrachadh, aidh, *s. m.* A shortening, abridging; an abridgment.

Giorrachadh, (a), *pr. part.* of giorraich. Shortening, abridging.

Giorrachan, ain, *s. m.* An abridger, a curtailer; an abridgment. *N. pl.* giorrachain.

Giòrradan, ain, *s. m.* A kind of periwinkle.—*Shaw.*

Giorrad, aid, *s. m.* Shortness; advancement in shortness. Gach là dol an giorrad, *every day growing shorter.*—*Macdon.* Thaobh a ghiorraid, *by reason of its shortness.*

Giorraich, *v. a.* Shorten, curtail, abridge. *Pret. a.* ghiorraich, *shortened; fut. aff. a.* giorraichidh, *shall shorten; fut. pass.* giorraichear, *shall be shortened.*—*Stew. Prov.*

Giorraichte, *p. part.* of giorraich. Curtailed, docked, shortened, abridged.

Giorraid, *a.* Shorter. Is giorraid e sin, *it is the shorter for that.*

Giorraideach, *a.* Having large buttocks or haunches.

Giorrte, *part.* (*Gr.* κυρτος, *crooked. Lat.* curtus.) Shortened, docked, curtailed.

Giort, *v. a.* Gird; tie, lace. *Pret. a.* ghiort, *girded; fut. aff.* giortaidh.

Giort, gioirt, *s. f.* (*Dan.* giord, *a hoop. Eng.* gird *and* girth.) A girth, a cingle or belly-band; a haunch, buttocks.

† Giosg, *s. m.* (*Ir. id.*) Barm, yeast.—*Shaw.*

Giosgach, *a.* Creaking; crashing; gnashing.

Giosgain, *s. m.* (*Ir. id.*) Barm.

Giosgan, ain, *s. m.* A creaking noise, as of a cart-wheel or door-hinge; a gnashing. Giosgan fhiacal, *gnashing of teeth.*—*Stew. N. T.*

† Giost. (*Ir. id.*) Barm or yeast.

† Giostaireas, eis, *s. m.* Old age.

Giostal, ail, *s. m.* (*Ir. id.* giostal. *Lat.* gestale.) A fact; a deed. Written also *geastal.*

Giota, ai, *s. m.* An appendage; dependance.

Girt, *s. f.* A defence or protection, a bulwark.—*Stew. Num. ref. Also,* a girth, a cingle.

Girtich, *v. a.* Defend; gird. *Pret.* ghirtich; *fut. aff.* girtichidh.

Gis, *s. f.* A guess, conjecture, venture. Bi gis, *at a venture;* leigh (no) dochdair bi gis, *a quack.*

Giseag, eig, *s. f.* A charm; a superstitious ceremony. *N. pl.* giseagan, *charms.* Far am bi cailleachan bithidh giseagan, *where old wives are there will be superstition.*—*G. P.*

Giseagach, *a.* Superstitious; superstitiously; ceremonious; like a charm.

Giseal, ail, *s. m.* (*Ir.* giseil.) A line.

Gisreag, eig, *s. f.* A charm, a superstitious ceremony. Written also *giseag.*

Gisreagach, *a.* See Giseagach.

Giuban. See Giubhan.

Giubhal, ail, *s. m.* (*Ir. id.*) The chirping of birds.

Giubhan, ain, *s. m.* (*Ir.* giuban. *W.* guybedin.) A fly.

Giubhas, ais, *s. m.* and *f.* Fir; pine. Giubhas nam mor shliabh, *the firs of the mountains.*—*Oss. Tem.* Craobh ghiubhais, *a fire-tree;* crann-giubhais, *a fir-tree;* bord giubhais, *deal.* Written also *giumhais.*

Giubhasach, aich, *s. f.* A fir-wood. Anns a ghiubhasach, *in the fir-wood.*

Giubhasach, *a.* Abounding in fir; like fir.

Giudal, ail, *s. m.* (*Ir.* giutal.) Prattle, tattle.

Giùgach, *a.* (*Ir. id.*) Jolt-headed; drooping the head sideways; drooping with cold; starving. Geocach giùgach, *wry-necked and jolt-headed.*—*Macint.*

Giùig, *s. f.* (*Ir. id.*) A jolt-head; a drooping of the head, as occasioned by a side blast; a shrinking of the body from cold. Tha gùig air gach duilean, *every creature droops with cold.—Macfar.*

GIÙLAIN, *v. a.* (*Ir. id.*) Carry, convey, bear, behave, suffer, put up with, endure. *Pret. a.* ghiùlain, *carried*, *fut. aff. a.* giùlainidh, *shall carry*. Ghiùlain i an laoch, *she conveyed the hero.—Oss. Gaul.* Giùlain le, *bear with, endure.—Stew. Rom.* Giùlain leam, *put up with me; fut. pass*, giùlainear

GIÙLAN, ain, *s. m.* (*Ir. id.*) A bearing, a carrying; carriage, conduct, bearing, behaviour; a funeral. Atharrachadh giùlain, *a change of conduct.—Stew. Pro.* Giùlan laochmhor, *heroic bearing.*

GIÙLAN, (a), *pr part* of giulain. Carrying, conveying, conducting; behaving. A giùlan a chlarsaich, *carrying his harp —Oss. Conn.*

† GIULLA, *s. m.* (now written *gille.*) A boy, a lad, a youth; a servant. Cia do thùinidh, a ghiulla? *where is thy dwelling, youth?—Fingalian Poem.* The diminutive [*giullan*] of this word is in frequent use.

GIULLACH, *a.* (*Ir. id*) Genial, fostering, cherishing

GIULLACHADH, aidh, *s. m.* (*Ir. id.*) A cherishing, a fostering, a nursing.

GIULLACHD, *s. f.* A cherishing, a nourishing, nourishment, nursing. Chum giullachd do ghruaig, *for the nourishing of thy hair.—Macdon.* Ruigidh an ro-ghiullachd air an ro-ghalar, *good nursing will remove a bad complaint.—G.P.*

GIULLAICH, *v. a.* Cherish, nourish, foster, rear. *Pret. a.* ghiullaich, *cherished*, *fut. aff. a* giullaichidh, *shall cherish* Giullaichidh e i, *he shall foster her.—Stew Eph. ref.*

GIULLAN, ain, *s m.* (*dim* of giulla.) A boy. Maide giullain, *a boy's staff.—Oss. N. pl.* giullain.

GIUNNACH, aich, *s. m* (*Ir. id.*) Hair.

GIÙRAIN, *gen. sing* and *n. pl.* of giuran

GIÙRAN, ain, *s. m.* (*Ir. id.*) The gills of a fish. Bric is ball-bhreac giùran, *trouts with spotted gills —Macdon.*

GIUS. A name given to a sow

GIUSAIDH, *s. f.* (*Corn.* gûysan, *an old sow*) A name given to a sow or pig.

† GIUSTA, *s. m* (*Ir. id.*) A can or tankard

GIUSTAL, ail, *s m.* The games or athletic exercises used formerly by the Irish at their *aonachs* [*aon-theachd*] or public meetings.—*Shaw.*

GIUTHAS, ais, *s. m.* Fir; a fir-tree Mar ghiuthas a lùb an doinionn, *like a fir bent by the storm.— Oss Fing* Gall-ghiuthas, *a pine —Stew. Is* Written also *giubhas.*

GIUTHASACH, aich, *s. f.* A fir-wood Teine an giuthasach chorr, *fire in the lofty fir-wood —Oss Fing.* Written also *giubhasach.*

GLAC, *v a.* (*Ir. id*) Catch, seize, snatch, apprehend, take, accept; take, as a city, take prisoner; feel. *Pret. a* ghlac, *catched, fut. aff. a.* glacaidh. Esan a ghlacas baile, *he who takes a town.—Stew. Pro*

GLAC, glaic, *s. m.* (*Ir. id*) The palm of the hand, a handful; (*Scotch*, glack, *handful*,) the arm; a grasp, a hold; a prong, a fork; a quiver; a dell, a narrow glen; a defile; (*Scotch*, glack, *a defile*) Sgaoil e a ghlacan, *he spread his arms.—Orr.* Fuar-ghlac a bhàis, *the cold grasp of death. —Mac'Lach* Is gann chitear tom no glac, *scarcely could hill or dell be seen.—Id*

GLACACH, aich, *s. f.* (*Ir. id*) A sprain of the wrist; an imposthume on the palm of the hand; a kind of pulmonary affection. In this last sense *glacach* is also called tinneas nan Dònullach, *the M'Donalds' disease*; there being a particular tribe of that clan which pretends to cure it by the touch, accompanied with the repetition of certain expressions.

GLACACH, *a.* (*Ir. id*) Grasping, catching, snatching; ready to seize; forked; full of dells or hollows.

GLACADAIR, *s. m, from* glac. (*Ir. id.*) A receiver; a seizer, one who catches.

GLACADAN, ain, *s. m.* (*Ir id.*) A repository; a trap.

GLACADH, aidh, *s. m.* (*Ir. id.*) A seizing; a receiving; a snatching; a catching; a grasp; a forked part; acceptance; feeling.

GLACADH, (a), *pr part* of glac; which see

GLACAG, aig, *s f.* (*dim.* of glac) A little palm, a little handful, a little dell, a bundle. Fàil nan glacag, *the fragrance of the dells.—Macfar. N. pl* glacagan, *dells.* Glacagan diomhair, *lonely dells —Macint.*

GLACAID, *s. f* A handful. *N. pl.* glacaidean. Glacaidean eorna, *handfuls of barley —Stew. Gen. D pl.* glacaidibh; *asp form*, ghlacaidibh Thug an talamh mach na ghlacaidibh, *the earth produced in handfuls —Stew. Ezek*

GLACAIDH, *gen. sing* of glacadh

GLACAIDH, *fut. aff. a.* of glac Shall catch See GLAC.

GLACAIL, *s. f.* (*Ir id*) Taking, catching, seizing, handling.

GLACAIR, *s. m* (*Ir. id*) An apprehender; a catcher.

GLACAIREACHD, *s f.* (*Ir. id.*) Impress; impressment, seizure; handling —*Shaw.*

GLACAIS, *s f.* A grasping, a wrestling, a grappling.

GLACAISEACH, *a.* Grasping, wrestling, grappling; athletic.

GLACAN, ain, *s m, dim* of glac (*Ir* glacoin) A little palm; a little grasp; a little dell; a bundle; a prong, a fork.

GLACANACH, *a.* (*Ir. id.*) Abounding in dells; forked

GLACAR, *fut. pass* of glac Shall be caught. *Glacar* is also used impersonally, the prep *le*, either simple or compounded, being understood, as *glacar* [leinn], *we caught*

GLACLACH, aich, *s m.* (*Ir. id*) A handful; a bundle. *N pl* glaclaichean.

GLAC-LEABHAR, air, *s m.* (*Ir id*) A pocket-book, a manual *N. pl* glac-leabhraichean

GLACTA, GLACTE, *p part.* of glac. Caught, seized, made prisoner. Cha d' fhuair coimheach riamh mi glacta, *a stranger never found me captive.—Fingalian Poem*

† GLADAIR, *s m* (*Ir id.*) A gladiator *N. pl.* gladairean

GLADAIREACHD, *s f* Gladiatorship; sword-fencing.

GLAFAIR, *s. m.* A babbler —*Shaw.*

GLAFARNACH, aich, *s m.* Noise, din; prating, chatting

GLAG, *s m.* (*Du.* klaag, *lament. Swed.* klagan, *complaint.*) A loud gabbling noise, loud talk.

GLAGACH, *a* Noisy, loquacious, garrulous, gabbling, blabbing.

GLAGAIR, *s. m.*, glag-fhear (*Ir id*) A noisy garrulous fellow. *N. pl* glagairean.

GLAGAIREACHD, *s f* Noisiness, garrulity

GLAGAIS, *s f* Loquacity, gabbling, prattle. *Asp. form*, ghlagais Is ann ort a tha' ghlagais! *how you do gabble!*

GLAGAN, ain, *s. m.* (*Ir id*) A mill-clapper. Glagan doruis, *the knocker of a door.*

GLAGANACH, *a.* Noisy, like a door-knocker, like a mill-clapper.

GLAGARRA, *a.* Loud; noisy; garrulous; flowing, sluggish —*Shaw.* Gu glagarra, *loudly*

GLAIB, *s f* (*Ir id*) A puddle or bog, dirty water.—*Shaw.*

GLAIBEACH, *a., from* glaib (*Ir id.*) Puddly, boggy.

GLAIC, *gen. sing* of glac; which see

GLAIC, *s f* (*Ir. id*) A handful, a grasp; a little glen

or dell; the palm or hollow of the hand. An ordag an aghaidh na glaic, *the thumb at variance with the palm.—G. P.*

GLAICEASACH, *a.* (*Ir. id.*) Athletic.

GLAICEIS, *s. f.* A grasping; a wrestling; a grappling.

GLAICEISEACH, *a.* Grasping; wrestling; grappling.

GLAIDEAN, ein, *s. m.* (*Ir. id.*) A glutton.

GLAIDEANACH, *a.* (*Ir. id.*) Gluttonous.

GLAIDEANACHD, *s. f.* (*Ir. id.*) Gluttony.

GLAIGEIS, *s. f.* Loquacity, gabbling, prattle.

GLAIM, *s. f.* (*Ir. id. Lat.* clamor.) A great noise; clamour, a common report; a pitiful complaint; a censure; a yelling, a howling; a yell, a howl; a large mouthful. Is olc an glaim tha muigh air, *there is a bad report abroad concerning him.* The Irish say the same.

GLAIMH, *s. f.* See GLAIM.

GLAIMHEAN, ein, *s. m.* A spendthrift. (*Ir.* glaimhin.)

GLAIMHICH, *v. n.* Roar, cry out.

GLAIMSEAR, ir, *s. m.* A voracious eater; a muncher.

GLAIMSEARACHD, *s. f.* Voraciousness; munching.

GLAINE, *s. f.* (*Ir. id. W.* goleini.) Cleanness; purity; brightness; clearness. Glaine na sìth, *the purity of peace.—Oss. Tem.* Glaine air mala na h-oidhche, *brightness on the brow of night.—Oss. Fing.*

GLAINE, *com.* and *sup.* of glan. (*Ir. id.*) More or most clean. See GLAN.

GLAINEACH, *a.* (*Ir. id.*) Pellucid; clean.

GLAINEACHD, *s. f.* (*Ir. id.*) Cleanness; brightness.

GLAINEAD, id, *s. m.* (*Ir. id.*) Cleanness; brightness.

GLAIS, *gen. sing.* of glas.

GLAIS, *v. a.* (*Gr.* κλεὶς, *a lock. Dor.* κλαΐς.) Lock; fold; clasp; fetter. *Pret. a.* ghlais, *locked; fut. aff. a.* glaisidh, *shall lock.*

GLAISE, *com.* and *sup.* of glas.

GLAISE, *s. f.* (*Ir. id.*) A pale or wan colour; a green colour; a grey colour; an azure hue; greenness; a shade; eclipse; verdure; *rarely*, poverty. Am min-fheur na ghlaise, *the rush in its greenness.—Stew. Job.* Glaise, *a shade.—Shaw.*

GLAISEACH, ich, *s. m.* (*Ir. id.*) Foam.

GLAISEACHD, *s. f.* Greyness; greenness; paleness; verdure; an eclipse.

GLAISEAD, eid, *s. m.* Increase in paleness, greenness, or greyness. A dol an glaisead, *growing more and more green or pale.*

GLAISEAN, ein, *s. m.* (*Ir. id.*) A kind of finch; a green linnet; a sparrow.—*Macd.* Glaisean daraich, *a greenfinch.—Shaw.* The *loxia chloris* of Linnæus. Glaisean seilich, *the bird called wagtail.*

GLAISEAR, *fut. pass.* of glais.

GLAIS-LEUN, -lein. (*Ir. id.*) Peppergrass; lesser spearwort.—*Shaw.*

GLÀM, glàim, *s. m.* (*Lat.* clam-o, *to cry.*) A cry, an outcry, a noise; a large mouthful.

GLÀM, *v. a.* Devour, gobble; seize eagerly; cry.

GLAMACH, *a.* (*Ir. id.*) Edacious; censorious.

GLÀMADH, aidh, *s. m.* (*Ir. id.*) A gobbling; a censuring.

GLÀMAIR, *s. m.* (*Ir. id. Lat.* clamor, *noise. Scotch*, glamar.) A noisy fellow; a glutton. *N. pl.* glàmairean.

GLÀMAIREACHD, *s. f.* Babbling, continued noisy talk; gluttony.

GLÀMH, *v. a.* Eat greedily; talk loudly.

GLAMH, glaimh, *s. m.* A catching greedily with the hands; a snatch. Thug e glamh orm, *he made a snatch at me.*

GLÀMHAIR, *s. m.* A glutton; a babbler. *N. pl.* glamhairean.

GLAMHAIREACHD, *s. f.* (*Ir.* glamaireacht.) Gluttony; continued babbling.

GLÀMHAN, ain, *s. m.* (*Ir.* glamhin.) A spendthrift; one who catches greedily at a thing. *N. pl.* glamhain.

GLAMHSA, *s. m.* A snapping of the mouth; a snatching greedily with the mouth; biting a mouthful, as of bread.

GLAMHSAIR, *s. m.* (*Ir. id.*) A murmurer.

GLAMHSAN, ain, *s. m.* (*Ir. id.*) A murmur; noise.

GLAN, *a.* Clean; pure; sincere; uncorrupted; clear; bright; radiant; resplendent; shrill. Bithibh glan, *be ye clean.—Stew. N. T.* Gath glan na h-òige, *the radiant beams of youth.—Oss.* A chlaidheamh glan gorm, *his bright blue sword.—Oss. Carricth.* Glan mar ghrian, *clear as the sun.—Stew. Song Sol.* Feadan glan ceòlar, *a shrill tuneful pipe.—Old Song.* Cuir ghlan-dholaidh, *spoil* or *destroy completely.* Dìreach glan, *exactly so.* Cha chòir an t-each glan a chur h-uige, *the willing horse should not be driven.—G. P. Com.* and *sup.* glaine *and* gloine. Is glaine measg nam mna, *purest among the women.—Oss. Fing.*

Gr. καλον and γλανη. *Dor.* γλαινα. *W.* glân. *Ir.* glan. *Corn.* glan. *Arm.* glan. *Germ.* klein. *Eng.* clean.

GLAN, *v. a.* and *n.* (*Ir.* glan.) Clean, cleanse, wipe, wash; purify, purge; brighten; weed. *Pret. a.* ghlan, *cleaned; fut. aff. a.* glanaidh, *shall clean.* Ghlan solus an eudan an righ, *joy brightened in the face of the king.—Oss. Tem.* Glanaidh i a beul, *she will wipe her mouth.—Stew. Pro.*

GLAN, (gu), *adv.* Cleanly; purely; brightly; completely; thoroughly. Chuir thu as gu glan, *thou hast completely destroyed.—Sm.* Gu glan, *clearly.—Id.*

GLANADAIL, *a.* Abstergent, cleansing, purifying.

GLANADAIR, *s. m.* A cleanser, as of clothes. *N. pl.* glanadairean.

GLANADAIREACHD, *s. f.* Cleansing; cleanliness; scrubbing; purification.

GLANADH, aidh, *s. m.* (*Ir. id.*) A cleansing, a cleaning, a weeding; a washing; a purification. Fuil a glanaidh, *the blood of her purifying.—Stew. Lev.*

GLANAIDH, *gen. sing.* of glanadh.

GLANAIDH, *fut. aff. a.* of glan. Shall or will clean. See GLAN.

GLANAIL, *a.* (*Ir.* glanamhail. *W.* glanawl.) Abstergent, cleansing, purifying, cleanly.

GLANAS, ais, *s. m.* (*Ir. id.*) Cleanness; purity.

GLANBHAN, ain, *s. m.* (*Ir.* glanmhan.) Clean wheat.

GLAN-BHÀRR, airr, *s. m.* A clean crop; a clean head of hair.

† GLANG, glaing, *s. m.* A shoulder.—*Shaw.*

GLAN-LABHRACH, *a.* Having a clear voice or distinct utterance.

GLAN-LABHRADH, aidh, *s. m.* Clearness of expression; clearness of voice.

† GLANLACH, aich, *s. m.* (*Ir. id.*) A fence; a dike.

† GLANLAICH, *v. a.* (*Ir. id.*) Fence, enclose; trench. *Pret. a.* ghlanlaich; *fut. aff. a.* glanlaichidh.

GLAN-RÙISGTE, *a.* Quite naked. Rinneadh do bhogha glanrùisgte, *thy bow was made quite naked.—Stew. Hab.*

GLANTA, *p. part.* of glan. (*Ir. id.*) Cleaned, cleansed, brightened. See GLAN.

GLANTAIR, *s. m.* A cleanser.

GLANTAIREACHD, *s. f.* Cleansing; purifying; weeding.

GLAN-THOILEACH, *a.* Curious.—*Shaw.*

GLAODH, glaoidh, *s. m.* A cry, a shout, a call; grief. Chluinnte a ghlaodh, *his cry was heard.—Orr. N. pl.* glaodhan, *cries.* Glaodhan bròin, *the cries of grief.—Ull.* Dean glaodh, *cry.* Glaodh choilich, *cock-crow.*

Glaodh, glaoidh, *s. m.* Glue; birdlime.
Gr. γλοιος *and* γλια. *Arm.* glu. *Ir.* glaodh. *Eng.* glue.

Glaodh, *v. a.* and *n.* Cry, shout; proclaim; proclaim banns; glue. *Pret. a.* ghlaodh, *cried; fut. aff. a.* glaodhaidh, *shall cry.* Ghlaodh e le glaodh mòr, *he cried with a loud voice.—Stew. Gen.*
Gr. καλεω, *to call,* and κλαιω. *Att.* κλαω; *to bewail.* *Ir.* glaodh.

Glaodhachadh, *s. m.* A proclamation; a proclamation of banns; gluing. Chaidh an glaodhachadh, *their marriage banns were proclaimed.*

Glaodhaich, *s. f.* (*Ir.* glaodhach.) A shouting; a crying; a proclaiming; a cry; a shout; a proclamation. Glaodhaich na muinntir, *the cries of the people.—Stew. Jam.*

Glaodhaich, (a), *pr. part.* of glaodh. Crying, shouting, bawling.

Glaodhan, *n. pl.* of glaodh; which see.

Glaodhan, ain, *s. m.* (*Ir. id.*) The pith of wood; *also,* pipes, tubes. Sùighidh an glaodhan, *the pith of wood shall suck the juice.—Macdon.*

Glaodhar, air, *s. m.* (*Ir. id.*) A noise; prating; a racket.

Glaodhran, ain, *s. m.* A rattle.

Glaodhta, **Glaodhte**, *p. part.* of glaodh. (*Lat.* † glutus.) Glued.

Glaoidh, *s. f.* (*Ir. id.*) A heap or pile.—*Shaw.*

Glaoim, *s. f.* A tingling sound in the ears.—*Stew.* 2 *K. ref.* A noise; a report, a common rumour.

Glaoine. See **Gloine.**

Glaoran, ain, *s. m.* (*Ir. id.*) Woodsorrel; the flower of woodsorrel.

Glaoranach, *a.* (*Ir. id.*) Like woodsorrel; abounding in woodsorrel.

Glaothar, *a.* (*Ir. id.*) Noisy; clamorous, prating.—*Shaw.*

Glaothar, air, *s. m.* A noise; clamour, prating.

Glaothran, ain, *s. m.* (*Ir. id.*) A rattle.

Glas, *v. a.* and *n.* (*Ir. id.*) Lock, as a door; clasp, fold, fetter; make grey; make pale; grow grey, pale, or green; dawn. *Pret.* ghlas; *fut. aff.* glasaidh. Glas an dorus, *lock the door.* Ghlas a mhaduinn, *the morning dawned.—Oss. Croma.* *Glas,* in the sense of *lock,* is also written *glais.*

† **Glas**, *s. m.* (*Ir. id.*) The sea; a wail.

Glas, glaise, *s. f.* A lock. (*Gr. Dor.* κλαϊς, *a lock and key.*) *Also,* a green surface; a green. *W.* clas, *a green surface.*

Glas, *a.* Grey; blue; green; pale or wan; poor. *Asp. form,* ghlas. Bu ghlas a chiabh, *grey were his locks.—Oss. Croma.* Tùr ghlas, *a grey tower.—Id.* A chnoca glas, *ye green hills.—Sm.* Is glas mo luaidh, *pale is [my love] the subject of my praise.—Oss. Com.* Cho glas ris a chàl, *as green as a kail-blade,* — said of a person whose visage is very pale.
Ir. glas. *W.* glas, *blue, green. Arm.* glas. *Corn.* glas, *blue, green.* Marc glas, *a grey horse. Arm.* march glas. Each glas, *a grey horse. Ir.* each glas.

Glasach, aich, *s. f.* Leaground; a fallow. *N. pl.* glasaichean.

Glasadh, aidh, *s. m.* A locking; a growing grey or pale; a making grey or pale.

Glasag, aig, *s. f.* (*Ir. id.*) Edible sea-weed; any kind of salad; a water-wagtail. *N. pl.* glasagan.

Glasagach, *a.* Abounding in edible sea-weed; abounding in salad.

Glasaidh, *fut. aff. a.* of glas. Shall lock. See **Glas.**

Glasail, *a.* (ghas-amhuil.) Pale, wan; greenish; greyish.

Glasair, *s. m.* (*Ir. id.*) A prater.—*Shaw.* *N. pl.* glasairean.

Glasan, ain, *s. m.* (*Ir. id.*) A sort of edible sea-weed; sea-wrack; any kind of salad.—*Shaw.*

Glasar, *fut. pass.* of glas. Shall be locked.

Glas-bhàn, *a.* (*Ir. id.*) Pale, palish.—*Shaw.*

Glas-charbadach, *a.* Having a locked jaw, causing a locked jaw.

Glas-charbaid, *s. f.* A locked jaw. Duine air am biodh glas-charbaid, *a man with a locked jaw.*

Glas-cheo, *s. m.* A grey mist.

Glas-chiabh, *s.* A lock of grey hair; grey hair.

Glasdachd, *s. f.*, *for* glasdaidheachd. (*Ir. id.*) Paleness; greyness.

Glasdaidh, *a.* (*W.* glasaiz.) Greyish; palish, wan.

Glas-eide, **Glas-eidhidh**, *s. f.* A grey shroud; a suit of grey clothes. Taibhse nan glas-eide, *the grey-shrouded spectre.—Oss.*

Glas-fhairge, *s. f.* A green sea. A ghlas-fhairge a sìor chòpadh, *the green sea perpetually foaming.—Macfar.*

Glas-fheur, -fheòir, *s. m.* Green grass.—*Shaw.*

Glas-fhoghnan, ain, *s. m.* A green thistle. An glas-fhoghnan sa bhruaich, *the green thistle on the steep.—Oss. Derm.*

Glas-ghort, -ghoirt, *s. m.* (*Ir. id.*) A green; a green plot of ground; fodder.

Glas-lamh, *s. m.* (*Ir. id.*) Manicles, fetters.

Glas-lann, -lainn, *s. m.* (*W.* glas-lan.) A green spot.

Glas-liath, *a.* Greyish.—*Shaw.*

Glas-mhagh, -mhaigh, *s. m.* (*Ir. id.*) A green field, a green plain.

Glas-mhaghach, *a.* Abounding in green fields.

Glas-mheur, *s. m.* Manicles; a thumb-screw.

Glas-mhuir, mhara, *s. f.* (*Ir. id.*) The green sea.

Glas-neul, -neoil, *s. m.* (*Ir id.*) A pale colour, a sallow or wan complexion; a grey cloud.

Glas-neulach, *a.* Having a pale hue, wan-complexioned, sallow; having grey clouds.

Glasra, ai. See **Glasradh.**

Glasrach, *a.* (*from* glas.) Green; having green groves or meadows; abounding in pot-herbs. Glasrach, raonach, *green and meadowy.—Macdon.*

Glasradh, aidh, *s. m.* (*Ir. id.*) A green grove; a pot-herb; verdure. *N. pl.* glasraidh. Caoin-ghlasradh ri taobh, *a pleasant grove by its side.—Oss. Carricth.*

Glasraich, *v. a.* Make green; make pale or wan; prepare green thread for use.—*Shaw. Pret.* ghlasraich; *fut. aff.* glasraichidh.

Glasraidh, *n. pl.* Pot-herbs; greens; salads; green groves.

Glasta, *p. part.* of glas. Locked; clasped.

Glas-thalamh, -thalmhainn, *s. c.* Lea or fallow ground. *N. pl.* glas-thalmhainnean.

Glas-uaine, *a.* (*Ir. id.*) Green, greenish, cerulean.—*Shaw.*

† **Gle**, *a.* (*Ir. id.*) Open; plain; pure; clean; good.—*Shaw.*

Gle, *adv.* (*Ir. id.*) Very; enough; perfectly. This word is prefixed to adjectives, giving them the force of the superlative degree. Gle gheal, *very white; white enough.* Gle mhaith, *very good,* or *good enough.*

† **Gleachas**, ais, *s. m.* (*Ir. id.*) A gallery.—*Shaw.*

Gleachd, *s. f.* (*Ir.* gleac.) A wrestling, a struggling; a struggle, a conflict, a wrestling match. Le mòr-ghleachd, *with much wrestling.—Stew. Gen.* Sluagh bu gharbh gleachd, *a people who fought fiercely.—Death of Oscar.* Tiucainn a ghleachd, *come to wrestle.* Written also *cleachd.*

GLEACHD, *v. n.* (*Ir.* gleac.) Wrestle, struggle; fight. *Pret. a.* ghleachd, *wrestled; fut. aff. a.* gleachdaidh, *shall wrestle.* Ghleachd mi ri mo phiuthair, *I wrestled with my sister.—Stew. Gen.* Chòmhlaich sinn 's a ghleachd, *we met and fought.—Oss. Duthona.*

GLEACHDACH, *a.* Full of ringlets; waving, as hair.—*Macint.* Wrestling, struggling. See also *cleachdach.*

GLEACHDADH, aidh, *s. m.* A wrestling; a struggling; a fighting; a wrestle.

GLEACHDAIR, *s. m.* (*from* gleachd.) A wrestler. *N. pl.* gleachdairean.

GLEACHDANAICH, *s. f.* A wrestling, a struggling; rivalry.—*R.*

GLEACHDAS, ais, *s. m.* Wrestling.

GLEADANAS, ais, *s. m.* Keeping, custody.

GLEADH, *v. a.* Keep. More frequently written *gleidh;* which see.

GLEADH, GLEADHNA, *s.* (*Ir. id.*) Tricks, sham, humour. —*Shaw.*

GLEADHADH. See GLEIDHEADH.

GLEADHAR, air, *s. m.* A rude blow, a buffet; noise.

GLEADHRACH, *a.* Noisy; rattling; giving heavy blows.

GLEADHRADH, aidh, *s. m.* A blow; a noise. Thug e gleadhradh dha, *he gave him a blow.*

GLEADHRAICH, *s. f.* (*Ir.* gleaghrach.) A loud rattling noise. Gleadhraich nan corn, *the rattling of the drinking cups.—Old Song.* Ciod a ghleadhraich th'ort? *why do you make such a noise?* is ann ort tha 'ghleadhraich! *what a noise you make!*

GLEADHRAN, ain, *s. m.* A rattling noise; a child's rattle. *N. pl.* gleadhrain.

GLEADHRANACH, *a.* Rattling, making a rattling sound.

GLEADHTACH, *a.* (*Ir. id.*) Frugal, saving; conservative; retentive. Written also *gleidhteach.*

GLEAMHSA, *s. m.* (*Ir. id.*) A slow long draught of liquor. —*Shaw.*

GLEAMHSACH, *a.* (*Ir. id.*) Slow, tedious; disagreeable. *Com.* and *sup.* gleamhsaiche.

GLEAMHSAN, ain, *s. m.* (*Ir. id.*) Continual talk; tiresome talk; a talkative person. *N. pl.* gleamhsain.

† GLEAN, *v.* See LEAN.

GLEANG, *s. m.* (*Eng.* clang.) A tinkling sound; a ringing sound, as of metal; clang; clangour.

GLEANGARSACH, *a.* (*Ir. id.*) Tinkling.

GLEANGARSAICH, *s. f.* A tinkling sound; clangour. Mar chiombal a ni gliongarsaich, *like a tinkling cymbal.—Stew. Cor.*

GLEANN, glinne, *s. m.* (*Corn.* glyn. *Ir.* gleann. *Scotch,* glen.) A valley, a glen. *Asp. form,* ghleann. Bho ghleann nan ruadh-bhoc, *from the valley of deer.—Orr.* Air feadh a ghlinne, *through the valley.—Oss. Derm. N. pl.* glinn, gleanna, gleannan, gleanntaidh, glinnte, *and* gleanntan.

GLEANNACH, *a., from* gleann. (*Ir. id.*) Full of valleys or glens.—*Macdon. Also,* steep; shelving.

GLEANNAIN, *gen. sing.* and *n. pl.* of gleannan.

GLEANNAN, ain, *s. m., dim.* of gleann. (*Ir. id.*) A little valley or glen; a defile. An gleannan modhar, *in a little peaceful valley.—Oss. Taura. N. pl.* gleannain.

GLEANNTAI', GLEANNTAIDH, GLEANNTAN, *n. pl.* of gleann. Glens or valleys. Beum sleibhe a sireadh gu gleanntaidh, *a mountain-torrent pouring to the valleys.—Oss.*

GLEANNTAIL, *a., from* gleann. (*Ir. id.*) Having valleys.

† GLEAR, *v. a.* (*Ir. id.*) Follow.

† GLEARRACH, *a.* (*Ir.* glearrthach.) Flexible, pliant.

GLEAS. See GLEUS.

GLEASD, *a.* See GLEUSD.

GLEASDACHD, *s.* See GLEUSDACHD.

GLEASLANN, ainn, *s. m.* (*Ir. id.*) A storehouse.

† GLEASTA, ai, *s. m.* Provision.

GLEASTAIR, *s. m.* A farrier.

GLEICEAN, ein, *s. m.* A shuttlecock. *N. pl.* gleicein.—*Macd.* and *Shaw.*

GLEICEANACH, *a.* Like a shuttlecock.

GLÈIDH, *v. a.* (*Gr.* κλειω. *Ir.* gleith.) Keep, save, preserve; tend, as cattle; detain. *Pret. a.* ghlèidh, *kept; fut. aff. a.* gleidhidh, *shall keep.* Gleidhidh mi do threud, *I will keep thy flock.—Stew. Gen.*

GLEIDHEADH, idh, *s. m.* A keeping, detaining, preserving; tending; industry; frugality.

GLEIDHEAR, *fut. pass.* of gleidh; which see.

GLEIDHIDH, *fut. aff. a.* of gleidh. Shall or will keep.

GLÉIDHTEACH, *a.* (*from* gleidh.) Frugal; saving; industrious. Gu glèidhteach, *frugally.*

GLEIDHTEACHAS, ais, *s. m.* Any thing saved or not spent; a store.

GLEIDHTEACHD, *s. f.* Frugality; industry; a disposition to hoard up.

† GLEILEACHD, *s. f.,* gle-ghealachd. (*Ir. id.*) Whiteness; pureness.

† GLEIRE, *s. f.* (*Ir. id.*) A choice; an election.

GLEITEAN, ein, *s. m.* (*Ir. id.*) A hard fight.

GLEITH, *v.,* more commonly written *gleidh.*

† GLEITHE, *s. f.* (*Ir. id.*) Grazing, feeding.

GLEITHIRE, *s. m.* (*Ir. id.*) A gadbee; a grazer.

GLEÒ, *s. m.* A fight, uproar, tumult, disturbance; a sigh. —*Shaw.* Co chuireadh orra gleò? *who could disturb them?* —*Old Song.*

† GLEODH, *v. a.* Cleanse, scour, polish. *Pret.* ghleodh, *cleansed; fut. aff. a.* gleodhaidh, *shall cleanse.*

GLEODH, gleodha, *s. m.* A cleansing, a scouring, a polishing; a sigh; a slumber; a groan.

GLEODHACH, *a.* (*Ir. id.*) Mournful.

GLEODHAMAN, ain, *s. m.* (*Ir. id.*) A drowsy stupid fellow.

GLEODHAMANACH, *a.* (*Ir. id.*) Drowsy, stupid.

GLEODHAMANACHD, *s. f.* (*Ir. id.*) Drowsiness, stupidity.

GLEOG, gleoig, *s. m.* A blow, a slap. Gleog san leth-cheann, *a slap on the side of the head.*

GLEOGAIR, *s. m.* A vain stupid fellow; a talkative fellow; an arrogant fellow. *N. pl.* gleogairean.

GLEOGAIREACHD, *s. f.* Arrogancy; talkativeness; awkward gesture.

GLEOGAMAN, ain, *s. m.* A stupid, drowsy fellow.

GLEOGH, *s.* See GLEODH.

GLEÒID, *s. f.* (*Ir. id.*) A slattern; a sloven. *N. pl.* gleòidean.

GLEOIDEACHD, *s. f.* (*Ir. id.*) Slovenliness.

GLEÒIDEIL, *a.* (gleòid-amhuil.) Slovenly; like a slattern.

GLEOIS, *s. f.* (*Ir. id.*) Babbling.

GLEÒISG, *s. f.* A talkative silly female.

GLEOISGEIL, *a.* (gleoisg-amhuil.) Like a silly female; apt to talk idly.

GLEÒITE, *a.* (*Ir. id.*) Neat, trim, tight; handsome; curious. —*Shaw.*

GLEÒMAN, ain, *s. m. from* gleodh. (*Ir. id.*) A sluggish man, a drowsy person. *N. pl.* gleomain.

GLEÒMANACH, *a.* (*Ir. id.*) Sluggish, drowsy. *Com.* and *sup.* gleomanaiche. Gu gleòmanach, *sluggishly.*

GLEÒMANACHD, *s. f.* (*Ir. id.*) Sluggishness, drowsiness; sluttishness.

GLEÒRAMAS, ais, *s. m.* (*Ir. id.*) Vain talk, idle boasting; a vain boaster, an idle talker.

GLEORANN, *s.* Cresses; nasturtium.

GLEOS, ois, *s. m.* (*Ir. id.*) Lamentation.

GLEÒSG, oisg, *s. f.* (*Ir. id.*) A silly woman.

GLEOSGACH, *a.* (*Ir. id.*) Silly, stupid.

GLEÒSGAIR, *s. m.* A vain stupid fellow. *N. pl.* gleosgairean.

GLEÒSGAIREACHD, *s. f.* (*Ir. id.*) Vanity; stupidity; stupid gesture.

GLEÒTHAN, ain, *s. m.* (*Ir. id.*) A clue.—*Shaw.* *N. pl.* gleothain.

GLEUS, *s. m.* and *f.* (*Ir. id.*) Order; trim; condition; strength; the lock of a gun; a form; furniture; a key or gamut; a work; preparation; readiness for action. Fiodhal air ghleus, *a violin in* [*tune*] *trim.* Ciod an gleus th'ort? *how art thou? in what condition of health art thou?* Thug aois dhiom gleus, *age has taken from me my strength.*—*Old Song.* Thannais na faoin-ghleus, *ghost of the empty form.*—*Oss.* Gu gleus bàis, *to the work of death.*—*Oss. Fing.* Chaidh e air ghleus, *he put himself in readiness.*—*Mac Lach.*

GLEUS, *v. a.* (*Ir. id.*) Put in order, prepare; trim; harness; put in tune, as a musical instrument. *Pret. a.* ghleus, *trimmed; fut. aff. a.* gleusaidh, *shall trim; pret. pass.* gleustadh. Dh'iarr e gun gleustadh chuid each, *he desired that his horses should be harnessed.*—*Mac Lach.*

GLEUSADH, aidh, *s. m.* (*Ir. id.*) A tuning of an instrument; a trimming; a preparing.

GLEUSADH, (a), *pr. part.* of gleus. Tuning; preparing; a trimming. A chruit ag a gleusadh, *the harp a-tuning.*—*Old Song.*

GLEUSAICH, *v. a.* (*from* gleus.) Prepare; trim. *Pret. a.* gleusaich, *trimmed; fut. aff.* gleusaidh.

GLEUSD, GLEUSDA, *a.* (*Ir. id.*) Diligent, industrious; keen; eager; tuned; prepared for action or for use; in humour; in good condition; ready for action. Giullan gleusda, *a diligent boy.* Coin ghleusda, *keen dogs.*—*Oss. Fing.* Bheil thu gu gleusda, *are you pretty well* or *tolerably well.*

GLEUSDACHD, *s. f.* (*Ir.* gleastacht.) Diligence, industriousness; keenness; eagerness; good humouredness; neatness; readiness.

GLEUSMHOR, *a.* Mannerly, orderly.

GLEUSTA, *p. part.* of gleus. (*Ir.* gleusta.) Diligent; keen; eager; tuned; prepared; in trim; in condition; braced; confirmed; bent, as a bow; cocked, as a gun. An cridhe ni thu gleusta, *their hearts thou wilt confirm.*—*Sm.* Cuilbhir gleusta na 'n laimh, *cocked guns in their hands.*—*Old Song.*

GLIADAR, air, *s. m.* (*Ir. id.*) Loquacity, pertness.

GLIADRACH, aich, *s. f.* (*Ir. id.*) A drab, a slattern.

GLIADRACH, *a.* (*Ir. id.*) Glittering; sprightly; wanton.

† GLIATH, *s. m.* (*Ir. id.*) War, battle.—*Shaw.*

GLIATHRACH, aich, *s. f.* A drab or common prostitute.

† GLIB, *s. f.* (*Ir. id.*) A ringlet; a slut.

GLIB, glibe, *s. f.* A glebe, or that portion of ground which the kirk allows her pastors.

† GLIB, *a.* (*Ir. id. Dan.* glib, *an accident.*) Slippery. Glib-shleamhuinn, *slippery with sleet.*—*Shaw* and *Macfar.*

GLIC, *a.* (*Ir. id.*) Wise, prudent, sagacious; steady; cunning; cautious. Bi glic, *be wise.*—*Stew. Pro.* Glic gun mhoille, *cautious, without dilatoriness.*—*Old Song.* *Com.* and *sup.* glice, *wiser, wisest.* Gu glic, *wisely.*

GLICEAD, eid, *s.* Advancement in wisdom; wisdom. A dol an glicead, *growing more and more wise;* air a ghlicead sa bheil e, *however wise he be.*

GLIDEACHADH, aidh, *s. m.* A moving, a stirring, a budging; motion. Cha b' urradh dha glideachadh, *he could not move.*

GLIDEACHD, *s. f.* Motion; commotion; the power of moving or stirring.

GLIDICH, *v. a.* (*Ir.* gliduigh.) Move, stir, budge. *Pret. a.* ghlidich, *moved; fut. aff. a.* glidichidh. Nach glidich thu? *will not you budge?* *Fut. pass.* glidichear, *shall be moved.*—*Stew. Is. ref.*

GLIFID, *s. f.* (*Ir. id.*) Noise; a voice.—*Shaw.*

† GLIN, *s.* See GLUN.

GLINN, *a.* (*Ir. id.*) Clear, manifest; *also, substantively,* the sky; light; a fortress.

GLINN, *n. pl.* of gleann. Valleys, glens. Rugadh tu sna glinn, *thou wert born in the glens.*—*Old Song.*

GLINNE, *gen. sing.* of gleann; which see.

† GLINNE, *s. f.* (*Ir. id.*) A habit; a cloak; bail.

GLINNEACH, *a.* (*Ir. id.*) Clear, manifest; pliable, flexible; full of valleys.

GLINNEACHADH, *a.* A making evident; a clearing up.

GLINNICH, *v. a.* and *n.* (*from* † glinn.) Make evident; clear up; observe closely.—*Shaw.* *Pret. a.* ghlinnich, *cleared.* Ghlinnich an là, *the day cleared up.*

GLINNICHTE, *p. part.* of glinnich. Made evident; cleared up.

GLINNIDH, *a.* (*Ir. id.*) Clear, manifest.

GLINNTE, *pl.* of gleann. Glens or valleys. A ruith gu glinnte, *running towards the valleys.*—*Orr.*

GLIOBACH, *a.* (*Ir. id.*) Hairy.

GLIOCAS, ais, *s. f.*, *from* glic. (*Ir. id.*) Wisdom, prudence; cunning; wit; steadiness; sagacity. Aig-san tha gliocas, *with him is wisdom.*—*Stew. Job.*

GLIOG, *s. m.* A tinkle.

GLIOG, *v. n.* Tinkle. *Pret.* ghliog, *tinkled.*

GLIOGACH, *a.* (*from* gliog.) Tinkling.

GLIOGAIR, *v. n.* Tinkle, tingle, ring. *Pret. a.* ghliogair, *tinkled; fut. aff.* gliogairidh.

GLIOGAR, air, *s. m.* (*Ir. id.*) A ringing, a tinkling noise; slowness.—*Shaw.*

GLIOGARACH, *a.* (*Ir. id.*) Making a tinkling sound, ringing.

GLIOGARSAICH, *s. f.* (*Ir. id.*) A continued tinkling noise.

GLIOGARSNACH, aich, *s. m.* (*Ir. id.*) A tinkling noise.

GLIOMACH, aich, *s. c.* (*Ir. id.*) A sloven; a slut; a long-limbed person; a lobster. Gliomach-spainnteach, *a craw-fish.*

GLIOMACH, *a.* (*Ir. id.*) Slovenly, sluttish, drabbish. *Com.* and *sup.* gliomaiche.

GLIOMACHAS, ais, *s. m.* Slovenliness, sluttishness.

GLIONG, *s. m.* (*Ir. id.*) A jingling noise, as of metal; a clang; clangour. Written also *gleang.*

GLIONG, *v. a.* and *n.* Make to jingle or clang; make a clang. *Pret. a.* ghliong; *fut. aff.* gliongaidh.

GLIONGACH, *a.* Tingling, tinkling, jingling; clanging.

GLIONGAN, ain, *s. m.* A tinkle, a tinkling or jingling noise; any thing which produces a tinkling sound.

GLIONGARAICH, *s. f.* A continued jingling noise.

GLIONGARAICH, *v. n.* Clang; make a jingling sound; tinkle. *Pret.* ghliongaraich, *made a jingling noise.* Ghliongaraich an claidheamh, *the sword clanged.*—*Mac Lach.*

GLIONGARSAICH, *s. f.* A loud clanging noise, as of cymbals. Written also *gleangarsaich.*

Gliosair, *s. m.* (*Ir. id.*) A prattling fellow, a tattler.—*Shaw*. *N. pl.* gliosairean.

Gliosaireachd, *s. f.* (*Ir. id.*) Prating.

Gliosdar, air, *s. m.* A clyster.

Gliosg, *s. m.* A glance; a twinkling. Ann an gliosg, *in a twinkling.*

Gliosgardaich, *s. f.* (*Gr.* γλιτχζος. *Lat.* gliscerus, *shining.*) A glancing or glittering light; a tremulous motion, or dangling; a ringing noise.

Gliostair, *s. m.* A clyster.—*Shaw*. *N. pl.* gliostairean.

Gliugail, *s. f.* (*Ir. id.*) Clucking, as a hen.

† **Gliumh**, *s.* (*Ir. id.*) Glue.—*Shaw*.

Gliusta, **Gliustach**, *a.* (*Ir. id.*) Slow.

Gliustachd, *s. f.* (*Ir. id.*) Slowness, tediousness.

† **Glo**, *s. m.* A veil, a covering, a hood. Hence *Beinn-ghlo*, (*i. e.* the hooded or cloud-capped mountain,) a mountain in Athol.

Glòbach, *a.* An epithet applied to a hen whose head is covered with down.

Glòbag, aig, *s. f.* A stupid quean. *N. pl.* glòbagan.

Gloc, *s. f.* A cluck, as of a hen; a cackle; loud confident talk; garrulity; a throat. Bu cheannach leam d'ubh air do ghloc, *dear-bought egg with so much cackling.*—*G. P.*

Glocach, *a.* Clucking; garrulous.

Glocail, *s. f.* A clucking; garrulity; loud prating.

Glocail, *a.* (gloc-amhuil.) Clucking; garrulous.

Glocair, *s. m.* (*Ir. id.*) A lubberly coward, a braggadocio; a chattering fellow. *N. pl.* glocairean.

Glocaireachd, *s. f.* Lubberliness; cowardliness; gasconading; chattering.

Glocan, ain, *s. m.* A sling; a fork; a wide throat.

Glocan, ain, *s. m.*, *dim.* of gloc; which see.

Glocar, *a.* (gloc-mhor.) *W.* cloçdar, *a clucking.* Apt to cluck; garrulous; apt to talk loudly and confidently.

Glochar, air, *s. m.* (*Ir. id.*) Hard respiration; asthma; a wheezing in the throat; a snoring.

Glocharnaich, *s. f.* Hardness of respiration; asthma; a continued wheezing in the throat.

Gloc-nid, *s. f.* A morning dram taken in bed.—*Shaw*.

† **Glog**, gloig, *s. f.* (*Ir. id.*) A soft lump.—*Shaw*.

Glogach, *a.* Skinny; flabby; lumpy.

Gloc-luinn, *s. f.* The rolling of the sea in a calm; the agitation of a vessel produced by such rolling.

Gloich, *s. m.* and *f.* A stupid person; a quean; an idiot.

Gloichd, *s. m.* and *f.* A stupid quean; an idiot; a slattern; a fool. Tha thu ad shean ghloichd le h-aois, *age has made an old fool of you.*—*Turn.*

Gloichdealachd, *s. f.* (gloichd-amhuileachd.) Sluttishness; queanishness; idioticalness.

Gloichdeil, *a.* (gloichd-amhuil.) Sluttish; queanish; idiotical.

Gloin, *v. a.* (*Ir. id.*) Glaze; vitrify.

Gloine, *com.* and *sup.* of glan. Cleaner, purer, purest. An t-òr a 's gloine, *the purest gold.*—*Stew. Song Sol.*

Gloine, *s. f.* (*from* glan.) Cleanness, purity, pureness; sincerity. Gloine lamh, *cleanness of hands.*

Gloine, *s. f.* (*Ir.* gloine, *glass.* *W.* glain, *a gem.* *Corn.* glaine, *glass.*) A glass; a pane of glass; a drinking glass; a glassful. Gloine uinneig, *a pane;* gloine uisge-beatha, *a glass of whiskey.* *N. pl.* gloineachean, *glasses.* Cinnidh uisge na ghloineachan cruaidh, *water shall turn into glass.*—*Macdon.*

The word *gloine* seems to be *glaoth-theine*, glued by fire. From the composition of this vocable, Dr. Smith infers, with much reason, that the Druids were no strangers to the making of glass; the knowledge of which art, he observes, they might have obtained from the first inventors, the Phœnicians. Dr. Smith presumes further, that the Druids were so perfect in the art, and so well acquainted with the properties of glass, as to apply it, with the most eminent success, to the purposes of astronomy. Mr. Huddleston, the very ingenious editor of "Toland's History of the Druids," touching this opinion, is somewhat sarcastic on Smith. He remarks that the telescopic hypothesis rests on a mistaken meaning of a quotation from Hecateus, who says, that the *Boreadæ bring the moon very near them;* and that the Boreadæ, even granting they were Druids, only asserted a prerogative which was common to all magicians, namely, "to bring down the moon;" and, consequently, that the allusion is made to incantation, and not to telescopes. All this does not in the least repel the opinion of Dr. S., which derives additional strength from Diodorus Siculus, who makes mention of an Hyperborean *island*, from which the moon was to be seen, *apparently* at a small distance from the earth, and exhibiting several inequalities and eminences on its surface. This is not the language of incantation, but a just description of the moon as seen through glasses of very considerable power.

Gloine nan Druidh. The Druids' glass, or the Druids' egg; by the Lowland Scots called *adderstanes.*

This amulet was in high esteem among the Druids. It was one of their distinguishing badges, and was accounted to possess the most extraordinary virtues. There is a passage in Pliny's Natural History, book xix., minutely describing the nature and properties of this amulet. The following is a translation of it:—"There is a sort of egg in great repute among the Gauls, of which the Greek writers have made no mention. A vast number of serpents are twisted together in summer, and coiled up in an artificial knot by their saliva and slime; and this is called *the serpent's egg.* The Druids say that it is tossed in the air with hissings, and must be caught in a cloak before it touch the earth. The person who thus intercepts it, flies on horseback; for the serpents pursue him until prevented by intervening water. This egg, though bound in gold, will swim against the stream. And as the magi are cunning to conceal their frauds, they give out that this egg must be obtained at a certain age of the moon. I have seen that egg as large and round as a common-sized apple, in a chequered cartilaginous cover, and worn by the Druids. It is wonderfully extolled for gaining law-suits, and access to kings. It is a badge which is worn with such ostentation, that I knew a Roman knight, a Vocontian, who was slain by the stupid emperor Claudius, merely because he wore it in his breast when a law-suit was pending."

My subscribers are referred to Huddleston's edition of Toland, for some very ingenious conjectures on the subject of this enigmatical account of the Druids' egg.

The amulets of glass and stone, which are still preserved and used with implicit faith in many parts of the Highlands, and are conveyed, for the cure of diseases, to a great distance, seem to have their origin in this bauble of ancient priestcraft.

Gloineach, *a.*, *from* gloine. (*Ir. id.*) Glossy, vitreous.

Gloineachadh, aidh, *s. m.* A glazing; a vitrifying; vitrification; a paning, as a window.

Gloinead, eid, *s. m.* (*from* gloine.) Cleanness, cleanliness; improvement in cleanness. A dol an gloinead, *growing more and more clean.* Is gloineid e an sgroth sin, *it is the cleaner for that scrubbing.*

Gloineadair, *s. m.* A glazier; a glassblower. *N. pl.* gloineadairean.

Gloineadaireachd, *s. f.* The business of a glazier; glassblowing; glazery.

Gloinich, *v. a.* (*Ir.* gloinigh.) Glaze; vitrify; pane, as a window. *Pret. a.* ghloinich, *glazed; fut. aff. a.* gloinichidh, *shall glaze.*

Gloinichear, *fut. pass.* of gloinich.

Gloinichte, *p. part.* of gloinich. Glazed; vitrified; paned.

Glòir, *gen. sing.* of glòr.

Glòir, *s. f.* (*Lat.* gloria. *Fr.* gloire. *Arm.* gloar. *Ir.* glòir.) Glory; praise; honour; a glorified state; talk. Ar gloir-ne, *our glory.*—*Stew. Thess.* Treun thair glòir, *powerful beyond all praise.*—*Old Song.*

Glòireachadh, aidh, *s. m.* A glorifying.

Gloiream, eim, *s. m.* (*Ir. id.*) Pomp, pageantry.

Gloireamach, *a.* (*Ir. id.*) Pompous. Gu gloireamach, *pompously.*

Glòireis, *s. f.* (*Lat.* gloriatio.) Boasting, prating, vain talk.

Glòireiseach, *a.* (*from* glòr.) Boastful, prating, verbose.

Glòireiseachd, *s. f.* Boastfulness, verbosity.

Glòirich, *v. a.* (*Ir.* gloirigh.) Glorify; raise to glory; honour. *Pret. a.* ghlòirich, *glorified; fut.* glòirichidh, *shall glorify.*

Glòirichte, *p. part.* Glorified; honoured.

Glòir-mhiann, *s. f.* (*Ir. id.*) Ambition; pride; desire for glory.

Glòir-mhiannach, *a.* (*Ir.* gloir-mhiannach.) Ambitious; proud; desirous of glory; vain-glorious. Fear glòir-mhiannach, *an ambitious man.*

Glòirmhor, *a.* Glorious; celebrated. A chumhachd gloirmhor, *his glorious power.—Stew. Col. Com.* and *sup.* gloirmhoire, *more* or *most glorious.*

Gloir-reim, *s. f.* Triumph; pomp, pageantry.—*Shaw.*

† **Gloislionta**, *a.* Crammed, stuffed; crowded; choke-full; thick-set.—*Shaw.*

Gloite, *s. f.* Gluttony.

Gloitear, eir, *s. m.* A glutton. *N. pl.* gloitearan.

Gloitearach, *a.* Greedy, gluttonous, voracious. Gu gloitearach, *greedily.*

Gloitearachd, *s. f.* Gluttony, voraciousness.

Glomar, air, *s. m.* (*Ir. id.*) A bridle.

Glomhar, air, *s. m.* An instrument put into the mouths of calves and lambs to prevent sucking.

† **Glomuin**, *s. f.* (*Ir. id. Scotch,* gloamin.) Evening.

Glonaid, *s. f.* (*Ir. id.*) A multitude, a crowd.

Glonn, *s. m.* (*Ir. id.*) An exploit; a deed; a loathing; a qualm; a calf. Oscar nam mor-ghlonn, *mighty Oscar.—Fingalian Poem.*

Glonnar, *a.* (glonn-mhor.) Mighty; heroic; *also,* loathing, qualmish.

Glonnrach, *a.* (*Ir. id.*) Glittering, resplendent.

Glonnradh, aidh, *s.* (*Ir. id.*) Fulgency, splendour.

Glòr, gloir, *s.* (*Ir. id.*) Speech, language, voice, utterance; noise; idle talk. C'àite am faighear glòr dhomh? *where can I find language?—Old Song.* Connal bu mhìn glòr, *Connal the mild in speech.—Oss.*

† **Glòr**, *a.* Clean, neat, trim; clear.—*Shaw.*

Glòrach, *a.* (*Ir. id.*) Noisy, clamorous, talkative, garrulous.

Glòrais, *s. f.* (*Ir. id.*) Prating.

Gloraiseach, *a.* Prating.

Glòramas, ais, *s. m.* (*Ir. id.*) Idle talk; boastful talk; *also,* a prater, a person who talks idly or at random. Written also *gleoramas.*

Glòrmhor. See **Glòirmhor**.

Glòtair, *s. m.* A glutton.

Glotaireachd, *s. f.* Gluttony.

† **Glotan**, ain, *s. m.* A bosom or breast.

Gloth, *s.* See **Glo**.

† **Gloth**, *a.* (*Ir. id.*) Wise, prudent, discreet.

Glothag, aig, *s. f.* (*Ir. id.*) Frog-spawn.

Glothagach, *a.* (*Ir. id.*) Abounding in frog-spawn; like frog-spawn.

Glothagach, aich, *s. f.* (*Ir. id.*) A quantity of frog-spawn.

† **Gluair**, *a.* (*Ir. id.*) Clear, bright, clean, gleaming; splendid.

† **Gluaireachd**, *s. f.* (*Ir. id.*) Clearness, brightness.

Gluais, *s. f.* (*Ir. id.*) A device, an invention—(*Shaw*); a gloss; interpretation.

Gluais, *v. a.* and *n.* (*Ir. id.*) Move, stir, bestir, walk; affect, agitate; afflict, provoke; proceed, advance, march. *Pret.* ghluais, *moved; fut. aff.* gluaisidh, *shall move.* Gluais gu comhraig, *bestir thyself for battle.—Oss. Croma. Pret. pass.* ghluaiseadh, *was moved.* Ghluaiseadh an righ, *the king was affected.—Stew. Sam.* Ghluais sòlas o fhocal, *comfort proceeded from his voice.—Oss.* Ghluais o'n ear madainn ghlan, *pure [radiant] morn advanced from the east.—Id.* Gluaisear leam, *I shall walk.—Sm.* Ni 'n gluaiseam gun mo ghaol, *I will not stir without my beloved.—Oss. Gaul.*

Gluaisdeach, *a.* Moving, stirring; agitating; causing motion; affecting, pathetic.—*Shaw.*

Gluaise, *s. f.* (*Ir. id.*) Neatness, trimness; cleanness.—*Shaw.*

Gluaiseadh. See **Gluasad**.

Gluaisear, *fut. pass.* of gluais.

† **Gluaisfear**. See **Gluaisear**.

Gluaisidh, *fut. aff. a.* of gluais; which see.

Gluaiste, *p. part.* of gluais. (*Ir. id.*) Moved, stirred; agitated, affected.

Gluarach, *a.* Pure; glorious; vociferous.

Gluasachd, *s. f.* (*Ir. id.*) Motion; power of motion; stirring; gesture; gait; movement; agitation; provoking; pathos. Thug thu gluasachd dhuinn, *thou hast given us the power of motion.—Mac Kellar's Hymn.* Gun ghluasachd, *motionless, unmoved.*

Gluasachd, (a), *pr. part.* of gluais. Moving, stirring; agitating, affecting, provoking. A gluasachd, *moving.—Stew. Pro. ref.*

Gluasad, aid, *s. m.* Motion; power of motion; stirring; moving; a movement; gesture, gait; agitation; a provoking. Gun ghluasad, *motionless, unmoved.* A gluasad 's a h-aogasg, *her motion and her appearance.—Mac Lach.* Gun ghluasad nunn na nall, *without moving hither or thither.—Id.*

Gluasad, (a), *pr. part.* of gluais. Moving, stirring; agitating, affecting, provoking. A gluasad a bhilean, *moving his lips.—Stew. Pro.*

Gluasadach, *a.* Moving; agitative; capable of motion; locomotive; creeping. Creutair gluasadach, *a moving creature.—Stew. Pro. ref.*

Gluasadh, aidh, *s. m.* A moving; agitation; motion; gait.

Gluasag, aig, *s. f.* The bird called a wagtail; a restless girl.—*Shaw.*

Gluasair, *s. m.* (*Ir. id.*) An interpreter.

Glucaid, *s. f.* (*Ir. id.*) A bumper.

Glug, *v. a.* Swallow with a gurgling noise; gulp; gurgle. *Pret. a.* ghlug, *gulped; fut. aff. a.* glugaidh, *shall gulp.* Ghlug e air h-uile deur dheth, *he gulped down every drop of it.*

Glug, gluig, *s. m.* (*Ir. id.*) A gurgling noise; the noise made in the throat by gulping any fluid; the noise of water when agitated in a vessel.

Glugach, *a.*, *from* glug. (*Ir. id.*) Stammering in speech, lisping; gurgling. *Com.* and *sup.* glugaiche.

Glugail, *s. f.* (*from* glug.) Gurgling, swallowed with a gurgling noise.

Glugair, *s. m.* (*from* glug.) A stammerer in his speech, a prater. *N. pl.* glugairean.

Glugaireachd, *s. f.* (*from* glugair.) The infirmity of lisping or stammering.

Glugan, ain, *s. m.*, *from* glug. (*Ir. id.*) A gurgling noise;

the gurgling noise of water against the side of a vessel; the noise of water when agitated in a confined vessel; the rolling of a ship at sea.

Gluganach, *a.*, *from* glugan. (*Ir. id.*) Rolling, like a ship; unsteady; tottering; gurgling.

Gluig, *a.* Rotten, unsound, or addle, as an egg. Ubh gluig, *an addle-egg*.

Glùin, *gen. sing.* of glùn; which see.

Gluine, *n. pl.* of glun. Knees. Mo ghlùine, *my knees.* —*Sm.*

Gluineach-bheag, *s. f.* Knot-grass.—*Macd.* and *Shaw.*

Glùinean, ein, *s. m.* A garter. *N. pl.* glùinein; *also, n. pl.* of glùn.

Glùineas, eis, *s. m.* The gout in the knee.

† **Gluing**, *s. f.* (*Ir. id.*) The shoulder.—*Shaw.*

Glùintean, *n. pl.* of glùn. Knees. *D. pl.* glùintibh. Air do ghlùintibh, *on thy knees.*

Glumag, aig, *s. f.* A deep pool; a deep hole. *N. pl.* glumagan.

Glumagach, *a.* Full of deep pools; full of deep holes.

Glumagan, ain, *s. m.* A deep pool; a deep hole. *Also, n. pl.* of glumag.

Glùn, glùin, *s. m.* A generation, a descendant; a step; a degree. Bean ghlùin, *a midwife.*

Glùn, glùin, *s. f.* A knee. Lubadh gach glùn, *let every knee bow.*—*Stew. O. T. N. pl.* glùine, glùinean, *and* glùintean. Mo ghlùine, *my knees.*—*Sm.* Gach uile ghlùintean, *every knee.*—*Stew. O. T.* Bean-ghlùin, *a midwife.* An leanabh nach foghlum thu ri do ghlùn cha 'n fhoghlum thu ri do chluais, *the child whom you teach not at your knee, you cannot teach when he comes to your ear.*—*G. P.*

W. glên. *Arm.* glin. *Corn.* glun. *Ir.* glun.

Glùnach, *a.* Having large knees; knock-kneed.

Glùnan, ain, *s. m.* (*dim.* of glùn.) A little knee; a garter. *N. pl.* glunain, *garters.*

Glùn-lùb, *v. n.* Kneel; courtesy, as a female. *Pret.* ghlùn-lub, *courtesied*; *fut. aff.* glùn-lubaidh, *shall kneel.*

Glùn-lùbach, *a.* Kneeling; genuflecting; courtesying. Mo chaileag ghlùn-lubach, *my courtesying maid.*—*Old Song.*

Glun-lubadh, aidh, *s. m.* A kneeling; a genuflection; a courtesy.

† **Glundas**, *a.* Bandy-legged; knock-kneed.

† **Glus**, gluis, *s. m.* (*Eng.* gloss.) Light, brightness.—*Shaw.*

Glusar, *a.* (*from* glus.) Bright, glossy.

Glut, *s. m.* Gluttony.

Glut, *v. n.* Eat gluttonously.

Glutach, *a.* (*from* glut.) Gluttonous.

Glutaich, *v.* Gormandise, eat greedily, glut. *Pret.* ghlutaich, *glutted*; *fut. aff.* glutaichidh, *shall glut.*

Glutair, *s. m.* (*Lat.* gluto.) A glutton. *N. pl.* glutairean.

Glutaireach, *s. f.* Gluttony.

Gnà. See **Gnàth.**

Gnàdran, ain, *s. m.* See **Gràdran.**

Gnàdranach, *a.* See **Gradranach.**

Gnàdranachadh, aidh, *s. m.*, written also *gradranachadh*; which see.

Gnàdranaich, *s. f.* See **Gradranach**, *s. f.* See **Gradranaich.**

Gnàdranaich, *v. n.* Prattle, chatter; cackle. See also **Gràdranaich.**

† **Gnais**, *s. f.* *Pars nefanda mulieris.*

Gnamhan, ain, *s. m.* (*Ir. id.*) A sea-snail; a periwinkle. *N. pl.* gnamhain.

Gnamhanach, *a.* Abounding in periwinkles.

Gnaoi, *a.* Pleasant, courteous; gentle; respectable.

Gnàs, gnais, *s. m.* (*for* gnathas.) Custom, fashion, habit, usage; experience. Fhir bu tighearnail gnàs, *thou whose habits were noble.*—*Turn.*

Gnàth, *s.* (*Ir. id.*) Manner, habit, practice, usage, fashion, custom; *rarely*, stature; the lowing of cows; a soothing voice. *N. pl.* gnàthanna, *usages*; *d. pl.* gnathannaibh. A réir an gnàth, *according to their manner.*—*Stew.* 1 *K.* Mar bu ghnàth leis, *as was his custom.*—*Ull.* Talla do 'n gnàth na cuirm, *a hall where feasting is frequent.*—*Oss. Tem.* Eòlach air gach gnàth, *acquainted with every custom.* —*Stew. Acts.* A ghnàth, *continually; usually.* Do ghnàth, *continually; usually.*

Gnàthach, *a.* (*Ir. id.*) Customary, common, usual, habitual, constant, continual; active; industrious. *Com.* and *sup.* gnàthaiche.

Gnàthachadh, aidh, *s. m.* (*Ir. id.*) A practising, a putting in practice; an habituating; a custom or manner, way, course. A reir gnàthachadh an t-saoghail, *according to the ways of the world.*—*Stew. Eph.*

Gnàthachadh, (a), *pr. part.* of gnàthaich; which see.

Gnàthaich, *v. a.* (*Ir. id.* *W.* gwnëyd.) Put in practice, practise; inure; exercise; accustom. *Pret. a.* ghnàthaich, *ruled*; *fut. aff. a.* gnàthaichidh. Na gnàthaich uachdranachd, *do not practise* [*authority*] *rule.*—*Stew. Lev.* Cha do ghnàthaich sinn briathran miodalach, *we used not flattering words.*—*Stew. Thess.*

Gnàthaichear, *fut. pass.* gnathaichear.

Gnàthaichte, *p. part.* of gnàthaich. Performed, practised; usual, accustomed, customary. San aimsir ghnàthaichte, *in the customary season.*—*Macfar.*

Gnàthail, *a.* Usual, customary; peculiar; proper.

Gnath-ainm, *s. m.* (*Ir. id.*) A usual or common name.

Gnàthanna, *n. pl.* of gnàth; which see.

Gnàthas, ais, *s. m.*, *from* gnàth. (*Ir. id.*) Usage, habit, custom; experience.—*Shaw.* A réir mo ghnàthais, *according to my custom.*

Gnàth-chainnte, *s. f.* Vernacular language.

Gnàth-chuimhne, *s. f.* (*Ir. id.*) Tradition.

Gnàth-eòlach, *a.* Having knowledge from experience; experienced.

Gnàth-eòlas, ais, *s. m.* (*Ir. id.*) Experience; knowledge got by experience.

Gnath-fhiabhras, ais, *s. m.* (*Ir. id.*) A constant fever; an unremitting fever.

Gnàth-fhocal, ail, *s. m.* A proverb, a by-word, a phrase. Bithidh e na ghnàth-fhocal, *he shall be a by-word.*—*Stew.* 1 *K.*

Gnàth-fhoclach, *a.* Proverbial.

Gnàth-fhuaim, *s. f.* A continued noise; a constant clack.

Gnàth-fhuaimneach, *a.* Making a continued noise.

Gnath-ghlas, *a.* (*Ir. id.*) Ever-green.

Gnath-urnuigh, *s. f.* Frequent prayer.—*Stew. Acts.*

Gnè, *s.* Kind, sort, species; temper or disposition; manner, form, appearance; complexion. (*W.* gne, *complexion.* *Ir.* gne.) *Also*, an accident or outward sensible sign.—*Shaw.* A reir a gnè, *after its kind.*—*Stew. O. T.* Ainnir bu mhìn gnè, *a virgin of the softest temper.*—*Oss. Fing.*

Gnè-mhill, *v. a.* Disfigure, deform.

Gnèth, *s.* See **Gnè.**

Gnèthealachd, *s. f.* Good nature, tender-heartedness, kindness; mannerliness; shapeliness.

Gnètheil, *a.* (gnèth-amhuil.) Good-natured, tender-hearted; shapely; mannerly. Gu gnètheil, *good-naturedly.*

† **Gnia**, *s.* (*Ir. id.*) Knowledge; a tree; a servant; a judge; a knowing person.

† **Gnic**, *s. f.* (*Ir. id.*) Knowledge.—*Shaw.*

Gniomh, *s. f.* (*Ir. id.*) A fact; a deed; a work; an office or business; an exploit; *rarely*, fear; a parcel; a division of land; the twelfth part of a plough-land. Chronaich mi an gniomh, *I blamed the deed.—Orr.* Gniomh a laimh, *the work of his hands.—Sm.* Cuir an gniomh, *perform, operate.—Macint.* Gniomh mna-glùine, *the office of a midwife.—Stew. Ex.* *N. pl.* gniomharan.

Gniomhach, *a.*, *from* gniomh. (*Ir. id. Lat.* gnavus.) Active; industrious; actual; busy; laborious; operative. An seillean gniomhach, *the busy bee.—Macfar.* *Com.* and *sup.* gniomhaiche.

Gniomhachas, ais, *s. m.* (*Ir. id.*) Doings; agency; business; activity.

Gniomhachd, *s. f.* (*from* gniomh.) Activity; industriousness; efficiency.

Gniomhaich, *v. a.* Perform, effect, operate, work. *Pret. a.* ghniomhaich, *performed; wrought; fut. aff. a.* gniomhaichidh, *shall work.* Ormsa ghniomhaich e beud, *to me he has wrought harm.—Mac Lach.*

Gniomhaiche, *s. m.* An agent, a doer.

Gniomhair, *s. m.* (gniomh-fhear.) An actor; an agent. *N. pl.* gniomhairean.

Gniomharach, *a.* (*Ir. id.*) Active; actual.

Gniomharan, *n. pl.* of gniomh. Deeds, doings, works, actions, exploits.

Gniomh-chomasach, *a.* (*Ir.* gniomh-chumasach.) Powerful; active.

† **Gnis**, *v. a.* (*Ir. id.*) Effect, bring to pass.

† **Gnithe**, *s. pl.* (*Ir. id.*) Transactions; business.

Gnò, *a.* (*Ir. id.*) Gloomy, surly, gruff; notable, remarkable, famous; jeering. Iomad bodachan gnò, *many a gruff old man.—Old Song.*

† **Gno**, *s. m.* (*Ir. id.*) Jeering, mocking; sea.

† **Gno**, *s. m.* Business. See **Gnothach**.

Gnòdh, *n.* Gloomy, surly, gruff; notable, remarkable, famous. Bu ghnòdh an geamhradh, *gloomy was the winter.—Old Song.*

Gnòdhan, ain, *s. m.* (*Ir. id.*) An angry frown; an angry groan; a noise; a moan.

Gnog, gnoig, *s. m.* (*Ir. id.*) A sudden shove; a rough shove; a jolt; a knock; a frown, a sulky look.

Gnogach, *a.* (*Ir. id.*) Pettish; sulky; frowning; jolting; knocking. *Com.* and *sup.* gnogaiche. Gu gnogach, *sulkily.*

Gnogag, aig, *s. f.* A pettish girl, a little sulky female.

Gnogaiseachd, *s. f.* Pettishness, sulkiness.

Gnoig, *gen. sing.* of gnog.

Gnòig, *s. f.* (*Ir. id.*) A frown, a gloom, a sulky look.

Gnòigeach, *a.* Frowning, gloomy, sulky.

Gnòigeag, eig, *s. f.* A sulky little female. *N. pl.* gnoigeagan.

Gnoimh, *s. f.* A visage; a grin; the nickname of a person who has a grinning countenance.

Gnos, gnois, *s. m.* (*Ir. id.*) A snout; a bill; a mouth; a ludicrous term for the mouth of a human being. Gnos muic, *the snout of a sow;* gnos tunnaig, *a duck's bill.*

Gnosach, *a.* (*from* gnos.) Snouty; having a large mouth. *Com.* and *sup.* gnosaiche.

Gnosair, *s. m.* A fellow with a large mouth; a blubber-lipped fellow. *N. pl.* gnosairean.

Gnosaireachd, *s. f.* (*from* gnos.) A mouthing; blubberliness.

Gnòsd, *s. f.* A lowing, a bellow; a snoring noise; a deep groan; a grunt. Ciod a dh' iarradh tu air bo ach a gnòsd? *what could you expect from a cow but a low?—G. P.*

Gnòsd, *v. n.* Low, bellow; snore. *Pret.* ghnosd, *lowed; fut. aff.* gnosdaidh, *shall low.*

Gnòsdaich, **Gnòsdail**, *s. f.* A lowing, a bellowing; a snoring noise.

Gnothach, aich, *s. m.* (*from* † gno.) *N. pl.* gnothaichean. See **Gnothuch**.

Gnothaich, *gen. sing.* of gnothach.

Gnothuch, uich, *s. m.* Business, an affair, a matter or circumstance; an errand; a call of nature. A gabhail gnothuich, *meddling, being a busy body.—Stew.* 1 *Thess.* A dol air ghnothuch, *going on an errand;* na biodh gnothuch agad ris, *having nothing to do with him.—Stew. Pro.* Ni e an gnothuch, *it will do;* tha gnothuch agam riut, *I have some business with you; I have something to do with you,* or, *to say to you;* dean do ghnothuch, *do your business; obey a call of nature;* gille gnothuichean, *an errand-boy;* gnothuch cabhagach, *a business which requires haste.—Stew.* 1 *Sam.* Rach air ghnothuch, *go on an errand;* ruith air ghnothuch, *run on an errand;* a dh' aon ghnothuch, *on purpose.* *N. pl.* gnothuichean.

Gnothuich, *gen. sing.* of gnothuch.

Gnothuichean, *n. pl.* of gnothuch. Affairs; errands.

Gnù, *a.* See **Gnò**.

† **Gnuach**, *a.* (*Ir. id.*) Leaky.

Gnùis, *s. f.* (*Ir. id.*) A face, visage; aspect; appearance. *Asp. form,* ghnùis. Sheall e 'm ghnùis, *he looked in my face.—Orr.*

Gnuis, *s. f.* (*Ir. id.*) Hazard, jeopardy; a notch.—*Shaw.*

Gnùis-bhrat, -bhrait, *s. f.* A veil for the face. Ghabh i gnùis-bhrat, *she took a veil.—Stew. O. T.*

Gnùis-fhionn, *a.* White-faced.

Gnuis-fhiosachd, *s. f.* Physiognomy. Fear gnuis-fhiosachd, *a physiognomist.*

Gnùis-fhiosaiche, *s. f.* A physiognomist. *N. pl.* gnuis-fhiosaichean, *physiognomists.*

Gnùis-mhalta, *s. f.* A modest countenance; a face expressive of softness of temper; having a modest countenance. Mo chaileag ghnùis-mhalta, *my modest-faced girl.—Old Song.*

Gnùis-mheall, *v. a.* (*Ir. id.*) Counterfeit, put on a false appearance, dissemble. *Pret. a.* ghnùis-mheall; *fut. aff. a.* gnùis-mheallaidh.

Gnùis-mheallach, *a.* (*Ir. id.*) Counterfeiting; apt to deceive from a fair exterior.

Gnùis-mhealladh, aidh, *s. m.* (*Ir. id.*) A dissembling, a counterfeiting; disguise or mask. Rinn iad gnùis-mhealladh, *they dissembled.—Stew. Gal.*

Gnùis-mhealltair, *s. m.* A dissembler.

Gnùis-nàire, *s. f.* (*Ir. id.*) Bashfulness, shamefacedness.—*Shaw.*

Gnùis-nàrach, *a.* (*Ir. id.*) Bashful, shamefaced. Gu gnùis-narach, *bashfully.*

Gnuis-nàrachd, *s. f.* Bashfulness, shamefacedness.

† **Gnumh**, *s. m.* (*Ir. id.*) A notch, a dent; a heap or pile.—*Shaw.*

† **Gnumh**, *v. a.* (*Ir. id.*) Heap up, pile, amass.

Gnumhail, *s. f.* (*Ir. id.*) Grunting, groaning.

† **Gnusadh**, aidh, *s. m.* (*Ir. id.*) A notch, a dent.

Gnùsadh, aidh, *s. f.* See **Gnùsd**.

Gnùsd, **Gnusdadh**, aidh, *s. m.* A low, a bellow; a snore;

a snoring noise; a grunt; the hollow roar of a bull; a deep groan. Leig e gnùsd as, *he bellowed, he groaned.*

GNÙSD, *v. n.* Low, bellow; grunt; make a hollow roar, as a bull; groan; snore. *Pret.* ghnùsd, *lowed*; *fut. aff.* gnusdaidh, *shall low.*

GNÙSDAICH, GNUSDAIL, *s. f.* Lowing, bellowing, roaring, as of a bull.

GNUSGALACH, *a.* Grunting.

Go, *prep.* To More frequently written *gu*, which see.

† Go, *s. m.* (*Ir id*) The sea; a spear.

Gò, *s m.* Guile, fraud, a lie; a blemish; an airy gait. *Asp form*, ghò. Do mhallachadh 's do ghò, *of cursing and of guile.—Sm* Dà reithe gun ghò, *rams without blemish.* —*Stew Ex*

GOB, guib, *s. m* A bird's bill, a beak; a snout; a name of contempt for a garrulous mouth, garrulity. Duilleag na ghob, *a leaf in its bill —Stew Gen* Gob crom, *a crooked bill —Macint* Gob circe, *a hen's bill.*

Ir gob *W.* gwp, *a bill* *Scotch*, gab. *Gr.* κοπις, *garrulous*

In the Hecuba of Euripides, Ulysses, who of all others had the gift of the gab, is thus described —ὁ ποικιλόφρων ΚΟΠΙς ἡδυλόγος, δημοχαριστης.—*Etym Mag*

GOBACH, *a.* (*Ir. id*) Billed, having a long bill, snouty; garrulous, prattling Gobach cireanach, *long-billed and crested —Macint* *Com* and *sup.* gobaiche, *more* or *most crested.*

GOBACH, aich, *s m* A kind of bird

GOBAG, aig, *s. f* (*Ir. id*) A dog-fish; a little bill, a garrulous female; a sand-eel *N. pl* gobagan. *D. pl.* gobagaibh

GOBAGACH, *a* (*Ir id*) Like a dog-fish; abounding in dog-fish, garrulous, as a female.

GOBAICHE, *com* and *sup* of gobach, which see

GOBAIR, *s m.* A talkative fellow, a gabbler, one who has the *gift of the gab* *N pl* gobairean; *d. pl.* gobairibh.

Gr κοβαλος, *a gabler*, and κοβαιρος, *a giber* *W* goaper.

GOBAIREACHD, *s. f.* Loquacity, garrulousness, the behaviour of a tattler

GOBAN, ain, *s m* (*Ir id*) A little bill, a garrulous mouth, a muffle, an external hindrance to speech

GOBANACH, aich, *s. m* (*Ir. id.*) A prater *N pl* gobanaiche.

GOBH, *v. a*, *provincial* for gabh; which see

GOBHA, *s. m* See GOBHADH.

GOBHA-DUBH, *s m* A water-ouzle.

GOBHAGAN, ain, *s m.* A titling. *N. pl.* gobhagain. Written also *gabhagan.*

GOBHADH, aidh, *s. m.* A blacksmith. *N. pl* goibhnean *for* gobhainnean. Gobhadh dubh, *a blacksmith* *Corn* gov du, *Arm* gof *Corn.* gov. *Ir* gobha

GOBHAIL, *gen sing.* of gobhal.

GOBHAINN, *s. m* A blacksmith. *N. pl* goibhnean, *smiths.*

GOBHAL, ail, *s. m* (*Ir id* *W.* gavyl) The forked part of any thing; the perinæum; a prop; a pillar or post; a fork, a prong; any furcated instrument; a descendant, a branch; a yoking; a day's labour Imirdh breug gobhal, *a lie requires a prop.* Written also *gabhal*

GOBHAL-REANG, *s f.* A pair of compasses More properly *gobhal-roinn.*

GOBHAL-ROINN, *s f* A pair of compasses. Leis a ghobhalroinn, *with the compass.—Stew Is.*

GOBHAR, air, *s. m.* A goat. See GABHAR.

GOBHAR-ADHEIR, *s f.* A snipe. See GABHAR-ADHEIR

GOBHÀRR, *s. m.* A periwig.

GOBHA-UISGE, *s. m.* The bird called a kingfisher; a water-ouzle, the *sturnus cinclus* of Linnæus.

GOBHLACH, *a.* Forked; bow-legged; astride, a-straddle. A marcach cas-gobhlach, *riding a-straddle*, clamhan gobhlach, *a kite.* *Com.* and *sup.* gobhlaiche.

GOBHLACHAN, ain, *s. m.* A swallow; an earwig; a young trout; a large minnow, *also*, the fish called a *parr* by the Scotch, and *samlet* by the English; it is the *salmulus* of naturalists. Gobhlachan gaoithe, *a swallow.*

GOBHLADH, aidh, *s. m.* The fork or furcated part of any thing; the perinæum; a prop; a pillar; a fork or prong.

GOBHLAG, aig, *s. f* A wooden fork or prong; any forked piece of timber; *in ridicule*, a bow-legged female. *N. pl.* gobhlagan.

GOBHLAN, ain, *s m* (*dim.* of gobhal) A little branch; a swallow; an earwig.

GOBHLAN-GAINMHICH, *s. m.* See GOBHLAN-GAINEIMH.

GOBHLAN-GAINEIMH, *s m* A sand-martin; the *hirundo riparia* of Linnæus

GOBHLAN-GAOITHE, *s m.* The *hirundo rustica* of Linnæus; a swallow Mar an gobhlan-gaoithe, *like the swallow.—Stew. Pro*

GOBHLAN-MARA, *s m.* A redshank.—*Shaw.*

GOBHLANNAIDH, *s. f.* A hollow between two hills.

GOBHTE, *p part.* See GABHTE.

GOC, *s m* A stop-cock *N. pl* gocan. Cha tig a soitheach le goc ach an deoch a bhios ann, *a stop-cocked barrel gives no better than it contains —G. P.*

GOCAMAN, ain, *s m.* (*Nor* gokman) An usher; a gentleman-usher; a warder, or domestic sentinel. *N pl.* gocamain

This officer was employed in the Hebrides in the time of Dr Martin, who makes mention of one whom he had seen at the house of Mac Neil of Barra His station was at the top of the house, where he was obliged to watch night and day, and strangers were never suffered to draw near the house until they returned satisfactory replies to his questions concerning the purport of their visit.

GÒD, gòid, *s m* (*Eng* † gaude.) Show, ornament; coquetry.

GÒDACH, *a* (*Ir. id*) Showy, dressy, coquettish; giddy. *Com* and *sup.* gòdaiche.

GODHAN, ain, *s m.* A cask, a barrel.

GOG, *s m* (*Ir. id*) A nod, a wagging of the head; (*W.* gogi, *shaking*,) a tittle, a syllable. Cha 'n e gog nan ceann a ni 'n t-iomram, *it is not the nodding of the head that makes the boat row —G. P.*

GOGACH, *a* (*Ir. id.*) Nodding; wagging, as the head; wavering, reeling.

GOGAID, *s. f.* A coquette; a giddy female; a stupid trull. *N. pl* gogaidean.

GOGAIDEACH, *a.* Coquettish, giddy, foolish; an epithet more commonly applied to a female

GOGAIDEACHD, *s f.* Coquetry, female finesse, womanish stupidity.

GOGAIL, GOGAILL, *s f.* A silly female, a stupid trull, a coquette, a doting female. *N. pl* gogailean.

GOGAILEACH, GOGAILLEACH, *a* Foolish, stupid, an epithet most commonly applied to a female.

GOGAILEACHD, GOGAILLEACHD, *s. f.* The behaviour of a silly female, low coquetry; dotage

GOGAILD, *s. f.* (*Ir. id.*) See GOGAIL.

GOGAIN, *gen. sing* and *n pl* of gogan.

GOGALLACH, aich, *s. f.* The cackling of poultry.—*Shaw*

GOGAN, ain, *s. m.* (*Scotch*, cogue.) A small wooden dish without handles, a kit; a pail; *rarely*, prating, cackling.

GOGAR, air, *s. m.* Light.

Gog-cheannach, *a.* (*Ir. id.*) Giddy, light-headed; shaking or nodding the head in walking, as a deer.—*Macint.*

Gog-gheadh, *s. f.* (*Ir. id.*) A small goose.

Gog-shùil, -shùl, *s. f.* (*Ir. id.*) A goggle-eye.

Gog-shuileach, *a.* (*Ir. id.*) Having wandering eyes; goggle-eyed.

Goibh, *s. f.* The letter *g*, the seventh letter of the Gaelic alphabet.

Goibheinn, *s. f.* A little hill.

Goibhneachd, *s. f.*, *i. e.* gobhainneachd. (*Ir. id.*) The trade of a blacksmith. Ris a ghoibhneachd, *working as a blacksmith.*

Goibhnean, *n. pl.* of gobhainn. Smiths.

Goibhrios, *s. m.* A false colour.

Goic, *s. f.* (*Ir. id.*) A scoff, a taunt; a tossing up of the head. Goic moit, *a cocking* or *tossing up of the head with a short neck.—Macdon.*

Goicealachd, *s. f.* A scornful tossing of the head.

Goiceil, *a.* (goic-amhuil.) Scoffing, taunting; scornfully tossing up the head.

Goid, *s. f.* Theft, stealing. Am bheil thu ri goid? *dost thou steal?—Stew. Rom.*

Goid, *v. a.* (*Ir. id.*) Steal, pilfer; creep softly. *Pret. a.* ghoid, *stole; fut. aff. a.* goididh, *shall steal.* Goididh an doinionn e, *the storm shall steal him.—Stew. Job.* Ghoid e orm, *he crept softly upon me.—Stew. Pro.*

Goideach, *a.* Inclined to pilfer.

Goideadh, idh, *s. m.* The act of stealing, theft, stealth.

Goideadh, 3 *sing.* and *pl. imper.* of goid. Goideadh e (no) iad, *let him* or *them steal.*

Goigean, ein, *s. m.* A coxcomb.

Goigeanachd, *s. f.* The behaviour of a coxcomb.

Goigleis, *s. f.* (*Ir. id. W.* goglais.) Tickling.

Goil, *v. a.* (*Ir. id.*) Boil; cook by boiling. *Pret.* ghoil, *boiled; fut. aff.* goilidh, *shall boil.*

† **Goil**, *s.* (*Ir. id.*) Prowress, chivalry.

Goil, goile, *s. f.* A stomach; appetite; a throat; a swarm, as of vermin; a boiling. Airson do ghoil, *for thy stomach.—Stew. Tim.* Air ghoile, *boiling; on the boil.—Stew. Job.* Air na goilean, *boiling;* gach anam air ghoil gu h-àr, *every soul boiling for bloodshed.—Mac Lach.*

Ir. goile. *W.* cwll, *stomach. Gr.* γύλιος, *cophinus cibarius. Lat.* gula, *a throat.*

Goileach, *a.* (*from* goil.) Boiling; hot, as boiling water. O choiribh ghoileach iochdrach, *from deep, boiling cauldrons.—Old Song.*

Goileachd, *s. f.* Flattery; gluttony; the conduct of a parasite.

Goileadh, idh, *s. m.* (*Ir. id.*) A boiling; a regurgitating; regurgitation.

Goileam, eim, *s. m.* (*Ir. id.*) Flattery; prattle; verbiage.

Goileamach, *a.* (*from* goileam.) Flattering; prattling. *Com.* and *sup.* goileamaiche. Gu goileamach, *pratingly.*

Goileamag, aig, *s. f.*, *from* goileam. (*Ir. id.*) A female prater, a prattling young girl.

Goileaman, ain, *s. m.* (*from* goileam.) A prater, a tattler. *N. pl.* goileamain.

Goileamhuin, *s. f.* (*Ir. id.*) Grief, sorrow.

Goilean, ein, *s. m.* (*from* goil, *stomach.*) A gourmand or greedy-gut; a parasite.

Goilean, *s. pl.* (*from* goil.) A state of boiling. Air na goilean, *boiling; very hot, as a liquid.*

Goileanach, *a.* (*from* goilean.) Parasitical; gluttonous; flattering.

Goilibheeir, *s. m.* A hashing-knife. This word is *provincial,* and seems to be a corruption of *cleaver.*

Goill, *s. f.* (*Ir. id.*) A hanging lip; a shapeless mouth, a distorted mouth; a face distorted with grief; a chop; a cheek; a sulky look; *rarely,* war; any cause of grief. Is ann air bha 'ghoill! *what a distorted mouth he had!*

Goilléach, *a.* (*from* goill.) Blubber-lipped; having a distorted mouth; sour-looking.

Goillear, ir, *s. m.* (goill-fhear.) A blubber-lipped person; a man with a distorted mouth.

Goillir, *s. m.* A Lewis bird, about the size of a swallow.

It is observed of this sea-bird, that it never comes ashore but in the month of January.

Goimh, *s. f.* (*Ir. id.*) A pang, a throb, anguish, agonising pain; a grudge; vexation; a storm; a frown. Do chridhe gun ghoimh, *thy heart without anguish.—Old Poem.* Ceann goimh air madainn earraich, *a spring morning has a frown.—G. P.*

Goimh-chridheach, *a.* Keen; ardent. Gu goimh-chridheach, guais-bheartach, *keenly and daringly.—Old Song.*

Goimheach, *a.* (*from* goimh.) Painful, throbbing.

Goimheil, *a.* (goimh-amhuil.) Sore, painful, throbbing; vexatious.

Goin, *s. f.* (*Ir. id.*) A wound, a hurt; a sting; a lance; a lancinating pain; *rarely,* delusion; paragraph. Cha b'fheairrd mo ghoin e, *my wounds were not the better for it.—Macfar.* Written also *guin.*

Goin, *v. a.* Wound, hurt; cause a sudden smarting; fascinate. *Pret. a.* ghoin, *wounded.* Ghoin e mi, *he wounded me. Fut. aff.* goinidh, *shall wound.*

Goineach, *a.* (*from* goin.) Painful, throbbing; prickly, stinging; agonising, vexatious; keen, eager. Gu goineach, *painfully. Com.* and *sup.* goiniche.

Goinead, eid, *s. m.* (*Ir. id.*) Painfulness; a throbbing; vexatiousness.—*Shaw.*

Goineag, eig, *s. f.* Pang, a twitching of pain.

Goineanta, *a.* Keen, piercing, wounding.

Goin-shùil, -shùl, *s. f.* A blasting eye; a fascinating eye. Goin shùil na righ-nathrach, *the fascinating eye of the cockatrice.—Old Song. N. pl.* goin-shùilean.

Goin-shùileach, *a.* Having a fascinating eye; having a blasting eye.

Goin-lamhach, *a.* A destructive hand; wounding with the hand.

Gointe, *p. part.* of goin. (*Ir. id.*) Bewitched; fascinated; *fay;* wounded.

Goir, *v. n.* Crow; squall, as a bird; call; name; talk loudly and pertly. *Pret. a.* ghoir, *crew; fut. aff. a.* goiridh, *shall crow.* Ghoir an coileach, *the cock crew.—Stew. N. T.* Fà mu'n goir a chorr, *the reason why the heron cries.—Oss. Derm.*

Ir. id. Gr. γηρυω *and* γαρυω, *to prate, to chirp, as a bird. Heb. Chald.* kara. *Syr.* karo, *to name.*

† **Goir**, *a.* Near. Hence goirid, *short.*

Goiream, 1 *sing. pres. aff.* of goir. I cry. *Also, for* goiridh mi, *I will cry.*

Goireas, eis, *s. m.* (*Ir. id.*) Moderation, a moderate quantity; cheer; apparatus; tools. Tha goireas agam, *I have a moderate quantity,* or *a sufficiency.*

Goireasach, *a.* (*Ir. id.*) Moderate; temperate; in moderate quantity; convenient. *Com.* and *sup.* goireasaiche, *more* or *most moderate.*

Goireil, *a.* Snug, convenient. Gu goireil, *snugly.*

Goirgeach, *a.* Foolish; doting.

Goirgeachd, *s. f.* (*Ir. id.*) Dotage; foolishness.

GOIRID, GOIRRID, *a.* (*from* †goir) Short; brief. (*Ir.* gairid *and* goirid.) An ceann ghoirid, *in a short time*, o cheann ghoirrid, *a short time since*, fear goirrid, *a man of low stature.*

GOIRIDH, *fut. aff. a.* of goir. Shall or will crow.

GOIRISEADH, idh, *s. m.* A target.

GOIRMEAN, ein, *s m* Wood. See GUIRMEAN.

GOIRNEAD, id, *s. m.* (*Ir. id.*) A gurnard.—*Shaw*

GOIRRIG, *s* A fool, a dolt.

GOIRSEADH, idh, *s. m.* A target —*Shaw.*

GOIRISINN, *s. f.* Horror, a tremour, a shuddering with fear or horror. Chuir thu goirisinn orm, *you made me shudder*

GOIRSINN, *s. f.* A crowing, a loud pert talking

GOIRRID See GOIRID

GOIRSINN, (a), *pr part.* of goir Crowing; talking loudly and pertly.

GOIRT, *a.* (*Ir. id*) Sore; sour; bitter; saltish, hard or sad; poor-spirited; narrow; mean. Le amghar goirt, *with sore distress* —*Sm* Acain ghoirt, *bitter sobbing.*—*Oss Gaul* Lionn goirt, *sour ale* Is goirt a chùis, *it is a hard case* —*Mac Luch* Goirt, *poor-spirited* —*Shaw*

GOIRT, *gen sing* of gort, which see.

GOIRT, *s. f.* (*Ir. id*) Famine. See GORTA.

GOIRT-BHRISEADH, idh, *s. m* A calamity; misery.

GOIRTE, *s f.* (*Ir. id*) Saltness, sourness.

GOIRTEACHADH, aidh, *s. m.* (*Ir. id*) The act of hurting; a souring.

GOIRTEAG, eig, *s f* A stingy female; a crab apple-tree. *N. pl* goirteagan

GOIRTEAN, ein, *s. m* (*Ir* goirtin) A little field; a little farm, a small patch of arable ground; a little corn-field *N. pl.* goirtein

GOIRTICH, *v a.* and *n.* Sour; leaven; hurt; grow sour. *Pret a* ghoirtich, *soured*, *fut. aff a* goirtichidh, *shall sour*, *fut pass.* goirtichear Goirtichear e, *he shall be hurt* —*Stew Ecc*

GOIRTICHTE, *p part* of goirtich Soured; leavened; hurt. Aran goirtichte, *leavened bread* —*Stew. Ex.*

GOISINN, *s f.* A gin, a trap —*Macd* *N pl.* goisinnean.

GOISINNEACH, *a.* Full of gins or traps; like a gin or trap; ensnaring.

† GOISTE, *s f* (*Ir id*) A halter; a snare —*Shaw.*

GOISTEACHD, *s. f* (*for* goistidheachd) Gossipping Cleamhnas am fagus is goisteachd am fad, *marriage at hand, and gossipping afar off.*—*G P*

GOISTIDH, *s. m* A gossip; a name given by a godfather to the father of a child to which he is sponsor *N. pl* goistidhean

GOISTIDHEACH, *a* Gossipping

GOISTIDHEACHD, *s f*, contracted *goisteachd*, which see

† GOITHNE, *s f* (*Ir. id.*) A lance, a spear, a quick gait —*Shaw*

† GOLADH, aidh, *s. m* (*It* gola) Gluttony.—*Shaw*

GOLAG, aig, *s f* (*Ir. id*) A budget. *N pl* golagan

GOLAIDH, *s f.* (*Corn.* golhan) A clumsy clasp-knife. *N pl.* golaidhean.

GOLG-HÀIR, *s. f* (*Ir id*) Lamentation, a loud wail. More properly *gul-ghàir*

GOL-GHAIREACH, *a* Lamenting, wailing; causing lamentation, mournful. More properly *gul-ghaireach.*

GOLLACH, *a.* Gluttonous

GÒMAG, aig, *s. f* A pinch, a nip. *N. pl.* gòmagan.

GÒMAGACH, *a.* Pinching, pinchy.

GON, goin, *and* gona, *s. m* A wound, a sting, a stab, a lance; a stinging, a stabbing, a lancing; a stinging pain, a throb; a charm; fascination. Naoidh gona, *nine wounds.* —*Old Song*

GON, *v a* (*Ir. id.*) Wound, sting, stab, lance; charm or fascinate. *Pret. a.* ghon, *fut. aff. a* gonaidh, *shall stab; fut pass* gonar. Gu ma h-ann a ghonar am fiosaiche! *may evil betide the prophet!*—*G. P*

GONACH, *a.* Wounding, stinging, stabbing; sharp, keen.

GONADAIR, *s. m.* A wounder, a piercer.

GONADH, aidh, *s m.* A lascinating, a bewitching or charming; fascination; a lancing, a stinging; a wound; a lancinating pain.

Gr ἀγων, *pain* *Eng.* agony. *Ir* gonadh.

GONADHAIRE, *s f.* A wounding, a stinging, a stabbing.

GONAIR, *s. m.* A wounder, a piercer.

GONAIS, *s. f.* (*Ir id.*) A sting, a prick, a wound.

GONAM, (*for* gonaidh mi) I will wound

GONTA, *p part.* of gon; which see.

† GOR, *s m.* and *f* (*Ir. id.*) Profit; laughter; pleasure. —*Shaw.* Pus, light; heat.

GÒRAG, aig, *s. f* A foolish female. Tapan gòraig air cuigeil crionta ig, *foolish woman's flax on the wise woman's rock.*—*G P.*

GÒRACH, *a.* (*Ir. id.*) Foolish, insane; mad Nur bha mi òg is gòrach, *when I was young and foolish* —*G. P.* Na innis do rùn do charaid gòrach, *tell not your mind to a foolish friend* —*Old Song.* *Com.* and *sup.* gòraiche.

GÒRACHD, *s. f* (*Ir. id.*) Foolishness, idiocy.

† GORAICEADH, idh, *s m.* A croaking, a croaking voice or shout.

GORAICEIL, *a* Croaking, screeching.

GORAICLEIS, *s. f.* Croaking; a shouting; a shout

GÒRAICHE, *s. f.* Foolishness, folly, insanity. Cha 'n 'eil ann ach a ghòraiche, *it is but folly.*

GÒRAICHE, *com* and *sup.* of gòrach; which see.

GÒRAICHEAD, eid, *s m.* Folly, foolishness, madness; increase in folly or madness. A dol an gòraichead, *growing more and more foolish* or *mad.*

GORAMHACH, *a* (*Ir. id.*) Greedy, hungry —*Shaw* Gu goramhach, *greedily.*

GORAMHACHD, *s f* (*Ir. id.*) Greediness, hunger, gluttony.

GORAMHAN, ain, *s m.* (*Ir id*) A hungry fellow, a glutton. *N pl* goramain

GORAN, ain, *s m* See GUIREAN.

GÒRG, *a.* (*Gr* γοργς.) See GARG

† GORGACH, *a* (*Ir id*) Foolish; peevish.—*Shaw*

† GORGACHAS, ais, *s m.* (*Ir. id*) Foolishness; peevishness, dotage

GORGAICH, *v a.* Hurt, injure, annoy.

GORGHLAN, *v a.* Weed, cleanse *Pret. a.* ghorghlan, *weeded.*

GORGHLANADAIR, *s m* A weeder.—*Shaw.*

GORM, guirm, *s.* A blue colour; azure colour; a green; a green spot of ground. Iall do ghorm, *a riband of blue.*—*Stew. Num*

GORM, *a* (*W* gwrm, *dun.* *Ir.* gorm, *blue*) Blue, azure, sky-coloured, green, verdant; *rarely*, great, illustrious; hot Na speuran gorm, *the blue heavens.*—*Orr.* Feur gorm, *green grass* *Com.* and *sup.* guirme.

GORM, *v. a.* and *n.* Make blue; make azure or green, as grass; grow blue, grow green, as grass. *Pret.* ghorm; *fut aff.* gormaidh. Ghorm am feur, *the grass grew green.*

Gormadh, aidh, *s. m.* A making blue; making green, as grass; growing blue; growing green, as grass, a blue or azure colour. Fo ghormadh nan sgiath, *beneath the blue colour of the shields.—Oss. Tem.*

Gorman, ain, *s. m.* A green knoll; blue bottle; indigo In this latter sense it is more frequently written *gurmean.*

Gormanach, *a.* Having green knolls

Gorm-bhallach, *a.* Spotted blue; blue-bossed. Cuchullin nam gorm-bhallach sgiath, *Cuchullin of the blue-bossed shields —Oss. Fing.*

Gorm-cheathach, ich, *s. m* and *f* Blue mist. An gorm-cheathach a snàmh, *the blue mist floating —Oss. Fing.*

Gorm-chruaidh, *s. f.* Blue steel; blue armour; a blue sword. Feachd nan gorm-chruaidh, *the blue-armed host. —Oss. Carricth.*

Gorm-eutrom, *a.* Light blue. Gùn gorm-eutrom, *a light blue colour.*

Gorm-ghlas, *a.* (*Ir. id. W.* gwrm-las.) Of an azure or blue colour, cerulean.

Gorm-mhac, -mhic, *s. m.* A brave servant, a sturdy domestic.—*Shaw.*

Gorm-phreas, -phris, *s. m.* (*Ir. id.*) A green bush. Gorm-phreas na bruaich, *the green bush of the bank —Oss. Dargo. N. pl.* gorm-phreasan.

Gorm-rod, -roid, *s m.* (*Ir. id*) A green path; a passage through the sea —*Shaw.* The track of a ship on the water.

Gorm-shùil, -shùl, *s. f.* A blue eye. A gorm-shùil a sealladh gu farasd, *her blue eye looking softly.—Oss. Com.*

Gorm-shuileach, *a.* Blue-eyed; *also*, a blue-eyed person. An gorm-shuileach treun, *the blue-eyed warrior.—Oss. Fing.*

Gorm-thalla, *s. m.* A blue hall; a blue land; a poetical name for the sky, often to be met with in the poems of Ossian.

Gorn, goirn, *s m.* (*Ir. id.*) An ember; a firebrand; the force of poison.—*Shaw* A murdering dart.

Gorrach. See Gorach.

Gorsaid, *s. f.* (*Ir. id*) A cuirass Cheangail e gòrsaid phrais, *he bound a brazen cuirass.—Mac Lach. N. pl.* gorsaidean.

Gorsaideach, *a.* Like a cuirass, wearing a cuirass

Gort, goirt, *s. m.* (*Ir. id.*) Standing corn; a crop of corn or grass; a field; a garden; the ivy. Written also *gart*; which see.

Gr χόρτος. *Lat.* hortus. *Ir.* gort. *Dan.* gaart *W.* gaard.

Gorta, ai, *s. f.* (*Ir.* gort.) Famine, hunger. Bha gorta san tir, *there was famine in the land.—Stew. Gen.* and *Ruth*

Gortach, *a.* (*Ir id.*) Hungry, starving; causing famine; sparing; greedy. Bliadhna ghortach, *a year of famine.* Cha 'n 'eil nàir aig a ghortach, *the hungry has no shame — G. P. Com.* and *sup.* gortaiche.

Gortachadh, aidh, *s. m.* (*Ir.* gortughadh.) A famishing; a souring; oppression; hurt, harm.

Gortadh, aidh, *s. m.* (*Ir. id.*) A famine. Airson a ghortaidh, *by reason of the famine.—Stew. Gen.*

Gortag, aig, *s. f* (*Ir. id.*) A crab-tree

Gortaich, *v a.* (*from* gort.) Famish, starve; sour; wrong, oppress *Pret.* ghortaich; *fut aff.* gortaichidh, *fut. pass.* gortaichear.

Gortaichte, *p. part* of gortaich. Famished, starved; soured; oppressed.

Gortaigheal, *s. m.* The universal language before the confusion of tongues at Babel.—Vide *Keating.*

Gortaladh, aidh, *s. m.* (*Ir. id*) Patching, mending.

Gortan, ain, *s. m.* (*Ir. id*) A hungry fellow.

Gortas, ais, *s. m.* Famine, hunger, starvation. Bhàsaich e le gortas, *he died of hunger.*

Gort-ghlan, *v. a* See Gart-ghlan

Gort-ghlanadh, aidh, *s. m* A weeding. More commonly written *gart-ghlan*

† **Gort-reabadh**, aidh, *s. m.* (*Ir. id.*) Misery.—*Shaw.*

Gortuich See Gortaich.

† **Gosda**, ai, *s. m.* (*Ir. id*) A ghost or spectre.

† **Gost-aois**, *a.* (*Ir. id*) Old age.—*Shaw*

† **Gost-aosmhor**, *a.* (*Ir. id.*) Aged.

† **Goth**, *a.* (*Ir id*) Straight, even.

† **Goth**, *s.* (*Ir id.*) A string, a dart. More properly *gath*, which see.

Gott, *s m.* (*Corn* goth, *pride*) An airy gait. Nach ann aig tha 'n gòth! *what an airy gait he has!* Thigeamaid a ghabhail gòth, *come let us walk about*

† **Goth**, *s. m.* (*Ir. id*) A vowel —*Shaw.*

Gòthach, *a.* Airy; having a smart or airy gait.

Gòthadh, aidh, *s. m* A smart gait.

Gothan, ain, *s m* (*dim* of goth) An airy youth

Gothanach, aich, *s. m* (*from* gòth.) A smart lively lad, a young man with an airy gait. *N pl* gòthanaich

Gothanach, *a.* (*Ir. id.*) Airy in gait, lively, smart; *also*, opprobious —*Shaw.*

Grab, *v a.* (*Ir. id*) Hinder, stop, prohibit, oppose; notch, indent; entangle. *Pret.* ghrab; *fut. aff. a.* grabaidh. Ghrab e maomadh na feachd, *he stopped the progress of the army —Mac Lach.*

Grabach, *a* (*Ir. id.*) Causing hindrance; entangling; opposing; notched, indented.

Grabadh, aidh, *s. m.* (*Ir. id*) A hindering, an opposing, a stopping; hindrance, entanglement, impediment, a notching or indenting.

Grabair, *s. m*, grab-fhear. (*Ir id*) A hinderer; an entangler; an opposer; a jester, a prattler; a droll. *N. pl* grabairean

Grabaireachd, *s. f.* (*Ir id*) Entanglement; opposition; idle talk; gibble-gabble.

Grabh, *v.* Grave, engrave, carve *Pret. a.* grabh, *graved, fut. aff.* grabhaidh, *shall grave.*

Grabhadair, *s m* (*Ir. id*) An engraver.

Grabhadaireachd, *s f* The business of an engraver.

Grabhail, *v. a.* Engrave, carve; embroider *Pret. a.* ghrabhail; *fut aff. a* grabhailidh.

Gr. γράφω, *write Germ* graben, *engrave. W.* crabu *Span.* gravar. *Eng. by met* carve.

Grabhailte, *p. part.* of grabhail. Engraved, carved. Obair ghrabhailte, *carved work.*

Grabhal, ail, *s m.* An engraving, carving; sculpture Obair ghrabhaladh, *carved.—Stew* 1 *K ref.*

Grabhalaiche, *s m.* An engraver

Grabhalair, *s m.* An engraver

Grabhalta, *a* (*Ir id.*) Graven, carved.

Grabhat, ait, *s. m* A cravat —*Turn.*

Grabh-lochd, *s m* A fault, an error, a blot —*Shaw.*

Grabh-lochdach, *a.* Faulty, full of errors, blotted

Grad, *a.* (*Ir. id*) Quick, sudden, speedy, soon, early, active, agile, clever, unexpected. Is grad do chaochladh, *thy death is early.—Oss Tem* Grad na ghnothuichibh, *quick* or *clever in his business —Stew. Pro ref* Gu grad, *quickly.*

Gràd, *a.* Ugly; nasty. *Com.* and *sup* gràide See also Grannd.

Gradag, aig, *s. f.* A short while; hurry. Ann an gradaig, *quickly, in a short time*

Gradan, ain, *s m*, *from* grad. (*Ir. id.*) Parched corn. Gràn gradain, *parched grains of corn.—Stew. Sam.*

Gradan was corn or meal prepared after the ancient custom of the Gael A woman sitting down, took a handful of corn, and holding it in her left hand by the stalks, she set fire to the ears, which were at once in a flame In her right hand she held a stick, with which she dexterously beat the grain at the very instant when the husks were quite burnt By this simple process, which is still followed in remote parts of the Highlands, corn may be cut down, dressed, winnowed, dried, ground, and baked, within half an hour In separating the meal from the husks, instead of sieves they made use of a sheep's skin stretched round a hoop, minutely perforated by a small hot iron The bread which is thus made is considered very salubrious, and is extremely pleasant to the palate of a Highlander Prepared in the same simple manner was the parched corn of holy writ, such as that which is mentioned in the book of Ruth

Grad-charach, *a* Nimble; fidgeting.—*Shaw.* Gu grad-charach, *nimbly*

Grad-chleas, *s m.* A hocus-pocus trick; a clever trick; a clever movement.

Grad-chleasach, *a* Nimble, agile Gu grad-chleasach, *nimbly*

Grad-chlisg, *v a* and *n* Startle; convulse. *Pret a* grad-chlisg, *startled*, *fut aff a* grad-chlisgidh, *shall startle*

Grad-chlisgeach, *a* Convulsed; convulsive; startling

Gradh, graidh, *s. m* (*Ir. id Gr* χαρις) Love, affection, charity, a beloved object *Asp form*, ghradh. Tha ghradh aig dh 'i, *he loves her. V. sing.* ghraidh. Thig-sa ghraidh! *come thou hither, my love!—Mac Lach.*

† **Gradh**, gradh, *s m.* (*Lat.* gradus *Ir.* gradh) A degree, a gradation; *adjectively*, noble; valiant; dear.

Gradhach, *a*, *from* gradh (*Ir. id*) Loving, fond, affectionate, amiable, dear, beloved An èilid ghradhach, *the loving hind—Stew. Pro.* A cneas gradhach, *her amiable form—Old Poem.* A chairde gradhach, *beloved friends.—Stew Rom.*

Gradhachadh, aidh, *s. m.* A loving, admiring, admiration.

Gradhachadh, (a), *pr part* of gradhaich. Loving; admiring

Gradhaich, *v a* (*from* gradh.) *Ir.* gradhuigh. Love, esteem. *Pret. a* ghradhaich, *loved*, *fut. aff a* gradhaichidh, *shall love.*

Gradhaichear, *fut pass.* of gradhaich Shall be loved. Gradhaichear e, *he shall be loved.*

Gradhaichte, *p. part.* of gradhaich. Beloved, admired.

Gradhail, *a* (*Ir* gradhamhuil.) Lovely.

Gradhaileachd, *s. f.* Loveliness

Gradhdan, ain, *s m.* See **Gràdran**.

Gradh-lasda, *a.* (*Ir. id.*) Fervent love.

Grad-leum, *s. m.* A quick spring or jump, a bound.

Grad-leum, *v n* Spring or jump quickly *Pret* ghrad-leum, *sprang*, *fut aff.* grad-leumaidh, *shall spring.* Ghrad-leum e, *he quickly sprang.*

Gradhmhoire, *com.* and *sup.* of gradhmhor.

Gradhmhor, *a* Loving, fond, affectionate. *Com* and *sup.* gradhmhoire Gu gradhmhor, *lovingly*

Gradhmhorachd, *s. f* Lovingness, fondness, affectionateness

Gràdran, ain, *s m.* A murmur; a peculiar complaining noise made by hens; a prolonged cackle; a chattering.

Gràdranach, *a.* Noisy, clamorous; cackling.

Gràdranaich, *s. f.* A continued chattering; a prolonged cackling or complaining noise, as hens are often heard to make; *also, adjectively*, noisy; cackling; clamorous.

Gràdranaich, *v. n.* Cackle; chatter; make a complaining, prolonged cackling, as hens are heard to utter.

Grad-theich, *v n.* Fly quickly. *Pret. a.* ghrad-theich; *fut aff a.* grad-theichidh, *shall fly.* Grad-theichidh a geilt, *her terror shall soon fly away.—Ull.*

Grad-thog, *v. a* Raise quickly. *Pret a.* ghrad-thog. Ghrad-thog mi siùil, *I quickly raised my sails.—Oss. Croma.*

† **Graf**, *v a.* (*Gr.* γραφω. *Ir* graf. *Eng. by met.* carve.) Write, inscribe; carve, engrave See **Grabh** or **Grabhail**.

Grafadh, aidh, *s. m.* (*Ir. id*) Engraving; writing.

Grafan, ain, *s. m.* (*Ir. id*) A grubbling-axe. *N. pl* grafain. Grafan bàn, *white horehound, ballota alba*, grafan dubh, *stinking horehound, ballota nigra.*

† **Grag**, graig, *s m.* (*Ir. id*) The noise of crows, cawing; croaking, a shout.

Gragair, *s. m.* (*Ir. id*) A glutton—*Shaw.* *N. pl.* gragairean

Gragallach, aich, *s. m.* (*Ir. id.*) The crowing or the clucking of a hen; the cawing or croaking of a crow.

† **Gragan**, ain, *s. m.* (*Ir. id*) A manor; a village; a district—*Shaw.*

Gragan, ain, *s m* (*Ir. id*) A bosom *N. pl.* gragain.

† **Grai**, *a* (*Arm* grai) Old.

From this very ancient Celtic vocable is derived γραιος and γραῖος. Hence the primitive inhabitants of Greece were called γραιοι, and also γραῖκοι, from another Celtic word *grec* or *groic*, which signifies *old* This name they received to distinguish them from the Hellenians, who were the descendants of Helen, the son of Deucalion, and who were of barbarous extraction

† **Graibh**, *s* (*Ir. id*) An almanack.

† **Graibhre**, *s f* (*Ir id*) A loud laugh; a word; utterance, a dignified expression

Gràichd, *s. f* A rough, scolding voice. Thug e gràichd air, *he spoke harshly to me*

Graideal, *s. f.* See **Groideal**.

Graidh, *s. m.* (*Ir. id*) A stud of horses, a drove of horses; a breed of mares. Written also *greigh*; which see.

Graidheach, aich, *s. m.* (*Ir. id*) A stallion. *N. pl.* graidheich

Graidheag, eig, *s f* (*Ir.* graidheog) A lovely young female; a beloved girl

Graidhean, ein, *s m.* A lover; a sweetheart *N. pl* graidhein.

Graidheanach, *a* Gallant; wanton; amorous.

Graideanachd, *s. f.* Gallantry; intrigue, amour

Graidhear, eir, *s. m* A lover.

Graige, *s f.* (*Ir. id*) Superstition.—*Shaw.*

Graigeach, *a.* Superstitious

Graigeachd, *s f.* (*Ir. id*) Superstition; superstitious usages.

Graigean, ein, *s m.* A glutton; a swag-bellied young person.

Graigeanach, *a* (*from* graigean.) Gluttonous

Graigeanachd, *s f.* Gluttony; the infirmity of a swag-belly

Graigeanas, ais, *s m.* Gluttony.

Graigh. See **Graidh**

Graigheach. See **Graidheach.**

Graillean, ein, *s m.* A cimeter.

Gràin, *s. f.* (*Ir. id.*) Loathing, disgust, abhorrence; abomination; deformity. Gràin do bhiadh, *a loathing for food.—Sm* Thusa le 'n gràin iodhala, *you who abhor idols.—Stew. Rom.* Is fearr na fochaid gràin, *the scorner is an abomination.—Stew. Pro.*

Gràin-abhall. See Gràn-ubhall.

Gràin-aigein. See Gran-aigein.

Gràineachadh, aidh, *s. m.* (*Ir. id.*) Loathing; defoedation; granulation.

Gràinead, eid, *s. m.* Ugliness; disgust.

Gràineag, eig, *s. f.* (*Ir.* graineog.) A hedge-hog, or urchin; a bittern; a wild duck.—*Stew. Zeph. N. pl.* gràineagan. Cruasachd na graineig; a proverb expressive of the folly of wordly-minded people, who part with all at the grave, as the hedge-hog is compelled to drop its burden of crab-apples at the narrow entrance of its hole.

Gràineagach, *a.* Abounding in hedge-hogs; like a hedge-hog, bristly.

Gràinealachd, *s. f.* Loathsomeness; hatefulness; abominableness; detestableness. *N. pl.* grainealachdan. Rinn e na gràinealachdan so, *he hath done these abominations.*—*Stew. Ezek.*

Gràineil, *a.* (gràin-amhuil.) Loathsome, abominable, detestable, nasty. *Com.* and *sup.* gràineile, *more* or *most detestable.* Nach graineile an duine? *is not man more abominable?*—*Stew. Job.*

Graing, *s. f.* Disdain, loathing, disgust; a frown.

Graingeach, *a.* (*from* graing.) Causing disdain; frowning.

Graingich, *v. a.* Loathe, disdain.—*Shaw. Pret. a.* ghraingich, *loathed.*

Gràinich, *v. a.* (*from* gràin.) Loath, hate; cause disgust; granulate. *Pret. a.* ghràinich, *loathed; fut. aff. a.* gràinichidh, *shall detest.*—*Old Song.* Ghràinich mi ris, *I detest him* or *it.*

Gràinichte, *p. part.* of gràinich. Loathed, detested.

Gràinne, *s. f.* A grain; seed corn; a small quantity of any grained or granulated substance; a small number, as of people. Gràinne do shiol, *a grain of seed.*—*Stew. Matt.* Gràinne mullaich, *the top grain on a stalk.*

Gr. γϱανον. *Lat.* granum. *W.* grawn. *Dan.* gran. *Du.* graan. *Arm.* greun. *Ir.* grain. *Teut.* graen. *Cron.* gronen. *Eng.* grain.

Gràinneach, *a.* (*Ir. id.*) Abounding in grain; granulous; granulated.

Gràinneachadh, aidh, *s. m.* A granulating; granulation.

Gràinnean, ein, *s. m.* (*dim.* of grainne.) A little grain, a single grain; a little quantity of any granulated or pulverised substance. Grainnean eorna, *a grain of barley; a little quantity of barley;* grainnean fùdair, *a little powder. N. pl.* grainneanan.

Corn. gronen. *W.* gronyn. *Arm.* greunan. *Ir.* grainean.

Gràinneanach, *a.* Grained, gritty, pulverised. *Com.* and *sup.* grainneanaiche, *more* or *most grained.*

Gràinnein, *gen. sing.* of grainne.

Gràinn-itheach, *a.* Granivorous. Eunlan grainn-itheach, *a granivorous bird.*

Grainne-mullaich, *s. f.* The top grain on a stalk.—*Shaw.*

Gràinnich, *v. a.* Pulverise, granulate. *Pret. a.* ghràinnich, *pulverise.*

Grainnse, *s. f.* A grange.

Grainnseach, ich, *s. f.* A corn farm; a grain farm; a grange. *N. pl.* grainnsich.

Grainnseag, eig, *s. f.* (*Ir. id.*) A cracknel; a hard brittle cake. *N. pl.* grainnseagan. Written also *crainnseag.*

Grainnseagach, *a.* (*Ir. id.*) Full of cracknels; having cracknels; like a cracknel.

Grainnsear, ir, *s. m.* A grieve, an overseer. *N. pl.* grainnsearan.—*Shaw.*

Grainnsearachd, *s. f.* The employment of a grieve, overseeing.

Gràip, *s. f.* A dung-fork. (*Scotch,* graip. *Teut.* greep *and* grepe, *a trident.*) *N. pl.* graipeachan.

Gràisg, gràisge, *s. f.* (*Ir. id.*) A rabble, a mob, the lowest of the people; *canaille, riff-raff.*

Gràisgealachd, *s. f.* Vulgarity; blackguardism.

Gràisgeil, *a.* (graisg-amhuil.) Low, vulgar, blackguardish.

Gramachadh, aidh, *s. m.* A fastening, a tightening; clenching; a grasping.

Grama-chos, -chois, *s. m.* A sure foot; sure-footing.

Grama-chosach, *a.* Sure footed. *Com.* and *sup.* gramachosaiche.

Gràmadach, aich, *s. m.* A grammar.—*Shaw.*

Gramag, aig, *s. f.* (*Ir. id.*) A hook; a buffoon; a jester. —*Shaw. N. pl.* gramagan.

Gramaich, *v. a.* Tighten, fasten; clench; grasp. *Pret. a.* ghramaich, *clenched; fut. aff. a.* gramaichidh, *shall clench.* Ris an do ghramaich an sealgair, *which the hunter grasped.* —*Old Poem.*

Gramaiche, *s. f.* A vice; pincers; a flesh-hook. *N. pl.* gramaichean.

Gramail, *a.* Firm; stout, vigorous; muscular; resolute; tightened, fastened, clenched. Thugaibh ionnsuidh ghramail, *make a vigorous onset.*—*Macfar. Com.* and *sup.* gramaile.

Gramaisg, *s. f.* (*Ir. id.*) A mob, a rabble.—*Shaw.*

Gramalachd, *s. f.* Firmness of body or mind; vigorousness; strength; muscular vigour.

Gramalas, ais, *s. m.* Firmness, whether of body or mind. Cha 'n fhacar do leithid air ghramalas, *thine equal for firmness was never seen.*—*Old Song.*

Gramasg, aisg, *s. m.* A morsel, a mouthful; a small bit of food.

Gran, ain, *s. m.* (*Ir. id.*) Hail; shot.

Gràn, gràin, *s. m.* Dried corn; grain. Gràn cruadhaichte, *dried corn.*—*Stew. Lev.* Gràn gradan, *parched corn.*—*Stew.* 1 *Sam.*

Gr. γϱανον. *Lat.* granum. *W.* grawn. *Ir.* gràin. *Du.* graan. *Dan.* gran. *Arm.* greun. *Corn.* gronen.

Gràn-abhal, ail, *s. m.* See Gràn-ubhall.

Gràinalach, aich, *s. f.* Grain.—*Shaw.*

Gran-aorrainne, *s.* The glanders.

Gràinda, Gràinnda, *a.* (*Ir.* granda.) Ugly, unseemly, nasty; shameful; ill-favoured; grim. Granda ri 'm faicinn, *ill-favoured, ugly to be seen.*—*Stew. Gen.* Is grannda leinn e, *we think it unseemly.*—*Macint.*

Grandachd, Granndachd, *s. f.* Ugliness; grimness; unseemliness; nastiness.

Granlach, aich, *s. m.* (*Ir. id.*) Corn, grain.—*Shaw.*

Gràn-lachan, ain, *s. m.* Lesser duck-meat; *lemma minor.*

Gràinna, *a.* See Grannda.

Grannaidh, *s. m.* (*Ir. id.*) Long hair.

Grant, *a.* Grey, green; *also,* the name Grant.

Gran-abhall, Gràn-abhall, ail, *s. m.* A pomegranate. *N. pl.* gran-ubhlan, *pomegranates.* Mar ghran-ubhall, *like a pomegranate.*—*Stew. Song Sol.*

Gràn-aigein, *s. m.* (*Ir. id.*) Common pile-wort, lesser celandine; the *ranunculus ficaria* of botanists.

Graoine, *s. f.* Joy; *adjectively,* joyful, bright.

Graoineachas, ais. See Greadhnachas.

Graoineag, eig, *s. f.* Irritation, provocation.

Graoineagaich, *v. a.* Provoke, irritate, incense.

Graollas, ais, *s. m.* Obscenity.

Graosda, Graosdach, *a.* (*Ir. id.*) Filthy, obscene.—*Shaw.*

Graosdachd, *s. f.* Filthiness, obscenity, ribaldry.—*Stew. Eph. ref. Shaw.*

Gràp, *v. a.* Climb.

Gràp, Gràpadh, aidh, *s. f.* (*Ir. id.*) A dung-fork.—*Shaw.* See also **Graip.**

Gràs, gràis, *s. m.* Grace, favour; divine favour. Ghràs Dhé, *God's grace.*
Lat. gratia. *Fr.* grâce. *Ir.* gràs. *It.* grazia.

Gràsaich, *v. a.* (*Ir. id.*) Give thanks.

Gràsail, *a.* (gràs-amhuil.) Gracious; graceful; merciful. Bean-ghràsail, *a gracious woman.*—*Stew. Pro.* Do'n ghrasail grasmhor, *to the graceful thou art gracious.*—*Sm.*

Gràsalachd, *s. f.* Graciousness; gracefulness; mercifulness.

Gràsda, *a.* Compassionate; gracious.

Gràsmhoire, *com.* and *sup.* of gràsmhor.

Gràsmhor, *a.* Gracious; merciful; full of grace. A Dhé ghràsmhoir! *gracious God!*

Gràsmhorachd, *s. f.* Graciousness.

Gràst, *a.* Ugly; compassionate.—*Shaw.*

Gràstachd, *s. f.* Ugliness; compassionateness.

Gràt, *s. m.* A grate.

Gràturnach, *a.* Noisy, clamorous. See **Gràdranach.**

Gràturnaich. See **Gradranach.**

Grathuinne, *s. f.* A while; a turn; some time. Eadar so is ceann ghrathuinne, *in a while after this;* gabh grathuinne deth, *take a while of it;* gabh do ghrathuinne deth, *take your turn of it;* grathuinne mhath, *a good while.*

† **Gré**, *s. m.* (*Ir. id.*) Nature, essence; *adjectively,* grey.

Greabhailt, *s. f.* (*Ir. id.*) A helmet.—*Shaw.*

† **Greach**, *s. m.* (*Ir. id.*) A nut.

Gread, Greadadh, aidh, *s. m.* (*Ir. id.*) A stroke; a blow; a wound; aridity; sorrow.—*Shaw.* Aobhar mo ghreadaidh, *the cause of my wound.*—*Turn.*

† **Gread**, *v. a.* Scorch; burn; torment; lash severely. *Pret. a.* ghread, *scorched; fut. aff.* greadaidh, *shall burn.*

Greadag, aig, *s. f.* (*Ir.* greadog.) A griddle or gridiron. *N. pl.* greadagan.

Greadan, ain, *s. m.* (*Ir. id. Old Swed.* graedda, *scorch.*) A parched crop; parched corn; a quarrel; large-grained snuff; a thumping; a blow; a creaking. Is goirt an greadan fhuair an duthaich, *the country has received a severe blow.*—*Old Song.* Thoir greadan air, *belabour it a while; strike awhile; give it* [*try it*] *a while.*

The snuff called *greadan* was made by pounding in a mortar the dried leaves of tobacco. It received its name, seemingly, from the resemblance of the mode of preparing it to that of *gradan;* which see.

Greadanach, *a.* (*Ir. id.*) Clamorous; obstreperous; fighting, thumping; babbling; chattering; quarrelsome.

Greadanachd, *s. f.* (*Ir. id.*) A parching of corn.

Greadanta, *a.* (*Ir. id.*) Vehement, hot, scolding; warm. Gu greadanta, *vehemently.*

† **Greadh**, greidh, *s. m.* (*Ir. id.*) A horse.—*Shaw.*

Greadh, *v. a.* (*Old Swed.* graedda, *bake bread.*) Prepare food, knead; winnow; thrash, thump. *Pret. a.* ghreadh; *fut. aff.* greadhaidh. A greadh na cuilm, *preparing the feast.*—*Oss. Derm.*

Greadhadair, *s. m.* A dresser of victuals; a winnower.

Greadhadaireachd, *s. f.* A dressing of food, or of grain; winnowing.

Greadhadh, aidh, *s. m.* (*Ir. id.*) A dressing of food, preparing; winnowing.

† **Greadhair**, *s. m.* (*Ir. id.*) A stallion.—*Shaw.*

Greadhaireachd, *s. f.* Covering a mare.

Greadhanachd, *s. f.* (*Ir. id.*) Drolling.

Greadharra, *a.* Pretty.—*Macd.*

Greadhnach, *a.* Joyful, glad; exulting; social; bright. An cùirtibh greadhnach, *in joyful courts.*—*Sm.*

Greadhnach, aidh, *s. m.* A merrymaking; adorning, making showy.

Greadhnachas, ais, *s. m.* Merriment, joy, sociality; pomp, solemnity, parade; brightness. Le mòr ghreadhnachas, *with much pomp.*—*Stew. Acts.*

Greadhuinn, *s. f.* A company, a band of men; a great number; a troop. Greadhuinn mun bhòrd, *a company around the table.*—*Old Song. Greadhuinn* is perhaps *greigh dhaoine,* or *greigh dh' fheoghainn,* a band of people.

Greallach, *a.* (*Ir. id.*) Dirty, nasty, filthy. *Com.* and *sup.* greallaiche.

Greallach, aich, *s.* (*Ir.* greallach.) Intestines; purtenance; pluck; a cart-saddle; a chain; clay. Nighidh tu a ghreallach, *thou wilt wash its entrails.*—*Stew. Ex.* Maille ri 'ghreallaich, *with its purtenance.*—*Id.*

Greallag, aig, *s. f.* A swing; a splinter bar. *N. pl.* greallagan.

Greallaich, *s. f.* Clay, mud, dirt, mire.

Grealsach, aich, *s. m.* (*Ir. id.*) A sort of fish called gilse. *N. pl.* grealsaich.

Gream, *s. m.* See **Greim.**

Greamaich, *v. a.* See **Greimich.**

Greamana. See **Greimeanna.**

† **Grean**, *s. m.* (*W.* graian. *Arm.* gruan. *Ir.* grean.) Gravel.

† **Grean**, *v. a.* (*Ir. id.*) Carve, engrave; emboss.

Greanachadh, aidh, *s. m.* An exhorting; exhortation.

Greanadh, aidh, *s. m.* An exhorting; exhortation.

Greanaich, *v. a.* Exhort. *Pret. a.* ghreanaich, *exhorted; fut. aff.* greanaichidh.

Greann, grinn, *s. m.* (*Ir. id.*) Hair standing on end; uncombed hair; a beard; a scowl; a gloom; a ruffled aspect; a noise, or clangour; hue; a blast; friendship, love; joke. Dh'fhàs air cith is greann, *he became angry and scowling.*—*Oss. Duthona.* Mar ghreann a bheireadh dà ord, *like the clangour of two hammers.*—*Old Poem.* Tha greann air an loch, *the surface of the lake is ruffled;* is iomad corp a chaochail greann, *many a body changed its hue.*—*Fingalian Poem.* Pòr is beadaraiche greann, *a race of the loveliest hue.*—*Macfar.* Mar ghreann reòtaidh, *like a wintry blast.*—*Old Song.*

Greannach, *a., from* greann. (*Ir.* greanach.) Bristly; hairy, shaggy; uncombed; rough; ruffled in the wind, as the surface of a lake. Aois ghreannach, *rough old age.*—*Mac Co.* Claigionn greannach, *a hairy scalp.*—*Stew. Ps. Com.* and *sup.* greannaiche.

Greannachadh, aidh, *s. m.* A bristling; a standing on end, as hair; a growing rough or shaggy.

Greannadh, aidh, *s. m.* (*Ir. id.*) A graving.

Greannaich, *v. a.* and *n.* Scowl; gloom; bristle; grow gloomy. *Pret.* ghreannaich; *fut. aff.* greannaichidh, *shall gloom.* Ghreannaich gach tulach, *every hillock has grown gloomy.*—*Macdon.*

Greannar, *a.* (*Ir.* grean-mhar.) Affable, facetious, witty; lovely, pleasant.

Greannarachd, *s. f.* (*Ir.* greannmharachd.) Affability; facetiousness; loveliness; discretion.

Greann-ghaoth, -ghaoithe, *s. f.* A boisterous wind; a rough breeze. Na greann-ghaoithe earraich, *than the winds of the vernal equinox.*—*Oss.*

Greannta, *a.* (*Ir. id.*) Neat, handsome, comely, becoming; carved, engraved. Gu greannta, *handsomely.*

Greanntachd, *s. f.* Neatness, handsomeness, comeliness; carved work.

Greanntasan, ain, *s. m.* Graving, carving.

Greap, *s. f.* A dung-fork.

Greas, *s. m.* Haste, despatch; *rarely*, a guest.

† **Gréas**, *s. m.* (*Ir. id.*) A guest; protection; a manner.

Greas, greise, *s.* See Greus.

Greas, *v. a.* and *n.* (*Ir. id.*) Hasten, despatch; promote; be quick, make haste. *Pret.* ghreas; *fut. aff.* greasaidh, *shall hasten.* Greas iuthaidh sìos, *speed an arrow downwards.—Oss. Com.* Greas ort, *make haste.—Stew. Gen* Ghreas i oirre, *she hasted.—Id.*

Grèas, *v. a.* See Greus.

Greasachadh, aidh, *s. m.* (*Ir. id.*) A hastening; inciting.

Greàsach, *a.* Common.

Greasachd, *s. f.* (*Ir. id.*) Hastening, despatch, hurry; preparation.

Grèasachd, *s. f.*, contracted for *greasaicheachd*, which see.

Greasachd, (a), *pr. part* of greas. Hastening, making haste. In some parts, the Gael say *greastachd*

Greasadh, aidh, *s. m.* A hastening, despatching

Greasaich, *v. a.* Hasten, incite

Greasaiche, *s. m.* (*Ir.* greasaidhe) A shoemaker; *also*, an embroiderer; an upholsterer. *N. pl* greasaichean

Greasaicheachd, *s. f.* The trade of a shoemaker; shoemaker's work; upholstery.

Greasailt, *s. f* (*Ir. id.*) An inn.—*Shaw.* *N. pl.* greasailtean.

Gréasair, *s. m.* (*Ir. id*) An innkeeper; a host. *N. pl.* greasairean.

Greasan, ain, *s. m.* (*Ir. id.*) A web.—*Shaw.*

Greasdachd, *s. f.* Hastening, despatch.

† **Greath**, *s. m.* (*Ir. id.*) A noise, a cry, a shout.

Greath, *v. a.* See Gréidh.

Greathlach, *s.* See Greallach

† **Gregh**, greigh, *s. m.* A dog Gach gregh bha na 'r mur, *every dog within our house —Old Song.*

Greid. See Gread.

† **Greideadh**, idh, *s. m.* (*Ir. id.*) A second stroke of infection.

Greideal, eil, *and* greidealach, *s f* (*Ir. id.*) A gridiron; a thin plate of iron for firing *bannocks.* Dubh na greidealach, *the smut of a gridiron*

Gréidh, *v. a.* Strike, thrash, beat; prepare victuals, knead, winnow. *Pret.* ghreidh, *thrash, fut. aff.* gréidhidh, *shall thrash.*

Gréidh, *s. m.* A beating, a thrashing Fhuair e a dheagh ghréidh, *he got a proper thrashing.*

Greidh, *s* See Greigh.

Gréidhte, *p. part.* of gréidh. Baked, kneaded; thrashed. Aran gréidhte, *baked bread.*

Greidlean, ein, *s m* A thin wooden instrument for turning *scones* on a gridiron; a name given to the Pleïades

Gréig, *s. f.* (*Ir. id.*) Greece.

Greigh, *s f.* A herd of horses, a stud. Greigh each air d'fhuarain ghorm, *herds of horses on the banks of the green fountains.—Macdon.*

Lat. grex. *Arm* gre, *a troop.* *Ir.* graidh *and* graidh *W.* gre, *a herd.*

Greigis, *s. f.* The Greek tongue.

Greillean, ein, *s. m.* A dagger; an old rusty sword.

Greim, *s. m.* A grasp, a hold; a bite; a morsel; a mouthful of food; a stitch; a pang, a gripe, a throb; a stitch in sewing; a difficult expression; a hard word. *N pl.* greimeana. Greim arain, *a morsel of bread —Stew. Gen.* and *Pro.* Greim bidh, *a bit of meat, a morsel of food.* Ann an greim, *fixed, held fast.—Stew.* 1 *K.* Greim an diabhoil, *devil's bit, scabiosa succisa.* Gabh greim, *take hold:* greim fola, *a pleurisy* Cha 'n 'eil greim ri ghabhail a dh' uisge no theine, *fire and water cannot be grasped — G. P.*—i. e. *fire and water are good servants, but bad masters.*

Greimeachadh, aidh, *s m.* (*Ir.* greamughadh) A catching; a holding; a griping

Greimeadh, idh, *s. m.* A grasping; biting.

Greimealtach, *a* Fixed; firm; holding fast

Greimeanna, *n. pl* of greim Grasps; holds, morsels, bits; pieces, gripes; sudden pains in any parts of the body

Greimeil, *a* Catching, apt to catch; firm, stout, capable of taking a firm grasp.

Greimich, *v a.* (*Ir* greamaich) Grasp, grapple, catch, fasten, adhere. *Pret. a.* ghreimich, *grasped, fut. aff. a* greimichidh, *shall grasp.* Cha ghreimich iad ri chéile, *they shall not adhere —Stew Dan*

Greimiche, *s m* A hook, a crook, a grapple; a vice. Greimiche fèòla, *a flesh-hook —Stew Rom*

Greimichte, *p part.* of greimich.

† **Greimisg**, *s f* (*Ir. id.*) Old garments; trash, trumpery, lumber —*Shaw.*

Gréine, *gen. sing.* of grian. Of the sun Éiridh na gréine, *sunrise;* luidh na gréine, *sunset;* talmhainnean cul na gréine, *countries having a southern latitude.*

Gréis, *v a* See Greus.

Gréis, *s.* See Greus.

Greis, *s f.* (*Ir id*) A while, a space of time; an attack; an action or engagement Greis air fiona is, greis air branndaidh, *a while at wine, a while at brandy — Macint.* Car greis, *for a while —Macdon* Fé na greis, *the interval action.—Oss* Thoir greis air d'obair, *work a while,* greis mhath, *a good while;* o cheann ghreis, *a while ago.*

† **Greis**, *s m.* (*Ir. id*) A champion—(*Shaw*), protection, pillage.

Greischill, *s f.* (*Ir id*) A sanctuary.

Gréise, *gen sing.* of greus

Greiseach, *a.* (*Ir id*) Soliciting, enticing.

Greiseachd, *s. f.* Solicitation, enticement —*Shaw*

Greisg, *s f* (*Ir. id*) Grease

† **Greistear**, ir, *s m* (*Ir. id.*) A carter. *N. pl* greistearan

† **Greit**, *s. m.* (*Ir. id.*) A champion, a warrior —*Shaw.*

† **Greith**, *s. f* (*Ir id*) A jewel, an ornament; dress

Greollach, aich, *s m* See Greallach.

Greugach, *a.* Grecian, Greek, *also*, a Grecian *N. pl.* Greugaich, *Grecians*

Greus, gréise, *s. m.* (*Ir. id.*) Embroidery, needlework; tambouring; fine clothes, furniture Greus obair, *embroidery,* obair ghréise, *embroidered work —Stew Ezek*

Greus, *v. a.* (*Ir id*) Embroider, adorn; dress *Pret a.* ghreus, *embroidered, fut aff a* greusaidh, *shall embroider*

Greusadh, aidh, *s. m* The act of embroidering, *also*, embroidery.

Greusaiche, *s m.* See Greasaiche

Greus-obair, -oibre, *s m.* Embroidered work; embroidery.

Grian, gréine, *s f.*, † gre, *nature* or *essence*, and theine, *fire.* (*Ir id*) The sun, the light of the sun. *Asp form,* ghrian, *sun.* A ghrian na h-og-mhaduinn! *thou son of early morn!—Oss Trathal* Eirigh na gréine, *sunrise,* luidh na greine, *sunset;* aomadh na grèine, *the oblique descending of the sun;* o nach d'eug thu mu 'n facas grian! *O that thou didst not die ere thou sawest the sun's light!*—*Mac Lach.* Gath grèine, *a sunbeam.*—*Oss.*

GRIAN, grein, *s.* (*Ir. id.*) The ground or bottom of the sea; the bottom of a lake or river; land.—*Shaw.*

GRIAN, *v. a.* Bask in the sun; expose to the sun. *Pret.* ghrian, *basked; fut. aff.* grianaidh, *shall bask.*

GRIANACH, *a.* (*Ir. id.*) Sunny, warm. Mu d' bhlathaibh grianach, *about thy sunny blossoms.*—*Macdon.* Dealbhan grianach, *idols.*—*Stew.* 2 *Chron. Com.* and *sup.* grianaiche.

GRIANACHADH, aidh, *s. m.* A drying, or a basking in the sun.

GRIANADH, aidh, *s. m.* A drying in the sun, a basking in the sun.

GRIANADH, (a), *pr. part.* Drying in the sun; basking. Pàirt san raon a grianadh, *some basking in the heath.*—*Macfar.*

GRIANAICH, *v. a.* (*from* grian.) Expose to the sun; bask. *Pret.* ghrianaich; *fut. aff.* grianaichidh.

GRIANICHTE, *p. part.* of grianaich. Dried in the sun.

GRIANAN, ain, *s. m.* (*Ir. id.*) A summer-house; a palace, or any royal seat; a court; a hall; a tent; a round turret; a sunny eminence; any place suited for exposing to the heat of the sun. An grianan còrr, *the beauteous hall was opened.*—*Fingalian Poem.* Grianan ard sam biodh na feidh, *the lofty eminence of deer.*—*Old Song.*

GRIANANTA, *a.* (*Ir. id.*) Sunny; exposed to the sun's heat; bright.

GRIANAR, *a.* (grianmhor.) Sunny; exposed to the sun's heat; bright, coloured by the sun.

GRIAN-BHEUM, *s. m.* A *coup de soleil.*

GRIAN-CHEARCALL, aill, *s.* A solar halo.

GRIAN-CHLACH, -chloich, *s. f.* (*Ir. id.*) A sun-dial.

GRIAN-CHRIOS, *s.* (*Ir. id.*) The Zodiac. Comharan na grèine-chrios, *the signs of the Zodiac.*

GRIAN-CHRIOSACH, *a.* Zodiacal.

GRIAN-CHUAIRTEAG, eig, *s. f.* A solar halo. *N. pl.* grian-chuairteagan.

GRIAN-DEATACH, GRIAN-DEATHACH, aich, *s. m.* Exhalation; vapour.

GRIAN-GHATH, *s. m.* A sunbeam. *N. pl.* grian-ghathan, *sunbeams; d. pl.* grian-ghathaibh. 'G an tiormachadh 's na grian-ghathaibh, *drying them in the sunbeams.*—*Macfar.*

† GRIAN-MHUINE, *s.* Blackberries.—*Shaw.*

GRIAN-NEOINEAN, ein, *s. m.* (*Ir.* gian-noinnin.) A turnsol or sunflower.

GRIANRACHADH, aidh, *s. m.* A drying in the sun; a basking; an exposing to the heat of the sun.

GRIANRAICH, *v. a.* (*Ir.* grianraigh.) Dry in the sun; bask; expose to the sun.

GRIAN-RIOCHD, *s. m.* An image of the sun; an image, an idol. *N. pl.* grian-riochdan.

GRIAN-SGÀIL, *s. f.* A parasol, an umbrella; any shade for the face against the sun's heat.

GRIAN-SGÀILEAN, ein, *s. m.* A little parasol; an umbrella.

GRIAN-SGAR, *s. m.* A chink, crack, or cleft, caused by the sun's heat.

GRIAN-SGARADH, aidh, *s. m.* A breaking into chinks by the sun's heat.

GRIAN-STAD, *s. m.* (*Ir. id.*) The solstice. Grian-stad gheamhraidh, *winter solstice;* grian-stad shamhraidh, *summer solstice.*—*Macdon.*

GRIANTACHD, *s. f.* A barren moor through which the river Spey runs. It is also called *Sliabh Ghrannas,* that is, *the heath of Grannius,* or *of the Sun.* Here are seen many Druidical circles of stone; and as the sun was an object of worship among the ancient Gael, as appears from an inscription dug out of the ruins of the Roman prætenture between the firths of Forth and Clyde, alluded to by Dr. John Macpherson in his Dissertations, it is presumable that the meaning here given is correct. Some say that the heath received its name from the clan Grant, who inhabit that country. The antiquarian already mentioned thinks it more probable that the Grants, in Gaelic called Granntaich, had their name from the country, and and not from a pretended Le Grand, as the genealogists of the tribe affirm.

GRIAN-THÌR, *s. f.* A sunny land. Grian-thir is uaine cota, *a sunny green-mantled land.*—*Macdon.*

† GRIB, *a.* (*Ir. id.*) Swift, quick.

GRIB, gribe, *s. f.* (*Ir. id.*) Hindrance, impediment; (*Gr.* γρῖφος, *a snare;*) dirt, filth; the feathers on the feet of birds; a manger.—*Shaw.*

GRIBEACH, *a.* Having feathers on the legs, as some fowls. Corr-ghribeach, *a heron.*

GRIBEACH, eich, *s. m.* (*Ir. id.*) A hunting nag. *N. pl.* gribeich.

GRIBEADH, idh, *s. m.* (*Ir. id.*) A manger.

† GRIBH, *s. m.* (*Dan.* grif. *Ir.* gribh.) A griffin, a warrior; a finger.

GRIBHEAG, eig, *s. f.* (*Ir. id.*) Haste, hurry, flurry; timidity. Written also *griomhag.*

GRIBHEAGACH, *a.* Hasty, in a hurry; flurried; timorous.

GRIBHEAN, ein, *s. m.* A griffin.

GRIBH-IONGACH, aich, *s. m.* A griffin.

GRIGEAG, eig, *s. f.* (*Ir. id.*) A pebble; a bead. *N. pl.* grigeagan.

GRIGEAGACH, *a.* Pebbled; like a bead; of beads.

GRIGLEACH, *a.* Clustered; in festoons, or in clusters.

GRIGLEACHAN, ain, *s. m.* A cluster of stars; a small constellation.

GRIGLEAN, ein, *s. m.* A group of stars; a name given to the Pleïades.

† GRIM, *s. f.* War, battle; a grey substance growing on stones.—*Shaw.*

GRIM-CHALLAIR, *s. m.* (*Ir. id.*) A herald.

GRIM-CHARBAD, aid, *s. m.* A war-chariot; the *currus falcatus* of the ancient Britons.

GRIM-CHLIATH, -chleithe, *s. f.* Hurdles used in sieges as a covert; a penthouse.—*Shaw.*

GRIMEIL, *a.* (grim-amhuil.) Warlike; skilful.

GRIMISGEAR, eir, *s. m.* A pedlar.

† GRIN, *s. f.* (*Ir. id.*) A piece or bit; a morsel.

GRÌN, grìne, *s. m.* A green; a green plot of ground. Air a ghrìn, *on the green. N. pl.* grìneachan, *greens.*—*Macint.*

GRÌNEAN, ein, *s. m.* (*dim.* of grin.) A green. Air na grìneanan gorm, *on the green plots.*—*Turn.*

† GRINN, *s. f.* (*Ir. id.*) A beard; a garrison; decency.

GRINN, *a.* (*Ir. id. Sax.* gearrian, *dress finely.*) Fine; beautiful; elegant; of an imposing appearance; neat, clean; artificial; workmanlike. Anart grinn, *fine linen.*—*Stew. Exod.* Do thigh grinn, *thy beauteous house.*—*Oss. Fing.*

GRINNEACH, ich, *s. m.* (*Ir. id.*) A young spark, a fop.—*Shaw.*

GRINNEACHADH, aidh, *s. m.* A dressing, a decorating; decoration; *also,* a striving, an effort.—*Shaw.*

† GRINNEADH, idh, *s. m.* (*Ir. id.*) A dying or perishing.—*Shaw.*

GRINNEAL, eil, *s. m.* (*Ir. id.*) The bottom or bed of a river, lake, or sea; a pool; a channel. Grinneal ghaineimh, *a bottom of sand.*—*Macint.* Lion air uchd ghrinneil, *a net on the bosom of the pool.—Macfar.* Cha ruiginn grinneal mo ghraidh, *I would not torment my love.—G. P.*

Grinneas, eis, *s. m.* (*Ir. id.*) Fineness; neatness; elegance; finery; delicateness. Am bòidhchead 's an grinneas, *in beauty and elegance.—Old Song.* Thaobh grinneis, *by reason of delicateness.—Stew. Deut.* Gha bhi luathas agus grinneas, *there cannot be expedition and neatness; quick and neat seldom meet.—G. P.*

Grinneasach, *a.* Fine, elegant; neat, clean. *Com.* and *sup.* grinneasaiche.

Grinnich, *v. a.* Adorn, dress; *rarely*, gather, pierce. *Pret. a.* ghrinnich, *adorned; fut. aff. a.* grinnichidh.

Griobh, *s. m.* (*Scotch*, grieve.) An overseer. *N. pl.* griobhan, *overseers.—Stew. Ex. ref.*

Griobhachd, *s. f.* Overseeing, superintendence.

Grioblas, *s. m.* (*Ir. id.*) Closeness.—*Shaw.*

Griògchan, ain, *s. m.* (*Ir. id.*) A constellation.

Griogchanach, *a.* Twinkling like stars; blazing, dazzling.

† **Griom**, *s. m.* (*Ir. id.*) War, battle.

Griom-challair, *s. m.* A herald; one who proclaims war or peace.

Griom-charbad, aid, *s. m.* A war-chariot; the *currus falcatus* of the ancient Britons.

Griomh, *s. m.* (*Ir. id.*) A nail; a talon, a claw.

Griòmh, *s. m.* A deed. More properly *gniomh;* which see.

Griomhach, *a.* (*Ir. id.*) Having claws or talons.

Griomhag, aig, *s. f.* Hurry, flurry; timidity. Foighidinneach gun ghriomhag, *patient without timidity.—Macfar.*

Griomh-shronach, *a.* Having an aquiline nose.

Griongal, ail, *s. m.* (*Ir. id.*) Care, sorrow; assiduity; industry.

Griongalach, *a.* (*Ir. id.*) Anxious; sorrowful; assiduous; industrious.

Griongalachd, *s. f.* (*Ir. id.*) Continued care; sorrowfulness; assiduity.

Grios, *a.* (*Ir. id.*) Entreat, beseech, implore; *rarely*, provoke; whet. *Pret. a.* ghrios; *fut. aff. a.* griosaidh, *shall beseech.* Grios air, *beseech him.*

Griosach, *a.* Imploring, supplicating.

Griosach, aich, *s. f.* (*Ir. id. Scotch*, grieshoch.) Hot embers; burning coals; the fire-side. Air a ghriosach, *on the embers.—Stew.* 1 *K.* Eadar a ghriosach 's an stairsneach, *between the fireside and the threshold.—Macint.*

Griosachadh, aidh, *s. m.* (*Ir.* griosughadh.) A frying; a stirring up, as of fire; provocation; excitement.

Griosadh, aidh, *s. m.* A beseeching, a solicitation; entreaty.

Griosaich, *v. a.* and *n.* Fry; grow hot; stir up, as a fire; provoke. *Pret.* ghriosaich; *fut. aff.* griosaichidh.

Griosaichte, *p. part.* Fried; kindled.

Grios-naimhdeas, eis, *s. m.* Inveterate enmity.

Grios-namhach, *a.* Inveterately hostile.

Griosta, *p. part.* of grios. (*Ir. id.*) Beseeched, implored; stirred up; provoked.

† **Grioth**, *s.* (*Ir. id.*) The sun.

Grìs, *s. f.* (*Ir. id.*) Tremour; terror; cuticular inflammation; pimples, pustules; fire.

Gris, *a.* (*Teut.* gris. *Fr.* gris. *Ir.* gris.) Grey.

Gris-dhearg, *a.* (*Ir. id.*) Roan colour; ruddy; liard; a colour mixed with red and grey. Gruaidh gris-dhearg, *a ruddy cheek.—Macint.*

Grìse, *s. f.* Grease; ointment for axle-trees.

Gris-fhionn, *s.* A mixture of white and black; black mixture; *also, adjectively*, grisled, spotted. Breac agus gris-fhionn, *spotted and grisled.—Stew. Gen.*

Grisg, *v. a.* (*Ir.* griosg.) Roast; fry. *Pret.* ghrisg, *roasted; fut. aff.* grisgidh.

Grisgean, ein, *s. m.* Roasted meat; boiled meat.—*Shaw.*

Grith, *s. f.* (*Ir. id.*) Knowledge; learning; outcry.

Gritheach, *a.* (*Ir. id.*) Learned; knowing; wise, discreet.—*Shaw.*

Gritheil, *s. f.* The grunting of young pigs.

Griun, *s. m.* (*Ir. id.*) A hedge-hog.—*Shaw.*

Griuthach, aich, *s. f.* The measles. Tha e 's a ghriuthach, *he is in the measles.*

Griuthlamhach, *a.* Quick, expert, ready-handed. Gu griuthlamhach, *expertly.*

Gròb, *v.* (*Goth.* gròb, *dig. Eng.* grub.) Join; join by serration; *also*, dig with the hands, grub.

Gròbach, *a.* (*Ir. id.*) Serrated; joined by serration; digging; grubbing.

Gròbadh, aidh, *s. m.* (*Ir. id.*) Serration; digging; grubbing; a joining by serration.

Grobais, *s. pl.* Mallows.—*Macd.*

Groban, ain, *s. m.* (*Ir. id.*) The top of a rock.

Grod, *a.* (*Ir. id.*) Rotten; putrid. Mar fhiodh grod, *like rotten wood.—Stew. Is.* Ubh grod, *a rotten egg. Com.* and *sup.* groide, *more* or *most rotten.*

Grod, *a.* Proud; smart.—*Shaw.*

Grod, *v. a.* and *n.* Rot; purify. *Pret. a.* ghrod, *rotted; fut. aff.* grodaidh, *shall rot.*

† **Grod**, groid, *s. m.* Foam.—*Shaw.*

Grodan, ain, *s. m.* (*Ir. id.*) A boat.—*Shaw. N. pl.* grodain.

Grodh, *s. m.* A lever, or crow.

Grodh-iarruinn, *s. m.* A crow of iron.

Grog, groig, *s. m.* A knock; a put with the head; a sudden shove or push; a pet, a huff.

Grogach, *a.* Knocking; putting; thumping; pettish; sulky. See also *gnogach.*

Groibleach, *a.* (*Ir. id.*) Long-nailed; having talons.

Groidheal, il, *s. m.* Coral.—*Macd.*

Groideal, groidle, *or* groidleach, *s. f.* A girdle or gridiron.

Gròigean, ein, *s. m.* An awkward handless fellow.

Gròigeanachd, *s. f.* Awkwardness, handlessness.

Groilean, ein, *s. m.* (*Ir. id.*) A bilboe.

Groilleach, ich, *s. f.* Coarse cloth.

Groimh, *s. f.* A grin; a visage; a nickname for a person with a grinning countenance.

Groiseaneach, *a.* (*Ir. id.*) Mouthed; snouty; garrulous.

Gròseid, *s. f.* (*Ir. id.*) A gooseberry.

Groisgeach, ich, *s. m.* (*Ir. id.*) A droll.—*Shaw.*

Grollan, ain, *s. m.* A cricket. Written also *greollan.*

Gronnsal, ail, *s. m.* A grunt.

Grontach, *a.* (*Ir. id.*) Corpulent, gross. *Com.* and *sup.* grontaiche.

† **Gron**, groin, *s. m.* (*Ir. id.*) A stain, a blot, or blemish.—*Shaw.*

Gronustal, ail, *s. m.* Brimstone, sulphur. Teine agus gronustal, *fire and brimstone.—Stew. Pro.*

Gropais, *s.* Mallows.

Gros, grois, *s. m.* (*Ir. id.*) A ludicrous term for the human mouth; a bill, as of a duck; a snout. Gros muic, *a sow's snout;* gros tunnaig, *a duck's bill.*

Grosach, *a.* Having a large mouth; thick-lipped; snouty. *Com.* and *sup.* grosaiche.

Grosadh, aidh, *s. m.* Twelve dozen.

Gròsaid, *s. f.* (*Scotch*, groset.) A gooseberry. Preas ghròsaid, *a gooseberry bush.*

Grosair, *s. m.* (*Ir. id.*) A grunter; a man with a large mouth; a blubber-lipped person.

Grosaireachd, *s. f.* (*Ir. id.*) Grunting; blubber-lippedness.

Grosanach, *a.* Mouthed, snouted.

Gròsd. See **Gnòsd.**

Gròt, groit, *s. m.* A groat. Is don' am pàigh an gròt, *a groat is but sorry pay.—Turn.*

Grothach, aich, *s. m.* See **Gnothach.**

Grothal, ail, *s. m.* (*Ir. id.*) Sand, gravel.

Grothalach, *a.* (*Ir. id.*) Sandy, gravelly; *also, substantively*, a gravel pit.

Grothan, ain, *s. m.* (*Ir. id.*) A purring; a moan, a groan, a complaining.

Grotonach, *a.* (*Ir. id.*) Heavy breeched, corpulent.

Gruag, gruaig, *s. f.* (*Ir. id.*) The hair of the head, especially of a female; a wig; a lock of hair; a woman; a wife. Le spìonadh an gruaig, *with tearing their hair.—Stew. Lev.* Gruag-bhréige, *a wig.*

Gruagach, *a.* (*Ir. id.*) Hairy; long-haired; having ringlets; womanly. *Com.* and *sup.* gruagaiche.

Gruagach, aich, *s. m.* and *f.* (*Ir. id. W.* gwreigen, *a little woman.*) A maid or virgin; a damsel; a bride's-maid; a bridegroom's-maid; a female spectre of the class of brownies, to which the Highland dairy-maids made frequent libations of milk; *rarely*, the chief of a place. Ghradhaich e 'ghruagach, *he loved the damsel.—Stew. Gen. N. pl.* gruagaichean. Na gruagaichean laoghach, *the pretty maids.—Macint.* Cha ghruagaichean gu léir air am bi 'm falt féin, *they are not all virgins who wear their own hair.—G. P.* This saying arose from the circumstance that young women in the Highlands were wont to be bareheaded until after marriage, or after child-bearing.

Gruagair, *s. m.* A hair-dresser.

Gruaidh, *s. f.* (*Ir. id. W.* gruz. *Corn.* grud.) A cheek; a brow; the temple, or side of the head; a liver. Coslas bàis na ghruaidh, *the paleness of death in his cheek.—Sm.* Do ghruaidhean, *thy temples.—Stew. Song Sol. ref.* Rughadh gruaidh, *a blush. N. pl.* gruaidhean.

Gruaidhean, *n. pl.* of *gruaidh*; which see.

Gruaidhean, ein, *s. m.* (*Ir. id.*) The liver.

Gruaidh-lagan, ain, *s. m.* A dimple on the cheek.

Gruaim, *s. f.* (*Ir. id.*) A gloom, a frown, or surly look; ill-humour; darkness. Fo dhoruinn 's fo ghruaim, *in sorrow and gloom.—Oss. Fing.* Luidh gruaim air Croma, *darkness settled on Croma.—Oss. Com.*

Gruaim-bheann, -bheinn, *s. f.* A dark hill; a gloomy mountain. O ghuaillibh nan gruaim-bheann, *from the shoulders of the gloomy mountains.—Macfar.*

Gruaimean, ein, *s. m.* (*from* gruaim.) A surly man; a man with a frowning visage; *also*, a frown, a gloom. An gnùis fo ghruaimean, *their visage* [*troubled*] *under a gloom.—Stew. Ezek.*

Gruaimean, *a.* Surly; frowning.

Gruama, *a.* (*Ir. id.*) Surly, stern, morose; dark, gloomy, cloudy, obscure.

Gruamach, *a.* (*Ir. id.*) Surly, stern, frowning, grim; gloomy, cloudy. Bu ghruamach an tuar, *stern was their aspect.—Oss. Fing. Com.* and *sup.* gruamaiche, *more* or *most surly.*

Gruamachd, *s. f.* (*Ir. id.*) Gloominess, cloudiness; surliness, sternness, grimness; a habit of frowning; a continual frown.

Gruamag, aig, *s. f.* (*from* gruaim.) A little frowning female.

Gruamaiche, *s. f.* Gloominess; gloom; sternness; surliness. Gruamaiche air na beanntaibh, *a gloom on the hills.—Macint.*

Gruamaiche, *a.*, *com.* and *sup.* of gruamach; which see.

Gruaman, ain, *s. m.* (*from* gruaim.) A gloom, a slight frown; a man who frowns. Na biodh oirbh gruaman, *let there not be a frown upon you.—Old Song.*

Grùan, **Grùbhan**, *s. m.* (*Ir. id.*) The liver.—*Stew. Ex. ref.*

Grùdair, *s. m.* (*Ir. id.*) A brewer, a distiller. *N. pl.* grudairean.

Grùdaireachd, *s. f.* (*Ir. id.*) The employment of brewing or distilling; a brewery, a distillery.

Grug, gruig, *s. m.* (*Ir. id.*) A wrinkle; a lie; straitness.

Grug, *a.* (*Ir. id.*) Morose; weak; wrinkled.—*Shaw.*

Grugach, *a.* (*Ir. id.*) Weak, feeble; wrinkled.

Grùid, *s. pl.* Grains; malt; sediment, dregs.

Grùideach, *a.* Full of grains; malty; full of dregs.

Grùig, *s. f.* Churlishness, inhospitality; a drooping look or attitude; a shrinking of the shoulders, as from cold.

Grullan, ain, *s. m.* (*Ir. id. Lat.* gryllus.) A cricket. *N. pl.* grullain. Written also *greollan.*

Grùmach, *a.* See **Gruamach.**

Grumadh, aidh, *s. m.* A groom.

Grunnachadh, aidh, *s. m.* A grounding; a sounding, a fathoming.—*Stew. Acts.* Cord grunnachaidh, *a sounding line.*

Grunnaich, *v. a.* Sound, fathom, ground. *Pret. a.* ghrùnnaich, *sounded*; *fut. aff. a.* grunnaichidh, *shall sound.*

Grunnadh, aidh, *s. m.* (*Ir. id.*) A heaping up, a gathering together, an accumulation.

Grunnan, ain, *s. m.* (*Ir. id.*) A little heap; a hillock.

Grnnnas, ais, *s. m.* See **Grunnasg.**

Grunnasg, aig, *s. f.* Groundsel. Grunnasg lionmhor, *abundance of groundsel.—Macint.*

Grunnd, gruinnd, *s. m.* Bottom, ground, foundation; the nether world; carefulness, economy. Grunnd am domhain, *the bottom of the deep.—Sm.* Grunnd a chleibh, *the bottom of his breast.—Mac Lach.* A chumhachdan dubha a ghruinnd, *ye gloomy divinities of the nether world.—Id.* *Dan.* and *Swed.* grund. *Du.* grond. *Germ.* grund. *Sax.* grund. *Scotch*, grund. *Eng.* ground.

Grunndachadh, aidh, *s. m.* A sounding; a filtering or straining.

Grunndaich, *v. a.* (*from* grunnd.) Sound, as water; defeculate; filter. *Pret. a.* ghrunndaich; *fut. aff. a.* grunndaichidh, *shall ground.*

Grunndail, *a.* (*from* grunnd.) Economical, frugal, careful; having a foundation; solid; sensible. Gu grunndail, *frugally.*

Grunndalachd, *s. f.* Good management; carefulness; solidity; sense.

Grunndalas, ais, *s. m.* Economy, frugality.

Grunndas, ais, *s. m.* Good management; carefulness; frugality; dregs or lees.

Grunndasach, *a.* (*from* grunndas.) Abounding in dregs; feculent. *Com.* and *sup.* grunndasaiche, *more* or *most feculent.*

Grunnd-lagh, *s. m.* (*Swed.* grund-lag.) A fundamental law.

Grunnd-luchd, *s. m.* Ballast.

Gruth, *s. m.* (*Ir. id.*) Curds. Cho gheal 's an gruth, *as white as curds.—Macfar.*

GRUTHACH, *a.* (*from* gruth.) Curdled or coagulated; like curds; curdling; curd-producing. A Bhealtuinn ghruthach, *curd-producing May.—Macfar.*

GU, *prep. governing the dat.* To, towards; till, until. Gu seilg nan sliabh, *to the mountain-chase.—Orr.* Gu crìche mo shaoghail, *till my life's end.—Oss.* Gu tuath, *northward;* gu deas, *southward;* air dol gu neoni, *gone to nothing.*

GU, *adv.* (*Ir.* go.) To. Gu bràth, *for ever;* gu la bhràth, *for ever;* gu dilinn, *for ever; till the deluge;* gu ruig, *until;* gu minic, *often;* gu siorruidh, *for ever;* gu suthainn, *for ever;* gu lèir, *altogether;* gu leòir, *enough;* bliadhna gu leth, *a year and a half.* When *gu* comes before an adjective, that adjective is thrown into the adverbial form; as, maith, *good;* gu maith, *well;* buileach, *effectual;* gu buileach, *effectually;* laidir, *strong;* gu laidir, *strongly.* *Gu* has often a similar effect on a noun substantive; as, beachd, *observation;* gu beachd, *clearly, evidently;* dearbh, *proof, conviction;* gu dearbh, *truly, indeed, certainly.*

GU, *conj.* That. Gu ma h-i a bhean sin, *may she be that wife.—Stew. Gen.* Gu ma toil leat, *may it please thee.—Sm.* Gu ma fad beò an righ! *long live the king!*

GUAG, guaig, *s. m.* and *f.* An unsettled, capricious person; a giddy, fantastical fellow. The Welsh say *guag ysprid*, a whim.

GUAGACH, *a.* Capricious, giddy, whimsical; *also,* crumpfooted. *Com.* and *sup.* guagaiche.

GUAIL, *gen. sing.* of gual; which see.

GUAILLE, *gen. sing.* of gualainn; which see.

GUAILLEACH, ich, *s. f.* A band tying the shoulders of dead men.

GUAILLEACHAN, ain, *s. m.* A companion; *also,* a shoulder-piece or mantle.—*Stew. Ex. ref.*

GUAILLEAN, (*for* guaillnean), *n. pl.* of gualainn. Shoulders.

GUAILLEAN, ein, *s. m.* (*from* gual.) A cinder; a dead cinder.

GUAILLEANACH, *a.* Full of cinders; like a cinder.

GUAILLEAR, ir, *s. m.* (*from* gual.) A collier. *N. pl.* guaillearan.

GUAILLEAR, eir, *s. m.* (*from* gualnain.) A comrade or chum.

GUAILLEARACHD, *s. f.* The employment of a collier; a colliery.

GUAILL-FHIONN, *a.* Having white or speckled shoulders, as a cow; a name given to a cow with speckled shoulders. —*Macint.*

GUAILLIBH, *d. pl.* of gualainn. Shoulders. Clann nan Gaidheal an guaillibh a chèile, *the Gael shoulder to shoulder.*

GUAILLICH, *v. a.* and *n.* Walk arm in arm, or hand in hand; elbow. *Pret.* ghuaillich, *elbowed; fut. aff. a.* guaillichidh, *shall elbow.*

GUAILLNEAN, *n. pl.* of gualainn. Shoulders, corners, angles.

GUAILLNEAN, ein, *s. m.* A cinder.

GUAIMEAS, eis, *s. m.* Neatness; snugness; quietness.

GUAIMEASACH, *a.* Neat; comfortable; quiet; snug. Gu guaimeasach, *neatly.*

GUAIRE, *s. f.* (*Ir. id.*) The hair of the head; the point of any thing; a bristle; roughness.

GUAIRSGEACH, *a.* Hairy; having hair on the head; bristly.

GUAIRTEAN, ein, *s. m.* (*properly* cuairtean.) A whirlwind; an eddy.

GUAIS, *s. f.* (*Ir. id.*) Danger; hazard; venture; enterprise.

GUAIS-BHEART, -bheirt, *s. f.* Enterprise; adventure; a dangerous enterprise; a hazardous attempt; a feat.

GUAIS-BHEARTACH, *a.* (*Ir. id.*) Enterprising; adventurous; hazardous; fool-hardy; daring. Gu goimh-chridheach guais-bheartach, *keenly and daringly.—Old Song.* *Com.* and *sup.* guais-bheartaiche.

GUAISMHOIRE, *com.* and *sup.* of guaismhor; which see.

GUAISMHOR, *a.* Dangerous, hazardous, critical; enterprising, daring, fool-hardy.

† GUAIT, *v.* Leave off; let alone; quit. *Pret. a.* ghuait; *fut. aff. a.* guaitidh.

GUAITEAL, eil, *s. m.* Desistance.

GUAL, guail, *s. m.* Coal; coals; a coal-fire. Deagh theine guail, *a good coal-fire.—Macfar.* Toll-guail, *a coal-pit;* gual fairge, *sea-coal.—Macd.*

Heb. gohal. *Arm.* glau. *Germ.* kole. *Ir.* gual.

GUALACH, *a.* (*Ir.* gualdha.) Full of coals; like coals.

GUALACHAN, ain, *s. m.* A stout young fellow. *N. pl.* gualachain.

GUALADAIR, *s. m.* (*from* gual.) A collier.

GUALAICH, *v. a.* Blacken, as with coal; burn into cinders; carbonize. *Pret.* ghualaich; *fut. aff.* gualaichidh.

GUALAICHTE, *p. part.* of gualaich. Burnt to a cinder; carbonized.

GUAL-BHRAN, ain, *s. m.* (*Ir. id.*) A fire-brand.

GUALLACH. See GUAILLEACH.

GUALAINN, *gen.* guaille *or* gualainne, *s. f.* (*Ir.* gualann. *Arm.* gonalen.) A shoulder, an arm; a corner, an angle. Soitheach air a gualainn, *a vessel on her shoulder.—Stew. Gen.* Gualainn deas an tigh, *the right corner of the house.* —*Stew.* 2 *K. ref.* Crios guaille, *a shoulder-belt.*

GUAMACH, *a.* Neat, tidy, well-formed; smirking; pleasant; careful. Beul guamach, *a smirking mouth.—Old Song.* Fàsach guamach, *a pleasant moor.—Macint.* *Com.* and *sup.* guamaiche.

GUAMAG, aig, *s. f.* A neat or tidy female; a smirking girl. —*Moladh Mhòraig.* *N. pl.* guamagan.

GUAMAGACH, *a.* Smirking, as a female; neat, trim, tidy.

GUAMAICHE, *com.* and *sup.* of guamach. More or most neat.

GUAMAICHEAD, eid, *s. m.* Neatness; improvement in neatness. A dol an guamaichead, *growing more and more neat.*

GUAMAISEACH, *a.* (*Ir. id.*) Quiet, comfortable.

GUAMNACH, aich, *s. m.* (*Ir. id.*) Lamentation.

GUANACH, *a.* (*Ir. id.*) Light, active; light-headed, giddy; unsteady, nodding, wavering. Maoisleach a chinn ghuanaich, *the light-headed roe.—Macint.* Air a chraig ghuanaich, *on the nodding rock.—Old Song.* *Com.* and *sup.* guanaiche.

GUANADH, aidh, *s. m.* Lightness, unsteadiness, giddiness.

GUANAIS, *s. f.* Lightness, unsteadiness, giddiness.—*Turn.*

GUANAISEACH, *a.* (*Ir. id.*) Light, active; light-headed; unsteady, nodding, wavering. Guanaiseach òg, *light-headed and young.—Macdon.*

GUANAISEACHD, *s. f.* Lightness; activity; light-headedness; unsteadiness.

GUANALAS, ais, *s. m.* Unsteadiness; light-headedness; wavering; strolling.

GUARAG-BHLEOTHAINN, *s. f.* A milch cow.

GUAS, guais, *s. m.* (*Ir. id.*) Danger, jeopardy.

GUASACHD, *s. f.* (*Ir. id.*) Danger, jeopardy; a perilous situation; a perilous adventure.

GUASACHDACH, *a.* (*Ir. id.*) Dangerous; perilous; hazardous; enterprising; painful. *Guasachdach* is used in this last sense in old medical manuscripts. *Com.* and *sup.* guasachdaiche.

† GUBHA. (*Ir. id.*) Lamentation; a battle, a conflict.

GUC, *s. m.* (*Ir. id.*) A sprout, bud, or germ; a bell, a

bubble; the flower of any leguminous vegetable. Barr-guc, *the flower of any leguminous vegetable, as of peas.*

Gucag, aig, *s. f., dim.* of guc. (*Ir.* gucog.) A bud, sprout, or germ; a bell; a bell-flower. *N. pl.* gucagan.

Gucagach, *a.* Belled, as a flower; in flower, as leguminous vegetables; having buds or blooms; clustering; curling, as a wave. Mar thonn gucagach, *as a curling billow.—Oss. Fing.*

† Gufarghoill, *s. f.* (*Ir. id.*) False testimony.

Gùg, guig, *s. m.* The cooing of a pigeon.

Guga, *s. m.* (*Ir. id.*) A St. Kilda goose; a fat fellow.—*Shaw.*

Gùgail, *s. f.* The clucking of a hen; the cooing of a pigeon.

Gugan, ain, *s. m.* (*Ir. id.*) A bud, a flower, a daisy.

Guganach, *a.* (*Ir. id.*) Budding, flowering; abounding in buds or in daisies.

Gugarnaich, *s. f.* The clucking of a hen.

Guidh, *v.* Beseech, implore; pray; imprecate. *Pret.* ghuidh, *prayed; fut. aff.* guidhidh, *shall pray.* Guidheam ort, *I beseech thee.—Sm.* Guidh mallachd air, *imprecate a curse on him;* guidh sìth, *salute.—Stew. Sam. ref.*

Guidhe, *s. f.* A prayer, an imprecation; intercession. Droch ghuidhe, *an imprecation.*

Guidheach, *a.* Prone to beseech; imploring. Sealladh guidheach, *an imploring look.*

Guidheachair, *s. m.* A supplicant; a petitioner; a swearer.

Guidheachan, ain, *s. m.* (*Ir. id.*) An earnest prayer; a petition; an imprecation.

Guidheadh, idh, *s. m.* A beseeching; an imprecating; an obsecration.

Guidheam, 1 *sing. imper.* of guidh. Let me beseech; *also, for* guidhidh mi, *I will beseech.*

Guil, *v. a.* and *n.* (*Arm.* guela. *Ir.* guil.) Weep, wail, or cry; mourn or lament. *Pret.* ghuil, *wept; fut. aff.* guilidh, *shall cry.* Aite anns an guileadh e, *a place where he might weep.—Stew. Gen.* Guilibh an laoch, *lament the hero.—Orr.*

Guilbinn, *gen.* guilbne, *s. m.* A curlew. *N. pl.* guilbnean.

Guilbneach, ich, *s. m.* A curlew. *N. pl.* guilbnich. Coire sam bi guilbnich, *a dell where curlews are found.—Macd.*

Guileag, eig, *s. f.* (*Ir. id.*) A singing, a chirping; warbling; a shout of joy; the note of the swan, exultation.—*Macint.*

Guileagag, eig, *s. f.* A chirping; a warbling; a cry of joy.

† Guilimne, *s. f.* Calumny, reproach.

Guilimneach, *a.* Calumnious, reproachful. Gu guilimneach, *calumniously.*

† Guilmnich, *v. a.* Calumniate, reproach.

Guilneach, ich, *s. m.* (*Ir. id.*) A curlew. *N. pl.* guilnich, *curlews.*

† Guimean, ein, *s. m.* (*Ir. id.*) A holy relic.—*Shaw.*

Guin, *v. a.* (*Ir. id.*) Cause a sudden pain; wound; sting; prick. *Pret. a.* ghuin; *fut. aff.* guinidh. Suil mheallach a ghuin mi, *an enticing eye that wounded me.—Old Song.*

Guin, guine, *s. f.* A stitch or sudden pain; a sharp lancinating pain; any momentary pain; a dart; a sting; a wound; trouble. Guin na ré, *the falling sickness.—Stew. Matt. ref.* *N. pl.* guinean.—*Stew. Is.*

Guin-chridheach, *a.* Ardent, keen. Guin-chridheach, guais-bheartach, *keen and daring.—Old Song.*

Guin-cheap, -chip, *s. m.* (*Ir. id.*) A pillory. *N. pl.* guin-cheapaichean.

Guineach, *a.* (*from* guin.) Sharp, keen, eager; wounding; lancinating; causing sudden pain; like a dart.

Guineach, ich, *s. m.* (*from* guin.) An arrow, a dart, a weapon. An guineach a lot a muineal, *the weapon that wounded her neck.—Oss. Derm.*

Guinneir, *s. f.* Epilepsy.

† Guin-scead, *s. m.* A scar.—*Shaw.*

Guin-sceadan, ain, *s. m.* A little scar.

Guir-bhris, *v. n.* (*Ir. id.*) Exulcerate; break out into pimples.

Guir-bhriseadh, idh, *s. m.* Exulceration.

Guirean, ein, *s. m.* A pimple, a pustule, a scab; *in derision,* a sickly-looking person. *N. pl.* guireanan. Atadh no guirean, *a swelling or a scab.—Stew. Lev.*

Arm. goron. *Box. Lex.* goryn. *Ir.* guirean.

Guireanach, *a.* (*from* guirean.) Pimply, pustulous, scabbed. *Com.* and *sup.* guireanaiche.

Guirm, *an inflection of the adjective* gorm; which see.

† Guirme, *s. f.* (*Ir. id.*) An inn.

Guirme, *com.* and *sup.* of gorm. (*Ir. id.*) Bluer, bluest.

Guirme, *s. f.* (*from* gorm.) Greenness, blueness. Guirme cneidh, *the blueness of a wound.—Stew. Pro.*

Guirmeachd, *s. f.* (*Ir. id.*) Blueness, greenness.

Guirmead, eid, *s. m.* Blueness, greenness; increase in blueness or greenness. A dol an guirmead, *growing more and more green.*

Guirmean, ein, *s. m., from* gorm. (*Ir. id.*) Indigo or blue; woad; any blue dye.

Guirmeanach, *a.* Like blue or indigo; abounding in woad.

Guirnead, eid, *s. m.* (*Ir. id.*) A gurnard.—*Shaw.*

† Guis, *v. n.* Flow, gush. *Pret.* ghuis, *flowed; fut. aff.* guisidh.

Guiseach, *a.* (*Ir. id.*) Leaky, full of chinks; not airtight, not water-tight.

Guiseag, eig, *s. f.* More frequently written *cuiseag.*

Guiseid, *s. f.* A gusset; clock of a stocking.—*Shaw.*

Guiseir, *s. m.* A stocking.

Guite, *s. f.* A sieve; a fan or hand-winnow for corn, and made of sheep-skin applied to a hoop, somewhat resembling the end of a drum. *N. pl.* guiteachan. Leis a ghuite, *with the fan.—Stew. Is.*

Guiteachan, *n. pl.* of guite. Hand-winnows.

Guiteanach, *a.* Bashful, timid.—*Shaw.*

Guitear, eir, *s. m.* (*Ir. id.*) A gutter; a sink, drain, or sewer. *N. pl.* guitearan.

Guiteas, eis, *s. m.* (*Ir. id.*) Denial, refusal.—*Shaw.*

Guiteirich, *v. a.* Drain, as a field; make sewers or drains. *Pret. a.* ghuiteirich, *drained.*

Guiteiriche, *s. m.* A drainer, a ditch-maker.

Guiteirichte, *p. part.* of guiteirich. Drained; having sewers.

Gul, guil, *s. m.* Weeping, lamentation. Am gu gul, *a time to weep.—Stew. Ecc.* Dean gul, *weep.* Written also and pronounced *gal.*

Gul, *v. a.* and *n.* See Guil.

Gulanach, *a.* Weeping, crying, mourning.

† Gulba, *s. m.* (*Ir. id.*) A mouth.

Gul-chaoin, *s. m.* (*Ir. id.*) Lamentation.

Gul-dheur, -dheòir, *s. m.* A tear.—*Shaw.*

Gul-ghair, *s. f.* A loud lamentation.

Gul-ghaireach, *a.* Weeping aloud.

Gum, *conj.* That, in order that. Gum faigh e, *that he will get.*

Gu 'm, (*for* gu am.) To their, to the. Gu 'm bailtean a

ghlacadh, *to take these towns;* gu 'm fearann a sgriosadh, *to lay waste the land.*

GUN, (gus an.) *conj.* That; till, until.

GUN, *prep.* (*Ir. id.*) Without. Gun amharus, *doubtless;* gun fhios, *without knowledge, in case, if perhaps.* Gun fhios am faic e thu, *in case he may not see you;* gun fhios nach faic e thu, *in case he may see you;* gun chàird, *incessantly, without rest;* is truagh gun thu agam! *Alas! that I am without thee!*—*Oss. Derm.* Gun fhios domh, *without my knowledge.*

† GUN, guin, *s. m.* (*Ir. id.*) A breach.

GU'N, (*for* gu an.) To the, to their.

GÙN, gùin, *s. m.* A gown; a woman's gown. Gùn oidhche, *a night-gown* or *bed-gown.* (*Ir.* gunna. *It.* gonna. *W.* gwn.) *N. pl.* gùnachan *or* gùintean.

GUNAIDEACH, *a.* Wicked, vicious; apt to push with the head, as a bull. Damh gunaideach.—*Stew. Ex. ref.*

GUNAIDEACHD, *s. f.* Viciousness.

GUNBHUINE, *s. f.* A dart; a javelin.—*Shaw.*

† GUNLANN, ainn, *s. m.* (*Ir. id.*) A prison; a pound for cattle.

† GUNN, guinn, *s. m.* (*Ir. id.*) A prisoner, a hostage.—*Shaw.*

GUNNA, ai, *s. m.* (*Ir.* gunn.) A gun or musket. Gunn' air dheagh ghleusadh, *a gun in good trim.*—*Mac Co.* Gunna mòr, *a great gun* or *cannon;* gunna glaic, *a fusee;* gunna caol, *a fusee, a fowling-piece.*—*N. pl.* gunnachan. Gunna caile, *a pop-gun;* gun spùtachain, *a squirt* or *syringe.*

GUNNA-BHIODAG, aig. A bayonet; a bayonet gun. Ur gunna-bhiodag rùisgte, *your bare bayonets.*—*Old Song.*

GUNNACH, *a.* Armed with a gun. Gunnach dagach, *armed with gun and pistol.*—*Old Song.*

GUNNAIR, *s. m.* (*from* gunna.) A gunner; a cannoneer; a musqueteer; a marksman.

GUNNAIREACHD, *s. f.* (*Ir. id.*) Shooting, firing; gunning; a shooting-match.

GUNN-BHUINE, *s. f.* (*Ir. id.*) A dart, spear, or javelin.

GUNNRAICH, *s. m.* An artilleryman.

GUNNRAIDH, *s. f.* Artillery.

† GUNRAGACH, *a.* (*Ir. id.*) Straying; apt to wander or go astray.

† GUNRAGADH, aidh, *s. m.* (*Ir. id.*) A straying, a wandering.

† GUNTA, *s. m.* (*Ir. id.*) A man of experience; a skilful man; a prying man.—*Shaw.*

† GUNTA. (*Ir. id.*) Wounded; pained; *also,* prepared.—*Shaw.*

GUNTACH, aich, *s. f.* (*Ir. id.*) Costiveness.—*Shaw.*

GUR, *conj.* (*Ir. id.*) That. Thuirt e gur maith e, *he said that it is good.*

GU 'R, (*for* gu ar.) To our, to us. Gu 'r dùthaich a mhilleadh, *to destroy our country;* gu 'r marbhadh, *to kill us.*

GU 'R, (*for* gu bhur.) To your. Gu 'r sgriosadh, *to destroy you.*

† GUR, guir, *s. m.* (*Ir. id.*) A blotch, a pimple; *anciently,* a man.

GUR, guir, *s. m.* (*Ir. id.*) A hatching, incubation; a brood of birds. Mar cheare a ni gur, *like a hen that hatcheth.*—*Stew. Jer.* Do 'n ghur rioghail, *of the royal blood.*—*Old Song.* Air ghur, *hatching.*

GUR, *v. n.* Hatch, incubate, or lie on eggs, as a fowl. *Pret.* ghur; *fut. aff.* guraidh. A gur air uighean, *hatching eggs.*—*Stew. Is.*

GURADH, aidh, *s. m.* (*Ir. id.*) A hatching, incubation.

GURAICEACH, ich, *s. m.* (*Ir. id.*) A blockhead.

GUR-CHLIATHACH, aich, *s.* A palisado.—*Shaw.*

GÙRD, *s. m.* A gourd.

GUR-LE-GÒG. Hatch with a song. This name has been given to the kind of cooing uttered during hatching time by the small sea-fowls called *Mother Cary's chickens.* See LUCHAIDH-FHAIRGE.

† GURNA, ai, *s. m.* (*Ir. id.*) A den, a cave, a place of concealment.

GURT, guirt, *s. m.* (*Ir. id.*) Pain, trouble; fierceness; *also, adjectively,* fierce, terrible.

GUS, *adv.* (*Ir. id.*) *prep.* and *conj.* Till, until; to; so that, in order that; as far as. Gus an crion a clach, *until the stone shall crumble.*—*Oss.* A bhliadhna gus an am so, *this time twelve month; a year ago.* A sheachduin gus an dé, *yesterday se'ennight.* Gus nach cluinnte leis a chliù, *in order that he might not hear his praise.*—*Oss. Tem.* *Gus,* when prefixed to a noun substantive without the article, generally has the dative case, otherwise it has a nominative case. Gus a chrioch, *to the end.*—*Stew. N. T.* Gus an sruth, *to the stream.*—*Stew. Deut.*

† GUS, guis, *s. m.* (*Ir. id.*) Weight, force; death; anger; deed; inclination.

GUS, *a.* (*Ir.* gus.) Sharp, keen, smart; strong.

GUSAR, *a.* See GUSMHOR.

GUSDAL, ail, *s. m.* (*Ir. id.*) A burden.—*Shaw.*

GUSGAL, ail, *s. m.* Loud lamentation, roaring, bawling. Cuiridh gusgal neach na bhreislich, *loud lamentation confounds one.*—*Macfar.*

GUSGALACH, *a.* Roaring; lamenting loudly.

GUSGALACHD, *s. f.* Continued roaring; loud lamentation.

GUSGAN, ain, *s. m.* A hearty draught.

GUSGAR, air, *s. m.* Roaring; loud wailing.

GUSGARLACH, aich, *s. m.* A keen sharp fellow.—*Shaw.* *N. pl.* gusgarlaich.

GUSMHÒR, *a.* Strong, powerful; capable; keen. Gu gusmhòr, *powerfully.* *Com.* and *sup.* gusmhoire.

GUSTAL, ail, *s. m.* A burden, a pledge.
W. guystel. *Lat.* gestale. *Ir.* gustal.

GUTACH, *a.*, more properly *cutach;* which see.

GUTALAICHE, *s. m.* A cuckold maker.

GUTH, *s. m.* A voice, a word; a report; a speech; mention; a vote; a vowel; a sound; an ill name; calumny; a bard. *N. pl.* guthan, *voices.* Guth caointeach, *a plaintive voice.*—*Oss.* Am meadhon a ghuth, *in the middle of his speech.*—*Oss. Croma.* Dean guth, *speak with me;* a ghutha Chona, *ye voices* [*bards*] *of Cona.*—*Oss. Carricth.* Guthan a bhàis, *the sounds of death.*—*Fingalian Poem.*

GUTHACH, *a.* (*from* guth.) Noisy, vocal; having a voice, having a vote.

GUTHAIT, *s. m.* (guth-àite.) The place of an oracle; a confessionary.—*Stew.* 1 *K.*

GUTHAN, *n. pl.* of guth; which see.

H.

H, (uath, *the white-thorn tree.*) The eighth letter of the Gaelic alphabet. It is used in the Gaelic, not properly as a letter, but as an aspiration When it is prefixed to a word beginning with a vowel, it has the same degree of aspiration with *h* in *hall, hurt*, as, na h-oighean, *the maids*, na h-oidhche, *of the night* *H* is also required between the negative *ni* and the following word, if it begin with a vowel; as, ni h-è, *not he*, ni h-eadh, *no*, ni h-iad, *not they*; ni h-eudar, *must not.* It is also used in the beginning of various interjections; as, haha! *an interjection of mirth;* hoilo! haibh! *interjections used in calling aloud to a person.* Hut! hud! *tut! pshaw!* Ho, ho!, *an interjection of defiance, and sometimes of disappointment.* H-ugad, *to thee; take care;* h-ugam, *to me*, h-ugaibh, *to you;*—said to persons when they are requested to take immediate care of their persons, as from a blow, or any impending danger. These words are also written respectively, *chugad, chugam, chugaibh.*

I.

I, (iogh) The ninth letter of the Gaelic alphabet. The Gael, differing from their brother Celts in Brittany and Cornwall, never use *i* as a consonant in the shape of *j* In this respect the Gaelic resembles the Greek and the ancient Latin, in which *j*, the consonant form of *i*, was never used as a distinct character The Gaelic *i* has two sounds: (1) both long and short, like *ee* in *deem*, as, sìn, *stretch*, cìr, *comb:* short, like *ee* in *feet*, as, bith, *existence*, sir, *seek* (2) Short and obscure, like *i* in *miss*, as, is, *am, art, is, are.*

I, *s pron.* (*Corn* hi *Arm* hi *Lat* ea) She, her Bhuail si i, *she struck her*, ise, *emphatic form of* i, *she, her*, in contradistinction to any other female, i fèin, *herself*

I, *s* An island.

Hind ey. *Heb.* i *or* ai *Island* ey *Du.* ey. *Barbarous Lat.* eia. *Sax.* †eia *Germ.* †ei *Swed* †oe *Ir* i

I Cholum chille, Iona, or St. Columba's Isle, in the Hebrides, was called *I* by way of eminence The far-famed monastery of this island, it is well known, was founded about the middle of the sixth century by St. Colum, or Columba, an Irish priest, who in a fit of displeasure had left his native country, after having involved it in three different wars According to Keating and Adamnan, he was of very high birth, but the cowl and tonsure presented to his eccentric mind charms superior to those of civil distinctions He was held in high estimation by the princes of Britain and of foreign countries, who often applied to him for deciding their controversies A curious circumstance related of him is, that he had a rooted aversion to cows, and would not suffer one to be seen within sight of his sacred tenements "Far am bi bo," he was wont to say, "bithidh bean, is far am bi bean bithidh malluchadh," *where there is a cow there is a woman, and where there is a woman there is swearing* This sentiment has, ever since, continued in the Gaelic language

The undisputed sacredness of the monastery was, no doubt, one reason why the remains of so many kings of various nations were crowded to this distant and lonely island the following very ancient prophecy may have been another —

Seachd bliadhna roimh 'n bhràth,
Thig muir thair Eirinn re aon tràth,
Is thair Ila ghuirm ghlais,
Ach snamhaidh I Cholum clèirach

A literal Translation

Seven years before the world's end
The sea shall come over Eirin at one tide,
And over green grassy Isla;
But I Colm shall float upon the flood

Saint Columba, of whom it is handed down that he uttered his discourses in verse to suit the taste of the people, uttered the following prediction in his last discourse to his disciples Every person who has read Dr Johnson's Tour to the Hebrides, cannot fail remarking the resemblance between the latter part of this prophecy, and the striking thoughts on the changes of human affairs in the illustrious tourist's description of Iona

An I mo chridhe, I mo ghraidh,
An àite guth manaich bithidh geum ba,
Ach mun tig an saoghal gu crìch
Bithidh I mar a bha

Literal Translation

In the isle of my heart, the isle of my love,
Instead of a monk's voice, there shall be the lowing of cattle;
But, ere the world comes to an end,
Iona shall flourish as before

† I, *s. f.* (*Ir* id) An art, a science; *also*, low, shallow.—*Shaw*

† IA, *s* (*Ir. id.*) Country. Hence, perhaps, comes the *ia* of the Latins, patria, Italia.

† IACH, eich, *s. m* (*Ir. id*) A salmon

IACH, *v n* (*Ir id*) Cry, scream, shout, yell, bawl. *Pret. a.* dh' iach, *cried*, *fut. aff a.* iachaidh, *shall cry*

IACH, èich, *s f.* (*Ir. id. Gr.* ἰαχη) A cry; a scream, a yell. *N pl* èich

IACHADH, aidh, *s m* A crying, a screaming, a yelling; a cry, a scream, a yell.

IACHAL, *s. m* A cry, a scream, a yell, a noise

IACHDAR, air, *s. m.* (*Ir. id.*) Bottom, foundation, basis; nether part. Iachdar-chànais, *bassus cantus in music.* Written also *iochdar*, which see

IACHDARACH, *a* Low; humble, inferior, nether; lower, lowest *Com* and *sup* iachdaraiche Written also *iochdarach.*

IAD, *pers pron.* (*Ir.* iad.) They, them Iad fèin, *themselves, they themselves*, iadsa, iadsan, *themselves*, iad sin, *those there*, iad so, *these here*, iad sud, *those yonder*

IAD, èid, *s m.* Jealousy. See EUD

IADACH, *a.* Jealous, suspicious See EUDACH.

IADACHADH, aidh, *s m* A jealous watching; jealousy.

IADAICH, *v a.* Watch jealously. *Pret. a.* dh' iadaich, *watched* Also written *eudaich*

IADAL, ail, *s m.* (*Ir. id*) A disease

IADH, *v. a* and *n* Surround; enclose, shut; wind; roll; join, bind; take a circuitous course, hover round. *Pret a.* dh' iadh; *fut. aff* iadhaidh, *shall surround.* Dh' iadh na tuillltean mi, *the floods surrounded me —Stew. Jonah.*

IADHACH, *a.* Surrounding; meandering, as a stream.

IADHADH, aidh, *s m.* (*Ir id*) A surrounding, a winding; a rolling; a fluttering round, a hovering round, a stretching, as of a bow, a circuit, a circumference; a circuitous course; a meander Iadhadh do thuil, *the winding of thy flood —Oss. Com.* Iadhadh do luing, *the circuit of thy ship. —Oss Fing.*

IADHADH, (a), *pr part.* of iadh Surrounding, winding, meandering; stretching, as a bow; rolling; moving round Ag iadhadh mu'n tràigh, *winding along the shore —Oss. Fing.*

A gorm-shùil ag iadhadh, *her blue eye rolling.—Id.* Bàs ag iadhadh mu 'shleagh, *death hovering about his spear.—Oss. Carthon.*

Iadhaidh, *fut. aff.* of iadh, which see.

Iadhaim, (*for* iadhaidh mi) I shall surround. Iadhaim ur braighde, *I will surround your captives.—Old Poem.*

Iadhar, *fut. pass.* of iadh. Shall be surrounded.

Iadh-lann, -lainn, *s. m.* (iadh *and* lann.) A corn-yard, any fenced place. *N. pl.* iadh-lainn *and* iadh-lannan.

Iadh-shlat, ait, *s. f.* (iadh *and* slat.) The ivy; honey-suckle. Mar iadh-shlat ri stoc aosda, *like an ivy to an aged trunk.*

Iadhta, **Iadhte**, *p. part.* of iadh. (*Ir. id.*) Surrounded; closed, hemmed.

Iadsa, **Iadsan**, *emphatic form* of iad.

† **Iagh**, *s. m.* (*Ir. id.*) An island.

Iain, *s. m.* (*Arm.* Yan.) The name John.

Ial, *s. m.* (*W.* ial, *clear.*) Light; a gleam of sunshine; a sunny interval between showers, age, time; generation.

Ialach, *a.* Sunny; having serene intervals, gleamy, as the sun in the interval of showers. Mòra nan aiteal ialach, *sunny Mora.—Oss. Duthona.*

Iall, éill, *s. f.* (*Ir. id. Dan.* oel.) A thong, a strip or string of leather, a latchet; a leash, a string; a riband; a lace. Iall bròig, *a shoe-string* or *latchet*, an iall ris an d'earb thu, *the string to which you trusted.—Ull.* Le h-éill ghuirm, *with a blue lace.—Stew. Exod.* Iall do ghorm, *a riband of blue.* *N. pl.* iallan.

Iallag, aig, *s. f.* (*dim.* of iall.) A thong, a shoe-tye, a latchet, a lace.

Iallach, *a.* Thongy, like a thong; like a latchet; in thongs, in strings; *also*, a thong, an assortment of thongs. An iallach cruaidh, *the hard thongs.—Ull.*

Iallan, ain, *s. m.* (*dim.* of iall.) A thong; a shoemaker's thread.

Iall-chasaidh, *s. f.* A martingale.

Iallachrann, *s. pl.* Shoes.—*Shaw.*

Iallag, aig, *s. f.* (*dim.* of iall.) A little thong, a thread; a shoemaker's thread.

Iallan, *n. pl.* of iall. Thongs, threads.

Ialtag, aig, *s. f.* A bat.—*Stew. Lev.* The *vespertinus murinus* of Linnæus. Ialtag anmoch, *a bat*, ialtag leathair, *a bat*, so also say the Irish. *N. pl.* ialtagan.

Ian, *s. m.* See **Eun**.

† **Ian**, *s. m.* (*Ir. id.*) A vessel; the blade of a weapon, a weasel.

Ianach, *a.* See **Eunach**.

Ianlaith. See **Eunlaith**.

Iapal, ail, *s.* Dispute.

† **Iar**, *prep.* (*Ir. id.*) After, second in order. Iar sin, *after that.*

† **Iar**, *s. m.* A bird.

Iar, *s.* West. An iar, *the west*, osag o'n iar, *a blast from the west.—Oss. Tem.* An iar-dheas, *the south-west*, an iar-thuath, *the north-west.*

† **Iar**, *a.* (*Ir. id.*) Dark, black, dusky.

Iarag, aig, *s. m.* (*Ir. id.*) A weasel, any little creature of a brownish hue; anguish, grief.

Iar-aois, *s. f.* An after age, a succeeding age, after times.

Iar-bhrò, *a.* (*Ir. id.*) Surviving, still alive.

Iar-bhleothann, ainn, *s. m.* (*Ir. id.*) After-milk.

Iar-bhreith, *s.* An after birth.—*Shaw.*

Iar-cheann, -chinn, *s. m.* (*Ir. id.*) The hind head; a noddle.

Iar-cheannsuidhe, *s. m.* A vice-president.

Iar-chleireach, ich, *s. m.* An under-secretary; an under-clerk. *N. pl.* iar-chleirich.

Iar-chleirsinneachd, *s. f.* An under-secretaryship; under-clerkship.

Iarchuan, ain, *s. m.* The west sea. *N. pl.* iar-chuantan, *western seas.*

Iar-dheas, *a.* (*Ir. id.*) South-west. Chum an iar-dheas, *to the south-west.—Stew. Acts.*

Iar-dhonn, *a.* (*Ir. id.*) Brownish, dusky; blackish, *also*, a brownish black.

Iar-dhraoi, *s. m.* (*Ir. id.*) A remnant; posterity.

Iar-fhlaitheachd, *s. f.* Viceroyalty; earldom, aristocracy.

Iar-fhlath, aith, *s. m.* A viceroy; a feudary lord, or a lord dependent on a greater; an earl.

Ir. iarla. *W.* iarll. *Corn.* arluth. *Old Dan. according to Wormius*, iarll, *baron*. *Swed.* iarler. *Old Sax.* eorl.

Iar-fhlath (pronounced *iurl*) is literally a secondary noble or chief, and hence evidently is derived the word *earl*, which is certainly not of Danish origin, as Dr Macpherson would have it. Among the northern nations the dignity of *iar-fhlath* was next to that of king, and it appears to have been in existence in the time of the Fingalians. Iar-fhlath Mùthan mor nan long, *the great earl of maritime Muthan.—Fingalian Poem.*

Iargaill, *s. f.* See **Iarguill**.

Iargain, *s. f.* See **Iargainn**.

Iargaineach, *a.* See **Iargainneach**.

Iargainn, *s. f.* Pain; distress, a groan; a dying groan, sediments; dregs. Written also *iarguinn.*

Iargainneach, **Iargaineach**, *a.* Painful; languishing, troubled; distressful; having sediment. Leabadh a thinneis iargainich, *the bed of his languishing sickness.—Stew. Ps.* Written also *iarguinneach.*

Iargainneachd, *s. f.* Painfulness; distress, the state of being troubled or distressed.

Iargalta, *a.* (*Ir.* iarculta.) Churlish; obstinate, backward, distressing.

Iargaltachd, *s. f.* Churlishness; obstinateness; backwardness.

Iargan, ain, *s. m.* Pain; a groan; sorrow.

Iarganach, *a.* Painful; pained; groaning; afflictive. Gu h-iarganach, *painfully.*

Iarganachd, *s. f.* Painfulness; afflictiveness, distress.

Iar-ghaoth, -ghaòithe, *s. f.* (*Ir. id.*) A west wind.

Iar-ghille, *s. m.* An under-servant; *also*, a minor. *N. pl.* iar-ghillean.

Iarguill, **Iarghuill**, *s. f.* Distress; calamity; strife, a battle, a skirmish.

Ir. id. *W.* argoll, *ruin.* *Gr.* ὀργίλος, *wrathful.* *Fr.* orgueil.

Iarguilleach, **Iarghuilleach**, *a.* (*Ir. id. Fr.* orgueilleux.) Troublesome, contentious, warlike.

Iarguinn, *s. f.* Trouble; affliction; a groan; the groan of a dying person; *also*, sediments, lees. Innis d' iarguinn, *tell thy trouble.—Orr.* Ionnsachadh làn iarguinn, *learning full of useless knowledge.—Old Song.*

Iarguinneach, *a.* Troubled, afflictive, troublesome, complaining.

Iarguinneachd, *s. f.* Continued trouble, troublesomeness.

Iargunach, *a.* See **Iarguinneach**.

Iarla, *s. m., contracted for* iar-fhlath; which see.

Iarlas, ais, *s. m.* (*Ir. id.*) An earnest penny, a pledge. *N. pl.* iarlasan, *pledges.* Written also *earlas.*

Iarmad, aid, *s. m.* (*Ir. id.*) A remnant or remainder, race, offspring, posterity. Iarmad mo shluaigh, *the remnant of* *my people.—Stew. O. T.* A chogadh ris an iarmad mheanbh, *to fight with the pigmy race.—Mac Lach.*

IARMADACH, *a.* Having remnants; in remnants; like a remnant; having posterity.

IARMAID, *gen. sing.* of iarmad.

IARMAILT, *s. f.* (*Ir. id.*) The firmament, air, skies, heavens. 'San iarmailt ùrair, *in the freshly green firmament.—Oss. Fin. and Lor.* Na h-iarmailtean, *the skies.*

IARMAIR, *s. f.* (*Ir. id.*) A remnant or remainder.

IARMART, airt, *s. m.* (*Ir. id.*) A result; consequence of an affair; riches; offspring.

IARMHEIRGHE, *s. f.* (*Ir. id.*) Matins; morning; rising early.

IARNA, IARNADH, aidh, *s. m.* A skain of thread; a measure of yarn; confusion.—*Shaw.*

IARNACHADH, aidh, *s. m.* An ironing; a smoothing, as of linen, with an iron.

IARNACHADH, (ag), *pr. part.* of iarnaich. Ironing, smoothing.

IARNACHAN, ain, *s. m., from* iarunn. (*Ir. id.*) An iron tool. *N. pl.* iarnachain.

IARNAICH, *v. a.* (*for* iarunnaich.) Iron; smooth linen by ironing. *Pret. a.* dh' iarnaich; *fut. aff. a.* iarnaichidh, *shall iron; p. part.* iarnaichte, *ironed.*

IARNAICHTE, *p. part.* of iarnaich. Ironed, as linen. Anart iarnaichte, *smoothed* or *ironed linen.*

IARNAIDH, *a.* Like iron; chalybeate; having an iron taste. Uisge iarnaidh, *chalybeate water.*

IARNAIR, *s. m.* An ironmonger.

IARNAN, ain, *s. m.* A skain; a measure of yarn; confusion. —*Shaw.*

IARR, *v. a.* (*Ir. id.*) Ask, demand; invite; inquire; seek, seach, look for; bid, desire. *Pret.* dh' iarr, *asked; fut. aff. a.* iarraidh, *shall ask.* Iarr e gu fleagh, *invite him to a feast.—Oss. Tem.* Dh' iarr iad Suilmhine, *they sought for Sulmina.—Orr.* Cha 'n fhaic 's cha 'n iarr iad, *they shall not see nor inquire.—Oss. Fing.*

Iarr, in the sense of *bidding* or *desiring*, has after it the preposition *air*, compounded or understood; as, iarr air, iarr orra, *desire him, desire them.*

IARRADAICHE, *s. m.* A probe; a feeler; a petitioner.

IARRADAIR, *s. m., from* iarr. (*Ir.* iarratoir.) A beggar, a petitioner.

IARRAIDH, IARRUIDH, *s. f.* An asking, a petitioning; requiring; searching; inquiring; invitation; request. Freagraidh cruachain an iarruidh, *the hillocks shall respond to their inquiries.—Oss. Tem.* Tha fhuil air a h-iarruidh, *his blood is sought.—Stew. Gen.* Ag iarruidh gu bealach, *moving towards the pass.—Old Song.*

IARRAIDH, IARRUIDH, *a.* Desirable, tolerable. An iarraidh ghleusta, *pretty well;* tha mi 'n iarruidh, *I am pretty well; I am so and so.*

IARRAIDH, IARRUIDH, *fut. aff. a.* of iarr. Shall ask. See IARR.

IARRAM, 1 *sing. imper.* of iarr. Let me ask; and 1 *sing. fut. aff. for* iarraidh mi, *I shall ask.*

IARSALACH, *a.* Covetous; *also*, a covetous person.

IARSCEART, eirt, *s. m.* (*Ir. id.*) The west; the north-west. —*Shaw.*

IARSCEARTACH, *a.* North-west; west.—*Shaw.*

IARSMACH, *a.* (*Ir. id.*) Generous.

IARSMADH, aidh, *s. m.* (*Ir. id.*) A remnant, a remainder; a relic; a burden; a New-Year's gift.—*Shaw.*

IARSPEALADH, aidh, *s. m.* After-grass; a second crop of grass.

IARTAICHE, *s. m.* (*from* iarr.) A probe; an importunate person; a dun; a petitioner; *also*, descendants, posterity, domestics.

IARTAS, ais, *s. m.* (*Ir.* iarratus.) A request, a desire, command; instance. Air d' iartas, *at thy request;* iartas beòil mhic Cumhail, *the verbal command of Fingal.—Fingalian Poem.* Iartas faoin, *a vain request.—Mac Lach.* Cha toill iartas achmhasan, *request bears no blame.—G. P.*

IARTHIR, *s. f.* A west country.

IAR-THUATH, *s.* North-west. An iar-thuath, *the north-west.—Stew. Acts.*

IAR-TOISEACH, ich, *s. m.* A captain of the rear-guard.

IARTUINNEAS, eis, *s. m.* Will, desire. B'e d' iartuinneas san am, *it was then thy desire.—Mack.*

IARUNN, uinn, *s. m.* Iron. Iarunn as an talamh, *iron out of the earth.—Stew. Job.* Gàd iaruinn, *an iron bar;* iarunn fàladair, *a sithe;* iarunn casaidh, *a crisping iron.* *Goth.* eisarn. *Cimbric*, iara. *Anglo-Sax.* isern *and* iren. *Span.* hierro. *Swed.* iarn. *Dan.* iern. *Ir.* iarrun. *Corn.* hoarn. *Arm.* uarn. *Manx*, iaarn.

IARUNNACH, aich, *s. m.* Iron; irons. Iarunnach seisearaich, *plough-irons.*

IASACHD, *s. f.* (*Ir. id.*) A loan; advantage; profit. Air iasachd, *in loan, borrowed.—Stew. Pro.* Gabhaidh e iasachd, *he will borrow.—Sm.*

IASACHDACH, *a.* Ready to give in loan; prone to ask in loan.

IASACHDAICHE, *s. m.* A creditor.

IASAD, aid, *s. m.* A loan; advantage; credit. Thug iad an iasad, *they gave on loan.—Stew. Ex. ref.* Millidh airc iasad, *necessity spoils credit.—G. P.*

† IASADACH, *a.* (*Ir. id.*) Squeamish.

† IASALACH, *a.* (*Ir. id.*) Easy; feasible; practicable.

IASALACHD, *s. f.* (*Ir. id.*) Frailty.

IASAN, ain, *s. m.* Petulance; sauciness; a petulant person.

IASANACH, *a.* Petulant; saucy.

IASANACHD, *s. f.* Petulance; sauciness.

IASG, eisg, *s. m.* (*Ir.* iasc.) A fish. Iasg dubh, *a name given to salmon on their return from the sea;* iasg air chladh, *fish at spawning.*

IASGACH, *a.* (*Ir. id.*) Abounding in fish.

IASGACH, *s. m.* See IASGACHADH.

IASGACHADH, aidh, *s. m.* The act of fishing.

IASGACHADH, (ag), *pr. part.* of iasgaich. Fishing, angling.

IASGACHD, *s. f., from* iasg. (*Ir. id.*) Fishing, angling; the art of angling; a fishery. Is daor cheannaich mi an t-iasgachd, *dearly have I bought the fishery.—Old Song.*

IASGAICH, *v. n.* (*from* iasg.) Fish, angle. *Pret. a.* dh' iasgaich, *fished; fut. aff. a.* iasgaichidh, *shall fish.*

IASGAIR, *s. m.* (*Ir.* iascair.) A fisher, an angler; a fisherman. *N. pl.* iasgairean. Iasgair cairneach, *an osprey.—Stew. Lev. ref. Ir.* iasgair cairneach. Iasgair diomhain, *a kingsfisher; an unsuccessful fisher.*

IASGAIREACHD, *s. f.* (*Ir.* iasgaireachd.) The employment of a fisher; the art of angling; the amusement of fishing.

IASGAIREAN, *n. pl.* of iasgair. Fishers.

IASGAN, ain, *s. m., dim.* of iasg. (*Ir. id.*) A little fish; a little shell-fish, a muscle. *N. pl.* iasgain.

IASGITHEACH, *a.* (*Ir. id.*) Piscivorous.

IASG-LOCH, *s. m.* (*Ir. id.*) A lake abounding in fish; a fish-pond.

IASG-LOCHAN, ain, *s, m.* A fish-pond. *N. pl.* iasg-lochain.

IASG-SHLAT, -shlait, *s. f.* A fishing-rod. Iasg-shlat sa cheituin, *a fishing-rod on spring.—Old Song.*

IASG-SLIGEACH, *s. m.* Shell-fish.

† **Iath**, *s. m.* (*Ir. id.*) Land.

Iath, *v.* More frequently written *iadh;* which see.

† **Ibh**, *s.* (*Ir. id.*) Country people; a tribe of people.—*Shaw.*

Ibh, *s. f.* Drink. Gun ibh, gun ith, *without meat or drink.*—*Oss. Gaul.* Hence *dibh;* which see.

† **Ibh**, *v. n.* (*Ir. id.*) Drink. *Pret. a.* dh' ibh; *fut. aff.* ibhidh, *shall drink.*

Ibhne, *s. f.* (*Ir. id.*) Drinking.

Ibhteach, *a.* Dry, droughty; soaking; that imbibes water.

Ic, ice, *s. f.* (*Ir. id.* *W.* iarc, *sane.*) A cure or remedy, balm; a supply, an eke. Ic airson a leòin, *balm for his wound.*—*Stew. Jer.* 'Gabhaibh ic, *take balm.*—*Id.*

'Ic, (*for* mhic), *gen.* and *voc. sing.* of Mac. Talamh 'ic Leòid, *the land of Mac Leod.*—*Old Song.* Chonail 'ic Cholgair! *Conal, thou son of Colgar!*—*Oss. Fing.*

Ic, *v. a.* (*Ir. id.*) Heal, cure; supply, eke. *Pret. a.* dh' ic, *eked; fut. aff.* icidh.

Iceach, *a.* (*Ir. id.*) Balmy; salutiferous; remedial; medicinal.

Iceadh, idh, *s. m.* (*Ir. id.*) The act of healing, curing, or remedying; a remedy; a supply, an eke.

Ich, *v. a.* Eat.—*Q. B. ref.* See **Ith**.

Ichd-air-neachd, *adv.* At any rate.—*Shaw.*

Ic-lus, luis, *s. m.* (*Ir. id.*) A medical herb.

Ic-lusach, *a.* Abounding in medical herbs.

† **Id**, *a.* (*Ir. id.*) Honest, good, just.—*Shaw.* *Also, substantively,* a ring.

Idearmanachd, *s. f.* Hydromancy.

† **Idh**, *s. f.* (*Ir. id.*) A wreath; a fine chain; a ridge; use.—*Shaw.*

Idhal, ail, *s. m.* More properly *iodhal;* which see.

† **Idid**, *a.* (*Ir. id.*) Cold, chill; *also,* an exclamation denoting cold.

Idir, *adv.* At all, yet. Mu ghabhas tu idir eudach, *if thou takest clothes at all.*—*Stew. Ex.* No idir air a bhruicheadh, *nor yet boiled.*—*Id.* Cha 'n 'eil e gu math idir, *he is not at all well;* cha deanainn idir e, *I would not do it on any account whatsoever.*

† **Idneadh**, *s.* Weapons, arms.

Idnearach, *a.* Prosperous; happy; merry. *Com.* and *sup.* idnearaiche. Gu h-idnearach, *prosperously.*

Idnearachd, *s. f.* Prosperousness; happiness; mirth.

† **Ifinn**, *s. f.* (*Ir. id.*) A gooseberry.

Ifreannta, *a.* Hellish; infernal; stygian; extremely wicked.

Ifrinn, *s. f.* Hell.
Arm. infern. *Corn.* ifarn. *Ir.* ifearn. *W.* yfern.

Ifrinn literally means the isle of the cold land, or clime, being a contracted form of *i-fuar-fhuinn.* The Celtic hell was a cold dark region, abounding in venomous reptiles and wild beasts, especially wolves. The Scotch Celts still retain the name, though well aware that cold forms no part of infernal punishment.

The following lines, quoted by Dr. Smith from an ancient Gaelic MS., illustrate the notions which our Celtic forefathers had of a place of punishment after death:—

" 'S mairg a roghnuicheas Ifrinn fhuar,
'S gur i uaimh nan driobhunn geur;
Is beag orm Ifrinn fhuar fhliuch,
Aite bith-bhuan is searbh deoch."

Ifrinneach, *a.* (*from* ifrinn.) Hellish; infernal; stygian; extremely wicked.

Ifrinneach, ich, *s. m.* A rake-hell. *N. pl.* ifrinnich.

Ifrionn, *s.* See **Ifrinn**.

Ifrionnach, *a.* See **Ifrinneach**.

† **Igh**, *s. f.* (*Ir. id.*) A ring.—*Shaw.*

Igh, *s. m.* (*Ir. id.*) Tallow; the fat of any slaughtered quadruped. Ghabh e 'n igh, *he took the* [*tallow*] *fat.*—*Stew. Lev.*

Igheach, *a.* (*Ir. id.*) Abounding in fat; fat, tallowy.

Ighean, inn, *s. f.* A daughter; a girl; a maid. Tiormaich ighean Thoscair, do dheòir! *dry, daughter of Toscar, thy tears!*—*Oss. Taura.* Nochd mna 's a h-ighinn, *the nakedness of a woman and her daughter.*—*Stew. Lev.* *N. pl.* igheanan.

† **Il**, ile, *s. m.* (*Ir. id.*) Plenty; difference; diversity; multitude; a compositive particle. More frequently written *iol;* which see.

Il-bheusach, *a.* More commonly written *iol-bheusach;* which see.

Il-cheardach, aich, *s. m.* See **Iol-cheardach**.

Il-chearnach, *a.* See **Iol-chearnach**.

Il-choimeasgta, *a.* See **Iol-choimeasgta**.

Il-chumasg, aisg, *s. f.* See **Iol-chumasg**.

Il-dhealbhach, *a.* See **Iol-dhealbhach**.

Ileach, ich, *s. m.* (*Ir. id.*) Ordure, dung.

Il-ghnetheach, *a.* See **Iol-ghnetheach**.

† **Ill**, *s. m.* (*Ir. id.*) Ill, ruin.

Ille, *for* a ghille. My lad. Illean biomaid sunntach, *my lads, let us be merry.*—*Turn.*

Illse, *com.* and *sup.* of iosal. Lower, lowest.

Illsich, *v. a.* Humble, demean; condescend; lower; subside. *Pret.* dh' illsich, *humbled; fut. aff. a.* illsichidh, *shall lower.* A dh' illsicheas e fein, *who demeans himself.*—*Sm.* Dh' illsich teine an righ, *the king's fire subsided.*—*Oss. Tem.* *Fut. pass.* illsichear; *p. part.* illsichte, *humbled, demeaned.*

Illsichear, *fut. pass.* of illsich. Shall be lowered.

Illsichte, *p. part.* of illsich. Lowered, humbled.

Im, ime, *s. m.* (*Ir. id.* *Arm.* aman.) Butter. Sruthain ime, *brooks of butter.*—*Stew. Job.*

Im-cheist, *s. f.* (ioma-cheist.) Perplexity, anxiety; dilemma, jeopardy. Ann an imcheist, *in perplexity.*—*Stew. Micah,* and *Oss. Dargo.*

Im-cheisteach, *a.* In perplexity; causing perplexity or doubt.

Im-chubhaidh, *a.* See **Iom-chuidh**.

Im-chubhaideachd, *s. f.* See **Iom-chuidheachd**.

† **Im-dheagal**, ail, *s. m.* Protection.

Im-dhearbh, *v.* See **Iom-dhearbh**.

Im-dhorus, uis, *s. m.* A back-door.

Imeach, *a.* (*from* im.) Buttery, abounding in butter; like butter; producing butter. Imeach càiseach, *abounding in butter and cheese.*—*Macfar.*

Imeachd, *s. f.* (*Ir.* im-theachd.) Walking; moving, coming, advancing; travelling; a course, pace, progress; departure. Bu ghrad a h-imeachd, *quick was her pace.*—*Mac Lach.* D' imeachd an saoghal chéin, *thy travelling in a distant world.*—*Orr.*

Imeachd, (ag), *pr. part.* of imich. Walking; coming, moving, advancing; travelling; departing. Ag imeachd an raoin, *traversing the heath.*—*Ull.* Cha 'n eil aon 'g an imeachd, *no one* [*walks on*] *traverses them.*—*Stew. Zeph.* Bi 'g imeachd, *be gone, be off.*

Imeachdan, ain, *s. m.* A child on leading-strings.

Imeall. See **Iomall**.

Imeasargain, *s. f.* A striking on all sides.

Imeasarganach, *a.* Striking on all sides

Imich, *v. a.* and *n.* Go; walk; be gone; depart; stir, budge; advance, come. *Pret* dh' imich, *went*; *fut. aff.* a. imichidh, *shall go.* Imich gu do shrutham diomhair, *begone to thy lonely streams*.—*Oss. Fin. and Lorm.* Dh' imich an laoch, *the hero has departed*.—*Oss Gaul.*

IMILEADADH, aidh, *s. m.* Unction

IMIR, *v. def* Must, need, require. An imir mi 'dheanamh? *must I do it?* Cha do thaisg riamh nach d' imir, *no man ever laid up a thing who did not find use for it.*—*G P* Imiridh mi e, *I shall need it*

IMIR, *s* See IOMAIRE

IMIRICH, *s. f.* (*Ir.* imirighe. *Lat* emigratio) Emigration; a flitting, a removal of abode. Chaidh iad imirich, *they emigrated*, or *changed their dwelling* Written also *imrich*, which see

IMIRICH, *v* Emigrate, change an abode. *Pret* dh' imirich, *emigrated*, *fut aff* a imirichidh, *shall emigrate*

IMLEACH, *a* Licking, apt to lick or lap with the tongue

IMLEACHADH, aidh, *s m* A licking, a lapping with the tongue

IMLEAG, eig, *s f* (*Lat* umbilica *Ir.* iomlacan) A navel. Eadar m' imleag 's m' àirnean, *between my navel and my reins*—*Death of Oscar.*

IMLEAGACH, *a* (*from* imleag) Umbilical; like a navel, of, or pertaining to, the navel

IMLICH, *v a* Lick or lap with the tongue *Pret a* dh' imlich, *licked*, *fut aff a* imlichidh. Imlichidh iad an duslach, *they will lick the dust.*—*Stew Mic* *Fut pass* imlichear, *shall be licked*, *p part* imlichte, *licked.*

IMLICHEAR, *fut pass* of imlich; which see

IMLICHTE, *p part* of imlich. Licked

IMNIDH, *s* (*for* iom-shniomh) Care, solicitude; sadness Gun imnidh gun eagal, *without care or fear*—*Old Song*

IMNIDHEACH, *a* (iom-shniomhach) Anxious, solicitous, uneasy; sad Gu h-imnidheach, *anxiously*

IMNIDHEACHD, *s f* Care, uneasiness.

IMPEACHADH, aidh, *s m* A persuading, a beseeching, a converting, a constraining

IMPICH, *v a* Persuade, constrain, beseech, convert *Pret. a* dh' impich, *converted*, *fut aff. a* impichidh, *shall convert*, *fut pass* impichear; *p part.* impichte, *converted* Written also *iompaich*, which see

IMPICHEAR, *fut pass* of impich

IMPICHTE, *p part* of impich Persuaded; converted

IMPIDH, *s f* (*Ir* *id*) A persuasion, entreaty, conversion, urging, constrainment, exhortation towards conversion, a twig, a rod. Cuir impidh air, *urge him*—*Stew 2 K* *N pl* impidhean, *d pl* impidhibh Le h-impidhibh, *with entreaties*—*Stew. Pro*

IMPIDHEACH, *a* Persuading, supplicatory, persuasive, constraining, urging; converting.

IMPIDHEACH, ich, *s m* A persuader; a petitioner; an intercessor, a converter

IMPIDHEACHD, *s f* Persuasion, petitioning; intercession

IMPIS, *s f* Likelihood An impis bhi sgàinte, *like to burst.*—*Macfar*

IMREUSON, oin, *s m* See IOMREUSON

IMREUSONACH, *a* See IOMREUSONACH.

IMREUSONAICHE, *s m* A wrangler See IOMREUSONAICHE.

IMRICH, *s f* A removal or change of abode, flitting, emigration. Air imrich, *emigrated*, chuir e imrich iad, *he removed them*—*Stew Gen.* Theid e imrich thar a chuan, *he shall emigrate beyond the sea.*—*Macfar.*

IMSEACH, *a* Revengeful, furious, enraged. Gu h-imseach, *furiously* *Com* and *sup* imsiche

IMSEACHD, *s. f.* Revenge, revengefulness.

IMSEACHAN, ain, *s. m.* Rage, fury

† IMSEACHTRACH, aich, *s m* A project.

IMTHEACHD, *s f* Walking, gait—*Stew Is* More frequently written *imeachd.*

IM-THUS, *s.* Progress; adventure

† IN, ine, *s. f.* A nail or claw. See IONGA.

† IN, *s. f.* A country; an island This vocable is now used only in composition with another word, as, *Albainn*, i e. *Alb-in*, the high country or island *Eirin*, i e. *Iarin*, the western isle, or Ireland.

INBH, inbhe, *s f* (*Ir. id*) Quality, rank, dignity, condition, station, state; size. An inbhe mhòir, *in great dignity*—*Stew. Ecc* Thainig e gu h-inbh, *he grew up in size* or *stature.* Ann an inbh mhath, *in a good state* or *condition.*

INBHEACH, *a*, *from* inbh. (*Ir id*) In high rank or condition, noble, exalted; sizeable; advanced in stature or condition, chief, ripe, mature. Duine inbheach, *a man of rank*, *a man high in office*, aite inbheach, *an exalted place.*—*Stew. Jam* *Com* and *sup* inbhiche. A b' inbhiche, *who was chief*—*Stew 1 Chr.*

INBHEACHAS, ais, *s. m* A fondness for being high in rank; a fondness for high office

INBHEACHD, *s f.* Height of rank or office; nobleness

INBHEAR, ir, *s. m* The confluence of two streams; the angular piece of ground which lies at the confluence of two waters

INBHEIRT, *s f.* A perfect birth—*Shaw*

INC, *s* A corruption of *ink*—*Mac Co.*

INEACH, INGHEACH, ich, *s. f* A block. See INNEACH.

INEACH, ich, *s. f.* (*Ir. id*) Generosity, hospitality; good management in housekeeping.

INEACHAIL, *a* (*i e.* ineach-amhuil) Generous, hospitable. Gu cairdeil ineachail, *friendly and hospitable.*—*Old Song.*

† INEACHRAS, ais, *s m.* (*Ir id*) A fair; a public meeting

INEALTA, *a* (*Ir id*) Neat, well-made; sprightly, handsome, elegant, adorned Deudan an ordugh finealta, *teeth in elegant array*—*R* Written also *finealta*, which see

INEALTACHD, *s f* (*Ir id*) Neatness; handsomeness; sprightliness; elegance Written also *finealtachd*, which see

INEALTAIR, *v a* Feed cattle, pasture, graze *Pret. a.* dh 'ionaltair, *fed*, *fut aff. a* inealtraidh, *shall feed* Ionaltair do mheannan, *feed thy kids*—*Stew Sol*

INEALTRACH, *a* (*Ir id*) Pasturing, grazing

INEALTRADH, aidh, *s m* A pasturing or grazing, pasturage. Caoraich san fhraoch ag inealtradh, *sheep pasturing on the heath.*—*R.*

INEALTRADH, (ag), *pr part* of inealtair

† INO, *s. f.* (*Ir id*) Force, compulsion, a stir, a neck of land, danger

INGEAR, ir, *s m.* (*Ir id.*) A level, a perpendicular, a mason's line; an anchor.

INGEARACH, *a* Perpendicular

INGHEAN, inghinn, *s. f.* (*Ir. id*) A daughter, a girl; a maid *N. pl.* inghean.in Nochd mna agus a h-inghinn, *the nakedness of a woman and her daughter.*—*Stew Lev ref.* An inghean ùr, *the blooming maid.*—*Old Poem.* Inghean céile, *a daughter-in-law*

† INGHILT, *s f.* (*Ir. id.*) Feeding, grazing, pasture.

IN-GHREIM, *s. m* A clutching grasp; a ravening; persecution, extreme avarice

In-ghreimeach, *a.* Clutching; ravenous; clawing; persecuting; avaricious; plundering.

Ingilt, *s. f.* Feeding, grazing; pasture.

Ingir, *s. f.* (*Ir. id.*) Sorrow, affliction.—*Shaw.* An anchor.

Inglan, *a.* (*Ir. id.*) Dirty, filthy, nasty.

Iniatar, air, *s. m.* (*Ir. id.*) A bowel or entrail.

Inich, *a.* Strong, sufficient; eager. Gu h-inich, *sufficiently.*

Inid, *s. f.* (*Ir. id.*) Shrovetide. Di-màirt inid, *Shrove-Tuesday.*

Inilt, *s. f.* (*Ir. id.*) Pasture, fodder.

Inilt, *v.* Feed cattle; pasture, graze.—*Shaw.*

Inirte, *s. f.* (*Ir. id. Lat.* inertia.) Laziness, inactivity, feebleness.

Inis, *s. f.* An island; a field to graze cattle in. More frequently written *innis;* which see.

Inis, *v. a.* More frequently written *innis;* which see.

† **Inis**, *s. f.* (*Ir. id.*) Distress, sorrow.

Iniso, *s. f.* (*Ir. id.*) A reproach.

Inisiol, *s. m.* A servant.

Inite, **Inithe**, *a.* Edible, eatable.

Inmhe, *s.* See **Inbhe**.

Inmheach, *a.* See **Inbheach**.

† **Inn**, I, us, we. This vocable is now used only in composition with a verb; as, dheanainn, *I would do;* bhuailinn, *I would strike.*

† **Inn**, *s.* (*Ir. id.*) A wave.—*Shaw.*

Inneach, ich, *s. m.* and *f.* (*Ir. id.*) Woof, or lining of cloth in weaving; a block; a curse. San dlùth no san inneach, *in the warp or woof.*—*Stew. Lev.* Is math an inneach a chlach gus an ruigear i, *the stone is a good block till you reach it.*—*G. P.*

† **Inneachas**, ais, *s. m.* (*Ir. id.*) Choice.

Inneachd, *s. f.* A blow.

Inneachadh, aidh, *s. m.* (*Ir. id.*) Agitating.

Inneadh, idh, *s. m.* (*Ir. id.*) Want, deficiency.

Inneal, eil, *s. m.* and *f.* (*Ir. id.*) An instrument, a tool, a machine; condition, state; deportment; order, array; attendance; dress, attire; service; restraint. Inneal bu shlinnteach fuaim, *a loud-sounding instrument.*—*Mac Lach.* Inneal cogaidh, *a weapon, arms;* inneal-ciùil, *a musical instrument.*—*Ull.* Inneal draghaidh, *a capstan;* inneal glacaidh, *a trap;* inneal fàsgaidh, *a press;* inneal iomchair, *a vehicle;* inneal mairbh, *an instrument of death;* inneal-smàlaidh, *an extinguisher.*

Innealaich, *v.* (*from* inneal.) Wield an instrument. *Pret. a.* dh'innealaich; *fut. aff.* innealaichidh.

Innealta, *a.* (*Ir. id.*) Neat; sprightly; elegant; well-made; handsome; active. Written also *finealta.*

Innealtachd, *s. f.* (*Ir. id.*) Neatness; sprightliness; elegance; handsomeness; activity.

† **Inneamh**, imh, *s. m.* (*Ir. id.*) Increase, augmentation.—*Shaw.*

Innean, ein, *s. m.* and *f.* (*Ir.* inneoin. *Corn.* anuan. *W.* einnion, *anvil.*) An anvil; a navel; *rarely*, the middle of a pool. Mar innean nan ord, *like the sounding of an anvil.*—*Old Poem.* Adharc innein, *the horn of an anvil.*

Innearach, *gen. sing.* of inneir.

Innearach, *a.* Full of dung.

Innein, *gen. sing.* of innean; which see.

Inneir, innearach, *s. f.* (*Ir. id.*) Manure, dung, ordure. Cairt innearach, *a dung-cart;* also, *a cart full of dung;* dùn innearach, *a dunghill.*

Innidh, **Innigh**, *s. pl.* (*Ir. id.*) Bowels, entrails, intestines; compassion. *D. pl.* innibh; *contracted* for innighibh. O t-innibh, *from thy bowels.*—*Stew. O. T.*

† **Innill**, *s. f.* (*Ir. id.*) A fort; a gin or snare.—*Shaw.*

Innilt, *s. f.* (*Ir. id.*) A handmaid; a maid-servant. Do bhan-oglach na h-innilt, *thy handmaid a servant.*—*Stew. Sam.*

Innis, *s. f.* Distress, misery.—*Shaw.*

Innis, innse, *s. f.* An island, an isle or islet. *N. pl.* innise, innsean, *and* innseachan, *islands.* Innis nan stuadh, *the island of waves.*—*Oss. Carricth.* Crathaidh innise, *islands shall tremble.*—*Oss. Tem.*

Arm. enes *and* enesan. *Ir.* inis. *W.* ynis. *Corn.* ennis.

Innis does not always signify an *island;* sometimes it means a *headland* or *promontory;* as, Craiginish, Deiginish, Treisinish, in Argyleshire; Mòrinish, in Breadalbane.

With the word *innis*, the Norwegian *noes* or *naes*, a *promontory*, and the termination *ness*, of many places in Scotland, as, Inverness, Tabertness, Stromness, have a strong affinity; so also have the Latin *nasum*, French *nez*, and the English *nose;* meaning the projecting feature. The Scotch *nes* also means a *promontory*, as do the Anglo-Saxon *naessa* and *nesse;* Old Swed. *noes;* Belg. *neus.*

Innis, *v. a.* Tell, relate, inform. *Pret.* dh'innis, *told fut. aff. a.* innsidh, *shall tell.* Innis d'iarguinn, *relate thy trouble.*—*Orr.* Innis dhomh, *tell me.*

Inniso. See **Inisg**.

Innleachd, *s. f.* (*Lat.* intellectus. *Ir.* innleachd.) Invention, ingenuity; contrivance, device. Droch innleachd, *a wicked contrivance.* *N. pl.* innleachdan. Dealbhmaid innleachdan, *let us devise devices.*—*Stew. Jer.* Cha'n fhiach duine gun neart gun innleachd, *a man is of little worth without strength or device.*—*G. P.* Gleidhidh airc innleachd, *necessity will make a shift.*—*Id.*

Innleachdadh, *a.* (*Ir. id.*) Ingenious, inventive; contriving; full of device or contrivance; sagacious. Gu h-innleachdach, *ingeniously.* *Com.* and *sup.* innleachdaiche.

Innleachdaiche, *s. m.* A contriver, an inventor, a deviser; an ingenious person.

Innleachdaiche, *com.* and *sup.* of innleachdach.

Innleachdail, *a.* See **Innleachdach**.

Innleachdair. See **Innleachdaiche**.

Innleachdan, *n. pl.* of innleachd. Inventions, devices, contrivances.

Innleag, eig, *s. f.* (*Ir. id.*) A child's doll.

† **Innlidh**, *s. f.* (*Ir. id.*) Forage.

Innlinn, *s. m.* Provender, fodder. Osciónn 'innlinn, *over its fodder.*—*Stew. Job.*

Innlis, *s. f.* (*Ir. id.*) A lamp, a lantern.

Innseach, *a.* Inclined to blab; *also*, insular, peninsular; abounding in islands.—*Macdon.*

Innseachan, *n. pl.* of innis. Islands. Na h-innseachan, *the Indies;* na h-Innseachan shuas, *the West Indies;* na h-Innseachan shios, *the East Indies.*

Innseadh, idh, *s. m.* (*Ir. id.*) A telling, a rehearsing or relating; a rehearsal or relation.

Innseadh, (ag), *p. part.* of innis.

Innseag, eig, *s. f.*, *dim.* of innis. (*Ir. id.*) An islet. *N. pl.* innseagan, *islets.* *Also*, little patches of arable ground, as in hilly or woody countries.

Innseagan, *s. pl.* Small plots of arable land, as in hilly ground, or in woods; *also*, islets.—*Macint.*

Innsean, *n. pl.* of innis. Islands, isles; Indies. Na h-Innsean shios, *the East Indies;* na h-Innsean shuas, *the West Indies.*

Innseannach, aich, *s. m.* (*from* innis.) An Indian; an islander. Innseannaich, *Indians.*

Innsear, *fut. pass.* of innis. Shall be told.

Innsgineach, *a.* Sprightly, lively, cheerful.

Innsgineachd, *s.f* Sprightliness, liveliness, cheerfulness.

Innsridh, *s. pl.* Effects, furniture, moveables

Innsrumaid, *s.f.* (*Ir.* ionstraiment *Lat.* instrumentum.) An instrument.

† **Innte**, *s f.* (*Ir. id.*) A kernel —*Shaw.*

Innte, *comp. pron.* (*Ir. id*) In her, within her; in her power.

Innteach, ich, *s. m.* (*Ir. id.*) A way, a road; a gate.

Inntil, *s.f.* (*Ir id*) A budget, a wallet; a satchel.—*Shaw*

Inntinn, *s.f* (*Lat* ingenium *Arm.* ingin. *Ir* inntinn, *Scotch*, ingyne) Mind, understanding, intelligence; ingenuity. Sùil bhur n'inntinn, *the eye of your minds.*—*Stew. Eph.* Inntinn dhùbailt, *a double mind*, a dh'aon inntinn, *with one mind* or *accord*

Inntinneach, *a*, *from* inntinn. (*Ir id.*) Mental, intelligent; high-minded, conceited, merry, sprightly. Bithibh inntinneach ceòlmhor, *be merry and musical.*—*Mac Co*

Inntinneachd, *s. f* (*Ir. id*) High-mindedness, conceitedness, sprightliness.

Inntinneas, eis, *s m.* Jollity.

† **Inntliomh**, *s* (*Ir id*) A treasury —*Shaw*

Inntreadh, idh, *s m* An entering, a commencing, entrance; a commencement.

Inntreas, eis, *s m.* (*Ir. id*) Entrance-money.

Inntrinn, *s. f* Entrance, admittance; commencement. Cha 'n 'eil inntrinn an so, *there is no entrance here*

Inntrinn, *v. n.* Enter; begin. *Pret.* dh'inntrinn, *entered*, *fut. aff.* inntrinnidh, *shall enter.*

Inntrinneadh, 3 *sing.* and *pl imper* of inntrinn Inntrinneadh e, *let him enter*, inntrinneadh iad, *let them enter*

Insgineach, *a.* (*Ir. id*) Sprightly, nimble. Gu h-insgineach ealamh, *sprightly and cleverly.*—*Old Song.*

Innsgineachd. See **Innsgineachd**.

Insgne, *s f* A sex, a gender; a speech

Intleachd, *s f* See **Innleachd**

Intleachdach, *a* See **Innleachdach**.

Intreabh, *s m* (*Ir id*) Want, poverty

† **Iob**, *s m* (*Ir id*) A lump of dough; *rarely*, death

Iobair, *v a* (iob-thoir.) Sacrifice, offer in sacrifice, make an offering *Pret a.* dh'iobair; *fut. aff a* iobairidh. Cha 'n iobair sibh, *ye shall not make an offering.*—*Stew Lev*

Iobairt, *s f* (*Ir* iodhbhairt) A sacrifice, an offering Faighear gu h-iòbairt tri uain, *let three lambs be got for sacrifice.*—*Mac Lach.*

Iobairt seems to be *iob-thoirt*, *literally*, an offering of a raw cake or a lump of dough, hence it has become an arbitrary term for any manner of sacrifice: iobairt fhion, *a wine offering*, *a libation*, iobairt losgaidh, *a burnt offering*

Iobradh, aidh, *s m.* The act of sacrificing, a sacrifice.

Iobradh, 3 *sing* and *pl imper* of iobair Iobradh e, *let him sacrifice*, iobradh iad, *let them sacrifice*

Iobram, 1 *sing imper.* of iobair. Let me sacrifice, *also for* iobraidh mi, *I will sacrifice*

Ioc, *s. m.* (*Ir. id*) Payment; requital; rent; remedy, compassion Ioc-eiric, *kindred-money; ransom*

Ioc, *v a.* (*Ir id*) Pay; render, requite; heal, cure, *rarely*, suffer, endure *Pret. a.* dh'ioc, *paid*, *fut. aff. a* iocaidh, *shall pay* Iocaidh iad umhla, *they shall pay a fine* *Fut. pass* iocar.

Iocach, *a*, *from* ioc. (*Ir. id.*) Ready to pay or requite.

Iocadh, aidh, *s. m.* A paying, a requiting, a payment, a requital.

Iocadh, 3 *sing.* and *pl. imper.* of ioc. Iocadh e, *let him pay*; iocadh iad, *let them pay.*

Iocaidh, *fut. aff. a.* of ioc. Shall pay.

Iocas, ais, *s. m.* (*Ir. id*) Payment, requital, remuneration.

Iochd, *s.f* (*Ir. id*) Pity, compassion, mercy, tenderness of heart; *rarely*, children. Gun iochd ri truaghain, *without pity to the helpless.*—*Mac Co.*

Iochdail, *a.* (iochd-amhuil) Merciful, compassionate, tender-hearted.

Iochdalachd, *s.f.* Mercifulness, compassionateness, tender-heartedness.

Iochdar, *a* (*from* iochd); more properly *iochdmhor;* which see.

Iochdar, air, *s m.* (*Ir. id*) Bottom, foundation, the lowest part of any thing or place. Iochdar na bruaich, *the bottom of the bank* —*Orr.* Iochdar nan cnoc, *the foundation of the hills* —*Sm.* Iochdar a ghlinne, *the lowest part* or *mouth of the valley*, tha e an iochdar, *he is beneath* The word of opposite meaning is *uachdar.*

Iochdarach, **Iochdrach**, *a.* Lower, lowest, nether, nethermost Ionad iochdrach na talmhainn, *the nether places of the earth.*—*Stew. Ez.* Seomar iochdrach, *a lower* or *nethermost chamber* —*Stew.* 1 *K.*

Iochdaran, ain, *s m.*, *from* iochdar. (*Ir. id*) An inferior; a subject; a subaltern; an underling. *N. pl.* iochdarain. The word of opposite meaning is *uachdaran.*

Iochdaranta, *a* (*Ir. id*) Deputed; tributary.

Iochdmhoire, *com* and *sup.* of iochdmhor. More or most merciful.

Iochdmhoire, *s f* Mercifulness, compassionateness.

Iochdmhoireachd, *s. f.* Mercifulness, compassionateness.

Iochdmhor, *s f.* (iochd-mhor.) Compassionate, merciful, tender-hearted Righrean iochdmhor, *merciful kings.*—*Stew.* 1 *K.* *Com.* and *sup.* iochdmhoire.

Iochdrach. See **Iochdarach**.

Ioc-luibh, *s.f* A medical herb. *N. pl.* ioc-luibhean.

Ioc-lus, -luis, *s. m.* (*Ir. id*) A medical herb; a healing herb Ioc-lus an aonaich, *the healing herb of the plain.*—*Oss Duthona*

Ioc-shlaint, *s f.* (*Ir id.*) A remedy; a cordial; balm; nectar, a healing draught Bainne mo chiocha mar iocshlainte, *the milk of my breasts as a cordial.*—*Oss. Gaul.* Beagan ioc-shlainte, *a little balm* —*Stew Gen.*

Ioc-shlainteach, *a.* Balsamic, remedial, cordial, benign.

Iodh, (I) The ninth letter of the Gaelic alphabet

Iodh, iodha, *s. f* (*Ir. id*) A cramp; a spasm; a rheumatic affection, a pang; a chain; a collar. *N. pl* iodhana, *spasms*, *rheumatic pains.* Written also *iogh.*

Iodhal, ail, *s. m* (*Ir. id. Gr.* εἴδωλον. *Lat.* idolus. *Fr.* idole.) Idol. *N. pl* iodhail *and* iodhalan, *idols*

Iodhalach, *a* Idolatrous

Iodhalachd, *s f.* Idolatry.

Iodhal-aoradair, *s. m* A worshipper of idols. *N. pl* iodhal-aoradairean.

Iodhal-aoradh, aidh, *s. m.* Idolatry, worship of images. Luchd iodhal-aoraidh, *idolaters.*—*Stew. Cor.*

Iodhan, ain, *s m.* (*Ir. id*) A spear, a pike; affection; obedience.

† **Iodhan**, *a.* (*Ir. id.*) Sincere; pure, clean.—*Shaw.*

Iodhanna, **Iodhannan**, *n pl* of iodh. (*Ir. id.*) Cramps; spasms. Written also *ioghana.*

† **Iodhlan**, *v. n.* (*Ir. id.*) Leap, skip

Iodhlan, ain, *s. m.* (*Ir. id.*) A leap, a hop or skip; a hero.

Iodhlanadh, aidh, *s. m.* (*Ir. id.*) A leaping, a skipping.

Iodhol, oil, *s. m.* An idol. *N. pl.* iodhoil, *idols.*—*Stew.* 1 *Chr.* See also Iodhal.

Iodhladair, *s. m.* An idolater. *N. pl* iodhladairean.

Iodhladaireachd, *s. f.* Idolatry.

† **Iodhna**, ai, *s. m.* (*Ir. id.*) A spear, a lance; a protection, a safeguard.—*Shaw.* Brightness, purity.

Iodhnach, aich, *s. m.* (*Ir. id.*) A gift.

Iodhnach, *a.*, *from* iodhna. (*Ir. id.*) Valiant, warlike, martial; like a lance or spear.

Iog, *s. f.* (*Ir. id.*) Deceit, cunning, *rarely*, a mother.

Iogach, *a.* Deceitful, cunning.

Iogan, ain, *s. m.*, *dim* of iog. (*Ir. id.*) Deceit, cunning; a bird's craw. Do 'n iogan, mhallachadh 's do ghò, *of deceit, cursing, and fraud.*—*Sm.*

Ioganach, *a.* (*Ir. id.*) Deceitful, false, treacherous; having a craw, as a bird; like a craw. Mionnan ioganach, *false oaths.*—*Sm.* Gu h-ioganach, *deceitfully.* *Com.* and *sup.* ioganaiche.

Ioganachd, *s. f.* (*Ir. id.*) Deceitfulness, falseness. Written also *iogarnachd.*

Iogara, *a.* Low, humble.

Iogaras, ais, *s. m.* (*Ir.* iogras) Uprightness, honesty.

Iogarnach, *a.* Deceitful, false, treacherous. Gu h-iogarnach, *deceitfully.* *Com.* and *sup.* iogarnaiche.

Iogarnachd, *s. f.* Deceitfulness, falseness, treacherousness.

Iogh (*Heb.* yod. *Gr.* ιωτα) The ninth letter (I) of the Gaelic alphabet, according to Irish grammarians.

Iogh, iogha, *s. m.* A cramp; spasm; rheumatic pains; a pang; a torment; any severe pain. *N. pl* ioghanna *or* ioghannan. Nach dean ioghannan do glacadh? *shall not pains seize thee?*—*Stew. Jer.*

Ioghanna, **Ioghannan**, *n. pl.* of iogh.

Ioghar, air, *s. m.* (*Gr.* ιχωρ) Pus or matter.

Ioghlacadh, *a.* Tractable, easily caught.

Ioghna, ai, *s. m.* Wonder, surprise; surprising. B'ioghna leis m' airm, *he was surprised at my arms.*—*Orr.* Is ioghna do thearnadh, *thy deliverance is surprising.*—*Ull.*

Ioghnadh, aidh, *s. m* See Ioghna.

Ioghoile, *s. f.* The pylorus, or lower orifice of the stomach.

Ioghrach, aich, *s. m.* A suppuration.

Ioghrachadh, aidh, *s. m.* A suppurating, a suppuration.

Ioghraich, *v. n.* (*from* ioghar.) Suppurate. *Pret. a.* dh'ioghraich; *fut. aff. a.* ioghraichidh, *shall suppurate.* Written also *iongaraich.*

Iogh ras, ais, *s. m.* (*Ir. id.*) Uprightness.

Iol, a *composite particle*, significant generally of diversity or variety.

Iol, *v. a.* (*Ir. id.*) Vary, change, chequer.

† **Iolacadh**, aidh, *s. m.* (*Ir. id.*) A burial.

Iolach, aich, *s. m.* (*Ir. id.*) A shout; mirth; a loud cry; *rarely*, damage; loss. An iolach ait is brònach fa seach, *the shout joyful and sad by turns.*—*Oss. Cathula.* Iolach bhròin, *a shout of grief.*

Iolachdach, *a.* (*from* iolach) Mirthful; shouting; disastrous.—*Com.* and *sup.* iolachdaiche.

Ioladh, aidh, *s. f.* Fun, merriment, merry-making. Cuir air ioladh, *make light of, make fun of.*

Ioladhach, *a.* (*Ir.* iolaghoch.) Merry; sprightly; humorous.

Iolagall, ail, *s. m.* Damage; a dialogue.

Iolaic, *v. a.* (*Ir. id.*) Bury.

Iolair, *gen* iolair *and* iolarach, *s. f.* (*Ir* iolar. *Germ.* adler) An eagle. Do luathas mar iolair, *thy speed like an eagle.* Aghaidh iolarach, *the face of an eagle.*—*Stew. Ezek.* Iolair-fhionn, *a gier eagle; a sea eagle;* the *falco ossifragus* of Linnæus. Iolair thimchiollach, *a gier eagle.* Iolair uisge, *an osprey;* the *falco haliætus* of Linnæus.—*Stew. Lev.* Iolair dhubh, *a ringtail eagle*, the *falco fulvus* of Linnœus. *N. pl* iolairean.

Iol-àireamh, eimh, *s. m.* (*Ir. id.*) Annumeration.

Iolair-shùil, -shùl, *s. f.* An eagle-eye. Iolair-shùil na gréin, *the eagle-eye of the sun.*—*Oss. Tem.*

Iolair-shùileach, *a.* Eagle-eyed.

Iòlair-thimchiollach, *s. f.* A gier eagle.—*Stew. Lev. ref.*

Iolann, ainn, *s. m.* (iodh-lann) A corn-yard. Sgreach na muic dol do 'n iolann, *the lowing of the cow on its way to the corn-yard.*—*G. P.*

Iolair-uisge, *s. f.* An osprey; the *falco haliætus* of Linnæus.—*Stew. Lev.*

Iolan, *a.* (*Ir. id.*) Sincere.

Iolanach, *a.* Ingenious; learned; skilful.

Iolanachd, *s. f.* Ingenuity; learning.

Iolar, air, *s. m.*, *perhaps* iol-thuar. (*Ir. id.*) Variety; diversity, much, plenty.

Iolar, *adv.* Down, below. Iolar shios, *down below.*

Iolarach, *gen. sing.* of iolair; which see.

Iolarach, *a.*, *perhaps* iol-thuarach. (*Ir.* iolardha.) Various, varied, variegated, chequered.

Iol-bheusach, *a.* (*Ir. id.*) Arch, sly; of various ways or humours; versatile; multifarious. Gu h-iol-bheusach, *archly.*

Iol-bhuadh, bhuaidh, *s. m.* (*Ir. id.*) A victory, a triumph.

Iol-bhuadhach, *a.* (*Ir. id.*) Victorious, triumphant, gaining many victories.

Iol-chainnteach, *a.* (*Ir. id.*) Polyglot; having many languages.

Iol-cheardach, aich, *s. m.* (*Ir. id.*) A jack of all trades.

Iol-chearnach, *a.* Polygonal; multangular.

Iol-chearnag, aig, *s. f.* A polygon; a multangular figure.

Iol-choimeasgta, *a.* Mixed, miscellaneous.

Iol-chosach, *a.* (*Ir. id.*) Many-footed.

Iol-chruthach, *a.* (*Ir. id.*) Changeable, assuming various shapes, as clouds, inconstant; various; comely, well-proportioned. Gu h-iol-chruthach, *changeably.*

Iol-chuire, *s. f.* (*Ir. id.*) Sadness; lamentation.—*Shaw.*

Iol-dhamhsadh, aidh, *s. m.* A promiscuous dance, a country dance; a ball.

Iol-danach, aich, *s. m.* (*Ir. id.*) A jack of all trades.

Ioldanach, *a.* Ingenious. Gu h-ioldanach, *ingeniously.*

Iol-dhathach, *a.* Of diverse colours, parti-coloured.

Iol-dhealbhach, *a.* (*Ir. id.*) Well-featured.—*Shaw.*

Iol-dhùil, *s. f.* (*Ir. id.*) Great desire, avarice.

Iol-fhilte, *a.* Complex, complicated.

† **Iolga**, *s. pl.* (*Ir. id.*) Tongs.

Iol-ghilleach, *a.* Complex.—*Shaw.*

Iol-ghineach, *a.* Heterogeneous. Gu h-iol-ghineach, *heterogeneously.*

Iol-ghleusach, *a.* Manifold, complicated.

Iol-ghnètheach, *a.* Diverse, various, of all sorts; many-coloured. Gu h-iol-ghnetheach, *diversely.*

Iol-ghonach, *a.* Inflicting various wounds, painful. Gu h-iol-ghonach, *painfully.*

IOL-GHRÀINEACH, *a.* Horrid; ugly; causing disgust.

† IOL-GHREASACH, aich, *s. m.* (*Ir. id.*) An inn; a lodging. —*Shaw.*

IOL-GHUTHACH, *a.* Of various tongues; polyglot; having a great compass of voice; having various voices, as a vocal mimic.

IOLLAN, *a.* (*Ir. id.*) Expert; mechanical.

IOLLANAICHE, *a.* A master of any art.

IOLLAPACH, *a.* Giddy.—*Shaw.*

IOL-LEABHAR, air, *s. m.* A volume. *N. pl.* iol-leabhraichean.

IOL-MHAOIN, *s.* Much goods or chattels.

IOL-MHAOINEACH, *a.* (*Ir. id.*) Opulent.

IOL-MHODHACH, *a.* (*Ir. id.*) Manifold, various.

IOL-PHOSADH, aidh, *s. m.* (*Ir. id.*) Polygamy, the circumstance of being often married.

IOL-PHOSDA, *a.* Often married.

IOL-SHIOLADH, aidh, *s. m.* (*Ir. id.*) A polysyllable.

IOL-SHLISNEACH, ich, *s. m.* A polygon; *adjectively*, polygonal.

IOM, an *insep. prep.* About; round; entire. Iomlàn, *quite complete;* iomghaoth, *a whirlwind;* iomshlainte, *perfect health;* iomcheist, *perplexity.*

IOMA, *a.* Many, much, numerous. Written also *iomad* and *iomadh.*

IOMA-BHIORACH, *a.* Prone to rebuke or check; causing a rebuke.

IOMACH, aich, *s. m.* A colt.

IOMACHAR, air, *s. m.* See IOMCHAR.

IOMA-CHAINNTEACH, *a.* Having many languages.

IOMA-CHEANNACH, *a.* Many-headed.

IOMA-CHEARNACH, *a.* Many-cornered.

IOMA-CHÉIN, *s. f.* Distance. O ioma-chéin, *from a distance.* —*Stew. Hab.* Written also *iom-chéin.*

IOMA-CHEIST, *s. f.* Doubt, perplexity. Written also *iomcheist.*

IOMA-CHIAN, *a.* Distant, far off; foreign, outlandish. Aitean ioma-chian, *outlandish places.*

IOMA-CHRITH, *s. f.* (*Ir. id.*) Trembling, tremour, violent tremour. Air iom-chrith chum dìoghailt, *trembling for revenge.*—*Mac Lach.*

IOMAD, *a.* (*Ir. id.*) Many, numerous, much. Iomad uair, *many an hour; many a time.*

IOMADACH, *a.*, *from* iomad. (*Ir. id.*) Numerous; in numbers; many: too much. Is iomadach seòrsa, *many a kind.* —*Macint.* Na slòigh gu h-iomadach, *the people in numbers.* —*Sm.*

IOMADACHADH, aidh, *s. m.* (*Ir. id.*) A multiplying; a numbering.

IOMADACHD, *s. f.* (*Ir. id.*) Multiplication; numerousness; multiplicity; abundance; plurality.

IOMADAICH, *v. a.*, *from* iomad. (*Ir.* iomadaigh.) Multiply, increase. *Pret. a.* dh'iomadaich, *multiplied; fut. aff. a.* iomadaichidh, *shall multiply.*

IOMADAIDH, *a.* and *s.* (*Ir. id.*) Manifold, several; superfluous; *also*, superfluity; multitude. Neònaid nan iomadaidh buaidh, *a pearl of manifold virtues.*—*Macfar.* Iomadaidh do shluaigh, *the multitude of thy people.* Is co maith na leòir is iomadaidh, *enough is as good as superfluity.*—*G. P.*

IOMADAIL, *a.* (iomad-amhuil.) Multipliable.

IOMADALACHD, *s. f.* (*Ir.* iomadamhlachd.) A multitude; abundance. Iomadalachd bhriathra, *a multitude of words.* —*Stew. Ecc.*

IOMADAN, ain, *s. m.* A changeable or fickle fellow; *also*, anxiety, solicitude, restlessness. Leòn no iomadan no bròn, *neither wound, nor anxiety, nor grief.*—*R.* Air iomadan, *adrift.*

IOMADANACH, *a.* (*from* iomadan.) Changeable, fluctuating; restless; moving to and fro; fickle; *also*, a fickle fellow. Gu h-iomadanach, *changeably. Com.* and *sup.* iomadanaiche.

IOMADANACHD, *s. f.* Changeableness; fickleness.

IOMA-DATHACH, *a.* (*Ir. id.*) Parti-coloured.

IOMADH, *a.* Many, much, numerous. Iomadh saoi as oigh, *many a hero and maiden.*—*Oss. Fing.*

IOMADHALL, aill, *s. m.* (*Ir. id.*) Sin, iniquity.

IOMAG, aig, *s. f.* A margin, a border.

IOMAGAIL, *s. f.* A dialogue; a dispute.

† IOMAGALLAIMH, *s. f.* (*Ir. id.*) A counsel, advice.

IOMAGAN, ain, *s. m.*, *from* ioma. (*Ir. id.*) Restlessness, anxiety, flitting.

IOMA-GHAOTH, ghaòithe, *s. f.* A whirlwind. Ioma-ghaoth fo sgiathaibh, *a whirlwind under his wings.*—*Oss. Gaul.*

IOMA-GNETHEACH, *a.* Parti-coloured; various; manifold; of various sorts.

IOMAGUIN, *s. f.* Perplexity, anxiety, distress, heaviness of mind, agony. Sheas i le h-iomaguin, *she stood perplexed.* —*Ardar.* An iomaguin ghéir, *in sore distress.*—*Id.*

IOMAGUINEACH, *a.* Perplexed; anxious; in distress; in agony; causing distress, pain, or anxiety. *Com.* and *sup.* iomaguiniche.

† IOMAIDH, *s. f.* (*Ir. id.*) Envy.

IOMAIGH, *s. f.* (*Ir. id.*) A border; open champaign ground.

† IOMAICH, *s. f.* (*Ir. id.*) A border; champaign country.

IOMAILL, *gen. sing.* of iomall; which see.

IOMAIN, *v. a.* (*Ir. id.*) Drive, as animals; conduct; drive any thing forward on the ground; kick gently forward, as a football; toss; whirl. *Pret. a.* dh'iomain; *fut. aff. a.* iomainidh, *shall drive.* Iomainidh iad, *they shall drive.*—*Stew. Job.* 'G an iomain sa chath, *driving them forward in battle.*—*Fingalian Poem.*

IOMAIN, *s. f.* (*Ir. id.*) A drove of sheep; a drove of black cattle; a sounder of swine. Gach iomain leatha féin, *every drove by itself.*—*Stew. Gen.* A leantuinn nan iomaine, *following the droves.*—*Id.* Le luirg-iomain, *with an ox-goad.*—*Stew. Jud.* Slat-iomain, *an ox-goad.*—*Stew. Jud. ref.*

IOMAINEACH, *a.* (*Ir. id.*) Coercive.

IOMAINICHE, *s. m.* A cattle-driver, a drover.

IOMAIR, *v. a.* Row; move; use or wield; play; game, *Pret. a.* dh'iomair, *wielded; fut. aff. a.* iomairidh, *shall wield.* Iomair am bàt, *row the boat.* An ramh is faisge iomair, *row the nearest oar.*—*G. P.* Iomair i san àrach, *wield it in the battle-field.*—*Oss. Dargo.*

IOMAIR, *v. def.* (*Ir. id.*) Must; need; require. *Pret.* dh'iomair, *must, or was obliged; fut.* iomairidh, *must or will be obliged.* Dh'iomair mi tòiseachadh, *I was obliged to begin;* an iomair e falbh? *must he go?* an d'iomair e falbh? *was he obliged to go?* an iomair mi falbh? iomairidh, *must I go away? yes;* iomairidh mise so, *I shall want this.*

IOMAIRE, *s. f.* (*Ir. id. Heb.* hamir.) A ridge or furrow; a ridge in ploughed land; a furrow. *N. pl.* iomairean. Iomairean cian, *long ridges.*—*Macfar.* Sna h-iomairibh cam, *in the crooked ridges.*—*Id.*

IOMAIREACHD, *s. f.* (*Ir. id.*) Courting.—*Shaw.*

IOMAIRG, *s. f.* Plundering; devastation; plunder; a skirmish.

IOMAIRICH, *s. f.* Emigration. See IMIRICH.

IOMAIRICH, *v. a.* (*from* iomaire.) Ridge; make a ridge, as in ploughed land; *also*, bear, carry; wield. *Pret. a.* dh' iomairich; *fut. aff. a.* iomairichidh, *shall bear.* A dh'iomairich sgiath, *who wore a shield.—Old Poem.*

Iomairichte, *p. part.* of iomairich. Ridged, as ploughed land; furrowed; borne, carried; wielded.

Ionmairidh, *inflection of* iomair. Shall be obliged. See **Iomair.**

Iomairt, *s. f.* (*Ir. id.*) Bustle; agitation; exertion; labour; playing; gaming; restlessness; fidgeting; conflict; a rowing. Iomairt nan laoch, *the exertions of the heroes.—Oss. Fing.* Iomairt nan lann, *the playing of swords.—Old Poem.* Iomairt nan tonn, *the agitation of the waves.—Oss.* Is ann ort a tha an iomairt! *how you do fidget!*

Iomairt, (ag), *pr. part.* of iomair. Rowing; moving; wielding; playing; using; making use of. Ag iomairt shaighde mar lainn, *using an arrow like a spear.—Orran.* Bheil thu ag iomairt so? *are you making use of this?*

Iomairteach, *a.* (*Ir. id.*) Playful; gamesome; bustling; agitating; fidgeting; restless. *Com.* and *sup.* iomairtiche, *more* or *most playful.*

Iomairtiche, *s. m.* A gambler; a bustling fellow.

† **Iomaith,** *v. a.* (*Ir. id.*) Check; rebuke.—*Shaw.*

Iomaith-fhear, -fhir, *s. m.* A man who rebukes or chides.

Iomall, aill, *s. m.* (*Arm.* ymyl. *Ir.* imeal.) A border, a boundary, extremity, verge, frontiers; a rim; a skirt; the edge or border of a vessel. Crùn òir da iomall, *a golden crown for its border.—Stew. Ex.* Iomall nan stuadh, *the boundary of the waves, the shore.—Oss. Fing.* Iomall soillse, *the skirts of day,* i. e. *twilight.—Id.* Iomall a chùirn, *the extremity* [*verge*] *of the rocks.—Oss. Carthon. N. pl.* iomaill; *d. pl.* iomallaibh. Gu iomallaibh na talmhainn, *to the ends of the earth.—Stew. Jer.* Iomall tràigh, *the sea-side.*

Iomallach, *a.* (*from* iomall.) Remote; on the frontiers; outermost; having borders; external. Anns na cearnaibh iomallach, *in the outermost corners.—Stew. Jer. Com.* and *sup.* iomallaiche, *more* or *most remote.*

Iomallaiche, *com.* and *sup.* of iomallach. More or most remote; outermost. O na h-aitibh a 's iomallaiche, *from the outermost parts.—Stew. Matt.*

Iomall-soillse, *s. m.* Twilight, *i. e.* the borders or skirts of day.—*Oss.*

Iomall-tràigh, *s. m.* The sea-side, the edge of the shore.

Iomaltar, air, *s. m.* (*Ir. id.*) A centre.

Iomansachd, *s. f.* (*Ir. id.*) Immensity.

Iomarach, aich, *s. f.* A border; a margin. Iomarach na banrighinn, *the Queensferry,*—a place in Scotland so called.

Iomarasg, aisg, *s.* (*Ir. id.*) A prophecy.

Iomarbhadh, aidh, *s. m.* (*Ir. id.*) A struggle, a strife; a skirmish; controversy, a debate; a lie, deceit; rowing; *also,* a comparison. Seachd oidhche ag iomarbhadh, *seven nights contending.—Fingalian Poem.*

Iomarbhas, ais, *s. m.* (*Ir. id.*) Sin; banishment; strife.—*Shaw.*

Iomarcach, *a.* (*Ir. id.*) Many, numerous; superfluous; redundant; excessive; oppressive. T-òigridh iomarcach, *thy numerous youth.—Sm.* A h-uisgibh iomarcach, *from many waters.—Id. Com.* and *sup.* iomarcaiche, *more* or *most numerous.* Gu iomarcach, *numerously.*

Iomarcaidh, *s. f.* (*Ir. id.*) Numerousness; abundance; superfluity.—*Shaw.*

Iomarchur, *s. m.* (*Ir. id.*) A rowing; a steering with oars; tumbling; wallowing; error.

Iomardadh, aidh, *s. m.* (*Ir. id.*) A reproach.

Iomarscleo, *s. m.*, more properly *iomarsgal;* which see.

Iomarsgal, ail, *s. m.* (*Ir. id.*) A wrestling, a struggling. Seachd lò ag iomarsgal, *seven days wrestling.—Old Poem.*

† **Iomartar,** air, *s. m.* (*Ir. id.*) A centre.

Iomartas, ais, *s. m.* (*Ir. id.*) Industry; motion; activity; bustling about; necessity.

† **Iomasgrach,** aich, *s. m.* (*Ir. id.*) An inn; a lodging-house; a lodging.

† **Iombath,** *s. m.* (*Ir. id.*) An adjoining sea; sea encompassing an island.—*Shaw.*

† **Iombath,** *v. a.* (*Ir. id.*) Overwhelm; fall into a swoon.—*Shaw.*

Iombathadh, aidh, *s. m.* (*Ir. id.*) Overwhelming; a swoon.

Iom-bhaidh, *s.* (*Ir. id.*) Excessive love.

Iom-bhuail, *v. a.* (*Ir. id.*) Strike frequently; thump; beat soundly. *Pret.* dh'iom-bhuail; *p. part.* iom-bhuailte.

Iom-bhualadh, aidh, *s. m.* (*Ir. id.*) A striking frequently; a thumping.

Iom-chainnteach, *a.* (*Ir. id.*) Expressive; talkative; polyglot.

Iomchair, *v. a.* (*Ir. id.*) Bear, carry; endure; behave; demean. *Pret. a.* dh'iomchair, *bore; fut. aff. a.* iomchairidh. A dh'iomchar fios do 'n sean righ, *to carry word to the aged king.—Mac Lach.*

Iomchan, ain, *s. m.*, more properly *iomchar;* which see.

Iomchaomhnas, ais, *s. m.* (*Ir. id.*) A question.—*Shaw.*

Iomchar, air, *s. m.* Behaviour, conduct, or bearing; a carrying; a moving; gait; a bier; a carriage. Iomchar nam beus, *moral conduct.* Iomchar uallach, *a stately gait.—Macint.* Fear iomchair arm, *an armour-bearer.—Stew. 2 Sam.*

Iomcharag, aig, *s. f.* (*Ir. id.*) A female porter.—*Shaw.*

Iom-chas, *v. n.* (*Ir. id.*) Murmur, complain.

Iom-chasaid, *s. f.* A complaint.

Iom-chathamh, *s. m.* A whirling drift. Thig iom-chathamh, *a whirling drift shall come.—Macfar.*

Iom-chein, *a.* Far off, remote; *also,* distance, remoteness. Dùchan iom-chèin, *remote countries.*

Iom-cheist, *s. f.* Perplexity, dilemma, anxiety. Ann an iom-cheist, *in perplexity.*

Iom-cheumnachadh, aidh, *s. m.* Perambulation, a walking round.

Iom-cheumnaich, *v. n.* Walk round, pace round, perambulate. *Pret. a.* dh'iom-cheumnaich.

Iom-chian, *a.* Distant, remote.

Iom-chlaidheamh, eimh, *s. m.* Sword-fighting, fencing.—*Shaw.*

Iom-chlaidheamhair, *s. m.* A sword-fighter, a fencer.

Iom-choimhead, id, *s. m.* Guarding, protecting.

Iom-choire, *s. f.* Reflection; blame; *also,* complement.

Iom-choireach, *a.* Apt to reflect or blame; accusing.

Iom-choirich, *v. a.* Blame, rebuke, or chide. *Pret. a.* dh' iom-choirich, *blamed.*

Iom-choirneach, *a.* (*Ir. id.*) Having many corners.

Iom-chomairich, *s. f.* A petition, a request, a favour; a farewell.

Iom-chomarc, airc, *s. m.* A present or donation.

Iom-chomhairle, *s. f.* Perplexity, doubt, dilemma; jeopardy. Ann an iom-chomhairle, *perplexed.—Stew. Cor.*

Iom-chomhairleach, *a.* Causing doubt or perplexity; perplexed.

Iom-chomhradh, aidh, *s. m.* (*Ir. id.*) A thesis.—*Shaw.*

Iom-chras, ais, *s. m.* (*Ir. id.*) Deportment, grace.

Iom-chubhaidh, *a.* (*Ir. id.*) Convenient, meet, proper, fit, suitable; expedient; decent, seemly. Tha so iom-chubhaidh, *this is expedient.—Stew. Cor. ref.* The contracted form is often in use. See **Iom-chuidh.**

IOM-CHUBHAIDHEACHD, *s. f.* (*Ir. id*) Convenience, suitableness, meetness; propriety, expediency; seemliness. Written also *iom-chuidheachd*

IOM-CHUIDH, *a.* (*Ir. id*) Convenient, meet, proper; expedient; suitable; decent, seemly Ann an am iom-chuidh, *in [good] proper time —Stew. Cor ref.* Iom-chuidh do 'n amadan, *seemly to the fool —Stew. Pro* Contracted for *iom-chubhaidh.*

IOM-CHUIDHEACHD, *s f.* (*Ir. id*) Convenience; convenientness, suitableness, meetness; propriety; expediency, decency. Contracted for *iom-chubhaidheachd.*

IOM-CHUIDHEAD, eid, *s. m* (*Ir id*) Convenience, suitableness, meetness, expediency

† IOM-DHA, ai, *s m.* (*Ir. id*) Anger; a bed or couch; a shoulder.

IOM-DHATHACH, *a.*, ioma *and* dath. (*Ir. id.*) Parti-coloured, many-coloured, variegated. Brat iom-dhathach, *a parti-coloured mantle —Macfar*

IOM-DHATHTA, IOM-DHATHTE, *part.* Dyed with various colours; many-coloured.

IOM-DHEARBH, *v a.* Prove, demonstrate. *Pret a* dh'iom-dhearbh, *demonstrated.*

IOM-DHEARBHADH, aidh, *s. m* A proof, a demonstration Bheir mi dhuit iom-dhearbhadh air, *I will give you a proof of it.*

IOM-DHEARBHAIL, *a* Demonstrative, capable of proof or demonstration

IOM-DHEARBHTA, *p. part.* Proved, proven, demonstrated

† IOM-DHEARG, *v. a* (*Ir id*) Rebuke, reprove, reproach, dispraise *Pret. a* dh'iom-dhearg, *reproved, fut. aff* iom-dheargaidh

† IOM-DHEARGACH, *a.* (*Ir. id.*) Prone to reprove or rebuke

IOM-DHEARGTA, *p. part.* (*Ir.* iom-dheargtha.) Reviled, reproved, rebuked

IOM-DHIOL, *s m.* A feast —*Shaw*

IOM-DHORUS, uis, *s m* (*Ir. id*) A lintel; a porch, a back door *N. pl.* iom-dhorsan

IOM-DHRUID, *v. a* (*Ir. id.*) Enclose, surround; besiege closely, hem in Tha iad air iom-dhruideadh, *they are on all sides hemmed —Macfar.*

IOM-DHRUIDEACH, *a* (*Ir id*) Surrounding, encompassing; hemming in; besieging

IOM-DHRUIDEADH, idh, *s. m.* (*Ir. id.*) A surrounding, encompassing; a siege, besieging.

IOM-EAGAL, ail, *s. m.* Terror, fright

IOM-EAGALACH, *a.* Fearful, terrible, frightful.

IOM-EUD, *s. f.* Jealousy, extreme suspicion

IOM-EUDAIR, *s m.* A jealous man, a suspicious man

IOM-EUDMHOR, *a.* Jealous, suspicious *Com* and *sup* iom-eudmhoire.

IOM-FHOCAL, ail, *s m.* Circumlocution.

† IOM-FHORAIL, *s f* (*Ir. id.*) Superfluity, extravagance, excess

† IOM-FHORRAN, ain, *s. m.* (*Ir. id*) A skirmish; a battle; a comparison.

IOM-FHUASGAILTEACH, *a.* Nimble.

IOM-FHUASGLACH, *a.* Apropos; good at a pinch.—*Shaw.*

IOM-FHULANG, aing, *s m.* (*Ir id*) Patience, forbearance.

IOM-GHABH, *v. a* Take; reduce; avoid.

IOM-GHABHAIL, *s. f.* Taking; reducing; shunning.

IOM-GHAOTH, ghaoith, *s f.* A whirlwind; an eddying wind. Iom-ghaoth fo' sgiathaibh, *a whirlwind under its wings. —Oss.*

† IOM-GHNÙIS, *s. f.* (*Ir. id*) Wonder

IOM-GHONACH, *a.* Giving many wounds; causing pains.

IOM-GHUIN, *s f.* A severe wound; agony.

IOM-GHUINEACH, *a.* Painful; causing a variety of pains; inflicting many wounds. Gu h-iom-ghuineach, *painfully*

IOMHACH, *a.* Envious.

IOMHADH, aidh, *s. m.* Envy —*Shaw.*

IOMHAIDH More frequently written *iomhaigh*, which see.

IOMHAIGH, *s. f.* (*Ir. id. Arm.* imaich. *Lat.* imago.) An image; a standing image; an idiom; a figure of speech. Iomhaigh mhòr, *a great image —Stew Da.* Cha tuig thu a h-iomhaigh, *you will not understand its idioms.—Old Song. N pl* iomh-aighean.

IOMHAIGHEACHD, *s. f.* Imagery.

† IOMHAS, ais, *s. m.* (*Ir. id*) Knowledge, judgment, learning

IOMLA, *a*, contracted for *iomluath*; which see

IOMLAG, aig, *s. f.* A navel. Do d'iomlaig, *to thy navel.—Stew. Pro* Written also *imleag.*

IOMLAID, *s. f.* (*Ir. id*) Exchange, barter; a moving; a gesture. Iomlaid chiomach, *exchange of prisoners.—Macfar.* Fear-iomlaid, *a broker*, luchd-iomlaid, *brokers,*

IOMLAID, *v a.* (*Ir. id*) Exchange, barter. *Pret. a.* dh' iomlaidh, *bartered; fut. aff. a.* iomlaididh, *shall barter.*

IOMLAIDEACH, *a.*, *from* iomlaid. (*Ir. id*) Exchanging, bartering; fickle, volatile, unsteady.

IOMLAIDEACHD, *s. f* (*from* iomlaid.) Exchange, barter; fickleness, volatileness, unsteadiness.

IOMLAIDEADH, idh, *s m.* An exchanging, a bartering, a changing; winding, rolling.

IOMLAIDICH, *v. a.* Exchange, barter. *Pret. a.* dh'iomlaidich, *exchanged.*

IOMLAINE, *com.* and *sup.* of iomlan. More or most perfect

IOMLAINE, *s. f.* (*Ir. id.*) Fulness, perfectness; maturity; integrity. Iomlaine na Diadhachd, *the fulness of the Godhead —Stew. Col,* Iomlaine cridhe, *integrity of heart,—Stew 1 K.*

IOMLAITEADH, idh, *s. m.* (*Ir. id.*) A rolling, a turning, a winding; see IOMLAIDEADH.

IOMLÀN, *a.* and *s.* Quite full, perfect, complete, entire; whole; all, the whole Duine iomlan, *a perfect man.* Fo iomlan blàth, *in full blossom —Macfar.* Dh'ith mi do 'n iomlan, *I have eaten of all.—Stew. Gen.* An t-iomlan diubh, *the whole of them.—Stew. Jer* Gu h-iomlan, *completely. Com.* and *sup* iomlaine.

IOMLANACHADH, aidh, *s. m.* The act of carrying to completion; a completing, a perfecting

IOMLANACHD, *s f.* Fulness, completion, completeness, perfectness, consummation; accomplishment, fulfilment. Iomlanachd nan Cinneach, *the fulness of the Gentiles'—Stew. Rom Ir.* iomlaineacht

IOMLANAICH, *v. a* Fulfil; complete, consummate. *Pret. a.* dh'iomlanaich, *completed, fut. aff. a.* iomlanaichidh, *shall complete.*

IOMLANAICHTE, *p part.* of iomlanaich. Consummated, perfected, completed

IOMLASGADH. See IOMLUASGADH.

IOMLAT, ait, *s. m.* (*Ir. id.*) Gesture.—*Shaw.*

IOM-LEABHAR, air, *s. m.* A volume. *N. pl.* iom-leabhraichean.

IOM-LEAG, aig, *s. m* More frequently written *iomlag* and *imleag*, which see.

IOM-LEAGACH, *a.* See IMLEAGACH.

IOM-LOISG, *v. a.* (*Ir. id*) Parch

IOM-LOSGADH, aidh, *s m.* (*Ir. id.*) Parching; adustion.

Iom-luadh, *v. n.* and *a.* Speak often or much; praise often or much.

Iom-luadh, aidh, *s. m.* Great praise; frequent speaking. Tha iom-luadh mòr air, *he is much spoken of.*

Iom-luagach, *a.* Apt to stray, wandering, straggling.

Iom-luagail, *s. f.* A straying, a wandering, a straggling.

Iom-luaidh, *s. f.* Great praise.

Iom-luainneach. See Iom-luaineach.

Iom-luaineach, *a.* Unsteady, restless, fickle, fidgeting.

Iom-luaineachd, *s. f.* Unsteadiness, restlessness, fickleness, fidgeting.

Iom-luaisg, *v. a.* Move often; move hither and thither; rock, as a vessel. *Pret. a.* dh'iom-luaisg, *rocked; fut. aff. a.* iom-luaisgidh, *shall rock.*

Iom-luaisgte, *p. part.* Moved hither and thither; rocked to and fro.

Iom-luas, ais, *s. m.* (*for* iom-luathas.) Lightness; freedom from light or burden; velocity. An do ghnàthaich mi iom-luas? *did I use lightness?—Stew.* 2 *Cor. ref.*

Iom-luasgach, *a.* (*Ir. id.*) Moving to and fro; agitating; rocking; tossing to and fro; fidgeting, restless, volatile. Gu h-iom-luasgach, *with a rocking motion.*

Iom-luasgadh, aidh, *s. m.* (*Ir. id.*) A moving or rocking to and from; commotion; agitation; restlessness.

Iom-luath, *a.* Fickle, changeable, inconstant, versatile. Is iom-luath an òige, *youth is changeable.—Mac Lach.*

Iomnaidh, *s. f.* Care; diligence; anxiety.

Iomnaidheach, *a.* Careful; anxious; solicitous.

Iomnaidheachd, *s. f.* Anxiousness, solicitude.

Iomnuachar, air, *s.* Polygamy.

Iomordadh, aidh, *s. m.* A reproach, expostulation.

Iomorran, ain, *s. m.* A comparison.—*Shaw.*

Iompachadh, aidh, *s. m.* A conversion, a change; a petitioning, a beseeching. Tha e air iompachadh, *he is converted;* tha i air a h-iompachadh, *she is converted.*

Iompachair, *s. m.* A converter. *N. pl.* iompachairean.

Iompachan, ain, *s. m.* A convert, a proselyte. *N. pl.* iompachain.

Iompaich, *v. a.* (*Ir.* iompoigh.) Change, turn; convert, as from vice to virtue; beseech, pray. *Pret. a.* dh'iompaich, *turned; fut. aff. a.* iompaichidh, *shall turn.* Co dh'iompaicheas e? *who will turn him?—Stew. Job.*

Iompaichear, *fut. pass.* Shall be changed, shall be converted. Iompaichear an uair gu blàthas, *the weather shall be changed to warmth.—Macfar.*

Iompaichte, *p. part.* of iompaich. (*Ir.* iompoighte.) Converted, as from vice to virtue; changed.

Iompaidh, *s. f.* (*Ir.* iompoidh.) A persuasion; a beseeching, an entreaty; a conversion. Cuir iompaidh orra, *persuade them.* Written also *impidh;* which see.

Iompaidh, (*for* iompaichidh.) Shall convert. An t-anam iompaidh e, *the soul he will convert.—Sm.*

Iompaidheach, *a.* Intercessory, mediatory; *also, substantively,* an intercessor, a petitioner, a converter.

Iompair, *s. m.* (*Ir.* impire.) An emperor. Iompair mòr nan nial, *the mighty emperor of the clouds.—Mac Lach.*

Iompaireachd, *s. f.* (*Ir.* impireachd.) An empire. An iompaireachd Bhreatunnach, *the British empire.*

Iompoich, *v. a.* Convert.—*Stew. Sam.* More properly *iompaich;* which see.

Iompoll, oill, *s. m.* An error.

Iomradh, *v.* (*Ir. id.*) Report, publish or divulge. *Pret.* dh'iomradh, *reported; fut. aff.* iomradhaidh, *shall report.*

Iomradh, aidh, *s. m.* (*Ir. id.*) A report or rumour; a saying; fame; memory; mention; abundance. Duine gun iomradh, *an obscure man.* As eugmhais iomraidh, *without fame.—Oss. Duthona.* Gun sgathadh e an iomradh, *that he would cut off their memory.—Sm.* Tha iomradh ann, *there is a report. N. pl.* iomraidhean.

Iomraich, *v. a.* and *n.* Carry away, remove; flit; emigrate. *Pret. a.* dh'iomraich. Cha 'n iomraich thu mo lann, *thou shalt not carry away my sword.—Oss. Fing.* See also Imirich.

Iomraideach. See Iomraiteach.

Iomraim, *v. a.* Row. *Pret. a.* dh'iomraim, *rowed.* Dh'iomraim na daoine, *the men rowed.—Stew. Jonah. Fut. aff.* iomraididh, *shall row.*

Iomraiteach, *a.* (*Ir.* iomraiteach.) Renowned, famed; much spoken of; made known by report. Iomraiteach san domhain, *declared* [*famed*] *throughout the earth.—Stew. Ex.* Iomraiteach ann an gniomharaibh arm, *renowned in feats of arms.—Old Legend.*

Iomrall, aill, *s. m.* Straying, wandering; error; departing. Chuimhnich mi m'iomrall, *I remembered my wandering.—Old Song.* Air iomrall, *astray.*

Iomrallach, *a.* Apt to go astray or wander; errant. *Com.* and *sup.* iomrollaiche.

Iomralladh, aidh, *s. m.* A straying, a wandering. Air iomralladh, *astray;* ag iomralladh, *straying.*

Iomrallaiche, *s. m.* A wanderer; a vagabond; a straggler.

Iomram, aim, *s. m.* (*Ir. id.*) Rowing.

Iomramh, aimh, *s. m.* (*Ir. id.*) A rowing, as of a boat. Ag iomhramh, *rowing.*

Iomramh, *v. a.* Row, as a boat. More frequently pronounced *iomair;* which see.

Iomramhaiche, *s. m.* (*Ir.* iomramhaidhe.) A rower.

Iomrasgal, ail, *s. m.* (*Ir. id.*) Wrestling.

Iom-reuson, oin, *s. m.* (*W.* amryson, *dispute.*) A verbal controversy, a wrangle, a dispute, an argument.

Iom-reusonach, *a.* Controversial, inclined to wrangle.

Iom-reusonaiche, *s. m.* A wrangler, a controversialist or disputant.

Iomrol, Iomroll, oill, *s. m.* (*Ir. id.*) See Iomrall.

Iomrolach, Iomrollach, *a.* See Iomrallach.

Iom-ruagach, *a.* Scattering; persecuting; pursuing; scaring.

Iom-ruagadh, aidh, *s. m.* (*Ir. id.*) Persecution; an irregular scattered pursuit; a rout; an invasion; a defeat.

Iomruagair, *s. m.* (*Ir. id.*) A persecutor, a pursuer, an invader.

Iom-ruaig, *v. a.* (*Ir. id.*) Persecute, pursue; disperse, rout; invade; defeat. *Pret. a.* dh'iomruaig, *routed; fut. aff. a.* iomruaigidh, *shall rout.*

Iomruaig, *s. f.* A pursuit; a scattered pursuit; a persecution; a sudden dispersion.

Iomruaigte, *p. part.* of iomruaig. Persecuted; routed, dispersed, scattered, scared.

Iomruin, *v. a.* Assign; appoint. *Pret. a.* dh'iomruin, *assigned; fut. aff.* iomruinidh, *shall assign.*

† **Iomsach**, *a.* (*Ir. id.*) Revengeful, enraged, furious.

† **Iomsachan**, ain, *s. m.* (*Ir. id.*) Rage, fury.

Iom-sgaoil, *v. a.* (*Ir. id.*) Disperse, scatter in various directions, scare, rout. *Pret. a.* dh'iom-sgaoil; *fut. aff. a.* iom-sgaoilidh.

Iom-sgaoileadh, idh, *s. m.* (*Ir. id.*) A dispersion, a scattering asunder, a scaring, a routing.

Iom-sgaoilte, *p. part.* of iom-sgaoil. Dispersed, routed, scattered.

Iom-sgaoiltear, eir, *s. m.* A disperser.

Iom-sgar, *v. a.* Disperse, separate, scare, rout. *Pret. a.* dh'iom-sgar, *dispersed; fut. aff. a.* iom-sgaraidh, *shall disperse.*

Iom-sgarach, *a.* Dispersing, separating, scaring, routing.

Iom-sgarachd, *s. f.* A separation, a dispersement, a scattering.

Iom-sgaradh, aidh, *s. m.* The act of separating, a dispersing, a dispersement.

Iom-sgoltadh, aidh, *s. m.* (*Ir id.*) Superfluity, excess.

Iom-shiubhail, *v. n.* Walk about, ramble, perambulate.

Iom-shiubhal, ail, *s. m.* A walking about, a ramble, a rambling.

Iom-shniomh, *s. m.* (*Ir.* imsniomh.) Care, anxiety; restlessness; convolution; a twisting; diligence.

Iom-shniomhach, *a.* Restless, uneasy; anxious; convolving, twisting; ghastly.

Iom-shruth, *s. m.* (*Ir. id.*) A counter-tide.—*Shaw.*

Iom-theachd, *s.*, more frequently written *imeachd;* which see.

Iom-thnùth, *s. m.* (*Ir. id.*) Zeal; envy.

Iom-throm, *a.* Very heavy.

Iom-thus, uis, *s. m.* Departure, migration; chance.

Iomuireadh, idh, *s. m.* (*Ir. id.*) Excess; exacting.—*Shaw.*

† **Ion**, *prep.* (*Ir. id.*) In. Tuadh ion na lamh, *an axe in his hand.*—*Old Poem.*

Ion, an *inseparable prep.* signifying fitness, worthiness. As ionmholta, *worthy to be praised;* ion-roghnaidh, *worthy to be chosen.*

Ion, *a.* Becoming, suitable, seemly, proper. 'N ion duinn 'n uair ar sàruchaidh? *becomes it us in the hour of distress?*—*Sm.*

† **Ion**, *s. m.* (*Ir. id.*) The sun; a circle.

Ionach, aich, *s. m.* (*Ir. id.*) A dirk.

† **Ionad**, *comp. prep.* (*from* † ion.) In thee. Now written *annad.*

Ionad, aid, *s. m.* A place; abroad; stead; room; office; position. *N. pl.* ionadan; *d. pl.* ionadaibh. An ionad naomh, *the holy place, sanctuary.*—*Stew. O. T.* O ionadaibh nam flath, *from the abodes of heroes.*—*Oss.* Ionad aoraidh, *a place of worship.*—*Mac Lach.* Ionad tasgaidh, *a storehouse, a granary.*—*Stew. Joel.* Ionad taimh, *a resting place.*

Ionadach, *a.* Local; representative; fond of one's place; *also*, a placeman.

Ionadas, ais, *s. m.* Locality.

Ionadh, aidh, *s. m.*, contracted for *ioghnadh;* which see.

Ionaid, *s. m.* A vicegerent.

Ionail, *v. a.* Wash, bathe, cleanse. *Pret. a.* dh'ionail, *washed; fut. aff. a.* ionailidh, *shall wash; p. part.* ionailte.

Ionaire, *s. f.* (*Ir. id.*) The most unexceptionable term for the male or female privities.—*Shaw.*

Ion-aiteachaidh, *a.* Habitable.

Ionaltair, *v. a.* and *n.* Pasture, feed, graze. *Pret.* dh' ionaltair, *pastured; fut. aff. a.* ionaltraidh, *shall pasture.* Ionaltraidh mi a ris, *I will feed* [*cattle*] *again.*—*Stew. Gen.*

Ionaltrach, *a.* Pasturing, feeding, grazing. Ainmhidh ionaltrach, *a beast of the pasture.*

Ionaltradh, aidh, *s. m.* (*Ir. id.*) A pasturing, a grazing; pasturage, pasture; a wandering, as of cattle on pasture ground. Cha 'n 'eil ionaltradh aca, *they have no pasture.*—*Stew. Joel.* Ionaltradh reamhor, *fat pasture.*—*Stew.* 1 *Chr.*

Ion-amhuil, *a.* (*Ir. id.*) Like, equal, the same, well matched.

Ionann, *a.* (*Ir. id. Arm.* unan, *one.*) Equal, similar, same. Ionannu agus sinn, *equal to us.*—*Stew. Matt.* Ionann is bhi rùisgte, *the same as if naked.*—*Old Song.* Uile ionann, *all the same, quite the same.*

Ionannach, *a.* Identical, equal, the same.

Ionannachd, *s. f.* Sameness, equality, identicalness.

Ionaol, *v. a.* (*Ir. id.*) Whitewash, plaster.—*Shaw.*

Ionar, air, *s. m.* (*Ir. id.*) A kind of mantle; the bowels.—*Macd.* and *Shaw.* A burden.

† **Ionaradh**, aidh, *s. m.* (*Ir. id.*) A clothing.

Ionarbhach, aich, *s. m.* A banisher, a destroyer.

Ionarbhadh, aidh, *s. m.* (*Ir. id.*) A banishing; banishment; expulsion.

† **Ion-bhaidh**, *s. f.* (*Ir. id.*) The time of a woman's bearing; parturition; a time or hour.—*O'Reilly.*

Ion-bholg, *v. a.* (*Ir. id.*) Swell; belly out, as a sail with wind.

Ion-bholgadh, aidh, *s. m.* (*Ir. id.*) A swelling, a bellying out.

Ion-bhreith, *s. f.* A perfect birth.

Ion-bhuadhach, *a.* Victorious, triumphant.

Ioncamas, ais, *s. m.* (*Ir. id.*) Usury, interest.

Ion-cheannachadh, *a.* Purchasable.

Ion-choimeas, *a.* (*Ir. id.*) Comparable, easily matched.

Ion-choimeasail, *a.* Comparable; equally respectable.

Ion-choimhead, *a.* (*Ir. id.*) Conservable, easily preserved.

Ion-choluinneadh, idh, *s. m.* (*Ir.* ioncholnadh.) A becoming incarnate; incarnation.

Ion-choluinnich, *v. n.* Become incarnate.

Ion-choluinnichte, *part.* Become incarnate; incarnate.

Ion-chomharaichte, *part.* Notable, conspicuous, easily discerned, remarkable.

Ion-chosanta, *v. a.* (*Ir. id.*) Defensible.

† **Ion-chosg**, *s. m.* (*Ir. id.*) Instruction; desire.—*Shaw.*

† **Ion-chosgair**, *s. m.* (*Ir. id.*) A teacher.

† **Ion-chrasal**, ail, *s. m.* (*Ir. id.*) Excitement.

Ion-chruinn, *a.* (*Ir. id.*) Homocentric.

Ion-dheanta, *a.* Practicable; feasible.—*Shaw.*

Ion-dioladh, *a.* Vendible.

Ion-diolaiche, *s. m.* One able to pay.

Ion-ditealta, *a.* Indictable.

Ionduile, *a.* Desirable.

Ionduthras, ais, *s. m.* Negligence.

Ion-fhir, *a.* Fit for a husband, marriageable.

† **Ion-fhorran**, ain, *s. m.* (*Ir. id.*) A fight, a skirmish.

Ionga, *s. m.* (*Ir. id. Arm.* ivin. *Lat.* unguis. *Span.* una.) A nail of the hand or foot; a claw, a talon, a hoof. Cha 'n fhàgar ionga dhiubh, *not a hoof of them shall be left.*—*Stew. Ex. N. pl.* ionganan, *nails.* Ionganan mar spuirean, *nails like claws.*—*Stew. Da.* Ionga eòin, *a bird's claw. Ir.* ionga éin. Ionga eich, *a horse's hoof.*

Iongach, *a.* Having claws or talons; having long nails, claws, or talons; hoofed; having strong hoofs; *also*, avaricious, miserly. Gu h-iongach, *avariciously. Com.* and *sup.* iongaiche.

Iongaideach, *a.* See **Iongantach**.

Iongantach, *a.* Wonderful, surprising, strange, curious, odd, remarkable; queer, droll. A bhearta iongantach, *his wonderful works.*—*Sm.* Fear iongantach, *a queer fellow. Com.* and *sup.* iongantaiche. Gu h-iongantach, *wonderfully.*

Iongantaiche, *com.* and *sup.* of iongantach.

Iongantais, *gen. sing.* and *n. pl.* of iongantas.

Iongantas, ais, *s. m.* (*Ir.* iongantus.) A wonder, a curiosity, a phenomenon, a miracle. Ghabh mi iongantas, *I wondered.* Tha thu 'cur iongantais orm, *you surprise me.* Nochdaibh iongantas, *shew a miracle.—Stew. Ex.* *N. pl.* iongantais *and* iongantasan, *wonders.* Meudaichear m'iongantais, *my miracles shall be multiplied.—Stew. Ex.*

Iongar, iongarach, *s. f.* Pus, matter. See **Ioghar**.

Iongarach, *a.* Abounding in purulent matter; like pus.

Iongaraich, *v. n.* Suppurate. See **Iogharaich**.

† **Ion-ghabh**, *v. a.* (*Ir. id.*) Manage; conduct, guide, lead; attack; reduce, subject.—*Shaw.*

Ion-ghabhail, *s. f.* (*Ir. id.*) Management, regulation, conduct; gesture; circumspection.—*Shaw.*

Ionghar, air, *s. m.* Pus; convenience.

Iongharach, *a.* Mattery, purulent; convenient.

Ion-ghnetheach, *a.* Homogeneous.

Ion-ghraidh, *a.* Lovely; becoming. Gu b'e nithe tha ion-ghraidh, *whatever things are lovely.—Stew. Phil.*

Ionglan, *a.* Dirty, nasty, unclean.

Iongna. See **Ionga**.

Iongnadh, aidh, *s. m.* Wonder, surprise, astonishment. Na biodh iongnadh ort, *be not surprised.—Stew. Ecc.*

Ionladh, aidh, *s. m.* Washing; a thing acceptable.

Ionlaid. See **Ionnlaid**.

Ion-lasda, *a.* Inflammable.

Ion-mhagaidh, *a.* Ridiculous.—*Shaw.* Gu h-ion-mhagaidh, *ridiculously.*

Ion-mhaith, *a.* Ignoscible, pardonable.

Ion-mhall, *a.* Slow; fatigued; *also*, slowness; fatigue.

Ionmhas, ais, *s. m.* (*Ir. id.*) A treasure. Ionmhas mòr, *much treasure.—Stew. Pro.* Mòran ionmhais, *much treasure.*

Ionmhasair, *s. m.* A treasurer. *N. pl.* ionmhasairean.

Ionmhasaireachd, *s. f.* The business of a treasurer.

Ionmhas-aite, *s. m.* A treasury. *N. pl.* ionmhas-aitean.

Ion-mheadhonach, *a.* Moderate, temperate, in mediocrity.

Ion-mheallta, *a.* Fallible, easily deceived. Gu h-ion-mheallta, *fallibly.*

Ionmholta, *a.* (*Ir. id.*) Praiseworthy, commendable, laudable, deserving, meritorious.

Ionmholtachd, *s. f.* Praiseworthiness, commendableness, laudableness, meritoriousness.

Ionmhuinn, *a.* (*Ir.* inmhuin.) Kind, courteous, debonair; dear, beloved; lovely; a beloved person. B'ionmhuinn le m'anam thu! *thou wert dear to my soul.—Ardar.* Mar is ionmhuinn leis, *as he loves.—Stew. Gen.* Sealladh ionmhuinn, *a lovely sight.—Macfar.* Ionmhuinn bhàn, *a fair-haired beauty.—Fingalian Poem.*

Ionmhuinneach, *a.* Beloved; lovely; amiable; courteous; desirable. Gu h-ionmhuinneach, *amiably.*

Ionmhuinneachd, *s. f.* (*Ir. id.*) The state of being beloved; endearment; courteousness.

Ionmhuinnich, *v. a.* Endear, make attached. *Pret.* dh' ionmhuinnich, *endeared.*

† **Ionn**, *prep.* (*Ir. id.*) Now written *ann.*

† **Ionnad**, *comp. prep.* (*Ir. id.*) Now written *annad.*

† **Ionnaibh**, *comp. prep.* (*Ir. id.*) In you. Now written *annaibh.*

Ionnail, *v. a.* Wash.

† **Ionnainn**, *comp. prep.* (*Ir. id.*) In us. See **Annainn**.

Ionnaltair, *s. m.* A bath.

Ionnam, **Ionnamsa**, *comp. pron.* In me. More commonly written *annam, annamsa.*

† **Ionnarachd**, **Ionnaradh**, aidh, *s. f.* (*Ir. id.*) A gift, a donation; a reward.

Ionnas, ais, *s. m.* A treasure. Written also *ionmhas.*

Ionnas gu, *conj.* So that; in so much that. *Ionnas gu* is also written *ionnas gum* and *ionnas gun*, according to the initial letter of the verb which follows it. Ionnas gum faic e, *so that he shall see;* ionnas gun do sgìthich iad, *so that they wearied themselves.—Stew. Gen.*

Ionndag, aig, *s. f.* See **Ionntag**.

Ionndagach, *a.* See **Ionntagach**.

Ionndraichinn. See **Ionndrain**.

Ionndrain, *s. f.* A straying, a wandering; missing; error. Air ionndrain, *a missing;* tha 'n òigh air ionndrain, *the maid is missing.—Orr.*

Ionndrain, *v. a.* Miss, feel the want of. *Pret.* dh' ionndrain, *missed; fut. aff. a.* ionndrainidh; *fut. pass.* ionndrainear, *shall be missing.—Stew.* 1 *K. ref.*

Ionnduras, ais, *s. m.* Chastity, purity.

Ionnlach, aich, *s. m.* (*Ir. id.*) A fault, a blemish; an accusation.

Ionnlaich, *v. a.* Complain; accuse.

Ionnlaid, *v. a.* Wash, bathe, cleanse; purify, purge. *Pret. a.* dh' ionnlaid, *washed; fut. aff. a.* ionnlaididh, *shall wash.*

Ionnlaid, *s. f.* (*Ir.* ionlat.) A bathing, a washing; an ablution; a bath; a purifying.

Ionnlaideach, *a.* Abluent, cleansing, purifying.

Ionnlaideachd, *s. f.* A bathing; a cleansing; purification; the state of being cleansed or purified.

Ionnlaidte, *p. part.* of ionnlaid. Washed, cleansed, purified.

Ionnlaigh, *s. f.* An accusation; a fault, a blemish.

Ionnoir, *s. pl.* (*Ir. id.*) The bowels or entrails.

Ionnrain, *v. a.* Count, reckon, calculate.

† **Ionnramh**, aimh, *s. m.* Service, attendance.

Ionnran, ain, *s. m.* (*Ir. id.*) An account, a reckoning.—*Shaw.*

Ionnsa, *a.* (*Ir. id.*) Dear, beloved. More frequently written *annsa;* which see.

Ionnrosg, oisg, *s. m.* (*Ir. id.*) A word.

Ionnsach, *a.* Sorrowful, fatal.—*Shaw.*

Ionnsachadh, aidh, *s. m.* Learning, education; instruction. Written also *ionnsuchadh.*

Ionnsaich, *v. a.* Learn; educate; instruct; train. See **Ionnsuich**.

Ionnsaichte, *p. part.* of ionnsaich. See **Ionnsuichte**.

Ionnsamhuil, *a.* Comparable; *substantively*, similitude.

Ionnsuchadh, aidh, *s. m.* Learning; education; training; instruction.

Ionnsuchadh, (ag), *pr. part.* of ionnsuich. Learning, educating, training.

Ionnsuich, *v. a.* Learn; teach; train; *rarely*, visit. *Pret. a.* dh' ionnsuich, *taught; fut. aff. a.* ionnsuichidh, *shall teach.* Ionnsuich a shlighean, *learn his ways.—Stew. Pro.*

Ionnsuichte, *a.* Learned; taught; trained; educated. Duine ionnsuichte, *a learned man.*

Ionnsuidh, *s. f.* (*Ir. id.*) A making towards a place or person in a hostile manner; an attack, an assault; an onset; an attempt; an invasion. Thoir ionnsuidh air, *make towards him;* thug iad ionnsuidh air na camhalaibh, *they fell upon the camels.—Stew. Job.* O ionnsuidh dhian ur nàmh, *from the fierce onset of your enemies.—Old Song.*

Ionnsuidh, [dh'], *prep.* To, towards; *literally*, to the approach, or onset. Dh' ionnsuidh tigh m'athar; *to my father's house*

IONNSUIDHLACH, ich, *s m* An aggressor, an invader.

IONNSUIDHEACH, *a* Aggressive; apt to attack.

† IONNTADH, *v. a* and *n.* Roll, turn, tumble, wallow; wind; scorn, slight —*Shaw*

IONNTAG, aig, *s. m* A nettle. Ionntag ghreugach, *fenugreek* —*Macd.* *N pl* ionntagan, *nettles.*

IONNTAGACH, aich, *s m.* Nettles, a crop of nettles, a place where nettles grow. Sealbhaichidh an t-ionntagach iad, *the nettles shall possess them.*—*Stew Hos*

IONNTAGACH, *a.* Full of nettles, like nettles

IONNTA, *comp. pron.* In them.—*Stew. Matt.* More commonly written *annta*

IONNTLAS, ais, *s. m* (*Ir. id*) Delight

IONÒLTA, *a* (*Ir. id.*) Potable, drinkable; palatable, as drink.

ION-PHEANASDA, *a* Punishable

ION-PHOSDA, *a.* (*Ir. id*) Marriageable.

IONRACAN, ain, *s. m.*, *from* ionraic. (*Ir. id.*) A just or upright person. An t-ionracan, *the just* —*Stew Job.*

IONRACAS, ais, *s m* and *f.* Righteousness, integrity, uprightness. Freagraidh m' ionracas, *my righteousness shall answer* —*Stew Gen.* Fear ionracais, *a righteous man*, luchd ionracais, *righteous people*, fear na h-ionracais, *the righteous man*, luchd na h-ionracais, *the righteous people*

† IONRACH, aich, *s m* (*Ir id.*) A medical tent —*Shaw.*

IONRACHAS, ais, *s. m.* See IONRACAS.

IONRADH, aidh, *s. m* A plundering; a laying waste; devastation Fear ionraidh, *a plunderer*

IONRADHACH, *a.* Devastating, laying waste, destroying; *also*, a plunderer, a depopulator.

IONRAIC, *a* (*Ir id*) Upright; honest; just, faithful, chaste. Duine ionraic, *a just man*, ionraic sna h-uile nithibh, *just in all things* —*Stew Tim* *Com* and *sup* ionraice Nur theid na meirlich a throd, thig daoine ionraic gu 'n cuid, *when thieves begin to scold, honest men come to their own* —*G P.*

IONRAICE, *com.* and *sup* of ionraic. More or most upright An ti is ionraice, *the most upright person* —*Stew Mic.*

IONRANACH, aich, *s m.* An accountant.

ION-ROGHNUIDH, *a* Worthy to be chosen, eligible. An ròd is ion-roghnuidh, *the way that should be chosen* —*Sm.*

IONRUIC, *a.* See IONRAIC

ION-RUITH, *a* Having an equal pace, running with equal speed. Each ion-ruith, *an equal-paced horse* —*Old Poem*

ION-SAMHUIL, *a.* (*Ir id.*) Like, such like; just like, comparable

IONSANACH, *a* (*Ir id*) Tardy.

ION-SGAMHACH, aich, *s. m.* A looseness of the skin

ION-SHIUBHAL, *a.* Passable.

ION-SMUAINEACH, *a.* Imaginable; supposable

IORAILTE, *s. f* Ingenuity

IORAILTEACH, *a.* (*Ir id*) Ingenious, inventive, well contrived. Am feadan ioraılteach, *the well-contrived flute* —*Moladh Mhòraig*

IORAILTEACHD, *s. f.* (*Ir. id*) Ingenuity; inventiveness

IORBALL, aill, *s.* (*Ir. id.*) A tail, a rump.—*Stew Deut. ref* More commonly written *earball*, which see.

† IORCALLACH, aich, *s. m* (*Ir. id.*) A strong robust fellow.

IORCHODACH, *a.* (*Ir. id*) Evil; mischievous; calamitous. More commonly written *urchoideach.*

IORDHALTA, *a.* (*Ir. id*) Certain; constant; continual.

IOR-DHALTACHD, *s. f.* (*Ir. id*) Certainty, constancy.

IORGAIL, *s f.* See IORGUIL.

IORGHAIL, IORGHUIL, *s. f.* Strife; fray; a battle; contest; tumult; skirmish. An tùs na iorghail, *in the front of battle.*—*Fingalian Poem* *Ir.* iorghuil, iarghail, *and* iorguil.

IORGHUILEACH, *a* (*Ir. id*) Quarrelsome, contentious, tumultuous. Gu h-iorghuileach, *contentiously*, *Com.* and *sup* iorghuiliche.

† IORGHUIS, *s f.* (*Ir. id*) A prayer, a request —*Shaw.*

IORGUIL, *s. f.* A fray, a strife, a contest, a battle; a tumult, a concourse.

IORGUILEACH, *a* Quarrelsome, contentious, tumultuous. Gu h-iorguileach, *contentiously*. *Com.* and *sup.* iorguiliche.

IORLANN, *s. m* (*Ir. id.*) A cellar, a buttery, a larder.

IORNA, *s f.* A yarn thread of a particular length; a spindle of yarn, a *hesp*, a *hank.*

IORNAN. See IORNA.

IORPAIS, *s f.* (*Ir id.*) A dropsy; restlessness

IORPAISEACH, *a* (*from* iorpais) Dropsical, restless. Gu h-iorpaiseach, *restlessly* *Com.* and *sup* iorpaisiche, *more* or *most restless.*

† IOS, *adv.* Down, east. Hence come the words *sios*, eastwards, downwards, and *shios*, east, down; and *a nios*, from the east, from below

IOSA, *s m.* The blessed name JESUS. Iosa Criosda, *Jesus Christ.*

† IOS, *v a.* (*Ir. id*) Eat, dine —*Shaw.*

† IOSADH, aidh, *s m* (*Ir. id.*) Eating.

IOSAL, *a* Low, lowly, humble; mean, downcast. An laoch tha iosal, *the hero who is laid low.*—*Oss.* A gorm-shuil iosal, *her blue eye downcast* —*Oss. Fing* Os-iosal, *clandestinely, privily* —*Stew. Gen.* *Com.* and *sup* isle *and* ilse.

Ir. isiol. *W.* isel. *Corn* izal. *Arm* isel

† IOSDA, ais, *s m.* (*Ir. id*) A house or dwelling

† IOSDAIL, *a.* (*Ir. id*) Convenient, commodious. Gu h-iosdail, *conveniently*

† IOSDAN, ain, *s m*, *dim.* of iosda (*Ir. id.*) A house or college

IOSDAS, ais, *s m.* (*Ir. id*) Entertainment; accommodating, lodging.

IOSGAID, *s f* (*Gr* ἰσχίς.) A thigh, a hip *N. pl.* iosgaidean.

IOSGAIDEACH, *a.* Having large thighs, having large hips; of, or belonging to, the thigh.

IOSGANN, ainn, *s m* A thigh, a hip *N. pl.* iosgannan, *thighs.* Mu' iosgannan, *about his thighs* —*Macint.*

IOSGANNACH, *a.* Having large thighs, having large hips; of, or belonging to, the thigh.

IOSLACHADH, aidh, *s m.* A lowering, a humbling

IOSLAICH, *v a* (*from* iosal) Lower, humble, degrade, demean, vouchsafe. See ISLICH.

IOSLANN, ainn, *s m.* A store-house, a buttery, a pantry.

IOSOIP, *s f.* Hyssop

IOSUID, *s m* A Jesuit. *N. pl.* iosuidean

IOSUIDEACH, *a.* Jesuitical

IOTA, IOTADH, aidh, *s m.* (*Ir.* iota) Thirst; drought, parchedness. Le 'n iota tarruing suas ruit, *in their thirst approaching thee* —*Macdon.*

IOTACH, *a.* (*Ir. id.*) Thirsty.

IOTAN, ain, *s m* Thirst.

IOTAR, *a.* See IOTMHOR

IOTAS, ais, *s. m* (*Ir id.*) Thirst.

Iotail, *a.*, *from* iot. (*Ir. id.*) Thirsty.

† **Ioth**, *s. m.* Corn.
Ir. ith. *W.* yd. *Corn.* iz. *Gr.* σιτος.

Ioth-chruinnich, *v. a.* Purvey, forage.

Ioth-ghaireach, *a.* (*Ir. id.*) Fertile, productive.

Ioth-ghaireachd, *s. f.* (*Ir. id.*) Fertility.—*Shaw.*

Ioth-lann, -lainn, *s. m.* (*Ir. id.*) A corn-yard; a barn; a granary. Written also *iadh-lann* and *iolann.*

Ioth-losgadh, aidh, *s. m.* (*Ir. id.*) A parching of corn; a blasting of a standing crop.

Iotmhoire, *com.* and *sup.* of iotmhor; which see.

Iotmhoireachd, *s. f.* Thirstiness, droughtiness, parchedness.

Iotmhor, *a.* Thirsty, droughty, dry; parched. Ma bhios e iotmhor, *if he be thirsty.*—*Stew. Pro. Com.* and *sup.* iotmhoire.

Iothros, ois, *s. m.*, ioth-ròs. (*Ir. id.*) Cockle; a corn-poppy; *papaver agrestis.*

† **Ir**, *s. f.* (*Ir. id. Lat.* ira.) Anger; a satire, a lampoon. —*Shaw.*

Ircilt, *s. f.* The side-post of a door.

Irchiullach, aich, *s. m.* A monster.

Ire, *s. f.* (*Ir. id.*) Ground, earth, land.

† **Ireall**, ill, *s. m.* (*Ir. id.*) A reply; a salutation; a greeting.

† **Ireas**, eis, *s. m.* An occursion or collision.

Irionn, *s. m.* (ire-fhonn.) A field; land, ground.

Iriosal, *a.*, ire, *earth, and* iosal, *low.* (*Ir. id.*) Humble, low, lowly; a lowly or humble person; mean. Iriosal agus air asail, *lowly, and on an ass.*—*Stew. Zech.* Na h-iriosal, *the humble.*—*Stew. Pro.*

Irioslachadh, aidh, *s. m.* Humiliation; the act of humbling or degrading; degradation, abasement, condescension.

Irioslachadh, (ag), *pr. part.* of irioslaich.

Irioslachd, *s. f.* (ire-iosalachd.) Humility, lowliness, humbleness; debasement, degradation; condescension. Irioslachd inntinn, *lowliness of mind.*—*Stew. Eph.*

Irioslaich, *v. a.* Humble, humiliate, abase; condescend. *Pret. a.* dh' irioslaich, *humbled; fut. aff. a.* irioslaichidh, *shall humble.* Irioslaich thu fèin, *humble thyself.*

Irioslaichte, *p. part.* of irioslaich. Humbled, abased, degraded.

Iris, *s. f.* (*Ir. id.*) A hen-roost. *N. pl.* irisean.

Iris, *s. f.* (*Ir. id.*) Brass; an era; a record; an assignation; a law; faith; a lover; a friend. Is trom eallach gun iris, *heavy is a burden that is not tucked on.*—*G. P.*

Iriseach, *a.* Just; equitable; lawful; judicious; like a roost.

Iriseas, eis, *s. m.* A present.

Irisleabhar, air, *s. m.* A commonplace-book.—*Shaw.*

Irisleachd. See **Irioslachd.**

† **Irr**, *s. f.* (*Ir. id.*) A tail, as of a fish; an end, a conclusion.

Irt, *s. m.* (*Ir. id.*) Death; *also,* St. Kilda.

Irteach, *a.* Of, or belonging to, St. Kilda.

Is, *conj.* (*Ir. id.*) And; as. Thusa is mise, *you and I;* ionnas is thusa, *as well as you.*

Is, *def. v.* (*Ir. id. Corn.* ez.) Am, art, is, are. Is mise an duine, *I am the man;* is tusa is trèine, *thou art the strongest.* —*Oss. Fing.* Is taitneach do ghuth, *pleasant is thy voice.* —*Oss. Tem.* Is sona do shluagh, *happy are thy people.*—*Oss. Fing.*

Isbean, ein, *s. m.* A sausage. *N. pl.* isbeanan.

Isbeanach, *a.* Like a sausage; full of sausages.

Ise, *s. pron.*, *emphatic form* of i. She, her. Ise fèin, *she herself.*

Isean, ein, *s. m.* A gosling, a chicken; a young fowl; a dirty child. *N. pl.* iseanan.

Iseanach, *a.* Like a gosling; dirty, as a child.

Isgeas, eis, *s. m.* A doubt.

Isle, *com.* and *sup.* of iosal. (*Ir. id.*) Lower, inferior, lowest. Cha 'n ìsle mise na sibhse, *I am not inferior to you.*—*Stew. Job.* A chuid a b' ìsle do 'n t-sluagh, *the lowest of the people.*—*Stew. K.*

Isleachadh, aidh, *s. m.* (*Ir.* isliughadh.) A humbling, a lowering, an abasement; condescension; a subsiding. Tha an amhainn air isleachadh, *the water has subsided.*

Isleachd, *s. f.* Lowness; abjectness; littleness; lowliness; condescension.

Islead, eid, *s. m.* (*Arm.* iselhat.) Lowness; abjectness; littleness; a growing lower. Chaidh mo mheamna an islead, *my imaginings became lower.*—*Old Song.* Air islead 's a bheil e, *however low he* or *it be.*

Islean, *s. pl.* People in middle or low life; plebeians. An uaislean is an ìslean, *their high and their low.*—*Mac Co.*

Islean, ein, *s. m.* A man in middle or in low life; a plebeian; an inferior; an underling.

Islich, *v. a.* Lower; bring or make low; humble; abase; condescend; subside. *Pret. a.* dh' ìslich; *fut. aff.* ìslichidh; *fut. pass.* ìslichear. Islichear iad, *they shall be brought low.*—*Stew. Job.* N' uair dh' ìslicheas farum a bhlàir, *when the noise of battle subsides.*—*Oss. Fing.*

Islichear, *fut. pass.* of ichlich; which see.

Islichte, *p. part.* of islich. Lowered, humbled, abased.

Israeleach, ich, *s. m.* An Israelite. *N. pl.* Israelich.

Ite, *s. f.* (*Ir. id.*) A feather; a quill; feathers, plumage, down; a wing; a fin. Ite eòin, *a bird's feather;* ite tombac, *a snuff-quill. N. pl.* itean *and* iteachan.

Iteach, *a.* (*Ir. id.*) Feathered; winged; plumed; finned; finny. Am bradan iteach, *the finny salmon.*—*Macfar.*

Iteach, ich, *s.* (*Ir. id.*) A flight; flying, as of a bird or an arrow; feathers, plumage, down. Le itich rèidh o thaifeid, *with direct flight from the bowstring.*—*Oss. Fing.*

Iteachan, ain, *s. m.* A small bobbin for yarn.

Iteag, eig, (*dim.* of ite.) A feather, a plume; a quill; a fin. *N. pl.* iteagan. Maille ri' iteagan, *along with its feathers.*—*Stew. Lev. ref.*

Iteagach, *a.* (*Ir.* iteogach.) Feathered, plumy, winged; feathery; finny. Gach eun iteagach, *every winged fowl.*—*Stew. O. T. Com.* and *sup.* itealaiche.

Iteal, il, *s. m.* A flying on wings, a fluttering of wings. Mar itil nan eun, *as the fluttering of birds.*—*Old Poem.*

Itealach, *a.* (*from* ite.) Flying, hovering, fluttering; winged.

Itealachadh, aidh, *s. m.* A flying; a flight.

Itealachadh, (ag), *pr. part.* of itealaich. Flying on wings, fluttering.

Itealachd, *s. f.* (*Ir. id.*) Advolation.

Itealaich, *v. n.* Fly, as a bird. *Pret.* dh' itealaich; *fut. aff.* itealaichidh. Eunlaith a dh' itealaicheas, *fowls that fly.*—*Stew. Gen. ref.*

Itean, *s. pl.* Fins; wings; quills. Gach ni air am bheil itean, *every thing that has fins.*—*Stew. Lev.*

Iteodha, **Iteotha**, *s. m.* Hemlock. Mar an iteotha, *like hemlock.*—*Stew. Hos.*

† **Ith**, *s.* Corn. Written also *ioth;* which see.

Ith, *v. a.* and *n.* (*Ir. id.*) Eat; gnaw or chew; devour; consume; corrode. *Pret. a.* dh' ith, *ate; fut. aff. a.* ithidh, *shall eat.* Cha 'n ith mi, *I will not eat.—Stew. Gen.* Ith suas, *eat up*, or *completely*.

ITH, *s.* Eating. See ITHEADH.

ITH-DHIAS, dhéise, *s. f.* An ear of corn.

ITHEADH, idh, *s. m.* An eating, a chewing, a gnawing; a corroding, a devouring; corrosion. Aran ri itheadh, *bread to eat;* an iolair a dheifricheas gu itheadh, *the eagle that hastens to eat.—Stew. Hab.*

ITHEADH, (ag), *pr. part.* of ith.

ITHEAM, 1 *sing. imper.* of ith. Let me eat; *or, for* ithidh mi, *I will eat.*

ITHEANNAICH, *s. f.* Eating; consumption of food. A réir itheannaich, *according to his eating.—Stew. Ex.*

ITHEAR, *fut. pass.* of ith. Shall be ate.

ITHIDH, *fut. aff. a.* of ith. Shall eat, chew, or consume.

ITH-IOMRADH, aidh, *s. m.* A backbiting, a slanderous report; a murmuring.

ITH-IOMRAITEACH, *a.* Slanderous, backbiting; abusive; murmuring.

† ITHIR, *s. f.*, ioth-ire. (*Ir. id.*) A corn-field; arable ground; the soil of land.

ITHTE, *p. part.* of ith. Eaten.

ITROS, *s. m.* (*Ir. id.*) A headland or promontory.

IUBHAR, air, *s. m.* (*Ir. id.*) Yew; a yew-tree. Written also *iughar.*

IUBHARACH, aich, *s. f.* (*Ir. id.*) An active female; a female archer; a boat; a place where yews grow; a group of yew-trees; a vessel under sail.

IUBHARACH, *a.* Made of yew; like yew; abounding in yews.

IUCHAIR, iucharach, *s. f.* (*Ir. id.*) A key; spawn; the row of fish; the screwed handle of a spinning-wheel. Ghabh iad iuchair, *they took a key.—Stew. Jud. N. pl.* iuchraiche, iuchraichean, *keys.* Iuchraiche rioghachd néimh, *the keys of the kingdom of heaven.—Stew. Matt.*

IUCHAR, air, *s. m.* (*Ir. id.*) The warm month; the dog-days. San iuchar chiatach, *in the pleasant dog-days.—Macfar.*

IUCHRAG, aig, *s. f.* A female fish; a spawner. *N. pl.* iuchragan.

IÙDHACH, aich, *s. m.* A Jew. *N. pl.* Iudhaich, *Jews.* Na h-Iudhaich, *the Jews.*

IUDHACH, *a.* Jewish.

† IUDICEACHD, *s. f.* Judgment.

† IUGH, *s. m.* A day.

IUGHAR, air, *s. m.* Yew; a yew-tree; a bow of yew. Craobh iughair, *a yew-tree.* Written also *iuthar;* which see.

IUGHARACH, aich, *s. f.* An active female; a female archer; a huntress; a place where yews grow; a group of yews.

IUGHRACH, *a.* Made of yew; like yew; abounding in yew. A bhogha iughrach, *his bow of yew.—Oss. Fin. and Lor.* Na h-oighean iughrach, *the daughters of the bow; huntresses.—Orr.*

IUGHRACH, aich, *s. f.* A place where yews grow.

IỲI, *s. f.* (*Gr.* ἰὸς.) An arrow. Written also *iùthaidh.*

† IUL, Iuil, *s. f.* The month of July.

IÙL, Iùil, s. *m.* (*Ir. id.*) Knowledge; a guide; way, course, direction; service, attendance; landmark. Ni mise dhuibh iùl, *I will be your guide.—Old Legend.* Glic gu h-iùil, *wise to guide* or *direct.—Mac Lach.* Chaill e an t-iùl, *he lost the course.—Oss. Duthona.*

IÙLACH, *a.* (*from* iùl.) Having knowledge; guiding, directing; rational.

IULADH, aidh, *s. m.* Sport, fun, merriment. Ri h-iuladh, *merrymaking.* See also IOLADH.

IÙLAG, aig, *s. f.* (*dim.* of iùl.) A mariner's compass.

IULAG, aig, *s. f.* A sprightly young female. *N. pl.* iulagan.

IULAGACH, *a.* Sprightly, light, cheerful; making short steps. *Com.* and *sup.* iulagaiche. Gu h-iulagach, *cheerfully.*

IÙLAR, *a.* See IULMHOR.

IULARACHD, *s. f.* See IÙLMHORACHD.

IÙLCHAIRT, *s. f.* A sea-chart; a guide.

IULLAG, aig, *s. f.* A sprightly female; a mincing gait; a female who minces when she walks.

IULLAGACH, *a.* Sprightly; mincing, or making short steps. Le ceumaibh iullagach, *with mincing steps.—Stew. Is.*

IÙL-MHOR, *a.* (*Ir. id.*) Wise; judicious; learned; polite. *Com.* and *sup.* iùlmhoire.

IUL-MHORACHD, *s. f.* Wisdom; judiciousness; politeness.

IUL-OIDHCHE, *s. f.* A star so called in the time of Ossian; *literally*, the night guide,—in allusion to the usefulness of stars in guiding benighted mariners, prior to the discovery of the magnet's properties. Iul-oidhche, tàr o'n speur, *guide of night, send thy light from the skies.—Oss. Dargo.*

IUMAIDH, *s. f.* Level ground; an open country; *also, adjectively*, having level ground.

IUMAIN. See IOMAIN.

IUMARACH, aich, *s.* A changing of place, a removing.

IUMHRACH, aich, *s. m.* (*Ir. id.*) A boat.

IUN, *s. m.* A naughty creature.—*Shaw.*

IUNADH, aidh, *s. m.* Wonder, surprise, strangeness. Written also *ioghnadh.*

IUNADH, *a.* Strange, wonderful; odd, curious.

IUNNDRAIN, *v. a.* Miss. See IONNDRAIN.

IUNDRAN, ain, *adv.* A missing, astray. See IONNDRAIN.

IUNNRAS, ais, *s. m.* (*Ir. id.*) A storm; a hurricane; the face of the skies. Iunnrais nan speur, *the hurricanes of heaven.—Macfar.*

IUNNSACHADH, aidh, *s. m.* See IONNSACHADH.

IUNNSAICH, *v. a.* Learn; teach; train; instruct; rear. *Pret. a.* dh' iunnsaich, *learned.* See IONNSAICH.

IUNNSAICHTE, *p. part.* of iunnsaich. See IONNSAICHTE.

IUR, *s.* More frequently written *iughar;* which see.

† IUR, *s. m.* Plunder; bloodshed; slaughter.—*Shaw.*

IÙRAN, ain, *s. m.* A sprout; the bud of a wild briar; a sort of luxuriant plant of which cattle are fond; *metaphorically*, a handsome youth; a hunter; a huntsman. Iùran na seilge, *hunter.—Ull.*

IÙRAS, ais, *s. f.* A felon or whitlow.

IURPAIS, *s. f.* Restlessness; fidgetting; dropsy.

IURPAISEACH, *a.* (*Ir. id.*) Restless; fidgetting; dropsical. Gu h-iurpaiseach, *restlessly. Com.* and *sup.* iurpaisiche.

IURRAM, aim, *s. m.* (*Ir. id.*) An oar-song; a boat song; tedious rhyme; a song sung during any kind of work, by way of lightening its burden; a fidgetting. Iurram a dhùisgeas an spiorad, *a spirit-stirring boat-song.—Macfar.* Iurram, *fidgetting.—Shaw.*

The *iurram*, or boat-song, seems to have been intended to regulate the strokes of the oars; so also, in ancient times,

——— stat margine puppis
Qui voce alternos nautarum temperet ictus,
Et remis dictet sonitum pariterque relatis,
Ad numerum plaudat resonantia cærula tonsis.

IURRAMACH, *a.* Like an oar-song.

IUSAN, ain, *s. m.* (*Ir. id.*) Giddiness, levity; a sudden whim.

IUSAN, ach, *a.* Giddy; light-headed, whimsical.

IUTHAIDH, *s. f.* [*pronounce* iùi.] *Gr.* ἰὸς.

IUTHAIR, *gen. sing.* of iuthar.

Iuthar, air, *s. f.* A yew-tree; yew. Iuthar beinne, *juniper;* iuthar talmhainn, *juniper.*

Laing is not correct when, in attacking the genuineness of the poems of Ossian, he asserts that the yew, so often mentioned in these works, is not a native plant of Scotland; for there are various places named after the yew, and have been so from time immemorial; as, *Gleniur*, i. e. *Gleann-iuthair*, or the glen of yews; *Dun-iur*, i. e. *Dun-iuthair*, or the mount of yews. These names, and many others, prove that the yew is indigenous, and that it was once abundant in the Highlands.

Iutharach, *a.* Made of yew; abounding in yew.

Iutharach, aich, *s. f.* A place where yews grow.

L.

L, l, luis, *the quicken tree;* for the Gael named their letters after natural objects and trees, when the names began with suitable initials. When it is preceded by itself, or by any other consonant, and followed by a broad vowel, as, *a, o, u*, it has a broad lingual sound, to which there is none like in the English language; as, *làn*, full; *lom*, bare; *lus*, an herb. When *l* is immediately followed by a short vowel, *e* or *i*, it is pronounced like the Italian *gl* in *gle* or *gli;* as, *litir*, a letter; *linn*, an age. Yet, in the case of nouns beginning with *l*, if the *masc. poss. pron.* go before, *l* is pronounced as in English; as, *a litir*, *his* letter; which differs essentially in sound from *a litir*, *her* letter. With regard to verbs beginning with *l*, the preterite is pronounced as in English; and in most other situations it is pronounced as *ll.*

Là, *gen.* la, *s. m.* (*Ir. id.*) A day; the space from evening to evening; one day; on a certain day; daylight. *N. pl.* lài, *days.* An là an diugh, *to-day, this day.—Stew. Gen.* Là a ghabh i anns an fhonn, *one day* [*on a certain day*] *she introduced into her song.—Oss. Fing.* Gu la, *till daylight;* là briagh, *a fine day;* là math, *a good day;* là fliuch, *a wet day;* là gailbheach, *a stormy day;* là seachduin, *a week day;* là dòmhnuich, *a Sunday;* an ath là, *the second day, the following day.—Stew. Acts.* Là càisge, *Easter;* la cainguis, *Whitsunday;* là fèill, *a feast-day, a fair-day, a festival: a holyday;* Là Mhuir, *Lady-day;* là bealtuinn, *May-day;* là na bliadhna ùr, *New-Year's-day;* là buain an lìn, *Nevermas, Græcæ Calendæ.* Là luain, *a Monday;* also, *a day that shall never arrive*, or *a day to which the moon gives light.* Do là, *by day;* laithean fèill, *days of folly;* la ceud fhèill Mhuire, *Purification-day.* Written also *làth* and *lò.*

† **La**, *prep.* With.

According to Shaw, this vocable is met with in old manuscripts, having the same meaning with the modern Gaelic *le;* which see.

† **Lab**, *s.* (*Lat.* labium. *Ir.* lab.) A lip.

Làb, laib, *s. m.* Dirt, mire; a puddle; a swamp or bog.

Làbach, *a.* Miry; dirty; swampy.

Làbail, *a.* (làb-amhuil.) Dirty; puddly.

Làban, ain, *s. m.* (*Ir. id.*) Mire; dirt; dirty work; drudgery.

Làbanach, aich, *s. m.* (*Ir. id.*) A dustman; a labourer; a plebeian; a draggler; a smearer; a dauber; a slovenly fellow. *N. pl.* làbanaich.

Làbanachadh, aidh, *s. m.* A dirtying, a smearing; a draggling.

Làbanachd, *s. f.* Labour; low dirty work; draggling.

Làbanaich, *gen. sing.* and *n. pl.* of làbanach.

Làbanaiche, *s. m.* A labourer; one who works among clay or puddly ground; a painstaking person; a plebeian; a draggler.

Làbanaich, *v. a.* Smear, daub, draggle. *Pret. a.* làbanaich; *fut. aff. a.* làbanaichidh.

Làbanta, *a.* (*Ir. id.*) Dirty, draggling, slovenly; like a plebeian, like a labourer, vulgar.

† **Labaonach**, *a.* Dissembling, pretending.

† **Labaonadh**, aidh, *s. m.* Dissimulation.

† **Labh**, laibh, *s. m.* (*Ir. id. Lat.* labium.) A lip. Hence *labhair*, speak.

Labhair, *v. a.* and *n.* (*from* †labh.) Speak, utter; talk; commune. *Pret. a.* labhair, *spoke; fut. aff. a.* labhraidh, *shall speak.* Labhair romhad, *speak on.—Stew. Gen.*

W. llavary. *Arm.* lavar *and* lavaret, *speak.* *Corn.* lavar; *speech.* In Vannes, *lavarour* means a tattler.

Labhaireach, *a.* Loud; utterable; loquacious; eloquent.

Labhairt, *s. f.* Speech, talk, conversation, discourse; language; utterance; voice; expression. Fear labhairt, *a spokesman, a speaker, an interpreter;* thair labhairt, *beyond expression;* droch labhairt, *bad speaking;* in the *Arm.* it is *drouch lavaret.*

Ir. id. *Corn.* lavar. *Arm.* lavar *and* lavaret.

Labhairt, (a), *p. part.* of labhair.

Labhairte, *p. part.* of labhair. Said, spoken. See **Labhair**.

Labhairteach, *a.* Inclined to speak; loud; utterable; expressible.

Labhairtiche, *s. m.* (*Arm.* lavarour, *a talker.*) An orator; a spokesman; a talkative fellow.

† **Labhar**, air, *s. m.* (*Ir. id.*) A laver, an ewer.

Labhar, **Labhara**, *a.* Loud, clamorous, loquacious, loud-sounding. Is fearr cù luath na teangadh labhar, *better is a nimble dog than a loud tongue.—Old Pro.* Written also *labhra;* which see.

Labhra, **Labhradh**, *a.* Loud, clamorous, loquacious, noisy. Cho labhra ri gaoith, *as loud as the wind.—Oss. Carricth.* Bu labhradh na caismeachd nan sonn, *louder than the warning of heroes.—Oss. Lod.* Labhradh, cealgach, *loquacious and cunning.—Old Song.*

Labhra, *s.* Lawers, a district of Breadalbane.

Labhrach, *a., for* labhaireach. (*Ir.* labhrach.) Loud, noisy, clamorous, loud-sounding; loquacious; eloquent. Is labhrach na builg fhàs, *shallows make a noise;* literally, *the empty bags are loud-sounding.—G. P.* A laoich labhraich! *thou eloquent hero!—Death of Carruil.*

Labhradh, *a.* See **Labhra**.

Labhradh, aidh, *s. m.* (*Corn.* lavra. *Arm.* lavar. *Ir.* labhradh.) A speaking, speechifying; speech, discourse. B'e labhradh mhill e, *speaking was his bane.—Old Song.* Urlabhradh, *utterance, elocution.*

Labhraiche, *s. m.* An orator; a spokesman; an elocutionist. Is balbh an labhraiche pongail, *mute is the distinct orator.—Old Song.*

Labhram, 1 *sing. imper.* of labhair. Let me speak; *or, for* labhraidh mi, *I will speak.*

Labhras, ais, *s. m.* A laurel or bay-tree; laurel, bay. An dearg labhras, *the laurel-tree;* crann labhrais, *a laurel-tree.*

Lat. laurus. *W.* lauryv. *Arm.* lore. *Fr.* laurier. *Ir.* labhras.

† **Lac**, *s. f.* Milk.

Lat. lac. *W.* llaeth. *Arm.* leth. *Ir.* lachd. *Span.* leche.

Lach, lacha, *s. m.* (*Ir. id.*) A wild duck, a wild drake. *N. pl.* lachaidh. Lach air lochan fuar, *a wild duck on a frigid lake.—Old Song.* Lach lochanach, *a dunter goose;* lach a chinn uaine, *a mallard;* lach ceann-ruadh, *the herb celendine.*

Lach, lacha, *s. m.* A reckoning at an inn, the expense of a penny wedding or public entertainment. Tog an lach, *raise* or *collect the reckoning.*

Lachach, *a.* (*from* lach.) Abounding in wild ducks or drakes; like a duck or drake. Coire lachach dràcach, *a dell abounding in ducks and drakes.—Old Song.*

Lachadair, *s. m.* A diver. *N. pl.* lachadairean.

Lachadh, aidh, *s. m.* (*Ir. id.*) A diving like a wild duck; *also*, a wild duck.

Lachag, aig, *s. f.* (*dim.* of lach.) A little wild duck or drake; a young wild duck or drake.

Lachaidh, *n. pl.* of lach. Wild ducks or drakes.

Lachair, *s. m.* A diver. *N. pl.* lachairean.

Lachan, ain, *s. m.* (*Ir. id.*) The common reed.

Lachar, air, *s. m.* (*Ir. id.*) A vulture; a large bird.

Lach-chinn-uaine, *s. m.* A mallard, or common wild duck, the *anas boschas* of Linnæus.

Lach-ceann-ruadh, *s. m.* The herb celendine.

† **Lachd**, *s. f.* (*Ir. id.*) Milk. See **Lac**.

Lachdainn, *a.* Homespun, grey, dun; clumsy.

Lachdan, **Lachdun**, *a.* Homespun, grey, dun; *also*, homespun grey cloth, *hodden grey.* Is com' leam na brigis lachdan, *I hate the grey breeches.—Old Song.*

Làd, làid, *s. m.* A load, a freight; a crowd; a volley. Written also *lòd;* which see.

† **Lad**, *s. m.* (*Ir. id.*) A water-course; a *lade.*

Lad, *s. m.* (*Germ.* laut. *Lat.* laud-o. *Eng.* loud.) Loud talk, clamorousness; *rarely*, a water-course.

Ladair, *gen. sing.* and *n. pl.* of ladar.

† **Làdar**, air, *s. m.* A thief, a robber.

Lat. latro. *Ir.* ladar. *Corn.* loder *and* lodar. *Arm.* lodhar *and* laer. *Goth.* lheider. *W.* lladron, *a robber. Gr.* λαθρα, *privately.*

Ladar, air, *s. m.* (*Ir. id.*) A ladle; a ladleful; a spoon; a scoop. *N. pl.* ladair. Gabh an ladar no'n taoman, *take the ladle or the laving dish.—Old Song.* Ni thu ladair, *thou shalt make spoons.—Stew. Ex.*

Ladarna, *a.* (*Ir. id.*) Bold, daring; impudently clamorous or loquacious. Ladarna is faoin, *rash and vain.—Oss. Carth.* Gu làmhach ladarna, *ready-handed and bold.—Old Song.*

Ladarnachd, *s. f.* Boldness; impudent loquacity.

Ladarnas, ais, *s. m.* (*Ir. id.*) Boldness; impudent loquacity.

Làdas, ais, *s. m.* Boldness in speech.

Làdasach, *a.* Bold in speech.

† **Ladh**, ladha, *s. m.* (*Ir. id.*) A sending, a mission, a deputation.

Ladhar, air, *s. m.* (*Ir. id.*) A hoof; a single hoof of a cloven-footed animal; a claw; a toe; a prong, a fork; a ludicrous name for a shanky leg. *N. pl.* ladhran. Gach aon a sgoilteas an ladhar, *every one that splits the hoof*, i. e. *cloven-footed.—Stew. Lev.* Sometimes written *laghar.*

† **Ladhna**, ai, *s. m.* Dumbness.

Ladhrach, *a.*, *from* ladhar. (*Ir. id.*) Hoofed; having large hoofs, having large claws, having large toes; forked, prouged; shanky; hasty. Tarbh ladhrach, *a bull with large hoofs.—Stew. Ps. ref.* Com. and *sup.* ladhraiche.

Ladhrag, aig, *s. f.* (*dim.* of ladhar.) A toe; a hoof; a fork; a prong.

† **Ladran**, ain, *s. m.* A robber, a highwayman; a thief.

Lat. latro. *Span.* ladron. *Ir.* ladron. *Corn.* loder *and* lodar. *Arm.* lodhar *and* laer. *W.* lladron. *Goth.* lheider, *a thief. Gr.* λαθρα, *privately.*

Ladurna, *a.* See **Ladarna**.

Lag, *v. n.* Faint; grow faint or weary; give up with fatigue. *Pret. a.* lag; *fut. aff. a.* lagaidh. Tra lag m' anam, *when my soul fainted.—Stew. Jonah.*

Lag, laig *and* luig, *s. m.* A hollow; a cavity; a pit; a dell. Lag a shléisde, *the hollow of his thigh.—Stew. Gen.* Dathanan gach luig, *the colour of every dell.—Macdon. N. pl.* lagan. Lagan loisgeach, *burning pits.—Mac Kellar's Hymn.*

Swed. laog, *low. Corn.* lakk, *a pit. Ir.* lag *and* log.

Lag, *a.* Weak; languid, faint; *also*, a feeble person. Lag ann airm, *weak in arms.—Oss. Tem.* Guth lag na h-oidhche, *the languid voice of night.—Id.* An cùis an laig, *in the cause of the weak.—Orr.*

Ir. id. W. llag, *loose. Pers.* llaca, *a weak person.*

Lagach, *a.* Full of dells, pits, or hollows.

Lagach, aich, *s. m.* A feeble person; a helpless person. *N. pl.* lagaich. Chaidh na lagaich o thaobh, *the feeble departed from him.—Oss. Tem.*

Lagachadh, (a), *pr. part.* of lagaich.

† **Lagadh**, aidh, *s. m.* Praise, fame, honour.

Lagadrag, aig, *s. f.* A thigh.

Lagaich, *v. a.* and *n.* (*Ir.* lagaigh.) Weaken; fatigue; grow weak; grow languid; become fatigued. *Pret. a.* lagaich; *fut. aff. a.* lagaichidh, *shall* or *will fatigue.* Na lagaich, *do not faint.—Stew. Heb.*

Lagaichte, *p. part.* of lagaich. Weakened, debilitated, fatigued.

Lagan, *n. pl.* of lag. Hollows, pits, cavities.

Lagan, ain, *s. m.* (*dim.* of lag.) A little hollow, a dell; a dimple, as on the cheek. Lagan na laimh, *the hollow of the hand;* lagan uaigneach, *a lonely dell.—Macint.* Lagan meachaire, *a dimple.*

Ir. logan. *Arm.* laguen, *a ditch. Scotch*, logan, *the pit of a kiln.*

Làgan, ain, *s. m.* (*Ir. id.*) Flummery; a kind of food much used by the Gael, and by the Lowland Scots called *sowens.* It is made by boiling the acidulated juice of oat-seeds to the consistency of a thick jelly.

Laganach, *a.* (*Ir. id.*) Full of little hollows or cavities; full of dells; like a dell.—*Macint.*

Làganach, *a.* Like flummery; abounding in flummery; of, or belonging to, flummery.—*Macdon.*

Lag-analach, *s.* An asthma; a gasp; *literally*, scantiness of breath.

Lag-chridhe, *s. f.* A faint heart; a chicken-heart; a dejected heart.

Lag-chridheach, *a.* Faint-hearted; feeble-minded; cowardly; dejected in heart or spirit. Dhoibhsan a tha lag-chridheach, *to them who are feeble-minded.—Stew. Thess.*

Lag-chridheachd, *s. f.* Faint-heartedness; cowardliness; dejectedness.

Lag-chuiseach, *a.* (*Ir. id.*) Feeble; faint-hearted; timid; unenterprising. Gu lag-chuiseach, *faint-heartedly.*

Lagh, lagha, *s. m.* Law; order; the stretch or bend of a bow. Lagh na dùthcha, *the law of the land;* bogha air lagh, *a bow on the stretch.—Sm. N. pl.* laghanna, *laws.* Mo laghanna, *my laws.—Stew. Gen.*

Gr. λογος, *word. Lat. barbarous*, laga, *law. Germ.* lage. *Island.* lag *and* laug. *Ang.-Sax.* lak *and* laga. *Corn.* laha. *Fr.* loi. *Dan.* low. *Swed.* lagh *and* lag, *order. Ir.* lagh. *Eng.* law.

Lagh, *v. a.* (*Ir. id.*) Pardon, forgive; acquit. *Pret. a.*

lagh, *forgave*; *fut. aff. a.* laghaidh, *shall forgive.* Lagh, guidheam ort! *forgive, I pray thee!—Stew. Gen. ref.*

LAGHACH. See LAOGHACH.

LAGHADH, aidh, *s. m.* (*Ir. id*) Remission; forgiveness; acquittal; the act or circumstance of pardoning or acquitting.

LAGHAICH, LAGHAIG, *v. a.* Permit, allow. Cha laghaig mi dhuit a dheanamh, *I will not suffer you to do it.*

LAGHAIL, *a.*, lagh-amhuil. (*Lat.* legalis. *Swed.* laga. *Ir.* lagh-amhail.) Lawful, legal, legitimate, rightful.

LAGHAILEACHD, *s. f.* Lawfulness, legality, rightfulness.

† LAGHAIRT, *s. f.* A lizard. *N. pl* laghairtean.

LAGHAR, air, *s. m.* See LADHAR.

LAGHDACHADH, aidh, *s. m* (*Ir* laghdughadh.) A diminishing, a decreasing; an abridging, a shortening; decrease, diminution

LAGHDAICH, *v. a* Diminish, lessen, subtract; demean; abridge, shorten. *Pret a.* laghdaich, *diminished; fut. aff. a.* laghdaichidh, *shall diminish, fut pass* laghdaichear, *shall be diminished*

LAGHDAICHEAR, *fut pass.* of laghdaich.

LAGHDAICHTE, *p part.* of laghdaich. Diminished

LAGHRAG, aig, *s f.* (*dim* of laghar.) See LADHRAG.

LAG-LAMH, -laimh, *s f* A weak hand; a pithless arm; weakness; helplessness

LAG-LAMHACH, *a.* (*Ir. id.*) Feeble-handed; weak, helpless. Mar thearmunn do 'n lag-lamhach, *a defence to the feeble.—Fingalian Poem*

† LAOSAINE, *s. f.* Freedom, liberty; remission.—*Shaw.*

LAGSAINN, *s f.* See LAIGSINN.

LAG-THAISDE, *s. f.* Abatement in a bargain.—*Shaw.*

LÀI, a *poetical abbreviation for* laithe or laithean, *n pl.* of la or làth. Days.

LAIB, *s. f.* Dirt, mire; a puddle; clay Cha 'n eil dorus gun laib, *there is no door without a puddle —G. P.*

LAIBHEIL, *a.* Dirty, miry, puddly.

LAIBH, *s. f.* Clay, mire, dirt —*Shaw.*

LAIBHIN, *s. f.* (*Ir. id*) Leaven or dough. Gun laibhin, *without leaven —Stew Ex.*

LAIBHINEACH, *a.* Like dough or leaven; made of dough; raw or unfired, as bread.

LAIBHREACH, ich, *s. f* A coat of mail. More properly written *lùireach.*

LAIBHRIG, *s. f.* A pier.—*Macd*

LAICHNEAS, eis, *s. m.* Joy.—*Shaw*

LAIDH, *v. n.* (*Ir. id* Gr λέχω) Lie, recline, couch, as a dog; set, as the sun. *Pret. a.* laidh; *fut. aff. a.* laidhidh, *shall lie.—Q. B. ref.* More frequently written *luidh.*

LAIDHE, *s. f.* A lying or reclining; a couching, as a dog; a setting, as of the sun. Dean laidhe, *lie down; couch.* Laidhe siùbhla, *childbed.* Written more frequently *luidhe,* which see.

LAIDHEACHAN, ain, *s. m* A snare or ambuscade, a lying in wait. Written also *luidheachan.*

LAIDH-SIÙBHLA, *s f.* Lying in childbed.

LAIDINN, *s f.* The Latin language. Ag ionnsuch' na Laidinn, *learning the Latin tongue*

LAIDINNEAR, ir, *s. m* A Latin scholar; a student in the Latin language. *N pl.* Laidinnearan.

LÀIDIR, *a.* (*Ir. id.*) Strong, powerful; able-bodied. Làidir mar na daragaibh, *strong as the oaks —Stew. Amos. Com.* and *sup.* làidire *and* treise, *more* or *most strong*

LÀIDIRE, *com.* and *sup.* of làidir Stronger, strongest.

LÀIDIREACHD, *s. f.* Strength; force.

LÀIDIREAS, eis, *s m* Strength; force.

LÀIDREACHADH, aidh, *s. m.* A strengthening, a growing strong.

LÀIDREAD, eid, *s m.* Improvement or increase in strength; convalescence. Air a làidread sa bheil e, *however strong he or it be*

LÀIDRICH, *v. a.* and *n.* (*Ir. id*) Make strong; grow strong

LAIG, *gen sing.* of lag; which see.

LAIGE, *com* and *sup.* of lag. Weaker, weakest Fear is laige lamh, *a man of the weakest arms —Oss. Carricth.*

LAIGE, *s f* (*Ir. id*) Weakness, debility, infirmity.

LAIGEAD, eid, *s. m.* Weakness; languor, increase in weakness or languor A dol an laigead, *growing weaker,* air laigeid a neart, *however weak his strength.—Old Poem*

LAIGHE, *s f* A spade, a shovel —*Shaw* *N. pl* laighean, *spades.*

LAIGHEAN, ein, *s m.* A spear

LAIGHEANN, inn, *s. m* The province of Leinster, in Ireland.—*Shaw.*

LAIGHEUR, eir, *s m* (*Ir.* laithgheir.) Verjuice.

LAIGSE, *s. f* (*from* lag.) Debility, weakness; languor, fatigue. Laigse nan lamh, *weakness of the hands —Oss Carthon.* A mo laigsibh, *from my weaknesses.—Stew 2 Cor*

LAIGSINN, *s. f.* Debility, weakness; fatigue, languor, *rarely,* liberty; remission. Mearachd agus laigsinn, *error and weakness —Macfar.*

LÀILT, *s f.* (*Ir id*) Clay, mould —*Shaw*

LÀILTEACH, *a* (*Ir id.*) Clayish; having mould.

LAIMH, *gen sing.* of làmh, which see.

LAIMH-BHASB, *v n* Fence, or practise the art of manual defence

LAIMH-BHASBAIREACHD, *s f.* Fencing, as with manual weapons.

LAIMH-CHEAIRDE, *s f.* A handicraft, any mechanical trade

LAIMH-CHEARD, -cheird, *s. m.* A mechanic, a tradesman *N. pl* laimh-cheairde.

LAIMHDEACHAS, ais, *s m.* Captivity, slavery.—*Shaw*

LAIMDHIA, -dhé, *s. m.* A household god.

LÀIMHICH, *v. a* Handle, touch; presume; take into custody. *Pret. a* làimhich. See LAMHAICH

LAIMH-FHOILEAD, eid, *s. m.* A handkerchief

LAIMH-RI, *prep.* Near, hard by, beside, at hand. An làimh ri, *near;* laimh ri tobar uisge, *near a well —Stew Gen* Laimh ris an abhainn, *near* or *by the river —Stew. Gen* Laimh rium, riut, rithe, rinn, ribh, riu, *near me, thee, her, us, you, them*

LÀIMHRIG, *s. f.* (*Ir. id*) A pier; a harbour; a ford.—*Shaw.*

LÀIMHSEACH, *a.* Apt to handle, finger, or feel.

LÀIMHSEACHADH, aidh, *s m.* A handling, a fingering; a feeling with fingers; a wielding, as of a manual weapon. Làimhseachadh lann, *handling of swords, a wielding of swords.* Láimhseachadh goirt, *a severe handling.—R S*

LAIMHSEACHADH, (a), *pr. part* of laimhsich; which see.

LAIMH-SGIATH, -sgeithe, *s. f.* A target or shield,

LAIMHSICH, *v. a.* (*Ir.* laimhsigh) Handle, finger, feel with the fingers; discuss, take in hand. *Pret. a* làimhsich, *felt; fut. aff. a* laimhsichidh, *shall* or *will feel* Gu 'n laimhsich mi thu, *that I may feel thee.—Stew Gen* *Fut sub.* laimhsicheas, *would* or *will handle.*

LAIMHSICHTE, *p. part.* of laimhsich. Handled, fingered, felt; discussed; taken in hand

LAIMH-THIONNACH, *a.* (*Ir. id*) Desirous, eager; given to chiromancy.

LÀINE, *s. f.* (*Ir. id.*) Fulness; completeness; repletion. Làine mara, *high water.*

LÀINE, *com.* and *sup.* of làn. Fuller, fullest.

LAINE, *s. f.* (*Ir. id.*) Gladness, merriment, cheerfulness. Written also *lainne.*

LAINEACH, *a.* (*Ir. id.*) Glad, joyful, merry. Gu laineach, *joyfully.*

LÀINEAD, eid, *s. m.* Fulness, repleteness; increase in fulness. A dol an làinead, *growing more and more full.*

LAINGEAN, *a.* Faithful; steady; stedfast.—*Stew. Ps. ref.*

LAINN, *gen. sing.* and *n. pl.* of lann; which see.

LAINNE, *s. f.* (*Ir. id.*) Cheerfulness, joy, merriment.

LÀINNEACH, *a.* (*Ir. id.*) Armed with a sword or spear; like a sword or spear.

LAINNEACH, *a.* Joyful, cheerful, merry.

LAINNIR. See LOINNIR.

LAINNTEAR, eir, *s. m.* A lantern. *N. pl.* lainntearan.

LAIPHEID, *s. f.* An instrument used to form horn-spoons. —*Shaw.*

LÀIR, *gen. sing.* of làr; which see.

LÀIR, làrach, *s. f.* (*Ir. id.*) A mare. Làir-asal, *a she-ass;* searrach seann làrach air greidh, *the foal of an old mare in the herd.*—*G. P.*

LAIR, *s. f.* (*Ir. id.*) The thigh; a haunch.—*Macd.* and *Shaw.*

LÀIR-ASAL, ail, *s. f.* A she-ass.

LÀIREACH. See LÀRACH.

† LAIRGE, *s. f.* A thigh; a haunch.

LÀIRIC, LÀIRICH, LÀIRIG, *s. f.* A moor; a hill; a burying place.

† LAIS, *s. f.* (*Ir. id.*) A hand; a flame.

† LAIS, *s. f.* An old word meaning a cry. *Arm.* lais: hence *lissus,* a mournful cry, taken from the twelve tables, according to Pezron.

LAISCEANTA, *a.* Flaming; inflammable; passionate; furious. Gu laisceanta, *passionately.*

LAISDE, *a.* Easy in circumstances, comfortable.

LAISDE, *s. f.* (*Ir. id.*) A latchet. *N. pl.* laisdean, *latchets.*

LAISDEACH, *a.* Having latchets or thongs; full of latchets; like a latchet.

LAISDEACHD, *s. f.* Easiness in circumstances, comfortableness.

LAISE, *s. f.* (*Ir. id.*) A flash, a flame.

LAISEACH, *a.* Flashing, flaming; inflammable.

LAISGEANTA, *a.* See LOISGEANTA.

LAISTE, *p. part.* of las. Kindled, lit. Laiste le boil chath, *kindled with ardour for battle.*—*Oss. Dargo.*

† LAITH, *s. f.* Milk.
Ir. id. *Fr.* lait. *Corn.* leath. *Lat.* lac.

† LAITH, *s. f.* (*Ir. id.*) Multitude; ale; a feast; stomach.

LÀITH, LAITHE, a *poetical abbreviation* of laithean. Tri laithe dhi na tosd, *three days was she silent.*—*Ull.*

† LAITHE, *s. pl.* (*Ir. id.*) A jeweller's scales.

LAITHEAN, *n. pl.* of làth. Days. *D. pl.* laithibh. Dubhra m' a laithibh, *darkness around his days.*—*Oss. Tem.*

LÀITHICH, *s. f.* Dirt, mire; puddle, kennel.

LAITHILT, *s. m.* (*Ir. id.*) A weighing with scales.

LAITHRE, *s. f.* (*Ir. id.*) A cow, a mare.—*Shaw.*

LAITHREACH. See LÀRACH.

LÀITHREACHD, *s. f.* Presence. Written also *lathaireachd;* which see.

LAITHRICH, *v. n.* (*Ir. id.*) Appear.

LAITIS, *s. f.* (*Ir. id.*) A lattice.

† LALACH, aich, *s. m.* (*Ir. id.*) A giant; a champion. *N. pl.* lalaich.

† LAMAIS, *s. m.* (*Ir. id.*) A poet.—*Shaw.*

LAMANTA, *a.* Menstruous. Té lamanta, *mulier menstruata.*

LAMH, laimh, *s. f.* A hand; an arm; a handle. Na cuiribh lamh ann, *lay not a hand on him.*—*Stew. Gen.* Lamh an uachdar, *the upper hand, superiority;* fhuair mi lamh an uachdar air, *I got the upper hand of him.* Air gach laimh, *on every hand.*—*Sm.* Cuir lamh ri, *sign, endorse;* fu laimh, *under-hand, privately.* Fu' laimh, *under his hand; under his command.*—*Stew. Gen.* Ann an laimh, *in custody.*—*Id.* Cum air do laimh, *stay thine hand.*—*Stew.* 1 *Chr.* Aig laimh, *at hand.*—*Oss. Tem.* Mu 'n laimh, *in hands; indifferently.* Fad o laimh, *afar off.*—*Stew. Ex.* Gabh as laimh, *engage, undertake;* as an laimh, *out of the hand; aside; off-hand; outright.*—*Stew. Num.* Lamh laidir, *a strong hand;* lamh dheas, *a right hand;* lamh chli, *a left hand;* lamh air laimh, *hand-in-hand.*
Gr. λαζω, λαβε, λαμβανω, *to take.* *Chin.* lao, *work with the hand.* *W.* llamh, *hand.* *Corn.* † lau. *Ir.* lamh. *Arm.* la, *pl.* llan. *Germ.* lan.

LÀMHACH, *a.* (*from* lamh.) Ready-handed; daring; presuming; having hands or handles.

LAMHACH, aich, *s. m.* (*Ir. id.*) The report of guns; military evolutions or manœuvres; shooting; slinging; casting. Lamhach fùdair, *firing.*—*Macint.* Luchd-lamhaich, *artillerymen; bowmen; slingers.*

LAMHACHADH, *a.* A handling, a fingering, a feeling, a groping.

LÀMHACHAIR, *a.* Ready-handed. Gu làmhachair strìtheil, *ready-handed and emulous.*—*Macfar.*

LÀMHACHAIREACHD, *s. f.* Ready-handedness.

LÀMHACHAS, ais, *s. m.* Firing of guns; military evolutions; artillery; dexterity; activity; management; groping, handling. Luchd-làmhachais, *artillerymen, bowmen,* or *archers.* Làmhachas làidir, *the strong hand; oppression; force.*—*Stew. Matt.*

LAMHADH, aidh, *s. m.* (*Ir. id.*) Handling, groping.

LAMHAGAN, ain, *s. m.* (*Ir. id.*) A handling, a groping.

LÀMHAICH, *v. a.* (*from* lamh.) Handle, feel, finger, grope; take in hand. *Pret.* làmhaich; *fut. aff. a.* làmhaichidh, *shall handle.*

LÀMHAICHTE, *p. part.* of làmhaich.

LÀMHAINN, *s. f.* (*Ir.* lamhann.) A glove, a gauntlet. Làmhainn iàrruinn, *a gauntlet.* *N. pl.* làmhainnean.

LÀMHAINNEAR, ir, *s. m.* A glover. *N. pl.* làmhainnearan.

LÀMHAIR, *s. m.* A shooter, a gunner.

LÀMHAIRT, *s. f.* A handling, a fingering.

LÀMHAN, ain, *s. m.* (*Ir. id.*) A glove, a gauntlet.

LAMH-ANART, airt, *s. m.* A hand-towel.

LAMHANNAN, ain, *s. m.* A bladder.—*Shaw.*

LAMHAS, ais, *s. m.* (*Ir. id.*) A glove.

LAMH-CHEAIRDE, *s. f.* (*Ir. id.*) A handicraft.

LAMH-CHEARD, -cheird, *s. m.* (*Ir. id.*) A tradesman, a mechanic. *N. pl.* lamh-cheird.

LAMH-CHEARDAIL, *a.* Mechanical; like a mechanic; ingenious.

LAMH-CHLAG, -chluig, *s. m.* A hand-bell. *N. pl.* lamh-chluig.

LAMH-CHLEAS, *s. m.* (*Ir. id.*) Legerdemain, sleight of hand.

LAMH-CHLEASACHD, *s. f.* (*Ir. id.*) The practice of legerdemain.

LAMH-CHLEASAICHE, *s. m.* A juggler or conjurer. *N. pl.* lamh-chleasaichean.

Lamh-chli, *s. f.* (*Ir. id.*) A left hand. Dh'ionnsuidh na laimh cli, *to the left hand.—Stew. Gen.*

Lamh-choille, *s. f.* (*Ir. id.*) A cubit Fichead lamh-choille, *twenty cubits.—Stew. Lev.*

Lamh-chomhart, airt, *s. m.* (*Ir. id.*) A clapping of hands —*Shaw.*

Lamh-chomhraig, *s m.* A combatant

Lamhdeanas, ais, *s. m* A restraint

Lamh-dheanta, *part.* Manufactured; made by hands. Timchioll-ghearradh lamh-dheanta, *circumcision made by hands.—Stew. Eph*

Lamh-dheantas, ais, *s. m.* Handiwork.

Lamh-dheas, *s. f.* A right hand Dh'ionnsuidh na laimh deise, *to the right hand.—Stew. Gen.*

Lamh-dhruidh, *s. m.* A palmister or chiromancer. *N. pl.* lamh-dhruidhean, *palmisters.*

Lamh-dhruidheachd, *s. f.* Chiromancy, palmistry.

Lamh-fhail, -fhàile, *s. f* A bracelet. Da lamh-fhàil, *two bracelets.—Stew. Gen. N. pl* lamh-fhailean, *bracelets —Id*

Lamh-ghlas, -ghlais, *s. f.* A manacle, a handcuff.

Lamh-ghreim, *s. f.* (*Ir. id.*) A handle.

Lamh-làidir, *s.* (*Ir. id*) A strong hand; force, oppression, compulsion. Leis an lamh-làidir, *with the strong hand.—Stew. O. T.*

Lamh-leigh, *s m.* (*Ir. id*) A surgeon —*Shaw.*

Lamh-leigheachd, *s. f* Chirurgery

Lamh-mhuileann, inn, *s. m.* (*Ir. id.*) A handmill. *N. pl.* lamh-mhuilinnean, *handmills*

† **Lamhnadh**, aidh, *s. m.* (*Ir. id.*) Nativity; a bringing forth.

Lamhnan, ain, *s m.* (*Ir id*) A bladder

Lamh-oibre, *s. m.* A workman, a labourer; a good workman.

Lamhrachan, ain, *s m.* A handle; a shaft. *N. pl.* lamhrachain.

Lamhrachdaich, *v. a.* and *n* Grabble; grope, handle clumsily.

Lamhrachdas, ais, *s. m.* A groping, a handling.

Lamhrag, aig, *s f* (*Ir. id.*) A silly woman, a dowdy.

Lamhragan, ain, *s. m.* (*Ir id.*) Handling, groping.

Lamhraich, *v. a.* and *n.* Grabble, grope; handle clumsily.

Lamh-rod, -roid, *s. m* A by-road, a footpath —*Shaw*

Lamhsaich, *v. a.* See **Làimhsich.**

Lamh-sgiath, -sgeithe, *s f.* (*Ir. id*) A shield; a small target.

Lamh-sgriobhadh, aidh, *s m.* A handwriting, a manuscript.

Lamh-sgriobhaidh, *s. f.* A handwriting, penmanship.

Lamh-sgriobhair, *s. m.* A clerk; an amanuensis. *N. pl.* lamh-sgriobhairean.

Lamh-speic, *s. f.* A handspike.

Lamhuinn, *s. f.* (*from* lamh.) A glove; a woollen glove. Lamhuinn iaruinn, *a gauntlet N. pl.* lamhuinnean, *gloves.*

Lamhuinneach, *a.* Having gloves; like gloves; gauntleted

Lamhuinnear, ir, *s m.* A glover. *N. pl.* lamhuinnearan.

Lamhuinnearachd, *s f.* The business of glovemaking.

Lamhuinnich, *v. a.* Provide with gloves; clothe the hands with gloves *Pret. a* lamhuinnich; *fut. aff. a.* lamhuinnichidh; *p. part.* lamhuinnichte

Lamhuinnichte, *p. part.* of lamhuinnich

Lamna, *s. m.* (*Ir. id.*) A space of time.

Lampa, *s. m.* A lamp.

Lampar, air, *s m.* (*Ir. id.*) A small bird, an unfledged bird

Lamprag, aig, *s. f.* A glow-worm.

Lamrag, aig, *s. f.* An ignorant silly woman; a dowdy.

Lamraig, *s. f* A black bird with white spots, supposed to be an Allenhawk.—*Shaw.*

Làn, làin, *s. m* Fulness; repletion, a swell, as of water; corpulence, *rarely*, a lane; a church Ann an làn aois, *in full age*, i. e. *in fulness of age.—Stew Job.* Is anns an abhuinn tha an làn! *what a swell there is in the river!* Is ann innte tha 'n làn! *how corpulent she is!* Làn mara, *high water*, làn beòil, *a mouthful*, làn broinn, *a bellyful*, làn dùirn, *a handful, a fistful.*

Làn, *a* Full; complete; filled; satisfied. Làn bha ré air tonn, *the moon was full on the waves.—Oss Lod* Làn bròin, *full of grief—Oss Gaul.* Gach clais làn le sruthan, *every furrow filled with tears —Id* Làn cheud do bhard, *a full* or *complete hundred of bards —Oss Tem.* Dearr làn, *quite full, brimful* Com and sup làine, *fuller, fullest*

Làn, in composition, signifies *quite, fully, completely, enough, well.* Làn deas, *quite ready*, gù lan mhath, *well enough, quite well.*

Lat p-len-us. *W* llawn. *Ir.* làn *Corn.* len. *Arm.* lan *and* leun.

Lànachd, *s f*, *from* làn (*Ir id*) Fulness, repletion, satiety; completion, fulfilment, abundance. Lànachd an tì, *the fulness of the Being.—Stew. Eph.* Lànachd do thruas, *abundance of compassion.—Mack*

Lànain, *s f* (*for* lanamhainn) A couple, a pair or brace; a married couple Gu mu buan do 'n lanain uasal! *long may the noble couple live!—Old Song.*

Lanamhainn, *s f.* (*Ir. id*) A couple, a brace or pair, a married couple.

Lanamhnas, ais, *s. m* Carnal copulation.—*Shaw.*

Lanamhuin, *s. f.* (*Ir. id*) A married couple.

Lan-aois, *s. m.* Advanced age.

Làn-chothrom, oim, *s. f.* A good opportunity; full weight. Tha 'n làn-chrothrom agad, *you have a good opportunity.*

Lan-chothromach, *a.* Quite convenient; of full weight.

Làn-chothromaich, *v a* Weigh thoroughly —*Stew. Job. P part.* làn-chothromaichte.

Làn-chriochnachadh, aidh, *s m.* A completing, a perfecting; a bringing to a full close, or final termination; a completion, accomplishment Written also *lan-chriochnuchadh.*

Làn-chriochnaich, *v. a.* (*Ir.* lain-chriochnaigh) Complete, accomplish, bring to a final close.

Làn-chriochnaichte, *p part.* of làn-chriochnaich. Brought to perfection or completion, quite finished

Làn-chrodha, *a* (*Ir. id*) Courageous —*Shaw.*

Làn-chruaidh, *a.* Quite hard, well tempered. Lannan làn-chruaidh, *well-tempered swords.—Fingalian Poem.*

Làn-chumhachd, *s f* (*Ir. id*) Plenipotence; discretionary power.

Làn-chumhachdach, *a.* (*Ir. id*) Plenipotent; *also, substantively*, plenipotentiary

Làn-deanta, *part.* (*Ir.* laindeanta) Quite complete, quite done or finished; perfectly trained Làn-deanta n airm, *well trained to arms.*

Làn-dearbhachd, *s f* (*Ir id*) Full of assurance or conviction; assuredness. Le làn-dearbhachd, *with full assurance.—Stew Thess*

Làn-dearbhadh, aidh, *s m* (*Ir. id*) A demonstration or proof, a complete trial; persuasion, conviction. Làn-dearbhadh air gach duine, *every man fully persuaded.—Stew. Rom.*

Lan-dearbhta, *p. part.* Fully proved; demonstrated; tried thoroughly.

Lan-deimhinn, *s. f.* (*Ir. id.*) Full assurance or certainty, firm persuasion. Bha lan-deimhinn aige, *he was fully persuaded.—Stew. Rom.*

Lan-dhearbh, *v. a.* (*Ir. id.*) Prove, demonstrate; try thoroughly, put to a true test. *Pret. a.* lan-dhearbh, *proved, fut. aff.* lan-dhearbhaidh, *shall prove.*

Làn-dhearbhta, *part.* Fully proven.

Lan-dùirn, *s. m.* A handful, a maniple.

Làn-dùlan, ain, *s. m.* An open challenge or defiance. Bheirinn làn-dùlan do d'naimh, *I would give an open challenge to thy foes.—Oss. Gaul.*

Làn-fhios, *s.* Full certainty; conviction; assurance. Tha làn-fhios agad, *thou knowest full well.—Stew. Tim.*

Làn-fhiosrach, *a.* Fully certain, quite aware, well assured. Tha mi làn-fhiosrach air, *I am quite certain of it.*

Làn-fhiosrachadh, aidh, *s. m.* Conviction; convincing; a making certain.

Làn-fhiosrachd, *s. f.* Decided conviction, full assurance.

Làn-fhiosraich, *v. a.* Make certain, make fully aware, convince.

† **Lang**, laing, *s. f.* (*Ir. id.*) Falsehood, treachery; a kind of fish.—*Shaw.*

Langach, *a.* (*Arm.* langach, *talkative.*) Slim, slender; *rarely*, false, treacherous. *Com.* and *sup.* langaiche, *more* or *most slim.* Gu langach, *slimly.*

Langach, aich, *s. m.* (*Ir. id.*) Ling.

Langaiche, *s. f.* Slimness, slenderness; falseness; *also*, a slender or slim person.

Langaid, *s. f.* (*Ir. id.*) A fetter for a horse. *N. pl.* langaidean.

Langaideach, *a.* Fettered, as a horse; like a horse's fetter.

Langain, *gen. sing.* of langan; which see.

Langair, *s. m.* (*Ir. id.*) The seam.—*Shaw* and *Macfar. Voc.* A glutton.

Langan, ain, *s. m.* (*Ir. id. Arm.* langach, *talkative.*) Noise, the noise made by deer; the bellowing of the hind after the deer; the monotony of the human voice; *also*, a breast. Langan bràghad, *the wesand.*

Langanaich, *v. n.* Bellow, as a deer, low; make a monotonous sound.

Langanaich, *s. f.* A bellowing, a lowing, a roaring; a continued and wearisome monotony.

Langan-bràghad, *s. m.* (*Ir.* laugan-brachad.) The wesand or windpipe.

Langar, air, *s. m.* (*Ir.* lang-fethir.) The seam; fetters or chains.—*Macfar. Voc.*

Langar-ileach, *s. m.* A lamprey.—*Shaw.*

Langasait, aite, *s. f.* A settee, a courtsey; a crouching.

Làn-ghealach, aich, *s. f.* A full moon. Solus na làn-ghealaich, *the full moon's light.*

Làn-ghuin, *s. f.* A period.

Làn-laghadh, aidh, *s. m.* Plenary indulgence.

Làn-luach, *s.* (*Ir. id.*) Full price. Air a làn-luach, *for its full price.—Stew. 1 Chr.*

Lan-mara, *s. f.* High tide, high water; a tide. Làn-mara le gealaich a thairneas, *the high tide caused by the attracting moons.—Old Poem.*

Lann, lainne, loinne, *s. f.* (*Ir.* lann. *W.* lainne, *a blade. Lat.* lanius, *a slaughterer.*) A sword; a knife; a blade; a lancet, a weapon; any bladed instrument. Lann liomhaidh, *a polished sword.—Oss. Gaul.* Lann thana, *a thin blade.—Oss. Tem.* *N. pl.* lainn *and* lannan. Tharruing iad an lainn, *they drew their swords.—Oss. Lod.* *D. pl.* lannaibh. Le lannaibh, *with lancets.—Stew. 1 K.* Lann Spainnteach, *a Toledo.—Turn.*

Lann, lainn, *s. f.* An enclosure; a house; a repository; a church; a scale, as of a fish; a scale or balance; a stud or boss; a gridiron; *rarely*, land, a veil. *N. pl.* lannan. Itean is lannan, *fins and scales.—Stew. Lev.* *D. pl.* lannaibh. Leantuinn ri do lannaibh, *sticking to thy scales.—Stew. Ezek.*

Corn. lannan, *enclosure.* *Ir.* lann. *Goth. Sax. Du. Eng. Teut. Germ. Swed. Run.* land. Also, *Heb.* lon, *to dwell.*

Lann, *v. a.* Put to the sword; exercise with the sword, fence with the sword. *Pret. a.* lann; *fut. aff. a.* lannaidh, *shall fence.*

Lannach, *a.* (*from* lann.) Scaly, as a fish; bladed; studded; bossy, bossed; like a scale, blade, stud, or boss. Am bradan lannach, *the scaly salmon.*

Lannadh, aidh, *s. m.* (*Ir. id.*) A putting to the sword; sword exercise, a peeling.

Lannaibh, *d. pl.* of lann; which see.

Lannair, *s. f.*, *from* lann. (*Ir. id.*) Radiance; glitter; splendour, a gleaming; light reflected on the blade of a sword, or any burnished metal surface; a great flame. Do shùil gun lannair, *thine eye without radiance.—Old Song.*

Lannair, *s. f.* A cow. *N. pl.* lannairean.

Lannaireach, *a.* (*Ir.* lannaireach *and* loineardha.) Gleaming, glittering, effulgent, radiant; beaming, shining; fond of sword exercise.

Lannaireachd, *s. f.* (*Ir.* loinearacht.) Continued gleaming, radiance, brightness; sword exercise.

Lannan, *n. pl.* of lann. Swords; scales, blades; weapons; bladed instruments.

Lannar, *a.* Bright, gleaming, beaming, radiant. Bu lannar a shnuadh, *bright was his aspect.—Oss. Gaul.*

Lann-bhuidhne, *s. f.* A garrison, a barrack.

Lanndaichean, *n. pl.* of lann. Enclosures.

Lanndair, *s. m.* A lanthorn.

Lann-ghorm, *a.* Blue-scaled, having blue scales. Bric lann-ghorm, *blue-scaled trouts.—Macdon.*

Lann-cleuta, *s. m.* An enclosed place; enclosure; a repository.

Lannrach, aich, *s. f.* (*Ir. id.*) A vast flame, a sudden conflagration; a blaze.

Lannrach, *a.* Gleaming, shining; burnished. Clogaidean lannrach, *gleaming helmets.—Old Song.*

Lannrachadh, aidh, *s. m.* A gleaming, a glittering, a glistening, a flaming.

Lannraich, *v. n.* Gleam, glitter, shine; blaze, bespangle. *Pret.* lannraich; *fut. aff. a.* lannraichidh, *shall gleam.*

Lannsaiche, *s. m.* A pikeman; a lancer. *N. pl.* lannsaichean.

Lannsair, *s. m.* A pikeman, a lancer.

Lanntair, *s. f.* (*Ir. id.*) A pantry; a partition. *N. pl.* lanntairean.

Làn-phunc, *s. m.* (*Ir. id.*) A full point or period.

Làn-sgrud, *v. a.* Examine minutely; catechise; consider fully. *Pret. a.* làn-sgrud; *fut. aff. a.* làn-sgrudaidh, *shall examine.*

Làn-sgrudadh, aidh, *s. m.* (*Ir. id.*) Minute examination; minute consideration.

Làn-shoilleir, *a.* (*Ir. id.*) Very clear; very bright; refulgent; evident; quite intelligible; notorious.

Làn-shoilleireachadh, aidh, *s. m.* A making clear; a brightening; making intelligible.

Làn-shoilleirich, *v. a.* and *n.* Make quite clear or intelligible; become bright; become quite evident.

Làn-shoillse, *s. f.* Perfect light; perfect day, broad day. Làn-shoillse na grèine, *the perfect* or *universal light of the sun;* làn shoillse na gealaich, *the light of the moon at full.*

Làn-shoillseach, *a.* Giving perfect light; giving general light.

Làn-shoillseachadh, aidh, *s. m.* A giving perfect light; a dispensing of general light.

Làn-shoillsich, *v. a.* Make quite clear or evident; give perfect or complete light. *Pret. a.* làn-shoillsich; *fut. aff. a.* làn-shoillsichidh.

Làn-shùil, -shùl, *s. f.* A full eye.

Làn-shuileach, *a.* (*Ir. id.*) Full-eyed. Mo chaileag lurach làn-shuileach, *my pretty full-eyed maid.—Old Song.*

Lantair, *s. m.* A partition wall.—*Stew.* 1 *K. ref.* *N. pl.* lantairean.

Làn-thoilich, *v. a.* Give complete satisfaction; please to the utmost. *Pret. a. id.*

Làn-tholl, -thuill, *s. m.* A perforation.

Làn-tlachd, *s. f.* (*Ir. id.*) Perfect liking; full contentment.

Lan-toil, *s. f.* (*Ir. id.*) Full satisfaction; concurrence; satiety.

Làn-toileach, *a.* (*Ir. id.*) Fully satisfied; quite willing; quite contented. Tha mi làn-toileach, *I am quite contented.*

Làn-toilichte, *p. part.* Fully or well pleased; quite satisfied; quite contented. Leis am bheil mi làn-toilichte, *in whom I am well pleased.—Stew.* 2 *Pet.*

Làn-tolladh, aidh, *s. m.* (*Ir. id.*) A perforation.

Làn-ughdarach, *a.* Plenipotent; *also, substantively,* a plenipotentiary.

Làn-ughdaras, ais, *s. m.* Full authority; discretionary power; plenipotence.

† **Laobh**, *a.* (*Ir. id.*) Partial; prejudicial.—*Shaw.*

Laoch, laoich, *s. m.* (*Ir. id.*) A hero, a champion; a term of approbation for a young man. *N. pl.* laoich.

Laochail, *a.*, (laoch-amhuil.) Brave, heroic; champion-like; enterprising; chivalrous.

Laochan, ain, *s. m.*, *dim.* of laoch. (*Ir. id.*) A young champion, a little hero; a would-be hero. Is sin thu fein, a laochain! *that is your sort, my little hero!* A boy is almost always addressed by this term. Ciod tha thu ag radh, laochain? *what sayest thou, boy?* *N. pl.* laochain.

Laochar, *a.*, *contr.* for laochmhor; which see.

Laoch-mhor, *a.* (*Ir. id.*) Heroic; chivalrous. Giùlan laoch-mhor, *heroic bearing* or *conduct.—Old Song.* Gu laoch-mhor, *heroically.* *Com.* and *sup.* laoch-mhoire.

Laochraidh, **Laochruidh**, *s. m.* and *f.* Heroes, warriors; militia; a band of warriors. Caoilte le' laochraidh, *Coilte with his warriors.—Ull.* Laochruidh Edoim, *the mighty ones of Edom.—Stew. Jer.* Dh'eugh an laochraidh gharg, *the band of fierce warriors has perished.—Old Song.*

Laodag, *s. f.* See **Lùdag**.

Laodhan, ain, *s. m.* (*Ir. id.*) The heart of a tree; the pith of wood; pulp; marrow. Brìgh a laodhan nam maoth-shlat, *juice from the pith of twigs.—Macint.*

Laodhanach, *a.* Pulpy; marrowy; having pith, as wood.

Laogh, laoigh, *s. m.* A calf; a fawn or young deer; a term of endearment for a child. Is binn guth laoigh a beinn, *pleasant is the voice of a fawn from the mountains.—Fingalian Poem.* Laogh feidh, *a fawn;* laogh alluidh, *a fawn.* Mo laogh geal, *my dear soul,* literally, *my white calf;* laoigh mo chridhe, *my darling;* laogh-fheòil, *veal;* laogh marbh, *a dead calf;* in the *Arm.* it is *lueou maru.* *Ir.* laogh. *Corn.* leauh. *W.* lho. *Manks,* leigh. *Arm.* lue *and* lueou.

Laòghach, *a.* (*from* laògh.) Abounding in calves or in fawns. Damhach, aghach, laòghach, *abounding in oxen, sturks, and calves.—Macdon.*

Laoghach, *a.* Beautiful; comely; pretty. An tulach laoghach an robh Taura, *the beautiful hill on which Taura stood.—Oss. Taura.* *Com.* and *sup.* laoghaiche, *prettier, prettiest.*

Laogh-alluidh, *s. m.* A fawn; *literally,* a wild calf.

Laoghan, ain, *s. m.* See **Laodhan**.

Laoghanach, *a.* See **Laodhanach**.

Laoghar, air, *s.* See **Ladhar**.

Laogh-feidh, *s. m.* A fawn.

Laogh-fheoil, *s. f.* Veal; *literally,* calf's flesh.

† **Laoi**, *s. m.* (*Ir. id.*) A day; hire; a tail; a song. Written *là* or *làth;* which see.

Laoidh, *s. f.* A hymn; a sacred poem; a poem in general; *adjectively,* exciting; animating. *N. pl.* laoidhean; *d. pl.* laoidhibh. Ann an laoidhibh, *in hymns.—Stew. Eph.* Leabhar laoidhean, *a hymn-book.*

Scotch, leid *and* luid. *Belg.* lied. *Island.* hliod, *a song.*

Laoidh, *v. a.* Exhort; admonish; excite, animate. *Pret. a.* laoidh, *exhorted; fut. aff. a.* laoidhidh, *shall exhort.*

Laoidheach, *a.* Hymnal; exhorting; admonishing; exciting.

Laoidheadh, idh, *s. m.* An exhortation; an advice; hymn-singing; exciting.

† **Laoi-leabhar**, air, *s. m.* (*Ir. id.*) A diary, a journal, a day-book. *N. pl.* laoi-leabhraichean.

Laoim, *gen. sing.* of laom.

Laoim, *v. n.* Lodge or fall flat to the ground, as standing corn. *Pret.* laoim; *fut. aff.* laoimidh, *shall lodge.*

Laoimte, *p. part.* of laoim. Lodged, or lying on the ground, as a corn-crop.

Laoineach, *a.* (*Ir. id.*) Elegant, handsome, neat, showy, stately. Og laoineach, *an elegant youth;* gu laoineach, *elegantly.* *Com.* and *sup.* laoinеach.

Laom, laoim, *s. m.* (*Ir. id.*) A blaze of fire; a sudden flame; a gleaming.

Laomach, *a.* (*Ir. id.*) Crooked; bent; curved, as the shores of a lake.—*Macdon.* *Also,* blazing, gleaming.

Laomachd, *s. f.* (*Ir.* laomdhachd.) Crookedness; winding; curvature.—*Shaw.* A gleaming.

Laomsgair, *a.* (*Ir.* laomsguire.) Great, vast, prodigious; abundant. Coire is laomsgaire bàrr, *a dell with abundant crops,* i. e. *a grassy dell.—Macdon.* Written also *laomsgiorra.*

Laomsgaireachd, *s. f.* Abundance, abundantness; prodigiousness. See also **Laomsgiorrachd**.

Laomsgiorra, *a.* Great, vast, prodigious; abundant. Written also *laomsgair.*

Laomsgiorrachd, *s. f.* Greatness, prodigiousness; abundantness.

Laos-bhoc, -bhuic, *s. m.* A castrated goat, a wether goat. *N. pl.* laos-bhuic.

Làpach, aich, *s. f.* (*Ir. id.*) A marsh, a swamp, a bog, a puddle.

Làpach, *a.* (*Ir. id.*) Swampy, marshy, or boggy; skinny; benumbed; frost-bitten; inactive; awkward. Cha bu làpach an ceannard, *their chief was not inactive.—Macfar.* Neó-làpach sa chomhstri, *clever in the contest.—Id.*

Làpachadh, aidh, *s. m.* A benumbing; a becoming benumbed; a becoming swampy or marshy. Tha mo lamhan air làpachadh, *my hands have become benumbed.*

Làpachas, ais, *s m.* Swampiness, bogginess; benumbedness, a failing; a mistake.

Lapadan, ain, *s. m.* (*Ir. id.*) A species of sea-fish.—*Shaw.*

Lapadh, aidh, *s. m* (*Ir id*) A paw; a claw; a clumsy fist

Lapaich, *v. a* and *n.* Benumb, be frost-bitten; become frost-bitten. *Pret. a. id. Fut aff.* làpaìchidh Fear nach lapaich clachan meallain, *a man whom hail cannot benumb.*—*Macdon.*

Lapaichte, *p part* of lapaich Benumbed; frost-bitten Lamhan lapaichte, *benumbed hands.*

Làr, làir, *s. m* Ground; floor; earth; a ground floor; middle, centre Do thùineadh fo lar, *thy dwelling under ground*—*Oss Lod* Le aghaidh gu làr, *with his face to the earth*—*Stew Gen* Air làr, *on the floor, on the ground*, lar, *a centre*—*Shaw* Neamh is làr, *heaven and earth.*—*Sm* Mu làr, *lost, abolished*, cur mu làr, *abolition*
Ir. làr *Corn* lèr *W.* llawr *Arm* leur. *Bisc.* lurra, *ground*

Làrach, aich, *s m* (*Ir id*) The site of a building; a vestige; old ruins; a field of battle D' aos-làrach, *thine aged site*—*Oss Taura* Thuit an sgiath san làraich, *the shield fell in the field of battle*—*Oss Lod.*

Larach, aich, *s m* A filly—*Shaw.* *N pl* laraich.

Lar-bhrat, -bhrait, *s m* A floor-cloth; a carpet.

Larum, uim, *s m* (*Ir* and *Eng. id*) An alarm, a warning.

Larumach, *a* Alarming; giving an alarm or warning.

Las, *v a* and *n.* Light, kindle, flame; inflame, burn, blaze, gleam *Pret a.* las, *fut aff. a* lasaidh, *shall light* Las an teine, *kindle the fire*, las a choinneal, *light the candle*, las sòlas an anam na h-oigh, *joy kindled in the maiden's soul*—*Oss Lod*
Ir id. *Swed* lysa, *to light* *Sam* lachas, *inflame*, and lus, *burn.* *Lat* luceo, *to shine*

Lasach, *a* Loose, loosened, slack; not firm; *also*, fiery; inflammable. *Com* and *sup* lasaiche
Corn and *Arm* lausq *Ir* lasach *Lat. by met.* laxus *Eng* lax

Lasachadh, aidh, *s m.* A loosening, a slackening, a relieving; relief, ease, relaxation. Air lasachadh, *loosened*, tha na teudan air lasachadh, *the strings have become loose*, fhuair e lasachadh, *he got relief*, beagan lasachaidh, *some relief, some ease, some relaxation.*

Lasachadh, (a), *pr* of lasaich; which see

Lasadh, aidh, *s. m* (*Ir id*) A kindling, a flaming or inflaming, a lighting, as of fire, a gleaming, a blazing; flame, a blaze; a flush, a blush, lust, a lace. Lasadh na h-oidhche, *the flame of night, a beacon*—*Oss Derm* A cur lasadh na gruaidhibh, *giving a flush to her cheeks*—*Old Poem*

Lasag, aig, *s. f* (*dim* of lasadh) A little flame, a little blaze, a combustible substance; a little or scanty fire; a short fit of passion; a dry faggot. *N pl* lasagan.

Lasagach, *a* Combustible, blazing, passionate

Lasaich, *v a* and *n* Loosen, slacken; intermit; give over, relieve; ease *Pret a* lasaich, *loosened*, *fut aff a* lasaichidh, *shall loosen* Lasaich an cord, *slacken the rope*, nach lasaich thu? *wo'n't you intermit*, or *give over? Fut. pass* lasaichear, *shall be loosened*

Lasaichear, *fut. pass* of lasaich, which see.

Lasaichte, *p part* of lasaich Loosened, slackened, relieved.

Lasail, *a*, las-amhuil (*Ir. id*) Fiery, inflammable.

Lasair, *gen* lasair *and* lasrach, *s f* (*Ir id. W.* llasair, *a blue colour.*) A flame, a blaze; a flashy young fellow, a spark Mar lasair air scòrr, *like a flame on a rock*—*Oss Fing.* Lasair feirg, *a flame of anger.*—*Oss. Tem.* O chumhachd na lasrach, *from the power of the flame.*—*Stew. Is.*

Lasair-choille, *s. f.* A goldfinch; a woodpecker.—*Shaw* and *Macd.*

Lasair-leana, *s.* (*Ir. id*) Lesser spearwort; *ranunculus flammula.*

Lasan, ain, *s. m.* (*Ir. id.*) Anger, passion; a fit of passion; a flame of wrath.—*Sm.* and *Q B. ref*

Lasanta, *a*, *from* lasan. (*Ir. id*) Passionate, fiery.

Lasantachd, *s. f.* (*Ir id.*) Passionateness, fieriness; habitude to anger.—*Shaw.*

Lasarach, aich, *s m.* (*Ir id*) Flames, flashes of light.

Lasarach, *a* (*Ir. id.*) Flaming, burning, gleaming; combustible; like a flame; passionate Teine lasarach, *a flaming fire.*—*Stew N T.* *Com* and *sup* lasaraiche.

Lasarachail, *a* Flaming, burning, gleaming; combustible.

Lasarachd, *s. f.* (*from* lasair.) Combustibleness, a tendency to kindle or flame.

Lasaradh, **Lasartha**, *a.* Flaming, burning, gleaming.—*Stew Gen.*

Lasd, laisd, *s. m.* (*Ir. id.*) A ballast, a lading—*Shaw.*

Làsdach, *a.* (*Ir id.*) Lordly, saucy; imperious. *Com.* and *sup* lasdaiche. Gu lasdach, *saucily.*

Làsdachd, *s f* (*Ir. id.*) Lordliness, imperiousness; sauciness

Làsdail, *a* (*Ir. id*) Lordly, imperious; saucy. Gu lasdail, *imperiously*

Làsdalachd, *s f.* (*Ir. id*) Lordliness; imperiousness; sauciness.

Lasgair, *s m* (*Ir. id*) A fop, a young spark, a beau.

Lasgaireach, *a* (*Ir. id*) Foppish, beauish.

Lasgaireachd, *s. f.* (*Ir. id.*) Foppishness, beauishness.

Lasrach, *a*, *contr.* for lasarach; which see.

Last, *s* See **Lasd.**

Lastain, *s f.* (*Ir. id*) A hem, a fringe, an edge—*Shaw.*

Lasuchadh, aidh, *s. m* See **Lasachadh.**

Lasuich, *v a.* See **Lasaich.**

† **Lat**, *s m* (*Ir. id*) A foot

Lath, latha, *s. m.* A day; daylight; one day, on a certain day. *N. pl.* laithe, laithean, *and* lathachan, *days* Gun latha, gun léirsinn, *without daylight or vision.*—*Oss Duthona* Air mo luasgadh gu latha, *rocked until daylight.*—*Ull* Air làth àraidh, *on a certain day*—*Stew Gen.* Na h-uile làth, *every day*; h-uile làth riamh, *every single day*; gach dolach làth, *every other day.* Bha lath eil' ann, *we have seen another day.*—*G P* Làth-breith, *a birth-day.*—*Stew Gen.* Gu là na siorruidheachd, *for ever.*—*Stew. 2 Pet. ref* Làth-fheill-Bride, *Candlemas*, Làth-bealtuinn, *May-day*, Làth-lùnasd, *Lammas-day*, Lath samhnadh, *Hallow-day*, Lath nollaig, *Christmas*, Làth ceud fheill Mhuir, *Purification-day*, Làth nan uile naoimhe, *All-saints'-day*, Làth Càisg, *Easter-day*; Làth aisig Righ Tearlach a dhà, *Restoration-day*, Làth fhéill Eoin, *St. John's-day, 27th Dec*, Làth fhéill Eòin baiste, *St. John's-day, 24th June*, Làth breith Muir, *Mary's nativity*, La na Crois naoimhe, *the day of the Holy Cross*, Làth fhéill-Mhàrtainn, *Martinmas*, Làth-fheill Mhicheil, *Michaelmas-day*, am foillseachadh, *or*, lath féill an Righ, *Epiphany*; Làth Dhaibhidh an naoimh, *St David's-day*, Làth Mhuir, *Lady-day*, Làth na bliadhna ùr, *New-Year's-day*; Lath sheachnaidh na bliadhna, *the day of the week on which the third of May falls.* On this day a Highlander seldom begins any work which he wishes to finish with expedition and success.

† **Lath**, laith, *s m.* (*Ir. id.*) A youth; a champion; a dog.—*Shaw.*

Làthach, aich, *s. m.* (*Ir. id.*) Mud, mire, mortar, clay; sea-weed; sea-ware; stuff drifted to the shores of a sea or lake; a swampy place; a puddle. Gun làthach, *without mire.—Stew. O. T.* Post an làthach, *tramp the mortar.—Stew. Nah.*

Làthachail, *a.* (lathach-amhuil.) Muddy, marshy, puddly; full of sea-weed or sea-ware.

Lathachan, *n. pl.* of lath. More properly *laithean.*

Làthail, *a.* (lath-amhuil.) *Ir.* laethamhail. Daily, quotidian. Aran lathail, *daily bread.—Stew. Matt.*

Lathailt, *s. f.* (*Ir. id.*) Method, knack. Fhuair mi 'n lathailt air, *I have got the knack of it.*

Lathailteach, *a.* (*Ir. id.*) Methodical, having the method or knack of doing any thing; becoming.

Lathailteachd, *s. f.* (*Ir. id.*) Methodicalness; method; seemliness.

Lathair, *s. f.* (*Ir. id.*) A victory.—*Macd.*

Làthair, *s. f.* (*Ir. id.*) Presence; company. As bhur làthair, *from your presence, absent from you,—Stew. Cor.* Thig crith na 'r lathair air treun-fhir, *the strong shall tremble in your presence.—Oss. Duthona.* As mo lathair! *away! out of my presence!*

Làthair, *a.* and *adv.* Present; alive; remaining; surviving; at hand; near. Cha'n'eil e làthair, *he is not in life; he is not present.* Cha làthair e, *he is not alive.* Gun chrioman làthair, *without a morsel remaining.—Macint.* Thoir làthair *produce, bring to view,* or *put down before one.* Thug i làthair im, *she produced butter.—Stew. Jud.*

Lathaire, *s. f.* A thigh.—*Shaw.*

Làthaireach, *a.* (*Ir. id.*) Present.

Làthaireachd, *a.* (*Ir. id.*) Presence; company. Mo làthaireachd, *my presence.—Stew. Ex.* A lathaireachd chorporra, *his bodily presence.—Stew.* 1 *Cor.*

† **Lathar**, air, *s. m.* (*Ir. id.*) An assembly; a narrative; knowledge; strength; vigour; acquisition; strength; a hidden meaning; a secret; a mystery; *also, adverbially,* near.

Làth-leabhar, air, *s. m.* A diary, a journal, a day-book.

Lathrach, aich. See **Larach.**

Le, *prep.* (*Ir. id.*) With, together with, in company with; by; by means of; on the same side with; in possession of; down with, or along with, as on a stream. Le troighibh rùisgte, *with bare soles.—Oss. Derm.* Sìth le d' anam, *peace with thy soul.—Oss. Tem.* Thomhaiseadh le Diarmad an torc, *the boar was measured by Dermid.—Oss. Derm.* Le mnaoi, *by means of a woman.—Stew. Pro.* Le so, *by the way;* le do chead, *by your leave.*

Le denotes property or possession; as, iadsan is le Croisd, *they who are Christ's.—Stew. Gal.* Na dealbhan bu le h-athair, *the pictures that were her father's.—Stew. Gen.*

Le also denotes feeling or opinion; as, b' fhad le Seumas an làth, *James felt the day tedious.*

Leab, **Leaba.** See **Leabadh.**

Leabach, *a.* Awry; awkward, staring.

Leabadh, **Leabaidh**, *gen.* leapach *or* leapa, *s. f.* (*Ir. id.*) A bed, a couch; the channel of a river. *N. pl.* leapaiche *or* leapaichean. Air an leabadh chrè, *on the bed of clay.—Orr.* A leabadh dhoilleir, *its gloomy channel.—Oss. Duthona.* Leabadh chloimh, *a feather-bed;* leabadh chonnlaich, *a straw-bed;* leabadh fhraoich, *a heather-bed.* Leabadh lùthaidh, *a folding-bed.—Macd.* Leabadh luachrach, *a rush-bed;* leabadh thogalach, *a folding-bed;* leabadh mhuill, *a chaff-bed;* leabadh chùl-beinc, *a bed intended for the promiscuous repose of the members of a family and of guests.* It was formed by the cottage wall on one side, and by the trunk of a tree or a plank on the other, with a sufficient quantity of heath, fern, or straw, and some blankets.

Leabag, aig, *s. f.* (*Ir.* leabog *and* leabhag.) A flap; any thing that hangs broad and loose; the leaf of a door; a Loch Lomond flounder, the *Pleuronectes Leviniæ* of naturalists. Leabag chearr, *a sole. N. pl.* leabagan.

Leabagach, *a.* Flappy, hanging loose; having flaps; folding, as a door. Dorus leabagach, *a folding-door. Com.* and *sup.* leabagaiche.

Leabag-chearr, *s. f.* A soal.—*Shaw* and *Macd.*

Leabaidh, *s. f.* See **Leabadh.**

Leabhadh, aidh, *s. m.* Reading. More properly *leughadh;* which see.

Leabhadh, aidh, *s. m.* A generation, a race.

Leabhar, *a.* (*Ir. id. Arm.* leffr.) Long; too long; trailing, as clothes; clumsy; tawdry. Còt leabhar, *a clumsy coat; com.* and *sup.* liuibhre.

Leabhar, air, *s. m.* (*Ir. id.*) A book, a volume. *N. pl.* leabhraichean, *books.* Leabhar ùrnuigh, *a prayer-book;* leabhar pòc, *a pocket-book;* an leabhar dearg, *the red-book;*—an old manuscript copy of the poems of Ossian, covered with red leather, which was given to Macpherson, the translator of Ossian, by Macdonald of Cnoidart; another MS. of the same description and name, was given by Macmhuirich, an Hebridean bard.

Lat. liber. *Fr.* livre. *Corn.* lifir *and* lyfir. *W.* llyvyr. *Arm.* levvr. In *Vannes, they say* leuar. *Bisc.* liburrua. *Ir.* leabhar.

Leabhar-cheangladair, *s. m.* A bookbinder.

Leabhair-cheangladh, aidh, *s. m.* Bookbinding.

Leabhar-cheanglair, *s. m.* A bookbinder. *N. pl.* leabhar-cheanglairean.

Leabhar-chlàr, -chlàir. Pasteboard; the boards of a book.—*Shaw.*

Leabhar-chòir, *s. f.* A copyright.

Leabhar-lann, -lainn, *s. m.* (*Ir. id.*) A library. *N. pl.* leabhar-lainn.

Leabhar-thrath-eachdraidh, *s. m.* A chronicle; a minute-book.—*Stew.* 1 *K. ref.*

Leabhrach, *a.* (*Ir. id.*) Bookish; full of books.

Leabhragan, ain, *s. m.* (*Ir. id.*) A library. *N. pl.* leabhragain.

Leabhraichean, *n. pl.* of leabhar. Books, volumes.

Leabhran, ain, *dim.* of leabhar. (*Ir. id.*) A little book; a manual. Contracted for *leabharan.* Leabhran fosgailte, *a little book open.—Stew. Rev.*

Leab-luidhe, *s. f.* Confinement to bed; a lying in bed.

Leab-luidheach, *a.* Bed-rid.

† **Leac**, *v. a.* Flay; destroy.—*Shaw.*

Leac, lic, *s. f.* A flag, a flat stone, a slab; a tomb-stone; a slate; a cheek; a declivity; a steep; a plate, as of metal. Fhliuch a dheur-shuil an leac, *his tearful eye bedewed the flag.—Ull.* Cha chàirich na seòid a leac, *the heroes shall not raise his tomb-stone.—Oss. Fin. and Lor.* Air leac Chromla, *on the steep of Cromla.—Id.* Og mhnaoi a b' aillidh leac, *a virgin of the fairest cheeks.—Id.* Mhaolaich an leac a bàrr, *the plate blunted its point.—Mac Lach.* Leac an teallaich, *the hearth-stone.* Leac an teintein, *the hearth.—Stew. Gen.* Leac eidhe, *a flake of ice;* leac eidhre, *a flake of ice;* the *Irish* say, leac oidhre. Leac lighe, *a grave-stone;* leac-shuaine, *a tile.*

Ir. leac. *Corn.* lech. *Arm.* lech. *W.* lhech, *a flag. Lat.* † lecchi, *a jaw-bone.*

Leacach, *a.* Abounding in flags or slabs; slaty; having declivities; having large cheeks; flat. Sròn leacach, *a flat nose.—Stew. Lev.*

Leacach, aich, *s. m.* The side of a hill.—*Macd.*

Leacachadh, aidh, *s. m.* A paving with flags or slabs of stone.

Leacadan, ain, *s. m.* A chin-cloth; a child's bib.

Leacadh, aidh, *s. m.* Destroying; a laying with flags.

Leacag, aig, *s. f.* (*dim.* leac.) A little flag; a slate. *N. pl.* leacagan.

Leacagach, *a.* Abounding in little flags or slates.

Leacaich, *v. a.* Pave with flags. *Pret. a.* leacaich; *fut. aff. a.* leacaichidh.

Leacaichte, *p. part.* of leacaich. Flagged, paved with flags.

Leacainn, **Leacuinn**, *s. f.* (*Ir.* leacain.) The side of a hill; a steep green surface; steep shelvy ground; a cheek. Lom gach leacainn, *the bare surface of each hill-side.—Macfar.* Sruth na leacainn, *the stream of the mountain-side.—Oss. Duth.* *N. pl.* leacainnean.

Leacainneach, *a.* Having steep surfaces; hilly; having large cheeks.

Leacan, ain, *s. m.* (*dim.* leac.) A little flag; *also*, wall pennywort.

Leacanta, *a.* Stiff; rigid; precise; exact; ceremonious; punctilious; neat.—*Macd.* Gu leacanta, *rigidly.*

Leacantachd, *s. f.* Stiffness; rigidness; preciseness; ceremoniousness; exactness; punctiliousness; neatness. Bheachdaich e le leacantachd, *he remarked with exactness.—Old Song.*

Leachd, *s. f.* See **Leac**.

Leachdach, *a.* See **Leacach**.

Leachdainn, **Leachduinn**, *s. f.* See **Leacainn**.

† **Leacht**, *s. f.* (*Ir. id.* *Lat.* lect-um *and* lect-io.) A lesson.

Leachtan, ain, *s. m.* (*Ir. id.*) A lecture; a lesson.—*Shaw.*

Leac-lighe, *s. f.* A grave-stone, a tomb-stone, a monumental slab.

Leac-ruiteach, *a.* Ruddy-cheeked. Ribhinn leac-ruiteach, ròsach, *a rosy, ruddy-cheeked girl.—Moladh Mhòraig.*

Leac-shuaine. A tile. Gabh leac-shuaine, *take a tile.—Stew. Ezek.* *N. pl.* lic-shuaine.

Leacta, *part.* Flagged, paved with flags or slabs.

Leac-uaighe, *s. f.* A grave-stone, a tomb-stone.

Leac-urlar, air, *s. m.* A paved floor; a pavement.—*Stew. Eth.*

Lead, *s. m.* Breadth. See **Leud**.

Leadain, *gen. sing.* and *n. pl.* of leadan.

Leadair, *v. a.* Abuse; tear; mangle; massacre; maim.

Leadairt, *s. f.* An abusing; a tearing; a mangling; a maiming; a massacring; a massacre. Air an leadairt le geur-lainn, *mangled with sharp swords.—Old Poem.* Ri leadairt chorp, *massacring bodies.—Id.*

Leadairt, *v. a.* Abuse; tear; mangle; maim; massacre.

Leadan, ain, *s. m.* (*Ir. id.*) Notes in music; litany; a head of hair; a ringlet; teasel, the *dipsacus fullonum* of botanists. A seinn' mo leadan, *singing my notes.—Old Song.* *N. pl.* leadain.

Leadanach, *a.* Musical; having ringlets; precise; belonging to the litany.

Leadan-liosda, *a.* Burdock.—*Shaw.*

Leadarra, *a.* Sharp; mangling; *also*, elegant. Gu leadarra, *elegantly.*

Leag, *v. a.* More frequently written *leig*; which see.

Leagadh, aidh, *s. m.* (*Ir. id.*) A falling; a fall; a throwing down. Roimh leagadh, *before a fall.—Stew. Pro.*

Leagaid, *s. m.* A legate; an offering.

Leagail. See **Leigeil**.

Leagh, *v. a.* (*Ir. id.*) Melt, dissolve, fuse, thaw; smelt. *Pret. a.* leagh, *melted*; *fut. aff. a.* leaghaidh, *shall melt.* Leagh mo chridhe, *my heart melted.—Orr.* Leaghaidh sneachd na shruthaibh, *snow will dissolve in streams.—Macfar.*

Leaghach, *a.* (*Ir. id.*) Soluble; colliquent.—*Shaw.*

† **Leaghad**, aid, *s. m.* A bandage, a band.

Leaghadair, *s. m.* (*from* leagh.) A melter; a smelter; a founder.

Leaghadaireachd, *s. f.* A melting; a smelting; a foundery.

Leaghadh, aidh, *s. m.* A dissolving or melting.

Leaghan, ain, *s. m.* (*Ir. id.*) Liquor, a liquid.

Leaghta, *p. part.* of leagh. Melted, dissolved. An iomhaigh leaghta, *the molten image.—Stew. Hab.*

Leaghtach, *a.* Dissolvent, colliquent, soluble.

Leaglaidh, *s. pl.* (*Ir. id.*) Rushes.—*Shaw.*

Leagta, *p. part.* of leag *or* leig. Let fall; thrown down; overthrown; overturned; felled; resolved; bent on. Leagta air dol maille ri, *resolved on going with her.—Stew. Ruth, ref.*

Lealg, *v. a.* Lick.

Lealgadh, aidh, *s. m.* Licking.

Leam, *comp. pron.* (*Ir. id.*) *contr. for* le mi. With me, in my company, by me; on my side, in my favour, in my mind or opinion. Marbhar leam e, *he will be killed by me*; am bi thu leam? *will you be on my side?* Is caomh leam ur dàn, *I deem your strain sweet.—Oss. Fin. and Lor.* Is cuimhne leam an laoch, *I remember the warrior.—Ull.* Leam fèin, *alone.—Id.* Leam is leat, *irresolute; fickle.—Sm.* and *Mac Lach.* Is nàr leam, *I am ashamed*; is maith leam e, *I am glad of it*; their leam, *methinks*; is coma leam e, *I do not like him* or *it*; *I am indifferent about him* or *it.*

Leam-leat, *s.* and *a.* Deceit; fickleness; irresolution; a person; irresolute; fickle.—*Sm.* and *Mac Lach.* Teanga leam-leat, *a deceitful tongue*; fear leam-leat, *a fickle fellow.*

† **Leamh**, leimh, *s. m.* (*Ir. id.*) A rower; an elm; an oar.

Leamh, *a.* (*Ir.* leamh.) Importunate, troublesome; greedy; saucy; simple, foolish; insipid; flattering; mealy-mouthed; jejune; raw. Blas leamh, *an insipid taste.* *Ir.* blas leamh.

Leamhach, *a.* Importunate; greedy; troublesome; saucy; simple; foolish; flattering; insipid to the taste.

Leamhachas, ais, *s. m. from* leamh. (*Ir. id.*) Importunateness; greediness; foolishness; insipidness; sauciness.—*Macd.*

Leamhan, ain, *s. m.* (*Ir. id.* *W.* lhuyven.) Elm; the elm tree; the inner rind of a tree: a rower; a moth; a night butterfly. Leamhan bog, *the horn-beam tree*; the *carpinus* of naturalists.

Leamhar, *a.* More properly *leabhar*; which see.

Leamh-dhàn, *a.* Forward; insolent; importunate; foolhardy. Gu leamh-dhàn, *forwardly.*

Leamh-dhànachd, *s. f.* Forwardness; vulgar insolence; importunateness; fool-hardiness.—*Shaw.*

Leamh-dhànadas, ais, *s. m.* See **Leamh-dhànachd**.

Leamh-ghaire, *s.* (*Ir. id.*) A smile.

Leamh-lachd, *s. f.* (leamh, *insipid*; lachd, *milk.* *Ir. id.*) Sweet milk; insipid milk.

Leamhnachadh, aidh, *s. m.* A stopping.—*Shaw.* Growing insipid.

Leamhnachd, *s. f.* Sweet milk; a corruption of *leamh-lachd*; which see.

Leamhnachd, *s. f.* Common tormentil, septfoil; the *tormentilla erecta* of botanists.

Leamhnaire, *s. m.* (*Ir. id.*) Coyness, bashfulness; foolish shame.

Leamh-narach, *a.* Coy, bashful. Gu léamh-nàrach, *coyly.*

Leamhrachdan, **Leamhragan**, ain, *s. m.* A stye or pimple on the verge of the eyelids.

Leamsa, *emphatic form* of leam. B' annsa leamsa dol eug, *I would gladly die.*—*Ull.* See **Leam.**

† **Lean**, *s. m.* (*Ir. id.*) Sorrow; ruin.—*Shaw.*

Lean, léin, *s. m.* (*Ir. id.*) A meadow; swampy ground.

Lean, *v. a.* (*Ir. id.*) Follow; adhere; pursue; imitate; trace. *Pret. a.* lean; *fut. aff. a.* leanaidh, *shall follow.* Lean mi thar muir is tìr thu, *I followed thee over sea and land.*—*Old Song.* Ri lic reòta lean a sàil, *its foot adhered to an ice-cold flag.*—*Oss. Derm.* Lean am fòghnan, *pursue the thistledown.*—*Oss. Gaul.*

Lean, *v. a.* Sprain. See **Leun.**

Leanabachd, *s. f.* See **Leanabaidheachd.**

Leanabaidh, *a., from* leanabh. (*Ir.* leanabaidhe.) Childish; infantile; pusillanimous. Nithe leanabaidh, *childish things.*—*Stew.* 1 *Cor.*

Leanabaidheachd, *s. f.* (*from* leanabh.) Childishness; pusillanimousness; nonage.

Leanabail, *a.* (leanabh-amhuil.) Childish, infantile; pusillanimous.

Leanabalachd, *s. f.* Childishness, nonage.

Leanaban, ain, *s. m.* (*Ir. id.*) A little child; a favourite child; a petted child; a spoiled child. M' aon leanaban, *my only child.*—*Mac Lach.* *N. pl.* leanabain.

Leanabanach, *a.* Childish, pucrile; infantile, infantine; pusillanimous; spoiled or petted, as a child. Gu leanabanach, *childishly.* *Com.* and *sup.* leanabaiche.

Leanabanachd, *s. f.* Childishness; puerility; pusillanimousness; nonage, childhood. Leanabanachd agus òige, *childhood and youth.*—*Stew. Ecc.*

Leanabanta, *a.* Childish, infantile. Gu leanabanta, *childishly.*

Leanabas, ais, *s. m.* Childhood, infancy.—*Macd.* Childish; pusillanimous. O t-aois leanabais, *from thy childhood.*—*Old Song.*

Leanabh, *gen.* leinibh, *s. m.* (*Bisc.* leinu.) A child, an infant. Theich an leanabh, *the child fled.*—*Orr.* Anam an leinibh, *the soul of the child.*—*Stew.* 1 *K.* Leanabh do ghaòil, *the infant of thy affection.*—*Oss. Gaul.* Leanabh altruim, *a foster-child.* Leanabh cìche, *a babe.*—*Macfar.* Leanabh diolain, *a bastard child.* Leanabh liughach, *a doll.*—*Shaw.* Leanabh mic, *a man-child;* leanabh nighinne, *a woman-child;* an leanabh nach foghlum thu ri do ghlùn, cha 'n fhoghlum thu ri d' chluais, *the child whom you tutor not at your knee, you cannot tutor when he reaches your ear; betwixt three and thirteen, bend the twig while 'tis green.*—*G. P.*

Leanabhan. See **Leanaban.**

Leanabuidh, *a.* See **Leanabaidh.**

Leanabuidheachd, *s. f.* See **Leanabaidheachd.**

Leanachd, *s. f.* A following; an adhering or sticking close to; a pursuing; a pursuit; adherence.

Leanachd, (a), *pr. part.* of lean. Following; adhering; pursuing. Ag am leanachd, *following me;* ag a leanachd, *following her;* ag an leanachd, *following them.*

Leanadar, an Irish inflection of *lean.* They followed.

Leanag, aig, *s. f.* A little plain or meadow. *N. pl.* lèanagan.

Leanail, *s. f.* See **Leanailt.**

Leanailt, *s. f.* A pursuing, a following; pursuit; an adhering; adherence. Ri leanailt ruaig, *following up the pursuit.*—*Old Song.*

Leanailteach, *a.* (*Ir. id.*) Adhering; following; adhesive; clammy; persevering; incessant. Gach peacadh leanailteach, *each adhering sin.*—*Sm.* Uisge leanailteach, *incessant rain;* leanailteach air obair, *persevering at work.*

Leanailteachd, *s. f.* Adhesiveness; adherence; perseverance; incessantness.

Leanamhain, *s.* (*Ir. id.*) Goods; substance; a spouse, a sweetheart; a pet; a concubine.

Leanar, *fut. pass.* of lean. Shall be followed. See **Lean.**

Leanartach, aich, *s. m.* The herb tormentil, or septfoil.—*Shaw.*

Lean-ghobhrag, aig, *s. f.* A snipe.—*Shaw.*

Leanmhuinn, *s. f.* (*Ir.* leanamhuin.) A following, a pursuing, a tracing; a pursuit; adherence; *rarely,* goods; substance. Luchd leanmhuinn, *followers, pursuers.*

Leanmhuinn, (a), *pres. part.* of lean. Following, pursuing, adhering, tracing. A leanmhuinn diomhanasa, *following vanities.*—*Stew. G. B.* Ag am leanmhuinn, *following me.*

Leanmhuinneach, *a.* Following, adhering, pursuing, tracing; adhesive; clammy; glutinous; *also, substantively,* a follower, an adherer.

Leanmhuinneachd, *s. f.* (*from* lean.) Adherance; adhesiveness; incessantness.

Leann, *s. m.* (*Ir. id.*) A sore; an ulcer; the humours of the body; *rarely,* a coarse cassock; a coat of mail. Leann-dubh, *melancholy.* *N. pl.* leanntan. Written also *lionn.*

Leann, leanna, *s. m.* (*Ir. id. W.* llyn.) Beer; ale. Deoch leanna, *a drink of beer or ale;* tigh-leanna, *an alehouse;* leann caol, *small beer;* leann làidir, *strong ale;* leann racadail, *ginger beer;* leann loisgte, *dregs from distilling whisky; dregs from which ale is brewed.*

Leannach, **Leannachadh**, aidh, *s. m.* Inflammation; suppuration; ulceration; a boil; an ulcer. Is leannachadh a th'ann, *it is an inflammation.*—*Stew. Lev.*

Leannachail, *a.* Ulcerous; suppurating; tending to suppuration; causing ulceration or suppuration; like an ulcer.

Leannaich, *v. n.* (*from* leann.) Suppurate; ulcerate. *Pret. a.* leannaich, *suppurated; fut. aff. a.* leannaichidh, *shall suppurate.*

Leannain, *gen. sing.* and *n. pl.* of leannan; which see.

Leannair, *s. m.* (*Ir. id.*) A brewer.

Leannan, ain, *s. m.* (*Ir.* leanan.) A mistress, a sweetheart, a concubine; *also,* a gallant; a beloved person; a pet; a darling. Leannan 'athar, *his father's concubine.*—*Stew. Gen.* Is cian mo leannan, *far away is my beloved.*—*Oss.* Leannan sìth, *a familiar spirit.*—*Stew. Deut.* *N. pl.* leannain.

Leannanach, *a.* Gallant; intriguing; wanton. *Com.* and *sup.* leannanaiche.

Leannanachd, *s. f.* (*from* leannan.) Gallantry; intriguing; courting; whoring; fornication; wantonness.—*Macint.* Ri leannanachd, *intriguing, making love.*

Leannan-sìth, *s. m.* A familiar spirit.—*Stew. Lev.* and *Deut.*

Leanndan. See **Leanntan.**

Leann-dubh, *s. m.* Melancholy; megrims. Leann-dubh air mo chridhe, *melancholy at my heart.*—*G. P.*

Leannra, **Leannradh**, aidh, *s. m.* A kind of fat soup; aleberry; sauce; condiment.

Leanntan, *s. pl.* Passions; the humours; the vapours.

Leanntras, ais, *s. m.* The vapours; the humours of the body.

Leantuinn, *s. f.* (*from* lean.) A following, a pursuing; an adhering; a tracing; a pursuit; adherence; imitation.

Leantuinn, (a), *pr. part.* of lean. Following, pursuing, tracing, adhering, imitating. Ag am leantuinn, *following me;* ag an leantuinn, *following them.*

Leapach, *gen. sing.* of leabadh.

Leapachan, ain, *s. m.* A bed-fellow.

Leapaichean, *n. pl.* of leabadh. Beds, couches.

† Lear, *a.* (*Ir. id.*) Clear; discernible. Now written *léir.*

Lear, *s. f.* (*Ir. id.*) The sea; the surface of the sea. Bhuail i gu lear, *she made towards the sea.—Orr.* Clos na min-lear uaine, *the repose of the smooth green sea.—Oss. Manos.*

Learach, *s.* See Leathar.

Learag, aig, *s. f.* A larch-tree; larch.

† Lear-dhromain, *s. m.* (*Ir. id.*) The ridge of a hill.—*Shaw.*

Learg, leirg, *s. f.* The rain-goose; a grey-coloured sea-fowl, which nestles near the water, and never rises during incubation.—*Shaw. Also,* a species of cormorant.

Learg, leirg, *s. f.* (*Ir. id.*) A sloping green or green slope; a little eminence; a plain field; *rarely,* a beaten path. Dearrsa air learg ciar, *a sunbeam on a dusky field.—Oss.*

Leargach, *a.* (*Ir. id.*) Steep; sloping; having many steeps or slopes.

Leargaidh, *s. f.* (*Ir. id.*) The slope of a hill; the side of any high eminence.

Leargann, ainn, *s. f.* (*from* learg.) A small sloping green field; the side of a green hill; steep pasture ground; the slope of a country side. Air taobh gach leargainn, *on every green hill-side.—Macint.*

Leargainneach, *a.* Sloping; steep; having steep pasture ground.

Leargair, *s. m.* A sluggard; a sailor.

Learguinn, *s. f.* See Leargainn.

Lear-mhadadh, aidh, *s. m.* (*Ir. id.*) A dog-fish. *N. pl.* learg-mhadraidh.

Lear-thaod, aoid, *s. m.* A spring-tide.

Lear-thoid, *s. m.* A football.

Lear-uinnean, ein, *s. m.* (*Ir. id.*) A sea-onion; a squill.

Leas, *s. f.* A flame; a spot; a blister. See Leus.

† Leas, *s. f.* A motive, a reason, a cause.—*Shaw.*

Leas, *s. m.* (*W.* lles. *Corn.* les. *Ir.* leas.) Good; improvement; benefit; *also,* reason, motive; *adjectively,* proper, fit. Cha ruig mi leas, *I need not;* cha ruig thu leas, *you need not.* Cha leas codal gu moch, *it is not fit to sleep till morn.—Fingalian Poem.* Is leas dhomh, *I ought.*

Leasach, aich, *s. m.* Runnet. Baigean leasaich, *a runnet-bag.*

Leasach, *a.* See Leusach.

Leasachadh, aidh, *s. m.* (*Ir.* leasughadh.) An improving, a benefiting; an improvement, amendment, amelioration; repair; correction. Chum leasachaidh, *for correction.—Stew. Tim.*

Leasachadh, (a), *pr. part.* of leasaich. Improving; amending, repairing, correcting.

Leasachail, *a.* Improvable; epispastic, escharotic.—*Shaw.*

Leasaich, *v. a.* and *n., from* leas. (*Ir.* leasuigh.) Improve; correct; rectify; repair; renew; manure. *Pret. a.* leasaich, *improved; fut. aff. a.* leasaichidh, *shall improve; fut. pass.* leasaichear. Leasaich do bheusan; *correct your morals;* leasaich an eibhle, *put fuel on the fire;* a bhean leasaich an stòp, *the woman who refilled the pot* or *tankard.—Old Song.*

Leasaichte, *p. part.* of leasaich. Improved, corrected, repaired; manured; *also,* runnetted, as milk.

Leas-ainm, *s. m.* (*Ir. id. Arm.* leshanv, *a surname.*) A nickname. *N. pl.* leas-ainmean.

Leas-ainmeach, *a.* (*Ir. id.*) Apt to give nicknames.

Leasan, ain, *s. m.* (*Fr.* leçon. *Arm.* lessen.) A lesson. *N. pl.* leasain.

Leas-athair, -athar, *s. m.* (*Ir. id.*) A step-father. *N. pl.* leas-aithrichean; *d. pl.* leas-aithrichibh.

Leas-bhrathair, *s. m.* A step-brother.—*Shaw.*

† Leasg, *s. f.* A hood; a rod; a spot of ground.

Leasg, *a.* Lazy, slothful; inactive, sluggish; loath. Leasg ann an gnothuichibh, *slothful in business.—Stew. Rom.* Cha leasg leam sgriobhadh, *I am not loath to write.—Stew. Phil.* Is leasg leam éiridh, *I am loath to rise. Com.* and *sup.* leisge.

W. llesg, *feeble. Ir.* leasg, *lazy. Germ.* leaseg. *Pers.* las *and* lase. *Hung.* lassan. *Teut.* lazzen.

Leas-ingean, -inginn, *s. f.* (*Ir. id.*) A step-daughter.

† Leas-luan, ain, *s. m.* (*Ir. id.*) A step-son.—*Shaw.*

Leas-luidhe, *s. f.* (*Ir. id.*) A reclining; a leaning.

Leas-mhac, -mhic, *s. m.* (*Ir. id.*) A step-son. *N. pl.* leas-mhic; *d. pl.* leas-mhacaibh.

Leas-mhathair, -mhathar, *s. f.* (*Ir. id.*) A step-mother. *N. pl.* leas-mhathraichean; *d. pl.* leas-mhathairichibh. Cha 'n oil leam cnead mo leas-mhathar, *I pity not the sob of my step-mother.—G. P.*

Leas-mhursaid, *s. f.* (*Ir. id.*) A gallon.—*Shaw.*

Leas-nighean, -nighinn, *s. f.* A step-daughter. *N. pl.* leas-nigheanan.

Leas-phiuthair, *s. f.* A step-sister. *N. pl.* leas-pheathraichean.

Leasrach, *s.* See Leasradh.

Leasradh, aidh, *s. m.* (*Arm.* lezron. *Ir.* leasra.) The thigh; the loins. *N. pl.* leasraidh. Thig righre o d' leasraidh, *kings will come from thy loins.—Stew. Gen.*

Leastair, *s. m.* An arrow-maker. *N. pl.* leastairean.

Leastaireachd, *s. f.* The occupation of an arrow-maker.

† Leastar, air, *s. m.* (*Ir. id.*) The furniture of a house; the vessels of a house; stale butter.

Leastar, air, *s. m.* (*Arm.* and *Corn.* leste. *Ir.* leastar.) A small boat; a cup; a vessel.

Hence the Greek λῃστρικοι (lestrikoi), *pirates;* and also Λαιστρύγονες, *the Lestrigons,* whom the poets of antiquity describe as cannibals, but who were in fact barbarous and rapacious pirates, infesting the Sicilian seas. Being born and brought up on board their vessels, they were suitably denominated λαιστρύγονες (lestrygones), i. e. *leastar-gin,* the race of ships. Hence it is evident that the Celtic language was once spoken in Greece, Italy, and Sicily.—See also *Malcolm's Antiquities.*

Leasuich, *v. a.* See Leasaich.

Leat, *com. prep.* With thee; by thee; to thee; along with thee; in thine opinion or estimation; in thy favour; you, yours. Luidhinn sinnte leat, *I would lie stretched with thee.—Ull.* Bithidh mi leat, *I will be with you.* Ciod their leat? *what think you?* Leam is leat, *irresolute; fickle, deceitful.—Sm.* and *Mac Lach.* An leat so? *is this yours?* So leat, *here's to you; here is your health.* Cha téid sin leat, *that will not succeed with you.* Coma leat e, *never heed him* or *it.*

Leath, *s.* Half. More frequently written *leth;* which see.

Leatha, *com. pron.* With her; by her; along with her; in her opinion; in her favour; hers. Gu luidhe leatha, *to lie with her.—Stew. Gen.*

Leathad, aid, *s. m.* (*perhaps* leth-fhad.) A declivity; a slope. Leathad nam beann, *the declivity of the hills.—Oss. Fing.* Ri leathad, *downwards, down hill;* a dol ri leathad, *going down hill;* cha lugha uchdach na leathad, *up hill is no longer than down hill.—G. P.*

Leathag, aig, *s. f.* The fish called plaice.

Leathann, *a.* Broad; spacious. Do sgiath leathann, *thy broad shield. Com.* and *sup.* leithne, *broader, broadest.* Ni 's leithne na 'n fhairge, *broader than the sea.*
W. lhydan. *Corn.* leden. *Arm.* ledan.

Leathagan, ain, *s. m.* Tangle, dilse.

Leathan ri leathan. A rule observed by most Gaelic and Irish writers. It prescribes that two vowels, contributing to form two different syllables, should both of them be of the same class of broad or of small vowels; as, *deànta*, and not *deante*, done.

Leathar, air, *s. m.* Leather; a hide. Leathar fionnta an daimh òig, *the hairy hide of a young ox.—Mac Lach.*
Dan. laer. *Arm.* ledr. *Teut.* lader *and* leer. *Sax.* lether. *Du.* leer. *Eng.* leather. *Also, Heb.* leor, *the skin.*

Leathrach, aich, *s.* Leather. Brògan leathraich, *leather shoes.*

Leathsa, *comp. pròn. (emph. form of* leath.) Hers; with her; in her favour. Is leathsa so, *this is hers;* tha mi leathsa, *I am on her side.*

Leatrom, uim, *s. m.* Weight, burden; grievance; pregnancy. Gach leatrom, *each weight.—Sm.*

Leatromach, *a.* Pregnant; burdensome. Dh' fhas i leatromach, *she became pregnant.—Stew. Gen. ref.* Written also *leth-tromach;* which see.

Le chéile, *adv.* Together. Dh' fhalbh iad le chéile, *they went away together.*

† **Leibeann**, inn, *s. m.* (*Ir. id.*) A long stride; a stretch. —*Shaw.*

Leibh. See **Libh.**

† **Leibheann**, einn, *s. f.* (*Ir. id.*) The deck of a ship; a scaffold, a gallery; the side of a hill.—*Shaw.*

Leibhitheach, ich, *s. m.* A Levite. *N. pl.* Leibhithich.

Leibhitheachail, *a.* Levitical.

Leibideach, *a.* Awkward; tawdry; shabby; vile; long-legged. Gu leibideach, *awkwardly.*

Leibideachd, *s. f.* Awkwardness; tawdriness; shabbiness.

Léic, leice, *s. f.* (*Ir. id.*) Neglect.—*Shaw.*

Leiceanta, *a.* (*Ir. id.*) Exact; neat; precise; elegant. Gu leiceanta, *precisely.*

Leiceantachd, *s. f.* (*Ir. id.*) Exactness; neatness; preciseness; elegance.

Leiceas, eis, *s. f.* A leek; leeks.—*Stew. Num.*

† **Leid**, *s. f.* A longing desire.

Leidig. See **Léidinn.**

Léidinn, *s. f.* A convoy for a short way.

Léidinn, *v. a.* Convoy, escort for a part of a journey.

Léig, *s. f.* (*Ir. id.*) A jewel, a gem; a league.—*Macd.* A lake in Ireland, so called by the Fingalian bards; *also*, the *gen. sing.* of leug; which see.

Leig, leige, *s. f.* (*Lat.* ligo.) A spade, a mattock.

Leig, *v. a.* Let fall; overturn; lay; place; lower, diminish. *Pret. a.* leig; *fut. aff. a.* leighidh. Leig as, *let go, loosen, set free;* leig an gunna, *fire the gun;* leig urchair, *fire a shot;* leig chead da, *let him alone;* leig a glaodh as, *he uttered a cry;* leig gu ràidhe, *refer, appeal, submit to arbitration;* leig taic, *lean;* leig cudthrom, *lean.—Stew. Heb.* Leig dhiot, *give over, cease.—Stew. Pro.* Leig sìos, *diminish, lower, lessen, let down.—Stew. Ex.* Leig ris, *discover; expose* or *make bare; acknowledge.* Leigidh mi ris, *I will discover.—Stew. Mic.* Leig bunaite, *lay a foundation;* leig d' anail, *rest, draw your breath;* leigibh bhur n-anail, *rest yourselves.—Stew. Gen.* Gun leigeadh Dia! *God grant!* Nar leigeadh Dia! *God forbid!*
When the preposition, simple or compounded, follows *leig*, it signifies *to permit.* Leig leis, *let him alone; permit him.* Leigidh mi sin leat, *I will allow you that; I will make that concession to you.* Leig ort, *let on thee; pretend.* Leig ort bhi tinn, *pretend to be sick.—Stew.* 2 *Sam.*
Sax. leegan. *Du.* leg. *Germ.* ligen, *lie. Goth.* ligan. *Belgic*, liggen *and* liggau. *Ir.* lig, *permit.*

Leigeadh, eidh, *s. m.* A letting; a letting down; a throwing down. Leigeadh na luaidhe, *a sounding.—Stew. Acts.*

Léigeas, eis, *s. f.* A leek; leeks.

Leigeil, *s. f.* A throwing down; a lowering; a letting fall; an overturn.

Leigeil, (a), *pr. part.* of leig.

Leigh, *s. m.* (*Ir.* liagh. *Dan.* laege. *Germ.* lech.) A physician. Feum air leigh, *need for a physician.—Stew. Matt. N. pl.* leighean.

Leigheadair, *s. m.* A pharmacopolist.

Leigheadaireachd, *s. f.* Pharmacy.

Leighean, ein, *s. m.* Instruction; erudition.—*Shaw.* Leighean spiosraidh, *spiceries.—Stew. Gen.*

Leigheanta, *a.* (*Ir. id.*) Proficient.

Leigheas, eis, *s. m.* (*Ir. id.*) A cure, a salve or medicine; a healing. Leighèas a dheanamh, *to work a cure; to heal. —Stew. Acts.*

Leigheasach, *a.* (*from* leigheas.) Medicinal; healing.

Leigheasaiche, *s. m.* A physician.

Leighis, *v. a.* Cure, heal; remedy. *Pret. a.* leighis, *cured; fut. aff. a.* leighisidh, *shall cure; fut. pass.* leighisear, *shall be cured.*

Leighiste, *p. part.* of leighis.

Leigh-lann, -lainn, *s. m.* A dispensary; an apothecary's shop.

Leigh-loisg, *v. a.* Cauterise.

Leigh-losgadh, aidh, *s. m.* A cautery; a caustic; a cauterising.

Léigis, *s. f.* A leek; leeks.

Léigiseach, *a.* Abounding in leeks; like leeks.

Leigte, *p. part.* of leig. Overturned; lowered; diminished.

Leigiun, uin, *s. m.* (*Ir. id.*) A legion.

Leim. See **Leum.**

Leimhe, *s. f.* Simplicity; folly; importunity.

Léin, léine, *s. f.* (*Ir. id. Lat.* læna, *the soldier's cloak.*) A shirt; a shift, a smock; a shroud. Tha e as a léin, *he has his coat off; he has nothing on but his shirt.* Léin iochdar, *an under-shirt;* lèin aifrionn, *a surplice. N. pl.* léintean, *shirts.* Gun chiste, gun léintean, *without coffins or shrouds.—Roy Stewart.* Léin anairt, *a linen shirt;* léin thuilinn, *a shirt of twilled linen.*

Léin-croich, *s. f.* A saffron shirt or mantle, so called from its being dyed with saffron.

This mantle was worn in former times by people of rank among the Gael, especially in the western isles. It was an upper garment, and consisted of twenty-four ells, tied round the middle by a belt, and reaching below the knees. A still more ancient dress was the *arrasaid* or *fearrasaid*, a woman's garment, which was tied round the waist, and fastened in front with a silver or brass buckle, and hung loosely to the ancle. It was a white plaid, with small stripes of black, blue, and red. See **Gaidheal.**

Leinibh, *gen.* and *voc. sing.* of leanabh. A leinibh chaoimh! *thou gentle child!—Orr.*

Leinibh luasgadh, aidh, *s. m.* A rocking, as of a cradle.

Leinn, *comp. pron.*, *for* le sinn. (*Ir.* linn.) With us, by us, to us; in our favour, on our side; ours. Thig leinn a Chrimòra! *come with us, Crimora!—Ull.* B' aithreach leinn, *it seemed strange to us.—Id.* An saibhreas so is leinn féin e, *these riches are ours.—Stew. Gen.* Bi leinn, *be on our side.*

Leinne, *emphatic form of* leinn.

Léinteag, eig, *s. f.*, *dim.* of léin. (*Ir.* leinteog.) A little shirt; a shroud.—*Old Song.* *N. pl.* leinteagan.

Léir, *a.* Visible; that can see; *also, substantively*, sight, perception. Sùilean leis nach léir, *eyes that cannot see.—Sm.*

Léir, [gu], *adv.* Altogether; completely. Neamh is làr gu léir, *heaven and earth together.—Sm.* Uile gu léir, *altogether.*

Léir, *v. a.* Torment; pain; harass; vex; oppress; pierce; thrill. *Pret. a.* léir, *tormented; fut. aff. a.* léiridh, *shall torment.* Léir, *pierce.—Shaw.*

Léir-chunntas, ais, *s. m.* A census, a general calculation.

Leire, *s. f.* (*Ir. id.*) Austerity, piety.

Léireadh, idh, *s. m.* A tormenting, a paining; a harassing; an oppressing; torment, oppression.

Leireadh, (a), *pr. part.* of léir. Tormenting, paining, oppressing, harassing. 'G an léireadh, *harassing them.—Oss. Dargo.* A léireadh nan sleisnean, *paining the thighs.—Macfar.*

Leir-fholach, aich, *s. m.* A canopy.—*Shaw.*

Leirg, leirge, *s. f.* (*Ir. id.*) A slope; an eminence; a plain; a field of battle; the surface of the sea; the deep, the sea; *rarely*, road, reason, motive. Dhìrich Gràine ri leirg, *Grana ascended the eminence.—Oss. Derm.* An géill mi san leirg? *will I yield in the field* [*of battle*]?—*Oss. Carricth.* Caidlidh san learg an laoch, *the hero shall sleep in the deep.—Ull.*

Léir-mheas, *s. m.* (*Ir. id.*) A general consideration; a full or general estimate; a general view; a census; balancing, weighing, pondering.

Léirse, *s. f.* Sight, vision; insight, knowledge; the sense of sight. Cha 'n 'eil a léirse aig, *he cannot see.*

Léir-sgrios, *s. m.* (*Ir. id.*) Destruction; utter destruction; carnage, massacre. An deigh an léir-sgrios, *after the destruction.—Orr.*

Léir-sgrios, *v. a.* Destroy, destroy utterly. *Pret. a. id.; fut. aff. a.* léir-sgriosaidh.

Léir-sgriosach, *a.* Destroying utterly; destruction. Gu léir-sgrios, *destructively.*

Léir-sgriosail, *a.* Utterly destructive.

Léirsinn, *s. f.* Vision, the sense of sight; insight, knowledge. A dalladh a leirsinn, *blinding his vision.—Oss. Duthona.* Snitheach gun leirsinn, *tearful and blind.—Oss. Fin and Lor.*

Leirsinneach, *a.* Visible; seeing; intelligent; enlightened. Gu léirsinneach, *visibly.*

Leirsinneachd, *s. f.* Visibleness; intelligentness; sagacity.

Leir-smuaine, *s. f.* A reflection; deep consideration.

Léir-thionail, *v. a.* Congregate; gather wholly together; muster.

Léir-thional, ail, *s. m.* A general assembly, a general gathering, a muster. Léir-thional eaglais na h-Alba, *a general gathering of the clergy of the kirk; a general assembly;* léir-thional chrodh, *a general gathering of black cattle.*

Léis, *gen. sing.* of lias.

Leis, *prep.* (*Ir. id.*) With; together with; along, down, as on a stream; by, by reason of; in favour of; to the leeward; belonging to. Leis an duine so, *with this man.—Stew. Gen.* Leis féin, *by himself;* leis an t-sruth, *down the stream;* leis an leathad, *down hill;* leis, *to the leeward.—Shaw.* Co leis thu? *whom do you belong to? whose child are you?*

Leis, *comp. pron.* With him, with it; in his favour, on his side, in his opinion. Leig leis, *let him* or *it alone; allow him* or *it.* Is aithreach leis, *he is surprised; he repents.* Bi leis, *be with him,* or *on his side.*

Léis-bheart, *s. f.* (*Ir. id.*) Armour for the thighs; trowsers.

Léis-bhrat, *s. m.* Trowsers.—*Macd.*

Leise, *s. f.* (*Ir. id.*) Happiness.

Leiseadh, aidh, *s. m.* (*Ir. id.*) Mocking.

Leisge, *com.* and *sup.* of leasg. Lazier, laziest. See **Leasg.**

Leisge, *s. f.* (*from* leasg.) Laziness, sloth, inactivity. Làmh na leisge, *the hand of sloth.—Stew. Pro.*
Ir. id. *Gr.* λέσχη, *idle chat.* *W.* llesgen, *a sluggish fit.*

Leisgean, ein, *s. m.* (*W.* llesgyn, *a weakling.*) A lazy person, a sluggard, a sloven. A leisgein! *thou sluggard!—Stew. Gen.*

Leisgeanachd, *s. f.* Indolence, sloth.

Leisgeanta, *a.* Lazy, indolent, slothful. Gu leisgeanta, *lazily.*

Leisgeil, *a.* (leisg-amhuil.) Lazy, slothful.

Leisgeul, -sgeil, *s.*, leth-sgeul. (*Ir.* leisgeul.) An excuse. Gabh mo leisgeul, *excuse me;* an leisgeul sin doibh, *their own affair be it.—G. P.*

Leisgeulach, *a.* Excusing; prone to excuse; apt to make excuses; excusable; excusatory; mediatory.

Leisgeulachd, *s. f.* Excusableness.

Leisgeulaiche, *s. m.* A mediator; an excuser.

Leistear, eir, *s. m.* An arrow-maker; a table. *N. pl.* leisteiran.

Leistearachd, *s. f.* The occupation of an arrow-maker.

Leite, *s. f.* (*Ir. id.*) Water-gruel.—*Shaw.*

Leith, *voc. sing.* of liath. Grey. A dhuine leith! *thou grey-headed man!*

Leithe, *com.* and *sup.* of liath. Greyer, greyest.

Leithe, *s. f.* (*Ir.* leth *and* leithe.) Greyness; mouldiness.

Leitheach, ich, *s. m.* (*Ir. id.*) A flounder, a plaice.

Leithead, eid, *s.* (*Ir. id.*) Greyness.

Leitheag, eig, *s. f.* A flounder.

Leithid, *s.* (*Ir.* leithid.) The like; equal; such. A leithid so, *the like of this;* leithid so rud, *such a thing as this;* cha 'n fhac mi riamh do leithid, *I never saw the like of you.* *N. pl.* leithidean; *d. pl.* leithidibh.

Leithne, *com.* and *sup.* of leathann. Broader, broadest.—*Stew. Job.*

Leithne, *s. f.* Breadth; broadness; extension.

Leithneachd, *s f.* Breadth; spaciousness; extension.

Leithnead, eid. Breadth.

Leithnich, *v. a.* Extend, enlarge; make broad, become broad. *Pret. a.* leithnich, *extended; fut. aff. a.* leithnichidh, *shall extend; fut. pass.* leithnichear; *p. part.* leithnichte, *extended.*

Leithnichte, *p. part.* of leithnich. Extended, enlarged.

Leithbheachas, ais, *s. m.* Unjust dealing; separation.

Leithbhreitheach, *a.* Partial, unjust.—*Shaw.* Perhaps *leth-bhreitheach.*

Leithbhreitheachd, *s. f.* Partiality. Perhaps *leth-bhreitheachd.*

Leithrinn, *s. pl.* Chains or fetters.

Leithse, *comp. pron.* By her, with her.—*Q. B. ref.* Written for *leathsa.*

Leith-sgeul, -sgeil, *s.*, *perhaps* leth-sgeul. (*Ir. id.*) An excuse, an apology. Gabh mo leith-sgeul, *excuse me.* Written also *leisgeul;* which see.

Leith-sgeulach, *a.* (*Ir. id.*) Prone to excuse or apologise; excusable.

Leith-sgeulachd, *s. f.* (*Ir. id.*) Excusableness.

Léitig, *s. f.* A convoy. Thoir léitig dha, *give him a convoy, convoy him.*

Léitig, *v. a.* Convoy. *Pret.* léitig; *fut. aff.* léitigidh.

Leitir, leitreach, *s. f.* (leathad-tìr.) A sloping shore; the side of a hill; a country side.

Le 'm, (*for* le am.) With their. Le 'm biodagaibh, *with their dirks.*

Le m' (*for* le mo) With me. Le m' each, *with my horse*

Le 'n, (le an.) With their.

Leo, *comp. pron* With them; in their company; by them; on their side, in their favour, in their opinion; theirs. Bha i brònach leo, *she was sorrowful in their company.—Ull.* Is boidheach leo am fàs, *beauteous in their estimation is their growth.—Id.* Is leo-san rìoghachd néimh, *theirs is the kingdom of heaven.—Stew N T* Leo féin, *by themselves, alone*; ciod their leo? *what is their opinion?*

Leob, *v. a* Tear in shreds, mangle

Leòb, leoba, *s m.* A shred, a peeling, a piece of any thin substance, as skin. Bhur bois gun leòb chraicinn, *your palms without a piece of skin —Macfar*

Leòbach, *a.* In shreds, flabby, skinny; ragged, tawdry *Com.* and *sup.* leobaiche

Leobhar, *a.* Long, tawdry, trailing; clumsy, not fitting; too long; as a piece of dress. Written also *leabhar.*

Leòd, leòid, *s m.* A cutting, a mangling, a maiming

Leòg, leòig, *s. m.* (*Ir id.*) A marsh or swamp.

Leògach, *a* (*Ir. id*) Marshy, swampy; slovenly, untidy, tawdry, clumsy *Com* and *sup.* leogaiche.

Leogan, ain, *s. m.* A slovenly, untidy fellow. *N pl* leoganach.

Leoganach, *a.* Slovenly, untidy, tawdry. *Com.* and *sup.* leoganaiche.

Leoganach, aich, *s. m.* A slovenly, untidy fellow. *N. pl.* leoganaich.

Leogarach, Leogaradh, *a.* (*Ir id*) Haughty, conceited, proud.

Leogh, *v.* More frequently *leagh*, which see.

Leoghan, ain, *s. m* A trowel.

Leoghantachd, *s. f.* Inconstancy.—*Shaw*

Leòghann, ainn, *s. m.* A lion. More frequently written *leomhann.*

Leòghas, *s.* The Isle of Lewis, one of the Western Isles

Dr Macpherson observes, that this name was given to the isle of Lewis by the Norwegians, who subdued the western isles of Scotland Certain it is that, in the Norse language, *lodhus* means a marsh, and that Lewis abounds in swampy grounds

Leoghasach, aich, *s. m.* A Lewis-man

Leòid, *gen. sing.* of leud; which see.

Leòide, *s. f.* Breadth, also, *Lude*, a district in Athol.

Leoideag, eig, *s f.* A disrespectful term for a female

Leoime, *s f.* Pride, self-conceit; foppishness, prudery, coquetry.

Leòin, *gen sing.* of leòn; which see.

Leòinte, *p part.* Wounded; maimed —*Stew. Is*

Leòir, *a.* (*Ir. id W.* llawer, *many. Corn.* leoar) Enough, sufficient Is leòir mo ghràs, *my grace is sufficient.—Stew Pro* Fhuair mi na 's leòir, *I have got enough*

Leòir, (gu), *adv* Enough.

Leom. See **Leam**

Leòmach, *a.* (*Ir id*) Foppish, airy, conceited of one's person, vain; prudish, flirting, prone to flirt *Com* and *sup.* leòmaiche.

Leòmachas, ais, *s* (*Ir. id.*) Foppishness; conceitedness; vanity; prudery.

Leòmag, aig, *s. f.* (*Ir. id*) A conceited airy girl; a prude. *N. pl.* leomagan.

Leomain, *gen. sing.* of leoman.

Leòmair, *s. m.* (*Ir. id*) A fop, a conceited fellow.

Leòmaireachd, *s. f.* Conceitedness, foppery; the behaviour of a fop

Leoman, ain, *s m* (*Ir.* leadhman) A moth —*Stew Job*

Leòmhan, ain, *s. m* A lion Leomhan treun, *a strong lion.—Sm. N pl.* leomhain, *lions.*

Gr λεων. *Lat* leo, *gen.* leon-is *Ir* leon *Eng.* lion *Arm* leòn *W.* llen *Bisc.* leoya. *It* leone *Fr.* lion *Sp.* leon. *Germ.* leu. *Dan* lowe *Sclav.* lev *Pol.* lew *Dal* law. *Arab.* levu *Heb.* lab, which is often pronounced lavi

Leomhanta, *a.* Lion-like; brave. Dà fhear leomhanta, *two lion-like men.—Stew* 1 *Chr.*

Leòn, leòin, *s. m* (*Arm* leun, *a hole*) A wound, a pang; severe distress; a sprain, a bruise. Mo leòn! *woe's me! N. pl.* leòintean

Leòn, *v a* Wound, maim; bruise; afflict *Pret. a* leòn, *wounded, fut aff a.* leònaidh, *shall wound*

Leònadh, aidh, *s. m* (*Ir id*) A wounding; a maiming, affliction

Leònta, *p. part* of leòn. Wounded, maimed, sprained, pained, afflicted Leònta gu bàs, *mortally wounded.—Stew Ez*

Leòntach, *a* Wounding, maiming; afflicting

Leòntachd, *s f, for* leomhantachd (*Ir id*) Bravery; brave actions; laxation, keeness of morals.

Leòr, *a* Enough, sufficient; sufficiency Ni 's leòr do bhainne, *enough of milk —Stew Pro*

Leòr-ghniomh, *s m* Satisfaction; a work of supererogation

Leòs, leòis, *s m* (*Ir. id*) Reproof, disclosure; a light, a blaze. In the latter senses it is most commonly written *leus*, which see

Leos. See **Leus**

Leothad, aid. See **Leathad.**

Le 'r, (le ar) With our, by our; belonging to our, in favour of our Le 'r cliù, 's le 'r creich, *with our fame and our spoils —Oss Gaul* Is leinn féin as le 'r cloinn e, *it is ours and our children's*

Le 'r, (*for* le ur *or* le bhur) With your, by your; belonging to your, in favour of your

Leth, *s m.* (*Ir.* leath) Half Leth na slighe, *the half of the way, midway —Oss Derm* Air leth, *apart, aside —Stew. Gen* Troidh gu leth, *a foot and a half*, leth mar leth, *half and half*, cuir as leth, *impute, charge*, tha mi' leth los, *I have half a mind*

Leth-ainm, *s. m* A nickname *N pl* leth-ainmean

Leth-ainmeach, *a* Inclined to nickname

Leth-a-mach, *s. m.* An outside; an exterior, external.

Leth-amadan, ain, *s m.* A ninny, a half-witted fellow.

Leth-a-muigh, *s. m* An outside or exterior On leth-a-muigh, *from without*

Leth-aon, -aoin, *s m.* A twin-child, a match, a fellow, one of a pair. *N. pl* leth-aona, *twins* Leth-aona na bolg, *twins in her womb.—Stew Gen.*

Leth-a-stigh, *s.* The inside, inward part, interior.—*Stew. Lev.*

Leth-bhliadhna, *s f* Half a year An ceann leth-bhliadhna, *at the end of half a year*

Leth-bhreac, *s m* An equal; a match, a fellow, one of a pair; a partner; half marrow; correlate. Cha 'n fhac mi riamh do leth-bhreac, *I never saw your equal*

Leth-bhreath, *s.* See **Leth-bhreith**

Leth-bhreith, *s. f.* Partiality; partial judgment, an unfair decision. Gun leth-bhreith, *without partiality.—Stew Jam.*

LETH-BHREITHEACH, *a.* Partial in deciding, unjust. Leth-bhreitheach anns an lagh, *impartial in the law.—Stew. Mal.*

LETH-BHRUICH, *a.* Half-boiled; parboiled.

LETH-BHRUICH, *v. a.* Half-boil, parboil. *Pret. a.* leth-bhruich; *fut. aff.* leth-bhruichidh, *shall half-boil.*

LETH-CHAILLTE, *a.* Half-lost; half-concealed; half-hidden. Leth-chaillte ann an nial, *half-lost* [*half-hidden*] *in a cloud.—Oss. Croma.*

LETH-CHÀIRT, *s. f.* The eighth part of a yard, half a quarter.

LETH-CHAOCH, *a.* Half-blood.

LETH-CHAR, *a.* Somewhat. Leth-char ocrach, *somewhat hungry.*

LETH-CHAS, -chois, *s. f.* One foot; a left foot. Tha e air leth-chois, *he has but one foot; he stands on one foot.*

LETH-CHEANN, *s. m.* The side of the head, the temples. Do leth-cheann, *thy temples.—Stew. Song Sol. ref.*

LETH-CHEANNACH, *a.* Sheepish, bashful.

LETH-CHEARCAL, ail, *s. m.* A semicircle. *N. pl.* leth-chearclan.

LETH-CHEARCLACH, *a.* Semicircular.

LETH-CHÉIL, *v. a.* Half-conceal, half-hide; see in part. *Pret. a.* leth-chéil; *fut. aff. a.* leth-chéilidh.

LETH-CHÉILTE, *part.* Half-concealed; half-hidden; seen in part.

LETH-CHLIATHAICH, *s. f.* The side of the human body.

LETH-CHODAL, ail, *a.* A dozing or slumber.

LETH-CHODALACH, *a.* Apt to doze; dozing, slumbering; narcotic, lethargic.

LETH-CHOS, -chois, *s. f.* One foot; left foot. Ag eiridh air leth-chois, *rising on one leg.—R.*

LETH-CHRUINN, *a.* Hemispherical, half round.

LETH-CHRUINNE, *s. f.* (*Ir.* leath-chruinne.) A hemisphere; a semicircle.

LETH-CHRUN, -chrùin, *s. f.* A half-crown, or a two shillings and sixpence piece. *N. pl.* leth-chrùintean.

LETH-CHUAIRT, *s. f.* A semicircle.

LETH-CHUAIRTEACH, *a.* Semicircular.

LETH-CHUID, *s. f.* A half share, a half; partiality.—*Shaw.*

LETH-DHEANTA, *part.* Half formed; half made, half finished. Leth-dheanta do mhùig, *half formed of mist.—Oss. Tem.*

LETH-DHEOMHAN, ain, *s. m.* A demi-demon. *N. pl.* leth-dheomhain.

LETH-EÒLACH, *a.* Half informed; half acquainted.

LETH-EUDACH, aich, *s. f.* A sheet of linen. *N. pl.* leth-eudaichean.

LETH-FHAICTE, *p. part.* Half seen; partly seen.

LETH-FHOCAL, ail, *s. m.* A by-word, a proverb, a trite saying; half a word. *N. pl.* leth-fhocail, *by-words.* Bithidh e na leth-fhocal, *he will be a by-word.—Stew.* 1 *K.*

LETH-FHOCLACH, *a.* Proverbial; fond of proverbs; like a proverb.

† LETH-OHRABAL, ail, *s. m.* (*Ir. id.*) A halfpenny.

LETH-INNIS, -innse, *s. f.* (*Ir.* leithinse.) A peninsula. *N. pl.* leth-innsean. Leth-innis Lochlinn, *the peninsula of Jutland;* leth-innis na Spàinn, *the peninsula of Spain.*

LETH-IOMALL, aill, *s. m.* A border.

LETH-IOMALLACH, *a.* Bordering.

LETH-LAG, *a.* Half tired, half fatigued.

LETH-LAMH, -laimh, *s. f.* One hand or arm; the left hand or arm. Air leth-laimh, *having but one hand* or *arm;* claidheamh na leth-laimh, *a sword in one hand.—Oss. Dargo.*

LETH-LEANN, -leanna, *s. m.* Small beer.—*Shaw.*

LETH-LEAPAICHE, *s. m.* A bed-fellow. Gheibh i leth-leapaiche, *she will get a bed-fellow.—Macfar.*

LETH-LUIDHE, *s. f.* A reclining, a leaning. Tha e na leth-luidhe, *he is reclining* or *leaning.*

LETH-MHÀS, -mhàis, *s. m.* A buttock, a thigh.—*Shaw.*

LETH-MUIGH, *s. m.* An exterior, outside; *adjectively,* external.

LETH-OINNSEACH, ich, *s. f.* A half-witted female.

LETH-OIR, *adv.* Sideways, edgeways.

LETH-PHUNT, -phuint, *s. m.* A half-pound, eight ounces. Leth-phunt sucair, *a half-pound of sugar.*

LETH-RANN, -rainn, *s. m.* A hemistich; a half.

LETH RI, *prep.* Towards. Leth ri éirigh na gréine, *towards the east, eastward.—Stew. Num.*

LETH-ROD, -roid, *s. m.* A by-road; a footpath.

LETH-ROSG, *s. m.* Purblindness.

LETH-ROSGACH, *a.* Purblind; blear-eyed.

LETH-RUADH, *a.* Somewhat red; reddish; brown.

LETH-SGOILTEAN, ein, *s. m.* A plank, a joist.

LETH-SHEISE, *s. m.* and *f.* A partner, a mate; a spouse; a beloved person. Mo leth-sheise, *my beloved.—Stew. Song Sol. ref.*

LETH-SHÙIL, -shùl, *s. f.* One eye. Tha e air leth-shùil, *he has but one eye.*

LETH-SHÙILEACH, *a.* Having but one eye; monocular.

LETH-TAOBH, *s. m.* A side; one side; apart, aside; a flitch; hysterics. Thionndaidh duine a leth-taobh, *a man turned* [*aside*] *to a side.—Stew.* 1 *K.* Thug e a leth-taobh e, *he took him aside.—Macdon.* Cuir air leth-taobh e, *put it on one side.*

LETH-TAOBHACH, *a.* Sideways.

LETH-TROM, -truim, *s. m.* A weight; a burden; a grievance; pregnancy. Gach leth-trom, *each weight.—Sm.* A leth-trom, *her pregnancy.—Turn.*

LETH-TROMACH, *a.* Weighty, burdensome; pregnant. Tha mise leth-tromach, *I am pregnant.—Stew. Gen.*

LETH-TRUIME, *s. f.* Oppression; counterweight; pregnancy.

LETH-UILEANN, inn, *s. m.* Half an angle; an acute angle; half sitting, reclining. Air leth-uileann, *leaning on one elbow.*

LEUB. See LEÒB.

LEUBAIDEACH, *a.* See LEIBIDEACH.

LEUBAIDEACHD, *s. f.* See LEIBIDEACHD.

LEUD, leòid, *s. m.* (*W.* llêd, *breadth. Lat.* latus, *broad.*) Breadth; extension; space; spaciousness. Leud a bhalla, *the breadth of the wall.—Stew. Ezek.* A réir leòid an tighe, *according to the breadth of the house.—Stew.* 1 *K.* Leud boise, *a handbreadth.—Sm.* Leud ròinneig, *a hair's-breadth.—Stew. Jud.* Air leud, *in breadth.—Stew.* 1 *K.* Cuig troidhean air leud, *five feet broad.*

LEUDACH, *a.* (*from* leud.) Spreading; extending; spacious; diffuse. Cainnt leudach, *diffuse language.*

LEUDÁCHADH, aidh, *s. m.* A spreading, an extending, a widening; a making broad or spacious; increasing; extension; increase in breadth.

LEUDAICH, *v. a.* (*Ir.* leathadaich.) Widen, extend, make broad or spacious; become wide or broad; enlarge; make diffuse. *Pret. a.* leudaich; *fut. aff. a.* leudaichidh, *shall widen.* Leudaich e air a chùis, *he enlarged on the subject.*

LEUDAICHTE, *p. part.* of leudaich. Widened, extended, enlarged; made spacious.

LEUG, léig, *s. m.* (*Ir.* liag.) A crystal; a jewel or gem; any precious stone; a meteor; *also,* a beloved person. Or no leug, *gold or crystal.—Stew. Job.* Leugan, *rubies,* or *precious stones of any kind.—Stew. Pro.* Mar leug theine, *like a meteor.—Fingalian Poem.* Mo leug phrìseil, *my precious jewel; my darling.—Old Song.*

There is a stone, or rather a crystal, called *leug*, which was in high request among the Gael during the ages of Popish superstition. Water poured upon it became straightway impregnated with peculiar medical virtues, which did not, however, extend beyond cattle. These stones are still in preservation, and in repute among the lower orders of Highlanders.

Leugach, *a.* (*from* leug.) Crystalline; like a jewel or gem; abounding in jewels; like a meteor.

Leugart, airt, *s. m.* A siege.—*Q. B. ref.*

Leugh, *v. a.* (*Lat.* lego. *W.* lleu *and* lleaw. *Ir.* leagh.) Read; peruse. *Pret. a.* leugh, *read; fut. aff. a.* leughaidh, *shall read.* Nach do leugh sibh? *have ye not read?*—*Stew. Matt.*

Leughadair, *s. m.* A reader. *Contr.* leughdair; hence *Lat.* lector. *N. pl.* leughadairean, *readers.*

Leughdaireachd, *s. f.* Reading.

Leughadh, aidh, *s. m.* (*Ir.* leaghadh.) A reading, a perusing; a perusal.

Leughadh, (a), *pr. part.* of leugh. Reading, perusing.

Leughair, *s. m.* A reader. Deagh leughair, *a good reader. N. pl.* leughairean, *readers.*

Leughaireachd, *s. f.* Reading. Thoir aire do'n leughaireachd, *take care of the reading.*—*Stew. Tim.*

Leughta, Leughte, *p. part.* of leugh. (*Lat.* lectus.) Read, perused.

Leum, leuma, léim, *s. m.* (*Ir. id.*) A leap, a bound, a spring, a frisk, a start. Leum gàbhaidh, *a desperate leap.*—*Ull.* Ruadh-bhoc nan leum, *the bounding roe.*—*Oss. Lodin.* Leum Chuchullin, *Cuchullin's leap*, or *loop's head, at the mouth of the Shannon.* Thoir leum, *leap.* Amhairc romhad mun toir thu do leum, *look before you ere you leap.*—*G. P.*

Leum, *v. n.* Leap, spring, bound, frisk, start; skip, hop. *Pret.* leum, *leaped; fut. aff. a.* leumaidh, *shall leap.* Leum air, *attack suddenly, seize greedily;* leum iad air a chreich, *they flew upon the spoil.*—*Stew. Sam.*

Leumadair, *s. m.* (*from* leum.) A jumper, a leaper; a dolphin.—*Shaw.* A spark or scale of iron.—*Macd. N. pl.* leumadairean.

Leumadaireachd, *s. f.* A continued jumping or leaping.

Leumadh, aidh, *s. m.* A leaping, a springing, a bounding, a frisking, a hopping.

Leumaidh, *fut. aff. a.* of leum. Shall or will start or jump.

Leumardaich, Leumartaich, *s. f.* Leaping, springing, frisking, hopping. Thòisich e air leumartaich, *he began to leap.*

Leumnach, *a.*, *from* leum. (*Ir. id.*) Bounding, jumping, frisking, hopping, starting, skipping; *also*, a creature that leaps, hops, or bounds. Fuaim nan carbad leumnach, *the noise of the bounding chariots.*—*Stew. Nah.* Arabach leumnach, *a prancing* or *bounding Arabian.*—*Old Song. Com.* and *sup.* leumnaiche.

Leumnach-uaine, *s. m.* (*Ir. id.*) A grashopper.

Leumnaich, *s. f.* A jumping, a springing, a bounding; a frisking, a hopping, a skipping.

Leumnaich, (a), *pr. part.* of leum. Jumping, springing, bounding, skipping, hopping. A leumnaich o nial gu nial, *bounding from cloud to cloud.*—*Oss. Gaul.* A minnean a leumnaich, *her fawn frisking.*—*Oss. Derm.*

Leun, *v. a.* Sprain the wrist or foot. *Pret. a.* leun, *sprained; fut. aff. a.* leunaidh, *shall sprain.*

Leun, *s. f.* A sprain of the wrist or foot.

Leun, lein, *s. m.* A swamp; swampy ground; a meadow; a field of luxuriant grass.

Leunach, *a.* Swampy, marshy. *Com.* and *sup.* leunaiche.

Leunadh, aidh, *s. m.* A spraining of the wrist or foot. Tha mo lamh air leunadh, *my wrist has got a sprain.*

Leus, leòis, *s. m.* (*Ir. id.*) A blaze, a flame; light; a torch; a fir-candle; a blister; a spot on the eye, a cataract. An dreach mar leòis, *their appearance like torches.*—*Stew. Nah.* Leus teine, *a flame of fire, a blaze.*—*Stew. Gen.* Duine aig am bheil leus, *a man who has a spot on his eye.*—*Stew. Lev.* Fo leus, *blind, having a cataract.*—*Oss. Croma. N. pl.* leòis *and* leusan. Leòis air a basaibh, *blisters on her palms.*—*Macfar.*

Ir. leus and les. *Armen.* louis, *a blaze.* *Swed.* lysa. *Sclav.* luzh, *light;* also, *Eng.* blaze.

Leusach, *a.*, *from* leus. (*Ir. id.*) Blazing, flaming, flashing; having blisters; spotted, as the eye. Sùil leusach, *a spotted* or *blemished eye.*

Leusachadh, aidh, *s. m.* (*Ir. id.*) A blistering; a flaming, a blazing.

Leusachail, *a.* Causing blisters, escharotic; apt to blister. Lamhan leusachail, *blistered hands;* also, *hands that are apt to blister.*

Leusaich, *v. a.* (*from* leus.) Blister, vesicate, make a flame. *Pret. a.* leusaich, *blistered; fut. aff. a.* leusaichidh; *p. part.* leusaichte, *blistered.*

Leusaichte, *p. part.* of leusaich. Blistered, vesicated. Lamhan leusaichte, *blistered hands.*

Leus-chnuimh, *s. f.* A glow-worm.

Leus-chnuimheach, *a.* Full of glow-worms; like a glow-worm; of, or belonging to, a glow-worm.

Leus-ghath, *s. m.* A ray of light; a sultry beam. *N. pl.* leus-ghathan.

† **Li**, *s. f.* (*Ir. id.*) The sea.—*Shaw.*

Li, *s. f.* (*Ir. id. Corn.* liu. *Arm.* liu *and* leou.) A tinge, a colour, a complexion; prosperity, happiness; a festival. A mhaise-mhna is aillidh li! *thou fair-faced beauty!*—*Fingalian Poem.* See also **Ligh**.

Lia, *s. m.* and *f.* (*Ir. id.*) A stream; a stone; hunger; a hog.

Lia, *a.* Grey. See **Liath**. Liath?

Liach, *s. f.* See **Liagh**.

Lia-chac, *s. m.* (*Ir. id.*) Hog's dung.—*Shaw.*

Liachd, *s.* (*Ir. id.*) A multitude, a great many.

Liachlan, ain, *s. m.* (*Ir. id.*) A spoonful.

Lia-chròth, *s. m.* A hog-sty.—*Shaw.*

Liadh, leidh, *s. f.* (*Ir.* liach.) A ladle; a large spoon; the blade of an oar. *N. pl.* liadhan, *ladles* or *spoons.*—*Stew. Jer.* Lan-leidh, *a ladleful.*

† **Lia-faile**, *s. f.* The stone called also *clach na cineamhuinn* (the fatal stone), on which the Scotch kings were wont to be crowned, now in Westminster Abbey.

The *lia fàil*, or, as some call it, the *liag fàil*, or *leug fàil*, was probably an invention of the Druids. It was the fatal chair on which the supreme kings of Ireland were inaugurated in the days of Druidism. From Ireland it was conveyed to Dunstaffhage in Scotland; thence, about the year 842, to Scone, by Kenneth II.; and, lastly, in 1300, by Edward to Westminster, where it still remains. How the lia fàil came to Scotland, whether by theft, fraud, or violence, is not ascertained. It possessed extraordinary virtues till the time of our Saviour's birth. When the rightful candidate sat on it, it emitted a strange noise, and appeared otherwise agitated in a surprising manner. All this was, no doubt, owing to the Druids, by whose clever jugglery the minds of men were then influenced and guided. It is not unlikely, then, that the lia fàil was lent to the Caledonians by their unsuspecting and generous brethren of Erin, in order to decide some question of royal right or legitimacy,—that the Caledonians detained it contrary to promise and justice,—and that the Irish thought it not worth the recovering, since its virtues had vanished at the commencement of the Christian era, or rather, perhaps, on the extinction of the Druidical order. Some time after its arrival in Scotland, a superstitious belief became attached to it,—that wherever the stone should be found, some one of the race should reign. This persuasion is not so old as the times of of Druidism.—I speak with deference where Toland differs in opinion. This able antiquarian has recorded an Irish rhyme, a "Druidical Oracle" respecting this most ancient monument, contained in the following words:—

Cioniodh scuit saor an fine,
Man ba breag an Faisdine.
Mar a bh' fhuighid an lia-fàil,
Dlighid flaitheas do ghabhail.

Translated into Latin by Hector Boethius.

Ne fallat fatum, Scoti, quocunque locatum
Invenient lapidem hunc, regnare tenentur ibidem.

English Translation.

Except old saws do feign,
And wizards' wits be blind,
The Scots in place must reign,
Where they this stone shall find.

Another.

Consider, Scot, where'er you find this stone,
If fates fail not, there fixed must be your throne.

LIAGAN, ain, *s. m.* (*Ir. id.*) An obelisk; a small stone.

LIAGH, leigh, *s. f.* See LIADH.

LIAGHDHEALG, *s.* A bodkin; a clasp; a button.

LIAN, *s.* A meadow. See LÒN.

LIAN. See LION.

LIANAICH, *s. f.* Sea-ware.—*Mac Co.*

LIAPHUTAG, aig, *s. f.* A hog's pudding; a sausage.

LIAS, léis, *s. f.* (*Ir. id.*) A thigh. Fuidh mo léis, *under my thigh.—Stew. Gen.*

LIAS, leis, *s. m.* (*Ir. id.*) A hut for calves or lambs.—*Shaw.*

LIATAS, ais, *s. m.* (*Ir. id.*) Mildew, blight, fustiness, lettuce.

LIATH, *a.* (*Gr.* λιῶς. *W.* lluyd. *Ir.* liath.) Grey, grey-haired; pale; mouldy. Màille liath, *grey-coloured armour.*—*Oss. Lod.* Falt liath, *grey hair;* each liath, *a grey horse.*—*Fingalian Poem.* A bhile a crith is iad liath, *his lips quaking and pale.—Oss. Tem.* Aran liath, *mouldy bread;*—the Irish say the same.

LIATH, *v. a.* and *n.* Make grey; grow grey; grow pale; grow mouldy.

LIATHACH, *a.* (*Ir. id.*) Greyish, grey; pale, blank.

LIATHACHADH, aidh, *s. m.* A growing grey; a making grey; a growing mouldy.

LIATHADH, aidh, *s. m.* (*Ir. id.*) A making grey; a growing grey or mouldy; a grey tinge.

LIATHAG, aig, *s. f.* A gilse, a fish of the salmon kind.

LIATHAN, ain, *s. m.* Marigold; the *chrysanthemum segetum* of botanists.

LIATHANACHD, *s. f.* Fustiness, mouldiness.

LIATH-BHÀN, *a.* (*Ir. id.*) Pale.

LIATH-BHUIDHE, *a.* (*Ir. id.*) Tawny.

LIATH-CHEARC, -chirc, *s. f.* (*Ir. id.*) A heath-hen. *N. pl.* liath-chearcan, *heath-hens.* Liath-chearcan fraoich, *heath-hens.—Old Song.*

LIATHDRAS, ais, *s. m.* Mustiness, mouldiness.

LIATH-FHEASGAR, air, *s. m.* Grey evening; evening; evening twilight.—*Oss. Tem.*

LIATH-GHATH, *s. m.* (*Ir. id.*) A violent dart.—*Shaw.*

LIATH-GHLAS, *a.* (*Ir. id.*) Hoary; bleak.

LIATH-GHORM, *a.* (*Ir. id.*) Azure, cerulean. Lear liath-ghorm, *the azure surface of the sea.* *Com.* and *sup.* liath-ghuirme.

LIATH-GHUIRME, *s. f.* An azure colour.

LIATH-LUIDNEACH, ich, *s. f.* The name given by the Fingalians to the banner of Dermid, the son of Duibhne.

LIATHLUS, luis, *s. m.* (*Ir. id.*) Mugwort; the *artemisia vulgaris* of botanists.

LIATH-LUSACH, *a.* Abounding in mugwort; like mugwort; made of mugwort.

LIATH-MHÙIG, *s. f.* Grey mist. Liath-mhùig nan tonn, *the grey mist of the waves.—Oss. Carricth.*

LIATHRADH, aidh, *s. m.* (*Ir. id.*) A sliding; a rolling; a sprinkling.

LIATH-REOTH, LIATH-REOTHADH, *s. m.* (*Ir.* liathreo.) Hoar-frost; like hoar-frost.—*Stew. Ex.*

† LIATHROID, *s f.* (*Ir. id.*) A ball; a roller; a knob; chaff.

LIATHRUISG, *s. f.* A fieldfare; the *turdus pilaris* of Gesner. Macdonald, in his Vocabulary, has it *liathtrosg.*

LIATUS, uis, *s. m.* See LIATAS.

LIBEAG, eig, *s. f.* More commonly written *leabag;* which see.

LIBEAGACH, *a.* See LEABAGACH.

LIBH, *comp. pron.* (*for* le sibh.) With you; together with you; on your side, in your favour; by you.

LIBHEADHAN, ain, *s. m.* (*Ir. id.*) A dowry.—*Shaw.*

LIBHEARN, eirn, *s. m.* (*Gr.* λιβυρνις. *Lat.* liburna. *Ir.* libhearn, *a ship.*) A ship, a galley; a habitation; dowry; cattle. Freothal mara ri taobh libheirn, *the whirl* [*eddy*] *of the sea round a ship.—Fingalian Poem.*

LIC, *gen. sing.* of leac; which see.

LICEAG, eig, *s. f.* A little slab.

LIDE, *s. f.* (*Ir. id.*) A jot, a tittle, a particle; an article, a letter; a little bit. Cha tuit lide, *nothing shall fall; a jot shall not fall.—Stew.* 2 *K.*

LIGEACH, *a.* Sly, cunning.

LIGH, *s. m.* (*Ir.* li. *Arm.* liv, liu, *and* leou, *colour.*) A colour, hue; a tinge, a complexion; *also,* prosperity; a festival. Ligh beo, *a lively colour; Arm.* liu beo. Ligh dubh [*bh* silent], *a black hue; Arm.* liu du. Ligh ruadh, *a red colour; Arm.* liu ru.

† LIGH, *v. a.* Lick.—*Shaw. Fut. aff. a.* lighidh.

LICHEACH, ich, *s. f.* (*Ir. id.*) A cow.

LIGHICHE, *s. m.* A physician. Nach leighis aon lighich? *cannot any physician heal?—Turn.*

LILE, *s. f.* A lily. See LILI.

† LILEADH, idh, *s. m.* (*Ir. id.*) A sucking, a licking.

LILI, LILIDH, and LILIGH, *s. f.* A lily. *N. pl.* lilidhean. Liligh, *a lily.—Stew. Hos.*
Lat. lilium. *Fr.* lis. *Germ.* lilean. *Du.* lilie. *Sclav.* lilia. *Boh.* lilium. *Hung.* liliom. *Bisc.* lilia. *Ir.* lile. *Eng.* lily.

LILIDHEACH, *a.* Abounding in lilies; like a lily; flexible.

† LILLEACH, *a.* (*Ir. id.*) Pliant, flexible.

LÌN, *gen. sing.* of lion; which see.

LÌN, *s. f.* (*Ir. id.*) A thread; a line; a series; score.
Gr. λινον. *Lat.* linum *and* linea. *Ir.* lin. *Teut.* lin *and* lein. *W.* llin. *Eng.* line. *Scotch,* ling.

† LIND, *s. m.* A disease.

LÌNEACHADH, aidh, *s. m.* A delineating, a delineation.

† LING, *v. n.* Skip; dart; go away.

LINGEADH, idh, *s. m.* (*Ir. id.*) A skipping, a flying off, a flinging, a darting.—*Shaw.*

LINGINNEACH, *a.* Somewhat round.

LÌNICH, *v. a.* (*from* lìn.) Line; delineate. *Pret. a.* lìnich, *lined; fut. aff. a.* lìnichidh, *shall line.*

LÌNIG, *s. f.* (*W.* llenig, *a veil.*) Lining. Dram mar lìnig cleibh, *a dram as a lining for the breast.—Macdon.*

LINN, *a.* (*Ir. id.*) Wet.

LINN, *s. f.* (*Ir. id.*) A generation; a race; a century; an age. Iomlan na 'linn, *perfect in his generation.—Stew. Gen.* Linn Lochlin, *the race of Lochlin.—Fingalian Poem.* O linn gu linn, *from age to age* N. pl. linntean Gu linn nan linntean, *from generation to generation* —*Stew. Is.*

LINNE, *comp. pron.* See LEINNE.

LINNE, *s f.* (*Ir. id*) A pool, a pond; an abyss; the deep; the sea; a lake; a strait; the entrance to a gulf. Air linne sheimh, *on a calm sea.*—*Oss. Derm.* *N. pl.* linnte, linntean, linneachan, *and* linntichean, *pools.* Rinn mi linntean, *I made pools.*—*Stew. Ecc.* Linne lìn, *a lint dam*, linne mhuilinn, *a mill-dam.*

W. llyn, *a pool.* *Du* lyn. *Arm.* lin. *Ir* linn. *Scotch*, linn. *Old Sax.* lin, *deep water* *Run.* ligna, *standing water*, *and* lind, *a well.* *Copt.* lein, *a river.* *Gr.* λιμνη, *a pool.*

Linn is formed from the root *an*, hence, too, *Len* and *Lenon*, rivers in Bretagne; *Lene*, a river in Languedoc, *Lenza*, in Lombardy, *Lenta*, in Abruzzo

LINNEAN, ein, *s. m*, *dim.* of lin. (*Corn* lynen. *Arm.* lignen.) A thread; a little line, a shoemaker's thread. Droch lìnnean, *a bad thread*, *Arm* droucq lignen. *N. pl.* linneanan.

LINNEACHAN, *n. pl.* of linn Pools, ponds. Linneachan airson éisg, *ponds for fish* —*Stew. Is.*

LINNEANACH, *a* Thready, in lines; having threads; like a thread or line; like a shoemaker's thread

LINNEARACH, aich, *s f.* A sea-green plant, often applied by the Hebrideans to the temples and forehead, to dry up the defluxions; and also to draw up the tonsils, which, among that people, are apt to swell at certain seasons

LINNOINEACH, *a.* Somewhat round.

LINNSGEARADH, aidh, *s m.* Genealogy.

LINNSEACH, ich, *s m.* One clothed in linen *N pl.* linnsichean.

LINNSEAG, eig, *s f*, *from* lin. (*Ir. id*) A shroud. *N. pl.* linseagan

LINNTE, LINNTEAN, *n pl.* of linn. Ages, generations Na linnte a dhùisgeas san òran, *the generations that shall awaken to the song* —*Oss. Gaul.* Gu linnte céin, *to distant ages.*—*Orr.*

LINNTE, LINNTEAN, LINNTICHEAN, *n. pl* of linn Pools, abysses; seas; lakes. An linnte dorcha, *in dark abysses.* —*Ard.*

LINTEACH, *a.* (*Ir id.*) Lineal.

LIOB, lioba, *s. m* A lip.

Lat. labium *Dan* lippe. *Swed.* lapp. *Ang.-Sax* lippe *Eng.* lip *Arm* lippe *Germ.* lepp *and* lipp. *It* labro *Sp.* labio. *Pers.* lib. *Jap* leepeer.

LIOBACH, *a.* (*from* liob.) Lipped; having large lips

LIOBAR, air, *s. m.* (*Ir. id*) A lubberly fellow, a slovenly fellow; an awkward man; a hanging or blubber lip.

LIOBARNACH, *a* Slovenly, awkward; *also*, a slovenly man.

LIOBART, airt, *s m.* A leopard.

LIOBASDA, *a.* Slovenly, untight, untidy, awkward. Gu liobasda, *untightly.*

LIOBASDACHD, *s. f.* Slovenliness, sluttishness, untidiness; awkwardness.

LIOBH, *v. a.* Smooth, polish, file, burnish, furbish. *Pret a.* liobh; *fut. aff a.* liobhaidh, *shall smooth.* Written also *liomh*; which see.

LIOBHACH, *a.* Smoothing, polishing, filing, burnishing; smooth, polished, burnished. Gu liobhach, *smoothly.*

LIOBHADH, aidh, *s. m.* A smoothing, a filing, a burnishing

LIOBHAG, aig, *s. f.* A floating weed seen in standing water

LIOBHAN, ain, *s. m.* (*from* liobh.) A file; any instrument for polishing a hard surface. Bha liobhan aca, *they had a file.*—*Stew. Sam. ref.* *N. pl* liobhain

LIOBHANACH, *a.* Like a file

LIOBHARA, *a.* (*Ir.* leabhar.) Filed, polished, smoothed, burnished

LIOBHARACHD, *s f.* The state of being smooth, filed, or burnished; smoothness; brightness.

LIOBHRAGACH, aich, *s. f.* A weed growing in standing water Written also *liobhagach*

LIOBHGHRUAG, aig, *s.* (*Ir. id.*) A wig.

LIOBHTA, LIOBHTE, *p. part.* of liobh. (*Ir.* liomhtha) Polished, filed, burnished. Umha liobhta, *polished brass.*—*Stew.* 1 *K.*

LIOBRACH, *a.* (*Ir. id.*) Thick-lipped.

LIOCADAN ain, *s. m.* (*Ir. id*) A chin-cloth.—*Shaw.*

LIOD, lioda, *s m* A lisp, a stammer in the speech.

LIODACH, *a*, *from* liod (*Ir. id.*) Lisping, stammering, as in speech. *Com* and *sup.* liodaiche

LIODAG, aig, *s. f* A girl who lisps. *N. pl.* liodagan.

LIODAICHE, *s m.* A man who lisps.

LIODAIR, *v a.* Tear, mangle, rend, bruise. *Pret. a.* liodair, *tore*, *fut. aff.* liodairidh, *shall tear.*

LIODAIRT, *s f* A tearing in pieces; a mangling, a bruising.

LIODAN, ain, *s m.* (*Ir. id.*) A litany —*Shaw.* Liodan an ùcadair, *teasel*, the *dipsacus fullonum* of botanists.

† LIOGAR, air, *s. m* (*Ir. id.*) A tongue

LIOGH, *s. f.* The blade of an oar.

† LIOGHA, *a* Brave; strong.

LIOGHACH, *a.* Strong; fair; fine; *also, substantively*, superiority.

LIOGHAIS, *s. f.* (*Ir. id*) Bravery, strength, ability.

LIOGHAN, ain, *s. m* (*Ir. id*) A trowel. *N pl.* lioghain.

† LIOGHAR, air, *s. m.* (*Ir. id*)

LIOMH, *v. a.* Smooth, polish, burnish, furbish. *Pret. a.* liomh; *fut. aff. a.* liomhaidh Liomhaibh na sleaghan, *furbish the spear.*—*Stew Jer.*

LIOMHA, LIOMHAIDH, *a.* (*Lat.* levis) Polished, glittering, burnished; sharp; whetted. An airm liomhaidh, *their polished arms* —*Oss. Gaul* Gun chlaidheamh liomhaidh, *without a sharp sword* —*Id.*

LIOMHARRA, *a.* Polished, glittering, burnished, bright.

LIOMHARRACHD, *s f.* Brightness; the state of being burnished or polished, as metal

LION, lìn, *s m.* (*Ir.* lion. *Dan.* lin. *Arm.* lin.) A net; a fishing-net, a snare; lining; number, quantity; a parcel. Lion iasgaich, *a fishing-net*, lion-obair, *net-work*, lion an damhain alluidh, *a cobweb*, lion eisirein, *a dredge*; lion iadhaidh, *a sweep-net, a drag-net*; am fear theid a ghnàmach le lion, gheibh e eun uair-eigin, *he who often spreads his net will sometimes catch a bird* —*G. P.* *N. pl.* liontan, *nets, snares.* Liontan airson mo chas, *snares for my feet.*—*Stew. Jer* A lion do'n Fheinn 's a bh'ann, *as many of the Fingalians as were present.*—*Old Poem.* Lion fear is fear, *one by one*; lion dithis is dithis, *two by two*, lion triùir is triùir, *three by three*, lion ceathrar is ceathrar, *four by four.*

LION, lìn, *s. m.* Flax, lint; linen. Bhuaileadh an lion, *the flax was smitten* —*Stew. Ex.* Curaichdean lìn, *linen hoods* or *bonnets.*—*Stew. Ez* Linne lin, *a lint dam*; la buain an lìn, *Nevermas, Græcæ Calendæ.* *N. pl.* liontan *and* liontaichean.

Lat. linum. *Ir.* lin. *Sp. It.* lino. *W.* llin, *lint, and* llian, *linen.* *Corn.* and *Arm.* lian. *Bisc.* linoa. *Teut.* lin. *Germ.* linon. *Eng* linen. *Sclav.* lan *Dal.* laon *and* lan *Swed* lien. *Germ* lein *Pol. Boh. Hung. Lus.* len.

LION, *v. a.* (*Arm.* leun, *fill.* *Gr* λιαν, *much.*) Fill; satisfy, satiate *Pret. a.* lion, *filled*, *fut aff. a.* lionaidh, *shall fill.* Lion i a soitheach, *she filled her vessel.*—*Stew Gen.*

Lionad, aid, *s. m.* Plenitude; fulness; repletion.

Lionadair, *s. m.* (*from* lion.) A funnel.—*Macd.* *N. pl.* lionadairean.

Lionadh, aidh, *s. m* (*Ir. id*) A filling; fulness. Lionadh mara, *the flowing of the tide.*

Lionadh, *pret. pass.* of lion Was filled, were filled. Lionadh an talamh le fòirneart, *the earth was filled with oppression.*—*Stew. Gen.* Lionadh, 3 *sing* and *pl. imper.* Lionadh e, iad, *let him, them, fill*

Lion-aodach, aich, *s m.* A sheet; linen

Lionar, *fut. pass* of lion. Shall be filled

Lionar, *a*, *for* lionmhor; which see.

Lionarachd, *s f.* See Lionmhoireachd.

Lion-bhrat, -bhrait, *s m* A sheet; a winding sheet Air fhilleadh san lion-bhrat, *wrapped in a winding sheet.*—*Macfar.*

Lioncaise, *s.* (*Ir. id.*) A tether, a spaniel; a line from the head to the fore-foot, or from the fore to the hind-foot of a beast.—*O'Reilly.*

Lionchar, *a.* (*Ir id*) Pleasing, delightful

Lion-eudach, aich, *s. m.* Linen cloth, linen Lion-eudach grinn, *fine linen.*—*Stew Pro.*

Lionmhoire, *com.* and *sup.* of lionmhor More or most numerous Ni 's lionmhoire na sinn, *more numerous than we are*—*Stew Gen*

Lionmhoireachd, *s f* Plentifulness, abundance; multiplicity, multitude Lionmhoireachd dheth, *abundance of it.*—*Macint* Thaobh lionmhoireachd, *by reason of multitude*—*Stew Gen.* Lionmhoireachd nan lamh mu 'n obair, *many hands make light work.*—*G P.*

Lionmhor *a* (*Ir. id*) Plentiful, numerous, abounding, abundant, copious Lionmhor ann lòn is dearg, *abounding in elks and red deer.*—*Old Poem* Cainnt lionmhor, *copious language.*—*Com.* and *sup* lionmhoire.

Lionmhorachd, *s f.* See Lionmhoireachd

Lionn, lionna, *s m* (*Ir. id* *W* llyn, *liquor*) Ale; beer, humour in the body Lionn caol, *small beer*, lionn làidir, *strong beer*, lionn goirt, *sour beer* Lionn stolda, *stale beer.*—*Macd.*

Lionnachadh, aidh, *s m.* See Leannachadh.

Lionnaich, *v. n* See Leannaich

Lionnan locraidh, *s m* A level—*Macd.*

Lionn-dubh, *s.* (*Ir. id*) Melancholy, gloomy fits, hypochondria, megrims. An lionn-dubh air a h-inntinn, *melancholy on her mind*—*Oss Gaul*

Lionn-dubhach, *a* Hypochondriac, despondent.

Lionn-luibh, *s m* The hop plant

Lionn-luibheach, *a* Abounding in hops; of, or pertaining to, hops

Lionn-ruadhaidh, *s m* (*Ir. id.*) Choler.

Lionn-tàtha, *s m* A strong cement used by the ancient Gael.

Lion-obair, -oibre, *s. f* (*Ir. id*) Network, chequerwork.—*Stew* 1 *K.*

Lion-oibriche, *s m.* (*Ir* lion-obraidhe.) A net-maker

Lionor, *a* See Lionmhor.

Lionradh, aidh, *s. m.* (*Ir. id.*) A thin mixed unsubstantial draught; insipid drink; juice; gravy; sauce; aleberry.

† Lionradh, aidh, *s. m* A web—*Shaw.*

Lionta, *p. part.* of lion. Filled, sated, full. See Lion.

Liontach, *a.* (*Ir. id.*) Satiating, sating, filling; full.—*Macint.*

Liontachd, *s. f.* (*Ir. id.*) Satiety, fulness; repletion.

Liontaibh, *d. pl.* of lion

Liontaidh, *a.* Full, satiated; plump. An grainnean liontaidh, *the plump grain*—*Macfar.*

Liontan, *n. pl.* of lion. Nets See Lion.

Lionte, *p. part.* of lior. Written also *lionta*; which see.

Liopard, aird, *s. m.* A leopard—*Stew. Jer.* and *Hos.* *N pl* liopardan.

Lios, *s. f.* (*Ir* lios. *W.* llys. *Arm* les, *a court* *Corn.* llys, *a manor-house.*) A court; a palace; a house, a fortified place; a garden. Lios luibhean, *a garden for herbs.*—*Stew.* 1 *K.* Lios àraich, *a nursery*, lios olaidh, *an olive garden*, lios rioghail, *a royal court* *Arm.* les roeyal. Lios iosal, *a low court.* *Arm.* les izel. *Ir.* lios iosal.

Lios, *s. m.* (*Ir. id*) An enclosure or stalls for cattle; the longing of a pregnant female, a dispute. *Lat.* lis

Liosadair, *s m* (*from* lios) A gardener. *N pl* liosadairean.

Liosadaireachd, *s. f.* The occupation of gardening, the business of a gardener

Liosadan, ain, *s. m.* (*dim.* of lios) A little garden.

Liosair, *s m.* (*Ir id*) A gardener; *also*, a garden. *N. pl.* liosairean

Liosda, *a* (*Ir. id*) Slow, tedious, lingering; stiff, importunate. Gu giosda, gu luath, *now slow, now quick.*—*Old Poem.* Leadan liosda, *burdock*

Liosdachd, *s. f.* (*Ir.* liostacht) Slowness, tediousness; stiffness, importunity, importunateness Airson a liosdachd, *for his importunity*—*Stew Luke.*

Liosdair, *s m.* A wrangler, a barrister; a pettifogger. *N. pl.* liosdairean.

Liosdaireachd, *s f.* Wrangling; pettifogging

Liosta, *a.* See Liosda

Liostair, *s m*, written also *liosdair*, which see.

Liotach, *a* Lisping Written also *liodach.*

Liotachd, *s f.* The infirmity of lisping. Written also *liodachd.*

Liotan, ain, *s m.* (*Ir. id.*) A litany.—*Macd*

† Liothach, aidh, *s. m.* A frightening; dismaying; a dismay.

Liothra, *s m* Hair—*Shaw.*

Lip, *s.* A lip.—*Q. B. ref.*

Lipinn, *s f.* (*Ir. id*) A small corn-measure, in Scotland called a lippy, of which four make a peck.

† Lis, *s. f.* Mischief, evil—*Shaw*

Lisg, *s. pl* The feelers of a fly.

† Lit, *s* Activity, celerity.—*Shaw.*

Lite, *s f.* (*Germ.* lid) Porridge, pottage; posset.

Liteach, *a* (*from* lite) Like porridge; relating to porridge.—*Macdon.*

Litir, *s. f* A pool, stagnant water A réidh-ghorm lith, *its smooth blue pools*—*Macfar.*

Lith, lithe, *s f* (*Ir. id.*) Aspect; colour; prosperity; festival; solemnity, pomp; a jewel; a tint, a die. Fear bu ghlaine lith, *a man of the fairest aspect.*—*Mac Lach.* Lith-dhonn caisfhionn, *brown and white-footed*—*Macfar.* Written also *ligh*, which see.

Litheadh, idh, *s m* (*Ir. id.*) A deluge; that part of a river where the water stagnates.

Lithear, ir, *s m. from* lith. (*Corn.* liuair.) A dyer.

Litheas, eis, *s m.* (*Ir. id.*) Solemnity; pomp—*Shaw.*

Litir, *gen.* litreach, *s. f* (*Lat.* litera. *Ir.* litir. *Arm.* lyzer.

Corn. lyzer.) A letter, a character in the alphabet; an epistle. Seanachd na litreach, *the oldness of the letter.—Stew. Rom.* Litir comhraig, *a challenge;* litir-ghrinnich, *a challenge;* litir dhealachaidh, *a bill of divorce;* litir ghaoil, *a love-letter;* litir leannanachd, *a love-letter, a billet-doux. N. pl.* litrichean, *letters; d. pl.* litrichibh.

LITIR-FHOGLUM, uim, *s. m.* Literature; lore.—*Old Poem.*

LITREACH, *gen. sing.* of litir; which see.

LITRICHEAN, *n. pl.* of litir. Letters.

LIUBHAIR, *v. a.* (*Lat.* libero.) Deliver, give up, surrender. *Pret. a.* liobhair, *delivered; fut. aff. a.* liubhraidh, *shall deliver.*

LIUBHRACH, *a.* Flaggy.

LIUBHRADH, aidh, *s. m.* A delivering, a giving up, a surrendering; a surrender.

LIUC, *s.* A shout, a noise.

LIUDAN, ain, *s. m.* A lever or crow; a gaveloc.

LIUDANACH, *a.* Like a lever.

LIÙG, liùig, *s. m.* (*Ir. id.*) A lame hand or foot; a sneaking gait; creeping.

LIUGACH, *a.* (*Ir. id.*) Lame-handed; lame-footed; sneaking; creeping.

LIÙGADH, aidh, *s. m.* (*Ir. id.*) A creeping; a sneaking; a creeping gait.

LIUGAIR, *s. m.* A cajoler.

LIUGAIREACHD, *s. f.* Cajoling.

† LIUGH, *s. f.* A cry, a shout.

LIUGHAD, *s.* and *a.* As many, an equal quantity. A liughad 's a theid mach, *as many as shall go out.*

LIUM, *comp. pron.; provincial* for leam; which see.

LIUMH, *s. m.* A cry.

† LIUN, *s. f.* (*Ir. id.*) Sloth, laziness, idleness; *also,* slothful, lazy.—*Shaw.*

† LIUNACHAS, ais, *s. m.* (*Ir. id.*) Idleness, sloth, laziness.

LIÙNASD, LIÙNASDAINN, LIUNASDAIL, *s. f.* Lammas.

LIUNCHLOS, *s. m.* Rest.—*Shaw.*

LIUNN, liunna, *s. m.* Ale. More commonly written *lionn.*

† LIUR, *s. m.* Noise, clamour, prating.

† LIURACH, *a.* Noisy, clamorous, prating.

LIURC, *s.* A pucker.

LIURC, *v. a.* Pucker.

LIUREACH, *a.* Puckered.

LIUTHAD, *a.* and *s.* As many, so many, equal quantity. A liuthad laoch 's a thainig, *when so many heroes came.—Old Poem.*

LIUTHAIR, *v. a.* (*Gr.* ἐλευθερόω.) Deliver, give up, surrender, set free. *Pret. a.* liuthair, *delivered; fut. aff. a.* liuthairidh, *shall deliver.*

LIUTHAIRTE, *p. part.* of liuthair. Delivered, surrendered, set free.

LIUTHARADH, *a.* A delivering, a giving up, a surrendering; a surrender.

LÒ, *s. m.* (*Ir. id.*) A day; a daylight; one day; on a certain day. More commonly written *là* and *làth;* which see.

† LO, *s. m.* (*Ir. id.*) A lock of wool; water.

LOB, loib, *s. m.* (*Ir. id.*) A puddle.

LOBAIS, *s. f.* (*Ir. id.*) Craft; ingenuity.

LOBANACH, *a.* Draggling; wallowing.

LOBANACHD, *s.* Draggling; frequent or continued wallowing; a drenching.

LOBANAICH, *s. f.* Draggling; wallowing; drenching.

LOBANAICH, *v. a.* Draggle; drench; wallow.

LOBARCAN, ain, *s. m.* A person drenched with rain or water; a diminutive person; a dwarf. *N. pl.* lobarcain.

LOBH, *v. n.* Rot, putrify, stink. *Pret. a.* lobh; *fut. aff. a.* lobhaidh, *shall rot.* Lobhaidh an abhainn, *the river shall stink.—Stew. Ex.*

LOBHACH, *a.* Rotten, stinking, fetid. Boladh lobhach, *a fetid smell.*

LOBHACHD, *s. f.* Rottenness, fetidness.

LOBHADAS, ais, *s. m.* Rottenness, fetidness.

LOBHADH, aidh, *s. m.* (*Ir. id.*) Rottenness, fetidness; stink; a putrifying, a stinking; putrefaction.

LOBHAIR, *gen.* and *voc. sing.* of lobhar; which see.

LOBHAIRCEAN, ein, *s. m.* A dwarf.

LOBHAR, air, *s. m.* (*Ir. id. Arm.* lovr.) A leper, a term of much personal contempt. Lagh do 'n lobhar, *a law to the leper.—Stew. Lev.*

LOBHARACH, LOBHRACH, *a.* Leprous. Lobhrach mar shneachda, *leprous as the snow.—Stew. Exod.*

LOBHARACHD, LOBHRACHD, *s. f.* Leprosy.

LOBHGACH, aich, *s. f.* A cow with calf.

LOBHRADH, aidh, *s. m.* A leprosy; a becoming leprous.

LOBHT, LOBHTA, *s. m.* (*W.* lloft. *Eng.* loft *and* aloft.) A gallery; a loft; a story; the highest floor; rooms on high; a garret; the part of a spinning wheel on which the spinner's foot rests. *N. pl.* lobhtan; *d. pl.* lobhtaibh. Do lobhta, *to a loft.—Stew.* 1 *K.* Le lobhtaibh iochdarach, *with lower stories.—Stew. Gen.*

LOBHTA, *p. part.* of *lobh.* Putrified, rotten, putrid; putrifying. Creuchd lobhta, *a putrifying sore.—Stew. Is.*

† LOC, *v. a.* (*Ir. id.*) Refuse; hinder.

† LOC, *s. m.* (*Lat.* loc-us, *a place. Ir.* loc.) A place.—*Shaw.*

LOCADH, aidh, *s. m.* (*Ir. id.*) Refusal; hindrance.

LOCAIR, *v. a.* Plane; smooth with a plane. *Pret. a.* locair, *planed; fut. aff. a.* locraidh.

LOCAR, air, *s. m.* A carpenter's plane. Locar dùirn, *a hand-plane;* locar gròbaidh, *a plough-plane;* locar sguitsidh, *a jack-plane;* locar dlùthaidh, *a jointer-plane;* locar-sgathaich, *shavings; spills of wood.*

LOCARACH, LOCRACH, *a.* Like a carpenter's plane; of, or belonging to, a plane.

LOCARADH, LOCRADH, aidh, *s. m.* A planing, working with a plane.

LOCARADH, LOCRADH, (a), *pr. part.* of locair. Planing. Saoir a locaradh 's a sabhadh, *carpenters planing and sawing.—Old Song.* Crann air a dheagh locradh, *a shaft well planed.—Old Song.*

LOCH, locha, *s. m.* A lake, a loch, an arm of the sea. Loch nan ruadhag, *the lake of roes.—Oss. Fing.* Loch Tath, *Loch Tay in Perthshire;* Loch Eireachd, *Loch-Erock in Inverness-shire;* Loch Aobh, *Loch-Awe in Argyleshire;* Loch Nios, *Loch Ness.*

Gr. λάκκος. *Lat.* lacus. *Germ.* lach, *pool. W.* llych, *lake. Manks,* luch. *Ir.* loch. *Arm.* lagen. *Bisc.* and *Fr.* lac. *Eng.* lake. *Sax.* and *Span.* lago. *Dal.* lokna. *Cop.* phalakkos. Also, *Heb.* lahh, *moisture. Chald.* lachah, *a marsh. Nor.* logus, *marsh;* and *Pers.* lacca, *a sea. Lugeus,* a lake in Illyria. *Luchnidus,* a lake in Macedonia. *Lucerne,* a lake in Switzerland. *Lucrin,* a lake in Campania.

† LOCH, *a.* (*Ir. id.*) Black, dark; every, all.—*Shaw.*

LOCHACH, *a.* Abounding in lakes.

LOCHADH, aidh, *s. m.* (*Ir. id.*) A fleece.

LOCHAIN, *s.* (*Ir. id.*) Sea-grass; sea-weed; sea-wrack.

LOCHAL, ail, *s. m.* The plant called brooklime.

LOCHAN, *n. pl.* of loch. Lakes.

† LOCHAN, ain, *s. m.* (*Ir id*) Chaff.—*Shaw.*

LOCHAN, ain, *s. m.* (*dim.* of loch.) A little lake, a pool. *N. pl.* lochain Lochain uisge, *pools of water.—Stew. Ecc.*

LOCHANACH, *a* Abounding in small lakes.

LOCH-ARMUNN, uinn, *s. m* A pigmy, a dwarf Written also *luch-armunn*

LOCHASAIR, *s.* A shower of rain

LOCHD, *s m.* (*Ir. id.*) A crime; a fault; a flaw or blemish, sin; a short sleep. Do lochd, *thy crime —Mac Lach. N.pl.* lochan, *our sins —Stew. Ez.*

LOCH-BHLEIN, *s* A flank. Written also *loch-lein.*

LOCHDACH, *a*, *from* lochd. (*Ir id*) Criminal; faulty; having flaws. Breith lochdach luath, *a faulty, hasty judgment.—Turn.*

LOCHDACHADH, aidh, *s m.* An injuring; a blaming, a censuring

LOCHCAICH, *v a* (*Ir* lochdaigh.) Blame, censure, injure. *Pret. a* lochdaich; *fut. aff. a.* lochdaichidh

LOCHDAICHTE, *p. part* of lochdaich Blamed, censured, injured.

LOCHLEIN, *s f., perhaps* loch-bhlein A flank, the region under the short ribs Air an lochlein, *on the flank.—Stew. Ex*

LOCHLINN, *s f.* The Baltic sea; *also*, Lochlin, or Scandinavia.

LOCHLINNEACH, ich, *s m* A Dane. Dubh-Lochlinneach, *a Dane*, fionn-Lochlinneach, *a Swede, a Norwegian.*

Some think that the proper orthography of this word is *Lochlannach*, from *loch*, lake, and *lann*, a Germano-Celtic word, meaning *land* If this opinion be correct, loch-lannach means a *lake-lander*, or one from the land of lakes

LOCH-MHAOIM, *s* The eruption of a lake

LÒCHRAN, ain, *s. m* A lamp, a torch, a flambeau; a light. *N pl* lochrain. Lasair nan lòchran, *the flames of the lamps —Oss Gaul* Na caith do lòchran, *spend not thy light —Id*

(*Ir id*) *Lat. by met.* lucerna *Goth* lukarn. *Arm.* luguern *Gr.* λυχνος. *Boh.* laûc, *a torch.*

LÒCHRANACH, *a* Full of lamps or torches; like a torch or lamp; lighted with lamps

LOCH-THAOMAIDHEAN, *s.* A burst of water from mountains

LÒD, loid, *s m.* (*Ir. id*) A puddle, a marsh or quagmire *N pl* lodan

LÒD, lòid, *s m.* (*Eng* load) A freight; a load; a volley; a cavalcade; bulk. Cuir gu càladh mi fein 's mo lòd, *put myself and my freight ashore —Old Song.* Leig iad lòd, *they fired a volley*, lòd sluaigh, *a cavalcade of people;* lòd-luach, *freightage.*

LÒDACHADH, aidh, *s m.* A freighting, a loading.

LODACHADH, aidh, *s. m.* A stagnating; a growing marshy or boggy.

LÒDAICH, *v a.* and *n.* Load, as a ship or a cart, grow bulky. *Pret. a.* lòdaich, *fut. aff. a.* lòdaichidh, *shall load, p. part.* lòdaichte, *loaded.*

LODAICH, *v. n.* (*from* lod) Stagnate; grow marshy or boggy. *Pret.* lodaich, *stagnated*, *fut aff.* lodaichidh, *shall stagnate.*

LÒDAIL, *a.* (*Ir. id*) Bulky, clumsy, cumbersome —*Macint.* Do chalpannan neo-lòdail, *thy neat legs.—Macfar.*

LODAIN, *s.* (*Ir. id.*) The privy parts; the flank

LODAN, ain, *s. m.* (*dim.* of lod. *Ir id*) A puddle, a little bog, a little marsh *N. pl.* lodain.

† LOG, loig, *s m.* (*Ir. id*) A pit or dike of water; a dungeon; a place —*Shaw.*

LOGAICHE, *s m.* A fool. *Ir.* logaidhe.

LOGAIRT, *s f.* Bad treatment; abuse; wallowing.

LOGAN, ain, *s m.* (*Scotch*, logan.) A small pit; a little hollow, the hollow of the hand—(*Shaw*), the side of a country; peace.

† LOGH. See LAGH.

LOGH, *s* (*Ir. id*) Renown

LOGHAILEACHD, *s. f.* Foolery, foolishness.

LOGHAN, ain, *s. m.* Indulgence, remission; jubilee.—*Shaw.*

LOGHMHOIREACHD, *s. f.* Stateliness; excellence; grandeur; famousness.

LOGH-MHOR, *a* (*Ir id.*) Famous, excellent; stately; majestic, grand; bright; valuable. *Com* and *sup.* loghmhoire.

LOIBEAN, ein, *s m.* A puddler; one who works in foul weather, one who works among puddly earth.

LOIBEANACHD, *s. f.* Working in foul weather; puddling.

LOIBHEACH, *a* Smelling fetidly, putrid, rotten. Tòchd loibheach, *a fetid smell.*

LOIBHEACHAS, ais, *s. m.* Fetidness, putridness

LOICEALACH, *a.* Doting; silly; foolishly fond. Gu loicealach, *dotingly*

LOICEALACHD, *s f.* Dotage; silliness; foolish fondness.

† LÒICH, *s f.* (*Ir id.*) A slattern; a trull; a place.—*Shaw.*

LOICHE. See LOICHEAD

LOICHEAD, eid, *s. m* (*Ir. id*) A lamp; a light; a torch; lightning; splendour *N. pl* loicheadan. *lamps.*

LOICHEADAIR, *s m* (*Ir. id*) A chandler.—*Shaw. N pl.* loicheadairean

LOIGEAR, eir, *s. m* An untidy or ragged person.

LOIGEARACHD, *s f.* Untidiness in dress

LOIME, *com.* and *sup.* of lom. More frequently written *luime.*

LOIME, *s. f*, *from* lom. (*Ir. id*) Bareness; baldness. More frequently written *luime*

LOIMIC, *s. f.* (*Ir id.*) A plaster for taking off hair.—*Shaw*

LÒIN, *gen sing.* of lòn. Of a diet See LON.

LÒIN, *gen. sing* of lon. Of a meadow.

† LOIN, *s f.* (*Ir. id.*) A little stream, a rivulet —*Shaw.*

LÒINEAG, eig, *s f.* A tuft of wool; a lock of wool, or of any such substance

LÒINEAGACH, *a* Like a tuft of wool; full of tufts of wool.

LÒINEAN, ein, *s m* A little meadow

LÒINEANACH, *a* Abounding in little meadows.

LOINEAR, eir, *s m.* Light; a gleam of light; a flash of light.—*Shaw.*

LOINEARACH, *a* Gleaming, shining; flashy; burnished. Written also *loinnreach*, which see.

LOINEARACHD, *s. f.* Brightness, effulgence. Written also *loinnreachd.*

LOINGEACH, *a.* (*Ir. id*) Nautical.

LOINGEAS, eis, *s. f.* (*Ir. id*) A ship; a barge; a shipping; a fleet. Loingeas chrannach, *a high-masted ship.—Ull. N. pl.* loingeasan

LOINGEASACH, *a.* (*Ir. id.*) Abounding in ships or in fleets.

LOING-BHRISEACH, *a.* (*Ir id*) Causing shipwreck.

LOING-BHRISEADH, idh, *s m.* (*Ir. id.*) Shipwreck.—*Shaw.* Written also *long-bhriseadh.*

LOING-SHAOR, -shaoir, *s. m.* (*Ir. id.*) A ship-carpenter. *N. pl.* loing-shaoir.

Loingsich, *v. n.* (*from* loingeas) Sail; set sail. *Pret. a.* loingsich; *fut. aff. a.* loingsichidh.

Loinid, *s. f.* (*Ir. id*) A churn-staff; a wooden instrument for frothing cream.

Loinideach, *a.* (*from* loinid) Like a churn-staff; belonging to a churning-staff, or a frothing-stick.

Loinidh, *s. f.* The sciatica; rheumatism. Gu h-olc leis an loinidh, *ill with the rheumatism.*

Loinig, **Loininn**, *s. f.* A lane for cattle. *N. pl.* loinigean *and* loininnean.

Loinn, loinne, *s. f.* A bladed weapon; the blade of a weapon. Dhùin an t-saill air an loinn, *the fat closed on the blade.—Stew. Jud.*

Loinn, loinne, *s. f.* (*Ir. id.*) Joy, gladness; fun, cheerfulness; good condition, fatness. Cha bhiodh loinn ach far am bi thu, *there is not joy but where thou art.—Macfar.*

Loinn, loinne, *s. f.* (*Ir. id. W.* llan.) A barn-yard; a corn-pen; a court; an area. Tobar na' loinn, *a well in his court.—Stew Sam. ref.*

Loinneach, *a.* (*Ir. id.*) Elegant; becoming; proper; neat; cheerful, joyful *Com* and *sup.* loinniche, *more* or *most elegant.*

Loinnearach. See **Loinnreach**.

Loinneas, eis, *s. m.* Elegance; neatness; seemliness; cheerfulness; sprightliness; wavering; rambling

Loinneil, *a.* (loinn-amhuil.) Elegant; pleasant; proper; neat; cheerful. Is loinneil dos gach doire, *cheerful are the tufts of every grove.—Macfar.* Ceòl loinneil, *cheerful music.—Macint.*

Loinnreach, *a.* Burnished; gleaming, bright, sonorous; loud; sounding; changing Ceann-bheairt loinnreach, *burnished helmets.—Oss. Taur.* Claidheamh loinnreach, *a gleaming sword —Stew. Nah.* Uile sholuis loinnreach neamha, *all the bright lights of heaven.—Stew Ezek*

Loinnreachd, *s. f.* Brightness, effulgence, sonorousness, loudness.

Loinnrich, *v. n.* Shine, gleam, glitter, sparkle *Pret.* loinnrich, *shone; fut. aff. a.* loinnrichidh, *shall shine.* Loinnrich iad mar dhath praise, *they shone* [*sparkled*] *like the colour of brass.—Stew Ezek.*

Lointean, *n. pl* of lòn; *d. pl.* lòintibh.

Loinseach, ich, *s. m* An exile

Loirc, *s. f.* (*Ir. id*) A gammon. Loirc do mhuic-fheoil, *a gammon of bacon.*

Loironeadh, idh, *s. m.* A stalk.

Loisceanta, *a.* See **Loisgeanta**.

Loise, *s. f.* A flame; *also, adjectively,* inflamed

Loiseam, eim, *s m.* Parade; grandeur; a company of gentry B' uallach do loiseam, *noble was thy company.—Turn*

Loisg, *v. a.* (*Ir id Arm.* lisqui.) Burn, scorch, scald, inflame; singe; parch; fire, as a gun or cannon. *Pret a* loisg, *burned; fut. aff. a.* loisgidh, *shall burn* Loisg iad tùis, *they burned incense —Stew. Jer.*

Loisgeach, *a.* Burning; inflammable; caustic; fiery, corroding.

Loisgean, ein, *s. m.* The herb called pimpernel—(*Macd*), a salamander.

Loisgeanta, *a.*, *from* loisg. (*Ir.* loisceanta.) Fiery; inflammatory; inflammable; flaming; keen; parching, scorching, blasting.

Loisgionn, *s. m.* A locust.

Loisgrean, ein, *s. m.* Burnt corn—(*Shaw*); corn burnt out of the ear instead of being threshed.

Loisgte, *p. part.* of loisg. (*Arm* losquet.) Burned, scorched, parched; inflamed; scalded. Ionadan loisgte, *parched places —Stew. Jer.* Tha so loisgte, *this is burned.* In the Armoric it is, *a so losquet.* Leann loisgte, *dregs from which ale is brewed.*

Loisid, *s f.* A kneading-trough.—*Macd. N. pl.* loisidean.

Loisidh, *s f* A flame.

Loisteach, ich, *s m.* (*Ir. id.*) A trough.

Loistean, ein, *s m* A lodging, a dwelling-place, a booth, a tent

† **Loisteil**, *a* (loist-amhuil.) Slothful, inactive.

Loistich-fuinidh, *s f.* A kneading-trough —*Shaw.*

Loit, *s. m.* See **Lot**

Loiteag, eig, *s f* (*Ir. id*) A nettle; a whore. *N pl* loiteagan

Loit-shealgair, *s. m.* A debauchee.

Lom, *v. a.* Shear; clip; strip, shave, make bare; fret. *Pret a* lom, *clipped; fut. aff. a.* lomaidh, *shall clip.*

Lom, *a.* Bare, naked; smooth; lean; open or exposed; bleak, *substantively,* a field O charragh lom na lear, *from the bare sea-rock —Oss. Tem* Lannan lom, *naked swords* Cho lom ri oigh, *as smooth as a virgin.—Oss. Fing.* Air an fhàich luim, *on the open field —Stew Ez. Com* and *sup* luime.

Lomadair, *s. m*, *from* lom. (*Ir.* lomadoir) A shaver, a shearer, a clipper, a plunderer. *N. pl.* lomadairean.

Lomadaireachd, *s f* Sheep-shearing; shaving; a plundering

Lomadh, aidh, *s. m.* (*Ir. id.*) A shaving, a shearing, a clipping; a plundering; a making bare; desolation; baldness.

Lomadh, (a) *pr. part.* of lom. Making bare; shearing, shaving.

Lomaich, *s. f* (*Ir* lomoigh) A shorn sheep.

Lomain, *s f.* (*Ir. id.*) A shield

Lomair, *s. m.* A barber, a shearer; a fleecer; a plunderer. *N. pl.* lomairean.

Lomair, *v a* Shear, as sheep; fleece. *Pret. a.* lomair, *fleeced; fut. aff. a.* lomairidh, *shall fleece*

Lomairt, *s. f* (*Ir id*) Sheep-shearing; a fleece; a peeling, shaving. Fear-lomairt, *a sheep-shearer;* luchd-lomairt, *sheep-shearers.* Luchd lomairt a chaorach, *his sheep-shearers.—Stew Gen.*

Lomairt, (a), *pr. part* and *inf* of lomair Shearing; to shear or fleece. A lomairt a chaorach, *to shear his sheep.—Stew. Gen*

Lomaisteach, *a.* (*Ir id*) Bare, bald, shorn; *also,* a bald man

Loman, ain, *s. m.* (*Ir. id*) An ensign, a banner; a shield. —*Shaw.* A bald man, *also,* a niggard; a knot in timber stripped of its bark. Gheibh an lomhan an lom-dhonas, *the niggard will receive misery.—G P.*

Lomanach, aich, *s m.* (*Ir. id*) A person of a meagre form; a bald man —*Shaw. N. pl.* lomanaich.

Lomar, *fut. pass.* of lom; which see

Lomar, air, *s. m.* A fleece *N pl* lomaran

Lomarach, *a.* Fleecy, woolly. Caoraich lomarach, *fleecy sheep. Com* and *sup* lomaraiche.

Lomardach, *a.* Naked, bare, uncovered Is bochd an ainis lomardach, *poor is the want that is naked.—G P.*

Lomardachd, *s f.* Nakedness, bareness.

† **Lomargain**, *s f* A devastation, a ravaging, a plundering, a fleecing

Lomarta, *part* of lomair. (*Ir* lomartha.) Shorn, fleeced. An treud lomarta, *the shorn sheep —Stew Song Sol*

Lomartair, *s. m* A shearer, a fleecer, a clipper.

LOMBAIR, *s f.* A bare surface; a field with a meagre crop of grass; *also, adjectively*, bare, unfertile.

LOM-CHOSACH, *a.* (*Ir id.*) Barefooted.

LOM-DHONAS, ais, *s m.* Misery, poverty

LOMHAIN, *s. f.* (*Ir. id.*) A leading-string

LOMHAINN, LOMHAIR, *s f* A leading-string; a cord or throng to lead a dog. Lomhainn chon, *a pack of hounds;* lomhair chon, *a pack of hounds.*

LOMHAR, *a.* Bright, effulgent, gleaming, glittering. Gu lomhar, *brightly*

LOM-LÀN, *a.* Quite full, brim full. Tobar lom-lan an cois na tràigh, *a brim full fountain on the shore.—Old Song.*

LOMNA, ai, *s m* A rope —*Shaw*

† LOMNAIR, *s m* (*Ir id.*) A harper.

LOMNOCHD, *a*, lom-nochd. (*Ir id*) Bare, naked, uncovered; *also*, nakedness. Bha iad lomnochd, *they were naked —Stew. Gen.* A cheann lomnochd, *his head bare.—Stew Lev.*

LOMNOCHDACHD, *s f.* Nakedness, bareness, the state of being uncovered.

LOMNOCHDAICHE, *s f.* (*Ir* lomnochduighe) Nakedness, bareness Written also *lomnochduiche*

LOMNOCHDAIDH, *s f.* (*Ir.* lomnochduighe.) Bareness, nakedness, nudity, bareness Lomnochdaidh na tire, *the* [*bareness*] *nakedness of the land.—Stew. Gen.* Written also *lomnochduidh*

LOMNOCHDUICHE, *s. f.* (*Ir.* lomnochduighe) Bareness, nakedness, nudity, barrenness. Do lomnochduiche, *thy nakedness —Stew Nah*

LOMNOCHDUIDH. See LOMNOCHDAIDH.

LOMPAIS, *s f.* Niggardliness; parsimony. Gun lompais, *without niggardliness.—Old Song.*

LOMPAS, *a.* (*Ir id*) Niggardly, sparing

LOMRACH, *a* (*Ir. id*) Fleecing, shearing; fleecy, woolly Caoraich lomrach, *fleecy sheep*

LOMRADH, aidh, *s m* (*Ir id*) A fleece; a fleecing, a shearing of sheep; effulgence, gorgeousness. Lomradh olla, *a fleece of wool.—Stew Jud.*

LOM-SGRIOS, *v a* Erase utterly, destroy; lay waste, sweep cleanly away *Pret a.* lom-sgriob, *fut aff a.* lom-sgriobaidh, *shall erase*

LOM-SGRIOB, *s. f* Desolation, a laying waste; a clean sweep; a sweepstake, complete erasure. Bheir mi lom-sgriob, *I will lay waste —Stew. Lev.*

LOMTA, *p. part.* of lom. Bared, made naked, stripped, fleeced, shorn, shaven

LÒN, lòin, *s. m. (Ir. id.)* A meadow *N pl* lòintean, *d pl* lòintibh 'G a thaomadh air lòintibh, *pouring it on meadows. —Oss*

LÒN, lòin, *s m.* (*Dan.* lon, *wages*) A diet, a dinner; a store, provision, food. Lòn do luibhibh, *a diet* [*dinner*] *of herbs —Stew Pro* Air bheag lòin, *on a scanty diet —Old Poem* Thug e dhoibh lòn, *he gave them provision —Stew Gen* An seann lòn, *the old store —Stew. Lev.* Lon siubhail, *viaticum*

The Gael of former times, like other ancient nations, had but one meal or diet a day, namely, the *lon* the terms, *diot, dinneir*, or *biadh-nòin*, and *suipeir*, are of modern date.

LON, loin, *s. m.* (*Ir. id.*) An ousel; a blackbird, an elk. Is binn guth loin, *sweet is the blackbird's strain.—Fingalian Poem* Lon dubh, *a blackbird.*

LON, loin, *s m* (*Ir id*) Greed, prattle; hunger; *also*, a rope of raw hides used by the people of St Kilda.

† LON, loin, *s. m.* (*Ir. id.*) A marsh, a morass; a pond, water

Anciently *lon* meant a *river*; hence, perhaps, *Lon-dun*, London, or, *the river-city.*

LONACH, *a.*, *from* lon. (*Ir. id*) Greedy, voracious; prattling; prone to tell secrets *Com.* and *sup.* lonaiche.

LÒNACH, *a.*, *from* lòn. (*Ir. id*) Meadowy; abounding in meadows; marshy; of, or pertaining to, food or provision. An coire lònach, *the meadowy dell.—Macdon. Com.* and *sup.* lònaiche.

LÒNACH, aich, *s. m.* A larder, a pantry.

LONACHD, *s. f*, *from* lon. (*Ir. id*) Greediness, voraciousness; talkativeness; the habit of tattling or of tale-telling.

LONAG, aig, *s f.* (*from* lon.) A tale-telling female; a prattling female *N. pl.* lonagan.

LONAGACH, *a* (*from* lonag) Like a tattling female; tattling, as a female.

LONAICHE, *s. f.* Prattling, tattling, tale-telling.

LONAICHE, *com* and *sup.* of lonach; which see.

LONAILT, *s. f* (*Ir. id.*) A pantry.

LONAINN, *s. f.* (*Ir.* loinin *Scotch*, loaning) A lane or passage for cattle.

LONAIS, aise, *s f.* Prattling; a disposition to tell tales; prating

LONAN, ain, *s. m* (*from* lon) A prattler; a tale-teller; *also*, prating, tale-telling Nach sguir thu do d' lonan? *wilt thou not cease thy prating?—Fingalian Poem. N. pl.* lonain

LON DUBH, -duibh, *s. m.* A blackbird; the *turdus merula* of Linnæus; an ousel. Nead an lon duibh, *the blackbird's nest*

† LONG, *v. a.* (*Ir. id*) Destroy; devour; worry. *Pret. a.* long, *fut aff a.* longaidh.—*Shaw.*

LONG, luing, *s f* (*Ir. id. W.* llong.) A ship; a barge. Gabh do long, *take thy ship.—Ull.* Aros nan long, *the abode of ships*, i e. *the ocean.—Oss Fing. N. pl.* longan; *d pl* longaibh. Mar na longaibh luatha, *like the fast-sailing ships —Stew. Job*

LONG, loing, *s m.* (*Ir. id.*) The fish called ling; *also*, a cup; a bed; a house; the breast.—*Shaw.*

LONGADH, aidh, *s m.* A supper; a meal or diet. *N. pl.* longaidh

LONGADH, aidh, *s m.* (*Ir. id*) A casting; a throwing; a devouring; a rocking.

LONGAIN, *s. f.* (*Ir. id*) A ship's crew.

LONGAS, ais, *s. m* (*Ir. id.*) Banishment; shipping.

LONG-BHÀTHADH, aidh, *s m* (*Ir. id*) Shipwreck.

† LONG-BHRAINE, *s. f.* (*Ir. id.*) The prow of a ship.—*Shaw.*

LONG-BHRISEACH, *a* Causing shipwreck; shipwrecking. Gailshionnan long-bhriseach, *shipwrecking storms.— Old Poem.*

LONG-BHRISEADH, idh, *s m* (*Ir. id*) Shipwreck. Rinn iad long-bhriseadh, *they made shipwreck.—Stew. Tim.*

LONG-CHEANNUICHE, *s f* A merchant-ship *N. pl.* luing-cheannuiche, *merchant-ships.* Mar longaibh cheannuiche, *like merchant-ships.—Stew. Pro.*

LONG-CHOGAIDH, *s. m.* (*Ir. id*) A ship of war, a man-of-war. *N. pl.* longan-chogaidh.

LONG-DHÌDEIN, *s. f.* A guard-ship.

LONG-FHADA, *s. f.* (*Ir. id*) A galley, *N. pl.* luing-fhada.

LONG-LÒDAIDH, *s. f.* A ketch

LONG-LÒDAIL, *s. f.* A ketch.

LONG-PHORT, -phuirt, *s m.* A harbour; a palace; a royal residence; a camp; a garrison; a tent. Is aithne dha gach long-phort, *he knows every harbour.—Macfar.* Cormac na long-phort, *Cormac in his camp.—Fingalian Poem.*

Long-phortach, *a.* Full of harbours, camps, or garrisons; of, or pertaining to, a harbour or garrison. A laoich làidir long-phortaich! *thou mighty hero of camps!—Fingalian Poem.*

Long-sgarach, *a.* Causing rifts in vessels.

Long-sgaradh, aidh, *s. m.* A rift in a ship or boat.

Long-shaor, -shaoir, *s. m.* (*Ir.* loing-shaor.) A carpenter; a ship-carpenter. *N. pl.* long-shaoir.

Long-spùille, *s. f.* Piracy. Luchd long-spùille, *pirates.*

Long-spùinneadair, *s. m.* A pirate or sea-robber; *literally*, a plunderer of ships.

Long-spùinneadh, idh, *s. m.* Piracy; the act of plundering ships.

Long-spùinnidh, *s. f.* A privateer; a pirate ship. *N. pl.* luing-spùinnidh.

Long-thogail, *s. f.* Ship-building.—*Shaw.*

Lonloingean, ein, *s. m.* The gullet, the throat; any pipe.

Lonn, loinn, *s. f.* (*Ir. id.*) A stake of wood; a bier-pole; timber laid under a vessel to facilitate the launching of it; a sword; a blade; a bar; *rarely*, anger, choler.

† **Lonn**, *a.* (*Ir. id.*) Strong, powerful.

† **Lonn**, loinn, *s. m.* (*Ir. id.*) A surge, a sea-swell; anger, choler.

Lonnachadh, aidh, *s. m.* An abiding, a dwelling or sojourning; continuance.

Lonnagan, **Lonnogan**, ain, *s. m.* A passionate young man.

Lonnrach, *a.* (*Ir. id.*) Shining, sparkling, glistering; bright, burnished; splendid; brave; *also, substantively*, a blaze; a gleam. Clachan lonnrach, *glistering stones.—Stew.* 1 *Chr.* Gu lonnrach, *splendidly. Com.* and *sup.* lonnraiche.

Lonnrachd, *s. f.* (*Ir. id.*) Brightness, effulgence; a gleaming.

Lonnradh, aidh, *s. m.* (*Ir.* loinreadh.) A gleaming, a glistering; a sparkling, a brightening.

Lonnraich, *v. a.* and *n.* (*Ir.* lonnraigh.) Make bright, burnish; grow bright; shine, gleam.

† **Lorc**, *a.* (*Ir. id.*) Fierce, cruel.

† **Lorc**, loirc, *s. m.* (*Ir. id.*) Murder; the cramp.—*Shaw.*

Lorc-chosgach, *a.* (*Ir. id.*) Antispasmodic.

Lor-daothain, *s.* (*Ir. id.*) Sufficiency, enough.

† **Lorg**, *a.* (*Ir. id.*) Blind.

Lorg, luirg, *s. f.* (*Ir. id.*) A staff; a crutch; a footstep; a trace, track, or print; a vestige; the stalk of a plant; the handle of a flail; the shaft of a banner; consequence; a troop, a band; progeny, offspring; a leg, a shin, a shank; the thigh; a woman. Ag aomadh air a luirg, *bending over his staff.—Oss. Fin. and Lor.* Air luirg an treud, *in the footsteps of the flock.—Stew. Song Sol.* Laoch air mo lorg, *a warrior in pursuit of me*, i. e. *in my track.—Oss.* Air lorg mo theachd, *since* [*in consequence of*] *my coming.—Stew. Gen.* Lorg iomain, *a goad;* cù luirg, *a terrier. N. pl.* luirg; *d. pl.* lorgaibh.

Lorg, *v. a.* Trace, follow by tracing, pursue; investigate. *Pret. a.* lorg, *traced; fut. aff. a.* lorgaidh, *shall trace.*

Lorgach, *a.* (*from* lorg.) Having a staff or crutch; like a staff or crutch; tracing, pursuing; searching.

Lorgachadh, aidh, *s. m.* (*from* lorgaich.) A tracing; a searching, a pursuing; a walking on crutches.

Lorgadh, aidh, *s. m.*, (*Ir. id.*) A searching; a tracing. Cù lorgaidh, *a terrier, a pointer.*

Lorgaich, *v. a.* (*from* lorg.) Trace, pursue, follow a footstep; walk on crutches. *Pret. a.* lorgaich; *fut. aff. a.* lorgaichidh.

Lorgaichte, *p. part.* of lorgaich. Traced, pursued, found out by tracing.

Lorgair, *s. m.* (lorg-fhear.) A tracer; a spy; one who pursues by tracing footsteps; a searcher; a pointer-dog; a slow-hound; a terrier. Lorgair mac luirg, *a character in Highland romance. N. pl.* lorgairean.

Lorgaireachd, *s. f.* (*Ir. id.*) A tracing; the habit of tracing; espionage.

Lorganach, aich, *s. m.* (*Ir. id.*) A sluggard. *N. pl.* lorganaich.

Lorgbheairt, *s. f.* (*Ir. id.*) Foot-harness; armour for the legs; covering for the legs and feet.

Lorg-iomain, *s. f.* A goad; a stick to drive cattle with. Le luirg-iomain, *with an ox-goad.—Stew. Jud.*

Los, *s. m.* (*Ir. id.*) Intention, purpose, design; account; sake; strength, virtue; effect, consequences; *rarely*, a tail, the point or end of a thing. Tha mi los dol dhachaidh, *I have a mind to go home;* tha mi a leth los, *I have half a mind.*

Losaid, **Losait**, *s. f.* (*Ir. id.*) A kneading-trough. *N. pl.* losaidean.

† **Losg**, *a.* (*Ir. id.*) Cripple; blind; dumb; *also*, a lame or blind person.—*Shaw.*

Losgach, *a.* Burning; inflammatory; apt to burn; corroding.

Losgadair, *s. m.* (*Arm.* losqadur.) A burner.

Losgadh, aidh, *s. m.* A burning; a scalding; a scorching; a parching; a kindling; a singeing; inflaming; a burn; a scald. Losgadh airson losgaidh, *a burning for a burning.—Stew. Ex.* Losgadh bhràghad, *the heartburn;* losgadh na grèine, *the scorching of the sun; the effect of the sun's heat on the human countenance.* Losgadh dealanaich, *a blasting by lightning.—Stew. Deut. ref.*

W. llosg, *heat. Arm.* losg. *Corn.* llosg. *Ir.* losgadh. *Teut.* loug, *a fire. Swed.* loghe. *Gr.* φλοξ, *a flame. Chin.* lo, *fire. Syr.* and *Carn.* osgan, *burnt.*

Losgan, ain, *s. m.* (*Ir. id.*) Childhood.

Losgann, ainn, *s. m.* (*Ir.* losgan.) A frog; the *rana temporaria* of Linnæus; a toad; a sledge.—*Macd. Rarely*, childhood. *N. pl.* losgainn. Theid na losgainn suas, *the frogs shall come up.—Stew. Gen.* Losgann nimhe, *a toad;* losgann buidhe, *a frog;* losgann dubh, *a toad;* the *rana bufo* of Linnæus.

Losgannach, *a.* Abounding in frogs or toads; like a frog or toad.

Losg-bhra-teine, *s.* A ducking or throwing of stones obliquely against the water, so as to make them rebound several times from the surface.

Losgunn, uinn, *s. m.* See **Losgann**.

Lot, lota, *s. m.* (*Ir.* lot. *Bisc.* lot.) A wound, a stab, a bruise, a hurt, a sore; *rarely*, a whore; wool; a leg; washing. Lot airson lotaidh, *wound for wound.—Stew. Ex. N. pl.* lotan, *wounds; gen. pl.* lot. Làn lot, *full of wounds.—Oss. Fing. D. pl.* lotaibh. Lot-urchair, *a gun-shot wound;* lot claidheimh, *a sword wound.—Stew. Rev.*

Lot, *v. a.* Wound, stab, bruise; hurt; *rarely*, commit fornication. *Pret. a.* lot; *fut. aff. a.* lotaidh. Lot i mòran, *she has wounded many.—Stew. Pro. Fut. pass.* lotar, *shall be wounded.* A lotadh mo chleibh, *wounding my breast.—Old Song.*

Lotach, *a.* (*from* lot.) Vulniferous; destructive; bruising, stabbing, maiming. Lannan lotach, *destructive swords.—Macdon. Com.* and *sup.* lotaiche.

Lotadh, aidh, *s. m.* (*Ir. id.*) A wounding, a stabbing, a bruising, a maiming; a stab, a wound, a bruise; *rarely*, fornication. Lot airson lotaidh, *wound for wound.—Stew. Ex.*

LOTAIDH, 3 *sing.* and *pl. imper a* of lot. Lotadh e, iad, *let him, them, wound* Also, *pret. pass. was wounded.* Lotadh ciocha geal Ghràine, *the fair breast of Gruna was wounded.—Oss. Derm.*

LOTADH, (a), *pr part* of lot; which see.

LOTAR, air, *s. m.* (*Ir. id*) A ruining; a mangling

LOTAR, *fut. pass.* of lot Shall be wounded. See LOT

† LOTH, *s m.* (*Ir. id*) A beard; sweat.

LOTH, *s m* and *f* A filly, a foal, a colt; a meal or diet. Loth asail, *an ass's colt.—Stew Gen.*

LOTHACH See LÀTHACH.

LOTHAG, aig, *s. f.* (*dim.* of loth) A young filly, foal, or colt; a little filly, foal, or colt. *N. pl* lothagan.

LOTHAINN-CHON, *s* A pack of hounds

LOTHAIR, *s. m.* (*Ir. id*) Lavender. Uisge an lothair, *lavender water.*

LOTHAL, ail, *s m.* The plant brooklime.

† LOTHAR, air, *s. m.* (*Ir id*) An assembly, a cauldron; a trough, a hound, cloth, raiment —*Shaw.*

† LU, *a* (*Ir id*) Little, small.

† LUA, *s. m* (*Ir id*) Water; an oath, a foot, a hand, a kick —*Shaw.*

LUACH, luacha, *s. m* (*Ir. id*) Value, worth, price, wages; Luach na lainn ud, *the value of that sword.—Oss. Derm* Bithidh cuimhne air do luach, *thy worth shall be remembered —Macfar.* Luach ciatach, *a goodly price.—Stew Zech* Luach saoithreach, *price of labour, hire, wages*, cha deanainn air mhòr luach e, *I would not do it for any consideration*, luach peighinn, *a pennyworth*, luach-saoraidh, *a ransom*, làn-luach, *full price —Stew.* 1 *Chr*

† LUACHAID, *s f.* (*Ir id*) Frost

LUACHAIL, *a.* (luach-amhuil) Rateable.

LUACHAIR, *s f.* (*Ir. id*) Splendour, brightness; a tempest.

LUACHAIR, *gen. sing* of luachar

LUACHAIRNEACH, ich, *s f.* (*Ir. id.*) A place where bulrushes, reeds, or rushes grow.—*Macd*

LUACH-AISIG, *s. m.* A ferryage, a water-fare Phaigh e 'n luach-aisig, *he paid the water-fare.—Stew Jon*

LUACHAR, *gen* luachair *and* luachrach, *s f.* A bulrush, a rush; the *scirpus palustris* of botanists Fàich na luachrach, *the rushy plain.—Oss Gaul* Caol-rath nan ald 's na luachair, *the vale of streams and rushes —Oss Tem*

LUACH-ARMUNN, uinn, *s. m* More properly *luch-armunn*, which see.

LUACHARN, airn, *s m* (*Ir. id. Lat.* lucerna) A lamp. See LÒCHRAN

LUACHMHOIRE, *com.* and *sup.* of luachmhòr More or most valuable.

LUACHMHOIREACHD, *s. f* (*Ir* luachmharachd) Valuableness, preciousness, excellence.

LUACHMHÒR, *a*, luach *and* mòr (*Ir.* luachmhar) Valuable, precious, excellent. Nithe luachmhor, *precious things.—Stew. Jer*

LUACHRACH, *gen. sing* of luachar.

LUACHRACH, *a*, *from* luachar (*Ir. id*) Full of rushes; rushy, like a rush; made of rushes. An glacag luachrach, *the rushy dell —Macint.* Raon luachrach, *a rush-covered meadow.—Orr.*

LUACHRACH, aich, *s. f* A place where rushes grow; a crop of rushes.

LUACH-PEIGHINN, *s. m.* A pennyworth. Deagh luach-peighinn, *a good pennyworth.*

LUACH-SAORAIDH, *s m* A ransom. A thug e féin na luach-saoraidh, *who gave himself a ransom.—Stew. Tim. ref.*

LUACH-SAOITHREACH, *s. m.* A reward, hire, wages.

† LUAD, luaid, *s. m.* A joint; the little finger.

LUADAIR, *s. m.* (*Ir. id*) A flax-wheel, the flier of a jack.

LUADAR, air, *s. m.* (*Ir. id.*) Motion, haste.

LUADH, luaidh, *s. m.* A fulling of cloth.—*Macint.* See LUATHADH.

LUADH, luaidh, *s. m.*, dh *silent.* (*Ir id. Span.* lua) Mention, panegyric, praise; conversation; rumour; talk; *rarely*, motion. Gun luadh ri éiridh, *without word of rising.—Ull* Mac mo luaidh, *the son of my praise.—Oss.* A luadh air sgeul mo ghradh, *his talk of* [*concerning*] *the tale of my love.—Oss Gaul.*

LUADH, *v a* (*Ir. id*) Mention; praise, converse.

LUADHADAIR, *s. m.* A fuller. *N. pl* luadhadairean.

LUADHADAIREACHD, *s f.* Fulling; the business of a fuller

LUADHADH, aidh, *s m* A mentioning; a praising; a fulling of cloth. For this last sense, see LUATHADH

LUADHAIRLE, *s f.* Motion, exercise.—*Shaw*

LUADHAR, *fut pass* of luadh. Shall be praised.

LUADH-GHÀIR, *s m.* A shout of joy; a loud laugh; joy. Written also *luagh-ghàir.*

LUADHMHOIRE, *com.* and *sup.* of luadhmhor.

LUADHMHOIREACHD, *s. f* The condition of being renowned.

LUADHMHOR, *a.* (luadh-mor.) Renowned, notable. Lanna luadhmhor, *renowned arms.—Old Poem.* Gu luadhmhor, *in a notable manner.* *Com.* and *sup.* luadhmhoire.

LUADHRADH, aidh, *s. m.* Fame, report.

LUADHRAICH, *v a* (*Ir.* luadhridh) Report, make renowned or notable.

LUADHREAL, eil, *s m* (*from* luadh, *praise*) Laurel. Coron luadhreil, *a coronet of laurel.*

LUAG, luaig, *s. f* A doll. Do luag a leinibh, *thy doll, my child.—Old Song.* *N pl* luagan.

LUAGH, luaigh, *s m.* (*Gr.* λογια. *Ir.* luadh.) Mention; talk See LUADH.

LUAGH-GHÀIR, *s. f.* (luadh-ghair.) A loud rejoicing; a shout of joy; a loud laugh, joy; *rarely*, a reward. Le luaghair, *with joy —Stew Zeph.*

LUAGHAIREACH, *a* Joyous, rejoicing, rejoicing loudly, or shouting with joy Sa chathair luaghaireach, *in the rejoicing city.—Stew. Zeph.*

LUAGHAIREACHD, *s f.* Continued joy; rejoicing.

LUAGHASACHADH, aidh, *s. m* A permitting, allowing; permission. Also written *luathasachadh.*

LUAGHLAS, ais, *s. m.* († lua, *hand*, and glas) A manacle, a handcuff, a fetter.

LUAGHSACHD, *s. f.* Permission; readiness to give permission

LUAGHSAICH, *v a* Permit, allow. *Pret. a.* luaghsaich, *permitted; fut. aff a.* luaghsaichidh, *shall permit.* Cha luaghsaich mi dhuit, *I will not allow you.* Also written *luathsaich.*

LUAGHSAICHTE, *p. part.* of luaghsaich. Permitted, allowed.

LUAGHUTA, *s. m* The gout; the gout in the fingers.

LUAIDH, *v* Mention; praise; make noted; full, as cloth *Pret. a id* ; *fut. aff.* luaidhidh, *shall mention.*

LUAIDH, luaidhe, *s f.* (*Dan* leey, *a song. Eng.* lay.) Praise; mention; a song or poem in praise of one; a beloved person; love; the subject of one's praise; lead. Gun fhilidh, gun luaidh, *without bard, without praise.—Oss. Tem.* Is glas mo luaidh, *pale is my beloved.—Oss. Com.* Cothrom luaidhe, *a weight of lead.—Stew. Zech.* Luaidh-ghorm, *blue lead.—Macint.* Luaidh chaol, *lead-drops, small shot;* citean luaidhe, *a lead-drop.*

LUAIDHE, *s. f.* (*Ir. id.*) Coition, copulation.

LUAIDHEACH, *a.* Laudable; giving praise; abounding in lead.

LUAIDHEACHD, *s. f., from* luaidh. (*Ir.* luaidheacht.) Praise; mention; frequent mention; love; reward; requital; renown.

LUAIDREAN, ein, *s. m.* (*Ir. id.*) A vagabond; *also,* vagary.

† LUAIGH, *a.* (*Ir. id.*) Cheerful, pleasant; *substantively,* buying; price.

LUAIGH, *s. f.* See LUAIDH.

LUAIGHEACHD, *s. f.* (*Ir. id.*) Requital, reward.—*Stew. Pro.* Written also *luaidheachd;* which see.

LUAILLEACH, ich, *s. m.* (*Ir. id.*) A mimic; a buffoon.—*Shaw.*

LUAILLEACH, *a.* See LUAILTEACH.

LUAILTE, *s. f.* Speed, despatch.

LUAILTEACH, *a.* (*from* luath.) Restless; volatile; full of gestures; rapid, swift. Written also *luathailteach.*

LUAILTEACHD, *s. f.* (*from* luath.) Restlessness; volatility; buffoonery; rapidity. Written also *luathailteachd.*

LUAILTICH, *v. a.* Accelerate, hasten, forward, promote.

LUAIMEAR, eir, *s. m.* A man with a voluble tongue; a prater; a tell-tale.

LUAIMEARACHD, *s. f.* Volubility of tongue; prating; tale-telling.

LUAIMH, *s. m.* (*Ir. id.*) An abbot.—*Shaw.*

LUAIMHNEACH, *a.* See LUAIMNEACH.

† LUAIMH-NIGH, *s. f.* A wave-offering.

LUAIMNEACH, *a.* (*Ir. id.*) Volatile; restless; fickle; ambulatory; skipping, frisking, hopping, jumping; *also,* a volatile or fickle man. Gu luaimneach, *restlessly. Com.* and *sup.* luaimniche.

LUAIMNEACHD, *s. f.* (*Ir. id.*) Volatility; restlessness; fickleness; unsteadiness; ambulatoriness; a propensity to skip or frisk; a habit of frisking or skipping; continued frisking, skipping, or hopping.

LUAIN, *s.* (*Ir. id.*) The loins, kidneys.

LUAIN, *gen. sing.* of luan. Dé luain, *Monday;* la luain, *a Monday.* See LUAN.

LUAINEACH, *a.* (*Ir. id.*) Volatile; fickle; unsteady; restless; changeable; flitting; ambulatory; always in motion; always running, as water. Tha thu gaoithe, luaineach, *thou art giddy and volatile.—Old Song.* Leabadh nan neula luaineach, *a bed of restless clouds.—Oss. Gaul.* Ceò luaineach, *restless* [*unsteady*] *mist.—Id.* Uisge luaineach an lòin, *the running stream of the meadow.—Old Song.*

LUAINEACHD, *s. f.* Volatility; fickleness; unsteadiness, changeableness, restlessness.

LUAIN-GHALAR, *s. m.* Nephritic pains; lunacy.

LUAIN-GHALARACH, *a.* Affected with nephritic pains; lunatic; causing nephritic pains.

LUAINTEAN, *a.* Nephritic.

LUAIREAGAN, ain, *s. m.* (*Ir. id.*) A grovelling person, a driveller. More properly *luaithreagan,* from *luaithre,* ashes. Bidh an luaireagan luaith na uallachan gille, *the child that grovelled in the ashes may be a strutting beau.— G. P.*

LUAIREAGANACH, *a.* (*from* luaithre.) Grovelling, wallowing; like a grovelling person. Amadan luaireaganach, *a grovelling idiot.*

LUAIREAGANACHD, *s. f.* The habit of grovelling; grovelling.

LUAIREANTA, *a.* See LUAITHREANTA.

LUAISD, *s. f.* A shovel, a stable-spade.

LUAISG, *v. a.* and *n.* (*Corn.* lask, *a cradle.*) Rock, swing, toss; wave, float; jolt; drive away. *Pret. a.* luaisg, *rocked; fut. aff. a.* luaisgidh, *shall* or *will rock.*

LUAISGTE, *p. part.* of luaisg. Rocked, tossed, swung.

LUAITH, *gen. sing.* of luath. Ashes. Also an *inflection* of luath, *swift;* which see.

LUAITHE, *com.* and *sup.* of luath. Quicker, quickest; faster, fastest. See LUATH.

LUAITHEAD, id, *s. m.* Swiftness, rapidity, quickness; increase in swiftness. A dol an luaithid, *growing more and more swift;* air luaithid sa bheil e, *however swift he be.*

LUAITHRE, *s. f.* (*Ir. id. Arm.* luder.) Dust, ashes. Gus an crion gu luaithre a chloch, *till the stone shall crumble into dust.— Oss. Gaul.* Ann an luaithre, *in ashes.— Stew. Jon.*

LUAITHREACH, *a.* (*Ir. id.*) Dusty; covered with dust; full of ashes; like ashes; *also, substantively,* a quantity of ashes.

LUAITHREADH, idh, *s. m.* (*Ir. id.*) A pulverising; dust, ashes. Luaithreadh a chas, *the dust of his feet.—Stew. Nah.*

LUAITHREANTA, *a., from* luaithre. (*Ir. id.*) Dusty; full of ashes; like ashes or dust; pulverised.

† LUAM, luaim, *s. m.* (*Ir. id.*) An abbot; a pilot.

† LUAMAN, ain, *s. m.* (*Ir. id.*) A veil.—*Shaw.* A small hand.

† LUAMH, luaimh, *s. m.* (*Ir. id.*) An abbot, a prior; a sneaking person; a corpse. *N. pl.* luaimh.

† LUAMHAIR, *s. m.* (*Ir. id.*) A pilot. *N. pl.* luamhairean.

† LUAMHNACHD, *s. f., from* luamh. (*Ir. id.*) An abbacy, a priory; an abbotship, a priorship.

LUAN, luain, *s. f.* The moon. Dé luain, *Monday;* la luain, *a Monday;* also, *a day enlightened by the moon,* i. e. *a day that shall never come.* Gu lath luain, *never.—R.*

Luan seems to be a contracted form of luath-an, *the swift planet.*

Gr. σελήνη. *Lat.* luna. *Ir.* luan. *W.* llun. *Fr.* lune.

† LUAN, luain, *s. m.* (*Ir. id.*) A loin; a kidney; a warrior. —*Shaw.* Luan-ghalar, *nephritic pains.*

† LUANAISG, *s. f.,* † lua, *foot,* and naisg. (*Ir. id.*) Chains for the legs.

† LUANASGACH, *a.* (*Ir. id.*) Chaining, fettering, binding; *also,* chained.

LUARACH, aich, *s. f.* (*Ir. id.*) A chain; a milching fetter; fetters.

LUARACH, *a.* Vulgar, common.—*Shaw. Com.* and *sup.* luaraiche.

LUAS, luais, *s. m.* (*Ir. id.*) Swiftness, speed. Do luas mar iolair nam beann, *thy speed like the mountain-eagle.— Ull.* Contracted for *luathas;* which see.

LUASACHADH, aidh, *s. m.* Permitting.

LUASACHAIL, *a.* That may be permitted.

LUASAICH, *v. a.* Grant, permit. *Pret.* luasich; *fut. aff.* luasaichidh; *fut. pass.* luasaichear, *shall be granted.* Luasaichear an costus, *the expense shall be granted.—Stew. Ezra.*

LUASAICHTE, *p. part.* of luasaich.

LUASGACH, *a.* Rocking, swinging, floating, tossing.

LUASGACHD, *s. f.* A rocking motion; continued rocking, swinging, or tossing.

LUASGADAIR, *s. m.* A swinger, a rocker. *N. pl.* luasgadairean.

LUASGADH, aidh, *s. m.* (*Arm.* lesisqel.) A rocking, a swinging, a tossing, a floating.

LUASGADH, (a), *pr. part.* of luaisg. Rocking.

Luasgan, ain, *s. m.* (*Ir. id.*) A cradle; childhood; a swing; a rocking or swinging motion. Gaoth 'chuireas luasgan air meoir a phris, *wind which shall cause the branches to shake.—Old Song.*

Luasganach, *a.* (*Ir. id.*) Rocking, swinging; unsteady, inconstant, restless. Am breac luasgannach, *the restless trout.—Macfar.* An òig luasganach, *inconstant youth.—Mac Lach.* Tonn luasganach, *a rocking wave.*

Luasganachd, *s. f.* (*Ir. id.*) Continued rocking or swinging; the amusement of swinging; unsteadiness, inconstancy.

Luasganaiche, *s. m.* (*Ir. id.*) One who rocks or swings.

Luasganaiche, *s. f.* A rocking motion; a swinging; a tossing in a swing.

Luath, *a.*, *from* †lua, *foot.* (*Bisc.* lehiath. *Ir.* luath.) Swift, fleet, quick, speedy, transient, soon. Luath mar fhìrein, *swift as an eagle.—Oss. Gaul.* Cho luath, *so soon, so quickly.—Stew. Gen.* Daraig is luaithe fàs, *an oak of the quickest growth.—Oss. Gaul.* Gu luath, *quickly, swiftly, soon.*

Luath, luaith, *s. f.* (*Ir. id.*) Ashes, dust; praise. In this last sense it is almost always written *luadh* or *luaidh.*

Luath, *v. a.* (*Ir. id.*) Hasten; make haste; move; full cloth; mill cloth. *Pret. a.* luath; *fut. aff. a.* luathaidh, *shall hasten.*

Luathach, *a.* Fulling, milling, as cloth; like ashes; full of ashes. Muileann luathach, *a fulling-mill.*

Luathachadh, aidh, *s. m.* A fulling, as of cloth; a hastening; a promoting or accelerating.

Luathadh, aidh, *s. m.* Hastening; moving.

Luathadh, aidh, *s. m.* A fulling or cleansing of cloth. Muileann luathaidh, *a fulling-mill.*

Where fulling mills are at a great distance, the waulking or fulling of cloth is performed by females in the following manner:—Six or eight (I have seen fourteen) take their stations, in an equal manner, on each side of a long frame of wattled work, or sometimes of a board ribbed longitudinally, and placed on the ground. Thereon is laid the wetted blanket or cloth which is to undergo the process of waulking. The women then kneel, and, with their arms, rub it firmly against the frame, with all their strength; singing loudly, at the same time, some mountain melody. When their arms grow tired, they very naturally have recourse to their legs; then, sitting upon the ground, and tucking their petticoats up to their knees, the cloth is forthwith under a course of more vigorous friction than before. As the work grows warm, the song grows louder and louder, even to a very yell; and at this stage of the process, a stranger coming unexpectedly upon them, and who had never heard of such a substitute for a fulling-mill, might well take them for the weird sisters engaged in some terrible incantation.

Luathaich, *v. a.* and *n.* Accelerate, hasten, hurry. *Pret. a.* luathaich; *fut. aff. a.* luathaichidh, *shall accelerate.* Luathaichidh i, *it hastens.—Stew. Ecc.* Luathaich ort, *make haste.—Stew. Song Sol. Fut. pass.* luathaichear.

Luathaichte, *p. part.* of luathaich.

Luathailt, *s. f.* Swiftness, quickness, rapidity, despatch.

Luathailteach, *a.* Swift, quick, rapid, expeditious; full of gestures; volatile. *Com.* and *sup.* luathailtiche.

Luathailteachd, *s. f.* Rapidity, swiftness, volatility.

Luathailtich, *v. a.* Accelerate, hasten, despatch, forward.

Luath-aireach, Luath-aireachail, *a.* Apprehensive, quick-witted.

Luatharan, ain, *s. m.* (*Ir. id.*) A sea-lark. *N. pl.* luatharain.

Luathas, ais, *s. m.*, *from* luath. (*Ir. id.*) Swiftness, rapidity, quickness, expedition. Luathas analach, *asthma.* Cha bhi luathas agus grinneas, *there cannot be expedition and neatness.—G. P. Luathas* is often contracted *luas.*

Luath-bhar, *a.* (*perhaps* luathmhor.) Expeditious, travelling quick, swift. Each liath luath-bhar, *a swift grey horse.—Fingalian Poem.*

Luath-bhàs, -bhàis, *s. m.* A sudden death; untimely death. Luath-bhàs m'athar ghaolaich, *the sudden death of my beloved father.—Orr.*

Luath-bhàt, *s. m.* (*Ir. id.*) A fly-boat.

Luath-bheulach, *a.* Gabbling; supple-tongued; talkative. Gu luath-bheulach, *talkatively.*

Luath-bhileach, *a.* Gabbling, prating, talkative. Gu luath-bhileach, *talkatively.*

Luath-chainnteach, *a.* (*Ir. id.*) Talkative.

Luath-choragach, *a.* Nimble-fingered; pilfering.

Luath-ghàir, -ghàire, *s. f.* (*Ir. id.*) A shout of triumph, a shout of joy, a loud rejoicing. Bithidh luath-ghàir ann, *there shall be a shouting.—Stew. Pro.*

Luath-lamhach, *a.* (*Ir. id.*) Ready-handed, quick-handed, dexterous; pilfering; covetous. Gu luath-lamhach, *dexterously.*

Luath-lamhachd, *s. f.* Ready-handedness; dexterousness; covetousness; knack; legerdemain.

Luath-long, -luing, *s. f.* A cutter; a fast-sailing ship.

Luath-mharc, *s. m.* (*Ir. id.*) A race-horse, a swif horse.

Luath-mharcachd, *s. f.* (*Ir. id.*) Swift riding; riding express.

Luath-mharcair, *s. m.* A rapid rider; an express. *N. pl.* mharcairean.

Luath-mhire, *s. f.* (*Ir. id.*) Gasconading, vaunting.—*Shaw.*

Luathraich, *v. a.* Hasten, accelerate, promote.

Luathsaich, *v. a.* Permit, allow; make an allowance. *Pret. a. id.; fut. aff.* luathsaichidh, *shall permit.* Cha luathsaich mi dhuit, *I will not permit you.*

Luathsachadh, aidh, *s. m.* Permission; an allowance.

Luathsachd, *s. f.* Permission; allowance.

Lùb, luib, *s. m.* (*Ir. id. Eng.* loop.) A noose, a loop; a tache; a winding; a maze; a meander; the curvature of a shore; a creek; cunning; craft; flexibleness; inclination; tendency; a bow; thong. *N. pl.* lùban. Lùban do ghorm, *loops of blue.—Stew. Ex.* Caothan nan lùban uaine, *green-winding Caothan.—Oss. Derm. D. pl.* lùbaibh. Tre lùbaibh cam, *through crooked windings.—Macfar.*

Lùb, *v. a.* (*Ir. id.*) Bend, stoop, bow, submit, yield; incline. *Pret.* lùb; *fut. aff. a.* lùbaidh, *shall bend.* Darag nach lùb, *an oak that will not bend.—Ull.* Lùb Fillean a bhogha, *Fillan bent his bow.—Oss. Tem.*

Lùbach, aich, *s. f.* A loop; a loop-hole; loops. *N. pl.* lùbaichean.

Lùbach, *a.*, *from* lùb. (*Ir. id.*) Bowing, bending, flexible, pliant; crooked, serpentine, winding, meandering; cringing; crafty; perverse. Slatag lùbach, *a pliant switch.* Nathair lùbach, *a crooked serpent.—Stew. Job.* Lùbach na theangaidh, *perverse in his tongue.—Stew. Pro.* Gu lùbach, *pliantly, craftily. Com.* and *sup.* lùbaiche.

Lùbadh, aidh, *s. m.* A bending, a bowing; a winding, a meandering; a yielding, submission. Cha d' rinn mi leat lùbadh, *I did not yield to thee.—Old Song.*

Lùbadh, (a), *pr. part.* of lùb; which see.

Lùbag, aig, *s. f.* (*dim.* of lùb.) A little loop; a little loop-hole; *also*, a measure of yarn. *N. pl.* lubagan.

Lùbaidh, *fut. aff. a.* of lùb; which see.

Lùbair, *s. m.* (*Ir. id.*) A crafty fellow; one who bends to every purpose; a cringing fellow.

Lùban, *n. pl.* of lùb; which see.

Lùban, ain, *s. m., dim.* of lùb. *(Ir. id.)* A bow, a bend; a loop; a little bow or bend; a little curvature; a meander.

Lùb-cheangal, ail, *s. m.* A hinge. *N. pl.* lùb-cheanglaichean.

† **Lubha**, *s. m.* (*Ir. id.*) The body; a corpse; praise, fame.

† **Lubhan**, ain, *s. m.* *(Ir. id.)* A lamb.

Lubh-ghort, -ghoirt, *s. m., perhaps* luibh-ghort. *(Ir. id.)* A garden.—*Shaw.*

Lubhra. See **Luibhre.**

Lubhrach, *a.* See **Lobhrach.**

Lub-lìn, *s. f.* *(Ir. id.)* A curved line.

Lùb-lìneach, *a.* (*Ir. id.*) Curvilinear.

Lùb-shruth, *s. m.* A winding stream.—*Macfar. N. pl.* lub-shruthan; *d. pl.* lùb-shruthaibh.

Lùbta, Lùbte, *p. part.* of lùb. Bent, made crooked, made to yield.

Luch, lucha, *s. m.* *(Ir. id.)* A mouse; the *mus musculus* of Linnæus; *rarely*, a prisoner, a captive. An eas agus an luch, *the weasel and the mouse.*—*Stew. Pro. N. pl.* luchaidh. Luch-fhrangach, *a rat;* luch feòir, *a field-mouse;* peasair nan luch, *vetches;* luch fairge, *a small Staffa bird resembling a swallow.* See **Luchaidh-fhairge.**

Luchag, aig, *s. f., dim.* of luch. (*Ir.* luchog.) A mouse; a little mouse. *N. pl.* luchagan.

Luchaidh, *n. pl.* of luch. Mice.

Luchaidh-fhairge, *s. pl.* Mother Cary's chickens; small black birds with crooked bills and webbed feet, resembling swallows in size, and found in vast numbers in the isle of Staffa, and throughout the Hebrides.

Shaw observes of these sea-fowls, that they go into holes like mice, and that when they are taken, a quantity of yellow oil falls from their bills. It has been remarked of them that they hatch their eggs by sitting on the ground about six inches from them, and, turning their heads towards them, make a cooing noise, called *gur le gùg*, 'hatch with a song,' day and night till the eggs are hatched. They are dreaded by mariners, who presage an approaching storm from their appearance. They collect during a tempest, and are seen sweeping with incredible swiftness along the wake of a ship They are common throughout the ocean; and are the same with the κυψελλοι, or *cypselli*, of the ancient seamen.—See **Pliny**, x. 30.

Luchair, *s. f.* *(Ir. id.)* A glittering colour; brightness; gleaming, glistering.—*Shaw.*

Luchaire, *s. f.* *(Ir. id.)* A mouser.—*Shaw.*

Lùchairt, airte, *s. f.* (*Ir. id.*) A court, a palace; a fort, a castle; a retinue. Lùchairt tighe an righ, *the palace of the king's house.*—*Stew.* 1 *K.* Mar chrannaibh lùchairte, *like the bars of a castle.*—*Stew. Pro.* Ionad lùchairt nan Gaidheal, *the place of retinue among the Gael.*—*Macfar.*

Luchairteach, *a.* Having palaces or courts; having forts or castles.

Luchar, air, *s. m.* (*Ir. id.*) Light.

Luch-armunn, uinn, *s. m.* (*Ir. id.*) A dwarf, a pigmy.

Luch-armunnach, *a.* Like a dwarf; pigmy.

† **Luchbhrac**, *s.* A white head of hair.

Luchd, *s. f.* (*Ir. id.*) A burden, a load, a freight, a cargo; *rarely*, a kettle, a cauldron. Luchd eartach, *a cart-load;* luchd luing, *a ship-load*, a *cargo.*

Luchd, *s.* (*Dan.* laug, *society. Ir.* luchd.) People, folks, company. Luchd-airde, *attendants, retinue.* Luchd-aiteachaidh, *inhabitants*—(*Stew. Hab.*); luchd-brathaidh, *spies*—(*Stew. Heb.*); *traitors;* luchd-ceannairc, *traitors, rebels*—(*Stew. Hab.*); luchd ceart-dheuchainn, *a jury;* luchd-comhairle, *advisers, counsellors*—(*Mac Lach.*); luchd-coimhid, *observers, spectators, overseers, attendants;* luchd-coimheadachd, *attendants, overseers;* luchd-ealaidh, *sportsmen; gay people*—(*Macfar.*); luchd-éisdeachd, *hearers,* luchd-eucoir, *unjust people, oppressors;* luchd-caladhainn, luchd-ealainn, *carpenters;* luchd-fairge, *mariners, seafaring people;* luchd-fiosachd, *wizards, soothsayers*—(*Stew. Lev.*); luchd-fòireignidh, luchd-fòireigin, *oppressors, extortioners*—(*Sm.*); luchd-gaòil, *lovers, beloved people;* luchd-leanmhuinn, *followers*—(*Stew. Eph.*); *pursuers;* luchd-malairt, *merchants*—(*Stew. Nah.*); luchd-millidh, *spoilers, destroyers, plunderers;* luchd-shaighead, *archers*—(*Stew. Job*); luchd-urrais, *sureties*—(*Stew. Pro.*); luchd-tiolpaidh, *cavillers;* luchd-tuaileis, *quarrelsome persons.*

Luchdach, *a.* Burdening, freighting, loading; ponderous.

Luchdachadh, aidh, *s. m.* A loading, a freighting, a burdening.

Luchdachadh, (a), *pr. part.* of luchdaich.

Luchdaich, *v. a.* (*from* luchd.) Load, burden. *Pret. a.* luchdaich, *loaded; fut. aff. a.* luchdaichidh, *shall load.*

Luchdaichte, *p. part.* of luchdaich. Loaded, laden. Luchdaichte le h-aingidheachd, *laden with iniquity.*

Luchdmhoire, *com.* and *sup.* of luchdmhor.

Luchdmhor, *a.* (luchd *and* mòr.) Heavy, laden, burdened; burdensome; capacious. *Com.* and *sup.* luchdmhoire.

Luch-lann, -lainn, *s. m.* (*Ir. id.*) A prison.

Luch-lein, *s. f.* A groin. Written also *loch-léin;* which see.

Luchuirt, *s. f.* A court, a palace; a castle, a fort; a royal retinue.

† **Lud**, *s. m.* (*Ir. id.*) A pond.

Lùdach, aich, *s. m.* (*Ir. id.*) A hinge. *N. pl.* lùdaich *and* lùdaichean, *hinges.*

Lùdag, aig, *s. f.* (*Ir.* ludagan *and* luadicin.) A little finger; a hinge; a little hinge; a joint. *N. pl.* ludagan, *hinges; d. pl.* lùdagaibh. Air a lùdagaibh, *on its hinges.*—*Stew. Pro. ref.* Mathair na lùdaig, *the ring-finger.*

Lùdaichean, *n. pl.* of ludach. Hinges.

Ludair, *v. a.* and *n.* Wallow, grovel; flounder; besmear with dirty water; roll in water. *Pret. a.* ludair, *wallowed; fut. aff.* ludairidh, *shall wallow.* Written also *luidir.*

Ludairt, *s. f.* (*Ir. id.*) Rolling in mire or water; wallowing; waddling in mire, as ducks.

Lùdan, ain, *s. m.* A hinge; the little finger. *N. pl.* ludanan, *hinges; d. pl.* ludanaibh. Dorus air a ludanaibh, *a door on its hinges.*—*Stew. Pro.*

Lùdanach, *a.* (*from* ludan.) Having hinges; like a hinge.

Ludar, air, *s. m.,* (*Fr.* loutre, *a water-dog.*) A slovenly person; a trull; fawning. *N. pl.* ludaran.

Ludarach, *a.* Slovenly, sluggish; wallowing, grovelling.

Ludarachd, *s. f.* Slovenliness, sluggishness; grovelling.

† **Ludasach**, *a.* Strong, powerful. *Com.* and *sup.* ludasaiche.

Ludh, *s. m.* (*Ir. id.*) Appearance; likeness; manner. Ludh an spioraid dol timchiol an drochaid, *go about the bridge as the ghost did.*—*G. P.*

Ludhar, *a.* (*Ir. id.*) Awkward; clownish; slovenly.

Ludragan, ain, *s. m.* (*Ir. id.*) An untidy person, a sloven, a slattern; a groveller; a shambling fellow.—*Shaw. N. pl.* ludragain.

Ludraganach, *a.* Untidy; grovelling.

Lùgach, *a.* (*Ir. id.*) Bow-legged.—*Macd.* and *Shaw.*

Lùgachd, *s. f.* The infirmity of bowed legs.

Lugadh, aidh, *s. m.* Thirst.

Lugaidh, *s.* (*Scotch,* luggie.) A little ansated wooden dish.

Lugan, ain, *s. m.* (*Ir. id.*) A sorry-looking fellow; a bow-legged man; a short crooked fellow.—*Shaw.*

Luganach, *a.* Shabby; sorry; bow-legged; of a mean personal appearance; *also*, a sorry fellow.

LUGH, *v.* (*Ir. id.*) Swear.—*Shaw.*

LUGH', *abbreviation* of lugha.

LÙGH, *s. m.* Pith; strength; power of motion. Phill a lùgh, *his strength returned.—Oss. Gaul.*

LUGHA, *com* and *sup.* of beag. (*Ir. id. Arm* lai.) Less, least. Is e is lugha na thusa, *he is less than you.* Am fear is lugha do 'n triùir, *the least of the three.* Air a chuid is lugha, *at the least.—Stew Gen.*

LUGHA, *s.* See LUGHADH.

LUGHACHAN, *n. pl* of lughadh. Oaths, imprecations, swearing.

LUGHAD, aid, *s. m.* (*Ir. id.*) Littleness. A dol an lughad, *growing less*, air a lughad, *however little it be*, air a lughaid sa bheil e, *however little he* or *it be.*

LUGHADH, aidh, *s. m.* An oath, an imprecation, swearing; want, thirst. *N. pl.* lughachan.

LÙGHADH, aidh, *s m.* Pith; strength; power of motion. A meòir gun lughadh, *her fingers without motion.—Ull.*

LUGHDACHADH, aidh, *s. m.* A diminishing, abating; diminution, abatement, a decreasing.

LUGHAICH, LUGHAIG, *v a* Permit, allow, swear. *Pret id*, *fut aff* lughaigidh, *shall permit.*

LUGHDAICH, *v a.* and *n*, *from* lugha (*Ir. id.*) Diminish, lessen, abate, decrease. *Pret a* lughdaich, *lessened*, *fut. aff a* lughdaichidh, *shall lessen.—Stew. Pro*

LUGHDAICHE, *s m* An abater.

LUGHDAIREACHD, *a.* Disparagement, abatement.

LÙGHMHOIRE, *com.* and *sup.* of lùghmhor

LÙGH-MHOR, *a* Vigorous, powerful, muscular; pithy. Leabadh nan laoch lùghmhor, *the bed of the powerful warriors.—Oss Derm. Com* and *sup.* lughmhoire. Written also *lùthmhor.*

LUGH'OR, *a.*, a *contraction* of lughmhor.

LUIB, *s f.* (*Ir id*) A corner; an angular turning; a winding, as of a stream, a meander; a creek; an eddy; a little glen. Luib, *a creek.—Stew Acts ref.* Luib na gaoith, *the eddy of the wind. Oss. Fin and Lor.* Luib, *a little glen.—Shaw.*

LUIBEACH, *a* (*from* luib.) Angular, meandering; having creeks; bending, as the shores of a lake.

LUIBEAN, ein, *s. m* A crafty fellow, one who can be made to bend to any purpose.

LUIBEANACHD, *s f* Craftiness.

LUIBH, *s. f* (*Ir. id.*) An herb; a weed, grass. Mar luibh a seargadh, *withering like an herb.—Oss. Gaul.* Luibh an liugair, *lovage.* Luibh nan tri bheann, *a plant of three leaves* or *of three corners.*

LUIBHEACH, *a.* (*Ir. id*) Full of herbs; full of weeds; botanic; herbal. Garaidh luibheach, *a botanic garden*, also, *a garden full of weeds.*

LUIBHEAN, ein, *s. m* (*dim* of luibh) A little herb; a blade of grass. Feur-luibhean gorm, *a green blade of grass.—Macfar.* Also, *N. pl* of luibh.

LUIBHEANACH, *a* Full of herbs; full of weeds; botanic, herbal.

LUIBHEANACH, ich, *s. m.* A botanist, a weeder, *also*, weeds, herbage.

LUIBHEANACHD, *s. f* Botany; herbage. Ri luibheanachd, *botanising.*

LUIBH-EOLACH, *a* Skilled in the virtues of herbs; skilled in the nature and formation of plants or herbs.

LÙIBH-EÒLAS, ais, *s. m.* Botanical knowledge; phytology.

LUIBH-GHORT, *s. m.* A garden, a green garden, a kitchen garden.

LUIBH-BHIAST, *s. m.* (*Ir.* luibh-phiast.) A caterpillar. *N. pl.* luibh-bheistean.

LUIBHNE, *s. f.* (*Ir. id.*) A dart, a spear; *also*, a shield; the fingers; the toes.

LUIBHNEACH, ich, *s m* (*Ir id.*) A weed.

LUIBHRE, *s. f* Leprosy; *also*, a coat of mail. Mar nochdar an luibhre, *as the leprosy appears.—Stew. Lev.*

LUIBH-SGÀILE, *s. f.* A gourd.—*Stew Jon.*

LUID, *s f* A rag; a trull; a slovenly female.

LUIDEACH, *a*, *from* luid. (*Ir. id*) Ragged.

LUIDEAG, eig, *s. f.* (*dim.* of luid) A rag; a young trull; a little slattern; *in ridicule*, a bank note. *N. pl* luideagan. Eudaichidh turra-chodal le luideagan, *drowsiness will clothe with rags.—Stew. Pro.*

LUIDEAGACH, *a.* (*Ir.* luideogach) Ragged. Na toir droch mheas air mac luideagach, *despise not a ragged boy.—G. P. Com.* and *sup* luideagaiche.

† LUIDH, *s. m.* A word of endearment.—*Shaw.* Perhaps a corruption of *a laogh.*

LUIDH, *s f.* A herb. More commonly written *luibh.*

LUIDH, *v n.* (*Dan.* lege, *a bed Ir.* luidh, *lie. Gr.* λήθω, *to conceal*) Lie, recline; settle, subside, as wind; perch; set, as the sun. *Pret. a.* luidh; *fut aff. a* luidhidh, *shall lie.* Luidh mi teann air, *I lay near him.—Oss. Lod.* Luidh an iolair air bàrr an teach, *the eagle perched on the top of the dwelling.—Oss Gaul.* Luidh a ghrian, *the sun has set*, luidh a ghaoth, *the wind has subsided.* Luidheadh ceò air Croma, *let mist settle on Croma.—Oss. Com.* Chaidh e' luidh, *he went to bed.* In some parts of the Highlands *luidh* is pronounced *laidh.*

LUIDHE, *s. f* (*Ir. id*) A lying, a reclining; a settling; a position, situation; a subsiding, as of wind; incubation; a setting, as of the sun; death. Mo mhac san torr na luidhe, *my son lying in the grave.—Oss. Fin and Lor.* Luidhe na grèine, *sunset.* A ghrian air luidhe, *the sunset.—Stew. Gen.* Tha e na luidhe, *he is lying, he is in bed.* Luidhe, *death.—Shaw.* Luidhe siùbhla, *childbed.—Stew. Micah, ref.*

LUIDHEACHAN, ain, *s m.* (*Ir id*) An ambush, a snare. *N pl.* luidheachain.

LUIDHEACHANACH, aich, *s. m.* One who lies in wait.

LUIDHEIR, *s. m* (*Ir. id*) A chimney, a vent; a flue. Toit as an luidheir, *smoke from the chimney.—Stew. Hos. N. pl.* luidheirean.

LUIDHINN, 1 *sing imper. sub.* of luidh. I would lie. Luidhinn sìnte leat, *I would lie stretched with thee.—Ull.*

LUIDHSA, LUIDHSE, (*for* luidh thusa) Lie thou.

LUIDIR, *v. a* Wallow; flounder; wallop; roll in water or mire; paddle; guddle. *Pret. a.* luidir; *fut aff a.* luidridh, *shall wallow.*

LUIDNEACH, *a.* Heavy, drooping, as with rain.

LUIDREACH, *a.* Wallowing, wallopping, paddling, guddling.

LUIDREADH, idh, *s m.* A wallowing; a floundering; a wallopping, a paddling; a guddling.

LUIDSE, *s m.* A heavy clumsy person.

LUIDSEACH, *a.* Heavy-heeled; clumsy.

LUIDSEAR, eir, *s. m.* A heavy clumsy person; a looby.

LUIG, *gen. sing* of lag. Of a dell. Dathannan gach luig, *the colours of every dell.—Macdon.*

LUIGEAN, ein, *s. m.* An inactive fellow; an untidy fellow.

LUIGEANACH, *a.* Inactive; untidy, unsmart.

LUIGEANACHD, *s f.* Untidiness, unsmartness; inactivity.

LUIGH, *s f.* A herb. More frequently written *luibh.*

LUIGH, *v. n.* Lie. See LUIDH. *Also*, tear; encourage, abet.

LUIGHE, *s. f.* (*Ir. id*) A proof; a cauldron, a kettle.

Luigheachd, *s. f.* Requital, recompense. Dia na luigheachd, *the God of recompense.—Stew. Jer.* Thoir luigheachd, *reward, requite.*

Luigheachdaich, *v. a.* Requite, recompense.

Luigheam, ein, *s. m.* (*Ir. id.*) A nave; a centre.

Luigheasach, aich, *s. m.* (*Ir. id.*) An allowance; *adjectively*, allowable.

Luiligheach, *s. f.* (*Ir. id.*) A milch cow.—*Shaw.*

Luim, an *inflection* of lom; which see.

† **Luim**, luime, *s. f.* (*Ir. id.*) Milk.

Luim-dheirg, *s. f.* The deep; deep water, the deep channel of a river. Bruach na luim-dheirg, *the verge of the deep.*

Luime, *s. f.* Bareness; bleakness; nakedness; a bare or smooth part. Luime a mhuineil, *the smooth of his neck.—Stew. Gen.*

Luime, *com.* and *sup.* of lom. Barer, barest. See **Lom.**

Luimead, id, *s. m.* (*Ir. id.*) Bareness, nakedness; barrenness; increase in bareness. A dol an luimead, *growing more and more bare.* Air a luimid is a bheil e, *however bare it be.*

Luimean, ein, *s. m.* (*Ir.* luimain.) A bare barren hillock; a spare-formed man; a target; a shield.

Luimeanach, *a.* Bleak; bare; abounding in bleak hillocks; like a bleak or barren hillock.

Luimlinn, *s. f.* (*Ir. id.*) A stream of milk.

Luimneach, *s.* Limerick in Ireland.

Luimneach, *a.* Active; brave; *also*, a standard-bearer or ensign. A laoich luimnich! *thou brave warrior!—Death of Carril.*

Luimneachd, *s. f.* Activity; bravery; an ensign-bearer.

† **Luin**, *s. f.* A sword; a spear; the blade of a weapon. Mac-an-luin, *the name of Fingal's sword*,—so called from Luno, the Scandinavian armourer who fabricated it.

Luing, *gen. sing.* of long; which see.

Luing-bhris, *v. a.* and *n.* Cause shipwreck; suffer shipwreck.—*Shaw.*

Luing-bhriseach, *a.* Causing shipwreck.

Luing-bhriseadh, idh, *s. m.* A shipwreck; a suffering of shipwreck.

Luingeas, eis, *s. f.* A ship; a navy. *N. pl.* luingeasan, *ships.*

Luingeasach, *a.* Abounding in ships; having a navy.

Luingios. See **Luingeas.**

Luiniasg, eisg, *s. m.* (*Ir. id.*) A sword-fish.

Luinne, *s. f.* (*Ir. id.*) Anger; impetuosity; *also*, mirth; melody.

Luinneach, *a.* (*Ir. id.*) Angry; *also*, mirthful, jovial—(*Shaw*); melodious; having swords.

Luinneag, eig, *s. f.* (*Ir.* luinnioc, *music.*) A ditty; a chorus; the burden of a song; a Gaelic song; a Highland catch. An uiseag 's a luinneag, *the lark and her song.—Macint.* Luinneag luaidh, *a poetical panegyric. N. pl.* luinneagan.

Luinneagach, *a.* Like a ditty; having Gaelic songs or catches.

Luinneanach, *a.* Tossing, floundering, paddling.

Luinneanachadh, aidh, *s. m.* A tossing, a floundering, a paddling.

Luinneanaich, **Luinnearaich**, *v. a.* and *n.* Flounder, paddle, wallop.

Luinneanaiche, **Luinnearaiche**, *s. f.* A continued floundering, a paddling, a wallopping.

Luinn-iasg, éisg, *s. m.* A sword-fish.

Luinnse, *s. m.* and *f.* An indolent person, a sluggard. *N. pl.* luinnsean.

Luinnseach, ich, *s. m.* (*Ir. id.*) A watch-coat; a heavy clumsy greatcoat.

Luinnsear, ir, *s. m.* A lounger; a lazy vagrant; a watchman. *N. pl.* luinnsearan.

Lùireach, ich, *s. f.* A coat of mail; a patched covering, a patched garment; an apron; harness. Càireadh gach fear a lùireach, *let each prepare his mail.—Oss. Duth.* A caramh nan lùireach, *repairing patched garments.—Macint.* Lùireach leathair, *a leathern apron;* eadar altaibh na lùireach, *between the joints of the harness.—Stew. 1 K.* Lùireach mhàilleach, *a coat of mail, an habergeon.—Stew. Ex.* Lùireach lannach, *a coat of mail; steel armour.—Stew. Sam. ref. N. pl.* lùirich.

Gr. λωρικιον. *Lat.* lorica. *Ir.* luireach. *W.* lhyrig.

Luirg, *gen. sing.* of lorg.

Luirg-bheairt, *s. pl.* Armour for the legs; a covering for the legs.

Luirgeann, inn, *s. f.* A shank; a shin; a long leg; a stalk; the gambrel or hind leg of a horse; a steep barren surface. Luirgeann luath, *a character in Highland romance. N. pl.* luirgne *and* luirgeannan. Luirgeannan os cionn a throidhibh, *legs above his feet.—Stew. Lev.* Luirgne cath, *spears.—Oss. Cathula.*

Luirgne, *n. pl.* of luirgeann; which see.

Luirgneach, *a.*, *for* luirgeannach. (*Ir. id.*) Long-legged, long-shanked, long-stalked. Lus luirgneach, *a long-stalked weed.—Macdon. Com.* and *sup.* luirgniche.

Lùiriste, *s. m.* A slovenly person, an untidy person. *N. pl.* luiristean.

Lùiristeach, *a.* Slovenly, untidy, lazy. Gu lùiristeach, *lazily.*

Luis, *s. f.* (*Ir. id.*) The quicken tree; the letter L of the Gaelic alphabet; *rarely*, a hand; drink.

Luis, *gen. sing.* of lus; which see.

† **Luis**, *v. n.* (*Ir. id.*) Dare; adventure.—*Shaw.*

Luisd, *s.* A slouch.

Luisean, ein, *s. m.* An herb, a little weed.

Luiseanach, *a.* (*Ir. id.*) Abounding in herbs or weeds.

† **Luisne**, *s. f.* (*Ir. id.*) A flame; a flash; a blush—(*Shaw*); a kind of beaten flax.

Luisreag, eig, *s. c.* A plant, a herb; a botanist; a female botanist; a female who knows the virtues of plants. *N. pl.* luisreagan.

Luisreagach, *a.* Abounding in herbs; dealing in herbs; botanical.

Lùithe, *s. f.* (*Ir. id.*) Swiftness.

Luitheach, *a.* (*Ir. id.*) Joyous.

Luitheach, *s. pl.* (*Ir. id.*) Veins, sinews.

Lùithreach, ich, *s. f.* See **Lùireach.**

† **Lulgach**, aich, *s. f.* (*Ir. id.*) A milch-cow.

Lumadheirg, *s. f.* The deep, deep water; the deep channel of a river.

Luman, ain, *s. m.* A covering, a plaid; a large greatcoat; a coarse covering; sackcloth. *N. pl.* lumain.

Lumanach, *a.* Having a coarse cover; like sackcloth.

Lumar. See **Lomar.**

Lumhair, *s. m.* (*Ir. id.*) A diver.—*Shaw.*

Lun, luin, *s. m.* An elk; a blackbird. More frequently written *lon.*

Lunasd, **Lùnasdainn**, **Lunasdal**, *s. f.* (*Ir. id.*) Lammas. More frequently written *lùnasd.*

Lundach, **Lunndach**, *a.* (*Ir. id.*) Lazy, sluggish, idle, lounging. An duine lunndach.—*Oss. Fin. and Lor. Com.* and. *sup* lunndaiche.

Lundair, Lunndair, *s. m.* (*Ir. id.*) A sluggard, a drone. Eirich a lundaire! *rise, thou sluggard!—Sm.* A lunndaire feuch a chorr! *behold the crane, thou sluggard!—Oss. Derm. N. pl.* lundairean.

Lundaireachd, Lunndaireachd, *s. f.* Laziness, sluggishness, sluggardliness.

Lung, *s.* See Long.

Lunn, luinn, *s. m.* (*Ir. id.*) A staff; a bar; the handle of an oar; the pole of a bier or litter; a wave; a bearer; a churn-staff; a vessel; a bond. Air lunn, *on a bar.—Stew. Num.* Cinn nan lunn, *the heads of the staves.—Stew. O. T. N. pl.* lunnan.

Lunnach, aich, *s. m.* (*Ir. id.*) An active youth.—*Shaw. N. pl.* lunnaich.

Lunnach, *a.* (*Ir. id.*) Helved; shafted; fitted with a handle; like a bar or shaft. Ramhan min lunnach, *smooth-handled oars.—Macfar.*

Lunnadh, aidh, *s. m.* An invading; a pressing on or forward; invasion.

Lunndach, *a.* See Lundach.

Lunndair, *s. m.* See Lundair.

Lunndraich, *v. a.* Thump, beat, trounce. *Pret. a.* lunndraich; *fut. aff. a.* lunndraichidh.

Lunndrainn, *s. f.* A personal beating, a thumping, a trouncing. Is e fhuair a lunndrainn! *what a trouncing he got!*

Lunnuinn, *s.* London.

According to Camden the etymology is *long*, vessel, and *din*, or *dun*, town, the town of ships. Tacitus and Ptolemy call it *Londinium*; Etienne des Villes, *Lindonian*; in the Acts of the Council of Arles, we see *Londinium*; in Marcellinus, *Lundinum*; in Bede, *Lundonia*; in Old Sax. Chron. *Lundone, Lundine, Lundune, Lundenbrig, Lundenburgh, Lundencaster*, and *Lundenric*.

Lupait, *s. f.* The name of one of St. Patrick's sisters, who came into Ireland along with him, and was sold into captivity in that part now called Louth.

Lur, *a.* Beloved; lovely; pretty; *also*, lovely object.

Lurach, *a.*, *from* lur. (*Ir. id.*) Lovely, comely, pretty; beloved. Is tu mo Mhàiri lurach! *thou art my pretty Mary!—Old Song.* D' fhalt donn, lurach, *thy comely brown locks.—Mac Co. Com.* and *sup.* luraiche.

Lurachan, ain, *s. m.* Ramps.—*Shaw.*

Lurag, aig, *s. m.* (*from* lur.) A pretty young female; a beloved girl. *N. pl.* luragan.

Luragach, *a.* Pretty; engaging, as a young female.

Luran, ain, *s. m.* (*Ir. id.*) A beloved young person. *N. pl.* lurain.

Luranach, *a.* (*Ir. id.*) Fond; gallant; *also*, a gallant.

Lùrdan, ain, *s. m.* (*Ir. id. Scotch*, lurdane.) A sly fellow; a worthless person.

Lùrdanach, *a.* (*Ir. id.*) Sly, cunning. *Com.* and *sup.* lùrdanaiche.

Lùrdanachd, *s. f.* (*Ir. id.*) Slyness, cunning, craftiness.

Lurg, Lurgadh, aidh, *s. m.* A shin, a shank; a shaft. Written also *luirgeann*.

Lurganach, aich, *s. m.* (*Ir. id.*) A shaft; a shank; *adjectively*, long-legged.

Lurgann, ainn, *s. f.* A shank, a shin, a long leg; a stalk; the gambrel or hind leg of a horse; a steep barren surface. *N. pl.* lurgainnean.

Lurg-bheairt, *s. f.* Greaves; armour for the legs.

Lùs, lùis, *s. m.* (*Ir. id.*) Pith; strength; contracted for lùthas.

Lus, luis, *s. m.* (*W.* llws *and* lhys. *Ir.* lus. *Corn.* † les *and* lusanan. *Arm.* lousaouen, *herbs. Dat.* lyssi, *a leaf. Fr.* lis, *lily. Alb.* lis, *a tree.*) A weed; an herb; a plant; a flower. *N. pl.* lusan, *weeds*; *d. pl.* lusaibh. Mar dha lus san drùchd, *like two flowers in the dew.—Ull.* Oighean Chaothain nan lus, *virgins of flowery Cona.—Id.*

Lus a bhalla, *pellitory of the wall*; lus a choire, *coriander*; lus a cholumain, *columbine*; lus garbh, *goose-grass*; lus riabhach, *common louse-wort*; Galium aparine; lus liath, *common lavender, lavendula angustifolia*; lus nan gorm-dhearc, *blackberry plant*; lus buidhe bealltuin, *marsh marigold*; lus nam mial, *mouse-ear, scorpion grass*; lus nam meal mòr, *common mallow, malva sylvestris*; lus a chromchinn, *daffodil*; lus nan cnapan, *great figwort, scorphularia nodosa*; lus Cholum-chille, *St. John's wort*; lus a chrùbain, *gentian*; lus an fhucadair, *teasel* or *fuller's thistle*; lus an fhograidh, *the herb called chase-the-devil*; lus bheathaig, *betony*; lus a phoine, *piony*: lus an t-siucair, *succory*; lus a mhealα, *honeysuckle*; lus mor, *spearwort, foxglove*; lus an liogair, *savage*; lus leth 'n t-samhraidh, *gilliflower*; lus na seilg, *spleenwort*; lus mhic cuimein, *cummin*; lus nan gràn dubh, *Alexanders*, the *Smyrnium olustratum* of botanists; lus nan tri bilean, *valerian, valeriana*; lus na siothchainnt, *loose-strife*; lus an t-saoidh, *fennel*; lus a phiobair, *dittany*; lus-Mhàiri, *marigold*; lus na h-oidhche, *nightshade*; lus nan leac, *the herb eyebright*; lus nan scòr, *clown's-all-heal*; lus nam braoileag, *whortleberry*; lus na smalaig, *smalage*; lus mhic-Righ-Bhreatuinn, *wild thyme*; lus an t-slan uchaidh, *ribwort*; lus mhic raonuill, *chase-the-devil*; lus nan laogh, *or* laogh-lus, *orpine, golden saxifrage*; lus nan cnamh, *samphire*; lus a chrois, *dwarf-honeysuckle*; lus nam muisean, *the primrose, primula veris*; lus an leusaidh, *a plant that raises blisters*; lus nan eithreag, *cloudberry-bush*; lus na fearnaich, *sundew, drosera*; lus na Spàinn, *pellitory of Spain*; lus na Fraing, *common tansey, tanacetum vulgare*; lus nan laoch, *rosewort*; lus gun mhathair gun athair, *a plant resembling flax, which grows in springs*; at a certain age its fibres lose their hold of the earth, and then it ascends to the surface, where it floats with its roots perpendicularly downwards. Lus cho chu'luinn nan carn, *a flower mentioned by Macdonald in his poem*, " Alt an t-siucair," with the English name of which I am not acquainted.

Lusach, *a. from* lus. (*Ir. id.*) Abounding in herbs or weeds; herbaceous; weedy. *Com.* and *sup.* lusaiche.

Lusairneach, ich, *s. f.* A place where weeds grow.

Lusan, *s. m.* (*dim.* of lus.) A little herb; a little flower; a young herb or flower.

Lusan, *n. pl.* of lus. (*Arm.* lousaouen.) Herbs; flowers; weeds.

Lusanach, *a.* (*from* lusan.) Abounding in herbs; herbaceous; flowery; herb-producing. An samhradh lusanach, *herb-producing summer.—R.*

Lus-chuach, -chuaich, *s.* A caterpillar.—*Stew.* 1 *K. ref.*

† Lusradh, aidh, *s. m.* (*Ir. id.*) A procession.—*Shaw.*

† Lusga, ai, *s. m.* (*Ir. id.*) The space of five years; a lustrum; infancy; a cave.—*Shaw.*

† Lusgadh, aidh, *s. m.* A lurking or skulking.

Lusgair, *s. m.* (*Ir. id.*) A troglodyte; a hermit. *N. pl.* lusgairean.

Lusgaireach, *a.* Like a troglodyte or hermit; lurking.

Lusgaireachd, *s. f.* Living retired in caves; solitariness.

Lusrach, *a.* Herbaceous; herbal. *Com.* and *sup.* lusraiche.

Lusradh, aidh, *s. m.* Herbage.—*Shaw.*

Lusrag, aig, *s. f.*, *from* lus. (*Ir. id.*) A charm wrought with herbs; a female who works cures with herbs; a female botanist. *N. pl.* lusragan.

Lusragan, ain, *s. m.* (*from* lus.) A botanist; an herbalist; an apothecary; a perfumer. *N. pl.* lusragain. Seòltachd an lusragain, *the art of the* [*herbalist*] *apothecary.—Stew. Ex. ref.*

Lustair, *s. m.* (*Ir.* lustaire.) A flatterer; a low cunning fellow.—*Shaw.* *N. pl.* lustairean.

Lustaireach, *a.* (*Ir. id.*) Flattering, cajoling, fawning.

Lustradh, aidh, *s. m.* A flattering, a cajoling, a fawning; flattery.

Luth, *s. m.* (*Ir. id.*) Longing, earnest desire.

Lùth, *s. m.* (*Ir. id.*) Vigour; pith; agility; muscular strength; a joint. (*Scotch*, lith, *a joint.*) Trèine agus lùth, *strength and agility.—Old Song.*

Lùth, *v. a.* (*Ir. id.*) Full or cleanse cloth. *Pret. a.* luth, *fulled; fut. aff. a.* lùthaidh, *shall* or *will full.*

Lùthach, *a.* Pithy; sinewy; muscular; agile; fulling; *also*, sinews, veins.

Lùthadh, aidh, *s. m.* A fulling of cloth. Muileann lùthaidh, *a fulling-mill.* See **Lucthadh.**

Lùthair, *s. m.* The name of Cuchullin's charioteer.

Luthar, *a.* (luthmhor.) Sinewy; muscular; pithy.—*Macint.*

Lùthas, ais, *s. m.* (*from* lùth.) Pithiness; strength; muscular vigour; agility; power of motion. Thug aois dhiom lùthas, *age has taken my pith away.—Old Song.* Lùthas ghairdean, *strength of arms.—Macfar.*

Lùth-chleas, *s.* (*Ir. id.*) Sleight of hand; a dexterous feat in jugglery; a chivalrous feat; legerdemain; a gambol; a frisking; athletic exercise. Lùth-chleas nan uan, *the frisking of lambs.—Old Song.* Lùth-chleasan, *agile movements; feats in legerdemain.*

Lùth-chleasach, *a.* Chivalrous; nimble, active, dexterous, agile.

Lùth-chleasachd, *s. f.* Chivalry; legerdemain; adroitness, dexterity, nimbleness, agility.

Lùth-chleasaiche, *s. m.* A conjurer, an adept in legerdemain; a chivalrous person.

Lùth-chuirt, *s. f.* A palace, a court. More frequently written *luchairt.*

Lùthdag, aig, *s. f.* A joint; a hinge; a thumb. *N. pl.* luthdagan, *hinges.* Lùthdagan do òr, *hinges of gold.—Stew.* 1 *K.* Written also *lùdag.*

Lùthmhoire, *com.* and *sup.* of luthmhor. (*Ir.* luthmhaire.) More or most muscular.

Lùthmhoireachd, *s. f.* (*Ir.* luthmhaireachd.) Muscular elasticity; strength; agility, activity.

Lùthmhòr, *a.* (luth *and* mòr.) Muscular, vigorous, athletic, active, agile. *Com.* and *sup.* lùthmhoire. Fear luath lùthmhor, *an active muscular man;* gu lùthmhor, *vigorously.*

M.

M, m, (muin, *the vine.*) The eleventh letter of the Gaelic alphabet. When *m* has its simple sound, it is articulated much the same as in other languages. Mòr, *great;* caman, *a club;* lom, *bare.* When *m* is aspirated, that is, when it is immediately followed by *h*, a new combination or letter is formed, somewhat like *v* in English; as, a mhusgaid, *the musket;* tamh, *rest.* Frequently, though never at the beginning of words, *mh* is pronounced like a nasal *oo;* as, ràmh, *an oar;* and sometimes *mh* is entirely mute in the middle and at the end of words; as, comhnard, *level;* domh, *to me.*

'M, (*for* am.) A form of the *def. art.* used before words beginning with a labial, especially if the preceding word ends with a vowel, or a vowel sound. Bhuail e 'm fear, *he struck the man;* dhòirteadh 'm fion, *the wine was spilt.*

'M, (*for* ann am.) In the. Taobh na creig 'm blàs na grèine, *beside the rock in the warmth of the sun.—Ull.*

'M, (*for* am.) It is placed before the future interrogative and affirmative, when it begins with a labial, and when the preceding word ends with a vowel or a vowel sound. Mu 'm bi na fir-dàn a luaidh, *whom the poets praise.—Oss. Fing.*

M', (*for* mo.) My. It is used before words beginning with a vowel or an aspirated consonant. M' anam a snamh an ceò, *my spirit floating in mist.—Ull.* M' fhear, *my man.* Ga m' chodal, *to my sleep.—Oss. Gaul.*

M'a, (*for* mu a.) About his or her; round his or her; concerning his or her. M'a shluagh, *about his people.—Oss. Fing.* A lamh m'a muineal, *his hand round her neck.—Oss. Duthona.*

Ma, *conj.* (*Corn.* and *Ir.* ma.) If. Ma 's e 's gu, *if it so be that;* ma 's e agus gu, *if it so be that;* ma 's cuimhne leat, *if you remember;* ma ta, *if so, if it so be, then. Ma* is joined to the *pres.* and *pret. aff.* and *fut. sub.*

Ma, *prep.* About, around; near. Ma rèir, *at liberty; loose!* More frequently written *mu;* which see.

† **Ma**, *s. m.* (*Ir. id.*) A breach.—*Shaw.*

Mab, maib, *s. m.* (*Ir. id.*) A fringe; a tassel; a stutter, a lisp.

Mabach, *a.*, *from* mab. (*Ir. id.*) Full of fringes; lisping, stuttering.

Mabadh, aidh, *s. m.* A stuttering, a lisping; a stutter or lisp. Cha 'n fhaigh fear mabaidh modh, *a stutterer is never respected.—G. P.*

Mabag, aig, *s. f.* (*dim.* of mab.) A little fringe. *N. pl.* mabagan.

Mabagach, *a.* (*from* mabag.) Full of fringes; tawdry. *Com.* and *sup.* mabagaiche.

† **Mac**, *a.* (*Ir. id.*) Clear, pure, clean.

Mac, mic, *s. m.* (*Arm.* moch. *Manx*, mack. *Germ.* mag.) A son; the Gaelic and Irish patronymic, *mac. N. pl.* mic; *d. pl.* macaibh. Mac cèile, *a son-in-law;* mac san lagh, *a son-in-law;* mac mic, *a grandson;* mac leabhar, *a copy, a volume;* mac-tire, *a wolf;* mac an dògha, *burdock;* mac an abar, *the ring-finger;* mac alla, *or* mac talla, *an echo,* i. e. *the son of the rock;* mac muirigheach, *the escallop fish;* mac na praisich, *whisky.*

† **Mac**, *v. a.* (*Ir. id.*) Bear, carry.—*Shaw.*

† **Macadh**, aidh, *s. m.* (*Ir. id.*) A bearing, a carrying.

Macail, *a.* (mac-amhuil.) Filial; affectionate.

Macaladh, aidh, *s. m.* Fostering after being weaned.—*Macfar. voc.*

Mac alla, *s. m.* An echo. Written also *mac talla.*

† **Mac-mna**, *s. f.* (*Ir. id.*) A handsome young female; a young girl.—*Shaw.*

Macan, ain, *s. m.*, *from* mac. (*Ir. id.*) A hero; a boy; a young son. Macan airson striopaich, *a boy for a harlot.—Stew. Joel. N. pl.* macain; *d. pl.* macanaibh. Lan do mhacanaibh, *full of boys.—Stew. Zech.*

Macanachd, *s. f.*, *from* macan. (*Ir. id.*) Heroism; ordering, directing.

Macanas, ais, *s. m.* Bravery, heroism.

Mac an dogha, *s. m.* Burdock.—*Shaw.*

Mac an Luin. The name of Fingal's sword, so called from its maker, Luno, an armourer of Scandinavia. B'e mac an Luin lann Mhic-Chumhail, *Mac an Luin was Fingal's sword.* —*Oss.*

Macanta, *a.* (*Ir. id. from* mac.) Mild, meek, gentle; submissive; kind, filial, honest; modest. A ta mise macanta, *I am meek.—Stew. Matt.* Gu macanta, *meekly.*

Macantachd, *s. f.* (*Ir. id.*) Meekness, mildness, gentleness, submissiveness; puerility. Spiorad na macantachd, *the spirit of meekness.—Stew.* 1 *Cor.* Ciùinichidh macantachd, *submissiveness will pacify.—Stew. Ecc. ref.*

Macantas, ais, *s. m.* (*Ir. id.*) Mildness, meekness, kindness, honesty, submissiveness, affectionateness.

Mac-fuirme, *s. m.* (*Ir. id.*) A poet of the second order.

Mach, A mach, *adv.* and *prep.* Out, without. Cuir mach e, *put him out;* mach air an dorus, *out of the door;* thoir mach ort, *get out;* tha e mach orm, *he is not on terms with me;* chuir iad mach air chéile, *they quarrelled;* rioghachdan mach, *foreign countries;* thoir am baile mach ort, *get out of doors.*

Macha, *s.* A Royston crow.—*Shaw.*

Machair, machrach, *s. f* (*Ir. id.*) perhaps *mach-thir* or *magh-thir.* A field, a plain; a name given by the Gael to the Lowlands of Scotland; any low-lying open country or champaign. Luibh na machrach, *the herb of the field.—Stew. Gen. N. pl.* machraichean. Air mhachair, *in the low country* or *Lowlands;* air feadh na machrach, *among the Lowlands.*

Macharach, *gen. sing.* of machair; often contracted *machrach.*

Mach-bhaile. A village in the suburbs of a great town. *N. pl.* mach-bhailtean, *suburbs.*

† Machd, *s. m.* (*Ir. id.*) A wave.

† Machdnach, aich, *s. m.* An observer.

† Machdual, ail, *s. m.* (*Ir. id.*) A sponge.—*Shaw.*

Machlag, aig, *s. f.* (*Ir. id.*) The womb or matrix. *N. pl.* machlagan.

Machlagach, *a.* Of, or pertaining to, the womb; bellying.

Machrach, *gen. sing.* of machair; which see.

Machraichean, *n. pl.* of machair. Open fields; champaign countries.

Machtra! An interjection.

Machuil, *s. f.* (*Lat.* macula. *Ir.* machuil.) A spot, a blemish.

Mac-leabhar, air, *s. m.* A volume, a copy. *N. pl.* macleabhraichean.

Macmeamnach, *a.* (*Ir. id.*) Imaginative, fanciful; belonging to imagination; having an imagination.

Macmeamnadh, aidh, *s. m.* (*Ir. id.*) Imagination; fancy.

Mac-muirgheach, *s. m.* The scallop fish.—*Shaw.*

Macnus, ùis, *s. m.* (*Ir.* macnas.) Wantonness; lewdness; mirth, diversion; festivity; fondness; kindness; prosperity. Neo-ghloine, macnus, *uncleanness, lewdness.—Stew. Gal.*

Macnusach, *a.* (*Ir.* macnasach.) Wanton, lewd, lascivious; merry; mirthful; jovial; festive. Tigh mòr macnusach, *a large festive house.—Old Song. Com.* and *sup.* macnusaiche.

Macnusachd, *s. f.* (*from* macnus.) Wantonness, lasciviousness; mirthfulness; festivity.

† Macraidh, *s. f.* (*Ir. id.*) A disease.—*Shaw.*

Macraidh, *s. f., collective.* (*Ir.* macra. *W.* macraidh.) Sons; young men. Written also *macruidh;* which see.

† Macrail, *a.* (*Ir.* macramhuil.) Like, as.

Macrail, *s. f.* A mackerel.

Macras, ais, *s. m.* (*Ir. id.*) Peevish, sobbing, peevishness.

Macrasach, *a.* (*Ir. id.*) Peevish, sobbing, sighing. *Com.* and *sup.* macrasaiche.

Mac-ratha, *s. m.* (*Ir. id.*) A child of fortune; a son of good luck. Is tu mac an ratha, *you are a lucky fellow.*

Macruidh, *s. f., collective; from* mac. (*Ir.* macra. *W.* macraidh.) A body of young men; sons; males; youngsters; children. A mhacruidh dheas, *the active young men.—Sm.* The terminations *ruidh* and *ruith* of collective nouns have an obvious affinity with the English termination *ry,* as in *cavalry, infantry;* and with the French *rie,* as in *cavalerie, infanterie;* as also with the Italian and Spanish terminations *eria* and *iero.*

Mac-samhladh, aidh, *s. m.* An equal; an equivalent; a fellow or match.

Mac-samhuil, *a.* (*Ir. id.*) Like as, such like, similar; *also,* the same, an equal; an emblem. Is mac-samhuil sin anam mo mhic, *such is the soul of my son.—Oss. Gaul.* A mhac samhuil cha 'n fhacas riamh, *his equal was never seen.* —*Fingalian Poem.*

Mac-samhuilt, *s. m.* (*Ir id.*) An equal, a compeer; a fellow or match; an emblem. Do mhac-samhuilt air misnich, *thy equal in courage.—Macfar.*

Mac-stroghha, *s. m.* A spendthrift.

Mactach, *a.* Pernicious; destructive.

† Mactadh, aidh, *s. m.* (*Ir. id. Lat.* macto.) A slaughtering, a massacre; a surprise.

Mac-talla, Mac-thalla, *s. m.* (*Ir. id.*) An echo; *literally,* the son of the rock, or the son of the hall. Mactalla 'snamh 's a ghleann, *echo floating in the valley.—Oss.*

Mac-thogail, *s. f.* Adoption.

Mac-tire, *s. m.* (*Ir. id.*) A wolf.

† Mad, *s. m.* (*Ir. id.*) A hand.

Madach, *a.* (*from* madadh.) Canine.

Mada, Madadh, aidh, *s. m.* (*Ir. id. Manx,* mawda.) A mastiff, a dog; the but-end of a gun. Cha charruich madadh a theanga, *a dog shall not move his tongue.—Stew. Exod.* Madadh allaidh, *a wolf;* madadh ruadh, *a fox;* madadh donn, *an otter.*

Madadh-alluidh, *s. m.* (*Ir. id.*) A wolf; *literally,* a wild dog. Mar mhadadh-alluidh, *like a wolf.—Stew. Gen. N. pl.* madaidh-alluidh, *wolves.—Stew. Zeph.*

The last wolf in Scotland is said to have been killed by the celebrated chieftain, Sir Ewen Cameron of Lochiel.

Madadh-donn, *s. m.* (*Ir. id.*) An otter; a brown mastiff.

Madadh-ruadh, *s. m.* (*Ir. id.*) A fox; a brown mastiff. *N. pl.* madaidh-donn.

Madainn, maidne, *s. f.* (*Ir.* madain. *Fr.* matin. *It.* matina.) Morning; Aurora. Nur dh' éireas madainn, *when morning rises.—Oss. Fing.* Air madainn, *on a morning;* 'sa mhadainn mhoich, *in early morn.—Orr.* Moch sa mhadainn, *early in the morning.*

Madainneach, *a.* Early, matutine, auroral.

Màdar, air, *s. m.* (*Ir. id.*) The herb madder, a dye.—*Mac Co.* Madar fraoich, *madder.*

† Madh, maidh, *s. m.* (*Ir. id.*) Ecstasy; a plain. Madh beag, *a little, a small share.—Shaw.* In the sense of plain it is now written *magh.*

† Madha, *a.* (*Ir. id.*) Unlawful, unjust.

Madhanta, *a.* (*Ir. id.*) Valiant; dexterous in the use of arms; *also,* coy. Sud am fear madhanta, *yonder is the hero dexterous in arms.—Old Poem.* Madhanta, *coy.—Shaw.*

Madhantachd, *s. f.* Valour; dexterity in the use of arms; coyness.

Madhar, air, *s. m.* See **Maghar**.

Madhm. See **Màm**.

† **Madhrail**, *s. f.* (*Ir. id.*) July.

Madrach, *a.* Like a dog or mastiff; doggish. Madrach-allaidh, *wolves.*

Madradh, aidh, *s. m.* (*Ir. id.*) A dog, a mastiff. *N. pl.* madraidh. Dh' imlich na madraidh 'fhuil, *the dogs licked his blood.—Stew.* 1 *K.* Madradh uisge, *an otter.—O'Reilly.* Madradh alluidh, *a wolf.*

Madraidh, *s. f., collective.* A number of dogs or mastiffs; the dog species.

Madrail, *a.* (madradh-amhuil.) Like a mastiff.

Madralachd, *s. f.* Doggishness.

Màg, maig, *s. f.* (*Ir. id.*) A paw; a claw; a ludicrous name for a clumsy hand. Màg an leomhainn, *the lion's paw.—Stew.* 1 *Sam. N. pl.* màgan.

Mag, *v.* (*Arm.* mag, *mock. Gr.* μωκος, *a mocker*, and μωκια, *derision.*) Mock, ridicule, scoff, jeer. *Pret. a.* mhag, *mocked; fut. aff.* magaidh, *shall mock.* This verb takes after it the *prep.* air, either simple or compounded. Mag air, *mock him;* mag orra, *mock them;* a magadh, *mocking.*

Magach, *a.* Scoffing, jeering, mocking; prone to scoff or mock.

Màgach, *a.* (*from* màg.) Having paws; like a paw or claw; belonging to a paw; having clumsy hands. *Com.* and *sup.* màgaiche.

Magadh, aidh, *s. m.* (*Gr.* μωκια. *Ir.* magadh.) Mocking, scoffing; ridicule, mockery. Ni amadain magadh, *fools make a mock.—Stew. Pro.* Ri magadh, *mocking.*

Magail, *a.* (mag-amhuil.) Scoffing, jeering; derisive.

Magair, *s. m.* (mag-fhear.) A mocker, a jeerer, a scorner. *N. pl.* magairean.

Màgair, *v. a.* and *n.* Creep; paw, finger clumsily. *Pret. a.* mhàgair, *crept; fut. aff. a.* màgraidh, *shall creep.*

Magairle, *s. f.* A testicle. *N. pl.* magairlean, *testicles; d. pl.* magairlibh.

Magairleach, *a.* Having testicles; having large testicles; like testicles; belonging to the testicles.

Magairlean, *n. pl.* of magairle.

Màgairt, *s. f.* Creeping.

Màgan, ain, *s. m., dim.* of màg. (*Ir. id.*) A little paw; a little clumsy hand.

Màgaran, ain, *s. m., from* màg. (*Ir. id.*) Creeping; moving on all fours; one who has a creeping gait.—*Stew.* 1 *K.*

Màgaran, *v. n.* Creep; move on all fours; walk with a creeping gait.

Màgarsaich, *s. f.* Creeping.

Magh, *s. f.* A field, a plain, a level country; a field of battle; a surface. Buaidh air magh, *victory in the field of battle.—Oss. Com.* Fuil air magh a sgeithe, *blood on the surface of his shield.—Oss. Gaul.* Righ nam magh, *king of the plains.—Oss.*

The king thus mentioned by the great poet of the Gael, was the king of the Maiatæ (*magh-aite*, level country), or the Lowlands of Scotland. The Scotch Celts, even at this day, scarcely know the Lowlands by any other name than *magh-thir*, or, as it is generally pronounced, *machair*, the land of plains.

Maghair, *s.* (*Ir. id.*) Ploughed land.

Magh aoraidh, *s. f.* A plain or field where Druidical worship was performed.

In this plain was a rude temple, such as is frequently seen in the Highlands, and elsewhere, consisting of a circle of rude massy obelisks, and standing, for the most part, perpendicular. Similar to these temples was that which Moses built, consisting of twelve stone pillars, as mentioned in Exod. xxiv. 4.

Ma-ghamhuinn, *s. f.* (magh-ghamhuinn.) A bear. *N. pl.* ma-ghamhuinnean *or* ma-ghamhnan.

Ma-ghamhuinneach, *a.* Bearish; like a bear.

Maghar, air, *s. m.* A word, expression; a bait for fish. 'G iasghachadh le maghar, *fishing with bait.—Old Song.*

† **Magh-fhal**, ail, *s. m.* (*Ir. id.*) A field-barrack.

† **Magh-lann**, -lainn, *s. m.* (*Ir. id.*) Field-barracks. *N. pl.* magh-lainn *or* magh-lannan.—*Shaw.*

Magh-shluagh, -shluaigh, *s. m.* People inhabiting low countries; Lowlanders.

Magh-suinne, *s. f.* Slavery.—*Shaw.*

Magh-uisge, *s. f.* A winter lake.—*Shaw.*

Maibean, ein, *s. m.* A mop; a tuft. Written also *moibean;* which see.

Maibeanach, *a.* Tufty, moppy. Written also *moibeanach.*

† **Maicne**, *s. pl.* (*Ir. id.*) Children, relations.

Maide, *s. f.* (*Ir. id.*) A stick; a staff; a cudgel; wood, timber. *N. pl.* maidean *and* maideachan. Cha mhaide balachain do shleagh, *thy spear is not a boy's staff.—Oss. Tem.* Maide singlidh, *a swingle staff.—Macd.* Maide slachdaidh, *a swingle stick;* maide stiùraidh, *a pot-stick, a thivel; the thiller or stick that moves the rudder of a boat or ship.—Shaw.* Maide measg, *a boy's top;* maide crois, *a crutch.—O'Reilly.* Maide-poit, *a thivel;* maide sniomhaidh, *a distaff.—Id.* Maide milis, *liquorice;* maide briste, *a pair of tongs;* literally, *a broken stick,* which in remote parts of the Highlands is used for a pair of tongs; hence, among many of the Gael, it has become an arbitrary term for that instrument.

Maideachan, *n. pl.* of maide; which see.

Maideag, eig, *s. f.* (*Ir.* maideog.) A pivot—(*O'Reilly*); a small shell; a periwinkle; the shell called by conchologists *concha veneris. N. pl.* maideagan.

Maidean, ein, *s. m.* (*dim.* of maide.) A little stick; a little piece of wood.

Maidean, *n. pl.* of maide; which see.

Maidh, *v.* See **Maoidh**.

Maidheach, maidhiche, *s. f.* A hare. *N. pl.* maidhichean. Written also *maigheach.*

Maidheag, eig, *s. f.* (*Ir.* maidheog.) A midwife. *N. pl.* maidheagan.

Maidhean, ein, *s. m.* Delay; irksomeness.

Maidheanach, *a.* Slow, tardy, irksome. Gu maidheanach, *tardily. Com.* and *sup.* maidheanaiche.

Maidheanachd, *s. f.* Slowness, tardiness, irksomeness.

Maidinn, *s. f.* More commonly written *madainn;* which see.

Maidne, (*for* madainne), *gen. sing.* of madainn; which see.

Maidneach, *a.* Matutine, early, auroral. Dh' éirich mi maidneach, *I rose early.*

Maidneachadh, aidh, *s. m.* A dawning, a drawing towards morning.

Maidneag, eig, *s. f.* (*from* madainn.) Aurora, or the morning star. Mar a mhaidneag san speur, *like the morning star in the heavens.—Old Song.*

Maidneagach, *a.* Auroral, like the morning star; of, or belonging to, the morning star.

Maidnean, ein, *s. m.* (*from* madainn.) A morning prayer; matins.

Maidnich, *v. n.* Dawn. *Pret.* mhaidnich, *dawned; fut. aff. a.* maidnichidh, *shall dawn.*

Màidse, *s. f.* A hudge; a shapeless lump; a turd. *N. pl.* maidsean.

Màidseach, *a.* (*from* màidse.) Hudgy, lumpy, shapeless, clumsy.

Màidsear, eir, *s. m.* (*prov.*) A major in the army. *N. pl.* maidsearan.

Màidsearachd, *s. f.* A majority, or the office of a major in the army.

Màio, *gen. sing.* of màg; which see.

Maig, *s. f.* (*Ir. id.*) An affected attitude and disposition of the head.

Maigeag, eig, *s. f.* A midwife.

Màigean, ein, *s. m.* A frog, a paddock; a child moving on all fours; a little fat fellow; a ludicrous term for a man with a creeping or a sprawling gait.

Màigeanach, *a.* (*from* màigean.) Creeping; frog-like; of, or pertaining to, a frog.

Màigeanachd, *s. f.* The act of creeping; a creeping gait.

Maigh, *s. f.* May. Eibhneach am mios Mhaigh, *joyous in the month of May.—Macfar.*

Maighdean, **Maighdeann**, inn, *s. f.* A maid or maiden, a virgin, a vestal; the last handful of a crop of oats that is cut up; a part of a spinning wheel. *N. pl.* maighdeanan *and* maighdinnean. Ma 's fios do mhaighdinnibh rùn maighdinn, *if maidens know a maiden's wish.—Old Song.* Maighdeann mhara, *a mermaid.*

Ir. id. Anglo-Sax. maegden. *Germ.* magatin *and* maitchen. *Du.* maagdeken. *Goth.* meden. *Sax.* mæden. *Eng.* maiden.

Maighdeanail, *a.* (maighdean-amhuil.) Modest; like a maid, vestal.

Maighdeanas, ais, *s. m.* (*from* maighdean.) Virginity, maidenhead. Comharan maighdeanais, *tokens of virginity;* thug e uaipe a maighdeanas, *he deflowered her.*

Maigheach, maighiche, *s. f.* A hare; the *mustela timida* of Linnæus. Tha maigheach neo-ghlan, *a hare is unclean.—Stew. Lev.* Cuilean maighiche, *a leveret. N. pl.* maighichean. Maigheach gheal, *a white or Alpine hare, the lepus hieme albus* of naturalists.

Màighean, ein, *s. m.* Delay; slowness, dilatoriness, laziness.

Màigheanach, *a.* Slow, dilatory, lazy, tedious. Gu maigheanach, *slowly. Com.* and *sup.* maigheanaiche.

Maigheanachd, *s. f.* Slowness, dilatoriness; laziness; tediousness.

Maighistir, **Maighstir**, (gh *silent*), *s. m.* A master; a teacher or tutor; a ruler. *N. pl.* maighstirean. Maighistir sgoile, *a schoolmaster;* maighistir-dannsaidh, *a dancing-master;* maighistir-sgriobhaidh, *a writing-master.*

Lat. magister. *It. Sp.* maestro. *Fr.* †maestre. *Du.* meester. *Germ.* meister. *Arm.* and *Corn.* maestr. *Ir.* maighistir. *Dan.* mester. *Teut.* meistar. *Dal.* mestar, *Carn.* moister. *Hung.* mester. *Boh.* mistr. *Pol.* mistrz.

Maighistireachd, **Maighstireachd**, *s. f.* (*Ir.* maighistiriocht. *Lat.* magistratus.) Mastery, superiority, rule, dominion. Cha ghnàthaich sibh maighistireachd, *ye shall not exercise mastery.—Stew. Lev. ref.*

Maighistireas, **Maighstireas**, eis, *s. m.* Superiority, mastery; sway; a mistress.

Maighistireil, *a.* (maighistir-amhuil.) Lordly, domineering; masterly. Gu maighistireil, *in a lordly manner.*

Maighre, *s. m.* (*Ir. id.*) A salmon; a salmon-trout; a shoal of salmon.

Maighneas, eis, *s. m.* (*Ir. id.*) A field.

Maildheach, *a.* Having large shaggy eyebrows.—*Macint.* Written also *mailgheach;* which see.

Màile, *s. f.* A mail, a helmet; a coat of mail; part of the geers of a loom called heedles. Maile an robh fuaim, *sounding helmets.—Oss. Fing.* Boillsge faoin a mhàile, *the faint gleam of his mail.—Oss. Com.* Written also *màille.*

Màileach, *a.* Mailed, covered with armour; having a helmet. Luireach mhàileach, *a coat of mail.* Written also *màilleach;* which see.

Màileid, *s. f.*, *from* mal. (*Ir. id.*) A wallet, a knapsack; a satchel; a bag or scrip; a budget; a ludicrous term for a capacious belly or a stomach. Bu ghionach do mhaileid; *greedy was thy stomach.—Macint. N. pl.* màileidean.

Màileideach, *a.* Having a wallet; like a wallet or knapsack; having a large belly.

† **Mailge**, *s. f.* (*Ir. id.*) A funeral pile.

Mailgheach, *a.* Having shaggy eyebrows; *also,* the Highland surname Malloch.

Mailghean, *s. pl.* Eyebrows. Mailghean a shùl, *his eyebrows.—Stew. Lev.*

Màilinn, mailne, *s. f.* The eyebrow; the space between the eyebrows, also termed *maolchair na mailne.*

Mailios, *s. f.* A wallet.

Perhaps the composition of this word is *mal Iosa,* i. e. Jesus's wallet. In former times, devout men made regular circuits among the Highlands, each with his wallet or bag, and begging alms for his poor brethren, which were asked and granted in the name and for the sake of Jesus.

† **Mailis**, *s. f.* (*Ir. id. Lat.* malitia. *Eng.* malice.) Ill-will.

† **Mailiseach**, *a.*, *from* mailis. (*Ir. id.*) Malicious. *Com.* and *sup.* mailisiche.

Mailisidh, *s. f.* A corruption of *militia.*

Maille, *s. f.* (*Ir.* maill.) Delay; hindrance; impediment. Written also *moille;* which see.

Maille, *com.* and *sup.* of mall. Slower, slowest. See **Mall**.

Màille, *s. f.* (*Corn.* mael, *steel.*) A ring; a mail, a helmet; also the name of an ancient Highland saint. Hence the parish of Kilmaly (of which Màille is the tutelary saint) derives its name.

Màilleach, *a.* Ringed; full of rings; like a ring; mailed; covered with armour. Luireach mhàilleach, *a coat of mail.*

Màilleach, ich, *s. f.* Mail or armour; a coat of mail. Gach màilleach throm, *every ponderous coat of mail.—Mac Lach.*

Mailleachan, ain, *s. m.* One of that order of spectral beings called by the Scots *brownie.* It is an inoffensive sprite; and Gaelic mythology records many useful services done by it to those families and individuals who were fortunate enough to procure its favours. See **Uruisg**.

Maillead, id, *s. m.* Slowness.

Maille ri, *comp. prep.* With, together, in company with. Maille rium, *with me;* maille riut, *with thee;* maille ris, *with him;* maille ri, *with her;* maille rinn, *with us;* maille ribh, *with you;* maille riu, *with them.*

Maillich, *v.* Slacken, delay, retard.

Mailmheasach, ich, *s. m.* Malmsey.

Maim. See **Màm**.

Maimseach, ich, *s. m.* A bubonocele.

† **Main**, *s. f.* (*Lat. It.* mane. *Ir.* main.) Morning; day.

† **Main**, *s. f.* (*Ir. id.*) See **Man**.

Màin, *gen. sing.* of màn. Of a hand.

† **Màin**, *v. n.* (*Gr.* μενω. *Lat.* maneo.) Remain; linger: stop. *Pret.* mhain; *fut. aff.* mainidh.

Mainchill, *s. m.* A sleeve.

Maindreach, ich, *s. m.* (*Ir. id.*) A hut, a booth; a fold.

Màineachdail, *a.* Neglectful; lingering; undevout.

Maineag, eig, *s. f.* (*Lat.* manica. *Ir.* maineog.) A glove. *N. pl.* maineagan.

† **Maineag**, eig, *s. m.* (*dim.* of màn.) A little hand. *N. pl.* maineagan.

† **Mainear**, eir, *s. m.* (*Ir. id.*) A manor.

Maineas, eis, *s. m.* (*Ir. id.*) A mistake, a bunder.—*Shaw.*

Mainidh, *s. f.* (*Gr.* μανια, *rage. Lat.* mania. *Ir.* mainigh.) Madness; rage; folly. Air mhainidh, *mad.*

Mainistear, eir, *s. m.* (*Lat.* monasterium.) A monastery. *N. pl.* màinistearan.

Mainneasach, *a.* Sluggish.

Mainnir, *s. f.* A fold for cattle, a pen; a prison; a booth. O'n mhainnir, *from the fold.—Stew. Heb. N. pl.* mainnirean.

Mainnireach, *a.* Having folds, pens, or prisons; like a fold, pen, or prison; belonging to a fold, pen, or prison.

Mainnireach, ich, *s. f.* A fold or pen; a booth, a prison. *N. pl.* mainnrichean; *d. pl.* mainnrichibh. Also written *manrach.*

Mainnis, *s. f.* (*Ir. id.*) Drawling; trifling; sluggishness. —*Shaw.*

Mainniseach, *a.* Drawling, sluggish. *Com.* and *sup.* mainnisiche.

Mainnreach, ich, *s.* A fold, a booth, a hut.—*Shaw.*

† **Mainse**, *s. f.* Maintenance, sustenance.

Mainsear, ir, *s. f.* (*Ir. id.*) A manger. *N. pl.* mainnsearan.

Mainnsearach, *a*, Having mangers; like a manger.

Main-obair, -oibre, *s.* Handiwork.—*Shaw.*

Mainse, *s. f.* (*Ir. id.*) Maintenance.

Mair, *a.* Alive, surviving. Am mair e? *is he alive? shall he live?* Cha mhair e, *he is not alive; he shall not live; it shall not last.*

Mair, *v. n.* (*Ir. id.*) Last, continue, endure; survive, live, exist. *Pret.* mhair; *fut. aff.* mairidh, *shall live.* Cha mhair e, *he will not live; he is not alive*; mairidh an iomradh, *their renown shall last.—Old Poem.*

Mairbhe, *inflection of* marbh; *also*, dead people. Na mairbhe cha mhol iad Dia, *the dead praise not God.—Sm.*

Mairbh-ghreim, *s.* A morphew.—*Shaw.*

Màireach, *s.* Morrow. Am màireach, *to-morrow;* màireach bithidh do righ gun ghleus, *to-morrow thy king shall be lifeless.—Oss. Fing.* An làth air mhàireach, *the next day;* an la 'r na mhàireach, *to-morrow, on the morrow.—Stew. Ex. ref.* Am màireach sin cha d' thig a choidh, *that morrow shall never come.—Old Song.* Moch am màireach, *to-morrow morning;* an la 'n deigh am màireach, *the day after to-morrow.*

Maireachdainn, *s. f.* Continuance; lasting; duration.

Mairealach, *a.* Benumbing. *Com.* and *sup.* mairealaiche.

Maireáladh, aidh, *s. m.* (*Ir. id.*) A benumbing, numbness.

Maiream, (*for* mairidh mi.) I shall or will last or live.

Maireann, *a.* (*from* mair.) Lasting, durable; surviving, existing. Is maireann a chliù, *lasting is his name.—Sm.* Ad dheigh cha bhi mi maireann, *I shall not long survive thee.—Ardar.* Tuille ni maireann do Gholl, *Gaul exists no more.—Oss. Gaul.* Am maireann da? *is he alive?*

Maireannach, *a.* (*Ir.* marthanach.) Everlasting; durable; long-lived. Beath mhaireannach, *everlasting life.—Stew. Rom.* Saibhreas maireannach, *durable riches.—Stew. Pro. Com.* and *sup.* maireannaiche.

Maireasail, *s. f.* (*Ir. id.*) Life.

Maireannachd, *s. f.* (*Ir.* marthanachd.) Durableness; continuance; long life.

Maireun, *s. m.* A small salmon.—*Shaw.*

Mairg, *s. f.* (*Ir. id.*) Woe; pity; folly. A mhairg dhuit! *woe to you! a pox take you!*

Mairg, *a.* Foolish, simple; woful, sorrowful. Is mairg a rinn thu e, *it is a pity you did it;* is mairg a dh' òladh branndaidh, *'tis a folly to drink brandy.—Old Song.*

Mairgeach, *a.*, *from* mairg. (*Ir. id.*) Woful, piteous, sorrowful. *Com.* and *sup.* mairgiche.

Mairgne, *s. f.* Woe.

Mairgneach, *a.* (*Ir. id.*) Woful, sorrowful. Gu mairgneach, *wofully. Com.* and *sup.* mairgniche.

Mairgnich, *v. n.* (*from* mairg.) Groan, sob; bewail, deplore. *Pret.* mhairgnich, *groaned; fut. aff. a.* mairgnichidh, *shall groan.*

Mairiche, *s. m.* A seaman or mariner; a marine. Chì am mairiche an uaigh, *the mariner shall see their graves.—Oss. Fing. N. pl.* mairichean. Written also *maraiche;* which see.

Mairidh, *fut. aff.* of mair. Shall or will last.

Mairionn, *a.* See **Maireann**.

Mairionnach, *a.* See **Maireannach**.

Mairiste, *s. f.* Cohabitation; copulation; a marriage; a match; a coupling; a spouse.

Mairisteach, *a.* (*from* mairiste.) Marriageable. Tha i mairisteach banail, *she is marriageable and modest.*

† **Mairl**, *v. a.* (*Ir. id.*) Bruise, pound, crumble. *Pret.* mhairl, *bruised.*

† **Mairn**, *v. a.* (*Ir. id.*) Betray. *Pret. a.* mhairn, *betrayed; fut. aff. a.* mairnidh, *shall betray.*

Mairn, *s. f.* (*Ir. id.*) A spying; a betraying.

Mairneach, ich, *s. m.* A betrayer.

Mairneal, eil, *s. m.* (*Ir. id.*) Delay; lingering. Na dean mairneal, *do not delay;* na cuir mairneal, *do not delay.*

Mairnealach, *a.* (*from* mairneal.) Apt to put off, dilatory, slow, tedious, slothful. Na bi mairnealach, *be not slow. Com.* and *sup.* mairnealaiche.

Mairnealach, aich, *s. m.* (*Ir. id.*) A sailor, a mariner. *N. pl.* mairnealaiche.

Mairnealachd, *s. f.* (*Ir. id.*) Dilatoriness, slowness, tediousness; slothfulness.

Mairnealaich, *v. a.* and *n.* Put off, procrastinate. *Pret. a.* mhairnealaich; *fut. aff.* mairnealaichidh.

Mairneamh, imh, *s. m.* (*Ir. id.*) A spy.

Mairt, *gen.* of mart.

Mairt, *s.* Matter; consequence; harm. An deomhan mairt, *the d—l may care.*

Mairt-fheoil, -fheola, *s. f.* Beef.

Mairthean, *a.* (*Ir. id.*) Lasting, durable; surviving; living. Fhad 's bu mhairthean thu, *as long as thou wert in existence.—Macint.* More frequently written *maireann.*

Mairtheanach, *a.* Lasting, durable, perpetual; surviving, in existence. An sealbh mhairtheanach, *the perpetual possession.—Stew. Lev.* More frequently *maireannach.*

Mairtheanachd, *s. f.* See **Maireannachd**.

Mairtireach, ich, *s. m.* (*Ir. id.*) A martyr.—*Stew. Rev. ref. N. pl.* mairtiriche.

Mairtireachd, *s. f.* (*Ir. id.*) Martyrdom; the fate of a martyr.

Màis, *gen. sing.* of màs; which see.

Mais, maise, *s. f.* (*Ir. id.*) A lump, a heap; an acorn.

Maise, *s. f.* (*Ir. id.*) Handsomeness, elegance, beauty, comeliness; bloom; grace; ornament. Oigh na maise! *thou maid of grace!—Old Poem.* Airson maise, *for beauty.—Stew. Ex.*

† **Maise**, *s. f.* (*Ir. id. Eng.* mess.) Food, victuals.

Maiseach, *a.*, *from* maise. (*Ir. id.*) Elegant, handsome, beautiful; graceful; having an imposing appearance. Maiseach na dealbh, *handsome in her person* or *form.—Stew. Gen. Com.* and *sup.* maisiche.

Maiseachadh, aidh, *s. m.* A beautifying, an adorning, a decking.

Maiseachail, *a.* (*from* maiseach-amhuil.) Elegant, handsome, beautiful, comely.

Maiseachd, *s. f.* (*Ir. id.*) Elegance, handsomeness, beautifulness, comeliness.

Maisealachd, *s. f.* (*Ir.* maiseamhlachd.) Elegantness, handsomeness, comeliness; delightfulness. Ann ad mhaisealachd, *in thy delightfulness.—Stew. Song Sol.*

Maisich, *v. a., from* mais. (*Ir. id.*) Deck, decorate, beautify. *Pret. a.* mhaisich, *decked; fut. aff. a.* maisichidh, *shall deck; fut. pass.* maisichear, *shall be decked.*

Maisiche, *com.* and *sup.* of maiseach. More or most comely.

Maisleadh, idh, *s. m.* (*Ir. id.*) Reviling; disparaging.

Maisteag, eig, *s. f.* (*Ir.* maisteog.) The mastich tree.

Maistir, *s. f.* (*Ir. id.*) A churn; *also,* urine.

Maistir, *v. a.* Churn, make butter. *Pret.* mhaistir, *churned; fut. aff. a.* maistirichidh, *shall churn.*

Maistirich, *v. a.* Churn. *Pret. a.* mhaistirich, *churned; fut. aff.* maistirichidh, *shall churn.*

Maistirichte, *p. part.* of maistirich. Churned.

Maistreadh, idh, *s. m.* The process of churning.

Maith, *a.* Good, virtuous, pious; becoming, pleasant; well; agreeable; excellent. Duine maith, *a good man.* Bean mhaith, *a virtuous wife.—Stew. Pro.* Is maith gheibhear thu, *you do well;* is maith fhuair thu, *you did well.* An maith thig e dhuit? *does it become thee? is it well for thee?—Stew. Jonah.* Is maith leam, *I desire;* is maith leam e, *I am glad of it.* Tha 'n t-earrach ann 's gur maith leam e, *it is spring, and I rejoice at it.—Old Song. Com.* and *sup.* fearr.

Ir. id. W. † mat. *Corn. Arm.* mad, mat. *Arab.* madi.

Maith, *s. f.* (*Turk.* mai, *good luck.*) Goodness, fruit; profit, benefit. Air son do mhaith, *for your benefit.*

Maith, *v.* (*Ir. id.*) Pardon, forgive; abate. *Pret. a.* mhaith, *pardoned; fut. aff. a.* maithidh, *shall pardon.* Maith, guidheam ort, *forgive, I pray thee.—Stew. Gen.* Cha mhaith mi peighinn, *I will not abate a penny.*

Maithe, *s. f., for* maitheanan. (*Ir. id.*) Chiefs, nobles, grandees, heroes. Maithe 'na Feinn, *the Fingalian chiefs.—Oss.* See also Maithean.

Maitheach, maithiche, *s. f.* See Maigheach.

Maitheachas, ais, *s. m.* (*Ir. id.*) Forgiveness, pardon, abatement; manure.

Maitheadh, idh, *s. m.* (*Ir. id.*) Forgiveness, pardon, abatement; slackening.

Maithean, *s. pl.* Nobles, chiefs, heroes; the principal chief, or best of any class of beings. Maithean an treud, *the principal of the flock.—Stew. Jer. D. pl.* maithibh. Gu maithibh Inisfàil, *to the chiefs of Inisfail.—Fingalian Poem.*

Maitheanas, ais, *s. m.* (*Ir.* maitheamhnas.) Pardon, forgiveness, remission of a penalty. Maitheanas peacaidh, *forgiveness of sins.—Stew. Eph.* Tha mi 'g iarruidh maithcanais, *I ask pardon;* maitheanas duit! *may God forgive you!*

Maitheas, eis, *s. m.* (*Ir. id.*) Goodness, kindness; bounty; druidism; sorcery. Arson a mhaitheas, *for his goodness.—Sm.*

Maitheasach, *a.* (*Ir. id.*) Good, benevolent.

Màithrean, ein, *s. f.* (*Ir. id.*) An aunt by the mother's side.

† Mal, mail, *s. m.* A king; a prince; a soldier; a poet. Seachd cathan do mhal-shluagh, *seven companies of soldiers.—Old Poem.*

Màl, màil, *s. m.* (*Ir. id. Arm.* mael, *gain. Scotch,* mail, *tribute.*) Rent, tribute, tax, subsidy. Ann am togail màil, *in the time of collecting rents.—Old Song.*

Màl, mala, *s. m.* See Mala.

Malabhar, air, *s.* (*Ir. id.*) Dwarf-elder.

Màlach, aich, *s. m.* (*Ir. id.*) A load.

Màla, Màladh, aidh, *s. m.* (*Arm.* màl. *Ir.* màla.) A satchel, a bag, purse, or scrip; a budget; a husk; a shell.—*Stew. 2 K. ref.* Mar mhàla piob, *like the bag of a pipe.—Macdon.*

Mala, Maladh, aidh, *s. f.* An eyebrow; a brow. Starno nam malar ciar, *dark eye-browed Starno.—Oss. Fing.* Mala na h-oidhche, *the brow of night.—Id.* Mala nan scorr, *the brow of the rock.—Oss. Tem.* Maladh cnoic, *the brow of a hill.—Stew. Luke. N. pl.* malaidhean.

Màladair, *s. m.* (*from* màl.) A tenant, one who pays rent.—*Shaw.* A farmer of the customs.—*Macd. N. pl.* maladairean.

Maladh, aidh, *s. m.* See Mala.

Malaid, *s. f.* (*Ir.* maloid.) A flail; a scourge; a thong. —*Shaw. N. pl.* malaidean.

Malaidhean, *n. pl.* of mala *or* maladh. Eyebrows.

Màlair, *s. m.* A merchant; a renter; a cottager holding of a farmer.

The *màlair*, or cottager, depends not for his whole support on farm labour; but may derive his sustenance from any handicraft of which he is master: the farmer of whom he holds, however, expects his aid during the season of harvest. *Màlair* is also a cottager who builds his hut on a barren spot of ground, and digs and cultivates patches around it, for which he pays no rent for a certain number of years.

Malairt, *s. f.* (*Ir. id.*) Exchange, barter; an exchanging, a bartering. Ri malairt, *exchanging, bartering;* a deanamh malairt, *exchanging.* Thoir am malairt, *give in exchange.*

Malairteach, *a.* (*Ir. id.*) Exchangeable, barterable; fond of bartering; pertaining to exchange or barter; mutual, reciprocal.—*Shaw. Com.* and *sup.* malairtiche.

Malairteach, ich, *s. m.* A barterer. Malairteach airgid, *a money-changer; a banker. Ir.* malartoir airgid.

Malairteachadh, aidh, *s. m.* (*Ir.* malairteachadh.) Exchanging, bartering.

Malairtich, *v. a.* (*Ir.* malairtigh.) Exchange, barter. *Pret. a.* mhalairtich, *bartered; fut. aff. a.* malairtichidh, *shall barter.*

Malairtichte, *p. part.* Exchanged, bartered.

Malart. See Malairt.

Malc, *v. a.* and *n.* (*Arm.* mallu.) Carry; bear; rot; putrify. *Pret.* mhalc, *rotted; fut. aff.* malcaidh, *shall rot.*

Malcach, *a.* Rotten; apt to rot; causing rottenness.

Malcadh, aidh, *s. m.* Rottenness, putrefaction; a carrying, a bearing.

Malcair, *s. m.* (*Ir.* malcthoir.) A porter; a bearer of burdens; a salesman. *N. pl.* malcairean.

Malcaireachd, *s. f.* A carrying; the business of a porter; porterage; selling; a sale.

Malcta, Malcte, *p. part.* of malc. Rotten, putrified, putrid.

Malda, *a.* See Malta.

Maldachd, *s. f.* (*from* malda.) See Maltachd.

† Mall, *a.* (*Lat.* malus.) Bad.

This is an old Celtic word; whence *mulluich* and *mallachd.*

Mall, *a.* Slow, dilatory, lazy; late; weak; pithless; dull, senseless. Mall chum feirge, *slow to anger.—Stew. Pro.* Mall a chluinntin, *slow of hearing, dull of hearing.—Stew. Acts, ref.* Is mall a chas, *pithless is his leg.—Ull.* Cha 'n 'eil mise ach mall, *I am but* [*weakly*] *weak. Com.* and *sup.* maille.

Ir. and *W.* mall, *slow. Lat.* moll-is. *Span.* muelle. *Fr.* mol *and* molle.

Mallachadh, aidh, *s. m.* A cursing or swearing; an oath; a curse; an imprecation. Ri mallachadh, *cursing.* Bheir e mallachadh orm, *he will bring a curse on me.*—*Stew. Gen.* Luchd mallachaidh, *swearers.*

Mallachd, *s. f.*, *from* mall. *(Ir. id.)* Modesty, gentleness, softness, mildness; debility.

Mallachd, *s. f.*, *from* † mall. *(Ir. id. W.* melltith.) A curse; an oath or imprecation. Seachd mallachd air Moirfhear Deorsa! *seven curses on Lord George!*—*Roy Stewart.* Mallachd-eaglais, *excommunication.*

Mallaich, *v. n.* Grow mild, grow calm or composed. *Pret. a.* mhallaich.

Mallaich, *v. a.* and *n.* *(Ir.* malluigh.) Curse; swear; execrate; imprecate. *Pret. a.* mhallaich, *swore; fut. aff. a.* mallaichidh, *shall swear.* Cha mhallaich mi 'n talamh, *I will not curse the earth.*—*Stew. Gen.* Written also *malluich.*

Mallaichte, *p. part.* of mallaich. Cursed, accursed. Mallaichte gu robh an corruich! *cursed be their wrath!*—*Stew. Gen.*

Mallan, ain, *s. m.* *(Ir. id.)* A mole.

Mall-bheurlach, *a.* *(Ir. id.)* Slow-spoken, drawling in speech.

Mall-bhriathrach, *a.* Slow or drawling in speech; not fluent in language; having feeble language.

Mall-cheumach, *a.* Slow; pacing slowly; having a feeble gait. Is mall-cheumach triall na gealaich, *slow is the moon's progress.*—*Ull.*

Mall-chodach, *s. m.* *(Ir. id.)* One who sups late.—*Shaw.*

Mall-dromach, *a.* *(Ir. id.)* Saddle-backed.

Mall-mhuir, *s. f.* *(Ir. id.)* A neap tide.

Mall-smuainteadh, aidh, *s. m.* *(Ir. id.)* Deep musing or study.—*Shaw.*

Mall-thriallach, *a.* Travelling slowly or feebly.

Malluchadh, aidh, *s. m.* Cursing, swearing; an oath, a curse, an imprecation. Written also *mallachadh.*

Malluich, *v. a.* and *n.* Curse, swear, imprecate. Written also *mallaich;* which see.

Malluichte, *p. part.* of malluich; written also *mallaichte;* which see.

Maloimh, *s. pl.* Mallows. A gearradh maloimh, *cutting down mallows.*—*Stew. Job.*

Malraich, *v. a.* Exchange, barter.

Malta, *a.* Mild, gentle; modest; calm, composed; lazy. Aghaidh mhalta, *a mild visage.*—*Macint.*
Ir. id. Gr. μαλακος. *W.* mallta. *Eng.* mild.

Maltachd, *s. f.*, *from* mall. *(Ir. id.)* Mildness, gentleness; modesty; calmness, composedness.

Maltag, aig, *s. f.* *(from* mall.) A mild female; a modest young female; a lazy female. *N. pl.* maltagan.

Maltagach, *a.* Mild or modest, as a female. Gu maltagach, *mildly.*

Maluidh. See **Mala**.

Màm, màim, *s. m.* A slowly-rising hill; any large round hill; a handful; as much of grain, or of any granulated or pulverised substance, as can be taken up between both hands; a hand, a fist; might; an eruption or sally; *rarely,* a breach; a gap or pass; a battle. Màm nan gleann, *the hills of the valleys.*—*Macint.* Hence *Mamlorn,* a forest in Argyleshire; and *Mammor,* a district in Lochaber. Mamsioc, *a rupture.* B' e sin am màm air mùin an t-saic, *that were the handful over and above the sack.*—*G. P.*

† **Mam**, *s. f.* A mother; a breast or pap; might, power.
Lat. mamma, *a pap. Heb.* am. *Ir.* mam, *id. Gr. Att.* μαμμια, *mother. Pers.* mama. *Spa.* mama. *Styr. Carn.* mama. *Alb.* meme. *Copt.* maa. *Malay,* maa.

Ma Màr, Mà Màrsa, *provincial expressions,* signifying, *on my word; by my troth.* Ma màr fhéin, *by my troth.*

Mamas, ais, *s. m.* *(Ir. id.)* Might, strength, power.

Mam-leighinn, *s. m.* A kind of moulter.—*Macfar. Voc.*

Mam-sichde, Mam-sioc, *s. f.* A rupture.

Mamuin, *s. m.* *(Ir. id.)* An instant.—*Shaw.*

† **Man**, main, *s. m.* A hand.
Ir. id. Gr. μανη. *Lat.* manus. *It.* mano. *Fr.* main.

Mán, main, *s. m.* A brook-bile, or an ulcerous swelling under the arm.—*Macfar. Voc.*

Man, *conj.* More frequently written *mun;* which see.

M' an, *(for* mu an.) About the; about their. Ag iadhadh m' an torr, *hovering about the hill.*—*Oss. Tem.* Dubhra m' an gruaidh, *gloom about their visage.*—*Id.*

† **Mana**, ai, *s. m.* *(Ir. id.)* A cause; a condition.

Mànach, aich, *s. m.* A monk, a friar; a conventual; a foreteller. An àite guth mànaich bithidh geum bà, *instead of friar's voice there will be the lowing of cows.*—*St. Columba's Prophecy. N. pl.* mànaich.
Gr. μοναχος. *Lat.* monachus. *Sax.* monec. *Du.* monik. *W.* mynach. *Ir. Corn.* and *Arm.* manach.

Mànachail, *a.* (manach-amhuil.) Monkish, friarly; conventual, monasterial; recluse; predicting.

Manachan, ain, *s. m.* *(Ir. id.)* The groin.—*Macd. N. pl.* mànachain.

Mànachas, ais, *s. m.* Monkishness; a monkish or conventual practice or observance.

Mànachd, *s. f.* *(Ir. id.)* The state or condition of a monk; monkishness; a cloister, a monastery.

Mànadh, aidh, *s. m.* An omen, a prediction; fate, lot. Mo mhànadh-sa, *my omen.*—*Stew.* 1 *K.*

Manadh, aidh, *s. m.* *(Ir. id.)* A trump at cards.

Managhise, *s. f.* († man, *hand, and* gise *or* geis, *spear.)* A spear.—*Shaw.*

Mànaich, *gen. sing.* and *n. pl.* of mànach.

Manaig, *s. f.*, *from* † man. *(Lat.* manica. *W.* maneg. *Corn.* manag.) A glove, a mitten. *N. pl.* manaigean, *gloves.*

Manaigeach, *a.* Gloved, having gloves on.

Manair. See **Mainnir**.

Mànaisteir, *s. f.* A monastery.
Lat. monaster-ium. *Ir.* manaisteir. *Turk.* manastir.

Manois. See **Managhise**.

Mànaran, ain, *s. m.*, *from* mànadh. *(Ir. id.)* A necromancer, a conjurer or enchanter; *also,* a melodious sound. In this last sense it is more frequently written *mànran;* which see.

Mànas, ais, *s. m.* *(Scotch,* mains.) A farm-stedding; a farm attached to a mansion-house or an estate, in olden times occupied by the proprietor.—*Jamieson.*

Mànas, ais, *s. m.* *(Ir. id.)* Strength, power.

† **Manchàin**, *s.* *(Ir. id.)* A tribute of the hand; gifts; presents given at wakes and funerals.

M'an cuairt, *prep.* and *adv.* See **Mu'n cuairt**.

† **Man-chnuimh**, *s. f.* *(Ir. id.)* A cheese-mite, a maggot.—*Shaw.*

Mandrag, aig, *s. f.* A mandrake. *N. pl.* mandragan.

Mandragach, *a.* Abounding in mandrakes; like a mandrake; of, or pertaining to, a mandrake.

Mang, maing, *s. c.* A deer of a year old; a fawn; a young hart.—*Stew. Song Sol.* Deceit; a bag; a budget; moroseness; sourness. Gleann san lionmhor mang, *a glen where harts abound.*—*Old Song.* Mang, *sourness.*—*Shaw.*

Mangach, *a.* *(from* mang.) Abounding in fawns or young harts; like a hart; of, or belonging to, a fawn or a hart; morose; sour; deceitful. Laoghach, mangach, maoisleach, *abounding in calves, deer, and roes.—Macdon.*

MANGAIL, *a.*, mang-amhuil. (*Ir. id.*) Deceitful, treacherous.

† MANGAIR, *s. m.* A taverner—(*Shaw*); a pedlar. *N. pl.* mangairean.

MANGAN, ain, *s. m.* A bear; a *corruption* of ma-ghamhuinn.

MANGANACH, *a.* Abounding in bears; of, or belonging to, a bear; bearish.

† MANN, mainn, *s. m.* (*Ir. id.*) Wheat; food; a wedge; an ounce; sin.

† MANN, *a.* (*Ir. id.*) Bad, naughty.—*Shaw.*

† MANNAR, air, *s. m.* (*Ir. id.*) Evil; loosening.

MANNDA, MANNTA, *a.* Stammering, stuttering; tongue-tied; lisping; demure, modest, bashful; *also*, one that stutters or lisps. Sheas e mannta neo dhàna, *he stood modest and unassuming.—Mac Lach.*

MANNDACH, MANNTACH, *a.* (*Ir. id.*) Stammering, stuttering, lisping; tongue-tied; demure, modest, bashful; *also*, one that stutters or lisps. *Com.* and *sup.* manntaiche.

MANNDACHD, MANNTACHD, *s. f.* (*Ir. id.*) The infirmity of stammering or stuttering; a lisping; bashfulness, demureness.

MANNDAIDH, *a.* Gagged.

MANNDAIR, MANNTAIR, *s. m.* (*Ir. id.*) A stutterer, a lisper; a demure person. *N. pl.* manndairean.

MANNTA, *a.* See MANNDA.

MANNTACH, *a.* See MANNDACH.

MANNTACHD, *s. f.* Written also *manndachd;* which see.

MANNTAIR, *s. m.* See MANNDAIR.

MANNTAL, ail, *s. m.* (*Gr.* μανδυς. *Du. Teut. Arm. Corn.* mantel.) A mantle, a robe.—*Shaw.*

MANNTAN, ain, *s. m.* Timidity, bashfulness, demureness; a lisp, a stutter. Crith manntain, *a bashful tremour.—Macfar.*

MÀNRACH, aich, *s. m.* (*Ir. id.*) A fold, a pen, a cattle-house; a gift. Am meadhon am mànrach, *in the midst of their fold.—Stew. Mic.* *N. pl.* manraichean.

† MANRACHD, *s. f.* (*Ir. id.*) A gift.—*Shaw.* Happiness. —*O'Reilly.*

MANRADH, aidh, *s. m.* (*Ir. id.*) Destruction.—*Shaw.*

MANRAICHIBH, *d. pl.* of manrach.—*Stew. Zeph.*

MÀNRAN, ain, *s. m.* (*Ir. id.*) A melodious sound; melody; a love-song or sonnet; amorousness; amorous discourse; a murmur. Mànran binn an òrain, *the sweet melody of song.—Oss. Taur.* Ri mànran ciùil, *singing a love-song.—Ull.*

MÀNRANACH, *a.* (*Ir. id.*) Melodious; musical; noisy; amorous. Oigh a bheòil mhànranaich, *maid of the melodious voice.—Old Song.*

MÀNRANACHD, *s. f.* (*Ir. id.*) Melodiousness; noisiness; musicalness; amorousness.

MANRAS, ais, *s. m.* (*Ir. id.*) Motion; noise.—*Shaw.*

MANTAG, aig, *s. f.* (*Ir.* mantog.) A bridle-bit, a gag, a muzzle.

† MAOCH, *s.* (*Ir. id.*) A bleaching-green.

MAODAL, ail, *s. m.* (*Ir.* meudal.) A paunch, a tripe; a stomach; a maw; the maw or craw of birds. An gialan agus an maodal, *their cheeks and the maw.—Stew. Deut.*

MAODALACH, *a.* Having a paunch; having a craw or maw; like a paunch or a maw; of, or belonging to, the paunch.

MAODH, *a.* More frequently written *maoth;* which see.

MAODHAICH, *v. a.* and *n.* More frequently written *maothaich.*

MAODHAIN, *gen. sing.* of maodhan.

MAODHADH, aidh, *s. m.* A moistening; a boasting; a reproaching; proclaiming.

MAODHAN, ain, *s. m.* See MAOTHAN.

MAODHANACH, *a.* Gristly; pectoral. See MAOTHANACH.

MAODHANACHD, *s. f.* Gristliness. See MAOTHANACHD.

MAODHAR, air, *s. m.* A fly, or any bait to catch fish.

MAODLACH, aich, *s. m.* A servant. *N. pl.* maodlaich.

MAOIDH, *v. a.* and *n.* Threaten; boast; envy; grudge; proclaim; bully; upbraid; cast up against one a favour bestowed on him. *Pret. a.* mhaoidh; *fut. aff. a.* maoidhidh. Mhaoidh sinn cath, *we proclaimed battle.—Old Poem.* Written also *maoith.*

MAOIDHEACH, *a.* Boasting; proclaiming; threatening; upbraiding; grudging. Written also *maoitheach.*

MAOIDHEACHAS, ais, *s. m.* Boasting; vain-glory; a threat; objection. See also MAOITHEACHAS.

MAOIDHEADH, idh, *s. m.* (*Ir. id.*) A boasting; a proclaiming; a threatening; a grudging; an upbraiding; a boast; a proclamation; a threat; a grudge. Nach dean maoidheadh, *who upbraideth not.—Stew. Jam.* Written also *maoitheadh.*

MAOIDHEAN, MAOIGHEAN, ein, *s. m.* Favour; a good work; personal influence or interest; entreaty; supplication. Deanaibh maoidhean air mo shon, *speak a good word for me; make interest for me.—Stew. Gen. ref.*

MAOIDHEANACH, MAOIGHEANACH, *a.* Having personal influence or interest; favoured; supplicatory. *Com.* and *sup.* maoidheanaiche.

MAOIDHM, *s. f.* See MAOIM.

MAOIL, an *inflection* of maol; which see.

MAOILE, *com.* and *sup.* of maol. Balder, baldest. See MAOL.

MAOILE, *s. f.* (*Ir. id.*) Baldness; bluntness; a promontory; a heap. Maoile nan cruach, *the baldness of the rocks.—Oss. Tem.* Sgaoil do mhaoile, *spread thy baldness.—Stew. Mic.*

MAOILEAD, eid, *s. m.* (*Ir. id.*) Baldness; bluntness; increase in baldness or bluntness. A dol am maoilead, *growing more and more bald;* air mhaoileid sa bheil e, *however bald he be; however blunt it be.*

MAOILEAN, ein, *s. m.* A brow; a bleak eminence; *in ridicule*, a stupid fellow.

MAOILINN, *s. f.* (*Ir. id.*) A summit; the ridge of a hill; a bleak pinnacle; a postern; a sea-maw. Thar a mhaoilinn bhàr-liath, *over the grey-coped postern.—Old Poem.* *N. pl.* maoilinnean.

MAOILINNEACH, *a.* (*Ir. id.*) Ridgy; topped, as a hill; pinnacled; having a bleak ridge or pinnacle; abounding in sea-maws; of, or belonging to, a sea-maw.

MAOIM, *s. f.* (*Ir.* maidhm.) Terror; flight; surprise; a sudden torrent; a sally; an impetuous onset. Le maoim, *with terror.—Macint.* Fa' mhaoim, *troubled, afraid.—Stew. Thess.* Maoim-sleibhe, *a water-spout, a mountain torrent.* Written also *maom;* which see.

MAOIMEACH, *a.* (*from* maoim.) Causing terror; causing mountain-torrents; like a mountain-torrent; boasting.

MAOIN, *s. f.* (*Ir. id.*) Wealth; goods; substance; a little quantity; *rarely*, love, esteem. Maoin a mhaighistir, *the goods of his master.—Stew. Gen.* An spreidh agus am maoin, *their cattle and their substance.—Id.*

MAOINEACH, *a.*, *from* maoin. (*Ir. id.*) Wealthy; substantial; productive; fertile. A bhealtuinn mhaoineach, *productive May.—Macfar.*

MAOIR, *gen. sing.* and *n. pl.* of maor; which see.

MAOIRSEACHD, MAOIRSNEACHD, *s. f.* Stewardship; an

officiary, or a district of landed property, under the management of a *ground officer*.

MAOIS, *s. f.* (*Ir. id.*) A bag or pock; a hamper; a burden; carriage; a measure of five hundred herrings; Indian maize. Maois èisg, *a measure of five hundred fish*; maois sgadan, *a measure of five hundred herrings.*

MAOISEACH, ich, *s. f.* (*Ir. id.*) A doe. Written also *maoisleach*; which see.

MAOISEACH, *a.* (*from* maois.) Like a bag or hamper; in measures of five hundred, as fish; like maize; like a roe or deer; abounding in roes.

MAOISEAG, eig, *s. f.* (*dim.* of maois.) A little hamper; a burden; a little pack; a scolding female; a heifer. *N. pl.* maoiseagan.

MAOISEAGACH, *a.* Scolding; prone to scold; like a bag or hamper.

MAOISLEACH, ich, *s. c.* A roe; a doe. Caraid na maoislich, *twin roes.—Stew. Song Sol.*

MAOISLEACH, *a.* Like a roe or doe; abounding in roes or does. Mangach maoisleach, *abounding in deer and roes.—Macdon.* A bhealtuinn mhaoisleach, *roe-producing May.—Macfar.*

MAOITH, *v. a.* and *n.* Threaten; boast; envy; grudge; proclaim; bully; upbraid; cast up past favours. *Pret. a.* mhaoith; *fut. aff. a.* maoithidh. Is fearr a mhaoith no' dhìbir, *it is better grudged than not had.—G. P.* Written also *maoidh.*

MAOITHE, *com.* and *sup.* of maoth; which see.

MAOITHE, *s. f.* (*Ir. id.*) Tenderness, softness.

MAOITHEACH, *a.* Boasting; vain-glorious; proclaiming; threatening; upbraiding; grudging.

MAOITHEACHAS, ais, *s. m.* A boast; vain glory; a proclaiming; a threat; a grudging; an objection.

MAOITHEADH, idh, *s. m.* A boasting; a proclaiming; a threatening; a grudging; a boast; a threat; a grudge.

MAOL, maoil, *s. m.* (*Ir. id.*) A promontory, a cape; as, *maol Chinntìre*, the promontory or mull of Kintyre; the brow of a rock; (*Corn.* moel, *a bald top*); the brow of the face; a servant; a bald head; a shaved or shorn monk. Mar chrainn ri maol carraig, *like trees on the brow of a rock.—Oss.* Hence, from the circumstance of their being shorn, various Highland saints received their names; as, *Maol-cholum*, St. Columba; *Maol-Iosa*, a saint of that name.

MAOL, *a.* (*Ir. id. Arm.* moal.) Bald; bare; hornless; blunt; easily imposed on; barren; bleak. Tha e maol, *he is bald.—Stew. Lev.* Maol, gun duilleach, *bare, without leaves.—Oss. Derm.* Iarunn maol, *blunt iron.—Stew. Ecc.* Mullach maol liath, *a bleak grey eminence.—Old Poem. Com.* and *sup.* maoile, *more* or *most bald.*

MAOLACHADH, aidh, *s. m.* A blunting; a making bald; a growing blunt or bald.

MAOLAG, aig, *s. f.* (*from* maol.) A name given to a cow without horns; *in ridicule*, a stupid female. *N. pl.* maolagan.

MAOLAICH, *v. a.* and *n.* (*Ir.* maolaigh.) Make bald or blunt; become bald or blunt; *rarely*, to allay or calm. *Pret. a.* mhaolaich, *blunted; fut. aff. a.* maolaichidh, *shall blunt.* Mhaolaich an leachd a bàrr, *the plate blunted its point.—Mac Lach.* Cha mhaolaich iad an ceann, *they will make bald their head.—Stew. Lev.* Mhaolaich mo chlaidheamh, *my sword become blunt.—Old Song.*

MAOLAICHTE, *p. part.* of maolaich. Made bald; made blunt.

MAOL-AIGEAN, -aigne, *s. f.* A dull comprehension; stupidity.

MAOL-AIGEANNACH, *a.* Dull of comprehension; stupid; blunt.

MAOL-AIGEANTACH, *a.* (*Ir. id.*) Blunt, stupid, dull.

MAOLAINN, *s. f.* A mule.

MAOLAN, ain, *s. m.* (*Ir. id.*) A beacon; a bleak eminence—(*Shaw*); that part of a pile which is above water in a fishing wear. *N. pl.* maolain.

MAOLANACH, *a.* Like a beacon; of, or belonging to, a beacon; abounding in beacons; bleak.

MAOLANACH, aich, *s. m.* A stake driven into the ground to support flakes for keeping cattle in a fold; the stake of a wooden fold or pen. *N. pl.* maolanaich.

MAOL-AODAINN, *s. f.* A bald brow; a bleak hill-side.

MAOL-AODAINNEACH, *a.* Bald; bleak-sided, as a hill.

MAOL-AODAINNEACHD, *s. f.* Baldness; bleakness.

† MAOLAS, ais, *s. m.* (*Ir. id.*) A sandal.

MAOL-BHATHAIS, *s. m.* A bald forehead.—*Stew. Lev.*

MAOL-BHATHAISEACH, *a.* Having a bald brow or forehead.—*Stew. Lev.*

MAOL-CHAIR, *s. f.* The space between the eyebrows; *also termed* maol-chair na mailne.

MAOLCHAR, *a.* Having a large space between the eyebrows.

MAOL-CHEANN, chinn, *s. m.* A bald head.—*Stew. Lev.* A stupid head. *N. pl.* maol-chinn.

MAOL-CHEANNACH, *a.* Bald-headed; stupid; bashful; sheepish.

MAOL-CHLUAS, -chluaise, *s. f.* A blunt or deaf ear.

MAOL-CHLUASACH, *a.* Tame, gentle; inactive.—*Shaw.* Dull of hearing.

MAOL-CHOLUM-CHILLE, *s. m.* St. Columba; *also*, St. Columba's attendant or servant. See MAOL.

MAOLCHRUACHD, *s. f.* A bald forehead or brow.

MAOL-CHRUACHDACH, *a.* Having a bald brow or forehead.—*Macint.*

MAOL-DHEARC, *s. m.* A mulberry. *N. pl.* maol-dhearcan. Craobh mhaol-dhearc, *a mulberry-tree.*

MAOL-DHEARCACH, *a.* Abounding in mulberries; like a mulberry; of, or pertaining to, a mulberry.

MAOL-DHEARCAG, aig, *s. f.* A mulberry. *N. pl.* maoldhearcagan.

MAOL-DOMHNUICH, *s. m.* A forest in Barra; the name Ludovick.

MAOLDORN, dùirn, *s. m.* (*Ir. id.*) A sword-hilt.—*Shaw.*

MAOL-FHAOBHAR, air, *s. m.* (*Ir. id.*) A blunt edge.

MAOL-FHAOBHRACH, *a.* (*Ir. id.*) Blunt, as a bladed instrument.

MAOL-IOSA, *s.* The name of a Highland saint who traversed the country bearing a wallet and collecting alms for his poor brethren. The Gaelic term *mailios*, a wallet, is perhaps derived from this name.

MAOL-OISINN, *s. f.* An obtuse angle; a rounded angle.

MAOL-OISINNEACH, *a.* Having the hair cut above the brows; bald-browed; having rounded receding angles.

MAOL-RUANAIDH, *s. f.* A nickname given to any giddy female who is fond of frequenting fairs, or any place of resort: hence the Gael say, Cha n' 'eil fèill no faidhir air nach fhaighear maoil-ruanaidh, *there is no fair or market where you see not maol-ruanaidh.*

MAOL-SNEIMHEALAS, ais, *s. m.* Carelessness; tawdriness; slovenliness, untidiness.

MAOL-SNEIMHEIL, *a.* Indifferent, careless; tawdry; slovenly, untidy.

MAOLUICH, *v. a.* and *n.* See MAOLAICH.

MAOLUIN, *s. f.* (*Ir. id.*) A mule.

MAOM, maoim, *s. f.* Fear, terror; a torrent; a pouring forth; a sally; an impetuous onset. Maom sleibh, *a sudden mountain-torrent caused by the bursting of a thunder-cloud.*

MAOM, *v. n.* Pour forth; burst forth; make a sally; make an impetuous onset. *Pret.* mhaom, *poured; fut. aff.* maomaidh, *shall pour forth.*

MAOMACH, *a.* Causing fright; pouring; impetuous, as a torrent.

MAOMADH, aidh, *s. m.* A pouring forth; a sally; an impetuous onset; a bursting, as a torrent. Ghrab e maomadh na feachd, *he stopped the onset of the host.—Mac Lach.*

MAOMADH, (a), *pr. part.* of maom. Pouring forth; bursting forth, as a stream; sallying; making an onset. Sruth a maomadh nan dàil, *a stream pouring towards them.—Old Poem.*

† MAON, maoin, *s. m.* (*Ir. id.*) A hero.

† MAON, *a.* Dumb, mute.—*Shaw. Com.* and *sup.* maoine.

MAONAG, aig, *s. f.* A bog-berry.

MAOR, maoir, *s. m.* An inferior civil officer; a bailiff; a steward; an underling agent superintending a portion of a gentleman's landed property; a baron. An ni a chuir na maoir a dh'ifrinn, *that which sent the officers to hell.—Old Saying.* Maor-baile, *a town-officer;* maor-eaglais, *a beadle; a church-officer; a churchwarden;* maor-siorram, maor-siorradh, *a sheriff's officer;* maor-rìgh, *a messenger-at-arms;* maor-striopaich, *a pimp* or *pander.—Shaw.* Maor-ghairm, *a herald.* Chruinnich e na maoir-ghairm, *he summoned the heralds.—Mac Lach.*

Ir. id. Corn. moar. *Arm.* maor. *Lat.* major. *W.* maer. *Eng.* mayor.

Formerly *maor* signified a *baron;* and in most oriental languages it means one of high degree. *Hind.* mor *and* moer, *a king. Syr. Chald.* mar, *a lord. Turk. Arab.* emir, *a prince. Pers.* mir *and* mirza, *a lord. Tart.* mir, *prince.*

MAORACH, aich, *s. m.* Shell-fish; a place where shell-fish are found. Clachan is maorach an aigeil, *the stones and shell-fish of the deep.—Macdon.*

MAORACH, *a.* Abounding in shell-fish.

MAORSAINNEACHD, *s. f.* (*from* maor.) A stewardship; an officiary, or that district of a gentleman's landed property which is under the inspection of a ground-officer or bailiff.

MAOSGANACH, aich, *s. m.* (*Ir. id.*) A hudge or shapeless trunk.

MAOSGANACH, *a.* Shapeless, hudgy, clumsy, full of hudges.

MAOTH, *v. a.* and *n.* (*Ir. id.*) Soften; smooth.

MAOTH, *a.* (*Ir. id.*) Tender, soft, gentle, delicate, smooth; tame, quiet; moist; enervated. Tha chlann maoth, *the children are tender.—Stew. Gen.* An osag mhaoth, *the gentle breeze.—Oss. Fing.* Gu maoth, *softly, gently.*

MAOTHACH, *a.* (*Ir. id.*) Lenitive, emollient; tender, gentle; soothing; moistening; enervating.

MAOTHACHADH, aidh, *s. m.* (*Ir.* maothughadh.) A softening; a smoothing; a taming; a becoming soft, tender, or smooth; a becoming tame; a moistening; irrigation; enervating.

MAOTHACHD, *s. f.* (*from* maoth.) Tenderness, softness; lenitiveness, gentleness; delicateness; smoothness; tameness; moistness.

MAOTHAG, aig, *s. f.* (*from* maoth. *Ir. id.*) An unformed egg; *also,* a delicate young female. *N. pl.* maothagan.

MAOTHAICH, *v. a.* and *n.* (*from* maoth.) Soften; mitigate; alleviate; enervate; tame; become soft; become enervated; grow exorable; grow less hardened or less cruel. *Pret. a.* mhaothaich, *softened; fut. aff. a.* maothaichidh, *shall soften; fut. pass.* maothaichear, *shall be softened.*

MAOTHAICHEAS, *fut. pass.* of maothaich.

MAOTHAICHTE, *p. part.* of maothaich. Softened, mitigated, alleviated; enervated; tamed.

MAOTHALACH, *a.* (*Ir. id.*) Lenitive, emollient; tender, soft. *Com.* and *sup.* maothalaiche.

MAOTHALACHD, *s. f.* (*Ir. id.*) Lenitiveness; tenderness, softness. Thaobh maothalachd, *by reason of tenderness.—Stew. Deut.*

MAOTHAN, ain, *s. m.* (*Ir. id.*) The chest or breast; a twig, an osier; a bud or tendril; a cartilage; a young person; a coward; any thing tender or soft; the *xiphoides,* the bone or gristle terminating in the lower end of the *sternum;* the gristle in the *scrobiculum cordis.* Cha ghearain i' maothan, *she will not complain of her chest.—Macint.* Gun mhaothan ri 'taobh, *without a tendril by her side.—Oss. Derm.* Gach maothan snitheach, *every tender maid weeping.—Death of Carril. N. pl.* maothain *and* maothanan.

MAOTHANACH, *a.* (*from* maothan.) Of, or belonging to, the chest; thoracic; like a twig or tendril; abounding in twigs; cartilaginous; slender in person.

MAOTHANACHD, *s. f.* Gristliness; limberness; tenderness; slenderness.

MAOTHAR, *a.* (*from* maoth.) Tender; smooth; quiet, peaceful; limber; mild; mannerly.

MAOTH-BHLAS, *s. m.* A mild taste; a sweet taste or flavour.

MAOTH-BHLASDA, *a.* Having a sweet or mild taste or flavour. Snothach maoth-bhlasda, *the sweet-tasted sap of trees.—Macfar.*

MAOTH-BHLATH, *s. m.* A soft or tender blossom. Mar mhaoth-bhlathan, *like the tender blossom.—Oss. Gaul.*

MAOTH-BHLÀTH, *a.* Lukewarm. See MEADH-BHLATH.

MAOTH-BHLÀTHAS, ais, *s. m.* Lukewarmness.

MAOTH-BHOS, -bhois, *s. m.* A soft palm of the hand. Do mhaoth-bhos bu ghrinne, *thy soft palm that was the fairest.—Old Song.*

MAOTH-CHLOIMH, *s. f.* Soft down; soft wool. Leabadh mhaoth-chloimh, *a bed of soft wool.*

MAOTH-LUS, -luis, *s. m.* A tender herb; a flower; grass. Mar mhaoth-lus fàsaidh tu, *like a flower thou shalt grow.—Sm. N. pl.* maoth-lusan.

MAOTHRAN, ain, *s. m.* (*from* maoth.) An infant, a child.—*Stew. Gen.* A twig, a tendril. *N. pl.* maothrain.

MAOTHRANACH, *a.* Infantile, tender, as an infant.

MAOTH-ROSG, -roisg, *s. m.* A soft eyelid, a tender eyelid; an eye expressive of a mild temper; a languid eye; a languid look. *N. pl.* maoth-rosgan.

MAOTH-ROSGACH, *a.* Having soft or tender eyelids; looking softly or mildly.

MAOTH-SHUIL, -shùl, *s. f.* (*Ir. id.*) A soft eye; a tender eye. *N. pl.* maoth-shuileach.

MAOTH-SHUILEACH, *a.* (*Ir. id.*) Tender-eyed; soft-eyed; ophthalmic.

MAOTH-SHÙILEACHD, *s. f.* (*Ir. id.*) Tenderness of the eyes; wateriness of the eyes.

MAOTHUICH. See MAOTHAICH.

MAR, *prep.* With, together with. Most frequently used in conjunction with the prep *ri,* either simple or compound. Mar ruinn san uair, *with us at that time.—Oss. Gaul.* Mar ris, *with him;* mar ri, *with her,*—having the same meaning with *maille ris, maille rithe.*

MAR, *prep.* and *conj.* (*Ir. Corn.* mar, *if.*) As; like as; like; if. Cha robh e mar mhìle dhomh, *he was not within a mile of me.* Is e is fhaisge mar dhà mhìle, *it is nearest by two miles. Mar,* when prefixed to a noun without the article, is a preposition, and commonly governs the dative. Mar nighinn, *as a daughter.—Stew. Sam.* Mar amhuinn mhòir, *like a great river.—Stew. Ps.* But if the noun have the article, it is governed as the nominative; as, Mar a ghrian, *like the sun;* mar uisge bhalbh, *like still waters.—Oss. Fin. and Lor.* Ni 's mo mar airde a chinn, *a head higher, higher by the height of the head.—Mac Lach* Mar gun, *as if,* mar gu, *as if,* mar gum b' ann, *as if it were,* mar gum b' eadh, *as it were;* mar aon, *together, as one;* mar an ceudna, *also,* mar chomhla, *together;* mar sin, *in that manner, as that, so,* dìreach mar sin, *exactly so, just so,* mar so, *thus, as this,* mar sud, *in your manner,* mar sin fhéin, *so and so.*

Mìr fhein, a provincial mode of expression, signifying *on my word, by my troth,* it is perhaps a corruption of Moire fhéin.

Mara, *gen. sing* of muir; which see

Marag, aig, *s. f.* (*Ir. id.*) A blood-pudding; a sausage, *in ridicule,* a pot-bellied person Marag dubh, *a blood-pudding hardened in smoke.* *N pl* maragan. Cha truagh cù is marag mu 'amhaich, *a dog is not to be pitied who has a sausage about his neck —G P.*

Maragach, *a.* Like a pudding; abounding in puddings, pot-bellied.

Maraiche, *s. m.* A mariner, a marine *N. pl* maraichean Is dorch' ars' am maraich' an oidhche, *dark, said the mariner, is the night —Oss. Duthona.*

Maraig, *gen. sing.* of marag; which see

Marain, *gen. sing.* of maran.

Maraiste, *s. f.* (*Lat* maritus, *husband*) A marriage; a match; a husband. *N. pl.* maraistean

Maraisteach, *a* Marriageable; fond of making matches.

Màran, ain, *s. m.* Entertainment; a feasting; a voice, a low voice; a murmur Le màran 's le mireadh, *with feasting and fun.—Old Song* Cumhach air lag mhàrain, *disconsolate, with a faint voice —Death of Carril.* *Màran* signifying a voice or murmur, ought perhaps to be *mànran.*

Maranach, *a* (*from* maran.) Hospitable; feasting; convivial; murmuring Bitheamaid maranach geanach, *let us be hospitable and good-humoured —Old Song.*

Mar an ceudna, *adv.* Also; too; in like manner.

Maranna, Marannan, *n pl.* of muir. Seas *—Stew. Gen. ref.*

Maraon, *adv* (mar *and* aon.) Together, in concert, as one. A ghluais iad maraon, *they moved together.—Oss Tem* Chì am mairiche an uaigh maraon, *the mariners shall see their graves as one.—Oss. Fing.*

Maras, ais, *s m* (*Ir. id*) A myriad; ten thousand —*Shaw.*

Marascal, Marasgal, ail, *s m.* (*Ir id*) A marshal; a master; a regulator; subjection. Marasgal feachd, *a field-marshal,* feachd-mharasgal, *a field-marshal* Cuir air droch mharasgal, *set a bad master over him.—Old Song.*

Marascalach, Marasgalach, *a.* Marshalling, like a marshal; of, or belonging to, a marshal.

Marasclachadh, Marasglachadh, aidh, *s. m.* A marshalling; a regulating, a superintending

Marasclachd, Marasglachd, *s. f.* Marshalling, regulation; superintendence, the office or rank of a marshal. Fuidh mharasglachd-san, *under his subjection. — Stew. 1 Pet. ref*

Marasglaich, *v. a.* Superintend; regulate; marshal *Pret. a.* mharasglaich; *fut. aff. a* marasglaichidh

Marbh, *a* Dead, lifeless, benumbed, torpid: spiritless; dull; vapid or stale, as beer. Duine marbh, *a dead man.* *Arm:* den maru Corp marbh, *a dead body.* *Arm* corf maru. In *Vannes,* they say, corf marv. Laogh marbh, *a dead calf.* *Arm.* lueou maru. Leann marbh, *stale beer* *Com* and *sup.* mairbhe

Ir marbh. *W.* marw. *Corn* marrow *Arm.* maru, maro, *and* marff.

Marbh, *s m.* A time of gloom or stillness Marbh na h-oidche, *the gloom* or *dead of night.* Marbh a gheamhraidh, *the dead of winter.*

Marbh, *v a.* Kill, massacre; make stale or flat. *Pret a* mharbh, *killed, fut. aff. a.* marbhaidh, *shall kill; fut pass* marbhar

Marbhach, *a* (*Ir. id.*) Deadly; destructive; poisonous, sanguinary, cruel *Com.* and *sup* marbhaiche

Marbhadair, *s m* A murderer, a slayer, a sanguinary warrior *N. pl.* marbhadairean

Marbhadh, aidh, *s m* (*Ir id*) A slaying, a butchering, a massacring, slaughter, massacre. Chum a mharbhaidh, *to the slaughter —Stew. Pro. ref.* Mortadh is marbhadh, *massacre.*

Marbhaibh, *d. pl.* of mairbhe To the dead. Also, 2 *pl imper a* of marbh, *kill ye.*

Marbhaiche, *s. m* A slayer, a murderer Gun teich am marbhaiche, *that the slayer may fly —Stew Num*

Marbhaidh, *gen sing* of marbhadh; also, *fut. pass* of marbh.

Marbhain, *gen sing* of marbhan; which see

Marbhaisg, *s. f* (marbh, *dead,* and fàisg, *squeeze*) A fatal end; a catastrophe; woe.

Marbhaisg ort is a common imprecation among both the Scotch and Irish Celts; and, as may be seen from the composition of the word *marbhaisg,* calls down death by drowning In such cases, the body was tied to a plank, and carried wet and dropping to the place of interment. Or, perhaps the orthography is *marbh-phaisg,* a shroud, if so, the imprecation merely invokes death, without any allusion to the manner of it

Marbham, 1 *sing imper* of marbh, *let me kill,* or for marbhaidh mi, *I shall kill.*

Marbhan, ain, *s m. from* marbh (*Ir id*) A dead body, a carcass Cha d' theid do mharbhan, *thy carcass shall not go —Stew 1 K* *N pl* marbhain.

Marbhanach, *a.* (*Ir id*) Like a carcass; full of carcasses, of, or belonging to, a carcass.

Marbhanta, *a, from* marbh (*Ir. id.*) Inactive, dull, spiritless, torpid; benumbed, lukewarm Gu marbhanta, *inactively, in a spiritless manner*

Marbhantachd, *s.* (*Ir id*) Inactiveness, dulness, deadness, spiritlessness, torpidness; lukewarmness

Marbh-aodach, aich, *s. m* Dead-clothes, a shroud

Marbh-aodaich, *v. a* Shroud; clothe or dress a dead body.

Marbhchras, ais, *s m* A carcass *N pl* marbh-chrasan

Marbh-dhruidh, *s m* A necromancer *N pl* marbh-dhruidhean.

Marbh-dhruidheach, *a* Necromantic.

Marbh-dhruidheachd, *s f.* (*Ir. id*) Necromancy.

Marbh-fhonn, -fhuinn, *s. m.* A funeral air, a dead march *—Oss. Tem.*

Mar-bhith, *prep* and *conj* Were it not Mar-bhith thusa, *were it not for you,* mar-bhith gun d' thàinig e, *were it not that he came*

Marbh-lath, *s. m* A dull heavy day; a still cloudy day

Marbh-lap, *v. n.* Become benumbed or frost-bitten, become torpid.

Marbh-lapach, *a* Benumbed, frost-bitten, causing torpor or paralysis.

Marbhnach, aich, *s. m* An epitaph, an elegy

Marbh-phaisg, *s f* (marbh *and* paisg, *wrap*) A death-shroud. Marbh-phaisg ort! *thy death-shroud on thee!*—a common imprecation among the Scotch and Irish Celts See also MARBHAISG.

MARBH-PHAISG, *v. a* Shroud, clothe with a shroud. *Pret a.* mharbh-phaisg, *fut. aff. a* marbh-phaisgidh

MARBH-PHAISGTE, *p part* of marbh-phaisg Shrouded, as a dead body

MARBH-PHASGADH, aidh, *s m* A shrouding. Air là do mharbh-phasgaidh, *on the day of thy shrouding.—Old Poem*

MARBH-RANN, rainn, *s f* (*Ir id.*) An epitaph, an elegy, a funeral song

MARBH-RANNACH, *a* Elegaic, funereal.

MARBH-SHRUTH, *s m* A still stream; that part of a river or stream the current of which is scarcely perceptible; the wake of a ship —*Shaw*

MARBHTACH, *a.* (*Ir* marbhthach) Deadly, destructive, baneful, sanguinary, cruel Làn do nimh marbhtach *full of deadly poison —Stew Jam Com* and *sup* marbhtaiche.

MARBHTACHD, *s f* Deadliness, destructiveness, banefulness, cruelty, bloodiness

† MARBRAID, *s f.* A fort —*Shaw N pl.* marbraidean

MARC, *s m* (*Chald.* merc *Germ* mark *W* marc *Arm.* and *Corn.* march *Ir* marc) A horse, a steed Le mharc uaibhreach ard-cheumach, *with his proud prancing horse —Oss Taura* Marc-choimhliong, *a horse race*, marc glas, *a grey horse Arm* march glas Marc Sasunnach, *an English horse Arm* march sauss. Marc dubh, *a black horse. Arm* march du.

MARCACH, aich, *s m*, *from* marc (*Ir id*) A rider, a horseman, a knight, a dragoon An t-each agus a mharcach, *the horse and his rider —Stew Ex* Gabh marcach, *take a horseman —Stew 2 K.* Marcach-dàin, *a rehearser of poetry, a person who attended the poet — O'Reilly. N. pl* marcaiche

MARCACH, *for* marcachadh

MARCACHADH, aidh, *s m* A riding, horsemanship.

MARCACHADH, (a), *pr part* of marcaich Riding Marcachadh nan tonn, *riding the billows —Old Poem* Written also *marcachd*

MARCACHD, *s f* (*Ir id*) Riding, horsemanship

MARCACHD, (a), *pr part* of marcaich Riding A marcachd na sine, *riding on the blast —Oss.*

MARCAICH, *v a* (*from* marc) Ride *Pret a* mharcaich, *rode, fut. aff* marcaichidh, *shall ride* Marcaichidh e le greadhnas, *he will ride joyously.—Ull.*

MARCAICHE, *s m.* (*from* marc.) A rider, a horseman; a dragoon, a knight *N pl* marcaichean Sgaoilidh am marcaichean iad fèin, *their horsemen shall spread themselves —Stew. Hab*

MARCAIR, *s m* (*W* marçawr *Corn* marhar) A horseman, a dragoon, a rider. *N pl.* marcairean Deagh mharcair, *a good rider*

MARCAIREACHD, *s f* Horsemanship Deagh mharcaireachd, *good horsemanship*

MARCAIS, *s m* A marquess.

MARCAISEACHD, *s f* A marquesate, riding, horsemanship

MARCAIT, *s f.* A market Air là marcait, *on a market-day. Mack.*

MARCLACH, aich, *s f* Provision, victuals —*Shaw*

MARC-LANN, -lainn, *s m* (*Ir id. W* marçlan) A stable

MARCREIL, *s f* Mackerel —*Shaw*

MARC-SHLUAGH, -shluaigh, *s. m.* (*Ir id. W.* marçawlu) Horsemen, cavalry, riders. Air am marc-shluagh, *on their horsemen —Stew. Ex.* A mharc-shluagh, *ye horsemen.—Stew. Jer.*

MARCUIS, *s* (*Ir. id.*) A marquess.

MARCUISEACHD, *s f* (*Ir. id*) A marquesate; riding; horsemanship.

MARG, mairg, *s. m* A mark in money, or thirteen shillings and fourpence. Marg fearainn, *a mark of land.*

MARGACH, *a* In marks, as money; like a fair or market.

MARGAD, aid, *s m.* See MARGADH.

MARGADH, aidh, *s. m.* (*Ir. id.*) A market; a fair. Anns a mhargadh, *in the market.—Stew. Matt.* Do mhargaidh, *thy fairs —Stew. Ezek.* Baile margaidh, *a market-town;* margadh na feòla, *the shambles* or *flesh-market.—Stew. 1 Cor* Margadh min, *a meal-market;* margadh chruidh, *the cattle-market*

MARGAIL, *a* (marg'amhuil.) Marketable; saleable

MARGAILEACHD, *s f.* Marketableness, saleableness.

MARGHAN, ain, *s m* A margin —*Shaw N. pl* marghain.

MARGLAICHE, *s m* A merchant.

MA' RI, *for* mar ri *or* maille ri; which see.

MARLA, *s m* (*Ir id*) Rich clay; that condition of lime called marl

MARLACH, *a.* Abounding in marl; like marl.

MARMHOR, MARMOR, oir, *s. m.* (*Ir* marmor. *Lat.* marmor) Marble. Clachan marmoir, *marble stones*

MARMHORACH, MARMORACH, *a* Of marble; like marble; abounding in marble.

MARMOR, oir, *s. m* See MARMHOR.

MARNIALACH, aich, *s m.* (mara, *gen sing* of muir, *sea*, and nial, *a cloud*) A pilot who foretells the state of the weather from the appearance of the sky, or from a certain arrangement or modification of clouds.

MARRACHADH, aidh, *s m.* An anchoring, a mooring; anchorage.

MARRAICH, *v. a* and *n* Moor, anchor, ride at anchor. *Pret a* mharraich, *anchored, fut. aff.* marraichidh

MARRAICHEADH, idh, *s. m* A bolt of iron or wood used for driving out another

MARRI, *prep* See MAR RI.

MAR RI, *prep* (*for* maille ri) With, together with, in company with Mar ri namhaid, *together with the enemy.—Oss Fing* Mar rithe, *along with her*, mar ria, *along with her.*

MARRIBH, *comp prep* See MAR RIBH

MAR RIBH, *comp. prep.* With you, together with you, along with you *Mar ribh* is more elegantly written *maille ribh.*

MARRINN, *comp prep.* See MAR RINN

MAR RINN, *comp prep* (*for* maille rinn.) With us, together with us, in company with us, on our side.

MARRIS, *comp. pron*, *for* maille ris (*Ir id*) See MAR RIS.

MAR RIS, *comp pron* (*Ir. id*) With him, along with him, together with him, on his side.

MARRIU, *comp prep* (*Ir id*) See MAR RIU.

MAR RIU, *comp prep.* (*for* maille riu.) With them, in company with them, on their side.

MARRIUM, *comp. prep.* (*Ir id*) See MAR RIUM.

MAR RIUM, *comp prep.* (*for* maille rium.) With me, along with me, in company with me, on my side, in my favour. In some parts of the Highlands they say *mar rum*

MARRIUT, *comp prep.* See MAR RIUT.

MAR RIUT, *comp. prep.* (*for* maille riut.) With thee, along with thee; on thy side. Some of the Gael say *mar rut.*

Màr-ros, *s. m.* (*Ir. id.*) Rosemary.

Marruit, *comp. pron.* (*for* maille ruit.) With thee, along with thee, on thy side.—*Stew. Gen.*

Marrum, *comp pron.* More properly *mar rium*, which see

Màrsadh, aidh, *s. m.* Marching; a march.

Marsal, ail, *s. m.* (*prov.*) A merchant; a shopkeeper *N pl.* marsalan.

Màrsal, ail, *s. m.* A marshal. Properly *marasgal*; which see

Màrsal, ail, *s m* Marching.

Marsalachd, *s. f.* (*prov.*) The business of shopkeeping.

Màrsaladh, aidh, *s. m.* A marching; a marshalling.

Marsan, ain, *s. m.* A merchant; a shopkeeper.

Marsantachd, *s f.* Merchandise; the occupation of a merchant

Mar sin, *adv.* In that way, in that manner; so, thus; in that direction. Ceart mar sin, *just so*, tha e mar sin, *he or it is so*, mar sin bha mi òg, *so was I in my youth* —*Old Poem.* Mar sin mairidh an iomradh, *thus their fame shall last.*—*Id* Mar sin fhéin, *just so*, *so so*

Mar so, *adv.* In this way, in this manner; thus, so. Is ann mar so tha 'chùis, *the case stands thus*, mar so chaith sinn an oidhche, *thus we spent the night* —*Oss*

Marsonta, *s. m.* A merchant.—*Macfar. Voc. N. pl* marsontan.

Marsontachd, *s. f.* Merchandise; the business of a merchant; shopkeeping.—*Stew Rev ref.*

Mar sud, *adv.* In that way or manner; in yon way or manner; in that direction. Mar sud agus, *if so, if it be so, then, so also.*

Màrt, mairt, *s. f.* (*Lat.* Martius *Ir.* Mart) The month of March.

Mart, mairt, *s. f.* (*Ir.* mart. *Scotch*, mart.) A cow. Dròbh nam mart, *the drove of cows* —*Macdon* Mart-geamhraidh, *a winter mart*, *a cow killed for winter food.*

Màrtain, *s f.* Martin, Martinmas. La fhéill Mhartain, *Martinmas-day*, or *the festival of St. Martin*

Martair, *s. m* A cripple; a maimed or mutilated person; *also*, one who maims.

Martanach, aich, *s. m* (*Ir.* martineach.) A cripple

Mart-bhainne, *s. f.* A milch cow. Dà mhart-bhainne, *two milch cows* —*Stew Sam.*

Mart-fheòil, -fheòla, *s. f.* (*Ir id.*) Beef.

Martraich, *v a* Maim, lame, mutilate. *Pret. a.* mhartraich, *maimed.*

Ma 's, *for* ma is. (*Ir. id.*) If. Ma 's è, *if it be; if it be he*; ma 's e agus, *if it be*, ma 's e agus gu, *if it be that, if it so be that*; ma 's fhior dha fhéin, *in his own belief.*

Mas, *conj.* Ere, before. Mas càn gur masgul e, *before it be cal'ed flattery.*—*Old Song.*

Màs, màis, *s m.* (*Ir. id*) A thigh; a hip; a buttock; a breech; a mace *N. pl.* màsan.

† **Mas**, *a* (*Ir id*) Excellent, handsome—(*Shaw*), round, heaped

Màsach, *a* Having large thighs or hips. Laoch plocach màsach, *a sturdy stout-thighed fellow* —*Macfar.*

Màsaolas, ais, *s m* A species of red berry.

Màsair, *s. m.* A mace-bearer.—*Macd.* A man with large thighs. *N. pl.* màsairean

Màsan, *n. pl.* of màs. Thighs, hips; buttocks

Màsan, ain, *s. m.* (*Ir. id*) Delay, dilatoriness, slowness; a reproof.

Màsanach, *a.*, *from* mas (*Ir. id*) Slow, dilatory, tedious. *Com* and *sup.* masanaiche. Gu masanach, *dilatorily.*

Masanachd, *s. f.* Dilatoriness, slowness, tediousness.

Masduidh, *s m.* (*Ir.* masdidh. *Arm* mastin. *Eng.* mastiff.) A large dog or mastiff. *N. pl.* masduidhean

Masduidheach, *a.* Like a mastiff.

Ma seach, *adv.* and *prep* Alternately; one by one; in turn; to and fro. A géilleadh ma seach, *yielding one by one.*—*Oss. Fing* Guil-sa ma seach, *sweep thou in thy turn.*—*Old Poem.* Fear ma seach, *one by one*

Ma seadh, *conj* (*Ir. id.*) If so, if it be so, then, in that case.

Masg, *v a* (*Ir id*) Infuse; mix; steep malt for brewing. *Pret. a.* mhasg, *infused*; *fut. aff. a.* masgaidh, *shall infuse.*

Masgadh, aidh, *s. m* (*Ir. id*) The process of infusing; a steeping, as of malt for brewing, an infusion. Ionad masgaidh, *a place for steeping malt.*

Masgair, *s. m.* (*Ir id*) One who steeps or infuses; a lump

Masgul, uil, *s m.* Flattery; cajoling Mas càn gur masgul e, *before it be called flattery* —*Old Song.*

Masgulach, *a.* Sycophantic; inclined to flatter or cajole; like flattery Gu masgulach, *in a sycophantic manner.*

Masgulachd, *s f* Sycophancy; the practice of flattery; a cajoling disposition.

Masgulaiche, *s. m.* A sycophant, a flatterer.

Masla, ai, *s. m.* See **Masladh.**

Maslach, *a* (*Ir. id*) Disgraceful, shameful, degrading, reproachful; slanderous. Iomchar maslach, *disgraceful conduct.*

Maslachadh, aidh, *s m.* An affronting; a reproaching; a degrading, scandalising, an affront; a reproach; degradation; slander Fhuair e 'mhaslachadh, *he was disgraced.*

Maslachadh, (a), *p part.* of maslaich. Affronting; reproaching; disgracing, degrading; shaming; slandering.

Masladh, aidh, *s. m* (*Teut* maschel, *a stain*) An affront, a reproach; a disgrace; scandal; shame A mhasladh, *his reproach* —*Stew. Pro.* Cha mhasladh sìth ri laoch, *peace with a hero is no disgrace.*—*Old Poem.* Masladh bith-bhuan, *everlasting shame.*—*Stew. Jer* Mo nàire 's mo mhasladh! *shame and confusion!*

Maslaich, *v a.* (*Ir.* maslaigh.) Affront, reproach; scandalise, slander, degrade *Pret. a.* mhaslaich, *fut aff. a* maslaichidh, *fut. pass* maslaichear, *shall be reproached.* Ma mhaslaichear sibh, *if ye be reproached.*—*Stew Pet.*

Maslaichte, *p. part.* of maslaich. Affronted, reproached; disgraced, degraded, shamed.

Maslail, *a.* (masladh-amhuil) Disgraceful

Maslain, *s f* Mastlin, mong-corn

Maslucuadh. See **Maslachadh**

Masluich See **Maslaich.**

Ma ta, *conj.* (*Ir id*) If so; nevertheless, then; however. Ma ta tha, *indeed it is; indeed he is* Bheil thu falbh? ma ta tha, *are you going? yes I am, yes indeed* Ni mise e ma ta, *I will do it then.* Ma ta gu dearbh, *indeed, verily*

† **Mata**, *a.* (*Ir. id*) Dark, gloomy; great —*Shaw.*

† **Mata**, ai, *s. m.* (*Ir. id*) A matrass.

Matag, aig, *s f.* (*Eng* mattock) A hoe, spade, or mattock —*Macd. N. pl* matagan

Matagach, *a.* Like a hoe, spade, or mattock

Math, *a.* Good, virtuous; becoming, pleasant, excellent; well; agreeable Duine math, *a good man*, (*Arm* den ma), là math, *a fine day*, là math-dhuit, *good day to you*, gu math, *well*, gu làn mhath, *quite well*, is math leam sin, *I am glad of that*, is math fhuair thu, *you did well* Written also *maith*, which see. *Com* and *sup* fearr.

Arab. madi, *good Germ* mod *Box Lex* mad *Ir*

math. *W.* † mat. *Corn* mat. *Arm.* mat *and* ma, *good. Chald Heb* matach *and* matah, *agreeable to the taste.*

MATH, maith, *s. m* (*Ir. id*) Good; profit; benefit; fruit; *rarely*, a hand Airson mo mhaith, *for my good.* Cha bhi cuimhne air a mhath a bha, *past kindness is not remembered.—G. P.* Written also *maith.*

MATH, *v a* (*Ir. id*) Pardon, forgive; abate; ameliorate; manure *Pret. a* mhath; *fut. aff. a* mathaidh. Am math thu dha? *wilt thou forgive him?* Math dhomh, *pardon me.*

MATHACHADH, aidh, *s m.* A manuring; manure; an improving

MATHADH, aidh, *s m* A pardoning, forgiving, abating, ameliorating

MATHAICH, *v. a.* (*from* math) Manure; improve, make good, ameliorate *Pret a.* mhathaich, *manured, fut. aff. a.* mathaichidh, *shall manure, fut. pass.* mathaichear, *shall be manured*

MATHAICHTE, *p. part* of mathaich. Manured, improved, made good

MATHAIM, (*for* mathaidh mi) I will forgive or abate

MATHAIN, *s f* (*Ir. id*) Mercy, disposal; good-nature

MÀTHAIR, màthar, *s. f.* A mother; a cause. *N. pl.* màithrichean, *mothers, d pl* màithrichibh, *to mothers,* màthair aobhair, *a first cause, a primary cause,* màthair-bhaile, *a metropolis* or *mother-city,* màthair-céile, *a mother-in-law,* màthair iongair, *the source of bile, the cause of suppuration.—Shaw* Mathair-baisde, *a godmother,* màthair na lùdaig, *the ring-finger,* màthair uisge, *a reservoir of water, a fountain head —Shaw*

Here it may be proper to observe, that a Highlander, in speaking to his mother, never says *a mhathair,* mother, but *a bhean,* woman On the other hand, when writing to her, or in apostrophising, he uses *a mhathair,* and not *a bhean*

Gr. μητηρ, *mother. Lat.* mater. *Pers.* mader *Syr.* mar. *Turk* mazer. *Malabar,* mada *and* mata. *Germ.* muter *Island.* mooder. *Ir* mathair *Eng* mother. *It* and *Span* madre. *Fr* mère *and* † metre. Plutarch in Iside, page 374, has "Isis quandoque *meyther* nominatur,"—Isis is sometimes called *meyther.*

† MATHAIR, *s f.* Gore, matter.

MÀTHAIREACHD, *s f.* (*Ir id*) The right of a mother.—*Shaw.*

MATHAIREAS, eis, *s m* Motherhood.

MATHAIREIL, *a* (mathair-amhuil.) Motherly; like a mother, tender Mac mathaireil, *a son like his mother*

MATHAIREILEACHD, *s f* Motherliness; female tenderness —*Shaw*

† MÀTHAN, ain, *s m* A twig, a sucker. Now written *maothan,* which see.

MATHANAS, ais, *s m* (*from* math.) Pardon, forgiveness. Written also *maitheanas,* which see.

MATHAR-MHORTADH, aidh, *s m* Matricide, or the murder of one's mother.

MATHAR-MHORTAIR, *s. m* A matricide, one who murders his or her mother

MATHAS, ais, *s m.* Goodness; benefit; bounty; business.

MATHASACH, *a* (*from* mathas) Benevolent, bountiful. Mathasach le céill, *bountiful with discretion —Old Song*

MATHASACHD, *s f.* Benevolence, bountifulness Cha 'n fhaicear do leithid air mhathasachd, *thy like for benevolence shall not be seen*

MATH-GHAMHUINN, -ghamhna, *s. m.* A bear Dà mhathghamhuinn bhainionn, *two she-bears —Stew.* 2 *K.* More properly *magh-ghamhuinn,* which see.

MATHSADH, aidh, *s m.* A doubt.—*Shaw.*

MATH-SHLOGH, oigh, *s.* (*Ir. id.*) A congregation.

MÉ, *a.* See MÉITH

MEABHADH, aidh, *s. m.* (*Ir. id.*) A defeat; a bursting.

MEABHAIR, *s. f.* See MEAMHAIR.

MEABHAL, ail, *s. m.* (*Ir. id.*) Fraud; deceit; shame; reproach.

MEABHALACH, *a.* (*Ir. id.*) Fraudulent; deceitful; shameful. *Com.* and *sup* meabhalaiche.

MEABHLACH, *a* See MEABHALACH.

† MEABHRA, ai, *s.* (*Ir. id.*) A fiction, a lie.—*Shaw.*

MEABHRACH, *a.* (*Ir. id*) Mindful; having a good memory.

† MEABHRACH, *a.* Cheerful, merry, pleasant. *Com.* and *sup.* meabhraiche. Gu meabhrach, *cheerfully.*

† MEABHRAICH, *v. a* Scheme, plan, commit to memory. *Pret. a.* mheabhraich, *schemed, fut. aff.* meabhraichidh.

MEABHRAICHTE, *p. part* of meabhraich Schemed, planned; committed to memory

MEACAN, ain, *s. m.* (*Ir id.*) A parsnip, a turnip; hire; reward; a small rod; a twig; a shoot; a plant. Meacan righ, *a parsnip,* meacan ragum, *horse-radish;* meacan sleibhe, *great bastard, black hellebore,* meacan roibe, *sneezewort;* meacan buidhe, *a carrot,* meacan raidich, *a carrot,* meacan ruadh, *a radish,* meacan uileann, *elecampane —Shaw* Is buan meacan na fòlachd, *lasting is the shoot which springs from malice.—G. P.*

MEACANACH, *a* Like a parsnip or a turnip; abounding in parsnips or turnips, of, or belonging to, parsnips or turnips.

† MEACH, *s f.* (*Ir id*) Hospitality.

MEACHAINN, *s f.* (*Ir id*) Abatement, as of rent—(*Macfar. Voc*), discount; luck-penny

MEACHAIR, *a* Pretty, beautiful, handsome; cheerful, sportive, talkative Meachair mar mhaighdinn, *pretty as a maid —Macint.* Gruaidhean meachair, *pretty cheeks. —Macfar*

MEACHDANN, ain, *s m.* A small rod; a twig.—*Macfar. Voc*

MEACHRÀN, ain, *s. m.* An officious person; an obliging person; an intermeddler *N. pl* meachrain

MEACHRANACH, *a* (*from* meachran.) Officious; interfering, intermeddling; ready to serve or oblige. *Com.* and *sup* meachranaiche, *more* or *most officious.* Gu meachranach, *officiously*

MEACHRANAICH, *v.* Interfere, intermeddle

MEAD, *s m.* (*Ir id.*) Size, bulk, extent, *also,* a measure. More commonly written *meud,* which see.

MEADACH, aich, *s m* (*Ir id*) A knife —*Shaw.*

MEADAG, aig, *s f* A knife. *N. pl* meadagan

MEADACHADH, aidh, *s m* See MEUDACHADH.

MEADAICH, *v a.* See MEUDAICH

MEADAR, air, *s. m, from* mead. (*Ir id*) A small ansated wooden dish, a *bicker,* a churn, a milk-pail.—*Shaw.*

The Irish *meadar* is of one piece, quadrangular, and hollowed with a chisel, the Highland *meadar* is, like the Lowland *luggie* or *bicker,* round, hooped, and ansated.

† MEADAR, air, *s. m* (*Ir. id. Gr.* μετρον. *Eng.* metre) Rhyme, verse

MEADARACH, *a* Like a *bicker,* ansated as a *bicker;* in verse or rhyme.

† MEADARACHD, *s f* Versification; modulation.

MEADARAICH, *v n* Versify, modulate *Pret. a.* mheadaraich, *versified, fut. aff* meadaraichidh, *shall versify; p. part* meadaraichte, *versified, in verse.*

MEAD-BHRONN See MEUD-BHRONN.

† MEADH, *s. m.* (*Ir. id Gr* μεθυ) Metheglin, mead.

MEADH, meidh, *s. f.* (*Ir. id.*) A balance, a scale. Air meidh, *in a balance —Stew. Ps.* See MEIDH.

† MEADHACH, ich, *s m* (*Ir. id.*) A stallion.

Meadhach, *a.* (*Ir. id.*) Fuddled with mead; like mead; abounding in mead; of, or belonging to, mead.

Meadhachan, ain, *s. m.* Force.

Meadhail, *s. f.* (*Ir. id.*) A carousal; a belly, a paunch.

Meadhaileach, *a.* Carousing; prone to carouse.

† **Meadhair**, *s. f.* (*Ir. id.*) Discourse; talk; mirth; a forewarning of future events.—*Shaw.*

Meadharach, *a.* (*Ir. id.*) Cheerful, lively, glad, festive. Brataichean meadharach, *cheerful banners.*—*Macdon.* Written also *meagharach.*

Meadharachd, *s. f.* Cheerfulness, liveliness, gladness; festiveness.

Meadh-bhlàth, *a.* Lukewarm. Do bhrigh gu bheil thu meadh-bhlàth, *because thou art lukewarm.*—*Stew. Pro.*

Meadh-bhlàthachadh, aidh, *s. m.* A warming, a making lukewarm.

Meadh-bhlàthaich, *v. a.* Make lukewarm.

Meadhon, oin, *s. m.* Middle, midst; a mean; centre; waist. Am meadhon nan tom, *in the midst of the hills.*—*Oss. Lod.* Mu d' mheadhon, *about thy middle* or *waist.*—*Macfar.* Meadhon là, *mid-day;* meadhon oidhche, *midnight. N. pl.* meadhona; *Arm.* moyennou.
Ir. id. Fr. moyen. *Corn.* mayn. *Eng.* mean.

Meadhonach, *a.* (*Ir. id.*) Intermediate, middlemost, middling; indifferent, so and so, in a middle state; instrumental.

Meadhonachd, *s. f.* (*Ir. id.*) Intermediateness; mediocrity; instrumentality.

Meadhona, **Meadhonan**, *n. pl.* of meadhon. Means.

Meadhon-là, *s. m.* Mid-day; noon. Air mheadhon-là, *at noon.*—*Stew. Gen.* Roimh mheadhon-là, *forenoon;* an deigh mheadhon-là, *in the afternoon.*

Meadhon-oidhche, *s.* Midnight. Mu mheadhon oidhche, *about midnight; at midnight.*—*Stew. Ex.*

Meadhrach, **Meadhrachdail**, *a.* Joyful, glad, festive.—*Turn.* Hospitable. *Com.* and *sup.* meadhraiche.

Meadhrachas, **Meadhrachdas**, ais, *s. m.* Gladness, joyfulness, festiveness.

Meadhradh, aidh, *s. m.* Gladness, joyfulness, ecstasy; ravishment. C' arson a bhios tu air do mheadhradh? *why wilt thou be ravished?*—*Stew. Pro. ref.*

† **Meag**, *s. m.* (*Ir. id.*) The earth.

Meag, meig *and* mig, *s. m.* (*Ir.* meadhg.) Whey. Deoch mhèig, *a drink of whey.*

Meagail, *a.* (meag-amhuil.) Serous; like whey; full of whey.

Meaghal, ail, *s. m.* The bark of a dog; an alarm; mewing, as of a cat.

Meaghailich, *s. f.* A barking; continued barking; mewing, as a cat. Thoisich e air meaghailaich, *he began to bark.*

Meaghar, air, *s. m.* Sport; mirth; cheerfulness; prettiness; festivity; pomp; speech; talk; memory. Meaghar chon, *the sport of dogs.*—*Fingalian Poem.*

Meagh-bhlàth, *a.* See **Meadh-bhlàth**.

Meaghlach, *a.* Glad, joyful; alarming; barking.

Meaghlachd, *s. f.* Gladness, joyfulness; a giving an alarm; frequent barking.

Meaghrach, *a.* (*from* meaghar.) Joyful; cheerful; lively; festive. Tigh meaghrach, *a festive mansion.*—*Old Song.* Gu meaghrach, *joyfully.*

Meaghradh, aidh, *s. m.* Gladness, joyfulness; sport; ecstacy. Ri meaghradh, *merrymaking.*

Meal, *v. a.* Enjoy; suffer, brook. *Pret. a.* mheal; *fut. aff. a.* mealaidh, *shall enjoy.* Gum meal 's gun caith thu e! *may you enjoy and live to wear it!* A mealtuinn, *enjoying.*

Meala, *gen. sing.* of mil; which see.

Meala, ai, *s. m.* (*Ir. id.*) Reproach; grief.—*Shaw.*

Mealach, *a.* Sweet, honeyed, like honey, abounding in honey, of honey; disposed to enjoy, brook, or bear. Snothach mealach, *the sweet sap of trees.*—*Macfar.* Do phòg mhear mhealach, *thy wanton, honeyed kiss.*—*Old Song.* Gu mealach, cìreach, *abounding in honey and wax.*

Mealadh, aidh, *s. m.* The act of enjoying; enjoyment.

Mealadh, (a), *pr. part.* of meal. Enjoying.

Mealag, aig, *s. f.* A smelt; the milt of a fish. *N. pl.* mealagan. In some parts *mealag* is pronounced *bealag.*

Mealagach, *a.* (*from* mealag.) Abounding in smelt; having milt, as fish; like milt.

Mealannan, *s. pl.* Sweetmeats.

Mealasg, aisg, *s. f.* (*Ir. id.*) Fawning; cajoling; clamorous joy; great rejoicing.

Mealasgach, *a.* (*Ir. id.*) Fawning; cajoling; clamorously joyful. *Com.* and *sup.* mealasgaiche.

Mealbh, **Mealbhag**, aig, *s. m.* and *f.* (*Ir. id.*) A satchel, a knapsack, a budget.

Meal-bhuc, *s. f.* A melon. *N. pl.* meal-bhucan, *melons.*—*Stew. Num.*

Meal-bhucach, *a.* Abounding in melons; like a melon; of, or belonging to, a melon.

Meal-bhucag, aig, *s. f.* A melon; a little melon. *N. pl.* meal-bhucagan, *melons.*

Meall, mill, *s. m.* (*Lat.* moles. *Ir.* meall. *W.* moel *and* mwl.) A lump; a knob; a boss; a heap; a hill; a hudge; any eminence; a bunch, a cluster. Meall eithe san fhuachd, *a lump of ice in the cold.*—*Ull. N. pl.* mill; *d. pl.* meallaibh. Ceathach mu na meallaibh, *mist around the hills.*—*Macint.* Meall fhighean, *a bunch of grapes.*—*Stew.* 1 *Sam.*

Meall, *v. a.* Allure, deceive, beguile; defraud or cheat; disappoint. *Pret. a.* mheall, *allured; fut. aff. a.* meallaidh. C'arson a mheall thu mi? *why hast thou beguiled me?*—*Stew. Gen.* Meallaidh gach neul a dhall-shùil, *every cloud deceive his dim eye.*—*Ull.*

Meallach, *a.* (*from* meall.) Knotty, knobby, bossy; full of lumps, hilly; alluring. *Asp. form,* mheallach, *the bossy shield.*—*Oss. Com.* Sùil mheallach, *an alluring eye.*—*Macfar. Com.* and *sup.* meallaiche.

Mealladh, aidh, *s. m.* (*Ir. id.*) A deceiving; a beguiling or defrauding; an alluring; deception; allurement; disappointment; goods; riches. Mealladh dòchais, *disappointment;* mealladh sùl, *ocular deception.*

Meallaidh, *fut. aff. a.* of meall; which see.

Meallain, *gen. sing.* and *n. pl.* of meallan.

Meallan, ain, *s. m.* (*dim.* of meall.) A little lump; a little knot or knob; a knoll; hail, hailstone. Clachan meallain, *hailstones;* bhuail saighdean ar sgiath mar mheallain, *arrows struck our shields like hail.*—*Oss. Duthona.* Meallan tachais, *a chilblain.*

Meallanach, *a.* Knotty, knobby, lumpy; having hillocks or knolls; like hail. Sian mheallanach, *a shower of hail, a hail-storm.*—*Macdon.*

Meallan tachais, *s. m.* A chilblain.

Meallar, *fut. pass.* of meall. Shall be deceived or allured.

Meall-shùil, -shùl, *s. f.* A leering eye; a winning or alluring look.

Meall-shùileach, *a.* Leering; having an alluring eye.

Meallta, *a.* and *p. part.* of meall. (*Ir.* meallta.) Deceived, cheated; mistaken, false. Tha thu meallta, *you are mistaken; you lie;* is tu is meallta an cùirt nan dia, *thou art* *the most false in the court of the gods.—Mac Lach.* Gu meallta, *falsely.*

MEALLTACH, *a., from* meall. (*Ir. id.*) Deceitful; alluring; disposed to cheat; false. Meidhean mealltach, *false weights; a false balance.—Stew. Pro.* Gu mealltach, *deceitfully.—Stew. Lev. Com.* and *sup.* mealltaiche.

MEALLTACHD, *s. f.* (*Ir. id.*) Deceitfulness; imposition, swindling.

MEALLTAIR, *s. m.* (*Ir.* mealltoir.) A deceiver, a cheat, a sharper, a swindler. *N. pl.* mealltairean, *cheats.*

MEALLTAIREACHD, *s. f.* (*Ir.* mealltoireachd.) Fraudulence, deceitfulness, swindling or imposition. Mealltaireachd mna, *the deceitfulness of woman.—Stew. Pro.* Luchd mealltaireachd, *deceivers, cheats, swindlers.*

MEALLTUINN, *s.* (*from* meal.) Enjoying, enjoyment.

MEALTUINN, (a), *pr. part.* of meal. Enjoying.

† MEAM, *s. m.* (*Ir. id.*) A kiss.

† MEAM, *v. a.* (*Ir. id.*) Kiss.—*Shaw.*

MEAMANACH. See MEAMNACH.

MEAMHAIR, *s. f.* (*Lat.* memoria. *Fr.* mémoire. *Ir.* meamhair.) Memory; remembrance; a memorandum.

MEAMHAIR, *v. a.* Remember, consider.—*Shaw. Also,* commit to memory; take a memorandum. *Pret. a.* mheamhair; *fut. aff. a.* meamhairidh.

MEAMHRACH, *a.* (*from* meamhair.) Mindful; having a good memory.

MEAMHRACH, aich, *s. m.* A record, a register.

MEAMHRAICH, *v. a.* Call to memory; scheme, plan, plot; mention; put in mind.—*Shaw. Pret. a.* mheamhraich; *fut. aff. a.* meamhraichidh.

MEAMHRAICHTE, *p. part.* Remembered; mentioned; considered of.

MEAMHRAN, ain, *s. m.* A membrane; a register; a memorandum.

MEAMNA, MEAMNADH, aidh, *s. m.* (*Ir. id.*) Imagination, fancy; pride; courage; vigour; animal spirits; high spirit; magnanimity. Lion meamnadh sinn uile, *proud joy filled all.—Fingalian Poem.* Mac-meamnaidh, *the imagination.*

MEAMNACH, *a.* Magnanimous, proud, high-spirited; strong; violent. Gu treun meamnach, *strong and proud.—Oss. Dargo.* Sitrich eacha meamnach, *the neighing of high-spirited horses.—Stew. Jer.* A beucaich gu meamnach, *roaring violently.—Old Poem. Com.* and *sup.* meamnaiche.

MEAMNADH, aidh, *s. m.* See MEAMNA.

MEAMRA, ai, *s. m.* (*Ir. id.*) A shrine, a tomb.

MEANACH, aich, *s. m.* See MIONACH.

MEANADH, idh, *s. f.* An awl. More commonly written and pronounced *minidh.*

MEÀNADH, aidh, *s. m.* A foreboding, a foretelling; fate; gaping, yawning.—*Shaw.*

MEANAIGEAN, *s. pl.* Gloves.

MEANAN, ain, *s. m.* (*Ir.* meànadh.) A yawn, a gape.

† MEANAN, *a.* (*Ir. id.*) Plain, clear.

MEANAN, ain, *s. m.* (*Ir. id.*) Sawdust; a yawn. Meanan cöinnich, *a species of scented wild herb.*

MEANANACH, *a.* (*from* meanan.) Full of sawdust; of sawdust; like sawdust; yawning, gaping.

MEANANAICH, *s. f.* A yawning, a gaping; a yawn, a gape; continued gaping. Thòisich e air meananaich, *he began to yawn;* is ann ort tha 'mheannaich! *how you do yawn!*

MEANBH, *a.* (*Ir. id. Gr. Att.* μινυος, *for* μικρος, *little. Arm.* menu.) Little, small; diminutive; pigmy; pulverised. Lusan meanbh, *little herbs.—Macfar.* A chogadh ris an iarmad mheanbh, *to fight with the pigmy race.—Mac Lach.*

MEANBH-BHITH, *s.* An animalcule.

MEANBH-CHRODH, -chruidh, *s.* Small cattle, as sheep and goats.

MEANBH-CHUILEAG, eig, *s. f.* A midge, a gnat. Meanbh-chuileag shamhraidh, *the summer gnat.—Macfar. N. pl.* meanbh-chuileagan, *gnats.*

MEANBH-CHUILEAGACH, *a.* Abounding in gnats.

MEANBH-CHÙIS, *s. f.* (*Ir. id.*) Parsimony; a trifling case.

MEANBH-CHUISEACH, *a.* (*Ir. id.*) Parsimonious; little-minded; curious.

MEANBHLACH, aich, *s. m., collective.* Dross; fragments, refuse.

MEANBH-PHEASAIR, -pheasrach, *s. f.* Millet; millet seed. —*Stew. Ezek.*

MEANBH-RIGH, *s. m.* A petty king. *N. pl.* meanbh-righrean.

MEANBH-SPREIDH, *s. f., collective.* Small cattle, as sheep and goats. Do 'n mheanbh-spreidh, *of the small cattle.— Stew. Lev. ref.*

MEANDANACH, aich, *s. m.* A mendicant.

MEANG, *s.* (*Ir. id.*) A blemish or spot; deformity; guile; craft; a branch. Gun mheang gun mheirg, *without blemish or rust.—Macdon.* Mo charaid gun mheang, *my guileless friend.—Old Song.*

MEANGACH, aich, *s.* (*Ir. id.*) Common cinque-foil; the *potentilla reptans* of botanists.

MEANGACH, *a.* (*from* meang.) Blemished; crafty, deceitful, cunning. *Com.* and *sup.* meangaiche, *more* or *most deceitful.* Gu meangach, *craftily.*

MEANGAIL, *a.* (meang-amhuil.) Blemished; deceitful; crafty; faulty. Gu meangail, *deceitfully.*

MEANGALACHD, *s. f., from* meang. (*Ir. id.*) Deceitfulness; blemishes; faultiness; sprouting, budding.

MEANGAN, ain, *s. m.* (*dim.* of meang.) A branch or bough; a twig. *N. pl.* meangain.

MEANGANACH, *a.* (*from* meangan.) Branchy; branching; full of branches; of, or belonging to, a branch. *Com.* and *sup.* menganaiche.

MEANGLAN, ain, *s. m.* A branch or bough; a twig. *N. pl.* meanglanan *and* meanglain, *branches.* Tri meanglain, *three branches.*

MEANGLANACH, *a.* Branchy, branching; full of branches; like a branch. *Com.* and *sup.* meanglanaiche.

MEANMA, MEANMADH, aidh, *s. m.* (*Ir. id.*) Courage; vigour; high spirit; fancy; magnanimity.

MEANMACH, *a.* (*Ir. id.*) Cheerful, high-spirited, courageous; fanciful; magnanimous. Gu meanmach, *courageously.*

MEANMACHADH, aidh, *s. m.* A cheering or inspiriting; an exhortation.

MEANMAICH, *v. a.* (*Ir.* meanmaigh.) Cheer, inspirit, exhort, or regale.—*Shaw.*

MEANMARACH, *a.* Spirited.

† MEANMARADH, aidh, *s. m.* (*Ir. id.*) Thought.—*Shaw.*

† MEANMLAIGE, *s. f.* (*Ir. id.*) Dullness; laziness; weakness.

MEANMUIN, *s. f.* (*Ir. id.*) Gladness, joy.

† MEANN, *a.* (*Ir. id.*) Clear; manifest; famous; dumb.

MEANN, minn, *s.* (*W.* myn. *Arm.* mynn. *Corn.* mynan, *a kid.*) A kid, a goat; *rarely, a* rib. Meann do 'n treud, *a kid from the flock.—Stew. Gen. Asp. form,* mheann. Dà dheagh mheann, *two good kids.—Stew. Gen.* Ceann a mhinn, *the head of the goat.—Stew. Lev. N. pl.* minn.

MEANNACH, *a.* (*from* meann.) Abounding in kids or goats; like a kid; of, or belonging to, a kid. A bhealtuinn mheannach, *kid-producing May.—Macfar.*

MEANNAD, aid, *s. m.* A place or room.

Meannan, ain, *s. m. dim.* of meann. (*Ir. id.*) A young kid, a little kid, a little goat; *rarely*, a rib. *N. pl.* meannain, *kids.* Ionaltair do mheannain, *feed thy kids.—Stew. Song Sol.* Meannan-athair, *a snipe.—Shaw.*

Meannanach, *a.* Abounding in young or little kids; like a young kid; frisky.

Meannanachd, *s. f.* Friskiness.

Meannd, Meannt, *s. m.* (*Sax.* minte. *Fr.* menthe. *Eng.* mint.) The plant called mint. Meannt fiadhaich, *wild mint.*

Meanntas, ais, *s. m.* Spearmint.

Meannrachd, *s. f.* (*Ir. id.*) Happiness, bliss, good luck.

Meantail, *s. f.* Deceit.—*Shaw.* Luchd meantail, *deceivers.*

Meantalach, *a.* (*Ir. id.*) Deceitful.

Meantalachd, *s. f.* (*Ir. id.*) Perfidy

Meantan, ain, *s. m.* (*Ir. id.*) A snipe.

Mear, *a.* (*Ir. id. Eng.* merry. *Sax.* merig.) Wanton; merry; cheerful; sudden or quick in motion. Eisdeadh a bhantrach mhear, *let the wanton widow listen.—Old Song.* Bha sibh mear, *ye were merry.—Stew. Jam.*

Meàr, *s.* A finger. More frequently written *meur;* which see.

Mearachd, *s. f.* (*Ir. id.*) Mistake; error, oversight; merriness. Mearachd agus laigsinn, *error and weakness.—Macfar.* Theagamh gur mearachd a bh'ann, *perhaps it was an oversight.—Stew. Gen.* Tha thu 'm mearachd, *you are mistaken;* mearachd céill, *madness; an error of judgment.*

Mearachdach, *a.* (*Ir. id.*) Erroneous, false, incorrect, misleading; mistaken. Barail mhearachdach, *an erroneous opinion;* a deanamh na meidhe mearachdach, *making the balances false.—Stew. Amos. Com.* and *sup.* mearachdaiche. Gu mearachdach, *erroneously.*

Mearachdaich, *v. a.* Mistake; miss; put wrong. *Pret. a.* mhearachdaich; *missed; fut. aff.* mearachdaichidh, *shall miss.*

Mearachdas, ais, *s. m.* (*Ir. id.*) Wantonness; merriness; mirth; liability to mistake.

Mearachdasach, *a.* (*Ir. id.*) Wanton; merry.—*Macint. Com.* and *sup.* mearachdasaiche.

† **Mearadh**, aidh, *s. m.* (*Ir. id.*) Affliction. *Heb.* mara, *to afflict.*

Mèaragan, ain, *s. m.* See **Meuragan**.

Mearagan, ain, *s. m.* (*from* mear.) A puppet; a puppet moving on springs. *N. pl.* mearagain.

Mearaich, *v. a.* and *n.* Err, mistake; go wrong; go astray. *Pret. a.* mhearaich; *fut. aff. a.* mearaichidh.

Mearaiche, *s. m.* A merry-andrew; a mountebank; a fool; a droll; a merry fellow.

Mearaichinn, *s. f.* Giddiness, insanity, delirium.

Mear-aithne, *s. f.* (*Ir. id.*) A slight or doubtful knowledge of a person.—*Shaw.*

Mearal, ail, *s. m.* Disappointment; error.

Mearalaich, *v. a.* Disappoint, put wrong. *Pret.* mhearalaich.

Mearalachadh, aidh, *s. m.* A disappointing; a disappointment; erring.

Mearalachd, *s. f.* (*Ir. id.*) Disappointment; error.

† **Mearbha**, ai, *s. m.* (*Ir. id.*) A lie; a fiction.

Mearbhal, ail, *s. m.* (*Ir. id.*) A mistake; random.—*Shaw.*

† **Mearc**, mearca, *s. f.* (*Ir. id. Lat.* merx.) Merchandise, wares, goods. Hence, perhaps, Mercurius (*i. e.* mearcurr), *Mercury, the god of merchandise.*

Mear-cheannach, *a.* Giddy, light-headed, insane.

Mear-chinn, *s. m.* Giddiness, insanity, delirium.

Mear-chunntadh, aidh, *s. m.* A miscalculation; a miscalculating, a misreckoning.

Mear-chunntas, ais, *s. m.* A miscalculation, a misreckoning.

Mear-dhàn, *a.* (*Ir. id.*) Fool-hardy.

Mear-dhànachd, *s. f.* (*Ir.* mear-dhanacht.) Fool-hardiness.

Mear-dhànadas, ais, *s. m.* Fool-hardiness; wanton rashness.

Mearganta, *a.* (*Ir. id.*) Sportive; wanton; brisk; obstinate. Mar reithe mearganta, *like wanton rams.—Sm.*

Meargantachd, *s. f.* (*Ir. id.*) Wantonness; sportiveness; obstinateness.

Meargantas, ais, *s. m.* (*Ir. id.*) Wantonness; sportiveness; briskness; obstinacy.

Mearghradh, aidh, *s. m.* (*Ir. id.*) Fondness; wanton fondness.

Mear-ghradhach, *a.* (*Ir. id.*) Fond; wanton. Gu mearghradhach, *wantonly.*

Mearle, *s. f.* Theft. More commonly written *meirle.*

Mearleach, ich, *s. m.* A thief. See **Meirleach**.

Mearsadh, aidh, *s. m.* Marching.

Mearsail, *a.* Stately in gait.

Mearsal, ail, *s. m.* Marching.

Mearsuinn, *s. f.* Strength; strong constitution; durableness. Perhaps *marsuinn.*

Mearsuinneach, *a.* (*Ir. id.*) Hardy; strong; durable; perpetual. See also **Marsuinneach**.

† **Meart**, *s. m.* (*Ir. id.*) A garment.

† **Meas**, *s. m.* A measure; a rod to measure graves.—*Shaw.* Hence perhaps *measair.*

Meas, *s. m.* Fruit; an acorn. Meas craoibh, *the fruit of a tree.—Stew. Gen*

W. mesen, *fruit. Arm.* mesan. *Ir.* meas.

Meas, *s. m.* (*Ir. id.*) Respect; opinion; conceit; reputation; fame; value; estimate; estimation. Cha robh meas aig air Cain, *he had no respect to Cain.—Stew. Gen.* Mu chall a mheas, *about the loss of his fame.—Oss. Fing.* A réir do mheas, *according to thy estimation.—Stew. Lev.* Tha meas aig dheth féin, *he has a conceit of himself;* cha tug mi meas freagairt air, *I did not give him the honour of a reply;* a réir do mheas-san, *according to thy opinion, fame,* or *estimate.*

† **Meas**, *s. m.* (*Ir. id.*) A weapon; a point or edge; a salmon; a pair of shears; wind; a fosterchild.—*Shaw.*

Meas, *v.* (*Ir. id.*) Consider; think; reckon; estimate; value; esteem; deem; presume; weigh; calculate; suppose; lay a tax or rate on. *Pret. a.* mheas; *fut. aff. a.* measaidh. Na measaibh, *think not.—Stew. Matt.* Measaidh an sagairt e, *the priest shall value it.—Stew. Lev.*

Measa, *com.* and *sup.* of olc. Worse, worst. Written also *miosa;* which see,

† **Measach**, *a.* (*Ir. id.*) Fishy.

Measadair, *s. m.* (*from* meas.) A valuer, an appraiser. *N. pl.* measadairean.

Measadaireachd, *s. f.* The business of appraising; the employment of an appraiser.

Measag, aig, *s. m.* (*Ir.* measg.) An acorn.

Measaidh, *fut. aff. a.* of meas; which see.

Measail, *a.* (meas-amhuil.) Respectable, reputable; respected, esteemed. Duine measail, *a respectable man.* Gu measail, *reputably.*

Measain, *gen. sing.* and *n. pl.* of measan.

Measair, measrach, *s. f.*, *from* † meas. (*W.* mesir. *Ir.* measaire. *Eng.* measure.) A tub; a just weight or measure. *N. pl.* measairean.

Measan, ain, *s. m* (*Ir.* and *Scotch*, *id.*) A lapdog, a little dog, a forward, impudent person.—*Macd.* Trod a mheasain 's a chùl ri làr, *the lapdog's bark with his back on the ground* —*G. P.*

Measar, *fut. pass.* of meas, which see

Measar, air, *s m* See Miosar

Measara. See Measarra.

Measarachd, *s. f.* See Measarrachd.

Measarra, **Measarrach**, *a.* Abstemious; temperate; moderate; sober; modest, continent. Bitheamaid measarra, *let us be sober.*—*Stew. Thess*

Measarrachd, *s f* (*Ir.* measardhachd) Abstemiousness; temperateness, soberness; continence; moderation, moderateness. Smuaineachadh am measarrachd, *thinking soberly.*—*Stew. Rom.*

Measarradh, *a* Abstemious, temperate; moderate; sober; continent Iadsan a chleachd bhi measarradh, *they who used to be abstemious.*—*Old Song.*

Measchaor, chaoir, *s m* A plummet; a sounding line —*Shaw*

Meas-chraobh, chraoibh, *s f* A fruit-tree. *N pl* meas-chraobhan.

Meas-chruinneachadh, aidh, *s. m* A gathering of fruit; a gathering of acorns.

Meas-chruinnich, *v* Gather fruit; gather acorns; gather corn.

Meas-chu, -choin, *s m.* A lapdog. *N. pl* meas-choin

Meas-chuilean, ein, *s m* A little lapdog, a young lapdog

Measg, *v. a.* Mix, mingle, stir about, move *Pret. a* mheasg, *moved*, *fut aff a* measgaidh, *shall mix.*
Gr μίγνω *Lat* misceo *It* mischio. *Arm W.* misgu. *Ir.* measg.

Measg, *prep for* am measg Among, amongst, in the midst Measg tannais a shluaigh, *among the spectres of his people* *Oss. Com.* Am measg na strì, *in the midst of battle* —*Oss Fing.* 'Nar measg-ne, *among us* —*Stew Job.* 'N ur measg-sa, *among you*, nam measg, *among them.*
W mysk *Arm* meask *Corn* mesk · *Ir* measg

Measgadh, aidh, *s m* The act of mixing; a stirring about, a mixture
Heb. masach, *a mixture* *Pun* meseg. *Pol* mieszan *Teut.* misken *Germ* mischen *Ir.* measgadh.

Measag, aig, *s f* (*Ir id*) An acorn

Measgadh, (a), *pr part* of measg Mixing; mingling, stirring about. A measgadh an geal-chobhar, *mixing the white foam.*—*Oss Tem*

Measgan, ain, *s m.* (*Ir id*) Butterwort; a small dish of butter

Meas-ghort, -ghoirt, *s m.* (*Ir. id*) A fruit-garden; an orchard —*Shaw*

Measgnachadh, aidh, *s m* A mixing, a stirring about; a mixture

Measgnaich, *v a* (*from* measg) Mix, mingle, stir about; copulate *Pret. a.* mheasgnaich, *mixed*, *fut. aff a.* measgnaichidh, *shall mix.* Mheasgnaich iadsan fìon, *they mixed wine* —*Mac Lach.*

Measgnaichte, *p part* of measgnaich Mixed

Measgta, **Measgte**, *p. part* of measg (*Lat.* mixtus) Mixed

Measra, **Measradh.** See Measarra *and* Measarradh.

Measraich, *v. a.* and *n.* Temperate, sober; become temperate or sober *Pret* mheasraich, *fut aff a* measraichidh, *p part.* measraichte.

Meat, **Meata**, *a* (*Ir. id.*) Cowardly, timid; feeble, faint-hearted. Sìol meata, *a timid race* —*Oss.*

Meatachadh, aidh, *s. m.* (*from* meat.) *Ir.* meatughadh: A dispiriting; an enfeebling; a growing timid, feeble, or faint-hearted.

Meatachd, *s. f.*, *from* meat. (*Ir. id.*) Timidity, cowardliness, faintheartedness; dismay; hindrance. An do thréig sinn le meatachd? *did we abandon with dismay?*—*Old Poem.*

Meatag, aig, *s. f.* (*Ir.* miotag.) A woollen glove; a mitten. *N. pl.* meatagan.

Meatagach, *a.* Provided with gloves; wearing gloves.

Meataghaich, *v a.* Provide with gloves. *Pret. a.* mheatagaich.

Meatagaichte, *p part.* Gloved Lamhan meatagaichte, *hands with gloves on.*

Meataich, *v. a.* and *n.* (*from* meat) Make effeminate; terrify; make spiritless, grow effeminate, timid, or terrified. *Pret* mheataich; *fut. aff.* meataichidh. Na meataicheadh gart a chuàin sibh, *let not the roaring of the sea terrify you.* —*Old Song.*

Meath, meatha, *s m* Decay, consumption; effeminacy. Meath-challtuinn, *southern-wood.*

Meath, *a.* (*Lat.* mitis. *Ir.* meath.) Meek, soft-hearted; despondent; effeminate; decaying

Meath, *v. a* and *n.* (*Ir id*) Soften with pity; affect; decay, wither, grow soft; grow effeminate. *Pret. a.* mheath, *softened; fut. aff. a.* meathaidh, *shall soften* Mheath i gach cridhe, *she softened every heart.*—*Ull.* Mheath foghara na machrach, *the harvest of the field has decayed.*—*Stew Joel.*

Meathach, *a* (*Ir. id*) Mild, tender, soft, effeminate; affecting; causing effeminacy; perishable, decaying; fat. *Com.* and *sup.* meathaiche. Written also *méidheach*; which see.

Meathach, aich, *s m.* (*from* meath) A degenerate person, a despondent person, a tender or excoriated part of the skin.

Meathachadh, aidh, *s. m.* A withering, a fading; a becoming effeminate, a rendering effeminate

Meathachan, ain, *s m* (*Ir. id.*) A glutton; an effeminate fellow

Meathadh, aidh, *s m* A withering or decaying; a shrinking; a degenerating; effeminacy; a desponding; despondency

Meathaich, *v a* and *n.*, *from* meath. (*Ir. id*) Soften, as with pity, affect; soften or make effeminate; grow mild; grow tender; grow effeminate. *Pret. a.* mheathaich; *fut aff. a* meathaichidh.

Meathanas, ais, *s m* (*Ir. id.*) Consumption.

Meathas, ais, *s. m*, *from* meath (*Ir id.*) Fat, fatness. —*Shaw.* *Also*, effeminacy

Meath-challtuinn, *s m* (*Ir id*) Southern-wood.—*Macd*

Meath-chridhe, *s. f* A faint heart; *also*, faintness of heart

Meath-chridheach, *a* Faint-hearted; effeminate. Tha sìth 'g am fhàgail meath-chridheach, *peace renders me effeminate* —*Macfar*

Meath-chridheachd, *s f.* Faint-heartedness, timidity.

Meath-chrith, *s f* A trembling from cowardice or from terror Sgaoilibh meath-chrith chath, *spread the dismaying tremour of battle.*—*Old Poem.*

Meath-ghaire, *s f* (*Ir id*) A smile.

Meath-ionnsuidh, *s. f.* A faint attack; a feeble onset; a spiritless invasion.

Meath-oidhirp, *s.* A faint endeavour. Thug e meath-oidhirp air, *he feebly attempted it.*

Meath-oidhirpeach, *a* Making a faint attempt; unenterprising

Meath-thinneas, eis, *s. m.* (*Ir. id.*) A consumption; a consuming malady; a debilitating sickness.

Meath-thogar, air, *s. m.* A faint inclination; indifference.

Meath-thogarach, *a.* Having a faint inclination; lukewarm in a cause; indifferent.

Meath-thogradh, aidh, *s. m.* A faint desire or inclination; lukewarmness; indifference.

Meathras, **Meatbas**, ais, *s. m.* Fat; grease.

† **Meide**, *s. f.* (*Ir. id.*) The neck.

† **Meideach**, eich, *s. m.* (*Ir. id.*) A stallion.—*Shaw.* *N. pl* meideich. Properly *meidh-each.*

Meideal, -eil, *s. m.* A medal.

† **Meidealach**, aich, *s. m.* (*Ir. id.*) A large knife; the leather hinge of a flail.

Méidh. See **Meath.**

Meidh, meidhe, *s. f.* A balance, a scale, a weight or measure. *N. pl.* meidhean. Meidhean ceart, *just balances.* —*Stew. Lev.* *D. pl.* meidhibh. Anns na meidhibh, *in the balances.*—*Stew. Job.* Written also *meigh.*

Meidhe, *s. f.* (*Ir. id*) A stump, stock, or trunk.—*Shaw.*

Meidheach, *a.* (*from* meidh) Like a scale or balance, of, or belonging to, a scale or balance; having scales, weights, or measures.

Méidheach, *a.* (*from* méidh.) Mild, tender-hearted, affectionate; effeminate; decaying, withering. A laoich mhéidhich! *thou mild hero!—Death of Carril*

Meidh-each, -eich, *s. m.* A stallion. *N. pl.* meidh-eich. —*Macd*

Meidheadair, *s m.* (*from* meidh) A balancer. *N. pl.* meidheadairean.

Meidhich, *v. a.* (*from* meidh.) Balance, weigh, or measure. *Pret. a.* mheidhich, *balanced; fut. aff. a.* meidhichidh

Meidhin, *s. f.* The middle, the midst.—*Shaw.*

Meidhinnean, *s.* Joints; hip joints. As na meidhinnean, *out of the hip-joint.*

Meidil, *s. f.* (*Ir. id*) A medlar.—*Macd.* *N. pl* meidilean. Crann meidil, *a medlar-tree*

Meidileach, *a.* Abounding in medlars; of, or belonging to, a medlar

Meigeadaich, *s f.* Bleating, especially that of a goat or kid. Le meigeadaich fhann, *with faint bleating*—*Macfar.*

Meigeadan, ain, *s. m* A goat, a kid. *N. pl.* meigeadain.

Meigeall, *v. n* Bleat, as a goat or kid.

Meigeallaich, *s. f.* A bleating, as of a goat or kid.

Meigh, meighe, *s. f.* (*Ir. id.*) A balance or scale: a weight or measure. A deanamh na meighe mearachdach, *making the scales false.*—*Stew. Amos.* Written also *meidh.*

Meigheach, *a.* See **Meidheach.**

Meighich, *v. a.* See **Meidhich.**

Méighlich, *s. f.* Bleating, as of a sheep. See **Méilich.**

Méighlich, *v a.* Bleat. *Pret.* mhéighlich; *fut aff.* méighlichidh, *shall bleat.*

Méil, *v n* Bleat, as a sheep. *Pret a.* mhéil; *fut. aff a.* méilidh.

Méil, *v. a.* Grind, as corn; pound; pulverise. *Pret. a.* mhéil, *ground.* Mhéil e gu smùr, *he ground it to powder.* —*Stew. Exod.* Méileadh mo bhean, *let my wife grind* —*Stew. Job.*

Gr. μυλλειν, *to grind.* *Lat.* molere. *Island.* and *Swed.* mala. *Dan.* male. *Arm* mala. *Goth.* malan. *Germ.* malen *and* mulen. *Heb.* mull *and* mil, *dust*,—all from the ancient word *mull* and *mill*, dust, still used among our brother Celts of Bretagne, in their dialect called the *Armoric.*

Méildear, *s. m.* See **Meiltear.**

Meildir, *s. f.* See **Meiltir.**

Méile, *s f.* (*Ir. id* *Lat.* mala, *a jawbone*) A hand-mill; a pestle; a stick for turning a quern; a jawbone. See **Muileann bràdh.**

Méileach, *a.* Of, or belonging to, a hand-mill, like a hand-mill; apt to faint with cold.

Méileachadh, aidh, *s. m.* (*Ir. id.*) A grinding with a hand-mill; a fainting with cold; reproaching.

Meileachd, *s. f.* (*Ir. id*) Reproach, abuse.

Méileadair, *s m* (*Span.* moledor.) A grinder; a miller; a hand-mill-grinder *N pl* méileadairean

Méileadaireachd, *s. f.* A grinding, the business of a grinder; hand-mill grinding.

Méileadh, eidh, *s. m.* A bleating, as of a sheep; *also*, a grinding or milling

† **Meilg**, *s. m* (*Ir. id*) Death; a pod; *also*, milk—*Shaw.*

Meilgeag, eig, *s f.* More properly *meiligeag*, which see

Méilich, *v. n.* Bleat, as a sheep, benumb. *Pret.* mhéilich, *bleated*, *fut. aff. a.* méilichidh, *shall bleat*

Méilich, *s. f* (*Ir.* meidhleach *and* meiligh.) Bleating, as of sheep. Méilich mhaoth, *soft bleating*—*Macfar.* Méilich nan caorach, *the bleating of sheep.*—*Stew Jud*

Méiligeag, eig, *s. f* A pea-pod; the pod of any leguminous vegetable. *N pl.* meiligeagan Meiligeag pheasrach, *the pod of a pea.*

Meiligeagach, *a.* Having pods; like a pod; abounding in pods A pheasair mheiligeach, *the podded pease.*—*Old Song.*

Meilis, *a.* See **Milis.**

Méill, *s f.* (*Ir. id.*) A clapper; a cheek; a blubber-lip; a swelled pendulous lip; an idiot.

Méilleach, *a.* Blubber-lipped; large-cheeked. *Com.* and *sup.* méilliche.

Méilleadh, idh, *s. m* (*Ir id.*) Incitement.

Méilleag, eig, *s f.* A blubber-lip, the bit of a bridle; a female with pouting lips. *N. pl* meilleagan

Meilleag, eig, *s f.* (*Ir. id.*) The outer rind of a tree

Meilleagach, *a* Blubber-lipped; having pouting lips

Méille-chartan, ain, *s. m* A violent itching in the sole of the foot.

Meillean, ein, *s. m.* (*Ir. id.*) Blame, reproach.

Méillear, ir, *s m.* A blubber-lipped fellow.

Meillg, *s. f* A rind, a pod

† **Meilliach**, *s f.* (*Ir. id*) The globe—*Shaw.*

Méilliceach, *a.* Blubber-lipped. *Com.* and *sup.* meilliciche.

Meillicean, ein, *s c* (*from* méill) A blubber-lipped person, a person with pouting lips.

† **Meilt**, *s f* (*Ir. id.*) Casting, hurling; grinding; chewing; consuming

Méilte, *p. part.* of méil Ground; grinded. Gràn méilte, *ground grain.*—*Stew Sam.* *Asp form*, mhéilte

Méiltear, eir, *s. m.* (*from* méil) A grinder; a miller *N. pl.* meilteirean, *grinders.*—*Stew. Ecc.*

Méiltearachd, *s. f.* Grinding; milling; the business or calling of a grinder or miller.

Meiltir, meiltreach, *s f.* Corn sent to be ground; grist, a mulcture, a fee for grinding grain.

Méin, *s. f.* (*Span.* mina, *mine.*) A mine; a vein of metal; ore, mien; (*Fr* mine. *Eng.* mien); air; mind; tenderness; fondness.

Meineabhag, aig, *s. f* A caressing, a fondling

Meineabhagach, *a.* Caressing, fondling; affectionate

Méineach, *a.* (*from* méin) Abounding in mines; full of ore or metallic strata; having a good mien; airy. *Com.* and *sup* méinich.

MÉINEALACHD, *s. f.* Tenderness; fondness; discreetness; affableness.

MÈINEAR, ir, *s. m.* A mineral; a miner; (*Du* myner, *a miner.*) a mineralogist, *also, adjectively,* mineral.

MÉINEARACH, *a* Mineralogical; *also, substantively,* a miner; a mineralogist.

MÉINEARACHD, *s. f.* Mining, mineralogy.

MÉINEIL, *a.* (méin-amhuil) Tender, affectionate, fond; discreet; affable, metal Gu méineil, *tenderly.*

MEINIGEAN, *s pl.* Gloves, mittens.
Corn. and *Arm* manag *and* manek. *Lat.* manica, *a hand-fetter.*

MEINM, *s. f* Courage, magnanimity. Cha robh meinm oirnne, *we had not courage*—*Macfar.*

MEINNEACH, *a.*, written also *meanmach*, which see.

MÉINN, *s f* (*Eng* mien *Fr* mine) Mien; good will, mercy, quality, kindness, tenderness; fondness, the surname Menzies Cia mordha a méinn! *how majestic her mien!*—*Mac Lach*

MEINNEACH, ich, *s f.* (*from* meinn) Mercy, pity; discreetness; fondness. Iolair gun mheinneach, *a ruthless eagle*—*Old Poem*

MEINNEACH, *a.* Merciful; pitiful; discreet; fond *Com* and *sup* meinniche.

MEINNEARACH, aich, *s m* A male of the clan Menzies Am Meinnearach, *the Menzies, the chieftain of the clan Menzies*

MÉINNEIL, *a* (meinn-amhuil) Affectionate, fond, affable, kindly, well-disposed

MEIRBH, *a.* (*Ir id*) Silly, spiritless, slow, tedious, feeble *Com* and *sup.* meirbhe.

MEIRBHE, *s f* (*Ir id.*) Silliness; spiritlessness, dulness, feebleness; slowness, tediousness, a lie

MEIRBHE, *com* and *sup* of meirbh, which see

† MEIRCEANN, inn, *s m.* (*Ir id*) A finger

MEIRDREACH, ich, *s f* (*Ir. id Lat.* meretrix) A whore

MEIRDREACHAS, ais, *s. m* (*Ir id*) Fornication

MEIRE See MIRE.

MEIREAN NAM MAGH, *s. m.* Agrimony.

MEIRG, *s.* Pity See MAIRG.

MEIRG, meirge, *s f.* (*Ir. id Corn Arm* marg, *rust*) Rust; a standard or banner. Cruaidhe gun mheirg, *armour without rust.*

MEIRG, *v. a* and *n* Rust *Pret* mheirg; *fut. aff. a* meirgidh, *shall rust.*

MEIRGEACH, *a.*, *from* meirg (*Ir id*) Rusty, rusted; causing rust, having banners; of, or belonging to, a banner

MEIRGEADH, aidh, *s. m* (*Ir id*) A rusting, rust

MEIRGEALI, ill, *s. m* (*Ir. id*) Roughness, ruggedness —*Shaw.*

MEIRGHE, *s f.* (*Ir* meirge.) A banner or standard; a pair of colours or flags; a band or troop, a company

MEIRGHEACH, *a.* (*from* meirghe) Having banners or flags; like a banner or flag.

MEIRGTE, *p part* of meirg. Rusted, covered with rust. Claidheamh meirgte, *a rusted sword.*

MEIRLE, MEIRLEADH, *s. f.* Theft, thieving, robbery.

MEIRLEACH, ich, *s. m*, *perhaps* meur-leamhach. (*Ir. id.*) A thief, a robber; a rogue, a rebel. *N. pl.* meirlich Far nach cladhaich na meirlich, *where thieves break not through*—*Stew Matt.* Meirleach, *a rogue, a rebel.*—*Shaw.*

MEIRLEACHAS, ais, *s. m* (*perhaps* meur-leamhachas) Theft, thieving; treason, rebellion.

MEIRNEAL, eil, *s. m.* (*Ir. id.*) A merlin.—*Shaw.*

MEIRSE, *s. f* (*Ir. id.*) A fine.

† MEIRTNEACH, *a.* (*Ir. id.*) Feeble; fatigued.

† MEIS, *a.* (*Ir id*) Bad, wicked.—*Shaw.*

† MEIS-CHEOL, -chiùil, *s m* (*Ir. id*) A singing; a modulation; music

MEISD, *s. f* Rust.

MEISDE, *s* (*for* measad *or* miosad.) Deterioration. A dol ain meisde, *growing worse and worse.*

MEISDE, a *mode of comparison* from olc Bad. Written also *misde*, which see.

MÈISE, *gen sing.* of mias; which see.

MÈISEAN, ein, *s. m.* A little plate

MEISGE, *s f.* (*Ir id.*) Drunkenness, tippling; tipsiness. Air mheisge, *drunk.* Written also *misge.*

MEISGEACH, *a* (*from* meisg.) Drunk, tipsy, intoxicating; fond of strong liquor. *Com.* and *sup.* meisgiche.

MEISGEAR, eir, *s m* A drunkard. *N pl.* meisgeirean.

MEISGEIREACHD, *s f* Habitual drunkenness

MEISLEAN, ein, *s. m.* Mastlin.

MEISNEACH, ich, *s.* More frequently written *misneach;* which see.

MEISNICH. See MISNICH.

MEITEAL, eil, *s m.* (*W* mettel.) Stuff; mettle. Feuch do mheiteal, *try your mettle.*

MEITEALACH, *a.* Made of metal; mettled; keen; smart; made of good stuff.

MÉITH, *v* See MEATH

MÉITH, *a.* (*Ir id.*) Fat, corpulent; soft; timid For the last two senses, see MEATH. Mias mhéith an t-sagairt, *the priests' fat mess*—*Old Saying.*

MEITHEACHD, *s. f.* (*Ir. id.*) Fatness; softness; timidity.

MEITHEALACH, aich, *s. m* (*Ir. id*) A fatling; a nursling

† MEITHLE, *s. f.* (*Ir. id.*) Reapers; crowds; concourse.

MEITHREAS, eis, *s m.* (*Ir. id.*) Kitchen-stuff; fatness.

MEO-BHLATH, *a.* Lukewarm. More properly *meadh-bhlàth;* which see.

MEO-BHLATHACHADH, aidh, *s. m* See MEADH-BHLÀTHACHADH.

MEO-BHLÀTHAICH, *v. a* Make lukewarm See MEADH-BHLÀTHAICH

MEOG, *gen.* meoig *and* mige. Whey. Written also *meag.*

MEOGACH, *a.* Like whey; abounding in whey See MEAGAIL.

MEOGAIL, *a* (meog-amhuil) Serous; like whey.

MEOGHAIL, *s. f.* (*Ir. id*) A medley, a mixture; a company, a mixed company

MEOGHAIR, *s f* (*Ir id*) Sport, fun, mirth; pomp, glory. Thug e là air meoghair chon, *he spent a day in the sport of hounds.*—*Fingalian Poem.*

MEOGHLACH, *a.* Mixed; confused, in a medley.

MEOGHRACH, *a* (*from* meoghair.) Merry, cheerful, sportive, sporting, lively, talkative. *Com.* and *sup.* meoghraiche, *more* or *most merry.*

MEOIR, *gen sing.* and *n. pl* of meur.

MEOMHAIR, *s f* (*Ir. id. Lat.* memoria. *Fr* mémoire) Memory.

MEOMHAIREACH, *a.* (*Ir. id.*) Mindful; having a retentive memory.

MEOMHAIRICH, *v. a.* Remember; mention; note; take a memorandum.

MEORACH, *a.* Meditating; pensive; gentle.

Meòrachadh, aidh, *s. m.* A meditating, a pondering; study; a remembering; meditation, remembrance.

Meòrachan, ain, *s. m.* A memorandum; a note-book; a record; minutes.

Meòraich, *v. a.* and *n.* Remember; mention; note; take or make a memorandum; meditate, ponder. *Pret. a.* mheòraich, *contemplated; fut. aff.* meòraichidh, *shall contemplate.*

Meòragan, ain, *s. m.* (*Ir.* meoracan.) A thimble. *N. pl.* meòragain. Also written *meuragan.*

Meòranach, aich, *s. m.* A memorandum, a memorial; a note-book; a record; minutes. *N. pl.* meòranaich.

Meothal, ail, *s. m.* Help.—*Shaw.*

Meud, *s. m.* (*Ir. id.*) Greatness, magnitude, largeness; size, dimension, extent, quantity, bulk; stature. Meud do ghairdean, *the greatness of thine arm.—Stew Ex.* Meud a bhròin, *the magnitude of his grief.—Oss. Fing.* Meud an t-saoghail, *the size of the world;* a dol am meud, *growing in size;* air mheud 's a bheil e, *however great he* or *it be, however much it be;* a mheud 's a tha làthair, *as many as are present; as many as are alive* or *surviving.*

Meudachadh, aidh, *s. m.* An enlarging, augmenting, adding; an addition, an enlargement.

Meudachadh, (a), *pr. part.* of meudaich. Enlarging, augmenting, adding to.

Meudachd, *s. f.* (*from* meud.) Extent, size, bulk; greatness; dimension; stature. *Asp. form*, mheudachd. Is ioghna leam a mheudachd, *I am surprised at its dimensions.*—*Oss. Derm.* Duine do mheudachd mhòir, *a man of great stature.—Stew. Num.*

Meudaich, *v. a.* and *n.* (*from* meud.) Enlarge, increase, multiply, grow in size; improve. *Pret. a.* mheudaich, *enlarged; fut. aff. a.* meudaichidh, *shall enlarge.* Meudaich mi do dhoilghios, *I will multiply thy sorrow.—Stew. Gen.* Meudaichidh tu a luach, *thou shalt increase its price.—Stew. Lev.* Mheudaich e, *it became large* or *larger.* Am fear nach meudaich an carn, gu meudaich e chroich, *he who will not add to the cairn, may he add to the gallows.—G. P.* For an explanation of this proverb, see Carn.

Meudaicheam, 1 *sing. imper. a.* of meudaich. Let me increase. *Also, for* meudaichidh mi, *I shall increase.*

Meudaichear, *fut. pass.* of meudaich; which see.

Meudaichte, *p. part.* of meudaich.

Meud-bhronn, *s. m.* Dropsy; pregnancy. Theasd e leis a mheud-bhronn, *he died of the dropsy.*

Meud-bhronnach, *a.* Dropsical; swag-bellied.

Meug, meig, *and* mige, *s. m.* (*Ir. id.*) Whey. See Meag.

Meugach, *a.* (*from* meug.) Serous; like whey; full of whey.

Meugail, *a.* (meug-amhail.) Serous; like whey.

Meunan, ain, *s. m.* (*Ir. id.*) A yawn, a gape.

Meunanach, *a.* (*from* meunan.) Yawning, gaping; addicted to yawning or gaping.

Meunanaich, *s. f.* The habit of yawning; a yawning. Ri meunanaich, *yawning;* thòisich e air meunanaich, *he began to yawn.*

Meunanda, *a.* See Meuranda.

Meur, meòir, *s. m.* (*Ir.* mear *and* meur.) A finger; a toe; a branch of a tree; a branch of a family; a branch of a river. *N. pl.* meoir. A meòir gun lùgha', *her fingers motionless.—Ull. D. pl.* meuraibh. Dh' fhàs i na ceithir meuraibh, *it became into four branches.—Stew. Gen.* Meur meadhonach, *middle finger.*

Meurach, *a.* Fingered; branchy; nimble-fingered.

Meurachadh, aidh, *s. m.* A fingering, a pawing; a growing into branches.

Meurag, aig, *s. f.* A pebble; a clue of yarn; a little or small finger.

Meuragan, ain, *s. m.* (*from* meur.) A thimble; a fingering, a handling. *N. pl.* meuragain, *thimbles.* Meuragan, *a handling* or *fingering.*

Meuraibh, *d. pl.* of meur.

Meuraich, *v. a.* and *n.* (*from* meur.) Finger, handle; branch. *Pret. a.* mheuraich, *fingered; fut. aff. a.* meuraichidh, *shall finger.*

Meuraichte, *p. part.* of meuraich. Fingered, handled; branched.

Meuran, ain, *s. m.* (*from* meur.) A thimble; a little branch; a small finger. *N. pl.* meurain.

Meuranach, *a.* Having thimbles; thimbled; like a thimble; branchy.

Meuranda, *a.* Tender, weakly, delicate.

Mhac, *asp. form* of mac. Son. A mhac, *his son.*

Mhacain, *voc. sing.* of macan. A hero, a champion. Also *gen. sing.* of mhacan, *asp. form* of macan. Bàs a mhacain, *the champion's death.—Old Poem.*

Mhachair, *voc. sing.* of machair. A level country. Also *asp. form* of machair; which see.

Mhacnus, uis, *s. m.*, *asp. form* of macnus; which see.

Mhadainn, *asp. form* of madainn. Morning. Anns a mhadainn, *in the morning.* Also *voc. sing.* of madainn. Mhadainn bhoidhche bhealtuinn! *thou beauteous morn of May!—Old Song.*

Mhàg, mhàig, *s. m.*, *asp. form* of màg; which see.

Mhag, *pret.* of mag. Mock. Mhag e orm, ort, orra, *he mocked me, thee, them.* See Mag.

Mhagh, *asp. form* of magh; which see.

Mhaighstir, *s. m.* See Maighstir.

Mhair, *pret. a.* of mair. Lasted; survived. Cha mhair an doinionn, *the storm will not last.—Oss. Gaul.* See Mair.

Mhaireann, *a.*, *asp. form* of maireann; which see.

Mhaise, *s. f.*, *asp. form* of maise; which see.

Mhaiseach, *a.*, *asp. form* of maiseach; which see.

Mhaith, *asp. form* of maith. Good. Is ceart cho mhaith leam so, *I like this just as well.* See Maith.

Mhall, *a.*, *asp. form* of mall; which see.

Mhallaich, *pret. a.* of mallaich. Cursed. See Mallaich.

Mhaoil, *asp. form* of maoil; an *inflection* of maol; which see.

Mhaoin, *s.*, *asp. form* of maoin; which see.

Mhaol, *a.*, *asp. form* of maol.

Mhaoth, *a.*, *asp. form* of maoth; which see.

Mhaothan, ain, *s. m.*, *asp. form* of maothan; which see.

Mhara, *asp. form* of mara; *gen. sing.* of muir; which see.

Mharbh, *a.*, *asp. form* of marbh; which see.

Mharbh, *pret. a.* of marbh. Slew, murdered. See Marbh.

Mhàs, mhàis, *s. m.*, *asp. form* of màs.

Mhaslaich, *pret. a.* of maslaich. Affronted; disgraced. See Maslaich.

Mhath, *asp. form* of math; which see.

Mhath, *pret. aff. a.* of math. Pardoned, forgave.

Mheadhon, *asp. form* of meadhon. Middle. Anns a mheadhon, *in the middle.*

Mheall, *pret. a.* of meall. Cheated, deceived. Mheall e mi, *he cheated me.*

Mheanbh, *asp. form* of meanbh; which see.

Mheann, *asp. form* of meann; which see.

Mhear, *a.*, *asp. form* of mear. Merry. See Mear.

Mheas, *pret. a.* of meas. Esteemed; valued; considered. See Meas.

Mheas, *asp. form* of meas; which see.

Mheasg, *pret. a.* of measg. Mixed. See Measg.

Mheat, *a.*, *asp. form* of meat; which see.

Mheath, *asp. form* of meath.

Mheidh, *asp. form* of meidh.

Mheirg, *asp. form* of meirg; which see.

Mheirg, *pret. a.* of meirg. Rusted. See Meirg.

Mheisge, *s. f.*, *asp. form* of meisge. Drunkenness. Air mheisge, *drunk.*

Mheisgear, *asp. form* of meisgear; which see.

Mheoir, *asp. form* of meoir, *gen. sing.* and *n. pl.* of meur.

Mheud, *s. m.*, *asp. form* of mheud. Air a mheud 's a bheil e, *however great it be; however much it be.* A mheud 's a tha, *as many as are.*

Mhi, *personal pron.*, *asp. form* of mi. I, me. An tusa rinn so? cha mhi; *was it you who did this? not I.*

Mhiann, *asp. form* of miann; which see.

Mhiannaich, *pret. a.* of miannaich; which see.

Mhic, *voc. sing.* of mac, and *gen. sing.* of mhac. A mhic mo mhic! *son of my son!—Old Poem.*

Mhill, *pret. a.* of mill. Spoiled, abused.

Mhillsich, *pret. a.* of millsich. Sweetened.

Mhillte, *asp. form* of millte, *p. part.* of mill. Spoiled.

Mhilltear. See Milltear.

Mhìn, *a.*, *asp. form* of mìn; which see.

Mhinic, *a.*, *asp. form* of minic. Frequent; often. Bu mhinic iomairt gheur-lann, *frequent was the play of sharp-edged swords.—Old Poem.*

Mhìnich, *pret. a.* of mìnich. Explained; smoothed. See Mìnich.

Mhionn, *pret.* of mionn. Swore. See Mionn.

Mhionnan, *asp. form* of mionnan.

Mhire, *asp. form* of mire.

Mhise, *asp. form* of mise, the *emphatic form* of mi. I, me.

Mhisge, *s. f.*, *asp. form* of misg. Drunkenness. Air mhisge, *drunk, tipsy.*

Mhisneach, *s.*, *asp. form* of misneach. Courage. Cha 'n'eil a mhisneach agam, *I have not the courage.* See Misneach.

Mhithich, *asp. form* of mithich.

Mhna, *asp. form* of mna, *gen. sing.* of bean; which see.

Mhnaoi, *asp. form* of mnaoi, *d. sing.* of bean; which see.

Mhnathan, *asp. form* of mnathan.

Mhò, *asp. form* of mò, *com.* and *sup.* of mòr. Greater, greatest. Cha mhò thu na esan, *thou art not greater than he;* b' e bu mhò do'n triùir, *he was the greatest of the three;* cha mhò thiubhram e, *neither will I surrender it.—Old Poem.*

Mhòid, *asp. form* of mòid; which see.

Mhòidich, *pret. a.* of mòidich; which see.

Mhòir, *asp. form* of mòir. See Mòr.

Mhol, *pret. a.* of mol. Praised; recommended. See Mol.

Mhòr, *a.*, *asp. form* of mòr; which see.

Mhòrachd, *s. f.*, *asp. form* of mòrachd; which see.

Mhòran, *asp. form* of moran; which see.

Mhòrchuis, *s. f.*, *asp. form* of mòrchuis; which see.

Mhuc, *asp. form* of muc; which see.

Mhùch, *pret. a.* of mùch. Smothered. See Mùch.

Mhùig, *asp. form* of mùig; which see.

Mhuir, *asp. form* of muir. Sea. Air mhuir, *on sea.* See Muir.

Mhusach, *a.*, *asp. form* of musach.

Mhusg, *asp. form* of musg; which see.

Mhùth, *pret. a.* of mùth. Changed.

Mi, *a compositive and negative particle.* Mi-naomh, *unholy;* mi-nàrach, *shameless.*

Mi, *pers. pron.* I, me.

Lat. Fr. and *Sp.* me. *Corn. It.* me *and* mi. *Ir.* me. *Gr.* μι *for* ἐμι. *Germ.* mich.

† **Mi**, *s. f.* (*Ir. id.*) A mouth; a month.

Miabhan, ain, *s. m.* Megrim.

† **Miach**, *s. m.* (*Ir. id.*) A bag, a budget; a satchel.

Miachair, *a.* (*Ir. id.*) Kind; loving, affable. Gu miachair, *kindly, affably.*

Miad, *s.* Extent. See Meud.

Miad, *s. m.* A meadow; a plain. Miad-fheurach, *having meadow-grass.—Macint.*

Miadaich. See Meudaich.

Miadan, ain, *s. m.* (*dim.* of miad.) A meadow; a plain. *N. pl.* miadain.

Miadanach, *a.* Meadowy; belonging to a meadow.

Miadar, air, *s. m.* A meadow; a plain.

Miad-fheur, -fheòir, *s. m.* Meadow-grass.

Miad-fheurach, *a.* Grassy; having long grass; like meadow-grass.—*Macint.*

Miadh, *s. m.* Honour, respect. Fionn a chuir miadh oirnne, *Fingal who honoured us.—Fingalian Poem.* Written also *miagh.*

Miadh, *s. m.* (mi, *neg. and* adh.) Misfortune, mishap, bad luck.

Miadhach, *a.* (*from* miadh.) Precious; respected; *also,* unfortunate.

Miadhail, *a.* Noble; honourable, precious.

Mi-adhartach, *a.* Backward; not inclined to advance or be forward; unprogressive.

Mi-adhartachd, *s. f.* Backwardness.

Mi-adhmhor, *a.* Unfortunate, unlucky, untoward; awkward. *Com.* and *sup.* mi-adhmhoire.

† **Miaduigh**, *s. f.* (*Ir. id.*) A hog, a sow.—*Shaw.*

Miag, *s. f.* A sly look, a smirk. Written also *miog.*

Miagach, *a.* Sly; looking slily; smirking. Written also *miogach.*

Miagail, *s. f.* Mewing, as a cat; caterwauling.

Miagh, *s.* Respect, honour, esteem; repute, fame. Gun mhiagh, gun mheas, *without fame, without respect.—Oss. Manos.* Ann am miagh, *in esteem, esteemed.*

Mi-agh, *s.* Disrespect, dishonour, disrepute; mishap; bad luck.

Miaghail, *a.* Respected, honoured; esteemed; famous; desirable, precious, valuable.

Miaghar, *a.* See Miaghail.

Miag-shùil, -shùl, *s. f.* A sly eye; a sly look; a smirking look.

Miag-shuileach, *a.* Giving a sly look; having a sly look.

Mial, *s. f.* (*Ir.* miol.) A louse. *N. pl.* mialan. Mial chaorach, *a sheep-tick;* mial chon, *a dog-tick;* mial mhara, *a whale;* mial iongnach, *a crab-louse;* mial spàgach, *a crab-louse; a crab-fish;* mial crion, *a moth* or *wood-louse;* miol balla, *a wall-louse;* mial goile, *a belly-worm.*

Mialach, *a.*, *from* mial. (*Ir.* miolach.) Lousy, pedicular. An galar mialach, *the phthyriasis,* or *lousy disease.*

Mialchu, choin, *s. m.* A greyhound. See Miolchu.

Mi-altrum, uim, *s. m.* Bad nursing. Cinnidh mac o mhi-altrum, ach cha chinn e o'n aog, *a son may grow from bad nursing, but cannot escape the grave.—G. P.*

Miamhail, *s. f.* A mewing, as of a cat. Ri miamhail, *mewing.*

MIAN. See MÉIN.

MIAN-FHAOILIDH, s. A yawn.

MIANN, s. (*Ir.* mian.) Desire; will; purpose, intention; inclination, love; appetite; delight; *also*, a thing desired or loved; a mole on the skin. Miann an aingidh, *the desire of the wicked.—Sm.* Tha mhiann orm falbh, *I have a mind to go;* bàs mo nàmh cha mhiann leam, *I desire not the death of my foes.—Orr.* Bu mhiann leis triall, *he chose to go.—Old Poem.* Cha 'n 'eil a mhiannsà suichte, *his appetite is not filled.—Stew. Ecc.* Miann mo shùil, *the delight of my eye.—Macfar.*

MIANNACH, a. (*from* miann.) Covetous; desirous; longing; greedy; desirable; pleasant. Is miannach dreach nam bliadhna dh' fhalbh, *pleasant is the appearance of the years that are gone.—Fingalian Poem.*

MIANNACHADH, aidh, s. m. A coveting; a longing.

MIANNACHAS, ais, s. m. (*Ir.* mianghas.) Desire; appetite; longing; greed; flavour.

MIANNACHASACH, a. Desirous.

MIANNAG, aig, s. f. (*from* miann.) A covetous female; a greedy girl. *N. pl.* miannagan.

MIANNAGACH, a. Desirous of trifles; covetous of dainties. *Com.* and *sup.* miannagaiche.

MIANNAICH, v. a. (*from* miann.) Desire, covet, lust after; long for; fix one's heart on. *Pret. a.* mhiannaich; *fut. aff. a.* miannaichidh, *shall covet.* Na miannaich, *do not covet.—Stew. Rom. ref.* Na miannaich a sgeimh, *lust not after her beauty.—Stew. Pro.*

MIANNAICHTE, p. part. of miannaich. Coveted; lusted after.

MIANNAR, a. See MIANNMHOR.

MIANNASACH, a. (*from* miann.) Covetous, greedy; lustful; longing, desirous. *Com.* and *sup.* miannasaiche.

MIANNASACHD, s. f. Covetousness, greediness; lustfulness.

MIANNMHOR, a. Covetous, greedy; lustful. *Com.* and *sup.* miannmhoire. Gu miannmhor, *covetously.*

MIANNMHOIREACHD, MIANNMHORACHD, s. f. Covetousness, greediness; appetibility.

MIANNUCHADH, aidh, s. m. See MIANNACHADH.

MIANNUICH, v. a. See MIANNAICH.

MIANNUICHTE, p. part. of miannuich. See MIANNAICH.

MI-AOGAS, ais, s. m. Unseemliness; uncomeliness; unlikeliness; a bad appearance.

MI-AOGASACH, a. Unseemly, unlikely, having a bad appearance, unbecoming. *Com.* and *sup.* mi-aogasaiche.

MIAPADH, aidh, s. m. Disgracefulness.

MIAPAIDH, a. Sad; disgraceful.

MIARBHAIL, s. See MIORBHUIL.

MIARBHAILEACH, a. See MIORBHUILEACH.

MIAS, mèise, s. f. (*Ir.* mias. *Goth.* mis. *Eng.* mess.) A plate; a dish; a charger; *rarely*, an altar. Geal-mhias mhor, *a large white plate.—Mac Lach.* Air mèise, *on a [plate] charger.—Stew. Acts.* *N. pl.* miasan.

MIASACH, a. (*from* mias.) Abounding in plates; like a plate or dish.

MI-BHAIGH, s. f. Cruelty; mercilessness; unfriendliness. Fear na mi-bhaigh, *the merciless man.—Old Poem.*

MI-BHAIGHEACH, a. Cruel, merciless, unfeeling. Gu mi-bhaigheach, *cruelly.*

MI-BHAIGHEIL, a. (mi-bhaigh-amhuil.) Cruel, merciless, unfeeling; unfriendly. Gu mi-bhaigheil, *cruelly.*

MI-BHAIL, s. f. Unthriftiness; extravagance.

MI-BHAILEACH, a. Unthrifty; extravagant. Gu mi-bhaileach, *unthriftily.*

MI-BHANAIL, a. Unwomanly; immodest. Bean mhi-bhanail, *an unmodest woman;* gu mi-bhanail, *immodestly.*

MI-BHANALAS, ais, s. m. Unwomanliness, immodesty.

MI-BHEUS, s. m. (*Ir. id.*) Immodesty, indecency; a misdeed; bad breeding, bad manners. Eiric nam mi-bheus a rinn, *a recompense for the misdeeds committed.—Mac Lach.* *N. pl.* mi-bheusan.

MI-BHEUSACH, a. (*Ir. id.*) Immodest, indecent; ill-bred, impolite. Fhir mhi-bheusaich! *thou ill-bred man!—Old Song.* *Com.* and *sup.* mi-bheusaiche. Gu mi-bheusach, *immodestly.*

MI-BHEUSACHD, s. f. Immodesty; bad breeding.

MI-BHLASDA, a. Insipid, tasteless, unsavoury, ill-tasted. Biadh mi-bhlasda, *unsavoury food;* do phogan mosach, mi-bhlasda, *thy nasty, tasteless kisses.—Old Song.*

MI-BHOIDHEACH, a. Not pretty, ugly, unhandsome; unseemly, unbecoming. Iomchar mi-bhoidheach, *unseemly conduct.*

MI-BHUAIDH, s. f. Unsuccessfulness in fighting; unluckiness.

MI-BHUAIDHEACH, a. Unsuccessful in fighting; unlucky.

MI-BHUAIREAS, eis, s. m. Quietness; harmlessness; tranquillity.

MI-BHUAIREASACH, a. Quiet in temper; not apt to provoke or trouble. Gu mi-bhuaireasach, *quietly.*

MI-BHUIDHEACH, a. Unsatisfied, greedy; unthankful, ungrateful. Do bhag mi-bhuidheach, *thy greedy guts.—Old Song.*

MI-BHUIDHEACHAS, ais, s. m. Unthankfulness, ingratitude.

MI-BHUILEACHADH, aidh, s. m. A misapplying; an abusing; a putting to a bad use; a squandering; a neglecting to improve.

MI-BHUILICH, v. a. Misapply; abuse; squander; misimprove. *Pret. a.* mhi-bhuilich, *misapplied; fut. aff. a.* mi-bhuilichidh, *shall misapply; p. part.* mi-bhuilichte, *misapplied.*

MI-BHUINEADH, idh, s. m. Despair, distrust.—*Shaw.*

MI-BHUNAILTEACH, a. Unsteady; unfounded; not firmly built, not firmly footed; changeable. Gu mi-bhunailteach, *unsteadily.*

MI-BHUNAILTEACHD, s. f. Unsteadiness; changeableness; want of foundation.

MIC, *gen. sing.* of mac. (*Ir. id.*) Of a son; *also, n. pl.* sons.

† MICHADAS, ais, s. m. An affront; ingratitude.—*Shaw.*

MI-CHAIDREACH, a. Unfriendly, unkind; unfond, unsociable. *Com.* and *sup.* mi-chaidriche.

MI-CHAIDREAMH, imh, s. m. Want of familiarity; unfriendliness; shiness; unsociableness.

MI-CHAIDREAS, eis, s. m. Unfriendliness; unsociableness, shiness.

MI-CHÀIRDEALAS, ais, s. m. Unfriendliness; unkindness.

MI-CHÀIRDEIL, a. Unfriendly; unkind. Gu mi-chàirdeil, *unkindly.*

MI-CHALMA, a. Feeble; not stout; of a slender form.

MI-CHAOIMHNE, s. f. Unkindness, unfriendliness.

MI-CHAOIMHNEALAS, ais, s. m. Unkindness, unfriendliness.

MI-CHAOIMHNEAS, eis, s. m. Unkindness, unfriendliness.

MI-CHAOMHNEIL, a. Unkind, unfriendly. Gu mi-chaoimhneil, *in an unfriendly manner.*

MI-CHAOMHAIN, v. a. Spend, squander. *Pret. a.* mhi-chaomhain; *fut. aff. a.* mi-chaomhnaidh, *shall squander.* Is baileach mhi-chaomhain thu do mhaoin, *completely hast thou squandered thy means.*

MI-CHEANALTA, a. Unhandsome; unbecoming or unseemly; untidy.

MI-CHEANNSA, a. (*Ir. id.*) Impudent.

Mi-chearmanta, *a.* Untidy, slovenly. Gu mi-chearmanta, *untidily.*

Mi-cheart, *a.* (*Ir. id.*) Not right; not proper; unjust.

Mi-cheartaich, *v. a.* Set out of order, misadjust. *Pret. a.* mhi-cheartaich; *fut. aff. a.* mi-cheartaichidh.

Mi-cheartas, ais, *s. m.* Injustice; impropriety.

Mi-chéill, *s. f.* (*Ir. id.*) Madness, insanity, folly. Tha thu air mhi-chéill, *thou art* [*mad*] *beside thyself.—Stew. Acts.*

Mi-chéilidh, *a.* (*Ir.* mi-chéillighe.) Foolish, unwise; imprudent; insane, mad. Inntinn mhi-chéillidh, *an insane mind.—Stew. Acts.* Gu mi-chéillidh, *madly, foolishly.*

Mi-chiall, -chéill, *s. f.* (*Ir. id.*) Folly, imprudence; insanity, madness; want of meaning. Am mi-chiall follaiseach, *their folly manifest.—Stew. Tim.*

Mi-chiallach, *a.* (*Ir. id.*) Foolish; imprudent; insane; without meaning. Gu mi-chiallach, *foolishly.*

Mi-chiat, *s. m.* A low opinion. Is mòr mo mhi-chiat deth, *I have a very low opinion of him.*

Mi-chiatach, *a.* Unseemly; ungainly; improper. Urr mi-chiatach, *an ungainly person;* giùlan mi-chiatach, *unseemly conduct.*

Mi-chineamhuinn, *s. f.* (*Ir. id.*) A misadventure; a mishap; mischance.

Mi-chineamhuinneach, *a.* (*Ir. id.*) Misadventurous; misfortunate.

Mi-chinnte, *s. f.* Uncertainty.

Mi-chinnteach, *a.* Uncertain.

Mi-chinnteachd, *s. f.* Uncertainty.

Mi-chion, *s.* Displeasure; aversion; dislike.

Mi-chiùin, *a.* Not calm, troubled, boisterous. Gu mi-chiùin, *boisterously.*

Mi-chiùineas, eis, *s. m.* Disquiet.

Mi-chlis, *a.* Inactive, inexpert; unclever.

Mi-chliù, *s. m.* (*Ir.* miochliù.) Dishonour, infamy, disrepute, defamation, dispraise, reproach. Lot agus mi-chliù, *a wound and dishonour.—Stew. Pro.* Mo mhi-chliù, *my reproach.—Stew. Gen.*

Mi-chliùiteach, *a.* (*Ir.* mochliuteach.) Infamous; dishonourable; reproachful; not renowned, obscure. Gu mi-chliùiteach, *infamously.*

Mi-chliùitich, *v. a.* Defame; disparage; bring into disrepute. *Pret. a.* mhi-chliùitich, *defamed; fut. aff.* mi-chliùitichidh, *shall defame.*

Mi-chneasta, *a.* (*Ir. id.*) Inhuman; unfeeling; uncivil; perilous; ominous. Gu mi-chneasta, *inhumanly.*

Mi-chneastachd, *s. f.* (*Ir. id.*) Inhumanity; incivility; perilousness; ominousness.

Mi-choidhis, *a.* Not indifferent; nice in appetite.

Mi-choingheallach, *a.* Unwilling to lend.

Mi-choingioll, *s.* Treachery, deceit.

Mi-chomhnard, *a.* Uneven, not level. Talamh mi-chomhnard, *uneven grounds.*

Mi-chompanta, *a.* Unsocial; morose.

Mi-chompantachd, *s. f.* Unsociableness; moroseness.

Mi-chompantas, ais, *s. m.* The state of being without a companion.

Mi-chothromach, *a.* Disproportionate; inconvenient; unjust.

Mi-chreideach, *for* mi-chreidmhach; which see.

Mi-chreideamh, imh, *s. f.* (*Ir. id.*) Unbelief; scepticism. Luchd mi-chreidimh, *sceptics.*

Mi-chreideas, eis, *s. m.* (*Ir. id.*) Want of credit; unbelief, incredulity.

Mi-chreideasach, *a.* (*Ir. id.*) Uncreditable, discreditable. Gu mi-chreideasach, *uncreditably.*

Mi-chreidimh, *s. f.* Unbelief, scepticism, infidelity. Airson am mi-chreidimh, *for their unbelief.—Stew. Rom.*

Mi-chreidmhach, Mi-chreidmheach, *a.* (*Ir. id.*) Unbelieving, sceptical. Bean mhi-chreidmhach, *an unbelieving wife.—Stew. Cor.*

Mi-chreidmhiche, *s. m.* An unbeliever; a sceptic; an infidel.

Mi-chridhealas, ais, *s. m.* Dejectedness, dulness, heartlessness.

Mi-chridheil, *a.* Dejected, dull, heartless, disheartened. Gu mi-chridheil, *dejectedly.*

Mi-chruinnealas, ais, *s. m.* Slovenliness, untidiness carelessness.

Mi-chruinneil, *a.* Untidy, slovenly, uncareful. Gu mi-chruinneil, *untidily.*

Mi-chuimhne, *s. f.* Heedlessness, carelessness, forgetfulness.

Mi-chuimhneach, *a.* Unmindful, forgetful, careless. Gu mi-chuimhneach, *carelessly.*

Mi-chuimhneachail, *a.* Unmindful, forgetful, careless. Gu mi-chuimhneachail, *forgetfully.*

Mi-chuineas, eis, *s. m.* A donation.—*Shaw.*

Mi-chuiseach, *a.* Modest, unassuming; attractive, bewitching; unenterprising.

Mi-chumachd, *s. f.* Shapelessness, clumsiness.

Mi-chumachdail, *a.* Unshapely; clumsy; not proportioned. Gu mi-chumadail, *clumsily.*

Mi-chumadail, *a.* Shapeless; clumsy; not handsome. Do chosan mi-chumadail, *thy shapeless legs.—Old Song.*

Mi-chumadh, aidh, *s. m.* Shapelessness, clumsiness.

Mi-chùram, aim, *s. m.* Remissness, carelessness, negligence.

Mi-chùramach, *a.* Careless, remiss, inattentive. Gu mi-churamach, *carelessly.*

Mi-dhàichealas, ais, *s. m.* Awkwardness; unhandsomeness.

Mi-dhàicheil, *a.* Awkward; unhandsome. Fear mi-dhàicheil, *an awkward man.*

Midhe, *s.* Meath in Ireland; a native of Meath.

Mi-dheabhaltach, *a.* Frugal.—*Shaw.*

Mi-dhealbh, *v. a.* Deform, misshape; take a bad likeness. *Pret. a.* mhi-dhealbh, *deform; fut. aff.* mi-dhealbhaidh, *shall deform.*

Mi-dhealbhach, *a.* (*Ir. id.*) Unmatched; unlikely; not well shaped; unseemly.

Mi-dhealbhaltach, *a.* Frugal.

† Mi-dheamhnas, ais, *s. m.* Honour, exaltation.

Mi-dheas, *a.* (*Ir. id.*) Awkward; inexpert; unhandsome; unstately in gait.

Mi-dhiadhachd, *s. f., for* mi-dhiadhaidheachd.

Mi-dhiadhaidh, Mi-dhiadhuidh, *a.* Ungodly, profane. Dhoibhsan a tha mi-dhiadhaidh, *to them who are ungodly.—Stew. Tim.*

Mi-dhiadhaidheachd, Mi-dhiadhuidheachd, *s. f.* Ungodliness, irreligion, profanity. An aghaidh mi-dhiadhuidheachd, *against ungodliness.—Stew. Rom.*

Mi-dhileas, *a.* (*Ir. id.*) Faithless; treacherous; dishonest. Gu mi-dhileas, *faithlessly.*

Mi-dhiongalta, Mi-dhiongmhalta, *a.* Not firm, not tight; insufficient.

Mi-dhiongaltachd, *s. f.* Insufficientness; want of firmness.

Mi-dhleasnach, *a.* (*contr. for* mi-dhleasdanach.) Undutiful; unfriendly. Gu mi-dhleasdanach, *undutifully.*

Mi-dhleasnas, ais, *s. m.* (*for* mi-dhleasdanas.) Undutifulness.

Mi-dhligheach, *a.* Unlawful; not according to its kind. Gu mi-dhligheach, *unlawfully.*

Mi-dhluigheil, *a.* Careless, inattentive.

Mi-dhòchas, ais, *s. m.* Despair, despondence; want of conceit.

Mi-dhòchasach, *a.* Despairing, desponding; not conceited.

Mi-dhoigh, *s. f.* Want of method; awkwardness; want of condition; want of health.

Mi-dhoigheil, *a.* Immethodical, awkward. Gu mi-dhoigheil, *immethodically.*

Mi-dhreach, *s. m.* (*Ir. id.*) An unseemly appearance; deformity; a bad look; an unpleasant exterior; a disfiguration.

Mi-dhreachadh, aidh, *s. m.* (*Ir. id.*) Disfiguring.

Mi-dhreachail, *a.* Deformed, disfigured; unpleasant to look at; having an unseemly exterior; disfiguring.

Mi-dhreachmhor, *a.* Unpleasant to look at; having an unseemly exterior; disfiguring; disfigured, deformed.

Mi-dhùrachd, *s. f.* Indifference, negligence, inattention.

Mi-dhùrachdach, *a.* Indifferent, negligent, inattentive.

Mi-earbsa, *s. m.* Distrust, suspicion.

Mi-earbsach, *a.* Distrustful, suspicious. *Com.* and *sup.* mi-earbsaiche.

Mi-éifeachd, *s. f.* Ineffectualness, inefficiency.

Mi-éifeachdach, *a.* (*Ir. id.*) Ineffectual; useless; vain. Gu mi-éifeachdach, *ineffectually.*

Mi-eireachdail, *a.* Ungenteel; unhandsome; ugly; unseemly. Giùlan mi-eireachdail, *unseemly conduct;* gu mi-eireachdail, *ungenteelly.*

Mi-eireachdas, ais, *s. m.* (*Ir. id.*) Ungenteelness; unseemliness; want of a pleasing exterior; deformity.

Mi-eudmhor, *a.* Unsuspicious; not inclined to jealousy; cold; disloyal; not zealous.

Mi-fhaiceallach, *a.* Inattentive; inconsiderate; unobservant. Gu mi-fhaiceallach, *inattentively.*

Mi-fhaicill, *s. f.* Inattention; want of observation.

Mi-fhallain, *a.* Unwholesome, unsound, unhealthy; rotten. Gu mi-fhallain, *unsoundly.*

Mi-fhallaineachd, *s. f.* Unwholesomeness, unsoundness; unhealthiness; rottenness.

Mi-fharasda, *a.* Not mild; ungentle; inquiet; turbulent.

Mi-fhasgach, *a.* Unshelterable; affording no shelter.

Mi-fhearail, *a.* (*Ir. id.*) Unmanly, soft, effeminate. Gu mi-fhearail, *in an unmanly manner.*

Mi-fhearalachd, *s. f.* Unmanliness, effeminateness, softness.

Mi-fhearalas, ais, *s. m.* Unmanliness, effeminateness, softness.

Mi-fhearghach, *a.* Not easily provoked; not causing provocation; unirritative.

Mi-fhein, *s. pron.* (*W.* myhun. *Arm.* ma hyny, *mine.*) Myself.

Mi-fhialachd, *s. f.* Unhospitableness; churlishness; unsociableness.

Mi-fhialaidh, *a.* (*Ir. id.*) Unhospitable; unsocial; churlish.

Mi-fhiù, *a.* Worthless, valueless.

Mi-fhiùachd, *s. f.* Worthlessness; demerit.

Mi-fhiughaireach, *a.* Spiritless, dull. Gu mi-fhiùghaireach, *spiritlessly.*

Mi-fhiùghaireachd, *s. f.* Spiritlessness, dulness.

Mi-fhiùghantach, *a.* Illiberal; niggardly. Gu mi-fhiùghantach, *illiberally.*

Mi-fhiùghantachd, *s. f.* Illiberalness; niggardliness.

Mi-fhiùghar, *a.* Spiritless, dull.

Mi-fhlathail, *a.* Ignoble; ungenteel; mean in appearance.

Mi-fhoighdinn, *s. f.* Impatience, restlessness.

Mi-fhoighdinneach, *a.* Impatient, restless. Gu mi-fhoighdinneach, *impatiently.*

Mi-fhortan, ain, *s. m.* Misfortune; mishap; bad luck. Claidheamh a mhi-fhortain, *the sword of mishap.—Sm.*

Mi-fhortanach, *a.* Misfortunate; unlucky. Gu mi-fhortanach, *unluckily. Com.* and *sup.* mi-fhortanaiche.

Mi-fhreagarrach, *a.* Unsuitable; not fitting; not answering.

Mi-fhreagarrachd, *s. f.* Unsuitableness, unfitness.

Mi-fhreasdalach, *a.* Improvident; unfavourable; unassisting. Gu mi-fhreasdalach, *improvidently.*

Mi-fhurachair, *a.* Careless, inattentive, unobservant. Gu mi-fhurachair, *carelessly.*

Mi-fhurachras, ais, *s. m.* Inattentiveness, unwatchfulness.

Mi-fhuran, ain, *s. m.* Churlishness; unsociableness; joylessness; disinclination to welcome or congratulate.

Mi-fhuranach, *a.* Churlish; unhospitable; backward to welcome or to congratulate. Gu mi-fhuranach, *churlishly.*

Mi-fhuras, *a.* Difficult, not easily done.

Mi-fhurasach, *a.* Impatient. Gu mi-fhurasach, *impatiently.*

Migeadaich, *s. f.* Bleating of goats.

Mi-ghean, *s. m.* (*Ir. id.*) Displeasure; discontent or dissatisfaction; disgust; discord; grudge. Fògraidh tu mi-ghean, *thou shalt banish disgust.—R.*

Mi-gheimnidh, *a.* Unchaste; incontinent; lewd. Gu mi-gheimnidh, *incontinently.*

Mi-gheimnidheachd, *s. f.* Unchasteness; incontinence; lewdness.

Mi-gheur, *a.* Blunt; stupid.

Mi-ghiùlan, ain, *s. m.* Improper conduct.

Mi-ghleidh, *s.* Mismanagement, want of frugality.

Mi-ghlic, *a.* (*Ir. id.*) Unwise, foolish, silly; rash; inexperienced. Gu mi-ghlic, *unwisely.*

Mi-ghliocas, ais, *s. m.* (*Ir. id.*) Imprudence.

Mi-ghloine, *s. f.* Uncleanness, filthiness.

Mi-ghnathach, *a.* Abusing; mischievous; unusual, uncommon.

Mi-ghnathachadh, aidh, *s. m.* An abusing; a misapplying.

Mi-ghnathachd, *s. f.* Bad usage; misapplying.

Mi-ghnathaich, *v. a.* Abuse; put to an improper use, misapply. *Pret. a.* mhi-ghnàthaich. Mhi-ghnathaich iad i, *they abused her.—Stew. Jud.*

Mi-ghnathaichte, *p. part.* of mi-ghnathaich. Abused; uncommon, unusual.

Mi-ghnètheil, *a.* Ill-tempered, ill-disposed; having a bad complexion; having a forbidding look.

Mi-ghniomh, *s.* (*Ir. id.*) A misdeed; mischief; lewdness. Luchd mi-gniomh, *evil doers.—Stew. Pet. N. pl.* mi-ghniomharan.

Mi-ghniomhach, *a.* (*Ir. id.*) Idle; misdoing; not industrious.

Mi-ghoireas, eis, *s. m.* Inconvenience; insufficiency.

Mi-ghoireasach, *a.* Inconvenient; insufficient; immoderate.

Mi-ghramail, *a.* Infirm; not muscular; unsteady; unstable.

Mi-ghramalas, ais, *s m.* Want of firmness; instability; want of resolution or mental decision.

Mi-ghreann, *s. m.* (*Ir. id.*) Loathing, disgust; disdain.

Mi-ghrunnd, *s* Want of industry; want of economy or frugality.

Mi-ghrunndail, *a* Unfrugal, not economical; not industrious.

Migiall, *v. n* Bleat, as a goat. *Pret.* mhigiall, *bleated.*

Migiallach, *a.* Bleating, as a goat.

Migiallaich, *s f.* The bleating of a goat.

Mi-inealta, *a* Inelegant, ungenteel, clumsy, unseemly.

Mi-iomchuidh, *a* Inconvenient; unbecoming, improper.

Mi-iomradh, aidh, *s m.* A bad report, a bad name; slander.

Mil, meala, *s f* Honey. Ith thusa mil, *eat thou honey* — *Stew Pro.* Soitheach meala, *a pot of honey* —*Stew* 1 *K* Also, *a honey-pot* Cir-mheala, *honeycomb.*
• *Gr.* μελι *Lat.* mel. *Fr* miel. *It* mele. *Ir.* mil *W.* mêl *Corn.* mel

Mi-labhrach, *a.* (*Ir.* mio-labharthach.) Impudent, forward, pert; *also*, sullen.

Mi-laghachadh, aidh, *s. m.* The act of abolishing or repealing a law; abolition.

Mi-laghaich, *v a* Abolish or repeal a statute *Pret a.* mhi-laghaich; *fut. aff* mi-laghaichidh.

Mi-laghail, *a.* Unlawful, illegal. Gu mi laghail, *unlawfully.*

Mi-laghaileachd, *s. f.* Unlawfulness, illegality.

Milbhir, *s. f.* (mil, *honey*, and † bir, *water. Ir. id*) Mead; metheglin.

Mil-dheoch, *s* Mead —*Macd.*

Mil-dheoghladh, aidh, *s. m.* Extracting of honey, sucking honey, as from flowers.

Mìle, *a.* A thousand. Measg mìle triath, *among a thousand heroes* —*Oss. Fing.* Lan mhìle, *a full thousand.* *N. pl* mìltean, *thousands.*
Lat. mille *Romaic* or *modern Gr.* μιλια *Bisc.* milla. *Sclav* millia. *Dal.* milya. *Pol.* mila. *Turk.* mil. *Boh.* mile. *W. Arm* mil *Ir* mìle. *Span* mil.

Mìle, *s. f.* A mile Da mhìle, *two miles;* deich mile, *ten miles,* mìle shlighe, *a mile of road, a mile in length,* clach mhìle, *a milestone* *N. pl.* mìltean.

Mileadh, idh, *s. m.* (*Ir. id. Lat* miles.) A soldier. See **Milidh**.

Mileag, eig, *s f.* A melon.

Mileanta, *a* Soldierly, brave; genteel; elegant; stately. Na ceannardan mileanta, *the brave chieftains.* An ceannsgalach mileanta, *the brave commander* —*Mac Vuirich.*

Mileantachd, *s. f.* Bravery; genteelness; handsomeness; stateliness

Mile-ghath, *s* Anxiety; hurry.

Milidh, *s. m.* (*Ir. id*) A hero; a renowned person Buillean a mhilidh, *the hero's blows.—Old Poem.* Cathan mhilidh, *the battles of heroes* —*Death of Carril.*

Mi-liosda, *a* Unimportuning, unsolicitous.

Mil-itheach, *a.* Mellivorous; pale, wan

Milis, *a.* (*Ir.* milis. *Corn.* melys, *sweet* *Gr* μελιττα, *a bee*, also, *an herb of which bees are fond.*) Sweet; savoury; flattering. Nithe milis, *dainties.—Stew. Pro.* Cainnt mhilis; *fair* or *flattering speech* *Com* and *sup.* milse. Aran milis, *any kind of sweet bread; gingerbread.*

Mill, *n. pl.* of meall. (*Ir. id.*) Lumps, knobs, hudges. See **Meall**.

Mill, *v. a.* (*Ir. id.*) Spoil or marr; abuse; make useless; destroy; ruin; violate. *Pret. a.* mhill, *spoiled; fut. aff. a.* millidh, *shall spoil.* Mhill iad mo cheum, *they marred my steps* —*Stew. Job*

Millcheo, *s. m.* (*Ir.* milcheo.) Mildew, blight.—*Stew.* 1 *K. ref.*

Milleadh, idh, *s. m.* (*Ir. id*) A destroying, spoiling, or damaging; defacing; damage; destruction, bane. Milleadh nam bochd, *the defacing of the poor.—Stew Pro.* Milleadh righre, *the bane of kings.* Tha e air a mhilleadh, *he* or *it is destroyed, he* or *it is abused.*

Millean, ein, *s. m* A tax.

Milliudh, *s.* A blasting or evil eye; a fascinating look.

Millse, *s. f.* (*Ir id*) Sweetness Millse nam bile, *the sweetness of lips* —*Stew Pro.*

Millse, *com* and *sup.* of milis. More or most sweet. Written also *milse.*

Millsead, id, *s. m.* Sweetness, increase in sweetness. Bha e ann mo bheul mar mhil air mhillsead, *it was in my mouth as honey for sweetness.—Stew. Ezek.* A dol am millsead, *growing more and more sweet.* Written also *milsead.*

Millte, *p part.* of mill. (*Ir. id.*) Spoiled, destroyed, made useless, violated

Millteach, *a*, *from* mill. (*Ir. id.*) Destructive; wasting; deadly; *substantively*, a wicked man. Mar uisge millteach, *like destructive waters.—Stew. Pro.* *Com.* and *sup.* milltiche.

Millteach, ich, *s. m* A tuft of luxuriant grass; verdant; grassy Bàrr a mhilltich, *the top of the grassy tufts.*—*Macint.* Gleann a mhilltich, *the grassy glen.—Id.*

Millteach, *a* Verdant, grassy. Maghanan millteach, *verdant meadows.—Old Poem.*

Millteachd, *s f.* Destruction, injury.

Millteanas, ais, *s. m* (*Ir. id*) A blunder, injury.

Milltear, *fut. pass.* of mill. Shall be destroyed.

Milltear, eir, *s. m.* (*Ir. id.*) A destroyer or spoiler; a waster; an oppressor. O shannt a mhillteir, *from the pleasure of the destroyer* —*Old Song.* Do 'n mhillteir mhòir, *to the great waster.—Stew Pro.* *N. pl.* milltearan.

Milltear, *imper. pass.* of mill.

Milltich, *s.* (*Ir. id.*) Tufts of good grass —*Shaw.*

Milltineachd, *s f.* Bravery, gallantry.

Millmheacan, ain, *s. m.* (*Ir. id*) A mallow. *N. pl.* millmheacain

Milneach, ich, *s. m.* (*Ir. id*) A thorn; a bodkin.

Mi-loinn, *s f.* Want of order; irregularity; impropriety.

Mi-loinnealas, ais, *s. m* Want of order; irregularity; impropriety.

Mi-loinneil, *a.* Disordered; irregular; disfigured; improper. Gu mi-loinneil, *without order.*

Milse, *com.* and *sup* of milis. Sweeter, sweetest. Ciod is milse na mile? *what is sweeter than honey?—Stew. Jud.*

Milseachadh, aidh, *s. m.* (*Ir. id*) A sweetening; a growing sweet.

Milseachd, *s. f.*, *from* milse. (*Ir. id*) Sweetness, savouriness; lusciousness; fragrance; flattery.

Milsead, id, *s. m.* (*Ir. id.*) Sweetness; increase in sweetness. Milsead caraid, *the sweetness of a friend;* a dol am milsead, *growing more and more sweet;* mar mhil air mhilsead, *like honey for sweetness;* air mhilsead 'sa bheil e, *however sweet it is;* is milsid an deoch an siucar, *drink is the sweeter for the sugar.*

Milsean, ein, *s. m.* (*Ir. id.*) Sweetmeat; any thing sweet;

a flatterer. *N. pl.* milseanan, *sweetmeats.* Milsean mara, *a kind of eatable sea-weed;* milsean crom-luis, *syrup of poppies.*

Milseanach, aich, *s. m.* A confectioner; a sweet-lipped person. *N. pl.* milseanaich.

Milseanta, *a.* (*Ir. id.*) Sweetened.

Milsich, *v. a.* (*from* milis.) Sweeten; mull; make savoury; make fragrant. *Pret. a.* mhilsich, *sweetened; fut. aff. a.* milsichidh, *shall sweeten.*

Milsichte, *p. part.* of milsich. Sweetened; mulled; made fragrant. Fion milsichte, *mulled wine.*

Mil-shliosnach, aich, *s.* (*Ir. id.*) A chiliaedron.

Mìlte, Mìltean, *pl.* of mìle. Thousands. *D. pl.* mìltibh. Aon do 'm mhìltibh cionta, *one of a thousand of my sins; one of my thousands of sins.—Sm.* Mìlte do mhuillionaibh, *thousands of millions.—Stew. Gen.*

Mi-mhacanta, *a.* Ungentle; not filial; dishonesty.

Mi-mhacantas, ais, *s. m.* Want of gentleness, want of meekness; dishonesty.

Mi-mhaighdinneil, *a.* Unwomanly, immodest, unbecoming a virgin, unmaidenly.

Mì-mhail, *a., contracted* for mi-mhodhail; which see.

Mi-mhaise, *s. f.* Unseemliness; unhandsomeness.

Mi-mhaiseach, *a.* Unhandsome, unseemly, uncomely. Gu mi-mhaiseach, *unhandsomely.*

Mi-mhalta, *a.* Not mild, not lenient; unkind; immodest.

Mi-mhaltachd, *s. f.* Want of mildness; unkindness; want of modesty.

Mì-mhar, *a., contracted* for mi-mhodhar; which see.

Mi-mheadhonach, *a.* Eccentric; not centrical; disproportionate.

Mi-mheadhonach, *s. f.* Eccentricity.

Mi-mheas, *s. m.* (*Ir. id.*) Disrespect; disregard; affront; indifference. Cuir air mi-mheas, *shew disrespect.*

Mi-mheas, *v. a.* Undervalue; shew disrespect.

Mi-mheasail, *a.* (*Ir. id.*) Disrespected; disrespectful. Gu mi-mheasail, *disrespectfully.*

Mì-mheasarrachd, *s. f.* (*Ir. id.*) Intemperance; immoderateness.

Mi-mheasarradh, *a.* (*Ir. id.*) Intemperate, immoderate.

Mì-mheasta, *a.* Vile, mean, ignoble, despised.

Mi-mhineachadh, aidh, *s. m.* A misinterpreting; a misinterpretation.

Mì-mhisneach, ich, *s. m.* Want of courage; discouragement. Cuir air mi-mhisneach, *discourage, dispirit.*

Mi-mhisneachail, *a.* Dispirited, dastardly, desponding, irresolute.

Mi-mhisnich, *v. a.* Discourage, terrify, damp the spirits.

Mi-mhodh, *v. a.* Act unpolitely towards one; reproach, revile, profane.

Mi-mhodh, -mhòidh, *s. m.* Incivility, disrespect, impoliteness, bad manners, impertinence; immodesty; an improper habit. Dad do mhi-mhodh, *aught of incivility.—Old Song.* Airde a mhi-mhoidh, *the height of impertinence.—Id.*

Mi-mhodhail, *a.* Unmannerly, ill-bred, uncivil, disrespectful, disgraceful. Gu mi-mhodhail, *impolitely.*

Mi-mhodhaileachd, *s. f.* Unmannerliness, impoliteness, impertinence, disrespectfulness. Do leithid air mi-mhodhaileachd, *thy equal in impertinence.—Old Song.*

Mi-mhodhar, *a.* Uncivil, ill-bred, impertinent, of unbecoming habits.

Mi-mhoil, *a., contracted* for mi-mhodhail; which see.

Mì-mhol, *v. a.* Dispraise or disparage. *Pret. a.* mhì-mhol; *fut. aff. a.* mi-mholaidh, *shall dispraise.*

Mi-mholadh, aidh, *s. m.* Dispraise, disparagement.

Mì-mhuinghinn, *s. f.* Diffidence; distrust.

Mìn, *a.* (*Ir. id.* W. man. *Gr.* μιννος *for* μικρος, *little.*) Smooth; calm, as the surface of water; soft, mild, gentle; plain; polished; tender, delicate; small or comminuted, as powder; *also, substantively,* a plain field. Clos na mìnlear, *the repose of the calm sea.—Oss.* Ainnir bu mhìn gné, *a maid of the softest temper.—Oss. Fing.* Bruthaidh tu ro mhìn, *thou wilt bruise very small.—Stew. Ex.* Buinibh gu mìn, *deal softly* or *gently.—Stew. Sam. Com.* and *sup.* mìne, *smoother, smoothest.* Ni 's mìne na oladh, *smoother oil.—Stew. Pro.*

Mìn, mìne, *s. f.* Meal; any comminuted or pulverized substance. Mìn mhìn, *flour—*(*Stew. O. T.*); *meal finely ground.* Soitheach mìne, *a vessel* [*barrel*] *of meal.—Stew.* 1 *K.* Mìn iarruinn, *iron filings.*

Mi-nadur, uir, *s. m.* Ill-nature, inhumanity.

Mi-nadurra, Mi-nadurrach, *a.* (*Ir.* mi-nadurtha.) Ill-nature; unnatural. Neoghloine mhi-nadurra, *unnatural impurity.—Stew.* 1 *Cor.*

Mi-nadurrail, *a.* Unnatural; ill-natured: inhuman.

Mi-nàire, *s. f.* (*Ir.* mio-nàire.) Shamelessness, immodesty, impudence.—*Stew. Eph.*

Mi-naireach, *a.* Shameless, impudent. Gu mi-naireach, *impudently.*

Minan, ain, *s. m.* Dross.

Mìn-aois, *s. f.* Minority.

Mi-naomh, *a.* Unholy, irreligious, profane, unsanctified, unpurified by holy rites. Do-dhaoinibh mi-naomh, *to ungodly men.—Stew. Tim.*

Mi-naomhachadh, aidh, *s. m.* A profaning, profanation.

Mi-naomhachd, *s. f.* Unholiness, profaneness.

Mi-naomhaich, *v. a.* Profane, unhallow, deprive of holiness. *Pret. a.* mhi-naomhaich; *fut. aff. a.* mi-naomhaichidh.

Mì-narach, *a.* Shameless, impudent. Gu mi-narrach, *shamelessly.*

Mìn-bhailtean, *s. pl.* Suburbs.

Min-bhallach, *a.* Having small spots, spotted, speckled. Laoigh mhìn-bhallach, *spotted calves.*

Mìn-bhar, air, *s. m.* Hemlock.—*Shaw.*

Mìn-bhean, -mhna, *s. f.* A tender name for a wife.

Mìn-bhileach, *a.* Smooth-lipped, fawning, flattering.

Mìn-bhradach, *a.* Light-fingered, prone to petty theft.

Mìn-bhraide, *s. f.* Larceny, petty larceny.

Mìn-bhriathar, air, *s. m.* A soft expression, a flattering word, a smooth word.

Mìn-bhriathrach, *a.* Flattering, smooth-worded.

Mìn-bhris, *v. a.* (*Ir. id.*) Pulverize, break into powder, crumble. *Pret. a.* mhìn-bhris; *fut. aff. a.* mìn-bhrisidh.

Mìn-bhriseadh, idh, *s. m.* A pulverizing, a crumbling.

Mìn-bhriste, *part.* Pulverized, powdered, crumbled.

Mìn-bhristeach, *a.* Pulverizing, crumbling; apt to crumble, pulverable.

Mìn-bhruich, *v. a.* Boil. *Pret. a.* mhìn-bhruich; *fut. aff.* mìn-bhruichidh.

Mìn-bhruth, *v. a.* Pound, pulverize, mince. *Pret. a.* mhìn-bhruth; *fut. aff.* mìn-bhruthaidh, *shall pound.*

Mìn-chagainn, *v. a.* Masticate; mump. *Pret. a.* mhìn-chagainn.

Mìn-chagnadh, aidh, *s. m.* Mastication; mumping.

Min-cheasnachadh, aidh, *s. m.* A scrutinizing, a close questioning, cross-examination.

Min-cheasnaich, *v. a.* Scrutinize, examine minutely, cross-examine. *Pret. a.* mhìn-cheasnaich; *fut. aff. a.* mìn-cheasnaichidh.

Min-chloch, -chloich, *s. f.* A smooth stone; a pumice stone. *N. pl.* mìn-chlochan

Min-chruth, *s. f* A delicate person or form; a smooth-skinned person.

Min-chruthach, *a.* Smooth-skinned, soft-complexioned, soft-featured.

Min-chuileag, eig, *s f* A gnat More frequently *meanbh-chuileag.*

Min-chuiseach, *a.* Particular, strictly punctual; particular about trifles; mean.

Min-chunntas, ais, *s m.* A particular account; a strict reckoning.

Min-dhealbh, *s m.* A miniature picture; a little image

Min-dhus, *s. m.* Powder, fine sand, dust —*Stew. Song Sol*

Min-dreach, *s m.* (*Ir.* id) A little image.

Min-duine, *s. m.* A manikin; a dwarf, a diminutive fellow

Mine, *com.* and *sup* of mìn, which see

Mine, *s f.* Pusillanimity; littleness; comminution, smoothness.

Mineach, *a.* (*from* mìn) Mealy, like meal, abounding in meal

Mineachadh, aidh, *s. m* (*Ir.* minughadh.) A smoothing, a polishing; a taming; a pulverizing, an explanation; illustration.

Mineachail, *a.* (mìneach-amhuil) Explanatory, illustrative

Mineachd, *s. f from* mìn (*Ir* id.) Smoothness; fineness; gentleness; softness

Minead, id, *s m* (*Lat.* minut-us.) Smoothness; minuteness, fineness, as of powder: increase in smoothness or fineness. A dol am mìnead, *growing smoother*, is mìnid a chlach gach buille, *a stone becomes more powdered at every blow.*

Mineag, eig, *s f* (*from* mìn) A gentle female; a female with mild dispositions, a smooth-skinned girl. *N. pl* mineagan.

Mineagach, *a* Gentle-tempered, as a female.

Min-eallach, aich, *s f* Small cattle.—*Shaw*

Minean, ein, *s. m* Dross, the small of coals, or of any drossy substance

Mineanach, aich, *s. m.* A manikin

Minear, *a.* Mealy; abounding in meal, producing meal.

Min-eargnas, ais, *s m* (*Ir.* id) Ignorance

Mineil, *a.* Mealy.

Mineite, *s f* A minute of time; a minute of proceedings; a moment Written also *mionaid*, which see.

Mineite, *s f* (*Ir* id) A small feather, a smooth feather. —*Shaw*

Mineiteach, *a* See Mionaideach.

Min-eolach, *a.* Thoroughly acquainted, minutely acquainted

Min-eolas, ais, *s m.* A minute or thorough acquaintance.

Min-fheur, -fheòir, *s. m* (*Ir* id.) Soft grass, smooth grass; closely shaven grass; a meadow; a flag, a bulrush. Mìn-fheur chaorach, *soft sheep-grass.* —*Macint.* Mìn-fheur, *a meadow.*—*Macd.* Mìn-fheur gun uisge, *a bulrush without water.*—*Stew. Job*

Min-ghaduigheachd, *s. f.* Larceny.

Min-gheal, *a.* Soft and fair. Mo chaileag bhuidhe mhìn-gheal, *my yellow-haired maid with skin so soft and fair.*—*Old Song.*

Min-ghearr, *v a.* Mince; hash. *Pret. a.* mhìn-ghearr, *hashed*, *fut. aff a.* mìn-ghearraidh.

Min-ghoideachd, *s. f* Petty larceny.

Min-iasg, -éisg, *s. f.* (*Ir.* id.) A minnow; the *cyprinus phoxinus* of Linnæus, small fish; a shoal of fish.

Minic, *a* See Minig.

Minich, *v. a.* (*Ir.* minigh.) Smooth; polish; tame; explain; paraphrase; make intelligible *Pret. a.* mhìnich, *smoothed; fut. aff. a.* mìnichidh, *shall polish.*

Minichear, *fut. pass.* of mìnich, *shall be polished*

Minichte, *p. part.* of mìnich. Smoothed; polished: explained, expounded

Minid, *s f.* (*Ir.* id.) The stomach; the stomach of a quadruped; runnet.

Minidh, *s. f* (*Ir.* meanadh) A shoemaker's awl. Tolladh e le minidh, *he will bore a hole with an awl* —*Stew. Ex* *N. pl.* minidhean

Minig, *a.* Frequent, often *Asp form,* mhinig. D' an-mhuinneachd mhinig, *thy frequent infirmities* —*Stew. Tim.* Is minig uair 's is tric, *many a time and oft*
Goth. maenig. *Ir.* minic. *W.* mynyk.

Minig, (gu), *adv.* Often, frequently.

Ministear, eir, *s. m.* A clergyman, a minister; a servant. *N pl.* ministearan

Ministearachd, *s f* Ministry; the profession of a clergyman

Ministreil, *a.* Ministerial.

Ministreileachd, *s f* Ministry, the business of a clergyman Ministreileachd air a h-earbsadh rium, *a ministry intrusted to me.*—*Stew. Cor*

Min-lach, aich, *s. f.* (*Ir.* id) The finest of grass —*Shaw.* *Also*, dross

Min-lamh, aimh, *s. m.* A soft hand; a soft arm.—*Oss.*

Min-lear, *s. f.* A calm sea Clos na mìn-lear uaine, *the repose of the calm green sea.*—*Oss.*

Minmhear, ir, *s m* Hemlock—(*Shaw*); the *conium maculatum* of botanists.

Minn, *n pl.* of meann Kids —*Stew.* 2 *Chr*

Minneach, ich, *s f* (*Ir.* id.) The herb mill-mountains; purging flax, *also*, falsehood.

Minnean, ein, *s m*, *dim.* of meann (*Arm* and *W.* mynin.) A young kid, a little kid; a young fawn *N pl.* minneinean. A minnean a leumnaich dlù dhi, *her fawn frisking beside her* —*Oss Derm.* Na minneinean laghach, *the pretty young kids* —*Macfar*

Minnicean, eig, *s f.* A kid's skin. Perhaps *minn-sheiceag.*

Minnicean, eig, *s m* A kid's skin. Perhaps *minn-sheicean.*

Minnseag, eig, *s f.* (*Ir* id) A young kid, a little kid.—*Shaw.*

Mi-nòs,-nòis, *s m.* A bad custom; misbehaviour; immodesty, unchastity. Mi-nòs a d' ghruaidhean, *immodesty in thy looks* —*Old Song.* Written also *mio-nos.*

Mi-nòsach, *a* Misbehaving; immodest, unchaste; morose.

Min-phroinnte, *p. part.* of mìn-phronn. Bruised, pounded, pulverized.

Min-phronn, *v a.* Pound, pulverize. *Pret a.* mhìn-phronn, *pounded*, *fut. aff. a* mìn-phronnaidh, *shall pound.* —*Stew.* 2 *K.*

Min-phronn, *a.* (*Ir.* id) Pounded, pulverized.

Min-rann, -roinn, *s. f.* (*Ir* id.) A short verse, a short poem; smooth verse.

Min-rosg, -roisg, *s m* (*Ir.* id.) A gentle eye, a soft eye.

Mìn-rosgach, *a.* (*Ir. id.*) Having a gentle eye; having a soft look.

Mìn-shùil, -shùl, *s. m.* (*Ir. id.*) A soft eye; a pink eye.

Mìn-shùileach, *a.* (*Ir.* mion-shuileach.) Soft-eyed; pink-eyed.

Mìn-uchd, *s. f.* A soft breast, a smooth breast. O 'mìn-uchd bàn, *from her soft fair breast.—Oss. Fing.*

Mìn-uchdach, *a.* Having a soft or smooth breast; smooth or soft-breasted.

Mio, *a neg. particle.* The Irish form of *mì.*

Miodair, *gen. sing.* and *n. pl.* of miodhar; which see.

Miodal, ail, *s. m.* (*Ir. id.*) Flattery, fawning; a fair speech. Le miodal tlà', *with smooth flattery.—Sm.* Luchd miodail, *flatterers.*

Miodalach, *a.* (*Ir. id.*) Flattering, fawning, smooth-lipped. Beul miodalach, *a flattering mouth.—Stew. Pro. Com.* and *sup.* miodalaiche.

Miodalair, *s. m.* (*Ir. id.*) A flatterer, a fawning fellow. *N. pl.* miodalairean.

Miodalaireachd, *s. f.* Sycophancy; the practice of flattery.

Miodar, air, *s. m.* A small ansated wooden dish, (see **Meadar**); *also*, pasture ground, a meadow. Neulaich paircean is miodair gu bàs, *parks and pastures have the colour of decay.—Macdon.*

Miodarach, *a.* Ansated, like a wooden dish; meadowy; having pasture ground.

Miodhair, *s. m.* A churl; a niggard. *N. pl.* miodhairean. Gu bheil am miodhair daonnachdail, *that the churl is bountiful.—Stew. Is.*

Miodhaireach, *a.* Churlish; niggardly. Gu miodhoireach, *churlishly.*

Miodhaireachd, *s. f.* Churlishness; niggardliness.

Miodhuil, *s.* (*Ir. id.*) Dislike, aversion.

Miog, *s.* A smirk, a smile; a sly look.

Miogach, *a.* Sly-looking, smirking, smiling; sparkling. A bhanaraich mhiogaich! *thou dainty maid with the laughing eye!—Macdon.* Sùil mhiogach bhoidheach, *a sly pretty eye.—Old Song.*

Miog-shùil, -shùl, *s. f.* A sly look; a smiling or laughing eye; an inviting eye; a leering eye.

Miog-shuileach, *a.* Sly-looking; smiling; having a smiling eye; having an inviting eye; leering.

Mi-oidhirpeach, *a.* Unindustrious; unendeavouring; unenterprising.

Miol, *s. m.* (*Ir. id.*) A louse. Written also *mial;* which see.

Miolach, *a.* (*Ir. id.*) Lousy; brutish. Written also *mialach.*

Miolag, aig, *s. f.* (*Ir. id.*) A melon; any small thing.—*Shaw.*

Miolan, ain, *s. m.* (*Ir. id.*) A lie.

Miolaran, ain, *s. m.* (*Ir. id.*) A soft wailing voice, a lament, a howl. Rinn e miolaran, *he howled.—Ull.*

Miolaranach, *a.* Howling, lamenting.

Miolaranaich, *s. f.* A continued howling; a wailing voice, a loud lament.

Miolasg, aisg, *s. f.* (*Ir. id.*) Flattery, fawning; keen desire.

Miolasgach, *a.* (*Ir. id.*) Flattering, fawning, cajoling; keenly desirous; restive. *Com.* and *sup.* miolasgaiche. Gu miolasgach, *in a flattering manner.*

Miolasgair, *s. m.* (*Ir. id.*) A flatterer, a fawning fellow. *N. pl.* miolasgairean.

† **Miolc**, *s.* (*Ir. id.*) Whey.

Miolc, *v. a.* Soothe, cajole, flatter. *Pret. a.* mhiolc, *soothed fut. aff. a.* miolcaidh, *shall soothe.*

Miolcach, aich, *s. m.* (*Ir. id.*) A churl, a clown.

Miolcach, *a.* Flattering, prone to fawn or flatter; clownish.

Miolcadh, aidh, *s. m.* Flattering, cajoling, soothing.

Miolcair, *s. m.* (*Ir. id.*) A cajoler.

Miolcaireachd, *s. f.* Flattery; the practice of flattery.

Miol-choille, *s. m.* (*Ir. id.*) A woodlouse.

Miol-chu, -choin, *s. m.* (*Ir. id.* *W.* mil-chi.) A greyhound.—*Stew. Pro.* *N. pl.* miol-choin. A mhiol-choin a caoineadh, *his greyhounds wailing.—Oss. Fing.*

Mioltag, aig, *s. f.* A fly; a gnat; a bat. Mioltag leathair, *a bat.—Shaw.* Written also *ialtag.*

† **Miomasg**, aisg, *s. m.* A lance, a spear, a javelin.—*Shaw.*

Miomhodh. See **Mi-mhodh**.

Mion, *a.* Punctual, exact; distinct; mean; small; *also*, a particle. See **Mionn**.

Mion, in composition, is used most frequently by the Irish, and *min*, by the Scotch, Celts.

† **Mion**, *s. m.* (*Ir. id.*) A diadem.—*Shaw.*

† **Mionach**, aich, *s. m.* (*Ir. id.*) Metal.

Mionach, aich, *s.* (*Ir. id.* *W.* monoch.) Bowels, guts, entrails. *Asp. form*, mhionach. Nighidh tu a mhionach, *thou wilt wash its entrails.—Stew. Ex.* *N. pl.* mionaichean. A pronnadh chorp is mhionaichean, *smashing bodies and bowels.—Macdon.*

Mion-acrach, **Mion-ocrach**, *a.* Voracious, ravenous; often hungry; having a false appetite.

Mion-acras, **Mion-ocras**, ais, *s. m.* Voraciousness, ravenousness; a false appetite, a craving for food. Mar mhion-acras leomhainn ghairg, *like the ravenousness of a fierce lion.—Mac Lach.*

Mionaid, *s. f.* (*Ir. id.*) A minute of time; a minute of proceedings; a moment. *N. pl.* mionaidean. Gach mionaid, *every moment.—Stew. Job.* Air a mhionaid, *this minute, this instant;* mionaidean comuinn, *a society's minutes;* mionaid no dha, *a minute or two;* da mhionaid, *two minutes;* trì mionaidean, *three minutes;* mionaid gu leth, *a minute and a half.*

Mionaideach, *a.* (*Ir. id.*) Minute, punctual, precise, particular.

Mionaideachadh, aidh, *s. m.* An inculcating; explaining; minute explanation; the act of taking down minutes.

Mionaidich, *v. a.* Inculcate; explain minutely; take down minutes.

Mionaigir, *s. f.* Vinegar.—*Macd.*

Mion-bhallach, *a.* Small-spotted, speckled. Laoigh mhion-bhallach, *spotted calves.—Macdon.*

Mion-chorrach, *a.* Very steep, precipitous.

Mion-chuiseach, *a.* See **Min-chuiseach**.

Mion-chunntas, ais, *s. m.* See **Min-chunntas**.

Miondan, ain, *s. m.* (*Ir.* miontan.) A small bird; a titmouse.

Mionn, *s. m.* (*Ir. id.*) A particle, a jot, an atom. Cha 'n 'eil mionn dhe m' rùn dhiot, *thou hast not a particle of my affection.—Oss. Fing.*

Mionn, *s.* (*Ir. id.*) An oath, a curse, swearing; the crown of the head; a skull; a diadem; a bell. *N. pl.* mionnan. Guth mionnan, *the voice of swearing.—Stew. Lev.* Mionnan eithich, *a false oath.—Id.* Thoir mionnan, *swear, give oath.* Gabh mionnan, *administer an oath.—Stew. Num.* Ceangal nam mionn, *the obligation of oaths.—Mac Lach.* *D. pl.* mionnaibh. Saor o m' mhionnaibh, *free from my oath.—Stew. Gen.* Mionnan is briathran, *cursing and swearing.* Mionn, *a diadem; a bell.—Shaw.*

Mionn, *v. a.* and *n.* Swear or curse; vow; give an oath. *Pret. a.* mhionn, *swore*; *fut. aff. a.* mionnaidh, *shall swear.*

Mionnach, *a.* Prone to swear; cursing, swearing; votive.

Mionnachadh, aidh, *s. m.* A swearing, a cursing, a vowing; an oath, a vow, an imprecation. Guth mionnachaidh, *the voice of swearing.*—*Stew. Lev.*

Mionnachadh, (a), *pr. part.* of mionnaich.

Mionnaibh, 2 *pl. imper.* of mionn. Swear ye. Also, *d. pl.* of mionn, *to oaths.*

Mionnaich, *v. a.* (*Ir.* mionnaigh.) Swear, curse, vow; administer an oath, give oath. *Pret. a.* mhionnaich, *swore.* Mhionnaich mi, *I swore.*—*Stew. Gen.* *Fut. aff. a.* mionnaichidh, *shall swear.*

Mionnaichte, *p. part.* of mionnaich. Sworn; cursed, accursed.

Mionnan, *n. pl.* of mionn; which see.

Mionnt, *s. m.* Mint, spearmint, peppermint. — *Macint.* Mionnt fiadhaich, *wild mint.*

Mionntan, ain, *s. m.* (*Ir. id.*) A wren, a tom-tit.

Mionntas, ais, *s. m.* Mint; spearmint; peppermint.—*Shaw.*

Mionntuinn, *s. f.* Mint; spearmint; peppermint.—*Macfar. Voc.*

Mi-onoir, *s. f.* (*Ir. id.*) Dishonour, disgrace.

Mi-onoirich, *v. a.* Dishonour. *Pret. a.* mhi-onoirich, *dishonoured.*

† Mionsa, *s. f.* (*Gr.* μηνος. *Lat.* mensis.) A month. Now written *mios;* which see.

Miontan, ain, *s. m.* (*Ir. id.*) A titmouse.—*Shaw.*

† Miorbhadh, aidh, *s. m.* A killing, a destroying.

Miorbhuil, *s. f.* A wonder, a miracle, a phenomenon, a prodigy.

From this word are evidently derived, *Eng.* marvel; *Fr.* merveille; *It.* maraviglia,—all signifying any thing wonderful. The Irish say *miorbhaille,* the Celts of Bretagne, *marvailh.* Dr. Smith ingeniously observes, that the right orthography is *miorbhe'il* or *meurbhe'il,* 'the finger of Bel,' signifying a wonder which could not have happened without the agency of Bel; the name under which the Druids worshipped the Divinity.

Miorbhuileach, *a.* (*Ir. id.*) Wonderful, marvellous, miraculous. *Com.* and *sup.* miorbhuiliche.

Miorbhuileachd, *s. f.* Wonderfulness, marvellousness.

Miortal, ail, *s. m.* Myrtle. Craobh-miortail, *a myrtle-tree.* *N. pl.* miortalan.

Miortalach, *a.* Abounding in myrtle; of myrtle; like myrtle.

Miortalach, Miortalnach, aich, *s. f.* A myrtle shrubbery; a myrtle thicket; a place where myrtles grow.

Miorun, uin, *s. m.* (*Ir. id.*) Ill-will, malice. Luchd mioruin, *malicious people.*—*Sm.* and *Macint.*

Mio-runach, *a.* Malicious. Gu mio-runach, *maliciously.*

Mios, *s. m.* Respect. More frequently written *meas;* which see.

Mios, *s. m.* A month; *rarely,* a moon; a plate or trencher: —in the two last senses it is commonly written *mias;* which see. *Asp. form,* mhios. O mhios dh' aois, *from a month old.*—*Stew. Num.* Fuil mios, *flowers, menstrual courses.*—*Stew. Lev.* Mios buidh, *July;* Mios dubh, *November, or the black month.* *Arm.* mis du. *W.* y mis du. Mios marbh, *December.* *Arm.* mis maru.

Gr. Æol. μεις for μην, *month.* *Boh.* meysc. *Pol.* miesiacz. *Sclav.* messez. *Span.* mes. *Corn. W. Arm.* mis. *It.* mese. *Fr.* mois. *Ir.* mios.

Mios, Miosa, *com.* and *sup.* of olc. Worse, worst. Riutsa ni 's miosa na riu-san, *with thee worse than with them.*—*Stew. Gen.* Ni 's miosa, agus ni 's miosa, *worse and worse;* a dol am miosa, *growing worse and worse;* am fear a's miosa, *the devil.*

Miosach, *a.* (*from* mios.) Monthly, menstrual. An galar miosach, *menstrual courses.*

Miosach, aich, *s. f.* The plant called purging-flax.—*Shaw.*

Miosachan, ain, *s. m.* (*from* mios.) An almanack, a calendar. *N. pl.* miosachain.

Miosail, *a.* Respected. More frequently written *measail;* which see.

Miosail, *a.* (*from* mios.) Monthly, menstrual.

Miosar, air, *s. m.* (*Fr.* mesure. *Eng.* measure.) The measure of a gun; a measure of meal. *N. pl.* miosairean. Taoisinn tri miosairean, *leaven three measures.*—*Stew. Gen.*

Miosarach, *a.* Having measures; abounding in measures; measuring.

Miosarachd, *s. f.* Measurement, mensuration.—*Shaw.*

Miosaraich, *v. a.* Measure. *Pret. a.* mhiosaraich; *fut. aff. a.* miosaraichidh.

Mioscais, Miosgais, *s. f.* (*Ir. id.*) Hate, spite, grudge.

Mioscaiseach, *a.* (*Ir. id.*) Spiteful, grudging, hating.

Mios-dhortach, *a.* Menstrual, flowing monthly.

Mios-dhòrtadh, aidh, *s. m.* Menstrual courses.

Miosgainn, *s. f.* See Miosguinn.

Miosgainneach, *a.* See Miosguinneach.

Miosgainneachd, *s. f.* See Miosguinneachd.

Miosgan, ain, *s. m.* A kitt, or small wooden vessel for containing butter. *N. pl.* miosgain.

Miosganach, *a.* Abounding in butter-kitts; like a butter-kitt; kittish; butter-making. A bhealtuinn mhiosganach, *butter-making May.*—*Macfar.*

Miosguinn, *s. f.* Spite, grudge, malevolence. Le miosguinn garg, *with bitter spite.*—*Old Song.* Luchd do mhiosguinn, *the people who have a spite against you.*—*R.*

Miosguinneach, *a.* Spiteful, grudging, malevolent. *Com.* and *sup.* miosguinniche.

Miosguinneachd, *s. f.* Spitefulness, malevolence, maliciousness.

Miosneach, ich. More frequently written *misneach;* which see.

Miosneachail, *a.* More frequently written *misneachail;* which see.

Miostadh, aidh, *s. m.* Mischief.

Miotag, aig, *s. f.* A mitten or worsted glove; fright, fear. Cha ghabh thu fuathas na miotag, *thou shalt not be afraid.* —*Old Song.*

Miotagach, *a.* Gloved; like a glove or mitten; full of gloves or mittens.

Miothag, aig, *s. f.* A bite; a pinching.

Miothagaich, *v. a.* Bite; pinch.—*Shaw.*

Miothar, *a.* Sordid, mean, abject, little or narrow.

Miotharachd, *s. f.* Sordidness, meanness, narrowness.

Miothlachd, *s. f.* Contempt, disrespect; discontent, displeasure; distress.—*Stew. 2 K.*

Mio-thlachdmhor, *a.* Disagreeable, contemptible; displeasing; impersonable.

Mìr, mire, *s.* (*Ir. id.* *Gr.* μειρος, *part.* and μειρω, *to divide.*) A bit; a piece or fragment; a part or portion; a bit of bread. Mìr fearainn, *a piece of ground.* — *Stew. Gen.* *N. pl.* mìrean *and* mìreannan; *d. pl.* mìribh. Gearraidh tu 'e na mhìribh, *thou shalt cut him in pieces.*—*Stew. Ex.* Crioman mire, *a bit of bread;* na h-uile mìr, *every bit, every whit;* mìr mòr, *a mess composed of chopped collops and herb seeds.*

Mir, *v. n.* Flirt, play, sport; wont. *Pret. a.* mhir; *fut. aff.* miridh, *shall flirt.*

Mir, *s. f.* A top or summit.—*Shaw.*

Mìr-còrr, *s.* See Mìr-mòr.

MIRE, *s. f.* A mow of hay or corn.

MIRE, *s. f.* (*Ir. id.*) Play, sport, diversion, mirth; levity, giddiness, transport; madness. Ri mire ghòraich, *indulging in foolish mirth.—Macfar.* Air mhire, *in a transport, in an excess of mirth.* Cuir air mhire, *transport with joy.*

MIREADH, idh, *s. m.* A flirting, a wantoning; mirth, play, pastime. Dh'éirich iad gu mireadh, *they rose to play.—Stew. Ex.* Air mhireadh, *going to excess in mirth, transported with joy.*

MIREADH, (a), *pr. part.* of mir. Flirting, sporting, merry-making. A mireadh ri, *flirting with.*

MIREAG, *s. f.* (*from* mire.) Pastime, sport, frisking; a playful girl, a wanton girl. Spreidh ri mireig, *cattle sporting.—Old Poem.* Is tric rinn mi riut mireag, *often have I sported with you.—Turn.*

MIREAGACH, *a.* Playful, frisky, sportive, wanton. Gu mireagach, *playfully.* Suilean mireagach, *wanton eyes.—Stew. Is.*

MIREAGACHD, *s. f.* Playfulness, sportiveness, wantonness.

MIREAN, ein, *s. m.* Frolicsomeness. Gille mircin, *a whirligig.*

MÌREAN, *s. m.* (*dim.* of mìr.) A little piece; a little more.

MIREANACH, aich, *s. m.* (*Ir. id.*) A bridle-bit.—*Shaw.*

MIREANACH, *a.* Lively, merry; causing mirth. Fonn mireanach, *a lively strain.—Macint.*

MIREANACHD, *s. f.* Liveliness, merriness.

MÌREANN, inn, *s. m.* (*Ir. id.*) A portion, a share.—*N. pl.* mireannan.

MÌREANNACH, *a.* In pieces, in portions, in shares; in splinters.

MÌREANNAICH, *v. a.* Shatter; portion, share. *Pret. a.* mhìreannaich, *shattered; fut. aff.* mìreannaichidh, *shall shatter.*

MÌREANNAICHTE, *p. part.* of mireannaich. Shattered, splintered; portioned.

MÌREANNAN, *n. pl.* of mìr. Pieces.

MIRE-CHATHA, *s. f.* Battle-frenzy; extreme individual fury in battle. A sgathadh cheann le mire-chath, *hewing heads in the fury of battle.—Macdon.* Bithibh air mhire-chath, *rage ye for battle.—Stew. Jer.*

MIRE-CHUTHAICH, *s. f.* Madness, frenzy, a transport of madness, raging madness.

MIRE-REOTHAIRT, *s. f.* The fury of a spring-tide; a violent spring-tide.

MIRE-SHRUTH, *s. m.* A rapid stream; a boiling impetuous current.

MI-REUSONTA, *a.* (*Ir.* mi-reusunta.) Unreasonable, irrational. Mi-reusonta agus olc, *unreasonable and wicked.—Stew.* 1 *Thess.* Gu mi-reusonta, *unreasonably.*

MI-REUSONTACHD, *s. f.* Unreasonableness, unconscionableness.

MIR-GUAILNE, *s. f.* A shoulder-piece.—*Stew. Ex.*

MI-RIAGHAILT, *s. f.* (*Ir. id.*) Confusion, unruliness; irregularity, informality; riot. Ughdar na mi-riaghailt, *the author of confusion.—Stew.* 1 *Cor.* Maighstir na mi-riaghailt, *the lord of misrule.*

MI-RIAGHAILTEACH, *a.* (*Ir.* miriaghalta.) Irregular, informal; unruly, disorderly; untractable; without rule; eccentric. Ag imeachd gu mi-riaghailteach, *walking disorderly.—Stew.* 2 *Thess.*

MI-RIAGHAILTEACHD, *s. f.* Irregularity, informality; unruliness, disorderliness; untractableness.

MI-RIAGHLADAIREACHD, *s. f.* Misgovernment, mal-administration.

MI-RIAGHLADH, aidh, *s. m.* A mismanaging; mismanagement; mal-administration.

MI-RIASANTA, *a.* Unreasonable, irrational; unconscionable. Gu mi-riosanta, *unreasonably.*

MI-RIASANTACHD, *s. f.* Unreasonableness, irrationalness; unconscionableness.

MI-RIOGHACHD, *s. f.* Anarchy; republicanism.

MI-RIOGHAIL, *a.* Unkingly; not becoming royalty; disloyal.

MI-RIOGHALACHD, *s. f.* Disloyalty, republicanism.

† MIRLE, *s. f.* (*Ir. id.*) A ball; a globe.—*Shaw.*

MIR-MÒR, *s.* A mess composed of chopped collops mixed with marrow and herb-seeds.

Gaelic poetry records that this was the favourite *morçeau* of Fingal, and his heroic ally Goll Mac-Mhuirn, *Gaul, the son of Morni,* who always sat on Fingal's right hand, and received the *mìr-mòr* over and above the customary ratio of the band of Caledonian warriors.

MIRR, *s. f.* Myrrh.

MI-RÙN, -rùin, *s. m.* Malice, ill-will. Luchd mo mhi-rùin, *the people of my hatred; they who hate me.—Sm.* Luchd mi-ruin, *malicious people.*

MI-RUNACH, *a.* Malicious, spiteful. Seachainn a mhuinntir mhi-runach, *avoid malicious people.—Old didactic Poem.* Gu mi-runach, *maliciously.*

MIS. More frequently written *mios;* which see.

MISD, MISDE, *com.* and *sup.* of olc. Worse, worst. Is misd e sin, *he is the worse for that. Asp. form,* mhisde. Cha mhisde thu sin, *you are not the worse for that.*

MI-SDIÙIR, *v. a.* Misguide, mislead; steer in a wrong course. *Pret. a.* mhi-sdiùir, *misguide; fut. aff. a.* mi-sdiùiridh, *shall misguide.*

MI-SDIÙIREADAIREACHD, *s. f.* Misguiding; mis-steering.

MISE, *emphatic form* of mi, *pers. pron.* (*Ir.* mise. *Goth.* mis.) I, me, myself, I myself. Seinnidh mise, *I will sing;* am buail thu mise? *will you strike me?* mise agus thusa, *I and thou;* co rinn e? mise, *who did it? I did.*

MISEACH, ich, *s. m.* (*Ir. id.*) A year-old goat; a young kid. *N. pl.* misich, *kids.* Gabhair, misich is òisgean, *goats, kids, and ewes.—Mack.*

MISG, misge, *s. m.* (*Arab.* mesck. *Pers.* mesk, *drunk.*) Drunkenness, tipsiness. Air mhisg, *drunk.—Stew. Jer.*

MISGEACH, *a.* (*Ir. id.*) Drunken. Fear misgeach, *a drunken man.*

MISGEALACHD, *s. f.* Drunkenness, tipsiness.

MISGEAR, eir, *s. m.* A drunkard, a tippler. Am misgear agus an geòcair, *the drunkard and the glutton.—Stew. Pro.*

MI-SGEINM, *s. f.* Untidiness, slovenliness, tawdriness.

MI-SGEINMEIL, *a.* Untidy, slovenly, tawdry. Gu misgeinmeil, *untidily.*

MI-SGEUL, -sgeòil, *s.* A false report.—*Shaw.* Tog mi-sgeul, *raise a false report.*

MI-SGIOBALTA, *a.* (*Ir. id.*) Untidy, slovenly, sluttish. Gu mi-sgiobalta, *untidily.*

MI-SGIOBALTACHD, *s. f.* (*Ir. id.*) Untidiness, slovenliness, sluttishness.

MI-SGOINNE, *s. f.* Carelessness, inattention, indifference; blameableness.

MI-SGOINNEIL, *a.* Careless, inattentive, indifferent; causing indifference or disdain. Gu mi-sgoinneil, *carelessly.*

MI-SHAMH, *a.* Rough, rugged; hard.—*Shaw.*

MI-SHEADH, *s. m.* Heedlessness, carelessness, inattention, indifference; indolence; senselessness.

MI-SHEADHAIL, *a.* (mi-sheadh-amhuil.) Heedless, indifferent; indolent; inattentive; senseless, weak.

MI-SHEADHAR, *a.* Heedless, inattentive; senseless, weak.

MI-SHEALBH, *s. m.* A cross, a disappointment.

MI-SHEALBHAR, *a.* Unfortunate, unlucky; unpropitious, disastrous. Gu mi-shealbhar, *unluckily.*

MI-SHEAMHAS, ais, *s. m.* Bad luck, mishap.

MI-SHEAMHSAR, *a.* Unlucky, ominous

MI-SHEÒL, *v. a.* Mislead, misguide; misdirect. *Pret. a.* mhi-sheòl; *fut. aff. a.* mi-sheòlaidh.

MI-SHEÒLADH, aidh, *s. m.* A misleading, a misguiding, a misdirecting.

MI-SHEÒLTA, *a* Not shifty, not ingenious; not dexterous, inexpert. Gu mi-sheòlta, *inexpertly*

MI-SHEÒLTACHD, *s f* Inexpertness, want of dexterity.

MI-SHEUN, *s m* Bad luck, mishap —*Shaw.*

MI-SHIOBHAILT, MI-SHIOBHALTA, *a* Uncivil, rude, unpolite, impertinent

MI-SHIOBHAILTEACHD, *s f* Incivility, rudeness, impertinence

MI-SHOCAIR, *s f* Uneasiness; uncomfortableness

MI-SHOCRACH, *a* Uneasy, uncomfortable; unstaid, not firmly situated Gu mi-shocrach, *uncomfortably.*

MI-SHONA, *a* Unhappy; unblest; unfortunate. Gu mi-shona, *unhappily.*

MI-SHUAIMHNEACH, *a.* Restless, troubled, uncomfortable, in confusion; causing trouble or confusion.

MI-SHUAIMHNEACHD, *s f.* Restlessness, uncomfortableness; trouble; disquiet

MI-SHUAIMHNEAS, eis, *s m.* Restlessness, uncomfortableness, trouble, disquietude Dh' fhaicinn mi-shuaimhneis, *to see trouble.—Stew. Jer*

MI-SHUAIRCE, *a* Uncivil, churlish, ungenerous. Gu mi-shuairce, *uncivilly* Fear mi-shuairce, *a churlish fellow.*

MI-SHUAIRCEAS, eis, *s m* Churlishness; ungenerousness; incivility; illiberality.

MI-SHÙGHAR, MI-SHUGHMHOR, *a.* Sapless, pithless.

MI-SHUIM, *s. m* Heedlessness, inattentiveness, neglect, indifference. Cuir air mi-shuim, *neglect, regard with indifference*

MI-SHUIMEIL, *a.* Heedless, inattentive, indifferent. Gu mi-shuimeil, *heedlessly*

MI-SHÙRD, *s.* Indolence, want of industry.

MI-SHÙRDAIL, *a* Unindustrious, inactive; indolent.

MI-SHÙRDALACHD, *s f.* Want of industry; habitual inactivity or indolence.

MISIMEAN DEARG, *s* The bogmint

MISIOMAIRT, *s f.* Foul or unfair play.

MISLEAN, ein, *s m* (*Ir id*) A wild flower; a kind of mountain-grass.

MISLEANACH, *a.* (*Ir. id*) Grassy, abounding in mountain-grass, vegetative; springing, as vegetables Glacag misleanach, *a grassy dell —Macfar.*

MISNEACH, ich, *s f.* (*Ir id*) Courage, spirit, manliness Thuit am misneach, *their courage fell —Macint.* Do mhac-samhailt air misnich, *thy equal in courage —Macfar.* Glac misneach, *take courage*, gabh misneach, *take courage*, cha 'n 'eil a mhisneach agad, *you have not the courage.*

MISNEACHADH, aidh, *s. m* An encouraging or exhorting; abetting, encouragement

MISNEACHAIL, *a* (misneach-amhuil.) Courageous, spirited, manly. Misneachail treubhach, *courageous and heroic —Macint.* Gu misneachail, *courageously.*

MISNEACHAIR, *s m.* An exhorter, an encourager.

MISNEACHAS, ais, *s. m.* Courage.

MISNEACHD, *s. f* Courageousness, spiritedness, manliness; habitual courage or manliness

MISNEIL, *a* Courageous, spirited, manly. Gu misneil, *courageously.*

MISNICH, *v. a.* and *n.* (*Ir.* misnigh.) Encourage; inspirit; enliven; become spirited; grow enlivened; refresh, cherish.

MISTE. See MISD or MISDE.

MI-STEIGHEALACHD, *s. f.* Unsteadiness; a tottering condition.

MI-STEIGHEIL, *a.* Unsteady, wavering; not having a good foundation.

MISTEAR, eir, *s m.* A cunning fellow; a deep designing fellow; an under-dealer.

MI-STIÙIR, *v a.* Mislead, misguide; steer in a wrong course *Pret. a.* mhi-stiùir, *misled*, *fut. aff. a.* mi-stiùiridh.

MI-STIÙIREADAIR, *s. m.* A misleader, a misguider; a bad steersman.

MI-STIÙRACH, *a.* Misleading, misguiding, mis-steering.

MI-STIÙRADH, aidh, *s. m.* (*Ir. id*) A misleading, a misguiding; bad steering; mismanagement, bad government.

MI-STIÙRANNAN, *s. pl.* Misdeeds; bad intentions; bad courses.

MI-STUAMA, *a.* Unchaste, immodest, immoderate, intemperate. Gu mi-stuama, *immodestly.*

MI-STUAMACHD, *s. f* Unchastity, immodesty; immoderateness, intemperance.

MITEAG, eig, *s. f* A mitten or worsted glove; a glove. Written also *meatag* or *miotag*

MITEAGACH, *a.* Like a mitten or glove; having mittens or gloves. More commonly written *meatagach* or *miotagach.*

MI-THABHACHD, *s f.* Weakness; silliness; inefficiency.

MI-THÀBHACHDACH, *a* Weak, unsubstantial, feeble; mean; uncomely Gu mi-thabhachdach, *weakly, ineffective.*

MI-THABHACHDAS, ais, *s. m.* Habitual silliness; habitual weakness, feebleness; meanness; uncomeliness; inefficiency.

MI-THAICEIL, *a.* Not stout; feeble, infirm; unable to give support; unsubstantial.

MI-THAICEILACHD, *s. f* Feebleness, infirmness, unsubstantialness

MI-THAING, *s f.* Lack of thanks; disinclination to thank; thanklessness

MI-THAINGEALACHD, *s f* Ingratitude, unthankfulness.

MI-THAINGEIL, *a* Ungrateful, unthankful, thankless; not easily satisfied or pleased Daoine mi-thaingeil, *unthankful men —Stew Tim.* Gu mi-thaingeil, *unthankfully.*

MI-THAITINN, *v* Dissatisfy, displease, offend. *Pret. a.* mhi-thaitinn, *displeased.* Mhi-thaitinn an radh, *the saying displeased —Stew Sam* *Fut. aff* mi-thaitnidh.

MI-THAITNEACH, *a* Unsatisfactory, displeasing, offensive; disagreeable; not giving satisfaction. Gu mi-thaitneach, *unsatisfactorily.*

MI-THAITNICH, *v.* Dissatisfy, displease, offend. *Pret. a.* mhi-thaitnich, *fut aff* mi-thaitnichidh

MI-THAPACHD, *s f.* Want of cleverness, inactivity, inexpertness, unalertness, slowness

MI-THAPADH, aidh, *s m.* Sluggishness, inactivity, *also*, a mishap

MI-THAPAIDH, *a* Not clever; not quick; sluggish, dull, inactive.

MI-THARBHACH, *a* Unprofitable; unsubstantial; without avail, fruitless; unfruitful, unproductive. Tha iad uile mi-tharbhach, *they are all unprofitable.—Stew. Rom.* Gu mi-tharbhach, *unproductively.*

MI-THARBHACHD, *s f.* Unprofitableness; unfruitfulness, unproductiveness

MITHEAN, *s. pl.* The vulgar peasantry. *D. pl.* mithibh.

MITHEAR, *a* Weak, crazy; infirm. Gu mithear, *crazily.*

MI-THEISD, *s. f.* (*Ir id*) Calumny.

MITHICH, *a.* Timous, opportune; *also*, time, fit season, due season. Is mithich 'iarruidh, *it is time to seek him.—Stew. Hos.* Is mithich tearnadh, *it is time to descend.—Macint.* Is mithich falbh, *it is time to be off;* rug i leanabh roimh 'n mhithich, *she was delivered before the time.*

MI-THLACHD, *s. f.* Dissatisfaction.—*Macint.* Discontentment; disgust; discord. Smachd air luchd mi-thlachd, *sway over the discontented.—Old Song.*

MI-THLACHDMHOR, *a.* Unhandsome; unpleasant; disgusting; not giving satisfaction. *Com.* and *sup.* mi-thlachdmhoire.

MITHLEANACH, *a.* Mischievous.

MI-THLUSAIL, MI-THLUSAR, *a.* Unkind; harsh; cruel; void of feeling or of affection.

MI-THLUSARACHD, *s. f.* Unkindness, harshness; cruelty.—*Shaw.*

MI-THOGARACH, *a.* Uninclined; averse; unwilling; backwark. Gu mi-thogarach, *unwillingly.*

MI-THOILE, *s f.* Want of will, want of inclination; unwillingness, backwardness.

MI-THOILEACH, *a.* Unwilling; dissatisfied, displeased, discontented. Gu mi-thoileach, *unwillingly.*

MI-THOILEACHADH, aidh, *s. m.* A displeasing, a dissatisfying; dissatisfaction.

MI-THOILICH, *v. a.* Displease, dissatisfy. *Pret a.* mhithoilich; *fut. aff. a.* mi-thoilichidh, *shall displease.*

MI-THOILICHTE, *p. part.* Displeased, dissatisfied, discontented.

MI-THRÒCAIR, *s. f.* Inclemency; cruelty.

MI-THRÒCAIREACH, *a.* Merciless, cruel. Gu mi-thròcaireach, *cruelly.*

MI-THRUACANTA, *a.* Uncompassionate, unfeeling.

MI-THRUACANTAS, ais, *s. m.* Uncompassionateness, want of feeling.

MI-THUIG, *v a.* Misunderstand, misapprehend, misconceive. *Pret. a.* mi-thuig, *misunderstood, fut. aff. a* mi-thuigidh, *shall misunderstand.*

MI-THUIGSE, *s. f.* Want of understanding, want of comprehension, senselessness.

MI-THUIGSEACH, *a.* Senseless, stupid, incapable of comprehending, unintelligent.

MI-THUIGSINN, *s. f.* A misconceiving or misapprehending; a misconception, a misunderstanding.

MITHUR, *a.* See MIÙGHAR or MIÙTHAR.

MI-UAIBHREACH, *a.* Not proud; condescending. Gu mi-uaibhreach, *condescendingly.*

MI-UAIGNEACH, *a.* Not solitary; not secret. Gu mi-uaigneach, *publicly.*

MI-UAILLE, *s. f.* Want of pride; humility; condescension; ignobleness.

MI-UALLACH, *a.* Not proud; humble, condescending.

MI-UASAL, *a.* Ignoble: ungenteel; unassertive of rank, not proud; condescending.

MIÙG, miùig, *s m.* Whey. Deoch mhiùig, *a drink of whey.*

MIÙGHAIREACHD, *s. f.* Penuriousness, niggardliness, meanness.

MIÙGHAR, *a.* Penurious; niggardly. Written also *miùthar.*

MI-ÙMHAL, *a.* Disobedient; unsubmissive, insubordinate; rebellious.

MI-ÙMHLACHD, *s. f.* Disobedience; unsubmissiveness; insubordination.

MIÙRAN, ain, *s. m.* A carrot. Miùran geal, *a parsnip.*

MIÙRANACH, *a.* Abounding in carrots or parsnips; like a carrot or parsnip.

MI-URRAM, aim, *s. m.* Dishonour, disrespect; disgrace.

MI-URRAMACH, *a.* Dishonouring, disrespecting; dishonourable, disrespectful.

MI-URRAMAICH, *v. a.* Dishonour, disrespect; disgrace, degrade. *Pret. a.* mhi-urramaich.

MIÙTHAIREACHD, *s f.* Penuriousness, niggardliness, meanness.

MIÙTHAR, *a* Penurious; mean. *Com.* and *sup.* miuthaire. Gu miùthar, *penuriously.*

MNA, *gen. sing* of bean. (*Ir id.*) Of a wife, of a woman. Gniomh mna-glùine, *the office of a midwife.—Stew. Ex.* Mna-bainnse, *of a bride;* guth mna-bainnse, *a bride's voice.—Stew Rev.*

MNAI, *n pl* of bean. Wives, women. Na mnai-glùine, *the midwives.—Stew. Ex.* Mnai chiùil, *women singers.—Stew. Ecc.*

MNAI'EALACHD, *s.* Womanliness, womanishness, effeminacy, modesty.

MNAOI, *d sing* of bean. To a woman, to a wife. Air do bhreth le mnaoi, *born of a woman.—Sm.* Thug e dha a nighean 'na mnaoi, *he gave him his daughter to wife.—Stew Gen.* Mar mhnaoi, *as a wife, to wife.—Id.*

MNATHAIBH, *d pl.* of bean. To wives, to women. See BEAN.

MNATHAIL, *a.* (mna-amhuil.) Womanly, womanish; modest; effeminate. Gu mnathail, *modestly.*

MNATHAILEACHD, *s. f.* Womanliness, modesty; womanishness, effeminacy.

MNATHAN, *n. pl.* of bean. Wives, women.

† MO, MODH, MOGH, *s. m.* (*Lat.* homo.) A man.—*Shaw.*

MO, *poss pron.* My, mine.
Ir. id. Arm ma. *Fr* ma. *It.* mio. *Scotch*, ma.

MÒ, *com* and *sup.* of mòr. (*Eng* † mo *and* † moe. *Sax*, ma.) Greater, greatest; taller, tallest. Ni 's mò na mise, *taller or greater than I, any more than me*, is e is mò dhibh uile, *he is the tallest of you all*, ni 's mò, *any more*, cha chuimhnich mi ni 's mò, *I shall remember no more.—Stew Heb.* Ni 's mò agus ni 's mò, *greater and greater;* ni bu mhò 's ni bu mhò, *greater and greater.—Stew. Jonah.* Cia 's mò na sin? *how much more than that?—Stew. Rom.* Cha mhò orm e na srabh, *I value him not a straw.*

MOB, *s f.* A mob; a tumult; a mop, a tuft.

MOBACH, *a.* Moppy, shaggy; tufty.

MOBAG, aig, *s f.* A young girl with moppy hair.

MOBAINN, *v a.* Tug, handle roughly. *Pret. a* mhobainn.

MOBAINN, *s f.* A tugging; a rough handling. Fhuair e' mhobainn, *he got himself roughly handled.*

MOCH, *a.* (*Ir id.*) Early, betimes, soon. Drùchd moch, *early dew.—Orr.* Moch an dé, *yesterday morning;* moch am màireach, *to-morrow morning*, moch an iar-thrath, *the morning after next*, o mhoch gu dubh, *from morning till night*, moch air bhò 'n dé, *the morning before last, two mornings ago.* Gu moch, *early;* gu moch sa mhadainn, *early in the morning;* anns a mhoch, *in early morning.* *Com.* and *sup.* moiche. In some parts of the Highlands *moch* is pronounced *much.*

MOCH-ABACHD, *s f.* Early ripeness; prematurity.

MOCH-ABAICH, *a.* Soon ripe; premature, precocious.

† MOCHD, *s. f.* (*Ir. id.*) Promotion, advancement.

MOCH-EIRIDH, *a.* Rising early; accustomed to rise early; *also, substantively*, early rising. Bi subhach, sùgradh, moch-eiridh, *be cheerful, temperate, and an early riser.—A Druidical Precept.* Rinn iad moch-eiridh, *they rose early.—Stew.* 1 *Sam.*

MO CHREACH! MO CHREACHADH! *interj.* Woe's me! alas!

MOCH-GHLAODH, *s. m.* An early cry. Chual na creagan a mhoch-ghlaodh, *the rocks heard his early cry.*—*Oss.*

MOCH-THRATH, *s.* (*Ir. id*) Morning, dawn. *Asp. form*, mhoch-thrath. Anns a mhoch-thrath, *early in the morning.*—*Stew. Song Sol.*

MÒD, mòid, *s.* (*Sax.* mote *and* mota. *Swed.* mote.) A court or meeting; a convention; a petty court; a baron baillie court; a court at which presides the agent of landed proprietors, to adjust differences among tenants, and to take cognizance of all abuses of any portion of his employer's property. *N. pl.* mòdan.

MÒDACH, *a.* (*from* mòd) Having meetings or courts; of, or belonging to, a court, fond of meetings.

† MODH, *s. m.* (*Ir. id*) A man; the male of any creature; a servant; work.

MODH, *s. m.* Manner; fashion; mode or method; good breeding. Air mhodh so, *after this manner.*—*Stew. Matt.* Air mhodh àraidh, *in a particular way.* *N. pl.* modhan *and* modhannan.
Ir. id. *Lat.* mod-us. *Fr.* mode. *Eng.* mode.

MODHAIL, *a.*, modh-amhuil (*Ir.* modh-amhail) Mannerly, moral, well-bred, courteous; delicate, mild; fashionable, modish. Dh' fhàs thu modhail, nàrach, *thou wert born mannerly and modest.*—*Old Song.*

MODHALACHD, *s. f.* (*Ir.* modhalacht) Mannerliness, good breeding; delicateness; courteousness; mildness.

MODHALAN, ain, *s. m.* (*Ir. id*) Red rattle.

† DODHAN, ain, *s. m.* (*Ir. id*) Childbirth; travail.

MODHANACH, *a.* (*Ir. id*) Moral, ceremonial; customary; well-principled. *Com.* and *sup.* modhanaiche.

MODHANAICHE, *com.* and *sup.* of modhanach.

MODHANAIL, *a.* (*from* modh.) Ethical, moral, ceremonial.

MODHANNAN, *n. pl.* of modh. Manners, principles; ethics; means, modes, ceremonies.

MODHAR, *a.* Quiet, peaceful, mild; mannerly, precise. Gleannan modhar, *a peaceful valley.*—*Oss. Tem.* *Com.* and *sup.* modhaire.

† MODH-DHAMH, -dhaimh, *s. m.* A plough-ox.—*Shaw.* *N. pl.* modh-dhaimh.

† MODH-LANN, -lainn, *s. m.* A tabernacle, a tent.

† MODH-MHARGADH, aidh, *s. m.* A slave-market.

MODH-SIOLAICH, *s. m.* A remnant of seed, a remnant of seed left to produce more.

MÒG, mòig, *s.* A paw; a broad clumsy foot; a clumsy hand. *N. pl.* mògan. Written also *màg*, which see.

MÒGACH, *a.* Having paws; having large paws, clumsy-footed; clumsy-handed, like a paw. *Com.* and *sup.* mògaiche.

MÒGACH, *a.* Shaggy, hairy, rough; *also*, a shaggy fellow, a shaggy creature. Mògach ladhrach, *shaggy and long-toed.*—*Macdon.* *Com.* and *sup.* mògaiche.

MÒGAICHE, *com.* and *sup.* of mògach; which see.

MOGAICHE, *com.* and *sup.* of mogach.

MOGAICHE, *s. f.* Shagginess, hairiness, roughness.

MOGAIN, *gen. sing.* and *n. pl.* of mogan.

MOGAL, ail, *s. m.* (*Ir. id*) A husk, a shell, as of fruit; a cluster, as of nuts; a branch; the skin of a boiled unpeeled potato; a globe. *N. pl.* mogalan; *d. pl.* mogalaibh. Cnothan as na mogalaibh, *nuts out of the husks.*—*Macfar.* Mogal na sùl, *the apple of the eye*, *the eyelid.*

MOGALACH, *a.* (*Ir.* magallach) Husky; husked; shelled, as nuts; like net-work; branchy; plenteous.

MOGAN, ain, *s. m.* (*Scotch*, mogan) An old hose or stocking worn without the foot, *hoggars*; boot-hose; a sock; a long sleeve for the arms, wrought like stockings; a defect in a thread. *N. pl.* mogain.

† MOGAN, ain, *s. m.* (*Ir. id*) A young hero.—*Shaw.*

MOGHAR, *a.* Soft, gentle, mild, quiet; mannerly; precise. Written also *modhar*.

MOGHNA, *s. m.* (*Ir. id*) A salmon.—*Shaw.*

MOGH-SAINE, *s. m.* (*Ir. id*) Slavery.

MOGH-SANTACHD, *s. f.* Slavery.

MOGHUL, uil, *s. m.* See MOGAL.

MOGLAIDH, *a.* (*Ir. id*) Soft.—*Shaw.*

MOGULACH, *a.* See MOGALACH.

MOIBEAL, eil, *s. m.* A broom, a brush or besom, a mop. *N. pl.* moibealan.

MOIBEAN, ein, *s. m.* A tuft; a mop. *D. pl.* moibeinibh. Canach na mhoibeiniba cabin, *mountain cotton in downy tufts.*—*Macdon.*

MOIBEANACH, *a.* In tufts, moppy.

MOIBEANAICH, *v. a.* Rub with a mop. *Pret. a.* mhoibeanaich; *fut. aff. a.* moibeanaichidh.

MOIBLEACH, *a.* Gnawing, chewing; half chewing, nibbling.

MOIBLEADH, idh, *s. m.* A gnawing, a chewing, a nibbling.

MOICHE, *com.* and *sup.* of moch, which see.

MOICHE, *s. f.* (*Ir. id*) Earliness, dawn.

MOICHEAD, eid, *s. m.* (*Ir. id*) Earliness. A dol am moichead, *growing earlier.*

MÒID, *v. a.* Vow, swear, devote. *Pret. a.* mhòid; *fut. aff. a.* mòididh.

MÒID, mòide, *s.* (*Ir. id*) A vow. Airson mòide, *for a vow.*—*Stew. Lev. ref.* *N. pl.* mòidean. Iocam mo mhòidean, *I will perform my vows.*—*Sm.* Written also *bòid*.

MÒID, *gen. sing.* of mòd.

MÒID, *s. f.* Height, size, bulk; dimensions. B' amhuil is crann giumhais a mhòid, *his height was like a pine.*—*Old Poem.* Mòid meamnaidh, *the height of courage.*

MÒIDE, *com.* and *sup.* of mòr. (*Ir. id.*) Greater, more. Is moide a ghlaodh e, *the more he cried.*

MÒIDEACH, *a.* (*Ir. id*) Vowing, votive, *also, substantively*, a votary. *N. pl.* mòidich, *votaries.*

MÒIDEACHADH, aidh, *s. m.* A vowing; a swearing.

MÒIDEADH, idh, *s. m.* (*Ir. id*) Vowing; devotion.

MOIDHEACH, moidhche, *s. m.* See MAIGHEACH.

MÒIDICH, *v. a.* Vow, swear; devote. *Pret. a.* mhòidich, *vowed*, *fut. aff. a.* mòidichidh, *shall vow*, *fut. pass.* mòidichear. Written also *bòidich*.

MÒIDICHTE, *p. part.* of mòidich. Vowed; devoted.

MÒIDTE, *p. part.* of mòid.

MÒIGEAN, ein, *s. m.* A squat, a plump person.

MÒIGEANACH, *a.* Squat, plump, fat.

MOIGH. More frequently written *muigh*, which see.

MOIGHEANAR, *a.* Happy; festive.—*Shaw.*

MOIGHRE, *a.* Stout, active, bouncing, handsome; *also*, a bouncing female.

MOIL, *s. f.* Hair matted together.—*Macfar. Voc.* A kind of black worm, a heap cast up.—*Shaw.*
Lat. moles, *a heap.* *Ir.* moil.

MOILEADAIR, *s. m.* A molester.

MÒILEAN, ein, *s. m.* (*Ir. id*) A little plump child, a diminutive rotund figure, a little lump; a bulb.

MÒILEANACH, aich, *s. m.* A little plump child; a diminutive rotund person, a little lump, a bulb.

MOILEANACH, *a.* Diminutive in person; plump and little; bulby.

MOILLE, *s. f.* (*Ir. id*) Delay; hinderance, stay, stoppage.

Na dean moille, *do not delay.—Stew. Gen.* Na cuiribh moille orm, *do not hinder me. Ir. id.*

Moilleach, *a.* Dilatory, tardy; *also*, pampering.

Moilt, *gen. sing.* and *n. pl.* of molt. More frequently written *mult.*

Moilteag, eig, *s f.* A comely little girl; a lusty little girl, *also*, lusty, low in stature.

Moim, *s f.* See **Maoim**.

Mòine, *s f.* (*W.* mawn. *Ir.* mòine.) Moss, peat; peats; a bog. Ris a mhòine, *making peats*, cruach mhòine, *a peat-stack;* poll mòine, *a peat-moss;* fòid mhòin, *a peat.*

Moineagag, aig, *s f.* (*Ir. id*) A pea or bean; a pod. *N. pl.* mioneagagan. Written also *meilligeag*

Moineasach, *a.* Tardy, dilatory; sedate, mild; dull, inactive. *Com.* and *sup.* moineasaiche.

Moineasachd, *s f.* Tardiness; dilatoriness; dulness; inactivity; sedateness; mildness.

Moin-fheur, -fheoir, *s. m.* Mountain grass; coarse meadow-grass, *rarely*, a meadow.

Moingeasach, *a.* See **Moineasach**.

† **Moingreult**, *s. f* A comet.—*Shaw.*

Moinig, *a.* Vain; boasting; trusting to.

Moinse, *s f.* (*Ir id*) A great pit; a peat-moss. *N. pl.* moinsean.

Moinseach, *a.* Abounding in large pits

Mòinteach, ich, *s f.* (*from* mòine) Moss; mossy ground; a moor; a peat-moss Mòinteach liath, *grey moss —Fingalian Poem.* A siubhal mòintich, *traversing the moors, traversing the moss.—Macint.* Amadan mòintich, *a dotterel.*

Mòinteachail, *a.* Mossy, moorish; marshy; fenny.

Mointidh, *a.* Moorish.

Moipeal. See **Moibeal**.

Moipean, ein, *s m* See **Moibean**.

Mòir, *inflection* of mòr; which see

Moirb, *s f.* (*Ir id*) An ant, a pismire, or emmet *N. pl.* moirbean.

Moircheart, cirt, *s m* (*Ir. id*) Justice; mercy.

Moire, *s f.* The Virgin Mary. Air Moire! *by St Mary!* Moire tha! *by St. Mary it is!* Moire cha 'n 'eil! *no, by St. Mary!*

The Gael scarcely utter a sentence without some such appeal to St. Mary.

Moireag, eig, *s. f.* A small shell. *N pl.* moireagan

Moireal, eil, *s f.* A borer, a wimble —*Macd* and *Shaw.* Written also *boireal.*

Moirealach, *a* Like a wimble; boring like a wimble.

Moireamas, *a provincial corruption of* Moire, *the Virgin Mary;* or it may be a mispronunciation of *moramas*, which is *m'oram*, or more correctly *m'urram*, or *air m'urram*, on my honour

Moir'ear, eir, *s m.* See **Moir-fhear**.

Moir'earachd, *s f* See **Moir-fhearachd**.

Mòireas, eis, *s. m* (*from* mòr) Haughtiness; pride, *also*, epilepsy.

Moireasach, *a.* Haughty; epileptic.

Moireasadh, aidh, *s m* The falling sickness

Moir-fhear, -fhir, *s. m.* An earl, a lord, a noble. Fhreagair moir-fhear, *a lord answered —Stew 2 K ref N. pl.* moir-fhearan.

Moir-fhearachd, *s f.* A lordship, an earldom

Moirneas, eis, *s. m.* A stream; great streams of water Mar mhoirneis do theine teinntich, *like a stream of smelted metal.—Old Poem.*

Moirneasach, *a.* (*Ir. id.*) Streamy, streaming.

Moirt, *s. f.* (*Ir. id.*) Dregs, lees —*Shaw.*

Moirteach, *a* Dirty; having dregs.

Moirteal, eil, *s m* (*Ir. id.*) A rafter, mortar; plaster; a cripple.

Moirtear, eir, *s. m* (*Ir id.*) A mortar. *N. pl.* moirtearan.

Moirteis, *s. f.* (*Ir. id*) A mortise; a tenon —*Shaw.*

† **Mois**, *s* (*Ir id Lat.* mos) A custom; a manner. Mois-leabhar, *a book on ethics.—Shaw.*

Moiseach, *a.* (*Ir id*) Snouty, sullen, surly.

Moisean, ein, *s. m.* A dirty fellow; a low rascally fellow. Written also *muisean.*

Moiseanach, *a.* Dirty; mean; rascally. Written also *muiseanach.*

Moit, *s. f* (*Ir. id.*) Shiness; sulkiness; pettishness; nicety; a short neck cresting up. Goic moit, *a cocking up of the head with a short neck —Macdon.* Bean gun mhoit, *a wife without sulkiness —Macfar.*

Moitealach, *a.* (*Ir id*) Shy, sulky; pettish, prudish.

Moitealachd. *s f* Shiness, sulkiness; pettishness; prudery; nicety.

Moiteil, *a* Shy, sulky; pettish, nice Maighdeann mhoiteil, *a sulky maid, a prude.—Old Song.*

Mol, *v a* (*Ir. id Corn. W* mawl) Praise; extol, recommend *Pret a.* mhol, *praised*, *fut aff. a* molaidh, *shall praise* Molaibh e, *praise him.—Sm.* Molam dhuibh, *I recommend to you —Stew Rom. ref.* Mholainn duit bhi falbh, *I would recommend to you to be going*, mholainn sin duit, *I would recommend that to you*, *I would advise you to that*

Mol, *s* (*Ir. id Gr.* μωλος and μωλος, *a battle*) A gathering; an assembly; a number, a beam, a heap.

† **Mol**, *a.* (*Ir. id.*) Loud, clamorous.—*Shaw.*

Molach, *a.* Rough, hairy; stormy. *Asp. form*, mholach. Cas mholach Bhràin, *the rough leg of Bran —Oss. Tem* Mar fhalluinn mholaich, *like a hairy garment —Stew. Gen* A mhuir mholach, *the stormy sea.—Oss. Com.* and *sup* molaiche

Molachan, ain, *s m.* (*from* molach.) A tuft of hair; a hairy place, a slough or bog; *also*, a vessel.

Moladh, aidh, *s. m* (*Ir. id. Pers. Arab.* moalakat, *in praise.*) A praising or extolling; praise, applause; recommendation. Moladh na h-ainnir, *the virgin's praise —Oss. Com* Cha dean mi tuille molaidh ort, *I shall not speak more in thy praise.—Macfar* Tha e air a dheagh mholadh, *he is well praised*

Molam, 1 *sing imper.* of mol. Let me praise, *also, for* molaidh mi, *I will praise* See **Mol**

Molan. See **Mulan**

Molanach. See **Mulanach**.

Molar, *fut pass* of mol; which see

Mo leon! *interj.* Woe's me! alas!

Moll, muill, *s. m.* (*Ir. id*) Chaff, dust, refuse, a station, a frame. Mar mholl ro ghaoith, *like chaff before the wind. —Sm.* Leabadh mhuill, *a chaff bed.*

Mollachd, *s. f* A curse. More frequently written *mallachd;* which see

Mollar, *i. e* **Mollmhor**, *a.* Abounding in chaff; like chaff.

Molltair, *s. f.* (*Ir. id*) A frame or mould for casting iron, or any substance in a molten state, a plasm. *N pl* molltairean

Moltair, *s f* (*Forensic Lat.* multura, *a fine*) Mill dues; a miller's toll, moulter Molltair ri phàigh, *moulter to pay —Old Song*

Mol-mhuilinn, *s. m.* The beam which turns round in a mill, and sets the whole in motion by means of the wheels thereto affixed.

Mol-olla, *s. m.* A ball of wool.—*Shaw.*

† Molrach, aich, *s. m.* (*Ir. id.*) A giant.

Molt, moilt, *s.* See Mult.

Molta, *p. part.* of mol. (*Ir. id.*) Praised, extolled.

Moltach, *a.* Praiseworthy, laudable, ready to praise.

Moltainneach, *a.* Panegyrical.

Moltair. See Molltair.

Moluach, aich, *s. m.* (*Ir. id.*) A marsh.

Momhar, Momharach, *a.* Stately, noble, pompous.

Mo'n. See Mu'n.

† Mon, moin, *s. m.* A truck.—*Shaw.*

Mona-bhuachaill, *s. m.* An allan hawk; a cormorant. Written also *muna-bhuachaill.*

Monach, *a.*, *from* mon. (*Ir. id.*) Wily.

Monach, *a.* Hilly, mountainous; moory.

Monachan, *s. pl.* Hills, mountains; moors.

Monadail, *a.* Hilly, mountainous; moory.

† Monadh, aidh, *s. m.* (*Ir. id. Fr.* monnoie.) Money.—*Shaw.*

Monadh, aidh, *s. m.* A hill, a mountain; a moor; an extensive common. Air feadh mhonaidh, *through the moor;* sa mhonadh, *in the hill;* mullach a mhonaidh, *the highest part of the moor.*

Heb. hhmin, *high.* *Jap.* mine. *Chin.* mon, *a summit.* *Chald.* manos, *a hill.* *Ir. Corn.* monadh. *W.* mynydh. *Lat.* mons.

Monaghair, *s. f.* A murmuring noise.

Monaidh, *gen. sing.* of monadh.

Monair, *gen. sing.* of monar.

Mo nàire! *interj.* Fie! for shame! Mo nàire ort! *fie upon you!* Mo nàire ort féin! *fie upon you!* Mo naire 's mo mhasladh! *O for shame!*

Monais, *s. f.* Slowness, dulness; sedateness.

Monaiseach, *a.* (*Ir. id.*) Slow, dilatory; dull; gentle, sedate. *Com.* and *sup.* monaisiche.

Monaiseachd, *s. f.* Slowness; dulness; gentleness; sedateness.

Monaistir, *s. f.* (*Ir. id. Lat.* monaster-ium.) A monastery. —*Shaw.*

Monar, air, *s. m.* (*Ir. id.*) A diminutive person or thing; a purling noise; a murmur; *rarely,* work.

Monaran, ain, *s. m.* (*from* monadh.) A species of mountain berry; a dogberry.—*O'Reilly.*

Monasg, aisg, *s. f.* (*Ir. id.*) Empty chaff; light dross; useless refuse.

Mong. See Muing.

Mongach, *a.* Fiery, red.

Mongair, *s. m.* A shaver, a clipper.

Mongach-mhear, *s.* Hemlock.—*Macd.*

Monlach, *a.* Hairy, rough, shaggy; brushy.

Monmhor, oir, *s. m.* (*Ir.* monmhar.) A murmur; uproar; complaint; grumbling; detraction. Gun mhonmhor, *without a murmur.*—*Stew. Phil.*

Monmhorach, *a.* Murmuring; noisy; grumbling; complaining.

Mo nuar! *interj.* (*Ir. id.*) Alas! alackaday! woe is the day!

Mop, moip, *s. m.* A mob; confusion; tumult; a mop, a tuft. Written also *mob.*

Mopach, *a.* Moppy; tumultuous; in mops or tufts; disordered, as hair.

Mopag, aig, *s. f.* A girl with disordered or uncombed hair.

Mòr, *a.* Great; noble, mighty; high in stature; large; corpulent; big, bulky; heavy; wide. An sluagh mòr, *the great, the nobility;* mòr-uisge a taomadh, *a great torrent pouring.*—*Oss. Com.* Tha truaighe an duine mòr air, *the trouble of man is heavy upon him.*—*Stew. Ecc.* 'G a sgaoileadh mòr, *spreading it wide.*—*Oss. Tem.* Tha mòr ort a dheanamh, *it is hard for thee to do it; you are not likely to do it;* eadar bheag is mhòr, *between great and small;* cha mhòr nach do thuit mi, *I had almost fallen;* tha iad mòr aig cheile, *they are great chums.* *Com.* and *sup.* mò. Duine mòr, *a great man; Corn.* dean maur; *Arm.* den maur; *W.* dyn mawr.

Corn. Arm. maur. *W.* mawr. *Ir.* mor. *Germ.* mor, *great.* *Eng.* more. *Hind.* mor, *a king.* *Syr.* mar, *a lord.* *Turk. Arab.* emir, *a prince.* *Pers.* mir, *a lord.* *Tar.* mir, *a prince.*

Mòrachd, *s. f.* Greatness; majesty; highness; excellency. Do mhòrachd rioghail, *your royal highness.*

Mòradh, aidh, *s. m.* (*Ir. id.*) Augmentation.

Mòraich, *v. a.*, *from* mòr. (*Ir.* moraigh.) Exalt, dignify, ennoble; magnify, enlarge. *Pret. a.* mhòraich, *exalted; fut. aff. a.* mòraichidh; *fut. pass.* mòraichear. Mòraichear t-ainm, *thy name shall be exalted.*—*Stew. Sam.*

Mòraichte, *p. part.* of mòraich.

Mòr-aigeantach, *a.* Magnanimous; high-minded; ambitious.

Mòr-aigeantachd, *s. f.* Magnanimousness; high-mindedness; ambitiousness.

Mòr-aigne, *s. f.* Magnanimity; ambition.

Mòrail, *a.* Majestic; great; magnificent; *substantively,* a triumph.

Morair, *s. m.* A lord. More properly *mor' ear,* or *mòr-fhear.*

Moraireachd, *s. f.* A lordship; an earldom.

Mòralach, *a.* (*Ir. id.*) Magnificent; majestic; proud; pompous; vain-glorious; powerful.

Mòralachd, *s. f.* (*Ir. id.*) Magnificence; greatness; majesty; excellence. Mòralachd rioghail, *royal majesty.* —*Stew. Chr.* Cainnt na mòralachd, *excellent speech.*—*Stew. Pro.* Mòralachd na shùil, *majesty in his aspect.*—*Mac Lach.*

Moralta, *a.* (*Ir. id.*) Moral.—*Shaw.*

Moraltachd, *s. f.* (*Ir. id.*) Morality.—*Shaw.*

Moram, *a corruption of* air m'urram. On my word, on my honour.

Moramas, *a corruption of* moram; which see.

Mòran, ain, *s.* and *a.* (*Ir. id.*) Many, much; a great number or quantity; a multitude; meadow-grass. Mòran spreidh, *much cattle.*—*Stew. Gen.* Air fàs na mhòran, *increased into a multitude.*—*Id.*

Mòr-aoibhneas, eis, *s. m.* (*Ir. id.*) Great joy.

Moraonach, aich, *s. m.* (*Ir. id.*) A great assembly; a market-place; a great heath or moor.

Mòr-bhaile, *s. m.* A great city, a metropolis. *N. pl.* mòr-bhailtean; *d. pl.* mòr-bhailtibh. Anns na mòr-bhailtibh, *in the great cities.*—*Stew. Gen.*

Mòr-bhuadhach, *a.* Heroic; conquering.

Mor-bhuaidh, *s. f.* Heroism; bravery; an heroic achievement. Fhir nam mòr-bhuadh! *thou conquering hero!*—*Ull.*

† Morc, *s. f.* A sow, a hog; *also,* great, huge.

Morcaich, *v. a.* and *n.* Corrupt, rot. *Pret.* mhorcaich, *corrupted; fut. aff.* morcaichidh.

Morcas, ais, *s. m.* Rottenness, corruption.

Morchlais, *s. f.* Magnificence.

Mòr-choluinneach, *a.* Corpulent; bulky.

Morchoinnde, *s. f.* A fleet.—*Shaw.*

Mòr-choinneal, -choinnle, *s. f.* (*Ir. id.*) A flambeau or torch.

Mòr-chridhe, *s. f.* A great heart; a generous heart; a brave heart; a high or noble mind.

Mòr-chridheach, *a.* (*Ir.* mor-chroidheach.) Great-hearted; generous; magnanimous.

Mòr-chuairt, *s. f.* A grand tour; a justiciary circuit. A deanamh mòr-chuairt na h-Eorpa, *making the great tour of Europe.*

Mòr-chùis, *s. f.* (*Ir. id.*) Pomp; grandeur; state; magnificence; pride; glory; exploit. Crionaidh do mhòr-chuis, *thy grandeur shall fade.—Oss. Trath.* Gun till thu le mòr-chuis, *that you may return with glory.—Oss. Fing.* Clann fhuilteach gun mhòr-chuis, *a bloody prideless clan.—Old Song.*

Mòr-chuiseach, *a.* (*Ir. id.*) Pompous, magnificent, stately; powerful; proud, haughty; heroic; vain-glorious. Bu mhòr-chuiseach a cheum, *proud was his pace.—Oss. Tem.*

Mor-chuisle, *s. f.* (*Ir. id.*) An artery; a great artery. *N. pl.* mor-chuislean.

† **Morcroid**, *s.* (*Ir. id.*) The highway.

Mòrdha, *a.* (*Ir. id.*) Great, noble, excellent, eminent; magnificent; majestic. Cia mordha d'ainm! *how [great] excellent is thy name!—Sm.* Cià mordha a meinn! *how majestic her mien!—Mach Lach.*

Mòrdhachd, *s. f.* (*Ir. id.*) See **Mòrachd**.

Mòr-dhail, *s. f.* (*Ir. id.*) A great assembly; a congress; a parliament; a diet. Mor-dhail Bhreatuinn, *the British parliament;* mor-dhail na Gearmailt, *the Germanic diet;* mòr-dhail shagart, *a conclave;* mor-dhàil Droma-céit, *the parliament of Dromceit,* in Derry; at which were present, Aodghan, king of the Scots, and St. Columba, abbot of Iona.—*Shaw.*

Mòrdhalach, *a.* (*Ir. id.*) Magnificent, proud, pompous, powerful.—*Mac Co.*

Mòr-dheigh, *s. f.* Aspiration; ardent desire; ardent fondness.

Mòr-dhòchas, ais, *s. m.* (*Ir. id.*) Sanguineness.

Mor'ear, eir, *s. m.* A lord; an earl; *literally,* a great man.

Mor'earachd, *s. m.* Lordship, earldom.

Mòr-fhaich, *s. f.* An extensive marsh; a sea-marsh.—*Shaw.*

Mòr-fhairge, *s. f.* (*Ir. id.*) An ocean; a great ocean; a high sea. Ri taobh na mòr-fhairge, *beside the great ocean.—Old Poem.*

Mòr-fhàs, *s. m.* Train oil.—*Shaw.* Great growth.

Mòr-fhlaithe, **Mòr-fhlaithean**, *n. pl.* of mòr-fhlath. Great chiefs; grandees; high-mightinesses; nobility.

Mòr-fhlath, -fhlaith, *s. m.* (*Ir. id.*) A great chief; a grandee.

Mòr-fhleadh, *s. f.* (*Ir. id.*) A great feast; epulation.

Mòr-fhliodh, **Mor-fhliogh**, *s. m.* Masterwort.—*Macd.* and *Macfar. Voc.*

Morgach, *a.* Rotten.

Morgachadh, aidh, *s. m.* Rottenness.

Morgadh, aidh, *s. m.* (*Ir. id.*) Corruption; rottenness.

Morgaich, *v. a.* and *n.* Corrupt, rot.

Morgantach, *a.* Magnificent.—*Shaw.* Gu morgantach, *magnificently.*

Morgantachd, *s. f.* Magnificence.

Mòr-ghairdeachas, ais, *s. m.* Rapture.

Mòr-ghaisge, *s. f.* (*Ir. id.*) Heroism.

Mòr-ghath, *s. m.* A large spear, a javelin; a fish-spear.

Mor-ghniomh, *s. m.* (*Ir. id.*) An exploit.

Mor-ghniomhach, *a.* (*Ir. id.*) Magnificent.

Mòr-ghràin, *s. f.* (*Ir. id.*) Abomination; detestation.

Mòr-inntinn, *s. f.* A great mind, a noble mind.

Mòr-inntinneach, *a.* High-minded; magnanimous; ambitious.

Mòr-inntinneachd, *s. f.* High-mindedness; magnanimity; ambitiousness.

Mòr-ioghnadh, aidh, *s. m.* Astonishment, amazement. Mòr-ioghnadh air gach neach, *astonishment on every one.—Stew. Jer.*

Mòrlanachd, *s. f.* (*Ir. id.*) Statute work done by tenants to their landlords.—*Macfar. Voc.*

Mòr-lannachd, *s. f.* A feat in swordmanship; carnage.

Mòr-lannair, *s. m.* A powerful swordsman.

Mòr-laoch, -laoich, *s. m.* A hero, a champion. An dà mhòr-laoch, *the two heroes.—Old Poem. N. pl.* mòr-laoich.

Mòr-leth-tromach, *a.* Far advanced in pregnancy.

Mòr-leth-tromachd, *s. f.* An advanced state of pregnancy.

Mòr-luach, *s. m.* A great price, great value. Cha deanainn air mhòr-luach e, *I would not do it for a great price,* or *reward.*

† **Mormanta**, *s. m.* Wormwood.—*Shaw.*

Mòr-mhaor, -mhaoir, *s. m.* A lord mayor; a lord high constable; a high steward, a high constable; a lord. *N. pl.* mòr-mhaoir.

Mòr-mheamnach, *a.* Proud; high-minded, high-spirited; aspiring; magnanimous.

Mòr-mheamnadh, aidh, *s. m.* Pride; high-mindedness; magnanimity.

Mòr-mheas, *s. m.* High esteem. Ann am mòr-mheas, *in high esteem.*

Mòr-mheas, *v. a.* (*Ir. id.*) Esteem greatly; value highly; magnify.

Mòr-mhuinntir, *s. f.* A multitude; a numerous household.—*Q. B. ref.*

Mòr-mhuirne, *s. f.* High spirit; mettle; gladness.

Mòr-mhuirneach, *a.* High-spirited, mettlesome; cheerful. Each mòr-mhuirneach, *a high-mettled horse.—Old Poem.*

Mòrnaich, *s. f.* (mòr-nithe.) A tolerable quantity.

Mornan, ain, *s. m.* (*Ir. id.*) A little timber dish. *N. pl.* mornain.

Morran, ain, *s. m.* A species of natural colewort growing by the sea-side.

Mòr-rath, *s. m.* Great luck; continued luck; prosperity.

Mòr-roinn, *s. f.* A province. *N. pl.* mor-roinnean. Ionmhas nam mòr-roinn, *the treasures of the provinces.—Stew. Ecc.*

Mòr-roinneach, *a.* Provincial; divided into provinces; of, or belonging to, a province.

Mòr-shàr, -shàir, *s. m.* A mighty hero. Lann a mhor-shàir, *the sword of the mighty hero.—Oss. Tem.*

Mòr-sheisear, *a.* Seven.—*Macfar. Voc.*

Mòr-shluagh, -shluaigh, *s. m.* A multitude; a host, an army.—*Stew. Ez.*

Mor-shoillse, *s. f.* Splendour.

Mort, *v. a.* Murder, massacre. *Pret. a.* mhort, *murdered; fut. aff. a.* mortaidh, *shall murder.*

Mort, *s. m.* Murder.
Swed. mord. *Germ.* mord *and* mort. *Low Germ.* moord.

Mortach, *a.* Murdering, massacring.

Mortachail, *a.* Murderous, sanguinary.

Mortadh, aidh, *s. m.* Murder; slaying; slaughter. Farmad is mortadh, *envy and murder.—Stew. Gal.* Na dean mortadh, *do not kill.—Stew. Ex.* Mortadh is marbhadh, *bloodshed and slaughter.*

Mortair, *s. m.* (*from* mort.) A murderer; mortar. Éiridh am mortair, *the murderer shall rise.—Stew. Job.* *N. pl.* mortairean.

Mortaireach, *a.* Murderous; like a murderer.

Mortaireachd, *s. f.* Murderousness; a massacring.

Mortal, ail, *s. m.* (*Ir. id.*) Mortar or lime.

Mort-fhear, -fhir, *s. m.* A murderer; *contracted* mortair.

Mòr-thìr, *s. f.* (*Ir. id.*) A continent, a main land; a great shore. Fàilte ort féin a mhor-thìr bhoidhche! *hail, thou beauteous main-land!—Mac Don.* Feadh mhòr-thìr is eilean, *among continents and islands.—Sm.* Mar neart na tuinne gu mor-thìr, *like a billow rolling in its strength to the main shore.—Old Poem.*

Mòr-thorrach, *a.* (*Ir. id.*) Prolific, fruitful; very big with child.

Mòr-thriath, -threith, *s. m.* A great prince; a great powerful chief.

Mòr-thuil, *s. m.* (*Ir. id.*) A deluge.

Moruach, aich, *s. m.* (*Corn. Arm.* morhuch. *Ir.* moruach.) A mermaid; a sea-monster.

Mòr-uachdaran, ain, *s. m.* (*Ir. id.*) A viceroy; a governor; a regent.

Mòr-uailse, *s. f.* High nobility. Chum a Mòr-uailse, Ban-Mharcuis Thulaich-bhardainn, *To the Most Noble the Marchioness of Tullibardine.*

Mòr-uaislean, *s. pl.* Nobility, grandees. Mòr-uaislean na dùthcha, *the nobility of the kingdom.*

Mòr-uasal, *a.* (*Ir. id.*) Noble in birth; of the highest rank in nobility; most noble.

Mòr-urranta, *a.* Bold; daring; self-confident. Gu mòr-urranta, *boldly.*

† **Mos**, *s. m.* (*Ir. id. Lat.* mos.) A manner, a fashion.

† **Mosach**, *a.* (*Ir.* mosdha.) Of, or belonging to, fashion or manner.

Mosach, *a.* (*Ir. id.*) Dirty; nasty; mean; of dirty habits; mean, niggardly; rough, bristly. Am béist mosach, *the dirty beast;* dh' fhàgadh tu fear mosach fialuidh, *thou wouldst render the mean man generous.—R.* *Com.* and *sup.* mosaiche.

Mosaiche, *com.* and *sup.* of mosach.

Mosaiche, *s. f.* Filthiness, dirtiness, nastiness.

Mosan, ain, *s. m.* (*Ir. id.*) Rough trash, as chaff; refuse.

Mosgail, *v. a.* and *n.* Awake, rouse, stir up. *Pret. a.* mhosgail; *fut. aff. a.* mosglaidh. Mhosgail e o 'aisling an laoch, *he awoke the hero from his dream.—Oss. Fing.* Mhosgail ardan, *haughty pride was roused.—Oss. Tem.* Mosglaidh iad o'n eug, *they shall awaken from death.—Macfar.*

Mosgain, *a.* Rotten; grey; mouldy; worm or moth-eaten. Fiaclan mosgain, *rotten teeth.—Macint.* Mar chraobha mosgain, *like grey* [*mossy*] *trees.—Oss. Duthona.* Mosgain maol gun duilleach, *grey and bare without foliage.—Oss. Derm.*

Mosgainneach, *a.* See **Mosguinneach**.

Mosgalach, *a.* Wakeful, watching, observant. *Com.* and *sup.* mosgalaiche.

Mosgalachd, *s. f.* Wakefulness; watchfulness, observance.

Mosgaltach, *a.* (*Ir. id.*) Wakeful, watchful, observant. *Com.* and *sup.* mosgaltaiche. Gu mosgaltach, *wakefully.*

Mosgaltachd, *s. f.* (*Ir. id.*) Wakefulness, watchfulness. *—Macd.*

Mo sgaradh! *interj.* Alas! woe's me!

Mosgladh, aidh, *s. m.* (*Ir. id.*) A rousing, a wakening; excitation. Fo mhosgladh feirge, *under the excitation of anger.—Oss. Tem.*

Mosgladh, (a), *pr. part.* of mosgail. Awakening, rousing, exciting. Na h-éildean a mosgladh, *the roes awakening.—Orr.*

Mosglaidh, *fut. aff. a.* of mosgail.

Mosguinneach, *a.* (*Ir. id.*) Devout; religiously inclined. Gu mosguinneach, *devoutly.* *Com.* and *sup.* mosguinniche.

Mosguinneachd, *s. f.* (*Ir. id.*) Devoutness.

Mosrach, *a.* (*Ir. id.*) Caressing coarsely; using indecent freedoms.

Mosradh, aidh, *s. m.* (*Ir. id.*) Coarse caressing or dalliance; maudlin civilities; indecent freedoms; brutal licentiousness.

† **Mota**, *s. m.* (*Ir. id.*) A mount, a mote.

† **Moth**, *s. m.* (*Ir. id.*) The male of any creature.

Mothach, *a.* Fertile, fruitful; pregnant.

Mothachadh, aidh, *s. m.* (*Ir.* mothughadh.) Feeling; perception; sense, sensibility.

Mothuchadh, (a), *pr. part.* of mothaich. Feeling, perceiving.

Mothachail, *a.* Perceptive; sensible; observant.

Mothaich, *v. a.* (*Ir.* mothaigh.) Feel, perceive; observe; know. *Pret. a.* mhothaich; *fut. aff. a.* mothaichidh, *shall feel.* Mhothaich sinn a meòir gun lutha, *we observed her fingers without motion.—Ull.*

Mothar, air, *s. m.* (*Ir.* mothar.) A loud and deep noise, murmur; a high sea; *rarely,* a park; a tuft of trees.

Mòthar, *a.* (*Ir. id.*) Mild, calm, composed, sedate; majestic; moving slowly and calmly; *also,* mettlesome. Bu mhòthar a beus, *mild was her demeanour.—Macint.* Oidhche mhòthar, *a calm night.*

Mòtharachd, *s. f.* Mildness; composedness; sedateness; calmness.

† **Moth-chat**, -chait, *s. m.* (*Ir. id.*) A tom-cat.

Mo-thruaighe! Woe's me! alas! Mo thruaighe mi! *woe's me!*

Mra, *for* mna; which see.

Mrathan, Mnathan, *n. pl.* of bean. Wives, women.—*Stew. Gen. ref.*

† **Mu**, *an ancient Celtic vocable,* long gone into disuse among the Gael; but in the Armoric it signifies, *shut the mouth.* It seems to be the root of the Greek μυω, μυστης, and μυστηριον.

Mù, *for* mò, *com.* and *sup.* of mòr.

Mu, *prep.* About, round about; concerning; for, on account of. Mu 'n tràth so am màireach, *about this time to-morrow.—Stew. 2 K.* A chomhachag ag iadhadh mu 'cheann, *the owlet winding about his head.—Oss. Taura.* Labhair e mu Iudas, *she spake concerning Judas.—Stew. N. T.* Oigh mu 'm bheil mo bhròn, *a maid for whom is my grief.—Oss.* Mu 'cairde, *on account of her friends.—Oss. Carricth.* An tìr mu thuath, *the north country; the country to the north.—Stew. Zech.* An tìr mu dheas, *the country to the south; the south country.—Id.* Mu dheireadh, *at last;* mu thiomchioll, *round about;* mu choinneamh, *opposite;* ciod mu bheil thu? *what are you about?*

Muabhraighe, *s. f.* A platform.

Muadh, muaidh, *s. m.* (*Ir. id.*) A form, a shape, an image; a cloud; *adjectively,* soft, moist.

† **Muadh**, *v. a.* Form, shape. *Pret. a.* mhuadh.

Muadhair, *s. m.* (*Ir. id.*) A rogue.

Muaidh, *a.* Shapely, well-formed; noble, good; soft,

tender; middle, midst. Loingeas mhuaidh, *a well-formed ship.—Old Poem.*

MUAL, muail, *s. m.* (*Ir. id.*) The top of a hill.

MUALACH, aich, *s. m.* (*Ir. id.*) A passage, a way; cow-dung.

MUBRAN, ain, *s. m.* (*Ir. id.*) Corn heated in the mow.

MUBRANACH, *a.* Heated, as corn in the mow.

MUC, muic, *s. f.* A sow, a hog, a pig; a perch. A mhuc a chaidh nigheadh, *the sow that was washed.—Stew. Pet.* Muc-mara, *a whale;* muc-bhiorach, *a porpoise;* muc-lochaidh, *a perch;* muc-shneachdaidh, *a heap of rolled snow. N. pl.* mucan; *d. pl.* mucaibh. *Ir.* muc. *W.* moch. *Corn.* moch. *Teut.* mocke.

MUC, muic, *s. f.* (*Ir. id.*) An instrument of war, whereby besiegers were secured in approaching a wall, like the Roman *pluteus* or *penthouse.* It was covered over with twigs, hair-cloth, raw-hides, and moved on three wheels.—*Shaw.*

MUCACH, *a.* (*Ir.* mucnach.) Swinish; hoggish; like a sow. A ghràisge mhucach, *the swinish mob.*

MUCACHAN, ain, *s. m.* A hoggish fellow.

MUCACHD, *s. f.* Swinishness, hoggishness; moroseness, grimness.

MUCAG, aig, *s. f.* (*Ir. id.*) A hip, the fruit of the dog-rose; *rarely,* a cup. *N. pl.* mucagan.

MUCAGACH, *a.* Abounding in hips, as a dog-rose; like a hip.

MUCAIBH, *d. pl.* of muc; which see.

MUCAIL, *a.* (muc-amhuil.) Swinish, hoggish.

MUCAIR, *s. m.* A swine-herd; a hoggish fellow. *N. pl.* mucairean.

MUCALACHD, *s. f.* Swinishness, hoggishness.

MUC-BHIORACH, aich, *s. f.* (*Ir. id.*) A porpoise. *N. pl.* mucan-biorach.

MUC-BHLONAG, aig, *s. f.* Hog's-lard.

MUC-BHUACHAILL, *s. m.* A swine-herd. *N. pl.* muc-bhuachaillean.

MUC-BHUACHAILLEACHD, *s. f.* Swine-herding.

MUCH, *a.* Early. See MOCH.

MÙCH, *v. a.* Smother, extinguish, quench, suffocate; press; pacify; mutter. *Pret. a.* mhùch, *fut. aff. a.* mùchaidh. Na mùchaibh an Spiòrad, *quench not the Spirit.—Stew. Thess.* Mùch fonn, *mutter an air.—Oss.*

† MUCHA, *s.* (*Ir. id.*) An owl.

MÙCHACH, *a.* Smothering, extinguishing, quenching; pressing, suffocating.

MÙCHADAIR, *s. m.* An extinguisher. *N. pl.* muchadairean.

MÙCHADH, aidh, *s. m.* (*Ir. id.*) A smothering, an extinguishing, a quenching; a suffocating; extinction, suffocation.

MÙCHAN, ain, *s. m.* (*Ir. id.*) A chimney, a vent. *N. pl.* muchain.

MUCH-EIRIDH. See MOCH-EIRIDH.

MU-CHOINNEAMH, *prep.* Opposite; over against.

MÙCHTA, MÙCHTE, *p. part.* of mùch. Extinguished, smothered, suffocated, quenched. Mùchte fo bhron, *suffocated, oppressed with grief.—Oss. Tem.*

MUCH-THRÀTH, *s. m.* Early morning, early dawn. See MOCH-THRATH.

MUC-INNIS, *s. f.* An old name for Ireland; the isle of whales.

MUC-LOCHAIDH, *s. f.* A perch; the *perca fluvialis* of Linnæus.

MUC-MHARA, *s. f.* A whale; a porpoise. Muca mara 'g ar seachnadh, *whales avoiding us.—Oss. Duthona.*

MUCNACH, *a.* (*Ir. id.*) Hoggish, swinish, morose.

MUCNACHD, *s. f.* (*Ir. id.*) Hoggishness, swinishness, moroseness.

MUCRAIDH, *s. f.* (*Ir. id.*) A sownder of swine; a gammon of bacon.

MUC-SNEACHDAIDH, *s. f.* A heap of rolled snow.

MUCUSG, *s. m.* Swine's grease.—*Shaw.*

MU D', *for* mu do. About thy.

MUDACH, *a.* (*Ir. id.*) Gross.

MUDAIDH, *a.* Dun-coloured.

MUDAN, ain, *s. m.* (*Ir. id.*) A cover, a covering.

MUDAN-CROICNE, *s. m.* A bit of skin to cover the lock of a gun.—*Shaw.*

MU DHÉIMHINN, *prep.* Concerning, about. Mu dhéimhinn so, *concerning this;* mu m 'dhéimhinn, *concerning me;* mu do dhéimhinn, *about thee;* mu 'dhéimhinn, *concerning him;* mu 'déimhinn, *concerning her;* m' ar déimhinn, *concerning us;* m' ur déimhinn, *concerning you;* mu 'n déimhinn, *concerning them.*

MU DHEIREADH, *adv.* At last, at length. Mu dheireadh thall, *at last.*

MUG, muig, *s.* A mug.

MÙGACH, *a.* (*Ir. id. Germ.* mucken, *speak indistinctly.*) Snuffling; speaking nasally; *also,* misty. O chùl nan sliabh mùgach, *from behind the misty mountains.—Oss. Tem. Com.* and *sup.* mùgaiche.

MÙGAIR, *s. m.* A snuffler.

MÙGAIREACHD, *s. f.* Snuffling.

MUGAN, ain, *s. m., dim.* of mug. (*Ir. id.*) A mug.

† MUGART, airt, *s. f.* (*Ir. id.*) Hog's flesh. A hog.—*Shaw.*

MÙGH, *v. a.* (*Ir. id.*) Change; alter; diversify; shift, turn; kill, destroy. *Pret. a.* mhùgh, *changed; fut. aff. a.* mughaidh. Written also *mùth;* which see.

MUGH, *s. m.* See MUGHA.

MÙGHA, MÙGHADH, *s. m.* A changing, an altering; a shifting, a turning; a decaying; change, difference, alteration; vicissitude; transition; novelty; change, or small money that may be given for larger pieces; decay; destruction. Tha mùgha air, *he is changed;* thoir dhomh mùgha crùin, *give me change for a crown;* thead a dhreach am mùgha, *its fashion shall perish.—Stew. Jam.*

MUGHARD, aird, *s. m.* Mugwort.

MÙGHTEACH, *a.* Changing; variable; inconstant, volatile, fickle; irresolute; unsteady, unsettled, giddy.

MÙGHTEACHD, *s. f.* Changeableness, variableness; inconstancy; fickleness; irresoluteness; unsteadiness.

MUIC, *gen. sing.* of muc.

MUICEANACH, ich, *s. m.* A plebeian.—*Shaw.*

MUICEIL, ealach, *s. f.* Pork. *Contracted for* muic-fheoil.

MUIC-FHEOIL, *s. f.* (*Ir. id.*) Pork.

MUICHE, *com.* and *sup.* of much.

MÙICHE, *s. f.* Dulness, sadness; mistiness; darkness; gloom. Ciod fà do mhùiche? *what is the cause of thy sadness?*

MUICHE, *s. f.* (*Ir. id.*) Earliness; a dawn. Anns a mhuiche, *in early morning.*

MUICNIS, *s. f.* (*Ir. id.*) The rope which ties a basket on a porter's back.

MÙIDH, *s.* A mane.

MUIDHE, *s. f.* A churn. Ri muidhe, *churning. N. pl.* muidheachan.

MÙIDHEACH, *a.* Having a mane; having a thick or a long mane.

MUIDSE, *s. f.* A linen or cambric cap worn by females. This word is a provincial corruption of the *Scotch* mutch.

MÙIG, *v. a.* and *n.* Smother, suffocate; quench; suppress; quash; grow gloomy or misty. *Pret. a.* mhùig, *smothered; fut. aff. a.* mùigidh, *shall smother.*

MÙIG, *s. f.* (*Ir. id. W.* mwg. *Corn.* mog.) A gloom, smoke, mist; a frown; a gloomy appearance, a gloomy sky. Torra fo mhùig, *mist-covered hills.—Oss. Tem.*

MÙIGEACH, *a.* Misty, gloomy, smoky; frowning; surly; scowling; reserved, shy. O chùl nan sliabh mùigeach, *from behind the misty mountains.—Oss. Tem.* Cha mhuigeach 'anam, *his mind is not gloomy.—Oss. Oinam.*

MÙIGEACHD, *s. f.* (*Ir. id.*) Mistiness, gloominess, smokiness; surliness.

MÙIGEAN, ein, *s. m., from* muig. (*Ir. id.*) A gloomy, churlish fellow; a churl, a grumbler; a mist.

MÙIGEANACHD, *s. f.* Gloominess, mistiness; churlishness.

MÙIGEIL, *a.* (*from* muig.) Misty, gloomy; churlish, reserved, shy. Gu muigeil, *gloomily.*

MÙIG-MHONADH, aidh, *s. m.* A misty mountain; a misty hill. Do mhùig-mhonadh féin, *thy own misty mountain.—Oss.*

MUIGH, *adv.* (*Ir. id.*) Out, outward, without. A muigh, *without.* An taobh a muigh, *the outside.*

MUIGH, *v. n.* Fail; falter; fall; be defeated; decay.—*Shaw.*

MUIGHE, *s. f.* A churn. Written also *muidhe.*

MUIGHTE, *p. part.* of mùgh. Changed, altered. See MÙGH.

MUIL, *s.* A promontory.

MUIL, muile, *s. f.* A mule. *N. pl.* muilidhean, *mules.—Q. B. ref. D. pl.* muilidhibh.—*Stew. Is.*

MUILCEANN, *s.* The root gentian; pennygrass; felwort.

MUILCEANNACH, *a.* Abounding in gentian or pennygrass; like gentian; of gentian, felwort, or pennygrass.

MUILCIONN, inn, *s.* See MUILCEANN.

MUILE, *s.* Mull in Argyleshire.

MUILEACH, ich, *s. m.* An inhabitant of Mull.

MUILEAG, eig, *s. f.* (*Ir. id.*) A little frog, a cranberry. *N. pl.* muileagan.

MUILEAGACH, *a.* Abounding in little frogs; abounding in cranberries.

MUILEANN, inn, *s. m.* A mill. Air cùl a mhuilinn, *behind the mill.—Stew. Ex.* Muileann min, *a meal;* muileann lìn, *a flax-mill;* muileann calcaidh, *a fulling-mill;* muileann gaoithe, *a wind-mill;* muileann lùathaidh, muileann luaidh, *a fulling-mill; a walk-mill;* muileann deilbh, *a warping-mill;* muileann brachaidh, *a malt-mill;* muileann bràdh, *a hand-mill* or *quern;* muilean snaoisein, *a snuff-mill. N. pl.* muilinnean, *contr.* muilnean.

Gr. μυλα. *Lat.* mola. *Mæso-Goth.* moulin. *Ang.-Sax.* mylen. *Ir.* muilleann. *Arm.* mulin. *W. Corn.* melin. *Germ.* malen. *Teut.* meulen *and* molen. *Fr.* moulin. *Dan.* molle. *Span.* molino.

MUILEANN BRÀDH, *s. m.* A hand-mill or quern.

The *bràdh* or *quern* was once the only mill for corn-grinding used in the Highlands of Scotland. It is still in use among the northern nations of Europe, and in many parts of Asia. This rude instrument is composed of two stones of granite. The undermost stone is about two feet in diameter, and commonly hollowed to the depth of six inches. This hollow is of equal depth and diameter. Within this is placed, horizontally, a smooth round flag about four inches thick, and so fitted to the cavity, that it can just revolve with ease. Through the centre of this revolving flag there is bored a hole for conveying the grain. In the lower stone, in the centre of its cavity, there is fixed a wooden pin on which the upper stone is placed in such exact equiponderance, that, though there be some friction from their contact, a little force applied will make the upper flag revolve for several times, when there is no grain underneath. On the surface of the upper flag, and near the edge, are two or three holes, just deep enough to hold in its place the stick by which it is turned round. The working of this mill was left to the women; two of whom, when the corn was properly dried (see GRADAN), sat squatting on the ground, with the *bràdh* betwixt them, and, singing loudly some mountain-melody, performed their work, the one turning round the upper flag with the thivel placed in one of the holes, and the other dropping the corn in through the large hole. This rude mill was common among the Celtic nations, from the earliest periods of their history of which we have any account that can be relied on; and, without question, it is to this simple instrument that we are to look for an explanation of our Saviour's prophecy of "two women grinding at a mill." In corroboration of this remark we have the authority of Dr. Clarke, who saw one worked in Nazareth, the earliest residence of Jesus Christ. "Two women," he observes, "seated on the ground opposite to each other, held between them two round flat stones, such as are seen in Lapland, and such as are in Scotland called *querns.* * * * * In the centre of the upper stone was a cavity for pouring in the corn; and by the side of this an upright wooden handle for moving the stone. As the operation began, one of the women, with her right hand, pushed this handle to the woman opposite, who again sent it to her companion; thus communicating a rotatory and very rapid motion to the upper stone; their left hands being all the while employed in supplying fresh corn, as fast as the bran and flour fell from the sides of the machine."

The law of Scotland attempted in vain to discourage the use of the *bràdh.* So far back as the reign of Alexander III., in the year 1284, it was enacted: "That na man shall presume to grind quheit, maisloch, or rye, with hand mylnes, except he be compelled by storm, and be in lack of mylnes quhilk should grind the samen. And, in this case, if a man grinds at hand-mylnes, he shall gif the threttein measure as multer; and gif any man contraveins this our prohibition, he shall tyne his hand-mylnes perpetuallie."

MUILEID, *s. f.* (*Span.* muleta, *a young mule.*) A mule; *also,* a mullet.—*Macd. N. pl.* muileidean.

MUILEIDEACH, *a.* Mulish; abounding in mullet.

MUILEIDEACHD, *s. f.* Mulishness; *also,* a bad smell.—*Shaw.*

MUILE-MHÀG, -mhàig, *s. f.* A frog.—*Macfar. Voc.*

MUILICHEANN, inn, *s. m.* A sleeve. *N. pl.* muilicheannan.

MUILICHEANNACH, *a.* Having sleeves; having long sleeves.

MUILIONN. See MUILEANN.

MUILL, *v. a.* Prepare, get ready.—*Shaw. Pret. a.* mhuill, *prepared; fut. aff.* muillidh, *shall prepare.*

MUILL, *gen. sing.* of moll; which see.

MUILLAIR, *s. m.* See MUILLEAR.

MUILLE, *s. f.* A mule.—*Shaw.*

MUILLEACH, ich, *s. m.* (*Ir. id.*) A puddle.

MUILLEAN, ein, *s. m.* A particle of chaff.

MUILLEAN, ein, *s. m.* A small bell.—*Shaw.*

MUILLEANACH, *a.* Abounding in particles of chaff.

MUILLEAR, eir, *s. m.* (muillinn-fhear, *contr.* muill'fhear or muillear.) *Germ.* müller. *Arm.* meilher, *a miller;* Muillear min, *a meal-miller;* muillear lìn, *a flax-miller;* muillear luathaidh, *a fuller of cloth. N. pl.* muilleirean.

MUILLEARACHD, *s. f.* The business of a miller; a grinding.

MUIL-LEATHANN, *a.* Flat-headed.—*Shaw.*

MUILLION, *a.* A million. *N. pl.* muillionan, *millions.* Muillionan do shluagh an fheòir, *millions of the tenants of the grass.—Macfar. D. pl.* muillionaibh. Mìlte do mhuillionaibh, *thousands of millions.—Stew. Gen.*

MUILLNEAN, ein, *s. m.* A particle of chaff.

MUILT, *gen. sing.* and *n. pl.* of mult.

MUILTEAG, eig, *s. f.* A species of small red berry. *N. pl.* muilteagan.

MUILT-FHEÒIL, *s. f.* Mutton. Deagh mhuilt-fheòil, *good mutton.*

MUIME, *s. f.* (*Germ.* mume.) A stepmother; a godmother; a nurse. Do mhuime chruaidh, *thy harsh stepmother.—*

Old Song. Fhuair i muime, *she got a nurse.—Stew. Gen. ref.* Muime chiche, *a nurse;* muime altrum, *a dry-nurse.*

Mùin, *gen. sing.* of mùn.

Muin, *s. f.* A name given by Irish grammarians to the eleventh letter (M) of the Gaelic alphabet.

Muin, *s. f.* The back; top; neck; a thorn; a bramble; a vine; part of a sheep's entrails; a mountain. Thog sinn an laoch air ar muin, *we lifted the hero on our backs.—Ull.* Air muin a cheile, *on each other's backs; upon each other.* Air do mhuin, *upon thee.*

Muin, (air), *prep.* Upon, above, on the top, on the back, mounted on. Air muin do chuirp, *upon thy back.—Mac Lach.* Air muin a mhonaidh, *on the top of the hill.* Chaidh e air a muin, *he had carnal connexion with her.*

Muin, *v. a.* Teach, educate, rear. *Pret. a.* mhuin, *taught; fut. aff. a.* muinidh, *shall teach.*

Mùin, *v. a.* Make water. *Pret. a.* mhùin; *fut. aff. a.* mùinidh.

Muince, *s. f.* (*from* muin.) A collar.—*Shaw.*

Muincheall, ill, *s. m.* A sleeve. *Ir.* mainchille; *perhaps* main-chéil, *from* † man, *hand*, and céil, *cover.*

Muincheallach, *a.* Sleeved; having long sleeves.

Muine, *s. f.* (*Ir. id.*) The redding; a thorn; a mountain; a whore.

Muineach, *a.* Of, or belonging to, the neck; necked; strong-necked; thorny. A mharc ghlas mhuineach, *his white, strong-necked horse.—Oss. Taura.*

† **Muineachadh**, aidh, *s. m.* (*Ir.* muiniughadh.) A taking possession; possession.

Muinead, eid, *s. m.* A collar; a necklace.

Muineadh, idh, *s. m.* A teaching, an instructing; instruction.

Muineal, eil, *s. m.* (*Ir. id. W.* mwnwel. *Lat.* monile, *a necklace.*) A neck; jaws. A lamh m'a muineal, *his hands about her neck.—Oss. Duthona.* Muineal na laimh, *the wrist.*

Muinealach, *a.* (*from* muineal.) Necked; long-necked; of, or belonging to, the neck; having large jaws.

Muinear, eir, *s. m.* (muin-fhear.) A teacher, an instructor. *N. pl.* muinearan.

Muineil, *gen. sing.* of muineal.

Muing, muinge, *s. f.* (*Ir. id. W.* mwng.) A mane. Muing eich, *a horse's mane.*

Muingeach, *a.* Having a mane; having a flowing mane; of, or belonging to, a mane.

Muinghial, *s. f.* (*Ir. id.*) The headstall of a halter or bridle.

Muinghialach, *a.* Having a headstall, as a bridle or halter.

Muinghinn, *s. f.* (*Ir. id.*) Trust; confidence; reliance; hope; security. Muinghinn ann ainm-san, *trust in his name.—Stew. Matt.* Dean muinghinn ann, *put trust in him.*

Muinghinneach, *a.* Confident; relying; hopeful; sanguine; secure. Muinghinneach asaibh, *confident of you.—Stew. Cor.* Gu muinghinneach, *confidently, securely.—Stew. Pro. Com.* and *sup.* muinghinniche.

Muinghinneachd, *s. f.* Confidentness, hopefulness, sanguineness.

Muinicheall, ill, *s. m.* A sleeve. *N. pl.* muinicheallan.

Muinicheallach, *a.* Sleeved; having long sleeves.

Muinighinn, *s. f.* See Muinghinn.

Muininn, *s. f.; contracted* for muinghinn; which see.

Muinle, *s. f.* A sleeve.—*Shaw. N. pl.* muinlean.

Muinmhear, ir, *s. m.* Hemlock.

Muinnidh, *s.* A mane.

Muinntearach, aich, *s. m.* See Muinntireach.

Muinntearas, ais, *s. m.* Service; servitude; kindness. Written also *muinntireas.*

Muinntir, *s. f.* (*Ir. id.*) People, folk, inhabitants; men; a household; servants; a family; a tribe or clan. Muinntir nach 'eil làidir, *folk who are not strong.—Stew. Pro.* Seachainn a mhuinntir mhi-runach, *shun malicious people.—Old Didactic Poem.* Muinntir do dhùthcha, *thy country-people;* a mhuinntir mo dhùthcha, *my country-people;* muinntir an tighe, *the people* or *inhabitants of the house;* muinntir a bhaile, *the towns-people.*

Muinntireach, *a.* Relating to a household; having a throng household; kind, friendly.

Muinntireach, **Muinntreach**, ich, *s. m.* and *f.* A servant, a hireling; an establishment of servants, a household. Muinntirich a' m' thigh, *servants in my house.—Stew. Ecc.* Rùn a mùinntreach, *the love of her household.—Mac Lach.*

Muinntireas, eis, *s. m.* Service, servitude; kindness.

Muinte, *p. part.* of muin. Taught, educated.

Muintear, eir, *s. m.* (*from* muin.) A teacher, an instructor. *N. pl.* muintearan.

Muir, *s. f.* (*Ir. id.*) Earth; leprosy; mortar.

Muir, mara, *s. f.* A sea, an ocean. Lean mi thar muir thu, *I followed thee over the sea.—Ull.* Air mhuir, *on sea;* taobh na mara, *the sea-side;* a mhuir mhòr, *the ocean;* a Mhuir Dubh, *the Black Sea;* a Mhuir Dhearg, *the Red Sea;* a Mhuir Bhuidhe, *the Yellow Sea;* Muir na Meadhonthìr, *the Mediterranean Sea;* airm mara, *a navy. Arm.* arm mar.

Lat. mare. *Germ.* meer. *Sclav.* morie. *Dal.* more. *Island.* mar. *Teut.* maer *and* maere. *Corn.* mor. *Ir.* muir. *Arm.* mar, mor, *and* var. Also, *Sax.* mere. *Fr.* mer, *a sea.* In the south of France they say *mare. Du* meer. *Dal. Croat. Boh. Lus.* more, *a sea. Sclav. Pol.* morze. *Goth.* marisaiv, *a pool. Du.* maras. *Fr.* mar-ais. *Eng.* morass, *a marsh. Tamoulic*, mari, *rain. Arab.* mara, *spring or spout, as water. Arab.* marakv, *a lake.* In some parts of *Africa*, marigots, *a marsh. O. Sax.* mars, merse, mere, *a lake;* hence Windermere and Mersey. *Du.* and *Teut.* meer, *a pool. Marinus*, a lake in Etruria; *Mar-ta*, a stream in Etruria; *Ismar-us*, a marshy track of country in Thrace; *Mor-awaw*, a river in Moravia; *Mura*, a river in Bavaria; *Morat*, a lake in Switzerland; *Margus*, a river in Old Persia; *Marsias*, a river in Bythinia; *Marea*, a lake in Egypt; *Morus*, a river in Dacia Vera.

Muirbhleachadh, aidh, *s. m.* (*Ir.* muirbhleaghadh.) Amazement.

Muirbhrinn, *s.* (*Ir. id.*) Scare-crows.

Muir-bhrùchd, *s.* (*Ir. id.*) A high tide.—*Shaw.*

Muir-chabhlach, aich, *s. f.* (*Ir. id.*) A squadron, a fleet.

Muircheartach, *s. m.* An Irish proper name of a man; *also*, expert.

† **Muir-chreach**, *s. f.* (*Ir. id.*) A wave; piracy; sea-plunder.

Muire, *s. f.* The Virgin Mary; St. Mary. Written also *Moire;* which see.

Mùire, *s. f.* (*Ir. id.*) A leprosy; a dry scab; scurvy.—*Macint.*

Mùireach, *a.* Leprous; a leprous person.

† **Mùireach**, ich, *s. m.* (*Ir. id.*) A sovereign; a sailor, a mariner; a marine.

Mùireadh, idh, *s. m.* (*Ir. id.*) A leprosy; a dry scab, scurvy.—*Macd.* Comhdaichte le mùireadh, *covered with leprosy.*

Muireadh, *s. f.; contracted* for muir-gheadh.

† Muirean, ein, *s f.* (*Ir. id.*) A woman, a young woman. —*Shaw*

Muireann, inn, *s. m* (*Ir id*) A fish-spear; a spear; a dart. *N. pl.* muireannan.

Muireannach, *a.* Like a spear or dart.

Muireil, *a.* (muir-amhuil.) Naval, maritime; like a sea.

Muir-fheachd, *s. f.* (*Ir id*) A fleet, a squadron.

Muirgeag, eig, *s. f.* (*Ir. id*) A frith, a narrow sea —*Shaw.*

Muirgheadh, *s. m* A wild goose, the *anas anser* of Linnæus.

Muirgheadh, *s f* (*perhaps* muir-ghath) A fish-spear; a trident. *N. pl* muirghean. Na muirghean reubach, *the murderous fish-spears* —*Macfar.*

† Muir-gheilt, *s f* (*Ir. id*) A mermaid.

Muir-gheoidh, *s pl* Wild geese

Muir-ghinneach, *a.* See Muirighinneach.

Muirgineach, *a* Dull, stupid *Com* and *sup.* muirginiche.

Muirgineachd, *s f* Dulness, stupidity.—*Shaw*

Muirgineas, eis, *s. m.* (*Ir. id*) Dulness, stupidity.

Muirorim, *s. f.* A naval engagement —*Shaw.*

Muirichinn See Muirighinn.

Muirighinn, *s. f* (*Ir. id*) A noise; a burden; a heavy charge, a family.

Muirighinneach, *a* (*Ir. id*) Burdensome; having a heavy charge, poor, numerous, as a family.

Muirirean, ein, *s m* A species of edible alga, with long stalks and long narrow leaves.—*Shaw.*

Muir-lan, -làin, *s m.* A high tide; high water

Mùirn, mùirne, *s f.* (*Ir id*) Cheerfulness, joy; delicateness, natural affection; a caress; fondness; a troop; a company Le furbhailt is le mùirn, *with welcome and joy* —*Oss Carthon.* Talla na mùirn, *the hall of hospitality* —*Mac Lach* Thaobh mùirn, *by reason of delicateness.*—*Stew. Deut*

Mùirneach, *a.* (*Ir. id*) Spirited, cheerful, joyous, pleasant, exhilarating, delicate, tender, beloved, fond, affectionate. Each mòr-mhùirneach, *a high-spirited horse.*—*Old Poem* An dùrdail mhùirneach, *the pleasant murmur* —*Macdon* Mac mùirneach, *a tender* [*affectionate*] *son.*—*Stew. Pro* Gu mùirneach, *tenderly, delicately* —*Id.*

Mùirneachd, *s f* The English channel.

Mùirneadh, idh, *s m* (*Ir. id*) A fondling, a caressing, a dandling.

Mùirneag, eig, *s f* (*Ir* muirneog) A cheerful girl; a beloved girl; an affectionate girl

Mùirneagach, *a* Cheerful, fond, affectionate, as a girl.

† Muirneamh, imh, *s m.* (*Ir id*) An overseer.

Mùirnean, ein, *s. m.* (*Ir.* muirnin) A beloved person; a darling; a cheerful young person; an affectionate young person; a minion

Mùirneanach, *a* Affectionate, cheerful, beloved, fond, caressing Gu mùirneanach, *lovingly*

Mùirnich, *v a* Caress, fondle, dandle, *also*, load, burden. *Pret. a* mhùirnich, *fut. aff a* mùirnichidh

Muirnin, *v a* Caress, fondle, dandle

Muir-reubann, ainn, *s. m.* Piracy.

Muirsgian, sgein, *s f.* A spout-fish

Muirsgianach, *a.* Like a spout-fish, abounding in spout-fish

Muir-spuinne, *s f.* Piracy Ri muir-spuinne, *committing piracy*

Muir-spuinnear, eir, *s. m* A pirate. *N. pl* muir-spuinnearan.

Muir-spuinnearachd, *s f.* Piracy; the practice of piracy.

† Muirt, *s. f.* (*Ir. id.*) Riches.

Muir-teachd, *s.* (*Ir. id.*) An unnavigable sea.—*Shaw.*

Muir-thachdar, air, *s. m.* Sea-chance.—*Macfar. Voc.*

Muir-thoradh, aidh, *s. m.* The product of the sea.

Muir-thuile, *s. f.* A high tide; an inundation occasioned by a high tide. *N. pl* muir-thuiltean.

Muiseach, *a.* (*Ir. id*) Surly.

Muiseadh, idh, *s. m.* A threat.

Muiseag, eig, *s. f.* A threat; severe treatment. Gach muiseag tha mi 'cluinntinn, *every threat I hear.*—*Mac Co*

Muiseagach, *a.* Prone to threat, threatening.

Muiseagadh, aidh, *s. m.* A threatening, a threat.

Muiseal, eil, *s m.* A curb, a check, a muzzle. Perhaps *muis-iall.*

Muisealach, *a.* Like a curb, like a muzzle; having a curb or muzzle.

Mùisean, ein, *s. m.* (*Ir. id*) A primrose; *primula veris.*

Muisean, ein, *s m* A low rascally fellow; a ramscallion; the devil. Fanaidh am muisean ri làth, *the devil will wait his day* —*G. P.*

Mùiseanach, *a.* Abounding in primroses, primrosy; like a primrose A choire mhùiseanaich! *thou primrosy dell!*—*Old Song*

Muiseanach, *a* Law; dirty; rascally.

Muisginn, *s. f.* An English pint. *N. pl.* muisginnean.

† Mùite, *a* (*Ir. id* *Lat* mutus) Dumb, mute.—*Shaw.*

Mùiteach, *a.* Changeable, variable, fickle, volatile; irresolute See also Mughteach

Mul, muil, *s m* (*Ir. id*) A conical heap, a mound; an axle; a multitude *N. pl.* mulan Mulan nan rotha, *the axletrees of the wheels* —*Stew.* 1 *K*

Mullach, aich, *s. m* (*Ir id*) A sea-calf.—*Shaw.* A puddle; water; an owl.

Mulach, aich, *s m* A summit More properly *mullach;* which see

Mulachag, aig, *s f* A cheese *N pl* mulachagan, *cheeses.* Mulachagan càise, *cheeses* —*Stew Sam*

Mulachagach, *a* Shaped like cheese; full of cheeses.

Mulachan, ain, *s. m* (*Ir* mulchan *Scotch,* mollachan.) A cheese *N pl* mulachain

Mulad, aid, *s m.* (*Ir id*) Grief, sadness, dejection, melancholy. A lionadh le mulad, *filling with grief.*—*Ardar,* Thig math a mulad, *good comes out of patience* —*G P.*

Muladach, *a., from* mulad (*Ir. id*) Sad, mournful, sorrowful, melancholy, grievous Muladach a ghnàth, *for ever sad* —*Sm* Is muladach an gnothach e, *it is a melancholy business. Com* and *sup* muladaiche.

Mulag, aig, *s f* (*Ir id*) A mule, a young mule; a little heap, a knoll, a patine, or the cover of a chalice. *N. pl.* mulagan.

Mulagach, *a* Hilly, knolly.

Mulaid, *gen sing* of mulad

Mulan, ain, *s m*, *dim* of mul. (*Ir id*) A little hill, a knoll, a heap, a conical hillock; a stack; a rick of hay or corn *N pl* mulain Mulain tomailteach, *bulky cocks of hay* —*Macfar*

Mulanach, *a* Knolly; like a knoll or hillock; full of ricks; like a rick, full of lumps

Mulart, airt, *s. m* Dwarf elder

Mulc, *v a* Push with the head, as a young calf; or with the snout, as a pig, shove; butt. *Pret a* mhulc; *fut. aff. a* mulcaidh.

Mulcach, *a* Apt to push or butt; pushing, butting; jostling.

Mulcadh, aidh, *s m.* A pushing or butting with the head,

as a young calf; a shoving, a jostling; a push, a shove, a jostle.

Mulcan, Mulchan, ain, *s. m.* A horned owl.

Mulghart, airt, *s.* The pole.—*Shaw.*

Mull, *s.* See **Maol.**

Mulcheann, inn, *s. m.* (mul, *axle*, and ceann, *end.*) The pole.

Mul-chu, *s. m.* The pole.—*Shaw.*

Mullach, aich, *s. m.* (*Ir. id.*) A top or summit; a height or eminence; a hill. Na mullach, *in her top.*—*Oss. Tem.* Mullach nan rionnag, *the height of the stars.*—*Stew. Job.* Mullach liath lom, *a grey bleak eminence.*—*Old Song.* Mullach an tighe, *the top of the house.* *N. pl.* mullaiche and mullaichean. Mullaiche nam beann, *the tops of the mountains.*—*Stew. Gen.* Air ar mullaichean, *on our heads.*—*Macint.* Clach-mullaich, *a top-stone, a corner-stone.*

Mullach dubh, *s. m.* Knapweed; *centaurea nigra.*

Mulladh, aidh, *s. m.* (*Ir. id.*) A mould.—*Shaw.* *N. pl.* mullaidbean.

Mullag, aig, *s. f.* (*Ir. id.*) The patine, or cover of a chalice. *N. pl.* mullagan.

Mul-mhagan, ain, *s. m.* A kind of large toad.—*Shaw.*

Mulp, mulpa, *s. m.* A lump; a knot.

Mulpach, *a.* Lumpy, knotty.

Mulpan, ain, *s. m.* (*dim.* of mulp.) A little lump; a little knot.

Mulpanach, *a.* Full of little lumps.

Mul-sneamh, *s. m.* Negligence.

Mul-sneamhach, Mul-sneamhail, *a.* Negligent.

Mult, muilt, *s. m.* (*W.* mollt. *Ir.* molt. *Arm.* maoud.) A wedder; a sheep. Mult réithe, *a tup.* *N. pl.* muilt.

Mu 'm, (*for* mu am.) About their, concerning their. Mu 'm bailtibh, *about their towns.*

Mu 'm, (*for* mu mo.) About my; concerning my. Mu 'm chomhnuidh, *about my dwelling.*—*Oss. Tem.*

Mu 'm, *conj.* Before; ere. Mu 'm faigh mi bàs, *before I die.*—*Stew. Gen.*

Mum, *conj.*; more correctly *mu'm*, which see.

Mu 'n, Mun, *conj.* Before that, ere; lest. Mu 'n robh ann sleibhte, *before hills existed.*—*Sm.* Mu 'n tig e, *before he comes.*

Mu 'n, (*for* mu an.) About the; concerning the, on account of the. Mu 'n triùir, *about the three.*—*Oss. Fing.* Mu 'n t-sonn, *on account of the hero.*—*Oss. Tem.*

Mu 'n, (*for* mu an.) About their; concerning their; on account of their.

Mun, *conj.*; more correctly *mu'n*; which see.

Mùn, muin, *s. m.* (*Ir. id.*) Urine, pissing. Dean do mhùn, *make water*; ri mùn, *pissing*; galar mùin, *the gravel.*

Mùn, *v.*; more properly *mùin.*

Munabhuachaill, *s. m.* A cormorant; an allan hawk; a diver.

Mùnach, *a.* Incontinent of urine.

Munadh, aidh, *s. m.* A hill. More frequently written *monadh.*

Munadh, aidh, *s. m.* (*Ir. id.*) Education, instruction; admonition. Deiseachd munaidh, *the ornament of education.*—*Old Song.*

Mùnadh, aidh, *s. m.* A making water.

Munar, air, *s. m.* (*Ir. id.*) A fact, a deed.—*Shaw.*

Munaran, *a.* (*Ir. id.*) Insignificant; *also*, a trifling thing; a trifling person.

† **Munata**, *s. m.* (*Ir. id.*) A champion.—*Shaw.*

Mu 'n cuairt, *adv.* and *prep.* Around; about; round about; by the circuit. Mu 'n cuairt domh, *around me, about me*, mu 'm chuairt, *around me*, mu d' chuairt, *around thee*, mu 'chuairt, *around him*, mu 'n cuairt da, *about him*, m'ar cuairt, *around us*, mu 'n cuairt duinn, *about us*, mu 'r cuairt, *around you*, mu 'n cuairt duibh, *about you.*

Mung, more properly *muing*, which see.

Mùnlach, aich, *s. m.* (*Ir.* munloch.) A puddle, mire, dirty water.

Munmhor, oir, *s. m.* See **Monmhor.**

Mu 'n seach, *adv.* and *prep.* Alternately; in return, to and fro. Fear mu 'n seach, *one by one, man by man.* M' obair a dol mu 'n seach orm, *my work increasing on my hands*, or *becoming greater than I can manage.*

Mur, *conj.* If not, unless. Mur bhiodh gu, *were it not that.*

Mur, *prov.* for mar.

Mùr, mùir, *s. m.* (*Ir. id.*) A wall, a tower, a hill; a fortification, a rampart; a house, a palace. Gach gregh bha na 'r mùr, *every dog in our house.*—*Old Song.* A caoidh 's a mhùr, *wailing in the hall.*—*Old Poem.* Mach-thir is mùr nan Gall, *the plains and palaces of strangers.*—*Old Song.* Mùr ollamh, *an academy.*—*Shaw.*

Lat. murus. *Lus.* mura. *Car.* myr. *Pol.* mur. *Belg.* *Du.* meuir. *Germ.* maur. *Ir.* mur. *W.* mur. *Da.* muur and mur.

† **Mùr**, *v. a.* Wall in; surround with a wall, fortify. *Pret.* a mhur, *fut. aff.* a mùraidh.

Murach, *a.* (*Ir. id.*) Walled.

Muran, ain, *s. m.* A kind of grass called bent; sea-reed grass, a carrot; *also*, rents.—*Shaw.*

Muranach, *a.* Like bent, abounding in bent. *Com.* and *sup.* muranaiche.

Murasg, aisg, *s. m.* A sea-shore; a marsh; a sea-marsh; a quick-sand.

Mur bhiodh, *conj.* Were it not, had it not been. Mur bhiodh thusa, *had it not been for thee.*

Mur bhiodh, (gu), *conj.* Were it not that; had it not been that.

Murcach, *a.* (*Ir. id.* Scotch, murky.) Sad, sorrowful, gloomy. *Com.* and *sup.* murcaiche.

Murcas, ais, *s. m.* (*Ir. id.*) Sadness, sorrowfulness, gloominess.

Mur-dhraidhean, ein, *s. m.* Agrimony.

Murlach, aich, *s. m.* A dog-fish.

Murlan, ain, *s. m.* (*Ir. id.*) A rough head; a rough top.

Murluinn, *s. f.* A kind of basket or hamper.

Murrach, *a.* (*Ir. id.*) Able, capable. Tha mi murraich air a dheanamh, *I am able to do it.* *Com.* and *sup.* murraiche. Ciod an ni is murraiche? *what is more capable?*—*Macfar.*

Murrachas, ais, *s. m.* (*Ir. id.*) Ability, superiority; capability.

Murrachd, *s. f.* Ability, capability, sufficiency.

Murraiche, *com.* and *sup.* of murrach. More or most capable. Is e is murraiche na thusa, *he is more able than you.*

Murraichе, *s. f.* (*Ir. id.*) Ability, capability, sufficiency, power.

† **Mursanach**, aich, *s. m.* (*Ir. id.*) A subject.—*Shaw.*

Mursanta, *a.* Servile.

† **Mursantachd**, *s. f.* (*Ir. id.*) Subjection.—*Shaw.*

Murt, *s. m.* (*Du.* moort.) Murder. See **Mort.**

Murtachail, *a.* Murderous; massacring. Written also *mortail.*

Murtadh, aidh, *s. m.* Murder, massacre. More frequently written *mortadh*; which see.

Murtair, *s. m.*, *from* murt. (*Du.* moorder.) A murderer. *N. pl.* murtairean. More frequently written *mortair;* which see.

† **Murtill**, *a.* (*Ir. id.*) Dull.—*Shaw.*

Murusg, uisg, *s. m.* Sea-shore; sea-marsh.

Mus, Mus an, *conj.* Before; before that; lest.

† **Mus**, *a.* Pleasant, agreeable, handsome.

Mùs, *a.* (*perhaps* mò is.) Too much; exceeding; exorbitant. Mùs làn, *too full.*

Musach, *a.* Nasty, ugly, filthy, of dirty habits. *Com.* and *sup.* mosaiche. Written also *mosach.*

Musag, aig, *s. f.* A dirty female; any dirty animal of the female kind. Co 'thàinig ach musag, *who came but the dirty creature.—Mach.*

Musaiche, *com.* and *sup.* of mosach.

Musaiche, *s. f.* Dirtiness, filthiness, nastiness, drabbishness.

Mu seach, *adv.* and *prep.* Alternately; in return; to and fro. Fear mu seach, *one by one, man by man;* a siubhal an domhain mu seach, *traversing the deep to and fro.—Old Poem.* Tha' obair dol mu seach air, *his work increases on his hands, becomes greater than he can manage.*

Musg, muisg, *s. f.* (*Ir. id.*) A musket. *N. pl.* musgan, *muskets.—Macint.*

Mùsg, mùisg, *s. f.* (*Ir. id.*) Rheum; gore of the eyes.

Musg, *v. n.* Grow mouldy or musty. *Pret.* mhusg; *fut. aff.* musgaidh.

Musgach, *a.* Like a musket; full of muskets; of, or belonging to, a musket; armed with a musket.

Mùsgach, *a.* Rheumy; mouldy; musty. *Com.* and *sup.* musgaiche.

Musgail, *v. a.* and *n.;* more frequently written *mosgail;* which see.

Musgalach, *a.* See Mosgalach.

Musgaltach, *a.* See Mosgaltach.

Musgaltachd, *s. f.* Watchfulness.

Mùsgan, ain, *s. m.* (*Ir. id.*) Horse-fish; rheum; mustiness; mouldiness; pith; the porous part of a bone.

Musganach, *a.* (*Ir. id.*) Rheumy; musty; mouldy; troubled.

Mùsganachd, *s. f.* (*Ir. id.*) Rheuminess; mustiness; mouldiness.

Musgladh, aidh, *s. m.* More frequently written *mosgladh;* which see.

Mustar, air, *s. m.* (*Ir. id.*) Self-sufficiency; muster.

Mustar-mhaighstir, *s. m.* A muster-master.

† **Musuinn**, *s. f.* (*Ir. id.*) Confusion, tumult, hurly-burly. —*Shaw.*

Mut, *s. m.* (*Ir. id.*) Any short thing.—*Shaw.*

Mutach, *a.* (*Ir. id.*) Short, thick, and blunt.

Mùtach, *a.* Mouldy; musty. *Com.* and *sup.* mùtaiche.

Mutag, aig, *s. f.* (*Ir. id.*) A kind of glove without fingers.

Mutaiche, *s. f.* Mouldiness; mustiness.

Mùtain, *gen. sing.* and *n. pl.* of mùtan.

Mutan, ain, *s. m.* A muff; a thick glove; a cover for a gun; an old musty rag; any thing worn by disease or time. *N. pl.* mutain.

Mùth, *v. a.* (*Lat.* muto.) Change, alter, diversify; give in exchange; shift, turn; destroy. *Pret. a.* mhùth, *changed; fut. aff. a.* mùthaidh, *shall exchange.* Mhùth e mo thuarasdal, *he changed my wages.—Stew. Gen.*

Mùth, *s. m.* A change, alteration, difference; vicissitude; novelty; a decaying; small money, which may be given for larger pieces. Air mhùth doigh, *in a different manner.*

Muthach, aich, *s. m.* A herd; a cowherd.

Mùtha, Mùthadh, aidh, *s. m.* A changing, an altering, a shifting; *also*, a change, alteration, difference; vicissitude; novelty.

Mùthaidh, *fut. aff.* of mùth. Shall or will change.

Muthairn, *s. f.* An ancle.—*Macd.* and *Shaw.* *N. pl.* muthairnean.

Muthairneach, *a.* Ancled; having large ancles.

Muthan, ain, *s. m.* Most frequently written *maothan;* which see.

Mùthar, *fut. pass.* of mùth. Shall be changed. See Mùth.

Mu-thimchioll, *prep.* About; round; around; *literally*, by the circuit. Mu m' thimchioll, *about me;* mu d' thimchioll, *about thee;* mu thimchioll, *about him;* mu timchioll, *about her;* m' ar timchioll, *about us;* m' ur timchioll, *about you;* mu 'n timchioll, *about them.*

N.

N, (nuin, *the ash.*) The twelfth letter of the Gaelic alphabet. It has various sounds: (1.) *N*, when immediately preceded by *i*, or when *i* is the last vowel of the same syllable, often sounds exactly as the French *n* in *guigne*, or the Italian *n* in *regno;* as, linn, *an age;* cùirn, *cairns;* nighean, *a daughter;* uinneag, *a window.* (2.) When *n* is in the beginning of a verb in the imperative mood, and followed by a broad vowel, as nochd, *shew;* or at the beginning of a masculine adjective, and followed by a broad vowel, as, naomh, *holy;* nuadh, *new;* it has no sound similar to it in English, but it accords exactly with the first *n* in the French *non*, no. The same remarks apply to the reduplicated *nn.* (3.) *N*, at the beginning of a feminine adjective, and followed by a long vowel; or in the preterites of verbs, whether aspirated or not, and followed by a long vowel; or in the end of words, and preceded by a long vowel, sounds as *n* in the English words *nor, not;* naomh, *holy;* naisg, *squeezed;* shnàg, *creeped;* làn, *full.* (4.) *N*, whether simple or aspirated, if followed by a short vowel, sounds like *n* in *seen, neat;* in the preterite, and in certain other tenses, as, nigh, *washed;* shniomh, *spun;* in the middle of words, as, sinidh, *shall stretch;* and in the end of words, as, min, *meal;* coin, *dogs.* Lastly; the monosyllable *an*, when the next word begins with *c* or *g*, sounds like *ng;* as, an cù, *the dog;* an gial, *the cheek.*

N, followed by a hyphen [n-], is introduced between the *poss. pron.* ar, *our*, and the following word, when it begins with a vowel; as, ar n-aithrichean, *our fathers.—Sm.* Nar n-òige, *in our youth.—Id.*

'N, (*for* an), *def. art.* The. 'N Tì tha glic, *the Being who is wise.—Sm.* Dh'imich 'n dreach àillidh, *the beauteous vision vanished.—Orr.*

'N, *d. sing.* and *pl.* of the *def. art.* an. To the.

'N, (*for* an), a *particle* which precedes the future tenses of verbs beginning with a dental. 'N dean mi e? *shall I do it?*

'N, *prep.* (*for* ann.) In. 'N tigh caol gun leus, *in the narrow dark dwelling.—Oss. Fing.* 'N cridhe 'n daoi, *in the heart of the wicked.—Sm.*

'N, *poss. pron.* (*for* an.) Their. Fo 'n sàil, *under their heels. —Oss. Fing.*

Na, *gen. sing. fem.* of the *article* an. Of the. Fo ghruaim na h-oidhche, *under the gloom of night.—Oss. Tem.* Also the *nom.* and *dat. pl.* Air na sliabhaibh, *on the mountains.—Id.*

Nà, *adv.* (*Ir. id.*) Than. Is fearr e na òr, *it is better than gold.—Stew. Pro.*

Na, (*for* ann.) In; within. 'Na d' shuain, *in thy sleep.—Oss. Fing.*

Na, *adv.* Not; nor; neither; or; it is also used optatively and imperatively. Na gluais nan còir, *move not in their direction.—Oss. Tem.* Na tuiteadh am fear òg, *let not the youth fall.—Id.*

Most languages have a similar negative to this. *Gr.* μη and μη. *Lat.* ne *and* ni. *Fr.* ne. *Dan.* ney. *Sclav.* ne. *Georgian*, no. *Ir.* na. *Corn. W. Scotch*, na. *Sp. It. Eng.* no. *Goth.* nih, niu, *and* ni.

'Na, denoting similarity, (*for* ann a.) Tha i 'na coigreach, *she is [as] a stranger.—Oss. Fing.* Goll na thorc ard, *Gaul like a huge boar.—Fingalian Poem.* Rinn e mi na m'athair, *he made me as a father.—Stew. Gen.*

'Na, (*for* ann a.) In his; in her; in its. 'Na chòmhradh 's 'na ghniomh, *in his words and actions.—Sm.* 'Na deigh bha mìle sonn, *in her suit were a thousand heroes.—Oss. Fing.*

Na, *rel. pron. pl.* (used without an antecedent.) Those who; those which; of those who; of them who; of such as. Tannais na dh'fhalbh, *the ghosts of those who have departed.—Oss. Fing.* Na sgrios a ghaillionn, *those which the storm has destroyed.—Macfar.*

Na, *rel. pron. sing.* (*for* an ni a.) A thing that; that which; what. Cha 'n 'eil agam na cheannaicheas e, *I have not what will buy it;* feuch na th'agad, *shew me what you have got.*

Na, *interrog. particle*, (*for* an do.) It is used in the same sense as *did, have, hast.* Na thuit thu 'n codal trom? *hast thou fallen into profound sleep?—Oss. Fing.*

Nàbachail, *a.* (*from* nàbuidh.) Neighbourly. Gu nàbuchail, *in a neighbourly manner.*

Nàbachas, ais, *s. m.* Neighbourhood; neighbourliness. Anns an nàbachas, *in the neighbourhood.*

Nàbachd, *s. f.* (*for* nabaidheachd.) Neighbourhood, vicinity. Anns an nàbachd so, *in this neighbourhood.*

Nàbaidh, *s. m.* A neighbour. See also **Nabuidh**.

Nàbaidheachas, ais, *s. m.* Neighbourhood; neighbourliness.

Nàbaidheachd, *s. f.* Neighbourhood.

Nàbuidh, *s. m.* A neighbour. Euslainte nach d' fhiosraich a nàbuidh, *a disease which his neighbour inquired not after.—Macfar.*

Dan. naboe. *Swed.* nabo. *Ir.* nàbadh.

Nàbuidheachd, *s. f.* Neighbourhood, vicinity.

Nach, *interrog.* and *neg. particle.* Not. Nach truagh leat mi? *dost thou not pity me?—Oss.* Tha e 'g radh nach tig e, *he says he will not come;* is beag nach do thuit mi, *I almost fell;* cha mhor nach do thuit mi, *I almost fell.*

Arm. nach. *Ir.* nach. *Lat.* neque, nec.

Nach, *rel. pron.* Who not; which not; that not. Fear nach trèig a chompanach, *a man who will not desert his comrade.*

Nach, *conj.* That not. Nach do thrèig a ghradh, *that his love did not vanish.—Oss. Fing.*

Na d', *for* ann do. (*Ir. id.*) In thy; in thine. Na d' fheirg, *in thy wrath.—Oss.*

Nad, *s.* (*Ir. id.*) The posteriors.

† **Nada**, *s.* (*Ir. id.*) Nothing.

Nàdar, air, *s. m.* Most frequently written *nadur.*

Nadarrach, *a.* See **Nadurrach**.

Nadur, uir, *s. m.* (*Ir. id.*) Nature, disposition, temper. Gnuis nàduir, *the face of nature.—Old Poem.* Thaobh nàduir, *by nature.—Stew. Eph.* Droch nàdur, *a bad temper.* *Arm.* droucq natur.

Nàdurra, *a.* (*Ir.* nadurtha.) Natural; humane, good-natured. Gradh nàdurra, *natural affection.*

Nàdurrach, *a.*, *from* nadur. (*Ir. id.*) Natural; good-natured. Deagh nàdurrach, *good-tempered;* math nàdurrach, *good-tempered.*

Nàdurail, *a.* (nadur-amhuil.) Natural.

† **Naibh**, *s. f.* (*Ir.* naebh. *Lat.* nav-is.) A ship.

† **Naibheag**, eig, *s. f.*, *dim.* of naibh. (*Ir. id.*) A little ship.

Naid, *s. m.* and *f.* (*Ir. id.*) A lamprey—(*Shaw*); a husband.

Naidheachd, Naigheachd, *s. f.* News. More properly written *nuaidheachd;* which see.

† **Nail**, *a.* (*Ir. id.*) Another.

Nail-bheul, -bheoil *s. m.* (*Ir. id.*) A bridle-bit.

Nàile, *s. m.* A Highland saint of that name. The Gael very frequently swear by, or rather assert in, the name of this saint. Nàile tha! Nàile cha 'n 'eil! *i. e.* air Nàile tha! air Nàile cha n' eil! *indeed it is! indeed it is not!* or, *by St. Nail it is! by St. Nail it is not!* Nàile fhein! *indeed! by my sooth!* Nàile fhéin theid mi dhachaidh! *by my sooth I shall go home.—Old Song.*

† **Naim**, *s. f.* (*Ir. id.*) A bargain, a covenant. *Hence* snaim *or* snaidhm, *a knot.*

Naimh, *gen. sing.* and *n. pl.* of namh; which see.

Naimhde, *gen. sing.* and *n. pl.* of nàmhaid.

Naimhdeach, *a.* (*from* nàmhaid.) Hostile, warlike; like an enemy; of, or belonging to, an enemy.

Naimhdealachd, *s. f.* Hostility; malice; viciousness.

Naimhdealas, ais, *s. m.* Hostility, enmity; malice, rancour, viciousness.

Naimhdean, *n. pl.* of nàmhaid. Enemies, adversaries, opponents.

Naimhdean, ein, *s. m.* (*Ir. id.*) An enemy.

Naimhdeanas, ais, *s. m.* (*Ir. id.*) Enmity, malice, viciousness.

Naimhdeas, ais, *s. m.*, *from* nàmhaid.) (*Ir. id.*) Enmity, hostility; rancorousness, malice.

Naimhdeil, *a.* (nàmhaid-amhuil.) Hostile; rancorous; vicious. Gu naimhdeil, *hostilely.*

† **Naindean**, ein, *s. m.* (*Ir. id.*) Valour; chivalry—(*Shaw*); a hero.

† **Naindeanach**, *a.* (*Ir. id.*) Valorous; chivalrous; *also*, a chivalrous person.

† **Naing**, *s. f.* (*Ir. id.*) A mother.—*Shaw.*

† **Naing-mhòr**, -mhòir, *s. f.* (*Ir. id.*) A grandmother.

'Nàird, (*for* nàirde) *adv.* Upwards, up, from below, on high; *literally*, to the height.

† **Naire**, *a.* (*Ir. id.*) Clean, neat, trim, tidy.

Nàire, *s. f.* (*Ir. id.*) Shame; disgrace; affront; bashfulness. Cha robh nàire orra, *they were not ashamed.* Fa nàire, *ashamed.—Stew.* 2 *Sam.* Ghabh i nàire, *she became ashamed;* air bheag nàire, *shameless;* mo nàire! *shame!* mo nàire ort! *shame on you!*

Nàireach, *a.*, *from* nàire. (*Ir. id.*) Bashful, sheepish; shameful.

Nàireachd, *s. f.* (*Ir. id.*) Bashfulness, sheepishness, shamefulness.

Nàirich, *v. a.* (*Ir.* nairigh.) Shame, affront, browbeat, insult. *Pret. a.* nàirich; *fut. aff. a.* nàirichidh, *shall affront; fut. pass.* nàraichear, *shall be brought to shame.—Stew. Pro.*

† NAISAIR, *s.* (*Ir. id.*) The old inhabitants of a country. *—Shaw.*

NAISG, naisge, *s. f.* A ring; a seal.

NAISG, *v. a.* Seal; make fast or secure; bind or tie. *Pret. a.* naisg, *bound; fut. aff. a.* naisgidh, *shall bind; fut. pass.* naisgear, *shall be bound.* Naisgeadh càch le càirdeas, *let the rest be bound with friendship.—Mac Lach.*

NAISGEAR, *fut. pass.* of naisg. Shall be bound; shall be sealed.

NÀISGIDH, *fut. aff. a.* of naisg. Shall bind or seal.

NÀISGTE, *p. part.* of naisg. Bound; tied; healed; secured.

NÀISINN. See NÀISTINN.

NÀISNEACH, *a.* Modest; continent; sober; temperate; shamefaced. Gu nàisneach, *modestly.*

NÀISNEACHD, *s. f.* Modesty, shamefacedness; continence; soberness, temperateness. Le nàisneachd agus stuaim, *with shamefacedness and sobriety.—Stew. Tim.*

NÀISTINN, *s. f.* Care; circumspection; wariness; modesty. Làn nàistinn, *full of circumspection.—Macfar.*

NÀISTINNEACH, *a.* Careful; circumspect; wary; modest.

NAITHEAS, eis, *s. m.* Hurt, harm, injury.

NAITHEASACH, *a.* Hurtful, harmful, injurious.

† NALL, *s. m.* (*Ir. id.*) A bridle.

NALL, *adv.* (*Ir. id.*) Hither; hitherward; to this side; from the other side; towards me; towards us. Thigeadh e nall, *let him come hither.—Oss. Tem.* A null is a nall, *hither and thither.*

† NALLUS, uis, *s.* See FALLUS.

NAM, *conj.* If. This conjunction is used before verbs beginning with any of the labials, *b, f, m, p.*

'NAM, 'N AM, (*for* ann am.) In their. 'Nam bailtibh, *in their towns.*

'NAM, 'N AM, (*for* ann mo.) In my. 'Nam dhosan liath, *in my grey locks.—Oss. Fing.*

NAM, *gen. pl.* of the *article.* Of the; of. It is used before nouns beginning with any of the labials, *b, f, m, p.* Mullach nam beann, *the pinnacles of the mountains.—Oss.* Feadh ghleanntai nam fàsach, *amid the glens of the forests.—Oss. Manos.* *Nam* often, especially with the poets, imparts to a substantive the force of its cognate or kindred adjective; as Fionghal nam buadh, (Fionghal buadhmhor,) *victorious Fingal.—Oss. Fingal.*

NÀMH, *poet. construction* for nàmhaid. *N. pl.* naimh *and* nàmhan. A measg nàmhan, *in the midst of enemies.—Old Poem.* O shàruchadh mo nàmh, *from the oppression of my enemies.—Sm.* A naimh 'g a threigsinn, *his enemies leaving.—Oss. Gaul.*

NÀMHACH, *a.* (*from* nàmh.) Hostile, inimical, inveterate. Gu nàmhach, *hostilely.*

NÀMHACH, aich, *s. m.* An enemy. Mar dhà nàmhach, *like two enemies.—Oss. Cathula.* *N. pl.* namhaich.

NÀMHACHAIL, *a.* (namhach-amhuil.) Hostile; inveterate, rancorous.

NÀMHACHAS, ais, *s. m.* Enmity, hostility; rancour.

NAMHADAS, ais, *s. m.* (*Ir. id.*) Fierceness, enmity.

NÀMHAID, namhaid, *and* naimhde, *s. m.* (*Ir. id.*) An enemy, an antagonist. Bha 'n nàmhaid sàmhach, *the enemy was quiet.—Oss. Fing.* *N. pl.* nàmhaidean *and* nàimhdean.

NÀMHAIDEACH, *a., from* nàmhaid. (*Ir. id.*) Hostile, inimical; inveterate, malicious; adverse. Torran nan laoch nàmhaideach, *the noise of the hostile heroes.—Fingalian Poem.*

NÀMHAIDEALACHD, *s. f.* Hostility; inveterateness, maliciousness; adverseness.

NÀMHAIDEAS, eis, *s. m.* Enmity, hostility; malice, rancour. Contracted *naimhdeas.*

NÀMHAIDEIL, *a.* (nàmhaid-amhuil.) Hostile, inimical. More frequently written *naimhdeil.*

NAN, *conj.* If. It is used before all verbs beginning with a vowel or a lingual consonant. Nan abairinn, *If I were to say;* nan deanainn, *if I were to do.*

NAN, *gen. pl.* of the *art.* an. Of the; of. Thaibhse nan sion, *ye spectres of the storms.—Oss. Gaul.* *Nan* is used before nouns beginning with a vowel or with a lingual consonant; and often, especially with the poets, it imparts to a substantive the meaning and force of its kindred adjective: Mòra nan cruaidh-learg (cruaidh-leargach), *shelving Mora.—Ull.* Cuan nan stuadh (cuan stuadhmhor), *the billowy ocean.*

'NAN, NA 'N, (*for* ann an.) In their. Gu h-iosal na 'n uir, *low in the dust.—Oss. Cathluno.* Sios nan còir, *downwards in their direction,* or, *towards them.—Oss. Tem.* Tha iad nan codal, *they are asleep.*

'N ANN. Is it? 'n ann a rìreamh? *really?*

NAOGAD, *a.* Ninety. Naogad fear, *ninety men.*

NAOGADAMH, *a.* Ninetieth.

NAOI, *a.* Nine.

Gr. ἐννέα. *Pers.* nuh. *Island.* niu. *Swed.* nijo *and* † nio. *Da.* ni. *Arm.* nae *and* nao. *Corn.* naou. *Ir.* naoi.

† NAOI, *s. f.* (*Ir. id.*) A hip; a man, a person; Noah.—*Shaw.*

NAOI-DEUG, *a.* Nineteen. Naoi-deug ar fhichead, *thirty-nine;* naoi fir dheug 'ar fhichead, *thirty-nine men.*

NAOIDH, *s. m.* (*Ir. id.*) A babe, an infant, a suckling.

NAOIDHEACH, *a.* Infantile, like a babe or suckling.

NAOIDHEACHAN, ain, *s. m.* (*from* naoidh.) (*Ir. id.*) An infant, babe, or suckling; a young child.

† NAOIDHEACHDACH, aich, *s. m.* A chief, a principal.—*Shaw.*

NAOIDHEAN, ain, *s. m., dim.* of naoidh. (*Ir. id.*) An infant, babe, or suckling; a bantling or urchin; bravery. Fhuair iad an naoidhean, *they got the infant.—Stew. Matt.* *N. pl.* naoidheanan, *infants.—Stew. Job.*

NAOIDHEANACH, *a.* (*Ir. id.*) Infantile, childish.

NAOIDHEANACHD, *s. f.* Infancy, childhood. Na naoidheanachd, *in his* or *her infancy.*

NAOIDHEANTA, *a.* (*Ir. id.*) Infantile, babyish, childish.

NAOIDHEANTACHD, *s. f.* (*Ir.* naoidhantachd.) Infancy, childhood, childishness.

NAOIMH, *gen. sing.* and *n. pl.* of naomh; which see.

NAOIMHIOS, *s. m.* (*Ir. id.*) November.

† NAOIMHIOSDADH, aidh, *s. m.* (*Ir. id.*) A sanctuary.—*Shaw.*

† NAOINEAL, il, *s. m.* (*Ir. id.*) Prowess; chivalry.—*Shaw.*

NAOINEAR, *a.* Nine persons in number.

NAOMH, naoimh, *s. m.* A saint, a holy person, a sanctified person. Airson nan naomh, *on account of the saints.—Stew. Rom.*

NAOMH, *a.* (*Ir.* naomhtha.) Holy, pious, divine, sanctified, sacred. Ceud thoradh naomh, *holy fruit.—Stew. Rom.*

NAOMHACHADH, aidh, *s. m.* A sanctifying, a consecrating; sanctification, consecration.

NAOMHACHAIL, *a.* (*from* naomh.) Sanctificatory.

NAOMHACHD, *s. f.* (*from* naomh.) Holiness, sanctification, sacredness. D' a naomhachd, *of his holiness.—Stew. Heb.* *Ir.* naomthachd.

NAOMHADH, aidh, *s. m.* (*Ir. id.*) Sanctifying, sanctification.

NAOMHAICH, *v. a.* (*Ir.* naomhaigh.) Sanctify, consecrate. *Pret. a.* naomhaich; *fut. aff. a.* naomhaichidh, *shall sanctify*; *fut. pass.* naomhaichear.

NAOMHAICHTE, *p. part.* of naomhaich. Sanctified, consecrated.

NAOMH-AITHIS, *v. a.* Blaspheme.—*Shaw.*

NAOMH-AITHIS, *s. f.* Blasphemy against saints.

NAOMH-AITHISEACH, *a.* Blasphemous.

NAOMH-CHISTE, *s. f.* (*Ir. id.*) A sacristy.

NAOMH-CHLEACHDAS, ais, *s. m.* (*Ir. id.*) A pious habit.

NAOMH-CHOISREAGADH, aidh, *s. m.* (*Ir. id.*) A consecrating; consecration.

NAOMH-CHOISRIG, *v. a.* Consecrate; set apart for religious purposes. *Pret. a.* naomh-choisrig; *fut. aff. a.* naomh-choisrigidh.

NAOMH-CHOISRIGTE, *p. part.* (*Ir. id.*) Consecrated.

NAOMH-DHEAN, *v. a.* Canonize; deify; sanctify. *No preterite; fut. aff.* naomh-ni.

NAOMH-DHEANAMH, *s. m.* A canonizing; a deifying; canonization.

NAOMH-DHEIRC, *a.* A collection made for the poor at church; a deodand; a pious gift or offering.

NAOMH-DHION, *v. a.* Give refuge in a sanctuary; take refuge in a sanctuary.

NAOMH-DHION, *s.* A sanctuary, an asylum.

NAOMH-DHIONACHD, *s. f.* The protection afforded by a sanctuary.

NAOMH-DHIONTA, *p. part.* Protected in a sanctuary.

NAOMH-DHIONTACH, *a.* Affording an asylum; having the privilege of protecting, as a sanctuary.

NAOMH-GHNAS, ais, *s. m.* Habitual piety.

NAOMH-GHOID, *s. f.* Sacrilege. Bheil thu ri naomh-ghoid? *dost thou commit sacrilege?*—*Stew. Rom.*

NAOMH-GHOIDEACH, *a.* Sacrilegious.

NAOMH-GHOIDICHE, *s. m.* A sacrilegious person.

NAOMH-MHALLACHADH, aidh, *s. m.* A blaspheming; blasphemy; profane swearing; excommunication; anathema.

NAOMH-MHALLACHAIR, *s.* A blasphemer, a profane swearer.

NAOMH-MHALLACHD, *s. f.* Blasphemy; excommunication; anathema.

NAOMH-MHALLAICH, NAOM-MHALLUICH, *v. a.* Blaspheme; anathematise; excommunicate.

NAOMH-MHALLUCHADH, NAOMH-MHALLACHADH, aidh, *s. m.* See NAOMH-MHALLACHADH.

NAOMH-ÒRAN, ain, *s. m.* (*Ir. id.*) A hymn, a sacred song, a psalm, an anthem. *N. pl.* naomh-orain.

NAOMH-REACHD, *s. f.* A divine law or precept; a holy ordinance; a canon law. Do naomh-reachd, *thy holy law.*—*Stew. Ps.* *N. pl.* naomh-reachdan.

NAOMH-SHLUAGH, -shluaigh, *s. f.* Holy people, saints.

NAOMH-THAISG, *s. f.* A sacristy; a vestry.

NAOMH-THRÉIG, *v. a.* Apostatize. *Pret. a. id.*; *fut. aff. a.* naomh-thréigidh, *shall apostatize.*

NAOMH-THRÉIGEACH, *a.* Apostatizing; inclining to apostasy; *also*, an apostate.

NAOMH-THRÉIGICHE, *s. m.* An apostate, a renegade.

NAOMH-THRÉIGSINN, *s. f.* Apostasy, secession.

† NAON, *a.* (*Ir. id.*) Certain; assured.—*Shaw.*

NAONAR, *a.* Nine in number; nine persons; the number nine.

NAOSG, naoisg, *s. m.* A snipe.—*Shaw.*

NAOSGACH, aich, *s. m.* (*Ir. id.*) A snipe. *N. pl.* naosgaich.

NAOSGACH, *a.* Abounding in snipes; like a snipe. Coire naosgach, *a dell abounding in snipes.*—*Macdon.*

NAOSGAIR, *s. m.* (*Ir. id.*) An inconstant man. *N. pl.* naosgairean.

NAOSGAIREACHD, *s. f.* Fickleness, inconstancy.—*Shaw.*

NAOTH, *a.* Nine. Written also *naoi;* which see.

NAOTHADH, NAOTHAMH, *a.* Ninth. An naothadh bliadhna, *the ninth year.*—*Stew. Lev.*

NAR, *conj.* Not; let not; may not. It is used optatively or imperatively. Nar leigeadh Dia! *God forbid!* literally, *may God not permit!*—*Stew. Rom.*

NÀR, *s. m.* (*for* nàire.) Shame, disgrace; affront.

NÀR, *a.* Shameful, disgraceful; affronted; ashamed; feeling affronted. Is nàr an gnothach e, *it is a shameful business.*

'NAR, (*for* ann ar.) In our. 'Nar smuainte, 'nar cainnte, 's 'nar gniomh, *in our thoughts, words, and actions.*—*Sm.* Thar sinn 'nar luidhe, *we are lying, we are a-bed;* tha sinn 'nar gaisgich, *we are heroes.*

'NAR, (*for* ann bhur.) In your. 'Nar fearann, *in your land.*

† NAR, *a.* (*Ir. id.*) Good; happy.

NÀRACH, *a.* (*from* nàire.) Bashful, modest; shameful, disgraceful. Aghaidh nàrach, *a modest countenance.*—*R.* Sgeith nàrach, *a shameful spewing.*—*Stew. Hab.* *Com.* and *sup.* naraiche.

NÀRACHADH, aidh, *s. m.* (*Ir. id.*) The act of affronting or of disgracing, an affront; a disgrace; causing shame.

NÀRAICH, *v. a.* Shame; affront; browbeat; insult; disgrace. *Pret. a.* nàraich, *affronted; fut. aff. a.* nàraichidh, *shall affront.*

NÀRAICHEAR, *fut. pass.* of nàraich. Shall be affronted.

NÀRAICHIDH, *fut. aff. a.* of nàraich. Shall affront.

NÀRAICHTE, *p. part.* Affronted, disgraced, insulted, browbeaten.

† NARD, naird, *s. m.* (*Ir. id.*) Skill; knowledge.

† NAS, nais, *s. m.* (*Ir. id.*) An anniversary; a band or tie; death—(*Shaw*); an assemby.—*O'Reilly.*

NAS, nais, *s.* A weasel. An nas agus an luch, *the weasel and the mouse.*—*Stew. Lev.* Written also *neas* and *eas.*

NASACH, *a.* Like a weasel; abounding in weasels.

† NASADH, aidh, *s. m.* (*Ir. id.*) A fair—(*Shaw*); an assembly. *N. pl.* nasaidhean.

† NASADH, aidh, *s. m.* (*Ir. id.*) Fame; reputation; report.

† NASADH, *a.* (*Ir. id.*) Noble, famous, noted.

NASG, naisg, *s. m.* A wooden collar; a chain; a ring; a band; a seal; store, provision.

NÀSG, *v.* Written also *nàisg;* which see.

NASGACH, *a.* Having a collar; like a collar; chained; full of rings; binding; obligatory.

NASGADH, aidh, *s. m.* A binding; an obliging; a chaining; a collaring; a sealing; an obligation; a tie or bond. Còir ort le nasgadh cléir, *a right to thee by the binding of a clergyman,* i. e. *by wedlock.*—*Old Song.*

NASGADH, (a), *pr. part.* of nasg.

NASGAIDH, (a), *adv.* (*perhaps* ann asgaidh, *as a gift.*) Gratis, for nothing; freely. A nasgaidh fhuair sibh, *freely ye received.*—*Stew. Matt.* Ni mo a dh' ith sinn an nasgaidh, *neither have we eaten for nothing.*—*Stew. Thess.*

NASGAIDH, *s. f.* A treasure; a gift.—*Shaw.*

NASGAIR, *s. m.* (*Ir. id.*) A surety.—*Shaw.*

NASGAR, air, *s. m.* A defence, fortification.

† NATH, *s. m.* (*Ir. id.*) Science, knowledge.—*Shaw.*

NATAR, air, *s. m.* Nitre.—*Stew. Jer.*

† NATHACH, *a.* (*Ir. id.*) Learned; *also*, dark, grey, gloomy.

NATHAIR, nathrach, *s. f.* The *coluber cerus* of Linnæus; a serpent, a snake, an adder, a viper. Nathair bhreac shligneach, *a spotted, scaly snake.*—*Mac Lach.* Nathair challtuinn, *a snake*, the bite of which is harmless. *N. pl.* nathraichean.

Lat. natrix. *Germ.* natter *and* nater. *Goth.* nadr. *Corn.* naddyr. *W.* nadyr. *Ir.* nathair.

NATHAIR-NIMHE, *s. f.* A poisonous serpent; an asp; an adder. Nathair-nimhe air an t-slighe, *an adder in the path.* —*Stew. Gen.*

† NATHAN, *a.* (*Ir. id.*) Noble; famous.

NATHRACH, *gen. sing.* of nathair.

NATHRAICHEAN, *n. pl.* of nathair. Serpents.

'N DÉIGH, *adv.* and *prep.* (*for* an deigh.) After; behind. 'N déigh tuiteam dha, *after it fell.*—*Oss. Fing.*

NE, *an emphatic adjection pl.* used with the *poss. pron.* ar, *our*, and put after substantives and adjectives. Ar mac-ne, *our son;* ar Dia gràsmhor-ne, *our gracious God.*

'N E, (*for* an e.) Is it? is it he? 'N e rinn so? *is it he who did thus?* Cha 'n e, *no*, i. e. *not he.*

NEABHAN, sin, *s. m.* (*Ir. id.*) A Royston crow; a raven. —*Shaw.*

NEACADAIR, *s. m.* A nectarine. Crann neacadair, *a nectarine tree.*—*Macd.* *N. pl.* neacadairean.

NEACADAIREACH, *a.* Abounding in nectarines; like nectarines.

NEACH, *s.* (*Ir. id.*) A person; a body; one; some one; *rarely*, an apparition. Neach eigin, *some person;* neach sam bi, *any body;* neach na neach eigin, *somebody or other;* gach neach, *every one.*

† NEACHDAR, *adv.* Neither; outwardly; without.

NEACHD, *s. f.* (*Ir. id.*) A tribe; a pledge.

NEACHDARACH, *a.* (*Ir. id.*) Neutral.

NEAD, nid, *s. m.* A nest. Ann am nead, *in my nest.*—*Stew. Job.* *N. pl.* nid.

Lat. nidus. *Fr.* nid. *Corn.* nied *and* nieth. *W. Arm.* nyth.

NEADACHADH, aidh, *s. m.* A nestling or housing in a nest; a building a nest.

NEADACHADH, (a), *pres. part.* of neadaich. Nestling.

NEADAICH, *v. n.* (*from* nead.) Nestle; lie snug, like a bird in its nest; build a nest. *Pret. a.* neadaich, *nestled; fut. aff. a.* neadaichidh, *shall nestle.*

NEADAICHTE, *p. part.* of neadaich. Nestled.

NEADAN, ain, *s. m.* (*dim.* of nead.) A little nest. A neadan creachta, *her little nest plundered.*—*Macfar.*

'NEADH. Is it?

NEAG, *v. a.* Notch, indent. Written also *feag.*

NEAG, *s. m.* (*Ir. id.*) A notch. See FEAG.

† NEAL, *a.* (*Ir. id.*) Noble.—*Shaw.*

NEAL, nèil, *s. m.* See NEÙL.

NEALLAIR, *s. m.* A rogue; a ramscallion. *N. pl.* neallairean.

NEALLAIREACHD, *s. f.* Roguery, rascality.

NEAMH, nèimh, *s. m.* Heaven; the skies. Drùchd nèimh, *the dew of heaven.*—*Stew. Gen.* *N. pl.* neamha. Oscionn nan neamh, *above the heavens.*—*Sm.*

Gr. νιφ-ω, νιφ-αω, νιφ-αω, *to veil*, νιφ-ος, *a cloud.* *Arm.* neff *and* nef. *Ir.* neamh. *W.* nèv, *heaven.* *Russ.* nebo. *Sclav.* nebu. *Pol.* niebo. *Dal.* nebo. *Bohem.* nebe. *Styrian* and *Carniolese*, nebo.

NEAMH, *the Irish form of the Gaelic negative prefix*, NEO.

NEAMHACH, aich, *s. m.* (*from* neamh.) A heavenly being. *N. pl.* neamhaich.

NEAMHACH, *a.; contr. for* neamhaidheach; which see.

NEAMHAIDH, *a.*, *from* neamh. (*Ir.* neamhdha.) Heavenly; divine; celestial. Ceòl neamhaidh, *heavenly music.*

NEAMHAIDHEACH, ich, *s. m.* A heavenly being.

NEAMHAIN, *s. f.* (*Ir. id.*) A pearl; *also, adjectively*, made of pearl; impetuosity. A cheann-bheart clochara neamhain, *his headpiece set with stones and pearls.*—*Fingalian Poem.*

NEAMHAINEACH, *a.* Abounding in pearl; like pearl.

NEAMHAIRD, *s. f.* (*Ir. id.*) Remissness.

NEAMHAN, ain, *s. m.* A raven, a crow.—*Shaw.*

NEAMHNAID, *s. f.* A pearl. Neamhnaid nan iomadaidh buadh, *a pearl of many virtues.*—*Macfar.* *N. pl.* neamhnaidean. See also NEAMHNUID.

NEAMHNAIDEACH, *a.* Abounding in pearls; pearly; like a pearl. Written also *neamhnuideach.*

NEAMHNUID, *s. f.* A pearl. *N. pl.* neamhnuidean; *d. pl.* neamhnuidibh. Air neamhnuidibh, *on pearl.*—*Stew. Job.*

NEAMHNUIDEACH, *a.* Pearly; like pearl. Written also *neamhnaideach.*

NEAMHUIDH, *a.* (*from* neamh.) See NEAMHAIDH.

† NEAN, *s. m.* (*Ir. id.*) An inch, a span; a wave.—*Shaw.*

NEANAIDH, *s. f.* A fond name for a grandmother.

This word is, I believe, local; but it may here be remarked, that the Celts of Bretagne have a word *nani*, meaning a grandmother; from which Pezron derives *nanaea*, the name of a famous goddess among the Persians.

NEANNTAG, aig, *s. f.* A nettle. More commonly written *ionntag* and *eanntag.*

NEAPAICIN, NEAPAIGIN, *s. f.* A napkin; a handkerchief. —*Stew. John.* Neapaicin pochd, *a pocket-handkerchief;* neapaicin amhaich, *a neckerchief.* *N. pl.* neapaicinean.

† NEAR, *s. m.* (*Ir. id.*) A wild boar.—*Shaw.*

† NEAR, *s. m.* Water; a river.

Heb. Pers. Arab. Chald. Sam. nahar, *a river.* *Turk.* nehri, *a river.* Naar, *a river in Old Persia;* Nehri, *a river in Tartary;* Naro, *a river in Illyricum;* Dinari, *a river in Georgia.*

'NEAR, (*for* an ear.) The east; the east point. 'Near dheas, *the south-east;* 'near thuath, *the north-east.*

NEARACH, *a.* Happy; lucky; prosperous. Is nearach an duine, *happy is the man.*—*Stew. Job.* *Com.* and *sup.* nearaiche. Gu nearach, *happily.*

NEARACHD, *s. f.* Happiness; luckiness; prosperity; *also*, happy, prosperous.

NEAR-ÀITE, *s. m.* A place frequented by wild boars.

† NEARNADH, aidh, *s. m.* A likening, a comparing; likeness, comparison.

NEART, neirt, *s. m.* (*Ir. id.* *W.* nerth.) Strength; power; pith; valour; *rarely*, a miracle. Neart nan dàn, *the strength of song.*—*Oss. Carricth.* Toiseach mo neirt, *the beginning of my strength.*—*Stew. Gen.* Neart a chuim, *the valour of his breast.*—*Old Poem.* Le uile neart, *with all his strength.*—*Mac Lach.* Le m' uile neart, *with all my strength;* neart teine, neart mara, is neart balaoich, *the strength of fire, the strength of the sea, and the strength of a foolish fellow.*—*G. P.*

NEARTACHADH, aidh, *s. m.* (*Ir.* neartughadh.) A strengthening; a confirming, a ratifying.

NEARTAICH, *v. a.*, *from* neart. (*Ir.* neartaigh.) Strengthen; confirm; ratify; establish. *Pret. a.* neartaich. Neartaich se e féin, *he strengthened himself.*—*Stew. Gen.* *Fut. aff. a.* neartaichidh; *fut. pass.* neartaichear.

Neartaichear, *fut. pass.* of neartaich. Shall or will be strengthened.

Neartaichte, *p. part.* of neartaich. Strengthened; confirmed.

Neartar, *a.* (*for* neartmhor.) Strong; powerful. Is neartar an sonn, *powerful is the hero.—Oss. Fing.*

Neartmhoireachd, *s. f.* Strength; powerfulness.

Neartmhor, *a.* Strong, powerful; robust. *Com.* and *sup.* neartmhoire.

Neartor, *a.*; contracted for *neartmhor.*

Neas, nise, *s. f.* (*Ir. id.*) A weasel, or the *mustela vulgaris* of naturalists; a hurt; a wound; a fortified hill.

† **Neas**, *s. m.* An isthmus, a promontory or headland.
Germ. naes; *the English termination* ness, as in Sheerness, Inverness, Stromness. The southernmost promontory of Norway is also called *Naes;* hence also the English word *nose*, i. e. *the projecting feature.* See Innis.

† **Neas**, *a.* (*Ir. id.*) Noble, generous, magnanimous; near, next.

Neas-abhag, aig, *s. f.* A ferret. *N. pl.* neas-abhagan, *ferrets.*

Neasachd, *s. f.* (*Ir. id.*) Nearness, propinquity, proximity. —*Shaw.*

† **Neasan**, ain, *s. m.* (*Ir. id.*) The next or nearest place.

Neasg, neisg, *s. m.* (*Ir. id.*) An ulcer; a tie; a bond; a stall. *N. pl.* neasgan.

Neasgaid, *s. f.* (*from* neasg.) An ulcer, a boil; a pustulous sore. *N. pl.* neasgaidean, *ulcers; d. pl.* neasgaidibh. Le neasgaidibh cràiteach, *with painful ulcers.—Stew. Job.* Neasgaidean fola, *piles, hæmorrhoids.—Stew. Sam.* Neasgaid chloich, *a stone bile.*

Neasgaideach, *a.* Ulcerous; full of ulcers; causing boils or ulcers.

† **Neasta**, *a.* (*Ir. id.*) Just, honest.—*Shaw.*

Neath, *s. m.* (*Ir. id.*) A wound.

† **Neathas**, ais, *s. m.* Manslaughter.

Neich, *a.* Good, noble, excellent.

Neid, *s.* A battle; a wound received in battle.

Néil, *gen. sing.* of neul.

Néilean, ein, *s. m.* (*dim.* of neul.) A little cloud.

† **Neimh**, *v. a.* and *n.* (*Ir. id.*) Corrupt, spoil.

† **Neimh**, neimhe, *s. f.* (*Ir. id.*) Brightness, splendour—(*Shaw*); a stain.

Neimh, *gen. sing.* of neamh.

Neimheach, *a.* Glittering, shining, bright, splendid.

Neimhead, eid, *s. m.* Consecrated ground; glebe land.

† **Neimheadh**, idh, *s. m.* (*Ir. id.*) A poem; science.—*Shaw.*

† **Neimhi**, *s. pl.* (*Ir. id.*) Ants' eggs.—*Shaw.*

Neimheileachd, *s. f.* Painfulness, soreness; venomousness; passionateness.

Neimhneach, *a.* (*Ir. id.*) Sore, painful; venomous; passionate.

Neimhneachas, ais, *s.* Soreness; venomousness; passionateness.

Néip, *s. f.* A turnip. *N. pl.* neipeis, *turnips.*

Neirt, *gen. sing.* of neart; which see.

† **Neith**, *s.* (*Ir. id.*) A fight, an engagement.—*Shaw.*

Neo, *a priv.* or *neg. particle*, which may be prefixed to most adjectives.

Neo, *adv.* Else, otherwise. Neo is truagh mo chàradh, *else poor is my condition.—Ull.* Air neo, *else, otherwise.*

Neo-abuich, *a.* Not ripe.

Neo-adhmhor, *a.* Unfortunate; unsuccessful; hapless; inglorious; joyless.

Neo-adhmhorachd, *s. f.* Unsuccessfulness; ingloriousness.

Neo-aghmhor, *a.* Unfortunate; unsuccessful; hapless; joyless; inglorious.

Neo-aire, *s. f.* Heedlessness, inattention, inadvertence; absence of mind.

Neo-aireach, *a.* Heedless, inattentive; absent in mind. Gu neo-aireach, *heedlessly.*

Neo-aireachail, *a.* Heedless, inattentive, inadvertent.

Neo-airidh, *a.* Unworthy, undeserving; worthless. Neo-airidh air peanas, *unworthy of punishment.*

Neo-airtnealach, *a.* Not sorrowful; joyful, cheerful. Aig eirigh dhuinn neo-airtnealach, *when we rose joyful.—Old Song.*

Neo-aithnichte, *a.* Unknown, unrecognised, undiscovered. Rioghachdan neo-aithnichte, *unknown kingdoms.—Macfar.*

Neo-aithreach, *a.* Impenitent; not contrite; not curious.

Neo-aithreachail, *a.* Uncontrite; impenitent; obdurate. Do chridhe neo-aithreachail, *thy impenitent heart.*

Neo-aithreachas, ais, *s. m.* Impenitence; obduracy; hardness of heart.

Neo-amharusach, *a.* Unsuspicious; indubitable. Gu neo-amharusach, *unsuspiciously.*

Neo-amharusachd, *s. f.* Unsuspiciousness; indubitableness.

Neo-amhluidh, *a.* Unlike, dissimilar. Bu neo-amhluidh du chòr-sa, *unlike was thy condition.—Orr.*

Neo-aogasach, *a.* Unseemly; unbecoming; not having a pleasant appearance or exterior.

Neo-aogasachd, *s. f.* Unseemliness; the want of a pleasant exterior.

Neo-aoibhinn, *a.* Sorrowful; joyless; downcast. An la neo-aoibhinn, *the joyless day.—Oss. Derm.*

Neo-aoibhneach, *a.* Sorrowful; joyless; downcast; cheerless. Gu neo-aoibhneach, *sorrowfully.*

Neo-aontachadh, aidh, *s. m.* A disagreeing; a disunion; dissentience; the act of disagreeing.

Neo-aontachail, *a.* Adverse, averse; disagreeing, disunited. Am prasgan neo-aontachail so, *this disunited mob.—Macfar.*

Neo-bhaigheach, *a.* Not sparing; cruel; unfeeling.

Neo bhaigheil, *a.* Cruel; merciless. Gu neo-bhaigheil, *mercilessly.*

Neo-bhàsmhoire, *com.* and *sup.* of neo-bhàsmhor.

Neo-bhasmhoireachd, *s. f.* Immortality. Ag iarruidh neo-bhasmhoireachd, *seeking immortality.—Stew. Rom.*

Neo-bhàsmhor, *a.* Immortal.

Neo-bheartach, *a.* Not rich.

Neo-bheartaichte, *part.* Unharnessed; unyoked.

Neo-bheathail, *a.* Lifeless, spiritless, inanimate.

Neo-bheus, *s. m.* (*Ir.* neamh-bheus.) Immodesty, immorality, indecency.

Neo-bheusach, *a.* Immoral; immodest, indecent. Gu neo-bheusach, *indecently.*

Neo-bhith, *s. f.* Non-existence; non-entity.

Neo-bhlasda, **Neo-bhlasta**, *a.* (*Ir.* neamh-bhlasta.) Tasteless, insipid; unsavoury. An ni a tha neo-bhlasta, *that which is unsavoury.—Stew. Job.*

Neo-bhlasdachd, **Neo-bhlastachd**, *s. f.* Tastelessness, insipidity, unsavouriness.

Neo-bhog, *a.* Not soft; not effeminate; hard; hardy.

Neo-bhoidheach, *a.* Not pretty; not becoming; unhandsome, unseemly.

NEO-BHRÀTHAIREIL, *a* Unbrotherly. Giulan neò-bhràthaireil, *unbrotherly conduct.*

NEO-BHRÀTHAIREILEACHD, *s. f.* Unbrotherliness

NEO-BHRÀTHRAIL, *a.* Unbrotherly.

NEO-BHRIGH, *s. f* Contempt, insignificance; want of substance; unimportance Cuir an neo-bhrigh, *set at naught, frustrate.*

NEO-BHUAIRTE, *part.* Undisturbed; untempted, untroubled, unprovoked.

NEO-BHUAN, *a.* (*Ir.* neamh-bhuan) Not lasting; transitory; evanescent.

NEO-BHUANACHD, *s f.* Transitoriness, momentariness, evanescence.

NEO-BHUIDHEACH, *a.* Unthankful

NEO-BHUNAILTEACH, *a.* Not well-founded, not having a sure foundation, unsteady, unfixed. Gu neo-bhunailteach, *unsteadily*

NEO-BHUNAILTEACHD, *s f.* Unsteadiness; the want of a sure foundation.

NEO-BHUNAITEACH, *a* Not well-founded; not having a sure foundation; unfixed, unsteady

NEO-CHAIRDEIL, *a* Unfriendly Gu neo-chairdeil, *in an unfriendly manner.*

NEO-CHAOCHLAIDEACH, NEO-CHAOCHLAIDHEACH, *a* Unchangeable, immutable Gu neo-chaochlaideach, *unchangeably*

NEO-CHAOCHLAIDEACHD, NEO-CHAOCHLAIDHEACHD, *s f.* Unchangeableness, immutability.

NEO-CHAOCHLUIDHEACH, *a.* Unchangeable, immutable. Tre dha ni neo-chaochluidheach, *by two immutable things —Stew. Heb.*

NEO-CHAOCHLUIDHEACHD, *s. f* Unchangeableness, immutability Neo-chaochluidheachd a chomhairle, *the immutability of his counsel.—Stew Heb*

NEO-CHABHRAIDEACH, *a* Not quarrelsome —*Stew Tim ref*

NEO-CHARRUICHTE, *part.* (*Ir* neamh-choruichte) Unstirred, unmoved

NEO-CHARRUIDHEACH, *a* Immovable, steady, fixed

NEO-CHARRUIDHEACHD, *s f.* Immobility, steadiness, fixedness

NEO-CHARTHANACH, *a* Uncharitable, unfriendly Gu neo-charthanach, *uncharitably*

NEO-CHEADAICHTE, *part* Not permitted, illicit, unlawful.

NEO-CHEALGACH, *a* Undesigning, not cunning, unfeigned; upright, sincere Creideamh neo-chealgach, *unfeigned faith —Stew. Tim*

NEO-CHEALGACHD, *s f* Unfeignedness, uprightness, unaffectedness

NEO-CHEANALTA, *a* (*Ir* neamh-cheanalta) Unhandsome, inelegant, indelicate

NEO-CHEANGAILTE, *p. part.* Unbound, disengaged

NEO-CHEANNSAICHTE, NEO-CHEANNSUICHTE, *part* Untamed, unconquered; unbridled; dissolute

NEO-CHEARBACH, *a* Tidy, trim, not tawdry, neat, not awkward in dress, exact

NEO-CHEART, *a* Not right, not proper, unjust.

NEO-CHEARTAICHTE, *part* Unadjusted, uncorrected.

NEO-CHIALLACH, *a* Foolish; stupid, imprudent, unmeaning

NEO-CHINNTE, *s f* Uncertainty, precariousness

NEO-CHINNTEACH, *a.* Uncertain, precarious, equivocal; indecisive Fuaim neo-chinnteach, *an uncertain sound.—Stew Cor*

NEO-CHINNTEACHD, *s f* Uncertainty, precariousness; doubtfulness, indecisiveness

NEO-CHIONT, *s m* (*Ir.* neamh-chiont.) Innocence; integrity; harmlessness. Am neo-chiont, *in my innocence —Sm.*

NEO-CHIONTACH, *a* (*Ir.* neamh-chiontach.) Innocent; harmless; spotless; unblamed; simple; *also*, an innocent person. Fuil nan neo-chiontach, *the blood of the innocent.* —*Stew Jer. Com* and *sup* neo-chiontaiche.

NEO-CHIONTACHD, *s. f.* Innocency; harmlessness; spotlessness.

NEO-CHIOSNAICHTE, *part* Untamed, unquelled; unconquered, unappeased.

NEO-CHÌRTE, *part.* Uncombed.

NEO-CHLAON, *a.* Not awry; not squinting; straight, upright; impartial, just.

NEO-CHLAON-BHREITHEACH, *a.* Impartial, fair in judging.

NEO-CHLAON-BHREITHEACHD, *s. f.* Impartiality or fairness in judging

NEO-CHLEACHDTA, *p. part.* Unaccustomed; unhabituated; uninured, unpractised

NEO-CHLÉIR, *s f* The laity.

NEO-CHLÉIREACH, ich, *s m.* A layman.

NEO-CHLÌ, *a.* Not awkward, not weak, dexterous; active.

NEO-CHNUASACHD, *s. f.* Indigestion.

NEO-CHNUASAICHTE, *part.* (*Ir.* neamh-chnuasaichte) Undigested, unchewed.

NEO-CHOIGILT, NEO-CHOIGILTEACH, *a.* Unthrifty, profuse.

NEO-CHOIMHEACH, *a.* Not strange; not shy, not difficult of access; affable, kind; not surly; frank, generous

NEO-CHOIMHEACHAS, ais, *s. m.* Want of shiness, affability, complacency.

NEO-CHOIMEASACH, *a* Incomparable.

NEO-CHOIMEASGTA, *a* (*Ir.* neamh-chumasgte.) Unmixed.

NEO-CHOIREACH, *a* (*Ir.* neamh-choirtheach) Blameless, inculpable. Bithidh sibhse neo-choireach, *ye shall be blameless —Stew. Gen.*

NEO-CHOISRIGTE, *part.* Unconsecrated, unhallowed.

NEO-CHOMAS, ais, *s m* (*Ir* neamh-chomas) Impotence; inability, debility

NEO-CHOMASACH, *a* Unable, impotent; impossible.

NEO-CHOMBANTA, *a.* Unsociable, uncompanionable.

NEO-CHOMHAIRLICHTE, *part* Unadvised, unresolved.

NEO-CHOMHNARD, *a.* Uneven in the surface, not level, not plain

NEO-CHOMPANTA, *a* Unsociable; uncompanionable Gu neo-chompanta, *unsociably.*

NEO-CHORDACH, *a.* Discordant.

NEO-CHORDADH, aidh, *s. m.* (*Ir* neamh-chordadh.) Disagreement, discordance; dissonance

NEO-CHOSLACH, *a* Unlike, dissimilar; unlikely. Cha 'n 'eil e neo-choslach, *it is not unlikely.*

NEO-CHOSMHUIL, *a* Unlike, dissimilar

NEO-CHOSMHUILEACHD, *s. f* Unlikeness; dissimilarity; unlikeliness.

NEO-CHOTHROM, oim, *s m* (*Ir* neamh-chothrom) Disadvantage; want of opportunity, disproportion.

NEO-CHOTHROMACH, *a.* Inconvenient; not opportune; disadvantageous, unjust

NEO-CHRÀBHACH, *a* Irreligious, impious, profane, *also*, not hypocritical Da dhaoinibh neo-chràbhach, *to profane men —Stew Tim.*

NEO-CHREIDEACH, ich, *s. m.* An infidel, an unbeliever, a sceptic *N pl* neo-chreidich.

NEO-CHREIDEACHD, *s f* Infidelity, scepticism.

NEO-CHRIOCHNACH, *a.* Unlimited, infinite, endless Sloinntearachd neo-chriochnaich, *endless genealogies —Stew. Tim.*

Neo-chriochnaichte, *part.* (*Ir.* neamh-chriochnichte.) Unfinished; undone; incomplete; unlimited.

Neo-chriochnuidheach, *a.* (*Ir.* neamh-chriochnuidheach.) Infinite, endless.

Neo-chriochnuidheachd, *s. f.* Infinitude; endlessness.

Neo-chrion, *a.* Not ungenerous; not little-hearted; liberal, generous, magnanimous. Gu fearail, neo-chrion, *manly and generous.—Old Song.*

Neo-chronail, *a.* Harmless.—*Stew. Ps. ref.*

Neo-chruadalach, *a.* Not hardy; not hard-hearted.

Neo-chruinn, *a.* Not round; not sane

Neo-chruinnichte, *part.* Ungathered, uncollected; unassembled; scattered.

Neo-chruthaichte, *part.* Uncreated, unformed.

Neo-chubhaidh, *a.* (*Ir.* neamh-chubhach.) Unseemly, unbecoming; unfit, improper

Neo-chuid, *s. f.* Poverty.—*Shaw.*

Neo-chuideach, *a.* Poor, indigent, improvident —*Shaw*

Neo-chuimhne, *s f.* (*Ir.* neamh-chuimhne.) Forgetfulness; heedlessness.

Neo-chuimhneachail, *a.* Forgetful; heedless

Neo-chuimseach, *a* Immoderate; intemperate; infinite

Neo-chùirteil, *a.* Uncourtly; uncourteous. Gu neo-chùirteil, *uncourteously.*

Neo-chumanta, *a.* (*Ir.* neamh-chumanta) Uncommon; unusual.

Neo-chùmhnantach, *a.* Unconditional, admitting of no conditions.

Neo-churaidh, *a.* Gentle

Neo-chùram, ain, *s m.* (*Ir.* neamh-chùram) Carelessness, inattentiveness, security.—*Macd.*

Neo-chùramach, *a.* (*Ir* neamh-churamach.) Careless, inattentive, inadvertent. Gu neo-chùramach, *carelessly*

Neo-churanta, *a* Unwarlike.

Neo-dhaichealachd, *s. f.* Unhandsomeness; want of genteelness; improbability.

Neo-dhàicheil, *a.* Unhandsome; ungenteel; improbable.

Neo-dhaingnichte, *part.* Unbound; unobliged; unengaged; unconfirmed; unratified

Neo-dhaonnach, *a.* (*Ir.* neamh-dhaonna.) Inhuman; inhospitable.

Neo-dhean, *v. a.* Undo.

Neo-dheas, *a.* (*Ir.* neamh dheas.) Not active; not neat

Neo-dhiadhaidh, *a* (*Ir.* neamh-dhiadhuidh) Ungodly, irreligious. See also **Neo-dhiadhuidh.**

Neo-dhiadhaidheachd, *s. f* Ungodliness; irreligion

Neo-dhiadhuidh, *a* Ungodly, irreligious Duine neo-dhiadhuidh, *an ungodly man.—Stew. Pro.*

Neo-dhiadhuidheachd, *s. f.* Ungodliness, irreligion, atheism.

Neo-dhìleas, *a* Unfaithful; faithless; unrelated Duine neo-dhìleas, *an unfaithful man.—Stew Pro* Gu neo-dhìleas, *faithfully.*

Neo-dhìllse, *s f.* Faithlessness; unfriendliness

Neo-dhìllseachd, *s. f.* Faithlessness; unfriendliness; non-relationship

Neo-dhiolta, *part.* Unpaid, unrequited, unrewarded; unrevenged.

Neo-dhiongalta, *a.* Not firm; not firmly bound, insufficient; not firmly fixed.

Neo-dhiongaltachd, *s. f.* Insufficientness; the state of not being firmly bound or firmly fixed; want of mental firmness

Neo-dhleasnach, *a.* Undutiful, unduteous; disobedient, irreverent

Neo-dhleasnas, ais, *s m* Undutifulness, disobedience, irreverentness.

Neo-dhligheach, *a.* Lawless; unlawful; illegitimate, undutiful Do dhaoinibh neo-dhligheach, *to lawless men —Stew. Tim*

Neo-dhuine, *s m* (*Ir.* neamh-dhuine) An insignificant fellow, an unmanly fellow, a nobody.

Neo-dhuinealachd, *s f* Unmanliness, effeminateness.

Neo-dhuinealas, ais, *s m.* Unmanliness, softness, effeminacy.

Neo-dhuineil, *a.* Unmanly, effeminate

Neo-dhùrachd, *s* (*Ir* neamh-dhurachd) Negligence, insincerity, irresoluteness.

Neo-dhùrachdach, *a.* Negligent, careless, insincere; irresolute Gu neo-dhùrachdach, *negligently*

Neo-eagallach, *a* (*Ir* neamh-eagolach.) Fearless; unappalled; bold, not skittish. Gu neo-eagallach, *fearlessly* *Com* and *sup* neo-eagallaiche

Neo-eagnaidh, *a* Foolish, ignorant, imprudent. Do dhaoinibh neo-eagnaidh, *to foolish men —Stew. Rom.*

Neo-eagnaidheachd, *s f* Foolishness; ignorance, imprudence.

Neo-ealanta, *a* (*Ir* neamh-ealladhanta) Inartificial; inelegant Gu neo-ealanta, *inartificially*

Neo-eid, *v a* Unclothe, disarray, strip - *Shaw*

Neo-éifeachd, *s f.* (*Ir* neo-efeachd) Ineffectualness, inefficiency, insufficiency, incapacity

Neo-éifeachdach, *a* Ineffectual; inefficient, incapable. Gu neo-éifeachdach, *ineffectually*

Neo-éisleanach, *a* Healthy, sound, spirited

Neo-éisleanachd, *s f* Healthiness, soundness, freedom from disease; spiritedness.

Neo-eòlach, *a* (*Ir* neamh-eolach) Ignorant, unacquainted, not expert; not cunning.

Neo-fhabhorach, *a* Unfavourable, not disposed to favour Gu neo-fhabhorach, *unfavourably*

Neo-fhaicinneach, *a* Invisible Gu neo-fhaicinneach, *invisibly* Written also *neo-fhaicsinneach.*

Neo-fhaicinneachd, *s f* Invisibleness. Written also *neo-fhaicsinneachd*

Neo-fhaicsinneach, *a* Invisible. Nithe neo-fhaicsinneach, *things invisible —Stew Col.*

Neo-fhaicsinneachd, *s f* Invisibility, invisibleness.

Neo-fhallain, *a* Unhealthy, unsound, unwholesome. Biadh neo-fhallain, *unwholesome food*

Neo-fhallaineachd, *s f.* Unsoundness, unhealthiness

Neo-fhallsa, *a* (*Ir* neamh-fhallsa) Not false, real, unfeigned Gu neo-fhallsa, *unfeignedly.*

Neo-fhallsail, *a* Not false, not deceiving; real unfeigning; fair.

Neo-fhasanta, *a.* (*Ir* neamh-fhasanta) Unfashionable, old-fashioned. Gu neo-fhasanta, *unfashionably.*

Neo-fheumail, *a* (*Ir* neamh-fheumail) Needless, unnecessary; useless, superfluous, unavailing. Is neo-fheumail sgriobh, *it is superfluous to write.—Stew. Cor* Gu neo-fheumail, *needlessly.*

Neo-fhiachail, *a* Valueless, trifling.

Neo-fhior, *a* Untrue. Gu neo-fhior, *untruly.*

Neo-fhios, *s m* Ignorance, want of information

Neo-fhiosrach, *a* Unconscious, not aware, ignorant, unintelligent Gu neo-fhiosrach, *unconsciously*

Neo-fhìreannach, *a.* Unrighteous; unjust; not ingenious; not faithful; wicked.

Neo-fhìreannachd, *s. f.* Unrighteousness; faithlessness; disingenuousness; wickedness; sinfulness.

Neo-fhìreantach, *a.* Unrighteous; unjust; disingenuous; unfaithful; wicked.

Neo-fhìreantachd, *s. f.* Unrighteousness; disingenuousness; wickedness. Ann an neo-fhìreantachd, *in unrighteousness.—Stew. Rom.*

Neo-fhoghainnteach, *a.* Not stout, not strong.

Neo-fhoghluimte, *a.* (*Ir.* neamh-fhoghlumte.) Ignorant; unlearned; untaught; rude. Neo-fhoghluimte ann an cainnte, *rude in speech.—Stew. Cor.*

Neo-fhoillsichte, *part.* Unrevealed, undiscovered.

Neo-fhoirfe, *a.* Imperfect; incomplete; insufficient.

Neo-fhoirfeachd, *s. f.* Insufficiency; incompleteness; imperfectness.

Neo-fhoirfidh, *a.* Imperfect; incomplete; insufficient.

Neo-fhoisneach, *a.* (*Ir.* neamh-fhoistineach.) Restless; impatient; uncomfortable; fidgetty; turbulent.

Neo-fhoisneachd, *s. f.* Restlessness; impatience; uncomfortableness; turbulence.

Neo-fhonnmhor, *a.* (*Ir.* neamh-fhonmhor.) Discordant, inharmonious, unmusical; dejected; not in humour.

Neo-fhonnmhorachd, *s.* Discordance, dissonance; dejectedness.

Neo-fhortanach, *a.* Unfortunate, unlucky.

Neo-fhreagarach, *a.* Unfit; not fitting; not corresponding; inapplicable.

Neo-fhreasdalach, *a.* Improvident; unfavourable; difficult. Gu neo-fhreasdalach, *improvidently.*

Neo-fhreasdalachd, *s. f.* Improvidentness; unfavourableness.

Neo-fhuras, *a.* Not easy, difficult; not patient; uneasy; *also, substantively,* difficulty.

Neo-fhurasach, *a.* Impatient; uneasy.

Neo-fhurasda, *a.* Not easy, difficult.

Neo-gharail, *a.* (*Ir.* neamh-gharamhuil.) Incommodious.

Neo-ghealtach, *a.* Not timid; unappalled; intrepid.

Neo-ghealtachd, *s. f.* Boldness; intrepidity.

Neo-gheamnaidh, **Neo-gheamnuidh**, *a.* Unchaste, incontinent, intemperate. Luchd neo-gheamnuidh, *incontinent people.—Stew. Tim.*

Neo-gheamnaidheachd, **Neo-gheamnuidheachd**, *s. f.* Unchasteness, incontinence, intemperateness.

Neo-gheimnidh, *a.* See Neo-gheamnaidh.

Neo-gheimnidheachd, *s. f.* See Neo-gheamnaidheachd.

Neo-ghean, *s. m.* Hatred; enmity; dislike; disaffection.

Neo-gheanmath, aith, *s. m.* Dissatisfaction; disapprobation; disaffection.

Neo-gheur, *a.* Blunt in edge, blunt in point; blunt in comprehension; dull, simple. Duine neo-gheur, *a simple man.—Stew. Pro.*

Neo-gheuraichte, *part.* Not sharpened; not soured; not leavened; unfermented. Aran neo-gheuraichte, *unleavened bread.—Stew. Gen. ref.*

Neo-ghlaine. See Neo-ghloine.

Neo-ghlan, *a.* (*Ir.* neamh-ghlan.) Unclean, impure, polluted. Ni sam bi neo-ghlan, *any thing unclean.—Stew. Lev.* Cairbh spreidh neo-ghloin, *the carcass of unclean cattle.—Id. Com.* and *sup.* neo-ghloine.

Neo-ghlic, *a.* (*Ir.* neamh-ghlic.) Unwise, foolish; witless; thoughtless. Anamain chrìne nan gniomh neo-ghlic! *thou little soul of deeds unwise!—Mac Lach.*

Neo-ghloine, *s. f.* Uncleanness; impurity; filth; pollution. Ma bheanas e ri neo-ghloine, *if he toucheth uncleanness.—Stew. Lev.*

Neo-ghluaiste, *part.* Unmoved; unagitated; unruffled.

Neo-ghluasadach, *a.* Immovable; undisturbed; unruffled. Bithibh neo-ghluasadach, *be ye immovable.—Stew. Cor.* Gu neo-gluasadach, *immovably.*

Neo-ghluasadachd, *s. f.* Immovableness.

Neo-ghnathach, *a.* (*Ir.* neamh-ghnathad.) Unusual; not customary; extraordinary; idle.

Neo-ghnàthachaidh, *a.* Impracticable.

Neo-ghnàthaichte, *part.* Unattempted; undone or unperformed; extraordinary; uncommon.

Neo-ghoireasach, *a.* Immoderate; intemperate; excessive; unfavourable.

Neo-ghoireasachd, *s. f.* Immoderateness; intemperateness; excessiveness.

Neo-ghoirt, *a.* Not sour; not sore.

Neo-ghoirteachadh, aidh, *s. m.* The process of taking away its acid from any substance; not fermenting; a not souring; a sweetening.

Neo-ghoirtich, *v. a.* Take off sourness; unacidulate; sweeten.

Neo-ghoirtichte, *part.* Unacidulated, sweetened; unleavened, unfermented. Aran neo-ghoirtichte, *unleavened bread.—Stew. Gen.* and *Ex.*

Neo-ghrad, *a.* Not quick; not sudden; slow; sluggish; dilatory. Is neo-ghrad a ghrian, *tardy is the sun.—Ull.* Gu neo-ghrad, *slowly.*

Neo-ghràsmhoireachd, *s. f.* Ungraciousness; unmercifulness.

Neo-ghrasmhor, *a.* (*Ir.* neamh-ghrasmhor.) Ungracious; unmerciful; without grace. Gu neo-ghràsmhor, *ungraciously.*

Neo-ghrinn, *a.* Inelegant; not fine; not showy. Gu neo-ghrinn, *inelegantly.*

Neo-ghrinneas, eis, *s. m.* Inelegance; lack of finery.

Neoid, *s. f.* (*Ir. id.*) A wound.

Neòil, *gen. sing.* and *n. pl.* of neul.

Neo-inbhich, *a.* Unripe; untimely; not come to maturity; not come to full growth. Gin neo-inbhich, *untimely birth.—Stew. Ecc. ref.*

Neoinean, ein, *s. m.* (*Corn.* neoinin.) A daisy. Glacag nan neoinean, *the daisy-covered dell.—Macfar.*

Neoineanach, *a.* Abounding in daisies; of daisies; like a daisy.

Neo-innleachd, **Neo-inntleachd**, *s. f.* Want of ingenuity; uninventiveness; non-contrivance.

Neo-innleachdach, **Neo-inntleachdach**, *a.* Not ingenious; uninventive; not contrivant; unartful, inexpert.

Neo-iochdmhoire, *com.* and *sup.* of neo-iochdmhor.

Neo-iochdmhoireachd, *s. f.* Pitilessness; want of mercy.

Neo-iochdmhor, *a.* Pitiless, unfeeling; merciless. Gu neo-iochdmhor, *pitilessly.*

Neo-iochdranach, *a.* Disobedient; insubordinate; disloyal.

Neo-iochdranachd, *s. f.* Insubordination; disobedience; disloyalty.

Neo-iogarra, *a.* Haughty, arrogant. Gu neo-iogarra, *haughtily.*

Neo-iogarrachd, *s. f.* Haughtiness; arrogance.

Neo-iomchubhaidh, *a.* See Neo-iomchuidh.

Neo-iomchuidh, *a.* Inconvenient; improper; unfit; unqualified; not commodious.—*Stew. Acts.*

Neo-iomlaineachd, *s. f.* Incompleteness, imperfectness; imperfection; incompletion.

Neo-iomlan, *a.* (*Ir.* neamh-iomlan.) Imperfect; incomplete; unfinished. Gu neo-iomlan, *imperfectly.*

Neo-iompaichte, *part.* Unconverted; unchanged.

Neo-ionann, *a* (*Ir.* neamh-ionann) Dissimilar, unlike, unequal; differing. Is neo-ionann duit e, *he is very unlike you.*

Neo-ionannachd, *s f.* Dissimilarity, inequality.

Neo-ionannas, ais, *s. m.* (*Ir.* neamh-ionannas) Dissimilarity, inequality.

Neo-ionmhuinn, *a.* (*Ir.* neimh-ionmhuin) Unlovely; unamiable; unbeloved; morose. Gu neo-ionmhuinn, *unamiably.*

Neo-ionmhuinneachd, *s f.* Unloveliness, the state of not being beloved; moroseness.

Neo-ionnsuichte, *a.* Unlearned, untaught, illiterate; rude; ignorant; untrained

Neo-iùlmhor, *a.* (*Ir.* neamh-iùlmhar) Untaught; ignorant; unskilful.—*Stew. Heb. ref*

Neo-laghail, *a.* Unlawful, illegitimate. Gniomh neo-laghail, *an unlawful action*

Neo-laghalachd, *s f.* Unlawfulness, illegitimateness.

Neo-lamhchair, *a.* Handless or inexpert; clumsy-handed, awkward.

Neo-lamchaireachd, *s. f.* Handlessness; inexpertness; want of dexterity

Neo-làthaireach, *a* (*Ir.* neamh-lathaireach.) Absent in person; apt to be absent or away.

Neo-lathaireachd, *s. f.* Absence of person.

Neo-leanabaidh, *a.* Not childish; manly.

Neo-leasaichte, *part* (*Ir* neamh-leasaichte) Uncorrected; unimproved; unamended.

Neo-lochdach, *a.* (*Ir.* neamh-lochdach. Unspotted, unblemished; faultless; sinless. Naomh agus neo lochdach, *holy and without blemish.—Stew. Eph.* Gu neo-lochdach, *unspottedly.*

Neo-loisgeach, *a.* (*Ir.* neamh-loisgeach. Incombustible; not corrosive; asbestive; uncaustical

Neo-luchdaich, *v. a.* Disburden, lighten. *Fut. aff.* neo-luchdaichidh.

Neo-luchdaichte, *p part* of neo-luchdaich. Disburdened; lightened.

Neo-mharbhach, **Neo-mharbhtach**, *a.* (*Ir.* neamh-mharbhthach) Immortal, not sanguinary.

Neo-mharbhachd, **Neo-mharbhtachd**, *s. f.* (*Ir.* neamh-mharbhthachd) Immortality.

Neo-mhealltach, *a.* Undeceiving; honest; undissembling.

Neo-mheangail, *a.* Unblemished.

Neo-mhearachdach, *a.* (*Ir.* neamh-mhearachdach.) Unerring; infallible. Gu neo-mhearachdach, *unerringly*

Neo-mheas, *s. m.* (*Ir.* neamh-mheas.) Disrespect; contempt.

Neo-mheàsail, *a.* Disrespected; contemptible Written also *neo-mhiosail*

Neo-mheasarra, *a.* (*Ir* neamh-mheasardha.) Intemperate; immoderate; excessive; beyond measure. Gradh neo-mheasarra, *intemperate love, whoredom.—Stew Ezek.*

Neo-mheasarrachd, *s. f.* (*Ir.* neamh-mheasarrdhacht.) Intemperateness; excess, immoderateness; excessiveness, immenseness Ann an neo-mheasarrachd, *in excess.—Stew. Pet.*

Neo-mheasgach, *a.* Incommiscible.

Neo-mheasgta, *a.* Uncompounded, unmixed

Neo-mheata, *a.* (*Ir.* neamh-mheata) Fearless; daring; stout.

Neo-mheatachd, *s. f.* Fearlessness; resoluteness.

Neo-mhìn, *a.* Unsmooth; rough-grained

Neo-mhiosail, *a.* Disrespected; contemptible. Written also *neo-mheasail.*

Neo-mhisgeach, *a* (*Ir.* neamh-mhisgeach.) Sober; not inclined to drunkenness or to tippling.

Neo-mhothachadh, aidh, *s. m.* (*Ir* neamh-mhothughadh.) Want of feeling; insensibility, stupidity, stupor.

Neo-mhothachail, *a.* Insensible; torpid; callous; unfeeling.

Neo-mhothuchadh, aidh, *s m* Want of feeling; insensibility; stupidity, stupor; callousness. Written also *neo-mhothachadh*

Neònach, *a.* Droll, capricious; eccentric; curious *Com.* and *sup.* neònaiche. Is neònach leam, *I was surprised.*

Neònachas, ais, *s. m.* A droll person; a curiosity; surprise, wonder Ghabh mi neònachas, *I was surprised.*

Neònaiche, *com* and *sup* of neònach.

Neònaid, *s f.* A pearl Written also *neamhnaid.*

Neònan, ain, *s. m* (*Corn.* neoinin) A daisy. *N. pl* neònain, *daisies* Neònain is sobhrach, *daisies and primroses —Old Song.*

Neònanach, *a.* Daisied; like a daisy. Glacag neònanach, *a daisied dell*

Neo-neach, *s m.* An insignificant person, a nobody.

Neo-neart, -neirt, *s. m* Pithlessness, feebleness.

Neo-neartar, *a* , *for* neo-neartmhor

Neo-neartmhor, *a* Weak; unwarlike; infirm *Com.* and *sup.* neo-neartmhoire.

Neo-neartor, *a.* (*for* neo-neartmhor) Weak; unwarlike; infirm Neo-neartor fo lann, *weak in wielding a sword.—Oss. Tem*

Neoni, *s.* (neo, *priv. and* nì) *Ir* neamhni Nothing; nonentity. Ged nach 'eil annam ach neoni, *though I am nothing —Stew. Cor.* Thig e gu neoni, *he or it will come to nothing.*

Neonich, *v. a* Annihilate, annul; neutralize; bring to nothing.

Neonitheach, *a* Trifling; of no account; valueless; inconsiderable; abortive.

Neonitheachd, *s. f* Nothingness, abortiveness.

Neo-oileanaichte, *part.* Untaught; illiterate.

Neo-oireamhnach, *a.* Unbecoming; inadequate; improper.

Neo-omhailleach, *a.* Heedless, careless.

Neo-onorach, *a* Ignoble, mean; dishonest; thievish, Duine neo-onorach, *a dishonest man.*

Neo-phòiteil, *a.* (*Ir.* neamh-phoit-amhuil) Sober, abstemious; not apt to go into excess in eating or drinking.

Neo-phòitearachd, *s. f.* Abstemiousness in drinking or in diet; sobriety; temperance

Neo-phrìs, *s. f* Want of value; uselessness, contemptibleness. Na cuir air neo-phrìs, *do not despise.—Stew Heb. ref*

Neo-rann-phairteach, *a* Incommunicable. Feartan neo-rann-phairteach, *incommunicable attributes —Stew Heb*

Neo-rann-phairteachd, *s. f* Incommunicableness

Neor-eisiomail, *s f.* Independence; the not being in one's reverence.

Neo-riaghailteach, *a.* Irregular, heteroclite; anomalous Gu neo-riaghailteach, *irregularly*

Neo-sgarail, *a.* Inseparable, not to be divided or parted

Neo-sgàthach, *a.* Not timid; fearless; undaunted or unappalled.—*Macint.* Bu neo-sgàthach an cùraidh, *unappalled was the hero —Old Song.*

NEO-SGEADAICH, NEO-SGEADUICH, *v. a.* Undress; unadorn, disarray.

NEO-SGEADAICHTE, NEO-SGEADUICHTE, *a.* Unadorned; disarrayed; undressed, stripped.

NEO-SGITHICHTE, *part.* Untired, unfatigued.

NEO-SHOOINNEAR, NEO-SGONNAR, *a.* Heedless

NEO-SHAILLTE, *a.* Unsalted; unseasoned; insipid.

NEO-SHALACH, *a.* (*Ir.* neamh-shalach.) Undefiled; unpolluted; clean; cleanly. An leabadh neo-shalach, *the bed undefiled.—Stew. Heb*

NEO-SHANNT, -shainnt, *s m* Want of desire; lack of ambition; loathing; squeamishness

NEO-SHANNTACH, *a* Not covetous; unambitious; loathing Macanta, neo-shanntach, *patient, not covetous.—Stew Tim.*

NEO-SHÀRACHAIDH, *a.* Unconquerable.

NEO-SHÀRAICHTE, NEO-SHÀRUICHTE, *part* Unoppressed, unharassed, unconquered.

NEO-SHEANNSAR, *a* Unlucky, ominous.—*Macint*

NEO-SHEANNSARACHD, *s f* Unluckiness, ominousness

NEO-SHEARGACH, *a.* Unblasting or unscorching, that does not wither; undecaying, unwithering

NEO-SHEARGACHTE, *part* Unwithered, unscorched, undecayed.

NEO-SHEARGTA, NEO-SHEARGTE, *part* Unwithered, unblasted, unscorched, undecayed

NEO-SHEASMHACH, *a* (*Ir* neamh-sheasmhach) Unstable; unsteady; not durable; inconstant. Neo-sheasmhach mar uisge, *unstable as water —Stew Gen*

NEO-SHEASMHACHD, *s. f* Instability; unsteadiness, inconstancy, transientness

NEO-SHOCRACH, *a.* Unquiet, restless, uncomfortable, not steady, not firmly placed.

NEO-SHOILLEIR, *a.* Indistinct, not clear, not bright, not transparent, not intelligible

NEO-SHOILLEIREACHD, *s f* Indistinctness, absence of light, the state of being dark or not bright, unintelligibleness

NEO-SHOIRBHEACHADH, aidh, *s m* Unsuccessfulness, the circumstance of not succeeding or prospering.

NEO-SHOIRBHEACHAIL, *a* Unsuccessful, unprosperous; unfortunate

NEO-SHOLARACH, *a* Improvident; shiftless; an improvident person Gu neo-sholarach, *improvidently*

NEO-SHÒLASACH, *a.* Joyless, delightless, mournful, sad

NEO-SHONA, *a* Unhappy, hapless; luckless An tìr neoshona so, *this luckless land.—Macfar*

NEO-SHONRUICHTE, *part.* Unresolved, undeterminate; indefinite, not remarkable

NEO-SHUAIMHNEACH, *a* Restless

NEO-SHUARRACH, *a.* Not insignificant, not valueless

NEO-SHUBHACH, *a* Joyless, comfortless Gun charaid, neoshubhach, *joyless, without a friend — Old Song*

NEO-SHUIDHICHTE, *part* Unsettled, unsteady; discomposed, unplanted

NEO-SHUILBHEAR, *a* Gloomy, cheerless, not merry, morose.

NEO-SHUIME, *s f* Carelessness, negligence, indifference Na cuir air neo-shuime, *despise not —Stew Heb*

NEO-SHUIMEALACHD, *s f.* Negligentness, inattentiveness, indifference.

NEO-SHUIMEIL, *a.* Negligent, indifferent, inattentive. Gu neo-shuimeil, *inattentively*

NEO-SHUNNTACH, *a* Dispirited, melancholy, spiritless; sullen, morose Gu neo-shunntach, *dejectedly*. *Com* and *sup* neo-shunntaiche.

NEO-SMIORAIL, *a.* Spiritless, dull. Daoine neo-smiorail, *spiritless men.—Oss. Fing*

NEO-SPÉISEIL, *a.* Underrating; careless; inattentive.

NEO-SPÒRSAIL, *a.* Not scornful; not prone to deride.

NEO-STRÀICEALACHD, *s. f.* Want of conceit; want of forwardness.

NEO-STRÀICEIL, *a.* Unassuming, unconceited; not forward.

NEO-STRUIDHEIL, *a* (*Ir.* neamh-straoigh-amhuil.) Not extravagant; frugal

NEO-THÀBHACH, *a.* Futile; pithless, weak; impotent; unimportant, immaterial; ineffectual; unprofitable; unavailable.

NEO-THÀBHACHD, *s. f.* Futility, pithlessness, weakness; unimportance, impotence, ineffectualness.

NEO-THABHACHDACH, *a.* Futile; pithless, unsubstantial; impotent, ineffectual, immaterial, unprofitable.

NEO-THABHAIRTEACH, *a.* (*Ir.* neamh-thabhartach.) Not inclined to give away; stingy, niggardly

NEO-THAIRBHE, *s f* Unfruitfulness, unproductiveness; unprofitableness; unavailableness; unsubstantialness.

NEO-THAITINN, *v* Displease, dissatisfy, disapprove. Neothaitinn i ris, *she did not satisfy him.*

NEO-THAITNEACH, *a.* Displeasing, dissatisfactory; unacceptable, disagreeable; unwelcome.

NEO-THARBHACH, *a* Unfruitful, unproductive; unsubstantial; unprofitable, fruitless; unavailable, unserviceable Fearann neo-tharbhach, *an unproductive farm*, ri oibribh neo-tharbhach, *with fruitless works.—Stew. Eph. Com.* and *sup* neo-tharbhaiche.

NEO-THARBHAICHE, *s. f.* Unfruitfulness; unproductiveness, unprofitableness; fruitlessness, unserviceableness.

NEO-THEAGAISTE, *part* Untaught, unlearned.

NEO-THEARUINNTE, *a* Insecure, unsafe; unprotected; unsaved Gu neo-thearuinnte, *insecurely.*

NEO-THEARUINNTEACHD, *s f.* Insecurity, unprotectedness.

NEO-THEÒMA, NEO-THEÒMADH, *a.* Unskilful, ignorant.

NEO-THETH, *a* Not hot, cool; not zealous.

NEO-THIMCHIOLL-GHEARRADH, aidh, *s m.* Uncircumcision

NEO-THIMCHIOLL-GHEARRTA, NEO-THIMCHIOLL-GHEARRTE, *a* Uncircumcised

NEO-THIOMCHIOLL-GHEARRADH, aidh, *s m* Circumcision. —*Stew. N. T.*

NEO-THIOMCHIOLL-GHEARRTA, NEO-THIOMCHIOLL-GHEARRTE, *a.* Uncircumcised Do dhuine neo-thiomchioll-ghearrte, *to one who is uncircumcised —Stew. Gen*

NEO-THOGARACH, *a* Uninclined; averse; reluctant; passionless Gu neo-thogarach, *reluctantly*

NEO-THOILE, *s f.* Want of inclination, nolition; unwillingness; reluctance

NEO-THOILEACH, *a.* Unwilling, disinclined; reluctant. Gu neo-thoileach, *unwillingly*

NEO-THOILEACHADH, aidh, *s m* A dissatisfying

NEO-THOILEACHAS-INNTINN, *s m* Dissatisfaction.

NEO-THOILEIL, *a* Stubborn, reluctant, perverse.

NEO-THOILEILEACHD, *s f.* Stubbornness, reluctantness; perverseness

NEO-THOILICH, *v a* Dissatisfy. *Fut. aff. a* neo-thoilichidh, *shall dissatisfy*

NEO-THOILICHTE, *part.* Dissatisfied, displeased, discontented. Neo-thoilichte leis, *dissatisfied with him* or *it*, iochdaran neo-thoilichte, *a malcontent.*

NEO-THOILTEANNACH, *a.* Undeserving; unworthy. See also NEO-THOILLTINNEACH

Neo-thoillteannas, ais, *s. m.* Undeservedness; unworthiness; demerit. Written also *neo-thoilltinneas.*

Neo-thoilltinneach, *a.* Undeserving; unworthy. Neo-thoilltinneach air bàs, *undeserving of death.*

Neo-thoilltinneas, ais, *s. m.* Undeservedness; unworthiness; demerit. A reir do neo-thoilltinneis, *according to thy demerit.*

Neo-thoinisgeil, *a.* Foolish; without common sense. Gu neo-thoinisgeil, *foolishly.*

Neo-thoirt, *s. f.* Indifference; negligence; contempt; disinclination.

Neo-thoirtealachd, *s. f.* Negligentness; indifference; carelessness; harmlessness.

Neo-thoirteil, *a.* Indifferent, negligent, careless; inattentive; causing no harm; causing no loss.

Neo-thoirt-fa'near, *s.* Inattentiveness.

Neo-thorrach, *a.* (*Ir.* neamh-thorthach.) Unfruitful, unproductive; barren; unprolific, not pregnant; past child-bearing. Ris a mhnaoi neo-thorraich, *to the barren woman.*—*Stew. Job. Com.* and *sup.* neo-thorraiche.

Neo-thorraiche, *s. f.* Unfruitfulness; unproductiveness; barrenness. Neo-thorraiche mo chuim, *the barrenness of thy womb.*—*Old Poem.*

Neo-thorraichead, id, *s. m.* Unfruitfulness; barrenness; increase in barrenness; female barrenness. A dol an neo-thorraichead, *growing more and more unfruitful* or *barren.*

Neo-thraigheach, *a.* Inexhaustible; that cannot be drained.

Neo-thràighte, *a.* Unexhausted; undrained.

Neo-thraoighte, *part.* Unexhausted; undrained.

Neo-thràthail, *a.* Unseasonable; late; untimely.

Neo-thròcaireach, *a.* (*Ir.* neamh-throcaireach.) Unmerciful, pitiless; relentless; callous.

Neo-thròcaireachd, *s. f.* Pitilessness; relentlessness, cruelty.

Neo-threòraichte, **Neo-threòruichte**, *a.* Not led; unconducted, undirected.

Neo-thruacanta, *a.* Uncompassionate, pitiless; unfeeling; unmerciful.—*Stew. Pro.* Is neo-thruacanta a ghnùis, *pitiless is his aspect.*—*Macfar.*

Neo-thruacantachd, *s. f.* Uncompassionateness; unmercifulness.

Neo-thruaillichte, *part.* Incorrupted; unspoiled or unmarred; unviolated; undefiled; unadulterated.

Neo-thruaillidh, *a.* (*Ir.* neamh-thruaillidh.) Incorruptible.—*Stew. Rom.* Incorrupted; undefiled; unadulterated.

Neo-thruaillidheachd, *s. f.* Incorruptibleness; incorruption; undefiledness; incorruptible purity.

Neo-thuasaideach, *a.* Not quarrelsome.—*Stew.* 1 *Tim.*

Neo-thuigse, *s. f.* Senselessness; absurdity; lack of judgment or common sense.

Neo-thuigseach, *a.* Senseless or foolish; unintelligent; irrational. Cinneach neo-thuigseach, *a foolish nation.*—*Stew. Rom.*

Neo-thuirseach, *a.* Not sad, not mournful; not causing sadness. Cha bhiodh a bhàs neo-thuirseach, *his death would not be without sorrow.*—*Old Song.*

Neo-thuisleach, *a.* Infallible; stable; established; not liable to fall or stumble.

Neo-thuisleachd, *s. f.* Infallibleness; stability; firmness.

Neo-thuiteamach, *a.* Infallible; unerring; unstumbling.

Neo-thuiteamachd, *s. f.* Infallibleness; infallibility; firmness.

Neo-uallach, *a.* (*Ir.* neamh-uallach.) Not proud, not vain, not conceited, not airy; humble, unambitious.

Neo-uasal, *a.* (*Ir.* neamh-uasal.) Mean, ignoble; unassertive of rank, not proud.

Neo-uidheam, *contr.* neo-uime, *s. f.* Undress; dishabille.

Neo-uidheamaichte, **Neo-uigheamaichte**, *part.* Undressed; unprepared; not ready.

Neo-uireasach, *a.* (*contracted for* neo-uireasbhuidheach.) Not poor; not needy; not dependent; not destitute.

Neo-uireasbhuidh, *s. f.* Absence of poverty; independence.

Neo-ullamh, *a.* (*Ir.* neamh-ullamh.) Unprepared; not ready; not done. Gum faigh iad sibh neo-ullamh, *that they shall find you unprepared.*—*Stew. Cor.*

Neo-ullamhachd, *s. f.* Unpreparedness, unreadiness.

Neo-umhailleach, *a.* Heedless, inconsiderate, inattentive, listless; without care or thought, secure. Gu neo-umhailleach, *heedlessly.*—*Stew. Ezek.* Samhach, neo-umhailleach, *quiet, without thought.*—*Stew. Jud.*

Neo-urchoideach, *a.* Harmless, safe; not troublesome; peaceful; innocent; quiet, tame.

Neul, neoil, *s. m.* A cloud. Mar neul ruiteach, *like a ruddy cloud.*—*Oss. Gaul.* Air chùl neòil, *behind a cloud.*—*Fingalian Poem. N. pl.* neoil; *d. pl.* neulaibh. Written also *nial.*

Gr. νεφελη, *a cloud. Lat.* nebula. *Germ.* nebel. *Arm.* niful *and* niul. *Corn.* niull. *Ir.* neul.

Neul, neòil, *and* néil, *s. m.* (*Ir. id.*) A trance or swoon; a fit; colour, aspect, appearance, complexion; *also,* light; a glimpse of light. Tha thu air neul an aòig, *you have the colour of death.*—*Old Song.* Caochladh neòil, *a change of appearance.*—*Macint.* A caochladh mo néil, *changing my complexion.*—*Old Song.*

Neulach, *a., from* neul. (*Ir. id.*) Cloudy, misty; cloud-covered; coloured. Anns an làtha neulach, *in the cloudy day.*—*Stew. Ezek.* An làthair nan laoch neulach, *in presence of the cloud-covered heroes.*—*Oss. Gaul.*

Neuladair, *s. m.* (*Ir.* neuladoir.) An astrologer; a meteorologist. *N. pl.* neuladairean.

Neuladaireachd, *s. f.* Astrology; meteorology: *also,* a sneaking and gazing about.—*Shaw.*

Neulaich, *v. a.* and *n.* (*from* neul.) Colour; gloss; assume a colour; grow cloudly. *Pret. a. id.; fut. aff. a.* neulaichidh. Neulaich paircean agus miodair gu bàs, *parks and meadows have the hue of decay.*—*Macd.*

Neular, *a.* (*for* neulmhor.) Having a good colour; coloured; well complexioned.

† **Neul-fhurtadh**, aidh, *s. m.* (*Ir. id.*) A slumbering.

Neulta, *n. pl.* of neul. Clouds; an assemblage of clouds. Neulta tiugh nan speur, *the thick clouds of heaven.*—*Sm.*

Neultach, *a.* (*from* neul.) Cloudy; misty. Là neultach, *a cloudy day.*

Neultachd, *s. f.* Cloudiness; mistiness; gloominess.

Neup, *s. m.* A turnip. Neupais, *turnips.*

Neupach, *a.* Abounding in turnips; like a turnip.

Ni, *s. m.* (*Ir. id.*) A thing, circumstance, affair, business; a deed, a fact; substance; cattle. *N. pl.* nithe *and* nitheannan. Ni sam bi, *any thing;* ni h-eigin, *something;* often contracted *ni' gin;* ni no ni' gin, *something or other;* neo-ni, *nothing;* beag nithe, *a little, a small quantity;* air bheag nithe, *almost, to a small degree;* ni math, *goodness, God;* a dheoin ni math, *God-willing;* air ghaol ni math, *for the love of God.*

Ni, *adv.* Not. Ni 'n guth mi o neul, *I am not a voice from a cloud.*—*Oss. Tem.* Ni 'm fear siubhail mi, *I am not a* *a traveller.—Id.* This negative requires *h* before an initial vowel Ni h-eadh (*i. e.* ni è), *no, nay, not so, it is not.—Stew. Gen.* Ni h-iad, *they are not, not they*

Gr. οὐ *and* μὴ *Lat.* ni *and* ne. *Goth.* ni *and* nih. *Corn.* and *W.* ni. *Sclav.* ne.

† NIA, *s. m.* (*Ir. id.*) A sister's son.

NI-BHEIL, *a.* Not, no *Ni-bheil* is properly the present of the negative mood of the auxiliary verb *bi*. As ni-bheil mi, thu, &c., *I am not, thou art not, &c.*

'N I, (*for* an i) Is it she? Cha 'n i, *it is not she.*

NI, *fut. aff. a.* of dean Shall or will do Ciod a ni mi? *what shall I do?* Ni e an gnothach, *it will do.*

† NIADH, *s. m.* (*Ir. id.*) A champion.

NIADHACHD, *s. f.* Bravery; chivalry.

† NIAL, *s.* (*Ir. id.*) A letter.—*Shaw.*

NIAL, *a.* A cloud, colour, complexion Crona nan nial, *cloudy Crona.—Oss. Com.* Carbad nan nial, *a chariot of clouds.—Macfar.* Written also *neul*, which see

NIALACH, *a.* Cloudy; misty; coloured. Written also *neulach.*

NIALADAIR, *s. m.* (*from* nial.) An astrologer, a meteorologist. *N. pl.* nialadairean

NIAL-EIDE, *s. f.* A mantle of clouds. Tràigh nan nial-eide, *the cloud-covered shore.—Ull.*

NIAMH, *s. m.* (*Ir. id.*) The brightness, colour, or appearance of any thing.—*Shaw.*

NIAMH, *a.* Beautiful

NIAMH, *v. a.* (*Ir. id.*) Gild; colour over; gloss. *Pret. id.*, *fut. aff. a.* niamhaidh.

NIAMHACH, *a.* (*Ir.* niamhtha.) Bright; pleasant; having a pleasant appearance.

NIAMHACHD, *s. f.* Brightness, pleasantness.

NIAMHAIL, *a.* Bright, pleasant.

NIAMH-GHAIRE, *s. f.* (*Ir. id.*) A smile.

NIAMHGHLAS, *a.* (*Ir. id.*) Greenish.—*Shaw.*

'NIAR, *s.* The west point; the west 'Niar dheas, *the south-west*, 'niar thuath, *the north-west*

'NIAR-MHÀINISTEAR, cir, *s. m.* Westminster.

NIAS See NEAS

† NIAT, *a.* (*Ir. id.*) Brave, valiant.

† NIATACHD, *s. f.* (*Ir. id.*) Bravery, valour.

NIATAL, ail, *s. m.* A reed *N. pl.* niatalan

NI-B'FHAIDE, *adv.* Longer; farther.

NIC, *s. f.* Daughter. This vocable is used in contradistinction to *Mac* in surnames, as, Seumas Mac Ghriogair, *James Mac Gregor*, Màire nic Ghriogair, *Mary Mac Gregory.*

NID, *gen. sing.* and *n. pl.* of neud.

† NÌD, *s. f.* (*Ir. id.*) Manslaughter.—*Shaw.*

NI 'D, (*for* ni iad.) They shall do

† NIDHE, *s.* (*Ir. id.*) Time.—*Shaw.*

† NIGH, nighe, *s. f.* (*Ir. id.*) A daughter, a niece. *W.* nith. *Corn.* noith, *a niece* Hence the modern word *nighean*

NIGH, *v. a.* Wash, bathe, cleanse, purify *Pret. a.* nigh; *fut. aff. a.* nighidh, *shall wash*, *p. part.* nighte.

NIGHEACHAN, ain, *s. m.* A washing of linen Bean nigheachain, *a laundress*, tigh nigheachain, *a washing-house* or *laundry*

NIGHEADAIR, *s. m.* (*Ir. id.*) A washer, a cleanser

NIGHEADAIREACHD, *s. f.* The occupation of washing, as of linen; the business of a laundress; bathing.

NIGHEADH, idh, *s. m.* A washing, a bathing; a purifying, a cleansing.

NIGHEADH, (a), *pr. part.* of nigh Bathing, washing, purifying, cleansing with water. Tha e 'g a nigheadh féin, *he is washing himself, he is bathing.*

NIGH-AITE, *s. f.* A bathing-place, a bath

NIGHEAN, nighinne, *s. f.* (*from* † nigh.) A daughter; a damsel; a term by which a young woman is addressed. Ghradhaich e 'n nighean, *he loved the damsel.—Stew. Gen.* Nighean céile, *a daughter-in-law.*

NIGHINNE, *gen. sing.* of nighean

NIGHTE, *p. part.* of nigh. Washed, bathed, cleansed; clean. A ghruaidh nighte le deòir, *her cheek bathed in tears.—Oss. Fing.*

Lat. nit-eo, nit-idus, *Fr.* nette, *clear* *Eng.* neat.

† NIGHTEAN, ein, *s. m.*, *from* nigh. (*Ir. id.*) Soap; a mixture of dung and urine for washing linen, used by the lower classes in Ireland, and the Highlands

NI'GIN, (*for* ni h-eigin.) Something. Ni na ni'gin, *something or other*

NI H-ANN, *adv.* No, not, nay, not so Ni h-ann mar tre' aon duine, *not as through one man.—Stew. Rom.*

NI H-È, *adv.* No, not; it is not so. Reubaibh bhur cridhe is ni h-è ur n-eudach, *tear your hearts and not your clothes.—Stew. Joel.*

NI H-EADH, *adv.* Nay, not; not so, it is not so

NI 'M, (*for* ni mi) (*Ir. id.*) I will do or make.

NI 'M, (*for* ni am) Not. Ni 'm faigh mi, *I will not get*

NIMH, *s. f.* (*Ir. id.*) A drop.

NIMH, nimhe, *s. f.* (*Ir. id.*) Poison; *rarely*, bitterness, sourness Nimh nan nathair, *the poison of serpents.—Stew. Job* Nathair nimhe, *an adder, a venomous serpent.*

NIMHEIL, *a.* (*i. e.* nimhe-amhuil) Poisonous, viperous, virulent, baneful Bha iad nimheil, *they were virulent.—Macdon.*

NIMHNEACH, *a.* (*Ir. id.*) Poisonous, virulent, viperous, baneful; peevish, passionate Tha shùil nimhneach, *his eye is baneful.—Sm.*

NIMHNEACHAN, ain, *s. m.* (*Ir. id.*) Rheumatism.—*Shaw.*

NIMHNEACHD, *s. f.* Virulence, banefulness

NIGIR, *a.* (*Ir. id.*) Sore; sick; bitter.

NI'NN, *for* nighinne. See NIGHEAN.

NINNEACH, *a.* Pleasant.—*Shaw.*

NIOM, (*for* ni mi) I shall or will do. Written also *ni'm.*

NIOMHACH, *a.* (*Ir. id.*) Bright; shining.—*Shaw.*

NIOMHAS, ais, *s. m.* (*Ir. id.*) Brightness, clearness, transparentness.

NIOMSA, (*for* ni mise) I will do.

† NION, *s. m.* (*Ir. id.*) A wave; a letter.—*Shaw.*

NIONACH, *a.* (*Ir. id.*) Pleasant; speckled, forked; catching.—*Shaw.* *Com.* and *sup.* nionaiche

† NIONADH, aidh, *s. m.* (*Ir. id.*) A prey; booty or plunder.—*Shaw.*

NIONAG, aig, *s. f.* (*for* nigheanag) A young daughter; a girl, a young girl; a little girl. Reic iad nionag, *they have sold a girl.—Stew. Joel.* *N. pl.* nionagan; *d. pl.* nionagaibh. Làn do nionagaibh, *full of girls.—Stew. Zech.*

NIOPAG, aig, *s. f.* (*Ir. id.*) A pinch, a nip.

NIOR, *adv.* (*Ir. id.*) Not; never. Anam nior thog, *who never lifted his soul.—Sm.*

NIOS, *adv.* (*Ir.* nios) From below; from the East.

NIOS, (a), *adv.* From below; from the East

NIOSGAID, *s. f.* An ulcer; a boil; any suppurating sore. *N. pl.* niosgaidean See NEASGAID.

NIOSGAIDEACH, *a.* Ulcerous; full of boils or ulcers; like an ulcer.

NIS, *adv.* (*Ir.* nis, *now.* *Dan.* nys, *lately.* *Arm.* neuze *and* neze, *then.*) Now, at this time

Nis, (a), *adv.* Now, at this time. A nis mata, *now then;* thig a nis, *come now.*

Ni's, (*for* ni is, *or* na is) Usually preceding an adjective, to express the comparative and superlative degree. Ni's fearr, ni's fhearr, *better;* ni's faide, ni's fhaide, *longer, any longer,* cha d' thig mi ni's fhaide, *I will not come any farther;* ni's miosa, *worse,* ni's mò, *greater, any greater, higher, larger, longer, any higher, any larger, any longer.*

Ni's, (*for* ni is.) A thing that is. Ni's fearr is urrainn duit fhaotainn, *the best thing you can get.*

Nise, *gen sing.* of neas; which see

Nitear, (*more properly* nithear,) *fut. pass.* of dean. Shall be done.

† **Nith**, *s f.* (*Ir. id.*) Slaughter; battle; manslaughter —*Shaw.*

Nithe, *n. pl.* of ni. Things, matters, business, affairs. Often written *nitheannan*

† **Nitheach**, *a.*, *from* nith. (*Ir. id*) Warlike

Nitheannan, *n. pl.* of ni. Written also *nithe.*

Nithear, *fut. pass.* of dean. Shall be done

Niùc, *s. m.* (*Scotch*, neuk) A corner or nook. *N. pl* niùcan.

Niùcach, *a.* Having corners or nooks.

'**Niugh**, *adv.* To-day A corruption of *an diugh.*

No, *adv.* and *conj* (*W* no *Ir.* no) Or, nor; else; otherwise. Teich, no fairich m' fhearg, *fly, or feel my wrath* —*Oss. Tem.* Cha 'n fhaic thusa no mise, *neither you nor I shall see.*

† **Nobhaidh**, *s f.* (*Ir. id*) A time, a season —*Shaw.*

Noch. More properly *nach;* which see

Nochd, *s. m.* Nakedness. A dh' fholach an nochd, *to conceal their nakedness* —*Stew Exod*

Nochd, *a* (*Corn* naydh.) Naked, bare, unclothed, unsheltered.

Nochd, *v. a.* Declare; reveal or disclose; shew; discover; make naked or strip; peel. *Pret a* nochd; *fut aff a* nochdaidh, *shall disclose.* Nochd caoimhneas, *shew kindness*

Nochd, an nochd, *adv* To-night, this night, this evening; *literally*, the [present] night. Is truagh mo chàradh an nochd, *wretched is my condition this night.—Ull*

Heb. noukh, *time of rest. Gr* νυκτος, *poet. dial.* νυκτα *or* νυχτα *Lat.* noct-u. *Franconian*, naht. *Goth.* nahts. *Germ.* nacht. *Pol* noc. *Bohem.* noc. *Dal* nooch *Styr.* and *Carn.* noch. *Anglo-Sax.* niht. *Fr.* †nuict. *Du* nagt *and* naecht. *Grisons*, neoch, *night. Span.* noche *Scotch*, nicht, *night. Ir.* nochd, *to-night*

Nochdach, *a.* Bare, naked; disclosing, revealing; stripping

Nochdachadh, aidh, *s. m.* A discovering, a revealing; a stripping or making bare.

Nochdadh, aidh, *s. m.* A declaring, a revealing, a discovering; a laying bare or naked, a stripping; a declaration; a revealment or discovery.

Nochdadh, (a), *pr. part.* of nochd; which see.

Nochdaich, *v a* (*Ir.* nochdaigh) Declare, reveal, or disclose, shew; strip; peel. *Pret. a. id.*, *fut aff a.* nochdaichidh.

Nochdaichidh, *fut. aff a.* of nochdaich. Shall declare.

Nochdaichte, *p. part.* of nochdaich Declared.

Nochdaidh, *gen. sing* of nochdadh, which see.

Nochdaidh, *fut. aff. a* of nochd Shall or will reveal. See **Nochd.**

Nochdam, 1 *sing. imper.* of nochd. Let me disclose. *Also, for* nochdaidh mi, *I shall* or *will disclose.*

Nochdar, *fut. pass* of nochd. Shall or will be disclosed.

Nochd-larach, aich, *s. m.* A laying waste, a desolation; a place that is laid waste Chum an dianamh nan nochdlaraich, *to make them a desolation.—Stew Jer.*

Nochdta, Nochdte, *p part* of nochd. Disclosed, uncovered, stripped, revealed

† **Nod**, *v. a.* Understand.

† **Nod**, *s m* (*Ir. id*) An abbreviation; a difficulty —*Shaw.*

† **Nod**, *s. m* (*Da.* nod.) Difficulty; emergency; need.

Nòdachadh, aidh, *s m* A grafting

† **Nodadh**, aidh, *s m.* (*Ir. id.*) Understanding.

Nòdaich, *v a.* (*from* nòd) Graft; knot —*Shaw. Pret a id*, *fut. aff a* nodaichidh, *shall graft*

Nòdaichte, *p part.* of nòdaich Grafted; knotted

Nòdair, *s m* A grafter, an abridger; a notary *N pl* nòdairean

Nodaireachd, *s f* The circumstance of abridging; the use of abbreviations, the business of a notary

† **Nodh**, *a.* (*Ir id*) Noble; excellent —*Shaw*

Nodha, *a.* New, fresh, recently made; novel; modern, not familiar Ur nodha, *quite new* Written more frequently *nomha* and *nuadh*

Noibhiseach, ich, *s. m.* A novice

Noigean, ein, *s. m* (*Scotch*, id) A cup; a wooden cup

Nòin, *s* Noon, noontide; the ninth hour of the day, according to the Roman calculation. Mar fhè nòin, *like the breeze of noon.—Oss.* Biadh nòin, *dinner,* trà noin, *noontide.*

W naun. *Ir* noin *Scotch*, none. *Lat.* nonus. *Dan* none, *an afternoon collation Lat* nona, *a meal-time among the Romans, about three in the afternoon.*

Nòin-dhorchadh, aidh, *s. m.* An eclipse of the sun —*Shaw.*

Nòinean, ein, *s m.* (*Corn* neoinin) A daisy.

Noineanach, *a* Full of daisies; of daisies

† **Nòin-reult**, *s. m* The evening star —*Shaw.*

Noir, *adv* East, eastward.

Nois, a noise, *adv.* (*Ir* nosa) Now, at this time. More frequently written *nis;* which see

Nòis, *gen sing* of nòs; which see.

† **Nois**, *a.* (*Ir. id*) Excellent; noble —*Shaw.*

Noisean, *s pl.* Trifles, bagatelles.

† **Noit**, *s.* (*Ir id*) A church; a congregation.

† **Noitheach**, *a.* (*Ir id*) Noble.—*Shaw*

Nollaig, *s f* (*Ir* nodhlag *W.* nadolig. *Fr* noel.) Christmas Làth nollaig, *Christmas-day.*

Nomha, *a* New, fresh, recently made, modern An lòn nomha, *the new store* —*Stew Lev.* Eudach nomha, *new clothes*, gealach nomha, *a new moon* —*Stew.* 2 *K.*

Pers. no, nou, *and* nau *Gr* νεος. *Æol.* νεϜος *Shans* navi *Lat* nov-us *It* nuov-o *Island* ny. *Swed.* ny *Dan* ny *Arm* neue *Fr.* neuf *and* nouv-eau *W* neuydh. *Corn.* nawydh. *Ir.* no *Sax.* neow. *Eng* new

Nonn, *adv.* More frequently written *nunn*, which see

† **Nos**, *a.* (*Ir id*) White; pure white; milk-white —*Shaw*

Norp, *s.* (*Ir. id*) Houseleek.—*Shaw Sempervivum tectorum.*

Nos, nois, *s. m.* (*Ir id*) Knowledge

Nòs, nòis, *s m* (*Ir id*) Custom, manner, habit, ceremony, biestings, or a cow's first milking after calving Cha bu nòs do Dhiarmad eagal, *Dermid was not wont to fear* —*Oss. Derm* Nòs luingeis, *a ship-dock*

† **Nos**, *a.* (*Ir. id*) White; clean; pure, purest white.

Nòsach, *a* (*from* nòs.) Adhering to customs; habitual, usual. *Com.* and *sup.* nosaiche.

Nòsachd, *s f.* Adherence to custom; habitude; customariness.

Nòsadh, aidh, *s. m* A liking; an approving —*Shaw.*

Nòsaich, *v a.* (*Ir id*) Enact; approve, practise; make customary *Pret. a.* nòsaich, *enacted, fut. aff.* nòsaichidh.

Nòsail, *a.* (nòs-amhuil) Usual, habitual; ceremonial.

Nòsalachd, *s. f.* Formality.

Nòsar, *a.* Usual, customary.—*Macint.* Juicy; soft; sappy. Feur nòsar, *juicy grass.* Na fiurain nòsar, *the juicy saplings.—Macfar*

Nòsara, *a.* See Nòsar

Not, *s. m.* (*Ir. id*) A bank note. *N. pl.* notaichean.

Nòthaist, *s m* and *f.* An idiot; a half-witted person *N. pl* nòthaistean

Nuachallachd, *s f* Astonishment

Nuachar, air, *s m.* and *f* (*Ir id*) A companion; a bride, a bridegroom —*Shaw.*

Nuadarra, **Nuadarrach**, *a.* Surly, sour, angry, sulky; gloomy Gu nuadarra, *sulkily*

Nuadarrachd, *s f.* Surliness, sulkiness, angriness

Nuadh, *a* (*Ir.* nua *and* nuadh) New, fresh; recent, modern, not habituated. Written also *nomha*, which see

Nuadhachadh, aidh, *s m* A renewing, a renovating; a renovation

Nuadhachd, *s. f* Newness, freshness, recentness, modernness, renovation; novelty. Nuadhachd beatha, *newness of life.—Stew N T.*

Nuadhaich, *v a* (*from* nuadh.) Renew, renovate. *Pret a.* nuadhaich; *fut aff a* nuadhaichidh, *shall renew.*

Nuadhaichte, *p. part* of nuadhaich. Renewed, renovated

Nuadharra, *a* Surly, sulky, angry, gloomy. Gu nuadharra, *gloomily*

Nuadharrachd, *s. f* Surliness, sulkiness, angriness; gloominess.

Nuadh-bheath, *s f.* A new life, a reformed life, an amended life

Nuadh-bhreith, *s. m.* A new birth

Nuadh-bhrioghachadh, aidh, *s m.* Transubstantiation

Nuadh-chreideach, ich, *s m* A novice; a proselyte. Gun bhi na nuadh-chreideach, *without being a novice.*

Nuadh-mhilidh, *s m* An untrained soldier, a raw recruit

Nuadh-theannsgnair, *s. m.* An innovator

Nuadh-theannsgnaireachd, *s. f* Innovation.

Nuadh-thionnsgantair, *s. m.* (*Ir* nuadh-thionsgantoir) An innovator

Nuadh-thionnsgnach, *a* Innovating, fond or innovation.

Nuadh-thionnsgnadh, aidh, *s. m.* An innovation

Nuaidhe, *com.* and *sup.* of nuadh, which see

Nuaidheachd, *s f* (*perhaps* nuadh-theachd) News; intelligence, a tale. Fear-nuaidheachd, *a newsmonger; a novelist* Is bochd an nuaidheachd, *sad is the tale—Macint.* Paipeir nuaidheachd, *a newspaper* *N pl* nuaidheachdan

Nuaigheachd, *s f*, more correctly *nuaidheachd*, which see.

Nuail, *s f.* (*Ir id*) A roar, a howl, a continued roaring or howling

Nuail, *v n.* Roar, howl. *Pret. a id., fut aff. a* nuailidh

Nuaimhneach, *a* Fearful.

'Nuair, *adv., for* an uair. (*Ir.* nuair.) When, at the time when, seeing that

Nuall, *a.* (*Ir. id*) Noble; famous

Nuall, nuaill, *s m.* (*Ir. id.*) A lament; a howl, a wail; a low; a loud murmur; a shriek; a freak; an opinion. Air cluinntinn nuall do thoirm, *on hearing thy wailing sound.—Macdon.* Nuall gun ghaoi, *a true saying.—Shaw.*

Nuallach, *a.* (*Ir. id*) Howling, wailing; roaring; freakish

Nualladh, aidh, *s. m.* (*Ir. id.*) A howling; a wailing; a roaring

Nuallaich, *s. f.* A howling; continued howling, a yelling; a howl, a yell.

Nuallaich, *v. n.* Howl; yell. *Pret.* nuallaich; *fut. aff. a* nuallaichidh, *shall howl.* Eighich agus nuallaich, *cry and howl.—Stew Ezek.*

Nuallan, ain, *s. m.* (*dim.* of nuall.) A lament, a wail; a howling; a lowing; a loud murmur; a continued loud sound; a shriek. Na taibhse ri nuallan, *the ghosts shrieking —Oss. Cathula.* Nuallan thonn, *the murmur of waves.—Ull* Nuallan bhò, *the lowing of cows —Macdon*

Nuallanach, *a* (*from* nuallan.) Howling; wailing loudly; skrieking; sounding, shrill. Piob nuallanach, *a loud-sounding pipe —Old Song.*

Nuallanaich, *s. f* A howling; a loud noise; a shrieking; a lowing Nuallanaich spreidh, *the lowing of cattle.—Old Song*

Nuallartach, *a* (nuall furtach.) Howling; roaring; lowing, shrieking; wailing loudly

Nuallartaich, *s f.* A continued howling; a continued roaring; a lowing; a shrieking.

Nuall-ghuth, *s. m* A howling voice; a roar, a howl.

Nuall-ghuthach, *a.* Howling, roaring, lowing; having a howling voice.

† **Nuallsan**, *a* (*Ir. id*) Noble, generous.—*Shaw*

Nualraich, *s. f.* Howling, roaring.

Nuamhanair, *s.* (*Ir. id.*) Embroidery.

Nuar, air, *s. m.* Woe; gloom; a frown

Nuar! *interj.* Alas! alackaday! Mo nuar! *alas!*

Nuarranta, *a* Gloomy, woful; surly, sulky. Gu nuarranta, *gloomily.* Mios nuarranta, *a gloomy month—Macfar.*

Nuarrantachd, *s. f.* Gloominess, wofulness; surliness, sulkiness

Nuas, **a nuas**, *adv.* From above, from on high; down, down hither; from the West

† **Nuathaigh**, *s.* (*Ir. id.*) Heaven.

Nuathar, air, *s m* A wedding—*Shaw.*

Nuig, (gu), *prep* (*Ir* nuige.) To, till, until; as far as. Gu nuig briseadh na fàire, *until daybreak—Stew. Gen.* Sinidh 'geugan gu nuig neamh, *its branches shall reach to [as far as] heaven—Old Song.* Gu nuig mo bhàs, *until my death* The Irish also say, *gu nuige mo bhàs.* Written also *gu ruig.*

Nuimhir, *s* (*Corn.* never. *Arm* niver. *Ir.* nuimhir.) A number. An niumhir deich, *the number ten.* In the Armoric it is *an niver decq.*

Nuimhireach, *a.* Numerous, numeral; *also*, an accountant, an arithmetician, a calculator. *N. pl.* nuimhirich.

Nuimhreachadh, aidh, *s m.* A numbering or computing.

Nuimhrich, *v.* (*Ir.* nuimhirigh) Number, calculate, compute. *Pret. a* nuimhrich; *fut. aff. a* nuimhrichidh, *shall number.*

Nuin, *s f* The ash-tree, *also*, the twelfth letter (N) of the Gaelic alphabet

† **Nuinean**, ein, *s m* (*Ir. id.*) A dwarf.

'N uiridh, *adv.* Last year. 'N uiridh *seems to be* an uair 'ruith, *the time* or *season that has gone by*

Null, **a null**, *adv.* Thither; to the other side; to the further side; beyond; over. Cuir do ghaisgeacha a null, send thy warriors thither.—Oss. Tem. A null 's a nall, *hither and thither, to and fro.* Written also *nunn;* which see.

Nuna, *s. m.* Hunger.

Nunn, a nunn, *adv.* (*Ir. id.*) Thither; to the other side; to the further side; beyond; over. Nach d'théid iad tharta nunn, *that they may not pass over them.—Sm.* A nunn agus a nall, *hither and thither.—Stew. Ex. ref.*

Dh'eubh e i nunn ri 'thaobh, *he called her over to his side.—Mac Lach.* The Irish say, *a nunn 'sa nall* in the same sense as the Gael do.

Nur, an uair. (*Dan.* naar. *Swed.* naer.) When.

'Nur, (*for* ann bhur.) In your. 'Nur n-inntinn is 'nur coluadar, *in your minds and conversations.—Sm.* Tha sibh 'nur cabhaig, *you are in a hurry.*

'Nuraidh, *adv.* See 'Nuiridh.

O.

O, (ogh *and* oir, *the spindle-tree.*) The thirteenth letter of the Gaelic alphabet. Ò, with the accent over it, sounds long and open, like o in *scòre;* as, còrr, *excellent;* òr, *gold;* tòchd, *a smell:* and short, like *o* in the Latin *forum;* as, forum, *noise.* It has also an obscure sound, like *o* in *cold;* long, as, tom, *an eminence;* and short, as, sodan, *gladness.* O, followed by *gh*, has a diphthongal sound, to which there is none similar in the English language; as, sogh, *ease;* roghainn, *choice.*

O, *interj.* O! oh! alas! an exclamation common to all people, ages, and languages.

O, *conj.* (*Ir. id.*) Since; seeing that; because.

O, *prep.* (*W.* o. *Lat.* à, è. *Ir.* o.) From; from whence; away from! *as a command.* O Chrona nan nial, *from cloud-capped Crona.—Oss. Com.* O thonn gu tonn, *from wave to wave.—Oss. Derm.* O 'n chuirm sibh! *away from the feast, you!—Oss. Tem.*

† **O, Ogh**, *s. m.* (*Ir. id.*) An ear.

† **Ob**, *s. m.* Hops.—*Shaw.*

Ob, òba, *s. m.* (*Ir. id.*) A bay, a harbour.

Òb, *v. a.* (*Ir. id.*) Refuse, deny, reject; shun. *Pret. a.* dh'òb; *fut. aff. a.* òbaidh, *shall refuse.* Dh'òb i, *she denied.—Stew. Gen. ref.* Na iarr comhrag, ach na h-òb i, *seek not battle, but shun it not.—Old Poem.* Na ith 's na òb cuid an leinibh bhig, *neither eat nor reject the child's food.—G. P. Fut. pass.* òbar.

Òbach, *a.* Refusing, denying, rejecting; shunning.

Obach, aich, *s. m.* One who refuses or shuns.

Obadh, aidh, *s. m.* (*Ir. id.*) A refusing, a denying, a rejecting; a shunning; a refusal, a denial; force; provocation.

Obag, aig, *s. f.* A hurry, a flurry; confusion; abruptness.

Obagach, *a.* Hurried, flurried; abrupt; causing hurry.

Obagaich, *s. f.* A flurry; confused anxiety; abruptness.

Obaig, *s. f.* A hurry, a flurry; confusion; abruptness.

Obain, *gen. sing.* and *n. pl.* of òban.

Obainn, *a.* Rash; hasty; sudden; nimble; quick; soon. Gu h-obainn, *suddenly, quickly.* More frequently written *obann.*

Obainne, *com.* and *sup.* of obann; which see.

Obainne, *s. f.* (*Ir. id.*) Rashness; hastiness; suddenness; nimbleness.

Obair, oibre, *s. f.* (*Ir. id.*) A work; labour; a bustle; a fuss. A dh'aon obair, *purposely;* rinn e dh'aon obair e, *he did it purposely* or *intentionally.* Obair chumta, *a task.—Stew. Ex.* Obair thrailleil, *servile work.—Stew. Lev.* Obair a 's anabhar, *a work of supererogation;* obair is ath-obair, *idle repetition of labour; doing work so carelessly that it must be done over again;* obair cheardail, *an engine, a machine, machinery, work made by engines;* obair-chreadha, *porcelain* or *China-work, earthenware-work, delf, a pottery;* obair-ghloine, *glass-work;* obair-ghréis, *embroidery, needle-work, tapestry.—Stew. Ex.* Obair-laimhe, *handiwork, hand-work,* in contradistinction to obair cheardail, or *engine-work;* obair-lìn, *net-work, chequer-work;* obair-lionain, *net-work, chequer-work;* obair-shnaidhte, *hewn-work;* obair-shnàthaide, *needle-work, embroidery.—Stew. Ex.* Obair-tharsuing, *chequer-work;* obair-theine, *fire-work;* obair-uaireadair, *clock-work;* obair-uchd, *breast-work, a parapet;* obair-uisge, *water-works, a jet;* obair-inntinn, *theory.*

Lat. opus *and* opera. *Span.* obra. *Bisc.* obra. *Ir.* obair. *Fr.* œuvre. *Corn.* and *Arm.* ober. Droch obair, *a bad work;* in Bretagne they say *droucq uber.*

Obair, *s.* A confluence. More correctly *abar;* which see.

Òbam, 1 *sing. imper.* of òb. Let me refuse. *Also, for* òbaidh mi, *I will refuse.*

Òban, ain, *s. m.* (*Ir. id.*) A bay, a small harbour; *also,* a village in Argyleshire, so named from its commodious harbour.

Òbanach, *a.* Abounding in bays or harbours.

Obann, *a.* Sudden; quick; soon; hasty; rash; nimble; agile. Eagall obann, *sudden fear.—Stew. Pro.* Obann le' bheul, *rash with his mouth.—Stew. Ecc. ref. Com.* and *sup.* obainne. Gu h-obann, *suddenly, quickly, unexpectedly.*

Obannachd, *s. f.* Suddenness; quickness; hastiness of temper.

Obar, air, *s. m.* A refusal, a denial.

Òbar, *fut. pass.* of òb. Shall be refused; shall be rejected; shall be shunned. Cha 'n òbar leis an gàbhadh, *he shall not reject the situation of plunder.—Orr.*

† **Obh**, *s. m.* Water. See Abh and Amh.

Obh, Obh! (*pronounced* obhou.) An interjection of wonder, grief, derision. O strange! alas! hey-day! away with! Perhaps it is a corruption of *aobh, aobh!*

† **Obhainn**, *s. f.* A river. Now written *abhainn;* which see.

Obhan, ain, *s. m.* (*Ir. id.*) Froth.

Obhanach, *a.* Frothy.—*Shaw.*

† **Obhann**, ainn, *s. m.* Fear, dread. Now written *uamhann.*

Obhraig, *s. f.* A collection made at church for the poor. This word seems to be a corruption of *naomh-dheirc,* a pious gift.

Obraichean, *n. pl.* of obair. (*Arm.* oubhraichan.) Works.

Obuinn, *a.* See Obann.

Obuinne, *s. f.* Rashness; suddenness. See Obainne.

† **Oc**, *s. m.* (*Ir. id.*) A poet.—*Shaw.*

† **Ocad**, aid, *s. m.* Permission, pleasure, will.

† **Ocaid**, *s. f.* (*Ir. id.*) Business; occasion.—*Shaw.*

Ocar, air, *s. m.* (*Ir. id. W.* ocyr.) Usury, interest, extortion. Le h-ocar, *with usury.—Stew. Pro.* Airgiod air ocar, *money lent on usury.—Stew. Deut.*

Ocarach, *a.* Usurious, extortive in money matters; of, or pertaining to, usury; *also,* a usurer. *Com.* and *sup.* ocaraiche.

Ocarachd, *s. f.* The practice of usury; usuriousness.

Ocarair, *s. m.* (ocar *and* fear.) A usurer, an extortioner.

Ocaras, ais, *s. m.* (*from* ocar.) The practice of usury;

hunger, in this latter acceptation, it is almost always written *ocras* or *acras*.

OCARASACH, *a*. Usurious, extortive; hungry; in this last sense, it is most commonly written *ocrach* or *acrach*; which see.

OCAS, ais, *s. m.* (*Ir. id.*) Interest; usury; annual rent.

OCH! *interj. of mental or bodily pain.* (*Corn.* och. *Ir.* och.) Ah! oh! alas! woe is me! Och! mo bhrathair! *ah! my brother!—Stew. O. T.* Och! a thighearna! *alas! Lord!—Stew. Jud.* Och! och! *an exclamation of bodily pain.*

OCHAIN! *interj.* Alas! Ochain! a laoigh, leig iad thu! *alas! my love, they have felled thee!—Old Song.*

OCHAIN NAN OCH! *interj.* Alas and alackaday!

OCHAL, ail, *s. m.* A moan, a howl, a wail; a moaning, a howling, a wailing.—*Shaw.*

OCHAS, ais, *s.* (*Ir. id.*) Mallows.

† OCHAS, ais, *s. m.* Itch. See TACHAS.

OCH IS OCHAIN NAN OCH ÉIRE! *An interjection of deep grief.—Fingalian Poem.*

OCH NAN OCHAIN! *interj.* Alas! alas! woe of woes! Och nan ochain! is trom a shuain! *alas! alas! heavy is his sleep!—Oss. Derm.*

OCHD, *s. m.* A bosom or breast. More frequently written *uchd;* which see.

OCHD, *a.* Eight.
Gr. οκτω. *Lat.* octo. *Belg.* acht. *Germ.* aht. *Anglo-Sax.* eahta. *Eng.* † eicht. *Scotch,* aucht.

OCHDACH, aich, *s. m.* (*Ir. id.*) A good key of voice; an octave.

OCHDAD, *a.* Eighty. Ochdad fear, *eighty men.*

OCHDAMH, *a.* Eighth. Air an ochdamh bliadhna, *on the eighth; on the eighth year.—Stew. Lev.*

OCHD-DEUG, *a.* Eighteen. Ochd bliadhna deug dh'aòis, *eighteen years of age.*

OCHDMHIOS, *s. m.* October; *literally,* the eight month.

OCHDNAR, *a.* Eight in number; applied chiefly to persons. Ochdnar dhaoine, *eight men.*

OCHD-OISINNEACH, *a.* Octangular; octagonal.

OCHD-OISINNEAG, eig, *s. f.* An octagon.

OCHD-SHLISNEACH, *a.* Eight-sided, octagonal, octangular.

OCHD-SHLISNEAG, eig, *s. f.* An eight-sided figure, an octagon.

OCHÒIN! *interj.* Oh! alas!

OCHÒIN FHÉIN, *interj.* Ah me! woe's me!

† OCHRA, *s. pl.* (*Ir. id.*) Shoes.—*Shaw.*

OCHRAS, ais, *s. m.* The gills of a fish.—*Shaw.*

OCRACH, *a.* (*Ir. id.*) Hungry, voracious, ravenous. Namhaid ocrach, *a hungry enemy.—Stew. Pro.* *Com.* and *sup.* ocraiche. Written also *acrach;* which see.

OCRAS, ais, *s. m.* (*Ir. id.*) Hunger, famine; usury; *rarely,* a bosom. Tha ocras orm, ort, orra, *I, thou, they, are hungry.* Air ocras, *an hungered.* Written also *acras.*

OCRASACH, *a.* Hungry, ravenous. *Com.* and *sup.* ocrasaiche.

OCRASAN, ain, *s. m.* (*from* ocras.) A hungry fellow, a glutton.

OD, *demons. pron.* That; yon, yonder; provincial for *ud;* which see.

O'D, or O D', (*for* o do.) From thy. O d' athair, *from thy father.*

† ODH, oidh, *s. m.* Music; the point of a spear; the sharp end of any thing.

ODHA, *s. m.* A grandchild; a nephew. Odha Iarla nam bratach, *the grandson of the Earl of banners.—Old Song.* *N. pl.* odhachan; see also ODHA.

† ODHALL, *a.* Deaf.—*Shaw.*

ODHAN, ain, *s. m.* Froth or foam.

ODHANACH, *a.* Frothy; foaming. D'alltan odhanach, *thy foaming streamlets.—Old Song.*

ODHANACHD, *s. f.* Frothiness, foaminess.

ODHANN, ainn, *s.;* more properly *aghann;* which see.

ODHAR, air, *s. m.* An abscess. Written also *othar.*

ODHAR, *a.* (*Ir. id.* *Gr.* ωχρος. *Eng.* ochre.) Pale, sallow; dun; yellowish. Do chorp odhar, *thy sallow carcass.—Macint.* *Com.* and *sup.* uidhre.

ODHARACH-MHULLACH, *s. f.* (*Ir. id.*) Devils-bit.

ODHARAG, aig, *s. f.* A scrat; a young cormorant. *N. pl.* odharagan.

ODHARAICH, *v. a.* and *n.* (*from* odhar.) Make dun, pale, or sallow; grow dun or sallow. *Pret.* dh'odharaich; *fut. aff. a.* odharaichidh.

ODHARAN, ain, *s. m.* (*Ir. id.*) The plant cow-parsnip, by botanists called *spondylium.*

ODHAR-BHÀN, *a.* Sallow; of a darkish white colour.—*Stew. Lev.*

ODH-MHEAS, *s. m.* (odh *and* meas.) Homage; great respect.—*Shaw.*

ODH-MHEASACH, *a.* Respectful; dutiful.

ODH-MHEASAIL, *a.* Respectable; much respected.

OFRAIDEACH, ich, *s. m.* An offerer, as of a sacrifice; a Druidical priest.—*Shaw.*

OFRAIL, *s. f.* (*Ir. id.*) An offering, oblation, or sacrifice.

OFRAIL, *v. a.* Offer, as in sacrifice. *Pret. a.* dh'ofrail, *offered; fut. aff. a.* ofrailidh, *shall offer.*

ÒG, *a.* (*Ir. id.*) Young, youthful. Òg ghaisgich! *thou youthful hero!—Oss. Com.* Mar sin bha mi òg, *so was I in my youth.—Old Poem.* Bean òg, *a young wife, a newly-married woman.* *N. pl.* òga. *Com.* and *sup.* òige.

ÒG, òig, *s. m.* A youth; a young child. Fo sgeir fhuaras òg, *under a cliff a youth was found.—Oss. Duthona.* Òig is duibhe gné, *youth of the darkest temper.—Oss. Com.*

ÒGACHD, *s.* (*from* òg.) Youth; youthfulness; virginity.

OGAIL, *a.* (òg-amhuil.) Youthful; youngish; having a youthful appearance.

ÒGAIN, *gen. sing.* of ògan. Of a youth.

ÒGAIR, *s. m.* A youth. Contracted for *òigfhear;* which see.

ÒGALACHD, *s. f.* Youthfulness; youth; the season of youth; the conduct of youth.

ÒGAN, ain, *s. m., dim.* of òg. (*Ir. id.*) A young man; a young branch; a twig; a tendril; a seedling. Ceud ògan aobhach, *a hundred joyous young men.—Orr.* Bàrr an ògain, *the top of the branch.—Macint.*

ÒGANACH, aich, *s. m.* (*Ir. id.*) A youth, a stripling, a minor. An t-òganach, *the youth.—Sm.* *N. pl.* òganaich. Marbhar an oganaich, *their young men shall be slain.—Stew. Jer.*

ÒGANACHD, *s. f.* (*Ir. id.*) Youth; youthfulness; the season of youth.

OG-BHEAN, -mhna, *s. f.* (*Ir.* òigbhean.) A young wife, a newly-married woman; a young woman. Òg-bhean, is faoin do bhruadar! *vain is thy dream, thou youthful wife!—Ull.*

ÒG-BHÒ, -bhoin, *s. m.* (*Ir. id.*) A young cow, a heifer.—*Shaw.*

ÒG-CHULLACH, aich, *s. m.* (*Ir. id.*) A young boar. *N. pl.* òg-chullaich.

OGH. One of the names of the thirteenth letter (O) of the Gaelic alphabet.

† OGH, ogha, *s. f.* (*Ir. id.*) A virgin; *also, adjectively,* pure; sincere; whole, entire.—*Shaw.*

OGHA, *s. m.* and *f.* A grandchild; a nephew. Ogha peathar is bhrathar, *a second cousin.* *N. pl.* oghachan. Clann no oghachan, *children or grandchildren.—Stew. Tim.*

Oghachd, *s. f.* (*Ir.* id.) Virginity.

Oghan, aim, *s m.* Polygraphy.

Oghan, ain, *s. m.* Froth or foam.

Oghanach, *a.* Frothy, foamy.

Oghar, *a.* Wan, dun, sallow. Written also *odhar;* which see.

Òglach, aich, *s. m.*, og-laoch. (*Ir.* id) A lad, a stripling; a soldier; a young hero; a man-servant; a vassal *N pl* òglaich. Ma 's òglaich sibhse thug gaol, *if ye be youths who have loved* —*Old Song* Ban-òg, *a handmaid, a maid-servant.*

Òglachas, ais, *s m* Slavery, servitude, vassalage; a sort of Irish verse, the fourth stage of human life, from the thirty-fourth to the fifty-fourth year of a person's age.

Òg-losgann, ainn, *s. m.* (*Ir.* og-losgain.) A tadpole, a little frog; a young frog

Ogluidh, **Ogluigh**, *a.* (*Ir.* id *Eng* ugly.) Dismal, gloomy; afraid; awe-struck, bashful

Ogluidheachd, **Ogluigheachd**, *s f.* Gloominess, awfulness; gloom, dread, bashfulness Làn ogluidheachd, *full of gloom* —*Orr.* Là ogluidheachd, *a day of gloominess* —*Stew. Joel.*

Òg-mhadainn, -mhaidne, *s f.* (*Ir.* id) Dawn, early morn.—*Macint*

Òg-mhadainneach, *a.* Early in the morning.

Òg-mhaise, *s. f.* Youthful beauty, youthfulness, handsomeness Co so na òg-mhaise? *who is this in his youthful beauty?*—*Ardar*

Òg-mhart, -mhairt, *s f.* (*Ir.* id.) A heifer, a young cow; young beef

Òg-mheur, -mheòir, *s. m* A young branch; *by a figure of speech,* a young person. Air bàrr nan òg-mheur samhraidh, *on the top of the young summer branches* —*Macfar.*

Òg-mhios, *s m.* June.—*Shaw*

Òg-mhnaoi, *s. f.* A young woman; a maid, a young wife, a newly-married wife Og-mhnaoi a b'aillidh leac, *a maid of the fairest cheeks* —*Oss.* Co do d' og-mhnaoi bheir furtachd? *who to thy young wife will give comfort?*—*Ull* Og-mhnaoi is *also the gen. sing.* of òg-bhean

Òg-narach, *a* Bashful, as youth, having the modesty or bashfulness of youth

Ògraidh, *s f.* See Oigridh

† **Oibid**, *s. f* (*Ir.* id) Submission, obedience

Oibne, *s f.* Quickness; suddenness Perhaps a contracted form of *obainne*

Oibneach, *a* Quick, sudden

Oibre, *gen sing.* of obair. Luchd oibre, *workmen, work-people.* See Obair

Oibreachadh, aidh, *s m.* (*Ir.* oibriughadh) A working, a labouring; a fermenting, a labour, fermentation Oibreachadh mhiorbhuile, *the working of miracles* —*Stew* 1 *Cor* Is goirt tha e air oibreachadh, *he is hard-worked*

Oibreachadh, (ag), *pr. part.* of oibrich.

Oibreachail, *a* Operative; effectual; laborious, industrious.

Oibrich, *v a.* and *n* (*Ir* oibrigh.) Work, labour, operate, effect by labour, ferment, mix, work to a due consistency, as lime or clay. *Pret* dh'oibrich, *wrought, worked*, *fut aff. a.* oibrichidh, *shall work.* Esan a dh'oibrich an go, *he who wrought the guile* —*Mac Lach* *Fut. pass.* oibrichear

Oibriche, *s m.* A workman, a labourer. Oibriche ealanta, *an ingenious workman* —*Stew Ex* Codal oibriche, *the sleep of a labourer.*—*Stew Ecc.*

Oibrichte, *p. part* of oibrich (*Ir* oibrightè) Wrought, operated, mixed; fermented Oibrichte le obair ghrèis, *wrought with needlework* —*Stew. Ex.*

Oich! Oich! *interj* of bodily pain. Oh! See Och

† **Oiche**, *s f.* (*Ir.* id. *Lat.* aqua) Water.

Oiche, *s f.* (a *contraction* of oidhche.) Night, evening, darkness

Oid, oide, *s m* (*Ir.* id) A stepfather; a fosterfather, a godfather, a teacher, *rarely*, a grandfather Oid altruim, *a fosterfather*, oid-baistidh, *a godfather*, oid-sgoile, *a schoolmaster* Oid-ionnsuich, *a teacher* —*Stew Pro* Oid-fhogluim, *a teacher.*—*Stew Gal* Oid-ciùil, *a music-master*, oid-dannsaidh, *a dancing-master*

Oid-altruim, *s m* A fosterfather; a nursing-father —*Stew Num*

Oid-baistidh, *s m.* A godfather.

Oid-ciùil, *s m.* A music-master.

Oid-dannsaidh, *s m* A dancing-master, a teacher of dancing

Oideachas, ais, *s m* (*from* oid) Instruction, education

† **Oideadh**, idh, *s m* (*Ir* id) Massacre, death —*Shaw*

Oideag, eig, *s f* A fillet *N pl* oideagan.

Oidean, ein, *s m* (*Ir* id) Love, tenderness; generosity, a degree of nobility

Oideas, eis, *s m*, *from* oid. (*Ir.* id) Instruction, tuition, education, counsel, advice

Oid-fhòghluim, *s m* A teacher, a schoolmaster Ar n-oid-fhoghluim, *our schoolmaster* —*Stew Gal*

Oidhche, *s f* (*Ir* id) Night, darkness, evening. 'San oidhche dhuibh dhoirch, *in the pitch-dark night.*—*Stew Pro* Ré na h-oidhche, *all night*, a là 's a dh'oidhche, *day and night*, beul na h-oidhche, *evening*, air feadh na h-oidhche, *during night*, meadhon-oidhche, *midnight*, meadhon na h-oidhche, *the middle of night*, marbh na h-oidhche, *the dead of midnight*, an oidhche an nochd, *this night*, oidhche mhath dhuit, *good night to you.* *N. pl* oidhchean, *nights* Oidhchean fadalach, *wearisome nights.* —*Stew Job ref* Sgreuchag oidhche, *a screech-owl*

Oidhche-mheirleach, ich, *s. m* A night-thief, a night-robber

Oidheachd, *s. f* (*from* oidhche.) A night's lodging, an entertainment

† **Oidheadh**, idh, *s m* (*Ir* id) Death

Oidheam, eim, *s m* A book, a slight or superficial notion of any thing, an idea, a hint

Oidheamach, *a.* Ideal, tractable.

Oidhearp, more commonly written *oidhirp*

Oidhearpach, *a.* Industrious, endeavouring, persevering

Oidheas, eis, *s m* A freestone

Oidhirp, *s f* An attempt, endeavour, trial, undertaking Dean oidhirp, *make an attempt*, thoir oidhirp, *make an attempt*, thug e oidhirp air, *he tried it*

Oidhirpeach, *a* Industrious, endeavouring, persevering

Oidhre, *s m* An heir; an heiress More frequently written *oighre*, which see.

† **Oidhre**, *s f* (*Ir* id) Ice; frost, snow See Eighe

Oidhreachd, *s f* See Oighreachd.

Oid-ionnsuich, *s m* An instructor, a guide Oid-ionnsuich a h-oige, *the guide of her youth.*—*Stew. Pro*

Oifig, *s f.* (*Ir* oific *Arm.* offich.) An office, a post, a situation Glacadh neach 'oifig, *let one seize his office* —*Sm*

Oifigeach, *a* (*Ir* oifigeach *Arm.* oifichur) Pertaining to office, official, fond of office, *also*, a man in office, an officer —*Stew Gen* *N pl* oifigich

Oifigeil, *a* (oifig-amhuil.) Official.

Oifrionn, inn, *s. m.* Mass. Written also *aifrionn.*

Oig, *s.* and *a.; an inflection of* òg; which see.

† **Oig**, *s. m.* A champion.—*Shaw.*

Oige, *com.* and *sup.* of òg. (*Ir. id.*) Younger, youngest.

Òige, *s. f.* (*Ir. id.*) Youth; the season of youth. Dean gàirdeachas a t-òige, *rejoice in thy youth.—Stew. Ecc.* Cha tuig òige aimbeart, *youth thinks not of want.—G. P.*

† **Oige**, *s. f.* A web. Written also *eige;* which see.

Oigeach, ich, *s. m.* A young colt; a stallion.—*Stew. Jer.* Written also *àigeach*, i. e. *aigh-each.*

Oigfhear, -fhir, *s. m.* A young man. Roghadh òigfhir, *a choice young man.—Stew. Sam.*

Oigh, oighe, *s. f.* (*Ir. id.*) A virgin; a young woman; *rarely*, a stag. *N. pl.* oighean. A thaobh oighean, *in regard to virgins.—Stew.* 1 *Cor.*

Oigh-cheòl, -chiùil, *s. m.* Virgin music; the musical voice of a virgin; virginals. Ni's ceòlmhor na oigh-cheòl, *more musical than a virginal.—R.*

† **Oighe**, *s. f.* (*Ir. id.*) Fulness; entireness.

Oighe, *s. f.* Ice; a file. See also **Eighe**.

Oigheach, *a.* Like a virgin; modest, bashful.

Oigheachd, *s. f.* Virginity; virgin modesty. A caoidh airson m' oigheachd, *bewailing my virginity.—Stew. Jud.*

Oigheam, ein, *s. m.* Obedience; homage.

Oighean, *n. pl.* of oigh; which see.

Oigheann, oighne, *s. f.* A pan; a cauldron. More frequently written *aghann;* which see.

Oigheannach, aich, *s. m.* A thistle.—*Stew. Gen. ref.* Written also *aigheannach.*

Oighidh, *s. m.* (*Ir. id.*) A guest.

Oigh-mara, *s. f.* A sea-nymph or nereid; a mermaid.

Oigh-nàir, *s. m.* Virgin modesty, virgin bashfulness.

Oigh-nàrach, *a.* Modest or bashful, as a virgin.

Oighneach, *a.* (*Ir. id.*) Generous.

Oigh-nighean, -nighne, *s. f.* An unmarried daughter; a virgin daughter.—*Stew. Is.*

Oighre, *s. m.* (*Lat.* hæres. *Ir.* oidhre.) An heir; an heiress. Oighre dligheach Dhundealgain, *the rightful heir of Dundealgan.—Fingalian Poem.* Beiridh bean mac, ach is e Dia ni 'n t-oighre, *a woman may bear a son, but God makes the heir.—G. P.*

Oighreachd, *s. f.*, *from* oighre. (*Ir. id.*) An estate; an inheritance. Oighreachd an fhir thréin, *the estate of the mighty chief.—Mac Lach.* Bheil oighreachd againne? *have we an inheritance?—Stew. Gen. Ir.* oidhreachd.

Oighreag, eig, *s. f.* A mountain-strawberry; a cloudberry; the rubus *chamæmorus* of botanists.

Oighreagach, *a.* Abounding in cloudberries; of, or relating to, cloudberries.

Oigimh, *s. m.* A stranger.—*Shaw.*

Oig're. See **Oigridh**.

Òigridh, *s. f.* (*collective.*) Youth; youngsters; a body of young men. Ghlaodh e ri òigridh, *he called to his youth.—Ull.* Tha an òigridh a crathadh an sleagh, *the youth are brandishing their spears.—Oss. Derm.*

Oil, *s. f.* (*Ir. id.*) Learning, education, tuition. Oil-thigh, *a school-house.* Oil I, *the Isle of Learning*, or *Holy Island*, so called from its having had, in remote ages, a renowned college.

Oil, *s. f.* (*Ir. id.*) A rock; a frightful precipice; reproach; infamy.—*Shaw.*

Oil, *v. a.* (*Ir. id.*) Teach, educate; train, bring up. *Pret. a.* dh'oil; *fut. aff. a.* oilidh. Ma dh'oil i clann, *if she has brought up children.—Stew. Tim.*

Òil, *v. a.* (*Ir. id.*) Drink; sip; absorb. *Pret. a.* dh'òil, *fut. aff. a.* òilidh. Òil h-uile deur dheth, *drink every drop of it.* Beagan uisge ri òl, *a little water to drink.—Stew. Gen.* Cha d'òil an sagart ach na bh' aige, *the priest drank no more than he had.—G. P.*

Oil-athair, -athar, *s. m.* A fosterfather. *N. pl.* oil-aithrichean, *fosterfathers.*

Oilbheum, bhéim, *s. m.* (*Ir.* oilbheim.) Reproach; scandal; offence; a stumble. Carraig oilbhéim, *a rock of offence.—Stew. Pet.*

Oilbheumach, *a.* Reproachful; causing offence or reproach; scandalous. *Com.* and *sup.* oilbheumaiche.

Oilbheumachd, *s. f.* Reproachfulness; scandalousness; scandalizing.

Oilbheumaiche, *com.* and *sup.* of oilbheumach.

† **Oilbhreo**, *s. m.* (*Ir. id.*) A funeral fire.—*Shaw.*

† **Oilcheas**, chis, *s. m.* (*Ir. id.*) Doubt; hesitation.—*Shaw.*

† **Oilcheasach**, *a.* (*Ir. id.*) Doubtful; hesitating; scrupulous.

Oile, *a.* Most frequently written *eile;* which see.

Oileamhnach. See **Oileanach**.

Oilean, ein, *s. m.* An island.—*Stew. Rev. ref.* More frequently written *eilein;* which see.

Oilean, ein, *s. m.* (*Ir. id.*) Education; nurture; breeding; honey-suckle. Gu bràth cha dealaich oilean riut, *never shall breeding forsake thee.—Old Song.* Theid dànadas gu droch oilean, *presumption will proceed to bad breeding.—G. P.*

Oileanach, *a.* (*Ir. id.*) Educating; nourishing; of, or pertaining to, education; insular.

Oileanach, aich, *s. m.* A student, a scholar, a pupil. *N. pl.* oileanaich.

Oileanaich, *v. a.* Teach, instruct; train, rear. *Pret. a.* dh'oileanaich; *fut. aff. a.* oileanaichidh.

Oilear, ir, *s. m.* (*Ir. id.*) A pilgrim; a traveller; a foreigner.—*Shaw.*

Oilearach, aich, *s. m.* (*Ir. id.*) A pilgrim; a traveller; a foreigner.

Oilearach, aich, *s. m.* A nursery.

Oilearadh, aidh, *s. m.* (*Ir. id.*) A pilgrimage; travelling.

Oileas, eis, *s. m.* Custom, use, habit, usage.

† **Oileasach**, *a.* Frequent; usual, customary.

Oilich, *v. a.* Frighten.—*Shaw.*

Oillmheidh, *s. f.* Balance or weight. *N. pl.* oillmheidhean.

Oillt, *s. f.* Terror; horror; detestation. Dlù-chrith air gach cnaimh le h-oillt, *every bone shaking with horror.—Mac Lach.*

Oillteachadh, aidh, *s. m.* A dreading; a detesting; a horrifying; horror; detestation. Tha e air oillteachadh, *he is horror-struck.* Tha mi air m' oillteachadh ris, *I am shocked at him.*

Oilltealachd, *s. f.* (*from* oillt.) Ugliness; terribleness; dreadfulness; detestableness.

Oillteil, *a.* (oillt-amhuil.) Shocking, horrible, detestable; disgusting, ugly; fearful. Lasan oillteil, *a fearful flame.—Oss. Duthona.* Craicionn oillteil, *ugly skin.—Old Song.*

† **Oilltheud**, -théid, *s. m.* A rope or cable. *N. pl.* oilltheudan.

Oilltich, *v. a.* (*from* oillt.) Regard with horror; shudder with horror; detest. *Pret.* dh'oilltich; *fut. aff.* oilltichidh. Gun oilltich gach linn gu bràth, *that every age may for ever detest.—Mac Lach.* Dh'oilltich mi ris, *I detest him, I am horrified at him.*

Oil! Oil! A cajoling address to an infant; an expression of derision at finery.

Oil-thigh, *s. m.* A school-house, an academy.—*Stew* 2 *Chr.* *N. pl.* oil-thighean.

Oil-thìr, *s. f.* A foreign shore; a strange country; a pilgrim. Written more frequently *eile-thìr.*

Oil-thìreach, ich, *s. m.* A stranger, a foreigner; a pilgrim. More frequently written *eile-thìreach.*

Oil-thìreach, *a.* Foreign; of, or belonging to, a pilgrim or a foreigner. See also Eile-thìreach.

Oil-thìreachd, *s. f.* Pilgrimage; the circumstance of being foreign.

Oil-threabhach, *a.* Valiant; truly brave. Gu h-oil-threabhach, *valiantly.*

Oil-threabhachd, *s. f.* Transcendant valour.

† Oin, *s. f.* (*Ir. id.*) A loan, a thing lent.—*Shaw.*

Oineach, *a.* (*Ir. id.*) Merciful, liberal. Gu h-oineach, *liberally.*

Oineach, ich, *s. m.* (*Ir. id.*) Mercy, liberality; a merciful person; a liberal person. Seirc is oineach, *benevolence and mercy.*—*Old Song.*

Oineachd, *s. f.* Mercy; liberality; mercifulness.

Oinneal, eil, *s. f.* (*Goth.* onael, *fire.* *Sax.* onaelan, *kindle.*) A house-fire.

Òinid, *s. c.* An idiot, a silly person, a stupid person. Slachdan an lamh òinid, *a batlet in the hand of an idiot.*—*Old Poem.*

Òinideach, *a.* Idiotical, foolish; of, or pertaining to, an idiot.

Òinideachd, *s. f.* Foolishness, simpleness.

Oinigh, *s. f.* (*Ir. id.*) A harlot. Air ghradh h-oinigh na tog trod, *raise not a quarrel for a harlot's sake.*—*Old Didactic Poem.* *N. pl.* oinighean.

Oinigheach, *a.* (*Ir. id.*) Whorish; like a harlot.

Oinigheachd, *s. f.* Whorishness; prostitution.

Oinmhid, *s. f.* (*Ir. id.*) An idiot.

Oinmhideach, *a.* Foolish, silly.

Oinmhideachd, *s.* Folly, silliness.

Oinmhidh, *s. m.* A fool, a nidget.

Oinnean, ein, *s. m.* An onion; a pebble.—*Shaw.* More commonly written *uinnean.*

Oinneanach, *a.* Like an onion, abounding in onions. Written also *uinneanach.*

Òinseach, ich, *s. f.* (*Ir. id.* *Arm.* ozeach, *a virago.*) An idiot; *also*, an abandoned woman. *N. pl.* òinseachan.

Oinseachail, *a.* (oinseach-amhuil.) Idiotical, foolish; whorish. Gu h-òinseachail, *foolishly.*

Oir, *gen. sing.* of òr. (*Ir. id.*) Of gold. Uair òir, *Aurora.*

Oir, *conj.* (*Ir. id.*) For; because that. Oir bhiodh sin na mhasladh, *for that would be a disgrace.*—*Stew. Gen.*

Òir, *s. f.* (*Ir. id.*) A hem; a fringe or border; edging; a boundary or limit. A leth oir, *sideways.* *N. pl.* oirean, *borders.*—*Stew.* 1 *K.*

Ir. oir. *Corn.* oir, *limit.* *Gr.* ὅρος, *limit*, and ὄρα. *Old Sax.* ora. *Fr.* † ore. *Lat.* ora.

Oir, *s. m.* (*Ir. id.*) The East point; East. A tìr an oir, *from the land of the East.*—*Old Poem.*

Oir, *s. f.* (*Ir. id.*) The spindle-tree; prickwood; the *euonymus vulgaris* of naturalists; the name of the thirteenth letter (O) of the alphabet.

Oir, *v. n.* Befit, become.

Oir, *a.* (*Ir. id.*) Fit, convenient, proper.

Oirbh, *comp. pron.* (*Ir.* oruibh.) On you; upon you; on you, as an obligation; in your possession. Cuiribh oirbh e, *put it on you;* na gabhaibh oirbh e, *take it not on you, take no heed of him* or *it.* Tha e oirbh a dheanamh, *you are obliged to do it;* ciod 'tha cur oirbh? *what ails you?* bheil dad aig oirbh? *has he any claim on you? are you in his debt?*

Oirbheart, *s.* (*Ir. id.*) Good actions, an exploit.—*Shaw.*

Oirbheartach, *a.* (*Ir. id.*) Great, gracious; doing great deeds. *Com.* and *sup.* oirbheartaiche.

Oirbhidinn, *s. f.* (*Ir. id.*) Honour, respect, veneration.

Oirbhidneach, *a.* (*Ir. id.*) Honoured, respected, venerated.

Oirbhir, *s. f.* (*Ir. id.*) Reproach, a curse, an armful.

Oirbhse, *emphatic form* of oirbh; which see.

Oirc, *s. f.* (*Ir. id.*) A lapwing.—*Shaw.*

Oirceadal, ail, *s. m.* (*Ir. id.*) Instruction; doctrine.

Oircean, ein, *s. m.* Now written *uircean;* which see.

Oirceart, eirt, *s. m.* (*Ir. id.*) A hurt, a bruise, a wound.

Oir-cheard, -cheaird, *s. m.* (*Ir. id.*) A goldsmith. Mac an òir-cheird, *the goldsmiths.*—*Stew. Ezra.* *N. pl.* òir-cheaird. See Or-cheard.

Oircheas, *s. m.* See Oirchios.

Oircheasach, *a.* (*Ir. id.*) Necessary, fit, proper; needy, in want, charitable. Written also *oirchiosach.*

Oircheasachd, *s. f.* (*Ir. id.*) Need, necessity; charitableness; *rarely*, a mess. Written also *oir-chiosachd;* which see.

Oir-chiabh, *s. m.* (*Ir. id.*) A yellow lock or ringlet; a golden lock or ringlet. See Or-chiabh.

Òir-chiabhach, *a.* (*Ir. id.*) Having yellow ringlets. See Or-chiabhach.

Oirchill, *s. f.* (*Ir. id.*) Provision reserved for the absent.—*Shaw.* A reward.

Oirchilleach, *a.* Bearing, carrying.

Òirchios, chise, *s. f.* Bounty; charity, an act of charity; *also, adjectively*, proper, meet.

Òirchiosach, *a.* Charitable, benevolent; needy; necessary; proper.

Òirchiosachd, *s. f.* Charitableness, benevolence; neediness, necessity, want.

Òir-chisde, *s. f.* A coffer; a treasury; a bank of gold, a precious magazine. *N. pl.* oir-chisdean.

Òir-chisdear, eir, *s. m.* A treasurer.

Oir-chneis, *s.* The foreskin.

Oir-chrios, *s. f.* A belt, an ornament; a gold necklace.

Oirde, *s. f.* (*Ir. id.*) A piece or lump; a splinter; order; improvement. Oirde fhiodha, *a log of wood.* *N. pl.* oirdean *and* oirdnean.

Oir-dhearc, *v. n.* Flourish; be famous. *Pret. a.* dh'oir-dhearc; *fut. aff. a.* oir-dhearcaidh, *shall flourish.*

Oirdhearc, *a.* See Oirdheirc.

Oir-dhearcas, ais, *s. m.* See Oirdheirceas.

Oirdheirc, *a.* (*Ir. id.*) Excellent; renowned, noble, honourable; worthy. Air nithibh oirdheirc, *on excellent things.*—*Stew. Pro.* Fhestuis ro oirdheirc! *most noble Festus!*—*Stew. Acts.*

Oirdheirceas, eis, *s. m.* (*Ir.* ordhearcas.) Excellence, excellency, nobleness, honourableness; worthiness; lustre. Oirdheirceas cumhachd, *the excellence of power.*—*Stew. Gen.* Oirdheirceas an eolais, *the excellency of knowledge.* *Stew. Ecc.*

Oirdneadh, idh, *s. m.* Ordination.

Oirdnean, *s. pl.* Splinters.

Oireachas, ais, *s. m.* (*Ir. id.*) Pre-eminence, superiority.

† Oireachdan, *s. pl.* Statutes; ordinances.—*Shaw.*

Oireachdas, ais, *s m* (*Ir. id*) An assembly.—*Shaw.*

Oiread. Now written *uiread*, which see

Oireadh, idh, *s m.* (*Ir id*) A befitting; a becoming.

† **Oireagail**, *s. f* A habitation, a waste house; a deserted house.

Oireamhan, ain, *s. m* (*Ir id*) Concord.

Oireamhnach, *a.* (*Ir. id.*) Meet, proper, expedient; accommodated. *Com.* and *sup.* oireamhnaiche.

Oireamhuin, *s. f.* (*Ir id*) Pertinence; influence; fitness

Oirean, *n. pl.* of oir Borders

Oirear, *a.* (*Ir. id*) Pleasant, agreeable; comely, becoming

Oireil, *a* (oir-amhuil) Meet, proper, becoming, seemly, comely; handsome Gu h-oireil, *becomingly.*

Oir-fheadhnach, *a.* Having excellent leaders, as an army

Oirfeid, *s f* (*Ir id*) Music, melody Oirfeid eagarach, *well-arranged music* —*Old Song*

Oirfeideach, *a* (*Ir id*) Musical, melodious, *also, substantively,* a musician

Oirgeadh, idh, *s m* (*Ir id*) Destroying

Oirghean, ein, *s m* (*Ir. id*) Destruction.

Oirghios, *s.* Cheer—(*Shaw*), a mess

Oirghreas, **Oirghreus**, ghreis, *s m* Embroidery, tapestry, needlework, tambouring, ornament.

Oirghreusach, *a* Embroidered

Oirghreusaiche, *s m.* An embroiderer.

Oiridh, *a* (*Ir id*) Meet, proper More frequently written *àiridh.*

Oiridh, *s pl* (*Ir id*) Devices wrought in gold

Oiris, *s f* (*Ir id*) A chronicle, delay, hindrance.

Oirle, *s f* A piece or fragment —*Shaw*

Òirleach, ich, *s f* (*Ir.* oirleach, ordlach) An inch, *also,* slaughter, massacre Nach caill aon òirleach, *that will not lose one inch* *Macfar.* *N. pl* òirlich Ceithir òirlich, *four inches.*—*Stew Jer*

Oir-lion, *v a* Increase *Pret. a* dh'oir-lion, *fut.* oir-lionaidh

Oir-mhiann, *s m* (*Ir id*) Avarice, covetousness.

Oir-mhiannach, *a* Avaricious, covetous

Oirmhid, *s f.* Credit, respect

† **Oirn**, *v a* (*Ir id*) Ordain, put in authority *Pret. a* dh'oirn; *fut. aff a* òirnidh.

Oirnealta, *a* (òir-inealta.) Elegant, neat; ornamental; beautiful, having an imposing exterior

Oirnealtachd, *s f.* (oir-inealtachd) Elegance, neatness, handsomeness; ornament

Oirneimh, *v a.* Shine with gold

Oirneis, *s f* (*Ir id.*) Furniture, chattels, instrument; tackling, *rarely,* a qualm of the stomach. Written also *airneis*

Oirnn, *comp pron* On us, upon us, over us, on us, as an obligation Bheil e oirnn a dheanamh, *he will make us do it*, tha e oirnn a dheanamh, *we are obliged to do it*, *it is our duty to do it*, togamaid oirnn, *let us bestir ourselves, let us be moving*, na gabhamaid oirnn e, *let us not heed him, let us take no notice of him*, thairis oirnn, *over us*

Oirnne, *emphatic form* of oirnn

Oirre, *comp pron.* On her, upon her, on her, *as a duty*, over her Cha 'n 'eil eagal oirre, *she is not afraid* —*Stew Pro* Tha e oirre a dheanamh, *she is bound or obliged to do it*, mòran uachdarain oirre, *many rulers over her* —*Stew. Pro* Chaidh e oirre, *he had carnal connexion with her*, dh'eirich e oirre, *he belaboured her*, togadh i oirre, *let her bestir herself, let her be off*: ciod tha 'cur oirre? *what ails her?*

Oir-thir, *s. f.* (*Ir.* oirthear) A coast, a shore; a border, a frontier; the east; an eastern country; the eastern world Oir-thir na h-Alba, *the coast of Scotland* —*Old MS.* Oir-thir ghaineimh, *a sand-bank*; bàth mòr aig oir-thir, *wrecks are frequent near the shore* —*G. P.*

Oir-thireach, *a.* (*Ir. id.*) Maritime; terminal; eastern.

† **Oirior**, *s m.* (*Ir. id*) The day after to-morrow. See **Iar-thrath** or **Ear-thrath.**

Oirp, *s* See **Oidhirp.**

Oisbheas, bheis, *s. m* (*Ir. id.*) An epicycle *N. pl.* oisbheasan

Oisbheasach, *a.* (*Ir. id.*) Like an epicycle; of, or belonging to, an epicycle.

Oisbhreag, eig, *s f* (*Ir. id.*) A hyperbole *N pl.* oisbhreagan.

Ois-cheum, *s m* Eminence, superiority

Ois-chreideamh, imh, *s f* (*Ir id*) Superstition —*Shaw.*

Òiseach, ich, *s f* An idiot; a female simpleton; a fool. Cha leannan òisich i, *she is not a fool's choice.*—*G. P.* Written also *òinseach*

Òiseachail, *a* (òiseach-amhuil) Idiotical, simple, as a female Gu h-òiseachail, *idiotically.*

Òisealachd, *s. f* Idiocy; female simplicity or foolishness.

Òisg, òisge, *s f* (*Gr* οἶς.) A sheep, a ewe. *N. pl* òisgean.

Òisgealachd, *s f* Sheepishness, foolishness

Òisgeil, *a.* (òisg-amhuil) Sheepish; silly Gu h-òisgeil, *sheepishly.*

Ois-sgriobhadh, aidh, *s m.* A superscription.

Oisin, *v a* (*for* ois-shin) Lie with the face upwards.

Oisinn, *s f* A corner; a nook, an angle Oisinn an tighe, *the corner of the house* —*Stew* 2 *K ref.* *N. pl.* oisinnean

Oisinneach, *a* Angular; having corners or nooks.

Oisinneag, eig, *s. f.* (*dim* of oisinn.) An angular figure; a little angle, a little corner or nook Tri-oisinneag, *a triangle*, ceithir-oisinneag, *a quadrangle, a parallelogram.*

† **Oisionair**, *s m* A tabard, a habit formerly worn over a gown —*Shaw*

Oisire, *s f* (*Ir id*) An oyster. *N pl.* oisirean

Oislin, *s pl.* Charms

† **Oistir**, *s. f* A door. See **Clann an oistir.**

Oistric, ice, *s. f.* An ostrich. Mar na h-oistrice san fhàsach, *like the ostriches in the desert.*—*Stew Lam*

Oit! oit! The exclamation of one who feels an unusual degree of heat

Oiteag, eig, *s f* A blast, a gust, a breeze, a squall. Oiteag, a carruch' an duilich, *a breeze stirring the foliage* —*Oss.* *N pl* oiteagan

Oiteagach, *a* Windy, blasty, squally Gaoth oiteagach, *a wind that comes in gusts or squalls*

Oitir, *s f.* A ridge or bank in the sea; a shoal; a promontory or headland, a rock projecting into the sea Oitir ghaineimh, *a sand-bank* —*Macd* Iad nan sreud air an oitir dhuinn, *they [standing] in ranks on the brown promontory.*—*Mac Lach*

† **Ol**, *v def.* (*Ir id*) Said. Dh'ol Fionn, *Fingal said.*—*Old Poem*

Òl, *v. a* Drink, sip; absorb. *Pret a* dh'òl; *fut aff.* òlaidh. Òlaidh e deoch, *he shall drink.*—*Sm.* Written also *òil.*

Òl, òil, *s m.* (*Dan.* el, *beer.*) Drinking, sipping, absorbing; drink.

Òl, (ag), *pr part.* of òil Drinking, sipping, absorbing.

Ola, ai, *s. m.* and *f.* Oil; olive; ointment. Ola chum soluis, *oil for light.—Stew. Ex.* Ola ungaidh, *anointing oil.—Id.* Written also *oladh.*

Arm. oleu. *Lat.* olea. *Teut.* olie. *Germ.* ol. *Ir.* ola.

Olabhar, air, *s. m.* A great army.

Olach, *a.* (*from* ola.) Oily, greasy.

Olach, *a.* Given to drink; tippling, sipping; absorbing.

Òlach, aich, *s. m.* A corruption of *òglach;* which see.

Olachan, ain, *s. m.* (*Ir. id.*) Immoderate drinking; a drinking-match; a carousal.

Oladh, aidh, *s. m.* (*Ir. id.*) Oil; olive; ointment. Measgta le h-oladh, *mixed with oil.—Stew. Lev.* Oladh fior-ghlan, *pure oil.—Id.* Corn-olaidh, *a cruse of oil, an oil cruse.—Stew.* 1 *K.* Oladh ungaidh, *anointing oil;* crann-olaidh, *an olive-tree.*

Arm. oleu. *Lat.* olea. *Span.* oleo. *Ir.* ola. *Germ.* ol. *Teut.* olie.

Oladh-bàis, *s. m.* Extreme unction.

Olaidh, *gen. sing.* of oladh; which see.

Olainn, *gen. sing.* of ollan.

Olann, ainn, *s. f.* Wool. Do lion no dh'olainn, *of linen or wool.—Stew. Lev.*

Swed. ull, *wool, and* ullen, *of wool. Ir.* olann, *wool. Eng.* woollen.

Òlar, *a.* Given to drink, tippling; sottish; absorbent.

Òlar, *fut. pass.* of òl. Shall be drunk.

Olart, airt, *s. m.* A hone. *N. pl.* olartan.

Olartach, *a.* Like a hone; performing the office of a hone.

† **Olartar**, air, *s. m.* (*Ir. id.*) A bad smell.—*Shaw.*

Olastair, *s. m.* (*Sax.* heolster.) A holster. *N. pl.* olastairean.

Olc, *a.* (*Swed.* elac. *Ir.* olc.) Wicked; mischievous; bad. Béist olc, *a wicked beast; also, a mischievous person;* lionn olc, *bad beer;* olc air mhath le càch e, *whether the rest take it well or ill.—Old Song. Com.* and *sup.* miosa. Is olc an airidh e, *it is a pity;* is tric fhuair olc-an-airidh car, *''tis a pity' has often been crossed.—G. P.*

Olc, uilc, *s. m.* (*Ir.* olc.) Mischief, evil; wickedness; harm or damage. Cha d' thig olc oirbh, *evil will not come over you.—Stew. Jer.* Is olc a fhuara sibh, *you have done wrong.—Stew. Gen.* Olc na cùis gu deireadh, *put off evil to the last.—G. P.* Ris an olc, *doing mischief. N. pl.* uilc. Na h-uilc, *the evils.—Sm.*

Olcas, ais, *s. m.* (*Ir. id.*) Badness; naughtiness; mischief. An samhuil air olcais, *their* [*like*] *match for badness.—Stew. Gen.* Chual thu' olcas, *thou hast heard its mischief.—Orr.*

Olchobhair, *s. f.* (*Ir. id.*) Pleasure; avarice.—*Shaw.*

† **Oll**, *a.* (*Ir. id.*) High; great; grand.

Olla, *a.* (*Ir. id.*) Woollen. Eudach olla, *woollen garments.—Stew. Lev.*

Olla, ai, *s. m.* A doctor. See **Ollamh**.

Ollabhar, air, *s. m.* A great host; a mighty army.

Ollach, *a.* Woolly, fleecy; like wool. Caoraich ollach, *fleecy sheep.—Macfar.*

Ollachail, *a.* (*contracted for* ollamhachail.) Rabbinical; lettered, literary.

Olladh, *a.* Woollen. Eudach olladh, *woollen clothes.*

Olladh, aidh, *s. m.* A doctor. See **Ollamh**.

Olladhaich, *v. n.* (*from* olladh.) Graduate; take the degree of doctor. Written also *ollamhaich;* which see.

Olladhaichte, *p. part.* of olladhaich. Graduated, as a physician.

Ollag, aig, *s. f.* (*Ir.* ollog.) Offal, refuse.

Ollaidh, *gen. sing.* of olladh.

Ollamh, aimh, *s. m.* (*Ir. id.*) A doctor of any faculty; a medical man, an apothecary; a learned man—(*Stew. Ecc.*); a chief bard. Ollamh Iùdhach, *a rabbi;* ollamh diadhachd, *a doctor in divinity;* ollamh leigheis, *a doctor in medicine;* ollamh lagha, *a doctor of laws.*

A succession of an order of literati named *ollamh*, existed in Mull from time immemorial, until after the middle of the last century. Their writings were all in Gaelic, to the amount of a large chestful. Dr. Smith says that the remains of this treasure were brought as a literary curiosity to the library of the Duke of Chandos, and perished in the wreck of that nobleman's fortune. The last of the order was the famous old Doctor John Breton, whose memory is preserved in the following words, inscribed on his tombstone in Iona:—

Hic jacet Johannis Betonus Mac-
Lenorum familiæ, Medicus,
qui mortuus est 19 Novembris, 1657,
Æt. 63. Donaldus Betonus fecit 1674.
Ecce cadit jaculo victricis mortis iniquæ
Qui alios solverat ipse mali.
Soli Deo Gloria.

Ollamhaich, *v. n.* (*from* ollamh.) Graduate, as a physician; teach. *Pret. a.* dh' ollamhaich; *fut. aff. a.* ollamhaichidh.

Ollamhaichte, *p. part.* of ollamhaich.

Ollamhain, *gen. sing.* and *n. pl.* of ollamhan. Of a doctor; of a bard; doctors, bards, literati; *also*, instruction.

Ollamhan, ain, *s. m.* A doctor, a medical man, a learned man, a bard of the first order. Ollamhan ri diadhachd, *a doctor in divinity;* ollamhan ri lagha, *a doctor of law;* ollamhan ri leigheas, *a doctor in medicine.*

Ollamhantas, ais, *s. m.* (*Ir. id.*) Professorship; superiority.

Ollamhnachd, *s. f.* (*Ir. id.*) Superiority; preparation.

Ollamhnaich, *v. a.* Instruct, teach, solemnize.

Ollanachadh, aidh, *s. m.* The act of instructing; instruction; a preparing; a preparation; a burying; a burial.

Ollanachd, *s. f.* Preparing the dead for interment; a funeral.

Ollanaich, *v. a.* Instruct; teach; prepare; make ready; solemnize; entomb. *Pret. a.* dh' ollanaich; *fut. aff. a.* ollanaichidh. Dhia ollanaich fein, *God, teach thou me thyself.—Old Poem.*

Ollanaichte, *p. part.* of ollanaich. Instructed; prepared; solemnized; entombed.

Ollas, ais, *s. m.* (*Ir. id.*) A boast.

Oll-dreug, dreig, *s. f.* A funeral pile; a bonfire; an *ignis fatuus.*

Oll-ghlor, -ghlòir, *s. m.* (*Ir. id.*) Bombast; fustain.

Oll-mhathas, ais, *s. m.* (*Ir. id.*) Great riches.—*Shaw.*

Oll-thuadh, aidh, *s. f.* (*Ir. id.*) A large axe; a battle-axe.

Olmhoireachd, *s. f.* Drunkenness, sottishness.

Òlmhor, *a.* Given to drink, tippling; drunken, sottish; absorbent. No feargach no òlmhor, *neither passionate nor given to drink.—Stew. Tit. Com.* and *sup.* òlmhoire.

† **Olom**, *a.* (*Ir. id.*) Crop-eared.—*Shaw.*

† **Oluidh**, *s. f.* (*Ir. id.*) A cow.

Oluinn, *gen. sing.* of olunn.

Olunn, uinn, *s. f.* Wool. Written also *olann.*

Omar, air, *s. m.* Amber; a cupboard; *also*, a trough. In this last sense, the common orthography is *amar;* which see.

Ombra, ai, *s. m.* (*Ir. id.*) Amber.

† **Omh**, *a.* (*Ir. id.*) Lonesome; unfrequented; solitary.

Omhaill, *s. f.* Heed, attention; care. Gabh omhaill, *pay attention;* ciod an omhaill th'ann? *what matters it?* cha 'n 'eil omhaill, *there is no matter;* ciod an omhaill th'agad? *what do you care?*

Omhailleach, *a.* Heedful; attentive; careful.

† **Omhan**, ain, *s. m.* (*Ir. id.*) Fear; froth; a sillabub.

† **Omhnach**, *a.*, *from* omhan. (*Ir. id.*) Terrible; frothy.

† **Omhnear**, eir, *s. m.* (*Ir. id.*) An embryo.—*Shaw.*

† **Omna**, ai, *s. m.* (*Ir. id.*) An oak; a lance, a spear.

† **Omoid**, *v. a.* (*Ir. id.*) Obey.

Omoideach, *a.* (*Ir. id.*) Obedient.

Omrann, ainn, *s. f.* A share; a division.—*Shaw.*

On, *conj.* Since, because, seeing that. On thainig thu, *since thou art come.*

O'n, (*for* o an.) From the, from their; away from the, absent from the, since the; away from their, since their. O'n tigh, *from home, abroad;* o'n aithrichibh, *from their fathers;* o'n doire tha'n sealgair, *the hunter is absent from the wood.*—*Oss. Carricth.* Is fhada o'n là, *it is long since the day.*—*Oss. Fing.*

† **On**, oin, *s. m.* (*Ir. id.*) A loan; a thing lent; sloth; a stain.—*Shaw.*

† **On**, oin, *s. m.* (*Ir. id.*) Advantage, profit; *also*, advantageous.

This is an ancient Celtic root, now gone into disuse among the Scottish Celts, but still preserved among the Celts of Erin. We have, however, derivatives from *on* in frequent use; as *sona*, i. e. *so-ona*, happy; and *dona*, i. e. *do ona*, bad. *On* seems to be the root of the Latin *bonus*, good.

Onadh, aidh, *s. m.* (*Lat.* unda.) A wave. See **Onfhadh**.

Onair, *s. f.* Honour; honesty. See also *onoir.*

Onairich, *v. a.* Honour; respect; esteem; reverence. Written also *onoirich.*

Onairichte, *p. part.* of onairich. Honoured; reverenced.

Onarach, *a.* Honourable; honorary; honest. Ball onarach, *an honorary member. Com.* and *sup.* onaraiche. More frequently written *onorach;* which see.

Onda, *a.* (*Ir. id.*) Simple, silly.

Ondhreug, eig, *s. f.* (*Ir. id.*) A meteor. Ondhreug uamharra, *a terrible meteor.*—*Fingalian Poem.*

Onfa, **Onfadh**, aidh, *s. m.* See **Onnfhadh** and **Anradh**.

Onfhadh, aidh, *s. m.* (*Ir. id.*) A storm at sea; a raging of the sea; a furious billow. Onfhadh na fairge, *the raging of the sea.*—*Stew. Jonah.*

† **Ong**, *a.* (*Ir. id.*) Clean; clear; bright.

† **Ong**, *s. m.* (*Ir. id.*) Sorrow; a sigh; a groan; healing; fire; a hearth.—*Shaw.*

Ong, *v. a.* Anoint. More frequently written *ung;* which see.

Ongadh, aidh, *s. m.* (*Ir. id.*) An anointing; unction, ointment. More frequently written *ungadh.*

† **Onn**, *s. m.* (*Ir. id.*) Furze; gorse. The letter O was formerly called *onn.*

† **Onn**, oinn, *s. m.* (*Ir. id.*) A stone; a horse.

Onnchon, oin, *s. m.* (*Ir. id.*) An ensign; a standard.

Onoir, *s. f.* Honour; nobleness of mind; respect, reverence; a mark of respect; honesty. Na h-òb is na iarr onoir, *seek not honour nor refuse it.*—*Old Didactic Poem.* Air m'onoir, *upon my honour;* cha 'n fhuiling an onoir clùd, *honesty will not endure patching.*—*G. P.*

Lat. honor. *Ir.* onoir. *Arm.* enor. *Fr.* honneur. *Corn.* annerh *and* onwr.

Onoirich, *v. a.* (*Ir.* onoirigh.) Honour; respect; revere. *Pret. a.* dh'onoirich; *fut. aff. a.* onoirichidh, *shall honour.*

Onoirichte, *p. part.* of onoirich. Honoured; respected; revered.

Onorach, *a.* (*Ir. id.*) Honourable; honorary; honest. Ball onorach, *an honorary member;* duine onorach, *an honourable man, an honest man.* Gu h-onorach, *honourably. Com.* and *sup.* onoraiche.

Onrachd, *s. f.* (*for* aonarachd.) Solitariness, loneliness; solitude; the state of being alone. Am fàg thu mi am onrachd? *wilt thou leave me in solitude? wilt thou desert me?*—*Ull.* Na onrachd, *by himself;* na h-onrachd, *by herself;* esan agus ise na'n onrachd, *he and she by themselves,* ' *solus cum sola.*'

Onrachdach, *a.* Solitary, lonely, alone; deserted, forlorn.

Onrachdan, ain, *s. m.* A lonely person; a deserted person; a forlorn person; a hermit; a widow; a widower.—*Macd.* An t-onrachdan a dhion, *to protect the forlorn.*—*Old Poem.*

Onrachdanach, *a.* Solitary, alone.

† **Or**, oir, *s. m.* (*Lat.* ora.) A coast, a border.—*Shaw.*

† **Or**, oir, *s. m.* (*Ir. id. Lat.* os, *gen.* oris.) A mouth, a voice, a sound.—*Shaw.*

Òr, òir, *s. m.* Gold. Òr fiorghlan, *pure gold.*—*Stew. O. T.* Gaol malluichte an òir, *the cursed love of gold.*—*Old Song.*

Lat. aur-um. *It.* oro. *Span.* ora *and* oro. *Bisc.* urrhe. *Manx,* aer. *Ir.* òr. *Fr.* or. *Arm.* aur. *Corn.* our. *W.* oyr.

Orabhar, *a.* Bushy, as hair; having yellow hair; having a yellow top; tipped with gold. Falt orabhar, *bushy hair.* —*Old Poem.*

Òrach, *a.* (*Ir. id.*) Golden; auriferous.

Òrachd, *provincial for* onrachd; which see.

Oracuil, *s. f.* (*Ir. id.*) An oracle.

Òradh, aidh, *s. m.* A gilding; gilding. Air òradh, *gilt.*

Orag, aig, *s. f.* A sheaf of corn. *N. pl.* oragan.

Oragan, ain, *s. m.* (*Ir. id.*) The herb organy.—*Shaw.* Wild marjoram; an organ.

Organach, *a.* Abounding in organy; like organy; of organy.

Òraid, *s. f.* (*Lat.* orat-io. *Ir.* òraid. *W.* araeth.) A speech; an harangue; a prayer. Rinn e òraid, *he made a speech.*—*Stew. Acts, ref.*

Òraideach, *a.* (*Ir. id.*) Like a speech or oration; fond of speechifying.

Òraideach, ich, *s. m.* (*Ir. id.*) A speaker, an orator, a declaimer. *N. pl.* òraidich.

Òraidear, ir, *s. m.* (*W.* arodawr, *historian. Lat.* orator, *a speaker.*) An orator, a declaimer.

Òraidich, *v. n.* Declaim, harangue, speechify. *Pret. a.* dh'òraidich.

Òrail, *a.* (òr-amhuil.) Golden; like gold; gilt.

Òrain, *gen. sing.* and *n. pl.* of òran.

Oraisd, *s. f.* An orange. *N. pl.* oraisdean.

Oraisdeach, *a.* Full of oranges; like an orange; fond of oranges.

Òran, ain, *s. m.* (*Ir. id.*) A song, a poem. An t-slige is an t-òran, *the shell and the song.*—*Ull.* Oran neamhuidh! *Hallelujah!* òran buachaill, *an eclogue;* òran luathaidh, *a catch.* Cha dean sinn òran deth, *we shall not make a song of it.*—*G. P. N. pl.* òrain. Fonn òrain, *the air of a song.*

Òranach, *a.* (*Ir. id.*) Fond of songs; having many songs; like a song; tuneful; fond of singing songs.

Òranaiche, *s. m.* A singer; a songster; a ballad-singer. Deagh oranaiche, *a good singer of songs.*

† **Orban**, ain, *s. m.* (*Ir. id.*) Patrimony.

Orbhaire, *s. f.* (*Ir. id.*) Mercy, goodness.—*Shaw.*

Òr-bhann, ainn, *s. m.* A lace of gold; a hinge of gold. *N. pl.* òr-bhannan.

Òr-bhannach, *a.* Having gold laces; having gold hinges.

Orbheart, eirt, *s. m.* A noble deed.

Orbheartach, *a.* Illustrious; performing noble deeds, magnanimous.

Òr-bhonn, -bhuinn, *s. m.* A gold piece or coin. *N. pl.* òr-bhuinn.

Or-bhuadhach, *a.* Noble, illustrious; victorious; triumphant.

Òr-bhuidhe, *a.* (*Ir. id.*) Yellow; yellow as gold. Thusa is òr-bhuidhe ciabh, *thou of the golden locks.—Oss.*

Òr-bhuidheach, ich, *s. m.* Or, or topaz in heraldry; the pure yellow in the arms of an earl or lord; or sol in that of a king or prince.

† **Orc**, *s. m.* (*Ir. id.*) A collop; the calf of the leg; a beagle.

† **Orc**, *s. m.* (*Ir. id.* *Corn.* orch, *supreme.*) A prince's son.

Orc, *s.* (*Ir. id.* *Span.* orco, *whale.*) A cramp; a salmon; a whale. Orc-innis, *the Orkneys*, or *the isle of whales.* Milton has, "The haunts of seals and *orcs* and sea-mews' clang."

† **Orc**, *v. a.* (*Ir. id.*) Kill, destroy.

Orcadh, aidh, *s. m.* A killing, a massacring; a destroying; destruction.

† **Orcain**, *s.* (*Ir. id.*) Murder, killing.

Orchan, ain, *s. m.* Incantation.

Òr-cheard, -cheird, *s. m.* (òr *and* ceard.) A goldsmith; a jeweller. Do'n òr-cheard, *to the goldsmith.—Stew. Pro.* *N. pl.* or-cheirde.

Òr-chiabh, *s.* A bright yellow lock of hair; golden locks.

Òr-chiabhach, *a.* (*Ir. id.*) Yellow-haired.

Òr-choilear, eir, *s. m.* A golden collar; a gold necklace.

Òr-chradh, aidh, *s. m.* Grief; sorrow.

Òr-chul, -chùil, *s. m.* Yellow hair; golden locks. Gu mu sàmhach a robh t-òr-chùl, *quiet be thy golden locks.—Oss. Derm.*

Orc-iasg, -eisg, *s. m.* (*Ir. id.*) A torpedo.—*Shaw.*

Ord, oird, *s. m.* (*Gr.* ὄρος.) A mountain.

† **Ord**, *s. m.* (*Ir. id.*) An order, a series. Hence *ordugh.*

Ord, ùird, *s. m.* (*Arm.* and *Corn.* orth.) A hammer; a mallet or maul; a part of a gun-lock; a piece or fragment. Ord agus claidheamh, *a maul and a sword.—Stew. Pro.* Mar fhuaim ùird, *like the noise of a hammer.—Fingalian Poem.* *N. pl.* ùird.

Ord, *s. m.* Death, manslaughter; *adjectively*, bold, valiant.

Ordachadh, aidh, *s. m.* See **Orduchadh**.

Ordag, aig, *s. f.* (*Ir. id.*) A thumb; a toe; the great toe; Air ordaig an laimh deise, *on the thumb of their right hand.—Stew. Ex.* Air ordaig an coise deise, *on the great toe of their right foot.—Id.* *N. pl.* ordagan. An ordag 'n aghaidh na glaic, *the thumb against the palm; the thumb at strife with the palm.—G. P.*

Ordagach, *a.* Having large thumbs or toes; digital.

Ordaich, *v. a.* See **Orduich**.

Ordail, *a.* (ord-amhuil.) Orderly, regular.

Ordan, ain, *s. m.*, *dim.* of ord. (*Ir.* ordin.) A little hammer or mallet. Generosity; dignity; a degree. *N. pl.* ordain.

Òr-dhuilleag, *s. f.* Gold leaf.—*Shaw.*

Ordon, *s. m.—Mac Co.* See **Ordugh**.

Ord-laoch, aoich, *s. m.* A hero.

Orduchadh, aidh, *s. m.* (*Ir.* ordughadh.) A commanding, ordering, ordaining, arranging; a command, an arrangement; appointment; ordination.

Orduchadh, (ag), *pr. part.* of orduich; which see.

Ordugh, uigh, *s. m.* (*Ir. id.* *Lat.* ordo.) A command, a decree; ordinance; order; arrangement; array. Fhuair e 'ordugh, *he got his orders;* do gach uile órdugh, *to every ordinance.—Stew. Pet.* Ordugh catha, *battle array.—Stew. Job.* Fiodh ann ordugh, *wood in order.—Stew. Ex.* Ordugh blàir, *battle order.—Mac Lach.* A dol an ordugh mu d' bhratach, *arranging around thy banner.—Macfar.*

Ordughail, *a.* (ordugh-amhuil.) Orderly, regular; formal.

Orduich, *v. a.* (*Ir.* orduigh.) Order, command, degree; ordain; prescribe; appoint. *Pret. a.* dh' orduich; *fut. aff. a.* orduichidh, *shall order.* Orduichidh uachdarain, *princes shall decree.—Stew. Pro.*

Orduichear, *fut. pass.* of orduich.

Orduichte, *p. part.* of orduich. (*Ir.* orduighte.) Ordered, commanded; decreed; ordained; appointed; prescribed; arranged.

Orgain, *s. f.* (*Ir. id.*) Slaughter; an organ.—*Shaw.*

Òr-ghruag, aig, *s. m.* Yellow hair.

Òr-ghruagach, *a.* (*Ir. id.*) Yellow-haired; a yellow-haired maid.

Or-lachadh, aidh, *s. m.* A bespewing.

Or-lasta, *a.* (*Ir. id.*) Shining, like burnished gold.

Or-lastail, *a.* Gleaming or shining, like burnished gold.

Or-leathair, *s. m.* An uncle by the father's side.

Or-loinneach, *a.* Extremely elegant; beautiful; highly finished; becoming.

Or-loinneachd, *s. f.* Extreme elegance.

Orm, *comp. pron.* (*Ir. id.*) On me, upon me, over me; in my possession; on me, *as a duty or obligation.* Cuir orm mo lùireach, *gird on me my mail.—Old Poem.* Cha 'n 'eil ni 'cur orm, *nothing ails me;* cha 'n 'eil dad agad orm, *you have no claim on me; I am nothing in your debt;* tha e orm a dhianamh, *I am obliged to it;* theid aig orm, *he will get the better of me;* fuirich orm, *softly, leisurely;* socair orm, *softly, leisurely.*

Or-mhadainn, *s. f.* The break of day; morning; Aurora.

Or-mhéin, *s. f.* Gold ore; a gold mine.

Or-mhéineach, *a.* Having gold ore; abounding in gold ore.

Ormsa, *emphatic form* of orm; which see.

Orn, *s. m.* (*Ir. id.*) Slaughter.

Ornaich, *v. a.* (*Ir. id.*) Adorn. *Pret. a.* dh'ornaich; *fut. aff.* ornaichidh.

Ornaid, *s. f.* (*Ir. id.*) Ornament.

Ornais, *s. f.* Nauseousness; a qualm.

Orp, *s. m.* A house-leek.—*Shaw.*

Orra, *comp. pron.* On them, over them; on them, *as an obligation;* on them, *as a claim;* in their possession; on her. Cuir orra e, *put it on them;* tha e orra a dheanamh, *they are bound to do it;* cha 'n 'eil ni agam orra, *I have no claim on them; they are not in my debt;* cha 'n 'eil sgillinn orra, *they have not a shilling in their possession;* cuir faire orra, *set a watch over them;* bheir mise orra a dheanamh, *I will make them do it;* theid agam orra, *I will get the better of them;* cha tugainn peighinn orra, *I would not give a farthing for them.* Orra, *on her.—Stew. Jer. ref.*

Orrachdan. See **Onrachdan**.

Orradh, aidh, *s. m.* A superstitious charm. *N. pl.* oraidhean.

Orraidheachd, *s. f.* Superstitious ceremonies, charms, enchantments.

Orrais, *s. f.* (*Ir. id.*) Squeamishness, a qualm.

Orraiseach, *a.* (*Ir. id.*) Squeamish, qualmish.

Orraiseachd, *s. f.* Squeamishness, qualmishness.

Orrar, air, *s. m.* (*Ir. id.*) A porch.—*Shaw.*

Orrasan, *emphatic form* of orra; which see.

Òrruidh, *a.* (*perhaps* òr-bhuidhe.) Yellow; golden. A ghrian, òrruidh sòir, *the sun like gold in the east.—Oss. Duthona.*

Òr-sgiathach, *a.* Golden-shielded, golden-winged. Dream òr-sgiathach, *a golden-shielded people.—Macdon.*

Òr-sheud, *s. m.* A golden jewel

Ort, *comp pron* (*Ir. id*) Upon thee, about thee, over thee; of, or concerning thee; on thee, *as an obligation.* Cuir ort e, *put it upon thee,* nach cluinn mi ort? *shall I not hear of thee?—Oss Tem* Ciod tha 'cur ort? *what ails thee?* tha e ort a dheanamh, *you are bound to do it,* bheil mi aige ort? *are you in his debt?* cha chuir e smad no smuairean ort, *it will not affect thee in the least,* is ann ort tha 'n iomairt! *how you do fidget!* gabhaidh mi ort, *I will thrash you,* cum ort, *contain yourself,* tog ort, *begone*

Ortsa, *emphatic form of* ort; which see.

Òs, òis, *s. m.* A deer, an elk. Aros nan òs, *the abode of deer.—Oss Fing*

Os, *prep.* (*Ir. id*) Above, over, upon, superior. Os m' uile aoibhneas, *above all my joy.—Sm* Os-cionn, *above, on the top,* os-aird, *openly, loudly,* os-iosal, *softly, quietly, privately,* os mo cheann, *above my head, superior to me,* os do cheann, *above thine head, superior to thee,* os an ceann, *above their head, superior to them*

Osadh, aidh, *s. m* (*Ir. id*) A desisting, a resting, a cessation Osadh còmhraig, *a parley* or *cessation of arms* *Ir* osadh comhraic

Osag, aig, *s f* A breeze, a gust, wind, a blast Osag a bhàis, *the blast of death — Oss. Carricth.* Tàifeid san osaig a fuaim, *a bow-string twanging in the wind.—Oss Com. N pl* osagan

Osagach, *a.* Blasty, windy, gusty, squally. Thàin gaoth osagach ga 'r siùil, *a wind came in gusts to our sails —Fingalian Poem.*

Osagan, *n pl* of osag Breezes, gusts, blasts.

Osan, ain, *s m.* (*Ir id*) A hose *N pl.* osain. Osain ghoirrid is gartainn, *short hose and garters —Macint.*

Osanach, *a* Having hose on Gu brògach osanach, *having shoes and hose on —Old Song*

Osanaiche, *s m* A hosier

Osann, ainn, *s m.* A sigh. Written more frequently *osunn* or *osnadh*

Osan preasach, *s* A very long plaited stocking, once worn (according, I believe, to Pennant) by the women in Breadalbane when in full dress.

† **Osar**, *a* (*Ir id*) Younger —*Shaw.*

Osar, air, *s m* (*Ir id*) A burden; a pack, preferment.

Osaraiche, *s m* (*Ir* ogsaraidhe) A porter, a carrier.

Os-barr, *adv.* and *conj* Besides; moreover Ceudan os bàrr, *hundreds besides —Old Song.*

Oscach *a.* Eminent, superior, excellent Gu h-oscach, *eminently Com* and *sup* oscaiche.

Oscar, air, *s m* (*Ir id*) A leap, a bound, a guest; a traveller; a ruinous fall, a champion, the motion of the hands in swimming, the son of Ossian.

Oscarr-lann, -lainn, *s m.* An hospital

Oscarra, **Oscarradh**, *a* (*Ir id*) Loud; energetic; emphatical, bold, renowned. Oscarra o 'm beul, *loud from their mouths.* Gu h-oscarra, *boldly.*

This word may probably refer to Oscar, the son of Ossian, and may mean *like an Oscar*, or *Oscar-like.*

Oscarrachd, *s f.* Loudness, emphasis; intrepidity; energy.

Oscardha, **Oscartha**, *a* More frequently written *oscarra*, which see

Os-cheumnachadh, aidh, *s m.* Superiority, pre-eminence, an excelling

Os-cheumnaich, *v. a.* Excel, exceed

Os-chrabhach, *a* Superstitious, hypocritical.

Os-chrabhadh, aidh, *s m* Superstition; hypocrisy

Os cionn, *prep*, more properly written *os ceann*; which see.

Òsda, *s. m.* (*Ir.* osda. *Span.* osdal, *an inn. Corn* osd, *a host.*) An inn; an alehouse. On tha sinn san tigh òsda, *as we are in the alehouse.—Old Poem.*

Osdadh. See Osda.

Òsdag, aig, *s f.* The landlady of an inn or alehouse

Òsdair, *s m*, osd-fhear. (*Ir* osdoir.) An innkeeper; a host or landlord.

Òsd-thighe, *s m.* An inn, a hotel, an alehouse *N. pl* osd-thighean.

Os-iosal, *adv* Softly, quietly, privately; secretly, covertly; underhand

† **Osgail**, *v a* Open. Now written *fosgail*, which see.

† **Osgailte**, *part* of osgail Opened, open. See Fosgailte.

Osgarach, *a.* Frail, brittle.—*Shaw.*

Osgarra See Oscarra.

Osgriobhan, ain, *s* Epigram.

Osmag, aig, *s. f.* A sigh, a sob; a slight sigh or sob.

Osmagach, *a* Sighing, sobbing.

Osmagail, ail, *s f* A sigh; sighing.

Osna, ai, *s. f.* A sigh, a sob, a groan; a breeze; a blast. Eiridh 'm osna, *my sighs shall rise.—Oss Croma* Osna choimheach, *a sharp breeze —Ull*

Osnach, aich, *s f.* (*Ir. id*) Carrion.

Osnach, *a*, *from* osnadh (*Ir.* osnadhbach) Troubled; sighing, sobbing Bu ghrad a h-imeachd 's i osnach, *quick was her pace as she sighed —Mac Lach*

Osnachail, *a.* Troubled; sighing, groaning.

Osnadh, aidh, *s m* (*Ir* osnadh.) A sigh, a sob, a groan; a breeze; a blast; *rarely,* a hair of the head. *N pl.* osnaidh.

Osnaich, *s f* (*Ir.* osnaidhe) Continued sighing; groans Ag osnaich leam fèin, *sighing in solitude —Roy Stewart.*

Osnaich, *v n.* (*Ir* osnaigh) Sigh, groan, sob *Pret. a* dh' osnaich, *fut aff.* osnaichidh, *shall sigh.* Dh' osnaich e gu geur, *he groaned bitterly.—Mac Lach.*

Osnaichean, *n. pl* of osnaich Sighs, groans; gusts of wind.

Osnaigh, *for* osnaidh, *n pl.* of osnadh; which see.

Ospag, aig, *s f* A sob, a sigh *N pl* ospagan

Ospagach, *a* Sobbing, prone to sob

Ospagail, *a.* (ospag-amhuil) Sobbing, sighing, apt to sob or sigh

Ospairn, *s f* A sob, a sigh; a struggle. Ag ospairn, *sobbing —Oss Tem.*

Ospairnich, *s f.* A sob, a sigh; sobbing, sighing; struggling An talamh ag ospairnich fo bhonn an cos, *the earth struggling under their feet —Fingalian Poem.*

Os-sgriobhadh aidh, *s m.* An epigram; a superscription.

Osta, *s m.* An inn, an alehouse. Written also *osda;* which see

Ostag, aig, *s. f.* A hostess; the landlady of an alehouse, inn, or hotel *N. pl* ostagan.

Ostair, *s. m.* (*Lat* host-is, *one who entertains.*) An innkeeper, an ostler.

Osunn, uinn, *s f* A sigh, a sob, a groan; a blast or gust of wind. Do spionna mar osunn Lodda, *thy strength like the blasts of Loda —Ull*

Otar, air, *s* Labour —*Shaw.*

Othail, *s. f.* Flurry; hurry; hubbub

Òthaisg, *s f.* A hog, a sheep one year old; *in ridicule,* a bashful person, a simpleton. *N. pl* òthaisgean

Othaisgeach, *a.* Like a sheep or hog; abounding in hogs, bashful, sheepish.

Othan, ain, *s. m* The froth of boiled whey or milk

OTHANACH, *a.* Frothy; foaming like boiled whey or milk. —*Macfar.*

OTHAR, *a.* (*Ir. id.*) Sick, wounded, maimed; weak

OTHAR, air, *s. m.* (*Ir. id.*) An abscess; labour, wages

OTHRAS, ais, *s. m.* (*Ir. id.*) Disease, an ulcer; a wound; ailment.—*Shaw*

OTHRASACH, *a* (*from* othras.) Diseased, wounded; sick.

OTHRASACH, aich, *s. m.* (*from* othras.) An hospital or infirmary.

ÒTRACH, aich, *s. m* (*Ir. id*) A dunghill; filth, dung Togaidh e o'n òtrach, *he will raise from the dunghill.*—*Sm.* Is làidir coileach air 'òtrach fhein, *the cock is strong on his own dunghill.*—*G P* *N pl* òtraichean.

ÒTRAICH, *gen sing.* of òtrach.

ÒTRAICHIBH, *d. pl* of òtrach

P.

P, p, (beith-bhog) The fourteenth letter of the Gaelic alphabet. It sounds like *p* in English; and when aspirated, that is, when it immediately precedes the letter *h*, it sounds like *f* in *fool*, or *ph* in *pharmacy* It is not ascertained from what natural object this letter derives its name Shaw considers it not improbable that it was thus named, from its being a soft way of expressing *b*; and that *p* was not in the Gaelic previous to our knowledge of the Latin It is certain that, like the labial letters of all languages, these letters were once used indiscriminately; for *pian* and *bian*, pain, *béist* and *péist*, beast, &c, are found in ancient manuscripts.

PAB, paib, *s m.* (*Scotch*, pab *and* pob) The refuse of milled flax; coarse tow.

PABHAIL, *s. f.* (*Ir. id*) A pavement; a causeway.

PAC, *s. m.* A pack; a wallet; a bundle; a knapsack; a budget *N. pl.* pacan.

Ir. id. Swed Germ. Eng. pack. *Arm.* pacq. *Anglo-Sax.* pocca.

PACACHADH, aidh, *s. m.* A packing up, a heaping up

PACADH, aidh, *s m* A packing.

PACAICH, *v. a.* (*Arm.* pacqaich, *baggage.*) Pack, load; heap up. *Pret. a.* phacaich; *fut. aff. a.* pacaichidh, *shall pack up.*

PACAINN, *v. a.* Pack up; load; heap up. *Pret. a.* phacainn; *fut. aff. a.* pacainnidh.

PACAINN, *s f.* A packing up, a loading; a heaping up

PACAIR, *s. m.* (pac-fhear.) A pedlar, a packman, a churl. *N. pl.* pacairean.

PACAIREACHD, *s. f.* (*Ir. id*) Pedling, hawking; the business of a pedlar

PACHARAN CHAPUIL, *s. m* Buckbean; marsh trefoil, *menyanthus trifoliata, trifolium paludosum*

PACHD, *s.* See PAC.

PACHD, *s. m.* A pack, a wallet. See PAC

PACHDAICH, *v. a.*, more frequently written *pacaich*, which see.

PACHDAIR. See PACAIR.

PACRAIDHE, *s. f.* Baggage, luggage.

PACLACH, ais, *s m.* An armful.

PADH, PADHADH, *s m.*; more properly *pathadh*, which see

PADHAL, ail, *s m.* (*Ir. id*) A ewer, a pail.

PÀG, pàig, *s. f.* (*provincial* for pòg) A kiss.

PÀGANACH, aich, *s. m* (*Ir. id.*) A heathen, a Gentile *N. pl.* pàganaich.

PÀGANACHD, *s. f.* (*Ir id*) Heathenism, Gentilism.

PÀGANTA, *a.* (*Ir. id*) Heathenish.

PAIDEIREAN, ein, *s m* (*dim.* of paidir) A bead, a string of beads; a rosary; a necklace of beads; beads *N. pl.* paideirein.—*Stew. Ex. ref.*

PAIDEIREANACH, *a.* Full of beads or of rosaries, wearing a rosary.

PÀIDH, *v. a* Pay; remunerate; requite *Pret a* phàigh; *fut aff.* pàidhidh, *shall pay.* Written also *pàigh*

PÀIDH, *s f.* Pay; payment; remuneration; requital. Written also *pàigh*

PÀIDHEADH, idh, *s m* A paying, a payment, a requiting, a requital

PAIDHIR, *s. f.* A pair; a couple, a brace. Paidhir dhag, *a brace of pistols.*—*Macint.* *N pl.* paidhrichean. Nam paidhrichibh, *in pairs.*

Du paar *Eng* pair *Sp.* par *Fr* paire

PAIDHIR, *v a* Pair, couple. *Pret* phaidhir; *fut. aff. a* paidhridh

PAIDIR, *s f.* (*Ir id Corn.* padar) The Lord's Prayer, paternoster; a bead Tha tuille is a phaidir aige, *he knows more than his beads*—*G. P*

PAIDIREAN, ein, *s m* (*Ir id. W* padaran.) A bead, a string of beads, a rosary, or beads on which the Romanists number their prayers; a necklace. *N. pl.* paidirein. See also PAIDEIREAN.

PAIDHRICH, *v. a.* Pair, couple

PAIDHRICHEAN, *n. pl.* of paidhir

PÀIGH, *v. a* Pay; remunerate, requite. *Pret* phàigh, *paid, fut aff a* pàighidh Pàigh t-fhiacha, *pay thy debts.*—*Stew. K ref.* Pàighidh mise thu, *I will pay you.*

PÀIGH, *s. m.* (*Du.* paai. *It Span* paga) Pay; payment, remuneration; requital Fhuair thu do phàigh, *you got your payment*, deagh phàigh, *good pay*; tha thu air do dheagh phàigh, *you are well paid.*

PÀIGHEADH, idh, *s m* The act of paying; pay, payment.

PÀIGH-MHAIGHISTIR, *s. m* A paymaster.

PÀIGH-MHAIGHISTIREACHD, *s f* Paymastership

PÀIGHTE, *p. part* of pàigh Paid, remunerated, requited Gaol gun bhi pàighte, *unrequited love*—*Old Song.*

PAILCHLOCH, -chloich, *s. f* (*Ir. id.*) Paving-stones.—*Shaw*

PAILIN, *s* (*Ir id*) A winding-sheet or shroud.

PAILLEART, eirt, *s m.* (*Ir id*) A slap given with the palm of the hand. *N. pl.* pailleartan

PAILLEARTACH, *a.* Ready to slap with the hand

PAILLEARTAICH, *v. a.* Slap with the hand.

PÀILLIUN, uin, PÀILLIUIS, *s. f.* A palace; a pavilion, a tent; a booth, a hut Dìomhaireachd a phàilliuin, *the darkness of his pavilion.*—*Stew Ps*

PAILLIUNACH, *a* Like a palace, or a pavilion, full of palaces or of pavilions

PAILLUIN, *s f.* A palace, a pavilion; a tent, a booth, a hut. Pailluin nan seòd a bh'ann, *the palace of departed heroes.*—*Oss. Fin and Lor.*

PAILM, *s. f* A palm; a palm-tree Pailm nan lamhaibh, *palms in their hands.*—*Stew. Rev*

PAILM-CHNUIMH, *s f.* A palmer-worm —*Stew. Joel*

PAILT, *a* (*Ir. id*) Plentiful, numerous; abounding; copious, fully Tùr pailt le céill, *a mind abounding in know-*

ledge.—Macint. Beannaich sinn gu pailt, *bless us abundantly.—Sm.* Tha e pailt cho àrd riumsa, *he is fully as tall as I am.*

Pailteas, eis, *s. m.* Plenty, abundance, enough. Pailteas arbhair agus fiona, *plenty of corn and wine.—Stew. Gen.* Tha am pailteas agam, *I have enough;* làn phailteas, *quite enough.*

† Pain, *s. f.* (*Ir. id.*) A cake; bread.

Pàineachadh, aidh, *s. m.* (*Lat.* pœna.) A punishing; a fining; a bailing; a punishment; a fine; bail, a security; insurance.

Pàineachadh, (a), *pr. part.* of pàinich.

Pàineachas, ais, *s. m.* (*Ir. id.*) A punishment; a penalty or fine; a bail, a security; insurance.

Paineal, eil, *s. m.* A pannel.

Pàinich, *v. a.* Punish; fine; bail; insure. *Pret. a.* phàinich; *fut. aff. a.* pàinichidh.

Pàinichte, *p. part.* of pàinich. Punished; fined; bailed; insured. *Asp. form,* phàinichte.

Painneal, eil, *s. m.* A pannel.—*Shaw.* *N. pl.* painnealan.

Painnidh, *a.* Strong; furious.

Painnteal, eil, *s. m.* (*Ir. id.*) A snare, a trap, a gin; a panther.

Painntear, eir, *s. m.* (*Ir. id.*) A snare, a trap, a gin; *also,* a panther.

Painntearach, *a.* Ensnaring; full of snares; like a snare; of, or belonging to, a snare.

Painntearach, aich, *s. m.* An ensnarer, a beguiler. *N. pl.* painntearaich.

Painntearachd, *s. f.* Entanglement; the practice of ensnaring or trepanning.

Painntin, *s. f.* A patten.—*Macd.*

Painntir, *s.* A snare, a trap, a gin. *N. pl.* painntirean.

Painntireach, *a.* Ensnaring, entrapping; inveigling, alluring.

Painntireach, ich, *s. m.* An ensnarer, a trepanner, a beguiler. *N. pl.* painntirich.

Painntireachd, *s. f.* Entanglement; a trepanning; the practice of beguiling.

Painntirich, *v. a.* Ensnare, trap, beguile. *Pret. a.* phainntirich; *fut. aff. a.* painntirichidh.

Painntirichte, *p. part.* Ensnared, entrapped, trepanned, inveigled.

Painte, *s. f.* (*Ir. id.*) A lace; a string to lace clothes.—*Shaw.*

Paipear, eir, *s. m.* Paper. Paipear sgrìobhaidh, *writing-paper;* paipear nuaidheachd, *a newspaper.* *N. pl.* paipearan.

Lat. papyrus. *Arm.* baper *and* paper. *Germ.* papyr. *Fr.* papier.

Pàirc, *s. f.* A park; an enclosed field; an enclosure; a field. *N. pl.* pàircean. Tha do phàirc air a dùnadh, *thy field is shut up.—Macfar.*

Teut. parck. *Germ.* parc. *Fr. W. Arm.* and *Corn.* parc. *Ir.* pairc. *Sax.* pearrac. *Eng.* park.

Pàirc, *v. a.* Enclose, as a field. *Pret. a.* phàirc; *fut. aff. a.* pàircidh.

Pàirceach, *a.* Abounding in fields or parks.

Pàirceachadh, aidh, *s. m.* A forming into parks.

Pàircich, *v. a.* Enclose a space of ground; wall round; confine within a park. *Pret. a.* phàircich; *fut. aff. a.* pàircichidh.

Pàircichte, *p. part.* of pairich. Enclosed, walled round, formed into a park; confined within a park.

Pairilis, *s. f.* Palsy or paralysis.

Pairinn, *s. f.* A paring of moss turf. *N. pl.* pairinnean.

Pàirt, *s. f.* (*Lat.* pars.) A part or portion, a share; *rarely,* kindred, relation; confederacy.

Pàirteach, *a.* In parts; in shares; having a share; ready to share; related; *substantively,* a partaker; a partner.

Pàirteachadh, aidh, *s. m.* A sharing, a dividing.

Pàirteachail, *a.* (pàirteach-amhuil.) Divisible, portionable.

Pàirteachas, ais, *s. m.* Participation; partnership.

Pàirtear, eir, *s. m.* A sharer, a partner; he who possesses or receives a part. *N. pl.* pàirtearan.

Pàirteil, *a.* Partial, kind. Iriosal pàirteil, *humble and kind.—Turn.*

Pàirtich, *v. a.* Impart, communicate; share, partake; portion, divide. *Pret. a.* phàirtich; *fut. aff. a.* pàirtichidh. Gu 'm pàirtich mi tiodhlac, *that I may impart a gift.—Stew. Rom.*

Pàirtiche, *s. m.* A partner; an associate; an abettor.

Pàirtidh, *s. f.* (*Swed. Ir.* parti.) A party. Is mi nach rachadh le pàirtidh, *I would not go with a party.—Turn.*

Pais, *s. f.* Passion; suffering. A Phais, *the Passion.—Macd.*

Pàisd, pàisde, *s. c.* (*Gr.* παις, *accusative Dor.* παιδα. *Pers.* peché.) A child, an infant. Written also *pàist.*

Pàisdealachd, *s. f.* Childishness; babyism.

Pàisdean, ein, *s. m., dim.* of pàisd. (*Ir.* paisdin.) A little child. Nur bha mi mo phàisdean, *when I was a little child.—Old Song.* Written also *pàistean.*

Pàisdean, *n. pl.* of pàisd. Children.

Pàisdeil, *a.* (pàisd-amhuil.) Childish, infantile, babyish.

Paisean, ein, *s. m.* A faint, a swoon. Chaidh i na paisean, *she fainted.* Cuiridh mi paisean ort, *I will knock you senseless;* paisean bàis, *a dead faint.*

† Paisg, *s. f.* (*Ir. id.*) Severe cold.

Paisg, *v. a.* and *n.* Swathe or swaddle; enwrap; shroud; starve with cold. *Pret. a.* phaisg; *fut. aff. a.* pàisgidh. Phaisg si i fèin, *she wrapped herself.—Stew. Gen.*

Paisgean, ein, *s. m.* A bundle, a pack.

Paisgearra, *s. f.* A midwife. *Pers.* Peshkari.

Paisgte, *p. part.* of paisg. Swathed, swaddled, wrapped, shrouded. *Asp. form,* phaisgte.

Pàist, *s. m.* See Pàisd.

Pàistean, ein, *s. m.* (*dim.* of pàist.) See Pàisdean.

Pait, *s. f.* (*Ir. id.*) A lump, a hunch; a protuberance.

Paiteach, *a.* (*Ir. id.*) Humpy, hunchy; having protuberances. *Com.* and *sup.* paitiche.

Pàiteach, *a.* (*Ir. id.*) Thirsty; athirst, droughty; parched. Bha mi pàiteach, *I was thirsty.—Stew. Matt. ref.* *Com.* and *sup.* pàitiche.

Paiteag, eig, *s. f.* Butter—(*Shaw*); a small lump of butter; a leveret.

Paitean, ein, *s. m.* A patten.

Paitrisg, *s. f.* A partridge.

Pàlas, ais, *s. m.* A palace.

Palltag, aig, *s. f.* A thump, a blow.

Palmair, Palmadair, *s. m.* A rudder—(*Shaw*); a pilot. Written also *falmadair.*

Pànair, *s. pl.* Beans. See also Pònair.

Pànaireach, *a.* Abounding in beans; like beans; of beans.

Panna, *s. m.* A pan.—*Shaw.*

Pannag, aig, *s. f.* A cake, a pancake.—*Macd.* Written also *bannag* and *bonnag.*

Pannagan, ain, *s. m.* A pancake.—*Macd.*

Pannal, ail, *s. m.* (*Ir. id.*) A crew; a band of men; a group of people; a company. Am pannal air a charraig, *the group on the rock.—Old Song.* Written also *bannal.*

PàPA, s. m. (Gr. παππα. Lat. papa. Du. paap.) A pope. Am papa, *the pope*; papa no Roimh, *the pope of Rome.*

PàPACHD, s. f. (*from* papa.) Popedom.

PàPANACH, aich, s. m. (*Ir. id.*) A papist, or Roman Catholic. *N. pl.* papanaich.

PàPANACHD, s. f. (*Ir. id.*) Popery; popedom.

PARABAL, ail, s. m. An ancient Celtic word, meaning a parable.—*Stew. Luke, ref.*

PARACAIT, s. f. (*Fr.* perroquet.) A parrot.—*Macd.*

PARALUS, uis, s. m. A parlour; a room to entertain in.—*Shaw.*

PARAS, ais, s. m. (*Span.* paraiso.) Paradise; heaven. A chuid do phàras da! *may he have his share of Paradise!*—a common ejaculation among the Gael when they hear of the death of a friend.

PARDAG, aig, s. f. A hamper for carrying things on both sides of a horse.

PARLADH, aidh, s. m. A parley.

PARN, s. m. (*Ir. id.*) A whale.

PARRAISTE, s. f., *provincial.* (*Ir. id.*) A parish.

PARR-RIABHACH NAN CEARC, s. m. A kite or glead.

PARTAN, ain, s. m. (*Ir.* and *Scotch,* partan.) A crab-fish; a crab-louse. A phartain spàgaich, *thou sprawling crab.*—*Turn. N. pl.* partain.

PARTANACH, a. (*from* partan.) Abounding in crab-fish or in crab-lice; like a crab-fish or crab-louse; greedy, rapacious.

PARTANACHD, s. f. Rapaciousness; extreme greed.

PASG, paisg, s. m. A wrapper; swaddling-cloth; a covering.

PASG, v. a. Wrap, swaddle, swathe; fold. *Pret. a.* phasg, *swathed; fut. aff. a.* pasgaidh.

PASGACH, a. Wrapping; swaddling; swathing; folding.

PASGADH, aidh, s. m. A wrapping, a swathing or swaddling; a folding, a binding up. Beagan pasgaidh, *a little folding.*—*Stew. Pro. ref.*

PASGADH, (a), *pr. part.* of paisg *or* pasg.

PASGAIRT, s. f. A pannier.

PASGAN, ain, s. m. (*Ir. id.*) A bundle, a wallet.

PASGAR, *fut. pass.* of pasg.

† PATA, s. m. (*Ir. id.*) A vessel; a hare.—*Shaw.*

† PATAN, ain, s. m. (*Ir. id.*) A leveret. *N. pl.* patain.

PATANTACHD, s. f. Thickness.—*Shaw.*

PATH, PATHADH, aidh, s. m. Thirst; thirstiness; drought; parchedness. Tha pathadh orm, *I am thirsty.*

PàTRAN, ain, s. m. A patron. *N. pl.* patrain.

PEABH-CHEARC, -chirc, s. f. A peahen. *N. pl.* peabh-chearcan.

PEABH-CHOILEACH, ich, s. m. A peacock. *N. pl.* peabh-choilich.

PEABH-EUN, -eòin, s. m. A pea-fowl; a peacock or peahen. A giùlan pheabh-eun, *carrying peacocks.*—*Stew. K. ref.*

PéAC, péic, s. m. (*Ir. id.*) Any sharp-pointed thing; the sprouting germ of any vegetable; a long tail.—*Shaw.*

PEAC', *for* peacadh; which see.

PéACACH, a. (*from* péac.) Fine, showy, gaudy; long-tailed. *Com.* and *sup.* péacaiche.

PEACACH, a. (*Ir. id.*) Sinful; *also,* a sinner. Duine peacach, *a sinful man;* slighe nam peacach, *the sinner's way.*—*Stew. Ps.*

PEACACHADH, aidh, s. m. A sinning, a transgressing.

PEACADH, aidh, s. m. (*Ir. id.*) Sin, transgression. Ri peacadh, *sinning;* ris a pheacadh, *sinning;* is mòr am peacadh e, *it is a great sin;* peacadh gine, *original sin;* gine-pheacadh, *original sin;* peacadh gniomh, *or* gniomh-pheacadh, *actual sin;* peacadh beag, *a peccadillo;* peacadh so-laghadh, *a venial sin;* peacadh collaidh, *incest.*

Heb. pischai. *Lat.* peccat-um. *Arm.* pechet. *W.* pechod. *Fr.* péché. *Corn.* pehad.

PEACAG, aig, s. f. A peacock. *N. pl.* peacagan. Written also *peucag.*

PEACAICH, v. n. (*Ir.* peacaigh.) Sin, transgress. *Pret. a.* pheacaich; *fut. aff. a.* peacaichidh. Pheacaich mi, *I have sinned.*—*Stew. N. T.*

PEACAIR, s. m. (peac-fhear.) A sinner. *N. pl.* peacairean.

PEACAIREACHD, s. f. The behaviour of a sinner.

PEALAID, s. f. A bare sheep-skin; a little ball, a pellet.

† PEALL, s. m. (*Ir. id.*) A horse; a couch or pallet; a veil.

PEALL, v. a. (*Ir. id.*) Mat, cover; teaze; pluck, pull asunder. *Pret. a.* pheall; *fut. aff. a.* peallaidh.

PEALLACH, a. (*Ir. id.*) Matted; covered with mats; teazing; having pallets or couches; shaggy. A shine pheallach! *thou shaggy old age!*—*Old Song.*

PEALLADH, aidh, s. m. (*Ir. id.*) A matting, a covering with mats; a teazing or plucking asunder.

PEALLAG, aig, s. f. A mat; coarse harness; cart harness; a veil, a covering; a coarse blanket; a slattern; an umbrella. *N. pl.* peallagan.

PEALLAGACH, a. Having a ragged harness, shaggy; drabbish or dirty, like a slattern. Na toir droch mheas air loth pheallagach, *despise not a shaggy colt.*—*G. P.*

PEALLAID, s. f. (*Ir. id.*) Pelt; skin stripped of its hair.

PEALTAG, aig, s. f. A clod.

PEAN, s. m. A pen. See PEANN.

PEANAIDEACH, a. That punisheth; punishable.

PEANAISTE, *part.* Punished.

PEANAR, air, s. m. A pen-case. *N. pl.* peanaran.

PEANAS, ais, s. m. (*Lat.* pœna. *Ir.* peanas. *Corn.* penys.) Punishment; chastisement; correction. Peanas cuirp, *corporal punishment;* peanas eaglais, *ecclesiastical punishment.*

PEANASACH, a. Liable to punishment, penal; prone to punish, vengeful; of, or relating to, punishment.

PEANASACHADH, aidh, s. m. The act of punishing; a punishment.

PEANASAICH, v. a. Punish, chastise, correct; torture. *Pret. a.* pheanasaich, *punished; fut. aff. a.* peanasaichidh.

PEANASAICHE, s. m. A punisher, a chastiser; an executioner.

PEANASAICHTE, p. *part.* of peanasaich. Punished, chastised, corrected.

PEANASAIL, a. (peanas-amhuil.) Penal; enacting punishment; deserving punishment; punishable.

PEANASDA, a. Penal.

PEANN, s. m. (*Ir. id. Lat.* penna.) A pen. Peann iaruinn, *an iron pen.*—*Stew. Jer.* Peann an sgriobhair, *a writer's pen.*—*Stew. Jud.*

PEANNAGAN, ain, s. m. (*Ir. id.*) A pen-case. *N. pl.* peannagain.

PEANNAID, s. f. Pain.

PEANNAIR, s. m. (peann-fhear.) A penman; a good writer. *N. pl.* peannairean.

PEANNAIREACHD, s. f. Penmanship.

PEANNAR, air, s. m. A pen-case. *N. pl.* peannaran.

PEANNSAIR, s. m. A fencer; a pair of pincers.—*Shaw.*

PEANNSAL, ail, s. m. A pencil. *N. pl.* peannsalan.

PEAPAG, aig, s. f. A pompion.

PEARLA, s. m. (Ir. id.) A pearl, a gem, a precious stone.

PEARLACH, a. (Ir. id.) Abounding in pearls and gems; like a pearl; plaited, corrugant.

PEARLAG, aig, s. f. (Ir. id.) A partridge. N. pl. pearlagan. —Shaw.

PEARLAICH, v. a. Bedeck with pearls or gems; plait, corrugate.

PEARLUINN, s. f. Fine linen, cambric, gauze, muslin.

PEARLUINNEACH, a. Like fine linen, cambric, or muslin; made of fine linen, cambric, or muslin.

PEARSA, s. m. A person; bodily shape. Do phearsa dheas ghrinn, *thy active, elegant form.*—*Old Song.* Pearsa eaglais, *a churchman, an ecclesiastic;* mìle pearsa, *a hundred persons.*

PEARSAICH, v. a. Personify; represent. *Pret. a.* phearsaich, *personified; fut. aff. a.* pearsaichidh; *p. part.* pearsaichte.

PEARSAL, ail, s. m. Parsley; *petroselinum vulgare.* More properly *pearsluibh.*

PEARSALACH, a. Abounding in parsley; of parsley; like parsley.

PEARSAN, ain, s. m. A person. Air pearsannaibh nan sagart, *on the persons of the priests.*—*Stew. Sam.*

PEARSANTA, PEARSONTA, a. Personable, having a portly figure; personal.

PEARSANTACHD, PEARSONTACHD, s. f. Personableness, portliness.

PEARSLUIBH, s. f. Parsley.

PEAS, s. m. A purse. Peas ghoidiche, *a cutpurse.*

PEASAIR, peasrach, s. f. (Ir. id. Fr. pesière, *a field of pease.*) Pease; a crop of pease. Eitean peasrach, *a grain of pease;* peasair each, *tares, vetches;* peasair luch, *lentiles;* peasair gheal, *white pease;* peasair fhiadhain, *vetches.*—*Stew. Ez.* Peasair chapull, *vetches;* peasair tuilbhe, *heath pease.* N. pl. peasraichean, *kinds of pease.*

PEASAN, ain, s. m. (Ir. id.) An impudent person; a sorry child; an imp; a brat; a puppy; a purse. N. pl. peasain.

PEASANACH, a. (Ir. id.) Pert, impudent; impish. Gu peasanach, *impudently.* Com. and sup. peasanaiche.

PEASANACHD, s. f. Pertness, impudence, petulance; impishness.

PEASANTA. See PEASANACH.

PEASANTACHD. See PEASANACHD.

PEASG, v. a. and n. Notch, gash; slash; make a slight incision; grow gashed or notched; burst, as the skin, with cold. *Pret. a.* pheasg; *fut. aff. a.* peasgaidh.

PEASG, s. f. A gash, a notch; an incision; a bursting of the skin, as with cold.

PEASGACH, a. Gashed, notched; full of incisions; burst, as the skin, with cold; causing gashes or notches; causing the skin to burst.

PEASGADH, aidh, s. m. A gash, a notch; a slight incision; a bursting of the skin. Tha do chasan air peasgadh, *the skin of thy feet is burst.*

PEAS-GHOIDICHE, s. m. A cutpurse.

PEASRACH, *gen. sing.* of peasair; which see.

PEASRAICHEAN, n. pl. of peasair. Kinds of pease; fields of pease.

PEAT, PEATADH, aidh, s. m. A pet; a tame animal.

PEATHAR, *gen. sing.* of piuthar. Of a sister.

PEATHRACHAS, ais, s. m. Sisterhood.

PEATHRAICHE, PEATHRAICHEAN, n. pl. of piuthar. Sisters.

PEGHINN. See PEIGHINN.

PÉIC, s. f. A long tail. Written also *peuc.*

PEIC, s. f. A peck; two gallons; the fourth part of a bushel.

PEICEAG, eig, s. f. (*dim.* of peic.) A peck. Cha 'n fhaigh sinn peiceag bhracha thogail, *we cannot brew a peck of malt.*—*Turn.*

PÉICEALLACH, a. Having a long tail.

PEICH, v. n. Snift with anger. *Pret. a.* pheich.

PEICHIL, s. f. A snifting with anger.

PEIGHINN, s. f. (Ir. pighinn.) A penny Scotch, or the fourth part of a shilling sterling; a penny. Airson peighinn, *for a penny.* N. pl. peighinnean.

PEIGHINNEACH, a. In pence; dapple.

PEIGHINN-RIOGHAL, s. f. Pennyroyal. Am bearnan bride is a pheighinn-rioghail, *the dandelion and pennyroyal.*—*Macint.*

PEILEAG, eig, s. f. Felt; any coarse cloth; a porpoise.

PEILEAGACH, a. Coarse, as cloth; like felt; made of felt.

PEILEID, s. f. A slap on the cheek.

PEILEIR, s. m. and f. (Ir. id. Corn. pel.) A ball; a bullet. Peileir tairneanaich, *a thunderbolt;* frasan dearg pheileir, *showers of red bullets.*—*Macdon.* N. pl. peileirean.

PEILEIR-LANN, -lainn, s. m. A cartouch; a place where balls are piled up.

PEILGHUIN, s. f. A pang; torment.

PEIL-GHUINEACH, a. Causing torment; painful, tormenting.

PEILIOCAN, ain, s. m. A pelican.

PEILISTEAR, eir, s. m. A quoit. (Gr. παλαιστρα. Lat. palæstra, *a place for manly exercise.*) N. pl. peilistearan.

PEILLICHD, s. f. Felt; any coarse cloth; a hut or booth used by the ancient Irish. These huts were made of earth and branches of trees, over which were laid the skins of beasts.

PEILLICHDEACH, a. Coarse or thick, as cloth; like felt; made of felt.

PÉIN, *gen. sing.* of pian; which see.

PEIN-DLIGHE, s. f. A penal law.

PEINGEALTACH, a. Cruel, tyrannical.

PEINGEALTACHD, s. f. Cruelty, tyranny.—*Q. B. ref.*

PEINTEAL, eil, s. m. (Ir. id.) A snare.—*Shaw.* N. pl. peintealan.

PEINTEALACH, a. Having snares; penurious.

PEINTEALACHD, s. f. Penuriousness.

PEIRCEALL, ill, s. A jaw, a jawbone; a corner, a nook; the abdomen. N. pl. peirclean. Ged robh a peirclean cruaidh, *though her jaws were hard.*—*Old Song.* D. pl. peirclibh. Mu 'pheirclibh, *about his jaws.*—*Macint.*

PEIRCEALLACH, a. Jawed; having large jawbones; large-cheeked; thin-faced; lantern-jawed.

PEIREADH, idh, s. m. Rage, fury.—*Shaw.*

† PEIREAGAL, ail, s. m. (Ir. id. W. perygl. Lat. periculum.) Danger; urgent necessity.

PEIRLEAG, eig, s. f. A partridge. N. pl. peirleagan.

PEIRLIN, s. (Ir. id.) Fine linen.

PEIRSE, s. f. (Ir. id.) A row, a rank; a perch in length. —*Shaw.*

PEIRSEACH, a. Formed into rows; well-ordered; divided into perches, as land.

PEIRTEALACH, a. Pert, impudent. Gu peirtealach, *pertly.* Com. and sup. peirteiliche.

PEIRTEALACHD, s. f. Pertness, impudence, effrontery.

PEIRTEIL, a. Pert, impudent.

PÉIST, s. More frequently written *béist.*

PEIST, s. f. (Ir. id. Lat. pestis.) A plague; loss; ailment.

Peit, *s. m.* A musician.

Peiteadh, idh, *s. m.* Music.

Peiteag, eig, *s. f.* (*Ir.* peiteog.) A vest or waistcoat. Peiteag riomhach, *a gorgeous vest.—Macint.* *N. pl.* peiteagan.

Peiteagach, *a.* Wearing a vest; of, or belonging to, a vest; like a vest.—*Macdon.*

Peisteal, eil, *s. m.* (*Ir. id.*) A pestle.

Peitean, ein, *s. m.* A short jacket.

Peitearlach, aich, *s. m.* (*Ir. id.*) The Old Law or Testament; sacred history.

Peitearlaichte, *a.* (*Ir. id.*) Versed in sacred history.

Peithir, *s. m.* A forester; a thunderbolt.

Peitseag, eig, *s. f.* (*Ir.* peisteog.) A peach. *N. pl.* peitseagan.

Peitseagach, *a.* Abounding in peaches; like a peach; of peaches.

Peòdar, air, *s. m.* (*Ir. id.*) Pewter; *in ridicule*, a *harum-scarum.*

Peòdarach, *a.* (*Ir. id.*) Of pewter; like pewter.

Peòdarair, *s. m.* (*Ir. id.*) A pewterer.

Peubar, *v. a.* Pepper. *Pret.* pheubar; *fut. aff. a.* peubaraidh.

Peubar, air, *s. m.* Pepper.

Gr. πιπερι. *Lat.* piper. *Pers.* † peperi. *Germ.* pfeffer. *Dal.* papar. *Lus.* peper. *Turk.* piber. *Javanese*, pepelini. *W.* puppur.

Peubarach, *a.* Peppery; like pepper; full of pepper.

Peubh-chearc, -chirc, *s. f.* A peahen. *N. pl.* peubh-chearcan.

Peubh-choileach, ich, *s. m.* A peacock. *N. pl.* peubh-choilich.

Peubh-eun, eòin, *s. m.* A pea-fowl; a peacock or peahen.

Peuc, péic, *s. m.* A long tail; any sharp-pointed thing; the sprouting germ of any vegetable.

Peucach, *a.* Long-tailed; gaudy, showy.

Peucag, aig, *s. f.* (*from* peuc.) A peacock, a peahen. *N. pl.* peucagan.

Peur, *s. m.* A pear. Craobh nam peur, *the pear-tree.—Stew. Sam. ref.* Craobh pheuran, *a pear-tree;* ubhlan is peuran, *apples and pears.*

Lat. pyrum. *Arm.* pêr. *W.* peren. *It.* pero. *Sp.* pera. *Fr.* poire. *Dan.* paere. *Du.* peer. *Germ.* byrn. In the South of France they say *perie* and *perien.*

Peurach, *a.* Abounding in pears; like a pear.

Peurlach, *a.* Corrugated, wrinkled.

Peurladh, aidh, *s. m.* A wrinkle.

Phac, *asp. form* of pac; which see.

Phac, *pret. a.* of pac. Packed, loaded; heaped up.

Phàidh. See **Phàigh**.

Phàigh, *pret. a.* of paigh. Paid, requited.

Phàiliun, *asp. form* of pàiliun; which see.

Phailt, *a.; asp. form* of pailt.

Phailteas, eis, *s. m.; asp. form* of pailteas; which see.

Phaipear, eir, *s. m.; asp. form* of paipear. Paper. See **Paipear**.

Phàirc, *s. f.; asp. form* of pairc; also, *voc. sing.* of pàirc.

Phairiseach, ich, *s. m.* A Pharisee. *N. pl.* Phairisich.

Phàirt, *s. f.; asp. form* of pàirt; which see.

Phàirtich, *pret. a.* of pàirtich; which see.

Phàisd, *asp. form* of pàisd; also *voc. sing.* of paisd.

Phaisg, *pret. a.* of paisg. Swathed, swaddled; wrapped; shrouded.

Phaisgte, *asp. form* of paisgte, *p. part.* of paisg. Swathed, swaddled; wrapped, shrouded.

Pheacadh, aidh, *s. m.; asp. form* of peacadh; which see.

Pheacaich, *pret. a.* of peacaich. Sinned, transgressed.

Pheacair, *s. m.; asp. form* of peacair; also *voc. sing.* of peacair.

Pheanas, ais, *s. m.; asp. form* of peanas; which see.

Phearsa, *asp. form* of pearsa.

Pheasair, pheasrach, *s. f.; asp. form* of peasair; which see.

Pheasg, *pret.* of peasg.

Pheathar, *asp. form* of peathar, *gen. sing.* of piuthair.

Pheighinn, *s. f.; asp. form* of peighinn; which see.

Phian, *pret.* of pian. Pained, tormented.

Phiantach, *a.; asp. form* of piantach; which see.

Phiantachail, *a.; asp. form* of piantachail.

Phic, *asp. form* of pic.

Phill, *pret. a.* of pill. Returned; caused to turn.

Phillear, *asp. form* of pillear.

Philleas, *fut. sub.* of pill; which see.

Phinnt, *asp. form* of pinnt; which see.

Phiob, *asp. form* of piob; also *voc. sing.* of piob.

Phiobair, *s. m.; asp. form* of piobair; also *voc. sing.* of piob

Phioc, *pret. a.* of pioc; which see.

Phiocaid, *s. f.; asp. form* of piocaid. A pickaxe. See **Piocaid**.

Phiorbhuic, *s. f.; asp.* of piorbhuic; which see.

Phiuthair, *asp. form* of piuthair; which see.

Phlaigh, *s. f.; asp. form* of plaigh; which see.

Phlaigheil, *a.; asp. form* of plaigheil. Contagious, pestilential, baneful, like a plague. Aimsir plaigheil, *pestilential weather.* See **Plaigheil**.

Phlaoisg, *pret. a.* of plaoisg; which see.

Phlàsdaich, *pret. a.* of plàsdaich. Plastered, bedaubed. See **Plàsdaich**.

Phleadhaich, *pret.* of pleadhaich.

Phloc, *asp. form* of ploc; which see.

Phloc, *pret.* of ploc. Bruised, mashed.

Phlosg, *s.; asp. form* of plosg. A breath, a gasp. Gun phlosg, *lifeless.* See **Plosg**.

Phlosg, *pret. a.* of plosg. Gasped; throbbed.

Phlosgail, *s. f.; asp. form* of plosgail; which see.

Phlosgartaich, *s. f.; asp. form* of plosgartaich. A panting, a sobbing.

Phlub, *asp. form* of plub; which see.

Phluic, *s. f.; asp. form* of pluic. A cheek.

Phlùr, *asp. form* of plùr.

Phòg, *asp. form* of pòg; which see.

Phòg, *pret. a.* of pòg. Kissed.

Phoit, *asp. form* of poit.

Pholl, phuill, *s. m.; asp. form* of poll; which see.

Phònair, *asp. form* of pònair; which see.

Phongail, *a.; asp. form* of pongail.

Phort, phuirt, *s. m.; asp. form* of port; which see.

Phòs, *pret. a.* of pòs. Married.

Phost, phuist, *s. m.; asp. form* of post; which see.

Phost, *pret. a.* of post. Tramped.

Phrab, *pret. a.* of prab. Entangled.

Phrais, *asp. form* of prais; which see.

Phramh, phraimh, *s. m.; asp. form* of pramh. A sleep, a nap. Do phramh, *thy sleep.* See **Pramh**.

Phrat, *asp. form* of prat; which see.

Phreas, phris, *s. m.; asp.* of preas; which see.

Phreas, *pret. a.* of preas. Wrinkled; grew wrinkled.

PHRIOB, *pret. a.* of priob. Winked; twinkled. See PRIOB.

PHRIOBACH, *a.*; *asp. form* of priobach.

PHRIONNSA, *asp. form* of prionnsa; which see.

PHRÌSEIL, *a.*; *asp. form* of prìseil; which see.

PHRÒIS, *pret.* of pròis. Cajoled, flattered.

PHRONN, *pret. a.* of pronn. Bruised, mauled. See PRONN.

PHRONNADH, aidh, *s. m.*; *asp. form* of pronnadh. A bruising, a mauling. Fhuair e a phronnadh, *he got himself mauled.*

PHRONNTA, *asp. form* of pronnta.

PHRONNUSG, uisg, *s. m.*; *asp. form* of pronnusg. Brimstone.

PHROP, *pret. a.* of prop; which see.

PHROSNAICH, *pret. a.* of prosnaich. Spurred, incited.

PHUBULL, uill, *s. m.*; *asp. form* of pubull; which see.

PHÙC, *pret. a.* of pùc. Pushed, shoved. See PÙC.

PHUIRT, *asp. form* of puirt, *gen. sing.* of port; which see.

PIAID, *s. f.* A magpie. Nead na piaid, *the magpie's nest.* More properly *pigheid*; which see.

PIAIDEACH, *a.* Abounding in magpies; like a magpie; piebald. See PIGHEIDEACH.

PIAN, péin, *s. m.* and *f.* Pain; a pang; torment; anguish; trouble or sorrow; punishment. Pian ifrinn, *the pains of hell.*—*Sm.* Gach gnè péin, *every kind of pain.*—*Id.* Cogadh nam pian, *afflictive war.*—*Mac Lach.* Ionad na péin, *the place of torment.*—*Dugald Mac Pherson.* *N. pl.* piantan *and* piantaidh.

Gr. ποινη. *Lat.* pœna. *Teut.* piin *and* pene. *Anglo-Sax.* pin. *Franconian,* pina. *Dan.* pine. *Fr.* peine. *Span.* pena. *Eng.* pain. *Ir.* pian. *Corn.* beyn *and* poan. *W. Arm.* poan *and* poen, *pain*; also, *Germ.* pein, *punishment.*

PIAN, *v. a.* (*Ir. id.*) Pain; torment; distress; annoy; punish. *Pret. a.* phian; *fut. aff. a.* pianaidh, *shall pain*; *p. part.* pianta.

PIANADAIR, *s. m.* A punisher; a tormentor.

PIANADH, aidh, *s. m.* (*Ir. id.*) The act of tormenting or paining; torment, pain, affliction, punishment.

PIANADH, (a), *pr. part.* of pian. Tormenting, paining; distressing, annoying; punishing. 'G ar pianadh, *tormenting us.*—*Stew. Matt.*

PIANAIL, *a.* (*from* pian.) Painful.

PIANAS. See PEANAS.

PIANTACH, *a.* (*from* pian.) Painful, tormenting; annoying; vexatious. Gu piantach, *painfully.* *Com.* and *sup.* piantaiche.

PIANTACHAIL, *a.* Painful; vexatious; afflictive.

PIANTACHAIR, *s. m.* A tormentor; a punisher. *N. pl.* piantachairean.

PIANTAICH, *v. a.* Cause pain; torment, afflict, punish. *Pret. a.* phiantaich; *fut. aff. a.* piantaichidh.

PIANTAICHTE, *p. part.* of piantaich. Tormented, pained; afflicted; annoyed; punished.

PIANTAIDH, *s. pl.* Pains, pangs, punishment. Ghlac piantaidh, *pains seized upon me.*—*Sm.*

PIANTAIL, *a.* Painful.

PIANTAN, *n. pl.* of pian. Pains.

PIASGACH, *a.* (*Ir. id.*) Rough, shaggy, hairy. Gu piasgach, *shaggily.*

PÌB, *s. f.* See PIOB.

PIBHINN, *s. f.* A lapwing. *N. pl.* pibhinnean.

PIBHINNEACH, *a.* Abounding in lapwings; like a lapwing; of lapwings.

PIC, *s. f.* (*Ir. id.*) A disorder in the tongue of fowls.

PIC, pice, *s. f.* A pickaxe. Pic na d' dhornaibh, *a pickaxe in thy fist.*—*Old Song.* Pic mheallach, *a Lochaber-axe.*—*Shaw.* Pic-thalmhainn, *mortar.*—*Q. B. ref.*

Anglo-Sax. becca. *Arm.* picq. *Fr.* pic. *Scotch,* pick. *Swed.* pigg, *a sting.* *Teut.* picken. *Du.* bicken. *Germ.* picken *and* bicken, *to sting.* *Germ.* picke, *a lance.*

The Macedonian lance was named *pica.* From *pic* evidently come the *Lat.* spica; *Sp.* espiga; and the English words, *pike, pick, beak.*

PIC, PICHD, *s. f.* Pitch. Comhdaich i le pic, *cover it with pitch.*—*Stew. Gen.* Pic-thalmhainn, *mortar.*—*Id.*

Gr. πισσα. *Lat.* pix. *Anglo-Sax.* pic. *W.* pyg. *Ir.* pic. *Arm.* pek. *Corn.* peg. *Fr.* poix. *Swed.* beck. *Span.* pez. *Ital.* pegola. *Sclav.* pekal. *Germ.* pech. *Franconian,* beh. *Belg.* pek *and* pick. *Scotch,* pick. In Lancaster and in other parts of Cheshire they say *picke.*

PIC, PICHD, *v. a.* Pitch; cover with pitch. *Pret.* phic; *fut. aff.* picidh.

PICEACH, *a.* Pitchy; like pitch; like a pickaxe.

PICEACHADH, aidh, *s. m.* A pitching or smearing with pitch.

PICEAL, eil, *s. m.* (*Ir.* picil.) Pickle. *N. pl.* picealan, *pickles.*

PICHD, *s. f.* See PIC.

PICIL, *v. a.* Pickle.—*Shaw.* *Pret. a.* phicil; *fut. aff. a.* picilidh.

PIGEAN, ein, *s. m.* (*Ir.* pigin. *W.* pigyn *or* piccyn.) A piggin, or small pail.

PIGHEID, *s. f.* A magpie; the *corvus pica* of Linnæus. A beicil mar phigheid, *bobbing like a magpie.* *N. pl.* pigheidean.

PIGHEIDEACH, *a.* Piebald; pied; abounding in magpies; like a magpie; of magpies.

PIGEADH, *s.* See PIGIDH.

PIGHE, *s. f.* See PITHE.

PIGIDH, *s. f.* (*Bisc.* pegar. *Scotch,* peg.) An earthen pot or pitcher; a can. *N. pl.* pigidhean. Bodach-phigidh, *an itinerant seller of earthenware.*

PILEIR, *s.* (*provincial.*) A pillar.

PILL, *v. a.* and *n.* (*Ir. id.*) Turn; return; turn away; cause to turn; turn aside. *Pret. a.* phill; *fut. aff. a.* pillidh. Pillidh a ghrian, *the sun will return.*—*Orr.* Pillidh freagradh mìn corruich, *a soft answer will turn away wrath.*—*Stew. Pro.*

PILL, *s. f.* (*Ir. id.*) A sheet; a covering. Pill chuiridh, *a sower's sheet.*

PILLEADH, idh, *s. m.* (*Ir. id.*) A turning; a returning; a return.

PILLEADH, 3 *sing.* and *pl. imper.* of pill.

PILLEAM, 1 *sing. imper.* of pill. Let me return; *or for* pillidh mi, *I will return.*

PILLEAN, ein, *s. m.* (*Ir.* pillin.) A saddle; a pad; a pillion; a pack-saddle.

PILLEAR, *fut. pass.* of pill. Shall return; shall be brought back.

PILLSEAR, eir, *s. m.* (*Ir. id.*) The fish called a pilchard.

PÌLLTEACH, *a.* Inclined to return; returning frequently.

PILLTINN, *s. f.* A returning; a return; a retrogression.

PILLTINN (a), *part.* Returning.

PINCEAN, ein, *s. m.* (*Ir. id.*) A gillyflower.

PINCHRANN, chroinn, *s. m.* A pine tree. *N. pl.* pinchroinn.

PINN, *v. a.* Pin; fasten with pins or pegs. *Pret. a.* phinn; *fut. aff. a.* pinnidh, *shall* or *will pin.*

PINNE, *s. f.* (*Ir.* pion.) A pin; a peg. Pinne na garmain, *the pin of the beam.*—*Stew. Jud.* Pinne cluaisein, *the dragpin of a cart.* *N. pl.* pinneacha *and* pinneachan, *pins.*—*Stew. Exod.*

PINNEACHADH, aidh, *s. m.* A pinning; a fastening with pins or pegs.

Pinneadh, idh, *s. m.* A pinning; a fastening with pins or pegs.

Pinneadh, (a), *pr. part.* of pinn. Pinning.

Pinnear, eir, *s. m.* (*Ir. id.*) An ink-horn; a pen-case.

Pinnich, *v. a.* Pin; fasten with a pin or peg. *Pret. a.* phinnich; *fut. aff. a.* pinnichidh.

Pinnichte, *p. part.* of pinnich. Pinned.

Pinnt, pinnte, *s. f.* (*Gr.* πινθα. *Germ.* pinte.) A pint, or two quarts. Bodach agus pinnt lionna, *a mutchkin of whiskey and a pint of ale.—Old Song.* Tri cheithreannan pinnte, *three quarters of a pint.—Stew. Lev. ref.* Stòp pinnte, *a quart pot. N. pl.* pinnteachean.

Pinteal, *v. a.* Paint.—*Shaw. Pret. a.* phinteal.

Pintealta, *a.* (*Ir. id.*) Painted.

Piob, pioba *or* pìb, *s. f.* A pipe; a bagpipe; a tube. A phiob mhòr, *the great Highland bagpipes;* piob na comhsheirm, *the union-pipes;* piob tombac, *a tobacco-pipe.* The Danes say *pibe tobak. N. pl.* pioban *and* piobachan. Piob-uisge, *a water-pipe;* piob-thaosgaidh, *a pump;* piob-shionnaich, *a pipe blown with bellows;* piob-leigidh, *the cock of a barrel;* piob-mhàla, *a bagpipe.*

Dan. pibe. *Swed.* pipa. *Du.* piep *and* pyp. *W.* pib. *Ir.* pib. *Corn.* piban, *a pipe. Germ.* pipen. *Island.* pipa, *a tube. It.* piva, *a flute. Sp. Bisc.* pipa, *a tunnel. Syr.* bibo, *a tube, a water-pipe,* and bebio, *an aqueduct. Arab.* bibib, *an aqueduct. Chald.* bib.

There are three kinds of bagpipes, the Highland, the Irish, and the Scottish. These instruments differ essentially in their tone and compass of sound; but they have this circumstance in common, that the air blown into them, and which gives them utterance, is collected into a bag, and is dislodged by the pressure of the performer's arm. Of these, the Highland pipe is, beyond comparison, the most magnificent. It consists of a large bag, to which is attached a pipe for the inflation of it; a chanter which furnishes the tenor part of the music; and three drones which sound a loud swelling bass. The sound of the drones is monotonous, and is in unison with the lowest note, save one, on the chanter. When the large drone is affixed, the noise is exceedingly loud, and well qualified for martial purposes. This instrument, as may be supposed, requires prodigious exertion of the lungs; and the piper is accordingly obliged to stand or walk when he plays on it. The compass of the bagpipe is not great. It has but nine notes in all, which are not capable of any variation by flats or sharps; so that they are natural. It is tuned by lengthening or shortening the drone, until the note desired is sounded.

The Gael are not to be accounted the inventors of this noble instrument, though they have improved upon it in such a degree as to render its music of a most martial character, and exclusively their own. The Norwegians had their *sueck-pipe* from time immemorial; yet it has been asserted that they borrowed it from the Caledonians. The Greeks had their ἀσκαυλης, or πυκαυλος, an instrument composed of an inflated bag, a chanter, and two drones. The peasants of Italy had, and still have, their *piva* and *cornumusa*, formed on the model of the ἀσκαυλης. Nero, who was an accomplished musician, is said to have greatly improved this instrument. There is still to be seen at Rome a sculpture, in basso-relievo, of the highest antiquity—a bagpiper, playing on his instrument like a Highlander.

Aristides Quintilianus observes, that the bagpipes were used among the Caledonians in the very early ages; yet the fragments of ancient Gaelic poetry which have come down to us make no mention of them; so if they existed in those times, they must have been in a very rude and unimproved condition. The *clarsach* and the *cruit* were the instruments of note among the old Gael; and these continued in vogue so long as their government was regular and their manners civilized. But when, in the course of time, dismemberment and distraction arose among them; when chieftainry, clanship, rivalry, and feud, usurped the place of law, subordination, and regular warfare, attention was turned to the bagpipe, which was introduced and speedily improved upon. It was soon found to be a most suitable instrument for spreading alarms, for collecting the clans with necessary speed, and for every exigency that might occur in the altered condition of their society. The bagpipe has been, for centuries past, the instrument of national music among the Gael; and in the Isle of Skye there was a college founded by the M'Leans and the M'Donalds, whither every performer who aspired to eminence resorted for instruction. The bagpipe is fast on the decline; and before the lapse of two centuries, it is likely that it shall, in its turn, give way to the long-neglected harp.

Piob, *v. n.* Pipe; squeak. *Pret. a.* phiob; *fut. aff. a.* piobaidh.

Piobach, *a., from* piob. (*Ir. id.*) Tubulous; tubular; fluted.

Piobadair, *s. m.* A pipe-maker; a bagpipe-maker. *N. pl.* piobadairean.

Piobadaireachd, *s. f.* Pipe-making; bagpipe-making.

Piobair, *s. m.*, piob-fhear. (*Ir. id.*) A Highland bagpiper; a piper of any description. *N. pl.* piobairean.

W. pibwr. *Du.* pieber. *Ir.* piobaire, *a piper. Du.* piber, *a fifer.*

Piobaireachd, *s. f.* (*Ir. id.*) The occupation of a bagpiper; piping; pipe-music; certain strains performed on the Highland bagpipe, wherein the Scottish Gael perceive much meaning, sentiment, and beauty, but which convey to the ears of a Lowland Scot or of a Southron, nothing but unintelligible and tremendous sounds.

Pioban, *n. pl.* of piob. Pipes; bagpipes.

Pioban, ain, *s. m., dim.* of piob. (*W.* piben. *Corn.* piban.) A little pipe; a tube; a reed; a little flageolet; the gullet or windpipe; the throat. *N. pl.* piobain.

Piobanach, *a.* (*from* pioban.) Tubulous; tubular; fluted.

Piobanta, *a.* Tubulous; tubular; fluted.

Piob-cheòl, chiùil, *s. m.* Pipe-music; bagpipe-music. Thig sibh le piob-cheòl, *you will come with pipe-music.—Old Song.*

Piobhar, air, *s. m.* A sieve; a honeycomb.—*Shaw.* A purse.—*O'Reilly.*

Piobull, uill, *s. m.* (*Gr.* βιβλος.) A Bible.

Pioc, *v. a.* Pick; peck; nip; pinch; nibble; dig with a pickaxe. *Pret. a.* phioc; *fut. aff. a.* piocaidh. Pioc an coimheach, *pinch the stranger.—G. P.* Pioc taingeadh, *pick a thank.—Old Song.*

Gr. πικω. *Goth.* pycan. *W.* and *Arm.* piga *and* pic. *Fr.* piquer. *Swed.* picka. *Belg.* pickan.

Pioc, *s. m.* and *f.* A nip or pinch with the nails or teeth; a pickaxe. Thoir pioc as, *pinch him.*

W. pig. *Arm.* bec. *Eng.* beak. *Belg.* beck. *Span.* pico. *It.* becco. The Greek πικος, *a woodpecker*, has an evident affinity with *pioc.*

Piocach, *a.* Pinching; pungent; nipping; nibbling; taunting.

Piocach, aich, *s. m.* A Pict. *N. pl.* Piocaich.

Piocadair, *s. m.* A nibbler; a carper.

Piocadh, aidh, *s. m.* (*Ir. id.*) A nipping; a pinching; a nibbling; a digging with a mattock.

Piocag, aig, *s. f.* (*from* pioc.) A small pair of nippers or pincers; a slight pinch; a taunting female. *N. pl.* piocagan.

Piocaich, *v. a.* Work or dig with a pickaxe. *Pret. a.* phiocaich; *fut. aff. a.* piocaichidh.

Piocaid, *s. f.* (*Ir. id.*) A pickaxe; a mattock; pincers.—*Macint.* A gheurachadh a phiocaid, *to sharpen his mattock.—Stew. Sam.*

Piocaidh, *fut. aff. a.* of pioc.

Piocair, *s. m.* (pioc-fhear.) A pikeman; one who digs with a pickaxe or mattock; a pioneer. *N. pl.* piocairean.

Piocaireachd, *s. f.* (*from* piocair.) The business of a pioneer; a digging with a pickaxe or mattock; the business of a pikeman.

Piocas, ais, *s. m.* A magpie.—*Shaw.*

Piochan, ain, *s. m.* One who wheezes in the throat.

PIOCHANACH, *a.* Wheezing; breathing with difficulty.

PIOCHANAICH, *s.f.* A wheezing in the throat. Ciod a phiochanaich th' ort? *why do you wheeze so?*

PIOCHDACH, aich, *s. m.* A Pict; a plunderer. *N. pl.* piochdaich.

PIOCHDACH, *a.* Pictish; given to plundering.

PIOL, *v. a.* Pull; pluck; tug. *Pret. a.* phiol; *fut. aff. a.* piolaidh.

PIOLACHADH, aidh, *s. m.* Plucking; digging out of the ground.

PIOLACHAIR, *s. m.* One who digs out of the earth.

PIOLACHAN, ain, *s. m.* A spaddle; an instrument to pluck or to dig with.

PIOLAICH, *v. a.* Pluck, dig. *Pret. a.* phiolaich; *fut. aff.* piolaichidh, *shall pluck; p. part.* piolaichte, *plucked.*

† PIOLAID, *s. f.* A palace; a prince's palace; a pillory.

PIOLLACH, *a.* Neat, trim, tidy; *also,* hairy. *Com.* and *sup.* piollaiche.

PIOLLACHD, *s. f.* Neatness, trimness, tidiness; *also,* hairiness.

PIOLLAIR, *s. m.* (*Ir. id.*) A pill.

PIOLLAISTEACH, *a.* Vexing; that vexes or troubles; teazing; annoying.

PIONAS. See PEANAS.

† PION-CHRANN, chroinn, *s. m.* A pine-tree.—*Shaw. N. pl.* pion-chroinn.

PIONSA, ai, *s. m.* (*Ir. id.*) Artifice, wile.

PIORAID, *s. m.* and *f.* A hat; a cap; a bonnet; a conical scull-cap; a parrot.—*Macdon.* A pirate.—*Shaw. N. pl.* pioraidean.

PIORAIDEACH, *a.* Like a bonnet; wearing a bonnet; conical; like a parrot; piratical.

PIORRA, PIORRADH, aidh, *s. m.* A squall; a blast; a pear. —*Shaw.*

PIOR-BHUIC, *s. f.* A wig or periwig. Gun bhonait gun phior-bhuic, *with bonnet or wig.—Macint.*

PIOS, piosa, *s. m.* A piece; a morsel or bit; a fragment or splinter; *also,* a silver drinking-cup; a fowling-piece. *N. pl.* piosan.

Arm. pez, *a piece. Ir.* piosa. *Span.* pieça. *Fr.* piece. *It.* pezzo. *Albanian,* piesse *and* piece. *Chald.* pas *and* pisah, *a piece,* and pesahh, *to break. Heb.* pissa. *Germ.* fetz, *a piece. Malay,* petza, *to break.*

PIOSACH, *a.* In pieces or fragments; splintering.

PIOSACH, aich, *s.*; more frequently written *piseach;* which see.

PIOSAN, ain, *s. m.* (*dim.* of pios.) A little piece.

PIOSARNACH, aich, *s. m.* (*Ir. id.*) Whispering.

PIOSARNACHD, *s. f.* (*Ir. id.*) Whispering.

PIOSTAL, ail, *s. m.* A pistol. Paidheir mhath phiostal, *a good brace of pistols.—Macfar. N. pl.* piostalan.

PIOTHAN, ain, *s. m.* A pie. Written also *pithean.*

PIRIDH, *s. f.* A top; a whirligig. *N. pl.* piridhean.

PISEACH, ich, *s. f.* Good luck; prosperity; fate; blessing; increase or produce; issue. Buaidh is piseach leat, *success and prosperity be with you.—Mac Co.* Am bi piseach oirre? *shall it prosper?—Stew. Ezek.* Piseach a bhilean, *the increase of his lips.—Stew. Pro.* Piseach mhath ort, *good luck to you; I wish you a good match.—G. P.* Cha do shaltair neach air a phiseach, *no one ever prevented his fate.* —*Id.*

PISEACHD, *s. f.*; more commonly written *piseach;* which see.

PÌSEAG, eig, *s. f.* A rag; a fragment of cloth, whether old or new. *N. pl.* pìseagan. Pìseag air toll, is e sin an tairbhe, ach pìseag air pìseig 's e sin an lùireach, *a patch on a hole is saving, but patch upon patch makes a ragged cloak.—G. P.*

PISEAG, eig, *s. f.* (*Ir.* piseog.) Sorcery, witchcraft; superstitious ceremony; a young moll-kitten. *N. pl.* piseagan.

PÌSEAGACH, *a.* In rags; in pieces, as cloth; ragged.

PISEAGACH, *a.* Superstitious; like a wizard; like a kitten.

PISEAGAICHE, *s. f.* A sorcerer; a wizard; a superstitious person.

PISEAN, ein, *s. m.* A tom-kitten. *N. pl.* piseinean *or* piseanan.

PISEARLACH, *a.* Juggling, conjuring. Cha 'n 'eil e pisearlach, *he is no conjuror.—G. P.*

PISEARNACH. See PIOSARNACH.

PIT, pite, *s. f.* (*Ir. id.*) A pit, a hollow—(*Shaw*); *θε μοστ κομμον ναμε φος θε σικρετ παρτς οφ α φιμαλε.*

PITEANTA, *a.* Effeminate.—*Shaw. Also,* lascivious, lewd.

PITEANTACHD, *s. f.* Effeminacy.—*Shaw. Also,* lasciviousness, lewdness.

PITHE, *s. f.* A pie.

PITHEAN, ein, *s. m.* A pie.

PITHEANNAN, *s. pl.* Pies; *also,* pastry.

PIÙIRNEACH, *a.* Full of pirns; like a pirn; of, or relating to, a pirn.

PIÙRN, piùirn, *s. m.* A pirn. *N. pl.* piùirnean. Piùrn le srann, *a noisy pirn.—Turn.*

PIUTHAIR, peathar, *s. f.* (*Corn.* piur.) A sister. Is i mo phiuthair i, *she is my sister.—Stew. Gen.* Clann do pheathar, *thy sister's children.—Old Song.* Ogha peathar is bhràthar, *second cousins. N. pl.* peathraichean; *d. pl.* peathraichibh. Piuthair chéile, *a sister-in-law;* piuthair athar, *an aunt,* or *father's sister;* piuthair mathar, *an aunt,* or *mother's sister; yet we say* piuthair m'athar, piuthair mo mhathar, *not* mo phiuthair athar, mo phiuthair màthar. Piuthair sean-athar, *a grand-aunt;* piuthair sean-mhathar, *a grand-aunt.*

PIUTHAIREIL, *a.* (piuthar-amhuil.) Sisterly.

PLABRAICH, *s. f.* A flapping or fluttering noise. Ri plabraich mu cheann brataich, *flapping about a flag-staff.— Old Song.*

PLACAID, *s. f.* (*Ir. id.*) A close timber vessel. *N. pl.* placaidean.

PLACANTACH, *a.* (*Ir. id.*) Coarse, rough. Gu placantach, *roughly.*

PLACANTACHD, *s. f.* (*Ir. id.*) Coarseness; roughness.

PLAGH, PLAGHADH, *s.* A glance; a momentary appearance. Written also *platha.*

† PLAC, plaic, *s. m.* (*Ir. id.*) A mouthful.

† PLAIC, *s. f.* (*Ir. id.*) A fine.—*Shaw.*

PLAICHID, *s. f.* A flagon.

PLAIDE, *s. f.* A blanket; coarse flannel; a plaid. Fo 'n phlaide, *under the blanket.—Old Song.* Còta plaide, *an under-petticoat of coarse flannel. N. pl.* plaideachan, *blankets.*

PLAID-LUIDHE, *s. f.* An ambush; a lying in wait. Deanamaid plaid-luidhe, *let us lie in wait.—Stew. Pro. ref.*

PLAID-LUIDHEACH, *a.* Lying in wait; like an ambush; fond of lying in wait; sculking; treacherous.

PLAIDSEACH, *a.* Squashing.

PLAIDSEADH, eidh, *s. m.* A squash.

PLAIGH, *s. f.* A plague or pestilence; an epidemic fever. Plaigh ro mhòr, *a very great plague.—Stew. Ex.* Plaigh sgaoilteach, *a spreading plague.—Stew. Lev.* A phlaigh uaine, *the yellow fever.*

Gr. Dor. πλαγα. *Lat.* plaga. *Swed.* plaoga. *Du.* plaghe. *Ir.* plaig. *Eng.* plague.

PLAIGHEACH, *a.* Pestilential; of, or belonging to, a plague or pestilence.

Plaigheil, *a.* (plaigh-amhuil.) Contagious; pestilential; like a plague or pestilence.

† **Plaitean**, ein, *s.m.* (*Ir.* plaitin.) The skull; a little head.

Plaitse, *s.f.* A squash; a squelch.

Plaitseach, *a.* Squashing; squelching.

Plam, *a.* (*Ir. id.*) Curdled.

Planait, *s.f.* A planet. *N. pl.* planaitean.

Plang, plaing, *s. m.* A plank; *also*, a plack, or two boddles; the third part of a penny. *N. pl.* plangan.
Gr. πλαξ. *Arm.* placq. *Germ.* plank. *Belg.* plank. *Fr.* planche. *W.* plange. *Corn.* plankan.

Plangach, *a.* Having planks; planked; made of planks; like a plank.

Plangaich, *v. a.* Provide with planks.

Plannt, plainnt, *s. m.* A plant. *N. pl.* planntan.
Ir. plannda. *Lat.* and *Sp.* planta. *Du.* planten.

Planntachadh, aidh, *s. m.* A planting; a plantation.

Planntachair, *s. m.* A planter. *N. pl.* planntachairean.

Planntaich, *v. a.* (*Ir.* planndaigh.) Plant; settle or establish a colony. *Pret. a.* phlanntaich; *fut. aff. a.* planntaichidh, *shall plant.*

Planntaireachd, *s. f.* The business of a planter.

Plaoisg, *v. a.* and *n.* Peel or skin; hull or unshell; uncover; disclose; open; burst; make a sound. *Pret. a.* phlaoisg; *fut. aff. a.* plaoisgidh; *p. part.* plaoisgte.

Plaosg, plaoisg, *s. m.* A shell; a husk; a peel; a rind; a sound; a noise. Cnothan is taine plaosg, *thinnest-shelled nuts.—Macint.* Gus am plaosg, *to the husk.—Stew. Num.* Plaosg buntàit, *a potato-skin.* *N. pl.* plaosgan.
Ir. plaosg. *Corn.* plysg. *W.* blisgyn. *Arm.* plyusken.

Plaosgach, *a.* (*Ir. id.*) Shelly; husky; having a rind; capsular; peeling; skinning; uncovering; glimmering; sounding; noisy. *Com.* and *sup.* plaosgaiche.

Plaosgadh, aidh, *s. m.* (*Ir. id.*) The act of shelling; a hulling; a peeling or skinning, as of a potato; an appearing; a discovering of one's self; opening, as of the eyes; a glimmering; a glimmering light; a sound.

Plaosgadh, (a), *pr. part.* of plaoisg.

Plapraich, *s.f.* See **Plabraich**.

Plàsd, plàsda, *s. m.* A parget or plaster; a daub. Plàsd dubh, *a medicated plaster.* Cha téid plàsd air bagairt, *a threat requires not a plaster.—G. P.*

Plàsd, *v. a.* Parget or plaster; daub; cover with lime or clay. *Pret. a.* phlàsd; *fut. aff. a.* plàsdaidh.

† **Plasda**, *a.* (*Ir. id.*) Feigned.—*Shaw.*

Plàsdach, *a.* (*Ir. id.*) Plastering; of a parget or plaster; daubing; *also*, a plaster.—*Shaw.*

Plàsdachadh, *a.* A plastering or pargeting; a daubing or smearing; a covering with lime or clay.

Plàsdachd, *s.f.* A plastering or pargeting; a daubing or smearing; a covering with lime or clay.

Plàsdaich, *v. a.* Plaster or parget; daub, smear; cover with lime or clay. *Pret. a.* phlàsdaich; *fut. aff. a.* plasdaichidh; *p. part.* plàsdaichte.

Plàsdair, *s. m.* (plàsd-fhear.) A plasterer. *N. pl.* plasdairean.

Plàsdaireachd, *s. f.* The occupation of a plasterer; the handiwork of a plasterer; a smearing or daubing.

Plàsdradh, aidh, *s. m.* (*Ir. id.*) A plastering, a pargeting; a besmearing; a covering with lime or clay.

Plàsdraich, *v. a.* Plaster or parget; daub, smear; cover with lime or clay. *Pret. a.* plàsdraich; *fut. aff. a.* plasdraichidh.

Plàsdrail, *s. f.* A plastering; a besmearing.

† **Plàt**, plàta, *s. m.* A plate.

Plath, platha, *s. m.* A glance; a twinkling; a moment; the momentary appearance of any thing, as of lightning; a flash; a meteor; a sudden gloom; a swoon; a gust. Ann am plath, *in a moment.—Stew. Ex.* A ghrian fu phlatha, *the sun under a sudden gloom.—Death of Carril.* Mar phlath dealanaich, *like a flash of lightning.—Stew. Ezek.* *N. pl.* plathan; *d. pl.* plathaibh.

Plathach, *a.* Glancing; flashing; transient; momentary; gusty. Roimh na gaothaibh plathach, *before the gusty winds.—Old Poem.*

Pleadh, pleadha, *s. m.* A digging; a dibbling; a spaddling.

Pleadhach, *a.* Digging; dibbling; made for digging or dibbling.

Pleadhag, aig, *s.f.* (*Ir.* pleadhog.) A dibble; a spaddle; a paddle. Bithidh pleadhag agad, *thou shalt have a paddle.—Stew. Deut.* *N. pl.* pleadhagan.

Pleadhagach, *a.* Like a dibble or spaddle; of a dibble, spaddle, or paddle.

Pleadhaich, *v.* (*from* pleadh.) Dig; dig out; work with a spaddle or dibble. *Pret. a.* phleadhaich; *fut. aff. a.* pleadhaichidh.

Pleadhaichte, *p. part.* of pleadhaich.

Pleadhain, *gen. sing.* and *n. pl.* of pleadhan.

Pleadhair, *s. m.* A dibbler; one who works or digs with a dibble or spaddle.

Pleadhan, ain, *s. m.* A dibble; a little oar; a paddle; a small spade.

Pleadhanachd, *s. f.* A paddling; a sculling; a dibbling; a digging with a spaddle.

Pleadhart, airt, *s. m.* A buffet; a blow or slap on the cheek.—*Macd.*

Pleaghan, ain, *s. m.* See **Pleadhan**.

Pleanais, *s. f.* A species of coarse linen.

Pleasg, pleasga, *s. m.* (*Ir. id.*) A noise; a crack; a crash; a loud blow.

Pleasg, *v. n.* Crack.

Pleasgach, *a.* Cracking; crashing; noisy; thumping.

Pleasgadh, aidh, *s. m.* A cracking; a crashing; a noise; a bursting; a breaking.

Pleasganach, *a.* Noisy; crashing; cracking; striking; breaking; bursting.

Pleat, pleata, *s. m.* A plait; a fold; a double. Féile nam pleat, *the plaited kilt.—Old Song.*

Pleat, *v. a.* Plait; fold; double; wreathe; braid. *Pret. a.* phleat; *fut. aff. a.* pleataidh.

Pleatach, *a.* Plaited; folded; doubled; wreathed. Folt pleatach, *braided hair;* féile phleatach, *a plaited kilt.*

Pleide, *s. f.* Spite; envy; insincerity; solicitation; begging. Fàilte gun phleide, *a sincere welcome.* — *Old Song.* Written also *bleide.*

Pleideil, *a.* (pleide-amhuil.) Spiteful; invidious; insncere; impertinent; begging. Written also *bleideil.*

Pleidear, eir, *s. m.* (pleide-fhear.) A spiteful person; a beggar; one who solicits impertinently. *N. pl.* pleideirean. Written also *bleidear.*

Pleiste, *s.* (*Ir. id.*) A testicle.

Pleòdar, air, *s. m.* Pewter; a harum-scarum; a soft, spiritless fellow.

Pleòdarach, *a.* Made of pewter; like pewter; abounding in pewter.

Pliadhach, *a.* (*Ir. id.*) Broad-footed.

Pliath-rod, -roid, *s. m.* A slipper.

Plibean, ein, *s. m.* (*Ir.* plibin.) A plover.

Ploc, pluic, *s. m.* (*Ir. id.*) A block; the block-head of a stick; a block-headed instrument; a round-head; a blockhead; a stopper; a bung; a large stump; a lump; a hunch; a cheek. Ploc chul-teallaich, *a lump of wood placed at the back of a fire.*

PLOC, *v a* Strike with a block, bruise; mash; strike on the head *Pret. a.* phloc; *fut. aff. a* plocaidh, *shall* or *will mash.*

PLOCACH, *a.* (*Ir id*) Blockish, lumpish; turgid; sturdy; full-faced. Laoch plocach, *a sturdy hero.—Old Poem.* An galar plocach, *the quinsy, the goitres.*

PLOCADH, aidh, *s m.* (*Ir id*) A bruising; a mashing with a block-headed instrument.

PLOCAIDH, *fut. aff a.* of ploc. Shall bruise or mash.

PLOCAIDH, *gen sing.* of plocadh

PLOCANTA, *a* Lumpish; blockish, round-headed; sturdy, full-faced.

PLOCANTACHD, *s f* Lumpishness; blockishness; doltishness, sturdiness.

PLOD, *v a* and *n* Scald, float, cause to float. *Pret a* phlod; *fut aff. a* plodaidh, *shall scald*

† PLOD, ploid, *s m.* (*Ir. id* *Fr* flotte *It.* flotta, *fleet.*) A pool, a fleet.

PLODACH, *a* (*Ir. id.*) Scalding, floating; like a float; of, or belonging to, a float

PLODACH, aich, *s m* A puddle, mire

PLODACHADH, aidh, *s m* Floating, buoyancy

PLODADH, aidh, *s m.* (*Ir id*) A scalding, a scald, a floating; a float, a fleet

PLODAG, aig, *s f.* Gruel; posset, warm posset Deoch phlodaig, *a drink of gruel*

PLODAICH, *v a* and *n* Scald; float, cause to float *Pret. a* phlodaich.

PLODAN, ain, *s. m.* (*Ir. id*) A small pool; a little float

PLODANACHD, *s f* (*Ir id*) Paddling, floating; guddling

PLODAR, PLODMHOR, *a* Buoyant, floating

PLOIDHISG, *s c.* A bumpkin; a booby; a simpleton, whether male or female. *N. pl.* ploidhisgean

PLOIDHISGEACH, *a* Doltish, stupid Balaoch ploidhisgeach, *a doltish fellow* Gu ploidhisgeach, *doltishly*

PLOIDHISGEAG, eig, *s. f* A doltish young female. *N. pl* ploidhisgeagan

PLOIDHISGEAN, ein, *s m* (*dim* of ploidhisg) A young bumpkin, a young booby, a doltish boy

PLOISG, *a.* (*Ir id*) Spongy; dry; elastic, inflammable, quick

PLOSG, ploisg, *s m.* (*Ir. id*) Life; breath, a throb; a gasp. Gun phlosg air dèile, *lifeless on the* [*plank*] *bier.—Old Song.*

PLOSG, *a* Quick

PLOSG, *v n* Pant, throb, gasp, sob *Pret.* phlosg, *panted, fut. aff* plosgaidh, *shall* or *will pant* Phlosg anam na chliabh, *his soul* [*heart*] *throbbed in his breast.—Mac Lach.*

PLOSGACH, *a* (*Ir. id*) Panting, throbbing, gasping; causing to pant or throb; like a pant or sob, quick, bold

PLOSGAIL, *s. f.* (*Ir. id*) A panting, a throbbing, a gasping, a pant, a throb, a gasp, a sound; a noise.

PLOSGAIL, (a), *pres part* of plosg Panting, throbbing, gasping M' anam a plosgail am innibh, *my soul panting within me.—Oss Gaul*

PLOSGARNACH, *a* Quick, bold, panting. *Com* and *sup* plosgarnaiche

PLOSGARNAICH, *s f.* Panting.

PLOSGARTACH, *a.* (*Ir. id*) Panting, throbbing; quick; bold; open.

PLOSGARTACHD, *s f.* Panting, gasping, throbbing

PLOSGARTAICH, *s. f.* Continued panting, sobbing, throbbing. Tha mo chridhe 's a phlosgartaich, *my heart is panting.—Old Song.*

PLOSGARTAICH, *v. n.* Sob, pant, throb, gasp. *Pret.* phlosgartaich.

PLUB, pluib, *s. m.* A lump, *in derision,* a round-head; a jolt-head; the noise made by the fall of a stone into water.

PLUB, *v. n.* Plump, like a stone into water. *Pret.* phlub; *fut. aff* plubaidh

PLUBACH, *a* (*from* plub) Jolt-headed; round-headed; chubby-headed.

PLUBAIR, *s. m.* (plub-fhear.) A jolt-headed fellow; a chubby-faced fellow. *N pl* plubairean.

PLUBAIS, *s. f.* Paddling; a paddling noise; a gurgling noise.

PLUBARTAICH, *s. f.* See PLUBRAICH.

PLUBRACH, *a.* (*Ir. id*) Making a plumping noise, floundering; puddling; gurgling; guggling.

PLUBRAICH, *s. f.* A plumping noise; a plunging; a puddling; a floundering; a guggling. Plubraich nan tonn, *the guggling of the waves.—Old Poem.* Na bric ri plubraich, *the trouts floundering.—Macdon.*

PLUC, pluic, *s m* (*Ir id*) A knot; a lump; a hunch; a tumour, a pimple, the rot among sheep; a bung. Pluc-mhaildheach, *beetle-browed.*

PLUC, *v a.* and *n.* Puff up the cheeks; knot; grow knotty. *Pret. a.* plucaidh, *fut aff. a* plucaidh.

PLUCACH, *a* (*from* pluc) Knotty; lumpish; hunchy; pimply; affected with the rot; chubby. Sròin phlucach, *a pimply nose.—Macint* An galar plucach, *the quinsy,* also, *the rot* *Com.* and *sup.* plucaiche.

PLUCADH, aidh, *s m.* (*Ir. id.*) A puffing of the cheeks; a knotting; a growing into knots, tumours, or pimples.

PLUCAIR, *s. m.* (*Ir id.*) A chubby-faced fellow. *N. pl.* plucairean.

PLUCAIREACHD, *s f.* (*Ir. id*) Chubbiness; *also,* impertinence.—*Shaw.*

PLUCAIS, *s. f.* A flux.

PLUCAN, *n. pl* of pluc. Knots; lumps; tumours; pimples.

PLUCAN, ain, *s m, dim.* of pluc. (*Ir. id.*) A little lump; a little tumour, a pimple; a little knot. *N. pl.* plucain.

PLUCANACH, *a* Full of little lumps; pimply; knotty.

PLÙCH, *v. a.* and *n.* Squeeze, press; throng; smother; constringe; mouth when eating *Pret.* phlùch; *fut. aff.* plùchaidh

PLÙCHADH, aidh, *s m* (*Ir. id*) A pressing, a squeezing; a thronging, a smothering; a mouthing in time of eating.

PLUIC, *s. f.* (*Ir.* pluice) A cheek. A seideadh pluic, *blowing up the cheek.—Sm* Pluicean, *cheeks.* Do phluicean mar na caoran, *thy cheeks like the service-berry.—Old Song* *D pl* pluicibh A' d' pluicibh, *i e.* ann do phluicibh, *in thy cheeks.—Macint*

PLUICEACH, *a* (*from* pluic.) Having large cheeks; chubby-faced; blub-checked

PLUIDEACH, *a.* Club-footed, splay or broad-footed.—*Macd.*

PLUINNSE, *s f.* A plunge, as in water.

PLUINNSEACH, *a* Plunging

PLUMANAICH, *s m* A plumping noise; a plunging, the dashing noise of waves

PLUMBAIS, *s* A plum, plums. Plumbais seargte, *prunes.* Craobh phlumbais, *a plum-tree.*

PLUMP, *s* A plump

PLUNDRAINN, *s. f.* Plunder, pillage, spoil; plundering. *Swed* plundring. *Germ* plundern. *Belg.* plundern.

PLUNDRAINN, *v a.* Plunder, pillage, spoil.

Plùr, plùir, *s. m.* *(Ir. id.)* A flower; a blossom; a nosegay; flour-meal or wheat-meal. *Asp. form*, phlùr. Do phlùr chruithneachd, *of flour-meal.—Stew. Ex.* *N. pl.* pluran, *flowers*.

Plùrach, *a.* (*from* plùr.) Flowery; mealy; like meal; pulverised.

Plùran, ain, *s. m.* *(Ir. id.)* A little flower; a flower; a blossom; a nosegay. Plùran seangan, *sheep sorrel; mountain clover*.

Plùran, *n. pl.* of plùr; which see.

Plùranach, *a.* (*Ir. id.*) Flowery; full of blossoms.

Plùranachd, *s. f.* (*Ir. id.*) Floweriness; botany; the business of a florist.

Plùranaiche, *s. m.* A botanist; a florist.

Pnamh. See Pramh.

Pobhuill, *s. f.* (*Ir. id.*) A poplar-tree. *N. pl.* pobhuillean.

Pobhuilleach, *a.* Abounding in poplar; of poplar.

Pobull, uill, *s. m.* A people; a populace; a nation; a tribe; a congregation. Do phobull taghta, *thy chosen people*.
Lat. popul-us. *Germ.* pobel, pöbel, *and* pofel. *Dan.* pöbel. *Fr.* peuple. *Ir.* pobal. *W.* and *Arm.* pobl.

Pobullach, *a.* Populous; of, or belonging to, the people. Duthaich phobullach, *a populous country*. *Com.* and *sup.* pobullaiche.

Pobullachd, *s. f.* Populousness.

Pòc, *s. m.* A pocket or pouch. Leabhar pòc, *a pocket-book;* airgiod pòc, *pocket-money*.

Poc, *s. m.* (*Du.* pok. *Scotch*, pock.) A bag, a little sack, a satchel. Poc min, *a meal-bag;* air a phoc, *begging*.

Pòc, *v. a.* Pocket or pouch; provide with a pocket. *Pret. a.* phòc; *fut. aff. a.* pòcaidh.

Poc, *v. a.* Put up in a bag or sack. *Pret. a.* phoc; *fut. aff. a.* pocaidh.

Pòcach, *a.* (*from* pòc.) Having pockets; having large pockets or pouches.

Pocach, *a.* Like a bag or sack; bagged.

Pòcachadh, aidh, *s. m.* A pocketing or pouching.

Pocachadh, aidh, *s. m.* A putting up in a bag or sack.

Pòcaich, *v. a.* Pocket or pouch; provide with pockets, as a coat. *Pret. a.* phòcaich; *fut. aff. a.* pòcaichidh.

Pocaich, *v. a.* (*from* poc.) Put up, as meal, into a bag or sack. *Pret. a.* phocaich; *fut. aff. a.* pocaichidh.

Pocain, *gen. sing.* and *n. pl.* of pocan; which see.

Pocair, *s. m.* (*from* poc.) A beggar.

Pòcait, *s. f.* A pocket or pouch. *N. pl.* pòcaitean.

Pòcaiteach, *a.* Having pockets; having large pockets; like a pocket; of a pocket.

Pocan, ain, *s. m.* (*dim.* of poc.) A little sack or bag; *also, in derision*, a little squat fellow. *N. pl.* pocain.

Pocanach, *a.* (*from* pocan.) Like a little bag or sack; squat; diminutive in person; stumpy; having a pock, bag, or satchel. Is fearr mathair phocanach na athair claidh'each, *better is a mother with a bag of victuals, than a father with a sword by his side.—G. P.*

Pocanta, *a.* Squat; squab; stumpy; diminutive. Do phearsa bagach pocanta, *your swaggy squat person.—Old Song*.

Pocantachd, *s. f.* Squatness; stumpiness; diminutiveness.

Pòg, pòig, *s. m.* A kiss. Is furtachd dhomh féin do phòg, *thy kiss is a comfort to me.—Turn.* *N. pl.* pògan, *kisses*. Pògan eas-caraid, *the kisses of an enemy.—Stew. Pro.*
Ir. pòg. *W.* poc. *Corn.* and *Arm.* pog *and* bocq, *a kiss*. *It.* bocca, *a mouth*. *Lat.* bucca, *a cheek*.

Pòg, *v. a.* (*Ir. id.*) Kiss. *Pret. a.* phòg; *fut. aff. a.* pògaidh, *shall kiss*. Thig agus pòg mi, *come and kiss me.—Stew. Gen.* *Fut. pass.* pògar.

Pògadh, aidh, *s. m.* A kissing; a kiss.

Pògaidh, *fut. aff. a.* of pòg. Shall or will kiss.

Pògair, *s. m.*, pòg-fhear. (*Ir. id.* *Arm.* pocqer.) A kisser; a gallant. *N. pl.* pògairean.

Pògaireachd, *s. f.* (*Ir. id.*) Kissing, frequent kissing, continual kissing.

Pògan, ain, *s. m.* (*dim.* of pòg.) A smack; a kiss.

Pòganta, *a.* Kissing; fond of kissing.

Pògta, *p. part.* of pòg. Kissed.

Poibleach, ich, *s. m.* (*Ir.* poibleoch.) Populace, a rabble, a mob; a plebeian.

Poibleach, *a.* Plebeian; of the populace; like a rabble.

Poibleachas, ais, *s. m.* Popularity.

Poicean, ein, *s. m.* A short squat fellow.

Poichean, ein, *s. m.* See Puichean.

Pòigean, *s. m.* (*dim.* of pòg.) A kiss, a smack. *N. pl.* pòigeanan. Thoir pòigean domh, *kiss me*.

Pòigeanach, *a.* Kissing, fond of kissing.

Poilleadh, idh, *s. m.* (*Ir. id.*) A boring, a piercing.

Pòinidh, *a.* A corruption of *poney*. Bu ghasd mo phòinidhse, *my poney was good.—Turn.*

Poir, *s.* A pore.

Poirse, *s. m.* (*Ir. id.*) A porch.

Pois, *v. a.* Haul, drag, lug. *Pret. a.* phais.

Pòisde, **Pòiste**, *p. part.* of pàs. Married. On is duine pòiste thu, *since you are a married man.—Turn.* Written also *pòsda*.

Poit, *s. f.* A pot, a cauldron. A phoit mhòr, *the great pot.—Stew.* 2 *K.* Poit dubh, *a still; a black pot;* poit chreadha, *an earthen pot;* poit luibhean, *a flower-pot;* poit-phlùran, *a flower-pot;* poit mhùin, *a chamber-pot;* poit leapach, *a chamber-pot;* poit thogalach, *a still;* poit ghlanaidh, *a fining-pot.—Stew. Pro.* *N. pl.* poiteachan. Poit na h-adhairc, *a ludicrous name for a tea-pot.*
Arm. pod. *Fr. Old Sax. Germ. Swed. Du. W. Ir.* pot *and* poite. *Hung.* pohat, *a cup*. *Greenlandese*, poyetach, *a porringer*. Hence also the *Lat.* potus *and* poto.

Pòit, *s. f.* Drinking, carousing, tippling; excess in eating or drinking.

Pòit, *v. n.* (*Lat.* poto.) Drink to excess, carouse.

Poit-chriadh, *s. f.* (*Ir. id.*) Potter's clay; a pot of clay, or an earthen pot. If the accent be on the first syllable, *poit*, it means potter's clay; if on *chriadh*, it signifies an earthen pot.

Pòiteach, *a.*, *from* pòit. (*Ir. id.*) Given to drinking, drunken.

Pòiteadh, idh, *s. m.* Tippling.

Poiteal, eil, *s. m.* A pottle. *N. pl.* poitealan.

Poitean, ein, *s. m.* (*dim.* of poit.) A little pot. *Ir.* poitin.

Poitear, eir, *s. m.* (pait-fhear.) A potter; a potmaker.

Pòitear, eir, *s. m.* (*Lat.* potor.) A drinker; a tippler, a drunkard; a gourmand. *N. pl.* pòitearan. Pòitearan fiona, *wine bibbers.—Stew. Pro.*

Pòitearach, *a.* Given to tippling, drunken.

Pòitearachd, *s. f.* (*Ir. id.*) The habit of tippling, drunkenness, carousing; excess in eating or drinking; banqueting; gormandizing. Ann am pòitearachd, *in banquetings.—Stew. Pet.*

Poitearachd, *s. f.* Pot making.

Pòl, pòil, *s. m.* A pall.

Polair, *s. m.* A sign; a searcher of holes and corners.—*Shaw.*

Polaireachd, *s. f.* A searching of holes and corners.

POLL, *s. m.* (*Ir. id.*) A nostril.—*Macd.* Hence *pollair*, a nostril. *N. pl.* pollan. *D. pl.* pollaibh. Ann am poll-aibh a shròine, *in his nostrils.—Stew. Gen. ref.*

POLL, puill, *s. m.* Mire, filth, mud; a puddle, a pool; a dark and deep part of any stream; deep stagnant water; a pond; a hole, a pit. Mar pholl nan sràid, *like the mire of the streets.—Stew. Zech.* Am fear a luidheas sa pholl togaidh e 'n làthach, *he who lies in the puddle will rise in dirt.—G. P.* Poll salainn, *a salt-pit.—Stew. Zeph.* Poll mòin, *a peat-moss;* poll damhair, *the rutting place of deer;* poll leathair, *a tanner's pool;* poll iasgaich, *a fish-pond, a pool where fish lie;* poll marcachd, *a road for ships;* poll acair-eachd, *a road for ships;* poll domhain, *a deep pool; Corn.* pol doun; *Arm.* poul don.

Gr. πηλος, *clay, a marsh. Dor.* παλος. *Arm.* poul *and* pull, *a ditch. Corn.* pol and polan. *W.* pull. *Germ.* pful. *Carribbees,* poulla, *a marsh. Anglo-Sax.* pul. *Belg.* poel.

† POLL, *s. m.* (*Ir. id.*) A pole of land, containing about sixty acres.

POLL, *v. a.* (*Ir. id.*) Hole, bore.

POLL-ACAIREACHD, *s. m.* A place for ships to ride in.

POLLACH, *a.* (*Ir. id.*) Holed; hollowed; fungous, porous.

POLLA-CHEANNACH, *a.* Jolt-headed.

POLLAG, aig, *s. f.* A fish called by the Scotch *powan*, and by Pennant *gwiniad;* the *salimo lavaretus* of Linnæus.

POLLAIR, *s. m., from* poll. (*Ir. id.*) A nostril. *N. pl.* pollairean, *nostrils. D. pl.* pollairibh. Gu 'r pollairibh, *to your nostrils.—Stew. Amos.*

POLL-LEATHAIR, *s. m.* A tanner's pool. *Arm.* poul lezr; z, *silent.*

POLL-MARCACHD, *s. f.* A road for ships.—*Macd. N. pl.* puill marcachd.

POLLTA, *p. part.* of poll. Bored.

PÒNAIDH, *s. m.* (*provincial.*) A poney. *N. pl.* ponaidhean.

PÒNAIR, *s. f.* (*Corn.* ponar. *Ir.* poneir.) Beans. Ponair agus gall pheasair, *beans and lentils.—Stew. Ezek.* Pò-nair fhrangach, *French beans;* pònair airneach, *kidneys;* pònair chapull, *marsh trefoil; buck-bean;* the *menyanthis trifoliata* of botanists.

PÒNAIREACH, *a.* Abounding in beans; like beans; of beans.

PONC, puinc, *s.* See PONG.

PONG, puing, *s. m.* (*Lat.* punctum. *Ir.* ponc. *W.* pwngc.) A point; an article. Written also *pung.*

PONGAIL, *a.* (pong-amhuil.) Punctual; exact; distinct; pointed. An labhraiche pongail, *the distinct orator.—Old Song.* Gu pongail, *punctually; distinctly.*

PONGAILEACHD, *s. f.* Exactness; pointedness; distinctness; punctuality.

PONG-LABHAIRT, *s. f.* Distinct utterance or articulation.

PONG-LABHRAICHE, *s. m.* A distinct articulator.

PÒR, pòir, *s. m.* (*Ir. id.*) Seed of any sort; a grain; corn; a race; a clan. Pòr cochullach, *pulse;* pòr nan gearr-mheann, *the race of young kids.—Macfar.* Pòr Dhiarmaid, *the race of Dermid,* i. e. *the Campbells.—Old Song.*

PÒRACH, *a.* (*from* pòr.) Abounding in seed, grain, or corn. —*Macint.*

† PORAISTE, *s. f.* A parish.—*Shaw.*

† PORAISTEACH, ich, *s. m.* A parishioner. *N. pl.* poraistich.

† PORC, *s.* A sow, a pig; pork. *N. pl.* porcan, *swine.*

Gr. πορκος. *Lat.* porcus. *Fr.* pourceau. *Ir.* porc. *Arm.* porc.

PORCAN, ain, *s. m.* (*dim.* of porc.) A little sow, a young sow, a pig.

PORCANTA, *a.* (*from* porc.) Piggish, swinish, porky.

PÒR-NIMHEACH, *a.* Radically venomous.

PÒRSAN, ain, *s. m.* A portion; a marriage portion.

PÒRSANAICH, *v. a.* Portion; give a marriage portion. *Pret. a.* phòrsanaich, *portioned.*

† PORT, *a.* (*Ir. id.*) Severe; fierce.

PORT, puirt, *s. m.* A port, harbour, or haven; a ferry. *N. pl.* puirt, *harbours; in* port; *wind-bound; weather-bound;* baile puirt, *a sea-port town.*

W. Ir. port, *a harbour. Bisc.* portua. *Lat.* portus. *It.* porto. *Fr.* port. *Sp.* puerto. *Germ.* port. *Dal.* porat. *Old Sax. Pol. Bohem.* port.

PORT, puirt, *s. m.* (*Ir. id.*) A tune, a strain; a fort; a garrison; a bank; the area of a place; a house; common food. Gabh port, *play a tune. N. pl.* puirt. Puirt mheara, *merry tunes.—Macint.*

PORT, puirt, *s. m.* A gate.

Port is not much used in this sense among the Scottish Celts; but we have *portair*, a doorkeeper, in frequent use.

W. porth, *a gate. Bisc.* porta *and* borta. *Lat.* porta. *Span.* puerta. *Fr.* porte. *Germ.* pforte. *Du.* poort. *Eng.* port. *Vulgar Greek,* πορτα.

PORTAIR, *s. m.* (*Ir. id.*) A ferryman; a doorkeeper; one who carries burdens for hire; *also*, the malt liquor, porter. *N. pl.* portairean.

PORTAIREACHD, *s. f.* (*Ir. id.*) Ferrying; the employment of a ferryman; the occupation of a doorkeeper; the carrying burdens or bearing messages for hire; ferryage; porterage.

PORTAN, ain, *s. m.* More frequently written *partan;* which see.

PORTAS, ais, *s. m.* (*Ir. id.*) The mass-book.—*Macd.*

PÒS, *v. a.* and *n.* (*Ir. id.*) Marry, wed; join in wedlock. *Pret. a.* phòs; *fut. aff. a.* pòsaidh, *shall marry.* Am pòs iad? *will they marry?*

PÒSACHAIL, *a.* Marriageable.

PÒSADH, aidh, *s. m.* (*Ir. id.*) A marrying or wedding; a marriage ceremony; a marriage; wedlock; a wedding. Toileach air do phòsadh, *willing to marry you.—Shaw.* Làth 'phòsaidh, *the marriage day.*

PÒSADH, (a,) *pres. part.* of pòs. Marrying, wedding; joining in wedlock.

PÒSAM, *for* pòsaidh mi, *I will marry.*

PÒSDA, *a.* and *part.* (*Ir. id.*) Married, wedded. Fear nuadh-phòsda, *a newly married man.*

PÒSGHEALL, *v. a.* Betroth or promise in marriage. *Pret.* phòs-gheall.

PÒSGHEALLADH, *a.* A betrothment; a promise of marriage.

POSLACH, aich, *s. m.* A bunch or tuft.—*Q. B. ref.*

POST, puist, *s. m.* (*Ir. id.*) A post or pillar.—*Q. B. ref.* A post in the army; a post or letter-carrier. *N. pl.* puist.

Bisc. posta, *a courier. It.* pasta. *Sp.* puesta. *Germ. Du. Eng.* post. *Boh.* posstæ. *Pol.* poszto. *Carinth.* poshta. *Sclav.* postha.

POST, *v. a.* Tread, trample, tramp. *Pret. a.* phost. *Fut. aff. a.* postaidh. Post an làthach, *tread the mortar.—Stew. Nah.*

PÒSTA, *p. part.* of pòs. Married, joined in wedlock. Mar nuadh-fhear pòsta, *like a fresh bridegroom.—Sm.*

POSTADH, aidh, *s. m.* A tramping with the feet, as in scouring clothes.

In scouring woollen clothes, or coarse linen, when strength of arms and manual friction are found insufficient, the Highland women put them into a tub, with a proper quantity of water; then, with petticoats tucked up a little way, they commence the operation of *posting*, which they continue until every part of the clothes receives an effectual cleansing. When three women are engaged, one commonly tramps in the middle, and the others tramp round her. This process is called *postadh*, and seems to a stranger almost as singular as the *luathadh*; which see.

Postan, ain, *s. m.* (*dim.* of post.) A little post.

Postanach, aich, *s. m.* (*Ir. id.*) A person with stout legs; that which has props.—*Shaw.*

Potair. See **Poitear.**

Potaireachd. See **Poitearachd.**

† **Poth**, potha, *s. m.* A batchelor.—*Shaw.*

Prab, *a.* Clever, active, quick.

Prab, *s. m.* (*Ir. id.*) Rheum, or the discharge from the corners of the eyes.

Prăb, *v. a.* Ravel; entangle; hamper; cumber; perplex. *Pret. a.* phrab; *fut. aff. a.* prabaidh.

Prabach, *a.* Ravelled; in knots; shaggy or dishevelled; out of order; as the hair of the head; unneat. *Com.* and *sup.* prabaiche.

Prabach, *a.* (*Ir. id.*) Blear; having humour about the eyes.

Prăbadh, aidh, *s. m.* A ravelling, or entangling; entanglement.

Prabair, *s. m.* (*Ir. id.*) A worthless fellow; an idle untidy fellow; a ramscallion; one of the rabble.

Pràbanach, aich, *s. m.* A comely young boy or lad.

Prabar, air, *s. m.* A rabble, a mob; the *canaille.* Am prabar porcanta, *the swinish multitude.*

Prabar, *fut. pass.* of präb. Shall be entangled, as thread.

Prablach, aich, *s. m.* Thread or hair entangled; any thing much entangled.

Prab-shuil, shùl, *s. f.* A blear eye; a rheumy eye. *N. pl.* prab-shuilean.

Prab-shùileach, *a.* Blear-eyed; having rheumy eyes.

Prabta, **Prabte**, *p. part.* of prab. Entangled.

Prac, praic, *s. m.* A kind of tax paid in the north of Scotland.

Pracais, *s. f.* Idle talk; irrelevant language.

Praidhinn, *s. f.* (*Ir. id.*) Earnest business; great haste; flurry.—*Shaw.*

Praidhinneach, *a.* Earnest; in great haste; flurried.—*Shaw.*

Praidhinneachd, *s. f.* Earnestness; the state of being in a great haste, or in a flurry.

Praimh, *gen. sing.* of *pramh;* which see.

Prainnseag, eig, *s. f.* (*Ir. id.*) A haggis; a bag pudding; the common name is *taigeis.*

Prais, praise, *s. f.* (*Ir. id.*) Brass; pot-metal.

Prais-bhallach, *a.* Well fortified, as if with brazen walls; strong, as a fortification; *also,* strong or brazen limbed.

Praiseach, ich, *s. f.* Broth; pottage; gruel; a kind of kail. Praiseach bhràthair, *English mercury; good Henry; wild spinach;* the *chenopodium* or *bonus Henricus* of botanists.

Ir. praiseach, *broth.* *W.* bresych. *Lat.* brassic-a, *cabbage.*

Praiseach, ich, *s. f.* (*Ir. id.*) A slut; a bawd; a pot; a crib; a manger. Mac na praisich, *whisky.*—*Turn.*

Praiseach, *a., from* prais. (*Ir. id.*) Brassy.

Praiseag, eig, *s. f.* A little pot.—*Macd.* *N. pl.* praiseagan.

Praisg, praisge, *s. f.* (*Ir. id.*) Pottage.

Praisiche, *s. f.* (*from* praise.) A brazier.—*Macd.* *N. pl.* praisichean.

Pràl, *v. n.* Beseech. *Pret. a.* phràl. *Fut. aff. a.* pràlaidh.

Pràlach, *a.* Beseeching; craving.

Pràladh, aidh, *s. m.* A beseeching.

Pramh, praimh, *s. m.* (*Ir. id.*) A sleep, a slumber, a nap; drowsiness. *Asp. form,* phramh. Madainn a dh'fhògras do phramh, *a morning that shall dispel thy slumber.*—*Oss. Derm.* Fo phràimh, *sleeping, slumbering;* a gabhail praimh, *taking a nap;* pramh chodail, *a nap.*

Pramhach, *a.* (*from* pramh.) Sleepy, drowsy, lethargic, slumbering, dozing.

Pramhachd, *s. f.* (*from* pramh.) Drowsiness, sleepiness, lethargy.

Pramhail, *a.* (pramh-amhuil.) Somniferous; narcotic; lethargic; sorrowful; disheartening.

Pramhaileachd, *s. f.* Somniferousness; lethargy; sorrowfulness; disheartedness.

† **Prann**, prainn, *s. m.* (*Ir. id.*) A wave.—*Shaw.*

Prantair, *s. m.* A hammer.

Prasach, aich, *s. f.* A manger; a crib; a stall. *Asp. form,* phrasach. Bithidh a phrasach glàn, *the crib shall be clean.*—*Stew. Pro.* Prasach each, *a horse-stall.*—*Stew.* 1 *K.*

Prasgan, ain, *s. m.* (*Ir. id.*) A flock; a herd; a gang; a mob, or rabble; a group of people. Am prasgan neo-aontachail so, *this disunited gang.*—*Macfar.*

Prasganach, *a.* (*Ir. id.*) Like a herd or flock; full of herds; like a gang or mob.

Prat, *s. m.* (*Scotch,* prat. *Swed.* spratt.) A prank, a trick. *N. pl.* pratan. Làn phrata, *full of tricks.*

Pratach, *a.* (*from* prat.) Pranky, tricky; mischievous. *Com.* and *sup.* prataiche.

Preab, *s. m.* (*Ir. id.*) A kick; a bounce; a start.

Preab, *v. a.* Kick; stamp with the foot; spurn. *Pret. a.* phreab; *fut. aff.* preabaidh. More frequently written *breab.*

Preabach, *a.* Kicking; stamping with the foot; spurning; apt to kick. Written also *breabach.*

Preabadair, *s. m.* (*Ir. id.*) A shoemaker. *N. pl.* preabadairean. More frequently written *breabadair.*

Preabag, aig, *s. f., dim.* of preab. (*Ir. id.*) A kick; a wince; *also,* a wincing mare.

Preabail, *s. f.* Stamping; kicking; spurning. See **Breabail.**

Preabair, *s. m.* (*Ir. id.*) One who kicks; a brave man.

Preabaireachd, *s. f.* (*Ir. id.*) Acting bravely; gallantry.

Preaban, ain, *s. m.* (*Ir. id.*) A patch, as on the shoe; a wincing horse; *rarely,* a court-yard. More frequently written *breaban.*

Preabanach, *a.* Patched, as a shoe; kicking; stamping; spurning. Written also *breabanach.*

Preabanachd, *s. f.* Continued stamping or kicking.

Preabanaiche, *s. m.* (*Ir.* preabanaidhe.) A botcher; a cobbler.

† **Preach**, *v. a.* and *n.* Grasp, hold, stand, stay; punish; crucify.—*Shaw.* *Pret.* phreach, *fut. aff.* preachaidh.

Preach, preacha, *s. m.* A grasp, a hold.

Preachach, *a.* Grasping, greedy, ravenous. Gu preachach, *greedily.*

Preachan, ain, *s. m., from* preach. (*Ir. id.*) A crow; a raven; a kite; a ravenous bird. *N. pl.* preachain. Preachan ingneach, *a vulture.*—*Stew. Lev. ref.* Preachan criosach, *a vulture.*—*Id.* Preachan (ceann-fhionn) ceannan, *an osprey;* preachan nan cearc, *a kite; a ringtail;* preachan ceirteach, *a kite.*

Preachanach, *a.* Ravenous, greedy; grasping; like a kite; abounding in kites or ravenous birds.

Preachanachd, s. f. Ravenousness, greediness, voracity.

Prealaid, s. m. (Ir. id.) A prelate, a bishop. N. pl. prealaidean.

† Preamh, s. m. (Ir. id.) A root, a stock; a tribe.

Preas, pris, s. m. A bush, a brier; a thicket; a cupboard. N. pl. pris and preasan. Mar phreas seargte, *like a withered bush.—Stew. Jer.* Ann am preas, *in a thicket.—Stew. Gen.* Cha deach car do theathair mu phreas, *your tether has not turned round the bush—G. P.;* said of a person who looks well. Preas dhearc, *a berry-bush;* preas dhearcag, *a berry-bush;* preas nan gearr-dhearc, *a barberry-bush;* preos ròs, *a rose-tree;* preas droighinn, *a thorn-bush;* mar phris droighinn, *like a thorn-bush.—Stew. Mic.* Preas-ghròsaid, *a gooseberry-bush;* preas fhiontag, *a cloudberry-bush;* preas deilgneach, *a barberry-bush;* preas nan smeur, *a bramble;* preas nan spiontag, *a currant-bush;* preas nan suidheag, *a raspberry-bush;* preas earnag, *a sloe-bush.*

Preas, preasa, s. m. (Ir. id.) A wrinkle, a corrugation, a rimple, a plait. N. pl. preasan.

Preas, v. a. and n. Wrinkle, corrugate, plait. *Pret. a.* phreas; *fut. aff. a.* preasaidh.

Preasach, a. Wrinkled, corrugated, plaited; wrinkling, rimpling; bushy; full of thickets; like a wrinkle; like a bush. Aghaidh phreasach, *a wrinkled face.*

Preasadh, aidh, s. m. A wrinkling; a wrinkle. Gun smàl, gun phreasadh, *without or wrinkle.—Stew. Eph.*

Preasag, aig, s. f. (dim. of preas.) A wrinkle; a little plait, a rimple; a little bush; a little thicket. N. pl. preasagan. Lan phreasag, *full of wrinkles.—Stew. Job.*

Preasagach, a. (*from* preasag.) Wrinkled, plaited, rimpled; full of wrinkles or plaits.

Preasan, ain, s. m. A free-will offering; a wedding boon.

Preasan, n. pl. of preas. Bushes; wrinkles.

Preasant, s. m. (Ir. id.) A present, a wedding present.

Preasarnach, aich, s. m. A shrubbery; a place full of bushes or thickets. N. pl. preasarnaich.

Preathal, ail, s. m. Dizziness; confusion; a stagger owing to dizziness or vertigo. Written also *breathal.*

Preathalach, a. Dizzy; confounded; bewildered; causing dizziness or confusion. Written also *breathal.*

Preathalachadh, aidh, s. m. A staggering; bewilderment, confusion.

Preathalaich, v. n. Stagger, as with dizziness; grow confounded or bewildered.

Priacail, s. f. (Ir. id.) Danger.—*Shaw.*

Prib, v. a. Wink. See Prioв.

† Pribhleid, s. f. (Ir. id.) Privilege.

Pribleach, a., *contracted for* priob-shuileach.

Pric, v. a. Sting, prick.—*Shaw. Pret. a.* phric; *fut. aff. a.* pricidh.

Priceadh, idh, s. m. A stinging, a pricking.

Priginn, s. f. (Scotch, priggin.) Haggling.

Primideach, a. Primitive; ancient; original; radical; not derived; focal. Focal primideach, *a radical word.*

Primideachd, s. f. Originality, primitiveness; radicalness.

Primidil, s. f. (Ir. id.) Firstlings; first produce or offering.—*Macd.*

Prìn, Prìne, s. m. A pin, such as is used for pinning clothes. N. pl. prìneachan. Prìn reamhar, *a blanket pin;* prìn iarruinn, *an iron pin.* The Danes say *iern-prin.* *Island.* prionn, *bodkin.* *Anglo-Sax.* prionn. *Dan.* prin, *a pin.* *Scotch,* preyne *and* prine.

Prìneachan, n. pl. of prìn. Pins.

Prìneachan, ain, s. m. A pincushion.

Priob, v. a. Wink; twinkle, as the eye. *Pret. a.* phriob, *winked; fut. aff. a.* priobaidh.

Priob, s. m. A wink, a twinkle of the eye. See also Priobadh.

Priobach, a. Winking, twinkling; having the habit of winking.

Priobadh, aidh, s. m. (Ir. id.) A wink, a twinkle; a winking, a twinkling. Ann am priobadh na sùl, *in a twinkling of an eye.—Stew. Num.*

Priobaid, s. f. (Ir. id.) A trifle; a bagatelle; a privet.—*Macd.* N. pl. priobaidean.

Priobarach, a. Brave, heroic. Gu priobarach, *bravely.* *Com.* and *sup.* priobaraiche.

Priobarachd, s. f. Bravery, heroism, gallant conduct.

Priobhaid, s. f. (Ir. id.) A secret; secrecy, privacy.

Priob-shuileach, a. Winking; having the habit of winking or twinkling.

Prioc, v. a. Prick or sting.

Priocadh, aidh, s. m. A pricking or stinging.

Priomh, a. (Lat. prim-us. Ir. priomh.) Prime; chief; capital; great; principal; etymon.

Priomhach, a. Principal; supreme, chief; fond of superiority; *also, substantively,* a favourite.

Priomhachd, s. f. (Ir. id.) Supremacy; principality; source.—*Macd.* Priomhachd a phàpa, *the pope's supremacy.*

Priomhadh, aidh, s. m. (Ir. id.) A primate.

Priomh-abhainn, -aibhne, s. f. A large river. *W.* prifafon.

Priomhair, s. m. (Lat. primarius.) A noble; a chief

Priomh-aithrichean, n. pl. of priomh-athair.

Priomh-arcal, ail, s. m. The main beam.

Priomh-athair, -athar, s. m. (Ir. id.) A patriarch; an ancestor; a primogenitor. N. pl. priomh-aithrichean. Am priomh-athair, *the patriarch.—Stew. Heb.*

Priomh-athaireach, a. Patriarchal.

Priomh-athaireachas, ais, s. m. (Ir. id.) A patriarchate.

Priomh-bhaile, s. m. A chief town, a capital, a metropolis. N. pl. priomh-bhailtean.

Priomh-bhard, -bhaird, s. m. (W. privard.) A chief bard, a poet laureate. N. pl. priomh-bhaird.

Priomh-chathair, -chathrach, s. f. A large city; a principal city. *W.* prif-caer.

Priomh-cheann, s. m. A supreme head.

Priomh-chiall, -chéill, s. f. Supreme or superior wisdom; great understanding.

Priomh-chlachair, s. m. An architect. N. pl. priomh-chlachairean.

Priomh-chlachaireachd, s. f. An architecture.

Priomh-chlàr, chlàir, s. m. (Ir. id.) An autograph and original.—*Shaw.*

Priomh-chlàrach, a. Autographical.

Priomh-chléireach, ich, s. m. A chief clerk; a protonotary. N. pl. priomh-chléirich.

Priomh-chleirsinneachd, s. f. The employment or office of a chief clerk.

Priomh-choslas, ais, s. m. (Ir. id.) An archtype.

Priomh-chrann, chroinn, s. m. A mainmast. N. pl. priomh-chrannan *or* priomh-chroinn.

Priomh-dhiùc, s. m. An archduke. N. pl. priomh-dhiùcan.

Priomh-dhruidh, s. m. (Ir. id.) An arch Druid. N. pl. priomh-dhruidhean.

PRIOMH-DHUINE, s. m. A noble, grandee; a chief. N. pl. priomh-dhaoine, *chiefs.—Stew. Acts.*

PRIOMH-EAGLAIS, s. m. A primitive church; high church; established church. N. pl. priomh-eaglaisean.

PRIOMH'EAR, ir, s. m., *for* priomh-fhear. (*Lat.* primarius.) A chief man; a noble; a chief.

PRIOMH-EASBUIG, s. m. An archbishop. N. pl. priomh-easbuigean.

PRIOMH-EASBUIGEACH, a. Archiepiscopal.

PRIOMH-EASBUIGHEACHD, s. f. An archbishopric; the dignity of an archbishop.

PRIOMH-FHÀIDH, s. m. (*Ir. id.*) A chief prophet. N. pl. priomh-fhaidhean.

PRIOMH-GHINEADAS, ais, s. m. Primogeniture. Thaobh còir priomh-ghineadais, *by right of primogeniture.*

PRIOMH-GHLEUS, s. m. A beginning; a foundation.—*Shaw.*

PRIOMHLAID, PRIOMHLAIT, s. m. A prelate. N. pl. priomh-laidean.

PRIOMHLAIDEACH, PRIOMHLAITEACH, a. Prelatical.

PRIOMHLAIDEACHD, PRIOMALAITEACHD, s. f. Prelacy.

PRIOMH-LAOCH, laoich, s. m. (*Ir. id.*) A hero of the first order. N. pl. priomh-laoich.

PRIOMH-LONG-PHORT, -phuirt, s. m. (*Ir. id.*) A royal residence; a principal sea-port town.

PRIOMH-LUINGEAS, eis, s. m. A first-rate ship; an admiral's ship. N. pl. priomh-luingeasan.

PRIOMH-PHRIONNSA, s. m. A prince royal. N. pl. priomh-phrionnsan.

PRIOMH-SHEÒL, shiùil, s. m. (*Ir. id.*) A mainsail. Thog iad am priomh-sheòl, *they raised the mainsail.—Stew. Acts.* N. pl. priomh-shiùil.

PRIOMH-SHLUAGH, -shluaigh, s. m. The aboriginal inhabitants of any country.

PRIOMH-SHONA, a. Supremely happy, supremely blessed.

PRIOMH-SHONAS, ais, s. m. Chief happiness. Is e am priomh-shonas a bhith creachadh, *their chief happiness is to plunder.—Macfar.*

PRIOMH-THÙS, thùis, s. m. An original; origin, foundation; principle; element.

PRIOMH-UACHDARAN, ain, s. m. (*Ir. id.*) A chief ruler. N. pl. priomh-uachdarain.

PRIOMH-UACHDARANACHD, s. f. (*Ir. id.*) Supremacy; supreme rule or authority.

PRIOMH-UGHDAR, air, s. m. An original author; an inventor. N. pl. priomh-ughdaran.

PRIOMPALLAN, ain, s. m. A beetle; a noise like that of a beetle. N. pl. priompallain.

PRIOMPALLANACH, a. Like a beetle; make a noise like a beetle.

PRIONNSA, PRIONNSADH, aidh, s. m. (*Ir. id.*) A prince. Ni mi e na phrionnsadh, *I will make him a prince.—Stew. 1 K. ref.* N. pl. prionnsan, prionnsaidh, *and* prionnsachan. Na prionnsachan, *the princes.—Stew. Zeph.*

PRIONNSACH, a. Princely, princelike.

PRIONNSACHAIL, a. Princely. Aros prionnsachail, *a princely mansion.*

PRIONNSACHD, s. f., (*from* prionnsa.) A principality, a princedom.

PRIONNSAIDH, s. pl. Princes.—*Q. B. ref.*

PRIONNSAIL, a. (prionnsa-amhuil.) Princely. Gu prionnsail, *in a princely manner.*

PRIONNSAILEACHD, s. f. Princeliness.

PRIONNT, s. m. (*Ir. id.*) Print. Ann am prionnt, *in print.*

PRIONNTAIR, s. m. A printer. N. pl. prionntairean.

PRIONNTAIREACHD, s. f. The profession of a printer; the employment of printing.

PRIOSAN, ain, s. m. A prison, a gaol. Ann am priosan, *in prison.*

Ir. priosun. *Corn.* brison. *Fr.* prison. *It.* prigione.

PRIOSANACH, aich, s. m. A prisoner, a captive. Na priosanaich uile, *all the prisoners.—Stew. Gen.*

PRIOSANACHADH, aidh, s. m. An imprisoning; imprisonment.

PRIOSANACHD, s. f. (*Ir. id.*) Imprisonment; captivity.

PRIOSANAICH, *gen. sing.* and *n. pl.* of priosanach.

PRIOSANAICH, v. a. Imprison; take captive. *Pret. a.* phriosanaich; *fut. aff. a.* priosanaichidh.

PRIOSANAICHTE, p. part. of priosanaich. Imprisoned; incarcerated; taken prisoner.

PRIOSUN, uin, s. m. More commonly written *priosan*; which see.

PRIS, *gen. sing.* and *n. pl.* Bushes, thickets.

PRÌS, prìse, s. m. A price, value, rate. Ciod a phrìs th' air so? *what is the price of this?* N. pl. prìsean.

Lat. pretium. *Fr.* prix. *It.* prezzo. *Sp.* precio.

PRÌSEACHADH, aidh, s. m. A valuing; a valuation; a prizing.

PRÌSEADH, idh, s. m. A valuing, a prizing; a valuation.

PRÌSEALACHD, s. f. Valuableness; dearness; value.

PRISEAN, ein, s. m. (*dim.* of preas.) A little bush; a little thicket.

PRÌSEAN, n. pl. of prìs. Prices.

PRÌSEIL, a. (prìs-amhuil.) Valuable, precious, dear.

PRÌSICH, v. a. (*from* prìs.) Value, estimate, prize, rate. *Pret. a.* phrìsich; *fut. aff. a.* prìsichidh; *p. part.* prìsichte.

† PROBHADH, aidh, s. m. (*Ir. id.*) A proof.

PROBHAID, s. f. Profit.—*Turn.*

PROBHAIDEIL, a. Profitable.

† PROBHAL, ail, s. m. (*Ir. id.*) A consul.—*Shaw.*

PROCADAIR, s. m. (*Ir.* procadoir.) An advocate. Procadair an righ, *a king's advocate.* N. pl. procadairean.

PROCADAIREACHD, s. f. Proctorship; the business of a proctor.

PROGHAIN, s. f. Care.—*Shaw.*

PROGHAN, ain, s. m. (*Ir. id.*) Dregs; lees; refuse.—*Macfar Voc.* Care, anxiety.—*Shaw.*

PROGHANACH, a. Having dregs or lees; full of refuse; in care or anxiety.

PROIMHIDH, a. (*Ir. id.*) Fat.

PROINN, s. f. (*Ir. id.*) A meal or diet; a dinner; *also,* voracity.

PROINNE, *com.* and *sup.* of pronn.

PROINNEACHADH, aidh, s. m. A dieting, a dining; a diet, a dinner.

PROINNICH, v. n. Dine; take a meal or diet. *Pret.* phroinnich; *fut. aff. a.* proinnichidh; *p. part.* proinnichte, *dined.*

PROINN-LANN, lainn, s. m. (*Ir. id.*) A dining-room, an eating-room, a refectory.

PROINNLIOS, s. m. (*Ir. id.*) A dining-room, an eating-room, a refectory.

PROINNTE, p. part. of pronn. Bruised; mauled; minced; pulverized.

PROINNTEACH, ich, s. (*Ir. id.*) A refectory; a dining-room.

PRÒIS, v. a. Flatter, cajole, put in good humour. *Pret. a.* phròis; *fut. aff. a.* phròisidh.

PRÒIS, pròise, s. f. Flattery, humouring, cajoling; pride;

niceness; ceremony. Bean gun phròis, *a wife without pride.—Macint.*

PROISDEAL, eil, *s. m.* A bottle. *N. pl.* proisdealan

PRÒISEACH, *a.* Apt to flatter, ready to humour; requiring flattery or humouring.

PRÒISEADH, idh, *s. m.* A flattering, a humouring, a cajoling.

PRÒISEAL, *a.* Bold; proud, nice

PRÒISEALACHD, *s. f.* Niceness; ceremoniousness; pride; a flattering; humouring

PRÒISEAN, ein, *s. m.* (*from* pròis.) One who flatters or humours, *also*, one who requires to be flattered, cajoled, or humoured

PRÒISEIL, *a.* (pròis-amhuil.) Requiring flattery or cajoling; proud, nice, ceremonious, proud

PRONN, proinn, *s. m.* (*Ir. id.*) Pollard—(*Shaw*), a dinner; food. Ghabh iad pronn is deoch, *they took food and drink.—Old Song*

PRONN, *v. a.* Pound or bray; grind, pulverize, bruise; mince, crush; maul, distribute; bestow *Pret. a.* phronn, *fut. aff. a.* pronnaidh. Ged phronn thu amadan, *though thou bray a fool.—Stew. Pro.* Thug e là air pronnadh òir, *he spent a day in distributing gold.—Fingalian Poem. Pronn*, distribute, should be written *bronn*

PRONN, *a.* (*Ir. id.*) Pulverized, pounded, smooth, in fragments. Siucar pronn, *moist sugar. Com.* and *sup.* proinne

PRONNACH, aich, *s. m.* Dross, any thing that is pulverized, *also, adjectively*, pounding, pulverizing; drossy; dividing, distributing, generous

PRONNADAIR, *s. m.* A pounder, a bruiser; a pestle. A pronnadair, *with a pestle.—Stew. Pro. ref. N. pl.* pronnadairean

PRONNADAIREACHD, *s. f.* The operation of pounding or bruising

PRONNADH, aidh, *s. m.* (*Ir. id.*) A pounding or bruising; a bruise; a splintering, a grinding, a mincing; distributing In this last sense *pronnadh* ought to be *bronnadh*

PRONNAG, aig, *s. f.* (*from* pronn.) Any thing pulverized or minced, dross

PRONNAGACH, *a.* Drossy; pulverized

PRONNAL, ail, *s. m.* A low murmur; a grumbling; a growl, an undertone. Written also *pronndal*

PRONNALACH, *a.* Murmuring, grumbling. Written also *pronndalach*

PRONNALAICH, *s. f.* A continued low murmur, a grumbling, a growling. Written also *pronndalaich*

PRONNAN, *s. pl.* Fragments, bits. Bris na 'n pronnan iad, *break them in bits*

PRONNAN, ain, *s. m.* A fragment, a bit, a splinter; one who divides, a generous person. *N. pl.* pronnain *and* pronnanan.

PRONNASG, aisg, *s. m.* Sulphur, brimstone. Crathar pronnasg, *brimstone shall be shaken.—Stew. Job*

PRONNASGACH, *a.* Sulphureous, sulphury, abounding in sulphur

PRONNASGAIL, *a.* (pronnasg-amhuil.) Sulphury, like sulphur

PRONN-BHIADH, bhidh, *s. m.* Fragments of nuts, minced meat

PRONNDACH, *a.* Pulverizing, bruising, splintering

PRONNDAL, ail, *s. m.* A low murmur; a low note, an undertone.—*Macint*

PRONNDALACH, *a.* See PRONNALACH.

PRONNDALAICH, *s. f.* See PRONNALAICH

PRONN-GHLÒIR, *s. f.* Small-talk, loquacity, tattle; whispering.

PRONN-GHLORACH, *a.* Loquacious, tattling, whispering.

PRONNTA, *p. part.* of pronn. Bruised, pulverized, pounded; crushed. Ni sam bi tha pronnta, *any thing that is crushed.—Stew. Lev*

PRONNUSG, uisg, *s. m.* Sulphur, brimstone.—*Stew. Rev.* Written also *pronnasg*.

PRONNUSGACH, *a.* Sulphurous; of sulphur; abounding in sulphur

PROP, pruip, *s. m.* (*Du.* proppa.) A support; a pillar; an undersetter, a prop.—*Q. B. ref.*

PROP, *v. a.* Prop, support, back, uphold. *Pret. a.* phrop; *fut. aff. a.* propaidh, *shall support.*

PROPADH, *s. m.* (*Ir. id.*) A supporting, a propping; a support, a prop

PROPAIDH, *fut. aff. a.* prop. Shall support.

PROPAINN, *v. a.* Prop, support, sustain. *Pret.* phropainn, *sustained*, *fut. aff.* propainnidh.

PROPAINNTE, *p. part.* Propped, supported, sustained.

PROPANACH, aich, *s. m.* (*Ir. id.*) A stripling, a sturdy lad. *N. pl.* propanaich. Am propanach àluinn, *the handsome stripling.—Turn.*

PROPTA, PROPTE, *p. part.* of prop. Propped, supported, upheld.

PROSDA, *a.* (*Ir. id.*) Strong, firm, stout.—*Shaw.*

PROSNACH, *a.* A stimulative; inciting, spurring, stimulant, encouraging.

PROSNACHADH, PROSNUCHADH, aidh, *s. m.* A stimulating, inciting; a spurring, an incitement, encouragement.

PROSNACHAIL, *a.* Encouraging, inciting, stimulating.

PROSNAICH, PROSNUICH, *v. a.* Invite, stimulate; encourage. *Pret. a.* phrosnaich, *fut. aff. a.* prosnaichidh.

PROSNAICHTE, PROSNUICHTE, *p. part.* of prosnaich. Invited, encouraged.

PROSNAN, ain, *s. m.* (*Ir. id.*) A company, a band, a group. *N. pl.* prosnain.

PROSNANACH, *a.* In companies, in bands, in groups.

PROTHAIST, *s. m.* (*Du.* proost.) A provost; *in derision*, a swag-bellied fellow. *N. pl.* prothaistean.

PRUCHLAIS, *s. f.* (*Ir. id.*) A den, a cave. Written also *bruchlais*

PRUIP, *gen. sing.* and *n. pl.* of prop. Props; undersetters.—*Stew. 1 K. ref.*

PUBAL, ail, *s. m.* Great water-dock; pestilence-wort, or butterbur.

PUBLICAN, ain, *s. m.* A publican. *N. pl.* publicain.

PUBULL, uill, *s. m.* (*W.* pabel.) A tent, a booth, a marquée, a tabernacle; a covering. *N. pl.* pubuill. Shuidhich iad am pubuill, *they pitched their tents.—Fingalian Poem.*

PUBULLACH, *a.* Tented; having booths; like a tent or booth; of, or belonging to, a tent or booth. Magh pubullach, *a tented field.*

PÙC, *v. a.* Push; shove, jostle. *Pret. a.* phùc, *pushed; fut. aff. a.* pùcaidh, *shall push*

PÙCADH, aidh, *s. m.* A pushing, a jostling, a shoving.

PÙCADH (a), *pr. part.* of pùc. Pushing, shoving, jostling

PÙCAID, *s. f.* A pimple, a scab, itch.—*Stew. Lev. ref. N. pl.* pucaidean.

PUCAIDEACH, *a.* Pimply; scabbed; having the itch.

PUCAIDEACHD, *s. f.* Scabbedness; itch.

PUCAIL, *s. f.* A pushing, a shoving, a jostling. Ciod a phùcail th' ort? *what are you pushing at?* is ann ort a tha phùcail, *how you do push.*

Pucan, ain, *s. m.* See Pocan.

Pùdar, air, *s. m.* (*Ir. id.*) Powder. Written also *fùdar;* which see.

Pùdarach, *a.* (*Ir. id.*) Powdered; powdery.

Pùdaraich, *v. a.* Powder, as the hair. *Pret. a.* phùdaraich.

Pùdaraichte, *p. part.* of pùdaraich. Powdered; covered with powder, as the hair.

Pùdhair, *s.* Power; *a local word.*

Pùdhar, air, *s. m.* (*Ir. id.*) Hurt, harm; a sore; a suppurating sore. See Pùthar.

Pudharachadh, aidh, *s. m.* Suppuration.

Puibleachadh, aidh, *s. m.* Publishing.

Puiblich, *v. a.* Publish; proclaim.

Puic, *s. f.* A bribe. *N. pl.* puicean, *bribes.*

Puiceach, *a.* Receiving a bribe; bribing; easily bribed; like a bribe.

Puicean, ein, *s. m.* (*Ir.* puicin.) A veil or cover over the eyes; blind-man's buff; a bribe.

Puicear, eir, *s. m.* (*Ir.* puiceoir.) One who gives bribes.

Puichean, ein, *s. m.* A little impudent stinking fellow—(*Shaw*); a sickly pithless fellow.

Puicneadh, idh, *s. m.* Blindfolding; imposition.

Puicne-screabhal, *s.* A spangle.—*Shaw.*

Pùidse, *s. f.* A pouch or pocket. Pùidse achlais, *a shoulder pocket;* pùidse briogain, *a breeches pocket;* pùidse uairead-air, *a fob.* *N. pl.* pùidsean *and* pùidseachan.

Puilpid, *s. f.* A pulpit.

Puincearn, eirn, *s.* (*Ir. id.*) A beam for measuring or weighing goods; the graduated beam.

Puingean, ein, *s. m.* A roll of butter.

Puinneag, eig, *s. f.* Sorrel; *N. pl.* puinneagan.—*Macd.*

Puinneagach, *a.* Abounding in sorrel; of sorrel; like sorrel.

Puinneagan, ain, *s. m.* Sorrel.

Puinneanach, aich, *s. m.* A belabouring; a beating or thrashing; a bruiser; a pugilist.

Puinneanachadh, aidh, *s. m.* A belabouring; a beating, a thrashing. Fhuair e phuinneanachadh, *he got himself thrashed.*

Puinneanaich, *v. a.* Belabour; beat; bruise. *Pret. a.* phuinneanaich; *fut. aff. a.* puinneanaichidh.

Puinse, *s. f.* Punch. Am puinse milis guanach, *the sweet heady punch.—Old Song.*

Puinseach, *a.* Of punch; like punch.

Puinsion, oin, *s. m.* Poison, venom; poisonous; *also,* a term of personal disgust, or contempt. Toradh puinsion, *poisonous fruit.—Stew. Deut. ref.* A phuinsion tha thu ann, *thou reptile that thou art.*

Puinsionach, *a.* Poisonous, venomous; baneful.

Puinsionachadh, aidh, *s. m.* A poisoning. Air a phuinsionachadh, *poisoned.*

Puinsionaich, *v. a.* Poison. *Pret. a.* phuinsionaich, *poisoned; fut. aff. a.* puinsionaichidh.

Puinsionaichte, *p. part.* of puinsionaich. Poisoned.

Puinsionta, *a.* Poisonous, venomous.

Puirleag, eig, *s. f.* (*Ir.* puirleog.) A crest; a tuft.

Puirleagach, *a.* Crested; tufted.—*Shaw.*

† **Puirneach**, ich, *s. m.* (*Ir. id.*) A hunter.

Puirt, *gen. sing.* and *n. pl.* of port; which see.

Puirtean, ein, *s. m.* (*dim.* of port.) A little haven or harbour; a little turret.

† **Puisg**, *v. a.* (*Ir. id.*) Beat, whip, lash.—*Shaw.* *Pret. a.* phuisg.

Puision, *s. m.* Poison, venom; *also,* venomous; a term of personal disgust. *Fr.* poison. In Vannes they say *pouison.*

Puisionach, *a.* Poisonous, venomous, baneful. Written also *puinsionach.*

Puiseonachadh, aidh, *s. m.* A poisoning. Air phuiseanachadh, *poisoned.*

Pusionaich, *v. a.* Poison. *Pret. a.* phuisionaich; *fut. aff. a.* puisionaichidh.

Puisionaichte, *p. part.* of puisionaich. Poisoned.

Puisionta, *a.* Poisonous, venomous, baneful.

Puist, *gen. sing.* and *n. pl.* of post; which see.

† **Puitric**, *s.* A bottle.—*Shaw.*

Pulag, aig, *s. m., contracted for* pulbhag. A round stone; a sizable round stone; *also,* a porpoise. *N. pl.* pulagain.

Pulagach, *a.* Full of round stones; like a round stone; of round stones. Contracted for *pulbhagach.*

Pula-mhullach, aich, *s. m.* A dome or cupola. *N. pl.* pula-mhullaichean.

Pulbhag, aig, *s. f.* A round stone; a sizable round stone. *N. pl.* pulbhagan.

Pulpaid, *s. m.* A pulpit.

Punan. See Punnan.

Punc, puinc, *s. m.* See Pung.

Puncail, *a.* See Pungail.

Puncaileachd, *s. f.* Written also *pungaileachd;* which see.

Pung, puing, *s. m.* (*Ir.* punc. *Lat.* punct-um. *Swed.* punkt.) A point; article; jot; tittle; whit.

Pungach, *a.* Pointed; having points.

Pungail, *a.* (pung-amhuil.) Punctual; exact; distinct; accurate.—*Macint.* Gu pungail, *punctually.*

Pungaileachd, *s. f.* Pointedness; punctuality; distinctness; exactness; accurateness; articulateness.

Pungalachd, *s. f.* See Pungaileachd.

Punglas, ais, *s. m.* Purple, melic-grass.

Punnan, ain, *s. m.* A sheaf of corn; a bundle of hay or straw; a burden, a fardle; a blast, as of a horn; a bittern.

Punnd, puinnd, *s. m.* A pound in weight; a pound sterling. Punnd Sassunnach, *an English pound in weight;* also, *a pound sterling.* *N. pl.* puinnd.

W. punt. *Lat.* pondo *and* pondus. *Scotch,* pund. *Germ.* pfundt. *Sclav. Pol. Corn. Hung.* funt.

Punntain. More frequently written *funntain;* which see.

Pùpaid, *s. f.* A pulpit.

Purgadair, *s. m.* Purgatory; a purifier.

Purgadaireach, ich, *s. m.* One undergoing the changes and pains of purgatory; *also, adjectively,* purgatorial.

Purgadaireachd, *s. f.* The state of purgatory; the changes of purgatory; the doctrine of purgatory.

Purgadaireadh, idh, *s. m.* Purgatory.

Purgaid, *s. f.* A purse; a dose of aperient medicine. *N. pl.* purgaidean.

Purgaideach, *a.* Laxative; purging, cleansing; vomitory.

Purgaideachd, *s. f.* Laxativeness; frequent purging.

Purpaidh, *s. f.* Poppy, purslain. Mar phurpaidh, *like the poppy.*

Purpail, *a.* Courageous; active.

Purpaileachd, *s. f.* Courage; activity.

Purr, *v. a.* Push; shove; jostle; thrust; put with the head. *Pret. a.* phurr; *fut. aff. a.* purraidh, *shall put.*

Purrach, *a.* Apt to push or shove; pushing, shoving, jostling, thrusting.

Purradh, aidh, *s. m.* (*Ir. id.* *W.* burth.) A pushing, a shoving, a jostling; a putting with the head; a thrust.

Rinn sibh an t-easlan a phurradh, *you have pushed the diseased.—Stew. Ezek.*

PURRADH (a), *pr. part.* of purr. Pushing, shoving, jostling, thrusting, butting. A purradh le adharcaibh, *pushing with his horns.—Stew. Ez.* Chunnaic mi an reithe a purradh le 'adhaircibh, *I saw the ram pushing.—Stew. Dan.*

PURRAGHLAS, ais, *s. m.* A name for a cat.

PURT, puirt, *s. m.* A fort, a tower, a town. See PORT.

PUS, puis, *s. m.* A mouth; a thick lip. See BUS.

PUS, *s. m.* (*Ir. id.*) A cat. Written also *bus*, which see.

PUSACH, *a.*, *from* pus. More frequently written *busach*, which see.

PUSACHAN, ain, *s. m.* (*Ir. id.*) A whining child.

PÙT, pùit, *s. m.* The young of moorfowl; a *pout*. *N. pl.* pùtan.

PUT, *s. m.* A push, a shove.

PUT, *v. a.* Push, shove, jostle, put with the head. *Pret.* phut, *pushed*; *fut. aff. a.* putaidh, *shall push.*

PÙTACH, *a.* (*from* pùt.) Like a young pout; moorfowl; abounding in young moorfowl; producing young moorfowl.

PUTACH, *a.* (*from* put.) Pushing, shoving, jostling.

PUTADH, aidh, *s. m.* A pushing, a shoving, a jostling; a butting, a push, a shove, a jostle, a put. Cha dean thu 'm putadh, *you will not make it out.*

PUTADH, 3 *sing.* and *pl. imper.* of put.

PUTAG, aig, *s. f.* A thowl, an oar pin; *also*, a pudding.—*Shaw.* *N. pl.* putagan.

PUTAGACH, *a.* Having thowls or oar pins, as a boat.

PUTAGAICH, *v. a.* Provide or furnish, as a boat, with thowls or oar pins.

PUTAGAICHTE, *p. part.* Furnished with oar pins, as a boat; thowled.

PUTAGAN, ain, *s. m.* A pudding, a pock-pudding.

PUTAIN, *gen. sing.* and *n. pl.* of putan; which see.

PÙTAN, ain, *s. m.* (*dim.* of put.) A young moorfowl, a pout; a young hare.—*Shaw.*

PÙTAN, *n. pl.* of pùt. Pouts, young moorfowl.

PUTAN, ain, *s. m.* A button. *N. pl.* putain. Putan dùirn, *a sleeve button.*

PUTANACH, *a.* Full of buttons; like a button.

PUTANACHADH, aidh, *s. m.* Buttoning.

PUTANACHD, *s. f.* Button-making.

PUTANAICH, *v. a.* Button. *Pret. a.* phutanaich, *buttoned*; *fut. aff. a.* putanaichidh, *shall button.*

PUTANAICHTE, *p. part.* of putanaich. Buttoned.

PÙTANTA, *a.* (*from* pùt.) Shy, as a young moorfowl; coy.

PÙTANTACHD, *s. f.* Shiness, coyness.

PUTAR, *fut. pass.* of put. Shall be pushed.

PÙTHAR, air, *s. m.* Hurt, harm; a sore, a suppurating sore; a grievous wound, a cause of sorrow. Is mòr ar pùthar, *great is our cause of sorrow.—Death of Carril.*

PUTHARACHADH, aidh, *s. m.* Suppuration.

† PUTRALL, aill, *s. m.* (*Ir. id.*) A lock of hair.—*Shaw.*

R.

R, r, (ruis, *the elder-tree*,) is the fifteenth letter of the Gaelic alphabet. In general, it sounds the same as in other languages; as, rach, *go*, mòr, *great*, rug, *caught*, where it has the same sound with *r* in *raw*, *more*, *rook*. But if in the same syllable *r* be preceded or followed by one of the small vowels, *e* or *i*, or by both, it has a sound to which there is none similar in the English tongue; but very much resembles that of *r* in the French word, prairie, *a meadow*; as, airidh, *worthy*, fir, *men*, feirg, *wrath*.

RA, *adv.* Very, exceeding, quite. More frequently written *ro*, which see.

† RA, *s. m.* A moving, a going, hence, rod, *a road.*

RÀBACH, *a.* (*Ir. id.*) Litigious, quarrelsome, plentiful; fruitful. *Com.* and *sup.* rabaiche.

RÀBACHAS, ais, *s. m.* Litigation, quarrelsomeness; plentifulness, fruitfulness. Fear ràbachais, *a litigious fellow*, luchd ràbachais, *litigious persons.*

RABAID, *s. f.* A rabbit. *N. pl.* rabaidean. Cuilean rabaid, *a young rabbit.*

RABAIDEACH, *a.* Abounding in rabbits, like a rabbit.

RÀBAIR, *s. m.* A quarrelsome, litigious fellow, a wrangler. Cha 'n 'eil ann ach ràbair òglaich, *he is but a wrangler of a fellow.* *N. pl.* ràbairean.

RÀBAIREACH, *a.* Quarrelsome, litigious, wrangling. Is e do ghnàth 'bhith ràbaireach, *you are always quarrelling.*

RÀBAIREACHD, *s. f.* Quarrelsomeness, litigiousness, wrangling, frequent or continued quarrelling.

RÀBAL, ail, *s. m.* A noise; a bustle.

RÀBALACH, *a.* Noisy, bustling.

RÀBALACHD, *s. f.* Noisiness; continued noise, continued bustle.

RABH, *pret.* of the auxiliary verb *bi*. Was. More frequently written *robh*; which see.

RÀBHACH, *a.* Giving a warning; giving a caution; admonitory, like a warning or caution, hinting.

RÀBHACHAIL, *a.* (rabhach-amhuil.) Admonitory; hinting, giving caution or warning, like a caution; fond of cautioning, or of warning.

RABHACHAN, ain, *s. m.* A beacon; a warning.

† RABHADAR, an Irish *inflection* of rabh. They were.

RÀBHADH, aidh, *s. m.* (*Ir. id. Du.* raab.) A caution; a warning, a hint, a precedent, an example. Bheir e rabhadh, *he will give warning.—Stew. Ezek.* Thoir rabhadh, *warn.*

RÀBHAN, ain, *s. m.* (*Ir. id.*) A rhapsody, a tedious repetition, a long prosing harangue; a spade.

RÀBHANACH, *a.* Rhapsodical, haranguing; *also*, an haranguer.

RÀBHANACHD, *s. f.* Rhapsody, an harangue.

RABHANAICHE, *s. m.* See RABHANAIR.

RÀBHANAIR, *s. m.* (rabhan'ear.) A rhapsodist; an haranguer; a proser. *N. pl.* rabhanairean.

RABHART, airt, *s. m.* Upbraiding.

RABHD, *s. m.* Idle talk, low, vulgar language; vapouring, a tedious harangue; *also*, an idle talker.

RÀBHDACH, *a.* Fond of idle talk; haranguing.

RABHDADH, aidh, *s. m.* Idle talk, vulgar language, vapouring, boasting; a boast.

RABHDAIR, *s. m.* One who indulges in idle talk; a verbose fellow; a vapourer, a gossip, a prater. *N. pl.* rabhdairean.

RABHDAIREACHD, *s. f.* Vulgar verbiage; verbosity; vapouring, prating, gossiping.

RABHLADH, aid, *s. m.* (*Ir. id.*) Boasting.

RÀC, ràic, *s. m.* (*Goth.* raca. *Arm.* rakkan.) A hay-rake. *N. pl.* ràcan.

Ràc, raic, *s. m.* A crash; a prolonged crash; the noise of cloth in the act of tearing; the noise of a sithe in the process of mowing; a prattling; a gushing; a shedding, as of tears; a croaking noise, as of crows.

† **Rac**, raic, *s. m.* (*Ir. id.*) A king or prince; a bag, a pouch.—*Shaw.*

Ràc, *v. a.* and *n.* Rake as hay; make a crashing noise; croak; rehearse; repeat. *Pret. a.* ràc; *fut. aff. a.* ràcaidh.

Ràcach, *a.* (*from* ràc.) Like a rake; crashing; noisy.

Racadal, ail, *s. m.* Horse radish; wild radish.

Ràcadh, aidh, *s. m.* A raking, as of hay; a crashing noise; the noise made by the tearing of cloth; a rake.

Ràcail, *s. f.* (*Arm.* straeal, *to crush.*) A continued crushing noise; frequent crushing; a discordant voice; a croaking.

Racain, *gen. sing.* and *n. pl.* of ràcan.

Ràcair, *s. m.* (*Ir. id.*) An impertinent prattler; a loud talker; a man with a discordant voice; a raker; a rehearser; a romancer; a talkative lying person. *N. pl.* ràcairean.

Racaireachd, *s. f.* (*Ir. id.*) Loud and idle prattling, impertinent language; vocal discordance; a raking; a rehearsing; romance; idle repetition; verbiage.

Ràcan, ain, *s. m., dim.* of ràc. (*Corn.* rakkan.) A little hay-rake; a harrow; noise; a croaking noise; a crash; mischief; bowling.

The harrow called *ràcan*, is used in the Hebrides. It consists of a block of wood with a few teeth, and is used in such places as will not admit of the use of the larger instrument. It is commonly tied to the horse's tail; but not unfrequently it is dragged along the surface by women and boys.

Ràcan, *n. pl.* of rac. Rakes, harrows.

Ràcanach, *a.* Like a rake or harrow; of, or belonging to, a rake or harrow; crashing; prating, dissonant, croaking.

Ràcanta, *a.* Crashing, noisy; loquacious; croaking.

Rach, *v. irr.* (*Ir.* rach.) Go, proceed, move, travel, walk. *Pret. a.* Chaidh, *went; fut. aff.* theid, *shall go.* Rach suas, *go west; go up* or *ascend. Pret. sub.* rachainn, *I would go. Pret. neg.* and *interrog.* deachaidh *and* deach, *did go.* An deach e suas? cha deach, *did he ascend? no.* Rach air ais, *go backward, wane, wither.*

Ràchadh, *imper.* of rach. Let go. Rachadh e, i, iad, *let him, her, them go*; also, *pret. sub.* of rach. Would go.

† **Rachail**, *s. f.* (*Ir.* rachoil.) A winding sheet.

Rachainn, 1 *sing. pret. sub.* of rach. I would go. Le fàilt rachainn na choinneamh, *with welcome I would go to meet him.—Oss.*

† **Rachall**, aill, *s. m.* A winding sheet.

Racham, 1 *sing. imper.* of rach. Let me go.

Rachar, (*from* rach.) Used impersonally. Rachar suas leam, leo, *I, they, went west*, or *ascended.*

Rachd, *s.* A law. More frequently written *reachd;* which see.

Ràchd, *s. m.* A rake for gathering hay. *N. pl.* rachdan. Written also *ràc.*

Ràchd, *s. m.* A crash; a prolonged crash; the noise made by the rending of cloth; the noise of a sithe in the process of mowing; a croaking; a prattling; a rake; a croaking noise; a gushing; a shedding, as of tears.

Rachd, *v. a.* Rake as hay; make a crashing noise; croak. Written also *rac;* which see.

Ràchdail. See **Ràcail.**

Rachdair. See **Ràcair.**

Ràchdan, ain, *s. m.* A rake, a harrow. *N. pl.* rachdain. Rachdain giuthais, *rakes of fir.—Macfar.* See **Ràcan.**

Rachdmhor, *a.* Handsome; tearful; *also*, legislative. O rosgaibh rachdmhoir an òg-thriath, *from the handsome eyes of the youthful chief.—Oss. Com.* and *sup.* rachdmhoire.

Ràd, raid, *s. m.* (*Dan. Goth.* rad, *a road.*) A road; a path. Written also *rathad* and *rod;* which see.

Radaireal, eil, *s. m.* A strolling; a wandering.

Ràdan, *n. pl.* of rad. Roads, paths.

Radan, ain, *s. m.* A rat; the *mus rattus* of Linnæus. *N. pl.* radain. Fuath radain, *ratsbane.*

Fr. rat. *Teut.* ratte, *rat. Ir.* radan. *Sp.* raton, *a hemouse.*

Radanach, *a.* Full of rats; like a rat; of rats.

Radan, uisge, *s. m.* A water-rat; the *mus amphibius* of Linnæus.

Radh, *s. m.* (*Ir. id. Gr.* ῥέω, *dico.*) A saying, a word; an expression; a speech. Radh do bheòil, *the word of thy mouth.—Mac Lac. N. pl.* radhan; *d. pl.* radhaibh. Iomradh air do radhaibh, *the report of thy sayings.—Stew.* 1 *K.*

Radh (ag), *pr. part.* of abair, *v. irr.* Saying, speaking. Ciod a tha thu 'gradh, *what are you saying.*

Radhadh, aidh, *s. m.* Instruction; a saying; expression. A faghail radhaidh, *receiving instruction.*

Radhainn, *s. f.* A saying, expression. Is sinn dh' fhaotadh a radhainn, *we had reason to say it.—Turn.*

Radharc, airc, *s. m.* (*Ir. id.*) The faculty of sight; seeing, sight. A faghail an radhairc, *receiving their sight.—Stew. Matt.* Radharc mo dha rosg, *the sight of my two eyes.—Oss.*

Radharcach, *a.* (*Ir. id.*) Having the faculty of sight; conferring the faculty of sight; observant.

Rag, *a.* (*Ir. id.*) Stiff; obstinate; inflexible; tight, as a rope; tough; dim. Amhach rag, *a stiff* or *stubborn neck.—Stew. Jer.* Ioma corp rag an raoin Ruairidh, *many a stiff corpse in the plain of Rory,* i. e. *in Killicrankie.—Old Song.* Sùil rag, *a dim eye.—Stew. Sam. ref. Com.* and *sup.* raige.

Rag, *s. m.* (*Ir.* rag. *Heb. Syr.* raka. *Goth.* raka.) A wrinkle; a term of personal contempt; a shabby fellow.

Ragach, *a.* (*Ir. id.*) Stiff, obstinate; tough; wrinkled. *Com.* and *sup.* ragaiche.

Ragachadh, aidh, *s. m.* A stiffening, toughening; a tightening, as of a rope; a wrinkling. Air ragachadh, *grown stiff* or *tough.*

Ragachail, *a.* Having a tendency to stiffen, toughen, or tighten; causing stiffness, toughness, or tightness.

Ragaich, *v. a.* and *n.* (*from* rag.) Stiffen, toughen, tighten or stretch, as a rope; grow stiff or tough; grow tight, as a rope. *Pret. a.* ragaich; *fut.* ragaichidh, *shall stiffen.*

Ragaichte, *p. part.* of ragaich. Stiffened, tightened, stretched, tense; toughened.

Ragaim, *s. f.* Sneezewort. Meacan ragaim, *or* roibhe, *sneezewort; common field pellitory;* the *ptarmica vulgaris pratensis* of botanists.

Ragair, *s. m.* One who uses violence; an extortioner, a villain, a rogue, a deceiver; an instrument for tightening a rope; one with a wrinkled face.

Ragaireach, *a.* (*Ir. id.*) Roguish, villainous, deceptive; using violence, extortive.

Ragaireachd, *s. f.* Roguishness, villainy, deceptiveness; violence; the practice of violence. Luchd na ragaireachd, *people of violence.—Sm.*

Rag-bheart, -bheirt, *s.* A mischievous deed.

Rag-bheartach, *a.* Perverse, headstrong, mischievous.—*Macd.*

Rag-bheartas, ais, *s. m.* Perverseness, obstinacy, mischief.

Rag-mhuinealach, *a.* Stiff-necked; stubborn; headstrong, perverse. Sluagh rag-mhuinealach, *a stiff-necked people*.—*Stew. Exod.*

RAG-MHUINEALACHD, *s. f.* Stubbornness, obstinacy, perverseness.—*Stew. Sam.*

RAG-ROTH, *s. m.* A torturing-wheel.

RAG-SHÙIL, -shùl, *s. f.* A dim eye. *N. pl.* rag-shùilean.

RAG-SHÙILEACH, *a.* Dim-eyed.

† RAIB, *s. f.* (*Ir. id.*) A turnip; a rope.—*Shaw.*

† RABH. Now written *robh*; which see.

RAIBLEACHAN, ain, *s. m.* A scullion.

RÀICHD, *s. f.* (*Ir. id.*) Idle talk; boasting; gibberish; impertinence.

RÀICHDEALACHD, *s. f.* Idleness in conversation; gibberish, boastfulness.

RÀICHDEIL, *a.* Inclined to talk idly.

† RAICNEACH, ich, *s. f.* (*Ir. id.*) A queen.

RÀID, *gen. sing.* of rad; which see.

RAIDE, *s. f.* Cunning, sliness. Luchd ràide, *cunning people*.—*Old Song.*

RAIDEACHAS, ais, *s. m.* (*Ir.* raiteachas.) Boastful speech; arrogant language, arrogance, pride, a saying; a report; a trial of skill.

RAIDEAG, eig, *s. f.* (*Ir.* raideog.) A myrtle.

RAIDEALACH, *a.* Cunning, sly; insidious. Gu raidealach.

RAIDEALACHD, *s. f.* Cunning, sliness.

RAIDEIL, *a.* Cunning, sly, insidious.—*Stew. O. T.*

† RAIDH, *s. f.* (*Ir. id.*) A radius.

RÀIDH, *v.* Threaten, appeal, look. *Pret. a.* ràidh, *threatened*; *fut. aff. a.* ràidhidh, *shall threaten*. Ràidh air, *threaten him*; ràidh e orm, *he threatened me.*

RÀIDH, raidhe, *s. m.* An umpire or arbiter; a judge; an appeal; a threat; a rank, as of soldiers, a speech; an entreaty, an intercession. Leig gu ràidhe, *bring to arbitration, submit to arbitration, appeal.* Thoir ràidh, *threaten.* Written also *ràith.*

RÀIDHE, *s. f.* A quarter of a year. See also RÀITHE.

RAIDHEAN, ein, *s. m.* (*Ir. id.*) A crowd or rabble.

RÀIDHEIL, *a.* (raidh-amhuil.) Quarterly. See RÀITHEIL.

† RAIDHMHEAS, eis, *s. m.* (*Ir. id.*) A dream, a romance, a cubit.—*Shaw.*

† RAIDHMHEASACH, *a.* (*Ir. id.*) Fabulous, romantic; gasconading.—*Shaw.*

RAIDHREACH, ich, *s. f.* (*Ir. id.*) A prayer, a petition, a request.

RAIDIS, *s. f.* (*Ir. id.*) Radish. *N. pl.* raidisean.

RÀIDSE, *s. m.* and *f.* An idle talker; a prater; verbiage.

RÀIDSEACH, *a.* Verbose; talking idly, prating.

RÀIDSEACHAS, ais, *s. m.* Idle talk, verbiage.

RAIGE, *com.* and *sup.* of rag.

RAIGEAD, eid, *s. m.* (*from* rag.) Toughness, tenseness, tightness, stiffness; increase in toughness or tenseness. *Raigead*, like all nouns ending in *ad*, derived from the comparative, is a kind of comparative noun. Is raigeid an cord an tarruing sin, *that pull has rendered the rope tighter.*

RAIGEALACHD, *s. f.* Impetuosity.

† RAIGH, *s. f.* (*Ir. id.*) Frenzy.

RAIGHE, *s. f.* An arm. Written also *ruighe*, which see.

RAIGHE, *s. f.* A rank or file of soldiers. Am builsgean ràighe Innistore, *in the midst of the ranks of Instore.*—*Old Poem.*

RAIGHEIL, *a.* (*from* raigh.) Frantic.

RAIGLEAR, eir, *s. m.* A ragged, untidy person.

RAILGE, *s. f.* A burial. More frequently written *reilig.*

RAILLIDH, *s. f.* A fight, a fray. This word is, I believe, local.

† RAIMH, *s. f.* (*Ir. id.*) Brimstone.—*Shaw.*

RÀIMH, *gen. sing.* and *n. pl.* of ràmh; which see.

RAIMHDEAS, eis, *s. m.* (*Ir. id.*) Fatness; greasiness.—*Shaw.*

RAIMHEAD. See REAMHAD.

RÀIN, *gen. sing.* of ràn.

RÀIN, *contracted for* ràinig; *pret.* of ruig, *v. irr.* Reached, arrived.

RÀINEACH, ich, *s. f.* (*Ir.* raithneach. *W.* rhedyn.) Fern; brake; the common female fern, the *filix femina vulgaris* of botanists; *also*, the name of a beautiful valley in the wilds of Perthshire, where the Gaelic language is spoken in its greatest purity. Raineach uaine, *green fern.*—*Oss. Duthona.* Mar rainich, *like fern*, goisean rainich, *a tuft of fern*; raineach muire, *common male fern*, the *filix major vulgaris.*

RAINEACHAIL, *a.* (raineach-amhuil.) Ferny, like ferns.

RÀINEAS, *inflection* of ruig. Reached, arrived. Ràineas tìr nam fionan trom, *I reached the land of clustering vines.*—*Mac Lach.*

RÀINIG, *pret.* of ruig. (*Ir.* rainidh.) Reached, arrived. Ràinig a gaoir mi, *her cries reached me.*—*Oss. Fin. and Lor.* Ràinig sinn easach na leacainn, *we reached the dark torrent of the steep.*—*Oss.*

RAIN-MHILL, *v. a.* Abolish; abrogate. *P. part.* rainmhillte.

RAINN, *gen. sing.* of rann; which see.

RAINN, *s. f.* A part or portion. More frequently written *roinn.*

RAINN AN UISGE, *s.* Eyebright.

RAINNSICH, *v. a.* Arrange, put in rows or ranks.

RAINNSICHEAN, *n. pl.* Ranges, rows, ranks.

RAINNSICHTE, *p. part.* of rainnsich. Arranged.

† RAIS, *s. f.* (*Ir. id.*) A path, a way.

RÀITE, *s. f.* Idle conversation; boasting; gibberish; verbiage; arrogant language; speech, language, one who talks idly. Bu tearc a ràite, *she spoke but seldom.*—*Oss. Gaul.*

RÀITEACH, *a.* Apt to talk idly; boasting; fluent; *also*, a desultory prater.

RÀITEACHAIL, *a.* Boastful; apt to prate; arrogant. Gu ràiteachail, *boastfully*; daoine ràiteachail, *boasters.*—*Stew. Gen.*

RÀITEACHAS, ais, *s. m.* (*Ir.* raidteachas.) Boastful speech, idle speech, desultory, unmeaning language; a lie; a report; an idle surmise; arrogance; a contest; a saying; a common saying, a speech. A ràiteachas, *his lies.*—*Stew. Jer.*

RÀITEACHD, *s. f.* Idle talk, verbiage; desultory prating. Luchd-ràiteachd, *idle talkers.*

RAITEAN, ein, *s. m.* (*Ir. id.*) Pleasure.—*Shaw.*

RÀITH, *s. m.* An umpire, a judge; an appeal, a threat; an entreaty; an intercession. *N. pl.* ràithean; *d. pl.* ràithibh. Leig gu ràith, *appeal.*

RAITH, *s. f.* (*Ir. id.*) Fern, brake.

RÀITHE, *s. f.* A quarter of a year. Ràithe sneachdach, reòtach, *a snowy, frosty quarter.*—*Macfar.*

RAITHEACH, *a.* Prone to threat, threatful; appealing.

RÀITHEACHD, *s. f.* A habit of threatening; minaciousness; the circumstance of appealing.

RÀITHEIL, *a.* (ràithe-amhuil.) Quarterly. An Raonsachadh Ràitheil, *the Quarterly Review.*

RAITHINN, *for* radh; which see.

Ràitse, *s. f.* Idle conversation; boasting; verbiage; a desultory prater.

Ramas, ais, *s. m.* (*Ir. id.*) Rhyme; romance.

Ramasach, *a.* Romantic; fabulous.

Ràmh, ràimh, *s. m.* An oar; a tree; a branch; a wood. *N. pl.* raimh *and* ramhan. Tairnibh bhur raimh, *pull your oars.—Ull.* Talamh nan ramh, *the country of woods.—Oss. Fing.*
Lat. ram-us, *a branch, and* rem-us, *an oar. Ir.* ramh. *W.* rhûyv. *Arm.* rava *and* rev. *Corn.* rev.

Ramh, *v. a.* (*Ir. id.*) Row a boat. *Pret. a.* ramh, *rowed; fut. aff. a.* ramhaidh, *shall row.*

Ramhach, aich, *s. f.* (*from* ramh.) A float or raft; a rowing; a rowing-match.

Ramhach, *a.* Having oars; woody; branchy.

Ramhachadh, aidh, *s. m.* A rowing; a furnishing with oars; a branching.

Ramhachd, *s. f.* (*from* ramh.) The employment of rowing; oar-making.

Ramhadair, *s. m.* (*Ir. id. Corn.* revador.) A rower; an oar-maker; *rarely*, a traveller. *N. pl.* ramhadairean.

Ramhadaireachd, *s. f.* The employment of rowing; oar-making.

Ramhadh, aidh, *s. m.* A rowing. Air a ramhadh, *rowed.*

Ramhaich, *v. a., from* ramh. (*Lat.* remig-o.) Row; supply oars; man with oars. *Pret. a.* ramhaich; *fut. aff. a.* ramhaichidh, *shall row.*

Ramhaiche, *s. m.* A rower. Gach ramhaiche fo' éislean, *each rower afflicted.—Oss. Duthona. N. pl.* ramhaichean, *rowers.* Do ramhaichean, *thy rowers.—Stew. Ezek.*

Ramhaichte, *p. part.* Furnished with oars; rowed.

Ramhair, *s. m.* ramh-fhear. (*Ir. id. W.* rhuyvur. *Corn.* revadar.) A rower. *N. pl.* ramhairean.

Ramhaireachd, *s. f.* (*Ir. id.*) The employment of rowing; oar-making.

Ramhan, *n. pl.* of ramh. Oars. See **Ramh**.

Ramhar, *a.* Fat. More frequently written *reamhar.*

Ramh-dhroighionn, -dhroighne, *s. f.* Buckthorn.—*Shaw.*

Ramh-long, luing, *s.* A galley. *N. pl.* ramh-longan.

Ramlair, *s. m.* A noisy fellow; a rambler.

Ramlaireachd, *s. f.* Noisiness; rambling.

Ràn, ràin, *s. m.* (*Ir. id.*) A loud cry; a shriek; a roar, a bellow. Leig e ràn as, *he roared;* dean ràn, *roar.*
Germ. rounen, *a murmur. Anglo-Sax.* runian. *Franconian,* runen. *Island.* runa.

† **Ran**, *s. m.* (*Heb.* ranach. *Egyptian,* ranah.) A frog.

Ran, rain, *s. m.* (*Ir. id.*) A crumb, a morsel; truth.—*Shaw.*

† **Ran**, *a.* (*Ir. id.*) Clear, evident; noble; nimble.—*Shaw.*

Ràn, *v. n.* Roar; cry aloud, as with pain; shriek; bellow; crash loudly. *Pret. a.* ràn; *fut. aff. a.* rànaidh, *shall roar; pret. sub.* rànadh, *would roar.* Ged rànadh sliabh, *though hills would roar.—Fingalian Poem.*

Rànaich, *s. f.* (*from* ràn.) A continued roaring; a shrieking; a crying aloud with pain; a bellowing. Rànaich na fairge mòir, *the roaring of the great sea.—Old Poem.*

Rànan, ain, *s. m.* A roar; a shriek; a cry; a bellow.

Ranc, rainc, *s. m.* More commonly written *rang;* which see.

Randach, aich, *s. m.* (*Ir. id.*) A partisan. *N. pl.* randaich.

Randonaich, *v. a.* Abrogate.—*Shaw.*

Rang, raing, *s. m.* (*Ir. id.*) A rank; a row; an order; a range; *rarely*, a wrinkle; the bank of a river. *N. pl.* rangan; *d. pl.* rangaibh. An taobh stigh do na rangaibh, *the inside of the ranges.—Stew. 2 K. ref.*
Ir. ranc, *a rank. Swed.* rang. *Dan.* rang. *Arm.* reng. *Teut.* rancke.

Rangach, *a.* (*Ir. id.*) In ranks or rows, in ranges; *rarely*, wrinkled.

Rangachadh, aidh, *s. m.* A putting in ranks or in rows; an arranging; arrangement.

Rangaich, *v. a.* Put in ranks or in rows; arrange. *Pret. a.* rangaich; *fut. aff. a.* raingaichidh.

Rangaichte, *p. part.* of rangaich. Put in order, arranged.

Rangair, *s. m.* A wrangler.

Rangan, ain, *s. m.* (*Ir. id.*) Sloth.

Rangan, *n. pl.* of rang. Ranks, rows.

Rann, rainn, *s. c.* (*Ir. id. Arm.* rann, *portion.*) A verse; a stanza; a song; rhyme; a poem; a catch; a section; a canto; a verse of a chapter; a portion or part; a bond or tie; a promontory.

Rannach, aich, *s. m.* (*Ir. id.*) A songster; a rhymer; a bard. *N. pl.* rannaiche.

Rannach, *a., from* rann. (*Ir. id.*) Metrical; versifying; *also,* distributed; in parts or portions.

Rannachd, *s. f.* Rhyme; metre; versifying; versification; a tale, a story; a satire.

Rannadh, aidh, *s. m.* A sharpening; a bringing to a point; a beginning.

Rannag, aig, *s. f.* A star. *N. pl.* rannagan.

Rannaich, *v. n.* Make verses; rhyme. *Pret. a.* rannaich; *fut. aff. a.* rannaichidh.

Rannaiche, *s. m.* A poet; a rhymer; a songster; a bard.

Rannaicheachd. See **Rannachd**.

Rannan, ain, *s. m.* The lowing of deer.—*Shaw.*

Rann-leabhar, air, *s. m.* Anthology.

Rannmheas, *s. m.* The scanning of verses.

Rann-phairt, *s. f.* (*Ir. id.*) Participation; a portion; a participle.

Rann-phairteach, *a.* (*Ir. id.*) Participating, sharing, apt to share; in shares.

Rann-phairteachadh, aidh, *s. m.* (*Ir. id.*) A participating; a giving a share.

Rann-phairteachail, *a.* Portionable; communicable; partaking of; prone to share.

Rann-phàirtich, *v. a.* Share; communicate; impart; divide into shares, portions, or sections. *Pret. a. id.; fut. aff.* rann-phàirtichidh.

Rann-phàirtiche, *s. m.* (*Ir.* rann-phartuiche.) A partaker, a sharer.

Rann-phàirtichte, *p. part.* of rann-phàirtich. Shared, communicated, imparted; divided into shares or sections.

Rannsachadh, aidh, *s. m.* A searching; a rummaging; an inspecting; a reviewing; a search; a minute examination; a review.

Rannsachair, *s. m.* A searcher; an examiner; a scrutinizer; an inspector; a reviewer. *N. pl.* rannsachairean.

Rannsaich, *v. a.* Search, rummage; examine, scrutinize; explore; review. *Pret. a.* rannsaich, *searched; fut. aff. a.* rannsaichidh, *shall search; fut. pass.* rannsaichear, *shall be searched.*

Rannsaichidh, *fut. aff. a.* of rannsaich. Shall or will search.

Rannsaichte, *p. part.* of ramsaich. Searched, examined, inspected, scrutinized, explored.

Rannsuchadh, aidh, *s. m.* See **Rannsachadh**.

Rannsuich, *v. a.* See **Rannsaich**.

Rannsuichte, *p. part.* of rannsuich. Searched, examined; inspected.

Rannta, *part.* Shared, divided.

Ranntachd, *s. f.* (*Ir. id.*) Versification, metre, poetry; jurisdiction; territory.

Rant, ranta, *s. m.* A rant; a noise; a confused dance.

Rantair, *s. m.* A ranter; a noisy fellow. *N. pl.* rantairean.

Rantaireachd, *s. f.* Ranting; noisiness. Is ann ort tha 'n rantaireachd! *how noisy you are!*

Rannuidheachd, *s. f.* See **Rannachd**.

Raod, *s. m.* A thing. More properly written *rud;* which see.

Raodhair, *s. f.* An upland plain or field; a down. *N. pl.* raoidhrichean.

Raogha, *s. m.* A choice. See **Rogha**.

Raoghnaich, *v.;* more frequently written *roghnaich.*

Raoic, *s. f.* A bellow, a roar; the voice of a deer. Written also *raoichd.*

Raoic, *v. n.* Bellow, roar; belch. *Pret. a.* raoic; *fut. aff. a.* raoicidh, *shall roar.* Mar a raoiceas leomhann, *as a lion roars.—Stew. Is.*

Raoichd, *s. f.* (*Ir. id.*) A bellow, a roar; the voice of a deer.—*Macint.* A belching noise; eructation.

Raoichd, *v. n.* Bellow, roar; bellow, as a deer; belch. *Pret. id.; fut. aff.* raoichidh, *shall bellow.*

Raoichdeach, *a.* Bellowing, roaring; making a belching noise; flatulent.

Raoichdeil, *a.* (raoichd-amhuil.) Bellowing, roaring; belching.

Raoichdeil, *s. f.* A bellowing, a roaring; a belching.

Raoimeach, *a.* Plundering.

Raoimeadh, idh, *s. m.* (*Ir. id.*) Depredation, plundering.

Raoin, *gen. sing.* of raon.

Raoineadh, idh, *s. m.* (*Ir. id.*) Triumph, victory.

Raoir, **Raoidhir**, (an), *adv.* (*Ir.* an reir.) Yesternight, last night, last evening.

Raomadh, aidh, *s. m.* (*Ir. id.*) Phlegm.

† **Raon**, *v. a.* Turn; change; tear, break.—*Shaw.*

Raon, raoin, *s. m.* (*Ir. id.*) A plain, a field, a green; an upland field or plain; a down. Air raoin nan sonn, *on the field of heroes.— Oss. Fing.* *N. pl.* raonaichean *and* raointean.

Raonach, *a.* Meadowy; having fields or greens; of a field or green; of an upland plain. Glasrach raonach, *abounding in green groves and meadows.—Macdon.*

Raonadh, aidh, *s. m.* (*Ir. id.*) A way, a road, a haunt; a breaking, a tearing, a changing.—*Shaw.*

Raonaichean, *n. pl.* of raon; which see.

Raosar, air, *s. m.* A currant.

Rap, ràpa, *s. m.* Any creature that digs, or that draws its food towards it, as cows; *also,* noise.—*Shaw.*

Ràpach, *a.* Noisy; slovenly; drivelling.

Ràpair, *s. m.* A noisy fellow; a slovenly fellow. *N. pl.* rapairean.

Ràpaireachd, *s. f.* Noisiness; slovenliness.

Ràpal, ail, *s. m.* (*Lat.* rabul-a, *a brawler. Eng.* rabble.) Noise, bustle. Cinneadh mhòr gun bhòsd gun ràpal, *a mighty clan without boast or noise.—Old Song.*

Ràpalach, *a.* Noisy, bustling. Gu ràpalach, *in a noisy manner. Com.* and *sup.* rapalaiche.

R' ar, (*for* ri ar.) By or beside our; to our. R'ar taobh, *by our side.* See **Ri**.

Ras, ràis, *s. m.* (*Ir. id.*) A shrub; underwood.

Ràsach, *a.* (*Ir. id.*) Shrubby; like a shrub; of shrubs.

Ràsachd, *s. f.* (*Ir. id.*) A shrubbery; shrubbiness.

Rasaiche, *s. f.* A gipsey; a hussy; a rambler; a rambling woman;—said mostly of a roving, lewd female.

Rasair, *s. m.* A rambler.

Rasaireachd, *s. f.* Rambling.

Ràsan, *n. pl.* of ràs. Shrubs; underwood; copses; brushwood.

Ràsan, ain, *s. m.* (*Ir. id.*) A grating discordant noise; unpleasant monotony; a monotonous speaker; *also,* a copse, a shrubbery.

Ràsanach, *a.* (*Ir. id.*) Discordant, monotonous, grating; *also,* a dull prosing speaker.

Ràsanachd, *s. f.* (*from* ràsan.) Monotony; tedious verbiage.

Ràsar, air, *s. m.* A razor.

Ras-chrann, -chroinn, *s. m.* (*Ir. id.*) A shrubbery tree.

Ras-chrannach, *a.* (*Ir. id.*) Abounding in shrub trees; made of shrub trees; *substantively,* a shrubbery.—*O'Reilly.*

Rasdach, aich, *s. m.* (*Ir. id.*) Churl.

Rasdail, *gen. sing.* of rasdal. Of a rake.

Rasdail, *v. a.* Rake together, as hay.

Ràsdal, ail, *s. m.* (*Lat.* rastell-um. *Arm.* rastel.) A rake for hay. Cho chruaidh ri ràsdal, *as hard as a rake;* ràsdal ghead, *a hand-harrow.* *N. pl.* ràsdalan *and* ràsdail, *rakes.*

Ràsdalach, *a.* Like a rake; that can be raked.

Ràsdaladh, aidh, *s. m.* A raking together, as hay; a gathering.

Ràsdaladh, (a), *pr. part.* of rasdail. Raking.

Ràsdalaiche, *s. m.* A raker of hay; one who works with a rake.

Rasgair, *s. m.* An idle talker.

Rasgaireachd, *s. f.* Idle talk.

Rasmhaol, aoil, *s. m.* A sea-calf.—*Shaw.*

Rastach, aich, *s. m.* See **Rasdach**.

Rastair, *s. f.* (*Ir. id.*) Great satiety.

† **Rat**, *s.* (*Ir. id.*) Motion.

Rath, *s. m.* (*Ir. Germ. id.*) Good luck; prosperity; success; good fame; character; surety; wages. Mo rath is mo chliù, *my character and renown.—Oss. Duthona.* Cha toir duine rath air éigin, *a man cannot force good luck.—G. P.* Cha tig rath ort, *you will not prosper.*

† **Rath**, *s. m.* (*Ir. id.*) A fortress; a village; an artificial mount; a steep place; a prince's seat; fern; a plain or cleared spot.

Rath, *s. m.* (*Lat.* ratis.) A raft. *N. pl.* rathan; *d. pl.* rathaibh. Chuir mi iad air falbh nan rathaibh, *I sent them off in their rafts.—Stew. K.*

Rathach, *a.* Prosperous, lucky, successful; like a float. Aiteam rathach, *a successful people.—Fingalian Poem.*

† **Rathach**, aich, *s. m.* (*Ir. id.*) The hough.—*Shaw.*

Rathachadh, aidh, *s. m.* A prospering, a succeeding; success, prosperity.

Rathad, aid, *s. m.* A road or highway; a path, a way, a track. Tre nàmh tha 'n rathad gu 'r loingeas, *the way to our ships lies through enemies.—Oss. Duthona.* Rathad mòr, *a high road.—Stew. Pro.* Rathad mòr an rìgh, *the king's high road;* rathaid mora, *highways.—Stew. Lev.* As an rathad, *out of the way; aside.—Oss. Duthona.* Air an rathad, *on the road, coming;* bhàrr an rathaid, *off the way.* Gabh do rathad, *begone;*—so the Latins said *cape viam.* A gabhail an rathaid, *travelling;* luchd gabhail an rathaid, *wayfarers;* ré an rathaid, *the whole way, all the way.*

Pers. rah. *Fr.* rade *and* route. *W.* rhyd. *Ir.* rod, *a road.* *Heb.* ratz. *Chald.* rahat, *to run.* *Arab.* rati, *to walk, and* rahhat, *one who runs.* *Germ.* raden. *Arab.* rats, *to run.*

Rathail; *a.* (rath-amhuil.) Fortunate, prosperous; famed; well-spoken of. Dream rathail, *a prosperous people.—Macdon.*

Rathamhnas, ais, *s. m* Prosperity; happiness.—*Shaw*

Rathan, ain, *s. m.* A surety; a twirl affixed to the *pirn* of a spinning-wheel; a pulley Fàg do chuid-throm air do rathan, *leave thy dependence on thy surety —Old Poem*

Rathanach, *a.* Having pullies —*Turn.*

Rath-mhoire, *com* and *sup.* of rath-mhor.

Rath-mhor, *a.* (*Ir.* rathmhar.) Fortunate, prosperous; reputed, noted. *Com.* and *sup.* rathmhoire.

Rath-sholus, uis, *s. m.* Between the front and back doors —*Shaw.*

Ratreut, *s. m.* A retreat.

Re, *prep.* (*for* ri.) To, at, by, of, against Eisd re m'ghuth, *listen to my voice.—Stew. Gen.* See Ri.

Ré, *s. m.* (*Ir. id.*) A space of time, duration; time, life, lifetime; a planet, the moon Ré an laoich, *the hero's life.—Oss. Gaul* Mar ré na h-oidhche, *like the moon of the night.—Oss. Duthona*

Rè, *prep.* During Rè tamuill, *for a time*; rè seal, *for a time, for a season*, dh' imich ri seal clann Mhuirn, *the sons of Morni have gone for a time.—Oss. Fin and Lor.* Rè na h-oidhche, *all night.—Stew. Job.* Rè 'n latha, *all day*, rè na bliadhna, *all the year, during the whole year*, rè an rathaid, *the whole way.*

Reab, *v. a.* See Reub.

Reabach, *a.* See Reubach.

Reabh, *s m.* (*Ir. id.*) A wile; a trick; cunning.

Reabhach, *a.* Subtle, cunning; *substantively*, one who plays tricks; a mountebank.

† **Reabhlanoar**, *a.* (*Ir. id*) Skipping, playing, sporting —*Shaw.*

Reabhradh, aidh, *s. m.* A skipping, a playing.

† **Reac**, *s. f.* (*Ir id.*) A woman, a damsel.

Reacar, *a.* Swift, hot; growing quick, strong —*Shaw.*

Reach, *v. n.*, *provincial for* rach, which see.

Reachd, *s. m.* A statute, a law, decree or ordinance, a command; command, power, authority; keen sorrow. Reachd do 'n uisge, *a decree to the rain —Stew. Job.* Chaill iad sealladh air gach reachd, *they lost sight of every law.—Mac Co.* Dream gun àireamh fo d' reachd, *people without number under thy command —Mac Lach.* *N. pl* reachdan. Mo reachdan, *my statutes —Stew O T* *Lat.* rect-um, *right. Eng.* † riht *and* reicht. *Germ.* recht. *Island.* rett *Swed.* raett. *Ir.* reachd *Sco.* richt.

Reachdach, *a.* (*Ir. id.*) Of, or belonging to, a law or statute; enactive; legislative; imperative; authoritative, strong; causing deep sorrow.

Reachdachadh, aidh, *s. m.* A legislating.

Reachdachd, *s. f.* Legislation; enaction.

Reachdadair, *s. m.* A legislator; a lawgiver.—*Q. B. ref.* *N. pl.* reachdadairean.

Reachdadaireachd, *s f.* Legislation; enaction; a decreeing.

Reachdaich, *v. n.* (*from* reachd.) Enact, legislate, ordain, decree, appoint. *Pret. a* reachdaich; *fut. aff. a.* reachdaichidh.

Reachdaichte, *p. part.* Enacted, ordained

Reachdail, *a* (reachd-amhuil) Lawful, legal, regular.

Reachdair, *s. m*, *from* reachd (*Germ* richter *Lat* rector *Ir.* reachdaire.) A legislator or lawgiver, a ruler; a rector; *rarely*, a dairyman.—*Shaw.* *N pl.* reachdairean.

Reachdairm, *s f.* A court of judicature.—*Shaw.*

Reachdar, *a* See Reachdmhor

Reachd-cheangail, *v. a.* Bind by decree, article; stipulate. *Pret. a. id*

Reachd-cheangailte, *a.* Bound by a decree; bound by a stipulation.

Reachd-dhaighneach, ich, *s m* A statute —*Macfar Voc.*

Reachd-dhaighneachadh, aidh, *s. m* The circumstance of binding by a decree or by stipulation, a fixing by law.

Reachd-dhaighnich, *v a* Bind by decree, fix by a law

Reachd-dhaighnichte, *p part* Bound by decree, fixed by law.

Reachd-mhathair, -mhathar, *s. f.* (*Ir. id*) A mother-in-law —*Shaw*

Reachd-mhòd, mhòid, *s. m* (*Ir. id.*) A court of law; a court of justice.

Reachdmhoire, *com* and *sup.* of reachdmhor

Reachdmhoireachd, *s f.* Stoutness; pithiness, rankness; substantialness, spiritedness, sorrowfulness

Reachdmhor, *a* Strong, stout, pithy, rank; substantial, spirited, sorrowful; commanding; imperative. Reachdmhor agus maith, *rank and good —Stew Gen.* Tha thu tarbhach reachdmhor, *thou art productive and substantial —Macfar.* *Com.* and *sup* reachdmhoire

Reachd-shaor, *a.* Licensed, authorised by law

Reachd-thabhairteach, *a* Lawgiving, legislating; fond of imposing laws, pertaining to legislation

Reachd-thabhairtear, eir, *s m* A lawgiver, a legislator *N. pl* reachd-thabhairtearan

Readan, ain, *s. m.* (*Ir. id*) A pipe; a reed; a wood-louse. *N. pl* readain

Readanach, *a* (*Ir id.*) Reedy, like a reed; full of wood-lice

Read-chord, -chuird, *s m.* The reins of a bridle

Readh, *a.* Tough, hard. Chagnadh e sleagh readh, *he would chew a tough spear.—Oss Derm.*

† **Readh-sgaoileadh**, idh, *s. m.* (*Ir. id.*) A flux.—*Shaw*

† **Reag**, reig, *s f.* (*Ir. id*) Night.

Reag-dhall, *a* (*Ir. id*) Purblind.—*Shaw.*

Reaghloraich, *a.* Resounding

Reall, *s*, more frequently written *reul.*

Realt, *s.*, more properly written *reult.*

† **Reamain**, *s. f* (*Ir. id*) A beginning —*Shaw.*

Reamhad, aid, *s m* Bulk, fatness.

Reamhair, *s. m* A traveller; a wayfaring man; a vagabond. *N. pl* reamhairean

Reamhar, *a* (*Ir id*) Fat, gross; thick; coarse Reamhar am feòil, *fat-fleshed.—Stew Gen.*

Reamhrach, *a.* Coagulative.

Reamhrachadh, aidh, *s m* (*Ir* reamhrughadh) A fattening, a feeding, grossness, fatness; coagulation.

Reamhrachail, *a* Fattening.

Reamhrachd, *s f.* (*from* reamhar) Fat, fatness, grossness. Reamhrachd na talmhainn, *the fat of the earth —Stew. Gen.* Reamhrachd muic mara, *blubber.*

Reamhrad, aid, *s m* Fatness; grossness —*Stew Job ref Also*, increase in fatness A dol an reamhrad, *growing more and more fat*

Reamhraich, *v a* (*Ir.* reamhraigh) Fatten; make fat, clot, concrete, coagulate. *Pret a id*, *fut. aff. a* reamhraichidh, *shall fatten.*

Reamhraichte, *p. part.* of reamhraich. Fattened, fed.

Rean, *s f.* (*Ir id.*) A span.

Reang, *v. a.* (*Ir. id.*) Starve. *Pret.* reang; *fut. aff.* reangaidh.

Reang, reanga, *s. m.* A rank or row; a rein or kidney. Air cùl reanga dhìslean, *behind the ranks of his friends.—Mac Lach.* Reanga, *reins.—Shaw.*

Reangach, *a.* In ranks or rows; having reins or kidneys; like a rein or kidney; wrinkled.

Reangadh, aidh, *s. m.* (*Ir. id.*) A starving; a putting in ranks or rows.

Reangair, *s. m.* A wrangler.

Reann, *s. m.* (*Ir. id.*) A star; land; soil; country. *N. pl.* rinn *and* reannan.

Reannag, aig, *s. f.* (*dim.* of reann.) A star; a starlet. *N. pl.* reannagan.—*Stew. Gen. ref.* Reannag-earbullach, *a comet;* an reannag tuathach, *the north star.*

Reannagach, *a.* Starry; spangled or studded. Oidhche reannagach, *a starry night.*

Reannair, *s. m.* (reann-fhear.) An astronomer. *N. pl.* reannairean.

Reannan, ain, *s. m., dim.* of reann. (*Ir. id.*) A star, a starlet. *N. pl.* reannain.

Reann-ghlan, *a.* Star-bright. Na rosgan reann-ghlan, *the star-bright eyes.—Fingalian Poem.*

† **Rear**, *s. m.* (*Ir. id.*) Provision.—*Shaw.*

Reas, reis, *s. m.* Rice.—*Macd.*

Reasan, ain, *s. m.* A reason. Written more frequently *reuson.*

† **Reasart**, airt, *s. m.* (*Ir. id.*) Preservation; health.

Reasbait, *s. m.* (*Ir. id.*) A beggar's brat.

Reasgach, *a.* (*Ir.* reascach, *tattling.*) Stubborn, perverse, or froward; skittish; restive; impatient. Dhoibhsan a tha reasgach, *to them who are froward.—Stew. Pet.* Each reasgach, *a restive horse. Com.* and *sup.* reasgaiche.

Reasgachd, *s. f.* Stubbornness, perverseness—(*Stew. Sam. ref.*); skittishness, restiveness, impatience.

Reasgaiche, *com.* and *sup.* More or most perverse, stubborn, or restive.

Reasgaichead, eid, *s. m.* Increase in stubbornness, restiveness, or impatience. It is also used as a comparative noun, as, Is reasgaicheid an t-each an spor, *the spur makes the horse more restive.*

Reasonta, *a.* See **Reusonta**.

† **Reatair**, *s. m.* (*Ir. id.*) A clergyman, a clerk.—*Shaw.*

Reatas, ais, *s. m.* (*Ir. id.*) Enmity, hatred.—*Shaw.*

Reath, *a.* Level, smooth. More frequently written *réidh;* which see.

Reath, reatha, *s. m.* (*Ir. id.*) A ram. More frequently written *reithe;* which see.

Reathach, *a.* Rammish; like a ram; rutting.

Reathachas, ais, *s. m.* Ramming, rutting; obstinacy; tuppishness. Written also *reitheachas.*

Reathlan, ain, *s. m.* A plain, a field; a level field. Reathlan nan laoch, *the field of heroes.—Oss. Tem.* More properly *réidhlean.*

† **Redhream**, *s. m.* (*Ir. id.*) A climate.

Reic, *s. m.* (*Ir. id.*) A selling, a sale, an auction. Reic agus ceannachd, *buying and selling.—Stew. Gen.*

Reic, *v. a.* (*Ir. id.*) Sell, dispose of. *Pret. a.* reic, *sold; fut. aff. a.* reicidh, *shall sell.* A reic airson greim arain, *who sold for a morsel of bread.—Stew. Heb.*

Reiceach, *a.* Selling, trucking; fond of trucking; saleable.

Reiceadair, *s. m.* (*Ir.* reacadoir.) A seller; an auctioneer; a broker. *N. pl.* reiceadairean.

Reiceadaireachd, *s. f.* Selling; auctioneering.

Reiceadh, eidh, *s. m.* A selling, a disposing of; a sale, an auction. Air a reiceadh, *sold.*

Reicear, *fut. pass.* of reic. Shall be sold. It is often used impersonally. Reicear [leam] e, *I sold him* or *it.*

Reicear, eir, *s. m.* A seller; an auctioneer.

Reic-chead, *s. m.* A license or permission to sell publicly.

Reic-cheadach, *a.* Licensed, authorised to sell.

Reicidh, *fut. aff. a.* of reic. Shall or will sell or dispose of.

Reicte, *p. part.* of reic. Sold.

Réide, *s. f.* Reconciliation, agreement, atonement. See **Réite**.

Réideach, *a.* Reconciling, fond of reconciling; clearing away obstruction, disentangling. See also **Réiteach**.

Reideachadh, aidh, *s. m.* A reconciling; a clearing away; a disentangling; reconciliation; union; clearance; disentanglement; harmony, union; a covenant.

Réideachair, *s. m.* A reconciler, an adjuster of differences, a mediator; one who clears away obstructions.

† **Reidh**, *s. m.* (*Ir. id.*) A rope; a withe. *N. pl.* reidhean.

Reidh, *s. m.* A plain; a meadow; level ground. Faoghaid an réidh, *the chase on the plain.—Oss. Fing.*

Réidh, *a.* (*Ir. id. Arm.* reih. *Teut.* reye, *arrangement.*) Level, smooth, plain; reconciled; appeased; conciliated; prepared; ready; in order; regular; disentangled; cleared of obstructions. Rathad réidh, *a plain road.—Stew. Pro.* Air buinne réidh, *on a smooth stream.—Macint.* Réidh ri' fear, *reconciled to her husband.—Stew. Cor.* Ni mi réidh e, *I will appease him.—Stew. Gen.* Am bi thu réidh? *will you be friends?* Reidh-dheudan, *regularly-set teeth.—Old Song.*

Reidheachd, *s. f.* Ready service; officiousness; smoothness, levelness; the state of being reconciled, or appeased; the state of being ready, or disentangled.

† **Reidheadh**, idh, *s. m.* Agreement; assent.—*Shaw.*

Reidh-labhairt, *s. f.* Eloquence; smooth eloquence.

Reidh-labhra, *a.* Eloquent; speaking with ease.

Reidhlean, ein, *s. m.* A smooth level green; a level field; a bowling-green.—*Macint.* Perhaps *reidhlann.*

Reidhleanach, *a.* Smooth or plain, meadowy.

Reidhir, (an), *adv.* Last evening, last night.—*Stew. Gen.*

Réidich, *v.* Reconcile; conciliate; appease; clear away; disentangle; adjust. *Pret. a.* réidich; *fut. aff. a.* réidichidh; *fut. pass.* réidichear.

Réidichte, *p. part.* of réidich. Reconciled, conciliated; propitiated; cleared of obstruction; disentangled; adjusted.

† **Reighlios**, *s.* A church, a shrine, a sanctuary.—*Shaw.*

† **Reil**, *a.* (*Ir. id.*) Clear, manifest.

† **Reil**, *s. m.* (*Ir. id.*) A star. See **Reul**.

Reileag, eig, *s. f.* (*Ir. id.*) A churchyard, a grave, a cemetery; a church.—*Shaw. N. pl.* reileagan.

Reileagach, *a.* Like a churchyard; having a churchyard; of a churchyard or cemetery.

Reilge, *s. f.* A churchyard, a grave, a cemetery; a church. Cha bhi dùil ri fear reilge, *there is no hope from the grave.*—*G. P.*

Reilteag, eig, *s. f.* A starlet; an astrolabe. *N. pl.* reilteagan.

Réilteagach, *a.* Full of starlets.

Reiltean, ein, *s. m.* (*dim.* of reil.) A starlet; an asterisk; an astrolabe. *N. pl.* réiltein.

Reim, *s. m.* (*Ir. id.*) Power, authority, sway; a progress; a series; a way; a band, a troop; equanimity.

From *reim*, power, probably comes *caithream*, a shout of triumph.

Reimeil, *a.* (reim-amhuil.) Bearing sway or authority;

persevering, constant, even-minded; even; rampant.—*Shaw.*

REIMHE, *s. f.* (*Ir. id.*) Fatness; grossness; pride.

REIMHEACH, *a.* (*Ir. id.*) Arrogant, forward; petulant; conceited.

REIMHEACHD, *s. f.* (*Ir. id.*) Arrogance, forwardness; petulance, conceitedness.

REIMSE, *s. f.* A club, a staff.

RÉIN, *s. f.* (*W.* Rhyn, *a great channel.*) The river Rhine.

Rein is a contraction of *reidh-an*, meaning a smooth water,—a most suitable name for the majestic Rhine. The name of every river in the world which ends in *n*, or which has *n* in the last syllable, may be derived from the root *an* (which see) or *ain*, meaning a flowing element, or water. This observation, if it be founded in truth, seems to afford a presumption that *an* is one of the few roots which have come down to us from the original language of man.

REING, REINGEAN, *s. pl.* The timbers of a ship.

RAINGEACH, ich, *s. m.* (*Ir. id.*) Ship timber; *also, adjectively,* abounding in ship timber, like ship timber, of ship timber.

RÉIR, *s. f.* (*Ir. id.*) Pleasure, inclination, will, desire. Ioma gille òg am réir, *many a youth fond of me.*—*Macfar.* Nam bithinn ad réir, *if I were of the same mind with thee.*—*Id.*

RÉIR, (a), *prep.* According to; in proportion. A réir d' iarrtais, *according to thy request* or *pleasure;* tha sinn réir chéile, *we are pleased with each other.*—*Macfar.* A rêir a chéile, *one with another.*

RÉIR, (do), *prep.* According to; in proportion. See also RÉIR (a).

RÉIS, *s. f.* (*Ir. id. Du.* reis, *a journey.*) A race; a chase; a span, nine inches long. Ruidh a réis, *running his race.*—*Sm.* Se lamhan-coille agus réis, *six cubits and a span.*—*Stew. Sam.* Cuir réis, *run a race;* feuch réis, *try a race.*

REISGHIOBHAR, air, *s. f.* A prostitute.—*Shaw.*

REISICHE, *s. m.* (*Ir.* reisidhe.) A rehearser, a romancer.—*Shaw.*

† REISMEIRDREACH, ich, *s. f.* (*Ir. id.*) A harlot, a street prostitute.

RÉITE, *s. f.* (*Ir. id.*) Reconciliation; agreement; atonement; settlement; a contract; adjustment; disentanglement. Ni e réite, *he will make atonement.*—*Stew. Lev.*

RÉITEACH, ich, *s. m.* A plain; any level place.

RÉITEACH, *a.* Reconciling; fond of reconciling; conciliating; clearing away obstructions; disentangling.

REITEACH, ich, *s. m.* See REITEACHADH.

RÉITEACHADH, aidh, *s. m.* (*Ir.* reiteach.) A reconciling; a conciliating; a disencumbering, a disentangling; a settling or adjusting; a reconciliation, a conciliation; a disentanglement; an adjustment. Réiteachadh pòsaidh, *a betrothment, a marriage contract.*—*Stew. Deut. ref.*

RÉITEACHAIL, *a.* Having a tendency to reconcile or conciliate; fond of reconcilement, fond of clearing away obstructions or entanglements.

RÉITEACHAIR, *s. m.* A reconciler, a conciliator, a propitiator, a mediator. *N. pl.* réiteachairean.

RÉITEACHD, *s. f.* The state of being reconciled; disentanglement.

RÉITH. See RÉIDH.

REITH, *v. a.* Leap, as rams on sheep.

REITHE, *s. m.* A ram. Reithe air a chulaobh, *a ram behind him.*—*Stew. Gen.* Reithe cogaidh, *a battering-ram;* reithe slachdaidh, *a battering-ram. N. pl.* reitheachan.

REITHEACH, *a.* (*from* reithe.) Rammish; like a ram; ruttish.

REITHEACHAS, ais, *s. m.* (*from* reithe.) Rammishness, tuppishness; ramming, rutting.

RÉITHEADH, idh, *s. m.* Ramming; the copulation of the ovile species.

REITHEADH, (a), *pr. part.* of reith. A mounting of sheep, as by rams. A reitheadh na spreidhe, *mounting the sheep.*—*Stew. Gen.*

REITHE-COGAIDH, *s. m.* A battering-ram. *N. pl.* reitheachan-cogaidh, *battering-rams.*—*Stew. Ezek.*

RÉITICH, *v. a.* (*from* réite.) Reconcile, conciliate, appease; clear away, disentangle; adjust. *Pret. a.* réitich; *fut. aff. a.* réitichidh.

RÉITICHTE, *p. part.* of réitich. Reconciled, conciliated, appeased; disentangled, disencumbered.

REO, *s. m.* Frost.

Arm. reau. In Vannes they say *reu. Ir.* reo. *W.* and *Corn.* rheu. *Germ.* rif *and* reif.

REOITHTE, *p. part.* of reoth. Frozen, congealed. Written also *reothta.*

REO-LEAC, -lic, *s. f.* A sheet of ice; ice. *N. pl.* reo-lic.

REO-LEAC, *v. n.* Congeal.

REOMHAD, *more correctly* romhad; which see.

REÒN, reòin, *s. m.* A span.—*Shaw.*

REO-SHRUTH, *s. m.* A frozen stream. Mar reo-shruth Lanna, *like the frozen stream of Lanna.*—*Oss. Fin. and Lor.*

REÒTA, *a.* Freezing; frosty; frozen. La reòta, *a frosty day;* ri la reòta 'coiseachd monaidh, *travelling a moor on a frosty day.*—*Old Song.*

REOTACH, *a.* Freezing; frosty. Ràithe sneachdach reòtach, *a snowy, frosty quarter.*—*Macfar. Com.* and *sup.* reòtaiche.

REÒTADH, aidh, *s. m.* A freezing or congealing; frost; congelation. Tigh reòtaidh, *an ice-house;* oidhche reòtaidh, *a frosty night;* air reòtadh, *frozen.*

REOTANACH, *a.* Stingy. Gu reotanach, *stingily.*

REOTANACHD, *s. f.* Stinginess.

REOTANDA, *a.* Stingy.

REOTH, *v. a.* and *n.* Freeze; congeal. *Pret.* reoth; *fut. aff. a.* reothaidh.

REOTH, REOTHADH, aidh, *s. m.* (*Corn.* reau.) Frost, congelation; a freezing, a congealing.

REOTHAIRT, RETHOIRT, *s. f.* (rè, *moon, and* toirt, *bringing.*) A spring tide. Sruth réthoirt, *a spring-tide stream.*—*Old Poem.*

REOTHTA, *p. part.* of reoth.

RÈ 'R, (*for* rè ar *or* rè ur.) During our, during your. Rè 'r là, *during our day, during our time.*

REUB, *v. a.* (*Ir. id.*) Tear, lacerate, mangle, wound; abuse. *Pret. a.* reub; *fut. aff. a.* reubaidh, *shall tear.* Reub e 'aodach, *he tore his clothes.*—*Stew. Gen.* Reub e shàil le mìle lot, *he mangled his heel with a thousand wounds.*—*Oss. Tem. Fut. pass.* reubar.

REUBACH, *a.* (*from* reub.) Tearing, lacerating; wounding, bruising.

REUBADH, aidh, *s. m.* A tearing, a wounding, laceration; a wound.

REUBAIDH, *fut. aff. a.* of reub. Shall tear.

REUBAINN, *s. f.* Robbing, robbery; plundering, freebooting. Ni mo ni thu reubainn, *neither shalt thou rob.*—*Stew. Lev.* Reubainn nan aingidh, *the robbery of the wicked.*—*Stew. Pro.* Luchd-reubainn, *freebooters, robbers.*

Heb. rab, *rob. Sax.* rypan, *to tear. Germ.* rauben, *to pillage. Dan.* raffuen. *Du.* roofen. *It.* rubare, *to rob.* We are told that *raubare*, a word found in the Salic law, means, *to take off by force.*

REUBAINNEACH, *a.* Plundering, robbing.

REUBAINNEACHD, *s. f.* The practice of plunder or of robbery, freebooting.

Reubainnear, eir, *s. m.* (reubainn-fhear.) A plunderer, a freebooter, a robber.

Reubair, *s. m.* (reub-fhear.) A plunderer, a robber; a tearer; a bruiser. *N. pl.* reubairean.

Reubaireachd, *s. f.* Robbery, plunder; a tearing, a lacerating.

Reubalach, aich, *s. m.* A rebel. *N. pl.* reubalaich.

Reubalach, *a.* Rebellious.

Reubaltach, aich, *s. m.* A rebel. *N. pl.* reubaltaich.—*Roy Stewart.*

Reubam, (*for* reubaidh mi.) I shall tear.

Reuban. See **Reubainn**.

Reubanair. See **Reubainnear**.

Reubar, *fut. pass.* of reub. Shall be torn.

Reubhag, aig, *s. f.* A lark. *N. pl.* reubhagan. Written also *riabhag.*

Reubta, *p. part.* of reub. Torn, mangled, wounded. Reubta le dealan, *wounded with lightning.—Oss. Gaul.*

Reud, *s. m.* A wood-louse; a timber-worm; a reed.

Reudan, ain, *s. m.*, *dim.* of reud. (*Ir. id.*) A wood-louse; a pedicular insect that eats through timber and paper; a timber-worm; a timber-moth; a reed. *N. pl.* reudain.

Reudan, *n. pl.* of reud.

Reudanach, *a.* (*from* reudan.) Full of timber-moths or timber-worms; like a timber-moth; reedy.

Reul, réil, *s. m.* (*Ir.* reull.) A star. Aon reul cha léir dhoibh, *not one star is visible to them.—Oss. N. pl.* reultan. Solus nan reultan, *starlight.—Ull.* Reul seachranach, *a planet.—Stew. 2 K.* Reul-na-madra, *the dog-star.—O'Reilly.*

This vocable is compounded of *ruith*, course, and *iul*, guide. If this be the true composition of *reul*, one is justified in inferring that the ancient Celts were not only not ignorant of navigation, but were in truth adventurous mariners, and could guide their course by the stars. Indeed, the Fingalian bards make frequent mention of *Iul Eirinn, Iul Lochlinn, Iul oidhche*, stars known to the Gaelic and Irish mariners by that name, and meaning the Guide to Eirin, the Guide to Scandinavia, the Guide of Night.

Reulach, *a.* (*from* reul.) Starry, sidereal, astral. Oidhche reulach, *a starry night.*

Reuladair, *s. m.* (*Ir.* reultoir.) An astronomer; a star-gazer; an astrologer. *N. pl.* reuladairean.

Reuladaireachd, *s. f.* Astronomy; astrology; star-gazing.

Reuladh, aidh, *s. m.* (*Ir. id.*) A declaration.—*Shaw.*

Reulag, aig, *s. f.* (*dim.* of reul.) A starlet. *N. pl.* reulagan.

Reulagach, *a.* Starry; studded.

Reul-airgiodach, *a.* Studded with silver. Claidheamh reul-airgiodach, *a silver-studded sword.—Mac Lach.*

Reul-dhruidh, *s. m.* An astrologer. *N. pl.* reul-dhruidhean.

Reul-dhruidheach, *a.* Astrological.

Reul-dhruidheachd, *s. f.* The occult science of astrology.

Reul-eolach, *a.* Versed in astronomy; versed in astrology.

Reul-eolas, ais, *s. m.* (*Ir. id.*) Astronomy; astronomical knowledge; astrology.

Reul-ghrigleach, *a.* Sidereal, astral; thick-set with constellations.

Reul-ghriglean, ein, *s. m.* A constellation; a group of stars, as those in the Bull's neck, called the Pleiades.

Reul-ghrigleanach, *a.* Sidereal, astral; thick-set with constellations.

Reul-sholus, uis, *s. m.* Star-light.

Reult, reilte, *s. f.* (*Ir. id.*) A star; a meteor. Air faicinn na réilte, *on seeing the star.—Stew. Matt.* An reult mhaidne, *the morning-star.—Stew. Pet. N. pl.* reultan.

Reultach, *a.* (*Ir. id.*) Starry, astral, sidereal. Oidhche reultach, *a starry night.*

Reultag, aig, *s. f.* (*dim.* of reul.) *Ir.* realtog. A starlet; an asterisk; a stud; an astrolabe. *N. pl.* reultagan.

Reultagach, *a.* Starry; studded.

Reultaich, *v. a.* Stud. *P. part.* reultaichte.

Reultair, *s. m.* An astronomer; a star-gazer; an astrologer.

Reultaireachd, *s. f.* Astronomy; star-gazing; astrology.

Reultan, ain, *s. m.* A starlet; an asterisk; a stud; an astrolabe.

Reult-bhuidheann, bhuidhne, *s.* A constellation.

Reult-chosgair, *s. m.* An astronomer; a star-gazer; an astrologer. *N. pl.* reult-chosgairean.

Reult-chuirt, *s. f.* The star-chamber.—*Shaw.*

Reult-iasg, -eisg, *s. m.* A fish with shining teeth.

Reum, reuma, *s. m.* (*Ir. id.*) Rheum; phlegm; catarrh; mucous saliva.

Reumach, *a.* (*Ir. id.*) Phlegmy; rheumatic; afflicted with catarrh.

Reumail, *a.* Constant; persevering; steady; having sway; phlegmatic. Steornadh reumail, *steady steering.—Old Poem.*

Reumalachd, *s. f.* Constancy; perseverance; steadiness; a phlegmatic temperament.

Reumhair, *s. m.* A traveller; a wayfaring man; a rover; a vagabond. *N. pl.* reumhairean.

Reumhaireachd, *s. f.* Travelling; wayfaring; roving; roaming.

Reusan, ain, *s. m.* (*Ir. id. Arm.* resoun. *Fr.* raison.) A reason, a cause, a motive, an argument. Written also *reuson.*

Reusanachadh, **Reusonachadh**, aidh, *s. m.* A reasoning or arguing; an expostulating; an argument; an expostulation.

Reusanachd, **Reusonachd**, *s. f.* Reasoning; an argument.

Reusanaich, **Reusonaich**, *v. a.* Reason, argue; think; expostulate. *Pret.* reusanaich; *fut. aff. a.* reusanaichidh. Reusonaich mi mar leanaban, *I reasoned [thought] as a child.—Stew. Cor.*

Reusanta, **Reusonta**, *a.* Reasonable, rational.

Reusantachd, **Reusontachd**, *s. f.* Reasonableness.

Ri, *prep.* (*Ir. id. Bisc.* ri, *at.*) To; with; on or during; in or in time of; at; by or beside; to or towards; in the direction of; of; against. Coslach ri cruaidh mo lainn, *like to the steel of my sword.—Oss. Tem.* Buinibh gu caoineil ri m' ghaol, *deal kindly with my love.—Oss. Fin. and Lor.* Maille ri, *together with*; ri la gaoithe, *on a windy day*; ri linn Thearlaich, *in the time of Charles*; ri uisge is gaoith, *in the time of rain and wind.—Old Legend.* Mar dhuilleig ri doininn, *like a leaf in the blast.—Id.* Na caomhaich ri sìth, *the friends at peace.—Oss. Cathluno.* Bha 'm feumach ri mo laimh, *the needy were at my side.—Oss.* Pillidh a ghrian ri doire, *the sun will return towards the grove.—Ull.* Gach sùil ri comhrag, *every eye in the direction of the battle.—Id.* Gun dùil ri pilleadh, *without hope of returning.* Ri bruthach, *up-hill*; ri leathad, *down-hill.* When *ri* comes immediately before a noun substantive, it often gives it the import of a *pr. participle.* An raineach ri turram 'sa ghaoithe, *the fern whistling in the wind.—Oss. Fin. and Lor.* A gnùis ri gàire, *her visage* *smiling.—Id.* *Ri* is also expressive of futurity; as, An tigh a tha ri thogail, *the house that is to be built.*

Ri, *adv.* As; like as. Cho chiùin ri aiteal, *as mild as a breath of wind.—Oss. Fing.* Cho ard ri stoirm, *as loud as a storm.—Id.*

Ria, *comp. pron.* To her; towards her; against her. Thubhairt mi ria, *I said to her.—Stew. Gen.* More commonly written *rithe.*

Riab. See **Reub.**

Riabhach, *a.* (*Ir. id.*) Brindled; greyish; darkish; brown; brownish. Righ nan torc riabhach, *king of the brindled boars.—Oss. Cathloda.* Sleagh riabhach, *a brown spear.—Oss. Tem.* Corr-riabhach, *a heron;* parr-riabhach nan cearc, *a kite.* *Com.* and *sup.* riabhaiche.

Riabhag, aig, *s. f.* (*Ir. id.*) A skylark; the *alauda arvensis* of Linnæus. Riabhag mhonaidh, *a titlark.* *N. pl.* riabhagan, *larks.*

Riabhag-choille, *s. f.* A woodlark; the *alauda arborea* of Linnæus.

Riabhag-mhonaidh, *s. f.* A titlark; the *alauda pratensis* of Linnæus.

Riabhaichead, eid, *s. m.* Brindledness; greyishness; brownishness; increase in brindledness or greyishness. A dol an riabhaichead, *growing more and more grey.*

Riabhan, ain, *s. m.* A handsome young stripling. *N. pl.* riubhain.

Riabhanach, *a.* Handsome; like a stripling.

Riach, *a.;* contracted for *riabhach;* which see.

Riachaid, *s. f.* A distributing, a dividing; a distribution, a partition; *also,* a controller.

Riachan, ain, *s. m.* (*Ir. id.*) Any thing grey.—*Shaw.*

Riachdail, *a.* Evident, manifest, clear.

Riachdailleas, eis, *s. m.* Necessity, want.—*Shaw.*

Riachdalas, ais, *s. m.* Clearness, manifestness.

Riachdanach, *a.* (*Ir. id.*) Immoral, impure; fond of sexual intercourse; needy, necessitous; necessary; needful; dutiful; incumbent.

Riachdanas, ais, *s. m.* Fornication; uncleanness; want, necessity; exigence; duty; necessaries.

Riadh, reidh, *s. m.* (*Ir. id.*) Interest; usury; rent; hire; a rib; a snare; *rarely,* correction; racing; taming; grief; a kind of capital punishment among the Irish.—*O'Reilly.* Airgiod air riadh, *money on usury.—Stew. Ex.* Na gabh riadh, *take no interest.—Stew. Lev.* Eich reidh, *hired horses.*

Riadhach, *a.* (*from* riadh.) Usurious; hired.

Riadhach, *a.* See **Riabhach.**

† **Riadhadh**, aidh, *s. m.* (*Ir. id.*) Hanging; a gallows.

Riadh-lann, -lainn, *s. m.* A house of correction.—*Shaw.*

Riadh-mhortair, *s. m.* A hired assassin; a bravo. *N. pl.* riadh-mhortairean.

† **Riagh**, *a.* (*Ir. id.*) Religious.

Riagh, *v. a.* (*Ir. id.*) Hang; crucify.

Riagh, reigh, *s. m.* (*Ir. id.*) A gallows; a cross; hence the opprobrious appellation, A mhic an reigh! *thou scape-gallows! improperly pronounced* a mhic an riaiche.

Riaghail, *s. f.* (*Lat.* regula.) A rule, a regulation; a law; government; direction.

Riaghail, *v. a.* (*Lat.* regulo.) Rule, govern, direct; settle, as by rule; arrange. *Pret. a.* riaghail; *fut. aff. a.* riaghlaidh. Riaghlaidh uachdarain, *princes shall rule.—Stew. Pro.* *Fut. sub.* riaghlas. A riaghlas cothrom, *who dispenses justice.—Macdon.*

Riaghailt, *s. f.* A rule or regulation; order; direction; a directory. *N. pl.* riaghailtean.

Riaghailteach, *a.* Regular, orderly, according to rule; peaceful; sober; moderate. *Com.* and *sup.* riaghailtiche.

Riaghailteachd, *s. f.* Regularity, orderliness; peacefulness; soberness.

Riaghailtich, *v.* Regulate, put in order, arrange, adjust; govern. *Pret. a. id.; fut. aff.* riaghailtichidh, *shall govern.*

Riaghailtiche, *com.* and *sup.* of riaghailteach.

Riaghailtichte, *p. part.* of riaghailtich. Regulated, put in order, adjusted; governed.

Riaghair, *s. m.* (*from* † riagh.) A hangman, an executioner; a scape-gallows; a rogue.

Riaghalta, *part.* (*Ir. id.*) Ruled, governed, managed, arranged; *rarely,* devout.

Riaghlach, *a.* According to rule, regular.

† **Riaghlach**, aich, *s. f.* (*Ir. id.*) An old woman.—*Shaw.*

Riaghlachadh, aidh, *s. m.* (*Ir.* riaghlughadh.) A regulating; a governing; a ruling; an arranging; a regulation; government; a rule; an arrangement.

Riaghladair, *s. m.* (*Ir.* riaghaltoir.) A ruler, a director, a manager, a regulator, a governor.—*Stew. Pro.* *N. pl.* riaghladairean.

Riaghladaireachd, *s. f.* A ruling, a directorship, a governorship, management, administration.

Riaghladh, aidh, *s. m.* (*Lat.* regula.) A rule, a direction, management; a ruling, a directing, a managing.

Riaghlaich, *v. a.* Rule, govern, manage, oversee; bring to order; arrange; direct. *Pret. id.; fut. aff.* riaghlaichidh. A riaghlaich os an cionn, *who ruled over them.—Stew. Ezra.*

Riaghlaichte, *p. part.* of riaghlaich. Ruled, managed; arranged, directed.

Riaghlair, *s. m.* (*W.* rheolwr.) A ruler, a manager, a director, an overseer. *N. pl.* riaghlairean.

Riaghlaireachd, *s. f.* Governing, managing, directing, overseeing; government, governance, management; directorship, governorship, administration.

Riaiche, *com.* and *sup.* of riach; which see.

Riamh, *adv.* More frequently written *riomh.*

Riamlach, aich, *s. m.* See **Driamlach.**

Rian, *s. m.* (*Ir. id.*) Form; fashion; order; management; good disposition or temper; a path, a footstep; a span; a sea. Rian nan arm, *the form of the armour.—Old Legend.*

Rianaiche, *s. m.* (*Ir.* rianuigh.) A wanderer, a traveller.

Rianaich, *v.* More properly *riaraich;* which see.

Rianail, *a.* (rian-amhuil.) Well-disposed; good-tempered; well-formed or fashioned.

Riar, *v. a.* Please; pleasure; satisfy; distribute.

Riar, *s. m.* (*Ir. id.*) Pleasure; will; desire; inclination; judgment; decree. A fhreasdal 's gach ni da 'riar, *to attend in every thing to her pleasure.—Mac Lach.* Mo riar, *my desire.—Stew.* 1 *K.*

Riarach, aich, *s. m.* A servitor.

Riarach, *a.* (*Ir. id.*) Ready to please; obliging; subservient; content, pleased; *also,* ready to participate; ready to share; dispensing.

Riarachadh, aidh, *s. m.* (*Ir. id.*) A sharing; a dispensing; a distributing; a pleasing: a satisfying; a distribution; satisfaction. Air a riarachadh, *distributed.*

Riarachadh, (a), *pr. part.* of riaraich.

Riarachas, ais, *s. m.* A distribution; one portion of a distribution.

Riarachd, *s. f.* (*Ir. id.*) A distribution; contentedness; satisfaction. Riarachd-inntinn, *contentment.—Shaw.*

Riaraich, *v. a.* Share; distribute; serve out; please; satisfy. *Pret.* riaraich; *fut. aff.* riaraichidh; *fut. pass.* riaraichear, *shall be divided.*

Riaraiche, *s. m.* A sharer; an econome; a dispenser of food.

Riaraichte, *p. part.* of riaraich. Shared; distributed; served; satisfied.

Riaraiste, *s. pl.* (*Ir. id.*) Arrears.

Riarta, *part.* Shared, served out, distributed; content.—*Shaw.*

Riasan, ain, *s. m.* See Riason.

Riasg, réisg, *s. f.* (*Ir. id.*) A moor; a heath.—*Macint.* A marsh, a fen; lay ground.

Riasgach, *a.* (*Ir. id.*) Moory; marshy; fenny; benty; stiff. *Com.* and *sup.* riasgaiche.

Riasgach, aich, *s. m.* (*Ir. id.*) Moorish ground; a moor; marshy ground. An riasgach as an dean damh rànan, *the moor whence rutting deer are heard.—Old Song.*

Riasgail, *a.* (riasg-amhuil.) Moorish; wild; indocile; untractable.

Riaslach, *a.* Tearing; mangling; criticising; apt to tear or mangle.

Riasladh, aidh, *s. m.* A tearing; a mangling; a criticising; a caressing. Oganach ga riasladh fo eachaibh, *young men mangled beneath horses.—Macfar.*

Riaslaich, *v. a.* Tear.

Riaslaiche, **Riaslair**, *s. m.* A tearer or mangler.

Riason, oin, *s. m.* (*Arm.* resoun. *Fr.* raison.) A reason, a cause, a motive, a ground, a principle; an argument. Written also *reuson.*

Riasonach, *a.* Fond of argument; reasonable.

Riasonachadh, aidh, *s. m.* Reasoning, arguing.

Riasonta, *a.* Reasonable, rational. Written also *reusonta.*

Riasontachd, *s. f.* Reasonableness, rationalness.

Riastadh, aidh, *s. m.* (*Ir. id.*) A welt.

Riastar, air, *s. m.* An insult; a drawing; a hauling.

Riastran, ain, *s. m.* An outrage; an insult. *N. pl.* riastrain.

Riastranach, *a.* Insulting; outraging; outrageous.

Riastranachd, *s. f.* Outrageousness; outrages.

Riatach, *a.* Illegitimate; foreign. *Com.* and *sup.* riataiche.

Riatachas, ais, *s. m.* Illegitimacy; outlandishness; the state of being foreign.

Riatachd, *s. f.* Illegitimateness; outlandishness.

Rib, *v. a.* Entangle; ensnare; separate the seed from flax. *Fut. aff. a.* ribidh; *fut. pass.* ribear; *p. part.* ribte, *entangled.*

Ribe, *s. f.* A snare, a gin; an ambuscade; entanglement; impediment; hair. Air ribe imichidh e, *he shall walk on a snare.—Stew. Job. N. pl.* ribeacha—(*Stew. Pro.*) *and* ribeachan. Ribeachan nan cuinneana, *the hairs of the nostrils.*

Ribeach, *a.* (*Ir. id.*) Ensnaring; entangling; full of snares; rough; hairy. Reithe ribeach, *a rough ram.—Stew. Dan.*

Ribeachail, *a.* Having a tendency to ensnare or to entangle.

Ribeachan, ain, *s. m.* A denticulated piece of wood used for separating flax from the seed.

Ribeachan, *n. pl.* of ribe; which see.

Ribeachas, ais, *s. m.* Ensnaring; the state of being ensnared.

Ribeachd, *s. f.* Ensnaring; the habit of ensnaring; a disposition to ensnare; entanglement.

Ribeadh, idh, *s. m.* An ensnaring; an entangling; the process of separating its seed from flax, by pulling it in handfuls through a denticulated piece of wood.

Ribeadh, *pret. pass.* of rib. Was ensnared. Also, 3 *sing.* and *pl. imper.* of rib.

Ribeag, eig, *s. f.* (*Ir. id.*) A hair; a whisker; a handful of flax; a dossil or pledget of lint; a rag; a tassel; a fringe. *N. pl.* ribeagan.

Ribeagach, *a.* Ragged; fringed; in dossils or pledgets; tasselled.

Ribear, *fut. pass.* of rib. Shall be entangled.

Ribear, eir, *s. m.* An ensnarer; a sharper. *N. pl.* ribeirean.

Ribh, *comp. pron.* To you; with you; against you. Cuirear so ribh, *this shall be added to you.—Stew. Matt.* Thig e ribh, *he* or *it will please you;* cha tig dad ribh, *no harm will happen to you.*

Ribheid, *s. f.* (*Ir. id. Germ.* ried.) A reed; a musical reed; the reed of a bagpipe, or of any wind-instrument; a pipe; a chanter; an oaten pipe. *N. pl.* ribheidean.

Ribheideach, *a.* (*Ir. id.*) Reedy; musical, canorous; fistulous.

Ribheideachd, *s. f.* Canorousness, melody.

Ribhinn, *s. f.* (*perhaps* righ-bhean.) A handsome young female; a maid. Ribhinn a b' àluinne snuadh, *a female of the fairest form.—Old Legend.* A ribhinn ùr! *thou blooming maid!—Old Poem.*

Ribleach, ich, *s. m.* (*Ir. id.*) Entanglement; any thing much entangled; knottiness; a long line or string.

Ribte, *p. part.* of rib.

Ricus, *s.* One of the names of the fifteenth letter (R) of the Gaelic alphabet.

Rideal, eil, *s. m.* (*Ir. id. Sax.* hriddle.) A riddle or coarse sieve; a sieve. Cho tollach ri rideal, *holed, as a riddle.—Macdon.*

Rideal, *v. a.* Riddle; winnow. *Pret. id.; fut. aff.* ridealaidh, *shall riddle.*

Ridealach, *a.* (*Ir. id.*) Like a riddle or sieve.

Ridealadh, aidh, *s. m.* (*Ir. id.*) A riddling or sifting of corn.

Ridealaich, *v. a.* Riddle; winnow; sift. *Pret. id.; fut. aff. a.* ridealaichidh, *shall riddle* or *winnow.*

Ridealaichte, *p. part.* of ridealaich. Riddled; winnowed; sifted.

Ridealair, *s. m.* (rideal-fhear.) A winnower; a sifter.

Ridir, *s. m.* (*Dan.* ridder. *W.* rhadyr. *Ir.* ridir. *Germ.* ritter: *hence also* rider: so eques *is a horseman or knight.*) A knight. Ridir beo-shlainte, *a Knight-bachelor.—Macd.* Ridir-oighreachd, *a Knight-baronet.—Macd.* Righdir spleadhach, *a Knight-errant.* Ridir a Chluarain, *a Knight of the Thistle,* (a British order). Ridir Phadruig an Naoimh, *a Knight of St. Patrick,* (a British order). Ridir a Ghartain, *a Knight of the Garter,* (a British order). Ridir a Chrainn Mhòir, *a Knight of the Grand Cross,* (a British order). Ridir feadhnach, *a Knight-commander* (of the Bath). Ridir co'lainneach, *a Knight-companion* (of the Bath). Ridir Dheorsa an Naoimh, *a Knight of St. George,* (a Russian order). Ridir Uilleim, *a Knight of King William,* (a Flemish order). Ridir Anna na Ban-naoimh, *a Knight of St. Ann,* (a Russian order). Ridir Aindreis an Naoimh, *a Knight of St. Andrew,* (a Russian order). Ridir na Geallaich ùir, *a Knight of the Crescent,* (a Turkish order). Ridir na Reannaig Tuathaiche, *a Knight of the North Star,* (a Swedish order). Ridir na h-Iolair Ruaidhe, *a Knight of the Red Eagle,* (a Prussian order). Ridir na h-Iolair Gile, *a Knight of the White Eagle,* (a Polish order). Ridir na h-Iolair Duibhe, *a Knight of the Black Eagle,* (a Russian order). Ridir an Leomhainn 's na Grèine, *a Knight of the Sun and Lion,* (a Persian order). Ridir na Lomairt Oir, *a Knight of the Golden Fleece,* (a Spanish order). Ridir a Chlaidheimh 's an Dùin, *a Knight of the Tower and Sword,* (a Portuguese order). Ridir Iolair nam beann, *a Knight* *of the Mountain-eagle*, an order of knighthood, which the Chevalier de St. George meant to have instituted, and to have conferred on all his adherents in Scotland, in the event of his being restored to the throne of his fathers.

Ridireach, *a.* Knightly; of, or belonging to, a knight; chivalrous.

Ridireachd, *s. f.* Knightliness; knighthood; chivalry.

Ridireil, *a.* (ridir-amhuil.) Knightly.

Rìfeid, *s. f.* A reed; the reed of any wind instrument. A rìfeid chiùil na bheul, *his musical reed in his mouth.*—*Macdon.* Written also *ribheid.*

Rìfeideach, *a.* Abounding in reeds; of reeds; fistulous.

† **Rig**, *s.* (*Ir. id.*) A spy.—*Shaw.*

Rig, *v.* More frequently *ruig;* which see.

Rigear, *fut. pass.* of rig.

Righ, *s. m.* A king. Righ nan uamhann, *the king of terrors.*—*Stew. Job.* It is also used as an exclamation in the sense of Lord; as, O Righ! *O Lord!* A Righ gleidh sinn! *Lord preserve us!* *N. pl.* rìghre *and* rìghrean.

Ir. righ. *W.* rhuy. *Arm.* roue *and* rhy. *Corn.* +ruy. *Fr.* roi. *It.* re. *Sp.* rey. *Lat.* rex. *Goth.* reiks. *Teut.* riech. *Germ.* reich. *Swed.* reck, (*according to Rudbeck*). *Lith.* ricke, *a lord.* *Alb.* reg. *Arab. Turk.* reys *and* rays, *prince.* *Heb. Ethiop.* rec, *a king.* *Raja* means *king* in the Shanscrit, and also in Sumatra, Malabar, and Ceylon. *Rae*, it is said, meant *king* among the ancient Babylonians; *eree* in Otaheite; and *rhio*, in the Sandwich Islands.

Rhea, which among the Greeks and Latins probably signified a lady, seems to have been derived from the old Celtic *ri* or *rhy.*

Righbhinn, *s. f.* A handsome young female—(*Macint.*); a lady of rank. *Perhaps* righ-bhean, *a queen.* Written also *ribhinn.*

Righbhinneach, *a.* Elegant; handsome, as a young female; ladylike.

Righ-chathair, chathrach, *s. f.* A throne; a metropolis, (being supposed to be the residence of a king). *N. pl.* righ-chathraichean.

Righ-chiste, *s. f.* A royal treasury. *N. pl.* righ-chistean.

Righ-cholbh, *s. m.* (*Ir. id.*) A sceptre.

Righ-choron, oin, *s. m.* (*Ir. id.*) A royal crown.

Righ-chrùn, ùin, *s. m.* A royal crown. *N. pl.* righ-chruintean.

Righ-dhail, *s. f.* (*Ir. id.*) A parliament; a congress of sovereigns.

Righ-damhna, *s. m.* A king designed; an heir-apparent to a kingdom.

Righdir, *s. m.* See **Ridir.**

Righe, *s. f.* A reproof; an arm: for the latter sense, see **Ruighe.**

Righeach, *s. f.* (*Ir.* rightheach.) An arm.

Righeachd, *s. f.* More frequently written *ruigheachd.*

Righeal-cuil, *s. m.* (*Ir. id.*) Stinking cranes-bill, *geranium robertianum.*

Righ-fheadhnach, aich, *s. m.* A generalissimo.

Righidir, *s. m.* See **Ridir.**

Righinn, *a.* (*Ir.* righin.) Tough; adhesive; clammy; viscid; stiff; lasting; drowsy; sluggish; dilatory. Chaidh sleaghan righinn a bhearnadh, *tough spears were hacked.*—*Death of Carril.* *Com.* and *sup.* righne.

Righ-lann, lainn, *s. m.* (*Ir. id.*) A palace, a royal court, a royal residence.

Righ-laoch, laoich, *s. m.* (*Ir. id.*) A prince; a good fellow; a respectable man.

Righ-mhortadh, aidh, *s. m.* Regicide.

Righ-mortair, *s. m.* A regicide. *N. pl.* righ-mhortairean.

Righ-nathair, -nathrach, *s. f.* (*Ir. id.*) A cockatrice; a serpent.—*Stew. Pro.* *N. pl.* righ-nathraichean.

Righne, *com.* and *sup.* of righinn. More or most tough.

Righneachadh, aidh, *s. m.* (*from* righinn.) A growing tough or clammy; a making tough or clammy.

Righneachas, ais, *s. m.* Tenacity; stiffness; toughness; delay.

Righneachd, *s. f.* Toughness; clamminess; viscidity; stiffness; drowsiness; sluggishness; *also*, a gift; a favour.—*Shaw.*

Righneas, eis, *s. m.* Tenacity; toughness.

Righnich, *v. a.* and *n.* (*Ir. id.*) Toughen; grow or make clammy or viscid; grow stiff; make stiff; delay. *Pret. a.* righnich, *toughened; fut. aff. a.* righnichidh.

Righnichte, *p. part.* of righnich. Toughened; stiffened; grown clammy or viscid.

Righ-phubull, uill, *s. m.* A royal pavilion; a tabernacle.

Rìghre, Rìghrean, *n. pl.* of righ. Kings. Righre o'd leasraidh, *kings from thy lions.*—*Stew. Gen.* Righrean na talmhainn, *the kings of the earth.*—*Sm.*

Righ-seisg, *s.* (*Ir. id.*) Greater burr-reed; *sparganium erectum.*

Righ-shlat, shlait, *s. m.* A sceptre. *N. pl.* righ-shlatan.

Righ-theachdair, *s. m.* (*Ir. id.*) An envoy; a royal embassy; an ambassador.

Rill, *v. a.* Sift or riddle; winnow. *Pret.* rill; *fut. aff. a.* rillidh.

Rilleadh, idh, *s. m.* A sifting; a riddling; a winnowing.

Rillean, ein, *s. m.* (*Ir. id.*) A riddle or coarse sieve.

† **Rimh**, *s.* (*Ir. id.*) Number.

† **Rimh**, *v. a.* (*Ir. id.*) Number, compute. *Pret.* rimh.—*Shaw.*

Rìmheach, *a.* (*perhaps* righ-mheach.) Gorgeous. More commonly written *riomhach;* which see.

Rimheadh, idh, *s. m.* (*Ir. id.*) Gorgeousness; pride. See **Riomhadh.**

Rìmhinn, *s. f.* A handsome young female; a lady. Written also *ribhinn.*

Rìmhinneach, *a.* Elegant; handsome, as a young female; ladylike.

Rinc, Ring, *v. a.* and *n.* (*Ir. id.*) Tear; pull; dance.

Rinceach, Ringeach, *a.* Tearing; pulling; parting; dancing.

Ringeadh, idh, *s. m.* (*Ir. id.*) A tearing; a dancing; a dance; hanging.—*Shaw.*

Ringeall, ill, *s. m.* (*Ir. id.*) A promise.

Ringear, eir, *s. m.* A dancer.

Ringheimhlean, *s. pl.* Chains.

† **Rinn**, *s. f.* (*Ir. id.*) Music; a foot; the stars.—*Shaw.* A headland; a tail.

Rinn, *s. f.* The point of a weapon. More frequently written *roinn.*

Rinn, *pret. a.* of dean. Did make; performed; accomplished. Is olc a rinn thu, *thou hast done ill.*—*Old Song.*

† **Rinne**, *s. f.* (*Ir. id.*) The understanding.—*Shaw.*

Rinne, *comp. pron.* To us; against us. Written also *ruinn;* which see.

Rinneach, *a.* (*Ir. id.*) Sharp, pointed.

Rinneadair, *s. m.* A carper; a spyfault.

Rinneadh, *pret. pass.* of dean. Was made or done. See **Dean.**

Rinneamh, eimh, *s. m.* The constellations.

Riob, *v. a.* Entrap, ensnare; entangle; inveigle. *Pret. a.* riob; *fut. aff. a.* riobaidh. Written also *rib.*

RIOB, *s m.* A snare, a trap; entanglement. *N. pl.* riobachan.

RIOBACH, *a.* Ensnaring; entangling; inveigling.

RIOBACHAN, ain, *s m* See RIBEACHAN.

RIOBADH, aidh, *s. m* (*Ir. id*) An ensnaring; an entangling; a snare; entanglement

RIOBAG, aig, *s. f* (*Ir. id.*) A patch, a clout; a rag; a ragged young female. *N. pl.* riobagan

RIOBAGACH, *a* Patched; clouted, ragged; tawdry *Com.* and *sup.* riobagaiche.

RIOBAID, *s. m* (*Ir.* roboid) A spendthrift. *N. pl.* riobaidean

RIOBAIDEACH, *a.* (*Ir* roboideach) Extravagant, prodigal —*Shaw.*

RIOBAIDEACHD, *s f* (*Ir* roboideachd) Extravagance

RIOBAIN, *s m* A riband, a sash or broad riband worn by females —*Stew Num ref*

RIOBHAID, *s f* A reed, the reed of a musical instrument; an oaten pipe Riobhaid chiùil, *a musical reed.—Macint* Written also *ribheid.*

RIOBHAIDEACH, *a* Reedy; canorous; musical; fistulous

† RIOBHAR, air, *s. m.* (*Ir id*) A sieve; a honeycomb —*Shaw* *N pl.* riobharan.

† RIOBHLACH, aich, *s m* (*Ir. id*) A rival *N. pl* riobhlaich —*Shaw.*

RIOBLACH, aich, *s. m.* A long line or string, an entangled string; entanglement, as of a string Tha 'n cord na rioblach, *the rope is quite entangled*

RIOBLACH, *a* Entangled, ragged; torn

RIOBLACHADH, aidh, *s. m* An entangling, an entanglement

RIOBLACHD, *s f* Entanglement, any thing much entangled.

RIOBLAICH, *v a* and *n* Entangle; involve; become entangled, as a rope. *Pret. a* rioblaich; *fut. aff. a.* rioblaichidh

RIOBTA, RIOBTE, *part.* of riob Entangled, ensnared, involved

RIOBTACH, *a.* Entangling; ensnaring, involving, apt to entangle or ensnare

† RIOCHOS, *s m* A king; rule.—*Fingalian Poem.*

RIOCHD, *s m* (*Ir id*) Shape; likeness, appearance, proportion; *as a preposition,* instead of. An riochd mairbh, *in the likeness of a dead man.—Ull.* A reir riochd gach aon diubh, *according to the proportion of each* —*Stew* 1 *K*

RIOCHDAICH, *v a* Represent, personate *Pret a id*, *fut aff* riochdaichidh, *p. part.* riochdaichte, *personated.*

RIOCHD-FHOCAL, ail, *s. m.* A pronoun *N pl.* riochdfhocail.

RIOCHDMHOR, *a.* Shapely, proportioned *Com* and *sup.* riochdmhoire

† RIODH, *s m* (*Ir id.* *Lat* radius) A ray or beam of light —*Shaw.*

RIOF, *s m* A reef. Riof a chur anns gach seòl, *to reef every sail —Old Song*

RIOGH, *s m* A king More frequently written *righ*

RIOGHACHADH, aidh, *s. m.* A reigning, a governing; governance; reign —*Stew. Chron.*

RIOGHACHADH, (a), *p part* of rioghaich

RIOGHACHD, *s. f.* (*Ir. id.* *Goth.* reiki. *Sclav* rieck) A kingdom, a dominion, a realm, an empire; government Is farsuing do rioghachd 's gur fial, *extensive is thy dominion, and hospitable* —*Mac Lach*

RIOGHAICH, *v a* Reign; rule or govern, as a king *Pret a.* rioghaich; *fut aff. a.* rioghaichidh. Rioghaich e dà bhliadhna deug, *he reigned twelve years.—Stew* 2 *K.* Rioghaichidh righrean, *kings shall reign.—Stew. Pro.*

RIOGHAIL, *a.* (riogh-amhail) Royal, kingly, regal, princely; loyal. Òg bu rioghail dreach, *a youth of a kingly appearance.—Mac Lach.* Lios rioghail, *a royal court; Arm.* les roeyal. Tigh rioghail, *a palace; Arm.* ty roeyal.

Lat. regal-is *Eng.* royal. *Fr.* royale. *Arm.* real and roeyal *Corn.* ryal.

RIOGHALACHD, *s. f.* Royalty, regality, majesty; regal pomp; princeliness.

RIOGHAN, ain, *s. f.* (*for* righ-bhean) A queen.—*Shaw.*

RIGH-BHUTH, *s. m.* A royal residence, a royal pavilion.

RIOGHLACH, aich, *s f.* (*Ir id*) An old hag.

RIOGH-LANN, lainn, *s m.* A palace, a royal residence. Written also *righ-lann*

RIOGH-LAOCH, laoich, *s. m* A prince; a good fellow; a respectable old man —*Shaw.*

RIOGH-NATHAIR, nathrach, *s. f* A cockatrice; a serpent. *N pl* riogh-nathraichean

RIOGH-PHUBULL, uill, *s. m.* A royal pavilion or tent. Written also *righ-phubull.*

RIOMH, *adv.* Ever; always; at any time. It is said of past time only Riomh o thoiseach an t-saoghail, *ever since the beginning of time*, an robh thu riomh san Roimh? *were you ever in Rome?* riomh roimh, *ever before*, na h-uile duine riomh agaibh, *every man of you.*

† RIOMH, *s m* (*Ir id*) A reckoning, a numbering, a computation

† RIOMH, *v a* (*Ir id.*) Number, compute. *Pret. id.*, *fut aff. a.* riomhaidh.

RIOMHACH, *a* (*perhaps* rioghmhach.) Regal; gorgeous, superb; precious, valuable; conceited. Do chulaidhean riomhach, *of superb apparel —Stew. Ezek.* *Com.* and *sup.* riomhaiche.

RIOMHACHAS, ais, *s. m.* Regality; gorgeousness, superbness; preciousness, valuableness.

RIOMHADH, aidh, *s m* Finery, gorgeousness, superbness; fondness; enumeration.

RIOMHAIR, *s m* (riomh-fhear) A computer, a reckoner, an arithmetician *N pl* riomhairean.

RIOMHAIREACHD, *s. f.* (*Ir. id*) Calculation, arithmetic.

† RION, *s. m.* (*Ir id*) A way, a road, a track.—*Shaw.*

RIONACHAS, ais, *s. m* Engraving; sculpture.

† RIONADAIR, *s m* (*Ir. id.*) A steward; a ruler, a director —*Shaw*

RIONAICH, *v. a* (*Ir* rionaigh.) Carve, engrave. *Pret. id.*

RIONAICHE, *s m.* A carver, an engraver. *N pl* rionaichean.

RIONAIDHEAS, eis, *s. m.* (*Ir id*) Sculpture, graving.

RIONAL, ail, *s m.* Carving, sculpture

RIONLUAS, ais, *s m* (*Ir. id*) Career

RIONNACH, aich, *s. m.* (*Ir.* rionghach.) A mackarel; a strong, robust man

RIONNACHAS, ais, *s m.* Graving; graven-work.

RIONNADH, aidh, *s m* (*Ir. id.*) Redness.—*Shaw.*

RIONNAG, aig, *s. f* (*Ir id*) A star, a starlet. Airde nan rionnag, *the height of the stars.—Stew. Job* More properly *reannag*, which see.

RIONNAGACH, *a* Starry; spangled; studded; like a star.

RIONNAIDH, RIONTAIDH, *s m* A satirist.

RIONNAL, ail, *s. m* Graving, graven-work.

RIOSTAL, ail, *s m.* A kind of plough used in the Hebrides, especially in Lewis, having a coulter formed like a sickle. It is sometimes drawn by one horse, and sometimes by two, according to the toughness of the soil. Its principal use is to draw a furrow before the large plough, which, without this expedient, would be retarded in its progress by stones, clods, and other obstacles.

RÌREADH, A RÌREADH, DA RÌREADH, DO RÌREADH, *adv.* Really; actually; indeed; seriously; verily; of a truth; certainly. A tha nam bantraichean da rìreadh, *who are widows indeed.—Stew. Tim.* Bheil thu rìreadh? *are you in earnest?* 'n ann rìreadh! *indeed! really!* Tha e cheart rìreadh, *he is in real earnest.*

RIS, *prep.* (*Ir. id.*) To; unto; at; beside; during; against; towards; exposed; bare, uncovered; meddling with. Cuir ris an àireamh, *add to the number;* ris an olc, *at mischief;* cuir teine ris an tigh, *set fire to the house;* ris an leathad, *down-hill;* ris a bhruthach, *up-hill;* tha do chraicionn ris, *thy skin is exposed;* leig ris, *disclose, divulge, confess;* ris an aimsir so, *during this weather;* na bi ris an each, *do not meddle with the horse;* laimh ris an tigh, *near the house.*

RIS, *comp. pron.* (*Ir. id.*) To him or it; with him or it; against him or it. Ciod do ghnothach ris? *what is your business with him? why do you meddle with him* or *it?* Cuir ris, *add to it, apply to it, ply your work;* feuch ris, *try him* or *it;* na bi ris, *do not molest him* or *it;* cha tig e ris, *it will not please him.*

RIS, A RIS, *adv.* Again; a second time; another time. Thig mi a ris, *I will come again.—Stew. N. T.* N' ann a ris? *again?* an tràs is a ris, *now and then.*

† RIS, *s. m.* (*Ir. id.*) A king; history; knowledge.—*Shaw.*

† RISEACH, ich, *s. m.* (*Ir. id.*) A romance; a story-teller. *N. pl.* risich.

RISEAN, ein, *s. m.* (*Ir. id.*) An historian.

RISGEANACH, aich, *s. m.* (*Ir. id.*) A brave soldier.—*Shaw.*

RIS-SAN, *emphatic form* of ris, *comp. pron.* See RIS.

RIST, *adv.* See RITHIST.

RISTEAL, eil, *s. m.* A kind of plough used in the Western Isles. See RIOSTAL.

† RITH, *s. f.* A course; a flight. See RUITH.

† RITHEADH, idh, *s. m.* (*Ir. id.*) A grove.

RITHINN, *a.* Tough; viscid; made of good stuff; durable. *Com.* and *sup.* rithne. See RIGHINN.

RITHIST, RITHISTICH, *adv.* Again; another time. A choigrich guil rithist, *stranger, weep again.—Oss. Gaul.* Thoir gaol do d' bhean rithistich, *love thy wife again.—Old Poem.* An tràs is a rithist, *now and then.*

RITH-LEARG, leirg, *s. m.* Extemporaneous rhyme.—*Shaw.*

RITHNEAS. See RIGHNEAS.

RITHNICH, *v. a.* and *n.* Make tough; grow ropy or viscous.

RIU, *comp. pron.* (*Ir. id.*) To them; against them; towards them; with them. Cuir riu, *add to them, ply them;* na bi riu, *do not molest them, do not meddle with them;* thig e riu, *he* or *it will please them;* cha tig dad riu, *no harm will befall them.*

† RIUBH, *s. m.* (*Ir. id.*) Sulphur.—*Macd.*

RIUM, *comp. pron.* (*Ir.* riom.) To me; towards me; with me. Na bi rium, *do not molest me, do not meddle with me;* thig e rium, *he* or *it will please me;* cha tig dad rium, *no harm will befall me;* rium riut, *a false person;* maille rium, *together with me.*

RIUM-SA, *emphatic form* of rium; which see.

RIUSAN, *emphatic form* of riu; which see.

RIUT, *comp. pron.* To thee; towards thee; with thee. Maille riut, *with thee;* co 'bha riut? *who was meddling with thee?* thig e riut, *he* or *it will please thee;* cha tig dad riut, *nothing will harm you;* thachair e riut, *he settled you, he gave you a proper dressing;* fear rium riut, *a false, double-dealing person.*

RIUTHA, *for* riu; which see.

RIUTSA, *emphatic form* of riut; which see.

RO', (*for* roimh), *prep.* and *adv.* Before; first.

RO', (*for* troimh.) Through. Ghluais geur na cruaidhe ro' cheann, *the weapon's edge passed through his head.—Oss. Tem.*

RO, *adv.* (*Ir. id.*) Very; much; too much; exceeding. When this adverb precedes an adjective, it communicates to it the same degree of comparison which *very* does to a noun in English; and, moreover, it throws it into the aspirated form, except it begins with *l, n,* or *r;* as, buan, *lasting;* ro bhuan, *very lasting;* cairdeil, *friendly;* ro chàirdeil, *very friendly;* daor, *dear;* ro dhaor, *very dear;* fearail, *manly;* ro fhearail, *very manly;* geur, *sharp;* ro gheur, *very sharp;* mall, *slow;* ro mhall, *very slow;* prìseil, *precious;* ro phrìseil, *very precious;* searbh, *bitter;* ro shearbh, *very bitter;* taitneach, *pleasant;* ro thaitneach, *very pleasant.* When the letter *s*, in the beginning of an adjective, is immediately followed by any consonant, except *l, r, n,* there is no aspiration. Thus we say, *ro sbairneil, ro sceilmeil, ro sgairteil, ro smiorail, ro spòrsail, ro stuama;* but we never say, *ro sleamhuinn, ro snitheach, ro sradach,* instead of *ro shleamhuinn, ro shnitheach, ro shradach. L* or *n*, at the beginning of adjectives which are preceded by *ro*, are pronounced much the same as in English; but when they are preceded by *s*, they have a sound to which there is none similar in the English or Scottish languages. Almost in every case where we wish to express a superlative degree, *ro* may be used, observing the directions just given.

RO-AIRE, *s. f.* Great care; great diligence. A toirt an ro-aire, *taking great care, looking diligently.—Stew. Heb.* Thoir an ro-aire air, *take great care of him* or *it.*

RO-AOIBHNEAS, eis, *s. m.* Great joy or gladness.

RÒB, ròib, *s. m.* A robe; shagginess. Ròb-bhrat, *a shaggy mantle.—Macfar.*

RÒBACH, *a.* Rough, shaggy. *Com.* and *sup.* ròbaiche.

ROBAIL, *s. f.* Robbery.

ROBAINN, *v. a.* Rob. *Pret. id.; fut. aff. a.* robainnidh.

ROBAINN, *s. f.* (*Ir.* robuin. *Germ.* rauben, *to pillage. Du.* rooven.) A robbery; plundering; *also,* a sale by auction; a roup. Robainn eaglais, *sacrilege.*

ROBAIR, *s. m.* (*Germ.* rauber. *Ir.* roboir. *Dan.* roffuer.) A robber. *N. pl.* robairean.

ROBAIREACHD, *s. f.* Robbery.

ROBH, *pret.* of bi. Was.

ROBH, robha, *s. m.* A roll of bread. *N. pl.* robhachan.

ROBHADH, aidh, *s. m.* (*Ir. id.*) A threat, a warning.

RO-BHAIGH, *s. m.* Great mercy.

ROBHAINN, *v. a.* Roll; roll together; wallow.

ROBHAIR, *s. m.* A roller.

† ROBHAR, *a.* (*Ir. id.*) Red.

† ROBHAR, air, *s. m.* (*Ir. id.*) A sieve.—*Shaw.*

RO-BHÀS, àis, *s. m.* (*Ir. id.*) A violent death.

RO-BHEUS, *s. m.* Good-breeding.

ROBUIST, *s. f.* (*Ir. id.*) Custody.

ROC, *s. m.* The tops of sea-weeds which appear above water.—*Shaw.*

RÒC, roic, *s. m.* (*W.* rhoç.) A hoarse sound; a hoarse or rough voice.

ROC, roic, *s. m.* A curl; a wrinkle; a fold; a plait. *N. pl.* rocan. Roc-eudainneach, *having a wrinkled face.—Mac Co.*

ROC, roic, *s. m.* A rock. *N. pl.* rocan.

Gr. ῥὼξ *and* ῥαχια, *a rock. Heb.* rach-as. *Chald.* racas. *Arab.* rek *and* rakahh. *Syr.* ragam. *Span.* roca. *It.* rocia. *Du.* rach. *Bisc.* rocha. *Arm.* roch. *Ir.* roc. *Fr.* roche *and* roc. In Languedoc they say *ro;* in Auvergne, *roh* and *ro;* in Dauphiny and Provence, *rocha;* in Franche-Comté, *roueche.*

ROCACH, *a., from* roc. (*Ir. id.*) Rocky; curly; wrinkled; plaited; dishevelled, as hair.

RÒCACH, *a.* Hoarse; having a rough voice.

RÒCAIR, *s. m.* A man with a hoarse voice.

ROCAIR, *s. m.* A customer; a common guest.

RÒCAIREACHD, *s. f.* Hoarseness of voice.

RÒCAIS, *n. pl.* of ròcas. Crows.

ROCAN, ain, *s. m.* (*Ir. id.*) A hut, a cottage; a plait; a little fold; a little wrinkle; a hood; a mantle; a surtout; a stumbling-block; a fray.

RÒCAN, ain, *s. m.* A hoarseness, a hoarse voice; a person with a hoarse or rough voice.

ROCANACH, *a.* (*Ir. id.*) Like a cot or hut; of a cot; mantled; hooded; plaited; folded; wrinkled.

RÒCANACH, *a.* Hoarse; having a hoarse voice; having a rough voice. *Com.* and *sup.* ròcanaiche.

RÒCANACHD, *s. f.* Hoarseness; a continued hoarse sound.

RÒCAS, ais. See RÒCUS.

ROC-EUDANN, ain, *s. m.* A wrinkled face.

ROC-EUDAINNEACH, *a.* Having a wrinkled visage.—*Mac Co.*

† ROCHALL, aill, *s. m.* (*Ir. id.*) A stumbling-block; a fray.

† ROCHAR, air, *s. m.* (*Ir. id.*) A killing, a slaughtering; slaughter.—*Shaw.*

ROCHDAIR, *s. m.* (*Ir.* rochtaire.) A customer; a visiter; one who haunts or often visits a place. Perhaps *ro-theachdair.*

† ROCHDAN, ain, *s. m.* (*Ir. id.*) A thicket.—*Shaw.*

ROCHDUIN, *s. f.* An ascent; arriving at; reaching.

RO'CHEILE, *adv.* (*for* troimh-cheile.) Confused; *also, for* roimh chéile, *done in a hurry.*

RO-CHRANN, ainn, *s. m.* A tall tree, a very tall tree. *N. pl.* ro-chrannan, ro-chroinn.

ROCHUAID, *s. f.* A lamprey.—*Shaw.* *N. pl.* rochuaidean.

ROCHUAIDEACH, *a.* Full of lampreys; like a lamprey; of lampreys.

ROCHUILLEACH, *a.* (*Ir. id.*) Terrible; very dangerous.—*Shaw.*

RO-CHÙRAM, aim, *s. m.* Great care; great anxiety or solicitude; vigilance.

RÒCUS, uis, *s. m.* A crow, a rook; the *corvus frugilegus* of Linnæus.

ROD, *s. m.* (*Ir. id.*) Sea-weed; a cast; a shot.

ROD, roid, *s. m.* A road, a way, a path, a track; a method. *N. pl.* reidean *and* ròdan; *d. pl.* roidibh *and* rodaibh. Rod mòr, *a high way;* rod mòr an righ, *the king's highway, the great military road;* rod réidh, *a plain road;* rod cartach, *a cart-road;* ré an roid, *all the way, the whole way;* taobh an roid, *the road-side.* Written also *rad* and *rathad;* which see.

Syr. rohot, *a course.* *Fr.* route, *a road.* *Arm.* rout. *Ir.* rod. *W. rhyd.*

RODACHD, *s. f.* A covering; a fence.

RODAIDH, *a.* Rotten; shrunken; having a rotten smell.

RODAIL, *a.* (*Ir. id.*) Prosperous; lancing; scarifying.—*Shaw.*

RODAIR, *s. m.* (rod-fhear.) A wayfaring man.

RODH, rodha, *s. m.* (*Ir. id.*) Water-edge; water-mark.—*Shaw.*

RO-DHOINIONN, inn, *s. m.* A tempest, a severe tempest.

RO-DHÙIL, *s. f.* (*Ir. id.*) Earnest hope; earnest expectation; jealousy. A réir mo ro-dhùil, *according to my earnest expectation.*—*Stew. Phil.*

RO-DHUINE, *s. m.* (*Ir. id.*) An excellent man; a nobleman; *also,* a commoner; a rogue.—*Shaw.* *N. pl.* ro-dhaoine.

RO-DHÙRACHD, *s. f.* (*Ir.* ro-dhuthrachd.) Great diligence; great care; much inclination.

† RODMUIN, *s. m.* (*Ir. id.*) A fox.—*Shaw.*

RO-EARAIL, *s. f.* Importunacy; earnest desire. Rinn e ro-earail, *he urged.*—*Stew. Gen.*

RO-EARBSA, *s. m.* Implicit trust, implicit confidence. Ro-earbsa, *implicit confidence in you.*—*Stew.* 2 *Cor.*

RO-EÒLAS, ais, *s. m.* Familiarity; intimacy; intimate knowledge or acquaintance.

RO-FHONN, *s. m.* (*Ir. id.*) An earnest longing, keen desire.

RO-FHUACHD, *s. m.* (*Ir. id.*) Severe cold. An ro-fhuachd a gheamhruidh, *in the severe cold of winter.*—*Old Song.*

ROGAINN, *v. a.* Pluck; tease; handle roughly.

ROGAINN, *s. f.* A rough handling. Fhuair e rogainn, *he got a rough handling.*

ROGAIR, *s. m.* A knave, a rogue. *N. pl.* rogairean.

ROGAIREACH, *a.* Roguish.

ROGAIREACHD, *s. f.* Knavery, roguery.

ROGH, *s. m.* (*Ir. id.*) An order; a custom; a wreath.—*Shaw.*

ROGH, *s. m.* Choice. See ROGHA.

ROGHA, ROGHADH, aidh, *s. m.* (*Ir. id.*) Choice; a selection; best part. Bu leatsa do rogha, *thine would be thy choice.*—*Oss. Fing.* Rogha do sheudar, *the best of thy cedar, thy choice cedar.*—*Stew. O. T.* Tharruing i sreang le rogha beachd, *she pulled the string with her best aim.*—*Ull.* Is tu rogha nam ban, *thou art the choicest of women.* Roghadh òigfhir, *a choice young man.*—*Stew. Sam.* Rogha is taghadh, *pick and choice.*

ROGHAINN, *s. f.* (*Ir.* roghain.) Choice; option; preference; a selection. Ma 's e do roghainn còmhrag, *if battle be thy choice.*—*Oss. Fing.* Is tu roghainn an t-sealgair, *thou art the best of hunters.*—*Macint.* Gabh do roghainn, *take thy choice;* roghainn mhac righ Eirin, *the choicest son of Eirin's king.*—*Fingalian Poem.* Gabh do roghainn, *take thy choice.*—*Stew.* 2 *Chr.*

ROGHAINNEACH, *a.* Eligible; optionable; preferable; optative; choosing; picking; selecting. *Com.* and *sup.* roghnaiche. Ma 's roghnaiche leat imeachd, *if thou preferest departing.*—*Fingalian Poem.*

ROGHLACH, aich, *s. m., perhaps* rogha-laoch. (*Ir. id.*) A choosing or selecting of soldiers; a body of picked soldiers.

† ROGHLACH, *a.* (*Ir. id.*) Angry, enraged.—*Shaw.*

† ROGHMHAL, ail, *s. m.* (*Ir. id.*) The election of a prince.—*Shaw.*

† ROGHMHAR, *a.* (*Ir. id.*) Valiant; very dangerous.

ROGHNACH. See ROGHAINNEACH.

ROGHNACHADH, aidh, *s. m.* (*Ir. id.*) A choosing; a selecting; a preferring; a selection; an election.

ROGHNAICH, *v. a.* Choose, pick out, select, prefer. *Pret. a. id.; fut. aff. a.* roghnaichidh, *shall choose.* Roghnaich dhuit féin, *choose for thyself.*—*Stew.* 2 *Sam.*

ROGHNAICHE, *com.* and *sup.* of roghainneach. More or most eligible; preferable. Is roghnaiche leam, *I would rather, I prefer.* Written also *roghnuiche.*

ROGHNAICHEAR, *fut. pass.* of roghnaich. Shall be chosen, picked out, or selected.

ROGHNAICHTE, *p. part.* of roghnaich. Chosen, selected, preferred. Written also *ròghnaichte.*

ROGHNUCHADH, aidh, *s. m.* See ROGHNACHADH.

ROGHNUICH, *v. a.* See ROGHNAICH.

ROGHNUICHE, *com.* and *sup.* of roghuinneach. More or most eligible, preferable. Is roghnuiche tuigse no airgiod, *understanding is preferable to* [*rather to be chosen than*] *silver.*—*Stew. Pro.*

ROGHNUICHTE, *p. part.* of roghnuich. Chosen, picked, selected, preferred.

ROGHUINN, *s. f.* See ROGHAINN.

Roghuinneach, *a.* See Roghainneach.

Roi', (*for* roimh), *prep.* Before; in front of; prior to; in preference to. Crithidh feachd roi' d' chruaidh, *hosts shall tremble before thy sword.—Oss Fing.*

Ròi', (*for* troimh), *prep.* Through. Roi' cham-chuislibh bhad chrann, *through the crooked veins of tufted trees—Macfar.*

Roi'ainmichte, *part.* (*for* roimh-ainmichte.) Forecited, already mentioned.

Roi-aithne, *s. f.* (*for* roimh-aithne.) Foreknowledge.

Roi'aithnich, *v.* (*for* roimh-aithnich.) Foreknow.

Roibean, ein, *s. m.* (*Ir.* roibin) A mustachio or whisker, a bushy beard; a small rope or cord, a mop.

Roibeanach, *a.* Having mustachios, whiskered, bushy, as a beard; ropy; moppy.

Roibeanachd, *s. f.* Bushiness, as of a beard, moppiness

Roibhe, *s. f.* (*Ir.* id) Sneezewort.

Roi'bheachd, *s f.* (*for* roimh-bheachd.) Foreknowledge, preconception, presentient.

Roi'bheachdach, *a.* (*for* roimh-bheachdach) Foreknowing, preconceiving, presentiment

Roi'bheachdail, *a* (*for* roimh-bheachdail.) Provident; cautious.

Roi'bhlas, ais, *s. m.* (*for* roimh-bhlas.) A foretaste, anticipation.

Roibne, *s. f.* A lance; a dart. *N pl.* roibnean.

Roibneach, *a.* Sharp, pointed; like a lance or dart; armed with a lance or dart.

Roi'bhriathar, air, *s m.* (*for* roimh-bhriathar) An adverb, a preface. *N pl* roimh-bhriathran

Roi'bhriathrach, *a* (*for* roimh-bhriathrach) Adverbial; prefatory.

Roic, *s. f.* (*W.* rhoç.) A roar, a bellow, a rift; a belching noise; the bellow of a deer More properly written *raoichd*

Roic, *v a* (*Ir.* id) Tear.

Ròice, *s. f.* Luxury; gluttony; a tearing; eating greedily; fondness for fat meat. Làn musaiche is ròice, *full of nastiness and gluttony.—Old Song.*

Ròiceach, *a.* (*from* ròice) Gluttonous, eating voraciously; fond of fat meats

Roiceach, *a* (*from* roic.) Bellowing, roaring; rifting, belching. An eas roiceach, *the roaring cascade.—Old Song*

Roiceil, *s. f* A roaring, a bellowing; a rifting, a belching

Roi'cheile, *adv.* Confused, higgledy-piggledy, done in a hurry; one before another, before each other.

Roi'chraicionn, inn, *s. m.* (*for* roimh-chraicionn) The foreskin. Written also *roi-chroicionn.*

Roichd, *s f.* See Raoichd.

† **Roid**, *s f.* (*Ir.* id.) A race; a force; momentum; a gale. —*Shaw.*

† **Roid**, *v. n* (*Ir.* id) Run fast. *Pret. a* roid, *fut. aff* roididh.

Heb. ratz. *Chald.* rahat, *to run.* *Germ* rad-en *Arab.* rats, *run.* *Syr.* reto, *walk.*

Roid, roide, *s m* (*Ir.* id.) Wormwood, gall.

Roid, *gen. sing.* of rod; which see

Roidean, ein, *s. m* Wildfire.

Roidhse, *s f.* A rinse. *N. pl* roidhsean *and* roidhseachan.

Roidhseach, *a.* Rinsing; scouring; acting as a rinse; like a rinse.

Roidhseachadh, aidh, *s m* A rinsing; a scouring, a scrubbing.

Roidhsich, *v. a.* Rinse; scour; scrub *Pret. a* roidhsich; *fut. aff. a.* roidhsichidh, *shall rinse*, *p part* roidhsichte, *rinsed.*

Roi'dhilinneach, *a* (*for* roimh-dhilinneach) Antediluvian

Roididh, *a.* Shrunken, rotten.

Roi'eolas, ais, *s. m.* (*for* roimh-eolas.) Foreknowledge, precognition.

Roighchd, *s* See Raoichd.

Roighne, *s f* Choice. See Roghainn

Roighneachadh, aidh, *s. m.* A choosing, a picking, or selecting; an election. Written also *roghnuchadh*; which see.

Roighnich, *v. a.* Choose. See Roghnaich.

Roighnichte, *p part* of roighnich. Chosen, selected, picked.

Roi'innis, *v* (*for* roimh-innis) Foretell, presage

Roi'innseadh, idh, *s m* (*for* roimh-innseadh) A foretelling, a prophesying, a presage

Ròil, *gen sing.* of ròl

Roi'lamh, *adv* (*for* roimh-laimh) Beforehand.

Roilbh, roilbhe, *s f* (*Ir* id) A mountain.

Roilbheach, *a.* (*Ir.* id) Hilly

Roileag, eig, *s. f.* A church; a burying-ground.

Roilean, ein, *s m* The snout of a sow.

Ròilean. See Ròithlean.

Roileanach, *a* (*from* roilean) Having a snout like that of a sow

Roille, *s. f* Darnel—*Shaw* *N. pl* roillean.

Roilleach, *a.* Abounding in darnels; like a darnel

Roimh, *s f.* The city of Rome

† **Roimh**, roimhe, *s f* (*Ir* id) Earth; soil; a family burying-ground.—*Shaw*

Roimh, *prep* (*Ir* id) Before, in front of, prior to; in preference to. Roimh sgrios theid uamhar, *before destruction goes pride—Stew Pro.* Roimh do ghnùis, *before thy face—Stew Matt* Roimh so, *before now, ere now, in time past*, co roimh? *before whom?* cuir roimh, *put before, prompt, dictate*, an làtha roimh, *the day before, the other day.*

Roimh-ainmichte, *part* Forecited, forementioned

Roimh-àithn, *v a.* Command previously, foreordain

Roimh-aithne, *s f* Foreknowledge, precognition

Roimh-àithne, *s f* A previous commandment, a former command or injunction.

Roimh-aithneachadh, aidh, *s. m.* A foreknowing, an anticipation; foreknowledge; anticipation

Roimh-aithnich, *v. a.* Foreknow, anticipate; foresee *Pret. a.* roimh-aithnich. An dream a roimh-aithnich e, *those whom he foreknew—Stew Rom* *Fut aff.* roimh-aithnichidh.

Roimh-aithnichte, *p part* of roimh-aithnich.

Roimh-bheachd, *s. f.* A presentiment, a preconception, foreknowledge; anticipation

Roimh-bheachdach, *a.* Preconceiving, foreknowing, anticipating.

Roimh-bheachdachadh, aidh, *s. m* A preconceiving, a foreknowing, precognition; foreknowledge, anticipation

Roimh-bheachdail, *a* Provident; cautious; foresightful, prescient

Roimh-bhlas, *s m.* A foretaste; anticipation

Roimh-bhriathar, air, *s. m* An adverb; a preamble, a preface.—*Shaw.*

Roimh-chéile, *adv.* Confused; in a hurry, hurriedly, higgledy-piggledy; one before the other, prematurely

ROIMH-CHEUM, *s. m.* Precedence; a generation before or past.

ROIMH-CHRAICIONN, inn, *s. m.* A foreskin. *N. pl.* roimh-chraicnean. Written also *roimh-chroicionn.*

ROIMH-CHROICIONN, inn, *s. m.* A foreskin. Feoil a roimh-chroicinn, *the flesh of his foreskin.—Stew. Lev.*

ROIMH-DHILINNEACH, *a.* Antediluvian; *also, substantively,* an antediluvian.

ROIMHE, *comp. pron.* Before him; in front of him; in preference to him. Dh'fhalbh e roimhe, *he went his way.—Stew. Gen.* Gabh roimhe, *oppose him* or *it, intercept him* or *it, stop his* or *its progress;* tha e 'cur roimhe, *he proposes;* cuir roimhe, *prompt him, dictate to him, put before him.*

ROIMHEACH, *a.* Roman; *also, substantively,* a Roman. *N. pl.* Roimhich.

ROIMH-EOLAS, ais, *s. m.* (*Ir. id.*) Foreknowledge, precognition, preconception, anticipation.

ROIMH-FHEUCHAINN, *s. m.* Foretaste; forecast.

ROIMH-GHEALL, *v. a.* (*Ir.* reamh-gheall.) Promise beforehand; pre-engage.

ROIMH-INNIS, *v. a.* Foretell, predict, tell beforehand. *Pret. a.* roimh-innis; *fut. aff.* roimh-innsidh.

ROIMH-INNSEADH, idh, *s. m.* A foretelling; divination; a telling beforehand.

ROIMH-LÀIMH, *adv.* Beforehand, before, afore, previously. A dh'ulluich e roimh-làimh, *whom he prepared afore.—Stew. Rom.*

ROIMH-LÒN, lòin, *s. m.* A viaticum.

ROIMH-MHEADHON-LA, *s. m.* The forenoon; *literally,* before the middle of the day.

ROIMH-ORDUCHADH, aidh, *s. m.* An ordering beforehand; a foreordaining. Air a roimh-orduchadh, *foreordained, ordered beforehand.*

ROIMH-ORDUICH, *v. a.* Order previously; order beforehand, foreordain, predestinate. *Pret. a.* roimh-orduich; *fut. aff. a.* roimh-orduichidh. Roimh-orduich e iad, *he foreordained them.—Stew. Rom.*

ROIMH-ORDUICHTE, *p. part.* of roimh-orduich. Foreordained, predestinated, ordered previously.

ROIMH-RADH, *s. m.* A preface, a preamble, a prologue.

ROIMH-RUITHEAR, eir, *s. m.* A forerunner.

ROIMH-RUITH-FHEAR, -fhir, *s. m.* A forerunner.—*Stew. Heb.*

ROIMH-SHEALL, *v. n.* Look forward; provide against.

ROIMH-SHEALLACH, *a.* Foresighted; provident; cautious; prospicient.

ROIMH-SHEALLADH, aidh, *s. m.* Foresight; caution; prospicience; a previous look or sight; a front view.

ROIMH-SHEALLTUINN, *s. f.* A looking before; a providing for; foresight; precaution.

ROIMH-SMUAINE, *s. f.* A forethought. *N. pl.* roimh-smuaintean.

ROIMH-SMUAINEACHADH, aidh, *s. m.* A thinking beforehand, forethought.

ROIMH-SMUAINTEACHAIL, *a.* Thinking beforehand; provident; cautious.

ROIMH-STALLAIR, *s. m.* A forestaller. *N. pl.* roimh-stallairean.

ROIMH-STALLAIREACHD. (*Ir. id.*) Forestalling.

ROIMH-THAGH, *v. a.* Forechoose; pre-elect; choose or select previously. *Pret.* roimh-thagh. *Fut. aff.* roimh-thaghaidh.

ROIMH-THAGHADH, aidh, *s. m.* A choosing beforehand; a pre-selection; a pre-election.

ROIMH-THAGHTA, *p. part.* Forechosen, pre-elected, chosen previously.

ROIMH-THEACHDAIR, *s. m.* A forerunner. *N. pl.* roimh-theachdairean.

ROIMPE, *comp. pron.* Before her; in front of her; in preference to her. Gabh roimpe, *go before her, stop her progress;* cuir roimpe, *prompt her, dictate to her.*

ROIMPE-SAN, *emphatic form* of roimpe.

ROIMSE, *s. f.* (*Ir. id.*) A pole; a stake. *N. pl.* roimsean.

ROIMSEACH, *a.* Like a pole or stake; of poles; inactive; *also, substantively,* an inactive person.

RÒIN, *gen. sing.* of ròn; which see.

RÒIN, *s. f.* The crest or the tail of any beast.

ROINN, *gen. sing.* of rann; which see.

ROINN, *s. f.* (*W.* rhan.) A share, part, or portion; a division; a sect; a class. Roinn da leth, *a bipartition. N. pl.* roinnean. A togail roinnean, *raising divisions* or *sects.—Stew. Rom.*

ROINN, *s. f.* (*Corn.* ryn. *Ir.* rinn, *a nib. Gr.* ῥιν, *a nose.*) A point; a nib; the point of any aculeated thing; a point of land or promontory. Roinn sleagh, *a spear-point.—Oss. Fin. and Lor.* Ròs air roinn nam fann-shlat, *a rose on the tip of the slender branches.—Macfar.* Roinn na roisg, *eye-bright;* also, *the apple of the eye.*

ROINN, *v. a.* (*Ir.* roinn.) Divide, share, distribute; point or aculeate. *Pret. a.* roinn; *fut. aff. a.* roinnidh; *fut. pass.* roinnear. Roinnidh an neo-chiontach, *the innocent shall divide.—Stew. Job.*

ROINN-BHEARRAG, aig, *s. f.* A bistoury.—*Macd.*

RÒINNE, *s. f.* (*Ir. id.*) Hair; horsehair; a hair; haircloth. Saic-eudach ròinne, *sackcloth of hair.*

RÒINNEACH, *a.* (*from* ròinne.) Hairy; rough; made of hair. Bian ròinneach a bhuic, *the hairy skin of the roe.—Old Song.*

ROINNEACH, *a., from* roinn. (*Ir.* rinneach.) Pointed; sharp-pointed; nibbed.

RÒINNEACH, ich, *s. m.* Hair; horsehair.

RÒINNEACHADH, aidh, *s. m.* A stuffing with hair; a fitting or dressing, as of fishing-hooks, with hair.

ROINNEACHADH, aidh, *s. m.* An aculeating or sharpening at the point.

RÒINNEACHD, *s. f.* Hairiness; roughness.

ROINNEADAIR, *s. m.* A divider.

ROINNEADH, idh, *s. m.* A dividing, a sharing; a division; a sect; a class; a portion.

RÒINNEAG, eig, *s. f.* (*dim.* of ròinne.) A hair. Cha tuit ròinneag, *not a hair shall fall.—Stew. Sam.* Leud ròinneig, *a hair's breadth.* Dheanadh tu teathair do ròinneig, *you would make a tether of a hair.—G. P. N. pl.* ròinneagan.

RÒINNEAGACH, *a.* Hairy; rough—(*Macint.*); full of hairs. *Com.* and *sup.* roinneagaiche.

ROINNEAR, *fut. pass.* of roinn. Shall be divided.

ROINNE-BHAIDHE, *s. f.* Haircloth.

RÒINNE-EUDACH, aich, *s. m.* Haircloth.

ROINN-GHEUR, *a.* Sharp-pointed. Fionn na sleagh roinn-gheur, *Fingal of the sharp-pointed spear.—Old Poem.*

ROINN-GHIAR, *a.* See ROINN-GHEUR.

RÒINNICH, *v. a.* (*from* ròinne.) Stuff with hair; provide with hair.

ROINNIDH, *fut. aff. a.* of roinn. Shall divide.

ROINN-PHAIRTEACH, *a.* Divisible; sharing, dividing.

ROINN-PHAIRTICH, *v. a.* Divide, share, distribute. *Pret. a. id.; fut. aff.* roinn-phàirtichidh.

ROINNSE, *s. f.* A rinse. *N. pl.* roinnseachan. See also ROIDHSE.

Roinnte, *p. part.* of roinn. Shared, divided, portioned.

Roi'orduchadh, aidh, *s. m.* (*for* roimh-orduchadh.) A fore-ordaining, an ordering beforehand, predestination.

Roi'orduich, *v. a.* (*for* roimh-orduich.) Foreorder, fore-ordain, predestinate.

Roi'orduichte, (*for* roimh-orduichte.) Ordered before, predestinated.

Roipe, *comp. pron.*; more frequently written *roimpe*; which see.

Roipeach, *a.* Extravagant; drunken.

Roipear, eir, *s. m.* (*Ir. id.*) A rapier; a tuck.—*Shaw.*

Roi'radh, *s. m.* (*for* roimh-radh.) A preface, a preamble; a prologue.

Ròis, *gen. sing.* of ròs.

Roisceal, eil, *s. m.* A sentence; a decree; a verdict.—*Shaw.*

Ròisd. See Ròist.

Roiseachan, ain, *s. m.* (*Ir. id.*) An instrument for bolling flax.

Ròiseadh, idh, *s. m.* Bolling of flax.

Ròiseal, eil, *s. m.* (*Ir. id.*) A boast; boasting; *also*, the lowest or most base.

Roisealach, *a.* (*Ir. id.*) Boasting; given to boast or vaunt.

Ròisealachd, *s. f.* A habit of boasting.

Ròiseid, *s. f.* (*Ir.* roisin.) Resin. Ròiseid fidhle, *fiddle-resin.*

Ròiseideach, *a.* Resinous; covered with resin.

Roisg, *gen. sing.* of rosg.

Roisg, *a.* (*Ir. id.*) Callow; unfledged.

Roisgeul, geòil, *s. f.* A fable, a romance.

Roisgeulachd, *s. f.* See Roisgeul.

Roisg-mheirleach, ich, *s. m.* (*Ir. id.*) A Tory; a burglar.

Roi'sheallach, *a.* (*for* roimh-sheallach.) Foresighted; provident; prospicient; cautious.

Roi'shealladh, aidh, *s. m.* (*for* roimh-shealladh.) Foresight; prospicience; a front view; a previous look or sight.

Roi'shealltuinn, *s. f.* (*for* roimh-shealltuinn.) A looking forward; providentness; prospicience.

† Roisre, *s. f.* (*Ir. id.*) Anger, choler; high spirits, exhilaration.

Roi'smuaine, (*for* roimh-smuaine.) A forethought. *N. pl.* roi'smuaintean.

Roi'smuaineachadh, aidh, *s. m.* See Roimh-smuaineachadh.

Roi'smuainich, *v.* See Roimh-smuainich.

Ròist, *v. a.* Roast, toast; scorch, parch. *Pret. a.* ròist; *fut. aff. a.* ròistidh, *shall roast*; *fut. pass.* ròistear. Cha ròist an leisgean, *the sluggard will not roast.*—*Stew. Pro.*

Roiste, *s. f.* (*Ir. id.*) A roach.

Ròiste, *p. part.* of ròist. Roasted, toasted; scorched, parched. Feòil ròiste, *roast meat.*

Roistech, ich, *s. m.* (*Ir. id.*) The fish called a roach. *N. pl.* ròistich.

Roistean, ein, *s. m.* (*Ir.* roistin.) A gridiron; a frying-pan.

Roit, *s. m.* Wormwood; gall.

† Roith, *s. f.* A wheel.

Roi'thagh, *v. a. for* roimh-thagh; which see.

Roi'thaghadh, aidh, *s. m.* See Roimh-thaghadh.

Roi'thaghta, *p. part.* (*for* roimh-thaghta.) Forechosen, pre-elected.

Ròithleach, *a.* (*from* † ròith.) Wheeling; hurling; having wheels; in rolls.

Roi'theachdair, *s. m.* (*for* roimh-theachdair.) A forerunner. *N. pl.* roi'theachdairean.

Ròithleagan, ain, *s. m.* A twirl; a little wheel; a little roll; a circle.

Ròithlean, ein, *s. m.* (*Arm.* rotalen.) A little wheel; the rim of a wheel; a pulley.

Ròithleanach, *a.* Having wheels.

Ròithlear, eir, *s. m.* (*Ir.* roithleoir.) A wheelwright; a cartwright; a roller.

Roithlearachd, *s. f.* Wheel-making; the business of a wheelwright or of a cartwright; rolling.

Roithre, *s. m.* (*Ir. id.*) A prater; a babbler.—*Shaw.*

Roithreachd, *s. f.*, *from* roithre. (*Ir. id.*) Prating, babbling; loquacity.

Ròl, ròil, *and* ròla, *s. m.* (*W.* rhol. *Arm.* roll. *Ir.* rol.) A roll; a volume; a swathe or roll of hay or grass; a list. *N. pl.* ròlan.

Ròl, *v. a.* (*Ir. id.*) Roll; rake into rolls, as hay. *Pret. a.* ròl; *fut. aff. a.* ròlaidh, *shall roll.* Ròl an treas tonn iad gu tràigh, *the third wave rolled them ashore.*—*Oss. Fin. and Lor.*

Ròlach, *a.* In rolls; in volumes.

Ròladh, aidh, *s. m.* (*Ir. id.*) A rolling; a raking into rolls, as hay; a roll, a swathe, a volume.

Ròlag, aig, *s. f.* (*dim.* of ròl.) A little roll; a swathe or roll of hay or grass; a little volume. A tionndadh ròlag sniomhanach, *turning the twisted rolls.*—*Macfar.* Ròlag fheoir, *a roll* or *swathe of hay* or *grass.* *N. pl.* ròlagan.

Rolag, aig, *s. f.* A roll of carded wool. *N. pl.* rolagan.

Ròlair, *s. m.* (*from* ròl.) A roller; a cylinder; a rule; one who rolls ground. *N. pl.* ròlairean.

Ròlaireachd, *s. f.* A rolling; a ruling; the employment of rolling ground.

Ròlan, ain, *s. m.* (*dim.* of ròl.) A roll; a volume. *N. pl.* rolain.

Ròmach, *a.* (*Ir. id.*) Hairy; rough; bearded; shaggy.—*Macint.* *N. pl.* romaiche.

Ròmachad. See Romaichead.

Ròmag, aig, *s. f.* A female with a beard; the *pudenda* of a female.

Ròmagach, *a.* Having a beard, as a female; hairy, rough, shaggy.

Ròmaiche, *com.* and *sup.* of romach.

Ròmaiche, *s. f.* Hairiness, roughness, shagginess.—*Macint.*

Ròmaichead, eid, *s. m.* Hairiness, roughness, shagginess; increase in roughness or hairiness. A dol an ròmaichead, *growing more and more hairy.*

Romhad, *comp. pron.* (*Ir. id.*) Before thee; in front of thee; in preference to thee; through thee; in opposition to thee. Romhad is mòr m'eagall, *great is my fear before thee.*—*Mac Lach.* Gabh romhad, *go on, go thy way, go about thy business*; labhair romhad, *speak on.*—*Stew. Gen.* Abair romhad, *say on.*—*Stew.* 1 *K.*

Romhad-sa, *emphatic form* of romhad.

Romhaibh, *comp. pron.* (*Ir.* romhuibh.) Before you, prior to you; in front of you; in preference to you; before your presence; through you; in opposition to you. Seasaidh mi romhaibh, *I will stand before you*, or *in front of you*; gabhaibh romhaibh! *begone! go your way!* gabhaidh e romhaibh, *he will go before you*; *he will intercept you*, or *stop your progress.*

Romhaibh-se, *emphatic form* of romhaibh.

Romhainn, *v. a.* and *n.* Roll; wallow.

Romhainn, *comp. pron.* Before us; prior to us; in our presence; in front of us; in preference to us; in opposition to us; through us. Sheas iad romhainn, *they stood before us.—Ull.* Gabhaidh e romhainn, *he will oppose us, he will intercept us, he will stop our progress.* Cuir romhainn, *prompt us, dictate to us.*

Romhainn-ne, *emphatic form* of rombainn.

Romhair, *s. m.* A rower; a rower or cylinder for levelling ground; a cylindrical rule; one who rolls ground. *N. pl.* romhairean.

Ròmhaireachd, *s. f.* Rowing; rolling or levelling ground.

Romham, *comp. pron.* Before me; prior to me; in front of me; in opposition to me; in preference to me; through me. Tha 'mi a cur romham, *I propose.—Stew.* 1 *K.* Theid mi romham, *I will go my way.*

Romhan, ain, *s. m.* (*Ir. id.*) French wheat; brank.—*Shaw.*

Ròmhanach, aich, *s. m.* (*Ir. id.*) A Roman. *N. pl.* Ròmhanaich.

Ro-mhar, *s. f.* (*Ir. id.*) Spring-tide; a full sea.

Ro-mheud, *s. m.* Excess; greatness. Ro-mheud 'aigheir 's a shòlais, *the excess of his joy and satisfaction.—Ull.*

Ro-mhiann, -mheinn, *s. m.* Earnest desire, keen desire.

Ro-mhòide, *s. f.* (*Ir. id.*) Excess; greatness.

† **Romhradh**, aidh, *s. m.* (*Ir. id.*) Sight.

Romhuibh. See **Romhaibh**.

Romnacois, *a.* Yellow and grey.—*Shaw.*

Rompa, *comp. pron.* (*Ir. id.*) Before them; in front of them; prior to them; in preference to them; in opposition to them; through them. Cuir rompa, *oppose them; prompt them; dictate to them;* gabh rompa, *stop their progress;* tha iad a cur rompa, *they propose or intend;* dh' imich iad rompa, *they went their way.—Stew. Acts.*

Ròn, ròin, *s. m.* (*Ir. id.*) A seal, a sea-calf; the hair of the mane or tail of a horse, or of a cow's-tail; (*W.* rhawn;) the rim of hair round the wooden instrument by which cream is commonly worked into froth.

† **Ron**, *a.* (*Ir. id.*) Strong-bodied.

Rònach, *a.* Hairy, shaggy; abounding in seals; like a seal. *Com.* and *sup.* rònaiche.

Rònadh, aidh, *s. m.* (*Ir. id.*) A club, a stake.—*Shaw.*

Rong, roing, *s. m.* (*Ir. id.*) A rung; a joining spar; a hoop; a clumsy staff; a dronish, lounging person. *N. pl.* rongan.

Rongach, *a.* Having rungs or spars; like a rung; dronish, lounging.

Rongair, *s. m.* A hoop-driver; a lounger. *N. pl.* rongairean.

Rongaireachd, *s. f.* Hoop-driving; sluggishness, dronishness.

Rongas, ais, *s. m.* A rung; a joining spar; a hoop; a clumsy staff; a stake; *in derision*, a dronish person.

Ronn, *s. m.* (*Ir. id.*) Slaver, saliva; rheum; a chain; a tie. *N. pl.* ronnan. Do ronnan, *thy slaver.—Macint.* A sileadh nan ronn, *slavering.—Macdon.* Piobair nan ronn, *a nickname for a bagpiper.*

Ronnach, *a.* (*Ir. id.*) Slavering; dirty with spittle; causing salivation. *Com.* and *sup.* ronnaiche.

Ronnachadh, aidh, *s. m.* (*Ir. id.*) A slavering, a salivating; slaver, salivation.

Ronnadh, aidh, *s. m.* A club, a staff.—*Shaw.*

Ronnag, aig, *s. f.*; more properly *reannag*; which see.

Ronnaich, *v. n.* and *n.* (*from* ronn.) Slaver, spit; salivate. *Pret. a.* ronnaich; *fut. aff. a.* ronnaichidh, *shall slaver.*

Ronnair, *s. m.* A slaverer; a slabberer. *N. pl.* ronnairean.

Ronnaireachd, *s. f.* Slavering, slabbering; a habit of slavering or slabbering.—*Moladh Mhòraig. Also*, salivation; distribution.

Ronn-chraos, *s. m.* A slavering or slabbering mouth. O dheudach no ronn-chraos, *from the teeth of thy slabbery mouth.—Old Song.*

Ronn-ghalar, air, *s. m.* Salivation, catarrh, rheumatism.

Ronnsachadh. See **Rannsachadh**.

Ro-oirdheirceas, eis, *s. m.* Excellency, great excellency. Airson ro-òirdheirceis eòlais, *for the excellency of knowledge.—Stew. Phil.*

Rop, *v. a.* Rope; bend or fasten with a rope; entangle, ravel. *Pret. id.; fut. aff. a.* ropaidh.

Ròp, ròip, *s. m.* A rope or cable. *N. pl.* ropan.

Goth. raip. *Anglo-Sax.* rap. *Ir.* rop. *Dan.* reeb. *Island.* reib. *Belg.* reeb *and* roop, *a rope. Lat.* rap-e, *pull.*

Ròpach, *a.* Ropy; furnished with ropes; made of ropes; moppy; entangled, ravelled. Gu crannach ròpach, *provided with ropes and masts.*

Ròpadair, *s. m.* (*Ir. id.*) A ropemaker or cordwainer. *N. pl.* ròpadairean.

Ròpadaireachd, *s. f.* Ropemaking, cordwaining.

Ròpadh, aidh, *s. m.* A rope; a binding or fastening with a rope.

Ropainn, *s. f.* A roup or sale by auction; a robbery. For this last sense, see **Reubainn** and **Robainn**.

Ropair, *s. m.* (*Ir. id.*) A rapier; a treacherous person.—*Shaw.* An auctioneer; a robber. For this last sense, see **Robair**.

Ròpan, ain, *s. m.*, *dim.* of rop. (*Ir. id.*) A little rope. *N. pl.* ropain.

Ro-phrìs, *s. f.* A great price; great value.

Ro-phrìsealachd, *s. f.* Excellence, great worth, preciousness; transcendent value.—*Stew. Phil. ref.*

Rort, roirt, *s. m.* (*Ir. id. Dan.* roort, *moved.*) A run, a race.

Rortadh, aidh, *s. m.* A flowing over.

Ròs, ròis, *s. m.* A rose; a flower; a disease called the rose. Ros-mhairi, *rosemary.*

Arm. rosen. *Lat.* rosa. *Hung. Dal. It. Span. Pol* rosa. *Boh.* ruoze. *Sclav.* rosha. *Du.* roose. *Germ.* rosen. *Ir.* and *Eng.* rose. *Swed.* ros. *Arm.* ros *and* rez. *Ir.* ros, *a rose.*

Ros, rois, *s. m.* and *f.* (*Ir. id.*) A promontory, an isthmus; *also*, a name given to the seed of flax, and various other vegetable substances; *rarely*, science, knowledge; arable land. Ros lin, *linseed.*

† **Ros**, *v. a.* (*Ir. id.*) Create; make.

† **Ros**, *a.* Pleasant; pretty; delightful.

Ròsach, *a.* Rosy; abounding in roses. Leac-ruiteach ròsach, *ruddy-cheeked and rosy.—Old Song.*

Ròsachd, *s. f.* Enchantment; a charm; witchcraft.

Rosad, aid, *s. m.* Mischance; fatuity; enchantment; charm; witchcraft. Dh'aindeoin gach rosaid dhuinn a dh'èreas, *in spite of every mischance that shall arise.—Turn.*

† **Rosadh**, aidh, *s. m.* (*Ir. id.*) A creating.

Ròsaich, *v. a.* Cover with roses; bedeck with roses.

Ròsaid, *s. f.* Resin. Rosaid fidhle, *fiddle-resin.* *N. pl.* rosaidean.

Ròsaideach, *a.* Resinous.

† **Rosal**, ail, *s. m.* (*Ir. id.*) Judgment.—*Shaw.*

Rosan, ain, *s. m.* (*Ir. id.*) A shrub.

Ròsann, ainn, *s. m.* (*Ir. id.*) A roasting.

Rosarnach, aich, *s. m.* (*Ir. id.*) A place where roses grow, a rose-garden.—*Macd.*

Rosbhan, ain, *s. m.* The apple of the eye. *N. pl.* rosbhain.

Ròs-bheul, -bhèil, *s. m.* A rosy mouth. Do ros-bheul tana, *thy thin rosy lips.—Old Song.*

Ròs-chrann, ainn, *s. m.* A rose-tree. Ròs-chrann gàraidh, *a garden rose-tree.—Macdon.*

Rosdadh. See **Rostadh.**

Ròsdadh. See **Ròstadh.**

Rosg, roisg, *s. m.* (*Ir. id.*) An eyelid, an eyelash; an eye, the eye-sight; dawn; understanding; *rarely*, prose. *N. pl.* rosgan; *d. pl.* rosgaibh. Mar Chairbre nan rosg gorm, *like blue-eyed Cairbre.—Oss. Tem.* Is lom an t-suil gun an rosg, *naked is the eye that wants an eyelash.—G. P.*

Rosgach, *a.* (*from* rosg.) Having large eyes; having large eyelids, or having large eyelashes; having handsome eyes; of, or pertaining to, the eyes or eyelids; dawning; clear-sighted; knowing.

Rosgadh, aidh, *s. m.* (*Ir. id.*) Eye-sight or vision; an eye; an eyelid, an eyelash; a looking; observation; dawn; dilution. Rosgadh na maidne, *the dawn of morn.—Stew. Job.*

Rosgail, *a.* (rosg-amhuil.) Clear-sighted.

Rosgal, ail, *s. m.* Joy, pleasure. Dh' éirich rosgal ad chridhe, *joy rose in thy heart.—Old Song.*

Rosg-catha, *s.* (*Ir. id.*) An incitement to battle; an address to an army.

Rosg-dhalladh, aidh, *s. m.* (*Ir. id.*) Blindness; mistake; error.

Rosg-fhradharc, airc, *s. m.* A sharp sight; a clear sight; vision.

Rosg-fhradharcach, *a.* Sharp-sighted, clear-sighted.

Rosglach, *a.* Joyful, glad, merry. *Com.* and *sup.* rosglaiche.

Rosglach, *a.* (rosg-shùileach.) Sharp-sighted, quick-sighted. *Com.* and *sup.* rosglaiche.

Rosg-shùileach, *a.* Sharp-sighted; having long eyelashes.

Ròs-mhàiri, *s. m.* The flower rosemary.

Rosta, *p. part.* of ròist. (*Ir. id.* *W.* rhòst.) Roasted; toasted. Feòil rosta, *roast meat.*

Ròstach, *a.* Roasting, toasting.

Ròstadh, aidh, *s. m.* Mishap.

Ròstadh, aidh, *s. m.* A roasting, as of meat; a roast; roast meat. Feòil air a ròstaidh, *flesh roasted.*

W. rhòst, *roasted.* *Ir.* rosta. *Germ.* rosten. *Teut.* rost. *Boh.* rosst. *Pol.* rozt.

Ròstadh, (a), *pr. part.* of ròist. Roasting; toasting, scorching. Thoir feòil 'g a ròstadh, *give flesh to roast.—Stew.* 1 *Sam.*

Ròtadh, aidh, *s. m.* A freezing; frost; hoar frost. Written also *reotadh*; which see.

† **Rotan**, ain, *s. m.* (*Ir. id.*) Redness.

Roth, rotha, *s. m.* A wheel; the rim of a wheel. *N. pl.* rothan, *wheels.* Eadar na rothan, *between the wheels.—Stew. Ezek.* *D. pl.* rothaibh. Roth gealaich, *a lunar halo*; roth gréin, *a solar halo.*

Shans. ratha. *Gr.* ῥοῖος, *strepitus.* *Lat.* rota, *a wheel.* *W.* rhod. *Arm.* rot. *Fr.* rouë. *Ir.* rhotha. *Franconian*, rad. *Belg.* rad.

Rothach, *a.* Rimmed, as a wheel; rotular.

Rothadair, *s. m.* (*from* roth.) A wheelwright.

Rothan, ain, *s. m.* (*dim.* of roth.) A little wheel; a little rim. *N. pl.* rothain.

Rothlas, ais, *s. m.* (*Ir. id.*) Evolution.

Ro-thoil, *s. m.* Great desire, willingness. Bha ro-thoil agam, *I was greatly desirous.—Stew. N. T.*

Rù, *s. m.* See **Rùn.**

Ruadh, ruaidh, *s. m.* (*Ir. id.* *Eng.* roe.) A deer; a roe or deer; a mountain deer; *rarely*, strength, virtue. *N. pl.* ruaidh. Na ruaidh o charn, *the deer from the rock.—Oss. Tem.* *D. pl.* ruadhaibh. Do ruadhaibh na fàsaich, *to the deer of the desert.—Id.*

Ruadh, *a.* Brown; red; reddish, red-haired; ruddy; *also*, strong. Each ruadh, *a brown horse.—Stew. Zech.* Caoir do theine ruadh, *gleams of red fire.—Old Poem.* Olla ruadh, *red-haired Olla.—Oss. Tem.* An Gille-ruadh, *Gilderoy*; an tuil ruadh, *the general deluge.* *Com.* and *sup.* ruaidhe.

Shans. rudhir. *Gr.* ἐρυθρός. *Teut.* and *Swed.* rod. *Germ.* roth. *Island.* rode *and* raudur. *Sax.* red. *Corn.* rydh. *Arm.* ryudh *and* ru. *Du.* rothe. *Sclav.* rumen. *Goth.* rodua. *Lat.* rufus, ruber, rutilus. *Fr.* rouge, *red.* *Scotch*, roy, *red-haired.*

Ruadhadh, aidh, *s. m.* A making red or brown; a becoming red, brown, or tanned; rusting. Mar ghàd air ruadhadh, *like a rusted bar.—Old Song.* Ruadhadh gréine, *a tanning occasioned by the sun.*

Ruadhag, aig, *s. f.*, *dim.* of ruadh. (*Ir.* ruadhog.) A young roe; a hind, a goat. An ruadhag a spioladh air d'uaigh, *the young roe browsing on thy grave.—Oss. Fing.* *N. pl.* ruadhagan.

Ruadhaich, *v. a.* and *n.* (*from* ruadh.) Embrown; become brown. *Pret. a. id.*; *fut. aff.* ruadhaichidh, *shall embrown.* Ruadhaich gach fonn, *every land became brown.—Macdon.*

Ruadhaichte, *p. part.* of ruadhaich.

Ruadhaig, *gen. sing.* of ruadhag; which see.

Ruadhain, *a.* Fusty.—*Macfar. Voc.*

Ruadhaineachd, *s. f.* Fustiness.

Ruadhair, *v. a.* Dig, delve; stir up; struggle; fight. *Pret. a. id.*; *fut. aff. a.* ruadhraidh. More properly written *ruamhair*; which see.

Ruadhan, ain, *s. m.* (*from* ruadh.) Ruddle; any substance that dies brown; reddishness, brownishness; a reddish or brown tinge. Bùrn glan gun ruadhan, *clean water without a brown tinge.—Macdon.*

Ruadhar, air, *s. m.* Digging, delving; stirring up; an onset, a skirmish; a heat; an expedition.

Ruadharadh, aidh, *s. m.* A digging or delving; a stirring; a fighting; an expedition.

Ruadharach, *a.* Digging, delving, stirring; fighting, skirmishing.

Ruadh-bhoc, -bhuic, *s. m.* (*Ir. id.*) A roebuck. Ruadh-bhoc nan leum, *the bounding roe.—Oss. Cathloda.* *N. pl.* ruadh-bhuic.—*Stew.* 1 *K.*

Ruadh-bhuidhe, *a.* (*Ir. id.*) Auburn; of a reddish yellow. Written also *buidhe-ruadh.*

Ruadh-bhuinne, *s. f.* Flood water; a brown torrent; a hill torrent embrowned by being impregnated with moss.

Ruadh-chailc, *s. f.* (*Ir. id.*) Ochre—(*Macd.*); ruddle.

Ruadh-chailceach, *a.* Ochreous; asphaltic.

Ruadh-chriadh, *s. m.* and *f.* (*Ir.* ruadh-chriot.) Ruddle.

† **Ruadh-laith**, *s. f.* Choler, *cholera morbus.—Shaw.*

Ruadh-laitheach, *a.* (*Ir. id.*) Choleric.

Ruadh-thuil, *s. f.* A hill torrent reddened with the moisture of mossy grounds; the general deluge. In this latter sense it is commonly written *an tuil ruadh.*

Ruagach, *a.* Persecuting; pursuing; putting to flight; scaring, dispersing; banishing; like a persecution; like a pursuit or flight.

Ruagadh, aidh, *s. m.* (*Ir. id.*) A persecuting, a pursuing, a scaring, a dispersing, a banishing; a chasing or hunting away; a persecution; a pursuit, a flight; a dispersion, a banishment.

Ruagadh, (a), *pr. part.* of ruaig. Persecuting, pursuing, putting to flight, dispersing; scaring; banishing. Sgrios 'g an ruagadh, *destruction pursuing them.—Ardar.*

RUAGAIR, s. m., *from* ruaig. (*Ir.* ruagaire) A persecutor; a pursuer; a hunter, an outlaw; an instrument to drive a thing from its place; a bar, a bolt; any instrument used for scaring birds or other creatures; a small bullet or slug; swan-shot *N pl.* ruagairean

RUAGAIREACHD, *s f* A pursuing, a persecution; a hunting, a chasing

RUAGALAICHE, *s f* A fugitive.

RUAGHAG, aig, *s f.* More correctly *ruadhag*, which see

RUAGHAN, ain, *s m* More properly *ruadhan*, which see

RUAICHILL, *v. a* Buy, purchase *Pret a* ruaichill, *fut* ruaichillidh.

RUAICHILLTE, *p. part* of ruaichill

RUAIDH, *gen* and *voc sing.* of ruadh; which see.

RUAIDH, *v. a.* Redden, embrown *Pret. a.* id, *fut aff* ruaidhidh

RUAIDHE, *com* and *sup.* of ruadh More or most red.

RUAIDHE, *s f.* Redness, brownness; reddishness, ruddiness; a disease so called Ruaidhe nan abhall 'n ad ghruaidh, *the ruddiness of apples in thy cheeks—Old Poem*

RUAIDHNEACH, ich, *s m.* (*Ir* id.) Hair

RUAIDHRINN, *s* (*Ir* id) Red points or edges

RUAIG, *s f* (*Ir* id) A flight, a pursuit; a precipitate retreat, a persecution, a chase, a hunt; a scaring away, a dispersion, a banishment Ruaig sionnaich, *a fox-chase*, ruaig an tuirc, *the boar-hunt—Oss. Derm.* Manos nan ruag, *the pursuing Manos—Fingalian Poem.* Ghabh iad an ruaig, *they took to flight*

RUAIG, *v a.* (*Ir.* id) Chase, hunt, pursue, put to flight; scare, disperse; persecute, banish *Pret. a.* ruaig, *fut aff a* ruaigidh Ruaigidh dorchadas, *darkness will pursue.—Stew. Nah* Ruaigeamaid an diugh, *let us hunt to-day—Oss Derm*

RUAIGIDH, *fut aff a* of ruaig

RUAIM, *s f.* (*Ir.* id) A fishing-line, a line

RUAIMLE, *s f.* (*Ir* id) A dirty pool; standing water impregnated with clay—*Shaw*

RUAIMLEACH, *a.* Muddy; agitated or disturbed, as water, agitating. Gu ruaimleach, *muddily*

RUAIMLEACHD, *s. f* Muddiness

RUAIMLICH, *v. a* Agitate or disturb water, or any fluid *Pret a* id, *fut. aff. a.* ruaimlichidh, *shall disturb*, *p part* ruaimlichte.

RUAIMNEACH, *a* Strong, robust; active

RUAIMNEACHD, *s f* Strength, robustness, activity.

RUAIN, *s f.* (*Ir.* id) A kind of weld which gives a reddish tinge or colour.

RUAINEACH, *a* (*Ir.* id) See RUAIMNEACH.

RUAINIDH, *a.* Red, reddish, strong, able, charitable—*Shaw* *Also*, a strong, boisterous fellow Maol-ruainidh, *a nickname applied to any female who is fond of places of public resort*

RUAINNE, *s. f* A hair. More frequently written *ròinne*, which see.

RUAIS, *s m.* (*Ir.* id.) A clown, a sluggish, stupid fellow, a noisy fellow. *N pl* ruaisean.

RUAISEALACHD, *s f.* Clownishness; disorderliness

RUAISEIL, *a* (ruais-amhuil.) Clownish, disorderly

RUAM, ruaim, *s m.* A kind of plant used in dying red.

RUAMH, ruaimh, *s. m* (*Ir.* id.) A spade—*Shaw.* *Hence* ruamhar, *a digging*.

RUAMHAIR, *v. a* (*from* ruamh.) Delve, dig, dress the surface, as of a garden; stir up; fight *Pret. a* id.; *fut aff a* ruamhairidh.

RUAMHAR, air, *s. m.* A digging or delving, a dressing the surface, as of a garden; a fight; a skirmish; an expedition.

RUAMHARADH, RUAMHRADH, aidh, *s. m.* A delving; a digging, a stirring up; a skirmishing

RUAMNACH, *a* (*Ir* id) Indignant, angry.

RUAMNADH, aidh, *s m.* A reproof, reprehension.

RUANACHD, *s f.* (*Ir.* id.) A romance; a strange tale; fiction; an harangue.

RUANAICHE, *s. m.* A romancer, an haranguer.

RUANAIDH, *a.* Red, reddish, strong, able; charitable; *also*, a strong, boisterous fellow.

RUANAIDH, *s. f.* (*Ir.* ruanaigh) Anger; darkness.

RUANAIL, *a* Lying; untrue, false; fictitious

RUAR, ruair, *s m* A digging, a delving, a stirring up; an expedition; a skirmish; a heat

RUARACAN, ain, *s m* A floundering; a groveller.

RUARACH, *a* See RUATHARACH.

RUARACH, aich, *s. m.* (*Ir* id) A liar, a romancer. Perhaps *ruanach*.

RUARADH, aidh, *s m* See RUATHARADH

RUATHAIR, *v a* Dig, delve, stir up More properly written *ruamhair*, which see.

RUATHAR, air, *s. m* (*Ir* id. *W* rhuthr, *a skirmish.*) An expedition, an invasion, a pillage; incursion, a skirmish; an onset, a rush, a heat, a digging or delving; (in the sense of delving, see RUAMHAR) Thug e ruathar gun chèill, *he made a furious rush.—Old Poem.*

RUATHARACH, RUATHRACH, *a* Digging, delving, stirring up, struggling, skirmishing; rushing, making an onset.

RUATHARACHADH, RUATHRACHADH, aidh, *s m.* A digging, a delving, a stirring up, a rushing, a making an onset.

RUATHARADH, RUATHRADH, aidh, *s m* A delving or digging, a skirmishing, a rushing, onset, a higgling. In the sense of delving, see RUAMHARADH.

RUB, *v a* (*W* rhubio *Ir* rub) Rub *Pret. a.* rub; *fut. aff* rubaidh, *shall rub*, *fut pass* rubar.

RUBACH, *a* Rubbing, prone to rub.

RUBADH, aidh, *s m* A rubbing, friction. Air a rubadh, *rubbed*

RUBAIR, *s. m* A rubber

RUBAN, *s m* A rubber

RÙBAN, ain, *s m.* A ruby. *N. pl* rùbain

RUBHAG, aig, *s f* A pulling or snatching violently

RUC, *s m.* See RUCHD.

RÙC, *s. m.* See RÙCHD.

RÙCAIL See RUCHDAIL or RÙCHAIL

RUCAN, ain, *s. m.* A conical heap of corn or hay.

RÙCAN, ain, *s. m* A wheezing in the throat

RÙCANACH, *a.* Wheezing.

RUCANACH, *a* Abounding in stacks of corn.

RUCAS, *s m.* (*Ir* id.) Fondness; keen desire; arrogance; pride, fawning, fondling, frisking Le rucas bhi 'g ad fhòirneadh, *arrogantly intruding thyself—Old Poem.*

RUCASACH, *a* Fond, keenly desirous, arrogant; fawning, fondling, frisking.

RUCASACHD, *s f.* Fondness, keen desire, arrogantness; a habit of fawning or fondling.

RÙCHAIL, *s f* A hoarse voice, hoarseness; any hollow, hoarse sound, a croaking, a rumbling, a grunting; a tearing or rending.

RUCHALL, aill, *s. m.* A fetter.

RUCHAN, ain, *s m* (*Ir* id) A hoarse noise, or a wheezing in the throat; the throat; the windpipe.

RUCHD, *v n.* Make a hoarse noise; shout, croak, grunt. *Pret. a.* ruchd; *fut aff. a.* ruchdaidh

Ruchd, *s. m.* A conical rick of hay or corn. *N. pl.* ruchdan.

Rùchd, *s. f.* A belch, a grunt; a clamour; *rarely*, a son. *Gr.* ερευγω, *rugio. Lat.* ructus. *W.* rhuch, *a belch. Ir.* rucht, *a clamour.*

Ruchd, *s. f.* (*Ir. id.*) A shape or form; a mask; a pig, a sow; entrails; a sigh, a groan, a lament.

Ruchdach, *a.* Abounding in ricks; like a rick.

Rùchdach, *a.* Hoarse; croaking; grunting.

Rùchdail, *s. f.* A hoarse noise; hoarseness of the voice; a croaking; a rumbling.

Ruchdan, ain, *s. m.* (*dim.* of ruc.) A little conical rick of hay or corn. *N. pl.* ruchdain.

Rùchdan, ain, *s. m.* The throat; a hoarse noise in the throat.

Rud, *s. m.* (*Ir.* rod.) A thing; matter, affair, circumstance; business; *pudendum; rarely*, a wood. It is used in contempt of any matter or production, and also of persons with contempt or pity. *N. pl.* rudan. Ciod rud a tha thu 'g radh? *what are you saying?* Rud mhosaich! *thou nasty thing!* Agus rud eile dheth, *and another thing, and more than that, moreover.* Mar thubhairt clag Scàin, an rud nach buin duit na buin da, *as the bell of Scoon rang, what belongs not to you, meddle not with.—G. P.*

The bell of Scoon, in this adage, means the Scotch law.

Rudach, *a.* Officious, meddling; trifling; particular about small matters. *Com.* and *sup.* rudaiche.

Rudan, *n. pl.* of rud. Things, matters. See Rud.

Rudan, ain, *s. m.* (*dim.* of rud.) A little thing, *pudenda juvenis.*

Rùdan, ain, *s. m.* (*Ir. id.*) A knuckle, a tendon. *N. pl.* rùdain.

Rùdanach, *a.* (*Ir. id.*) Knuckly, having large knuckles; of, or belonging to, a knuckle.

Rudha, Rudhadh, aidh, *s. m.* See Rugha.

Rudhain, *a.* Musty.

Rudhrach, aich, *s. m.* A sojourner; a tenant; a darkening; darkness—(*Shaw*); a gloomy countenance.

Rudhrach, *a.* (*Ir. id.*) Searching or groping; scrambling; long, straight.

Rudhrachas, ais, *s. m.* Length—(*Shaw.*); obscurity.

Rug, *pret. a.* of *v. irr.* beir. Caught; overtook; bore or bare. Rug e orra, *he overtook them.—Stew. Gen.* Rug iad clann, *they bare children.—Stew. Gen.*

Rug, ruig, *s. m.* and *f.* (*Ir. id.*) A wrinkle; a plait.—*Shaw.*

Rugach, *a.* (*Ir. id.*) Wrinkled; plaited. Aghaidh rugach, *a wrinkled face.*

Rugadh, aidh, *s. m.* A rush towards any common property; a greedy grasping at any thing; a cheap purchase, a good bargain.

Rugadh, *pret. pass.* of beir. Was or were caught or overtaken; was or were born. Rugadh air, *he was caught* or *overtaken;* ón rugadh mi, *since I was born.*

Rugadh, aidh, *s. m.* An old person; a person with a wrinkled face.

Rugair, *s. m.* A bar; a latch.—*Shaw.*

Ruganta, *a.* Stout, muscular; tough; made of good metal.

Rugantachd, *s. f.* Stoutness; toughness.

Rugh, rugha, *s. m.* The herb rue.

Rugha, Rughadh, aidh, *s. m.* A blush; a flush; a cape; a promontory or headland; a hanging. Rugha do ghruaidh, *the flush of thy face.—Ull.* Rughadh nàire mu 'ghruaighe, *a blush of shame on his cheek.—Mac Lach.* Rughadh gruaighe, *blushing, shamefacedness;* mar a chuan air ruadh-rugha, *like the sea on a brown headland.—Fingalian Poem.* Rughadh, *a hanging.—Shaw.*

Rughach, *a.* Blushing; bashful; having capes or headlands; like a cape or headland.

Rughadh. See Rugha.

Rughaich, *v. a.* and *n.* Blush, flush; cause to blush. *Pret. a.* rughaich; *fut. aff. a.* rughaichidh.

Rughteach, *a.* Florid, ruddy, rosy-cheeked, flushed in the face.

Ruibeach, *a.* See Riobach.

Ruibean, ein, *s. m.* A riband; a silken tape.

Ruibeanach, *a.* Ribanded; covered with ribands; decked with ribands.

Ruibeanaich, *v. a.* Adorn with ribands; provide with ribands. *P. part.* ruibeanaichte.

Ruibh, *comp. pron.* See Ribh.

† **Ruibh**, ruibhe, *s. f.* Sulphur.—*Shaw.*

Ruibhne, *s. f.* (*Ir. id.*) A lance, a spear. *N. pl.* ruibhnean.

Ruibhneach, *a.* (*Ir. id.*) Armed with a lance or spear; like a lance or spear; of, or belonging to, a spear or lance; strongly guarded; *also, substantively*, a man armed with a spear; a lancer. *N. pl.* ruibhnich, *lancers.*

Ruic, *s. f.* (*Ir. id.*) A fleece.

Ruice, *s. f.* (*Ir. id.*) A reproach; a rebuke—(*Shaw*); a defeat; a red shade; a blush occasioned by shame.

Ruiceach, *a.* Reproaching; rebuking, reproving.

Ruiceach, *a.* Exalting, lifting up.

Ruichealt, eilt, *s.* (*Ir. id.*) Close concealment.

Ruideach, *a.* Glib, flowing.

Ruideal, eil, *s. m.* (*W.* rhydilh.) A riddle or coarse sieve. Written also *rideal;* which see.

Ruideasach, *a.* Frisky, playful, gamboling. Bu ruideasach gamhainn is laogh, *playful were the stirks and calves.—Old Song.*

Ruideis, *s. f.* (*Ir. id.*) A frisking, a gamboling, a capering, a leaping. Ri ruideas luath mu d' lòin, *nimbly frisking about thy meadows.—Macdon.*

Ruidh, *v. a.* and *n.* See Ruith.

Ruidh, *s. f.* See Ruith.

Ruidhe, *s. f.* A shaling.

† **Ruidheadh**, idh, *s. f.* (*Ir. id.*) A reproof; a censure; a ray.—*Shaw.*

Ruidhil, *v. a.* (*Sax.* reol.) Hurl; roll; reel; twirl. *Pret. a.* ruidhil; *fut. aff. a.* ruidhilidh.

Ruidhil, *gen.* ruidhle, *s. f.* (*Goth.* reol, *a reel.*) A hurl; a wheel; a Scotch dance called a reel. Ruidhil thulachan, *a kind of Highland reel from which females are commonly excluded. N. pl.* ruidhlean *und* ruidhleachan.

Ruidhleadh, idh, *s. m.* A hurling, a rolling, a reeling; a hurl, a roll, a reel.

Ruidhlean, ein, *s. m.* A wheel of any vehicle, a little wheel. *N. pl.* ruidhleanan.

† **Ruidhleas**, *a.* (*cont. for* ro-dhileas.) Very faithful.

Ruidhte, *s. f.* Drunkenness, revelling, rioting.

Ruidhtear, *s. m.* A drunkard, a reveller, a riotous person. *N. pl.* ruidhteirean.

Ruidhteireachd, *s. f.* Drunkenness, revelling, rioting. Ann an ruidhteireachd, *in rioting.—Stew. Rom.*

Ruidigh, *a.* Glad, cheerful, merry.

Ruidigheachd, *s. f.* Gladness, cheerfulness, merriness.

Ruig, *s. m.* A half-castrated ram, a ridgeling. *N. pl.* ruigeachan.

Ruig, *v. a.* and *n.* Reach; arrive at; hold forth; stretch out; attain to. *Pret. a.* ruig; *fut. aff. a.* ruigidh, *shall*

reach. Cha ruig thu air, *you cannot reach it*; cha ruig thu leas, *you need not.*
Sax. raecan. *Du.* reic. *Germ.* reichean. *Belg.* rayken.

RUIG, (gu), *prep.* As far as, until, to.

RUIGEACHD, *s. f.* Castration; the state of being castrated.

RUIGEACHD, *s. f.* A reaching, an attaining, an arrival.

RUIGEAS, *fut. sub.* of ruig. Shall reach. Mu ruigeas tu, *if you shall reach* or *arrive.*

RUIGHE, *s. f.* (*Ir.* ruigh. *Arm.* ri.) An arm; the arm from the wrist to the elbow. Dh' éirich a ruighe geal, *her fair arm rose.—Oss. Lodin.* Bac na ruighe, *the hollow of the arm.*

RUIGHE, *s. f.* A shepherd's cot; a *sheeling* or hut built in the midst of hill pasture, where cattle are tended during the summer months; called also *bothan airidh.*

RUIGHEACH, *a.* Having strong arms; having handsome arms; abounding in shepherds' huts.

RUIGHEACHD, *s. f.* A reaching, an attaining to, an arrival; a mental trial.

RUIGHEACHD, (a), *pr. part.* of ruig. Reaching, arriving, attaining. A ruigheachd gu neamh, *reaching to heaven.—Stew. Gen.*

RUIGHEANAS, ais, *s. m.* (*Ir. id.*) Brightness. See RUITHEANAS.

RUIGHINN, *a.* See RIGHINN.

RUIGIDH, *fut. aff. a.* of ruig. Shall reach or arrive.

RUIGINN, 1 *sing. pret. sub.* of ruig. I would reach.

RUIGLEAN, ein, *s. m.* A ridgeling, a half-castrated goat.

RUIGLEANACH, *a.* Like a ridgeling, castrated; abounding in ridgelings; of, or belonging to, a ridgeling.

RUIGSINN, *s. f.* A reaching, an arriving, an attaining; an arrival.

RUIGSINN, (a), *pr. part.* of ruig. Reaching, arriving, attaining.

RUIGSINNEACH, *a.* Accessible; attainable.

RUIM, *gen. sing.* of rum; which see.

RUIMNEACH, ich, *s. m.* A marsh.

RÙIN, *gen. sing.* of rùn; which see.

RÙINE, *s. f.* Secrecy, mystery; private intimation. *N. pl.* rùintean.

RUINIGIL, RUINIGIN, *s. f.* Dangerous navigation.

RUINN, *comp. pron.* (*Ir.* rinne.) To us. Na bi ruinn, *do not meddle with us, do not molest us*; cuiridh iad ruinn, *they will ply us; they will try our mettle; they will add to us*; an Spiorad a cur ruinn, *the Spirit applying to us*; cha tig e ruinn, *he* or *it will not please* or *satisfy us*; cha tig ni ruinn, *no harm shall befall us.*

RUINN, *s. f.* More properly *roinn*; which see.

RÙINNE, *s. f.* More commonly written *roinne*; which see.

RUINNEACH, ich, *s. m.* Grass.

RUINNEADH, idh, *s. m.* (*Ir. id.*) Consumption; detersion, cleansing.

RUINNS, *v. a.* Rinse; scourge.

RUINNSE, *s. f.* A rinse; a whip, a scourge.—*Shaw.*

RUINNSEAR, eir, *s. m.* A rinser; a searcher.

RUINNSICH, *v. a.* Rinse; scour; whip, scourge. *Fut. aff.* ruinnsichidh.

RUINNSINN, *s. f.* A rinsing.

RUINNTE, *part.* More properly *roinnte*; which see.

RUIRE, *s. m.* (*Ir. id.*) A knight; a champion; a lord.

RUIREACH, ich, *s. m.* A champion; a knight; an exile. *N. pl.* ruirich.

RUIREACH, ich, *s.* An old name of the river Liffy, in Ireland.

RUIREACH, *a.* Famous.

RUIREACHAIL, *a.* Championlike; knightly; famous.

RUIREACHAS, ais, *s. m.* Lordship, dominion; renown; bravery.

RUIS, *s. f.* (*Ir. id.*) The elder-tree; one of the names given to the fifteenth letter (R) of the Gaelic alphabet; *rarely*, a way, a road.

RUISCEANTA, *a.* More properly *ruisgeanta*; which see.

RUISEALACHD, *s. f.* Hastiness, rashness; disorder.

† RUISEAN, ein, *s. m.* A luncheon.

RUISEANTA, *a.* (*Ir. id.*) Hasty, rash; disorderly.

RUISEIL, *a.* Rash, hasty, precipitate; disorderly. Gu ruiseil, *rashly.*

RÙISG, *s. f.* A small boat made of bark; *also, n. pl.* of rùsg, *peelings.*

RUISG, *s. f.* (*Ir. id.*) A skirmish; a fray, a fight.—*Shaw.*

RÙISG, *v. a.* Peel, shell, husk; clip; strip; fleece; undress; excoriate; disclose; unsheathe; make bare; *rarely*, shave; chafe; gall; tear, rend. *Pret. a.* rùisg; *fut. aff. a.* rùisgidh, *shall make bare.* Rùisg e stiallan geala, *he peeled white streaks.—Stew. Gen.* D' easbhuidh do namhaid na rùisg, *disclose not thy wants to an enemy.—G. P.* Ruisgidh brù bràghad, *the belly will strip the back.—Id.*

† RUISG, *v. a.* Smite, strike, pelt. *Pret. a.* ruisg; *fut. aff.* ruisgidh.—*Shaw.*

RÙISGEACH, *a.* Caustic, escharotic.

RÙISGEAN, ein, *s. m.* A vessel made of the bark of trees.

RUISGEANTA, *a.* Fond of fighting or frays, quarrelsome.

RÙISGIDH, *fut. aff. a.* of rùisg.

RUISG-SHUILEACH, *a.* See ROSG-SHUILEACH.

RUISG-SHÙL, *s. pl.* Eyelashes, eyelids.

RÙISGTE, *p. part.* of ruisg. Peeled; husked; shelled; stripped; undressed, naked; unsheathed. Ruisgte agus lomnochd, *stripped and naked.—Stew. Mic.*

RUIT, *s. f.* (*Ir. id.*) A javelin.

RUITEACH, *a.* Ruddy; rosy-cheeked; florid. Mar neul ruiteach, *like a ruddy cloud.—Oss. Gaul.* Bha e ruiteach, *he was florid.—Stew. Sam.* *Com.* and *sup.* ruitiche.

RUITEACHAN, ain, *s. m.* A ruby. *N. pl.* ruiteachain, *rubies.—Stew. Lam.*

RUITEACHD, *s. f.* Ruddiness, floridness.

RUITEAG, eig, *s. f.* Redness; a slight tinge of red.

RUITEAN, ein, *s. m.* An ankle-bone; a fetlock, a pastern; a dirty grovelling child.

RUITH, *v. a.* Run; race; course; retreat; flow; rush. *Pret. a.* ruith; *fut. aff.* ruithidh, *shall run.* Is maith a ruith sibh, *you have run well.—Stew. Gal.* Ruithidh e orm, *he will run upon me.*

RUITH, ruithe, *s. f.* (*Arm.* red. *Ir.* rioth *and* rith.) A running, a racing; a flowing, as of a stream; a rushing; a run, a race; a pursuit; a course; a flight, as of an army; a flux; an army, a troop. Gille ruithe, *a footman, a runner, a forerunner*; ruith na cuthaig, *an April-fool's errand*; ruith air theas, *a running to and fro, as cattle do in hot weather*; leig ruith dha, *let it run; let it flow.*

RUITHEACH, *s. m.* (*Ir. id.*) A handcuff.

RUITHEACH, *a.* (*from* ruith.) Running; flowing; fluent; moving; on the march. Uisge ruitheach, *running water*; canmhuinn ruitheach, *fluent language.—Old Song.*

RUITHEAN, *a.* (*Ir. id.*) Red-hot; blazing.

RUITHEAN, ein, *s. m.* (*Ir. id.*) Delight, pleasure.—*Shaw.*

RUITHEANAS, ais, *s. m.* (*Ir. id.*) Brightness; splendour, glitter.

RUITHIL, *v. a.* See RUIDHIL.

RUITHIL, ruithle, *s. f.* See RUIDHIL.

Ruithlean, ein, *s. m.* (*Arm.* rotelen.) A little wheel, a little rim. See also Ruidhlean.

Ruithleanach, *a.* Having wheels or rims; having little wheels or rims.

Ruithneadh, idh, *s. m.* A flame.

Ruith-sgiùrsadh, aidh, *s. m.* Running the gauntlet.

Ruithteach, *a.* (*from* ruith.) See Ruitheach.

Ruithteach, *a.* (*from* rutha.) Florid, ruddy, rosy-cheeked. Perhaps *rughaiteach.*

Ruithteachd, *s. f.* Floridness, ruddiness. Perhaps *rughaiteachd.*

Rùladh, aidh, *s. m.* A slaughtering; a slaughter or massacre.

Rum, ruim, *s. m.* (*Swed. Ir.* rum.) A room or chamber; room or place; a floor. Rum cùil, *a back-room;* rum beòil, *a front-room;* dean rum, *make room.* *N. pl.* rumaichean, *rooms.*

Rumach, aich, *s.* A marsh; a quagmire, a slough; a puddle. *N. pl.* rumaichean; *d. pl.* rumaichibh.

Rumachail, *a.* (rumach-amhuil.) Marshy, boggy.

Rumaich, *v. n.* Make room, give place, stand aside. *Pret. a.* rumaich; *fut. aff. a.* rumaichidh.

Rumail, *s. f.* A rumbling noise.

Rumhar, air, *s. m.* A mine.—*Shaw.*

Rumpal, ail, *s. f.* A rump. A sgoltadh chorp gu'n rumpail, *splitting bodies to their rumps.—Macdon.*

Rumpalach, *a.* Rumped; having a large rump; of a rump.

Rùn, rùin, *s. m.* Love, fondness, desire; affection; inclination; accord; purpose, intention, design; determination; *also,* a person beloved. Cha 'n 'eil bheag do m' rùin duit, *you have nought of my love.—Old Poem.* Tir mo rùin, *the land of my affection.—Mac Lach.* Gun rùn, *without inclination.—Stew. Pro.* Mo rùn geal òg, *my fair, young, beloved one.—Old Song.* A dh'aon rùn, *of one mind, with one accord, unanimous.* *N. pl.* rùinte *and* rùintean. Thig rùinte gu neoni, *purposes come to naught.—Stew. Pro.*

Rùn, rùin, *s. m.* A secret, a mystery; secrecy. *N. pl.* rùinte *and* rùintean.

Corn. Arm. Goth. runa, *a mystery.* *Germ.* rune. *W.* rhin. *Anglo-Sax.* run *and* rune. *Old Sax.* girunu, *mystery.*

Ollaus Wormius, whose erudition cannot be questioned, has an elaborate dissertation on the origin of the Runæ, in the beginning of his work on Runic literature. It would have shortened or facilitated his inquiries had he known, or rather had it occurred to him, that in the Gaelic, Irish, and Armoric dialects of the Celtic, *rùn* signifies a *secret* or *mystery.* Indeed, the Cimbric term *runa,* which signifies hieroglyphics, seems to be quite explanatory of Runæ, characters which were but a mysterious and hieroglyphical mode of writing used by the priests of the ancient Goths. The Runic hieroglyphics are, perhaps, the *secreta literarum* mentioned by Tacitus *de Mor. Germ.* When the Germans afterwards learned the use of letters they, very naturally, called their alphabet Runæ. See *Gloss. Goth. ad Voc. Runa.*

Rùnach, aich, *s. c.* (*from* rùn.) A beloved person; a mistress; a confidant. *N. pl.* rùnaich.

Rùnach, *a.* (*from* rùn.) Trusty, confident; partial, fond; purposing; dark, mysterious; mystical: hence *Runic.* See Rùn.

Rùnachadh, aidh, *s. m.* A purposing; a designing; a determining; a loving.

Rùnaiche, *s. m.* (*Ir.* runaighe.) A confidant; a discreet person; a beloved person.

Rùnaich, *v. a., from* rùn. (*Ir.* runaigh.) Design; purpose; mean; intend; determine. *Pret. a.* runaich; *fut. aff.* runaichidh, *shall design.* An deadh-ghean a rùnaich e, *the good pleasure he has purposed.—Stew. Eph.*

Rùnaichte, *p. part.* of rùnaich. (*Ir.* runaighte.) Designed; determined; definitive.

† **Rùn-airm**, *s. m.* (*Ir. id.*) A council-chamber.—*Shaw.*

† **Runbhocan**, ain, *s. m.* (*Ir. id.*) A pretence.—*Shaw.*

Run-chléireach, ich, *s. m.* (*Ir. id.*) A secretary; a private secretary. *N. pl.* run-chléirich.

Run-chléireachd, *s. f.* The business of a private secretary.

Run-chléirsneachd, *s. f.* Secretaryship; private secretaryship.

Run-diomhair, *s. m.* (*Ir. id.*) A mystery; a secret purpose; a private intention. An run-diomhair so, *this mystery.—Stew. Rom.*

Run-diomhaireach, *a.* Mysterious; mystical; plotting.

Rùn-phàirteach, *a.* (*Ir. id.*) Communicable; apt to disclose a secret or one's mind; *also, substantively,* one who partakes of a secret.

Rùn-phàirteachadh, aidh, *s. m.* A disclosing of a secret; a disclosing of one's mind or purposes; a disclosure of a secret; a partaking of a secret.

Rùn-phàirtich, *v. a.* Disclose a secret, disclose one's mind; partake of a secret; consult, advise with.

Rùn-sheòmar, air, *s. m.* A council-chamber. *N. pl.* rùn-sheòmraichean.

Rupail, *s. f.* A rumbling sound; a continued rumbling.—*Shaw.*

Rurgaid, *s. f.* (*Ir.* rurgoid.) Rhubarb.

Rurgaideach, *a.* Abounding in rhubarb, like rhubarb, of rhubarb.

† **Rus**, ruis, *s. m.* (*Ir. id.*) Knowledge, skill; wood.—*Shaw.* Purple.—*O'Reilly.*

Rùsg, rùisg, *s. m.* A fleece; a peeling; a cover; rind, bark; a husk; a shell. *N. pl.* rùsgan; *d. pl.* rùsgaibh. Neòil nan rùsgaibh bàn, *clouds in white fleeces.—Macfar.*

Goth. rusg. *W.* rhysg. *Ir.* rusg. *Corn.* risk *and* rusk. *Arm.* rusk, *the bark of a tree.*

† **Rusg**, *v. a.* Beat, strike, pelt. *Pret. a.* rusg; *fut. aff. a.* rusgaidh.

Rùsgach, *a.* (*Ir. id.*) Peeling, fleecing; excoriating, epispastic; stripping; *also,* fleecy; having many rinds, as an onion; crustaceous. Caoraich rùsgach, *fleecy sheep.—Macfar.* Reithe garbh-rùsgach, *a thick-fleeced ram.—Mac Lach.*

Rùsgadh, aidh, *s. m.* (*Ir. id.*) A peeling, a husking, a shelling; a fleecing; a stripping or undressing; a making bare or naked; an excoriating; an excoriation; a fleece; a husk; an unsheathing. Rùsgadh air bhasaibh, *excoriations on the palms.—Macfar.* Rùsgadh lann air gach taobh, *unsheathing of swords on every side.—Fingalian Poem.*

Rùsgadh, (a), *pr. part.* of rùisg; which see.

Rùsgail, *a.* Epispastic.

Rùsgan, ain, *s. m.* A little fleece; a piece of skin peeled off; an excoriated place; a small boat made of bark.

Ruslach, *a.* Scratching, excoriating.

Rusladh, aidh, *s. m.* A scratching. Bhiodh rusladh leis na h-ionghan ann, *there would be scratching with the nails.—Mac Co.*

† **Rustaca**, *a.* (*Ir. id.*) Rustic, rude, clownish.—*Shaw.*

† **Rustach**, aich, *s. m.* (*Ir. id.*) A rustic, a boor; a churl. *N. pl.* rustaichean.

Rustan, ain, *s. m.* (*Ir. id.*) A hillock, a hudge, a lump; a heap.

Ruta, **Rutadh**, aidh, *s. m.* A ram; *also,* a herd, a rout; a tribe of people.

Ruth, *s. m.* Salary, wages, hire; the fish called hornback.

Rutha, **Ruthadh**, aidh, *s. m.* A point of land, cape, or promontory, a flush (*Gr.* ῥυτις) Written also *rugha*, which see

RUTHACH, *a* Having capes or headlands; abounding in capes or headlands; flushed

RUTHADH, aidh, *s. m.* See RUTHA.

RUTHARACH, *a* (*Ir. id*) Quarrelsome; fighting.

RUTHARACHD, *s f.* (*Ir. id*) Quarrelsomeness; continued or frequent fighting

S.

S, s, (suil *and* sail, *the willow*) The sixteenth letter of the Gaelic alphabet It has two sounds (1) It sounds like *sh* in *sheet*, when it is preceded or followed by *e* or *i*, whether immediately or with a lingual intervening; as, bris, *break*, sir, *seek*, fàisg, *squeeze*; sion, *a blast*. (2) In every other situation it sounds like *s* in *salt*, *sack*; as, sac, *a sack*, sona, *happy*, srac, *tear*, cas *or* cos, *a foot* But when *s* is immediately followed by *h*, there is only an aspirated articulation heard, as, a shùil, (*pron.* a hùil), *his eye*, shuidh, (*pron* hui), *sat* Lastly, *sh* are altogether quiescent when they are followed by either of the liquids *l*, *n*, as, shleuchd, *worshipped*, shnamh, *swam* *S*, when preceded by the letter *t* with a hyphen (*t*-), is quiescent, as, san t-sabhal, *in the barn*, an t-sluaigh, *of the people*.

S', (*for* so), *demonstrative pron* This Am baile s', *this town*

'S, (*for* is), *def. v* Am, art, is, are.

'S, (*for* agus) And

The following lines, of inimitable beauty, exemplify the contracted forms of the preceding words *is* and *agus*

Ach 's léir leat, a sholuis an là,
Taibhse Thrathail na cheo glas,
Tra dh' eireas e 'd dhearsa tra nòin,
'S a bhios ceo air binnein nan sleibhte
'S taitneach le d' dhearsa leabadh nan treun
'S ceò éide nan laoch gàbhaidh
'S tric thu blà air leabaidh Threinmhòir,
'S ag éiridh air lic Thrathail —*Oss Truthal*

Thou dost behold, O light of day,
The ghost of Trathal in his misty shroud,
When it rises in thy noontide beam,
And when the mist is on the mountain tops
Pleasant to thy rays are the graves of heroes,
And the cloudy mantle of warriors fierce
Often art thou warm on the bed of Trenmor,
And rising on Trathal's tomb

'SA, (*for* agus a) And his; and her

'SA, *for* anns a (*Ir id*) In the Mar dharaig 'sa ghleann, *like an oak in the valley* —*Ull*

SA, *an emphatic adjection* A mhac-sa, *his son*, do mhac-sa, *thy son*.

† SAB, *a* (*Ir id*) Strong, able, *also*, *substantively*, death, a bolt, a bar.

SABADH, aidh, *s m* Squabble, quarrel.

SABAID, *s. f.* (*Ir. id.*) A quarrel, a row or fray, a fight *N. pl* sabaidean.

SÀBAID, *s f* Sabbath. A choimheadas an t-Sàbaid, *that keepeth the Sabbath* —*Stew Is.*

Gr. σάββατον *Lat* sabbatum *Goth* sabbatu. *Ir* saboid.

SABAIL, *s* (*Ir. id*) A granary, a barn —*Shaw.* Now written *sabhal*, which see

SÀBAILT, *s f.* See SÀBAID.

SABH, saibh, *s. m* A salve, an ointment for a sore, *also*, sorrel, a spittle, a bolt, the bar of a gate Sabh-shùl, *eye-salve.*—*Stew. Rev.* Sabh-tairnidh, *ointment for extracting matter from a sore.*

SÀBH, sàibh, *s m* (*Dan.* sawe.) A saw. Sabh laimh, *a hand-saw* *N pl.* sàibh *and* sàbhan. Le sàbhan, *with saws* —*Stew. Chr.* Le sàibh, *with saws* —*Stew.* 1 *K.* Sabh-sgriob, *a hand-saw*, sabh-dùirne, *a hand-saw*, *a whip-saw*.

SÀBH, *v a* Saw, work or cut with a saw. *Pret a.* shàbh; *fut aff a* sàbhaidh, *shall saw*, *p. part.* sabhta.

SÀBHACH, *a.* Unctuous; healing, *also*, cutting, as a saw.

SABHACH, *a* Abounding in sorrel; like sorrel; of sorrel; quarrelsome; quarrelling.

SÀBHADAIR, *s m.* A sawyer *N pl* sàbhadairean, *sawyers*

SÀBHADAIREACHD, *s. f.* The process of sawing; the business of a sawyer

SABHADH, aidh, *s m* Sorrel; a quarrel

SÀBHADH, aidh, *s m.* A sawing Air a shabhadh, air a sabhadh, air an sàbhadh, *sawn*; muileann sàbhaidh, *a sawmill*, slochd sàbhaidh, *a sawpit*

SÀBHADH, (a), *pr part.* of sàbh Sawing Saoir locaradh 's a sàbhadh, *joiners planing and sawing*

SABHAIL, *gen sing* of sabhal

SÀBHAIL, *v a* (*Ir. id*) Save, protect, spare; preserve; use frugally or sparingly *Pret. a.* shàbhail, *fut. aff a* sàbhailidh, *fut pass* sàbhailear.

SABHAIL, *v a* Store up in a barn *Pret. a.* shabhail.

SÀBHAIL, *s f.* A saving, a protecting, a sparing, protection; frugality

SÀBHAILEACH, *a* Saving, preserving; sparing, frugal, careful Gu sàbhaileach, *frugally*. *Com.* and *sup.* sàbhailiche.

SÀBHAILEACHD, *s f* Parsimony, frugality, economy.

SABHAILICHE, *s m.* A frugal man, an economist; a preserver.

SÀBHAILT, *a* Safe; secure Sàbhailt air tìr, *safe on land.* —*Old Song* An calaidhean sàbhailt, *in secure harbours.* —*Mac Co*

SÀBHAILTE, *p part* of sabhail. Saved, preserved, delivered.

SÀBHAILTEACHD, *s f* Safeness; secureness.

SÀBHAIR, *s m* (sàbh-fhear) A sawyer *N pl* sàbhairean.

SÀBHAIREACHD, *s f.* The process of sawing, the business of a sawyer.

SABHAIRLE, *s. m* (*Ir id*) A cur, a mastiff —*Shaw.*

SABHAL, ail, *s m* (*Ir* sabhail.) A barn, a granary. Siol san t-sabhal, *seed in the barn* —*Stew Hag* *N. pl.* saibhlean, *barns* Bhriseadh na saibhlean, *the barns were broken down* —*Stew Joel*

SÀBHALACH, *a.* (*Ir id*) Saving; frugal; preserving. Gu sàbhalach, *frugally*. *Com.* and *sup.* sabhalaiche

SÀBHALACHD, *s f* Parsimony; frugality; economy.

SÀBHALADH, aidh, *s m.* A saving, a sparing; a protecting; frugality; protection, preservation Chum an sàbhaladh, *to protect them* —*Macint.*

SÀBHALADH, (a), *pr. part* of sàbhail. Saving, sparing; preserving, delivering.

SÀBHALAICHE, *s. m.* A frugal person; *also*, a protector, a preserver or saviour.

SÀBHALTACHD, *s f.* Security, safety; protection.

SÀBHAN, ain, (*dim.* of sabh) A little saw. *N. pl.* sabhain.

SABHAN, ain, *s. m* A cub, a cur, a young mastiff.—*Shaw.*

SÀBHAN, *n pl* of sabh; which see.

Sabhas, ais, *s. m.* (*Ir.* sabhsa.) Sauce.—*Shaw.*

Sabhdair, *s. m* A stroller, a lounger. *N. pl* sabhdairean.

Sabhdaireachd, *s. f.* Strolling, lounging.

Sabhlach, *a.* Healing; like a salve; unctuous

Sabhlaich, aich, *s. m.* (*Ir id*) A spittle.

Sabhladh, aidh, *s. m.* A salve; a healing ointment; *also*, a stirring up, as corn in a barn

Sabhsach, *a.* Full of sauce; like sauce; of sauce

Sabhsaich, *v. a.* Sauce. *Pret. a* shabhsaich, *sauced.*

Sabhsaichte, *p. part.* of sabhsaich. Sauced.

Sabhsair, *s. m* One who makes sauce, a sausage.—*Macd.* and *Shaw. N. pl* sabhsairean.

Sabhsaireachd, *s. f.* Sauce-making; sausage-making.

Sabhul, uil, *s. m.* See **Sabhal**.

Sac, *v. a* Sack, put up in sacks or bags *Pret. a.* shac; *fut. aff. a.* sacaidh.

Sac, saic, *s. m.* A sack, a pock or bag; a measure of corn consisting of five bushels, a measure of coals consisting of three bushels, a burden, *in derision*, a short, fat fellow *N. pl.* saic. Sac mine, *a meal-sack, a sack of meal*, sac drona, *a back load, a man's load*, sac imrich, *a load of furniture at a flitting*, sac uisge-bheatha, *a pack-saddle with a cask of whisky on each side*, sac-bhrathair, *a pack-saddle.*

The word *sac* is found with very little variation in almost all languages, and signifying the same thing; the supposition, therefore, is not unreasonable, that it is one of the few words which have come down to us from the original language of man

Heb. Chald. sac, *a sack* *Arab.* sagari. *Copt* pisok, *a pannier.* *Gr.* σακκος, *a sack.* *Lat* saccus. *It* sacco. *Span.* saco *and* saca *Belg* sack. *Fr.* sac *Du.* zak. *Swed.* sack. *Goth.* sack. *Germ.* sack. *Dan Nor.* saek. *Sclav. Carn.* shakel *Hung* saak. *Turk* sak. *Georgian*, sako. *Anglo-Sax.* saecc *and* sacc. *Ir* sac *W* sach *Corn.* zah. *Arm.* sach *Bisc.* sac

Sacach, *a.* Like a sack, short and corpulent

Sacachadh, aidh, *s. m.* A sacking or putting up in a sack; a pressing into a sack

Sacachadh, (a), *pr. part* of sacaich.

Sacadh, aidh, *s. m.* A putting up in a sack, a pressing into a sack.

Sacaich, *v. a.* (*from* sac.) Press into a sack; put in a sack; fill to satiety. *Pret. a.* shacaich; *fut. aff a.* sacaichidh.

Sacaichte, *p. part.* of sacaich. Laid up in a sack, as grain; bagged; filled to satiety.

Sacaid, *s. f.* (*Scotch*, sacket.) A little sack or bag *N pl.* sacaidean.

Sacail, *s. f.* (*Germ.* shekel. *Carn.* shakel. *Sclav.* shakel, *a sack.*) A bagging, a putting up in a bag

† **Sacair**, *s. m* (*Ir. id.*) A priest.

Sacan, ain, *s. m., dim.* of sac. (*Ir. id*) A little sack; a short corpulent fellow; *also*, an unmannerly fellow —*Shaw N. pl* sacain.

Sacanta, *a* Corpulent, squat; like a sack or pock

Sacantachd, *s. f* Corpulence; squatness.

Sacarbhuig, *s f.* (*Ir. id*) A confession

Sacbut, uit, *s.* A sackbut.—*Stew. Dan*

† **Sach**, *v. a.* (*Ir. id.*) Sack or besiege.—*Shaw.*

Sachd. See **Sac**.

Sachdachadh, aidh, *s m* See **Sacachadh**.

Sachdadh, aidh, *s. m.* See **Sacadh**.

Sachdaich, *v a.*: written also *sacaich*; which see

Saclan, ain, *s m.* A standard.—*Shaw.*

Sacraidhe, *s. f.* Baggage, luggage.

Sacrail, *s. f.* (*Ir. id.*) A sacrifice

Sacramainte, *s f.* A sacrament, the eucharist Làth sacramainte, *a communion-day, a day appointed for partaking of the Lord's Supper*

Sac-shrathair, -shrathrach, *s. f.* (*Ir id*) A pack-saddle

Sadach, aich, *s m.* (*Ir id*) Saw-dust, mill-dust, dust of any description —*Macd*

Sadadh, aidh, *s m* (*Ir. id*) A dusting, a beating.

Sadadh, *v a.* Dust, beat or brush dust out of cloth, brush dust away

Sadaich, *s f.* A whisk —*Macd*

Sadhail, *a* (*Ir id*) Pleasant.

Sadhail, *s f* (*Ir id*) Neglect, delight, a good house —*Shaw*

Sadhal, ail, *s m.* (*Ir id* *Sax* sadl) A saddle *N pl* sadhalan

Sagart, airt, *s m* (*Ir id* *Lat* sacerdos *Shan* sacradas) A priest, a churchman *N. pl* sagairtean Cha 'n fhiach sagart gun chléireach? *what is a priest without a clerk?*—*G. P*

Sagartach, *a* (*Ir id*) Priestly, clerical

Sagartachd, *s f.* (*Ir id.*) Priesthood Sagartachd sior-ruidh, *everlasting priesthood* —*Stew Ex*

Sagartail, *a* (sagart-amhuil) Priestly or priestlike, sacerdotal; *rarely*, pious, holy

† **Sagh**, saigh, *s f.* A bitch —*Shaw*

† **Sàgh**, *v a* (*Ir. id*) Drink, suck; guzzle —*Shaw* Perhaps *sàth*

Saghail, *s f.* An attack.

† **Saghain**, *s f* A bitch.

Saghal, *a* Nice; tender —*Shaw*

Saghalachd, *s. f* Delight; content; voluptuousness.

Sagharlachd, *s. f* Delight; content, satisfaction —*Shaw*

† **Saghmhair**, *s m.* (*Scotch*, syvour) A sink, a kennel.

Sags-bheurla, *s f.* The English language; the Anglo-Saxon.

Sagsunn, uinn, *s* (sags-fhonn.) England; *literally*, the land of Saxons: *pronounced* Sasunn

Sagsunnach, aich, *s m.* (*Corn* zaznak.) An Englishman, a Saxon. *N. pl* Sagsunnaich.

Saibh, *gen. sing* of sabh

Saibhir, *a.* (*Ir.* saidhbhir) Rich, opulent, fertile, plentiful. Saibhir ann an tròcair, *rich in mercy* —*Stew. Eph.*

Saibhir, *v. a.* and *n* Make wealthy; become wealthy.

Saibhire, *com* and *sup.* of saibhir.

Saibhireach, *a.* Enriching; fertile *Com* and *sup* saibhiriche.

Saibhireachd, *s f* Richness, opulence; abundance, plenty. Saibhireachd na sìth, *the abundance of peace* —*Sm.*

Saibhlean, *n. pl* of sabhal. Barns, granaries.

Saibhreas, eis, *s m* (*Ir.* saidhbhreas) Riches, wealth, plenty. Saibhreas agus urram, *riches and honour* —*Stew Pro.* The word of contrary meaning is *daibhreas*

Saibhrich, *v. a* and *n* Enrich or make wealthy; become rich *Pret. a.* shaibhrich, *enriched*, *fut aff. a* saibhrichidh

Saibhrichte, *p. part.* of saibhrich. Enriched

Saic, *gen sing* and *n pl* of sac

Saic-dhiollaid, *s f.* A pack-saddle

Saic-eideadh, idh, *s m* Sackcloth; a clothing in sackcloth

Saic-eudach, aich, *s. m* (*Ir id*) Sackcloth Saic-eudach air mo chroicionn, *sackcloth on my skin* —*Stew Job*

Sàich, *s f* (*Ir id*) Plenty, a bellyful, *also*, *adjectively*, sated. Contracted, perhaps, for *sàthaich*.

† Saide, *s. f.* A seat, a couch. *N. pl.* saidean. *Ir. id. Lat.* sedes. *It.* sedia. *Germ.* sett.

Saidealach, *a.* (*Ir.* saidolach.) Bashful; sheepish; easily duped. Gu saidealach, *sheepishly*. *Com.* and *sup.* saidealaiche.

Saidealachd, *s. f.* Bashfulness; sheepishness; simplicity.

Saidealta, *a.* Bashful; easily duped or imposed on; sheepish; blunt.—*Macfar. Voc.*

Saidealtachd, *s. f.* Bashfulness; sheepishness; simplicity. Gun saidealtachd gun uamhann, *without bashfulness or fear.*—*Old Song.*

Saidh, *s. f.* A treasury; the prow of a ship—(*Shaw*); *also,* a bitch; mildness.

Saidhbhir, *a.* (*Stew. Gen. ref.*); more frequently written *saibhir.*

† Saidhiste, *s. f.* (*Ir. id.*) A seat.

Saidseach, ich, *s.* A wallet.

Saifear, ir, *s. m.* Sapphire-stone.

Saifearach, *a.* Abounding in sapphire; like sapphire; of sapphire.

Saigean, ein, *s. m.* (*Ir. id.*) A short, squat fellow. *N. pl.* saigeanan.

Saigeanach, *a.* Short and squat in stature.

Saigeanach, aich, *s. m.* A person of a low, squat stature. *N. pl.* saigeanaich.

Saigeannta, *a.* Short in stature, squat.

† Saigh, *s. f.* A sharp edge, a sharp point.
This vocable seems to be the root of *saighead*, an arrow.

Saighdeach, *a.* Arrowy; pointed.

Saighdeadh, idh, *s. m.* A darting or shooting forward.

Saighdeadh, (a), *pr. part.* of saighead. Darting; shooting. Nathair a saighdeadh air lom, *a serpent darting forward on the plain.*—*Mac Lach.*

Saighdear, eir, *s. m.* (*Ir.* saigheadoir. *Lat.* sagittarius.) A soldier; *literally*, an archer. Saighdear-coise, *a foot-soldier;* saighdear-fairge, *a marine;* saighdearan dearg, *red-coated soldiers; red-coats;*—a name given to the government soldiers during the disturbances in 1715 and 1745, in contradistinction to the soldiers of Prince Charles, who were, commonly, called *saighdearan dubh.*
Saighdear (saighead-fhear) means an archer, as has already been said. The standing armies of the Gael had, at one time, no other weapons of offence than bows and arrows; hence, in process of time, *saighdear* became an arbitrary term, and now signifies a soldier of any description.

Saighdearachd, *s. f.* Soldiership; brave actions; the army; the profession of a soldier.

Saighdearail, *a.* (saighdear-amhuil.) Soldierlike; brave; martial; warlike.

Saighead, eid, *and* saighde, *s. f., from* † saigh. (*Ir. id.*) An arrow, a dart. Thuit an saighead gu faoin, *the arrow fell harmless.*—*Orr.* Ag iomairt saighde mar lainn, *using an arrow as a spear.*—*Id. N. pl.* saighdean; *d. pl.* saighdibh.
Ir. saighead. *Lat.* sagitt-a. *It.* saetta. *Arm.* and *W.* saeth. *Corn.* seth.

Saighead, *v. n.* (*W.* saethu.) Dart or shoot forward; move swiftly. *Pret. a.* shaighead; *fut. aff.* saigheadaidh *and* saighdidh.

Saigheadair, *s. m.* An archer; an arrow-maker; a soldier. See Saighdear.

Saigheas, eis, *s. m.* (*Ir. id.*) Oldness, antiquity.

Saighnean, ein, *s. m.* Lightning; a hurricane.

Sail, *s. f.* (*Ir. id.*) A beam, a joist; common willow. *N. pl.* sailthean.

† Sail, *v. a.* Salute.

Sàil, *v. a.* Provide with heels, as shoes. *Pret.* shàil; *fut. aff. a.* sàilidh.

Sàil, sàl, sàlach, *s. f.* A heel. *N. pl.* sàiltean, *heels.* Bruthaidh tusa 'shàil-san, *thou shalt bruise its heel.*—*Stew. Gen.*
Corn. saudl. *Ir.* sail. *Swed.* sala. *Arm.* seuzl, *heel. W.* saile, *groundwork.*

Sàil, *s. f.* Brine; the sea. See Saile.

† Sàil, *s. f.* A guard, a custody.—*Shaw.*

Sail-bhreaghadh, aidh, *s. m.* A rejoicing.

Sàil-bhruth, *s. m.* A bruise on the heel.

Sailchead, eid, *s. m.* Dirtiness; defilement, dirt—(*Stew. Jam.*); increase in dirtiness. A dol an sailchead, *growing more and more dirty.*

Sàil-chuach, aich, *s. m.* (*Ir.* sal-chuach.) A violet; a pansy. *N. pl.* sàil-chuachan. Coille is guirme sàil-chuach, *a wood where violets are bluest.*—*Old Song.* Written also *fàil-chuach.*

Sail-chuachadh, *a.* Abounding in violets; like a violet; of violets.

Sail-chuachag, aig, *s. f.* A young violet, a little violet. Sail-chuachag air uachdar d' fheòir, *young violets on the tops of thy grass.*—*Macfar.*

Sàile, *s.* Salt water; brine; sea. Air sàile rachainn thàiris leat, *I would cross the sea with you.*—*Old Song.*
Chald. sal. *Lat. Span.* sal. *It.* sale. *Finlandese,* sal. *Fr.* sel. *Teut.* salz. *Pol.* sal. *Lusat.* soll. *Bohem.* sul. *Dal.* szol. *Ir.* sàile. *Germ.* salz.

Sàileach, *a.* Having heels; *also,* briny, salt.

Saileag, eig, *s. f.* (*dim.* of sail.) A young willow, a little willow; a little beam or joist. *N. pl.* saileagan.

Sàileag, eig, *s. f. dim.* of sàil. (*Ir. id.*) A heel-piece; a little heel. *N. pl.* sàileagan.

Sàilean, ein, *s. f.* An arm or branch of the sea; a bay. Perhaps *sailinn*, i. e. *saile-linn.*

Sàileanach, *a.* Abounding in bays or in friths; like a bay or frith; of a bay or frith.

Sàileas, eis, *s. m.* (*Ir. id.*) Salt water; the sea.—*Shaw.*

Saileid, *s. f.* Sallad.

Sàil-ghille, *s. m.* A footman, a page. *N. pl.* sàil-ghillean.

Sailinn, *s. f.* (saile-linn. *Ir.* sailin.) A deep bay; an arm of the sea; a frith. *N. pl.* sailinntean.

Saill, *v. a.* (*Ir. id.*) Salt, pickle, cure, season. *Pret. a.* shaill; *fut. aff. a.* saillidh, *shall salt; fut. pass.* saillear.

Saill, saille, *s. f.* Fatness; fat, grease; pickle; brine. Do shaill na talmhainn, *of the fatness of the earth.*—*Stew. Gen. ref.* Fillean saille, *collops of fat.*—*Stew. Job.*

Sailleach, *a.* Fat; abounding in fat; greasy; corpulent. *Com.* and *sup.* sailliche, *more* or *most fat.*

Sailleach, ich. (*Ir. id.*) Willow.

Sailleachd, *s. f.* Fatness; fat; greasiness; corpulence.

Sailleadh, idh, *s. m.* The process of salting or pickling.

Saillean, ein, *s. m.* A sort of paste used by weavers to smooth their thread.

Saillear, *a.* (saillmhor.) Fat; lusty; greasy; corpulent.

Saillear, *s. m.* (*Ir. id.*) A salter; a pickler; a salt-cellar; a vessel for storing up salted fish. *N. pl.* saill-leirein.

Saillear, *fut. pass.* of saill. Shall be salted.

Saillearach, *a.* Of, or belonging to, a salter or pickler.

Saillearachd, *a.* The business of a salter or pickler.

Saillmhor, *a.* Fat; abounding in fat; greasy; pickled. *Com.* and *sup.* saillmhoire.

Saillte, *p. part.* of saill. Salted, seasoned; salt, briny; pickled. Bùrn saillte, *salted water.*
Ir. id. Swed. salt. *Goth.* and *Scandinavian,* salz.

W. halen. *Anglo-Sax.* sealt. *Corn.* selliz, *salt.* *Germ.* salz, *salt water.*

Saillteachd, *s. f.* Saltness. Saillteachd d'uisgeachan, *the saltness of thy water.—Old Poem.*

Sailm, *gen. sing.* and *n. pl.* of salm.

Sailm-dharaich, *s. m.* A decoction of oak-bark.

Sailmeachd, *s. f.* Psalmody.

Sailm-uchd, *s. m.* An ointment, of which fresh butter and healing herbs are the principal ingredients.

Sail-spiorad, aid, *s. m.* A guardian spirit.

Sàilteachadh, *a.* A tracing or following footsteps.

Sàiltean, *n. pl.* of sàil. Heels; steps; vestiges; footsteps.

Sailtheach, *a.* (*from* sail.) Beamed or joisted; like a beam or joist.

Sailthean, *n. pl.* of sail. Beams, joists. Sailthean a sheòmra, *the beams of his chambers.—Sm.*

Sailtich, *v. a.* (*from* sail.) Provide with beams or joists. *Pret. a.* shailtich; *fut. aff. a.* sailltichidh.

Sàiltich, *v. a.* (*from* sàil.) Follow by tracing the footsteps. *Pret. a.* shàiltich; *fut.* sàiltichidh.

Sailtichean, *s. pl.* Hatches; steps.

Sailtichte, *p. part.* of sailtich. Provided with beams or joists.

Sàiltichte, *p. part.* of sàiltich. Heeled; provided with heels, as shoes.

† **Saim**, *a.* (*Ir. id. Sax.* seme. *W.* saim, *tallow.*) Rich.—*Shaw.*

Saimh, *v.* (*Ir. id. Lat.* suavis.) Quiet, still; mild, pleasant; sweet. *Asp. form,* shaimh. Ri oidhche shaimhe, *on a quiet night.—Oss. Derm.*

† **Saimh**, *s. m.* (*Ir. id.*) A pair, a brace, a couple.—*Shaw.*

Saimh, saimhe, *s. f.* (*Ir. id.*) Pleasure, delight; ease, luxury; repose, quietness, peacefulness. An lear an saimh shuaine, *the sea in profound repose.—Oss. Duthona.* Saimh na h-oidhche, *the quietness of night.—Oss. Fin. and Lor.*

Saimh-bhreathach, *a.* Producing twins.

Saimh-bhriathar, air, *s. m.* A flattering speech; smooth language.

Saimh-bhriathrach, *a.* Flattering; cajoling.

Saimh-bhriathrachas, ais, *s. m.* Cajoling language.

Saimh-chealg, cheilg, *s. f.* (*Ir.* saimh-chealgadh.) Hypocrisy.

Saimh-chealgach, *a.* Hypocritical.

Saimheach, *a.* Luxurious; fond of ease; fond of pleasure.

Saimheachas, ais, *s. m.* Luxury; fondness of ease or pleasure.

Saimheachd, *s. f.* Love of pleasure; a state of luxury or pleasure; a luxurious habit.

Saimhghrios, *v. a.* (*Ir. id.*) Allure, entice.

Saimh-ghriosach, *a.* Alluring, enticing.

Saimh-ghriosadh, aidh, *s. m.* (*Ir. id.*) Allurement.

Saimhiche, *s. m.* A votary of pleasure; *also*, votaries of pleasure.

Saimhneachadh, aidh, *s. m.* (*from* † saimh.) A yoking; a coupling.

Saimhnich, *v.* Couple; yoke. *Pret. a.* shaimhnich, *yoked;* *fut. aff.* saimhnichidh.

Saimhnichte, *p. part.* of saimhnich. Coupled; yoked.

Saimhrigheach, *a.* Easy, satisfied, quiet, content.

Saimhrigheachd, *s. f.* Ease, quiet, satisfaction.

Saimhsealair, *s. m.* A counsellor. *N. pl.* saimhsealairean.

† **Sain**, *v. a.* (*Ir. id.*) Vary, alter, change. *Pret. a.* shain.

Sain, *a.* (*Ir. id. Lat.* sanus.) Sound; healthy.

† **Sain-chreach**, *a.* Healed; sound.

Saindrean, ein, *s. m.* A seat; society.—*Shaw.*

† **Saine**, *s. f.* Variety; variation; soundness; *also*, sedition; discord.

Sain-fhios, *s. m.* A mark; a proof; etymology.

Sainnseal, eil, *s. m.* A handsel; a new-year's gift.

Sainnsealaiche, *s. m.* One who gives a handsel.

Sainnt, *gen. sing.* of sannt; which see.

Sainnt, sainnte, *s. f.* Covetousness. More frequently written *sannt;* which see.

Sainre, *s. f.* A reddish purple; sanguine colour; flesh colour.

Sainntreabh, eibh, *s. m.* (*Ir. id.*) A family; a house.

Sair, *gen. sing.* and *n. pl.* of sàr.

Sàir-bhrigh, *s. f.* An attribute.

Sàir-fhios, *s. m.* Certain knowledge. More frequently written *sàr-fhios.*

Sairdeal, eil, *s. m.* A sprat. *N. pl.* sairdealan.

Sairdealach, *a.* Abounding in sprats; like a sprat; of sprats.

Sàisde, *s. f.* Sage; mountain or wild sage.

Sàisdeach, *a.* Of sage; like sage; abounding in sage.

Saith, *s. c.* A horse; a bitch; a backbone; a haft; a treasure; a thrust; a piercing; a space; a multitude; a swarm.

Saith, *a.* Vulgar, vile; cheap.

Sàitheach, *a.* Full, satisfied, glutted, sated; replete; stabbing. Tha mi sàitheach dheth, *I am sated with it.*

Sàitheachd, *s. f.* Fulness, satiety; repletion; gormandizing; frequent stabbing.

Saitheas, eis, *s. m.* Cheapness; vileness.—*Shaw.*

Sàithich, *v. a.* and *n.* Fill, satiate, glut; grow full or satiated. *Pret. a.* shàithich. *Fut. aff. a.* saithichidh.

Sàithichte, *p. part.* of sàithich. Filled, satiated, glutted; replete.

Sàithte, *p. part.* of sàth. Stabbed, pierced, thrust. An sleaghan sàithte san leirg, *their spears thrust in the plain.* —*Mac Lach.*

Sal, sail, *s. m.* Dirt, filth; dross, dust; a spot or blemish. Co dh'ionnlaid dhiubh gach sal, *who cleansed them of all filth.* —*Sm.* Mar shal, *like dross.—Stew. Ps.* Air sal an raoin, *on the dust of the plain.—Mac Lach.* Sal-cluaise, *ear-wax.* *Anglo-Sax.* sale. *Germ.* sal. *Ir.* sal, *dirt.* *Eng.* soil. *Corn.* sal, *vile.*

Sàl, sàil, *s. m.* Sea; salt-water. A leum thar an t-sàl, *bounding over the sea.—Old Poem.*

Salach, *a., from* sal. (*Ir. id. Germ.* sal.) Dirty, unclean, foul, nasty; polluted, defiled; troubled or agitated, as a fluid. Bithidh e salach, *he shall be defiled.—Stew. Lev.* Cuan salach nan garbh-thonn, *the troubled billowy ocean.—Ull.* Fuil shalach, *polluted* or *foul blood.—Old Song.*

Salachadh, aidh, *s. m.* (*Ir.* salchadh.) A dirtying, a defiling, a soiling; filth; defilement.

Salachadh, (a), *pr. part.* of salaich.

Salachar, air, *s. m.* (*Ir.* salchar.) Filth, dirt, dung, excrements; filthiness, dirtiness, grossness, corruption; dross. *Asp. form,* shalachar. O gach uile shalachar, *from all filthiness.—Stew. Cor.* Written also *salchar;* which see.

Sàlag, aig, *s. f.* (*from* sàil.) A heel-piece. *N. pl.* sàlagan.

Salaich, *v. a.* (*Ir.* salaigh.) Defile; make dirty; spoil; pollute, contaminate. *Pret. a.* shalaich; *fut. aff. a.* salaichidh; *fut. pass.* salaichear, *shall be defiled; p. part.* salaichte, *defiled.*

Salaichte, *p. part.* of salaich. Defiled; made dirty; spoiled.

Salaid, *s. f.* (*Fr.* salade.) Salad.—*Macd.*

Salainn, *gen. sing.* of salann; which see.

Salainneach, *a.* Salting; communicating a salt taste.

SALAINNEACHADH, aidh, *s. m.* A salting, a pickling, a seasoning.

SALAINNICH, *v. a.* Salt, pickle, season. *Pret. a.* shalainnich, *salted.*

SALANN, ainn, *s. m.* Salt. An fhairge shalainn, *the salt sea.—Stew. Gen.* Poll salainn, *a salt-pit.—Stew. Zeph.* Bacaid shalainn, *a salt-bucket.*

Ir. salann *or* salan. *Lat.* sal, *salt*, and salin-us. *Span.* sal. *Fr.* sel. *Gr. by met.* ἅλς. *W.* halen. *Arm.* halon. *Corn.* holan.

SALANNACH, *a.* Abounding in salt.

SALANNAN, ain, *s. m.* A salt-pit; a salt-pool. *N. pl.* salannain.

SALCHADH, aidh, *s. m.* See SALACHADH.

SALCHAR, *s. m.* (*Ir. id.*) Filth, dirt; filthiness; dross; dung, excrements; filthiness, dirtiness; grossness, corruption. O 'n salchar, *from their filthiness.—Stew. Pro.* Salchar on airgiod, *dross from the silver.—Stew. Pro.*

SÀL-CLUAIS, *s. m.* Ear-wax.

† SALL, saill, *s. m.* Bitterness; satire; invective; a lampoon.

† SALLAN, ain, *s. m.* Singing; harmony.

SALLTAIR, *s. m.* A chaldron; a Scotch measure of sixteen bolls; an English measure of thirty-six bushels.

SALM, sailm, *s. c.* A psalm. *N. pl.* sailm; *d.pl.* salmaibh. Ann an salmaibh, *in psalms.*

SALMACH, *a.* Like a psalm; of psalms; full of psalms.

SALMADAIR, *s. m.* A psalm-book; a psalmist; a songster; a chorister. *N. pl.* salmadairean. Salmadair chraoibh dhlu-dhuillich, *the songster of the leafy tree.—Macdon.* Salmadair binn, *a sweet psalmist.—Stew. 2 Sam.*

SALMAIR, *s. m.* (*Ir. id.*) A psalmist; a chorister; a precentor; a clerk. *N. pl.* salmairean.

SALMAIREACHD, *s. f.* Psalm-singing; the office of a clerk or precentor; the business of a clerk.

† SALT, sailt, *s. m.* (*Ir. id.*) Colour.—*Shaw.*

SALTAIR, saltrach, *s. f.* (*Ir. id.*) Psaltery; a psalter; a saltmonger; *also*, the title of several Irish traditionary records, as, *Saltair na Teamkrach. N. pl.* saltairean.

SALTAIR, *v.* (*Ir. id. Germ.* schalten.) Tread, trample. *Pret. a.* shaltair, *trod; fut. aff.* saltraidh, *shall tread* or *trample.* Saltraidh e, *he will trample.—Stew. Mic.*

SALTAIRT, *s. f.* (*Ir.* saltuirt.) A treading, a trampling.

SALTAIRT, (a), *pr. part.* saltar. Treading, trampling.

SALTRAICH, *s. f.* A treading, a trampling; a continued trampling; a tramp, a tread. Chluinnte an saltraich astar cian, *their tread was heard a great way off.— Fingalian Poem.*

SALTRAICH, *v.* Tread, trample. *Pret. a.* shaltraich, *trod; fut. aff. a.* saltraichidh.

SALTRAICHTE, *p. part.* of saltraichidh. Trodden, trampled on.

SALTRAIDH, *fut. aff. a.* of saltair. Shall or will trample or tread.

† SAM, *s. m.* (*Ir. id.*) The sun.

SAMH, saimh, *s. m.* (*Ir. id.*) Rest, ease; pleasure; quietness; shelter; a quiet spot; *rarely*, the sun. A gorm lasadh am samh na-h-innse, *bluely flaming in the shelter of the isle.—Oss. Cathula.*

SAMH, saimh, *s. m.* That part of sorrel which bears seed.

SÀMHACH, *a.*, *from* samh. (*Ir. id.*) Quiet, silent; unmoved, undisturbed; peaceful, calm; pleasant, mild; easy. An oidhche sàmhach, *the night quiet.—Ull.* C'uime tha thu cho samhach? *why art thou so silent?—Oss. Tem.* Gu mu samhach a robh d'òrchul, *quiet be thy golden locks.—Oss. Derm. Com.* and *sup.* samhaiche.

SAMHACH, aich, *s.* (*Ir.* samhthach.) A handle; a haft; a shaft; the edge of a weapon. Samhach tuaidh, *the handle of a hatchet*—(*Macd.*); *the edge of a hatchet.—Shaw.* Samhach sgein, *the haft of a knife.*

SAMHACHAN, ain, *s. m.* A soft, quiet person.

† SAMHADH, aidh, *s. m.* A congregation.

SAMHAIL, *a.* (*Ir. id.*) Like; like as; resembling; equal.

SAMHAILT, *s. f.* A resemblance; a likeness; image; an apparition.

SAMHAIN, *s. f.* Pleasure; satisfaction.

SAMHAINN, samhna, *s. f.* See SAMHUINN.

SAMHAIRCEAN, ein, *s. m.* A primrose.

SAMHALTAN, ain, *s. m.*, *from* samhladh. (*Ir. id.*) An emblem, a hieroglyphic.

SAMHALTANACH, *a.* Emblematical; having emblems or hieroglyphics.

SAMHAN, ain, *s. m.* A little dog; the plant *savin* or *sabina.*

SAMHARCAN, ain, *s. m.* (*Ir.* samharcain.) A primrose.

SAMHAS, ais, *s. m.* Delight, pleasure, satisfaction; ease.

SAMHASACH, *a.* (*Ir. id.*) Causing delight or pleasure; agreeable; causing satisfaction; undisturbed, at ease. *Com.* and *sup.* samhasaiche.

SAMHASAICHE, *s. m.* A suttler.—*Shaw.*

SÀMHCHAIR, *s. f.* Quietness, calmness, tranquillity. An samhchair sheas an righ, *the king stood tranquilly.—Oss. Tem.*

SAMHLA, ai, *s. m.* See SAMHLADH.

SAMHLACH, *a.* (*from* samhla.) Likening, comparing; spectral; typical.

SAMHLACHADH, aidh, *s. m.* (*Ir.* samhlughadh.) A comparing, a likening; a comparison, a likeness, similitude; image, type; analogy; an emblem.

SAMHLACHADH, (a), *pr. part.* of samhlaich. Likening, comparing. 'G am shamhlachadh, *comparing me.*

SAMHLACHAIL, *a.* Typical, emblematical, analogical, hieroglyphical.

SAMHLACHAS, ais, *s. m.* (*Ir. id.*) A resemblance, similitude, comparison, analogy; example, pattern. Samhlachas an ti ud, *the similitude of that being.—Stew. Rom. ref. N. pl.* samhlachasan; *d. pl.* samhlachasaibh. Gun robh sibh 'nar samhlachasaibh, *that you were examples.—Stew. Thess. ref.*

SAMHLADH, aidh, *s. m.* A resembling, a comparing; a resemblance or likeness; a pattern or sample; a shape, form, or appearance; an apparition; a comparison, analogy, similitude; a slender person. Samhladh na h-altarach, *the pattern of the altar.—Stew. 2 K. ref.* Samhladh nam briathar fallain, *the form of sound words.—Stew. N. T.* Baoth-shamhla nam marbh, *the dread apparition of the dead.—Oss. Tem.*

SAMHLAICH, *v. a.* Liken, compare, assimilate, resemble. *Pret. a.* shamhlaich, *likened; fut. aff. a.* samhlaichidh; *p. part.* samhlaichte.

SAMHLUCHADH, aidh, *s. m.* See SAMHLACHADH.

SAMHLUICH, *v. a.* See SAMHLAICH.

SAMHLUTH, *a.* (*Ir. id.*) Brisk, active.

SAMHNA, *gen. sing.* of samhuinn.

SAMHNADH. See SAMHUINN.

SAMHNAG, aig, *s. f.* A bonfire; a fire or blaze which is kindled on the evening of the first of November. *N. pl.* samhnagan. See SAMHUINN.

SAMHNAGACH, *a.* Having many bonfires.

SAMHRA, *s. m.* See SAMH-THRÀ.

SAMHRACH, *a.* Like summer; warm.

SAMHRACHAIL, *a.* Estival; bringing summer; like summer.

SAMHRADH, aidh, *s. m.* (samh-thràth, *pleasant season.*) Summer. Aghaidh na grèine samhraidh, *the visage of the summer's sun.—Oss. Duth.* Seomar samhraidh, *a summer parlour.—Stew. Jud.* Tigh samhraidh, *a summer-house, a grotto, an arbour, a bower.* Toiseach an t-samhraidh, *the beginning of summer.*

SAMHRAG, aig, *s. f.* Trefoil; clover; shamrock. *N. pl.* samhragan. Written also *seamhrag.*

SAMHRAGACH, *a.* Abounding in trefoil or in shamrock; like trefoil or shamrock; of trefoil or shamrock.

SAMHRAIDH, *gen. sing.* of samhradh.

SAMHSA, SAMHSADH, aidh, *s. m.* Sorrel-weed; sauce.

SAMHSACH, *a.* Abounding in sorrel; like sorrel; of sorrel.

SAMHTHACH, aich, *s. m.* (*Ir. id.*) A handle or helve.

SAMHUIL, *a.* (*Lat.* similis.) Like, as, such; *also, substantively,* likeness, resemblance, a match; image; representation. An samhuil so do nithibh, *such like things.—Stew. Jer.*

SAMHUILT, *s. f.* A resemblance, likeness, image; a match; a representation; an apparition; a slender person.

SAMHUINN, samhna, *s. f.* The first evening of November; Hallowe'en; All Saints'-tide, Hallow-tide. Oidhche shamhna, *Hallowe'en.* Siubhal na samhna dha, *never may he return,* i. e. *may he pass as Hallowmas passed.—G. P.*

Samhuinn was one of the great Druidical festivals, which took place in the beginning of winter, when a fire was regularly kindled, called the fire of peace (*samh-theine*). The fires which are kindled in many parts of Scotland on Hallowe'en, are the remains of this ancient superstition.

SAMPLAIR, *s. m.* An example; a sample. Mar shamplair, *as a sample.*

SAMPULL, uill, *s. m.* An example.

SAMRAG. See SEAMRAG.

SAN, *for* anns an. (*Ir. id.*) In the. Mar bhruaich san duibhre, *like a precipice in the dark.—Oss. Com.*

'SAN, (*for* agus an.) And the. An diugh 'san dé, *to-day and yesterday.*

† SAN, *a.* (*Ir. id.*) Holy.

SAN. An emphatic adjective. A mhac-san, *his son;* a mac-san, *her son.*

† SAN, *v. a.* Release; dissolve.—*Shaw.*

† SANADH, aidh, *s. m.* A releasing; a dissolving.

SANARC, airc, *s. m.* (*Ir. id. Lat.* sandaraca.) Red orpiment.

SÀNAS, ais, *s. m.* (*Ir. id.*) A warning; a hint; a low sound, a whisper; a private sign; peace; augury; a greeting; a salute; a glossary; etymology. Bheir e sanas le' chois, *he [speaketh] giveth a hint with his foot.—Stew. Pro.* Mar shànas do gach tìr, *as a warning to every country.—Mac Lach. N. pl.* sànasan.

SÀNASACH, *a.* Warning; hinting; whispering; greeting or saluting.

SÀNASAN, ain, *s. m.* (*Ir. id.*) A glossary; etymology; a private hint; a low whisper; a warning.

SÀNASANAICHE, *s. m.* (*Ir.* sànasanuidhe.) An etymologist.

† SANCT, *a.* (*Ir. id. Lat.* sanctus.) Holy, pious, sacred.

† SANCTAIR, *s. m., from* † sanct. (*Ir.* sanctoir.) A sanctuary. *N. pl.* sanctairean.

† SANNADH, aidh, *s. m.* Looseness.—*Shaw.*

SANNT, sainnt, *s. m.* (*Ir.* saint.) Inclination, desire; carnal inclination; greed; covetousness; ambition. Esan a dh' fhuathaicheas saunt, *he who hates covetousness.—Stew. Pro.* O shannt a mhilltir, *from the ambition of the destroyer.—Old Song.* Sannt bidh, *appetite for food;* tha shannt orm, *I intend;* dh' éirich sannt air, *a carnal affection awoke in him;* sannt gniomh, *inclination to work.* Sannt gun sonas éiridh an donas da, *hapless greed ill betides.—G. P.*

SANNTACH, *a.* (*Ir.* santach.) Greedy, covetous; lustful; ambitious. Sanntach air buannachd, *greedy of gain.—Stew. Pro.* Duine sanntach, *a covetous man.—Stew. Eph. Com.* and *sup.* sanntaiche.

SANNTACH, aich, *s. m.* (*from* sannt.) A covetous person.

SANNTACHADH, aidh, *s. m.* A coveting, a lusting, a wishing for; covetousness, lust, desire. Air sanntachadh dha, *after he coveted.*

SANNTACHD, *s. f.* (*from* sannt.) Covetousness, greediness; ambitiousness; lustfulness.

SANNTAICH, *v. a.* (*Ir.* santaigh.) Covet, lust, desire eagerly, long for. *Pret. a.* shanntaich; *fut. aff. a.* sanntaichidh. Sanntaichidh e gu mòr, *he will covet greedily.—Stew. Pro. Fut. sub.* sanntaicheas; *fut. pass.* sanntaichear.—*Stew. Pro.*

SANNTAICHTE, *p. part.* of sanntaich.

SANNTUICH. See SANNTAICH.

SANT, *s. m.* A squelch.

SANTAIR, *s. m.* A stroller, a lounger. *N. pl.* santairean.

SANTAIREACHD, *s. m.* Strolling, lounging.

SAOBAN, ain, *s. m.* A swing; a swinging or waving to and fro.

SAOBANACH, *a.* Swinging; like a swing.

SAOBANACHADH, aidh, *s. m.* A swinging, as on a rope.

SAOBANACHD, *s. m.* Swinging, as on a rope.

SAOBANAICH, *s. f.* Swinging, as on a rope.

SAOBANAICH, *v. a.* Swing. *Pret.* shaobanaich, *swung; fut. aff. a.* saobanaichidh.

SAOBANAICHTE, *p. part.* of saobanaich. Having been swung.

SAOBH, *a.* (*Ir. id.*) Foolish; deranged, mad, silly; apt to err or to be led astray; erroneous; dim; blind.

SAOBH, *v. a.* (*Ir. id.*) Infatuate, lead astray; charm, amuse. *Pret. a.* shaobh; *fut. aff. a.* saobhaidh.

SAOBHADH, aidh, *s. m.* Foolishness; infatuation; derangement; error; a going aside—(*Smith*); amusement.

SAOBH-ADHRADH, aidh, *s. m.* Superstition.

SAOBH-CHAINNT, *s. f.* (*Ir. id.*) Prattle, gabble, idle talk.

SAOBH-CHAINNTEACH, *a.* Prattling, gabbling; prone to prate or to talk foolishly.

SAOBH-CHIALL, -chéill, *s. f.* (*Ir. id.*) Folly, nonsense, stupidity.

SAOBH-CHIALLACH, *a.* (*Ir. id.*) Foolish, nonsensical, stupid.

SAOBH-CHOIR, *s. f.* (*Ir. id.*) A whirlpool. *N. pl.* saobh-choirichean.

SAOBH-CHOIREACH, *a.* Having whirlpools.

SAOBH-CHOMHRADH, aidh, *s. m.* Foolish talk, prattle. Luchd-saobh-chomhraidh, *foolish talkers.*

SAOBH-CHOMHRAITEACH, *a.* Prattling, inclined to prattle.

SAOBH-CHRABHACH, *a.* Hypocritical, insincere, false-hearted; superstitious.

SAOBH-CHRABHADH, aidh, *s. m.* (*Ir. id.*) Hypocrisy; superstition.

SAOBH-CHRABHAIR, *s. m.* A hypocrite.

SAOBH-CHREIDEACH, *a.* Superstitious; heterodox; apt to be blown about by any wind of doctrine; credulous; hereditary; *also,* a superstitious person; a credulous person; a heretic. Duine a bha na shaobh-chreideach, *a man who was an heretic.*

SAOBH-CHREIDEAMH, imh, *s. m.* (*Ir. id.*) Superstition; heterodoxy; heresy—(*Stew. Acts, ref.*); a wild opinion. Aimhreite is saobh-chreidimh, *seditions and heresies.—Stew. Gal.*

SAOBH-CHREIDICHE, *s. m.* A superstitious or credulous person; a heretic.

SAOBH-FHAIDH, *s. m.* A false prophet.

SAOBH-GHLÒR, ghlòir, *s. m.* Idle talk, chit-chat, small talk.

Saobh-mhiann, *s. m.* Punctiliousness; foolish desire; idle ambition

Saobh-mhiannach, *a* Punctiliousness; foolishly ambitious.

Saobh-nos, nòis, *s m* (*Ir. id*) A bad practice, a foolish habit; bad habits; bad breeding; anger; indignation.

Saobh-nosach, *a* (*Ir. id.*) Having bad habits or practices; morose, peevish; ill-bred.

Saobh-sgeul, sgeòil, *s. f* (*Ir. id*) An idle story; a romance or novel; an improbable fiction

Saobh-sgeulachd, *s f* An idle story, a romance. *N pl.* saobh-sgeulachdan

Saobh-sgeulaiche, *s m.* An idle story-teller; a romancer, a novelist

Saobh-sgriobhadh, aidh, *s. m.* Bad writing; a libel, a libellous composition *N. pl* saobh-sgriobhaichean.

Saobh-sgriobhair, *s. m.* A libeller *N pl.* saobh-sgriobhairean

Saobh-shruth, *s. m* An eddying tide; an eddy

Saobh-smuaineadh, idh, *s m.* Conceit; a whim; an extravagant thought.

Saod, saoid, *s m* A state or condition; care; attention; a track or journey Ciod an saod a th'ort? *how do you do?*

Saodach, *a* In good condition or health, driving, as cattle

Saodachadh, aidh, *s m* A driving of cattle, as to pasture, a conducting or guiding, a taking care of, a tending

Saodachadh, (a), *pr. part* of saodaich Driving, as cattle to pasture, conducting; tending A saodach' a chruidh, *driving the cattle*

Saodaich, *v a.* Drive, as cattle; conduct, guide, tend. *Pret a* shaodaich; *fut aff. a* saodaichidh, *shall drive*

Saodaichear, *fut pass* of saodaich

Saodaichte, *p part* of saodaich Driven, as cattle to the pasture

Saodar, *a* See **Saodmhor**

† **Saodh**, *s* (*Ir id*) Pain

Saodmhoireachd, *s f* Prosperousness; good condition of health or fortune

Saodmhor, *a* In good condition of health or fortune, prosperous, well, attentive. *Com.* and *sud* saodmhoire

Saoduchadh, aidh, *s. m* See **Saodachadh**

Saoduich, *v a* See **Saodaich**

Saoghal, ail, *s m* (*Ir. id Lat* seculum) A world; life, existence, lifetime; an age, a generation, subsistence, living O thoiseach an t-saoghail, *from the beginning of the world —Stew Matt* Ré fad mo shaoghail, *during my whole lifetime.—Old Song* Curam an t-saoghail, *worldly care*, c'aite air an t-saoghal a bheil e? *where in the world is he?* air fad an t-saoghail, *throughout the world*, air feadh an t-saoghail, *throughout the world* Cha mhath an saoghal an sealg, *hunting is but a poor living —G P*

Saoghalach, *a* (*from* saoghal) Worldly, terrestrial, mundane Fad-shaoghalach, *long-lived* Gearr-shaoghlach, *short-lived Com* and *sup* saoghlaiche

Saoghalachd, *s. f.* Worldliness; long life

Saoghalan, ain, *s m* (*Ir. id*) An old man

Saoghalta, *a* (*from* saoghal) Worldly, worldly-minded, secular, terrestrial Foghlum saoghalta, *worldly wisdom. —Stew. Col*

Saoghaltachd, *s f.* Worldliness, worldly-mindedness.

Saoi, Saoidh, *a.* (*Ir id. W.* syw, *learned*) Generous, heroic, good; godly Fagaidh tu falamh an duine saoi, *thou wilt leave empty the generous man.— Old Song.* The word of opposite signification is *daoi*, so *soillcir*, *doillcir*, *saibhreas*, *daibhreas*, and many words beside.

Saoi, Saoidh, *s m* (*Ir id.*) A generous man; a nobleman; a hero; a worthy; a man of letters; a tutor or preceptor. Tra chì mac an Luin saoi na airc, *when Fingal's sword sees a hero in distress —Oss. Manos. N. pl.* saoidhean Gearrar na saoidhean sios, *the warriors shall be cut down — Old Poem.*

Saoibh, *a* Peevish, morose; mad, foolish.

Saoibhneach, *a.* Peevish, morose, joyless. *Com.* and *sup.* saoibhniche.

Saoibhneas, eis, *s. m.* Peevishness, moroseness, joylessness. *—Oss. Oinam.*

Saoibhneasach, *a.* Causing peevishness, moroseness, or joylessness.

Saoibh-sgeul, sgeoil, *s m* (*Ir. id*) A fable

Saoidh, *s. m.* See **Saoi**

Saoidh, sàidh, *s f.* (*Dan.* höe, *hay*) Hay *Asp form*, shaoidh A gearradh na sàidh, *mowing the hay-grass*

Saoidheadair, *s. m.* A hay-cutter; a hay-maker *N. pl.* saoidheadairean.

Saoidheadaireachd, *s. f.* Hay-cutting; hay-making.

Saoidhean, *n. pl* of saoi *or* saoidh, which see.

Saoil, *v* (*Ir id*) Think, suppose, imagine; seem. *Pret* shaoil, *fut. aff. a* saoilidh, *shall think.* Shaoil mi, *I thought*; an saoil thu? *think you? do you imagine?* an saoil mi c'àite am bheil e, *I wonder where he or it is*, c'àite an deach e, an saoil thu? *where has he gone, think you?* Shaoileas gu b'e Lochlann a dh'éirich, *it was supposed that Lochlin arose.— Ull.*

Saoileam, (*for* saoilidh mi) I will think; *also, imper.* let me think

Saoilear, *fut pass* of saoil Shall be thought

Saoilidh, *fut aff a.* of saoil. Shall or will think.

Saoilsinn, *s f* A thinking, a supposing, or imagining

Saoilsinn, (a), *pr. part.* of saòil Thinking, supposing, imagining A saoilsinn bhi 'g ad fhaicinn, *supposing to be seeing you.—Ull.*

Saoiltinn, more properly *saoilsinn*, which see.

Saoimeach, *a* Easy, comfortable; having nothing to do; exempt from toil More properly *soimeach.*

Saoimeachd, *s. f.* Comfortableness, exemption from labour. More properly *soimeachd.*

Saoi-oileanta, *a.* Well-trained, well-bred; educated. Each saoi-oileanta sith-fhada, *a well-trained bounding steed.— Fingalian Poem*

Saoir, *gen sing* of saor; which see

Saoire, *com* and *sup* of saor, which see

Saoiread, eid, *s. m* Cheapness, advancement in cheapness A dol an saoiread, *growing cheaper and cheaper.*

Saoirse, *s f* (*Ir id*) Freedom, cheapness; release

Saoirseach, ich, *s m.* A freeman

Saoirseach, *a.* (*Ir id.*) Free, voluntary, cheap.

Saoirsinneachd, *s. f* The trade of a carpenter or joiner.

Saoith, *s m.* (*Ir. id*) A tutor, a preceptor; a guardian; a man of letters

Saoithealachd, *s f* Generosity.

Saoitheil, *a.* (saoith-amhuil) Expert, generous, skilful, learned

Saoithreach, *a* Toiling, industrious, painstaking; plodding, servile; toilsome, difficult Gu saoithreach sgith shuidh Garna, *Garno sat down toiling and tired.—Oss. Cathluno.*

Saoithreach, *s f.* Labour, fatigue, work; *also, gen. sing.* of saothair.

Saoithreach', *for* saoithreachadh; which see.

Saoithreachadh, aidh, *s. m.* Working, labour, taking pains; a dressing, as of soil; tillage, toil. Le saoithreachadh, *with working.—Stew. Thess.*

Saoithreachadh, (a), *pr. part.* Working, labouring; dressing, as soil; tilling. A shaoithreach na talmhainn, *to till the ground.—Stew. Gen* 'G a shaoithreachadh, *to dress it.—Id.*

Saoithreachail, *a* (saoithreach-amhuil) Painstaking, laborious, toilsome; plodding—*(Macint)*; requiring much pains; requiring care or labour. Is fhearr a bhi sona na saoithreachail, *better have luck than labour.—G. P.*

Saoithrich, *a* See Saothraich

Saoithriche, *s m.* A painstaking person, a labourer, a working man; a plodder, a tiller of the ground

Saor, saoir, *s m*, *from* †saoth, *work, and* fear, *man (Ir. id W.* saer) A carpenter or joiner Mar thuaidh an glaic saoir, *like a hatchet in the hands of a carpenter.—Mac Lach.* Mac an t-saoir, *the carpenter's son.—Stew. Matt.*, also the surname *Macintyre. N. pl.* saoir. Saoir a locaradh, *carpenters planing*, saor chairtean, *a cartwright*, saor chuidhlean, *a wheelwright*, saor mhuilnean, *a millwright*, saor fheuna, *a cartwright*, saor charbad, *a coachmaker*, saor chlach, *a stonecutter, a stonehewer* or *polisher*

Saor, *v. a.* (*Ir. id*) Save; redeem; deliver; rescue; set at liberty; acquit, disentangle. *Pret. a* shaor; *fut. aff. a.* saoraidh A shaor mi, *who redeemed me.—Stew. Gen* Saoraibh an duine sàruichte, *deliver the oppressed man.—Stew. Jer.*

Saor, *a.* (*Ir. id*) Free, at liberty, ransomed, delivered; exempt, cheap; except; save. Clann na mna saoire, *the children of the free woman.—Stew Gal* Uine shaor, *vacation, leisure time*; saor o, *except* Saor o na dh'ith na h-òganaich, *except that which the young men have eaten.—Stew O. T.* Gu saor, *freely, cheaply. Com.* and *sup.* saoire.

Saorach, *a.* Freeing, ransoming, exempting; cheapening.

Saorachadh, aidh, *s m.* A freeing, or setting at liberty, a ransoming; an acquittal; a cheapening

Saorachd, *s f.* The state of being free, freed or ransomed; acquittance, cheapness

Saoradh, aidh, *s. m* (*Ir id*) A redeeming, a ransoming, a setting at liberty, emancipation; cheapness, redemption, deliverance, acquittal, rescue Am fear-saoraidh, *the Redeemer.*

Saoradh, (a), *pr. part.* of saor, which see

Saoraich, *v a* Set at liberty, ransom; acquit, rescue, cheapen *Pret a.* shaoraich, *fut aff a* saoraichidh, *p. part* saoraichte.

Saoraichte, *p part.* of saoraich.

Saoranach, aich, *s. m* A freeman, a freedman, a burgess *—Macd. N. pl* saoranaich.

Saoranachd, *s. f* The state of being free; the condition of a freedman, the state or a burgess.

Saor-chlann, *s f.* Freemen.

Saor-chloch, oich, *s m.* A stonemason.

Saor-chridheach, *a.* Candid; open-hearted; unbetrothed. Gu saor-chridheach, *candidly.*

Saor-chridheachd, *s. f.* Candour; candidness; open-heartedness.

Saor-chuairt, *s f.* Circulation, free circulation Saor-chuairt na fola, *the free circulation of the blood.*

Saor-dhail, *s. f* (*Ir. id*) Acquittance, cheapness; freedom.

Saor-dhalach, *a.* (*Ir. id*) Cheap; free.—*Shaw*

Saor-inntinneach, *a.* Thinking freely, having liberty of conscience.

Saor-inntinneachd, *s. f.* Free-thinking, liberty of conscience

Saor-inntinniche, *s m* A free-thinker

Saorsa, *s. m.* See Saorsadh.

Saorsachd See Saorsainneachd

Saorsadh, aidh, *s m.* Freedom, liberty; free-will, deliverance.

Saorsainn, **Saorsuinn**, *s. f* Redemption, salvation, deliverance; acquittal, cheapness.

Saorsainneachd, *s. f* The office of a redeemer, or deliverer; the circumstance of redeeming, saving, or acquitting; the state of being redeemed, saved, or acquitted; the business of a carpenter Tha e 'g ionnsuchadh na saorsainneachd, *he is learning the business of a carpenter.*

Saorsanach, aich, *s m* A helper at work—*(Shaw)*, an unhired workman, a freeman *N pl.* saorsanaich

Saor-sheilbh, *s f.* Freehold

Saor-thabhairt, *s f* A giving freely or voluntarily

Saor-thabhartair, *s m* One who gives freely, voluntarily, or gratuitously *N pl* saor-thabhairteirean.

Saor-thabhartas, ais, *s m.* A free gift, a free-will offering.—*Stew Lev*

Saor-thoil, *s f.* Free will

Saor-thoirt See Saor-thabhairt.

† **Saoth**, *v a* Punish *Pret. a.* shaoth, *punished*, *fut aff.* saothaidh, *shall punish.*

† **Saoth**, saoith, *s. m* (*Ir id*) Labour, work; pains, trouble; punishment; a disease or ailment Hence *saothair* and *saor*, i. e *saoth-fhear.*

Saothach, aich, *s. m* (*Ir id*) A dish; a vessel; a ship. Saothach ionnlaid, *a washing-basin* See Soitheach.

† **Saothach**, *a.* Castigatory

Saothachan, ain, *s. m.* (*dim* of saothach.) A little dish, a plate.

Saothadh, aidh, *s. m* Exculpating; exculpation

Saothair, *s m.* (saoth-fhear) A punisher, a torturer; a labourer, a diseased man

Saothair, saoithreach, *s f*, *from* † saoth. (*Ir* saothar, *labour*, *Bisc* sari, *wages*) Labour, trouble, pains, service, work, drudgery, the labour or pains of childbed Saothair a nasgaidh, *unpaid labour, service without wages.—Stew. Jer* Ceud thoraidh do shaoithreach, *the first-fruits of thy labour.—Stew Ex* Bha saothair chruaidh oirre, *she was in hard labour.—Stew. Gen* Air bheagan saoithreach, *having little trouble, having little work, taking little pains.—Macint* Is saothair leis, *he thinks it a hard matter.—Stew. Pro* Ri saothair, *taking pains, in travail*; gabh saothair air, *take pains on it*, caith do shaothair, *bestow thy labour in vain*, a dh'aindeoin do shaoithreach, *in spite of all thy trouble or pains*, fiach saoithreach, *wages, reward.*

Saotharcan, *s. m.* A species of grey plover

Saoth-dhamh, dhaimh, *s m* A labouring ox. *N pl* saoth-dhaimh.

Saothmhor, *a.* Toilsome, laborious, drudging; difficult. *Com.* and *sup.* saoth-mhoire

Saothmhorachd, *s. f.* Toilsomeness.

Saoth-phurt, uirt, *s m* An imposthume.

Saothrach, *a* Toiling, industrious, drudging; painstaking; plodding, servile, toilsome; difficult.

Saothrachadh, aidh, *s m* Working, labouring, plodding, toil, tillage.

Saothrachail See Saoithreachail

Saothraich, *v. a.* and *n* (*from* † saoth) Toil, labour; plod, take pains; dress, as soil; till *Pret. a* shaothraich, *fut aff. a* saothraichidh. Saothraichidh e air a shon féin —*Stew Pro.*

Saothraiche, *s. m.* (*Ir.* saothraidhe.) A labourer, a working man; a painstaking man; a plodder.

Saothruich, *v.* See Saothraich.

Sapair, *s. f.* Sapphire.

Sapaireach, *a.* Of sapphire.

Sàr, sàir, *s. m.* (*Ir. id.*) A hero; an excellent man; a worthy. *N. pl.* sàir. Chualas le sàr a ghuth, *a hero heard his voice.—Oss. Tem.* A shàir! *thou hero!—Id.* Also Sir. *Russ.* tsàr, *an emperor. Phœn.* and *Chal.* sar or zar, *a prince.* Diodorus Siculus calls the queen of the Massagetæ, who, according to Ctesias, cut off Cyrus's head, *Zarina;* and the Russian name *Tsarina* was, till of late, the title of the Empress of all the Russias.

Sàr, *a.* (*Ir. id.*) Excellent, matchless; noble, brave. Sàr cheannard nan sàr laoch, *the matchless leader of matchless heroes.—Oss. Fing.*

Sàr, sàir, *s. m.* A stoppage, hinderance, or prevention. Cuir sàr san obair, *put a stop to the work.* Cha do chuir sàr nach d' fhuilinn sàr, *nobody gives provocation but gets it in return.—G. P.*

Sàr, *a particle.* (*Ir. id. Germ.* sehr.) This compositive particle expresses a superlative degree, and changes into the aspirated form the initial consonant of the word to which it is prefixed. Sar-mhaith, *very good;* sar-mhaiseach, *exceeding handsome;* sar-dhuine, *an excellent man;* sàr-ghniomh, *an exploit;* sàr-bheachd, *penetration, deep thought, a very good thought.*

Sàr, sàir, *s. m.* A louse.

Sàr-ab, *s. m.* (*Ir. id.*) A chief abbot.

Sàr-abuich, *a.* Quite ripe.

Sàrach, *a.* Lousy; *also*, opposing, putting a stop to.

Sàrach', **Sàruch'**, *for* sàrachadh.

Sàrachadh, aidh, *s. m.* A harassing, an oppressing; a fatiguing or tiring; a conquering; a perplexing; oppression; conquest; victory; extortion; infringement; a violent rescue; an illegal rescue. Tha e air a shàrachadh, *he is oppressed* or *distressed.*

Sàrachadh, (a), *pr. part.* of saraich. Harassing, oppressing; conquering; wronging; rescuing violently or illegally; infringing; fatiguing.

Sarachail, *a.* Oppressive; requiring pains or trouble.

Sàrachair, *s. m.* (*Ir. id.*) An oppressor, a harasser; a conqueror; an extortioner; an infringer; one who rescues violently or illegally.

Sàradh, aidh, *s. m.* An obstacle, an opposition, a stop. Chuir thu sàradh anns na Fionntaibh, *thou hast opposed the Fingalians.—Old Poem.* Cuiridh sinn sàradh san ealaidh, *we shall put a stop to the fun.—Old Song.*

Sàrag, aig, *s. f.* (*dim.* of sàr.) A louse. *N. pl.* sàragan.

Sàragach, *a.* Lousy.

Sàraich, *v. a.* (*Ir.* saraigh.) Oppress, harass; conquer; put to trouble; wrong, injure; fatigue; rescue violently or illegally. *Pret. a.* shàraich; *fut. aff. a.* sàraichidh.

Sàraichte, *p. part.* of sàraich. (*Ir.* saraighte.) Oppressed, harassed; conquered; troubled, perplexed; injured; fatigued; rescued violently or illegally.

Sàr-bhan, *s. f.* An excellent woman.

Sàr-bheachd, *s. f.* A good thought, a deep thought.

Sàr-bhuille, *s. f.* A heavy blow.

Sàr-bhuilleach, *a.* Giving heavy blows; heavy-handed.

Sardail, *s. m.* A sprat.

Sàr-dhuine, *s. m.* An excellent man, a worthy. *N. pl.* sàr-dhaoine, *worthies.*

Sàr-fhear, fhir, *s. m.* An excellent man.

Sàr-fhios, *s. m.* Certain knowledge. Tha sar-fhios agam, *I know quite well.*

Sàr-laoch, -laoich, *s. m.* A great hero. *N. pl.* sar-laoich.

Sàr-mhaise, *s. f.* Exceeding handsomeness.

Sàr-mhaiseach, *a.* Exceeding handsome.

Sàr-mhaith, *a.* Exceeding good, excellent.

Sar-ògan, ain, *s. m.* An excellent young woman.

Sàruchadh, aidh, *s. m.* See Sàrachadh.

Sàruchail, *a.* See Sàrachail.

Sàruich, *v. a.* See Saraich.

Sàruichte, *p. part.* of saruich. See Saraichte.

Sàr-umhal, *a.* Most obedient.

Sàs, *v.* Lay hold of, fasten on; grasp, grapple. *Pret. a.* shàs; *fut. aff. a.* sàsaidh, *shall lay hold of.* Shàs i na laimh, *it fastened his hand.—Stew. Acts.* Na chéile shàs iad, *they grasped each other.—Oss. Cathluno.*

Sàs, *s. m.* An instrument; means; arms; engines.—*Shaw.*

Sàs, *s. m.* Difficulty; distress; trouble; custody; a grasp, a grapple; *also, adjectively*, fast; laid hold of; straitened; distressed; *rarely*, capable. An sàs teann, *in sore trouble, sorely distressed.—Oss. Gaul.* Tha 'n cosan an sàs, *their feet are* [*fast*] *ensnared.—Sm.* A gheug an sàs na laimh, *the branch grasped in his hand.—Oss. Dargo.*

Sàsach, *a.* Satiating, saturating; causing satiety or repletion; glutting; apt to grasp; apt to fasten on; of a grasping disposition.

Sàsachadh, aidh, *s. m.* A filling, a satiating; repletion; greediness. Tha e air a shàsachadh, *he is satiated.*

Sàsachd, *s. f.* Satiety, repletion, saturation; cloyment, sufficiency, abundance; greediness. Sàsachd an t-saibhir, *the abundance of the rich.—Stew. Ecc.*

Sàsadh, aidh, *s. m.* Satisfaction; comfort; content; sufficiency; fulness.

Sàsaich, *v. a.* (*Ir.* sasaigh.) Fill, satisfy, satiate; glut, gorge, saturate, cloy. *Pret. a.* shàsaich; *fut. aff. a.* sàsaichidh.

Sàsaichte, *p. part.* of sasaich. (*Ir. id.*) Satiated, satisfied, glutted, gorged, saturated.

Sasamh, aimh, *s. m.* Amends; satisfaction; pleasure.

Sàsda, **Sàsdach**, *a.* (*Ir. id.*) Easy, at leisure; easy-minded.

Sàsdachd, *s. f.* Easiness; indolence; sauciness.

Sasdadh, *a.* Easy; indifferent; easy-minded; *also, substantively*, ease; indifference; easy-mindedness.

Sasgunn, uinn, *s.* (*Germ.* Sachsen, *Saxon.*) England.

Sasgunnach, aich, *s. m.* (*Corn.* Zaznak.) An Englishman; a Saxon. *N. pl.* Sasgunnaich.

Sasgunnach, *a.* (*pronounce* Sassunnach.) English, Saxon.

Sàs-mhort, *s. m.* A massacre, a revengeful murder.

Sàsmhortach, *a.* A massacring, murdering from revenge.

Sàsmhortadh, aidh, *s. m.* Massacre, a revengeful murder.

Sàs-mhortair, *s. m.* A murderer, a revengeful murderer.

Sàsuchadh. See Sàsachadh.

Sàsuich. See Sàsaich.

Sàth, *s. m.* (*Ir. id.*) Plenty, satiety, sufficiency; repletion; fill; food; a thrust; a stab; a push. Dh'ith sinn gu 'r sàth, *we ate to satiety.—Stew. Ex.* Bhur sàth, *your fill.—Stew. Lev.* Olaibh bhur sàth, *drink your fill.*

Sàth, *v. a.* Thrust, stab, pierce; push, shove. *Pret. a.* shath; *fut. aff. a.* sàthaidh, *shall thrust.* Shàth e na bhroinn e, *he thrust it into his belly.—Stew. Jud. Fut. pass.* sàthar. Sàthar sleagh troimhe, *he shall be pierced with a spear.—Stew. Ex.*

† **Sathach**, aich, *s. m.* (*Ir. id.*) More frequently *soitheach;* which see.

Sàthach, *a.* (*Ir. id.*) Satiated, sated, full, filled; repleto; satisfied; causing satiety; thrusting, stabbing, piercing, pushing. Cha 'n 'eil sibh sàthach, *ye are not satiated.—*

Stew. Hag. Bithidh sibh sàthach, *you will be satisfied.*—*Stew. Lev.* Sàthach agus ocrach, *full and hungry.*—*Stew. Phil.* Sàthach builleanach, *giving thrusts and blows.* —*Old Song.*

SÀTHADH, aidh, *s. m.* (*Ir. id.*) A thrusting, a shoving, a pushing, a piercing; a thrust, a pierce, a stab, a shove.

SATHAIRN, SATHUIRN, *s. f.* (*Ir. id.*) Saturday. Di-Sathairn, *Saturday*; air la Sathairn, *on a Saturday.* Deireadh nan seachd Sathairn ort, *the end of seven Saturdays be upon you.*—*Old Saying.*

Sathuirn is a smoothing of *Sadurn* or *Sadorn*, a name given by the ancient Celts to Saturn, a warlike Titan monarch. The Latins rendered this name *Saturnus*, powerful, warlike. The various branches of the Celtic nation still call Saturday, or *dies Saturni*, with but little variation, *di Sadurn*; and the Celts of Brittany call Thursday, or *dies Jovis*, *Di Jou.*

SÀTHAR. See SÀTH.

SB and SP are sometimes used indiscriminately.

SBAIRN, *s. f.* (*Ir. id.*) Emulation; rivalry; a struggle; strife; stress; agony; exertion; contest; a wrestle. Ged ni fear sbairn, *though a man strive.* More frequently written *spairn.*

SBAIRNEACH, *a.* Emulous; rivalling; striving, struggling; causing emulation, stress, or exertion; requiring exertion. Written more commonly *spairneach.*

SBAIRNEIL, *a.* (sbairn-amhuil.) Emulous; striving, struggling; exerting; wrestling; difficult; requiring exertion; agonizing.

SBREAMB, *v. a.* Tighten clothes about one; confine one's self with tight clothes.

SBREAMBANACH, *a.* Drawing one's clothes tightly about one.

SBROGAILL, *s. f.* (*Ir. id.*) The dewlap of a beast; a crop, a craw; a double chin; a cock's comb or crest.

SC and SG are, for the most part, used indiscriminately by Gaelic writers.

SCABALL, aill, *s. m.* (*Lat.* scapula. *Ir.* scabal.) A helmet; a hood; a scapular—(*Shaw*); a guard for the shoulder, used by the ancient Caledonians.

SCABAR, *a.* Thin.—*Shaw.*

† SCABHAISTE, *s. f.* Advantage.

SCÀBHAL, ail, *s. m.* A scaffold; a booth; a shop; a hut; a screen covering the entrance at a door. *N. pl.* scabhalan.

SCÀBHAL, ail, *s. m.* A cauldron; a kettle; a baking-trough; a large bowl. *N. pl.* scàbhalan.

SCAD, *s. m.* (*Swed.* skada, *harm. Scotch,* skaith.) Loss; harm; grief; woe. Mo scad! *woe's me!*

SCAFA, *s. m.* A skiff; a cock-boat.

Gr. σκαφη, *a boat,* σκυφος sometimes means a *ship. Lat.* scapha. *Germ.* schiff, *a ship. Anglo-Sax.* scyp. *Franconian* and *Eng.* skiff. *Belg.* schip. *Island.* skip. *Swed.* skep. *Ir.* scaff.

SCAFALD, aild. See SCAFALT.

SCAFALL, aill, *s. m.* (*Ir. id.*) A scaffold—(*Macd.*); *also,* a booth; a hut; a shop.

SCAFALLACH, *a.* Scaffolded; having scaffolds; full of scaffolds.

SCAFALLACHADH, aidh, *s. m.* The act of erecting a scaffold.

SCAFALLACHD, *s. f.* Scaffolding.

SCAFALLAICH, *v. a.* Erect a scaffold.

SCAFALT, ailt, *s. m.* A scaffold. *N. pl.* scafaltan.

SCÀIL, *s. f.*; more frequently written *sgàil*; which see.

SCAILC, *s. f.* See SGAILC.

† SCAILP, *s. f.* A den, a cave. *N. pl.* scailpean.

SCÀIN, more frequently written *sgàin*; which see.

SCAIR, *s. f.* Any place where a thing is laid to dry.

SCAIREACHD, *s. f.* A creaking; a shrieking.

SCAIREAP, eip, *s. m.* Lavishness, extravagance.—*Macd.*

SCAIREAPACH, *a.* Lavish, extravagant.

SCAIRT, scartach, *s. f.* The caul; a midriff; a shout; a shriek; a thick tuft of shrubs or branches. An scairt os cionn nan airnean, *the caul above liver.*—*Stew. Ex.*

SCAIRTEACH, *a.* Having a large caul; like a caul; of, or belonging to, a caul; shouting; shrieking.

SCAITEACH, *a.* See SGAITEACH.

SCÀL, scàil, *s. m.* A baking-trough—(*Stew. Ex. ref.*); a large bowl; a kettle; a cauldron.

† SCĂL, scail, *s. m.* A man; a champion.

SCALAG, aig, *s. m.* (*from* scal.) A man-servant; a farm-servant; *rarely*, an old man.

SCALAICHEAN, *s. pl.* Scales, balances.

SCÀLAN, ain, *s. m.*, more frequently written *sgàilean*; which see.

SCALLD. See SGALLD.

SCALLACH, *a.* Bald.

SCALLACHAN, ain, *s. m.* An unfledged bird. *N. pl.* scallachain.—*Shaw.*

SCAMHAN, ain, *s. m.* A villanous person; a term of great personal contempt.

SCAMH-GHLONN, oinn, *s. m.* A villanous prank; a shabby action.

SCANN, scainn, *s. m.* and *f.* A membrane; a multitude; a swarm. *N. pl.* scannan. Written also *sgann*; which see.

SCANNACH, *a.* Membranaceous; filmy; swarming; in swarms or multitudes.

SCANNAL, ail, *s. m.* See SGAINNEAL.

SCANNALACH, *a.* See SGAINNEALACH.

SCANNAN, ain, *s. m.* (*dim.* of scann.) A little membrane; a thin membrane; a film; a little swarm; a group. Scannan saille, *a caul.*—*Shaw. N. pl.* scannain.

SCANRA, SCANNRA. See SCANNRADH.

SCANRACH, SCANNRACH, *a.* Dispersing, scattering, scaring, routing; terrifying.

SCÀNRADH, SCÀNNRADH, aidh, *s. m.* A dispersing, a scattering, a scaring; a rout, dispersion; persecution; a confusion; a surprise; a fright. See also SGANRADH.

SCÀNRAICH, SCÀNNRAICH, *v. a.* Disperse, scatter, scare, rout. *Pret. a.* scànraich, *scattered*; *fut. aff. a.* scanraichidh. See also SGANRAICH.

SCÀNRAICHTE, SCANNRAICHTE, *p. part.* Dispersed, scattered, routed, scared; confounded; persecuted. See also SGANRAICHTE.

SCANRAIDH, *s. f.* Dispersement through fear or astonishment.

SCAR, *v. a.* and *n.* Separate, part; wound, torment; split. More frequently written *sgar*; which see.

SCARA, SCARADH, aidh, *s. m.* A separating; a wounding; a tormenting; a separation; a wound; torment; woe; a blow; a mark, as of a blow. Fo chomhara scara na còmhraig, *under the marks of the wounds of battle.*—*Oss. Calth. and Col.* Mar sgaradh shaoghalta! *my earthly woe! woe's me!* Written also *sgara* and *sgaradh.*

SCARACHDAINN, *s. f.* A separating; a separation; a wounding; a tormenting. Written more frequently *sgarachdainn.*

SCARADH, (a), *pr. part.* of scar. Separating, parting; splitting; wounding; tormenting. Cinnn ga 'n scaradh, *heads a wounding.*—*Old Song.* More frequently written *scaradh.*

SCARAIL, *a.* (scar-amhuil.) Separable. See SGARAIL.

† SCARAIT, *s. f.* (*Ir.* scaroit.) A table-cloth.

SCARBH, scairbh, *s.* (*Dan.* skarv.) A cormorant; a shag.

—*Stew. Lev.* The *pelecanus graculus* of Linnæus. *N. pl.* scarbhan.

SCARBHACH, *a.* Like a cormorant; abounding in cormorants; of cormorants

SCARBHAN, ain, *s. m.* (*dim.* of scarbh.) A little cormorant; a young cormorant.

SCARLAID, *s. f.* Scarlet. Còt scarlaid, *a scarlet coat*, ligh scarlaid, *scarlet colour.* In *Bretagne* they say *liou scarladd* *Arab.* yxquerlet *Turk* iskerlet. *Teut* schaerlaet *Arm.* scarladd *Germ* schaerlach. *Island.* skarlatz *Belg* scharlaken *Swed* scharlakan. According to Pezron the root of this word is Celtic —*See Pezron, Antiq Celt.*

SCARLAIDEACH, *a* Like scarlet, of scarlet

SCARTHANAICH, *s f* Dawn; twilight; *literally*, the parting of light and darkness Ann an scarthanaich an là, *in the dawn of day* —*Stew. Jud*

SCÀTH, *s*, more frequently written *sgàth*, which see.

SCÀTHACH, *a.* See SGÀTHACH

SCÀTHAN, *s m* A mirror. Written also *sgàthan.*

SCEACH, *s f.* A hawthorn, a white-thorn; a brier, a bramble

SCEACHAG, aig, *s f.* (*dim* of sceach) A hawthorn-berry, a haw *N pl.* sceachagan

SCEACHAGACH, *a* Abounding in hawthorn-berries, of hawthorn-berries

SCEALB. See SGEALB

SCEALLAN, ain, *s m.* Wild mustard; a kernel *N pl* sceallain See also SGEALAN

SCEALLANACH, *a* Abounding in wild mustard, of wild mustard, having a kernel.

SCEAP, scip, *s f* See SGEAP.

SCEATH. See SGEITH.

SCEILE, *s. f.* (*Ir id*) Misery, pity —*Shaw*

SCEILM, *s f.* Boasting, vain-glory; tattle; neatness or tidiness in dress, an impudent, prattling person.

SCEILMEIL, *a* (sceilm-amhuil.) Boasting; tattling; impudently garrulous, tidy, smart

SCEIMH, sceimhe, *s f* Beauty, ornament; handsomeness, seemliness, a scheme, a draught. Written also *sgeimh.*

SCEIMHEACH, *a* Beautiful, handsome; blooming *Com.* and *sup* sceimhiche

SCEIN, *gen sing* of scian

SCEINM, *s f*, more frequently written *sceilm* and *sgeilm.*

SCEINMNEACH, *a* Swift, quick, nimble —*Shaw*

SCEINNEADH, eidh, *s. m* An eruption, a gushing forth; a bouncing.

SCÉINNEADH, idh, *s m.* Packthread; twine Cord scéinnidh, *a packthread*

SCEIR, *s f*, more commonly written *sgeir*, which see

SCEIREACH, *a.* See SGEIREACH.

SCEIRMEIS, *s. f* A skirmish —*Macd.*

SCEIRMEISEACH, *a.* Skirmishing, like a skirmish, of skirmishes

SCEIRMEISEACHD, *s f* Continued or frequent skirmishing

SCEITH. See SGEITH.

SCEOT, sceoit, *s m.* (*Lat.* scutum) A shield or target

SCIAMH, sceimh, *s*, more frequently written *sgiamh*

SCIAMHACH, *a.* See SGIAMHACH.

SCIAN, scein, *s. f.* A knife Scian-phinn, *a penknife* — *Stew. Jer* Scian achlais, *or* scian ochlais, *a Gaelic armpit dagger, commonly used in close quarters.* See also SGIAN.

SCIATH, sceithe, *s f.*, more frequently written *sgiath*, which see.

SCIATHACH, *a* See SGIATHACH.

SCIATHANACH See SGIATHANACH.

† SCILLE, *s. f.* Fright, terror. Hence *Scylla*, the name of a rock half way between Italy and Sicily, so frightful to ancient mariners.

† SCINN, *v n* Spring, as water; gush —*Shaw*

SCIOB. See SGIOB.

SCIOBAL, ail, *s m.* A barn, a granary; the skirt of a robe; the fold of a mantle; a mantle, a garment

SCIOB, *s. f.* A scoop

SCIOPAIR, *s m* A skipper, a mariner. *N. pl.* sciopairean. —*Stew* 1 *K. ref.*

SCIORBHA. See SGIORBHA.

SCIORR, *v. n.* Slip, stumble, slide; run a risk Written also *sgiorr.*

SCIORD See SGIORT.

SCIORRADH, aidh, *s. m.* A slipping, a stumbling, a sliding; a risking; a slip, a stumble, a risk. Written also *sgiorrail;* which see.

SCIORRAIL, *a.* See SGIORRAIL.

SCIORT, *v. a.* Squirt. *Pret. a.* sciort, *squirted.* See SGIORT.

SCIORTAN, ain, *s m.* See SGIORTAN.

† SCIOT, *s m.* An arrow, a dart.

This is a Celto-Sythian vocable, and seems to be the root of the word *Scythæ*, Scythians, literally *archers.*

SCIOTH, *s. m.* A partition; a partition of wattled work.

† SCIOTH, *a* See SGÌTH.

SCIOTHAS See SGITHEAS.

SCIÙR, *v a.* Scour, purge, cleanse More frequently written *scùr* or *sgùr*, which see

† SCIÙRLONG, *s m.* A fugitive, a deserter —*Shaw.*

SCIÙRS, *v. a* Whip, scourge; scare, scatter, or disperse; persecute; pursue *Pret* sciùrs, *fut. aff a.* sciùrsaidh, *shall scourge.* See SGIÙRS.

SCIÙRS, *s. m* A lash, a whip, or scourge, a scaring, a scattering, a forcible dispersement; woe; affliction, persecution; pursuit Sciùrs do 'n each, *a whip for the horse* —*Stew. Pro* See also SGIÙRS.

SCIÙRSACH, *a* Lashing, whipping, scourging; scaring, scattering, dispersing, persecuting, pursuing.

SCIÙRSA, SCIÙRSADH, aidh, *s. m* A lash, a scourge; a lashing, a scourging, a scaring, a scattering; a persecuting.

SCLABHACHD, *s f.* Slavery, bondage.

SCLABHADH, aidh, *s m.* (*Ir. id* *Fr* esclave) A slave, a bondsman

SCLABHAIDHEACHD, *s f.* Slavery, bondage, servitude.

SCLAMH, *v a.* Seize greedily; snatch, usurp. *Pret. a. id.*, *fut aff. a* sclamhaidh

SCLAMHACH, *a* Apt to snatch or to take away by force; greedy.

SCLÀMHACHD, *s f* A seizing greedily or violently; usurpation

SCLÀMHADH, aidh, *s m.* A seizing; a snatching with violence, usurpation

SCLÀMHAIR, *s m* A usurper, one who seizes violently. *N. pl.* sclamhairean.

SCLEAD, *s m* A slate —*Macd* *N. pl.* scleadan. Tigh sclead, *a slated house.*

SCLEADACH, *a* Slaty, slated, abounding in slates.

SCLEADAIR, *s. m.* A slater. *N. pl* scleadairean.

SCLEADAIREACHD, *s f.* The business of a slater.

SCLEADAR, *a.* Slaty, laminar

SCLEÒ, *s. m.* Vapour, mist; shade; darkness; idle talk;

rodomontade; a romance; verbiage; falsehood; high puffing; fustian; a spectre; a struggle; misery; compassion. Tannas a shuidheas air scleò, *a ghost who reclines on mist.—Oss. Fing.* Scleò air neòil nan gleann, *a spectre on the clouds of the valleys.—Id.* Scleò nan curaidhean, *the struggle of the heroes.—Old Poem.* Iomar-scleo, *a contest maintained with various success.—Id.* Ri scleò, *speaking at random, telling lies.* Written also *sgleò.*

Scleòid, *s. m.* and *f.* A silly person; one who is easily imposed on; one who indulges in idle talk.

Scloid, *s. f.* Filth.—*Shaw.*

Scloing, *s. f.* Snot. Written also *sgloing.*

Scloingean, ein, *s. m.* Snot. *N. pl.* scloingeanan.

Scloingeanach, *a.* Snotty, filthy. Do shroin plucach scloingeanach, *thy carbuncled snotty nose.—Old Song.*

Sclongaid, *s. f.* Snot. *N. pl.* sclongaidean.

Sclongaideach, *a.* Snotty.

Scòd, scòid, *s. m.* Pride; airiness; coquetry; a sheet of a sail; a corner of a cloth.

Scòdail, *a.* (scòd-amhuil.) Proud; airy. Also written *sgòdail.*

Scòid, *s. f.* (*Ir. id.*) A neck.

Scòideas, eis, *s. f.* Pride; airiness; coquetry; flirting. Written also *sgòideas.*

Scòideasach, *a.* Proud; airy; coquettish; flirting. Written also *sgòideasach.*

Scòideasachd. See Sgòideasachd.

Scoil, *s. f.* (*Arm.* scol.) A school; *also,* education. Written also *sgoil;* which see.

Scoilear, eir, *s. m.* (*Arm.* scolaer.) A scholar; a schoolman; a good scholar. *N. pl.* scoilearan, *scholars.* Also written *sgoilear.*

Scoilearachd, *s. f.* Scholarship.

Scoilt, *v. a.* See Sgoilt.

Scoiltean, ein, *s. m.* See Sgoiltean.

† Scoit, *s. f.* (*Lat.* scut-um. *Arm.* scoet.) A shield or target.

Scoitiche, *s. m.* A mountebank or quack.

Scolb, *s.* A prick, a prickle; a skirmish with knives and dirks; *also,* a spray or wattle used in thatching with straw; a splinter. See also Sgolb.

Scolt, sgoilt. See Sgolt.

Scoltach, *a.* Cracking, splitting; apt to crack or split; causing to crack or split. See Sgoltach.

Scoltadh. See Sgoltadh.

Scor. See Sgor.

Scoradh, aidh, *s. m.* See Sgoradh.

Scoraid. See Sgoraid.

Scornach. Written also *sgornach;* which see.

Scornan. Written also *sgornan.*

Scorr, *s. m.* A rock; a cliff; a pinnacle; a concealed rock jutting into the sea; the tail of a bank; a notch or mark made by the stroke of a knife or any sharp instrument. Crainn gheugach nan scorr, *the branchy trees of the rocks.—Oss. Fing.* Mar lasair air scorr, *like a flame on a pinnacle.—Id.* See Sgor.

Scorrach, *a.* Rocky, cliffy. *Com.* and *sup.* scorraiche.

Scorr-bheann, bheinn, *s. f.* A rocky mountain; a projecting cliff; a blasted cliff.—*Oss. Tem.* Written also *sgòr-bheann;* which see.

Scòrr-bheannach, *a.* Rocky, cliffy.

Scorr-shruth, *s. m.* A rocky stream.—*Oss. Tem.* *N. pl.* scorr-shruthach.

† Scot, *a.* Little; contemptible.

† Scotan, ain, *s. m.* A small flock; a group of people.

Scot-bheurla, *s.* The Scotch tongue.—*Shaw.*

Scoth, *s. m.* A flower; the choice part of any thing; a disease; a small boat: for this last sense, see Sgoth.

Scrabach, *a.* See Sgrabach.

Scraideach, *a.* See Sgraideach.

Scraideag, eig, *s. m.* A diminutive female. *N. pl.* scraideagan.

Scraideagach, *a.* Diminutive; shabby; puny.

Scraidean, ein, *s. m.* A diminutive fellow; a shabby-looking fellow.

Scraideanach, *a.* Diminutive; shabby; puny.

Scràiste, *s. m.* A sluggish person; a sluggard; *also,* sluggishness.

Scràisteach, *a.* Sluggish, slovenly; *also, substantively,* a sluggard or sloven. Gu scraisteach, *sluggishly. Com.* and *sup.* scraistiche.

Scràisteachd, *s. f.* Sluggishness, slovenliness, laziness.

Scràistealachd, *s. f.* Sluggishness, slovenliness, laziness.

Scràisteil, *a.* (scraiste-amhuil.) Sluggish, slovenly, lazy. Gu scraisteil, *sluggishly.*

Scrait, sgraite, *s. f.* A rag.

Scraiteach, *a.* Ragged, shabby.

Scraiteag. See Scraideag.

Scraitean. See Scraidean.

Scrath, *v. a.* and *n.* Peel; take off the skin or rind; pare a surface; excoriate. *Pret. a.* scrath; *fut. aff. a.* scrathaidh.

Scrath, *s. m.* The skin or peel of any thing; a rind; a husk; a turf, a sod.

Scrathach, *a.* Skinny; having a thick skin or rind; having many rinds, as an onion.

Scrathail, *a.* (scrath-amhuil.) Tearing, destroying; destructive; terrible. Mar thonn scrathail, *like a destroying billow.—Old Poem.*

Screab, *s. m.* A scab; the itch; the mange. Written also *sgreab.*

Screabach, *a.* Scabbed; itchy; mangy. Written also *sgreabach.*

Screach. See Sgreach.

Screachach, *a.* See Sgreachach.

Screachadh, aidh, *s. m.* See Sgreachadh.

Screachag, aig, *s. m.* A jay; a young female that shrieks. Screachag choille, *a jay;* screach oidhche, *a screech-owl.* Written also *sgreachag.*

Scread, *s.* A shriek, a cry, a shout; any shrill jarring noise; a creaking noise. Written also *sgread.* Leig i sgread aisde, *she shrieked.*

Screadach, *a.* Shrieking, crying, shouting; making a loud discordant noise; creaking.

Screadachan, ain, *s. m.* A little squaller; a shrieking child.

Screadail, *s. f.* Continued shrieking. See Sgreadail.

Screadan, ain, *s. m.* The noise of any thing in tearing; a creaking or grating noise; a clashing noise; a scream, a shriek. Screadan nan lann, *the grating* or *clashing of swords.—Oss. Lodin.* Screadan eun, *the scream of birds.—Oss. Tem.* Written also *sgreadan.*

Screadanach, *a.* Creaking, clashing; screaming, shrieking.

Screamh, screimh, *s. m.* Abhorrence, disgust. Tha thu 'cur screamh orm, *you disgust me.*

Screamhach, *a.* Abhorrent, disgustful.

Screamhach, *a.* Disgusting.

Screapal, ail, *s. m.* A scruple.

Screataidh, *a.* See Screitidh.

Screatachd, *s. f.* See Scréitidheachd.

Scréitidh, *a.* Abhorrent, abominable, disgusting. See also Sgréitidh.

Scréitidheachd, *s. f.* Abhorrentness; abominableness, disgustfulness.

Screuch. See Screach or Sgreach.

Scribhinn, *s. f.* A rugged, rocky side of a hill.

Scribhinneach, *a.* Rocky; having a rocky side, as a mountain.

Scribhinneachd, *s. f.* Rockiness, ruggedness.

Scrid, scride, *s. m.* (*Ir. id.*) A breath; the least breath of life or air; the least sign of life. Cha d'fhàg e scrid ann, *he left not a breath of life in him.*

Scrin, scrine, *s. f.* A shrine. *N. pl.* scrineachan, *shrines. Germ.* schrein. *Belg.* schryn. *It.* scrigno. *Fr.* escrine. *Swed.* skryn. *W.* ysgrin. *Ir.* scrin.

Scrineach, *a.* Having a shrine, like a shrine; of shrines.

Scrìob, *v.* Scratch, scrape; make a furrow; a currycomb. *Pret.* scriob; *fut. aff. a.* scriobaidh. Written also *sgriob.*

Scrìob, *s. f.* A scratch, a scrape; a furrow; a currycombing. Thoir scriob, *make a furrow;* also, *take a round; take a turn.* Written also *sgriob.*

Scrìobach, *a.* Scratching, scraping; furrowing; currycombing. See also Sgriobach.

Scriobach, aich, *s. m.* The itch.

Scriobachan, ain, *s. m.* A scraper; a wooden instrument for raking ashes. Scriobachan na luaithre, *a wooden fire-shovel.*

Scrioban, ain, *s. m.* A currycomb; a scraper; any instrument for scraping.

Scriobanach, *a.* Like a scraper; like a currycomb.

Scriobh, *v. a.* Write; compose. *Pret. a.* scriobh, *wrote; fut. aff. a.* scriobhaidh. Scriobh iad, *write them.—Stew.* Written also *sgriobh;* which see. *Swed.* skrifva. *Gr.* σκαριφω. *Germ.* schreiben. *Anglo-Sax.* scrifen.

Scriobhadair, *s. m.* A writer; a clerk, scribe; a notary; a penman. *N. pl.* scriobhadairean.

Scriobhadh, aidh, *s. m.* A writing; writing; penmanship. Deagh scriobhadh, *good writing. N. pl.* scriobhaichean, *writings.*

Scriobhaichean, *s. pl.* Writings.

Scriobhainn, *s. f.* See Sgriobhainn.

Scriobhainnear, eir, *s. m.* (*Eng.* scrivener.) A writer, a clerk, scribe, or notary.

Scriobhair, *s. m.*, scriobh-fhear. (*Swed.* skrifvare.) A writer, a scribe, a clerk; a penman. *N. pl.* scriobhairean.

Scriobhaireachd, *s. f.* The business of writing; the business of a writer, clerk, or notary; penmanship.

Scriobham, 1 *sing. imper.* of scriobh. Let me write; *also, for* scriobhaidh mi, *I will write.*

Scriobhta, **Scriobhte**, *p. part.* of scriobh. (*Arm.* scrit.) Written, recorded, registered.

Scriobhuinn, *s. f.* A bill or evidence; writings. *N. pl.* scriobhuinnean, *bills, writings.*

Scrios, *s. m.* See Sgrios.

Scrios, *v.* More frequently written *sgrios;* which see.

Scriosach, *a.* See Sgriosach.

Scriosadair, *s. m.* More frequently *sgriosadair;* which see.

Scriosadaireachd, *s. f.* See Sgriosadaireachd.

Scriotachan, ain, *s. m.* A little squaller. Also written *sgreadachan.*

Scròb, *v. a.* Scratch. *Pret.* scrob; *fut. aff.* scrobaidh, *shall scratch.* Written also *sgròb;* which see.

Scròbach, *a.* Scratching; inclined to scratch.

Scròbadh, aidh, *s. m.* A scratching. See also Sgròbadh.

Scròban, ain, *s. m.* The crop or craw of a bird. Written also *sgròban.*

Scròbanach, *a.* Having a crop or craw; having a large craw; of craws. Also written *sgròbanach;* which see.

Scrobha, *s. m.* A screw. *N. pl.* scrobhachan. Written also *sgrobha.*

Scrubair, *s. m.* A scrub; a miser. *N. pl.* scrubairean.

Scrubaireachd, *s. f.* Scrubbishness; niggardliness.

Scrud, *v.* See Sgrud.

Scuab, scuaib, *s. f.* A besom or broom; a brush; a sheaf. See Sguab. *Arm.* scuba, *a brush. Span.* escoba. *Lat.* scopa.

Scuab, *v. n.* See Sguab.

Scuabach, aich, *s. f.* A besom or broom; a brush. *N. pl.* scuabaichean. See Sguabach.

Scuabach, *a.* Sweeping, brushing; cleanly.

Scuabachan, ain, *s. m.* (*dim.* of scuabach.) A little brush or besom.

Scuabadh, aidh, *s. m.* A sweeping, a brushing.

Scuàbag, aig, *s. f.* (*dim.* of scuab.) A little sheaf; a little broom or besom.

† **Scud**, scuid, *s. m.* A ship. Hence the English sea term *scud.* Some etymologists derive this vocable from the Greek χεδια. *Arm.* sgytt, *a boat. Swed.* scutta. *Island,* skiut. *Ir.* scud.

Scud, *v. a.* Cut off; abscond; cut off at a blow. See Sgud.

Scùd, scùid, *s. m.* A scout, a spy. See also Sgùd.

Scudach, *a.* Cutting off; absconding.

† **Scuite**, *s. m.* A wanderer.

Scuits. See Sguits.

Sculag, aig, *s. m.* See Sgalag.

Scumadair, *s. m.* See Sgumadair.

Sdà, *s. m.* See Stà.

Sdad, *v. a.* and *n.* See Stad.

Sdad, *s. m.* See Stad.

Sdaid, *s. f.* See Staid.

Sdaidheir, sdaidhreach, *s. f.* A stair. *N. pl.* sdaidhrichean. See Staidheir.

Sdeall, *s.* See Steall.

Sdeig, *s. f.* A steak. See Steig.

Sdeòc, *s. f.* An idle female; a female who is fond of staring idly at persons. Written also *steòc.*

Sdeud, *s.* See Steud.

Sdiall, *s. m.* See Stiall.

Sdiolan, ain, *s. m.* A thread. See Stiolan.

Sdiorap, aip, *s. m.* A stirrup. *N. pl.* stiorapan.

Sdiotach, aich, *s.* A name given to a cat.

Sditidh, *s.* A name by which a cat is called.

Sdiùir, *v. a.* Steer. See Stiùir.

Sdiùradh, aidh, *s. m.* A steering, a directing, a guiding; steerage; guidance. See Stiùradh.

Sdoc, sduic, *s. m.* More properly *stoc;* which see.

Sdod, sdoid, *s. m.* Sulkiness; a pet; a sulky fit.

Sdodach, *a.* Sulky; pettish. Gu sdodach, *sulkily. Com.* and *sup.* sdodaiche.

Sdodan, ain, *s. m.* A sulky child; a pettish person.

Sdodanach, *a.* Sulky, pettish, peevish. Gu sdodanach, *sulkily.*

Sdodanachd, *s. f.* Sulkiness; peevishness.

Sdoilean, ein, *s. m.* See Stoilean.

Sdòirean, ein, *s. m.* A sour, sulky fellow.

Sdòireanach, *a.* Sulky; boorish.

Sdór. An expression used to incite a bull towards a cow.

Sdùrd. See Stùrd.

'Se, (*for* is e.) It is he or it. 'Se rinn so, *it is he who did this.* 'N esa rinn so? 'se, *is it he who did this? yes.*

Se, *pers. pron.* (*Ir. id. Heb.* se.) He; it. This vocable is, in all respects, equivalent to *è;* and, in general, it is used where the personal pron. *e* immediately follows it; and, in such instances, it seems to be employed to prevent an awkward hiatus. Bhuail se e, *he struck him* or *it.*

Sè, Sea, *a.* Six. Sè fichead mìle, *one hundred and twenty thousand.—Stew. Jon.*
Heb. ses *and* sis. *Ethiop.* and *Pers.* ses. *Tonq.* sau. *Fr.* six. *It.* sei. *Lat.* sex. *Span.* seijs. *Bisc.* sey. *Ir.* sè.

Seab, *v. a.* Creep softly; sneak. *Pret.* sheab, *sneaked.* Sheab e orm, *he crept softly upon me.*

Seabach, *a.* Creeping softly.

Seabadh, aidh, *s. m.* A creeping softly.

Seabair, *s. m.* A sly, sneaking fellow. A sheabair, *thou sneaker.* See also Seapair.

Seabaireachd, *s. f.* Slyness, sneaking.

Seabh, *s. m.* A quid of tobacco. Tombac seabh, *chewing tobacco. Seabh* is perhaps a corruption of the English word *chew.*

Seabhag, aig, *s. f.* (*Ir.* seabhas. *W.* hebog.) A hawk, a falcon; the spleen. An seabhag a rèir a gne, *the hawk after its kind.—Stew. Lev.* Is duilich seabhag dheanamh do 'n chlamhan, *a carrion kite will make a bad hawk.—G. P. N. pl.* seabhagan.

Seabhagach, *a.* (*Ir.* seabhacach.) Like a hawk or falcon; abounding in hawks or falcons; of hawks or falcons.

Seabhagail, *a.* (*Ir.* seabhacamhuil.) Like a hawk or falcon.

Seabhagair, *s. m.* (*Ir.* seabhacair. *W.* hebogydd.) A falconer. *N. pl.* seabhagairean.

Seabhagaireachd, *s. f.* Falconing; the business of a falconer.

Seabhagan, ain, *s. m.* The call of a hawk; a place where hawks are kept.

Seabhag-oidhche, *s. f.* A night-hawk.—*Stew. Lev.*

Seabhaid, *s. f.* Wandering. Air sheabhaid, *astray.*

Seabhaid, *v. n.* Wander, stray; go astray. *Pret. a.* sheabhaid, *wandered; fut. aff.* seabhaididh.

Seabhaideach, *a.* (*Ir.* seabhoideach.) Wandering, straying, apt to go astray.

Seabhaideachd, *s. f.* Aptness to go astray or wander; a wandering disposition; the state of being astray.

Seabhais. See Seabhas.

Seabhaiseach. See Seabhasach.

Seabhaiseachd. See Seabhasachd.

Seabhas, ais, *s. m.* Weariness; fatigue; labour; wandering; strolling; a stroll.

Seabhasach, *a.* (*Ir. id.*) Weary, fatigued; laborious; wandering, straying; discursive. *Com.* and *sup.* seabhasaiche.

Seabhasachd, *s. f.* Laboriousness, fatigue, weariness; a wandering; the state of being astray; discursiveness. Tha mi sgìth le seabhasachd, *I am tired of wandering.*

† **Seabhrach**, *a.* (*Ir. id.*) Certain, sure, true.

Seac, *v. a.* and *n.* (*Ir. id.*) Wither, scorch, dry, parch; waste, decay. *Pret.* sheac; *fut. aff. a.* seacaidh. Seacaidh geugan nan crann, *the branches of the trees shall wither.—Macdon.*

Seac, *a.* Withered, scorched, dried, parched; decayed, sapless, marcid. Meanglain seac, *withered branches.*
Lat. sicc-us. *Bisc.* siccua. *It.* secco. *Span.* sec-o. *Arm. W.* sech. *Corn.* sekh, *dry, withered. Sclav.* suchu. *Pol.* succhi, *dry. Chald.* sak, *to dry.*

Seacach, *a.* Causing to wither; apt to wither. Written also *seachdach.*

Seacachadh, aidh, *s. m.* A parching, a scorching; a drying, a withering. Tha e air seacachadh, *it has become withered.*

Seacadh, aidh, *s. m.* A withering, a parching, a scorching; a scorching heat; a scorched or withered part. Fo sheacadh na grèine, *under the scorching heat of the sun.—Oss. Tem.* Air seacadh nan raon, *on the withered surface of the upland fields.—Oss. Tem.* Air seacadh, *withered.*

Seacadh, (a), *pr. part.* of seac. Withering, parching, scorching. Written also *seachdadh.*

Seacaich, *v. a.* and *n.* (*from* seac.) Wither, parch, scorch; dry up for want of moisture. *Pret. a.* sheacaich; *fut. aff. a.* seacaichidh, *shall wither.*

Seacaichear, *fut. pass.* of seacaich.

Seacaichte, *p. part.* of seacaich. Withered, parched, scorched.

Seacamh, aimh, *s. m.* A helmet or headpiece. Ceud seacamh 's ceud bheairt bholgach, *a hundred helmets, and as many bossy bucklers.—Oss. Taura.*

Seacanta, *a.* (*Ir. id.*) Parched, withered; apt to parch or wither; apt to grow parched or withered.

Seacd, *a.* More properly *seac* or *seachd;* which see.

Seacd, *v. a.* and *n. Pret. a.* sheachd; *fut.* seachdaidh. See Seac or Seachd.

Seacdach, *a.* See Seacach.

Seacdadh. See Seacadh.

Seacdaich, *v. a.* and *n.* More properly *seacaich* or *seachdaich;* which see.

Seacdaichte, *p. part.* More properly *seacaichte* or *seachdaichte;* which see.

† **Seach**, *s. m.* (*Ir. id.*) A turn; alternation.

Seach, *adv.* and *prep.* Past, gone by; aside, or out of the way; in comparison of; in preference to. Deo grèine a chaidh seach, *a sunbeam that has gone by.—Oss. Cathluno.* Rach seach, *go by, go past;* seach neach fo 'n ghrèin, seach m' athair deurach, *in comparison of any under the sun, in comparison of my mourning father.—Ull.* Snamh seach geallach na h-oidhche, *swimming past the moon of night.—Oss. Fin. and Lor.* Fear seach fear, *one man from another;* seach a chèile, *one from another;* cha 'n aithne dhomh h-aon seach a chèile, *I know not one from another;* san dol seach, *in passing, en passant;* mu seach, *alternately;* mun seach, *alternately;* seach a chèile, *one by, past,* or *from another.*

† **Seach**, *v. a.* (*Ir. id.*) Shun; pass by.

Seachad, *adv.* and *prep.* Past, gone by; by; aside; out of the way. Rach seachad, *go by;* an oidhche a dol seachad, *the night going past.—Oss. Taura.* Cuir seachad mo sgiath, *put aside my shield.—Oss.* Seachad orm, *past me;* dol seachad, *passing;* san dol seachad, *in passing, en passant;* air dol seachad, *past, gone by.*

† **Seachad**, *v. a.* Deliver, surrender.—*Shaw.*

Seachadach, *a.* Parsimonious; frugal; hoarding; traditionary.

Seachadachd, *s. f.* Parsimony; frugality; a disposition to hoard; hoarding; tradition.

Seachadadh, aidh, *s. m.* A laying up or storing; a tradition.

Seachadaich, *v. a.* Put aside; avoid; hoard.

Seachadas, ais, *s. m.* Tradition. *N. pl.* seachadais. Seachadais dhaoine, *the traditions of men.—Stew. Col.*

Seachaid, *v. a.* Lay up, store, hoard; deliver, surrender. *Pret. a.* sheachaid; *fut. aff. a.* seachaididh, *shall hoard.*

Seachaideach, *a.* Laying up, storing; frugal; delivering, surrendering.

Seachaideachd, *s. f.* A disposition to hoard; frugality; a hoarding.

Seachain, *s. pl.* Idle tales; an allegory.

Seachain, *v. a. (Ir. id.)* Shun, avoid; abstain from; stray. *Pret. a.* sheachain; *fut. aff. a.* seachnaidh, *shall shun.* Seachain i, *avoid it.—Stew. Pro.* Seachnaidh duine a bhrathair, ach cha seachain e 'choimhearsnach, *a man may do without a brother, but not without a neighbour.—G. P.*

Seachainteach, *a.* Allegorical; dismal; ominous; shunning; to be avoided.

Seacham, *comp. prep.* Past me. *Emphatic form,* seacham-sa.

Seachantach, *a.* (*Ir. id.*) Evitable, avoidable; apt to shun or avoid; shunning; wandering, straying. *Com.* and *sup.* seachantaichè.

Seachantachd, *s. f.* (*Ir. id.*) Avoidableness; a tendency to wander.

Seacharan, ain, *s. m.* More frequently written *seachran;* which see.

Seach-bhriathar, *s. m.* An allegorical saying.

Seachd, *a.* (*Ir.* seacht. *Arm.* seich.) Seven. Seachd geallaich chaidh tharram, *seven moons* [*months*] *passed over me.—Ull.* Rè sheachd bliadhna, *during seven years;* gabhaidh tu nan seachdaibh, *thou wilt take* [*them*] *in sevens.—Stew. Gen.* Seachd sgìth, *quite tired.*

Seachd, *a.* Withered, scorched, parched; decayed. See **Seac.**

Seachd, *v. a.* and *n.* Wither, scorch, parch; grow withered; decay. *Pret. a.* sheachd; *fut. aff.* seachdaidh.

Seachdach, *a.* Withering, scorching, parching; causing to wither. Written also *seacach.*

Seachdachadh, aidh, *s. m.* A growing withered; a causing to wither.

Seachdadh, aidh, *s. m.* A withering, a scorching, a parching; a scorched or withered part; a growing withered or parched. Air seachdadh, *withered.* Written also *seacadh;* which see.

Seachdaich, *v. a.* and *n.* Wither, scorch, parch; grow withered or parched. *Pret. a.* sheachdaich; *fut. aff. a.* seachdaichidh, *shall scorch.* Written also *seacaich.*

Seachdaich, *v. a.* (*from* seachd.) Arrange into sevens; septuplicate; septimate. *Pret. a.* sheachdaich; *fut. aff. a.* seachdaichidh.

Seachdaichear, *fut. pass.* of seachdaich. Shall be withered.

Seachdaichte, *p. part.* of seachdaich. Withered, scorched, blasted.

Seachdain, *s. f.* A week. See **Seachduin.**

Seachdaineach, *a.* Hebdomadal, weekly. Also written *seachduineach.*

Seachdamh, *a.* (*from* seachd.) Seventh; *also,* a seventh part. An seachdamh là, *the seventh day.—Stew. Ex.* An seachdamh la deug, *the seventeenth day.*

Seachd-deug, *a.* (*Ir.* seacht-deag. *Arm.* seichtec.) Seventeen. Seachd fir dheug, *seventeen men;* seachd fir fhichead, *twenty-seven men.*

Seachd-dùbailt, *a.* Septuple or sevenfold.

Seachd-fillte, *a.* Sevenfold.

Seachd-mhios, *s.* September.

Seachdnar, *a.* Seven in number. Seachdnar dhaoine, *seven men in number.*

Seachd-reultan, *s. pl.* The Pleïades.

Seachd-rinn, *s. pl.* The Pleïades.

Seachd-shlisneach, *a.* Heptagonal; *also,* a heptagon.

Seachd-shlisneag, eig, *s. f.* A heptagon.

Seachduan, ain, *s. m.* A fold.

Seachduin, *s. f.* (seachd, *seven, and* ùin, *a period of time.*) A week, seven days. Coimhlion a seachduin, *fulfil her week.—Stew. Gen.* Seachduin bho 'n diugh, *this day sennight;* eadar so 's ceann seachduin, *in a week's time;* la seachduin, *a week-day;* seachduin na luaithre, *Ember-week.*

Seachduineach, *a.* Weekly; hebdomadal.

Seach-labhair, *v. n.* Allegorise; speak allegorically. *Pret. a.* sheach-labhair; *fut. aff. a.* seach-labhairidh.

Seach-labhairt, *s. f.* Allegorising; speaking allegorically; an allegory.

Seach-labhrach, *a.* (*Ir. id.*) Allegorical; speaking allegorically; prone to speak allegorically.

Seach-labhradh, aidh, *s. m.* (*Ir. id.*) An allegory; allegorical speaking.

Seachlan, ain, *s. m.* A warren.—*Shaw.*

Seach-luidh, *v. n.* Lie apart; lie aside.

Seach-luidhe, *s. m.* A lying apart.

Seach, (ma), *adv.* Alternately; in return. Fear ma seach, *man by man; one by one; each in rotation.* Written also *mu seach.*

Seach, (man). Alternately; in rotation. Uair man seach, *time about;* grathuinn man seach, *while about.* Written also *mun seach.*

Seachmhall, aill, *s. m.* Digression; partiality; oblivion.

Seachmhallach, *a.* Digressive; oblivious; forgetful.

Seachmhallachd, *s. f.* Oblivion: forgetfulness.

Seach, (mu), *adv.* Alternately, in return; in rotation. Fear mu seach, *one by one; man by man.*

Seach, (mun), *adv.* Alternately, in return; in rotation. Fear mun seach, *man by man; one by one;* gabh tarruing mun seach dheth, *take while about of it;* tha d' obair dol mun seach ort, *your work is increasing on your hands; your work is increasing more than you can manage.*

† **Seachnab**, aba, *s. m.* (*Ir. id.*) A prior.

Seachnach, *a.* Avoidable; shunning, avoiding.

Seachnachadh, aidh, *s. m.* Avoiding, shunning.

Seachnadh, aidh, *s. m.* A shunning or avoiding; a wanting, a missing.

Seachnaich, *v. a.* Avoid; shun; miss; escape. *Pret.* sheachnaich; *fut. aff.* seachnaichidh; *p. part.* seachnaichte.

Seachnaichte, *p. part.* of seachnaich. Shunned.

† **Seachrach**, *a.* (*Ir. id.*) Dirty.

Seachrain, *v. n.* Go astray, wander, err. *Pret.* sheachrain.

Seachrain, *gen. sing.* of seachran.

Seachran, ain, *s. m.* (*Ir. id.*) A straying; a wandering; an error. Seachran air luim na fàsaich, *straying on the bleakness of the desert.—Oss. Conn.* Air seachran, *astray, out of one's course;* na leig dhomh dol air seachran, *let me not go astray.—Sm.* Gach maraich air seachran, *every seaman out of his course.—Oss. Duthona.* Seachran a mhiann, *the wandering of desire.—Stew. Ecc.* Mo sheachran, *my error.—Stew. Job.*

Seachran, (a), *pr. part.* Wandering, going astray; straying, erring. A' seachran gu h-iar, *wandering towards the west.—Oss.*

Seachranach, *a.* (*Ir. id.*) Wandering, straying, erring; wrong; causing error; prone to stray or to err. Reul seachranach, *a wandering star, a planet*—(*Stew.* 2 *K.*); also, *a comet;* rathad seachranach, *a by-road.—Stew. Jud.*

Seachranachd, *s. f.* A tendency to go astray; the state of being astray; error.

Seach-rod, -roid, *s. m.* (*Ir. id.*) A by-road, a by-path. *N. pl.* seach-rodan.

Seac-theinn, *s. f.* A severe illness; a mortal sickness. Bha thu fo sheac-theinn, *thou wert mortally sick.—Old Song.*

Seac-thinn, *a.* Mortally sick; severely indisposed.

Seac-thinneas, eis, *s. m.* A severe illness; mortal sickness.

Sead, *s. m.* See **Seud**.

† **Sead**, *s. m.* A way, a road; a seat.—*Shaw.*

Seadair, *s. m.* (*Ir. id.*) A dolt; a sneaking fellow.

Seadaireach, *a.* Sneaking.

Seadaireachd, *s. f.* Sneaking.

† **Seadal**, ail, *s. m.* A short space of time.

Seadh, *adv., for* is e. (*Ir. id.*) It is, it is so; yes, yea; be it so. Seadh gu dearbh, *yes, indeed;* seadh, seadh mata, *well, well then;* seadh! *indeed!* ma seadh, *if so; then;* moire seadh, *yes indeed; by St. Mary, it is so.*

Seadh, *s. m.* (*Ir.* seagh.) Sense or meaning; care, attention; esteem, respect, value; a discourse or dialogue; the crop or craw of a bird. Gabh seadh, *pay attention;* seadh-suiridh, *a love-token.*

† **Seadh**, *a.* (*Ir. id.*) Strong, stout.—*Shaw.*

† **Seadh**, *v. a.* Esteem, prize, value; saw, plane.

Seadhach, *a.* (*Ir.* seaghach.) Attentive; sensible; fit; courteous; gentle.

Seadhail, *a.* (seadh-amhuil.) Attentive; careful; fit; courteous; sensible; respectful.

Seadhar, *a.* (*for* seadhmhor.) Attentive; careful; heedful.

Seadharachd, *s. f.* Attentiveness.

Seadh, (ma). If so, if it be so, then. A deiream ma seadh, *I say then.—Stew. Rom.*

Seadhmhor, *a.* Attentive; careful; heedful. *Com.* and *sup.* seadhmhoire.

Seadhmhorachd, *s. f.* Attentiveness.

Seadh-suiridh, *s. m.* A love-token.

Seagall, aill, *s. m.* (*Gr.* σικαλη. *Arm.* segal. *Fr.* seigle.) Rye. An cruithneachd agus an seagall, *the wheat and the rye.—Stew. Ex.*

Seagallach, *a.* (*from* seagall.) Abounding in rye; of rye.

Seagh, *s. m.* More frequently written *seadh.*

Seagha, *a.* Curious; ingenious.—*Shaw.*

Seaghach, *a.* (*Ir. id.*) Gentle, courteous; soft, mild. A seinn luinneaga seaghach, *singing gentle ditties.—Old Song.*

Seaghas, ais, *s. m.* Wood.

Seaghlan, ain, *s. m.* An old man; an infirm person; a pithless person; a column, a post; *rarely,* a king.

Seaghlanach, *a.* Infirm; stiff; columnal.

Seal, *s. m.* A seal. More properly *seul;* which see.

Seal, *s. m.* (*Ir. id.*) A space of time, a while, a season; a course, a turn. Re seal, *for a season;* dh' imich ri seal clann Mhuirn, *the sons of Morni have gone for a season.—Oss. Fin. and Lor.* Seal mu 'n thuit e, *a while before he fell.—Oss. Calth. and Col.*

Sealach, (*from* seal.) Momentary, transitory; lasting but a season.

* 493

Sealadach, *a.* (*from* seal.) Transitory; alternate; by turns.

Sealaidheach, *a.* Transitory.

Sealaidheachd, *s. f.* Transitoriness, alternation; vicissitude; change.

Sealan, ain, *s. m., dim.* of seal. (*Ir. id.*) A short while, a short space; a sheep-louse; a halter or rope for execution.

Sealanta, *a.* (*Ir. id.*) Rigid.—*Shaw.* Gu sealanta, *rigidly.*

Sealantas, ais. Rigidness.

Sealbh, seilbh, *s. f.* (*Ir. id.*) Possession; inheritance; property; stock; cattle; a drove or herd of cattle; a field; luck; *rarely,* a pretence, colour. Sealbh chaorach, *a stock of sheep;* sealbh chrodh, *a possession* or *stock of black cattle.—Stew. Gen.* Faigh sealbh, *obtain possession;* gabh sealbh, *take possession.*

Sealbhach, *a.* Possessive.

Sealbhachadh, aidh, *s. m.* (*Ir.* sealbhaghadh.) Possession, property; a possessing, an enjoying, inheriting.

Sealbhachadh, (a), *pr. part.* of sealbhaich. Possessing, inheriting.

Sealbhadair, *s. m.* (*from* sealbh.) A possessor, an owner, a proprietor, occupant. Sealbhadair neimh, *the possessor of heaven.—Stew. Gen. N. pl.* sealbhadairean.

Sealbhadaireachd, *s. f.* Possessorship, ownership.

Sealbhadh, aidh, *s. m.* A possessing, an inheriting; a possession.

Sealbhag, aig, *s. f.* Sorrel. Do shealbhag 's do luachair, *thy sorrel and thy rushes.—Macdon.* Sealbhag nam fiadh, *round-leaved mountain-sorrel.*

Sealbhagach, *a.* Abounding in sorrel; of sorrel; like sorrel. Gu seamragach sealbhagach, *abounding in shamrock and sorrel.—Old Song.*

Sealbhaich, *v. a. from* sealbh. (*Ir.* sealbhaigh.) Possess, inherit, own, enjoy. *Pret. a.* shealbhaich; *fut. aff. a.* sealbhaichidh.

Sealbhaiche, *s. m.* A possessor, an inheritor, an owner, a proprietor, an occupant.

Sealbhaichear, *fut. pass.* of sealbhaich. Shall be possessed; *it is used also impersonally, as,* sealbhaichear leam, *I shall possess.*

Sealbhaichte, *p. part.* of sealbhaich. Possessed.

Sealbhaidh, *s. f.* An encountering; an encounter.—*Shaw and Mac Co.*

Sealbhan, ain, *s. m.* A little possession, a little inheritance; a great number, a multitude; a drove, a group of animals; a throat. An sealbhan chéile air uchd an t-srutha, *in each other's throat on the breast of the stream.—Oss. Dargo. N. pl.* sealbhain.

Sealbhar, *a.* (*for* sealbh-mhòr.) Prosperous, lucky, propitious.

Sealbharachd, *s. m.* Prosperousness, propitiousness, good luck; the possession of property.

Sealbhmhoireachd, *s. f.* Propitiousness, prosperousness, luckiness; the possession of property.

Sealbhmhor, *a.* (sealbh-mòr.) Propitious, prosperous, lucky; having much property or possession. Ged bhithinn cho sealbhmhor, *though I were possessed of as much property. Com.* and *sup.* sealbhmhoire.

Sealg, seilg, *s. f.* (*Ir. id.*) A hunt, a chase; hunting; fowling, hawking; the milt of swine; the spleen of man or beast; a bellyache. Is aoibhinn an obair an sealg, *the chase is a joyous occupation.—Old Song.* Sealg-bhata, *a hunting-pole.*

Sealg, *v. a.* and *n.* (*Ir. id. Heb.* shalach, *to drive away.*) Hunt, chase; take or catch by hunting; fowl, hawk. *Pret.*

shealg, *hunted; fut. aff. a.* sealgaidh, *shall hunt.* Sealg dhomh sithionn, *hunt venison for me; take me venison.—Stew. Gen.*

SEALGACH, *a.* Hunting, chasing, fowling, venatic, hawking; fond of hunting; having spleen; splenetic.

SEALGADH, aidh, *s. m.* A hunting, a chasing, a fowling; a hunt, a chase.

SEALGADH, (a). Hunting, chasing, fowling. A sealg' a bhràthar, *hunting his brother.—Stew. Mic.*

SEALGAG, aig, *s. f.* A certain bitter herb.

SEALGAIR, *s. m.*, sealg-fhear. (*Ir. id.*) A hunter or huntsman; a fowler, a falconer; a sportsman; a gamekeeper, a forester. Shealgaire nan ciar-thorc! *thou hunter of the dusky boars!—Oss. Fing.* Sealgair a theab, *an unsuccessful hunter. N. pl.* sealgairean.

SEALGAIREACH, *a.* Like a huntsman or hunter.

SEALGAIREACHD, *s. f.* Hunting, hawking, falconing, fowling; the business of a huntsman, hawker, or fowler.

SEALL, *v. n.* (*W.* selw.) Look, behold, see, observe. *Pret. a.* sheall; *fut. aff. a.* seallaidh, *shall look.* Seallaidh mi ri, *I will look toward.—Stew. Jon.* Seall orm, *look on me.* Dhia seall oirnn! *Lord, have pity on us! Fut. sub.* shealllas, *shall look.* Am fear nach seall roimhe, cha seall e na dheigh, *he who looks not before him, will not look after him.—G. P.*

SEALL! Lo! behold! Seall! an gaisgeach treun a teachd, *lo! the conquering hero comes.—Fingalian Poem.*

SEALLA, *s. m.* See SEALLADH.

SEALLADH, aidh, *s. m.* (*Ir. id. Corn. Arm.* sell.) A look; a gaze; a prospect; a view; a sight; a vision; a supernatural sight; a short while. Sealladh ard, *a proud look.—Stew. Pro.* Gabh sealladh, *take a view;* an sealladh Dhé, *in the sight of God.—Stew. Gen.* Sealladh nan sùl, *the sight of the eyes.—Stew. Ecc.* As an t-sealladh, *out of sight;* a dol as an t-sealladh, *going out of sight; growing lean or emaciated, wasting in person;* fear seallaidh, *a seer;* luchd seallaidh, *seers.—Stew. 2 K.* As mo shealladh, *out of my sight.* For *sealladh*, in the sense of *supernatural sight*, see TAIBHSDEARACHD.

SEALLADH-CÙIL, *s. m.* A back look; a looking behind; a back view. Le ceumaibh mall 's le sealladh-cùil, *with slow steps, and lingering looks behind.—Oss. Gaul.*

SEALLADH-NASACH, *a.* A raree-show.—*Shaw.*

SEALLADH-TAOIBH, *s. m.* A side look; a side view. Le sealladh taoibh bu mhòr an aire, *with side looks they watched attentively.—Oss. Manos.*

SEALLAN, ain, *s. m.* (*dim.* of sealladh.) A short sight; a glance; a short while. Seallan beag, *a little while.—Stew. Heb.*

SEALL-FHIOS, *s.* Ocular proof, certainty. Tha seall-fhios agam air, *I am quite certain of it.*

SEALLTACH, *a.* Looking, gazing, staring; cautious, circumspect.

SEALLTUINN, *s. m.* A looking, observing, a viewing; a look, an observation, a view.

SEALLTUINN, (a), *pr. part.* of seall.

SEALTAIDH, *s. m.* A Highland poney.

† SEALTUIR, *s. m.* A sword.—*Shaw.*

SEAM, *s. m.* A mote, an atom; any small object.

SEAMACH, *a.* Warning; hinting; winking.

SEAMADH, aidh, *s. m.* A caution; a warning; a winking. Thug mi seamadh dhuit, *I gave thee warning.*

SEAMAN, ain, *s. m.* (*Ir. id.*) A stout little fellow; a nail, a pin; a small nail rivetted. *N. pl.* seamannan.—*Q. B. ref.*

SEAMANACH, *a.* Stout, firm; jolly; rivetted, as a nail.

SEAMANACHD, *s. f.* Stoutness, firmness, jolliness.

SEAMAR. See SEOMAR.

SEAMH, *a.* Mild, calm; modest, gentle; peaceful; slim, slender, small.

SEAMHACH, *a.* Mild, calm; modest, gentle; peaceful; producing mildness, calmness, or peace; slim, slender. Gu seamhach, *mildly. Com.* and *sup.* seamhaiche.

SEAMHACHD, *s. f.* Quietness; mildness; gentleness; modesty.

SEAMHAIDH, *a.* Fine; small; subtle; mild, gentle.

SEAMHAS, ais, *s. m.* Good luck; prosperity.

SEAMHASACH, *a.* Lucky.

SEAMHASACHD, *s. f.* Luck; continued good luck.

SEAMHASAIL, *a.* (seamhas-amhuil.) Lucky, fortunate, prosperous. Gu seamhasail, *luckily.*

SEAMHASAIR, *s. m.* A lucky or fortunate man.

SEAMHASAR, *a.* Lucky, fortunate; bringing good luck; boding good luck. Gu seamhasar, *luckily.*

SEAMH-MHEAS, *s. m.* Mellow fruit.

SEAMRAG, aig, *s. f.* (*Ir.* seamrog.) Shamrock, trefoil, clover.

This herb is worn on St. Patrick's day by all true Irishmen, in memory of the tutelary saint of their country.

SEAMRAGACH, *a.* Abounding in shamrock; of shamrock. Seamragach, sealbhagach, *abounding in shamrock and sorrel.—Old Song.*

SEAMSAG, aig, *s. f.* A small nail or peg; wood sorrel; *oxalis acetosella.*

SEAN, *a.* Old, aged; antique, ancient. An sean laoch, *the aged warrior.—Orr.* Fhuair e bàs na shean duine, *he died an old man.—Stew. Gen.* O shean, *of old. Com.* and *sup.* sine. Cha sean do 'm shean, 's cha 'n òg do m' òig thu, *you are neither old with my old, nor young with my young;* i. e. *as you are not my relation, I will have nothing to do with you.—G. P.*

Heb. Chald. sen, zken. *Arab. Eth.* chen. *Lat.* sen-ex. *Ir.* sean, *old. W.* shen.

SEÀN, *s. m.* A jewel. See SEUN.

† SEAN, seana, *s. m.* (*Lat.* cœna.) A supper.

† SEAN, *s. m.* Prosperity, happiness. Cuir a shean, *squander.*

SEAN, *v.* Refuse; *also*, enchant; bless. See SEUN.

SEANACACH, *a.* Crafty; shifty, wily: *hence* seannach or sionnach, *a fox.*

SEANACAR, *a.* (*from* sean.) Old-fashioned; looking old. Aodan co seanacar ri creag, *a face seemingly as old as the rocks.—Old Song.*

SEANACH, *a.* (*from* sean.) Crafty; lucky.

SEANACHAIDH, *s. m.* (*Ir.* seanchuidhe.) An antiquarian; a genealogist; a historian; a recorder.—*Stew. 2 Sam.*

The Seanachaidh were the chronologers, genealogists, and historians of the Celtic nations.

SEANACHAS, ais, *s. m.* (*Ir.* seanchas.) Antiquities; history; a chronicle; genealogy; a narration; conversation; talk. Luchd-seanachais, *genealogists;* also, *talkers.—Stew. Ezek.* Cron seanachais, *an anachronism.*

SEANACHD, *s. f.* (*from* sean.) Oldness; antiquity, ancientness. Seanachd na litreach, *the oldness of the letter.—Stew. Rom.*

SEANADAIR, *s. m.* (*from* seanadh.) A charmer, a conjurer. *N. pl.* seanadairean.

SEANADAIREACHD, *s. f.* A charming, a conjuring; the business or art of a conjurer.

SEANADH, aidh, *s. m.* (*Ir. id.*) A denying, a refusing; a refusal; a charm; a blessing; a synod, a senate, a council of elders. Comhairle an t-seanaidh, *the deliberation of the senate.—Macfar.*

Seanagar. See Seanacar.

Seanaiche, *s. m.* A senator, a member of parliament; a member of a synod; an antiquarian.

Seanailtireas, eis, *s. m.* A decree.

Sean-aimsir, *s. f.* Olden time.

Sean-aimsireil, *a.* Old-fashioned; antique.

Seanair, *s. m.*, sean-fhear. (*Ir.* seanoir. *W.* henwr.) An elder, a presbyter; a senator, a member of parliament; an ancient bard; a Druid.

Seanaireach, *a.* Presbyterian, senatorial; *substantively,* a presbyterian.

Seanaireachd, *s. f.* (*Ir.* seanoireacht.) Presbyterianism; old age, dotage; the fifth stage of human life, from 64 to 84 years of age; *rarely,* bird-catching.

Seanait, *s. f.* A senate. *Lat.* senat-us. *Ir.* seanaid. *W.* and *Corn.* senedh.

Sean-aòis, *s.* (*Ir. id.*) Old age. Na shean-aòis, *in his old age;* na sean-aòis, *in her old age;* nan sean-aòis, *in their old age.*

Sean-ar, *s. m.* (*Heb.* senar, *Noah's mount.*) Old land.

Seanarasg, aisg, *s. m.* A proverb or old saying.

† **Seanas,** ais, *s. m.* Shortness of sight.—*Shaw.*

Seanasach, *a.* Genealogical; skilled in genealogy.—*Mac K.*

Seanasan, ain, *s. m.* Etymology.

Sean-athair, -athar, *s. m.* (*Ir. id.*) A grandfather; an aged father; an ancestor. Sean-athair an t-sean-athar, *a great-grandfather.* *N. pl.* sean-aithrichean.

Sean-athaireachd, *s. f.* Ancestry.

Sean-bhean, mhna, *s. f.* (*Ir. id.*) An old woman; often, the oldest woman of a village. Tigh na sean-mhna, *the old woman's house.* *N. pl.* sean-mhnathan.

Sean-bheanachd, *s. f.* Anility.—*Shaw.*

Seanchaidh. See Seanachaidh.

Seanchas. See Seanachas.

Sean-chomhar, air, *s. m.* An old token; a monument.

Sean-chuimhne, *s. f.* Tradition; genealogy.

Sean-chuimhneach, *a.* Traditional; genealogical.

Seanda, *a.* Old, antique, old-fashioned.

Seandachd, *s. f.* Age; antiquity, oldness.

Sean-duine, *s. m.* An old man; often, the oldest man of a village. Na sean-daoine, *the old men; the men of old.*

Sean-fhear, -fhir, *s. m.* An old man; an elder, a presbyter; a dotard.

Sean-fhearachd, *s. f.* Presbyterianism; dotage, senility.

Sean-fhocal, ail, *s. m.* An old saying, a proverb or adage. —*Macint.* A reir an sean-fhocail, *according to the adage;* mar their an sean-fhocal, *as the old saying runs.* *N. pl.* sean-fhocail.

Sean-fhoclach, *a.* Proverbial; fond of proverbs.

Seang, *a.* (*Ir. id.*) Slender, slim; small; small-bellied; gaunt; hungry; nimble; agile. A seang chorp, *her slender body.*—*Macfar.* Each seang séiteach, *a small-bellied, snorting steed.*—*Old Poem.* Tri choin sheanga, *three gaunt hounds.*—*Oss. Fin. and Lor.* Cha tuig an sàthach an seang, *the fed understand not the hungry.*—*G. P.*

Seang, *v. a.* and *n.* Make slender or slim; grow slim or slender. *Pret. a.* sheang; *fut. aff.* seangaidh.

Seangach, *a.* Slender in body; slim; causing bodily slenderness.

Seangachadh, aidh, *s. m.* A making slender; a reducing in shape; a growing slender.

Seangaich, *v. a.* and *n.* (*from* seang.) Make slender or slim; reduce in bodily bulk; grow slender; grow gaunt. *Pret. a.* sheangaich; *fut. aff. a.* seangaichidh, *shall grow slender.*

† **Seangal,** *a.* (*Ir. id.*) Wise; prudent; shrewd.—*Shaw.*

Seangan, ain, *s. m.* (*Ir. id.*) An ant, emmet, or pismire; *in derision,* a slender person. Imich chum an t-seangain, *go to the ant.*—*Stew. Pro.* *N. pl.* seanganan *and* seangain.

Seanganach, *a.* Abounding in ants; of ants.

Seangan-mhathair, *s. f.* The mother of a great grandfather or great grandmother.

† **Seanghain,** *s. m.* (*Ir. id.*) A conception, or a child near the time of its birth.—*Shaw.*

Sean-ghille, *s. m.* An old bachelor. *N. pl.* sean-ghillean.

Sean-ghin, *s. m.* A child begotten in old age.

Sean-lith, *s.* Happiness.—*Shaw.*

Sean-mhathair, mhathar, *s. f.* A grandmother; an aged mother. A chomhnuich ad shean-mhathair, *which dwelt in thy grandmother.*—*Stew. Tim.*

Seanmhor, *a.* See Seunmhor.

Seann, *a.* Old, aged; ancient, antique. Seann laoich nach d'imich gu blàr, *aged warriors who went not to battle.*—*Mac Lach.* Tha e na sheann duine, *he is an old man;* an seann duine, *the old man; the oldest man of a village.*

Seannach, aich, *s. m.* (*Ir. id.*) A fox. *N. pl.* seannaich. Tha tuill aig na seannach, *foxes have holes.*—*Stew. N. T.* Cha mhair an seannach ri shìr ruith, *a fox cannot hold out a chase for ever.*—*G. P.*

Seannachaich, *v. n.* Play the fox. *Pret. a.* sheannachaich.

Seannachail, *a.* (seannach-amhuil.) Foxlike; cunning.

Seannachan, ain, *s. m.* A young fox, a little fox; a term of personal contempt.

Sean-nòs, *s. m.* An old custom, an old habit, an old usage.

Sean-nòsach, *a.* Fond of old customs; retaining old habits; old-fashioned.

Seannsair, *s. m.* A chanter; the drone of a bagpipe; a pipe. *N. pl.* seannsairean. A gleusadh 'sheannsairean, *tuning his pipes.*—*Macint.*

Seannsaireachd, *s. f.* Chanting.

Seannsalair, *s. m.* A chancellor.—*Macd.* *N. pl.* seannsalairean.

Seannsalaireachd, *s. f.* A chancellorship.

Seannsa, *s. m.* Luck.—*R. S.*

Seannsar, *a.* Lucky; prosperous.

Sean-radh, *s. m.* (*Ir. id.*) An old saying, an adage. *N. pl.* sean-ràite.

Sean-sgeul, -sgeòil, *s. m.* An old tale; a legend.

Sean-sgeulach, *a.* Archaiological.

Sean-sgeulachd, *s. f.* An old tale; a legend; a tradition; archaiology.

Sean-sgeulaiche, *s. m.* An archaiologist.

Seanta, *part.* See Seunta.

Seantaidh, *a.* (*from* sean.) Primitive, primeval.

Sean-tiomnadh, aidh, *s. m.* The Old Testament.

Sèap, *v. n.* Sneak; slink; flinch; crouch; pursue closely. *Pret. a.* shèap; *fut. aff. a.* seapaidh, *shall sneak.* Sheap e air falbh, *he slunk away.*

Seapach, *a.* Sneaking; crouching; flinching; also, a sneaking fellow. *Com.* and *sup.* seapaiche.

Sèapadh, aidh, *s. m.* (*Ir. id.*) A sneaking; a crouching; a flinching.

Sèapair, *s. m.* (seap-fhear.) A sneaking, slinking fellow; a mean fellow; a crouching fellow. *N. pl.* seapairean. A sheapaire! *thou slinking fellow!* Cha 'n fhuirich ach seapair, *none but a sneaking fellow will stay.*—*G. P.*

SEAPAIREACHD, *s. f.* A habit of sneaking or slinking; meanness.

SEARADAIR, *s. f.* (*Ir.* searadoir. *Arm.* serruider.) A towel, a hand-napkin. *N. pl.* searadairean, *towels.*

† SEARB, seirb, *s. m.* (*Ir. id.*) Theft, larceny.

SEARBAID, *s. f.* A rower's seat in a boat.—*Shaw.*

SEARBH, *a.* (*Ir. id.*) Bitter; sour; sharp; severe; harsh; sarcastic. Maille ri luibhibh searbh, *with bitter herbs.*—*Stew. Ex.* Glaodh ro shearbh, *a very bitter cry. Com.* and *sup.* seirbhe.

SEARBH, *v. a.* and *n.* Sour; embitter; acidulate; grow sour. *Pret. a.* shearbh, *embittered; fut. aff. a.* searbhaidh, *shall embitter.*

SEARBHACH, *a.* Causing sourness; sharp; severe.

SEARBHACHADH, aidh, *s. m.* A growing sour or bitter; a growing sharp or severe; a making sour.

SEARBHAD, aid, *s. m.* Sourness; harshness; severity; increase in sourness. A dol an searbhad, *growing more and more sour.*

SEARBHADAIR, *s. m.* See SEARADAIR.

SEARBHADAS, ais, *s. m.* (*Ir. id.*) Bitterness; sourness; a bitter; harshness or severity; sharpness; harshness of taste or sound. Piob ri searbhadas, *a pipe making a harsh sound.* —*Old Poem.*

SEARBHADH, aidh, *s. m.* A making sour; an embittering; a pickling; a growing sour, severe, or harsh.

SEARBHAG, aig, *s. f.* A pickle; a bitter sarcastic female.

† SEARBHAN, *s. pl.* Oats.—*Shaw.*

SEARBHAN, ain, *s. m.* A tribute.

SEARBHANT, aint, *s. f.* (*Fr.* servante.) A servant-maid; a house-maid; a kitchen-maid. *N. pl.* searbhantan.

SEARBHANTACHD, *s. f.* The condition of a female servant; the handiwork of a female servant.

SEARBHAS, ais, *s. m.* (*Ir. id.*) Sourness; bitterness; harshness, severity; asperity. Searbhas m' anam, *the bitterness of my soul.*—*Stew. Job.*

SEARBHASACHD, *s. f.* Sourness; bitterness; harshness; severity; asperity.

SEARBH-BHRIATHAR, air, *s. m.* A bitter saying; a sarcasm.

SEARBH-BHRIATHRACH, *a.* Bitter in language; sarcastic.

SEARBH-GHLÒIR, *s. f.* Vain glory; boasting; raillery; sarcastic language; cacophony.

SEARBH-LUIBH, *s. m.* A bitter herb; wormwood. Chuir e air mhisg mi le searbh-luibhean, *he hath made me drunken with wormwood.*—*Stew. Lam.*

SEARBHÒS, ois, *s. m.* A deer, a roe, a stag.—*Shaw.*

SEARBH-RADH, *s. m.* A bitter saying; sarcasm; cacophony. *N. pl.* searbh-raite.

SEARBH-RAITEACH, *a.* Bitter in language; sarcastic.

SEARBHTA, *p. part.* of searbh. Soured; embittered; acidulated; pickled.

SEARBHTACH, *a.* Causing sourness; embittering; acidulating.

SEARBH-UBHAL, *s. m.* A tart apple; a crab-apple; coloquintida. *N. pl.* searbh-ubhlan.

† SEARC, seirc, *s. f.* Now written *seirc*; which see.

SEARCAG, aig, *s. f.* More frequently written *seirceag.*

SEARCAIL, *a.* See SEIRCEIL.

† SEARCALL, aill, *s. m.* Flesh; delicate meat; the best part of flesh-meat.

SEARG, seirg, *s. m.* (*Ir. id.*) A pithless man; a pithless beast; an insignificant person; a person or beast shrivelled with age or infirmity.

SEARG, *a.* (*Ir. id. Gr.* Ξηρος.) Dry; withered, shrivelled.

SEARG, *v. a.* and *n.* (*Ir. id.*) Wither; dry; scorch; blast with heat, drought, or cold; grow withered; grow dry or scorched; pine away. *Pret. a.* shearg; *fut. aff.* seargaidh, *shall wither; fut. neg.* searg. Ni 'n searg ur cuimhne mar lus, *your fame shall not wither like an herb.*—*Oss. Cathula.*

SEARGACH, *a.* Blasting, scorching, withering; apt to become withered or blasted.

SEARGADH, aidh, *s. m.* A withering, a scorching, a blasting. Air seargadh, *withered.* Ma bhios seargadh ann, *if there be blasting.*—*Stew.* 1 *K.*

SEARGADH, (a), *pr. part.* of searg. Withering, blasting, scorching. A seargadh air an tràigh, *withering on the shore.*—*Oss. Gaul.*

SEARGAICH, *v. a.* and *n.* Cause to wither, scorch, parch, or blast; grow withered, scorched, or blasted. *Pret. a.* sheargaich; *fut. aff.* seargaichidh, *shall wither.*

SEARGAICHEAR, *fut. pass.* of seargaich.

SEARGAICHTE, *p. part.* of seargaich. Withered, parched, scorched, blasted.

SEARGANACH, *a.* Dried up, withered, blasted; *also,* a shrivelled person.

SEARGTA, SEARGTE, *p. part.* of searg. Withered, parched, scorched, blasted. Fraoch seargte, *withered heath.*—*Orr.*

SEARMOIN, *s. f.* (*Ir. id.*) A sermon. Dean searmoin, *preach.* Cionnas ni iad searmoin? *how can they preach?* —*Stew. Rom.*

SEARMOINICH, *v.* Preach, deliver a sermon. *Pret. a.* shearmoinich, *preached.* Shearmoinich e siothchainnt, *he preached peace.*—*Stew. Eph.*

SEARMONACHADH, aidh, *s. m.* A preaching.

SEARMONACHADH, (a), *p. part.* of searmoinich. A searmonachadh soisgeil na sìth, *preaching the Gospel of peace.*—*Stew. Rom.*

SEARMONAICHE, *s. m.* A preacher. Deadh shearmonaiche, *a good preacher;* gun searmonaiche, *without a preacher.*—*Stew. Rom.*

SEARN, *v. a.* Loose, untie.—*Shaw.*

SEARN, *s. m.* (*Ir. id.*) A youth, a stripling.—*Shaw.*

SEARNACH, *a.* Dissolvent, separable.

SEARNADH, aidh, *s. m.* A yawning; a stretching of the limbs; extension.—*Shaw.* *Also,* loosening; dissolving.

SEARPAN, ain, *s. m.* An order; a custom; a swan.—*Shaw.*

SEARR, *s. m.* A colt, a foal. Hence *searrach.*

SEARR, *s. m.* (*Ir. id.*) A sickle, a sithe; a phial.

SEARR, *v. a.* Yawn, stretch the limbs; reap, mow; shear; slaughter, massacre. *Pret.* shearr; *fut. aff.* searraidh, *shall yawn.*

SEARRACH, aich, *s. m.* (*from* searr.) A foal, a filly, a colt. *N. pl.* searraich. Deich searraich, *ten foals.*—*Stew. Gen.* Càmhail le 'n searraich, *camels with their colts.*—*Id.* Chunnaic mi searrach 's a chulaobh rium, *I saw a foal from behind.*—*G. P.*

A Gael considers it a bad omen to have a back view of the first foal or grazing quadruped he sees on any year.

SEARRACH, *a.* Edged; pointed; sharp, like a hook, like a sithe.

SEARRACHACH, *a.* Abounding in foals, fillies, or colts. Coire searrachach uanach, *a dell where foals and lambs abound.*—*Macdon.*

SEARRACHAIL, *a.* (searrach-amhuil.) Like a foal or filly; slender-footed, as a foal. Each searrachail, *a slender-footed horse.*—*Old Poem.*

SEARRAG, aig, *s. f.* (*Ir.* searrog.) A bottle; a phial; a leathern bottle; a cup. *N. pl.* searragan. Thraoghainn mo shearrag, *I would drain my bottle.*—*Old Song.* Da uanan is searrag dhonn, *two lambs and a brown cup.*—*Mac Lach.*

Searragach, *a.* Like a bottle or phial; full of bottles or phials.

Searragaich, *v.* (*from* searrag.) Bottle; lay up in bottles.

Searragaichte, *p. part.* of searragaich. Bottled; laid up in bottles.

Searraich, *s. f.* The herb pilewort; the *ranunculus ficaria* of botanists.

Searr-fhiacall, aill, *s. m.* A sharp tooth.

Searr-fhiaclach, *a.* Having teeth like a sickle.—*Macd.*

Searr-shùil, shùl, *s. f.* A squint-eye.—*Shaw.*

Searr-shùileach, *a.* Squint-eyed.

Sears, *v. a.* Charge or load, as a gun. *Pret.* shears, *charged.*

Searsadh, aidh, *s. m.* A charge, as of a gun.

Searsainn, *v. a.* Charge or load a gun. *Pret. a.* shearsainn, *charged.*

† **Searthonn**, uinn, *s. m.* A chief poet; a prince; art; knowledge.

Seas, *s. m.* (*Ir. id.*) A plank for stepping into a boat; a bench made on a hayrick, by cutting off part of the hay.

Seas, *v. n.* and *a.* (*Ir. id.*) Stand; stop; endure; last; maintain or stand by. An seas triath na h-Eirinn? *shall the princes of Eirinn stand?*—*Oss. Tem.* Seas an còir, *maintain their* [*cause*] *right.*—*Stew.* 1 *K.* Seas beagan, *stop a little;* cha 'n fhad sheasas e, *he* or *it will not stand* or *last long.*

Seasach, *a.*, *for* seasamhach; which see.

Seasachas, ais, *s. m.* A truce—(*Shaw*); sitting; standing-room.

Seasadh. More frequently written *seasamh;* which see.

Seasaidh, (*for* seasamhaidh), *fut. aff.* of seas, *shall stand.*—*Stew. Ps.*

Seasam, 1 *sing. imper.* of seas. Let me stand. *Also for* seasaidh mi, *I will stand.*

Seasamain, *s. f.* Jessamine.

Seasamh, *v. n.* Stand; rise up; stop; endure; last. *Pret. a.* sheasamh; *fut. aff. a.* seasamhaidh.

Seasamh, aimh, *s. m.* A standing; a footing; cessation; an enduring or lasting; continuance; stability. Laoch na sheasamh, *a hero standing.*—*Oss.* Air dhroch sheasamh chas, *on uncertain footing.*—*Mac Co.* Dean seasamh, *stand up;* éirich do sheasamh, *rise up standing.* Cha bhi seasamh aig droch bheart, *there is no stability in mischief.*—*G. P.* Seasamh chlaidheimh, *standing on one's head.*

Seasamh, (a), *pr. part.* of seas.

Seasamhach, *a.* Durable; lasting; steadfast; constant; having a good footing; sure-footed. Gu seasamhach, *steadfastly.* *Com.* and *sup.* seasamhaiche.

Seasamhachd, *s. f.* Durableness; steadfastness; constancy.

Seasda, *s. m.* (*Ir. id.*) A defence.—*Shaw.*

Seasdan, ain, *s. m.* (*Ir. id.*) A shout; a hunter's cry.

Seasdar, air, *s. m.* Defence; peace.

Seas-dubh, duibh, *s. m.* A standish.

† **Seasg**, seisg, *s. m.* (*Ir. id.*) A reed; a sedge; burr-reed.

Seasg, *a.* (*Ir. id.*) Barren; dry; yielding no milk; unprolific. Crodh seasg, *barren cattle, cattle that yield no milk;* cìochan seasga, *dry breasts.*—*Stew. Hos.* Ni mo bhios e seasg, *neither will he be barren.*—*Stew. Ex.*

Seasgach, *a.* Causing barrenness; barren. Beinn sheasgach nam fuaran, *the barren mountain of springs.*—*Old Song.*

Seasgachd, *s. f.* Barrenness; a herd of barren cattle.

Seasgad, *a.* Sixty.

Seasgaich, *s. f.* (*Ir.* seasgaidhe.) A barren cow.

Seasgair, *a.* (*Ir. id.*) Comfortable; in easy circumstances; warm and dry; sheltered; cozy; soft; effeminate; still; calm.

Seasgair, *s. m.* One in comfortable circumstances; a cozy person; an effeminate person; one who thrashes corn by the bulk. *N. pl.* seasgairean.

Seasgaireach, *a.* Comfortable, easy; warm and dry; cozy; sheltered; snug—(*Macint.*); effeminate; delightful. Gu seasgaireach, *comfortably, snugly.*

Seasgaireachd, *s. f.* Comfortableness; ease; warmth; coziness; snugness. An seasgaireachd, *at ease.*—*Sm.* Luchd na seasgaireachd, *people who are in easy circumstances.*—*Stew. Ps.*

Seasgan, ain, *s. m.* (*Ir. id.*) A handful or shock of gleaned corn; a truss of gleaned corn; gleanings of corn; land that has been gleaned. *N. pl.* seasgana *or* seasganan, *gleanings.* Seasgana t' fhogharaidh, *the gleanings of thy harvest.*—*Stew. Lev.*

Seasganach, aich, *s. m.* (*Ir. id.*) A bachelor. *N. pl.* seasganaich.

Seasganach, *a.* (*from* seasgan.) In handfuls or shocks, as gleaned corn.

Seasganachd, *s. f.* Celibacy.

Seasgann, ainn, *s. m.* A fenny country, a marsh; a bog-reed.

Seasgannach, *a.* Marshy.

Seasgar, *a.* (*Ir. id.*) Soft, effeminate; still, calm; comfortable; dry and warm; snug. *Com.* and *sup.* seasgaire.

Seasg-bho, -bhoin, *s. f.* (*Ir. id.*) A barren cow; a heifer.

Seasg-chorp, -chuirp, *s. m.* (*Ir. id.*) A barren body; constitutional barrenness.

Seasg-chorpach, *a.* (*Ir. id.*) Constitutionally barren; unprolific.

Seasglach, aich, *s. m.* Barren cattle.

Seasmhach, *a.*, *for* seasamhach. (*Ir. id.*) Durable; steadfast; fixed; firm; constant; established. Aite-comhnuidh seasmhach, *a fixed place of abode.*—*Stew. Cor.* Bithidh gach focal seasmhach, *every word shall be established.*—*Id.* *Com.* and *sup.* seasmhaiche.

Seasmhachd, *s. f.* (*Ir. id.*) Durableness; steadfastness; firmness; fixedness; constancy. Seasmhachd bhur cridhe, *the steadfastness of your hearts.*—*Stew. Col.*

Seasrach, aich, *s. m.* (*Ir. id.*) A lad, a youth.—*Shaw.*

Seasunta, *a.* Prosperous. Gu seasunta, *prosperously.*

Seasuntachd, *s. f.* Prosperity.

Seat, seata, *s. m.* A skinful, a bellyful; a quean.

Seathadair, *s. m.* A skinner. *N. pl.* seathadairean.

† **Seathadh**, aidh, *s. m.* A skin, a hide.—*Shaw.*

Seathadh, *a.* Sixth. An seathadh mac, *the sixth son.*—*Stew. Gen.*

† **Seathar**, *a.* (*Ir. id.*) Strong; able; good.—*Shaw.*

† **Seathar**, air, *s. m.* (*Ir. id.*) A library; a study.

Seatharach, *a.* Divine.

Seathbhog, uig, *s. f.* Marjoram.

Seathnar, *a.* Six, six in number. Seathnar mhac, *six sons.*—*Stew. Gen.*

Secel, eil, *s.* A shekel.

† **Segh**, *s.* (*Ir. id.*) Milk; a buffalo; a moose-deer.

Seic, *s. f.* Sack-wine.—*Macd.*

Seic, *s. f.* A hide or skin; the peritoneum—(*Shaw*); a bone. Seic an tairbh, *the skin of the bull.*—*Stew. Ex. ref.*

A dh'aindeoin do sheic, *in spite of your skin.* *N. pl.* seicean *and* seiceachan.

Seiceach, *a.* Having a thick skin or hide; of a skin or hide.

Seicean, ein, *s. m.* A pellicle; a film; the skull; the pellicle of the brain—(*Shaw*); a membrane which covers the intestines.

Seiceanach, *a.* Filmy; having a pellicle.

† **Seich**, *s. m.* (*Ir. id.*) A combat; an adventurer.—*Shaw.*

Seiche, *s. f.* A hide or skin. Written also *seic;* which see.

Seichim, *s. m.* Shechem-wood.

Seicil, seicle, *s. f.* (*Lat.* secula, *a sithe. Eng.* sickle.) A hatchel; a flaxcomb. *N. pl.* seiclean.

Seicil, *v. a.* Hatchel: dress or comb flax. *Pret. a.* sheicil, *hatchelled; fut. aff. a.* seiclidh.

Seicilte, *p. part.* of seicil. Hatchelled or hackled.

Seicleadh, idh, *s. m.* The process of hatchelling or flax-combing. Lion air a dheadh sheicleadh, *flax well dressed.*

Seiclear, eir, *s. m.* A hatcheller or flax-dresser. *N. pl.* seicleirean.

Seiclear, *fut. pass.* of seicil. Shall be combed or dressed, as flax.

Seiclearachd, **Seicleireachd**, *s. f.* The business of flax-dressing or hackling.

Seid, seide, *s. f.* A surfeit; a bellyful; a tympany; a full belly; a truss; a bed spread on the ground, by the Lowland Scots called *shakedown;* voluptuousness. *N. pl.* seideachan. Sop as gach seid, *a wisp from every truss.*—*G. P.*

Séid, *v. a.* and *n.* (*Ir. id.*) Blow, puff; breathe, pant. *Pret. a.* shéid; *fut. aff. a.* séididh, *shall* or *will blow.* Shéid adharc Fhinn, *Fingal's horn blew;* séid suas, *blow up, puff up. Pret. sub.* shéideadh. Gach oiteag a shéideadh, *every blast that would blow.*—*Oss.*

Séide, *s.* See **Seideadh**.

Séideach, *a.* Blowing, puffing; windy, blustering.

Séideadh, idh, *s. m.* (*Ir. id.*) A blowing, a puffing; a blast; wind; a panting, a breathing.

Séidean, ein, *s. m.* A blowing; a blow or puff; a panting; anhelation.

† **Seidean**, ein, *s. m.* (*Ir. id.*) A quicksand.—*Shaw.*

Séideil, *s. f.* A continued blowing or puffing; a blast; a panting; anhelation.

Seideir, *s. f.* Cider.—*Macd.*

Seideireach, *a.* Abounding in cider; of cider.

Seidhir, *s. f.* A chair, a seat; a chaise. *N. pl.* seidhrichean, *seats, chaises.* Seidhir reidh, *a hired chaise;* seidhir da laimh, *an arm-chair.*

Seidhrichean, *n. pl.* of seidhir.

Séidich, *s. f.* Blowing, panting.

Séididh, *fut. aff. a.* of séid. Shall or will blow.

Séidrich, *s. f.* A blowing; a panting; anhelation; a blustering, as of wind. Written also *séitrich:* which see.

Séidte, *p. part.* of séid. Blown; blown up.

† **Seigh**, *s. f.* A hawk.—*Shaw. N. pl.* seighean.

† **Seigheann**, inn, *s. m.* (*Ir. id.*) A champion; a warrior. —*Shaw.*

† **Seighear**, eir, *s. m.* (*Ir. id.*) A falconer. *N. pl.* seigh-earan.

† **Seighnean**, ein, *s. m.* (*Ir. id.*) A hurricane, a tempest; lightning.

Seilbh, seilbhe, *s. f.* (*Ir. id.*) Possession; property; a herd or drove of cattle; farm-stock. Gabh seilbh, *take possession;* rach na sheilbh, *take him* or *it in hand.*

Seilche, *com.* and *sup.* of salach.

Seilcheag, eig, *s. f.* A snail. An t-seilcheag agus am famh, *the snail and the mole.*—*Stew. Lev. N. pl.* seilcheagan.

Seilcheagach, *a.* Abounding in snails; snailish; of snails.

Seile, *s. f.* (*Ir. id. Gr.* σιαλος.) Spittle, saliva.

Seileach, *a.* (*Ir. id.*) Slavering; spitting; salivous; mucous.

Seileach, ich, *s. f.* (*Ir. id. Corn.* helak. *W.* helig.) A willow; a willow copse; a place where willows grow. Seileach an t-shruthain, *the willow of the brook.*—*Stew. Lev.* Slat seilich, *a willow switch.*

Séileadach, aich, *s. m.* (*Ir. id.*) A pocket-handkerchief. Perhaps *seile-eudach.*

Seileadan, ain, *s. m.* (*Ir. id.*) A spitting-box; a pocket-handkerchief.

Séileann, einn, *s. m.* (*Ir. id.*) A sheepked or tick.

Seileannach, *a.* Abounding in sheepkeds or ticks; like a sheepked.

Seileid, *s. f.* A bellyful; a surfeit; a big belly.

Seileir, *s. m.* A cellar. *N. pl.* seileirean.
W. seileir. *Ir.* seileir. *Fr.* cellier. *Arm.* cellyer *and* ceilher.

Seileireach, *a.* Cellular; having cellars.

Seilg, seilge, *s. f.* (*Ir. id.*) A hunt, a chase; hunting; venison. Iùran na seilge, *the huntsman.*—*Oss. Gaul.*

Seilg, *gen. sing.* of sealg.

Seilich, *v. n.* Spit; slaver. *Pret. a.* sheilich; *fut. aff. a.* seilichidh.

Seilicheag, eig, *s. f.* A snail. *N. pl.* seilicheagan. Chunnaic mi'n seilcheag air an lic luim, *I saw a snail on the bare stone*—(*G. P.*)—a bad omen among the Gael.

Seilicheagach *a.* Snailish; abounding in snails.

Seilicheagag, *n. pl.* of seilicheag.

Seilisdeir, *s. m.* (*Ir.* siolastar.) A sedge; a flag; yellow flower-de-luce. *N. pl.* seilisdeirean.

Seilisdeireach, *a.* Sedgy; abounding in sedges or flags.

Seillean, ein, *s. m.* (*Ir. id.*) A bee; a humble-bee. Seillean diomhain, *a drone-bee.*—*Macd.* Seillean a diogladh chluarain, *the bee sucking a thistle-flower.*—*Macdon. N. pl.* seilleanan, *bees; d. pl.* seilleanaibh. Làn do sheilleanaibh, *full of bees.*—*Moladh Mhòraig.*

Seilleanach, *a.* (*from* seillean.) Abounding in bees.

Seilliunn, uinn, *s. m.* A sheepked, or tick; also written *seileann.*

Seilt, *s. f.* (*Ir. id.*) A dropping; a drivelling; a slavering; salivation; mucus.

Seilteach, *a.* Slavering; causing salivation; mucous.

Seilteachd, *s. f.* The infirmity of slavering; ooziness; salivation; a course of salivation.

Seiltichean, *s. pl.* Scrofulous sores.

Sèim, *s. f.* A squint; *also,* squinting. Séim-shuileach, *squint-eyed.*

Seimh, *a.* Quiet, calm, mild, peaceful, gentle; soft, kind; smooth; *rarely,* little; single. San fhairge sheimhe, *in the calm sea.*—*Oss. Cathula.* Seimh gu robh do thamh, *soft be thy repose.*—*Oss. Fin. and Lor.* An Seimh-an, *i. e.* an Seimh-amhuinn, *the Seine in France* (see **An**). Gu seimh, *quietly, softly, smoothly. Com.* and *sup.* seimhe.

Seimhe, *s. f.* Quietness, calmness, mildness, peacefulness; gentleness, softness, kindness; smoothness.

Seimheach, *a.* Causing quietness, calmness, or mildness; quiet, calm, mild.

Seimheachadh, aidh, *s. m.* Calming.

Seimheachd, *s. f.* Quietness, calmness, mildness, peacefulness; peaceableness, gentleness, kindness. Tre mhacantas agus sheimheachd, *through meekness and gentleness.—Stew. 2 Cor.*

SEIMH-MHEAS, *s. m.* Mellow fruit.

SEIMHICH, *v. a.* and *n* Quiet, calm, soothe, smooth, grow quiet or calm; grow kind, soft, or gentle. *Pret.* sheumhich; *fut. aff a.* seimhichidh.

SEIMHICHTE, *p. part.* of seimhich.

SEIMHIDE, *s. f* A snail. *N. pl* seimhidean.

SEIMHIDH, *a.* See SEIMH.

SEIMLEIR, *s f.* (*Ir. id.*) A chimney; a vent. *N. pl.* seimleirean.

SEIMLEIREACH, *a.* Having chimneys; of chimneys; chimneyed.

SEIMLEIRICHTE, *p. part.* of seimleirich. Chimneyed.

SEINN, *v a* (*Ir.* sein) Sing; warble; carol; ring, as a bell. *Pret. a.* sheinn, *fut. aff a.* seinnidh, *shall sing.* Seinn le h-aoibhneas, *sing with joy —Stew. Job.*

SEINN, *s m.* A singing; a warbling; a ringing, as of a bell La seinn do chluig, *the day of thy* [*bell-ringing*] *funeral.—Old Song.*

SEINNEADAR, an Irish *inflection* of seinn. Shall sing, shall be sung

SEINNEAM, 1 *sing. imper* of seinn Let me sing *Also for* seinnidh mi, *I will sing.*

SEINNEAR, *fut. pass* of seinn Shall or will be sung.

SEINNIBH, 2 *pl imper.* of seinn.

SEINNSEARACHD, *s f.* Ancestry. See SINNSEARACHD.

SEIPEAL, eil, *s. m.* A chapel.—*Shaw.*

SEIPEALACH, *a.* Having chapels, of or relating to, a chapel

SEIPINN, *s f.* A chopin, a quart *N. pl.* seipinnean

SEIPINNEACH, *a.* In chopins, containing a chopin.

SEIRBH, *inflection* of searbh; which see.

SEIRBHE, *com* and *sup.* of searbh More or most bitter See SEARBH.

SEIRBHE, *s. f.* (*Ir. id*) Bitterness; sourness, crabbedness; moroseness; asperity Gach uile sheirbhe, *all bitterness.—Stew. Eph.*

SEIRBHEACHD, *s f* See SEIRBHE.

SEIRBHEAD, id, *s m* Bitterness, sourness, crabbedness, moroseness; increase in bitterness. A dol an seirbhead, *growing more and more bitter.*

SEIRBHEIS, *s. f.* Service, work, labour, use. Seirbheis chruaidh, *hard* or *grievous service.—Stew. K.*

SEIRBHEISEACH, ich, *s. m.* (*from* seirbheis) A servant, a domestic. Seirbheiseach do chìs, *a servant to tribute —Stew. Gen.*

SEIRBHEISEACHD, *s f.* The condition of a servant, the business of a servant

SEIRC, seirce, *s f.* (*W.* serch. *Ir.* searc) Benevolence, charity; affection Seirc is oineach, *benevolence and mercy —Old Song* Céilichidh seirc aimeamh, *charity conceals evil.—G. P.*

SEIRCEAG, eig, *s f.* (*from* seirc.) A beloved young female; a mistress; a sweetheart; a benevolent young female *N. pl* seirceagan

SEIRCEALACHD, *s. f.* Benevolence; the practice of benevolence.

SEIRCEAN, ein, *s. m.* (*from* seirc.) A beloved person, a darling; *also*, a jerkin. A seircean-se a rug i, *the beloved* [*choice*] *one of her who bore her.—Stew Song Sol*

SEIRCEAR, eir, *s. m.* A wooer—(*Shaw*); a benevolent man, a charitable man

SEIRCEIL, *a.* (seirc-amhuil) Charitable, benevolent; affectionate, fond; dutiful. Gu seirceil, *charitably.*

SEIRDEAN, ein, *s. m.* (*Ir.* seirdin) A pilchard.

SEIRDEANACH, *a* Abounding in pilchards, like a pilchard.

SEIREAN, ein, *s m* A shank, a leg; *in derision*, a person having small legs. *N pl* seireanan

SEIREANACH, *a* Having spare shanks.

SEIRG, *s f* Clover, trefoil —*Shaw*

SEIRG, *inflection* of searg; which see.

SEIRG, seirge, *s f* A withering, a shrivelling; a decay or consumption

SEIRGEAN, ein, *s m* (*Ir. id.*) A shrivelled person, a sickly person, a consumptive person; a shrunken form, a jerkin

SEIRGLIDH, *a.* Withered, *also, substantively*, a withered person.

SEIRGNE, *s f* A consumptive person, marcour; *adjectively*, sickly.

† SEIRIC, *a.* Strong, able

SEIRIC, *s* (*Ir id Lat.* seric-um) Silk; superfine silk —*Shaw*, and *Macpherson's Introduction.*

SEIRICEACH, *a* (*from* seiric) Silken, silky.

SEIRICEAN, ein, *s m.* (*Ir. id*) A silkworm.

SEIRM, *s. f.* Music, melody.

SEIRMEACH, *a.* (*from* seirm.) Melodious; musical, harmonious

SEIRMEIL, *a* See SEIRMEACH

SEIRSEALACH, *a* (*Ir id.*) Strong, robust, *also, substantively*, a robust person

SEIRSEALACHD, *s f.* (*Ir. id*) Strength, robustness

SEIRSEAN, ein, *s. m* A robust man.

SEIRSEANACH, aich, *s. m* An auxiliary; an unhired workman. *N. pl.* seirseanaich

SEIRT, seirte, *s f* Strength, power.—*Shaw.*

SEIRTEIL, *a.* Strong

† SEIS, *s.* Skill, knowledge.

SEIS, seise, *s m* (*Ir id*) Pleasure, delight; satisfaction, treat, entertainment; a fit match, one's equal or match, a company, a noise, a tumult, a bustle, *also* used in the sense of what agrees ill or well with one. Is olc an seis dhuit e, *it is bad for you*, am fear aig am bi maighstir bithidh seis aige, *he who has a master has found his match —G. P.*

SÉISD, *v a* Besiege, invest *Pret. a* shéisd, *fut* séisdidh, *shall besiege*, *fut pass* séisdear

SÉISDE, *s f* A siege, a tune or air; the chorus or burden of a song Cuir séisde, *besiege*, fo shéisde, *under a siege. N. pl* seisdean

SÉISDEACH, *a.* Besieging, investing

SÉISDEACHD, *s f.* The state of being besieged; a siege, frequent or continued besieging

SÉISDEADH, idh, *s. m.* A besieging; a siege Seisdeadh Ierusaleim, *the siege of Jerusalem —Stew. Ezek.*

SÉISDEADH, (a), *pr. part* of séisd Besieging, investing Dol g' an séisdeadh, *going to besiege them —Macint.*

SEISEACH, *a* (*Ir id*) Pleasurable, delightful, satisfying, agreeable, noisy, tumultous; libidinous

SEISEACHD, *s. f* Pleasure, delight; continued pleasure, sensuality, entertainment, a treat, noisiness

SEISEAN, ein, *s m* (*Ir* seisiun) A session of college; a kirk-session, or a petty court in the kirk, consisting of the clergyman, who presides, the parish schoolmaster, who acts as clerk, and the elders, assizes, a court. Cuir air an t-seisean, *summon before a kirk-session.*

SEISEAR, *a.* Six. Eireadh seisear ghleusta, *let six active men rise.—Macdon.* Seisear fhear, *six men —Stew Ezek*

SEISEIL, *a.* (seis-amhuil.) Pleasant; humane; mild. Gu seiseil, *pleasantly.*

† SEISEILBH, *s. f.* Talk, discourse.

SEISG, seisge, *s. f.* (*Ir. id.* *W.* hesk.) A sedge; a bog-reed.

SEISGEACH, *a.* Sedgy; abounding in bog-reeds.

SEISGEAD, eid, *s. m.* (*Ir. id.*) Barrenness.

SEISGEANN, inn, *s. m.* A fenny country; an extended marsh; a bog-reed. Also written *seasgann.*

SEISICH, *v. a.* (*from* seis.) Treat, entertain; match. *Pret. a.* sheisich; *fut. aff. a.* seisichidh.

SEISREACH, ich, *s.* A plough; a plough of four or of six horses: a team; quarter-land. Seisreach fearainn, *a plough of land;* millidh aon each an t-seisreach, *one horse will break a team.—G. P.*

SEIST, seiste, *s. f.* A bed; a couch. Seist-luachrach, *a bed of rushes.—Old Song.*

SÉIT, *v. a.* See SÉID.

SEITEACH, seitche, *s. f.* (*Ir. id.*) A wife.

SEITHE. See SEICHE.

SEITHIR, seithreach, *s. f.* A chair; a coach or chaise. *N. pl.* seithrichean; *d. pl.* seithrichibh.

SÉITRICH, *s. f.* (*Ir.* seitrigh.) A puffing, a blowing, a panting; a blustering; anhelation; sneezing. Is faoin séitrich na doininn, *vain is the blustering of the blast.—Oss.*

† SEO, *s. m.* (*Ir. id.*) Substance.—*Shaw.*

SEOBHAG, aig, *s. f.* A hawk.—*Stew. Lev. ref.* Written also *seabhag.*

SEOC, seoic, *and* seoca, *s. m.* The plume of a helmet.

SEOCACH, *a.* Plumed or plumy, as a helmet.

SEOCAN, ain, *s. m.* (*dim.* of seoc.) The plume of a helmet. Leig e 'n seocan air aghaidh, *he let the plume drop on his visage; he covered his forehead with the plume.—Oss. Duthona.*

SEOC DA LEIG, *s.* A corruption of John de Liege, and meaning a kind of clasp-knife, of which that person was the inventor.

SEOCHLAN, ain, *s. m.* A person who is feeble and awkward in using his hands; a pithless fellow; an old man.

SEOCHLANACH, *a.* Feeble and awkward in the use of one's hands; pithlessness.

SEOCHLANACHD, *s. f.* Feebleness and awkwardness in manual exertion.

SEÒD, seòid, *s. m.* (*Ir. id.*) A jewel. More frequently written *seud;* which see.

† SEOD, *s.* (*Ir. id.*) A cow; property.

SEÒG, *v. a.* Dandle; swing to and fro; shake laterally; hobble. *Pret. a.* sheòg; *fut. aff. a.* seògaidh.

SEÒGACH, *a.* Dandling; swinging; shaking.

SEOGAL, ail, *s. m.* Rye. See SEAGAL.

SEÒGAN, ain, *s. m.* (*Scotch,* shog.) A swinging motion; a pendulous motion; a hobbling.

SEÒGANAICH, *s. f.* A dandling; a swinging; a shaking to and fro; a hobbling; a pendulous motion.

SEÒID, *s. m.* A hero, a warrior, a chief, a noble; *also,* heroes, chiefs, nobles; *likewise,* jewels. Mu uaigh an t-seòid, *about the hero's grave.—Oss. Carthon.* Seoid aonaich, *a fairing.*

† SEOID, *a.* (*Ir. id.*) Strong.—*Shaw.*

SEÒL, *s. m.* A way, method, or expedient; a direction, a guidance; a weaver's loom. Seòl teichidh, *a way to escape.—Stew. Jer.* Air an t-seòl so, *in this manner;* thoir seòl dha, *direct him;* cuir seòl air, *arrange, set in order, make preparation.*

SEÒL, siuil, *s. m.* A sail, a ship. *Asp. form,* sheòl. M' anam mar sheòl san doinionn, *my soul like a sail in the storm.—Ull.* Crann siùil, *a mast;* seòl mòr, *a mainsail.—Stew. Act. ref.* Seòl toisich, *a foresail;* seòl uachdrach, *a topsail;* seòl meadhonach, *a mainsail.*
Ir. id. *W.* hwyl. *Dan.* sejl. *Eng.* sail.

SEÒL, seoil, *s. m.* A shawl.

SEÒL, *v. a.* (*Ir. id.*) Sail; navigate; direct, guide, conduct; instruct. *Pret. a.* sheòl; *fut. aff. a.* seòlaidh. Sheòl sinn o charraig nan tùr, *we sailed from Carricthura.—Oss. Manos.* Seòlaidh fireanntachd, *righteousness will direct.—Stew. Pro.* Seòl sinn le d' sholus, *guide us with thy light.—Oss. Manos.* Seòl an rod dha, *point out the way to him.*

SEÒLACH, *a.* Guiding, directing; willing to guide; full of expedients; ingenious; shifty. Gu seòlach, *ingeniously. Com.* and *sup.* seòlaiche.

SEÒLADAIR, *s. m., from* seòl. (*Ir.* seòladoir.) A seaman, a navigator, a steersman. *N. pl.* seòladairean.

SEÒLADAIREACHD, *s. f.* The business of a sailor; a sea-life; sailing, navigation, steering. Bha seòladaireachd cunnartach, *sailing was dangerous.—Stew. Acts.*

SEÒLADH, aidh, *s. m.* (*Ir. id.*) A sailing; a guiding, a directing; a steering; navigation; guidance, direction.

SEÒLADH, (a), *pr. part.* of seòl. Sailing; guiding, directing; steering. Air farr-bheinn a seòladh, *sailing along the mountain ridge.—Oss.* A seòladh an roid, *shewing the way.*

SEÒLAIREACHD, *s. f.* (*Ir. id.*) Sailing, navigation.

SEÒLAM, 1 *sing. imper.* of seòl. Let me sail. *Also, for* seolaidh mi, *I will sail* or *guide.*

SEÒL-BHÀT, *s. m.* A pilot-boat. *N. pl.* seòl-bhàtaichean.

SEÒL-BHAT, *s. m.* A goad; a staff for driving cattle. *N. pl.* seòl-bhataichean.

SEÒL-CHRANN, -chroinn, *s. m.* (*Ir. id.*) A mast.

SEÒL-CHRANNACH, *a.* Having masts; having high masts.

SEÒL-MARA, *s. m.* (*Ir. id.*) A tide.—*Shaw.*

SEÒL-MEADHONACH, aich, *s. m.* A mainsail. *N. pl.* siùil-meadhonach.

SEÒL-MÒR, *s. m.* (*Ir. id.*) A mainsail. *N. pl.* siùil-mora, *mainsails.*

SEÒL-MULLAICH, *s. m.* A top-gallant.

SEÒLTA, *a.* (*from* seòl.) Ingenious; having shifts or expedients; artful, wily; skilful, wise; methodical; set in order. Buineamaid gu seòlta, *let us deal wisely.—Stew. Gen.*

SEÒLTACHD, *s. f.* Ingeniousness; artfulness, wiliness, guile; method; arrangement. Ghlac mi le seòltachd, *I caught with guile.—Stew. 2 Cor.*

SEÒL-TOISICH, *s. m.* A foresail. *N. pl.* siùil-toisich, *foresails.*

SEÒL-UACHDRACH, *s. m.* A topsail. *N. pl.* siùil-uachdrach.

SEÒMAIR, *gen. sing.* of seòmar.

SEÒMAIREACHD, *s. f.* Chambering.

SEOMALTA, *a.* Large, bulky.

SEÒMAR, air, *s. m.* (*Ir.* seomra.) A chamber, a room, a parlour, an apartment. An treas seòmar, *the third apartment.—Stew. 1 K.* *N. pl.* seòmraichean. Ni thu seòmraichean, *thou shalt make rooms.—Stew. Gen.* Seòmar àraich, *a nursery;* seòmar aoidheachd, *a banquet-room, a dining-room;* seòmar eudachaidh, *a vestry;* seòmar culaidh, *a vestry, a robing-room;* seòmar suidhe, *a sitting-room, a parlour, a waiting-room;* seòmar leapach, *a bed-room;* seòmar samhraidh, *a summer-parlour.—Stew. Jud.* Seòmar cùil, *a back-room;* seòmar beòil, *a front-room.*

SEÒMARACH, *a.* Having chambers, rooms, or apartments; *also,* cellular, vascular.

SEÒMRADAIR, *s. m., from* seòmar. (*Ir. id.*) A chamberer; a rake; a chamberlain. *N. pl.* seòmradairean.

Seòmradaireachd, *s. f.* Chambering; raking; the business or office of a chamberlain. Seòmradaireachd agus macnus, *chambering and wantonness.—Stew Rom*

Seonadh, aidh, *s. m.* Augury, sorcery, druidism —*Shaw*

Seonaidh.

According to Martin, *Seonaidh* is the name of a water-spirit, which the inhabitants of Lewis used to propitiate by a cup of ale, in the following manner —The inhabitants of the island came to the church of St. Mulway, each man carrying his provisions Every family gave a pock of malt, and the whole was brewed into ale One of their number was chosen to wade into the sea up to the middle, carrying in his hand a cup filled with ale When he reached a proper depth, he stood still and cried aloud "Seonaidh! I give thee this cup of ale, hoping that thou wilt be so good as to send us plenty of sea-ware for enriching our ground, during the coming year." He then threw the ale into the sea This ceremony was performed in the night-time On his coming to land, they all repaired to church, where there was a candle burning on the altar There they stood still for a time, when, on a signal given, the candle was put out, and straightway they adjourned to the fields, where the night was spent mirthfully over the ale Next morning they returned to their respective homes, in the belief that they had insured a plentiful crop for the next season

Seòrsa, *s m.* A sort, a kind, a species *N. pl* seòrsachan

Seorsda, Sforta, *provincial* for seorsa.

Seotanachd, *s. f.* Laziness, indolence.

Seotanta, *a.* Lazy, indolent. Leasg seotanta, *lazy and indolent.—Mac Co* Gu seotanta, *lazily.*

Seothag, aig, *s f* A hawk —*Shaw* Written also *seabhag* and *seobhag.*

Sè-shlisneach, *a.* Hexagonal; *also, substantively,* a hexagon.

Sè-shlisneag, eig, *s f.* A hexagon; a hexagonal figure.

Seud, *s. m.* (*Ir.* sead.) A jewel; a precious stone; an instrument; *rarely,* a way or path. O 's tu mo sheud, gur tu! *O thou art my jewel, that thou art!—Old Song. Asp. form,* sheud Mar sheud ghointe, *like a destructive instrument —Old Poem. N pl* seudan Seudan òir is seudan airgid, *jewels of gold and jewels of silver —Stew Ex.*

Seudach, *a* Like a jewel; abounding in jewels, of jewels; jewelled

Seudachadh, aidh, *s m* A bedecking with jewels.

Seudachan, ain, *s m* A jeweller; a jewel-box or repository for jewels, a jewel-house, a museum *N. pl* seudachanan.

Seudaich, *v. a* Adorn with jewels *Pret a* sheudaich, *fut. aff.* seudaichidh.

Seudair, *s. m.* (seud-fhear) A jeweller. *N. pl.* seudairean

Seudaireachd, *s f.* The occupation of a jeweller.

Seud-lann, -lainn, *s m.* A jeweller's shop; a jewel-house. —*Shaw.*

Seudraidh, *s f.* Jewellery; a collection of jewels

Seoghal, ail, *s m.* (*Lat.* sigill-um) A seal Now written *seul*

Seul, seula, *s. m* (*Ir.* seala. *Corn.* siel) A seal. Sheulaich iad le 'sheul, *they sealed with his seal.—Stew.* 1 K

Seul, *v. a.* Seal *Pret a.* sheul, *fut. aff. a.* seulaidh, *shall seal.*

Seulach, *a.* Having seals; sealed; of seals.

Seulachadh, aidh, *s m* A sealing

Seulaich, *v a.* Seal *Pret. a* sheulaich; *fut aff. a.* seulaichidh, *shall seal.* Sheulaich i iad, *she sealed them.—Stew.* 1 *K.*

Seulaichear, *fut. pass.* of seulaich. Shall be sealed.

Seulaichte, *p. part.* of seulaich. Sealed.—*Stew Job. Asp. form,* sheulaichte.

Seulta, *p. part.* of seul Sealed.

Seumar, air, *s. m.*, *provincial* for seòmar; which see

Seumasach, aich, *s. m.* A Jacobite

Seun, *s m* (*Ir* id.) A charm; an amulet; a charm for protection; prosperity; good luck.

Seun, *v a* Deny, refuse, decline, forbear, refrain, conceal; bless, make sacred, defend from the power of enchantment *Pret a* sheun, *denied, fut aff a* seunaidh Sheun i, *she denied —Stew. Gen* Sheun na h-oighean, *the maidens forebore —Oss Derm.* Sheun a ghealach i fèin fo neulaibh, *the moon concealed herself under a cloud —Oss Gaul*

Seunach, *a* Apt to deny or to refuse; denying, refusing; forbearing, defending from enchantment; conjuring, having charms or amulets, like a charm or amulet, of charms or amulets.

Seunachd, *s f* A denial, a refusal, forbearance; defence from enchantment

Seunadair, *s m* (*from* seun) One who refuses, a conjurer; a defender from enchantment.—*Stew Deut N pl* seunadairean

Seunadaireachd, *s f* Conjuration, enchantment, a charming

Seunadh, aidh, *s m* (*Ir id*) A denying, a refusing, a hiding; a forbearing, a defending from enchantment or charming, a denial, a refusal, concealment; defence from enchantment, augury, druidism

Seunadh, (a), *p part* of seun

Seunail, *a* (seun-amhuil) Like a charm or amulet; enchanting, *also,* happy; prosperous.

Seun-bholadh, aidh, *s. m.* A stench —*Shaw*

Seunmhoire, *com* and *sup* of seunmhor

Seunmhoireachd, *s f* Enchantment; the state of being enchanted

Seunta, *p part* of seun. (*Ir. id*) Denied, refused; hidden, concealed; defended from enchantment; having a charm for protection; charmed, bewitched; sacred

Seuntas, ais, *s m* (*Ir id*) A denial; concealment, a charm, enchantment, the property of an amulet, *also,* a stench

Sg *and* Sc are very often used indiscriminately

Sgà, *s m* Fear, timidity, sake. Tha mi fo sgà, *I am afraid,* air sgà d'ainm, *for thy name's sake,* air mo sgà-sa, *on my account, for my sake* Written also *sgàth,* which see.

Sgab, *v a.* See Sgap

Sgabag, aig, *s f.* A winter-mart; beef slain for winter-food; beef

Sgabagan, *n. pl* of sgabag Beeves.

Sgabaiste, *s f* (*Ir id*) Robbery, felony, rapine.

Sgabaisteach, *a* Committing robbery or rapine; felonious Gu sgabaisteach, *feloniously*

Sgaball, aill, *s. m* A helmet or headpiece, a hood or scapular, a cauldron. *N pl* sgaballan.

Sgaballach, *a.* Wearing a helmet, like a helmet, of helmets.

Sgabard, aird, *s* A sheath or scabbard.

Sgabh, *s. m.* (*Ir. id*) Sawdust.

Sgabhaiste, *s f* Advantage, good

Sgabhal, ail, *s. m.* See Scabhal

Sgabhrach, *a* (*Ir. id.*) Club-footed; splay-footed.

Sgabhrachd, *s f* The infirmity of a club-foot

Sgabull, uill, *s. m* See Sgaball

Sgabullach, *a* See Sgaballach

Sgach, (*for* agus gach, *or* is gach) And each, and every

Sgach, (*for* anns gach) In each, in every Sgach am, *always, at every time.—Stew Pro* Sgach àit, *in every place.—Sm*

Sgad, *s m* Loss; ruin; mischance Mo sgad! *woe's me! my ruin*
Germ shad. *Franconian*, scado. *Anglo-Sax.* scathe. *Scotch*, skaith

Sgadan, ain, *s. m.* (*Ir. id.*) A herring. Sgadan garbh, *the fish called alewife* *N. pl.* sgadain.

Sgadanach, *a.* Abounding in herrings, like a herring Buntàtach, feòlar, sgadanach, *abounding in potatoes, flesh, and herrings.—Macfar.*

Sgafair, *s m* A bold-hearted man. *N. pl* sgafairean.

Sgafal, **Sgafald**, *s. m.* A scaffold. *N. pl.* sgafaldan

Sgafaldach, *a* Having scaffolds; scaffolded.

Sgafaldaich, *v a* Erect scaffolds.

Sgafanta, *a* (*Ir id*) Bold, in good spirits; hearty

Sgafantas, ais, *s m* Boldness; in good spirits

Sgafara, *a* Lively, in good spirits, alert, active.

Sgag, *v a* Split; crack; burst; shrink, *also*, cleanse, winnow, filter *Pret* sgag; *fut aff a* sgagaidh

Sgagach, *a* (*from* sgag) Apt to split or crack, as the surface of any thing, causing to split or crack, full of splits, cracks, or clefts, cleansing; filtering, winnowing. Teas sgagach samhraidh, *the cracking heat of summer —Old Poem*

Sgagadh, aidh, *s m* (*Ir id*) A splitting or cracking; a bursting, a split, crack, or fissure on the surface of any thing, a cleansing, a filtering; a winnowing; a filter; a winnow

Sgagaidh, *fut aff.* of sgag Shall or will split

Sgagait, *s m* A split or crack, as on the surface of deal, a fissure, a cleft

Sgagaite, *a* Split; cracked, burst; cleansed; filtered; winnowed

Sgagaiteach, *a.* Full of splits, cracks, or clefts; causing splits, cracks, or clefts

Sgaifean, ein, *s m* A term of personal contempt.

† **Sgaifir**, *s f* The stern of a ship —*Shaw*

Sgaighnean, ein, *s m* A hand-winnow, or a winnowing-fan

Sgaigte, *p part* of sgag, which see

Sgàil, *v. a.* Shade, overshade, darken, cast a shade, eclipse. *Pret* sgàil, *fut. aff. a* sgàilidh.

Sgail, sgaile, *s f* (*Ir id*) A flame, a flash, brightness —*Shaw.*

Sgàil, sgàile, *s f* (*Dan* skiul, *shelter*) A shade, a shadow; a mask, a veil, a curtain, a spectre Sgàil a bhais, *the shadow of death —Stew Job* *N pl* sgàilean *and* sgàileachan Sgàilean nan sonn o shean, *the spectres of departed heroes —Fingalian Poem* An sgaileachan, *their curtains —Stew Jer.*

Sgailc, sgailce, *s f.* A dram, a morning-dram; a bumper of spirituous liquor, a loud momentary noise, a smart report; baldness.

Sgailclach, *a* Making a loud report

Sgailcearra, *a.* (*Ir id*) Loud, as a report, hard, giving hard blows; causing a loud explosion, explosive

Sgàile', *for* sgaileadh; which see.

Sgaile, *s f.* (*Ir id*) A printing type

Sgàileach, *a*, *from* sgaile. (*Ir id.*) Shady, shading, shadowy, masked, veiled; spectral.

Sgàileachadh, aidh, *s. m.* A shading; a veiling, a masking

Sgàileachd, *s. f* Shadiness, shadowiness; darkness, the state of being veiled or masked

Sgàileadair, *s. m.* A masker, a shade. *N pl.* sgàileadairean.

Sgàileadh, idh, *s m.* A shading, a shadowing; a veiling, a masking.

Sgàileadh, (a), *pr. part.* of sgàil Shading, veiling, masking. Neul 'g a sgàileadh, *a cloud veiling it.—Oss. Cathluno.*

Sgàileag, eig, *s. f.* (*Ir id*) A little shade; a thin shade or veil; an umbrella; a fan; *also*, a little dish; a plate.—*Shaw.*

Sgàilean, ein, *s m*, *dim* of sgàil. (*Ir.* sgàilin) A thin shade or veil; a fan; an umbrella; an arbour. *N. pl.* sgaileanan

Sgàileanach, *a.* Shady; veiling; like a shade or veil; like a fan; like an umbrella; full of arbours; filmy

Sgàileanachd, *s f.* Shadiness, shadowiness; filminess.

Sgàilich, *v. a.* (*from* sgàil) Shade, veil, mask. *Pret. a.* sgàilich; *fut. aff* sgàilichidh.

Sgàilichte, *p part* of sgàilich Shaded, veiled, masked.

Sgailleag, eig, *s f.* A blow or slap with the palm of the hand. *N. pl.* sgailleagan.

Sgailleagach, *a.* Striking with the palm of the hand; slapping

Sgailleas, eis, *s m* (*Ir. id.*) Disdain.—*Shaw.*

Sgailleasach, *a.* (*Ir id.*) Disdainful. Gu sgailleasach, *disdainfully.*

Sgaillte, *p. part.* of sgallt. (*Ir.* sgallta) Scalded.

Sgaillteach, *a* Scalding

† **Sgailp**, sgailpe, *s. f* A den, a cave

† **Sgailpeach**, *a.* Abounding in dens or caves.

Sgailtean, ein, *s m.* See **Sgoiltean.**

Sgàin, *v a* and *n* (*Ir. id*) Burst, split, cleave, tear asunder, rive or rend. *Pret. a.* sgàin; *fut aff a* sgàinidh, *shall burst.*

Sgaindear, eir, *s m.* (*Ir id*) A division

Sgàineach, *a.* Apt to burst, split, or cleave, causing to burst, split, or cleave; bursting, splitting, cleaving; tearing asunder.

Sgàineadh, idh, *s m.* A bursting, a splitting, a cleaving; a riving, a tearing asunder, a burst, a split, a cleft, a rent.

Sgàineadh, 3 *sing* and *pl. imper.* of sgàin Sgaineadh e, iad, *let him, them, burst*

Sgainne, *s. f* A sudden irruption or sally; an attack; a flaw

Sgainneal, eil, *s. m* (*Ir.* scannail) Scandal, calumny. Thog thu oirnn sgainneal, *thou hast calumniated us.—Old Song.*

Sgainnealach, *a* (*Ir* scannalach) Calumnious, slanderous, reproachful. Gu sgainnealach, *calumniously.*

Sgainnealachadh, aidh, *s m* (*Ir* scanlughadh.) A calumniating, a slandering, a reproaching.

Sgainnealachadh, (a), *pr. part* of sgainnealaich. Calumniating, slandering, reproaching

Sgainnealaich, *v. a* Scandalize, calumniate; reproach.

Sgainnealaichte, *p part* of sgainnealaich. Scandalized, calumniated; reproached

Sgainnearach, *a.* Scattering, dispersing, scaring; persecuting.

Sgainnearadh, aidh, *s m* A scattering, a dispersing, a scaring, a persecuting; a sudden dispersion, a persecution.

Sgainneart, eirt, *s m* Dispersion, dispersement; a swing; a persecution, a trial of strength. Faiceamaid sgainneart ghlan, *let us see a fair trial of strength —Old Poem.*

Sgainneartach, *a* Dispersing; persecuting; powerful.

Sgainnir, *v a.* and *n* Scatter, disperse; persecute; *Pret a.* sgainnir; *fut aff. a.* sgainniridh. Sgainnir sibh iad, *you dispersed them.—Stew. Ezek.*

Sgainnir, *s. f.* Dispersion; persecution; defamation. Gun bheum, gun sgainnir, *without blame or defamation.*

Sgàinte, *p. part.* of sgàin. Burst, split, cleft, torn asunder. Sgàinte o chéile, *burst asunder.—Sm.*

Sgàinteach, *a.* (*Ir. id.*) Apt to burst, split, or rive; causing to burst, split, or rive; bursting, splitting, riving.

Sgaip, *v. a.*; more properly *sgap*; which see.

Sgaipte, *p. part.* of sgap; which see.

Sgair, *s. m.* Any place where a thing is laid to dry.—*Shaw.*

Sgàird, sgàirde, *s. f.* (*Ir. id.*) A flux, a dysentery, a loose stool; skit; *rarely*, a smock. Sgaird fola, *a bloody flux.*

Sgàirdeach, *a.* Habitually loose in the bowels; afflicted with a flux or dysentery.

Sgàirdeachd, *s. f.* The state of being afflicted with dysentery.

Sgaireach, *a.* Prodigal; *also, substantively*, a prodigal.

Sgàireachd, *s. f.* A crying out; a shrieking.

Sgaireap, eip, *s. m.* (*Ir.* sgairiop.) Lavishness, extravagance.

Sgaireapach, *a.* Lavish, extravagant. Gu sgaireapach, *lavishly.*

Sgairn, *s. f.* A shriek; a confused noise; a howling, a growling. B' fhad chluinnte an sgairn, *their howling was heard afar off.—Old Poem.*

Sgairneach, *a.* Shrieking; howling; growling.

Sgairneach, ich, *s. m.* A rocky hill-side; a rocky, sloping surface; loose or loosened rocks; *also*, a continued howling. Sgairneach o chreagaibh ard, *loosened rocks from lofty precipices.—Oss. Dargo. N. pl.* sgairnich. In the former class of meanings, I am not aware that there is a single term in the English language to express the true signification of *sgairneach.*

Sgairp, *s. f.* (*Ir. id.*) A scorpion. *N. pl.* sgairpean.

Sgairpeach, *a.* Like a scorpion; full of scorpions; of scorpions.

Sgairt, *v. n.* Shout, cry, roar, bawl, shriek. *Pret.* sgairt; *fut. aff.* sgairtidh.

Sgairt, sgairte, *s. f.* (*Ir. id.*) A loud shout or cry, a roar, a shriek; a caul, a midriff; a tuft of trees or branches; a bush; activity, bustle. Thoir sgairt, *cry aloud.* An sgairt thug Fionn as, *the shout which Fingal gave.—Oss. Duthona.* Sgairt an cridhe, *the caul of their hearts.—Stew. Hos.* Thàinig e le sgairt, *he came with a bustle.—Oss.*

Sgairteach, *a.* Shouting, roaring, shrieking, clamorous; active; bustling; having a large caul.

Sgairteachadh, aidh, *s. m.* A shouting, a roaring, a shrieking; a bustling motion.

Sgairteachd, *s. f.* Continued shouting, roaring, or bawling, a shrieking; a shout, a roar, a shriek. Na tannais a sgairteachd, *the spectres shrieking.—Oss. Gaul.* Ri sgairteachd, *shrieking.* Sgairteachd gheur, *a piercing shout* or *cry.—Mac Kellar's Hymn.*

Sgairteadh, idh, *s. m.* A shouting, a roaring, a bawling, a shrieking; a bustling motion.

Sgairtealachd, *s. f.* Activity; boldness of manner; vigorousness; a bustling turn.

Sgairtear, eir, *s. m.* (*Ir.* sgairteoir.) A bawler, a crier. *N. pl.* sgairtearan.

Sgairteil, *a.* (sgairt-amhuil.) Active; bold in manner; vigorous; bustling.

Sgairtich, *v. n.* (*from* sgairt.) Shout, roar, bawl, shriek. *Pret. a.* sgairtich; *fut. aff.* sgairtichidh, *shall shout.* Sgairtich mo nighean, *my daughter shrieked.—Stew. G. B.*

Sgaite, (*for* sgaithte), *p. part.* of sgath. Pruned, lopped off, cut off; dispersed; destroyed.

Sgaite, *s. f.* A short angry rebuke; a cut; a snarl; *in derision*, a short-tempered person. Thug e sgaite orm, *he rebuked me angrily, he snarled at me.*

Sgaiteach, *a.* (*Ir. id.*) Sharp, keen, cutting, piercing; destructive; stormy, blustering; shabby. Mar chlaidheamh sgaiteach, *like a sharp sword.—Sm.* Cainnte sgaiteach, *cutting language;* gaoth sgaiteach, *a piercing wind, a blustering wind.* Gu sgaiteach, *sharply, cuttingly.*

Sgaiteachd, *s. f.* Sharpness, keenness; asperity.—*Macint.*

Sgaith, *s. f.* A flower.

Sgaithean, ein, *s. m.* A small shadow.—*Shaw.*

Sgal, *v. n.* Shriek, yell, howl loudly, squall. *Pret. a.* sgal; *fut. aff. a.* sgalaidh, *shall howl.* Cha sgal cù roimh chnaimh, *a dog will not howl if struck with a bone.—G. P.*

Sgal, *s. m.* A shriek, a yell, a loud howl, a squall; the swell of a bagpipe. Sgal a chuilein, *the loud howl of his dog.—Orr.* Sgal gaoithe, *a squall of wind. N. pl.* sgalan. Le trì sgalan dh'imich anam, *with three shrieks his soul departed.—Oss. Com.*

Swed. sqwala *and* skal. *Germ.* schall. *Franconian*, skall. *Eng.* squall. *Ir.* sgal.

† **Sgal**, *s. m.* (*Ir. id.*) A man; a champion; a calf.

Sgàl, sgàil, *s. m.* (*Ir.* sgala.) A baking-trough; a tray. *Dan.* skaal, *a drinking-cup.*

Sgalach, *a.* Shrieking, yelling, howling, squalling; apt to shriek, yell, howl, or squall.

Sgàladh, aidh, *s. m.* A baking-trough.

Sgalag, aig, *s. m.* (*from* † sgal.) A farm-servant. Sgalag is eich ghniomhach, *a farm-servant and work-horses. N. pl.* sgalagan.

Swed. † skalk. *Gloss. Keron.* scalch. *Germ.* schalk. *Franconian*, scalc. *Anglo-Sax.* scalc, sceal*c*. *It.* scalco. *Barbarous Lat.* scalcus. *Ir.* sgalog.

Sgalag is evidently derived from † *sgal*, man, a term which is in common use among the Irish Celts. There does not seem to be strong enough ground for the supposition of Dr. Jamieson, that this word must have been introduced into the Hebrides by the Norwegians.

Sgàlain, *s.* Weighing-scales; weights.

Sgalan, ain, *s. m.* (*Ir. id.*) A scaffold; a hut.

Sgalanta, *a.* Loud-sounding; loud and shrill. Piob sgalanta, *a loud-sounding pipe.—Macint.*

Sgalantachd, *s. f.* Sonorousness.

Sgalartaich, *s. f.* A howling, a yelling; a howl, a yell. Bu tric sgalartaich ar con, *frequent was the howling of your dogs.—Orr.*

† **Sgaldach**, aich, *s. m.* (*Ir. id.*) A stubble.—*Shaw.*

Sgaldruth, *s. m.* (*Ir. id.*) A fornicator.

Sgall, *v. a.* (*Ir. id.*) Scald; trouble, disturb.—*Shaw.*

Sgallach, *a.* (*Ir. id.*) Bald; troublesome. *Com.* and *sup.* sgallaiche.

Sgallachd, *s. f.* (*Ir. id.*) Baldness; troublesomeness; disturbance.

Sgalladh, aidh, *s. m.* A scalding; a scald. Fhuair e sgalladh, *he got himself scalded.*

Sgallagach, aich, *s. m.* Birdseed.—*Shaw.*

Sgallais, *s. f.* (*Ir. id.*) Derision, ridicule, mocking. Ri sgallais, *deriding.*

Sgallaiseach, *a.* Deriding, ridiculing; given to ridicule; opprobrious.

Sgallaiseachd, *s. f.* The practice of ridicule.

Sgallaisich, *v. a.* Deride, ridicule. *Pret. a. id.*

Sgallt, *v. a.* Scald. *Pret. a.* sgallt; *fut. aff. a.* sgalltaidh.

Sgallta, *a.* (*Ir. id.*) Scalded, burned; bare, bald.—*Shaw.*

Sgalltach, *a.* Scalding; apt to scald.

Sgàm, sgàim, *s. m.* A spot; a spot on linen; ironmould.

Sgamail, *s. pl.* Scales.

Sgamal, ail, *s. m.* (*Ir. id.*) Exhalation—(*Shaw*); scum; phlegm.

Sgamh, *s. m.* Dust, dross. Sgamh eighe, *filings.*—*Macd.*

Sgamh, sgaimh, *s. m.* (*Ir. id.*) A lobe of the lungs. *N. pl.* sgamhach.

Sgamhach, *a.* Having good lungs; of lungs; pulmonary.

Sgamhag, aig, *s. f.* A wry mouth.

Sgamhan, *s. pl.* (*Ir. id.* *W.* ysgyfaint.) Lungs; lights; liver; *also*, a term of personal contempt. Anns an sgamhan, *in the liver.*—*Stew. Ezek.*

Sgamhanach, *a.* Pulmonary; having strong lungs.

Sgamhar, air, *s. m.* (*Ir. id.*) Sawdust.—*Shaw.*

Sgamh-chnaimh, *s. f.* (*Ir.* scamh-chnaoi. A consumption of the lungs.

Sgamh-ghalar, air, *s. m.* A consumption of the lungs.

Sgann, sgainn, *s. m.* (*Ir.* sgann.) A membrane; a multitude; a swarm; a parcel.

Sgannal. See **Sgainneal**.

Sgannan, ain, *s. m.* (*dim.* of sgann.) A little membrane; a pellicle; the caul; a group of people; a little parcel.

Sgannanach, *a.* Membranaceous.

Sganrach, **Sgannrach**, *a.* Dispersing, scattering, scaring, routing, dispelling; terrifying; persecuting; like a dispersion, rout, or persecution.

Sganradh, **Sgannradh**, aidh, *s. m.* A dispersing, a scattering, a scaring, a routing, dispelling; dispersion; a rout; a persecution; confusion; surprise, fright.

Sganradh, **Sgannradh**, (a), *pr. part.* Dispersing, scattering, scaring, routing, dispelling; persecuting; terrifying. A sganradh doininn, *dispelling the storm.*—*Oss.*

Sganraich, **Sgannraich**, *v. a.* Disperse, scatter, scare, rout, dispel; persecute; terrify. *Pret. a. id.*; *fut. aff.* sganraichidh.

Sganraichte, **Sgannraichte**, *p. part.* of sganraich; which see.

Sganraidh, **Sgannraidh**, *s. f.* Dispersement through astonishment or fear; a sudden dispersion, astonishment; defamation.

Sgaog, sgaoig, *s. c.* A giddy young female; a light-headed person. *N. pl.* sgaogan.

Sgaogach, *a.* Giddy, volatile, fickle, flighty. Caileag sgaogach, *a giddy girl.* *Com.* and *sup.* sgaogaiche.

Sgaogan, ain, *s. m.* (*dim.* of sgaog.) A giddy young person.

Sgaoganachd, *s. f.* Giddiness, volatileness, flightiness, fickleness.

Sgaoil, *v. a.* (*Ir. id. Scotch*, skel, *spill.*) Spread, enlarge; dishevel; scatter, disperse, dispel; loose, untie; unfold, reveal, divulge; destroy; dismiss; stretch; unsew. *Pret. a.* sgaoil, *fut. aff. a.* sgaoilidh. Sgaoil, a Dheirg, do sgia! *O Dargo, spread thy shield!*—*Ull.* Sgaoil do mhaoile, *enlarge thy baldness.*—*Stew. Micah.*

Sgaoile, *s. f.* Dispersion; a scattered state; looseness. Cuir fa sgaoile, *scatter; divulge.*

Sgaoileach, *a.* Causing to spread or scatter; dishevelling; loosening; unfolding, divulging; diffuse.

Sgaoileadh, idh, *s. m.* (*Ir.* scaoileadh.) A spreading, a scattering, a dishevelling, a dispersing, a loosening; an unfolding, a revealing, a divulging; a destroying; dispersion; diffusion. Bu chian air sgaoileadh, *far asunder was our dispersion.*—*Death of Ossian.*

Sgaoileadh, (a), *inf.* and *pr. part.* of sgaoil; which see.

Sgaoilear, *fut. pass.* of sgaoil. Shall be spread. See **Sgaoil**.

Sgaoilidh, *fut. pass.* of sgaoil.

Sgaoilte, *p. part.* of sgaoil. (*Ir. id.*) Spread, dispersed, scattered, dishevelled; loosened, untied; divulged. Cuirm sgaoilte, *a banquet spread out.*—*Oss. Tem.*

Sgaoilteach, *a.* Apt to spread or scatter; apt to untie or loosen; apt to divulge, spread abroad; diffuse; profuse. Cainnt sgaoilteach, *diffuse language.* Fear b' fhad sgaoilteach cliù, *a man of widely spread fame.*—*Mac Lach.*

Sgaoilteachd, *s. f.* A proneness to spread or scatter; a proneness to loosen or divulge; diffuseness; profuseness.

Sgaoim, *s. f.* (*Dan.* skam, *confusion.*) Terror, fright, fear; a start; skittishness. Co so na sgaoim o Mhealmhor? *who is this* [*coming*] *in terror from Mealmor?*—*Ardar.*

Sgaoimeach, *a.* Terrified; timid, skittish; causing to start.

Sgaoimeachd, *s. f.* Timidity, skittishness.

Sgaoimear, *a.* Timid, skittish.

Sgaoll, sgaoill, *s. m.* Fright; shiness, timidity.

Sgaollair, *s. m.* A shy or timid man; any shy creature. *N. pl.* sgaollairean.

Sgaollaireachd, *s. f.* Shiness, timidity.

Sgaollmhor, *a.* Timid, shy. *Com.* and *sup.* sgaollmhoire.

Sgaollmhorachd, *s. f.* Timidity, shiness.

Sgaoth, sgaoith, *s. m.* (*Ir.* sgaoth *and* sgaoidh.) A swarm; a flight of birds; a crowd, a multitude. Sgaoth eunlaith, *a flight of birds.*—*Oss. Gaul.*

Sgaothan, ain, *s. m.* (*Ir. id.*) A chamber-pot.

Sgap, *v. a.* (*Ir. id. Scotch*, skel, *spill.*) Scatter; spread; disperse; squander. *Pret. a.* sgap; *fut. aff. a.* sgapaidh, *shall scatter.* Sgapaidh e gach olc, *he will scatter every evil.*—*Stew. Pro. ref.* *Fut. pass.* sgapar. Sgapar siol, *seed shall be scattered.*—*Macfar.*

Sgapach, *a.* Apt to scatter, spread, or disperse; apt to squander; scattering, spreading, dispersing, squandering; diffuse.

Sgapadair, *s. m.* (*from* sgap.) A disperser; a disseminator. *N. pl.* sgapadairean.

Sgapadh, *pret. pass.* of sgap. Was scattered or dispersed. Sgapadh iad, *they were scattered.* Sgapadh Lochlann o chéile, *Lochlin was dispersed.*—*Ull.*

Sgapadh, 3 *sing.* and *pl. imper.* of sgap. Sgapadh e, iad, *let him, them, scatter.*

Sgapadh, aidh, *s. m.* (*Ir. id.*) A scattering; a spreading; a squandering; a dispersing, a routing; a dispersion, a rout.

Sgapaidh, *fut. aff. a.* of sgap. Shall or will scatter. See **Sgap**.

Sgapair, *s. m.* (*from* sgap.) A scatterer, a disperser; a squanderer; a disseminator. *N. pl.* sgapairean.

Sgapaireachd, *s. f.* A scattering; dispersion; a routing; extravagance.

Sgapta, **Sgapte**, *p. part.* Scattered, spread abroad, dispersed, routed; squandered. Mo mhuinntir sgapta, *my dispersed people.*—*Stew. Zeph.*

Sgar, *s.* See **Sgaradh**.

Sgar, *v. a.* and *n.* Separate, part, tear asunder; wound, afflict, torment, harass, gall; unfold for drying. *Pret. a.* sgar; *fut. aff. a.* sgaraidh.

Sgarach, *a.* Separating, parting; schismatic; tearing asunder; wounding, afflicting, harassing.

Sgarachduinn, *s. f.* A separating, a parting, a tearing asunder; a harassing; a separation.

Sgaradair, *s. m.* (*from* sgar.) A separator, a tearer asunder; a harasser, a tormentor.

Sgàradaireachd, *s. f.* Separation; schism.

Sgaradh, aidh, *s. m.* A separating, a parting; a tearing asunder; a harassing, a tormenting; woe, distress; a separation; a faction; a dissension; a division; schism. Tha sgaradh nar measg, *there are divisions among you.—Stew 1 Cor.* Mo sgaradh, *woe's me.*

Sgaradh, (a), *pr part.* of sgar, which see

Sgarar, *fut. pass* of sgar. Shall be separated Ni 'n sgarar mo chorp o Dhearg, *my body shall not be separated from Dargo.—Ull.*

Sgarbh, sgairbh, *s m.* (*Dan.* skarv) A cormorant; a heron. *N. pl.* sgarbhan. Trod nam ban mu 'n sgarbh, is an sgarbh air an loch, *the women scolding* [*disputing*] *who shall have the heron, and the heron on the lake.—G. P.*

Sgarbh, sgairbh, *s. m.* Shallow water, a ford

Sgarbh, *v. a.* Wade, cross a river by a ford

Sgarbhach, *a.* Abounding in cormorants, like a cormorant; of cormorants

Sgar-bhoc, *s m.* Scurvy

Germ. scharbock *Belg* scheurbuick. *Swed.* skorbiug.

Sgarbhocach, *a.* Scurvied, like a scurvy.

Sgard, sgaird, *s. m* A flux, looseness of the bowels, skit.

Sgard, *v. n.* Squirt, pour, sprinkle

Sgardach, *a.* Loose in the bowels, squirting, pouring, sprinkling.

Sgardadh, aidh, *s m* A squirting, a syringing; a pouring, a sprinkling.

Sgardair, *s m.* (*Ir.* sgardaire.) One afflicted with weakness of the bowels; a squirt; a syringe, a water-gun

Sgarlaid, *s f* Scarlet. See Scarlaid

Sgarnail, *s. f* A screaming, a shrieking.

Sgat, sgait, *s m.* A skate.—*Shaw.*

Sgath, *v. a.* Prune, lop, cut off; cut down, destroy *Pret a* sgath, *fut. aff. a.* sgathaidh, *shall cut down.*

Sgàth, *s.* (*Ir. id*) Fear; fright, timidity; bashfulness; disgust, squeamishness, account, sake; a shadow; a shade, veil, or covering A gabhail sgàth, *taking fright*, air sgàth, *for the sake of*, na dh' fhuiling Troidh air a sgàth! *what Troy suffered on his account!—Mac Lach* Tha thu 'cur sgàth orm, *you make me squeamish.*

Sgath, *s. m* A large bundle of rods tied closely together, and used in some parts of the Highlands for a door, threshed or scutched flax

Sgath'. See Sgàthadh.

Sgathach, *a* Pruning, cutting down, lopping; destroying, skirmishing; *also, substantively*, prunings, loppings

Sgàthach, *a.* Timid; bashful, afraid; shadowy, shady, covering; causing fear Bha mi sgàthach, *I was afraid —Stew. Job.*

Sgàthachan, ain, *s m* (*from* sgàth.) A tail; *ἡ πυγὴ ποδή*

Sgàthachas, ais, *s m.* Fear; timidity; bashfulness

Sgathadh, aidh, *s m.* A pruning, a lopping, a cutting down; abnudation; destruction, loss; a shred, a segment; a skirmishing, a bickering. Air a sguthadh gun iochd, *cut down without pity —Oss. Gaul* Cha d' fhuair sgathadh nach d' fhuiling nàir, *they never met with loss who did not suffer blame.—G. P.*

Sgathag, aig, *s f* Trefoil in flower —*Shaw*

Sgathagach, *a.* Full of trefoil in flower.

Sgathair, *s. m.* A spruce fellow, a beau *N pl* sgathairean

Sgàthan, ain, *s m* (*from* sgath, *shadow.*) *Ir* scathan A mirror or looking-glass; a gazing-stock A réidh-ghorm lith mar sgàthan, *her smooth blue pools like mirrors —Macfar.* Is math an sgàthan sùil caraid, *a friend's eye is a good mirror —G. P*

Sgatharra, *a.* Pruning, lopping; cutting down

Sgath-bhard, aird, *s. m.* A satirist, a lampooner

Sgath-bhardachd, *s f.* Satire, lampooning, ribaldry

Sgath-lann, -lainn, *s m.* A shed, a booth, a tent; a shop, a cover; a penthouse

Sgàth-thigh, *s m* A porch —*Stew. Mark*

Sgathta, Sgathte, *p. part.* of sgath Pruned, lopped off, cut down

Sgé, *poetical contraction for* sgiath A shield, a wing, a shelter An sgé na h-innis, *in the shelter of the isle —Oss Gaul*

Sgeach, *s* A haw, the berry of the hawthorn; a bush, bramble, or brier, a bust.

Sgeachag, aig, *s f*, *dim* of sgeach. (*Ir. id*) A haw, or the red berry of the hawthorn. *N pl* sgeachagan, *haws*

Sgeachagach, *a* Abounding in haws or hawthorn berries, like a haw; of haws Mios sgeachagach, *the month of hawthorn berries —Macdon.*

Sgeachagan, *n pl* of sgeachag Haws.

Sgeachanach, *a* Bushy; brambly.

Sgeachrach, *a* Prickly; full of briers or brambles, of briers or brambles

Sgeachradh, aidh, *s m.* A prickle, a brier or bramble.

Sgeach-spionnan, ain, *s m* A gooseberry-bush —*Shaw*

Sgead, *s.* A speck, a white spot, an ornament

Sgeadach, *a* Fond of dress; speckled, sky-coloured, cirrocumulated. Neul sgeadach, *a cirrocumulus cloud.*

Sgeadachadh, aidh, *s m* A bedecking or adorning, a dressing or clothing, ornament, dress; clothes Sgeadachadh gu leòir, *enough of ornament —Macint*

Sgeadachadh, (a), *inf.* and *pr part.* of sgeadaich

Sgeadachail, *a* (sgeadach-amhuil) Ornamental, beautifying, fond of ornament, fond of dress

Sgeadachair, *s. m.* One who adorns or beautifies, a garnisher, a decker

Sgeadaich, *v a* Bedeck, adorn, beautify; dress, clothe, garnish *Pret a* sgeadaich; *fut aff a* sgeadaichidh, *shall adorn*, *fut pass* sgeadaichear.

Sgeadaichear, *fut pass* of sgeadaich Shall be bedecked or adorned Sgeadaichear na lòin, *the meadows shall be adorned —Macfar*

Sgeadaichte, *p part* of sgeadaich, which see

Sgeadas, ais, *s. m.* (*Ir id*) Ornament, decoration, dress; spottedness, speckledness

Sgeadasach, *a.* Ornamental, decorating, fond of dress; spotted, speckled Breac le neòil sgeadasach, *spotted with cirrocumulus clouds —Fingalian Poem*

Sgeal See Sgeul.

Sgealachd, *s f* See Sgeulachd

Sgealag, aig, *s. f.* Wild mustard *Shaw.*

Sgealagach, aich, *s. m* Wild mustard

Sgealagach, *a* Abounding in wild mustard-seed, of wild mustard-seed

Sgealan, Sgeallan, ain, *s m* (*Ir id*) Wild mustard—(*Macd*), a kernel—(*Macfar Voc*), a slice —*Shaw*

Sgealanach, Sgeallanach, *a* Abounding in wild mustard, having a kernel; in slices, like wild mustard, like a kernel, of wild mustard

Sgealb, sgeilb, *s* (*Ir.* scealp. *Germ* schalp) A splint, a splinter, piece, or fragment, a cliff, a sherd. Air sgeilb creige, *on the fragment of a rock.—Oss. Cathluno.* Sgealb, *a cliff —Shaw.* Sgealb a thogas teine, *a sherd that lifteth fire —Stew Is N. pl* sgealban, *d pl* sgealbaibh Chaidh am bàt na sgealbaibh, *the boat went into fragments* or *splinters.—Old Song.*

SGEALB, *v. a.* and *n.* Splinter, smash, break into fragments; split, tear; snatch. *Pret. a.* sgealb; *fut. aff. a.* sgealbaidh.

SGEALBACH, *a.* (*from* sgealb.) Splintering, smashing; cleaving; rending; snatching; apt to break into fragments; in splinters; smashed.

SGEALBADH, aidh, *s. m.* A splintering, a smashing, a breaking into fragments; a cleaving; a splinter, a fragment, a rent; a snatching, a plucking.

SGEALBAG, aig, *s. f.* (*dim.* of sgealb.) A little splinter; a little fragment; a little rock; a pinch. *N. pl.* sgealbagan.

SGEALBAGACH, *a.* In small splinters or fragments; breaking into splinters.

SGEALB-CHREUG, *s. f.* A splintered cliff. Airde nan sgealbchreug, *the pinnacles of the splintered cliffs.—Old Poem.*

SGEALB-CHREUGACH, *a.* Full of splintered rocks or cliffs.

SGEALLAG, aig, *s. f.* Wild mustard. Written also *sgealag.*

SGEALLAGACH, aich, *s. m.* Wild mustard; a quantity of wild mustard.

SGEALLAN, ain, *s. m.* See SGEALAN.

SGEALLANACH. See SGEALANACH.

SGEALP, sgeilp, *s. m.* See SGEALB.

SGEALP, *s. m.* A slap or blow with the palm of the hand.

SGEALP, *v. a.* Slap or strike with the palm of the hand. *Pret. a.* sgealp; *fut. aff.* sgealpaidh.

SGEALPACH, *a.* Slapping or striking with the palm of the hand.

SGEALPARRA, *a.* (*from* sgealp.) Loud, piercing, shrill; smart, as a report. Piob sgealparra Mhic Cruimein, *the loud-sounding pipes of Mac Crimean.—Old Song.* Braidhe sgealparra, *a smart report;* cainnt sgealparra, *loud and articulate utterance.*

SGEALPARRACHD, *s. f.* Loudness; shrillness; smartness; as of a report.

SGEAMH, sgeimh, *s. m.* Polypody.—*Shaw. Polypodium vulgare.*

SGEAMH, *v. a.* Reproach. *Pret. a.* sgeamh; *fut. aff.* sgeamhaidh.

SGEAN, sgéin, *s. m.* A fright; terror; astonishment; wildness; a wild look; a mad look. Ghabh an t-each sgean, *the horse took fright;* air sgean, *gone off in a fright, as a horse.*

SGEANA, *inflection of* sgian. Mar sgeana, *as knives.—Stew. Pro.* See SGIAN.

SGEANACH, *a.* Apt to take fright, as a horse; wild, furious; having a wild look. Each sgeanach, *a wild* or *timid horse.*

SGEANADH, aidh, *s. m.* See SGEAN.

SGEANN, *v. n.* Gaze, stare, glare. *Pret. a.* sgeann; *fut. aff. a.* sgeannaidh, *shall gaze.* Sgeann e orm, *he stared at me;* sgeann a shùilean na cheann, *his eyes glared in his head.*

SGEANN, *s. m.* A gaze, a stare, a glare.

SGEANNACH, *a.* Gazing, staring, glaring, apt to gaze, stare, or glare.

SGEANNADH, aidh, *s. m.* A gazing, a staring, a glaring; a gaze, a stare, a glare.

SGEANNAG, aig, *s. f.* A staring female.

SGEANNAIR, *s. m.* (*from* sgeann.) A gazer, a starer. *N. pl.* sgeannairean.

SGEAP, sgeapa, sgip, *s.* A hive; a handwinnow; a skep. Cròdhaidh fuarachd iad nan sgeap, *cold shall hem them in their hives.—Macdon.* Sgeap sheillean, *a bee-hive. N. pl.* sgeapaichean. *Gr.* σκέπω, *to cover. Germ.* schapp, *a storehouse. Sax.* scephen. *Eng.* skep, *a hive.*

SGEAPAICHEAN, *n. pl.* of sgeap.

SGEARACH, *a.* Happy.

SGEARACH, aich, *s.* A square.

SGEARADH, aidh, *s. m.* A stage-play.

SGEARAIL, *a.* Happy.

SGEARAILEACHD, *s. f.* Happiness.

SGEATH, *v.* See SGEITH.

SGEATHACH, *a.* Emetic. See SGEITHEACH.

SGEATH-CHOSG, *s. m.* An anti-emetic.

SGEATHRACH, aich, *s. m.* A vomit.

SGEATHRAICH, *v. n.* Vomit; spew.

SGEI', *poetical abbreviation* of sgeithe; *gen. sing.* of sgiath; which see.

SGEIG, *v.* Mock, deride, taunt; scorn. *Pret.* sgeig; *fut. aff.* sgeigidh, *shall scorn.* Sgeigidh gach aon, *every one shall deride.—Stew. Zeph.*

SGEIG, sgeige, *s. f.* (*Ir.* sgige *and* sgeig.) Mockery, derision, ridicule; a taunt; scorn; buffoonery; waggery. Ball-sgeige, *a laughing-stock.—Stew. Jer.*

SGEIGEACH, *a.* Prone to mock, deride, or ridicule; prone to scorn; scornful; taunting; waggish.

SGEIGEACH, ich, *s. m.* A mocker, a derider; a taunter, a scorner; a wag; a buffoon or zany.

SGEIGEAR, eir, *s. m.* (sgeig-fhear.) A mocker, a derider; a taunter, a scorner; a wag, a buffoon; a gander.

SGEIGEIL, *a.* (sgeig-amhuil.) Prone to mock or ridicule; taunting, scorning.

SGEIGEIREACHD, *s. f.* Mockery, derision; a habit of taunting; waggery; waggishness, buffoonery.

SGEIGIDH, *fut. aff. a.* of sgeig. Shall or will mock.

SGÉIL, sgéile, *s. f.* (*Ir. id.*) Misery; pity; calamity; disaster. Mo sgéil! *alas!*

SGEIL, *s. f.* (*Island.* skill.) Skill; knowledge, learning; skilfulness, dexterity; shelling grain. Fear gun sgeil, *a man without skill;* air bheag sgeil, *ignorant.*

SGÉIL, *gen. sing.* of sgeul; which see.

SGEILC, *s. f.* A smart explosion; a loud report; a pop. Sometimes written *sgailc.*

SGEILCEARRA, *a.* Smart or loud, as a report or explosion. Braidhe sgeilcearra, *a loud report.*

SGEILEACH, *a.* Pitiable, pitiful.

SGEILEIL, *a.* (sgeil-amhuil.) Skilled; knowing; intelligent; skilful, dexterous; *also* written *sgileil;* which see.

SGEILEIT, *s. f.* A skillet or little boiler. *N. pl.* sgeileitean.

SGEILM, *s. f.* (*Germ.* skelm, *prattle. Dan.* skielm, *a knave.*) Prattle, garrulity; tale-telling; vain-boasting, vain-glory; a tell-tale; an impertinent prater; neatness or tidiness in dress.

SGEILMEARRA, *a.* Prattling, garrulous; neat, trim, or tidy in dress; quick, nimble.

SGEILMEIL, *a.* (sgeilm-amhuil.) Prattling, garrulous, talkative; vain-glorious; neat, trim, or tidy in dress; quick, nimble.

SGEILMEILEACHD, *s. f.* Prattling; garrulousness; talkativeness; neatness, tidiness.

SGEILP, *s. f.* (*provincial.*) A shelf. *N. pl.* sgeilpeachan.

SGEILP. See SGEALP.

SGÉIL-THEACHDAIR, *s. m.* A tale-bearer, a bringer of news. *N. pl.* sgéil-theachdairean.

SGEIM, *s. f.* Foam.

SGEIMH, *s. f.* (*Ir.* sceimh.) Ornament; beauty; handsomeness; personal elegance; a scheme, draught, or schedule.

Sheas iad nan sgeimh, *they stood in their beauty.—Oss. Carricth.* Sgeimh an naomhachd, *the beauty of their holiness.—Sm.* Sgeimh ard, *high bloom, good plight or habit of body.*

Sgeimh, *v. a.* Adorn, beautify; make a draught or scheme; skim, scum.

Sgeimheach, *a.* (*from* sgeimh.) Ornamental; handsome; elegant; like a scheme or draught. Maise sgeimheach an caoin-chruth, *the exquisite beauty of their fair forms.—Oss. Cathula.*

Sgeimhich, *v. a.* Adorn, bedeck, beautify.

Sgeimhle, *s. f.* (*Ir. id.*) Surprise, alarm; a skirmish.

Sgeimhlich, *v.* (*Ir. id.*) Surprise, alarm; skirmish, bicker.

Sgéimhnidh, *a.* (*Ir. id.*) Clean; fierce.

Sgéin, *gen. sing.* of sgeun *or* sgean; which see.

Sgein, *s. f.* (*Ir. id.*) A hiding-place.

Sgeineil, *a.* Neat, tight.

Sgeing, *s. f.* A bounce, a start.

Sgeingach, *a.* Bouncing; starting.

Sgeinm, *s. f.* Prattle; talkativeness; impertinent garrulity; a garrulous *person*; a tell-tale; (*more frequently written sgeilm* in the foregoing meanings;) neatness or tidiness in dress; taste in dress; a tidy person.

Sgeinmeach, *a.* Garrulous; tidy; smart; nimble; quick.

Sgeinmeachd, *s. f.* Garrulousness; tidiness; smartness; nimbleness.

Sgeinmeil, *a.* (sgeinm-amhuil.) Garrulous; tidy, neat, tasteful in dress.

Sgéinne, *s. f.* Pack-thread.

Sgeinneadh, idh, *s. m.* An eruption; a gushing forth; a sally; a bouncing; a sliding.

Sgeir, *s. f.* (Skir-os, *a rocky isle in Greece.*) A rock, a cliff; a rock in the sea; a sharp flinty rock. O sgeir thirim bha sùil 's a glaodh, *from a dry rock she looked and cried.—Oss. Fin. and Lor.* *N. pl.* sgeirean.

Sgeireach, *a.* (*from* sgeir.) Rocky, cliffy, flinty.

Sgeireag, eig, *s. f.* (*dim.* of sgeir.) A little rock, a little cliff; a sea rock; a sharp rock; a sharp splinter of a rock; a splinter of a stone. *N. pl.* sgeireagan.

Sgeireagach, *a.* Rocky, cliffy, stony; full of splinters of stones; apt to break into splinters.

Sgeith, *v. a.* (*Lat.* sateo. *Ir.* sceith.) Vomit; spew; spawn. *Pret. a.* sgeith; *fut. aff. a.* sgeithidh, *shall spew.* Sgeithibh, agus tuitibh, *spew and fall.—Stew. Jer.*

Sgeith, sgeithe, *s. m.* A vomiting, a spewing; a spawn; the stuff that is vomited; a vomit. Na 'sgeith, *in his vomit.—Stew. Is.* Sgeith rionnaig, *a falling* or *shooting star;* a clammy coagulated substance, somewhat transparent, which is seen on meadows, and vulgarly supposed to be the substance of which a falling star is composed.

Sgéith, *v. a.* Cut out or shape, as cloth. *Pret. a.* sgeith; *fut. aff. a.* sgéithidh.

Sgeith-chosg, *s. m.* An emetic.

Sgeitheach, *a.* Nauseous; causing vomiting; spawning.

Sgeitheadh, idh, *s. m.* A vomiting; a spawning; a vomit; spawn.

Sgeith-rionnaig. See **Sgeith.**

Sgeithrich, *s. f.* A vomit; vomiting.

Sgeithte, *p. part.* of sgéith. Spewed or vomited.

Sgéithte, *p. part.* of sgéith. Shaped. Obair sgéithte, *a task.*

† **Sgeò**, *s. m.* (*Ir. id.*) Understanding.—*Shaw.*

Sgeòc, sgeòic, *s. m.* A long neck; the neck of a bottle or phial.

Sgeòcach, *a.* Long-necked, as a phial or bottle.

Sgeòcag, aig, *s. f.* A long-necked female. *N. pl.* sgeòcagan.

Sgeòcan, ain, *s. m.* (*dim.* of sgeòc.) The neck of a phial or bottle; *in derision*, a long neck.

Sgeòil, *gen. sing.* of sgeul; which see.

Sgeolach, aich, *s. f.* One of the cups of Fingal.

Sgeudach, *a.;* written also *sgeadach;* which see.

Sgeudachadh, aidh, *s. m.* See **Sgeadachadh.**

Sgeudaich, *v. a.* Written also *sgeadaich;* which see.

Sgeul, *gen.* sgeòil *or* sgeile, *s. f.* (*Ir. id.*) A tale; a story; a fable; news; a narrative. Tha mise le d' sgeul fo mhulad, *I am full of grief at thy tale.—Ull.* Choigrich na sgéile truaighe, *stranger of the mournful tale.—Oss.* A deanamh sgeile, *making a tale; telling a tale or falsehood;* also, *narrating, uttering a speech.—Sm.* Air sgeul, *found.—Stew. N. T.* Innis sgeul, *tell a tale, relate a story;* thoir sgeul, *bring news, carry news.*

Sgeulach, *a.* Like a tale; having tales; fond of relating tales. Cha robh sgeulach nach robh breugach, *there never was a tale-bearer who told not some falsehoods.—G. P.*

Sgeulachd, *s. f.* (*Ir. id.*) A tale, a story; a fable; a legend; a history; historical narration; archaiology. Sgeulachda shean bhan, *old wives' tales.—Stew. Tim.* Gun aire thoirt da sgeulachdaibh, *without heeding fables.—Id.*

Sgeulaiche, *s. m.* (*Ir.* sgeulaidhe.) A reciter of tales, fables, or legends; a newsmonger; an historian; an archaiologist. *N. pl.* sgeulaichean.

Sgeul-theachdair, *s. m.* (*Ir. id.*) A tale-bearer. *N. pl.* sgeul-theachdairean.

Sgeun, sgein, *s. m.* (*Ir. id.*) Fright, terror, astonishment; wildness; a mad look. Dh' fhalbh an t-each air sgeun, *the horse ran off in fright.*

Sgeunach, *a.* Timid, skittish, wild, as a horse; apt to run off in fright, as a horse.

Sgeunail, *a.* (sgeun-amhuil.) Pruned, neat, in order.—*Shaw.*

Sgia, *s. f.* See **Sgiath.**

Sgialachd, *s. f.* See **Sgeulachd.**

Sgiamh, *v. n.* and *a.* Squeak, squeal; beautify, adorn.

Sgiamh, sgeimh, *s.* (*Ir.* sciamh.) Beauty; handsomeness, elegance; ornament, dress, decoration; a squeak, a squeal.

Sgiamhach, *a.* (*Ir.* sciamhach.) Beautiful, fair, lovely; handsome, elegant; ornamental; adorned. Sgiamhach mar a ghealach, *fair as the moon.—Stew. Song Sol.* *Com.* and *sup.* sgiamhaiche.

Sgiamhachd, *s. f.* Beautifulness; loveliness; handsomeness; elegance; ornament; the state of being adorned.

Sgiamhaich, *v. a.* Beautify, adorn, bedeck, dress, clothe. *Pret. a.* sgiamhaich; *fut. aff. a.* sgiamhaichidh.

Sgiamhaiche, *com.* and *sup.* of sgiamhach; which see.

Sgiamhaichead, eid, *s. m.* Beautifulness, handsomeness; increase in beauty.

Sgiamhail, *s. f.* A squall; a mewing, as of a cat; a squeak, any squalling noise.

Sgiamhail, *a.* Squally; squeaking; mewing, as a cat.

Sgiamh-ard, aird, *s. m.* High bloom.

Sgiamh-òradh, aidh, *s. m.* A gilding.

Sgian, *gen.* sgeine *or* sgine, *s. f.* (*Arab.* skian. *W.* ysgien. *Ir.* sgian. *Sax.* sagene.) A knife. *N. pl.* sgeinichean *and* sginichean. Sgian ri d' scornan, *a knife to thy throat.—Stew. Pro.* Sgian-achlais, *a large pocket-knife;* once much worn by the Gael, and put to various uses: it was particularly serviceable in close fight. Sgian bearraidh *or* sgian bhearraidh, *a razor;* sgian bùird *or* sgian bhùird, *a* *table-knife;* sgian collaig *or* sgian chollaig *a chopping-knife;* sgian pronnaidh *or* sgian phronnaidh, *a chopping-knife;* sgian pheann, *a pen-knife;* sgian phinn, *a pen-knife.*

SGIAN-ADHAIRCEACH, *a.* Sharp-horned, as a sheep.

SGIAN-ADHAIRCEACH, ich, *s. f.* A name given to a sheep with sharp horns.

SGIAP, *v. a.* Sweep off; carry off with celerity; pass over with celerity; skip. *Pret. a.* sgiap; *fut. aff. a.* sgiapaidh. Sgiap e leis e, *he swept it off with him.*

SGIAP, *s. m.* A sweep; swift motion; a skipping.

SGIAPACH, *a.* Sweeping; moving with celerity; skipping.

SGIATH, sgeithe, *s. f.* (*Ir. id.*) A wing or pinion; a wing of a house or of an army; a shield, target, or buckler; shelter, protection. Sgiath iolair, *an eagle's wing.* Sgiath chòlainn mo dheagh Oscair, *the shield of my brave Oscar's comrade.—Oss. Gaul.* Feadh bholg a sgeithe, *around the boss of his shield.—Oss. Dargo. N. pl.* sgiathan, *wings.* Air tuilteach gaoithe sgaoil i sgiathan, *on a flood of wind she spread her wings.—Id.*

Gr. σκαιὰ, *a left hand,* and σκιὰ, *shade. Corn.* sgeth, *shadow. Ir.* sciath, *shield, wing. Nor.* skia, *a cloud.*

SGIATHACH, *a., from* sgiath. (*Ir. id.*) Winged, as a bird; winged, as a house; shielded; having shields; giving shelter or protection; streaked with white. Gach eun sgiathach, *every winged fowl.—Stew. Gen. ref.*

SGIATHACH, aich, *s. m.* A cow with white streaks on her side.

SGIATHAIBH, *d. pl.* of sgiath. Air sgiathaibh gaoithe, *on the wings of wind.—Ull.*

SGIATHAN, ain, *s. m.* A fan.

SGIATHAN, *n. pl.* of sgiath. Wings; shields, targets, or bucklers.

SGIATHANACH, aich, *s. m.* A native of the Isle of Skye.

SGIATHANACH, *a.* Winged; belonging to Skye; of Skye. An t-eilean Sgiathanach, *the Isle of Skye; the winged island.*

The name of this island has given room to much ingenious conjecture. Mr. Toland, in his History of the Druids, supported by his very ingenious editor, Mr. Huddleston, as well as by Dr. Smith of Campbeltown, are disposed to trace the name to a remote antiquity, and will have it that the island was so called, from its containing the famous winged temple of Apollo, which he is said to have had among the Hyperboreans. *Sgiath* is a pure Celtic term, signifying *wing.* In support of the conjecture of these eminent antiquarians, it has been justly observed, that ὑπερβόρειοι, *Hyperboreans,* was a name given to the islanders or Hebridians by the ancient mariners, from their being so far north from the Gades or the Straits of Gibraltar. Diodorus Siculus, too, in describing the Hyperboreans of the isles (not those of the Continent who inhabited the northern parts of Europe from Scythia, or Tartary and Russia, westward to Scandinavia, or Sweden and Norway inclusive), says, that "of all the other deities they worshipped Apollo the most"—Τον Απολλω μαλιστα των αλλων θεων παρ' αυτοις τιμᾶσθαι.—*Lib.* ii. *cap.* 130. Unquestionably this is a proof that the Hyperboreans (the Boireadbach) did worship Apollo; and the striking resemblance of the Celtic *grian,* sun, and *Grannus,* one of the names of that divinity, may be mentioned as affording additional corroboration. Respecting the winged Hyperborean temple, there are the ruins of a spacious edifice still shewn in the Isle of Skye, which is supposed to be the remains of the building in question. It cannot be doubted that such a building did exist. Eratosthenes, already mentioned, one of the most learned chronologers, and one of the most accurate geographers of his time, speaking of Apollo's arrow, with which he slew the Cyclops, and in honour of which one of the northern constellations (*saighead, sagitta,*) has been named, says of the arrow, Εκρυψε δε αυτο εν Ὑπερβορεοις ου και ὁ ναος ὁ πτερινος, *He hid it among the Hyperboreans, where there is a winged temple.* But πτερινος here presents a little barrier; as ναος πτερινος may be either a *winged* temple or a temple *made of wings;* πτερινος being translatable either way. This difficulty Mr. Toland *flies* over cleverly, and says, if he (Eratosthenes) meant the former, the ruins correspond with the epithet πτερινος; if the latter, where can feathers be found in such abundance and variety as among the western islands, where many of the inhabitants pay their rent with them, and have profit besides?

Others will have it, that the island received its name from the Norwegians, after their conquest of it and the neighbouring isles; and that it signifies the cloudy island, from the Norse *skia,* a cloud. The least learned opinion on this subject is the most probable; which is, that the isle was so called from its northern promontories, Waterness and Toterness, which shoot out into the sea, and exhibit to mariners the appearance of wings.

SGIATH-CHATHA, *s. f.* A battle shield. Ciod ach do sgiath-chatha mo dhìdean? *what but thy battle-shield is my defence.—Oss.*

SGIATH-SHÙILEACH, *a.* (*Ir. id.*) Wall-eyed.

† SGIB, *s. f.* A hand, a fist.

SGIBEACH, *a.* Spruce, trim, tidy, neat. Gu sgrideil sgibeach, *lively and spruce.—Macint.*

SGIBEARNAG, eig, *s. f.* A hare.—*Shaw.*

SGIBHEAL, eil, *s. m.* Eaves of a roof.—*Shaw.*

SGIBID, *s. f.* A pastime, by the Lowlanders called *tig.*

SGIG. See SGEIG.

SGIL, *s. m.* Skill, knowledge, learning; skilfulness; *also,* the process of shelling grain.

SGIL, *v. a.* Shell grain, separate grain from the husk. *Pret. id.; fut. aff.* sgilidh.

SGILDAIMHNE, *s. m.* A minnow.—*Macd.* and *Shaw.*

SGILEAM, *s.* See SGEILM.

SGILEIL, *a.* Skilful.

SGILLEAG, eig, *s. f.* A small pebble.—*Shaw.*

SGILLINN, *s. f.* A shilling; a penny. Sgillinn Albannach, *a Scotch penny;* sgillinn Shassunach, *a shilling.* Gun uiread is sgillinn, *without so much as a penny.—Mac Co.* Da sgillinn is bonn sea, *twopence halfpenny. N. pl.* sgillinnean.

Germ. schilling. *Anglo-Sax.* scylling. *Franconian,* scelling. *Sax.* schillingh.

SGILM, *s. f.* See SGEILM.

SGILMEIL, *a.* See SGEILMEIL.

SGIMHEAL, eil, *s. m.* A penthouse.

SGIMILEAR, eir, *s. m.* A scambler; an intruder. *N. pl.* sgimilearan.

SGIMILEARACHD, *s. f.* Scambling, impertinent; intrusion.

SGINEADH, idh, *s. m.* A leap, a skip.—*Shaw.*

SGINEAG, eig, *s. f.* (*Ir.* sgineog.) A flight.

SGINEAL, eil, *s. m.* (*Ir. id.*) A leap, a skip, a start.

SGINEALACH, *a.* Leaping, skipping, starting.

SGINICHD, *s. f.* A squeezing, a pressing, a hugging with force.

SGINICHD, *v. a.* Squeeze, press, hug with force. *Pret. id.; fut. aff.* sginichdidh.

SGIOB, *v. a.* Sweep quickly away. More properly *sgiap;* which see.

† SGIOB, sgib, *s. m.* (*Ir. id. Dan.* skib.) A ship.

SGIOB, *s.* See SGIAP.

SGIOBACH, *a.* Like a ship or boat; having ships or boats; of ships or boats; *also,* tidy, spruce, trim.

SGIOBADH, aidh, *s. m.* A ship's crew or company; a boat's crew.

SGIOBAIDH, *a.* Tidy, neat, spruce; trim in person.

SGIOBAIR, *s. m.,* sgiob-fhear. (*Du.* schipper.) A pilot, skipper, or helmsman; a master of a ship. *N. pl.* sgiobairean.

SGIOBAIREACHD, *s. f.* The business of a pilot, skipper, or helmsman.

SGIOBAL, ail, *s. m.* (*Ir.* sciobal, *barn. Heb.* schibal, *an ear of corn.*) A barn, a granary. *N. pl.* sgiobalan, *barns.*

Sgìobal, ail, *s. m.* A garment, mantle, or vestment; the skirt of a mantle; the fold of a mantle. Thairis tha i sgaoileadh a sgiobail, *over him she spreads her mantle.—Oss. Cathula.* Air sgiobal na gaoithe, *on the skirts of the wind.—Oss. Duthona.*

Sgiobalach, *a.* (*from* sgiobal.) Having barns or granaries, of barns or granaries; mantled, robed; having a long garment or folding robe; skirted, as a garment.

Sgiobalta, *a.* Tidy, neat, spruce, trim, tight, active. Gu sgiobalta, *tidily.*

Sgiobaltachd. Tidiness, neatness, spruceness, trimness; tightness; activity.

Sgiobarnag, aig, *s. f.* A hare.

Sgiobul, uil, *s. m.* See **Sgiobal**.

Sgiogair, *s. m.* A jackanapes. *N. pl.* sgiogairean.

Sgiogaireachd, *s. f.* The behaviour of a jackanapes.

Sgiol, *v. a.* Shell grain; separate corn from the husk. *Pret. a.* sgiol; *fut. aff. a.* sgiolaidh.

Sgioladh, aidh, *s. m.* A shelling of grain.

Sgiolam, aim, *s. f.* A loquacious, forward girl; a tale-telling person. See **Sgeilm**.

Sgiolamail, *a.* (sgiolam-amhuil.) See **Sgeilmeil**.

Sgiolan, *s. pl.* Groats, hulled barley.

Sgiolladh, aidh, *s. m.* Decidence.

Sgiolta, *a.* and *part.* Shelled or separated from the husk, as grain; light, nimble; neat, spruce, trim; active; bald. Gràn sgiolta, *hulled grain*; am buicean sgiolta, *the light young roe.—Macint.* Gillean sgiolta nan comhdach, *striplings neat in their attire.—Mac Co.*

Sgioltachd, *s. f.* Lightness, nimbleness; neatness, trimness; activity.

Sgiomlair, *s. m.* A frequent intruder on one's hospitality. *N. pl.* sgiomlairean.

Sgiomlaireachd, *s. f.* Frequent intrusion on one's hospitality.

Sgiop, *s. f.* A scoop.

Sgiorbha, *s. m.* Gall.

Sgiord, *v. a.* Squirt, purge. *Pret.* sgiord; *fut. aff.* sgiordaidh.

Sgiordach, *a.* Squirting, purging.

Sgiordan, ain, *s. m.* A syringe, a watergun.

Sgiorr, *v. n.* (*Ir.* sciorr.) Slip, stumble, slide; run a risk.

Sgiorrach, *a.* Running a risk, escaping narrowly, fool-hardy; apt to slip or stumble.

Sgiorradh, aidh, *s. m.* (*Dan.* skeer, *befall.*) An accident, a mischance; a risk, sudden danger; harm, mischief.

Sgiorrail, *a.* (sgiorr-amhuil.) Accidental, risking, calamitous; mischievous.

Sgiorran, ain, *s. m.* A stumbler; one who runs a risk; a slight risk; a slip, a slight accident.

Sgiorr-fhocal, ail, *s. m.* A random expression, an ill-timed expression, a *lapsus linguæ.*

Sgiorrta, *a.* (*Ir.* sgiortha.) Slipped, fallen.

Sgiorrtachd, *s. f.* Frequent risking; fool-hardiness, liability to accident.

Sgiort, sgiorta, *s. m.* (*Swed.* skiorrte. *Dan.* skiorte, *a shirt.*) A skirt. Sgaoil mi mo sgiort, *I spreading skirt.—Stew. Ez. N. pl.* sgiortan, *skirts.—Stew. Nah.*

Sgiort, *v. a.* Skirt, edge, border. *Pret. id.*, *fut. aff.* sgiortaidh, *shall* or *will skirt.*

Sgiortach, *a.* Skirted, having a long skirt, like a skirt; bordered. Geal sgiortach, *white-skirted.—Macdon.*

Sgiortachadh, aidh, *s. m.* A skirting, a bordering, the act of furnishing with a skirt or border.

Sgiortadh, aidh, *s. m.* A skirting, a bordering; a skirt, a border.

Sgiortaich, *v. a.* Skirt, border. *Pret. id.*, *fut. aff.* sgiortaichidh, *shall skirt.*

Sgìos, *s. m.* Fatigue, weariness, lassitude, toil. A chlann an sgìos! *ye sons of toil.—Oss. Gaul.* Ar saothair 's ar sgios-ne, *our labour and fatigue.* Written also *sgìtheas.*

Sgioth, *s. m.* A partition of wattled rods.—*Shaw.*

Sgiothas, ais, *s. m.*, *contracted* sglos, which see.

Sgiothlaich, *s. f.* A haunch.—*Shaw.*

Sgìre, *s. f.* A parish. More frequently written *sgìreachd.*

Sgìreachd, *s. f.* (*Sax.* scyre, *shire.*) A parish. Cruinneachadh sgìreachd, *the gathering of a parish.—Old Song. N. pl.* sgìreachdan.

Sgìreachdail, *a.* (sgìreachd-amhuil.) Parochial, belonging to a parish.

Sgìreachdair, *s. m.* A parishioner. *N. pl.* sgìreachdairean.

Sgistear, eir, *s. m.* A prater, a talkative fellow; a droll. *N. pl.* sgistearan.

Sgistearachd, *s. f.* Prating, drollery.

Sgite, *s. f.* (*Ir. id.*) The fish called maiden-ray.

Sgìth, *a.* Tired, fatigued, weary, wearied. Tha mi sgìth 's mi leam fhéin, *I am weary and alone.—Old Song.* Seachd sgìth, *quite tired.*
Arm. scuith. Corn. squyth *and* skèth. *Ir.* scith *and* sgith.

Sgitheach, sgìtheche, *s. f.* A blackthorn, a thorn, a brier, a thicket of blackthorn. Sgìtheach an fhàsaich, *the thorn of the wilderness.—Stew. Jud.* Reas sgìthche, *a blackthorn bush.*

Sgìtheachadh, aidh, *s. m.* A tiring, a fatiguing, a growing weary or fatigued. Air sgìtheachadh, *fatigued.*

Sgìtheas, *s. m.* Fatigue, weariness, lassitude. *Contracted* sgios, which see.

Sgìthich, *v. a.* and *n.* Tire, weary, fatigue, grow tired, weary, or fatigued. *Pret. a.* sgìthich, *fut. aff. a.* sgìthichidh. Sgìthich sibh e, *you have wearied him.—Stew. Mal.* Na sgìthich d' a smachdachadh, *grow not weary of his correction.—Stew. Pro.*

Sgìthichte, *p. part.* of sgìthich. Tired, wearied, fatigued.

Sgiuganaich, *s. f.* Whimpering. Thòisich e air sgiuganaich, *he began to whimper.*

Sgiulta, *a.* See **Sgiolta**.

Sgiultachd, *s. f.* See **Sgioltachd**.

Sgiurdan, ain, *s. m.* A squirt, a syringe.

† **Sgiurlong**, oing, *s. m.* (*Ir. id.*) A fugitive, a deserter.—*Shaw.*

Sgiùrs, *v. a.* Scourge, whip, lash; scare or scatter suddenly, persecute; pursue. *Pret. a. id.*, *fut. aff. a.* sgiùrsaidh, *shall* or *will scourge.* Sgiùrsaidh e gach mac, *he scourges every son.—Stew. Heb.*

Sgiùrs, *s. m.* A scourge. See **Sgiùrsadh**.

Sgiùrsach, *a.* Scourging, lashing, persecuting; inclined to scourge, lash, or persecute; like a scourge or lash, like a persecution; of a scourge or lash, of a persecution.

Sgiùrsadh, aidh, *s. m.* (*Ir.* sciùrsa.) A scourging, a whipping, a lashing; a persecuting, a scourge, a whip or lash, a persecution. Sgiùrsadh na teanga, *the scourge of the tongue.—Stew. Job.* Ruith sgiùrsadh, *running the gauntlet.*

Sgiùrsadh, *pret. pass.* of sgiùrs. Was scourged, 3 *sing.* and *pl. imper.* sgiùrsadh e, sgiùrsadh iad, *let him scourge, let them scourge.*

Sgiùrsadh, (a), *inf.* and *p. part.* of sgiùrs; which see.

Sgiurt. See **Sgiort**.

Sgiut, *v. a.* Scatter. *Pret. a.* sgiut; *fut. aff.* sgiutaidh, *shall scatter.*

Sglàbh, sglaibh, *s. m.* (*Fr.* esclave.) A slave; a bondsman. *N. pl.* sclàbhan.

SGLABHAICHE, *s. m.* A slave. *N. pl.* sglabhaichean.

SGLÀBHAIDHEACHD, *s. f.* Slavery; servitude.

SGLAIGEAN, ein, *s. m.* A draught tree; the beam of a wain.

SGLAMH, *v. a.* (*Ir. id.*) Seize violently or greedily; grasp; snatch; clutch. *Pret. id; fut. aff. a.* sglamhaidh.

SGLÀMH, *v. a.* Scold; use abusive language; wrangle. *Pret. id.; fut. aff. a.* sglàmhaidh, *shall scold.*

SGLAMHACH, *a.* Greedy; snatching; grasping; clutching; apt to seize greedily or graspingly. Gu sglamhach, *greedily.*

SGLÀMHACH, *a.* Abusive; scolding, wrangling; foul-mouthed.

SGLAMHACHD, *s. f.* Greediness; inclination to grasp, snatch, or clutch greedily.

SGLÀMHACHD, *s. f.* Abusiveness; a habit of scolding or wrangling; abusive language.

SGLAMHADH, aidh, *s. m.* A seizing violently; a grasping or snatching greedily; a clutching; a greedy grasp or snatch, a clutch.

SGLÀMHADH, aidh, *s. m.* A scolding; an abusing; a wrangling; a scold; abuse; a wrangle.

SGLAMHAICH, *v. a.* Engross to one's self; monopolize.

SGLAMHAID, *s. m.* (*Ir. id.*) A glutton.

SGLAMHAIR, *s. m.* A greedy fellow, a grasper, a snatcher; a usurper.

SGLÀMHAIR, *s. m.* A scolder, an abusive, foul-mouthed fellow. *N. pl.* sglamhairean.

SGLAMHAIREACHD, *s. f.* Greediness; a propensity to grasp, snatch, or clutch; usurpation.

SGLÀMHAIREACHD, *s. f.* Abusiveness; scolding, wrangling.

SGLÀMHRACH, *a.* Abusive; scurrilous; scolding, wrangling.

SGLAMHRADH, aidh, *s. m.* Verbal abuse; a scold; a harsh reprimand; a wrangle; ribaldry. Is e fhuair a sglamhradh, *he got himself abused* or *scolded.*

SGLAMHRUINN, *s. f.* Verbal abuse; a scold; a harsh reprimand; a person who is addicted to scolding.

SGLAMHRUINNEACH, *a.* Abusive; scurrilous; apt to scold or rebuke harshly.

SGLEAD, *s. m.* A slate. Tigh sglead, *a slated house. N. pl.* sgleadan. See also SCLEAD.

SGLEADACH, *a.* Slated; slaty; abounding in slates. Written also SCLEADACH.

SGLEADAIR, *s. m.* A slater, a tiler; a slate-quarrier. *N. pl.* sgleadairean.

SGLEADAIREACHD, *s. f.* The occupation of a slater; a slate-quarry.

SGLEAFART, airt, *s. m.* A slap or blow with the open hand.

SGLEAFARTAICH, *v. a.* Strike with the open hand.

SGLEAMHAS, ais, *s. m.* A scroyle; a term expressive of much personal contempt.

SGLEAMHASACH, *a.* Scroylish; mean.

SGLEAMHRAIDH, *s. m.* A stupid, untidy fellow; a low, ignorant fellow; a bumpkin. *N. pl.* sgleamhraidhean.

SGLEAMHSA, *s. m.* A mean fellow.

SGLEAP, sglèip, *s. m.* Ostentation; awkwardness.

SGLEAPACH, *a.* Ostentatious; vaunting; awkward. Gu sgleapach, *ostentatiously.*

SGLEAPAIR, *s. m.* An ostentatious fellow; a silly vaunter; an awkward, sprawling fellow. *N. pl.* sgleapairean.

SGLEAPAIREACHD, *s. f.* Ostentatiousness; silly vaunting; awkwardness.

SGLEAT, *s. m.* A slate. *N. pl.* scleatan. Tigh scleat, *a slated house;* craig sgleat, *a slate-quarry.*

SGLEATACH, *a.* Slated, slaty; abounding in slates; thin, as a slate or flag.

SGLEATAIR, *s. m.* (sgleat-fhear.) A slater, a tiler; a slate-quarrier. *N. pl.* sgleatairean.

SGLEATAIREACHD, *s. f.* The business of a slater; the employment of house-slating; a slate-quarry; a slate-work.

SGLEÒ, *s. m.* A vapour or mist; shade, darkness; idle talk, boasting, rodomontade; verbiage; romance, falsehood; high puffing, pompous words, fustian; a spectre; a struggle; misery, compassion. Written also *scleò;* which see.

SGLEÒID, *s. m.* and *f.* A sloven, a slattern, a drab or slut; filth; a silly fellow. *N. pl.* sgleòidean.

SGLEOIDEACH, *a.* Like a sloven, drabbish, sluttish, filthy; silly. Gu sgleòideach, *drabbishly. Com.* and *sup.* sgleòidiche, *more* or *most drabbish.*

SGLEÒIDEIL, *a.* (sgleoid-amhuil.) Slovenly, drabbish, sluttish; filthy; silly.

SGLEINNSEARD, *s. m.* A kind of scon. *N. pl.* sgleannsardan.

SGLIGEAN, ein, *s. m.* A speckled or spotted creature.

SGLIGEANACH, *a.* Speckled, spotted.—*Shaw.*

SGLIURACH, aich, *s. f.* A slattern, a slut; a gossip; a whore.

SGLIURACHD, *s. f.* Sluttishness; gossiping; whorishness.

SGLOINGEAN, ein, *s. m.* Snot, snivel, mucus; a term of personal contempt.

SGLOINGEANACH, *a.* Snotty, snivelling.

SGLOINGEANACHD, *s. f.* Snottiness; a habit of snivelling.

SGLONGACH, *a.* Slimy, mucous.

SGLONGAID, *s. f.* Snot, snivel, mucus; a term of personal contempt.

SGLONGAIDEACH, *a.* Snotty, snivelling, mucous.

SGLONGAIDEACHD, *s. f.* Snottiness; a habit of snivelling.

SGOB, *v. a.* Pluck from; tug, pull; scoop out. *Pret. id.; fut. aff. a.* sgobaidh.

SGOBACH, *a.* Plucking, tugging, scooping; apt to pluck.

SGOBADH, aidh, *s. m.* A plucking, a tugging, a pulling; a pluck, a tug, a pull.—*Macfar.*

SGOBALLACH, aich, *s. m.* A piece, a morsel.—*Shaw.*

SGOCH, *v. a.* Make an incision.

SGOCH, *s. m.* A cut; a slit; an incision.

SGOCHACH, *a.* Full of cuts, slits, or incisions; causing cuts or slits.

SGÒD, sgòid, *s. m.* Conceit, airiness, affectation; vanity, foppery, pride; lordliness; command, rule; a lappet; the corner of a cloth; the sheet of a sail; the corner of a sail. Ainnir gun sgòd, *a maid without conceit.*—*R.* Cainnt gun sgòd, *language without affectation.*—*Mac Lach.* Fuidh d' sgòid, *under thy rule.*—*Macint.* Crann sgòid, *a ship-boom.*

SGÒDACH, *a.* Conceited, airy, vain, affected, foppish, proud, lordly.

SGÒDAG, aig, *s. f.* A conceited girl; an airy or affected female; a coquette. *N. pl.* sgòdagan.

SGÒDAIL, *a.* (sgòd-amhuil.) Conceited, airy, affected, foppish, proud, showy.

SGÒDAN, ain, *s. m.* (*dim.* of sgòd.) A corner of a cloth; a sheet of a sail.

SGÒID, *gen. sing.* of sgòd; which see.

SGÒID, sgòide, *s. f.* A shirt; a lappet.

SGÒIDEAG, eig, *s. f.* A vain, airy girl; a coquette. *N. pl.* sgòideagan.

SGÒIDEAGACH, *a.* Vain, airy, as a girl; coquettish; showy.

SGÒIDEAS, eis, *s. m.* Vanity, airiness; conceit, foppery; show, pageantry.

SGÒIDEASACH, *a.* Vain, airy, conceited, foppish; flirting; showy; formal; fond of pageantry.

SGÒIDEIL, *a.* (sgòid-amhuil.) Vain, airy, conceited, foppish; flirting; showy; formal; fond of show or pageantry.

Sgoignean, ein, *s. m.* A fan.

Sgoil, sgoile, *s. f.* (*Ir.* scoil. *Corn. Arm.* scol. *Lat.* schol-a.) School; education. Cha 'n 'eil sgoil aig, *he has no education;* tigh sgoile, *a schoolhouse;* tighe na sgoile, *the schoolhouse;* maighstir sgoile, *a schoolmaster.*

Sgoileam, eim, *s. m.* Loquacity, prattle; impertinent garrulity.

Sgoileamach, *a.* Loquacious; prattling; impertinently garrulous.

Sgoilear, eir, *s. m.* (sgoil-fhear.) A scholar, a student; a schoolman. Deagh sgoilear, *a good scholar.*

Arm. scolaer *and* scolyer, *a scholar. Corn.* skylur. *Ir.* scoilair.

Sgoilearach, *a.* Scholastic, learned, like a scholar.

Sgoilearachd, *s. f.* Scholarship, learning, education.

Sgoilearan, *n. pl.* of sgoilear. (*Corn.* skylurion. *Ir.* scoilairean.) Scholars; students.

Sgoileisteach, *a.* Scholastic.

Sgoilmrich, *v.* Chatter, prate.

Sgoilmrich, *s. f.* Chatter, prating.

Sgoil-oide, *s. m.* A schoolmaster; an usher.

Sgoilt, *v. a.* and *n.* Split, rive; cleave; burst, crack. *Pret. a.* sgoilt; *fut. aff. a.* sgoiltidh, *shall split; fut. sub.* sgoilteas, *shall cut.* An ti a sgoilteas fiodh, *he who cleaves wood.—Stew. Ecc. Fut. pass.* sgoiltear, *shall be split.* Sgoiltear na gleannta, *the valleys shall be cleft.—Stew. Mic.* Sgoiltidh suil a chlach, *an evil eye will split a stone.—G. P.*

Sgoilte, *a.* and *p. part.* of sgoilt. Split, riven, cleft; burst, cracked.

Sgoilteach, *a.* Splitting, riving, cleaving; bursting, cracking; causing to split or burst; apt to split.

Sgoilteadh, 3 *sing.* and *pl. imper.* of sgoilt.

Sgoiltean, ein, *s. m.* (*from* sgoilt.) A splinter, a cleft; a billet of wood; a slit; the half of a square neckerchief; a slit stick used by children to throw pebbles with.

Sgoiltear, *fut. pass.* of sgoilt. Shall be split or riven; shall burst.

Sgoiltear, eir, *s. m.* A splitter of wood. *N. pl.* sgoiltearan.

Sgoinnear, *a.* Heedful.—*Shaw.*

Sgoithean, ein, *s. m.* The prime or best part of any thing.

Sgoitiche, *s. m.* A mountebank; a quack. *N. pl.* sgoitichean.

Sgoitidheachd, *s. f.* Quackery.

† **Sgol**, sgoil, *s. m.* (*Ir.* sgol. *Islandic*, skiola.) A skull.

Sgolag, aig, *s. f.* and *m.* An olive-tree; *also*, a rustic, a servant. In the last two senses it is more frequently written *sgalag.*

† **Sgol**, sgoil, *s. m.* Loud laughter.

Sgolaisteach, *a.* (*from* sgoil.) Scholastic.

Sgolb, *s. m.* A spray or wattle used in thatching a house; a splinter; a prick or prickle; a skirmish or fight with knives or dirks; a doubt.

Sgolbach, aich, *s. m.* A spray or wattle used in thatching houses.

Sgolbach, *a.* Prickly, prickled; splintered; splintering.

Sgolbanach, aich, *s. m.* A youth, a stripling.—*Shaw. N. pl.* sgolbanaich.

Sgolbanta, *a.* Thin, slender; apt to break into splinters.

Sgolbantachd, *s. f.* Thinness, slenderness; aptness to break in splinters.

† **Sgol-ghàire**, *s. f.* Loud laughter; a horse-laugh.

Sgolt, sgoilt, *s. m.* (*Ir.* sgoilt.) A split, a slit, a cleft, a rent. *N. pl.* sgoltan.

Sgoltach, *a.* Splitting, slitting, cleaving, riving; apt to split, cleave, rive, or burst.

Sgoltadh, aidh, *s. m.* A splitting, a slitting, a cleaving, a rending, a riving; a bursting; a split, a slit, a cleft, a rent, a rift; a burst. *N. pl.* sgoltan; *d. pl.* sgoltaibh. Ann an sgoltaibh na creige, *in the clefts of the rock.—Stew. Song Sol.*

Arm. squeltren, *the noise of splitting wood.*

Sgoltadh, (a), *inf.* and *pr. part.* of sgoilt. To split; splitting.

Sgomhal-sgarach, *a.* Astride, astraddle.—*Shaw.*

Sgonn, sgoinn, *s. m.* A dunce; a trifler; a prater.

Sgonnag, aig, *s. f.* A hasty word; a *flatus.*

Sgonnair, *s. m.* A dunce; a trifler, a whiffler; a prater; a rascallion. *N. pl.* sgonnairean.

Sgonnaireachd, *s. f.* The behaviour of a dunce or trifler; trifling, whiffling, prating.

Sgonnasach, *a.* Trifling, whiffling, prating.

Sgonnasachd, *s. f.* A habit of trifling, whiffling, or prating.

Sgonn-bhalach, aich, *s. m.* A dunce, a trifler, a rascallion. *N. pl.* sgonn-bhalaich.

Sgonn-labhair, *v.* Prate, blab foolishly.

Sgonn-labhairt, *s. f.* Prating, blabbing.

Sgonnsa, *s. m.* A sconce.

Sgor, *v. a.* Scarify, scratch, erase; lance; cut in pieces.

Sgòr, sgoir, *s. m.* A rock, a cliff; a hidden sea-rock; a notch or mark made by a sharp instrument; a stud of horses or mares.—*Shaw.* Written also *scor.*

Island. sgòra, *a cut* or *notch. Ir.* scor. *Dan.* skaar. *Swed.* skaer, *scattered rocks. Germ.* schor, *high.*

Sgorach, *a.* Scarifying, erasing; rocky, cliffy; full of notches.

Sgoradh, aidh, *s. m.* A scarifying, an erasing, a scratching, a scoring; a scarification, an erasure; a scratch, a score.

Sgoradh, (a), *inf.* and *pr. part.* of sgor; which see.

Sgoranach, aich, *s. m.* A young man, a stripling. *N. pl.* sgoranaich.

Sgor-bheann, -bheinn, *s. f.* A cliffy rock, a blasted rock, a rocky mountain, a projecting cliff. See also *scor-bheann.*

† **Sgor-chailbhe**, *s. f.* (*Ir. id.*) The epiglottis.—*Shaw.*

Sgor-éild, *s. m.* A hill frequented by roe-deer; an upland rock.—*Ull.*

Sgor-fhiacail, -fhiacla, *s. m.* A buck-tooth. *N. pl.* sgor-fhiaclan, *buck-teeth.*

Sgor-fhiaclach, *a.* Buck-toothed.

Sgorn, sgoirn, *s. m.* A throat, windpipe, gullet. *N. pl.* sgornan. An scornan fosgailte, *their throats open.—Sm.* Sgorn srathrach, *the pin* or *peg of a straddle.—Shaw.*

Sgornach, aich, *s. m.* A throat, a windpipe, or gullet.

Sgornan, *n. pl.* of sgorn. Throats, windpipes, or gullets; it is also rendered as the singular number.

Sgorthanach. See **Sgoranach.**

Sgòt, sgòit, *s. m.* Conceit. More frequently written *sgòd;* which see.

† **Sgot**, sgoit, *s. m.* (*Ir. id. Eng.* scot. *Dan.* skot, *tax.*) A shot or reckoning; part or portion of a reckoning.

Sgotan, ain, *s. m.* A little flock.—*Macfar. Voc.*

Sgoth, *v. a.* (*Ir. id.*) Pull.

Sgoth, *s. m.* A small boat; a skiff; a flower; a son; the prime or best part of any thing; a disease. Imich ad sgoth, *depart in thy skiff.—Oss. Gaul.* Sgoth-long, *a yacht.*

Sgothadh, aidh, *s. m.* A pull.

Sgothag, aig, *s. f.* A small yacht, a cutter.

Sgoth-long, luing, *s. f.* A yacht. *N. pl.* sgoth-longan.

Sgrabach, *a.* (*Ir. id. Dan.* scrape, *a reproof.*) Rough, shaggy; rugged; rare.

Sgrabachan, ain, *s. m.* Roughness.

Sgreabhag, aig, *s. f.* A crust, a scab.

Sgrabanach, *a.* Rough, shaggy; rugged; rare, scarce.—*Shaw.*

Sgrabanachd, *s. f.* Roughness, shagginess; ruggedness.

Sgragall, aill, *s. m.* Tinfoil, goldleaf; a spangle.

Sgragallach, *a.* Like tinfoil or goldleaf; spangled.

Sgraideach, *a.* Diminutive; of a shabby exterior.

Sgraidshàbh, *s.* A hand-saw.

Sgraideag, eig, *s. f.* A diminutive female; an ugly female. *N. pl.* sgraideagan.

Sgraideagach, *a.* Ugly and diminutive, as a little, ugly female.

Sgraidean, ein, *s. m.* An ugly little fellow.

Sgraideanach, *a.* Diminutive and ugly; having an ugly diminutive person.

Sgrailleadh, idh, *s. m.* Offensive language.

Sgraing, sgrainge, *s. f.* A frown, a gloom; a forbidding look; a gloomy appearance. Aghaidh gun sgraing, *a face without a frown.—Old Song.*

Sgraingeach, *a.* Frowning, gloomy; having a frowning or forbidding visage.

Sgraingean, ein, *s. m.* A fellow with a frowning or gloomy visage.

Sgràist, sgràiste, *s. m.* and *f.* (*Ir. id.*) A sluggard, a slothful person. *N. pl.* sgraistean.

Sgràisteach, *a.* Sluggish, slothful, indolent. *Com.* and *sup.* sgràistiche.

Sgràisteachd, *s. f.* (*Ir. id.*) Sluggishness, slothfulness, indolence.

Sgràisteag, eig, *s. f.* A sluggish or slothful young female, a sloven.

Sgràistealachd, *s. f.* Sluggishness, slothfulness, slovenliness.

Sgràisteil, *a.* (sgràist-amhuil.) Sluggish, slothful, indolent. Gu sgraisteil, *sluggishly.*

Sgrait, *s. f.* A rag. *N. pl.* sgraitean *or* sgraiteachan.

Sgraiteach, *a.* (*from* sgrait.) Ragged, tattered, shabby. Gu sgraiteach, *raggedly.* *Com.* and *sup.* sgraitiche.

Sgraiteachd, *s. f.* (*from* sgrait.) Raggedness, shabbiness.

Sgraiteag, eig, *s. f.* A ragged female; a shabbily-dressed female. *N. pl.* sgraiteagan.

Sgraitean, ein, *s. m.* A ragged fellow; a shabbily-dressed fellow. *N. pl.* sgraiteanan.

Sgraith, *s. f.* A turf; a green sod; greensward.

Sgraithte, *p. part.* of sgrath. Peeled; pared, as a surface; stripped of bark or covering; excoriated.

Sgram, *v. a.* Wipe off.

Sgrath, *v. a.* and *n.* Peel; pare, as a surface; strip off, as bark or any covering; excoriate. *Pret. a.* sgrath; *fut. aff. a.* sgrathaidh, *shall peel.*

Sgrath, *s. m.* (*Eng.* †scraw.) A peel, skin, or rind of any thing; the bark of a tree; the coat of an onion; a scale; a turf; a green sod; greensward.

Sgrathach, *a.* Having a peel, skin, or rind; having many skins or coats, as an onion; having a strong skin or rind; peeling, excoriating.

Sgrathaich, *v. a.* Peel, skin; pare, as a surface; strip off, as bark; a coat or covering; excoriate.

Sgrathaichte, *p. part.* of sgrathaich. Peeled, skinned; pared, as a surface; stripped of bark, coat, or covering; excoriated.

Sgrathail, *a.* Peeling, paring; destructive; tearing.

Sgreab, *s. m.* A scab, a crust, or scurf; mange, itch.

Sgreabach, *a.* Scabbed, crusted; mangy, itchy; affected with mange or itch.

Sgreabhal, ail, *s. m.* A favour given by a newly-married couple; an annual tribute of threepence, paid at the command of the monarch by the petty princes of Ireland to St. Patrick.

Sgreach, *v. n.* (*Ir.* sgriach.) Shriek, screech, scream; whoop; cry with a loud and shrill voice; crunk. *Pret. a.* sgriach, *shrieked; fut. aff. a.* sgreachaidh.

Sgreach, *s. m.* A shriek, a screech, a piercing cry, a scream. Leig i sgreach aisde, *she shrieked.*
Island. skraeka. *Dan.* skraek. *Swed.* skrik *and* skrika. *Dan.* skrige. *Corn.* skriga. *Ir.* screachadh.

Sgreachach, *a.* Shrieking, screeching, screaming; apt to shriek or screech.

Sgreachadh, aidh, *s. m.* A shrieking, a screeching, a screaming; a whooping; a shriek, a screech.

Sgreachag, aig, *s. f.* (*from* sgreach.) A jay; *also*, a shrill-voiced female. *N. pl.* sgreachagan. Sgreachag oidhche, *an owl.—Stew. Is.* Sgreachag-choille, *a jay; the corvus glandericus* of Linnæus. Sgreachag reilge, *an owl.*

Sgreachagach, *a.* Like a jay; of jays.

Sgreachail, *s. f.* Shrieking, screeching; a screaming; a crunking. Is ann ort tha 'n sgreachail! *how you do shriek!*

Sgreachan, ain, *s. m.* (*from* sgreach.) A person who shrieks; a person with a shrill voice; a vulture. Sgreachan criosach, *a vulture;* sgreachan iongnach, *a vulture.*

Sgread, *s. m.* (*Ir. id.*) A shriek, a scream; a harsh, shrill sound; a grating sound; a creaking noise; a crashing or clashing noise; a squall; a bawling.

Sgread, *v. n.* Shriek, screech, scream; make a harsh, shrill sound; creak; clash; squall.

Sgreadach, *a.* Shrieking, screeching; creaking; making a grating noise; squalling; crashing; clashing.

Sgreadachan, ain, *s. m.* A little squalling creature; a squalling child.

Sgreadadh, aidh, *s. m.* A shrieking, a screeching; a creaking, a grating; a squalling; clashing; a shriek, a screech; a creak; a grating noise; a squall.

Sgreadag, aig, *s. f.* A shrieking female; a shrill-voiced female; sour drink.

Sgreadail, *s. f.* A shrieking, a screaming; a loud creaking; a grating noise; a crashing or clashing noise. Taibhse a sgreadail, *spectres shrieking.—Oss. Gaul.* Screadail an lanna, *the clashing of their swords.—Oss. Conn.*

Sgreadair, *s. m.* (sgread-fhear.) A crier; a bawler; one with a shrill voice.

Sgreadalach, *a.* Shrieking, screaming, bawling, crying; creaking, grating, clashing.

Sgreadan, ain, *s. m.* The noise of cloth when tearing; a grating noise, a clashing noise; a bawler; a shrill-voiced fellow. Cruaidh a sgreadan air cruaidh, *steel grating on steel.—Oss. Fing.*

Sgreagan, ain, *s. m.* (*Ir. id.*) Hard, rocky ground.

Sgreaganach, *a.* Bleak, barren; hard, rocky. Talamh sgreaganach, *hard, rocky ground.*

Sgreamh, sgreimh, *s. m.* Disgust; a disgusting object, a disgusting sight; abhorrence, loathing. Ghabh e sgreamh, *he took a disgust.*

Sgreamhail, *a.* (*i. e.* sgreamh-amhuil.) Disgusting, abominable.

Sgreamhaileachd, *s. f.* Disgustfulness, abominableness.

† **Sgreapal**, ail, *s. m.* A scruple in weight.—*Shaw.*

† **Sgreapalach**, *a.* In scruples of weight.

† **Sgreastadh**, aidh, *s. m.* Destruction.

Sgreat, *s. m.* Disgust, abhorrence, abomination.

Sgreatachd, *s. f.*, contracted for *sgreataidheachd;* which see.

Sgreataidh, *a.* Disgusting, abhorrent, abominable; terrible, dreadful, horrible. Bu sgreataidh an namh e, *he was a dreadful enemy.—Oss. Corm.*

Sgreataidheachd, *s. f.* Disgustfulness, abhorrence; abomination; dreadfulness, horribleness, frightfulness.

Sgreath, *s.* See Sgreamh.

Sgreathail, *a.* Disgustful, abhorrent, abominable; dreadful, horrible, frightful.

Sgreig, *v. a* Fry.

Sgréitidh, *a.* See Sgreataidh.

Sgreiteachd, *s. f.*, contracted for *sgreitidheachd.* See Sgreatachd.

Sgriach, *s.* See Sgreach.

Sgriachail, *s. f.* See Sgreachail.

Sgribhinn, *s. f.* A rugged slope; a rugged, sloping shore.

Sgribhinneach, *a* Having rugged slopes; having rugged, sloping shores

Sgribhisg, *s.* Notes, comments

Sgrid, sgride, *s. f.* A voice; a breath; a breath of life, a sign of life; a breath of air.

Sgrideil, *a.* (sgrid-amhuil.) Lively, vivacious, sprightly. Gu sgrideil sgibeach, *lively and spruce.—Macint.*

† **Sgrin**, sgrine, *s. f.* (*Ir. id. Dan* skrin) A shrine.

Sgriob, *v. a* Scratch; scrape; furrow; comb or curry, as a horse; engrave, write; carve *Pret. a* sgriob, *fut. aff a* sgriobaidh Mar charraig a sgriob an dealan, *like a rock furrowed by lightning.—Oss. Fin. and Lor.*

Sax. screapan. *Du.* scrobben. *Swed.* scrap.

Sgriob, *s m* (*Ir. id*) A scratch, a scrape; a furrow; a cart-rut; an itching of the lip, superstitiously supposed to precede a feast, or a kiss from a favourite; a short excursion. Sgriob croinn, *the furrow of a plough*, thoir sgriob mu 'n cuairt, *take a turn round, take a circuit*, sgriob dibhe, *an itching of the lip supposed to precede a dram;* sgriob pòig, *an itching of the lip supposed to precede a kiss*

Sgriobach, *a.* Scratching, scraping; furrowing, prone to scratch.

Sgriobach, aich, *s m* The itch, mange, scurvy Duine aig am bheil sgriobach, *a man who has the scurvy —Stew. Lev. ref*

Sgriobachan, ain, *s. m.* (*from* sgriob) A wooden fire-shovel; a kind of rake without teeth, a scraper

Sgriobadan, ain, *s m.* (*from* sgriob) A scraper, a nutmeg-grater.

Sgriobaidh, *fut. a.* of sgriob Shall or will scratch

Sgriobair, *s m.* (*Ir. id*) A scraper, a scratcher, a grater; a graving tool.

Sgriobaireachd, *s. f.* Continued scraping or scratching, working with a graving tool.

Sgrioban, ain, *s m.* (*from* sgriob.) A currycomb, a hoe; a wool-card; a rake; a scraping. Gheibh cearc an sgriobain rud-eigin, *the scraping hen will get something —G P.*

Sgriobar, *fut pass* of sgriob. Shall be scratched.

Sgriobh, *v. a.* Write, record; compose; engrave *Pret. a.* sgriobh; *fut. aff. a.* sgriobhaidh, *shall write.* Sgriobh sios, *write down, record, register.*

Gr. γραφω. *Lat.* scribo *Swed.* skrifva. *Arm* scriva

Sgriobh, *s. m.* Writing, penmanship; composition, engraving.

Sgriobhach, *a.* Fond of writing; writing, penning, engraving.

Sgriobhadair, *s m* A writer, a clerk, a notary. *N. pl.* sgriobhadairean.

Sgriobhadh, aidh, *s. m.* (*Ir.* scrid.) A writing, a composing, an engraving; writing, penmanship, hand-writing. B'e 'n sgriobhadh sgriobhadh Dhé, *the writing was the writing of God —Stew. Ex.* Lamh-sgriobhaidh, *a hand-writing*, fà-sgriobhadh, *an appendix.*

Sgriobhadh, *pret. pass* of sgriobh. Was written. Also, 3 *sing.* and *pl. imper.* Scriobhadh e, iad, *let him* or *them write.*

Sgriobhainn, *s f.* A bill; a writ, evidence.

Sgriobhainnear, eir, *s. m* (*Arm.* scrivagner.) A scrivener, a notary, a clerk, a writer.

Sgriobhair, *s m* (sgriob-fhear) A writer, a clerk, a penman. *N pl* sgriobhairean.

Sgriobhaireachd, *s f* The business of a writer, clerk, or notary, the profession of writing; penmanship.

Sgriobhar, *fut pass* of sgriobh Shall be written It is also used impersonally

Sgriobh-lochd, *s. m* A fault in writing —*Macd.*

Sgriobhta, Sgriobhte, *p part* of sgriobh. Written, recorded, registered

Arm scrivet, scrihuet, *and* scrit, *writing. Du.* and *Germ* shrift

Sgriobhtach, *a* Writing; fond of writing; writing frequently

Sgriobtuir, *s* (*Arm.* scritur *Ir.* scriobhtuir.) Scripture. *N. pl* sgriobtuirean

Sgrioch, *s* A scratch; a score, a line; a furrow.

Sgrioch, *v. a.* Scratch, score, notch, draw a line or furrow *Pret id.*, *fut aff. a.* sgriochaidh.

Sgriodan, ain, *s m.* The channel of a mountain-torrent, a mountain-torrent

Sgriodanach, *a* Full of channels; like a mountain; like a torrent; of torrents.

Sgrios, *s f.* (*Ir.* scrios) Destruction, ruin, a slip, a stumble.

Sgrios, *v. a.* (*Ir.* scrios) Destroy, ruin, abolish, cut off, consume, annihilate; slip, stumble; sweep the surface from any thing. *Pret. a.* sgrios; *fut. aff. a* sgriosaidh, *shall destroy.* Sgrios thu an daoi, *thou hast destroyed the wicked.—Sm* Sgrios mo chos, *my foot slipped.*

Sgriosach, *a.* Destructive, ruinous, wasteful; slippery: apt to stumble Mar uisge sgriosach, *like destructive water. —Stew Pro. ref* *Com* and *sup* sgriosaiche

Sgriosadair, *s m* (*Ir* scriostair) A destroyer, a pillager, one who lays waste *N. pl.* sgriosadairean.

Sgriosadaireachd, *s f.* Destroying, continued pillaging or wasting; annihilation

Sgriosadh, aidh, *s m.* A destroying, a wasting; a pillaging, a sweeping off the skin or surface of any thing, a slipping, a stumbling, destruction, waste, pillage; a slip, a stumble

Sgriosadh, (a), *pr. part* of sgrios Destroying, wasting, pillaging; slipping, stumbling

Sgriosail, *a.* (sgrios-amhuil) Destructive, ruinous

Sgriosar, *fut. pass.* of sgrios Shall or will be destroyed, abolished, or cut off

Sgriosta, *p. part* of sgrios.

Sgriotachan, ain, *s. m* A little squalling creature, an infant.

Sgròb, *v. a.* Scratch, scrape; scrawl. *Pret. a.* sgròb, *fut. aff a.* sgrobaidh

Sax screopan. *Swed.* scrap *Du* scrobben, *rub hard*

Sgròbach, *a* Scratching, scraping, scrawling

Sgròbadh, aidh, *s. m* A scratching, a scraping, a scrawling; a scratch, a scrawl.

Sgròban, ain, *s m.* (*Ir.* scroban.) The crop of a bird, a craw, a gizzard

Sgrobanach, *a.* Having a crop, craw, or gizzard, having a large crop, craw, or gizzard; of crops, craws, or gizzards.

Sgrobha, *s. m.* A screw; a corkscrew. *N. pl.* sgrobhan *and* sgrobhachan.
Dan scruve *Swed.* skruf. *Du.* scroeve.

Sgrobhach, *a.* Twisted like a screw; spiral

Sgrodha, *s m.* A screw; a corkscrew. *N pl.* sgrodhan *and* sgrodhachan. Written also *sgrobha.*

Sgrodhach, *a.* Twisted like a screw; spiral. Written also *sgrobhach*

Sgrog, sgroig, *s m.* A ludicrous term for the head or neck; a hat; a bonnet; a skull-cap.

Sgrogach, *a.* Having a hat or bonnet.

Sgrogag, aig, *s. f.* An old cow; an old ewe; an oath

Sgrogan, ain, *s. m* A skull-cap.

Sgroig, *gen sing* of sgrog

Sgroigean, ein, *s m* A ludicrous term for a short neck, or for a short-necked person; a hat; a bonnet

Sgròill, *v. a.* Peel, pare, excoriate *Pret. a* sgròill, *fut aff a* sgròillidh.

Sgròille, *s f.* A peeling, a paring; any part that is torn off a skinned or coated surface.

Sgròilleach, *a* Peeling, paring; excoriating; in peels or in parings

Sgròilleag, eig, *s f* (*dim* of sgròille) A peel or peeling, a paring, any part that is torn from a coated surface *N pl* sgròilleagan

Sgròilleagach, *a.* In peelings or parings; apt to peel, pare, or excoriate

Sgroth, *s m* A turf, a sod, a sward; a pull or tug; a rough handling; a scouring; a long rhyme.

Sgrothach, *a.* Turfy; apt to pull, tug, or handle roughly, scouring

Sgrothadh, aidh, *s m* A turf, a sod, or sward, a pull or tug, a scouring.

Sgrubail, *a* Scrupulous, hesitating —*Macfar. Voc*

Sgrubair, *s m.* (*Dan* srubet, *mean*) A scrub, a niggard *N pl* scrubairean Cha sgrubair e 's an tigh òsda, *he is not a scrub in the alehouse* —*R*

Sgrubaireachd, *s f.* Scrubbishness, niggardliness

Sgruball, aill, *s m* A scruple or doubt. *N pl.* sgruballan

Sgruballach, *a* Hesitating, scrupulous

Sgrud, *v. a* (*Ir* scrud) Examine, catechise, question, pry, search. *Pret. id*; *fut. aff. a.* sgrudaidh

Sgrudachadh, aidh, *s m* An examining, a questioning; a prying, a searching; an examination, a search, investigation.

Sgrudach, *a* Examining, catechising, questioning; prying, searching, inquisitive; investigating

Sgrudadh, aidh, *s. m.* (*Ir* scrudadh) An examining, a catechising, a questioning; a prying, a searching; an examination, a search; inqusitiveness, curiosity, investigation.

Sgrudadh, (a), *pr part.* of sgrud Examining, questioning, prying, searching A sgrudadh gach ionaid, *searching every place.*—*Stew Pro.*

Sgrudaich, *v a* Examine, catechise, or question, search, pry, investigate

Sgrudaichte, *p part* of sgrudaich. Examined, catechised; searched, investigated

Sgruibleach, ich, *s m.* Rubbish, refuse

Sgruigean, ein, *s. m* A ludicrous term for the neck; a short-necked person Rug i air a sgruigean air, *she grasped him by the neck* —*Old Song*

Sgruigeanach, *a* Short-necked

Sgruinge, *s f.* An ensign.—*Shaw*

Sgruit, *s. m* and *f.* A thin, meagre person; an old, hard-featured person; an old man; a niggard. *N. pl.* sgruitean.

Sgruiteach, *a* Thin, meagre in person; niggardly.

Sgrut, sgruit, *s. m.* A thin, meagre fellow; an old man; a niggard.

Sgrutach, *a.* Thin, meagre, old; niggardly. *Com.* and *sup.* sgrutaiche.

Sguab, *v a* (*Ir* scuab. *Arm* scuabaf) Sweep; brush; bind up in sheaves, move quickly or with a sweep. *Pret a* sguab, *swept*, *fut aff a.* sguabaidh, *shall sweep.* An àrach is tric a sguab e, *oft did he sweep the battle-field.* —*Oss. Duthona*

Sguab, sguaib, *s. f.* A besom; a floor-brush; a sheaf of corn; sweepings; refuse. Mar leus ann an sguaib, *like a flame on a sheaf;* sguab aodaich, *a cloth-brush;* sguab làir, *a floor-brush*, sguab urlair, *a floor-brush* Sguab deannaich, *a whisk.*—*Macd. N. pl.* sguaban.
Ir sguab, *a besom. Arm.* sguba *Span.* escoba. *Old Celtic,* skybo *and* skuba *Lat.* scopa, *a besom.*

Sguabach, aich, *s. f.* A besom or floor-brush. *N. pl.* sguabaichean

Sguabach, *a* (*from* sguab) Sweeping, brushing, cleansing; moving with a sweep.

Sguabachan, ain, *s m* A little brush or besom.—*Shaw.*

Sguabadh, aidh, *s m* (*Ir id*) A sweeping, brushing; a sweeping motion; sweepings; refuse.

Sguabadh, (a), *inf* and *pr. part.* of sguab To sweep or brush; sweeping, brushing, moving with a sweep Meòir a sguabadh na cruit, *fingers [sweeping] moving nimbly along the harp-strings* —*Oss. Trathal.*

Sguabag, aig, *s. f* (*dim.* of sguab.) A little besom or brush; a whisk; a little sheaf; a female that moves with a sweeping gait. *N. pl.* sguabagan.

Sguabaichean, *n pl* of sguabach, which see.

Sguab-ghàbhaidh, *s. f.* The name of the banner of Oscar the son of Ossian.

Sguabhair, *s. f* A square.—*Macdon. N pl* sguabhrean.

Sguab-lion, lîn, *s f* (*Ir.* scuab-lion) A sweep-net, a drag-net *N. pl.* sguab-liontan.

Sguabta, *p. part.* of sguab Swept, brushed

Sguaibte, *p part* of sguab. Swept, brushed.

Sguain, sguaine, *s. f.* and *m.* (*Ir id*) A train, a tail; a swarm, a crowd

Sguair, *s. m.* A squire, an esquire.

Sgùd, sgùid, *s. m* A scout or spy. *N pl* sgudan, *spies.*

† **Sgud**, sguid, *s m* A ship
Arm squytt, *a boat. Swed* scutta, *scudding, as a ship.*

Sgud, *v. a* (*Swed* skudda, *shake off.*) Cut off at a blow; hew down; walk quickly *Pret a* sgud; *fut. aff. a* sgudaidh, *shall cut off*

Sgùdach, *a.* Spying; apt to spy

Sgudach, *a* Cutting of, hewing down at a blow; walking quickly or with a sweeping gait

Sgùdachd, *s. f* Espionage; a habit of spying; frequent spying, or scouting

Sgudadh, aidh, *s m* A cutting off at a blow; a hewing down at a blow, a sweeping gait.

Sgudag, aig, *s f* A female with a sweeping gait; an active tidy girl

Sguibhir, *s m* A squire, an esquire —*Shaw* and *Macd.*

Sguiblich, *v. a* Tuck up *P. part.* sguiblichte, *tucked*

Sguileach, ich, *s. f.* Rubbish, refuse —*Shaw*

Sgùilean, ein, *s m* A large coarse basket made of willow twigs; a hamper

Sguille, *s. f* (*Ir. id*) A kitchen-boy; a scullery.

Sguilleir, *s. m* A scullery.

Sguir, *v. a.* and *n.* (*Ir. id*) Cease, leave off, terminate; settle. *Pret. a.* sguir, *ceased*, *fut aff a.* sguiridh, *shall cease.* Sguir ruaig an·tuirc, *the boar-chase has ceased*—*Oss. Derm.* Nach sguir thu? *wilt not thou leave off?*

Sguiridh, *fut. aff. a.* of sguir. Shall or will cease.

Sguirt, *s. f.* (*Swed.* skiorrte, *a skirt.* *Ir* sguirt.) A lap, a skirt; a shirt, a smock—*Macd.*

Sgùirte, *p part* of sgùr. Scoured, cleansed, purged.

Sguirteach, *a* Skirted; having a skirt, shirt, or smock.

Sguite, *s. m.* A wanderer.

Sguiteal, eil, *s m.* A scuttle.

Sguitlear, eir, *s. m.* A low menial drudge.

Sguitlearachd, *s. f.* Menial drudgery, scullery

Sguits, *v. a* Switch; lash, thrash, beat; dress flax. *Pret. a.* sguits, *switched*, *fut. aff. a* sguitsidh, *shall switch.*

Sguitseach, *a.* Switching, lashing, thrashing, beating; dressing, as flax.

Sguitseach, ich, *s. f.* A wanton female, a prostitute. *N. pl.* sguitsichean.

Sguitseadh, idh, *s. m.* A switching, a lashing, a whipping, a thrashing, a beating; a dressing, as of flax. Deireadh mo sgéil mo sguitseadh, *the end of my tale will be whipping,* i. e. *confess and be hanged.*—*G. P.*

Sguitsear, eir, *s m.* A beetle; a thrasher, a dresser of flax

Sgulan, ain, *s m.* An old man; a little old man.—*Shaw.*

Sgùlan, ain, *s. m* A hamper; a coarse basket; a creel. Written also *sgùlean.*

Sgùm, *s. m.* Scum, froth

Sgùmach, *a.* Scummy, frothy

Sgumadair, *s. m.* One who scums or skims; a scummer. *N. pl* sgumadairean.

Sgumadaireachd, *s. f* The business of scumming; continued scumming.

Sgumhara, *a.* Fat.

Sguman, ain, *s. m.* An untidy head-dress, a rick of corn—(*Macfar. Voc*), the train tied up; a skimming-dish.—*Shaw*

Sgumrag, aig, *s. f.* A young slattern, a cinder-wench; a sort of fire-shovel. *N. pl.* sgumragan

Sgumragach, *a.* Slovenly; like a slattern

Sgùr, *v. a.* (*Goth.* scur) Scour, burnish; cleanse, purge, purify. *Pret. a.* sgùr; *fut. aff. a.* sgùraidh, *shall purge*

Sgur, *s. m.* Ceasing, leaving off, desisting; termination, conclusion. Buidheachas gun sgur, *thanks without ceasing.*—*Stew. Thess* Gun sgur, *unceasingly.*

Sgùrach, *a.* Scouring; burnishing, cleansing, purging, purifying.

Sgurachd, *s f* A ceasing, a leaving off, a finishing, a conclusion.

Sgùradh, aidh, *s m.* A scouring; a burnishing; a cleansing, a purging, a purifying; a scour. Claidheamh nach d' fhuair a sguradh, *a sword that never was scoured*—*Macint.*

Sgùrainn, *s. f* Scouring-water; water in which much soap has been dissolved in the course of clothes-washing; by the Scotch Lowlanders called *graith.*

Sgur-eild, *s.* A hill which roes frequent, an upland rock.—*Ull.*

Sgurr. See Sgorr.

Sgut. See Sgud.

Sgùt, sgùit, *s. m* See Sgùd.

Sgutach, *a* Cutting off at a blow; hewing down at a blow; moving nimbly; walking with a sweeping motion Written also *sgudach.*

Sgùtachd, *s f* Espionage; a habit of spying; frequent spying or scouting.

Sgutachd, *s. f.* Continued cutting; a sweeping gait, nimble motion.

Shàbh, *pret. a.* of sàbh. Sawed.

Shàbhail, *pret a.* of sabhail; which see.

Shabhal, ail, *s m*, *asp. form* of sabhal. Barn. O shabhal, *his barn*

Shàbhaladh, (a), *inf* of sabhail. To save.

Shaibhir, *a*, *asp. form* of saibhir, which see.

Shaibhreas, eis, *s. m.*; *asp form* of saibhreas. Riches O shaibhreas, *his riches.*

Shaighead, eid, *s. f*, *asp. form* of saighead, which see

Shàil, shàlach, *s f*, *asp form* of sail A heel Reub a shàil, *his heel was lacerated*—*Oss Derm*

Shaill, *pret a.* of saill. Salted, pickled, seasoned.

Shaillte, *p. part* of saill. Salted, seasoned. See Saill

Shaimh, *a*, *asp form* of saimh; which see.

Shaithich, *pret a* of sàithich Filled, satiated.

Shalach, *a.*, *asp form* of salach; which see

Shalaich, *pret a.* of salaich Defiled, soiled See Salaich.

Shaltair, *pret. a* of saltair. Trampled

Shamhach, *asp. form* of samhach, which see.

Shamhladh, *asp form* of samhladh; which see.

Shamhlaich, *pret. a* of samhlaich; which see.

Shamhradh, *asp form* of samhradh, which see.

Shannt, shainnt, *s m.*, *asp form* of sannt; which see

Shanntach, *a.*, *asp form* of sanntach.

Shanntaich, *pret. a.* of sanntaich; which see.

Shaobh, *a.* See Saobh.

Shaodaich, *pret. a* of saodaich. Drove, as cattle See Saodaich.

Shaoghal, ail, *s. m.*, *asp form* of saoghal; which see

Shaoi, *a.* See Saoi.

Shaoil, *pret.* of saoil, which see.

Shaoileas, *fut sub.* of saòil. Would think. It is also used impersonally. Shaoileas gu b'e Lochlinn a dh'eirich, *it was thought that Lochlin rose*—*Ull.*

Shaoilte, *inflection* of saoil Would think. Shaoilte gum b'oinid e, *one would think him an idiot.*—*Ull*

Shaoir, *asp. form* of saoir, which see.

Shaoithreachadh, (a), *inf.* of saoithrich; which see

Shaor, *pret.* of saor, which see.

Shaor, *asp. form* of saor. See Saor

Shàr, *asp. form* of sàr, which see

Sharachadh, (a), *inf.* of sàraich; which see

Shàraich, *pret.* of sàraich. Oppressed. See Sàraich

Shàraichte, *asp. form* of sàraichte, *p. part.* of saraich, which see.

Shàs, *pret* of sàs; which see.

Shàsaich, *pret. a.* of sàsaich Satiated, glutted

Shàsaichte, *p. part* of sàsaichte, which see

Shàth, *pret. a* of sbàth; which see

Shè, *asp. form* of sè. Six A shè uiread, *six times as much.*

Sheac, *pret. a* of seac. Withered

Sheachd, *asp. form* of seachd. Seven. A sheachd uiread, *seven times the number, seven times as much*

Sheachd, *pret.* of seachd

Sheachran, ain, *s. m.*, *asp. form* of seachran

Shealbhaich, *pret a* of sealbhaich, which see

Shealbhar, *asp form* of sealbhar.

Shealg, *pret.* of sealg, which see.

SHEALGAIRE, *voc. sing.* of sealgaire. See SEALGAIR.

SHEALL, *pret. a.* of seall. Looked, beheld, gazed.

SHEALLADH, aidh, *s. m.; asp. form* of sealladh.

SHEALLAS, *fut. sub.* of seall. Shall look. Tra sheallas i farasd, *when she looks mildly.—Ull.*

SHEALLTUINN, (a), *inf.* of seall. To look. See SEALL.

SHEAMH, *asp. form* of seamh; which see.

SHEAN, *asp. form* of sean. Old. O shean, *of old*; bho shean, *of old.*

SHEANACHAS, ais, *s. m.* See SEANACHAS.

SHEANG, *asp. form* of seang; which see.

SHEAP, *pret. a.* of seap. Sneaked. See SEAP.

SHEAPACH, *a.: asp. form* of seapach; which see.

SHEARBH, *asp. form* of searbh.

SHEARG, *pret. a.* of searg. Withered.

SHEARGACH, *a.; asp. form* of seargach; which see.

SHEARGAICH, *pret. a.* of seargaich. Embittered. See SEARGAICH.

SHEARGTA, *p. part.* of searg; which see.

SHEAS, *pret. a.* of seas. Stood; stopped.

SHEASAMH, *s. m.; asp. form* of seasamh. Standing. Tha mi 'mo sheasamh, *I am standing;* tha thu 'd sheasamh, *thou art standing;* tha e na sheasamh, *he is standing;* tha e na seasamh, *she is standing.*

SHEASAMHACH, *a.; asp. form* of seasamhach.

SHEASG, *asp. form* of seasg.

SHÉID, *pret.* of séid. Blew. Shéid osag o 'n aonach, *a blast from the desert blew.—Oss. Gaul.* See SÉID.

SHEIDEADH, *pret. sub.* of séid. Would blow. Gach osag a sheideadh, *every breeze that would blow.—Oss. Gaul.* Also *pret. pass.* was blown.

SHEILBH, *asp. form* of seilbh; which see.

SHEILEACH, *asp. form* of seileach.

SHEILICH, *pret. a.* of seilich; which see.

SHEILLEAN, ein, *s. m.; asp. form* of seillean; which see.

SHEIMH, *asp. form* of seimh; which see.

SHEINN, *pret. a.* of seinn. Sung.

SHEÒL, *pret. a.* of seòl. Directed, guided, sailed.

SHEÒL, *asp. form* of seòl; which see.

SHEÒLTA, *a.; asp. form* of seolta.

SHEUL, *pret. a.* of seul. Sealed.

SHEUN, *pret. a.* of sheun; which see.

SHIAN, *pret. a.* of sian. Screamed, shrieked.

SHIAP, *pret.* of siap; which see.

SHIAR, *asp. form* of siar. West. See SIAR.

SHIL, *pret.* of sil. Dropped; rained.

SHÌN, *pret. a.* of sìn. Stretched. Shìn an righ a cheum, *the king stretched his pace,* or *hastened.—Oss. Cathula.*

SHINE, *asp. form* of sine, *com.* and *sup.* of sean. Older, oldest. Am fear bu shine, *the oldest. W.* hin.

SHINNSEARAN, *asp. form* of sinnsearan, *n. pl.* of sinnsear; which see.

SHÌNTE, *asp. form* of sìnte, *p. part.* of sìn.

SHIOL, *voc. sing.* of siol. Race. Shiol na leirg, *ye sons of the ocean.—Ull.* Also *asp. form* of siol; which see.

SHIOS, *asp. form* of sios. East; below.

SHIR, *pret.* of sir; which see.

SHIUBHAIL, *pret. a.* of siubhail. Departed, travelled; died; vanished. Shiubhail e, *he died;* shiubhail an dreach, *the vision vanished.—Oss.*

SHIÙIL, *asp. form* of siùil; which see.

SHIUNNSAIR, *asp. form* of siunnsair. A chanter. A shiunnsair, *his chanter.*

SHIURSAICH, *voc. sing.* of siùrsach; which see.

SHLACHD, *pret.* of slachd. Beat, thrash, thump; strike with a batlet.

SHLACHDAINN, *s. f.: asp. form* of slachdainn; which see.

SHLÀINTE, *s. f.; asp. form* of slainte; which see.

SHLÀINTEIL, *asp. form* of slainte. See SLAINTEIL.

SHLÀN, *asp. form* of slàn; which see.

SHLÀNAICH, *pret.* of slànaich. Healed.

SHLAT. See SLAT.

SHLEAGH, *asp. form* of sleagh. A spear. Càireadh gach fear a shleagh, *let each adjust his spear.—Oss. Duthona.*

SHLEIBHTE. See SLÉIBHTE.

SHLEUCHD, *pret.* of sleuchd.

SHLIABH, *asp. form* of sliabh; which see.

SHLIGE, *asp. form* of slige.

SHLIGEACH, *asp. form* of sligeach; which see.

SHLIGHE, *s. f.; asp. form* of slighe; which see.

SHLIGNEACH. See SLIGNEACH.

SHLIOCHD, *asp. form* of sliochd; which see.

SHLIOGARRA, *asp. form* of sliogarra.

SHLIOS, *asp. form* of slios. See SLIOS.

SHLISEAGAICH, *pret.* of sliseagaich. Planed. See SLISEAGAICH.

SHLOC, SHLOCHD. See SLOC or SLOCHD.

SHLOIGH, *asp. form* of sloigh, *n. pl.* of sluagh. See SLUAGH and SLOIGH.

SHLOIGHTIRE, *voc. sing.* of sloightir; which see.

SHLOINN, *asp. form* of sloinn; which see.

SHLUAGH, aigh, *s. m.; asp. form* of sluagh; also *voc. sing. O Shluagh!* an exclamation of surprise, having much the same import with *O dear! O Lord!* See SLUAGH.

SHLUAGHMHOR, *asp. form* of sluaghmhor.

SHLUAISD, *pret. a.* of sluaisd. Shovelled; shoved aside.

SHLUGACH, *asp. form* of slugach.

SHLUGAN, ain, *s. m.; asp. form* of slugan; which see.

SHLUIG, *pret. a.* of sluig. Swallowed. See SLUIG.

SHNÀG, *pret. a.* of snàg. Creeped; sneaked. See SNÀG.

SHNÀGAIRE, *voc. sing.* of snàgair; which see.

SHNAIDH, *pret. a.* of snaidh. Hewed. See SNAIDH.

SHNAIDHTE, *asp. form* of snaidhte; which see.

SHNAIM, *pret. a.* of snaim. Tied, knotted. See SNAIM.

SHNÀMH, *pret.* of snamh.

SHNÀS, *pret. a.* of snàs; which see.

SHNIOMH, *pret. a.* of sniomh. Spun, twisted, See SNIOMH.

SHOC, *asp. form* of soc; which see.

SHOCAIR, *asp. form* of socair; which see.

SHOCRACH, *asp. form* of socrach; which see.

SHOCRAICH, *pret. a.* of socraich. Established, founded, made steady. See SOCRAICH.

SHOGH, *asp. form* of sogh; which see.

SHOILLEIR, *asp. form* of soilleir; which see.

SHOILLSICH, *pret. a.* of soillsich. Illuminated, enlightened, brightened. See SOILLSICH.

SHOIRBHEAS, eis, *s. m.; asp. form* of soirbheas; which see.

SHOITHEAMH, *asp. form* of soitheamh; which see.

SHÒLAS, ais, *s. m.; asp. form* of sòlas; which see.

SHOLUS, uis, *s. m.; asp. form* of solus. Light. See SOLUS.

SHON, *asp. form* of son; which see.

Shonas, ais, *s. m.; asp. form.* of sonas. Happiness. See Sonas.

Shonraich, *pret. a.* of sonraich. Determined, resolved; appointed.

Shonraichte, *p. part.* of sonraich.

Shòr, *pret.* of sòr; which see.

Shrachd, *pret. a.* of srachd; which see.

Shrann, *pret.* of srann; which see.

Shrath, *s. m.; asp. form* of srath.

Shreang. See Sreang.

Shròn, *asp. form* of sròn; which see.

Shruth, *s. m.; asp. form* of sruth.

Shuaicheantas, ais, *s. m.; asp. form* of suaicheantas. A banner. See Suaicheantas.

Shuaimhneas, eis, *s. m.; asp. form* of suaimhneas; which see.

Shuain, *s. f.; asp. form* of suain. Sleep, slumber. O shuain an éig, *from the sleep of death.—Oss. Derm.*

Shuarach, *asp. form* of suarach; which see.

Shuas, *asp. form* of suas.

Shuath, *pret. a.* of suath. Rubbed; stirred about. See Suath.

Shubhach, *a.; asp. form* of subhach; which see.

Shubhachas, ais, *s. m.; asp. form* of subhachas.

Shubhailc, *asp. form* of subhailc.

Shubhailceach, *a.; asp. form* of subhailceach.

Shùg, *pret. a.* of sùg. Sucked; imbibed. See Sùg.

Shuidh, *pret.* of suidh. Sat. See Suidh.

Shuidhich, *pret.* of suidhich.

Shuidhichte, *p. part.* of suidhichte, *p. part.* of suidhich. See Suidhichte.

Shuigeartach, *asp. form* of suigeartach.

Shùil, shùl, *s. f.; asp. form* of sùil.

Shuilbhear, *asp. form* of suilbhear.

Shuim, *s. f.; asp. form* of suim; which see.

Shuinn, *voc. sing.* of sonn. A hero.—*Oss. Derm.*

Shult. See Sult.

Shumain, *asp. form* of sumain; which see.

Shùrdag, *s. f.; asp. form* of sùrdag.

Si, *pers. pron.* (*Ir.* si. *Goth. W.* hi.) She; it. *Si* is never used like *i*, to denote the objective after the active verb. We say, phòs e i, *he married her;* not *phòs e si.*

'Si, (*for* is i.) It is she. 'Si rogha nam ban òga, i, *she is the choice of damsels.—Old Song.*

'Si, (*for* is i, *or* agus i.) And she; as she; whilst she. 'Si seòladh gu triagh nan nial-eide, *whilst she sails to the cloud-covered shore.—Ull.*

Sia, *a.* Six. Sia-deug, *sixteen;* sia thar fhichead, *twenty-six;* sia fichead, *six score;* sia ceud, *six hundred.*

Siab, *v. a.* Wipe off, rub off, cleanse. *Pret. a.* shiab, *wiped; fut. aff. a.* siabaidh, *shall wipe.* A shiabadh a sùl, *to wipe her eye.—Oss. Dargo.*

Siab, *s. m.* A wipe; a rub; a cleansing; a flinching. Thug e siab dha, *he gave him a wipe.*

Siabach, *a.* Wiping; rubbing; cleansing; flinching; sarcastic; cutting.

Siabadh, aidh, *s. m.* The act of wiping; the act of rubbing or cleansing; a wipe, a rub; a cleansing; a flinching.

Siabadh, (a), *pr. part.* of siab. Wiping, rubbing, cleansing.

Siabair, *s. m.* (*from* siab.) A wiper, a rubber, a cleanser; a sarcastic fellow.

Siabh, *v. a.* Written more frequently *siab;* which see.

Siabhach, *a.* More frequently written *siabach.*

Siabhadh, aidh, *s. m.* A wiping, a rubbing, a cleansing; a wipe, a rub. See also Siabadh.

Siabuinn, *gen. sing.* of siabunn.

Siabunn, uinn, *s. m.* Soap. Cha n' fhàgadh siabunn geal i, *soap could not whiten her.—Old Song.*

Chald. savaun, spun, *and* sapon. *Syr.* tsapano. *Arab.* saban, sabun. *Malay.* sabon. *Gr.* σηπων *and* σαπων. *Lat.* sapo. *Dan.* seepe. *Du.* seap *and* soap. *Island.* savun. *Germ.* sepfen. *Turk.* saboun *and* sapoun. *Gipsey language*, sapuni. *Span.* xabon. *Fr.* savon. *Arm.* sabun. *W.* sebon. *Corn.* seapan *and* seban.

Siabunnach, *a.* Soapy; of soap.

Siach, *v. a.* Sprain; filter. *Pret. a.* shiach, *sprained; fut. aff. a.* siachaidh, *shall sprain.*

Siachadh, aidh, *s. m.* A spraining; a sprain; a filtering.

Sia-chearnach, *a.* Hexangular. Written also *sé-chearnach.*

Sia-chearnag, aig, *s. f.* A hexangle; a hexangular figure.

Siad, *pers. pron.* (*Ir. id.*) They. This pronoun is another form of *iad;* but it is not, like *iad*, employed to denote an object after an active verb. This form of the personal pronoun is used in such expressions as the following: Mharbh siad iad, *they killed them;* shrachd siad iad, *they killed them.* The Gael do not say *mharbh iad siad, shrachd iad siad.*

'Siad, (*for* is iad.) It is they; they were the persons.

'Siad, (*for* is iad, *or* agus iad.) And they, as they, or while they.

Siad, *v. n.* Sneak, skulk.

Siadair, *s. m.* A sneaking fellow; a mean-skulking fellow; a looby, a numskull. *N. pl.* siadairean.

Siadaireachd, *s. f.* Sneakingness; meanness; stupidity.

Siadhail, *s. f.* Sloth, sluggishness.—*Shaw.*

Siadhan, ain, *s. m.* A state of confusion; *also, adjectively,* confused, topsy-turvy.

Siaman, ain, *s. m.* See Sioman.

Siamarlan, ain, *s. m.* A factor or land-agent.

Sian, sìne, *s.* (*Ir.* sian, *sound. Lat.* son-us.) A scream, a shriek, a roar; a sound; a voice. *N. pl.* siantan.

Sian, sìne, *s.* A storm, a blast; rain; a charm or spell; an amulet.

Sian, *v. n.* Shriek, scream, yell; roar. *Pret. a.* shian; *fut. aff. a.* sianaidh, *shall shriek.* Shian na taibhsean, *the spectres shrieked.—Ull.*

Sianach, *a.* Screaming, shrieking, yelling; roaring; stormy; showery; like a charm or spell; of charms or spells.

Sianachd, *s. f.* A screaming, a shrieking, a yelling; a roaring; storminess; continued showers or blasts.

Sianaiche, *s. m.* One who screams, shrieks, yells, or roars.

Sianail, *a.* (sian-amhuil.) Screaming, shrieking, yelling; roaring; stormy; showery.

Sianar, *a.* (*for* sianmhor.) Stormy; showery. O mhonadh sianar, *from a stormy hill.—Oss. Tem.*

Sianas, ais, *s. m.* Hate; hating.

Siansach, *a.* Harmonious; melodious; pleasant; *also,* doleful.

Siansadh, aidh, *s. m.* Harmony; melody; pleasantness.

Siantan, **Sianntan**, *n. pl.* of sian; which see.

Siap, *v. a.* Wipe away, rub off; flinch. Written also *siab.*

Siapach, *a.* See Siabach.

Siapadh, aidh, *s. m.* See Siabadh.

Siapunn, uinn, *s. m.* Soap. Written also *siabunn;* which see.

Siar, *adv.* (*Ir. id.*) West; western. Soir na siar, *neither* *east nor west.—Oss. Gaul.* Gu tràigh siar, *to a western shore.—Ull.*

SIAR, *adv.* Obliquely; aside; sideways; onwards. Fuil is fallus a srutha' siar, *blood and sweat running obliquely.—Oss. Cathluno.* Ruith e siar le tartar, *he rushed onwards with a noise.—Old Poem.*

SIAR-SHÙIL, shùl, *s. f.* A squint-eye; an oblique or side look.

SIAR-SHUILEACH, *a.* Squint-eyed.

† SIASAR, air, *s. m.* (*Ir. id.*) A session, the sitting of a court, assizes.—*Shaw.*

SIA-SHLISNEACH, *a.* Six-sided; hexagonal.

SIA-SHLISNEAG, eig, *s. f.* A six-sided figure, a hexagon.

SIAT, *s. m.* A tumour, a swelling; a puffing up.—*Shaw.*

SIAT, *v. a.* Swell; puff up. *Pret. a.* shiat, *swelled; fut.* siataidh, *shall swell.*

SIBH, *pers. pron.* (*Ir. id.*) Ye, you.

SIBHEALTA, *a.* (*Ir. id.*) Civil, obliging, compliant, complaisant, affable, mannerly, courteous. Gu sibhealta, *civilly.* Laochan sibhealta, *a civil lad.—R.* Written also *siobhailt;* which see.

SIBHEALTACHD, *s. f.* (*Ir. id.*) Civility, obligingness, complaisantness, affableness, courteousness.

SÌBHEILT, *a.* More frequently written *siobhailt* or *sìbhealta;* which see.

SIBHRHEILTEACHD, *s. f.* Civility, complaisance, affability. Written also *siobhaltachd* or *sìbhealtachd.*

SIBHSE, *emphatic form* of sibh. (*Ir. id.*) Ye, you.

SIBHT, *s. f.* A shift, a scheme, a plan, a contrivance; industry; a subterfuge.

SIBHTEACH, *a.* Full of shifts, schemes, or plans; contrivant. —*Shaw.*

SIBHTEALACHD, *s. f.* Providentness; contrivance.

SIBHTEIL, *a.* (sibht-amhuil.) Full of shifts or plans; shifting; contrivant; provident.

SIC, SICHD, *s. m.* A sudden personal onset; a sudden effort to take hold of one; a sudden grasping; the inside of the skull. Thug e sichd air, *he made a sudden effort to catch him;* rug e le sic, *he grasped suddenly.—Old Song.*

† SIC, *a.* (*Ir. id. Lat.* siccus.) Dry, parched, droughty.

SICIR, *a.* Prudent; steady; not easily imposed on; sagacious.

SICIREACHD, *s. f.* Prudence; steadiness; sagaciousness.

SÌD, side, *s. m.* and *f.* (*Swed.* siden, *silk. Arm.* seyz. *Du.* zyde.) Silk; weather. Truscan do shìde, *a clothing of silk.—Stew. Pro.*

SID, *s. m.* A lair, as of a bear.

SID, *adv.* (*for* sud.) Yonder, there. This is a North Highland form of *sud,* and by some ranked among the demonstrative pronouns.

SÌDEACH, *a.* Silky, silken.

SÌDEACHD, *s. f.* Silkiness.

SIDHEADH, idh, *s. m.* (*Ir. id.*) A blast.—*Shaw.*

† SIDHEANG, *s. m.* Infamy.

† SIDHICH, *v. a.* Prove.—*Shaw.*

SÌGH, *a.* See SÌTH.

SIGHEANN, sighne, *s. f.* Venison. More frequently written *sitheann;* which see.

SIGHEAR, eir, *s. m.* A mountaineer.

SÌGHICH, *s. m.* and *f.* A fairy. See SÌTHICH.

† SIGHIN, *s. f.* (*Ir. id. Lat.* signum.) A sign, a token.

SIGHINICH, *v. a.* Sign, mark.—*Shaw.*

† SIGIR, *s. f.* Silk.—*Shaw.*

SIGIREUN, *s. m.* A silkworm.

† SIGLE, *s. f.* (*Lat.* sigillum. *Ir.* sigle.) A seal.

† SIGNEAD, eid, *s. m.* (*Ir. id.*) A signet.

SIL, *v. a.* and *n.* Drop; fall in drops, as a liquid; drip; shed; rain. *Pret. a.* shil, *dropped; fut. aff. a.* silidh, *shall drop.* Shil mo chainnt orra, *my words dropped on them.—Stew. Job.* Silidh mo dheòir, *my tears shall fall.—Oss. Taura.* Silidh an là, *the day will rain.*

SIL, sile, *s. f.* (*Gr.* σιαλος, *a spittle.*) A drop; a spittle; an issue. Sil na sul, *a tear, a dropping of the eye.*

SÌL, *gen. sing.* of sìal.

SÌL, sile, *s. f.* A shower; a heavy shower; a grain—(for this last sense, see SÌOL). Breac an t-sìle, *the bird called a wagtail.*

SÌL, *v. n.* Shower; rain in heavy showers. *Pret. a.* shìl, *showered; fut. aff. a.* silidh, *shall shower.*

SÌLEACH, *a.* Rainy, showery. Aimsir shìleach, *showery weather.*

SILEADH, idh, *s. m.* (*Ir. id.*) A dropping, as of a liquid; a shedding; an issuing; a drop; an issue.

SILEADH, 3 *sing.* and *pl. imper.* of sil.

SÌLEADH, 3 *sing.* and *pl. imper.* of sìl.

SILEADH, (a), *pr. part.* of sil. Dropping; raining, showering; shedding; a weeping. A sùil a sileadh, *her tears falling. —Oss. Cathula.* A sileadh dheur, *shedding tears.—Ull.*

SÌLEADH, (a), *pr. part.* Showering heavily.

SILEAG, eig, *s. f.* (*dim.* of sil.) A little drop. *N. pl.* sileagan.

SILEAGACH, *a.* In drops; falling in little drops; dripping.

SÌLEAN, ein, *s. m.* (*dim.* of sìl *or* siol.) A little grain.

SILIDH, *fut. aff. a.* Shall or will drop.

SILIN, *s. f.* A cherry.—*Shaw.*

SILTE, *s. f.* (*Ir. id.*) A drop; a spittle; an issue. *N. pl.* siltean.

SILTEACH, *a.* Dropping, dripping; oozing; tearful; moist; issuing, as matter from a sore; scrofulous; thin; fading. Is iomadh sùil tha silteach, *many an eye is tearful.—Macint.* Cneadh silteach, *a scrofulous issue;* silteach, *fading.—Shaw.*

SILTEACH, ich, *s. m.* A running issue; a scrofulous issue; an oozing; a discharge; flowers; a person afflicted with scrofulous sores. Silteach o fheòil, *an issue from his flesh. —Stew. Lev.* Airson a shiltich, *on account of his issue.—Id.* Laithean a siltich, *the days of her discharge.—Id.*

SILTEACHD, *s. f.* Continued dropping or oozing; a scrofulous habit.

SIMIDE, *s. f.* A mallet, a rammer. *N. pl.* simidean.

SIMIDEACH, *a.* Like a hammer or rammer; of a hammer or rammer.

SIMILEAR, eir, *s. f.* A chimney. Mullach an t-simileir, *the chimney-top.*

SIMONACHD, *s. f.* Simony.

SIMONAICHE, *s. m.* A man guilty of simony.

SIMPLICH, *v. a.* Simplify. *Pret. a.* shimplich, *simplified; fut. aff. a.* simplichidh, *shall simplify.*

SIMPLIDH, *a.* (*Ir. id.*) Simple, plain, unaffected, meek; mean; unalert. Daoine simplidh ciùin, *men meek and mild.—Sm.*

SIMPLIDHEACHD, *s. f.* (*Ir.* simplidheacht.) Simplicity, simpleness; plainness; unaffectedness; meekness; meanness; unalertness. Na biodh simplidheachd oirbh, *let there be no meekness in you.—Macfar.*

SIN, *demons. pron.* That, those, there. An duine sin, *that man;* sin thu, *there you are;* o sin, *since, since that time; thence,* or *from that place;* o sin suas, *from that time forward;* mar sin, *in that way* or *manner;* sin ri radh, *that is to say;* a sin thu! *be off with you;* ciod sin? *what is that?* Sin agad e, *there you have him* or *it;* (*perhaps,* is sin agad e.) Sin thu fhéin, *that is your sort; that is like yourself;* mar sin fhéin, *so and so; just so*, mar sin sios e, *and so on.*

SIN, (a), *adv.* (*Ir. id.*) Then; on that occasion; there, in that place, in that manner. An sin fhéin, *in that very place, on that very occasion* or *time*. Sin mar thainig an gaisgeach, *in that manner came the hero* —*Fingalian Poem*

SIN, *v. a* and *n.* (*Ir. id*) Stretch; lengthen, prolong, grow in stature; extend; lie at full length, reach a thing to another *Pret. a* shin, *fut. aff. a.* sinidh, *shall stretch.* Shininn mo lamh, *I would stretch my hand* —*Old Poem* Sinidh e a laithean, *he will prolong his days.*—*Stew Pro*

SINE, *gen. sing.* of sion; which see

SINE, *s.f.* A blast; stormy weather

SINE, *com.* and *sup.* of sean. Older, oldest

SINE, *s.f.* Age. A shine chas-aodainneach, *wrinkled age* —*Old Song*

SINE, *s f.* An udder. More frequently written *sinne*.

SINEAD, eid, *s. m.* Age; advancement in age A reir an sinead, *according to their* [*birth*] *age*, a dol an sinead, *growing older and older.*

SINEADH, idh, *s m* A stretching, a lengthening, a prolonging, a protracting, extending, a lying at full length; a reclining; a delaying. Do laithean gun dùil ri sìneadh, *thy days without hope of being lengthened* —*Oss Derm* Na shìneadh dlu dh' i, *stretched beside her* —*Ull* Na shìneadh air uileann, *reclining*

SINEADH, (a), *pr part* of sin.

SINGIL, *v. a.* Dress flax, prepare flax for the hatchel, belabour, or give a thrashing *Pret a* shingil; *fut aff. a.* singlidh.

SINGILEAR, eir, *s. m.* One who prepares flax for the hatchel. *N. pl.* singlearan

SINGILEARACHD, *s. f.* The preparing of flax for the hatchel

SINGILTE, *a.* Single; alone, not double; having one plait, unmixed.

SINGILTE, *p. part.* of singil. Dressed or prepared for the hatchel, as flax.

SINGLEADH, idh, *s m.* A preparing of flax for the hatchel; a belabouring, a thrashing.

SINGLIDH, *fut aff. a* of singil.

SINIDH, *fut. aff. a.* of sin. Shall or will stretch See SIN.

SINN, *pers. pron.* (*Ir. id*) We, us Bhuail sinn e, *we struck him*; bhuail e sinn, *he struck us.*

SINNE, *emphatic form* of sinn.

SINNE, *s.f.* An udder, a teat, a pap, a dug. *N. pl* sinneachan.

SINNEACH, *a.* Having large udders or teats

SINNEACH, ich, *s. f.* A wen.—*Shaw*

SINNEAN, ein, *s m.* (*dim.* of sinne.) A little udder, teat, or dug.

SINNSEAR, eir, *s. m* (*Ir.* sinsior) An ancestor *N pl* sinnsearan.

SINNSEARACHD, *s. f.* (*Ir.* sinsireacht) Ancestry; seniority; eldership; a right by succession; descent; progeny Mo shinnsearachd, *my ancestry, my fathers.*—*Stew. Gal* Gun sinnsearachd, *without descent* —*Stew. Heb.*

SIN-SEAN-ATHAIR, *s m* A great-grandfather.—*Macd*

SIN-SEAN-MHATHAIR, *s. f.* A great-grandmother.—*Macd.*

SINTE, *p part* of sin. (*Ir id*) Stretched, lengthened, extended, reached; grown in stature Sinte leat san t-slocad, *stretched with thee in the grave.*—*Ull*

SINTEACH, *a.* Stretching; stretched; long, growing fast in stature; long, tall; straight.

SINTEAG, eig, *s. f.* (*from* sin.) A stride; a long pace; a straight line. *N. pl.* sinteagan

SINTEAGACH, *a* Striding; bounding; bouncing.

SINTIN, (*for* siantan), *n. pl.* of sian, which see

SIOBAG, aig, *s. f* A puff of the mouth, a whiff.

SIOBAID, *s. f.* A scallion, an onion, the plant called *sybou*.

SIOBAIDEACH, *a.* Abounding in scallions, onions, or in sybows; of scallions, onions, or sybows

SIOBANN, ainn, *s. m.* The plant called *sybow.*

SIOBHAG, aig, *s f.* A straw *N. pl.* siobhagan.

SIOBHAGACH, *a.* Abounding in straws, like a straw

SIOBHAILT, *a.* Civil, obliging; affable; mannerly, courteous —*Macint* Gu siobhailt, *civilly*

SIOBHAILTEACHD, *s f.* Civility; affability, mannerliness; courteousness

† SIOBHAS, ais, *s m* (*Ir. id.*) Rage, fury, madness.—*Shaw*

† SIOBHASACH, *a* Raging, furious, mad.

† SIOC, *s m* Frost, the umbilical region.—*Shaw*

† SIOC, *v* (*Ir id. Lat.* sicco, *to dry*) Freeze, dry up, grow hard *Pret. a* shioc; *fut. aff a* siocaidh

† SIOCAICHTE, *part* Frozen, dried up, grown hard; obdurate —*Shaw*

SIOCAIR, *s m* A motive, a reason, a natural; an opportunity —*Shaw*

SIOCHAICH, *v. a* and *n.* Compose, pacify, assuage; grow composed or calm. *Pret a* shiochaich, *fut. aff. a* siochaichidh

SIOCHAICHE, *s m* A peacemaker

SIOCHAIL, *a* Peaceful, peaceable, quiet; causing peace or quietness, prosperous Gu siochail, *peacefully.*

SIOCHAILEACHD, *s. f* Peacefulness; peaceableness; peacemaking.

SIOCHAINNT, *s. f.* (sìth o chainnt.) Silence, tranquillity, peace.

SIOCHAINNTEACH, *a* Silence; silent, tranquil, peaceful.

SIOCHAIR, *s m.* An insignificant person; a diminutive, trifling person, a diminutive creature; a varlet; a brat. A shiochair! *thou brat!* *N. pl* siochairean.

SIOCHAIREACHD, *s f* Personal insignificance; diminutiveness of person or figure

SIOCHATH, *s f.* (sìth o chath.) Peace, tranquillity, silence.

SIOD, sioda, *s f* (*Span* seda.) Silk. Le sgiathaibh sioda, *with wings of silk.*—*Macfar* Truscan do shioda, *clothing of silk* —*Stew Pro. ref.*

SIODACH, *a* Silky, silken

SIODACHD, *s. f.* Silkiness

SIODAIL, *a.* (siod-amhuil.) Silky, like silk

SIOG, sioga, *s. m* (*Ir. id*) A streak, a rick —*Shaw.*

SIOGACH, *a* Streaked, ill-coloured, ill-shaped; inactive

† SIOGAIDH, *s. m.* A fairy; a pigmy *N pl* siogaidhean

† SIOGAIL, *a* (*Ir id.*) Streaked; striped.—*Shaw*

SIOGAISDEACH, *a* Long and shapeless in person, having long limbs, tough

SIOGAISDEACHD, *s f* Shapelessness of person, toughness.

SIOL, sil, *s m.* (*Ir id*) Seed, corn; issue; children, a tribe, a clan. Am an t-sil chur, *sowing time* —*Stew Lev* Eadar do shìol-sa agus a siol-sa, *between thy seed and her seed*, a shìl nam fonn, *ye children of the song*, i e *bards* —*Oss Fing* Siol ginidh, *seed of copulation* —*Stew Lev* Siol-lann, *a granary* *N pl* sioltan, *d pl.* sioltaibh Do shioltaibh, *to seeds* —*Stew. Gal.*

SIOL, *v* Sow, drop; spell; drivel.—*Shaw* *Pret.* shiol, *fut. aff* siolaidh.

SIOL, siola, *s. m.* A gill; a syllable, a dropping; the prow of a ship.

Siolach, *a.* (*from* siol) Having progeny, prolific; having seed; *also, substantively*, offspring, a descendant. Siolach aluinn nan speur, *the handsome offspring of the skies.—Mac Lach.*

Siolachadh, aidh, *s. m.* A filtering, a clarifying; a clarification; a breeding, a generating, a propagating

Siolachan, ain, *s m.* (*Dan* sil, *a hair-sieve Ir.* sioltaghan *and* siolthan, *a strainer*) A strainer, a filterer, a searce.

Sioladair, *s. m* A sower—*Stew. Matt*); a seedsman. *N. pl* sioladairean.

Sioladaireachd, *s f* The employment of sowing, the business of a seedsman

Sioladh, aidh, *s m* A syllable, a gill, a dropping; the prow of a ship —*Shaw*

Sioladh, aidh, *s m.* A breeding, a generating; a sowing; a race, offspring

Sioladh, *v. a* and *n* (*Arm* sizla. *Swed* sila.) Strain, filter, cause to subside; cleanse, as a fluid, tranquillize, subside, settle, as any disturbed fluid, become composed *Pret a* shioladh, *fut. aff a* siolaidh Sioladh m' anam o stri, *let my soul subside from struggle.—Oss. Fing* Sioladh am bainne, *pass the milk through a strainer*; leig leis sioladh, *let it subside.* Written also *siolaidh*

Siolag, aig, *s f* A strainer

Siolag, aig, *s f* (*dim* of siol) A gill. *N. pl.* siolagan

Siolagach, *a* In gills, fond of drams; tippling.

Siolaich, *v. a.* and *n* (*from* siol) Breed, produce, generate, spring, as seed, engender, propagate; be fruitful *Pret. a.* shiolaich, *fut. aff a* siolaichidh. O Dhiarmad shiolaich clann nach gann, *from Dermid sprang a numerous race —Old Song.* Siolaichibh, *propagate, be fruitful — Old Song.*

Siolaidh, *fut aff.* of sioladh, which see.

Siolaidh, *gen. sing.* of sioladh

Siolaidh, *v. a* and *n* (*Arm* sizla *Swed* sila) Strain, filter, clarify, cleanse, cause to subside, settle, as a disturbed fluid; tranquillize, compose; subside, become composed *Pret a* shiolaidh, *fut aff a.* siolaidh Shiolaidh confadh lot gu sìth, *the rage for wounds was changed to peace —Mac Lach*

Siolaidh, *s f* Race, offspring —*Macfar. Voc Also*, a stallion

Siolan, ain, *s m* A strainer, a filter *N pl* siolanan

Siolar, *a* (*for* siolmhor) Abounding in seed, prolific, productive, generative, fruitful.

Siolarnach, *a.* Snoring, snorting —*Shaw*

Siolastair, *s m* More frequently written *seilistear;* which see

Siol-chonnlach, aich, *s m* Fodder.—*Shaw*

Siol-chuir, *v. a.* (*Ir* siolchur) Sow *Pret a.* shiolchuir, *sowed, fut. aff. a.* siolchuiridh, *shall sow* Shiolchuir e san tìr, *he sowed in the land.—Stew Gen P part.* siolchuirte, *sown.*

Siol-chur, -chuir, *s m* Sowing.

Siol-ginidh, *s m* Seed of copulation —*Stew Lev*

Siol-lann, lainn, *s m* A granary.

Siolman, ain, *s m.* Refuse of corn Cha 'n eil ann a 's miosa na siolman, *there is no refuse worse than that of the corn pickle*—(*G. P.*); said of mean gentry

Siolmhoire, *com* and *sup.* of siolmhor, which see.

Siolmhoireachd, *s f.* Fruitfulness, generativeness, productiveness

Siolmhor, *a.* (*Ir.* siolmhar) Abounding in seed; prolific, productive, generative, fruitful. *Com.* and *sup.* siolmhoire.

Siolradh, aidh, *s. m* Breed, race, offspring.—*Shaw.*

Siolraich, *v. a* Breed, generate, propagate. *Pret. a.* shiolraich; *fut. aff. a.* siolraichidh.

Siolruin, *s. f.* A diæresis.

Siolta, *s m.* A teal —*Shaw*, and *Macd.*

Sioltachan, ain, *s. m.* A strainer. More frequently written *siolachan*

Sioltaiche, *s. f.* A goosander; the *mergus serrator* of Linnæus. *N pl* sioltaichean.

Siol-triabh, eibh, *s m.* A family

† **Siolt-shuileas**, eis, *s m.* A running of the eyes.—*Shaw.*

Siomaguad, guaid, *s. m.* Evasion; a shuffle; a subterfuge; equivocation

Siomaguadach, *a.* Evasive, shuffling, equivocating.

Siomaguadachd, *s. f.* A habit of evading, shuffling, or equivocating.

Siomaid, aide, *s. f.* A mallet, rammer, or rolling-pin. *N. pl.* siomaidean

Siomaideach, *a.* Like a rammer, mallet, or rolling-pin.

Sioman, ain, *s. m* A rope of straw or hay; a rope, a cord; *in derision*, a tall shapeless fellow. Grad fhighear na siomain, *quickly are the straw ropes twisted —Macfar.* Corr-shiomain, *an arcuated stick used for making straw ropes.* Cho mear ri ceann siomain, *as merry as a rope's end —G. P.*

Siomanach, *a.* Like a rope of straw or hay; having ropes of hay or straw, as a rick.

Siomanaiche, *s m.* One who makes ropes of hay or straw.

Siomrag, aig, *s f* See **Seamhrag** or **Seamrag**.

† **Sion**, sine, *s f.* A chain, a tie, a bond.

Sion, sine, *s f* A storm, a blast, rain; snow; weather. Daora nan sion, *stormy Dora —Oss. Cath.* Mar chritheach san t-sìne, *like an aspen bitter blast —Ull* Nur thuiteas an t-sion gu tlàth, *when the rain falls gently.—Oss. Fing. N pl* siontan, *storms, d. pl* siontaibh. Tannas air eide' le siontaibh, *a spectre shrouded in storms —Oss. Duthona.*

† **Siona**, *s. m* (*Ir* id) Delay —*Shaw.*

Sionaidh, *s. m* A prince, a lord, a noble; a chief. *N. pl.* sionaidhean.

Sionail, *a* (sion-amhuil) Stormy, blasty; rainy

Sionan, ain, *s* The Shannon, a river in Ireland.

Sion-bhuailte, *part* Weather-beaten.

Sion-bhuailteach, *a* Exposed to the weather.

Sion-bhualadh, aidh, *s m.* A beating of wind or weather.

† **Sionn**, *adv.* In this place, here —*Shaw*

Sionnach, aich, *s m* (*Heb* shinne) A fox, the *canis vulpes* of Linnæus *N pl.* sionnaich, *foxes* Tha tuill aig na sionnaich, *foxes have holes —Stew N T*

Sionnachair, *s m* A fox-hunter *N pl* sionnachairean

Sionnachas, ais, *s m* (*from* sionnach.) Craftiness, low cunning

Sionnachla, *s m.* A weather-gaw.—*Shaw.*

Sionnadh, aidh, *s m* (*Ir id*) A reproof, a rebuke; a scoff.—

Sionnsair, *s m* A chanter, the chanter of a bagpipe. Sgaladh nan sionnsar, *the piercing sound of the chanters.— Old Song N pl* sionnsairean

Sionnsaireach, *a* Having a chanter; like a chanter; of a chanter

Sionnsaireachd, *s f* Chanting; playing on a chanter.

† **Sionradhach**, *a* Single.

† **Sionsa**, *s. m* (*Ir. id*) A censer —*Shaw.*

Sion-steud, *s m* A driving blast. A casgadh sion steuda nan speur, *calming the driving blasts of heaven.—Oss Manos.*

Siontach, *a* Stormy, blasty, rainy, showery; snowy

Siontachd, *s f* Storminess, raininess, showeriness, snowiness.

Siontaibh, *d. pl.* of sion; which see.

Siontan, *n. pl.* of sion. Storms. See Sion.

Sior, *a.* (*Ir. id*) Continual, ever, long, lasting.

This vocable is often prefixed to a word to denote continuance or perpetuity.

Sior, (gu), *adv.* Ever, for ever; continually, eternally. Thuit mo ghrian gu sior, *my sun has set for ever.—Ull.*

Sior-atharrachadh, aidh, *s. m.* Variableness, changeableness; continual fluctuation; continual shifting.

Siorbhai, *s. m.* Thievery, theft.

Sior-bheo, *a.* Everliving; everlasting, evergreen.

Sior-bhraoilich, *s. f.* Continued loud noise, a constant rattling; constant clattering.

Sior-bhualadh, aidh, *s. m.* A continued striking; constant thumping.

Sior-bhuan, *a.* Everlasting, eternal.

Sior-bhuantachd, *s. f.* Eternity of being; eternity of existence.

Sior-bhuantas, ais, *s. m.* Durableness.

Siorcall, aill, *s. m.* (*Ir. id. Lat.* circul-us.) A circle.—*Shaw. N. pl.* siorcallan.

Siorcallach, *a.* Circular; circled.

Siorcallaichte, *p. part.* Circled, encircled, surrounded.

Sior-chainnt, *s. f.* Garrulity, constant prating.

Sior-chainnteach, *a.* (*Ir. id.*) Extremely garrulous; continually talking.

Sior-chainnteach, ich, *s. m.* A constant tattler, a babbler.

Sior-chas, *v. n.* Turn to and again.—*Shaw.*

Sior-chasach, *a.* Running to and fro; walking frequently.

† **Siorda**, ai, *s. m.* A great favour or present.—*Shaw.*

Siordan, ain, *s. m.* A rattling noise; a rustling noise.

Siordanach, *a.* Making a rattling noise, rustling.

Sior-éighe, *s. f.* A continued crying, shouting, or shrieking.

Sior-éigheach, *a.* Crying, shouting, or shrieking continually.

Sior-ghàir, *s. f.* Continued laughter, frequent laughter; continued noise or clamour.

Sior-ghlac, *v. a.* (*Ir. id.*) Gripe; handle roughly, grasp frequently.—*Shaw.*

Sior-ghlac, aic, *s. m.* A gripe, a rough handling; a frequent grasping.

Sior-ghnàth, *s. m.* Continual use; constant habit or practice.

Sior-ghnathaich, *v. a.* Use often, use much; practise frequently. *Pret. a.* shior-ghnathaich; *fut. aff. a.* sior-ghnathaichidh; *fut. pass.* sior-ghnàthaichear.

Sior-iarruidh, *s. f.* Importunity; constant or urgent petitioning.

Sior-iarruidheach, *a.* Importunate, troublesome, by reason of frequent requests or petitions.

Sior-imrich, *s. f.* Transmigration.

Sior-lamhach, *a.* Long-handed.—*Shaw.*

Sior-loisg, *v. a.* Burn perpetually or eternally. *Fut. aff. a.* sior-loisgidh.

Sior-losgach, *a.* Burning perpetually or eternally.

Sior-losgadh, aidh, *s. m.* Everburning; eternal fire.

Sior-mhaireannach, *a.* Everlasting; eternal; immortal; durable.

Sior-mhaireannachd, *s. f.* The state of being everlasting or eternal; immortality; durableness.

Sior-òl, *s.* Hard drinking, frequent drinking.

Sior-osd, *v. n.* Gape or yawn frequently.

Siorrachd, *s. f.* A shire or county, the office of sheriff. Cha n'eil siorrachd do 'n d' théid thu, *there is no shire you can go to.—Old Song.*

Siorradh, aidh, *s. m.* A sheriff.

Siorralach, aich, *s. m.* Broomrape.—*Shaw.*

Siorram, aim, *s. m.* A sheriff.

Siorramachd, *s. f.* A shire or county; the office of sheriff.

Siorruich, *v. a.* (*Ir.* siorraidh.) Eternize, immortalize, perpetuate. *Pret. a.* shiorruich, *eternized*; *fut. aff. a.* siorruichidh, *shall eternize.*

Siorruidh, *a.*, sior-ruith, *ever running.* (*Ir.* siordhaidhe.) Ever, eternal, everlasting. *Asp. form*, shiorruidh. Mar sheilb, *as an everlasting possession.—Stew. Gen.*

Siorruidh, (gu), *adv.* For ever. Gu suthain siorruidh, *for ever and ever.*

Siorruidheachd, *s. f.* Eternity; immortality; perpetuity. O shiorruidheachd, *from eternity.—Stew. Pro.* O shiorruidheachd gu siorruidheachd, *from eternity to eternity.*

Siorsan, ain, *s. m.* Pleasant or good news.—*Shaw.*

Siorsanach, *a.* Slow, tedious, *also, substantively*, a slow, tedious person.

Sior-shileach, *a.* Dropping or dripping continually.

Sior-shileadh, idh, *s. m.* A continual dropping.—*Stew. Pro.*

† **Siort**, *v. a.* Strike. *Pret.* shiort, *struck.*

† **Siortair**, *s. m.* (*from* siort.) An executioner.—*Shaw. N. pl.* siortairean.

Siorthoireas, eis, *s. m.* A request.

Sior-uaine, *a.* Evergreen; *also, substantively*, an evergreen.

Sior-uisge, *s. m.* A running stream; a perennial fountain; constant rain.

Sior-uisgeach, *a.* Abounding in running streams or perennial fountains; raining continually.

Sios, *adv.* (*Ir. id.*) East, eastward, down, downward, future. Rach sios, *go east, go down*, leig sios, *let down, furl* or *strike, as a sail*, leig iad an seòil sios, *they struck sail.—Stew. Acts.* Cluinnidh aimsir sios air cliù, *future time shall hear our praise.—Oss. Carricth.* Sios is suas, *east and west, up and down, to and fro; backwards and forwards, topsyturvy.* *Asp. form*, shios, *east, in the east, down, below.* Cuir sios, *put eastward* or *downward; send eastward* or *downward, humble, abase.*

† **Siosa**, *s. m.* (*Ir. id.*) A court, a parliament.—*Shaw.*

Siosal, *s.* The name Chisholm.

Siosalach, aich, *s. m.* One named Chisholm.

Siosar, *gen.* siosair *and* siosarach, *s.* A pair of scissors, sheers. *N. pl.* siosaran.

Siosarach, *a.* Like scissors or sheers; of scissors or sheers.

Siorsanaich, *s. f.* Hissing.

Siosma, *s. m.* (*Ir. id.*) Schism; a secession, a private conference; a whisper.

Siosmach, *a.* Schismatic; conferring privately; whispering.

Siosmair, *s. m.* A schismatic, a seceder, a whisperer. *N. pl.* siosmairean.

Siosmaireachd, *s. f.* A schismatising, a seceding, a secession; whispering.

Siota, *s. m.* An ill-bred child, a petted or spoiled child.

Siotach, *a.* Ill-bred, as a petted child, pampered; *also, substantively*, an ill-bred person, a pampered person.

Siotaidh, *s. f.* A trifle, a jot.—*Shaw.*

Sioth, *s. f.* Peace. Written also *sìth*, which see.

Sioth, *a.* Spiritual, unearthly; belonging to spirits.

Siothadh, aidh, *s. m.* See Sith.

Siothaich, *s.* See Sithich.

Siothamh, aimh, *s. f.* Peace; rest. Seallaidh siothaimh. *sights of peace.—Stew. Ezek.*

Siothann, *s. f.* Venison. More frequently written *sitheann*.

Siothchail, *a.* (siothchath-amhuil.) Peaceable; peaceful, quiet; placable; causing peace; prosperous. An deigh sin siothchail, *then peaceable.—Stew. James.* Gu siothchail, *peaceably.*

Siothchaileachd, *s. f.* Peaceableness, peacefulness, quietness, placableness.

Siothchainnt, *s.* (sìth o chainnt.) Silence; peace, tranquillity. Shearmoinich e siothchainnt, *he preached peace.—Stew. Eph.*

Siothchainnt, *s. f.* Salutation; peaceful language.

Sioth-chainnteach, *a.* Peaceful, quiet, tranquil; causing peace or quietness; pacific. Gu sioth-chainnteach, *peacefully.*

Sioth-chainnteach, *a.* Using peaceful language; speaking peace; peace-speaking.

Sioth-chainntiche, *s. m.* A peacemaker.

Siothchath, *s. m.* (sìth o chath.) Peace, or abstainment from war. Written also *siochath.*

Sioth-choimheadaiche, *s. m.* A constable. See also Sìth-choimheadaiche.

Siothlaich, *v. a.* and *n.* Strain, filter; cleanse; settle or subside, as an agitated fluid. *Pret. a.* shiothlaich, *filtered.*

Sioth-shaimh, *s. f.* Peaceful rest, soft repose; supineness. An sioth-shaimh luidhidh mi, *I will lie in peaceful rest.—Sm.* Written also *sith-thaimh.*

Sioth-shaimheach, *a.* Enjoying peaceful rest.

Sioth-shaimheachd, *s. f.* The enjoyment of peaceful rest or of sound repose.

Sìr, *a.* (*for* sior.) Ever. It is often prefixed to words, and signifies perpetuity or continuance. Sìr dhol an aghaidh, *continually going forward.—Stew. Sam.*

Sir, *v. a.* (*Ir. id.*) Seek, look for, search; want; ask, request, beg. *Pret. a.* shir, *sought; fut. aff. a.* siridh, *shall seek.* Sir air, *ask of him;* shir i oirbhse, a fhlatha, *she asked of you, ye nobles.—Fingalian Poem. Fut. sbu.* shireas. Esan a shireas, *he who seeketh.—Stew. Matt.* Ciod a tha thu sireadh? *what do you want? what do you look for?*

Sir-bhuain, *v. a.* Cut, shear, or mow frequently.

Sìr-bhualadh, aidh, *s. m.* A frequent or continual striking.

Sìr-chleachd, *v. a.* Exercise often, train to. *Pret. a.* shìr-chleachd.

Sireach, *a.* Seeking, searching; prying; scrutinous; *also,* lean, poor.—*Shaw.*

Sìr-chainnt, *s. f.* Garrulity, constant prating.

Sir-chainnteach, *a.* Garrulous; talking continually.

Siread, eid, *s. m.* (*from* sir.) A ferret.

Sireadach, *a.* Like a ferret; abounding in ferrets.

Sireadan, ain, *s. m.* (*from* sir.) A probe.

Sireadh, idh, *s. m.* A seeking, a looking for, a searching; asking; a requesting, a begging, a petitioning; a request, a petition.

Sìreamh, eimh, *s. m.* A disease.

Sìr-shileadh, idh, *s. m.* A continual dropping.

Siris, *s. f.* A cherry. *N. pl.* sirisean. Thuit an t-siris, *the cherry has fallen.—Macdon.*

Siriseach, *a.* Like a cherry; abounding in cherries; of cherries.

† Sist, *s.* A time, a while.

Sisteal, eil, *s. m.* A cistern; a flaxcomb.—*Shaw.*

Sistealach, *a.* Having cisterns; having flaxcombs; like a cistern; like a flaxcomb.

Sit-sit! *interj.* Hush!

Site, *s. f.* A sheet, as of paper. *N. pl.* siteachan. Site phaipeir, *a sheet of paper.*

Siteach, *a.* Sheeted, in sheets; of sheets; like a sheet.

Siteag, eig, *s. f.* A nice young female. *N. pl.* siteagan.

Siteagach, *a.* Nice, as a young female; effeminate.

Sitealachd, *s. f.* Cunning, craftiness.

† Sitearn, eirn, *s. m.* A harp.

Siteil, *a.* Cunning, crafty, designing.—*Stew. Gen. ref.*

Sìth, *a.* Spiritual, like a spirit. Daoine sìth, *fairies.*

Sìth, *s. f.* (*Ir. id. Goth.* sib.) Peace; stillness, quietness, rest from war; reconciliation. Cha mhasladh sìth ri laoch, *peace with a hero is no disgrace.—Old Poem.* Chuir Ronan fàilt shìth air an aosda, *Ronan gave a salutation of peace to the aged man.—Orr.*

Sith, sithe, *s. f.* A shock, a sudden onset; a sudden attempt to grasp or bite; a stride; a gnash. Sith nan còp corndhubh, *the shock of round black bosses.—Fingalian Poem.*

Sith-aigean, aigne, *s. f.* A mind disposed to peace; a tranquil mind.

Sith-aigeantach, *a.* Disposed to peace, placable; tranquil in mind.

Sìthamh, aimh, *s. m.* Quiet repose; unbroken rest.—*Oss. Tem.*

Sìthain, *s.* (*perhaps* sìth-thuin *or* sìth-dhun, *fairies' dwelling, fairies' knoll.*) A green knoll or hillock, tenanted, according to superstitious belief, by fairies. *N. pl.* sithainean. Dh' odharaich na sithainean feòir, *the grassy knolls have become dun.—Macdon.*

Sith-bheath, *s. f.* Immortality.

Sith-bheo, *a.* (*Ir. id.*) Eternal; immortal; perennial. Plùran sith-bheo, *a perennial flower.*

Sìth-bhollsair, *s. m.* A herald, one who proclaims peace. *N. pl.* sith-bhollsairean.

Sìth-bhollsaireachd, *s. f.* A proclaiming of peace; the business or office of a herald of peace.

Sìth-bhrfitheamh, eimh, *s. m.* A justice of the peace.

Sìth-bhriseadh, idh, *s. m.* A breaking of the peace; a disturbance; rebellion.

Sìth-bhristeach, *a.* Peace-breaking; riotous, rebellious; *also, substantively,* a riotous person; a rebel.

Sith-bhrog, *s. f.* A fairy; a fairy residence, fairyland.

Sith bhruach, aich, *s. f.* A fairy hill. *N. pl.* sith-bhruachan

Sith-bhruth, *s. m.* A fairy residence; fairyland. Mar cheol o shìth-bhruth, *like music from fairyland.—Old Song.*

Sith-bhuan, *a.* Eternal, immortal; perpetual, perennial.

Sith-bhuantachd, *s. f.* Eternity, immortality.

Sìthchail, *a.* Peaceable, placable, peaceful, tranquil; peace-bringing.

Sìth-chainnt, *s. f.* A salutation; words of peace, peaceful language.

Sìth-chainnteach, *a.* Saluting, speaking peacefully.

Sith-cheangail, *v. a.* Join in a confederacy; bind over to keep the peace.

Sìth-cheanglach, *a.* Confederative; binding over to keep the peace.

Sìth-cheangladh, aidh, *s. m.* A confederation; a binding over to keep the peace.

Sìth-cheanglaiche, *s. m.* One who joins in a confederacy; one of a confederacy; one who binds over to keep the peace. *N. pl.* sìth-cheanglaichean.

Sìth-choimheadaiche, *s. m.* A constable; one who keeps the peace.

Sith-dhuine, *s. m.* A fairy. *N. pl.* sith-dhaoine, *fairies,* literally, *peacemakers.*

Sith-dhun, dhuin, *s. m.* A fairy knoll; a Druidical term, meaning a mount of peace or reconciliation, that is, a place of worship.

The Druid who performed his ceremonies of worship on these knolls was called *sithiche*, i. e. *peacemaker*. In process of time, and long after the extinction of Druidism, *sith-dhun* came to signify *a fairy mount*; and this meaning it still preserves.

Sitheadh, idh, *s. m.* A bending, a sloping, a declining.—*Shaw.*

Sitheal, *s. m.* A trowel—(*Macd.*); a drinking-cup; a body.—*Shaw.* *N. pl.* sithealan.

Sitheann, sithinn, *and* sithne, *s. f.* Venison. Gun uireas air sitheann no frith, *without want of venison or forest.*—*Oss. Dargo.* Ith do m' shithinn, *eat of my venison.*—*Stew. Gen.*

Sitheannach, *a.* Abounding in venison; of venison.

Sith-fhad, *a.* Long-limbed; striding; bounding; prancing.

Sith-fhad, *s. m.* The name of one of Cuchullin's chariot horses—(*Oss. Fing.*); a long stride; a bound; a prance.

Sith-fhear, fhir, *s. m.* A strong man.—*Shaw.*

Sith-ghaoth, ghaoithe, *s. f.* A whirlwind. The fairies were supposed to cause this wind in order to raise themselves into the air, hence the name: literally, *fairy-wind.*

Sithghlic, *a.* Politic; cunning.

Sith-ghliocas, ais, *s. m.* Policy; cunning, artfulness.

Sithich, *v. a.* and *n.*, *from* sith. (*Ir. id.*) Calm, pacify, assuage, reconcile—(*Stew. Num. ref.*); grow calm, grow pacified, grow reconciled.

Sithich, *s. m.* A fairy; an elf. *N. pl.* sithrichean. This word seems to be derived from *sith*, and literally means *a peacemaker.*

The *sithich* is the most active sprite of Highland mythology. It is a dexterous child-stealer, and is particularly intrusive on women in travail. At births many covert and cunning ceremonies are still used to baffle the fairy's power, otherwise the new-born infant would be taken off to Fairyland, and a withered brat laid in its stead. They are wantonly mischievous, and have weapons peculiar to themselves, which operate no good to those at whom they are shot. A clergyman of the kirk, who wrote concerning Fairyland about the end of the seventeenth century, says of these weapons, that "they are solid earthly bodies, nothing of iron, but much of stone, like to a yellow soft flint spar, shaped like a barbed arrow-head, but flung like a dart with great force." This belief, as well as most Highland superstitions, are traceable to the early ages of the British Druids, on whose practices they are founded.

Sithionn, *s. f.* See Sitheann.

Sith-mhaor, mhaoir, *s. m.* A constable, a peace-officer, a policeman; a watch.

Sith-mhaorsainneachd, *s. f.* The jurisdiction of constable.

Sithnne, *s. f.* A teat, a pap, a nipple, an udder. *N. pl.* sithneachan. Written also *sinne.*

Sithnneach, *a.* Having teats or udders; having large teats or udders.

Sithnneachan, *n. pl.* of sithnne. Teats, paps, udders.

Sith-sheirc, *s. f.* Constant affection.

Sith-sheircell, *a.* Constant affection.

Sitig, *s. f.* A dunghill.

Sitrich, *v. n.* (*Ir. id.*) Neigh; bray; sneeze. *Pret. a.* shitrich, *neighed; fut. aff.* sitrichidh, *shall neigh.*

Sitrich, *s. f.* (*Ir.* seitreach *and* sitreach.) A neigh; a bray; a sneeze; a neighing; a braying; a tittering. Ri sitrich mar eachaibh, *neighing like horses.*—*Stew. Jer.*

Siu. See So.

Siubhail, *v. n.* Depart, go; travel, walk, stroll; fly; vanish; expire. *Pret.* shiubhail, *went; fut. aff.* siubhlaidh, *shall go.* Siubhlaidh mi rùisgte, *I will go stripped.*—*Stew. Mic.* Siubhlaidh an t-saighead, *the arrow shall fly.*—*Oss. Fin. and Lor.* Shiubhail an dreach aillidh, *the beauteous vision vanished.*

Siubhal, ail, *s. m.* A departing, a going, a moving, a travelling, a walking, a strolling; departure; death; motion; a course; swiftness; travel; a flight; a measure or time in music between fast and slow; a looseness of the bowels. Do laoich air siubhal, *thy heroes departed* or *dead.*—*Oss. Derm.* Air siubhal 's na cuantaibh, *our course in the seas.*—*Oss. Gaul.* Mar shiubhal saighde, *like an arrow's flight.*—*Id.* Mar shiubhal nan long, *like the course* or *motion of ships.*—*Oss. Lodin.* Gorm shiubhal Lubair, *the blue* [*stream*] *course of Luba.*—*Oss. Tem.* Fear siubhal, *a traveller.* Siubhal na samhnadh dha, *let him pass as Hallowmas did*, i. e. *never to return.*—*G. P.*

Siùbhal, ail, *s. m.* Travail. Luidhe siùbhal, *childbed.*

Siubhalach, *a.* See Siùbhlach.

Siubhalaiche, *s. m.* A traveller, a wayfaring man; a pedestrian; a stroller.

Siubhlach, *a.* (*from* siubhal.) Travelling, moving, migrating; flitting; restless; transient; departing; speedy, swift. Aighean siubhlach, *restless deer.*—*Macint.* Sgaoth shiùbhlach nan corr, *the migrating swarm of cranes.*—*Mac Lach.* *Com.* and *sup.* siùbhlaiche.

Siubhlachd, *s. f.* Continued travelling, moving, or flitting; restlessness; transientness; speediness; pedestrianism.

Siubhladh, aidh, *s. m.* Travelling; departure, death; motion; looseness of the bowels. See Siubhal.

Siubhlaiche, *s. m.* A traveller, a wayfaring man, a pedestrian, a stroller.

Siuc, *a.* (*Ir. id.* *Lat.* siccus.) Dry, parched, scorched.

Siucar, air, *s. m.* Sugar. Siucar pronn, *pounded sugar, moist sugar.*—*Macdon.* Siucar candaidh, *candied sugar;* siucar dubh, *black sugar;* siucar geal, *white sugar;* alt an t-siucair, *a stream immortalized by Macdonald, in a descriptive poem so called.*

Pers. schukur. *Gr.* σακχαρ, σακχαριον. *Lat.* saccharum. *Swed.* socker. *Germ.* zucker *and* sucker. *Dan.* sucker. *Arm.* sawgr. *Fr.* sucre. *Eng.* sugar.

Siucarach, *a.* Saccharine, sweet; of sugar.

Siùdain, *gen. sing.* of siùdan.

Siùdain, *s. m.* Swing, toss, dandle, fondle, rock; nod. *Pret. a.* shiùdain; *fut. aff.* siùdainidh.

Siùdan, ain, *s. m.* A swing; a tossing, a rocking; any instrument for swinging or rocking on.

Siùdanach, *a.* (*from* siùdan.) Swinging, tossing, dandling, rocking; fond of swinging, tossing, or dandling.

Siùdanachadh, aidh, *s. m.* A swinging, a tossing, a dandling, a rocking.

Siùdanachd, *s. f.* Continued swinging, tossing, dandling, or rocking; the amusement of swinging.

Siùdanaich, *v. a.* (*from* siùdanach.) Swing, toss, dandle, rock, fondle. *Pret. a.* shiùdanaich; *fut. aff. a.* siùdanaichidh.

Siùil, *gen. sing.* and *n. pl.* of seòl. Of a sail; sails. Ar siùil breid-gheal, *our white-spreading sails.*—*Ull.*

Siùlmhor, *a.* Bright; cheerful; delightful. More commonly written *suilbhear.*

Siumrag, aig, *s. f.* See Seamrag.

Siunas, ais, *s. m.* Lovage.—*Shaw.*

Siunnsair, *s. m.* A chanter; the chanter of a bagpipe. *N. pl.* siunnsairean.

Siunnsaireachd, *s. f.* Chanting, playing on a chanter.

† **Siunnsa**, *s. m.* (*Ir. id.*) Sense.

† **Siuir**, *s. f.* A sister.

(*Ir. id.* *Lat.* soror. *Fr.* sœur. *Corn.* sywr *and* hywr.

Siurdan, *v. n.* Rattle; rustle; make a noise. *Pret.* shiurdan.

Siurdan, ain, *s. m.* A rattling noise; a rustling noise.

Siurdanach, *a.* Rattling; noisy; rustling.

Siùrdanachd, *s. f.* A continued rattling; a continued rustling noise.

Siùrdanadh, aidh, *s. m.* A rattling; a rustling; a rattling noise; a rustling noise.

Siùrsach, aich, *s. f.* A whore, a strumpet. *N. pl.* siursaichean. Written also *siùrtach.*

Siùrsachail, *a.* (siùrsach-amhuil.) Whorish, whorelike.

Siùrsachd, *s. f.* Whoredom, prostitution. Dean siùrsachd, *commit whoredom.* See also Siùrtachd.

Siùrsaich, *gen. sing.* of siùrsach.

Siùrsaichean, *n. pl.* of siùrsach; which see.

Siùrtach, aich, *s. f.* A whore, a strumpet. *N. pl.* siùrtaichean.

Siùrtachail, *a.* (siùrtach-amhuil.) Whorish, whorelike.

Siùrtachd, *s. f.* Whoredom, prostitution. Rinn i siùrtachd, *she played the whore, she prostituted herself.—Stew. Jud.* Written also *siùrsachd.*

Siurtaich, *gen. sing.* of siurtach.

Siùrtaichean, *n. pl.* of siùrtach. Whores.

Siùrtag, aig, *s. f.* A bound; a bounce; a stride; a caper; a sudden sally; a skipping.—*Shaw.* Written also *sùrtag.*

Siùrtagach, *a.* Bounding; bouncing; striding; capering; sallying; skipping.

Siùsan, ain, *s. m.* A humming noise; a whisper; *also,* the name Susan.

Siusanach, *a.* Humming; whispering.

Siusanadh, aidh, *s. m.* A humming; a whispering; a hum; a whisper.

Siusarnadh, aidh, *s. m.* A whispering.

Siusarnaich, *s. f.* Whispering.

Slàbag, aig, *s. f.* A slut, a slattern. *N. pl.* slabagan.

Slàbair, *s. m.* A sloven; a draggler; one who works among mire. *N. pl.* slàbairean.

Slàbaireachd, *s. f.* Slovenliness; working amongst mud or mire; miriness.

Slàban, ain, *s. m.* A sloven; a draggler.

Slàbanach, *a.* Slovenly; dirty, miry.

Slabhag, aig, *s. f.* The lining of a horn. *N. pl.* slabhagan.

Slabhagan, ain, *s. m.* A species of edible sea-weed, gathered from rocks, but differing from dilse or *duilliasg* —*Shaw.*

Slabhraidh, *s. f.* (*Ir.* slabhradh.) See Slabhruidh.

Slabhraideach, *a.* Chained; like a chain; of chains. Written also *slabhruidheach.*

Slabhruidh, *s. f.* A chain; a pothook; a pothanger or chain slung over a kitchen fire, as a convenience for boiling or for dressing food. Tinne na slabhruidh, *a link of the chain.* Obair shlabhruidh, *chainwork.—Stew.* 1 *K. N. pl.* slabhruidhean. Ann an slabhruidhean, *in chains.—Stew. Nah.*

Slac, *v. a.* See Slachd.

Slacair, *v. a.* Beat, bruise, maul. See also Slachdair.

Slacair, *s. m.* (slac-fhear.) A beater, a bruiser. See also Slachdair.

Slacairt, *s. f.* Beating, as with a mallet; bruising; mauling. See also Slachdairt.

Slacan, ain, *s. m.;* written also *slachdan;* which see.

Slacanaich, *v. a.* (*from* slacan.) See Slachdanaich.

Slacraich, *s. f.* See Slachdraich.

Slachd, *v. a.* (*Germ.* slacht, *a beating.*) Beat, thrash, maul, bruise; beat with a batlet. *Pret. a.* shlachd; *fut. aff. a.* slachdaidh, *shall beat.*

Salachdach, *a.* Prone or inclined to beat, thrash, maul; or bruise.

Salachadh, aidh, *s. m.* A beating, a thrashing, a mauling; a bruising; a beating with a batlet.

Slachdadh, (a), *pr. part.* of slachd. Beating, thrashing, mauling, bruising. A slachdadh sgeire, *beating a rock.— Oss. Derm.*

Slachdainn, *s. f.* A beating, a thrashing, a mauling, or bruising. Fhuair e 'shlachdainn, *he got a thrashing.* Thoir a dheagh shlachdainn da, *give him a proper thrashing.*

Slachdainn, *v. a.* Beat, thrash, maul, bruise; beat with a batlet. *Pret. a.* shlachdainn; *fut. aff. a.* slachdainnidh.

Slachdair, *v. a.* Beat, thrash, bruise, maul; strike with a batlet. *Pret. a.* shlachdair.

Slachdair, *s. m.* A beater, a thrasher, a bruiser, a mauler; one who strikes with a batlet. *N. pl.* slachdairean.

Slachdaireachd, *s. f.* A continued beating, bruising, or mauling; a striking with a batlet.

Slachdairt, *s. f.* A beating, a thrashing, a bruising, a mauling; a beating or thrashing with a batlet.

Slachdan, ain, *s. m.* (*from* slachd.) A beetle; a batlet; a wooden instrument for beating clothes with; a bat. Slachdan aig oinid, *a beetle in an ideot's hand.—Macfar.* Slachdan druidheachd, *a magic wand.—Shaw.*

Slachdanaich, *v. a.* Beat, bruise, thrash; beat with a batlet or beetle. *Pret. a.* shlachdanaich; *fut. aff. a.* slachdanaichidh.

Slachdanaich, *s. f.* (*from* slachdan.) A beating, a bruising, a thrashing; a beating with a batlet.

Slachdarsaich, *s. f.* A beating, a thrashing, a mauling; a continued beating or thrashing; a buffeting. Slachdarsaich nan tonn, *the buffeting of the waves.—Old Poem.*

Slachdraich, *s. f.* A beating, a bruising, a thrashing, a mauling; a continued beating or thrashing; a buffeting. Slachdraich nan sonn, *the bruising blows of the heroes.— Fingalian Poem.* Slachdraich a chuain uaibhrich, *the buffeting of the proud ocean.—Macdon.*

Slachdran, ain, *s. m.* A battering-ram.

Slachduinn, *s. f.;* written also *slachdainn;* which see.

Slad, slaid, *s. f.* Theft, larceny, robbery. Ceal-shlad, *sacrilege.*

Slad, *v. a.* (*Ir. id.*) Steal, rob. *Pret. a.* shlad; *fut. aff. a.* sladaidh, *shall steal.*

Sladach, *a.* Thievish; robbing, plundering. Gu sladach, *like a thief* or *robber.*

Sladachd, *s. f.* Thievishness, robbery, plunder; the practice of theft or robbery. Gun dad sladachd, *without any theft.—Macdon.*

Sladadh, aidh, *s. m.* The act of thieving, robbing, or plundering; theft, robbery.

Sladaiche, *s. m.* (*Ir.* sladaighe.) A thief, a pilferer, a robber. *N. pl.* sladaichean.

Sladair, *s. m.* (slad-fhear.) A thief, a pilferer, a robber, a plunderer. *N. pl.* sladairean.

Sladaireachd, *s. f.* Thievishness, robbery, plundering. Ceal-shladaireachd, *sacrilegiousness.*

Slad-mharbh, *v. a.* Rob and murder; murder in order to conceal a robbery.

Slad-mharbhadh, aidh, *s. m.* Robbery and murder.

Sladmhoireachd, *s. f.* Theivishness, robbery.—*Shaw.*

Slad-mhortadh, aidh, *s. m.* The double crime of robbery and murder; murder committed in order to effect or to conceal robbery.

Slad-mhortair, *s. m.* One who commits the double crime of robbery and murder; one who commits murder to effect or to conceal robbery.

Slad-mhurt, *v. a.* See Slad-mhort.

Slad-mhurtadh, aidh, *s. m.* See Slad-mhortadh.

Slad-mhurtair, *s. m.* Written also *slad-mhortair.*

Sladta, Sladte, *p. part.* of slad. Stolen, robbed, plundered.

Slag, slaig, *s. m.* (*Scotch, id.*) A spoonful of any inspissated substance, as porridge; flummery.

Slagan, ain, *s. m.* Curdled milk; any inspissated substance.

Slaib, *s. f.* (*Ir. id.*) Mire, mud; a puddle; mire by the side of a stream.

Slaibeach, *a.* Miry; muddy; of dirty habits; puddling in mire; draggling.

Slaibear, eir, *s. m.* (slaib-fhear.) A dirty fellow; one who cares not to avoid mire; a draggler; one who works in mire or mud.

Slaibearachd, *s. f.* Draggling.

† **Slaibhre**, *s. f.* (*Ir. id.*) A purchase.—*Shaw.*

Slaibhreas, eis, *s. m.* (*Ir. id.*) Chains; servitude; bondage; the state of being in chains.

Slaid, slaide, *s. f.* (*Ir. id.*) Theft, robbery.

Slaid, *v. a.* Steal, rob, plunder. *Pret. a.* shlaid; *fut. aff. a.* slaididh. Shlaid i uam mo chlì, *she stole away my strength.—Old Song.*

Slaideach, *a.* Thievish, robbing, plundering.

Slaidear, eir, *s. m.* (*from* slaid.) A thief, a robber, a plunderer. *N. pl.* slaidearan.

Slaidearachd, *s. f.* The practice of theft or of robbery.

Slaidse, *s. f.* A lash; a stroke with a lash.

Slaidse, *v. a.* Lash; whip. *Pret. a.* shlaidse, *lashed; fut. aff. a.* slaidsidh, *shall lash.*

Slaidseach, *a.* (*from* slaidse.) Lashing, whipping; prone to lash.

Slaidseanta, *a.* Stout, robust.

Slaidsearachd, *s. f.* A lashing, a whipping.

Slaidte, *p. part.* of slaid. Stolen, robbed, plundered,

Slaighdean, ein, *s. m.* (*Ir. id.*) A cold, a cough.—*Shaw.*

Slaighre, *s. f.* A sword, a cimeter. *N. pl.* slaighrichean.

Slaim, slaime, *s. f.* A booty or plunder; much booty; a heap.—*Shaw.*

Slaimeach, *a.* Having prey or booty; of prey or booty; in heaps.

Slàine, *com.* and *sup.* of slàn; which see.

Slàinead, eid, *s. m.* Wholeness, entireness; health; convalescence. A dol an slàinead, *growing more and more whole* or *healthy.*

Slainnte, *s. f.* See Slàinte.

Slàinte, *s. f., from* slàn. (*Ir. id.*) Health; soundness; a healing virtue; salvation; a health or toast. Bheil thu ad shlàinte? *are you in health?* Slàinte na sgiathaibh, *health [healing] in his wings.—Stew. Mal.* Chum bhur slàinte, *for your salvation.—Stew. N. T.* Air do shlàinte, *your health, à votre santé;* air ur slàinte, *your healths;* slàinte leat, *farewell,* i. e. *health be with you;* deoch slàinte, *a toast* or *health in drinking;* dh'òl iad mo dheoch slàinte, *they drank my health;* thig mi thaobh mo shlàinte, *I will come if I be well,* or *if my health permit.*

Slainnteach. See Slainnteil.

Slainntealachd, *s. f.* Healthfulness; benignity.

Slàinteil, *a.* (slainte-amhuil.) Healthy, wholesome, salubrious, salutary; benign. Gu slainnteil fallain, *healthy and sound.*

Slait, *a.* (*Ir. id.*) Strong; robust.

Slam, *v. a.* Teaze, pluck, or card wool. *Pret. a.* shlam; *fut. aff. a.* slamaidh.

Slam, slaim, *s. m.* (*Ir. id.*) A lock of hair; a flock or tuft of wool; slime.

Slamach, *a.* Teazing; plucking, as wool; carding; in locks, as hair; in flocks, as wool.

Slamach, *a.* Clotty.

Slamaich, *v. n.* Clot, curdle. *Pret.* shlamaich; *fut. aff.* slamaichidh.

Slamaichte, *p. part.* of slamaich. Clotted.

Slamag, aig, *s. f.* (*dim.* of slam.) A little lock of hair; a little flock of wool. *N. pl.* slamagan. D'òrchul na shlamagan bachlach, *thy yellow hair in curled locks.—Moladh Mhòraig.*

Slamagach, *a.* In little locks, as hair; in little flocks or tufts, as wool.

Slaman, ain, *s. m.* (*Ir. id.*) Coagulated milk not separated from the whey.

Slamanach, *a.* Coagulated or curdled, as milk; like coagulated milk; producing curds. A bhealtuinn shlamanach, *curd-producing May.*

Slamanachd, *s. f.* The state of being curdled; coagulation; a tendency to coagulate.

Slaman-ceathaich, *s. m.* A light dry mist; a stratus-cloud, or fall-cloud.

Slamban, ain, *s. m.* (*Ir. id.*) Curdled milk not separated from the cream. Written also *slaman.*

Slambanach, *a.* See Slamanach.

Slambanachd, *s. f.* See Slamanachd.

Slamhach, aich, *s. f.* A frothstick, or an instrument for frothing cream.—*Shaw.*

Slamhan, ain, *s. f.* An elm.—*Shaw.*

Slamhagan, *s. pl.* Locks of hair or of wool.

Slamhanach, *a.* Abounding in elms; of elms; made of elm.

† **Slan**, slain, *s. m.* A defiance, a challenge. Now writtten *dùlan* or *dùbhlan.*

Slàn, *a.* (*Ir. id.*) Whole, entire, unbroken; safe or unhurt; sound, healthy; healed. Slàn gum pill thu, *safe may you return.—Oss. Gaul.* Ighean nan òr-chleachd, an slàn duit? *maid of the golden locks, art thou well?—Oss. Cathula.* Gu slàn fallain, *safe and sound, in perfect health.* Gu mu slàn a robh thu, *well mayst thou be.* Tha e beo slàn, *he is alive and well.* Oighean boidheach, slàn leibh, *ye pretty maidens, farewell.—Ardar.* Slàn leibh, *farewell,* seems to be either a contraction, or a corruption of *slàinte leibh. Com.* and *sup.* slàinte.

† **Slanach**, *a.* (*from* † slan.) Defying, challenging; ready to defy or challenge; of a defiance or challenge.

Slànach, *a.* Healing, curing; having a healing virtue; salubrious, salutary.

Slànachadh, aidh, *s. m.* A healing, a curing; a remedying; a growing whole; a repairing; a saving.

Slànachadh, (a), *pr. part.* of slànaich. Healing, curing; repairing or making whole; mending.

Slànadh, *s. m.* (*Ir. id.*) Healing; saving; salvation; securities.

Slànaich, *v. a.* and *n., from* slàn. (*Ir.* slanaigh.) Heal, cure, remedy; make whole, mend, repair; grow whole; grow well. *Pret. a.* shlànaich, *healed; fut. aff. a.* slànaichidh, *shall heal; fut. pass.* slànaichear, *shall be healed.* Written also *slànuich.*

Slànaichear, *fut. pass.* of slanaich. Shall be healed.

Slànaichidh, *fut. aff. a.* of slànaich.

Slànaichte, *p. part.* of slànaich. Healed, cured, mended.

Slàn-lus, luis, *s. m.* (*Ir. id.*) The herb ribwort; the *plantago lanceolata;* any medicinal herb. *N. pl.* slàn-lusan.

Slàn-lusach, *a.* Abounding in ribwort; of ribwort; abounding in medicinal herbs.

Slànuchadh, aidh, *s. m.* (*Ir.* slanughadh.) A healing, a curing, a remedying; a growing whole; a repairing, a mending; a saving. Written also *slanachadh.*

Slànuich, *v. a.* and *n.* (*from* slàn.) Heal, cure, remedy; make whole; mend, repair; grow whole; grow well. *Pret. a.* shlànuich, *healed; fut. aff. a.* slànuichidh. Written al o *slànaich.*

Slànuichear, *fut. pass.* of slànuich. Shall be healed.

Slànuichidh, *fut. aff. a.* of slànuich. Shall heal; shall grow whole.

Slànuichte, *p. part.* of slànuich Healed, cured; made whole; mended.

Slànuighear, ir, *s. m.* (*Ir* slànaigtheoir.) A saviour; the name given to Jesus Christ.

Slaòd, slaòid, *s m* (*Ir. id*) A raft; a float; a trail, a trailing burden; a drag, a sledge; a term of contempt for a lazy, untidy person, murder.
Ir. slaod *It* slitta, *a sledge. Dan.* slaed. *Eng.* sled

Slaod, *v. a* Drag, trail, pull, draw; walk with a trailing gait. *Pret. a* shlaod, *dragged, fut. aff. a.* slaodaidh.

Slaodach, *a* (*from* slaod.) Dragging, trailing, pulling; slovenly, sluggish, having a sluggish gait; untidy

Slaodadh, aidh, *s m* A dragging, a trailing, a pulling; a raft, a float; a trailing burden, a drag, a sledge, a sluggish gait

Slaodail, *s f.* A continued dragging, trailing, or pulling

Slaodail, *a.* (slaod-amhuil) Dragging, trailing, pulling, like a raft, like a drag.

Slaodair, *s. m*, *from* slaod. (*Swed.* slaetti, *a trollop*) A slovenly fellow, a sloven, a sluggard; an untidy fellow *N pl* slaodairean.

Slaodaireachd, *s f.* Slovenliness, sluggishness; untidiness

Slaodan, *n pl.* of slaod, which see

Slaodan, ain, *s. m.* (*dim.* of slaod) A little raft, a little float; a little trailing burden

Slaodan, ain, *s m* A cold, a cough; the rut of a cart-wheel —*Shaw*

Slaodanach, aich, *s m* A slounging fellow

Slaodrach, aich, *s m* A hinge, a foundation

Slaoichd, *s* and *a.* A large piece, as of bread, a clumsy slice; *adjectively*, inverted, lying —*Macfar Voc*

Slaoid, *gen sing* of slaod; which see

Slaòid, *v. a.* Drag, trail, pull, walk with a trailing gait. *Pret a* shlaoid; *fut. aff a.* slaoididh, *shall drag.*

Slaoighte, *s f.* Roguery, dishonesty Written also *sloighte*

Slaoighteil, *a* See Sloighteil.

Slaoightir, *s m* See Sloightir

Slaoightireachd, *s f* See Sloightireachd.

Slaoit, *s.* Dirt, filth

Slaonasadh, aidh, *s m.* (*Ir. id.*) A tragedy

Slaop, slaoip, *s m* Slovenliness, sluggishness

Slaopach, *a.* Slovenly, sluggish, awkward, tawdry; untidy; drawling; unclean Beul is neo-shlaopach glòir, *a mouth whose speech is* [*drawling*] *not elegant* —*Mac Lach*

Slaopachd, *s f.* Slovenliness, sluggishness, awkwardness, tawdriness; untidiness, a habit of drawling, uncleanness.

Slaopair, *s. m* (*Ir.* slapaire *Du* slabberen) A sloven, a sluggard; an awkward, untidy fellow, a drawler.

Slaopaireachd, *s f.* Slovenliness, sluggishness; awkwardness

Slaot, slaoit, *s m* Dirt, dross—(*Stew Is ref*), a raft, a drag, in these last meanings it is more frequently written *slaod*, which see

Slaotan, ain, *s m* A cold.—*Shaw.*

Slapach, *a.* Sluttish, drabbish; lukewarm

Slapag, aig, *s f* A slut, a drab, a slattern. *N. pl.* slapagan Written also *slabag.*

Slapagach, *a* Sluttish, drabbish.

Slapair, *s. m.* A sloven, a sluggard; one who works in mud. *N. pl.* slapairean

† **Slapar**, air, *s. m* A skirt; the train of a long robe.

Slaparach, *a.* Having a long skirt or train, as a robe.

Slaparaich, *s f.* (*Ir. id.*) Din

Slasdach, *a.* Envying; invidious; having a grudge

Slasdachd, *s f.* Envy; a grudge —*Shaw.*

Slat, slait, *s f.* (*Ir. id.*) A rod, a wand, a switch; a lineal yard; the penis. *N. pl.* slatan, *rods, d. pl.* slataibh. Slatan glas do 'n chritheach, *green rods of the poplar;* slat bhrogaidh, *a goad*, slat-iasgaich, *a fishing-rod*, slat-iomain, *a goad*, slat-mhara, *dilse*, slat-mharcachd, *a riding-switch*, slat-reul, *an astrolabe;* slat-rioghail, *a sceptre;* slat sgiùrsaidh, *a lash, a scourge*, slat-shiùil, *a sailyard*, slat shuaicheantais, *a mace, a flag-staff*, slat-thombais, *a yard, an ell-wand*, eadar an t-sùgh 's an t-slat, *between the bark and the tree.*—*G P.*

Slatach, *a.* Abounding in rods, wands, or switches; like a rod, wand, or switch; pliant, as a switch; in rods or wands; in yards; branchy, branching, sprouting. Na fiùrain slatach, *the pliant tendrils* —*Macfar*

Slatag, aig, *s f* (*dim.* of slat) A little rod, wand, or switch; a tendril or twig. *N. pl* slatagan.

Slatagach, *a.* Abounding in little rods, wands, switches, tendrils, or twigs.

Slatail, *a* (slat-amhuil) Straight, upright; tall, stately; limber; wanton.

Slataileachd, *s. f.* Uprightness; talness, stateliness; wantonness

Slatan, ain, *s m* (*dim* of slat.) A little rod, a little wand.

Slatan, *n. pl* of slat Rods, wands, switches See Slat.

Slatarra, *a.* Straight; tall; upright.—*Shaw*

Slat-iasgaich, *s. f.* A fishing-rod.

Slat-iomain, *s f.* A goad. Slat-iomain dhamh, *an ox-goad* —*Stew Jud ref.*

Slat-mhara, *s. f* Dilse, tangles *N pl* slatan-mara. Carraig nan slata-mara, *the dilse-covered rock.*—*Oss. Cathula.*

Slat-sgiùrsaidh, *s. f.* A lash, a scourge Fuaim na slait-sgiùrsaidh, *the sound of the lash* —*Stew Nah. N. pl.* slatan-sgiùrsaidh

Slat-shuaicheantais, *s f* A mace; a sceptre; a flag-staff, a banner-staff Slat-shuaicheantais do neart, *the sceptre of thy power.*—*Sm.*

Slat-thomhais, *s f.* Any rod used for superficial measurements, a yard, an ell-wand, a pole

Sleachd, *a* More frequently *sleuchd*, which see.

† **Sleachd**, *v. a.* Cut, dissect, lance; scarify.—*Shaw.*

Sleachdadh, aidh, *s. m* A cutting; a dissecting; a lancing, a scarifying

Sleag, *v n* Sneak, drawl. *Pret a* shleag; *fut aff.* sleagaidh.

Sleagach, *a* Sneaking, drawling. Gu sleagach, *sneakingly. Com.* and *sup.* sleagaiche.

Sleagadh, aidh, *s m* A sneaking; a drawling —*Shaw.*

Sleagair, *s. m* A sneaking fellow; a drawler. *N. pl.* sleagairean.

Sleagaireachd, *s f* A habit of sneaking, the behaviour of a sneaking fellow, drawling

Sleagan, ain, *s. m* (*Ir id*) A shell

Sleagh, sleigh, *s f.* (*Ir id*) A spear, lance, or javelin. *N. pl* sleigh *and* sleaghan O bheum na sleagh, *from the wound of the spear* —*Orr.* Thog sinn sleigh, *we lifted spears* —*Oss Tem*

Sleaghach, *a* (*from* sleagh.) Armed with a spear or dart; like a spear or dart; of a spear or dart.

Sleaghair, *s m* (sleagh-fhear) A spearman. *N. pl.* sleaghairean

Sleaghaireachd, *s f* Shooting with a spear; spearing; fighting with spears

Sleaghan, ain, *s m* (*Ir id*) A kind of turf-spade; an iron instrument for digging; a spaddle; a little spear

Sleaghan, *n pl.* of sleagh Spears

Sleamhainn, *a* (*Ir.* sleamhain *Germ* schliefen, *to glide.*) Slippery; smooth; plain.

Sleamhan, ain, *s. m.* (*Ir id*) An elm-tree.

Sleamhanach, *a.* Abounding in elms; like an elm; of elms.

Sleamhna, *com.* and *sup.* of sleamhainn. More or most slippery.

Sleamhnachadh, aidh, *s. m.* (*Ir.* sleamhnughadh.) A sliding; a gliding; a slipping; slipperiness. Written also *sleamhnuchadh.*

Sleamhnachadh, (a), *pr. part.* of sleamhnaich. Sliding; gliding; slipping. Written also *sleamhnuchadh.*

Sleamhnachd, *s. f.* (*i. e.* sleamhainneachd.) Slipperiness; smoothness.

Sleamhnad, aid, *s. m.* Smoothness.

Sleamhnaich, *v. a.* and *n.* (*Ir.* sleamhnaigh.) Make slippery; make smooth; slide; slip; stumble; glide; move imperceptibly. *Pret. a.* shleamhnaich; *fut. aff. a.* shleamhnaichidh, *shall slide.* Written also *sleamhnuich.*

Sleamhnuchadh, aidh, *s. m.* See Sleamhnachadh.

Sleamhnuich, *v. a.* and *n.* Make slippery; make smooth; slide; slip; stumble; glide; move softly and imperceptibly. *Pret. a.* shleamhnuich, *slipped; fut. aff. a.* sleamhnuichidh, *shall slip.* Cha shleamhnuich mo cheum, *my foot shall not slide.—Sm.*

Sleamhuinn, *a.* (*Ir.* sleamhuinn.) Slippery; smooth.

Sleant, *s.* (*Ir. id.*) A tile.

Sleantach, aich, *s. m.* A flake; a slice.—*Shaw* and *Stew. Job. ref.*

† **Sleas**, sleis, *s. m.* A mark; a sign; a ridge; a side: in this last sense, see Slios.

Sleasd, *v. a.* Smear, bedaub, bespawl. *Pret.* shleasd; *fut. aff.* sleasdaidh.

Sleasdach, *a.* Smeary, dirty.

Sleasdaich, *v. a.* Smear, bedaub, bespawl. *Pret.* shleasdaich; *fut. aff.* sleasdaichidh; *p. part.* sleasdaichte.

Sleasdaireachd, *s. f.* A smearing, a bedaubing, a bespawling.

Sleasg, *v. n.* Crack, split. *Pret. a.* shleasg.

Sleasgach, *a.* Cracking, splitting; causing to crack or split; apt to crack or split.

Sleasgadh, aidh, *s. m.* (*Ir. id.*) A cracking, a splitting; a crack, a split.

Slèibh, *gen. sing.* of sliabh. Of a hill or mountain.

Slèibhte, *n. pl.* of sliabh. Hills, mountains. Slèibhte nan carba ciar, *the mountains of dusky roes.—Orr.* Slèibhte ceò, *mountains of mist.—Oss.*

Sleibhteach, *a.* Hilly, mountainous; of hills; of mountains.

Sleimhne, *s. f.* Slipperiness; smoothness.

Sleimhne, *com.* and *sup.* of sleamhainn or sleamhuinn, *more or most slippery.*

Sleimhneach, *a.* Slipping; slippery; smooth.

Sleimhneachd, *s. f.* Slipperiness; smoothness.

Slèis, *gen. sing.* of slias.

Sleisde, *gen. sing.* of sliasaid. Of a thigh.

† **Sleithe**, *s. f.* (*Ir. id.*) A section, a division; a cutting.

Sleogach, *a.* Qualmish, queasy.

Sleogadh, aidh, *s. m.* Qualmishness.

Sleuchd, *v. n.* (*Ir.* sleachd.) Bow down, kneel, worship. *Pret. a.* shleuchd; *fut. aff. a.* sleuchdaidh. Shleuchd iad, *they worshipped.—Stew.* 1 *K.*

Sleuchdadh, aidh, *s. m.* (*Ir.* sleachdadh.) A bowing down, a kneeling, a worshipping.

Sliabh, slèibh, *s. m.* (*Ir. id.*) A hill, a mountain, a mount, a moor; moorish ground; heathy ground. Air mullach nan sliabh, *on the top of the hills.—Stew. Mic.* Sliabh an t-siorraidh, *Sheriffmoor. N. pl.* sleibhte. Sleibhte creagach coillteach, *rocky wooded mountains.—Oss. Duthona.*

Sliabhair, *s. m.* (sliabh-fhear.) A mountaineer; a Highlander. *N. pl.* sliabhairean.

Slias, slèis, *s. f.* A thigh; the coarse part of a thread. *N. pl.* sliasan.

Sliasach, *a.* Having large thighs; of, or belonging to, the thigh.

Sliasaid, *gen.* slèisde, *s. f.* A thigh. Fuidh shliasaid a mhaighstir, *under his master's thigh.—Stew. Gen.* Lag a shleisde, *the hollow of his thigh.—Id. N. pl.* sleisdean.

Sliaspair, *v. a.* Daggle, draggle. *Pret. a.* shliaspair, *draggled.*

Sliaspair, *s. m.* A daggler, a draggler.

Sliaspairt, *s. f.* Daggling, draggling; covering or besmearing with mud.

Sliast, *s. m.* A ledge in a loom.

Sliastan, ain, *s. m.* A ledge in a loom.

Slìb, *v. a.* See Sliob.

Slige, *s. f.* A shell; a drinking-shell; a scallop-shell; a splinter of earthenware; the scale of a balance; a bomb. Chaidh an t-slige is an t-òran mu 'n cuairt, *the shell and the song went round.—Ull. N. pl.* sligeachan. Chaidh e na shligeachan, *it broke into splinters;* slige-chreachainn, *a scalloped shell;* slige-chreadha, *a potsherd;* slige-neamhuinn, *a mother of pearls, the shell of the pearl-fish;* slige-thomhais, *the scale of a balance.*

Sligeach, *a.* (*from* slige.) Shelly; abounding in shells; of shells; like a scale; like a bomb; of a bomb.

Sligeachan, *n. pl.* of slige. Shells; splinters of earthenware; scales.

Sligeadachd, *s. f.* Conchology.

Sligeadair, *s. m.* A conchologist. *N. pl.* sligeadairean.

Sligeadh, idh, *s. m.* Fomentation.

Sligean, ein, *s. m., dim.* of slige. (*Ir. id.*) A little shell; a little scale or balance; a little splinter.

Sligeanach, *a.* Spotted; sky-coloured; cirrocumulated; scaled.

Sligearnach, *a.* Made of shells; full of shells.

Sligeart, eirt, *s. m.* A pumice-stone. *N. pl.* sligeartan.

Slige-chreachainn, *s. f.* A scalloped shell, in former times used for drinking. Làn na slige-chreachainn, *the fill of the scalloped shell.—Macint.*

The custom of drinking out of shells is of great antiquity, and was very common among the ancient Gael. Hence the expressions so often met with in the Fingalian poets, "the hall of shells," "the chief of shells," "the shell and the song." The scallop-shell is still used, in drinking strong liquors, at the tables of those gentlemen who are desirous to preserve the usages of their ancestors.

Slige-chreadha, *s. f.* A potsherd. Ghabh e slige-chreadha, *he took a potsherd.—Stew. Job.*

Slige-neamhuinn, *s. f.* A mother-of-pearl; a pearl-fish shell.

Slige-thomhais, *s. f.* The scale of a balance.

Slighe, *s. f.* (*Ir. id.*) A way, road, or path; a track. Is i so an slighe, *this is their way.—Stew. Ps.* An t-slighe, *the way. N. pl.* sligheachan.

Sligheach, *a., from* slighe. (*Ir.* slightheach.) Artful, cunning, sly; fertile in schemes, shifts, or stratagems.

Sligheadair, *s. m.* An artful scheming fellow; one who is fertile in devices or stratagems. *N. pl.* sligheadairean.

Sligheadaireachd, *s. f.* (*Ir.* slightheadoireachd.) Artfulness, cunning, sliness; fertileness in schemes, shifts, or stratagems; the practice of stratagems.

Sligneach, *a.* Spotted; cerulean; sky-coloured; green; scaly. *Asp. form,* shligneach. Nathair bhreac shligneach, *a spotted green serpent.—Mac Lach.*

Slim, *a.* (*Ir. id. Eng.* slim.) Lean, slender.

Slinn, slinne, *s. f.* (*Ir. id.*) A weaver's reed or slay; a flat stone; a tile—(*Shaw*); a flag.

Slinnchrann, chrainn, *s. m.* An ensign-staff, a flag-staff.

Slinneag, eig, *s. f.* A shoulder; a shoulder-blade. A chuid nach 'eil air an t-slinneag tha e air a chliathaich, *what is not on the shoulder may cover the ribs.—G. P.*

Slinnean, ein, *s. m.* and *f* (*Ir. id*) A shoulder; a shoulder-blade *N pl.* slinneinean. An slinnean deas, *the right shoulder.—Stew. Ex*

Slinneanach, *a* Having large shoulders; of the shoulder; of the shoulder-blade. Fear slinneanach leathann, *a large-shouldered, broad-built man.—Mac Co*

Slinneanach, aich, *s m* A large-shouldered man

Slinnteach, ich, *s f* Housetiles; a quantity of tiles

Sliob, *s m* A polish, a gloss

Sliob, *v a* (*Ir id*) Smooth, polish; gloss, varnish, besmear, daub, spatter, cover. *Pret. a* shliob, *fut aff a* sliobaidh Shliob i e le làthaich, *she daubed it with slime —Stew Gen* Sliob bodach is sgròbaidh e thu, *stroke a sorry fellow and he will scratch you —G. P.*

Sliobach, *a* Smoothing, polishing; glossy; besmearing, daubing, spattering

Sliobachadh, aidh, *s m* A smoothing, a polishing, a glossing, a besmearing, a daubing, a spattering

Sliobadh, aidh, *s m* A smoothing, a polishing, a glossing, a besmearing, a daubing, a spattering; a polish, a gloss, a varnish

Sliobadh, 3 *sing* and *pl imper.* of sliob; which see

Sliobaich, *v a* Smooth, polish, gloss, varnish; besmear, daub, spatter *Pret a.* shliobaich, *glossed, fut aff. a.* sliobaichidh, *shall gloss*

Sliobaichte, *p part* Smoothed, polished, glossed, varnished, besmeared, daubed

Sliob-cheannach, *a* Having smooth hair, glossy-haired Anna chioch-chorrach, shliob-cheannach, *round-breasted, glossy-haired Anna.—Old Song.*

Sliobradh, aidh, *s m* Glossiness; a draught

Sliobta, *p part* of sliob Polished, smoothed, varnished, glossed

Sliochd, *s m* (*Ir.* sliochd, *a race Dan* slaegt) Offspring, race, posterity, seed; a tribe or clan, a multitude; a troop, a rout, a track or print.

Sliochdach, *a* Having numerous descendants, prolific, generative, populous, in tribes, having tracks.

Sliochdar, *a. for* sliochdmhor

Sliochdmhor, *a* Having many descendants, prolific, populous

Sliodach, *a* Cunning, artful. Gu sliodach, *cunningly Com* and *sup* sliodaiche.

Sliog, *s f* A shell More frequently *slige*, which see

Sliog, *s m.* (*Ir id.*) A polish, a gloss

Sliog, *v a* (*Du.* sleych, *smooth. Eng* sleek) Stroke; caress, smooth, gloss, lubricate *Pret a* shliog; *fut aff a* sliogaidh, *shall stroke*

Sliogach, *a.* Smooth, glossy; silky; lubricated; sleek; stroking; caressing; smoothing; fawning; testaceous.

Sliogadh, aidh, *s. m* A stroking; a caressing, a smoothing, a glossing; a gloss; a lubricating; a fawning, a caress

Sliogadh, (a), *pr part.* of sliog Stroking; smoothing, caressing, fawning; glossing; a making sleek, lubricating A sliogadh an ula, *stroking their beard —Oss Dargo*

Sliogan, ain, *s m* A shell, a bomb, a cup, a hulk, a scale

Slioganach, *a* Dappled

Sliogard, aird, *s m* A crust; a pumice-stone —*Shaw*

Sliogardach, *a* Crusty, hard.

Sliogarnach, *a* (*from* sliog.) Made of shells, shelly

Sliogarra, *a* Smooth, glossy; silky, lubricated; sleek.

Sliogarrachd, *s f* Smoothness; glossiness, silkiness, sleekness

Sliogta, *p. part* of sliog. Stroked; smoothed; caressed; glossed, lubricated, fawned.

Sliom, *a.* (*Ir. id. Eng* slim) Slim, sleek; smooth; glossy, slippery, lubricated Na bric shliom, *the sleek fish —Macdon.*

Sliom, *v. a.* Smooth; gloss; flatter. *Pret.* shliom; *fut. aff* sliomaidh.

Sliomach, *a* Sleek, smooth, glossy; slim

Sliomachd, *s f.* Sleekness; smoothness; glossiness; slipperiness; slimness

Sliomaich, *v a.* Make sleek, smooth, or glossy; lubricate. fawn, flatter. *Pret a.* shliomaich; *fut. aff. a* sliomaichidh, *shall make sleek*

Sliomair, *s. m.* A filcher, a thief, a flatterer. *N. pl.* sliomairean.

Sliomaireachd, *s. f.* Filching.

Slionc, *v a.* Beat.

Sliop, sliopa, *s.* A lip.—*Macd* and *Shaw. N. pl.* sliopan

Sliopach, *a.* Lipped, blubber-lipped.

Sliopag, aig, *s. f.* A thick-lipped young female. *N. pl.* sliopagan.

Sliopair, *s. m* A blubber-lipped fellow *N pl.* sliopairean.

Slios, *s m.* (*Ir. id.*) A side or flank, the side of a country; a limb; a coast; a border, an edge. An stoirm eididh ri slios carraig, *the dreadful tempest beating against the side of the rock —Oss. Manos.* Slios nan liath-bheann, *the side of the grey hills —Oss Fing* Slios a sgeith, *the edge of his shield — Oss Fing* Is fhad slios na bliadhna, *the whole year is a long stretch.—G P.*

Sliosach, *a* Having many sides; multilateral, having a border.

Sliosag. See Sliseag

Sliosda, *a* (*Ir. id*) Fair courteous; flattering, fawning.

Sliosdachd, *s. f* Fairness, courteousness; flattery.

Sliosmhor, *a* Glossy, polished; extensive, as a country side.

Sliosnach, *a* Having sides; lateral, multilateral; angular.

Slis, *v a.* Slice; chip, shave, as wood *Pret. a.* shlis; *fut. aff.* slisidh.

Slis, slise, *s f* (*Ir. id.*) A slice, a chip, a spill; a lath; a thin board. *N. pl.* slisean —*Macd* and *Shaw.*

Slis-cheumnach, *a.* Apt to make a digression.

Slis-cheumnaich, *v. n* Make a digression.

Sliseag, eig, *s f., dim* of slis. (*Ir. id.*) A shaving of wood; a chip or spill of wood; a thin slice of any thing; the temple, the upper part of the head. *N. pl.* sliseagan. Far am bi saoir bithidh sliseagan, *where carpenters are there will be shavings.—Old Saying*

Sliseagach, *a* Full of shavings, chips, or spills, full of slices, easily planed, as wood; of shavings, of chips or spills; in slices.

Sliseagachadh, aidh, *s. m* A chipping or planing of wood, a slicing

Sliseagaich, *v a* Plane; cut off in chips or spills; slice. *Pret a* shliseagaich, *planed, fut aff. a.* sliseagaichidh, *shall plane*

Sliseagaichte, *p. part* of sliseagaich Planed; cut off in chips or spills, sliced

Sliseagan, *n pl.* of sliseag Wood-shavings, chipping-spills.

Slisneach, ich, *s* (*Ir id.*) A quantity of wood-shavings, chips, or spills, scales

Sliucanach, *a* Horned.—*Shaw.*

Slob, sluib, *s. m* A puddle, a plash, a little pool.

Slobach, *a.* Puddly, plashy

Sloban, ain, *s m* (*dim.* of slob.) A puddle, a plash, a little pool

Sloc, sluic, *s m* (*Ir id.*) A pit; a ditch; a hollow; a dell; a den, a dungeon; a grave, a pool; a marsh Written also *slochd*, which see.

Slocach, *a.* Full of pits or ditches, full of hollows or dells; full of dens or dungeons; full of pools or marshes. See also Slochdach.

Slocachadh, aidh, *s m* See Slochdachadh.

Slocaich, *v. a.* See Slochdaich.

Slocan, ain, *s. m.* (*dim.* of sloc.) A little pit; a little ditch; a little hollow or dell; a little pool.

Slochd, sluichd, *s. m.* A pit; a ditch; a hollow; a dell; a den; a dungeon; a grave; a pool; a marsh. Ann an slochd éigin, *in some pit.—Stew. Gen.* Tumaidh tu mi san t-slochd, *thou shalt plunge me in the ditch.—Stew. Job.* Cho-fhreagair gach slochd, *every dell echoed.—Ull.* San t-slochd so, *in this dungeon.—Stew. Gen.* Sìnte san t-slochd, *stretched in the grave.* Slochd-guail, *a coalpit.*

Sloc-shàbhaidh. A sawpit.

Slochdach, *a.* (*from* slochd.) Full of pits or ditches; full of hollows or dells; full of dens, caves, or dungeons; full of pools; full of marshes; like a pit or ditch; like a den; like a dungeon.

Slochdachadh, aidh, *s. m.* A digging of pits, ditches, dens, or dungeons.

Slochdaich, *v.* (*from* slochd.) Dig a pit; make a ditch; draw a ditch. *Pret. a.* shlochdaich, *dug; fut. aff. a.* slochdaichidh, *shall dig.*

Slochdaichte, *p. part.* of slochdaich.

Slochdan, ain, *s. m.* (*dim.* of slochd.) A little pit or ditch; a little hollow; a little dell; a little cave or den; a little pool.

Slochdanach, *a.* Full of little pits or ditches; full of little hollows or dells; full of little caves or dens.

† **Sloch-sine**, *s. f.* A flake of snow.

Slod, sloid, *s. m.* (*Ir. id.*) A little pool, a little puddle, a little standing water.

Slodach, *a.* Full of little pools or puddles.

Slodan, ain, *s. m.* A little pool, a little puddle, a little standing water.

Slodanach, *a.* Full of little pools or puddles.

Slodhag, aig, *s. f.* The lining of a horn.—*Macfar. Voc.*

Slodhagach, *a.* Lined, as a horn.

Slogair, *s. m.* A gulf.

Slogan, ain, *s. m.* (*Scotch*, slogan.) A war-cry.

Every clan, and many districts, had their own war-cry. *Crogun an fhithich,* the raven's rock, the war-cry of the Macdonells. *Craig eileachaidh,* a rock at the mouth of the Spey, the war-cry of the Grants. *Croit ubh,* or *craig dhubh,* the black rock, the war-cry of the Macphersons. *Loch Sloigh,* in Arrochar, the war-cry of the Macfarlanes. *Ard Chaillich,* the war-cry of the Macgregors. *Tulaich ard,* the war-cry of the Mackenzies. *Carn na cuimhne,* the war-cry of Braemar. *Fraoch,* the war-cry of that tribe of the Macdonells called Macdonalds.

Sloidhe, *s. f.* (*Ir. id.*) A section, a division.

Slòigh, *gen.* slogh, *s. pl.* People; an army; a host; armies; hosts. Tàir nan slògh, *the reproach of the people.—Sm.* Sloigh Loch lainn, *the hosts of Lochlin.*

Sloìghre, *s. f.* A sword, a cimeter.

Sloighte, *s. f.* Roguery, dishonesty, cozening; *also,* rundross from the ore of metal.

† **Sloighte**, *part.* Beaten. Obair sloighte, *beaten-work.*

Sloighteil, *a.* (sloighte-amhuil.) Roguish, dishonest, cozening.

Sloightir, *s. m.* (sloighte-fhear.) A rogue, a rascal, a dishonest person; a cozener. *N. pl.* sloightirean.

Sloightireachd, *s. f.* Roguery, rascality; the practice of dishonesty; cozening.

Sloinne, *s. f.* (*Ir. id.*) A surname; a patronymic. Ciod a's sloinne duit? *what is your surname?*

Sloinn, *v. a.* (*Ir. id.*) Surname. *Pret. a.* shloinn; *fut. aff. a.* sloinnidh; *fut. pass.* sloinnear, *shall be surnamed.* Co uaith a shloinneadh i? *from whom was she surnamed?—Old Song.* Sloinnidh se e féin, *he will surname himself.—Stew. Is.*

Sloinne, *s.* See Sloinneadh.

Sloinneach, *a.* Clannish; fond of genealogy.

Sloinneachail, *a.* Genealogical.

Sloinneadh, idh, *s. m.* A surnaming; a surname. Tha e air a shloinneadh, *he is surnamed;* tha i air a sloinneadh, *she is surnamed;* thug mi sloinneadh ort, *I surnamed you.—Stew. Is.*

Sloinneadh, 3 *sing.* and *pl. imper.* of sloinn.

Sloinnear, *fut. pass.* of sloinn. Shall be surnamed.

Sloinnich, *v. a.* Surname; give a surname. *Pret. a.* shloinnich; *fut. aff. a.* sloinnichidh, *shall surname.*

Sloinnte, *p. part.* of sloinn. Surnamed.

Sloinnte, *s. f.* Genealogy. Nuair dh'airmheadh an sloinnte, *when their genealogy was reckoned.—Stew.* 1 *Chron.*

Sloinntear, ir, *s. m.* A genealogy. *N. pl.* sloinntearan.

Sloinntearach, *a.* Genealogical.

Sloinntearachd, *s. f.* Genealogy. Sloinntearachd neo-chriochnaich, *endless genealogies.—Stew. Tim.*

Sloitir, *s. m.* See Sloightir.

Sluagh, sluaigh, *s. m.* (*Ir. id. Gr.* λαὸς. *W.* llu.) A people; multitude; folk; a host; an army. Moran sluaigh, *much people. Asp. form,* shluagh. Tosdach sheas a shluaigh, *silent his people stood.—Oss. Duthona.* Sluagh-coise, *infantry; pedestrians.* Sluagh-marcachd, *cavalry; riders.* O shluagh! an exclamation, having much the same import with *O dear! O Lord! N. pl.* slògh.

Sluaghar, *a. for* sluaghmhor; which see.

Sluaghmhoire, *com.* and *sup.* of sluaghmhor.

Sluaghmhoireachd, *s. f.* Populousness.

Sluaghmhor, *a.* Populous. No sluaghmhor, *populous No.—Stew. Nah. Com.* and *sup.* sluaghmhoire.

Sluaigh, *gen. sing.* of sluagh.

Sluaigheachd, *s. f.* (*Ir. id.*) An expedition—(*Shaw*); population.

Sluaisd, *v. a.* (*for* sluasaid.) Shovel; shove aside with a spade or shovel. *Pret. a.* shluaisd; *fut. aff. a.* sluaisdidh, *shall shovel.*

Sluaisd. See Slusaid.

Sluaisdeach, *a.* Shovelling; shoving.

Sluaisdeachadh, aidh, *s. m.* A shovelling; a raking or shoving aside with a spade or shovel.

Sluaisdeachd, *s. f.* Working with a spade or shovel.

Sluaisdich, *v. a.* Shovel. *Pret. a.* shluaisdich, *shovelled; fut. aff. a.* sluaisdichidh, *shall shovel.*

Sluaisdichte, *p. part.* of sluaisdich. Shovelled.

Sluasaid, *s. f.* (*Ir.* sluasad.) A shovel; a spade. Mile sluasaid is caib, *a thousand shovels and spades.—Old Song. N. pl.* sluasaidean. Na sluasaidean, *the shovels.—Stew. Jer. Sluasaidean* is often contracted *sluaisdean.*

† **Sluch**, *v. a.* (*Island.* slock, *quench.*) Quench, extinguish; stifle; overwhelm.

† **Sludhach**, aich, *s. f.* (*Ir. id.*) A horn.—*Shaw.*

Sludhagan, ain, *s. m.* A horn; the lining of a horn.

Sludraiche, *s. f.* (*Ir. id.*) A foundation.

Slugach, *a.* Apt to swallow or ingulf; gulping, swallowing.

Slug, sluig, *s. m.* (*Ir. id.*) A gulp.

Slugadh, aidh, *s. m.* A swallowing, ingulfing; a gulping.

Slugair, *s. m.* (*Ir. id.*) A glutton; a hard drinker; *also,* a spendthrift.—*Shaw. N. pl.* slugairean.

Slugaireachd, *s. f.* Gluttony; greedy swallowing; extravagance.

Slugaite, *s. m.* A quicksand; a slough; a muddy place. *N. pl.* slugaitean.

Slugan, ain, *s. m.* (*Ir.* slugthan.) A little deep pool; a deep pool in a stream; a whirlpool; a throat or gullet; a gorge. Bha leum dlù aig slugan carraig, *he sprang quickly into the pool of the rock.—Oss. Fing.*

SLUGANACH, *a* Abounding in deep pools; having a large throat, greedy or gluttonous; swallowing; gulping.

SLUGANACHD, *s. f.* Gluttony, greediness

SLUG-GHAINEAMH, eimh, *s m* A quicksand.

SLUG-PHOLL, -phuill, *s m.* (*Ir. id*) A whirlpool —*Shaw.* *N. pl.* sluig-phuill

SLUIC, *gen. sing.* and *n pl* of sloc; which see

SLUICHD, *gen. sing* and *n pl* Of a pool, pit, or hollow, of a dell, pools, pits, hollows, dells. Tha cnuic is sluichd 'g am freagairt, *hills and dells re-echo to them* —*Oss Cathluno.*

SLUIG, *v. a.* (*Dan* sluigear, *to devour. Ir* slug, *swallow.*) Swallow, engorge, ingulf, gulp down; devour. *Pret. a.* shluig, *swallowed, fut aff. a* sluigidh Shluig e daoine, *it devoured men.—Stew. Ezek*

SLUIGEAR, *fut pass.* of sluig Shall be swallowed.

SLUIGIDH, *fut aff a* of sluig. Shall or will swallow.

SLUIGEAN, ein, *s m* A little glutton; the neck of a bottle

SLUIGTE, *p part.* of sluig Swallowed, engorged, ingulfed; gulped down, devoured. *Asp. form,* shluigte.

SLUINN, *s. f.* A telling, a declaring.

† SLUS, *v a* Dissemble; counterfeit *Pret. a* shlus

SMACHD, *v a* Chastise, correct; rule; keep under subjection; keep in awe; discipline; reprove *Pret a.* smachd, *fut aff a* smachdaidh

SMACHD, *s m* (*Ir id*) Chastisement, correction; rule; discipline; authority, as of a master over a pupil, reproof, awe, subjection Smachd airme, *military discipline, the rule of arms* —*Oss Tem* Cuir fuidh smachd, *bring into subjection* —*Stew* 1 *Cor* Cum smachd air, *keep him under subjection*

SMACHDACH, *a* Prone to chastise or correct, ruling, lording; keeping in awe or under subjection *Com* and *sup* smachdaiche.

SMACHDACHADH, aidh, *s m* (*Ir* smachdughadh.) A chastising or correcting, a keeping in awe or under subjection, chastisement, correction, severe reproof, rule, awe, subjection Smachdachadh o leanabh, *correction from a child* —*Stew. Pro*

SMACHDAICH, *v a* Chastise, correct, or punish; keep in awe, keep under subjection, reprove severely, rule *Pret a* smachdaich; *fut. aff a* smachdaichidh, *shall punish* Smachdaich le slataibh, *chastise with rods.*—*Stew* 1 *K* Smachdaichidh mi na daoine, *I will punish the men* —*Stew. Zeph*

SMACHDAICHTE, *p. part* of smachdaich. Chastised, corrected, punished; brought under subjection

SMACHDAIL, *a.* (smachd-amhuil) Disciplinary; lordly, authoritative, commanding, overbearing

SMACHDAIR, *s. m.* A disciplinarian, an authoritative person, one who overbears. *N. pl* smachdairean

SMACHD-BHANN, ainn, *s m* A penal law, a code of criminal law

SMACHD-LANN, -lainn, *s m* A house of correction —*Shaw*

SMACHDUCHADH, aidh, *s m*, more properly *smachdachadh*; which see

SMACHDUICH, *v a.* See SMACHDAICH

SMAD, *s m* A particle, a jot, a small portion of any thing; smut, soot Cha chuir e smad orm, *it will not affect me in the least.*

SMÀD, *v a* and *n* Boast; beat away; intimidate, scare *Pret a.* smàd; *fut. aff a* smàdaidh.

SMADACH, *a* (*from* smad) Sooty, smutty.

SMÀDACH, *a* (*from* smàd) Prone to boast; prone to beat off, intimidating, scaring

SMÀDADH, aidh, *s. m* Boasting

SMÀDAIL, *a* Boastful; threatening; intimidating, scaring.

SMADAN, ain, *s. m.* (*dim.* of smad.) Soot; smut; a particle of soot or smut, a jot, a particle.

SMADANACH, *a.* (*Ir id.*) Smutted; sooted, dusty.

SMÀG, *v. a.* and *n* Paw; grope, go on all-fours. *Pret. a.* smàg; *fut aff a* smàgaidh

SMÀG, smàig, *s. f.* A paw; *in derision,* a clumsy palm, a clumsy foot. *N. pl* smàgan. Air smàgan, *on all-fours.*

SMÀGACH, *a* Pawed, having large paws, clumsy-footed; pawing, groping

SMÀGACHADH, aidh, *s. m* A pawing, a groping, a moving on all-fours.

SMÀGAICH, *v. a.* and *n.* Paw, grope, creep, move on all-fours. *Pret a.* smàgaich

SMÀGAIL, *s. f.* A groping, a pawing; a creeping, or moving on all-fours

SMÀGAIR, *s. m.* A creature with paws; a clumsy-fisted fellow; a clumsy-footed fellow; one who gropes, creeps, or moves on all-fours.

SMÀGARSAICH, *s f.* Pawing, groping, creeping, moving on all-fours

SMAICHD See SMACHD.

SMAIDSEART, eirt, *s m.* An active young fellow

SMÀIG, *gen. sing.* of smàg.

SMÀIGEAN, ein, *s m* A frog. *N pl.* smàigeinean Cluich nan smàigean, *leapfrog.*

SMÀIGEANACH, *a.* Like a frog; full of frogs; creeping, groping.

SMÀIGEANACHD, *s f.* Creeping, groping; a creeping gait.

SMÀIL, *v a* Snuff or top, as a candle; knock down, dash to the ground. *Pret a* smàil; *fut aff. a.* smàilidh; *fut. pass.* smàilear, *p. part* smàilte.

SMÀIL, *gen* and *voc sing.* of smàl

SMÀL, *v. a* See SMÀIL

SMÀL, smàil, *s m* (*Ir.* smol) The snuff of a candle; an infirm or sickly person *N pl* smàlan

SMAL, smail, *s m.* A spot, a blot, or blemish; sorrow; vexation; dimness, a cloud; gloom; obscurity. Smal cha 'n 'eil annad, *thou hast no spot.*—*Stew. Song Sol.* Gheibh e smal, *he will get a blot.*—*Stew. Pro.* Fu smal, *extinguished* —*Oss Gaul* Cionnas a thàinig smal air an òr? *how has the gold become dim?*—*Stew Lam.*

SMÀLADAIR, *s. m* (*Ir* smaladoir) A pair of snuffers; an extinguisher, a candle-snuffer *N. pl.* smàladairean, *snuffers* —*Stew Jer*

SMÀLADAIREACHD, *s f* The business of a candle-snuffer.

SMÀLADAN, ain, *s m* A pair of snuffers, an extinguisher.

SMÀLADH, aidh, *s m.* A snuffing, as of a candle; extinguishing, as of a candle or fire; a quenching; a knocking down

SMÀLADH, (a), *pr. part.* of smàil Snuffing or topping a candle; extinguishing or quenching a flame, knocking down. A smàladh an teine fo' shlneadh, *quenching the fire with its weight* —*Oss. Taura.*

SMALAG, aig, *s f.* The play called fillip.

SMALAN, ain, *s m* (*from* smàl) Grief, vexation, sorrow; dimness, gloom; dust; a particle of dust. Tha Minla fu smalan, *Minla is absorbed in sorrow.*—*Oss. Duthona.*

SMALAN, ain, *s. m* A hillock; a little blow, a fillip

SMÀLANACH, *a.* Grieved; vexed; sorrowful; gloomy; grievous, vexatious; full of hillocks.

SMÀLANACHD, *s f* Sorrowfulness, grievousness, vexatiousness, gloominess

SMÀL-SHOITHEACH, -shoithche, *s m.* An extinguisher — *Stew Ex* Smàl-shoithchean

SMAOGAL, ail, *s m* (*Ir. id*) A husk or hull. —*Shaw.* Smaogal chnò, *the husk of a nut.*

SMAOGALACH, *a* Husky; having a husk or hull

Smaoin. See Smuain.

Smaointe. More frequently written *smuainte;* which see.

Smaointean. See Smuaintean.

Smaointeachadh, aidh, *s. m.* See Smuainteachadh.

Smaointich, *v. a.* Think, consider; ponder, meditate; purpose, intend, devise. *Pret. a.* smaointich; *fut. aff.* smaointichidh, *shall think.* A smaointean a smaointich e, *his purposes that he purposed.—Stew. Jer.*

Smaolach, aich, *s. m.* A thrush, an ouzle.—*Shaw.*

Smaosdrach, aich, *s. m.* A cartilage, a gristle.

Smaosrach, aich, *s. m.* Gristle or cartilage.—*Shaw.*

Smarag, aig, *s. f.* (*Ir. id.*) An emerald. *N. pl.* smaragan.

Smaragach, *a.* Abounding in emeralds; like an emerald; of emeralds.

Smeac, *s. m.* (*Ir. id.*) A smack, a kiss; a fillip with the finger.

Smeacadh, aidh, *s. m.* A palpitation; a panting—(*Shaw*); smacking with the lips.

Smeach, smeacha, *s. m.* A chin; a neck; a fillip. *N. pl.* smeachan.

Smeachach, *a.* Chinned; having a peaked chin; having a long neck.

Smeachan, ain, *s. m.* (*dim.* of smeach.) A little chin; a chin; a person with a peaked chin.

Smeachanach, *a.* Chinned; having a peaked chin.

Smear, *s. m.* (*Ir. id. W.* mer.) Marrow, pith; animal spirits, sprightliness. See Smior.

Smeàr, smèara, *s. m.* A bramble-berry. See Smeur.

Smeàrach, *a.* Pawing, fingering, or handling clumsily; groping; full of bramble-berries; of bramble-berries. See also Smeurach.

Smearachadh, aidh, *s. m.* A groping; a pawing, a fingering, or handling awkwardly; a fumbling; a greasing, a smearing. Written also *smeurachadh.*

Smearachan, ain, *s. m.* A kitchen-brat, a lick-plate.

Smeàrachd, *s. f.* Continued groping, fumbling; greasing, smearing.

Smearag, aig, *s. m.* A brambleberry. *N. pl.* smearagan. See also Smeurag.

Smeàraich, *v. a.* Grope, paw, finger awkwardly, feel; fumble; grease, smear. *Pret. a.* smearaich; *fut. aff. a.* smearaichidh. Written also *smeuraich.*

Smearaiche, *s. f.* The second swarming of a hive.

Smearalas, ais, *s. m.* See Smioralas.

Smèaroid, *s. f.* A coal, a burning coal, a hot ember.

Smeat, smeata, *s. m.* A simper, a smile.

Smeatach, *a.* (*Ir.* smutach.) Simpering; snouty; short-snouted.

Smeatadh, aidh, *s. m.* A simpering; a simper; a snout.

Smeatag, aig, *s. f.* A simpering young female; a flat-nosed young female. *N. pl.* smeatagan.

Sméid, *s. f.* (*Ir. id.*) A nod, a wink, a beckoning.

Sméid, *v. n.* Nod, wink, beckon; make a private sign to; hiss. *Pret. a.* sméid, *nodded; fut. aff. a.* sméididh.

Sméideach, *a.* (*from* sméid.) Nodding, beckoning, making private signs; hissing; *also, substantively,* one who nods, beckons, or makes private signs.

Sméideadh, idh, *s. m.* (*Ir. id.*) A nodding, a beckoning, a winking; a hissing; a nod, a beckon, a wink; a hiss.

Sméideadh, 3 *sing.* and *pl. imper.* of sméid; which see.

Smeig, *s. f.* See Smig.

Smeigead. See Smigead.

Smeil, *s. f.* A pale look, a ghastly look.—*Shaw.*

Smeileach, *a.* Pale, ghastly, puny.

Smeileag, eig, *s. f.* (*from* smeil.) A pale, puny female. *N. pl.* smeileagan.

Smeilean, ein, *s. m.* A pale, ghastly-looking fellow.

Smeirne, *s. f.* A spit, a broach.

Smeoirn, smeoirne, *s. f.* The point of a dart or spear. Eadar smeoirn agus gàinne, *between dart and arrow.—Old Song.*

Smeoirneach, *a.* (*from* smeoirn.) Sharp; pointed; like a spear's point; pointed, as a dart or spear.

Smeòr, *v. a.* Smear, anoint, grease; tar sheep. *Pret. a.* smeòr; *fut. aff. a.* smeòraidh.

Smeòrach, aich, *s. f.* (*Ir. id.*) A mavis; the *turdus musicus* of Linnæus; a linnet; the name of a dog. Uiseag is smeòrach, *the lark and the mavis.—Macdon.* Ceileir na smeòrach, *the warbling of the mavis.—Oss. Derm.* Cha dean aon smeòrach samhradh, *one swallow will not make a summer.—G. P.*

Smeòrach, *a.* Smearing, anointing; greasy, tallowy.

Smeòrachadh, aidh, *s. m.* A smearing, an anointing; a greasing, a tarring.

Smeòradair, *s. m.* A smearer, an anointer; one who smears or tars sheep. *N. pl.* smeòradairean.

Smeòradaireachd, *s. f.* Smearing; the employment of smearing or tarring sheep.

Smeòradh, aidh, *s. m.* A smearing, an anointing; a tarring or smearing of sheep; unction.

Smeòraich, *v. a.* Smear; anoint; tar, as sheep. *Pret. a.* smeòraich; *fut. aff. a.* smeòraichidh, *shall smear.*

Smeòraichte, *p. part.* of smeòraich. Smeared, anointed, tarred.

Smeur, smeura, *s. m.* (*Ir. id.*) A bramble-berry; a black-berry; any fruit resembling a bramble-berry. Craobh nan smeur, *a mulberry-tree.—Stew. Sam.*

Smeurach, *a.* Full of bramble-berries; full of berries; of bramble-berries; groping, fumbling.

Smeurachadh, aidh, *s. m.* A groping, a fingering awkwardly; a pawing; a feeling, a fumbling.

Smeurachan, ain, *s. m.* A kitchen-brat, a lick-plate; a bone-picker.

Smeurachd, *s. f.* Continued groping; a habit of groping or of fingering awkwardly; a fumbling. Written also *smearachd.*

Smeurag, aig, *s. f.* (*dim.* of smeur.) A bramble-berry. *N. pl.* smeuragan.

Smeuragach, *a.* Full of bramble-berries; of bramble-berries.

Smeuraich, *v. a.* and *n.* Grope, feel, handle awkwardly, fumble. *Pret. a.* smeuraich; *fut. aff. a.* smeuraichidh, *shall grope.* Smeuraichidh iad san dorchadas, *they shall grope in the dark.—Stew. Job.*

Smeuraichidh, *fut. aff.* of smeuraich.

Smeuran, *n. pl.* of smeur. Bramble-berries. See Smeur.

Smeur-phreas, -phris, *s. m.* A bramble. *N. pl.* smeur-phreasan.

Smeur-phreasach, *a.* Abounding in brambles; of brambles.

Smiar, *s.* See Smeur.

Smid, *s. f.* A syllable, a word. Gun smid, *mute, mum;* gun smid chainnt, *without a syllable of speech.—Sm.* Gun smid tha ceann na h-eòlais, *speechless is the head of knowledge.—Old Song.*

Smig, smige, *s. f.* A chin; a smile; mirth. *N. pl.* smige-achan, *smiles.*

Smigeach, *a.* Chinned; having a large chin; smiling; mirthful.

Smigead, eid, *s. m.* A chin.—*Macd.*

Smigeadach, aich, *s. m.*, smig-eudach. (*Ir. id.*) Chin-cloth.

Smigeadh, idh, *s. m.* A smiling; a smile; mirth.

Smigean, ein, *s. m.* (*dim.* of smig.) A little chin; mirth; a smile.

Smileach, ich, *s. f.* A nightingale. *N. pl.* smilichean.

SMIODAM, aim, *s. m.* Spirit; pluck; animal spirits; smartness; stamina. Cha 'n'eil smiodam annad, *you have no pluck.*

SMIODAMACH, *a.* Having spirit or pluck; having animal spirits; having stamina.

SMIOL, smiola, *s. f.* A nightingale.—*Shaw.*

SMIOLACH, *a.* Abounding in nightingales; of nightingales; sweet, as a nightingale's voice.

SMIOLACH, aich, *s. m.* A nightingale.

SMIOLAG, aig, *s. f.* (*dim.* of smiol.) A young nightingale; a nightingale. *N. pl.* smiolagan.

SMIÒR. See SMEÒR and SMIÙR.

SMIOR, *s. m.* (*Ir. id. W.* mer.) Marrow; pith; strength; pluck; animal spirits, vivacity; the best part of any thing. Le smior, *with marrow.*—*Stew. Job. N. pl.* smioran; *d. pl.* smioraibh. An smiornibh a chnamh, *in the strength of his bones.*—*Old Song.*

SMIORACH, *a.* Abounding in marrow, pithy; of marrow.

SMIÒRACH, *a.* See SMEORACH.

SMIORACHAN, ain, *s. m.* A kitchen-brat; a lick-plate; a bone-picker.

SMIORADH, aidh, *s. m.* See SMEORADH.

SMIORAIL, *a.* (smior-amhuil.) Manly, active, brisk, lively; having marrow, pith, or pluck; like marrow.

SMIORALACHD, *s. f.* (*from* smior.) Habitual manliness; habitual activity, briskness, or liveliness.

SMIORALAS, ais, *s. m.* Manliness, activity, briskness, liveliness, pluck. Cha 'n' fhac mi do leithid air smioralas, *I never saw your like for manliness.*

SMIOT, *s. m.* (*Ir. id.*) An ear; a small portion of any thing; a particle; a box or blow.

SMIOTACH, *a.* Crop-eared; of, or belonging to, the ear.

SMIOTAG, aig, *s. f.* A hand or glove without fingers.

SMIOTAN, ain, *s. m.* A fillip; a small ear.

SMIST, *v. a.* Smite.

SMISTE, *s. f.* A pestle.

SMISTEADH, idh, *s. m.* A smiting, a pounding.

SMISTEAN, ein, *s. m.* A short thick stick, a cudgel; a pestle.

SMIÙR, *v. a.* Smear, grease, anoint; daub; tar or smear sheep. *Pret. a.* smiùr; *fut. aff. a.* smiùraidh.

SMIÙRACH, *a.* Smearing, greasing, anointing, daubing, tarring; apt to smear, grease, or daub; greasy.

SMIÙRADAIR, *s. m.* A smearer; one who smears or tars sheep. *N. pl.* smiùradairean.

SMIÙRADAIREACHD, *s. f.* The employment of sheep-shearing; the business of a sheep-shearer.

SMIÙRADH, aidh, *s. m.* A smearing, a greasing, an anointing, a daubing; smearing or tarring of sheep. Cha dean smiùradh ur saoradh, *tarring will not save you.*—*Mac Co.*

SMOD, smoid, *s. m.* Dirt, dust, smut.

SMOD, smoid, *s. m.* Drizzling rain; a moist haze; a creeping mist.

SMÒDACH, *a.* Drizzling; moist; hazy; misty.

SMODACH, *a.* Dirty, dusty, smutty.

SMODAN, ain, *s. m.* A little spot or blemish; smut, dirt. Gun smur gun smodan, *without dust or spot.*—*Old Song.*

SMÒDAN, ain, *s. m.* Drizzling rain, moistness; haze; haziness.

SMODANACH, *a.* Spotted, soiled, dirty.

SMÒDANACH, *a.* Drizzly, moist, hazy, misty.

SMÒDANACHD, *s. f.* Drizzliness; haziness.

SMÒG, smoig, *s. m.* Written also *smàg;* which see.

SMÒGACH, *a.* (*from* smog.) See SMAGACH.

SMÒGACHADH, aidh, *s. m.* A groping, a pawing. Written also *smagachadh.*

SMÒGAICH, *v. n.* Paw, grope, feel. Written also *smagaich.*

SMÒGAIRNEACH, ich, *s. m.* A creature with large paws—(*Macint.*); *also, adjectively,* having large paws, large-boned.—*Shaw.*

SMÒGARSAICH, *s. f.* A pawing; awkward groping.

SMOIGLEACH, *a.* Smutted, soiled, dirty.

SMOIGLEADH, idh, *s. m.* Smut, dirt.

SMOIT, smoite, *s. f.* Sulkiness, techiness; a sulky fit.

SMOITEACH, *a.* Sulky, techy.—*Shaw.*

SMOITEACHD, *s. f.* Habitual sulkiness or techiness.

SMOL, *s. m.* (*Ir. id.*) A weaver's shuttle.

SMÒL, *s.* More frequently written *smàl;* which see.

SMOLACH, aich, *s. m.* A ember; a thrush.

SMÒLADAIR, *s. m.* See SMÀLADAIR.

SMÒLADAN, ain, *s. m.* See SMÀLADAN.

SMOLASG, aisg, *s. m.* Dross, refuse, sweepings.

SMOLDACH, aich, *s. m.* A nightingale.

SMOT, *v. n.* Snuffle.

SMOT, *s. m.* A mouthful; a pluck.

SMOTACH, *a.* Snuffling.

SMOTAIL, *s. m.* A snuffling. Ciod an smotail a th' ort? *why do you snuffle so?*

SMOTAN, ain, *s. m.* A block, a log, a stock.

SMOTAN, ain, *s. m.* A mouthful; a pluck.

SMUAIN, smuaine, *s. m.* A thought; a notion, fancy; reflection; imagination; prudence, presence of mind. *N. pl.* smuainte *and* smuaintean.

SMUAINEACH, *a.* (*from* smuain.) Thoughtful; pensive; fanciful; reflecting; prone to reflect, prudent.

SMUAINEACHADH, aidh, *s. m.* A thinking, a fancying, a reflecting, a meditating, an imagining; a thought, a fancy, an imagination; a meditation.

SMUAINEACHADH, (a), *pr. part.* of smuainich.

SMUAINEACHAIL, *a.* Thoughtful, pensive; cautious, considerate.

SMUAINEADH, idh, *s. m.* A thought, a notion, a fancy; an opinion; a reflection; an imagination; sedateness, pensiveness; a device.

SMUAINICH, *v. a.* Think, consider, reflect; ponder, meditate; imagine; suppose; devise. *Pret. a.* smuainich; *fut. aff. a.* smuainichidh, *shall think.*

SMUAINICHEAR, *fut. pass.* of smuainich.

SMUAINICHIDH, *fut. aff. a.* of smuainich. Shall or will think.

SMUAINTE, SMUAINTEAN, *n. pl.* of smuain. Thoughts, notions, fancies, reflections, imaginations. Is tric sibh am smuainte, *often are you in my thoughts.*—*Oss. Derm.* Smuaintean a chridhe, *the thoughts of his heart.*—*Stew. Gen.*

SMUAINTEACH, *a.* Thoughtful, pensive; sedate; contemplative; considerate; cautious.

SMUAINTEACHADH, aidh, *s. m.* (*Ir.* smuaintiughadh.) The exercise of thinking; a fancying; a thought, a reflection, a fancy; meditation.

SMUAINTEACHAIL, *a.* Thoughtful, pensive; sedate; contemplative; considerate, cautious.

SMUAINTEADH, idh, *s. m.* See SMUAINEADH.

SMUAINTICH, *v. a.* (*Ir.* smuintich.) Think, consider, ponder; meditate; imagine, suppose, devise, purpose, intend. *Pret. a.* smuaintich; *fut. aff. a.* smuaintichidh.

SMUAIREAN, ein, *s. m.* (*Ir. id.*) A dejecting thought; a vexing thought; sorrow, vexation. Gun smuairean ro' dhoininn, *heedless of the storm.*—*Oss. Corm.* Cha chuir e smuairean orm, *it will not vex me in the least; it will not cost me a thought.*

SMUAIREANACH, *a.* (*from* smuairean.) Apt to be dejected; apt to be vexed; dejected, vexed; causing dejection, causing vexation.

SMUAIREANACHD, *s. f.* Dejectedness, pensiveness, vexation.

SMUAIS, *v. a.* Break in pieces, splinter, smash. *Pret. a.* smuais; *fut. aff. a.* smuaisidh, *shall smash.*

SMUAIS, *s. f.* Shivers, splinters, smashing; grease intermixed in the bone, marrow. Chaidh e na smuais, *it went into shivers.*

Smuaiseach, *a.* Smashing, shivering, splintering; greasing; greasy; full of marrow; of marrow.

Smuaisich, *v. a.* Smash. *Pret. a. id.* smashed; *fut. aff. a.* smuaiscichidh, *shall smash.*

Smuaisichte, *p. part.* of smuaisich. Smashed.

Smuaisrich, *s. f.* Smashing; fragments.

Smùc, smùic, *s. m.* A snivel; a snore, a nasal sound.

Smùcach, *a.* Snivelling; snoring; uttering nasal sounds.

Smùcail, *s. f.* A snivelling, a snoring; a snore; nasal utterance.—*Macd.* Ciod an smùcail a th' ort, *why do you snivel so?*

Smùcan, smùchan, ain, *s. m.* Smoke. *Gr.* σμύχω, *lento igne sine flamma consumere.*

Smùcanach, **Smùchanach**, *a.* Smoking, smoky.

Smùchanaich, *s. f.* A snivelling, a snoring; nasal utterance.

Smùdan, ain, *s. m.* A ring-dove or wood-pigeon; smoke; smoke made for a signal. Mar smùdan an coille fhas, *like a ring-dove in a desert wood.—Oss.* Tha smùdan fein an ceann gach foid, *its own smoke is at the top of every turf.—G. P.*

Smùdan, ain, *s. m.* A particle of dust; a mote, block, a log, soot, smut.

Smùdanach, *a.* Abounding in ring-doves or wood-pigeons; of wood-pigeons; smoking, smoky.

Smug, smuig, *s. f.* (*Ir. id.*) A spittle; a snot, mucus. Smug na cuthaig, *woodsare, cuckoo's spittle.*

Smug, *v. a.* and *n.* Spit, snot. *Pret.* smug; *fut. aff. a.* smugaidh.

Smugach, *a.* (*from* smug.) Spitting, having a habit of spitting; snotty.

Smugadair, *s. m.* (*Ir. id.*) A bespawler; a handkerchief.

Smugadanaich, *s. f.* Spitting.

Smugadh, aidh, *s. m.* A spitting.

Smugaid, *s. f.* (*from* smug.) A spittle; phlegm; saliva. Tilg smugaid, *spit;* smugaid a thilgeadh, *to throw a spittle. Stew. Job.* Smugaid na cuthaig, *woodsare, or that froth or kind of spittle which is observed on herbs, as lavender, sage, or on brier-sprouts, in summer. N. pl.* smugaidean.

Smugaideach, *a.* Spitting often; salival.

Smugaideachd, *s. f.* Salivation; a habit of spitting.

Smugaidean, *n. pl.* of smugaid.

Smugaid na cuthaig, *s. f.* Woodsare, a frothy exudation observed in summer on herbs, as lavender, or sage, and also on grasses, as clover.

Smugail, *s. f.* Mucus, snot.

Smùid, *s. f.* (*Ir. id.*) Smoke; vapour; fume; mist. A cur smùid, *smoking as a peat-fire before it flames. N. pl.* smùidean; *n. pl.* smùidibh. Anam nan laoch dol suas nan smùidibh, *the souls of heroes ascending in mists.—Orr.*

Smùid, *v. n.* (*Ir. id.*) Smoke, fume, exhale. *Pret. a.* smùid; *fut. aff. a.* smùididh, *shall smoke.*

Smùideach, *a.* Smoky, vapoury, fuming, exhaling.

Smuidean, ein, *s. m.* A particle of dust, a mote.

Smuideanach, *a.* Dusty, having particles of dust.

Smùideil, *a.* (smùid amhuil.) Smoky, vapoury, effluvious.

Smùidre, *s. pl.* Clouds, as of smoke or dust; exhalation; mist. Smùidre ceathaich, *clouds of mist.—Oss. Taura.*

Smùidreach, *a.* Smoking, smoky. Air son dà earr nan aithinnean smuidreach so, *for the two tails of these smoking firebrands.—Stew. Is.*

Smùidrich, *s. f.* Smoke, mist; a volume or a cloud of smoke; a smoking. Le smùidrich ghlas, *with grey smoke.—Oss. Conn.* Neula dùis nan smùidrich dhorcha, *clouds of dust like dark smoke.—Orr.*

Smùig, *s. f.* (*Ir.* smug.) Snot, phlegm, mucus; dirt, filth; a snout.

Smuigeach, *a.* Snotty, phlegmy, mucous; dirty; filthy.

Smuigeadach, aich, *s. m.* (*Ir. id.*) A pocket-handkerchief.

Smùinteachadh. See **Smuainteachadh.**

Smùintich, *v.* See **Smuaintich.**

Smuir, *s. f.* (*Ir. id.*) A beak; a snout.—*Shaw.*

Smùir, *s.* A particle of dust; an atom; dust, ashes, earth; a blot, a spot, a blemish. Fo smùir, *under dust.—Oss. Tem.* Dealradh na gréin gun smùir, *the splendour of the spotless sun.—Id.*

Smùirneach, *a.* Full of dust, dusty, atomy; drossy.

Smùirnean, ein, *s. m.* (*dim.* of smùir.) A mote, atom, or particle of dust. An smùirnean, *the mote.—Stew. Matt.*

Smùirneanach, *a.* Full of motes; dusty.

Smùirneanachd, *s. f.* Dustiness; the state of being full of motes.

Smuis, *s. f.* Marrow, pith; sweat; sap; the gristle of the nose. Smuis is aisnichean, *marrow and ribs.—Macdon.* Smuis air a gharbh ghairdean, *sweat on his brawny arm.—Macfar.* Written also *smuais.*

Smuiseach, *a.* Having marrow or pith; sweating; stirring up, exciting; moving.

Smuisean, ein, *s. m.* A name importing much personal contempt.

Smuit, *s. f.* (*Ir. id.*) A nose, a bill or beak, a snout.

Smulc, *s. m.* (*Ir. id.*) A snout; a surly look.

Smulcach, *a.* Snouty; having a surly look.

Smulan, ain, *s. m.* A lump of wood.

Smulcair, *s. m.* (*from* smulc.) A person having a surly look; a boxer.

Smulcanta, *a.* Snouty; having a surly look.

Smùr, smùir, *s. m.* Dross, dust; ashes; a blot or blemish. Gun smùr gun smodan, *without spot or blemish.—Old Song.*

Smùr, *v. a.* Bedaub. See **Smiùr.**

Smùrach, *a.* Drossy, dusty; having blots, spots or blemishes.

Smùrach, aich, *s. m.* (*Ir. id.*) Dross, dust. Smurach mòin, *peat dross.*

Smut, *s. m.* A flat nose; a peaked chin.

Smutach, *a.* Snouty, having a short snout, having a peaked chin; saddle nosed.

Smutag, aig, *s. f.* A flat nosed, or saddle-nosed female.

Smutan, ain, *s. m.* (*Ir. id.*) A log, a block.

Sna, (*for* anns na.) In the. Aogas na doininn sna neulaibh, *the appearance of storms in the clouds.—Orr.*

Sna, (*for* anns an do.) In which, where. Carraid sna tharruing mi lann, *a battle in which I drew my sword.—Oss. Fing.* A chluain sna chuireadh an cath, *the plain where the battle was fought.—Id.*

'Sna, (*for* is na *or* agus na.) And the; and not. Na fleasgaich òg sna caileagan, *the young men and women.—Old Song.* Falbh 'sna fan, *go and wait not.*

Snàd, snàid, *s. f.* See **Snàthad.**

Snadh, snadh, *s. m.* (*Ir. id.*) A sup.—*Shaw.*

Snàdh, snàdha, *s. m.* Thread, yarn.

Snadhach, *a.* Sappy, juicy.

Snadhadh, aidh, *s. m.* (*Ir. id.*) Protection, defence; a guardian-angel.

Snàdhainn, *s. f.* See **Snàthainn.**

Snàdhainneach, *a.* See **Snàthainneach.**

Snadh-ghairm, *s. f.* (*Ir. id.*) An appellation; a naming; an appeal.

Snadhm. See **Snaidhm.**

† **Snag**, snaig, *s. f.* The hiccup.—*Shaw.*

Snăg, snaig, *s. f.* A woodpecker. *N. pl.* snagan.

Snàg, snàig, *s. m.* One with a creeping gait, one whose motions are slow.

SNÀG, *v. n.* (*Sax.* snaga, *a serpent. Eng* snake.) Creep, sneak; crawl; steal softly. *Pret. a.* shnàg; *fut. aff. a.* snàgaidh; *pret. sub.* shnàgas. Gach ni a shnàgas, *every creeping thing.—Stew. Lev*

SNAGACH, *a.* Full of woodpeckers, like a woodpecker, of a woodpecker.

SNÀGACH, *a.* Creeping, sneaking; crawling; stealing softly

SNÀGADH, aidh, *s m.* A creeping, a crawling, a sneaking.

SNÀGAIR, *s m* (snàg-fhear) A creeper, a crawler; a sneaking fellow. Snàgair daraich, *a woodpecker, a snarler. N pl* snàgairean.

SNAGAIRDICH, *s f* A gnashing, a grating of the teeth Snagairdich fhiocal, *gnashing of the teeth —Stew Matt ref*

SNÀGAIREACH, *s. f.* A creeping, a crawling, a sneaking; a habit of creeping or crawling, a habit of sneaking, a sneaking habit.

SNÀGAN, ain, *s m.* A creeping or crawling; a creeping motion, one who creeps; a crawler, one with a creeping gait.

SNÀGAN, ain, *s m*, *dim* of snag, which see.

SNĂGAN, ain, *s. m.* (*Ir. id.*) A short drink or draught.—*Shaw.*

SNÀGANAICH, *s. f* Creeping, crawling.

SNAGAN-DARAICH, *s m* A woodpecker

SNAGARDACH, aich, *s m* A woodpecker. *N pl.* snagardaich.

SNÀGARDAICH, *s f* Creeping, crawling.

SNAGARRA, *a.* Alert, clever, smart Gu snagarra, *alertly.*

SNAGARRACHD, *s f.* Alertness, cleverness, smartness

SNAGARTAICH, *s f* A gnashing or grating of the teeth

SNAG-LABHAIR, *v a.* Stammer or hesitate in speech

SNAG-LABHAIRT, *s f.* (*Ir id*) Stammering; a stammer in speech

SNAG-LABHAIRTICHE, *s. m.* A stammerer in speech

SNAIDH, snaidhe, *s f* A slice; a lopping; a chip

SNAIDH, *v a.* Hew, carve, whet; slice, lop; defalcate; protect, patronize. *Pret. a* shnaidh, *fut. aff. a.* snaidhidh Snaidh dà chlàr, *hew two tables —Stew Ex* Written also *snaigh*, which see

SNAIDHEACH, *a* Hewing, carving, whetting, slicing, lopping, defalcating

SNAIDHEADAIR, *s. m.* A hewer of stone. a carver, a whetter, one who lops, a defalcator *N. pl* snaidheadairean, *hewers of stone —Stew* 1 *Chron.*

SNAIDHEADAIREACHD, *s. f* Stone hewing; carving; cutting in chips

SNAIDHEADH, idh, *s. m* A hewing, a carving, a blocking; a whetting, a slicing, a lopping, a defalcation Snaidheadh fiodha, *a carving of wood —Stew Ex* Snaidheadh chlacha, *a hewing of stone*

SNAIDHEARACHD, *s. f* Hewing of stone, carving, cutting in chips.

SNAIDHM, *s* See SNAIM

SNAIDHTE, *p part* of snaidh Hewn, carved, graven, whetted, sliced, lopped off, defalcated, polished Clacha snaidhte, *hewn stone —Stew* 1 *K.* See also *snaighte*

SNĂIG, *s f* (*Scotch,* sneck) The latchet of a door *N pl* snaigeachan. Cuir an t-snaig air an dorus, *sneck the door*

SNĂIG, *v. a.* Latch or sneck as a door.

SNÀIG, *v n.* Creep, crawl, sneak; steal softly *Pret a.* shnàig; *fut. aff. a* snàigidh, *shall creep* Written also *snàg*

SNÀIGEACH, *a.* Creeping, crawling; sneaking; having a creeping gait.

SNAIGEACHAN, *n pl.* of snaig.

SNÀIGEADH, idh, *s. m.* A creeping, a crawling; a sneaking

SNÀIGEADH, (a), *pr. part* of snàig. Creeping, crawling, sneaking. A snàigeadh air an talamh, *creeping on the earth —Stew Gen.*

SNÀIGEAN, ein, *s. m.* A reptile, a creeping thing; one with a creeping gait *N. pl.* snaigeanan.

SNÀIGEANACH, *a.* Creeping; having a creeping gait.

SNÀIGEANACHD, *s. f.* Creeping; a creeping gait

SNAIGH, *v. a.* (*Ir* snoigh) Cut; hew; carve, grave, lop, whet, slice, polish *Pret a* shnaigh; *fut. aff. a.* snaighidh, *shall hew.* Snaighibh dhomhsa bogha, *cut a bow for me —Ull* Written also *snaidh.*

SNAIGHEACH, *a.* Cutting, hewing, carving, graving, whetting; lopping.

SNÀIGHEACH, *a.* (*Ir. id.*) Creeping, crawling; sneaking; having a creeping gait. Beothach snàigheach, *a creeping thing, a reptile.*

SNAIGHEADAIR, *s. m* A stone-hewer; a graver, a carver, a lopper; a defalcator. *N. pl.* snaigheadairean

SNAIGHEADAIREACHD, *s. f.* Hewing of stone; graving, carving.

SNĂIGHEADH, idh, *s m.* A cutting, a hewing, a carving, a graving, a lopping, a whetting, a polishing

SNAIGHTE, *p. part* of snaigh (*Ir.* snoighte.) Hewn, cut, carved, graven, polished, whetted, sliced, lopped; defalcated. Clach shnaighte, *a hewn stone*, clachan snaighte, *hewn stones*, iomhaigh shnaighte, *a graven image.—Stew. Hab* Briathran snaighte, *polished words.—Old Song.*

SNAIM, *s m* (*Ir* snaidhm) A knot; a tie; a difficulty, a puzzle Daoine a dh' fhuasgladh gach snaim, *men who would solve every difficulty —Mac Lach.* Cuir snaim, *tie a knot*

SNAIM, *v a* Knot, tie, fasten, bind, fetter *Pret. a.* shnaim, *bound*, *fut aff a* snaimidh, *shall bind.*

SNAIMEACH, *a.* Knotty.

SNAIMEADH, idh, *s. m* A knotting, a fastening with a knot.

SNAIMEANACH, *a* Knotty; nodous.

SNAIMEANACHD, *s. f* Knottiness.

SNAIMEAS, eis, *s m.* A rout, a multitude.

SNÀITH, *v. a.* Thread *Pret. a.* shnàith

SNÀITH, *s. f.* (*Ir. id.*) A thread, a filament.

SNÀITHNE, *s f* (*contracted for* snàthainn.) A thread, a string, a cord Snàithne tri fillte, *a string of three plaits or folds —Stew. Ecc.* Snàithne tomhais, *a measuring line —Stew Job N. pl.* snàithnean.

SNAITHNEACH, *a.* Thready, in threads, in strings, in cords

SNÀMH, *v a* and *n* (*Ir id.*) Swim, float *Pret a.* shnàmh; *fut aff a.* snàmhaidh, *shall swim* Snàmhaidh I Cholum clàraich, *the isle of Columba* [*of the harp*] *shall float —Old prophecy.*

SNAMH, snaimh, *s m* The slimy track of a snail.

SNÀMH, snàimh, *s m.* Swimming, the art of swimming and floating Math air an t-snàmh, *good at swimming;* cuir air snàmh, *cause to float* or *swim, deluge*, cuirear an tìr air snàmh, *the land shall be* [*deluged*] *soaked —Stew. Is.*

SNÀMH, (a), *p. part* of snamh Swimming, floating. A snamh air gaoith, *swimming on wind —Oss. Fing.* Mactalla a snàmh sa ghleann, *an echo floating in the valley.—Id.*

SNÀMHACH, *a* Floating, swimming, addicted or prone to swim; prone by nature to swim, as fish, or amphibious animals. A bhileag shnàmhach, *a long weed that lies on the surface of water*

SNÀMHACH, aich, *s. f.* Slow swimming; slow sailing; floating.

SNÀMHACHAN, ain, *s m.* (*from* snamh.) A float; a raft *N. pl* snàmhachain, *rafts.—Stew* 1 *K ref.*

SNÀMHADH, aidh, *s. m.* A swimming, a floating:

SNÀMHADH, 3 *sing* and *pl imper. a.* of snamh. Snamhadh e, iad, *let him* or *them swim.*

SNÀMHAICHE, *s. m* A swimmer, a good swimmer. Chaill

mi snàmhaiche a chaolais, *I have lost the swimmer of the frith.—Old Song.*

SNÀMHAIDH, *gen. sing.* of snàmhadh.

SNÀMHAIDH, *fut. aff. a.* of snàmh. Shall swim or float.

SNÀMHAIR, *s. m.* A swimmer. *N. pl.* snàmhairean. Deadh shnàmhair, *an expert swimmer.*

SNÀMHAN, ain, *s. m.* (*Ir. id.*) Slow sailing, slow swimming, floating; a float; a creeping.

SNAMHLUATH, *a.* (*Ir. id.*) Swift in swimming; swift swimming.

† SNAOI, *s. f.* (*Ir. id.*) A bier; *rarely*, flowing; running.

SNAOIDH. See SNAIDH.

SNAOIS, *s. f.* A slice. *Macd.*

SNAOISEACH, *a.* In slices.

SNAOISEAN, ein, *s. m.* (*Ir.* snaoisin. *Sax.* niezan, *sneeze.*) Snuff; a pinch of snuff; powder. *Asp. form*, shnaoisean. Mo roghainn do shnaoisein, *my choice of snuff.—Macint.*

SNAOISEANACH, *a.* Snuffy; fond of snuff; snuffling; powdered or pulverized.

SNAOISEANACHD, *s. f.* The habit of snuff-taking; calcination.

SNAOISEANADH, idh, *s. m.* (*Ir.* snaoisineadh.) Calcination.

SNAOISICH, *v. a.* (*from* snaois.) Slice. *Pret. a.* shnaoisich, *sliced; fut. aff. a.* snaoisichidh, *shall slice.*

SNAOISICHTE, *p. part.* of snaoisich. Sliced.

SNAOISEIN, *v. a.* Calcine, pulverize.

SNAOMANACH, *a.* Stout, jolly.

SNAOMANACH, aich, *s. m.* A stout fellow; a jolly fellow. *N. pl.* snaomanaich.

SNAP, *v. a.* Pull a trigger; miss fire. *Pret. a.* shnap; *fut. aff. a.* snapaidh.—*Macint.*

SNAPACH, *a.* Apt to miss fire, as a gun; that fireth; that strikes fast.—*Shaw.*

SNAPAIREACHD, *s. f.* Snapping; a snapping sound, such as that caused by the flint of a gun-lock.

SNAS, snàis, *s. m.* (*Ir. id.*) The slimy track of a snail.

SNÀS, *s. m.* (*Ir. id.*) Decency; regularity; elegance; neatness; colour, aspect or appearance; analysis, analyzing. Cuir snas air, *put a good appearance on it, make it neat;* biorraid bu loinntreach snàs, *a gleaming helmet.—Mac Lach.* Snàs-obair, *neat handiwork.*

SNÀS, *v. a.* Cut; dissect; lop; trim; prune, analyze, criticise. *Pret. a.* shnàs; *fut. aff. a.* snàsaidh.

SNÀSACH, *a.* Making neat, trim, or regular; pruning, lopping, neat, trim, elegant.

SNÀSACHADH, aidh, *s. m.* A making neat or regular; a trimming, a lopping, a pruning; a criticising, an analysis.

SNÀSACHD, *s. f.* (*from* snàs.) Neatness, elegance, trimness, spruceness; a trimming, a making neat, criticism; a lopping, or cutting down.

SNÀSADAIR, *s. m.* A dissector, a trimmer or pruner; a critic; an analizer. *N. pl.* snasadairean.

SNÀSADAIREACHD, *s. f.* Dissecting; analyzing.

SNÀSADH, aidh, *s. m.* A cutting, a dissecting, a lopping, a trimming, an analysis.

SNÀSAICH, *v. a.* Cut, dissect; trim, lop tastefully, as a hedge or tree; prune; analyse, criticise. *Pret. a.* shnàsaich; *fut. aff.* snàsaichidh, *shall dissect.*

SNÀSAICHEAR, *fut. pass.* of snàsaich. Shall be cut.

SNÀSAICHIDH, *fut. aff. a.* of snasaich; which see.

SNASDA, *a.* See SNASTA.

SNASDA, *s. m.* (*Ir. id.*) Colour.

SNÀSMHOIRE, *com.* and *sup.* of snàsmhor; which see.

SNÀSMHOR, *a.* (*Ir.* snasmhar.) Trimmed, lopped; neat, elegant, decent; accurate—(*Macint*); *also*, brave. Cainnt shnàsmhor, *accurate* or *elegant language. Com.* and *sup.* of snàsmhor.

SNÀSTA, *a.* (*Ir. id.*) Trimmed, lopped, pruned; neat, elegant; accurate; *also*, brave, gallant. Deud geal snàsta, *a white elegant tooth.—Old Song.*

SNÀSTACH, *a.* Trimming, lopping, pruning; criticising.

SNÀTH, snàth, *s. m.* (*Ir. id.*) Yarn; thread; a line.—*Macint.* Snàth-bursaid, *worsted-thread;* snàth-fuaidhle, *sewing-thread;* snàth sioda, *silk-thread.*

SNÀTH, *v. a.* Thread, string. *Pret. a.* shnàth; *fut. aff. a.* snàthaidh, *shall thread.*

SNATH, *v. a.* Sup.

† SNATHA, *s. m.* (*Ir. id.*) Easing, a riddance from pain; *also*, grief, trouble.—*Shaw.*

SNÀTHAD, aide, *s. f.* (*Ir. id. Manks.* sned. *Arm.* nados.) A needle. Crò snàthaide, *the eye of a needle.—Stew. Matt. N. pl.* snàthadan.

SNÀTHADACHAN, ain, *s. m.* (*Ir. id.*) A needle-case. *N. pl.* snàthadachanan.

SNÀTHADAIR, *s. m.* (*Ir.* snathadoir.) A needlemaker. *N. pl.* snàthadairean.

SNÀTHAINN, snàithne, *s. f.* A thread, a string, a skein, a line. Snàthainn ascaird, *a thread of tow.—Stew. Jud. N. pl.* snàithnean.

SNAITHNEAN, ein, *s. m.* (*dim.* of snàthainn.) A little thread; a string, a skein.

SNEACHD, *s. m.* (*Ir.* sneachd. *Germ.* schnee.) Snow. O thir an t-sneachd, *from the land of snow.—Oss. Fing.* Ris an t-sneachd, *snowing;* sneachd is reotha, *snow and frost.*

SNEACHDA, ai, *s. m.* See SNEACHD or SNEACHDADH.

SNEACHDACH, *a.* Snowy; like snow. Ràithe sneachdach bhuaireasach, *a snowy stormy quarter.—Macfar. Asp. form*, shneachdach.

SNEACHDADH, aidh, *s. m.* Snow. Ann uisgibh sneachdaidh, *in snow water.—Stew. Job.* Là sneachdaidh, *a snowy day.—Stew.* 1 *Chr.* Ris an t-sneachdadh, *snowing;* a cur an t-sneachdaidh, *snowing;* muc shneachdaidh, *a huge snow-ball.*

SNEACHDAIL, *a.* (sneachd-amhuil.) Snowy.

SNEACHDAR, *a.* Snowy; like snow.

SNEAG, *s. m.* A notch, a nick; a dent, a cut.

SNEAGACH, *a.* Notched, notching.

SNEAGAICH, *v. a.* Notch; dent, indent. *Pret. a.* shneagaich; *fut. aff. a.* sneagaichidh.

SNEAGAIREACHD, *s. f.* A notching, indentation; a cutting or whetting with a knife.

SNEAGH, sneigh, *s. m.* (*Ir. id.*) A nit.—*Shaw.*

SNEAGHACH, *a.* Full of nits; like nits; of nits.

SNEAGHAN, ain, *s. m.*, *provincial form* of seangan. An ant.

SNEAMH, sneimh, *s. m.* A nit.—*Macfar. Voc.*

SNEAMHACH, *a.* Full of nits, nitty; like nits, of nits.

† SNEIDH. See SNEIGH.

SNEIDHE, *s. f.* Sadness, vexation.

† SNEIGH, *a.* Straight, direct—(*Shaw*); little, small.

SNEIDHE, *s. f.* See SNIDHE.

SNIDH, *s. f.* (*Ir. id.*) A nit.

SNIDH, *v. n.* (*Ir. id.*) Ooze through, drop, distil; let in water. *Pret. a.* shnidh; *fut. aff. a.* snidhidh, *shall ooze.* Snidhidh an tigh troimh, *the house droppeth through.—Stew. Ecc.*

SNIDHE, *s. f.* (*Ir.* sneidhe, *sorrow.*) Rain oozing through the roof of a building; a drop, a tear; sorrow. Written also *snithe.*

SNIDHEACH, *a.* Oozing, as rain through a roof; not water proof, as a house; weeping, sad, moist with tears. Written also *snitheach.*

Snidheadh, idh, *s. m.* An oozing, a dropping; a shedding of tears; sadness.

Snig, *s. f.* A nit.

Sniomh, *v. a.* and *n.* (*Swed.* sno.) Spin, wind yarn; twist, twine, wring; curl; wrench. *Pret. a.* shniomh, *spinned; fut. aff. a.* sniomhaidh, *shall twist; fut. neg.* sniomh, *shall spin.* Cha sniomh iad, *they do not spin.—Stew. Matt.* Shniomh e an t-sleagh a lamhan, *he twisted the spear from his hands.—Oss. Cathula.* Sniomhaidh e 'cheann deth, *he will wring its head off.—Stew. Lev.* Ar cridhe air an sniomh, *our hearts entwined.—Ull.*

Sniomh, *s. m.* A spinning, a winding of yarn, a twisting, a twining, a twist, a twine; a curl or ringlet; a wrench; sadness. Deagh shniomh, *good spinning;* math ar an t-sniomh, *good at spinning;* a shealgair is aillidh sniomh, *thou huntsman of the comely ringlets.—Fingalian Poem.*

Sniomh, (a), *pr. part.* of sniomh. Spinning, winding, twisting, twining. Mar shruthaibh dhealain a sniomh sa chéile, *like streams of lightning, twisted together.—Oss. Cathluno.*

Sniomhach, *a.* (*from* sniomh.) Spinning, winding, twisting, twining; tending to twist or twine.

Sniomhachan, ain, *s. m.* (*Ir. id.*) A spinner.

Sniomhachas, ais, *s. m.* Spinning, spun yarn.

Sniomhadair, *s. m.* A spinner; a cordwainer. *N. pl.* sniomhadairean.

Sniomhadh, aidh, *s. m.* A spinning, a winding, a twisting, a twining.

Sniomhaiche, *s. m.* A spinster. *N. pl.* sniomhaichean.

Sniomhaidh, *gen. sing.* of sniomhadh.

Sniomhaidh, *fut. aff. a.* of sniomh. Shall spin or twist.

Sniomhain, *a.* (*Ir. id.*) Curling, twisting, gyrous, spiral, winding. Cùl sniomhain, *curled hair;* air staidhrichibh sniomhain, *on winding stairs.—Stew.* 1 *K.*

Sniomhaineach, *a.* See **Sniomhanach**.

Sniomhair, *s. m.* (*from* snoimh.) A spinner; a cordwainer; *also,* a wimble.—*Macd. N. pl.* sniomhairean.

Sniomhaireachd, *s. f.* The business of a spinner; the business of a cordwainer.

Sniomhanach, *a.* Plaited, twisted, braided; gyrous. Ciabh sniomhanach, *a plaited ringlet.—Old Song.*

Sniomhta, Sniomhte, *pr. part.* of sniomh. Spun, twisted.

Snisean, ein, *s. m.* See **Snaoisean**.

Snith, *v. a.* Ooze through; drop, distil; weep. Written also *snidh;* which see.

Snithe, *s. f.* Rain oozing through the roof of a house; a tear. Written also *snidhe.*

Snitheach, *a.* Oozy, not waterproof; tearful, moist with tears; sad. Tigh snitheach, *a house which is not waterproof;* snitheach gun léirsinn, *tearful and blind.—Ull.* T-aos-chiabha snitheach, *thy aged locks moist with tears.—Id.*

† **Sno**, *s. m.* (*Ir. id.*) Visage—(*Shaw*); appearance, colour.—*O'Reilly.*

Snòd, snòid, *s. m.* (*Scotch,* a snood.) The twisted hairs which are fastened to a fishing-hook.

Snòdach, *a.* (*from* snòd.) Snooded, as a fishing-hook.

Snodh, snodha, *s. m.* A smile. Snodh-ghàire, *a smile.*

Snodhach, aich, *s. m.* (*Ir. id.*) Sap, juice, the sap of trees, especially of birch. Written also *snothach;* which see.

Snoidh. More frequently written *snaidh;* which see.

Snot, *v. n.* Smell, snuffle, snort; suspect. *Pret. a.* shnot, *snuffled; pret. a.* snotaidh.

Snotach, *a.* Smelling, snuffling, snorting; inclined to smell, snuffle, or snort; suspicious.

Snotadh, aidh, *s. m.* A smelling, a snuffling, a snorting; suspicion.

Snotadh, (a), *pr. part.* of snot. Smelling, snuffling, snorting; suspecting. A snotadh bhileagan, *smelling the leaves.—R.*

Snotail, *s. f.* A continued smelling, snuffling, or snorting.

Snothach, aich. Sap, juice, especially the sap of trees. Thig snothach fuidh 'n chairt, *sap shall come under the bark.—Macint.* Dìridh snothach o'n fhreumhaich, *sap shall climb from the roots.—Macfar.* Is geal gach nodha gu ruig snothach an fhearna, *every thing new is white, even to the bark of the alder.—G. P.;* alder when newly peeled is white, but it turns red in a short time.

Snuadh, snuaidh, *s. m.* (*Ir. id.*) Hue, colour; aspect, appearance; complexion; a river, a brook; blood; the hair of the head. Duchomar bu ghruamaiche snuagh, *Duchomar of the frowning aspect.—Oss. Fing.* Air tréigsinn a shnuaidh, *having changed its colour.—Macfar.*

† **Snuadh**, *v. n.* (*Ir. id.*) Flow, as a stream.—*Shaw.*

Snuadhach, *a.* Having a good colour, aspect, or complexion.

Snuadhaich, *v. a.* Give a good face or appearance to; adorn. *Pret. a.* shnuadhaich; *fut. aff. a.* snuadhaichidh.

Snuadhaichte, *p. part.* of snuadhaich. Adorned, bedecked.

Snuadhar, *a.* (*for* snuadhmhor.) Having an imposing appearance; likely, well-looked, personable; pleasant to behold, comely, elegant. A shobhrach, is snuadhar do ghnùis, *O primrose, pleasant is thy appearance.—Macdon.* Snuadhar treun, *personable and strong.—Death of Ossian.*

† **Snuadh-chlais**, *s. f.* (*Ir. id.*) The channel of a river.—*Shaw. N. pl.* snuadh-chlaisean.

Snuadhmhor, *a.* Having an imposing exterior; likely, well-looked, personable, pleasant to behold, comely, elegant.

Snuim. See **Snaim**.

Snuisean, ein, *s. m.* Snuff, a pinch of snuff.

Ir. snisin. *Swed.* snus, *snuff. Sax.* niezan, *sneeze.*

Snuiseanach, *a.* Snuffy, fond of snuff; snuffing, snuffling.

Snuiseanachd, *s. f.* The habit of snuff-taking; a habit of snuffling.

So, *demons. pron.* (*Ir. Heb.* so. *Arm.* ze *and* zeo.) This, this here; these, these here. An t-àite so, *this place.—Oss. Tem.* Tréig so, *leave this* [*place.*]—*Id.* Gu so, *until now; to this place;* gu so bu treun e, *until now he was strong.—Oss. Fing.* C'arson so? *why so?—Stew. Sam.* A so suas, *hence forward;* a so, *hence; Arm.* a so. Amhuil mar so, *even as this; Arm.* evel ma so. Amhuil so, *like this; Arm.* evel ze *or* evel zeo. Amhuil mar an duine so, *even as this man. Arm.* evel ma zeo den.

So, *adv.* Here, here is. So, *here, take this;* so, so, *here, here; come, come;* so agad e, *here you have him* or *it;* so am fear, *here is the man;* so leat, *here is to you, here is your health;* so an t-aite, *here is the place.* In the last instances *so* seems to be *is so.*

So, (an), *adv.* (*Pers.* enja *or* eenja.) Here; in this case or instance, hither. Gabh clos an so, *here take repose.—Oss. Fing.* An so's an sud, *here and there.*

So, *insep. prep.* (*Ir. id.*) Easily, gently, softly, aptly. This word is never used but in composition; and then its meaning is the reverse of *do;* as, so-dheanamh, *easily done;* do-dheanamh, *not easily done;* so-lùbaidh, *flexible;* do-lùbaidh, *inflexible.*

† **So**, *a.* (*Ir. id.*) Young.

† **Soadh**, *s.* (*Ir. id.*) A bed, a couch; a turning, a returning, a return; an eclipse.

So-aireamh, *a.* (*Ir. id.*) Easily numbered; numerable, computable.

So-aithneach, *a.* (*Ir. id.*) Easily known or recognised, conspicuous.

† So-alt, s. (Ir. id.) A good leap.

So-aomaidh, a Easily bent, flexible; easily persuaded, exorable.

So-atharrachadh, a. Alterable; easily moved.

So-atharruichte, part. Alterable.

Sobha, s. m. (Ir. id.) The herb sorrel.—Shaw. Sobha-talmhainn, strawberries.

Sobhaladh, aidh, s m., more properly so-bholadh. Fragrancy, sweet scent.

So-bheus, s. m. Good-breeding. N pl so-bheasan, good-manners.

So-bheusach, a. Well-bred.

So-bhinntichte, a. (Ir. so-bhintighthe) Coagulable, easily curdled.

So-bhlasda, a (Ir. id) Savoury, tasty.

So-bhogachaidh, a. Moveable; pliable, easily softened.

So-bholadh, aidh, s. m (Ir. id) A pleasant smell.

So-bholtanachd, s. f. (Ir. id.) Fragrancy.

Sobhrach, aich, s. m (Ir id.) A primrose Sobhrach am bruachaibh nan allt, a primrose in the banks of the streams.—Macfar.

Sobhrach, a. Abounding in primroses, like a primrose. Glachdag biolarach sobhrach, a dell abounding in cresses and primroses.—Macfar.

Sobhrachan, ain, s m A young primrose.

Sobhraide, s. f. (Ir. id) Sobriety; mildness, gentleness

So-bhriste, a. (Ir. id.) Frangible, brittle.

So-bhristeachd, s. f Brittleness; weakness

So-bhròn, òin, s. m. (Ir. id.) Pleasant sorrow; melancholy pleasure.

So-bhuailteach, a. (Ir. id.) Easily hit, easily struck.

Soc, v. a. Fit a plough with a coulter; provide with a socket; point.

Soc, suic, s m. A coulter, a sock; a beak; a chin; a snout; a point; a socket Soc croinn, the coulter of a plough, a geurachadh shuic, sharpening his coulter —Stew. Sam. Cloidhean soc ri soc, swords point to point.—Fingalian Poem.
Dan sok. Arm. soc. W. swch. Corn soch. Germ. sochs Ir. soc. Scotch, sock, a coulter

Soc, s. m. Silence.

Socach, aich, s. m. Soccage.

Socach, a. Coultered as a plough, socked; beaked, snouted; having a peaked chin; pointed, like a coulter; like a beak or snout.

Socadh, aidh, s. m. A coulter; a socket, a sock—(Stew Ex.); a fastening, a coulter to a plough.

† Socaiche, s f. (Ir. socaidhe.) An army, a host, a multitude.

† Socail, s. f. Ease, rest, tranquillity; mildness —Shaw.

Socail, a (Ir. socamhuil) Easy, mild, gentle.

Socain, gen. sing. of socan.

Socair, a. (Ir. id.) Easy, at leisure; tranquil, comfortable; safe.

Socair, s. f. (Ir socra) Ease, rest, leisure, mildness; tranquillity; comfort, a prop, a rest. Air do shocair, at leisure, leisurely, bheil thu air do shocair? are you at leisure? socair, socair, at leisure, at leisure; n pl socairean. Socairean an tighe, the rests of the house —Stew 1 K.

Socait, s. f. A socket N. pl socaitean, sockets —Q B. ref.

Socàiteach, a. Socketted, like a socket.

† Socalach, a. Easy, at rest, mild.—Shaw.

Socal, ail, s. m. Ease, tranquillity.

Socan, ain, s. m. (dim. of soc.) A little coulter; a little sock; a little beak, chin, or snout; a little rest or prop, a fieldfare; a big-bellied little man.

Socarach, a. contracted socrach; which see

† Sochaidh, s f. An army, a host, a multitude —Shaw.

Sochair, s. (Ir sochar, blessing Heb. sacar, hire) A benefit; a favour; emolument, privilege, comfort, ease N. pl sochairean; d pl. sochairibh

So-chairdeach, a. Nearly related, intimately acquainted

So-chairdean, s pl. Friends, intimate friends

So-chairdeas, eis, s. m. Friendship, intimate friendship

Sochaireach, a. Prone to confer a benefit, obliging, lucrative; yielding profit, easy minded; right Written also socharach

Sochaireachd, s. f Obligingness, lucrativeness, easy-mindedness.

Sochairean, n pl Benefits, blessings

So-chaochlaideach, a. Easily changed, changeable.

So-chaochlaidh, a. Easily changed, changeable, convertible

Sochar, air, s m. See Sochair

Socharach, a (Ir. id) Obliging, ready to favour, lucrative, easy minded; simple; right

So-chasta, a (Ir. id.) Handy, manageable —Shaw.

Sochd, s. See Soc

† Sochd, s m (Ir. id) Silence, peace, quietness.

Sochdair. See Socair.

So-chiùnachadh, a. Easily appeased, placable, exorable

Sochladh, aidh, s. m. (Ir sochla) Fame, character —Shaw

Sochladh, a Sensible.

So-chlaoidhte, a. Easily conquered

So-chlaonadh, aidh, s. m Aptness to bend, flexibility, aptness to go astray, towardness —Shaw

So-chlaonadh, aidh, s. m. Flexibleness.

So-chloiste, a. (Ir. id) Audible.

So-chloistinn, s. f. Audibleness.

So-chluinntinn, a. Audible, easily heard, also, substantively, audibleness.

Sochmadh, a (Ir id) Abstemious.

Sochmhor, a. Abstemious.

So-chnàmh, a. Easy of digestion, digestible

So-chnàmhaiche, s m One who has a good digestion

So-chnàmhta, a. (Ir. id) Easy of digestion, digestible.

So-chobhaiste, a. (Ir id) Conformable.

Sochois, s m A learned man.

So-chomharaichte, a. Easily distinguished, observable, conspicuous

So-chomhairleach, a. Easily advised.

So-chomhairlich, a Easily advised, easy to be entreated —Stew. Jam

So-chomhradhach, a (Ir. so-chomhraidh) Conversable, affable, complaisant

So-chomhraiteach, a. Conversable; affable.

† So-chonradh, aidh, s m (Ir id.) Cheapness

So-chordach, a. (Ir id) Agreeable.

So-chosmhal, a. (Ir id) Conformable.

Sochraid, s. f. A multitude of people

So-chramhta, a Digestible, easy of digestion.

So-chreidimh, s f. Credulity

So-chreideamhach, a Credulous; also, substantively, a credulous person.

So-chridheach, a. Good-natured, tender-hearted, soft-hearted

So-chridheachd, s f. Good-nature; cordiality, kindness

So-chumta, *a.* Mouldable, easily shaped.

Socrach, *a.*, *from* socair. (*Ir. id.*) Steady, established, firmly footed, fixed; at ease, at leisure; comfortable; slow in moving, not easily hurried; sedate; calm, quiet, smooth, plain; equal. Feachd bu shocrach ceum, *a host of the steadiest step*, or *marching in time.*—*Mac Lach.* Tha 'chridhe socrach, *his heart is fixed.*—*Sm.* Gu socrach, *leisurely, coolly, softly*, gabhaidh mi an t-slighe gu socrach, *I will lead the way [at leisure] softly.*—*Stew. Gen.*

Socrachadh, aidh, *s. m.* (*Ir.* socrughadh.) A making steady, an establishing; an appointing; a tranquillising; tranquillity, comfort.

Socrachd, *s. f.* Steadiness; undisturbedness.

Socradh, aidh, *s. m.* (*Ir.* socra.) Ease, leisure, tranquillity, calmness, smoothness.

Socraich, *v. a.* (*from* socair.) Make steady; establish; found, fix or place on a firm footing or foundation, appoint, determine; stand at ease; stand firm, quiet, compose, assuage, appease. *Pret. a.* shocraich; *fut. aff. a.* socraichidh, *shall make steady.* Socraichidh mi mo smuaintean, *I will fix my thoughts.*—*Sm.* Shocraich iad uile air an lòn, *they all stood firm on the plain.*—*Mac Lach.*

Socraichear, *fut. pass.* of socraich.

Socraichidh, *fut. aff. a.* of socraich. Shall make steady, establish, or found. See Socair.

Socraichte, *p. part.* of socraich, which see.

Socras, ais, *s. m.* Ease, tranquillity.

Socul. See Socal.

Sod, soda, *s. m.* (*Ir. id.*) Boiled meat, the noise of water when meat is boiling in it.

Sod, soid, *s. m.* A sod, a stout corpulent person; a clumsy awkward person, *in derision.* Is tric a chinn an cneadach 's a dh' fhalbh an sodach, *often does the puny grow, and the stout decay.*—*G. P.*

Sodach, *a.* Sodish, clumsy, awkward, untidy.

Sodail, *gen. sing.* of sodal.

Sodair, *v. a.* and *n.* Trot.

Sodair, *s. m.* A stout man; a clumsy awkward fellow, a strong clumsy quadruped, *also*, a trotting horse.—*Macd.* *N. pl.* sodairean.

Sodaireachd, *s. f.* Stoutness of person, clumsiness.

Sodal, ail, *s. m.* (*Ir. id.*) Flattery, fawning, pride, arrogance. Luchd sodail, *flatterers.*

Sodal, *a.* (*Ir. id.*) Flattering, fawning, proud, arrogant.

Sodalach, *a.*, *from* sodal. (*Ir. id.*) Flattering, fawning, parasitical, proud, luxurious, epicurean. Gu sodalach, *fawningly.* *Com.* and *sup.* sodalaiche.

Sodalach, aich, *s. m.* A flatterer, a fawning fellow, a cajoler; a parasite.

Sodalachd, *s. f.* The practice of flattery, luxury, epicurism.

Sodalaich, *s. f.* Continued or frequent flattery, fawning, or cajoling.

Sodalaich, *v. a.* Flatter, fawn, soothe, cajole. *Pret. a.* shodalaich, *flattered*; *fut. aff. a.* sodalaichidh.

Sodan, ain, *s. m.* (*Ir. id.*) Joy, gladness, shewing itself by gestures. Làn sodain, *full of joy.*—*Oss. Fin. and Lorm.*

Sodanach, *a.* (*from* sodan.) Joyful, glad, cheerful.—*Macint.* Gu sodanach, *gladly.* *Com.* and *sup.* sodanaiche.

† Sodar, air, *s. m.* (*Ir. id.*) A trot, a trotting, a trotting pace; *also*, sodder.—*Shaw.*

Sodarnach, aich, *s. m.* (*Ir. id.*) A strong clumsy person, a strong clumsy beast.—*Macfar. Voc.*

Sodarnach, *a.* (*Ir. id.*) Strongly built in person, clumsy, able to trot; strong and sound for marching.

† Sodh, *s. m.* (*Ir. id.*) A turning, a winding, a changing; an eclipse.

† Sodh, *v. a.* (*Ir. id.*) Turn.

† Sodhan, *a.* Prosperous.—*Shaw.*

So-dhealbhach, *a.* (*Ir. id.*) Well formed, handsome.

So-dheanamh, *a.* Easy, easily done, practicable, possible.

So-dheanta, *a.* Easy, easily done, practicable, possible.

So-dhearbhta, *a.* Evincible, demonstrable, easily proved.

So-dhionta, *a.* Easily defended, defensible.

So-dhochanta, *a.* Easily hurt or damaged.

So-dhruidte, *a.* Easily shut.

Sodrach, aich, *s. m.* (*Ir. id.*) A trotting, a trotting pace.

Sodsag, aig, *s. f.* A pillion.

So-fhaghail, *a.* Attainable; easily got.

So-fhaicinn, So-fhaicsinn, *a.* Easily seen, apparent, evident, conspicuous.

So-fhaicsinneach, *a.* Visible, conspicuous.

So-fhaotainn, *a.* Easily got, acquirable, attainable.

So-fholach, *a.* Easily hidden, concealable.

Sogh, *s.* (*Ir. id.*) Luxury, pleasure, joy, luxurious ease; riot, delicacies, dainties; sumptuousness, prosperity. Esan a ghradhaicheas sogh, *he who loves pleasure.*—*Stew. Pro.* Sogh nan oigh, *the joy of maidens.*—*Old Song.* Sogh san là, *riot in the day time.*—*Stew. 2 Pet.* Sogh rioghail, *royal dainties.*—*Stew. Gen.*

Soghach, *a.* (*from* sogh.) Luxurious, delicate, sumptuous; prosperous.

Soghail, *a.* (sogh-amhuil.) Luxurious; fond of delicacies; sumptuous, cheerful, prosperous. Biadh sòghail, *delicate* or *sumptuous food.*—*Stew. Lam.* Gu soghail, *deliciously, sumptuously.*—*Stew. Pro.*

Sogh-aimsir, *s. f.* Calm weather, fair weather, pleasant weather.—(*Macd.*); a season of pleasure.

Soghainn, Soghan, *a.* Pleasant, agreeable, cheerful.

Soghainn, *s. f.* A kind of paste used by weavers to smooth their threads.

Soghair, *s. m.* (sogh-fhear.) A votary of pleasure; an epicure, an epicurean.

Soghairfachd, *s. f.* Luxuriousness, sumptuousness; epicurism, epicureanism.

Soghalachd, *s. f.* Luxuriousness, sumptuousness.

Soghar, (*for* soghmhor.) Luxurious, sumptuous.

Soghchù, choin, *s. m.* A greyhound, a hound-bitch.

So-ghiùlan, *a.* Easily born or carried; easily suffered, sufferable; portable.

So-ghlacaidh, *a.* Easily caught, easily taken.

So-ghlacta, *a.* (*Ir.* so-ghlactha.) Easily caught or taken.

So-ghluaiseach, *a.* Moving easily, put in motion with little impetus.

So-ghluaiste, *a.* Easily moved, changeable, variable.—(*Stew. Pro.*); wavering, fickle.

So-ghluasad, *a.* Easily moved, easily removed, changeable.

Soghmhar. See Soghmhor.

Soghmhor, *a.* (*Ir.* soghmhar.) Luxurious, sumptuous, prosperous. *Com.* and *sup.* soghmhoire.

So-ghnaidh, *a.* (*Ir. id.*) Fair, comely, handsome.

So-ghniomh, *s. m.* A good deed.

So-ghniomhach, *a.* Doing a good deed, beneficent.

So-ghnùis, *s. f.* A fair face, a comely face.

So-ghnùiseas, eis, *s. m.* (*Ir. id.*) Comeliness, beauty.—*Shaw.*

So-ghointe, *a.* (*Ir. id.*) Easily hurt, bruised, or wounded; vulnerable.

So-ghradh, aidh, *s. m.* (*Ir. id.*) Great fondness, sincere attachment, or affection.—*Macint.* Luchd mo sho-ghraidh, *the people whom I sincerely love.*—*Old Song.*

So-ghradhach, *a.* (*Ir. id.*) Beloved, tenderly beloved; affectionate; acceptable. Mhic Fhinn sho-ghradhaich, *son of beloved Fingal.—Fingalian Poem.* Le cridhe so-ghradhach, *with an affectionate heart.—Old Song.* So-ghradhach, *acceptable.—Shaw.*

So-ghradhaich, *v. a.* Love tenderly.

So-ghradhaichte, *p. part.* Loved tenderly.

† **Soghsur**, uir, *s. m.* (*Ir. id.*) Fatness.

† **Soir**, *s. f.* (*Ir. id.*) The hand.—*Shaw.*

Soibh, *a compositive particle*, sometimes used for *so;* which see.

Soibheus, *s. m.* (*Ir. id.*) Good-breeding. *N. pl.* soibheusan, *good-manners.*

Soibheusach, *a.* (*Ir. id.*) Well-bred, mannerly; courtly.

Soi-bhriste, *a.* (*Ir. id.*) Easily broken, brittle, frail.

Soi-bhristeachd, *s. f.* (*Ir.* soibhristeacht.) Brittleness, weakness.

Soibhsgeul. See **Soisgeul.**

Soicead, eid, *s. m.* (*Ir. id.*) A socket.

Soicheal, eil, *s. m.* (*Ir. id.*) Joy, mirth.—*Shaw.*

Soichealach, *a.* Joyful, mirthful, gay; causing joy or mirth.

Soichealachd, *s. f.* Joyfulness, mirthfulness, gaiety. Luchd na soichealachd, *the gay.*

Soi-chinealta, *a.* (*Ir. id.*) Noble, high-born.

So-chinealtachd, *s. f.* (*Ir. id.*) Nobility, high-birth.

Soi-chinealtas, ais, *s. m.* Nobility, high-birth.—*Shaw.*

† **Soichle**, *s. f.* Joy, mirth, pleasure, gaiety.

Soideal, eil, *s. m.* Rudeness, ignorance.

Soidealach, *a.* Rude, ignorant.—*Shaw.* *Com.* and *sup.* soidealaiche.

Soidealachd, *s. f.* Rudeness, ignorance.

Soidealta, *a.* (*Ir. id.*) Rude, ignorant.

Soidealtachd, *s. f.* (*Ir.* soidealtacht.) Rudeness; ignorance.

Soidhineach, *a.* Liberal. Gu soidhineach, *liberally.*

Soighdear. More properly *saighdear:* which see.

Soighdearachd. See **Saighdearachd.**

Soighead. More properly *saighead;* which see.

Soigheam, eim, *s. m.* (*Ir. id.*) A precious stone or gem.

† **Soighidh**, *s. f.* (*Ir. id.*) An attack.

Soighlear, eir, *s. m.* (*Ir.* soighleir.) A jailor.

Soighme, *s. f.* (*Ir. id.*) A thunder-bolt; a flash of lightning.

Soighnean, ein, *s. m.* (*Ir. id.*) A puff of wind, a thunder-bolt, a flash of lightning.

Soighneas, eis, *s. m.* Pleasure, delight.

Soighniomh, *s.* (*Ir. id.*) A good deed or action.

Soighniomhach, aich, *s. m.* A benefactor.

† **Soil**, *s.* (*Ir. id.*) The sun.

Soil-bheachd, *s.* (*Ir. id.*) A jest.—*Shaw.*

Soil-bheum, *s. m.* A flash of lightning; a thunderbolt; a *coup de soleil.*

Soilbhir. See **Suilbhear.**

Soilbhire. See **Suilbhire.**

Soileach. See **Seileach.**

Soi-leaghta, *a.* Fusible.

Soileas, eis, *s. m.* (*Ir. id.*) Officiousness—(*Shaw.*); flattery.—*Macdon.*

Soileasach, *a.* Officious; flattering.

Soileasachd, *s. f.* Officiousness.

† **Soilfeachd**, *s. f.* (*Ir. id.*) A charm.

Soilleag, eig, *s. f.* (*Ir. id.*) A willow, a sallow.—*Shaw.* *N. pl.* soilleagan.

Soilleagach, *a.* Abounding in willows or sallows; like a willow or sallow.

Soilleir, *a.* (*Ir.* soileir.) Clear, bright, lucid; clean, transparent, limpid; evident, manifest, intelligible; discernible. Là soilleir, *a bright-day;* cridhe fìreannach soilleir, *a true and clean heart.—Old Song.* *Com.* and *sup.* soilleire.

Soilleire, *com.* and *sup.* of soilleir. Brighter, brightest.

Soilleireachadh, aidh, *s. m.* A clearing, a brightening, a cleaning; a making intelligible; illustration, explanation.

Soilleireachd, *s. f.* Clearness, brightness; effulgence; cleanness; transparentness, limpidness; intelligibleness; day-light, dawn. Mu'n t-soilleireachd, *about dawn.*

Soilleirich, *v. a.* and *n.* Clear, brighten, clean; make intelligible, elucidate, enlighten. *Pret. a.* shoilleirich; *fut. aff. a.* soilleirichidh, *shall enlighten.* Shoilleirich an là, *the day brightened up.*

Soilleirse, *s. f.* (*Ir. id.*) An axiom.

Soillse, *s. f.* (*Ir. id.*) Clearness, brightness, effulgence; elucidation; a light, a luminary. Gun fhiughair ri madainn no soillse, *without hope of morning nor light.—Oss. Gaul.* A shoillse maiseach, *ye beauteous luminaries.—Orr.* Soillse na sùl, *the herb eye-bright.—Macd.*

Soillseach, *s.* (*Ir. id.*) Bright, clear, transparent, shining, causing light; causing to brighten or clear up. Neul soillseach, *a bright cloud.—Stew. Job.*

Soillseachadh, aidh, *s. m.* A brightening, a clearing up, a lightening; a shining; an elucidation; an explanation.

Soillseachadh, (a), *pr. part.* of soillsich.

Soillseachd, *s. f.* Brightness, clearness, effulgence; transparentness.

Soillseadh, idh, *s. m.* A shining, a brightening, a lightening, a gleaming; a brightness; a gleam.

Soillseadh, (a), *pr. part.* Shining, brightening, lightening, gleaming. A braghadh a soillseadh mar ghealach, *her neck shining like the moon.—Oss. Derm.* A shoillseadh, *to shine.*

Soillsean, ein, *s. m.* A taper.

Soillsich, *v. a.* and *n.* (*Ir. id.*) Brighten, clear up, shew forth; enlighten, gleam. *Pret.* shoillsich; *fut. aff. a.* soillsichidh. Shoillsich an là', *the day cleared up;* nach soillsich tuille do chlaidheamh, *shall thy sword gleam no more.—Oss. Gaul.* *Fut. pass.* soillsichear.

Soillsichear, *fut. pass.* of soillsich.

Soillsichidh, *fut. aff. a.* of soillsich. Shall brighten.

Soillsichte, *p. part.* of soillsich.

Soillse na sùl, *s. f.* The herb eye-bright.—*Macd.*

Soimeach, *a.* (so-imeach.) Easy, good-natured; not skittish, comfortable, in easy circumstances; having little or nothing to do. Is soimeach fear-fearainn ach is sona fear ceirde, *the landed man is at ease, and the tradesman well off.—G. P.*

Soimeachan, ain, *s. m.* A good-natured person.

Soimeachd, *s. f.* Easiness, goodness of temper; comfortableness; easiness of circumstances, idleness, freedom from labour.

Soimh, *a.* Quiet, peaceable; good-natured; tame; comely. Gu samhach soimh, *quietly and peaceably.* Written also *soitheamh.*

Soimhe, *s. f.* See **Saimhe.**

Soimheagan, ain, *s. m.* A soft, good-natured person.

Soimhneach, *a.* Quiet; agreeable.

Soimhneas, eis, *s. m.* Reconciliation; fretting.

Soin, *v. a.* Sound; make a noise.

Soin, soine, *s. f.* (*Lat.* sonus. *Ir.* soin.) A sound, a noise—(*Shaw*); esteem; comeliness.—*Macfar. Voc.* and *Shaw.*

Soinchearb, s. (*Ir. id.*) Synalœpha.—*Shaw.*

Soineach, a. Noisy.

Soineachas, ais, s. m. Noisiness, noise.

Soinealachd, s. f. Comeliness, handsomeness.—*Macfar. Voc.*

Soineann, inn, s. m. See Soinionn.

Soineanta, a. (*Ir. id.*) Serene, as weather; pleasant; comely, meek; good-tempered.

Soineantachd, s. f. Serenity, pleasantness; comeliness; meekness.

Soineas, eis, s. m. (*Ir. id.*) Sulkiness.—*Shaw.*

Soineil, a. (soin-amhuil.) Comely, handsome,; esteemed, estimable. *Asp. form*, shoneil. Bu shoineil le Deardshul an t-òg, *the youth were esteemed by Dardala.—Fingalian Poem.*

Soinionn, s. f., i. e. so-shion or son-shion. (*Ir.* soinean. *W.* hinon.) Calm weather, sunshine; *also*, a blast—(*Shaw*); gaiety, cheerfulness.

Soinionnach, a. Calm, as weather; shining; pleasant; gay, cheerful.

† Soinmheach, a. (*Ir. id.*) Happy; fortunate.

† Soinneach, eich, s. m. (*Ir. id.*) A racehorse.—*Shaw.*

Soinneachd, s. f. Starting.

So-innseadh, a. Effable, expressible; easily told or described.

So-iomchaire, *com.* and *sup.* of so-iomchar. More or most portable; tolerable or endurable. Is so-iomchaire a bhitheas, *it will be more tolerable.—Stew. Mat.*

So-iomchar, a. (*Ir.* so-iomchair.) Portable, easily carried; tolerable or sufferable; easily endured; easy. Tha mo chuinge so-iomchar, *my yoke is easy.—Stew. Mat. Com.* and *sup.* so-iomchaire.

So-iompach, a. Easily converted; convertible; converting with ease.

So-iompaichte, *p. part.* Easily converted.

Soipean, ein, s. m., *dim.* of sop. (*Ir.* soipin.) A little wisp, a little handful, as of hay or straw.

Soipeanach, a. In little wisps or handfuls, as of hay or straw.

Soir, s. f. (*Ir. id.*) The east.

Soir, a. East, eastern; easterly, eastward. Soir na siar an aghaidh an aonaich, *nor east nor west on the face of the hill.—Oss. Gaul.* Na sleibhtean soir, *the eastern hills.—Oss. Cathluno.*

Soirbh, a. (*Ir. id.*) Affable, easy; calm, quiet, pliable; prosperous; languid. Righ math soirbh, *a good, quiet king.—Old Song. Com.* and *sup.* soirbhe.

Soirbhe, s. f. (*Ir. id.*) Affability; ease; calmness, quietness; pliableness; prosperousness; languidness.

Soirbhe, *com.* and *sup.* of soirbh.

Soirbheachadh, aidh, s. m. A prospering, a favouring, a succeeding; prosperity, success; a growing affable, calm, or quiet.

Soirbheachadh, (a), *pr. part.* of soirbhich.

Soirbheachd, s. f. (*Ir. id.*) Affableness; calmness, quietness; easiness; prosperity.

Soirbheas, eis, s. m. (*Ir. id.*) Prosperity, success; a fair wind. Saoghal fad is soirbheas, *long life and prosperity.—Old Song.* La an t-soirbheis, *the day of prosperity.—Stew. Ecc.* Tha 'n soirbheas air caochladh, *the fair wind has changed.—Old Song.* Soirbheas math leat, *good speed to you:* cha 'n éirich soirbheas leis, *he will not prosper.* The word of opposite meaning is *doirbheas.*

Soirbheasach, a. Prosperous, successful, thriving; favourable; having a fair wind. Tùrus soirbheasach, *a prosperous journey.—Stew. Acts.* Gaoth shoirbheasach, *a fair or favourable wind.*

Soirbhich, v. n. Prosper, succeed, thrive; come speed. *Pret. a.* shoirbhich; *fut. aff. a.* soirbhichidh, *shall prosper.* Ma shoirbhicheas tu, *thou dost prosper.—Stew. Gen.*

Soirbhichidh, *fut. aff. a.* of soirbhich.

Soirbhriste, a. (*Ir. id.*) Ductile.

Soirch, a. Clear, bright; light; conspicuous.

Soirche, s. f. Clearness, brightness; light; conspicuousness; joy.

Soirche, *com.* and *sup.* of sorcha. Clearer, brighter.

Soircheachd, s. f. (*Ir.* soircheacht.) Clearness, brightness.

Soirchead, eid, s. m. Clearness, brightness, increase in clearness or brightness. A dol an soirchead, *growing more and more clear.*

Sŏire, s. f. A vessel, a bag, a leathern bottle. Soire na cloinne, *the womb, the matrix.*

Sŏireadh, idh, s. m. and f. A vessel, a bag; a leathern bottle. Lionar gach soire le fion, *every bottle shall be filled with wine.—Stew. Jer.*

Sŏireag, eig, s. f. (*dim.* of sŏire.) A little vessel, a little bag. *N. pl.* soireagan.

Soireanach, aich, s. m. A fat jolly person.

Soireann, inn, s. f. See Soirionn.

Soireanta, a. See Soirionta.

Soiridh, a. (*Ir.* soireidh.) Convenient; agreeable.

Soirionn, inn, s. f. (*Ir. id.*) Serene weather, serenity, pleasantness; comeliness; meekness. Written also *soinionn.* The word of opposite meaning is *doirionn* or *doinionn.*

Soirionta, a. Serene; pleasant; comely; meek; cheerful; good-tempered.

Soirn-liadh, -leidh, s. f. (*Ir.* soirn-liach.) A baker's peel.

Soirthe, s. f. See Soire.

Soise, s. f. (*Ir. id.*) Alteration, change.

Soisgeul, sgeil, s. (so-sgeul *or* sogh-sgeul, *tidings of joy.*) Gospel; glad tidings. Leig thu 'n soisgeul air di-chuimhne, *thou hast neglected the Gospel.—Macint.*

Soisgeulach, aich, s. m. An evangelist.

Soisgeulach, a. Evangelical; of, or belonging to, the gospel.

Soisgeulachd, s. f. A tale or tidings of joy; evangelism; evangelical preaching.

Soisgeulaich, v. n. Bring or bear good news; preach the gospel. *Pret. a.* shoisgeulaich; *fut. aff. a.* soisgeulaichidh.

Soisgeulaiche, s. m., sogh-sgeulaiche. (*Ir.* soisgealaidhe.) An evangelist; a bringer of good news. *N. pl.* soisgeulaichean; *d. pl.* soisgeulaichibh. Droing gu bhi nan soisgeulaichibh, *people to be evangelists.—Stew. Eph.*

Soisgeulta, a. *Ir. id.*) Evangelical.

Soi-shinte, a. Ductile, pliable.

Soishion, s. Freedom, privilege.

† Soisil, a. Proud, haughty.—*Shaw.*

† Soision, a. Younger.—*Shaw.*

Soisle, s. f. (*Ir. id.*) Brightness.

Soistean, ein, s. m. (*Ir. id.*) A good habitation, a residence.

So-ith, a. Edible; palatable.

Soithchean, *n. pl.* of soitheach.

Soitheach, soithche, s. m. (*Ir. id.*) A vessel; a dish; a wooden dish; a pitcher; a ship. *N. pl.* soithichean; *d. pl.* soithchibh. Ann an soithichibh cloich, *in vessels of stone.—Stew. Ex.* Soithichean òir, *vessels of gold.—Stew. II Chr.* Clùd nan soithchean, *a dishclout.*

Soitheagan, ain, s. m. A soft, good-natured person.

Soitheamh, a. Quiet, peaceable; good-natured, tame; comely. Tha thu soitheamh banail, beusach, *thou art quiet, modest, and mannerly.—Old Song.* Mo laochan soitheamh sìbhealta, *my good-natured, civil lad.—R.*

Soithleag, eig, s. f. (*Ir. id.*) A circle.

Soithleagan, ain, s. m. (*dim.* of soithleag.) A little circle.

Soithmheannach, a. Covetous.

Soithneach, a. (*Ir.* soithinneach.) Desirous.

SOITHNICH, *v. a.* Allure, entice; desire. *Pret. a.* shoithnich, *allured.*

SOITHNICHTE, *p. part.* of soithnich Allured

SOL, *conj* Ere, before that.

† SOL, *s. m.* The sun. Though *sol* has gone into disuse among the Gael, it is retained in the word *solus*, sometimes written sòlas, *light*, *i. e.* sol-las, *sun-light.* *Lat.* sol. *Corn.* sol *and* sul. *Ir* sul *Span. Goth. Swed* sol. *It.* sole. *Fr.* soleil *Dan.* soel

SO-LABHAIRT, *a.* Expressible The word of opposite meaning is *do-labhairt.*

SO-LABHRACH, *a.* (*Ir.* so-labhartha.) Speaking with facility; expressible; affable

SO-LABHRACHD, *s. f.* (*Ir.* so-labharthachd) Eloquence, affability.

SO-LABHRADH, *a.* (*Ir. id*) Affable; exorable, expressible.

SOLADH, aidh, *s. m.* (*Ir. id.*) Profit

SO-LAGHACH, *a.* (*Ir.* solaitheach) Venial, pardonable.

SO-LAGHACHD, *s. f.* Venialness, pardonableness.

SOLAIMTE, *a* Solemn Gu solaimte, *solemnly.*

SOLAIMTEACHD, *s. f.* Solemnity.

SOLAIR, *v. a.* (*Ir id*) Provide, procure; gather; shift for; prepare. *Pret a* sholair; *fut. aff. a.* solairidh Na solairibh òr, *provide not gold.—Stew. Mat.*

SOLAIREACH, *a* Provident, procuring, gathering; getting; catering; purveying

SOLAIREACHD, *s. f.* Providentness; the business of a purveyor; catering.

SOLAITHEACH, *a.* Venial.

SOLAMANTA, *a.* Solemn; solemnized.—*Shaw* Gu solamanta, *solemnly.*

SOLAMANTACHD, *s. f.* Solemnity; solemnization. La solamantachd, *a day of solemnity.*

SOLAMH, *a.* (so *and* lamh.) Quick, ready, dexterous.—*Shaw.*

SOLAMUIN, *s. f* Solemnity.—*Shaw.*

SOLAR, air, *s m.* Provision, any thing that is purveyed; a gathering, a getting, providing, or procuring; purveying; a shifting for; a catering. Dean solar, *provide, cater* Mur dean duine solar, *if a man does not provide.—Stew Tim*

SOLAR', *for* solaradh.

SOLARACH, *a.* Provident, catering, purveying. Fear solarach, *a provident man.*

SOLARACHADH, aidh, *s. m.* A providing or catering.

SOLARADH, aidh, *s m.* A providing; a getting, a gathering, a catering, a purveying. Am gu solaradh, *a time to get*—*Stew. Ecc. ref.* Fear solaraidh, *a purveyor*, luchd solaraidh, *purveyors.*

SOLARADH, (a), *pr. part.* of solair. Providing, getting, gathering, catering, purveying. A solar' dhearc da h-àl, *gathering berries for its young.—Oss. Gaul.*

SOLARAICH, *v. a.* (*from* solar.) Provide, get, gather; acquire; cater; purvey; shift for; prepare. *Pret. a.* sholaraich.

SOLARAICHE, *s. m*, *from* solar. (*Ir.* solaraidhe.) A provider, a caterer, a purveyor.

SOLARAICHIDH, *fut. aff. a* of solaraich.

SOLARAICHTE, *p part.* of solaraich

† SÒLAS, ais, *s. m.* (*Gr.* σόλος, *a quoit.*) A round ball thrown into the air, perhaps in honour of the sun, *also*, a quoit.

SÒLAS, ais, *s. m.*, *from* † sol, *sun.* (*Ir.* solas. *Gr.* σέλας.) Light; knowledge. Written also *solus*, which see.

SÒLAS, ais, *s. m.* (*Ir. id.*) Comfort, consolation, mental pleasure. Chual an sluagh le sòlas cridhe, *the people heart with heart felt comfort.—Mac Lach.* Thoir sòlas, *comfort*, gun sòlas, *comfortless* *N. pl* sòlasan, *comforts.—Stew Is*

SÒLASACH, *a. from* sòlas. (*Ir. id*) Comfortable, consolatory; pleasant to the mind. *Com* and *sup* solasaiche.

SÒLASACH, *a* (*from* sòlas.) Luminous, shining; full of light See also SOLUSACH.

SÒLASACHADH, aidh, *s. m.* A comforting, a consoling; comfort, consolation.

SÒLASACHADH, aidh, *s. m.* A lighting, a shining, a kindling, contracted *soillseachadh*

SÒLASAICH, *v a.* Console, comfort. *Pret* a. shòlasaich, *fut aff. a* sòlasaichidh, *shall comfort*

SÒLASAICHIDH, *fut aff a* of sòlasaich.

SÒLASAICHTE, *p part* of sòlasaich Consoled, comforted

SOLASDA, SOLASTA, *a* (*Ir. id*) Bright, luminous, inflammable Gu solasda, *luminously*

SOLASDACHD, SOLASTACHD, *s f.* (*Ir. id*) Brightness, luminousness, inflammableness

SO-LEAGHADH, *a* Easily melted, easily dissolved, soluble

SO-LEAGHTA, *a* Easily melted; easily dissolved, soluble, colliquable

SO-LEAGHTACH, *a* Easily melted; easily dissolved; that can melt or dissolve easily

SO-LEIGHEAS, *a.* Curable, medicable, easily cured. Leòn so-leigheas, *a medicable wound*

SO-LEÒINTE, *a* Vulnerable —*Shaw and Macfar. Voc.*

SÒ-LEÒNADH, *a.* Vulnerable, easily wounded.

SO-LEÒNTA, *a* (*Ir. id*) Vulnerable.

SO-LEUGHADH, *a.* Legible,

SO-LEUGHTA, *a* Legible, easily read.

SOLL, *s m* (*Ir id*) Bait for catching fish.

SOLLACH, *a.* Jolly, stout; comely, handsome; personable

SOLLACHD, *s. f* Jolliness, stoutness, comeliness, handsomeness; personableness

SOLLAIN, *s. f.* Rejoicing, gladness, mirth; a hearty welcome Là sollain, *a day of rejoicing, a feasting day*, said of Christmas and New Year's day

SOLTA, *a* Comely A ghnuis sholta, *the comely countenance* —*Old Song.*

SOLTANAS, ais, *s m* Jollity, mirth

SO-LÙBACHD, *s f.* Flexibility; exorableness

SO-LÙBAIDH, *a* Flexible, exorable.

SO-LUGHADH, *a* (*Ir* so-laghadh) Venial, pardonable

SOLUS, uis, *s. m.* (*from* † sol, *sun*) Light; knowledge; the moon; a heavenly body, *rarely*, a quoit. Solus bristeach nan reultan, *the broken* [*twinkling*] *light of the stars*—*Ull Asp. form*, sholus. Caomhain do sholus, a Ghrian, *spare thy light, O Sun.—Oss Gaul.* An solus ùr, *the new moon*, an solus làn, *the full moon*, caochladh an t-soluis, *the change of the moon*; rach a mo sholus, *go out of my light.*

SOLUSACH, *a.* (*from* solus) Luminous, shining, gleaming Written more frequently *soillseach.*

SOLUSACHD, *s. f.* Luminousness. Written more frequently *soillseachd*; which see.

SOLUSMHOR, *a* Luminous.—*Shaw*

† SOMA, *s. f.* (*Ir id.*) A flock of swans; learning

SOMACHAN, ain, *s m.* (*Ir id*) A soft, good-natured, innocent person.

SOMAIN, *s f.* Wealth.

SOMAINEACH, *a.* Rich, wealthy.

SOMALTA, *a.* (*Ir. id*) Bulky, stout; personable, comely; easy gentle; negligent, generous, liberal. *Asp. form*, shomalta Do 'n àg-mhnaoi shomalta, *to the comely maid.—Macint*

SOMALTACHD, *s. f.* (*Ir. id.*) Bulkiness, stoutness, personableness, comeliness; easiness; gentleness; negligence; generousness; abundance

Somaltas, ais, *s. m.* See Somaltachd.

So-mharbhachd, *s. f.* Mortality.

So-mharbhta, *a.* Mortal; easily killed

So-mhiannach, *a* Desirable

Sòmhlach, *a.* Crowding; pressing together; abridging, lessening.

Sòmhlachadh, aidh, *s m.* A packing close, a pressing together, a lessening in bulk, an abridging, an abridgement, an abbreviation. Written also *sumhlachadh.*

Sòmhlachadh, (a) *pr part* of sòmhlaich.

Sòmhlaich, *v. a.* Pack close, press together, lessen in bulk, abridge, abbreviate *Pret. a* shòmhlaich ; *fut. aff. a.* somhlaichidh See also Sùmhlaich. The word of opposite meaning is *dòmhlaich.*

Sòmhlaichear, *fut pass* of sòmhlaich. Shall be pressed together, or abridged

Somhlaichidh. *fut aff. a* of somhlaich.

Sòmhlaichte, *p part* of somhlaich

Somhlan, *a.* Safe, secure, sound, unhurt.

Somhlanachd, *s. f* Safeness, secureness, soundness.

So-mhuinte, *a.* Tractable, manageable.

Son, *s m* (*Ir id.*) Sake, cause, stead, account Air son cloinn nan daoine, *for the sake of mankind*, c'arson? *why, on whose account?* c'arson so, *why so?* c'arson sin, *why so?* air mo shon, *on my account, in my stead, for my sake*, air mo shon-sa, *for me, as for me, for my part* —*Stew. Gen* Air mo' shon-sa dheth, *as for me, as for my part of it*, air mo shon féin, *as for myself, as for my own part*, air mo shon féin deth, *as for my own part of it*, air a son, *for her, for her sake*, air a shon, *for him, for his sake*, air son so, *on this account*, air shon so uile, *for all this, for all that* —*Stew Lev.* Air bhur son, *for your sake, on your account*, air an son, *for their sake, on their account*, air an son-sa dheth, *as for them, as for their part of it*, air shon sin, *on that account, nevertheless.*

† Son, soin, *s m.* (*Lat.* sonus *Ir* son) A sound, a voice; a word; good, advantage, a stake, a beam.—*Shaw*

† Son, *a.* Tall.

Sona, *a.* (*Ir. id*) Happy, blessed; prosperous, lucky, fortunate Is sona mise, *happy am I.*—*Stew Gen* Is sona thu, a thìr, *blessed art thou, O land!*—*Stew Ecc* Cha toir muir na mon' a chuid o dhuine sona, *neither seas nor mountains can bar the lucky.*—*G. P.*

Sonadh, *a.* See Sona

Sonairte, *s. f* (*Ir. id*) Strength; courage

Sonann, ainn, *s m., perhaps* son-fhonn. (*Ir. id.*) A fertile land, a good soil.

Sōnas, ais, *s. m* Vexation, annoyance. Cuir sōnas, *vex, disoblige, put into a pet.*

Sŏnas, ais, *s m.* (*Ir id.*) Happiness, bliss; prosperity, luck Sonas an lorg na caitheamh, *good luck follows the liberal.*—*G P.* Sannt gun sonas, éiridh an donas da, *hapless greed will not succeed.*—*G. P.*

Sonn, suinn, *s. m.* (*Ir. id*) A hero; a champion; a stout man, a bait to catch fish, a club, a staff, a stake An sonn, *the hero* —*Oss N. pl.* suinn. Mar na suinn, *like the heroes* —*Oss. Trathal.* Lochlinn nan sonn, *warlike Lochlin.* —*Oss Lodin.*

Sonn, *v. a* Pierce; thrust; oppress. *Pret.* shonn, *pierced*; *fut aff. a.* sonnaidh, *shall pierce.* Ann am bhith 'sonnadh chlaigeanna, *while piercing skulls.*—*Turn*

Sonnach, aich, *s. m* A palisade; a castle; a wall. Dail nan sonnach, *the plain of palisades.*

Sonnadh, aidh, *s. m.* (*Ir. id.*) A contention, strife; a thrusting, a pierce, a thrust, a pierce, oppression.

Sonn-mharcach, aich, *s. m.* An aide-de-camp; a courier on horseback.

Sonnta, *a*, *from* sonn. (*Ir. id*) Heroic, bold, courageous; merry; confident.

Sonnta, *p. part.* of sonn.

Sonntach, *a.* See Sonnta.

Sonntachd, *s. m.* Heroism; boldness, courageousness; confidence; mirth.

Sònrach, *a* Special, particular, specific; remarking.

Sonrachadh, aidh, *s. m.* A specifying, a particularizing; a determining; an appointing; a making out; a noting; a remarking; specification; a determination

Sonrachadh, (a) *pr part.* of sonraich

† Sonraic, *a.* (*Ir. id*) Righteous

Sonraich, *v. a.* Specify, particularize; determine; mark out; note, remark. *Pret. a.* shonraich, *specified*; *fut. aff. a* sonraichidh; *fut. pass.* sonraichte.

Sònraicheam, 1 *sing. imper. a* of sonraich Let me specify; *also, for* sonraichidh mi, *I will specify.*

Sònraichear, *fut. pass.* of sònraich Shall be specified, shall be determined

Sònraichidh, *fut. aff. a.* of sònraich. Shall or will specify.

Sònraichte, *p. part* of sonraich. Specified, particularised; determined; appointed, marked out; remarked. *Asp. form,* shònraichte Air an la shonraichte, *on the appointed day.* —*Stew Pro.*

Sònraichte, Sonruichte, *a* Certain, particular, special, peculiar, noted, notable, notorious. Duine sònraichte, *a certain man* Cairde sònraichte, *particular friends* —*Stew. Pro* Sluagh sònraichte, *a peculiar people.*—*Stew. Jan.* Bha adharc shònruichte aige, *he had a notable horn.*—*Stew. Dan* Sònruichte airson droch-bheart, *notorious for wickedness.* Gu sònruichte an duine so, *particularly, this man.* Gu sònraichte, *particularly, in particular, especially*

Sontach, *a* See Sonnta.

Sonuidh, *a.* (*Ir. id.*) Lucky; propitious.

Sop, *s. m.* (*Ir. id.*) A wisp or handful of hay or straw; a bundle; the top or crest of a hen or any other bird. *N. pl.* sopan Sop fodair, *a wisp of straw*; sop as gach seid, *a wisp from every truss.*—*G. P.*; said of those who have nothing but what they borrow.

Sopag, aig, *s f, dim.* of sop (*Ir.* sopog.) A wall; a wisp of straw; a small bundle of straw for thatching

Sopan, ain, *s m.* (*dim.* of sop) A little wisp; a little handful, as of hay or straw. Sopan säidhe, *a wisp of hay*

† Sopar, air, *s m* (*Ir. id*) A well See Tobar

So-phroinnte, *a.* Easily pulverized.

So-phronnaidh, *a.* Easily pulverized.

So-phronnta, *a* Easily pulverized.

Soplach, aich, *s. m.* (*Ir. id.*) A wisp or handful of hay or straw.

Soplach, *a.* (*Ir. id.*) Full of straw; useless; insignificant. —*Mdcfar. Voc*

Sop-reic, *s. m* The sign of a tavern or inn; the sign of a shop.

† Sor, *s. m.* (*Ir id.*) A louse

Sòr, *s. m.* (*Ir. id*) Stop; hesitation.

Sòr, *v. n.* Hesitate, scruple. *Pret. a.* shòr; *fut. aff.* sòraidh, *shall hesitate.* Cha shòr e do mharbh, *he will not hesitate to kill you.* Dream nach sòradh builleanan, *people who would not hesitate to strike* —*Old Song.*

Sòrach, *a.* Hesitating, scrupulous.

Sorachda, Sorachta, *a.* (*Soracte,* a mountain in the Faliscan territory; now Monte di S. Silvestro.) Acervated, accumulated, heaped.

Sòradh, aidh, *s. m.* Hesitation, scrupulousness.

Sorachadh, aidh, *s. m.* The act of acervating; accumulation.

Soraich, *v. a.* Accumulate, heap up.

Soraideadh, idh, *s. m.* Salutation.

Soraidh, *s. f.* A blessing; a parting blessing; compliments salutation; a farewell; success, health, happiness. Soraidh le bordachd, *farewell to poetry.—Old Song.* Soraidh leat, a ghraidh, *farewell, thou beloved.—Death of Carril.* Soraidh slàn do 'n ailleagan, *health to the maiden.—Old Poem.* Soraidh leat, is improperly, yet frequently, pronounced *sòr leat.*

Soraidh, *a.* (*Ir. id.*) Happy, successful.

† **Sorb,** soirb, *s. m.* (*Ir. id.*) A fault or blemish; *also, adjectively,* foul, dirty.

Sorb, *v. a.* (*Ir. id.*) Foul, pollute. *Pret. a.* shorb.

Sorbach, *a.* Foul, polluted; faulty.

Sorbachadh, aidh, *s. m.* A polluting.

Sorbaich, *v. a.* Pollute.

Sorb-aorachas, ais, *s. m.* (*Ir. id.*) A satyr, a lampoon.

Sorb-chàineadh, idh, *s. m.* A satire, a lampoon.

† **Sorb-charn,** airn, *s. m.* (*Ir. id.*) A dunghill.—*Shaw.*

Sorc, *s. m.* (*Ir. id.*) Delight, pleasure.

Sorcair, *s. m.* A cylinder. *N. pl.* sorcairean.

Sorch, *s. m.* (*Ir. id.*) An eminence; a heap.

Sorcha, *a.* (*Ir. id.*) Light; clear; evident, manifest. The word of opposite meaning is *dorcha.*

Sorchaich, *v. a.* (*from* sorcha.) Enlighten; make clear light, or manifest; heap up. *Pret. a.* shorchaich; *fut. aff. a.* sorchaichidh, *shall enlighten.* The word of opposite meaning is *dorchaich.*

Sorchaichidh, *fut. aff. a.* of sorchaich.

Sorchaichte, *p. part.* of sorchaich. Enlightened; made clear, light, or manifest; heaped up.

Sorchàin, *s. f.* A satire, a lampoon; scurrilous rhyme; slander.

Sorchan, ain, *s. m.* A stool; a support; a little eminence. Sorchan leigidh, *a trestle or gawntree. N. pl.* sorchain.

Sorchanach, *a.* (*from* sorchan.) Like a stool; having little eminences.

Sord, *s.* More frequently written *sùrd;* which see.

Sordail, *a.* (sord-amhuil.) More frequently written *sùrdail;* which see.

So-reamhrachadh, *a.* Easily fattened; coagulable.

So-reamhraichte, *a.* Coagulable.

So-réiteach, *a.* Easily arranged; easily adjusted; easily disentangled, as a string; reconcileable.

So-riaghladair, *s. m.* A mild governor, a lenient ruler; one who rules with facility.

So-riaghladh, So-riaghlaidh, *a.* Easily governed, easily managed; governable, manageable.

Sorn, soirn, *s. m.* (*Ir. id.*) A snout; a disagreeable visage; the fire-place of an oven or kiln; the flue of an oven or kiln. Sorn-ràc, *an oven-rake or baker's peel.;* sorn-bhaidh, *Stornaway,* i. e. *the snout or nose of the bay.*

Sornach, *a.* (*from* sorn.) Snouty; long-chinned; having a flue; peevish, ill-natured. *Com.* and *sup.* sornaiche.

Sornair, *s. m.* (sorn-fhear.) A baker; a long-chinned person; a peevish fellow.

Sornaireachd, *s. f.* (*Ir. id.*) The business of a baker.

Sornairean, *n. pl.* of sornair,

Sornan, ain, *s. m.* (*Ir. id.*) A skate fish.—*Shaw, Macd. and Mac. Voc.*

Sornan, ain, *s. m.* (*dim.* of sorn.) A little snout; a little chin; a little flue; a hillock.—*Shaw.*

Sornanach, *a.* Abounding in skate-fish; of skate-fish; like a skate-fish; having little hillocks.

So-roinneadh, *a.* Divisible.

So-roinnte, *a.* Divisible, separable.

Sòrsa. See **Sort.**

Sòrt, soirt, *s. m.* (*Dan.* sort. *Arm.* seurt. *Ir.* sort.) Sort, kind, species.

Sortan, ain, *s. m.* (*Ir. id.*) Praise, glory; a shout.

Sorthan, ain, *s. m.* (*Ir. id.*) Reproof; prosperity.—*Shaw.*

Soruidh. Written also *soraidh;* which see.

So-ruigheachd, *a.* Attainable, easily reached.

So-ruigsinn, *a.* (*Ir. id.*) Attainable.

Sos, *s. m.* A mixture of food for dogs or swine.

Sos, *s. m.* Cessation; giving over; knowledge.

Sosadh, aidh, *s. m.* (*Ir. id.*) A dwelling, an abode.

† **Sosar,** *a.* (*Ir. id.*) Younger, youngest.—*Shaw.*

So-sdiùradh, So-sdiùraidh, *a.* Manageable, governable; easily guided or steered.

So-sgoltadh, So-sgoltaidh, *a.* Easily cleft or split; fissible.

So-sgoilte, *a.* Easily cleft or split; fissible.

So-shamhlachadh, *a.* Comparable; applicable; easily matched.

So-shàruichte, *a.* Easily oppressed; easily conquered.

So-sheachanta, *a.* Easily avoided; easily shunned.

So-sheachnadh, So-sheachnaidh, *a.* Avoidable; easily shunned or avoided.

So-sheòlta, *a.* (*Ir. id.*) Navigable; easily guided or directed.

So-shìneadh, *a.* Easily stretched.

So-shìnte, *a.* Ductile, as wire; easily stretched.

So-shìnteachd, *s. f.* Ductility.

† **Sosta,** *s. m.* (*Ir. id.*) An abode, a dwelling-house.—*Shaw.*

Sostan, ain, *s. m.* (*Ir. id.*) A noise; a cry.—*Shaw.*

Sostanach, *a.* (*Ir. id.*) Noisy, clamorous.

Sostanachd, *s. f.* Noisiness; clamorousness.

Sot, *v. a.* Boil any thing overmuch.

Sotal, ail, *s. m.* See **Sodal.**

Sotalach, *a.* See **Sodalach.**

Sotalaich. See **Sodalaich.**

Sòth, *s. m.* More frequently written *sogh;* which see.

Sòthail, *a.* See **Soghail.**

Sothan, *s. m.* (*Ir. id.*) A spruce fellow.

So-thaosgadh, So-thaosgaidh, *a.* Exhaustible; easily drawn or drained.

So-tharruing, *a.* (*Ir.* so-tharrangtha.) Easily drawn; ductile.

So-theagasg, *a.* Easily taught; docile.

So-theanndadh, *a.* Easily turned.

So-tholladh, So-thollaidh, *a.* Perforable, easily bored.

So-thruaillidh, *a.* Corruptible.

So-thuigse, *s. f.* Comprehension.

So-thuigsinn, *a.* (*Ir.* so-thuigsionn.) Easily understood; intelligible.

Sotlaidh, *s. f.* Harm, damage; *also, adjectively,* bad, naughty.

Sotsach, *a.* Plump, fat, chubby.

Sotsag, aig, *s. f.* A plump young girl; a pillion.

So-uisgeach, *a.* (*Ir. id.*) Moist, watery; apt to be moist.

So-uisgidh, *a.* Easily watered; having an affinity for moisture.

Spac, spaca, *s. m.* A sudden exertion, as in wrestling. Spac cleachdaidh, *wrestling, a wrestling match.* Tha iad a cur spac cleachdaidh, *they are wrestling.*

Spachadh, aidh, *s. m.* A plucking by the roots.

Spad, spaid, *s. m.* (*Ir. id.*) A clod, a turf.—*Shaw.*

Spad, spaid, *s. f.* (*Ir. id.*) A spade.—*Shaw.*

Spad, *v. a.* Fell; knock down; strike flat to the ground; kill; flatten. *Pret. a.* spad; *fut. aff. a.* spadaidh.

Spadach, *a.* Full of clods or turf; of clods, of turf; like a spade; of a spade; felling, knocking down; flattening; prone or ready to bruise; ready to fell or strike to the ground.

Spadadh, aidh, *s. m.* A digging with a spade; a felling; a bruising; a flattening; a killing.

Spadadh, (a), *pr. part.* of spad. Felling; knocking down; striking to the ground; flattening; killing. A spadadh chorp chasagach, *felling long-coated bodies.*—*Old Song.*

Spadag, aig, *s. m.* A fillip; a knock-down blow; a kind of play.—*Macd.* *N. pl.* spadagach.

Spadagach, *a.* Filliping; knocking down.

Spadaiche, *s. m.* A feller; a bruiser; a pugilist. *N. pl.* spadaichean.

Spadaidh, *fut. aff. a.* of spad. Shall or will knock down.

Spadail, *gen. sing.* of spadal.

Spadair, *s. m.* (spad-fhear.) A feller; a bruiser; a pugilist. *N. pl.* spadairean.

Spadaireachd, *s. f.* Frequent or continued felling, bruising or knocking down; pugilism.

Spadal, ail, *s. m.* (*Ir. id.*) A spaddle, a ploughstaff.—*Shaw.*

Spadalach, *a.* Like a spaddle; like a ploughstaff.

Spadanach, aich, *s. m.* A sluggard; *adjectively*, slow, sluggish.

Spadanta, *a.* (*Ir. id.*) Slow, sluggish; mean, niggardly. —*Macfar. Voc.*

Spadantachd, *s. f.* (*Ir. id.*) Slowness, sluggishness; meanness; niggardliness.—*Shaw.*

Spadar, *fut. pass.* of spad; which see.

Spad-chluas, -chluais, *s. f.* A flat ear; a dull ear. *N. pl.* spad-chluasan.

Spad-chluasach, *a.* (*Ir. id.*) Flat-eared; somewhat deaf. —(*Shaw and Macfar. Voc.*); *substantively*, a flat-eared person, a deaf person.

Spad-chos, choise, *s. f.* A flat foot, a plain sole. *N. pl.* spad-chosan.

Spad-chosach, *a.* (*Ir. id.*) Flat-footed, plain-soled; *substantively*, a splay-footed person.

Spad-fhocal, ail, *s. m.* A vaunt; a vaunting expression; a gasconade; rhodomontade.

Spad-fhocalach, Spad-fhoclach, *a.* (*Ir. id.*) Gasconading; ostentatious.

Spad-fhoclair, *s. m.* A gasconader; a braggadocio.

Spad-phluic, *s. f.* (*Ir. id.*) A blub cheek, a chubby face.

Spad-phluiceach, *a.* (*Ir. id.*) Blub-cheeked, chubby-faced; *substantively*, a blub-cheeked person; a chubby-faced person.

Spad-shròin, -shròna, *s. f.* A flat nose.—*Shaw.*

Spad-shròineach, *a.* (*Ir. id.*) Flat-nosed; *substantively*, a flat-nosed person.

Spadta, Spadte, *p. part.* of spad. Felled; knocked down, laid flat.

Spad-thalamh, -thalmhainn, *s. m.* Unproductive ground; fallow ground.

Spad-thinneas, eis, *s. m.* (*Ir.* spaid-thinneas.) Epilepsy; lethargy.

Spàg, *v. a.* Fold up the leaves of a book; distort a shoe.

Spag, *s.* The fold of the leaf of a book, occasioned by improper usage; the distortion in a shoe, occasioned by walking awry.

Spàg, spàig, *s. f.* (*Ir. id.*) A ham; a claw or paw; the foot of a cloven-footed quadruped; *in derision*, a clumsy foot; a club-foot; a long flat foot; a plain sole. *N. pl.* spàgan. Oscionn a spàgan, *above his feet.*—*Stew. Lev. ref.* Spàgan dubha, *hams dried in smoke.*

Spàgach, *a.* (*Ir. id.*) Like a ham, of hams; having claws; having paws; club-footed; broad-footed; out-toed.—*Macd. Shaw*, and *Macfar. Voc.*

Spàgach, *a.* Folded up, as the leaves of a book, by improper usage; distorted, as a shoe.

Spàgair, *s. m.* (spag-fhear.) A club-footed fellow; a fellow with an awkward sprawling gait; a flat-soled person. *N. pl.* spàgairean.

Spàgair tuinn, *s. m.* The bird called little grebe. The name *spàgair tuinn* seems to be a corruption of *spàg ri tòin*; which see.

Spàgaireachd, *s. f.* An awkward, sprawling gait.

Spagh, spagha, *s. m.* A swathe of mown grass. *N. pl.* spaghan.

Spaghach, *a.* In swathes, as mown grass; having a good swathe.

Spagluinn, *s. f.* (*Ir. id.*) Ostentation; show; conceit.

Spagluinneach, *a.* Ostentatious; showy; conceited; *also*, an ostentatious, conceited person.

Spagluinneachd, *s. f.* Ostentatiousness; showiness; conceitedness.

Spàg ri tòin, *s.* The water-fowl called little grebe; the *colymbus auritus* of Linnæus.

Spàid, spàide, *s. f.* A spade; a clod or turf; a sluggard; a drug; carrion; an eunuch. *N. pl.* spaideachan. *Ir. id. Gr.* σπάδων, *an eunuch. Lat.* spado. *Fr.* spadon.

† Spàid, *a.* Dull, heavy; dead, insipid; unfruitful.

Spaide, *s. f.* Show, ostentation; foppery; sluggishness.

Spaideal, eil, *s. m.* A spaddle; a plough staff.—*Macd.*

Spaidealachd, *s. f.* (*Ir.* spaid-amhuileachd.) Showiness; gawdiness; foppishness; sluggishness.

Spaideil, *a.* (spaid-amhuil.) Showy, gawdy; foppish; *also*, sluggish.—*Shaw.*

Spaid-fhion, -fhiona, *s. m.* (*Ir. id.*) Flat or dead wine.

Spaidhir, spaidhreach, *s. f.* (*Ir. id.*) The pocket-hole of a gown or petticoat; a petticoat; a placket.

Spaidsear, eir, *s. m.* A stroller, a saunterer, a rambler.

Spaidsearachd, *s. f.* Walking, sauntering, promenading, stalking. Written also, by metathesis, *spaisdearachd.*

Spaidsearan, *n. pl.* of spaidsear.

Spaidseirich, *v. n.* Walk, saunter, promenade. Written also *spaisdeirich.*

Spaid-thalamh, thalmh, ainn, *s. m.* (*Ir. id.*) Unproductive ground.

Spàig, *s. f.* (*Ir. id.*) A lame leg.

Spàil, *v. a.* Swaddle, swathe, wrap up. *Pret. a.* spàil; *fut. aff. a.* spàilidh. Written also *spéil.*

Spàileach, *a.* Swaddling, swathing, wrapping up.

Spàileachadh, aidh. The act of swathing.

Spàileadh, idh, *s. m.* A swaddling; a swathing; a wrapping up. Written also *speileadh.*

Spàilich, *v. a.* Swathe.

Spailleachd, *s. f.* Vain glory, ostentation; conceitedness; foppery. Written also *spaillichd.*

Spailleachdail, *a.* Vain-glorious, ostentatious, conceited.

Spailleachdair, *s. m.* A vain-glorious man; an ostentatious man; a fop; a vaunter. *N. pl.* spailleachdairean.

Spailleadh, idh, *s. m.* A check; an abuse—(*Shaw*); a fall.—*O'Reilly.*

Spailliceach, *a.* Vain-glorious. Gu spailliceach, *vain-gloriously. Com.* and *sup.* spailliciche.

Spailliceil, *a.* See **Spaillichdeil**.

Spaillichd, *s. f.* Vain glory, ostentation, conceit; foppery.

Spaillichdealachd, *s. f.* Vain-gloriousness; ostentatiousness; conceitedness; foppery.

Spaillichdeil, *a.* (spaillichd-amhuil.) Vain-glorious; ostentatious; conceited; foppish. Oganach spaillichdeil, *a foppish fellow.*

Spaillichdear, eir, *s. m.* (spaillichd-fhear.) A vain-glorious man; an ostentatious man; a vaunter; a fop; an egotist.

Spailp, spailpe, *s. f.* (*Ir. id.*) Pride; conceit: a beau—(*Macfar. Voc.*); a smack or kiss; a lie; *also, adjectively,* notable.—*Shaw.* Spailp d' fhear-tighe, *the pride of thy landlord.—Macfar.*

Spailpean, ein, *s. m.* (*Ir.* spailpin.) A conceited person; a beau; a fop; an intruder; *also, a rascal.*

Spailpeanta, *a.* Conceited, foppish.

Spailpear, eir, *s. m.* A beau; a fop; a spruce fellow; an intruder. *N. pl.* spailpearan.

Spailpearra, *a.* Conceited, beauish, foppish. Gu spailpearra, *conceitedly.*

Spailpearrachd, *s. f.* Conceitedness, foppishness.

Spailpeil, *a.* (spailp-amhuil.) Proud, airy, conceited, beauish, foppish; spruce; notable. Ag éiridh gu spailpeil a dhamhsadh, *rising beauishly to dance.*

Spàin, spàine, *s. f.* (*Ir.* sponog *and* spàin.) A spoon. *N. pl.* spainean.—*Stew. Ex. ref.* and *Lev. Also,* spàineachan, *spoons.* Làn spàine, *a spoonful.* Spàin aòil, *a trowel.—Macd.*

Spàin, (an), *s. f.* Spain.

Spàineach, *a.* (*from* spàin.) Like a spoon; of spoons.

Spàineachan, *n. pl.* of spàin. Spoons. Written also *spàinean*

Spàinean, *n. pl.* of spàin. Spoons.

Spàinis, *s. f.* The Spanish language.

Spàinneach. See **Spàinteach**.

Spàinteach, ich, *s. m.* A Spaniard. a Spanish sword or toledo. *N. pl.* Spàintich, *Spaniard.* Is lionmhor spainteach air thaobh clìth orra, *many a sword hangs by their side.—Turn.*

Spàinteach, *a.* Spanish. Fion Spàinteach, *Spanish wine.*

Spairiseach, *a.* Conceited; strutting; airy in gait.

Spairiseachd, *s. f.* Conceitedness; a strutting gait.

Spairn, *s. f.* (*Ir. id.* A log of wood.—*Shaw.*

Spairn, *s. f.* (*Ir. id.*) Emulation; a struggle; an effort; a wrestle; agony. Spairn nan laoch, *the struggle of the heroes.—Oss. Fing.* Spairn a chleibh, *the agony of his breast.—Id.* Spairn a bhàis, *the struggle of death, mortal strife.—Id.* Dean spairn, *strive.*

Spairn, *v. n.* Strive, struggle, wrestle.—*Shaw.*

Spairneach, *a.* Emulous; struggling; striving; making an effort; wrestling; causing emulation, struggle, or strife.

Spairneachd, *s. f.* Emulousness; rivalry; continued or frequent emulation; wrestling. Dh' éirich gu spairneachd na suinn, *the champions got up to wrestle.—Death of Carril.*

Spairneadh, idh, *s. m.* (*Ir. id.*) A wrestling; a contest; exertion.

Spairneag, eig, *s. f.* A shell or couch. *N. pl.* spairneagan.

Spairneagach. *a.* Abounding in shells or conchs; of shells; like a shell or conch.

Spairnealachd, *s. f.* Emulousness.

Spairneil, *a.* (spairn-amhuil.) Emulous; striving; difficult; arduous; troublesome; herculean. Gu spairneil, *emulously.*

Spairnidh, *fut. aff. a.* of spairn.

Spairt, spairte, *s. f.* (*Ir. id.*) A turf, a clod; a splash of water; an inspissated fluid—(*Shaw*); a violent knocking down; a smash, a smashing; a daub, a daubing. *N. pl.* spairtean; *d. pl.* spairtibh. Le spairtibh ùire, *with clods of dust.—Stew. Job.*

Spairt, *v. a.* Splash, spatter, or daub; knock down; throw to the ground with violence; smash. *Pret. a.* spairt; *fut. aff. a.* spairtidh, *shall splash.* Spairt i e le làthaich, *she daubed it with lime.—Stew. Ex. ref.*

Spairt, *a.* Thick.—*Macfar. Voc.*

Spairteach, *a.* Splashing, daubing; causing to splash; smashing.

Spairteachd, *s. f.* Frequent or continued splashing, daubing, or smashing.

† **Spaisd**, *v. n.* Walk, parade, saunter, stroll.

Spaisdear, eir, *s. m.* (*from* † spaisd.) A saunterer, a stroller, a rambler. *N. pl.* spaisdearan.

Spaisdearach, *a.* (*Ir.* spaisteardha.) Walking, parading, sauntering, strolling, rambling.

Spaisdearachd, *s. f.* (*Ir.* spaisteorachd.) Walking, parading, promenading, sauntering, strolling; a ramble. Bha e 'spaisdearachd, *he was walking.—Stew. Dan.* Aite spaisdearachd, *a promenade, a walk.—Stew. Ezek.* Tha mi dol a ghabhail ceum spaisdearachd, *I am going to stroll about a little.*

Spaisdrich, *v. n.* Walk, parade, saunter, stroll, ramble. *Pret. id.; fut. aff. a.* spaisdrichidh, *shall walk.*

Spaisean, ein, *s. m.* A term of contempt for a boy.

Spàl, spàil, *s. m.* (*Ir.* spol. *Du.* spoel.) A weaver's shuttle. Spàl figheadair, *a weaver's shuttle.—Stew. Job.*

Spàlach, *a.* (*from* spàl.) Like a shuttle.

Spàladair, *s. m.* A shuttle-maker. *N. pl.* spàladairean.

Spàlag, aig, *s. f.* (*Ir.* spalog.) A pod; the cod or husk of any leguminous vegetable. *N. pl.* spalagan.

Spàlagach, *a.* Podded; having a large pod, cod, or husk; of pods, cods, or husks.

† **Spall**, *v. a.* Beat, strike.

Spalla, ai, *s. m.* (*Ir. id.*) A wedge, a pinning in building; a fragment of a stone or wall.—*Shaw.*

Spalladh, aidh, *s. m.* See **Spalla**.

Spallair, *s. m.* An espalier. Spallairean, *espaliers.*

Spalpair, *s. m.* See **Spailpear**.

Spang, spaing, *s. f.* A span.

Spangachadh, aidh, *s. m.* A spanning.

Spangaich, *v. a.* Span. *Pret. a. id.; fut. aff.* spangaichidh; *p. part.* spangaichte.

Spaoil, *v. a.* Swaddle, swathe, wrap up. Written also *spéil.*

Spaoileach, *a.* Swaddling, swathing, wrapping up.

Spaoileadh, idh, *s. m.* A swaddling or swathing; a wrapping up. Brat spaoilidh, *a swaddling band.*

Spàr, *s. m.* A roost; a joist, a beam. *N. pl.* sparan. Spàr chearc, *a hen-roost.*

Spăr. See **Sparr**.

Spàrach, *a.* Having a roost; like a roost; joisted; roosted, perched, as on a roost.

Sparan, ain, *s. m.* A crisping-pin.

Sparasach, *a.* Beauish, foppish; strutting. Written also *spairiseach.*

Sparasachd, *s. f.* See **Spairiseachd.**

Spàrdan, ain, *s. m.* A roost. Air an spàrdan, *on the roost.—Roy Stewart.*

Spàrdanach, *a.* Having a roost; like a roost; roosted; perched, as on a roost.

Sparn, spairn, *s. f.* More frequently written *spairn*; which see.

Spàrr, *s. m.* (*Ir. id.*) A roost; a joist, a beam.—*Shaw. N. pl.* spàrran. Spàrr nan cearc, *a hen-roost.*

Spărr, *s. m.* A spar; a nail.—*Shaw. N. pl.* sparran.

Spărr, *v. a.* (*Ir. id.*) Drive; dash or push forward; fasten; nail; rivet; enforce; inculcate. *Pret. a.* sparr; *fut. aff. a.* sparraidh. Sparr thu do chròg, *thou didst dash thy feet.—Macint.*

Spàrrach, *a.* Having a roost; like a roost; joisted; perched, as on a roost.

Spărrach, *a.* Driving; shoving; dashing; nailing; rivetting; inculcating; enforcing.

Spărradh, aidh, *s. m.* (*Ir.* sparra.) A driving; a dashing; a shoving; a shove; a nailing; a rivetting; an enforcing; an inculcating; a charge; a positive order; a nail; a rivet. Thoir sparradh, *give a charge.* Thug e sparradh dhoibh, *he gave them a charge.—Stew.* 2 *K.* and *N. T.* Cuir sparradh, *give a charge.* A cur sparradh orra, *charging them.—Stew. Tim.* Teann-sparradh, *a strict injunction; a firm nailing or rivetting.*

Sparrag, aig, *s. f.* (*Ir. id. Gr.* σπάραγμα, *frustum rei dilaceratæ.*) The bit of a bridle—(*Sm.*); a nail; a rivet. *N. pl.* sparragan.

Sparragaich, *a.* (*from* sparrag.) Having a bit, as a bridle; nailed; rivetted.

Sparragaich, *v. a.* Drive; nail; rivet; inculcate; charge strictly; bridle, curb. *Pret. a.* sparragaich; *fut. aff. a.* sparragaichidh.

Sparragaichte, *p. part.* of sparragaich.

Spărran, ain, *s. m.* A bolt, a bar. Sparran doruis, *the bolt of a door.*

Spàrsan, ain, *s. m.* (*Ir. id.*) The dewlap of a beast; *in contempt,* a flaccid hanging lip; a diminutive little fellow; a dry stalk.

Spàrsanach, *a.* Having a dewlap; having a flaccid lip.

Spart, spairt, *s. m.* (*Ir. id.*) A clod.

Spat, *s. m.* (*Ir. id.*) A flap.

Speac, *s.* (*Ir. id.*) A spoke, a bar.

Speacach, *a.* Having spokes or bars, as a wheel or a gate.

Speacaich, *v. a.* (*from* speac.) Provide with spokes or bars.

Speach, speacha, *s. m.* and *f.* A wasp. *N. pl.* speachan.

Speach, speacha, *s. m.* A blow; a kick; froth; the play called fillip.—*Macd. N. pl.* speachannan, *blows.* Laoich a bhuaileadh speachannan, *heroes who deal blows.—Macdon.*

Speachair, *s. m.* One who kicks.

Speachannach, *a.* Waspish, peevish, cross; vicious; dealing blows.

Speachanta, *a.* (*from* speach.) Waspish, fretful, peevish, cross; vicious. Gu speachanta, *waspishly.*

Speachantas, ais, (*from* speach.) Waspishness, fretfulness, peevishness, crossness; viciousness.

Speacharra, *a.* Waspish, fretful, peevish, cross; vicious, nimble, agile. Gu speacharra, *waspishly.*

Speacharrachd, *s. f.* Waspishness, fretfulness, crossness; nimbleness.

Speaclairean. See **Speuclairean.**

Speal, speala, *s. f.* (*Ir. id.*) A scythe; a mowing-hook; a short while at any kind of work; a short fit of vigorous exertion. Thoir speal air an obair, *bestow a short while on the work.*

Speal, *v. a.* (*Ir. id.*) Mow, cut down. *Pret. a.* speal; *fut. aff. a.* spealaidh.

Spealach, *a.* (*Ir.* spealdha.) Like a scythe; like a hook; cutting down, mowing.

Spealadair, *s. m.* (*Ir.* spealadoir.) A mower, one who mows with a scythe—(*Macd.*); a scythe. *N. pl.* spealadairean.

Spealadaireachd, *s. f.* (*Ir.* spealadoireachd.) The occupation of mowing.

Spealadh, aidh, *s. m.* A mowing; a shelling.

Spealain, *s. pl.* (*Ir. id.*) Shavings.

Spealair, *s. m.*, speal-fhear. (*Ir. id.*) A mower; one who cuts down or mows fast. *N. pl.* spealairean.

Spealaireachd, *s. f.* A mowing, a cutting down; a hewing down.

Spealanta, *a.* (*Ir. id.*) Quick, ready, acute; clever; cutting; ready spoken. Gu spealanta, *quickly, acutely.*

Spealantachd, *s. f.* (*Ir. id.*) Quickness, acuteness; cleverness.

Spealg, *s. f.* A splinter, a fragment. *N. pl.* spealgan; *d. pl.* spealgaibh. Chaidh e na spealgaibh, *it went into splinters.*

Spealg, *v. a.* and *n.* Splinter, smash, break in pieces; split, cleave; chip, shive; go into splinters. *Pret. a.* spealg, *splintered; fut. aff. a.* spealgaidh, *shall* or *will splinter.* Spealgaidh mi, *I will break in pieces.—Stew. Is.*

Spealgach, *a.* Splintering, smashing, splitting, cleaving, shiving; full of splinters; splintered.

Spealgach, aich, *s. f.* A quantity of splinters, fragments, shives, or chips.

Spealgadh, aidh, *s. m.* A splintering, a smashing, a breaking in pieces; a splitting or cleaving; a chipping, a shiving; a splinter, a shive, a chip.

Spealgair, *s. m.* (*from* spealg.) One who splits or splinters. *N. pl.* spealgairean.

Spealgan, *n. pl.* of spealg. Splinters, fragments, shives.

Spealgarra, *a.* Splintering.

Spealp, speilp, *s. m.* Armour; a belt; conceit, foppery.

Spealpair, *s. m.* A beau, a fop, a spruce fellow.—*Mac Co. N. pl.* spealpairean. See also **Spailpear.**

Spealpaireachd, *s. f.* Beauishness, foppery, spruceness. Written also *spailpearachd.*

Spealparra, *a.* Beauish, spruce. Gu spealpearra, *beauishly.*

Spealparrachd, *s. f.* See **Spealpaireachd.**

Spealt, *v. a.* Cleave, split, shiver; strike with violence; smash, clash. *Pret. a.* spealt, *split; fut. aff. a.* spealtaidh, *shall cleave.*

Spealtach, *a.* Cleaving, splitting, shivering, shiving, chipping, smashing; clashing; apt to cleave, split, or go into shivers.

Spealtachd, *s. f.* A cleaving, a splitting, a shivering, a shiving, a chipping.

Spealtadh, aidh, *s. m.* A cleaving, a splitting.

Spealtair, *s. m.* (spealt-fhear.) A cleaver, a smasher, a bruiser; an instrument for cleaving. *N. pl.* spealtairean.

Spealtaireachd, *s. f.* Continued or frequent cleaving, smashing, or splintering; a violent striking; a clashing. Lainn ri spealtaireachd, *swords clashing.—Macdon.*

Spealtan, ain, *s. m.* A fragment, a splinter, a shiver; a shive, a chip. *N. pl.* spealtain.

Spealt-chleas, *s. m.* A giving blow for blow; mutual violence.

Spealt-chleasachd, *s. f.* Reciprocal violence.

Spearl, *v. a.* Spoil.

Spearlach, *a.* Spoiling.

Spearladh, aidh, *s. m.* Spoliation.

Spearrach, aich, *s. m.* (*Ir.* spearthach.) A hamstring—(*Macfar. Voc.*); a kind of fetter for cattle.—*Shaw.* Cuir spearrach, *hamstring.*

Spearrachadh, aidh, *s. m.* Hamstringing.

Spearraich, *gen. sing.* of spearrach.

Spearraich, *v. a.* Hamstring; fetter cattle. *Pret. a. id.*; *fut. aff. a.* spearraichidh; *p. part.* spearraichte, *hamstrung.*

Spearraichear, *fut. pass.* of spearraich.

Spearraichte, *p. part.* of spearraich.

Speic, speice, *s. f.* (*Swed.* spik. *Ir.* speic.) A spike, a long nail; a spar; a bar; a prop; a blow. *N. pl.* speicean, *blows.* Is iad a bhuaileas speicean, *they will strike blows.*—*Mac Co.*

Speic, *v. a.* Spike; spar; prop; strike. *Pret. a.* speic; *fut. aff. a.* speicidh, *shall spike.*

Speiceach, *a.* Spiked; sparred; nailing; striking.

Speiceadh, idh, *s. m.* A spiking, a nailing.

Spéid, *s. f.* (*Ir. id.*) A speat; a mountain torrent.

Spéid, spéide, *s. f.* Speed, progress. Cha tig e spéid, *he will make no progress.*

Spéideach, *a.* Like a speat or mountain torrent.

Spéideach, *a.* Making speed, making progress.

Spéideil, *a.* Coming speed; busy; industrious.

Speidhil, *v. n.* Slide, slip; skate. *Pret. a. id.*; *fut. aff. a.* speidhlidh, *shall slide.*

Speidhleadh, idh, *s. m.* A sliding, a slipping; skating; a slide, a slip; a stumble.

Speidhleireachd, *s. f.* The amusement of sliding or skating.

Spéidich, *v. a.* and *n.* Speed, cause to make speed. *Pret. a.* spéidich; *fut. aff. a.* spéidichidh.

Speil, *s.* (*Ir. id.*) Cattle; flocks; herds.

Spéil, *v. n.* Slide, slip; skate. *Pret.* spéil; *fut. aff.* spéilidh, *shall slide.*

Spéileach, *a.* Apt to slide or slip.

Spéileadh, idh, *s. m.* A sliding; a skating; slipping; stumbling; a slide; a slip; a stumble. Ri spéileadh, *skating.*

Spéilearachd, *s. f.* See Speileireachd.

Spéilean, ein, *s. m.* A slippery place; a place to slide on.

Spéileireachd, *s. f.* The amusement of sliding or skating; frequent slipping or stumbling.

Spéill, *v. a.* Swaddle, swathe, wrap up. *Pret. a.* spéill; *fut. aff. a.* spéillidh; *fut. pass.* spéillear; *p. part.* speillte, *swaddled.*

Spéilleach, *a.* Swaddling, swathing, wrapping up.

Spéilleadair, *s. m.* A swaddler, a swather. *N. pl.* spéilleadairean.

Spéilleadh, idh, *s. m.* A swaddling, a swathing, a wrapping up. Brat-spéillidh, *a swaddling band.*

Spéillear, *fut. pass.* of spéill. Shall be swaddled.

Spéillidh, *fut. aff. a.* of spéill. Shall or will be swaddled.

Spéillte, *p. part.* of spéill. Swaddled, swathed, wrapped up.

Spéilp, *s. f.* (*Ir. id.*) Armour; a belt—(*Shaw*); pride, foppery, conceit.

Speilteir, *s. m.* Zinc.

Spéir, speire, *s. f.* (*Ir. id.*) A hough, a ham, a hoof; a claw, a paw; the leg or foot of the human body; *in derision,* a sparrow-hawk; spades at cards. Cha 'n fhàgar speir dhiubh, *not a hoof shall be left.*—*Stew. Ex. ref.* *N. pl.* speirean *and* speireachan.

Spéir, *gen. sing.* of speur; which see.

Spéireach, *a.* (*from* speur.) Having houghs or hams; clawed; hoofed; slender-limbed; shanky; like a hawk.

Speiread, eid, *s. m.* Spirit.—*Macfar.* More frequently written *spiorad;* which see.

Speireag, eig, *s. f.* (*Ir.* speireog.) A hawk; a sparrow-hawk; a slender-limbed girl; any slender-limbed creature of the feminine gender; a shank. *N. pl.* speireagan.

Speireagach, *a.* Like a hawk; slender-limbed; shanked; having claws.

Speirean, ein, *s. m.* (*dim.* of speir.) A spindle-shank.

Speirge, *s. f.* See Speireag.

Spéir-sheabhag, aig, *s. f.* A sparrow-hawk.—*Mack.* *N. pl.* speir-sheabhagan. The *falco nisus* of Linnæus.

Spéis, *s. f.* Esteem, respect; affection, love, attachment, fondness, liking, endearment. Thoir spéis, *shew respect, love.* Tra bheir mi spéis, *when I respect.*—*Sm.* Thug thu do spéis do Art, *you gave your affection to Ardar.*—*Ardar.*

Spéiseal, *a.* See Spéiseil.

Spéisealachd, *s. f.* See Spéiseileachd.

Speisealta, *a.* (*Ir.* spesialta.) Becoming, comely; having a good appearance; handsome; clean; in order; tight. Gu speisealta, *becomingly, handsomely.*

Speisealtachd, *s. f.* Comeliness, seemliness, handsomeness; cleanness.

Spéiseil, *a.* (speis-amhuil.) Esteemed; fond; seemly; cleanly; tight; tidy. Tha thu agam ro spéiseil, *I esteem you very much.*—*Old Song.*

Spéiseileachd, *s. f.* Fondness, attachment; the circumstance of being esteemed; seemliness; cleanliness; tightness; tidiness.

Speuclair, *s. m.* An optician; a spy-glass, an eye-glass.

Speuclaireachd, *s. f.* The business of an optician.

Speuclairean, *s. pl.* Eye-glasses or spectacles.

Speuclairiche, *s. m.* An optician.

Speur, spéir, *s. m.* The sky, the firmament, the heavens. Mar dhealan nan speur, *like the lightning of the skies.*—*Oss. Gaul.* Mar theine spéir, *like the fireball of the sky.* *N. pl.* speuran; *d. pl.* speuraibh.

Ir. spéir, *the sky.* *Gr.* σφαῖρα. *Eng.* sphere. Perhaps *speur* may have an affinity with ζέφυρος.

Speurach, *a., from* speur. (*Ir.* speurgha.) Aerial, atmospheric, celestial.

Speuradair, *s. m.* (*from* speur.) A stargazer, an astronomer, an astrologer, a meteorologist. *N. pl.* speuradairean.

Speuradaireachd, *s. f.* Stargazing, astronomy, astrology, meteorology.

Speuraibh, *d. pl.* of speur; which see.

Speuran, *n. pl.* of speur. Skies, heavens.

Speur-eòlach, *a.* Versed in astronomy, versed in astrology.

Speur-eòlas, ais, *s. m.* Astronomy; astrology; meteorology.

Speur-ghlan, *s. m.* (*Ir. id.*) A clear sky—(*Macfar. Voc.*); a clear sky.—*Shaw.*

Spial. See Spiol.

Spian, *v. a.* See Spion.

Spic, spice, *s. f.* (*Ir. id.*) A spike, a long nail, a spar.

Spiceach, *a.* Like a spike, like a nail, like a spar; full of spikes, nails, or spars.

Spìd, spide, *s. f.* Spite, malice; reproach, censure; shame, infamy. Gach dochair is gach spìd, *every mischief and malice.*—*Sm.*

Ir. spid. *Du.* spyt. *Eng.* spite. *Dan.* spids, *sharp.* *Eng.* spit.

Spìdeach, *a.* Spiteful, malicious; shameful; reproachful, contemptible. Gu spìdeach, *spitefully.*

Spìdeachas, ais, *s m.* Spitefulness.

Spìdeag, eig, *s f.* A spiteful young female; a delicate, slender creature. *N. pl.* spideagan.

Spìdeag, eig, *s f* A nightingale; a robin-redbreast; a slender creature *N pl.* spìdeagan

Spìdeagach. *a* Spiteful, as a young female.

Spìdeagach, *a* Abounding in nightingales; like a nightingale; of nightingales, melodious

Spìdeal, eil, *s m* (*Ir id*) A hospital, a charitable foundation, a spittal.

Spìdealachd, *s f* (*Ir.* spidamhlachd) Spitefulness, maliciousness; shamefulness, reproachfulness; contempt

Spìdeil, *a*, spìd-amhuil. (*Ir.* spìdamhuil) Spiteful, malicious; reproachful, infamous, despicable, shameful Gu spìdeil, tailceasach, *spitefully and reproachfully.—Sm* Leis am bu spìdeil duais foill, *who despised the wages of deceit —Old Song*

Spìdeileachd, *s f* See Spìdealachd

Spid-shuileach, *a* Purblind —*Shaw*

Spig, *v a* Mock, scoff

Spigeil, *a.* Mocking, scoffing

Spile, *s f.* A wedge.—*Shaw*
Ir. spile. *Arm* spilhen, *a pin* *Du* spijlen *Eng* spill, *a shiver of wood*

Spiligean, ein, *s. m* A grain, as of corn

Spiligeanach, *a* Having grains, as of corn

Spìlle, *s. f.* A certain measure of yarn.

† **Spin**, *s.* (*Ir id* *Lat.* spina) A thorn

Spineil, *a.* (spin-amhuil) Thorny.

Spìnn, spinne, *s f.* A certain measure of yarn. *N. pl* spìnnteau.

Spìnnle, *s. f.* See Spìlle

Spìoc, *s f* Niggardliness, meanness.

Spìocach, *a* Niggardly, mean, miserable Gu spiocach, *in a niggardly manner.* *Com.* and *sup.* spiocaiche

Spìocadh, aidh, *s m* Niggardliness, meanness Tha thu air d'itheadh le spiocadh, *thou art eaten up with niggardliness.*

Spiocaid, *s. f.* A spigot.

Spìocair, *s m.* A niggard, a churl *N pl* spiocairean.

Spìocaireachd, *s f* Niggardliness, meanness, churlishness.

Spiochag, aig, *s f* (*Ir id*) A purse, a bag.—*Shaw.* *N pl.* spiochagan.

Spiochagach, *a.* Like a purse; of a purse

Spìochan, ain, *s m* (*Ir id*) A wheezing in the throat, a person who has a wheezing in his throat

Spiochan, ain, *s. m.* A purse, a bag

Spiochanach, *a* (*from* spiochan) Like a purse; of a purse.

Spiochanaich, *s. f.* A frequent or continued wheezing in the throat

Spiod. See Spìd

Spiol, *s. m.* See Spioladh.

Spiol, *v a* Snatch, pluck, tug; tease, carp, grasp, browse. *Pret. a* spiol; *fut. aff. a* spiolaidh, *shall pluck, fut pass* spiolar, *shall be plucked.*

Spiolach, *a.* Snatching, plucking, tugging, teasing, carping; browsing; grasping; apt to snatch, pluck, tug, or grasp.

Spioladair, *s. m* One who plucks or tugs; a teaser, a carper; a pair of pincers or nippers.—*Macd.* *N. pl.* spioladairean

Spioladaireachd, *s. f.* Plucking, tugging; frequent or continued plucking or tugging.

Spioladh, aidh, *s m.* A snatching, a plucking, a tugging; a carping; a grasping; a browsing; a snatch, a pluck, a tug, a grasp. Thoir spioladh air, *pluck him or it.*

Spioladh, (a), *pr. part.* of spiol. Snatching, plucking, tugging; teasing; carping; grasping; browsing. An ruadhag a spioladh air d' uaigh, *the roe browsing on thy grave.—Oss Fing.*

Spiol-bhòta, *s. m.* A boot jack

Spiolgan, ain, *s. m* A plucking, a tugging, nippers.

Spion, *v a* Pull, pluck; tear away, tear from the root; drag. *Pret. a.* spion, *pulled. fut aff a.* spionaidh, *shall pull. fut pass* spionar, *shall be pulled.*

Spion an eidheann o'craoibh,
Spion an iolair o ciar-chreich,
Spion an leanabh a mhàthair ghaoil,
Ach na spion o m' ghaol mise

Pull the ivy from its tree,
Pull the eagle from its dusky prey,
Tear the infant from its mother dear,
But tear not me from him I love.—*Ardar*

Spionach, *a.* Pulling, plucking, tearing, dragging; apt to pull, apt to pluck, apt to tear, apt to drag.

† **Spionad**, aid, *s. m.* A sinew

† **Spionadach**, *a.* Sinewy.

Spionadair, *s m.* One who pulls or plucks; one who tears or drags; nippers.

Spionadh, aidh, *s m* A pulling, a plucking, a tearing away, a dragging, a pull, a pluck, a tear; *also,* motion, action.—*Shaw.*

Spionadh, 3 *sing* and *pl.* of spion; *pret. pass* of spion. Was pulled or torn away. Mar ghiumhas a spionadh le srann-ghaoth ard, *like a pine torn up by the boisterous wind —Oss.* Spionadh, *pret sub* of spion, *would pull.*

Spionadh, (a), *pr part.* of spion. Pulling, plucking, tearing, dragging

Spionadh, *fut. aff a.* of spion Shall or will pluck

Spionan, ain, *s m* (*Ir. id*) A gooseberry-bush; grossularia.

Spionar, *fut pass* of spion Shall or will be plucked or torn.

Spionn', (*for* spionna *or* spionnadh.) Strength. Commonly written with an apostrophe when the following word begins with a vowel Gun spionn' ad laimh, *without strength in thine arm.—Ull.*

Spionna, **Spionnadh**, aidh, *s m.* (*Ir. id*) Strength, force, might, pith, power. Ciod e spionnadh an laoich? *what is the hero's strength?—Oss*

Spionnar, *a* (spionn-mhor) Strong, powerful, pithy.

Spiontachan, ain, *s m.* (*Ir. id*) A searcher.

Spiontag, aig, *s. f* (*Ir.* spiontog) A currant; a gooseberry. *N pl.* spiontagan.

Spiontagach, *a* Abounding in currants; of currants

Spiorad, aid, *s. m.* (*Lat* spiritus *Arm.* sperod.) A spirit, a ghost; sprightliness, spirit, heart; animal spirits. Spiorad bréige, *the spirit of falsehood.—Stew Mic.* Spiorad briste, *a broken spirit* or *heart.—Stew. Pro.* An Spiorad Naomh, *the Holy Ghost* Droch spiorad, *an evil spirit. Arm.* droucq spered Spiorad beo, *a lively spirit* *Arm* spered beo. *N. pl.* spioradan.

Spioradail, *a* (spiorad-amhuil,) Spiritual, sprightly, lively, Ghocas spioradail, *spiritual understanding.—Stew. Col.*

Spiorsag, aig, *s f* (*Ir* spiorsog) A sparrow-hawk.

Spios, *s m.* Spice.—*Macfar Voc.* and *Shaw.*

Spios, *v. a.* Spice.

Spiosach, *a.* Spicy, spiced.

Spiosachadh, aidh, *s. m* A spicing; an embalming.

Spiosachan, ain, *s. m.* A spice-box; an embalmer.

Spiosadach, *a.* Spicy, spiced.

Spiosaich, *v. a.* Spice; embalm.

Spiosrach, *a.* Spicy, spiced; perfuming; abounding in spices Fion spiosrach, *spiced wine*

Spiosrachadh, aidh, *s. m.* The progress of perfuming or embalming.

Spiosrachan, ain, *s m.* An embalmer

Spiosrachd, *s. f.* Embalming, perfuming; spicery; perfumery; the state of being embalmed or perfumed

Spiosradhach, *a.* (*contracted* spiosrach.) Spiced. Fion spiosradhach, *spiced wine.—Stew. Song Sol.*

Spiosraich, *v. a.* Spice, embalm, perfume. *Fut aff. a.* spiosraichidh, *shall perfume.*

Spiosraiche, *s. m.* An embalmer, a perfumer. *N. pl.* spiosraichean.

Spiosraichear, *fut. pass.* of spiosraich. Shall be embalmed.

Spiosraichidh, *fut. aff a.* of spiosraich Shall embalm

Spiosraichte, *p. part* of spiosraich. Embalm, perfumed.

Spiosraidh, *s. f.* Spices, spiceries. Spiosraidh chum ola ungaidh, *spices for anointing oil.—Stew. Ex.*

Spiothag, aig, *s. f.* A small stone, a pebble; a flake. *N. pl.* spiothagan

Spiothagach, *a.* Full of small stones; pebbled; of pebbles.

Spiothair, *s. m.* A spy, a scout.—*Shaw.* *N. pl* spiothairean

Spiothaireachd, *s f* Spying; frequent spying.

Spiric, *s f.* A spire, a steeple, a pinnacle. *N. pl.* spiricean.

Spiriceach, *a.* (*from* spiric.) Like a spire, like a steeple; full of spires.

Spiricean, ein, *s. m.* (*dim.* of spiric.) A little spire; a spiracle.

Spiriceanach, *a.* Having spires; pinnacled.

Spiris, *s. f.* (*Ir. id*) A sort of hammock, a hen-roost —*Shaw.* and *Macfar. Voc* *N. pl.* spirisean.

Spiriseach, *a.* (*from* spiris) Elevated, as a roost; like a roost; like a hammock.

Spirlinn, *s f.* (*Ir. id.*) A fall; a chance.

Spirseag, eig, *s. f.* A sparrow-hawk. *N. pl.* spirseagan.

Spirseagach, *a.* Like a sparrow-hawk; abounding in sparrow-hawks.

Spiteal, il, *s. f.* A spittal.

Spitheag, eig, *s f.* See **Spiothag.**

Spithear, eir, *s. m.* An emissary; a scout.

Spiul, *v. a.* See **Spiol.**

Spiulgan, ain, *s. m.* (*Ir. id*) A picking, a plucking, nippers.

Splad, *v. a.* Slam; shut, as a door, with violence.

Splad, *s. m.* A fall; a falling forward; a tumble; a falling flatly on the ground; a noise, as of a door shutting. Thuit e le splad, *he fell heavily on the ground;* dhùin e 'n dorus le splad, *he slammed the door with violence.*

Splaidse, *s. f.* A squash.

Splaidseach, *a.* Squashing

Splang, splaing, *s. m.* A sparkle, a blaze, a flash of fire; a flake. Splang céill, *a spark of understanding.*

Splangadh, aidh, *s. m.* A sparkling, a blazing, a flashing.

Splangaid, *s. f.* Snot; mucus; phlegm.—*Macd.* *N. pl.* splangaidean.

Splangaideach, *a* Snotty; phlegmy.

Splangaideachd, *s f.* Snottiness; phlegminess.

Spleachd, *v. n* See **Spleuchd.**

Spleachdair, *s. m.* See **Spleuchdair.**

Spleadh, spleadha, *s m.* (*Ir id*) Vainglory, fiction, romance; boasting; flattery; dependance; exploits

Spleadhach, *a* (*Ir. id*) Vainglorious, fictitious, romantic; verbose, boasting; flattering. Ridir spleadhach, *a knight-errant*

Spleadhachas, ais, *s m* Vainglory; fiction, romance; a feat, boasting; flattery; dependance; hyperbole

Spleangaid, *s f.* (*Ir. id.*) Snot, mucus; phlegm.

Spleangaideach, *a.* Snotty; phlegmy

Spleoid, *s m* (*Ir id*) Satan.

Spleuchd, *a* Stare, gaze *Pret a* spleuchd, *gazed, fut aff a.* spleuchdaidh, *shall* or *will gaze.*

Spleuchd, *s. m.* A stare, a gaze. Is ann ort a tha 'n spleuchd! *how you do stare!*

Spleuchdach, *a* Staring, gazing; apt to stare or gaze

Spleuchdadh, aidh, *s m* A staring, a gazing; a stare, a gaze.

Spleuchdair, *s. m* A starer, a gazer; an idle starer; an eye-glass. *N. pl.* spleuchdairean.

Spleuchdaireachd, *s f.* A habit of staring or gazing.

Spleuchdairean, *n. pl* of spleuchd Starers, gazers; *also,* eye-glasses or spectacles.

Splionach, aich, *s m* An ill-thriven animal.

Spliùchan, ain, *s m* A bladder, a leather purse; a tobacco pouch Spliùchan tombac, *a leathern tobacco pouch.*

Spliùchanach, *a* Like a tobacco pouch.

Spliudrach, aich, *s. m.* Bad beer, swipes

Spliùgach, *a.* Splay-footed.

Spliùgan, ain, *s. m.* A splay-footed person.

Spluig, *s. f.* A wry mouth, as is occasioned by crying.

Spòc, *s. m.* A spoke, as of a wheel.

Spòcach, *a.* (*from* spòc.) Having spokes.

Spoch, *v. a.* Rob, spoil; provoke, affront.—*Shaw*

Spochadh, aidh, *s m.* Depredation; provocation

Spòdh, *v. a* Geld, castrate. *Pret a.* spodh, *castrated, fut. aff a.* spodhaidh, *shall castrate.* *Gr.* σπαδῶν. *Lat.* spado, *eunuch.* *Eng* spay

Spodha, *s m.* A gelding, a castrating, a spaying; castration.

Spodhadair, *s. m.* A gelder. *N pl* spodhadairean

Spodhadaireachd, *s f.* The operation of gelding, the business of a gelder.

Spodhadh, aidh, *s. m.* A gelding or castrating; a spaying; castration

Spodhaidh, *fut. aff. a.* of spodh

Spodhta, *p part* of spodh.

Spòg, spòig, *s. f.* A paw, a claw, a foot; a clumsy leg, *in derision; also,* the spoke of a wheel *N. pl* spògan, *claws.* —*Macint.* and *Mack.* Written also *spàg*

Spògach, *a.* (*from* spòg) Having paws, having claws; clumsy-footed. Written also *spàgach;* which see.

Spoid, *s. f.* (*Ir. id.*) A hasty word.

Spòl, spòil, *s. m.* More frequently written *spàl.*

Spold, *s. m.* A piece of meat, a joint of meat. Spold laòigh, *a loin of veal —Macd.*

Spoldaich, *s pl.* Slain bodies, carcases.

Spoilinn, *s f.* (*Ir. id.*) A small joint of meat.

Spolla, *s. m.* A joint of meat; a fragment. Spolla laoigh, *a joint of veal.—Shaw.*

Spolt, *v. a.* Tear, mangle; abuse; sprinkle; bespatter. *Pret. a.* spolt; *fut. aff. a.* spoltaidh, *shall tear.* Spoltaidh e an fhaodail le ghial, *he will tear the found booty with his jaw.*—*Mac Lach.*

Spoltach, *a.* Tearing, mangling; abusing; sprinkling; apt to tear, mangle, or devour.

Spoltadh, aidh, *s. m.* A tearing, a mangling; abusing; sprinkling, bespattering.

Spoltaidh, *fut. a.* of spolt; which see.

Spòn. See **Spàin.**

Spònag, aig, *s. f.* A spoon, a little spoon.

Spong, spoing, *s. f.* A sponge; touchwood; tinder; a niggard, *in contempt.*

Gr. σπόγγος. *Lat.* spongia. *Arm.* spoinche. *Corn.* spong. *Ir.* sponc *and* spong. *Eng.* sponge.

Spongail, *a.* (spong-amhuil.) Spongy; niggardly, parsimonious.

Spongach, *a.* Spongy, like a sponge; niggardly, parsimonious. *Com.* and *sup.* spongaiche.

Spongail, *a.* Niggardly.

Spongair, *s. m.* A niggardly fellow; a churl. *N. pl.* spongairean.

Spongaireachd, *s. f.* Niggardliness, the conduct of a niggard.

Spongairean, *n. pl.* of spongair.

Spongalach, *a.* Parsimonious, niggardly; churlish.—*Macfar. Voc.* Gu spongalach, *parsimoniously.* *Com.* and *sup.* spongalaiche.

Spongalachd, *s. f.* Parsimonious, niggardliness.

Spŏr, *v. a.* Spur on, incite, goad. *Pret. a.* spor; *fut. aff. a.* sporaidh.

Spŏr, spuir, *s.* A spur; the spur of a cock; the talon or claw of a fowl; a gun-flint; *also,* a goad, an incitement. Spor anns am bi bearn, *a notched flint.*—*Macint.* *N. pl.* spuir *and* spuirean. Spuir air a spògan, *spurs on his legs.*—*Macint.* Agus 'iongannan mar spuirean, *and his nails like claws.*—*Stew. Dan.*

Sax. spura *and* spur. *Dan.* spore. *Swed.* sporre. *Du.* spoor. *Ir.* spor. *Eng.* spur.

Spŏrach, *a.* Spurred, as a horseman; having spurs, talons, or claws; like a spur or talon; having flints; like a flint; apt to grasp; of a grasping disposition.

Spŏradair, *s. m.* (*Ir.* sporadoir.) A spurrier, a spur-maker; a flint-cutter.

Spŏradaireachd, *s. f.* Spur-making; flint-cutting; greediness.

Spŏradh, aidh, *s. m.* A spurring, an inciting, a goading; an incitement, a goad.

Spŏradh, 3 *sing. imper.* of spor. Sporadh e, *let him spur.*

Spŏraidh, *fut. aff. a.* of spŏr. Shall or will spur.

Sporan, *n. pl.* of spor.

Spŏran, ain, *s. m.* (*Ir.* sparan.) A purse. *N. pl.* sporain, *purses.* Bithidh aon sporan againn, *we shall have one purse.*—*Stew. Pro.* Sporan molach, *a Highland purse,*—a shaggy purse formerly worn by the Scotch Highlanders. It is made of the skin of badgers and of other animals. It is fastened by a belt round the middle, and hangs down in front, with tassels dangling to it. In this purse they kept their money, when they had it, and their tobacco.

Spòrs, *s. m.* Sport, diversion, fun; game; pastime; mockery, scorn; pride. Spòrs do na chì mi, *a sport to all who see me.*—*Sm.* Luchd an spòrs, *scorners.*—*Id.* Dean spòrs do, *make sport of.*

Spòrsach, *a.* Sporting; fond of sport; playful; funny; causing sport or diversion; prone to deride or to scorn. *Com.* and *sup.* spòrsaiche.

Spòrsail, *a.* (spòrs-amhuil.) Foppish, beauish; sportful, funny; deriding, jeering; haughty. Gu spòrsail, *foppishly.*

Spòrsaileachd, *s. f.* See **Spòrsalachd.**

Spòrsalachd, *s. f.* Foppishness, beauishness; a habit of jeering or deriding; sportfulness; haughtiness, conceitedness. Fear spòrsalachd, *a fop.*

Spot, *s. m.* (*Flemish,* spotte.) A spot, speck, or blemish; a spot or place. *N. pl.* spotan; *d. pl.* spotaibh. Air an spot, *on the spot, immediately;* gun spot, *spotless.*

Spotach, *a.* Spotted, speckled. Gu spotach, *spottedly.*

Spot, *v. a.* Spot.

Spotag, aig, *s. f.* (*dim.* of spot.) A little spot or blemish.

Spotagach, *a.* Spotted, blemished.

Spotaich, *v. a.* Spot, speckle, blemish. *Pret. a.* spotaich; *fut. aff. a.* spotaichidh.

Spotaichear, *fut. pass.* of spotaich.

Spotaichte, *p. part.* of spotaich. Spotted, speckled

Spoth, *v. a.* (*Ir. id.*) Geld, cut, or castrate; spay. *Pret. a.* spoth, *gelded;* *fut. aff. a.* spothaidh, *shall geld.* Written also *spodh.*

Spothadair, *s. m.* (*Ir.* spothadoir.) A gelder. *N. pl.* spothadairean.

Spothadaireachd, *s. f.* The operation of castrating, the business of a gelder.

Spothadh, aidh, *s. m.* A gelding, a cutting or castrating; a spaying; castration.

Spothaidh, *fut. aff. a.* of spoth.

Spothar, *fut. pass.* of spoth.

Spothta, *p. part.* of spoth.

† **Sprac**, spraca, *s. m.* (*Ir. id.*) A spark; life; motion.

Spracach, *a.* Strong, vigorous.

Spracadh, aidh, *s. m.* Strength, vigour, exertion.

Spraic, *s. f.* (*Ir. id.*) A harsh reprimand; a frown; an imperious mandate; *also,* vigour, exertion; an effort; sprightliness.

Spraiceach, *a.* (*from* spraic.) Inclined to reprimand; frowning; passionate; scolding; imperious; *also,* vigorous; sprightly.

Spraicealachd, *s. f.* Frequent scolding; a habit of frowning; passionateness; imperiousness; arbitrariness; vigorousness; much exertion; frequent exertion.

Spraiceil, *a.* (spraic-amhuil.) Scolding; reprehensive; frowning; passionate; imperious; arbitrary; vigorous.

Spraid, *s. f.* (*Ir. id.*) A blast, a puff; the report of a gun.

Sprăidh, spraidhe, *s. m.* A loud blast; a loud report; a shot; a crack; an explosion.

Spraidheach, *a.* Blasty, blustering; causing a loud report, explosive.

Spraidheil, *a.* (spraidh-amhuil.) Blasty, blustering.

Spreadh, spreadha, *s. m.* (*Ir. id.*) A crack; a rude onset; a sudden onset, as of two fowls fighting; a sudden shock; a stirring up; a provocation.

Spreag, *v. a.* Provoke; reprove; enforce. *Pret. a. id.*; *fut. aff. a.* spreagaidh, *shall reprove;* *fut. pass.* spreagar.—*Stew.* 1 *Cor. ref.*

Spreagach, *a.* Reproving; prone to reprove or rebuke.

Spreagachadh, aidh, *s. m.* A reproving; a provoking.

Spreagadh, aidh, *s. m.* (*Ir. id.*) A stirring up; provocation; reproof; a sudden blow.

Spreagaich, *v. a.* Reprove; provoke.

Spreagaichidh, *fut. aff. a.* of spreagaich.

Spreagail, *a.* Bold; active; smart.

Spreagair, *s. m.* A provoker; an inciter.

Spreagaireachd, *s. f.* Provoking; provocation.

Spréid, *v. a.* Spread. *Pret. id.; fut. aff.* spréididh, *shall spread.*

Spreidh, *v.* See **Spreigh**.

Spréideach, *a.* Spreading; apt to spread, diffuse.

Spréidh, spreidhe, *s. f.* (*Ir.* spre) Cattle, a herd; a marriage portion. Fa-chomhair sùl na spreidhe, *opposite to the eyes of the cattle.—Stew. Gen.* Buachail na spreidhe, *the shepherd —Oss Cathluno.*

The Gael, like other ancient people, were wont to give cattle, as portions, to their daughters; hence *spreidh* comes to signify a marriage portion. Tacitus, *de Mor Germ* observes, that this usage was common among the German tribes, who resembled the ancient Gael in various ways

Spreidheach, *a.* Abounding in cattle; rich in cattle

Spréidte, *p. part.* of spréid. Spread out.

Spreig, *v. a.* Scold, blame, accuse, enforce, press; stir up, prompt. *Pret. a.* spreig; *fut. aff a* spreigidh, *shall scold.*

Spreige, *s. f.* A scold, a reproof, an accusation. Chum spreige, *for reproof.—Stew Tim.*

Spreigeach, *a.* Inclined to scold, blame, or accuse; enforcing; expressive; forcible.

Spreigeadh, idh, *s m.* A scolding, a blaming; an accusation; an enforcing, a pressing; a stirring up; a prompting, a scold, a blame; an accusation.

Spreigealachd, *s. f.* A habit of scolding; undauntedness, boldness; activity.—*Macfar. Voc*

Spreigear, *fut. pass* of spreig.

Spreigearra, *a.* Scolding; smart in speech; expressive, forcible. Beurla spreigearra, *expressive English.—Old Song.*

Spreigearrachd, *s f.* Scolding; smartness of language, expressiveness of speech.

Spreigeil, *a.* (spreige-amhuil.) Scolding; accusing, apt to scold; undaunted, bold; active.

Spreigeileachd, *s f.* See **Spreigealachd**

Spreigh, *v. a.* and *n* Part, separate, scatter, disperse; dismiss; burst suddenly. *Pret a.* spreigh; *fut. aff. a.* spreighidh.

Spreighich, *s. f.* A parting, a separating, a scattering, a dismissing; a bursting. A snamh le spréighich bhàrr thonn, *parting the surface of the waves in swimming —Old Poem.*

Spreigidh, *gen. sing.* of spreigeadh

Spreigidh, *fut. aff a.* of spreig.

Spreilleach, *a* Blubber-lipped

Spreilleachd, *s f.* The deformity of blubber-lips.

Spreilleag, eig, *s f.* A blubber-lipped female.

Spreillear, eir, *s. m.* A blubber-lipped fellow.

Spreòchan, ain, *s. m.* A weakling; an infirm old person. More frequently applied to an old female. Spreòchan truagh cailllich, *an infirm old woman.*

Spreòchanach, *a.* Weak, infirm, feeble Gu spreochanach, *feebly.*

Spreòchanachd, *s. f.* Weakness, infirmity

Spreòchanta, *a.* Weak, infirm. Gu spreòchanta, *weakly, infirmly.*

Spreodadh, aidh, *s m.* A cavilling; a censuring.

Spreoid, *v. a.* Cavil, censure.

Spreoid. See **Spreoit.**

Spreòit, *s. m.* An useless thing; an idler, a drone; a fragment—(*Shaw*), *also*, a bowsprit

Spreotadh See **Spreodadh**

Sprineag, eig, *s. f* (*Ir. id*) A pebble.—*Shaw* *N. pl* sprinneagan.

Sprineagach, *a.* Pebbly.

Spriong, *s. m* A wrinkle

Spriong, *v a.* Wrinkle, corrugate —*Shaw*

Sprionnach, *a.* Wrinkling, corrugating.

Spriongadh, aidh, *s. m* A wrinkling.

Sprios, spriosa, *s m* (*Ir. id.*) A twig or wicker—(*Shaw*), a bramble.

Spriosach, *a.* Abounding in twigs, like a twig; of twigs or wicker.

Spriosan, ain, *s m*, *dim* of sprios (*Ir. id*) A small twig or wicker, a bramble; a poor diminutive creature. Also, *n pl* of sprios

Spriosanach, *a* Like a twig, diminutive; slender.

Spriuchar, air, *s. m* (*Ir id.*) A sting

Spriunnan, ain, *s m* (*Ir. id*) A currant —*Shaw.*

Spriunnanach, *a* Abounding in currants; of currants.

Spriùtan, ain, *s m.* A finger-end; *in ridicule*, a finger, a hard finger. *N pl.* spriùtain.

Spriùtanach, *a* Hard-fingered

Sproch, sprocha, *s. m.* (*Ir. id.*) Robbery.

Sprochadh, aidh, *s m* Robbing.

Sprochaill, *s f.* A dewlap, the crop of a bird. *N pl.* sprochaillean

Sprochailleach, *a.* Having a dewlap; having a crop, as a fowl, like a dewlap, like a crop or craw

Sprochair, *s. m.* (sproch-fhear) A robber. *N. pl.* sprochairean.

Sprochaireachd, *s. f.* Robbery; the commission of robbery.

Sprochd, *s. m.* (*Ir. id.*) Sadness, sorrow, dejection; a lament. Ciod so a chuir m' anam fo sprochd? *what is this that has brought sadness on my soul?—Oss Gaul.* Tog sprochd an laòich, *raise the hero's lament —Ull.*

Sprochdach, *a* Causing sadness, dejected, sorrowful

Sprochdalachd, *s. f.* Sadness, dejectedness, mournfulness

Sprochdail, *a* (sprochd-amhuil) Sad, dejected, mournful

Sprochdaileachd. See **Sprochdalachd.**

Sprodh, sprodha, *s. m* (*Ir.* sproth) A sprat *N. pl.* sprodhan.

Sprodhach, *a* Abounding in sprats; like a sprat, of sprats

Sprodhan, ain, *s. m.* (*dim.* of sprodh.) A young sprat.

Sprogaill, *s. f.* (*Ir. id.*) A dewlap, a crop or craw. *N. pl.* sprogaillean.

Sprogailleach, *a* Having a dewlap, having a large dewlap, like a dewlap; having a crop or craw, having a large crop or craw, like a crop or craw

Spronnan, ain, *s m.* A crumb, *also, plurally*, crums, fragments, refuse. Written also *sprunnan*

Spronnanach, *a.* Crummy, in crums or fragments.

Sproth, *s. m.* (*Ir id.*) A sprat.

Spruacach, *a* Pettish.

Spruacanach, *a.* Pettish.

Spruacanachd, *s. f.* Pettishness.

Spruan, ain, *s m.* Brushwood—(*Macd*), firewood.

Spruanach, aich, *s. f.* A quantity of brushwood.

Spruanach, *a.* Abounding in brushwood, like brushwood, of brushwood.

Spruidhean, ein, *s. m.* A claw, a paw, a clutch. *N. pl.* spruidheanan, *paws;* in derision, *the fingers.*

Spruidheanach, *a.* Clawed, having paws, having long hard fingers.

Spruidheanachd, *s. f.* A pawing, or fingering clumsily.

Spruille, *s. f.* (*Ir. id.*) Crums, fragments; dross, refuse.

Spruilleach, ich, *s. f.* A quantity of crums or fragments; a quantity of dross.

Spruilleag, eig, *s. f.* A small scrap, a fragment; offal.

Spruilleagach, *a.* In crums or in fragments.

Spruis, *s. f.* Spruce fir. This is, I believe, a local word.

Spruisealachd, *s. f.* Spruceness, tidiness, trimness.

Spruiseil, *a.* Spruce, tidy, trim. Gu spruiseil, *tidily.*

Sprunnan, *s. m.* A crum; *also, plurally,* crums, fragments; dross, refuse.

Sprunnanach, *a.* In crums; crummy.

Spuaic, *v. a.* Bruise; maul. *Pret. id.; fut. aff.* spuaicidh.

Spuaic, **Spuaichd**, *s. f.* (*Ir. id.*) Callosity; a callous tumour; a blue mark; pettishness; the pinnacle of a tower.

Spuaiceach, *a.* Bruising; mauling; pinnacled.

Spuaicearra, *a.* Bruising; mauling; pinnacled; pettish.

Spuaichdeach, *a.* Callous, as a tumour; pinnacled; pettish.

Spuaiche, *s. f.* (*Ir. id.*) A pet; pettishness.

Spuaicheach, *a.* (*Ir. id.*) Pettish.

Spud, *s. m.* (*Ir. id.*) Balderdash.

Spuidreach, ich, *s. m.* Slip-slop.

Spùill, *v. a.* Spoil; rob, plunder. *Pret. a.* spùill, *spoiled; fut. aff. a.* spùillidh, *shall spoil.*

Spùille, *s. f.* (*Lat.* spolium. *It.* spoglie.) Spoil, plunder, prey. Gheibh sibh ur toil spùille, *you shall get enough of spoil.*

Spùilleach, *a.* Spoiling, plunderous, predatory.

Spùilleadair, *s. m.* A spoiler, a plunderer. *N. pl.* spùinneadairean.

Spùilleadaireachd, *s. f.* Robbery, plundering.

Spùilleadairean, *n. pl.* of spuilleadair.

Spùilleadh, idh, *s. m.* A spoiling, a plundering; spoil, plunder.

Spùillear, eir, *s. m.* A robber, a plunderer.

Spùillear, *fut. pass.* of spùill. Shall or will be spoiled or plundered.

Spùillearachd, *s. f.* Robbery, plundering.

Spùillearan, *n. pl.* of spùillear.

Spùille-chogadh, aidh, *s. m.* A predatory warfare.

Spùillinn, *s. f.* Plunder, booty, spoil; a plundering, a spoiling; burglary, robbery.

Spuing, spuinge, *s. f.* Sponge; tinder; touchwood; a niggard, *in derision.* *N. pl.* spuingean, *sponges.* Cho tioram ri spuing, *as dry as tinder.* Written also *spong.* *Gr.* σπόγγος. *Lat.* spongia. *Arm.* spoinche. *Corn.* spong. *Ir.* spong.

Spuingealachd, *s. f.* Sponginess; parsimoniousness, niggardliness.

Spuingeil, *a.* Spongy; parsimonious, niggardly.

Spùinn, *v. a.* Spoil, plunder, rob. *Pret. a.* spùinn, *spoiled; fut. aff. a.* spuinnidh, *shall rob; fut. neg.* spùinn. An spùinn duine Dia? *shall a man rob God?—Stew. Mal.*

Spùinne, *s. f.* Spoil, plunder, booty. Lionaidh sinn le spùinne, *we shall fill with spoil.—Stew. Pro. ref.*

Spùinneach, *a.* Spoiling, plundering, plunderous.

Spùinneadair, *s. m.* A spoiler, a plunderer, a robber. *N. pl.* spùinneadairean.

Spùinneadaireachd, *s. f.* Spoiling, plundering, robbery; the practice of robbery.

Spùinneadairean, *n. pl.* of spùinneadair.

Spùinneadh, idh, *s. m.* A spoiling, plundering, or robbing; spoil, booty, robbery.

Spùinnear, *fut. pass.* of spùinn. Shall or will be spoiled or plundered.

Spùinnear, eir, *s. m.* A robber or plunderer.

Spùinnearachd, *s. f.* Robbery, plundering.

Spùinnearan, *n. pl.* of spùinnear.

Spuir, *gen. sing.* and *n. pl.* of spor.

Spuirean, *n. pl.* of spor.

Spuirse, *s. f.* (*Ir. id.*) Milkweed; spurge; the *euphorbia exigua* of botanists.

Spuirseach, *a.* (*from* spuirge.) Abounding in spurge or milkweed, like spurge or milkweed, of spurge or milkweed.

Spùis, spùise, *s. f.* A pocket. *N. pl.* spùisean.

Spult, *v. a.* Splash, bespatter, sprinkle; tear, mangle. *Pret. a.* spult; *fut. aff. a.* spultaidh; *fut. pass.* spultar.

Spult, *s. m.* A splash, a sprinkling.

Spultach, *a.* Splashing, bespattering; sprinkling; tearing, mangling, devouring.

Spultadh, aidh, *s. m.* A splashing, a sprinkling; a tearing, a mangling.

Spultadh, (a), *pr. part.* of spult. Splashing, sprinkling; mangling; devouring. Tha thu 'g am spultadh, *you splash me.*

Spultaidh, *fut. aff. a.* of spult.

Spultair, *s. m.* One who splashes or bespatters; a tearer, a mangler.

Spultaireachd, *s. f.* Splashing, bespattering, sprinkling; tearing, mangling.

Spultairean, *n. pl.* of spultair.

Spultar, *a.* Apt to splash or bespatter.

Spultar, *fut. pass.* of spult.

Spungail, *a.* Niggardly; churlish.

Spungair, *s. m.* A niggard; a churl. *N. pl.* spungairean.

Spungaireachd, *s. f.* Niggardliness; churlishness.

Spungairean, *n. pl.* of spungair.

Spungalachd, *s. f.* Niggardliness.

Spuran. See **Sporan**.

Spursan, ain, *s. m.* (*Ir. id.*) A gizzard; giblets.

Spursanach, *a.* Having a gizzard; of gizzards or giblets.

Spùt, *v. a.* and *n.* (*Lat.* sputo.) Spout, pour, squirt. *Pret. a.* spùt; *fut. aff. a.* spùtaidh.

Sput, *s. m.* (*Ir. id.*) An eunuch.

Spùt, spùit, *s. m.* (*Ir. id.*) A spout; a spout of water; a torrent; a cascade; a pour of rain; *in contempt,* bad drink, slip-slop, hog-wash. *N. pl.* spùtan; *d. pl.* sputaibh. Gach sruthan na spùtaibh, *every streamlet in spouts.—Macint.* Tobraiche nan spùtaibh dian, *fountains [gushing] in impetuous torrents.—Macfar.*

Spùtach, *a.* Spouting; spouty; squirting; pouring; sloppy.

Spùtachan, ain, *s. m.* A squirt, a syringe. Gunna spùtachain, *a syringe.*

Spùtadh, aidh, *s. m.* A spouting; a pouring; a squirting; a spout; a pour of water; a torrent; a cascade.

Spùtaidh, *fut aff.* of spùt. Shall or will spout

Spùtan, ain, *s. m.* (*dim.* of spùt.) A little spout, a little cascade, a rill; *also*, a syringe —*Macd.*

Spùtanach, *a.* Full of little spouts, or cascades; squirting; like a syringe.

Spùtar, *fut. pass.* of spùt.

Spùtarsaich, *s f.* Slip-slop.

Sràbh, sràibh, *s. f.* A straw; plenty. *N pl.* srabhan. Eòin a cruinneachadh shràbh, *birds gathering straws.*—*Macfar.*

Sràbhach, *a.* Full of straws, strawy; made of straws; like a straw; plentiful; squandering

† **Srabhan**, ain, *s. m* Superfluity.—*Shaw.*

Srac, *v.* See **Srachd**.

Sracair. See **Srachdair**

Sracanta, *a.* See **Srachdanta**

Srachd, *v. a* (*Ir id*) Tear, rend, pull, cut asunder; rob, spoil, plunder. *Pret. a.* shrachd, *tore*, *fut. aff. a* srachdaidh, *shall tear*

Srachda, ai, *s m.*; written also *srachdadh;* which see.

Srachdach, *a.* Apt to tear; full of rents.

Srachdadh, aidh, *s. m.* A tearing, a rending, a pulling, a cutting asunder, a robbing, a spoiling; a fissure; a tear or rent; robbery, spoil; extortion; a young twig, a shoot, a sprout. Ro shrachdadh nan nial, *through the fissures of the clouds* —*Oss Gaul.*

Srachdair, *s. m.* (srachd-fhear.) A tearer; an extortioner, a champion —*Macd.* *N. pl* srachdairean.

Srachdaireach, *a.* Tearing, rending, given to extortion; given to fighting.

Srachdaireachd, *s f.* The habit of tearing, continued or frequent tearing; extortion; hard fighting —*Macd.*

Srachdanta, *a.* Tearing; oppressing; apt to extort, stout, vigorous.

Srad, sraid, *s m.* (*Ir.* srad.) A spark of fire, a drop *N. pl.* srada *or* sradan Mar dh' eireas na srada suas, *as the sparks fly upwards.*—*Stew Job*

Srad, *v. n.* Spark, emit sparks, sparkle *Pret.* shrad; *fut. aff.* sradaidh

Sradach, *a.* Sparky, full of sparks

Sradadh, aidh, *s m* A sparking, a sparkling.

Sradag, aig, *s f.* (*dim.* of srad) A little spark of fire. Beum nan sradagan, *a stroke that causes sparks* —*Macdon*

Sradagach, *a.* (*from* sradag) Sparky; full of sparks, apt to emit sparks.

Sràid, sraide, *s. f.* (sreach-àite) *Ir* sraid A street, a lane, a walk, a promenade. Air an t-sràid, *on the street* —*Stew. Pro.* *N. pl* sraidean Mar pholl nan sràidean, *like the mire of the streets.*—*Stew. Zech.* Gabh sràid, *take a walk.*

Sràideach, *a.* Full of streets; having fine streets; like a street; of streets.

Sràideachd, *s f.* Sauntering; promenading.

Sraideag, eig, *s f* A mat —*Shaw.* *N. pl.* sraideagan.

Sràidean, *n pl.* of sràid Walks, lanes

Sràidean, ein, *s m.* (*dim* of sràid) A little walk, a lane.

† **Sraidean**, ein, *s. m* A shepherd's bag —*Shaw*

Sràidear, eir, *s. m.* (sràid-fhear) A saunterer, a lounger *N. pl.* sraidearan

Sràideas, eis, *s. m.* Sauntering, lounging; walking, promenading.

Sràideireachd, *s. f.* Sauntering, lounging; promenading; a promenade.

Sràid-imeachd, *s. f.* A sauntering, a lounging; walking, a promenading. A sràid-imeachd, *walking.*—*Stew. Gen. ref.*

† **Srait**, *s f* A tax, a fine —*Shaw*

Sraith. See **Sreath**

Sramh, sraimh, *s m.* (*Ir. id*) Milk gushing from the teat of a cow

Srann, *v. n.* Make a loud humming noise; twang, snore *Pret. a* shrann; *fut. aff a* srannaidh, *shall twang.*

Srann, srainn, *s m.* A loud humming noise, a snore; a twanging noise; the noise made by wind, as among the cordage of a ship, the noise of a bowstring; the impetus of one walking fast; the noise produced by swift aerial motion; the loud strain of a bagpipe *Stew.* in *Eccles* has *srann* in the sense of enchantment. Srann na sìne, *the noise of the blast* —*Oss Gaul.* Piob is beachdail srann, *a pipe of the cheering strain.*—*Old Song*

Srannach, *a* Humming loudly; snoring, whizzing.

Sranna-ghaoth, -ghaòithe, *s f.* A loud-sounding wind.—*Ull.* See also **Srann-ghaoth**.

Srannail, *a* (srann-amhuil) Humming loudly, snoring, snorting, neighing, whizzing

Srannail, *s f* A loud humming, a snoring; a snorting, a neighing, a whizzing, a continued hum; a continued snoring, a continued whizzing Srannail a chuid each, *the snorting* [*neighing*] *of his horses* —*Stew. Jer*

Srannan, ain, *s. m.* (*Ir* sranan) A humming noise; a whizzing noise, great hoarseness; rattling in the throat Srannan sèididh, *a sort of whirligig.*

Srannartaich, *s. f.* A snoring, a snorting Thòisich e air srannartaich, *he began to snort*

Srannchan, ain, *s m* (*from* srann) A humming-board; a thin notched piece of wood, attached at one end to a string, and making a loud humming noise when moved with a swift vertical motion

Srannraich, *s. f.* A loud humming noise; a snoring; a snorting; a loud hoarse noise Beachan gheug ri srannraich, *the bees of the branches humming* —*Macd.*

† **Sraodh**, sraodha, *s m.* A sneeze.

Sraoil, *v. a.* Tear *Pret.* shraòil, *fut. aff.* sraòilidh.

Sraòileach, *a* Apt to tear; given to tear; easily torn

Sraoileag, eig, *s f* A species of berry, a quean, a dirty hussy, a spark of fire. *N pl* sraoileagan

Sraoileagach, *a* Queanish, sluttish; sparkling, as fire

Sraòin, sraòine, *s f* A huff, a pet.

Sraoineis, *s f.* A huff, a pet, a swell of petulance or pride.

Sraoineiseach, *a* Huffish; petulant, pert, querulous.

† **Sraon**, *v a* Turn, scatter —*Shaw*

Sraonadh, aidh, *s. m.* A huff; the impetus of one walking fast, quick motion.

Sraonais, *s f* A huff, a swell of petulance or pride.

Sraonaiseach, *a.* Huffish, petulant, querulous Gu sraonaiseach, *huffishly.*

Sraonaiseachd, *s f.* Huffishness, petulance; pertness, querulousness.

† **Srath**, sratha, *s m* A general fine, a tax —*Shaw.*

Srath, sratha, *s. m* (*Ir.* srath *and* sratha. *Corn.* strath *Scotch*, strath.) A valley, a mountain valley, the bottom of a valley; a low-lying country through which a river rolls; the low inhabited part of a country, in contradistinction to its hilly ground, a dell, *rarely*, marshy ground Srath Oisein nam Fiann, *the valley of Fingalian Ossian* —*Old Song* Luchd àiteachaidh an t-sratha, *the inhabitants of the valley* —*Stew Jud* Eas is àille srath, *a waterfall in a pretty dell* —*Old Poem* *N. pl.* srathan

Srathach, *a* (*from* srath) Abounding in *straths* or valleys

Srathachadh, aidh, *s. m* The act or the circumstance of imposing a general fine; a taxing; taxation

† **Srathaich**, *v a.* Impose a general fine; tax.

Srathair, srathrach, s. f. (*Ir.* srathar.) A cartsaddle, a packsaddle; a straddle. Cuir an t-srathair air an each, *put the cartsaddle on the horse;* a cur na srathrach air an each, *putting the cartsaddle on the horse. N. pl.* srathraichean.

Srathair, *s. m.* A stroller, a lounger. *N. pl.* srathairean.

Srathan, ain, *s. m.* (*dim.* of srath.) A little valley or *strath.*

Srathanach, aich, *s. m.* An inhabitant of a valley or *strath. N. pl.* srathanaich.

Sread, sreada, *s. m.* A rank or row, a long line; an order or class; a layer; a swathe or roll, as of grass; a herd, a flock; a troop, a cavalcade; a round or circle. Nan sread air an oitir, [*people*] *in ranks on the promontory.—Mac Lach.* See also **Sreath.**

Sreadach, *a.* In ranks, rows, or lines; in herds or flocks; in swathes or rolls, as grass.

Sreadachadh, aidh, *s. m.* The act of arranging in rows, ranks, or lines.

Sreadaich, *v. a.* Arrange in rows or lines; arrange in classes. *Pret.* shreadaich; *fut. aff. a.* sreadaichidh.

Sreadaichte, *p. part.* of sreadaich. Arranged or drawn out in rows or lines; arranged in classes.

Sreadh. See **Sreath.**

† **Sreamh**, *v. n.* Stream, flow.

† **Sreamh**, sreimh, *s. m.* A stream, a spring.

Sreamh-shuil, -shùl, *s. f.* A blear eye.

Sreamh-shuileach, *a.* Blear-eyed. A shine shreamhshuileach, *blear-eyed old age.—Old Song.*

† **Srean**, *s. m.* A wheezing.—*Shaw.*

Sreang, *v. a.* Extend; draw out into threads; tear.—*Shaw.*

Sreang, sreing, *s.* (*Ir.* srang.) A string, a line; a rope or cord. Tharruing i 'n t-sreang le rogha beachd, *she drew the string with her best aim.—Ull.* Sreang-rioghailt, *a plumb-line* or *plummet;* sreang-stiùiridh, *a stern-rope, a stern-line;* sreang-tart, *a loadstone;* sreang-thomhais, *a measuring-line, a surveyor's line* or *chain.—Stew.* 2 *K.* Sreang-lion, *a casting-line.*

Sreangach, *a.* (*Ir. id.*) Full of strings or threads; full of lines; stringy, thready; like a string, like a line; lineal; strung, threaded.

Sreangaich, *v. a.* String; bend with strings; suit with strings; draw out into threads; make subtile. *Pret.* shreangaich.

Sreangan, ain, *s. m.* (*dim.* of sreang.) A little string, a little thread, a little rope or line.

Sreanganach, *a.* Full of little threads or strings; stringy.

Sreang-art, airt, *s. m.* (*Ir.* sreang-art.) A loadstone.—*Shaw.*

Sreangartach, aich, *s. m.* A tall raw-boned man, *in derision.*

Sreangartach, *a.* Like a loadstone, magnetic.

Sreang-lion, *s. m.* A casting-net. *N. pl.* sreang-liontan.

Sreang-riaghailt, *s.* A plumb-line, a plummet; a ruling line; a mason's parallel line.

Sreang-thomhais, *s. m.* A measuring line; a surveyor's line.—*Stew.* 2 *K.*

Sreath, sreatha, *s. m.* (*Ir.* sraith.) A rank or row; a long line; a roll or swathe, as of grass; an order, a class; a layer; a round, a circle. Ann dà shreath, *in two rows.—Stew. Lev. N. pl.* sreathan; *d. pl.* sreathaibh. Le sreathaibh, *with rows of jewels.—Stew. Song Sol.*

On stated occasions of carousal, it was customary among the old Gael to sit in a circle, which they called *sreath* or *sreadh.* The cup-bearer filled the cup to the brim at every round, and, however potent the liquor might be, it was cleared off at a draught. These scenes of intemperance lasted not unfrequently for three days! It was deemed effeminacy in any one of the circle to retire sober. I have somewhere read, that, at such drinking-matches, it was usual for two men to be in attendance at the door with a litter, to carry off to bed every individual as he fell senseless from his chair.

Sreathach, *a.* (*from* sreath.) In ranks or rows; in lines; in rolls or swathes; in classes; lineal; full of ranks or rows; full of rolls or swathes.

Sreathachadh, aidh, *s. m.* A putting in ranks or rows, a drawing up in lines; a rolling into swathes, as grass.

Sreathaich, *v. a.* Plant in rows or ranks; draw up in rows or ranks.

Sreathaichte, *p. part.* of sreathaich. Put in rows or ranks; draw up in lines.

Sreathail, *a.* (sreath-amhuil.) In rows, in lines; in rolls; in classes.

Sreathainn, *s. f.* Straw on which corn is laid when on the kiln.

Sreathal, ail, *s. m.* That is in rows.

Sreathan, *n. pl.* of sreath; which see.

Sreathan, ain, *s. m.* The filmy skin which covers an unborn calf; vellum.

Sreathan, ain, *s. m.* (*dim.* of sreath.) A little row or rank.

Sreathnaich, *v. a.* (*Ir. id.*) Wet, moisten; spread out, extend.

Sreathnaichte, *p. part.* of sreathnaich. (*Ir. id.*) Wetted, moistened; spread out.

Sreothart, airt, *s.* (*Ir.* sraoth.) A sneeze.

Sreothartach, *a.* Sternutative; apt to sneeze.

Sreothartaich, *s. f.* (*Ir.* srothfurtach.) A sneeze; sneezing; continued sneezing; frequent sneezing. Rinn an leanabh sreothartaich, *the child sneezed.—Stew.* 2 *K.* Thòisich e air sreothartaich, *he began to sneeze.*

Srian, *v. a.* Bridle, curb, restrain. *Pret. a.* shrian; *fut. aff. a.* srianaidh, *shall bridle.*

Srian, sréine, *s. f.* (*Ir. id.*) A bridle; a curb; restraint. Srian do'n asal, *a bridle for the ass.—Stew. Pro.*

Srianach, *a.* Bridled; like a bridle; of a bridle; ringstreaked. Each srianach ceumnach, *a bridled prancing horse.—Old Poem.* Am bras-each srianach, *the highmettled bridled steed.—Oss. Taura.* An seillean srianach, *the ring-streaked bee.—Macdon. Com.* and *sup.* srianaiche.

Srianachd, *s. f.* Ruling or managing by means of a bridle; the state of being ring-streaked.

Srianadh, aidh, *s. m.* A bridling; a curbing, a checking; a pulling down the power of an enemy.

Srianta, *a.* Reined, curbed, checked.

Sriut, sriuite, *s. f.* A quick rehearsal, as of rhyme; a speech rapidly delivered; a long tedious rhyme.

Sriutach, aich, *s. f.* A quick rehearsal, as of rhyme; a speech rapidly delivered; tedious rhyme.

Sriutach, *a.* Rapid in rehearsing.

Sriutaiche, *s. m.* (*from* sriut.) One who rehearses rapidly; a rhymer. *N. pl.* sriutaichean.

Sriutan, ain, *s. m.* A long and quick repetition of news or poetry.—*Shaw.*

Srobach, *a.* Apt to push, thrust, or shove.

Srobadh, aidh, *s. m.* A pushing, a thrusting, a shoving; a push, a thrust, a shove.

† **Sroghall**, aill, *s.* (*Ir. id.*) A whip or lash. *N. pl.* sroghallan.

Sròil, *gen. sing.* of sròl; which see.

Sròin, sròine, *and* sròna, *s. f.* A nose; a nostril; a headland or promontory. Anail a shròine, *the breath of his nostrils.—Stew. Job.* *Sròin* is also written *sròn* in the nominative.

Sròine, *gen. sing.* of sròin.

Sròine, Sroinean, Sròintean, *s. pl.* of sròin. Noses. Sròine gun aileadh annt, *noses without the sense of smell.* —*Sm.*

Sròineach, *a.* (*from* sròin) Large-nosed, sharp-nosed; apt to smell, snuff, or snuffle; sharp-scented, nasal; having headlands or promontories; like a nose; like a headland.

Sròineachadh, *a.* A smelling, a snuffing, a snuffling, a snorting.

Sròineag, eig, *s. f.* (*dim.* of sròin.) A little nose; a little promontory. *N. pl.* sròineagan. Written also *srònag.*

Sroineagach, *a.* Having numerous promontories or jutting points.

Sroineagraich, *s. f.* A smelling, a snuffing; a snuffling, a snorting.

Sròinean, *a.* White-nosed; *a corruption of* sròin-fhionn.

Sròinean, ein, *s. m.* (*from* sròin.) A horse's noseband

Sròineil, *a.* (sròin-amhuil) Nasal

Sròineiseach, *a.* Smelling, snuffling, snorting; apt to smell, snuffle, or snort.

Sròineiseachd, *s. f* A habit of smelling, snuffling, or snorting.

Sròin-eudach, aich, *s. m.* A pocket-handkerchief

Sròin-fhionn, *a* White-nosed, as a quadruped

Sroin-iall, -éill, *s f* The noseband of a horse's halter.

Sròinich, *s f* A snuffing, a snuffling, a snorting; a hard breathing; a panting Sròinich ar cuim, *the hard breathing of our breasts* —*Death of Carril*

Sròinich, *v. n.* Snuff, snuffle, snort; breathe through the nostrils; pant.

Sròintean. See **Sròine.**

Sròl, sroil, *s m.* (*Ir. id.*) Silk, satin, gauze, a crape; a sash, a flowing riband; a streamer. Cha 'n iarr mi siod na sròl, *I will ask neither silk nor satin* —*Macfar* *N pl.* sròlan *and* sròltan; *d. pl.* sròlaibh *or* sroltaibh Le 'n sioda 's le 'n sròltaibh, *with their silks and their sashes* —*Mac Co.* Sròl-bhratach, *a pennon of silk, a streamer.*

Sròl-bhratach, aich, *s* A silk pennon or banner.

Sròl-bhratach, *a* Having pennons or banners of silk or satin.

Sròlach, *a* (*from* sròl) Like silk or satin, like gauze or crape; flowing, as a riband, sash, or streamer; made of silk or satin.

Sròn, sròin, *s. f* A nose; a nostril, a promontory or headland. See **Sròin.**

Srònach, *a.* Large-nosed, sharp-nosed; sharp-scented; apt to smell or snuff; nasal; having headlands or promontories

Srònag, aig, *s f.* (*dim.* of sròn) A little nose; a little headland or promontory; any prominent or projecting part of a rock or hill. Feadh nan srònagan, *among the jutting rocks.*—*Moladh Mhòraig.*

Srònagach, *a.* Having numerous headlands or promontories; jutting, as rocks.—*Macint.*

Srònagraich, *s f.* A smelling, a snuffing; a snorting

Srònail, *a* (sròn-amhuil) Nasal.

Srònaiseach, *a.* Apt to smell; smelling, snuffling, snorting.—*Macint.*

Srònaiseachd, *s f* A habit of smelling, snuffling, or snorting. Ciod an srònaiseachd th' ort? *why do you snuffle so?*

Srònan, ain, *s. m.* A horse's noseband.

Sròn-fhionn, *a.* Having a white nose, as a black sheep

Sroth, more frequently written *sruth.*

Srothan, ain, *s m.* See **Sruthan.**

Sruamach, *a.* (*Ir. id.*) Streamy; powerful in armies, having great armies.

Sruamach, aich, *s. m.* A meeting of streams

Srub, *v a.* Suck, draw in; snuff, inhale, imbibe. *Pret a* shrub; *fut. aff. a.* srubaidh, *shall suck in.*

Srubach, *a* Apt to suck or inhale, snuffing; sucking, inhaling, imbibing.

Srubadh, aidh, *s m* A sucking, an inhaling, an imbibing

Srubag, aig, *s f* A mouthful of any liquid.—*Macfar Voc.*

Srubair, *s m* A sucker; the sucker of a pump, one who gulps or drinks greedily. *N pl* srubairean.

Srubaireachd, *s f* A sucking; a frequent sucking; a gulping; a drinking greedily.

Sruban, ain, *s m* A cockle—(*Macd*), a drawing or sucking in —*Shaw.*

† **Srudhar,** *a* In small pieces

† **Sruith,** *s f* Knowledge, discerning.

Srùlach, *a.* Flowing, as a streamlet; full of little streamlets; gurgling, purling Crònan t-easain srùlaich, *the murmur of thy purling cataracts.*—*Macdon.*

Srùlag, eig, *s m.* A rill or rivulet. *N. pl.* srùlagan.

Srùlagach, *a.* Abounding in rills, purling

Sruth, *v. n* Flow, stream, pour; drop, derive. *Pret a* shruth, *flowed, fut aff a* sruthaidh, *shall flow.*

Sruth, srutha, *s m* (*Ir. id.*) A stream or current; a river, a torrent; a brook; a fountain; a tide; *rarely,* a man of letters, an ecclesiastic. Bhris fàire air monadh nan sruth, *dawn broke on the hill of streams.*—*Oss Gaul.* Sruth bhliadhnai, *the stream of years* —*Old Poem* Onfha na sruth, *the rage of torrents.*—*Oss. Tem.* *N pl* sruthanna *and* sruthaidh Sruthanna na beatha, *the fountains of life* —*Stew Pro.*

Sruthach, *a.* (*from* sruth) Streaming, streamy, flowing; dropping, as a liquid.

Sruthadh, aidh, *s. m* A streaming, a flowing, a dropping.

Sruthadh, (a), *pr. part.* of sruth Streaming, flowing A sruthadh le bainne, *flowing with milk.*—*Stew Ex.*

Sruthaibh, *d. pl.* of sruth. To streams. See **Sruth.**

Sruthaibh, 1 *pl. imper. a.* of sruth Stream ye.

Sruthaidh, *fut aff. a* of sruth. Shall stream.

Sruthail, *v. a.* (*from* sruth) *Ir id.* Wash, rinse, cleanse, scour. *Pret a* shruthail, *washed, fut aff. a.* sruthailidh, *shall wash*

Sruthain, *gen sing* and *n pl.* of sruthan. Of a rill.

Sruthan, ain, *s m* (*dim* of sruth) A little stream or current; a streamlet, a rivulet *N pl* sruthain Tharta tha na sruthain a breabail, *over them the streams gurgle.*—*Oss* Sruthan anrach na h-aoise, *the mournful streamlets* [*tears*] *of age* —*Oss. Gaul*

Sruthan, *n. pl.* of sruth Streams, currents, tides; fountains

Sruthanach, *a.* Full of streamlets; like a rill; purling, gurgling.

Sruth-chlais, *s. f.* (*Ir. id.*) A conduit, a canal, the bed of a river or stream, a channel —*Shaw.* Sruth-chlais, *a conduit.*—*Stew 2 Sam* *N pl* sruth-chlaisean

Sruth-chlaiseach, *a* Like a conduit or canal, full of channels.

Sruthlach, *a.* Cleansing, rinsing, washing, scouring, scrubbing; that has the quality of cleansing, washing, or scouring.

Sruthladh, aidh, *s m* A cleansing, rinsing, a washing, scouring, or scrubbing; a dirty streamlet

Sruthladh, (a), *pr part.* of sruthail

Srùthlag, aig, *s f* A rivulet, a rill, water conducted through a pipe; a small spout of water falling from a pipe *N. pl* sruthlagan

Srùthlagach, *a.* Abounding in rills; like a rill.

Stà, *s. m.* Use, utility; service, serviceableness; profit. Gun stà, *useless.*—*Sm.*

Stabh, *v. a.* To stave. *Pret. a.* stabh; *fut. aff. a.* stabhaidh, *shall stave.*

† **Stabh**, stabha, *s. m.* A vessel.

Stabhach, *a.* A straddle, striding; wide-forked; asunder. —*Shaw.*

Stabhaich, *v. n.* Straddle.—*Shaw.*

Stàbull, uill, *s. m.* A stable, a stall. *N. pl.* stabullan. Gille stàbuill, *a stable-boy.*
Lat. stabulum. *Cop.* stabla. *Sp.* establo. *Arm.* staoul. *It.* and *Teut.* stalle. *Eng.* stable *and* stall.

Stac, *v. a.* Deafen; drive stakes into the ground; make a false step. *Pret. a.* stac; *fut. aff. a.* stacaidh.

Stac, staca, *s. m.* (*Sax.* staca, *a stake. Ir.* stac.) A stake or post driven into the ground; a pillar, a column; a little eminence; a false step, a hobbling step; a halt; a cliff, a rock; a stack; a thorn. Stac, *a stake.* Tha stac chrùbaich ann, *he has a halt in his pace.* A leumnaich o stac gu stac, *bounding from rock to rock.*—*Oss. Dargo.*

Stacach, *a.* Deaf; full of stakes; pillared; columnar; full of impediments; full of little eminences; hirpling; lame; hobbling; dull of hearing; causing deafness; rugged; rocky; thorny; full of heaps; coacervated.

Stacachadh, aidh, *s. m.* A heaping up; coacervation.

Stacadh, aidh, *s. m.* A deafening; a driving stakes into the ground; a pillar; a false step; a hobbling step; a stack.

Stacaich, *v.* Heap up; coacervate. *Pret. id.; fut. aff.* stacaichidh.

Stacan, ain, *s. m.* (*dim.* of stac.) A knoll; a little stake or post; a little pillar; a false step; a little halt; a little stack.

Stacanach, *a.* Full of little eminences; knolly; rugged; full of impediments. Cnocanach stacanach, *knolly and rugged.*—*Macint.*

Stacarsaich, *s. f.* Tramping or walking awkwardly.

Stad, *v. a.* and *n.* (*Swed.* stadt. *Ir.* stad.) Stop, stay, stand, wait for; cease, desist; rest. *Pret.* stad, *stopped; fut. aff.* stadaidh, *shall stop.* An uair a stad i, *when it* [*stopped*] *rested.*—*Stew. Num.* Nach stad thu? *will not you stop* or *stand?*

Stad, *s. m.* (*Swed.* stadt. *Ir.* stad.) A stop, a pause; an interruption, delay; a period. Cuir stad air, *put a stop to him* or *it;* cuir gu stad, *put a stand.* A chos a chuir eilde gu stad, *his leg that set deer to a stand.*—*Ull.* Gun stad, *without delay, incessantly;* dean stad, *stop.*

Stadach, *a.* Apt to stop, pause, or delay; obstructive, impeding.

Stadachd, *s. f.* A stopping, a pausing, a delaying, a waiting for; obstruction, impediment. Ciod an stadachd a th'ort? *why do you stop* or *delay?*

Stadadh, aidh, *s. m.* A stopping, a pausing, a delaying; an obstructing or impeding; a stop, a pause, a delay; obstruction, impediment.

Stadadh, *pret. sub.* of stad. Would stop. Nan stadadh e, *if he would stop.*

Stadaich, *s. f.* An impediment; an obstacle.

Stadaidh, *gen. sing.* of stadadh.

Stadaidh, *fut. aff. a.* of stad. Shall or will stop.

Stadail, *s. f.* A stopping, a pausing, a delaying, a lingering; frequent stopping, pausing, or lingering.

Stàdail, *a.* Stately, portly, proud, pompous. Gu stàdail, *in a stately manner.* Written more frequently *stàideil;* which see.

Stadar, *fut. pass.* of stad. Shall be stopped.

Stàdh, stàdha, *s. m.* Use, utility, service; work, working; the stays of a ship. Cha 'n eil stàdh ann, *there is no use in him;* gun stàdh, *useless.* Ar stàdh 's ar tarruing cum fallain, *preserve our stays and our haulyards.*—*Macfar.*

Stadhar, *a.* Useful, serviceable; good at working, industrious.

Staduit, *s. f.* A statute. *N. pl.* stàduitean.

Stàduiteach, *a.* Of a statute.

Staid, *s. f.* (*Lat.* stat-us. *Arm.* stat *and* stad. *Ir.* stad.) Condition, state, rank; a furlong (*Lat.* stadium); a craft; a wile. Ann an droch staid, *in a bad state.*

Stàidealachd, *s. f.* Stateliness, portliness, self-importance, pompousness of manner. Written also *stàideileachd.*

Stàideil, *a.* (staid-amhuil.) Stately, portly, self-important, having a portly gait. Is stàideil sios is suas a cheum, *stately was his pace to and fro.*—*Mac Lach.*

Stàideileachd, *s. f.* Stateliness, portliness, self-importance.

Staidheir, staidhreach, *s. f.* (*Sax.* staeger. *Ir.* staighre.) A stair. 'N àird an staidheir, *up stairs.* Mullach na staidhreach, *the top of the stair.*—*Stew.* 2 *K.* Staidheir shniomhach, *a winding stair;* staidheir shniomhain, *a winding stair. N. pl.* staidhrichean, *stairs; d. pl.* staidhrichibh. Air staidhrichibh sniomhach, *on winding stairs.*—*Stew.* 1 *K.* Written also *staigheir.*

Staidhineach, *a.* Having stays; like stays.

Staidhinean, *s. pl.* Stays.

Staidhre, *s. f.* See **Staidheir**.

Staidhreach, *a.* Having stairs; having many stairs; storied.

Staidhreach, *gen. sing.* of staidheir.

Staidhrichean, *n. pl.* of staidheir. Stairs.

Staigean, ein, *s. m.* A stout little fellow.

Staigeanach, *a.* Having a stout and squat person; *substantively,* a squat fellow.

Staigeanachd, *s. f.* Squatness of person; the gait of a stout, squat person.

Staigheir, staighreach, *s. f.* (*Sax.* staeger.) See **Staidheir**.

† **Stail**, *s. f.* A throw.—*Shaw.*

Stailc, *v. a.* Drive forward; press or push forward or onward; prick. *Pret. a.* stailc; *fut. aff. a.* stailcidh.

Stailc, *s. f.* A driving, pressing, or pushing forward; a pricking; a stop, an impediment; stubbornness; a prick; a thorn.

Stailceach, *a.* Apt to drive or push forward; pressing or pushing forward; prickly, thorny.

Stailcidh, *fut. pass.* of stailc. Shall or will press forward.

Stailcneach, *s. f.* Stubble; the standing roots of burnt heath.

Stailinn, *s. f.* (*Sax.* stal. *Du.* stael.) Steel. Farum ar stailinn, *the noise of our steel.*—*Oss. Duthona.*

Stàilinneach, *a.* (*from* stailinn.) Of steel; like steel; steel.

Stàilinnich, *v. a.* (*from* stailinn.) Harden, as iron; convert into steel. *Pret. a.* stàilinnich, *steeled; fut. aff. a.* stàilinnichidh, *shall steel.*

Stàilinnichte, *p. part.* of stailinnich. Steeled; hardened.

Stàin, *s. f.* (*Corn.* stian. *Ir.* stan.) Tin.—*Shaw.*

Staing, stainge, *s. f.* (*Scotch,* stank. *Arm.* stancq. *Corn.* stancq.) A ditch, a trench. *N. pl.* staingean, *ditches.* Staing dhomhain, *a deep ditch.*—*Stew. Pro. Arm.* stancq doun, *a deep ditch.*

Staingeach, *a.* Full of ditches or trenches.

Staingich, *v. a.* (*from* staing.) Dig a ditch or trench. *Pret. id.; fut. aff. a.* staingichidh.

Staingichte, *p. part.* of staingich. Ditched, trenched. Talamh staingichte, *trenched ground.*

Staipeal, eil, *s. m.* A stopple.

Stair, *s. f.* Noise, confusion, tumult, strife; *also*, history. Euchdach an stair, *deadly in strife.—Old Poem.*

† **Stairiceach**, *a.* Light.—*Shaw.*

Stairearaich, *s. f.* A rattling noise; a loud rumbling; a roaring. Clachan meallain le stairearaich, *hailstones with a rattling noise.—Macfar.* Written also *stairirich.*

Stairirich, *s. f.* A rattling noise; a rumbling; a roaring. Stairirich nan cliath, *the rattling noise of harrows.—Macfar.* A stairirich measg charraige, *roaring among the rocks.—Oss. Cathula.* Written also *stairearaich.* Stairirich a rothan, *the rattling of her wheels.—Stew. Jer.*

Stairn, *s. f.* Loud noise, clamour, confusion. Ri stairn, *making noise.*

Stairneach, *a.* Noisy, clamorous.

Stairseach. See **Stairsneach.**

Stairsneach, ich, *s.* A threshold. Cos-ulla' na luidh air an stairsnich, *Cosula lying on the threshold.—Oss. Gaul. N. pl.* stairsnichean.

Stal, stail, *s. m.* (*Ir. id.*) A stallion.—*Shaw.*

Stalac. See **Stalc.**

† **Stalacach**, *a.* Gazing, staring.

Stalan, ain, *s. m.* (*dim.* of stàl.) A stallion.

Stalc, stailc, *s. m.* (*Teut.* starc, *starch.*) Starch; a stare.

Stalc, *v. a.* Dress, as a fishing-hook; fix, as a line to a hook; stalk or hunt deer; starch; stare, gaze. *Pret. a.* stalc; *fut. aff. a.* stalcaidh.

Stalcach, *a.* Stiffening, starching; stiff, starched; staring, gazing.

Stalcadair, *s. m.* Starch. *N. pl.* stalcadairean.

Stalcadh, aidh, *s. m.* A stiffening or starching; a staring; a gazing; a dressing, as a fishing-hook; a fixing, as a fishing-line to a hook; a fowling; a stalking.

Stalcair, *s. m.* (*Ir. id.*) A fowler; a deer-stalker; a starer, a gazer; a dresser of hooks; an arrow-maker. *N. pl.* stalcairean.

Stalcaireachd, *s. f.* The occupation of a fowler; deer-stalking; a habit of staring; frequent staring or gazing; the business of dressing fishing-hooks.

Stalda, *a.* Stale.—*Shaw.*

Stamac, aic, *s.* A stomach; appetite. *N. pl.* stamacan, *stomachs.*

Lat. stomachus. *Arm.* stomocq. *Fr.* estomac.

Stamh, staimh, *s. m.* Tangle, dilse.—*Macd. Shaw,* and *Macfar. Voc.*

Stamh, staimh, *s. m.* The isle of Staffa.—*Shaw.*

Stamha, *s. m.* A vase.

Stamnadh, aidh, *s. m.* A managing; a taming; a making pliable.

Stamnaidh, *a.* Manageable; tame; pliable.

Stàn, *adv.* Up. Thig stàn, *come up.*

Stanard, aird, *s. m.* Stint; a yard-wand; a yard; the upright piece of wood to which is affixed the rock of a spinning-wheel. Gun stanard, *without stint.—Mac Co. N. pl.* stanardan.

Stang, staing, *s. m.* (*Scotch*, stank. *Arm.* and *Corn.* stancq, *a ditch.*) A ditch, a trench; a peg, a pin. *N. pl.* stangan.

Stangach, *a.* Full of ditches or trenches; trenched; drained, as land; pettish; having upright horns. Gabhair nan adhaircean stangach, *the upright-horned goats.—Macfar.*

Stangach, aich, *s. m.* A beast with upright horns.

Stangaich, *v. a.* Dig a ditch or trench. *Pret. a.* stangaich; *fut. aff. a.* stangaichidh.

Stann, **Stannt**, *s. m.* A tub; a meal-tub; a vat. *N. pl.* stannan.

Staof, *a.* (*provincial.*) Stiff.

Staofainn, *s. f.* (*provincial.*) Starch.

Staòig, *s. f.* A steak; a collop; a piece of meat. *N. pl.* staoigean.

Staòigeach, *a.* In steaks or collops; like a steak or a collop.

Staoin, *s. f.* Pewter; tin; a lazy, inactive person, *in derision.* D' uile staoin, *all thy tin.—Stew. Is.*

Staoineach, *a.* Abounding in pewter or tin; of pewter or tin.

Staon, *a.* (*Ir. id.*) Oblique; awry; bent; inclined.—*Shaw.*

Staon, *v. a.* Bend; incline; make awry. *Pret. a.* staon; *fut. aff. a.* staonaidh.

Staonach, *a.* Apt to bend; oblique; awry; crooked. *Com.* and *sup.* staonaiche.

Staonadh, aidh, *s. m.* (*Ir. id.*) A bending; an inclining; a making awry; a bend; an inclination; a bias.

Staonaich, *v. a.* Bend; make oblique or awry; incline. *Pret. a.* staonaich; *fut. aff. a.* staonaichidh.

Staonard, aird, *s. m.* A crick in the neck.—*Shaw.*

Staonta, *a.* Bent; inclined.

Stap, stapa, *s. m.* (*Du.* stap.) A step, as of a stair; the step of a dance; a step or pace. *N. pl.* stapan.

Stapach, *a.* Having steps; stepping, pacing.

Stapal, ail, *s. m.* A lamp.

† **Staplan**, ain, *s. m.* The noise of the sea.

Stàpull, uill, *s. m.* A stable. *N. pl.* stàpuill. See **Stàbull.**

Stapull, uill, *s. m.* (*Ir.* stapal.) A bar, a bolt, a staple; a link, a torch. *N. pl.* stapuill. Na stapuill iaruinn, *the iron bolts.—Sm.*

Stapullach, *a.* Having bars, bolts, or staples; like a bar, bolt, or staple.

Starbhan, ain, *s. m.* A noise; a rustling noise.

Starbhanach, aich, *a.* Stout, robust; steady, firm; noisy, rustling. *Com.* and *sup.* stàrbhanaiche, *stouter, stoutest.*

Starbhanach, aich, *s. m.* A stout, robust man. Dithis starbhanach, *two robust men.—Macdon. N. pl.* starbhanaich.

Starbhanachd, *s. m.* Stoutness, robustness; steadiness, firmness.

Starbhanaich, *s. f.* Continued noise; continued rustling noise.

Starn, stairn, *s. m.* An upstart. *N. pl.* stairnean.

Starnach, *a.* Like an upstart.

Starr, *v. a.* Propel; push with a jerk. *Pret.* starr; *fut. aff. a.* starraidh.

Starrach, *a.* Propelling; pushing.

Starr-shuileach, *a.* Squint-eyed.

Stàt, stàit, *s. m.* See **Staid.**

Stàtail, *a.*; more frequently written *stàideil;* which see.

Stàtalachd, *s. f.* See **Stàidealachd.**

Stàtuis, *s. f.* A statute.

Steabhag, aig, *s. f.* (*Ir. id.*) A staff, a stick; a club.—*Macd. N. pl.* steabhagan.

Gille steabhaig, (Ir. *giolla stenfaig*), was a foot-messenger or letter-carrier, who ran from place to place with a long staff in his hand.

Steach, *adv.* (anns an teach, *in the house.*) *Ir. id.* Within, in; in the house, into the house. Cuir steach e, *put him in;* bheil e steach? *is he within? is he in the house?* So also **Stigh**, (anns an tigh), *within.* Likewise in the

Hebrew, מבית, *within*.—*Gen*. ch. vi. 14. *Steach* is also written *a steach*.

† STEACH, *v. n.* Enter.—*Shaw*.

STEAFAG, aig, *s. f.* A staff, a stick, a club.

STEALL, *s. m.* A spout; a sudden pour of rain; a heavy shower; a gush of water, as from a squirt or pipe; a torrent. Mar steall aonaich, *like a mountain-torrent*.—*Oss. Taura*.

STEALL, *v. a.* and *n.* Spout, as from a squirt or pipe; a cascade; gush; pour water; squirt. *Pret. a.* steall; *fut. aff. a.* steallaidh.

STEALLACH, *a.* Spouting, squirting; gushing suddenly, as water; inclined to spout, squirt, or gush; showery.

STEALLADH, aidh, *s. m.* A spouting, a squirting, a gushing; a spout; a sudden gush of water from a pipe or squirt; a heavy, sudden shower.

STEALLADH, (a), *pr. part.* of steall. Spouting, squirting, gushing; showering heavily; pissing. A stealladh bainne ann an cuachain, *spouting milk into a pail*.—*Old Song*.

STEALLAIR, *s. m.* (*Ir. id.*) A squirt, a syringe; a cascade. *N. pl.* steallairean.

STEAR, *s. m.* A rude blow.

STEARNAL, ail, *s. m.* A bittern; the lesser tern, or the *larus minutus* of Linnæus; the sign of an inn or an alehouse. Stearnal tigh òsda, *an innkeeper's sign*.—*Shaw*.

STEIC-BHRÀGHAD, aid, *s.* (*Ir.* steic-bhràghad.) The windpipe, the weasand.—*Macd*.

STEIDH, *s. f.* A foundation; a basis; ground. Steidh-dhaingnich na fìrinn, *the ground of truth*.—*Stew. Tim.* Steidh teagaisg, *a text*. Written also *steigh*; which see.

STEIDH-DHAINGNICH, *s. f.* A foundation; a basis; ground. Steidh dhaingnich na firinn, *the ground of truth*.—*Stew. Tim.*

STEIDHEACH, *a.* Having ground for a foundation; having a strong foundation.

STEIDHEACHADH, aidh, *s. m.* A grounding; a laying a foundation. Air dhuibh bhi air bhur steidheachadh, *on your being grounded*.—*Stew. N. T.* Written also *steigheachadh*.

STEIDHICH, *v. a.* Lay a foundation. *Pret. a.* steidhich; *fut. aff. a.* steidhichidh. Written also *steighich*.

STEIDHICHTE, *p. part.* of steidhich. Founded, grounded.—*Stew. Col.*

STEIDH-TEAGAISG, *s. f.* A text, the subject of a sermon.

STÉIG, stéige, *s. f.* (*Ir. id.*) A steak; a collop; a piece of meat. *N. pl.* stéigeach.

STÉIGEACH, *a.* In steaks or collops.

STEIGH, *s. f.* A foundation; a basis; a ground. Steigh-dhaingnich, *a foundation*; steigh-teagaisg, *a text*. See also STEIDH.

STEIGHICH, *v. a.* See STEIDHICH.

STEIGHICHTE, *p. part.* of steighich. See STEIDHICHTE.

STÉIGICH, *v. a.* (*from* stéig.) Cut into steaks or into collops. *Pret. a.* stéigich; *fut. aff. a.* stéigichidh; *p. part.* stéigichte.

STEILLE, *s. f.* (*Ir. id.*) Lustiness, stoutness; ruddiness; laziness; looseness, laxativeness.

STEILLEACH, *a.* Lusty, stout; ruddy; lazy; loose, laxative.

STEILLEAN, ein, *s. m.* A gawn-tree or trestle. *N. pl.* steillean.

STEILLEAR, eir, *s. m.* A lusty, lazy fellow. *N. pl.* steillearan.

STEINNEIL, *a.* Keen, ardent, eager; emulous, endeavouring.

STÉINLE, *s. f.* (*Ir. id.*) The itch; the mange; an ulcer. Tha 'n stéinle ort, *thou hast the itch*.

STÉINLEACH, *a.* Itchy, itched; mangy, ulcerated.

STEINLEACHADH, aidh, *s. m.* A becoming mangy; an ulcerating; itch; mange; an ulcer; ulceration.

STEINLEACHD, *s. f.* The state of being affected with the itch, mange, or ulcer.

STÉINLICH, *v. n.* Ulcerate. *Pret. a.* stéinlich; *fut. aff.* stéinlichidh, *shall ulcerate*; *p. part.* stéinlichte, *ulcerated*.

STEOLL; more properly *steall*; which see.

† STEORN, *s. m.* A star.
Gr. ἀστὴρ. *Lat.* astrum. *Maeso-Goth.* stairno. *Island.* stiorna. *Swed.* † stierno. *Dan.* stierno. *Anglo-Sax.* steorra. *Arm.* steren.

† STEORN, *v. a.* Steer by the stars; regulate, manage, govern.

STEORNACH, *a.* Starry; steering; regulating, managing, governing.

STEORNADH, aidh, *s. m.* (*from* steorn.) A steering by the stars; a regulating, a managing, a governing. Fear-steornaidh, *a steersman*; *a ruler*. Luchd steornaidh nan crioch, *the rulers of the land*.—*Mac Co.*

STEORNAIDH, *fut. aff.* a. of steorn. Shall or will steer or govern.

STEORNAIDH, *gen. sing.* of steornadh.

STEUD, steuda, *s. m.* A race; a steed; a wave, a surge. Cuir steud, *run a race*. Fonn nan steud 's nan ribhinn oigh, *the land of steeds and virgins fair*.—*Mac Lach.* Sgaoth eunlaith air steuda sàil, *a flight of birds on the briny billows*.—*Oss. Gaul.* Thoir steud, *take a run* or *race*. Chuir siad nan steud iad, *they set them running*.—*Old Song*.

STEUD, *v. n.* Run speedily. *Pret. a.* steud; *fut. aff. a.* steudaidh.

STEUDACH, *a.* Speedy, swift; billowy.

STEUDADH, aidh, *s. m.* A race, a running; a wave, a billow, a surge.

STEUD-EACH, eich, *s. m.* A swift horse; a race-horse; a war-horse. Ar steud each san t-sliabh, *the war-horse in the mountain*.—*Oss. Fing.*

STIALL, *v. a.* and *n.* Streak, stripe; cut into stripes. *Pret. a.* stiall; *fut. aff. a.* stiallaidh.

STIALL, *s. m.* (*Ir. id.*) A streak, a stripe. Mar stialla soluis, *like streams of light*.—*Oss. Cathula.* Stialla geala, *white stripes*.—*Stew. Gen.*

STIALLACH, aich, *s. m.* A stripe, a streak; the split of a plank; a chop taken from any thing.—*Shaw*.

STIALLACH, *a.* (*from* stiall.) Streaked, striped; brindled; in streaks, in stripes; tearing in shreds. Spreidh stiallach, *streaked cattle*.

STIALLADH, aidh, *s. m.* A streaking, a striping; a tearing in pieces or in shreds; a streak, a stripe.

STIALLAICH, *v. a.* Streak, stripe; rend in pieces or in stripes. *Pret. a.* stiallaich; *fut. aff.* stiallaichidh, *shall stripe*; *fut. pass.* stiallaichear, *shall be striped*.

STIALLAICHTE, *p. part.* of stiallaich. Streaked, striped; rent into shreds or stripes.

STIC, *s.* A pole or stake; *in derision*, a long-legged person.

STIC, *s. f.* (*Du.* stik.) A stitch in sewing; a slice; *also*, a staff. Cuir stic, *sew a stitch*. *N. pl.* sticean.

STIC, *v.* Stick, adhere, cleave to. *Pret. a.* stic; *fut. aff.* sticidh, *shall* or *will stick*.

STICEACH, *a.* Clammy, adhesive, glutinous.

STICEADH, idh. A sticking, cleaving, or adhering to; adherence.

STICEAN, ein, *s. m.* (*dim.* of stic.) A little stitch in sewing; a little slice; a little staff.

STIGH, *adv.* (anns an tigh.) In, within. Tha iad stigh air cheile, *they are reconciled*.

Still, *v. a.* and *n.* Push suddenly and violently; move swiftly; divide. *Pret. a.* still; *fut. aff. a.* stillidh.

Still, *s. f.* Swift motion; violent and sudden exertion. Earb na still air astar, *the roe bounding swiftly afar.—Oss. Conn.*

Stim. See Stiom.

Stinleag, eig, *s. f.* A hasp or clasp of yarn; a staple; the hinge of a trunk. *N. pl.* stinleagan.

Stinleagach, *a.* In hasps or clasps, as yarn; having staples; hinged.

Stiog, *s. m.* A steak; a piece of meat.

Stiol, *s. m.* A thread; a string.

Stiolan, ain, *s. m.* (*dim.* of stiol.) A little thread; a little string.

Stiom, stioma, *s. m.* A snood; a hair-lace; a riband; a belt; a brace; a wreath; a streak, a stripe. *N. pl.* stioman. A gruag na stioman dualach, *her hair in flowing ringlets.—Old Poem.* Stioman dh'obair shlabhraidh, *wreaths of chainwork.—Stew.* 2 *K.*

Stiomach, *a.* Like a snood or hair-lace; like a riband; like a belt; streaked, striped.

Stiopain, *s. f.* A stipend.

Stiopall, aill, *s. m.* A steeple.

Stiorap, aip, *s. f.* A stirrup. *N. pl.* stiorapan.

Stiorapach, *a.* Having stirrups; like a stirrup.

Stirean, ein, *s. m.* A sturgeon; an insignificant person, *in derision. N. pl.* stireanan.

Stireanach, *a.* Like a sturgeon; abounding in sturgeons; of sturgeons.

Stiubhard, aird, *s. m.* A steward.—*Stew. Is. N. pl.* stiubhardan.

Stiùbhart, *s.* The surname Stewart.

Stiùbhart, airt, *s. m.* (*Ir.* stiobhard.) A steward. *N. pl.* stiùbhartan.

Stiùbhartach, aich, *s. m.* A steward. *N. pl.* stiùbhartaich, *stewards.*

Stiùbhartachd, *s. f.* Stewardship; the business of a steward.

Stiùir, *s. f.* (*Swed.* styre. *Ir.* sduir.) A stern, helm, or rudder; a guide; a rule. Air an stiùir, *at the stern;* fear stiùir, *a helmsman;* fear na stiùir, *the helmsman. Stiùir* has sometimes *stiùireach* in the genitive. Fear na stiùireach, *the steersman.—Macdon. N. pl.* stiùireadh.

Stiùir, *v. a.* Steer, guide, direct, manage, rule. *Pret. a.* stiùir, *steered; fut. aff. a.* stiùiridh, *shall steer.* Stiùir mo cheum, *direct my steps.—Sm.*

Swed. styra, *steer. Dan.* styre. *Belg.* stieren. *Germ.* stiuran. *Goth.* stiuran. *Ir.* stiùr.

Stiùireach, *a.* Having a stern; steering, guiding. Written also *stiùradh.*

Stiùireadair, *s. m.* (*Swed.* styrare.) A steersman or pilot; a director. *N. pl.* stiùireadairean. See also Stiùradair.

Stiùireadaireachd, *s. f.* A steering or piloting; the business of a pilot; steerage. Written also *stiùradaireachd.*

Stiùireadh, idh, *s. m.* A steering or piloting; a managing; management, direction, guidance. Written also *stiùradh;* which see.

Stiùireadh, 3 *sing.* and *pl. imper.* of stiùir. Stiùireadh e, *let him steer;* stiùireadh iad, *let them steer.* Also *pret. sub.* of stiùir.

Stiùr, *v. a.* See Stiùir.

Stiùradair, *s. m.* (*Swed.* styrare.) A steersman, a pilot; a director. Ge b'e aird is miann leis an stiùradair, *whatever point the steersman pleases.—Stew. Jam. N. pl.* stiùradairean.

Stiùradaireachd, *s. f.* A steering or piloting; the business of a pilot; steerage.

Stiùradh, aidh, *s. m.* A steering, a directing, or guiding; direction, management. Fo stiùradh boirionnaich, *under management of a woman.—Macfarlane's Translation of Galgacus's Speech.* Written also *stiùireadh.*

Stob, stuib, *s. m.* A thorn, a prickle; a sharp-pointed stick; a thrust or stab.

Stob, *v. a.* Stab, thrust, push.

Stòb. See Stòp.

Stobach, *a.* (*from* stob.) Prickly, thorny.

Stobadh, aidh, *s. m.* A pricking; a stabbing; a thrusting; a stab; a lunge.

Stobadh, (a), *pr. part.* of stob.

Stobh, *v. a.* Stew; crop; cut. *Pret. a.* stobh; *fut. aff. a.* stobhaidh, *shall stew.*

Stobhach, *a.* Stewing; cropping; cutting.

Stobhadh, aidh, *s. m.* A stewing; a cropping; a cutting; a stew.

Stobhta, *p. part.* of stobh. Stewed; cropped.

Stoc, stuic, *s.* (*Sax.* stoc, *a trunk. Ir.* stoc.) A stock; a root, a trunk of a tree; capital; store; a sounding-horn; a trumpet; a post, a pillar; a cravat; a cravat-stiffener; a stock or pack of cards. Ged bhàsaich a stoc, *though its stock [trunk] should die.—Stew. Job.* Chualas stoc Fhionnaghail, *Fingal's horn was heard;* stoc leapach, *a bed-post; a bed-side;* stoc luing, *a gun-wall;* stoc cuibhle, *the stock of a spinning-wheel.*

Stoca, *s. m.* A wallet-boy; one who attends a rider, and carries his wallet; a stocking.—*Shaw.*

Stocach, *a.* Having a stock; having a trunk, as a tree; like a stock or trunk; having posts or pillars; like a sounding-horn or trumpet.

Stocach, aich, *s. m.* (*Ir. id.*) An idle fellow who lives about the kitchens of great people, and will not work for his own support.—*Shaw.*

Stocadh, aidh, *s. m.* A sounding, as of a horn or trumpet; the flourish of a trumpet; a benumbing; a growing stiff. Stocadh nam buadh, *the flourish of victory.—Old Poem.*

Stocadh, aidh, *s. m.* A stocking; a foot-boy, a wallet-boy. *N. pl.* stocaidh. Stocaidh gheal air do chalpa, *white stockings on thy legs.—Macdon.*

Stocaich, *v. a.* and *n.* Stock; grow stiff or benumb. *Pret. a.* stocaich; *fut. aff. a.* stocaichidh.

Stocaidh, *s. f.* A stocking.—*Macfar. Voc.*

Stocainn, *s. f.* A stocking. *N. pl.* stocainnean. Figheadair stocainn, *a stocking-weaver.*

Stocainneach, *a.* Like a stocking; wearing stockings. Brògach stocainneach, *wearing shoes and stockings.*

Stocainnean, *n. pl.* of stocainn.

Stocainnich, *v. a.* Provide with stockings; put on stockings. *Pret. a. id.; fut. aff.* stocainnichidh; *p. part.* stocainnichte.

Stocainnis, *s. pl.* Stockings.

Stocair, *s. m.* (stoc-fhear.) *Ir. id.* One who sounds a horn; a trumpeter. *N. pl.* stocairean.

Stocaireachd, *s. f.* Frequent or continued blowing, as of a horn; the business of a trumpeter.

Stocnaich, *v. a., for* stocainnich; which see.

Stocnais, *s. pl.* Stockings.

Stod, stoid, *s. m.* A pet, a fit of peevishness. Ghabh e 'n stod, *he took the pet.*

Stodach, *a.* Pettish, peevish. Gu stodach, *pettishly. Com.* and *sup.* stodaiche.

Stodag, aig, *s. f.* A pettish or peevish young female. *N. pl.* stodagan.

Stoich, *s. f.* A stink.

Stoid, *s. f.* A pet, a fit of peevishness.

Stoideag, eig, *s. f.* A pettish or peevish girl. *N. pl.* stoideagan.

Stoidhil, *s. f.* A style; a title. An stoidhil ùr, *the new style of computing time:* an seann stoidhil, *the old style.*

Stoilean, ein, *s. m.* *Membrum mas.*

Stoileanach, *a.* Lewd; lecherous; bawdy.

Stoipeal, eil, *s. m.* A stopple; a plug. *N. pl.* stoipealan.

Stoipealach, *a.* Like a stopple; having a stopple.

Stoipealaich, *v. a.* Provide with a stopple.

Stoir, *s. pl.* Stepping-stones.—*Shaw.*

Stóirean, ein, *s. m.* A sulky fellow.

Stòiridh, *s. f.* A story, a tale; a story in height. *N. pl.* stòiridhean.

Stoirm, *s. f.* (*from* toirm.) A storm or tempest. Chuireadh leis an stoirm gu fè, *he changed the tempest to a calm.*—*Sm.* Mar stoirm ghailbhich mheallain, *like a heavy storm of hail.*—*Oss. Cath.* *N. pl.* stoirmean.
Ir. stoirm. *Du.* storm. *Old Sax.* stourm. *W.* ystorm. *Germ.* sturm *and* storm. *Eng.* storm.

Stoirmeach, *a.* (*from* stoirm.) Stormy. Aimsir stoirmeach, *stormy weather.*

Stoirmeachd, *s. f.* Storminess; stormy weather.

Stoirmeil, *a.* (stoirm-amhuil.) Stormy, tempestuous; manly. Gaoth stoirmeil, *a stormy wind.*—*Stew. Acts.*

Stoirmeileachd, *s. f.* Storminess, tempestuousness; manliness.

Stòite, *a.* Projecting, prominent. A ciochan stòite, *her prominent breasts.*—*Old Song.*

Stòl, stoil, *s. m.* A stool; a seat; a stool of repentance. *N. pl.* stòlan, *stools; d. pl.* stolaibh. Air na stolaibh, *on the stools.*—*Stew. Ex.* Stol chos, *a foot-stool;* air an stòl, *on the stool of repentance; doing penance; undergoing church discipline.*
Sax. stòl. *Swed.* stol. *Goth.* stol. *Ir.* sdol *and* stol.

Stòlda, *a.* Sedate, composed; staid; settled; steady; tame; slow; at leisure. Stòlda na 'cleachdaibh, *composed in her demeanour.*—*Old Song.* *Com.* and *sup.* stòilde. Thusa bu stòilde ann ad bheus, *thou who wert staid in thy manners.*—*Old Song.*

Stonta, *s.* A tub, a vat.

Stop, *v. a.* Stop; plug. *Pret. id.; fut. aff. a.* stopaidh.

Stòp, stuip, *s. m.* (*Dan.* stob, *a mug.*) A wooden vessel like a flagon; a measure of liquor; a pot. Leasaich an stòp, *replenish the pot;* stòp muisginn, *a mutchkin;* stòp pinnt, *a pint measure;* stòp siolaig, *a gill pot.* *N. pl.* stuip.

Stopainn, *v. a.* Stop; restrain.

Stòr, stòir, *s. m.* (*Ir. id.*) Store, ammunition; treasure; a hoard; a quantity of goods; a magazine; a store-house.

Stòr, *v. a.* Store, treasure, hoard up, lay by; furnish, replenish. *Pret. a.* stòr, *treasured; fut. aff. a.* storaidh.

Stòr. A word used to incite a bull towards a cow.

Stòrach, *a.* Hoarding, treasuring, saving; inclined to hoard; having a treasure or hoard; rich; having goods or ammunition.

Stòras, ais, *s. m.* (*Ir. id.*) Store, treasure, riches, money.

Stòrasach, *a.* Wealthy, rich; having ammunition, full of stores.

Stot, *v. a.* and *n.* Rebound, as a ball, from the ground.

Stotail, *s. f.* A rebounding from the ground.

Strabaid, aide, *s. f.* A low drab; a street-prostitute. *N. pl.* strabaidean.

Strabaideach, *a.* Drabbish; whorish. Gu strabaideach, *drabbishly.*

Strabaideachd, *s. f.* Drabbishness; whorishness.

Stràc, stràic, *s. m.* A strickle; a stripe; a ruler used to strike grain to a level with a dish; a blow; a thrash; a crashing sound. *N. pl.* stracan. Fhuair e stràc, *he got a blow.*

Stràc, *v. a.* Strike or beat violently; thrash; strike corn level with a dish, by applying a rule diametrically along the rim. *Pret. a.* stràc; *fut. aff. a.* stràcaidh.

Strac, *v. a.* (*Ir.* stroc. *It.* straciare.) Tear, rend. *Pret. a.* strac; *fut. aff. a.* stracaidh. See also **Srachd**.

Stracach, *a.* Apt to tear; easy to tear; inclined to tear.

Stràcach, *a.* Striking, thumping, thrashing; prone to thump or thrash; like a strickle; of strickles.

Stracadh, aidh, *s. m.* A tearing, a rending.

Stràcair, *s. m.* A gossip, a tattling fellow; a bruiser, a thrasher. *N. pl.* stracairean.

Stràcaireach, *a.* Inclined to gossip or tattle; inclined to bruise, thump, or thrash.

Stracaireachd, *s. f.* Gossiping; visiting; tattling.

Stracaireachd, *s. f.* A continued tearing; frequent tearing.

Strachd, *v. a.;* written also *srachd;* which see.

Stràchd, straichd, *s. m.* A strickle; a rude blow; a crashing noise.

Strachdach, *a.* See **Stracach**.

Stràchdach, *a.* See **Stràcach**.

Stràchdair, *s. m.* A gossip, a tattling fellow; a bruiser, a thrasher. *N. pl.* strachdairean.

Strachdaireachd, *s. f.* Continued tearing; frequent tearing; extortion.

Stràchdaireachd, *s. f.* Continued beating; frequent thrashing; hard fighting.

Stragh, straigh, *s. m.* An arch, a vault. *N. pl.* straighean.

Stràic, stràice, *s. f.* Pride, haughtiness, conceit. Mar sin a bhitheas luchd na stràice, *so shall fare the proud.*—*Macfar.*

Stràiceach, *a.* Proud, haughty, conceited. Gu straiceach, *conceitedly.* *Com.* and *sup.* stràiciche.

Stràicealachd, *s. f.* Pride, haughtiness, conceitedness.

Stràicean, ein, *s. m.* A truncheon; a baton; a conceited fellow.

Stràiceil, *a.* (straic-amhuil.) Proud, haughty, conceited.

† **Straif**, *s. f.* A sloe-bush.

Stràill, *s. f.* Delay, neglect; a carpet; a mat, a rug.—*Shaw* and *Macd.* *N. pl.* stràillean.

Stràill, *v. n.* Tear in pieces; pluck. *Pret. a.* straill; *fut. aff. a.* stràillidh.

Stramp, *v. a.* (*Du.* strampe.) Tramp; trample; tread on; stamp with the foot. *Pret. a.* stramp; *fut. aff. a.* strampaidh, *shall tramp.*

Strampach, *a.* Tramping; trampling; prone to tramp or trample; prone to tread; stamping with the foot.

Strampail, *s. f.* A tramping; a trampling; a treading; a stamping with the foot.

Strangach, *a.* Plucking; twitching; quarrelsome; confused; lazy.

Strangadh, aidh, *s. m.* A plucking; a twitching; a quarrelling; a pluck; a twitch; a quarrel; confusion; laziness.

Strangair, *s. m.* (*Ir. id.*) A lazy fellow; a contentious, quarrelsome fellow. *N. pl.* strangairean.

Strangaireachd, *s. f.* Laziness; contentiousness, quarrelsomeness.

Strangalach, *a.* Contentious, quarrelsome, perverse. Gu strangalach, *contentiously.* *Com.* and *sup.* strangalaiche.

Strangalachd, *s. f.* Contentiousness, quarrelsomeness, strife; a skirmish, a contest; frequent skirmishing or fighting.

STRANN. See SRANN.

STRANNRAICH, s. f. A whizzing noise; a snorting; a loud hoarse sound. Strannraich nan speur, *the loud noise of the heavens.—Macfar.*

STRAOILE, s. f. A rude heavy blow; a thump, a buffet *N. pl.* straoilean *and* straoileannan. Le straoileannan trom, *with heavy blows —Mac Lach.*

STRAOILEACH, a. Striking rudely or heavily.

STRAOILEADH, idh, s. m. See STRAOILE

STRAOILEAG, eig, s m A slovenly female, a dragtail.

STRAOILEID, s. f. (*Ir. id.*) A slattern.

STRAOILICH, s. f. Loud hammering noise; a rattling noise, as of metal.

STRAON, v. n. Stumble, tumble, slip, slide; go awry.

STRAONACH, a Prone to tumble, causing to tumble; awry, oblique.

STRAONADH, aidh, s. m. A stumbling, a slipping; a turning.

STRAPADH, aidh, s. m. (*Ir. id*) A strap, a latchet

STRAPAINN, v a. Strap.

STRATH, s. m. The stay betwixt the topmast and foremast, whereby it is supported.

STRATH, s m. See SRATH

STREACHLADH, aidh, s m. (*Ir. id*) A laceration

STREACHLAN, ain, s. m (*Ir. id*) A band, a garter

STREAP, streapa, s m A climbing; strife; struggle. Leinn dearbhar streap nan lann, *we shall try the strife of swords. —Mac Lach.*

STREAP, v a Climb, scale, mount with difficulty, clamber. *Pret. a. id., fut aff. a* streapaidh, *shall climb* Streapaidh an duine glioc, *the wise man shall scale —Stew Pro.* Thar ròs-chrann gàraidh cha streap iad, *they shall not climb the rose-tree of the garden —Macdon*

STREAPACH, a. Fond of climbing, scrambling, clambering.

STREAPADH, aidh, s. m. A climbing, a scrambling upwards

STREAPADH, (a), *pr. part.* of streap Climbing

STREAPAG, aig, s. f. A conflict, a squabble, a skirmish; a passionate female.

STREAPAGACH, a. Fond of squabbling, of, or belonging to, a squabble.

STREAPAID, s f. A squabble, a skirmish, a strife. *N pl* streapaidean

STREAPAIDEACH, a Prone to squabble, quarrelsome; litigious. *Com.* and *sup* streapaidiche.

STREAPAIDEACHD, s. f Quarrelsomeness, contentiousness

STREAPAIDH, *fut. aff. a.* of streap Shall or will climb.

STRI, STRIGH, s. f. (*Swed Dan* strid *Arm* striva) Strife, contention; rivalry; contest, battle. Is coma leam stri, *I dislike strife.—Ull* Stri nam fonn, *the contest of strains, musical competition —Oss. Fing.* Stritha ard, *loud-sounding battles —Oss. Tem.* Dean stri, *strive*, cha dean e stri, *he will not strive.—Stew. Mat.* Cuir strigh, *strive.*

STRIALL, s. m A stripe, as of cloth, a shred

STRIALL, v. a Cut into stripes, as cloth.

STRIALLACH, a. In stripes, or shreds.

STRIANACH, aich, s m A badger. *N. pl.* strianaich

STRIGH, v. Strive, struggle; contend, emulate.

STRIGHMHOR, a. (*Corn* strifor.) Emulative, contentious.

STRILLEAN, ein, s m A mop

STRILINN, s. (*Ir. id.*) A garter

STRIOC, s. (*Ir. id*) A streak

STRIOCACH, a. (*Ir. id.*) Streaked

STRIOCHD, s. m. A yielding, submission, obeisance, a bow. Dean striochd, *yield.*

STRIOCHD, v. n. (*Ir.* strioc) Yield, submit, bow, cringe *Pret a. id, fut aff. a.* striochdaidh. An gaisgeach nach striochd, *the hero who will not yield —Oss Fing.*

STRIOCHDACH, a. Submissive, submitting; prone to yield; causing to submit or yield.

STRIOCHDADH, aidh, s. m (*Ir* striogadh) A submitting, submission, obedience

STRIOCHDAR, a. Submissive, under submission.

STRIOLLA, s m (*Ir id*) A girth, a girdle.

STRIOP, s. Whoredom.

STRIOPACH, aich, s f. (*Ir id*) A harlot, a bawd Mar ri striopach, *as with a harlot —Stew. Gen.* *N pl* striopaichean, *harlots*

STRIOPACHAIL, a (striopach-amhuil) *Ir.* striopamhail Whorish Le mnaoi striopachail, *by means of a whorish woman —Stew Pro*

STRIOPACHAS, ais, s m. (*Ir id*) Whoredom, prostitution, fornication. Rinn i striopachas, *she has played the harlot —Stew. Gen.* Torrach le striopachas, *with child by whoredom —Id.* Air a lion le striopachas, *filled with fornication —Stew. Rom* Fear striopachais, *a whoremonger — Stew Eph*

STRIOPAICH, *gen. sing.* of striopach, which see.

STRITH. See STRI

STRITHA, n. pl of strith See STRI

STRITHEIL, a (strith-amhuil) Emulous Gu saoithreachail stritheil, *emulous, careful and emulous —Macfar*

STRITHMHOR, a See STRIGHMHOR.

STROBAID, s f. A strumpet *N. pl* strobaidean.

STROBAIDEACHD, s f Whoredom, whoring

† STRODA, s. (*Ir. id*) A strand, a shore.

STROGH, s Extravagance, prodigality

STROGHAIL, a. (strogh-amhuil) Extravagant, prodigal, profuse, lavish. Gu stroghail, *extravagantly.*

STROGHAIR, s m. A prodigal, a spendthrift *N. pl.* stroghairean.

STROGHALACHD, s Prodigality, extravagance

STROIC. See STRAC or SRAC

STROIDH, v See STRUIDH.

STROIDHEIL, a. See STRUIDHEIL.

STRUIDH, v a Spend, squander, waste. *Pret a. id, fut aff a* struidhidh, *shall spend* Struidh e ar n-airgiod, *he hath spent our money —Stew Gen.*

STRUIDHE, STRUIGHE, s. f. Extravagance, waste, profusion Luch struidhe, *extravagant people*

STRUIDHEALACHD See STRUIDHEILEACHD

STRUIDHEAS, eis, s m Extravagance, waste

STRUIDHEASACH, STRUIGHEASACH, a Extravagant, prodigal, wasteful Gu struidheasach, *wastefully* *Com* and *sup* struidheasaiche

STRUIDHEIL, STRUIGHEIL, a Extravagant, profuse, wasteful.

STRUIDHEILEACHD, STRUIGHEILEACHD, s f Extravagance, profusion, wastefulness

STRUIDHEAR, STRUIGHEAR, eir, s. m. A spendthrift or prodigal. *N. pl* struidhearan

STRUMPAID, s f. A strumpet *N pl* strumpaidean

STRUTH, strutha, s. f (*Ir id Dan.* struds *Swed* struss) An ostrich.

STRUTHACH, a. Like an ostrich, of, or belonging to, an ostrich; abounding in ostriches

STUADH, stuaidh, s (*Ir id*) A billow or wave; undulation; a gable; a pillar, *rarely*, a street, a scroll O stuaidh an t-sàil, *from the briny billow —Oss Gaul* Iomall nan stuadh, *the shore —Oss Fing* Stuadh osnig air an fheur, *the grass undulating with the breeze —Oss Tem.* *N. pl.* stuaidh *and* stuadhan, *d pl.* stuadhaibh

Mar stuadhaibh deataich, *like pillars of smoke.—Stew Song Sol.*

STUADHACH, *a.* (*from* stuadh) Tempestuous, billowy Ruith sinn ro 'n chuan stuadhach, *we sailed before* [*drifted on*] *the tempestuous sea —Oss Duthona*

STUADH-BHEANN, -bheinn, *s f.* A stormy hill, a mountain. Mullach nan stuadh-bheann, *the top of the stormy hills —Oss Manos.*

STUADH-BHRAGHAIDEACH, *a* Stiff-necked

STUADH-GHLAS, *a* Having green waves, as the sea A mhuir stuadh-ghlas, *the green-waved sea.—Ull*

STUADH-GHREANNACH, *a* Tempestuous, as the sea

STUADHMHOR, *a* Stormy; proud; high-spirited. Each stuadhmhor, *a proud-spirited horse —Old Poem*

STUAGH, stuaigh, *s m* See STUADH

STÙAGHAR, *a.*, *for* stuadhmor

STUAIC, *s f* A little hill, a projecting cliff, a little promontory

STUAIDH, *s f* A flock, a herd Da uan as an stuaidh mhòir, *two lambs from the great flock —Mac Lach*

STUAIDH, *gen sing* of stuadh

STUAIDH-BHEUMNACH, *a* High-spirited; quick-paced Each stuaidh-bheumnach, *a quick-paced horse —Fingalian Poem*

STUAIGH, *s. f* See STUAIDH

STUAIM, stuaime, *s f* Modesty; moderation, temperance; continence; *rarely*, air, mien Geal-laimh na stuaim, *the fair hand of modesty —Oss* Macantas is stuaim, *meekness and temperance —Stew Gal*

STUAMA, STUAMADH, *a.* Modest, temperate; continent, moderate in appetite or desire

STUAMACH, *a* See STUAMA

STUAMACHD, *s f* Moderation, temperateness; continence

STUBH, stubha, *s m* Stuff, substance, matter, pith; strength, mettle; corn Diadh stubh, *good stuff*

STÙC, stùic, *s m* and *f.* A little hill projecting from a greater; a rock, a steep Dhìrich Fionnghal an stùc, *Fingal ascended the hill —Oss Duthona* Aig bun na stùic, *at the foot of the rock —Macint.* *N pl* stùic; *d pl* stùcaibh. An sealgair air stùcaibh, *the hunter on the rocks —Oss Cathula*

STÙCACH, STÙCHDACH, *a* Hilly, rocky, rugged, having projecting cliffs or jutting precipices; *also*, stiff, rigid, horned *Com* and *sup* stùcaiche

STÙCAN, ain, *s m*, *dim.* of stùc. (*Ir id*) A little hill, a conical hill

STÙCANACH, *a.* Having little hills; having projecting cliffs.

STÙC-BHEANN, -bheinn, *s f* A rocky mountain, a precipitous hill A siubhal nan stùc-bheann, *travelling rocky mountains —Old Song*

STÙCHD, *s* See STÙC

STÙIC, STÙICHD, *s f* The scowling side-look of a bull or any large quadruped

STUIC, *gen sing* and *n pl* of stoc; which see

STUIDEAR, eir, *s m* A student; a study. *N pl* stuidearan.

STUIDEARACHD, *s f* Study

STUIG, *v a* Incite or spur on to fight, as dogs *Pret a id.*, *fut aff. a* stuigidh, *shall incite*, *fut pass* stuigean

STUIRICHD, *s f* A pinnacle

STÙR, stùir, *s m* Dust Daoimean nach gabh stùr, *diamond that catches no dust —Old Song* Cuir stùr riu, *disperse them, scatter them as dust*

STÙRACH, *a.* Dusty.

STÙRD See STÙRT.

STURRACH, *a.* Rugged, uneven. *Com.* and *sup.* sturraiche.

STURRAG, aig, *s. f* A pinnacle, a butting cliff.—*Macfar. Voc.*

STURRAGACH, *a* Full of pinnacles, pinnacled.

STURRANTA, *a.* (*Ir id.*) Thick, gross, fat

STÙRT, stùirt, *s m.* Sulkiness, sullenness; pride, a disease in sheep Làn stùirt as gruaim, *full of sullenness and gloom —Old Song*

STÙRTAIL, *a* (sturt-amhuil.) Sulky, sullen, morose; proud. Gu stùrtail, *sulkily.*

STÙRTAILEACHD, *s. f.* Sulkiness, sullenness, moroseness, intractableness.

STUTH, stutha, *s. m* Stuff, substance; matter, pith; strength; mettle, corn Stuth na Tòiseachd, *the stuff of Ferntosh*, or *whisky.—R.* Deagh stuth, *good stuff.*

STUTHAIL, *a.* (stuth-amhuil.) High-mettled; of good stuff; tough; pithy, hardy.

† SUADH, *a* Mild, gentle, mannerly *Ir. id* *Lat.* suavis. *It.* soave. *Fr.* suave.

† SUADHAS, ais, *s m.* (*Lat.* suavitas.) Mildness, mannerliness

SUACAN, ain, *s. m.* An earthen pot or vessel, an earthen furnace. Suacan crè, *an earthen furnace —Sm*

† SUADH, *a* (*Ir id*) Prudent, discreet.

† SUADH, suaidh, *s. m.* An advice, a counsel; a learned man

SUADH, *v* See SUATH.

SUADHADH, aidh, *s m* See SUATHADH.

SUAIB See SUAIP

SUAIBHREACH, *a* Gentle, quiet; not proud; easy.

SUAICHEANTA, *a.* Easily known, remarkable; conspicuous by reason of dress or badge, banner or armorial bearings Eididh suaicheanta, *a well-known dress, a conspicuous dress.*

SUAICHEANTACH, *a* Armorial

SUAICHEANTAICHE, *s. m.* A standard-bearer.

SUAICHEANTAS, ais, *s m.* A standard, a banner, colours; a cockade; an armorial ensign, an escutcheon; a portent. Dha 'm bu shuaicheantas giumhas? *whose cockade was the fir-crop?—Old Song*

SUAIDHTE, *p part.* of suadh. See SUAITHTE

SUAIGH, *a.* (*Ir id*) Prosperous

SUAIL, SUAILL, *a* (*Ir id* *W.* sal) Inconsiderable, little, insignificant, mean

SUAILMHEASTA, *a* Homely, ordinary.

† SUAIM, *s f.* (*Ir id*) A tone, accent, voice —*Shaw.*

SUAIMHNE, *s. f.* Quietness, peace.

SUAIMHNEACH, *a.* (*Ir id.*) Composed, quiet, gentle, peaceable; safe, secure Gu suaimhneach, *composedly. Com* and *sup.* suaimhniche

SUAIMHNEAS, eis, *s m* (*Ir id.*) Rest, tranquillity, quietness, calmness, peace Thug e dhuibh suaimhneas, *he gave you rest —Stew 1 Chr* Greim tioram agus suaimhneas, *a dry morsel and quietness —Stew. Pro.*

SUAIMHNEASACH, *a* (*Ir id.*) Quiet, calm, peaceable, sedate Is suaimhneach an ribhinn òg, *sedate is the young maiden.—Old Song*

SUAIMHNICH, *v n* Take rest, be at rest, take ease

SUAIN, suaine, *s. f* Sleep; profound sleep. *Asp. form*, shuain O shuain an éig, *from the sleep of death —Oss. Gaul*

Ir suan *Dan* sovn *Lat* somnus *Anglo-Sax.* swǽfan *and* swaefian

SUAINAIRM, *s m* (*Ir.* suan-airm) A dormitory.—*Shaw.*

SUAINE. Sweden

SUAINEACH, *a* Sleepy, lethargic, narcotic.

SUAINEAMH, eimh, *s m* (*Ir. id*) The confluence of rivers.

SUAINEARTACH, *a* Sound asleep; narcotic

Suain-ghalar, air, *s. m.* (*Ir.* suan-ghalar.) Lethargy, habitual drowsiness.

Suainmhor, *a.* Inclining to sleep, sleepy, narcotic.

Suainmhorachd, *s. f.* Sleepiness.

Suaip, *s. f.* A likeness; a resemblance. Tha suaip mhor aig ris, *he has a great resemblance to him.*

Suairce, *a.* (*Ir. id.*) Civil, complacent, affable; kind, generous. Suairce, siobhailte, *affable and civil.—Macint.* Le giùlan suairce, *with generous conduct.—Old Poem.*

Suairceas, eis, *s. m.* (*Ir. id.*) Civility, complaisance, affability; kindness. Gun suairceas ri damhaich, *without kindness to strangers.—Mac Co.*

† **Suaiteachd**, *s. f.* (*Ir. id.*) Fatigue; a tempering or mixing together.

Suaitheantas, ais, *s. m.* (*Ir. id.*) See **Suaicheantas**.

Suaithte, *p. part.* of suath. (*Ir.* suaite.) Rubbed; stirred about as posset; kneaded, mixed.

Sual, *a.* (*Ir. id.*) Famous.

† **Sual**, suail, *s. m.* (*Ir. id.*) A wonder.—*Shaw.*

Suanach, aich, *s. m.* A covering, a garment, a plaid. Gun suanach, *without covering.—Macint.*

Suantach, *a.* (*from* suain.) *Ir. id.* Lethargic, drowsy, narcotic.

Suarach, **Suarrach**, *a.* (*Ir. id.*) Insignificant, contemptible, trifling, mean, abject, indifferent; of no account, valueless, silly. Dealbh suarrach, *a despised idol.—Stew. Jer.* Tha 'm bord suarrach, *the table is contemptible.—Stew. Zech.* Mnaoi shuarrach, *silly women.—Stew. Tit.* Cuir suarrach, *set at nought*; na cuir suarrach, *despise not.—Stew. Pro.* *Com.* and *sup.* suarraiche.

Suarachas, **Suarrachas**, ais, *s. m.* Insignificance, meanness; indifference, contempt.

Suarcas, ais, *s. m.* (*Ir. id.*) Wit; drollery.

Suarraiche, *com.* and *sup.* of suarrach. More or most insignificant.

Suarraiche, *s. f.* (*Ir.* suaraighe.) Insignificance, cheapness.

Suarraichead, eid, *s. m.* Increase in meanness; deterioration; diminution in value. A dol ann suarraichead, *growing more and more valueless.*

Suarraicheas, eis, *s. m.* Insignificance, neglect, indifference.

Suas, **a suas**, *adv.* (*Ir. id.*) Up, upwards, from below; west, westwards. Dh' eirich suas fuaim nam foun, *up rose the sound of the song.—Oss. Carricth.* Suas leis, *up with him* or *it*; sìos is suas, *east and west, up and down, to and fro*; dean suas, *make up*; *constitute*; cuir suas, *exalt, promote*; tog suas, *rear, educate.*

† **Suas**, suais, *s. m.* Urbanity.

Suas-mhol, *v. a.* (*Ir. id.*) Extol, magnify, exalt; flatter, puff up.

Suath, *v. a.* (*Ir. id.*) Rub; stir about; as posset, or any such inspissated substance; knead; mix; temper. *Pret. a.* shuath; *fut. aff. a.* suathaidh, *shall rub*; istric suathadh adhorn, *often is he rubbing his fists.—Old Poem.*

Suathadh, aidh, *s. m.* (*Ir. id.*) A rubbing, attrition, friction; a stirring about, as of any inspissated fluid; a mixing, a kneading. Mortair gun suathadh, *untempered mortar.*

Sùbailt, *a.* (*Arm.* soubl.) Supple, flexible, agile. Spiorad subailt, *a flexible mind.* (*Arm.* spered soubl.) Gu sùbailt, *with agility.*

Subaiste, *s. f.* A mouth.

Subas, ais, *s. m.* A mess of wild berries and milk.

Sùbh, *s. m.* See **Sùgh**.

Subh, subha, *s. m.* Pleasure, delight; joy, mirth.

Subhach, *a. from* subh. (*Ir. id.*) Glad; cheerful, merry. Bi subhach am meadhon do dheur, *be cheerful in the midst of thy tears.—Oss. Fin.* and *Lor.* Bha iad subhach, *they were merry.—Stew. Gen.* *Com.* and *sup.* subhaiche.

Subhachas, ais, *s. m.* (*Ir. id.*) Pleasure, joy; cheerfulness, mirth. Am bi subhachas agam, *shall I have pleasure.—Stew. Gen.* Deireadh an t-subhachais sin, *the end of that* [*mirth*] *laughter.—Stew. Pro.*

Subhailce, ailce, *s. f.* (*Ir. id.*) Virtue, moral excellence. Bean na subhailce, *a virtuous woman.—Stew. Pro. ref.* chum gloir agus subhailce, *to glory and virtue.—Stew.* 2 *Pet.* *N. pl.* subhailcean; *d. pl.* subhailcibh.

Subhailceach, *a.* (*Ir. id.*) Virtuous; of, or pertaining to, virtue. Co gheibh bean shubhailceach? *who can find a virtuous woman?—Stew. Pro.* Gu subhailceach, *virtuously.—Id.*

Subhan, ain, *s. m. from* sùbh. (*Ir. id.*) Juice, sap; water impregnated with the juice of corn seeds, of which is made a kind of coagulated food, by the Lowland Scots, called *sowens.*

Subhar, *a.* A contraction of *sùbhmor*; which see.

Subh-chraobh, -chraoibh, *s.* A raspberry bush; any bush which yields berries.

Subh-craoibh, *s.* A raspberry; rasps.

Subhlach, aich, *s. m.* (*Ir. id.*) Juice pressed out of apples and other fruit; liquor.

Subh làir, *s.* A strawberry. Subhan làir, *strawberries.*

Sùbhmhor, *a.* See **Sughmhor**.

Subh-thalmhainn, *s.* (*Ir. id.*) A strawberry.

Sùblachadh, aidh, *s. m.* A making supple, or flexible.

Sùblaich, *v. a.* and *n.* Make supple, or flexible; grow flexible. *Pret. a.* shùblaich, *made flexible*; *fut. aff.* sublaichidh, *shall make supple.*

Sùblaichte, *p. part. of* sublaich. Made flexible.

Sucar, **Suchdar**, air, *s. m.* See **Siucar**.

Sucarach, *a.* Saccharine.

Such, *s. m.* A whispering noise.

Suchadh, aidh, *s. m.* A wave.

Suchadh, aidh, *s. m.* Suction, evaporation.

Suchan, ain, *s. m.* (*Ir. id.*) A sucker.

Sud, (*perhaps* is ud.) *demonstrative pron.* *Ir. id.* Yon, yonder; that, there; *also*, lo! so, in that manner. Ciod sud? *what was that? what was yon?* Sud an lamh a thogas an t-sleagh, *here is the hand that will lift the spear.—Oss. Fing.* Sud mar chiteadh an Greugach, *so was the Grecian seen.—Mac Lach.* We say *sud* very often as an incitement: sud, sud, *come, come.*

Sudag, aig, *s. f.* (*Ir. id.*) A cake.

† **Sudh**, *a.* (*Ir. id.*) Secure.

Sùdh. See **Sùgh**.

Sudhar, **Sudhmhor**, *a.* See **Sughmhor**.

Sudral, ail, *s. m.* (*Ir. id.*) Light; a candle.

Sug, *v. a.* Suck, imbibe; attract. *Pret. a.* shùg, *sucked*; *fut. aff. a.* sùgaidh, *shall suck*; sùgaidh e nimh, *he will suck poison.—Stew. Job.*

Sax. sucan. *Anglo-Sax.* sycan *and* sucan. *Du.* suyken. *Germ.* saugen. *Fr.* sugan. *Belg.* zugen. *Fr.* succer. *It.* succhiare, *to suck.*

Sùgach, *a.* (*Ir. id.*) Sucking; attraction.

Sugach, *a.* (*Ir. id.*) Cheerful, merry. Is tu am fear sugach, *a merry fellow art thou.—R.* Fhir shugaiche, *thou merry fellow.*

Sugachas, ais, *s. m.* (*Ir. id.*) Mirth.

Sùgag, aig, *s. f.* The bloom of clover, so called from its containing a honeyed juice.

Sùgadh, aidh, *s. m.* A sucking, suction; an imbibing; attraction.

Sugaidheachd, *s. f.* Joyousness.

Sùgair, *s. m.* A droll; a mountebank; a merry fellow. *N. pl.* sugairean.

Sùgaireachd, *s. f.* Drollery, buffoonery.

Sugan, ain, *s. m.* (*Ir. id.*) A rope of straw or hay.—*Heb.* Sugar, *a band for the neck.*

Sùgh, súgha, *s. m.* Juice, sap; substance; broth; a berry; a wave. Sùgh nan gràn-ubhall, *the juice of the pomegranates.—Stew. Song Sol.* Sùgh ann am poit, *broth in a pot.—Stew. Jud.* Druim nan sùgh, *the backs of the waves.—Mac Lach. N. pl.* sùghan; *d. pl.* sùghaibh, a ceann ris na sùghaibh, *her head against the billows.—Macfar.*

Ir. id. Lat. succus, *juice. W.* syg, *sap. Arm.* sygan. *Fr.* suc, *juice.*

Sùghach, *a.* Juicy; abounding in berries.

Sùghar, **Sùghmhor**, *a.* Juicy, sappy; moist; billowy.

Sugh-dharaich, *s.* (*Ir. id.*) Misletoe.

Sùghmhorachd, *s. f.* Juiciness, sappiness; succulence.

Sùgradh, aidh, *s. m.* (*Ir. id.*) Merriment, play, sport. Dh' eirich cuid gu sùgradh, *they rose to play.—Stew. Ex.* Ri sùgradh, *in sport.—Stew. Pro. ref.* and *Macfar.* Mu shùgradh, *about mirth;* nighean donn an t-sùgraidh, *thou brown-haired sportive maid.—Old Song.* A sùgradh ri mhnaoi, *sporting with his wife.—Stew. Gen.*

Suibhealas, ais, *s. m.* A spunging, a sharking.

Suibheallan, ain, *s. m.* A parasite.

Suidh, suidhe, *s.* The beam or joist of a building. *N. pl.* suidhean.

Suidh, *s. m.* (*Ir. id.*) A hero, a champion.

Suidh, *v. n.* (*Goth.* sie. *Ir.* suidh). Sit down. *Pret. a.* shuidh, *sat; fut. aff. a.* suidhidh, *shall sit.*

Sùidh, *v. a.* Soot; cover with soot; season by exposing to smoke; *also* suck, imbibe. *Pret. a.* shùidh, *sooted; fut. aff.* sùidhidh, *shall or will soot;* written also *sùith.*

Sùidh, suidhe, *s. m.* Soot. See also **Sùith**.

Suidhe, *s. m.* A sitting, a sederunt, a session. Dean suidhe, *sit down;* suidhe bidh, *a meal.—Macd.*

Suidheachadh, aidh, *s. m.* A planting; a setting; establishing; situation; posture; position. Suidheach' inntinn, *gravity.—Stew. Tit.*

Suidheag, eig, *s. f.* (*W.* syvi. *Corn.* sevi.) A strawberry. *N. pl.* suidheagan.

Suidheagach, *a.* Abounding in strawberries.

Suidheagan, *n. pl.* of suidheag.

Suidheagan, ain, *s. m. from* suidhe. (*Ir.* suidheachan. *Arm.* sichen.) A place of sitting; a seat of turf or stone; a rustic seat.

Suidhealachd, *s. f.* (*Ir. id.*) Gravity.

Suidheann, einn, *s. m.* (*Ir. id.*) A ship's cable.

Suidhe-bhalaoch, oich, *s. m.* A chimney-sweeper.

Sùidhich, *v. a.* (*from* suidh.) Plant, set, settle; pitch, establish, appoint; agree or make an appointment; repose. *Pret. a.* shuidhich, *planted; fut. aff. a.* suidhichidh, *shall plant;* shuidhich e 'bhùth, *he planted his tent.—Stew. Gen.* Suidhich faire, *place a watch.—Stew. Jud.* Shuidhich iad eatorra fein, *they made an appointment among themselves.—Stew. Job.*

Suidhichear, *fut. pass.* of suidhich, *shall be.* Planted or settled.

Suidhichte, *p. part.* of suidhich. Planted, set, settled; pitched, established, appointed; determined, fixed; stationary; grave, sedate; composed, steady. Air an la suidhichte, *on the appointed day.—Stew. Pro.* Tha 'laithean suidhichte, *his days are determined.—Stew. Job.* Suidhichte air dol maille ri, *set,* or *resolved on going with her.—Stew. Ruth.* Is còir do na mnaibh bhi suidhichte, *the wives ought to be grave.—Stew. Tim.*

Sùidhte, *p. part.* of sùidh. Sooted; seasoned or dried in smoke, as bacon.

Suigeart, eirt, *s. m.* Gladness, cheerfulness; frisking. Olamaid slainnte Thearlaich le suigeart, *let us drink Charles's health with gladness.—Old Song.* A dol le suigeart do 'n choille, *going frisking to the wood.—Macfar.*

Suigeartach, *a.* Glad, cheerful, frisky, joyful. *Com.* and *sup.* suigeartaiche. Gu suigeartach, *gladly.*

Sùigh, *v. a.* Suck, imbibe, attract. *Pret. a.* shùigh, *sucked; fut. aff. a.* sùighidh, *shall suck;* sùighidh an glaodhan an sùgh, *the pith shall suck the juice.—Macdon. P. part.* suighte.

Sùigh. See **Sùith**.

Sùigh-bhalaoch, *s. m.* A chimney-sweeper.

Suigleadh, idh, *s. m.* (*Ir. id.*) Snot.

Suil, *s.* The sixteenth letter (S) of the Gaelic alphabet.

Suil, *conj.* (*Ir. id.*) Before that, ere.

Sùil, sùl, *s. f.* (*Ir. id.*) An eye; a look; regard; aspect; hope, expectation; a loophole; *rarely* tackle. *N. pl.* sùilean. Tha 'n sùil ri lear, *their eye is towards the sea.—Ull.* Thugaibh sùil o 'r neòil, *look down from your clouds.—Fingalian Poem.* Mòralachd na 'shùil, *majesty in his aspect.—Mac Lach.* Bha sùil aca rium, *they had an eye on me,* or, *waited for me.—Stew. Job.* Tha sùil agam ris, *I hope for him;* tha sùil agam air, *I have an eye on him;* droch shùil, *an evil eye.—Stew. Pro.* Sùil rag, *a dim eye.—Stew. Sam. ref.* sùil bhiorach, *a sharp eye;* sùil gheur, *a sharp eye.*

Suilbhear, *a.* (*Ir.* suilbhir.) Cheerful, merry. Laoich nan gorm-shùil suilbhear, *hero of the cheerful blue eye.—Old Poem. Com.* and *sup.* suilbhire. Gu suilbhear, *cheerfully.*

Suilbhearach, *a.* Cheerful, merry. *Com.* and *sup.* suilbhiriche.

Suilbhearachd, *s. f.* (*Ir.* suilbhireacht.) Cheerfulness, merriness.

Sùil-bheum, -bheuma, *s. m.* (*Ir.* sùilbeim.) The blasting influence of an evil eye. *N. pl.* sùil-bheumannan.

Suilbheumach, *a.* Having an evil eye; blasting with the eye.

Suilbhire, *com.* and *sup.* of suilbhear. More or most cheerful.

Suilbhire, *s. f.* Cheerfulness; mirth.

Suil-chritheach, *s. m.* A bog; a quagmire.

Sùileach, *a.* Ocular; like an eye; eyed; having many eyes; sharp-sighted; having large eyes; of, or belonging to, the eye.

Sùileag, eig, *s. f.* (*dim.* of sùil.) A little eye; a little loop; a little orifice.

Sùileagach, *a.* Full of little eyes or orifices; full of loopholes.

Sùilean, *n. pl.* of sùil; which see.

Suilleag, eig, *s. f.* A bell or bubble.—*Macd. N. pl.* suilleagan.

Suilleagach, *a.* Full of bells or bubbles.

Sùil-leigh, *s. m.* An oculist.

Sùil-leigheas, eis, *s. m.* An eye-salve.

Suil-mhargach, *a.* Forestalling.

Suil-mhargaidh, *s.* A forestaller.—*Macfar. Voc.*

Sùil-radharc, *s.* (*Ir. id.*) Fascination; foresight; the sense of sight; vision; fate.

Sùil-radharcach, *a.* Fascinating; having the sense of sight.

Suim, *s. m.* (*Ir. id. Isl.* soome.) Respect, regard; consideration, attention; a sum, amount. Cha bhi suim aig dh'eiric, *he shall not regard a ransom.—Stew. Pro.* Cha 'n eil suim ann dhomhsa, *it makes no matter to me.—Stew. Gal.* Mar diol sinn an suim cheart, *if we pay not the right sum.—Mac Lach.* Gabh suim, *pay attention.*

Suimeil, *a.* (suim-amhuil.) Regardful, respectful, considerate, attentive. Gu suimeil, *regardfully.*

Suimeileachd, *s. f.* Regardfulness, respectfulness, considerateness, attentiveness.

Suineann, *s.* Stammering.

Suinn, *gen. sing.* and *n. pl.* of sonn; which see.

Suipeir, *gen.* suipeir *and* suipearach, *s. f.* A supper. An deigh na suipeir, *after supper.—Stew. Cor.*

Suire, *s. f. sing* and *pl.* (*Ir. id.*) A nymph; mermaids; nereids; sea-nymphs.

Suireadh, idh, *s. m.* See Suirtheadh.

Suiriche, *s. m.* (*Ir.* suirighe.) A wooer; a fool.

Suirthiche, *s. m.* (suire thaghaiche, *a nymph-chooser.*) A lover, a suitor. *N. pl.* suirthichean.

Suirtheadh, idh, *s. m.* (suire-thagh, *nymph-choosing.*) Courting or wooing. 'g a suirtheadh gu cùirteil, *wooing her courteously.—Macdon.* Is trian suirtheadh samhladh, *to be given to a woman is one third of the way to win her.—G. P.*

Sùiste, *s. f.* (*Ir. id.*) A flail. *N. pl.* suistean.

Sùisteachadh, aidh, *s. m.* A threshing with a flail.

Sùisteachd, *s. f.* (*Ir. id.*) The employment of a thresher; threshing.

Sùistear, eir, *s. m.* One who threshes with a flail. *N. pl.* sùistearan.

Sùith, *v. a.* Soot; cover with soot; season or dry in smoke. *Pret a.* shùith, *sooted; fut aff. a.* sùithidh, *shall soot; p. part.* sùithte, *sooted, seasoned in smoke.*

Sùithe, *s. m.* (*Ir.* suth *and* suthaighe. *Du.* soet.) Soot. Neul an t-sùithe, *the colour of soot.—Macint.*

Sùitheach, *a.* Sooty; full of soot; of, or belonging to, soot.

Sùithe-bhalaoch, oich, *s. m.* A chimney-sweeper. *N. pl.* sùithe-bhalaoich.

Sùithte, *p. part.* of sùith; which see.

† **Sul**, suil, *s. m.* The sun.
Ir. id. Corn. sol *and* sul. *Lat. Span. Goth. Swed.* sol. *It.* sole. *Dan.* soel.

Sùl, *gen. sing.* of sùil.

Sulair, *s. m.* A St. Kildan bird; a Soland goose.—*Macd. N. pl.* sulairean.

Sulaireach, *a.* Like a Soland goose; full of Soland geese; of, or belonging to, a Soland goose.

Sùlas, ais. See Sòlas.

Sùl-bheachd, *s. f.* Watchfulness; eye-sight. Air gach taobh tha sùl-bheachd, *on every side there is watchfulness.—Mac Lach.*

Sulchair, *a.* Hearty, hospitable, affable. Gu sulchair, *heartily.*

Sulchaireachd, *s. f.* Heartiness, hospitableness, affableness.

Sul-fhradharc, *s.* Fascination; foresight; eye-sight; fate.

Sùl-fhradharcach, *a.* Fascinating; foresighted; foreseeing.

Sùlmhor, *a.* Quick-sighted. *Com.* and *sup.* sulmhoire. Gu sulmhor, *in a quick-sighted manner.*

Sùl-radharc, *s.* See Suil-radharc.

Sùl-radharcach, *a.* See Suil-radharcach.

Sult, *s.* (*Ir. id.*) Fatness, fat; *also*, mirth, jest, joy. Do shult na talmhainn, *of the fatness of the earth.—Stew. Gen.*

Sultach, *a.* Fat.

Sultar, *a.* See Sultmhor.

Sultmhoireachd, *s.* Fatness.

Sultmhor, *a.* (*Ir.* sultmhur.) Fat, lusty, corpulent, jolly; fertile; pleasant, jocose. *Com.* and *sup.* sultmhoire.

Sum, suim, *s. m.* A sum; *also*, as much grazing ground as will suffice four sheep; *a sowme.*

Sumag, aig, *s. f.* A packsaddle; the cloth of a packsaddle; a pad.—*Macint. N. pl.* sumagan.

Sumagach, *a.* Like a packsaddle; of, or belonging to, a packsaddle.

Sumaid, aide, *s. f.* (*Eng.* summit.) A wave or billow; a ridge. *N. pl.* sumaidean.

Sumaideach, *a.* Billowy; stormy as the sea; ridgy.

Sumain, aine, *s. f.* A wave or billow. Cha siùil na sumaine glas, *the blue billows are not sails.—Oss. Cathula. N. pl.* sumainean. Chaidh do shumainean tharrum, *thy waves went over me.—Stew. Jon.*

Sumaineach, *a.* Billowy, flowing; causing waves.

Sumhail, *a.* Tight, tightly bound; packed closely; strait-laced; not bulky. Gu sumhail, *tightly;* written also, *somhail.*

Sumhaileachd, *s. f.* Tightness.

Sumhlachadh, aidh, *s. m.* A bending tightly; a packing close; a pressing together; a tightening; a diminishing in bulk; an abridgment.

Sumhlaich, *v. a.* (*from* sumhail.) Bend tightly; pack closely; press together; tighten; diminish in bulk; abridge. *Pret. a.* shumhlaich, *packed closely; fut. aff. a.* sumhlaichidh; *fut. pass.* sumhlaichear.

Sumhlaichte, *p. part.* of sumhlaich.

Sumach, aich, *s. m.* A plaid.

Sunais, *s. f.* Lovage.

Sunn, *s.* A wall.

Sunnailt, *s. f.* A likeness, a resemblance; a comparison; a match. Sunnailt t-eugais, *the likeness* [*match*] *of thy face.—Old Song.*

Sunnd, *s. m.* Joy, mirth, gladness.

Sunndach, *a.* (*Ir.* sonntach.) Joyous, glad, merry; good-humoured.—*Macint.* Gu sunndach, *good-humouredly. Com.* and *sup.* sunndaiche.

Sunndan, ain, *s. m.* (*dim.* of sunnd.) A short fit of gladness; a sudden emotion of joy.

Sunn-ghaoth, -ghaoithe, *s. f.* A boast, a gasconade.

Sunn-ghaothar, *a.* Boastful; vain, blustering. Gu sunnghaothar, *boastfully.*

Sunnt. See Sunnd.

Sunrach, *a.* (*Ir. id.*) Particular, special.

Sunraich, *v. a.* Appoint, ordain, determine, order; mark out. See Sonraich.

Sunraichte. See Sonraichte.

Suntaidh, *a.* Quick.

Sùr, *a.* (*Arm.* sùr. *Teut.* suer *and* soer.) Sour.

Sùrag, aig. *s. f.* Wood-sorrel.

Sùragach, *a.* Abounding in wood-sorrel; like wood-sorrel.

Sùrd, *s.* Industry; alertness, cleverness; preparation or bestirring for work or business. Cuir sùrd ort, *bestir thyself, prepare thyself for business.*

Sùrdag, aig, *s. f.* A bound, a stride, a bounce, a caper. A gearradh shùrdag, *cutting capers, bounding.—Macdon.* and *Macint.* A teachd le sùrdag, *coming with a bound.—Macfar. N. pl.* surdagan.

Surdagach, *a.* Bounding; striding; bouncing; apt to bound or bounce. An eilid shurdagach, *the bounding roe.*

Surdagaich, *v. n.* Bound, stride, bounce. *Pret. a.* shurdagaich, *bounded; fut. aff. a.* surdagaichidh, *shall bound.*

Surdail, *a.* (surd-amhuil.) Industrious, active, clever; pushing, shifty. Gu surdail, *industriously.*

Surdalachd, *s. f.* (*from* sùrd.) Industriousness, activity, alertness.

Surram, aim, *s. f.* A snoring noise, as of one asleep.

Surtag, aig, *s. f.* See Surdag.

Susbuin, *s. f.* (*Ir. id.*) Substance; strength; stamina; virtue.

Susdalach, **Sustalach**, *a.* Prudish, affected, coy, shy. Caileag shusdalach, *a shy girl. Com.* and *sup.* susdalaiche.

Susdalachd, **Sustalachd**, *s. f.* Prudishness, affectedness, coyness.

Sùth, sùtha, *s. m.* See Sùgh.

Sùthag, aig, *s. f.* A strawberry, a raspberry.

Suthain, *a.* (*Ir. id.*) Eternal, everlasting; *rarely*, prosperous. Gu suthain siorruidh, *for ever and ever.*

Suthaineachd, *s. f.* (*Ir.* suthaineacht.) Eternity. A thus na suthaineachd, *from all eternity.*

Sùth-bhrigh, *s. f.* Decoction, juice, extract, essence.

Sùth-bhrigheach, *a.* Juicy.

Sùth-bhrighear, **Sùth-bhrighmhor**, *a.* Juicy.

Sùthmhoire, *com.* and *sup.* of sùthmhor.

Sùthmhor, *a.* (*Ir.* suthmhor.) Juicy, sappy. *Com.* and *sup.* sùthmhoire.

Suthmhorachd, *s. f.* Juiciness, sappiness.

T.

T, t, (tin.) The seventeenth letter of the Gaelic alphabet. T, not aspirated, has two sounds: (1.) Nearly like *t* in *town;* or exactly like *t* in the Italian, *tocco,* or in the French, *toucher.* (2). A slender sound, like *ch* in *cheek;* as, tighinn, *coming;* saillte, *salted.* When aspirated, it sounds like *h* in *him;* as, thainig, *came.* It is silent in the middle of words, in the end of long syllables, in some tenses of certain verbs irregular, and in *thu* and *thusa;* as, maitheas, *goodness;* maoth, *gentle;* an d' thainig thu? *art thou come?*

T- is placed between the *def. art.* and the *nom. sing. mas.* of most nouns beginning with a vowel. Is mi féin an t-aonaran truagh, *a poor solitary being am I.—Oss. Taura.* An t-eug a strigh ris, *death struggling with him.—Id.*

T- is also inserted between the *def. art.* and any noun beginning with s followed by a vowel or a liquid. Mun d' thainig an t-saighead is an t-sìne, *before the arrow and the blast came.—Ardar.* An t-sloc a rinn casan nan aoidhean, *the pit made by the feet of strangers.—Oss.* Toirm an t-sruthain, *the purling of the stream.—Oss. Conn.*

T' and T- are often used for the *poss. pron.* do, *thy*, before words beginning with a vowel, or with a quiescent consonant; as, Tog t-or-cheann, *lift thy golden head.—Orr.* T-airde mar dharraig, *thy height like an oak.—Ull.* See almost every chapter of Stewart's Translation of the Old Testament.

T', *for* ta *or* tha, *pres. ind.* of the *aux. verb,* bi, *be.* Am, art, is, are.

Ta, *pres. ind.* of bi. Am, art, is, are.

† **Ta**, *s. m.* Water; *also*, the Tay.

Tabaid, *s. f.* (*Arm.* tabut.) A fight; a squabble; a conflict; a broil. *N. pl.* tabaidean.

Tabaideach, *a.* Quarrelsome, fond of squabbles, causing squabbles; of, or belonging to, a quarrel or squabble.

Tabaideachd, *s. f.* Quarrelsomeness, fondness for squabbling.

Tabar, air, *s. m.* A timbrel, a tabor. *N. pl.* tabaran.

Tabh, taibh, *s.* The ocean; a sea; a sort of fishing net.

Tabhach, *a.* Marine; *also*, strong, lusty.

Tabhach, aich, *s. m.* (*Ir. id.*) A sudden eruption; a forcing, a pressing.

Tabhachd, *s. f.* (*Ir.* tadhbhacht.) Substance; stoutness; comeliness; valour; effect; benefit. Taisbeinibh ur tabhachd, *show your valour.—Old Song.* B' i bhlath-ghrian do thabhachd, *the warm sun was thy benefit.—Macdon.*

Tabhachdach, *a.* (*Ir.* tabhachdach.) Stout, comely, substantial; effectual, effective; beneficial. Gu tabhachdach, *effectually. Com.* and *sup.* tabhachdaiche.

Tabhain, *v. n.* (*Ir.* tafain.) Bark, yelp. *Pret. a.* thabhain, *barked; fut. aff. a.* tabhainidh, *shall bark.*

Tabhair, *v. irr.* (*Ir. id.*) Give, bestow, grant; bring. *Pret.* thug, *gave; fut. aff.* bheir. Do 'm bhriathraibh tabhair aire, *give ear to my words.—Sm.* Tabhair mach, *bring out; produce.* Gach craobh a bheir mach meas, *every tree that yields fruit.—Stew. Gen.* Tabhairinn, *I would give.* Written also *thoir.*

Tabhaiream, 1 *sing. imper.* of tabhair. Let me give.

† **Tabhairn**, *s. f.* A tavern, an inn; a sea.
Lat. taberna. *Arm.* tavarn. *Teut.* taverne. *Ir.* tabhairne, *a tavern.*

Tabhairt, *s. f.* A giving or granting; a grant, a gift, a bestowal. A tabhairt, *giving; granting;* tabhairt an geall, *pledging; mortgaging.*

Tabhairteach, *a.* Liberal, generous; ready to give; dative. Gu tabhairteach, *liberally. Com.* and *sup.* tabhairtiche.

Tabhairteachd, *s.* Liberality, generosity; a readiness to give or bestow.

Tabhairtear, eir, *s. m.* A giver, a donor. *N. pl.* tabhairtearan.

Tabhal, **Tabhall**, aill, *s. m.* (*Lat.* catapulta.) A sling from which stones were cast; *rarely*, a chief. Crann tabhail, *the shaft of a sling.*

† **Tabhal**, ail, *s. m.* A plank; a board; a chief.

Tabhan, ain, *s. m.* (*Ir.* tafan.) A bark, a yelp.

Tabhanaich, *v. n.* Bark, yelp. *Pret. a.* thabhanaich, *barked; fut. aff.* tabhanaichidh, *shall bark.*

Tabhanaich, *s. f.* Barking, yelping; continued barking. Thoisich an cu air tabhanaich, *the dog began to bark.*

Tabhartach, *a.* (*Ir.* tabharthach.) Bountiful, generous.

Tabhartan, ain, *s. m.* A leader, a general. *N. pl.* tabhartain.

Tabhartas, ais, *s. m.* (*Ir. id.*) An offering; a present, or gift; a boon. Tabhartas luaisgte, *a wave-offering.—Stew. Exod.* Tabhartas dibhe, *a drink-offering.—Id.* Tabhartas togta, *a heave-offering.—Stew. Num.* Tabhartas Bhenuis, *the gift of Venus.—Mac Lach.*

Tabhram, (*for* tabhaiream), 1 *sing. imper.* of tabhair. Let me give.

Tabhuan, *a.* Persevering; *substantively*, perseverance.

Tabhuanachd, *s. f.* Perseverance.

Tabhuil, *a.* In order.

Tabhull, uill, *s.* See **Tabhal**.

Tabhuin, *v. n.* Bark, yelp. Written also *tabhain.*

Tabhun, uin, *s. m.* (*Ir.* tafan.) A bark, or yelp Written also *tabhan.*

Tabhunaich, *s. f.* Barking or yelping; continued or frequent barking.—*Macint*

Tabhunaich, *v. a.* (*from* tabhun) Bark, yelp. *Pret. a* thabhunaich; *fut. aff. a.* tabhunaichidh, *shall bark.*

Tac, *v. a.* See **Tachd**.

Tac, *s.* A tack, or small nail; a peg, a prop; a surety. *Eng.* tack. *Corn. Arm.* tach. *Span* tachuela *and* tacho, *little nails*, the Latin *patagum*, too, means, according to Nonnius, a little golden skewer used by the Roman ladies

Tac, *s. m.* A time; a lease.

Tacaid, *s. f.* (*from* tac) *Ir id Arm Corn* tach. A tack, or small nail; a peg; a large-headed nail for ornament; a stud, or knob; a stitch, or sudden pain. *N pl.* tacaidean; *d. pl.* tacaidibh; le tacaidibh airgid, *with silver studs.—Stew. Song Sol.* Bhuail tacaid mi, *a pain has seized me.—Old Song.*

Tacaideach, *a.* (*from* tacaid.) Full of nails, causing sudden pain, agonizing. Brògan tacaideach, *shoes with tacks in their soles and heels.*

Tacaidich, *v. a.* Stick full of tacks. *Pret. a.* thacaidich.

Tacail, *a.* (*Ir. id.*) Strong, solid, able

Tacain, *s. f.* A while, a short space of time; also *gen. sing.* of tacan.

Tacan, ain, *s m.* (*from* tac.) A while, a short space of time. Tacan mun do sheòl sinn, *a while before we sailed.* —*Old Song.* Eadar so is ceann tacain, *in a little time hence.*

Tacar, air. See **Tachdar**.

Tachair, *v.* (*Ir. id*) Meet, happen, or come to pass *Pret.* thachair, *met; fut. aff.* tachairidh, *shall happen.* Thachair dhomh dol, *I happened to go —Stew Ruth.* Tachair ri, *oppose, resist;* tachair ris, *oppose him, match him;* tachair air, *meet him.* Is truagh mar a thachair, *sad is the occurrence.—Macint*

Tachairidh, *fut. aff* of tachair.

Tachairt, *s. f.* A meeting; opposition, or the act of opposing. Fhuair e tachairt ris, *he met with his match.*

Tachairt, (a), *pr. part.* of tachair. • Meeting, happening; opposing Leig dhomhsa tachairt ris an laoch, *let me oppose the hero.—Oss. Tem.*

Tachais, *v. a* Scratch; remove an itching sensation by rubbing. *Pret. a.* thachais; *fut. aff* tachaisidh, *shall scratch.*

Tachan, ain, *s. m.* A kind of martin

† **Tachar**, air, *s. m* (*Ir. id.*) A fight, a skirmish, a squabble

Tacharan, ain, *s. m* (*Ir. id.*) A spectre, a ghost; a feeble, timid person; an orphan. *N. pl* tacharain.

Tachas, ais, *s. m.* (*Ir.* tochus) Itch, mange; an itching Tachas tiorram, *scurvy.—Stew. Lev.*

Tachasach, *a.* Itchy, mangy; itching. Cluasan tachasach, *itching ears.—Stew. Tim*

Tachd, *s. m.* See **Tachdadh**.

Tachd, *v. a.* and *n.* (*Ir* tacht.) Choke, strangle *Pret. a* thachd, *choked; fut. aff.* tachdaidh, *shall choke, fut. pass.* tachdar, *shall be choked.*

Tachdach, *a.* Causing strangulation; suffocating.

Tachdadh, aidh, *s. m.* (*Ir.* tachtadh.) Strangling; suffocation; *rarely*, a promise, security. Is fearr le m' anam tachdadh, *my soul chooseth strangling —Stew. Job.*

Tachdaidh, *fut. aff* of tachd.

Tachdar, *fut. pass.* of tachd Shall or will be choked

Tachdar, air, *s. m.* (*Ir. id. Heb.* dagar, *to collect, heap*) Provision, fish, multitude; *also*, gleaning Tachdar mara 'cur làn 's gach lion, *sea-fish filling every net.—Old Song*

Tachdarach, *a.* Having provision, relating to provision.

Tachdrach, *a* See **Tachdarach**

Tachdta, Tachdte, *p part* of tachd. Choked, strangled

Tachraidh See **Tachairidh**.

Ta 'd, (*poetical contraction* of ta iad.) They are. Ta 'd truaillidh, *they are corrupt.—Sm.* Ta 'd nan eire, *they are a burden —Id*

† **Tad**, *s m.* (*Ir. id*) Lowness of spirits; a thief.

Tadaidh. See **Tàlaidh**.

† **Tadhach**, *a.* (*Ir id*) Unsavoury.

Tadhach, aich, *s m* A ledge. Eadar na tadhacha, *between the ledges —Stew* 1 *K*

Tadhaill, *v.* Visit, haunt See **Taoghail**.

Tadhal, ail, *s m* (*Ir id*) A flesh-hook; the sense of feeling.

Tadhasg, aisg, *s. m* News, information.

Tadhlach, aich, *s* (*Ir. id*) A swelling or pain in the wrist

Tafach, *a* Craving.

Tafach, aich, *s m* An exhortation.

Tàg, *s m* A blow on the cheek.

Tagair, *v. a.* (*Ir. id*) Plead, claim, dispute, debate. *Pret. a* thagair, *fut aff* tagraidh Tagraidh e 'n cùis, *he will plead their cause.* Thagaireadh am fireann, *the righteous would dispute —Stew. Job. Fut pass* tagrar.

Tagairt, *s f* A claiming; a pleading, a debating; a plea

Tagar, air, *s. m.* (*Ir. id*) An order, a course.

Tagarach, *a.* Fond of pleading; debating

Tagaradh, aidh, *s m.* See **Tagradh**.

Tagarair, *s. m* (*Ir.* tagarthoir) A pleader, a disputant, a claimant.

Tagh, *v. a* (*Ir.* togh) Choose, select *Pret* thagh, *chose, fut. aff. a* taghaidh, *shall choose.*

Tagha. See **Taghadh**.

Taghach, *a* Elective; choosing.

Taghadair, *s m* An elector; a chooser; a selector *N pl* taghadairean

Taghadaireachd, *s. f* The business of an elector, an electing; an electorate

Taghadh, aidh, *s. m.* (*Ir* togha) The act or the circumstance of choosing, a choice, selection; election. Roghadh is taghadh, *pick and choice* Luchd taghadh, *or* luchd tagha, *electors*, the body-guard of a Highland regiment was also so called. This band consisted of chosen men, and all of the same clan They fared at the same table with the chieftain; and each enjoyed his hospitality according to his deserts.

Taghadraidh, *s. f.* An electorate

Taghadroinn, *s. f* An electorate

Taghaidh, *fut aff. a.* of tagh. Shall choose.

Taghairm, *s. f* (*Ir* togharm) A sort of divination, an echo; a petition; a summons.

The divination by the *taghairm* was once a noted superstition among the Gael, and in the northern parts of the Lowlands of Scotland When any important question concerning futurity arose, and of which a solution was, by all means, desirable, some shrewder person than his neighbours was pitched upon, to perform the part of a prophet This person was wrapped in the warm smoking hide of a newly-slain ox or cow, commonly an ox, and laid at full length in the wildest recess of some lonely waterfall The question was then put to him, and the oracle was left in solitude to consider it Here he lay for some hours with his cloak of knowledge around him, and over his head, no doubt, to see the better into futurity, deafened by the incessant roaring of the torrent, every sense assailed, his body steaming, his fancy was in ferment, and whatever notion had found its way into his mind from so many sources of prophecy, it was firmly believed to have been communicated by invisible beings who were supposed to haunt such solitudes.

TAGHAIRMEACH, *a.* Responsive, prophetic, oracular; echoing.

TAGHALL. See TAOGHALL.

TAGHAR, air, *s. m.* (*Ir. id.*) A distant noise.

TAGH-GHUTH, *s. m.* (*Ir.* toghuth.) A vote or suffrage, a voice at an election.

TAGHTA, TAGHTE, *pr. part.* of tagh. (*Ir.* toghta.) Chosen; select; choice. Or taghta, *choice gold.*—*Stew. Pro.* Daoine taghta, *chosen* or *picked men;* also, *the elect.*

TAGLUINN, *s. f.* A contest, a squabble; animosity. Luchd tagluinn, *quarrelsome persons.*

TAGLUINNEACH, *a.* Quarrelsome, squabbling; contestable.

TAGRACH, *a.* (*for* tagarach.) Pleading, advocating; claiming; prone to plead or to claim; relating to pleading.

TAGRADAIR, *s. m.* A pleader, an advocate; a claimant. *N. pl.* tagradairean.

TAGRADAIREACHD, *s. f.* The business of a pleader or advocate.

TAGRADH, aidh, *s. m.* A pleading; advocating; a claiming.

TAGRAIDH, *fut. aff.* of tagair.

TAIBEAN, ein, *s. m.* Tabby.

TAIBHLEAS, eis, *s. m.* A backgammon table, the game of backgammon.

† TAIBHREADH, idh, *s. m.* A dream.—*Shaw.*

TAIBHREAL, eil, *s.* Laurel. More properly *laibhreal* or *laibhreas;* which see.

TAIBHREALACH, *a.* Abounding in laurel; of, or belonging to, laurel.

TAIBHSE, *s. m.* (*Ir. id. Arab.* tabish.) A ghost or apparition; a vision. *N. pl.* taibhsean. Taibhsean an t-sleibh, *the ghosts of the moor.*—*Oss. Fin. and Lor.* A thaibhse! togaibh leibh e, *ye ghosts! bear him along with you.*—*Ull.*

TAIBHSDEAR, eir, *s. m.* A seer, or one gifted with the second sight. *N. pl.* taibhsdearan.

TAIBHSDEARACHD, *s. f.* (*from* taibhse.) The second sight, or the faculty of seeing otherwise invisible objects.

I consider that some account of the Highland seers, and of their predictions, will not here be misplaced nor unacceptable.

At the sight of a vision of this kind, Dr. Martin observes, the eyelids of the gifted person were erected, and the eyes continued staring till the vision disappeared. If an object is seen in the morning, it will be accomplished in the afternoon; if at noon, on that very day; if in the evening, that very night; and if after candles are lit, on that night for certain. If a shroud is seen about a person, it foretells approaching death; and the time of it is more or less distant, according to the height at which the shroud is observed on the body. If it be seen about the middle, death is not expected within a twelvemonth; if as high as the head, it is not many hours distant. To see a spark of fire falling on one's arm, foretells that a dead child shall be seen in the arms of that person. To see a chair empty at the time a person sits in it, is a sure sign of approaching death to that person. Seers did not observe supernatural appearances at the same time, though they might happen to be in the same apartment; but when one of them who saw a vision, touched any number of his brethren, they all saw it as well as the first.

Having said this much of seers, and of the second sight, it may be amusing to many, to know how far the prophecies and the fulfilments agreed. For this purpose I select an instance or two recorded by an English nobleman in the seventeenth century, who, previous to his going to the Highlands, was one of the sturdiest unbelievers in the second sight.

"SIR,—I heard very much, and believed very little, of the second sight; yet its being assumed by severall of great veracitie, I was induced to make inquirie after it, in the year 1652, being confined to abide in the North of Scotland, by the English usurpers. * * *

" * * * I was travelling in the Highlands, and a good number of servants with me, as is usual there. One of them going a little before me, entering into a house where I was to stay all night, and going hastily to the door, he suddenly stept back with a screech, and did fall by a stone which hit his foot. I asked what the matter was, for he seemed to be very much frighted. He told me very seriously that I should not lodge in that house, because shortly a dead coffin would be carried out of it, for many were carrying of it when he was heard to cry. I neglecting his words, and staying there, he said to the other servants he was sorry for it, and that surely what he saw would come to pass. Tho' no sick person was then there, yet the landlord died of ane apoplectick fit before I left the house.

" * * * I shall trouble you with but one more which I thought the most remarkable of any that occurred to me. In January 1652, Lieut. Col. Alex. Munro, and I, were in the house of one Wm. M'Leud, of Ferinlea, in the county of Ross. He, the landlord, and I, were sitting on three chairs neir the fire; and in the corner of the great chimney there were two islanders, who were that *very night* come to the house, and were related to the landlord. While the one of them was talking to Munro, I perceived the other to look oddly toward me. From his look, and his being an islander, I conjectured him a seer, and asked him what he staired at? He answered me by desiring me to rise from the chair, for it was ane unluckie one. I asked him why? He answered, because there is a dead man in the chair next to me. Well, said I, if he be in the next chair to me, I may keep mine own. But what is the likeness of the man? He said he was a tall man with a long grey coat, booted, and one of his legs hanging over the arme of the chair, and his head hanging dead on the other side, and his arm backward, as if it was broken. There were some English troops then quartered near that place, and there being at that time a great frost after a thaw, the country was covered all over with yce. Four or five of the English ryding by this hous some two hours after the vision, while we were sitting by the fire, we heard a great noise, which proved to be those troopers, with the help of other servants, carrying in one of their number, who had a very mischievous fall, and had his arme broke; and falling frequently in swooning fits, they brought him into the hall, and set him on the verie chair, and in the verie posture that the seer prophecied. But the man did not die, though he recovered with great difficulty.

"Among the accounts given me by Sir Norman M'Lud, there was one worthy of special notice, which was thus:—There was a gentleman in the isle of Harris, who was always seen by the seers with an arrow in his thigh. Such in the isle who thought these prognostications infallible, did not doubt but he would be shot in the thigh before he died. Sir Norman told me that he heard it the subject of their discourse for many years. At last he died without any such accident. Sir Norman was at his burial at St. Clement's Church in the Harris. At the same time the corpse of another gentleman was brought to be buried in the verie same church. The friends on either side came to debate who should first enter the church, and in a trice from words they came to blows. One of the number, who was armed with a bow and arrows, let one fly among them. (Now everie familie in that isle have their burial place in the church in stone chests, and the bodies are carried in open biers to the burial place.) Sir Norman having appeased the tumult, one of the arrows was found shot in the dead man's thigh. To this Sir Norman was a witness.

"These are matters of fact which, I assure you, are truely related."—*Succinct Accompt of my Lord Tarbolt's Relations, in a Letter to the Hon. Robert Boyle, Esquire, of the Predictions made by Seers, whereof himself was Ear and Eye-witness.*

I have seen a work on the second sight, by one who styles himself 'Theophilus Insulanus,' wherein is recorded a great variety of cases where these visions were exactly fulfilled, and in so satisfactory a way, that many of the Highland clergy became believers in the existence of this faculty. Either Dr. Beattie must not have been aware of this circumstance, or he threw out a galling sarcasm when he said that none but the most ignorant pretended to be gifted with the second sight.

These cases of shadowy prediction will enable the reader to balance the conflicting opinions entertained on the curious subject of the second sight; the one by Dr. Beattie of Aberdeen, and the other by the celebrated Dr. Samuel Johnson. The former ascribes this pretended faculty wholly to the influence of physical causes on superstitious and uninstructed minds. He thinks that long tracts of mountainous deserts, covered with dark heath, and often obscured by misty weather, narrow valleys, thinly inhabited, and bounded by precipices resounding with the fall of torrents, the mournful dashing of waves along the friths and lakes that intersect the country, the grotesque and ghastly appearance of such a landscape by the light of the moon, must diffuse a gloom over the fancy, which may be compatible enough with occasional and social merriment, but cannot fail to tincture the thoughts of a native in the hour of silence and solitude: that it is not wonderful if persons of a lively imagination, immured in deep solitude, and surrounded with the stupendous scenery of clouds, precipices, and torrents, should dream (even when they think themselves awake) of those few striking ideas, with which their lonely lives are diversified, of corpses, funeral processions, and other subjects of terror; or of marriages, and the arrival of strangers, and such like matters of more agreeable curiosity: that none but ignorant people pretend to be gifted in this way, and that in them it may be nothing more, perhaps, than short fits of sudden sleep or drowsiness, attended with lively dreams, and arising from bodily disorder, the effect of idleness, low spirits, or a gloomy imagination. Nor is it extraordinary, he observes, that one should have the appearance of being awake, and should even think one's self so, during those fits of dozing; that they should come on suddenly, and while one is engaged in some business. The same thing happens to persons much fatigued, or long kept awake, who frequently fall asleep for a moment, or for a long space, while they are standing, or walking, or riding on horseback: add but a lively dream to this slumber, and (which is the frequent effect of disease) take away the consciousness of having been asleep, and a superstitious man may easily mistake his dream for a waking vision. Beattie disbelieves the prophetical nature of the second sight; and does not think it analogous to the operations of Providence, nor to the course of nature, that the Deity should work a miracle in order to give intimation of the frivolous matters which were commonly predicted by seers; and that these intimations should be given for no end, and to those persons only who are idle and solitary, who speak Gaelic, or who live among mountains and deserts.

To these objections it has been powerfully replied by Dr. Johnson, that by presuming to determine what is fit, and what is beneficial, they presuppose more knowledge of the universal system than man has hitherto attained; and therefore depend upon principles too complicated and extensive for our comprehension, and that there can be no security in the consequence when the premises are not understood: that the second sight is only wonderful because it is rare, for, considered in itself, it involves no more difficulty than dreams, or perhaps the regular exercise of the cogitative faculty: that a general opinion of communicative impulses, or visionary representations, has prevailed in all ages and nations: that particular instances have been given with such evidence as neither Bacon nor Bayle have been able to resist; that sudden impressions, which the event has verified, have been felt by more than own or publish them; that the second sight of the Hebrides implies only the local frequency of a power which is no where totally unknown; and that where we are unable to decide by antecedent reason, we must be content to yield to the force of testimony. By pretension to second sight, no profit was ever sought or gained. It is an involuntary affection, in which neither hope nor fear are known to have any part. Those who profess to feel it do not boast of it as a privilege, nor are considered by others as advantageously distinguished. They have no temptation to feign, and their hearers have no motives to encourage the imposture.

Taibhsean, *n. pl.* of taibhse.

Taibhsear. See Taibhsdear.

Taibhsearachd, *s. f.* See Taibhsdearachd.

Taibhseil, *a.* (taibhse-amhuil.) Ghostly, ghastly, spectral.

† **Taibhsich**, *v. n.* (*Ir.* taibhsigh.) Reveal; appear; seem. *Pret. a.* thaibhsich; *fut. aff.* taibhsichidh.

Taic, taice, *s. m.* Support; a prop; leaning; dependence. Cum taic ris, *support him; patronize him.* Laoich ri sleaghan an taic, *heroes leaning on their spears.—Ull.* Shuidh iad ri taic, *they sat leaning backwards.—Mac Lach.* An taice, *leaning—(Stew. Song. Sol.); also,* in conjunction, near.

Taiceachd, *s. f.* Great exertion.

Taiceadh, idh, *s. m.* A supporting; a recommending; a depending; dependence.

Taiceil, *a.* (taic-amhuil.) Stout; firm, solid.

Taid, Taitidh, *s. m.* (*W.* tad. *Arm.* tât. *Scotch,* dad.) An infantile name for a father.

Taid, (*a poetical contraction of* a ta iad.) They are.

Taidhean, ein, *s. m.* (*Ir. id.*) A troop, a multitude, a cavalcade; a mill-pond.

Taidhleach, *a.* (*Ir. id.*) Splendid; delightful; pleasant. *Com.* and *sup.* taidhliche.

Taidhleachd, *s. f.* (*Ir. id.*) Splendidness; pleasantness.

Taif, *s.* (*from* † ta.) The ocean. An taif fo bhruailean, *the sea* [*in agitation*] *in a storm.—Oss. Fing.*

Swed. haf, *whence* haven. To the Celtic root *ta* may be traced the names of all waters which begin with *ta* or *tam.*

Taifeid, *s. f.* A bow-string. Taifeid san osaig a fuaim, *a bow-string sounding in the wind.—Oss.* Fo thaifeid theann, *under a tight bow-string.—Oss. Tem.*

Taifeid, *s. f.* Taffety.—*Macd.*

† **Taifnichte**, *part.* Driven away by force.

† **Taig**, *s. f.* (*Ir. id.*) Custom.

Taigeis, *s. f.* A haggis, or kind of blood-pudding, much relished by the Scotch and Gael. It is made up of various ingredients, and has been named by the celebrated Burns, in an ode addressed to it, the chieftain of the pudding race.

Taigeis, *s. f.* The scrotum.

Tail, *a.* Solid, substantial.

Tailce, *s. f.* (*Ir. id.*) Force, vigour.

Tailceanach, *a.* (*Ir. id.*) Stately.

Tailceas, eis, *s. m.* Contempt; reproach; spite; provocation. Com' an dean iad tailceas ort? *why do they reproach thee?—Sm.*

Tailceasach, *a.* Contemptuous, reproachful; spiteful.—*Sm.* Gu tailceasach, *contemptuously. Com.* and *sup.* tailceasaiche.

Tailceasachd, *s. f.* Contemptuousness; reproachfulness; spitefulness.

Taile, *s. f.* Solidity, substance, matter; means; a lump, wages.

Taileabart, airt, *s. m.* A halbert.—*Macd. N. pl.* taileabartan.

Taileasg, eisg, *s. f.* Sport, game, mirth; chess, backgammon, draughts. Gun taileasg, gun cheòl, *without mirth or music.—Old Song.* Cluich air thaileasg, *playing at chess.—Macint.*

Taileil, *a.* (taile-amhuil.) *Ir. id.* Substantial, solid.

Taileileachd, *s. f.* Solidness, substantialness.

† **Tailgean**, ein, *s. m.* (*Ir. id.*) A holy offspring; a religious soldier of God.

Tailisg, *s. f.* A war instrument.

† **Taille**, *s. f.* (*Ir. id. Gr.* τέλος, *tax. Fr.* taille.) Wages, tax, tribute.

Tàillear, eir, *s. m.* A tailor. Tailear gun eolas, *an ignorant tailor.—Mac Co.*

Tailleireachd, *s. f.* The business of a tailor.

Taillse, *s. m.* A spectre or apparition.

Tailm, *s. m.* An instrument or utensil; a snare, a gin.—*Macd.*

Tailmsich, *s. f.* A noise, confusion, bustle.

Tailp, *s. f.* A bundle, bunch.

Taim, (*Ir. id.*) *poetical contraction of* ta mi *or* tha mi. I am. Taim sgith le m' osnaigh, *I am weary with groaning.—Sm.*

† **Taim**, *s. f.* (*Ir. id.*) A town.

Taimh, *gen. sing.* of tamh.

Taimh, *s. f.* (*Ir. id.*) Death; mortality; fainting.

Taimhleac, -lic, *s. f.* (*Ir.* taimhleacht.) A grave-stone; *literally,* the stone of rest; a heap of stones, collected on the spot where a person has been killed or buried.

Taimhleasg. See Taileasg.

Taimhneul, -neoil, *s. m.* (*Ir. id.*) A slumber; a trance, or swoon; ecstasy. Thuit e ann an taimh-neul, *he fell into a swoon.*

Taimhneul, *v. n.* Slumber; fall into a sleep, fall into a swoon.

Taimhneulach, *a.* Like a slumber, like a trance or swoon; of, or belonging to, a slumber or trance.

Tain, *s. f.* (*Ir. id.*) Water. Folach tain, *water parsnip.*

Tàin, *s. f.* Cattle, cows, flocks—(*Macint.*); land, country. *N. pl.* taintean. A chreach 's a mhor thàintean, *his booty and his numerous flocks.—Old Poem.*

Taine, *com.* and *sup.* of tana; which see.

Taine, *s. f.* Thinness, slenderness, leanness.

Tainead, eid, *s. m.* (*Lat.* tenuitas.) Thinness, tenacity; increase in thinness. A dol an tainead, *growing more and more thin.* Ar cunntas dol an tainead, *our numbers growing less numerous.—Old Song.*

† **Taineantach**, *a.* Darting a double ray, corruscating.

Taing, *s. f.* (*Ir. id. Goth.* danc. *Eng.* thank.) Thanks; gratitude; obligation. Taing is buidheachas duit, *many thanks to you;* gun taing dhuit, *without thanks to you, in spite of you.*

Taingealachd, *s. f.* Thankfulness, gratefulness.

Taingeil, *a.* (taing-amhuil.) Thankful, grateful. Gu taingeil, *thankfully.*

Tainistear, eir, *s. m.* A second son; a regent, a governor; a lord, a peer; the third name of dignity among the ancient Caledonians.

Tainisteireachd, *s. f.* Regency; dynasty; thanisty.

Tainstre, *s. pl.* Ancient laws or regulations.

Tainntean, ein, *s. m.* (*perhaps* toinntean.) A thread.

Tainnteanach, *a.* Thready, filmy, viscous.

Tainte, *s. f.* (*Ir. id.*) Booty, prey, spoil.

Tàintean, *n. pl.* of tàin; which see.

Taip, *s. f.* (*Ir. id. W.* taip, *a rock. Eng.* top. *Scotch*, tap.) A mass or lump; a rock.

Malcolm, a most ingenious antiquary, observes, that in Terra Firma, in South America, there is a hill called Tapaconti. This word is compounded of *taip*, a rock, *connadh*, wood; and *ti*, the Kilda word for great. This word, and many others (see *ti, an, ab,* &c.) seen throughout this work, seem to prove that America was peopled from the old world.

† **Tair**, *prep.* Over, beyond. Now written *thar.*

Tàir, tàire, *s. m.* (*Ir. id.*) Disgrace; contempt; reproach. Tàir cha do rinneas air neach, *I treated no man with contempt.—Old Poem.* Fuidh thàir, *despised.—Stew. Job.* Gun taise, gun tàir, *without effeminacy or reproach.—Mac Co.*

Tairbeart, eirt, *s. m.* A peninsula.

Tairbeartach, *a.* Peninsular.

Tairbh, *gen. sing.* and *n. pl.* of tarbh.

Tairbhe, *s. f.* (*Ir. id.*) Gain, profit, advantage; avail, benefit. Nithe gun tairbhe, *things without profit.—Stew. Jer.* Tairbhe eucorach, *unjust gain;* tairbhe cha dean t-òrchul rèidh, *thy smooth yellow hair cannot avail.—Mac Lach.*

Tairbhealach, aich, *s. m.* (*Ir. id.*) A defile, a pass, a narrow valley, a mountain valley; *rarely*, a ferry.

Tair-bheart, -bheirt, *s. m.* A liberal action. *N. pl.* tairbheirt *and* tairbheartan.

Tairbheartach, *a.* (*Ir. id.*) Liberal, beneficial; fruitful, profitable.

Tairbheirt, *s. f.* (*Ir. id.*) Turpentine.

Tàir-chainnt, *s. f.* Reproachful language, vituperation.

Tàir-chainnteach, *a.* Reproachful, vituperative. Gu tairchainnteach, *reproachfully.—Stew. Jud.*

Tairchheadal, ail, *s. m.* A prophecy.

Tair-chreich, *s. f.* Desert; merit.

Tàireach, *a.* Vile.

Tàireachd, *s. f.* Contemptuousness, reproachfulness, baseness; long life.

Tàiread, eid, *s. m.* Vileness, contempt; increase in contempt. A dol an tàiread, *growing more and more contemptible.*

Taireag, eig, *s. f.* (*Ir. id.*) Provision; preparation.

Tairealachd, *s. f.* See **Tairealachd.**

Tairéam, eim, *s. m.* Dispraise, disparagement.

Taireamach, *a.* Disparaging.

Tairean, ein, *s. m.* (*Ir. id.*) A descent.

Taireasg, eisg, *s. f.* A spade for cutting turf; a file; a saw.

Taireasg-luaithre, *s.* Sawdust.

Tàireil, *a.* (tàir-amhuil.) Contemptuous, reproachful; degrading, disgraceful; despised, disgraced, base, vile. A chainnt tàireil, *his speech contemptible.—Stew. 2 Cor.* Tàireil na shuilibh, *despised in his sight.—Stew. Gen.* Gach ni bha tàireil, *every thing that was vile.—Stew. Sam.*

Taireileachd, *s. f.* Contemptuousness, reproachfulness, disgracefulness, vileness.

Taireis, *adv.* (tar eis, *on the track.*) *Ir. id.* After, afterwards, afterhand. Taireis mo chur san uaigh, *after I am in my grave.—Sm.*

Tairg, *v. a.* (*Ir. id.*) Offer; bid; nail. *Pret. a.* thairg; *fut. aff. a.* tairgidh, *shall offer; fut. pass.* tairgear, *shall be offered.* Tairgear uan geal diutse, a ghrian! *a white lamb shall be offered to thee, O sun!—Mac Lach.*

Tairgeadh, idh, *s. m.* (*Ir. id.*) An endeavour; a going, a passing; a nailing.

Tairgeam, (*for* tairgidh mi.) I shall or will offer.

Tairgear, *fut. pass.* of tairg.

Tairgeug, geuga, *s. m.* A graft.

Tairgheag, eig, *s. f.* (*Ir. id.*) An imp, a brat.

Tairgheal, eil, *s. m.* An offering, an oblation.

Tairgre, *s. f.* (*Ir. id.*) A prophecy.

Tairgreach, *a.* Prophetic; soothsaying, rhyming.

Tairgreachd, *s. f.* A prophecy, a proverb.—*Stew. Is. ref.*

Tairgse, *s. f.* An offer. Thoir tairgse, *make an offer;* cuir na thairgse, *put in his offer.*

Tairgseach, *a.* Offering, ready to offer a price.

Tairis, *a.* Trusty, faithful; acceptable; loving, kind. Cha tairis leam ur faoilte, *your invitation is not acceptable to me.—Old Poem.* Guth tairis nam bard, *the mild voice of bards.—Oss. Tem.*

Tairise, *s. f.* (*Ir. id.*) Trustiness, fidelity; attachment; kindness.

Tairiseach, Tairisneach, *a.* Trusty; faithful; loyal.

Tairiseachd, Tairisneachd, *s. f.* Trustiness, fidelity; attachment; kindness. Deagh thairisneachd, *good fidelity.—Stew. Tit.*

Tairisean, ein, *s. m.* (*Ir.* tairisin.) A cross band or tye. *N. pl.* tairiseanan.

Tairisiomh, *a.* Dear, intimate, trusty, friendly.

Tairleach, *s. m.* A moisture.

Tairlearach, *a.* (tair *and* lear.) *Ir. id.* Transmarine.

Tairm, *s. f.* (*Ir. id.*) Necromancy.

Tairmcheall, ill, *s. m.* (*Ir. id.*) A circuit.

Tairn, *v. a.* (*for* tarruing.) Draw; pull; attract; nail. *Pret. a.* thairn, *drew; fut. aff.* tairnidh, *shall draw.* Tairnibh ur ràimh, *pull your oars.—Ull. Fut. pass.* tairnear.

Tairneach, *a.* (*for* tarruingeach.) Pulling, drawing; attractive, alluring. Le briathraibh tairneach, *with enticing words.—Stew. Col.*

Tairneach, ich, *s. m.* Thunder; a thundering noise. Tra ni tairneach neamh am bualadh, *when the lightning of heaven smites them.—Oss. Dargo.*

Tairneach, *a.* Thundering. Mar thannas air sleibhte tairneach, *like a ghost on the thundering mountains.—Oss. Cathula.*

Tairneanach, aich, *s. m.* Thunder; a thundering noise. Tairneanach agus clach mheallain, *thunder and hail.—Stew. Ex.* Peileir tairneanaich, *a thunderbolt.*

Tairng, *v. a.* Nail, fasten with nails. *Pret a.* thairng, *nailed; fut. aff.* tairngidh Tha d' fhardoch air a tairngeadh, *thy dwelling [coffin] is nailed.—Old Song*

Tairnge, *s. pl* (*Ir.* tairnge, *a nail.*) Nails, pegs.

Tairngire, *s. f.* A promise.

Tairngte, *p. part.* of tairng. (*Ir.* tairngthe) Nailed, *also, for* tarruingte, *drawn*

Tairnich, *v. n.* (*Ir. id*) Thunder; make a thundering noise. *Pret. a.* thairnich, *fut. aff.* tairnichidh.

Tairp, *s. m.* A clod.

Tairpeach, *a.* (*Ir. id*) Strong; grand, pompous; cloddy.

Tairseach, ich, *s. m.* (*Ir. id.*) The hinge of a door; a threshold.

Tairsgian, sgein, *s. f.* A spade for cutting turf.

Tair-shliabhach, *a.* Transmontane.

Tais, *a.* (*Ir. id.*) Soft, moist, wet, not hardy; remiss; relaxed; pitiful. *Com.* and *sup* taise.

Taisbean, *v. a.* See Taisbein.

Taisbean, ein, *s. m.* A revelation; a vision; an apparition; an appearance, a figure.

Taisbeanach, *a.* Of, or relating to, a revelation; revealing, discovering; of, or belonging to, an apparition or vision.

Taisbeanadh, aidh, *s. m.* (*Ir. id.*) A revealing, a revelation; evidence; demonstration; a demonstrating; an appearing, appearance.

Taisbeanar, *fut. pass.* of taisbean.

Taisbeanta, *a.* and *p part.* of taisbean. Revealed, discovered, shewn, presented. Aran taisbeanta, *shew-bread.—Stew. Ex.* The Irish say *aran taisbeanta*, in the same sense

Taisbein, *v. a.* Reveal, discover, shew. *Pret a.* thaisbein; *fut. aff.* taisbeinidh. Taisbein do chaoimhneas, *shew thy kindness.—Sm.*

Taisbeinte, *p. part.* of taisbein. Revealed, discovered, shewn; made evident.

Taisc, *s. m.* See Taisg

Taiscealach, *a.* Espying, viewing.

Taiscealladh, aidh, *s m.* A betraying.

Taisdeal, eil, *s. m.* A journey, a travel, a march; a voyage *N. pl.* taisdealan.

Taisdealach, *a.* Journeying, travelling; itinerant; like a traveller; of, or belonging to, a journey.

Taisdealach, aich, *s. m.* (*from* taisdeal) A traveller; a pedestrian, a pilgrim, a saunterer. *N pl.* taisdealaich Taisdealach bochd rùisgte, *a poor and naked traveller.—Old Song.*

Taisdealachd, *s f.* Travelling; pedestrianism; pilgrimage; sauntering, lounging.

Taisdealaiche, *s. m.* A traveller; a pedestrian; a pilgrim; a saunterer, a lounger.

Taise, *com* and *sup* of tais

Taise, *s. pl.* (*Ir. id*) Dead bodies; relics of saints.

Taise, *s. f.* (*Ir. id.*) Softness; moistness; effeminacy; timidity, weakness Gun taise, gun fhaitcheas, *without effeminacy or dread —Old Song*

Taiseachadh, aidh, *s m.* The act of softening or moistening; a growing effeminate, a making effeminate; softness; effeminacy.

Taiseachadh, (a), *pr. part* of taisich Softening, moistening, making effeminate. Air an taiseachadh le smior, *moistened with marrow.—Stew. Job.*

Taiseachd, *s. f.* (*Ir. id.*) Softness, moisture; effeminacy, timidity.

Taisead, eid, *s m.* Softness, moistness, timidity; increase in softness or timidity. A dol an taisead, *growing more and more soft or timid.*

Taiseag, eig, *s. f.* (*Ir. id.*) Restitution.

Taisealbh, *v. a.* (*Ir. id.*) Personate or represent.—*Shaw.*

Taisealbhadh, aidh, *s. m.* (*Ir. id.*) A representation, a likeness; exhibition.

Taisg, taisge, *s. f.* (*Ir. id. Swed* taska, *a pocket*) A reconnoitring, a spying; a stake, a pledge, or deposit, a saving; a treasure.

Taisg, *v. a* (*Ir id*) Lay aside, or lay up, treasure, hoard, inter. *Pret a* thaisg; *fut aff.* taisgidh, *shall lay up.* Taisg m' aitheanta, *lay up my commandments.—Stew Pro. Fut pass* taisgear, *shall be hoarded* Taisgear gach claidheamh na thruaille, *let every sword be put up into its sheath —Mac Lach*

Taisg-arm, *s m* An armoury

Taisgeach, ich, *s m* A hoard, a treasure; a saving; a pose; a thing given in charge. An taisgeach maith sin, *that good thing committed to you —Stew Tim.*

Taisgeach, *a.* Saving, frugal, hoarding.

Taisgealadh, aidh, *s. m* Prognosticating.

Taisgear, *fut. pass.* of taisg; which see

Taisg-eide, *s f.* A shroud, or winding-sheet.

Taisg-eudach, aich, *s. m.* A shroud, or winding-sheet.

Taisg-eudaich, *s. m.* A wardrobe

Taisgidh, *s f* (*Ir. id*) A trunk.

Taisill, *s f.* (*Ir. id*) Trespass; damage.

Taisg-inntinn, *s f.* Reservedness; equivocation, mental reservation.

Taisg-ionad, aid, *s. m.* A storehouse, a treasury. *N pl.* taisg-ionadan.

Taisgte, *p. part* of taisg Hoarded, laid up, buried.

Taisich, *v a.* (*from* tais) Soften, moisten; make effeminate; flinch, or shrink with fear. *Pret. a.* thaisich, *softened, fut. aff.* taisichidh, *shall moisten.* Nuair thaisicheas bròn iad, *when grief softens them —Oss. Tem* Cridhe nach taisich roimh fhuathas, *a heart that will not shrink before any thing fearful.—Mac Lach.*

Taisichte, *p part* of taisich. Softened, moistened, made effeminate.

Taisleachadh, aidh, *s m.* The act of wetting or moistening, or making damp; a bathing; a making effeminate.

Taislich, *v a.* and *n* (*Ir id.*) Wet, soften, moisten; bathe; grow effeminate *Pret a* thaislich; *fut aff* taislichidh

Taislichte, *p. part.* of taislich. Wetted, softened, moistened; bathed

Taist, *s f* (*Ir id*) A tache, button, loop, catch.

Taisteag, eig, *s. f* (*Ir id*) A moment

Taisteal, eil See Taisdeal.

Taistealach. See Taisdealach

Taistearachd, *s f* See Taibhsdearachd

† **Tait**, *s* (*Ir. id.*) Pleasure, *also*, mercury.

Taithleach, *a* (*Ir. id*) Quiet, peaceable, *also, substantively*, peace, quietness

Taite, *s f.* A beginning, a commencement.

Taiteach, ich, *s. m.* Abuse, reproach.

Taithris, *a* See Tairis.

Taithleach, *a.* (*Ir id.*) Quiet, peaceable, bright, pleasant; handsome, *substantively*, an excuse.

Taithneadh, idh, *s m* Splendour, brightness.

Taitinn, *s. f.* Pleasure, satisfaction.

Taitinn, *v* Please, satisfy, be acceptable. *Pret* thaitinn, *pleased, fut. aff.* taitinnidh or taitnidh, *shall please.* Thaitinn e rium, *he or it pleased me.*

TAITNEACH, *a* (*from* tait) Pleasant, grateful, or acceptable; satisfactory; becoming Is taitneach d' fhuaim, *pleasant is the sound.—Oss. Tem* Dh' fhalbh am fàil a bha taitneach, *the grateful odour has gone.—Macdon* Toil thaitneach Dhe, *the acceptable will of God.—Stew. Rom.* Seud taitneach, *a precious jewel.—Stew. Job. Com.* and *sup* taitniche Ma 's e 's taitniche leat, *if it be more agreeable* [*seem good*] *to thee —Stew* 1 *K.*

TAITNEACHD, *s f* Pleasantness; delight; delightfulness, satisfaction Ann ad thaitneachd, *in thy delights.—Stew. Song Sol*

TAITNEADH, idh, *s m* Satisfaction; pleasure. Tionndaidh e gu do thaitneadh, *it will turn to thy satisfaction.— Old Song*

TAITNEAS, eis, *s m* Satisfaction; pleasure.

TAITNICHE, *com* and *sup* of taitneach; which see.

TAITNIDH, *fut aff* of taitinn.

TÀL, tàil, *s m.* (*Ir. id*) A carpenter's adze or axe, a cooper's adze. Tàl deis, *a kind of plane used for the right side*, tàl cùil, *a small plane used for the left side*, tal fuinn, *a hoe*

TAL, *s f* (*Ir id*) A dropping

TALACH, *a* (*Ir id*) Apt to complain, apt to grudge; querulous, murmuring, prone to reproach

TALACH, aich, *s m.* (*Ir id*) A complaint, a murmur; dispraise. Cha 'n eil reuson talaich agam, *I have no reason to complain*

TALACHADH, aidh, *s. m.* A complaining; a complaint, a murmuring, a murmur, disparagement.

TÀLADH, aidh, *s m* (*Dan* talen, *speech*) The act of caressing, a stroking; a rocking, as of a child to sleep; a taming, a domesticating, enticing, a making attached, an elegy.

TÀLADH, (a), *pr. part* of tàlaidh Caressing, stroking, lulling asleep A tàladh ma ghaoil, *caressing my love.—Old Song*

TALAG, aig, *s f.* A roach

TÀLAIDH, *v. a* Caress, cajole; soothe; stroke, tame; entice, rock asleep, as a cradled infant. *Pret a* thàlaidh; *fut. aff* tàlaidh; *fut. sub.* thàlaidheas Ma thàlaidheas peacaich thu, *if sinners entice thee —Stew Pro Fut pass* tàlaidhear. Talaidhear e, *he shall be enticed.— Stew* 1 *Jam.*

TALAIDHTE, *p. part.* of talaidh. Caressed, cajoled, soothed; stroked, tamed; enticed; rocked asleep.

TALAMH, talmhainn, *s m.* (*Ir id*) Earth, ground, land, soil; country Thugadh mi do 'n talamh, *I was taken to their country —Oss. Gaul* Aghaidh na talmhainn, *the face of the earth*, talamh tioram, *dry land.*

TÀLAN, ain, *s m* (*Ir.* tallan) A talent, whether of money or of mind, feats in arms, chivalry. *N. pl.* talain *and* talantan

TALBAN, ain, *s m.* A partition.

TALC, tailc, *s* (*Ir id*) Force, strength; courage; vigour.

TALCANTA, *a.* (*Ir. id*) Strong, stout; sturdy; proud, prancing

TALCARRA, *a* Strong, stout, sturdy; proud, prancing. Gu talcarra, *stoutly.*

TAL FUINN, *s m* A hoe.

TAL-FHRADHARC, airc, *s.* Caution, foresight.

TAL-FHRADHARCACH, *a.* Cautious, foresighted.

TALGADH, aidh, *s. m.* A quieting, a pacifying; pacification.

TALGANTA. See TALCANTA.

† TALL, *v.* (*Ir id. Fr.* tailler.) Cut.

† TALL, talla, *s m.* Theft

TALLA, ai, *s m* (*Ir. id. Arm.* tall *Gr.* αὐλη, *hall.*) A hall, a house; a court; a rock; the cleft of a rock; a tower; an echo. Talla nan sian, *the hall of storms.* Mac talla 'snamh sa ghleann, *echo floating in the valley —Oss. Tem.*

TALLACH, *a.* Having halls or courts; of, or belonging to, a hall.

TALLADH, aidh, *s m* (*Ir. id.*) A cutting off, a lopping.

† TALLAIR, *s. m* A thief, a robber.

TALMHAIDH, TALMHUIDH, *a.* Earthly, terrestrial, earthy; powerful, strong-bodied. An cruinne talmhaidh, *the terrestrial globe.*

TALMHAIDHEACHD, *s. f* Earthliness.

TALMHAINN, *gen. sing.* of talamh

TALMHANTA, *s. m.* A mineral —*Macfar. Voc.*

TALMHANTACH, *a.* Mineralogical.

TALMHANTACHD, *s f.* Mineralogy.

TAL-RADHARC, airc, *s m.* Wariness, caution.

TAL-RADHARCACH, *a.* Wary, cautious.

TA 'M, (*for* a ta mi) I am.

† TAMACH, *a.* (*Ir. id.*) Dull, slow.—*Shaw*

TÀMAILT, ailte, *s f* Disgrace, reproach; disparagement; an indignity, an affront Thoir tamailt, *disgrace*. dean tamailt, *disparage* Cha d' thug thu dhoibh tamailt, *thou didst not disgrace them —Mac Co* Osunn thamailte nan laoch, *the heroes' sigh at their disgrace.—Fingalian Poem.* Ball tamailte, *an object of disgrace.—Mac Lach.*

TÀMAILTEACH, *a.* Disgraceful, degrading; reproachful; indignant. *Com* and *sup.* tamailtiche.

TÀMAILTEACHADH, aidh, *s m* A disgracing or degrading; disgrace, disdain, degradation, debasement.

TÀMAILTICH, *v. a* (*from* tamailt) Disgrace, degrade; affront, reproach. *Pret a.* thàmailtich; *fut aff.* tàmailtichidh.

TAMAN, ain, *s m* (*Ir. id*) The trunk or body of any thing.

TAMH, taimh, *s. m.* (*Ir. id*) Rest, leisure, quietness; delay, idleness; ocean; plague, ecstasy. Na feidh nan tamh air sgur-eild, *the deer at rest on their rocks.—Ull.* C'aite an tamh dhuit? *where is thy place of rest?—Oss Fin. and Lor.* Bheil thu ad thamh? *are you at leisure?* Tamh, *ocean —Macfar. Voc.*

TAMH, *v. n.* Rest, repose; settle. *Pret.* thamh; *fut. aff.* tamhaidh. San am bu chòir dhomh tamh, *when I ought to repose —Sm*

TAMHACH, *a.* Fond of rest, supine, indolent, sluggish; causing ease or rest.

TAMHACH, aich, *s m* (*Ir. id.*) A dolt.

TAMHACHADH, aidh, *s. m* A reposing, a quieting; a settling.

TAMHAICH, *v. n* Take rest, repose, recline; tranquillize, settle. *Pret. a* thamhaich; *fut aff.* tamhaichidh.

TAMHACHD, *s f.* Rest, repose, tranquillity, a settled state; an abode.

TAMHAICHE, *s m.* An inhabitant, a resident, a lodger, *N. pl* tamhaichean

TAMH-AIRNEIS, *s f* Furniture that is immoveable, fixtures.

TAMH-AITE, *s. m.* A place of rest, an abode.

TAMHAM, (*for* tamhaidh mi) I will rest.

TAMHAN, ain, *s. m.* (*Ir. id.*) A block, a stock, a trunk; a dolt

TAMHANACH, aich, *s m* (*Ir. id.*) A blockhead, a dolt, an inactive fellow *N. pl* tamhanaich.

TAMHANACH, *a* (*Ir id*) Splenetic, vapourish; doltish, sluggish.

TAMHANACHD, *s f* Stupidity, doltishness; inactivity; sluggishness.

TAMHANTA, *a.* Slow, sluggish, doltish

TAMHANTACHD, *s f.* Slowness, sluggishness, doltishness.

Tamhantas, ais, *s. m.* Slowness, sluggishness, doltishness.

Tamhasg, aisg, *s. m.* (*Ir. id.*) A fool; a dwarf or pigmy.—*Macfar. Voc.*

Tamhasgach, *a.* Foolish; doltish; dwarfish.

Tamh-leac, -lic, *s. f.* A grave-stone; stones heaped on a place where a person has been found dead, or has been buried.

Tamh-shuain, *s. f.* (*Ir. id.*) A trance; an ecstasy; a profound sleep.—*Macfar. Voc.*

Tamul, Tamull, uill, *s. m.* (*Ir. id.*) A short while, a short time, a space or distance. Tamul dh' i na tàmh, *she being a short while silent.*—*Ull.* Tamul as is a thaic re sleagh, *at a little distance, leaning on a spear.*—*Oss. Gaul.* Re tamuil, *for a little while.*—*Stew. Job.* An ceann tamuill, *in a short time.*—*Stew.* 1 *K.* Car tamuil bhig, *for a short time.*—*Stew.* 2 *Pet. ref.*

'Tan, *adv.* When, at the time.—*Macfar. Voc.*

Tàn, tain, *s. m.* Cattle; a head of black cattle; a flock of sheep; farm stock.

Tàn, tàin, *s. m.* A country; a territory; ground, land, earth. *Ir. id.* Gr. *τανα*, *land. Madag.* tane. *Chin.* tien. *Malay*, tana.

'Tan, land, is not much in use among the Gael. It is seen, however, in all names of countries ending in *tania;* as Britannia, Aquitania, Lusitania. *Tan*, signifying earth or ground, gave the name *Titans* (*Ti-tàn*), dwellers in the earth, to those people of antiquity who, in preference to the open air, lived in the subterraneous caverns in which Europe once abounded. The opposition made by the Italian Titans, descendants of Hellen, son of Deucalion, to the northern invaders, whose generals took the name of gods, gave rise to the fabled war between the gods and the giants. Ti-tans, as may be seen, is a pure Celtic name, meaning literally an *earth-being*, or subterraneous being; they were also called Gigantes, from *γηγινς*, another Celtic term (Cé-gin, *earth-born*,) in Greek characters.

Tana, *a.* (*Ir.* tanaidhe. *Arm.* tanan. *Corn.* tanan. *Eng.* thin.) Thin; slender; lean; attenuated; not numerous; liquid. A teachd le 'lainn thana, *coming with his thin sword.*—*Ull.* Tana o la gu la, *lean from day to day.*—*Stew. Sam.* *Com.* and *sup.* taine.

Tanachadh, aidh, *s. m.* A thinning; a rarifying; a diluting; dilution.

Tanadh, *a.* See **Tana**.

Tanaich, *v. a.* and *n.* (*from* tan.) Make thin, slender, or lean; attenuate; rarify; grow thin, slender, or lean; grow attenuated; grow rarified. *Pret. aff.* thanaich; *fut. aff.* tanaichidh, *shall make thin; fut. pass.* tanaichear, *shall be thinned.*

Tanaichear. See **Tanaich**.

Tanaichte, *p. part.* of tanaich. Thinned, attenuated, diluted, rarified.

† **Tanais**, *s. f.* (*Ir. id.*) A parable.

Tànaiste, *s. m.* (*from* † tan.) A dynast, a thane, a prince; a governor of a country.

Tànaisteach, *a.* Dynastic; governing; surveying.

Tànaisteachd, *s. f.* A dynasty, a thanistry; a form of government, under which the oldest of a family was entitled to succeed to the sovereignty or lordship on the death of the reigning prince or lord, in whose lifetime the *tanaiste* was commander-in-chief.

Tanalach, *a.* (*Ir. id.*) Short-winded.

Tanalach, aich, *s. m.* Shallow water.—*Macfar. Voc.*

Tànas, ais, *s. m.* (*from* tàn.) Dominion, lordship.

Tancard, aird, *s. m.* (*Ir. id.*) A tankard.

Tangnach, *a.* Malicious; treacherous.

Tangnachd, *s. f.* (*Ir. id.*) Malice, grudge; fraud.—*Macfar. Voc.*

Tangnadh, aidh, *s. m.* Treachery, deceit.

† **Tann**, *s. m.* (*Ir. id.*) A prince.

Tann, (*for* a ta ann.) Who exists, who appears; who is present. 'S e is airde t' ann, *he is the highest that exists.*—*Sm.*

Tannalach, *a.* (*Ir. id.*) Bellowing; extremely painful.

Tannaladh, aidh, *s. m.* (*Ir. id.*) Bellowing; agony.—*Macfar. Voc.*

Tannas, ais, *s. m.* A spectre or apparition. *N. pl.* tannais. Feuch tannas dorch air creig, *behold a dark spectre on the hill.*—*Oss. Duthona.* Tannais fhuar a sgreadail, *grisly spectres shrieking.*—*Oss. Fing.*

Tannasach, *a.* Like a spectre; of spectres.

Tannàsg, aisg, *s. m.* See **Tannas**.

Tannàsgach, *a.* See **Tannasach**.

Taobh, *v. a.* (*Ir. id.*) Side with or favour, be partial. *Pret.* thaobh; *fut. aff.* taobhaidh. Taobh ruim, *side with me.*—*Macfar.*

Taobh, *s. m.* (*Ir. id. Arm.* tu.) A side; support, or countenance; partiality, favour; a flank; a direction, place, or quarter. Tannais a sgairteachd gach taobh dheth, *spectres shrieking on every side of him.*—*Oss. Gaul.* Bhuail e 'chruaidh na taobh, *he thrust his steel into her side.*—*Oss. Fing.* Cum taobh ris, *favour or countenance him;* taobh na strì, *the flank of battle.*—*Oss.* Ciod an taobh an téid mi? *which way shall I go?* taobh sam-bi, *any whither.*—*Stew.* 1 *K.* Da 'm thaobhsa, *as for me, as for my part.*—*Stew. Gen.* An taobh beoil, *the front part.* A thaobh, *aside, astray.*—*Stew. Num.* Cuir gu taobh, *put aside;* cuir a thaobh, *put aside.* An taobh air chùil, *the hinder part;* an taobh chùil, *the back part, behind; backward.* Sheall e thaobh a chùil, *he looked backwards.*—*Mac Lach.* A thaobh, *by reason of;* taobh ri taobh, *side by side;* taobh na mara, *the sea side;* taobh tìr, *a shore, the water's edge;* as an taobh thall, *from the other side; Arm.* eus an tu all.

Taobhachadh, aidh, *s. m.* A leaning to a side or a party; a countenancing.

Taobhachd, *s. f.* (*Ir. id.*) Partiality; faction; presumption.

Taobhadh, aidh, *s. m.* (*Ir. id.*) A commission; a trusting; a relying.

Taobhaich, *v. a.* (*from* taobh.) Favour or side with, countenance, be partial to. *Pret. a.* thaobhaich; *fut. aff.* taobhaichidh. Taobhaich rium, *favour me.*

Taobhaichte, *p. part.* of taobhaich.

Taobhair, *s. m.* A partisan; an apostate.

Taobh a mach, *s. m.* The outside.

Taobhan, ain, *s. m.* (*Ir. id.*) A beam or rafter; a rib or small beam laid on the rafter of a house.

Taobh a muigh, *s. m.* The outside; *also*, without, outward.

Taobh a steach, *s. m.* The inner side.

Taobh a stigh, *s. m.* The inner side; *also*, within, inward. Taobh stigh an tighe, *the inner side of the house.*

Taobh-bhreith, *s. m.* Partiality; a partial or unjust decision; *also*, an unjust or partial judge.

Taobh-bhreitheach, *a.* Partial; unjust in deciding.

Taobh-cheum, -cheim, *s. m.* A side-step; a digression.

Taobh-cheumnach, *a.* Apt to digress, digressing.

Taobh-ghabhail, *s. f.* (*Ir. id.*) A secret fondness; a hankering attachment.

Taobh-gheal, *a.* (*Ir. id.*) White-sided.

Taobh-ghlas, *a.* Grey-sided. O charraig thaoibh-ghlais, *from a grey-sided rock.*—*Oss. Tem.*

Taobh-ghorm, *a.* Green-sided, blue-sided. Coire taobh-ghorm, *a green-sided dell.*—*Macdon.*

Taobh-ghreim, *s.* (*Ir. id.*) A stitch in the side; a pleuritic affection. *N. pl.* taobh-ghreimeannan.

Taobh-ghreimeach, *a.* Pleuritic.

TAOBH-LEIS, *s. m.* (*Ir. id.*) The lee-side.

TAOBH-SHLIGHE, *s. f.* (*Ir. id.*) A bye-path, a foot-path leading parallel to a highway. *N. pl.* taobh-shlighean.

TAOBH-SHLIGHEACH, *a.* Having bye-roads.

TAOBH-SHRUTH, *s. m.* An eddying tide, or back-water.

TAOBH-THOIR, *s. m.* A creditor; a commissary.—*Macfar. Voc.*

TAOBH-THROM. (*Ir. id.*) Pregnant.

TAOBH-THRUIME, *s. f.* Pregnancy.

TAOBH-TIR, *s.* (*Ir. id.*) The edge of the shore; a district.

TAOD, taoid, *s. m.* (*Ir. id.*) A rope or cable; a rope of hair; a halter. *N. pl.* taodan. Ar crainn is ar taodan, *our sails and our cables.*—*Macfar.*

TAODACH, *a.* (*Ir. id.*) Having ropes or cables; like a rope; of ropes; haltered; stubborn.

TAODACHAN, ain, *s. m.* (*Ir. id.*) A stubborn creature.

TAODAN, ain, *s. m.* (*dim.* of taod.) A little rope or cable; also *n. pl.* of taod.

TAODH, *s. m.* (*Ir. id.*) Woollen yarn.

TAODHAIR, *s. m.* (*Ir. id.*) An apostate. *N. pl.* taodhairean.

TAODHAIREACH, *a.* Apostatical.

TAODHAIREACHD, *s. f.* Apostasy.

TAOG, taoig, *s. f.* A fit of passion; frenzy.

TAOGHAIL, *v.* Frequent, repair to; visit, call on. *Pret.* thaoghail; *fut. aff.* taoghlaidh. An sealgair na sleibh cha taoghail, *the hunter shall not frequent the moors.*—*Ull.* Written also *taothal.*

TAOGHAILL, *gen. sing.* of taoghall.

TAOGHALACH, *a.* Frequenting, visiting; fond of frequenting.

TAOGHALL, aill, *s. m.* A frequenting, a visiting; a visit; a game at golf, foot-ball, or *shinty.* Cuir taoghall, *play at foot-ball;* cuir 'thaoghaill, *drive home, as a foot-ball.*

TAOGHAN, ain, *s. m.* A badger. *N. pl.* taoghain.

TAOGHANACH, *a.* Like a badger; full of badgers; of badgers.

TAOGHAS, ais, *s. m.* A grave.

TAOGHLAM, (*for* taoghlaidh mi.) I shall frequent or visit.

† TAOI, *a.* (*Ir. id.*) Ready; silent; mild; *substantively,* a birth; a trope; a turning.

TAOIG, *s. f.* A fit of passion; frenzy.

TAOIGEACH, *a.* Infuriate, frantic.

TAOIGHIN, *s. f.* A mill-pond.

TAOIM, *s.* (*Ir. id.*) Water in a ship or boat, bilge-water—(*Macfar. Voc.*); a dash of water.

TAOIMEACH, *a.* Leaky, not water-tight, as a ship or boat.

TAOINNEADH, idh, *s. m.* A crispation.

TAOIS, taoise, *s. f.* (*Ir.* taos.) Dough or leaven. Taois ghoirt, *sour leaven.*—*Stew. Ex.* and *Lev.*

TAOISEACH, ich, *s. m.* (*Ir. id.*) A leader or commander. Bu lionmhor taoiseach na luidhe, *many a hero was laid low.*—*Old Poem.* Now written *toiseach.*

TAOISINN, *v. a.* Leaven, knead. *Pret. a.* thaoisinn; *fut. aff.* taoisnidh. Taoisinn trì miosairean, *leaven three measures.*—*Stew. Gen.*

TAOISNEACH, *a.* Like leaven or dough; of leaven.

TAOISNEACHADH, aidh, *s. m.* The process of leavening.

TAOISNICH, *v. a.* (*from* taois.) Leaven, knead. *Pret. a.* thaoisnich, *leavened; fut. aff.* taoisnichidh, *shall leaven; p. part.* taoisnichte.

TAOISNICHTE, *p. part.* of taoisnich.

TAOLAMACH, aich, *s. m.* A parricide. *N. pl.* taolamaich.

TAOM, taoma, *s. m.* (*Ir. id.*) A pouring of any liquid, an overflow, a torrent; a fit of sickness; a passion, frenzy; water that leaks through a vessel. *N. pl.* taoman; *d. pl.* taomaibh. An tuil a teachd na taomaibh, *the flood coming in torrents.*—*Old Poem.* Thainig uisge na thaomaibh, *rain came in torrents.*

TAOM, *v. a.* (*Ir. id. Scotch,* toom. *Dan.* tom.) Pour, overflow; shed; empty; throw water out of any vessel. *Pret. a.* thaom; *fut. aff.* taomaidh. Tra thaom na filidh an ceòl, *when the bards poured forth their strains.*—*Oss. Derm.*

TAOMACH, *a.* Emptying; apt to overflow; subject to fits.

TAOMACHADH, aidh, *s. m.* An overflowing, an outpouring.

TAOMADH, aidh, *s. m.* A pouring; an overflowing; an overflow; an effusion; a flood; a fit of sickness. Fo thaomadh dheoir, *under a fit of tears.*—*Oss. Fing.*

TAOMADH, (a), *pr. part.* of taom. Pouring, overflowing; emptying; laving. Air tràigh a taomadh, *pouring on the shore.*—*Oss. Fing.*

TAOMAICH, *v. a.* Pour out, throw out, empty, as a vessel or cart, of any thing that can be poured out of it; unload. *Pret. a.* thaomaich, *emptied; fut. aff. a.* taomaichidh, *shall empty.* Thaomaich iad an saic, *they emptied their sacks.*—*Stew. Gen.* Taomaich a chairt, *unload the cart.*

TAOMAICHTE, *p. part.* of taomaich. Emptied; unloaded.

TAOMAIR, *s. m.* A pump; one who works at a pump. *N. pl.* taomairean.

TAOMAIREACHD, *s. f.* Working at a pump.

TAOMAN, ain, *s. m.* (*from* taom.) A small wooden vessel for throwing water out of boats; a vessel to lave with. Gun seòl, gun ramh, gun taoman, *without sail or laving dish.*—*Old Song.* Gabh an ladar no 'n taoman, *take the ladle or laving dish.*—*Id. N. pl.* taomain.

TAOM-BOILE, *s. f.* A fit of frenzy; a raging passion.

TAOM-BOILEACH, *a.* Frantic, raging with passion or anger.

TAOSG, *v. a.* (*Ir. id.*) Pour; pump, drain, empty; effuse, circumfuse. *Pret. a.* thaosg; *fut. aff.* taosgaidh. A taosgadh a dui-neoil air gleanntai', *pouring her dark clouds on the valleys.*—*Oss.* A chorruich a taosgadh, *his wrath pouring forth.*—*Mac Lach.*

TAOSGACH, *a.* Pouring; overflowing; apt to overflow; brimful.

TAOSGADH, aidh, *s. m.* (*Ir. id.*) A pouring; an overflowing; a pumping, a draining; an overflow.

TAOSGAICHE, *s. m.* (*Ir. id.*) One who works at a pump.

TAOSGAIR, *s. m.* (*Ir.* taosgoir.) One who works at a pump. *N. pl.* taosgairean.

TAOSGAIREACHD, *s. f.* Pumping; labouring at a pump.

TAOSGTA, taosgte, *p. part.* of taoisg. (*Ir.* taosgtha.) Pumped, emptied, drained.

TAOTHALL, aill, *s. m.* A frequenting, a haunting, a visiting; a haunt or place of resort; a game at golf or the foot-ball. Aite taothaill, *a place of resort.*—*Stew. Is. ref.*

TAP, *s. m.* (*Ir. id.*) A tuft of wool or dressed flax fixed to a distaff.

TAPACHD, *s. f.*; *for* tapaidheachd. (*Ir.* tapacht.) Cleverness; alertness; activity; manliness.

TAPADH, aidh, *s. m.* Cleverness; alertness; activity; manliness; manhood. Cuimhnicheadh gach aon a thapadh, *let each remember his manhood.*—*Ull.*

TAPAG, aig, *s. f.* A slight accident; a slip.

TAPAIDH, *a.* (*Ir. id.*) Clever, alert, active; manly. Clann feardha tapaidh, *an active manly clan.*—*Macdon.* Bi tapaidh, *be clever, be quick.*

TAPAN, ain, *s. m.*; *dim.* of tap. (*Ir. id.*) A little tuft of wool or flax on a distaff; a tuft of flax added to a larger quantity to make up a deficiency in weight.

TAPANTA, *a.* Clever, capable, quick. Gu tapanta, *cleverly.*

TAPAR, air, *s. m.* (*Ir. id.*) A taper.

Tapais, *s. f.* A carpet.

Taplach, aich, *s. m.* A repository for small things.—*Macfar. Voc.*

Taplaich, *s. f.* A wallet; a repository of small things.

Taponta, *a.* See Tapanta.

Tar, *prep.* (*Sax.* thwyr.) Beyond, over, across, athwart; on the other side.

Tàr, *v. a.* and *n.* Go; send; come; descend; befall; prepare. *Pret. a.* thàr; *fut. aff.* tàraidh. Iul-oidhche tàr o'n speur do sholus, *star of night, send thy light from the skies.—Oss. Dargo.* Thàr e mach, *he went out.—Stew. Gen.* Na tàradh neul air Carraigthura, *let not a cloud descend on Carricthura.—Oss. Carricth.* Gus an tàr dhomh bàs is uaigh, *till death and the grave be my lot.—Mac Lach.*

Tàr, *s. m.* A belly. See Tàrr.

Tar, *a.* Active, quick, clever.—*Shaw.*

Tarachair, *s. f.* An auger, a gimblet.

Tarachd, *s. f.* Activity; going, coming.

Tàraidh, *fut. aff.* of tàr.

Tàran, ain, *s. m.* An apparition; the apparition of an unchristened child. *N. pl.* tàrain.

Taranach, *a.* Spectral.

Tarang, aing, *s. f.* A nail.—*Stew. Is.* *N. pl.* taraingean or tairngean.

Tarbh, tairbh, *s. m.* A bull. *N. pl.* tairbh. Mòran tharbh, *many bulls.—Sm.* Tarbh uisge, *a sea-bull* or *cow*; tarbh tàna, *a parish bull*; croicionn tàirbh, *a bull's hide*; *Arm.* crochen taru.

Phen. thor, *a bull.* *Chald. Syr. Sam.* tor *and* taur. *Heb.* thora *and* tor. *Arab.* taur *and* tauro. *Runic*, tarffur. *Gr.* ταυρος. *Lat.* taurus. *Span.* and *Manx*, tarv. *It.* toro. *Arm.* taru. *Corn.* tarv. *Ir.* tarbh.

Tarbhach, *a.* (*Ir. id.*) Like a bull; *also*, profitable, fruitful, productive; pithy, substantial; effectual. Am faod duine a bhi tarbhach? *can a man be profitable?—Stew. Job.* Cainnt tharbhach, *pithy language.—Mac Lach.* Buille tarbhach, *an effectual* or *decisive blow.—Macfar. Com.* and *sup.* tarbhaiche.

Tarbhachd, *s. f.* (*Ir.* tarbhacht.) Gain, profit; fruitfulness; productiveness.

Tarbhaich, *v. n.* (*Ir. id.*) Gain, profit; grow gainful; grow fruitful; reap gain, profit, or advantage. *Pret.* tharbhaich; *fut. aff.* tarbhaichidh.

Tarbhaichead, eid, *s. m.* Fruitfulness; improvement or advancement in fruitfulness. A dol an tarbhaichead, *growing more and more fruitful.*

† **Tarbhaidh**, *s. f.* Hinderance; an impediment; misfortune.

Tarbhan, ain, *s. m.* (*Ir. id.*); *dim.* of tarbh. A little bull; a young bull.

Tarbhanta, *a.* (*Ir. id.*); *from* tarbh. Like a bull; fierce, stern, boorish; bull-faced.

Tarbhas, ais, *s. m.* (*Ir. id.*) A surfeit.

Tar-bheir, *v. a.* (*Ir. id.*) Transfer; carry over.

Tarbh-tana, *s. m.* (tarbh-tain.) *Ir. id.* A parish bull, a bull which is the property of a district.

† **Tar-chonair**, *s. f.* (*Ir. id.*) A ferry.

Tarcuis, *s. f.* Contempt, reproach, scorn, despite. Dean tarcuis, *reproach* or *despise*; an dean thu tarcuis? *wilt thou despise?—Stew. Rom.* Luchd tarcuis, *spiteful people.—Id.*

Tarcuiseach, *a.* Contemptuous, reproachful, scornful, despiteful. Gu tarcuiseach, *reproachfully.* *Com.* and *sup.* tarcuisiche.

Tarcuisich, *v. a.* (*from* tarcuis.) Despise, contemn, revile, scorn. *Pret. a.* tharcuisich; *fut. aff.* tarcuisichidh; *p. part.* tarcuisichte.

Tareis, *prep.* (tar *and* eis, *or* tar *and* greis.) After, afterwards.

Tar-fhradharc, airc, *s. m.* A squinting look, a looking askance; a leer or ogle.

Tar-fhradharcach, *a.* Having a squint, goggle-eyed; looking askance; leering, ogling.

Targadh, aidh, *s. m.* (*Ir. id.*) A governing or ruling; government, rule; an assembly.

Targaid, *s. f.* (*Sax.* targa.) A shield or target. Mile targaid, *a thousand targets.—Stew. Song. Sol.*

The target of the Gael was orbed, and made of light wood, with a single covering of tough leather, or, if thin, with several folds, and studded with brass, iron, or silver, according to the condition or means of the wearer.

Targaideach, *a.* Like a target; of a target; armed with a shield.

Targair, *v. a.* Foretell, bode. *Pret. a.* thargair; *fut. aff.* targraidh.

Targhan, ain, *s. m.* A noise.

Targrach, *a.* Foretelling; prophetic.

Targradh, aidh, *s. m.* A foreboding, a prediction.

Targraiche, *s. m.* A foreboder. *N. pl.* targraichean, *foreboders.*

Tarladh, *def. verb*, 3 *sing.* and *pl. imper.* (*Ir.* tarla.) Happen, befall, meet. Tarladh e, *let it happen.* Nur a tharladh sibh cuideachd, *when you met together.—Old Song.*

Tarladh, aidh, *s. m.* (*Ir. id.*) A draught; a leading in of corn or hay.

Tarlaid, *s. f.* A female drudge or slave. *N. pl.* tarlaidean.

Tarlaideach, *a.* Drudging, as a female.

Tarlaidh, *fut. aff.* of tarladh. Shall or will befall, or meet.

Tàrmach, aich, *s. m.* A ptarmigan. Tàrmach breac na beinn, *the spotted ptarmigan of the mountain.—Old Song.*

This is a rare species of moorfowl, seen on the tops of the highest Highland hills. The size of the ptarmigan is nearly that of grouse, and its colour light grey; but in winter it is perfectly white. It is a very shy and timid bird; but when the sportsman comes upon it by surprise, it is daunted even to stupidity, and has not always the courage even to fly from danger.

Tàrmachan, ain, *s. m.* See Tàrmach.

Tarmadh, aidh, *s. m.* (*Ir. id.*) A dwelling.

Tarmaich, *v. n.* Dwell, reside, lodge. *Pret.* tharmaich; *fut. aff.* tarmaichidh. Ann am airnibh tharmaich mo niosgaid, *in my reins my ulcer resides.—Macfar.* Ceann anns an do tharmaich gliocas, *a head where wisdom dwelt.—Old Poem.*

Tarman, ain, *s. m.* (*Ir. id.*) See Torman.

Tàrmanach, aich, *s. m.* See Tarmachan.

Tarmun, uin, *s. m.* (*Ir. id.*) A sanctuary, an asylum. Perhaps *tearmunn.*

Tarmunach, *a.* Affording a sanctuary or asylum.

Tarnadair, *s. m.* An innkeeper. *N. pl.* tarnadairean.

Tarnadaireachd, *s. f.* The occupation of an innkeeper.

Tarnaid, *s. f.* A tavern.

Tarnaidh, (*for* tarruingidh.) Shall or will draw.

Tarnochd, *s. f.* (*Ir. id.*) Nakedness; the secret parts.

Tarnochd, *a.* (*Ir. id.*) Naked.

Tarp, *s. m.* A clod; a lump of earth or clay.

Tarpach, *a.* (*Ir. id.*) Cloddy; bulky; weighty.

Tarpachd, *s. f.* (*Ir. id.*) Bulkiness.

Tarpan, ain, *s. m.* A cluster; a crab-fish. *N. pl.* tarpain.

Tarpan, ain, *s. m.* (*dim.* of tarp.) A little clod.

Tarpanach, *a.* Cloddy.

Tarr, *s. m.* (*Ir. id.*) A tail; an extremity; the lowest part of the belly. Breac tarr-gheal, *a white-bellied trout.—Macdon.*

TARRACH, a. Fearful, timid; horrible.

TARRACH, aich, s. m. A girth; a crupper.—Macfar. Voc. and Macd.

TARRACHAN, ain, s. m. (Ir. id.) A glutton.

TARRADH, aidh, s. m. (Ir. id.) Se TARRAGH.

TARRADH, v. See TARRAGH.

TAR-RADHARC, airc, s. m. (Ir. id.) A squint; a leer.

TAR-RADHARCACH, a. Squinting, leering; goggle-eyed.

TARRAG, aig, s. f. A nail; a stud; N. pl. tarragan.

TARRAGACH, a. Full of nails, like a nail; of nails.

TARRAGH, aigh, s. m. (Ir. tarradh.) A conveying of corn to the barn or yard, a drawing; a leading; a frequent going to and from a place. Féisd an tarraigh, *the feast of the in-gathering.*—Stew. Ex.

TARRAGH, v. a. Convey corn from the field to the yard.

TARRAIG, *gen. sing.* of tarrag.

TARRAING, v. a. See TARRUING.

TARRAN, ain, s. m. A nail.—Macint.

TARRANACH, a. Like a nail, full of nails.

TARRANG, aing, s. f. A nail, a stud. N. pl. tarraingean, *cont.* tairngean, *nails*, tarrang na leth-cheann, *a nail in his temple.*—Stew. Jud.

TARRANG-ART, s. f. The compass-needle; a loadstone, a magnet.

TARR-FHIONN, a. White-bellied; white-tailed; having white buttocks.

TARR-GHEAL, a. White-bellied, white-tailed. Breac tàrr-gheal, *a white-bellied trout.*—Macdon.

TARRUING, v. a. (Sax. tacran.) Draw, pull; teaze; allure, entice, extract, distil; approach, draw near; aim. *Pret.* tharruing; *fut. aff.* tarruingidh. Tarruing do ghealchlaidheamh, *draw thy bright sword.*—Ull. Tharruing i 'n t-sreang le rogha beachd, *she pulled the string with her best aim.*—Id. Tarruing le d' chlàrsaich dlù, *draw near with thy harp.*—Oss. Duthona. Tha 'n laoch a tarruing a bhuille. Tarruing suas, *draw up*; tarruing suas ri, *take up acquaintance with, cultivate acquaintance, approach.*

TARRUING, s. m. A draught, a pull, a drag, a haulyard; an alluring, or enticing, attraction; a while, a time, a turn. Tarruing éisg, *a draught of fishes*, ar stàdh's air tarruinge, *our stays and our haulyards.*—Macfar. Air a cheud tarruing, *at the first, at once*, gabh do tharruing féin deth, *take your own turn of it*; is e so mo tharruing-sa, *this is my turn or while*, adh'aon tarruing, *at once, at one time.*—Stew. Jud. Tarruing dubailt, *double distilled liquor*, tarruing air ais, *revulsion, retraction.*

TARRUINGEACH, a. Drawing, alluring, attractive.

TARRUINGTE, p. part. of tarruing. (Ir. tarrangtha.) Pulled, drawn, enticed; extracted, distilled.

TARSNAN, ain, s. m. (*from* tarsuingean.) A cross-bar, a spoke, a cross-beam, a transom. N. pl. tarsnain.

TARSNAIN, *gen. sing.* and *n. pl.* of tarsnan.

TAR-SHOILLEIR, a. Transparent.

TAR-SHOILLSEACH, a. Transparent.

TAR-SHOILLSEAN, ein, s. m. A transparency.

TAR-SHOLUS, uis, s. m. Transparentness.

TART, tairt, s. m. (Ir. id. Swed. torst.) Thirst, drought, parchedness. Ann an ocras agus tart, *in hunger and thirst.*—Stew. 2 Cor. Trid fearainn tairt, *through a land of deserts.*—Stew. Is. Tha tart orm, *I thirst*, or, *am thirsty.*

† TARTAN, ain, s. m. (Ir. id.) A hillock; a clod; tartan.

† TARTANACH, a. (Ir. id.) Hilly; cloddy; of plaid.

TARTAR, a., *for* tartmhor; which see.

TARTAR, air, s. m. A noise, clangor; a loud-swelling sound; clamour, hurry. A thartar mar thuinn a slachdasgeire, *his noise like a wave buffeting a rock.*—Oss. Derm. Theirinn an righ na thartar eiti', *the King descended in the clangor of his arms.*—Oss. Duthona.

TARTARACH, a. Noisy, loud; having a swelling sound; forward, magnanimous. Dha 'm bu thartarach piob, *whose pipe loudly sounded.*—Old Song. Tartarach, *magnanimous.*—Macfar. Voc. *Com.* and *sup.* tartaraiche.

TARTARACHD, s. f. Noisiness, loudness; forwardness; magnanimity.

TARTHAIL, s. f. (Ir. id.) Help; assistance.

TARTMHOR, a. (Ir. tartmhor.) Thirsty; droughty; dry, parched. Ma bhios e tartmhor, *if he be thirsty.*—Stew. Pro. *Com.* and *sup.* tartmhoire.

TARTMHORACHD, s. f. Great or continued drought, parchedness, droughtiness.

TAR-UINNEAG, eig, s. f. (Ir. id.) A casement. N. pl. tar-uinneagan.

TÀSAN, ain, s. m. (Ir. id.) A tedious drawling discourse; a plaintive harangue; monotony; a whining sermon; one who speaks in a drawling manner; a plaintive or a tedious haranguer.

TÀSANACH, a. (Ir. id.) Slow or tedious in speaking; plaintive, whining, monotonous.

TÀSANACHD, s. f. (Ir. id.) Slowness, or tediousness in discourse, monotony; presbyterian cant.

TÀSANAICHE, s. f. (Ir. tasanaidhe.) A term of ridicule for a tedious whining orator.

TASART, airt, s. m. Reproach; a rebuke; calumny. Fo thasart, *under reproach.*—Stew. Neh.

TASDAIL, s. f. (Ir. id.) A trial.

TASDAN, ain, s. m. A groat. N. pl. tasdain.

TASG, s. m. (Ir. id.) A job; a task; a report; a character. N. pl. tasgan.

TASGAIDH, s. f. A laying up or hoarding; a treasuring; a hoard, a treasure. Is tu mo thasgaidh 's mo rèir, *thou art my treasure and my love.*—Old Song.

TASGAIR, s. m. (Ir. id. W. tasgwr.) One who assigns a job or task; a taskmaster, a slave.

TASGAL, ail, s. m. Money offered for the discovery of cattle *lifted* by Highland freebooters.

There have often been instances of vassals, and even clans, taking an oath never to receive such money; and to put to death every person who should receive it. They took this oath in a solemn manner, over a drawn dirk which they kissed, saying, 'If we break this our oath, may we perish by this weapon, or by any other.'

TASPULLACH, a. Witty, sarcastic.

TASPULLACHD, s. f. Wit, witticism; a sarcasm.

† TAST, s. m. (Ir. id.) A rein-deer.

TATH, s. m. Slaughter; bail, security.

TATH, s. The Tay.

† TATH, s. m. (Ir. id.) A lord, slaughter; cement.

TÀTH, v. a. (Ir. id.) Solder, cement; join. *Pret. a.* thàth, *soldered*, *fut. aff. a.* tàthaidh, *shall or will solder.*

TÀTHACH, a. Having the quality of soldering; cementing.

TATHACH, aich, s. m. A visiter, a guest, a stranger. M' aoidheachd ag iarruidh tathaich, *my hospitality in quest of a guest.*—Oss. Manos. Bu tric tathaich o thuath, *frequent were visiters from the north.*—Old Legend.

TÀTHADH, aidh, s. m. A cementing, a joining, a soldering.

TÀTHADH, (a), *pr. part.* of tàth. Cementing, joining, soldering.

TATHAICH, *gen. sing.* of tathach.

TATHAICH, v. n. Resort to, frequent; visit; crave; exact; profit. Is tric a thathaich thu i, *often didst thou resort to her.*—Mac Co. A tathaich bhailtean, *visiting*, or, *frequenting cities.*—Stew. Hos.

Tathaich, *s. f.* A resorting to, or frequenting; a visiting; a craving.

Tathaiche, *s. m.* A frequenter, a visitor, an acquaintance, a guest.

Tathaicheadh, idh, *s. m.* A frequenting, a visiting; a craving.

Tàthaidh, *fut. aff. a.* of tath; which see.

Tàthair, *s. m.* (*Ir. id.*) A joiner; a sluggish fellow.

Tàth-bheum, *s.* (*Ir. id.*) A mortal blow; anciently the exercise of casting stones or darts from the Crann-tabhuil, which corresponded to the Roman catapulta.

Tath-bhuille, *s. m.* A mortal blow.

Tathlach. See Talach.

Tathlan, ain, *s. m.* A reproach; calumny.

Tathta, Tathte, *p. part.* of tath. Soldered, cemented, joined.

Tathuich. See Tathaich.

Tathunn, uinn, *s. m.* (*Ir.* tathfan.) A bark or yelp; the bay of a deer.

Tathunnaich, *s. f.* Barking, yelping.

Té, *s. f.* A woman; any object animate or inanimate, to which we ascribe the feminine gender. An té b'òige, *the younger woman.—Stew. Gen.* In Grelman's Collection of Gipsey words, *tsche* means *a girl.*

Teabh, *s.* A quid of tobacco; perhaps a corruption of *chew.*

Teabhach, *a.* Renowned; brave. Gu teabhach, *bravely; com.* and *sup.* teabhaiche, *more or most brave.*

Teabhachd, *s. f.* Fame, glory, exploit; bravery. Aite am meadhon or theabhachd, *joyful in the midst of his fame.—Oss. Trathal.* Càn anns an dàn an teabhachd, *celebrate their exploits in song.—Orr.*

Teacair, *s. m.* (teachd-fhear.) See Teachdair.

Teach, *s. m.* A house, a dwelling-place; a home. Theach mo ghaoil, *home of my heart.—Oss. Fing.* Na teach diamhair, *in her lonely dwelling.—Orr.*

Gr. τοῖχος, τεῖχος, *a wall*, and τεγος. *Lat.* tectum, *house. It.* tetto. *Etrurian*, tshec, *a temple.* *Germ. Pol.* dach, *a house. Swed.* taak. *Teut.* theki. *Old. Sax.* thece. *Arm.* tec. *Ir.* teach.

Teachd, *s.* (*contracted for* tigheachd.) *Ir. id.* An arrival, a coming, an approach. Is ait ceum do theachd, *joyous is the step of thy approach.—Oss. Trath.* Teachd mun cuairt na bliadhna, *the expiration of the year.—Stew.* 2 *Sam.* Air teachd, *come;* a teachd, *coming;* tha an raineach uaine air teachd thairt, *the green fern has grown over her.—Oss. Derm.*

Teachd, (a), *pr. part.* of the *irr. v.* thig. Coming, arriving, approaching. A teachd o 'n chath, *coming from battle.—Ardar.*

Teachdadh, aidh, *s. m.* A closing.

Teachdair, *s. m.* (teachd-fhear.) *Ir. id.* A messenger; an envoy; a despatch; intelligence or news. Bhuail teachdair a bhàis thu, *the messenger of death has smote thee.—Old Song.* Teachdair coise, *a foot-messenger;* teachdair eich, *an express, a courier.* *N. pl.* teachdairean, *messengers.—Stew. Pro.*

Teachdaireach, *a.* Of, or pertaining to, a messenger or courier.

Teachdaireachd, *s. f.* (*Ir.* teachdaireacht.) A message, an embassy, a legation, an errand; intelligence or news. Air theachdaireachd, *on an embassy;* teachdaireachd a chuir moran gu truaighe, *an intelligence that has caused sorrow to many.—Fingalian Poem.*

Teachd-a mach, Teachd mach, *s. m.* A coming out or egress; expenditure, increase.

Teachd an tìr, *s. m.* Food; maintenance; diet; livelihood. A theachd an tìr, *his food.—Stew. Pro.* Gun teachd an tìr gun bhiadh, *without diet or food.—Macdon.*

Teachd a steach, Teachd steach, *s. m.* Coming-in; an income; a revenue.

Teachd a stigh, Teachd stigh, *s. m.* Coming-in; an income; a revenue. Teachd a stigh mòr, *a great revenue.—Stew. Pro.*

Teachmuail, *s. f.* (*Ir. id.*) Affliction; sickness.

Tead. See Teud.

Teadarnach, *a.* (*Ir. id.*) Revengeful.

Teadhair, teadhrach, *s. f.* A cart-rope; a tether. *N. pl.* teadhraichean.

Teadhraichean, *n. pl.* of teadhair.

Teagair, *v. a.* Provide; collect, gather. *Pret. a.* theagair; *fut. aff. a.* teagairidh, *shall or will provide.*

Teagamh, aimh, *s.* Doubt, uncertainty; hesitation; suspense; perplexity; a doubtful question; a difficulty. Gun teagamh, *without doubt;* fear rèitich gach teagamh, *the clearer of every difficulty.—Old Song.* Ann an teagamh, *in doubt.*

Teagamhach, *a.* Doubtful, uncertain; in suspense; perplexed; suspicious, distrustful; sceptical. Gu teagamhach, *doubtfully. Com.* and *sup.* teagamhaiche.

Teagamhachd, *s. f.* Doubtfulness; doubt; uncertainty; scepticism.

Teagamhaiche, *s. m.* A doubter, a sceptic.

Teagamhaiche, *com.* and *sup.* of teagamhach.

Teagaisg, *gen. sing.* of teagasg.

Teagaisg, *v. a.* Teach, educate. *Pret. a.* theagaisg, *taught; fut. aff.* teagaisgidh, *shall teach.* Teagaisg iad do d' mhic, *teach them to thy sons.—Stew. Deut. Fut. pass.* teagaisgear; *p. part.* teagaisgte, *taught.*

Teagaisgeach, *a.* Didactic, instructive.

Teagaisgear, *fut. pass.* of teagaisg.

Teagaisgte, *p. part.* of teagaisg.

Teagar, air, *s. m.* (*Ir. id.*) Provision; a purchase; warmth.

Teagarach, aich, *s. m.* A purchase; *adjectively*, warm, snug.

Teagasg, aisg, *s. m.* (*Ir. id.*) Teaching, instruction; doctrine; a text; *also*, Druidism; sorcery. Gun teagasg, *without instruction.—Stew. Pro.* Le gach uile ghaoth teagaisg, *with every wind of doctrine.—Stew. Eph.*

Teagasgach. Didactic, instructive.

Teagasgair, *s. m.* (*Ir.* teagasgthoir.)

Teagasgaireachd, *s. f.* The employment of a teacher.

† **Teagh**, *s. m.* A house, an apartment; *hence*, teaghlach, *a family.*

Teaghas, ais, *s. m.* (*Ir. id.*) A small room, a closet.

Teaghlach, aich, *s.* († teagh *and* sluagh.) *Ir. id. W.* teulu. A family; a clan or tribe; race or progeny; a household. *N. pl.* teaghlaichean. Uile theaghlaiche na talmhainn, *all the families of the earth.—Stew. Gen.*

Teaghlachail, *a.* (*W.* teuluacol.) Domestic; of, or belonging to, a family.

Teagmhach. See Teagamhach.

Teagmhachd, *s. f.* See Teagamhachd.

Teagmhaiche, *s. m.* (*from* teagamh.) A sceptic.

Teagmhail, *s. f.* (*Ir. id.*) Strife, a battle; interference, meddling, expostulation; retribution, revenge; a meeting; rencounter.

Teagmhaileach, *a.* Contentious; contending; striving.

Teagmhaiseach, *a.* (*Ir.* teggmhuiseach.) Accidental; liable to chance or accident; at a venture, at random.

Teagmhaiseachd, *s f* The state of being liable to chance or accident.

Teagmhas, ais, *s m.* (*Ir.* tagbhais) Chance, an accident, a guess, a venture; any thing done at a venture, or at random Thaobh teagmhais, *at a venture, at random.—Stew.* 1 *K ref.* Am agus teagmhas, *time and chance — Stew Ecc ref*

Teagmhuil, *s f.* See Teagmhail.

Teagmhus, uis See Teagmhas.

Teagnach, *a* (*Ir id*) Using force or violence, making an exertion; difficult. *Com* and *sup* teagnaiche.

Teagnadh, aidh, *s m* (*Ir. id*) Striving, forcing; violent exertion.

Teagradh, aidh, *s m.* Provision, acquisition.

Teagradh, 3 *sing* and *pl imper* of teagair

Teagram, 1 *sing imper* of teagair Let me provide; *also, for* teagraidh me, *I will provide*

† **Tealla**, *s.* (*Gr.* τιλος, *dung* *Lat* tellus, *earth*) Earth

Teallach, aich, *s. m* A hearth, a furnace; a forge, an anvil Leac an teallaich, *the hearth —Stew Gen ref* Do luaith theallaich, *of the ashes of a furnace.—Stew Ex* Air cruaidh theallaich, *on a hard anvil —Oss Fing* Clach ceann an teallaich, *a large flag which stands behind a fire in Highland cottages* *N pl* teallaichean

Teallachag, aig, *s f* (*from* teallach) *Ir.* teallachog A domestic concubine; a master's favourite servant maid

Teallaich, *gen sing* of teallach

Teallaid, *s. f* A stout woman, a drab *N pl* teallaidean.

Teallaideach, *a* Drabbish, sluttish

Teallrach, *a* Profuse

Teallsan, ain, *s. m* Philosophy, erudition, a philosopher, a learned man

Teallsanach, aich, *s m* A philosopher, a learned man. *N pl* teallsanaich Cha 'n eil crabhach, teallsanach no sagart, *there is neither hypocrite, philosopher, nor priest —R*

Teallsanachail, *a* Philosophical; erudite

Teallsanachd, *s f* Philosophy, erudition

Teallsanair, *s m* A philosopher, a learned man

Teamhaidh See Tiamhaidh

Teamhachd, *s f* See Tiamhachd

Teamhair, *a* (*Ir id*) Pleasant, delightful, pleasant to the eye

Teamhaireachd, *s f* Pleasantness, delightfulness

Teampull, uill, *s m* (*Ir id*) A temple, a church

Teampullach, *a.* Like a temple, or, belonging to a temple, *substantively*, a churchman, a templar

Teanachdas, ais, *s. m* A deliverance from imminent danger; a defence Co is urrainn teanachdas, *who can be a defence.—Old Song.*

Teanail, *v a* See Tionail.

Teanalach, *a.* See Tionalach.

Teanaladh, aidh, *s. m.* See Tionaladh

Teanalaiche, *s. m* See Tionalaiche

Teanga, ai, *s. f* See Teangadh.

Teangach, *a.* Loquacious; tongued; lingual Gu teangach, *loquaciously*

Teangachd, *s. f.* Loquaciousness, philology.

Teangadh, aidh, *s f.* A tongue; a language. Teangadh mhìn, *a smooth tongue*, *n pl* teangaidh *and* teangaidhean Le teangaidh bhreugaich, *with lying tongues —Sm.*

Teangaiche, *s m* A linguist *N. pl* teangaichean.

Teangair, *s m* An orator, a linguist. *N. pl.* teangairean.

Teangaireachd, *s. f.* Oratory; philology.

Teangas, ais, *s m.* A pair of pincers

Teann, *a.* Tight; tense; strait, close; stiff, rigid, strict; near; narrow; like a miser; firm; besieged. Bhris e 'n iall theann, *he broke the tight thong.—Mac Lach.* Teann air sheas ainnir, *near him a virgin stood —Oss. Tem.*

Ir teann, *tight* *Gr* τινω, *to stretch.* *Lat.* tendo. *W.* tynnu, *to draw.* *Arm.* tenna

Teann, (gu), *adv.* Tightly, tensely, straitly, closely; stiffly; strictly, miserly; firmly A thaibhse a lean sinn gu teann, *ye spectres who closely pursued us —Ull.*

Teann, *v a* and *n.* (*Ir.* tean) Go; proceed; come; move; tighten, straiten; press together. *Pret a* theann; *fut. aff a* teannaidh Teann suas, *proceed westwards;* theann i ri lasadh a chrùisgein, *she proceeded to light the lamp.—Old Song.* 'G a theannadh mu 'pheirclibh, *tightening it about his jaws.—Macint.* Theann i an lomradh, *she pressed together the fleece.—Stew Jud.*

Teanna, *s m* Enough, sufficiency; abundance; a surfeit. Tha mo theanna agam, *I have enough*, is mairg a rachadh air bhannaig, is a theanna aig fein, *it is pitiful to ask when one has enough of his own —G. P.*

Teannach, aich, *s m* (*Ir. id*) A guiltless person

Teannachadh, aidh, *s. m* A tightening, binding, or squeezing, a besieging, a strait, a siege Tha mi an mo theannachadh, *I am straitened*

Teannachadh, (a), *pr part* of teannaich. Binding, fastening, tightening Gùn ag a theannachadh mu d' mheadhon, *a gown drawn tightly about thy waist.—Old Song*

Teannachair, *s m* (*Ir id*) A pair of pincers, tongs, a vice *N pl* teannachairean.

Teannachan, ain, *s m.* A press; a pair of pincers; a vice *N pl* teannachain

Teannadh, aidh, *s m.* A tightening, a straitening, a pressing, stiffness, rigidness; a proceeding or moving towards any thing, a sufficiency, enough, for the last two senses, see *teanna*, or *teann-shàth.*

Teannaich, *v a.* (*from* teann) Tighten; straiten; bind, squeeze, crush, crowd, oppress; besiege; clasp, clench. *Pret. a* theannaich, *fut aff. a.* teannaichidh. Theannaich iad e, *they besieged it —Stew.* 2 *K* *Fut. pass.* teannaichear. Cha teannaichear do cheumanna, *thy steps shall not be straitened —Stew Pro.* *P. part* teannaichte, *straitened*

Teannair, *s m* (*from* teann.) A squeezing press; a tightener; an oppressor; the roaring of the sea in a cave.

Teannas, ais, *s m* (*Ir id*) Austerity

Teannchair, *s. m.* A pair of pincers; a pair of tongs.—*Stew.* 1 *K. ref* *N pl* teannchairean.

Teanndach, *a* Oppressive, afflictive

Teanndachd, *s. f* Oppression, hardship; affliction or trouble *N pl* teanndachdan, *d pl* teanndachdaibh. O theanndachdaibh, *from troubles —Stew. Pro.*

Teanndaich, *v a* Oppress, afflict; grasp, clench; confine. *Pret. a.* theanndaich, *fut aff* teanndaichidh; *p. part* teanndaichte

Teann-dhruid, *v a* Grasp, clench, hold fast; confine closely; besiege. *Pret a.* theann-dhruid, *grasped; fut. aff.* teann-dhruidh

Teann-fhàisg, *v. a.* (*Ir.* teanfaisg.) Squeeze hard, wring. *Pret a* theann-fhaisg; *fut aff* teann-fhaisgidh; *p. part.* teann-fhàisgte.

Teann-fhasgadh, aidh, *s m* A hard squeezing, or wringing.

Teann-ghlac, *v. a.* Grasp, or hold fast. *Pret. a* theann-ghlac, *fut. aff. a.* teann-ghlacaidh.

Teann-ghlacach, *a.* Grasping firmly.

Teann-ghlacadh, aidh, *s. m.* A grasping firmly; a powerful grasp.

Teann-ghlacta, **Teann-ghlacte**, *p. part.* Grasped, or clenched firmly.

Teann-lamh, aimh, *s. m.* (*Ir. id.*) A tinder-box; fire.

Teannradh, aidh, *s. m.* (*Ir. id.*) A shewing; a manifestation; a discovery.

Teann-shàth, *s.* A surfeit, fill; abundance; sufficiency. Olaidh mi mo theann-shath, *I will drink my fill.—Old Song.* A theann sath aig, *he* or *it has quite enough.* See also **Teanna.**

Teannta, *a.* (*Ir. id.*) Joined together; pressed together; tight.

Teanntachd, *s. f.* (*Ir.* teannta.) Oppression, hardship; distress, trouble. Ann an teanntachd, *in time of trouble.—Stew.* 1 *Ch.* Written also *teanndachd.*

Teanntaich, *v. a.* See **Teanndaich.**

Tearadh, aidh, *s. m.* A contention.

Tearainn. See **Tearuinn.**

Tearb, *v. a.* Separate, part, divide. *Pret. a.* thearb; *fut. aff.* tearbaidh, *shall separate.* Written also, *tearbaidh.*

Tearb, *s. m.* See **Tearbadh.**

Tearbach, *a.* Divisible; separable; apt to divide or separate.

Tearbachd, *s. f.* Divisibleness.

Tearbadh, aidh, *s. m.* A dividing, separating, or parting; a division; a separation. Ghabh mi tearb' o 'n treud sin, *I separated from that flock.—Macfar.*

Tearbaidh, *v. a.* Separate, part, divide. *Pret. a.* thearbaidh; *fut. aff.* tearbaidh. Thearbaidh e na h-uain, *he separated the lambs.—Stew. Gen.*

Tearbhadh. See **Tearbadh.**

Tearc, *a.* (*Ir. id.*) Few, rare, scarce. Bu tearc a ràite, *few were his words.—Oss. Gaul.* Cha tearc sinn mar laoich na Feinn, *we are not few, like Fingal's heroes.—Oss. Duthona.*

Tearcad, aid, *s. m.* Fewness, scarceness, rareness; increase in scarcity. A dol an tearcad, *growing more and more scarce.*

Tearcadh, aidh, *s. m.* Fewness, scarceness.

Tearc-eun, -eoin, *s. m.* A phœnix; *literally*, a rare bird; *rara avis.*

Tearm, *s.* A noise made by trampling.

Tearmunn, uinn, *s. m.* (*Ir. id.*) Protection, safety; defence; a place of security, a sanctuary. Thoir tearmunn, *defend;* òg a thoirt tearmunn, *young to defend.—Old Poem.* Dean tearmunn, *protect.* A chion tearmunn, *for want of protection.—Stew. Job.*

† **Tearmunn**, uinn, *s. m.* (*Ir. id. Lat.* terminus.) A limit or boundary.

Tearmunnach, *a.* Affording protection.

Tearmunnachd, *s. f.* Protection.

Tearmunnair, *s. m.* A protector, a patron.—*Macd.* and *Macfar. Voc. N. pl.* tearmunnairean.

Tearmunnaireachd, *s. f.* Protection.

Tearnach, *a.* Condescending; descending; apt to descend; *also, for* tearuinteach, *giving protection.*

Tearnachd. See **Tearuinteachd.**

Tearnadh, aidh, *s. m.* (*Ir.* tearnadh, *convalescence.*) Descending, descent; sinking; deliverance; protection. Is ioghna do thearnadh, *thy deliverance is wonderful.—Ull.* A tearnadh, *descending;* an curach a direadh 's a tearnadh, *the bark rising and sinking.—Oss. Fin.* and *Lor.*

Tearnadh, (a), *pr. part.* of teirinn.

Tearnar, *fut. pass.* of tearuinn. Shall be saved. Tearnar e, *he shall be saved.—Stew. Rom.*

Tearr, tearra, *s. f.* Tar, pitch.

Tearr, *v. a.* Smear with tar or pitch. *Pret. a.* thearr; *fut. aff.* tearraidh.

Tearrach, aich, *s.* A crupper.

Tearrachd, *s. f.* A bitter remark, a sarcasm.

Tearrachdail, *a.* (tearrachd amhuil.) Sarcastic.

Tearradh, aidh, *s. m.* A tarring or pitching. Gath tearradh, *a whitloe*, or, *felon.*

Tearraid, *s. m.* A police officer; a messenger at arms.—*Macfar. Voc.*

Tearraideach, *a.* Of, or belonging to, a messenger at arms.

Tearraideachd, *s. f.* The business of a police officer, or of a messenger at arms.

† **Tearran**, ain, *s. m.* (*Ir. id.*) Anger, vexation.

Tearuinn, *v. a.* Save, preserve, protect. *Pret. a.* thearuinn, *defended; fut. aff.* tearuinnidh, *shall preserve; fut. pass.* tearuinnear, *shall be saved; p. part.* tearuinnte, *saved.*

Tearuinnear. See **Tearuinn.**

Tearuinnte, *p. part.* of tearuinn. Saved, preserved, protected; safe, secure. Bithidh e tearuinnte, *he shall be safe.—Stew. Pro.*

Tearuinteach, *a.* Protecting, preserving, saving.

Tearuinteachd, *s. f.* Security, safety; salvation. Ann an tearuinteachd, *in safety.—Stew. Job.*

Tearuntachd, *s. f. Stew. Lev. ref.* See **Tearuinteachd.**

Teas, *s. m.* Heat, warmth. Teas an tà, *the heat of the day.—Stew. Gen.* Teas na grein, *the sun's heat;* ruithe air theas, *running to and fro, as cattle are seen to do on a hot day.*
Chal. desun, *burn to a cinder. Old Per.* atesh, *fire. Modern. Per.* tes, *heat. Thibet.* tsa. *Turk.* ates, *heat*, *and* teslik, *anger. W.* tes, *heat. Ir.* teas. *Corn. Arm.* tês.

† **Teas**, *s.* (*Ir. id.*) A message.

Teasach, aich, *s. f.* (*from* teas.) A fever. Airde teasaich, *the height of a fever;* teasach bhuidhe, *a yellow fever. N. pl.* teasaichean.
Ir. teasbhach, *a fever. W.* tesaç, *or*, tesach, *fulness of heat. Arm.* tisicq.

Teasaich, *v. a.* and *n.* (*from* teas.) Warm, heat; become warm or hot. *Pret. a.* theasaich, *warmed; fut. aff. a.* teasaichidh. This verb is not much in use.

Teasaichte, *p. part.* of teasaich. Warmed, heated.

Teasair, *s. m.* (*Ir. id.*) A messenger.

Teasairg, *v. a.* (*Ir.* teasarg.) Save, protect, defend; rescue. *Pret. a.* theasairg, *saved; fut. aff.* teasairgidh, *shall save; p. part.* teasairgte.

Teasairgeach, *a.* Saving, protecting, rescuing.

Teasairginn, *s. f.* (*Ir.* teasairgin.) Deliverance, a rescue; salvation. Chum ar teasairginn, *for our deliverance.—Stew. N. T.*

Teasairgte, *p. part.* of teasairg. Delivered, saved, rescued; safe.

Teasbhach, *a.* (*Ir.* teasmhach.) Sultry, warm; *also, substantively*, sultriness.

Teas-bhat, *s. m.* A hot-bath.

Teas-bhatach, *a.* Abounding in hot-baths; of, or belonging to, a hot-bath.

Teasd, *v. n.* Die, expire. *Pret. a.* theasd, *died; fut. aff.* teasdaidh, *shall die.*

Teasd, *s. m.* A witness.

Teas-fhailce, *s. f.* A hot-bath.

† TEASG, *v. a.* Cut or lop off; prune; wound. *Pret. a.* theasg, *wounded; fut aff. a.* teasgaidh, *shall wound; pret. pass.* theasgadh, *was wounded.* Is ioma ceann a theasgadh leis, *many a head was wounded by him.—Fingalian Poem.*

TEASGADH, aidh, *s. m.* (*Ir. id.*) A cutting down.

† TEASGAL, *a.* (*Ir. id.*) A scorching, blasting wind.

TEAS-GHAOTH, aoithe, *s. f.* (*Ir. id.*) A parching wind.

TEAS-GHRADH, -ghraidh, *s. m.* A fervent love; ardent affection.

TEAS-GHRADHACH, *a.* Cherishing a fervent love; loving ardently or affectionately.

TEAS-GHRADHAICH, *v. a.* Love ardently or tenderly. *Pret. a.* theas-ghradhaich, *loved tenderly; fut. aff. a.* teas-ghradhaichidh.

TEAS-GHRADHAICHTE, *p. part.* of Teas-ghradhaich. Ardently loved.

TEAS-GHUIREAN, ein, *s. m.* A pimple.

TEAS-LOISGEACH, *s. m.* A fervid or burning heat.

TEASTAIL, *s. f.* (*Ir. id.*) Want, defect.

TEASTAS, ais, *s. m.* (*Ir. id.*) A report.

TEAS-THUMAIT, *s. f.* A hot-bath.

TEATH, *a.* See TETH.

TEATHAIR. See TEADHAIR.

TEATHAR, air, *s. m.* A guiltless person.

TEICH, *v. n.* Fly or run away; retreat; keep off, or aside. Theich iad o'n fhàsach, *they fled from the desert.—Oss. Duthona.*

Arm. teichet, *fly.* *Ir.* teich. *Sclav.* tecchi, *run,* and tec, *a race.* *Styr.* and *Carn.* techen, *run.* *Alban.* ticune, *a flight.* *Dalm.* techy.

TEICHEACHD, *s. f.* A running away; a retreating; a flight.

TEICHEADH, idh, *s. m.* A running away, a retreating; a retreat, a flight. Gabh an teicheadh, *take to flight;* air theicheadh, *on flight;* cuir air theicheadh, *put to flight.*

TEICHEADH, (a), *p. part.* of teich. Running away, retreating.

TÈID, *fut. neg.* and *interrog.* of Rach. An téid thu maille rium? *will you go with me?* nach téid thu mach? *will you not go out?* Written also, though not very properly, *d' thèid,* as if *do thèid.*

† TEIL, *s. f.* (*Ir. id.* *Arm.* teile, *dung.*) Fertile ground.

TEILE, *s. f.* (*Ir. id.*) A lime, or linden tree.

TEILEACH, *a.* A lime or linden; full of limes; *substantively,* a place where limes grow.

TEILEAG, eig, *s. f.* (*dim.* of teile.) A little lime-tree; a young lime.

TEILEAGACH, *a.* Abounding in little limes.

TEILG, *more properly* tilg; which see.

TEILICH, *v. a.* (*Ir. id.*) Refuse, deny, conceal. *Pret. a.* theilich, *denied; fut. aff. a.* teilichidh, *shall deny; p. part.* teilichte.

TEILIS, *s. f.* (*Ir. id.*) A house.

TEILLEACH, *a.* Blub-cheeked.—*Macd.*

TEILM, *s. f.* (*Ir. id.*) A dart; an arrow.

TEIMH, *s. m.* Death; a curtain; a cover.

TEIMHEIL, *a.* (*Ir.* teimheal.) Dark, gloomy, obscure.

TEIMHEILEACHD, *s. f.* Darkness; gloom; obscurity.

TEINE, *s. m.* A fire, a flame, a conflagration. Chunnas teine a bhàis, *the flame of death was seen.—Oss. Fing.* Taobh an teine, *the fire-side;* cuir ri theine, *set on fire;* teine adhair, *lightning;* teine dé, *a ring-worm;* teine éibhneis, *a bonfire;* teine sionnachain, *Will-o'-the-wisp;* teine eigin, *a forced fire* (see TEINE EIGIN); teine math, *a good fire;* *Arm.* tan mad.

Arm. Corn. W. tan. *Ir.* teine, *fire.* *Eng.* tine. *Sax.* tynan, *kindle.* *Teine* is perhaps a contraction of *teithin,* or *teitin, i. e.* Titan, *the sun.*

TEINE ADHAIR, *s. m.* Lightning; a thunder-bolt; a fire-ball; any luminous meteor. Thig teine adhair is torunn na 'dheigh, *lightning shall come, and thunder after it.—Macdon.*

TEINE-AOIBHNEIS, *s. m.* A bonfire.

TEINE CHRIOS, *s. m.* An iron for striking fire from a flint.

TEINE DÉ, *s. m.* Herpes; a ring-worm; a certain scorbutic affection of the skin.

TEINE-DHEALAN, *s. m.* Phosphoric light, emitted from putrid fish, or rotten wood.

TEINEASACH, *a.* (*Ir.* teithneasach.) Fiery, hot, impetuous, hasty. *Com.* and *sup.* teineasaiche.

TEINEASACHD, *s. f.* Fieriness; impetuousness; hastiness.

TEINE-ÉIBHNEIS, *s. m.* A bonfire.

TEINE EIGIN, *s. m.* A forced fire, a fire of necessity; a fire produced by friction.

The *teine eigin* was considered an antidote against the plague, the murrain, and all infectious diseases among cattle. Dr. Martin gives the following account of it: "All the fires in the parish were extinguished, and eighty-one married men, being deemed the proper number of men for effecting this purpose, took two planks of wood, and nine of them were employed by turns, who, by their repeated efforts, rubbed the planks against each other, till the heat thereof produced fire; and from this forced fire each family was supplied with new fire. No sooner was the fire kindled than a pot filled with water was put thereon, which was afterwards sprinkled on people who had the plague, or on cattle who had the murrain; and this process was said to be followed with invariable success."

TEINEIL, *a.* (teine amhuil.) Fiery, hot, ardent, passionate. Gu teineil, *passionately;* ro theineil an strì, *very fiery in battle.—Oss. Tem.*

TEINE SIONNACHAIN, *s. m.* A vapour shining without heat, seen during night in marshy ground, and called Will-o'-the-wisp, and Jack-with-the-lantern.

TEINIDH, a. (*from* teine.) Hot, fiery, impetuous, inflammatory.

TEINIS, *s. f.* Tennis.

TEINIS-CHÙIRT, *s. f.* A tennis-court.—*Macd.*

TEINN, teinne, *s. f.* Distress, trouble, difficulty; hardship; strait; perplexity, jeopardy; haste, hurry. Aimsir teinne is trioblaid, *the time of distress and trouble.—Sm.* Ghlaodh iad nan teinn, *they cried in their trouble.—Id.* Anns an teinne, *in the straitness.—Stew. Jer.* Teinn mo chridhe, *my heart's grief.—Sm.*

TEINNBHEALACH, *a.* (*Ir. id.*) Perverse, obstinate, contumacious.

TEINNTEACH, *a.* (*Ir. id.*) Fiery, hot, inflammatory, combustible; impetuous in temper. Mar amhuinn theinntich, *like a fiery furnace.—Sm.*

TEINNTEACH, ich, *s. m.* Lightning.

TEINNTEACHD, *s. f.* Fieriness, inflammatoriness, combustibleness.

TEINNTEAN, ein, *s. m.* (*from* teine.) *Ir.* tinntean. A fire-place, a forge, a furnace. Leac an teinntein, *the hearth.—Stew. Gen.*

TEINNTEANACH, *a.* Having a fire-place, forge, or furnace; of, or belonging to, a fire-place, forge, or furnace.

TEINNTIDH, *a.* (*Ir.* tinntighe.) Fiery, inflammatory, combustible; hot-tempered. Mar chaoiribh teinntidh o 'n chladach, *like fiery gleams from the beach.—Fingalian Poem.*

TEINTREACH, *s. pl.* Sparks of fire; flashes of light or fire; *adjectively,* fiery, combustible, hot-tempered. *Com.* and *sup.* teintreche.

Teirbeirt, *s. f.* A bestowing or distributing; a sending forth. Air theirbheirt teine nan neul, *when clouds send forth their lightning.—Fingalian Poem.*

Teirce, *com.* and *sup.* of Teare. Fewer, fewest.

Teirce, *s. f.* (*Ir. id.*) Fewness; poverty; rareness, scarceness.

Teircead, eid, *s. m.* Fewness, rareness, scarceness; increase in poverty, or in scarceness. A reir teirceid nam bliadhna, *according to the fewness of the years.—Stew. Lev.* A dol an teircead, *growing more and more rare.*

Teirceas, eis, *s. m.* Fewness; scarceness.

Teireadh, idh, *s. m.* A recommendation.

Teirig, *v. n.* (*Ir.* teiric. *Gr.* τείρω. *Lat.* tero, *to spend.*) Wear out, spend, exhaust, come to an end; go, repair to. *Pret.* theirig; *fut. aff.* teirigidh. Gus an teirig an là, *till the day comes to an end.—Stew. Job.* Theirig steach da h-ionnsuidh, *go in unto her.—Stew. Gen.* Na teirig san oidhche amach, *walk not out at night.—Old Didactic Poem. P. part.* teirigte, *worn out, run out, at an end.*

Teirigidh, *fut. aff.* of teirig. Shall wear out.

Teirigte, *p. part.* of teirig; which see.

Teirinn, *v. n.* Descend, come down, alight; dismount. *Pret. a.* theirinn, *descended; fut. aff.* teirinnidh, *shall descend.*

Teiris, *v. a.* and *n.* Tame, quiet, as unruly cattle; stop; be at peace; said to quell cattle when they fight or are unruly.

Teirm, *s. f.* A term, a condition; a season, a while. *N. pl.* teirmean. Air na teirmean sin, *on these terms.*

Teut. termiin, *a boundary.* *Arm.* termen. *Gr.* τερμονς. *Lat.* terminus. *Teirm* once meant a limit of land, as well as of time; being a contracted form of the Armoric *termen*, compounded of ter, *land*, and men, *a stone*. There is no practice more common to all ages and countries, than that of fixing the limits of land by means of a stone.

Teirmeasg, eisg, *s. m.* A mishap, a misfortune. Teirmeasg ort, *a pox take thee, a plague take thee.*

Teirmeasgach, *a.* Unfortunate.

Teirt, *s. f.* (*Ir. id.*) Sunrise.

Téis, *s. f.* (*Ir. id.*) A strain; the air to which any song or poem is sung; diligence. Bu ghrinn thu 'thogail na téis, *thou wert good at raising a strain.—Old Song.*

Teismeid, *s. f.* A last will or testament. Dean do theismeid, *make your will.*

† **Teist**, *s. m.* (*Lat.* testes. *Ir.* teist.) A witness; a drop.

Teisteanas, ais, *s. m.* An attestation, a testimonial, a certificate.

Teisteadh, idh, *s. m.* A defection, a falling off.

Teisteas, eis, *s.* Testimony. Teisteas Dé, *the testimony of God.—Sm.*

Teisteil, *a.* Chaste; having a good character. Gu teisteil, *chastely.*

Teith, *a.* See Teth.

Teithneas, ais, *s. m.* (*Ir. id.*) Haste.

Teithneasach, *a.* Hasty; in haste.

Teò, **Teoth**, *v. a.* Warm. *Pret.* theò, *warmed; fut. aff.* theothaidh, *shall warm;* theo a chridhe, *his heart warmed.—Stew.* 1 *K.*

Teo-chridheach, **Teoth-chridheach**, *a.* Warm-hearted, affectionate. Teo-chridheach da cheile, *affectionate towards each other.—Stew. Rom.*

Teoithe, *com.* and *sup.* of teth. Hotter, hottest.

Teoithead, id, *s. m.* Increase in hotness; heat. A dol an teoithid, *growing more and more hot.*

Teoilteach, *a.* (*Ir. id.*) Warm-hearted.

Teoiteachan, ain, *s. m.* (*Ir. id.*) A warming-pan.

† **Teol**, *s. m.* Plenty; substance; *also*, a thief.

Teoma, *a.* Expert, active, clever; shrewd. Teoma ann an cogadh, *expert in war.—Stew. Song. Sol.*

Teomachd, *s. f.* Expertness, activity, cleverness; manhood; shrewdness. Ann an gaisge is ann an teomachd, *in valour and manhood. Mac Co.*

Teom-chridheach, *a.* Tender-hearted, compassionate, affectionate.

Teom-chridheachd, *s. f.* Tender-heartedness, compassionateness, affectionateness.—*Stew. Phil.*

Teòr, teòir, *s. m.* (*Ir. id.*) A mark or limit; a sign or token.—*Stew. Deut. ref.*

Teotachan, ain, *s. m.* A warming-pan; a chafing-dish.—*Macfar. Voc.*

Teoth. See Teo.

Teoranta, *a.* Definite.

Teorchan, ain, *s. m.* (*Ir. id.*) The space of three hours.

Teothadh, aidh, *s. m.* A warming, a chafing, a heating.

Teothadh, (a), *pr. part.* of teo *or* teoth. Warming, chafing.

Teothachadh, aidh, *s. m.* A warming, chafing, or heating.

Teothachadh, (a), *pr. part.* of teothaich. Warming, heating.

Teothaich, *v. a.* and *n.* (*from* teoth.) Make warm, grow warm. *Pret. a.* theothaich; *fut. aff.* teothaichidh, *shall warm.*

Teothaichte, *p. part.* of teothaich. Warmed.

Teth, *a.* (*Ir. id. Teut.* tet, *burnt.*) Hot, scalding; warm, sultry; *rarely*, smooth, fine. Teth-loisgeach, *burning hot, scalding hot;* gu tinn teth, *feverishly hot.*

Teuchd, *s. m.* A feat or exploit; heroism. Duine a dheanadh teuchd, *a man who could perform an exploit.—Macint.*

Teuchdach, *a.* Supremely valiant, heroic.

Teud, *v. a.* Supply, as an instrument of music, with strings. *Pret.* theud; *fut. aff.* teudaidh.

Teud, teuda, *s. m.* (*Ir.* tead.) The string of a musical instrument; a harp, any stringed instrument; a chord, a string; a rope. Feadh thorman gach teuda, *amid the music of every string.—Ull.* Mairidh e 'm fonn nan teud, *he will live in the music of the harp.—Oss. Gaul.* Inneal binn nan teuda deich, *a melodious ten-stringed instrument.—Sm.* Clarsach gun teud, *a stringless instrument.—Oss. Fing.*

Teudach, *a.* Stringed; having many strings.

Teudach, aich, *s. f.* An assortment of musical strings; the strings of a harp; a quantity of strings.

Teudaiche, *s. m.* (*Ir.* teudaidhe.) A harper. *N. pl.* teudaichean.

Teudan, ain, *s. m.; dim.* of teud. (*Ir.* teidin.) A little musical string; also *n. pl.* of teud.

Teud-cheòl, -chiùil, *s. m.* The music of a stringed instrument. Bu bhinne na teud-cheòl a guth, *sweeter than harp-music was her voice.—Old Poem.*

Teud-chleas, *s. m.* A feat in rope-dancing.

Teud-chleasachd, *s. f.* Rope-dancing.

Teud-chleasaiche, *s. m.* (*Ir.* teid-cleasaidhe.) A rope-dancer.

Teug-bhoil, *s. f.* A battle, a strife; severe affliction. Tùs na teug-bhoil, *the front of battle.—Old Poem.* Written also *teugmhail.*

Teug-bhoileach, *a.* Warlike, contentious; afflictive.

Teugmhail. See Teug-bhoil.

Teugmhaileach, *a.* See Teug-bhoileach.

† **Teul**, *s. m.* (*Ir. id.*) A subterraneous passage.

Teum, *v. a.* Bite; sting; cut or taunt. *Pret. a.* theum, *bit; fut. aff. a.* teumaidh, *shall bite.* Teumaidh nathair e, *a serpent shall bite him.—Stew. Ecc. Fut. pass.* teumar, *shall be bitten; p. part.* teumta, *bitten.*

Teum, teuma, *s. m.* A bite; a mouthful, a morsel; a taunt, a sarcasm. Teum arain, *a morsel of bread.*

Teumach, *a.* Prone to bite.

Teumadh, aidh, *s. m.* A biting, a bite.

Teumaidh, *fut. aff.* of teum; which see.

Tha, *asp. form* of ta, *pr. aff.* of the *aux. v.* bi. Am, art, is. are.

Thabhair, *v. a.* Give, grant, bestow. Contracted *thoir;* which see.

Thachair, *pret.* of tachair. Met, happened. See Tachair.

Thabhairt, (a), *inf.* of tabhair *or* thabhair.

Thairbhse. See Taibhse.

Thaic, *asp. form* of taic.

Thaim, *poetic contraction* of tha mi. I am. Ged thaim a nois gun chàil, *though now I be feeble.*—*Oss.*

Thàin, *for* thainig. See Thig.

Thàinig, *pret.* of thig; which see.

Thair, *prep.* Over, above, beyond, to the other side. Thair gach té, *beyond or above all women.*—*Mac Lach.* See also Thar.

Thairis, *prep.* (*Ir.* tairis.) Over, above, beyond, athwart; to the further side; at an end; remaining, over and above. Gach ni a bhios thairis, *every thing that remains;* chaidh mi thairis orra, *I went beyond,* or *excelled them;* thoir thairis, *give over;* thug e thairis, *he overfatigued himself.*

Thairt, Thairte, *comp. pron.* Over her, above her, beyond her, across her. Raineach uaine a teachd thairt, *green fern growing over her.*—*Oss. Derm.*

Thall, *adv.* Beyond, on the other or further side, opposite, yonder, at a little distance. Tannais a sgreadail a thall, *ghosts screaming opposite.*—*Oss. Fing.* Thall 's a bhos, *hither and thither, here and there, on all sides.*

Th'ann, (*for* tha ann *or* ta ann.) Exists, is there, is in that place. Guth Dheirg is e th'ann, *it is the voice of Dargo that is there.*—*Ull.* Co th'ann? *who is it?* Ciod th'ann? *what is it? what is in that place?*

Thannas, *asp. form* of tannas; which see.

Thaobh, *asp. form* of taobh; which see.

Thaobh, (a), *prep.* Concerning, touching; by reason of; on account of; as for; aside; astray. Thaobh tuairmeis, *at a venture.*—*Stew.* I *K.* A thaobh tubaist, *by accident;* dol a thaobh, *going aside* or *astray; apostatizing.*

Thaom, *pret.* of taom.

Thapadh. See Tapadh.

Thar, *prep.* Over, across, to the further side, beyond. Tharr bharraibh nan tonn, *over the tops of the waves.*—*Ull.* Thar 'uaigh ag aomadh, *bending over his grave.*—*Oss. Fin. and Lor.* Thar a chòir, *superfluous, too much.*—*Stew. Lev.*

Thar a chéile, *adv.* In disorder, in confusion; stirred about; agitated; deranged, crazed. Cuir thar a chéile, *confuse, disarrange, drive mad.*

Tharad, *comp. pron.* (*for* thairis ort.) Over thee, across thee, beyond thee.

Tharam, *comp. pron.* (thairis orm.) Over me, across me, beyond me. Seachd gealaich chaidh tharam, *seven moons passed over me,* i. e. *I spent seven months.*—*Ull.*

Tharladh, *pret.* of *v. def.* tarladh. Came to pass, befell.

Tharlas, *fut. sub.* of *v. def.* tarladh. Shall have happened or met; shall happen or meet. Tra tharlas doibh an céinthir, *when they meet in a foreign land.*—*Oss.*

Tharruinn, *comp. pron.* (*for* thairis oirnne.) Over us, across. Theid tharruinn an sruth le caoirean bròin, *the stream shall pass over us with a melancholy murmur.*—*Oss. Derm.*

Tharruing, *pret.* of tarruing.

Tharta, *comp. pron.* (*for* thairis orra.) Over them, across them. Tharta tha na sruthain a breabail, *over them the streams are gurgling.*—*Oss. Dargo.*

Thartar, *asp. form* of tartar; which see.

Theab, *def. v.* (used through all the persons of the preterite.) Had almost, had nearly, was near to, was nearly, was almost. Theab e tuiteam, *he had almost fallen.* Theab mi, thu, e, *I, thou, he, had almost.*

Theabhachd, *asp. form* of teabhachd.

Theach, *asp. form* of teach.

Theag', Theagamh, *adv.* Perhaps, perchance, peradventure. Theag gur eòl dhuit an lann so, *perhaps thou knowest this sword.*—*Oss. Dargo.* Theagamh gur mearrachd a bh'ann, *perhaps it was an oversight.*—*Stew. Gen.*

Thearnadh. See Tearnadh.

Theich, *pret.* of teich. Theicheas, *fut. sub.;* theichinn, 1 *sing. imp. sub.* I would fly. See Teich.

Théid, *fut. aff.* of rach. Shall or will go. Théid sinn air chùl, *we shall vanish.*—*Oss. Fing.* Theid do bhàth, *thou shalt be drowned;* theid do chrochadh, *thou shalt be hanged;* theid am marbh, *they shall be killed.* See Rach.

Theine, *asp. form* of teine.

Theinntich. See Teinnteach.

Their, *fut. aff. a.* of abair; which see.

Theirbeirt. See Teirbeirt.

Theireadh, *imp. sub.* of abair. Would say.

Theiream, (*for* their mi.) I will say.

Theirear, *fut. pass.* of abair. Shall be said.

Theirig, *pret. a.* of teirig.

Theirinn, *pret. sub.* of abair. I would or could say. See Abair.

Theirteadh, *sub. pass.* of abair. Could or would be said.

Theò, Theòth. See Teo.

Theòthaich, *pret.* of teòthaich.

Thi, *asp. form* of ti; which see.

Thig, *fut. aff.* of thig. Shall come. Thig Treunmor le 'dhoininn, *Treunmor shall come in his tempest.*—*Ull.* Thig e rium, *it will please me;* thig uait, *come forward,* said in defiance.

Thigeadh, 3 *sing.* and *pl. imper.* of thig. Let come. Thigeadh e, iad, *let him* or *them come;* also, *pret. sub.* of thig, *would come; ought, would become.* Thigeadh e nam faodadh e, *he would come, if allowed;* thigeadh duit a dheanamh, *you ought to do it.*

Thigeam, *imper.* of thig. Let me come; *also, for* thig mi, *I shall or will come.*

Thigheachd. See Tigheachd.

Thighearna. See Tighearn.

Thiginn, 1 *sing. pret. sub.* of thig. I would come.

Thill, *pret.* of till. Returned. Thill na laoich nan caogadaibh, *the heroes returned in bands of fifties.*—*Fingalian Poem.*

Thilleas, *fut. sub.* of till; which see.

Thimchioll, (mu), *prep.* Around, about, in a circuit, concerning. Mu thimchioll da cheud, *about two hundred;* mu m' thimchioll, *about me;* mu 'thimchioll, *about him;* mu 'n timchioll, *about them.* Do bhreacan mu d' thimchioll, *thy plaid about thee.*—*Old Song.*

Thìr, *asp. form* of tìr.

Thirim, *for* thioraim, *asp. inflection of* tioram. Dry, parched, barren. O'n sgeir thirim bha 'sùil 's a glaodh, *from the barren pinnacle she looked and wailed.*—*Oss. Fin. and Lor.*

Thisd! *interj.* Hush!

Thiugh. See Tiugh.

Thiughaich, *pret.* of tiughaich; which see.

Thlà, *asp. form* of tlà; which see.

Thnù, *asp. form* of tnù, *s. m.* Envy, malice.

Thog, *pret. a.* of tog. Lifted, raised, elevated; educated, reared. See Tog.

Thogail, *asp. form* of togail.

Thogail, (a), *infin.* of tog; which see.

Thogair, *pret.* of togair; which see.

Thogas, *fut. sub.* of tog.

Thogradh. See Togradh.

Thoil. See Toil.

Thoilich, *pret.* of toilich.

Thoill, *pret. a.* of toill. Deserved, merited.

Thoinneamh, (a), *infin.* of toinn *or* toinneamh.

Thomhais, *pret. a.* of tomhais.

Thoinnte, *asp. form* of toinnte, *p. part.* of toinn.

Thoir, (*contracted for* thabhair.) Give, bestow, grant, deliver. *Pret. a.* thug; *fut. aff.* bheir; *fut. neg.* toir. Thoir air, *compel him; persuade him;* thoir orra, *compel them;* thoir aire, *attend, observe;* thoir an aire, *take care, observe;* thoir leum, *jump;* thoir ionnsuidh, *attack, make an onset;* thoir thairis, *give up; resign or abdicate; surrender;* thoir buidheachas, *give thanks;* thoir oidhirp, *attempt;* thoir stigh, *bring in; tame; cultivate;* thoir stigh ort, *get in with you, get into the house;* thoir an dorus ort, *go to the door;* thoir aichmheil, *avenge;* thoir suas, *yield, cede, surrender, abdicate;* thoir breith, *judge, decide;* thoir an geall, *bet, pawn, pledge, mortgage;* thoir comhairle, *advise;* thoir as, *take out; fly, escape;* thoir as thu fein, *fly, deliver thyself*—(*Stew. Pro.*); thoir na casan asad, *take to your heels;* thoir na buinn asad, *take to your heels;* thoir smachd, *chastise, rebuke;* thoir géill, *yield, submit, obey;* thoir thairis e, *bring him over; overfatigue him;* thug e thairis, *he knocked himself up;* thoir ceum, *make a step, step;* thoir mach, *take out; descry, spy;* thoir tuairmeas, *guess.* Thugaibh am monadh oirbh, *betake yourselves to the mountains.*—*Stew. Jos.* Cha tugainn srabh ort, *I value you not a straw.* *Pret. pass.* thugadh, *was given.*

Thoiseach, *asp. form* of toiseach.

Thonn, *asp. form* of tonn; which see.

Thorman, *asp. form* of torman; which see.

Thorr, *asp. form* of torr.

Thorran, *asp. form* of torran.

Thréig, *pret.* of tréig; which see.

Threigsinn, (a), *infin.* of treig. To leave, forsake, or abandon.

Thréine, *asp. form* of tréine; which see.

Threise, *asp. form* of treise; which see.

Throid, *pret. a.* of troid; which see.

Throisg, *pret.* of troisg.

Thruaighe. See Truaighe.

Thruim, *asp. form* of truim, an *inflection* of trom; which see.

Thrus, *v. a.* of trus. Gathered; collected; bundled.

Thrusdair, *voc. sing.* of trusdar.

Thu, (*asp. form* of tu), *pers. pron.* Thou; thee.

Pers. tou *and* tu, *thou.* *Dor. and Æol.* τυ. *Lat.* tu. *Goth.* thu. *Isl.* thu. *Swed.* tu *and* du. *Dan.* du. *Du.* u. *Sax.* tho *and* thu. *Germ.* thu *and* du. *Arm.* to *and* hu. *Ir.* tu.

Thuadh, *asp.* of tuadh.

Thuaineal, *asp. form* of tuaineal. Giddiness; dizziness, vertigo. Ghlac e an t-aos-dharach na thuaineal, *he grasped an aged oak in his dizziness.*—*Oss. Dargo.* See Tuaineal.

Thuaiream, *asp. form* of tuaiream.

Thuairmeas, *asp. form* of tuairmeas.

Thuairmeis, (mu), *adv.* About, near the number of. Mu thuairmeis dheich mìle, *about ten thousand.*

Thuarasdal. See Tuarasdal.

Thuath. See Tuath.

Thubhairt, *pret.* of abair.

Thubhradh, *pret. pass.* of abair; which see.

Thugad, *comp. pron.* To thee, unto thee. Thugad-sa, *unto thee.*—*Stew. Ps.* *Thugad*, is often said to those whom we wish to warn of immediate personal danger.

Thugar, (*from* thoir *or* tabhair), *used impersonally.* Was brought; *also*, bring. Thugar an so beagan uisge, *bring here a little water.*—*Stew. Gen.*

Thugas, (*for* thugadh.) See Thoir.

Thugtar, *imper. pass.* of thoir *or* tabhair.

Thuig, *pret. a.* of tuig. Understood.

Thuige, *prep.* (*for* chuige *or* h-uige.) To, towards. Thuige sin, *thither.*—*Stew. Ecc.*

Thuigeadh, 3 *sing.* and *pl. imp. a.* of tuig.

Thuiginn, 1 *sing. pret. sub.* of tuig. I would understand.

Thuigse, *asp. form* of tuigse; which see.

Thuigsinn, (a), *pr. infin.* of tuig. To understand.

Thuil, *asp. form* of tuil. Bhruchd cuimhne na bha mar thuil, *the remembrance of the past rushed like a flood.*—*Oss. Dargo.*

Thuill. See Toll.

Thuille, **Thuilleadh**, *adv.* Moreover, beside; over and above; more, nay more. Thuilleadh air bhur boidibh, *beside your vows.*—*Stew. Lev.* Do thuilleadh sluagh, *of more people.*—*Stew. Sam.* Thuille air so, *moreover;* thuille air sin, *moreover.*

Thuillead. See Tuillead.

Thuilteach, *asp. form* of tuilteach.

Thuinn, *s.* (*asp. form* of tuinn.) Wave, billow. A h-anam mar thuinn a luasgadh, *her mind agitated like a billow.*—*Oss. Gaul.* See Tonn.

Thuir, *v. sing.* of tùr; which see.

Thuireadh, *asp. form* of tuireadh; which see.

Thuirleas, *sub. pret.* of tuirl. Shall descend. Tra thuirleas m'anam an ceo, *when my spirit shall descend in the mist.*—*Oss. Gaul.*

Thuirling, *pret.* of tuirling; which see.

Thuirt, *contraction for* thubhairt; which see.

Thuislich, *pret. a.* of tuislich; which see.

Thuit, *pret. a.* of tuit. Fell, stumbled. See Tuit.

Thuiteadh, *imp. sub.* of tuit. Would fall.

Thuiteas, *fut. sub.* of tuit. Would fall.

Thul-chuiseach, *asp. form* of tul-chuiseach.

Thun, *prep.* and *adv.* To, unto, almost. Greasam le sleagh thun mo ghaoil, *I will hasten with a spear to my beloved.*—*Oss. Derm.* Thun mo mhic, *to my son.*—*Oss. Gaul.* Thun tuiteam, *almost falling.*

Thurram. See Turram.

Thùrus, *asp. form* of tùrus; which see.

Thusa, *pers. pron.; emphatic form* of thu. Thou, thee.

Thut. An expression of impatience.

Tì, *s. m.* A rational being. An tì 's àirde, *the Supreme Being; voc.* A thì! *O thou Being!* A thì tha 'stiùradh na cruinne! *O thou who governest the globe.*—*Macfar.*

Malcolm has the following observations on the word *ti.* "In St. Kilda," he says, "*ti* means *great.* The old name of Hispaniola is Hayti. Now *I* is an island; as, *I choluim chille,* Icolmkil. A Southron would pronounce *i* ay *or* ai, and *ti,* great, would be *ayti,* or the great island. Among the Caribs, *di* means a great person; and among the Gael, *Dia* is God. The striking resemblance between many West Indian, American, and Celtic terms, may be seen under An, Ab, and elsewhere throughout this work.

Ti, *s. m.* (*Ir. id.*) Intention, design, purpose. Bha 'thi air mise a sgrios, *his design was to slay me.—Orr.*

Tiachair, *s. m.* (*Ir. id.*) A naughty person; *also, adjectively,* perverse.

Tiachdaidh, *s. m.* A customer; a resorter, a haunter; a guest.

Tiadhan, ain, *s. m.* (*Ir. id.*) A little hill, a mound; a stone, a testicle; an otter. *N. pl.* tiadhain.

Tiadhanach, *a.* Full of little hills or mounds.

Tiag, *s. m.* (*Ir. id.*) A wallet; a vessel.

Tiaghas, ais, *s. m.* A mansion.

Tiamhachd, *s. f.* Gloominess, solitariness, sonorousness.—*Macfar. Voc.*

Tiamhaidh, *a.* (*Ir.* tiamhdha.) Gloomy, solitary, lonely; dark; quiet; sonorous. Nach tiamhaidh tosd an oidhche, *how gloomy and quiet is the night!—Oss. Gaul.* Gu tiamhaidh, *solitarily.*

Tiamhaidheachd, *s. f.* Gloominess, solitariness, sonorousness.

Tiarmail, *a.* Sagacious; prudent; thoughtful; sedate. Gu tiarmail, *sagaciously.*

Tiarmalachd, *s. f.* Sagaciousness; prudence; thoughtfulness; sedateness.

Tiarrach, aich, *s. m.* (*Ir.* tiarrthach.) A paunch; a tripe.

† Tias, *s. m.* (*Ir. id.*) A tide.—*Shaw.*

Tiasgadal, ail, *s. m.* (*Ir. id.*) Industry; contrivance.—*Shaw.*

Tibearsan, ain, *s. m.* (*Ir. id.*) A springing, a sprouting; overflowing.

Tibhe, *s. f.* A gibe.

Tibheach, ich, *s. m.* A giber.

Tibhearsean, ein, *s. m.* A spouting, an overflowing; a spunging.

Tibh-fhiacal, ail, *s. m.* (*Ir. id.*) A fore-tooth.

† Tibhre, *s. m.* (*Ir. id.*) A fool; one who laughs or giggles much.

Tibhreach, *a.* (*Ir. id.*) Foolish; giggling.

Tibhreadh, idh, *s. m.* A springing, a flowing.

Tig, *fut. neg.* and *interrog.* of thig. Shall come. Written also *d'thig.*

Tigh, tighe, *s. m.* A house, a mansion or dwelling-house. Mullach an tighe, *the top of the house;* ceann-tighe, *the head of a house or family; the head of the branch of a family.* Tigh-arm, *an armoury, a dépôt.* Gu bhi na thigh-arm, *to be an armoury.—Stew. Song. Sol.* Tigh-bainne, *a dairy;* tigh-cànach, *a custom-house;* tigh-cise, *a custom-house;* tigh-malairt, *an exchange;* tigh-caol, *a narrow house* or *grave.* Sìth ann do chriadh-thigh caol, *peace in thy cold mansion of clay.—Oss.* Tigh-chearc, *a hen-house;* tigh-faire, *a watch-house;* tigh-aire, *a watch-house; a house where vigils are held over a corpse;* tigh-cluiche, *a theatre;* tigh-eiridinn, *a poor-house; an hospital;* tigh-cùinnidh, *a mint;* tigh-cuthaich, *a madhouse;* tig-òsd, *an inn*—(*Stew. Gen.* and *Acts*); *also, an alehouse;* tigh-lionn, *an alehouse;* tigh-beag, *a necessary;* tigh-nigheachain, *a laundry;* tigh-mhànach, *a convent, a monastery;* tigh-tasgaidh, *a store-house*—(*Stew.* 1 *Chr.*); tigh-màile, *a hired house;* na thigh-màile fein, *in his own hired house*—(*Stew. Acts*); tigh-sgoile, *a schoolhouse;* tigh smachduchaidh, *a house of correction*—(*Stew. Jer.*); tigh-stòr, *a magazine* or *granary, a storehouse;* tigh-taimh, *an inn*—(*Stew. Ex.*); tigh-teth, *a hothouse;* tigh-tairn, *an inn*—(*Macint.*); tigh-togalach, *a brewery, a brewing-house.* As an tigh, *out of the house; Arm.* eus an ty. Aig an tigh, *at home, at the house;* in *Vannes* they say *ag an ty.* Tigh rioghail, *a palace; Arm.* ty roëyal. Ann mo thigh, *in my house; Arm.* en ma ty. Ann do thigh, *in thy house; Arm.* en da ty.

Gr. τοῖχος *and* τειχος, *a wall,* τεγος, *a house. Ir.* tigh *and* teagh. *W.* tŷ. *Corn.* tshyi. *Arm.* ti *and* ty.

Tighe, *gen. sing.* of tigh.

Tigheachd, *s. f.* Coming, arriving; an arrival, an approach. Ann dochas ri d'thigheachd, *in hopes of thy coming.—Ull.* Often contracted *teachd;* which see.

Tigheadas, ais, *s. m.* (*from* tigh.) Housekeeping; husbandry; residence. Fionn na thigheadas samhraidh, *Fingal in his summer's residence.—Old Legend.*

Tighean, ein, *s. m.* A bag or satchel.

Tighean, *n. pl.* of tigh.

Tighearn, arna, *s. m.* A lord; a baronet; a name given to any proprietor, however insignificant.

Tighearn is always written by the Gael with *gh:* and I do not think it advisable to deviate in this instance from the common orthography, though I am persuaded that the Irish *tiarna* is a more correct form of the word. It is evidently the same with *terna* of the Chaldaic, τυραννος of the Greek, *tyrannus* of the Latin, and *teyrn* of the Welch and Armoric. This being the case, the *gh* seems to have been introduced into this word and its derivatives by the ancient rehearsers of Gaelic poetry, or by Gaelic poets themselves, in order to make up three syllables. A similar epenthesis occurs in the first verse of the Iliad.

Tighearnachd, *s. f.* Lordship.

Tighearnail, *a.* (tighearn-amhuil.) *W.* teyrnawl. Lordly, haughty; domineering.

Tighearnas, ais, *s. m.* (*from* tighearn.) *W.* teyrnas. *Ir.* tiarnas. Lordship, mastery, supremacy, power, dominion, superiority; jurisdiction. Tighearnas le h-an-iochd, *mastery with rigour.—Stew. Lev. ref.* Cha 'n eil tighearnas aig bàs oirbh, *death has no dominion over you.—Stew. Rom.*

Tigheas, eis, *s. m.* (*Ir. id.*) *from* tigh. Housekeeping; husbandry.

Tigheasach, *a.* (*Ir. id.*) Domestic, fond of domestic life; fond of housekeeping; of, or belonging to, housekeeping.

Tighinn, *s. m.* Coming, approaching; an arrival, an approach. Cha n' fhaicear ni 's mo do thighinn, *thy coming shall be seen no more.—Death of Carril.*

Tighinn, (a), *pr. part.* of thig. Coming, approaching.

Tighinn stigh, *s. m.* A coming in; entrance; an income or revenue.

Tileadh, idh, *s. m.* (*Ir. id.*) A ship's poop.

Tilg, *v. a.* (*Ir.* tealg *and* teilg.) Throw, cast, fling; produce, yield, or bring forth; shoot; fire, as with a gun; vomit. *Pret. a.* thilg, *threw; fut. aff.* tilgidh, *shall throw.* Tilg t-aran, *cast thy bread.—Stew. Ecc. Fut. sub.* thilgeas. Gach craobh a thilgeas meas, *every tree that yields fruit.—Stew. Gen. ref.* Tilg crann, *cast lots;* tilg smugaid, *spit. Fut. pass.* tilgear, *shall be thrown; p. part.* tilgte.

Tilgear, *fut. pass.* of tilg; which see.

Tilgte, *p. part.* of tilg. Thrown, cast; shot. Tilgte air an t-slighe, *cast upon the highway.—Stew.* 1 *K.*

Tilig. See Tilg.

Till, *v. n.* Turn; return, come back. *Pret.* thill; *fut. aff.* tillidh. Cha till mi, *I shall not return.—Oss. Fing.* Ged phillea Mac Leoid cha till Mac Cruimein, *though Mac Leod shall return, Mac Crummin shall never.—Old Song.*

Tilleadh, idh, *s. m.* A turning, a returning, a return.

Tillidh, *fut. aff.* of till.

Tìm, *s. f.* (*Swed.* timme, *hour.*) Time; season. Ann am bliadhna thìm, *in a year's time;* tìm an earraich, *the spring season.*

Tìmbuail, *s. f.* A cymbal.

Timchioll, *v.* (*Ir.* timchill.) Surround, encompass. *Pret. a.* thiomchioll; *fut. aff.* timchiollaidh.

Timchioll, *prep.* (*Ir.* timchioll.) Round about, in a circuit. Mu thimchioll, *around; concerning;* timchioll orm *around me.*

Timchiollach, *a.* Circuitous; circular.

TIMCHIOLLADH, *s. f.* Circuitousness, circularity; tending towards circularity.

TIMCHIOLLADH, aidh, *s. m.* A surrounding.

TIMCHIOLL-GHEARR, *v. a.* Circumcise, cut around. *Pret.* thimchioll-ghearr; *fut. aff.* timchioll-ghearraidh.

TIMCHIOLL-GHEARRADH, aidh, *s. m.* (*Ir.* timchill-ghearradh.) Circumcision, a cutting round.

TIMCHIOLL-GHEARRTA, *p. part.* of timchioll-ghearr. Circumcised.

TIMCHIOLL-SGRIOBH, *v. a.* Write around.

TIMCHIOLLTA, *p. part.* of timchioll. Surrounded.

† TIME, *s. f.* (*Ir. id.*) Fear; heat; pride; dignity.—*Shaw.*

† TIMEACH, *a.* Timid; hot; proud.

TIMEIL, *a.* (tim-amhuil.) Timely; timorous.

TIMHEAL, eil, *s. m.* (*Arm.* teval.) Darkness; a glimmering or shady light.

TIMHEALACH, *a.* (*Ir. id.*) Dark; glimmering; gloomy.

TIN, *s.* The seventeenth letter (T) of the Gaelic.

TINEACH, ich, *s. m.* (*Ir. id.*) Kindred.

TINGEALACH, ich, *s. m.* House-leek.

TINN, *a.* (*Ir. id. Eng.* tine, *trouble.*) Sick; faint. Tinn le fiabhrus, *sick with a fever.*—*Stew. N. T.* Bha fonn an oran tiamhaidh tinn, *the strain of their song was plaintive and sad.*—*Ull.* Tha e gu tinn, *he is sick;* gu tinn teth, *sick and feverish. Com.* and *sup.* tinne.

TINNE, *s. f.* (*from* teann.) Tightness; severity, rigidness.

TINNE, *com.* and *sup.* of teann. Tighter, tightest.

TINNE, *s. f.* (*Ir. id.*) The link of a chain; a chain. *N. pl.* tinneachan.

TINNEANACH, *a.* Liable to fits, subject to fits.

TINNEANAS, *s. m.* (*from* tinn.) Fits.

TINNEAS, eis, *s. m.* (*Ir. id.*) Sickness, disease. Leabadh a thinneis, *the bed of his sickness.*—*Stew. Ps.* Tinneas na gealaich, *lunacy;* tinneas feachd, *army-sickness;* tinneas sgoile, *truantship;* tinneas-caitheimh, *consumption.*

TINNEASACH, *a.* Sickly, distempered; frail; evil.

TINNEASACHD, *s. f.* Sickness, sickliness; the misfortune of being subject to fits.

TINNEAS-AN-RIGH, *s. m.* The scrofula.

TINNEAS-CLOINNE, *s. m.* Pains of parturition; travail—(*Stew. Gen.*); distempers of children.

† TINNEASNACH, *a.* (*Ir. id.*) Stout, strong; having stout ribs.

TINNREAMH, *s. m.* (*Ir. id.*) Service.

TINNTEAGAL, ail, *s. m.* (*Ir. id.*) Corruption.

TINNTEANAS, ais, *s. m.* Great haste.

TIOBAIR, *s. f.* A spring, a fountain, a draw-well. *N. pl.* tiobraichean.

TIOBAIRT, *s. f.* (*Ir.* tiobar *and* tiobrad.) A spring, a fountain, a draw-well; a cistern. As do thiobairt, *from thy cistern.*—*Stew. Pro. N. pl.* tiobairtean.

TIOBAIRTEACH, *a.* Abounding in springs; of, or belonging to, springs.

TIOBAR, air, *s. f.* (*Ir. id.*) A spring-well or fountain, a draw-well. *N. pl.* tiobair.

TIOBARSAN, ain, *s. m.* A springing; streaming; dropping.

TIOBRACH, *a.* Abounding in spring-wells; of, or belonging to, springs.

TIODAL, ail, *s. m.* (*Ir. id.*) A title. *N. pl.* tiodalan.

TIODALAICH, *v. a.* Entitle, confer a title. *Pret.* thiodalaich; *p. part.* tiodalaichte.

TIODHLAC, aic, *s. m.* A gift or present, a donation; an offering; a funeral, interment.

TIODHLACADH, aidh, *s. m.* (*Ir.* tiodhlacadh, *gift.*) A granting or bestowing; a gift; the act of burying; an interment. Tiodhlacadh ann an diomhaireachd, *a gift in secret.*—*Stew. Pro.* A tiodhlacadh, *bestowing; burying.*

TIODHLAIC, *v. a.* (*Ir.* tiodhlac, *present.*) Bestow, present; bury. *Pret. a.* thiodhlaic, *buried.* Thiodhlaic an laoch a chù, *the hero buried his dog.*—*Old Poem. Fut. aff.* tiodhlacaidh, *shall bury; p. part.* tiodhlaichte, *buried.*

TIOGAIR, *s. m.* A tiger. *N. pl.* tiogairean.

TIOGAIREACH, *a.* Like a tiger, fierce like a tiger.

† TIOGH, *a.* (*Ir. id.*) Late.

TIOLAM, aim, *s. m.* A snatch; a sudden attempt at biting.

TIOLAMACH, *a.* Snatching, prone to snatch or bite.

TIOLP, *v. a.* Snatch, grasp at. *Pret.* thiolp, *snatched; fut. aff. a.* tiolpaidh, *shall snatch.*

TIOLPACH, *a.* Carping, snatching; apt to carp or to snatch; captious, cavilling.

TIOLPADAIR, *s. m.* A critic; a carper; a superficial critic; a cut-purse. *N. pl.* tiolpadairean.

TIOLPADAIREACHD, *s. f.* Criticising; a carping.

TIOLPADAN, ain, *s. m.* A cut-purse.

TIOLPADH, aidh, *s. m.* A snatching, a grasping suddenly or eagerly; a carping; captiousness. Luchd tiolpaidh, *cavillers.*

TIOM, *s. f.* Time; *also*, thyme.—*Macd.*

TIOM, *a.* (*Ir. id.*) Tender, mild, soft; timid; delicate; compassionate, warm-hearted. Crithidh feachd nach tiom, *hosts that are* [*not timid*] *valiant shall tremble.*—*Oss. Fing.*

TIOM, *v. a.* and *n.* Soften, assuage.

TIOMACH, *a.* Soft, delicate, timid; merciful, warm-hearted.

TIOMACHADH, aidh, *s. m.* A softening, a melting into tears; a becoming timid; softness, timidity, mercifulness.

TIOMACHD, *s. f.* (*Ir. id.*) Softness, tenderness.

TIOMADH, aidh, *s. m.* Softness, delicateness; melting into tears; a softening with grief; timidity; warm-heartedness; dejection. Iomadh ceud fo thiomadh, *many a hundred dejected.*—*Old Song.* Thàinig tiomadh air suilean Fhionn, *Fingal's eyes melted into tears.*—*Oss. Taura.*

TIOMAICH, *v. a.* and *n.* (*from* tiom.) Soften or make effeminate; become softened; become exorable; intimidate; become afraid. *Pret. a.* thiomaich; *fut. aff. a.* tiomaichidh, *shall soften.* Laoch nach tiomaich, *a hero who shall not become afraid.*—*Macdon.*

TIOMAIN, *s. f.* (*Ir. id.*) A driving; a proceeding.

TIOMAIRG, *v. a.* (*Ir. id.*) Collect, gather.

TIOMAL, ail, *s. m.* (*Ir. id.*) An ambit.

TIOMALLAIR, *s. m.* (*Ir. id.*) A glutton.

TIOMALTAS, ais, *s. m.* (*Ir. id.*) Victuals.

TIOMARGADH, aidh, *s. m.* (*Ir. id.*) A collection; a translation.

TIOMARNADH, aidh, *s. m.* (*Ir. id.*) A command.

† TIOMAN, *v. a.* (*Ir. id.*) Give, bestow; drive; turn off, thrust off, push.

TIOMANTA, *part.* (*Ir. id.*) Given, bequeathed.

TIOMANTAIR, *s. m.* (*Ir. id.*) One who bequeaths.

TIOMBHAIGH, *s. f.* False fellowship.

TIOM-BUAIL, *s. f.* A cymbal.

TIOM-CHAINNT, *s. f.* (*Ir. id.*) Circumlocution.

TIOMCHAIR, *a.* (*Ir. id.*) Tender-hearted.

TIOM-CHRIDHE, *s. m.* A warm heart; *also*, compassion, mercy. Cuiribh oirbh tiom-chridhe, *put on compassion.*

TIOM-CHRIDHEACH, *a.* Warm-hearted, compassionate, merciful.

TIOM-CHUAIRT, *s. f.* (*Ir. id.*) A visit; a bishop's visit; a justiciary circuit; a periodical visit or return; a friendly visit; a cycle; a circle.

TIOM-CHUAIRTEACH, *a.* Periodical; circular.

TIOMGHAIR, *v. a.* (*Ir. id.*) Ask, request.

TIOMGHAIRE, *s. f.* (*Ir. id.*) A request, a petition.

TIOMHAIDH. See TIAMHAIDH.

TIOMHAIDHEACHD, *s. f.* See TIAMHAIDHEACHD.

TIOMNA. See TIOMNADH.

TIOMNACH, *a.* Of, or belonging to, a will; testatory.

TIOMNACH, aich, *s. m.* (*Ir. id.*) A bequeather, a testator.

TIOMNADH, aidh, *s. m.* A will or testament; a covenant. An Tiomnadh Nuadh, *the New Testament;* an Sean Tiomnadh, *the Old Testament.*

TIOMNAICH, *v. a.* (*Ir.* tiomnaigh.) Bequeath. *Pret. a.* thiomnaich; *fut. aff.* tiomnaichidh, *shall bequeath.*

TIOMNADH, *v. a.* (*Ir.* tiomna.) Deliver up; bequeath; surrender. *Pret.* a. thiomnadh, *bequeathed; fut. aff.* tiomnaidh, *shall bequeath; fut. pass.* tiomnar, *shall be bequeathed.*

TIOMNAIR, *s. m.* A testator; a legator. *N. pl.* tiomnairean.

TIOMNAM, (*for* tiomnaidh mi.) I shall or will bequeath.

TIOMPAN, ain, *s. m.* (*Ir. id. Lat.* tympanum.) A timbrel; a harp; the drum of the ear; a drum; a kitchen-jack. Tiompan na laimh, *a timbrel in his hand.—Stew. Ex. N. pl.* tiompain.

TIOMPANACH, aich, *s. m.* A performer on the timbrel; a harper; a drummer; a minstrel.

TIOMPANACH, *a.* Of, or pertaining to, a timbrel or harp.

TIOMPANACHD, *s. f.* Beating on a timbrel; the noise of a timbrel.

TIOMPANAICHE, *s. m.* (*Ir.* tiompanuidhe.) A performer on the timbrel; a harper; a minstrel.

TIOMSAICH, *v. a.* (*Ir. id.*) Collect, bring together.

TIOMUIN, *s. f.* (*Ir. id.*) A dedication; a giving up.

† TION, *s. m.* (*Ir. id.*) A beginning.

TION, *a.* (*Ir. id.*) Soft.

TIONAIL, *v. a.* and *n.* (*Ir.* tionad.) Gather, assemble, collect. *Pret. a.* thionail, *gathered; fut. aff.* tionailidh, *shall gather; fut. pass.* tionalar; *p. part.* tionailte, *gathered.*

TION, *v. n.* (*Ir. id.*) Melt, dissolve. *Pret.* thion.

TIONADH, aidh, *s. m.* (*Ir. id.*) A melting, a dissolving.

TIONAILEACH, *a.* Causing to collect or assemble; prone to assemble or to gather; fond of gathering.

TIONAILTE, *p. part.* of tionail.

TIONAL, ail, *s. m.* (*Ir.* tional.) A gathering; an assembly or assemblage; a collection. Tional nan nial, *a gathering of the clouds.—Oss. Tem.* A thaobh an tionail, *concerning the collection.—Stew.* 1 Cor.

TIONALACH, *a.* Causing to collect or assemble; prone to assemble; fond of gathering.

TIONALADH, aidh, *s. m.* The act of gathering, an assembling, a collecting, a gathering; an assembly, a collection.

TIONALADH, (a), *pr. part.* of tionail. Gathering, assembling, collecting. A tionaladh bhioran, *gathering sticks.—Stew.* 1 K.

TIONAS, ais, *s. m.* (*Ir.* tionus.) A tan-yard.

TIONC, *v. a.* (*Ir. id.*) Save, deliver, free; attend. *Pret. a.* thionc; *fut. aff. a.* tioncaidh, *shall save.*

TIONCACH, *a.* Saving, bringing about deliverance or freedom.

TIONCADH, aidh, *s. m.* (*Ir. id.*) The act of saving or delivering; deliverance, liberation.

TIONCAICHE, *s. m.* (*Ir.* tioncaidhe.) A deliverer, a saviour.

TIONCHOSG, *s. m.* Instruction.

TIONRAMH, aimh, *s. m.* Attendance.

TIONG, *s.* A tingle, as of a bell.

TIONG, *v. a.* Tingle.

TIONGAIL, *s. f.* A tingling, a tingle; frequent or continued tingling.

† TIONNAR, air, *s. m.* A sleep, a slumber.

TIONNDADH, aidh, *s. m.* A turning; a turning round or back.

TIONNDADH, *v. a.* and *n.* Turn, return, or come back. *Pret. a.* thionndadh, *turned; fut. aff. a.* tionndaidh, *shall* or *will turn.* Tionndadh rium, *turn towards me.—Macfar.* Tionndadh a leth-taobh, *turn aside.—Stew. Jam.*

TIONNSGAIL, *v. a.* Contrive, invent, devise, plot. *Pret. a.* thionnsgail, *contrived;* tionnsgailidh, *shall contrive.*

TIONNSGAIN, *s. f.* A beginning; an element; a contrivance.

TIONNSGAIN, *v. a.* (*Ir.* tionnsguin.) Contrive, invent, devise; commence. *Pret. a.* thionnsgain; *fut. aff. a.* tionnsgnaidh.

TIONNSGALACH, *a.* Contrivant, ingenious; adventurous; diligent, industrious.

TIONNSGANTACH, *a.* (*Ir.* tionsgantach.) Contrivant, ingenious; adventurous; diligent, industrious. *Com.* and *sup.* tionnsgantaiche.

TIONNSGANTACHD, *s. f.* Contrivance, ingeniousness; diligence.

TIONNSGANTAIR, *s.* (*Ir.* tionsgantoir.) A deviser, a contriver; a beginner.

TIONNSGLACH, *a.* See TIONNSGALACH.

TIONNSGNACH, *a.* (*for* tionnsgnathach.) *Ir.* tionsgantach. Contrivant, ingenious; adventurous; industrious.

TIONNSGNACHD, *s. f.* Ingeniousness; adventurousness; industry.

TIONNSGNADH, aidh, *s. m.* An invention, a project, a device, a design; a beginning, a commencement; an element. Le droch thionnsgnadh, *with bad design.—Old Song.*

TIONNSGNAIR, *s. m.* A deviser, a contriver; a beginner.

TIONNSGNATH. See TIONNSGNADH.

TIONNSGRADH, aidh, *s. m.* A dowry, a portion; a reward.

† TIONRAMH, aimh, *s. m.* (*Ir. id.*) Attendance.

TIONSAN, ain, *s. m.* (*Ir. id.*) A drop.

TIONSGADAIL, *s. f.* (*Ir. id.*) A managing.

TIONSGRA, *s. m.* (*Ir. id.*) Wages, a reward, a dowry.

TIONTANAS, ais, *s. m.* (*Ir. id.*) Haste, speed, expedition.

TIOPAL, ail, *s. m.* (*Ir. id.*) A water-spider.

TIOPARSAN, ain, *s. m.* A flowing, a streaming.

TIORADH, aidh, *s. m.* A drying; a scorching.

TIORAIL, *a.* (*Ir.* tioramhuil.) Sheltered; warm, snug; commodious, convenient; homely. Gath tiorail na greine, *the warm sun-beam.—Macfar.*

TIORAIME, *com.* and *sup.* of tioram; also written *tirime;* which see.

TIORAM, *a.* (*from* tìr, *earth.*) Dry; parched; seasoned. Greim tioram, *a dry morsel.—Stew. Pro.* O'n sgeir thirim, *from the dry rock.—Oss. Fin. and Lor. Com.* and *sup.* tioraime *and* tirime.

TIORAMACH, *a.* (*Ir. id.*) Dry, thirsty.

TIORAMACH, aich, *s.* Drought, thirst.

TIORAMACHADH, aidh, *s. m.* A drying, a parching, a seasoning. Cuir air thiormachadh, *set to dry.*

TIORAMACHAIL, *a.* (*Ir.* tioramach-amhuil.) Desiccative, absorbent.

TIORAMACHD, *s. f.* (*Ir.* tiormachd.) Drought, dryness, thirst; a continuance of dry weather.

TIORAMAICH, *v. a.* and *n.* (*Ir.* tiormaich.) Dry, parch, season. *Pret. a.* thiormaich; *fut. aff.* tiormaichidh, *shall dry; p. part.* tioramaichte, *dried.*

TIORAMAICHTE, *p. part.* of tioramaich; which see.

TIORAMALACHD, *s. f.* Drought, thirst; avidity.

TIORAMAN, ain, *s. m.* (*Ir. id.*) Water thickened with oatmeal.

TIORANACH, aich, *s. m.* A tyrant.

TIORANTA, *a.* Tyrannical, oppressive.

Tiorc, *v. a.* Save, deliver, free. *Pret. a.* thiorc, *saved; fut. aff.* tiorcaidh.

Tiorcach, *a.* Working or bringing about deliverance.

Tiorcadh, aidh, *s. m.* A liberating, a delivering.

Tiormaich. See Tioramaich.

Tiorman, ain, *s. m.* See Tioraman.

Tiorraid, *s. f.* (*Ir. id.*) A robe, a mantle.

Tiort, tiorta, *s. m.* (*Ir. id.*) An accident, a chance, a mischance; a risk.

Tiortach, *a.* (*Ir. id.*) Accidental; causing or leading to accidents; liable to accidents.

Tiortachd, *s. f.* Liability to accident.

Tioruirse, *s. f.* (*Ir. id.*) A remnant.

Tiot, tiota, *s. m.* A minute; a moment; a trice; a short while. Ann an tiota, *in a moment.—Stew. Job.* Thig an so car tiota, *come hither a little while.*

Tiotach, *a.* Momentary.

Tiotadh. See Tiot.

Tiotag, aig, *s. f.* (*dim.* of tiot.) A very short while, a minute, a trice.

Tiotal, ail, *s. m.* (*Ir. id.*) See Tiodal.

Tiotalaich. See Tiodalaich.

† **Tiotan**, ain, *s. m.* (*Ir. id.*) The sun, Titan.

Tiotan, ain, *s. m.* (*dim.* of tiot.) *Ir. id.* A little while.

Tìr, tìre, *s. f.* A country, a region, a territory; land in opposition to water; a shore, a beach, a coast. San tìr chéin, *in the distant country.—Orr.* Tìr aineoil, *a strange land.—Stew. Gen.* Air tìr, *on land, on dry ground;* rach air tìr, *go ashore;* an tìr mhòr, *the Continent.* Tìr fo thuinn, *Flanders, Holland.—O'Reilly's Vocabulary.*

Lat. terra. *Fr.* terre. *Corn. W. Arm.* tir. *Ir.* tior and tir. In *tìr* we have the root of the *Gr.* τειρω, and the *Lat.* tero, *to crumble or wear, as dry earth.* Hence also the *Gr.* τερσω and τερσω, *to dry.* Hence also the *Gaelic* tioram, *dry,* through the medium of the *Irish* tior.

† **Tircean**, ein, *s. m.* (*Ir.* tircan.) Meaning, signification, exposition.

Tirceanas. See Tircean.

Tìreach, *a.* (*from* tìr.) *Ir.* tiorrthach. Territorial; of, or belonging to, a country; of the same country; *substantively,* a countryman; a patriot.

Tìreachadh, aidh, *s. m.* A colonizing; colonization; a colony.

Tìreachas, ais, *s. m.* (*Ir. id.*) A colony; a colonizing; colonization.

Tirealachd, *s. f.* Homeliness.

Tireil, *a.* (*Ir.* tir-amhuil.) Homely, snug, comfortable.

Tìrich, *v.*, (*from* tìr.) *Ir. id.* Colonize, settle, bring to land. *Pret. a.* thìrich, *settled; fut. aff.* tìrichidh, *shall settle; p. part.* tirichte.

Tirim. See Tioram.

Tiseadh, idh, *s. m.* (*Ir. id.*) A coming.

Tisean, ein, *s. m.* (*Ir. id.*) A grudge.

Tìr-mòr, *s. f.* A continent. More commonly *mòr-thir;* which see.

Tirpean, ein, *s. f.* (*Ir.* tirpinn.) A houseleek.

Tirleach, ich, *s. m.* (*Ir. id.*) Demesnes; mansion-house.

† **Tit**, *s. f.* (*Ir. id.*) The earth.

Tìth, *s.* An eager desire; eagerness; keenness; forwardness.

Titheach, *a.* (*from* tìth.) *Ir. id.* Eagerly; desirous; eager; keen; earnest; willing; sharp; forward. Gu titheach, *keenly.* Titheach chum uilc a ghnàth, *ever eager for mischief.—Ull.*

† **Tithinn**, *s.* (*Ir. id.*) The sun.

Tiu; more properly *tiugh;* which see.

Tiubhair, *v. a.* (*Ir. id.*) Give, grant; present; deliver; give up. *Pret. a.* thiubhair, *gave; fut. aff.* tiubhraidh, *shall give.* Thiubhair i 'gradh, *she gave her love.—Fingalian Poem.* Gun tiubhradh e dh 'i, *that he would give her.—Stew. Mat.*

Tiubhrach, *a.* Prone to give; generous.

Tiubhrachadh, aidh, *s. m.* A giving or granting; a presenting; a delivering; a giving up; a grant.

Tiubhradh, aidh, *s. m.* (*Ir. id.*) A giving or granting; a grant, a gift.

Tiubhraich, *v. a.* Give, grant; present, deliver, give up. *Pret. a.* thiubhraich, *gave; fut. aff. a.* tiubhraichidh, *shall give up.* Tiubhraich dhomh aon do d' dha shleagh, *give me one of thy two spears.—Oss. Trathal.*

Tiubhthachd, *s. f.* (*Ir. id.*) Sloth.

Tiubruid, *s. f.* (*Ir. id.*) A well, a cistern.

Tiucainn, **Tiugainn**, *v. def.* Come.

Tiuchag, aig, *s. f.* (*Ir. id.*) A pore.

Tiuchan, ain, *s. m.* A pore.

† **Tiugh**, *s. m.* (*Ir. id.*) The end.

† **Tiugh**, *a.* (*Ir. id.*) Latter, last.

Tiugh, *a.* (*Ir. id. W.* tew. *Arm.* teo, *thick. Eng.* tough. *Scotch,* teuch.) Thick; close; dense; gross; clumsy; dull; foggy; hazy; squab; corpulent.

Tiughachadh, aidh, *s. m.* (*Ir.* tiughuchadh.) A thickening, a condensing, a coagulating; condensation, coagulation.

Tiughad. See Tiuighead.

Tiughadas, ais, *s. m.* (*Ir. id.*) Thickness; closeness; denseness; grossness; solidity; consistence.

Tiughaich, *v. a.* and *n.* (*from* tiugh.) Thicken, condense, coagulate; grow thick, gross, or dense. *Pret. a.* thiughaich, *thickened; fut. aff. a.* tiughaichidh, *shall thicken; p. part.* tiughaichte, *thickened.*

† **Tiugh-bhagh**, *s. n.* (*Ir. id.*) Late drinking.

Tiughalach, aich, *s. m.* (*Ir. id.*) The thickest part of liquids.

Tiughalachd, *s. f.* See Tiughalach.

† **Tiugh-lath**, *s. m.* The last day.

Tiuighe, *s. f.* Thickness, denseness, grossness; dulness; solidity; consistence.

Tiuighe, *com.* and *sup.* More or most thick.

Tiuighead, eid, *s. m.* (*Arm.* teoahat.) Thickness, grossness, dulness; increase in thickness or in grossness. A dol an tiuighead, *growing more and more thick;* air thiuighead sa bheil e, *however thick it be;* is tiuighid e sin, *that has rendered it more thick.*

Tiunnal, ail, *s. m.* A match, likeness, comparison. Tiunnal t-aogais is tearc ri fhaotainn, *the match of thy face is seldom found.—Old Song.*

Tla, **Tlàth**, *a.* (*Ir. id.*) Soft, mellow; sounding mellow; mild, meek; smooth, tranquil, gentle; balmy; feeble. Aoibhir-Chaomha na gnuise tla, *mild-visaged Evercoma.—Oss. Gaul.* Caoireall le 'chruit thlà, *Carril with his softly-sounding harp.—Oss. Duthona.* Bu tlath a gorm-shuil, *soft was her blue eye.—Oss. Fing.* Céilte fo 'tlàth-chiabhan, *concealed under her soft locks.—Oss. Tem. Com.* and *sup.* tlaithe. Ni 's tlaithe na oladh, *smoother than wool.—Stew. Pro.* Nur thuiteas an t-sian gu tlàth, *when the shower falls gently.—Oss. Fing.*

Tlachd, *v. a.* (*Ir. id.*) Colour; polish.

Tlachd, *s. f.* (*Ir. id.*) Satisfaction; comfort, pleasure, delight; honour; liking; beauty; the earth; *rarely,* a garment; colour; market; a burial. Gabhaidh mi tlachd, *I will take pleasure.—Sm.* Togaibh cuimhne Orla le tlachd, *extol with honour the memory of Orla.—Oss. Fing.*

Tlachdaich, *v. a.* (*Ir. id.*) Inter. *P. part.* tlachdaichte, *interred.*

TLACHD-AIRM, s. m. (Ir. id.) A market-place.

TLACHDAR, a. See TLACHDMHOR.

† TLACHD-BHAILC, s. m. (Ir. id.) A market-town.

TLACHD-BHEIRT, s. f. (Ir. id.) Geography.

† TLACHD-BHOG, s. m. (Ir. id.) A quagmire, a quicksand.

† TLACHD-BHUTH, s. m. (Ir. id.) A booth or tent at a fair.

TLACHD-EOLAS, ais, s. m. Geography; geographical knowledge.

TLACHD-GHRABHACHD, s. f. (Ir. id.) Geography.

TLACHD-GHRABHAICHE, s. f. A geographer.

TLACHDMHOIRE, com. and sup. of tlachdmhor.

TLACHDMHOIREACHD, s. f. Handsomeness, comeliness, pleasantness.

TLACHDMHOR, a. (Ir. tlachdmhur.) Handsome; goodly; comely; becoming; pleasant. Leanabh tlachdmhor, *a goodly child.—Stew. Ex.* Tlachdmhor do dhuine, *becoming in a man.—Stew. Ecc.*

TLACHD-SGRIOBHADH, aidh, s. m. Geography.

TLACHD-SGRIOBHAIR, s. m. A geographer.

TLACHD-SHEIST, s. f. (Ir. id.) A strawberry.

TLACHD-SHUBH, s. m. A strawberry.

TLACHD-THOMHAISEACH, a. Geometrical; of, or belonging to, geometry.

TLACHD-THOMHAS, ais, s. m. (Ir. id.) Geometry.

TLACHD-THOMHASAIR, s. m. A geometrician.

TLAIM. See TLÀM.

TLÀITHE, com. and sup. of tlath. See TLÀ.

TLÀM, tlàim, s. m. A handful, as of wool. Tlàm do chloimh nan caorach, *a handful of wool.—Macint.*

TLÀM, v. a. (Ir. id.) Teaze or pluck, as wool; handle. *Pret. a.* thlàm; *fut. aff.* tlàmaidh, *shall teaze.*

TLÀMACH, a. Teazing or plucking.

TLÀMADH, aidh, s. m. The process of plucking or of teazing, as of wool. Co-thlamadh, *a mixing.*

TLAMADH, (a), pr. part. of tlàm. Teazing, plucking; handling.

TLÀS, s. m. (Ir. id.) A merry trick.

† TLÀS, s. m. (Ir. id.) Cattle; a fair.

TLÀS, tlàis, s. m. Mildness, softness, mellowness, tenderness; smoothness; tranquillity. Tionndadh ascaoin na sìne gu tlàs, *turn the inclemency of the blast to mildness.—Macfar.*

TLÀTH, a. See TLÀ.

TLASACH, aich, s. m. (Ir. id.) A fair.

TLÀ-THAISLICH, v. a. Bedew; moisten.

TLATHAS. See TLÀS.

TLI, s. m. (Ir. id.) Colour; feature.

TLIOCHD, s. m. (Ir. id.) A beginning.

TLIOCHDAN, ain, s. m. (Ir. id.) Hoarseness.

TLIOCHDANACH, a. Hoarse; causing hoarseness.

TLU, TLUGH, s. m. (Ir. id.) A pair of tongs.

TLÙS, tlùis, s. m. Kindness, compassion, mildness; a lie; cattle. Fheara bu mhor tlùs is baigh, *ye heroes noted for compassion and mercy.—Oss. Cathula.* Thig tlùs is blàthas, *mildness and warmth shall.—Macint.* Tlùs nan speur, *the kindness of the skies.—Macfar.*

TLUSACH, aich, s. m. A dissembler, a liar.

TLÙSAIL, a. (tlus-amhuil.) Kind, compassionate, tender, mild; false. Gu tlùsail, *kindly.*

TLÙSAILEACHD, s. f. Kindness, compassion, tenderness, mildness.

TLÙSAIR, s. m. A kind, compassionate man.

TLÙSAIREACHD, s. f. Kindness, compassionateness, tenderness.

TLUSAR, a. See TLUSMHOR.

TLUSMHOIRE, com. and sup. of tlùsmhor.

TLUSMHOIREACHD, s. f. Kindness, compassionateness, mildness.

TLÙSMHOR, a. Kind, compassionate, mild, tender. Gu tlusmhor baigheil, *kindly and compassionately.—Macfar.*

TNÙ, TNÙTH, tnùtha, s. m. (Ir. id.) Envy, malice, grudge; avarice; indignation; zeal, bigotry; fire; longing. Am fianuis tnutha, *before envy.—Stew. Pro.* Do mhòr-chridhe gun tnùth, *thy great heart without malice.—Old Song.*

TNUTH. See TNÙ.

TNÙTHACH, a. (*from* tnuth.) *Ir. id.* Envious, malicious, jealous; *also, substantively,* an envious person, a jealous person, a rival.

TNUTHADH, aidh, s. m. (Ir. id.) A conflict.

TNÙTHAR, *for* tnuthmhor.

TNÙTHMHOR, a. Envious, malicious, jealous. Gu tnùthmhor, *enviously.* *Com.* and *sup.* tnùthmhoire.

† TOB, s. m. (Ir. id.) Surprise.

TOBAC, s. m. Tobacco.

† TOBAN, ain, s. m. (Ir. id.) A hood or cowl.

TOBAR, air, s. m. A well, a spring, or fountain. Beul an tobair, *the mouth of the well.—Stew. Gen.* *N. pl.* tobraichean *and* tobraiche. Tobraiche na beatha, *the fountains* [issues] *of life.—Stew. Pro. ref.*

TOBAR-BAISTIDH, s. m. A font, a baptistry.

TOBAR-FIOR-UISGE, s. m. A spring-well, a living spring; a perennial spring.

TOBAR-TÀIRNE, s. m. A draw-well.

TOBH, s. m. A rope or cable; a hoe. Tobh cartach, *a cart-rope;* tobh corcaich, *a hempen rope:* affined to *tobh* are the *Du.* towe; *Dan.* too; *Eng.* tow.

† TOBHACH, aich, s. m. (Ir. id.) A wresting; a compelling; inducing.

† TOBHACH, a. (Ir. id.) Sudden, surprising.

TOBHT, TOBHTA, s. A rower's bench; a clod; a turf.

TOBRAICHE, TOBRAICHEAN, n. pl. of tobar.

TOCADH, aidh, s. m. Prosperity.

TOCH, TOCHA, s. m. (Ir. id.) The hough; a fit of crying; love.

TOCH, v. a. Hamstring, hough. *Pret. a.* thoch, *hamstring; fut. aff. a.* tochaidh, *shall hamstring.*

TOCHACH, a. Houghed; of, or belonging to, the hough.

TOCHADH, aidh, s. m. The act of hamstringing.

TOCHAIL, s. f. A mine, a quarry; a digging.

TOCHAIL, v. a. (Ir. id.) Dig, delve; mine, quarry. *Pret. a.* thochail, *dug; fut. aff.* tochailidh, *shall dig.* Thochail iad slochd, *they dug a pit.—Sm.* *P. part.* tochailte, *dug, delved, quarried.*

TOCHAILLEACH, a. Rooting out, extirpating; digging; *substantively,* one who digs.

TOCHAILLEACH, ich, a. (Ir. id.) Mineral.

TOCHAILLICHE, s. m. (*from* tochaill.) A miner; a pioneer.

TOCHAILTE, p. part. of tochail. (Ir. tochalta.) See TOCHAIL.

TOCHAILTEAR, eir, s. m. A miner, a quarrier.

TOCHAIR, v. a. Invite; wind up, as yarn.

TOCHALAICHE, s. m. A miner, a digger, a delver.

† TOCHAR, air, s. m. (Ir. id.) A causeway, a pavement; a crowd.

TOCHAR, air, s. m. A dowry or marriage portion. See also TOCHRADH.

TOCHAR, v. a. Give a dowry or marriage portion. *Pret.* thochar.

TOCHARACH, a. Having a large dowry.

TOCHARAIS. See TACHARAIS.

Tocharas. See Tacharas.

Tocharaiste, *p. part.* of tocharais.

Tochas. See Tachas.

Tòchd, *s. m.* (*Ir. id.*) A smell. Deagh thòchd, *a good smell;* droch thochd, *a bad smell.*

Tochd, *s. m.* (*Ir. id.*) A fit; a trance; silence; a bed-tick.

Tòchd, Tochdach, *a.* (*Ir. id.*) Still, silent.

Tochdail, *a.* (*Ir. id.*) Still, silent.

Toch-fhearg, eirge, *s. f.* Silent rage, smothered wrath.

Toch-fheargach, *a.* Raging in silence.

Tochladh, aidh, *s. m.* (*Ir. id.*) A digging, a mining, a quarrying; a pit, a mine, a quarry, a grave.

Tochmhaire, *s. f.* (*Ir. id.*) A marriage treaty.

Tochradh, aidh, *s. m.* A marriage portion or dowry. A rèir tochraidh' nam maighdean, *according to the dowry of the virgins.—Stew. Ex.*

Tochrais, *v. a.* Wind or reel yarn. *Pret.* thochrais, *wound; fut. aff.* tochraisidh; *p. part.* tochraiste.

Tochraiste, *p. part.* of tochrais. Wound up, as yarn. Snàth tochraiste, *wound up yarn.*

Tochras, ais, *s. m.* The reeling or winding up of yarn or thread.

Tochuil. See Tochail.

Tochus, *s. m.* (*Ir. id.*) Possessions, property.

Tocsaid, *s. f.* A hogshead. *N. pl.* togsaidean.

Tod, *s. m.* (*Ir. id.*) A clod, a sod.

Todan, ain, *s. m.* A small clod.

Todhachd, *s. f.* (*Ir. id.*) Silence.

Todhail, *s. f.* (*Ir. id.*) Destruction.

Todhar, air, *s. m.* A field manured by a moveable fold; bleaching.

Todhas, ais, *s. m.* (*Ir. id.*) Silence.

Tofas, ais, *s. m.* (*Ir. id.*) Topaz.

Tog, *v. a.* (*Ir. id.* In *Malabar,* toger.) Lift, carry; raise, build, construct; extol; take away; exact, as a tribute; cheer; stir up; rear; brew; distil. *Pret. a.* thog, *lifted; fut. aff.* togaidh. Tog sprochd an laoich, *raise the hero's lament.—Ull.* Le gliocas togar tigh, *with wisdom an house is built.—Stew. Pro.* Cha tog piob na taileasg mi, *neither bagpipe nor mirth shall cheer me.—Mac Co.* Togaidh duine fiar aimhreite, *a perverse man stirs up strife.—Stew. Pro.* Togaidh an làth, *the day will clear up;* tog ri, *ascend, repair to;* nur thogamaid ri gleann-Caothain, *when we used to repair to the vale of Cona;* tog suas, *lift up, rear, educate;* tog ort, *lift on there, begone, be off;* c'aite thog thu ort? *whither are you bound?* tog cùis, *appeal;* tog lionn, *brew beer;* tog uisge beatha, *distil whisky.*

Togail, togal, *and* togalach, *s. f.* (*Ir.* togbhail.) A lifting, a carrying, a raising; the act of building; a building or structure; a carrying off tribute; a stirring up; a rearing, a brewing, a distilling; a levying, a levy. Togail spreidhe, *a rearing of cattle; a carrying off of cattle.* Tha bhò air an togail,—said of a cow having the appearance of starvation. Tha thu air do thogail, *you are very much taken with.* Ceann na togail, *the head of the levy.—Stew. 1 K.* Togail lionn, *a brewing of beer;* tigh togalach, *a brewing-house.*

Togail, (a), *pr. part.* of tog.

Togair, *gen. sing.* of togar.

Togair, *v. a.* (*Ir. id.*) Desire, wish, covet. *Pret. a.* thogair; *fut. aff.* togairidh, *shall desire.* Nach togair suidhe, *who desire not to sit.—Stew. Ps.* Ma thogras tu, *if you desire or like.*

Togam, 1 *sing. imper.* of tog. Let me raise. *Also for* togaidh mi, *I shall* or *will raise.*

Togar, *fut. pass.* of tog. Shall or will be lifted.

Togar, air, *s. m.* (*Ir. id.*) Desire; will; a wish; pleasure; inclination.

Togarach, *a.* (*Ir. id.*) Covetous, desirous, wishful; willing; joyful; having a bias or propensity. Gu togarach, *wishfully. Com.* and *sup.* togaraiche.

Togarachd, *s. f.* Covetousness, wishfulness; willingness; propensity. Togarachd bhur n-inntinn, *the willingness of your minds.—Stew.* 1 *Cor.*

Togbhail. See Togail.

Toghaidh, *s. f.* Attention; respect; care; liking.

Togh. See Tobh.

Togh, *v.* Choose. See Tagh.

Toghadh. See Taghadh.

Togladh, aidh, *s. m.* (*Ir. id.*) A sacking; destroying.

Togradh, aidh, *s. m.* (*Ir.* togra.) A coveting, a desiring, willing, or wishing; a desire, a wish, a propensity.

Togram, *for* togradh mi. I shall or will desire.

† **Toi,** *a.* (*Ir. id.*) Silent, mute; gentle.

Toibheum, toibheuma, *and* toibheim, *s.* (*Ir.* toibheim.) Slander, scandal, reproach, aspersion; blasphemy; blemish. A faotainn toibheim, *receiving blasphemy.—Stew. Rom.* Luchd toibheim, *blasphemers.*

Toibheumach, *a.* Slanderous, scandalous; reproachful; railing; blasphemous. Casaid thoibheumach, *a railing accusation.—Stew. Pet.* Briatharan toibheumach, *blasphemous words;* daoine toibheumach, *blasphemous men.* Gu toibheumach, *slanderously, blasphemously.—Stew. Tim. Com.* and *sup.* toibheumaiche.

Toic, toice, *s. f.* (*Ir. id.*) Wealth, riches; means, substance; a support, a prop. Written also *taic.*

Toice, *s. f.* An opprobrious name for a worthless female.

Toiceach, *a.* (*from* toic.) *Ir. id.* Wealthy, rich, substantial; propping; swelled up with arrogance or with conceit.

Toiceil, *a.* (toic-amhuil.) Wealthy, substantial. Toiceil de chrodh 's de chaoraich, *wealthy in cattle and sheep.—Old Song.*

Toichd, *s. f.* (*Ir.* tochd.) A bed-tick or ticken.

Toiche, *s. f.* (*Ir. id.*) Fate, destiny.

† **Toiche,** *a.* (*Ir. id.*) Wall-eyed.

† **Toichead,** eid, *s. m.* (*Ir. id.*) An arrest.

† **Toicheall,** ill, *s. m.* (*Ir. id.*) A journey—(*Shaw*); a departure.

Toicheasdal. See Toichiosdal.

Toicheum, *s. f.* (*Ir. id.*) A slow pace.

Toicheumach, *a.* (*Ir. id.*) Gradual, step by step.

Toichiosdal, ail, *s. m.* (*Ir. id.*) Arrogance, presumption; opinionativeness; a party; a faction; a cause; an army.

Toichiosdalach, *a.* Arrogant, presumptuous; opinionated.

† **Toichneadh,** idh, *s. m.* (*Ir. id.*) A fast, a vigil.

† **Toid,** *a.* (*Ir. id. Lat.* tot *and* totus.) Whole, entire; *substantively,* the whole.

† **Toideadh,** *a.* (*Ir. id.*) Thankful.

Toidhchd. See Toichd.

† **Toidhearnadh,** aidh, *s. m.* Punishment.

Toigh, *s.* Love, fondness; desire; attention. Is toigh leam Dia, *I love God.—Stew. Ps.* Esan is toigh leis, *he whom he loves.—Stew. Pro.* Toigh, *attention.—Macfar. Voc.*

Toigh, *a.* (*Ir. id.*) Dear, beloved; agreeable. *Com.* and *sup.* docha, *more* or *most dear.*

Toigheach, *a.* (*from* toigh.) *Ir. id.* Fond of, cherishing a fondness, susceptible of fondness; attentive, careful. *Com.* and *sup.* toighiche.

Toigheachd, *s. f.* (*Ir. id.*) A concession, yielding; noting, illustrating; a coming.

TOIL, toile, *s. f.* (*Ir id. Gr.* θέλω, *volo.*) Will, desire, pleasure, inclination. Deagh thoil, *good-will*, tha mo thoil agam, *I have enough*, bithidh do thoil ri dheanamh agad, *you will have enough to do.*

TOILEACH, *a* (*Ir. id*) Willing, desirous, voluntary; glad Cridhe toileach, *a willing heart.—Stew. Ex* Gu toileach, *willingly —Stew. Pro* Toileach air do phòsadh, *willing to marry you.—Stew* Tha mi toileach, *I am willing, I agree, I assent*

TOILEACHADH, aidh, *s m.* (*Ir* toiliughadh) A pleasing

TOILEACHAS, ais, *s. m* Gladness, willingness.

TOILLEACH-INNTINN, *s f* Comfort, mental pleasure, satisfaction.

TOILEACHAS-INNTINN, *s m* Mental pleasure, satisfaction, peace of mind, contentment.

TOILEAS, eis, *s m.* (*Ir. id*) The will, willingness.

TOILEIL, *a* (toil-amhuil) Wilful, obstinate, *also*, willing, voluntary Le irioslachd thoileil, *with voluntary humility. Stew Col* Gu toileil, *wilfully*

TOILICH, *v a.* (*from* toil) *Ir id.* Please, satisfy, content; indulge, gratify; agree, assent to *Pret. a.* thoilich; *pleased; fut aff* toilichidh, *shall please*, *p. part.* toilichte, *pleased* Ma thoilicheas tu, *if you like*

TOILICHTE, *p. part.* of toilich Pleased, satisfied, contented, gratified. Bha e toilichte, *he was contented.—Stew. Lev.*

TOIL-INNTINN, *s f* Contentment, satisfaction, inward pleasure

TOILL, *v a* (*Ir* tuill) Deserve, merit *Pret a* thoill, *deserved*, *fut aff* toillidh, *shall deserve.* Thoill thu peanas, *you deserve punishment*, gun seachnadh e 'm bàs a thoill, *that he might avert the death he merited —Mac Lach* Dheagh-thoill thu e, *you well deserved it*

TOILLIDH, *fut. aff.* of toil

TOILLTEACH, *a.* (*Ir id*) Meritorious, deserving.

TOILLTEANAS, ais, *s. m.* (*Ir. id*) Desert, whether good or ill

TOILLTINN, *s f* (*Ir. id*) Desert, demerit A toilltinn, deserving

TOILLTINNEACH, *a* Deserving, deserved, meritorious Gu toilltinneach, *deservedly* *Com* and *sup* toilltinniche

TOILTEACH, *a.* (*Ir. id*) Voluntary, willing

TOILTEALACHD, *s f* Willingness.

TOILTEIL, *a.* Willing, obstinate

† TOIMHIL, *s. f.* (*Ir id*) Eating

TOIMHSLACHAN, ain, *s m* A riddle, a puzzle, a hard question, a parable Chuir e 'mach toimhseachan, *put forth a riddle.—Stew Ez* *N pl.* toimhseachain, *d pl.* toimhseachanaibh Le toimhseachanaibh, *with hard questions — Stew Ez ref*

† TOIMHNEAMH, imh, *s f.* (*Ir id*) A womb

TOIMHSEACH, ich, *s m.* (*Ir. id*) A farm

TOIMHSEAGAN, ain See TOIMHSEACHAN

TOIMHSEAL, TOIMHSEIL, *a.* (*Ir. id*) Judicious, sagacious, sensible

TOIMHSEAN, *s pl* Weights, measures, scales, or balances Toimhsean fìreannach, *just weights —Stew Lev.*

† TOIN, *s f* (*Ir id Gr.* τόνος) Tone, accent

TOINEADH, idh, *s. m.* (*Ir. id.*) A thaw, thawing

TOINEAL, èil, *s m.* (*Ir. id*) A trance; astonishment

TOINEAMH, imh, *s. m* (*Ir id*) A salmon; a monument

TÒIN, TONA, *s f* (*W* tin. *Ir.* toin.) The bottom; the breech, a measure Tòin an diabhuil duibh —*Macvuirich*

TOIN-CHLODHACH, aich, *s m.* (*Ir.* tonchlodhach) A turncoat.

TÒIN-CHRUAIDH, *s. f* A method of inflicting punishment, by which a person is raised a little from the ground, and suffered to fall on his breech; it is now known only in childish pastimes

TOINISG, *s f.* (*Ir. id.*) Understanding, judgment, discretion. Fear gun toinisg, *a man without judgment.*

TOINISGEACH, *a.* (*Ir. id*) Intelligent, rational, reasonable.

TOINISGEIL, *a* (toinisg-amhuil) Intelligent, rational, reasonable; having a sound judgment.

TOINN See TOINNEAMH.

TOINNEALAS, ais, *s m.* Prosody

TOINNEAMH, *v. a.* Twist, plait, twine; wreath, writhe, wrench *Pret. a.* thoinneamh, *twisted*, *fut. aff.* toinneamhaidh; *pr. part.* toinnte *and* toinneamhte, *twisted.*

TOINNEAMH, eimh, *s m* (*Ir. id*) A twist, a plait, a twine; a wreathing, a twisting, a plaiting, a twining, *rarely*, death

TOINNEAMH, (a), *p. part.* of toinn, *or*, toinneamh Twisting, plaiting, twining.

TOINNEAMHAICHE, *s m* A twister; an instrument that twists or twines

TOINNTE, *s. f* A thread of yarn

TOINNTE, *p part* of toinneamh, *or*, toinn. Twisted, plaited, twined, wreathed 'Fhalta tana toinnte, *his thin plaited hair —Oss Taura* Anart toinnte, *twined linen.—Stew. Ex*

TOINNTEAN, ein, *s m* (*dim.* of toinnte.) A thread. Toinntean snath-fuaidheil, *sewing thread*

TOINNTE-LÌN, *s* (*Ir id*) A spindle.

TOIR, *v*, *for* tabhair, which see.

† TOIR, *s f* (*Ir id*) A churchyard

TOIR, *s f.* (*Ir id*) Help

TÒIR, *s f* A pursuit, a chase, persecution, a diligent search, a party in pursuit Air tòir nam bochd, *persecuting the poor —Sm.* An tòir, *in pursuit, following, in consequence —*An tòir air, *in pursuit of him.—Stew Pro* Air feachd, air thòir, 'san tuasaid, *in the ranks, in the pursuit, or in battle —Old Poem.*

† TOIRB, *s f.* Fuel

TOIRBEART See TOIRBHEART

TÒIREACH, *a* Prone to pursue, or to persecute, like a pursuit or persecution, of, or belonging to, a pursuit, or a persecution; *substantively*, a pursuit, a diligent search, a persecutor.

TÒIREACHD, *s f* A pursuing, a persecuting, a pursuit, a persecution; frequent or continued pursuit, or persecution. Cha do rinn iad tòireachd, *they did not pursue —Stew. Gen*

TÒIRBHEART, eirt, *s.* A bountiful or liberal action.

TÒIRBHEARTACH, *a* Gracious, bountiful, liberal; munificent Bhuin e rium gu tòirbheartach, *he dealt graciously with me —Stew Gen* *Com* and *sup* toirbheartaiche.

Tòirbheartach may perhaps mean *munificent as Thor, (cho beartach ri Tòr,)* a Celto-Germanic God of that name

TOIR-BHEARTAS, ais, *s m* (*Ir id*) Graciousness, bounty, liberality; munificence, tradition; a dose Rium dean toirbheartas, *act with bounty towards me —Sm*

TOIRBHEIR, *v a* (*Ir id.*) Give up, deliver; dispense; transfer

TOIRBHEIRT, *s. f.* (*Ir id.*) A giving up, a delivering; a dispensing; a transferring; a tranference, an oblation, an offering

TOIRBHEIRTEACH, *a.* Bountiful, liberal.

TOIRBHLEASGADH, aidh, *s m.* (*Ir. id.*) A rumbling.

TOIRBHREITH. See TOIRBHEIRT

Toirchim, *s. f.* Numbness, deadness. Toirchim suain, *a dead sleep.*

Toirchimeach, *a.* (*Ir. id.*) Stupid; benumbed.

Toirchimeachd, *s. f.* (*Ir. id.*) Stupidity, numbness; confinement in a tower.

Toirchios, *s.* (*Ir. id.*) A conception, fœtus; increase; plenty.

Toirdeas, eis, *s. f.* (*Ir. id.*) Dotage.

Toireachd, *s. f.* (*Ir. id.*) Pursuit, search.

Toireamh, eimh, *s. m.* (*from* torr.) An elegy; a plowman.

Toireannach, *a.* Impetuous. *Com.* and *sup.* toireannaiche.

Toireannachd, *s. f.* Impetuousness.

Toireim, *s. f.* (*Ir. id.*) A stately gait.

Tòireis, *s. f.* (*Ir. id.*) Keen inquiry; anxiety.

Toireiseach, *a.* (*Ir. id.*) Anxious.

Toirghill, *s. f.* (*Ir. id.*) A sufficient pledge.

Tòirich, *v. a.* (*from* tòir.) *Ir.* tòirigh. Pursue, chase, persecute, search after. *Pret. a.* thòirich, *persecuted; fut. aff.* tòirichidh, *shall persecute; p. part.* toirichte, *persecuted.*

Tòiriche, *s. m.* (*from* tòir.) A persecutor, a pursuer. *N. pl.* toirichean.

Tòirichte, *p. part.* of tòirich.

Toiriosg, *s. f.* (*Ir. id.*) A handsaw; a file.

Toir-leum, -leuma, *s. m.* (*Ir. id.*) A prodigious leap; a summerset.

Toir leum, *v. n.* (*Ir. id.*) Make a prodigious leap; throw a summerset.

Toirm, *s.* (*Ir. id.*) Noise; thunder; a murmuring sound. Toirm chogaidh, *the noise of battle.—Stew. Ex.* Toirm seillein an aonaich, *the murmur of the mountain bee.—Oss. Tem.*

Toirmeasg, eisg, *s. f.* (*Ir. id.*) A forbidding, a hindering; a prohibition; a hinderance, an impediment.

Toirmeasgach, *a.* (*Ir. id.*) Apt to hinder or forbid.

Toirmeasgachd, *s. f.* (*Ir. id.*) The habit or the practice of forbidding.

Toirmeasgadh, aidh, *s. m.* (*Ir. id.*) The act or circumstance of forbidding; prevention. A toirmeasgadh, *forbidding.*

Toirmisg, *v. a.* (*Ir.* toirmeasg.) Forbid; hinder; inhibit; obstruct. *Pret. a.* thoirmisg, *fut. aff. a.* toirmisgidh, *shall forbid.*

Toirmisgte, *p. part.* of toirmisg. (*Ir.* toirmisgthe.) Forbidden, hindered, inhibited. Am meas toirmisgte, *the forbidden fruit.*

Toirmrich, *s. f.* Noise; a murmuring sound; clangor. Toirmrich gharbh nan cuairteagan; *the brawling noise of the eddying streams.—Macfar.*

Toirn, *s. f.* (*Ir. id.*) A great noise, a sound.

Toirn, *s. f.* (*Ir. id.*) A fiery oven, a fiery furnace.

Toirneach. See Tairneach.

Toirneadh, idh, *s. m.* (*Ir. id.*) Respect, deference; a raising, a constructing.

Toirneamh, eimh, *s. m.* Punishment.

Tòirnich, *v.* Season a cask or any wooden vessel; rumble, make a noise. *Pret. a.* thoirnich; *fut. aff. a.* tòirnichidh.

Toirrichead, eid, *s. m.* Pregnancy; fruitfulness; increase in pregnancy, or in fruitfulness. A dol an toirrichead, *growing more and more pregnant.*

Toirricheas, eis, *s. m.* (*Ir.* toirrichios.) Pregnancy, conception; fruit, fruitfulness. Thug e toirricheas dhi, *he gave her conception.—Stew. Ruth.*

Toirrse, *s. f.* A lump; a torch.

Toirt, *s. f.* (*Ir. id.*) Value; quantity; bulk; strength; harm; reluctance; sadness; a cake. Dh' imich e mu 'n ordugh le toirt, *he obeyed the order reluctantly.—Mac Lach.* An deomhan toirt, *the d—l may care.*

Toirt, *s. f.* (*for* tabhairt.) A giving, granting, or bestowing; a grant.

Toirtealachd, *s. f.* (*Ir.* tairteamhlacht.) Bulkiness; strength, stoutness; fruitfulness. Mòr-churaidh 'n toirtealachd, *a hero in strength.—Old Song.*

Toirtean, ein, *s. m.* (*Ir.* toirtine.) A thin cake.

† **Toirtean**, *a.* (*Ir. id.*) Useful, serviceable.

Toirteil, *a.* (toirt-amhuil.) *Ir.* toirtheamhail. Strong, stout, bulky; destructive; fruitful. Am meadhon a chath thoirteil thruim, *in the midst of the destructive heavy strife.—Oss. Cathluno.*

Toirt-thairis, *s. f.* A surrender; a giving up through despair or fatigue; despair; extreme fatigue.

Toirtheach, *a.* (*Ir. id.*) Fruitful.

Toirthealachd, *s. f.* Fruitfulness.

Toirtis, *s. f.* (*Ir. id.*) A tortoise.

† **Toisc**, *s. f.* (*Ir. id.*) Good-will.

† **Toiscidh**, *s. f.* (*Ir. id.*) Will, desire.

Toiseach, ich, *s. m.* (*Ir.* tosach.) Beginning, origin; precedence; front, or van; original; *also*, a leader. O thoiseach an t-saoghail, *from the beginning of the world;* air thoiseach air, *before him.—Sm.* A toirt toisich, *giving precedence.—Stew. Rom.* O thoiseach gu deireadh, *from beginning to end.*

Toiseach, (an). First; in the first place; previously; at first. Nur thog thu 'n toiseach do mhor-sgiath, *when first thou didst carry the spacious shield.—Oss. Tem.*

Tòiseachadh, aidh, *s. m.* A beginning, a commencing, a commencement.

Toiseachail, *a.* (toiseach amhuil.) Fond of precedence.

Toiseachd, *s. f.* Commencement; priority; precedence.

Toisg, *s. pl.* (*Ir. id.*) Back-teeth, grinders, tusks; *also, in the singular*, proper time or season—(*Macfar. Voc.*); a thing; a circumstance—(*Shaw*); a business, a work; wholesome administration.

Toisgealta, *a.* Left, sinister. Dorn toisgealta a mhilidh, *the left fist of the hero.—Old Poem.*

Toisgeil, *a.* (*Ir.* toisg-amhuil.) Left, sinister.—*Macfar. Voc.*

Toisgeileach, *a.* Left-handed.

Tòisich, *v.* Commence, begin, set to. *Pret. a.* thòisich; *fut. aff.* tòisichidh, *shall begin; fut. pass.* toisichear.

Toisiche, *s. m.* A leader, a chief, a prince; a primate, a nobleman. Hence the surname Mac-an-tòisiche, *Macintosh.*

Tòisichear, *fut. pass.* of toisich. Shall be begun; *also, used impersonally*, toisichear [leam], *I began.*

† **Toisidh**, *s. pl.* (*Ir. id.*) Shoes.

Tòit, *s.* (*Ir. id.*) Smoke, vapour; *rarely*, a fragment; a rick of corn. Mar lasair 's an toit ag a cuartachadh, *like a flame surrounded by smoke.—Oss. Cathluno.* Tòit as an luidheir, *smoke from the chimney.—Stew. Hos.*

† **Toit**, *a.* (*Ir.* toit. *Lat.* tot and totus.) Whole, entire.

Tòit, *v.* (*Ir. id.*) Perfume; smoke.

Tòiteach, *a.* (*Ir. id.*) Smoky, vapoury.

Toiteachan, ain, *s. m.* (*Ir. id.*) A vent, a chimney.

Toiteadh, idh, *s. m.* (*Ir. id.*) Roasting, fumigation.

Tòitean, ein, *s. m.* (*Ir. id.*) A flame, a conflagration.

Toitean, ein, *s. m.* A collop, a steak; a bit of flesh roasted on embers.

Toiteanach, *a.* Like a collop, full of collops, of collops.—*Macdon.*

Toitear, *a* (*Ir. id.*) Lumpy.

Tòiteil, *a* (toit-amhuil.) Smoky.

Toitheastal. See Toichiastal.

Toithleannan, ain, *s m.* (*Ir. id.*) A paramour; a concubine.

Toitreach, ich, *s. m.* A conflagration

† **Tol**, *s. m* (*Ir id*) A churchyard

† **Tola**, *s. m.* (*Ir. id*) A church officer; superfluity; sleep

† **Toladh**, aidh, *s. m.* (*Ir. id.*) Destruction—(*Shaw*), sleep

Tolg, tuilg, *s m* (*Ir id*) A hollow, a bruise, as on the surface of laminated metal vessels; the sinkings of any undulating surface, a colour; a wave; *rarely*, a bed, a crevice, pride.

Tolgach, *a* Full of hollows; full of bruises, as a plate of metal Abounding in colours; showy, gaudy; proud, haughty, inconstant Uaillse tholgach an fhasain, *the gaudy pride of fashion.—Old Song*

Toll, *v a* (*Ir id Arm* toulla.) Bore, pierce, or perforate, make a hole; dig a hole or pit *Pret. a.* tholl, *bored, fut. aff.* tollaidh, *shall bore.* Tollaidh e le minidh, *he shall bore with an awl —Stew. Ex*

Toll, tuill, *s. m.* (*W* twll *Arm* toull *Corn Ir.* toll) A hole, a bore, a crevice, a pit, cave, or den; *rarely*, a head; a wicket Rinn e toll, *he bored a hole;* toll-torraidh, *a wimble-hole*, toll-torain, *a wicket.—Macd.* Toll-guail, *a coal-pit*, toll-gaineimh, *a sand-pit*, toll-cluaise, *a touch-hole*, toll-coinein, *a rabbit-borrough*, toll domhain, *a deep hole*, *Arm.* toull don

Tollach, *a.* (*Ir.* tollthach.) Boring, perforating; full of holes

Tolladair, *s. m.* (*Ir* toller.) A borer, a piercer; a wimble; stone-borer. *N pl* tolladairear

Tolladaireachd, *s. f* Boring

Tolladh, aidh, *s. m.* A boring or piercing; a digging of holes or pits.

Tollair, *s. m.* (*Ir* toller.) A borer, a piercer; a foxhound *N. pl* tollairear, *borers*, *Arm.* tolleryen.

Toll-bhuth, *s m.* A tolbooth, or prison —*Macd*

Toll-choinein, *s. m.* A rabbit-hole.

Toll-cluaise, **Toll-cluaisein**, *s. m.* A touch-hole

Toll-gaineimh, *s m* A sand-pit

Toll-guail, *a* A coal-pit

Tollta, *p part* of toll Bored, pierced; full of holes.

Tolltach, *a* Full of holes or bores, full of pits; causing holes Cho tolltach ris an rideal, *as full of holes as a riddle —Macdon*

Tolm, tuilm, *s m.* (*Ir. id*) A hillock, a mound, a knoll. Cho-fhreagair gach tolm is creag, *every hillock and grove resounded.—Oss. Conn*

Tolman, ain, *s m.* (*dim.* of tolm.) A little hill, a knoll; a mound

Tolmanach, *a.* Knolly; full of knolls or mounds

Tom, tuim, *s. m* (*Ir id*) An eminence; a green eminence; a knoll, a hillock, a bank; a grave; a conical knoll; a bush, a tuft, a thicket; *rarely*, the plague. Dosain is tuim nan ruadhag, *the thickets and hillocks of roes —Oss Fing*

Gr τύμβος *Lat.* tumulus. *Arm.* tumbe. *Ir* tom *W.* tom, and tiom

Tom, *v a* (*Ir id*) Dip, immerse, drench, bathe. *Pret a* thom, *dipped, fut. aff.* tomaidh, *shall dip* Tomadh e a chos, *let him dip his foot.—Stew. Deut ref*

Tomach, *a* (*Ir. id*) Bushy, tufty.

Tomad, aid, *s. m* Size, bulk, dimension

Tomadach, *a.* Sizable, bulky, causing bulk

Tomadachd, *s. f.* Sizableness, bulkiness.

Tomadh, aidh, *s. m* A dipping, an immersing, a drenching, a bathing; a dip, an immersion, a drenching

Tomaidh, *fut. aff.* of tom.

Tomald, **Tomalt**, ailt, *s m* Size, bulk, dimension. Garbh ann tomailt; *bulky.—Macdon.*

Tomaltach, *a.* See Tomadach

Toman, ain, *s m.* (*dim.* of tom) *W.* tomen. A little knoll or mound; a little tuft or bush. Da thoman uaine fo dharaig, *two green knolls of oak.—Oss. Fing.*

Tomanach, *a* (*Ir. id.*) Full of knolls or mounds; bushy; tufty.

Tomanta, *a* Rude.

Tombac, *s m.* Tobacco; snuff Tombac *seabh*, tombac cagnaidh, *tobacco;* feuch tombac, *give me some tobacco, or some snuff.*

Tòmh, *v. n.* Point with the finger *Pret. a* thomh, *pointed; fut aff. a.* tomhaidh, *shall point;* tomh ris, *point at him.*

Tomhadh, aidh, *s m.* A pointing with the finger.—*Stew. Is.*

Tomhail, *s. f* Terror, fright Tra dh' iadhas tomhail, *when terror surrounds —Oss. Duthona.*

Tomhail, *a* Vast, terrible —*Oss. Tem*

Tomhaileach, *a* Vast, terrible; frightful.

Tomhaileachd, *s f* Vastness, terribleness, frightfulness.

† **Tomhailt**, *v a.* (*Ir id.*) Eat.

Tomhais, *v a* (*Ir id*) Measure, weigh, balance; fathom; sound, guess, unriddle *Pret. a.* thomhais, *measured; fut aff.* tomhaisidh, *shall or will measure.* Tomhais e le troidhibh rùisgte, *measure it with bare soles.—Oss. Derm. Fut pass shall be measured.*

Tomhaisean, *s pl* Weights, scales, balances.

Tomhaiste, *p. part.* of tomhais. Measured, weighed, fathomed

Tomhartaich, *s. f.* Uncertainty, hesitation. Tha mi san tomhartaich, *I am hesitating.*

Tomhas, ais, *s m.* (*Ir id*) A measure, a weight, a balance, a scale, measurement, mensuration, a riddle; a hint; a mood or mode in music. Tomhas dubailte, *double measure —Stew Jer.* Thar tomhas, *beyond measure*, tomhas cruithneachd, *a measure of wheat.—Stew. Rev.*

† **Tomhladh**, aidh, *s.* (*Ir. id.*) The milk of a cow.

Tomlachd, *s* (*Ir. id.*) Thick milk, curds

† **Tomhradh**, aidh, *s. m* (*Ir.* tomhra) Protection

† **Tomhraiche**, *s.* (*Ir.* tomhraidhe) A protector; a patron.

Tomnach, aich, *s m.* A testator

Tòn, tona See Tòin

Tònach, *a* Having large hips, having a large breech.

Tònach, aich, *s m.* (*Ir. id*) A shirt, a garment—(*Shaw*), a bath

Tònag, aig, *s f.* A clew of yarn; a term of ridicule for a squat waddling female

Tonalas, ais, *s. m.* Cringing, adulation.

Tonaso, *s.* A ball of yarn.

† **Tonc**, *s. m.* (*Ir id*) A chain

Ton-chlodhach. See Toin-chlodhach.

Ton chruaidh See Tóin chruaidh.

† **Tonda**, *a.* Stubborn

Tònlagan, ain, *s m* (*Ir. id*) Sliding on the breech.

Ton-lodanach, *a.* Having a fawning or cringing spirit.

Ton-lodanadh, aidh, *s. m* A fawning or cringing; a soliciting, fawning, solicitation

Tonn, *v. n.* (*Ir. id.*) Undulate

Tonn, tuinn, *and* tuinne, *s. m.* and *f.* (*Ir id.*) *Corn. Arm. W.* ton.) A wave, billow, or surge; *rarely*, a hide. Tonn air traigh leis fein, *a lonely wave on the shore.—Ull.* and *Oss. Asp. form.* thonn. Nuallan thonn, *the noisy waves. Ull. N. pl.* tonnan. Chadh do thonnan tharum, *thy waves went over me.—Stew. Jon.*

Tonnach, aich, *s. m.* (*Ir. id.*) A mound, a rampart, a barrier.

Tonnach, *a.* (*Ir. id.*) Wavy, billowy, tempestuous, undulating. An fhairge ghlas thonnach, *the blue billowy ocean.—Macfar.*

Tonnadh, aidh, *s. m.* (*Ir. id.*) A vomiting; a death by poison.

Tonnag, aig, *s. f.* A small square of tartan, or of any coarse woollen stuff, used as a loose covering for the shoulders, and worn by women; a mantle.

Tonnag, aig, *s. f.* (*dim.* of tonn.) A little wave. Nuair thogadh tu tonnag, *when thou wouldst raise a little wave. Old Song.*

Tonnan, ain, *s. m.* (*dim.* of tonn.) *Ir. id.* A little wave.

Tonnan, *n. pl.* of tonn; which see.

Tonn-ghluasad, aid, *s. m.* Undulation.

Tonn-luaisg, *v. n.* Toss or rock on the waves; pitch or keel, as a vessel. *Pret. a.* thonn-luaisg; *fut. aff. a.* tonn-luaisgidh.

Tonn-luasgach, *a.* Causing a reeling motion, as of a ship at sea.

Tonn-luasgadh, aidh, *s. m.* The rocking or heaving of a vessel on the water; the pitching or keeling of a ship.

Top, *s. m.* (*Ir. id.*) A top; a tuft. Top circe, *a tuft on the head of a hen.*

Topach, *a.* Topped or tufted; having a tuft on the top of the head. Cearc thopach, *a tufted hen.*

Topainn, *s. f.* A teazing, or pulling by the hair.

Topar, air, *s. m.* (*Ir. id.*) A taper.

† **Tor**, *a.* Heavy.

† **Tor**, *s. m.* A bush; a shrub; a lord—(*Shaw*); a crest; a bull; a pursuer; fear; a sovereign, a lord; a tower, a steeple, a castle; weariness.

Torach, *a.* See **Torrach**.

Tòrachd, *s. f.* (*Ir.* toruigheachd.) Pursuit, chase, persecution; a tracing; strict search; retaliation. Fuileachdach san tòrachd, *bloody in the chase.—Death of Carril.* Tha tòrachd orm, *I am pursued.—Old Poem.* Luchd tòrachd, *pursuers, persecutors.—Stew. Jos.*

Toradh, aidh, *s. m.* An auger or wimble; an iron for boring stones; an answer. Toll toraidh, *an auger hole.*

Toradh, aidh, *s. m.* Fruitfulness. See **Torradh**.

Torag, aig, *s. f.* (*Ir. id.*) A wench.

Torail, *a.* See **Torrail**.

Torain, **Torair**, *s.* (*Ir.* torain.) A worm, a grub; vermin in corn. Mar lus is torair 'g a reubadh, *like an herb that worms devour.—Oss. Manos.*

Toralachd, *s. f.* See **Torralachd**.

Toran, àin. See **Torrail**.

Toras, ais, *s. m.* (*Ir. id.*) Weariness; a journey; a lord.

Torb, *s. m.* (*Ir. id.*) A throng; a rout.

Torc, tuirc, *s. m.* A boar, a hog; a wild boar; a whale; *rarely*, a collar; the heart, the face. Tomhais an torc, *measure the boar.—Oss. Derm.* Torc nimhe, *a wild boar.—Ull.* Lorg nan torc, *the track of whales.—Oss. Tem.* Torc alluidh, *a wild boar.*
Ir. id. W. turch. *Corn. Arm.* tourch, *and* torch.

Torchair, *gen. sing.* of torchar.

Torchair, *v. a.* Kill by knocking, or by throwing down; pierce; perish; happen. *Pret. a.* thorchair, *killed*; *fut. aff. a.* torchairidh. Thorchair leis an inghean, *by him the maiden fell.—Fingalian Poem.*

Torchair, *s. m.* (*Ir. id.*) A leveller.

Torchar, air, *s. m.* (*Ir. id.*) A fall; death.

Torc-mhuineal, eil, *s. m.* (*Ir.* torc-mhuin.) A hog's neck; a boar's neck.

Torchar, air, *s. m.* A mortal fall; a hurt by a fall.

Tor-chathair, -chathrach, *s. f.* A throne. *N. pl.* tor-chathraichean.

Tordhan, ain, *s. m.* (*Ir. id.*) An elegy.

Torgan, ain, *s. m.* (*Ir. id.*) A musical sound; noise, din, rattle.

Torlais, *s.* A person who talks at random.

Tormach, aich, *s. m.* (*Ir. id.*) Increase; the feeding of cows a short time before and after calving.

Tormachadh, aidh, *s. m.* Increasing.

Tormadh, *a.* (*Ir. id.*) Pregnant, growing big.

† **Tormaich**, *v. a.* Magnify, increase, enlarge.

Torman, ain, *s. m.* A musical sound; melody; murmur; a stringed musical instrument, a harp; the drone of a Highland bagpipe. Is ait leo torman do chlar, *pleasant to them is the music of thy harp.—Oss. Manos.* Torman an torrain, *the murmur of the thunder.—Oss. Conn.*

Torman, ain, *s. m.* The herb called clary.—*Macd.*

Tormanach, *a.* (*Ir. id.*) Murmuring; making a musical murmur; rumbling.

Torman-ciùil, *s. m.* A harp, a stringed musical instrument. A thorman-ciùil na laimh chli, *his harp in his left hand.—Oss. Duthona.*

† **Torn**, *s. m.* A kiln, a furnace, an oven; a lord.

Tornail, *s. f.* Knocking one thing against another.

Tornair, *s. m.* (*Ir. id.*) A turner.

Tornamh, aimh, *s. m.* (*Ir. id.*) Humiliation; descent.

Toroisg, *s. f.* A hand-saw; a file.

† **Torr**, *s. f.* (*Ir. id.*) A belly.

Torr, *s. m.* A tower, a castle; an eminence; a mound, a hill, a rock; a tomb or grave. 'N e 'n torr so t-aois làrach, *is this mound thine aged site.—Oss. Taura.* O thorr-thir an t-sneachd, *from the hills of the land of snow. Oss.* Mo chlann san torr, *my children in the tomb.—Oss. Fin.* and *Lor.*

Torrach, *a.* Towery; full of eminences.

Torrach, *a.* Fruitful; pregnant. Dh' fhàs i torrach, *she became pregnant.—Stew. Gen.* *Com.* and *sup.* torraiche.

Torrachas, ais. See **Torraicheas**.

Torradh, aidh, *s. m.* An auger. See **Toradh**.

Torradh, aidh, *s. m.* Produce; fruit, fruitfulness; pregnancy; benefit, profit. Torradh trom, *much produce.*

Torradh, aidh, *s. m.* A heaping or piling up; a burying, a burial; a heap.

Torraghan, ain, *s. m.* A murmur; a purling noise.

Torrghanach, *a.* Murmuring, purling.

Torraich, *v. a.* and *n.* (*Ir.* toirrchigh.) Impregnate; make fruitful; conceive, become pregnant; become fruitful. *Pret. a.* thorraich; *fut. aff.* torraichidh, *shall conceive; pret. pass.* thorraicheadh. Thorraicheadh i, *she conceived, Stew. Gen. ref.*

Torraiche, *com.* and *sup.* of torrach. More or most fruitful.

Torraiche, *s. f.* Fruitfulness; pregnancy.

Torraichead, eid, *s. m.* Fruitfulness, pregnancy; increase in fruitfulness, or in pregnancy. Tha i dol an torraichead, *she grows more and more fruitful.*

Torraicheas, eis, *s. m.* (*from* torrach.) Conception, pregnancy, fruitfulness. Meudaichidh mi do thorraicheas, *I* *will increase thy conception.—Stew. Gen.* Torraicheas anabuich, *an embryo, a fœtus, untimely birth —Stew. Job.*

TORRAIL, *a.* Fertile; productive; prolific

TORRAILEACHD, *s. f.* Fertility; productiveness

TORRAMH, *s. m* A pilgrimage

TORRAN, ain, *s. m.* (*dim* of torr) A little hill; an eminence, a rising ground; a mound; a grave

TORRAN, TORRANN, ain, *s m.* (*Ir.* toran *Arm. W.* toran.) Thunder; a rumbling noise, a murmur. Torman an torrain, *the noise of the thunder —Oss. Conn.* Torran na sine, *the murmur of the blast —Oss. Trath.*

TORRANACH, *a* Thundering; noisy, sounding like thunder.

TORR-CHATHAIR, -chathrach, *s. f.* A citadel, a fortress; a throne *N. pl.* torr-chathraichean, *citadels.*

TORRTHAIR, *s m.* A monster; a dwarf.—*Macfar. Voc.*

TORRUNN See TORRAN

TORRUNNACH, *a* Thundering, noisy; sounding like thunder Le buille thorrunnach, *with a thundering blow —Mac Lach.*

TOR-STOL, *s. m.* (*Ir. id*) A chair of state.

TORT, *s. m.* (*Ir id*) A cake; a little loaf.

TORTAIL, *a.* (*Ir. id.*) Strong, stout; tight, firm.

TORTAILEACHD, *s f* Strength, stoutness, tightness, firmness.

TORTAOBH, *s.* (*Ir. id*) Confidence.

TÒS, *s* Beginning, commencement, origin; front, foremost; part, *written also,* tùs, which see.

TÒS, (an), *adv* At first, sooner; in the beginning, at the commencement; in the first place.

TOSD, *a.* Quiet, silent, still Nach tosd an oidhche, *how silent is the night!—Oss Gaul*

TOSD, *s m.* Silence, quietness, stillness Tosd na h-oidhche, *the silence of night —Oss. Gaul.* Sheas iad nam balbh thosd, *they stood still and silent.—Mac Lach.* Bi d' thosd, *be quiet —Stew. Jos.* Tha iad nan tosd, *they are silent.*

TOSDACH, *a.* (*from* tosd) *Ir. id.* Silent, quiet, causing silence or stillness Dearg gu tiamhaidh tosdach, *Dargo lonely and silent.— Ull.* Talla tosdach na dichuimhne, *the quiet land of forgetfulness —Oss Cathluno.*

TOSDACH, (gu), *adv.* Silently, quietly, calmly.

TOSDACHD, *s. f.* Silence, quietness, peacefulness

TOSDAICH, *v a.* and *n* Make quiet, silence; confute; grow quiet or silent *Pret. a.* thosdaich; *fut. aff.* tosdaichidh. Tosdaicheam, *I will put to silence, fut. pass* tosdaichear, *shall be silenced*

TOSG, toisg, *s m.* A tusk, a back-tooth or grinder; a gash, a cut *N. pl.* tosgan

TOSGACH, *a.* Tusky; like a tusk

TOSGAIR, *s m.* (*Ir. id*) An ambassador—(*Macfar. Voc*), *N pl* tosgairean.

TOSGAIREACHD, *s. f* An embassy.

TOSGAL, ail, *s m* Arrogance.

TOSGAN, *n pl.* of tosg, which see

TOSTAL, ail, *s. m.* (*Ir. id*) Arrogance, presumption.—*Macfar. Voc.*

TOSTALACH, *a.* (*Ir. id.*) Arrogant, presumptuous Gu tostalach, *arrogantly Com* and *sup.* tostalaiche.

† TOT, toit, *s m* (*Ir. id*) A wave, a sod, a turf—(*Shaw*); a woman

† TOTA, *s. m.* (*Ir id*) A rower's bench.

† TOTH, totha, *s. m* (*Ir. id.*) A female — (*Shaw*), *pudenda muliebria.*

† TOTHBHALL, bhuill, *s* (*Ir. id.*) *Pudenda muliebria.*

TOTH, *s. m.* Fume; a puff of smoke.

TOTHACHD, *s. f.* (*Ir. id.*) Validity; substance.

TOTHAIR, *s. m* (*Ir. id.*) A freebooter

TRA, *adv.* When, while, whilst; as soon as. Tra chroch e 'n talamh, *when he hung the earth.—Sm.* Tra sguab iad an àrach, *when they scoured the field.—Ull.*

TRA, *s m.* (*W.* tro.) Time; season; day, hour. See also TRÀTH.

TRÀBHACH, aich, *s f.* (*Ir id.*) Stuff driven by the waves to the shore; stuff left on the banks of a river by a flood.

† TRACHD, *s. m.* (*Ir. id.*) A tract, a treatise, history, narration; a report.

TRÀCHD, *v* Negotiate; traffic, treat; handle *Pret. a.* thràchd, *negotiated, fut. aff.* tràchdaidh, *shall negotiate.*

TRÀCHDACH, *a.* Negotiations, trafficking, negotiators.

TRÀCHDADH, aidh, *s. m.* A negotiating, a trafficking; a negotiation, a traffic; purposing

TRACHDAIL, *s. f.* (*Ir. id*) A negotiation.

TRACHDAIR, *s m.* An historian, a recorder; one who writes treatises. *N pl.* trachdairean.

TRACHDAIREACHD, *s* The business of an historian; history; writing of treatises.

TRACHDALACHD, *s f.* (*Ir. id*) History—(*Macfar. Voc.*), negotiation.

TRACHLACH, *a* (*Ir id*) Fatiguing, laborious

TRACHLADH, aidh, *s m.* (*Ir. id.*) Fatigue—(*Macfar. Voc.*); loosening.

TRACHLAICHE, *s. m.* A drudge; one employed at dirty, laborious work; a squanderer.

TRADAN, ain, *s. m* A scolding person; a quarrelsome person.

TRADANACH, *a.* (*Ir. id.*) Scolding, quarrelsome, litigious. —*Macfar. Voc.*

TRADH, *s. m* (*Ir. id*) A lance, a spear.

TRÀ FEASGAIR, *s. m.* Eventide.

TRAGH, *v n.* (*Ir* traigh.) Subside, settle, ebb See TRAOGH.

TRAIDEACH, ich, *s. m* (*Ir id.*) A warrior.

TRAIDH. See TROIDH.

TRAGHADH, aidh See TRAOGHADH

TRAIGH, tragha, *s. f.* (*W* traeth. *Ir.* traigh) The sea-shore; the shore of a lake or river; the reflux or ebbing of the tide. Dh' iarr i 'n tràigh, *she repaired to the shore.— Ull.* Onfha na tràgha, *the raging billows of the shore — Id.* Ghios na trâgha, *to the shore —Id* Mar thràigh fhuaimear a chuain, *like the noisy reflux of the sea.—Oss. Fing.*

TRAIGH, *s. m.* (*Ir. id.*) Strength; a lazy person.

TRÀIGH-CHEUM, *s* A path along the shore of a sea or lake.—*Macfar. Voc.*

TRAIGHEANACH, aich, *s. m.* (*Ir id.*) A lazy person.

TRAIGH-GHEADH, -gheoidh, *s* A shore-goose; a goose that is fed on shore. Guilbnich as tràigh-gheoidh, *curlews and shore-geese —Macdon.*

TRAIGHIDHEACH, *a* (*Ir. id.*) Tragical.

TRAIGH-MARA, *s. f.* A sea-shore; an ebbing of the sea.

TRAIGHTE, *p. part.* of traigh. Subsided; ebbed, as the tide; settled, as a disturbed fluid; dry, as land from which the tide has receded An talamh traighte, *the dry land.—Sm.*

TRAILL, *s. f.* (*Ir. id.*) A kneading-trough; a tray.

TRAILL, traille, *s. m.* and *f* A slave, a bond-man, or bond-maid; a labourer, a drudge; a hard-wrought servant *N. pl.* tràillean do thraillean, *thy bondmen —Stew. Lev* Mar thraillean, *like slaves —Mac Co.*

Ir. tràill, *a slave. Dan.* trael. *Sax.* thrael. *Germ.* trill. *Eng.* thrall.

Tràilleach, *a.* (*Dan.* traelagtig) Servile, slavish.

Traillеachd, *s. f.* (*Ir.* traillidbeacht.) Slavery, bondage; drudgery, slavishness.

Traillealachd, *s. f.* Slavery, bondage; drudgery, slavishness. Traillealachd na Roimh, *the bondage of Rome.* —*Translation of Galgacus's Speech*

† **Traillear**, eir, *s m.* (*Ir. id.*) A baker.

Trailleas, eis, *s f.* (*Ir. id*) Slavery

Traillеil, *a* (traill-amhuil) Slavish, servile; in bondage, enslaved. Obair thràilleil, *servile work* —*Stew. Lev.*

Tràillidh, *a.* (*Ir. id*) Slavish, servile, enslaved.

Traillidheachd, *s f.* (*Ir. id*) Slavery, slavishness, hard service. Traillidheachd t-athar, *the hard service of thy father.*—*Stew.* 1 *K. ref.*

Traill-luingeas, eis, *s. f.* A galley; a convict ship.

Traineadh, idh, *s. m.* (*Ir. id.*) A culling, a choosing.

Trainnse, *s. f.* (*Ir. id.*) A trench, a drain.

Trainnsear, eir, *s. m* (*Scotch*, trunscheour) A plate or trencher.

Traisg, *v. n* Fast, abstain from food; observe a fast; be hungry. *Pret a* thraisg, *fasted, fut aff. a.* traisgidh, *shall fast.* C'arson a thraisg sibh, *why do you fast?*—*Stew. Is.* Written also, *troisg.*

Traisgeach, *a* Of, or belonging to, a fast.

Traisgidh, *fut. aff. a.* of traisg

Traisgte, *a.* Cross, cross-grained.

Tràit, *s f.* (*Ir id*) A cataplasm.—*Macfar. Voc*

Tràiteach, *a.* Of, or belonging to, a cataplasm; like a cataplasm.

Tràith. See **Tràigh.**

Trall, *s. f.* A drab, a trull.

Trang, *a.* (*Germ.* drang *Swed Dan.* trang, *close*) Throng; close; on good terms, very intimate

Trà-nòin, *s m* Mid-day, noon. Ri ceòl tra-nòin, *singing at noon* —*Mac Lach.*

Trannsa, *s. m.* (*Scotch*, trance) A passage, or entrance.

Traogh, *v. a* and *n.* Ebb, as the sea, subside, as a flood; settle, as a disturbed fluid; pacify; abate. *Pret. a.* thraogh, *subsided, fut aff. a.* traoghaidh, *shall subside* Thraogh na h-uisgeacha, *the waters subsided.*—*Stew Gen.* Traoghaidh tiodhlacadh fearg, *a gift will pacify anger* —*Stew. Pro. ref.*

Traoghach, *a.* Subsiding soon; tending to ebb, or to abate.

Traoghadh, aidh, *s. m.* A subsiding, an ebbing of the tide; a settling, as of an agitated fluid; an assuaging; assuagement.

Traoghta, *p part* of traogh. Subsided, ebbed, dried up; settled, as any agitated fluid.

Traoidhte, *s f.* Treachery, treason, deceitfulness

Traoidhtear, eir, *s m.* A traitor. *N. pl.* traoidhtearan

Traoidhtearachd, *s. f* Treason; the practice of treason.

Traoill, *s. f.* (*Ir. id*) Cant.

Traon, traoin, *s. m* A rail; a corn-crake.

Traonair, *s. m.* (*Ir. id*) An idler

Traonaireachd, *s f.* (*Ir id.*) Leisure; vacancy

Trapan, ain, *s m.* (*Ir. id*) A cluster, a group —*Macfar. Voc.* and *Shaw.*

Trapan, ain, *s. m.* A cluster, a bunch

Trapanach, *a.* Clustering, clustered, in groups.

Tràs, Trasa, *adv.* (*for* tràth so, *the present time*) Now, at present.

Tràs, (an), *adv.* Now, at present.

Trasd, trasda, *s m.* (*Ir. id*) A cross, thwart, or disappointment.

Trasda, *a.* Cross; laid across.

Trasdach, *a.* Cross, crosswise

Trasdachd, *s. f.* (*Ir id*) Crossness

Trasg, traisg, *s m.* A fast. Dh' éigh iad trasg, *they proclaimed a fast.*—*Stew. Jon* Ri trasg, *fasting* —*Stew Is* Là traisg, *a fast day.* Written also, *trosg*

Trasgadh, aidh, *s m* The circumstance of fasting; a fast Written also, *trosgadh.*

Trasgaìr, *v. a.* Kill, oppress; overwhelm

Trasgairt, *s f* (*Ir id.*) Abrogation, oppression; overthrow.

Trasgar, air, *s m* (*Ir* trasgradh.) Destruction; oppression; a great fall.

Trasgradh, aidh, *s. m* (*Ir id.*) Destruction, oppression, a killing, an oppressing

Trasnan, ain, *s m.* (*Ir id*) A ledge; a cross-beam.

Tràth, tràtha, *s m.* (*Ir. id*) Time, season; day, hour, prayer-time Focal na thràth, *a word in season.*—*Stew Prov.* An ceann an naoi tràth, *at the end of the ninth day* —*Fingalian Poem* *N. pl.* trathan, *d. pl.* tràthaibh. Sna tràthaibh ceart, *in the proper seasons* —*Macfar.* Trath-noin, *mid-day, noontide.*—*Oss. Trath* Tràth-bidh, *meat-time*, tràth-feasgair, *eventide, evening*, trath-urnuigh, *prayer-time*

Trathadair, *s. m.* (*from* tràth) A timepiece *N. pl* tràthadairean

Tràthail, *a.* (tràth-amhuil) Early, soon; in time, in good or proper time.

Tràth-bidh. See **Tràth.**

Tràth-feasgair See **Tràth.**

Trathnan, ain, *s m* (*Ir. id.*) A little stalk of grass

Trath-nòin. See **Tràth.**

Tràth urnuigh See **Tràth**

Tre, *prep* (*Ir. id.*) Through; by means of. Tre aineolas, *through ignorance* —*Stew. Lev.* Tre mo chleith, *through my casement* —*Stew Pro. ref*

Treabh, treibh, *s. f* (*Ir. id*) A tribe, or clan; a farmed village; *also*, tilling; agriculture

Treabh, *s.* (*Sax.* thraf *Scotch*, thraive, *Swed* † trafwe.) Two cocks of corn, consisting each of twelve sheaves.

Treabh, *v. a* Till, plough, cultivate. *Pret. a* threabh, *tilled, fut aff. a* treabhaidh, *shall till.* Cha treabh an leisgean, *the sluggard will not plough* —*Stew Pro.* Iadsan a threabhas euceart, *they who plough iniquity.*—*Stew. Job*

Treabhach, aich, *s* (*Ir id.*) Winter cresses, *Eryssimum barbara.*

Treabhachail, *a* Agricultural; arable.

Treabhachas, ais, *s m* Agriculture, husbandry; a specimen of ploughing. Is sibhse treabhachas Dhé, *ye are the husbandry of God.*—*Stew*, 1 *Cor.*

Treabhachd, *s f* Agriculture, husbandry.

Treabhadh, aidh, *s. m* (*Ir id*) Ploughing, tilling; tillage, agriculture, husbandry. Treabhadh nam bochd, *the tillage of the poor. Stew. Pro* Treabhadh choirce, *corn-husbandry*, treabhadh eorna, *barley-husbandry*, talamh treabhaidh; *plough land, arable land.*

Treabhadh, (a), *pr. part* of treabh.

Treabhaiche, *s. m* (*from* treabh.) A ploughman, or tiller of ground; a husbandman, a peasant Bha e na threabhaiche, *he was a tiller of the ground.*—*Stew. Gen.* *N. pl* treabhaichean

Treabhailt, *s. f.* A mill-hopper, *in ridicule*, a bulky female

Treabhair, *s. m* (*Ir. id*) A surety.

Treabhaireachd, *s. f.* (*Ir. id.*) Husbandry

Treabhair, *s. m.* (*Ir. id.*) A ploughman, a tiller; a homestall, a homestead.

Treabhlachd, *s. f.* (*Ir. id.*) A family; a household.—*Shaw.*

† **Treabhar**, air, *s. m.* (*Ir. id.*) The tide; activity; choice.

Treabhar, *a.* (*Ir. id.*) Discreet; skilful.

Treabhta, **Treabhte**, *p. part.* of treabh. Plowed, tilled, cultivated.

Treachail, *v. a.* Dig; dig deep; fatigue; oppress with labour, overwork. *Pret. a.* threachail; *fut aff. a.* treachailidh. Chladhaich e slochd is threachail e, *he dug a ditch, and dug it deep.*—*Sm.*

Treachailte, *p. part.* of Treachail. Dug, digged; fatigued with labour; overwrought. Clachan treachailte le 'm buinn, *stones dug up with the feet.*—*Death of Carril.*

Treachdair, *s. m.* An historian.

Treachlach, aich, *s. m.* A squanderer.

Treachladh, aidh, *s. m.* A digging; a fatiguing; fatigue, hardship.

† **Tread**, treid, *s. m.* A scold, a quarrel. Hence the English word *threat.* Aristophanes uses the word θρεττε in the sense of quarrelling: his commentator says he got it from the barbarians. It is now written *trod.*

Tread, *s. m.* A trade.

† **Treadhan**, ain, *s. m.* (*Ir. id.*) A fast of three days; an ebb; want; a louse.

Treadhanas, ais, *s. m.* (*Ir. id.*) Abstinence.

† **Treagh**, *s. m.* (*Ir. id.*) A spear.

Trealaich, *s. f.* Lumber, trash; a mixed heap of valueless articles; tackling. Trealaich cath, *the lumber of battle.*—*Macfar.*

Trealais, *s. f.* (*Ir. id.*) The spleen.—*Macfar. Voc.*

Trèalamh, aimh, *s. m.* (*Ir. id.*) Indisposition, weakness; apparel, furniture.

Treall, *s. m.* (*Ir. id.*) A short space; a while.

Treallach, aich, *s. m.* Lumber; trash.

Treaman, ain, *s. m.* (*Ir. id.*) An alien.

Trean, *v. a.* Train, as soldiers.

Treanadh, aidh, *s. m.* Lamentation, wailing; Whitsuntide, the week from Thursday preceding, to that following Whitsunday.

Trean ri trean, *s. m.* The bird called corn-crake.—*Macdon.* and *Macfar. Voc.*

Treananta, *a.* (*Ir. id.*) Triangular.

Treanta, *p. part.* Trained or disciplined as soldiers.

Trearach, aich, *s. m.* (*Ir. id.*) An artificer.

Treartha, ai, *s. m.* Art, science.—*Macfar. Voc.*

Treartiiach, *a.* Artificial; skilled in arts; scientific.

† **Treas**, treis, *s. m.* (*Ir. id.*) A skirmish, a battle; adversity.

Treas, *a.* (*Ir. id.*) Third. An treas la, *the third day;* an treas fear, *the third man;* san treas aite, *in the third place.*

Treasa, *com.* and *sup.* of treun. Stronger, strongest.

Treasaid, *s. f.* A third crop.

Treas-barr, *s. m.* A third crop.

Treas-cuid, *s. f.* A third part.

† **Treasdach**, *a.* Sure-footed; thorough pacing. Each treasdach luath-bhar, *a sure-footed, quick-pacing horse.*—*Fingalian Poem.*

Treasg, treisg, *s. m.* Groats, or hulled oats; draff; brewers' grains.

Treas-tarruing, *s. f.* Triple distilled spirits, triple distilled whisky; a third time.

Treathaid, *s. f.* A stitch or sudden pain.—*Macfar. Voc.*

Treathaideach, *a.* Painful; paining by sudden twitches.

† **Treathan**, ain, *s. m.* (*Ir. id.*) A wave; sea; high water; a foot; a trace.

Treathnach, aich, *s. m.* (*Ir. id.*) A gimblet; a foot.

Treibhdhireach, *a.* Upright, righteous, virtuous, sincere; honest, faithful. Duine treibhdhireach, *an upright man;* treibhdhireach agus gun tuisleadh, *sincere and without offence.*—*Stew. Phil.*

Treibhdhireas, eis, *s. m.* Uprightness; sincerity; honesty.

Treibhse, *s. f.* (*Ir. id.*) Room, place, stead.

Treibhseach, *a.* (*Ir. id.*) Apt to change.

Treibhseachd, *s. f.* (*Ir. id.*) Changeableness.

Tréig, *v. a.* (*Ir. id.*) Leave; forsake; depart from; desert. *Pret. a.* thréig, *forsook; fut. aff. a.* tréigidh, *shall forsake.* Threig e comhairle, *he forsook advice.*—*Stew.* 1 *K.* Treig olc, *depart from evil.*—*Stew. Pro.* Gaoth a thogas is a threigeas an dos, *wind that agitates the bush and leaves it.* —*Oss. Lod.* *P. part.* treigte, *left, forsaken, abandoned.*

Tréigeach, *a.* Apt to forsake, desert, or abandon.

Tréigeadh, idh, *s. m.* A forsaking, a deserting, an abandoning; abandonment, desertion.

Tréigeal, *s. m.* A departure; molasses.

Tréigean, ein, *s. m.* Leaving, forsaking; abandonment.

Treigear, *fut. pass.* of tréig.

Treigheannas, ais, *s. m.* (*Ir. id.*) Fasting; abstinence.

Treigsinn, *s. f.* (*Ir. id.*) A quitting, forsaking, or abandoning; abandonment, desertion.

Tréigsinn, (a), *pr. part.* of tréig. Leaving, quitting, forsaking. Mo chàil a treigsinn, *my strength failing.*—*Oss. Derm.*

Tréigsinneach, *a.* Apt to forsake, abandon, or desert; *substantively*, a deserter.

Tréigte, *p. part.* of tréig. Forsaken, abandoned, deserted; forlorn.

Tréin, *gen.* of treun.

Tréine, *s. f.* (*Ir. id. W.* tren.) Strength, might, power. A thréine, *his might.*—*Stew.* 1 *K.* Mar threine tuinne, *like the strength of a wave.*—*Fingalian Poem.*

Tréine, *com.* and *sup.* of treun. (*Ir. id.*) Stronger, strongest. Sibhse bu tréine sna gleanntai, *you were the strongest in the valleys.*—*Oss. Cathluno.*

Treinnse, *s. f.* (*Ir. id.*) A trench.

Treis, treise, *s. f.* (*Ir.* treimhse.) A while, a space of time; distance of place. Treis mhath, *a good while;* o cheann treise, *a while ago;* treis air astar, *a good way off.*

Treise, *com.* and *sup.* of treun. Stronger, strongest. Is tu 's treise na mise, *thou art stronger than I.*—*Stew. Jer.* Iadsan is treise, *those who are strongest.*—*Stew. Gen.*

Treise, *s. f.* (*Ir. id.*) Strength, force; power, vigour; a trial of strength; battle; trial; adversity. A treise 'g a fàgail, *her strength forsaking her.*—*Oss. Gaul.* Treise Ghuill na éide staillinn, *Gaul's strength in his mail of steel.*—*Id.* Dh'eug mo threise, *my vigour has died away.* —*Oss. Derm.* Garbh-fhraoch anns gach treise, *fierce wrath in every battle.*—*Fingalian Poem.*

Treiseil, *a.* (treise-amhuil.) Strong, powerful, vigorous.—*Macfar. Voc.*

† **Tréite**, *s. f.* (*Ir. id.*) Embrocation.

Treith, *s. f.* Accomplishment; qualification.

Treith, *gen. sing.* and *n. pl.* of triath; which see.

† **Treithe**, *s. f.* (*Ir. id.*) Ignorance; weakness.

Treitheach, *a.* (*Ir. id.*) Accomplished, learned.

Treodas, ais, *s. m.* (*Ir. id.*) Food.

TREOIR, s. f. Strength, might; vigour; direction—(*Macfar. Voc.*); a troop.

TREOIR, s. An instrument for forming the heads of nails.

TREÒRACHADH, aidh, s. m. A leading, conducting, or guiding. Tha mi air mo theorachadh, *I am conducted.*

TREÒRACH, a. Active.

TREORACHADH, (a), pr. part. of treoraich. Leading, conducting, guiding.

TREORACHÀIR, s. m. A leader, a conductor, a guide.

TREÒRAICH, v. a. Lead, conduct, guide; direct. *Pret. a.* threoraich; *fut. aff. a.* treoraichidh, *shall guide.*

TREORAICHE, s. m. A leader, a conductor, a guide. *N. pl.* treoraichean.

TREORAICHEAR, *fut. pass.* of trèoraich.

TREORAICHEAR, eir, s. m. (*Ir.* treoraigtheoir.) A leader, a conductor, a guide.—*Macfar. Voc.*

TREORAICHTE, *p. part.* of treoraich. Led, conducted, guided.

TREORAN, ain, s. m. (*Ir. id.*) A little active child.

TREORAN, s. (*Ir. id.*) Three parts.

TRESG, s. f. Groats.—*Macfar. Voc.* More properly *treasg*; which see.

TREUBH, treubha, s. m. (*Lat.* tribus.) A tribe, a clan; kin; a family. Aon treubh do d'mhac, *one tribe to thy son.*—*Stew.* 1 *K.* *N. pl.* treubhan.

TREUBHACH, aich, s. m. (*from* treubh.) One of a tribe or clan.

TREUBHACH, a. Clannish; in tribes or clans; relating to a clan; powerful; gallant; valiant. Fhuaradh gu treubhach i, *she was found valiant.*—*Sm.* Na fir threubhach, *the valiant men.*—*Roy Stewart.*

TREUBHACHAS, ais, s. m. Valour.

TREUBHACHD, s. f. Clannishness; bravery, gallantry.

TREUBHAICHE, *com.* and *sup.* of treubhach. More or most valiant.

TREUBHAICHE, s. m. One of a tribe or clan.

TREUBHAICHEAD, id, s. m. Bravery, gallantry; improvement or advancement in bravery. A dol an treubhaichead, *growing more and more brave;* air a threubhaichead sa bheil iad, *however brave they be.*

TREUBHAN, ain, s. m. (*Ir. id.*) A tribune. *N. pl.* treubhain.

TREUBHANTAS, ais, s. m. Valour, gallantry, courage; magnanimity. Ni sinn treubhantas, *we shall act valiantly.*—*Sm.* Bearta treubhantais, *deeds of valour.*—*Id.*

TREUBHAS, ais, s. m. Valour, courage. Innis da mo threubhas, *tell him of my courage.*—*Oss. Dargo.*

TREUBHUN, uin, s. m. (*from* treubh.) A tribune.

TREUD, treuda, s. m. (*Ir.* tread.) A flock or herd of cattle; followers; a band of men. Gleidhidh mi do threud, *I will feed thy flock.*—*Stew. Gen.* Thuirt e ri a threud, *he said to his [flock] followers.*—*Sm.* Mar fhuaim tuinne bha gach treud, *each band was like a roaring wave.*—*Fingalian Poem.* *N. pl.* treudan; *d. pl.* treudaibh.

TREUDACH, a. Gregarious; in herds or flocks; of, or belonging to, a flock or herd.

TREUDAICHE, s. m. (*from* treud.) A keeper of cattle; a shepherd—(*Macfar. Voc.*); a cowherd, a swineherd.

TREUN, a. (*W.* treun. *Ir.* trean.) Strong, powerful; brave, magnanimous. Bha sibh treun thar ghloir, *you were brave beyond praise.*—*Old Song.* *Com.* and *sup.* treine *and* treise.

TREUN, trein, s. m. A strong man, a warrior, a hero; a champion. Na feithibh an treun, *wait not for the hero.*—*Ull.*

TREUNACHAS, ais, s. m. (*Ir. id.*) Valour.

TREUNAD, aid, s. m. Strength; bravery; increase in strength or in bravery. A dol an treunad, *growing more and more strong;* air a threunad sa bheil e, *however strong he be.*

TREUNADAS, ais, s. m. (*from* treun.) Strength; bravery; manhood; mightiness. A taomadh do threunadais, *pouring thy strength.*—*Oss. Fing.* D' ard threunadas, *thy high mightiness.*

TREUNAS, ais, s. m. (*from* treun.) *Ir.* treanas, *strength.* *W.* trenus, *impetuous.* Strength, might; bravery, courage. A taomadh a threunais, *pouring his strength.*—*Oss. Fing.*

TREUN-DHÀN, -dhàin, s. m. An epic or heroic poem.

TREUNEAR, ir, s. m. (treun-fhear.) *Ir.* trein-fhear. A strong man; a hero; a champion. *N. pl.* treunir. Dhùisg na treunir lasair, *the heroes kindled a flame.*—*Oss. Duthona.*

TREUN-LAOCH, -laoich, s. m. A strong warrior; a hero, a champion. Mo lann an uchd nan treun-laoch, *my sword in the breasts of warriors.*—*Oss. Cathluno.* *N. pl.* treun-laoich.

TREUNTAS, ais, s. m. Strength; power; magnanimity. Thréig iad an treuntas, *they have forsaken their magnanimity.*—*Old Song.*

TREUN-THOISGEACH, a. Brave with expedition; performing exploits in quick succession.

TRI, a. Three. Tri làithe dhi na tosd, *three days was she silent;* dha na tri, *two or three.*
Shans. traya. *Gr.* τρεῖς. *Lat.* tres. *It.* tre. *Fr.* trois. *Teut.* drii. *Belg.* drie. *Germ.* drei, thri, *and* dri. *Anglo-Sax.* threo *and* thry. *W. Arm. Ir.* tri.

† TRIABHALL, aill, s. m. (*Eng.* travel. *Fr.* travaille.) A journey. Now written *triall.*

TRIACHAN, ain, s. m. (*Ir. id.*) A sock or shoe.

TRIADH. See TRIATH.

TRIALL, s. m. (*Ir. id.*) A journey; a travelling; a way; expedition, a march; design. Dh' aom e 'thriall, *he bent his way.*—*Oss. Fing.* Triall na gealaich, *the moon's journey, the moon's path.*—*Ull.* Mun criochnaich e 'thriall, *before he ends his journey.*—*Macdon.* Triall nan cùraidh, *the heroes' march.*—*Mac Lach.* Air mo thriall, *on my way.*

TRIALL, v. n. and a. (*Ir. id.*) Travel, journey; traverse; march; go, be gone, be off; imagine, devise, plot. *Pret. a.* thriall; *fut. aff.* triallaidh.

TRIALLACH, a. (*from* triall.) Itinerant; travelling; fond of walking; of, or relating to, a journey.

TRIALLADH, aidh, s. m. A travelling or journeying; a journey.

TRIALLAICHE, s. m. (*from* triall.) A pedestrian; a traveller; a wayfaring man.

TRIALLAIR, s. m. (triall-fhear.) A pedestrian; a traveller; a wayfaring man.—*Macfar. Voc.*

TRIAMH, a. Third. An triamh fear, *the third man.*

TRIAMHAIN, a. (*Ir. id.*) Weary.

TRIAMHNADH, aidh. Weariness.

TRIAMHNUIN, s. f. Lamentation.

TRIAMHUINEACH, a. (*Ir. id.*) Mournful.

TRIAN, s. (*Ir. id.*) A third, a third part; particle; a district. Trian a chliù, *the third part of his fame.*—*Oss. Tem.* Gearr ar as dà thrian, *two thirds shall be cut off.*—*Stew. Zech.* An treas trian, *the third part.*—*Id.* Chluinnte gu 'thrian am fonn, *the strain was imperfectly heard.*—*Oss. Tem.* Trian do shoillse, *a particle of light.*—*Oss.*

TRIANACH, a. (*from* trian.) *Ir. id.* Three by three; of the third part.

TRIANAID, s. f. The Holy Trinity. An Trianaid Chruithear, *the Godhead.*

TRIANTAN, ain, s. m. A triangle. *N. pl.* triantain.

TRIANTANACH, a. Triangular.

TRIARACH, a. (*Ir. id.*) Thirdly.

TRIATH, a. (*Ir. id.*) Noble; valuable; weak.

TRIATH, treith, s. m. (*Ir. id.*) A lord, a noble, a prince; a chief or chieftain; a hero; a leader; *rarely,* a hillock;

a wave. Coimeas do 'n charraig an triath, *like a rock is the hero.—Oss. Fing.* *N. pl.* treith, triaith, *and* triatha. Thog na triaith sleagh a bhàis, *the chiefs lifted the spears of death.—Oss. Tem.* Triatha Mhorbheinn, *the chiefs of Morven.—Id.*

TRIATHACH, *a.* (*Ir. id.*) Lordly, triumphant.

TRIATHACH, aich, *s. m.* (*Ir. id.*) A trophy.

TRIBUAIL, *v. a.* Handle or finger a stringed musical instrument; strike. *Pret. a.* thribuail; *fut. aff.* tribuailidh, *shall handle.* Thribuail am bard a chruit, *the bard handled the harp.—Oss. Fin. and Lor.*

TRIC, *adv.* (*Ir. id.*) Often, frequently; frequent. Gu tric, *frequently.* Is minic uair 's is tric, *many a time and oft.*

TRICE, *com.* and *sup.* of tric. Oftener, oftenest.

TRICEAD, *a.* Thirsty.

TRICEAD, eid, *s. m.* Frequency; a growing more frequent. A dol an tricead, *growing more and more frequent.*

TRI-CHEANNACH, *a.* Tricipital.

TRI-CHOSACH, *a.* Three-footed, tripedal; *also*, a tripod.

TRI-CHUAIRT. Three times, thrice.

TRID, *prep.* (*Ir. id. W.* trid, *that tends through.*) Through, by means of. Da thrid, *through it* or *him.—Stew. Mic.* Tridsan, *through him;* da tridsa, *through her.—Stew. Gen.* D' an tridsan, *through them.—Id.* Trid amach, *throughout;* trid a cheile, *promiscuously; helter-skelter.*

TRID-AMHARTAN, ain, *s. m.* Mishap; ill luck.

TRI-DEUG, *a.* (*Corn.* tredhek. *Ir.* trideag. *Lat.* tredecim.) Thirteen. Tri fir dheug, *thirteen men;* tri clachan deug, *thirteen stones.*

TRID-SHOILLEIR, *a.* Transparent.

TRID-SHOILLSE, *s. f.* (*Ir. id.*) A transparency.

TRID-SHOILLSEACH, *a.* (*Ir. id.*) Transparent.

TRID-SHOILLSEACHAN, ain, *s. m.* (*Ir. id.*) A transparency.

TRID-SHOILLSEACHD, *s. f.* Transparentness.

TRID-SHOILLSEAN, ein, *s. m.* A transparency.

TRI-FHOGHAIR, *s. f.* (*Ir. id.*) A triphthong.

TRI-FICHEAD, *a.* Sixty. Tri fichead 's a h-aon, *sixty-one;* tri fichead 's a deich, *seventy;* tri fichead deug, *two hundred and sixty;* tri fichead 's a h-aon deug, *sixty-one;* tri fichead 's a tri-deug, *seventy-three.*

TRI-FILLTE, *a.* Threefold, triple.

TRILEAN, ein, *s. m.* A quavering sound; a warbling.

TRILEANTA, *a.* Quavering, warbling; trifling. See TRIOLANTA.

TRILIS, trilse, *s. f.* (*Ir. id.*) Luxuriant locks; bushy hair. A cleachdadh ri 'n trilsibh, *struggling with their luxuriant locks.—Old Song.*

TRILISEACH, *a.* (*Ir. id.*) Luxuriant, or bushy, as hair.

TRILLEACHAN, ain, *s. m.* A grey plover.

TRILLEACHAN TRÀIGH, *s. m.* Collared oyster-catcher.—*Shaw.*

TRILLSEAN, ein, *s. m.* (*Ir. id.*) A small torch, a flambeau, a lamp, a lantern.

TRILLSIDH, *s. f.* (*Ir. id.*) A torch, a lamp.

TRI MHEURACH, aich, *s. m.* Any instrument with three prongs, a three-pronged fork; a trident.—*Stew. Sam.*

TRINNSE, *s. f.* (*Ir. id.*) A trench.

TRINNSEAR, eir, *s. m.* A trencher or plate.

TRIOBLAID, TRIOBLOID, *s. f.* (*Ir. id.*) Trouble, distress, calamity. Le trioblaid chruaidh, *with hard trouble.—Sm.* La mo thriobloid, *the day of my trouble.—Id.*

TRIOBLAIDEACH, TRIOBLOIDEACH, *a.* Afflictive, distressing, distressful; calamitous; vexatious; afflicted, distressed.

TRIOBLAIDICH, TRIOBLOIDICH, *v. a.* Afflict, distress, trouble; vex.

TRIOCH, *s.* The hooping-cough.

TRIOCHAD, *a.* Thirty.

TRI-OISINNEACH, *a.* Triangular.

TRI-OISINNEAG, eig, *s. f.* A triangle; a triangular figure.

TRIOLANTA, *a.* Quavering, warbling; trifling, inconsiderable. Le d' phuirt thriolanta, *with the warbling strains.—Macfar.*

TRIOLLACHAN, ain, *s. m.* A grey plover—(*Macd.*); a schemer. Written also *trilleachan.*

TRIOLLACHAN-TRÀIGH, *s. m.* Collared oyster-catcher.

TRIOM, *comp. pron.* (*for* tromham.) Through me; through my means.

TRIOMAN, ain, *s. m.* (*Ir. id.*) Great toadstool.

TRIOM-SA, *emphat. form* of triom. Through me, by means of me.—*Stew. Pro. ref.*

TRIONAID, *s. f.* See TRIANAID.

TRIOPAL, TRIOPALL, aill, *s. m.* (*Ir. id.*) A bunch, cluster, or festoon. *N. pl.* triopaill. Triopaill fionain, *clusters of the vine.—Stew. Pro. ref.*

TRIOPALACH, TRIOPALLACH, *a.* (*Ir. id.*) Bunchy, clustered, in festoons; trim, tidy.

TRIOSGAN, ain, *s. m.* Household stuff.

TRI-RAMHACH, *a.* Three-oared; *substantively*, a trireme.

† TRIST, *a.* (*Ir. id. Lat.* tristis.) Sad; tired; *substantively*, a curse.

TRI-THEUDACH, *a.* Three-stringed. Inneal tri-theudach, *a three-stringed instrument.—Stew. Sam.*

TRI UAIREAN. Thrice, three times; three o'clock; three hours.

TRIUBHAS, ais, *s. f.* See TRIUGHAS.

TRIUBHASACH, *a.* Wearing trowsers.

TRIUGH, *s. f.* The hooping-cough or chin-cough.

TRIUGHAS, ais, *s. f.* (*Ir.* trius. *W.* trws.) Trowsers, pantaloons; breeches and stockings in one piece of dress. Triughas lìn, *linen breeches.—Stew. Ezek.*

TRIUINE, *s. f.* (*Ir. id.*) Poverty.

TRIÙIR, *a. pl.* (*Ir.* triur.) Three, three in number. Rug mi dha triuir mhac, *I bore him three sons.—Stew. Gen.*

TRIUIREAN, ein, *s. m.* A sheep's purl.

TRIUN, *s. m.* A poor person; *adjectively*, poor.

TRO', *for* troimh.

TROBHD, *v. def.* Come.

This word is used only in conversation.

TROCAIR, *s. f.* (*Ir. id.*) Mercy, compassion, pity; pardon. Trocair is aille leam, *I will have* [*prefer*] *mercy.—Stew. N. T.*

TROCAIREACH, *a.* (*Ir. id.*) Merciful, compassionate; pitiful. Gu trocaireach, *mercifully.*

TROCAIREACHD, *s. f.* (*Ir. id.*) Mercifulness, compassionateness, willingness to pardon.

TROCAIRICHE, *com.* and *sup.* of trocaireach. More or most merciful.

† TROCH, *s.* (*Ir. id.*) A short life.

TROCHLADH, aidh, *s. m.* (*Ir. id.*) A loosening.

TROD, *s. m.* (*Swed.* trata, *to quarrel. Ir.* treid, troid, *a scold.*) A scold, a reprimand; a scolding; a quarrel, a struggle or contention; strife, battle; a starling. Fhuair e 'throd, *he got a scold.* Cridhe nach sgithich an trod, *a heart that will not tire in battle.—Old Poem.*

TROD, *v.* See TROID.

TRODACH, *a.* (*Ir. id.*) Scolding; apt to scold or reprimand; quarrelling; struggling.

TRODADH, aidh, *s. m.* A scolding.

TRODAG, aig, *s. f.* A scolding female. *N. pl.* trodagan.

Trodan, ain, *s. m.* (*Ir. id.*) A quarrel.

Trodanach, *a.* (*Ir. id.*) Quarrelsome.

Trogbhail, *s. f.* A dispute, quarrel, or wrangle. Na tog trogbhail air an aineol, *raise not a quarrel with a stranger.*—*Old didactic Poem.*

† **Trogh**, *s.* (*Ir. id.*) Children.

Troghan, ain, *s. m.* (*Ir. id.*) A raven.

Troghbhail, *s. f.* A quarrel.

Troich, *s. m.* (*Ir. id.*) A dwarf, a pigmy; a diminutive, hump-backed person; a coward. Duine tha na throich, *one who is a dwarf.*—*Stew. Lev.*

Troicheil, *a.* (troich-amhuil.) Dwarfish; hump-backed.

Troid, *v. n.* Scold; rebuke; wrangle. *Pret. a.* throid, *scolded; fut. aff. a.* troididh, *shall scold.* Throid i ris, *she scolded him.*

Troidh, *s. f.* A foot, the sole of the foot; a foot in length; *rarely*, sorrow. *N. pl.* troidhean; *d. pl.* troidhibh. Tomhais e le troidhibh rùisgte, *measure it barefooted.*—*Oss. Derm.* Oscionn a throidhean, *above his feet.*—*Stew. Lev.*

Troidheach, ich, *s. m.* (*Ir.* troightheach.) A footman; a pedestrian; a foot-soldier.

Troigh. See **Troidh**.

Troigh, *a.* (*Ir. id.*) Short-lived.

Troightear. See **Traoidhtear**.

Troightearachd. See **Traoidhtearachd**.

Troimchill, *s. f.* (*Ir. id.*) A sanctuary.

Troime. (*Ir. id.*) See **Truime**.

Troimeachd, *s. f.* (*Ir. id.*) Heaviness.

Troimh, *prep.* (*W.* trw *and* trwy.) Through, from side to side. Troimh mo chleith, *through my casement.*—*Stew. Pro.*

Troimhe, *comp. pron.* Through him, through it.

Troimh-lot, *v. a.* Pierce, give a mortal wound. *Pret. a.* throimh-lot; *fut. aff. a.* troimh-lotaidh, *shall pierce; fut. pass.* troimh-lotar.

Troimpe, *comp. pron.* Through her.

Troinnsear, eir, *s. m.* (*Scotch*, trunscheour.)

Troisg, *v. n.* (*Ir. id.*) Fast; observe a fast, observe a rigid abstinence from food; be hungry. *Pret. a.* throisg, *fasted; fut. aff. a.* troisgidh. 'N uair a throisg e, *when he had fasted.*—*Stew. Mat.*

Troisgeach, *a.* (*Ir. id.*) Fasting; rigidly abstinent, given to fasting; severe, rigid.—*Macfar. Voc.*

Troisgeachd, *s. f.* Fasting, the practice of fasting.

Troisgeadh, idh, *s. m.* A fasting; a fast.

Troiste, *s. f.* (*Ir. id.*) A three-footed stool.

Troite. See **Traoidhte**.

Troitear. See **Traoidhtear**.

Troitearachd. See **Traoidhtearachd**.

Troll, *s.* (*Ir. id.*) Corruption.

† **Trom**, *s. m.* (*Ir. id.*) Blame, rebuke.

Trom, *a.* (*W.* trwm. *Ir.* trom.) Heavy, weighty, ponderous; deep or profound, as sleep; oppressive; sad, dejected, melancholy. Eallach throm, *a heavy burden.* Dh' fhagadh mise gu truagh trom, *I was left wretched and sad.*—*Ull.* Is trom a shuain, *profound is his sleep.*—*Oss. Derm.* An sealladh trom, *the sad spectacle.* Am fonn a briseadh gu trom, *the strain breaking mournfully.*—*Oss. Tem.* Diogbhailt throm, *severe vengeance.*—*Mac Lach. Com.* and *sup.* troime *and* truime.

Tromachadh, aidh, *s. m.* A making heavy, a loading; an oppressing; a making sad or dejected.

Tromachadh, (a), *pr. part.* of tromaich.

Tromaich, *v. a.* (*from* trom.) Make heavy; aggravate; oppress; deject, make melancholy. *Pret. a.* thromaich; *fut. aff.* tromaichidh; *fut. pass.* tromaichear.

Tromaichte, *p. part.* of tromaich. Made heavy; oppressed.

Troman, ain, *s. m.* (*Ir. id.*) The wood of the bore-tree. See **Droman**.

Troman, ain, *s. m.* (*Ir. id.*) A weight, a great weight.

Tromara, **Tromarach**, aich, *s. m.* (*Ir. id.*) A client.

Trom-bhanòglach, aich, *s. f.* (*Ir. id.*) A female client.

Trombhod, oid, *s. m.* (*Ir. id.*) The herb vervain.—*Macd.*

Trom-bhuail, *v. a.* Strike heavily, strike hard. *Pret.* throm-bhuail; *fut. aff. a.* trom-bhuailidh; *fut. pass.* trom-bhuailtear. Trom-bhuailtear leis, *shall be struck by him.*—*Sm.*

Trom-bhuidheann, -bhuidhne, *s. f.* (*Ir. id.*) A tribe of vassals, a clan.

Trom-chasair, *s. m.* (*Ir. id.*) A heavy shower.

Trom-chodal, ail, *s. m.* Heavy or deep sleep.

Trom-chodal, ail, *s. m.* A deep sleep; lethargy.

Trom-chodalach, *a.* Sleeping heavily; causing deep sleep; lethargic.

Trom-chodalaiche, *s. m.* A lethargic person.

Trom-chuis, *s. f.* An important case.

Trom-chuiseach, *a.* (*Ir. id.*) Important, of great concern.

Tromhad, *comp. pron.* Through thee. *Emphatic form*, tromhadsa, *through thee; Ir.* treodsa.

Tromhaibh, *comp. pron.* Through you.

Tromhainn, *comp. pron.* Through us.

Tromham, *comp. pron.* Through me.

Trom-inntinn, *s. f.* A heavy or dejected mind; heaviness of mind.—*Macfar. Voc.*

Trom-inntinneach, *a.* Dejected, melancholy. Gu trom-inntinneach, *dejectedly.*

Trom-lighe, *s. f.* (*i. e.* trom-luidhe.) The nightmare; a weight on the heart or spirits; distracting grief. Gach maraiche air seachran le trom-lighe, *each mariner forgetting [leaving] his course with grief.*—*Oss. Duthona.*

Trom-luidh, *v. n.* (*Ir. id.*) Overlay.

Trom-luidhe, *s. m.* Overlaying; the nightmare.

Trom-mhathair, -mhathar, *s. f.* (*Ir. id.*) A matron.

Trom-oglach, aich, *s. m.* (*Ir. id.*) A client.

Tromp, troimp, *and* truimp, *s. f.* (*Ir.* trump *and* tromp.) A trumpet; a trump, a jew's-harp.

Trompa, *comp. pron.* Through them. *Emphatic form*, trompasan.

Trompaid, *s. f.* A trumpet. *N. pl.* trompaidean.

Trompair, *s. m.* (tromp-fhear.) *Ir.* trompadoir. A trumpeter; a player on the jew's-harp. *N. pl.* trompairean.

Trompaireachd, *s. f.* Trumpeting; the business of a trumpeter; playing on the jew's-harp.

Trom-shuain, *s. f.* Profound sleep, lethargy.

Trom-tric, *a.* Pell-mell.

Trom-thuradh, *s. m.* (*Ir. id.*) A great draught.

Troraid, *s. f.* A spire; a steeple.—*Macd.*

Trosdail, *a.* (*Ir.* trosd-amhuil.) Serious, sedate; demure; dull.

Trosdalachd, *s. f.* Seriousness; demureness.

Trosdan, ain, *s. m.* (*Ir. id.*) A pace; a foot—(*Macfar. Voc.*); a support or prop, a crutch.

Troso, troisg, *s. m.* (*Ir.* trosga.) A codfish—(*Macd.*); a religious fasting—(*Macfar. Voc.*); a booby.

Trosg, troisg, *s. m.* A fast, a religious fast; fasting.

St. Paul, in his Epistle to the Colossians, ch. ii. v. 23, writes *εθελοθρησκια*, a voluntary fast, a superstitious fast. A Gael of Scotland would call it *toil-throsg*, or *toil-thrusg*. The correspondence is too striking to require comment.

Trosgach, *a.* Like a codfish; abounding in codfish; of, or belonging to, a codfish; like a booby; fasting.

TROSGADH, aidh, *s. m.* A fasting, a religious fast. Gairmibh trosgadh, *proclaim a fast.—Stew.* 1 *K.*

TROSGAIR, *s. m.* (trosg-fhear.) Cod-fishing; fasting, frequent or continued fasting.

TROSGAN, *s.* (*Ir. id.*) Goods, chattels.

TROSLOG, oig, *s. f.* (*Ir. id.*) A hop, a limp.

TROSNAN. See TROSTAN.

TROSTAN, ain, *s. m.* A pace; a foot; a support or prop; a pillar; a stilt, a crutch. *N. pl.* trostain. Cuig trostain, *five pillars.—Stew. Ex. ref.*

TROST, *s. m.* (*Ir. id.*) A sturdy little fellow; a dwarf.

TROSTACH, *a.* (*Ir. id.*) Sturdy; dwarfish.

TROT, *v. a.* and *n.* Trot. *Pret.* throt, *trotted; fut. aff. a.* trotaidh, *shall trot.*

TROT, trota, *s. m.* A trot. Cuir an t-each na throt, *put the horse a trotting.*

TROTAIL, *s. f.* A trotting; a jogging motion.

TROTAIR, *s. m.* One who trots.

TROTAIREACHD, *s. f.* Continued trotting.

TROTH, *s. m.* A taint.

TROTHACH, *a.* Tainted.

† TRU, *s.* (*Ir. id.*) A face; a fall.

TRUACANTA, *a.* (*Ir. id.*) Pitiful, compassionate, tender-hearted.

TRUACANTACHD, *s. f.* Pitifulness, compassionateness, tender-heartedness.

TRUACANTAS, ais, *s. m.* Compassion, pity.

TRUADH; more frequently *truagh;* which see.

TRUADHAN, ain. See TRUAGHAN.

TRUAGAILEACH, *a.* Compassionate.

TRUAGH, *a.* (*Ir. id. W.* truan, *render piteous.*) Poor; wretched; lean; sad, sorrowful, mournful. Duine truagh, *a poor man;* mo sgeul thruagh, *my sad tale.— Ull.* Comhara truagh a bhàis, *the mournful* [*marks*] *appearances of death.—Oss. Tem.* Gu truagh trom, *wretched and sad;* is truagh leam thu, *I pity you;* is truagh mar thachair, *sad is the occurrence.—Macint. Com.* and *sup.* truaighe.

TRUAGHAILEACH, *a.* Compassionate, tender-hearted.

TRUAGHAILEACHD, *s. f.* Compassionateness, tender-heartedness.

TRUAGHAN, ain, *s. m.* (*from* truagh.) *Ir. id. W.* tryan. A wretched or distressed person; an object of pity; a child of misfortune. Na saruich an truaghan, *oppress not the distressed.—Stew. Pro.* Cuis an truaghain, *the cause of the wretched.—Id.*

TRUAGHANACHD, *s. f.* Wretchedness, unfortunateness, pitiableness.

TRUAGHANTA, *a.* (*from* truaghan.) *Ir. id.* Wretched, pitiable, lamentable.

TRUAGHANTACHD, *s. f.* Wretchedness, unfortunateness, pitiableness.

TRUAGHAS. See TRUAS.

TRUAGH-MHEILEACH, *a.* Compassionate.

TRUAIGHE, *s. f.* (*Ir. id.*) Wretchedness, misery; calamity; pity. Tuireadh a thruaighe, *the sad tale of his calamity.—Oss. Fin. and Lor.* Mo thruaighe! *woe's me!* Mo thruaighe thu! *woe unto thee!—Stew. Ecc.* Mo thruaighe sunn! *woe unto us!—Stew. Sam.* Mo thruaighe iad! *woe unto them!—Stew. Hos.*

TRUAIGHE, *com.* and *sup.* of truagh.

TRUAIGHMHEIL, *s. f.* Compassion, compassionateness.

TRUAIGHMHEILEACH, *a.* Compassionate.

TRUAILL, *v. a.* (*Ir.* truaill.) Pollute; violate chastity; defile; adulterate; sheath. *Pret. a.* thruaill, *polluted; fut. aff.* truaillidh, *shall pollute.* Cha truaill sibh sibh fein, *you shall not defile yourselves.—Stew. Lev.* Truaill do chlaidheamh, *sheath thy sword.*

TRUAILL, truaille, *s. f.* (*Ir.* truail.) A sheath, a scabbard; *rarely,* a carcass. Tha 'n lann san truaille, *the sword is in the scabbard.*

TRUAILLEACH, ich, *s. m.* (*Ir. id.*) A sheath.

TRUAILLEACH, *a.* Polluting, defiling, violating.

TRUAILLEADH, idh, *s. m.* A polluting, a violating or deflowering, a defiling; pollution, deflowerment, defilement; adulteration; corruption; profanity. Sruth glan gun truailleadh, *a stream pure and unadulterated.—Ross.*

TRUAILLEACHADH, aidh, *s. m.* (*Ir.* truailleaghadh.) A polluting, defiling, or adulterating; pollution, defilement; adulteration.

TRUAILLEACHD, *s. f.* See TRUAILLIDHEACHD.

TRUAILLEAN, ein, *s. m.* A niggard.

TRUAILLEANACH, aich, *s. m.* (*Ir. id.*) A miser.

TRUAILLICH, *v. a.* (*Ir.* truailligh.) Pollute, unhallow; deflower; adulterate; profane. *Pret. a.* thruaillich, *polluted; fut. aff.* truaillichidh, *shall pollute.*

TRUAILLIDH, *fut. aff. a.* of truaill.

TRUAILLIDH, *a.* Polluted, defiled, contaminated; corrupt; corruptible; miserable; wretched; dismal. Bha 'n talamh truaillidh, *the earth was corrupt.—Stew. Gen.* Duine truaillidh, *a corrupt man.—Stew. Rom.*

TRUAILLIDHEACHD, *s. f.* (*Ir.* truaillidheacht.) Pollution, corruption; wretchedness, miserableness; pollutedness. Ri truaillidheachd thubhairt mi, *I said to corruption.—Stew. Job.*

TRUAILLTE, *p. part.* of truaill. Polluted, defiled; adulterated; deflowered. Aran truaillte, *polluted bread.—Stew. Mal.*

TRÙAN, ain, *s. m.* A trowel.—*Macd.*

TRUAS, truàis, *s. m.* (*Arm.* truez.) Compassion, pity; wretchedness; leanness; poverty. Truas do 'n duine bhochd, *pity for the poor man.—Stew. Pro.* Gabh truas, *take pity.*

TRUDAIREACHD, *s. f.* Filthiness, nastiness; obscenity.

TRUDANACH, aich, *s. m.* A wrangler.

TRUDAR, air, *s. m.* A filthy person, an obscene person; a stammerer.

TRUID, *s. m.* A starling. An truid 's am brùdhearg, *the starling and redbreast.—Macint.*

TRUID, *s. f.* A field of battle; strife, battle. Cearr am measg truid, *awkward in the midst of strife.—Old Song.*

TRUIDEAG, eig, *s. f.* A starling.

TRUIDREACH, ich, *s. m.* Melody, warbling; chirping, chattering, twittering.

TRUIME, *s. f.* (*Ir. id.*) Heaviness, weight, dejection.

TRUIME, *com.* and *sup.* of trom.

TRUIMEACHD, *s. f.* Heaviness, weight, sadness.

TRUIMEAD, eid, *s. m.* Heaviness; increase in weight; faintness, dejectedness. A dol an truimead, *growing more and more heavy.*

TRUIMID, *comparative form* of truime. Heavier. Is truimid e sin, *that has rendered it heavier.*

TRUINNSE, *s. f.* (*Ir. id.*) A trench.

TRUINNSEAR, eir, *s. m.* (*Ir. id.*) A trencher or plate; a salver.

TRUINNSICH, *v. a.* (*Ir.* truinsigh.) Trench; inclose. *Pret. a.* thruinnsich, *trenched; fut. aff. a.* truinnsichidh; *p. part.* truinnsichte.

TRUIS-BHRAGAD, aid, *s. m.* A necklace.

TRUISEALACH, *a.* Lascivious, carnal. More correctly *drùisealach.*

Truisealachd, *s. f.* Lasciviousness, lust. Ann an truisealachd, *in lasciviousness.—Stew.* 1 *Pet. ref.*

Trumadas, ais, *s. m.* Heaviness, faintness, dejectedness.

Trup, *s. f.* A troop.

Trupair, *s. m.* (*Ir.* tropeir.) A trooper.

Trus, *s.* A girdle; a girt; a bundle.

Trus, *v. a.* Gather, collect; bundle; truss; reprimand; go to; repair to. *Pret. a.* thrus; *fut. aff.* trusaidh. Thrus do chinneadh ri chéile, *thy kind gathered together.—Old Song.* A thrusadh lus mu bhun nan stùc, *to gather herbs at the foot of the rocks.—Old Song.* Trus ort, *be off, be gone*; a trusadh do 'n tigh osda, *repairing to the alehouse. —Old Song.*

Trusach, *a.* Gathering, collecting, bundling, trussing.

Trusach, aich, *s. m.* (*Ir. id.*) A sheaf.

Trusadh, aidh, *s. m.* (*W.* trwsa, *a packet.*) A gathering, a collecting, a bundling; a collection, a bundle.

Trusaite, *s. m.* A wardrobe; a lumber-room.

Trusalachadh, aidh, *s. m.* A girding up; a preparing, a making ready.

Trusaladh, aidh, *s. m.* A girding up, a preparing, a bestirring.

Trusalaich, *v. a.* Gird up; prepare, make ready, bestir. *Pret. a.* thrusalaich, *girded up*; *fut. aff. a.* trusalaichidh; *p. part.* trusalaichte.

Truscan. See Trusgan.

Trusdaireachd, *s. f.* Dirtiness of person, dirtiness of manners or of conversation; filthiness; filth, dirt, trash.

Trusdar, air, *s. m.* A dirty person, an indecent or obscene person, a clown; a drab; dirt, filth, trash.

Trusdarnach, aich, *s. m.* (*Ir. id.*) A stammerer.

Trusgan, ain, *s. m.* (*Ir. id.*) A garment, a shroud; a vesture, a mantle; a covering; clothes; *also*, a smelt; furniture, chattels; a man's privy parts. An trusgan do dhealan, *in a shroud of lightning.—Oss. Tem.* Trusgan air cruit an aonaich, *a mantle* [*grass*] *on the ridge of the moon.—Macint.*

Trusgar, air, *s. m.* (*Ir. id.*) Oar-weed.

Truslag, aig, *s. f.* A leap.

Trùth, trùtha, *s. f.* A shrew; a beastly being; a beast.

Truthdaireachd, *s. f.* Dirtiness, slovenliness, filthiness, obscenity.

Truthdar, air, *s. m.* A dirty person, an indecent or obscene person; a sloven; a slattern.

Tu, *pers. pron.* Thou. *Asp. form*, thu. Nan tigeadh tu, *if thou wert to come.*

Gr. Dor. and Æol. τυ. *Lat.* tu. *Pers.* tou *and* tu. *Shans.* twau. *Goth.* thu. *Swed.* tu *and* du. *Dan.* du. *Germ.* thu *and* du, u. *Isl.* thu. *Anglo-Sax.* tho. *Fr.* tu. *It.* tu. *Arm.* te, to, *and* hu. *W.* ti. *Ir.* tu.

Tuachail, *a.* Prudent; wise; cunning.

Tuadh, tuaidh, *s. f.* (*Ir. id.*) An axe or hatchet; *rarely*, renown. Mar thuaidh an glaic saoic, *like an axe in the grasp of a carpenter.—Mac Lach.* Written also *tuagh.*

Tuadh-catha, *s. f.* (*Ir. id.*) A battle-axe.

Tuadh-fhola, *s. f.* A fleam, an instrument for bleeding cattle.

Tuagh, tuaigh, *s. f.* An axe or hatchet. Iarunn na tuaigh, *the iron of the hatchet, the axe-head.—Stew.* 2 *K.*

† **Tuagha**, *s. pl.* (*Ir. id.*) Hooks, crooks; hinges.

Tuaicheal, eil, *s. m.* Dizziness; vertigo.

Tuaichealach, *a.* Causing dizziness or vertigo; vermicular.

Tuaichle, *s. f.* (*Ir. id.*) Augury; enchantment.

Tuaifear, ir, *s. m.* (*Ir. id.*) A boor.

Tuaileachd, *s. f.* (*Ir.* tuaileacht.) Twilight.

Tuaileas, eis, *s. m.* (*perhaps* tuath-chleas.) Calumny, defamation; disorder. Fear tuaileis, *a tale-bearer.—Stew. Pro.* Luchd tuaileis, *slanderers.—Stew. Tim.*

Tuaileasach, *a.* (*Ir. id.*) Calumnious, defamatory, reproachful; turbulent. Luchd tuaileasach, *calumnious persons, false accusers.—Stew. Tim.* Gu tuaileasach, *calumniously. Com.* and *sup.* tuaileasaiche.

Tuaileasachd, *s. f.* Calumniousness, tale-bearing; the practice of calumny.

Tuaileasag, aig, *s. f.* (*Ir. id.*) A scold; a foul-mouthed female; a disorderly, quarrelsome female.

Tuailte, *s. f.* A towel; a hand-towel.

Tuailteach, *a.* Like a towel; furnished with towels.

Tuailtear, eir, *s. m.* A weaver of towels. *N. pl.* tuailtearan.

Tuailtearachd, *s. f.* The business of towel-weaving, the occupation of a towel-weaver.

Tuaim, *gen. sing.* of tuam; which see.

Tuaim, *s. f.* See Tuam.

Tuaineal, eil, *s. m.* (*Ir. id.*) Dizziness, vertigo. Ghlac e 'n t-aosdharach na thuaineal, *in his dizziness he grasped the oak.—Oss. Dargo.*

Tuainealach, aich, *s. m.* Dizziness, vertigo.

Tuainealach, *a.* Causing dizziness.

Tuair, *gen. sing.* of tuar; which see.

† **Tuair**, *v. a.* (*Ir. id.*) Bode, portend, predict.

Tuair, *s. f.* A northern exposure. See Tuathair.

Tuaiream, eim, *s. m.* (*Ir.* tuairim.) A guess; opinion; aim, venture; vicinity; neighbourhood; nearness. Sloigh mu 'r tuaiream, *hosts around you.—Oss. Cathula.* Thaobh tuaireim, *at venture, at random.—Stew.* 1 *K. ref.* Thuit i mu 'thuaiream, *she fell beside him.—Oss. Cathluno.*

Tuaireap, eip, *s. f.* A squabble; a fray; a fight; confusion; tumult.

Tuaireapach, *a.* Squabbling; fighting; causing squabbles; tumultuous; disorderly. *Com.* and *sup.* tuaireapaiche.

Tuairgin, *s. f.* (*Ir. id.*) A hatchel; a washing-staff.

Tuairgne, *s. f.* Confusion, tumult, riot; a squabble, fray, or fight. Ughdar na tuairgne, *the author of confusion.—Stew.* 1 *Cor.*

Tuairgneach, *a.* Tumultuous; causing riot or uproar; disorderly. Gu tuairgneach, *tumultuously.*

Tuairisg, *s. f.* (*Ir. id.*) A symbol, a character.

Tuairmeachadh, aidh, *s. m.* A guessing; a venturing; arming.—*Macfar. Voc.*

Tuairisgeul, -sgéil, *or* -sgeóil, *s. m.* A bad report; defamation. Tuairisgeul bréige, *a false report.—Stew. Ex.* Tuairisgeul mhòran, *the defaming of many.—Stew. Jer.*

Tuairisgeulach, *a.* Defamatory, raising bad reports.

Tuairmich, *v. a.* Guess; conjecture; venture; aim. *Pret. a.* thuairmich; *fut. aff.* tuairmichidh.

Tuairmeis, *s. f.* A guess, a conjecture; a venture; an opinion. Thaobh tuairmeis, *at a venture.—Stew.* 1 *K.*

† **Tuairn**, *s. f.* (*Ir. id. Arm.* tuairn. *Gr.* τόρνος.) A turning-loom.

Tuairnean, ein, *s. m.* (*Ir. id.*) A mallet; a beetle.

Tuairnear, eir, *s. m.* A turner. *N. pl.* tuairnearan.

Tuairnearachd, *s. f.* The employment or occupation of turning; the trade of a turner.

Tuaisdeach, *a.* (*Ir. id.*) Slovenly, untidy, unseemly.—*Macfar. Voc.* Gu tuaisdeach, *in a slovenly manner.*

Tuaisdeachd, *s. f.* Slovenliness, unseemliness.

Tuaith, *inflection* of tuath; which see.

Tuaith, *s. f.* (*Ir. id.*) A territory; a lordship.

Tuaithcheall, *s.* (*Ir. id.*) Skill, sagacity.

Tual, *s.* (tuath-ùil.) A fatal or an unprosperous course; a moving from east to west by the north; unlucky; ominous; left, sinister, awkward; backward.

TUAL, *a.* Noted, remarkable either for good or evil; awkward.

TUALACHD, *s. f.* (*Ir. id.*) Possibility.

TUALAING, *a.* (*Ir. id.*) Able.

TUALAING. See FULAING.

TUALAING, *s. f.* (*Ir. id.*) Patience.

TUAL-BHEART, *s. pl.* Exploits; base deeds. Colguil nan tual-bheart, *Colgul of base deeds.—Old Poem.*

TUAL-CHAINNT, *s. f.* Ribaldry, jargon.

TUAM, tuaim, *s. f.* A tomb, a grave; a cave; a moat; a mound; *rarely*, a farm. Codal nan tuam, *the sleep of the grave.—Oss. Cathula.* Ula nan tuam, *the grass* [*beard*] *of the mounds. N. pl.* tuaim; *d. pl.* tuamaibh. As na tuamaibh, *from the tombs.—Stew. Mat.*

Tuam or *tom* seems to be the root of the Greek τυμβος, the Latin *tumulus*, and also of *cumulus*, which is but another form of *tumulus*. *Tuam* literally signifies a *ditch*, and consequently a *grave*. The graves of the good and the brave in ancient times, especially among the Gael, were formed of coped heaps of earth; and those of malefactors of coped heaps of stone.

TUAMACH, *a.* Abounding in graves or mounds; like a grave; of, or relating to, the grave.

TUAMAICH, *v. a.* (*from* tuam.) Entomb. *Pret. a.* thuamaich, *entombed; fut. aff. a.* tuamaichidh, *shall entomb.*

TUAMAICHTE, *p. part.* of tuamaich. Entombed.

TUAMANN, *a.* (*Ir. id.*) Fierce; morose.

TUA-PHOLL, -phuill, *s. m.* (*Ir. id.*) A whirlpool.—*Shaw.*

TUAR, tuair, *s. m.* (*Ir. id.*) Foreboding; omen; hardship; shade; colour; countenance; complexion; food; house; fear; life. Gné sam bi thuair, *every kind of hardship.—Macfar.* Faileus mu 'n tuar, *a shade upon their countenance.—Oss. Tem.* Mar thuar na soillse, *like the appearance of light.—Id.* Iongantas m' an tuar, *wonder at their fear.* Gun teach gun tuar, *without house or life.—Fingalian Poem.*

TUARAGAN, ain, *s. m.* (*Ir. id.*) A bleacher.

TUARAIL, *a.* (tuar-amhuil.) Hardy, stout, firm; having a northern exposure.

TUARAISGEUL. See TUAIRSGEUL.

TUARASDAL, ail, *s. m.* (*Ir.* tuarusdal.) Wages, hire, fee, salary. Ainmich do thuarasdal, *appoint thy wages.—Stew. Gen.*

TUARASDALAICH, TUARASDALUICH, *v. a.* Engage for hire; hire. Thuarasdaluich mi thu, *I hired you.—Stew. Gen. Pret.* thuarasdalaich; *fut. aff.* tuarasdalaichidh.

TUARASDALAICHE, *s. m.* A hireling; *also*, one who hires.

TUARG, *s. m.* (*Ir. id.*) A beetle; a maul.

TUARGAN, ain, *s. m.* Discontent, dissatisfaction, sedition; misunderstanding; a squabble; a beating.

TUARGANACH, *a.* Discontented, dissatisfied; squabbling.

TUARGANACHD, *s. f.* Discontentedness, dissatisfaction.

TUARGNACH CATHA, *s. m.* A field-marshal, a generalissimo.

TUARGNADH, aidh, *s. m.* Discontent, dissatisfaction, sedition; misunderstanding.

TUASAID, *s. f.* A squabble, fray, or quarrel; a wrangle; a fight; contention. Air thòir air tuasaid, *in the pursuit or in battle.—Old Song.* Tuasaid ghaoth agus chrag, *the battle of winds and rocks.—Fingalian Poem.*

TUASAIDEACH, *a.* Quarrelsome; causing squabbles or quarrels; brawling, wrangling, tumultuous. Gun bhi tuasaideach, *without being a wrangler.—Stew. Tim.*

TUASAIDEACH, *s. f.* Squabbling, quarrelsomeness, wrangling.

TUASGAIL, *v. a.* Loosen. Written also *fuasgail*; which see.

TUASGAILTE, *p. part.* of tuasgail.

† TUASGEART, *a.* (*Ir. id.*) North, northern.

TUASGLACH, *a.* Apt to untie or loosen; loosening.

TUASGLADH, aidh, *s. m.* A loosening; a looseness of the bowels.

TUASGLAGADH, aidh, *s. m.* (*Ir. id.*) A releasing; a loosening; a dissolving.—*Shaw.*

TUATH, *a.* (*Ir. id.*) North, northern. An taobh tuath, *the north side, the north country, the north.* Gu tuath, *to the north, northward.*

TUATH, *s. f.* (*Ir.* tuath.) Tenantry; the aggregate number of any land proprietors, farmers, or peasants; peasantry; laity; country-people.

TUATHACH, aich, *s. m.* (*Ir.* tuaitheach.) A north-countryman; a North-Highlander; *rarely*, a lord; a proprietor. *N. pl.* tuathaich.

TUATHACHD, *s. f.* (*Ir. id.*) A lordship; a proprietorship; a sovereignty.

TUATHAIR, tuathrach, *s. f.* (tuath-thìr.) A northern exposure; a country-side lying towards the north.

TUATHAL, *a.* (*contracted* tual.) *Ir. id.* Ominous; unlucky; sinister; left; backward; awkward; *also*, brave. O sheal-ladh an laoich thuathail, *from the sight of the brave hero. Oss. Tem.*

TUATHANACH, aich, *s. m.* (*from* tuath.) A farmer, a peasant; a layman.—*Macd. N. pl.* tuathnaich.

TUATHANACHAS, ais, *s. m.* Husbandry, agriculture.

TUATHANACHD, *s. f.* Husbandry, agriculture; the condition of a farmer or peasant. Tuathanachd Dhé, *the husbandry of God.—Stew. 2 Cor.* Bu toigh leis tuathanachd, *he loved agriculture.—Stew. 2 Chr.*

TUATH-CHEATHARNA, *s. f.* Yeomanry; peasantry; common people. Neach do 'n tuath-cheatharna, *one of the common people.—Stew. Lev.* Is lionmhor ur tuath-cheatharna, *numerous are our peasantry.—Old Song.*

TUATH-FHRAS, ais, *s. m.* A northern blast.

TUATH-GHAOTH, -ghaoithe, *s. f.* A north wind.

TUATH-GHAOTHACH, *a.* Aquilonial. Mios thuath-ghaothach, *an aquilonial month.—Macfar.*

TUATHLACH, *a.* Ominous; unlucky; awkward; left-handed.

TUATHLACHD, *s. f.* Ominousness; unluckiness; awkwardness; rusticity.

TUATHLAN, ain, *s. m.* (*from* tuath.) An awkward, ungainly person; a boor; a rustic; a plebeian. *Ir.* tuathallan.

TUATHRACH, *gen. sing.* of tuathair.

TUATHRACH, *a.* Having a northern exposure.

TUBAG, aig, *s. f.* A vat; a tub. *N. pl.* tubagan.

TUBAGACH, *a.* Like a vat or tub; of, or belonging to, a vat or tub.

TUBAG-SHILIDH, *s. f.* A dropping-tub.—*Macfar. Voc.*

TUBAIST, aiste, *s. f.* (*Ir. id.*) Mischance, accident; misfortune, calamity; mischief. Thig tubaist air, *mischief shall befall him.—Stew. Gen.* Thaobh tubaiste, *by accident.*

TUBAISTEACH, *a.* (*Ir. id.*) Accidental; unlucky; unpropitious; unfortunate; calamitous. *Com.* and *sup.* tubaistiche.

TUBAISTEACHD, *s. f.* Accidentalness; unluckiness; calamitousness.

TUBAIT, *s. f.* A tippet. Tubaitean, *tippets.*

TŬBH, tubha, *s.* (*Ir. id.*) Thatch; any stuff, as straw, heath, or fern, wherewith the roof of a house is covered; opposition. Tha do thigh mòr gun tubh, *the great house is without thatch;* tigh tubha, *a thatched house.*

TUBH, *v. a.* Thatch. *Pret. a.* thubh, *thatched; fut. aff.* tubhaidh, *shall thatch.*

TUBHACH, *a.* Thatched; like thatch.

Tubhadair, *s. m.* (*from* tubh.) *Arm* toer. A thatcher. *N. pl.* tubhadairean.

Tubhadaireachd, *s. f.* The employment of thatching; the business or occupation of a thatcher.

Tubhailt, *s. f.* A towel. Tubhailt bùird, *a table-cloth.*—*Macd.*

Tubhailtear, eir, *s. m.* A towel-weaver.

Tubhailtearachd, *s. f.* Towel-weaving.

Tubhta, Tubhte, *part.* Thatched. Tigh tubhta, *a thatched house.*

Tuca, ai, *s. m.* (*Ir. id.*) A tuck, a rapier.—*Shaw.*

Tùcadair, *s. m.* A fuller of cloth.—*Macd.* *N. pl.* tucadairean.

Tùcadaireachd, *s. f.* The fulling of cloth; the trade of a fuller.

Tùch, *v. a.* and *n.* Extinguish; smother, as a flame, by covering it; quench; grow hoarse. *Pret. a.* thùch; *fut. aff.* tùchaidh.

Tùchach, *a.* Causing hoarseness.

Tùchadh, aidh, *s. m.* An extinguishing, a smothering; hoarseness.

Tùchan, ain, *s. m.* Hoarseness; a fit of hoarseness occasioned by cold, or by exertion of the voice. Le tùchan is le cnatan, *with hoarseness and cold.*—*Old Song.*

Tùchanach, *a.* Causing hoarseness; hoarse; guttural. Le thorman tùchanach, *with his hoarse murmurs.*—*Macint.*

† **Tuchd**, *s.* (*Ir. id.*) A form; time; season.

Tùchta, Tùchte, *p. part.* of tùch. Made hoarse, affected with hoarseness; extinguished or smothered, as a flame.

Tudan, ain, *s. m.* A small heap of any thing; a tuft, as of wool; a turd.

Tufag, aig, *s. f.* A foist; a stench.

Tug, *pret. neg.* and *interrog.* of tabhair; which see.

Tugadh, *pret. aff. neg.* and *interrog. pass.* of tabhair. Was given.

Tugaid, *s. f.* (*Ir. id.*) Cause, reason.

Tugh, *v. a.* See Tubh.

Tugh, tugha, *s. m.* See Tubh.

Tughadair. See Tubhadair.

Tughadaireachd, *s. f.* See Tubhadaireachd.

Tugtadh, *pret. sub. pass.* of tabhair. Should be given, or be taken away.

Tuidhle, *a.* (*Ir. id.*) Pleasant.

† **Tuidhme**, *s. f.* (*Ir. id.*) A confederacy, a conjunction. —*Shaw.*

Tuig, *v. a.* (*Ir. id.*) Understand, perceive, discern. *Pret. a.* thuig, *understood*; *fut. aff.* tuigidh; *fut. pass.* tuigear, *shall be understood.* Thuig e do chridhe, *he understood thy heart.*—*Stew.* 2 *Sam.*

Tuigeam, (*for* tuigidh mi.) I shall understand.

Tuigear. See Tuig.

Tuigse, *s. f.* (*Ir. id.*) Understanding, judgment, knowledge, skill. Faigh tuigse, *get understanding.*—*Stew. Pro.*

Tuigseach, *a.* (*Ir. id.*) Intelligent, judicious, knowing, rational, prudent, skilful. Duine tuigseach, *an* [*intelligent*] *wise man.*—*Stew. Pro.* Tuigse nan daoine tuigseach, *the understanding of the prudent.*—*Stew.* 1 *Cor.* Gu tuigseach, *intelligently.* *Com.* and *sup.* tuigsiche.

Tuigsinn, *s. f.* The circumstance of understanding or perceiving.

Tuigsinn, (a), *pr. part.* of tuig. Understanding, perceiving.

Tuigsinneach, ich, *s. m.* A knowing person.

Tuil, tuile, *s. f.* (*Darien*, doulah.) A flood, a deluge; a heavy rain, a torrent; overflowing of running waters; a tide. Bhrùchd cuimhne mar thuil, *memory burst forth like a flood.*—*Oss. Dargo.* An tuil a bha 'm chridhe thràigh i, *the flood in my heart has ebbed away.*—*Oss. Derm.* An tuil ruadh, *Noah's flood.* *N. pl.* tuilte *and* tuilteachan.

Tuil-bheum, -bheuma, *s.* A torrent; a torrent caused by the bursting of a thunder-cloud; a thunder-shower. Tha iad mar thuil-bheum, *they are like a torrent.*—*Old Poem.*

Tuil-cheanach, aich, *s. m.* (*Ir. id.*) A handsel.

Tuil-dhorus, uis, *s. m.* A flood-gate; the lock of a canal. *N. pl.* tuil-dhorsa, tuil-dhorsan. Tuil-dhorsa nan neamh, *the* [*flood-gates*] *windows of heaven.*—*Stew. Gen.*

Tuileudach, aich, *s. m.* (*Ir. id.*) An apron.

Tuilich, *v. a.* (*from* tuil.) *Ir.* tuiligh. Inundate, flood, overflow. *Pret. a.* thuilich, *flooded*; *fut. aff.* tuilichidh.

Tùilinn, *s. f.* Twilled linen. Léin thùilinn, *a shirt of twilled linen.*

Tuiliop, *s.* (*Ir. id.*) A tulip.—*Macd.*

Tuill, *gen. sing.* and *n. pl.* of toll. Of a hole; holes, caves, pitfalls. Tuill an fhirich, *the mountain-caves.* — *Oss. Cathula.* See Toll.

Tuille, Tuilleadh, *adv.* More; any more; any longer; any further, in regard to time. Cha bhi mi am onrachd tuille, *I shall be lonely no more.*—*Old Poem.* Tuille cha léir dhuit Oscar, *Oscar thou shalt see no more.*—*Oss. Gaul.* Tuilleadh gu bràth, *any more for ever.*—*Stew. Ecc.*

Tuille, Tuilleadh, *com.* of mòran. (*Ir. id.*) More, a greater number, a greater quantity, more numerous. Tuille is ceud fo ùir, *more than a hundred under ground.* —*Oss. Tem.* Tuille is a chòir, *more than enough, too much, more than his due*; tuille is ni 's leòir, *more than is sufficient, too much*; tuille is ni bu leoir, *more than was enough.* —*Stew. Ex.* A thuille ris, *in addition to it, more thereto.* —*Stew. Lev.* A thuille air sin, *moreover, in addition to that*; tuilleadh fòs, *yet more*; ciod tuilleadh? *what more?* —*Stew. Heb.*

Tuillead, eid, *s. m.* A greater quantity, an additional quantity. Gheibh thu an tuillead, *you will get the more*; a thuillead air sin, *over and above that.*

Tuille eile, *conj.* Furthermore, moreover, nay more.

† **Tuiltin**, *s.* Merit; demerit. See Toiltinn.

Tuilm, *gen. sing.* and *n. pl.* of tolm; which see.

Tuilm, tuilme, *s. f.* An elm; an oak; *pudenda muliebria.*

Tuil-mhaoim, *s. f.* A sudden deluge, a torrent, a mountain-torrent, caused by the bursting of a thunder-cloud, or by the rapid melting of snow. Mar leaghas sneachd na thuil-mhaoim, *as snow melts in torrents.*—*Old Song.* Tuil-mhaoim sleibh, *a mountain-torrent.*—*Macdon.*

Tuil-ruadh, aidh, *s. f.* Noah's flood.

Tuilte, Tuilteachan, *n pl.* of tuil; which see. *Ir. id.*

Tuilteach, *a.* (*Ir. id.*) Flooding, inundating; causing a flood; deluging.

Tuilteach, ich, *s. m.* (*Ir. id.*) A flood. Air tuilteach gaoithe sgaoil i 'sgiathan, *on a flood of wind she spread her wings.*—*Oss. Dargo.*

Tuim, *gen. sing.* of tom; which see.

Tuimpe, *s. f.* (*Ir. id.*) A turnip.

Tùin, *v. n.* Dwell, reside. *Pret.* thùin, *dwelt.*

Tùin, *s. f.* A dwelling-place.

Tùineach, ich, *s. m.* A dwelling or abode; a lodger, a resident. An i cois na creig do thùineach? *is the foot of the rock thy dwelling?*—*Oss. Fin. and Lor.*

Tùineachadh, aidh, *s. m.* A dwelling or residing; residence.

Tùineachadh, (a), *pr. part.* of tùinich.

Tùineachas, ais, *s. m.* A dwelling-place, a home.

Tùineadh, idh, *s. m.* A residing or dwelling; a residence, a dwelling-place; a receptacle. Tuineadh nan treun, *the* *dwelling of heroes.—Mac Lach.* A tuineadh an truscan a chomhraig, *dwelling in the skirts of battle.—Oss. Lod.*

TÙINEAS, eis, *s. m.* An abode, a house, a receptacle. Tùineas nan sleagh, *the abode of spears.—Oss. Fing.*

TÙINEASACH, *a.* Of, or belonging to, an abode; residing, inhabiting.

† TUINGE, *s. f.* (*Ir. id.*) An oath.

TÙINICH, *v. n.* Dwell, reside, lodge, stay, sojourn, inhabit. *Pret.* thùinich, *dwelt; fut. aff.* tuinichidh, *shall dwell.*

TÙINICHE, *s. m.* A dweller, a lodger.

TUINIDHE, *s. f.* A den.

TUINNEAMH, eimh, *s. m.* (*Ir. id.*) Death.

TUINNEAS, eis. See TÙINEAS.

TUINNEASACH, *a.* Causing death.—*Macfar. Voc.*

TUINN, tuinne, *gen. sing.* of tonn.

TUIR, *v. a.* Relate, rehearse with a mournful cadence; accompany a rehearsal with a mournful air. *Pret. a.* thùir; *fut. aff.* tùiridh, *shall rehearse.* Tùir an aithris neo-aghmhor, *rehearse the hapless tale.—Oss. Cathluno.*

† TUIR, *s. m.* (*Ir. id.*) A lord; a pillar.

TÙIR, *gen. sing.* and *n. pl.* of tùr.

TUIRBHEACH, *a.* (*Ir. id.*) Bashful, modest.—*Shaw.*

TUIRC, *gen. sing.* and *n. pl.* of torc.

TUIRE'. See TUIREADH.

TUIREADH, idh, *s. m.* A lament, a wail; lamentation; a request; a melancholy narrative; mourning; a dirge; a death-song; an elegy. Ciod fà do thuiridh? *what is the reason of thy lament?—Ull.* Le tuire' glaoidh thog e 'cheann, *with a wailing voice he raised his head.—Oss. Gaul.* Dh' èisd sinn ri tuireadh a thruaighe, *we listened to the sad narrative of his woe. N. pl.* tuireannan; *d. pl.* tuireannaibh. Nan tuireannaibh, *in their lamentations.—Stew. 2 Chr.*

TUIREAN, ein, *s. m.* (*Ir. id.*) A troop; a multitude.—*Shaw.*

TUIREANN, inn, *s. m.* (*Ir. id.*) A spark from the anvil; lightning; wheat; a troop; a crowd.

TUIREANNAN. See TÙIREADH.

TUIREASG, TUIRIOSG, *s. m.* An axe; a saw. An ardaich an tuireasg e fein? *shall the axe exalt itself?—Stew. Is.*

TUIREASGACH, *a.* Like an axe or saw; performing the part of an axe or saw.

TUIREASGAICHE, *s. m.* One who works with an axe or saw.

TUIRGINN, *s. f.* A flood; a beetle; a wash-staff.

TUIRIDH, *s. f.* (*Ir. id.*) A request; an elegy; a pillar.

TUIRIGHIN, *s. f.* (*Ir. id.*) A pillar; a supporter; a conquest.

TUIRIOSG, *s. m.* See TUIREASG.

TUIRL, *v. n.* Descend, come down, dismount. *Pret.* thuirl; *fut. aff.* tuirlidh, *shall descend.* Tuirleadh e, *let him descend.* Tuirlibh a thaibhse, tuirlibh air ghlas-sgiathaibh ur ceo, *descend, ye ghosts, descend on the grey wings of your mist.—Ull.*

TUIRLEADH. See TUIRL.

TUIRLEUM, *v. n.* Leap down; leap; fall upon. *Pret. a.* thuirleum; *fut. aff.* tuirleumaidh.

TUIRLEUM, *s. m.* A leap, a jump; a great leap; an onset; a contest. B'e sud an tuirleum teann, *that was a severe contest.—Old Poem.*

TUIRLIBH, *inflection of* tuirl; which see.

TUIRLING, *v. n.* (*Ir. id.*) Descend, come down, dismount. *Pret. a.* thuirling; *fut. aff.*

TUIRLING, *s. f.* A descent, a coming down; a slope, a declivity.

TUIRLINN. See TUIRLING.

TUIRMHEACH, *a.* See TUIRBHEACH.

TUIRMHEACHD, *s. f.* (*Ir. id.*) Modesty.

TUIRSE, *s. f.* (*Ir. id.*) Sorrow, sadness; melancholy, dejection; a dirge, an elegy. Is mòr fà mo thuirse, *great is the cause of my sorrow.—Oss. Fin. and Lor.* Bu trom a tuirse is bu chian, *heavy and long was her sorrow.—Ull.* Tuirse nam bard, *the dirge of the bards.—Oss. Tem.*

TUIRSEACH, *a.* (*Ir. id. Arm.* truhëus.) Sorrowful, mournful, sad, melancholy; causing sorrow or sadness. Cha 'n ioghna mise a bhi tuirseach, *no wonder that I be sorrowful.—Oss. Fin. and Lor.* Bu tuirseach tearc a làithe, *sad and few were his days.—Orr.* Gu tuirseach, *sorrowfully. Com.* and *sup.* tuirsiche. Bu tuirsiche gu mòr Ronan, *far more sad was Ronan.—Orr.*

TUIRSICH, *v.* (*Ir.* tuirsigh.) Make sorrowful or sad.

TUIRSICHE, *com.* and *sup.* of tuirseach.

TUIRSNEACH, *a.* Troubled, heavy in mind.

TUIRSNEADH, idh, *s. m.* Trouble, heaviness of mind.—*Macint.*

TÙIS, *s. f.* (*Ir. id. Lat.* thus.) Incense; frankincense; *rarely,* a jewel; a king; a noble. Altair na tùis, *the altar of incense.—Stew. Ex.* Tulach na tùis, *the hill of frankincense.—Stew. Song Sol.*

TÙIS, *gen. sing.* of tùs.

TUISDEACH, ich, *s. m.* (*Ir. id.*) A parent.

TÙISEACH, ich, *s. m.* (*Ir. id.*) A leader, a commander.

TÙISEAR, eir, *s. m.* A censer. Gabhaidh a tùisear, *he will take a censer.—Stew. Lev.* Tùisear òir, *a golden censer.—Stew. Rev.*

TUISG, *gen. sing.* and *n. pl.* of tosg.

TUISILL, *v. n.* Fall; slip; stumble; deliver; bring forth. *Pret.* thuisill; *fut. aff.* tuislidh.

TUISLE, *s. f.* A fall; a slip; a stumble; a trespass; a delivery; a bringing forth.—*Macfar. Voc.*

TUISLEACH, *a.* Apt to fall, slip, or stumble; infirm, fallible; slippery.

TUISLEACHADH, aidh, *s. m.* A stumbling, a falling.

TUISLEACHADH, (a), *pr. part.* of tuislich.

TUISLEADH, idh, *s. m.* (*Ir. id.*) A stumbling, a slipping, a falling; a stumble, slip, or fall; decay; offence; a delivery. Treibhdhireach agus gun tuisleadh, *sincere and without offence.—Stew. Phil.*

TUISLEAG, eig, *s. f.* A fall, a slight fall, a slip; a jump, a leap.

TUISLEAGACH, *a.* Desultory; leaping; skipping; slipping; stumbling.

TUISLICH, *v. n.* (*Ir.* tuisligh.) Stumble, slip, fall; commit an error; deliver, bring forth. *Pret.* thuislich; *fut. aff.* tuislichidh. Tuislichidh mo luchd-tòir, *my persecutors shall stumble.—Stew. Jer. Pret. sub.* thuislicheas. Ma thuisleachas tu, *if thou fallest.*

TUISLICHTE, *p. part.* of tuislich. (*Ir.* tuislighte.) Overturned, overset; fallen; delivered.

TUISMEACH, *a.* Stumbling, slipping, sliding, falling.

TUISMEACHAN, ain, *s. m.* An accoucheur.

TUISMEACHD, *s. f.* A stumble; frequent stumbling or falling.

TUISMICH, *v. n.* Stumble, slip, slide, fall; deliver, bring forth. *Pret. a.* thuismich, *stumbled; fut. aff.* tuismichidh.

† TUIT, *s.* (*Ir. id.*) The flat of any thing.

TUIT, *v. n.* (*Ir. id.*) Fall, stumble; sink; subside; set, as the sun; befall, happen. *Pret. a.* thuit, *fell; fut. aff.* tuitidh, *shall fall.* Fad o' dhachaidh thuit do ghradh, *far from home thy beloved has fallen.—Ull.* Thuit an oidhche, *the night fell.—Oss. Fin. and Lor.* Tuitidh a ghaoth, ach mairidh ar cliù, *the wind shall subside, but our fame shall last.—Oss. Duthona.* Thuit mo ghrian gu sìor, *my sun has set for ever.—Ull.* On a thuit dhuinn, *since it has befallen us.—Old Song.* Cha tuit e, *he shall not fall;* nach tuit e? *shall he not fall?* A tuiteam air 'uchd, *falling on his breast.—Oss. Derm.*

TUITEADH, *imp. sub.* of tuit. Should fall. Also, 3 *sing.* and *pl. imper.* tuiteadh e, *let him fall.*

TUITEAM, eim, *s. m.* A fall, a stumble; an overturn. Tri 'n tuiteam-san, *through their fall.—Stew. Rom.* Tuiteam oidhche, *nightfall.*

TUITEAM, 1 *sing. imper.* of tuit. Let me fall. *Also for* tuitidh mi, *I will fall.*

TUITEAM, (a), *pr. part.* of tuit; which see.

TUITEAMACH, *a.* (*from* tuiteam.) *Ir.* tuisteamach. Fallible; apt to fall or stumble; causing to fall or stumble; frail; ruinous; accidental; contingent. An tinneas tuiteamach, *epilepsy.*

TUITEAMACH, aich, *s. f.* Epilepsy.

TUITEAMACHD, *s. f.* Fallibility; liableness to fall; contingence.

TUITEAMAS, ais, *s. m.* Chance, accident; occurrence; contingency; lot; falling sickness, epilepsy. Am agus tuiteamas, *time and chance.—Stew. Ecc.* Tinn leis an tuiteamais, *ill with epilepsy; lunatic.—Stew. Mat.* Gach droch thuiteamas, *every evil occurrence.—Stew.* 1 *K.* An dàil gach tuiteamais, *to face every lot or accident.—Smith's Address to a Highland Regiment.*

TUITEAM-OIDHCHE, *s. m.* Nightfall.

TUITEAN, ein, *s. m.* A badger.—*Macd.*

TUITEAR, *fut. pass.* of tuit. Shall be made to fall; *also used impersonally.*

TUITHTEAR, eir, *s. m.* A tutor, a preceptor.

TUITHTEARACHD, *s. f.* Tutorage, tuition, the employment of a preceptor.

TUITIDH. See TUIT.

† TUL, tuil, *s. m.* (*Ir. id.*) A beginning; a face; a fashion; a relique; a flood.

TUL, *s. m.* (*Ir. id. Heb.* tel.) A hillock.

TULACH, *s. m.* (*from* tul.) A little hill, a knoll, a mound, a green eminence; the top of a gentle rising ground. Sliabh nan tulach, *the hill of green knolls.—Oss. Derm.* An tulach laoghach an robh Taura, *the pretty eminence on which Taura stood.—Oss. Taura.* Chàirich sinn san tulaich an laoch, *we interred the hero in the hill.* Tulaich ard, *the war-cry of the Mackenzies.*

TULACHACH, *a.* Knolly.

TULACHAN, ain, *s. m.* (*dim.* of tulach.) *Ir.* tulchan. A little green eminence, a little knoll or conical hill, a mound; a tomb. Tha iad uile nan tulachain, *they are all in their* [*green mounds*] *graves.—Oss. Gaul.*

TULACHANN. See TULCHANN.

TULAG, aig, *s. f.* (*Ir.* tullog.) The fish called pollock.—*Macfar. Voc.*

† TULAGADH, aidh, *s. m.* A change of labourers.

TULAGACH, *a.* Abounding in pollocks; of, or belonging to, a pollock.

TULAGAN, ain, *s. m.* (*Ir. id.*) A rocking.

TULAICH, *gen. sing.* and *n. pl.* of tulach.

TULAICHEAN, *n. pl.* of tulach; *also,* the name of a certain Highland dance.

TUL-AIGNE, *s. f.* Intention, purpose, motive.

TULAN, ain, *s. m.* (*Ir. id.*) A kettle.

TUL-BHREAC, *a.* Spotted, speckled, freckled.

TUL-BHROICNEACH, *a.* (*Ir.* tul-bhreicneach.) Freckled.

TULC. See TULG.

TULCACH, *a.* See TULACHACH.

TULCHAINN, *gen. sing.* of tulchann.

TULCHAINNEACH, *a.* Having high gable walls; gabled.

TULCHANN, ainn, *s. m.* The gable wall of a house; the end wall of a house; the stern of a ship; the hinder part of a person.

TULCHLAON, *v. a.* (*Ir. id.*) Slant, slope, form in a zig-zag line.

TULCHLAON, *a.* Slanting, sloping, in a zig-zag.

TUL-CHLAONACH, *a.* (*Ir. id.*) Tending to a slope; sloping gently; in a zig-zag line.

TUL-CHLAONACHD, *s. f.* (*Ir. id.*) A slanting; a gradual descent; a declivity; zig-zagging.

TULCHOIR, *a.* (*Ir. id.*) Obstinate.

TUL-CHOMHRAIC, *s. f.* (*Ir. id.*) An assembly.—*Shaw.*

TULCHROM, *a.* Slant, sloping.

TUL-CHROMADH, aidh, *s. m.* A slanting, a sloping; a slant or slope.

TULCHUIS, *s. f.* Perseverance; confidence, boldness.—*Macfar. Voc.*

TULCHUISEACH, *a.* Persevering; plodding; bold; confident. O'n eascar thulchuiseach, *from the persevering foe.—Sm.*

TULG, tulga, *s. m.* (*Ir.* tolg.) A bruise or hollow on the surface of any laminated metal surface; the hollow between billows; the sinking of any undulating surface; a jolting. Tulg tuinn, *the rocking of waves.*

TULG, *v. a.* and *n.* Make a hollow, as on the surface of a plate of metal; rock; move; jolt. *Pret.* thulg; *fut. aff.* tulgaidh, *shall rock.*

TULGA. See TULGADH.

TULGACH, *a.* Having bruises, as the surface of a plate of metal; causing bruises, as on a metal surface; variable, inconstant, as the surface of agitated water; causing a jolting or rocking motion.

TULGADH, aidh, *s. m.* A bruising, as of a metal surface; a rocking motion, as caused by agitated water; undulation; a jolting; a moving; a rocking. Le tulgadh tuinne air mo luasgadh, *rocked by the motion of billows.—Ull.* Gun tulgadh, *firm, motionless, unshaken, unmoved.*

TULGAN, ain, *s. m.* A rocking motion, as caused by agitated water; a little bruise, as on a metal surface.

TULGANACH, *a.* Hilly, knolly.

TULM. See TOLM.

TULMAN, ain, *s. m.* A little hill, a knoll. *N. pl.* tulmain *and* tulmanan. Timchioll thulmanan dhiomhair, *around lonely knolls.—Macdon.* Written also *tolman.*

TULMANACH, *a.* Knolly. Written also *tolmanach.*

TUL-RADHARC, airc, *s. m.* (*Ir. id.*) Foresight, providence.

TUL-RADHARCACH, *a.* Foresighted.

TUM, *v. a.* (*Ir. id.*) Dip, immerse, duck; steep; bathe. *Pret. a.* thum; *fut. aff.* tumaidh. Thum iad an còta san fhuil, *they dipped the coat in the blood.—Stew. Gen.* A chos ag a tumadh sa chaochan, *his foot dipping in the brook.—Oss. Cathula.*

TUMA, ai, *s. m.* (*Ir. id.*) A tomb.

TUMA. See TUMADH.

TUMADH, aidh, *s. m.* A dipping, an immersing, a ducking; a dip, an immersion.

TUMADH, (a), *pr. part.* of tum. Dipping, immersing; bathing.

TUMAIR, *s. m.* (*Ir.* tumthair.) A bather, a dipper, one who immerses; a diver. *N. pl.* tumairean.

TUMAITE, *s. m.* A bath, a bathing-place.

TUMTA, TUMTE, *p. part.* of tum. (*Ir.* tumtha.) Dipped, immersed, bathed, steeped.

TÙNAICH, *v. n.* Dwell, inhabit, reside, lodge, sojourn. *Pret. a.* thùnaich; *fut. aff.* tùnaichidh, *shall dwell.*

TÙNAICHE, s. m. A lodger, a resident, an inhabitant.

TÙNAIDH, s. m. A house, abode, or dwelling place; a retreat or receptacle. Tùnaidh 'n còs nan sliabh, *a retreat in the mountain-caves.—Oss. Fing.*

TÙNAIDH, v. a. Inhabit, dwell. *Pret.* thùnaidh; *fut. aff* tunaidh. Thusa tha 'tùnaidh air sliabh, *thou who dwellest on the hill.—Oss. Fing*

TUNN, v. a. Tun or barrel.

TUNNA, s.m. (*Swed id. Ir* tonna.) A tun. *N.pl.* tunnachan

TUNNADAIR, s. m. A tunning-dish; a funnel; a tunner —*Macd. N. pl.* tunnadairean.

TUNNADAIREACHD, s f. Tunning or barrelling.

TUNNAG, aig, s f A mantle. See TONNAG.

TUNNAG, aig, s. f. A duck. Tunnag fhiadhaich, *a wild duck N. pl.* tunnagan.

TUNNAG-FHIADHAICH, s f. A wild duck.

TUR, a. Complete, whole, entire, total; *rarely*, dry. Chuir e tur stad air m'aiteas, *he has put a complete stop to my joy.—Old Song.* Gu tur, *completely, altogether, quite, entirely.* Struidh e gu tur ar n'airgiod, *he hath quite spent our money.—Stew. Gen*

TUR, tuir, s. m (*Ir. id*) A desire, inclination, heaviness; petition Tur thilgeadh, *an inclination to vomit.*

TÙR, tùir, s. m. Genius, mind, understanding; a tour or journey. Inntinn is ùr nam fear, *the mind and genius of the heroes.—Mac Lach.* Ghocas agus tùr, *wisdom and understanding.—Stew Ex* Is e do thùr a bha beachdail, *thy mind was observant.—Macint.* Ghabh sinn tùr is tamh is fois, *we travelled and took our rest.—Fingalian Poem.*

TÙR, tùir, s. m. A tower or turret. Tra dh' fhàsas sean gach tùr is talla, *when every tower and hall shall grow old. —Oss. Trath*

Arab. thar, *tower, and* tour, *hill. Pers. Armen.* tar, *hill. Syr* thur, *hill Heb* thur *and* thor, *a hill Gr.* τυρος, τυῤῥις, *and* τυρσος, *a tower,* in Suidas. *Lat* turris. *Dan* tur *Swed.* tor. *Dal.* turan. *Anglo-Sax.* tor *and* torr *Teut.* torre. *It.* torre. *Ir.* tùr. *Arm* twr *and* tur Strabo observes, that the ancient Moors called Mount Atlas, *dyr.*

TÙR, v a Invent, devise, plan; conceive, frame *Pret a.* thùr, *devised, fut aff* tùraidh, *shall devise.* A thùr oibre ealanta, *to devise cunning work.—Stew. Ex. ref.* A thùras olc, *that devises evil.—Stew. Pro. ref.*

TÙRACH, a (*from* tùr) Towery, towering; turretted; intelligent, ingenious.

TÙRACHADH, aidh, s. m. A towering; tower-building.

TURACHAN, ain, s. m. (*Ir. id*) A big-bellied person.

TURADAN, ain, s. m. A little heap; a nodding, as in sleep

TURADH, aidh, s. m. (*Ir. id.*) Fair or dry weather. Tha 'n là na thuradh, *the day is fair.*

TÙRAICH, v Tower, build towers; fortify with towers; invent, devise. *Pret.* thùraich, *towered, fut. aff* tùraichidh, *shall devise, p. part.* tùraichte.

TÙRAIL, a. (tur-amhuil) Ingenious, intelligent, skilful. Gach duine tùrail, *every skilful man.—Stew. Chr*

TURAIT, s f. (tùr-aite.) *Pers* touraat. *Eng.* turret. A tower or turret. Turait an luchd-faire, *the tower of the watchmen, the watch-tower.—Stew. 2 K.* Turait-faire, *a watch-tower.*

TURAITEACH, a Turretted; like a turret.

TURAM See TURRAM.

TURAMAN, ain, s. m A nodding, as in sleep; a shaking, a vibrating, a tottering, a moving.

TURAMANAICH, v. n. Nod in sleep; shake, vibrate, totter, move.

TURAMANAICH, s. f. A nodding, as in sleep; a tottering or shaking; a vibrating, vibration.

TURAS, ais. See TÙRUS.

TURASGAR, air, s. m. (*Ir. id*) Sea-weed. *Macfar. Voc.* and *Shaw.*

TURBHAIDH, s. f. (*Ir. id.*) A mischance, a misfortune.

TURCACH, aich, s. m. A Turk.

TURCACH, a. Turkish.

TURCAID, s. f. A blacksmith's pincers, hoof-pincers. *N. pl.* turcaidean, *pincers.*

TURCHAR, air, s m. (*Ir. id*) Riches, wealth.

TUR-CHODAIL, v n. Slumber.

TUR-CHODAL, ail, s. m. Slumber, dozing; lethargy. An sgrios a' tur-chodal, *their destruction slumbering.—Stew. 2 P*

TUR-CHODALACH, a Slumbering, dozing, lethargic.

TUR-CHOMHRAC, aic, s. m. An assembly

† TUR-GHABHADH, aidh, s. m. (*Ir. id*) Iniquity.

TUR-GHABHALACH, a Iniquitous, guilty.

TÙR-GHABHAIL, s. f. (tùr, *journey; and* gabhail) A course, a journey. Most frequently applied to the sun's course. *Fr.* tour, *the artificial day.*

TUR-GHUIN, s. f. Destruction. Gu dean thu ar tur-ghuin, *that thou canst effect our destruction Fingalian Poem.*

TURLACH, aich, s. m. (*Ir. id.*) A bonfire, a great fire; conflagration; ground covered with water. Mu thùrlach aobhach na féisde, *around the joyous banquet-fire.—Oss. Conn.*

TURLOCH, s m (*Ir. id.*) A brook; a place where water lodges in winter.

TUR-LOM, v n. Make quite bare; strip naked; glean. *Pret. a.* thur-lom; *fut. aff.* tur-lomaidh, *shall make bare.* Cha tur-lom thu d' fhion-lios, *thou shalt not glean thy vineyard.—Stew. Lev.*

TUR-LOM, a. Quite bare, naked.

TUR-LOMADH, aidh, s. m. A making quite bare; a stripping

TÙRN, tùirn, s. m. A job, a work, a turn. Droch thùrn, *a bad job.*

† TURNADH, aidh, s m. (*Ir. id*) An escape; a spinning wheel

TÙRNAICHE, s f. (*Ir.* turnaidhe, *minister*) One who is employed in jobs.

† TURNAMH, aimh, s. m. (*Ir. id.*) A descent, humiliation, rest

TURNAIR, s. m. A turner.

TUR-OINNSEACH, ich, s f. A mere idiot.

TURRA-CHODAIL, v. n. Slumber, doze

TURRA-CHODAL, ail, s m. Slumber; a slumbering, dozing; drowsiness; a lethargy Eudaichidh turra-chodal le luideagan, *drowsiness will clothe with rags.—Stew. Pro.*

TURRA-CHODALACH, a. Slumbering, dozing; lethargic; causing drowsiness.

TURRA-CHODALAICHE, s m A person afflicted with habitual drowsiness, or lethargy.

TURRAG, aig, s f (*Ir. id.*) A conflict; a wench.

TURRAIG, s. f (*Ir. id*) A push, a thrust.

TURRAM, aim, s m A soft murmur, a whisper, a low whispering noise An raineach ri turram sa ghaoith, *the fern whispering in the wind.—Oss. Fin. and Lor.* Tha' e na thurram suain, *he is in sound sleep.—Old Poem.*

TÙRSA, TÙRSADH, aidh, s m. Sadness, dejection, melancholy.—*Macfar. Voc.*

TÙRSACH, a. Sad, dejected; melancholy—(*Macfar. Voc.*) Gu tùrsach, *sadly, heavily, mournfully, in a mournful manner.* Arsa Fionn gu tùrsach, *said Fingal sorrowfully.—Oss. Duthona.*

TÙRSACHD, *s. f.* Sadness, melancholy, dejection, heaviness.

TURSARAIN, *s. f.* Greater stitch-work. Stellaria holostea.

TURSGAIR, *s. f.* (*Ir. id.*) Equipage.

TURSGAN, *s. pl.* Implements.

TURTAN, ain, *s. m.* (*Ir. id.*) A sod, a turf.

TURTUR, uir, *s. m.* A turtle. *N. pl.* turturan; *d. pl.* turturaibh. A thabhartas do thurturaibh, *his offering of turtles.—Stew. Lev.*

TÙRUS, uis, *s. m.* and *f.* (*Ir. id.*) A journey, a travel, a voyage; a course. Tha 'n turus mòr, *the journey is great.—Stew.* 1 *K.* Turus soirbheasach, *a prosperous journey. Stew. Rom.* Chriochnaich mi mo thùras, *I have finished my journey.—Stew. Tim.* Turas mhath leat, *a good journey to you. N. pl.* tùrusan.

TÙRUSACH, *a.* Of, or pertaining to, a journey or voyage; pedestrian.

TÙRUSACH, aich, *s. m.* A traveller, a pilgrim.

TÙRUSACHD, *s. f.* Travelling; pedestrianism; pilgrimage.

TÙRUSAICHE, *s. m.* (*from* tùrus.) A traveller, a pilgrim; a pedestrian.

TÙRUSAN, ain, *s. m.* (*Ir. id.*) A traveller, a pilgrim.

TURÙSGAR, *s.* Giblets; equipage.

TÙS, tùis, *s. m.* (*Ir. id.*) A beginning, a commencement, an origin; the foremost part, as the front or van of an army. An tùs m' aimsir bha mi baoth, *in the beginning of my life I was foolish.—Old Song.* Tùs na teugbhoil, *the front of battle.—Fingalian Poem.* Helen tùs ar craidh, *Helen the origin of our sorrow.—Mac Lach.* Air thùs, *at first, foremost;* air thùs a shloigh, *in front of his army.—Mac Lach.* Air thùs is air thoiseach, *first and foremost.*

TUSA, *emphat. form* of tu. (*Ir. id.*) Thou. Is tusa aon diubh, *thou art one of them.—Oss. Duthona.*

TUS-AINM, *s. m.* A patronymic.

TUS-AINMEACH, *a.* Patronymic.—*Macfar. Voc.*

† TUSARNACH, aich, *s. m.* (*Ir.* tus-ornach.) A parricide.

TUSG, tuisg, *s. f.* A tooth, a tusk, a fang—(*Sm.*) *N. pl.* tuisg. Tuisg nan leomhann, *the lions' teeth.—Stew. Ps.* See also TOSG.

TUSGACH, *a.* (*from* tusg.) Having large teeth; tusky, fanged.

† TUSGAIRN, *s. f.* (*Ir. id.*) Fiction.

† TUSGARNADH, aidh, *s. m.* (*Ir. id.*) Fiction.—*Shaw.*

TUS-MHUINNTIR, *s. f.* Aborigines, or earliest inhabitants of a country.

TUT! An expression indicative of impatience.

TÙT, *s.* A silent *flatus; also,* a stink.

TÙTACH, *a.* (*Ir.* tùtach, *dirty.*) Stinking; breaking wind silently. *Com.* and *sup.* tutaiche.

TÙTACH, aich, *s. f.* A sounding horn. See also DUBHTACH.

TÙTAICHE, *com.* and *sup.* of tùtach.

TUTHAN, ain, *s. f.* (*Ir. id.*) A slut.

TÙTHT, *s.* See TÙT.

TUTHTACH. See TÙTACH.

U.

U, (uir.) The eighteenth and last letter of the Gaelic alphabet. According to the Irish Grammarians it takes its name from *uir*, heath; or from *iubhar*, yew. It has three sounds: long, like *oo* in *moon;* as, tùr, *a tower;* stùr, *dust;* short, like *u* in *push;* as, ur, *a child;* urram, *honour;* short and obscure, like *u* in *rut, cup;* as, mur, *if not;* gun, *without;* mun, *before.*

UA, *prep.* (*Ir. id.*) From.

UABHAIS, *gen. sing.* of uabhas.

UABHANN, ainn, *s. m.* Fright, terror, horror. Ghabh mi uabhann, *I was horrified.*

Ir. uabhann. *W.* ovan. *Arm. Corn.* oun. *Bisc.* owna.

UABHANNACH, *a.* Frightful, terrible, horrible. Gu h-uabhannach, *frightfully. Com.* and *sup.* uabhannaiche.

UABHAR, air, *s. m.* (*Ir. id.*) Pride, insolence; pomp; heat—(*Macfar. Voc.*); Luchd uabhair mhalluichte, *the cursed proud.—Sm.* Airson an uabhair, *for their pride.—Stew. Zeph.* See also UAMHAR.

UABHARACH, *a.* (*Ir. id.*) Proud, haughty, arrogant; terrible. Gu h-uabharach, *proudly. Com.* and *sup.* uabharaiche, *more or most proudly.*

UABHARR, *a.* Proud, haughty, insolent; raging; terrible. Stoirm uabharr steuda Lochlainn, *the raging storms of the waves of Lochlin.—Ull.* See also UAMHAR.

UABHAS, ais. See UAMHAS.

UABHASACH. See UAMHASACH.

UABHEIST, *s. m.* A monster, a wild beast. Mar uabheist anns na cuantaibh, *like a monster in the seas.—Stew. Ez. N. pl.* uabheistean.

UACHDAR, air, *s. m.* (*Ir. id.*) The top, surface, or upper part of any thing; cream. O uachdar gu h-iochdar, *from top to bottom;* an uachdar carraigh, *on the surface of a rock.—Orr.* An uachdar, *above, aboard;* an uachdar fa seach is an iochdar, *above and below alternately.—Oss. Fin. and Lor.* Lamh an uachdar, *superiority, upper-hand, the upper grapple in wrestling;* Uachdar-tìre, *Ochtertyre,* a place in Perthshire.

UACHDAR, air, *s. m.* (*Ir. id.*) Mountain sanicle.

UACHDARACH, UACHDRACH, *a.* (*Ir. id.*) Uppermost, highest; creamy, producing cream. A Bhealtuinn uachdrach, *cream-producing May.—Macfar. Com.* and *sup.* uachdaraiche.

UACHDARACHD, UACHDRACHD, *s. f.* Supremacy, superiority.

UACHDARAICHE, UACHDRAICHE, *com.* and *sup.* See UACHDARACH.

UACHDARAN, UACHDRAN, ain, *s. m.* (*from* uachdar.) *Ir. id.* A ruler, a governor, a superior, a prince. A bhios na uachdaran, *who shall be a ruler.—Stew. Mic.* Ni mi e na uachdaran, *I will make him a prince.—Stew.* 1 *K. N. pl.* uachdarain.

UACHDARANACHD, UACHDRANACHD, *s. f.* (*Ir. id.*) Rule, dominion, government, superiority, supremacy, principality. Bithidh uachdaranachd agad air, *thou shalt rule over him.—Stew. Gen.* Biodh uachdranachd aca, *let them have dominion.—Id.*

UADH, uaidh, *s. f.* See UAGH.

UADHACH, *a.* See UAGHACH.

UADHAIDH. See UAGHAIDH.

UADH-CHRITHE, *s. f.* Horror, dread, terror.

UAGH, uaigh, *s. f.* (*Ir. id.*) A cave, a cavern, a den; dread; terror.

UAGHACH, *a.* Full of caves, caverns, or dens; dreadful, terrible.

Uaghaidh, *s. f.* A cave, cavern, or den. *N. pl.* uaghaidhean.

Uaghidheach, *a.* Full of caves or dens.

Uaibh, *comp. pron.* (*Ir. id.*) From you, from amongst you. Ciod a tha uaibh? *what do you want?* Thigibh uaibh, *come forward*, an expression of defiance.

Uaibhreach, *a.* (*Ir. id.*) Proud, haughty, insolent; airy; superb, gorgeous. Buailidh e an t-uaibhreach, *he strikes the proud.*—*Stew. Job.* Piuthar uaibhreach reul nan speur, *the gorgeous sister* [*the moon*] *of the heavenly bodies.*—*Oss. Fing.* Na h-uaibhrich, *the proud.*—*Stew. Pro.* Gu h-uaibhreach, *proudly.*—*Stew. Mic. Com.* and *sup.* uaibhriche.

Uaibhreachas, ais, *s. m.* Pride, haughtiness, insolence, arrogance. Làn uaibhreachais a d' shaothair, *full of pride at thy work.*—*Old Song.*

Uaibhreachd, *s. f.* Pride, haughtiness, insolence, arrogance.

Uaidne, *s. f.* The stilt of a plough.—*Macfar. Voc.*

Uaigh, *s. f.* (*Ir. id.*) A grave, a tomb; a den, a cavern. Crimin aig uaigh an laoich, *Crimina at the hero's grave.*—*Ull. N. pl.* uaighean.

† **Uaigh-reir**, *a.* (*Ir. id.*) Having arbitrary sway; *substantively*, arbitrary sway.

Uaigneach, *a.* (*for* uaignidheach.) *Ir.* uaigneach. Lonely, solitary, lonesome, secret; deserted; private. Bile nan sruthan uaigneach, *the banks of the lonely streamlets.*—*Oss. Fin. and Lor.* Nan teach uaigneach, *in their lonely mansion.*—*Oss. Taura.* Gnothuch uaigneach, *private business, a private message.*—*Stew. Jud.* Gu h-uaigneach, *solitarily.*—*Macdon. Com.* and *sup.* uaigniche.

Uaigneas, eis, *s. m.* (*Ir. id.*) Loneliness, lonesomeness, retirement, privacy. Mar thonn an uaigneas, *like a lonely wave.*—*Oss. Fin. and Lor.* An uaigneas, *in secret, in a retired place.*—*Macint.*

Uaignidh, *a.* Lonely, solitary, secret; deserted.

Uaignidheach, *a.* Lonely, solitary, lonesome, secret; deserted. Gu h-uaignidheach, *secretly.*—*Stew. Job.*

Uaignidheas, eis, *s. m.* Loneliness, lonesomeness, retirement, privacy. An uaignidheas, *in secrecy.*—*Stew. Mat.*

† **Uail**, *s. f.* (*Ir. id.*) A wail, a howl, a lament.

Uaill, *a.* Proud; famous.

Uaile, uaille, *s. f.* Pride, conceit, foppery; boasting; fame; dignity; a howl. Dean uaill, *boast, pride thyself*; am fear a ni uaill, *he who boasts himself.*—*Stew. Pro.* A dh' arduich t-ionnsuchadh chum uaille, *whom learning has raised to dignity.*—*Macfar.* C' aite am bheil aobhar-uaille, *where is there cause for boasting?*—*Orr.*

Uailleach, *a.* See **Uallach**.

Uailleag, eig, *s. f.* (*from* uaill.) A conceited female.

Uaillean, ein, *s. m.* A fop, a coxcomb.

Uailleanachd, *s. f.* Foppery.

Uailleart, eirt, *s. m.* A howl.

Uailleartach, *a.* Howling.

Uaill-fheart, *s. m.* A deed of renown; a howl.

Uaill-fheartach, *a.* (*Ir.* uaillfeartach.) Illustrious, renowned; ostentation; howling.

Uaillich, *v. a.* (*Ir.* uailligh.) Elevate; make proud or vain; roar, howl. *Pret. a.* dh' uaillich; *fut. aff.* uaillichidh, *shall elevate.*

Uaill-mhiann, *s. m.* (*Ir. id.*) Ambition; fondness for rank or distinction.—*Macfar. Voc.*

Uaill-mhiannach, *a.* (*Ir.* uaillmhianach.) Ambitious; fond of rank or distinction.—*Macfar. Voc.*

Uaillse, *com.* and *sup.* of uasal. See **Uaisle**.

Uaillsean. See **Uaislean**.

Uaim. See **Fuaim**.

Uaim, *s. f.* (*Ir. id.*) A weaver's harness; union; embroidery.

Uaimh, *s. f.* (*Ir. id.*) A grave, a den, a cave; a grotto. Ma 's carraig no uaimh do chomhnuidh, *whether a rock or cave by thy dwelling.*—*Ull. N. pl.* uaimhean.

Uaimheach, *a.* Full of graves, full of dens or caverns.

Uaimhneach, *a.* Terrible, dreadful. Gu h-uaimhneach, *terribly. Com.* and *sup.* uaimhniche.

Uaimhneachd, *s. f.* Terribleness, dreadfulness.

Uaimhnich, *v. a.* Terrify. *Pret. a.* dh' uaimhnich; *fut. aff.* uaimhnichidh.

Uain, *s. f.* (*Ir. id.*) A loan; a pin, a peg.

Uain, *gen. sing.* and *n. pl.* of uan; which see.

Uainceann, inn, *s. m.* Lambskin.—*Macfar. Voc.*

Uainceannach, *a.* Of, or pertaining to, lambskin; like lambskin.

Uaine, *a.* (*Ir.* uaithne.) Green; livid. Mar iurain uaine am bogha na frois, *like a green tendril in the rainbow.*—*Oss. Fin. and Lor.* Dhealain uaine a bhàis, *thou livid lightning of death.*—*Oss. Com.* Ogain, nam breacan uaine, *the green plaided youths.*—*Old Song.*

Uaine, *s. f.* (*Ir.* uaithne.) Greenness, lividness; the green sickness, menstrual courses; safety; a wooden pin.

Uaine, *com.* and *sup.* of uaine. More or most green.

Uainead, eid, *s. m.* Greenness, lividness; increase in greenness. A dol an uainead, *growing more and more green.*

Uainealach, *a.* Verdant.—*Macint.*

Uainealachd, *s. f.* Verdure, greenness.

Uainn, *comp. pron.* (*Ir. id.*) From us, from amongst us; off us. Ciod a tha uainn, *what want we?* tha uainn bhi falbh, *we want to be gone, we had better be gone.*

Uainne, *emphat. form.* of uainn; which see.

Uainnearas, ais, *s. m.* (*Ir. id.*) Retirement.

Uaipe, *comp. pron.* From her; off her, descended from her. Ciod a tha uaipe? *what does she want?*

Uaipe-san, *emphat. form.* of uaipe. From her.

Uaircheas, is, *s. m.* (*Ir. id.*) A cock-boat.

Uair, *s. f.* An hour; season; time; weather; one time, once; once on a time. An uair, *the hour, one o'clock, when*; uair eiridh iad gu neamh, uair theid iad gu domhainn sios, *one time they mount to heaven, another time they go down to the deep.*—*Sm.* An uair gàbhaidh, *in the time of danger.*—*Ull.* Air uairibh, *sometimes, at times*; Chluinntear a bròn air uairibh, *her grief was heard at times.*—*Ull.* Thug mi i 'n uaigneas uair, *I once took her apart.*—*Macint.* Na uairean, *sometimes, at times*; 'n uair, *when*; uairibh, *sometimes.*

Lat. hora. *It.* ora. *Fr.* heure. *Hung.* ora. *Dal.* ura. *Germ.* uhr. *Eng.* hour. *Scotch*, hoor *and* heur. *Ir.* uair. *Arm.* eur *and* ur. *Du.* uur. *Corn.* ur. *W.* awr.

Uair-eigin, **Uair 'gin**, *adv.* Sometime, sometime or other. Uan na uair-eigin, *sometime or other.*

Uaireach, *a.* Needless, useless, insignificant, unimportant, unnecessary. Is uaireach dhuit, *it is needless for you*; ni mo is bean uaireach mise, *nor am I a woman without importance.*—*Old Poem.*

Uaireach, *a.* (*from* uair.) Horary, hourly.—*Macfar. Voc.*

Uaireachan, ain, *s. m.* A timepiece.

Uaireadair, *s. m.* (*from* uair.) A watch, a timepiece, a clock. *N. pl.* uaireadairean.

Uaireadair-gaineimh, *s. m.* A sand-glass.

Uaireadair-gaineamhain, *s. m.* A sand-glass.

Uaireadair-gealaich, *s. m.* A moon-dial.

Uaireadair-greine, *s. m.* A sun-dial.

Uaireadairiche, *s. m.* A clockmaker; a watchmaker.

Uaireil, *a.* (uair-amhuil.) Hourly, horary. *Ir.* uair-amhail. *Lat.* horalis. *W.* awrawl.

Uairibh, *adv.* Sometimes, at times.

Uairibh, (air), *adv.* Sometimes, at times. See **Uair.**

Uair-lan, ain, *s. m.* A sun-dial.

Uair-òir, *s.* Aurora, morning; *literally*, the golden-hour.

Aurora itself seems to be *aurea hora*, the golden hour, a name descriptive of the golden hue of the eastern clouds in early morning.

† **Uais**, *a.* (*Ir. id.*) Noble, well descended.—*Shaw.*

Uaisle, *com.* and *sup.* of uasale. (*Ir. id.*) More or most noble.

Uaisle, *s. f.* Nobility.

Uaisleachadh, aidh, *s. m.* (*Ir. id.*) An ennobling, a dignifying.

Uaisleachadh, (ag), *pr. part.* of uaislich. Ennobling, exalting.

Uaisleachd, *s. f.* Nobility, gentility; pride.

Uaislean, *s. pl.* (*Ir. id.*) Gentry, nobility, nobles. Dh' ionnsaidh nan uaislean, *to the nobles.—Stew.* 1 *K.*

Uaislich, *v. a.* (uaisligh.) Ennoble, exalt, dignify. *Pret. a.* Dh' uaislich; *fut. aff.* uaislichidh, *shall ennoble; fut. pass.* uaislichear, *shall be ennobled.*

Uaislichte, *p. part.* of uaislich. Ennobled, exalted, dignified.

Uait, *comp. pron.* (*Ir. id.*) From thee, from off thee, descended from thee. Thig uait, *come forward*, said in defiance; ciod a tha uait? *what do you want?* tha uait a bhi falbh, *you had better be gone.*

Uaith, Uaithe, *comp. pron.* From him, from it. Ciod a tha uaith? *what does he want?* thigeadh e uaithe, *let him come forward*, said in defiance; Ciod bheir la uaith, *what a day may bring forth.—Stew. Pro.* Chuige is uaith, *to and fro.*

Uaithe-san, *emphat. form* of uaith.

Uallach, *a.* (*from* uaille.) *Ir. id.* Conceited, airy, proud, arrogant, vain-glorious; ostentation; gallant. Cathuil uallach 'teachd, *gallant Cathula coming.—Oss. Cathula.* Gu h-uallach, *proudly. Com.* and *sup.* uallaiche.

Uallach, aich, *s. f.* (*Ir.* ualach.) A burden, a load, an oppressive weight; a heavy charge. Is eutrom an t-uallach, mo ghradh, *light is the burden, my love.—Oss. Gaul.* Uallach an tighe, *the charge of the house.—Stew.* 1 *K.* Is trom an uallach an aois, *age is a heavy burden.—G. P.* More frequently written *eallach;* which see.

Uallachadh, aidh, *s. m.* A burdening, a loading, or encumbering.

Uallachadh, aidh, *s. m.* A making conceited or arrogant, a becoming conceited, airy, or arrogant.

Uallachag, aig, *s. f.* A coquette—(*Macfar. Voc.*); an airy, conceited girl. *N. pl.* uallachagan.

Uallachan, ain, *s. m.* (*Ir. id.*) A showy stripling; a gallant; a coxcomb; a fop; a swaggerer.

Uallachas, ais, *s. m.* Conceit; airiness; vanity; gallantry; foppery; *rarely* lewdness.

Uallachd, *s. f.* Conceitedness, airiness, showiness, ostentation.

Uallaich, *v. a.* (*Ir.* ualaigh.) Load, burden. Dh' uallaich, *loaded; fut. aff.* uallaichidh, *shall load; p. part.* uallaichte.

Uallaich, *v. a.* and *n.* Make conceited, become conceited.

Uallair, *s. m.* A coxcomb.

Uam, *comp. pron.* From me; away from me. Com' a spionadh thusa uam, *why wert thou torn from me.—Ull.* Uam sumainte nam blàr, *from me be* [*away with*] *the thoughts of battles.—Oss. Gaul.* Uam grian is madainn is samhradh, *far from me be sun, morn, and summer.—Oss. Derm.* A sìor acain na bheil uam, *aye deploring them who are away from me.—Old Poem.* Tha sin uam, *I want that.*

Uamh, uamha, *s. f.* (*Ir.* uamh.) A cave, a cavern, a den; a grave. Uamh-thalmhainn, *a subterraneous cavern; Ir.* uamh-thalmhan.

Uamhach, *a.* Full of caves or caverns; cavernous.

Uamhaidh, *s. f.* A cave, cavern, or den. *N. pl.* uamhaidhean.

Uamhaidheach, *a.* Full of caves or caverns; like a cave or cavern.

Uamhainn, *gen. sing.* of uamhann; which see.

Uamhais, *gen. sing.* of uamhas.

Uamhann, ainn, *s. m.* Dread, terror, dismay; horror; amazement. Righ nan uamhann, *the king of terrors.—Stew. Job.* Uamhann a bhlàir, *the terror of battle.—Fingalian Poem.* Tuitidh uamhann orra, *amazement shall fall on them.—Stew. Ex.*

Uamhann, *a.* Dreadful, terrible, horrible. Chaidh Fionn a sìos le tartar uamhann, *Fingal descended with terrible noise.—Oss. Manos.*

Uamhannach, *a.* (*from* uamhann.) Dreadful, terrible, horrible, shocking. Le tartar uamhaunach na mara, *with the dreadful noise of sea.—Fingalian Poem.* Gu h-uamhannach, *dreadfully. Com.* and *sup.* uamhannaiche.

Uamharr, uamharra, *a.* Proud, arrogant; terrible, direful, shocking; loathsome, abominable; excessive.

Uamharrach, *a.* See **Uamharr.**

Uamharrachd, *s. f.* Pride, arrogance; direfulness; loathsomeness; abominableness; excessiveness. Chunnaic mi uamharrachd, *I saw* [*a horrible thing*] *abomination.—Stew. Jer.*

Uamharradh, *a.* Proud; abominable; direful; disgustful, loathsome, excessive.

Uamhas, ais, *s. m.* (*Ir.* uathmhas.) Dread, horror, dismay, astonishment.

Uamhasach, *a.* (*Ir.* uathmhasach.) Dreadful, awful, horrible; astonishing; shocking. *Com.* and *sup.* uamhasaiche.

Uamhasachd, *s. f.* Dreadfulness, horribleness; astonishment; abominableness.

Uamhunn. See **Uamhann.**

Uamhunnach, *a.* See **Uamhannach.**

Uan, uain, *s. m.* A lamb. *N. pl.* uain. Leum cnocain beag mar uan, *little hills leaped like lambs.—Sm.* Croicionn uain, *a lambskin; Arm.* crochen oan.

Gr. accusative, ὄϊν. *Sclav.* ouen. *Ir.* uan. *Arm.* oan. *Corn.* oñ.

Uanach, *a.* Agnal; like a lamb; abounding in lambs; lamb-producing. Bhealtuinn uanach, *lamb-producing May.—Macfar.*

Uanachd, *s. f.* (*Ir. id.*) Yeaning.

Uanan, ain, *s. m.* (*dim.* of uan.) A little lamb, a young lamb. Uanan do dh' uachdran nan Dia, *a young lamb to the chief of the gods.—Mac Lach.*

Uan-càisg, *s. m.* A paschal lamb.

Uapa, *comp. pron.* From them, from amongst them; away from them. Thainig mi uapa, *I came from them;* ciod a tha uapa? *what do they want?* Thigeadh iad uapa, *let them come forward*, said in defiance; tha uapa bhi falbh, *they had better be gone.*

Uapa-san, *emphat. form* of uapa.

Uarach-mhullaich, *s. f.* (*Ir. id.*) The herb devil's-bit.—*Macfar. Voc.*

UARAN, ain, *s. m.* (*Ir. id.*) Fresh water.

UAS, *s. m.* A crown or ornament of silver worn by that order of poets next to the *ollamh*.

UASAL, *a.* (*Ir. id.*) Noble, high-born; genteel; proud; precious; *also* a gentleman. Chàr uasail, *thou noble* [*friend*] *ally.—Oss. Fing.* Oscionn chlach uasal, *above* [*precious stones*] *rubies.—Stew. Pro.* Duine uasal, *a gentleman.*

UASAL, ail, *s. m.* A nobleman; a gentleman. Uasail, *sir;* uasail ionmhuinn, *dear sir;* so also say the Irish.

† UATH, uaith, *s. m.* (*Ir. id.*) Earth; hawthorn; small number, retirement.

† UATH, *a.* (*Ir. id.*) Solitary, alone, single, lonesome; terrible.

UATHA, *comp. pron.* From them. Uatha-san ceannaichidh sibh, *from them ye shall buy.—Stew. Lev.*

UATHAIL, *a.* (*Ir.* uath-amhuil.) Solitary, single.

UATHA-SAN, *emphatic form* of uatha.

UATHBHASACH, *a.* (*Ir. id.*) Dreadful, terrible; shocking, direful. Cia uathbhasach an t-àite so, *how dreadful is this place!—Stew. Gen. Contracted* uabhasach.

UBAG, aig, *s. f.* Incantation; a charm or spell; a superstitious ceremony.

UBAGACH, *a.* Enchanting; like a charm; superstitious.

UBAGAICH, *v. a.* Subdue by charms or spells; enchant. *Pret. a.* dh' ubagaich, *enchanted; fut. aff. a.* ubagaichidh, *shall enchant.*

UBAGAICHE, *s. m.* One who subdues by charms or philters.

UBH, *s. m.* An egg; *rarely,* the point of a weapon. *N. pl.* uibhean, *eggs.* A blàiteachadh nan ubha, *hatching the eggs.—Macfar.*

Gr. ὠὸν. *Lat.* ovum. *It.* uovo. *Teut.* ey *and* eye. *Arm.* uy. *Belg.* ey. *Germ.* ey. *Fr.* œuf. *Manks,* ov. *W.* uy *and* wy. *Corn.* oy. *Ir.* ugh.

UBHACH, *a.* (*Ir. id.*) Oval; like an egg; full of eggs; egg-producing; pointed.

UBHAGAN, ain, *s. m.* (*from* ubh.) A pancake, a custard.

UBHAIL, *a.* (*Ir.* ugh-amhuil.) Oval.

UBHAL, UBHALL, aill, *s. m.* (*Ir. id.*) An apple. Crann ubhall, *an apple tree.—Stew. Song. Sol. N. pl.* ùbhlan. Mios nan ubhlan, *the month of apples.—Macfar.*

UBHAL-GHORT, -ghoirt, *s. f.* An orchard; a garden.

UBHAL NA COISE, *s. m.* The ancle.

UBHAL NA LEISE, *s. m.* The hip-bone.

UBHAL NA SÙL, *s. m.* The apple of the eye. Mar ubhal do shùl, *the apple of thine eye.—Stew. Pro.*

UBHLA, UBHLADH, aidh, *s. m.* A fine, a penalty; a tax, a tribute; impost. Cuirear ùbhla air, *he shall be* [*fined*] *punished.—Stew. Ex.*

UBHLACH, *a.* Abounding in apples; of, or belonging to, an apple.

UBHLAN, *n. pl.* of ubhal.

ÙCADAIR, *s. m.* (*Ir.* ùcair.) A fuller of cloth, a napper of cloth. *N. pl.* ùcadairean.

ÙCADAIREACHD, *s. f.* The business of a fuller of cloth; fulling.

UCAID, *s. f.* (*Ir. id.*) Occasion.

UCAIN, *s. f.* (*Ir. id.*) Harshness.

ÙCAIR, *s. m.* A fuller of cloth; a napper of cloth. *N. pl.* ùcairean.

ÙCAIREACHD, *s. f.* The business of a fuller of cloth.

UCHANAICH, *s. f.* Sobbing, groaning.—*Macfar. Voc.*

UCHD, *s. m.* (*Ir. id. Gr.* οχθη.) A breast or bosom; a lap; intercession. Ann uchd a mhor fhir, *in the warrior's breast.—Ull.* Uchd nan cruach, *the breast of the mountains.—Oss. Trath.* Beul ri beul, is uchd ri h-uchd, *mouth to mouth, and breast to breast.—Oss. Cathluno.* Ri h-uchd feuma, *encountering emergency.—Smith's address to a Highland regiment.* Ri h-uchd cruadail, *breasting difficulty.—Id. N. pl.* uchdan. Na h-uchdan, *the breasts.—Stew. Lev.*

UCHDACH, *a.* (*from* uchd.) Pectoral; thoracic; steep, precipitous.

UCHDACH, aich, *s. m.* (*from* uchd.) *Ir. id.* A short steep ascent; a steep; a steep portion of a high-road; an up-hill road; a breastplate; a stomacher; a meadow. Gun uchdach a dhìreadh, *without climbing an ascent.—Macint.* Sgoilt i 'n uchdach phrìseil, *she split the precious breastplate.—Mac Lach. N. pl.* uchdaich. Uchdaich Ghibeah, *the meadows of Gibeah.—Stew. Jud.*

† UCHDALL, *a.* High, erect; *Germ.* uchell; hence *Oichil,* a chain of mountains in the Lowlands of Scotland.

UCHDAN, ain, *s. m.* (*from* uchd.) A short steep ascent; a steep portion of road; an up-hill road; a hillock; a sob. *N. pl.* uchdain *and* uchdanan. Aird nan uchdanan, *the top of the hillocks.—R.*

UCHDANACH, *a.* Full of steep ascents, or of hillocks—(*Macint.*); steep or uneven, as a highway; *also* sobbing.

UCHDANACHADH, aidh, *s. m.* A sobbing, sighing, groaning.

UCHDANAICH, *v. n.* Sob, sigh, groan. *Pret. a.* dh' uchdanaich.

UCHDANAICH, *s. f.* Frequent sobbing; sobbing or groaning.

UCHDAS FHIADHAIN, *s. m.* Common mallow.

UCHDAS-FRANCACH, *s. m.* Dwarf mallow.

UCHD-ARDACH, *a.* High-breasted; high-chested. Eun uchd-ardach, *a high-breasted bird.—Macdon.*

UCHD-BHÀN, *a.* Fair-breasted.

UCHD-GHEAL, *a.* White-breasted.

UCHD-CHRIOS, *s. m.* A breastband; a stomacher.

UCHD-EIDIDH, *s. f.* (*Ir. id.*) A breastplate; armour for the breast. Air son na h-uchd-eididh, *for the breastplate.—Stew. Ex.*

UCHD-EUDACH, aich, *s. m.* (*Ir. id.*) A breastplate.

UCHD-MHAC, -mhic, *s. m.* An adopted son.—*Macfar. Voc.*

UCHD-MHACACH, *a.* Of, or belonging to adoption.

UCHD-MHACACHADH, aidh, *s. m.* The circumstance of adopting; adoption.

UCHDMHACACHD, *s. f.* Adoption; frequent adopting. A feitheamh ris an uchd-mhacachd, *waiting for the adoption.—Stew. N. T.*

UCHDMHACAICH, *v. a.* Adopt as a son. *Pret. a.* dh' uchdmhacaich, *adopted; fut. aff. a.* uchdmhacaichidh, *shall adopt; fut. pass.* uchdmhacaichear, *shall be adopted.*

UCHDMHACAICHTE, *p. part.* of uchdmhacaichte. Adopted.

UCHD-RUADH, *a.* Red-breasted, brown-breasted. Am banal uchd-ruadh, *the red-breasted covey.—Macdon.*

UCSA, *s. m.* The name given to an ass in its fourth year.

UD, *demons. pron.* (*Ir. id.*) Yon, that there, that yonder. Thall ud, *over there;* am baile ud thall, *that tower yonder.*

UDAGOC, *s. m.* A woodcock.

UDAIL, *v. a.* and *n.* Cause to totter or waver; toss; move backwards or forwards; flounder.

UDAIL, *a.* Wavering; tottering; tossing; slow; inhospitable. Cha b' udail thu a measg chàich, *thou wert not slow among the rest.—Old Song.*

UDAL, ail, *s. m.* Distress, jeopardy; wavering; tossing.—*Macfar. Voc.*

UDAL, (ag). Wavering, tossing, tottering; moving to and fro as any light substance in an eddy. Ag udal cuain, *tossing on the ocean.—Ull.*

UDALACH, a. (*from* udal.) Wavering, tossing, tottering; removing from place to place; causing distress or jeopardy.

UDALAN, ain, s. m. A swivel —*Macfar. Voc.* *N. pl.* udalain.

UDARAG, aig, s. m. (*Ir. id.*) A woodcock.

UDHAR, air, s. m. (*Ir. id*) A wound, a sore, an ulcer, or bile.—*Macfar. Voc.*

UDHARACH, a. Sore, ulcerous.

UDLAICHE, s. m. An old hart. —*Macfar. Voc.* *N. pl.* udlaichean.

UDLAIDH, a. (*Ir. id.*) Lonely; morose; churlish; gloomy. —(*Macfar. Voc*); tigh udlaidh, *a lonely house.*—*Macint.*

UGADH, aidh, s m. (*Ir. id*) A birth —*Shaw.*

UGAN, ain, s. m. The throat; the upper part of the breast. —*Macfar. Voc.* Crithe-chiùil air m' ugan, *warbling in my throat* —*Old Song.*

UGH, uigh, s. m. An egg. Gealagan uigh, *the white of an egg.*—*Stew Job* *N pl* uighean, *eggs*, a gur air uighean, *sitting on eggs* —*Stew. Jer.* *Ugh* is more properly written *ubh*, agreeably to the analogy of many other languages. See UBH.

UGHDAR, air, s. m (*Ir. id. Lat.* auctor. *Fr* auteur) An author. Ughdar na mi-riaghailt, *the author of confusion* —*Stew.* 1 *Cor.*

UGHDARACH, a. Authentic; having an author; of, or belonging to, an author; authoritative.

UGHDARACHD, s. f. Authorship; authenticity; authority.

UGHDARAICH, v. a. (*from* ughdar.) Authorize, empower; own as an author. *Pret a.* dh' ughdaraich, *authorized; fut aff. a* ughdaraichidh, *shall authorize.*

UGHDARAICHTE, p part of ughdaraich. Authorized, empowered; owned as a work by its author.

UGHDARAS, ais, s m. (*Ir id. Lat* auctoritas) Authority; power. Cha 'n e nach eil ughdarras againne, *not that we have not power.*—*Stew.* 2 *Thess. ref.*

UGHDARASACH, a. (*Ir. id*) Authentic; authoritative

UIBEACH, a Round, globular, rotund, circular.

UIBEACHD, s. f. Roundness, circularity, globularity, rotundity.

UIBH, *gen.* and *sing* of ubh; which see.

UIBHIR, s. m. (*Ir. id*) Number, quantity; sum, account. Chuireadh sios an uibhir, *the number was put down* —*Stew.* 1 *Chr.* Uibhir ri càch, *as much as the rest.*—*Old Poem*

UIDEAL, eil, s. m. A wavering, a tottering; a moving to and fro; jeopardy. Gun sibh bhi fa uideal, *without your being moved* or *shaken.*—*Stew. Thess. ref.* Written also *udal*, which see.

UIDEALACH, a Wavering, tottering; causing to wave or totter; in jeopardy

UIDH, v. a Favour, countenance; take part *Pret* dh' uidh, *favoured, fut aff* uidhidh, *shall favour* Cha n' uidh thu leis, *thou shalt not favour him* —*Stew. Ex.*

UIDH, uidhe, s. f (*Ir.* uidhe) A degree; a span; a stage; a way, a journey, *also*, care, attention; a hearing. Uidh air 'n uidhe, *step by step, by degrees*

UIDHEAM, eim, s. m. Dress, decoration; order, preparation; furniture, harness, equipage Uidheam a phàilliuinn, *the furniture of the tabernacle.*—*Stew O. T.* Gun arm gun uidheam, *without arms or dress.*—*Death of Carril.* See also UIGHEAM.

UIDHEAMACHADH. See UIGHEAMACHADH

UIDHEAMAICH. See UIGHEAMAICH.

UIDHEAMAICHTE. See UIGHEAMAICHTE.

UIDH-GHILLE, s m. (*Ir.* uigh-ghiolla.) A footman; an errand-boy.

UIDHIS See UIS.

UIG, uige, s f (*Ir id*) A jewel; a precious stone; a pebble; *rarely*, knowledge, ingenuity.

† UIGE, s f. (*Ir. id*) Carded wool to be spun for clothes, a web. Hence it means the spinning out of a poem, or a story.

UIGEACH, a Abounding in jewels or precious stones, like a jewel or precious stone

UIGEAN, UIGEANN, einn, s. m. (*Ir id.*) The forepart of the neck

UIGH, *gen sing* of ugh

UIGH, uighe, s f A degree; a space; a stage, a journey, desire, wish, delight, visage; care, thought, attention, partiality; a leaning to. Uigh air uigh phill a ghean, *by degrees his spirits returned* —*Ull* An uigh ri triall, *then desire fixed on departing* —*Oss. Dargo.* Ol is ceòl air uigh gach fir, *drinking and music were the delight of each hero* —*Oss. Gaul* *Uigh*, in the sense of *aghaidh*, seems to be a contracted form of *aghaidh*

UIGH, *gen sing* of ugh

UIGHEACH, ich, s. m (*from* uigh) A traveller

UIGHEAM, eim, s. m (*Ir.* ugham.) Dress, decoration, order, preparation, furniture, harness, equipage. Tha e na làn uigheam, *he is in full-dress*, a dol an uigheam, *dressing, preparing.* See also UIDHEAM

UIGHEAMACHADH, aidh, s m Dressing, decorating; preparing, decoration; furniture, equipage

UIGHEAMAICH, v. a (*from* uigheam.) Dress, decorate, equip, prepare; get in order. *Pret. a* dh' uigheamaich, *fut aff. a* uigheamaichidh; *p part* uigheamaichte.

UIGHEAMAICHIDH, *fut act.* of uigheamaich Shall or will prepare

UIGHEAMAICHTE, *p. part.* of uigheamaich. (*Ir.* ughamtha) Prepared, dressed, decorated, equipped

UILC, *gen. sing.* and *n. pl.* of olc (*Ir. id.*) Of evil; evils, ills Na h-uilc, *the evils.*—*Sm.*

UILD, *gen sing.* and *n. pl.* of ald; which see

UILE, a All; whole; every. Uile air chaochladh, *all changed* —*Ardar.* Bhur n-uile chùram, *all your care.*—*Stew* 1 *Pet* Uile gu léir, *altogether, completely, wholly*, gu h-uile, *altogether, completely, wholly*, a choille gu h-uile làn duillich, *the wood completely full of foliage* —*Macdon*

Gr ὅυλος *and* οὖλος. *Swed. Eng.* all. *Teut* heel *Arm* oll. *Ir* uile.

UILEACH, a. Universal; general.

UILEACHD, s. f. (*from* uile.) *Ir. id* Universality; generality

UILEANN, s f; *gen* uille *and* uilinne An elbow; an angle or corner Uileann Dheirg air slios a sgeith, *Dargo's elbow was on the side of his shield*, or, *leaning on his shield* —*Ull* Air uilinn nan leac, *on the corners of the flags* —*Oss Conn*

UILEANNACH, a. (*from* uileann) *Ir.* uilleannach.) Elbowed, cornered; angled.

UILEANNACH, aich, s. m. The lowest branch of a deer's horn.—*Macfar. Voc*

UILEAR, a Unnecessary.

UILE-BHEANNAICHTE, UILE-BHEANNUICHTE, *part.* Truly blessed, completely blessed

UILE-BHEIST, s m. A monster, a hideous wild beast Mar uile-bheist mhi-chiallach, *like a mad monster* —*Old Song*

UILE-BHUADHACH, a Victorious, triumphant.

UILE-CHINNTEACH, a Quite certain, unerring; all-sufficient

Uile-chumhachd, *s. f.* (*Ir. id.*) Omnipotence.

Uile-chumhachdach, *a.* (*Ir. id.*) All-powerful, omnipotent, almighty. An t-Uile-chumhachdach, *the Almighty.*

Uile-dhionoghalta, *a.* All-sufficient.

Uile-fhaicsinneach, *a.* All-seeing, omniscient.

Uile-fhaicsinneachd, *s. f.* Infinite vision, omniscience.

Uile-fhiosrach, *a.* All-knowing, omniscient.

Uile-fhiosrachd, *s. f.* Omniscience.

Uile-ghlic, *a.* All-wise.

Uile-ghliocas, ais, *s. m.* Infinite wisdom.

Uile-ice, *s. m.* Misletoe; a nostrum; a panacea.—*Macd.* *Arm.* oll-yiach. *W.* ol-hiach. *Ir.* uile-iceach.

This is an ancient Druidical term, as we may learn from Pliny, who says of the misletoe, that the Druids "called it by a word that signifies in their language *all heal*:" *Omnia sanantem appellantes suo vocabulo.*—Lib. xvi. ch. 44. The Druids gathered the misletoe on the tenth of March. Toland supposes that Virgil (*Æn.* lib. vi.) alludes to the ceremony of consecrating the misletoe, where he makes mention of the *golden branch.* Pliny, in the 16th book of his Nat. Hist., is particular in his description of the misletoe. The following is a translation of it:—"The Druids (so they call their magi) hold nothing in such sacred respect as the misletoe, and the tree on which it grows, provided it be an oak. They select certain woods of oak, and they do not perform any sacred rite without the leaf of that tree; so that hence it is likely they have been called Druids, explaining the name from the Greek, Δρυς, Drus, *oak;* Druidæ, *Oakites.*" Whatever grows on that tree, more than its natural growth, they think has been sent from heaven, and is a proof that the tree has been chosen by God himself. However that [species of misletoe] is very rarely found, and when found it is sought after with great devotion; and especially at the sixth moon, which is the beginning of their months and years, and when the tree has passed its thirtieth year, because it has already abundant vigour, though not half-grown. They call it by a word signifying in their own language, ALL-HEAL; and having prepared sacrifices and feasts under the tree, they bring up two white bulls, whose horns are then first bound; the priest in a white robe ascends the tree, and cuts it off with a golden knife: it is received in a white sheet. Then, and not till then, they sacrifice the victims, praying that God would render his gift prosperous to those on whom he had bestowed it. When misletoe is given as a potion, they are of opinion that it can remove animal barrenness, and that it is a remedy against all poisons.

Uile-iomlan, *a.* All-perfect.

Uile-iomlanachd, *s. f.* All-sufficiency; infinite perfection.

Uile-ionadach, *a.* Omnipresent.

Uile-ionadachd, *s. f.* Omnipresence.

Uile-lathaireach, *a.* Omnipresent.

Uile-lathaireachd, *s. f.* Omnipresence.

Uile-leirsinneach, *a.* All-seeing.

Uile-leirsinneachd, *s. f.* The divine perfection of seeing all things.

Uile-shlugach, *a.* All-devouring.

Uilidh, *a.* All. Gu h-uilidh, *altogether, completely, wholly.*

Uilinne. See **Uileann.**

Uilinneachd, *s. f.* (*Ir. id.*) Elbowing; side by side.

Uille, *gen. sing.* of uileann.

Uille, *gen. sing.* of uillidh.

Uillidh, uille, *s. m.* Oil. *Gr.* ἔλαιον. *Teut.* olie. *Fr.* huile. *Box. Lex.* eli.

Uillnean, *n. pl.* uileann. Elbows; arms.

Uilt, *gen. sing.* and *n. pl.* alt. Of a joint; joints. Uilt a shliasad, *the joints of his thighs.*—*Stew. Ecc.*

Uilt, uillt, *gen. sing.* and *n. pl.* of alt. Of a stream or torrent; torrents.

† **Uim**, *s. m.* (*Ir. id. Lat.* humus.) The earth.—*Shaw.*

Uim-chealllach, aich, *s. m.* Any close private place.

Uim-chladh, *s. m.* Circumvallation.

Uim-dhruid, *v. a.* (*Ir.* um-dhruid.) Enclose; besiege; shut up close.

Uim-ghlac, *v. a.* (*Ir.* um-ghlac.) Gripe, grasp, embrace.

Uime, *prep.* About, concerning, respecting, regarding.

Uime, *comp. pron.* About him; concerning him or it.

Uimeach, ich, *s. m.* A brazier.

Uime sin, *adv.* Therefore, on that account, concerning that, on that head.

Uimhir, *s. m.* Number; amount; sum; equal quantity. *W.* nuimhir. *Ir.* uimhir. *Lat.* numerus.

Uimhir, *adv.* As many; as much. Uimhir ri so, *as much as this.*

Uimhreach, *a.* Numerous, plenteous.

Uimhreachail, *a.* Arithmetical, numeral, numerical.

Uimhreachan, ain, *s. m.* (*from* uimhir.) An arithmetician.

Uimhseann, einn, *s. m.* The ash; the wood or timber of the ash. Craobh uimhseinn, *an ash-tree.*

Uimite, *a.* (*Ir. id.*) Corpulent.

Uimpe, *comp. pron.* (*Ir. id.*) About her; around her; concerning her.

Uim-sheol, *v. a.* Circumnavigate.

Uim-sheoladh, aidh, *s. m.* Circumnavigation.

Uim-sheoladair, *s. m.* A circumnavigator.

Uim-shruth, *s.* Circumfluence.

Ùine, *s. f.* (*Ir.* uain.) Time, season. Caith t-ùine le feidh an aonaich, *spent your time with the mountain-deer.*—*Oss. Fin. and Lor.* Ar n-ùine a ruith air sgiathaibh, *our time flying on wings.*—*Orr.* Cha 'n eil ùine agam, *I have no leisure.*

Uineachd, *s. f.* Leisure, vacation.

† **Uineamh**, *s. m.* (*Ir. id.*) Strength.

Uine-shaor, *s. f.* Leisure, vacation.

Uinge, *s. f.* (*Ir. id.*) An ounce.

Uinich, *s. f.* Hurry, bustle; confusion, disturbance.—*Macfar. Voc.* Le mòran ùinich, *with much bustle.*—*Macint.*

Uinneag, eig, *s. f.* A window. Na uinneig bha ian na h-oidhche, *in his window was the bird of night.*—*Oss. Conn.* A gearradh mach uinneaga, *cutting out windows.* —*Stew. Jer.*

Uinneagach, *a.* Windowed; having many windows; of, or belonging to, a window.

Uinneagachadh, (ag), *pr. part.* of uinneagaich. Making windows, cutting out windows.

Uinneagaich, *v. a.* Make windows; provide with windows, insert windows. *Pret.* dh'uinneagaich; *fut. aff.* uinneagaichidh.

Uinneagaichte, *p. part.* of uinneagaich. Windowed.

Uinnean, ein, *s. m.* An onion. *N. pl.* uinneanan, *onions.* —*Stew. Num.* *Ir.* unniun. *Fr.* ognon. *Arm.* ouignoun.

Uinneanach, *a.* Like an onion; of onions; full of onions; producing onions.

Uinneanaich, *v. a.* Provide with onions.

Uinnseann, einn, *s. m.* The ash; the wood or timber of the ash-tree.

Uipear, eir, *s. m.* A clown or boor; a churl, a surly fellow. *N. pl.* uipeirean.

Uipeireach, *a.* Clownish, boorish; churlish, surly.

Uipearachd, *s. f.* Clownishness, boorishness; churlishness, surliness.

Uir, *s. m.* The eighteenth and last letter (U) of the Gaelic alphabet.

Uir, *s. f.* (*Ir. id. Corn.* oar *and* uor.) Earth, soil, mould, land, dust; a mound; *figuratively*, a grave; *also*, fire Thogas an ùir tharta, *the earth was raised over them* — *Oss. Cathluno.* An ùir thioram, *the dry land* —*Stew Gen. ref.* Togsa m' ùir, *raise thou my grave.*—*Oss. Fing* Fo 'n uir, *in the dust, under the ground, in the grave*.

Uircean, ein, *s. m.* A pig; a young pig; grice.

Uirceanach, *a.* Like a pig; of a pig; abounding in pigs.

Uir-chomhnuidh, **Uir-chònnuidh**, *s. m.* A dwelling of clay; a grave or tomb. Thogadh ùir-chomhnuidh do 'n laoch, *a tomb was raised for the hero.*—*Oss.*

Uird, *gen. sing.* and *n. pl.* of ord; which see.

Uire, *com.* and *sup.* of ùr; which see.

Uire, *s f.* Freshness; greenness.

Uiread, eid, *s. m.* Greenness; increase in greenness. A dol an ùiread, *growing more and more green.*

Ùiread, *s. m.* (*Ir. id*) An equal quantity; an equal number, *adjectively*, as much; as many; so much. A dha uiread arain, *twice as much bread.*—*Stew. Ex.* Leth uiread, *half as much.*—*Id* Uiread as chum a bhéil, *so much as to his mouth.*—*Stew. Pro* Gun uiread as sgillinn, *without so much as a penny* —*Mac Co.* Uiread is so, *as much as this.*

Uireas, eis, *s. m.* Bail, security; warrant; want Gun uireas air siothainn no frithe, *without want of venison or forest.*—*Oss Dargo.* *Uireas*, in the sense of *bail* or *security*, is more frequently written *urras*.

Uireasbhach, *a.* (*Ir* uireasbach) See **Uireasbhuidheach**.

Uireasbhuidh, *s. f.* (*Ir.* uireasbadh.) Want, indigence, lack, poverty; abjectness; deficiency. D'uireasbhuidh, *thy want.*—*Stew. Pro.*

Uireasbhuidheach, *a.* Indigent, needy, abject, beggarly, deficient Duine uireasbhuidheach, *an indigent man* Ceud-thoiseach uireasbhuidheach, *beggarly elements.* — *Stew. Gal.*

Uireasbhuidheach, ich, *s. m.* An indigent man, a beggar

Uir-fhamh, *s. m.* A mole; the *talpa europæus* of Linnæus Dùcan uir-fhamh, *a mole-hill.*

Uirghioll, ill, *s. m* Eloquence; utterance—(*Macfar. Voc.*), language; delivery; narration, history; command.

Uirghiollach, *a.* Eloquent.

Uir-ghreann, *s. m.* Puberty.

Uir-ghreannach, *a* (*Ir. id*) Adolescent; at the age of puberty

Uir-ghreannachd, *s. f.* (*Ir id*) Puberty, ripeness of age

Uiridh. See **Uirigh**.

Uiridh, (an), *adv* Last year An time so 'n uiridh, *this time last year.*—*Macint* *An uiridh* seems to be *an uair a ruith.*

Uirigioll, ill, *s. m* Eloquence; utterance; delivery; language; narration; history; command. Uirigioll cruaidh, *difficult utterance* —*Sm* Cha 'n eil cainnte no uirigioll, *there is neither language nor speech* —*Id.*

Uirigh, *s. f.* A couch, a bed. Le deuraibh m' uirigh uisgichim, *with tears I will water my couch.*—*Sm* *N pl.* uirighean; *d. pl* uirighibh. Air an uirighibh, *on their couches.*—*Stew Amos.*

Uir-iosal, *a.* (ùir, *dust, and* iosal, *low.*) *Ir. id.* Lowly, humble; mean, base, cringing

Uir-isle, *s. f.* (*Ir. id*) Lowliness; meanness

Uir-islich, *v. a.* (*Ir.* uirisligh) Debase, hamble, cast down; disparage. *Pret a.* dh'uirislich, *debased*, *fut. aff.* uirislichidh.

Uir-islichte, *p. part.* of uir-islich,

Uirlios, *s. m.* (*Ir. id*) A garden; a walled garden

Uirneas, eis, *s. m.* (*Ir id*) A furnace.

Uirneasach, *a.* Having furniture; of, or belonging to, furniture; furniture.

Uirre, *comp. pron.* See **Oirre**.

Uis, *s.* Use, utility, service. Ged tha mi 'deanamh uis deth, *though I make use of it.*—*Macint.* Gun uis, *useless.*

Uisdealachd, *s. f.* Supplication.

Uiseag, eig, *s. f* *Ir.* uiseog A lark; the *alauda arvensis* of Linnæus Sgiath na h-uiseig, *the lark's wing* —*Oss Com* Guth na faoin-uiseig, *the voice of the lonely lark* — *Oss. Taura.*

Uiseagach, *a.* Like a lark; abounding in larks.

Uisealachd, *s f.* Usefulness, utility.

Uisfil, *a.* (uis-amhuil) Serviceable, useful Gu h-uiseil, *usefully.*

Uisge, *s m* Water, rain; a shower; a river; a stream. *N. pl* uisgeachan. Mar uisge ri h-aonaich, *like a stream over the hill.*—*Ull* Fior-uisge, *a running stream.* Mar uisge balbh a ghlinne, *like the noiseless waters of the valley* —*Oss. Fin. and Lor.* Uisge beatha, *whisky.* *N. pl.* uisgeacha *or* uisgeachan. Uisgeacha na dile, *the waters of the flood.*—*Stew Gen*

Turk su *and* schuy, *water* *Belg* esck *and* asch *Old Brit.* isca *Corn. Arm.* isge. *Ir.* uisg. *Esk*, the name of a river in Scotland.

It was as common with the ancient Britons as it is with the Highlanders of the present times, to give rivers the name of *uisge*, which the Romans, in accordance with the terminations of their own language, wrote *isca* and *asca* These words were retained, in a contracted form, in the English language, in the names *ask*, *esk*, *osk*, which, in process of time, ran into a metathetic form, *ax*, *ex*, *ox*, signifying *water*, and still retained in the names of certain streams in England

Uisgeach, *a.* Watery; pluvial; causing rain

Uisgeacha, **Uisgeachan**, *n. pl.* of uisge; which see

Uisgeachadh, aidh, *s m.* The act of watering or moistening.

Uisgeachadh, (ag), *pr. part.* of uisgich.

Uisgealachd, *s f.* Wateriness, swampiness, moistness.

Uisge-beatha, *s m.* Whisky Uisge beatha baothal, *whisky four times distilled.*

Uisge-caisreachd, *s* A kind of holy water formerly drank by the Gael at Christmas, and believed to be a preservative against the machinations of evil spirits and witchcraft, until the next anniversary.

Uisgeil, *a.* (uisge-amhuil) Watery, swampy, fenny, moorish.

Uisge-nimhe, *s m.* Sulphuric or vitriolic acid, aqua fortis.

Uisgich, *v a* (*from* uisge) *Ir* uisgigh Water; moisten, wet *Pret. a.* dh'uisgich, *watered; fut aff a* uisgichidh, *shall water.* Dh'uisgich Apollos, *Apollos watered* —*Stew 1 Cor*

Uisgidh, *n pl* of uisge. Waters; rivers Na h-uisgidh dorcha, *the dark waters* —*Sm.*

Uisgidh, *a.* (*from* uisge.) Watery—(*Macfar. Voc*), swampy; blear.

Uisge-oillt, *s. f.* Hydrophobia.

Uisge-ruith, *s.* A running water or stream. Osciomn nan uisge-ruith, *above the running water.*—*Stew. Lev*

Uistre, *s. m.* An oyster

Ula, **Uladh**, aidh, *s m.* (*Ir.* ulcha, *a beard* *Gr* οὖλος, *heavy curled hair*) A beard, *figuratively*, long grass. 'Fholt is ula feadh na gaoithe, *his hair and beard streaming in the wind.*—*Oss. Manos* Uladh aosda air uchd, *his aged beard on his breast.*—*Oss. Taura* Ri fead an ula na h-uaimh, *whistling in the long grass of the cavern.* — *Oss Manos*

Ulach, aich, *s m.* (*Ir* ulcha) A beard.

Ulach, *a.* Bearded

Uladh, aidh, *s. m.* See **Ula**

Uladh, aidh, *s m* A fine, mulct; tax, impost Cuir ùladh, *lay a fine*

Uladh, aidh, *s.* (*Ir id.*) A jerk.

ULAG, aig, *s. f* A pulley. *N. pl* ulagan.

ULAGACH, *a.* Having pullies, like a pulley; of, or belonging to, a pulley.

ULAIDH, *s f.* (*Ir id*) A hoard, a treasure; a treasure found; a packsaddle. Chaill sinn an t-sàr ulaidh, *we have lost the precious treasure —Macfar* M' ulaidh, *my darling, my treasure —Macfar Voc.*

ULAINN, *s f.* A charnel-house.

ULARTAICH, *s f.* Howling, roaring Ulartaich nam buachaillean, *the shepherds' howling.—Stew Zech.* Written also *ulfhartaich.*

ULCHADH, aidh, *s. m* (*Ir.* ulcha) A beard.

ULFHARTAICH, *s f* Howling, roaring. Làn ulfhartaich, *full of howling —Stew Deut.*

ULLACHADH, aidh, *s. m* A preparing; preparation

ULLACHADH, (ag), *pr. part.* of ullaich Preparing

ULLAG, aig, *s. f* As much of meal or of any pulverized substance as can be lifted between the thumb and two fingers, *also*, a mouthful of meal, a kind of multure — *Macfar Voc*

ULLAICH, *v a* (*for* ullamhaich) Prepare, make ready, adjust, put in order. *Pret a.* dh'ullaich, *prepared; fut aff.* ullaichidh, *shall prepare, fut. pass.* ullaichear, *shall be prepared*

ULLAICHTE, *p part.* of ullaich. Prepared, made ready, adjusted.

ULLAMH, *a* (*Ir. id*) Ready, in readiness; finished, done, over Bheil thu ullamh? *are you ready?* Ullamh chum urchoid, *ready for mischief;*—the Irish say the same.

ULLAMHACHD, *s f.* Readiness, completeness; completion;

ULLAMHAICH, ULLMHUICH, *v. a* Prepare, make ready, adjust, put in order. *Pret a.* dh'ullmhuich, *fut aff* ullmhuichidh Ullmhuichidh mise thu, *I will prepare thee. —Stew. Ezek*

ULLMHUICHTE, *p part* of ullmhuich. Prepared, made ready.

ULLDACH. See ULLTACH

ULLTACH, aich, *s* (*Ir.* ulltach) An armful; a burden carried within the fold or grasp of the arms; a bundle. Ulltach feòir, *an armful of grass* Rinn i adhart do 'n ulltach bu tirime, *she made his shroud of driest [grass].— Oss Fin and Lor.*

ULLUICH See ULLOICH

ULLUICHTE, *p. part* of ulluich. See ULLAICHTE.

ULTACH, aich, *s m* An Ulsterman

UMAD, *comp pron* (*Ir id*) About thee, around thee, respecting thee; upon thee; on thine account

UMADAIL, *a.* Boorish; unsocial

UMADH, aidh, *s. m* A withe used to fasten the door of a cow-house

UMAIBH, *comp pron* About you, around you, concerning you, on your account. Fuidh amharus umaibh, *in doubt about you.—Stew. Gal*

UMAIDH, *s m* An ignorant boor, a booby, a fellow of vulgar manners San duine chòir cha bhi ach umaidh, *the worthy man shall be deemed a boor —Old Song*

UMAINN, *comp. pron* (*Ir. id*) About us, around us, concerning us; on our account Dh'iadh iad umainn, *they surrounding us.—Oss. Duthona*

UMAM, *comp pron.* About me, around me; concerning me, on my account

UMAR, air (*Ir id.*) See AMAR.

UMARLAID, *s f* A vulgar bulky female

UMASTAR, air, *s m.* (*Ir. id.*) Circumference

UM-DHRUID. See UIM-DHRUID

UM-GHLAC. See UIM-GHLAC.

UMHA, *s m* (*Ir id*) Brass; copper. Airgiod is umha, *silver and brass —Stew. Ex.*

UMHACH, *a.* Brazen; of copper.

UMHADAN, *s m* A brazier; a copper-smith; a tinker.

UMHADAIREACHD, *s. f.* The trade or business of a brazier or of a copper-smith; braziery.

UMHAIL See UMHAILL.

UMHAILEACH, *a.* See UMHAILLEACH.

UMHAILL, *s. f* (*Ir. id*) Heed, consideration, attention; doubt, suspicion. Gun umhaill do 'n lot, *heedless of the wound —Oss. Cathluno.* Na biodh umhaill agaibh, *do not heed —Stew Song Sol* Gun umhaill, *without suspicion, heedless*, cha 'n eil umhaill, *there is no matter;* ciod an umhaill th'agadsa? *what matters it to you? what business is it of yours?* cuir umhaill, *suspect.*

UMHAILLEACH, *a.* Heedful, attentive, considerate, careful; suspicious, scrupulous. Gu h-umhailleach, *heedfully.*

UMHAILLEACHD, *s. f* Heedfulness, attentiveness, a habit of attention, suspiciousness

UMHAL, *a.* (*Ir id. Corn* huvel. *Lat.* humilis) Submissive, obedient, subordinate; humble, lowly Umhal an cridhe, *lowly in heart —Stew. Mat.* Umhal do lagh, *obedient to law.—Stew. Rom.*

UMHLA. See UMHLADH.

UMHLACH, *a.* Apt to impose a fine; relating to a fine.

UMHLACHADH, aidh, *s. m.* (*Ir.* umhlughadh.)

UMHLACHAIL, *a.* Liable to penalty or fine; penal.

UMHLACHD, *s f* (*Ir. id.*) Obedience, submission, submissiveness, humbleness, obeisance; the practice of imposing penalties; taxation. Rinn iad ùmhlachd, *they made obeisance —Stew Gen* Umhlachd a chreidimh, *the obedience of faith —Stew. Rom.*

UMHLADH, aidh, *s f* A fine or penalty; a tax, tribute, or impost Iocaidh iad umhladh, *they shall pay a fine — Mac Lach*

UMHLAICH, *v. a.* (*Ir.* umhlaigh.) Humble, humiliate; make submissive. *Pret a.* dh'umhlaich, *humbled; fut aff* umhlaichidh, *shall humble.* Umhlaich thu féin, *submit thyself —Stew Gen*

UMHLAICHTE, *p part.* Humbled.

UMHRUISG See URUISG.

UMHRUISGEACH, *a* See URUISGEACH

UMPA, *comp pron* About them, round them; respecting them, concerning them Eudach saic umpa, *sackcloth about them.—Stew. Jon*

UMPAIR, *s. m* An umpire, an arbiter, a judge.—*Macfar, Voc N. pl* umpairean

UMPAIREACH, *a* Like an umpire or arbiter, of, or belonging to, an umpire or arbiter

UMPAIREACHD, *s f* The employment of an umpire or arbiter; arbitration

UMURLAID, *s m.* A vulgar bulky female.—*Macfar. Voc.*

UNAICH, *s. f* Hurry, bustle, confusion, struggle, rivalry; disturbance. Le mòran unaich, *with much bustle.—Macint.*

UNAMAID, *s f* (*Ir id*) A salve

UNFAIRT, *v n* (*Ir. id*) Toss, wallow; tumble. See AONAIRT

UNFAIRT, *s. f.* (*Ir id.*) A tossing; a wallowing or tumbling See AONAIRT.

UNG, *v. a.* Anoint, besmear, daub. *Pret. a.* dh'ung, *anointed, fut. aff. a.* ungaidh, *shall anoint, fut. pass.* ungar.

UNGA, ai, *s m.* An ingot.

UNGA, ai, *s m.* Brass, copper. Airgiod is unga, *silver and brass.—Stew Ex ref* and *Lev.*

Ungadh, aidh, *s. m.* (*Ir. id.*) An anointing; *also*, ointment, unguent. Ungadh deireannach, *extreme unction.* Ungadh bàis, *extreme unction.—Macfar. Voc.* Oladh ungaidh, *oil for anointing.*

Ungaidh. See **Ung.**

Ungar. See **Ung.**

Ungta, Ungte, *p. part.* of ung. (*Ir.* ungtha.) Anointed; besmeared, bedaubed. Aon ungta Dhe, *the anointed one of God.—Sm.*

Unnsa, *s. m.* An ounce.
Lat. uncia. *Fr.* once. *Teut.* onçu. *Arm.* onç.

Untas, ais, *s. m.* (*Ir. id.*) A windlass.

Untasach, *a.* Of, or belonging to, a windlass; like a windlass.

Upag, aig, *s. f.* A shove, a push, a thrust.

Upagach, *a.* Shoving, pushing, thrusting.

Upagaich, *v.* Push, shove, thrust; jostle, jolt. *Pret.* dh' upagaich.

Upagaich, *s. f.* A pushing, a shoving, a thrusting; a jostling.

Upairneach, *a.* Bustling; noisy.

Upairneachd, *s. f.* Bustle; continued or frequent bustle or noise.

Ur, *s. m.* (*Arm.* ur, *a man.*) A child; a person. *N. pl.* urachan. Ur bheag, *an infant.*

† **Ur**, *s. m.* (*Ir. id.*) Mould; heath; a beginning.

Ur, *s. m.* (*Gr.* οὐρα, *a tail.*) A tail; a harm; a border or brink; heath. Ur, *heath.—Statist. Acc. Blair Athol.*

Ur, *a.* (*Ir. id.*) Fresh; new; recent. Osag ùr nan sliabh, *the fresh breeze of the mountains.—Oss. Lodin.* Righ ùr, *a new king.—Stew. Ex.* Truscan ùr, *a new garment.—Stew.* 1 *K.* Ur nomh, *quite new.*

Ur, (as), *adv.* Anew; afresh; again; a second time. Am bròn as ùr, *in grief anew.—Oss. Tem.* Sgaoil cuirm as ùr, *the feast was spread a second time.—Oss. Fing.*

Ur, (*for* bhur.) *poss. pron.* Your. Aobhar ur bròin, *the cause of your grief.—Ull.* Togaibh ur siùil, tairnibh ur raimh, *raise your sails, pull your oars.—Id.*

Urach, aich, *s. m.* A bottle; a pail.

Ùrachadh, aidh, *s. m.* A freshening, a refreshing; a recommencing; refreshment; recommencement, renewal.

Urachadh, (ag), *pr. part.* of ùraich.

Urachair, *a.* See **Furachair.**

Ùrachd, *s. f.* Newness; freshness; strangeness. Bheil ùrachd nuaidheachd agad? *have you got any news?*

Urachdag, aig, *s. f.* A thowl. *N. pl.* urachdagan.

Urag, aig, *s. f.* (*dim.* of ur.) A little child.

Ùraich, *v. a.* and *n.* (*from* ùr.) Refresh, renew; become fresh, make fresh; strive. *Pret. a.* dh'ùraich, *refreshed; fut. aff.* ùraichidh, *shall refresh.* Cha 'n ùraich mo gheug am feasd, *my branch shall never become fresh.—Ardar.* Nur dh'ùraicheas an strì, *when the battle renews.—Oss. Fing.*

Ùraichte, *p. part.* of uraich. Made fresh; renewed; refreshed.

Uraidh, (an). See **Uiridh**, (an).

Ùrail, *a.* (ùr-amhuil.) Fresh; flourishing; juicy.—*Macfar. Voc.*

Uraireachd, *s. f.* Freshness; greenness; verdure; juiciness; coolness.—*Macint.*

Uran, ain, *s. m.* (*Ir. id.*) A welcome; courtesy; affability. See **Furan.**

Uranach, *a.* See **Furanach.**

Ùranach, aich, *s. m.* (*from* ùr.) An upstart.—*Macd.*

† **Uranach**, *a.* (*Ir. id.*) Ignoble; conversant.

Uranachd, *s. f.* (*Ir. id.*) The condition of an upstart; cold bathing; conversation.

Uranta, *a.* See **Urranta.**

Urar, *a.* (*for* urmhor.) Fresh; green; verdant; juicy; flourishing. San iarmailt ùrair, *in the freshly green firmament.—Oss. Fin. and Lor.* A choillteach ùrac, *the green wood.—Oss. Cathula.*

Urard, aird, *s. m.* High ground; a place situated on high ground.

Urbhallach, aich, *s. m.* The herb devil's-bit.

Ur-bharrach, aich, *s.* Green branches, green foliage.

Urbheachd, *s. f.* An after-thought.

Ur-bhlath, *s.* A blossom; a flower; a fresh blossom.

Ur-bhlaith, *a.* (*Ir. id.*) Fruitful; abounding in blossom.

Urc, *s. m.* (*Ir. id.*) An inclosure; a fold.

Urchail, *s. pl.* (*Ir. id.*) Fetters or chains.

Urchailte, *s. pl.* (*Ir. id.*) Fettered, chained.

Urchair, *s. f.* A shot; a cast; a throw; the report of a gun. Urchair gunna, *a gun-shot;* beul ri urchair gunna as, *about a gun-shot off;* thoir urchair, *throw or cast;* leig urchair, *fire a shot.*

Urchaireachd, *s. f.* A shooting; a throwing or casting, as of a stone; the amusement of shooting or firing.

Urchall, aill, *s. m.* (*Ir. id.*) Hinderance; a spaniel.

Ur-chleas, *s. m.* A feat; a clever action.

Ur-chleasach, *a.* Active, nimble, quick in performing feats.

Ur-chleasachd, *s. f.* Activity, nimbleness; legerdemain; juggling.

Ur-chleasaiche, *s. m.* An adept in legerdemain; a juggler or conjurer.

Urchoid, *s. f.* (*Ir. id.*) Harm, mischief; adversity, calamity; loss; accident; violence. Ann an latha d'urchoid, *in the day of thy calamity.—Stew. Pro. ref.* La na h-urchoid, *the day of adversity.—Stew. Ecc.* Le urchoid, *with violence.—Stew. Gen. ref.* Written also *urchuid.*

Urchoideach, *a.* (*Ir. id.*) Mischievous; calamitous; detrimental; adverse.

Urchoill, *s. f.* A green wood. Mòra nan urchoill, *green-wooded Mora.—Oss. Tem.*

Urchoir. See **Urchair.**

Urchoireachd. See **Urchaireachd.**

Urchosg, oisg, *s. m.* (*Ir. id.*) An antidote, a preservative against any evil.

Ur-chrann, ainn, *s. m.* A green tree; a fresh tree; a fresh or green branch; a flourishing tree. Mar ùr-chrann uaine, *like a flourishing green tree.—Sm.*

Urchuid, *s. f.* Harm, mischief; adversity, calamity, loss, accident; damage, violence. Urchuid air urchuid, *mischief on mischief.—Stew. Ezek.*

Urchuideach, *a.* See **Urchoideach.**

Urchullach, aich, *s. m.* A heifer of a year and a half old.

Urchur, uir, *s. m.* (*Ir. id.*) A shot; a throw or cast; a gun-shot. More frequently *urchair.*

† **Urdail**, *s. f.* (*Ir. id.*) A collection; a large share.

Ùr-dharaig, *s. f.* A young oak; a flourishing oak. Sgaoilidh do chliùsa mar ur-dharaig, *thy fame shall spread like the flourishing oak.—Oss. Duthona.*

Ur-dhubhadh, *s. m.* (*Ir. id.*) An eclipse—(*Macfar. Voc.*); a darkening. Ur-dhubhadh na grèine, *an eclipse of the sun;*—the Irish say the same.

Ur-fhalluinn, *s.* A new robe or garment. Thigibh oighrean, le ùr-fhalluinn, *come, ye maidens, with a new garment.—Ull.*

Ur-fhas, *s. m.* A sprout; a bud; a shoot; a new growth; a fresh growth.

Ur-fhas, *v. n.* Sprout, bud, or shoot; grow afresh. *Pret. a.* dh' ùr-fhas; *fut. aff.* ur-fhàsaidh. Ur-fhàsaidh si, *it will grow again.—Stew. Job.*

Ur-fhasach, *a.* Casting sprouts or buds; producing sprouts, buds, or shoots.

Ur-ghairdeachas, ais, *s. m.* (*Ir. id.*) Great rejoicing; congratulation.

Urghais, *s. f.* (*Ir. id.*) Exchange; alteration.

Ur-ghorm, *a.* Freshly green. Ag ionaltiadh fhasach urghorm, *grazing on the freshly virid field.—Macfar.*

Urgra, *s. m.* (*Ir. id.*) A battle; a loss.

Urla, *s. m.* A floor. More frequently written *urlar;* which see.

Urla, urladh, aidh, *s. m.* (*Ir. id.*) A front or forehead; a visage or countenance; an aspect; a bottom; a place lying low among hills; a lock of hair; the breast. Air urla ghleann, *in the bottom of the valleys.—Oss. Fing.* M' urla 'g eiridh ard, *my breast rising high.—Oss. Lodin.*

Ur-labhairt, *s. f.* (*Ir.* ur-labhair.) Graceful speaking, rhetoric, eloquence, oratory.

Ur-labhairteach, *a.* Eloquent; rhetorical; oratorical. *—Macfar. Voc.*

Ur-labhairteachd, *s. f.* Elocution; rhetoric; oratory.

Ur-labhairtear, eir, *s. m.* An orator, a rhetorician; a graceful speaker.

Ur-labhrach, *a.* Eloquent, rhetorical.

Ur-labhradh, aidh, *s. m.* Eloquence, rhetoric; graceful utterance. Anns gach ùr-labhradh, *in all utterance.—Stew. Rom. Cor.*

Urlach, *a.* Having long hair; having ringlets or curls. Cas-urlach, *curled.—Macdon.*

Urladh. See **Urla.**

Urlaich, *v. a.* Hate, detest. Dh' urlaich i ris, *she detests him.*

† **Urlaidh**, *s. f.* A skirmish.

Urlaim, *s. f.* Readiness, preparation.—*Macfar. Voc.*

Urlaimh, *a.* (*Ir.* urlamh.) Neat, trim, tidy; ready-handed; quick in reading.—*Macfar. Voc.*

Urlaimh, *s. f.* (*Ir. id.*) Readiness; preparation.

Urlamaich, *v. a.* Prepare, make ready.—*Macfar. Voc.*

Urlamhas, ais, *s. m.* (*Ir. id.*) Possession; captivity.

Urlàn, *a.* (*Ir. id.*) Very full.

Urlann, ainn, *s. m.* (*Ir. id.*) A staff.

Urlar, air, *s. m.* (uir-lar.) *Ir. id.* A floor; a groundfloor; a pavement; the ground; the earth; a floor of earth or clay; a low place or bottom among hills. Urlar-arbhair, *a corn-floor.—Stew. Hos.* Urlar-bualaidh, *a threshing-floor.—Id.* Urlar chlach, *a pavement of stones.—Stew.* 2 *K.* Urlar bhord, *a deal-floor.*

Urlarachadh, aidh, *s. m.* The act of flooring, or laying a floor.

Urlaraich, *v. a.* Lay a floor; floor. *Pret. a.* dh' urlaraich, *floored; fut. aff. a.* urlaraichidh, *shall floor. P. part.* urlaraichte, *floored, having a floor.*

Urlaraiche, *s. m.* One who lays a floor; one who mines or prepares clay or earth for a floor.

Urlaraichte. See **Urlaraich.**

Urlatach, aich, *s. m.* (*Ir. id.*) A tumbler, a stage-player.

Urlataidh, *s. f.* (*Ir. id.*) Agility.

Urloisgeach, *a.* Fervent, keen, zealous; causing or promoting zeal.—*Macfar. Voc.*

Urlosgadh, aidh, *s. m.* Fervour, zeal, keenness.

Ùr-luachair, -luachrach, *s. f.* (*Ir. id.*) Green rushes, young rushes.—*Macfar. Voc.*

Ùr-mheangan, ain, *s. m.* A young branch; a twig. Ur-mheangan nan carn, *the young branches of the rocks.—Macfar.*

Ùrmhoireachd, *s. f.* Freshness, greenness, juiciness, newness.

Ùrmhor, *a.* Fresh, green; juicy; flourishing; recent. *Com.* and *sup.* ùrmhoire, *more* or *most green.*

Urnuigh, *s. f.* (*Ir.* urnaighe.) A prayer, a petition. Mil-tean urnuigh 'g ad leanachd, *a thousand prayers following thee.—Macfar.* Urnuigh an Tighearna, *the Lord's prayer;* dean urnuigh, *pray;* ri urnuigh, *praying;* ag urnuigh, *praying.*

Urr. See **Ur.**

Urra, **Urradh**, aidh, *s. m.* A person; a child; a being; power; strength; a good author; authority; a defendant at law; a chieftain; *adjectively,* able, capable. Urra 'chuireas leam, *a person who will aid me.—Sm.* Cha 'n urradh iad a thogail, *they cannot lift him.—Oss. Derm.* Is urradh dhomh, *I am able.*

Urrach, aich, *s. m.* A pull or haul; a pulling.

Urrachdag. See **Urachdag.**

Urrad, *a.* and *s.* As much, as many; so much, so many. Na h-urrad cheannais oirnne, *so much superiority over us.—Macfar.* Written also *uiread;* which see.

Urrag, aig, *s. f.* A little child; written also *urag.*

Urrail, *a.* Confident, self-sufficient; bold, impudent, forward.—*Macfar. Voc.*

Urraim, *gen. sing.* of urram.

Urrainn, *s. f.* and *a.* (*Ir. id.*) An author, authority; ability, power; a stay, a support. Sgeul gun urrainn, *a tale without an author;* na bi ad urrainn anns a bhréig, *be not the author of a lie.—Old Didactic Poem.* Cha 'n urrainn duit éiridh, *you cannot rise.*

Urralachd, *s. f.* Confidence, self-sufficiency; boldness, impudence.

Urram, aim, *s. m.* (*Ir. id.*) Respect, honour; deference; worship; significance, signification. Beartas agus urram, *riches and honour.—Stew. Pro.* A toirt urraim, *giving honour.—Stew. Jud.*

Urramach, *a.* (*Ir. id.*) Honourable; noble; honorary; reverend, worshipful; worthy, respected, distinguished. Bha e na b' urramaiche, *he was more honourable.—Stew. Gen.* Tha 'ainm urramach, *his name is reverend.—Sm.* Ball urramach, *an honorary member.*

Urramachd, *s. f.* (*Ir. id.*) Honourableness; nobleness; respectfulness; homage; submission; the state of being reverend.

Urramaich, *v. a.* (*Ir.* urramaigh.) Respect, honour, revere; worship, adore. *Pret. a.* dh' urramaich, *respected; fut. aff.* urramaichidh.

Urramaiche, *com.* and *sup.* of urramach; which see.

Urramaichte, *p. part.* of urramaich. Respected, honoured, revered.

Urranta, *a.* Bold, daring, dauntless; powerful; capable; confident in one's own strength or capacity. Fir meamnach urranta, *high-spirited and powerful men.—Mac Co.* and *Macdon.* Gu h-urranta, *boldly.*

Urrantachd, *s. f.* Boldness, dauntlessness, confidence in one's own strength or capacity.—*Macfar. Voc.*

Urras, ais, *s. m.* (*Ir.* urrudhas.) Security, surety; warrant; bail; caution; one who becomes bail for another; a bondsman, a bondswoman. Ma tha thu 'n urras, *if you are in surety.—Stew. Pro.* Theid mise an urras air do shon, *I shall go bail for you;* theid mise an urras ort, *I will warrant you.*

Urrasach, *a.* (*Ir.* urrudhasach.) Requiring bail or security; *also,* bold, daring, self-confident.

Urrasachd, *s. f.* The practice of becoming bail; insurance; *also*, boldness, intrepidity, self-confidence. Dàn leis an urrasachd, *bold with the confidence.—Stew.* 2 *Cor.*

Urrasail, *a.* (Urras-amhuil.) Bailable, admitting bail. Cionta urrasail, *a bailable offence.*

Urrasair, *s. m.* An insurer.

Ursa, *s. m.* A bear. *Lhuyd.*

Ursach, *a.* Bearish; full of bears.

Ursachd, *s. f.* Bearishness; a bearish temper.

Ursag, aig, *s. f.* (*Ir.* ursag.) A she-bear, a little bear, a young bear.

Ursainn, *gen. sing.* of ursann.

Ursan, ain, *s. m.* (*Ir. id.*) A defender.

Ursann, ainn, *s. m.* (*Ir.* ursain.) The sidepost of a door—(*Macfar. Voc.*); a support, a prop, a pillar. Air an da ursainn, *on the two sideposts.—Stew. Ex. N. pl.* ursainnean. Ursainnean do fhiondruinn, *sideposts of polished bone.—Fingalian Poem.*

Ursann-chatha, *s. m.* A support in time of war; a bulwark in battle; a chief, a champion; the ranks of an army in battle order. Chi mi tri ursanna chatha, *I see three champions.—Oss. Cathula.* Bristear leis ursanna chatha, *the ranks of battle shall be broken by him.—Id.*

Ursgar, air, *s. m.* (*Ir. id.*) A loud bawl.

Ursgartach, *a.* Sweeping cleanly.

Ursgartadh, aidh, *s. m.* A sweeping cleanly; sweepstakes.

Ursgeul, -sgéil, or -sgeoil, *s. m.* A tale, fable, or romance; a novel; a tale of later times, a modern tale.

Ursgeulachd, *s. f.* A tale of modern times; a romance.

Ursgeulaiche, *s. m.* A romancer; one who relates tales of modern times.

Ur-shneachd, *s. m.* Fresh snow, new-laid snow. Mar ùr-shneachd air bharraibh gheug, *like new-laid snow on the branches.—Ardin.*

Urspeal, *v. a.* Cut or mow down quickly.

Urspealach, *a.* Cutting or mowing down quickly.

Urspealachd, *s. f.* The process of cutting or mowing down.

Urspealaiche, *s. m.* One who cuts or mows down; a destroyer.

Ursuinn. See **Ursann.**

† **Ursul**, uil, *s. m.* (*Ir. id.*) A pair of tongs.

Ùruisg, *s. m.* (*perhaps* urr-uisge.) A brownie, or a being who was supposed to haunt lonely dells, moorland lakes, and waterfalls. He seems to have had the qualities of man and spirit curiously commingled.

Some have compared this class of imaginary beings to the satyrs of the ancients; but without reason, since they had no disposition, nor any point of character in common, excepting a fondness for solitude, which the *ùruisg* possessed only at certain seasons of the year. About the end of harvest he became more sociable, and hovered about farm-yards, stables, and cattle-houses. He had a particular fondness for the products of the dairy, and was a fearful intruder on milkmaids, who made regular libations of milk or cream to charm him off, or to procure his favour. He could be seen only by those who had the second-sight; yet I have heard of instances where he made himself visible to persons who were not so gifted. He is said to have been a jolly personable being, with a broad blue bonnet, flowing yellow hair, and a long walking-staff. Every manor-house had its *ùruisg*: and in the kitchen, close by the fire, was a seat which was left unoccupied for him. The house of a proprietor on the banks of the Tay is, even at this day, believed to have been haunted by this sprite, and a particular apartment therein has been for centuries called *seomar Bhrùnaidh*, Brownie's room. When irritated through neglect or disrespectful treatment, he would not hesitate to become wantonly mischievous. He was, notwithstanding, rather gainly and good-natured than formidable. Though, on the whole, a lazy, lounging hobgoblin, he would often bestir himself in behalf of those who understood his humours, and suited themselves thereto. When in this mood, he was known to perform many arduous exploits in kitchen, barn, and stable, (*nec cernitur ulli,*) with marvellous precision and rapidity. These kind turns were done without bribe, fee, or reward; for the offer of any one of these would banish him for ever. Kind treatment was all that he wished for; and it never failed to procure his favour.

In the northern parts of Scotland the *ùruisg's* disposition was more mercenary. Brand, in his description of Zetland, observes, that "not above forty or fifty years ago almost every family had a *brownie*, or evil spirit so called, which served them, to which they gave a sacrifice for his service; as when they churned their milk, they took a part thereof, and sprinkled every corner of the house with it for Brownie's use: likewise, when they brewed, they had a stone which they called *Brownie's stane*, wherein there was a little hole, into which they poured some wort for a sacrifice to Brownie. They also had stacks of corn which they called *Brownie's stacks*, which though they were not bound with straw ropes, or any way fenced as other stacks used to be, yet the greatest storm of wind was not able to blow away straw off them."

The brownies seldom discoursed with man, but they held frequent and affectionate converse with one another. They had their general assemblies too; and on these occasions they commonly selected for their rendezvous the rocky recesses of some remote torrent, whence their loud voices, mingling with the water's roar, carried to the ears of wondering superstition detached parts of their unearthly colloquies. In a certain district of the Highlands, Peallaidh *an spùit*, Slochdaill *a chùirt*, and Brunaidh *'n easain*, were names of note at those congresses; and they still live in legends which continue to amuse old age and infancy.

Uruisgeach, *a.* Like a brownie; haunted by brownies.

† **Us**, *s. m.* (*Ir. id.*) News; a story.

Usa, **Usadh**, (*for* fhusa), *com.* and *sup.* of furas. Easier, easiest. Is usa radh na chur an gniomh, *it is easier said than done.*

Usachd, *s. f.* Power; facility.

Usaid, *s. f.* (*Ir. id.*) Use.

Usgadh, aidh, *s. m.* (*Ir. id.*) Goose-grease.

Usgàr, air, *and* usgarach, *s. m.* (*Ir. id.*) A jewel, a pearl; an ornament, a necklace. Usgar do 'n òr, *an ornament of gold.—Stew. Pro. N. pl.* usgraichean. Thug e leis usgraichean, *he took with him ornaments.—Stew. Jud. D. pl.* usgraichibh. Le usgraichibh, *with jewels.—Stew. Song Sol.*

Usgarach, aich, *s. m.* Jewellery.

Usgaraiche, *s. m.* A jeweller.

Usgaraidh, *s. f.* Jewellery.

Usgar-bhraghad, *s. m.* A necklace; a jewel for the neck. —*Macfar. Voc.*

Usgar-laimhe, *s. m.* A bracelet; a jewel for the hand or wrist.—*Macfar. Voc.*

Usgar-mheur, *s. m.* A jewelled ring.

Usgraichean. See **Usgar.**

Usgraidh. See **Usgaraidh.**

† **Uslainn**, *s. f.* (*Ir. id.*) Play, sport.—*Shaw.*

† **Uslainneach**, *a.* (*Ir. id.*) Cheerful, brisk, merry; nimble.—*Shaw.* Gu h-uslainneach, *cheerfully.*

Uspag, aig, *s. f.* (*Ir. id.*) A pang; sudden pain. *N. pl.* uspagan.

Uspagach, *a.* Causing pangs, or sudden pains.

Uspan, ain, *s. m.* (*Ir. id.*) A huge, a shapeless lump or heap—(*Macfar. Voc.*); *in derision*, a clumsy fellow.

Uspairn, *s. f.* Emulation; strife, struggle, contention.—*Macfar. Voc.*

Uspairneach, *a.* (*Ir. id.*) Emulous; causing emulation; striving, struggling.

Uspairneachd, *s. f.* (*Ir. id.*) Emulation; the practice of emulation; strife, contention.

Uspairniche, *s. m.* An emulous person.

Usuireachd, *s. f.* (*Ir. id.*) Usury.

Utag, aig, *s. f.* (*Dan.* utak, *a reproof.*) A shove, a push, a jostle; strife, confusion, uproar.

Utagach, *a.* Apt to push, shove, or jostle, clamorous, noisy, confused, in disorder

Utagachadh, aidh, *s. m.* A pushing, shoving, or jostling; the act of raising noise, clamour, or confusion

Utagachadh, (ag), *pr. part.* of utagaich.

Utagaich, *v. a.* (*from* utag) Push, shove, jostle.

Uth, *s. m* (*Gr.* οὖθαρ.) An udder. Le 'n uthaibh làn, *with their udders distended.—Macdon.*

Uthach, *a* Having udders; having large udders; relating to an udder

Uthaibh, *d. pl* of uth.

Uthard, *adv.* Up, above, up there, up yonder, above there, above yonder. Uthard shuas, *up aloft*, uthard ud, *up yonder.*

Utlaiche, *s m.* An old hart Utlaiche nan cnoc, *the hart of the mountains.—Mac Lach*

Utlaidh, **Utluidh**. See **Udlaidh**.

Utrais, *gen. sing.* of utras.

Utraiseach. See **Utrasach**.

Utras, ais, *s m.* Molestation; restlessness; fidgeting; uneasiness.

Utrasach, *a.* Restless, uneasy, fidgeting; troublesome, vexatious.—*Macfar. Voc.*

Utrasachd, *s f.* Restlessness, uneasiness, fidgeting, troublesomeness, vexatiousness.

Utrasaiche, *com.* and *sup* of utrasach. More or most restless, or uneasy.

Utrod, oid, *s m.* A cattle-road *N pl.* utrodan.

Utrodach, *a.* Having a road for cattle; of, or belonging to, a cattle-road.

SUPPLEMENT.

A.

Abhadh, aidh, *s. m.* (*Ir. id.*) An abode; a lampoon or satire.

Abharach, aich, *s. m.* (*Ir. id.*) A manly youth.

Abhastrach, aich, *s. m.* (*Ir. id.*) The barking of a dog.

Abhlach, aich, *s. m.* (*Ir. id.*) A carcase.

Ab-mhathair, *s. f.* (*Ir. id.*) A mother-abbess. *N. pl.* ab-mhathraichean.

Abag, aig, *s. f.* (*Ir. id.*) A voice.

† **Abran**, ain, *s. m.* (*Ir. id.*) A song, a poem, an ode. *N. pl.* abrain.

Absaloid, *s. f.* (*Ir. id.*) Absolution.

Acnamhach, aich, *s. m.* (*Ir. id.*) The food of a labourer.

Acobhair, *s. f.* (*Ir. id.*) Avarice, penury.

Acrasach, *a.* (*Ir. id.*) Hungry.

Acsal, ail, *s. m.* (*Ir. id.*) An angel; *adjectively*, generous, noble.

Adhaill, *s. f.* (*Ir. id.*) A precipice.

Adhair, *s. f.* (*Ir. id.*) Fire.

† **Adhar**, air, *s. m.* (*Ir. id.*) Snow, frost.

Adhartar, air, *s. m.* (*Ir. id.*) A dream.

Adhas, ais, *s. m.* (*Ir. id.*) Good, prosperity.

Adhbhas, ais, *s. m.* (*Ir. id.*) A garrison.

Adhnàir, *s. m.* Villany; confusion; shamefacedness.

Agamh, aimh, *s. m.* (*Ir. id.*) A doubt; suspicion.

Agart, airt, *s. m.* (*Ir. id.*) Revenge; quarrel.

Aghnas, ais, *s. m.* Pleading, argumentation.

Aghradhaidh, *s. m.* (*Ir. id.*) Expostulation; challenging.

† **Aicne**, *s. f.* (*Ir. id.*) Nature.

Aicre, *s. f.* (*Ir. id.*) Inheritance, patrimony.

Aidhe, *s. f.* (*Ir. id.*) A monition; a house; a fortress.

Aidhear, eir, *s. m.* A cracking of the skin from being exposed to the weather.

Aidhne, *s. f.* (*Ir. id.*) Age; an advocate.

Aigeal, eil, *s. m.* (*Ir. id.*) The bottom of a valley.

Aighne, *s. m.* (*Ir. id.*) A prophet; a pleader.

Aileas, eis, *s. m.* (*Ir. id.*) A pleasant country.

Aillis, *s. f.* (*Ir. id.*) A cancer, a spreading sore.

Aillseach, *a.* (*Ir. id.*) Negligent.

Aillseag, eig, *s. f.* (*Ir. id.*) A caterpillar.

Aimheagan, ain, *s. m.* (*Ir. id.*) An abyss.

Aimrios, *s. m.* (*Ir. id.*) Error.

† **Aincidh**, *s. f.* (*Ir. id.*) A doubt.

† **Aincis**, *s. f.* (*Ir. id.*) A skin or hide.

Ainle, *s. f.* An insect with four legs and a winged tail, always living on trees.

Ainteach, *s. m.* Religious abstainment from eating flesh.

Airceas, eis, *s. m.* (*Ir. id.*) Maturity.

Airchis, *s. f.* (*Ir. id.*) A pledge; a meeting.

Airealach, *a.* (*Ir. id.*) Feeble.

Airghir, *s. f.* (*Ir. id.*) A cow-calf.

Airnean, ein, *s. m.* (*Ir. id.*) A watching at night.

Airneas, eis, *s. m.* (*Ir. id.*) Watchfulness.

Airneasach, *a.* (*Ir. id.*) Watchful.

Aisge, *s. f.* (*Ir. id.*) A present or gift.

Aitheadh, idh, *s. f.* A stealing away or retiring privately; elfshot.

Aiteas, eis, *s. m.* (*from* àite.) *Ir. id.* A dwelling-place.

Aiteasach, *a.* Glad, joyful.

Aithreach, ich, *s. m.* (*Ir. id.*) A farmer.

Aithreas, eis, *s. m.* (*Ir. id.*) Repentance.

Aithrin, *s. f.* (*Ir. id.*) A sharp point; a satirizing tongue.

Allas muire, *s. m.* (*Ir. id.*) St. John's wort.

Alltas, ais, *s. m.* (*Ir. id.*) Wildness; savageness.

† **Alluin**, *s. m.* (*Ir. id.*) Time.

Amaran, ain, *s. m.* (*Ir. id.*) Distress; a bungler.

Ama, *s. m.* (*Ir. id.*) The *hame* of a horse-collar.

† **Amhach**, aich, *s. m.* A vulture.

Amhad, aid, *s. m.* (*Ir. id.*) Rawness; crudeness. Air amhad, *however raw.*

Amhlach, *a.* (*Ir. id.*) Voracious.

Amhladh, aidh, *s. m.* (*Ir. id.*) Voracity.

Amhail, *s. f.* (*Ir. id.*) Evil, mischief.

† **Amhailt**, *s. f.* (*Ir. id.*) Death.

Amhall, aill, *s. m.* (*Ir. id.*) A visit.

Amhdhadh, aidh, *s. m.* Permission; a permitting.

Anach, aich, *s. m.* (*Ir. id.*) A path; anger; a washing.

Anairt, *a.* (*Ir. id.*) Soft, tender, mild, gentle; humane.

Anart, airt, *s. f.* (*Ir. id.*) A draught causing death.

An-duile, *s. f.* (*Ir. id.*) Inordinate desire; avidity.

Anglas, ais, *s. f.* (*Ir. id.*) Chalk and water.

Annamh, aimh, *s. m.* (*Ir. id.*) A wilderness.

Anradh, aidh, *s. m.* (*Ir. id.*) A boon, a petition.

Anraidh, *s. m.* A champion.

Ansgairt, *s. f.* (*Ir. id.*) A thicket.

† **Aodh**, *s. f.* Fire.

† **Aodh**, *s. m.* A liver; an eye.

Aoibhe, *s. f.* (*Ir. id.*) Neatness, elegance.

Aoineach, *a.* (*Ir. id.*) Fasting.

Aoireadh, idh, *s. m.* (*Ir. id.*) The corner of a sheet or sail.

Aol-phlàsd, *s. m.* (*Ir. id.*) A parget or plaster.

Aonach, aich, *s. m.* (*Ir. id.*) A fair, an assembly; a prince; a hill.

Arach, aich, *s. f.* (*Ir. id.*) A bier; a gallows.

Arachas, ais, *s. m.* (*Ir. id.*) Strength; might.

Arachdas, ais, *s. m.* (*Ir. id.*) Strength.

Armail, *s. f.* (*Ir. id.*) Arms, weapons; an armoury.

ARMHORACH, aich, s m. A native of Bretagne. N. pl. armhoraich.

ARRAIS, s f. (Ir. id.) Joy, pleasure; a streaming, a running

ARTACH, aich, s m. (Ir. id) A quarry.

ASGAL, ail, s. m. (Ir. id.) Flowing of the tide, conference.

ASTAL, ail, s. m (Ir. id.) A javelin, a spear or pike; a pike-staff, a chip or lath.

ATHACH, aich, s. m. (Ir. id) Fermentation.

ATHAIR LIATH, s m (Ir. id.) Mountain sage.

ATHAS, ais, s m (Ir. id) Victory.

ATHMHAOLTAS, ais, s. m. (Ir. id) Shame

B.

BAC, s. m. (Ir id) A spade or shovel.

BACADH, aidh, s. m (Ir. id.) Cow-dung

BACAS, ais, s m (Ir. id.) A captive, a hostage

BACHLADH, aidh, s m (Ir. id.) The head of a stick

BACHLACH, aich, s. m. (Ir. id.) A cudgeller

BAILT, s m A belt, a cingle.

BAIRCEAN, s pl. Cross-sticks or side-timbers in a house, between the rafters.

BAIRN, v a (Ir. id.) Judge, assure, warrant

BAISLEACH, ich, s m. Heavy rain; a stone where women were wont to wash.

BALL-NASG, aisg, s. m. (Ir. id) A ligament connecting the bones at the joints to prevent dislocation; the joints; the limbs.

BANAIDEACH, a. (Ir. id) Serious.

BANN, s m (Ir id) A band of men, a marching or journeying; an interdict.

BANNAG, aig, s. f. A cake. Mo bhannag ort, *a method of asking a new-year's cake*

BANNSACH, aich, s m A dart, an arrow.

BANSGOTH, s m (Ir id) A son-in-law.

BAOS, s m (Ir id) Fornication, caprice; frenzy, wickedness

BAOSACH, a. Wanton; capricious

BAOSRADH, aidh, s m Vanity

BAOTHANTAS, s m Folly, simplicity

BEALGACH, aich, s m. An interpreter

BEANNACH, aich, s m (Ir id) A fork

BEANNACHAN, ain, s m (Ir id) A cuckold

BEAN-EIGIN, s f (Ir. id) A rape

BEANN, s f (Ir id) Regard, attention, *rarely*, a bone, the arms of a cross.

BEARTAR, air, s m. A cart; a shot; a stroke

BEAS, s m Rent, tax, tribute

BEASGNAICH, v. a. (Ir id) Agree, accommodate

BEILBHEAN RUADH, s. m (Ir. id) A buzzard

BEILLEAN, ein, s m. (Ir id) Blame, reproach

BEINNSE, s f A bench, a seat

BEOTHACHAN, ain, s m (dim. of beothach) Ir id A little beast.

BEUL BREAGH, a (Ir id) A flattering mouth; flattery

BIATACHAS, ais, s m (Ir. id) Food, victuals, nourishment

BIORACH, aich, s m (Ir id) A colt, a boat.

BIORAICHE, s. m. (Ir. id) A steer, a young bullock

BIRICHE, s. m. A filly

BIRIDE, s f. A breeding-cow; a shrew

BISLACH, ich, s f. The crisis of a disease

BLADAR, air, s. m (Ir id) Flattery, the act of flattering or coaxing

BLADARACH, a. (Ir. id.) Flattering, coaxing

BLAGAIR, s m. A blast, a puff, a boaster.

BLAGAIREACHD, s. f. (Ir. id.) Boasting

BLAODHAGACH, a. (Ir id.) Noisy, garrulous.

BLASDAG, aig, s. f. (Ir. id) A sweet-mouthed female.

BLÀTHACH, a (Ir. id) Flowery.

BLÀTHADH, aidh, s. m (Ir id) Politeness; smoothness.

BLÀTHAN, ain, s m. (*from* blàth) A small flower; a little blossom

BLIOCHD-FOCHADAN, s m. (Ir id.) Common sowthistle; *sonchus oleraceus.*

BLOING, s. f. (Ir. id) A bubble

BLUNAG See BLONAG.

BOCAIL, s. f. (Ir. id.) Ostentation.

BOCHDRACH, aich, s m A beggar.

BODAN, ain, s m. Cat's tail; reed-mace. *Typha angustifolia* Bodan dubh, *great cat's-tail. Typha latifolia*; bodan measgain, *common butterwort. Yorkshire sanicle, pinguicula vulgaris.*

BOID, s m (Ir id) A bottle.

BOID, a (Ir. id) Neat trim.

BOIDEAL, eil, s. m. (Ir. id) A pudding

BOINEAN, ein, s m (Ir. id) A bud or sprout.

BOLAN, ain, s f. (Ir. id) A full-grown cow.

BOLGAN, ain, s m (Ir id) A frock

BOLSTAR, air, s m A bolster *Not good Gaelic.*

BOLTANACH, a Rank; olefactory.

BOMAN, ain, s. m A boast, a bounce.

BORD UISGE, s. m A flood-gate

BORRAN, ain, s m (Ir id) Anger

BOSAN, ain, s. m A purse

BRACAN, ain, s. f A glove, a gauntlet, a handcuff

BRADACH, aich, s. m. (Ir id) A thief

BRAGHAIRT, s f (Ir id) A bundle, a truss or pack.

BRAID, s f A mountain, a mountainous country

BRAICHEAS, eis, s. m (Ir id) Refuse of malt; malt from which the juice has been extracted.

BRAIDHIN, s f A quern

BRAINEACH, ich, s m The prow of a ship

BRAOSDAIL, a. Gaping, gazing

† BRAS, s m Prosperity, increase

† BRAS, s m. A lie; a romance; a covering for the head.

BRASACH, a. (Ir id) Nimble, lively, sudden

BRASAIR, s m (Ir id) A sycophant.

BRASGAN, ain, s. m A mob

BRATH, s. m A remnant, a fragment, a spy; a lie; dependence.

BRAT-LAIMH, s m A hand-towel.

BREACHDAN, ain, s m. Fresh butter.

BREALL, s. m. A knob at the end of either of the sticks of a flail

BREALLAN, ain, s. m. (Ir. id) A vessel.

† BREAS, a (Ir. id) Great, mighty, prosperous, comely.

BREASAIL, a. Great, mighty, princely.

BREID, s f. (Ir. id.) Frize; a coarse kind of woollen cloth.

Breiseachan, ain, *s. m.* (*Ir. id.*) A still.

Breolaid, *s. f.* Delirium.

Brideag, eig, *s. f.* (*Ir. id.*) An image of St. Bridget, used on the eve of that Saint by unmarried girls, with a view to discover their future husbands.

Brion, *s. m.* (*Ir. id*) Inquietude, dissatisfaction.

Brionn, *s. m.* (*Ir. id*) A fiction, a lie.

Briosglan, ain, *s. m.* A skirret; silver weed; wild tansey, goose-grass; the *potentilla anserina* of botanists.

Brobh, *s. m.* Round-rooted bastard cypress; the *scirpus maritimus* of botanists

Brobhadan, ain, *s. m* (*Ir. id*) A grasshopper

Brocach, *a.* Dirty, ill-scented; odious.

Brollaich, *s. f.* (*Ir. id.*) Boldness, confidence.

Bronn, *s. f.* (*Ir. id*) A quern.

Broth, *s. m.* (*Ir. id.*) Flesh; corn; a mole, a ditch; a fire; straw.

Brothlach, aich, *s. m.* A pit made in the ground, in which the ancient Gael dressed their food.

Bruid, *s. f* (*Ir. id*) A thorn; anxiety.

Bruighseach, ich, *s. f.* (*Ir id.*) A womb with young.

† **Buac**, *s. m.* (*Ir. id*) A liquor prepared for bleaching, mist, a cap of mist on a hill.

Buacais, *s. f.* (*Ir id*) Confusion.

Buacharan, ain, *s. m.* Dry cow's dung, used by the poorer sort of Scotch and Irish Gael for fuel.

Buadan, ain, *s m* (*Ir. id.*) The bone in a horn.

Buadhachas, ais, *s. m.* (*Ir id*) Victory, triumph.

Buadhairt, *s. f.* (*Ir id*) Trouble

Buaic, *s. f* (*Ir id.*) A pinnacle.

Buaig, *s f.* (*Ir. id*) A cup, a chalice.

Buaileachan, ain, *s m.* (*from* buaile.) *Ir. id* A milker of cows, a place where cows are milked

Buailteach, ich, *s. m.* (*Ir id*) A dairy-house.

Buarach, aich, *s. m.* (*Ir id*) The early feeding of cows; rising to feed cows.

Buarachan, ain, *s. m.* A cow-herd

Buine, *s f.* The set-off in basket-making; the thick welt or border in finishing any wicker-work.

Buinnean, ein, *s. m.* (*Ir. id*) A shoot, a young twig.

Buinnse, *s* A bundle; a bunch.

Buinnseal, eil, *s m.* A bundle, a bunch.

Buiseal, eil, *s. m.* (*Ir. id.*) A bushel

Busag, aig, *s. f.* (*from* bus) A kiss

C.

Cab, *s. m.* (*Ir id.*) The bit of a bridle.

Cac an airgid, *s m* (*Ir. id.*) Litharge.

Cabhag, aig, *s f.* (*Ir id*) A kind of pillory.

Caibe-sgraith, *s. m.* A breast-plough

Caifean, ein, *s. m.* A trifling, diminutive fellow; a dandiprat.

Caifeanach, *a.* Trifling; diminutive; pithless

Caig, *v. a* Tease, disturb *Pret.* chaig; *fut aff* caigidh, *shall tease.* Caig air, *tease him*

Caigill, *v. a* Lay up; cover the fire.

Caile-circein, *s. f.* (*Ir id*) A shuttlecock.

Caimean, ein, *s m.* (*Ir id*) Reproof, blame, reproach.

Cairneach, *a.* (*Ir. id*) Fleshy.

Caise, *s. f.* (*Ir. id*) The privy parts of a female.

Caistean, ein, *s. m* (*Ir. id*) A crafty fellow.

Caiteach, ich, *s. m.* A winnow-sheet; the mainsail of a ship.

Caith, *s. m.* (*Ir. id.*) *Pudendum virile.*

† **Calb**, *s m.* (*Ir id*) The head.

Calc, *a.* (*Ir. id.*) Hard, obdurate.

Calchearcain, *s m* (*Ir id.*) A shuttlecock.

Camar, air, *s m.* (*Ir id*) A soft, foolish person

Camaran, ain, *s. m.* (*Ir. id*) An idiot.

Cananach, aich, *s. m.* (*Ir. id.*) A canon; canonist.

Caobhan, ain, *s. m.* (*Ir. id*) A little bough or twig.

Caodachan, ain, *s. m.* An infant beginning to walk.

Caoidh, *s. f.* Decency.

Caoineas, eis, *s. m* (*Ir. id*) Lamenting.

Caoinleach, ich, *s. m.* (*Ir. id.*) Corn-stubbles

Caolach, aich, *s m.* Wattles.

Carsan. See **Carrasan**.

Catail, *a.* (cat-amhuil) Cross, crabbed.

Cathach, *a.* (*Ir. id.*) Chaffy.

Ceadach, aich, *s. m.* (*Ir. id*) Coarse cloth

Ceal, *s m.* (*Ir id*) A covering; fine flour; sickness; prophecy

Ceallach, aich, *s m.* (*Ir. id.*) Contention; war, strife.

Cean-aois, *s f* (*Ir. id*) Old age

Ceann, cinn, *s. m.* Harvest home For other significations, see the Dictionary.

Ceannair, *s m.* (*Ir. id*) A leader.

Ceannasg, aisg, *s.* (*Ir. id*) A headstall, a band; government, ruling

Ceap, *s m* (*Ir. id.*) A rallying point in battle

† **Cearnair**, *s. m.* (*Ir. id*) A conqueror.

† **Ceart**, *s m* (*Ir id.*) A rag, an old garment

† **Ceas**, *s m.* (*Ir id*) A kiss

Ceasan, ain, *s. m.* The coarse wool of the flank.

Ceothallan, ain, *s. m.* A stupid fellow.

Ciallach, aich, *s. m* (*Ir id*) A lover

Cinnseach, ich, *s m.* (*Ir id*) Want.

Ciochair, *s m.* (*Ir. id*) A stingy man.

Ciolag, aig, *s f.* Provision, store

Ciolar, air, *s. m.* Linsey woolsey.

Ciomach, *a.* (*Ir. id*) Restless

Ciomach, aich, *s. m* A restless fellow.

Cionmhor, *a* Lovely.

Cipean, ein, *s. m.* A stick or dibble for planting

Clabhrachan, ain, *s m* A babbler.

Clab-sholus, uis, *s. m* (*Ir id*) Twilight

Clannadh, aidh, *s m.* (*Ir. id.*) Interment, a child's portion

Cleod, *s m.* (*Ir. id*) A horse-fly.

Cliamach, aich, *s. m.* (*Ir. id*) A lobster, a ragged child; a surly fellow.

Cliath, *s. f.* (*Ir. id*) The treadles of a loom

Clith, *s m.* (*Ir. id*) A desire of copulation in cattle

Cluain lin, *s f.* Corn spurry, *spergula arvensis.*

Cluas, cluais, *s f.* (*Ir. id.*) Gladness, joy.
Cluas liath, *s. f.* A certain medicinal herb.
Cludag, aig, *s. f.* (*Ir. id*) Concealment; a store
Cnamhag, aig, *s. f.* A maggot.
Cnapain, *s m.* (*Ir. id*) A louse.
Cnocair, *s m* (*Ir. id.*) A crabbed little fellow
Cochlach, aich, *s. m* (*Ir. id*) Hair-lace.
Cochlach, *a* (*Ir id*) Braided. Ciabhan cochlach, *braided hair*
† **Cod**, *s m* (*Ir. id*) A part, a piece. Now written *cuid*
Codarsnachd, *s f* (*Ir. id.*) Contrariety
Cogairseach, ich, *s m* (*Ir. id*) A whisperer.
Cogar, air, *s m* (*Ir. id.*) An insurrection; a conspiracy
Coidheis, *a.* (*Ir id*) Commodious, convenient.
Coilt, coilte, *s f* (*Ir. id*) A heifer
Coimheas, *s m.* Coolness, indifference; equality, comparison
Coimhneas, eis, *s. m* Neighbourhood
Coindreach, *s m* (*Ir id.*) Impediment, restriction, mischief, instruction; direction.
Coireach, ich, *s m* (*from* coir.) *Ir. id* A guilty person.
Coirean coilich, *s m* Wild campion, *lychnis dioica*
Coiseantach, aich, *s m.* A protector
Coisreach, ich, *s. m.* (*Ir id.*) A feast
Colach, **Collach**, *a* (*Ir. id*) Incestuous; sinful, wicked
† **Comach**, aich, *s m* (*Ir id*) A tax, a toll
Comharbas, ais, *s. m* (*Ir id*) Succession
Comh-chòsach, *a* (*Ir id*) Concave
Comh-fhlannas, ais, *s m* Consanguinity
Compan, ain, *s. m* (*Ir id*) See **Companach**
† **Conair**, *s f* (*Ir. id*) A haven, a crown
Conga, *s m* (*Ir id*) The antlers of a buck
Congart, airt, *s m* (*Ir id*) Command
Congbhalach, *a* (*Ir. id*) Tenacious
Congbhalas, ais, *s. m* (*Ir id*) A stay, a help, support.
Contraill, *s f* (*Ir id.*) Opposition
Còraichean, *n pl* of còir; which see.
Coraicheas, eis, *s m* (*from* còir) *Ir. id* Surety, protection.
Corcan, ain, *s m* (*Ir. id*) A small boat
Corcran, ain, *s. m* (*Ir. id*) A small pot
Cormach, aich, *s m.* (*Ir id.*) A brewer
Corrach, aich, *s. m* Ground under which there is decayed wood
Corpan, ain, *s m* (*dim* of corp) A little body; a miserable body; a corpuscle
Corthachd, *s. f.* Lassitude
Cosar, air, *s m.* (*Ir. id*) A coat, a mantle
Cosnach, aich, *s m.* (*Ir id*) A defendant
Cosrach, *s m* (*Ir id*) Fetters.
Cotharach, aich, *s. m.* Water scorpion-grass
Crabhaidh, *a.* Frail, not stout
Creasach, aich, *s m.* (*Ir. id.*) Spear *N pl* creasaichean
Creasan, ain, *s. m* Faith
Creathair, *s. m.* (*Ir id*) An extortioner *N pl* creathairean.
Crinlam, eim, *s. m.* A fall.
Crineamh, eimh, *s f.* Fate, destiny
Criodair, *s m.* (*Ir. id.*) A fondler *N pl* criodairean
Crislean, *s. pl* Sinews.
Croiligh, *s. f.* Pain, infirmity
Croiteach, *a* Gibbous

Crosag, aig, *s. f.* A small cross; a small cup; perverseness.
Crotal coille, *s. m.* Lungwort; the *muscus pulmonarius* of botanists.
Crotan, ain, *s. m.* Purple, dyer's lichen.
† **Cruach**, *a.* (*Ir. id.*) Red
Cruach luachair, *s. m.* (*Ir. id*) Dwarf club-rush; the *scirpus cespitosus* of botanists.
Cruadhaig, *s f.* Distress; necessity.
Cruadhail, *s. f.* (*Ir. id.*) Danger; hardship; inhumanity
Cruadhalachd, *s f* (*Ir. id.*) Hardness, niggardliness, rigour.
Cruadhalta, *a.* (*Ir. id.*) Hard, niggardly, inhuman.
Cruadhchradh, aidh, *s m* Austerity
Crubhasg, aisg, *s. f.* (*Ir. id.*) A crimson colour.
Crubheoin, *s. m.* The herb birdsfoot; the *trifolium ornithopodioides* of botanists.
Crubh-leomhainn, *s. m.* Common lady's-mantle; common vervain, the *alchemilla vulgaris* of botanists.
Crucach, aich, *s. m.* (*Ir. id.*) A heap.
Cruinneach, ich, *s. f.* (*Ir id.*) Dew; mist; fog.
Cruinneagan, ain, *s m.* (*Ir. id.*) A mass, a heap.
Cruinnean, ein, *s. m.* (*Ir. id.*) A tuft.
Cruisgean, ein, *s m.* (*Ir id*) A jug, a small pitcher.
Crùistean, ein, *s m.* (*Ir. id*) A little lamp or cruse
Cruiteachan, ain, *s m* A dwarf, a hunchback
Cruscadh, aidh, *s. m* (*Ir. id*) A box, a small coffer.
Cuairsgiath, -sgeith, *s. f.* (*Ir. id.*) A crooked target.
† **Cuaith**, *s f.* (*Ir. id*) The country
Cuan, ain, *s. m* (*Ir id*) Deceit, a multitude
Cuarag, aig, *s f.* (*Ir. id.*) A knapsack
Cuartach, *a* (*Ir. id*) Current.
Cuideag, eig, *s f.* (*Ir. id.*) A spider.
† **Cuig**, *s. f* A counsel, an advice; a secret, a mystery.
Cuileann tràigha, *s. m* (*Ir. id*) Sea-holly; the *eryngium maritimum* of botanists
Cùil-fhionn, *a* (*Ir id*) Fair-haired.
Cuille, *s f* Black cloth; a quill.
Cuillsean, ein, *s m* (*Ir. id*) The quilt or tick of a bed
Cuimhas, ais, *s. m* (*Ir id*) The list of cloth
Cuimhealta, *a* Bruising.
Cuimreach, ich, *s m* (*Ir id*) An assistant
Cuineal mhuire, *s m* Great white mullen; hag's taper; lady's fox-gloves; cow's lungwort; the *verbascum thapsus* of botanists
Cuineas, eis, *s m* (*Ir. id*) Rest, quiet
Cuinneag mhione, *s f* (*Ir id.*) Wild angelica; the *angelica sylvestris* of botanists
Cuinsear, eir, *s m* A poniard
Cuirceag, eig, *s f* A hive *N. pl.* cuirceagan.
Cuirpean, ein, *s m* A crupper.
Cuirpear, eir, *s m* A carper
Culair, *s f.* (*Ir id.*) The throat; a palate, chops
Cumailt, *s f* (*Ir id*) A touching; a wiping
† **Cumal**, ail, *s m.* (*Ir. id*) Three cows, the value of three cows.
Cungantach, *a.* (*Ir id*) Helpful
Cungantair, *s m.* (*Ir. id*) A helper, an assistant
Cunnadh; more properly *connadh*, which see
† **Cur**, *s m.* (*Ir. id.*) Present time; fatigue, surety, pledge.
Curaid, *s m* (*Ir. id.*) A curate.

D.

Dabhar, air, *s. m.* (*Ir. id.*) A bucket; a pitcher.
Daigear, eir, *s. m.* (*Ir. id.*) A dagger, a poniard.
Daoineas, eis, *s. m.* (*Ir. id.*) Manliness
Daorchlann, *s. f.* (*Ir. id.*) Slaves; servants; plebeians
Daosgar, air, *s. m.* (*Ir. id.*) Refuse; remainder.
Daosgar, *a.* (*Ir. id.*) Unteachable.
Darsan, ain, *s. m.* A murmur.
Dartach, aich, *s. m.* (*Ir. id.*) A two-year-old bull
† **Deach**, *a.* Profitable
Deachlach, *a.* (*Ir. id.*) Hard, difficult
Deacrach, *a.* See **Deacair**.
Deacrachd, *s. f.* (*Ir. id.*) Difficulty; hardship
Deann, *s. m.* (*Ir. id.*) A gibe; mist
Dearach, aich, *s. m* Destruction, pillage.
Dearg, *a.* (*Ir. id.*) Bitter, severe, intense, inveterate.
Deatachan, ain, *s. m* A chimney.
Deil, deile, *s. f.* (*Ir. id.*) A cow's udder
Deilin, *s. f.* (*Ir. id.*) A trespass.
† **Deirbh**, *s. f.* (*Ir. id.*) A churn.
Diasair, *v. a.* Glean. *Pret. a.* dhiasair, *gleaned*, *fut aff.* diasraidh.
Didhiol, *s. m.* (*Ir. id.*) Arrears.
Dilghean, *s. m.* (*Ir. id.*) Affection; suppression
Dilse, *s. f.* (*Ir. id.*) A sea-plant.
Dimheas, *s m.* (*Ir. id.*) Great honour, high esteem, scarcity of fruit
Dimheasach, *a.* (*Ir. id.*) Proud; contemptuous; servile.
Dimhinn, **Dimhineachd**, *s. f.* (*Ir. id.*) Provision, caution; heed; confidence.
Dimhnidheach, *a.* (*Ir. id.*) Sad Gu dimhnidheach, *sadly*.
Dimhnidheachd, *s. f.* Sadness
Dimholtair, *s. m.* (*Ir. id.*) A slanderer.
Dimreas, eis, *s f* (*Ir. id.*) Want, necessity.
Dineach, ich, *s. m* (*Ir. id.*) A salutary draught
Dineudach, aich, *s. m.* (*Ir id.*) A frock
† **Dinge**, *s. f.* (*Ir. id.*) Thunder.
Dingir, *s. m.* A pavior's rammer.
† **Dinimh**, *s. f.* (*Ir. id.*) Weakness, diminution
Dinseadh, idh, *s. m* (*Ir. id.*) Contempt.
Diobhalach, *a.* (*Ir. id.*) Robbed, spoiled; ablative
Diobhalachd, *s. f.* Ablation
Diobhaladh, aidh, *s m.* (*Ir. id.*) Damaging; annoying
Diobhar, air, *s. m.* Disrespect; omission.
Diobhlach, *a* (*Ir. id*) Prodigal. *Com* and *sup* diobhlaiche.
Diobhlachd, *s. f.* (*Ir. id.*) Prodigality.
Diobhlas, ais, *s. m.* (*Ir. id.*) Prodigality.
Diochrach, *a.* (*Ir. id*) Diligent, zealous
Diogan, ain, *s. m.* (*Ir. id.*) Grief
Diogar, *a.* Eager, intent, vehement
Dioghaoth, aoithe, *s. f* (*Ir id*) A blast in corn
Dioghart, airt, *s. m* (*Ir. id*) A decollation.
Dioghlais, *s. f.* (*Ir. id*) Abuse, defamation
Dioghlus, uis, *s. m* Darkness
Dioghras, ais, *s. m* Zeal, uprightness

Diolainteach, ich, *s m* (*Ir id.*) A bachelor.
Diolgad, aid, *s. m.* Forgiveness; remission
Diolmhaoin, *s f* (*Ir. id*) Alimony.
Dioltair, *s m.* (*Ir. id.*) A seller.
Diolunta, *a* (*Ir id.*) Valiant; hospitable, generous. Gu diolunta, *generously*
Diomhran, ain, *s m* (*Ir. id.*) A mystery.
Dionàire, *s f* (*Ir id*) Shamelessness.
Dionaireach, *a* (*Ir. id*) Shameless
Dionasach, *a* (*Ir id*) Ardent. *Com.* and *sup.* dionasaiche Gu dionasach, *ardently*
Dioncharn, -chuirn, *s. m.* A fort
Dionghair, *s f* A tribute, a benevolent succour
Dionoglachas, ais, *s m* Heroism
† **Diormach**, *a* (*Ir id*) Unfit to walk.
Dirreachdas, ais, *s. m.* Gelding.
Dis, *a.* Incapable of bearing cold; careful against cold
Diugadh, aidh, *s. m* Clucking, as of a hen
Diùid, *s f* (*Ir id*) Pain, sorrow.
Diurnach, aich, *s m.* (*Ir id*) One who drinks or swills.
Dleachd, *s. f.* (*Ir id*) A toll, a right, a due.
Dleachdair, *s m* (*Ir. id*) A lawgiver
† **Dlomh**, *s. m.* (*Ir. id.*) Refusal
Dlug, dluig, *s f* (*Ir. id.*) Avarice; penury.
Do-bhuidheachas, ais, *s m.* Ingratitude, unthankfulness.
Dochraidh, *s. f.* Lust
Dochraid, *s f.* (*Ir. id.*) Servitude.
Do-dheantas, ais, *s. m* Impracticability
Do-dhuine, *s. m.* A bad man, a rogue. *N pl* do-dhaoine
Doghaltas, ais, *s. m* (*Ir. id.*) Revenge
Do-ghleusadh, *a* (*Ir. id*) Untuneable
Doghnasach, *a* (*Ir id*) Ill-favoured
Dòid-gheal, *a.* White-handed
Doigheil, *a* (dogh-amhuil.) Decent, well-appointed
Doighleug, eig, *s f* A touchstone
Doireanta, *a.* Sullen, dogged
† **Doiriata**, *a.* (*Ir id*) Lewd
Dòirtear, eir, *s. m.* One who spills.
Doit, *s f.* (*Ir id*) A grain of an inebriating quality that grows among corn
Doithchearnas, ais, *s m* (*Ir. id*) Churlishness, niggardliness, abhorrence.
Do-lamhach, *a* Not easily handled, *also, for* da-lamhach, *ambidexterous.*
Do-lamhachd, *s f* Ambidexterity
Donadas, ais, *s m* (*Ir id*) Evil; miserableness
Donn-ruadh, *a* Of a bay or chesnut colour
Dorcan, ain, *s m* (*Ir id*) A yearling bull-calf
Dornasg, aisg, *s m* (*Ir id.*) A manacle
Dorrtha, *a* See **Dorrach**
Do-sheoladh, *a.* Innavigable; that cannot be guided or directed.
Do-sgaoilte, *a* (*Ir id.*) Not easily spread, indissoluble; inevitable.
Do-sgathach, *a.* (*Ir. id.*) Improvident, extravagant Gu do-sgathach, *improvidently*.

DRABHAS, ais, *s. m.* Dirt

DRABHASACH, *a.* Dirty.

DRAOTH, draotha, *s m.* (*Ir. id*) A pull, a tug, a pluck

DRAOTHADH, aidh, *s. m* (*Ir. id*) A pulling, a tugging, a plucking

† DREACHD, *s f* A draught or pattern, a poem.

DREANACH, *a* (*Ir. id*) Despicable

DREASAIL, *s pl* (*Ir. id*) Shreds, small teats.

DRIUBHLACH, aich, *s. m* (*Ir. id*) A cowl

DROBHLAS, ais, *s m* Misery.

DROCH, *s. m* A moth or worm in wood or cloth.

DROCHDAIL, *s. pl* (*Ir. id.*) Bad news.

DROCH-CHLEACHDAS, ais, *s. m.* Malpractice.

DROCH-NOS, *s m* A bad habit

DROCH-SGEUL, -sgeil, *s. m* Bad news; detraction.

DROMACHD, *s f.* (*Ir. id.*) Affirmation

DROMAN, ain, *s. m.* The back-band of a horse when in a cart.

DUALACHAN, ain, *s m* (*Ir id*) A toil-maker

DUBHAS, ais, *s. m* Sorrow.

DUBHAN CEANN-CHOSACH, *s m* Common self-hail, all hail, devil's bit; the *prunella vulgaris* of botanists.

DUBHRAS, ais, *s m* A gloomy wood.

DUILLEAN, ein, *s. m.* A spear.

DUILLEAG-BHAITE BHÀN, *s f.* White water-lily, the *nymphæa alba major lymphatica* of botanists

DUILLEAG MHAITH, *s f.* Nipple-wort, dock-cresses; the *lopsana communis* of botanists

DUILLEAG MHIN, *s. f.* See DUILLEAG MHAITH

DULIASG NA H-AIBHNE, *s.* Broad-leaved pond-weed; the *potamogeton natans* of botanists.

E.

EA-CONN, *s. m.* (*Ir id*) Madness, fury

EACHRANN, ainn, *s m* A bramble; an impediment, a stumbling-block

EADAILIS, *s f* (*Ir id*) The Italian language

EADARLAMH, aimh, *s. m* (*Ir. id*) Temporary happiness

EADRADH, aidh, *s m* (*Ir id*) A division, lust, adultery

EALA BHUIDHE, *s f* St John's wort

EALADHANTACH, *a* (*Ir id*) Artificial

EALADHANTAIR, *s m* (*Ir id*) An artificer.

EANGACH, aich, *s. m* A babbler

EARAIS, *s f.* (*Ir id*) A tail

EARGNADH, aidh, *s m* Devastation, destruction

EARLACH, *a.* (*Ir id.*) Diffusive

EARNADH, aidh, *s m* (*Ir id*) A redemption, payment, assessment, promulgation; extension, prophecy

EARNAIL, *s f* (*Ir id.*) An endowment; a department of any science.

EARRAIDEACH, *a.* (*Ir id*) Erroneous.

EASADH, aidh, *s m.* (*Ir id*) Sickness, disease.

EASAIR, *s f* (*Ir. id*) Excess.

EASBADH, aidh, *s. m* (*Ir. id*) Vanity, idleness

† EASGAR, air, *s m* The plague, a grain of corn, a kernel.

EASARGAIN, *s. f* (*Ir. id*) Contrition.

EASBUIG BHÀN, *s. m* Greater daisy, ox-eye daisy; the *chrysanthemum leucanthemum* of botanists

EIGEANTACH See EIGINNEACH

EIGHRE See EIGH

EILNICH, *v. a* Corrupt, spoil, violate. *Pret. a.* dh'eilnich.

EIMHEACH, *a* Nimble, swift

EINNID, *s f.* (*Ir. id.*) Generosity

EIRICEIL, *a* Heretical.

EITHRE, *s f* The tail of a fish

F.

FAIDEAG, eig, *s. f* (*Ir id*) A green plover. *N. pl.* faideagan.

FAIL, *s f.* (*Ir. id*) A den, a hogstie

FAINNEAL, eil, *s m* A fannel, or handful of straw used for thatching

FAIRCLE, *s f* (*Ir. id.*) The uppermost, extremity, choice

FAIRNEACHD, *s f.* (*Ir. id*) A meeting

FÀLADAS, ais, *s m.* Spite, hatred

FALLAINEAS See FALLAINEACHD

FALLSAN, ain, *s m.* (*Ir id*) A sluggard *N pl* fallsain.

FALLSANACH, aich, *s m* A falsifier.

FALLUINNG MHUIRE, *s f* Common lady's-mantle, the *alchemilla vulgaris* of botanists

FAOCHAG, aig, *s f* (*Ir. id*) A weaver's thrum

† FAOILEACH, ich, *s m* Supplement

† FAOL, faoil, *s m* A prop, a support; a whelp, patience, forbearance

FAOSGNACH, *a.* (*Ir. id.*) Auspicious

FARACH, aich, *s. m* (*Ir. id*) A mallet, a beetle

FARACH DUBH, *s. m.* Great fig-wort, kernel-wort, the *scrophularia nodosa* of botanists

FARCAN, *s. m.* (*Ir. id*) A corn on hands or feet

FÀSACH, *a.* (*Ir id*) Desert, desolate

FASACH, aich, *s m* (*Ir. id*) Stubble, the grassy headland of a ploughed field.

† FASG, faisg, *s. m.* (*Ir. id*) A prison; a band, a bond.

FASGAIR, *s. m* A keeper, a jailor.

FASLACH, aich, *s. m* Instigation.—*Shaw*

FATHAN, ain, *s. m.* (*Ir id*) Coltsfoot; the *tussilago farfara* of botanists

FEACHDNACH, aich, *s m* Prosperity, luck; manhood.

FEADAIR, *s. m* A whistler; a piper

FEADHAN, ain, *s m.* The leader of a flock of wild geese.

† FEARACH, *a* (*Ir. id*) Wild.

FEARSACH, *a* (*Ir id*) Full of little ridges in the sand.

FEOCHAN, ain, *s m* Decay.

FEORAS, ais, *s m.* The spindle-tree

FEOTHAN, ain, *s. m* (*Ir. id*) A dormouse.

FIADHAN, ain, *s. m.* Wildness, evidence

FIAG, FIAGA, *s pl.* Rushes peeled and prepared; candle-wicks.

FIAL, *a.* (*Ir. id.*) Modest, good.

FIALAS, ais, *s. m.* (*Ir. id.*) A tribe.
FIALTAS, ais, *s. m* Protection.
FILLTE, *a.* Treacherous
† FINEACH, *a.* (*Ir id.*) Frugal
FINEAL MHUIRE, *s. m* Flix-weed, the *sysimbrium sophia* of botanists.
FITHREACH, ich, *s m* (*Ir. id*) Sea wreck.
FIORADH, aidh, *s. m* (*Ir id.*) Satisfaction, comfort; completion; sufficiency.
† FLAITH, *s f.* (*Ir. id.*) Milk
† FLAITH, *s. m.* (*Ir. id*) A kind of strong beer
FLAITHEANAS, ais, *s. m* Heaven, sovereignty, dominion
FLEANN UISGE, *s. m* Various-leaved water-crowfoot; the *ranunculus aquaticus* of botanists
FLIODH, *s. m.* A kind of medical herb
FLIUCHPAS, ais, *s m* Moisture
FOCHAS, ais, *s. m.* (*Ir. id.*) Mallows
FOGAIR, *s f.* (*Ir id*) A proclamation, a command
FOGHAIL, *s. f.* (*Ir. id.*) Grief, vexation.
FOGHAIRT, *s. f.* (*Ir. id*) A chasing, a pursuing; a banishing
FOGHLADH, aidh, *s m* (*Ir id.*) Robbery, trespass
† FOILCHEAS, *a* (*Ir id.*) Dark, obscure; *substantively*, a mystery
FOILEUM, *s f.* (*Ir id*) A leap, a skip, a bounce
† FOILLE, *s. f.* (*Ir id*) Smallness, littleness.
FOILLSEACH, *a.* (*Ir. id*) Declaratory.
† FOINEALL, ill, *s. m* (*Ir. id*) A fool
FOIRBHEACH, ich, *s m.* (*Ir id*) An elder.
FOIRBHEART, eirt, *s. m* (*Ir. id*) Help, assistance
FOIRBHEARTACH, aich, *s. m.* (*Ir. id*) An assistant
FOIRBHREITH, *s f.* (*Ir id*) Prejudice.
FOIREANN, einn, *s. m.* (*Ir. id*) A crowd, a multitude.
FOIRNEACHAN, ain, *s m.* (*Ir. id*) A roller
FOISEAD, eid, *s. m.* (*Ir. id.*) A faucet
FOLABH. See FOLBH or FALBH.
FOLABHRADH, aidh, *s. m.* (*Ir id*) An insidious question.
FOLCADH, aidh, *s. m* (*Ir. id.*) A ley of potash.
† FOLLACH, aich, *s m.* (*Ir id*) A covering; a garment, military colours
FOLLASGAIN, *s f* Wood crow-foot, the *ranunculus auricomus* of naturalists.
FOLTACH, aich, *s. m* (*Ir id*) A vassal, a hireling
FONNSAIR, *s m* (*Ir id*) A cooper.
FORAIL, *s f* (*Ir id*) An offer; a gift.
FORAS, ais, *s m.* (*Ir id*) An armistice, depth; foundation, bottom
FORBACH, aich, *s m* (*Ir. id.*) A funeral entertainment
FORCHAN, ain, *s m* (*Ir. id*) Instruction, a sermon
FORGHALL, aill, *s m* (*Ir id*) A lie, a fable, a romance
FORLAMHAS, ais, *s m* Force, power, conquest, pain, superfluity.
FORMAIL, *a* (*Ir id*) Shapely, sightly
FORMAN, ain, *s m* (*Ir id*) A sound or noise
FOROIDEAS, eis, *s m.* Tradition; elements of knowledge
FOROIDEASACH, *a* Traditionary, elemental, elementary
FORRAN, ain, *s m* (*Ir. id*) Oppression, destruction.
FORRANACH, *a.* (*Ir. id*) An oppressor
FOSRADH, aidh, *s m* (*Ir id*) A dwelling, knowledge; dissolution, releasing; a bed; a clasp, a cramp
FOTHACH, aich, *s m.* A cry, a shout.
FRAOCHAN, ain, *s. m* (*Ir. id*) A whortle-berry, a bilberry.
FREACADAN See FREICEADAN.
FREACAIR, *s. f.* Attendance.
FRIOGHAN, ain, *s. m.* A barb
FRIOSG, *a* (*Ir. id*) Nimble, active
FROMHACH, aich, *s m* (*Ir. id.*) A glutton.
FUAGAIRT, *s f.* (*Ir. id*) Adjuration, warning
FUARACHAS, ais, *s. m* Coldness
FUASAN, ain, *s m* (*Ir. id*) A gainsaying, contradiction
FUASGAR, air, *s m.* A dispersion, a total rout.
FUINEACHAN, ain, *s. m.* (*from* fuin) *Ir. id.* A baker
FUIREANN, inn, *s f* (*Ir id*) Ballast.

G.

GABHAIL, *s. f.* Barm, colonization, peopling.
GABHAR, air, *s m.* (*Ir. id*) Light, illumination; conflict.
GAIDHEAL, *s. m* A British or Irish Celt
GAIRGHEAN, ein, *s. f.* (*Ir id*) A niece, crow-foot
GAIRGRE, *s. f.* (*Ir. id.*) A pilgrim's habit.
GAIRMEACH, *a* Appellative; that calls.
GAIRTEAG, eig, *s. f.* A crab-tree; the *pyrus malus* of botanists
GAISIDH, *s. f.* (*Ir id*) A stream, a current.
GALAN, ain, *s. m.* (*Ir. id.*) A sudden blast, a sudden glimpse; chivalry.
GALBHAIDH, *s. f.* Heat, warmth
GALGADH, *a.* Stout, valiant.
GALLAN-GREANNCHAIR, *s m* Colt's-foot, the *tussilago farfara* of botanists.
GALLRACH, *a* (*Ir. id*) Infectious.
GALRADH, aidh, *s. m.* Infection, disorder.
GAMAIRLE, *s. m* A foolish fellow.
GAMASACH, *a.* Proud in gait.
GAOIS, *s. f.* (*Ir. id*) Wisdom.
GAOLAN, ain, *s. m.* (*from* gaol) A beloved person.
GARBH, gairbh, *s. m.* (*Ir. id*) A scab, warfare; courage.
GARBH-LUS, uis, *s m* Hay-ruff, catch-weed, goose-grass, the *gallium aparine* of botanists
GARMACH, aich, *s m* (*Ir id*) A grandson.
† GARSAN, ain, *s m* (*Ir. id* *Fr.* garçon) A young lad.
† GASACH, *a.* (*Ir. id*) Angry, indignant.
GASDAIR, *s m.* An active man, a prater.
GATACHAN, ain, *s m* (*Ir. id*) A little boy
GEALBHAN SGIOBUILL, *s m.* (*Ir id*) A bunting
GEALDRUIDH, *s. m.* Round-leaved sun-dew; the *drosera rotundifolia* of botanists.
GEAMACH, *a.* (*Ir. id.*) Blear-eyed
GEARAN, ain, *s. m.* (*Ir id*) The herb dog's-ear
GEARBAG, aig, *s f.* (*Ir id*) A scab
GEARCACH, aich, *s. m.* A nestling, an unfledged bird
GEATRACH, *a* (*Ir. id*) Fearful, timid
GEOIS, *s. f.* (*Ir id*) A flat belly
GIG, *s f.* (*Ir id*) Tickling
GILLE-MÙCHAIN, *s. m.* A chimney-sweeper.
GIOB, *s. m.* (*Ir. id*) A pull, a pluck.
GIOBAG, aig, *s f.* A gipsy; a largess, a boon
GIOGAIR, *s. m* An uneasy person

GIOLCACH, aich, *s. m.* A reed, a place where reeds grow. Giolcach sleibhe, *common broom*, the *spartium scoparium* of botanists

GIOSGACH, aich, *s m* Wavering; a wavering fellow

GIOSGANACH, aich, *s. m.* A waddler

GIUSTAG, aig, *s. f.* A thick-bodied girl

GLAISFACH, ich, *s m* (*Ir. id*) Foam

GLANGACH, *a* (*Ir id*) Broad-shouldered

GLASAIR COILLE, *s m* Wood betony.

GLLACAIR, *s. m* (*Ir. id.*) A shout, a loud cry

GLEIRE, *s f* (*Ir. id*) Chastity

GLEORAG, aig, *s f* A lark.

GLEORAN, ain, *s m* (*Ir id*) Cuckoo flower

GLOMAR, air, *s m* A bridle

GLODH, *s m* Slime

GLODHACH, aich, *s m.* The slimy matter coming from a cow before calving.

† GLOTH, *s f* A veil

† GLOTH, *a* (*Ir. id*) Wise, discreet

GLUCAID, *s f.* (*Ir id*) A bumper

GLUINEACH DHEARG, *s f* Climbing knot-grass

GLUINEACH DHUBH, *s f* Climbing knot-grass, the *polygonum convolvulus* of botanists

GLUINEACH MHOR, *s f.* Spotted knot-grass, the *polygonum persicaria* of botanists.

GLUINEACH THETH, *s f* Water knot-grass, lake-weed

GLUNGAN, ain, *s m* (*Ir id*) A clink

GOIDNICH, *s f.* Theft, stolen goods

GOIRGEACH, *a* (*Ir id*) Foolish, doting

GONADAIR, *s m* One who wounds

GONTACH, aich, *s. m.* (*Ir. id.*) An old coarse coverlet.

† GORADH, aidh, *s m* (*Ir id*) A blush, heat, a warming, whipping

GORMAN, ain, *s m* Blue-bottle, the *centaurea cyanus* of botanists

† GRAB, *s m* (*Ir id*) A tooth, a dent, a notch

GRAFAN BÀN, *s m* White horehound, the *ballota alba* of naturalists

GRAFAN DUBH, *s. m.* Stinking horehound; the *ballota niget* of botanists.

GRAIGEANAS, ais, *s m* Gluttony.

GRAN AIGLIN, *s. m.* Common pilewort; lesser celandine; the *ranunculus ficaria* of botanists

GRAN LACHAIN, *s m* Lesser duck meat; the *lemma minor* of botanists.

GRAOLTAS, ais, *s m.* (*Ir id*) Obscenity.

† GREACHD, *s. f* (*Ir id*) An outcry.

GREADAIR, *s m* A warming-pan

GREAS, GREASACH, *a.* (*Ir id*) Usual

† GREID, *s f.* (*Ir id*) A stroke

GREIMIRE, *s m.* (*Ir. id.*) A grappling-hook, pincers

GRÉIS, *v. a* (*Ir id.*) Grease *Pret a* ghréis, *greased; fut. aff. a* gréisidh; *p. part* grèiste

GRÉISE, GRÉISG, *s f* (*Ir id*) Grease

GRÉISTE, *part.* Greased, brocaded, embroidered.

GRIANRACHD, *s f* (*Ir. id*) The warmth of the sun; sun-rising

GRINN, *s f* (*Ir id*) A piece or morsel; decency

GRINN, *a* (*Ir. id*) Neat, clean, pleasant; serious, attentive

GRIOCAS, ais, *s m* (*Ir id*) A rumbling noise.

GRIODAR, air, *s. m.* (*Ir. id*) A great noise

GRIOSAIR, *s m* A frying-pan

GROIG, *s f* (*Ir id*) A scrawl.

GROILEAN, ein, *s m* (*Ir id.*) A bilboe.

GROMAG, aig, *s. f* (*Ir id*) A prating girl.

GROPADH, aidh, *s m* A gulley, a server

GROTÒNACH, *a* (*Ir id*) Heavy-breeched, corpulent

GUAMAN, ain, *s m* (*Ir. id*) A cheek

GUAN, guain, *s m* A fool

GUIS, *s f.* (*Ir. id*) A leek

GURRAN, ain, *s m* (*Ir id*) Grunting, lowing, bellowing.

GUSTAL, ail, *s m* (*Ir id*) Protection; ability, affluence.

GUSRAG, aig, *s f* A clumsy girl

GUTALACH, aich, *s m.* (*Ir. id.*) An adulterer

GUTALAG, aig, *s f* (*Ir id*) An adulteress

I.

IAR-FHEUR, -fheòir, *s m* (*Ir id*) After-grass

† IAIL, *s* God forgive you!—*Shaw*

IAN, *s m* A vessel; the blade of a sword

IAPAL, ail, *s m* Controversy

IARAG See EIREAG

IARN-AOIS, *s. f* The Iron age

IARNAIR, *s m* An ironmonger

IARNAIREACHD, *s f* The business of an ironmonger

IARNALLACH, aich, *s f* (*Ir id*) An after-birth, secundine

' *alchemilla*D, *s f* (*Ir. id.*) Facility.

m (*Ir id*) Dung, ordure

FAOCHAG, aig, *s*

† FAOILEACH, ich (*Ir id*) Diversity, difference

† FAOL, faoil, *s*, *s. m.* (*Ir. id*) Protection, a protector forbearance

'I, *s f* (*Ir id*) A journey, decession, de-

FAOSGNACH, *a* (*I*

m. (*Ir id*) The navel

FARACH, aich, *s m* *r. id*) A perfect birth

FARACH DUBH, *s* (*Ir. id*) A level, a perpendicular; a chain *scrophularia* measure with.

INGEARACH, *a* (*Ir id*) Level, perpendicular.

INGEALTAS, ais, *s m* Pasture ground, ground fit for feeding cattle

INILT, *s f* (*Ir id*) Fodder.

INIS, *s f* (*Ir. id*) Distress, misery

INNLEAG, eig, *s f* A child's baby

INNTINNEAS, eis, *s m* (*Ir id*) Jollity

† IODHAN, ain, *s m* (*Ir id*) A pike, spear, javelin; affection, obedience, a confirming

† IODHNACH, aich, *s m* (*Ir id*) A gift

IOLDANACH, aich, *s m.* (*Ir. id*) A jack-of-all-trades.

IOLDANACH, *a* (*Ir id*) Ingenious *Com* and *sup* ioldanaiche

IOL-MHAITHEAS, eis, *s m* Much good, great advantage.

† IOMADHALL, aill, *s m* (*Ir id*) Guilt, iniquity

IOMAIREAG, eig, *s. f* (*Ir. id*) A skirmish

IOMLOSGADH, aidh, *s m* (*Ir id*) Adustion.

IOMLOISG, *v a.* Parch. *Pret. a* dh'iomloisg, *fut. aff. a.* iomloisgidh.

IOMRASGAL, ail, *s. m* Wrestling.
† IONCHOSG, oisg, *s. m.* (*Ir. id.*) Impediment, hinderance.
IONCHRASAL, ail, *s. m.* (*Ir id*) Excrement.
† IONNAR, air, *s. m.* (*Ir. id*) A gift.
IONNTLAS, ais, *s m.* (*Ir. id*) Delight
IONSANACH, *a.* (*Ir. id.*) Tardy.
ION-THOLLTA, *a.* (*Ir. id*) Penetrable; easily bored.
IOSDAN, ain, *s. m* (*Ir. id.*) A cottage

L.

† LABHACHD, *s. f.* (*Ir id.*) Matter
LACHAN, ain, *s. m.* (*Ir id.*) The common reed
LACHAR, air, *s. m* (*Ir id*) A vulture, a large bird.
LAINNEACH, *a.* Gleaming, coruscant.
LAINNEIL, *a.* Buxom, handsome
LAINNREACH. See LOINNEACH
LAMHACHAS, ais, *s. m.* (*Ir. id.*) Grovelling
LAMHAGAN, ain, *s m* (*from* lamh) *Ir. id.* A glove
LAMHAN CAT LEACAINN, *s m* Common navel-wort, the *umbilicus veneris* of botanists
LAMHNAN, ain, *s m.* (*Ir. id*) A bladder
LANG, laing, *s m* (*Ir. id*) A feast
LANGAN, ain, *s. m.* (*Ir. id.*) A shotten fish.
LAN-TORRACH, *a.* (*Ir id*) Full, pregnant.
LAOIDHEAN, ein, *s. m* (*Ir. id*) Pith, pulp, marrow
LAOIDHEANACH, *a* (*Ir. id.*) Pithy, pulpy.
LEADANACH, aich, *s m* (*Ir. id*) A cloth-dresser
LASADH, aidh, *s. m* (*Ir. id*) Lust.
LEAGAIT, *s m* (*Ir. id.*) A legate; an offering
LEAMHADH, aidh, *s m.* (*Ir id*) Marshmallows, the *althæa* of botanists.
LEASG, leisg, *s f.* The rain-goose
LÉIR-SGRIOSTA, *part* Destroyed, ruined; ravaged, defaced
LEOGARADH, aidh, *s m.* (*Ir id*) Haughtiness
LIATHAN, ain, *s m.* Common marigold, the *chrysanthemum segetum* of botanists
LIOGADH, aidh, *s m* A whetting, a sharpening.
LIOMHADAIR, *s. m* A burnisher; a polisher.
LION NA H-AIBHNE, *s f* Various-leaved water-crowfoot; the *ranunculus aquatilis* of botanists.
LION NA BANN-SÌTHE, *s f.* Fairy-flax; purging-flax; the *linum catharticum* of botanists.
LIONN-RUADH, *s. m.* (*Ir. id.*) Choler.
† LOBHAR, air, *s m.* (*Ir. id*) Work, a day's work
LOCHD, *s f.* (*Ir. id.*) A nap, a wink of sleep
LOINGEACH, *a* (*Ir id.*) Nautical.
LOINGEAS, eis, *s m* (*Ir. id*) An exile
LOINGSEACH, ich, *s m* A mariner. *N. pl* loingsich
LOIST, *s f* A pillion, a pannel; a sloven.
LOIT, *s f* (*Ir. id*) A whore
LOMAN, ain, *s m* A knot in timber, a piece of timber stripped of its bark
LOMRADH, aidh, *s m.* (*Ir. id*) Effulgence; gorgeousness
LONAILT, *s. f* (*Ir. id*) A storehouse, a repository.
LONGADAN, ain, *s m* (*Ir. id*) A swing-swong
LONGAIR, *s f* A ship's crew.
LOTHACH See LÀTHACH.
LUACHAIR, *a* (*Ir id*) Bright, resplendent.
LUACHAIR, *s f.* Splendour, brightness, a tempest.
LUAILLEACH, *a.* Mimicking, full of gestures
LUAIN, *s pl* (*Ir id*) The loins, kidneys
LUAITHREACH, *a* Expeditious, active
LUAMAIR, *s m.* (*Ir. id*) An astronomer, a navigator, a pilot
LUAMAN, ain, *s m* (*Ir id.*) A little hand
† LUAN, luain, *s m* (*Ir. id*) A greyhound; a woman's breast
LUASGAN, ain, *s m* (*Ir. id.*) Childhood
LUATHRACHD, *s f.* Forwardness, quickness
LÙBAG, aig, *s. f.* (*Ir id*) A tenter.
LÙDAGAN, ain, *s m* (*Ir. id*) The little finger.
LUIBHNEACH, ich, *s m* (*Ir id*) A weed; a quantity of weeds
LUIDEACH, *a* (*Ir id*) Ragged
LÙIDEAN, ein, *s. m* (*Ir id*) The little finger.
LUIGHNE, *s pl* Javelins, spears
LUISTE, *s m* (*Ir id*) A slouch, a sluggard, a clown; a straw pannel
† LUMHAN, ain, *s m* A lamb
LURGAINNEACH, *a.* Long-legged
LURGANACH, *a.* (*Ir. id*) A shaft
LUSDADH, aidh, *s. m.* Flattery.

M.

MAC GUN ATHAIR, *s m* Lesser duck-meat; the *lemna minor* of botanists.
MACHALL UISGE, *s. m.* Water avens, the *geum rivale* of botanists.
MAGAR, air, *s m.* A word, an expression
MAIGEAG, eig, *s. f.* (*Ir. id*) A midwife
MALACH, aich, *s. m.* (*Ir. id.*) A load.
MANDAL, ail, *s. m.* (*Ir. id*) Anger, roughness
MAOLAS, ais, *s. m* (*Ir. id*) A sandal
MARBHACHD, *s. f.* (*Ir. id.*) Languor, languishment
MARBHAN, ain, *s. m.* (*Ir id.*) The margin of a book.
MARCAN, ain, *s. m* A horse
MASAG, aig, *s f* A small red berry
MEACAN DUBH, *s m.* Comfrey; the *symphytum officinale* of botanists
MEACAN DUBH FIADHAIN, *s. m.* Bugle, the *ajuga reptans* of botanists.
MEACAN AN RIGH, *s. m* Common parsnip; the *pastinaca sativa* of botanists
MEACAN SLEIBHE, *s. f.* Great bastard black hellebore; the *helleborus niger fœtidus* of botanists
MEACAN-TOBHACH, *s. m.* Great common burdock, burr; cloth-burr, the *bardana major* of botanists

Mealaidh, s. m. (Ir. id.) A reaper.
Mealcair, s. f. (Ir. id.) A hasty pudding
Meallach, a. (Ir. id.) Soft; fat, rich; rank.
Meantan, ain, s. m. (Ir. id.) A snipe
Mearadh, aidh, s. m. (Ir. id.) Affliction.
Meilleadh, idh, s. m. Inciting; incitement; encouragement
Meillean, ein, s. m. Blame, reproach.
Meilt, meilte, s. f. (Ir. id.) Grinding, mastication, consuming.
Meirse, s. f. (Ir. id.) Smallage
Meoran, ain, s. m. (Ir. id.) A thimble.
Miach, s. m. (Ir. id.) A measure
Mianach, a. Abounding in ore
Miann, s. m. A mole on the skin
Mi-fhonn, s. m. Indifference; lowness of spirits
Mi-fhonnmhor, a. Indifferent; low in spirits.
Mighleidh, s. f. (Ir. id.) Abuse.
Millsean-monaidh, s. m. (Ir. id.) Bog honey-suckle
Millsean, ein, s. m. The milt
Millteach, ich, s. m. (Ir. id.) A wicked man, a destroyer.
Millteachd, s. f. Destruction, injury, abuse.
Millteanas, ais, s. m. (Ir. id.) A blunder
Milltean, ein, s. m. A prodigal
Milltearachd, s. f. Destruction, injury, abuse.
Milseanta, a. Sweetened.
Milineach, a. (Ir. id.) Brave, gallant.
Millneachd, s. f. (Ir. id.) Bravery
Minneach, ich, s. m. (Ir. id.) A lie.
Miodarach, aich, s. A kind of ansated wooden dish
Miolan, ain, s. m. (Ir. id.) A lie.
Miongradh, aidh, s. m. (Ir. id.) A gnawing
Miothag-bhuidhe, s. f. Wood night-shade; the *solanum dulcamara* of botanists
Misnealachd, s. f. Courageousness
Modhalan, ain, s. m. Red-rattle
Moiltean, ein, s. m. A hogrel
Moineag, eig, s. f. (Ir. id.) Bogberry
Moircheas, eis, s. m. (Ir. id.) The falling sickness
Moirteal, eil, s. m. (Ir. id.) A cripple
Molan, ain, s. m. (Ir. id.) A little heap, a hill, a brow
Monach, a. (Ir. id.) Cunning.
† Mong, s. m. (Ir. id.) An edge, a border.
Mongair, s. m. (Ir. id.) A shaver, a trimmer, a clipper.
Mongar, air, s. m. Roaring.
Moran, ain, s. m. (Ir. id.) Meadow saxifrage
Mor-dhochas, ais, s. m. Sanguineness
Mothrach, aich, s. m. (Ir. id.) A damp woody place.
Muaidh, s. f. (Ir. id.) A sound, a cloud.
Mualach, aich, s. m. (Ir. id.) A way or passage; cow-dung
Mucachan, ain, s. m. (from muc) Ir. id. A clown, a hoggish fellow
Muchag, aig, s. f. (Ir. id.) Broom-rape
Muclach, aich, s. m. A herd of swine
Mudan, ain, s. m. (Ir. id.) A cover, a slight covering.
Muilleach, ich, s. m. A puddle.
Muinchinn, s. m. (Ir. id.) A headland, a sea-coast.
† Muine, s. f. (Ir. id.) A whore; a mountain; a thorn; a bramble.
Muineadh, idh, s. m. (Ir. id.) Affability, good behaviour.
Muin-sheud, s. m. (Ir. id.) An ouch.
Muirbhleasg, s. m. (Ir. id.) Stupidity; amazement.
Muirbhrinn, s. pl. (Ir. id.) Scarecrows; termagants
Muireachan, ain, s. m. (Ir. id.) A bulwark.
Muire oigh, s. f. The Virgin Mary
Muirghabhal, ail, s. m. (Ir. id.) An arm of the sea.
Muirineach, ich, s. m. Sea mat-weed.
Muirtis, s. f. (Ir. id.) A mortice.
Muiseach, a. (Ir. id.) Surly
Mulabhar, air, s. m. Dwarf-elder; the *sambucus humilis* of botanists.
Mulach, aich, s. m. (Ir. id.) Puddle water, dirt, an owl.
Mulard, aird, s. m. (Ir. id.) A drake.
Mullach dubh, s. m. Knapweed, the *centaurea nigra* of botanists
Mullan, ain, s. m. (Ir. id.) A mole; a kind of milking-vessel
Mùnaichte, *part* Be-p——d; be-mired
Murach dubh, s. m. (Ir. id.) A blackmoor.
Mur-bhuachaill, s. m. A diver. *N pl.* mur-bhuachaillean.
Murlach, aich, s. m. The bird called kingsfisher

R. Cameron:

N

Nagair, a. (Ir. id.) Comely, handsome
† Naireach, a. (Ir. id.) Brave; generous
Nairne, s. f. Purity, chastity, modesty
Nais, s. f. (Ir. id.) A furnace, a fire-hearth in a forge
Naodhan, ain, s. m. (Ir. id.) A well or fountain.
Naoidhean, ein, s. m. (Ir. id.) Bravery
Naomhag, aig, s. f. (Ir. id.) A coble
Naomh oigh, s. f. (Ir. id.) The Blessed Virgin, a nun
Narrach, a. (Ir. id.) Cross, ill-tempered
Nàsach, a. See Nòsach.
† Neabhaidh, s. m. (Ir. id.) An enemy.
† Neachd, s. f. (Ir. id.) A tribe, a family.
Neamhachd, s. f. Heavenliness
Neamhail, a. (neamh-amhuil) Heavenly
Neamhain, s. f. Impetuosity; violence, activity
† Nean, s. m. (Ir. id.) An inch; a span; a wave.
Neas, s. m. (Ir. id.) A tool for making earthen pots
Neimh, s. f. Poison See Nimh
† Neoid, a. (Ir. id.) Strong, stout, thick; penurious; scanty; wicked
Niadh, a. (Ir. id.) Strong; *substantively*, honour; veneration.
† Niogharach, a. (Ir. id.) Constant.
Nionadh, aidh, s. m. (Ir. id.) Childbearing.
Noigean, ein, s. m. A measure of a quarter of a pint.
Nosarachd, s. f. (Ir. id.) Custom; modishness.
Nuadhas, ais, s. m. (*from* nuadh.) The first of any thing; biestings.
Nuall, nuaill, s. m. (Ir. id.) Praise.
Nuallach, a. (Ir. id.) Freakish.
Nuallach, aich, s. m. (Ir. id.) A germander.

O.

OCHRAS, ais, *s. m.* (*Ir. id*) The gills of a fish
OGHAM, *s. m.* The occult manner of writing used by the ancient Gael.
OIBNEACH, *a.* Sudden, quick. *Com.* and *sup.* oibniche.
OIDEAN, ein, *s. m.* (*Ir. id.*) A degree of nobility.
OIDHEAS, eis, *s. m.* Instruction; counsel.
OIGHNEACH, *a.* (*Ir. id*) Liberal, generous
OINIDH, *a.* (*Ir. id*) Generous, liberal, magnanimous
OINSEACHD, *s f.* (*Ir. id*) Whoredom.
OIRBHIR, *s. f.* (*Ir. id.*) Reproach, a curse.
OIRCEAS, eis, *s. m* (*Ir. id*) A mess
OIRCHILL, *s f* (*Ir id*) Concealment, ambush.
OIRCHIND, *s f* (*Ir. id*) Providence
OIREAMHAN, ain, *s m* Concord, agreement, union
OIRNEADH, idh, *s m* (*Ir id*) Ordination
ÒRACH, *a.* Auriferous.
ORBAN, ain, *s m.* (*Ir. id*) A patrimony
† ORC, *v a.* (*Ir id*) Murder
† ORCAIN, *s f* (*Ir id*) Murder
† ORD, *s. m* Death; manslaughter; *adjectively*, bold, valiant.
ORDAN, ain, *s m* (*Ir id*) Generosity; dignity, solemnity, a small hammer, a degree; music.
ORD-LAOCH, aoich, *s m* (*Ir id*) A hero
ORNAIL, *s f* (*Ir id*) The upper part of a door-case
ORNAID, *s f* (*Ir id*) An ornament
ORNAIDEACH, *a* Ornamental
OSADH, aidh, *s m* (*Ir. id*) Concord, confederacy.
† OSAR, air, *s m.* Exaltation, preferment
OSNACH, aich, *s m* Carrion
OSNADH, aidh, *s. m* (*Ir id*) The hair of the head
† OSRAN, ain, *s m* (*Ir id*) Peace

P.

PAIDEAG, eig, *s f.* (*Ir id*) A torch made of tallow lapped upon linen.
PAIL. See PARHAIL.
† PAIN, *s f* (*Ir id*) Bread, a cake.
PAIPEAN BÀN, *s. m.* White garden-poppy, the *papaver album sativum* of botanists
PAIPEAN RUADH, *s m.* Red poppy
PAIPEAN DUBH, *s m* Black garden-poppy, the *papaver nigrum sativum* of botanists
PÀIRTEACH, ich, *s. m* A partaker, a partner.
PÀIRTEACHAS, ais, *s m* Partnership, association
PALTAG, aig, *s f* A thump, a blow.
PARDAG, aig, *s f.* A hamper used in mountainous places for carrying things on both sides of a horse
† PARN, *s. m* (*Ir. id*) A whale.
PEIRSILL, *s f* Parsley Peirsill mhòr, *smallage*, the *apium palustre* of botanists.
† PEIST, *s f.* A pestilence, ailment, loss
PIOLAIR, *s f* A pillar
† PIONNSARACH, *a.* (*Ir id*) Wily, cunning
† PIONNSARACHD, *s f* Wiliness
PIOSARNACH, aich, *s m* (*Ir. id.*) A whisper
PITEAG, eig, *s. f.* (*Ir id.*) An effeminate person
PLAB, *s. m.* (*Ir. id*) Smut; a spot, a fillip
PLABAIR, *s. m.* (*Ir. id*) A babbler.
PLACAIR, *s. m* A chubby-faced fellow; a glutton
POBAL, ail, *s m* Butter-burr; the *tussilago petastes* of botanists
POCAIR, *s. m.* A beggar
POICHEAN, ein, *s m.* A pithless diminutive fellow
POIR, *s f.* (*Ir. id.*) A pore
POIT-CHAMAG, *s. f.* A pothook.
PONAIR CHAPULL, *s m* Marsh-trefoil; buck-bean, the *menyanthis trifoliata* of botanists
† PONT, *a.* (*Ir. id*) Fierce, cruel, vehement
PORT GUNNA, *s. m.* (*Ir id*) A loophole
PRAGHAIN, *s. f.* (*Ir id.*) Care, anxiety.
PRAISEACH, *a.* (*Ir. id.*) Brassy.
PRAISEACH BHRATHAR, *s m.* English mercury; wild spinach, the *chenopodium* of botanists.
PRAISEACH BHUIDHE, *s m* Wild cabbage; nape, the *brassica* of botanists
PRAISEACH FEIDH, *s. m* Bastard mustard, the *thlapse arvense* of botanists
PRAISEACH FIADHAIN, *s m* Common wild goose-foot orache; the *chenopodium album* of botanists.
PRAISEACH GARBH, *s. m.* Wild mustard; charlock, the *sinapis arvensis* of botanists
PRAISEACH GLAS, *s m* Fig-leaved goose-foot, the *chenopodium serotinum* of botanists
PRAISEACH MHIN, *s m.* Wild orache; the *atriplex hastata* of botanists
PRAISEACH A BHALLA, *s m* Wall goose-foot; the *chenopodium murale* of naturalists
PRAISEACH MARA, *s m* Sea goose-foot; glasswort, the *chenopodium maritimum* of botanists.
PRAISEACH TRÀGHA, *s m.* Sea colewort; the *cramba maritima* of botanists
PRAISGL, *s f* (*Ir id.*) Pottage
PREACHAIN, *s f* The bones taken out of pork for the purpose of making bacon
PREASTAIDH, *a.* Unable to bear cold; timid
PRIBHLEID, *s f* (*Ir. id*) A privilege
PRIOBAICHE, *s m* (*Ir id.*) A blinkard
PRIOBHAID, *s. f.* (*Ir id*) Privacy, secrecy
† PROBHADH, aidh, *s m* (*Ir id*) A proof.
PROIMBEALLAN, ain, *s. m.* (*Ir. id.*) A drone-bee, a beetle
PROIMHIDH, *a* (*Ir id*) Fat
PROISEAL, *a* (*Ir id*) Bold; proud; nice.
† PRONN, *v a.* (*Ir id*) Give, bestow
† PRONNADH, aidh, *s m* (*Ir id*) A giving, a bestowing
PUINNEARN, eirn, *s m* (*Ir id*) A beam for measuring or weighing goods; the graduated beam.
PUINTEALTA, *a.* (*Ir. id.*) Precise; punctual
PUNAN, ain, *s. m.* A bittern; a blast, the sound of a horn.
PURPAIL, *a* Punctual, accurate

R.

RABHACHAN, ain, s. m. A beacon
RAIBEACH, a. (Ir. id.) Loose
RAIGH, s. f. Frenzy.
RAINAS, ais, s. m. A romance, a fable
RAIPLEACHAN, ain, s. m. A scullion
RANNAIR, s. m. (Ir. rannoir W. rhannur) A distributer
RAOB, v. a. (Ir. id.) Tear, rend; prop
RAOBACH, a. (Ir. id.) Tearing, rending.
RAOBACHD, s. f. (Ir. id.) Tearing, excess, gluttony
RASDACH, a. (Ir. id.) Churlish, unpolite. *Com.* and *sup.* rasdaiche
RASDAIR, s. f. (Ir. id.) Great satiety
RATHAN, ain, s. m. (Ir. id.) A bunch; a bundle
REABHACH, a. (Ir. id.) Joyful.
REABHACH, aich, s. m. One who plays tricks, a mountebank
REAMHAIS, s. f. (Ir. id.) Foretelling, prognostication
REANGACH, a. (Ir. id.) Wrinkled
REUSONTAS, ais, s. m. (Ir. id.) Ratiocination
RIADRANACH, aich, s. f. (Ir. id.) An old maid, a cast-off mistress
RIAGHALTACHD, s. f. (Ir. id.) Regularity; religiousness
RIARACH, aich, s. m. (Ir. id.) A servitor.
RIDLAG, eig, s. f. Sweet myrtle, a small shrub
RIGHEAL RIGH, s. m. (Ir. id.) Stinking cranesbill
RIGHNEAS, eis, s. m. (Ir. id.) Delay
RIGH-THEACH, s. m. (Ir. id.) A royal residence, a palace
RINGEALL, ill, s. m. (Ir. id.) A promise
RIOMSACHAN, ain, s. m. (Ir. id.) A searcher
RIONNACHD, s. f. (Ir. id.) A burial, interment.
RISEAN, ein, s. m. (Ir. id.) An historian
RITHNEAS, eis, s. m. (Ir. id.) Slowness, delay
ROB, s. m. (Ir. id.) Any beast that digs up the earth with its snout.
ROBHÀS, ais, s. m. (Ir. id.) A violent death.
ROILBH, roilbhe, s. f. (Ir. id.) A mountain.
ROILBHEACH, a. (Ir. id.) Hilly
ROILLEACHAN, ain, s. m. (Ir. id.) A rolling-stone
ROIMHSE, s. f. (Ir. id.) Sin, iniquity
ROISGEACH, a. (Ir. id.) Wise.
ROSGACH, a. Wise, knowing.
RÒSAG, aig, s. f. (Ir. id.) A rose-tree
ROS LACHAIN, s. m. Lesser duck-meat; the *lemma minor* of botanists
RÒTHLAG. See RÒLAG
RUAIDH-RINN, s. (Ir. id.) Red points or edges.
RUAINEACH, a. (Ir. id.) Fierce; forward.
RUAMNACH, a. (Ir. id.) Indignant.
† RUCHD, a. (Ir. id.) Vehement; *substantively*, a sow, a pig, entrails; a groan; a lamentation.
RUIMFANACH, ich, s. m. A marsh
RUIMHE, s. f. (Ir. id.) A reproof, a reproach.
RUIREACH, a. (Ir. id.) Famous.
RUTHARACH, a. (Ir. id.) Quarrelsome
RUAGAIR, s. m. A fugitive, an outlaw.
RUAIDHLE, s. m. (Ir. id.) A poor worn-down creature
RUAINN, s. f. (Ir. id.) Water in which dye-stuff is boiled.
RUANAIDH, a. (Ir. id.) Red sorrel.
RUBHAG, aig, s. f. (Ir. id.) A thong of hemp or flax, a shoemaker's wax-end
RUIBH, s. f. (Ir. id.) Rue
RUINTEALAS, ais, s. m. Darnel.
RUIPLEACHAN, ain, s. m. A gor-bellied fellow
RUMAIL, s. f. A convulsion
RUSTAG, aig, s. f. (Ir. id.) A bear.
RUTH, s. m. (Ir. id.) A chain, a link

S.

SABHALTACHD, s. f. Security, safety, protection
SACRAIL, s. f. (Ir. id.) A sacrifice
SAIGHLEAS, eis, s. m. (Ir. id.) An age, old age
† SAINEAS, eis, s. m. (Ir. id.) Sedition
SAINEIL, a. Graceful, beautiful, handsome, various
SAIRSE, s. f. (Ir. id.) A sieve
SAISDE BHEAG, s. f. Small garden sage, the *salvia hortensis major vulgaris* of botanists
SAISDE CHNUIC, s. f. Mountain-sage, the *salvia Alpina* of botanists
SAISDE COILLE, s. f. Wood-sage, the *salvia agrestis* of botanists
SAMHACHAN, ain, s. m. (Ir. id.) A soft quiet person.
SAMHADH, aidh, s. m. An edge, as of a hatchet
SAMHNAS, ais, s. m. (Ir. id.) Anger.
SANNADH, aidh, s. m. A loosening, a separating
SAOBH-GHLORACH, a. Gabbling
SAOILEACHDAINN, s. f. (Ir. id.) A thinking; thought, reflection.
SAOIRE, s. (Ir. id.) Festivals, holidays
SAORSACHADH, aidh, s. m. A cheapening
SAORSAICH, v. a. Cheapen *Pret. a.* shaorsaich, *cheapened*; *fut. aff. a.* saorsaichidh, *shall cheapen*, *p. part.* saorsaichte.
SAOR-CHLOICH, s. m. (Ir. id.) A mason
SAOTHACHAN, ain, s. m. (Ir. id.) A dish; a plate
SAOTHAIL, a. Laborious, toilsome, painstaking
SARAG, aig, s. f. (Ir. id.) A gloss
SASAMH, s. m. (Ir. id.) Pleasure, satisfaction.
SÀSDA, a. (Ir. id.) Satisfied, grateful
SÀTHOIDE, s. m. (Ir. id.) A preceptor
SDODACH, a. (Ir. id.) Restive
SEAGHAS, ais, s. m. (Ir. id.) A wood
SEALAN, ain, s. m. (Ir. id.) A halter for execution.
SEALANACH, aich, s. m. (Ir. id.) An executioner, a villain, a meagre man or beast
† SEALLADH, aidh, s. m. A cell.
SEAMAR BHÀN, s. f. Trefoil; white clover; white honey-suckle, the *trifolium repens* of botanists

Seamar chapuill, *s. f.* Purple trefoil; broad-leaved clover; the *trifolium pratense* of botanists.

Seamar chre, *s. f.* Male speedwell; the *veronica officinalis* of botanists.

Seamar mhuire, *s. f.* Female pimpernel; yellow wood loose-strife; the *anagallis fœmina* of botanists.

Seamhrag, aig, *s. f.* A small nail or peg; wood-sorrel.

Seananach, aich, *s. m.* (*Ir. id.*) A wasp.

Seannachan, ain, *s. m.* (*Ir. id.*) A wily fellow.

Sean-talamh, *s. m.* (*Ir. id.*) Fallow-land.

† **Searnach**, *a.* (*Ir. id.*) Dissolvent, separable.

† **Searnadh**, aidh, *s. m.* (*Ir. id.*) Dissolution, separation.

Sear-shuil, *s. f.* (*Ir. id.*) A squint-eye.

Seasaothar, air, *s. m.* (*Ir. id.*) A rower's bench in a boat.

Seasdan, ain, *s. m.* A shout; a hunter's cry.

Seasgach, aich, *s. f.* (*Ir. id.*) A dry cow.

Seicean, *s. m.* (*Ir. id.*) The membrane that covers the guts.

Seilide, *s. f.* (*Ir. id.*) A snail.

Seimhean, ein, *s. m.* Black-headed bogrush; the *schœnus nigricans* of botanists.

† **Seire**, *s. f.* (*Ir. id.*) Food.

Seireach, *a.* (*Ir. id.*) Liberal of food.

Seirsean, ein, *s. m.* (*Ir. id.*) A robust person.

Seis madraidh, *s. f.* Great burr-reed; the *sperganium erectum* of botanists.

Seoladh, aidh, *s. m.* (*Ir. id.*) The first semi-metre of a verse.

Sgamall, aill, *s. m.* Scum; phlegm.

Sgaballach, aich, *s. m.* A wardrobe-keeper.

Sgaindear, eir, *s. m.* A division, dissension.

Sgairg, *s. f.* (*Ir. id.*) A stony gravelly bottom.

Sgalaid, *s. f.* (*Ir. id.*) Noise.

Sgamh, *s. m.* A wry mouth.

Sgaoilteag, eig, *s. f.* (*Ir. id.*) A sheet; a winding-sheet.

Sgaothan, ain, *s. m.* (*Ir. id.*) A chamber-pot.

Sgathach, aich, *s. m.* (*Ir. id.*) A fence made of loppings.

Sgardach, aich, *s. m.* Vomiting; a squirt; a bunch of furze or thorns placed before the tap in a mask kieve.

Sgfarach, aich, *s. m.* (*Ir. id.*) A square.

Sgàthan, ain, *s. m.* A gazing-stock.

Sgiatan, ain, *s. m.* A dart.

Sgillian, *s. pl.* The scales of a fish.

Sgineidrach, *a.* Skittish.

Sgioballan, ain, *s. m.* A brush for sweeping cattle with.

Sgiorrag, aig, *s. f.* A flatus.

Sgiolmhor, *a.* Talkative. *Com.* and *sup.* sgiolmhoire.

Sgirbh, *s. f.* (*Ir. id.*) A rocky ford; a stony bottom.

Sgoige, *s. f.* The throat.

Sgoigeach, *a.* Guttural.

Sgrab, *v. a.* (*Ir. id.*) Erase; scratch; write.

Sgraban, ain, *s. m.* (*Ir. id.*) A currycomb.

Sgoloair, *s. m.* (*Ir. id.*) A scold. *N. pl.* sgolgaireau.

Sgonasach, *a.* Eager, greedy.

Sgram, *s. m.* (*Ir. id.*) A snatch; a snap.

Sgramain, *s. m.* (*Ir. id.*) An extortioner.

Sgreabhag, aig, *s. f.* (*Ir. id.*) A crust.

Sgreagar, *a.* Rocky.

Sgreig, *s. f.* (*Ir. id.*) Rocky ground.

Sgribeag, eig, *s. f.* (*Ir. id.*) A small griddle.

Sgrog, sgroig, *s. f.* An old cow or ewe.

Sgruibleachan, ain, *s. m.* A scribbler.

Sgruigean, ein, *s. m.* The neck of a bottle.

Sgrutach, aich, *s. m.* (*Ir. id.*) The itch.

Sguirb, *s. f.* (*Ir. id.*) Cessation.

Sguirbeadh, idh, *s. m.* A condemning; condemnation.

Siachair. See Siochair.

Sidhe, *s. f.* (*Ir. id.*) A blast.

Silteachan, ain, *s. m.* A still; a distiller.

Siogan, ain, *s. m.* A gizzard.

Siollan, ain, *s. m.* A skinny, meagre creature.

Sion, *s. m.* A whisper; a phenomenon; brightness; a warning.

Siosdan, ain, *s. m.* (*Ir. id.*) A hunter's cry.

Siothlan, ain, *s. m.* (*Ir. id.*) A strainer; a sack.

Sistealach, aich, *s. m.* (*Ir. id.*) A flax-dresser; a wool-comber.

Sistealachd, *s. f.* (*Ir. id.*) Flax-dressing; wool-carding.

Sistealair, *s. m.* A flax-dresser; a wool-comber.

Siunan, ain, *s. m.* (*Ir. id.*) A vessel made of straw to hold meal.

Siurdan, ain, *s. m.* (*Ir. id.*) Tattle.

Siurran, ain, *s. m.* (*Ir. id.*) Giddiness; drunkenness; a watery mist.

† **Slabhar**, *a.* (*Ir. id.*) Narrow.

Slaimean, ein, *s. m.* A dirty person.

Slamair, *s. m.* One who eats voraciously.

† **Slaod**, *s. m.* (*Ir. id.*) Murder, slaughter; a pulley or crane.

Slaodrach, aich, *s. m.* (*Ir. id.*) Foundation.

Slaod-theine, *s. m.* A wasting or consuming fire; a great fire in which many persons were consumed.

Sleant, *s. m.* A tile.

Sliasaid, *s. f.* (*Ir. id.*) The coarse part of a thread.

Sliasd, **Sliasdan**, ain, *s. m.* (*Ir. id.*) A ledge in a loom.

Slonnadh, aidh, *s. m.* Cattle.

Sludrach, aich, *s. m.* (*Ir. id.*) A foundation.

Smaile, *s. f.* A blow, a buffet.

Smeirne, *s. f.* A spit; a broach.

Smiste, *s. f.* (*Ir. id.*) A mallet.

Smol, *s. f.* (*Ir. id.*) A weaver's shuttle.

Smugadair, *s. m.* (*Ir. id.*) A pocket-handkerchief.

Smuit, *s. f.* A nose, a bill, a beak.

Smulag, aig, *s. f.* (*Ir. id.*) A fillip with the fingers.

Smulc, *s. m.* A snout; a surly look.

Smulcach, *a.* Snouty; surly.

Snoghach, *a.* (*Ir. id.*) Beautiful.

Socan, ain, *s. m.* (*Ir. id.*) A big-bellied man; a field-fare.

Sodarach, *a.* Trotting.

Soimhneach, *a.* Peaceable; agreeable.

Sòimhneas, eis, *s. m.* Fretting; reconciliation.

Soighne, *s. f.* (*Ir. id.*) Pleasure, delight.

Soineach, *a.* (*Ir. id.*) Noisy.

Soisealach, *a.* Airy; hearty; proud.

Soislean, ein, *s. m.* A firm or bold standing.

Sonnadh, aidh, *s. m.* A fort, a garrison.

Sopag, aig, *s. f.* A small bundle of straw.

Sortan, ain, *s. m.* (*Ir. id.*) A shout.

Spadanach, aich, *s. m.* A sluggard. *N. pl.* spadanaich.

Spaid, *s. f.* (*Ir. id.*) A drug; a sluggard; an eunuch.

Spailleadh, idh, *s. m.* (*Ir. id.*) A fall.

Spailp, *s. f.* (*Ir. id.*) A kiss; a lie.

Sparsan, ain, *s. m.* (*Ir. id.*) A diminution.

† **Spart**, *a.* Heavy, dull, dense.

Spearag, aig, *s. f.* (*Ir. id.*) A sparrowhawk.

Spliot, *v. a.* Dash or throw carelessly aside.
Spliudrach, aich, *s. m.* *(Ir. id.)* Bad beer.
Spoid, *s. f.* *(Ir. id.)* A hasty word.
Spoidear, eir, *s. m.* *(Ir. id.)* A hasty person.
Spursan, ain, *s. m.* *(Ir. id.)* A diminutive person.
Sràideachan, ain, *s. m.* A saunterer; a vagabond.
Sraidheag, eig, *s. f.* *(Ir. id.)* A cake.
Srang, sraing, *s. m.* *(Ir. id.)* A frown.
Sram, *s. m.* Matter running from the eyes.
Sràmach, *a.* Blear-eyed.
† Sreabhan, ain, *s. m.* *(Ir. id.)* A cake.
Sreangair, *s. m.* *(Ir. id.)* A sneaking half-starved fellow.
Sruaic, *s. f.* *(Ir. id.)* A pustule.
Sruan, sruain, *s. m.* *(Ir. id.)* A kind of triangular frame on which bread is set to bake before the fire.
Srubh, srubha, *s. m.* *(Ir. id.)* A snout.
Srubhag, aig, *s. f.* A cake baked before the fire.
Stabh, stabha, *s. m.* *(Ir. id.)* An iron vessel chained to a well by the way-side.
Stalcair, *s. m.* *(Ir. id.)* A pacing-horse; a bully; a robust fellow.
Stànadair, *s. m.* A tinker, a tin-smith.
Steallair, *s. m.* A faucet.
Stiopas, ais, *s. m.* Drowsiness.
Stocainnte, *a.* Stiff, or numbed, as the legs are after sitting for a long while.
Strach, *s. m.* An arch, a vault.
Streachail, *v. a.* *(Ir. id.)* Lacerate. *P. part.* streachailte.
Striochlan, ain, *s. m.* *(Ir. id.)* A rag; any valueless thing.
Stroighean, ein, *s. m.* Mud and straw mixed for a wall.
Stroill, *s. f.* *(Ir. id.)* Delay.
Stuacach, *a.* *(Ir. id.)* Gruff, boorish, churlish.
Stùcair, *s. m.* A stiff, conceited fellow; a churl. *N. pl.* stucairean.
Suag, suaig, *s. f.* A rope, a cable.
Suagair, *s. m.* A rope-maker.
Suaill, *s. f.* *(Ir. id.)* A small quantity.
Suaim, *s. f.* *(Ir. id.)* Sound.
Suaile, *a.* *(Ir. id.)* Weary, weak, pale, dejected.
† Suall, *a.* Famous, renowned; *substantively*, a wonder.
Suaiteachan, ain, *s. m.* *(Ir. id.)* A mixer; a kneader.
Sualach, *a.* *(Ir. id.)* Famous, admirable.
Suanaran, ain, *s. m.* A sleeper.
† Subhallach, *a.* *(Ir. id.)* Religious.
Sugan, ain, *s. m.* *(Ir. id.)* A straw collar for cattle.
Suileasg, eisg, *s. f.* *(Ir. id.)* An osier.
Sumair, *s. m.* *(Ir. id.)* A gulf; a whirlpool; a sucker; a swallower; a drinker; a glutton; the sucker of a pump.
Sunn, *s. m.* *(Ir. id.)* A puff; a blast; a push; a fortification.
Sunnach, aich, *s. m.* *(Ir. id.)* A strong fort; a milching place; a summit.
Sunn-ghaoth, aoithe, *s. f.* *(Ir. id.)* A high wind.
Suthan, ain, *s. m.* A booby, a dunce; small beer.
Surabhan, ain, *s. m.* Southernwood.

T.

† Tab, *s. m.* *(Ir. id.)* A start.
Tabar, air, *s. m.* *(Ir. id.)* A tabor; a timbrel.
Tabhuich, *v. n.* Profit; exact. *Pret.* thabhaich.
Tabhul, uil, *s. m.* *(Ir. id.)* A horse-fly.
Tacadh, aidh, *s. m.* *(Ir. id.)* Prosperity.
Tach, *s. m.* Value, estimation.
Tag, *v. a.* *(Ir. id.)* Deliver.
Tagarach, aich, *s. m.* A pretender, a claimer.
Taghal, ail, *s. m.* *(Ir. id.)* A feeling, touching, the sense of feeling.
Taibheirt, *s. f.* *(Ir. id.)* Disparagement.
† Taibhseach, *a.* *(Ir. id.)* Proud.
† Taibhseachan, ain, *s. m.* *(Ir. id.)* A proud person; a coquette.
† Taibhseachd, *s. f.* *(Ir. id.)* Proudness; coquetry.
Taiceachd, *s. f.* *(Ir. id.)* Reliance.
Taircheall, ill, *s. m.* *(Ir. id.)* An act, action.
† Tairgeadh, idh, *s. m.* *(Ir. id.)* Collecting; a collection.
Tairis, *v. a.* and *n.* Love; come; stay, remain. *Pret. a.* thairisg; *fut. aff.* tairisgidh.
Taisgeachan, ain, *s. m.* A storekeeper.
Taisgeadh, idh, *s. m.* *(Ir. id.)* A store; wealth.
Taisgealach, aich, *s. m.* *(Ir. id.)* A pilgrim; a passenger.
Taisgealachd, *s. f.* *(Ir. id.)* Pilgrimage.
Taisgidh, *s. f.* *(Ir. id.)* A trunk; a hoarding, a laying up.
Taisill, *s. f.* Trespass; damage; injury; injustice.
Taithleachas, ais, *s. m.* *(Ir. id.)* Excusation.
Talcais, *s. f.* Contempt.
Talchar, air, *s. m.* *(Ir. id.)* Obstinacy.
Talcharach, *a.* Obstinate.
Tamhan, ain, *s. m.* *(Ir. id.)* The spleen.
Tamaidh, *s. m.* *(Ir. id.)* A slothful person.
Tànaiste, *s. m.* The heir-apparent to a prince.
Tànaisteas, eis, *s. m.* *(Ir. id.)* Dominion.
Taobhach, *a.* (*from* taobh.) *Ir. id.* Partial.
Taobhan, ain, *s. m.* A patch or clout on the side of a *brogue*.
Tarail, *s. f.* *(Ir. id.)* A visit.
Tarar, air, *s. m.* An augre, a piercer.
† Tasgail, *a.* *(Ir. id.)* Renowned.
Tasgal, ail, *s. m.* A great wave.
Tasgalachd, *s. f.* *(Ir. id.)* The rolling of the sea.
† Tath, *s. m.* *(Ir. id.)* A lord; a ruler; anger.
Teaghlachan, ain, *s. m.* (*from* teaghlach.) *Ir. id.* A domestic.
Teagail, *s. f.* *(Ir. id.)* A house, a habitation.
Teagair. See Teagar.
Tealrachd, *s. f.* Profusion, extravagance.
Tealtachd, *s. f.* *(Ir. id.)* Simplicity.
Tealtaidh, *a.* Silly; cowardly.
Teamhair, *s. f.* *(Ir. id.)* A covered or shaded walk on a hill.
Teangan, ain, *s. m.* *(Ir. id.)* A tongue; a language.
Teanntan, ain, *s. m.* *(Ir. id.)* A press.
† Teas, *s. m.* *(Ir. id.)* A sound.
† Teasd, *s. m.* *(Ir. id.)* A report.
Teasdail, *s. f.* *(Ir. id.)* Want.
† Teilm, *s. f.* *(Ir. id.)* Great terror.

Teisbeirt, *s f.* Increase, growth.
Tiachair, *a.* (*Ir. id.*) Perverse, ill-disposed; sickly; weary under a burden.
Tiachag, aig, *s. f.* A small bag.
Tiarpan, ain, *s. m.* (*Ir. id.*) A testicle.
Tibearsan, ain, *s. m.* (*Ir. id.*) A still.
Tibheadh, idh, *s. m.* (*Ir. id.*) Laughter; joking; shunning; quickness.
Tigheach, *a.* (*from* tigh.) *Ir id.* Domestic
Tigheadasach, *a.* (*Ir. id.*) Diligent; busied about housekeeping; hospitable
† **Tinneasach**, *a.* (*Ir id.*) Stout, strong, *literally*, strongly ribbed
Tionchair, *s. f.* Attendance.
Toibhre, *s. f.* (*Ir. id.*) A fancy, an illusion.
Tomair, *s. m.* (*Ir id.*) Protection; a protector; a dipper
Tollachan, ain, *s m* (*from* toll) A piercer *N pl* tollachain
Tomhadh, aidh, *s m* (*Ir. id.*) A threat; a frown.
Tomradh, aidh, *s. m* (*Ir. id.*) Fustian; bombast
Totarnachd, *s. f.* (*Ir. id.*) Stuttering, stammering
Traogh, *a.* (*Ir. id.*) Empty; ebbed.
Treanas, ais, *s. m* Abstinence.
Trudarnach, aich, *s. m.* A stammerer.
Truimpleasg, *s m.* (*Ir. id.*) Fulmination, explosion
† **Trull**, trulla, *s m.* (*Ir. id.*) A head.
Trusdar, air, *s m.* Dirt, filth, dust.
Trusdarnach, aich, *s m.* (*Ir. id.*) A stammerer.
Trusdromach, aich, *s. m.* (*Ir. id.*) A busy-body.
Trusgan, ain, *s. m.* (*Ir. id.*) The privy parts.
Tuacaird, *s f.* A winding of yarn.
Tuaradh, aidh, *s. m.* (*Ir id.*) A sauce.
Tuaslach, aich, *s. m.* One who releases
Tuchraidh, *s f.* (*Ir. id.*) The appointed time; critical time
Tuilcheanach, aich, *s m.* (*Ir. id*) A handsel
Tuile talmhainn, *s. m.* (*Ir id*) Bulbous crow-foot, butter-cup, the *ranunculus bulbosus* of botanists.
† **Tuilm**, *s. f* (*Ir id*) A gift.
Tuirbheach, *a* (*Ir id*) Shamefaced, bashful
Tuireanta, *a* (*Ir id*) Pregnant
Tuirginn, *s f* (*Ir id*) A flood, a broad, squat person, a wash-staff; a bottle.
Tuiridh, *s f* (*Ir id*) A pillar, a support; a request
Tulchair, *s. m* (*Ir. id*) An emulator
Tulpaist, *s f* (*Ir id.*) An avenue; a walk before a door
Tulscan, ain, *s m* (*Ir id*) A spreading; a loosening, a bursting
Tum-dhias, *s f* (*Ir id*) A bushy ear of corn
Turachan, ain, *s m* A big-bellied person, a ranter; a beggar.
Tusgarnach, aich, *s m* A libeller, a story-teller.
Tuslang, aing, *s m* A wrestling
Tusornachd, *s f* (*Ir id*) Whispering.

U.

Uaim, *s. f.* (*Ir. id*) Embroidery
Uainnearach, *a.* Secret, retired.
Uaimeach, *a* (*Ir. id*) Solitary *Com* and *sup* uaimiche
Uainnearas, ais, *s. m.* Secrecy, retirement
Uaiseach, ich, *s m* (*Ir id.*) A hero. *N pl.* uaisichean
Uamh, uaimh, *s m.* (*Ir id*) Ornament.
Uanachd, *s. f.* (*Ir. id.*) Earning.
Uaslaid, *s. f.* (*Ir. id.*) Gentleness, redemption
Ucas fhiadhain, *s. m.* Common mallow, the *malva sylvestris* of botanists.
Ucas fhrangach, *a.* Dwarf mallow; the *malva rotundifolia* of botanists.
Uchdach, aich, *s m* (*Ir id*) A cleff in music.
Udhachd, *s. f.* (*Ir. id.*) A will or testament; a confession
Uilidh, *s. f.* (*Ir. id*) A lake.
Uilleann, inn, *s. m.* Honeysuckle.
Uireagal, ail, *s. m.* Dread, terror.
Uireagalach, *a* (*Ir id*) Terribly afraid.
Uisgrian, ein, *s. m.* (*Ir. id.*) An aqueduct
Uisiarach, aich, *s m.* (*Ir id*) A petitioner.
Unach, aich, *s m.* A bleaching, a washing
† **Urach**, aich, *s. m* (*Ir. id.*) Earth; beginning, contention, a bottle; a pail, a small tub.
Uran, ain, *s m.* (*Ir id*) A cold bath.
Urard, *a.* Very high, *substantively*, a high place
Urgais, *s f* (*Ir id*) An exchange, an alteration
Urghart, airt, *s m* (*Ir id*) Bad luck, misfortune, victory.
Urlainn, *s f.* (*Ir id*) The staff of a spear
Urlarach, aich, *s m* (*Ir. id*) A close housekeeper.
Urrlach, *a* (*Ir id*) Having thick or bushy hair
Urmach, aich, *s m.* (*Ir. id.*) An armoury
Ursnaidhin, *s. m.* (*Ir id*) A pin or jack to fasten the cords of a harp.
Usgarach, *s m.* A separation *N. pl* usgaraichean

AN

ENGLISH-GAELIC DICTIONARY.

AN

ENGLISH-GAELIC DICTIONARY.

A.

A, *a.* Ceud litir na h-aibidil.

A. Giorrachadh airson Artium, *nan ealadhain; agus airson* Anno, *anns a bhliadhna; ann am bhliadhna.* A.D., *ann am bhliadhna an t-Slànuighfhir.* A.N., *o chruthachadh 'n t-saoghail; roimh meadhon là.* A.U.C., *o leigeadh bunaite na Roimh.*

A, *a.* Ag. Go a fishing, *rach a dh'iasgachadh.* What art thou doing? *ciod tha thu a deanamh?* A walking, *ag imeachd.*

A, in some vulgarisms, is differently expressed. Two acres a man, *da acair am fear;* once a year, *uair sa bhliadhna.*

Aback, *adv.* Air ais, an comhar chùil.

Abacot, *s.* Seorsa boineid a b' àbhaist bhith aig righribh Shasuinn.

Abacus, *s.* Bord cunntais, clàr cunntais, clach mhullaich.

Abactors, *s. pl* Creachadairean, spùinneadairean; robairean; luchd reubainn; luchd creich.

Abaddon, *s.* An diabhol.

Abaft, *adv.* Gu deireadh; o'n chrann gu deireadh luinge (no) bàta; eadar an crann mor 's an stiùir.

† Abaisance, *s.* Umhlachd; modh; beic; stnochd.

Abalienate, *v.* Thoir thairis cuid aon neach do neach eile.

Abalienation, *s.* Toirt thairis cuid aon neach do neach eile.

Abandon, *v. a* Tréig, fàg; cuir cùl ri; diobair, cuitich, thoir thairis; leig dhiot; dealaich ri. He abandoned her, *threig se i.*

Abandoned, *part.* and *a.* (*Forsaken*), tréigte, fagte; diobairte; cuitichte; (*wicked*), mallaichte; millte; caillte, aingidh, olc, cionntach; coirpte; peacach; curt.

Abandonment, *s.* Treigsinn; fàgail, diobairt, toirt thairis.

Abase, *v. a.* Islich, irioslaich, cuir sios Abased, *islichte irioslaichte*, he shall be abased, *islichear e.*

Abasement, *s.* Isleachadh, isleachd, irioslachadh; (*as of rent*), meachainn

Abash, *v. a.* Nàirich, nàraich, cuir gu h-ambluadh, cuir gu nàir. Abashed, *nàraichte*, *fu nàir.*

Abate, *v a.* and *n.* Lughdaich, beagaich; islich, leig sios; ciùinich; fàs ciùin; traogh diosg; rach an lughaid.

Abatement, *s* Lughdachadh, beagachadh; meachainn; isleachadh; ciùineachadh; traoghadh, diosgadh, leigeil sios.

Abater, *s.* Lughdaiche, beagaiche; fear isliche, fear isleachaidh.

Abba, *s.* Athair

Abbacy, *s.* Abaideachd, abaiteachd; còir abaite, seilbh abaite; fearann abaite; inmhe aba; abachd

Abbess, *s* Ban-aba; ban riaghlaidh abaite.

Abbey, *s* Abaid, abaite, cill-mhànach, mainistear.

Abbot, *s.* Ab, aba.

Abbreviate, *v a* Giorraich, gearr goirrid, aithghearraich. Abbreviated, *giorraichte ; aith-ghearraichte.*

Abbreviation, *s.* Giorrachadh; aithghearrachadh.

Abbreviator, *s* Giorradair Abbreviators, *giorradairean.*

A. B. C An aibideal; an *eubsaidh;* ceud leabhar cloinne.

Abdicate, *v. a.* Leig dhiot, thoir suas; thoir thairis; fàg, dealaich ri; diobair còir, diobair dreuchd (no) oifig, (no) inbhe.

Abdication. Toirt suas, fàgail, tréigsinn, diobairt còrach, dealachadh ri dreuchd, dealachadh ri oifig no ri inbhe.

Abditive, *a* Céileadail, ceileadach

Abdomen, *s.* Iochdair a chuirp, iochdar na bronn; com

Abduce, *v. a.* Thoir as, thoir air falbh; tarruing air falbh

Abduction, *s* Toirt air falbh, tabhairt as; tarruing air falbh

Abecedarian, *s* Fear teagaisg na h-aibidil, neach a tha 'g ionnsuchadh na h-aibidil.

Abed, *adv.* San leabaidh, na laidhe, na luidhe, air do lluidhe

Aberrance, Aberrancy, *s.* Seachran, seacharan; iomral; iomrol; mearachd.

Aberrant, *a.* Seachranach; iomrolach; mearachdach.

Aberration, *s* Seachran, treigsinn slighe; iomrol, dol a thaobh; allaban.

Abet, *v.* Brosnuich, prosnuich; brog, stuig; cuir air aghaidh; cuidich, aontaich; coghain. Abet me, *cuir leam, cuidich mi, seas ri m'chùl, tagair mo chùis; cuin taobh rium.*

† Abetment, *s.* Brosnuchadh, prosnuchadh; aontachadh, cuideachadh; coghnadh.

Abetter, Abettor, *s* Brosnuchair; fear aontachaidh; aontaiche; cùl-taice.

Abhor, *v.* Fuathaich; gràinich; oilltich; dubh-ghràinich; gairisnich. Abhorred, *fuathaichte*

Abhorrence, Abhorrency, *s.* Fuath, gràin, oillt; dubhghrain, sgreat, sgreatachd, sgreite, fuathachadh, gràineachadh.

Abhorrent, *a.* Fuathach, graineil, oillteil, dubh-ghraineil, sgreataidh, sgreitidh.

Abhorrer, *s* Fuathadair, gràineadair.

Abide, *v. n* Fan, fuirich, stad, feith; tamh; gabh comhnuidh, tùinich; buanaich mair; dean foighidinn, glac foighidinn. Abide by a person, *cum taobh ri neach*

Abide, *v. a.* Giùlan; fuiling, fuilig.

Abider, *s.* Fear tamha, fear comhnuidh, fear tùiniche.

Abiding, *s.* Fuireach, fuireachadh, fanachd, fantuinn, stadachd, tamh, comhnuidh, buanachadh; marsuinn, maireachdainn.

Abject, *a.* Suarrach, miothar, gràineil, truaillidh, diùbhaidh, ainniseach; neo-spioradail.

Abjectedness, *s.* Suarrachas, ainnis; uireasbhuidh, truaghanachd.

Abjection, Abjectness, *s.* Ainniseachd; miothaireachd, tàireileachd, tràilleileachd; bochduinn; ìsleachadh, lagchridheach, truime inntinn.

Abjectly, *adv.* Gu suarrach, gu h-ainniseach, gu miothar, gu gràineil; gu truaillidh, gu diùbhaidh, gu taireil, gu tràilleil.

Abjectness. See Abjection.

Ability, *s.* Comas, cumhachd, clithe, tréine. Abilities, *caileachd.*

Abintestate, *a.* Aig am bheil oighreachd gun tiomnadh.

Abjuration, *s.* Fréiteachadh, aicheadh, aitheach, eitheach, mionnuchadh; cùl-mhionnachadh. Abjuration oath, *cùl-mhionnan.*

Abjure, *v.* Mionnaich, fréitich, àicheadh, aicheun; cùl-mhionnaich.

Ablactate, *v.* Cuir air diol; cuir bhàrr na ciche; coisg.

Ablation, *s.* Tabhairt air falbh.

Able, *a.* Comasach, cumhachdach, foghainteach, làidir, heartmhor, urrainn, treòrach, murrach; teoma, sgileil; beartach. He was not able, *cha b'urradh dha, 'cha b'urrainn e;* as well as I was able, *mar b'fhearr a dh'fhaotainn; mar b'fhearr b'urrainn mi;* I am able to do it, *tha mi murrach air a dheanamh.*

Able-bodied, *a.* Laidir, treun, neartmhor, foghainteach, calma, taiceil.

Ableness, *s.* Murrachas, tréine, spionnadh.

Ablegate, *v.* Cuir air theachdaireachd, cuir air thùras.

Ablegation, *s.* Cur air theachdaireachd, cur air thùras.

Ableness, *s.* Comasachd; neart, tréine laidireachd, urraineachd.

Ablepsy, *s.* Doille, dalladh, cion léirsinn, cion fradhairc, neo-leirsinneachd.

† Ablocate, *v.* Leig mach air riadh.

Abluent, *a.* Ionnladach, nighteach; a glanadh, a nigheadh.

Ablution, *s.* Ionnlad, nighe, nigheadh, nigheachan, glanadh, saoradh o chionnt.

Abnegate, *v.* Aicheadh, diult, seun, òb, seachain.

Abnegation, *s.* Aicheadh, diùltadh, seunadh, seachnadh.

Abnodation, *s.* Sgathadh chraobh na phreas.

† Abnormity, *s.* Mi-dhaichealachd, droch cumadh.

† Abnormous, *a.* Mi-dhàicheil; neo-chumadail.

Aboard, *adv.* Air bord, air luing, air uachdar.

Abode, *s.* Comhnuidh, tamh, aite comhnuidh, aite tamha; fardoch, aros tuinidh, tuineas, cleithe, dachaidh; fuireach, tamhachd, tuineachas.

Abode, *v. a.* Fiosaich, fàisnich; innis roimh làimh; aragarraich, àitich.

Abodement, *s.* Fiosachadh, fiosachd, faisneachd, innseadh roimh làimh; màn-adh, tinnsgiodal, aragarradh; comhar; sanas.

Abolish, *v. a.* Dubh amach; cuir as do, sgrios, cur mu làr; mio-laghaich, cuir a mugha; mill; rain-sgrios; randonaich. Abolished, *mio-laghaichte, dubhte a mach.*

Abolishable, *a.* Ri chur as, ri chur a mugha, so chur as, so chur mu làr, so dhubh amach.

Abolisher, *s.* Sgriosadair; mi-laghachair.

Abolishment, *s.* Sgrios, sgriosadh; cur as, cur a mugha, sgriosadaireachd.

Abolition, *s.* Cur mu làr, cur a mugha, sgriosadh, mio-laghachadh.

Abominable, *a.* Fuathach, oillteil, gràineil, sgreamhail; salach, truaillidh, neoghlan, deistinneach, sgreataidh, sgreitidh; uamharra.

Abomination, *s.* Fuath, oillt, gràin, sgreamh; sgreat, sgreatachd; culaidh ghràin, cùis fhuatha, fà deistinn; sal; truaillidheachd, neo-ghloine, deistinneachd, sgreitidheachd, sgreataidheachd; uamharrachd, dubh-ghráinealachd; aingidheachd, coirbteachd.

Abominableness, *s.* Grainealachd, oilltealachd, sgreamhalachd, deistinneachd, fuathalachd, sgreat.

Abominably, *adv.* Gu gràineil, gu h-oillteil, gu sgreamhail, gu deistinneach, gu sgreataidh.

Abominate, *v. a.* Fuathaich, gràinich, oilltich, dubh-ghràinich.

Aborigines, *s.* Priomh-shluagh, priomh-mhuinntir, fine dhùthchusach, ceud luchd-aiteachaidh tìre. The Aborigines of Scotland, *na Gaidheal.*

Abortion, *s.* Torradh anabuich, aisead neo-thìmeil, aisead ro'n mhithich, breith anabuich, breith neo-thìmeil, breith roi' laimh, tigheachd neo-thìmeil; faoin-bhreith; an-torras.

Abortive, *a.* Roi 'n mhithich, roi 'n tìm, neo-thìmeil, mu 's trath, anabuich, an-torrach, neonitheach; air a bhreith roi 'n am.

Abortively, *adv.* Gu neo-thìmeil, gu h-anabuich, gu h-anntorrach, gu mi-thìmeil, gun torradh, gu faoin.

Abortiveness, *s.* Anabuchadh; anntorras; dìth torraidh, torradh neo-choimhlionta.

Abortment, *s.* See Abortiveness.

Above, *prep.* Os cionn, thar, thair; a bhàrr air; ni 's airde ni 's mo, thairis air, tuille is, tuille na, a thuilleadh air, àrd os cionn. He sat above me, *shuidh e os mo cheann;* above all, *os cionn nan uile, gu h-araid, gu h-araidh, os cionn gach ni, 's a cheud aite;* over and above, *a thuille air sin; thuille na còrach.* He is above doing that, *cha b'fhiach leis sin a dheanamh.*

Above, *adv.* Shuas, uthard, os ceann; gu h-ard, an àird, nàird, sna speuraibh, anns an adhar. From above, *bho 'n airde, os airde; nuas.*

Above board, *adv.* Os cionn bùird, an lathair dhaoine, a lathair, san t-sealladh, am fiadhnuis shùl, gun chleith, gun fholach, gun fhoill; gu h-aon-fhillte.

Above cited, *a.* A thubhradh, a sgriobhadh, As above cited, *mar a thubhradh.*

Above ground, *a.* Os cionn talmhainn, fathast beò.

Abound, *v. n.* Cinnich, fàs, bi pailt, soirbhich, bi saibhir.

About, *prep.* Mu, mu chuairt, mu 'n cuairt, mu thimchioll, mu dheimhinn, tiomchioll, fagus da, do thaobh, a thaobh, uime; a bhuineas do. About ten thousand, *mu dheich mìle;* about noon, *mu mheadhon là;* they were speaking about you, *bha iad a bruidhinn mu d' dhéimhinn;* throw your plaid about you, *cuir do bhreacan mu 'n cuairt duit;* about me, *mu 'n cuairt domh, mu m' dheimhinn;* about him, *uime, mu 'n cuairt dà, mu 'thimchioll, mu 'dheimhinn;* about them, *umpa, mu 'n cuairt doibh;* about her, *uimpe, mu 'n cuairt di, mu deimhinn, mu timchioll;* about whom, *cia uime;* go about a thing, *uidheamaich, deasaich, cir sùrt, rach an seilbh ni;* about to fly, *air bheul teiche;* what are you about? *ciod mu bheil thu?*

About, *adv.* Mu chuairt; gu cruinn, gu cuartach, gu cearclach, gu timchiollach; fogus air, fogus do, am fagus, am fagusg; an so 's an sud, gach taobh; air gach taobh, fad mu chuairt; air falbh. Bring about, *thoir mu 'n cuairt;* come about, *thig mu 'n cuairt.*

Abracadabra, *s.* Giseag Arabach, òrra, eolas leighis air a bhrith-ghalar.

Abrade, *v. a.* Gearr dheth, sgath, lom air falbh, bearr; sgiol.

Abrasion, *s.* Gearradh, sgathadh, bearradh, suathadh, sgioladh.

Abreast, *adv.* Taobh ri taobh; comh-uchdachail, uchd ri h-uchd, nan càraid.

Abridge, *v. a.* Giorraich, beagaich, lughdaich, cuingich, cutaich, sumhlaich, somhlaich, dìthich. Abridged, *giorr-aichte, cutaichte;* abridged of, *dìthichte.*

Abridger, *s.* Giorrachan, giorradair, cuingeachair; sumh-lachair.

Abridgement, *s.* Giorradan; giorrachadh, cuingeachadh, sumhlachadh, beagachadh, lughdachadh.

Abroach, *adv.* Air bheul ruith a mach, a dol mu sgaoil.

Abroad, *adv.* A mach, a muigh, an taobh muigh, o'n tigh, thall, mu sgaoil, gu farsuing, am farsuingeachd, an tìr eile, air aineol, air ainiul; fod as, an cein, 's na riogh-achdan mach; gu fad farsuinn; (*here and there*), air gach taobh; (*in sight*), a lathair, san t-sealladh. Run abroad, (as a person), *ruith a mach, ruith sios is suas;* (as a re-port), *ruith mu sgaoil, sgaoil.*

Abrogate, *v. a.* Mio-laghaich; trasgair; ais-ghairm, neo-dhean; cuir an neo-bhrigh, cuir mu làr lagh, cuir as lagh. Abrogated, *mio-laghaichte.*

Abrogation, *s.* Mio-laghachadh, trasgradh.

Abrupt, *a.* Briste, creagach, carrach, carraigeach; aith-ghearr; corrach, cas; obann, obuig, cabhagach; grad, biorach; sgoilte.

Abruption, *s.* Cas-bhriseadh, sgoltadh; grad dhealachadh; sgaradh, sgarachduinn.

Abruptly, *adv.* Gu creagach, gu carrach; gu cas.

Abruptness, *s.* Graide, caise, cabhag, obainne; corra-bhristeachd; garbhalachd.

Abscess, *s.* At, othar, uthar, màn, màm, neasgaid, meall, còs galarach 'sa chorp.

Abscind, *v. a.* Gearr dheth, sgath as, sgud.

Abscission, *s.* Gearradh, sgathadh, sgudadh.

Abscond, *v. n.* Foluich thu fein; rach am fògradh, teich; rach air theicheadh.

Absconder, *s.* Fògarrach, fuagarrach, fear fuidh choille, coilltear.

Absence, *s.* Neo-lathaireachd; (*of mind*), dìth mothaich, neo-aire, cionaire, dlùth smuaineachadh; mi-shuim.

Absent, *a.* Neo-lathaireach; gun bhi làthair, a fiadhnuis, as an fhianuis; (*in mind*), neo-aireach; dearmadach; dlùth smuaineach, trom-smuaineach.

Absent, *v. a.* Cum as an lathair, cum as an rathad; cum air falbh; na tig an làthair, séachain an lathair.

Absentee, *s.* Dìth-lathaireàch; fear nach eil san duthaich.

Absinthiated, *part.* Searbh, searbhaichte, air bhlas na burmait, air bholadh na burmait.

† **Absist**, *v. n.* Seas air falbh; seas, seasamh, stad, sguir, thoir thairis, leig dhiot.

Absolve, *v.* Lagh, math, saor; criochnaich, coimhlion. Absolved, *laghta, laghte.*

Absolute, *a.* Coimhlion, iomlan, saor; ceannasach; neo-cheangailte; gun chumha.

Absolutely, *adv.* Gu h-iomlan; gu tùr; gu saor, gu neo-cheangailte, gun chumha, gun cheangal, gun chumhnant.

Absoluteness, *s.* Saorsachd, iomlanachd, neo-cheangailt-eachd; aintighearnas.

Absolution, *s.* Mathadh, laghadh; mathanas, maitheanas, absaloid.

Absolutory, *a.* Maitheach, saorsach, o buileachadh maith-eanais.

† **Absonant**, *a.* Baoth; mi-reusanta, neo-thuigseach; neo-chordach.

† **Absonous**, *a.* Baoth; mi-reusanta, nach eil a cordadh ri reuson.

Absorb, *v. a.* Sùgh, sùig; sluig, òl. Absorbed, *sughta, sùigte, òilte.*

Absorbent, *a.* Tiormachail, tioram; sùigheach.

Absorbent, *s.* Leigheas a thiormaicheas àitidheachd a cholla.

Absorpt, *part.* Tiormaichte, sughta, sùigte, sluigte.

Absorption, *s.* Tiormachadh; sughadh, slugadh.

Abstain, *v. n.* Treig, fàg, seachain, fuirich o, cum o, fan o.

Abstemious, *a.* Stuama, geimnidh, measarra, measarradh.

Abstemiously, *adv.* Gu stuama, gu geimnidh, gu measarra.

Abstemiousness, *s.* Stuaime, stuamachd, geimnidheachd, geamnachd, measarrachd.

Absterge, *v. a.* Siab, glan; rub.

Abstergent, *a.* Siabail, glanail.

Abstersion, *s.* Srabadh, glanadh; rubadh.

Abstinence, *s.* Trosgadh, trasgadh, trasg; stuaime; meas-arrachd; seachnadh.

Abstinent, *a.* Trosgach, trasgach; stuama; measarra, measarradh.

Abstract, *v. a.* As-tharruing; thoir brigh a ni, roinn; eadar dhealaich; sumhlaich, cuingich.

Abstract, *s.* As-tharruing brìgh; suim; gearrachadh; cutachadh; sumhlachadh.

Abstract, *a.* Eadar-dhealaichte, sgarta, dorch, do-thuig-sinn, deacair.

Abstracted, *p. a.* Dealaichte; eadar-dhealaichte; glan; dorch, do-thuigsinn, deacair.

Abstraction, *s.* Dealachadh, eadar-dhealachadh, atharr-achadh; as-tharruing; (*of mind*), neo-aire, domhain-bheachdachadh.

Abstruse, *a.* Do-thuigsinn, doilleir, dorcha, duilich, deac-air, cruaidh.

Abstrusely, *adv.* Gu doilleir, gu dorcha, gu duilich, gu deacair, gu cruaidh.

Abstruseness, *s.* Doilleireachd, doirche, deacaireachd.

Absurd, *a.* Mi-reusonta, amaideach, baoth, neo-thuigseach, mi-chiallach, neo-fhreagarrach.

Absurdity, *s.* Mi-reusontachd, amaideachd; mi-reuson, mi-chiallachd, mi-fhreagarrachd.

Absurdly, *adv.* Gu mi-reusonta, gu h-amaideach, gu mi-fhreagarrach.

Abundance, *s.* Pailteas, lionmhoireachd, saibhireachd.

Abundant, *a.* Pailt, lionmhor; saibhir.

Abundantly, *adv.* Gu pailt, gu lionmhor, gu saibhir.

Abuse, *v.* Mi-ghnàthaich, mi-ghleidh; mi bhuilich; (*de-ceive a person*), meall; thoir an car a; (*carnally*), truaill; (*in word*), sglanrainn; (*in action*), mill; droch càirich; beubanaich.

Abuse, *s.* Mi ghnathachadh; mi-ghleidh; mealladh; truaill-eadh; sglanruinn, milleadh, droch-caramh; beubanachd; tàirealachd, droch cainnte, seirbhe cainnte.

Abused, *p.* Mi ghnathaichte; sglànruinte; meallta; truaillte; millte; beubanaichte.

Abuser, *s.* Mi-ghnathachair; mealltair, cuilbheartair; tru-aillear; fear searbh-bhriathrach.

Abusive, *a.* Mi-ghnathachail; sgainnealach, searbh-chainnt-each, searbh-bhriathrach.

Abusively, *adv.* Gu mi-ghnathachail; gu sgainnealach, gu searbh-chainnteach, gu searbh-bhriathrach.

Abusiveness, *s.* Sgainnealachd, tàirealachd; droch cainnte.

† **Abut**, *v.* Coinnich, comhdhail, ruig.

Abutment, *s.* Comhdhail.

† **Abuttal**, *s.* Crioch fearainn, crioch tìre, iomall fearainn.

Abyss, *s.* Aigean, dubh aigean; slochd gun ghrunnd; grinneal; (*hyperbolically*), doimhne, doimhneachd uisge mu chridhe na cruinne; (*in the language of theology*), ifrinn.

Acacia, *s.* Ainm seorsa craoibhe; leigheas Eiphiteach.

Academical, *a.* Oil-thigheil; sgoileil, sgoileisdeach.

Academian, *s.* Aoileanach, sgoilear.

Academician, *s.* Sgolaisdeach; oileanach; fear teagaisg ann an ard-sgoil.

Academy, *s.* Tigh munaidh, tigh foghlum, ard-sgoil; tigh oilein, mòr-sgoil, scolaisd; colaist; comunn chum leas foghluim agus ealadhain.

Acanaceous, *a.* Biorach, stobach, geur.

Acanthus, *s.* Seorsa luibh.

Acatalectic, *s.* Rann dìreach.

Accede, *v.* Aontaich le; dluthaich ri; coird.

Accelerate, *v. a.* Defrich, luathaich, cuir an cabhaig; greas; cuir air adhairt. Accelerated, *deifrichte, luathaichte.*

Acceleration, *s.* Luathas, cabhag, deifir; greasachd, greasdachd; luathachadh.

† Accend, *v. a.* Las, fadaidh; beothaich, cuir ri theine.

† Accension, *s.* Lasadh, fadadh, beothachadh.

Accent, *v.* Snàs-labhair, pong-labhair; (*in poetry*), cainnte, briathran.

Accent, *s.* Blas cainnte, snàs-labhairt, guth-ghleus, fonn.

Accentuate, *v.* Labhair gu pongail, labhair gu snàsmhor, labhair gu gleusda.

Accentuation, *s.* Pong-labhairt, snàs-labhairt.

Accept, *v.* Gabh, gabh ri, gabh stigh; (*in a juridical sense*), aontaich, coird ri.

Acceptability, *s.* Taitneachd; ciat, ciatachd.

Acceptable, *a.* Taitneach, ciatach, freagarrach.

Acceptableness, *s.* Taitneachd, ciatachd, freagarrachd.

Acceptably, *adv.* Gu taitneach, gu ciatach, gu freagarrach.

Acceptance, *s.* Taitneachd, gabhail ri; deadh-thoil.

Acceptation, *s.* Ciall, seadh.

Accepter, *s.* Gabhaltair, gabhadair, fear a ghabhas ri.

Access, *s.* Comas dol, rathad, rod, slighe, cead, ruigsinn, ruigheachd; meudachadh, meudachd, cinneas. There is no getting an access to it, *cha n'eil seòl ruigheachd air.*

Accessariness, *s.* Aontachadh, aontachd, co'pairteachd.

Accessary, *a.* Aontach, comh-pairteach.

Accessible, *a.* So-ruigheachd, so-ruigsinn, ruigsinneach.

Accession, *s.* Meudachadh; teachd.

Accessory, *a.* Barrachd; thuillead.

Accessory, *s.* (*In law.*) Comh-pairtiche an ciont, aontachair; comh-chiontaiche.

Accidence, *s.* (*a corruption of accidents.*) Priomh-leabhar cainnte.

Accident, *s.* Sgiorradh, tuiteamas, mi-shealbh, tubaist; ciall, seadh.

Accidental, *a.* Sgiorrail, tuiteamach, tubaisteach, mi-shealbhar; teagamhach neo-chinnteach.

Accidentally, *adv.* Gu sgiorrail, gu tuiteamach; thaobh sgiorradh, thaobh tuiteamais, thaobh tubaiste.

Accidentalness, *s.* Sgiorralachd, tuiteamachd, tubaisteachd, buailteachd do sgiorradh, buailteachd do thuiteamas, buailteachd do thubaist.

† Accipient, *s.* Gabhadair.

Acclaim, *s.* Caithreim, gair, luath-ghair, ard-mholadh.

Acclamation, *s.* Gàir, gàirdeachas, luath-ghair, caithream, conghair.

Acclivity, *s.* Bruthach, uchdach, uchdan; leargann.

Acclivious, *a.* Corrach, uchdachail.

Accolent, *s.* Fear aiteachaidh crìche.

Accommodable, *a.* Freagarrach; goireasach.

Accommodate, *v. a.* Cum ri; freagarraich, goireasaich; ceartaich; dean réidh; àitich.

Accommodate, *a.* Freagarrach, ceart, cubhaidh.

Accommodation, *s.* Freagarrachd, goireas, ceartachadh; aiteachd, rum.

Accompany, *v. a.* Rach le, rach maille ri, rach cuid ri, lean ri, rach an cuideachd, thig an cuideachd, rach an compailt. They who accompany, *iadsan a tha dol an cuideachd.*

Accomplice, *s.* Pairteach, pairtiche, comh-phairtiche, comh-chionntaiche, comh-oibriche, fear aontachaidh.

Accomplish, *v.* Coi'lion, comhlion; thoir gu crìche; crìochnaich; breaghaich, sgeadaich; deasaich, feartaich.

Accomplished, *part.* and *a.* Coimhlionta, crìochnuichte; air teachd gu crìche; ullamh, deas; sgeadaichte; breaghaichte; feartaichte.

Accomplisher, *s.* Criochnachair; fear criochnaich; fear criochnachaidh.

Accomplishment, *s.* Coimhlionadh, criochnachadh; (*of mind*), cail, feart, buaidh.

Accompt, *s.* Cunntas, meas.

Accomptant, *s.* Fear cunntais, cunntair, fear àireimh.

Accord, *v. n.* Còird, freagair, comh-chòird, aontaich; dean coimh-sheirm.

Accord, *v. a.* Reitich, dean reidh.

Accord, *s.* Co'chordadh, comh-chordadh; comh-bhann; réite; comh-aontachd; cairdeas deòin; (*in music*), comh-sheirm. With one accord, *a dh'aon rùn, dh'aon inntinn.*

Accordance, *s.* Cordadh, co'chordadh, comh-sheirm, comh-fhreagarrachd; cairdeas.

According, *prep.* A reir, do reir. According to their kind, *a réir an gné, a réir an seòrsa;* according to my word, *a réir m'fhocaill.*

Accordingly, *adv.* A reir sin.

Accost, *v. a.* Cuir fàilte; labhair ri, bruidhinn ri.

Accostable, *a.* Fosgailte; suairce.

Account, *s.* Cunntas, aireamh; meas; urram; inbhe; cùis; reuson; doigh; aithris; sgeul; mìneachadh. On any account, *air aon doigh;* of great account, *prìseil; daor; gaolach;* a man of no account, *fear gun urram;* on that account, *air son sin, air shon sin;* on his account, *air a shonso;* on my account, *air mo shon, air mo shon-sa;* on their account, *air an son, air an son-sa.*

Account, *v. a.* Meas; cuir as leth; innis, cunnt; thoir cunntas; bi freagarrach.

Accountable, *a.* Freagarrach.

Accountant, *s.* Cunntair; fear àireimh.

Account-book, *s.* Leabhar cunntais.

Accoutre, *v.* Eid, uidheamaich, uigheamaich; armaich; deasaich.

Accoutrements, *s. pl.* Acfhuinn, buill-acfhuinn; beairt, airneis, armachd, eididh cogaidh.

Accredited, *a.* Creideasach.

Accretion, *s.* Cinneachduinn, fàs, toradh; fàs a thaobh leanailteachd.

Accretive, *a.* Cinneachdail, torach.

Accroach, *v.* Clic, tarruing h-ugad le clic, le dubhan, no le cromag.

Accrue, *v. n.* Cuir ri; thig; sruth. Much good will accrue to you, *thig mòran maith a d'ionnsuidh.*

Accumulate, *v.* Carn suas, cruach, cruinnich; cnuasaich; tionail, cuir ri cheile; torr. Accumulated, *carnte suas, cruinnichte; cnuasaichte, tionailte.*

Accumulation, *s.* Carnadh, cruinneachadh, cnuasachadh, tionaladh; cur ri chéile.

Accumulative, *a.* Cruinneadach, cruachadh, cnuasadach; cruinneachail; tionalach.

Accumulator, *s.* Carnair, cruinneachair, fear cruinneachaidh, cnuasair, tionalair.

Accuracy, *s.* Pongalachd, pongalas, ceartachd, sicireachd, soilleireachd, snàsmhoireachd; freagarrachd.

Accurate, *a.* Pongail, ceart, sicir; dìreach, snasmhor; freagarrach, cinnteach.

Accurately, *adv.* Gu pongail, gu ceart, gu sicir; gu snàsmhor; gu freagarrach.

Accurateness, *s.* Pongalachd, ceartachd, sicireachd, snasmhoireachd, freagarrachd.

Accurse, *v. a.* Malluich; guidh mallachd, dìt. Accursed, *malluichte; airidh air mallachd; fuathach; oillteil; aingidh.*

Accusable, *a.* Buailteach do chron, airidh air dìteadh; ciontach.

Accusation, *s.* Caisead, casaid; cuis dhìtidh; grieomh tagraidh; gearan; coir, cronachadh. A false accusation, *casaid bhréige.*

Accuse, *v. a.* Dean casaid; dìt, gearain; coirich, cuir coir air; cronaich; cuir as leth. He accused him falsely, *rinn e casaid bhréige air.*

Accused, *part.* Coirichte, cronaichte.

Accuser, *s.* Casaidiche, ditear, gearainiche; fear ditidh, tagrair, fear tagraidh.

Accustom, *v.* Cleachd, gnathaich; dean. Accustomed, *cleachta, gnathaichte, deanta, deante*; accustomed to war, *deanta ri cogadh.*

Accustomable, *a.* Gnàthach, cumanta, fasanta, cleachdar, cleachdmhor.

† **Accustomance**, *s.* Cleachdainn, nos, gnath, fasan, àbhaist.

Accustomarily, *adv.* A ghnath, gu cumannta; an cumantas.

Accustomed, *a.* Tric, minic; gnathaichte; cleachda, cleachta.

Ace, *s.* Aon; an eus air na cairtibh, *mar, eus a chridhich, eus an doimein*; ro bheagan do ni sam bi, smad; smùirnean.

Acerb, *a.* Searbh, garg, goirt, geur.

Acerbity, *s.* Searbhas, seirbhe, gairgead, géire, geurad; goirteas.

† **Acervate**, *v. a.* Carn suas, cruach.

† **Acervation**, *s.* Carnadh, cruachadh, cnuasachadh, tionaladh.

Acescent, *a.* Searbh, garg, goirt; geur; leth-char searbh, leth-char goirt.

Acetous, *a.* Searbh, goirt, geur, garg.

Ache, *s.* Cradh, pian; guin; craon; goimh, goirteas, greim. Tooth-ache, *cnuimh fhiacail*; belly-ache, *coiliginn*; head-ache, *ceann goirt*; an extreme ache of a boil, *goimh neasgaid.*

Ache, *v. n.* Mothaich cradh (no) pian; bi goirt.

Achieve, *v.* Dean, cuir an gniomh; criochnaich; coisinn, buidhinn; coimhlion.

Achievement, *s.* Gaisge; gniomh euchdach, beart, morghniomh euchdach, deanadas; suaicheantas.

Achiever, *s.* Gaisgeach; fear euchdach; beartair; deanadair.

Aching, *s.* Pian; mi-fhoisneachd; reasgachd.

Aching, *a.* Goirt; piantachail; cronach.

Acid, *a.* Searbh, garg, goirt, geur.

Acid, *s.* Searbh-ni; searbhag, geurag, goirteag.

Acidity, *s.* Searbhas, seirbhe, gairgead, géire, goirteas, goirtead, geurad, searbhad.

Acidness, *s. f.* Searbhachd, gairgeachd, geurachd, goirteachd.

Acidulate, *v. a.* Searbhaich, gargaich, geuraich, goirtich. Acidulated, *searbhaichte, goirtichte, geuraichte.*

Acknowledge, *v. a.* Gabh ri, aitich, aidich; aithnich, dean aithne, deonaich. Acknowledged, *aitichte, aidichte; aithnichte; deonaichte.*

Acknowledgment, *s.* Aiteachadh, aideachadh; aithneachadh; aidmheil.

Acme, *s.* Mullach, bàrr, airde, spiric, spiricean.

Acorn, *s.* Cno dharaich, darcan.

Acoustics, *s.* Claisneachd, claisteachd; ìoc-shlainnt chluas; cluas-ice.

Acquaint, *v.* Innis, thoir fios, foillsich, nochd, dean aithnichte.

Acquaintance, *s.* Eolas, caidreamh; cleachd; urr eòlais; caidreach. I have no acquaintance with him, *cha n' eil eòlas sam bi agam air*; an acquaintance of mine, *aon do mo luchd eòlais.*

Acquainted, *a.* Eolach; cleachda, cleachta, cleachte. Acquainted with him, *eòlach air.*

Acquest, *s.* Coisneadh; buannachd, tairbhe, teagnadh.

Acquiesce, *v.* Geill, striochd, aontaich, comh-aontaich; gabh ri; tamhaich.

Acquiescence, *s.* Géilleadh, striochdadh, aontachadh; tamhachadh, umhlachd, gabhail ri.

Acquire, *v.* Coisinn, faigh, buannaich.

Acquirable, *a.* So-fhaotainn; so-chosnaidh.

Acquired, *part.* and *a.* Coisinnte, buannaichte.

Acquirement, *s.* Coisneadh, cosnadh, buannachadh, buannachd; tairbhe; teagnadh; *(of mind)*, càileachd, feart, buaidh.

Acquisition, *s.* Coisneadh, cosnadh, buannachadh; tairbhe; buannachd, teagnadh.

Acquit, *v.* Saor, lagh, fuasgail, leig fa sgaoil; giulain. Acquit yourself handsomely, *giùlain thu fein gu h-eireachdail.*

Acquittal, *s.* Saoradh, saorsadh, fuasgladh.

Acre, *s.* Acair fearainn.

Acrid, *a.* Teth, loisgeach; searbh, garg, goirt.

Acrimonious, *a.* Geur, searbh; loisgeach, sgaiteach.

Acrimony, *s.* Geurad, searbhad, searbhas, gairgealachd; sgaitichead.

Acritude, *s.* Searbhas, geurad.

Acromatical, *a.* Mor-fhoghluimte.

Acronical, *a.* Ag eiridh agus a luidh comhluath ris a' ghrian.

Acrospire, *s.* Feusag sìl, gineag.

Across, *adv.* Tarsuing.

Acrostic, *s.* Cros-dhàn, rann tarsuing.

Act, *v. a.* and *n.* Dean; gnathaich; dean cleas; cleasaich; cluich.

Act, *s.* Gniomh, tùrn, reachd; euchd; cleas; achd, reachd; earann. Acts, *gniomharan.* A great act, *euchd*; a wicked act, *droch thùrn, droch ghniomh.*

Action, *s.* Gniomh, turn, obair; *(battle)*, cath, baiteal, blàr. An action at law, *cuis lagha, cuis tagraidh.*

Actionable, *a.* Peanasail; mi-laghail; neo laghail.

Active, *a.* Tapaidh, grad, ealamh, deas, fuasgailte, tuasgailte; smiorail, surdail; beòthail, beò; ruaimneach, ùrchleasach; teoma, deanadach, gniomhach.

Activeness, *s.* Tapachd, tapadh, ealamhachd, smioralas, beothalachd, ruaimneachd.

Activity, *s.* Tapachd, tapadh, ealamhachd, beothalachd, ruaimneachd; deanadachd.

Actor, *s.* Fear cluiche, cleasaiche.

Actress, *s.* Bana chleasaiche; bean-chleasaiche.

Actual, *a.* Cinnteach, dearbhta, fior; gniomha. Actual sin, *peacadh gniomha.*

Actuality, *s.* Cinnteachd, dearbhachd.

ACTUALLY, *adv.* Gu cinnteach, gu dearbh, gu fior.

ACTUARY, *s.* Cléireach cùirt.

ACTUATE, *v.* Brosnaich, brosgail; beothaich; neartaich.

ACTUATED, *part.* Brosnaichte, beothaichte, neartaichte.

ACUATE, *v.* Geuraich, bioraich, thoir roinn.

ACULEATE, ACULEATED, *a.* Geur, biorach, stobach; bioragach.

ACUMEN, *s.* Bior, binnean; *figuratively*, géire, geurad inntinn.

ACUMINATED, *a.* Biorach, binneanach, geur.

ACUTE, *a.* Geur, biorach; guineach; brais, dealasach; carach; smiorail, beò, beothail, sgaiteach; sicir.

ACUTELY, *ad.* Gu geur, gu biorach, gu guineach, gu brais, gu dealasach; gu smiorail, gu sgaiteach.

ACUTENESS, *s.* Géire, geiread, geurad; graidead; géire inntinn; tuigse; sicireachd, beothalas, sgaiteachd.

ADAGE, *s.* Gnàth-fhocal, sean-fhocal, leth-fhocal.

ADAMANT, *s.* Daoimean; leug, seud.

ADAMANTINE, *a.* Daoimeanach, leuganta; cruaidh.

ADAPT, *v.* Freagarraich, dean freagarrach; sonraich; ceartaich.

ADAPTATION, *s.* Freagarrachd, sonachadh, sunrachadh, ceartachadh; ceartachd.

ADD, *v. a.* Cuir ri, meudaich; leasaich. Add to this, moreover, *thuille air so.*

ADDECIMATE, *v.* Deicheamhaich, tog deicheamh.

ADDER, *s.* Nathair, nathair nimhe. Adders, *nathraichean.*

ADDIBLE, *a.* So mheudachadh, so chur ri.

ADDICE, *s.* Seorsa tuaigh, tàl.

ADDICT, *v. a.* Thoir suas; liòbhair, aom; cleachd, coisrig.

ADDICTED, *a.* Cleachta; air a thoirt suas, liobhairte; coisrigte; deigheil air. Addicted to vice, *cleachta ri h-olc;* addicted to drinking, *deigheil air an òl.*

ADDICTION, *s.* Tabhairt suas, toirt suas, liobhradh, coisrigeadh.

ADDITION, *s.* Meudachadh, cur ri, cur suas, aircamh, fàs.

ADDITIONAL, *a.* Barrachd, tuille, oscionn.

ADDLE, *a.* Breun, lobh, grod; gluig, fàs, seasg, neo-thorrach. An addle-egg, *ubh gluig;* an addle-head, *ceann àrcain.*

ADDLE, *v. a.* Dean fas, dean gluig, dean seasg.

ADDLE-PATED, *a.* Gaoithe, gog-cheannach; eutrom, falamh, fàs.

ADDRESS, *v. a.* Uidheamaich, ullamhaich, deasaich thu fein chum obair, cuir sùrt; labhair ri, bruidhinn ri; sgriobh; guidh.

ADDRESS, *s.* Deaslabhairt; sèoltachd; guidh; modh; modhalachd; sgil.

† ADEMPTION, *s.* Toirt an falbh.

ADEPT, *a.* Teoma, sgileil.

ADEPT, *s.* Teomach, fear teoma.

ADEQUATE, *a.* Ionann, comh-ionann; freagarrach; lathailteach; cothromach; iomchuidh.

ADEQUATELY, *adv.* Gu h-ionann; gu freagarrach; gu lathailteach, gu h-iomchuidh; gu cothromach.

ADEQUATENESS, *s.* Freagarrachd, lathailteachd, iomchuidheachd.

ADHERE, *v.* Lean ri, dluthaich, stic. Adhere to him, *lean ris.*

ADHERENCE, *s.* Leanachd, leantuinn, leanmhuinn, dlùthachadh, dlu-leanachd; *figuratively*, rioghalachd, dìllse do 'n righ, seasamhachd inntinn.

ADHERENT, *a.* Leanailteach.

ADHERENT, *s.* Leanmhuinniche, fear leanmhuinn.

ADHERER, *s.* Fear leanmhuinn, leanmhuinniche, fear leanachd, fear leantuinn.

ADHESION, *s.* Leanailteachd; leanachd, leanmhuinn.

ADHESIVE, *a.* Leanailteach, sticeanta.

ADHIBIT, *v.* Deàn feum, uidhis, cuir gu uidhis, cuir gu feum.

ADHIBITION, *s.* Uidhis, feum, stà.

ADJACENCY, *s.* Fogasachd, fagasachd, faigse, dlùs.

ADJACENT, *a.* Fogus, fagus, dlùth am fogus; thall; laimh ri.

ADJECT, *v.* Cuir ri, co-chuir; measg, coimeasg; cuir a steach.

ADJECTION, *s.* Cur ri; co-chur, measgadh, coimeasgadh.

ADJECTIVE, *s.* Buaidh-fhocal, feart-fhocal, for-bhriathar; far-bhriathar.

ADJECTIVELY, *adv.* Mar bhuaidh-fhocal, mar fheart-fhocal.

ADIEU, *adv.* Dia leat; slainnte leat, slàn leat; beannachd leat; soraidh leat; sar leàt.

ADJOIN, *v.* Cuir ri, stic ri, tàth, dlùthaich, dlùth.

ADJOURN, *v. a.* Cuir dheth; dàilich; cuir dàil, cuir dheth gu làth eile; sìn.

ADJOURNMENT, *s.* Dàil, dàileachadh; cur dheth.

ADIT, *s.* Uamh; uamh-rod; rod fo'n talamh.

ADJUDGE, *v.* Thoir breith, thoir binn; dit; breithnich; orduich mar bhreitheamh.

ADJUDGMENT, *s.* Breith, breitheanas, binn.

ADJUNCT, *a.* Aonaichte; air chur ri, dlùthaichte.

ADJUNCT, *s.* Ni a bhuineas do ni eile; buntuinneas.

ADJURATION, *s.* Mionnachadh, gabhail mionnan; mionniarruidh; guidhe, griosadh.

ADJURE, *v. a.* Mionnaich, gabh mionnan; earalaich an ainm Dhé, guidh, grios.

ADJUST, *v.* Ceartaich, ceartuich, cuir an ordugh; dean freagarrach, dean cothromach, riaghailtich.

ADJUSTMENT, *s.* Ceartachadh, cothromachadh; cuir an ordugh; riaghailteachadh.

ADJUTANT, *s.* Fear cuideachaidh, fear còghnath; oichear coghnaith, oifigeach do 'n gnothach pàigh thoirt do shaighdearaibh.

ADJUTANCY, *s.* Inbh oicheir còghnaidh; deadh riaghailt.

ADJUVANT, *a.* Cuideachail.

ADMEASUREMENT, *s.* Tomhas, ceart-thomhasadh.

ADMENSURATION, *s.* Tomhas, ceart-thomhasadh.

ADMINISTER, *v.* Fritheil, dean seirbheis; tabhair, thoir, builich, riaghail, riaghailtich.

ADMINISTRATION, *s.* Frithealadh; riaghladh; uachdranachd, riaghailtearachd.

ADMINISTRATIVE, *a.* Frithealach.

ADMINISTRATOR, *s.* Riaghladair; frithealachair, fritheiliche, fear a riaghlaicheas gnothuichibh agus cuid neach sam bi a theasd gun teismeid.

ADMIRABILITY, *s.* Iongantasachd, uamhasachd; neonasachd.

ADMIRABLE, *a.* Iongantach; ionmholta, cliùiteach eagmhaiseach, neonach; uamhasach.

ADMIRABLENESS, *s.* Iongantachd, eagmhaiseachd, ionmholtachd, cliùiteachd, neonachd.

ADMIRABLY, *adv.* Gu h-iongantach, gu h-ionmholta, gu h-eugmhaiseach.

ADMIRAL, *s.* Ard-mharaiche; ceann-feadhna cabhlaich, ceannard cabhlaich, luingeas ard-mharaiche. Admirals, *ard-mharaichean.*

ADMIRALTY, *s.* Buidheann riaghlaidh na cabhlaich; an tigh anns an cum buidheann riaghlaidh na cabhlaich coinneamh.

ADMIRATION, *s.* Iongantas; mor-mheas.

Admire, *v. a.* Gabh iongantas, gabh neonachas; amhairc le h-iongantas; amhairc le mor-mheas; mothaich meas (no) urram, gradhaich.

Admirer, *s.* Fear ioghnaidh; urramair; speisear, graidhear, graidhean, fear gaoil, ceistean.

Admissible, *a.* Ceadachail; luigheasach; a dh' fheudas inntrinn.

Admission, *s.* Inntrinn, comas inntrinn; ceadachadh; luigheasachd.

Admit, *v.* Ceadaich, deonaich, gabh, leig stigh.

Admittance, *s.* Cead inntrinn, comas inntrinn; ceadachadh, deonachadh.

Admitted, *part.* Ceadaichte, deònaichte; gabhte steach.

Admix, *v.* Coimeasg.

Admixtion, *s.* Coimeasg, cumasg.

Admixture, *s.* Coimeasg, cur troimh cheile

Admonish, *v. a* Comhairlich, earalaich, teagaisg, thoir rabhadh. Admonished, *comhairlichte earalaichte, teagaisgte.*

Admonisher, *s* Comhairliche, teagasgair; fear comhairle

† **Admonishment**, *s* See **Admonition**.

Admonition, *s* Comhairle, earail, rabhadh, teagasg. Give him an admonition, *thoir comhairle dha.*

Admonitory, *a* Comhairleach, teagasgach, rabhach; teagasgail, rabhail

Adnoun, *s.* See **Adjective**.

Ado, *s.* Othail, iomairt, iurpais, saothair, eas-ordugh, tuairgne, mùch Much ado about nothing, *moran iomairt mu neoni;* what ado there is in the court, *is ann tha 'n iomairt sa chùirt*, with much ado, *le moran saothair; air éigin;* I had much ado to manage him, *Is gann b' urradh dhomh a chur gu taic.*

Adolescence, *s.* Oige, ùr-fhas

Adopt, *v.* Uchdmhacaich; gabh Adopted, *uchdmhacaichte;* an adopted son, *uchd-mhac.*

Adopter, *s.* Uchdmhacair.

Adoption, *s.* Uchdmhacachd, gabhail h-ùige neach féin.

Adorable, *a.* Urramach, airidh air aoradh, aoradhail, airidh air ard-mheas, gloirmhor, ionmholta.

Adorableness, *s.* Urramachd, aoradhalachd; ard-mholadh; ard-mheas

Adoration, *s.* Aoradh; ard-urram, urram naomh.

Adore, *v. a.* Aor, thoir aoradh, dean aoradh; urramaich, thoir urram, gradhaich.

Adorer, *s.* Aoradair; gràdhair; fear gaoil, ceistean, fear an gaol.

Adorn, *v.* Sgeadaich, breaghaich, uigheamaich, éid, dean snàsmhor, sgiamhaich; busg; busgainn, ardaich. Adorned, *sgeadaichte, breaghaichte, uigheamaichte, sgiamhaichte, busgainnte; ardaichte.*

Adornment, *s.* Sgeadachadh, breaghachadh, uigheamachadh, sgiamhachadh, busgainn

Adown, *adv* A bhàn, bhàn, sios, air làr.

Adrift, *adv.* Leis; leis an t-sruth; air iomadan; leis a ghaoth.

Adroit, *a.* Seolta, teoma, lamhach, lamhchar deas.

Adroitness, *s.* Seoltachd, teomachd, lamhchaireachd.

Adry, *a.* Tioram, an diosg; pàiteach, tartmhor

Adscititious, *a.* Barrachd, tuille

Advance, *v. a.* Cuir air adhairt, cuir air aghaidh, ardaich; mòraich, roghnaich, leasaich; luathaich.

Advance, *v. n.* Dluthaich, thig am fagus, thig air d-adhairt, thig air d' aghaidh, teann; cinn; thoir tairgeas.

Advance, *s* Dluthachadh, teannadh; meudachadh; leasachadh, arduchadh, cinntinn. Advance money, *earlas*

Advanced, *part.* Ardaichte, arduichte; meudaichte, leasaichte, mòraichte.

Advantage, *s.* Buidhinn, tairbhe; coisinn, buannachd, proidhit, sochair, leas, math, maith, fath; cothrom; lamh an uachdar, barrachd; sgabhaiste. It is for your advantage, *is ann airson do leas tha e*, what advantage is it to you? *ciod an tairbhe th' agad as?* you have the advantage of him, *tha 'n cothrom agad air.*

Advantage, *v. a.* Dean maith, leasaich, proidhitich; ardaich

Advantage-ground, *s.* Cothròm talmhainn.

Advantageous, *a.* Tarbhach, iomchuidh, feumail; uidhiseil, proidhiteil.

Advantageousness, *s* Tairbhe, tarbhachd, iomchuidhcachd, feumalachd, uidhisealachd, buannachd.

Advantageously, *adv.* Gu tarbhach, gu h-iomchuidh, gu feumail.

Advent, *s.* Teachd; teachd an t-Slànuigh'ir; nollaig, mios cràbhaidh.

Adventitious, *a.* Tuiteamach, tubaisdeach.

Adventure, *s.* Tuiteamas, teagmhais, teagmhas; tubaist, feuchainn, deuchainn, tuairmeas, tuairmse; cunnart, baoghal By adventure, *a thaobh tubaiste*

Adventure, *v.* Feuch ri, thoir deuchainn.

Adventurer, *s* Teagmhasair, baoghlair

Adventurous, *a.* Dàn, misneachail; teagmhaiseach; cunnartach, baoghlach.

Adventurously, *adv.* Gu dàn, gu misneachail; gu baoghlach, gu teagmhaiseach.

Adverb, *s.* Ceann-bhriathar; ceann-fhocal.

Adverbial, *a* Ceann-bhriathrach, ceann-bhriathrail.

Adversary, *s.* Nàmhaid, nàmh, eas-caraid.

Adverse, *a* Mi-shealbhar; ann aghaidh; tarsuing; crosda, mi-fhabhorach, neo-aontachail; dochainneach; contarach sgriosail, naimhdeil, namhaideil. Adverse to me, *am m' aghaidh.*

Adversity, *s* Amhghar, teinn, dosgainn, dosgainneachd; airc; cruaidh-chas, dochann; aindeas. He is in adversity, *tha e na airc*, adversity tries friends, *feuchaidh cruaidh-chàs caraid.*

Advert, *v* Thoir aire, fidrich, beachdaich; gabh suim.

Advertence, *s* Aire, beachd, suim, omhaill.

Advertent, *a* Aireachail, beachdail, suimeil; omhailleach.

Advertise, *v. a* Thoir sanus; thoir fios, gairm, glaodh, innis, foillsich, thoir rabhadh

Advertised, *part* Gairmte, foillsichte.

Advertiser, *s.* Sanasair; gairmear, glaodhair, rabhadair.

Advertisement, *s.* Sanas, gairm, glaodh, rabhan, rabhadh follaiseach.

Advice, *s.* Comhairle, sànas, fios, seoladh; rabhadh. Advice boat, *bàt fad.*

Advisable, *a.* Glic; crionna, sicir; iomchuidh; freagarrach.

Advisableness, *s.* Crionnachd; sicireachd; iomchuidheachd, freagarrachd

Advise, *v. a.* Comhairlich, thoir comhairle; innis, cuir fios, thoir fios

Advise, *v. n* Cuir comhairle; gabh comhairle, smuainich

Advised, *part.* Comhairlichte; sicir, glic, crionna

Advisedly, *adv* Gu crionna, gu sicir; a dheóin, a dh'aon deòin, a dh' aon obair.

Adviser, *s.* Comhairliche, fear comhairle; comhairleachair.

Adulation, *s.* Sodal, miodal, bleid, goileam, brosgal

Adulator, *s.* Sodalair, sodalaiche, bleidire, brosgalair, fear bleideil, fear sodalach.

Adulatory, *a.* Sodalach, miodalach, bleideil, beulchar, goileamach, brosgulach.

Adult, *a* Air fàs, air teachd gu h-aois, air teachd gu h-inbhe, mòr; fearail

Adult, *s.* Duine deante; gille; urr air teachd gu h-aois, no gu h-inbhe

† **Adulterate**, *v.* Dean adhaltranas; truaill, truailich.

Adulterate, *v.* Dean adhaltranas, truailich, truaill, mill; cuir dholaidh, coimeasg.

Adulterate, *a* Truaillichte, millte.

Adulterateness, *s.* Truaillidheachd, truailleachd

Adulteration, *s.* Truailleachadh; truailleachd.

Adulterer, *s.* Adhaltranaiche, adhaltranach; fear adhaltruis.

Adulteress, *s.* Ban-adhaltranaiche.

Adulterine, *s* Urr adhaltruis

Adulterous, *a.* Adhaltranach, adhaltrasach. An adulterous child, *urr adhaltruis.*

Adultery, *s* Adhaltras, adhaltranas

Adultness, *s* Fearachas; boirionnas.

Adumbrant, *a* Sgàileach, sgàileanach; duibhreach.

Adumbrate, *v* Sgàilich, dorchaich, duibhrich

Adumbration, *s.* Sgaileachadh, duibhreachadh.

Aduncity, *s.* Caimead.

Adunque, *a* Cam, crom, cromagach, dubhanach

Advocacy, *s.* Tagradh, leithsgeul, didean.

Advocate, *s* Tagrair, tagradair, fear tagraidh, fear lagha; leithsgeulaiche In scripture, *eadar-ghuidhear*

Advocation, *s.* Tagradh, tagrachd, eadar-mheadhonachd.

Advolation, *s* Itealachd

Advolution, *s.* Ròladh, ruithleadh.

Advoutry, *s.* Adhaltras, adhaltranas.

Advowee, *s.* Neach aig am bi beathan eaglais ri thoirt seachad do neach eile.

Advowson, *s* Còir air eaglais a bhuileachadh air diadhair.

Adust, *a.* Loisgte, seargte, tioram; iom-loisgte

Adustible, *a.* So-loisgte, so-sheargte, so-chrionadh.

Adustion, *s.* Iom-losgadh; losgadh, seargadh

Adze, *s* Tàl

Æra, *s* Ceann aimsir.

Aerial, *a.* Adharail, adhorach; athaireil, gaothar, spioradail, ard An aerial being, *bith adharail, spiorad.*

Ærugo, *s* Meirg.

Aerology, *s* Adhar-iùl, adhar-eolas

Aeromancy, *s.* Adhar-eolas, adhar iùl.

Aeronaut, *s* Adhar-sheoladair.

Aeroscopy, *s* Adhar-amharc

Aerostation, *s* Adhar-sheoladaireachd.

Æthiops mineral, *s.* Beo-airgiod is pronnusg.

Ætites, *s* Clach iolair.

Afar, *adv.* An céin, am fad, fad air falbh, fad as

Affability, *s* Suairceas, caoimhneas; caoimhnealas, deagh ghloir, cuirtealachd, so-chomhradhachd

Affable, *a.* Suairc, caoimhneil, cùirteil; seimh, so-chomhradhach, modhail, deagh-ghloireach.

Affableness, *s.* Suairceas, caoimhnealachd, cuirtealachd, modhaileachd.

Affably, *adv.* Gu suairc, gu caoimhneil, gu cùirteil, gu modhail.

Affair, *s* Gnothach, cùis, rud; gnothach graidh. Their own affair be it, *a leithsgeul sin doibh féin.*

Affect, *v* Drùigh; feuch ri, streap ri, oidhripich; (*make a show*), gabh ort, leig ort, (*love*), gradhaich. It did not affect him in the least, *cha do dhrùigh e air a bheag, cha do chuir a smad air.*

Affectation, *s.* Coslas fallseil; faoin choslas, faoin leanachd, baoth-choslas, baoth-leanachd, foirmeileachd; pongaileachd; baoth-ghradh; ceigeineachd.

Affected, *part.* and *a.* Buailte; deante le mòran sgleò; foirmeil; rudach, ceigeineach. Well affected, *cairdeil, dileas;* (*with disease*), buailte le galar. How stands he affected? *ciamar tha 'dhùrachd?*

Affectedness, *s.* Foirmeileachd, pongaileachd; ceigeineachd

Affecting, *a.* Muladach, tuirseach, brònach; truagh.

Affection, *s* Gradh, gaol, aigne, càil; dealas, caileachd; fulang; (*disease*), galar, eucail, tinneas Governed by his affections, *air a stiuradh le 'aignibh*, he has every person's affections, *tha deagh rùn gach neach aig*, without affection, *gun chàil, gun mhothachadh*, evil affection, *droch dhùrachd, droch aigne.*

Affectionate, *a* Teo-chridheach; caomh-chridheach; caoimhneil, truacanta, gaolach, deothasach.

Affectionately, *adv.* Gu teo-chridheach, gu caomh-chridheach, gu caoimhneil, gu gaolach, gu truacanta, gu deothasach

Affectionateness, *s.* Teo-chridheachd, tiom-chridheachd, caoimhnealachd, gaolachd, truacantachd.

Affectioned, *a.* Aomta

Affective, *a* Carraideach, truagh, muladach; piantach

Affiance, *s.* Ceangladh, ceangal pòsaidh; bun, dochas, muinghinn earbsa.

Affiance, *v a* Geall ann am pòsadh; cuir dòchas; cuir earbsa. Affianced, *geallainte.*

Affidavit, *s* Mionnan; teisteas; buàthar, focal

Affied, *a.* Gealltuinte, cumhnantaichte, ceangailte.

Affiliation, *s.* Uchd-mhacachd; uchdmhacachd

Affined, *a* Càirdeach, dileas

Affinity, *s.* Cairdeas, dìllse; daimh pòsaidh; cleamhnas, chamhnas Contract affinity, *dean cleamhnas.*

Affirm, *v a.* Cuir an céill, càir; dearbh; foillsich; aidich; daingnich, dean cinnteach. Affirm a decree, *daingnich reachd*, affirmed, *dearbhte, foillsichte, daingnichte*

Affirmable, *a* Daingneachail, dearbhail, so-dhaingneach

Affirmance, *s.* Daingneachd, dearbhadh

Affirmant, *s* Dearbhair, fear daingneachaidh.

Affirmation, *s.* Daingneachadh, dearbhadh, briathrachadh, contigairt.

Affirmative, *a* Daingneachail, dearbhach, dearbhail. One holds the affirmative, the other the negative, *their an darna fear tha, is am fear eile cha n' eil.*

Affirmed, *part.* Dearbhte; dearbhta; foillsichte; aidichte, daingnichte.

Affirmer, *s* Fear-daingneachaidh; fear dearbhaidh; daingneachair, dearbhadair.

Affix, *v.* Cuir ri, ceangail ri; tàth; ic, ioc. Affixed, *ceangailte ri*

Affix, *s* Ie-shiol, ic

Afflict, *v. a* Cradh, pian, sàruich, claoidh, leòn Afflicted, *cradhte, saruichte, claoidhte, leointe, leònta.*

Afflictedness, *s* Cradhachd, pian, saruchadh, claoidh, leòn; airc, truaighe, an-shocair, amhghar, bròn, muladachd.

Afflicter, *s* Cradhair, piantair, saruchair, claoidhear; fear-saruchaidh.

Affliction, *s* Amhghar, anshocair, bròn, truaighe, mulad; doilghios, pian, airc, leòn.

Affluence, *s.* Beartas, beairteas, pailteas, saibhreas, maoin,

Affluent, *a.* Beartach, beairteach, pailt, saibhir.

AFFLUX, AFFLUXION, s. Lionadh, sruthadh

AFFORD, v. Thoir, thabhair, builich; thoir a mach; bi comasach, bi murrach.

AFFOREST, v. Coilltich, frithich; fàsaich, tionndadh talamh gu frith, na gu fàsach.

AFFRANCHISE, v. Saor, saoraich, saorsaich, saoranaich.

AFFRAY, s. Tabaid, caonnag, tuasaid, còmhstrigh, tuairgne

AFFRIGHT, v. a. Cuir eagal, geilt, oillt, no fuath air neach, fuathasaich.

AFFRIGHT, s. Eagal, oillt, geilt, uamhann; sgeun.

† AFFRIGHTFUL, a Eagallach; oillteil, umhannach, uamhasach.

AFFRONT, v. Aghaidbich, thoir aghaidh, thig aghaidh ri h-aghaidh; naraich, maslaich, tarcuisich He was affronted, *ghabh e nair, fhuair e 'nàrachadh, fhuair e 'mhuslachadh*, affronted, *nàraichte, maslaichte*

AFFRONT, s Nàrachadh, masladh, tàir, spid, tarcuis. Take affront, *gabh gu dona, gabh gu soithich*

AFFRONTER, s. Narachair, maslachair.

AFFRONTING, a. Tarcuiseach, maslachail, spideil; tàireil.

AFFUSE, v. Doirt air, taom air.

AFFUSION, s Dortadh, taomadh

AFFY, v. Geall ann am pòsadh, cuir dochas, cuir muinghinn; cuir earbsa, cuir bun

AFIELD, adv. A mach, o 'n tigh.

AFLAT, adv. Air làr, air an talamh, comhad ris an làr.

AFLOAT, adv. Air snamh, air phlod; *figuratively*, anns an t-sealladh, ag imeachd.

AFOOT, adv. Air chois, air falbhan, do chois, as an leabadh Set afoot, *tog, cuir air chois.*

† AFORE, prep Roimh, air thoiseach air

AFORE, adv. Roimh; a chian, an tùs; air thùs

AFOREHAND, adv. Roimh-laimh

AFORE-MENTIONED, a. A thubhradh, a dubhradh, a sgriobhadh, air a roimh-radh.

AFORETIME, adv. O shean, o chian.

AFRAID, a. Eagallach, gealltach He is afraid of you, *tha eagal air romhad*, he is afraid, *tha e 'gabhail eagaill*, *tha eagal air.*

AFRESH, adv. As ùr, gu h-ur, a ris, as an nomha, as an nuadh He began afresh, *thòisich e as ùr*

AFRONT, adv. Air thus, an tùs, air thoiseach, an aghaidh

ASTERN, adv. An comhar an stiùir, gu deireadh

AFTER, prep. and adv. An deigh, an tòir; a réir. After that, *an deigh sin;* after me, *am dheigh*, after him, *na dheigh*, after her, *na deigh*, after us, *na 'r deigh*, after you, *n' ur deigh*, after them, *na 'n deigh;* after all, *an deigh na h-uile, an deigh sin uile; fadheoidh, mu-dheireadh*, after my own way, *a réir mo sheòl féin*, after this manner, *air an doigh so, air an seòl so;* a little while after, *beagan an deigh sin*, after a day or two, *an deigh làth na dhà*, one after another, *fear an deigh chéile.*

AFTER-AGES, s. Linntean ri teachd, an t-am ri teachd, an t-al ri teachd

AFTER-ALL, adv. An deigh sin uile; fadheoidh, mudheireadh; air a' cheann thall.

AFTERBIRTH, s. Ath-bhreith.

AFTERCLAP, s. Ath-bhuille.

AFTERCOST, s. Ath-chosdas

AFTERCROP, s. Ath-bhàrr, an dara bàrr

AFTER-ENDEAVOUR, s Ath-oidhirp

AFTERGAME, s. Ath-chluich.

AFTERLOVE, s. Ath-ghradh.

AFTERMATCH, s. Ath-bharr.

AFTERNOON, s Deigh mheadhon làtha

AFTERPAINS, s. Ath-thinneas, ath-thinneas cloinne

AFTERPART, s. Deireadh.

AFTERTASTE, s. Ath-bhlas, blas a dh' fhanas an deigh òl

AFTERTHOUGHT, s Ath-smuaine.

AFTERTIMES, s Amanna ri teachd, linntean ri teachd, aimsir ri teachd

AFTERTOSSING, s. Ath-thulgadh tuinne.

AFTERWARD, adv An deigh sin, an deigh laimh.

AGA, s. Oifhichear Turcach.

AGAIN, adv A ris, ris, a rithist, rithistich, air an laimh eile, uair eile, am eile; fathast, fhathast; air ais, an aghaidh Again and again, *iomad uair, uair is uair.*

AGAINST, prep (*Contrary*), an aghaidh, (*opposite*), mu chomhar; (*referring to time*), fa-chomhair, air cheann, (*over against*), thàll Against thee, *ann ad' aghaidh*, straight against us, *calg dhìreach na 'r n-aghaidh*, I am not against it, *cha n' eil mi na aghaidh*, against the grain, *an aghaidh chuilg*, against one's will, *a dh' aindeoin*, against Monday, *air cheann Di luain*, (*in provision for*), fa chomhair.

AGAPE, adv. Le beul fosgailte, gu craosach, gu spleucach

AGARIC, s. Seorsa cungaidh leigheis

AGAST, a Air uamhann, fo uamhann, fo eagall

AGATE, s Agait, clach phrìseil

AGE, s. Aois, linn, al, ùine, aois duine; uine cheud bliadhna. He has come to age, *thainig e gu h-inbhe;* six years of age, *sè bliadhna dh'aois;* great age, *aosmhorachd, aoismhoireachd*, of the same age, *comh-aoismhor, comhshean.*

AGED, a Aosmhor, sean, aosda.

AGEDLY, adv. Gu h-aosmhor, gu h-aosda.

AGENCY, s Gniomhachas, deanadas, gilleachas. Free agency, *saor-ghniomh, saor-thoil.*

AGENT, s. Gniomhaich; fear gnothuich; sgriobhair; fear ionaid, riochdfhear.

AGENT, a. Gniomhach, deantach

AGGENERATION, s Dlùth-chinneas, dluth-fhas.

AGGERATE, v Carn suas, cruinnich, torr.

† AGGLOSE, a Carnach, torrach, tomanach, tolmach

AGGLOMERATE, v Cearslaich, ceirslich; ceartlaich

AGGLUTINATE, v. Glaodh ri chéile, stic ri chéile, glaodhaich.

AGGLUTINATION, s Glaodhadh; sticeadh

AGGRANDIZE, v. Ardaich, uaillsich, meadaich, moraich, inbhich.

AGGRANDIZED, part Ardaichte, arduichte, uaillsichte, meudaichte; moraichte, inbhichte.

AGGRANDIZEMENT, s Ardachadh, arduchadh, uaillseachadh, meudachadh, inbheachd

AGGRANDIZER, s. Arduchair

AGGRAVATE, v. Antromaich, meudaich.

AGGRAVATION, s Antromachadh, meudachadh

AGGREGATE, v a Cruinnich, cnuasaich, torr, carn; dluthaich ri chéile, cnapaich

AGGREGATE, s An t-iomlan.

AGGREGATION, s. Cruinneachadh, torradh, cnuasachadh torr, cnuasachd

AGGRESS, v. Buail an toiseach, cionntaich an toiseach.

AGGRESSION, s Bualadh an toiseach, ceud-chionnt, ceud-choire

AGGRESSOR, s. An ti bhuaileas an toiseach, an ti choiricheas an toiseach, coireach, cionntaiche Who was the aggressor? *co bu choireach?*

Aggrievance, *s.* Buaireadh; dochann, saruchadh; cron; ciurradh.

Aggrieve, *v.* Buair, dean eucoir; eucoirich, dochainn, sàruich. Aggrieved, *buairte, dochannaichte, eucoirichte.*

Aggroup, *v. n.* Co-thionail; co' chruinnich.

Aghast, *a.* Fu' uamhann, fo eagal.

Agile, *a.* Lùthar, luthmhor, luath, clis, cleasmhor, brisg, beothail, deas; tapaidh, smiorail, smearail.

Agility, *s.* Luathas, luthmhorachd; beothalachd, smioralachd, tapachd.

Agio, *s.* An diubhair tha eadar cùinn agus airgiod paipeir.

Agitable, *a.* So-ghluasad, so-charuchaidh, so-charuichte; gluasadach.

Agitate, *v. a.* Gluais, caruich, oibrich cuir troimh chéile; buair; cnuasaich, fidrich.

Agitation, *s.* Gluasachd, gluasadh, gluasad, dian-ghluasad, caruchadh; buaireas, buaireadh, oibreachadh; troimh cheile, mi-shuaimhneas; cnuasachd, fidreachadh.

Agitator, *s.* Gluasadair; fear gniomh; fear gnothuich.

† Agminal, *a.* Buidheannail, buidheannach.

Agnail, *s.* Gath-tearra.

Agnation, *s.* Sliochd o aon athair.

† Agnition, *s.* Aideachadh.

Agnomination, *s.* Ciallachadh.

Ago, *adv.* Seachad, seach, roimh so, a chaidh. Two years ago, *o cheann da bhliadhna;* long ago, *o cheann fad;* it is not long since he died, *cha n' eil fad on theasd e.*

Agog, *a.* Eutrom, gaoithe, amaideach; togarrach, teth.

Agoing, *a.* Air siubhladh.

† Agone, *adv.* Seach, seachad.

Agonistes, *s.* Dorn, chùraidh; fear a ni comhrag airson airgid.

Agonize, *v.* Pian, cradh, cradhaich; curaich.

Agony, *s.* Pian, cradh; curadh, guin, geur-ghuin; amhghar cruaidh-ghleachd; craon, spairn a bhàis. Full of agony, *lan péin.*

Agouty, *s.* Beothach beag ruadh a tha fàs anns na h-Innseachan shuas; tha e mu thomad coinein; agus cha n'eil aig ach da fhiacal anns gach peirceall.

Agrarian, *a.* Fàicheach.

Agree, *v.* Coird, aontaich; comh-choird; reitich. Are you agreed, *bheil sibh toilichte; bheil sibh réidh;* agree on, *sonraich;* they agreed upon a day, *shonraich iad latha.*

Agreeable, *a.* Freagarrach, taitneach; ciatach.

Agreeableness, *s.* Freagarrachd; taitneachd, ciatachd; coslachd, cordachd.

Agreeably, *adv.* Gu freagarrach, gu taitneach, gu ciatach; a réir, do réir.

Agreed, *part.* Sonruichte; aontaichte; toilichte.

Agreement, *s.* Cordadh, comh-chordadh; (*reconciling*), réite, reiteadh; (*in tune*), comh-sheirm; (*proportion*), samhladh; comh-fhreagarrachd; (*bargain*), cumhnant, bann.

Agrestic, *a.* Fàicheil.

Agricultural, *a.* Treabhachail, tuathanachail.

Agriculture, *s.* Treabhachas, tuathanachd; tuathanachas, fearas tighe.

Agriculturist, *s.* Treabhaiche, tuathanach.

Agrimony, *s.* Geurag bhileach; a gheurag bhileach, murdhraidhean.

Aground, *adv.* Air; air traigh, air làr. The boat has run aground, *chaidh am bàt air;* he run himself aground, *chaidh e troimh a mhaoin.*

Ague, *s.* Fiabhrus; crith-fiabhrus; crith; fiabhrus critheach. A fit of ague, *taom fiabhruis.*

Aguish, *a.* Fiabhrusach, critheach; critheanach.

Aguishness, *s.* Fiabhrusachd, critheanachd.

Ah! *interj.* Ah! mo thruaigh.

Aha! *interj.* Aha; focal fochaid, (*no*) tàire.

Ahead, *adv.* An ceann; air thoiseach.

Aheight, *adv.* An airde, shuas, uthard.

Aid, *v.* Cuidich, coghain, cobhair, cabhair; dean coghnadh le, dean cobhair le, cum taic.

Aid, *s.* Cuideachadh, còghnadh, cobhair; taic; cis; deolaidh.

Aide-de-camp, *s.* Dian-chomhla.

Aider, *s.* Fear-coghnaidh; fear-cobhair; fear cuideachaidh.

Aidless, *a.* Gun chobhair, gun chòghnadh, gun taic, gun chuideachadh, anfhann; uireasbhach.

Aiery, *s.* Nead seabhaig.

Ail, *v. a.* and *n.* Pian, cradh; gearain, mothaich pian, fairich pian. What ails you? nothing, *ciod a tha cur ort? cha n' eil dad; ciod dh' fhairich thu? cha d' fhairich dad.*

Ail, *s.* Tinneas, galar, eucail.

Ailing, *a.* A gearain. He is ailing, *tha e a gearain.*

Ailment, *s.* Tinneas, eucail, galar.

Aim, *v.* Comharaich, beachdaich, gabh cuimeis, cuir ri sùil; (*design*), iarr, sir. I aim at your good, *tha mi ag iarruidh do leas;* they aim at high things, *tha sùil aca ri nithibh ard.*

Aim, *s.* Beachd; rùn; meann, oidhirp; barail; seol.

Air, *s.* Athar, adhar; àile; iarmailt; speuran; (*wind*), gaoth, feochan; (*smell*), tòchd, fàile; (*music*), fonn, ceòl; (*publicity*), foillseachd, follaiseachd; (*appearance*), coslas, neul, aogas, gne; (*gait*), sgòd, gò, uallachd. In the air, *anns an adhar;* an air of wind, *feochan gaòithe;* taking the air, *a gabhail na gaòithe, a gabhail sràid;* it has taken air, *chaidh e fo sgaoileadh:* he has the air of a gentleman, *is mòr a tha do choslas an duine uasail aig.*

Air, *v. a.* Cuir ri gaoth; teò, teòthaich; blàthaich.

Air-bladder, *s.* Entroman gaoithe; (*in fish*), mealag, bealag.

Air-built, *a.* Faoin; diamhain; faileusach.

Air-hole, *s.* Toll gaòithe.

Airiness, *s.* (*Of a place*), gaotharachd; farsuingeachd; fallaineachd; (*of a person*), faoineachd, eutruimead, beothalachd, sgòd, uallachd.

Airing, *s.* Spaidseireachd, spaisdearachd, gabhail na gaoithe; sràideasachd, cnocaireachd. Take an airing, *gabh sràid.*

Airling, *s.* Gaothan; urr eutrom, gaoithe.

Airpump, *s.* Taoman adhair, piob-thaosgaidh athar.

Airy, *a.* (*In person*), gaoithe, gaothaidh, eutrom, aotrom, faoin; stàideil; cridheil; (*place*), gaothar, fosgailte; fallain; (*thin*), tan, adharail; gaoithe, faoin.

Aisle, *s.* Meadhon eaglais.

Akin, *a.* Cairdeach; aileas; coslach.

Alabaster, *s.* Oillbhastair, seorsa cloich fhinealta, ro fhuras ghearradh, agus mur is tric geal.

Alack! *interj.* Mo thruaighe! och! mo chreach!

Alackaday! *interj.* Mo thruaigh! mo chreach! och!

Alacriously, *adv.* Gu h-aighearach, gu cridheil; gu h-aigeantach, gu h-aoibhneach, gu tapaidh, gu smearail; gu suilbhir.

Alacrity, *s.* Aighean, aighearachd; cradhealas; aigeantas, aigeantachd; suilbhireachd, tapachd; smioralachd; beothaileachd, toileachas, misneach.

Alamode, *adv.* Anns an fhasan, a réir an fhasain.

Aland, *adv.* Air traigh, air tir, air cladach, air talamh tioram.

Alarm, *s.* Caismeachd; rabhadh, sanas; maoim, fuathas; faireachadh; eagal. Sound an alarm, *buail caismeachd;* an alarm bell, *clag rabhaidh;* alarm post, *cnoc-faire;* false alarm, *faoin-eagal.*

Alarm, *v. a.* Buail caismeachd; thoir rabhadh, thoir sanas; cuir eagall air, buair.

Alarming, *a.* Eagalach, fuathasach; oillteil.

Alas! Mo thruaighe! mo chreach! mo leòn! mo nuar!

Alas! alas! Mo thruaighe! och agus ochain! och nan ochain! ochain nan och! och agus ochain nan och! och agus ochain nan och éire!

Alate, *adv.* A chianamh, o cheann ghoirrid.

Alb, *s.* Léin aifrionn.

Albany, *s.* Albainn.

Albeit, *adv.* Gidheadh, giodh.

Albion, *s.* Breatunn; Albainn.

Albugineous, *a.* Mar ghealgan uibh; air am bheil an galar sùl.

Albugo, *s.* Galar araid san t-sùil.

Alcanna, *s.* Dath-luibh Eiphiteach.

Alchymist, *s.* Leaghadair mheiteala; fear leaghaidh mhiotailtean.

Alchymy, *s.* Eolas air aon mhiotailt a thionndadh gu miotailt eile; seorsa meiteal do 'n deanar spàineachan.

Alcohol, *s.* Branndi ioma-tharruingte; uisge baoghal.

Alcoran, *s.* Piobal nan Turcach.

Alcove, *s.* Puball; puball riomhach.

Alder, *s.* Fearna. An alder tree, *craobh fhearna.*

Alderman, *s.* Aon do riaghlairean baile mhòir.

Aldern, *a.* Fearna, fearnach.

Ale, *s.* Leann, lionn, liunn. New ale, *leann ùr;* strong ale, *leann laidir;* small ale, *leann caol;* stale ale, *leann goirt.*

Aleberry, *s.* Leann teth.

Alebrewer, *s.* Grùdair.

Alecost, *s.* Seorsa luibh.

Alegar, *s.* Leann geur; leann goirt, leann geur (no) goirt.

Alehouse, *s. m.* Tigh leanna, tigh osda.

Alehouse-keeper, *s.* Fear tigh lionna, grùdair.

Alembic, *s.* Poit thogalach.

† **Alength**, *adv.* Air fhad.

Alert, *a.* Furachair, deas, ullamh; smiorail; beothail; ealamh; grad; beadaidh; lonach.

Alertness, *s.* Furachras, furachaireachd; smioralas, beothalachd; ealamhachd, beadaidheachd.

Alewife, *s.* Bean tigh-lionna, ban-ghrudair.

Alexipharmic, *a.* Nimh-fhògrach.

Algebra, *s.* Seorsa cunntais Arabach.

† **Algid**, *a.* Fuar; fionnar; reòtaidh.

† **Algidity**, *s.* Fuachd; fionnarachd.

Algorism, *a.* Cùnntas.

† **Alible**, *a.* Susbuinneach.

Alien, *s.* Coigreach, allmharach, gall.

Alien, *a.* Coigreach, allmharach.

Alienable, *a.* So-thoirt o, so-thoirt thairis.

Alienate, *v.* Tar-thoir, thoir thairis; thoir inntinn a thaobh.

Alienation, *s.* Tar-thoirt; toirt a thaobh; tarruing a thaobh; cur cùl; caochladh graidh.

Alight, *v.* Tuirling, tuirleum, teirinn; thig bhàn, thig a nuas.

Alike, *adv.* Cosmhal, coslach, ionann, comh-ionann; gun diubhar. All alike, *uile ionann.*

Aliment, *s.* Biadh, lon, teachd-an-tìr, aran; beathachadh, tighinn suas; connlach.

Alimental, *a.* Biadhach, beathachail, aranach, lònail; lònach.

Alimentation, *s.* Biadhachadh; beathachadh.

Alimony, *s.* Beo-shlainnte sgar-mhna.

Aliquant, *a.* Còr-phairteach.

Aliquot, *a.* Cuid dhireach.

Alish, *a.* Leannach, lionnach; air bhlas an lionna.

Alive, *a.* Beo, lathair; beothail, spioradail, smiorail, mothachail. Alive and well, *beò slàn;* is he alive? *bheil e beo? am beo e? bheil e làthair?* whilst I am alive, *fhads is beò mi.*

Alkali, *s.* Cal-shalainn; ni sam bi a dh'oibricheas air dha bhi air a chur le uisge geur.

Alkanet, *s.* Seorsa luibh.

All, *a.* Uile: gu léir. Every one in particular, *gach, gach uile, gach fear;* in general, *na h-uile;* all day, *re 'n làth;* all the world over, *air fad an t-saoghail;* with all my heart, *le m' uile chridhe;* make all the haste you can, *bi cho luath 's is urrainn duit, dean an deifir is luaithe is urradh dhuit;* it is all one, *tha e uile ionann;* all the while, *ré na tìme;* it is all one to me, *tha e uile ionann dhomhsa;* it is all over, *tha e criochnaichte;* it is all over with him, *tha e dheth;* all at once, *a dh'aon bheum;* alltogether, *mu chomhlath;* wholly, *gu h-uile, gu tur;* by all means, *air na h-uile cor;* on all fours, *margarsanaich;* for all you, *a dh'aindeoin ort;* at all, *idir;* All Saints Day, *làth nan uile naomh.*

Alla, Allah, *s.* Focal Turcach a ciallachadh *Dia.*

Allay, *v. a.* Caisg, coisg, lughdaich; truaillich miotailtean.

Allay, *s.* Droch mheiteal; droch-mhiotailt.

All-bearing, *a.* Uile-thorrach.

All-cheering, *a.* Uile-bheothachail.

All-conquering, *a.* Uile-bhuadhach.

All-consuming, *a.* Uile-mhillteach, leir-mhillteach, leir-sgriosail.

All-devouring, *a.* Uile-itheach, uile-shlugach, uile-mhillteach.

Allegation, *s.* Abradh, radh; tagradh, dearbhadh; contagairt, leithsgeul.

Allege, *v.* Abair, abair mar leithsgeul; tagair; dearbh; foillsich; deimhinn, deimhinnich, contagair, cuir an ceill, cum a mach.

Allegeable, *a.* A dh'fhaotar a radh, a dh'fheudar a thagradh.

Alleger, *s.* Dearbhadair, tagradair.

Allegiance, *s.* Dìliseachd, dillseachd, ùmhlachd, do 'n lagh.

† **Allegiant**, *a.* Dilis do righ, umhal.

Allegoric, *a.* Samhlachail; seach-labhrach, dealbhach.

Allegorically, *adv.* Gu samhlachail, gu seach-labhrach, gu dealbhach; gu dorcha.

Allegorize, *v.* Samhlaich, seach-labhair.

Allegory, *s.* Samhladh; seach-labhairt.

Allelujah, *s.* Focal Eabhruidheach a ciallachadh *Molaibh Dia.*

Alleviate, *v. a.* Eutromaich; lughdaich; coisg, caisg; ciùinich, traoigh. Alleviated, *eutromaichte; lughdaichte; coisgte, caisgte; ciùinichte; traoighte.*

Alleviation, *s.* Eutromachadh; lughdachadh; cosgadh, casgadh; ciùineachadh; traoghadh.

Alley, *s.* Sràid gàraidh; lonuinn, lonaig; clobhsa; sraid-chumhann; frìth-shràid.

ALL-FOURS, *s* Seorsa cluich air chairtean. On all-fours, *a smògarsanaich.*

ALL-HAIL, *v.* Gu mu slan robh sibh; fàillte is furan, slàinte uile.

ALLIANCE, *s* (*By blood*), cairdeas, daimh, dillseachd; (*by marriage*), chamhnas, cleamhnas, (*of states*), caidreamhas; càirdeas.

ALLICIENCY, *s.* Tarruing

ALLIED, *a.* Cairdeach, daimheil; an caidreamhas; réidh

ALLIGATE, *s.* Co'cheangail; tàth ri chéile.

ALLIGATION, *s.* Co'cheangladh; co'thàth

ALLIGATOR, *s* Cròghall mhor.

ALLISION, *s.* Comh-bhualadh.

ALL-KNOWING, *a* Uile-fhiosrach.

ALLOCATION, *s* Co'chur, cur ri chéile.

ALLOCUTION, *s* Labhairt; comh-labhairt; comh-luadar.

ALLODIUM, *s* Saor-sheilbh

ALLONGE, *v.* Sàth; put, starr

ALLOO, *v* Stuig, mar choin chum faoghaid.

ALLOT, *v.* Pairtich, roinn, riaraich, riaruich, sonruich, orduich, tomhais mach do neach Allotted, *pairtichte, roinnte, riaraichte, sonruichte, orduichte.*

ALLOTMENT, *s.* Pairt, cuid, codach, roinn, earann, cuibhrionn, pairteachadh, roinneadh, riarachadh, orduchadh

ALLOTTED, *part.* See ALLOT.

ALLOTTERY, *s.* Pairt cuid, roinn, earann

ALLOW, *v. a.* Ceadaich, leig le, deònaich, thoir cead, thoir comas Allow him to depart, *leig leis falbh*, he is not allowed, *cha n'eil chead aige, cha n'eil comas aige*

ALLOWABLE, *a* Ceadachail, ceaduichte; ceart, laghail.

ALLOWABLENESS, *s* Cead, comas, laghaileachd

ALLOWANCE, *s* Cead, comas; saorsadh, saorsuinn; (*gift*), tabhartas, deonachas, gean maith, cuibhrionn, cuid, pàirt roinn, duais, mathalachd.

ALLOWED, *a* Ceadaichte, deonaichte, air bhuileachadh, ceart, laghail.

ALLOY, *s.* Droch mhiotailt; laghdachadh

ALL-SUFFICIENCY, *s* Uile-chomasachd, uile-iomlanachd.

ALLUDE, *v.* Ciallaich, cialluich, sanasaich

ALLUMINATE, *v* Dealbh, dàth

ALLUMINOR, *s.* Dealbh-liobhadair

ALLURE, *v* Meall, thoir a thaobh, buair; (*wheedle*), tàlaidh

ALLUREMENT, *s* Mealladh, buaireadh

ALLURER, *s* Meallair, mealltair, buairear, buaireadair, fear tàlaidh, tàladhaiche

ALLURINGLY, *adv.* Gu mealltach, gu buaireach, gu taladhach

ALLUSION, *s* Ciallachadh, sanas, coimeas

ALLUSIVE, *a.* Ciallach, ciallachail, sànasach, sanasail.

ALLUVION, *s.* Feudal aimhne.

ALL-WISE, *a* Uile-ghlic.

ALLY, *v* Dean cleamhnas, dean caidreamhas, dean daimh

ALLY, *s* Caraid, caidreamhach; bann-charaid, chamhuinn

ALMANACK, *s* Miosachan

ALMIGHTINESS, *s* Uile-chumhachd

ALMIGHTY, *a* Uile-chamhachdach. The Almighty, *An t-Uile-chumhachdach*

ALMOND, *s* Amon, cno ghreugach Almonds (*in anatomy*), *fàircagan*

ALMONER, *s* Déirc-roinneadair, fear-coimhid déirc.

ALMONRY, *s.* Amraidh, tigh-coimhid déirc

ALMOST, *adv* Ach beag, air bheag; cha mhòr; gu h-inbhe bhig There is not a day almost but he comes, *is gann tha là nach tig e*: the corn is almost ripe, *tha 'n t-arbhar thun a bhi abuich, cha mhor nach eil an t-arbhar abuich*, he almost killed him, *theab e a mharbh; cha mhòr nach do mharbh se e.*

ALMS, *s.* Déirc, déircean Give alms, *thoir déirc*; alms basket, *cliabh-dhéirc.*

ALMS-DEED. Déirc; tabhartas carthannach. Alms-house, *tigh nam bochd.*

ALMS-MAN, *s.* Déircear; deirciche; duine bochd, baigeir.

ALMUG-TREE, *s* Crann almuig.

ALNAGE, *s.* Slat-thomhais.

ALOES, *s* Leigheas fuasglach.

ALOFT, *prep* Suas, 'nairde; gu h-ard.

ALOFT, *adv.* Shuas, uthard.

ALOGY, *s.* Mi-reuson, neo-thuigse.

ALONE, *a.* Aonar, aonarach, aonaranach, singilte. He is alone, *tha e na aonar*, she is alone, *tha i na h-aonar*; let him alone, *leig leis, leig chead da, com' leat e*

ALONG, *adv* Air fhad, air fad. Along with, *comhlath ri, cuid ri*, along the river, *ri taobh na h-aibhne*, all along, *re na tìme so, gu so, gus an am so.*

ALOOF, *adv* Air falbh, am fad, an céin, greis as; ni 's mo air fuaradh Stand aloof, *seas air falbh, cum agad féin.*

ALOUD, *adv* Gu labhradh; gu h-ard, gu h-osgarra

ALPHA, *s* (*Greugais*) A cheud litir do 'n Aibidil Ghreugach; an ceud ni, tùs, toiseach

ALPHABET, *s* Abidil, aibitil, aiblit; *eubsaidh*, Is e sin ri radh, *a, b, c.*

ALPHABETICAL, *a.* Aibidileach, aibliteach.

ALPHABETICALLY, *adv.* A réir ordugh na h-aibidil.

ALPINE, *a.* Ailpeach.

ALREADY, *a* Cheana, a cheanadh.

ALSO, *adv.* Mar an ceudna, cuideachd, fòs.

ALTAR, *s.* Altair.

ALTARAGE, *s* Airgiod altrach.

ALTER, *v. a.* Atharraich, tionndadh, mùth, mùgh, caochaih. *Altered*, atharraichte

ALTERABLE, *a* So-atharrachadh, so-thionndadh, so-mhùgh, so-atharraichte.

ALTERATION, *s* Atharrachadh, mùth, mùgh, caochladh.

ALTERCATION, *s.* Connsach, connsachadh, conspuid; tuaircap, tuasaid, trod, comhstrigh, tabaid, deasboireachd.

ALTERNATE, *a.* Mu 'n seach; malairteach.

ALTERNATE, *v* Mùth; iomhlaidich, malairt, dean ma 'n seach.

ALTERNATELY, *adv* Ma 'n seach

ALTERNATION, *s.* Mùth, iomlaideachd; malairt

ALTERNATIVE, *s.* Atharrachadh, mùgh seòla.

ALTHOUGH, *conj* Ged, gidheadh.

† ALTILOQUENCE, *s* Ard-ghlòir, gloireis, glòrais.

ALTIMETRY, *s* Ard-thomhas, aird-thomhas.

† ALTISONANT, *a* Ard-fhogharach.

ALTITUDE, *s* Airde.

ALTOGETHER, *adv.* Gu léir, gu tur, uile gu léir, air fad.

ALUM, *s.* Falm, falam

ALUMINOUS, *a* Falmach; falmanta.

ALWAYS, *adv.* An comhnuidh, daonann, am bidheantas, a ghnath, do ghnath; gun sgur, gun chàirde

AM, *v* Tha mi, ta mi; Is mi I am learned, *tha mi ionnsaichte*, I am sick, *tha mi tinn*, as far as I am able, *cho math 's is urrainn mi, mar is fearr a dh'fheudas mi*, as well as I am, *cho mhath riumsa*

AMABILITY, *s.* Gradhachd; gaolachd, ionmhuinneachd.

Amain, *adv.* Gu dian; le neart; le treise; le fior spionnadh; a dh'aindeoin.

Amalgam, *s.* Comh-leaghan.

Amalgamate, *v.* Comh-leagh.

Amalgamation, *s.* Comh-leaghadh.

Amandation, *s.* Dol air ghnothuch.

Amanuensis, *s.* Sgriobhair, run-sgriobhair; fear a sgriobhas mar dheachdas duine eile.

Amaranth, *s.* Seorsa luibh.

Amaritude, *s.* Searbhas, searbhad, seirbhe; goirteas; géire, geurad.

Amassment, *s.* Carnadh, cruachadh; cnuasachadh; cruinneachadh, torradh.

Amass, *v. a.* Carn suas; cruach; cnuasaich, cruinnich; cuir ri chéile, torr.

Amaze, *s.* Ioghnadh, iongantas, eagal, amhluadh, uamhann.

Amaze, *v.* Cuir ioghnadh air; cuir fu eagal, cuir fu amhluadh.

Amazedness, *s.* Ioghnachd; iongantas; amhluadh; uamhann, uamhannachd.

Amazement, *s.* Eagal, amhluadh, uamhann, oillt.

Amazing, *a.* Iongantach, miorbhuileach.

Amazon, *s.* Ban-ghaisgeach, ban-churaidh.

Ambages, *s.* Cuairt-radh; iom-fhocal; gloireis.

Ambagious, *a.* Glòireiseach, glòraiseach.

Ambassador, *s. m.* Teachdair, teachdair righ; righ-theachdair; ard-theachdair.

Ambassadress, *s.* Ban-theachdair.

Ambassage, *s.* Teachdaireachd.

Amber, *s.* Omar; bith brisg buidhe soilleir, a gheibhear mach shios air an tràigh mu dheas do mhuir Lochlinn.

Amber-head, *s.* Paidirean omair.

Amber-drink, *s.* Deoch air dhath an omair.

Ambergris, *s.* Seorsa cungaidh-leigheis cubhraidh, air dhath na luaithe, agus a leaghas mar chéir.

Ambidexter, *s.* Fear deas-lamhach; fear leam-leat.

Ambidexterity, *s.* Deas-lamhacd; leam-leat.

Ambidexterous, *a.* Deas-lamhach; leam-leat; cealgach.

Ambient, *a.* Iadhach; cuairteach, iom-chuairteach.

Ambiguity, *s.* Amharusachd; doilleireachd, teagmhachd, neo-chinnte, dùbailteachd.

Ambiguous, *a.* Dorcha, doilleir; da-chiallachail; teagmhach; dùbailte, neo-chinnteach.

Ambiguousness, *s.* Amharusachd; doilleireachd; teagmhachd; neo-chinnte; dùbailteachd.

Ambilogy, *s.* Cainnte dhùbailt, dorch-chainnt.

Ambit, *s.* Cuairt.

Ambition, *a.* Glòir-mhiann, mòr-aigne, ard-aigne, deigh air urram.

Ambitious, *a.* Glòir-mhiannach, mòr-aigneach, ard-aigneach.

Ambitude, *s.* Cuairt, uim-chuairt, iom-chuairt, tiom-chuairt.

Amble, *v. n.* Falaraich, rach air falaireachd.

Amble, *s.* Falaireachd, siubhal eich eadar trot agus ceum.

Ambrosia, *s.* Lòn dhé nan Cinneach, deoch neamhuidh.

Ambrosial, *a.* Ro-mhilis, ro-chubhraidh, ro-bhlasda.

Ambry, *s.* (*for* almonry.) Amraidh; pantraidh.

Ambulation, *s.* Spaisdeareachd, spaidseireachd, sraideiseachd; falbhan, siubhladh.

Ambulatory, *a.* Cuartachail; spaisdeireach, sraideiseach; siùbhlach.

Ambury, *s.* Flioghan.

Ambuscade, *s.* Plaid-luidhe; feall-fholach, luidheachan.

Ambush, *s.* Luidheachan, plaid-luidhe, feall-fholach.

Ambustion, *s.* Losgadh, sgaltadh.

Ameliorate, *v.* Leasaich, mathaich, dean ni 's fearr.

Amelioration, *s.* Leasachadh, mathachadh.

Amen, *adv.* Gu mu h-amhuil a bhitheas, mar sin biodh e.

Amenable, *a.* Freagarrach; buailteach.

Amend, *v. a.* and *n.* Leasaich, ath-leasaich; dean ni 's fearr; càirich, fàs ni 's fearr.

Amend, *s.* Diol.

Amender, *s.* Leasachair, ath-leasachair, diolair.

Amendment, *s.* Leasachadh; ath-leasachadh.

Amend, *s.* Diol; dioladh.

Amenity, *s.* Ciatachd; boidhchead; tlachdmhoireachd.

Amerce, *v.* Umhlaich; cuir ùmhladh; leig cìse, (no) càin; dean peanas air.

Amerced, *a.* Umhlaichte; peanasaichte.

Amercement, *s.* Umhlachadh, umhladh, paineachadh, cìse, càin.

Amethodical, *a.* Mi-riaghailteach; neo-sheolta.

Amethyst, *s.* Seorsa buaidh-chloich.

Amiable, *a.* Taitneach, aluinn; so-ghradhach; gradhach, maiseach.

Amiableness, *s.* Aluinneachd, gradhalachd.

Amicable, *a.* Cairdeil; caoimhneil; suairce.

Amicableness, *s.* Cairdealachd; cairdealas; caomhnealachd; suairceas.

Amicably, *adv.* Gu cairdeil; gu caoimhneil; gu suairce.

Amice, *s.* Cuid do chulaidh shagairt.

Amid, **Amidst**, *prep.* Air feadh, a measg, am meadhon.

Amiss, *adv.* Gu h-olc, gu docharach, gu mearrachdach; a an rathad; dona; olc, mi-cheart. It is not amiss, *cha n'eil e dona.*

Amissing, *adv.* Air iunndrainn, air chall.

Amission, *s.* Call, calldach.

Amity, *s.* Cairdeas, gradh, co'chordadh, cordadh; réite.

Ammunition, *s.* Storas feachd; fudar is luaithe; uidheam gunnaireachd.

Amnesty, *s.* Maitheanas coitchionn; leir-laghadh.

Among, **Amongst**, *prep.* Air feadh, am measg. Among friends all things are common, *am measg chairdean tha gach nì coitchionn*; among us, *n'ar measg*; among you, *n'ur measg*; among them, *na 'm measg*; from among, *o measg*; from among you, *o ur measg*; from among them, *o am measg.*

Amorist, *s.* Gaolair, gradhair; slatair, leannan.

Amorous, *a.* Gradhach, gaolar; slatail, ceisteanach, suireachail, leannanach, teth.

Amorousness, *s.* Gaolarachd; ceisteanachd; leannanachd; slataileachd.

Amort, *a.* Trom, marbhanta, mi-mhisneachail, neoshuundach, neo-thogarrach.

Amount, *s.* Suim, meud, an t-iomlan, cunntas. The amount came to this, *thainig an t-iomlan gu so.*

Amount, *v.* Ruig; thuig. The sum total will amount to this, *thig an t-iomlan gu so.*

Amour, *s.* Leannanachd dhiomhair; suireadh, cuis leannanachd.

Amphibious, *a.* Dà-bheothach, da-bheathach; a thig beo air uisge is air tire.

Amphibiousness, *s.* Da-bheathachas, da-bheothachas.

Amphibological, *a.* Teagmhach; amharusach; dubailt; ioma-chiallach.

Amphibology, *s.* Teagmhachd; amharusachd; dubailteachd; ioma-chiallachd.

Amphibolous, *a.* Iol-thilgte; agail; a null is a nall; teagmhach.

Amphitheatre, *s.* Tigh-cluiche, tigh sùgradh, lann-amhairc, cuairt-lann amhairc.

Ample, *a.* Mòr; farsaing, farsuing; leudach, meudmhor; fiùghantach, foghainteach.

Ampleness, *s.* Meudachd, farsuingeachd, leudachd, fiùghantachd.

Ampliate, *v.* Meudaich; farsuingich, leudaich.

Ampliation, *s.* Meudachadh; farsuingeachd; leudachd.

Amplification, *s.* Meudachadh, farsuingeachd, leudachadh, leudachd.

Amplifier, *s.* Meudachair; leudachair.

Amplify, *v. a.* Meudaich, leudaich; farsuingich.

Amplitude, *s.* Meud, leud; farsuingeachd; mòrachd, airde, inbhe; pailteas.

Amply, *adv.* Gu mor, gu pailt, gu saibhir.

Amputate, *v. a.* Gearr, snàs.

Amputation, *s.* Gearradh, snàsadh.

Amulet, *s.* Seun, sian cloch buaidh.

Amuse, *v.* Toilich; breug; meall.

Amusement, *s.* Breugadh, mealladh, miodal, caitheamh-aimsir; spuirt, ealaidh, sugradh, cridhealas; fearas-chuideachd.

Amuser, *s.* Miodalaiche, breugair, meallair.

Amusive, *a.* Meallach, breugach, miodalach.

Anabaptist, *s.* Anabaisteach.

Anacathartic, *a.* Sgeitheach.

Anachorite, *s.* Aonaranach; manach.

Anachronism, *s.* Cron-seanachais.

Analeptic, *a.* Comh-fhurtachail; neartachail.

Analogize, *v.* Minich le cosmhalachd, samhlaich.

Analogous, *a.* Coslach, cosmhuil samhlach.

Analogy, *s.* Cosmhuileachd, coslachd; coslas; samhladh; samhlachadh.

Analysis, *s.* Snàsadh; tur-rannsachadh, bun-rannsachadh.

Analytical, *a.* Snasach; tur-rannsuchail; bun-rannsuchail.

Analyze, *v. a.* Snàs; tur-rannsuich; bunn-rannsuich; thoir air ais chum a cheud inbhe.

Anarch, *s.* Fear mi-riaghailt; fear aimhreit, fear buaireis; fear-eas-ordugh.

Anarchical, *a.* Mi-riaghailteach; aimhreiteach; buaireasach, eas-ordughach.

Anarchy, *s.* Mi-riaghailt; aimhreit; buaireas; easordugh.

Anastomosis, *s.* Alt-cheangal.

Anathema, *s.* Mallachd eaglais.

Anathematize, *v.* Guidh mallachd eaglais air, thoir mallachd eaglais air.

Anatocism, *s.* Ocar; an-ocar.

Anatomical, *a.* Corp-shnasach; corp-shnasadail; corp-rannsuchail.

Anatomist, *s.* Snasair, snasadair, corp-shnasaiche; corp-shnasadair, corp-shnasair.

Anatomize, *v. a.* Corp-shnàsaiche, snàsaich.

Anatomy, *s.* Corp-shnasadh, corp-rannsuchadh, corp-shnasadaireachd, snasadaireachd.

Ancestor, *s.* Sinnsear; athair. Ancestors, *aithrichean, sinnsearan.*

Ancestry, *s.* Sinnsearachd; siol.

Anchor, *s.* Acair, achdair. Anchor-hold, *greim-acair.*

Anchor, *v.* Acairich.

Anchorage, *s.* Acairseid, acarsaid; càla, caladh.

Anchored, *part.* Acairichte.

Anchorite, *s.* Dithreabhach, aonaranach; mànach.

Anchovy, *s.* Seòrsa eisg-mara.

Ancient, *a.* Sean, aosda; seannda, arsaidh; sean aimsireil.

† Ancient, *s.* Suaicheantas, suaitheantas; bratach, sròl; fear brataich.

Anciently, *adv.* O shean, o cheann fada, roimh so.

Ancientness, *s.* Seanndachd; arsaidheachd; aosmhorachd.

Ancientry, *s.* Seanndachd.

Ancients, *s.* Sean daoine.

And, *conj.* Agus, is, as. And so forth, *agus mar sin sios e?* and please God, *a dheòin Dia;* how can we enter and not be seen? *cia mar a theid sinn steach, gun air faicinn?* I will go and see, *theid mi dh'fhaicinn;* I will go and see him, *theid mi 'g a fhaicinn.*

Andiron, *s.* Iarunn-biora.

Androgynal, *a.* Firionn-boirionn.

Androgynous, *a.* Firionn-boiriom.

Androgynus, *s.* Urr firionn-boirionn.

Anecdote, *s.* Sgeul; ur-sgeul, gearr-sgeul.

Anemometer, *s.* Gaoth-mheigh, àil-mheigh; inneal chum déine na gaoithe a thombsadh.

Anemone, *s.* Plùr na gaoithe.

Anent, *prep.* Mu dheimhinn, mu thimchioll; an coinneamh.

Aneurism, *s.* At-chuisle.

Anew, *adv.* As ùr, as a nuadh, as nomh; as thoiseach; as ùr 's as thoiseach, a ris, a rithist, uair eile.

Anfractuous, *a.* Lùbach, carach, fiar; neo-dhìreach.

Angel, *s.* Aingeal, bith neamhuidh.

Angelica, *s.* Aingealag; seorsa planda.

Angelic, *a.* Ainglidh, neamhuidh; neamhail; aingealach, aingealail.

Angelical, *a.* See Angelic.

Angelicalness, *s.* Ainglidheachd, neamhalachd, neamhuidheachd.

Anger, *s.* Fearg; feisge; diom; corruich; buath; mi-thlachd; teinntidheachd, teinnteachd. *Angar,* (provincial).

Anger, *v.* Feargaich, cuir fearg air; cuir feirg air; corruich, buair, cuir miothlachd air, cuir mi-ghean.

Angle, *s.* Cearn, cùil, uilinn, oisinn, cearnag.

Angle, *s.* Cungaidh iasgaich.

Angle, *v.* Iasgaich, iasgaich le slait.

Angler, *s.* Iasgair, iasgair-slait; iasgair dubhain.

Anglicism, *s.* Bearlachd.

Angrily, *adv.* Gu feargach, gu crosda, gu diomach, gu mi-gheanach, gu mi-thlachdmhor.

Angry, *a.* Feargach, diomach, teinnteach; mi-gheanach, mi-thlachdmhor crosda, sgaiteach; (*in surgery*), guineach, goimheach.

Anguish, *s.* Pian, cradh, craon, claoidh, doruinn, amhghar.

Anguished, *a.* Pianaichte, cradhta, doruinnichte.

Angular, *a.* Cearnach, oisinneach; cùileach.

Angularity, *s.* Cearnachd, oisinneachd; cùileachd.

Angulated, *a.* Cearnaichte, cearnta, oisinnichte.

Anhelation, *s.* Séitrich, seideadh, plosgartaich, osmagail, àinich, séitean.

† Anhelose, *a.* Séitealach, plosgartach, osmagach, aineach.

Anights, *adv.* Anns an oidhche, an deigh dhorch' oidhche; air feadh na h-oidhche.

Anil, *s.* Lus a ghuirmein.

Anility, *s.* Sean bheanachd; cailleachas, cailleachantas.

Animable, *a.* So-bheothachadh, beothachail.

Animadversion, *s.* Achmhasan, coire, cronachadh; tearrachd; aire, beachdachadh; peanas.

Animadversive, *a.* Achmhasanach, coireachail, cronachail, tearrachdail; beachdail.

Animadvert, *v.* Cronaich, achmhasanaich, coirich, tearrachdaich; faigh coire, faigh cron; gabh beachd; ceasnuich.

Animadverter, *s.* Cronachair, achmhasanaiche, tearrachdair.

Animal, *s.* Ainmhidh, beothach, beathach; bith; baoghlan.

Animal, *a.* Ainmhidheach.

Animalcule, *s.* Meanbh-bhith

Animate, *a.* Beo; beothail, beathail.

Animate, *v.* Beothaich, beathaich, mosgail; suilbhirich; cuir misneach.

Animated, *part.* and *a.* Beothaichte; beo, beothail, spioradail; brisg, togarrach, smiorail, cridheil.

Animation, *s.* Beothalachd, beothalas, spiorad; deò; brisgeachd, togarrachd.

Animative, *a.* Beothachail, beathachail.

Animator, *s.* Beathachair.

† **Animose**, *a.* Teth, breis, dian, borb, feargach, misneachail

Animosity, *s.* Feirge, feargachd; mi-run, fuath, tnu, gamhlas, buirbe.

Anise, *s.* Ainis, seorsa luibh.

Anker, *s.* Buideal, gòthan, gingean tunna; mutharn; soitheach a chumas mu thuairmeis ochd gallana.

Ankle, *s.* Caol na coise, aobrann, aobrunn. Ankles, *aobrannan.*

Annalist, *s. m.* Eachdraiche; seanachaidh.

Annals, *s. pl.* Eachdruidhean, meanbh-eachdruidh; seanachas; eachdraidh o bhliadhna gu bliadhna

Annals, *s.* Aifrionn ann darna ceud airson anamaibh nam mairbh, no airson nam beò.

Annex, *v.* Cuir ri, ceangail ri, tàth, ic, ioc.

Annexed, *a.* Ceangailte; tàthta.

Annexation, *s.* Tathadh, ic, ceangal, ceangladh.

Annihilable, *a.* Neonitheach; so-sgriosadh, so-mhilleadh

Annihilate, *v.* Cuir gu neo ni, sgrios, tur-sgrios; mill.

Annihilation, *s.* Sgrios, tur-sgrios, leir-sgrios; neonitheadh.

Anniversary, *a.* Bliadhnail.

Anniversary, *s.* Cuimhneachan bliadhnail, cuirm bliadhnail, † beirbheis.

Anno domini. Bliadhna an Tighearna.

Annotate, *v a.* Minich; comharaich.

Annotation, *s.* Mineachadh; comharachadh.

Annotator, *s* Mineachair.

Announce, *v.* Innis, gairm; dean follais, glaodh, foillsich, cuir an céil, craobh-sgaoil.

Annoy, *v.* Cuir dragh, cuir mio-thlachd, buair, docharaich, cuir moille, cuir campar, faranaich, gonaich.

Annoyance, *s.* Dragh, mio-thlachd, buaireadh; gonadh, moille, campar, faran.

Annoyer, *s.* Buaireadair; gonadair.

Annual, *a.* Bhliadhnail, uair sa bhliadhna.

Annually, *adv.* Bbliadhna gu bliadhna, bliadhnail, gach bliadhna.

Annuitant, *s.* Neach aig am bheil na h-uibhir sa bhliadhna.

Annuity, *s.* Na h-urrad 's a bhliadhna; bliadhnachas.

Annul, *v.* Dubh a mach, cuir air cùl, thoir air ais, neodhean.

Annular, *a.* Fàinneil; cuairteach, cruinn, cearclach.

Annulet, *s.* Fàinneag

Annullible, *a.* So-dhubh-amach.

Annumerate, *v.* Cuir ri, ath-chuir, meudaich, iol-aireamh

Annumeration, *s.* Iol-aireamh, meudachadh.

Annunciate, *v* Innis, foillsich, dean aithnichte, thoir sgeul, thoir nuaidheachd.

Annunciation day, *s.* La féill Mhuir.

Anodyne, *a.* Lasachail, athaiseil, furtachail.

Anoint, *v* Ung; coisrig, smiùr; sliob.

Anointed, *a* Ungta, coisrigte; sliobta; smiùirte.

Anointer, *s* Ungair, ungadair; smiùradair

Anomalous, *a.* Mi-riaghailteach.

Anomaly, *s.* Mi-riaghailt.

Anomy, *s.* Lagh-bhriseadh.

Anon, *adv.* An tràs is a ris, an dràsd 's a rithist; air uairibh, na uairean; gu grad, gu brath, an gradaig.

Anonymous, *a.* Neo-ainmeach, neo-ainmichte

Another, *a* Eile; aon eile, aon a thuilleadh, fear eile One after another, *fear an deigh chéile;* they killed one another, *mharbh iad a chéile*, they like one another well, *as ro thoigh leo chéile;* one with another, *a réir chéile*, another way, *rod eile.*

Ansated, *a.* Cluasach.

Answer, *v* Freagair, thoir freagairt, thoir freagradh, toilich. Answer for, *bi freagarach*, *rach an urras.*

Answer, *s.* Freagradh, freagairt; (*to a letter*), fios-freagairt.

Answerable, *a.* Freagarach; ionann; co'ionann

Answerableness, *s* Freagarachd.

Answerably, *adv.* Gu freagarach.

Answerer, *s* Freagarair, fear-freagairt.

Ant, *s* Seangan; sneaghan.

Antagonist, *s.* Eas-caraid, nàmhaid; fear conspoid; comh-strithear; co-sheise.

Antaloic, *a* Lasachail, a choisgeas pian.

Ante, *adv.* Roi', roimh, ro.

Anteact, *s.* Roi' ghniomh.

Ante-ambulation, *s.* Roi' imeachd, tus-imeachd.

Antecede, *v* Rach air thoiseach, rach roimh.

Antecedence, *s.* Teachd air thoiseach, tùs-imeachd.

Antecedent, *a.* Roimh, an toiseach.

Antecedently, *adv.* Roimh-laimh.

Antechamber, *s* Seomar aghaidh, seomar taobh, foisheomar.

Antecursor, *s* Gille ruithe, roimh-theachdair

Antedate, *v.* Sgriobh la do 'n mhios tuille is tràthail; roimh-bhlais.

Antediluvian, *a.* Roimh 'n tuil, roimh 'n dìle, roimhthuilteach, priomh-aimsireach

Antediluvian, *s.* Roimh-thuilteach.

Antelope, *s.* Seors gabhair le adharc chrom

Antemeridian, *s* Roimh mheadhon-làtha.

Antemundane, *a.* Roi' thoiseach an t-saoghail

Antepast, *s.* Roimh-ghabhail, roi' bhlas, roi' eolas

Antepenult, *s* An sioladh mu dheireadh ach a dhà

Anterior, *a.* Roimh, roimh laimh.

Anthelmintic, *a.* Durag-mharbhach

Anthem, *s* Laoidh; naomh-òran; oran neamhuidh.

Anthill, *s* Tom sheangan.

Anthology, *s* Comh-chruinneach do phlùran, comh chruinneach rann; rann leabhran.

Anthony's fire, *s.* Tinneas an righ; teine dé

Anthypnotick, *a* Brosgaltach.

Anti. An aghaidh. Is focal Greugach e so, nach faicear ach co' cheangailte ri focal eile.

ANTIACID, *a* Geur-chosgach, garg-chosgach.

ANTIC, *s.* Neonachas, cleas, cluich; baoth-chleasaiche; lùth-chleasaiche.

ANTIC, *a.* Neonach, cleasach; baoth, iongantach, tuaisteach

ANTICHAMBER, *s.* Foir-sheomar, seomar-aghaidh, mach-sheomar

ANTICHRIST, *s.* Anacriosd

ANTICHRISTIAN, *a* Ana-criosdach; ana-criosduigh; mi-chreideach.

ANTICHRISTIANITY, *s.* Ana-criosduidheachd.

ANTICHRONISM, *s* Cron-seanachais.

ANTICIPATE, *v.* Roimh-bhlais; roi' mheal; gabh roimh laimh; glac.

ANTICIPATION, *s* Roimh-bhlas; roimh bhlasdachd; roi' mhealtuinn, gabhail roimh laimh; roimh-bharail

ANTICONVULSIVE, *a.* Math an aghaidh an tuiteamais

ANTICOURTIER, *s.* Fear an aghaidh na cùirt; ana-chuirtear

ANTIDOTAL, *a.* Urchosgach.

ANTIDOTE, *s* Ur-chosg, cosg-leigheas; leigheas an aghaidh nimhe

ANTIFEBRILE, *a.* Fiabhras-chosgach.

ANTIMONARCHICAL, *a* Neo-aon-fhlaitheach, neo-aon-fhlaitheachdail

ANTIMONARCHICALNESS, *s.* Neo-aon-fhlaitheachd

ANTIMONY, *s.* Seorsa méine, sonruichte airson leigheas

ANTINEPHRITIC, *n* Airn-sgrudach.

ANTINOMY, *s.* Atharrachadh eadar da lagh.

ANTIPARALYTIC, *a.* Crith-chosg, math airson a pharailis.

ANTIPATHETICAL, *a* Fuathar, gràineil, mi-thlachdmhor.

ANTIPATHY, *s* Fuath, gràin, mio-thlachd.

ANTIPESTILENTIAL, *a* Cas-chosgach, plaigh-chosgach.

ANTIPHRASIS, *s* Car-fhocal, car-bhriathar

ANTIPHRASTIC, *a.* Car-fhoclach, car-bhriathrach

ANTIPODAL, *a.* Cas-bhonnach, cos-bhonnach

ANTIPODES, *s.* Cas-bhonnaich, cos-bhonnaich.

ANTIPOPE, *s* Pàp air eigin.

ANTIQUARIAN, *s.* Arsaidhear, arsair, arsfhear.

ANTIQUARY, *s.* Arsaidhear; arsair, arsfhear.

ANTIQUITY, *s* Arsaidheachd, arsachd, arsaireachd; seann-dachd; aimsir chéin

ANTIQUATE, *v* Arsaidh, arsaich.

ANTISPASMODIC, *a.* Iodh-chosgach

ANTITHESIS, *s.* Trasd-bhriathar, trasd-chainnte, crosg-chainnt, trasdachd

ANTITYPE, *s* Samhladh

ANTITYPICAL, *a.* Samhlachail

ANTLER, *s.* Cabar feidh; uileannach, meur crochd feidh

† ANTRE, *s* Uamh, garaidh, slochd, brocluinn.

ANVIL, *s.* Innean.

ANXIETY, *s* Ro-chùram, cur, curadh, iomaguin, iomluasg, dearmail, triobloid, buaireadh; smuairean

ANXIOUS, *a.* Cùramach, iomaguineach, iom-luasgach, dear-malach, trioblòideach, buaireasach, mi-fhoisneach Anxious about, *cùramach mu* (no), *mu thimchioll*, do not be anxious, *na bithibh cùramach, na biodh curam oirbh.*

ANY, *a* Aon, air bith, sam bi, gach Any more, *tuille, tuilleadh*, any one of you, *aon agaibh, aon air bith agaibh*, without any danger, *gun chunnart air bi, gun chunnart sam bi* Is any body there? *bheil gin an sin?* Is any one of them alive? *bheil neach beò dhiu?* Any further, *n' is mò, tuille*, any longer, *ni 's fhaide, ni 's mò*, any more, *tuille*, any where out of the way, *an aite sam bi as an rathad*, at any time, *uair sam bi, uair eigin.*

AORIST, *a.* Neo-shònraichte, neo-shuidhichte.

AORTA, *s* Cuisle-chinn; chuisle mhòr

APACE, *adv.* Gu h-ealamh, gu grad, gu cabhagach, gu diair, gu brais, gu teann.

APART, *adv.* Gu taobh, a leth-taobh, air leth; gu h-uaig-neach, o chàch.

APARTMENT, *s* Seomar, aite-comhnuidh, carann do thigh-còmhnuidh

APATHY, *s.* Cian-mhothuchaidh, neo-mhothachadh.

APE, *s.* Apa, apag; fear fanoid; magair

APE, *v* Mag, fanaid; thoir dheth.

APEAK, *a.* Biorach, binneanach, spiriceach.

APERIENT, *a.* Fuasglach, fosglach, tuasglach, sgùrach.

† APERT, *a.* Fosgailte; fuasgailte.

APERTION, *s* Fosgladh, bearn, sgoltadh, bealach, cab

APERTNESS, *s.* Fosglachd, fosgailteachd

APERTURE, *s.* Fosgladh, toll, sgoltadh, bearn

APEX, *s* Binnean, bàrr; fior-bharr ni sam bi

APHELION, *s.* An t-aite do chuairt réil, anns am faide e o 'n ghrian; grian choimadh.

APHONY, *s.* Bailbhe.

APHORISM, *s* Rùn suidhichte, ràite, àithne, riaghailt choit-chionn sean-fhocal

APIARY, *s.* Sgeap sheillein, tigh-sheillein, beach-lann.

APIECE, *adv.* Am fear, gach fear, gach h-aon, gach neach; am beothach. A penny a piece, *sgilinn am fear*

APISH, *a.* Fochaideach, magail; ciatach, gaoithe, faoin; gòrach; mireagach, mear

APISHLY, *adv.* Gu fochaideach, gu magail, gu gaoithe, gu faoin, gu gòrach.

APISHNESS, *s.* Fochaideachd, magaileachd; baoth-chleas-aidheachd, faoineachd

A PIT PAT, *adv* A plosgartaich.

APLUSTRE, *s* (L) Bratach luing, long-shuaicheantas

APOCALYPSE, *s.* Foillseachadh, taisbeanadh, taisbean, tais-bein

APOCALYPTICAL, *a.* Foillseachail, taisbeanach

APOCRYPHA, *s* A mheud sin do 'n phiobull is nach eil cinntealas co sgriobh e.

APOCRYPHAL, *a.* Teagmhach; neo-chinnteach.

APOCRYPHALNESS, *s* Teagmhachd; neo-chinntealas.

APOGEE, *s* An t-ionad sin ann cuairt réil, anns am faide e o na ghrian

APOLOGETICAL, *a.* Leithsgeulach.

APOLOGIZE, *v.* Gabh leithsgeul

APOLOGIZE, *s.* Ur-sgeul, faoin-sgeul; modh-sgeul, (no) sgeul a theagasgas modhannan.

APOLOGY, *s* Leithsgeul; tagradh, dion.

APOPHTHEGM, *s* Rogh-radh, gnath-fhocal

APOPLECTIC, *a* Spad-thinn; buailteach do spad-thinneas.

APOPLEXY, *s* Spad-thinneas; balbh-thinneas

APORRHŒA, *s.* Sioladh, sumgadh

APOSTACY, *s* Dealachadh o chreideamh; tuisleachadh; naomh-threigsinn, naomh-thuisleachadh; aith-chreideamh.

APOSTATE, *s* Naomh-thuisleachair; naomh-threigeach

APOSTATIC, *a* Naomh-threigeach; aith-chreidmheach.

APOSTATIZE, *v.* Tuislich, tréig creideamh.

APOSTEMATE, *v.* Iongaraich.

APOSTEMATATION, *s.* Iongarachadh.

APOSTEME, APOSTUME, *s.* Iongarachadh.

APOSTLE, *s.* Abstol

APOSTLESHIP, *s* Abstolachd.

Apostolical, *a.* Abstolach.

Apostrophe, *s.* Gearra-chomhar, no comhar gu bheil litir no litrichean air am fagail mach a focal; mar *roi'* airson *roimh*, *co'* airson *comh*.

Apothecary, *s.* Olladh, leigh, lusragan, fear reicidh leigh-easan.

Apotheosis, *s.* Dia-dheanamh.

Apotome, *s.* Corlach.

Apozem, *s* Suth, sùgh; sugh-bhigh.

Appal, *v.* Cuir eagal, cuir oillt, cuir geilt.

† **Appalment**, *s* Eagal, sgàth, oillt, geilt, fiamh.

Appanage, *s* Talamh tainisteireachd, fearann tainistridh.

Apparatus, *s.* Uigheam, acfuinn, acfhuinn; airneis, cungaidh, treallaidh; gairreas

Apparel, *s.* Aodach, eideadh, eididh, uidheam, uigheam; earradh

Apparel, *v.* Aodaich, cudaich, éid; uigheamaich, comhdaich; breaghaich, sgiamhaich, earr.

Apparent, *s* Soilleir, dearbhta, dearbhte, cinnteach, cosmhal, coslach, follaiseach, comharaichte, sònruichte

Apparently, *adv.* A reir coslais

Apparition, *s.* Tannasg, taibhse, fuath, fuathas; sealladh; ailinse; bòchdan; bodach; sìthich.

Apparitor, *s.* Maor eaglais, beideal, beadal

† **Appay**, *v.* Toilich.

† **Appeach**, *v.* Cronaich, achmhasanaich, thoir achmhasan, dìt, thoir binn.

Appeachment, *s.* Cronachadh, cuis-dhitidh, achmhasan; diteadh, binn.

Appeal, *v* Leig gu ràithe, tog cùis; thoir fianuiseach, tarruing fianuis.

Appeal, *s.* Cuis-thogail; leigeil gu ràithe.

Appealant, *s* Cùis-thogair; neach e leigeas gu ràithe.

Appear, *v. n.* Thig san t-sealladh, bi san t-sealladh; thig lathair; bi soilleir; leig a làthair; plaoisg. It appears to me, *is i mo bharailse.*

Appearance, *s* Teachd a lathair; coslas, cugas; neul; teachd am follais, foillseachadh, sealladh; taibhse. He has the appearance of death, *tha neul an aoig air.*

Appeasable, *a* So-chiùineachaidh; so-chiùineachail; ciùineachail; furas chiùineachadh.

Appease, *v a.* Ciùinich, traoigh, tragh, réitich; dean sìth.

Appeaser, *s.* Ciùineachair; traghadair, réiteachair.

Appellation, *s.* Ainm; tiotal.

Appellative, *a.* Gairmeach; ainmeachail; tiotalach.

Append, *v.* Croch ri, cuir ri.

Appendage, *s.* Buntuinneas; crochadas; fath-rud.

Appendix, *s.* Leasachadh, fath-sgriobhadh.

Appertain, *v* Buin do ni no neach.

Appertenance, *s.* Buntuinneas.

Appetence, *s.* Miann, deothas, ocras, acras, ciocras, fonn; sannt; miann-feòlmhor.

Appetibility, *s* Miann-mhoireachd; deothasachd.

Appetible, *a.* Miannmhor, deothasach.

Appetite, *s* Ocras, acras, *stamac*, deothas, ciocras, miann, càs; sannt. I have no appetite for food, *cha n'eil sannt bidh orm.*

Appetition, *s.* Miann, deothas, sannt.

Appetitive, *a.* Miannach, deothasach, sanntach, lonach, ocrach, acrach.

Applaud, *v.* Mol, ard-mhol, bos-mhol, bas-mhol; bos-ghair, bos-ghaird.

Applauder, *s.* Moladair, bos-mholadair

Applause, *s.* Moladh, ard-mholadh, cliù, alladh, meas; luadh ainm; bos-ghair; bos-ghairdeachas; luadh-ghair, caithreim. Vain applause, *faoin-chliù*

Apple, *s* Ubhall, abhall Apples, *ubhlan;* a crab-apple, *ubhall fiadhain*, the apple of the eye, *ubhall na sùl*, an apple-woman, *cailleach ùbhlan*

Appliance, *s* Co'chur.

Applicable, *a* So-shamhlachaidh; a luidheas air neach. This name is applicable to you, *luidhidh an t-ainm so ortsa.*

Application, *s.* Co'chur, comh-chur; samhlachadh, dichioll, aire, dian-smuaineachadh.

Applicative, *a.* Dichiollach, aireachail.

Apply, *v* Co'chuir, cuir ri; cuir ris; dean feum; feuch ri, bi dìchiollach Apply your mind, *leig d'inntinn*, (agree), *luidh* This applies well to you, *is math luidheas so ruit* (*no*) *ort ;* (as a petitioner,) *sir, iarr.*

Appoint, *v* Sonraich, sunraich, runaich, ainmich; orduich, socraich, suidhich, deasaich, dean suas

Appointed, *part.* Sonraichte, sunraichte, runaichte, ainmichte, orduighte, socraichte, suidhichte, deasaichte; taghta; aontaichte. An appointed day, *là suidhichte.*

Appointment, *s.* Sonrachadh, sunrachadh; rùnachadh; ainmeachadh, ordughadh; socrachadh, suidheachadh; deasachadh; taghadh; aontachadh; bann; cordadh; ordugh; decrèut; airneis; duais. By appointment, *a réir cordaidh, a réir orduigh.*

Apportion, *v a* Roinn, riaraich, pairtich. Apportioned, *roinnte, riaraichte, pàirtichte*

Apportionment, *s.* Roinn, roinneadh, riarachadh, pairteachadh.

Appose, *v.* Ceasnuich, ceasnaich, rannsuich.

Apposite, *a.* Ceart, deas; freagarrach, iomchuidh.

Appositely, *adv.* Gu ceart, gu deas, gu freagarrach, gu h-iomchuidh.

Appositeness, *s.* Ceartas, deise; freagarrachd, iomchuidheachd.

Apposition, *s.* Dluth-chur, cur taobh ri taobh.

Appraise, *v.* Meas, cuir luach (no) prìs air ni.

Appraiser, *s* Measair, measadair, luachadair; fear meas. Appraisers, *measadairean.*

Appraisement, *s.* Measadaireachd, measadh.

Appreciate, *v.* Meas, prìsich; cuir luach, gradhaich.

Appreciation, *s.* Meas, prìs, luach; measadaireachd.

Apprehend, *v. a.* Glac, cuir lamh air, sàr, tog; tuig, bi fo eagal; cuir amharus.

Apprehender, *s* Glacadair, beachdadair; smuainteachair

Apprehensible, *a.* So-ghlacadh, so-thuigsinn

Apprehension, *s.* Tuigse; barail; mothachadh, amharus, eagal; glac.

Apprehensive, *a.* Tuigseach, eagalach, mothachail, amharusach, fu eagal.

Apprehensiveness, *s.* Tuigseachd, eagalachd, mothachaileachd, amharusachd

Apprentice, *s.* Foghlumach, foghluinn.

Apprenticeship, *s.* Ùine foghluim.

Apprize, *v.* Thoir fios, thoir sanas, dean aithnichte, dean follaiseach, thoir rabhadh, innis, cuir an céill.

Approach, *v n* Dluthaich am fagus, thig am fagus; teann

Approach, *s.* Dluthachadh am fagus, teachd, slighe; (*of a foe*), ionnsuidh.

Approachable, *a.* So-ruigheachd.

Approachless, *a.* Do-ruigheachd, do theachd am fagus.

Approachment, *s.* Dlùthachadh am fagus, teachd, tighinn.

Approbation, s. Taitneachd; tlachd ciat; gean maith; cead; moladh; dearbhadh.
Appropinquate, v. Dluthaich, theirig am fogus, thig am faisge, (no) am fagus.
Appropriable, a. A dh' fhaodas neach a ghabhail mar a chuid féin.
Appropriate, v. Gabh; cuir air leth; cuir ris; gabh mar do chuid féin, gabh h-ugad féin.
Approvable, a. Taitneach; cliùiteach, airidh air cliù.
Approval, s. Gean maith; taitneadh, deagh thoit.
Approve, v. Tagh, gabh tlachd; dearbh; mol.
Approved, a. Dearbht; dearbhta molta; deuchainnichte. Thoroughly approved, *làn dearbhte.*
Approvement, s. Dearbhadh; moladh.
Approver, s. Dearbhadair; moladair.
Approximate, a. Fogas, dlù; dlùth, am fochair.
Approximate, v. Druid am fagus, dlùthaich am fagus.
Approximation, s. Dlùthachadh.
Appulse, s. Bualadh.
Appurtenance, s. Buntuinneas.
Apricot, s. Seorsa meas.
April, s. Aibreann, Abraon, Diblinn; mios meadhon an earraich; an ceathramh mios do'n bhliadhna.
Apron, s. Apran, aparan; broineag, bronnag; dion bhréid.
Aproned, a. Apranaichte.
Apron-man, s. Fear-oibre, fear ceairde.
Apt, a. Deas, ealamh, ullamh; tapaidh; grad, brisg, deonach, freagarrach; buailteach, iomchuidh.
Apt, v. Dean iomchuidh, dean freagarrach.
Aptate, v. a. Dean iomchuidh, dean freagarrach.
Aptitude, s. Iomchuidheachd, freagarrachd; aomadh, ullamhachd.
Aptly, adv. Gu h-iomchuidh, gu freagarrach, gu lathailteach.
Aptness, s. Iomchuidheachd, freagarrachd; aomadh; ullamhachd, miann.
Aqua fortis, s. Uisge teinntidh, uisge baothal.
Aquatic, a. Uisgeach, uisgearradh; fas san uisge, uisgidh.
Aqua vitæ, s. Branndi; uisge beatha.
Aqueduct, s. Piob uisge, pioban uisge; feadan uisge; sput; srùlag.
Aqueous, a. Uisgidh; uisgeil.
Aqueousness, s. Uisgidheachd; uisgealachd.
Aquiline, a. Crom, crom-shronach.
Arabian, a. Arabach.
Arabic, s. Cainnt nan Arabach.
Arable, a. So-threabhadh; treabhaidh. Arable ground, *talamh treabhaidh.*
Arack, Arrack, s. Seorsa dibhe laidir a bheirear as na h-Innseachan shios.
Aration, s. Ar, treabhadh, treabhachas.
Araneous, a. Mar eididh an damhan alluidh, faoin.
Arbalist, s. Crois-bhogha.
Arbiter, s. Raithe; breitheamh.
Arbitrable, a. An-toileil; an-smachdail, ceann-laidir; so-bhreith.
Arbitrament, s. Toil; àilghios, breith.
Arbitrarily, adv. Gu h-antoileil; gu h-an-smachdail, gu h-àilghiosach.
Arbitrary, a. An-toileil, an-smachdail, ailghiosach; ceannlaidir, aintighearnail.
Arbitrate, v. Thoir breith; bi mar ràithe.
Arbitration, s. Ràithe; sonrachadh; suidheachadh.

Arbitrator, s. Breitheamh.
Arboreous, a. Craobhach, coillteach.
Arboret, s. Craobhag.
Arborist, s. Craobhadair; maor coille.
Arbour, s. Sgàilean, sgàile-bhothan; suidheagan fo dhubhradh craoibh.
Arbuscle, s. Ras-chrann.
Arbute, s. Lus-shùgh làir.
Arc, s. Bogha; pàirt do chearcall.
Arcanum, s. Diomhaireachd, run-dhiomhair, diùbhras.
Arch, s. Bogha, pairt do chearcall, bogha drochait, druimbhogha; ceannard.
Arch, v. a. Boghaich; lùb.
Arch, a. Priomh; ard; pratach; mear, sunntach, beothail; eolach, cuilbheartach, ceabhachdach; carach, sligheach.
Archæology, s. Seann-sgeulachd.
Archaism, s. Sean-fhocal; dubh-fhocal.
Archangel, s. Priomh-aingeal; ardaingeal; lubh.
Archangelic, a. Priomh-aingleach, ard-aingleach; a bhuineas do ard-aingeal.
Archbishop, s. Priomh easbuig, ard easbuig.
Archbishopric, s. Priomh-easbuigeachd, priomh-easbachd; ard-easbuigeachd, priomh-easbachd.
Archchanter, s. Ard-chantair.
Archdeacon, s. Ard-fhrithealaiche, ard-fhrithealachair, fear ionad ard-easpuig.
Archdeaconry, s. Ard-fhrithealachadh, ard-fhrithealachd.
Archdruid, s. Coi-bhi, coibhi Druidh.
Archduke, s. Priomh-dhiùc, ard-dhiùc, prionnsa rioghail; ard-fhlath.
Archdutchess, s. Priomh-bhan-diùc, ard bhan-diùc; tiotal nighnne, no peathar ard-dhiùc.
Arched, part. Boghaichte.
Archer, s. Fear bogha, boghadair. Archers, *fir bhogha.*
Archery, s. Boghadaireachd.
Arches-court, s. Cùirt ard-easbuig.
Archetypal, a. Priomh-choslach, priomh-shamhlachail.
Archetype, s. Priomh-choslas, priomh-shamhladh; ceadthus, dealbh.
Architect, s. Priomh-chlachair; ard-chlachair.
Architecture, s. Priomh-chlachaireachd, ard-chlachaireachd.
Archives, s. Eachdruidh, eachdraidh; leabhar-lann.
Archness, s. Cuilbheartachd; seoltachd; pratachd; géiread.
Archprelate, s. Ard-easbuig.
Arctation, s. Cumhangachadh; priosantachd.
Arctic, a. Tuathach, tuath; mu thuath, gu tuath.
Arcuate, a. Boghaichte; lubte, crom.
Arcuation, s. Boghachadh; lubadh, cromadh.
Arcubalister, s. Crois-bhoghair.
Ardency, s. Teas, déine, teas-ghradh, dian-ghradh.
Ardent, a. Dian, dianasach, teas-ghradhach; càirdeil; garg. Ardently, *gu dian, gu dianasach, gu teas-ghradhach, gu garg.*
Ardour, s. Teas; teas-ghradh; durachd; déine; gradh, miann; misneach.
Arduous, a. Ard; duilich, doilich, deacair, cruaidh; neo-fhuras, neo-fhurasda.
Arduousness, s. Duilichead; duilicheadas; deacaireachd; cruadhas; neo-fhurasachd.
Are, v. Tha, ta; bheil. They are, *tha iad;* are they? *bheil iad?* how are you? *cia mar tha thu?*
Area, s. Ionad fosgailte; cùirt; clobhsa, ùrlar, rum.

Arefaction, *s.* Tiormachadh.
Arefy, *v.* Tiormaich.
Arena, *s.* Gaineamh, gaineach.
Arenaceous, *a.* Gaineamhach.
Arenulous, *a.* Gaineamhach.
Argent, *a.* Airgiodach; geal, air dath airgid.
Argil, *s.* Creadh, creuch; poit-chriadh.
Argue, *v. a.* Arguin; co'reusonaich, co'riasonaich; connsaich, troid, deasboirich; dearbh; aom; geurain
Arguer, *s.* Arguiniche; reusonaiche; deasboiriche; connspoidiche.
Argument, *s.* Argumaid, reuson, reusonachd; connsach, deasboireachd; connspuid; brigh-cainnt, brigh-sgriobhaidh.
Argumental, *a.* Arguineach, reusonach, deasboireach, connspoideach.
Argumentation, *s.* Arguineachd, reusonachd, riasonachd, deaspoireachd.
Argute, *a.* Geur; beulaiseach; binn.
Arianism, *s.* Teagasg Ariuis, neach a chum mach nach bu cho'ionann Criosd ri Dia, ach gum b' e am bith cruthaichte a b' airde.
Arid, *a.* Tioram, tioramaichte; cruaidh, cruaidh-thioram; treabhte, greadte.
Aridity, *s.* Tiormachd; tiormalachd, greadadh.
Aries, *s.* An reithe, aon do chomharan a Ghrian-chrios.
Arietate, *v.* Put (no) purr mar ni reithe.
Arietation, *s.* Putadh, purradh; bualadh, slachduinn.
Arietta, *s.* Luinneag.
Aright, *adv.* Ceart; gu ceart; gun chron, gun lochd, gun mhearachd.
Ariolation, *s.* Faisneachd, faidheadaireachd.
Arise, *v* Eirich, éirich; éirich suas, dìrich
Arisen, *part.* Air éiridh.
Arista, *s.* Calg, colg.
Aristocracy, *s.* Iar-fhlaitheachd, ear-fhlaitheachd; flaitheachd.
Aristocrat, *s.* Iar-fhlaithiche.
Aristocratic, **Aristocratical**, *a.* Ear-fhlaitheach.
Arithmancy, *s.* Fiosachd le cunntas.
Arithmetic, *s.* Cunntas, àireamhachd.
Arithmetical, *a.* Aireamhachail; uimhreachail, nuimhreachail.
Arithmetician, *s.* Cunntair, àireamhair, uimhreachan, fear-àireamh.
Ark, *s.* Airc, ciste; long; airc Noe; airc nan Iudhach.
Arm, *s.* (*Of the body*), gairdean; (*of the sea*), sàilean, sàil-linn, loch-sàile, frithe; caolas; (*a bough*), meur, meang-lan, bogha; *figuratively*, treòir, cumhachd, neart, treine. Arm's length, *fad gairdein*; having long arms, *gairdeanach*, *fad-lamhach*, an armful, *ultach*: an armpit, *lag na h-achlais*, take up in thine arms, *tog ann ad aslaich*
Arm, *v.* (*Take arms for war*), tog airm, éirich; tog armachd, (*put on arms*), armaich, rach fo armachd, arm, éid le h-airm.
Armada, *s* Cabhlach cogaidh, feachd mara, feachd fairge.
Armament, *s.* Feachd; *mar is tric*, cabhlach (no) feachd mara.
Armature, *s.* Armachd, airm.
Armed, *a.* Armaichte.
Armed chair, *s.* Cathair da laimh.
Armental, *a.* Greigheach; crodhach; buidhneach; bannalach.
Armhole, *s.* Lag na h-achlais, achlais, asgail, asguil
Armiger, *s.* Armair, gille airm.

Armigerous, *a.* Armach.
Armillary, *a.* Fàinneach.
Arminianism, *s.* Teagasg Arminiuis, neach a chum mach gu bheil saor-thoil agus saorsadh choitchionn ann.
Armipotence, *s.* Tréine airm, cumhachd, buadhalachd
Armipotent, *a.* Treun, cumhachdach, buadhach, fearail.
Armisonant, *a.* Fuaimneach, gliongach
Armistice, *s.* Eineach, fosadh o chomhrag car ùine, fosadh comhraig
Armlet, *s.* Gairdean beag; eididh gairdein, armachd gairdein
Armorial, *a.* Suaicheantach.
Armour, *s.* Armachd, airm; buille airme.
Armourer, *s.* Armadair, gobhainn arm, arm-cheard, fear dheanamh airm.
Armoury, *s* Tigh-arm; arm-lann.
Armour-bearer, *s.* Gille-airm, fear iomchair arm.
Armpit, *s.* Lag na h-achlais, achlais, asguil, asgail.
Arms, *s.* Airm, buill airm; cath; cogadh, suaicheantas. Deeds of arms, *feart*, *gaisge*, call to arms, *gairm chum cath* (*no*) *chum cogaidh*; they are up in arms, *tha iad air éiridh*, fire-arms, *airm-theine*; by force of arms, *le h-eigin*, *a dh'aindeoin*
Army, *s.* Feachd; armailt; sluagh. Armies, *feachdan*, *armailtean.*
Aromatic, *a.* Boltrach, deagh-bholtrach, deagh-aileach, cubhraidh, spiosrach
Aromatics, *s* Boltrachais, spiosraidh.
Aromatize, *v.* Boltraich, spiosraich, cubhraich; milsich. Aromatized, *boltraichte*, *spiosraichte*, *cubhraichte.*
Arose, *pret.* of arise. Dh'éirich; dhìrich.
Around, *adv.* and *prep.* Mu 'n cuairt, timchioll, air gach lamh, air gach taobh, mu thimchioll
Arouse, *v.* Dùisg, mosgail; brosnuich; beothaich.
Arow, *adv.* Ann an sread, ann an sreath; gu dìreach, gu comhad (comh-fhad)
Aroynt, *adv* Bi falbh, bi triall, tog ort, trus ort, imich, gabh romhad, gabh do rathad.
Arquebuse, *s* Gunn caol, gunn glaic.
Arrack, *s* Scorsa uisge beatha a nithear anns na h-Innseachan shios
Arraign, *v* Dìt, cronaich, casaid, cuir casaid, coirich.
Arraignment, *s.* Dìteadh, cronachadh; casaid, coireachadh
Arrange, *v* Cuir an ordugh, cuir an uidheam, réitich; cuir an lathailt Arranged, *ann ordugh*, *uidheamaichte*, *deas*, *ullamh*, *réitichte.*
Arrangement, *s* Ordugh, uidheam, reiteachadh.
Arrant, *a.* Dona, olc, danardha, dannara; fior; cinnteach. An arrant rogue, *fior-chrochair*, *crochair as an aghaidh*
Arrantly, *adv.* Gu dona, gu h-olc, gu dannara, gu fior, gu cinnteach.
Arras, *s.* Obair ghreanta shnàthaid, obair ghréis.
Array, *s.* Sread, sreath, ordugh; eide, eididh, eudach, culaidh, earradh, uidheam In battle array, *an ordugh catha*, out of array, *troimh-chéile*, *air feadh chéile*
Array, *v a.* Cuir an ordugh, dean réith, éid, earr, eudaich, comhdaich, uidheamaich, sgeadaich, sgiamhaich.
Arrear, *adv* An deigh; air dheireadh, an deigh-laimh, mo dheireadh.
† **Arrearage**, *s* Corlach, iarmad paigh, deir-ainfhiach. Pay an arrearage, *paigh deir-ainfhiach.*
Arrears, *s* Fiachan gun phaigh, iarmad pàigh, iarmad dioladh; deir-ainfhiach.
Arreptitious, *a.* Sguabte air falbh; fuadaichte, air snàgadh steach.

ARREST, *v. a.* Glac, dean greim, cuir an laimh, cuir an sàs; grab, bac, stad; cuir bac, cuir stad, dàilich, cuir dàil.

ARREST, *s.* Glacadh, greim; lamh; bac, bacadh, stad, moil

ARRET, *s.* Decreùt, breith.

ARRIDE, *v.* Fochaid, mag, fanaid, dean fochaid, dean mag, dean sgeig, dean fanaid

ARRIERE, *s.* Deireadh feachd.

ARRIVAL, *s* Teachd, tighinn, ruigsinn, ruigheachd.

ARRIVE, *v.* Ruig, rach gu tìr We arrived on shore, *ràinig sinn tìr.*

ARROGANCE, *s.* Uaille, uallachd, uabhar, ardan, an-danadas, ceannardas, rucais, spairiseachd.

ARROGANT, *a* Uallach, uabharach, ardanach, an-dàn, ceannardach, spairiseach; beadaidh, barpail

ARROGANTLY, *adv* Gu h-uallach, gu h-uabharach, gu h-ardanach, gu h-an-dàna, gu ceannardach, gu spairiseach, gu beadaidh, gu barpail

ARROGATE, *v.* Gabh d'ionnsuidh, agair; iarr còir, togair

ARROSION, *s* Cnamhadh, itheadh, creimeadh.

ARROW, *s.* Saighead, guin

ARROWHEAD, *s* Ceann saighid

ARSE, *s* Tòin Whip his arse, *gréidh a thòin, gabh air a thòin*, hang an arse, *bi mall, bi mairnealach*

ARSENAL, *s.* Arm-lann, tigh arm; tigh tasgaidh, tigh taisg; tigh stòir

ARSENIC, *s* Mèin mharbhtach; airsneag

ART, *s* Ealadhain, ceaird, eolas, cuilbheart, seòl, seòltachd, iùl, fios, sgil; lathailt You have not the art of it, *cha n'eil an seol agad air, cha n'eil an lathailt agad air*, the black art, *an dubh-chleasachd*, a master of arts, *cearraiche*

ART, *v.* Tha; is; bheil Thou art mad, *tha thu air a chuthach*, thou art the man, *is tusa an duine*, art thou there? *bheil thu an sin?*

ARTERIAL, *a* Cuisleachail, cuisleach. Arterial blood, *fuil mhòr-chuisleach.*

ARTERIOTOMY, *s.* Gearradh-chuisle.

ARTERY, *s* Cuisle-mhòr; mòr-chuisleach.

ARTFUL, *a* Seolta, ealanta, cuilbheartach, eolach; teoma, sligheach

ARTFULLY, *adv* Gu seolta, gu h-ealanta; gu cuilbheartach, gu teoma

ARTFULNESS, *s.* Seoltachd, teòmachd, cuilbheartachd, cuilbheart

ARTHRITIC, *a.* Altail; gutach

ARTHRISIS, *s.* Alt-thinneas, alt-ghalar, alt-eucail

ARTICHOKE, *s.* Farusgag

ARTICLE, *s.* Airteagal, ponc, pong, leth-fhocal, reachd, (*head of discourse*), ceann-teagaisg, (*of peace*), cumhnant; teirm, (*of marriage*), bann, ceangal, (*a joint*), alt, tàth Break articles, *bris cumhnant* (*no*) *teirm*

ARTICLE, *v.* Cumhnantaich; ceangail, dean teirmean, coird; reachd-cheangail, banntaich, bann-cheangail. Articled, *ceangailte*

ARTICULAR, *a.* Altail, altach.

ARTICULATE, *a.* Pongail, ramnte; so-thuigsinn, soilleir

ARTICULATE, *v a.* Labhair gu pongail, pong-labhair; reitich, reachd-cheangail, bann-cheangail, dean teirmean, cumhnantaich

ARTICULATELY, *adv.* Gu pongail.

ARTICULATENESS, *s* Pongalachd, pongaileachd

ARTICULATION, *s.* Ceangladh, alt, alt-cheangladh, (*in grammar*), pong-labhairt

ARTIFICE, *s* Cealg, ceilge, cuilbheart, prat; car; seol; innleachd, ealadhain, ceaird Full of artifice, *lan ceilge.*

ARTIFICER, *s.* Cealgair, cuilbheartair; fear ceirde; fear ealadhain, fear oibre.

ARTIFICIAL, *a.* Innleachdach; ceardail; ealadhanta.

ARTIFICIALLY, *adv.* Gu h-innleachdach, gu h-ealanta.

ARTIFICIALNESS, *s.* Ceardaileachd, ceardalachd.

ARTILLERY, *s.* Gunnraidh; gunnachan mòra.

ARTISAN, *s.* Fear ceirde; fear ealadhain

ARTIST, *s* Fear ealadhain; fear teoma, fear sgileil

ARTLESS, *a.* Neo-sheolta, mi-theoma, aineolach, simplidh, gun chealg, gun char

ARTLESSLY, *adv* Gu neo-sheolta, gu mi-theoma, gu h-aineolach, gu simplidh, gu nadurra

ARTLESSNESS, *s* Neo-sheoltachd; mi-theomachd; mi-chealgachd, simplidheachd

ARUNDINEOUS, *a.* Giolcach; gainneach.

AS, *conj.* (*Implying time of action*), nur, nuair, an uair; an am; air do. As I stood at the door, *nur sheasamh mi aig an dorus*, as I was coming down, *air dhomh bhi teurnadh.* As, (*in comparisons, and answering to* so, such, &c.) *mar.* As, (*in one part of a sentence answering to* so *in another,*) *mar, ceart mar, air mheud is.* As you said, so it fell out, *mar a thubhairt thu, thachair e, ceart mar thubhairt thu, thainig e gu crìche.* As that was troublesome, so this was pleasant, *air mheud is gun robh sin draghail, bha so taitneach* As, (*in the latter clause of a sentence answering to* so, *or* as great, much, little, soon, fast,) *agus, as, is, 's.* As soon, and with as little trouble as you can, *cho luath agus le cho bheag di agh's a dh'fhaotas tu*, as fast as I could, *cho luath agus a b'urrainn mi* As, (*redoubled, with an adverb betwixt, and the particles* it is, they be, &c.), *air, as, is, a mheud as, air mheud as* As rich as you are, he would not care a pin for you, *cha tugadh e prìn ort, air bheartaichead 's a bheil thu;* all this is thine, great as it is, *is leatsa so air a mhòid, is leatsa so air a mheud 's a bheil e* As, (*answering to* so, as, *where equality or comparison is intimated,*) *mar, ann, as, agus, cho mhath ri, cho mhath as, cho mhor ri.* They are as fools, *tha iad mar amadain* (*no*) *nan amadain.* By night as well as by day, *an oidhche cho mhath ris an là*, they see by night as well as by day, *is léir leo san oidhche cho mhaith is anns an la* (*no*) *cho mhaith san oidhche as anns an là* I loved you as a brother, *ghradhaich mi thu mar bhrathair.* As, (*signifying* accordingly, proportionably as,) *mar, a réir.* As you deserve, *a réir do thoilltinneis*, as I ought, *mar bu chòir dhomh.* As, (*which thing*) She did as she was desired, *rinn e mar chaidh iarruidh oirre.* As, (*for* if,) *mar is, ma is* As I live, *mar is beo mi*, as you love me, *mar is toigh leat mi, ma 's toigh leat mi.* As for, *a thaobh, air son;* as for you, *air do shonsa dheth*, as being, *mar*, as far as, *fhad 's a, cho fad ri, co fhad ris*, as far as I can see, *fhad 's as leir dhomh;* as far as Breadalbane, *cho fad ri Bràidalbainn* As if, as though, *mar gu b' eadh, mar gu 'm b' ann* As if he were my brother, *mar gu bu mo bhrathair e* As it were, *mar, mar gu 'm b' ann, mar gu m' b' eadh* As long as, *fhad 's a*, as large as, *cho mor ri, co mhor ri*, as many as, *na h-uimhir as, a mheud as* (*no*) *agus, a liuthad agus,* (*no*) *as* As many years as he lived, *a liuthad bliadhna as a bha e beò* As often as, *co minic agus, cho tric agus*, as soon as, *nur, cho luath agus, cho luath 's*, as soon as ever, *ceart cho luath, cho lom luath*, as well as, *cho mhaith ri;* as yet, *fòs, fathast, fhathast, fhastaich*, as lean as a rake, *cho chruaidh ri ràsdal*, as sure as death, *cho chinnte is am bàs, cho fior ris a bhàs*, such as it is, *mar tha e.*

ASAFŒTIDA, *s.* Bith-breunach, breun-bhith.

ASBESTINE, *a* Neo-loisgeach.

ASBESTOS, *s* Seorsa cloich leacanta nach gabh losgadh no milleadh le teine

ASCARIDES, *s* Seorsa duraig.

Ascend, *v.* Dìr, dìrich, éir, éirich; tog ri, rach n' aird, rach suas, theirig suas (no) n' àird.

Ascendancy, *s.* Ceannas, carrachd, drughadh, smachd; lamh an uachdar. He got the ascendancy over him, *fhuair e lamh an uachdar air.*

Ascendant, *s.* Ceannas, barrachd, smachd; lamh an uachdar; airde; a mheud sin do 'n ghrian-chrios 's a bhios an uachdar air uair sam bi.

Ascendant, *a.* Ann uachdar, uachdrach, ard.

Ascendency. Faic Ascendancy.

Ascension, *s.* Eiridh, dol suas, dol 'n airde, dìreadh, eiridheachd; ardachadh.

Ascension-day, *s.* La deas-ghabhail, Féill deich laithean roimh Chaingis, mar chuimhneachan air dol suas Chriosd gu neamh.

Ascent, *s.* Uchdach, uchdan, bruthach, airde.

Ascertain, *v.* Faigh a mach; dean cinnteach, dearbh; faigh fios; foraisich; socraich, tomhais

Ascertainable, *a.* So-dhearbhadh, so-fhaotainn mach.

Ascertained, *a.* Dearbhte; cinnteach; socraichte.

Ascertainer, *s.* Dearbhair, dearbhadair; fear a ni cinnteach, (no) a shocraicheas.

Ascertainment, *s.* Riaghailt, riaghail, tomhas.

Ascetic, *a.* Diadhaidh, crabhach, cruaidh-chrabhach.

Ascetic, *s.* Dithreabhach, di-threamhach, aonaran.

Ascites, *s.* Seorsa meud-bhronn.

Ascititious, *a.* Seasachail.

Ascribable, *a.* A dh' fhaotas chur as leth; so-chur as leth

Ascribe, *v. a.* Cuir as leth, thoir do Ascribe to yourself, *gabh h-ugad fein.*

Ash, *s.* Uinseann. An ash-tree, *craobh uinsinn*, wild ash, *craobh chaoran.*

Ashamed, *a.* Fu' nair, fu amhluadh; nàraichte, nàr. He is ashamed, *tha e 'gabhail nàire*, I am ashamed of you, *tha mi 'gabhail nàire asad.*

Ash-coloured, *a.* Dubh-liath, air dhath an uinseann.

Ashen, *a.* Uinsinn; uinseannach.

Ashes, *s.* Luath, luaithre, duslach, luaithreach

Ashlar, *s.* Clach-shreathal, clach mar a thig i as a ghairbheal.

Ashore, *adv.* Gu tìr, gu traigh; air tìr, air traigh.

Ash-wednesday, *s.* Di ciadain na luaithre.

Ash-weed, *s.* Seorsa luibh, luibh na luaithre.

Ashy, *a.* Luathach, luaithreach; air neul na luaithre; glas, glasdaidh.

Asia, *s.* Aon do chearnan na cruinne.

Aside, *adv.* Gu taobh, a leth-taobh; leis féin; o chàch, fiar.

Asinine, *a.* Asalach.

Ask, *v. a.* Iarr, sir; feòraich, guidh, athchuinge, asluich; farraid, faoinich, faoineachd, fiosraich, thoir cuireadh Ask of him, *feòraich dheth; asking, a sireadh, a feorachadh.* You will get it for the asking, *gheibh thu e chionn iarraidh.*

Askance, *adv.* Gu taobh, a leth-taobh, càm, neo-dhìreach.

Askant, *adv.* Gu taobh, a leth-taobh, air leth-taobh, fiar, cam.

Asker, *s.* Iarradair, guidhear, aslachair, ath-chuingear, ath-chuingiche.

Asker, *s.* Beothach uisge.

Askew, *adv.* Gu taobh, fiar, a leth-taobh

Aslant, *adv.* Claon, fiar, gu taobh.

Asleep, *adv.* Aig fois, an codal, an suain. He is asleep, *tha e na chodal, tha e na shuain;* one of my legs is asleep, *tha 'n codal deilgeachan am chos;* fast asleep, *an turram suaine.*

Aslope, *adv.* Trasd, fiar, leth-fhad, leth-bhruthach.

Asp, *s.* Nathair nimhe.

Asp, Aspen, *a.* Critheann, critheach.

Asparagus, *s.* Creamh-mac-feidh.

Aspect, *s.* Dreach, coslas, eugas, tuar; gné; neul; sealladh, gnuis; amharc, aghaidh, beachd.

Aspectable, *a.* Faicsinneach, leirsinneach, anns t-sealladh

Aspection, *s* Amharc, sealladh, sealtuinn.

Aspen, *s* Critheann, critheach. An aspen-tree, *crann-critheann.*

Aspen, *a.* Critheann, crithcannach.

Asperate, *v. a.* Garbh, garbhaich, dean garbh, dean neo-chòmhnard.

Asperity, *s.* Gairbhe, garbhad; gairgead; sgaiteachd; beumnachd, sglàruinn, sglamhruinn, crosdachd, cainnteachd

Asperous, *a.* Garbh, neo-chomhnard.

Asperse, *v. a.* Maslaich, beum, dean tàir, dean spìd, tarcuisich, càin.

Aspersion, *s.* Spultadh, crathadh; masladh, tàir, spìd, càin, cùl-chàin, tarcuis, tuaileas, beum.

Asphaltic, *a.* Ruadh-chailceach, lachdach, pronnusgach; piceach.

Asphaltos, *s.* Seorsa bith so-lasadh; lachd air uachdar na mara mairbhe far an robh Sodom agus Gomorrah.

Asphaltum, *s.* Pic-chlach.

Asphodel, *s.* Seorsa lili; plannt.

Aspic, *s.* Seorsa nathrach.

Aspirate, *v.* Pong-labhair, labhair gu somolta, (no) gu làidir.

Aspirate, *a.* Somolta.

Aspiration, *s* Mor-dheigh, mor-mhiann, ard-mhiann; geall, cis, plosgartaich; labhairt shomolta, labhairt a mach.

Aspire, *v.* Bi an geall air, dìr ri, ruig air, oidhirpich.

Aspirer, *s* Fear mòr-mhiannach; fear a tha 'n geall air bhith ni 's airde no tha e

Aspiring, *a.* Mor-mhiannach, ard-mhiannach, mòr-aigneach

Asquint, *adv.* Claon; cam, fiar. Looking asquint, *a sealltuinn claon.*

Ass, *s* Asal, asail, *figuratively*, baothair, baoghlan, amadan, amhlair.

Assail, *v.* Thoir ionnsuidh air, éirich air; buail air; leum air; labhair ri.

Assailable, *a.* So-bhualadh.

Assailant, *s.* Buaileadair; gearr-choilear, ionnsuidhear.

Assailer, *s.* Buaileadair; ionnsuidhear

Assassin, *s.* Mortair, murtair, marbhadair, foill-mhortair, duine-oircneach.

Assassinate, *v.* Mort, murt, marbh; mort an uaigneas (no) le foill.

Assassinate, *s* Mortadh, murtadh, marbhadh, foill-mharbhadh, dean foill-fholach, dean plaid-luidhe

Assassination, *s.* Foill-mhortadh, foill-mharbhadh.

Assassinator, *s.* Foill-mhortair, mortair, murtair.

Assation, *s* Ròstadh, ròst; toiteadh.

Assault, *s.* Ionnsuidh; droch oidhirp, oidhirp naimhdeil; ruadhar The first assault, *a cheud ionnsuidh*, go assault (as bitches), *rach air ghasair.*

Assault, *v. a.* Thoir ionnsuidh; thoir oidhirp naimhdeil, thoir ruadhar; leum air, buail air.

Assay, *s.* Feuchainn, deuchainn; deacaireachd, cruaidhchàs, ceasnachadh.

Assay, *v.* Feuch ri, thoir deuchainn, thoir oidhirp, tòisich. He assayed, *dh'fheuch e ri; thug e deuchainn.*

Assayer, *s.* Feuchadair.

Assecution, *s.* Faotainn.

Assemblage, *s.* Cruinneachadh, tional, co' thional; coinnamh; sèanadh, màd; comh-dhail.

Assemble, *v.* Cruinnich, teonail, tionail, comh-theanail.

Assembled, *part.* Cruinnichte, teanailte, tionailte; an ceann chéile.

Assembly, *s.* Cruinneachadh, comh-chruinneachadh, tional, tionaladh, coi' thional, teanal, teanaladh, mòd coinneamhsùgraidh, seanadh; conlan, coisridh gu sugradh; dannsadh, bàl.

Assent, *s.* Aontachadh, cead; cordadh, géilleadh.

Assent, *v.* Aontaich, co' aontaich, géill. He assented, *dh' aontaich e.*

Assentment, *s.* Aontachadh, co' aontachadh.

Assert, *v.* Dearbh; briathar, briathraich, beachd, daingnich; tagair, càir, càirich.

Assertion, *s.* Briathar, focal, dearbhadh, dearbhadh soilleir.

Assertive, *a.* Dearbhach, briathrach, tagràch.

Assertor, *s.* Dearbhair, dearbhadair, briathradair, tagradair.

Assess, *v.* Leig cìs, (no) càin, tog cìs, meas.

Assessment, *s.* Cìs, càin, meas, cìs-leagadh.

Assessor, *s.* Cìs-mhaor, cìs-thogair; cis leigear.

Assets, *s.* A mheud sin do mhaoin urr mharbh is a chuirear air leth chum 'fhiachan a phàigh.

Assever, *v.* Briathraich; mionn, mionnuich.

Asseveration, *s.* Briathar, mionnan follaiseach, mionnadh.

Asshead, *s.* Burraidh, umaidh, baoghlan, baothair amhlair; amadan, gurraiceach, ceothallan.

Assiduity, *s.* Dìchioll, dìchiollachd, dùrachd, buan-dhùrachd.

Assiduous, *a.* Dìchiollach, dùrachdach, buan-dhurachdach, tul-chuiseach, *bisidh.*

Assiduously, *adv.* Gu dichiollach, gu durachdach, gu buan-dhurachdach.

Assign, *v.* Comharaich; ainmich; sonraich; dean thairis do neach eile.

Assignable, *a.* So-dheanamh thairis, so-bhuileachadh; comharachail.

Assignation, *s. m.* Comhdhail, coinneamh. Hold an assignation, *cum coinneamh.*

Assigned, *part.* Builichte, air dheanamh thairis.

Assignee, *s.* Fear a ni gnothuch an riochd neach eile.

Assigner, *s.* Sonrachair, ainmeachair.

Assignment, *s.* Toirt thairis, liobhradh; buileachadh.

Assimilate, *v.* Co' choslaich; coimeasg.

Assimilation, *s.* Co' choslachd; coimeasgadh.

Assist, *v.* Cuidich, coghain, cobhair, cabhair, foir, furtaich; dean coghuadh, dean cobhair, dean foir, dean furtachd. Assist me, *cuidich mi; cuidich leam, foir orm, dean cabhair orm.*

Assistance, *s.* Cabhair, coghnadh, cuideachadh, foir, furtachd.

Assistant, *s.* Fear-coghnaidh; fear cuideachaidh.

Assistant, *s.* Còghnach, co' ghnathach, cuideachail, furtachail.

Assize, *s.* Cuirt cheartais; riaghail thomhas.

Assize, *v.* Sonraich tomhas (no) luach (no) prìs ni.

Assizer, *s.* Tomhas-riaghladair.

Associable, *a.* So-chompanta; so-thàth, so-cheangladh.

Associate, *v. a.* Dlùth-cheangail, tàth; cum conaltradh, dean companas.

Associate, *s.* Companach; comhlann; combach; fearpàirt, pàirtiche, fear comh-roinn, caidreamhach.

Association, *s.* Co' chòrdadh; companachd, companas, compantas, pàirteachas; bann, bannalas, caidreamh.

Assort, *v.* Cuir an ordugh, réitich, dean reidh.

Assortment, *s.* Ordugh, réiteachadh; cungaidh; airneis.

Assuage, *v.* Ciùinich, eutromaich, siochaich, traogh, tràgh, caisg, coisg, lughdaich.

Assuagement, *s.* Ciùineachadh; traoghadh; lughadachadh; cosgadh, socair, fois, sith, siothchainnt.

Assuager, *s.* Ciùnachair, traoghadair, cosgair, cosgadair.

Assuasive, *a.* Ciùineach, traoghach, cosgach.

Assuefaction, *s.* Cleachd, nòs, cleachduinn, àbhaist.

Assuetude, *s.* Cleachd, nos, àbhaist.

Assume, *v.* Gabh, gabh ort, togair; gabh h-ugad fein; tog, glac.

Assumer, *s.* Duine togarach; fear leamh.

Assuming, *a.* Ladarna, dàn, stràiceil; ceannasach, smachdach.

Assumption, *s.* Gabhail, togail, arduchadh. Assumption-day, *là arduchaidh Mhuire.*

Assurance, *s.* Dearbhachd, dearbh-bheachd, làn-dearbhachd; cinntealas, cinnteachd; dànachd, dànadas; beadaidheachd, beag-narachd.

Assure, *v.* Dean cinnteach, thoir dearbh-bheachd.

Assured, *a.* Cinnteach; dearbh-bheachdaichte. I am assured of it, *tha mi cinnteach as.*

Assuredly, *adv.* Gu cinnteach, gun teagamh.

Assuredness, *s.* Cinntealas.

Assurer, *s.* Cinnteadair; dearbh-bheachdair.

Asterisk, *s.* Rionnag; an comhar *.

Asterism, *s.* Co'shoillse, grigleachan, griglean.

Astern, *adv.* Focal maraiche a ciallachadh, *gu deireadh, san deireadh.*

Asthma, *s.* Gainne analach, cuing analach, luas analach; caitheamh, eiteach.

Asthmatic, Asthmatical, *a.* Air a bheil luas-analach; séidrich, dlù-shéidrich; crion-sgamhanach.

Astonish, *v. a.* Cuir ioghnàdh air, cuir breathal air, cuir uamhann air, cuir eagal air. I astonished him, *chuir mi ioghnadh air.*

Astonished, *a.* Fu ioghnadh, fu bhreathal, fu uamhann, fu eagal, fu amhluadh, air làn ciambainn.

Astonishing, *a.* Iongantach, miorbhuileach, eagallach, uamhasach.

Astonishingness, *s.* Iongantachd, miorbhuileachd, uamhasachd.

Astonishment, *s.* Ioghnadh, iongantas, breathal, uamhann, eagal, amhluadh, maoidhm; oillt.

Astound. See Astonish.

Astraddle, *adv.* Gobhlach, cas-gobhlach.

Astral, *a.* Reulach, reultach, rionnagach, reulagach.

Astray, *adv.* Air iomrol, air seachran, am mearachd; bhàrr an rathaid, as an rathad; air eòlas. He went astray, *chaidh e air seachran.*

Astrict, *v.* Teann, teannaich, ceangail.

Astriction, *s.* Teannachadh, ceangladh, teannadh; crupadh.

Astrictive, *a.* Teannachail, ceanglach, crupach.

Astride, *adv.* Cas-gobhlach, gobhlaisdeach.

Astringe, *v.* Crup, trus, ceangail.

Astringent, *a.* Ceangailteach, ceanglach, teannaidh, crupach.

Astrography, *s.* Reul-chunntas, reul-eolas.

Astrolabe, *s.* Slat-réil, inneal chum airde na greine 's nan rionnag a thomhas air muir.

Astrologer, *s.* Speuradair, reuladair, réul-dhruidh.

Astrology, *s* Speuradaireachd, reuladaireachd, reul-dhruidheachd, reul-eolas

Astronomer, *s.* Reuladair.

Astronomical, *a.* Reuladach.

Astronomy, *s.* Reuladaireachd; reul-eolas; eolas mu astar, meud agus siubhal nan reultan

Astro-theology, *s.* Reul-dhiadhaireachd.

Astute, *a.* Eòlach, seòlta, cuilbheartach, sligheach, carach

Asunder, *adv* As a chéile, o chéile; gu sgaoilte.

Asylum, *s.* Dìdean, tearmunn, dion-aite, ionad tearmuinn duis-chùil.

At, *prep.* Aig; air, ann. At home, *aig an tigh*, at sea, *air mhuir*, at school, *san sgoil*, at a distance, *air astar, greis as, greis air falbh*, at church, *san eaglais, aig an t-searmoin*, at the beginning, *an toiseach, an tùs, air thùs*; at the door, *aig an dorus*, at first sight, *air a chéud sealladh*; at one blow, *le aon bhuille*; at my desire, *air m' iarrtas*, at your pleasure, *air d'dùlghios, fo do sgòd*, at a venture, *a thaobh tuairmeis*, at hand, *am fogus, aig laimh*; at all, *idir*, at best, *air a chuid is fhearra*, at least, *air a chuid is lugha*, at most, *air a chuid is mò, air a chuid is fhaide*; at leisure, *socair, air athais*, at your leisure, *air ad athais, air do shocair*; at her leisure, *air a h-athais, air a socair*; at last, *mu dheireadh, mu dheireadh thall*, at that time, *an sin, air an uair, air an am sin*, at present, *air an uair, an tràths, an dràsdaich, an ceart-uair*, at once, *air aon tarruing, mu chomh-luath, dh'aon tarruing*, at the worst, *air a chuid is miosa*

Ataraxy, *s.* Samhchair, siochainnt, ciùineas.

Ate, *pret. of* eat. Dh'ith.

Atheism, *s.* Dia-aicheadh, mi-chreidsinn mu Dhia, ana-creidsinn.

Atheist, *s* Dia-aicheanaich, ana-creidmheach, ana-creideach.

Atheistical, *a* Dia-aicheanach, ana-creideach, mi-naomh.

Atheous, *a.* Mi-naomh.

Athirst, *adv.* Pàiteach, tartmhor, iotmhor, air pathadh. Are you athirst? *bheil thu pàiteach?*

Athletic, *a.* Laidir, calma, carachdach; beothail; fuasgailte

Athwart, *adv.* and *prep.* Crosgach, tarsuing, trasd, cearr, dòcharach; air feadh.

Atilt, *adv.* A leth-taobh, aomte mar shoitheach chum a thaomachadh.

Atlas, *s.* Leabhar cé-dhealbhair; seorsa sioda airson eudach boirionnaich

Atmosphere, *s.* Aile, adhar, athar, an t-àile a tha cuartachadh na cruinne.

Atmospheric, *a.* Aileach, atharach; athar.

Atom, *s* Dadmun, neoni, smùirneag.

Atomical, *a.* Dadmunach

Atomist, *s.* Dadmunaiche, teallsanach a chumas mach gun do rinneadh an saoghal o chruinneachadh dhadmun

Atomy, *s.* Dadmun.

Atone, *v.* Aontaich, còird; thoir diol; seas an riochd neach eile, dean réite.

Atonement, *s.* Dioladh; réite, tabhartas peacaidh.

Atop, *adv.* Air mullach, air bàrr.

Atrabilarious, *a.* Lion-dubhach, dubhach, dubhleannach; dubh-laitheach, dubh-neulach.

Atrabilariousness, *s.* Dubh-lionn, dubh-leann, lionn-dubh, truime-inntinn.

Atramental, *a* Dubh

Atrocious, *a.* Aingidh; fuileach, fuilteach, ain-iochdmhor, garg, an-trom, ciontach, curt.

Atrociousness, *adv.* Gu h-aingidh, gu ro-aingidh, gu fuileach, gu fuilteach, gu h-aniochdmhor, gu h-antrom, gu ciontach, gu ro-chiontach.

Atrociousness, *s* Aingidheachd; an-iochd; fuilteachd, an-iochdmhorachd.

Atrocity, *s.* Aingidheachd; an-iochd, ana-barrachd; fuileachd, buirbe, gairge

Atrophy, *s* Caoile, caitheamh.

Attach, *v.* Glac, dean greim; tàlaidh; dean deighcil, lean, dlùth-lean

Attachment, *s* Deigh, tlachd, gradh; tairisneachd, spéiscalachd, leanmhuinn, 'leanachd, leantuinn; dlùth-leanachd, leanmhuinneachd; dilseachd, glacadh

Attack, *s* Ionnsuidh; bualadh; ruadhar, ruathar, foir-neart, foirreigin, † forlonn.

Attack, *v a* Thoir ionnsuidh, thoir ruadhar, leim air, buail air, cum comh-dhail.

Attacker, *s.* Ionnsuidhear; ruatharaiche, fear fóirneirt, fear foireigin.

Attain, *v* Coisinn, buidhinn, faigh, buannaich; beir, ruig

Attainable, *a.* So-choisneadh, so-fhaotainn; so-ruigsinn.

Attainder, *s.* Diteadh; masladh.

Attainment, *s* Buannachd, coisinn; feart, buaidh, càile; ruigsinn, faotainn.

Attaint, *v.* Dìt, maslaich, easurramaich, truaill.

Attainted, *a.* Ciontach, dìte; maslaichte

Attaint, *s.* Masladh, cionnt, diteadh, truailleadh.

Attainture, *s.* Achmhasan, masladh, toibheum

Attaminate, *v a.* Truaill, mill, salaich.

Attemper, Attemperate, *v a.* Coimeasg; baisd; truaill, deasaich.

Attempt, *s.* Oidhirp, deachainn, feuchainn; ionnsuidh Make an attempt, *thoir oidhirp, thoir deuchainn.*

Attempt, *v.* Thoir oidhirp, dean oidhirp, thoir deuchainn, feuch ri

Attempter, *s* Oidhirpeach, deuchainniche, ionnsuidhear.

Attend, *v.* Feith air, fritheil do, fritheil air; bi furreach, (no) fuireachail fan, fuirich, thoir an aire Attend on him, *feith air*, attend to him, *thoir an aire air, (no) dha, thoir aire dha.*

Attendance, *s* Feitheamh, frithealadh, fritheal, fuireachadh, comhaideachd; coimheadachd, aire, seirbheis.

Attendant, *s.* Fear-fritheil, fear-frithealaidh, seirbhciseach Attendants, *luchd feithealaidh, seirbheisich.*

Attendant, *a* Leanadail, an lorg, maille ri; co-imeachadh

Attent, *a* Aireachail, fuireachail, furachair

Attention, *s* Aire, beachd, aire dhùrachdadh, cùram, faicill, seadh, suim, spéis, urram.

Attentive, *s.* Aireachail; furachair, cùramach, faiceallach, durachdach, aireach; seadhar, seadhail, suimeil Be silent, but attentive, *bi ad thosd, is bi ad chom*

Attentively, *adv* Gu h-aireachail, gu furachair, gu curamach, gu faiceallach, gu durachdach, gu seadhar, gu suimeil

Attentiveness, *s.* Furachras, faiceallachd, suimeileachd

Attenuant, *a.* Tanachadh, tanachail, tana; caol.

Attenuate, *v. a.* Tanaich, caolaich, dean tana; dean caol.

Attenuate, *a.* Tana, caol, tanaichte, caolaichte.

Attenuation, *s.* Tanachadh, caolachadh.

Atter, *s.* Iongar.

Attest, *v.* Thoir fianuis, thoir teisteas; dean teisteas, dean fianuis; tog fianuis, tarruing fianuis; briathraich, gairm air.

Attest, *s.* Fianuis, teisteas, teisteannas.

Attestation, *s.* Fianuis, teisteas, teisteannas; còmhdach.

Attic, *a.* Grinn, dreachmhor; uachdrach.

Attire, *v.* Eid, eudaich, aodaich, earr, comhdaich; clùthaich, sgeudaich; sgiamhaich.

Attire, *s.* Eididh, eudach, aodach, earradh, culaidh; comhdach; sgeudachadh; cuimhne fèigh.

Attitude, *s.* Suidheachadh; seasamh; suidhe; sgiamh.

Attorney, *s.* Fear lagha; sgriobhair, sgriobhadair.

Attorneyship, *s.* Sgriobhaireachd.

Attract, *v.* Tarruing; sreang, meall, buair, tàladh.

Attraction, *s.* Tarruing; dlùth-tharruing, dlùth-thairneadh, cumhachd tarruing, mealltachd.

Attractive, *a.* Tarruingeach, tairneach; tàladhach; buaireach, mealltach, dlù-thairneach.

Attractiveness, *s.* Tarruingeachd, tairneachd; dlùthairneachd.

Attributable, *a.* So-chur as leth.

Attribute, *v.* Cuir air, cuir as leth.

Attribute, *s.* Buaidh; feart; càile; cumhachd; subhailc; clù.

Attrition, *s.* Caitheamh, suathadh, rubadh; doilghios, aithreachas.

Attune, *v.* Gleus, cuir am fonn.

Auburn, *s.* Dubh-dhonn, buidhe ruadh, donn.

Auction, *v. a.* Reic, creic, rop, reic am follais, do 'n neach is airde a thairgeas.

Auction, *s.* Ropainn, creic, reic, reiceireachd.

Auctioneer, *s.* Reiceadair, creiceadair, ropainnear, ropadair.

Aucupation, *s.* Eunadaireachd, sealg.

Audacious, *a.* Dàn, danarra; beag-narach, miobhail, mimhodhail, stràiceil.

Audacity, *s.* Dànadas, danarrachd; beag-narachd, mimhodhaileachd, stràiceileachd.

Audible, *a.* So-chluinntinn, so-chlaistinn, so-chlaistinneach, ard-ghuthach, osgarra, labhradh, soilleir; ard.

Audibleness, *s.* So-chlastinn; osgarrachd.

Audibly, *adv.* Gu labhradh, gu h-osgarra, gu h-ard.

Audience, *s.* Eisdeachd, co'thional; claistinn.

Audition, *s.* Claisneachd, cluinntinn.

Auditor, *s.* Claisniche; fear èisdeachd.

Auditory, *s.* Eisdeachd, coi-thional; luchd èisdeachd, ionad èisdeachd.

Auditory, *a.* Claisneach, claistinneach.

Auditress, *s.* Ban-chlaisniche.

† **Auf**, *s.* Umaidh, baothair, amadan.

Auger, *s.* Toradh; boireal.

Aught, *pro.* Dad, ni, ni sam bi, ni air bi.

Augment, *v.* Cinn, fàs, meudaich, cuir ri.

Augment, *s.* Meudachadh; cinneachdainn, fàs.

Augmentation, *s.* Meudachadh; cinneachdainn; leasachadh.

Augur, *s.* Eun-dhruidh; fàidh, fiosaiche; dreallanaiche, faistinnear.

Augur, *v.* Dean faisneachd; dean fiosachd; innis le comharan.

Augurate, *v.* Dean fàisneachd; dean fiosachd; innis le comharan.

Auguration, *s.* Eun-dhruidheachd; fàisneachd, fiosachd; faidheadaireach.

Augurer, *s.* Eun-dhruidh; fàidh, fiosaiche.

August, *a.* Mor; mòrach; mòralach, mordha; flathail; rioghail; ard-urramach; naomha.

August, *s.* Liùnasd; ceud mios an fhogharaidh.

Augustness, *s.* Mòrachd, mòralachd; flathaileachd; rioghaileachd; osgarrachd.

Auletic, *a.* Piobach.

Aulic, *a.* Cùirteach, rioghail; flathail.

Aunt, *s.* Piuthar athar, piuthair màthar.

Auricle, *s.* Cluas; leabag.

Auricula, *s.* Seorsa plùir.

Auricular, *a.* Cluasach; diùbhrasach; diomhair, cogarach.

Auriferous, *a.* Òrach.

Aurora, *s.* A mhaduinn; an Uair-òir; a bhan-Dia a dh' fhosgladh dorsaibh na madainn, seorsa luibh.

Aurora Borealis, *s.* Na fir-chlis.

Auscultation, *s.* Eisdeachd, claistinn, claisneachd, caisdeachd.

Auspice, *s.* Druidheachd, manadh; drùghadh; dion, faosgnadh, tuar, tarraghail.

Auspicial, *a.* See Auspicious.

Auspicious, *a.* Aghmhor, fortanach, sona, sealbhar, faosgnach.

Auspiciousness, *s.* Aghmhorachd, fortanachd, sonas, sealbharachd, faosgnachd, sealbharachd.

Austere, *a.* Tuaiteal, cruaidh; geur-theann; geur, garg; searbh; guù, gnò, bodachail, smachdail.

Austerely, *adv.* Gu tuaiteal, gu cruaidh; gu geur, gu garg; gu guù; gu bodachail, gu smachdail.

Austereness, *s.* Tuaitealachd, cruadhas; teannas, smachd, ain-iochd, géire, searbhas, seirbhe.

Austerity, *s.* Tuaitealachd, cruadhas; teannas, smachd, geurad, geire, gairge; seirbhe, searbhas.

Austral, *a.* Deas, deiseil, deiseal, a laimh na h-airde deas.

Australize, *v. n.* Imich gu deas, gabh gu deas; deasshiubhail.

Austrine, *a.* Deas, deiseil, deisearach.

Authentic, *a.* Fior, fireannach, ughdaraichte.

Authentical, *a.* Fior, fìreannach; ughdarail.

Authenticity, *s.* Fireannachd; ùghdaralas, ughdaraileachd.

Author, *s.* Ughdar; urradh; urrainn.

Authoritative, *a.* Ughdarrach; smachdail; beachdail; ceannasach.

Authoritatively, *adv.* Gu h-ughdarrach; gu smachdail, gu ceannasach.

Authority, *s.* Ughdarras, cumhachd, riaghladh, smachd; dion, cùl-taice; teisteas; (*leave*), cead, comas. I have authority to do it, *tha cead* (*no*) *comas agam a dheanamh.*

Authorize, *v.* Thoir ughdarras, thoir cumhachd; thoir cead, thoir comas; sonraich, socraich; dearbh; creid; thoir creideas.

Autograph, *s.* Priomh-chlar.

Automatical, *a.* Fein-ghluasach, féin-ghluasadach.

Automaton, *s.* Féin-ghluaisear.

Automatous, *a.* Fein-ghluasadach, fein-ghluasach.

Autopsy, *s.* Dearbhadh-sùl; fradharc sùl.

Autumn, *s.* Foghar: fogharadh.

Autumnal, *a.* Fogharach, fogharall; fogharaidh, foghrachail.

Auxesis, *s.* Meudachadh; leasachadh.

Auxiliar, Auxiliary, *a.* Còghnachail, còghnathach, cuideachail; cuideachaidh.

Auxiliar, Auxiliary, *s.* Fear-còghnaidh, fear-cuideachaidh, cuideachair, coghnadair.

Avail, *v. n.* Buidhin, buannaich, coghain; cuidich; dean tairbhe, dean stà; dean feum. It did not avail me, *cha do reim e feum, stà, (no) tairbhe dhomh.*

Avail, *s.* Buidhin, buannachd, tairbhe, stà, feum, piseach. Without avail, *gun tairbhe, gun sta, gun fheum.*

Available, *a.* Tarbhach, tairbheach, buannachdail, feumail.

Availableness, *s.* Tairbhe, tarbhachd, buannachd.

Availably, *adv.* Gu tarbhach, gu buannachdail, gu feumail; gu buidhneach, gu piseachail.

Avant-guard, *s.* Toiseach réismeid, toiseach feachd.

Avarice, *s.* Sannt, gion, miùthaireachd, spiocaireachd, spiocachd, spiocaichead, leibideachd, dulchann.

Avaricious, *a.* Sanntach, gionach, miùthar, spiocach; leibideach.

Avast, *adv.* (*focal maraiche.*) Cum air do laimh, stad, seas, is leòir e; sguir.

Avaunt, *int.* Bi triall, bi falbh, gabh romhad, thoir an rothad ort; bi trus, cum agad fèin.

Avel, *v.* Spiol air falbh, spion air falbh.

Avenage, *s.* Cìos coirce, càin coirce.

Avenge, *v.* Diol; thoir aichmheil, dean dioghaltas, dean peanas. Avenge us on them, *diol sinn orra.*

Avengeance, *s.* Dioladh, aichmheil, dioghaltas, peanas.

Avenged, *part.* Diolte.

Avengement, *s.* Diol, dioladh, dioghaltas; peanas.

Avenger, *s.* Doladair, dioghaltair; peanasaich; aichmheiliche.

Avenue, *s.* Sràid, rod; sraid agus craobhan air gach taobh dhi, sraid-chumhann; *bothar*, craobh-shlighe.

Aver, *v.* Briathraich, cáir, cáirich, abair.

Average, *s.* Eadar dha anabharr, a réir chéile; cìs ceannaiche.

Averment, *s.* Briathar, focal, mionn, teisteas.

† **Averruncate**, *v.* Spion as an fhreumh, (no) as a bhun.

Aversation, *s.* Fuath; gràin.

Averse, *a.* Fuathmhor, fuathach; neo-shealbhar, neo-fhabhorach, ann aghaidh, neo-thoileach.

Aversely, *adv.* Gu fuathach; gu neo-shealbhar, gu neo-fhabhorach, gu neo-thoileach.

Averseness, *s.* Ain-deoineachd, miothlachd; fuath, gràin.

Aversion, *s.* Fuath, gràin, miothlachd, gamhlas.

Avert, *v. a.* Cum air falbh, cuir gu taobh, tionndadh air falbh; seachain, till, pill.

Aviary, *s.* Eunadan, eun-ionad, eun-lann.

Avidity, *s.* Gion, gionachd, gionaichead; glamhaireachd, deothasachd.

Avise, *s.* Rabhadh, fios; fios air thoirt le litrichean.

† **Avize**, *v.* Thoir rabhadh; comhairlich, smuainich.

Avocate, *v. a.* Gairm air falbh, gairm a leth taobh.

Avocation, *s.* Leth-obair; gniomh, gnothach; gairm air falbh, gairm a leth-taobh.

Avoid, *v.* Seachain, seachuin; tar as; rach as; fàg, cuitich, cuir cùl; cuir a mach, sgeith, tilg; cac; falamhaich, falmhaich.

Avoidable, *a.* So-sheachnadh; so-sheachanta; so-fhàlamhachadh.

Avoidableness, *s.* So-sheachantachd.

Avoidance, *s.* Cur a mach, seachnadh; claise.

Avoided, *part.* Seachainte; cuitichte; falmhaichte.

Avoider, *s.* Seachnair; fear seachnaidh.

Avoidless, *a.* Do-sheachnadh, do-sheachanta; nach gabh seachnadh.

Avolation, *s.* Itealachadh, itealachd; dol as; fuadach; ruith air falbh.

Avouch, *v.* Aidich, thoir teisteas, thoir fianuis, fìreannaich.

† **Avouch**, *s.* Aideachadh, aidmheil, teisteas; fianuis.

Avoucher, *s.* Aidmheileach, aideachair; fianuis.

Avow, *v.* Nochd, aidich, leig ris; foillsich, fìreannaich, mionn, briathraich.

Avowable, *a.* So-nochdadh, so-aideachadh, a dh' fhaotas nochdadh, a dh' fhaotas aideachadh.

Avowal, *s.* Nochdadh, aidhmheil fhollaiseach; aideachadh, foillseachadh.

Avowed, *part.* Nochdta, nochdte; foillsichte; aidmhichte, aidichte.

Avowedly, *adv.* Gu follaiseach; as an aghaidh.

Avower, *s.* Fìreannachair.

† **Avowtry**, *s.* Adhaltras, adhaltranas.

Avulsion, *s.* Spionadh; spioladh, reubadh.

Await, *v.* Feith air; feith ri; fuirich; fritheil air. Punishment awaits him, *tha peanas a feitheamh air.*

Awake, *v.* Dùisg, fairich, mosgail.

Awake, *a.* Am faireach; duisgte. He is awake, *tha e na fhaireach;* she is awake, *tha i na faireach;* they are awake, *tha iad nam faireach;* he is wide awake, *tha e na gheal fhaireach;* she is wide awake, *tha i na geal faireach.*

Award, *v. a.* Thoir, thabhair, builich; sonraich le breith, orduich.

Award, *s.* Breith, dìteadh, binn.

† **Aware**, *v.* Bi faiceallach; thoir aire.

Aware, *a.* Faicilleach, faiceallach, aireachail, aireach; furachair. I came on him when he was not aware, *thainig mi air gun fhios da.*

Away, *adv.* Air falbh; as; gun bhi lathair. Away with him, *air falbh, leis;* away with you, *thoir an rathad ort, bi falbh;* I cannot away with this, *cha n' urrainn mi so fhulachdainn.*

Awe, *s.* Eagal, fiamh, uamhas; mor-mheas, ard-urram.

Awe, *v. a.* Cuir eagal air.

† **Awe-band**, *s.* Urras.

Awful, *a.* Eagallach, uamhasach, fuathasach.

Awfully, *adv.* Gu h-eagallach, gu h-uamhasach.

Awfulness, *s.* Eagallachd, uamhasachd.

Awhile, *adv.* Grathuinn, greis, tachdan, tacain.

Awkward, *a.* Cearbach, neo-chuimir, neo-chruinneil, slaopach, slaodach, luidseach, loigearach, luidireach; neo-theoma, neo-lamhchair; neonach.

Awkwardly, *adv.* Gu cearbach, gu neo-chruinneil, gu slaopach, gu luidseach.

Awkwardness, *s.* Cearbachd; neo-chuimireachd; neo-chruinnealachd, slaopachd, slaodachd, luidseachd; luidireachd, loigearachd.

Awl, *s.* Minidh.

Awless, *a.* Neo-eagalach; neo-urramach; neo-mheasail.

Awn, *s.* Colg (no) calg arbhair.

Awning, *s.* Bàt-phubull, bàt-bhuth.

Awoke, *pret.* of awake. Dhuisg, mhosgail.

Awork, *adv.* Aig obair.

Awry, *adv.* Cam, fiar; gu cam, gu fiar; a leth-taobh; gu neo-dhìreach.

Axe, *s* Tuadh; tàl A Lochaber axe, *pic mheallach.*

Axilla, *s.* Asgail; aslaich.

Axiom, *s.* Dearbh-bhriathar, dearbh-radh, soilleirse.

Axis, *s* Aisiol

Axle, Axletree, *s.* Aisiol; acastair; mul.

Axunge, *s.* Muc-bhlonag.

Ay, *adv.* Seadh, is e.

Aye, *adv.* A ghnàth, do ghnàth; daonann, daonalt, an comhnuidh; am bidheantas; gu brath, gu siorruidh, gu suthain siorruidh, gu bràth siorruidh; gun sgur, gun chàirde; am feasd.

Azure, *a.* Gorm, liath-ghorm, gorm eutrom.

B.

B, An dara litir do 'n Aibideal.

Baa, *v. n* Méilich mar chaor.

Baa, *s* Méilich

Baal, *s.* Beil, Dia nan Druidhean, dia bréige, iodhol.

Babble, *v* Gioraig; dean gobais, dean lonais, dean goileain; dean biolasg.

Babble, *s* Giorag, gobais, lonais, gob, faoin-chomhradh, glag; luath-chainnt, faoin-chainnt, luath-bhileulachd, biolasg.

Babbler, *s* Gobair, glagair; breugair.

Babe, *s* Naoidhean, naoidhe, leanabh, leanabh beag

Babery, *s.* Deideag, ailleagan.

Babish, *a* Leanabaidh, leanabanta, faoin

Baboon, *s.* Apa, apag

Baccated, *a* Cluigeanach, dearcach.

Bacchanalian, *s.* Poitear, misgear; misgear tuaireapach.

Bacchanals, *s.* Poit, meisge.

Bacciferous, *a.* Dearcach, dearcagach.

Bachelor, *s* Gille, sean ghille, fleasgach, fear gun phòsadh, diolaineach. Batchelor's button, *fear suiridh, gioban suiriche*

Bachelorship, *s.* Gilleadas, fleasgachd

Back, *s* Druim, muin; cruit; croit; droman; cùl, cùlthaobh, culaobh; dronnan, dronnag. The back of the head, *cùl a chinn*, behind your back, *air do chùlaobh;* take on your back, *thoir air do dhruim, thoir air do mhuin*, the back-bone, *cnaimh na droma*, the backside, *culaobh, an taobh ar chùil*, (of the body), *tòin*, put back to back, *cuir cul ri cùl.*

Back, *v. a.* Neartaich, cuir suas, cuir le; cuir leis, cum taic, cum taobh; dion, còghain; cuidich; (*back, as horse*), suidh air, marcaich, bris

Back, *adv* Air ais, air chùl, air chulaobh; a ris Come back, *thig air ais, thig air d' ais*

Backbite, *v.* Cain, cùl-chain, cul-chaineadh

Backbiter, *s.* Fear-cùl chàinidh. Backbiters, *luchd cul-chàinidh*

Backbiting, *s* Càineadh, cùl-chàin, sgainneal.

Backdoor, *s* Dorus cùil

Backfriend, *s.* Caraid cùil; namhaid

Backgammon, *s.* Tailcasg, taimhleasg

Backhouse, *s.* Tigh-cùil, tigh-beag.

Backpiece, *s.* Eididh droma; eididh cùil

Backroom, *s* Seomar cùil; seumar cùil.

Backside, *s.* Taobh cùil; taobh ar chùil; clobhsa; cùlthaobh; deireadh; (*of the body*), tòin.

Backslide, *v.* Cùl-sleamhnaich; tuislich.

Backslider, *s* Cul-sleamhnachair, tuisleachair, naomhthreigeach

Backsliding, *s.* Cul-sleamhnachadh, tuisleachadh, naomhthreigsinn.

Backstairs, *s.* Staidhir cùil; staidhrichean cùil.

Backstaff, *s* Slat réil.

Backstays, *s.* Staidhinnean cùil, stàdh.

Backsword, *s.* Claidheamh cùil.

Backward, *adv.* Air ais, an comhar chùil, an comhar a dheiridh.

Backward, *a.* Neo-thoileach; neo-shunndach, mall; diombach; deireanach, mairnealach

Backwardly, *adv.* Gu neo-thoileach, gu mall, gu diombach, gu deireanach, gu h-eithich, gu mairnealach.

Backwardness, *s.* Mi thoile; moille; diombachd; deireanachd, mairnealachd.

Bacon, *s* Muic-fheoil chrochte; muic-fheoil chruaidh shaillte. Save your bacon, *thoir an aire ort fein.*

Bad, *a.* Olc, aingidh, droch bhcartach, dona; droch; coirpte; curt; ciurrail, sgriosail; neo-shlainnteil, tinn. A bad man, *duine aingidh, droch dhuine;* a bad day, *la olc, droch làth.*, bad luck, *droch-fhortan, mi-fhortan, tubaist*

Bade, *pret.* of bid. Dh' iarr. Bade for, *thairg.*

Badge, *s.* Comhar, comharadh, suaicheantas.

Badger, *s* Broc, brochd As shy as a badger, *cho fiat ri broc.*

Badly, *adv.* Gu h-olc, gu h-aingidh, gu dona, gu coirpte; gu ciurrail; gu tinn, gu soithich. Badly off, *gu dona dheth*

Badness, *s.* Olcas, donadas, aingidheachd; coirpteachd.

Baffle, *v.* Fairtlich; meall; thoir an car a; seachuin.

Baffle, *s.* Fairtleachadh; mealladh

Baffler, *s.* Fairtleachair.

Bag, *s* Sac, sachd, poc, pochd, pocan, sacaid, bag, màla, màladh, màileid; baigean; brù; sporan, ugh A rennet bag, *baigean leasaich*, a cloak bag, *mailiosa.*

Bag, *v.* Sacaich, pocaich; lion. Bag or swell out, *bagaich*, bagged up, *sacaichte.*

Bagatelle, *s.* Faoineas, faoin-rud; ni suarrach gun luach

Baggage, *s* Airneis, cungaidh, imrich, bagaisd. A worthless woman, *buobh*

Bagnio, *s.* Tum-aite, tum-ionad; aite nighe; drùs-thigh, fothrag thobair

Bagpipe, *s* Piob-mhàlaidh; piob-mhor. See Piob.

Bagpiper, *s* Piobair. Bagpipers, *piobairean*

Bagpiping, *s.* Piobaireachd.

Bail, *s* Urras, paineachas. Go bail, *rach ann urras.*

Bail, *v.* Gabh air urras; thoir urras, rach an urras.

Bailable, *a* Urrasail; a dh' fhaotar a thoirt a mach air urras

Bailiff, *s.* Maor, maor-righ; gribh, stiùbhard.

Bailiwick, *s.* Baillidheachd; cuibhrionn fearainn; stiùbhardachd.

Bait, *s.* Baghte; (*on a hook*), bìdheag; biorìasg; bìthean, maghar; (*refreshment*), lon, (no) biadh air tùras; (*enticement*), mealladh; soll.

Bait, *v.* Gabh biadh, gabh baghte; cuir biadh (no) bìdheag an dubhan; meall; stuig coin, stuig; thoir ionnsuidh; thoir ruadhar; (*bait with dogs*), ruaig, conartaich.

Baiting-place, *s.* Tigh lionna.

Baize, *s.* Pluc-aodach; clo caiteanach, aodach plucanach, aodach caiteanach.

Bake, *v.* Fuin; deasaich (no) greidh biadh ann an amhuinn; cruadhaich le teas (no) le teine; ròsd.

Bakehouse, *s.* Tigh-fuinidh.

Baken, *part.* Fuinte; cruadhaichte

Baker, *s.* Fuineadair. Bakers, *fuineadairean*.

Balance, *s.* Comh-cothrom; meidh; meidh-chothroim; toimhsean; na th' eadar dha chunntas; (*the scale*), slige.

Balance, *v.* Comh-chothromaich; tomhais le meidh.

Balancer, *s.* Tomhasair, meidheadair.

Balcony, *s.* For-uinneag.

Bald, *s.* Maol; gun fhalt; lom, lomnochd, lomnoch, sgailceach; sgiolta, maol-cheannach; gun fhiù, gun bhrìgh

Balderdash, *s.* Bàilisdearachd; glòirmeas, gleòrmas, earraghloir, faoin chomhradh, goileam; mi-thuigse, spud, spagadaghlog.

Baldly, *adv.* Gu maol; gu lomnochd; gu neo-bhrighmhor.

Baldness, *s.* Maoilead, lomnochdaidh, luimead; sgailc.

Baldric, *s.* Crios, stiom, beilt; cearcal; grian-chrios.

Bale, *s.* Bàthar; trusag; ceanglachan; ni sam bi truste chum iomchar; truaighe, donas, bròn.

Bale, *v. a.* (*focal maraiche*) Taom uisge a bat (no) luingeas.

Bale, *v. a* Trus, trus suas, ceangail suas mar thrusaig

Baleful, *a.* Dona, dòineach; millteach, ciurrail, sgriosail; olc; droch mhuinte, mi-shealbhar; truagh, bronach, dubhach

Balefulness, *s.* Millteachd, donas; sgriosalachd, truaighe, bròn.

Balk, *s.* (*a beam*) Sail; spàr, suithe; (*disappointment*), mealladh dochais, mealladh; (*in agriculture*), balc, bailc, iomaire.

Balk, *v.* Meall, thoir an car a, grab; diùlt; seachain.

Ball, *s.* Ball, nì cruinn air bi; an cruinne cé; peileir; (*a dance*), dannsa, caithris, rant, bàl, bannal dannsaidh. The ball of the eye, *ubhal na sùl*; the ball of the leg, *ubhal na coise;* a musket-ball, *peileir gunna, peileir musga*, a snowball, *caob shneachdaidh, muc shneachdaidh.*

Ballad, *s* Oran faoin, fonn; balanta.

Balladsinger, *s* Fear òrain, oranaiche; balantaiche

Ballast, *s.* Balaiste; na h-urrad luchd is a ni eithear freagarrach gu seòladh

Ballast, *v. a.* Balaistich; gleidh còmhnard mar bhàt, grunnd-luchdaich.

Ballate, *s.* Seorsa dannsaidh.

Balloon, *s.* Bat adhair; àile-eithear, aile-churach; (*in architecture*), peileir mullaich, (*in fire-works*), cracairneòil.

Ballot, *s.* Ball-taghaidh, ball-tagha; ball roghnachaidh; crannchur, taghadh (no) roghnachadh le buill àraidh.

Ballot, *v.* Tagh le buill roghnachaidh, crann-chuir.

Balm, *v. a.* Ung, ic, ìoc; ciùinich, maothaich

Balm, *s.* Ice, ìoc-shlainnt, sugh phlannt cubhraidh.

Balmy, *a.* Ioc-shlainnteach; maoth, sùghar, milis, tlàth; bogar; cùbhraidh.

Balneary, *s.* Failc; ionad failcidh; tum-aite; seomar ionnlaid.

Balsam, *s.* Oladh, oladh ungaidh, uineamaid.

Balsamic, *a.* Iocshlainteach; ungail, bogar, olach.

Baluster, *s.* Stùc; carradh beag, post

Balustrade, *s.* Stùc-shread, sread do phuist.

Bamboozle, *v. a.* (*a cant word.*) Meall; thoir an car a.

Ban, *s.* Bann; gairm, glaodh; mallachd; mallachadh, bac, bacadh

Ban, *v.* Mallaich, malluich; molluich

Band, *s.* Bann, ceangal, bann bhragaid; truis bhragad, coilear; bannal; dròbh, lòd, bròd; cuideachd, stiom; crios

Band, *v a.* Bann, ceangail.

Bandage, *s.* Ceangal, stiom; cuaran.

Bandbox, *s.* Bogsa paipeir; cisteag.

Bandit, *s.* Fogaraiche.

Banditti, *s pl* Creachadairean, luchd-spùinnidh, robairean.

Banditto, *s.* Creachadair, spùinneadair; robair.

Bandog, *s.* Mastuidh; cù mòr.

Bandoleer, *s* Adhrac bheag fhùdair.

Bandrol, *s.* Sròl, bratach.

Bandy, *s.* Caman; maide cam; cromag.

Bandy, *v. a.* Tilg null is a nall, tilg h-uige is uaithe

Bandyleg, *s.* Cam-chos, crom-chos

Bandylegged, *a* Cam-chosach, crotach.

Bane, *s.* Puinsion; nìmhe; sgrios; donas, dochann.

Baneful, *a* Puinsionta, nìmhe; sgriosail, millteach; nimheil; dochannach.

Banefulness, *s* Puinsion, puinsiontachd; millteachd; sgriosalachd, dochannachd

Banewort, *s* Lus na h-oidhche; an deagha.

Bang, *v* Bual, straoidhil, slachduinn, splad.

Bang, *s* Buille; straoidhle; steur, gleog

† **Bangle**, *v. a.* Caith chuid is a chuid.

Banish, *v a.* Fogair, fuadaich, cuir air falbh; cuir as an rioghachd; cuir as an duthaich, cuir air fògradh

Banishment, *s* Fogradh, fuadachadh, fògairt.

Bank, *s* Bruach aibhne; uchdan beag; banc; oitir, beinc; ionad a ghleidh airgid A bank of oars, *alach raimh*

Banker, *s* Bancair, fear gleidhidh ionmhais (no) airgid

Bankrupt, *a.* Briste, ain-fhiach.

Bankrupt, *s.* Fear briste, fear nach diol ain'-fhiach.

Bankrupt, *v.* Bris.

Bankruptcy, *s.* Briseadh

Banner, *s.* Bratach, suaicheantas, meirghe.

Bannian, *s.* Culaidh maidne, trusgan maidne, gùn oidhche

Bannock, *s.* Bonnach; breacag, aran. A bannock of oatmeal, *bonnach coirce.*

Banquet, *s.* Cuirm; cuilm, fèist; bancait; fleadh, fleagh, feisd, ròic.

Banqueter, *s* Fèistear, poitear.

Banqueting, *s.* Feisteireachd, poitearachd, cuirm

Bansticle, *s* Biorag lodain

Banter, *v.* Fochaid, fanaid, mag; dean fochaid, dean fanaid.

Banter, *s* Fochaid, fochaid; mag, sgeig.

Banterer, *s.* Fochaidiche, magair, sgeigear.

Bantling, *s.* Leanabh, naoidhean, pàisde; maothran, niochran.

Baptism, *s* Baisteadh.

Baptismal, *a.* Baisteach, baistidh. A baptismal font, *a mar baistidh.*

Baptist, *s.* Baistichte; ana-baistiche.

Baptistry, *s* Ionad baistidh, tobar baistidh.

Baptize, *v.* Baist. Baptized, *baiste*, he was baptized, *bhaisteadh e.*

Bar, *v.* Crann; glais, dùin; bac; gabh roimh; cum, cum air ais

Bar, *s* Bacadh; crann, glas; (*where causes are pleaded*), crannag.

Barb, *s.* Calg, colg, gath saighde, guin saighde; corran, rinn, roinn, ribheag, riobhag

Barb, *v. a* Bioraich; riobhagaich, ribheagaich.

Barbacan, *s.* Daighneach, toll gunna.

Barbarian, *s* Allmharaiche, fiadh-dhuine, duine borb.

Barbarian, *a* Allmharach, fiadhaich; borb, neo-fhiosrach; aineolach.

Barbarism, *s* Fiadh-radh, fiadh-bhriathar; borb-radh, borb-bhriathar; brùidealachd

Barbarity, *s.* Ain-iochd, mi-chneastachd, buirbe, gairge.

Barbarous, *a* Fiadhaich, borb, borbarra, mi-chneasta, garg; an-iochdmhor.

Barbarously, *adv.* Gu h-ain-eolach; gu borb, gu fiadhaich; gu borbarra, gu mi-chneasta, gu garg.

Barbed, *p a* Armaichte; colgaichte, riobhagaichte, ribheagaichte, gathaichte

Barber, *s.* Bearradair; barbair

Barberry, *s.* Barbrag A barberry bush, *preas nan gearr dhearc*, *preas deilgneach*

Bard, *s.* Bard, filidh, fear dàn, aoisdàn.

Bare, *a.* Lom, lomnochd; rùisgte, simplidh, bochd, uireasbhuidheach, uireasbhach; gann ;(*lean*), truagh, cruaidh; (*only*), amhàin.

Bare, *v a.* Lom, rùisg

Bare, *pret.* of bear Rug, bheir.

Barebone, *s* and *a.* Sgroingean, sgruit, ràsdal; bochd, caol, tana

Barefaced, *a.* Beag-narach, miobhail, mi-mhodhail; dàn; peasanach

Barefacedly, *adv* Gu beagnarach, gu mio-bhail, gu mimhodhail, gu dan

Barefacedness, *s* Beagnarachd; miobhaileachd, mimhodhaileachd, peasanachd

Barefoot, *a.* Caslom, coslom, casruisgte, cosruisgte; gun bhrog gun osan

Bareheaded, *a* Ceann lom, gun bhoineid; gun churachd

Barely, *adv* Gu lom, gu lomnochd, gu rùisgte, gu gann. He can barely live, *is gann is urradh dha tighinn beo*

Bareness, *s* Lomnochdaidh, truaighe, luime, uireasbhuidheachd, uireasbhachd, bochduinn.

Bargain, *s.* Cordadh, co-chordadh; co' cheangal, cùmhnant, malairt, bargan, ceannach; luach peighinn.

Bargain, *v.* Coird, co-choird; cumhnantaich; malairtich; barganaiche

Bargainer, *s* Cumhnantaich, ceannaich, malairtiche, barganaiche.

Barge, *s* Bàt aigheir, bàt fada, bat deich-ràmhach Bargeman, *fear-bàta*

Bark, *s.* (*of a tree*) Cairt; rùsg, sgrath; rùsg craoibh; (*a boat*), barc, bàt, curach, eithear; (*of a dog*), tathun.

Bark, *v.* Tathun, dèan tathun; comhartaich.

Barker, *s* Cairtear, fear a bheir cairt bhàrr chraobhan

Barking, *s.* Tathunaich.

Barley, *s.* Eòrna.

Barley-brake, *s.* Seorsa cluiche.

Barleycorn, *s* Grain eorna, grainnean eorna, eitean eorna, an treas cuid dh' oirleach.

Barm, *s.* Beirm, deasguinn, deasgainn.

Barmy, *a* Beirmeach, deasguinneach.

Barn, *s.* Sabhal, sobhal; sgiobal; tigh tasgaidh. Barns, *saibhlean.*

Barnacle, *s.* Seorsa eòin cosmhal ri geadh; seorsa faòich; inneal each-leigh chum each a ghlacadh air a shròin.

Barometer, *s.* Aile-mheidh, athar-mheidh.

Barometrical, *a.* Àile-mheidheach.

Baron, *s.* Baran, ridir, righidir.

Baronage, *s.* Baranachd, ridireachd.

Baroness, *s.* Ban-bharan; ban-righidir.

Baronet, *s.* Tighearn; ridir; ridir-beo-shlainnte.

Barony, *s.* Baranachd.

Baroscope, *s.* Aile-mheidh.

Barouche, *s.* Seorsa carbaid; carbad fosgailte

Barracan, *s.* Seorsa camlait.

Barracks, *s* Ceithreannan shaighdearan.

Barrator, *s.* Siostair; tagluinniche; fear connspuide; fear aimhreite.

Barrel, *s.* Bairill; soitheach fiodha, feadan gunna.

Barrel-bellied, *a.* Bronnach, bagach, baganta.

Barren, *a.* Seasg, aimrid, neo-thorrach; gun sliochd; gainmheach, gainmhidh; fàs; gann; tiorram gun bhrigh, trùagh.

Barrenness, *s.* Seasgachd; seisge, aimrideachd; neo-thorrachas, neo-thorraichead; caoile; tainead, gainne, bochduinn

Barricade, *s.* Daingneach; bac; balladh bacaidh, babhunn.

Barricade, *v. a* Dùin; druid; crann; sparr, daingnich; daighnich.

Barricado, *s.* Daingneach, daighneach.

Barricado, *v* Daingnich, daighnich; druid suas, duin.

Barrier, *s* Daingneach, balladh bacaidh; crioch, bachann, babhunn, crioch; gàrradh criche.

Barrister, *s.* Fear lagha, fear tagraidh, tagarair.

Barrow, *s* Barradh; barradh laimhe, cuidhle-barradh.

Barrow, *s.* Muc, uircean, bainbh.

Barter, *v* Mùth, malairtich, thoir am malairt, iomlaid, suaip.

Barter, *s.* Mùthadh, mùghadh, malairt, malairteachd; iomlaid, ceannachadh, ceannuigheachd

Barter, *s.* Malairtiche; iomlaidiche, ceannuiche.

Base, *s.* Steidh, steigh, bun, bunait, iochdar.

Base, *a* Suarrach, miùthar; truaillidh, diblidh, bochd; diolain; neo-fhiachail, tàireil; nàr, sloighteil, (*in sounds*), borbhanach.

Base, *v.* Truaillich, mill.

Baseborn, *a.* Bochd, diblidh, iosal, diolain.

Basely, *adv.* Gu suarrach, gu miùthar; gu truaillidh, gu diblidh; gu bochd, gu neo-fhiachail, gu tàireil, gu sloightell.

Baseness, *s.* Suarrachd, suarraichead, suarrachas, miùtharachd; truaillidheachd; diblidheachd, bochduinn; tàirealachd; sloightearachd; neo-fhiachalachd; (*of sound*), borbhanachd.

Bashaw, *s.* Fo-uachdaran; fear ardanach stràiceil.

Bashful, *a.* Nàrach, adhach, mallta; modhail, beusach, beusmhor; saidèalta; leth-cheannach.

Bashfully, *adv.* Gu nàrach, gu h-adhach, gu mallta, gu beusach, gu beusmhor; gu saidealta.

Bashfulness, *s.* Nàrachd, nàire, adhachd, malltachd, modhaileachd, beusmhorachd; saidealtachd.

Basilik, *s.* Talla; cùirt; eaglais rìomhach.

Basilicon, *s.* Sabh leigheis, sabh tairnidh, acfhuinn leigheis.

Basilisc, *s.* Righ-nathair; nathair nimhe.

Basin, *s.* Soitheach uisge, *beasan*, soitheach ionnlaid, aghann, mias; achdair-pholl, lochan beag.

Basis, *s.* Steidh, steigh, bun, bunait, cloch-bhun, cloch-bunaidh; iochdar.

Bask, *v.* Grianraich; dean bolg ri grein

Basket, *s.* Croidhle, croidhleag, cliabh, bascaid, basgait, sgùilean, ceis, caiteag. Nothing can fall from an empty basket, *cha tuit caoireag a cliabh falamh.*

Basket-hilt, *s.* Dorn-chur.

Basket-maker, *s.* Cliabhair, cliabhadair; croidhlear.

Bass, *s.* Brat; glun-bhrat, cos-bhrat

Bass, *a.* (*In music.*) Faic Base.

Bassock, *s.* Glun-bhrat.

Bassoon, *s.* Torm-fheadan, borbh-fheadan.

Bass-viol, *s.* Torm-fhidheall; beus.

Bastard, *s.* Leanabh diolain, urr dhiolain, drùth-leanabh

Bastard, *a.* Diolain; neo-laghail; truaillidh; fallsa

Bastarded, *a.* Diolainichte.

Bastardize, *v* Dialainich, diolanaich.

Bastardly, *adv.* Gu truaillidh, gu neo laghail, gu fallsa

Bastardy, *s.* Diolanas; neo-laghaileachd; truailleachd; truaillidheachd

Bastinade, *v.* Buail, buail le bat, straoighil; singil, gabh air, slachduinn; fuaigh, fuaidhil.

Bastinade, *s.* Bualadh, straoighleadh, singleadh, slachduinn; fuadhladh, fuaidheal.

Bat, *s* Bat; guidseal, caman; (*in zoology*), ialtag, ialtag anmoch; dioltag.

Batch, *s* Fuineadh, greadh; dorlach air a dheasachadh (no) air fhuineadh.

Bate, *v.* Lughdaich; lughadaich; math; sgath; thoir air falbh; dean plocaireachd

Bate, *s* (*for* debate.) Connsuchadh, connspoid.

† **Batement**, *s.* Lughdachadh.

Bath, *s.* Tum-aite, tum-ionad, aite-ionnlaid, aite nigh bat, failc; soitheach ionnlaid, soitheach tumaidh

Bathe, *v. a.* Nigh; tum, ionnlaid, taislich.

Bathed, *part.* Nighte, tumta, tumte, ionnlaidte, taislichte

Bating, *prep.* Saor o; ach

Batlet, *s.* Slachdan.

Batoon, *s* Bat, slachdan, caman.

Battalia, *s.* Ordugh catha, ordugh blàir, sread cogaidh.

Battalion, *s.* Cuideachd, buidheann; aireamh shaighdearan eadar cuig agus a h-ochd-ceud; earann feachd.

Batten, *v.* Reamhraich; mathaich; biath.

Batter, *s.* Buail, slachdainn; tilg sios, leig sios

Batter, *s.* Soghainn; seorsa druidhleagain air a dheanamh le min mhin, uisge, is uibhean airson charaiceagan

Battering-ram, *s.* Reithe cogaidh; reithe slachdaidh, reithe slachdainn, slachdran.

Battery, *s.* Slachdainn, slachdarsaich; uchd-dhaingneach, (*in law*), ionnsuidh, bualadh.

Battle, *s.* Cath, blàr, conas, comhrag; tuasaid, caonnag, baiteal, feachd, earann feachd The front of battle, *tùs catha, tùs blàir;* the midst of battle, *builsgean còmhraig;* a hard battle, *cruaidh-chath;* draw up in battle order, *cuir an ordugh blàir;* a pitched battle, *blàr*, a battle-field, *blàr cath.*

Battle-array, *s.* Ordugh catha, ordugh blair.

Battle-axe, *s.* Tuagh catha.

Battledoor, *s* Straoidhleagan

Battlement, *s* Farra-bhalladh; barr-bhalladh, uchd-bhalladh, leth-bhalladh.

Baubee, *s.* Bonnsè, bonnsia.

Bavaroy, *s* Seorsa clòc

Bavin, *s.* Bioran, maide; bruthan connaidh, cualag chonnaidh.

Bawble, *s.* Faoin-rud, faoineachd, deideag.

Bawd, *s.* Siùrsach, striopach

Bawdily, *adv* Gu draosdach, gu drabasta; gu siùrsachail

Bawdiness, *s* Draosd, draosdachd, draosdaireachd, drabastachd, mi-gheamnuidheachd

Bawdy, *a* Draosdach, drabasta, salach

Bawdy-house, *s* Tigh-siùrsaich; drùs-lann.

Bawl, *v.* Eigh, glaodh; sgreach, sian.

Bawsin, *s* (*In zoology*), broc

Bay, *a.* Buidhe, buidhe ruadh, donn

Bay, *s.* Camus, geoth, geòdh, loch; sailean, sailinn, bàgh, (*a tree*), laibhreal.

Bay, *s.* Càs, cuglıann; iomcheist, teinne.

Bay, *v* Tathun, tathunaich.

Bayard, *s.* Each donn, each buidhe-dhonn

Bay-tree, *s* Craobh laibhreil, craobh laibhreis.

Bay-window, *s* Uinneag bogha.

Bayonet, *s.* Gunna-bhiodag.

Bdellium, *s* Bith cubhraidh.

Be, *v.* Bi Shall be, *bithidh;* you are too young to be there, *tha thu tuille is òg gu bhi an sin*, let him be, *leig leis, leig chead da*, to be out, *a bhith a mach; a bhith am mearrachd*, be without it, *bi as a dhìth*, so be it, *mar sin bithcadh e.*

Beach, *s* Traigh, cladach, tìr

Beached, *a.* Air tìr, air tràigh, air cladach, air a chladach

Beacon, *s.* Cusbair amhairc, tigh soluis; leus; leus mara

Bead, *s.* Paidirean, citean paidirein, paidir A bead-roll, *sreang phaidirean.*

Beadle, *s.* Beadal; maor eaglais, cleireach eaglais, fear cluig.

Beagle, *s* Tollair, tobhlair, cuilean lorgaidh

Beak, *s.* Gob, beic, ruthadh, rughadh.

Beaker, *s.* Copan gobach; meadar.

Beal, *s.* Neasgaid, guirean, iongarachadh.

Beal, *v.* Iongaraich.

Beam, *s.* Sail; meidh, tomhas, cabar, adharc feidh, (*of light*), gath soluis, baoisg, dearsadh; (*a weaver's beam*), gairmean, garmain

Beaming, *a.* Baoisgeach, baoisgeil, dearrsach, gairmeanach, dealrach.

Beaming, *s* Baoisgeadh, dearrsadh, dealradh.

Beamy, *a.* Dearrsach, dealrach, binneach, adhairceach; cabrach, craunach.

Bean, *s.* Pànair, pònair.

Bear, *s* Math-ghamhuinn; magh-ghamhuinn, mangan A constellation called the lesser Bear, *drag-bhod.*

Bear, *v a.* and *n.* Giulain, iomchair, prop, cum suas, cum taic ri, fuilig, fiuling; (*as a woman*), beir, gin, (*as the earth*), thoir uaith; (*win*), coisinn, buidhinn. Bear with me, *giulain leam, fuiling leam*

Beard, *v.* Beir air feusag neach; aghaidhich; riobhagaich

Beard, *s.* Feasag, feusag, feosag; colg, roinn, (*of a hook*) riobhag, ribheag

Bearded, *a.* Feusagach, feosagach; molach ròmach; colgach, calgach; biorach, riobhagach, ribheagach; riobhagaichte.

Beardless, *a.* Lom; gun fheusag; òg

Bearer, *s* Fear iomchair, fear giùlain, fear cumail suas; craobh thorrach.

Bearherd, *s.* Buachaill mhagh-ghamhuinn

Bear-fly, *s* Seòrsa cuileig

Bearing, *s* (*Conduct*), giùlan, iomchar, dol mach, caithbeatha; (*of a child*), beirsinn; (*of a ship*), gabhail

Beast, *s* Beathach, beothach, béisd, béist; biast; ainmhidh, brùit, brùid; *an cumantas*, beothach ceithir chosach sam bi, air am bheil olainn no fionnadh Beasts, *beothaichean*, *ainmhidean*, *béistean*, *brùidean;* thou dirty beast! *a bheothaich mhosaich!* a wild beast, *fiadh-bheist*, a great beast, *uamh-bheist*

Beastliness, *s.* Beothachaileachd, béisdealachd, béistealachd, brùideileachd, neo-ghloine, sailche.

Beastly, *a* Beothachail, béisteil, brùiteil, neo-ghlan, salach, draosda, drabasta

Beat, *v. a.* Buail; gabh air, straodhil, gréidh, lundrainn, slachd, slachdainn, (*overcome*), fairtlich, buadhaich, (*bruise*), pronn; (*beat out of countenance*), cuir gu nàir, cuir nàir air, nàraich; (*beat in upon, as rain*), sil, snith; (*beat with the fist*), dorn, dornaich; (*beat to powder*), minphronn; (*beat to the ground*), smàil gu talamh.

Beat, *s.* Buille.

Beaten, *part.* Buailte, greidhte, slachdainnte. He is beaten, *tha e buailte, tha e air a bhualadh*, (no) *air a ghréidh*, a beaten path, *frith-ròd, aisridh, aisridh chos, rod deanta*

Beater, *s.* Bualadair, buailtear.

Beatific, *a* Adhmhor, beannuichte, sona.

Beatification, *s* Beannuchadh.

Beatify, *v* Beannaich, beannuich, dean sona; dean aoibhinn.

Beating, *s* Bualadh, straoidhleadh, gréidh, slachduinn. The beating of a sore, *guin*, a quick palpitation, *plosgartaich*, *frith-bhualadh cuisle.*

Beatitude, *s.* Sonas, admhorachd, ard-shonas, beannuchadh.

Beau, *s.* Spailpear, fear spairiseach, leannan, suiriche.

Beauish, *a* Spailpeach, spairiseach, sgòdail, leòmach, ciatach, riomhach

Beauteous, *a.* Bòidheach, laghach, lurach, maiseach, deadhmhaiseach; aluinn, sgiamhach, grinn, dreachmhor, eireachdail.

Beauteously, *a.* Gu boidheach, gu maiseach, gu deaghmhaiseach, gu h-aluinn, gu sgiamhach, gu dreachmhor, gu h-eireachdail

Beautiful, *a.* Boidheach, laghach, maiseach, deaghmhaiseach, sgiamhach, dreachmhor, aluinn, eireachdail, ciatach, grinn.

Beautifully, *adv.* Gu boidheach, gu laghach, gu maiseach, gu deagh-mhaiseach, gu sgiamhach, gu dreachmhor, gu hàluinn, gu h-eireachdail, gu ciatach, gu grinn

Beautifulness, *s.* Boidheachas, boidhche, maiseachd, maise, deaghmhaise, dreachmhorachd, eireachdas, àluinneachd, grinnead.

Beautify, *v. a* Sgiamhaich, dean boidheach, dean dreachmhor, dean àluinn, (no) grinn, cuir dreach air, cuir eireachdas air, dean grinn.

Beauty, *s.* Boidhichead, maise, eireachdas, dreach, sgiamh; oigh eireachdail, rimhinn.

Beauty-spot, *s* Spot maise, ball-seirc

Beaver, *s.* Dobhran; dobhar-chu; biast dubh; madadh donn; beathadach, seorsa aid; leabag clogaide.

Becafico, *s.* Seorsa eòin.

Becalm, *v.* Ciùinich, siothchaich, slochaich, féithich.

Became, *pret.* Dh'fhas, chinn.

Because, *conj.* A chionn, a bhrìgh, do bhrigh, bhrìgh, air a shon so, fa chùis

Bechance, *v. n.* Tachair, thig gu crìche, tuit, éirich.

Beck, Beckon, *v. n.* Sméid, caog. Beckon him, *sméid air.*

Beck, Beckon, *s* Smeide, caogadh, caog.

Becloud, *v. a.* 'Dorchaich, doilleirich, duibhrich.

Become, *v.* Fas, cinn, bi iomchuidh, bi freagarrach; thig do He will become rich, *fàsaidh e beartach*, it well becomes you, *is math thig e dhuit*, what became of him? *ciod a thainig air?*

Becoming, *a.* Eireachdail, cubhaidh, ciatach, taitneach, tlachdmhor; beusach; fas, cinntinn Well-becoming, *deagh-mhaiseach.*

Becomingly, *adv.* Gu h-eireachdail, gu taitneach, gu tlachdmhor.

Bed, *s.* Leabaidh, leabadh; uiridh, uirigh; airteal; fardoch, aros, pòsadh, clais uisge, amar uisge, claise aibhne; geadag. Go to bed, *rach a luidh, thoir do leabadh ort*, put to bed, *cuir luidh*, a chaff-bed, *leabadh mhuill*, a feather-bed, *leabadh chlòimh*, a straw bed, *leabadh thogalach*, she is brought to bed, *tha i na luidh siùbhladh.*

Bed, *v a.* Cuir luidh; cuir chodal; luidh le; cuir, planndaich, suidhich.

Bedabble, *v.* Spult, fliuch, ludair, ludairt.

Bedaggle, *v a.* Salaich, clabar. Bedaggled, *salaichte.*

Bedaub, *v a* Sliob, eabair; beubanaich.

Bedchamber, *s.* Seomar leapach.

Bedclothes, *s* Plaideachan; eudach leapach.

Bedding, *s.* Leabadh, leabaidh; airneas leapach.

Bedeck, *v. a.* Sgiamhaich, sgeaduich; òr; breaghaich, uidheamaich, uigheamaich, deasaich; éid, maisich; snàs, dearrsaich.

Bedehouse, *s.* Tigh-eiridinn, tigh-bhochd.

Bedew, *v.* Driuchd, taislich, tlà-thaislich, fliuch.

Bedfellow, *s.* Coimh-leabaich.

† **Bedight**, *v.* Sgiamhaich, uigheamaich, uidheamaich. See **Bedeck**.

Bedim, *v.* Dall; dorchaich; doilleirich

† **Bedizen**, *v* Sgiamhaich, éid, uigheamaich

Bedlam, *s* (*for* Bethlehem.) Tigh-cuthaich.

Bedlamite, *s* Urr chuthaich, urr air chuthach.

Bed-post, *s* Post leapach, stump leapach

Bed-presser, *s.* Lunndair, leisgean, droll.

Bedraggle, *v* Salaich.

Bedrench, *v. a.* Fliuch, tum, tom, lobanaich.

Bedrenching, *s.* Fliuchadh, tumadh, tomadh, lobanaich.

Bedrid, *a.* San leabaidh. She is bedrid, *tha i na leabaidh.*

Bedrop, *v.* Sil, fliuch; spot, breacaich

Bedstead, *s.* Leabaidh; stoc-leapach.

Bedtime, *s.* Trà leapach, am codail, tràth dol a luidh.

Bedung, *v.* Innearich; math, mathaich, leasaich

Bedward, *adv.* Dh'ionnsuidh (no) thun na leapach.

Bedwarf, *v.* Cutaich, gearr

Bee, *s.* Seillean, beach. A swarm of bees, *sgaoth sheillean.*

Beech, *s.* Faibhile, crann faibhile, craobh fhaibhile.

Beef, *s.* Mart-fheoil; feoil dàimh, feòil tairbh; damh, mart, mart-geamhruidh; sgabag.

Bee-hive, *s.* Sgeap, sgeap-sheillean. Bee-hives, *sgeap-aichean.*

Been, *part.* Air bhith, iar bhith. I have been often there, *bha mi gu minic an sin.*

Beer, *s* Beòir, leann, liunn, lionn, leann caol. Fresh beer, *leann ùrr;* strong beer, *leann laidir;* sour beer, *leann goirt.*

Beet, *s.* Bitis.

Beetle, *s.* (*Fly*), daol dubh; dubh-chuile; (*mallet*), fairc, fairche, farachan; slachdan.

Beetle, *v. a.* and *n.* Fairc; slachdanaich; buail mach, croch a mach.

Beetle-browed, *a.* Ploc-mhalach; maildheach, ploc-mhaildheach; gruamach.

Beetle-headed, *a.* Baoth, baothaireach, umaidheach, ploc-cheannach, poll-cheannach.

Beetling, *a.* Crochach, an crochadh

Beeves, *s. pl.* Mairt, daimh, spreidh, crodh, bà; sgabagan.

Befal, *v.* Eirich, tuit, thig gu crich, tachair. Evil will befall you, *eirichidh olc dhuit;* evil befell you, *dh'eirich olc dhuit, is olc mar a thachair dhuit.*

Befit, *v.* Freagair, freagraich, bi freagarrach, dean iom-chuidh; thig do. This will befit you, *thig so gu maith dhuit.*

Befool, *v.* Dean amadan do; cuir air bhaothaireachd.

Before, *prep.* and *adv.* Roimh, ro, roi; air toiseach; air thoiseach; air beulaobh; mus an, mu 'n, mu 'm, (*in presence of*), an làthair; an lathaireachd; (*sooner*), ni 's trath-àil. Before me, *romham, air thoiseach orm, ann mo lathair;* before thee, *romhad, air thoiseach ort, ann do làthair;* before him, *roimhe;* before her, *roimpe,* before you, *romh-aibh;* before them, *rompa;* before the house, *air beulaobh an tighe,* before the judge, *an làthair a bhreitheimh,* before my eyes, *mu chomhar mo shùilibh,* before you were born, *mu 'n do rugadh tu;* before I die, *mu 'm faigh mi bàs,* before now, *roimh so;* before then, *roimh sin;* the day before, *an là roimh,* the day before yesterday, *an là roimh 'n dé;* before all things, *roimh nan uile nì, roimh na h-uile nì, gu h-àraid, gu h-araidh,* beforehand, *roimh laimh,* before the time, *roimh an am, roimh 'n mhithich, roimh mhithich,* never before, *riomh roimh.*

Befoul, *v.* Salaich.

Befriend, *v.* Cuidich, còghain, dean caoimhneas, nochd cairdeas.

Befringe, *v.* Riobagaich; faim; greus

Beg, *v. a.* Guidh, grios, iarr, asluich; iarr deirc. I begged of him, *Ghuidh mi air, ghrios mi air.*

Began, *v.* Thòisich. Faic Begin.

Beget, *v.* Gin, gein, faigh clann Begotten, *ginte, geinte*

Begetter, *s.* Gineadair.

Beggar, *s.* Deirceach, iarradair, bleideire, bochd, *baigeir;* deòradh; truaghan, feumanach, ditheach

Beggar, *v. a.* Thoir gu bochduinn, thoir gu dìth.

Beggarliness, *s.* Feum, uireasbhuidheachd, lochduinn; diblidheachd; truaghanachd, feumanachd, baigeireachd, mitharachd, truaillidheachd, aimbeartas

Beggarly, *a.* Diblidh, feumach, bochd uireasbhach, uireasbhuidheach; aimbeartach, truagh, diblidh, mùthara, truaillidh

Beggarly, *adv.* Gu h-uireasbhuidheach, gu feumach, gu diblidh, gu bochd, gu truagh, gu mùthar, gu truaillidh.

Beggary, *s.* Uireasbhuidh, feum, bochduinn, aimbeart.

Begging, *s.* Baigeireachd. He went a begging, *chaidh e air bhaigeireachd.*

Begin, *v. a.* and *n.* Tòisich, tionnsgain, inntrinn. Began, thòisich; I am to begin, *tha mi dol a thoiseach,* begin afresh, *tòisich as ùr,* since the world began, *o thòiseach an t-saoghail,* the work has begun, *tha 'n obair air tòiseachadh,* I have just begun, *tha mi air ùr thoiseachadh.*

Beginner, *s.* Ughdar; tùsair, toiseachair, tionsgnair.

Beginning, *s.* Tùs, toiseach, tòiseachadh; ceud-thoiseach, ceud-aobhar. The beginning of the year, *toiseach na bliadhna;* from the beginning of spring, *o thoiseach an earraich,* a fresh beginning, *ùr thòiseachadh,* from the beginning to the end, *o thoiseach gu deireadh.*

Begird, *v.* Crioslaich, ceangail, druid; iom-dhruid.

Begler-beg, *s.* Rioghladair Turcach.

Begnaw, *v.* Cneim, creim, ith, ith air falbh, cnamh.

Begone, *interj.* Bi falbh! bi triall! imich! tog ort!

Begot, *pret* of beget. Ghin, ghein.

Begotten, *part.* Ginte; air ghineadh, air ghintinn An only begotten child, *aon ur-cloinne,* my only begotten, *m'aon ghin,* my only begotten son, *m'aon duine cloinne,* my first begotten child, *mo cheud ghin cloinne, mo cheud ur cloinne*

Begrease, *v. a.* Créis, geir, salaich, rub le créis, no le geir.

Begrime, *v. a.* Salaich; dubhaich, dubh.

Beguile, *v.* Meall; breug, cuir seachad; thoir an car a, thoir a thaobh.

Begun. Faic Begin.

Behalf, *s.* Sgàth, cuis; taobh. In behalf, *as leth, arson, airson, air sgàth, air taobh,* on my behalf, *as mo leth, air mo thaobh.*

Behave, *v.* Giùlan, gnathaich; iomchair. Ill-behaved, *droch mhuinte,* well-behaved, *deadh-mhuinte, beusach.*

Behaviour, *s* Iomchar, giùlan; caith-beath, dol mach, gnathachadh, beus, modhanna. Good behaviour, *deadh iomchar, deagh chaith-beatha, deagh bheus.*

Behead, *v. a* Dì-cheann; dì-cheannaich; thoir an ceann de

Beheld. Faic Behold.

Behemoth, *s.* Oilphaint; each uisge.

Behest, *s.* Iarrtas, aithne, ordugh, reachd; *comannt.*

Behind, *prep* and *adv* Air chùl, air cùl, air chulaobh, air culaobh, an deigh, air dheireadh, air deireadh; as an t-sealladh, as an radharc, air falbh; gu taobh; air ais, (*remaining*), a lathair. Behind me, *air mo chulaobh, a m' 'dheigh,* behind my back, *air mo chùlaobh,* behind-hand, *an dheireadh, an deigh-laimh*

Behold, *v.* Faic, seall, dearc, amhairc, beachdaich. Behold them, *faic iad.* He beheld me, *chunnaic e mi.*

Behold! Faic! seall! feuch!

Beholden, *a.* An comain; mar fhiachaibh. I am beholden to you, *tha mi ad chomain*

Beholder, *s.* Fear amhairc. Beholders, *luchd amhairc*

Beholding, *s.* Scealltuinn, amharc, beachdachadh.

Behoof, *s.* Uidhis, buannachd, tairbhe, *prodhait.* In my behoof, *as mo leth.*

Behoveful, *a.* Uidhiseil, buannachdail, tairbheach; dligheach, cubhaidh.

Behove, *v.* Bi cubhaidh, bi freagarrach (no) iomchuidh It behoves me, *is cubhaidh dhomh, is coir dhomh*

Being, *s* Bith; nàdur; beath; creutair, ur. Our being, *air bith,* habitation, *aros, tigh;* before I was in being, *mu 'n do rugadh mi,* the greatest Being (God), *an Tì a 's airde, am Fear is fhearr*

Being, *part* Bith Our being here, *ar bhith an so,* being it is so, *on is ann mar sin a tha chùis,* I being dead, *air dhomh bhith marbh,* for the time being, *air an uair, san am tha lathair.*

Belabour, *v.* Buail, buail gu h-inich; greidh, slachdainn, luinnsich, lundrainn; eirich air, gabh air, singil.

Belated, *a.* Anmoch. I was belated, *bha mi anmoch; thuit an oidhche orm.*

Belay, *v.* Fàth-fheith; dean plaid-luidhe; (*am measg mharaich,*) ceangail ball.

Belch, *v.* Brùchd, raoichd; dioghrog.

Belcher, *s.* Brùchdair, raoichdear.

Beldame, *s.* Bansgal, sean-bhean, sean chailleach, cailleach chrosda, cailleach chànranach.

Beleaguer, *v.* Druid, iom-dhruid, cuairtich, cuir séisd, iadh.

Beleaguering, *s.* Druideadh, iom-dhruideadh, cuairteachadh, séisd, seisdeadh.

Belfounder, *s.* Clogadair.

Belfry, *s.* Clog-aite, clag-ionad, clogas, stiopul.

Belie, *v.* Cùl-chàin, maslaich, breugaich.

Belief, *s.* Creideamh; barail; creideas; creud. Of little belief, *air bheag creidimh;* hard of belief, *do chreideamhach;* easy of belief, *so-chreidmheach;* according to my belief, *a reir mo bharail.*

Believable, *a.* So-chreidsinn; creideasach.

Believe, *v.* Creid; thoir creideas; earbas; saoil; smuainich; bi 'n dùil, bi 'n dòchas. I believe, *tha mi a creidsinn, creideam, tha mi 'n dùil;* I believe you, *tha mi 'g ad chreidsinn;* I verily believe you, *tha mi 'g ad dheagh chreidsinn;* make him believe it, *thoir air a chreidsinn, thoir a chreidsinn air.*

Believer, *s.* Creideach, creidmheach; criosduigh.

Believingly, *adv.* Gu creideach, gu creidmheach, gu sochreideach.

Belike, *adv.* Maith dh'fhaoidte, dh'fhaoidte, theagamh, a reir coslais.

Bell, *s.* Clog, clag; cluigean; suilleag, bolg. An alarm-bell, *clag caismeachd.*

Belle, *s.* Aigh-riomhach; nighean eireachdail, rimhinn.

Belled, *a.* Cluigeanach, cluigeanaichte.

Belles-lettres, *s.* Foghlum uasal, ard-fhoghlum; ardoilean.

Bell-fashioned, *a.* Cluigeanach.

Bellied, *a.* Bronnach, bagach; leth-tromach.

Belligerent, *a.* Cogach.

Bellow, *v.* Geum, beuc, bùir, bùirich, raoichd, langanaich; glaodh; ràn.

Bellowing, *s.* Beucaich; beucail; glaodhaich; rànaich; (*of deer*), bùireadh, bùirich, raoichd, raoichdil; langan.

Bellows, *s.* Balg, bolg, balg séid, balg séididh, builgean.

Belluine, *a.* Brùideil.

Belly, *s.* Brù; bolg; bag; machlag. Your eyes are bigger than your belly, *is mò do shùilean no do bhrù;* a little belly, *bronnag, bolgan;* big-bellied, *bronnach, bragach;* (as a woman), *leth-tromach;* a belly-ful, *lan bronn, seat, làn;* belly-ache, *coiliginn;* belly-band, *giort, bronnach;* fair words fill not a fool's belly, *cha dean a ghloir bhoidheach an t-amadan sathach.*

Belly, *v.* Balgaich, bolgaich, bagaich.

Belly-ache, *s.* Coiliginn, bru-ghoirt.

Bellyful, *s.* Lan-bronn; seat; sath, teann-shath.

Belly-god, *s.* Craosair, geocair.

Belly-pinched, *a.* Acrach, ocrach, air acras, ciocrach.

Belman, *s.* Fear cluig; beadal; gairmair.

Belock, *v.* Glais, dùin, druid.

Belong, *v. n.* Buin. Does this belong to you? *am buin so dhuitse?* who does this belong to? *co dà bhuineas so?*

Beloved, *a.* Gradhaichte, ionmhuinn. Dearly beloved, *ro-ionmhuinn, ro-ghradhaichte;* she is beloved by him, *is ionmhuinn leis i.*

Below, *prep.* and *adv.* Fo, fodh, fodha, fu, fuidh; ni 's isle, ni 's ìlse; gu h-iosal; air thalamh; iolar, shios, sios, a bhàn; iochdrach; an iochdar. Below me, *fum, fodham;* below thee, *fodhad;* below her, *foidhpe;* below you, *fodhaibh;* below them, *fodhpa;* put it below, *cuir sios e, cuir a bhàn e;* it is below, *tha e shios, tha e iolar;* from below, *os iosal, a nuas, n'àirde;* the places below, *na h-ionadan iochdrach;* I would think it below me to do it, *cha b'fhiach leam a dheanamh.*

Belswagger, *s.* Drùsair; drùsdar.

Belt, *s.* Crios; beilt. A shoulder-belt, *crios-guaille.*

Beltmaker, *s.* Criosadair. Beltmakers, *criosadairean.*

Belwether, *s.* Clag mhult.

Belying, *s.* Cùl-chàin, masladh.

Bemad, *v.* Cuir air bhreathas, cuir air chuthach.

Bemire, *v.* Eabair, salaich, luidir; spult.

Bemiring, *s.* Eabradh, salachadh, luidreadh, spultadh.

Bemoan, *v.* Caoidh, gearain, guil, dean cumhadh, dean bròn.

Bemoaner, *s.* Caoidhear, gearanaiche, cumhadair.

Bemoaning, *s.* Caoidheadh, gearain, cumhadh, gul, bròn.

Bemoil, *v.* Eabair, luidir, salaich.

Bench, *s.* Beinc, suidheagan; beinnse, cathair breitheimh; fora; Breitheamhna. The King's Bench, *Beinc an Righ.*

Bench, *v. a.* Beincich; cuir air beinc.

Bend, *v. a.* Lub, crom, cam, dean cam; (*to a certain point*), stiùir; (*bend your mind*), leig d'inntinn, suidhich d'inntinn; (*subdue*), ceannsaich, smachdaich.

Bend, *v. n.* Sonraich, sunraich; géill; lùb; fas cam (no) crom.

Bend, *s.* Lùb, lubadh, luib; car, crom, cromadh; plaigh.

Bendable, *a.* So-lùbaidh; so-chromadh; so-chamadh; a lùbas; a ghabhas lùbadh; lubach.

Bended, *a.* Lubte, crom, cam. With bended knees, *le glùintean lùbte.*

Bender, *s.* Lùbair; lùbadair.

Beneath, *prep.* and *adv.* Fo, fodh, fodha; fuidh; fu; gu h-iosal; air thalamh, iolar, sios, shios; a bhàn; an iochdar, iochdrach.

Benedictine, *s.* Mànach.

Benediction, *s.* Beannachd, beannachadh; taing, buidheachas.

Benefaction, *s.* Gean maith, oirchiseachd, deadh thùrn, maitheas.

Benefactor, *s.* Deagh charaid, fear cùl-taic, fear oirchiseach.

Benefactress, *s.* Ban-oirchisiche.

Benefice, *s.* Beathachadh.

Beneficed, *a.* Beathaichte.

Beneficence, *s.* Fiughantas, fialachd, fialaidheachd, maitheas, oirchios, cairdeas.

Beneficent, *a.* Fiughantach, fial, fialaidh, oirchiseach, mathasach.

Beneficial, *a.* Tarbhach; sochaireach; maith, math, buannach, feumail, uidhiseil.

Beneficially, *adv.* Gu tarbhach, gu sochaireach, gu maith, gu buannach, gu feumail.

Benefit, *s.* Tairbhe, sochair, coisinn, maithe, feum, uidhis; co-ghnadh; stà gniomh, buannachd; deagh thùrn, *proidhit.*

Benefit, *v.* Tairbhich, coisinn, dean feum, dean stà, dean co'ghnadh.

Benet, *v.* Eangaich; iadh; paintirich.

Benevolence, *s.* Deagh-ghean, deagh-thoil, gean maith; seirc, fiùghantas, mathasachd.

Benevolent, *a.* Seirceil, fiùghantach, mathasach.

Bengal, *s.* Seorsa eudaich air dheanamh le siod agus le rôinne.

Benight, *v.* Dorchaich, duibhrich.

Benighted, *part.* and *a.* Dorchaichte; anmoch, aineolach.

Benign, *a.* Caoimhneil, caoin, caomh, cairdeil, trocaireach, gràsmhor; fabhorach; còir, fial, fialuidh; math, slainnteil.

Benignity, *s.* Caoimhnealas, caoinealachd, caomhachd, cairdeas, cairdealas, caoimhne, grasmhoireachd, trocair, fabhor, fialachd, fialuidheachd, slainntealachd.

Benignly, *adv.* Gu caoimhneil, gu caoin, gu caomh, gu cairdeil, gu fial, gu fialuidh, gu grasmhor.

† **Benison**, *s.* Beannachd.

Bent, *s.* Lùb, lùbadh, aomadh, crom, cromadh; (*inclination*), rùn, togar, rùn suidhichte, toil, aom 'inntinn, seorsa feòir monaidh; muradh. The bent of your mind, *togar* (*no*) *aomadh d'inntinn.*

Bent, *a.* Lubta, lubte, camaichte, cam, crom. He is bent on going away, *tha e 'n càs air falbh, tha e 'n geall air falbh;* his mind is bent upon it, *tha inntinn suidhichte air;* bent many ways, *ioma-charach;* not to be bent, *do lùbaidh.*

Benum, Benumb, *v. a.* Funtuinn, funnduinn, meilich.

Bepinch, *v.* Pioc, gòmagaich.

Bepiss, *v.* Mùin.

Bequeath, *v.* Tiomnadh, fàg le tiomnadh. I bequeath, *tiomnam.*

Bequeather, *s.* Tiomnadair.

Bequest, *s.* Dìleab.

Berattle, *v.* Dean stairn, dean gleadhraich.

Bereave, *v.* Thoir air falbh, thoir uaith, thoir o; spùinn, spùill, creach.

Bereavement, *s.* Spùinneadh, spùilleadh.

Bereft, *a.* Spùinnte, spùillte.

Bergamot, *s.* Seorsa peura; seorsa snuisein.

Berlin, *s.* Seorsa coisde (no) carbaid.

Bernardine, *s.* Seorsa mànaich.

Berry, *s.* Dearc, dearcag, sùbh. A little berry, *dearcag;* crowberry, *eidhreag;* cloudberry, *broidhleag;* serviceberry, *caoran;* currantberry, *rusar, dearc-fhrancach;* a gooseberry, *gròsaid;* a juniperberry, *dearcag aitinn;* a strawberry, *suibheag làir;* a raspberry, *suibheag;* a brambleberry, *smeurag;* a white-thornberry, *sgeachag.*

Berth, *s.* Aite, oifig, (no) post air mhuir; acarsaid.

Beryl, *s.* Seorsa cloich phriseil.

Bescreen, *a.* Sgàil, sgàilich; duibhrich.

Beseech, *v.* Guidh, iar gu durachdach, grios, asluich. Beseech him, *guidh air, grios air;* I beseech thee, *guidheam ort;* I besought thee, *ghrios mi ort.*

Beseem, *v.* Bi freagarrach, bi cubhaidh. It beseems, *is cubhaidh, is ceart, is còir.*

Beseeming, *a.* Freagarrach, cubhaidh, ceart.

Beset, *v.* Cuairtich, iadh, druid, iom-dhruid; fàth-fheith; cuir dragh, cuir moille air.

Beset, *a.* Cuairtichte, druidte.

Beshrew, *v.* Guidh mallachd; mallaich.

Beside, Besides, *prep.* and *adv.* Laimh ri, fagus air, fogus do, ri taobh; a thuille, a thuille air so (no) sin, a bhàrr air sin, fòs. Beside me, *laimh rium, fagus domh;* besides the bridge, *fogus air an drochait, ri taobh na drochait;* he is beside himself, *tha e thar a chéill,* (*no*) *gòrach.*

Besiege, *v.* Cuir séisd ri, iom-dhruid; cuairtich.

Besieger, *s.* Séisdear.

Besieging, *s.* Seisdeadh, cuairteachadh, iom-dhruideadh.

Besmear, *v.* Salaich, eabair, luidir; smiùr, sliob.

Besmeared, *a.* Salaichte; smiùrte, sliobte.

Besmoke, *v.* Dean dubh le deathach, croch anns an deathach (no) san t-sùidhe.

Besom, *s.* Sguab, sguabach.

Besot, *v. a.* Fag gun tùr, fàg gun toinisg; cuir air mheisg.

Besought. Faic **Beseech**.

Bespangle, *v.* Lannair, loinnir, lannaich.

Bespatter, *v.* Spùlt le salchair (no) poll, salaich; cuir thairis le salchair, càin.

Bespattering, *s.* Spultadh, salachadh; càineadh.

Bespawl, *v.* Smugarsaich.

Bespawler, *s.* Smugadair.

Bespeak, *v.* Dean guth air son; orduich; gabh; solair; innis; cuir an céill, nochd.

Bespeckle, *v.* Ballaich, breacaich, breac; spot.

Bespeckled, *a.* Ballaichte, breacaichte, breac; spotach.

Bespew, *v.* Sgeith, tilg.

Bespice, *v.* Spiosraich.

Besprinkle, *v.* Spult; crath air, taislich.

Besprinkling, *s.* Spultadh, crathadh; taisleachadh, fliuchadh.

Best, *a.* Is fearr. What had we best do? *ciod is fhearr dhuinn dheanamh?* I will do my best, *ni mi mar is fhearr is urrainn mi;* to the best of my knowledge, *mar is fhearr is fhiosrach mi.*

Bestain, *v.* Salaich, truaill, dubh, spot.

Bestead, *v.* Tairbhich, dean feum. That will not bestead you much, *cha mhòr is fheairrde thu sin.*

Bestial, *a.* Brùideil, brùiteil, béisteil; mosach, musach; feolmhor.

Bestiality, *s.* Brùiteileachd; mosaiche; feòlmhoireachd.

Bestink, *v.* Dean droch bholadh, dean droch fhail, dean tochd.

Bestir, *v. a.* Carraich, gluais, mosgail, grad-ghluais, dean cabhag. Bestir yourself, *cuir car dhiot.*

Bestow, *v. a.* Thoir, thabhair, builich, bairig; tiodhlaic. Bestow pains, *gabh saothair.*

Bestowed, *part.* Builichte, bairigte, tiodhlaicte, air thabhairt.

Bestower, *s.* Tabhartair, buileachair, tiodhlacair.

Bestowing, *s.* Tabhairt, toirt, buileachadh, tiodhlacadh.

Bestowment, *s.* Tabhartas, gibht, tiodhlac.

Bestraught, *a.* Gòrach, air dhearg-chuthach.

Bestrew, *v. a.* Sgap, sgainnir, sgaoil.

Bestride, *v. a.* Rach gobhlach, rach cas gobhlach; marcaich; ceum thair.

Bestrown, *part.* Sgapte, sgapta, sgaoilte.

Bet, *s.* Geall.

Bet, *v.* Cuir geall, cuir an geall. What will you bet? *ciod a chuireas tu an geall?*

Betake, *v.* Gabh; rach; tog ort; imich; falbh. They betook themselves to fighting, *ghabh iad dh'ionnsiudh na caonnaig;* he betook himself off, *dh'fhalbh e, thog e air.*

Beteem, *v.* Thoir, thabhair, builich, bairig.

Bethink, *v.* Cuimhnich, cuimhnich agad, cuimhnich ort; smuainich, smaoinich; smuaintich, beachdaich.

Bethinking, *s.* Cuimhneachadh, smuaineachadh, beachdachadh.

Bethlehem, *s.* Tigh cuthaich.

Bethral, *v. a.* Traillich; buadhaich air, fairtlich air.

Bethump, *v.* Buail, stroidhil, éirich air.

Betide, *v. n.* Tachair, eirich, thig gu crìche. Woe betide you! *droch nuaidheachd ort!*

Betime, betimes, *adv.* Moch, much, moch-thràth, much-thràth; gu trathail, gu moch; sa mhadainn.

Betoken, *v.* Ceallaich, feuch. That betokens evil, *is comhar uile sin.*

Betony, *s.* Lus mhic Bheathaig, glasair coille.

Betray, *v.* Brath; meall; nochd, feuch. That betrays a bad intention, *tha sin a feuchainn droch dhùrachd.*

Betrayer, *s* Brathair, brathadair, fear brathaidh; traoightear, mealltair

Betrim, *v.* Deasaich, snàsaich, uigheamaich, sgiamhaich, sgeadaich, busg, busgaich, busgainn.

Betroth, *v.* Ceangail, dean ceangal-pòsaidh; geall ann am pòsadh.

Better, *a.* A 's fearr, ni 's fearr, a 's fhearr, ni 's fhearr is fhearr. The better plan, *an seòl is fhearr*, better and better, *ni 's fhearr agus ni 's fhearr*, it were better to be dead, *b' fhearr a bhith marbh*, it is the better for that, *is fheairrd e sin*, *is e sin 'fheothas;* what is one man better than another? *ciod is fhearr aon duine no duine eile?* grow better, *cinn ni 's fhearr, rach am feothas.*

Better, *s* Uachdaran; feothas, feabhas.

Better, *v* Leasaich; dean ni 's fearr, thoir am feothas He bettered; *leasaich e*, bettered, *leasaichte.*

Between, *prep.* Eadar, anns a mheadhon, san eadar mheadhon. Between us, *eadaruinn;* between you, *eadaraibh*, between them, *eatorra*, between the two, (indifferent), *eadar an da chuid*, between ourselves, *eadaruinn féin*, between whiles, *gach dolach uair, an tràths is a ris, air uairibh, na uairean.*

Betwixt, *prep.* Eadar.

Bevel, *s.* Riaghailt clachair.

Beverage, *s.* Deoch.

Bevy, *s.* Ealtuin, ealt eun, sgaoth; (*of quadrupeds*), greidh, dròbh; (*of people*), bannal, cuideachd, bròd, lòd.

Bewail, *v.* Caoidh, dean tuireadh, caoin, guil.

Beware, *v.* Thoir an aire, gabh curam, bi faicilleach.

Beweep, *v.* Guil, caoin, caoidh

Bewet, *v.* Fliuch, taislich, dealtaich, uisgich

Bewilder, *v. a.* Cuir air seachran; rach thar a cheile; cuir an ceo, cuir air iomral, cuir an iom-cheist.

Bewildered, *a.* Air seachran, thar a cheile; ann an ceo, an am brath cheo.

Bewitch, *v.* Cuir buitseachd; cuir druidheachd.

Bewitcher, *s.* Druidh, buitseach

Bewitchery, *s.* Buitseachd, buitseachas; druidheachd.

Bewray, *v* Brath, meall, innis, nochd, leig ris; truaill, salaich.

Bewrayed, *a.* Brathte, meallta, truaillte, salaichte

Bewrayer, *s* Brathair, brathadair, traoidhtear; mealltair

Bewraying, *a.* Mealltach, traoidhteil; lonach.

Bey, *s* Uachdaran Turcach.

Beyond, *prep.* Thall, air an taobh thall, air taobh thall; thar. Beyond measure, *anameasarrach*, beyond calculation, *thar cunntas*, go beyond, *rach null, rach thairis, rach thar.*

Biangulous, *a.* Dà-oisinneach, da-uilinneach.

Bias, *s.* Togar; togradh; toil, aomadh, taobh.

Bias, *v. a.* Aom; cudthromaich.

Bib, *v* Òl, pòit.

Bib, *s* Smig-bhrat, breid-uchd leinibh.

Bibacious, *a* Olar, pòiteil, misgeach.

Bibber, *s.* Poitear, misgear, meisgear.

Bible, *s.* Pioball.

Biblical, *a.* Pioballach, diadhuidh; a bhuineas do 'n phioball, (no) do-dhiadhuidheachd.

Bibulous, *a.* Còsach; olar; craosach.

Bicipital, *a.* Da-cheannach.

Bicker, *v.* Dean caonnag, dean tabaid, dean tuasaid, connsaich.

Bickerer, *s.* Tabaidiche, tuasaidiche.

Bickering, *s.* Caonnag, tabaid, tuasaid; connsachadh.

Bicornous, *a.* Da adhairceach, da bheannach.

Bid, *v* Iarr, aithn; orduich; (*invite*), cuir, thoir cuireadh; (*offer a price*), tairg, thoir tairgeas; tairg luach. Bid adieu, *gabh slainnte le, gabh cead do.*

Bidden, *part* Cuirte, air chuireadh; air iarraidh Not bidden, *gun chuireadh, gun iarruidh, gun sireadh*

Bidder, *s* Tairgear, tairgsear; fear cuiridh.

Bidding, *s.* Iarrtas, aithne; ordugh, ailghios; earail; cuireadh At your bidding, *air d' iarrtas;* bidding of banns, *gairm pòsaidh.*

Bide, *s.* Fuirich, fan, stad còmhnuich; buanaich, mair, fulaing, giùlan.

Bidental, *a* Dà-fhiaclach.

Biding, *s* Fuireachadh, fanachd; àros, fardoch

Bier, *s.* Cobhan, ciste mhairbh; carbad; cairbh-charbad.

Biestings, *s.* Nòs, nùs, ceud bhainne, bainne nòis, bainne nùis.

Biferous, *a.* A bheir da bhàrr sa bhliadhna.

Big, *a* Mòr, meudmhor, domhail, reamhar, (*with child*), torrach, leth-tromach, (*swollen*), atmhor; (*proud*), sgodail, leomach, ardanach, mòr-inntinneach Big words, *briathran atmhor*

Bigamist, *s* Fear aig am bheil da bhean.

Bigamy, *s.* Posadh dùbailt.

Bigbellied, *a* Bronnach, bagach.

Bigly, *adv.* Gu sgodail, gu leomach, gu h-ardanach, gu h-atmhor

Bigness, *s.* Meud, tomad, tomald.

Bigot, *s* Baoth-chreidiche; dall-chreidmhiche, tnuthair.

Bigotted, *a.* Teas-ghradhach, dall-eudmhor; baoth-ghradhach.

Bigotry, *s.* Baoth-chreidimh; dall-chreidimh, dall eud; baoth-ghradh, teas-ghradh.

Big-swollen, *a.* Atmhor; thun sgàineadh

Bilander, *s.* Luingeas ceannuiche.

Bilberry, *s* Dearcag mhonaidh, braoileag.

Bilbo, *s.* Groilean, claidheamh beag, cloidhean; gearra-chlaidheamh.

Bilboes, *s.* Ceap, ceap air bord luing

Bile, *s.* Domblas; neasgaid, iongrach, iongrachadh; leannachadh

Bilge, *s.* Leud iochdair luing; bulg.

Bilge, *v.* Bris, mar ni luingeas, air craig, leig stigh uisge.

Bilingsgate, *s* Droch sheanchas, cainnt dhrabasta; trod; bardachd.

Bilinguous, *a* Da-chainnteach.

Bilious, *a.* Domblasach, domblasda.

Bilk, *v. a.* Meall, thoir an car a; bris le foill.

Bill, *s.* (*of a bird.*) Gob, beic; (*in money*), bann airson airgid A bill of exchange, *bann iomlaid, bann sgriobhaidh, bann a bheir coir do neach airgiod fhaotainn an aite sònraichte*, bill of parcels, *cunntas ceannachaidh;* (an axe), *sgian sgathaidh, bearr-sgian;* a bill of divorce, *bann dealachaidh.*

Bill, *v.* Pòg.

Billet, *s.* Creamhchdan; bileit, papeir beag; litir.

Billet, *v.* Thoir ceithreamhnan do shaighdear, cuir saighdear air cheithreamhnan.

Billet-doux, *s.* Litir leannanachd; litir gaoil.

Billiard, *s.* Seorsa cluiche air bord, le buil bheag is le lorgan.

Billow, *s.* Tonn, sumain, sumaid. Billows, *tonnan.*

Billowy, *a.* Tonnmhor, sumaineach, gailbheach, garbh, molach. A rough sea, *muir ghailbheach, muir mholach; garbh chuan.*

Binary, *a.* Dùbailt, dual.

Bin, *s.* Ciste.

Bind, *v.* Ceangail, naisg, cuibhrich; teannaich; thoir air; bac. Bind hand and foot, *ceangail eadar lamhan is chosan;* bind by benefits, *cuir fu chomainibh.*

Binder, *s.* Ceangladair, ceanglair, fear ceangail, fear ceanglaidh; teannachair.

Binding, *s.* Ceangal, ceangladh, cuibhreach, cuibhreachadh; teannachadh, crios, nasgadh.

Binocle, *s.* Gloine-amhairc dhùbailt.

Binocular, *a.* Da-shuileach.

Biographer, *s.* Beò-eachdraiche, beath-eachdraiche.

Biography, *s.* Beò-eachdraidh, beath-eachdraidh.

Bipartite, *a.* Da-phairteach.

Bipartition, *s.* Pàirteachadh; roinn da leth.

Biped, *s.* Bith air dha chois; beothach da-chosach, dachosach.

Bipedal, *a.* Da-chosach; da throidh air fad (no) air leud.

Bipennated, *a.* Da-sgiathach.

Birch, *s.* Beithe. A birch-wood, *coille-bheithe.*

Birchen, *a.* Beithe. A birchen wood, *coille bheithe.*

Bird, *s.* Eun, eunlan, eunlaith. A young bird, *garrag.*

Birdbolt, *s.* Seorsa saighde.

Birdcage, *s.* Eunadan.

Birdcatcher, *s.* Eunadair.

Birdcherry, *s.* Fiodhag.

Birdgander, *s.* Seorsa geòidh.

Birdlime, *s.* Bigh eoin.

Bird's-foot, *s.* Crubh eòin.

Birth, *s.* Breith; siol; sinnsearachd. By birth, *a thaobh brath;* from his birth, *on rugadh e;* of high birth, *uasal;* of low birth, *iosal;* new birth, *ùr-bhreith;* untimely birth, *torrachas anabuich.*

Birthday, *s.* La breith. The King's birthday, *làth breith an Righ, co' ainm la breith an Righ.*

Birthright, *s.* Còir-bhreith.

Biscuit, *s.* Briosgaid, breacag bhrisg chruithneachd.

Bisect, *v.* Gearr na dha leth; leth; dean dà leth, sgoilt.

Bisection, *s.* Gearradh na dha leth; sgoltadh.

Bishop, *s.* Easpuig, fear easpuig.

Bishopric, *s.* Easpachd, easpuidheachd, sgìreachd easpuig.

Bismuth, *s.* Seorsa miotailt.

Bissextile, *s.* Bliadhna leumaidh.

Bistoury, *s.* Sgian leigh, corc leigh; roinn-bhearrag.

Bisulcous, *a.* Ladhrach, aig am bheil ladhran sgoilte.

Bit, *s.* (*Of a bridle*), spearrag, aill-bheul, cabstar; (*a little portion*), crioman, criomag, mìre beag, mìrean; greim, pioc; daochal. You shall not get a bit, *cha n' fhaigh thu crioman,* (*no*) *pioc;* a tit-bit, *toitean.*

Bit. See **Bite.**

Bitch, *s.* Galladh; baobh, bidse; sagh.

Bite, *v.* Teum, tiolam; gearr; beum; meall, thoir an car a; creim, criom.

Bite, *s.* Teum, tiolàm, gearradh; beum, creim, criom; sgobadh, spoineadh.

Biter, *s.* Teumair; tiolamair, beumair; mealltair, sgobair.

Bitter, *a.* Goirt, garg, searbh, teth, geur; guineach; beumnach; brònach.

Bitterly, *adv.* Gu goirt, gu garg, gu searbh, gu geur, gu guineach, gu bronach.

Bittern, *s.* Stearnall, gràineag, sgarbh, scarbh, corra-ghrian.

Bitterness, *s.* Seirbhe, searbhadas, searbhas; gairge, géire, mi-run, gamhlas, fuath, tnù, droch nadur; sprochd, doilghios; dubhachas.

Bitumen, *s.* Pic; bith.

Bivalve, *a.* Da-dhuilleach, da-dhuilleagach; da leabagach.

Blab, *v.* Dean lonais, bi lonach, bi luath-bheulach.

Blab, *s.* Lonag; glabair; sgileam.

Black, *a.* Dubh; dorch; dubhach; brònach, aingidh. Black and blue, *dubh-ghorm;* black-browed, *gruamach;* a black mouth, *bus dubh;* black-mouthed, *dubh-ghrosach;* somewhat black, *leth-char dubh.*

Black, *s.* Dubh. The black of the eye, *dubhagan na sùl.*

Black, *v.* Dubh, dubhaich, dorchaich.

Blackberry, *s.* Dearcag dhub; smeurag.

Blackbird, *s.* Lon dubh, lon.

Black-brown, *a.* Dubh dhonn.

Black-browed, *a.* Gruamach; dorch.

Black-cattle, *s.* Crodha, spreidh.

Blacken, *v.* Dubhaich, dubh, dean dubh; fas dubh; dorchaich; tog droch sgeul; tog droch cliù, (no) droch alladh; càin, cùl-chàin.

Blackened, *a.* Dubhaichte; dorchaichte.

Blackening, *s.* Dubh, dubhadh; dubhadan.

Blackguard, *s.* Sgonn-bhalaoch crochair.

Blacking, *s.* Dubhadan, dubh. Shoe-blacking, *dubh nam bròg.*

Blackish, *a.* Leth-char dubh.

Blacklead, *s.* Luaidhe dhubh.

Blackmail, *s.* Dubh-chis.

Blackness, *s.* Dubh, duibhe, duibhead, doirche; aingidheachd.

Blackpudding, *s.* Marag dhubh. Blackpuddings, *maragan dubha.*

Blacksmith, *s.* Gobha, gobhainn, gobhainn dubh.

Blackthorn, *s.* Airneag, preas airneag; doighionn dubh.

Bladder, *s.* Aotraman, eutroman, bolg, balg; guirean, leus.

Blade, *s.* (*Of grass*), duilleag, bileag; (*of corn*), dias, diasag, geamhar; (*of a sword*), lann; lainne; loinn; (*a youth*), lasgair. Bladebone, *cnaimh slinnean.*

Bladed, *a.* Duilleagach, bileagach; lannach.

Blain, *s.* Guirean, neasgaid, plucan, leus.

Blamable, *a.* Coireach, ciontach, airidh air achmhasan.

Blamableness, *s.* Coire, ciont.

Blame, *s.* Coire, oilbheum, lochd, cron. Without blame, *gun choire, neo-chiontach;* lay the blame on him, *cuir a choire air.*

Blame, *v.* Coirich, cronaich; maslaich; cuir choire air; troid. You are to blame, *tha thu ri choireachadh.*

Blamed, *part.* Cronaichte, coirichte.

Blameless, *a.* Neo-chiontach; neo-choireach, neo-lochdach; glan, treibhdireach gun chionnt, gun choire, gun lochd.

Blamelessness, *s.* Neo-chiontachd; tréibhdhireas.

Blameworthy, *a.* Coireach; airidh air achmhasan.

Blanch, *v. a.* Gealaich, dean geal; rùisg, sgrath; (*evade*), seachain, cuir gu taobh.

Blanched, *a.* Gealaichte, geal; bàn.

Bland, *a.* Caoin, caoimhneil, seimh; ciuin, tlàth; maoth; bog.

Blandish, *v.* Miniich, ciùinich; breug

Blandisher, *s.* Miodalaiche, sodalaiche.

Blandishment, *s.* Miodal, sodal, sogh-chomhradh, ciùin-chomhradh, tlà-bhriathar, goileam; gaol beul breagh.

Blank, *a.* (*Pale*), ban, glasdaidh, (*out of countenance*), nàr, fu amhluath; rughteach; (*empty*), fàs, falamh; geal, gun sgriobhadh. Point blank, *as an aghaidh, caol direach*

Blank, *s.* Ionad fàs (no) falamh; dl-sgriobhadh; crann faoin.

Blank, *v* Cuir gu nair, nàraich, cuir fu amhluath

Blanket, *s* Plaide, plaideag, *blangait; (a child's blanket)*, faicean.

Blare, *v.* Glaodh, bùir, bùirich, raoichd; leagh, mar choinneal

Blaspheme, *v.* Dia-mhaslaich, naomh-chàin, labhair toibheum, masluich

Blasphemer, *s.* Dia-mhlaslachair, toibheumaiche, oilbheumaiche, fear toibheuma

Blasphemous, *a.* Toibheumach; oilbheumach, naomh chainteach, maslach, baoth-bhriathrach.

Blasphemously, *adv.* Gu toibheumach, gu naomh-chainteach, gu maslach

Blasphemy, *s* Toibheum, oilbheum Dia-mhasladh, Dia mhaslachadh, masladh, baoth-bhriathar.

Blast, *s.* Sian, sion; osag, oiteag, séide, seideadh; fuar-ghreadadh, braidhe; (*a sound*), sgal; (*blight*), millcheò

Blast, *v* Loisg, searg, doth; cuir gu neo-ni; mill, cuir oillt air.

Blasted, *a.* Loisgte, seargte, dòthte; millte

Blatant, *a* Geumnaich

Blaze, *s* Leus, lasair; solus lasrach; soillseachadh; drilinn

Blaze, *v. a* and *n* Leus, las, lasraich, soillsich, leagh air falbh mar ni coinneal; (*publish*), sgaoil, innis, dean aithnichte, foillsich

Blazer, *s* Iomradair, fabhraiche, fear a sgaoileas iomradh.

Blazing, *a* Leusach, lasach, soillseach, drilinneach.

Blazon, *v* Sgiamhaich, sgeadaich, breaghaich; foillsich; dean aithnichte, gairm, mol, ard-mhol, cliùich; cliùthaich, ardaich, meudaich.

Blazonry, *s* Suaicheantachd

Bleach, *v.* Gealaich, bànaich, dean geal, dean bàn Bleached, *gealaichte*, bleached linen, *anart gealaichte.*

Bleacher, *s* Gealachair, fear gealaich, fear gealachaidh.

Bleaching, *s* Gealach, gealachadh

Bleak, *a.* Lom, fuar; neo-thorrach, di-threabhach; cruaidh; ard; bàn, glasdaidh; gun tuar. He grew bleak, *dh' fhas e bàn*

Bleakness, *s* Luime, fuarad, di-threabhachd; cruaidhe; glasdaidheachd.

Blear, Bleared, *a.* Ròsbach, ròsb-shuileach, brach-shuileach, sreamhshuileach, rùisgte, prabach, dall, dorcha, uisgidh, lag.

Blear, *v* Ròsbaich, sreamhaich; dean rosb-shuileach (no) brach-shuileach

Bleat, *v.* Meadhail, meidhlaich, meidhlich, dean meadhal; (*like a goat*), migeanaich

Bleating, *s.* Meadhlaich, meidhlich; migeanaich.

Bleb, *s.* Leus, bucaid, guirean

Bleed, *v. a.* Caill fuil, sruth fuil; tarruing fuil.

Bleeding, *s.* Call fola, sruth fola.

Blemish, *s.* Gòid, gaoid; ciurr, ciurram; sal; sgainneal, tàir.

Blemish, *v.* Mill, ciurr; salaich; càin, sgainneal.

Blench, *v.* Clisg, siab air falbh; bac

Blend, *v* Measg, coimeasg; cuir air feadh chéile.

Bless, *v.* Beannaich, dean sona, sochairich, dean aoibhneach; dean adhmhor, dean soirbheasach, mol; glòirich, coisrig He blessed me, *bheannaich e mi.*

Blessed, *a* Beannuichte, sona, sonadh, adhmhor; aoibhneach, aoibhinn, naomh.

Blessedly, *adv.* Gu beannaichte, gu sona, gu h-adhmhor, gu h-aoibhneach.

Blessedness, *s.* Sonas, ard-shonas; ard aoibhneas; sochaireachd, neamhuidheachd; naomhachd.

Blessing, *s.* Beannachd, beannachadh, sochair, tairbhe; buannachd. Invoke a blessing, *guidh beannachd.*

Blest, *part.* Beannaichte; ard-shona; naomh, neamhuidh.

Blew, *pret.* of blow. Shéid. Faic Blow.

Blight, *s* Mill-cheò; fuar-dhealt

Blight, *v a* Searg, mill, sgrios, cuir as da

Blighted, *part. a.* Seargta, seargte, millte.

Blind, *a* Dall, gun léirsinn; dorch, aineolach; diomhair; do-fhaicsinn; do fhaotainn. The blind, *na doill*

Blind, *v. a* Dall, dorchaich; meall, thoir an car a.

Blind, *s.* Sgàile; dall-bhrat, sgàile shùl; leithsgeul meallta

Blindfold, *a* Dall; le suilibh comhdaichte (no) folaichte.

Blindman's-buff, *s* Dallan dàite.

Blindness, *s.* Doille; dorchadas, aineolas

Blindworm, *s.* Nathair bheag nimhe.

Blink, *v.* Caog, priob, sméid

Blinkard, *s.* Caogair, priobair.

Blinking, *s* Caogadh, priobadh, sméideadh

Bliss, *s.* Ard-shonas, mor-shonas, ard-shubhas, fior-shonas.

Blissful, *a.* Ard-shona, subhach; fior-shona, aoibhinn, eibhinn, làn aiteis

Blister, *s* Leus, bolg, bucaid, guirean, plucan

Blister, *v* Leus, bolgaich, tog leus (no) bolg.

Blithe, *a* Sunntach, ait, mear, suilbhear, aobhach, beothail; cridheil; biolagach, suigeartach

Blithely, *adv* Gu sunntach, gu h-ait, gu mear, gu suilbhear, gu h-adhbhach, gu beothail, gu cridheil, gu biolagach, gu suigeartach

Blitheness, Blithesomeness, *s.* Sunnt, aiteas, mire, suilbhearachd, beothaileachd, cridhealas; suigeartachd.

Blithsome, *a.*, Faic Blithe.

Bloat, *a.* At; séid, fàs atmhor; boc, boch

Bloated, *a* At-te, seidte suas, air atadh.

Block, *s.* Ploc; creamhchda, creamhchdan; ceap, ealag, meach; ulag, fear gun tuigse; bac A stumbling block, *ceap tuislidh*

Block, *v.* Bac, dùin, druid.

Blockade, *v.* Iom-dhruid, cuairtich.

Blockade, *s.* Iom-dhruideadh, cuairteachadh.

Blockhead, *s.* Umaidh, sgonn, sgonn-bhalaoch, baoghlan, baothair, burraidh, gurraichdeach, amhlair.

Blockish, *a* Umaidheach, baothaireach

Block-tin, *s.* Staoin, iarrunn geal

Blood, *s* Fuil; cinneach, teaghlach, cinneadh, sliochd gineal, siol; mortadh, marbhadh; beath; (*temper*), nadur, gne; (*a fop*), spailpear, sùgh ni sam bl.

Blood-guiltiness, *s.* Mortadh.
Blood-heat, *s.* Fuil-theas, teas colla.
Bloodhound, *s.* Cù luirg; lorgair.
Bloodily, *adv.* Gu fuilteach, gu marbhtach.
Bloodless, *a.* Neo chiontach an mortadh; bàn; glas; marbh.
Bloodshed, *s.* Dort-fola, marbhadh, àr, mortadh.
Bloodshot, *a.* Dearg; dearg le fuil bhriste.
Bloodsucker, *s.* Geala, deala, dealag; creadhal; mortair.
Bloodthirsty, *a.* Fuilteach, marbhtach, mortach, borb.
Bloodvessel, *s.* Cuisle, cuisleag.
Bloody, *a.* Fuilteach, marbhtach, mortach, borb.
Bloody flux, *s.* Galar gasda.
Bloody-minded, *a.* Borb, neo-thruacanta.
Bloom, *s.* Blàth. In bloom, *fu bhlàth;* in the full bloom of her life, *fu làn bhlàth a h-aimsir.*
Bloom, *v.* Cuir mach blàth, thig fu bhlàth.
Blossom, *s.* Blàth.
Blossom, *v.* Cuir a mach blàth; thig fu bhlàth.
Bloomy, *a.* Blàitheach, blaitheanach; urar; ruighteach.
Blot, *v.* Dubh; salaich; maslaich; duaichnich; *blot out,* dubh a mach.
Blot, *s.* Sal, smal, salchar; tàir, masladh; cron; lochd, breòn, grabhlochd. A blot on the forehead cannot be hid, *an cron a bhios san eudan, cha 'n fhaodar fholuch.*
Blotch, *s.* Guirean, bucaid, builgean, leus.
Blote, *v.* Croch anns an deathach (no) anns an t-sùidhe.
Blow, *s.* Buille, straoidhle, stèar; gleadhar; sgealp.
Blow, *v. a.* and *n.* Séid; plosgaich; seid suas, at; bi fu bhlàth. Blow out, *séid as, cuir as;* blow up, *boch.*
Blowse, *s.* Caile reamhar phluiceach, moigean.
Blowsy, *a.* Pluiceach, ruighteach, dearg-ghruaidheach; loisgte le gréin.
Blubber, *s.* Reamhrachd muic mara.
Blubber, *v.* Dean ulfhart, bi air at le caoineadh.
Bludgeon, *s.* Guitseal, bat goirrid garbh, slacan.
Blue, *a.* Gorm.
Bluebottle, *s.* Brog na cuthaig, curachd na cuthaig, gorman.
Blue-eyed, *a.* Gorm-shuileach.
Blueness, *s.* Guirme; guirmead.
Bluff, *a.* Gnò, gnù, gruamach; reamhar, sultmhor; soireanach, pluiceach, mòr.
Blunder, *s.* Mearrachd, aimhreidh.
Blunder, *v.* Mearachdaich, dean mearachd, rachd am mearachd.
Blunderbuss, *s.* Scorsa gunna, gunna goirrid, gunna glaic.
Blunderer, *s.* Mearachdair.
Blunderhead, *s.* Baoghlan, umaidh, corracheann.
Blunt, *a.* (*In edge*), maol, neo-gheur, gun fhaobhar; (*in understanding*), maol, baoghalta, gun sgairt, gun mhodh, gun ghéiread; (*in manner*), mi-mhodhail.
Blunt, *v.* Maolaich, dean maol.
Bluntly, *adv.* Gu maol; gu baoghalta; gu mi-mhodhail; gu neo-cheannasach.
Bluntness, *s.* Maolad; maoilead; cion-faobhair; (*of manner*), baoghaltachd, mu mhodhaileachd; neo-spràicealachd; cion-modh.
Blunt-witted, *a.* Maol, baoghalta, neo-gheur.
Blur, *s.* Sàl; spot; smàl; tàir, masladh.
Blur, *v.* Salaich; dubh; maslaich.
Blurred, *a.* Salaichte, dubhta, maslaichte.
Blush, *v.* Rughaich; deargaich; rughaich le nàir. He blushed, *thainig rughadh nàire na ghruaidh.*
Blush, *s.* Rughadh; deirge, rughadh gruaidh.
Bluster, *v.* Dean collaid, dean stairirich; dean rabhd; bragainn; dean ràn (no) toirm, mar ni gaillshion.
Bluster, *s.* Collaid; rabhd; bragainn; spad-fhocal; stairirich, toirm; gaillshion; séidrich; bollsgaireachd.
Blusterer, *s.* Rabhdair; spad-fhoclaiche; glagair; bollsgair.
Bo, *interj.* Bo!
Boar, *s.* Torc; cullach; fiadh-chullach.
Board, *s.* Bord; deile; planc; (*a table*), bord; (*a council*), mòd; cùirt. On board of ship, *air bord luing.* (*Board,* or *boarding*), bord, cairteal.
Board, *v. a.* Bordaich, deilich, planc; plancaich; thoir ionnsuidh; rach a dh'aindeoin air bord luinge; rach air bord; cuir air bhord.
Boarder, *s.* Bordair, fear air bhord; cairtealaiche.
Boarding-school, *s.* Sgoil bùird.
Board-wages, *s.* Diol lòin, diol beathachaidh; na h-urrad airson cheithreannan agus teachd-an-tìr.
Boarish, *a.* Torcach; mucail, mucanta; reasgach; garg, ain-iochdmhor; brùideil; near, niar.
Boast, *s.* Bòsd, bòst; bosdainn; brag, bragainn; spagluinn, uaill, glagaireachd, spaillichd; rabhd; ràite, ràiteachas; gloc; goirsinn.
Boast, *v. n.* Bòsd, bragainn; dean bòsd, dean uaill, (no) spagluinn, dean ràite.
Boaster, *s.* Bòsdair, bragair; spagluinniche, glagair, rabhdair.
Boastful, *a.* Bòsdail; spagluinneach; mor-chuiseach, uaibhreach; ràiteach, spaillichdeach, spaillichdeil, stràiceil; uallach; morghaileach.
Boastingly, *adv.* Gu bòsdail, gu spagluinneach, gu mor chuiseach, gu h-uaibhreach; gu raiteach, gu spaillichdeil, gu stràiceil.
Boat, *s.* Bàt, eithear, sgòth, barc, culaidh, coite, curach; biorlinn; corcan, grodan. A pleasure-boat, *bàt aigheir;* a boatman, *fear aiseig;* a boat-song, *iurram.*
Boatman, *s.* Fear aiseig, fear bàta.
Bob, *v.* Buail, slachduinn; meall, mag, fochaid.
Bob, *s.* Cluigean, crochadan, luinneag.
Bobbin, *s.* Iteachan.
Bob-cherry, *s.* Seorsa cluiche-cloinne.
Bob-tailed, *a.* Cutach; gearr-earbullach.
Bode, *v.* Fàisnich, fastinnich, manaich; taragair, dean fiosachd.
Bodement, *s.* Faisneachd, faistinn, manadh, taragradh, roinnseadh.
Bodice, *s.* Staidhinnean, cliabh boirionnaich.
Bodiless, *a.* Neo-chorporra; spioradail; àileanta; truagh an-fhann.
Bodilessness, *s.* Neo-chorporrachd, spioradaileachd.
Bodily, *adv.* Corporra.
Bodily, *a.* Gu corporra.
Bodkin, *s.* Dealg, dealgan; snàthad tharruing.
Body, *s.* Corp, colluinn; creutair; urr; neach, gin; meall; (*substance*), bith; brigh; (*strength*), spionna, treòir, neart; (*company*), buidheann, bannal. Any body, *urr sam bi, neach air bi;* a little body, *urrag;* a dead body, *corp, cairbh;* a body of infantry, *coisridh;* a body of cavalry, *eachraidh;* somebody, *urr 'gin, neach h-eigin;* strong-bodied, *laidir, colma.*
Bog, *s.* Boglach, cathar; criathrach, criarach; gaorasglach; féith.
Boggle, *v.* Clisg; teagamh; bi an ioma-chomhairle.
Boggler, *s.* Gealtair; teagmhaiche.
Boggy, *a.* Bog, cathrach; féitheach.

Bog-house, *s.* Tigh oiche, tigh beag, tigh cac
Bog-mint, *s* Meismean dearg.
Bog-reed, *s.* Seasgan.
Boil, *v a* and *n.* Bruich, goil; fiuch, greadh, deasaich; cuir air ghoil
Boiled, *part.* and *a* Air ghoil, bruich, bruichte, greadhte, deasaichte. Half-boiled, *leth-bhruich.*
Boiler, *s* Coire, poit; goileadair, *ccatal.*
Boiling, *s.* Goil, air a ghoil
Boisterous, *a* Gailbheach, gaothar, stoirmeil, buaireasach; fuathasach, borb, ard-labhrach.
Boisterously, *adv* Gu gailbheach, gu stoirmeil, gu gaothar, gu borb, gu buaireasach, gu fuathasach, gu h-ard-labhrach
Bold, *a.* Dàna, ladurna; misneachail, duineil, oscarra, laidir, foghainnteach, treubhach.
Bold-faced, *a.* Dana, beag-nàrach.
Boldly, *adv.* Gu dana, gu ladurna, gu misneachail, gu h-oscarra, gu duineil, gu foghainnteach, gu treubhach
Boldness, *s* Dànachd, dànad, dànadas; ladurnachd, misneach, duinealas, cruadal, treubhantas.
Boll, *s* Bolla
Bolster, *s* Adhartan, bodhstair, cluasag, cearchall
Bolster, *v* Cluasagaich, cum suas, cum taobh
Bolt, *s.* Crann; glas; saighead; peilear taimeanaich, ceangal, cuibhreach
Bolt, *v. a.* Crann, glais; fastaidh; leum; criathraich, ridil, † glan.
Bolter, *s* Criathar mìn
Bolus, *s.* Seorsa leigheis
Bomb, *s.* Toirm; gunna toirm-shlige; seorsa gunna mòr as an tilgear steach, do bhaile no dhaighneach sam bi, slige chruinn dearr lan do nithe millteach, a sgàineas agus a mhilleas gach ni a bhios am fagus
Bombard, *v.* Thoir ionnsuidh le toirm-shlige
Bombasin, *s.* Seorsa eudaich.
Bombast, *s* Ard-ghlor, sgleò, spagluinn; gloireàm, ard-ghleadhraich.
Bombast, *a* Ard-ghlorach, spagluinneach, ard-bhriathrach
Bombketch, *s.* Luingeas toirm-shlige, luingeas air nach drùigh toirm-shlige
Bombilation, *s.* Gleadhraich, toirm; fuaim
Bombus, *s* Toirm, fuaim, dranndan
Bonaroba, *s.* Striopach
Bond, *s* Ceangal, cuibhreach, bann, bruid, braighdeanas Bonds, *ceanglaichean, cuibhrichean*, enter into bonds, *rach an urras*
Bond, *a* Tràilleil, daor, am bruid Bond and free, *daor agus saor*
Bondage, *s* Braighdeanas, bruid, traillealachd, daorsadh, daorsa. In bondage, *ann am braighdeanas, ann am bruid*, free from bondage, *saor o bhraighdeanas*
Bondmaid, *s.* Ban-tràill, tràill
Bondman, *s* Daor-oglach, traill-oglach, tràill.
Bondsman, *s* Urras.
Bone, *s* Cnaimh, craimh. What breeds in the bone cannot be taken out of the flesh, *na ghineas sa chraimh, cha d'thoirear as a chraicean*, the back-bone, *cnaimh na droma*, the cheek-bone, *peirceall*, shin-bone, *lurgainn.*
Bonefire, *s.* Teine éibhneis, samhnag, gealbhan.
Boneless, *a* Gun chnaimh; gun chnamhan.
Boneset, *v.* Suidhich cnaimh.
Bonnet, *s* Boineid, bioraid, ceann-chòmhdach, currachd
† **Bonnily**, *adv* Gu boidheach, gu h-aillidh, gu greannar, gu maiseach, gu laoghach, gu dreachmhor; gu suilbhear.
Bonny, *a.* Bòidheach, aillidh, greannar, lurach, maiseach, laoghach, dreachmhor, tlachdmhor, eireachdail, ceanalta; suilbhear.
Bonny clabber, *s* Blathach goirt.
Bony, *a.* Cnamhach, cnaimheach; laidir, garbh, calpanta.
Booby, *s* Umaidh, baoghlan, baothair, burraidh, amadan, asal; cun mòr.
Book, *s* Leabhar Without book, *gun leabhar; air chuimhne, air chridhe.*
Book, *v.* Cuir sios, cuir an leabhar.
Bookbinder, *s.* Leabhar cheanglair, fear cheangal leabhraichean
Bookish, *a* Deidheil air leughadh (no) air leabhraichean
Book-keeper, *s.* Sgriobhair, cléireach, fear ghleidheadh chùnntas.
Book-keeping, *s.* Leabhar-choimhead, an doigh air an gleidhear cunntas.
Book-learned, *a.* Foghluimnte, faoghluimnte.
Bookmate, *s.* Co-sgoilear; co' fhoghlumaiche
Bookseller, *s* Leabhar-lannair, leabhar-reiceadair.
Book-worm, *s.* Reudan leabhair; fear toigheach mu fhoghlum, leughair gun toinisg.
Boom, *s.* Crann sgòid
Boom, *v* Ruith mar luingeis, boch (no) at mar thonn.
Boon, *s* Gibhte, tabhartas; saor-thabhartas, gean maith, tiodhlac; guidhe, (*as a gift*), mar ghibhte, mar thabhartas.
Boon, *a.* Mear, sunntaich, cridheil, aobhach, ait.
Boor, *s* Balaoch, uipear, umaidh, trusdar; baothair, burraidh, bodach
Boorish, *a.* Balaochail, umadail, uipearach, mi-mhodhail, droch-oileanaichte, umaidheach, baothaireach, bodachail.
Boose, *s.* Buaile, buathal.
Boot, *v.* Tairbhich; beartaich, buannaich, dean feum (no) stà.
Boot, *s* Bòt, cosbheairt. Boots, *bòtan*
Boot, *s* Buannachd, coisinn, tairbhe, feum. Something to boot, *rud eigin thuille na còrach.*
Boot-hose, *s.* Mogan; gearr-osan.
Booth, *s.* Bùth, bothag, bothan, loistean, sgailean; mainreach.
Bootless, *a* Gun fheum, gun stà, neo-fheumail, neo-tharbhach, diomhain, faoin.
Booty, *s.* Cobhartach, creich, creach, plundrainn, spùinneadh, spùilleadh.
Bo-peep, *s.* Dìdeagaich
Borable, *a.* So-tholladh.
Borachio, *s* Misgear, meisgear, poitear, searrag leathair.
Borage, *s.* Seorsa plannta, am borrach.
Bordal, *s* Drùis-lann, tigh siùrsachd
Border, *s* Foir, oir, faim, bile, fraidhe; (*of a country*), crioch, iomall; eirthir, (*of a river*), taobh, bruach.
Border, *v.* Faim, foir, iomallaich; ruig. Bordered, *iomallaichte, faimte.*
Borderer, *s.* Criochadair
Bore, *v* Toll
Bore, *s.* Toll; (*of a gun*), cailibhear.
Bore. Faic **Bear.**
Boreal, *a* Tuathach; tuath; gu tuath, mu thuath.
Boreas, *s* Gaoth thuath; tuath-ghaoth.
Boree, *s.* Dannsa francach.
Borer, *s* Tolladair
Born, *part.* Air gin, air bhreith, ginte, beirte. Since I was born, *on rugadh mi*, well-born, *uasal;* base-born, *iosal, dìblidh, diolain;* he was born and brought up in the Highlands, *rugadh is a thogadh e sa Ghaidhealtachd*

Borne, *part.* Giùlainte, iomchairte. Not to be borne, *do-ghiulan, do-iomchar.*

Borough, *s.* Baile-margaidh.

Borrow, *v.* Gabh iasad, gabh coingheall; sir an coingheall; thoir o

Borrower, *s.* Iasadaiche, coingheallaiche, fear a gheibh an coingheall, fear a shireas an coingheall

Boscage, *s* Coille, doire, coillteach.

Bosky, *a.* Coillteach, craobhach, crannach; doilleir, duibh-reach; garbh, atmhor.

Bosom, *s* Uchd, brollach, broilleach, cridhe, gaol; glac The bosom of the deep, *uchd na doimhne*, the wife of my bosom, *bean ma ghaòil*

Bosom, *v.* Gabh san uchd; céil, glac gu gaolach

Boss, *s.* Còp, còpan; tarrag, reultag.

Botanic, *a.* Luibheach

Botanist, *s.* Lusragan

Botany, *s.* Lus-eòlas, luibh-eòlas.

Botch, *s.* Guirean, bucaid, neasgaid bheag; clùtaireachd.

Botch, *v.* Clùt; càirich gu neo-shnàsmhor.

Botcher, *s.* Clutair, creideir.

Botchy, *a.* Clùtach, neo-chearmanta.

Both, *a.* Le chéile, an dithis, an do chuid.

Both, *conj* Faraon, maraon, araon; mar an ceudna, co maith.

Bots, *s* Seorsa duraig a gheibhear ann am mionach eich.

Bottle, *s* Searrag, botal, buideal; boiteal; urach, proisdeal.

Bottle, *v a* Searragaich, botalaich, buidealaich, boitealaich.

Bottle-screw, *s* Sgrobha, bidhis

Bottom, *s.* Iochdar, grunnd, bunait, bun; srath, gleann; doimhne; grunnal; tòin; cearsail, cearslag; tònag; luing At the bottom, *aig a ghrunnd*, the bottom of a mountain, *iochdar* (*no*) *bun monaidh;* from top to bottom, *o cheann gu bun;* a bottom of thread, *cearsail, tònag*

Bottom, *v.* Suidhich, bunaich, grunndaich, socraich.

Bottomless, *a* Gun ghrunnd; gun iochdar The bottomless pit, *slochd an dubh-aigein*

Bough, *s.* Meur, meanglan, meangan

Bought, *pret* and *pass. part* of buy Cheannaich; ceannaichte

Bought, *s.* Tinne, cnòt; cromadh, luib.

Bouillon, *s* Brot, sugh, sùbh, brìgh.

Bounce, *s* Leum, sùrdag, bòsd, bagradh, bagairt, spagluinn, crac, crachd, braidhe.

Bounce, *v.* Leum, sùrdagaich, bagair, dean bòsd, breab

Bouncer, *s.* Bòsdair; fear spagluinneach, fear spaillichdeil. A bouncing lad, *bun balaoich*, a bouncing lass, *bun caile*

Bound, *s.* Iomall, crioch, foir, eir-thir, foir-iomall; ceann, comhar; comharadh, leum, ath-leum The rough bounds, *na garbh-chriochan*, a bound or mill-stone, *clach muilinn*

Bound, *v.* Leum, ath-leum, fri-leum, surdagaich; iomallaich, foir

Bound, *pret.* of bind Ceangailte, cuibhrichte I am bound to do it, *tha e orm a dheanamh.*

Bound, *a* Dol. Whither are you bound? *c'aite a tha thu dol?*

Boundary, *s.* Crioch, foir, iomall, eir-thir, foir-iomall, ceann, banc, cloch-criche.

Boundless, *a* Neo-chriochnach, gun chrioch, gun cheann.

Boundlessness, *s.* Neo-chriochnachd

Bound-stone, *s* Clach criche, clach-chleasachd.

Bounteous, *a.* Fial, fialuidh, fiughantach, còir, tabhartach, tiodhlacach; mathasach; toirbheirteach, oirdheirc.

Bounteousness, *s.* Féile, fialachd, fiùghantachd, mathasachd, toirbheirteas.

Bountiful, *a* Fial, fialaidh, fiùghantach, mathasach, tabhartach, tiodhlacach, toirbheirteach

Bountifully, *adv* Gu fial, gu fialaidh, gu fiùghantach, gu mathasach, gu toirbheirteach

Bountifulness, *s.* Féile, fialachd, fialaidheachd, fiughantachd.

Bounty, *s.* Fiùghantas, tòirbheirteas, gibhte, tabhartas, tiodhlac

Bourn, *s.* Crioch, iomall, foir, allt, sruthan.

Bouse, *v* Òl, poit, dean an-bharr òil.

Bousy, *a* Olar, poiteach, misgeach, meisgeach, geòcach, air mheisge, air an daoraich

Bout, *s* Grathuinn, speal, greis, car; oidhirp, deuchainn A merry bout, *carr sunndach*

Bow, *v.* Lùb, crom, cam, striochd, géill, dean umhlachd, bruth, saruich.

Bow, *s* Bogha; lùb, lùbadh, crom, cromadh, umhladh, striochd, géill A fiddle-bow, *bogha fidhle*, an archer's bow, *bogha-saighde*, a rainbow, *bogha frois*, a bowman, *saighdear, leistear*, a bow-maker, *boghadair*

Bowelless, *a* Ain-iochdmhor, neo-thruacanta, cruadalach, mi-thruacanta

Bowels, *s pl* Innigh, mionach, caomhalachd, truacantachd, cridhe, com My bowels were moved for him, *ghluais m' innigh air a shon, bha mo chridhe fo bhuaireas leis.*

Bower, *s* Bothan samhruidh, sgàilean; suidheagan sgaileach; achdair.

Bowery, *a* Sgàileach, sgàileanach, fionnar, dubharach

Bowl, *s.* Ból, cuach, copan, cop. A little bowl, *bólan.*

Bowl, *s.* Ball

Bow-legged, *a.* Spad-chosach, cam-chasach.

Bowling-green, *s.* Reidhlean

Bow-line, *s.* Sron-teud.

Bowman, *s.* Boghadair, saighdéar

Bowsprit, *s* Crann-uisge, crann-spreòite.

Bowstring, *s* Sreang-bogha

Bowyer, *s.* Saigheadair, boghadair, fear bogha.

Box, *s* Bocsa, cobhan; cisteag, buille, straoidhle, gleadhar Poor's-box, *bocsa nam bochd*

Box, *v* Buail, straoidhil, dornaich.

Boxer, *s* Dornair, dorn-laoch, dorn-churaidh

Boxing, *s* Dornaireachd, caonnag

Boy, *s* Giullan, balachan, òganach, leanabh gille Boys will have toys, *fàr am bi giullain bi gorraiche.*

Boyhood, *s* Oige.

Boyish, *a.* Balachail, leanabaidh, leanabail, leanabanta, socharach, faoin, mar ghiullan.

Boyishly, *adv* Gu balachail, gu leanabail, gu leanabanta, gu socharach, gu faoin

Boyishness, *s.* Balachantachd, leanabantachd, leanabaidheachd, faoinead

Brabble, *s* Tuasaid, iomairt, buaireas, connsach, aimhreit.

Brabble, *v* Connsaich

Brabbler, *s* Tuasaidiche; fear buaireis; fear aimhreite

Brace, *v.* Gramaich, teannaich, ceangail

Brace, *s* Ceangal, bann, stiom.

Brace, *s.* Paidhir, caraid, deise, dithis

Bracelet, *s.* Lamh-fhailc; usgar laimh.

Bracer, *s.* Stiom, ceangal, teannachair, giort, ni sam bi a theannaicheas (no) a neartaicheas

BRACHIAL, *a.* Gairdeanach.

BRACHYGRAPHY, *s.* Gearr-sgriobhadh, sgriobhadh goirrid.

BRACK, *s.* Bearn, briseadh.

BRACKISH, *a.* Saillte, leth-char saillte; leth-char goirt.

BRAD, *s.* Tarrag gun bhonait; tairnean urlair.

BRAG, *v.* Bragainn, bòst, bòsd, dean uaill, dean spagluinn, dean maoitheadh, dean ràiteachas.

BRAG, *s.* Brag, bòsd; uaill, raiteachas; seorsa cluiche air chairtibh.

BRAGGADOCIO, *s.* Bragair, bòsdair, ràite; fear spagluinneach; fear spad-fhoclach.

BRAGGART, BRAGGER, *s.* Bragair, fear bòsdail, raite; spagluinniche, spad-fhoclair.

BRAID, *v.* Figh, dualaich, pleat.

BRAID, *s.* Dual, pleat.

BRAIN, *s.* Eanachainn, eanachaill; tuigse, inntinn.

BRAIN, *v.* Cuir an t-eanachainn a; marbh.

BRAINISH, *a.* Borb; brais, cas.

BRAINLESS, *a.* Baoghalta; maol; amaideach, lag, faoin.

BRAIN-PAN, *s.* Claigeann, claigionn, plub.

BRAIN-SICK, *a.* Tinn san tuigse; eutrom, gaoithe; gòrach; thar chéill.

BRAIN-SICKNESS, *s.* Tinneas tuigse.

BRAIT, *s.* Daoimeau neo-mhìnichte.

BRAKE, *s.* Cliath mhòr; droighionnach; sgitheach; seicil; amar fuinidh; raineach; cabstar.

BRAKY, *a.* Biorach, deilgneach, garbh.

BRAMBLE, *s.* Preas nam smeur; preas nan suigheag. A bramble-berry, *smeurag.*

BRAN, *s.* Garbhan, càth a chruithneachd; bràn.

BRANCH, *s.* Meur, meanglan, geug; sliochd; cabar.

BRANCH, *v.* Sgaoil, meur-sgaoil; sgiamhaich.

BRANCHER, *s.* Geugair.

BRANCHLESS, *a.* Gun mheur, gun mheanglan; gun gheug, gun sliochd; lom.

BRAND, *v.* Comharaich le iarunn teth, loisg.

BRAND, *s.* Comhar, tàir-chomhar; mi-chliù; aithinne; comhar cluais.

BRANDED, *p. part.* Loisgte le h-iarunn; sgainnilichte; maslaichte.

BRANDISH, *v.* Crath.

BRANDY, *s.* Branndi, deoch laidir.

BRANGLE, *v.* Connsaich, dean comh-strigh, dean brionglaid.

BRANGLE, *s.* Connsachadh, comh-stri; brionglaid, aimhreit.

BRANK, *s.* Seorsa cruithneachd.

BRANNY, *a.* Garbhanach; cochullach.

BRASIER, *s.* Umhadair; ceard-umha. Brasiers, *umhadairean.*

BRASIERY, *s.* Umhadaireachd; obair umha.

BRASIL, *s.* Fiodha a ni dath dearg.

BRASS, *s.* Umha, prais.

BRASSY, *a.* Umhach, praiseach.

BRAT, *s.* Garrach; ablach; focal tàireil.

BRAVADO, *s.* Bòsd, brag, bragainn, bragaireachd, spagluinn; maoitheadh; uaill; bagradh.

BRAVE, *a.* Misneachail, foirteil, gaisgeil; fearail, dàn; dùlanach; cruadalach, tabhachdach, foghainteach; faobhach, mòr-chuiseach, treubhanta.

BRAVE, *s.* Cùraidh, laochan; baoth-churaidh; bòsd, brag.

BRAVE, *v.* Dulanaich, thoir dùlan, maoidh.

BRAVELY, *adv.* Gu misneachail, gu gaisgeil, gu fearail, gu dàn, gu dùlanach, gu cruadalach, gu tabhachdach, gu foghainteach, gu faobhach.

BRAVERY, *s.* Misneach, gaisge, fearalas, mòr-chuis, cruadal, cùrantachd, tàbhachd, spiorad, treubhantas; tréine.

BRAVO, *s.* Mortair, riadh-mhortair.

BRAWL, *v.* Dean brionglaid (no) tuaireap; dean cànran, dean tuaiseid, dean comh-strì.

BRAWL, *v.* Brionglaid, tuasaid, comh-stri, aimhreit, cànran, caoirean.

BRAWLER, *s.* Fear tuaireapach, fear tuasaideach, fear tuaiseid, fear aimhreite.

BRAWLING, *a.* Brionglaideach, tuasaideach; cànranach, caoireanach.

BRAWN, *s.* Cruaidh-fheòil tuirc; gairdean; calpa; meud; neart; torc; cullach.

BRAWNINESS, *s.* Neart; treise; spionnadh; cruadalas; culpantas.

BRAWNY, *a.* Neartmhor, laidir, gramail; feitheach, calpach, cruaidh-ghreimeach.

BRAY, *s.* Rann asail, langan, raoichd, beuc, buireadh.

BRAY, *v.* Pronn, bruth; ràn; beuc, raoichd.

BRAZE, *v.* Càirich (no) tàth le h-umha; praisich, umhaich.

BRAZEN, *a.* Praise; praiseil; umhach, cruaidh; dàn.

BRAZEN-FACED, *a.* Dàna, beagnàrach, ladurna, danarra.

BRAZENNESS, *s.* Praiseileachd; beagnarrachd; dannaras.

BREACH, *s.* Beum, bealach; briseadh, bearn; fosgladh; srachd, connsachadh.

BREAD, *s.* Aran; beathachadh, biadh, lòn.

BREAD-CORN, *s.* Coirce; siol do 'n deanar aran.

BREADTH, *s.* Leud.

BREAK, *v.* Bris, sgealb; crac, sgoilt. Break them to shivers, *bris iad nam bloighdean;* break out, *bris a mach;* break up, *sguir; sgaòil;* break with him, *cuir a mach air.*

BREAK, *s.* Fosgladh; briseadh; bealach, bearn; sgealbadh, sgoltadh, fàilneachadh.

BREAKER, *s.* Sumain; marannan, bris-thonn, tuinn bhuaireaseach a slachdainn sgeir no oitir.

BREAKFAST, *s.* Bris-throsg, diot, diot bheag, biadh maidne, greim maidne, ceud-thomhailt.

BREAM, *s.* Seorsa éisg.

BREAST, *s.* Uchd, brollach, broilleach; cliabh; langan; coguis, cridhe; cioch. On the breast, *air chiche.*

BREAST-BONE, *s.* Cliathan.

BREAST-HIGH, *a.* Aird-uchd; cho ard ris a bhroilleach, gu ruig an uchd.

BREAST-KNOT, *s.* Uchd-riomhadh.

BREASTPLATE, *s.* Uchd eididh.

BREASTWORK, *s.* Obair uchd.

BREATH, *s.* Anail; beath; (*of wind*), deò, feochan.

BREATHE, *v. n.* Séid, tarruing anail; (*rest*), leig d' anail, gabh fois.

BREATHING, *s.* Seideadh; clochar, tarruing analach; urnuigh dhiomhair, fois, fosadh.

BREATHLESS, *a.* Gun anail, gun deo, marbh; tosd; balbh; as an anail, an cabhaig.

BREECH, *s.* Màs, tòin; brigis, briogais; earr gunna, stoc gunna.

BREECHES, *s.* Briogais, brigis, briogan.

BREED, *v.* Gin, àraich; beir, siolaich; tog; tionnsgain.

BREED, *s.* Siol, sliochd; àlach; seorsa, silidh; luchd, teaghlach, bròd.

BREEDING, *s.* Beus, modh, oilean; ionnsachadh; eolas teagasg; gnathachadh; beathachadh.

BREEZE, *s.* Tabhul.

BREEZE, s. Gaoth, soirbheas, feochan, drothan, osag, osunn, oiteag, fo'ghaoth.
BREEZY, a. Gaothar, fionnar, osagach, oiteagach, drothanach.
BRETHREN, s. Braithrean.
BREVIARY, s. Leabhar urnuigh.
BREVIATE, s. Giorrachadh, as-tharruing; cunntas gearr.
BREVIATURE, s. Giorrachadh.
BREVITY, s. Giorrad, aithghearrad.
BREW, v. Tog, dean togail; bruith; dealbh ni; tionsgain, cnuasaich.
BREWER, s. Grùdair, fear togalach, cormach, cuirmeach.
BREWHOUSE, s. Tigh-togalach.
BREWIS, s. Brathas.
BRIBE, s. Cumha, briob, duais eucoir, duais claonaidh.
BRIBE, v. Briob, ceannaich le duais.
BRIBER, s. Briobair, briobadair.
BRIBERY, s. Briob, cumha; duais bhratha; briobaireachd.
BRICK, s. Clach-chreadha; criadh-chlach; fòid chreadha; builionn.
BRICK-DUST, s. Criadh-dhusladh, criadh-dhùs, criadh-dhuslach.
BRICK-KILN, s. Uamh-chreadha; àth chreadh-chlach; àth chlacha creadha.
BRICKLAYER, s. Criadh-chlachair.
BRICKMAKER, s. Criadh-losgair.
BRIDAL, a. Pòsaidh; pòsach.
BRIDAL, s. Pòsadh; banais; maraiste.
BRIDE, s. Bean bainnse.
BRIDE-CAKE, s. Bonnach bainnse; aran bainnse; bonnach bean (mna) bainnse.
BRIDEGROOM, s. Fear bainnse.
BRIDEMAID, s. Gruagach bean (mna) bainnse; maighdeann, bean choimheadachd.
BRIDEMAN, s. Fleasgach fir bainnse.
BRIDEWELL, s. Gainntir; tigh smachdachaidh; carcar, priosan, rioghlann, toll buth.
BRIDGE, s. Drochaid, drochaite; uachdar na sròn.
BRIDLE, s. Srian; aghastar; smachd; ceannsal.
BRIDLE, v. Srian; smachdaich; ceannsaich; cum stigh; stiùir.
BRIDLE-BIT, s. Mireanach.
BRIDLE-CUTTER, s. Dioghladair.
BRIDLE-HAND, s. Lamh sréine.
BRIEF, a. Goirrid; gearr, athghearr, cuimear.
BRIEF, s. Gearr-fhoirm; gearr-sgriobhadh.
BRIEFLY, adv. Gu gearr, gu goirrid, gu h-aithghearr.
BRIEFNESS, s. Ath-ghearrad, ath-ghoirrid, giurrad.
BRIER, s. Dreas, dris; crioch. Out of the brier into the thorns, *as an dris anns an droighionn.*
BRIERY, s. Dreasach, driseach, deilgneach; criochar.
BRIGADE, s. Buidheann; earann shaighdearan; bannal, bragàd.
BRIGADIER, s. Ard-chaiptean, ard-chaptan, ceannard feodhna, ceannard slògh, ard-cheannard airm; ceann-feadhna, ceann-feodhna.
BRIGAND, s. Creachadair, spùinneadair, robair; meirleach.
BRIGANDINE, BRIGANTINE, s. Long da chrann; lùireach mhàilleach.
BRIGHT, a. Dealrach, dearrsach, soilleir, soillseach, glan, lannradh; drilinneach; liobhta, liobhte; eanachainneach, inntinneach, tapaidh; toinisgeil.
BRIGHTEN, v. a. Soillsich, dearrsaich, glan, soilleirich, liobh; fàs soilleir, fàs suilbhear.
BRIGHTLY, adv. Gu dealrach, gu dearrsach, gu soilleir, gu lonradh, gu liobhte; gu h-inntinneach; gu h-eanchainneach.
BRIGHTNESS, s. Dealradh, dearrsadh, soillse; soilleireachd; lonnraichead; glòir; tapachd; geur-thoinisg; géire géiread.
BRILLIANCY, s. Lannaireachd, lonnraichead, dealradh, dearrsadh, soillse.
BRILLIANT, a. Lannaireach, dealrach, soillseach.
BRILLIANT, s. Soillsean; buaidh chlach.
BRIM, s. Beul, bile, oir, foir; bruach uisge; taobh tobair; iomall.
BRIMFUL, a. Lomlàn, dearr-làn.
BRIMMER, s. Cuach lomlàn.
BRIMSTONE, s. Pronnusg, pronnasg, grunnastal, pronaistear.
BRIMSTONY, a. Pronnusgach, pronnasgach, grunnstalach.
BRINDED, a. Stiallach, riabhach, riathach.
BRINE, s. Sàil; muir, uisg mara; deur.
BRING, v. Tabhair, thabhair, thoir, beir. Bring to pass, *thoir gu criche;* bring forth, *beir; cuir lathair;* bring off, *thoir dheth;* bring over, *thoir thairis; iompaich;* bring under, *ceannsaich.*
BRINGER, s. Fear breith; fear giùlain.
BRINISH, a. Sàileanta; salainneach; saillte, goirt.
BRINK, s. Foir, oir, taobh, bruach, bile, fraidhe. The brink of a river, *bruach aimhne;* on the brink of a precipice, *air fior fhaobhar creig;* on the brink of death, *ris a bhàs.*
BRISK, a. Briosg, brisg, mear; smiorail, smearail, beò; beathail, beothail; ealamh, clis, tapaidh.
BRISKET, s. Brollach, broilleach.
BRISKLY, adv. Gu brisg, gu mear, gu smearail, gu beò, gu beothail, gu h-ealamh, gu clis, gu tapaidh.
BRISKNESS, s. Beothalachd, smearalas, smeoralas, tapachd; graidead.
BRISTLE, s. Frioghan; greann, colg; calg.
BRISTLE, v. Frioghanaich, greannaich.
BRISTLY, a. Frioghanach; greannach; feargach; colgach; rómach.
BRITISH, a. Breatunnach.
BRITTLE, a. Brisg; breoite; lag; so-bhriseadh.
BRITTLENESS, s. Brisgead, maothalachd.
BROACH, s. Bior; leug, seud; broiste, bràiste.
BROACH, v. Bris air, fosgail; leig ruithe.
BROACHED, part. Briste, fosgailte.
BROACHER, s. Fosgaldair; tionnsgnair, tionnsgnadair; ùghdar.
BROAD, a. Leathann; farsuing; mòr; fosgailte; drabasta. A mile broad, *mìl air leud.*
BROAD-CLOTH, s. Aodach leathann.
BROADNESS, s. Leud, farsuingeachd.
BROAD-SHOULDERED, a. Slinneanach.
BROADSIDE, s. Taobh luing; lod a gach gunna air taobh luinge.
BROADSWORD, s. Claidheamh mòr, claidheamh leathann, claideamh da laimh.
BROADWISE, adv. An comhar a thaoibh.
BROCADE, s. Siod air a ghreusadh.
BROCADED, a. Greusta, greusta mar shiod.
BROCCOLI, s. Seorsa càil.
BROCK, s. Broc, brochd; taoghan.
BROCKET, s. Mang, fiadh òg.
BROGUE, s. Brog Ghàileach; bròg-éill; droch bhlas cainnt.
BROIDER, v. Greus.
BROIDERER, s. Greusair, greusadair.

BROIDERY, s Greusadaireachd, gréis; greus-obair.

BROIL, s. Tuasaid, tabaid, caonnag, buaireas, streapaid; droch cord; iorgail, aimhreite, *mob*

BROIL, v Ròist; bruich, grisg.

BROKE, *pret.* of break. Bhris, spealg, bhruan

BROKEN, *part* Briste, spealgta, bruanta.

BROKENHEARTED, a. Brischridhcach, tuirseach, trom.

BROKENNESS, s. Breoiteachd; fior-aithreachas

BROKER, s. Faithilteur; fear a ni gnothuch airson neach sam bi

BROKERAGE, s Tuarasdal faithilteir.

BRONZE, s Umha, prais

BROOCH, s Broiste, braiste, seud, leug.

BROOD, v. Gur, guir, suidh air uibhean; beachd-smuainich; bi-bheachdaich

BROOD, s. Gur, àlach; siol, bròd.

BROODY, a Torrach, siolach

BROOK, s Allt, alltan; sruth, sruthan; bùrn.

BROOK, v Giulain, fulaing; fuluing; meal.

BROOK-LIME, s Lochal

BROOM, s Bealuidh, bealaidh; sguab, sguab urlair Common broom, *giolcach sleibhe.*

BROOMSTAFF, s Cas sguabaich, maide-sguabaich.

BROOMSTICK, s. Cas sguabaich, maide sguabaich

BROOMY, a Bealuidhcach, lan bealaidh, mar bhealaidh

BROTH, s Brot, eunbhrigh, eunbhruithe, sùgh feola, bràcan

BROTHEL, s Drùth lann, tigh siursaich, tigh siùrsachais

BROTHER, s Brathair, dearbh-bhràthair

BROTHERHOOD, s Brathaireachas, brathaireachd, comunn

BROTHERLY, *adv.* Bathaircil

BROUGHT Faic BRING

BROW, s. Clar aodainn, aodann, eudann; aghaidh, cnuaichd, mala, maladh, rosg, (*edge of a high place*), faobhar, bruach

BROW-BOUND, a Crùnta

BROWBEAT, v Nàraich, buadhaich, faigh lamh 'n uachdar

BROWN, a Donn

BROWNISH, a Leth-char donn, iardhonn, donnach

BROWNNESS, s. Donnad, duinnead

BROWN STUDY, s. Dubh-smuaine, dubh-bheachd, smuaintean airsnealach

BROWSE, v Bileagaich; creim, creim preasarnach, thig beò air preasarnach no air duilleagan

BROWSE, s Bileagan craoibh, preasail, preasarnach

BROW-SICK, a. Tinn, dubhach, mi-chridheil

BRUISE, v Pronn, bruth, mìn-phronn, greidh

BRUISE, s Pronnadh, bruthadh, breothadh, ciurradh

BRUISER, s Pronnadair, bruthadair, dornair

BRUISING, s Pronnadh, bruthadh; caonnag

† BRUIT, s Bruidheann; fabhradh

BRUMAL, a Geamhrail

BRUNETTE, s Nigheann donn

BRUNT, s. Buille, straoidhle, ionnsuidh

BRUSH, s Sguab; sguabachan, sguab aodaich; *bruis*

BRUSH, v Sguab, *bruisinn.* Brush away, *sguab air falbh*

BRUSHER, s Sguabair.

BRUSHWOOD, s Frith-choille, preasarnach, dlù-phreasarnach, crionach, rasan.

BRUSHY, a. Molach, ròmach, frioghanach, giobach, greannach

BRUSTLE, v. Crac, dean starbhanaich

BRUTAL, a. Brùideil, béisteil; salach; mucail; borb, garg, ain-iochdmhor, allmharra, neo-thoinisgeil; umaidheach, miolach; gràineal.

BRUTALITY, s. Brùidealachd, buirbe; ain-iochd; allmharachd.

BRUTALIZE, v. Dean all-mhara, dean fiadhaich.

BRUTALLY, *adv.* Gu brùideil; gu borb, gu garg; gu h-ain-iochdmhor.

BRUTE, s Brùid, ainmhidh, beathach, beothach, béist.

BRUTE, a Brùideil, ainmhidheach, béisteil, fiadhaich, borb, ain-iochdmhor, allmharra, neo-thoinisgeil, aineolach.

BRUTISH, a Brùideil, béisteil, borb, fiadhaich; neo-thuigseach, allmharra, aineolach; feolmhor; salach; gràineil.

BRUTISHNESS, s. Brùidealachd, béistealachd; umaidheachd; buirbe; ain-iochdmhoireachd

BUBBLE, s Builgean, bolg, guc, gucag, buiccan, suilleag; mealladh.

BUBBLE, v Meall.

BUBBLER, s. Mealltair; ceabhchdair.

BUBO, s. Drùth-neasgaid

BUBONOCELE, s Mamsioc

BUCK, s Boc, boc earba, damh, damh-feidh, cull-bhoc

BUCK, v Bùir, dàir, reithich

BUCKET, s Cuinneag; cur-ghalan, stòb.

BUCKLE, s Bucal; clasp, cnaire; cuailean

BUCKLE, v Bucal, buclaich; clasp, cuaileanaich, crom, lùb; géill

BUCKLER, s Sgiath

BUCKLER, v Eid le sgiath, dion, cum suas.

BUCKRAM, s Leathar buic, boc leathar

BUCKTHORN, s Ramh-dhroighionn; sgitheach; preas deilgneach

BUCOLIC, s Bua-choilleag, bo-choilleag, oran buachaill, coilleag

BUD, s Urfhàs, fiùran, maothan; gineamhuinn, gineag, boinean, gucag

BUD, v Gin; thig fo urfhàs, thig fo dhuille

BUDGE, v Gluais, carraich, glidich; imich aong

BUDGER, s Gluasair, glideachair.

BUDGET, s Balg, bolg, poc, maileid, mach; taisgeach, spriuinhachan, stòr, stòras

BUFF, s Croicionn bo-allaidh, craiceann fiadh-thairbhe

BUFFALO, s Bo-alluidh, tarbh-alluidh, agh allaidh, fiadhtharbh

BUFFET, s. Boiseag, sgailleag, gleadhar, seorsa àmraidh.

BUFFET, v a Buail, dornaich; slachdainn

BUFFETER, s Dornair; slachdair; buailtear.

BUFFETING, s. Bualadh; (*of waves*), dosraich.

BUFFLE, s Faic BUFFALO

BUFFLEHEADED, a Poll-cheannach, ploc-cheannach; amaideach, baoth

BUFFOON, s. Cleasaiche, fear aincheirt, sgeigear, baoth chleasaiche

BUFFOONERY, s Ain-cheart, sgeigearachd, baoth-chleasachd.

BUG, s Seorsa miol

BUGBEAR, s Bòcan, cuis eagail, eaga. meallta.

BUGLE, s Dubhtach; stoc; tromp

BUGLOSS, s Boglus.

BUILD, v Tog.

BUILDER, s Clachair; fear togalach

BUILDING, s Tigh, aitreabh; togail

BULB, s Meacan, meallan; bun; stoc

BULBOUS, a Meacanach, meallanach, plucanach; bunach, stocach.

Bulge, *v.* Fuasgail; brùchd mach; leig stigh uisg mar ni luing.
Bulk, *s.* Tomad, tomald, meud; domhlas, dùmhlas; buc, buchd; sùlt; mor-chuid, garbh-chuid.
Bulkhead, *s.* Claraidh (no) sgealan ann an luing.
Bulkiness, *s.* Tomald, tomad, meud; tomaldachd, tomadachd, meudachd, domhalachd, dùmhalachd.
Bulky, *a.* Mòr, tomadach, tomaldach, domhail, dumhail, bucail, sultmhor.
Bull, *s.* Tarbh; (*in the popish church*), achd Pàpa; (*in speech*), mearachd; (*in a scriptural sense*), namhaid garg, fuilteach. A two-year-old bull, *dartan.*
Bullace, *s.* Airneag, bulaistear.
Bullbaiting, *s.* Conairt tharbh; cath eadar tarbh is coin; coineart.
Bull-beef, *s.* Tairbh-fheòil.
Bull-calf, *s.* Laogh firionn; dorcan; umaidh, baoghlan; sgonn.
Bulldog, *s.* Cù feoladair, madadh, mastaidh; tarbhmhadadh.
Bullet, *s.* Peileir.
Bulletin, *s.* Nuaidheachd cùirt.
Bull-eyed, *a.* Lan-shuileach; sgeannach.
Bullhead, *s.* Sgonn gun tolnisg, umaidh, baoghlan.
Bullion, *s.* Airgiod no òr neo-chùinte.
Bullition, *s.* Goil.
Bullock, *s.* Damh; tarbh òg.
Bully, *s.* Bragair, bòlsgair, maoidhear; dorn-churaidh; fear gleadhrach, fear tuasaideach; rabhdair.
Bully, *v.* Bragainn, maoidh, dean straic, bagair; goir.
Bulrush, *s.* Luachair, cuilc, buigneach, boigean, bog luachair, bog bhuinne.
Bulwark, *s.* Badhann, babhunn; daighneach; dion; duncatha, †girt.
Bulwark, *v.* Daingnich, dion.
Bum, *s.* Deireadh, ceann deiridh, tòin.
Bumbailiff, *s.* Maor-righ.
Bump, *s.* Cnap, meall; at; buille; straoidhle; gleadhar, gleothar, gleog.
Bumper, *s.* Sgailc, glucaid, gloine dearr-làn.
Bumpkin, *s.* Balaoch, umaidh, bromanach, ploighisg, gleosgair, sgleamhraidh.
Bun, *s.* Seorsa arain milis.
Bunch, *s.* Meall, cnap; baguid; buinnse; poslach; snuim; cluigean; gas; dos; borr.
Bunch, *v.* At; baguidich; buinnsich.
Bunchbacked, *a.* Crotach; crom-shlinneanach.
Bunchy, *a.* Cnapach; baguideach, buinnseach; cluigeanach, gasach, dosach.
Bundlé, *s.* Trusgan, ceanglachan, glacan, glaclach; aslachan, achlasan; paiggean, buinnseal, buindeal, braghairt.
Bundle, *v.* Trus, ceangail suas.
Bung, *s.* Stoipeal, staipeal, ploc, pluc, arcan buideil.
Bung, *v.* Stoipealaich, ploc, plocaich.
Bunghole, *s.* Beul mòr, beul.
Bungle, *v.* Mill; dean gu neo-chearmanta, dean gu cearbach; càirich; clùd.
Bungle, *s.* Tuafaireachd.
Bungled, *a.* Millte.
Bungler, *s.* Tuafair; fear ceirde gun eireachdas, bunglair, fear cearbach, amaran.
Bunter, *s.* Stràill, boirionnach salach, siùrsach.
Bunting, *s.* Gealag bhuachair, gealbhan sgiobuill.
Buoy, *s.* Fleodruinn; bolladh stiùraidh.
Buoy, *v.* Cum an uachdar, cum air an t-snamh, plodaich.
Buoyancy, *s.* Plodaireachd, plodadh, air snamh.
Buoyant, *a.* Plodach, air an t-snamh, air snamh; eutrom, snamhach.
Bur, *s.* Dearcan suiriche, gioban suiriche; cliadan.
Burden, *s.* Eallach, uallach, eire, luchd; lòd; trom, truime, eirbheirt, beirt, gusdal; (*of a song*), luinneag.
Burden, *v.* Tromaich, luchdaich, eallaich; muirnich.
Burdensome, *a.* Trom, luchdmhor, luchdar, cudthromach; cruaidh; do-ghiùlan, doilghiosach.
Burdock, *s.* Mac-an-dogha.
† **Burg**, *s.* Borg, burg; tigh; baile maigaidh.
Burganet, *s.* Seorsa clogaide, bioraid.
Burgh, *s.* Baile margaidh.
Burgher, *s.* Bùirdeasach, saoranach; burgair; tamhaich baile margaidh.
Burglar, *s.* Meirleach, gaduiche, goidiche, tigh-spuinneadair.
Burglary, *s.* Meirle, gaduidheachd; robaireachd, spùilinn, tigh-spùinneadaireachd.
Burgomaster, *s.* Ard-bhùirdeasach, ard-bhurgair, ceannbhurgair.
Burial, *s.* Adhlac, adhlacadh, tiodhlac, tiodhlacadh; torradh; ollanachadh, tlachdadh.
Burier, *s.* Adhlacair, tiodhlacair; torradair.
Burlesque, *v.* Dean fanaid, dean sgeig, cuir air ioladh, mag, fochaid.
Burlesque, *s.* Cainnt bhallsgach, fearas chuideachd, fanaid, sgeige; magadh, ioladh, abhachd.
Burlesque, *a.* Cridheil; sunntach, abhachdach; iongantach, neonach.
Burliness, *s.* Meud, tomad, sult; farum, stairn; glòrmas, gleòrmas.
Burly, *a.* Mòr, tomadach, sultmhor, dòmhail.
Burn, *v.* Loisg, cuir ri theine, sgaillt, doth, gread, tiormaich, seargaich.
Burn, *s.* Losgadh, losg, sgaillt, dothadh, doth, greadadh.
Burnet, *s.* Loisgean.
Burning, *s.* Teine, leus; lasair, losgadh, lasadh, deargiasadh, lasarra.
Burning, *a.* Teth, loisgeach; teinntidh, dian-theth, deothasach.
Burning-glass, *s.* Teine losgaidh.
Burnish, *v.* Lòinnrich, grinnich, glan, soilleirich; sgùr; liobh, liobhraich.
Burnisher, *s.* Loinnreachair, glanadair, liobhadair, sgùradair.
Burnt, *a.* Loisgte; seargta; teth.
Burr, *s.* Leapag na cluais.
Burrow, *v.* Toll, toll coinein; †burg; baile margaidh.
Burrow, *v.* Toll, cladhaich.
Bursar, *s.* Bòrsair.
Burse, *s.* Tigh malairt; bòrsadh.
Burst, *v.* Sgàin, sgoilt; sgag.
Burst, *s.* Sgaineadh, sgoltadh, grad-bhriseadh; sgag.
Burstenness, *s.* Mam-sioc.
Burt, *s.* Seorsa eisg.
Burthen. Faic **Burden.**
Bury, *v.* Adhlaic; cuir san uaigh, cuir fo 'n talamh, cuir san ùir, folaich; ceil; tiodhlaic. Buried, *adhlaicte.*
Bush, *s.* Preas, dos, gas, goiscan, gasan, meanglan; tom.
Bushel, *s.* Ceithreamh, ceathramh, feorlan, mioch.
Bushy, *a.* Preasach, dosach, gasach, meanglanach, duslu-

ingeach, rasach; (*as hair*), dualach, bachlach, bachlagach, coisreagach, mobach.
BUSILY, *adv.* Gu cabhagach, gu gniomhach; gu bisidh
BUSINESS, *s.* Gnothach; gniomh; cuis; ceaird; obair; rud A man of business, *fear gnothuich*, he will do his business (destroy), *foghnaidh e dha.*
BUSKIN, *s* Leth-bhòt, seorsa osain.
BUSKY, *a.* Coillteach, craobhach.
BUSS, *s.* Pòg, pòigean, pogan.
BUSS, *v a* Pog
BUSS, *s* Curach, eithear, bat iasgaich.
BUST, *s* Dealbh, dealbh aghaidh, cruth aghaidh; dealbh cinn agus guaille, cairbh-theine.
BUSTARD, *s* Coileach Turcach
BUSTLE, *s* Othail, uinidh, uinich, buaireas, iorghuill, cabhag, obair, iomairt, sgairt, deanadas.
BUSTLE, *v* Iomairt, oibrich; dean iomairt.
BUSTLER, *s* Fear sgairteil, fear deanadach, duine iorghuilleach
BUSY, *a* Gniomhach, deanadach, bisidh, dichiollach, meachranach, rudach, leamh.
BUSY-BODY, *s.* Biodanach, briollsgair; neach a ghabhas gnothuch ri rud nach buin dà, lonag; sgileam.
BUT, *conj* Ach, mur, gidheadh, fathast. But for, *mur bhiodh*, but it, *ach ma*, but seldom, *ach ainmig*, but for him, *mur bhiodh esan*
BUT, *s.* Crioch, iomall, (*a measure*), butta, da thogsaid, tunna, (*a mark*), comhar, (*of a gun*), bun, stoc, ceann. One on whom a jest is passed, *ball abhachd.*
BUT, *v.* Put, purr, mu'c, sath, stailc.
BUTCHER, *s.* Feoladair, brothair
BUTCHER, *v.* Marbh, cosgair, casgair, reub, beubanaich, mort, àraich
BUTCHERLY, *a.* Maibhtach, cruaidh-chridheach, borb, aniochdmhor, fuilteach.
BUTCHERY, *s* Feoladaireachd, tigh brothaidh.
BUTCHER'S BROOM, *s.* Calg bhrudhainn.
BUT-END, *s.* Ceann, stoc, bun
BUTLER, *s* Buidealair, barra-dhriopair.
BUTLERSHIP, *s* Buidealaireachd.
BUTTER, *s* Im, caiteag, paiteag Fresh butter, *breachdan.*
BUTTER, *v* Sliob le im
BUTTERBUMP, *s.* Stearnal.
BUTTERFLY, *s.* Dealbhan dé, dealman dé, dealan de, dearbadan, feileagan
BUTTERMILK, *s* Blàthach, bainne goirt, bainne muighe.
BUTTERTOOTH, *s.* Clàr-fhiacal
BUTTERWORT, *s.* Bodan measgain.
BUTTERY, *a.* Imeach, bogar, reamhar.
BUTTERY, *s.* Tigh bainne; pantraidh
BUTTOCK, *s.* Màs, tiugh a mhàis, ceòs, to nan, gead, buisgin, tòin, ceann deiridh.
BUTTON, *s.* Cnap, putan.
BUTTON, *v.* Putanaich.
BUTTON, *s.* Seorsa eisg mara
BUTTONHOLE, *s.* Toll cnaip, toll putain.
BUTTRESS, *s* Bonn, bunachur, tarrabhalladh, prop, taic.
BUXOM, *a.* Meamnach, eutrom, beothail, subhach, macnusach, leannanach, mear.
BUXOMLY, *adv* Gu meamnach, gu h-eutrom, gu beothail, gu subhach, gu macnusach, gu leannanach
BUXOMNESS, *s.* Meamnachd, beothalachd, subhachas, macnusachd, leannanachd, mire.
BUY, *v* Ceannaich, ruaichill.
BUYER, *s.* Ceannachair, fear ceannachaidh.
BUZZ, *v* Dean diurrasan; dranndanaich; dean siusan, (no) durdan, dean cronan, crònan, crònanaich, dean torman
BUZZ, *s* Diurasan, dranndan, siusan, durdan, durdail, cronan, torman, monmhor, borbhan
BUZZARD, *s.* Seobhag, clamhan; siadair, sgonn-bhalach, beilbhean ruadh.
BY, *prep.* Le, tre, trid, an deigh, air, a réir; (*near*), fogas air, laimh ri, dlu do; (*past*), seachad, seach. By ourselves, *leinn féin*, by some means, *air sheòl eigin, air mhodh eigin*, by all means, *air na h-uile cor*, by chance, *a thaobh tubaist*, by what means, *ciod an doigh*, by degrees, *chuid is a chuid, uigh air an uigh*, by little and little, *chuid is a chuid*, by heart, *air chuimhne, air chridhe;* by such a day, *air cheann leithid so làth*, by and by, *a chlisge*, by the by, *le so;* by the way, *air an rathad; le so*, by day, *an àithne an là*, day by day, *gach dolach là;* by the river's side, *ri taobh na h-aibhne;* drop by drop, *diotag air dhiotag*, by the time he arrived, *air cheann da teachd*
BY-AND-BY, *adv.* A chlisge, an ceann ghoirrid; an cais, gu goirrid
BY-END, *s* Gnothach diomhair.
BYLAW, *s* Frith-lagh
BYNAME, *s.* Frith-ainm, leth-ainm.
BYPATH, *s* Frith rod, leth rod, leth-rathad
BYROAD, *s.* Frith rod, leth-rod, leth rathad, frith-rathad, crois-shlighe
BYSTANDER, *s* Fear amhairc.
BYSTREET, *s* Frith-shraid, sraid-leth-taoibh
BYWORD, *s.* Gnath-fhocal, leth-fhocal, for-fhocal.

C.

C, An treas litir do 'n Aibideal.
CAB, *s* Tomhas Eabhrach a chumas tri bodaich Altainnach
CABAL, *s* Eolas diomhair nan Eabhrach; beul-aithris nan Iudhach, coinneamh dhiomhair
CABAL, *v* Cum coinneamh dhiomhair
CABALIST, *s* Ollamh Judhach, aon eolach air beul-aithris nan Iudhach.
CABALISTICAL, *a* Diomhair.
CABARET, *s.* Tigh òsda, tigh lionna; tigh mòr.
CABBAGE, *v.* Goid piseagan, (no) mireannan aodaich.
CABBAGE, *s* Càl cearslach, fuigheal aodaich
CABBAGE-TREE, *s* Seorsa craoibh.
CABBAGE-WORM, *s* Durag chàil, bradag chàil
CABIN, *s* Seomar luing, lantair, bùth, bothag; caban, buailt.
CABINET, *s* Cisde, cisteag, airc, cobhan, clòsaite, bothan.
CABINET COUNCIL, *s* Comhairle dhiomhair. A member of the cabinet council, *ball na comhairle diomhair.*
CABLE, *s.* Taod, cord luing; sron-teud, oil-theud.
CACAO, *s* Bainne-chnò
CACHECTIC, *a.* Euslan, breoite, tinn, neo-fhallain.

Cachexy, *s.* Euslainnte; tinneas.

Cackle, *v.* Gloc, giùthail; cànnrain, glagain; gair, goir.

Cackle, Cackling, *s.* Gloc, glocail, giuthail, gaireachdaich; (*of geese*), canran, gànnraich.

Cacodemon, *s.* Deamhan, droch-spiorad.

Cadaverous, *a.* Cairbheach, marbhanach, conablachail; lobhta, breun, malcta.

Caddis, *s.* Catas; sgroilleach lìn; seorsa duraig.

Cade, *a.* Maoth, mallta, muirneach; bog; tais.

Cadence, *s.* Tuiteam, ìsleachadh; fonn ìsleachadh; fonn.

Cadent, *a.* Tuiteamach.

Cadet, *s.* Brathair òg; deóin-shaighdear; fear a ghabhas anns an arm an nasguidh, an dùil ri post fhaotainn.

Cadger, *s.* Marsonta, marsal, marsan, ceannaiche, fear pac; fear a bheir im is caise do 'n mhargadh.

Cade, *s.* Riaghlair Turcach; portair (no) fear iomchair Albannach.

Cag, *s.* Buideal beag, bairill a chumas ceithir galanaibh.

Cæcias, *s.* Gaoth a tuath.

Cage, *s.* Eunadan; gainntir, carcar; cròilean.

Cage, *v.* Cuir an eunadan; gainntirich.

Caitiff, *s.* Slaoightir; cealgair, sgonn-bhalach, eagonach.

Cajole, *v.* Miodalaich, breug, meall, dean giodal, dean sodal, (no) liùghaireachd, dean beul breagh.

Cajoler, *s.* Miodalair, miodalaiche, mealltair; liugair, sodalaiche; miolcair.

Cajolery, *s.* Miodalachd, sodalachd, liùgaireachd, miolcaireachd.

Cake, *s.* Bonnach, dearnagan, breacag, caraiceag, abhlan; builionn; bairghean.

Cake, *v. n.* Cruadhaich.

Calamanco, *s.* Seorsa aodaich olla.

Calamine, *s.* Seorsa talmhainn a thionndas copar gu prais.

Calamitous, *a.* Mi-shealbhar, dòineach, doruinneach, dosgainneach, truagh; gàbhaidh, gàbhach, anshocrach, ain-deiseach; mi-aghmhor, neo-shona; goirt; olc; sgriosail.

Calamity, *s.* Doruinn, dosgainn, uaigh, gàbhadh, calldach; anshocair.

Calamus, *s.* Cuilc, giolc, giolcag; cléite, cuille; peann.

Calash, *s.* Seorsa carbaid aigheir; culaidh chinn.

Calcareous, *a.* Gaineamhach, gaineachaidh.

Calceated, *a.* Brògach; crudhach.

Calcination, *s.* Luaithreachadh, bleith.

Calcine, *v.* Luaithrich; loisg gu luaithre.

Calcography, *s.* Gearradh air umha, umh-ghrabhaladh.

Calculable, *a.* So-chunntadh, so-aireamh.

Calculate, *v.* Cunnt, aireamh, meas, cuir ri chéile; riomhair; nuimhrich.

Calculation, *s.* Cunntas, aireamh, riomhar; nuimhreachadh, cothromachadh.

Calculator, *s.* Fear meas, cunntair, aireamhair, riomhair.

Calculous, *a.* Clachach, gaineamhach, gaineachaidh, garbh, criadhach, grinnealach, cruaidh, doirneagach.

Calculus, *s.* Clach-fhuail.

Caldron, *s.* Coire, poit mhòr; dean-choire; lothar, beille, bruin.

Calefaction, *s.* Blathachadh; teòthadh; leasachadh, blaiteachadh, blàthas, teas.

Calefactive, *a.* Teòthach; blàiteach.

Calefy, *v.* Blathaich, blaitich, teòth, teòthaich.

Calendar, *s.* Miosachan.

Calender, *s.* Crann teanntaidh.

Calender, *v.* Mìnich aodach ann an crann teanntaidh; crann-theannaich, mìnich, liosraich.

Calends, *s.* A cheud la do gach mìos a réir aireamh nan Roimheach.

Calf, *s.* Laogh; calpa na coise; baothair, baoghlan.

Caliber, *s.* Cailbhir; toll gunna.

Calice, *s.* Cop, cup, copan.

Calico, *s.* Aodach cotain.

Calid, *a.* Teth, blath; teinntidh, sgaillteil, loisgeach.

Calidity, *s.* Teas, ro-theas, dian-theas.

Calif, *s.* Righ (no) Iompair Turcach, ard-shagairt do chreideimh Mhathomeid.

Caligation, *s.* Dorchadas, doilleireachd, duibhre.

Caliginous, *a.* Dorcha, doilleir, ceothar, gruamach.

Caligraphy, *s.* Sgriobhadh boidheach.

Calix, *s.* Copan.

Calk, *v.* Calc.

Calker, *s.* Calcair, calcadair, fear calcaidh.

Call, *v.* Gairm, goir, thoir cuireadh; cuir; thoir ainm; (*call aloud*), glaodh, gairm, goir, eigh, eubh. What do they call him? *c'ainm th'air? c'ainm their iad ris? c'ainm e?*

Call, *s.* Gairm, goir, glaodh; eigh, gairmeadh; iarrtas; cuireadh; ceaird.

Calling, *s.* Gairmeadh, glaodh, éigh; ceaird, ealdhain.

Callipers, *s.* Gobhalroinn cham; inneal a thomhas shoithchean.

Callosity, *s.* Cruaidh-at; calunn.

Callous, *a.* Cruaidh, neo-mhothachail; tiugh.

Callow, *a.* Ruisgte mar gharrag, lom, gun chloimh.

Calm, *a.* Ciùin, samhach; seimh, tosd, tosdach; suaimhneach, sìochail; feitheil, soimeach, socrach.

Calm, *v.* Ciùinich, ciùnaich, sìothchaich; coisg, caisg, leig, socraich.

Calm, *s.* Ciùineas, samhchair, tosd, seimhe, suaimhneas, sìth, siòchath, siochainnt, socair; féith.

Calmer, *s.* Ciùnadair.

Calmly, *adv.* Gu ciùin, gu samhach, gu seimh, gu tosd, gu tosdach, gu suaimhneach, gu socrach.

Calmness, *s.* Ciùine; ciùineas; samhchair; socair; seimhe, sìth, fois, tamh.

Calorific, *a.* Blaiteach, teòthach.

Caltrops, *s.* Seorsa inneil-cogaidh.

Calumniate, *v.* Maslaich, dean tair, cul-chain, dean casaid bhréig, tog tuaileas, beum.

Calumniation, *s.* Cùl-chain, càineadh, tàir, tuaileas, sgainneal, beumadh.

Calumniator, *s.* Fear cùl-chainidh, tuaileasaiche, sgainnealaiche, cul-chàineadair.

Calumnious, *a.* Tuaileasach, tàireil, sgainnealach.

Calumny, *s.* Casaid bhréig, tuaileas, mi-sgeul, cul-chaineadh, sgainneal.

Calve, *v.* Beir laogh. The cow has calved, *rug a bhò laogh.*

Calvinism, *s.* Teagasg an roi-orduchadh a réir Chalbhin.

Calvinist, *s.* Fear leanmhuinn Chalbhin; Calbhineach.

Cambric, *s.* Pearluinn; lion eudach finealta, a rinneadh an tus ann am bail sa mhòr-thir ris an goirear *Cambray*.

Came. See Come.

Camel, *s.* Camhal, ainmhidh Arabach.

Camelot, Camlet, *s.* Camlait; aodach air a dheanamh do shioda agus dh' olainn.

Cameleon, *s.* Ainmhidh beag a mhuthas a dhath gu minic.

Cambrated, a. Boghta, boghte
Cameration, s. Boghadh, lubadh
Camlet See Camelot
Camomile, s Camambhil, cambhil, luibh leigheis.
Camois, a Spad-shronach, spadta.
Camp, s Camp, fos-longphort, dun
Camp, v. Campaich, dean camp
Campaign, s. Am cogaidh, machair, comhnard, an ùine a sheasas saighdearan ri cogadh ann aon bhliadhna.
Campaniform, a. Cluigeanach
Campanulated, a. Cluigeanach
Campion (wild), s Coirean
Can, s Soitheach cuach, cop, copan
Can, v (*I can*), feudaidh mi, is urrainn mi, is urradh dho As fast as can be, *cho luath 's a dh'fhaotas.*
Canaille, s Gràisg, prabar, a chuid is isle do 'n t-sluagh.
Canal, s Cladh-shruth, cladh-amhainn, cladh-uisge, guitear; pioban Canal-coal, *seorsa guail.*
Canary, s Fion a Chuan-iar l.
Canary, s. Eun ceilearach as a Chuan-iar-l.
Cancel, v Dubh a mach, mill, cuir gu neo-bhrigh. Cancelled, *dubhte a mach*
Cancellated, a Tarsuinnichte, dubhte a mach
Cancelled, a Dubhte a mach, millte, neo-bhrighichte, air a chur gu neo-bhrigh
Cancer, s Cruban, partan, (*a sore*), buirbean, ailse, goirteas cnamhach.
Canceration, s. Buirbeanachadh.
Cancerous, a Buirbeanach, ailseach, cnamhach
Candent, a. Teath dearg; dian theth
Candid, a Ceart, fireannach, ionraic, neo-chealgach; direach; geal
Candidate, s. Iarradair, co' iarradair, fear iarruidh no oifig
Candidly, s Gu ceart, gu fireannach; gu h-ionruic, gu dìreach; gu h-onorach, gu saor, gu soilleir.
Candidness, s. Ceartas, fireanntachd, ionracas
Candify, v Dean geal, gealaich
Candle, s Coinneal, coillinn, lòchran; soillse, solus
Candleholder, s Coinnealdair; fear gun stà.
Candlelight, s Solus coinnle, solus còille.
Candlemas, s. Feill-Bride, an fhéill-Bride.
Candlestick, s. Coinnlear, coìllear.
Candlestuff, s. Géir, igh, blonag
Candle-waster, s Mac-strogha, mac-struidhe
Candour, s. Fìrinn, ionracas, deagh-ghnèth
Candy, v. Canndaidh
Cane, s Slat, slatag, bat, lorg, cuilc, giolc, lainn, bior; seorsa cuilc as an tig siucar
Cane, v a Buail, slataich, sguitse, sguitsich, gabh air neach le bat
Canine, a Conach, madaidheach
Canister, s Caiteag, cisteag, bocsan a chumail *tea*, bascaid
Canker, s Cnamhuinn; durag, cnuimheag; meas-chnuimh; bratag, meirgeadh; ròs fiadhaich.
Canker, v Cnamh, ith, mill; leannaich; feargaich.
Canker-worm, s Cnamh-chnuimh
Cannibal, s Fear a dh'itheas feoil duine, duine itheach; fiadh-dhuine.
Cannon, s. Gunnadh mòr, *canan.* Cannon-ball, *peileir gunna mhoir, peileir canain.*
Cannonade, v. Gunnraich; gunnairich; *cananaich*

Cannonading, s. Gunnaireachd, lamhachas.
Cannonier, s. Gunnair; gunnadair.
Cannot. Cha 'n urradh, cha 'n urrainn; nach urradh, nach urrainn I cannot, *cha 'n urradh dhomh, cha 'n urrainn mi*, cannot I? *nach urradh dhomh? nach urrainn mi?*
Canoe, s. Coite, biorlinn, curach, curach Innseanach.
Canon, s. Riaghail eaglais, cleir-lagh, naomh-riaghailt, naomh reachd, na Sgriobtuirean
Canon-bit, s. Cabstar.
Canonical, a. Riaghailteach, cleir-laghail Canonicals, *eididh na cléir.*
Canonist, s. Fear teagaisg lagha na h-eaglais.
Canonization, s. Naomh-dheanamh; naomhachadh; coisreagadh.
Canonize, v. Naomh dhean, naomhaich, coisrig
Canopy, s. Ceann-bhrat, crom-chomhdach, comhdach rioghail
Canorous, a Ceòlar, ceòlmhor, fonnmhor; ard, ceilearach.
Cant, s. Gràisg-chomhradh; sgleò; ràsanachd; langan; ràite; beurla bodaich
Cant, v Càn; rasanaich; seinn; langanaich.
Cantata, s Oran, ceòl tiomhaidh, fonn.
Cantation, s. Seinn, càntaireachd.
Canter, s. Cealgair; ràsan, fear fuar-chrabhaidh, falaireachd
Canterbury-gallop, s. Falaireachd.
Cantharides, s Cuileag Fhrancach, cuileag Spàinnteach
Canticle, s. Oran naomh, laoidh, luinneag, càntaig; dàn Sholaimh
Canting, a Crabhach, fuar chrabhach, cealgach; ràsanach; (*affected*), ceigeach, ceigeanach.
Cantle, v Gearr na mhìribh
Cantle, Cantlet, s. Mìre, fuigheal, fuighleach, iarmad, bloidh
Canto, s. Earann do dhàn; duan, dàn.
Canton, s. Earann duthcha, srath, taobh duthcha; fineadh, clann, muinntir.
Canton, v. Roinn fearann (no) dùthaich.
Canvass, s Caineab, caineab-aodach, canbhais, aodach siùil, clùd siolaidh; iarraidh, sireadh, dian-shireadh; rannsachadh
Canvass, v Sir, iarr, rannsuich, ceasnaich
Cany, a Cuilceach, giolcanach
Canzonet, s Oran, duan, dan, luinneag
Cap, s. Ceap, curachd, boineid, bonaid; ceannasg, beannag, bioraid, bigean; barr croinn luinge. Cap-a-pie, *o cheann gu cois, o mhullach gu bonn*
Cap, v Ceapaich, ceap, curaichdich, boineidich
Capability, s. Comasachd, murrachas, urrainneachd, freagarrachd.
Capable, a. Comasach, murrach, urrainneach, freagarrach, teoma, iomchuidh, fiosrach
Capacious, a. Mor, farsuinn, farsuing, leudmhor; barrasgaoilteach; *rùmar*
Capaciousness, s. Farsuingeachd, fairsneachd, leud, leudachd, meudachd.
Capacitate, v. Ullamhaich, comasaich, deasaich.
Capacity, s. Comas, murrachas; càile, tuigse, toinisg; inbhe, staid, leud, *rùm*
Caparison, s. Each-aodach, each-eididh riomhach.
Cape, s. Rugha, roinn, maol, ceann; (*of dress*), bannbhràighe, trusgan uachdair.

Caper, *s.* Leum, surdag, dannsa; leumartaich; seorsa dearcaig shearbh.

Caper, *v.* Leum, dean mire, danns, dean beiceiseach

Capering, *s.* Leumartaich, leumnaich, mire, danns; beiceiseach, beiceartach, ruideis

Caperer, *s.* Leumadair, leumnaiche, dannsair, damhsair.

Capillaceous, *a.* Roinneach, (no) caol mar ròinneig.

Capillament, *s.* Feusag, feosag, gaoisd, ròinne.

Capillary, *a.* Roinneagach; caol; feusagach

Capital, *a.* Priomh; ard; corr, grinn, gasd; ciontach, bàs-thoilltinneach

Capital, *s.* Ard bhaile, priomh-chathair, priomh bhaile; calpa, litir mhòr; earras.

Capitation, *s.* Cunntas ceann.

Capitular, *s.* Caibidealach.

Capitulate, *v.* Geill air chumha, striochd air chumha

Capitulation, *s.* Teirm-striochd; teirm-ghéill; réite, cumhnantan, teirmeannan

Capon, *s* Coileach spoghte

Caprice, *s* Dòchas, mùthteachas; gl; faoineis, neonachas, iongantas, taom mac meamna.

Capricious, *a* Dòchasach, muthteach; faoin, faoineiseach, neònach, iongantach, gogaideach, gaoith

Capriciously, *adv.* Gu dòchasach, gu mùthteach, gu faoin, gu neonach, gu gogaideach, gogaill.

Capriciousness, *s.* Dòchasachd; muthteachd; faoineachd; faoineiseachd; gogaideachd, gogailleachd

Capricorn, *s* Aon do chombara na Grein-chrios; grian-stad gheamhraidh.

Capsicum, *s.* Seorsa peupair

Capstan, *s.* Undais luing, inneal draghaidh, inneal tog-alach

Capsular, *s* Fàs mar chisteig, cisteil

Capsulated, *a.* Ceisdichte; ceisdealaichte

Captain, *s.* Ceann feadhna, ceann feodhna, ceannard feadhna; caiptean, ceannard luinge, comanntair. Captain of the rear-guard, *iar-toiseach*

Captaincy, *s.* Feadhnachd, ceannardachd, inbhe caiptein, comannta

Captainship, *s.* Inbhe cinn-feadhna, ceannardachd; ceann-feadhnachd, comannt

Captation, *s* Suireadh; miodal, goileam

Caption, *s* Glac, glacail, glacadh; beirsinn, cur an lamh.

Captious, *a* Crosda, cainnteach, buaireasach, aimhreiteach, frionasach, feargach; reasgach; dian

Captiously, *adv.* Gu crosda, gu cainnteach, gu buaireasach, gu h-aimhreiteach, gu frionasach, gu feargach, gu reasgach, gu dian.

Captiousness, *s f* Crosdachd, cainnteachd, buaireasachd, aimhreiteachd, frionasachd, feargachd, reasgachd, déine, friotharachd.

Captivate, *v* Buail le gaol (no) le mor-dheidh; ceannsaich; thoir am bruid (no) am braighdeanas, traillich

Captive, *s.* Ciomach, ciomaidh; priosanach, daor-oglach, tràill; braighe

Captivity, *s* Ciomachas, priosanachd; trailleachd; daorsadh, bruid, braighdeanas.

Captor, *s.* Glacadair, fear glacaidh

Capture, *s.* Glacadh, glacail; creach, creich, spùille, spuilinn; spuinne, cobhartach.

Capuched, *part* Curacaichte.

Capuchin, *s.* Brathair bochd; fàlluinn mna, ceann aodach mna, curachd

Car, *s.* Carn; cairt; carr; carbad, feun, cuingrach

Carabine, *s.* Gunna marcaiche; gunna beag; olastair; gunna glaic, gunna cutach, gearra-ghunna.

Carabineer, *s.* Olastairiche, gearra-ghunnair

Caravan, *s* Bannal thùrusaiche oir-thireach, iomchar mòr

Caravansary, *s.* Tigh osda, tigh aoidheachd san aird an ear.

Caraway, *s* Carbhaidh.

Carbuncle, *s.* Carmhogal, seorsa seuda, a bheir solus anns dorchadh mar eibhleig, plucan, guirean, bucain, bucaid.

Carbuncled, *a* Lan charmhogala, dearg mar charmhogal, plucanach, guireanach, bucaideach.

Carbuncular, *a.* Carmhogalach; dearg mar ghuirean

Carcanet, *s* Paidrean, muin-sheud, muinge

Carcass, *s* Cairbh, conablach, closach, carcais; corp marbh, truaill

Carcelage, *s* Tuarasdal fir coimhid carcair

Card, *s* (*Of paper*), cairt; (*for wool*), card; sgrioban Playing at cards, *cluich air chairtean*, a pack of cards, *stoc chairtean.*

Card, *v.* Card, ciom; cir cloimh (no) ascard (no) olainn

Carder, *s* Cardair, ciomair, cireadair; (*at cards*), fear chairtean, cearraiche.

Cardiac, *a* Beathalach, cridhealach, ath-bheothachail, beothachail, ioc-shlainnteach, brosnachail, neartachail, aontachail

Cardialgy, *s.* Losg-bhràghaid.

Cardinal, *a* Priomh, ard, inbheach, sònruichte. The cardinal points, *ceithir airdean an athair, ear, iar, deas, tuath*, the cardinal virtues, *na priomh chàilean, crionnachd, stuaim, ceartas, agus cruadal*

Cardinal, *s* Priomh-dhiadhair Pàpanach.

Care, *v* Gabh suim, thoir aire, gabh curam I do not care for you, *tha mi coma ort*, what care I? *ciod an omhail th'agamsa? ciod sin domhsa?*

Care, *s.* Cùram, aire, iomaguin, carc; toigh, proghain, omhaill, seadh, suim; dìchioll, faicill, furachras Take care, *thoir 'n aire*, take care that you do it, *feuch gun dian thu e*

Care-crazed, *a.* Iomaguineach, ro-churamach, bi-chùramach

Careen, *v* Calc, càirich eu-dionadh luinge

Career, *s* Aite réis, cùrsa, réis, roid; ruithe, cruaidh-ruith, siubhal le srann; deannadh.

Career, *v* Ruith, cruaidh-ruith, imich le luathas

Careful, *a.* Cùramach, aireachail, iomaguineach; seadhoil, suimeil, dicheallach, faiceallach, toigheach, friochnamhach, furachair

Carefully, *adv* Gu curamach, gu h-aireachail, gu h-iomaguineach, gu seadhail, gu suimeil, gu dicheallach, gu faiceallach, gu furachair, gu h-onihailleach

Carefulness, *s* Cùram, aire, curamachd, suimealachd, faicilleachd, faiceallachd, seadhalachd, furachras, dichioll, dichiollachd

Careless, *a.* Neo-chùramach, neo-aireach, neo-aireachail, neo-fhaicilleach, neo-shuimeil, mi-sheadhail, mi-sheadhar, neo-fhurachair, neo-dhichiollach, dearmadach, dichuimhneach

Carelessly, *adv* Gu neo-chùramach, gu neo-aireachail, gu neo-fhaicilleach, gu neo-shuimeil, gu mi-sheadhail, gu neo-dhichiollach, gu dearmadach

Carelessness, *s* Neo-churam, cion-aire, mi-shuim, mi sheadh, dearmad, dichuimhneachd

Caress, *v* Dean beadradh, dean briodal, beadraich, briodalaich; glac gu gaolach, caidir

Caress, *s* Beadradh, briodal, caidreamh

Cargo, *s.* Luchd luing, lòd luing, luchd; lòd.

Caricature, *s.* Baoth dhealbh; dealbh tuaisteach.

Caries, *s.* Lobh, lobhadas, breunadas, groide.

Carious, *a.* Lobh, lobhta, lobhach, loibheach, breun, grod mosgain.

† **Cark.** See **Care.**

Carl, *s.* Bodach.

Carman, *s.* Cairtear.

Carminative, *a.* Follasach, failseach, lusragach; a sgaoileas gaoth cuim.

Carmine, *s.* Dearg, corcur.

Carnage, *s.* Marbhadh, àr, mortadh, murtadh, casgradh, sgrios, beubanachd.

Carnal, *a.* Feòlmhor, collach; corporra, mi-gheimnidh, ana-miannach.

Carnally, *adv.* Gu feòlmhor, gu collach, gu corporra, gu mi-gheimnidh, gu h-anamiannach.

Carnality, *s.* Feòlmhorachd, collaidheachd; mi-gheimnidheachd.

Carneous, *a.* Feòlach; sultmhor, reamhar.

Carnival, *s.* Di mairt inid; cuirm, feist, aimsir, sollain.

Carnivorous, *a.* Feoil-itheach, glutach, glàmhach, clamhanach, faoghaideach. Carnivorous birds, *faoghaidiche.*

Caroche, *s.* Carbad.

Carol, *v.* Céileir, seinn gu binn, beinneagaich; mol; glòirich.

Carol, *s.* Oran molaidh, oran aoibhneis; luinneag.

Carousal, *s.* Féill, cuirm, fleagh.

Carouse, *v.* Ol, òil, poit, ol gu h-anabarra, ruiteirich.

Carouse, *s.* Ol, pòit; ruite, ruitearachd; cuirm, fleagh.

Carouser, *s.* Poitear, meisgear, ruitear.

Carp, *s.* Carmhanach uisge.

Carp, *v.* Coirich, cronaich, faigh coire, faigh cron; achmhasanaich, faigh fabht, creim; connsaich.

Carpenter, *s.* Saor; † ailtear, drothlair; saor chairtean.

Carpentry, *s.* Saorsainneachd.

Carper, *s.* Creamadair; cronachair.

Carpet, *s.* Brat urlair, cas-bhrat, stràille, làr-bhrat.

Carping, *a.* Cronachail, cainnteach, crimeagach, creimeach.

Carriage, *s.* Carbad, feun; coisde, carr, carn, cairt; inneal giùlain, inneal iomchair; (*behaviour*), beus, dolmach, caith-beatha; gnathachadh, modhanna.

Carrier, *s.* Cairtear, fear-iomchair, fear-giùlain; portair; teachdair.

Carrion, *s.* Cairbhe, closach, ablach, conablach, marbhan; eug-bhroth.

Carrot, *s.* Curran, miuran; carrait; cearracan.

Carroty, *a.* Ruadh; dearg. Carroty hair, *falt ruadh.*

Carry, *v.* Giùlain, iomchair, beir, thoir; (*gain*), coisinn, faigh.

Carry-tale, *s.* Lonag; sgileam.

Cart, *s.* Cairt, feun, carbad, carn, carr. Cart load, *lòd, luchd, carr-luchd;* cart road, *rod cartach.*

Cart, *v.* Cairt, cairtich.

Cartel, *s.* Cairteal; cordadh mu iomlaid chiomach.

Carter, *a.* Cairtear, feunadair; greistear, greasadair.

Cart-horse, *s.* Each cartach, gearran; feunaidh.

Cartilage, *s.* Maothan.

Cartilaginous, *a.* Maothanach.

Cartoon, *s.* Dealbh; dealbh air scròl mòr paipeir.

Cartouch, *s.* Peilear-lann; bocsa pheilearan.

Cartridge, *s.* Searsadh gunna, soire a chumas aon urchair, urchair.

Cart-rut, *s.* Lorg cartach, aile chuibhleachan.

Cartulary, *s.* Cairt-lann.

Cartwright, *s.* Saor, saor-chairtean, saor-fheuna.

Carve, *v.* Grabh; gearr air fiodha, (no) air cloich, snàs; gearr fiadh, riaraich, Carved, *grabhta; greanta.*

Carver, *s.* Grabhadair, gearradair, snàsadair, snaitheadair.

Carving, *s.* Grabhadh, gearradh, snàsadh, snaitheadh, grabhadaireachd, gearradaireachd, snàsadaireachd, snaitheadaireachd.

Caruncle, *s.* Feoil bhrùite, plucan, meall.

Cascade, *s.* Eas, spùt, leum uisge, sruth eas.

Case, *s.* Truaill, comhdach; duille; cochall; sgrath.

Case, *v.* Truaillich; comhdaich, duillich; sgrath.

Case, *s.* Staid, inbhe, inmhe; cor, cal; cùis, nì; rud, gnothach. In good case, *ann an deagh chal;* as the case stands, *mar a tha chùis;* in case that, *air eagal gu, an d' eagal gu;* I pity your case, *is truagh leam do chor;* put the case it be so, *leig gur ann mar sin a tha.*

Case-harden, *v.* Cruadhaich, cruadhaich an sgrath a muigh.

Case-knife, *s.* Golaidh.

Casement, *s.* Far-uinneag; tar-uinneag, uinneag air ludannan.

Caseous, *a.* Càiseach.

Cash, *s.* Airgiod ullamh.

Cashier, *s.* Fear coimhead airgid.

Cashier, *v.* Cuir air falbh; diobair; ceadaich, diolg.

Cask, *s.* Bairill; buideal, godhan, gingean, togsaid; tunna.

Cask, Casque, *s.* Clogaid, ceann bheairt; bioraid.

Casket, *s.* Cisteag, bocsan; seud-lann, cofra.

Cassia, *s.* Spiosraidh.

Cassiowary, *s.* Eun mòr Innseanach.

Cassock, *s.* Cosag, casag.

Cast, *v.* Tilg; cuir; cunnt, àireamh; dealbh, cruthaich; dìt, diobair; tionsgainn, cnuasaich. Cast out, *cuir a mach;* cast up a vapour, *cuir smùid;* cast water about, *spairt uisge mu 'n cuairt;* casting the hair, *a cur an fhionna.*

Cast, *s.* Tilgeadh; urchair; dealbh; dìteadh; buille; car; gné, seorsa, tuar. Near a stone's cast, *teann air* (*no*) *beul ri urchair cloich.*

Cast, *s.* Seòrsa; gineadh, fineadh.

Castaway, *s.* Tréigeanach, diobarach, neach tréigte, (no) caillte.

Castaway, *a.* Gun sta, gun fheum, sean.

Caster, *s.* Tilgear; dealbhadair, cruthadair; dìtear; fiosaiche.

Castigate, *v.* Smachdaich, peanasaich, buail, greidh, saoth.

Castigation, *s.* Smachd, peanas, saothadh, bualadh; oilean.

Castigatory, *a.* Smachdail, peanasach, saothach, buailteach.

Casting-net, *s.* Lion iasgaich, lion uisge, lion tilgidh.

Castle, *s.* Caisteal, dùn, daingneach, caislean.

Castlery, *s.* Buille mu thuaiream.

Castling, *s.* Torraicheas anabuich.

Castor, *s.* Dobhran, dobhar-chu; ainm reult.

Castrate, *v.* Spogh, spoth; gearr. Castrated, *spoghte.*

Castration, *s.* Spoghadaireachd; spoghadh, spothadh; gearradh.

Casual, *a.* Tuiteamach, neo-chinnteach, teagamhach, tubaisdeach.

Casualty, *s.* Tuiteamas, tubaisd.

Casuist, *s.* Aithne-chuisiche, fear-lagha.

Casuistical, *a.* Aithne-chuiseach.

Casuistry, *s.* Aithne-chuiseachd.

Cat, *s.* Cat. Cat-o'-nine-tails, *sgiùrs, tàs, cuip;* the idle man will put the cat into the fire, *cuiridh fear na thamh an cat san teine.*

Catachresis, *s.* Andualarasg.

Cataclysm, *s.* Tuil, dil, dilinn.

Catalogue, *s.* Ainm-chlar; ainm-lit.

Catamountain, *s.* Cat fiadhaich.

Cataphract, *s.* Marcair fo làn armaibh.

Cataplasm, *s.* Plàsd; trait.

Catapult, *s.* Inneal a thilg chlacha.

Cataract, *s.* Eas, spùt, leum uisge; galar sùl, doille.

Catarrh, *s.* Ronn ghalar; carrasan.

Catarrhal, *a.* Carrasanach.

Catastrophe, *s.* Crioch, ceann thall; deireadh; crioch uamharra; tubaist, duaidh.

Cat-call, *s.* Sgiamhail.

Catch, *v.* Glac, beir air; rib; toilich. Catch at, *thoir sic; thoir ionnsuidh.*

Catch, *s.* Glacadh, glacail, greim, beirsinn; ribeadh, breith; tairbhe, buannachd; (*a song*), luinneag, duanag; oran luathaidh; (*a cheat*), mealltair.

Catcher, *s.* Glacair, glacadair; fear glacaidh, ribeadair.

Catching, *a.* Gabhaltach, glacach, deas gu glacadh; gionach, lonach; geur; beumach.

Catchpoll, *s.* Maor righ, maor.

Catechetical, *a.* Ceasnachail, sgrudail, ceisteach.

Catechism, *s.* Leabhar cheistean, leabhar ceasnachaidh, ceisteachan.

Catechist, *s.* Ceasnachair, sgrudair.

Catechize, *v.* Ceasnaich, sgrud.

Catechizer, *s.* Ceasnachair, sgrudair.

Catechumen, *s.* Ùr-Chriosduigh; ceisteanaiche.

Categorical, *a.* Dearbh-chinnteach; freagarrach; neo-theagamhach.

Category, *s.* Rang; sreath; cùis.

Catenate, *v.* Ceangail cuibhrich.

Catenation, *s.* Ceangladh, cuibhreachadh.

Cater, *v.* Solar; teanail, cuir ri chéile, ceannaich.

Cater, *s.* An ceithreamh air chairtean; an ceithreamh air dhìstean.

Caterer, *s.* Solaraiche, fear solair.

Cateress, *s.* Ban solaraiche.

Caterpillar, *s.* Burrus, luschuach, duil-mhial, ailseag, bolb, cnuimh-chàil.

Catership, *s.* Solar, solarachd, tionaladh.

Caterwaul, *v.* Piochair; dean miadhail; miadhail, mi-amhail, sgiamh.

Cates, *s.* Biadh, lòn.

Catgut, *s.* Teud fidhle; seorsa aodaich.

Cathartic, *a.* Sgùrach, purgaideach, glanach, faisgneach, ionnlaideach.

Cathedral, *s.* Priomh-eaglais, ard-eaglais, eaglais easbuig; cathair easbuig.

Catheter, *s.* Piob-màin.

Catholic, *a.* Coitchionn, coitchionnta, cumanta. A Roman catholic, *pàpanach.*

Catholicism, *s.* Coitchionnachd, coitchionntachd; cumantachd.

Catholicon, *s.* Cungaidh leighis cumanta.

Catoptrics, *s.* Ais-shoillseadh, ais-dhealradh.

Cattle, *s.* Spreidh, crodh, tàin, drobh; callach, maoin, ceathra; airneas, stoc; tlas. Small cattle, *meanbh-spreidh.*

Cattle-dealer, *s.* Dròbhair.

Caudle, *s.* Deoch mna siùbhla; plotag.

Caught, *part.* Glacte.

Caul, *s.* (*A piece of dress*), bréid; currac; lion obair gruaige; (*of the body*), sgairt.

Cauliferous, *a.* Cuisleanach, cuiseagach.

Cauliflower, *s.* Càl-gruaidheam, càl-colaig.

Caulk, *v.* See Calk.

Cause, *s.* Aobhar, cùis; reuson; riasan; fàth, cionfàth; cas, tagradh; son; cealtair; teagmhadh, damhna, iomreuson; taobh, pairtidh. For this cause, *air son so, air shon so, air an aobhar so;* in his cause, *air a shon, na aobhar, ann a aobhar;* without cause, *gun aobhar, gun reuson;* a cause at law, *cuis lagha;* for what cause? *c'arson?* for that cause, *air son sin, air an aobhar sin.*

Cause, *v.* Dean, thoir gu criche; orduich; thoir air, aom, tog.

Causeless, *a.* Gun aobhar, gun reuson, gun chionfàth.

Causeway, *s.* Cabhsair; tochar.

Caustic, *a.* Loisgeach, cnamhteach.

Caustic, *s.* Cungaidh leigheis loisgeach.

† **Cautel**, *s.* Rabhadh, sanas; faicill.

Cautelous, *a.* Cuilbheartach, eòlach, aireach, faicilleach.

Cauterization, *s.* Losgadh; leigh-losgadh.

Cauterize, *v.* Loisg, leigh-loisg; doth.

Caution, *s.* Sànas, rabhadh; comhairle; aire, curam, faicill; (*pledge*), urras; earlas.

Caution, *v.* Thoir sanas, thoir rabhadh, comhairlich.

Cautionary, *a.* Ann urras, ann geall, am paineachas.

Cautious, *a.* Sicir, faicilleach, faiceallach, curamach, glic, crionna, crionnda, aireachail, furachair.

Cautiously, *adv.* Gu sicir, gu faicilleach, gu faiceallach, gu cùramach, gu glic, gu crionna.

Cautiousness, *s.* Sicireachd, faicill, faicilleachd, faiceallachd, curamachd, gliocas, crionndachd.

Cavalcade, *s.* Lòd sluaigh, tasgar, drobh, bannal.

Cavalier, *s.* Marcair; ridir; marcaiche spairiseach; fear a chum taobh ri Rì Tearlach a h-aon.

Cavalier, *a.* Uaibhreach, sparaiseach, spairiseach, ardanach; stràiceil, treun.

Cavalierly, *adv.* Gu h-uaibhreach, gu spairiseach, gu h-ardanach, gu stràiceil.

Cavalry, *s.* Marc-shluagh, eachraidh, eachruidh.

Cavate, *v.* Cladhaich, toll, pleadhaich, slocaich.

Cavation, *s.* Cladhachadh, tolladh, pleadhachadh, slocachadh.

Cave, *s.* Uamha, uadha, uamhaidh, uadhaidh, còs, toll, sloc, slochd, brochdlùinn; fuachasach; † blotlach.

Caveat, *s.* Bac, bacadh; sànas, rabhadh, comhairle.

Cavern, *s.* See Cave.

Cavernous, *a.* Uamhach, slocach, còsach; lan shlochd; coireach.

Cavil, *v.* Connsaich, cunnuilich, deaspoirich; dean connspoid.

Cavity, *s.* Lag, sloc, coire, uagha.

Caw, *v.* Ròc.

Cease, *v.* Sguir; stad, coisg, cuir stad, leig dhiot.

Ceaseless, *a.* Bitheanta, an comhnuidh, a ghnàth, do ghnath, gun sgur, am bitheantas, am bidheantas, gun fhois, gun chrioch.

Cecity, *s.* Doille, cion leirsinn.

CECUTIENCY, *s.* Dorchadas, doillead, doilleireachd.
CEDAR, *s.* Seudar.
CEDE, *v.* Tiomnaidh, liobhair, thoir suas, thoir thairis; géill.
CEIL, *v.* Linig, plastaich (no) aolaich taobh stigh tighe.
CEILING, *s* Linig, tighe; mullach, bràighe.
CELANDINE, *s.* An ceann ruadh. Lesser celandine, *gran aigein.*
CELATURE, *s.* Rionaidheas, rionachas, rionail.
CELEBRATE, *v* Mol, ard-mhol; chùich; dean iomraiteach; coimhead, cum
CELEBRATED, *a.* Cliùiteach, ainmeil, iomraiteach
CELEBRATION, *s.* Coimhead (no) cumail féill, cuimhneachadh follaiseach, moladh, ardmholadh; cliuthachadh; cuimhneachan
CELEBRIOUS, *a.* Cliùiteach, ainmeil, iomraiteach, allail, comharraichte, mor-chliùiteach
CELEBRITY, *s* Cliù, ainm, ainmeileachd, alladh, iomradh, iomraiteachd; moladh
CELERITY, *s* Luathas, cabhag.
CELESTIAL, *a* Neamhuidh, ainglidh, naomh, atharail
CELIBACY, *s* Gilleadas, gun phòsadh, staid shingilte; diolanas.
CELIBATE, *a* Singilte mar ghille neo-phòsda
CELL, *s* Uamh-sheomar, slochd, cill, còsag, còsan, *seileir*
CELLAR, *s* Ionad tasgaidh, seileir, speansa.
CELLULAR, *a* Seileireach; còsagach.
† CELSITUDE, *s* Airde; inbhe
CEMENT, *s.* Cnadh-cheangal, liunn-tàthaidh; mortair; bann; ceangal.
CEMENT, *v* Tàth, ceangail, dlùthaich ri cheile, stic
CEMENTATION, *s.* Tathadh, ceangladh, dluthachadh, stic.
CEMENTER, *s* Tathair, tathadair, ceanglair, sticeadair
CEMETERY, *s* Cladh, cill, ait-adhlaic, reilig
CENOTAPH, *s* Fas-charn; clach-cuimhne, clach-cuimhne airson neach a chaidh adhlac' an céin
CENSE, *s* Cìs, càin, màl, earc, cion, comhach.
CENSER, *s* Tuiseir, sionnsa, soitheach-tuis, aghann theine
CENSOR, *s* Achmhasanaiche, smachdair; fear cronachaidh; oingeach a measg nan Roimheach
CENSORIOUS, *a* Achmhasanach, coireachail, trodach; diombach, cànranach
CENSORIOUSNESS, *s* Achmhasanachd, coireachaileachd, cànranachd.
CENSURABLE, *a* Airidh air achmhasan, ciontach, coireach, ri choireachadh.
CENSURE, *v* Coirich, cronaich, achmhasanaich, dìt; faigh coire, faigh fabhta; trod ri *Censured,* coirichte, achmhasanaichte, cronaichte
CENSURE, *s* Coire, cronachadh, achmhasan; trod, casaid, tàir; mi-chliù, casurram, breith, barail, dìt, binn.
CENSURER, *s* Coireachair, cronachair, achmhasanaiche.
CENT, *a.* Ceud, ciad.
CENTAUR, *s* An saighleadair, aon do chomharaibh a ghrianchrios
CENTAURY, *s.* A cheud bhileach
CENTENARY, *s* Ceud bliadhna.
CENTESIMAL, *a* An ceudamh
CENTIFOLIOUS, *a* Ceud-dhuilleach, ceud-dhuilleagach; aig am bheil ceud duilleag
CENTRAL, *a.* Meadhonach, teis air-mheadhonach
CENTRE, *s* Meadhon, teis air-mheadhon; teis-meadhon; builsgean, iomlag, imleag, ceartlar, iomaltar
CENTRIC, *a* Meadhonach, anns a mheadhon

CENTRIFUGAL, *a.* Meadhon-sheachnach.
CENTRIPETAL, *a.* Meadhon-aomach.
CENTUPLE, *a* Ceud fillte, ceudach.
CENTURIATE, *v.* Ceudaich, ciadaich, roinn na cheudaibh.
CENTURION, *s.* Ceannard cheud; feadhna; caiptean
CENTURY, *s* Aireamh cheud bliadhna.
CEPHALALGY, *s* Ceann-goirt.
CEPHALIC, *a.* Math airson ceann goirt.
CERASTES, *s.* Nathair adhairceach
CERATE, *s.* Sabh leigheis; oladh-céireach
CERATED, *a* Céirichte, céireach.
CERECLOTH, *s.* Aodach céireach, aodach mairbh.
CEREMENT, *s* Aodach céirichte, aodach céireach, céir-bhrat, aodach mairbhe; marbh-phaisg.
CEREMONIAL, *a.* Gnathach, deas-ghnathach; foirmeil; riaghailteach.
CEREMONIAL, *s.* Gnàth; deas-ghnath; foirm, riaghailt, modh.
CEREMONIOUS, *a* Foirmeil; modhail; siobhailt
CEREMONY, *s* Deasghnath, modh, riaghailt, foirm. *Ceremonies,* deas-ghnathanna, modhanna
CERTAIN, *a* Cinnteach, dearbh, dearbhte, deimhin, beachdaidh; follaiseach, gun teagamh; soilleir; riaghailteach; suidhichte; sonruichte.
CERTAINLY, *adv.* Gu cinnteach, gu dearbh, gu deimhin, gun teagamh, air chinnte.
CERTAINTY, *s.* Cinnte, cinntealas, dearbhadh, làn-dearbhadh, dearbh-chinnte
CERTIFICATE, *s.* Teisteanas; dearbhadh, teisdeas
CERTIFY, *v.* Teistich, dearbh, teisteanaich, deimhinich; thoir fios, dean cinnteach.
CERTITUDE, *s* Cinnte, cinntealas, làn dearbhadh, dearbhchinnte
CERVICAL, *a.* Muinealach
CERULEAN, *a* Gorm, speur-ghorm; liath-ghorm
CERULIFIC, *a.* Gorm-dhathach
CERUMEN, *s.* Sal-cluais; céir-cluais.
CERUSE, *a.* Luaidh gheal.
CESS, *s.* Cìs, càin, màl.
CESSATION, *s* Sgur, sgurachd, sgurachdainn, stad, stadachd, fosadh, tamh, anail. Cessation of arms, *fosadh airm, fosadh cogaidh*
CESSIBLE, *a.* So-thoirt thairis; so-theitheach.
CESSION, *s* Géill, geilleachduinn, teicheadh, dol gu taobh (no) as an rathad, dol air chùl
CESTUS, *s.* Crios maighdinn, crios geimnidh; cearcall truaillidh
CETACEOUS, *a* Orcach, mar mhuic-mara.
CHAD, *s* Scorsa éisg
CHAFE, *v* Blathaich, blàitich, teòth, rub, suath, feargaich, brosnuich, cuir air bhoil, + boltraich.
CHAFE, *s* Teas, blathas, corruich, fearg, feirge, ardan, farran; boil, cuthach, *angar,* dot
CHAFER, *s.* Scorsa daoil
CHAFF, *s.* Moll, caithleach, càth, lochair, ni suarrach
CHAFFER, *v n.* *Prig,* ceannaich; plocairich, tagluinnich; dean suaip; tròc, *baraganaich.*
CHAFFERER, *s* Fear tagluinneach, plocair, fear roinn, ceannaiche, marsonta, baraganaiche.
CHAFFERY, *s* Prigeireachd, plocaireachd, tagluinn, marsontachd, tròcainn.
CHAFFWEED, *s* Catluibh
CHAFFY, *a* Mollach, mollar, càthar, càthach, muilleach; salach; eutrom, suarrach, olc
CHAFING-DISH, *s.* Teòiteachean, aghann teine.

Chagrin, *s.* Droch ghean, droch-fhonn, mothlachd; frionas, iomaguin, friothaireachd, farran; an-shogh, trioblaid; buaireas; tuirse.

Chagrin, *v. a.* Farranaich; goirtich, pian, cuir mothlachd; feargaich, buair; tuirsich, brosnaich

Chagrined, *part* Farranaichte, goirtichte, pianta; feargaichte, buairte, brosnuichte

Chain, *s.* Slabhruidh, cuibhreach, ceangal; geamhladh, arach.

Chain, *v. a.* Cuibhrich, ceangail, geamhlaich, geimhlich; tràillich.

Chain-pump, *s.* Piob-thosgaidh mara.

Chain-shot, *s.* Urchair shlabhruidh, peilearan air an ceangal ri chéile le slabhruidh

Chain-work, *s.* Obair shlabhruidh.

Chair, *s.* Cathair, suidheagan, seidhir. *Chairs*, cathraichean, seidhrichean

Chairman, *s.* Fear suidhe; ceann suidhe; riaghlair comuinn, ard-shuldhear; portair.

Chaise, *s.* Carbad, carr, cathair, seidhir, coisde, *coidse*

Chalcographer, *s.* Umha-ghrabhair.

Chalder, *s.* Salltair, tomhas shé bolla deug.

Chaldron, *s.* Tomhas shea buiseal deug 'ar fhichead

Chalice, *s.* Cop, cup, copan, bòl; cuach, corn; cupan comanaich.

Chalk, *s.* Caile.

Chalk-cutter, *s* Càile-thochailtear.

Chalk-pit, *s.* Toll cailce; sloc cailce.

Chalky, *a.* Cailceach, geal

Challenge, *s.* Dùlan, cairteal dùlain

Challenge, *v.* Dùlanaich, cuir gu dùlan, dànaich, togair, conspoid; iarr gu comhrag deise; cronaich, cocrich.

Challenger, *s.* Dulanaiche.

Chalybeate, *a.* Iarunnaidh; iarnaidh; stailinneach, air bhlas iaruinn (no) stailinn.

Cham, *s.* Uachdaran Tartarach.

Chamade, *s.* Drumaireachd.

Chamber, *s.* Seomar, seumar, aitreamh, rum, seomar uachdrach.

Chamberer, *s.* Seomradair, seomarair, seumradair; slatair, drùisear

Chamber-fellow, *s.* Co'sheomaraiche, companach.

Chamberlain, *s.* Fear-ionaid uachdarain; seomaraiche; sgriobhadair, sgriobhair, scumarlan; cailteanach

Chambermaid, *s.* Caileag sheomair, ban-sheomraiche.

Chamber-pot, *s.* Fualan, amar mùin.

Chamblet, *v.* Eug-samhlaich.

Chameleon, *s.* Dearc luachair a mhuthas an dath

Champer, *v* Claisich, cladhaich, bùraich.

Champer, *s.* Clais.

Chamois, *s.* Seorsa gabhair.

Chamomile, *a.* Cam-bhile

Champ, *v.* Caguinn, creim, gearr, teum.

Champaign, *s* Magh, machair, reidh, còmhnard, apainn; cars; seorsa fiona

Champaign, *a* Combnard, réidh, iosal, fosgailte.

Champignon, *s.* Balg losgain

Champion, *s.* Cùraidh, gaisgeach, laoch, laochan, treunlaoch, fiann-laoch, dion, dionair, cathaiche, milidh, saighdear; luan, fiallach, † arg, † asgath

Chance, *s.* Tuiteamas, tuiteam, teagamhas, sealbhar, mishealbhadh, cineamhainn, tubaisd, gàbhail, cunnart, † cadaim; fortan. *By chance*, thaobh tubaisd, thaobh tuiteamais.

Chance, *v.* Tachair, tuit, eirich. It chanced, *thachair e.*

Chancel, *s.* Ionad altarach, ionad na seirbheis.

Chancellor, *s.* Ard-chomhairleach, ard-bhreitheamh, seannsalair. The lord chancellor, *morair nan seul.*

Chancery, *s.* Mòd ceartais, cùirt a cheartais, cùirt na còrach.

Chancre, *s.* Drùis-ghuirean, clap.

Chandelier, *s.* Coinnleir meurach.

Chandler, *s.* Coinnealdair, coilleadair, fear dheanamh choinnlean

Change, *v. a.* Mùth, caochail, atharraich, malairtich, leasaich, tionndadh, carruich.

Change, *s.* Mùth, mùthadh, caochladh, atharrach, malairt, leasachadh, carrachadh, annas; briseadh. Change of the moon, *idireug*

Changeable, *a.* Muthteach, caochlaideach; so-mhuthadh, so-chaochlaidh, neo-shuidhichte, neo-bhunailteach, neosheasmhach, luaineach, siubhlach, iomluath, gaoithe

Changeableness, *s.* Muthteachd, caochlaideachd, luaineachd, siubhlachd, neo-bhunailteachd, neo-sheasamhachd, iomluathas

Changeful, *a.* Muthteach, caochlaideach, neo-chinnteach, so-mhuthadh, so-chaochlaidh, neo-bhunailteach, luaineach, siubhlach, iomluath

Changeling, *s.* Urr luaineach, gaothan; urr shlthichean, oinseach, amadan.

Changer, *s.* Muthadair, malairtiche, brisear.

Channel, *s.* Aigean, clais, grinneal, grionnal, caolas, sruth-chlais, cneas mara.

Chant, *v* Càn, seinn; tuir; seinn laoidh, gabh òran, gabh ceòl.

Chant, *s.* Cànadh, oran, seinn, ceilear, ceòl, comh-sheirm

Chanter, *s* Càntair, oranaich, fear ciùil, ceòlraiche; (*a pipe*), seannsair, siunnsair, cuislean.

Chanticleer, *s* Coileach.

Chanting, *s.* Càntaireachd, seinn, ceòl, comh-sheirm

Chantress, *s.* Ban-oranaiche, ban-chantair.

Chaos, *s* An dubh-choimheasg; an coimeasg as an do chruthaicheadh an saoghal a reir barail nan sean Ghintealach, mi-riaghailt.

Chaotic, *a* Coimeasgach, mi-riaghailteach, thair a cheile

† **Chap**, *s.* Feag, sgolt, cab, sgag; peirceall. Full of chaps, *sgagach*

Chape, *s.* Crambaid, crambait.

Chapel, *s.* Cillinn, caibeal, tigh aoraidh; *seapail.*

Chapeless, *a.* Gun chrambaid.

Chapelry, *s.* Fearann caibeil.

Chaperon, *s.* Seorsa curaichd.

Chapiter, *s.* Ceann puist, ceann colmhuin.

Chaplain, *s.* Ministear tighe, ministear teaghlaich; ministear feachd.

Chapless, *a.* Peircleach, peirceallach, caol-pheirceallach.

Chaplet, *s.* Fleasg, blàth-leasgaidh, blath-fhleasg, coron; tutag chloimh air ceann peubh-choilich.

Chapman, *s.* Ceannaiche, marsan, marsonta; buthan, fear-ceirde

Chaps, *s.* Craos, gros, beul

Chapter, *s.* Caibdeal, caibdeil; coinneamh cléire priombeaglais.

Char, *s.* Obair làtha; tùrn.

Char, *v.* Fath-loisg, dean obair là.

Character, *s* Cliù, ainm, iomradh; (*a letter*), litir; comhar, comharradh; (*person*), neach, pearsa. A bad character, *droch chliù*

Characteristic, *a.* Cosmhuil, coslach.

Characterize, *v.* Thoir cliu air neach, innis, cuir an céill, sgriobh, grabh, grabhail

Characterless, *a.* Gun chliù, gun ainm

Charcoal, *a* Gual fiodha, fiodh-ghual.

Charge, *v.* Earb, meas, tathaich, cosd, cost; cronaich, coirich, cuir as leth, orduich, aithne, cuir impidh, thoir sparradh; (*a gun*), *seurs*, lion; luchdaich; (*load*), eallaich; luchdaich; cuir lòd air; (*attack*), thoir ionnsuidh air, leum air. I charge you, *tha mi cur impidh ort*, charge strictly, *thoir sparradh*, *thoir teann sparradh*

Charge, *s* (*Trust*), earbsadh, cùram, geard, (*cost*), cosd, cosdas; (*impeachment*), cronachadh, coireachadh, cur as leth; (*of a gun*), lòd, scarsadh; (*attack*), ionnsuidh, sic, ruathar; (*office*), dreuchd; (*a load*), luchd, lòd, eallach, uallach, cothrom, cudthrom; (*order*), àithne, impidh, sparradh, ordugh, comannt. Under my charge, *fo m' chùram*, *fo mo chomannt*, lay it not to my charge, *na agair orm e*, to my charge, *as mo leth*

Chargeable, *a* Cosdail, daor, stroghail; struidheil; ciontach, coireach; freagarach

Chargeableness, *s.* Cosdas, daorad, stroghalachd

Chargeably, *adv* Gu cosdail, gu daor.

Charger, *s* Mias, (*horse*), each, steud-each

Charily, *a.* Faicilleach, faiceallach, aireachail, curamach, grunndail.

Chariness, *s* Faicill, faicilleachd, cùram, grunndalas, crionndachd

Chariot, *s* Carbad, feun, cobhair, carr, † creadradh.

Charioteer, *s* Carbadair, feunadair, drubhair; carbair, corbair.

Charitable, *a.* Carthanach, seirceil, caoimhneil, fiùghantach, iochdmhor, truacanta

Charitableness, *s* Carthanachd, carthan, seirc, seirceilcachd, caoimhnealachd, fiùghantachd

Charitably, *adv* Gu carthanach, gu seirceil, gu caoimhneil, gu fiùghantach, gu h-iochdmhor, gu truacanta

Charity, *s* Carthan, gradh, seirc, deagh-ghean, déirc, deagh-thoil, oirchios Charity conceals faults, *ceilichidh seirc ainneamh*

Chark, *s.* Guaillean

Charlatan, *s.* Cleasaiche, baoth-chleasaiche; feall-leigh, sotalaiche

Charlatanry, *s* Cleasachd; baoth-chleasachd, sotal, feall

Charles's wain, *s.* An ceata cam

Charm, *v* Cuir druidheachd, seunaich, cuir buitseachd, cuir geasachd, cuir fo' gheasaibh; suaimhnich; toilich.

Charm, *s.* Druidheachd; buitseachd, gisreag, giseag, geasachd, seun, geas, geasadaireachd

Charmer, *s* Druidh, seunadair, geasadair, suaimhniche, luisreagan, (*lover*), graidhean.

Charming, *a.* Ro-thaitneach, ro-ionmhuinn, gradhach, grinn

Charnel, *a.* Cairbheach.

Charnel-house, *s* Tigh chnaimhean

Chart, *s.* Cairt, cairt-iùil.

Charter, *s.* Cairt, còir, comas, céad, aonta

Chartered, *a.* Ceadaichte, cairtichte.

Charter party, *s.* Paipeir co' chumhnanta

Charman, *s* Baitsear.

Charwoman, *s* Borionnach air pàigh latha.

Chary, *a* Sicir, glic, curamach, faiceallach.

Chase, *s.* Ruaig, sealg, seilg, faoghaid, fiadhach, fiadhachd; tachdar. Open country, *faiche.*

Chase, *v.* Ruaig, fuadaich, lean, dlu-lean, cruaidh-lean

Chaser, *s* Ruagair; sealgair.

Chasm, *s.* Sgolt, sgoltadh, fosgladh, faslach; sgaineadh, an-sgaineadh; bearn.

Chaste, *a.* Geamnuidh, geimnidh, stuama; ceannsach, glan, teisteil, gasta, neo-thruaillte, neo-thruaillidh; fiorghlan; macanta, ionruic.

Chasten, *v* Peanasaich, smachdaich, buail; saoth, cuir fu' smachd.

Chasteness, *s.* Geamnachd, geamnaidheachd, geumnidheachd, stuaim, ceannsachd; glaine, macantas, ionracas.

Chastisement, *s.* Peanas, smachd, smachdachadh, falatas; bualadh, gréidh, caraist

Chastiser, *s.* Peanasair, smachdair, smachdachair.

Chastity, *s.* Geimnidheachd, geimneachd, teistealachd, stuaim; ceannsachd, glaine, macantas, ionracas

Chat, *s.* Comhradh, bruidhinn, cracaireachd; gobais, giorag, biolasg, caibeis, ceilir, seanachas; (*of brushwood*), slatag.

Chat, *v.* Bruidhinn, dean comhradh, dean cracaireachd, dean gobais.

Chattel, *s.* Maoin, earras, airneis, feudail

Chatter, *s.* Dean gobais, dean goileam; sgeilmrich, gnàdaranaich.

Chatterer, *s.* Gobair, sgeilm, cabair, gioragaiche

Chatwood, *s.* Bradhan; connadh.

Chaw, *v* Cagain, cnamh, creim.

† **Chawdron**, *s.* Mionach, greallach.

Cheap, *a.* Saor, neo-luachmhor, neo-phrìseil, cunnarach.

Cheapen, *v.* Saoraich, dean saor; prig, dean plocaireachd, dean tagluinn, prìsich

Cheapness, *s* Saorad, saoiread, luach-peighinn

Cheat, *s* Feall, foill; car; prat, mealltair, slaoightir.

Cheat, *v* Meall, thoir an car a.

Cheater, *s* Mealltair, slaoightir.

Check, *v* Bac, cum air ais; grab cronaich, acmhasanaich.

Check, *s.* Bac, moille; grabadh, cronachadh, cron, achmhasan; fuath; aodach breac (no) stiallach

Checker, **Chequer**, *v.* Eag-samhuilich; breacaich

Checker-work, *s.* Obair eag-samhuil.

Cheek, *s* Gruaidh, leac, pluic; leth-cheann.

Cheek-tooth, *s.* Culag, fiacal cùil

Cheer, *s* Cuirm, biadh; goireas; cridhealas, mire, ealaidh, aighear, toil inntinn.

Cheer, *v* Thoir misneach, brosnuich, sòlasaich, comhfhurtaich, dean suilbhear, dean aobhach

Cheerer, *s.* Misneachair, brosnachair, fear sòlais.

Cheerful, *a* Suilbhear; cridheil, ait, aobhach, sunntach, aigeantach, aighearach, mear, eutrom, suigeartach, seiseach

Cheerfully, *a.* Gu suilmhear, gu cridheil, gu h-ait; gu h-aobhach, gu sunntach, gu h-aigeantach, gu mear, gu suigeartach.

Cheerfulness, *s* Suilbhearachd, suilbhire, suilmhearachd, cridhealas, aiteas, aighear, sunnt, toil-inntinn, aigeantachd, suigeartachd, sùgradh.

Cheerless, *a* Neo-shuilmhear, dubhach, neo-chridheil, trom, tuirseach, neo-ait, marbhanta

Cheery, *a.* Suilmhear, ait, cridheil, sunntach

Cheese, *s* Càise

Cheese-cake, *s.* Bonnach càise.

Cheese-press, *s.* Fiodhan, ballan binntich, ballan binnteachaidh

Cheesy, *a* Càisear

Cherish, *v.* Altruim, araich, tog, cum suas; misnich; sliog.

Cherisher, *s* Altrumair; misneachair; fear misneachaidh, fear coghnaidh; cul-taic

Cherry, *s* Siris. Cherry-tree, *crann siris*, *craobh shiris.*

CHERRY-CHEEKED, *a.* Ruiteach, dearg; gruaidh-dhearg.
CHERUB, *s.* Aingeal, spiorad neamhuidh.
CHERUBIC, *a.* Ainglidh
CHERVIL, *s* Cos uisge.
CHESLIP, *s.* Corra-chòsag, corra-chòsach; cailleach chòsach.
CHESNUT, *s.* Geinm-chno, geinm-chnù. A chesnut tree, *craobh gneinm-chnù.*
CHESS-MAN, *s.* Fear fòirn.
CHEST, *s.* Ciste, cobhan; cofra; maothan, uchd.
CHEVALIER, *s.* Ridir, righidir, treun-laoch.
CHEVERIL, *s.* Meann, minnigeag.
CHEW, *v.* Cagain, creim, cnamh; cnuasaich.
CHEWING, *s.* Cagnadh, creimeadh, cnamhadh; cnuasachd.
CHICANE, *s.* Feall, foill, car, innleachd, briongiaid charrach.
CHICANER, *s.* Fear tagluinneach, brionglaidiche.
CHICANERY, *s.* Feall, foill, car, innleachd, brionglaideachd.
CHICK, CHICKEN, *s.* Eun circe, eireag; isean.
CHICKEN-HEARTED, *a* Gealtach, cladhaireach, tais.
CHICKEN-POX, *s.* Breac òtraich
CHICK-PEA, *s* Peasair luch.
CHICKWEED, *s* Fliogh
CHIDDEN, *part.* Achmhasanaichte, cronaichte, coirichte.
CHIDE, *v.* Troid ri, achmhasanaich, cronaich, coirich, maslaich, tagair.
CHIDER, *s* Trodair, achmhasanaich, cronachair
CHIDING, *s.* Trod, achmhasan, cronachadh, coireachadh, glamras.
CHIEF, *a.* Priomh, ard, urramach; corr, mòr, flathail, uasal, araidh.
CHIEF, *s.* Ceann, ceannard, ceann cinnidh, ceann feadhna, ceann feodhna, sionaidh, riaghladair, priomh-dhuine, flath.
CHIEFLESS, *a.* Gun cheann feadhna, lag, neo-threubhanta.
CHIEFLY, *adv.* Gu h-araidh, gu h-urramach; gu h-ard.
CHIEFTAIN, *s* Ceannard, ceann cinnidh, ceann fine, ceann feadhna, ceann feodhna; comanntair.
CHILBLAIN, *s.* Cusb, fuachd-ghuirean; fuachdan, meallan tachais.
CHILD, *s.* Leanabh, naoidhean, pàisde, pàisdean, urr, urrag, maothran. A bastard child, *urr dhiolain*, children, *clann*, an only child, *aon-ghin, aon-ghin cloinne*; with child, *torrach, leth-tromach*; a child on strings, *imeachdan*, an ill-bred child, *siota.*
CHILDBEARING, *s.* Breith-cloinne.
CHILDBED, *s* Luidhe-siùbhladh, laidhe-siùbhladh, leabadh-shiùladh.
CHILDBIRTH, *s.* Breith cloinne, aisead.
CHILDHOOD, *s* Leanabaidheachd, leanabachd, naoidheanachd; luasganachd.
CHILDISH, *a.* Leanabaidh, leanabanta; faoin
CHILDISHNESS, *s.* Leanabaidheachd, leanabantachd, faoineas.
CHILDLESS, *a* Gun chlann, gun shiochd, neo-thorrach.
CHILIAD, *s.* Mìle.
CHILIARCH, *s* Ceannard mhìle.
CHILL, *a* Fuar, fionnar, fionn-fhuar; air gridcadh; tuirseach, dubhach.
CHILL, *s* Fuachd, crith-fhuachd; fionnarachd
CHILL, *v. a.* Fuaraich, fionnaraich; mi-mhisnich
CHILLINESS, *s* Fuaire, cion-teas, fonail; ball-chrith, crith-fhuachd.
CHILLNESS, *s.* Fuachd, fionnarachd, ball-chrith.
CHILLY, *a.* Fuar, fionnar, fionn-fhuar; fiunnar; reòt, reotaidh.
CHIME, *s.* Co'sheirm, fonn; gliong, gliongarsaich; fuaim.
CHIME, *v.* Dean co'sheirm, co'sheirmich, co'choird; gliong

CHIMERA, *s.* Faoin-smuaine, baoth-dhòchas; neònachas, amaideas, faoineas, faòineachd, diomhanas.
CHIMERICAL, *a.* Faoine, baoth, amaideach, diomhain
CHIMNEY, *s.* Simileir, luidheir, mùchan, sorn. Chimney corner, *cùil, taobh 'n teine.*
CHIMNEY-PIECE, *s.* Sùidhe-bhalaoch; gille-mùchain
CHIN, *s* Smig.
CHINA, *s* Oir-chriadh; soithichean finealta creadha
CHINCOUGH, *s.* An t-sriuth-chasd.
CHINE, *s.* Cnaimh na droma, druim, cliathag
CHINK, *s* Sgag, gag, sgàineadh, sgoltadh, bruchag, bearn, crac.
CHINK, *v.* Gliong, gleang
CHINKY, *a.* Sgagach, sgàinteach, sgoltach, bruchagach, bearnach
CHINTS, *s.* Seorsa aodaich canaich a thig as na h-Innseachan shios
CHIP, *v* Sliseagaich, sgath, pronn, dean meanbh; spealg, sgealb
CHIP, *s.* Sliseag; slios, stiall, sdiall; (*of stone*), spealg, sgealb, sgeireag.
CHIPPING, *s.* Sliseag; slios, spealg, sgealb.
CHIROGRAPHER, *s.* Sgriobhair, lamh-sgriobhair
CHIROGRAPHY, *s.* Sgriobhadh, lamh-sgriobhadh
CHIROMANCER, *s.* Lamh-dhruidh, lamh-fhiosaiche, dearnadair.
CHIROMANCY, *s.* Lamh-dhruidheachd, lamh-fhiosachd, dearnadaireachd.
CHIRP, *v.* Bid, dean bìdil; ceileir, ceileirich, biog.
CHIRPER, *s* Bìdear; ceileiriche; biogair.
CHIRPING, *s* Bìdeil, ceileir; biogail.
CHIRURGEON, *s.* Leigh, lighiche, lamh-leigh, dearg-leigh; taithleigh.
CHIRURGERY, *s* Lamh-leigheachd, dearg-leigheachd.
CHISEL, *s.* Gilcab, gilb.
CHIT, *s* Leanabh; fochann, foichlean.
CHIT-CHAT, *s.* Cracaireachd, bruidhinn, faoin chòmhradh.
CHITTERLINGS, *s* Mionach, greallach.
CHITTY, *a* Leanabaidh, leanabanta, faoin.
CHIVALROUS, *a.* Ridireach, treubhach, euchdmhor
CHIVALRY, *s* Ridireachd, treubhantachd, euchd, mòr-ghniomh, treunas
CHOCOLATE, *s.* Cnò na craoibh cocoa; sugh bhainne-chnothan.
CHOICE, *s* Taghadh, roghadh, roghainn; tocha; a chuid is fearr, brod. Pick and choice, *roghadh is taghadh*, take your choice, *gabh do roghainn*
CHOICE, *a.* Taghta, taghte; luachmhor; roghnuichte; curamach, grunndail
CHOIR, *s.* Ionad-ciùil; comh-cheòl, comh-chàntaireachd; luchd seinn, luchd ciùil, bannal ciùil, fioch.
CHOKE, *v* Tachd, mùch; dùin suas, druid seas Choked, *tachte*, he was almost choked, *theab e bhi tachdte.*
CHOKE, *s* Feusag farusgaig
CHOKER, *s* Tachdair, muchadair.
CHOLER, *s.* Fearg, corruich, ardan, lasan fearg
CHOLERIC, *a* Feargach, cas, cainnteach, crosda, ardanach, dranndanach, cabhagach; diomach, diombach, droch-mheineach, mithlachdmhor
CHOOSE, *v.* Tagh, roghnaich
CHOOSER, *s.* Taghadair, roghnachair.
CHOP, *v.* Sgud, sgath, gearr, pronn, spealg, sgealb
CHOP, *s* Spealg, sgealb, bloighde, pronnan; colag, toitean; sgolt, sgag, gag.

Chop-house, *s.* Tigh-ith.
Choppin, *s.* Seipinn.
Chopping, *a.* Cnaparra, cnapanta sultmhor, reamhar, bunach, fallain, mòr, tàbhachdach.
Chopping-block, *s.* Ineach; ealag.
Chopping-knife, *s.* Sgian colaig, sgian pronnaidh, *goll-bheir.*
Choppy, *a.* Tollta, tollach, tolltach; gagach, sgagach, sgoilte; brisg.
Chops, *s* Craos, beul, peirceall.
Choral, *a.* Co'sheirmeach
Chord, *s.* Teud innil ciùil, sreang.
Chorister, *s.* Comh-cheolraiche.
Chorographer, *s.* Cé-ghrabhair
Chorography, *s.* Cé-ghrabhachd.
Chorus, *s* Comh-cheòl, comh-sheinn, luinneag, fonn òrain
Chose, *pret.* of choose. Thagh, roghnaich.
Chosen, *part* Taghta, taghte, roghnaichte.
Chouse, *v.* Meall, thoir an car a.
Chouse, *s.* Mealladh, car, prat; umaidh.
Chrism, *s.* Oladh, ungadh.
Christ, *s.* Chriosd; an Slànuighfhear, an t-eadar-mheadhonair, Mac Dhé.
Christen, *v* Baisd, baist.
Christendom, *s.* A Chriosdachd. Throughout Christendom, *air feadh na Criosdachd.*
Christening, *s* Baisteadh
Christian, *s.* Criosduigh.
Christian, *a.* Criosduigheach, Criosdail.
Christianity, *s* Criosduigheachd, an creidimh Criosduigh.
Christianise, *v.* Iompaich thun a chreidimh Chriosduigh.
Christian name, *s.* Ainm baistidh, ainm Criosduigh.
Christmas, *s.* Nollaig.
Christmas-box, *s.* Column
Christ's thorn, *s* Scorsa droighne
Chromatic, *a* Dathach.
Chronic, **Chronical**, *a.* Maireannach, mairionnach; fadalach; buan.
Chronicle, *s.* Eachdraidh, seanachas, meanbh-eachdraidh, cuimhneachan.
Chronicler, *s.* Eachdair, eachdairiche, eachdraiche, seanachaidh; beolaiche.
Chronologer, *s.* Eachdraiche, seanachaidh
Chronology, *s.* Am-àireamh, aireamh aimsir; am chunntas, ùine-chunntas, ùineadaireachd
Chronometer, *s.* Uaireadair.
Chubbed, *a.* Pluiceach, pluiceanach, moigeanach, ploccheannach
Chuck, *v.* Gloc, gaganaich, gràdranaich; diugadh
Chuck, *s.* Gloc, gagan, gràdran, glocail; gradranaich; diug
Chuckle, *v.* Gloc; gràdranaich.
Chuckle, *s.* Gloc, glocail; diugadh
Chuff, *s.* Burraidh, ceothallan, umaidh, baoghlan, bodach.
Chuffiness, *s* Maol-cheannachd, burraidheachd, ceothallanachd, umaidheachd, baoghlanachd.
Chuffy, *a* Bodachail, gnò, gnù, ceothallanach, umaidheach.
Chum, *s.* Companach, combach, co'sheomaraiche.
Chump, *s* Ploc, ceann, ceap fiodha
Church, *s* Eaglais, tigh aoraidh, teampull; cill, co'thional, † durtach

Church attire, *s.* Culaidh eaglais, culaidh cléir; eudach caomhanta.
Churchman, *s.* Cléireach, pearsa eaglais, ministear
Churchwarden, *s.* Maor eaglais
Churchyard, *s.* Cladh, clachan, cill, aite adhlaic, ìonad torraidh.
Churl, *s.* Bodach; umaidh, burraidh, iargaltaiche; sgonn.
Churlish, *a.* Bodachail, umaidheach, umadail, iargaltach, gnò; borb; gionach; neo-shiobhailt, neo-aoidheil; crosda, cainnteach, doicheallach, gruamach.
Churlishly, *adv* Gu bodachail, gu h-umaidheach, gu h-umadail, gu h-iargaltach, gu gnò, gu borb, gu gionach; gu crosda, gu doicheallach.
Churlishness, *s.* Umaidheachd, iargaltachd, buirbe, neo-shiobhailteachd, crosdachd; doicheallachd.
Churm, *s.* Toirm, straoidhlearachd, gleadhraich.
Churn, *v.* Dean muighe, maistir; dean im.
Churn, *s.* Muighe, deirbh; cuinneag.
Chyle, *s.* Am biadh na shùgh geal anns a ghoil, mu'm fàs e na fhuil
Chymist, *s.* Teas-fheallsanach.
Chymistry, *s.* Teas-fheallsanachd.
Cibarious, *a* Biadhar, airson itheadh.
Cicatrice, *s* Aile, athailte, creuchd-lorg, leòn-lorg, comhar, sliochd
Cicatrization, *s.* Leigheas.
Cicatrize, *v.* Leighis
Cicurate, *v.* Ciùnaich, ceannsaich; mìnich, càtaich, criataich
Cicuration, *s.* Ciunachadh, ceannsachadh, mineachadh; criatachadh.
Cider, *s.* Sùgh nan ubhlan, ubhal-bhrigh.
Cierge, *s.* Coinneal adhlaic
Ciliary, *a.* Fabhrach, fabhrantach, rosgach
Cilicious, *a.* Roinneach, molach, ròmach, fionnach, gaoisteach.
Cimeter, *s.* Claidheamh crom, cloidhean, graillean, slaighre.
Cincture, *s* Bann, ceangal, crios; eachdrath, cearcall; lann; iadhlann; gàraidh.
Cinder, *s.* Guaillean; luath, luaithre.
Cinder-wench, *s* Sgumrag; cailleach luaithre
Cineration, *s.* Luaithreachadh.
Cineritious, *a.* Luaithreach.
† **Cingle**, *s.* Giort, tarrach, crios
Cinnabar, *s* Basgart
Cinnamon, *s.* Càineal
Cinque, *s.* Cùig, còig.
Cinquefoil, *s.* Seamrag chuig bhileach; cuig bhileach.
Cinque ports, *s.* Na cùig calaidh is dlùithe do 'n Fhrainc.
Cion, *s.* Fàilean, ur-fhàs, fiùran, maothan, meangan, meanglan, gineag.
Cipher, *s.* Comhar (no) figeir ann an cunntas, an litir O; fear gun fhiù, caifean.
Cipher, *v* Aireamh, cunnt.
Cipherer, *s.* Cunntair.
Ciphering, *s* Aireamh, cunntas, cunntaireachd.
Circinate, *v.* Cearcail.
Circle, *s.* Cearcal, siorcall, cuairteag; cuairt; beachd; fainne; (*company*), cuideachd, conaltradh, bannal; (*enclosure*), iadh-lann.
Circle, *v.* Cuartaich, cuairtich, cearcail, iadh, druid.
Circled, *a.* Cuartaichte, cuairtichte; cearclaichte; cruinn, cearclach.

Circling, *a.* Cearclach, cruinn; cuairteagach.

Circuit, *s.* Cuairt; fainne, coron, crùn, cuairt nam breitheamhna, cuairt nam morairibh dearg.

Circuiteer, *s.* Cuairtiche.

Circuitous, *a.* Cruinn; cuairteach; mu 'n cuairt.

Circular, *a.* Cruinn; cearclaichte, siorcullach.

Circularity, *s.* Cruinnead.

Circulate, *v.* Cuir mu 'n cuairt; cuir fa sgaoil.

Circulation, *s* Cuairt-imeachd; cruinn-ghluasad; cuairteachadh; ath-philltinn; sgaoileadh.

Circumambient, *a.* Cuairteach, cuairteanach, iadhach.

Circumcise, *v.* Timchioll-ghearr. Circumcised, *timchioll-ghearrte.*

Circumcised, *part.* Timchioll-ghearrte, timchioll-ghearrta

Circumcision, *s.* Timchioll-ghearradh

Circumference, *s.* Cruinne; cuairt-lìn, cuairte; cearcall, uime-astar.

Circumferentor, *s* Scorsa inneal tomhais.

Circumfluence, *s.* Uime-shruthadh.

Circumfluent, *a* Uime-shruthach; uime-lionach.

Circumforaneous, *a* Iomrolach

Circumfuse, *v.* Sgaoil, taosg, doirt, uime-dhoirt; iomasgaoil, spliot.

Circumfusion, *s.* Sgaoileadh, taosgadh, dortadh, uime-dhortadh.

Circumgyrate, *v* Ruithil.

Circumgyration, *s.* Ruithleadh.

Circumition, *s.* Cuairt-imeachd, dol mu 'n cuairt

Circumjacent, *a.* Fogus, fagus, dlu do, mu 'n cuairt.

Circumlocution, *s.* Cuairt, bhriathar, neo-dheas-labhairt, uime-labhairt.

Circumlocutory, *a.* Cuairt-bhriathrach, uime-labhradh.

Circummured, *a* Daingnichte mu 'n cuairt; ballach, uime-bhallach, uime-dhruidte.

Circumnavigate, *v.* Uime-sheòl, seòl mu 'n cuairt, cuairt-sheòl

Circumnavigator, *s* Cruinne-sheòladair.

Circumplication, *s* Uime-fhilleadh.

Circumposition, *s.* Cuairt-shuidheachadh, uime-shuidheachadh.

Circumrotation, *s.* Ruithleadh cuibhleadh

Circumrotaory, *a.* Ruithleach, cuibhleach.

Circumscribe, *v.* Cughannaich, druid, uime-dhruid, iomadhruid; ceannsaich.

Circumscription, *s.* Cughannachadh, druideadh, uime-dhruideadh, ioma-dhruideadh.

Circumspect, *a* Faicilleach, furachair, faireachail, aireachail, sicir, crionna, cùramach.

Circumspection, *s.* Faicill, faiceallachd, furachras, aire, sicireachd, crionnachd, cùram.

Circumspectly, *adv.* Gu faiceallach, gu furachair, gu faireachail, gu sicir, gu crionna, gu cùramach

Circumspective, *a.* Faicilleach, furachair, faireachail, aireachail, sicir, crionna, curamach.

Circumstance, *s.* Cùis, gnothach, rud, ni; cor; inbhe

Circumstanced, *a* Suidhichte, air chor.

Circumstant, *a* Cuairteach; iadhach.

Circumstantial, *a.* Tubaisdeach; araidh, sonruichte, suidhichte, pongail pungail.

Circumstantiate, *v.* Innis gu riochdail (no) gu pongail

Circumvallate, *v* Daighnich, daingnich; druid, iomachladhaich, uime-chladhaich

Circumvallation, *s.* Daighneachadh, daingneachadh, daingneach.

Circumvent, *v.* Meall, thoir an car a, diobair.

Circumvention, *s.* Mealladh, feall, foill, cealg, ceilg, fallsachd

Circumvolation, *s.* Uime-itealaiche.

Circumvolution, *s.* Uim-ròladh, dol mu 'n cuairt.

Circumvolve, *v.* Uime-ròl, ròl, ruidhil.

Circus, *s.* Preaban, cùirt; cuairt ionad chuairt-chleasan

Cisalpine, *a.* Tar-Ailpeach

Cist, *s.* Ciste; còmhdach.

Cistern, *s.* Amar, soitheach, tobar; sisteal

Citadel, *s.* Caisteal, caisdeal, dùn, daingneach, arm-lann

Cital, *s* Bardainn, rabhadh, sànas; gairm, achmhasan; comhdachadh; *suman*, provincial.

Cite, *v.* Gairm, orduich iarr.

Citer, *s.* Rabhadair, gairmear; bollsair

Citizen, *s.* Saor-fhear, cathaireach, fear mhuinntir baile

Citrine, *a* Odhar, buidhe, mar shìtron.

Citron, *s.* Sìtron, scorsa limaid

City, *s.* Cathair; baile, dùn; †duam. Cities, *cathraichean, bailtean.*

Civil, *a* Còir, siobhailt, siobhalta, suairc; caoimhneil, modhail; daonach, daonachdach; seolta, eòlach; duthchasach Civil law, *reachd dùthcha, lagh rioghachd*, civil war, *cogadh eadar muinntir na h-aon rioghachd.*

Civilian, *s.* Ollamh ann an Lagh na Roimh.

Civility, *s.* Siobhailteachd, siobhaltachd, suairceas, caoimhne, caoimhnealas, modhalachd, daonachd; saorsainn.

Civilize, *v.* Ciùnaich, oil, teagaisg, ceannsaich; smachd Civilized, *ceannsaichte, grinn, suairc, ciùin.*

Clack, *s.* Clag, glag; clabar, gnath-fhuaim.

Clad, *pret.* and *p part.* Comhdaichte, eudaichte, sgeadaichte

Claim, *v.* Iarr, sir, agair, tagair, cuir stigh airson, agair còir, tathaich Claimed, *air a thagradh*

Claim, *s.* Agradh, agartas, tathaich.

Claimable, *a* A dh' fhaotas agradh, so-thagradh.

Claimant, *s* Tagradair, tagarair, fear tagraidh, agartair, aon a thagras, fear agairt

Clamber, *v.* Streap, streap air éigin, dreap.

Clamminess, *s* Leanailteachd, righineachd, rithineachd

Clammy, *a.* Leanailteach, righinn, rithinn, stuceach, bitheanta.

Clamorous, *a* Fuaimreach, ard ghuthach; eigheach, eubhach, glaodhach; gàireach, blaoghach; sgairteach, bruidhneach, sostanach

Clamour, *s.* Fuaim, gàire, gaoir, gairtheach, ansgairt, glaodhaich, eigheachd, fos-ghàir, ard-ghlaodhaich.

Clamp, *s.* Clabhdan, mir, pàitse.

Clan, *s* Clann, fine, cine, cinneadh, teaghlach.

Clandestine, *a* Diomhair, sàmhach, gun fhios, uaigneach, seapach.

Clandestinely, *adv* Gu diomhair; gu samhach, gu h-uaigneach, gun fhios, os iosal.

Clang, *s* Gleang, gliong, fuaim.

Clangour, *s.* Gleangarsaich ghiongarsaich, gleang, gleangail, fuaim.

Clank, *s* Gleang, gliong; ard-stairirich.

Clank, *v.* Gleang, gliong.

Clanking, *s* Gleangail, gliongail.

Clap, *v* Bosbhuail, bois, bois-ghair, mol; buail air; clapainn.

Clap, *s.* Braidhe, coigeal; deanna; (*in surgery*), clab.

CLAPPER, *s.* Teangadh cluig; clagan muilinn, clagan, glagan.
† CLAPPER-CLAW, *v.* Troid; sglamhraich; mi-ghnathaich.
CLARET, *s.* Fiona dearg Francach.
CLARIFICATION, *s.* Siothladh, glanadh, soilleireachadh, siolachadh.
CLARIFY, *v.* Glan, siolaidh, siolaich, soilleirich.
CLARION, *s.* Stoc, adharc, buabhall, tromp, trompaid.
CLARITUDE, *s.* Soilleireachd; glaine, glainead; dealrachd, loinreachd.
CLARITY, *s.* Soilleireachd; glaine, glainead, dealrachd, loinreachd.
CLARY, *s.* Torman.
CLASH, *v.* Cuir an aghaidh, buail, sgeilc.
CLASH, *s.* Stathrum; fuaim, straplaich, sgeilc.
CLASP, *s.* Clic, broiste, braiste, clasb, crampaid.
CLASP, *v.* Glac, teann-ghlac; druid, gramaich; greimich; teannaich.
CLASP, *s.* Sgian druididh, golaidh.
CLASS, *s.* Earann, roinn, sreath, rang; ordugh; seorsa, treubh; clann, cinneadh.
CLASS, *v.* Cuir ann ordugh, roinn, riaghailtich, sreadaich.
CLASSIC, *s.* Ughdar measail, ard-ughdar.
CLASSIC, CLASSICAL, *a.* Ughdarach, ughdarail.
CLATTER, *v.* Dean gleadhraich, (no) straoidhlearachd; glag.
CLATTER, *s.* Gleadhraich, gàirich, gaòir, fuaim.
CLAUDICATE, *v.* Dean crupach (no) bacach, bacaich.
CLAUSE, *s.* Earann, cuibhrionn, roinn.
CLAUSTRAL, *a.* Mànachail.
CLAUSURE, *s.* Druideadh, dùnadh.
CLAVATED, *a.* Cnapach, meallach, meallanach, plucanach.
CLAVE, *pret.* of cleave. Sgoilt.
CLAVICLE, *s.* Cnaimh-coileir, cromag-ghuaille.
CLAW, *s.* Mòg, màg, smàg, cròg, cràg, iongna.
CLAW, *v.* Tachais, sgriob, sgròb, suath, rub, reub.
CLAWED, *a.* Mògach, màgach, smàgach, crògach, cràgach, iongnach.
CLAY, *s.* Criadh, creach; lathach; duslach, dusladh.
CLAY-COLD, *a.* Fuar mar chreadh; marbh, gun deò.
CLAYEY, *a.* Criadhach, creuchaidh, marbh, eugmhor.
CLAYPIT, *s.* Toll creadh, poll creuch; toll creuch.
CLEAN, *a.* Glan; finealta; nighte; neo-chiontach, gasta; geimnidh.
CLEAN, *v.* Glan, nigh, ionnlaid; cairt.
CLEANLINESS, *s.* Glaine; glainead, eireachdas, sgeinm, greantachd.
CLEANLY, *a.* Glan, neo-shalach; finealta; sgeinmeach; sgilmeil; grinn, eireachdail.
CLEANNESS, *s.* Glaine; finealtachd, sgeinm, sgilmeileachd, greantachd; neo-chiontachd.
CLEANSE, *v.* Glan, nigh, ionnlaid, sgùr, gealaich; cairt.
CLEANSED, *a.* Glan, nighte, ionlaidte, sgurta, sgurte; gealaichte.
CLEANSER, *s.* Glanadair, sgùradair, gealadair.
CLEAR, *a.* (*Bright*), loinnreach, dealrach, soilleir, geal, glan, soillseach; (*manifest*), soilleir; so-fhaicinn; (*transparent*), glan, soilleir, soillseach, trid-shoilleir, trid-shoillseach; (*innocent*), neo-lochdach, glan, ionraic, neo-chionntach; (*free*), saor, glan, réidh; (*distinct*) pongail, so thuigsinn, riachdail; reitichte. He came off free, *thainig e dheth saor.*
CLEAR, *v. a.* Soilleirich, reitich, dean reidh, fuasgail; glan; soillsich; (*clarify*) siothlaidh, siolaidh, saor. The day clears up, *tha 'n la 'togail, tha 'n la 'soilleireachadh*; cleared, *siolaidhte.*
CLEARANCE, *s.* Saoradh, saorsadh, saorsainn, fuasgladh: teisteas luinge o thigh na cìse.
CLEARER, *comp.* and *sup.* Glaine, soilleire, gile.
CLEARLY, *adv.* Gu soilleir, gu riachdail, gu glan, gu beachd, gu h-ionraic, gu saor, gun chosd.
CLEARNESS, *s.* (*Brightness*), loinnreachd, lannair, dealreachead, soilleireachd; soillse, trid-shoilleireachd; (*from fault*), ionracas, treibhdhireas.
CLEAR-SIGHTED, *a.* Geur-shuileach, biorach, geur, fradharcach, léirsinneach.
CLEAVE, *v.* Lean ri, dlù lean, stic ri; sgoilt, spealt, sgealb, spealg. Cleft, *sgoilte, spealgte.*
CLEAVER, *s.* Sgoltair, sgoiltear, spealtair, sgealbair, spealgair; sgian sgoltaidh, sgian (no) tuadh feoladair, *goilibhear.*
CLEF. (*In music*), Uchdach.
CLEFT, *s.* Sgolt, sgoltadh, gag, sgag, sgaineadh, crachd crac; sgoiltean.
CLEMENCY, *s.* Baigh, tròcair, iochd, caomhalachd, caoimhneas, seimhe, macantas, iochdalachd.
CLEMENT, *s.* Baigheil, tròcaireach, iochdmhor, caomh, caomhail, caoimhneil, seimh, macanta, ciùin, ceannsaidh, cinealta.
CLERGY, *s.* Cléir, cliar. The clergy, *a chléir.*
CLERGYMAN, *s.* Ministeir, pears, eaglais; sagairt; cléireach; eaglaiseach.
CLERICAL, *a.* Cliarach; cléireachail; sagairteil.
CLERK, *s.* Cléireach; sgriobhair, sgriobhaiche, sgriobhadair.
CLERKSHIP, *s.* Cléirsinneachd, cleireachd, sgriobhaireachd.
CLEVER, *a.* Tapaidh; deas; smearail, smiorail; sgileil, ullamh, teoma, clis; eòlach.
CLEVERLY, *adv.* Gu tapaidh, gu deas, gu smearail, gu sgileil, gu h-ullamh, gu tioma, gu clis.
CLEVERNESS, *s.* Tapachd; tapadh; deise, smearalas, teomachd, eòlas.
CLEW, *s.* Cearsle; cearsla; tònag, riaghailt.
CLEW, *v.* Cearsail, tacharais, toinneamh, toinn.
CLICK, *v.* Gliog, diog.
CLICKET, *s.* Glagan doruis.
CLIENT, *s.* Tromara; duisghille; dusair; fear a chuireas a chuis an lamh fir-lagha.
CLIFF, *s.* Craig, creag, sgor-bheann, stùc; craig chorrach; cnoc, binnean, sgeir, sgealb.
CLIMATE, *s.* Dùthaich; an t-àileadh; an aimsir.
CLIMAX, *s.* Dreimear; direadh.
CLIMB, *v.* Streap, dreap, dìr, dìrich.
CLIME. See CLIMATE.
CLINCH, *v.* Teann, teannaich, duin an dorn; lub.
CLINCH, *s.* Gearr-bhriathar; doilleireachd cainnte.
CLINCHER, *s.* Gramaiche.
CLING, *v.* Lean ri, croch ri; stic, † searg, sùigh, tiormaich.
CLINGY, *a.* Leanailteach, sticeach, rithinn.
CLINIC, *a.* Euslan, tinn, an-shocrach.
CLINK, *v.* Gliong, gleang.
CLINK, *s.* Giong, gleang, gliongan; bualadh, straoidhle, fuaim.
CLIP, *v.* Glac; bearr, gearr, lom, rùisg, lomair.
CLIPPER, *s.* Bearradair, gearradair, lomradair.
CLIPPING, *s.* Bearradh, gearradh, lomadh; rùsgadh, lomairt; piseag.
CLITORIS, *s.* Brillean.

Cloak, *s.* Clòc, cloc; fallainge; trusgan uachdrach; folach, falach, céile; sgàil; leithsgeul.

Cloak, *v.* Falluingich; folaich, ceil.

Cloak-bag, *s* Màileid, mailios.

Clock, *s.* Tràthadair, uaireadair; daol dubh.

Clockmaker, *s.* Uaireadairiche.

Clockwork, *s.* Obair uaireadair.

Clod, *s.* Fòid, faob, sod, clod, caob; †tarp, spairt; meall talmhain (no) creadha; umaidh.

Clod, *v.* Clod.

Cloddy, *a.* Clodach, caobach, foideach, faobach; salach, làthachach.

Clog, *v.* Amail, bac, tromaich, luchdaich, antromaich.

Clog, *s* Amaladh, amal, truime, luchd, eallach, uallach; brog mhaide.

Cloggy, *a.* Amalach; sticeach, trom, antrom.

Cloister, *s* Dion-bhothan; ionad bhan-naomh.

Cloisteral, *a.* Aonaranach, diadhaidh, manachail.

Cloistress, *s* Ban-naomh, cailleach dhubh.

Close, *v* Druid, dùin, criochnaich, comh-dhùin Close upon, *coird*, enclose, *iadh, cuairtich; tàth, cuir ri chéile.*

Close, *s.* Clobhsa, cuirt; clos, mainnir, †eacra; (*end*), crioch, fluid, ceann thall, combdhunadh, ceann-deiridh, deireadh.

Close, *a.* Dùinte, iadhte, druidte, glaiste; (*secret*), diomhair, uaigneach; folaichte; (*reserved*), dùinte, fad thall, seolta, eolach; cuilbheartach; (*dark*), dorcha; (*fast*), teann, cughann, cumhann; gramail; (*thick*), tiugh, dluthaichte; (*sultry*), blàth, bruich; (*near*), dlu, fogus, fagus.

Closebodied, *a.* Teann.

Closehanded, *a.* Cruaidh, sanntach, gionach, cruadalach, sgroingeanach, spiocach.

Closely, *adv.* Gu dùinte, gu teann, gu glaiste; gu h-uaigneach; gu seòlta, gu h-eolach, gu cuilbheartach, gu cughann; gu tiugh.

Closeness, *s.* Cughannachd, dùinteachd; diomhaireachd, uaigneachd; aonaranachd; gion, sannt; foigse, foigseachd.

Closer, *s.* Criochnuighear, criochnachair, fear criochnachaidh.

Closet, *s.* Clòsaid, seomar beag, seomar cùil

Closestool, *s.* Ceal-stòl

Closure, *s.* Dùnadh, druideadh; iadh-lann; crioch, comhdhunadh.

Clot, *v.* Slamaich. Clotted, *slamaichte*

Clot, *s.* Rag, meall cruaidh.

Cloth, *s.* Aodach, eudach; eideadh; clo; clóth, comhdach, cealt Clothes, eudach, trusgan.

Clothdresser, *s.* Leadanach; fear dheasachaidh aodaich.

Clothe, *v* Aodaich, eudaich, eid, comhdaich, sgeadaich uidheamaich; clùthaich, †ionair, faith. He shall be clothed, *sgeadaichear e, eudaichear e*, clothed, *aodaichte*

Clothes, *s.pl.* Aodach, eudach, trusgan, culaidh, uidheam.

Clothier, *s.* Marsonta aodaich; fear dheanamh aodaich, clòdair, clothadair.

Clothiery, *s.* Clothadaireachd.

Clothwork, *s.* Figheadaireachd; figheachas.

Clotpoll, *s.* Burraidh, umaidh, baoghlan; amhlair, céothallan.

Clotter, *v.* Slamaich; rag, reamhraich; cruadhaich; reoth.

Clotty, *a.* Slamach; slamaichte; reothte.

Cloud, *s.* Neul; dubh-neul; gruaim; doirche, dorchadas; duiseal, dubhachas, doilleireachd; duiseal.

Cloud, *v.* Neulaich; dorchaich, doilleirich.

Clouded, *a.* Neulach; gruamach, dorch; doilleir, duaichnidh, duisealach, duisnealach.

Cloudless, *s* Soilleir, gun neul.

Cloudy, *a* Neulach, neulmhor, gruamach, dorch, doilleir, duaichnidh, neo-shoilleir; dubhach, muladach.

Cloudily, *a.* Gu neulmhor, gu gruamach, gu dorch, gu doilleir, gu duaichnidh.

Clough, *s* Sgeir, sgor-bheann

Clout, *s.* Clùd, clùt; luideag, cearb, pìseag; (*on a shoe*), breaban

Clout, *v* Clùd, clùt, càirich. Clouted, *cairichte, clùdte*

Clouted, *part.* *Corruptly used for* clotted; which see.

Clouterly, *a* Cearbach

Clove, *pret* of cleave. Sgoilt, spealg, sgealb.

Clove, *s.* Clo-mheas, seorsa spiosraidh

Cloven, *part.* Sgoilte, roinnte, eadar-dhealaichte. Clovenfooted; speireach, ionga-sgoilte.

Clover, *s* Seomrag, seamrag, seamhrag, trì bhileag; seirg, *clòbhar.*

Clown, *s.* Umaidh, burraidh bodach, balaoch; fear gun oilean, gun bheus, tuathanach; amadan.

Clownish, *a.* Umaidheach, burraidheach, bodachail, balaochail, mi-mhodhail; brùideil, aineolach, neo-thuigseach.

Clownishness, *s* Umaidheachd, burraidheachd; mimhodhaileachd; brùidealachd.

Cloy, *v a* Sàsaich, lion; sleog, cuir gais air

Cloyment, *s.* Sàsachadh, làn, teann-shath, teann-sath.

Club, *s.* Caman; iomainiche; guitseal; slacan, †caoirle; (*company*), bannal, comunn, cuideachd; (*share*), lach, roinn, cuibhrionn

Club, *v.* Cuir cuid ri chéile; roinn costas.

Clubfooted, *a.* Sgabhrach; brod-chosach

Clubheaded, *s.* Ploc-cheannach.

Club-law, *s.* Lamh laidir; lagh airm.

Clubrush, *s.* Cruach luachair.

Cluck, *v* Gloc, gràdranaich, dean gloc (no) glocail, dean gradran, diug.

Clucking, *s.* Glocail; diugadh

Clump, *s* Creamhacan; coille-bheag; doire, bad, badan coille

Clumps, *s.* Baothair, burraidh, amadan, gleosgair, guraiceach.

Clumsily, *adv* Gu neo-chearmanta, gu cearbach, gu luidseach, gu gleosgach, gu neo-ghreannta, gu neo-lamhchair; gu faobach.

Clumsiness, *s* Neo-chearmantachd, cearbachd, luidseachd gleosgachd, neo-ghreanntachd neó-lamhchaireachd.

Clumsy, *a.* Neo-chearmanta, neo-chuimeir, luidseach, cearbach, gleosgach, neo-ghreannta, neo-lamhchair, faobach, bréin, neo-ghrinn; neo-theoma, neo-lathailteach.

Clung, *pret.* of cling; which see.

Clung, *a* Caol; truagh, seargte.

Cluster, *s.* Bagaid, baguid, bagaist; cluigean, dos, triopaill, triopuill; (*group of animals*), greidh, cròilean, droilean; (*of people*), co' chruinneachadh; lòd, dròbh, bannal, cuideachd

Cluster, *v.* Bagaidich, cluigeanaich; dosraich

Clustery, *a.* Bagaideach, baguideach; cluigeanach, dosach; dosrach, triopuilleach.

Clutch, *v* Sglamh, thoir sglamh; glac, greimich, gramaich

Clutch, *s.* Greim, glaic, smàg, cròg, lamh, màg, ionga. Clutches, *smàgan, crògan.*

Clutter, *s.* Stairn, farum, fuaim, stathrum, glaodhar

Clyster, *s.* Seorsa sgiort; sgiort-cuim.

COACERVATE, *v.* Cruach, stocaich, cnuasaich.

COACERVATION, *s.* Cruachadh; stacachadh, cnuasachadh, cnuasachd, tionaladh; cruach.

COACH, *s.* Carbad aigheir, car, cathair, *coidse.*

COACHHOUSE, *s.* Tigh carbaid; *tigh coidse.*

COACHMAKER, *s.* Carbair.

COACHMAN, *s.* Carbadair, fear carbaid.

COACTION, *s.* Aineart; éigin, eigneachd, lamh-laidir.

COACTIVE, *a.* Aineartach; eigneachail, eigneach.

COADJUMENT, *s.* Co' cho-ghnadh, comh-chuideachadh, co' oibreachadh.

COADJUTOR, *s.* Fear-co'ghnaidh, fear cuideachaidh; comh-oibriche.

COADUNITION, *s.* Coimeasgadh.

COAGMENT, *v.* Co' thionail, cuir ri chéile, cruach, cnuasaich.

COAGMENTATION, *s.* Co' thionaladh, cruach, cnuasachd.

COAGULABLE, *a.* So-bhinnteachaidh, so-bhinntichte; so-shlamachaidh.

COAGULATE, *v.* Binntich, slamaich, tiughaich.

COAGULATIVE, *a.* Binnteachail, slamachail.

COAL, *s.* Gual; guaillean.

COALERY, *s.* Guailleareachd, obair-ghuail, toll guail, sloc-guail.

COALESCE, *v.* Comh-fhàs, comh-chinn; coimeasg, aontaich; bann.

COALESCENCE, *s.* Comh-fhàs; coimeasgadh, aontachadh; binnteachadh, slamachadh.

COALHOUSE, *s.* Tigh guail.

COALMINE, *s.* Slochd guail, toll guail.

COALWORK, *s.* Guailleireachd, obair ghuail.

COALY, *s.* Gualach, gualaidh; guailleanach.

COARCT, COARCTATE, *v. a.* Cughannaich, teannaich, daighnich; dluthaich; tiughaich.

COARSE, *a.* Garbh; neo-fhinealta, *cursa;* neo-ghrinn; neo-mhìre; (*in manners*), mi-mhodhail, borb, neo-shiobhailt, doirbh, gnò.

COARSELY, *adv.* Gu garbh, gu neo-fhinealta; gu mi-mhodhail, gu borb.

COARSENESS, *s.* Gairbhe, gairbhead, neo-fhinealtachd; tiughad, mi-mhodhaileachd, mi-mhodh, buirbe.

COAST, *s.* Tìr, cladach; tràigh, eirthir, slios; còrsadh, crioch; taobh, iomall.

COAST, *v.* Còrsaich, seol dlù do thir.

COASTER, *s.* Corsaiche, corsair.

COASTING, *s.* Corsaireachd, seòladh fagus air tìre.

COAT, *s.* Còt; sgannan, còmhdach; falluinge, (*vesture demonstrative of office*), eide, eidiuh, aodach; (*of a beast*), calg, colg, fionnadh. A long coat, *cosag, cot leabhar;* a short coat, *cot goirrid;* a female's under coat, *còt iochdair, cot bùn.*

COAT, *v.* Comhdaich; cuibhrig; eid, spréid, faluingich.

COAX, *v. a.* Dean sodal, dean miodal, breug.

COAXER, *s.* Sodalaiche, miodalair.

COB, *s.* Ceann, mullach, bàrr, gob.

COB, *s.* Seorsa eoin mara; damhan alluidh.

COBBLE, *v.* Cairich, clùd, breidich.

COBBLER, *s.* Brògair, fear charamh shean-bhròg, clùdair.

COBBLING, *s.* Brògaireachd; cludaireachd.

COBIRON, *s.* Bota, bota-iaruinn, iarunn laimh.

COBNUT, *s.* Seorsa cluiche cloinne.

COBSWAN, *s.* Priomh ealadh, ealadh an tùs na h-ealt.

COBWEB, *s.* Lion damhain alluidh, eididh damhain, eididh figheadair fodair.

COBWEB, *a.* Faoin, fann, lag, anfhann, so-bhriseadh.

COCCIFEROUS, *a.* Dearcach, dearcagach, caorach.

COCHINEAL, *s.* Coiseineil, ruaidhmre, dath-sgarlaid.

COCHLEARY, *a.* Sgrobhach, faochagach.

COCK, *s.* Coileach; (*weathercock*), coileach-gaoithe; (*of a barrel*), goc; (*of an arrow*), riobhag, ribheag; (*of a gun*), acfhuinn, achduinn; (*of a man*), bod; (*a leader*), laoch, feadhna, feodhna, ceann-feadhna; (*of hay*), còil, cuidhleag, curachdag, rucan; (*of a hat or bonnet*), cocainn.

COCK, *v.* Tog suas gu peirteil; cocainn; (*cock hay*), cuidhle; (*strut*), imich gu spairiseach.

COCKADE, *s.* Cocàd, dos, suaicheantas.

COCKATRICE, *s.* Righ-nathair, nathair nimhe, nathair chìreach, † suil-mhalari.

COCKBAWD, *s.* Siùrsach, siùrsdach, striopach.

COCKBOAT, *s.* Curach, còit, sgoth, corcan.

COCKBROTH, *s.* Eun-bhrigh; eun-bhruith.

COCK-CROWING, *s.* Goir-choilich, gairm-choilich.

COCKER, *s.* Gleachdair choileach.

COCKER, *v.* Breug, tàladh.

COCKEREL, *s.* Coileach òg, eun coilich.

COCKFIGHT, *s.* Cog-choileach, cath-choileach. The cock-fight day, *là cog nan coileach.*

COCKHORSE, *adv.* Air muin eich.

COCKLE, *s.* Cogal, iothros; eanntag, eanntagach; (*in ichthyology*), sruban, coilleag, dubh-iasgan.

COCKLED, *a.* Coilleagach, srubanach.

COCKLESTAIRS, *s.* Staidhir, chuairteach.

COCKLOFT, *s.* Garait, spàr.

COCKMATCH, *s.* Cog-choileach.

COCKNEY, *s.* Lunnuinneach, fear a mhuinntir Lunnuinn.

COCKSCOMB, *s.* Gaothan, lasgair.

COCKSURE, *a.* Lan chìnnteach.

COCKSWAIN, *s.* Maighstir bata.

COCOA, *s.* Seorsa croinn pailm.

COCTILE, *a.* Bruitheach, bruith, bruich; fuinte.

COCTION, *s.* Bruitheadh bruicheadh; fuineadh, cnàmh.

COD, *s.* (*Fish*), Bodach ruadh, trosg; (*a husk*), cochall, cochull, spalag, rusg, meiligeag, mcinigeag; plaosg, (*of the testicles*), magairle, magairlean.

CODE, *s.* Leabhar; riaghailt, lagh.

CODICIL, *s.* Fàth-sgriobhadh teismeid, leasachadh tiomnaidh.

CODLE, *v.* Leth-bhruich, droch-dheasaich.

COEFFICACY, *s.* Comh-éifeachd.

COEFFICIENCY, *a.* Comh-obair, comh-oibreachadh.

COEFFICIENT, *a.* Comh-oibreachail.

COEMPTION, *s.* Comh-cheannachadh, comh-cheannachd.

COEQUAL, *a.* Comh-ionann.

COEQUALITY, *s.* Comh-ionannachd, leth-bhreacas.

COERCE, *v.* Bac, ceannsaich, smachd, cum air ais; iomain.

COERCION, *s.* Bacadh, ainneart, cumail air ais ceannsal, smachd.

COERCIVE, *a.* Bacach, smachdach, ceannsalach; iomaineach.

COESSENTIAL, *a.* Comh-stuthach; comh-bhitheach.

COESSENTIALITY, *s.* Comh-stuthachas, comh-bhith.

COETANEOUS, *a.* Comh-aosmhor; comh-aois; comh-aosda.

COETERNAL, *a.* Comh-shiorruidh, comh-bhibhuan.

COETERNITY, *s.* Comh-shiorruidheachd, comh-bhibhuantachd.

COEVAL, *a.* Comh-aosmhor, comh-aois, comh-aosda, san aon linn, comh-linnteach.

Coexist, *v.* Comh-bhith; mair beò ionann ri
Coexistence, *s.* Comh-bhith.
Coexistent, *a.* Comh-bhitheach; comh-chinneasach, comh-fhasach.
Coffee, *s.* Seorsa dearcaig Arabaich.
Coffeehouse, *s.* Tigh-osda araidh.
Coffer, *s.* Cobhan; cisteag, cobhan ionmhais, aire, carcar.
Coffin, *s.* Cisde mairbh.
Cog, *v.* Meall, thoir an car a; tàladh, breug.
Cog, *s.* Fiacal; fiocal rotha muilinn.
Cogency, *s.* Neart, spionnadh, lamh làidir, cumhachd, ain-neart.
Cogent, *s.* Neartmhor, neartar, laidir, treun, éifeachdach; cumhachdach.
Cogger, *s.* Sodalaiche, miodalaiche, fear goileamach.
Cogglestone, *s.* Doirneag.
Cogitable, *a.* So-bheachdachadh, so-smuaineachadh.
† **Cogitate**, *v.* Beachdaich, smuanich; smuaintich.
Cogitation, *s.* Beachdachadh, smuainteachadh, smuaine-achadh, breithneachadh, smu'airean, curam.
Cogitative, *a.* Beachdachail, smuainteachail.
Cognation, *s.* Cinneach, cinneadh; daimh, cairdeas, caidreamh.
Cognition, *s* Fios, beachd, aithne; eòlas; geur-mhoth-achadh; deuchainn.
Cognizable, *a.* Buailteach do bhreitheanas, airidh air fheachainn; freagarrach; neo-laghail
Cognizance, *s.* Cunntas, ùghdaras, comhar.
Cognominal, *a.* Sloinnteachail.
Cognomination, *s.* Sloinne, cinneadh.
Cognoscible, *a.* So-aithneachadh.
Cohabit, *v.* Comhnuich; comh-thuinich, luidh le.
Cohabitant, *s.* Comhnuiche, fear-comhnuidh; comh-thuiniche.
Coheir, *s.* Comh-oighre.
Coheiress, *s.* Comh-bhan-oighre.
Cohere, *v.* Co-chroch, co-lean, stic ri.
Coherence, *s.* Comh-chrochadh; leanailteachd, righne-achd.
Coherent, *a.* Sticeach, leanailteach; righinn, rithinn.
Cohesion, *s.* Leanailteachd, righneachd.
Cohesive, *a.* Leanailteach, sticeach, righinn, rithinn
Cohort, *s.* Buidheann shaighdearan, aireamh chuig ceud.
Coif, *s.* Deise-cinn, currachd, cuailean, bréid; ceap, bonaid.
Coifure, *s.* Deise-cinn.
Coil, *s.* Trus, trusag; cuidhleag; còil cruinneachadh, tu-aireap; tabaid.
Coil, *v.* Trus; cuidhle; còil robhainn sa cheile; cruinnich.
Coin, *v.* Cùin.
Coin, *s.* Cùin, cùinne; airgiod cùinte, airgiod.
Coinage, *s.* Cùineadh, cùinneadh.
Coincide, *v.* Tachair; coird, co' choird, aontaich.
Coincidence, *s.* Tachairt, cordadh, comh-chordadh; aont-achadh.
Coincident, *a.* Comh-thachairteach, comh-fhreagarach.
Coindication, *s.* Comh-thuaradh, comh-innseadh,
Coiner, *s.* Cuinnear, cùintear.
Coistril, *s.* Cladhair.
Coit, *s.* Peilistear, leac peilisteir.
Coition, *s.* Leannanas, coimhreatain; slataireachd; (*of poultry*), chathadh.
Coke, *s.* Guaillean

Colander, *s.* Siolachan, criathar, criabhar, dlochd, dlochdan.
Colation, *s.* Sioladh, glanadh, siolachadh.
Colature, *s.* Sioladh, siothlachadh, glanadh.
Cold, *a* Fuar, fuaraidh, fionn-fhuar, fionnar; (*indifferent*), neo-sheadhar, coidhis; coimheach, neo-chairdeal, neo-fhaoilidh, (*chaste*), gast, geimnidh; (*of temper*), neo-ghrad, neo-chas He who feels cold let him clothe, *am fear leis am fuar, fuaidheadh e.*
Cold, *s* Fuachd, cnatan, casd; slaotan; fuarachd, fionn-arachd
Coldly, *adv* Gu fuar, gu fuaraidh; gu fionn-fhuar, gu fionnar, neo-sheadhar, coidhis, coimheach, gu neo-chaird-eil, neo-fhaoilidh; gu gast; gu geimnidh.
Coldness, *s.* Fuachd, fuaraidheachd, funtuinn, reòtadh, mi-sheadh; neo-churam; coimheachas; cion-seirc, geimn-idheachd.
Cole, *s* Càl.
Colewort, *s.* Cal, còlbhairt.
Colic, *s.* Coiliginn, brù-ghoirt, goirteas mionaich.
Collapse, *s.* Co' thuiteam, co' dhunadh.
Collar, *s.* Coileir, fàil-mhuineil; muinge, muin-theud, teud-bhraghad; nasg, bann-muineil
Collarbone, *s.* Cnaimh na guaille.
Collate, *v.* Coimeas, coimheas, cuir ri chéile, cuir an ordugh.
Collateral, *a.* Taobh ri taobh.
Collation, *s.* Bladh, lòn; coimeas, cur ri chéile.
Collator, *s.* Coimheasair, coimheasadair.
Collaud, *v.* Comh-mhol.
Colleague, *s.* Comh-oibriche, companach, comh-phairtiche; gualliche.
Collect, *v.* Teanail, tionail, cruinnich, cnuasaich, comh-thionail; tog.
Collect, *s.* Urnuigh aimsir; urnuigh ghearr bhrighar
Collectaneous, *a.* Tionailte; coimeasgte.
Collected, *a* Tionailte, tianailte, cruinnichte, cruinn, an ceann a chéile; cearamanta; sicir.
Collection, *s.* Tional, teanal, tionaladh, teanaladh; coimh-thional; cruinneach, cruinneachadh; comh-chruinneach-adh, cnuasachd; (*for the poor*), deirc; naomh-dheirc; obhraig. A corruption perhaps of *naomh-dheirc.*
Collective, *a.* Cruinnichte, tionailte, teanailte.
Collectively, *adv* Gu cruinn, gu léir, gu h-iomlan
Collector, *s.* Cruinneachair, trusadair, tionalaiche, fear trusaidh; cis-thogair, fear-togalach.
College, *s.* Oil-thigh, Ard-sgoil, tigh-oil, colaisd, ard-thigh foghluim.
Collide, *v.* Buail, sgeilc.
Collier, *s.* Guaillear, gualadair, gual-thochailtear; luingeas guail. Colliers, *guaillearan*
Colliery, *s.* Guaillearachd, obair-ghuail.
Colliflower, *s.* Càl-còlag.
Colligation, *s.* Comh-cheangladh; comh-cheangal, comh-bhannachadh, comh-fhastadh.
Colliquable, *a.* So-leaghadh
Colliquant, *a.* Leaghach, comh-leaghach.
Colliquate, *v.* Leagh, comh-leagh; bogaich, taislich
Colliquation, *s.* Leaghadh, comh-leaghadh; bogachadh, taisleachadh.
Colliquefaction, *s.* Leaghadh, comh-leaghadh.
Collision, *s* Comh-bhualadh, sgeilc, braidhe.
Collocate, *v.* Suidhich, àitich
Collocation, *s* Suidheachadh, suidheach, àiteachadh

Collocution, *s.* Comhradh, bruidhinn, cracaireachd.

Collop, *s.* Toitean, colag, staoig.

Colloquial, *a.* Comhraidh, cainnteach, bruidhneach.

Colloquy, *s.* Comhradh, bruidhinn, cracaireachd, comh-labhairt; cainnte; conaltradh.

Colluctation, *s.* Gleachd, comh-ghleachd, spairn; spid, gamhlas.

Collusion, *s.* Cealg-chordadh, comh-aontachadh.

Collusive, *a.* Cealgach, fealltach, mealltach, pratach, carach.

Colly, *s.* Dubhadan guail, dubhadh guail.

Collyrium, *s.* Sabh-shùl.

Colon, *s.* (*In punctuation*), Pung, lan-phung.

Colon, *s.* (*In anatomy*), Caolan.

Colonel, *s.* Coirneal, cath-mhilidh; ceannard mile, fear-ceannard, réismeid.

Colonize, *v.* Aitich, tìrich, bruidhich; suidhich ceathara.

Colony, *s.* Aiteachas, bruidheachd.

Colorate, *a.* Daithte, lighte.

Coloration, *s.* Dathadh, dathadaireachd.

Colorific, *a.* Dathach.

Colossus, *s.* Dealbh mòr; cruth mòr.

Colour, *s.* Dath, neul, dreach, tuar, ligh; céileadh, sgàil, leithsgeul. Colours, (*ensigns*), bratach, suaicheantas, meirghe.

Colour, *v.* Dath; céil; gabh leithsgeul.

Colourable, *a.* So-dhathadh.

Coloured, *a.* Daithte; dàicheil; eug-samhuil.

Colouring, *s.* Dathadh; dath, ligh; leithsgeul.

Colourless, *a.* Gun dath; bàn; glasdaidh; trid-shoilleir.

Colours, *s.* Bratach, suaicheantas, suaitheantas, meirghe.

Colt, *s.* Searrach, oigeach, biriche, loth, lothag, clibeag; gaothan òg.

Coltish, *a.* Mear; meamnach; beiceiseach; drùiseil.

Coltsfoot, *s.* An gallan greannchair; fathan.

Coltstooth, *s.* Biorag, bireag.

Columbine, *s.* Lus a cholamain, lus a choluim.

Column, *s.* Stùc, colmhuinn, post; uaithne, seaghlan, rang, bannal, cuideachd; (*of a book*), leth-thaobh duilleig.

Coma, *s.* Galar codail; turrachdal, suaine-ghalar.

Comate, *s.* Combach, companach.

Comatose, *a.* Codalach, turra-chodalach; trom.

Comb, *v.* Cìr; ciom; card.

Comb, *s.* Cìre; (*of a cock*), cìrean; (*honeycomb*), cire-mheal.

Combat, *s.* Comhrag, comhrag deise; tuasaid, gleachd; baiteal, batailte.

Combat, *v.* Comhraig, cuir an aghaidh; thoir ionnsuidh, cathaich.

Combatant, *s.* Comh-ghleacadair, gleacair, namhaid, laoch, cùraidh, milidh, † adhlan.

Comber, *s.* Cìreadair; cardair.

Combination, *s.* Bann; comh-bhann, comh-chomhairle; comh-bhoinn.

Combine, *v.* Comh-aontaich; comh-choird, coird.

Combined, *a.* Comh-aontaichte, dluthaichte ri chéile, ceangailte; ann an comh-bhoinn.

Combless, *a.* Gun chìse, gun chìrean.

Combustible, *a.* Faloisgeach, grad-loisgeach, so-loisgeach, leusach, lasarra.

Combustion, *s.* Losgadh, falosgadh.

Come, (*a word of exhortation.*) So, sud, greas. Come, be of good cheer, *so, tog do mhisneach.*

Come, (*a word of reconciliation.*) So so, sud sud. Come come, let us be friends, *so so, bitheamaid réidh.*

Come, *s.* Thig, tiucainn; teann, dluthaich; trobhd. When we come to die, *nur thig sinn dlù do 'n bhàs;* come about, *thig mu 'n cuairt, thig gu criche;* what are you come about? *ciod mu bheil air tighinn, ciod mu 'n d'thàinig thu;* come back, *pill, thig air ais;* come back soon, *thig air d'ais a chlisge;* come at, *ruig;* come in, *thig a steach, thig a stigh, intrinn;* come on, *thig air d'adhairt, thig air d'aghaidh;* to come, *ri teachd, ri tighinn;* come to pass, *tachair, thig gu criche;* it will come to pass, *tarlaidh e;* come again, *thig a ris;* come down, *thig a bhàn, thig a nuas, teirinn;* come forth, *thig a mach;* come off well, *thig dheth gu maith;* come out here, *thig a mach an so;* when all comes to all, *mu dheireadh, air a cheann thall, mu dheireadh is mu dhiù;* come near, *thig am fagus, druid am fagus;* he will come to by degrees, *thig e h-uige chuid is a chuid;* come short of, *thig gearr air;* come with child, *fas torrach;* come together, *cruinnich, tionail;* come to hand, *thig gu laimh.*

Comedian, *s.* Cluicheadair, cleasaiche.

Comedy, *s.* Dealbh-chluiche, cluiche anns am bheil beusan an t-sluaigh air am feuchainn.

Comeliness, *s.* Tabhachd, maise, eireachdas, seamhachd, breaghachd, dàichealachd, tlachd, sgiamh, boidhicheas, deagh-mhaise.

Comely, *a.* Tabhachdach, maiseach, eireachdail, seimh, breagh, grinn, dàicheil, tlachdmhor, sgeamhail, bòidheach, sgiamhach; ciatach, cubhaidh.

Comely, *adv.* Gu tabhachdach, gu maiseach, gu h-eire-achdail, gu seimh, gu breagh, gu grinn, gu dàicheil, gu tlachdmhor, gu sgiamhail, gu boidheach, gu sgiamhach, gu ciatach, gu cubhaidh.

Comer, *s.* Teachdair.

Comet, *s.* Rionnag iomrolach.

Comfiture, *s.* Millsean.

Comfort, *v.* Furtaich, comh-fhurtaich, sòlasaich, beothaich; thoir aiteas.

Comfort, *s.* Furtachd, comh-fhurtachd, sòlus, aiteas, cabh-air, cobhair, socair, toileach inntinn.

Comfortable, *a.* Sòlasach, taitneach, socrach, tiorail.

Comforter, *s.* Solasaiche, comh-fhurtair; an Spiorad Naomh.

Comfortless, *a.* Dubhach, gun sòlas, gun chomh-fhurt-achd.

Comic, *a.* Neonach, iongantach, atharrach, cleasach; mear, cridheil, abhachdach.

Comical, *a.* Neonach, iongantach, atharrach, mear, cridheil, ait; abhachdach.

Comeliness, *s.* Neonachas; àbhachdas, cleasachd.

Coming, *s.* Teachd, tighinn, tarruinn dlù (no) am fagus.

Coming, *s.* Tighinn stigh, teachd stigh, teachd a steach, màl.

Comity, *s.* Cùirtealachd, modhaileachd, siobhailteachd.

Comma, *s.* Pongan ann an sgriobhadh mar so (,).

Command, *v.* Orduich, àithn, iarr; thoir ordugh, thoir àithne, riaghail; † tiomairn.

Command, *s.* Ordugh, aithne, iarrtas; cumhachd; ughd-darras, ceannas, ceannartas, ceannardas; rioghladh, com-annt, congart. At your command, *air d'iarrtas, fo do chomannt, fo do sgòd.*

Commander, *s.* Uachdaran, ceann feadhna, ceannard; caiptean; slachdan cahhsair. Commander-in-chief, *tu-airgneach càtha.*

Commandress, *s.* Ban-uachdran; ban-cheannard.

Commemorable, *a.* Ri chuimhneachadh, airidh air chuimh-neachadh.

COMMEMORATE, *v.* Cuimhnich, cum cuimhne.
COMMEMORATION, *s.* Cuimhneachan, cuimhne.
COMMEMORATIVE, *a.* Cuimhneachail.
COMMENCE, *v.* Tòisich, tionnsgain.
COMMENCEMENT, *s.* Toiseach, toiseachadh, tionnsgnadh, tùs.
COMMEND, *v.* Mol, cliùthaich; earb, tiomnadh.
COMMENDABLE, *a.* Ionmholta, airidh air moladh, cliùthar.
COMMENDABLY, *adv.* Gu h-ionmholta.
COMMENDATION, *s.* Moladh, cliù, cliùth, teireadh, deagh theisteannas.
COMMENDATORY. Moladach, moltach.
COMMENDER, *s.* Moladair.
COMMENSURABILITY, *s.* Comh-thomhaiseachd.
COMMENSURABLE, *a.* Comh-thomhaiseach, comh-fhreagarach, comh-chruinn, comh-ionann.
COMMENSURATION, *s.* Comh-thomhas.
COMMENT, *v.* Mìnich, cuir an céil, leudaich.
COMMENTARY, *s.* Mìneachadh; soilleireachadh; eachdraidh; meanbh-eachdraidh.
COMMENTATOR, *s.* Mìneachair, fear mìneachaidh.
COMMENTER, *s.* Mìneachair; leudachair.
COMMENTITIOUS, *a.* Fallsa, breugach, faoin.
COMMERCE, *s.* Comh-cheannachd; geilios, malairt, comh-mhalairt, comh-chaidreamh; conaltradh, comh-thorrachd, caigleachd; ceaird; seorsa cluiche air chairtean.
COMMERCE, *v.* Comh-cheannaich; comh-mhalairt; cum caidreamh, cum conaltradh.
COMMERCIAL, *a.* Comh-chaidreach, comh-mhalairteach, malairteach, ceairdeil.
COMMINGLE, *v.* Coimeasg.
COMMINUTE, *v.* Pronn, méill, mìn-phronn.
COMMINUTION, *s.* Pronnadh, méilleadh.
COMMISERABLE, *a.* Truagh, diblidh.
COMMISERATE, *v.* Gabh truas ri.
COMMISERATION, *s.* Truas; comh-mhothachadh, truacantas, tròcair.
COMMISSARISHIP, *s.* Coimisearachd, coimisdearachd.
COMMISSARY, *s.* Coimisear, coimisdear.
COMMISSION, *s.* Barantas, ughdarras; earbsadh; oifig.
COMMISSION, *v.* Barantaich, ughdarraich, thoir comas, thoir ughdarras, earb.
COMMISSIONER, *s.* Ughdarraiche, fear aig am bheil ùghdarras.
COMMISSURE, *s.* Tàthadh, comh-thàthadh.
COMMIT, *v.* Earb, tiomnadh; cuir an laimh; gainntirich; gnathaich, cuir cionnt an gniomh.
COMMITMENT, *s.* Priosanachadh, priosanachd, cur an laimh.
COMMITTEE, *s.* Comunn riaghluidh, cuideachd riaghlaidh.
COMMITTEE, *s.* Ciontach.
COMMIX, *v.* Coi'mheasg; cuir feadh chéile, measg, measgnaich.
COMMIXTURE, *s.* Coimeasgadh.
COMMODIOUS, *a.* Iomchuidh, freagarrach; feumail; garail; rùmar, ceart, cubhaidh; uibhseil.
COMMODIOUSLY, *adv.* Gu h-iomchuidh, gu freagarrach, gu garail, gu ceart, gu cubhaidh.
COMMODIOUSNESS, *s.* Iomchuidheachd, freagarrachd, feumalachd.
COMMODITY, *s.* Leas, tairbhe, maith, proidhit; iomchuidhead; bàrr, bàthar, gleus, cungaidh, nì, maoin.
COMMODORE, *s.* Ceannard cabhlaich, ard-mharaiche.
COMMON, *a.* Cumanta, cumaint, coitchionn; gnathaichte, follaiseach, àbhaisteach; minic, dìblidh, iosal. Common people, *sluagh cumaint, prabar, gràisge, gasradh, tuath.*
COMMON, *s.* Talamh coitchionn.
COMMONAGE, *s.* Ionaltradh, còir ionaltraidh.
COMMONALTY, *s.* Tuath, tuath-cheatharna, an cumanta, an sluagh; gasradh, prabar, gràisg.
COMMONER, *s.* Tuathanach, ceatharnach, duine cumaint (no) cumanta; ball thigh na *Tuath-chomhairle;* Sgoilear don dara sreath ann an *Oxford;* † siursach.
COMMONITION, *s.* Comhairle, rabhadh, sanas.
COMMONLY, *adv.* Gu cumanta, gu cumainte, gu tric, gu minic, gu bidheanta, gu coitchionnta, an cumantas, mar is tric, mar is gnàth, mar is cumainte.
COMMONNESS, *s.* Cumantas, bidheantachd, coitchionntachd.
COMMONPLACE, *a.* Cumanta, cumainte; minic.
COMMONPLACE-BOOK, *s.* Iris-leabhar, aithris-leabhar.
COMMONS, *s.* Tuath; sluagh cumainte, prabar, gràisge; a chomhairle iochdrach ann tigh na *parlamaid;* biadh, lòn, comh-lòn ann an ard-sgoilean.
COMMONWEALTH, *s.* Comh-fhlaitheachd; comunn.
COMMOTION, *s.* Buaireas, tuasaid, brionglaid, eas-ordugh, aimhreit, connsach, comhstri, tabaid, dùsgadh.
COMMUNE, *v.* Labhair, comh-labhair, cum comunn (no) conaltradh.
COMMUNICABLE, *a.* Rann-phàirtichte, so-bhuileachadh.
COMMUNICANT, *s.* Fear comanaich, comanaiche. Communicants, *luchd-comanaich, muinntir comanaich.*
COMMUNICATE, *v. a.* and *n.* Innis, cuir an céill; comh-labhair, thoir, thabhair, tabhair, builich; foillsich; gabh comanach.
COMMUNICATION, *s.* Comh-chaidreamh; comh-innseadh, comh-labhairt, comhradh, comhluadar, conaltradh.
COMMUNICATIVE, *a.* Comhradhach, comhraiteach; bruidhneach; neo-dhùinte; beulchar, gobach, lonach, peilpeanta.
COMMUNION, *s.* Comhluadar, conaltradh, comunn, comh-chomunn, companas, caidreamh, aonachd; suipeir an Tighearna.
COMMUNITY, *s.* Comh-fhlaitheachd; comh-shealbh, comh-sheilbh, comhrannaich.
COMMUTABILITY, *s.* Comh-chaochlaideachd; co-mhalairteachd, comh-iomlaideachd.
COMMUTABLE, *a.* Comh-chaochlaideach, co-mhalairteach, comh-iomlaideach, so-iomlaideach, so-mhùghadh; so-mhùthadh.
COMMUTATION, *s.* Co-chaochladh, co-mhalairt, co-iomlaid, co-mhùghadh, co-mhuthadh.
COMMUTE, *v.* Caochlaidh, malairt, iomlaidich, mùth.
COMPACT, *s.* Co-cheangal, co-cheangladh; bann, cùmhnant, cordadh, co-chordadh, réite, *bargan,* bealtair.
COMPACT, *v.* Ceangail, daingnich, daighnich, naisg; co-thàth, cuir ri cheile; cumhnantaich.
COMPACT, *a.* Teann, daingeann, diongmhalta; cruinn, cearmanta; dùinte; ceangailte; bucar, tàthte; gearr, goirrid, ath-ghearr.
COMPACTLY, *adv.* Gu teann, gu daingeann, gu diongmhalta, gu cruinn, gu cearmanta; gu gearr.
COMPACTNESS, *s.* Daingnead, diongmhaltas, cearmantas.
COMPACTION, *s.* Comh-thàthadh.
COMPANIABLE, *a.* Céilidheach, fial, faoilidh.
COMPANION, *s.* Companach, combach; guailliche, guailleachan, fear comuinn, co-laoch. A knight-companion, *ridir comh-lainn.*
COMPANIONABLE, *a.* Companta, fial, faoilidh.
COMPANIONSHIP, *s.* Companas compantas, caidreamh.
COMPANY, *s.* Cuideachd, coisridh, comhluadar, conaltradh;

bannal, buidheann, meadhail; compailt; (*of soldiers*), cuid-eachd, buidheann, ceatharn, † coib.

Company, *v.* Cum conaltradh ri, co-cheimnich.

Comparable, *a.* Ion-choimeas, ion-samhlaichte, co-choimeasail.

Compare, *v.* Coimeas, samhluich, samhlaich. With what shall I compare you? *ciod ris an coimeas mi thu? ciod an cosmhalachd ris an coimeas mi thu?*

Compare, *s* Coimeas, samhladh, coslas.

Comparison, *s.* Coimeas, coimeasachadh, samhladh, coslas, comh-shamhladh, cosmhalach, samhlachadh. Beyond comparison, *thar na h-uile samhladh; as an t-sealladh,* without comparison, *gun choimeas*

Compart, *v* Roinn, pàirtich, co-phàirtich; cuir an ordugh

Compartiment, *s.* Earann; roinn, pàirt, cuid.

Compartition, *s.* Pàirteachadh; cuid, pàirt

Compass, *v.* Cuairtich, cuartaich, iadh; druid, seisd; beachd; glac; faigh.

Compass, *s* Cuairte, cuairteag, cearcal, cruinne; crioch, rum; comas; iùl, combaist

Compasses, *s.* Gobhalreang, gobhal-roinn, inneal roinn

Compassion, *s* Truas, iochd, truacantas; ath-thruas; comh-mhothachadh; tròcair.

Compassionate, *a.* Truacanta, iochdmhor, ath-thruasach; baigheil, trocaireach; caomh, caomhail, tiom-chridheach

Compassionate, *v.* Gabh truas ri

Compassionately, *adv* Gu truacanta, gu h-iochdmhor, gu baigheil, gu trocaireach, gu caomh, gu tiom-chridheach.

Compatibility, *s.* Freagarrachd, comh-fhreagarrachd; cubhaidheachd, iomchuidheachd.

Compatible, *a.* Freagarrach, comh-fhreagarrach, cubhaidh, iomchuidh.

Compatibleness, *s.* Freagarrachd, comh-fhreagarrachd, iomchuidheachd.

Compatibly, *adv.* Gu freagarrach, gu cubhaidh, gu h-iomchuidh.

Compatriot, *s.* Comh-thìreach.

Compeer, *s.* Companach, combach, co-aois, co-bhrathair, co-oibriche.

Compeer, *v n* Bi co-ionnan; bi freagarrach, bi cosmhuil.

Compel, *v.* Eignich, comh-éignich, thoir air, iomain, diong, ruaig, diobair Compel him to do it, *thoir air a dheanamh,* I will compel him to do it, *bheir mi ort a dheanamh,*

Compeller, *s.* Eigneachair.

Compend, *s.* Giorrachadh, gearr-fhoirm.

Compendious, *a.* Gearr, cuimir, goirrid, ath-ghoirrid.

Compendium, *s.* Giorrachadh, giorrachan

Compensate, *v* Ioc, pàigh, diol, comh-dhiol, co-leasaich, sàsaich, toilich. Compensated, *paighte, diolte*

Compensation, *s* Ioc, iocadh, pàigh, dioladh, co-leasachadh, tuarasdal, diol-thuarasdal

Comperendinate, *v.* Dàilich, cuir dheth, ath-lathaich.

Comperendination, *s.* Dàil, cur dheth; ath-lathachadh.

Competence, *s.* Cuimse; cuibhseach, goireas; (*in law*), comas, ùghdaras.

Competent, *a.* Freagarrach, iomchuidh, cubhaidh, cuimseach, goireasach; (*qualified*), murrach; comasach.

Competently, *adv.* Gu freagarrach, gu iomchuidh, gu cubhaidh, gu cuimseach, gu goireasach, gu leòir, gu murrach, gu comasach.

Competition, *s.* Co-dheuchainn, stri, strigh, comh-stri, co-dhreimeas.

Competitor, *s.* Comh-dheuchainniche, deuchainniche, comh-shuiriche.

Compilation, *s.* Cur ri chéile; comh-chruinneachadh, cnuasachd.

Compile, *v.* Cuir ri cheile, cruinnich, comh-chruinnich, tionail, cnuasaich.

Compiler, *s* Comh-chruinneachair, tionalaiche.

Complacence, Complacency, *s* Aoidhealachd, suairceas mhodhaileachd, tlachd, aiteas, sòlas, soirbheas, suigeart, caomhalachd, siobhaltachd, taidhleachd.

Complacent, *a.* Aoidheil, suairc, modhail, tlàth, caoimhneil, caomhail, soirbh; siobhailt, so-chomhraidhach.

Complain, *v* Gearain, casaid, dean casaid; caoidh; cumha, dean bron What do you complain of? *ciod a tha thu gearan?* complain of him, *dean casaid air.*

Complainer, *s.* Gearanaiche, casaidiche, fear casaid. Complainers, *luchd gearain, luchd casaid.*

Complainant, *s* Casaidiche.

Complaint, *s.* Gearain, casaid; tinneas, eucail; urchòid; cumhadh, caoidh, ocain, eagnach, cuadan. Make a complaint, *dean gearan (no) casaid.*

Complaisance, *s.* Siobhaltachd, modhaileachd, suairceas, caoimhneas

Complaisant, *a.* Siobhailt, sibhealta, modhail, suairc, caomhnail, tlà, cùirteil.

Complaisantly, *adv* Gu siobhailt, gu sibhealta, gu modhail, gu suairc, gu caoimhneil, gu cùirteil, gu tlà.

Complement, *s.* Làn-àireamh, luchd; iomlanachd, foirfeachd.

Complete, *a* Iomlan, foirfe, coimhlionta; slàn, ullamh, deas.

Complete, *v a.* Foirfich, iomlion, coimhlion, criochnaich; thoir gu criche. Completed, *coimhlionta, criochnaichte, ullamh, deas.*

Completely, *adv.* Gu foirfe, gu coimhlionta, gu h-iomlan; gu léir, gu tur.

Completeness, *s* Foirfeachd, iomlaine, iomlanachd, coimhliontachd; abachd

Complex, *a.* Iom-ghnetheach; iol-fhillte, deacair, duilich; innleachdach, do-thuigsinn.

Complexion, *s.* Tuar, gné, neul, dreach, aghaidh.

Complexure, *s.* Filleadh.

Compliance, *s.* Aontachd, aontachadh, aomadh, striochd, geilleadh

Compliant, *a* Aontachail, soimeach; soitheamh, suairc, striochdail, siobhailt.

Complicate, *a.* Iol-fhillte; ioma-gnethach; duilich, do thuigsinn.

Complicate, *v* Comh-fhill, figh, cas, pleat; rib.

Complication, *s.* Comh-fhilleadh, iol-fhilleadh; figheadh; ribeadh.

Complier, *s.* Aontachair, fear aontachaidh

Compliment, *s.* Sodal, miodal; comh-ghàirdeachas; moladh; tiodhlac, gibhte Compliments, *beannachd, soraidh.* Give him my compliments, *thoir mo bheannachd dha.*

Compliment, *v* Mol, dean sodal (no) goileam, dean modh.

Complimental, *a.* Co-ghairdeachail, miodalach, sodalach

Complimentary, *a* Co-ghairdeach; miodalach.

Complimenter, *s* Miodalaiche, sodalaiche, fear miodalach, fear miodail

Complore, *v* Comh-ghuil, comh-chaòin

Comply, *v.* Aontaich, aom, géill, striochd.

Comport, *v. n.* and *a* Freagair; giùlain, iomchair.

Comport, *s.* Giùlan, iomchar, beus, dol mach, caith-beatha.

Comportable, *a.* Freagarrach, ceart, cubhaidh, iomchuidh.

COMPORTANCE, *s.* Giùlan, iomchar, beus, dol mach, caith-beatha.

COMPOSE, *v. a.* Comh-chuir, cuir ri chéile; co-dhluth, co-ghleus, deasaich; (*settle*), siochaich, socraich, sioladh, coisg, caisg.

COMPOSED, *a.* and *part.* Samhach, ciùin, tiamhaidh, tosd, bìth; siochainnteach, ciùinichte; coisgte; sonraichte, suidh-ichte; comh-dhlùthte.

COMPOSEDLY, *adv.* Gu samhach, gu ciùin, gu tiamhaidh, gu tosd, gu bìth.

COMPOSEDNESS, *s.* Samhchair, ciùineas, tosdachd.

COMPOSER, *s.* Ughdar, sgriobhair, deasachair; clodhair.

COMPOSITION, *s.* Sgriobhadh; obair sgriobhte, co-mheasg-adh, co-chordadh; comh-dhluthadh.

COMPOSITOR, *s.* Clodhair.

COMPOST, *v.* Math, mathaich, inneirich, leasaich.

COMPOST, COMPOSTURE, *s.* Mathach, inneir, leasachadh.

COMPOSURE, *s.* Riaghailt; suidheachadh, ciùineas; sioch-ath, samhchair; cordadh.

COMPOTATION, *s.* Comh-òl, pòit-poitearachd; ruite; ruitear-achd.

COMPOUND, *v.* Coimeasg, measg; coird ri luchd-fhiachan.

COMPOUND, *a.* Coimeasgte; iom-ghnetheach.

COMPOUND, *s.* Coimeasgadh.

COMPOUNDABLE, *a.* So-choimeasg.

COMPOUNDER, *s.* Coimeasgair; fear cordaidh, fear réite, ràithe.

COMPREHEND, *v.* Tuig; coimhsich; cum; gabh a stigh.

COMPREHENSIBLE, *a.* So-thuigsinn.

COMPREHENSION, *s.* Tuigse, toinisg, inntinn, eolas; urr-ainneachd, comas.

COMPREHENSIVE, *a.* Tuigseach, toinisgeil, inntinneach; làn; seadhar, ciallach; farsuing, leudmhor.

COMPREHENSIVELY, *adv.* Gu làn, gu farsuing, gu leudmhor.

COMPRESS, *v.* Faisg, naisg, teannaich, dluthaich; bruth, co-bhruth, glac gu gaolach; cughannaich.

COMPRESS, *s.* Cuaran.

COMPRESSIBLE, *a.* Fàisgeach; so-fhàsgadh, so-nasgadh, so-theannachadh, so-bhruth, so-chughannadh.

COMPRESSION, *s.* Teannadh, teannachadh, fàsgadh, nasgadh, bruthadh.

COMPRISE, *v.* Cum, gabh.

COMPROBATION, *s.* Teisteas, comh-theisteas, teisteannas; làn-dearbhadh.

COMPROMISE, *s.* Co-chordadh, comh-bhann, *bargan.*

COMPROMISE, *v.* Co-choird, réitich, dean suas.

COMPROVINCIAL, *a.* Comh-dhuthchasach.

COMPT, *s.* Cunnt, aireamh, uimhir.

COMPULSATORY, *a.* Aindeonach, eigneach, strìgheil.

COMPULSION, *s.* Aindeonachd, eigneachd, strìgh, iomain.

COMPULSORY, *a.* Eigneach, eigneachail.

COMPUNCTION, *s.* Agartas, agartas coguis, aithreachas.

COMPUNCTIOUS, *a.* Aithreachail.

COMPUNCTIVE, *a.* Agartach.

COMPUTABLE, *a.* So-aireamh, so-chunntadh, a dh' fhaodar àireamh.

COMPUTATION, *s.* Aireamh, cunntas; meas.

COMPUTE, *v.* Aireamh, cùnnt; nuimhir, nuimhrich, meas.

COMPUTE, *s.* Aireamh, cunntas; meas.

COMPUTER, *s.* Aireamhair, cunntair; measadair.

COMRADE, *s.* Companach, combach, baigheach, guaille-achan; co-oibriche, co-shaothairiche.

CON. Focal Laitin a chìthear gu minic anns a Bheurla, agus a tha co-ionann ri *comh* no *coimh* anns a Ghailic.

CONCATENATE, *v.* Ceangail, co-cheangail, co-chuibhrich.

CONCATENATION, *s.* Co-cheangladh, co-chuibhreachadh.

CONCAVE, *a.* Cuasach; cuachach.

CONCAVITY, *s.* Cuasachd.

CONCEAL, *v. a.* Céil, céilich, folaich, cuibhrich, còmhdaich, gleidh uaigneach, caon. Concealed, *folaichte, céilte.*

CONCEALABLE, *a.* So-cheileadh, so-fholach.

CONCEALER, *s.* Ceileadair, feir céile, fear falaich.

CONCEALMENT, *s.* Céilt, folachan, folach, folachadh, diomh-aireachd.

CONCEDE, *v.* Geill, aontaich, ceadaich, fulaing, leig le. I will concede this to you, *leigidh mi so leat;* conceded, *aontaichte, ceadaichte.*

CONCEIT, *s.* Smuain, smaoine, dochas; beachd; barail; spéis, meas; uaill; fein-spéis.

CONCEIT, *v.* Smuainich; baralaich, creid, saoil.

CONCEITED, *a.* Uaibhreach, àrdanach, danarradh, leòmach, sgodail, uallach, féin-speiseil; ceann-laidir.

CONCEITLESS, *a.* Baoghalta.

CONCEIVABLE, *a.* So-smuaineachadh, so-shaoilsinn; so-chreidsinn.

CONCEIVE, *v.* Bronn-ghabh, gin, fastorrach (no) leatromach; smainich, smuaintich, smaointich, saoil, beachdaich, tuig, tionsgain.

CONCEIVER, *s.* Beachdadair, beachdair.

CONCENTRATE, *v.* Comh-chruinnich.

CONCENTRIC, *a.* Comh-chearclach, comh-chruinn.

CONCEPTACLE, *s.* Soitheach.

CONCEPTION, *s.* Bronn-ghabhail, gineamhuinn, torraicheas; barail, beachd-meas, smuain, dochas, aithne, eolas, tuigse, † cupar.

CONCEPTIOUS, *a.* Gineadach, torrach.

CONCERN, *v. a.* and *n.* Buin do, gabh gnothach, gabh curam.

CONCERN, *s.* Cùram; seadh, suim, aire; mulad; cuis, gnothach, rud. Of great concern, *cudthromach;* of small concern, *faoin, gun diù.*

CONCERNING, *prep.* Mu, mu thimchioll, mu dheimhinn, uime, air, reir, do réir, a thaobh.

CONCERNMENT, *s.* Gnothach.

CONCERT, *v.* Dealbh, (no) socraich gu h-uaigneach; gabh comhairle.

CONCERT, *s.* Caidreamhas; (*in music*), comh-sheirm.

CONCERTATION, *s.* Comh-strìgh; droch cordadh.

CONCESSION, *s.* Géilleadh, géilleachdainn; ceadachadh, buileachadh, tabhairt, toirt suas, tiomnadh, leigeil.

CONCH, *s.* Slige, faoch, spairneag.

CONCILIATE, *v.* Dean réidh, réitich; buingin.

CONCILIATION, *s.* Réite.

CONCILIATOR, *s.* Réiteachair, fear réite, reitear.

CONCILIATORY, *a.* Réiteachail.

CONCINNITY, *s.* Cubhaidheachd; iomchuidheachd; freagarr-achd, sgeamnaidheachd; maise, gleusdachd.

CONCINNOUS, *a.* Cubhaidh, iomchuidh; maiseach; freag-arrachd, sgeamnaidh, gleusda, gasda; boirionta; finealta, ceanalta, ciatach.

CONCISE, *a.* Goirrid, gearr, ath-ghoirrid, cuimir, cutach.

CONCISENESS, *s.* Giurrad, cutaichead; aith-ghiorrad.

CONCISION, *s.* Gearradh, sgathadh, sgriosadh.

CONCITATION, *s.* Dùsgadh, masgladh; brosnachadh, pros-nachadh, brogadh, stuig.

CONCLAMATION, *s.* Gaire, comh-ghaire, buaireas, glaodh-aich.

Conclave, *s.* Seomar uaigneach; an t-ionad anns an cruinnich priomh shagartan Eaglais na Roimhe; coinneamh dhiomhair.

Conclude, *v.* Comh-dhùin, criochnuich; sònraich, sùnraich, beachdaich.

Conclusible, *a* So-shonrachadh.

Conclusion, *s* Comh-dhunadh, crioch, earr, deireadh, ceann deiridh, ceann thall; fuinn; † tionnriomh.

Conclusive, *a* Sonrachail; criochnach, comh-dhùnach.

Concoct, *v.* Cnamh; abuich, glan.

Concoctible, *a* So-chnamh.

Concoction, *s.* Cnamhadh; abuchadh; inmheachd.

Concolour, *a.* Aon-dathach.

Concomitancy, *s.* Comh-cheumnachadh, co-imeachd.

Concomitant, *a* Comh-cheumnach

Concomitant, *s* Companach; fear comhaideachd, fear coimeachd; buntuinneas

Concord, *s.* Cordadh, co-chordadh, comh-aontachd, sìochath, sìth, ciùineas, socair, (*in music*), comh-sheirm.

Concordance, *s.* Cordadh, Clar-innse a phiobuill.

Concordant, *a.* Comh-chordach; comh-aontach; freagarrach; comh-sheirmeach.

Concordate, *s.* Bann, ceangal; coinneamh, dail, cruinneachadh.

Concorporate, *v* Co-chruinnich, co-thionail, co-chorpaich.

Concourse, *s.* Comh-chruinneachadh, comh-dhail, coinneamh; bròd, lòd, bannal, iorgail

Concremation, *s* Losgadh, comh-losgadh.

Concretion, *s.* Comh-chinneas, comh-fhàs.

Concrete, *v* Cruadhaich, slamaich, binntich

Concrete, *a.* Cruadhaichte, slamaichte, binntichte.

Concretion, *s.* Cruadhachadh, slamachadh, binnteachadh; grudh.

Concubinage, *s.* Siùrsachas, striopachas; leannanachd, meirdreachas.

Concubine, *s* Siursach, siùrtach, striopach, leannan, teallachag, toigh-leannan, bean-dhiolain, meirdreach

Concupiscence, *s* Ana-mhiann, an-shannt, an-togradh, baois, fonn ana-mhiannach; an-toil.

Concupiscent, *a* Ana-mhiannach, an-shanntach, an-togarach, an-toileach, baoiseach

Concupiscible, *a.* Deigheil, miannach, togarach, sanntach.

Concur, *v.* Aontaich, co-aontaich.

Concurrence, *s.* Aontachadh, aonachd, comh-aontachadh; toil, deòin, cead; còghnadh, cuideachadh

Concurrent, *a.* Aontachail; comh-aontach

Concussion, *s.* Crithe, crathadh, criothnachadh

Condemn, *v.* Dit, coirich, cronaich, daor, binn.

Condemnable, *a* Airidh air diteadh, so-dhiteadh, coireach.

Condemnation, *s* Diteadh, binn.

Condemner, *s* Fear ditidh, ditear.

Condensate, *v.* Tiughaich, dlùth, dluthaich, dumhlaich, teannaich.

Condensation, *s* Tiughachadh, dluthachadh, dùmhlachadh

Condense, *v.* Tiughaich, fas tiugh, dùmhlaich

Condense, *a.* Tiugh, dòmhail, dùmhail, trom

Condensity, *a.* Tiughad, tiughead.

Condescend, *v* Irioslaich; islich; striochd, géill; aontaich.

Condescending, *a.* Iriosal, aontach, aontachail, suairc; cuirteal, caomh.

Condescension, *s* Deòin-isleachd, aontachd, suairceas, striochdadh, geilleadh.

Condescensive, *a* Iriosal, suairc, cùirteal, caomh, caoimhneil.

Condign, *a.* Toilltinneach; cothromach; freagarrach.

Condiment, *s.* Ainlean, sabhs; searbhe, leannradh.

Condisciple, *s.* Comh-sgoilear.

Condite, *v.* Saill.

Condition, *s.* Staid, inbhe, cor; modh; cùmhnant, cumha; riochd, gné, rùn, achd.

Condition, *v.* Reitich, socraich, cumhnantaich.

Conditional, *a.* Air chumhnanta, air chumha, eachdail.

Conditionally, *adv.* Air chumhnant, air chumha.

Condole, *v* Comh-ghuil, comh-chaoin.

Condolement, *s* Truas, bròn, mulad, sprochd, tuirse, tuireadh.

Condolence, *s.* Comh-ghul, comh-chaoin, comh-bhròn, truas.

Conduce, *v.* Coghain, cuidich.

Conducive, *a.* Cuideachail.

Conduct, *s.* Beus, iomchar, caith-beatha, giulan, gluasad, dol mach; conbharsaid; sdiuradh; riar; treòrachadh, léidinn.

Conduct, *v.* Treòraich, stiùir, marasglaich; gluais; giùlain.

Conductor, *s.* Treòrachair; fear stiùraidh; fear-seòlaidh, marasglaiche, ceann feadhna, ceannard.

Conductress, *s* Bean-stiùraidh.

Conduit, *s.* Piob, piob uisge, guiteir, sruth-chlais, dobharchlais.

Cone, *s.* Bioraid; circan clogaid.

Confabulation, *s.* Comhradh, buidhinn, cracaireachd.

Confabulatory, *a* Comhraiteach, bruidhneach.

Confection, *s* Biadh milis, millseadh, millseanachd; coimeasg.

Confectionary, *s.* Millseanachd.

Confectioner, *s.* Millseanaiche.

Confederacy, *s* Comh-bhoinn, comh-bhann; comhairle; comh-cheangal, sìth-cheangal.

Confederate, *a* Comh-bhoinneach, comh-bhannach, ceangailte, co-cheangailte.

Confederate, *s.* Companach, combach, fear rùin, fear comh-bhoinn.

Confederate, *v* Co-aontaich, comh-changail, beasnaich; dean comh-bhoinn

Confer, *v* Labhair, bruidhinn ri, comh-labhair; (*bestow*), builich, thoir, thabhair, tiodhlaic; coimeas.

Conference, *s* Comh-labhairt, comhradh, bruidhinn.

Confess, *v.* Aidich, faoisid, faosaid; gabh ri Confessed, *aidichte, am follais, soilleir.*

Confessedly, *adv.* Gun teagamh, gu soilleir

Confession, *s.* Aideachadh, faosaid, aidmheil.

Confessor, *s.* Aideachair, faosaidear; sagart aidmheil.

Confest, *a.* Follaiseach, soilleir.

Confidant, *s.* Fear rùin.

Confide, *v.* Earb ri, cuir muinghinn.

Confidence, *s.* Earbsadh, earbsa, muinghinn, dànachd, misneach; rùn, dochas, dùil, deadlas, sonntach, tortaobh.

Confident, *a.* Earbsach, muinghinneach, dàn, misneachail; dochasach, runach, cinnteach, dearbh-chinnteach, sonnta.

Confident, *s* Fear rùin, fear cridhe.

Confidential, *a.* Dileas, earbsach, tairis.

Confidently, *adv.* Gu h-earbsach, gu muinghinneach, gu dochasach; gu sonnta.

Configuration, *s* Co-chum, cumachd.

Confine, *s* Crioch, bruach, comh-bhruach, iomall, ceann.

CONFINE, *a.* Dlù, fagus.
CONFINE, *v.* Dùin, druid, gainntirich, ceangail, cuibhrich; priosanaich; ceannsaich; cughannaich, iadh, cuairtich.
CONFINEMENT, *s.* Dùnadh; gainntireachd, priosanachd, priosanachadh, cuibhreachadh, cuibhreachd, fo chuibhreach.
CONFINES, *s.* Criochan, iomaill, iomallan.
CONFINITY, *s.* Fagsachd, fagasachd; faigse, dlùthas; nàbachd, nabuidheachd, coimh-fhearsnachd.
CONFIRM, *v.* Daighnich, daingnich, comh-dhaighnich, coneartaich; dearbh, comh-dhearbh; socraich.
CONFIRMABLE, *a.* Daingneachail, so-dhaingneachadh, sodhearbhadh, dearbhail, dearbhadail.
CONFIRMATION, *s.* Daingneachadh, comh-dhaingneachadh, comh-dhearbhadh, dearbh-theisteas.
CONFIRMER, *s.* Dearbhair, dearbhadair.
CONFISCATE, *v.* Arfuntaich
CONFISCATION, *s.* Arfuntachd; call maoin.
CONFLAGRANT, *a.* Comh-losgach, comh-lasach
CONFLAGRATION, *s* Comh-losgadh; comh-lasadh; teine, losgadh.
CONFLATION, *s.* Comh-shéideadh; leaghadh.
CONFLEXURE, *s.* Bogha, lùbadh, camadh.
CONFLICT, *v.* Cath, cathaich, strìgh, comhraig, gleac, spairn.
CONFLICT, *s.* Cath, blàr, strìgh, comh-strìgh, comhrag, gleic, spairn; baiteal, tuasaid, † coinbhliochd.
CONFLUENCE, *s.* Inbhear, cumar, comar, co-shruth, abar; (*of people*), lòd, muinntir, comh-chruinneachadh, cruinneach.
CONFLUENT, *a.* Comh-shruthach.
CONFLUX, *s.* (*Of waters*), inbhear, comar, abar; (*of people*), tionaladh, comh-thional; dròbh, lòd, buidheann.
CONFORM, *a.* Coslach, cosmhal, cosmhuil.
CONFORM, *v a.* and *n.* Aontaich, strìochd géill; co-aontaich; co-chum.
CONFORMABLE, *a.* Cosmhal, cosmhuil, co-ionann; freagarrach, cubhaidh, iomchuidh, do réir, soitheamh; co-aontachail, maith-nadurrach
CONFORMATION, *s.* Comh-chruth, cruth, cumadh, cumachd
CONFORMIST, *s.* Co-aontachair; fear a dh'aontaicheas leis an Eaglais easbuigheach.
CONFORMITY, *s.* Coslas, comh-choslas, samhlachd, eugas; aontachd, freagarrachd, co-aontachadh.
CONFOUND, *v.* Cuir air aimhreidh, cuir troimh chéile; buair; cuir gu h-amhluadh, nàraich, cuir gu nàire, claoidh.
CONFOUNDED, *a.* Buairte, claoidhte, naraichte, fo amhluadh; graineil; oillteil, anabarrach, fuathasach, maslach, nàr.
CONFOUNDEDLY, *adv* Gu graineil, gu h-oillteil, gu h-anabarrach, gu fuathasach, gu maslach, gu nàr.
CONFOUNDER, *s* Buaireadair; fear aimhreite, milltear.
CONFRATERNITY, *s.* Brathaireachas, comh-bhrathaireachas.
CONFRICATION, *s* Comh-shuath, comh-rubadh, suath, rubadh.
CONFRONT, *v.* Aghaidhich, cuir aghaidh ri h-aghaidh, coimeas. Confronted, *aghaidh ri h-aghaidh, aghaidhichte.*
CONFUSE, *v.* Cuir thar a chéile, cuir air aimhreidh; buair, nàraich, cuir gu nàir. *Confused*, thar a chéile, fu nàir, nàr, fu amhluadh.
CONFUSEDLY, *adv.* Thar a chéile, troimh chéile, gu mi-riaghailteach, gu buaireasach, gu cabhagach
CONFUSION, *s.* Eas-ordugh, mi-riaghailt, streapag, buaireadh, tuairgne; nàir, amhluadh; claoidh, milleadh; cabhag; uamhas.

CONFUTE, *v.* Cuir mach; tosdaich, cuir samhach.
CONFUTABLE, *a.* So-chur mach
CONFUTATION, *s* Cur a mach, cur samhach, breugaich
CONGE, *s.* Modh, beic; umhlachd, strìochd; cead.
CONGE D'ELIRE, *s.* Comas Easbuig a thaghadh
CONGEAL, *v.* Cruadhaich, reotaich, ragaich, cuisnich, slamaich
CONGEALED, *s.* Cruadhaichte, reòta, rag, slamaichte.
CONGEALABLE, *a.* So-shlamachadh.
CONGEALMENT, *s.* Slamachadh
CONGELATION, *s.* Reoth, reothadh; reòtadh; slamachadh
CONGENIAL, *a.* Cosmhal, cosmhuil, co-nadurra, co-ghinte
CONGENIABLY, *s* Cosmhalachd, co-choslachd.
CONGENITE, *a.* Co-ghinte, co-nadurra.
CONGER, *s.* Ca-ran creig, creagag, easg mhor, easg mar, easg shiùileach
CONGERIES, *s.* Cruach, dunan, dùn, carn, cruinneach.
CONGEST, *v a.* Cruach, cruinnich, cuir ri chéile, carn.
CONGLOBATE, *v.* Ceartlaich, ceirslich.
CONGLOBATE, *a.* Cruinn, ceartlach, ceirsleach, ceartlaichte, ceirslichte
CONGLOBE, *v.* Ceartlaich, dean cruinn
CONGLOBERATE, *a.* Ceartlach, ceartlaichte, cruinn mar bhall.
CONGLUTINATE, *v.* Glaodh, tàth, cuir sa chéile; comh-thàth.
CONGLUTINATION, *s.* Glaodhadh, tàthadh, comh-thàthadh, slànuchadh
CONGRATULANT, *a* Comh-ghairdeachail.
CONGRATULATE, *v* Dean comh-ghairdeachas, comh-fhàiltich; † cargair
CONGRATULATION, *s.* Comh-ghairdeachas; fàilte, comh-fhàilte.
CONGRATULATORY, *a.* Comh-ghairdeach, miodalach.
CONGREGATE, *v a* and *n.* Coi-thionail, co-thionail, tionail, teanail; coinnich, cruinnich, co-chruinnich Congregated, *teanailte, an ceann a chéile*
CONGREGATION, *s* Teanal, tional, tionaladh, teanaladh, cruinneachadh; comh-thionaladh, comh-theanal, clochar; carn, dùn.
CONGRESS, *s.* Coinneamh, co-thional; cruinneachadh, mòd, † dàil, comhrag, tuasaid.
CONGRESSIVE, *a.* Co-thionalach; comhragach.
CONGRUENCE, CONGRUITY, *s* Cordadh, co-chordadh, freagarrachd, comh-fhreagarrachd, comh-fhreagartas, lathailteachd
CONGRUOUS, *a* Freagarrach, co-fhreagarach, lathailteach
CONICAL, *a.* Barrachaol, biorach, spiriseach
CONJECTURAL, *a.* Baralach, barailcach, teagamhach, neo-chinnteach, amharusach
CONJECTURE, *s.* Barail; foir-bhreith; amharus, teagamh, tuairmeas, toimhseach
CONJECTURE, *v.* Baralaich, thoir barail, thoir tuairmeas
CONJOIN, *v. a.* and *n.* Tàth, comh-thath, cuir sa chéile, comh-cheangail, dluthaich; aontaich
CONJOINT, *a.* Comh-cheangailte; comhrannaich.
CONJOINTLY, *adv* Gu ceangailte, an comhrannaich, cuideachd, le chéile; gu pairteachail
CONJUGAL, *a.* Céileach, pòsach, posadach, pòsdail, posda, maraisteach
CONJUGATE, *v.* Comh-cheangail, comh-dhlùthaich, comh-bheartaich

CONJUGATION, s. Paidhir, caraid, cupall, deise; comh-bheartachadh, comh-cheangal.

CONJUNCTION, s. Aontachd, aonachd; coinneamh; bann; comh-bhoinn.

CONJUNCTIVE, a. Dluthaichte, aonaichte.

CONJUNCTLY, adv. An còmharnaich, an comhrannaich, an comhroinnich.

CONJUNCTURE, s. Eigin, càs, gàbhail, iom-cheist; am son-ruichte; co-cheangal.

CONJURATION, s. Druidheachd, fiosachd, beul-dhruidh-eachd, asarlachd; doilbheachd; co-mhionnachadh.

CONJURER, s. Cleasaiche, druidh; fiosaiche. He is no conjurer, *cha 'n eil e pisearlach*

CONJURE, v. Grios, guidh, aslaich, asluich; cuir buitse-achd, cuir fu gheasaibh

CONJUREMENT, s. Griosadh, guidheadh, aslachadh

CONNASCENCE, s Comh-bhrath, comh-bheirsinn.

CONNATE, a Comh-ghinte

CONNATURAL, a Comh-nadurra

CONNECT, v. Dlùthaich, ceangail, cuir ri chéile, tàth. Connected, *dlùthaichte, ceangailte, cairdeach, dìleas, dlù an daimh.* He is connected with him, *tha e cairdeach dha, tha daimh aig ris*

CONNECTIVE, a. Dlùthach, ceanglach

CONNECTIVELY, adv. Ann an co-bhoinn, an comhrannaich, sa chéile.

CONNEX, v. Tàth, comh-thàth, comh-cheangail.

CONNEXION, s Comh-thathadh; ordugh; ceangal, aon-achd; cairdeas, daimh.

CONNIVANCE, s. Sméideadh, caogadh, aontachadh.

CONNOISSEUR, s. Breith, fear fiosrach, fiosraiche.

CONNUBIAL, a. Pòsach, maraisteach

CONOID, s. Birichean

CONQUASSATE, v. Comh-chrath.

CONQUER, v. Buadhaich, ceannsaich, fairtlich, faigh lamh an uachdar, sàraich, sàruich, claoidh; cuir an teich air, islich, cuir fo, tràillich.

CONQUERABLE, a So-sharuchadh; so-chlaoidh.

CONQUEROR, s. Buaidhear, buaidh-laoch, gaisgeach, treun-laoch; saruchair, claoidhear, cosgraiche

CONQUEST, s Buaidh, buaidh-larach, claoidh, sàrachadh, lamh an uachdar; cosgairt; † cod, gabhaltas

CONSANGUINEOUS, a. Càirdeach.

CONSANGUINITY, s. Cairdeas, daimh, dlù-chairdeas; co-fhlannas

CONSCIENCE, s. Comh-fhios, coguis, cogais; coinseas.

CONSCIENTIOUS, a. Coguiseach, ionraic, onorach, treibh-dhireach, cothromach, ceart.

CONSCIONABLE, a Reusanta, reusantach, ceart

CONSCIOUS, a. Fiosrach, eolach, fein-fhiosrach, coimh-fhiosach.

CONSCIOUSLY, adv Gu lan-fhiosarch, gu coimh-fhiosach

CONSCIOUSNESS, s Fein-fhios, fein-fhiosrachd

CONSCRIPT, a. Co-sgriobhta

CONSCRIPTION, s. Comh-sgriobhadh.

CONSECRATE, v. Coisrig, naomhaich, beannaich

CONSECRATED, a. Coisrigte, naomhaichte, naomh, beann-aichte.

CONSECRATION, s. Coisreagadh, naomhachadh, naomhachd, beannachadh, naomh-choisreagadh

CONSENT, s. Aontachadh; toil, cead; cordadh. Without his consent, *gun a chead.*

CONSENT, v. Aontaich, géill; thoir cead, ceadaich, leig le.

CONSEQUENCE, s. Buile, toradh, deanmhas; co-lorgadh, co-leanachd; leantuinneas; crioch; ceann thall, ceann deiridh, deireadh; feumalachd, cudthrom; fiù. The consequence of your doings, *toradh do dheanadais;* of no consequence, *gun fhiù*, of great consequence, *cudthromach.*

CONSEQUENT, a. Leantuinneach, teachd an lorg.

CONSEQUENTIAL, a. Leantuinneach; criochnachail; spàir-iseach; uallach, dòchasach

CONSERVABLE, a. So-ghleidh, so-choimhead, ion-choimhead.

CONSERVATION, s. Coimhead, dion, gleidh, gleidheadh, gleadh

CONSERVATIVE, a. Coimheadach, dionach, gleadhtach.

CONSERVATOR, s Coimheadaiche; fear-coimhid.

CONSERVATORY, s. Taisg-ionad; tigh-stòr.

CONSERVE, v. Coimhead, dion; canndaich; millsich, siuc-araich; scarbhaich.

CONSERVE, s Millsean air a dheanamh do shugh meas air a bhruitheadh le siucar.

CONSIDER, v. a. and n. Smuainich, smuaintich, smaointich, beachdaich, beachd-smuainich, thoir faimear; cuimhnich; diol, paigh.

CONSIDERABLE, a. Mòr, an iarruidh mhòr; fiachail, fiù, luachmhor, measail, cudthromach.

CONSIDERABLY, adv. Gu mor; an iarruidh; gu cud-thromach.

CONSIDERATE, a Smuaineachail, smuainteach, smuainte-achail, smaointeachail, sicir, crionna, glic, ciallaidh, suidh-ichte, ciùin

CONSIDERATELY, adv. Gu smuainteachail, gu sicir, gu crionna, gu glic, gu ciallaidh, gu suidhichte

CONSIDERATENESS, s. Crionnachd, sicireachd.

CONSIDERATION, s. Smuaine, beachd; crionnachd, glìocas, ciall, cnuasachd; cudthrom; dioladh; pàigh; meas, suim.

CONSIGN, v. Earb, thoir thairis, thoir suas; tiomnadh, cui-tich, tar-bhuilich.

CONSIGNED, part. Earbte, tarbhuilichte.

CONSIGNMENT, s. Earbsadh, toirt thairis, tiomnadh, tar-bhuileachadh, comh-earbsadh.

CONSIMILAR, a Comh-chosmhuil.

CONSIST, v. n Bi ann, bi lathair; cum.

CONSISTENCE, s. Staid, tainead, tiughad; cruth, cumadh, cumachd; freagarrachd, cubhaidheachd, cordadh; reim, reimeileachd

CONSISTENT, a. Lathailteach; tiugh; cordach, comh-chor-dail; cubhaidh, freagarrach, rianail

CONSISTENTLY, adv. Gu lathailteach, gu cubhaidh, gu freagarrach, gu rianail

CONSISTORY, s. Cuirt eaglais, cléir-mhòd.

CONSOCIATE, s Companach, combach.

CONSOCIATION, s. Companas, conaltradh; comh-bhoinn.

CONSOLABLE, a Furtachail

CONSOLATION, s. Sòlas, furtachd, comh-fhurtachd.

CONSOLATOR, s. Comh-fhurtair.

CONSOLATORY, a Comh-fhurtachail, furtachail, sòlasail, sòlasach

CONSOLE, v Comh-fhurtaich, furtaich, sòlasaich, thoir solas, thoir comh-fhurtachd

CONSOLER, s. Comh-fhurtair, sòlasaiche.

CONSOLIDATE, v. a. and n. Daingnich, daighnich, cruadh-aich, teannaich, neartaich, co-ghreimich.

CONSOLIDATION, s. Daighneachadh, daingneachadh, cru-adhachadh, teannachadh.

CONSONANCE, CONSONANCY, s. Co-sheirm; comh-fhuaim; freagarrachd, comh-fhreagarrachd; cordadh, comh-chor-dadh; cairdeas, réite

Consonant, *s.* Co-fhoghair.
Consonant, *a.* Freagarrach, comh-fhreagarrach, aon-ghuthach.
Consonous, *a.* Aon-ghuthach; comh-sheirmeach; freagarrach.
Consort, *s.* Companach; leth-bhreac; céile; bean phosda, fear posda; aonachd.
Consort, *v.* Cuir ri chéile, cùir cuideachd; pòs.
Conspicuity, *s.* Faicsinneachd, follaiseachd.
Conspicuous, *a.* So-fhaicsinn, soilleir, follaiseach, follais; sorcha; ballardach, fiodhnasach; ainmeil, cliùiteach, ard, inbheach, oirdheirc, uasal.
Conspicuously, *adv.* Gu follaiseach, gu soilleir.
Conspicuousness, *s.* So-fhaicsinneachd, soilleireachd, follaiseachd, soirche; ainmeileachd, cliù, òirdheirceas, airde.
Conspiracy, **Conspiration**, *s.* Co-rùnachadh, co-mhionnachadh, ceannairc, feall, foill, cealg-chomhairle, foill-rùn, traoidhte-choinneamh.
Conspirator, *s.* Co-rùnaiche, co-mhionnaiche, fealltair, traoidhtear.
Conspire, *v.* Co-rùnaich, co-mhionnaich; ceannaircich, foillich; cogair.
Constable, *s.* Sith-mhàor, sìth-chomheadaiche, *constabull.*
Constableship, *s.* Sith-mhaorsainneachd, sith-choimhead-achd, *constabullachd.*
Constancy, *s.* Seasmhachd, neo-chaochlaideachd, buanachadh, buanachd, marsuinn, bunailteachd, maireannachd; diongaltachd; cinnteas.
Constant, *a.* Seasmhach, neo-chaochlaideach, buan, maireannach, mairionnach, mairionn, maireann, bunaiteach, bunailteach, diongalta, daingeann, laidir; cinnteach; sonraichte, bidheanta, cunbhalach.
Constantly, *adv.* Gu seasmhach, gu buan, gu maireann, gu maireannach; an comhnuidh, an cumaint, an cumaint 's an comhnuidh, am bidheantas, gun sgur, gun chairde, gun toirt thairis.
Constellation, *s.* Comh-shoillse, griglean, grigleachan, comh-reult; † rinnreim.
Consternation, *s.* Eagal, uamhas, oillt, uamhunn; iongantas, ioghnadh, mor-ioghnadh.
Constipate, *v.* Dòmhlaich, dùmhlaich; tiughaich; daighnich, druid suas, teannaich.
Constipation, *s.* Domhlachadh, tiughachadh; daingneachadh cuim.
Constituent, *s.* Sònrachair, sùnrachair, taghadair.
Constitute, *v.* Dean suas, dean, orduich, co-shuidhich, co-dhealbh; tog, sonraich (no) tagh chum oifig.
Constitution, *s.* Co-dhealbhadh, co-shuidheachadh, reachd, dealbh; nàdur; (*of body*), cal, càil, gleus.
Constitutional, *a.* Laghail, reachdail, rioghail, nadurra; càileil.
Constrain, *v.* Co-éignich, eignich, aindeonaich; truaill, truaillich; glac, bruth, fàisg; naisg, ceangail.
Constrainable, *a.* So-eigneachadh; so-bhruthadh; so-nasgadh.
Constrainer, *s.* Eigneachair.
Constraint, *s.* Aindeoin, breith air éigin, éigin, eigneachadh, aineart, bacadh, cughannachd.
Constrict, *v.* Ceangail, co-cheangail, crub; cughannaich, domhlaich, mùch.
Constriction, *s.* Crupadh, co-chrupadh; fasgadh.
Constrictor, *s.* Nasgair; fàsgair, mùchadair.
Constringe, *v.* Crup, comh-chrup, comh-dhaighnich.
Constringent, *a.* Crupach, daingneachail.
Construct, *v.* Tog, comh-thog; dealbh, comh-dhealbh.
Construction, *s.* (*In building*), togail, comh-thogail; dealbh, comh-dhealbh; (*meaning*), mìneachadh, seadh, ciall.
Constructive, *a.* Togail.
Construe, *v.* Cuir sa chéile; mìnich, eadar-theangaich.
Constuprate, *v.* Truaill.
Constupration, *s.* Truailleadh, siùrsachd, siùrsachas, striopachas.
Consubstantial, *a.* Comh-stuthail, comh-nadurra, comh-bhrigheil.
Consubstantiality, *s.* Comh-stuthachd.
Consubstantiation, *s.* Comh-stuthachadh, comh-bhrigh-eachadh.
Consubstantiate, *v.* Comh-stuthaich, comh-bhrighich, co-dhaighnich.
Consul, *s.* Probhal, ard-uachdaran Roimheach; fear a chuireadh do bhaile-puirt eilthireach, chum ceartas fhaicinn aig ceannaichean no duthcha do 'm buin e, a mheud dhuibh 's a sheòlas do 'n chàla cheudna.
Consulship, *s.* Probhalachd.
Consult, *v.* Gabh comhairle, cuir comhairle, sir comhairle; rannsuich.
Consultation, *s.* Comh-chomhairle, comhairle, rùn phairteachadh. Holding a consultation, *a cumail comhairle.*
Consumable, *a.* So-chaitheamh, so-sgriosadh.
Consume, *v.* (*Spend*), caith, cosd, cuir a' shean; cnamh; (*destroy*), sgrios; cuir as do; mill; (*decay*), searg, crion; méil, corb, bronn. Consumed, *caithte; sgriosta.*
Consumer, *s.* Milleadair, milltear, sgriosadair; struidhear.
Consummate, *a.* Iomlan; foirfe; sàr, còrr; tur, fior. A consummate hero, *sàr-ghaisgeach, sàr-laoch;* a consummate rascal, *fior chrochair, tur-chrochair.*
Consummate, *v.* Criochnaich, iomlanaich, foirfich; coimhlion.
Consummation, *s.* Iomlanachd, foirfeachd, crioch; bàs.
Consumption, *s.* Caitheamh, cosd, sgrios, cnamh, milleadh; éiteach, tinneas caitheimh, meath-thinneas, sgamh-chnuimh.
Consumptive, *a.* Caithteach, cnamhtach, cnaimhteach; millteach, sgriosail, sgriosach.
Consumptiveness, *s.* Caithteachd.
Contabulate, *v.* Plancaich, déil, deilich.
Contabulation, *s.* Deileachadh.
Contact, *s.* Beanachd; comh-bhualadh.
Contagion, *s.* Plaigh; càs; galar plaigheil (no) gabhailteach; gabhaltachd.
Contagious, *a.* Plaigheil, galarach, gabhailteach, gabhaltach; puinsionta.
Contagiousness, *s.* Plaighealachd; gabhailteachd.
Contain, *v. a.* and *n.* Cum, gabh; bac; bi geimnidh; bi stuaim. I cannot contain myself, *cha n'urrainn mi cumail orm;* it contained two pints, *chum e da phinnt.*
Contaminate, *v.* Truaill, truaillich; salaich; † sorb.
Contaminated, *a.* Truaillte, truallichte, salaichte, truaillidh, salach.
Contamination, *s.* Truailleadh, truaillidheachd, salachadh.
Contaminator, *s.* Truailliche.
Contemn, *v. a.* Tarcuisich, maslaich, dearmad, dearmadaich; dean tair, dean dì-meas, dean tarcuis, dean spid; cuir air chùl, cuir ar dearmad. Contemned, *tarcuisichte, maslaichte.*
Contemner, *s.* Fear tarcuis, tarcuisiche, di-measair, spidcar. Contemners, *luchd tarcuis.*
Contemplate, *v.* Beachdaich, beachduich; beachd-smuainich; seall, smuainich, meoraich.
Contemplation, *s.* Beachdachadh, beachdalachd, smuain, smuaineachadh, smuainteachadh, beachd-smuainteachadh, airsge.

Contemplative, *a.* Smuainteachail, beachdail, smuairean-ach, stuidearra.

Contemporary, *a.* Comh-aimsireil, comh-linneach, comh-aosmhor.

Contemporary, *s.* Comh-aois.

Contempt, *s.* Dìmeas, tàir, tarcuis, spìd, dearmad; mi-mheas, mi-mhodh, mi-shuim, eas-onoir; magadh, fanaid; dìblidheachd.

Contemptible, *a.* Suarrach, dìblidh, truagh, faoin; gun fhiù, air bheag meas; fuathach, di-measta.

Contemptibly, *adv.* Gu suarrach, gu dìblidh, gu truagh, gu faoin, gu dimeasach.

Contemptibleness, *s.* Suarrachas, suaraichead, dìblidh-eachd, truaighe.

Contemptuous, *a.* Tàireil, tarcuiseach, spìdeil, dearmad-ach; mi-mhodhail, magach, fanaideach.

Contemptuousness, *s.* Tairealachd, tarcuiseachd, dear-madachd, mi-mhòdhaileachd, tàire, tarcuis, mi-mhodh.

Contend, *v.* Strìgh, cathaich, spairn, dean ùinich; (*argue*), cum a mach. He contended, *chathaich e;* he contended or argued, *chum e mach.*

Contender, *s.* Cùraidh, gaisgeach, laoch, milidh.

Contending, *s.* Strìgh, comh-strìgh, spairn, ùinich, conns-achadh, connsach.

Content, *a.* Toilichte; buidheach, riaraichte; toileach; sàsaichte. Content with my lot, *toilichte le mo chor;* I am quite content, *tha mi làn toilichte.*

Content, *v.* Toilich, taitinn, riaraich, dean buidheach.

Contented, *part.* Toilichte; buidheach; riaraichte; sas-aichte; neo-ghearanach. Nature is contented with few things, *tha Nàdur toilichte le* (*beagnaich*) *beag nithe;* easily contented, *so-thoileachadh, so-riarachadh.*

Contention, *s.* Strìgh, comh-stri, comh-strìgh, spairn; connsach, connsachadh, tabaid, tuasaid, tagluinn, dealas, connspoid, cath, aimhreite, dreann; gleac, iarguill, caon-nag, uspairneachd, cur mach, iom-reuson, ciasal, † ceallach.

Contentious, *a.* Connsachail, tabaideach, tuasaideach, dealasach, tagluinneach, connspoideach, aimhreiteach, dreannach, iarguilleach, iorghuilleach; uspairneach, crosda, caonnagach, cainnteach, cas.

Contentiousness, *s.* Tabaideachd, tuasaideachd, dealas-achd, connspoideachd, iarguilleachd, uspairneachd.

Contentless, *a.* Neo-thoilichte, neo-bhuidheach, diom-bach (diombuidheach), gearanach.

Contentment, *s.* Toileachas inntinn, toil-inntinn; toil-eachadh.

Contents, *s.* Bladh-leabhair; clar-innsidh.

Conterminous, *a.* Comh-chriochach, comh-iomallach.

Contest, *v.* Cuir an aghaidh, cathaich; spairn.

Contest, *s.* Strì, strìgh, comh-strì, spairn, comh-spairn, connsach, tagluinn, tuasaid, tabaid, dealas; cath, comhrag, iorghuil, gleac; caonnag, iom-reuson, comh-lan; ionnsuidh.

Contestable, *a.* Tagluinneach, tuasaideach, tabaideach, dealasach.

Context, *s.* Comh-theagasg.

Context, *a.* Fighte, dualaichte.

Contexture, *s.* Figheadh, dualadh; pleatadh, obair fhighte.

Contiguity, *s.* Dlùthas, foigse, fogusachd.

Contiguous, *a.* Dlù, dlùth, fogus, fagus, fa-chomhair, laimh ri.

Continence, Continency, *s.* Géimnidheachd, stuaim, stuamachd, malltachd, measarachd, ceannsachd.

Continent, *a.* Geimnidh, stuam, stuamadh, mallta, meas-arra, ceannsach, gasda.

Continent, *s.* Mòr-thir; tir-mòr.

Contingence, Contingency, *s.* Teagmhas, tuiteamas, tuiteamachd, tubaisd.

Contingent, *a.* Teagamhach, tuiteamach, neo-chinnteach, tubaisdeach.

Contingent, *s.* Tuiteamas, tubaisd.

Contingently, *adv.* Gu tubaisdeach, thaobh tubaisd.

Continual, *a.* Maireannach, mairionn, buan, bi-bhuan, bi-dheanta, do-ghnàth, a ghnàth, gun sgur, gun chàirde, cion-mhairionn, cion-mhaireannach.

Continually, *adv.* Daonalt, daonanta, an comhnuidh, a ghnath, do ghnàth, gu bidheanta, gun chàirde, an cu-maint.

Continuance, *s.* Maireachduinn, marachduinn, marsuinn, maireannachd, buanachd; fuireachadh.

Continuation, *s.* Buanachadh; fadachadh. In continua-tion, *air aghaidh.*

Continue, *v.* Fuirich, fan, buanaich, stad; rach air adhairt.

Continued, *p. a.* Minic, tric.

Continuedly, *adv.* Gu minic, gu tric, gun chàird, gun stad, gun chlos, daonanta.

Continuer, *s.* Buanachair.

Continuity, *s.* Fogasachd, foigse, foigseachd, dlùthas.

Contort, *v.* Toinneamh, sniomh.

Contortion, *s.* Toinneamh, sniomhadh, car.

Contraband, *a.* Mi-laghail, toirmisgte, neo-cheadaichte.

Contract, *v. a.* and *n.* Co-tharruing, giórraich, lughdaich; (*betroth*), ceangail, geall, pòsadh; (*shrink*), trus; crion, crup; (*agree*), coird, barganaich, cumhnantaich.

Contract, *s.* Cordadh, cumha, cumhnant, teirm, cor; co-cheangal; ceangal, † doithir. A marriage contract, *ceangal, ceangal pòsaidh.*

Contractible, *a.* So-chrupadh.

Contraction, *s.* Comh-thrusadh, giorrachadh, crupadh, comh-chrupadh, aith-ghearrad, gearradh.

Contractor, *s.* Cùmhnantaiche, barganaiche; ceannach-adair.

Contradict, *v. a.* Cuir an aghaidh, àicheadh.

Contradiction, *s.* Aicheadh, friothradh, aghaidh; contar; *a contradiction in terms*, comh-aicheadh bhriathra.

Contradictory, *a.* Aicheadhach, eìthich, friotharach, con-tarach, neo-fhreagarrach.

Contradistinction, *s.* Tur-dhiubhair; eadar-dhealachadh.

Contradistinguish, *v.* Eadar-dhealaich, diubharaich.

Contrariety, *s.* Neo-freagarrachd, neo-lathailteachd, neo-rianaileachd; codarsnachd, † contrailleachd.

Contrariwise, *adv.* Gu neo-aontachail, gu contrarach.

Contrary, *a.* Neo-aontachail, neo-rianail; naimhdeil, con-trarach, contrailleach; neo-fhreagarrach, an aghaidh. On the contrary, *air an lamh eile, an aghaidh sin.*

Contrast, *s.* Eu-coslas; coimeas.

Contrast, *v.* Coimeas, cuir an aghaidh.

Contravene, *v.* Cuir an aghaidh, bac, gabh roimh, frith-chuir.

Contravention, *s.* Cur an aghaidh, bacadh, aghaidh, frith-chur.

Contributary, *a.* Comh-chiseach.

Contribute, *v.* Cuir stigh, cuir leis, comh-thabhair, comh-bhuilich; cuir air adhairt, luathaich, cuidich.

Contributing, *part.* A cuideachadh, a comh-thabhairt, a comh-bhuileachadh.

Contribution, *s.* Comh-thoirt, comh-thabhairt, comh-bhuileachadh; (*for the poor*), naomh-dheirc; tionaladh.

Contributive, *a.* Cuideachail.

Contributor, *s.* Cuideachair, fear còghnaidh.

CONTRITE, *a.* Brùite, aithreachail, brònach, dubhach; caithte, comh-bhrùite.

CONTRITION, *s.* Aithreachas, briseadh-crìdhe, bròn, dubhachas, dubh-aithreachas; mèileadh, bléith.

CONTRIVABLE, *a.* So-dhealbhadh, so-thionsgnadh.

CONTRIVANCE, *s.* Innleachd, dealbh, dealbhadh, seòl, ealdhain.

CONTRIVE, *v.* Tionsgain, dealbh; sònraich; comh-mhionnaich.

CONTRIVER, *s.* Tionsgnaiche, dealbhadair, innleachdaiche.

CONTROL, *s.* Smachd, bac, ceannsachadh, ughdarras, cumhachd, maighistearas, lamh an uachdar.

CONTROL, *v.* Smachd, smachdaich, ceannsaich, iompaich.

CONTROLLABLE, *a.* So-smachdadh, so-cheannsachadh.

CONTROLLER, *s.* Riaghlair, smachdair.

CONTROLMENT, *s.* Smachd, ceannsachd, riaghailt, lamh an uachdar; aghaidh.

CONTROVERSIAL, *s.* Connsachail, connspoideach, iom-reusonach, arguinneach, tagluinneach.

CONTROVERSY, *s.* Connsach, connsachadh, connspoid, iom-reuson, argumaid, arguinn, tuasaid, tagluinn, eagsamhlas; fuarnadh.

CONTROVERT, *v.* Cuir an aghaidh; connsaich, reusonaich.

CONTROVERTIBLE, *a.* So chur an aghaidh.

CONTROVERTIST, *s.* Fear connsachaidh, iom-reusonaiche, comh-riasonaiche.

CONTUMACIOUS, *a.* Dùr, reasgach, ceann-laidir, eas-umhal, neo-urramach; tagluinneach, crosda, crosanta, do-lùbadh.

CONTUMACIOUSNESS, *s.* Dùiread, reasgachd, ceann-laidireachd, eas-umhlachd, tagluinneachd, crosdachd.

CONTUMACY, *s.* Reasgachd, eas-umhlachd; ceann-laidireachd, tagluinn.

CONTUMELIOUS, *a.* Tàireil, maslach, tarcuiseach, nàr, tuaileasach, toibheumach, sgainnealach, mi-mhodhail; sglamhrach.

CONTUMELY, *s.* Tàir, masladh, tarcuis, nàir, tuaileas, toibheum, sgainneal, mi-mhodh, sglamhradh, mi-chliù, athais, beillean, spreigeadh, iom-dheargadh.

CONTUSE, *v.* Pronn, bruth. *Contused*, proinnte, pronnta.

CONTUSION, *s.* Pronnadh, bruthadh, leòn, goirteachadh.

CONUNDRUM, *s.* Beum, gearradh.

CONVALESCENCE, CONVALESCENCY, *s.* Feobhas, feabhas, dol am feobhas; brotachadh, ur-shlainnte.

CONVALESCENT, *a.* A dol am feobhas, a brotachadh.

CONVENE, *v.* Tionail, teanail, cruinnich, comh-chruinnich, comh-theanail, comh-thionail. *Convened*, tionailte, cruinnichte, cruinn, an ceann a chéile.

CONVENER, *s.* Cruinneachair; gairmeadair.

CONVENIENCE, *s.* Iomchuidhead, iomchuidheachd; socair, cothrom; coidhiseachd.

CONVENIENT, *a.* Iomchuidh, *i. e.* iom-chubhaidh; cothromach; freagarrach; coidheis; amail; goireasach.

CONVENIENTLY, *adv.* Gu h-iomchuidh; gu cothromach; gu freagarrach; gu goireasach.

CONVENT, *s.* Tigh mhànach, tigh chailleacha dubha, tigh bhan-naomh, manaistear; abaid, abait; cill.

CONVENTICLE, *s.* Coinneamh, comh-thional, cruinneachadh, coinneamh dhiomhair; coinneamh chum aoraidh; tigh-aoraidh.

CONVENTION, *s.* Cruinneachadh, comh-thional, comh-theanal, mòd, coinneamh; comh-dhàil; seanadh, feis; comhbhoinn, bann, cumhnant, cordadh car uine araidh.

CONVENTIONAL, *a.* Cumhnantaichte, comh-bhannach.

CONVENTUAL, *s.* Mànach, aba, brathair-bochd, cailleach dhubh, ban-naomh.

CONVENTUAL, *a.* Manachail, dìthreabhach, aonaranach diadhuidh.

CONVERGE, *v.* Comh-aom; comh-ruith.

CONVERSABLE, *a.* Comhradhach, comhraiteach, suilbhear; bruidhneach, caoimhneil, caidreamhach.

CONVERSABLY, *adv.* Gu comhradhach, gu comhraiteach, gu suilbhear, gu caoimhneil, gu caidreamhach.

CONVERSANT, *a.* Eolach, fiosrach, teoma.

CONVERSATION, *s.* Còmhradh, bruidhinn, cainnt, conbharsaid, comh-labhairt, cracaireachd; (*communion*), caidreamh, comhluadar, conaltradh; comunn; (*behaviour*), beus, caithbeatha, giùlan, iomchar, dol mach.

CONVERSE, *v.* Comhradh, bruidhinn, labhair, dean còmhradh, dean bruidhinn, dean guth; comh-labhair.

CONVERSE, *s.* Comhradh, bruidhinn, cracaireachd; comhluadar, conaltradh, communn, caidreamh; eòlas. Hold converse, *cum conaltradh.*

CONVERSION, *s.* Iompachadh, leasachadh-beatha; mùth, atharrachadh, tionndadh, pilleadh, pilltinn.

CONVERSELY, *adv.* Air mhuth doigh, air atharrachadh doigh.

CONVERT, *s.* Iompachan.

CONVERT, *v. a.* and *n.* Iompaich; leasaich, atharraich, tionndadh (no) pill chum maith, pill.

CONVERTER, *s.* Iompachair, fear iompachaidh.

CONVERTIBLE, *s.* So-iompachadh, iompachail, a ghabhas iompachadh.

CONVEX, *a.* Cruinn, dronnach, dronn-chruinn, dronn-chuairteach, uchdachail.

CONVEXED, *a.* Dronn-chruinn.

CONVEXITY, *s.* Dronn-chruinnead; uchdach.

CONVEXO-CONCAVE, *a.* Dronn-chuachach.

CONVEY, *v.* Giùlain, iomchair; treòraich; tar-thoir, tarthabhair, thoir thairis; thoir.

CONVEYANCE, *s.* Giulan, iomchar; caraiste; inneal iomchair; tar-thoirt, tar-bhuileachadh, tiomnadh-maoin.

CONVEYANCER, *s.* Tar-thabhairtear; sgriobhair araidh.

CONVEYANCING, *s.* Tar-thabhairt, tar-bhuileachadh.

CONVEYER, *s.* Portair; cairtear; fear iomchair.

CONVICT, *v.* Dìt; cuir ciont as leth; glac; di-chòmhdaich, fallsaich.

CONVICT, *s.* Ciontach, priosanach, urr air dhìteadh.

CONVICTION, *s.* Dìteadh; agartas; geur-mhothachadh; soilleireachadh.

CONVINCE, *v.* Thoir dearbh, dean cìnnteach; soilleirich; dìt.

CONVINCIBLE, *a.* So dhearbhadh, so-chur a mach.

CONVINCING, *a.* Soilleir; do chur an aghaidh, dearbhach, comhdachail.

CONVINCINGLY, *adv.* Gu soilleir, gu riochdail, gu cinnteach, gun teagamh.

CONVIVIAL, *a.* Fleaghach, fleaghail, cuirmeach, cuirmeil, fial, subhach, aighearrach; sunntach, taitneach, caidreamhach.

CONVOCATE, *v. a.* Cruinnich, teanail, tionail, comh-chruinnich, comh-ghairm, thoir gairm cruinneachaidh.

CONVOCATION, *s.* Cruinneachadh, teanaladh, comh-chruinneachadh, comh-ghairm, còmh-dhail, mòd.

CONVOKE, *v. a.* Cruinnich, teanail, tionail, comh-chruinnich, comh-ghairm, thoir gairm cruinneachaidh.

CONVOLVE, *v. a.* Comh-ròl, comh-ruidhil, toinneamh. *Convolved*, toinnte.

Convoy, *v. a.* Léidich; léidinn, thoir léidinn, comh-cheimnich, comh-sheòl; dìon; *geardainn.*

Convoy, *s.* Léideachadh; léidinn, dìon, dìdean, *geard.*

Convulse, *v. a.* Grad-chlisg, uspairn; oibrich; buair.

Convulsion, *s.* Uspairneachd, grad-chlisge; buaireas.

Convulsive, *a.* Clisgeach, uspairneach.

Cony, *s.* Coinean, rabait. Cony borough, *toll conein.*

Coo, *v.* Dùrd, dean dùrdail; ceileir.

Cook, *v.* Greadh, deasaich biadh.

Cook, *s.* Còcair, cochdair.

Cookery, *s.* Còcaireachd. Cooking, *ri còcaireachd.*

Cook-maid, *s.* Ban-chocair.

Cool, *a.* Fuar, fuaraidh, fionnar, fionn-fhuar, fiunnar; neo-thlùsar, coimheach, neo-dheothasach, neo-reasgach.

Cool, *s.* Fionnarachd, fiunnarachd. The cool of even, *fionnarachd an fheasgair.*

Cool, *v.* Fuaraich, fionnaraich, fiunnaraich; coisg, caisg.

Cooler, *s.* Fuarachair, soitheach fuarachaidh.

Coolly, *adv.* Gun bhlàthas, gun theas; gu coimheach, gu ciùin.

Coolness, *s.* Fuachd, fionnarachd, coimheachas, coimheas.

Coom, *s.* Sùidhe; sal, salachar, duslach, sal-rotha.

Coomb, *s.* Tomhas ceithir cheathrannan.

Coop, *s.* Cùb; bairill; crò, cròth, cròilean, lann, fàl, fang.

Coop, *v.* Cùb; cròth, fang, priosanaich.

Cooper, *s.* Cùbair, fear dheanamh shoithchean; fonnsair; *the business of a cooper,* cùbaireachd.

Co-operate, *v.* Comh-oibrich, còghain; cuidich.

Co-operation, *s.* Comh-oibreachadh, còghnath, coghnadh; comh-obair.

Co-operative, *a.* Cuideachail.

Co-operator, *s.* Comh-oibreachair, cuideachair, fear coghnaidh.

Co-optation, *s.* Comh-mhiannachadh.

Co-ordinate, *a.* Co-ionann, taobh ri taobh, comh-inbheach.

Co-ordination, *s.* Co-ionannachd; comh-inbheachd.

Coot, *s.* Seorsa tunnaig fhiodhaich; dubh-lach, dubhlachadh. *Coots,* dubh-lachaidh.

Cop, *s.* Bàrr, ceann, mullach; *top.*

Coparcenary, *s.* Comh-oighreachas, comh-roinn dh'oighreachd shinnseara.

Coparcener, *s.* Comh-oighre.

Copal, *s.* Seorsa ròsaid.

Copartner, *s.* Comh-phairtear, comh-phairtiche, combanach.

Copartnership, *s.* Comh-phàirteachd, comh-roinn.

Cope, *s.* Currac; giobal; curac mhànach; ni sam bith leis an comhdaichear an ceann, brat no ni a sgaoilear thar cheann, mar chuasach nan neamha.

Cope, *v.* Barraich, cuir barran air ni; dean strìgh (no) spairn; connsaich, gleac.

Copier, *s.* Sgrìobhair; fear a leanas eisiomlair.

Coping, *s.* Barran; mullach.

Copious, *a.* Lionmhor, pailt; làn, iomadach; saibhir; briathrach.

Copiously, *adv.* Gu lionmhor, gu pailt, gu làn, gu iomadach, gu saibhir; gu briathrach.

Copiousness, *s.* Lionmhaireachd, pailteas, làine; saibhreas; briatharachas.

Copist, *s.* Eisiomlairiche; ath-sgrìobhair.

Copped, *a.* Barraichte, barranaichte.

Copper, *s.* Umha, *copar,* unga; coire mòr, coire togalaich.

Copperas, *s.* Copar, coparas.

Copper-nose, *s.* Sròin-dhearg.

Copper-plate, *s.* Clo-chlàr.

Coppersmith, *s.* Ceard-umha.

Copper-work, *s.* Umhadaireachd; umha-lann, ceardach-umha.

Coppery, *a.* Umhach.

Coppice, *s.* Frith-choille, dlù-choille, preasarnach.

Coppled, *a.* Barra-bhiorach, binneanach; spiriceach.

Copse. See Coppice.

Copulate, *v.* Ceangail, cuplaich; caraidich, measgnaich; rach cuideachd mar theid firionn as boirionn.

Copulation, *s.* Ceangladh; cuplachadh; caraideachadh; leannanas, comh-riatain.

Copy, *s.* Ath-sgrìobhadh, dùblachadh; amhladh, samhladh, eisiomlair, eiseimpleir, leth-bhreac, mac-leabhar.

Copy, *v.* Ath-sgrìobh.

Copyright, *s.* Leabhar chòir.

Coquet, *v.* Dean bòilich, dean beadradh; meall le beadradh.

Coquetry, *s.* Leannanachd, faoin-bheadradh.

Coquette, *s.* Sgòdag, gogaid.

Coracle, *s.* Curach, curachan, eathar, sgòth, barc.

Coral, *s.* Coireal, croimheal, coradhan, groidheall.

Coralline, *a.* Coirealach.

Corant, *s.* Seorsa dannsaidh.

Corban, *s.* Croidhle-deirce; tiodhlac, deirc, gibht.

Corbel, *s.* Croidhle; niùc an am balladh airson dhealbhan.

Cord, *s.* Cord, ròp, taod, teathair, lòmainn, sugan, teud, sreang, cabal, gad; ball; connadh, cruach chonnaidh ochd troidhean air fad, ceithir air airde, is ceithir air leud.

Cord, *v.* Cord, rop, taodach, teathairich, ceangail, naisg.

Cordage, *s.* Cordail, cùird luingeis.

Cordial, *a.* Cridheil; treibhdhireach; beothachail, athbheothachail. Cordially, *gu cridheil gu suilbhear, gu toileach, gu treibhdhireach.*

Cordial, *s.* Ioc-shlainnte; deoch-bheathail, deoch-bhlasda; ni a ni suigeartach.

Cordiality, *s.* Cridhealas; dubhrachd, gradh-carthannachd, meas, treibh-dhireas.

Cordovan, *s.* Leathar eich, leathar Spainnteach.

Cordwain, *s.* Leathar.

Cordwainer, *s.* Brogair, greusaiche; dualadair.

Cordwood, *s.* Connadh, connadh cruachte.

Core, *s.* Cridhe; cuairsgean; iongar.

Coriaceous, *a.* Leatharach.

Coriander, *s.* Lus a choire, coireaman.

Corinth, *s.* Spiontag, dearcag Fhrancach.

Cork, *s.* Arcair, àrc; stoipeal searraig, crann àrcain.

Corky, *a.* Arcanach, àrcach; eutrom, gaoithe.

Cormorant, *s.* Sgarbh; muna-bhuachaill; craosair.

Corn, *s.* Arbhar, gràn, gort, pòr, coirce; meall air na h-ordagan. Corn-field, *achadh;* corn-floor, *urlar bualaidh, urlar sabhuil;* corn-flower, *curac na cuthaig.*

Corn, *v.* Saill; granaich.

Corn-muse, *s.* Seorsa piobain.

Corneous, *a.* Adhairceach.

Corner, *s.* Oisinn, niùc, cearn, uilinn; buailt, foir, mial.

Corner-stone, *s.* Clach oisinn, cearbag.

Cornerwise, *adv.* Air oisinn, air uilinn.

Cornet, *s.* Inneal ciùil; fear brataich eachraidh; buabhall.

CORNETER, s. Buabhallaiche, buabhall; ceatharn each.
CORN-FIELD, s. Achadh.
CORN-FLOOR, s. Urlar sabhuil, urlar bualaidh.
CORN-FLOWER, s. Brog na cuthaig; currac na cuthaig.
CORNICE, s. Barra-bhailc, barra-mhaise; mullach carra.
CORNICLE, s. Adhairceag
CORN-LAND, s. Talamh treabhaidh.
CORN-MILL, s. Muileann min.
CORN-PIPE, s Pioban; feadan arbhair
CORN-POPPY, s. Beilbheag.
CORN-SPURRY, s. Cluain lin
CORNUCOPIA, s. Adharc shaibhreis, adharc barraichte le meas agus ùbhlan ann an lamhaibh ban De.
CORNUTED, a. Adhairceach
CORNUTO, s. Fear ban-adhaltranaiche.
CORNY, a. Cruaidh mar adhairc, adhairceach; arbharach.
COROLLARY, s. Comh-dhunadh, suim; comh-leanadas
CORONAL, a. Coronach; fleasgach.
CORONAL, s. Coron, crùn, fleasg, fleasgadh, blàth-fhleasgaidh, cruinneacan
CORONATION, s Righ-chrùnadh, crùnadh, crùnachadh
CORONER, s. Coronair; fear do 'n dleasdanas fhaotainn a mach, as leth an righ, cia mar a fhuair neach air bi bàs ro 'n am.
CORONET, s. Coron, crùn, fleasg, blath-fhleasgadh, cruinneacan.
CORPORAL, s. Corplàir; ceannard ochdnar, an t-oichear is isle anns an arm, oifigeach iosal air bord luinge
CORPORAL, a. Corporra, corporradh, colla, collgha, collaidh. Corporally, *gu corporra*
CORPORALITY, s. Corporrachd; collaidheachd, coluinneachd.
CORPORATE, s. Aonaichte, aontaichte; coitchionn.
CORPORATION, s. Comh-chorp; comunn, bannal
CORPOREAL, a. Corporra; collaidh, colluinneach
CORPS, s. Buidheann, bannal, cath-bhuidheann.
CORPSE, s. Corp, corp marbh, cairbhe, marbhanach
CORPULENCE, s Reamhrachd, sultmhorachd, sult, feolmhorachd, feolmhoireachd; domhalas, tiughad, gairbhe, làn.
CORPULENT, s Reamhar, sultmhor, sultar, feolmhor, feolar, domhail, dumhail; làn; tiugh, garbh, promhaidh, cruambar, daillidh, grontach.
CORPUSCLE, s. Corpan, dad, dadmun.
CORPUSCULARIAN, s Dadmunach
CORRADE, v. Rub, suath.
CORRADIATION, s Co-dhealradh, co-dhearrsadh.
CORRECT, v. Leasaich; ceartaich, cuir ceart, feobhasaich; cronaich, smachd, smachdaich; greidh.
CORRECT, a. Ceart, ceartaichte; snasmhor; deas, ullamh; freagarrach; pongail, sicir.
CORRECTION, s. Ceartachadh, leasachadh; smachd, smachdachadh; cronachadh; riadh; peanas House of correction, *smachd-lann, tigh, smachd.*
CORRECTIVE, a. Ceartachail, smachdachail; cronachail
CORRECTLY, adv. Gu ceart, gu snàsmhor; gu freagarrach, gu pongail.
CORRECTOR, s. Ceartachair, smachdachair, smachdadair
CORRELATE, s. Comh-charaid, leth-bhreac
CORRELATIVE, a. Comh-dhìlleas, comh-chàirdeas
CORREPTION, s Cronachadh, trod
CORRESPOND, v. Freagair, comh-fhreagair; cum caidreamh suas.

CORRESPONDENCE, s. Comh-fhreagairt; caidreamh, conaltradh, comunn.
CORRESPONDENT, a. Freagarrach, lathailteach, comh-fhreagarrach.
CORRESPONDENT, s. Caidreamhaiche, comh-fhreagairtear, comh-fhreagraiche.
CORRESPONSIVE, s. Freagarrach, comh-fhreagarrach
CORROBORANT, a. Neartachail, daingneachail, daighneachail
CORROBORATE, v Neartaich, comh-neartaich, daighnich, comh-dhaighnich, dearbh, deimhinich.
CORROBORATION, s Neartachadh; dearbhadh, déimhineachadh
CORRODE, v Ith, cnàmh, caith, creim, loisg
CORRODENT, a. Cnamhach, caithteach, loisgeach
CORRODIBLE, a So-chnamh, so-chaitheamh, so-losgadh
CORROSION, s. Cnàmh, cnàmhadh, caitheamh, creimeadh, losgadh
CORROSIVE, a. Cnàmhach, caitheach, caithteach, losgach; geur, searbh, goirt
CORROSIVELY, adv. Gu cnàmhach, gu caithteach.
CORROSIVENESS, s. Cnamhachd, caithteachd, géiread.
CORRUGANT, s. Preasach, preasagach, casach, peurlach, spriongach
CORRUGATE, v. Preas, cas, spriong, peurlaich.
CORRUGATION, s. Preasadh, casadh, spriongadh, peurladh
CORRUPT, v. Truaill, truaillich, mill; morcaich, grod.
CORRUPT, a (*Tainted*), truaillidh, coirpidh, (*rotten*), morcaidh, lobhta, morcach, grod, musgach, (*wicked*), olc, aingidh, coirpte, peacach, mibheusach, droch, fiar
CORRUPTER, s. Truaillear, truailleadair, milltear.
CORRUPTIBLE, a. Truaillidh, so-thruaillidh.
CORRUPTION, s. Truaillidheachd, coirpidheachd, morcas, morcaidheachd, lobhadh; groide, + fulrath; iongar.
CORRUPTLY, adv. Gu h-aingidh, gu h-olc, gu coirpte.
CORRUPTNESS, s. Truaillidheachd, coirpidheachd, morcaidheachd, lobhadh, dubhailc, aingidheachd.
CORSAIR, s Còrsair; mar-spuinneadair.
CORSE, s Corp, cairbhe, marbhanach, carcais
CORSELET, s. Uchd-eideadh; eideadh-uchd, eide-uchd
CORTICAL, a. Cairteach, sgrathach.
CORUSCANT, a. Dealrach, dearrsach, drilinneach, lannaireach, loinnreach, lasach
CORUSCATION, s. Dealradh, dearrsadh, drilinn, lannaireachd, leus
CORYMBIATED, a Dearcach, dearcagach.
COS, s. Cloch-gheurach, clach liobhraidh
COSIER, s. Clùdair, cearbair.
COSMETIC, a. Sgeadachall; naisneach, liomhach, grinneadach, ni sam bi a ni glan no grinn, grinneadas.
COSMICAL, a. A dh' éireas is a loidheas comh-luath ris a ghrian.
COSMOGONY, s. Cé-chruthachadh, cé-dhealbhadh.
COSMOGRAPHER, s Tlachd-sgriobhair, cé-sgriobhair.
COSMOGRAPHY, s. Tlachd-sgriobhadh, cé-sgriobhadh, domhain-ghrabhadh.
COSMOPOLITAN, s Iomrolaiche; fear gun dachaidh sam bi ach an saoghal mor, fear a tha aig an tigh 's na h-uile aite.
COSSET, s Uan a thogar a cuman, peat.
COST, s. Cosd, cosdadh; pris, fiach, luach, struidh, strodha.
COST, v. Cosd, cost. How much cost it? *cia meud a chosd e?*
COSTAL, a. Aisneach

Costard, *s.* Ceann; ubhal cruinn.

Costive, *a.* Com-dhaingean, teann sa chom

Costiveness, *s* Daighneachadh cuim

Costliness, *s.* Cosdas, costas, prìscalachd, daorad; luachmhorachd, greadhnachas, grinneas

Costly, *a* Cosdail, prìseil, daor, luachmhor, greadhnach, grinn.

Costmary, *s.* Costag a bhaile gheamhruidh

Costume, *s* Eide, eideadh, culaidh, eudach, aodach, deise.

Cot, *s* Bothan, bothag; cròth, coite, caban, seorsa leapach

Cot, *s.* Caile-bhalaoch.

Cotemporary, *a* Co-aosmhor, comh-aimsireil

Cotemporary, *s* Comh-aois. My cotemporary, *mo-chomh-aois*

Coterie, *s* Cuideachd, comunn, bannal.

Cotillon, *s.* Scorsa dannsaidh.

Cotland, *s* Croite

Cotquean, *s* Caile bhalach, balach chailean

Cottage, *s* Bothan, bothag, cròth, coite, caban, †iosdan

Cottager, *s* Coitear, croitear

Cotton, *s* Canach, canaichean, cotan; cadas, canur, craobh chanaich

Couch, *v a* and *n* Crùb, crùban, dean crùban, luidh, dean luidhe, crom, lùb sios, cuir luidhe, folaich, ceil, (*couch as a spear*), socraich

Couch, *s.* Luidheagan, langasaid, uiridh, leabadh; spiris, spàr, suidhe, colcag, colcaidh, coisir; sreath, breath

Couchant, *a.* Sìnnte, na luidhe, na chrùban

Couched, *a.* Folaichte, céilte.

Cough, *s* Casd, casdaich, casadaich, cnatan, fuachd, cothan, fothach

Cough, *v a* and *n.* Casd, dean casd.

Could, *imperf. pret.* of can B' urradh, b' urrainn. I could, *b' urradh dhomh*

Coulter, *s.* Soc, sochd, coltar

Council, *s.* Comhairle, comhdhail, mòd, coinneamh, seanadh

Counsel, *s* Comhairle, scòladh, crionnachd; diomhaireachd; (*in law*), comh-airliche, fear tagraidh.

Counsel, *v.* Comhairlich, seòl.

Counsellor, *s* Comhairliche, caraid; fear tagraidh, fear lagha.

Count, *v.* Cùnnt, aireamh, cuir ri chéile, dean aireamh; innis, meas, cuir as leth.

Count, *s.* Cunntas, aireamh, uimhir, lach.

Count, *s* Iarla, iar-fhlath, morair

Countable, *a.* So-aireamh, so-chunntadh

Countenance, *s* Gnùis, aghaidh, aodann, eudann, coslas, fiamh, dreach.

Countenance, *v* Cum cul ri, cum taobh ri, cum taic ri.

Countenancer, *s* Caraid, taic, cul-taic, fear cùl-taic.

Counter, *s.* Droch-airgiod; airgiod, bùth-chlàr

Counter, *adv* An aghaidh, gu calg dhìreach

Counteract, *v* Cuir an aghaidh, bac.

Counterbalance, *v* Comh-thromaich, comh-chothromaich

Counterbalance, *s.* Comh-thromachadh, comh-chothrom.

Counterbuff, *s.* Ath-bhuille; buille eile, buille air ais.

Counterbuff, *v.* Ath-bhuail, buail air ais.

Counterchange, *s* Malairt, comh-mhalairt

Countercheck, *v.* Gabh roimh, bac, stad.

Counter-evidence, *s.* Comh-theisteas, comh-fhianuis.

Counterfeit, *v. a.* Fallsaich; cùin; dean coslach, gnuismheall.

Counterfeit, *a* Fallsa; gnùis-mheallta; fuar chrabhach; meallta, mealltach, cealgach; breugach.

Counterfeit, *s.* Fallsair, cealgair, breugair.

Countermand, *v.* Ais-ghairm, ais-orduich; cuir an aghaidh, gabh ro, bac.

Countermand, *s.* Ais-ordugh; ais-aithne.

Countermarch, *v.* Pill, till mar ri feachd.

Countermarch, *s.* Pilleadh, pilltinn, feachd-philltinn.

Countermark, *v.* Ath-chomharaich.

Countermark, *s.* Ath-chomhar.

Countermine, *v.* Comh-tholl, tar-tholl

Countermine, *s.* Tar tholl.

Counterpane, *s.* Cubhrainn, cubhraig.

Counterpart, *s.* Leth-bhreac; comh-phairt.

Counterpoise, *v.* Comh-chothromaich, cothromaich.

Counterpoise, *s.* Cothrom, co-chothrom

Countertide, *s* Ath-sruth, ais-shruth, saobh-shruth.

Countess, *s.* Ban-mhorair; ban-iarla

Counting-house, *s* Tigh cunntais, tigh-gnothuich, oiche.

Countless, *a.* Do-àireamh, do-chùnntadh; do-innseadh, thar cùnntas.

Country, *s* Dùthaich, tìr, talamh, fearann, fonn, tlachd; tuath. A pleasant country, *aileas*

Country, *a* Duthchail, tuathail, tuaitheach, bodachail, balachail, rastach, bromanach, aineolach.

Countryman, *s* Fear-dùthcha; tuathanach, gnàisear, ceatharnach, bodach, balaoch, sgalag, bromanach. My countryman, *m' fhear-dùthcha.*

County, *s.* Siorrachd, siorramachd

Couple, *s* Paidhir, cupall, caraid, deise, cuingear, dithis; fear agus bean.

Couple, *v.* Paidhirich, cuplaich, caraidich, pòs, ceangail dithis ri cheile, coimhlich.

Coupled, *a.* Paidhirichte, cuplaichte.

Couplet, *s* Ceathramh, caraid, rann; paidhir. A couplet of doves, *paidhir cholaman.*

Courage, *s.* Misneach, treubhantas, curantas, cruadal, spiorad; curaisd, smiòr, smiòralas, cingeachd; tapadh

Courageous, *a* Misneachail, treubhanta, cruadalach, spioradail, caraisdeach, smiorail, cingeach, tapaidh, curanta, curantach

Courageously, *adv* Gu misneachail, gu treubhanta, gu cruadalach, gu spioradail, gu smiorail, gu curanta

Courageousness, *s.* Misneach, treabhantach; gaisge, curaisdeachd; curantachd.

Courier, *s.* Teachdair, gille ruithe.

Course, *s.* Cursa, reis, ruithe, réim, comhruith; (*race ground*), ionad réise, aite comh-ruithe; (*of life*), iomchar, giùlan, beus, caith-beatha, dol a mach; (*of a ship*), gabhail, cursa luinge; (*of food*), riarachadh Of course, *air chinnte.*

Course, *v a.* and *n.* Ruith, steud, cursaich, ruaig, cuir na ruith, cuir na steud, sealgaich, sealg

Courser, *s* Each réise, steud-each, each cùrsa

Courses, *s* Mios-shruth, sileadh cuim

Coursing, *s.* Fiadhachd, sealg, sealgaireachd, faoghaid

Court, *s.* Cuirt, mùr, pàiliunn, lùth-chairt, lùth-chuirt, ionad còmhnuidh righ, righ-lann; breaslann; (*flattery*), miodal, sodal; (*of justice*), reachd airm, cuirt-cheartais, mòd; (*hall*), talla, lios, cùirt, (*area*), blobhsa, cùirt; preaban. Court-day, *la-cùirt*, a court of judicature, *reachd-airm, reachd-mhòd.*

Court, *v.* Suirtheadh, dean suirtheadh; sir am pòsadh; aslaich; iarr.

Court-cards, *s.* Cairtean dùbailt.

Court-dresser, *s.* Sodalaiche, miodalaiche.

Courteous, *a.* Cùirteil, modhail; flathail, caoimhneil, suairce.

Courteousness, *s.* Cùirtealachd, modhaileachd; beus.

Courtesan, *s.* Siùrsach, striopach, strabaid.

Courtesy, *s.* (*Obeisance*), beic, beichd.

Courtesy, *s.* (*In manners*), modhaileachd, suairceas, deagh-bheus, siobhaltachd, deagh-ghean, siobhaltachd; suairceas; tlachd.

Courtezan, *s.* Siursach, striopach; strabaid, meirdreach.

Courtier, *s.* Suiriche; cùirtear.

Court-leet, *s.* Mòd.

Courtlike, *a.* Modhail, beusach; miodalach.

Courtliness, *a.* Modhaileachd, cùirteas, furan, caomhalachd, suairceas, flathaileachd.

Courtship, *s.* Suireadh, suirtheadh; leannanachd, gaol.

Cousin-german, *s.* Comh-ogha; caraid. Cousins-german, *clann brathar athar* (*no*) *màthar, clann peathar athar* (*no*) *màthar.*

Cove, *s.* Uamha, uagha, uamhaidh; còmhdach; fasgadh; geodha, camus, bagh, òban.

Covenant, *s.* Cumha, cùmhnant, cunradh, ceangal, comh-cheangal; *bargan;* achd, cor, gniomh.

Covenant, *s.* Cumhnantach, cunraich, ceangail, co-cheangail.

Covenanter, *s.* Cumhnantaiche, cùnraiche.

Covenous, *a.* Cuilbheartach, eolach, cealgach, pratail.

Cover, *v.* Còmhdaich, cuibhrig, folaich, céil; sgàil, fuan, dion; gur.

Cover, *s.* Còmhdach, brat, cubhrainn, cuibhrig, sgàil; fàluing; fasgadh; croicionn; (*a sheath*), truaill, dùbla, dùbladh.

Coverlet, *s.* Cùbhraig, cùbhrainn, brat-leapach.

Covert, *s.* Dion, dìdean, fasgadh, comhdach, brat, garadh; aite folaich; dubhradh.

Covert, *a.* Diomhair, folaichte, falaichte, céilte.

Coverture, *s.* Dion, didean.

Covet, *v. a.* Sanntaich, miannaich, iarr gu durachdach.

Covetous, *a.* Sanntach, miannach, gionach, lonach; ciocrach, maoin-chiocrach, iognach. Covetously, *gu sanntach, gu miannach.*

Covetousness, *s.* Sannt, miann, gion, an-shannt, dulchanachd.

Covey, *s.* Sgaoth eun, ealt, ealtuin.

Covin, *s.* Cealg-chordadh.

Cow, *s.* Bò, ba, mart, laithre, †fearb, †agh, †tearc.

Cow, *v.* Mi-mhisnich.

Coward, *s.* Cladhair, gealtair; cailleach.

Cowardice, *s.* Cladhaireachd, gealtaireachd, meatachd; eagal, geilte.

Cowardliness, *s.* Cladhaireachd, gealtaireachd, gealtachd, meatachd.

Cowardly, *a.* Cladhaireach, gealtach, meata, eagalach, cailleachanta, cailleachail, tais, bog, neo-smiorail, neo-dhuineal.

Cower, *v.* Dean cruban, crùb.

Cowherd, *s.* Buachaill, buachaill bhò.

Cowherding, *s.* Buachailleachd.

Cowhouse, *s.* Bàich, bo-lann, bò-thigh, buaile, buailidh.

Cowkeeper, *s.* Buachaill.

Cowl, *s.* Currac, bioraid, bonaid.

Cowparsnip, *s.* Odharan.

Cowslip, *s.* Seorsa plùrain.

Coxcomb, *s.* Cirean coilich; goigean, spaillicear.

Coy, *a.* Malta, banail, beusach; geimnidh bandaidh; gealtach, sgaolar; coimheach; samhach, bìth.

Coyly, *adv.* Gu matta, gu banail, gu beusach, gu gealtach, gu coimheach, gu samhach, gu bìth.

Coyness, *s.* Maltachd, banalachd, geimnidheachd, bandaidheachd, gealtachd, sgaolarachd.

Cozen, *v.* Meall, thoir an car a. He cozened him completely, *thug e 'n glan char as.*

Cozenage, *s.* Feall, feill, mealladh, mealtaireachd; mealltachd, fallsachd, cuilbheartachd, slaoighte, slaoightearachd, ceilge, cealgaireachd.

Cozener, *s.* Mealltair, cealgair, fallsair, slaoightear, fealtair.

Crab, *s.* Partan; crùban, tarpan; ubhal fiadhain; cainntean, duine crosda, doirbh.

Crab, *a.* Goirt, searbh. A crabcherry, *searbh-shiris.*

Crabbed, *a.* Crosda, cainnteach, searbh, doirbh, cringeanach, mi-nosach, sgiorrail, droch-mhéineach, dranndanach. A crabbed little fellow, *cainntean, cnocair.*

Crabbedly, *adv.* Gu crosda, gu cainnteach, gu searbh, gu doirbh.

Crabbedness, *s.* Crosdachd, cainnteachd, seirbhe, doirbhe, cringeanachd.

Crab-tree, *s.* Goirteag, craobh ubhlan fiadhain.

Craber, *s.* Radan uisge.

Crack, *s.* (*Split*), sgolt, crac, crachd, sgàin, gag, bearn, leasg.

Crack, *s.* (*Noise*), crac, braidhe, spreadh, blocadh, torman, fuaim; stairn; sgonnag, sginneag.

Crack, *v.* (*Split*), crac, sgàin, sgoilt, gog, sgag, beairn, sgar.

Crack, *v. a.* and *n.* (*Noise*), crac, dean braidhe; bòsd. Crack your whip, *crac do chuip;* it cracked, *leig e crac as.*

Crackbrained, *a.* Gòrach; gogaideach, gogailleach; neo-shuidhichte; oinnseachail; amaideach.

Cracker, *s.* Gleòrmas, glòramas; rabhdair; cracair.

Crackhemp, *s.* Crochair.

Crackle, *v.* Crac, dean cracail, dean briosgarnaich.

Crackling, *s.* Cracail; briosgarnachd; diorrasanaich.

Crackling, *s.* Croinnseag, gràiseag; breacag.

Cradle, *s.* Creadhal, craidheal.

Cradle-clothes, *s.* Aodach creadhlach.

Craft, *s.* Ceaird; seoltachd; innleachd, cuilbheart, gangaid, gabhdadh.

Craftily, *adv.* Gu seolta, gu cuilbheartach, gu carach, gu mangach, gu cealgach, gu fealltach, gu sligheach.

Craftiness, *s.* Cuilbheartachd, ceilge, foill, feall, gabhdachd, mang, fallsachd, cluainteararachd, seoltachd.

Craftsman, *s.* Fear-ceairde; fear ealdhain.

Crafty, *a.* Cuilbheartach, cealgach, carach, lubach, fealltach, gabhdach, mangach, fallsail, cluainteach, ceabhacach, innleachdach, seòlta, eolach, sligheach.

Crag, *s.* Craig, creug, cragan; cul na h-amhaich.

Cragged, *a.* Cragach, creugach, craganach, garbh; stùcach, stacach.

Craggedness, *s.* Garbhalach.

Craggy, *a.* Cragach, creugach, craganach, garbh; stùcach, stacach.

Cram, *v.* Dinn; sparr, pùc, lion, stailc; sàsaich.

Crambo, *s.* Cluich rannachd.

Cramp, *s.* Iodha; orc; bac, bacadh; gramaiche; corbaidh.

Cramp, *a.* Duilich, cruaidh, deacair, do-fhuasgladh, doirbh, do-dheanamh.

CRAMP, *v* Grab, bac, ceangail, cuibhrich, amail.
CRAMPFISH, *s* Oro-iasg, craimb-iasg.
CRAMPIRON, *s.* Gramaiche.
CRANBERRY, *s* Muileag
CRANE, *s.* Corr, corra-riabhach, corra-mhonaidh, corra-ghriobach; feadan (no) pioban crom
CRANIUM, *s.* Claigeann, claigionn
CRANK, *s.* Crangaid; slighe charach.
CRANKLE, *v a* Lùb, ruith mach is stigh an luibibh.
CRANKLES, *s.* Luibean, meallan, dùnain
CRANKNESS, *s* Slainnte, fallaineachd, neart, treòir
CRANNIED, *a* Tollta, tolltach, sgàinteach, sgoltach, gagach, sgagach, bruchagach
CRANNY, *s* Toll, sgàineadh, gag, sgagadh, bruchag, peasg, sgoltadh
CRAPE, *s* Sròl.
CRAPULENCE, *s* Meisge, meisgearachd, meisge-thinneas
CRAPULOUS, *a.* Meisgeach, air mhcisge
CRASH, *s* Broidhle, stairn; bruan, géisg
CRASH, *v.* Bruan, dean géisg It crashed, *leig e geisg as*
CRASS, *a.* Tiugh.
CRASSITUDE, *s.* Tiughad
CRATCH, *s.* Prasach
CRATER, *s* Cup, bòl, gòblaid.
CRAVAT, *s* Brat-muineil, neapaicinn amhaich; bann-bhràghaid, stoc
CRAVE, *v* Aslaich, aithchuing, grios, guidh; sir; tathaich, tagair; bi an càs. Crave a debt, *tathaich ain-fheach.*
CRAVEN, *s* Fùidsidh, cladhair, gealtair.
CRAVEN, *a* Gealtach; dìbìdh.
CRAVER, *s.* Aslachair; tathaichear, tagairtear, tagrair.
CRAUNCH, *v* Pronn, cagain, cnuas.
CRAW, *s* Sgròban, goile, geuban
CRAWFISH, *s* Ciomach aibhne.
CRAWL, *v* Snag, ealaidh, snàgain.
CRAWLER, *s.* Snàgair, màgran
CRAWLING, *a* Snàgach, ealadhach, màgranach, màgach.
CRAWLING, *s.* Snagadh, snagarsaich, ealadh, màgran.
CRAZE, *v* Bris, bruth, broth, bruan, pronn, an-fhannaich, cuir thar chéill
CRAZED, *a* Gòrach, breòite.
CRAZINESS, *s.* Laigse, laigsinn, breòiteachd, crioplachd, an-fhannachd, anmhuinneachd
CRAZY, *a* Briste, breoite, anfhann, anmhann, lag, fann, mall, gòrach.
CREAK, *v.* Sgread, diosgain, fead, géisg.
CREAK, *s* Sgread, diosgan, diosgail, géisg, geisgeil, sgreadail.
CREAM, *s* Ceath, uachdar
CREAMFACED, *a,* Bàn, bandaidh, gealtach
CREAMY, *a* Ceathar, uachdrach.
CREASE, *s.* Preas, preasag
CREASE, *v.* Preas
CREATE, *v.* Cruthaich, dealbh; gin, thoir a mach, dean.
CREATION, *s* Cruthachadh, dealbhadh, deanamh. The creation, *an domhain, an saoghal, an cruinne cé.*
CREATIVE, *a* Cruthadach, cruthachail, dealbhach, ginead-ach, torrach.
CREATOR, *s* Cruthachair, dealbhair, The Creator, *an Cruith-fhear.*
CREATURE, *s.* Creutuir, creutair, duil, bith, ainmhidh, ainbhith, beathach, beothach, an duine.
CREDENCE, *s.* Creideas.

CREDENDA, *s* Creud; creidimh.
CREDENTIAL, *s.* Teisteannas, teisteas; litir-molaidh.
CREDIBILITY, *s.* Creideas, cosmhalachd; coslas.
CREDIBLE, *a.* Creideasach, coslach, so-chreidsinn; airidh air chreidsinn, fior, fireannach.
CREDIBLENESS, *s.* Creideasachd, coslas.
CREDIT, *s.* Creideas; cliù; creideamh, teisteas, firinn, earbsadh. Without credit, *gun chreideas;* give credit, *thoir creideas.*
CREDIT, *v.* Creid, thoir creideas; earb a.
CREDITABLE, *a.* Creideasach; measail.
CREDITABLENESS, *s* Creideasachd, deagh ainm, deaghchliù.
CREDITABLY, *adv* Gu creideasach, gu measail.
CREDITOR, *s.* Fear creideis, creideasaiche, iasachdaiche.
CREDULITY, *a.* Baoghaltachd, neo-amharusachd.
CREDULOUS, *a* Baoghalta, so-chreideamhach, neo-amharusach, faoin.
CREED, *s.* Creud.
CREEK, *s* Rugha, bagh, lub, lulb, camus, òban, geòth, geòdh, port, poll-marcachd.
CREEKY, *a.* Rughach, baghach, lubach, luibeach, camusach, obanach, geòthach
CREEP, *v* Snàg, ealaidh, màgrain, crùb, crom, striochd
CREEPER, *s.* Snagair, magranaiche, crùbair.
CREEPHOLE, *s.* Toll, dion, leith-sgeul; scòladh
CREMATION, *s.* Losgadh
CRENATED, *a* Feagaichte, feagach.
CREPITATE, *v.* Crac, dean cracail
CREPITATION, *s* Cracail.
† CREPUSCULE, *s.* Breac-sholus, tuaileachd.
CRESCENT, *s.* Bogha; gealach ur.
CRESCIVE, *a.* Fàsadach, gineadach
CRESS, *s.* Biolair Dock cresses, *duilleag mhaith.*
CRESSET, *s* Tigh-soluis, tigh faire.
CREST, *s* Circan; top; dos; curac, puirleag; gearradh airm; leoime, sgòd, ardan, uaille.
CRESTED, *a* Circanach, cireach, dosach, puirleagach.
CRESTFALLEN, *a.* Trom, gun spiorad, neo-mhisneachail.
CRETACEOUS, *a.* Cailceach, caelceil.
CREVICE, *s.* Toll, crac, sgoltadh, gag, sgàineadh, fosgladh.
CREW, *s* Sgiobadh, bannal, foirne, cuideachd, lamhan sgibe, muinntir luinge; bròd, gràisg.
CREWEL, *s.* Cearsla do shnàth toinnte
CRIB, *s* Prasach, mainnsir, gribeadh; buaile; bothan.
CRIB, *v* Druid, duin suas, fang.
CRIBBAGE, *s.* Seorsa cluiche air chairtean
CRIBBLE, *s.* Criathar, ruideal
CRIBRATION, *s* Criathradh, ruidealadh
CRICK, *s.* Geisge dorus, diosgan, diosgail, giosgan; pian san amhaich.
CRICKET, *s.* Cuileag theallaich, greollan, grollan.
CRICKET, *s* Seorsa cluiche air creutaig.
CRICKET, *s* Creupan, stòl iosal.
CRIER, *s* Gairmeadair; bollsair, fear-gairm, eubhadair, éigheadair
CRIME, *s* Cion, lochd, coire, cront, peacadh, ciont, fabhda, cuisean
CRIMELESS, *a.* Neo-chiontach, neo-lochdach, neo-choireach; glan.
CRIMINAL, *a.* Ciontach, lochdach, coireach, peacach, aingidh.
CRIMINAL, *s.* Ciontach, peacach; crochair.

Criminally, *adv.* Gu ciontach, gu lochdach, gu coireach, gu peacach; gu h-aingidh.

Crimination, *s.* Coireachadh, cur as leth, dìteadh.

Crimp, *a.* Brisg, so-bhriseadh, so-phronnadh.

Crimple, *v. a.* Preas; crup.

Crimson, *s.* Cro-dhearg; dearg-ghonn. Crimson colour, *crubhasg.*

Crimson, *v.* Deargaich.

Cringe, *v.* Crup, dluthaich ri cheile, crùb; dean ùmhlachd, lùb, striochd, dean sodal.

Cringe, *s.* Striochd neo-dhuineil.

† **Crinigerous**, *a.* Romach, roinneach, molach, gaoisdeach, gaoisneach.

Crinkle, *v.* Fas preasach (no) preasagach, preas.

Cripple, *a.* Crùbach, bacach, gun luth nan cas.

Cripple, *s.* Crioplach; urr chrupach.

Crisis, *s.* Cruadhas; faochaidh; am cunnartach; airde tinneis. The fever is at a crisis, *tha'n teasach na h-airde.*

Crisp, *a.* Brisg; so-phronnadh; bachlagach, caisreagach, cuachach, dualach; cùirneanach, camagach, snìomhain, clìbeach, rocanach, rocach.

Crispated, *a.* Toinnte, bachlaichte, dualaichte.

Crispation, *s.* Casadh, dualadh, caisreagachd, cuachadh.

Crispy, *a.* Cuachach, dualach, bachlach.

Criterion, *s.* Cuspair deuchainn; dearbh; crois-riaghlaidh.

Critic, *s.* Breitheamh; teallsanach, ceasnachair; rannsachair; tiolpadair.

Critical, *a.* Pongail; lèirsinneach, beachdaidh; cunnartach; èigneach, èigeantach; cronachail.

Criticise, *v.* Rannsuich, geur-rannsuich; breathnaich; gearr; cronaich, faigh coire.

Criticism, *s.* Rannsachadh, geur-rannsachadh; gearradh, cronachadh, coireachadh, achmhasan, geur-bhreith.

Critique, *s.* See **Criticism**.

Croak, *v.* Dean ròc mar ni fitheach.

Croak, *s.* Ròc, rocan, rocail, rùcail, goraicleis.

Crocitation, *s.* Ròcail, rùcail.

Crock, *s.* Soitheach creadha, croc, cuach creadha.

Crockery, *s.* Eathraichean creadha, criadhachd.

Crocodile, *s.* Croghall.

Crocus, *s.* Seorsa plùraìn; crò, croch.

Croft, *s.* Croite, acair, goirtean; loinn.

Crofter, *s.* Croitear.

Crone, *s.* Cailleach; sean chaor.

Crony, *s.* Caraid, combach, sean chompanach, caraid dìleas; guaillìche.

Crook, *s.* Cromag, croman; slabhruidh, lorg buachaill; caman; lùb, lùib, car, tionndadh.

Crook, *v.* Crom, cam, lùb, fiar.

Crookback, *s.* Croitean, croman, crotair, troich.

Crookbacked, *a.* Crotach, crom.

Crooked, *a.* Crom, cam, lùbach, lùbta, feachdta, neo-dhìreach, crotach, corranta.

Crookedness, *s.* Cruime, caime, fiaire, fiarad; duaichneachd; reasgachd.

Crop, *s.* (*Of a bird*), sgròban, goile, geuban; (*of land*), bàrr; arbhar, fochann, torradh; foghar. The land produced a plentiful crop, *thug am fearann bàrr pailt uaith.*

Crop, *v.* Bearr, gearr, sgud; sgath; buain.

Cropful, *a.* Sathach, làn, buidheach.

Cropper, *s.* Columan sgròbanach.

Crosier, *s.* Bachull easpuig.

Croslet, *s.* Croiseag.

Cross, *s.* Crois; crosg; croich; crann ceusaidh; (*mischance*), earchall, tubaisd, doirbheas, campar, mi-shealbh. A small crop, *crosag.*

Cross, *a.* Crosgach, traisgte, tarsuing, tarsuinn; trasda; (*in temper*), crosda, doirbh, catail; cringeanach, aithghearr, cas, crosanta; reasgach, eithich, diùrrasach, searbh, mi-shealbhar.

Cross, *prep.* Thar, thairis, tarsuing.

Cross, *v. a.* and *n.* Cuir crosgach, cuir tarsuing; croisg, crois; rach thar, rach thairis; dubh a mach, sgrioch a mach. Cross the river, *rach thar an amhainn, croisg an amhainn.*

Crossbow, *s.* Crois-bhogha.

Crossbowman, *s.* Crois-bhoghadair.

Cross-examination, *s.* Crosg-cheasnachadh, cruaidh-cheasnachadh, cruaidh-sgrudadh.

Cross-examine, *v. a.* Crosg-cheasnaich, cruaidh-cheasnaich, cruaid-hsgrud.

Crossgrained, *a.* Crosda, eithich, mi-ghnètheil, leamh, draghail, reasgach; trasdach.

Crossness, *s.* Crosgachd; tarsuingeachd, trasdachd, tairsneachd; crosdachd; cainnteachd, doirbheas, reasgachd, cringeanachd, friothaireachd, cealg. A fit of crossness, *crosag.*

Cross-staff, *s.* Slat-reul.

Crosswind, *s.* Gaoth-tharsuing.

Crotch, *s.* Gobhal; croman, forc.

Crotchet, *s.* Prop; seorsa comhar ann an ceòl-sgriobhadh; dòchas, faoin-dhòchas.

Crouch, *v. n.* Crùb, crom; striochd; sleuchd; dean miodal; meath-chrom.

Crouching, *a.* Crubach, striochdach; sleuchdach, miodalach.

Crouching, *s.* Crubadh, striochdadh, sleuchdadh, miodal.

Croup, *s.* Braman; (*a disease*), crup.

Crow, *v.* Goir, gairm, glaodh; dean gloc, dean raite (no) raiteachas. The cock crew, *ghoir an coileach.*

Crow, *s.* Ròcas, feannag, cnaimheach; † duis. A hooded crow, *feannag ghlas.*

Crow, *s.* (*Of iron*), geimhleag.

Crow, *s.* Goirsinn, goir, gairm, glaodh, gloc, raiteachas. Cock crow, *goir choilich, gairm choilich.*

Crowd, *s.* Lòd sluaigh, buidheann, bannal, iorgail, domhladas sluaigh.

Crowd, *v.* Domhlaich, dumhlaich, mùch; teannaich, lion.

Crowd, *s.* Cruit, seorsa innil ciùil.

Crowder, *s.* Cruitear, cruiteag.

Crowfoot, *s.* Fleann uisge. Wood crowfoot, *follasgain, gairgheam*; various-leaved water-crowfoot, *lion na h-aibhne.*

Crown, *s.* Crùn, coron; fleasg, blàth-fhleasgaidh; mullach a chinn; (*in money*), crùn; (*dignity*), onoir inbhe, urram; sgeadachadh.

Crown, *v. a.* Crùn; sgeadaich; àrduich, dìol; crìochnuich.

Crucial, *a.* Crosgach, trasda, tarsuing.

Cruciate, *v. a.* Ceus; croch; cradh.

Crucible, *s.* Praiseach, poit leaghaidh.

Crucibler, *s.* Ceusadair.

Crucifix, *s.* Crois, crann-ceusaidh; dealbh chriosd air a chrann.

Crucifixion, *s.* Ceusadh.

Crucify, *v.* Ceus, croch, cuir neach gu bàs le chasaibh agus a lamhaibh a thairneadh ri crann, cradh, preach, gallruich.

Crude, *a.* Amh, neo-bhruich, anabuich, glas, searbh, goirte; neo-chriochnuichte

Crudeness, *s.* Amhachd, amhad, anabachd, anabuidheachd.

Crudity, *s* Amhachd, amhad, anabachd, glasdachd.

Crudle, *v. n.* Binntich, slamanaich, slamaich, slambanaich, fas na ghrudh, sgath, reamhraich *Crudled*, binntichte

Cruel, *a.* Borb, garg, cruaidh-chridheach, ain-iochdmhor, fuilteach; neo-dhàonnach, cruadalach, deineasach, deineachdach; eu-trocaireach, fòirneartach, foireigneach, neo-thruacanta, aingidh

Cruelty, *s.* Buirbe, gairge, ain-iochd, neo-dhaonachdas, eu-trocair, deineasachd, foirneart, foireigin.

Cruet, *s.* Searrag bheag, searrag fhion-gheur.

Cruise, *s* Cuach, crusaidh, crùisgean

Cruise, *s* Seòladh, cùrsachd, seoladh an toir namhuid (no) an toir creich

Cruise, *v.* Seol, cùrsaich, bi a cùrsachd

Cruiser, *s* Seoladair, cùrsair

Crum, Crumb, *s* Bruanag, spruilleach, crioman, criomag, pronnag, spronnag, spronnan, pronnan

Crumble, *s* Bruan, pronn, bris

Crumby, *a.* Bruanagach, criomanach, pronn, pronnanach, maoth, brisg

Crump, *a* Crotach, cruiteach, crom.

Crumple, *v. a* Cas, preas, criopagaich.

Crunkle, *v.* Sgreach, dean caoirean mar chorr

Crupper, *s.* Cruipean, cisleach, cuirpean, braman

Crural, *a* Luirgneach, cosach, seireanach

Crusade, *s* Cogadh na crois, seorsa cùin

Crush, *v.* Bruth, pronn, much, bris, mill, pùc, stramp, sàruich.

Crush, *s* Bruthadh, pronnadh, mùchadh, briseadh, pucadh, strampadh

Crust, *s.* Slige, sgrath; uachdar pithein, rùsgadh, carr, creim

Crust, *v.* Sgrathaich; carraich, carr, creim

Crustaceous, *a* Sligeach, rùsgach, carrach

Crustiness, *s.* Crosdachd, doirbhe, gruamaiche

Crusty, *a.* Sgrathach, rusgach, crosda, doirbh, gruamach, doimhe.

Crutch, *s* Lorg, trosnan, treostan, bat, cuaille, steafag, lorg-chomhnaidh.

Cry, *v* Eigh, eubh, glaodh, gairm, sgairt, beuc, ràn, blaodh, sgreach, sgread; (*weep*), guil, dean gul; (*cry down*), cronaich, coirich

Cry, *s.* Eigh, eubh, glaodh, gairm, sgairt, beuc, ran, blaodh, sgreach, sgread, fuachas, ulfhart; (*of dogs*), tathunn, tathunnaich, (*weeping*), gul, caoineadh, caoidh, tuireadh, gul-chaoin.

Crying, *s* Eighich, glaodhaich, gairmeadh, sgairteachd, beucail, rànaich, blaodhaich, sgreachail, sgreadail, ulfhartaich; (*weeping*), gul, caoineadh, caoidh, tuireadh. She fell a crying (weeping), *thoisich i air gul*

Cryal, *s.* Còrr-riabhach

Cryptæ, *s.* Càsàn.

Cryptic, *a.* Diomhair, folaichte, falaichte, céilte.

Crystal, *s.* Criostal

Crystal, *a* Criostalach, soilleir, trid-shoilleir.

Cub, *s.* Cuilean, measan, ainm taireil airson balachain no caileig

Cub, *v. a.* Beir.

Cube, *s* Ceithir-chearnag; ceathraman

Cube, *v.* Triplich.

Cubical, *a.* Ceathramanach.

Cubiform, *a.* Ceathramanach

Cubit, *s.* Lamh-choille, bann-lamh, ruighe-mheas; ochd òirlich dheug, uilinn.

Cuckold, *s* Fear ban-adhaltranaiche, gutalach, beannachan.

Cuckold, *v.* Truaill bean fir eile.

Cuckoldy, *a.* Truagh, diblidh.

Cuckold-maker, *s.* Gutalaiche.

Cuckoldom, *s.* Adhaltranas; gutalachd

Cuckoo, *s.* Cuthag; cuach, cuag.

Cuckoo-flower, *s* Bròg na cuthaig, gleoran.

Cuckoo-spittle, *s.* Smugaid no cuthaig

Cucullate, *a* Curacaichte.

Cucumber, *s* Cularan, cucambar.

Cud, *s* Cìr. Chew the cud, *cnamh a chìr.*

Cuddle, *v.* Curaidh, crùb, dean curaidh, dean crùban, dean beadradh.

Cuddy, *s* Guraiceach, baoghlan, balaoch.

Cudgel, *s.* Guitseal, cuidseal, bat, bat feannsaireachd.

Cudgel, *v.* Buail le bat; straoidhle, stear, greidh.

Cudweed, *s* Cnamh-lus, lus a chìre.

Cudwort, *s* Cat-luibh.

Cue, *s* Earball; ciabh, ciabhag, sànas; cuid, cuibhrionn.

Culrpo, *s* Corp

Cuff, *s.* Buille, stroidhle, stear, boiseag, deilseag, goilleag, dorn.

Cuff, *v. a.* Buaill, stroidhle, deilsich, dornaich, gréidh.

Cuff, *s* (*Sleeve*), muinle, muinicheall, muilicheann.

Cuirass, *s.* Uchd-eide, uchd-eididh, uchd-bheart.

Cuirassier, *s* Saighdear an uchd-eididh, trupair uchd-bheartaichte.

Cuish, *s* Cois-bheart, màs-bheart

Culinary, *a* Cearnach, citsinneach

Culdees, *s.* Coilltich, céiltich.

Cull, *v. a.* Tagh, roghnaich.

Culler, *s* Taghadair, roghnachair.

Cullion, *s* Sgonn-bhaolach.

Cully, *v.* Meall.

Cully, *s* Fear air a mhealladh le striopaich

Culpability, *s* Coire, coireachd, ciont.

Culpable, *a* Coireach, ciontach, airidh air achmhasan, airidh air peanas.

Culpableness, *s* Coire, ciont

Culpably, *adv* Gu coireach, gu ciontach, gu h-eucorach.

Culprit, *s* Ciontach, priosanach, ciomach.

Cultivate, *v* Treabh, ar, thoir stigh, dearg, builich; aitich, leasaich, mathaich *Cultivated*, treabhté Cultivated land, *talamh treabhte*

Cultivation, *s* Treabhadh, ar; leàsachadh, buileachadh; mathachadh, àiteachadh; fearachas-tighe, oilean, ionnsachadh.

Cultivator, *s* Treabhair, treabhaiche, tuathanach, leasachair, fear tighe.

Culture, *s.* Treabhadh, ar; mathachadh, leasachadh

Culver, *s* Colaman, smùdan.

Cumber, *v. a.* Fàsaich, tromaich, bac, amail, bith mar eallach; cuir moille, cuir dragh air

Cumber, *s* Fàsachadh, truime, bac, amal, moille, dragh.

Cumbersome, *a.* Fàsachail, amalach, draghail, trom, fòirneartach

Cumbersomeness, *s.* Fasachaileachd, draghalachd; foirnearteachd, amalachd, amailteachd, bac, amal.

Cumbrous, *a.* Draghail, trom, amalach, foirneartach.

Cumin, *s.* Lus mhic cuimein.

Cumulate, *v.* Carn, torr, cruach, cuir ri chéile, teanail, cnuasaich, cruinnich.

Cunctation, *s.* Dàil, mairnealachd, mairneal, ath-lathachadh.

Cuneal, *a.* Geinneach, geinneil

Cuneated, *a.* Geinneil, mar gheinne

Cunning, *a.* Seolta, sligheach, cuilbheartach, còlach, carach, mangach, gabhdach, ceabhachdach, cluainteach; sgileil, ionnsuichte, glic. A cunning man, *duine glic, druidh, fiosaiche.*

Cunning, *s* Seoltachd, sligheachd, cuilbheart, cuilbheartachd, mang, gabhdadh, cluaine, sgile, ionnsuchadh, gliocas.

Cunningly, *adv* Gu seolta, gu cuilbheartach, gu sligheach, gu gabhdach, gu ceabhachdach

Cunningman, *s.* Druidh; fiosaiche, fear fiosachd.

Cup, *s.* Cup, cop, copan, cupan, cuach, cuachag, corn, creachann, slige, noigean, searrag

Cupbearer, *s* Gille-cupain, gille corn.

Cupboard, *s.* Corn-chlar, corn-stial, clar shoithichean

Cupboard, *v* Taisg, cuir suas, cuir seachad.

Cupgossip, *s* Cuirmeag

Cupidity, *s* Sannt, miann, fonn

Cupola, *s.* Cuach-mhullach

Cupreous, *a* Coparach, copardha.

Cur, *s.* Cu, madadh, measan, ainm taireil airson duine

Curable, *a.* So-leigheas.

Curableness, *s.* So-leigheasachd

Curacy, *s.* Fo-mhinistearachd; fo-shagartachd

Curate, *s* Fo-shearmoiniche, ministear frithealaidh Sasunnach, fo-shagart sglreachd.

Curative, *a* Slànach, leigheasach.

Curb, *s* Cabstan, cabstar, muiseal, ceannsachadh, smachd, bac, amal.

Curb, *v. a.* Smachdaich, ceannsaich, bac, cum stigh, cum air ais, cum fodha.

Curd, *s.* Gruth, bainne binntichte, slamban, slaman, slagan

Curd, *v. a.* Binntich; slamaich, sgath, reamhraich.

Curdle, *v. a* and *n* Gruthaich, binntich; slamaich, sgath, reamhraich; fas na ghruth.

Curdy, *a.* Gruthach, binntichte, slamach, slamanach, slagach, slaganach

Cure, *s.* Leigheas, cneasachadh, cungaidh leigheis, ice

Cure, *v. a* Leighis, slànuich; (*meat*), saill; gleidh.

Cureless, *a* Do-leigheas, do-shlanuchadh, nach gabh leigheas (no) slanuchadh.

Curer, *s.* Leigh, leigheasair, slanuchair.

Curfew, *s.* Clog an teine; clog nan ochd uairean dh' oidhche, a sheinneadh ri am Righ Uilleam nam buadh, mar ordugh chum gach teine a mhùchadh agus gach solus a chur as, gus an la 'r na mhàireach.

Curiosity, *s* Ciadlus; feòrachas; iongantas, neònachas.

Curious, *a.* Iongantach, neonach, ciadlusach, innleachdach, ceanalta, ainmig; cuairealta; pongail, si cir.

Curiously, *adv* Gu h-iongantach, gu neonach, gu ciadlusach, gu h-innleachdach; gu h-ainmig; gu cuairealta; gu pongail, gu sicir.

Curl, *v. a.* and *n.* Cas, toinneamh, dual, dualaich, caisreagaich; sniomh.

Curl, *s.* Caisreag, clearc, bachlag, camag; dual fuilt, ciabh, ciabhag, cuailean, cuach, cuach-fhalt.

Curled, *a.* Caisreagach, clearcach, bachlach, dualach, camagach, ciabhach, ciabhagach, sniomhanach; toinnte, amalach, cornach.

Curlew, *s* Guilbinn, guilbneach, guilneach.

Curmudgeon, *s.* Sglamhaiche, sgroingean, spiocair

Currant, *s.* Dearc fhrangach, *raosar*

Currency, *s.* Cuairteachadh, cuairteachd, ruithe, biruithe, iomlaideachd

Current, *a* Cuartach, iomlaideach, ullamh; deas; bidheanta, gnathaichte, cumaint, fasanta, coitchionn

Current, *s.* Sruth, cas-shruth, buinne-shruth, (*in navigation*), seol-mara

Currently, *adv* Gu cumaint, gu coitchionn, an cumantas, gu fasanta

Curricle, *s* Carbad air dha rotha

Currier, *s* Sudar, fear dheasachadh leathair.

Currish, *a* Madail; brùideil, searbh, doirbh, coimheach, crosda, neo-shiobhailt

Curry, *v.* Deasaich leathar, buail; greidh, (*curry-horse*), cìr, rub, (*in kindness*), criataich, giogail, (*flatter*), dean miodal (no) goileam

Currycomb, *s* Sgrioban, each-chìr, cìr eich

Curse, *v a* Mionn, mionnaich, malluich, mollaich, guidh mallachd Curse you, *mollachd ort*

Curse, *s* Mionn, mionnachadh, mallachd, mollachd, droch-ghuidhe, cascaoin, an-fhocal, dròch-comhdhail, buaireas, cràdh *Cursed*, mallaichte, mollaichte. It is not worth a curse, *cha n' fhiach e mallachd*

Cursed, *a.* Mollaichte, malluichte, fuathasach, aingidh, mi-naomh; draghail, buaireasach

Cursedly, *adv* Gu truagh, gu h-antruagh, gu nàr, gu-fuathasach, gu curt.

Cursing, *s.* Mionnachadh, mallachadh, mollachadh.

Cursorily, *adv* Gu cabhagach, gu luath, gu grad; gu neo-fhearteil.

Cursory, *a* Cabhagach, deifireach, luath, grad; neo-churamach; neo-fhearteil

Curst, *a* Crosd, cas, cainnteach, dranndanach, curt.

Curt, *a* Gearr, goirrid, cutach, gearr-earbullach, stumpach

Curtail, *v. a* Giorraich, beagaich, cutaich, earraich, dean cutach, dean duitseach.

Curtailed, *a* Giorraichte, beagaichte, cutach, gearr-earbullach, earraichte; (*as a cock*), dùitseach

Curtailment, *s* Giorrachadh, beagachadh, cutachadh, earrachadh

Curtain, *s.* Cùirtean, brat; corais, croch-eididh leapach. Curtain-lecture, *trod leapach, trod a bheir bean phosda do 'fear na 'luidhe*

Curtain, *v. a* Cuirteanaich, brataich, croch le cùirteinibh

Curvated, *a.* Crom, cam, lùbta, lùbte, carrach.

Curvation, *s.* Cromadh, crom, camadh, lùbadh, car, luib.

Curvature, *s* Cromadh, camadh, cruimead, lùbadh, luib

Curve, *v a* Crom, cam, lùb

Curve, *a* Crom, cam, lùbach, neo-dhireach

Curve, *s* Cromadh, camadh, lubadh, luib, car

Curvet, *s* Cruinn-leum, sùrdag

Curvilinear, *a.* Cam-lineach, cam, crom, lubach.

Curvity, *s.* Cromad, caimead, cromadh, luib.

Cushion, *s* Pillean, adhartan, bog-shùidheagan.

Cusp, *s.* Bior na gealuich ùir

Cuspated, *a* Biorach mar dhuilleig

Custard, *s.* Ubhagan, uibheagan

Custody, s. Coimhead, cul, dingir, lamh, geard, cùram; gleidh; dion. In custody, *ann laimh.*

Custom, s. Cleachd, nòs, gnath, àbhaist, gnàthachadh, fasan; † geis; màl, càin, cìs. *Customs,* cleachdna, àbhaistean A bad custom, *droch chleachd, droch fhasan,* according to custom, *a reir an fhasain;* as the custom is, *mar tha 'm fasan,* it is my custom, *is gnath leam, is àbhaist domh,* as is my custom, *mar is àbhaist domh,* pay custom, *pàigh cìs,* custom-house, *tigh-cìse, tigh-càin.*

Customable, a. Tric, minic, cumaint

Customarily, *adv.* Gu cumaint, gu minic, gu coitchionta, am bidheantas, an cumantas.

Customer, s. Teachdaiche.

Cut, v. a Gearr, (*cut or slice*), snaidh; (*cut and mangle*), beubanaich, (*cut or lop*), sgath, (*cut the hair*), bearr, bearraich; (*cut off at a blow*), sgud, (*cut corn*), buain, (*cut or geld*), spoth, (*cut or grave*), grabh; (*cut out, as a seamstress*), sgeath, dealbh, cum Cut off the head, *dicheannaich,* he is cut to the heart, *tha e air a ghonadh na chridhe,* cut short, *giorraich.* (*Cut out or surpass*), gearr mach, faigh barrachd

Cut, s Gearradh; grabhadh, leòn; aith-ghearradh; dealbh, cumadh.

Cutaneous, a. Craicneach, croicneach

Cuticle, s. Sgrath thana, fa-rusgadh, croiceann, craiceann croicnean

Cutlass, s. Gearra-chlaidheamh, claidheamh cutach.

Cutler, s. Sgianadair, fear dheanamh sgeinichean.

Cutpurse, s. Gearra-sporan, meirleach.

Cutter, s. Sgoth luath; barc a bhuineas do na chis-lann; gearradair.

Cut-throat, s. Mortair, gearra-mhuineil.

Cut-throat, a. Fuilteach, fuileachdach, borb.

Cutting, s. (*Of cloth*), cludag, pìseag; (*of wood*), sliseag, spealg.

Cuttle, s Fear-cùl-chàinidh.

Cycle, s. Cuairteag, cuairt, cearcall.

Cyclopædia, s Cuairt-iùl

Cygnet, s. Ealadh òg; isean eala.

Cylinder, s. Sorcair, rothlair, robhair.

Cylindrical, a. Sorcaireach.

Cymar, s. Fàluing, sgàilean.

Cymbal, s. Tiom-buail, tiompan, gliongan.

Cynic, a. Doirbh, an-daonna, brùideil.

Cynic, s. Teallsanach doirbh.

Cynicalness, s. Doirbhe, an-daonnachd, brùidealachd.

Cynosure, s An tuath-rionnag, leis an stiùir na seoladairean.

Cypress, s. Cuphair, cann cuphair.

Czar, s. Sàr-righ, ainm Iompair *Russia.*

Czarina, s Ban Iompair *Russia.*

D.

D, s An ceathramh litir do 'n Aibideal D D. *Ollamh re diadhachd,* L D *Ollamh re lagh,* M D. *Ollamh re leigheas*

Dab, v. a Buail, frith-bhuail, buail gu fòil

Dab, s Meall, meallan, pluc, plucan, buille, sgailleag; seorsa fleogain; (*in low colloquy*), fear ceairde, fear teoma.

Dabble, v. a and n Fliuch, spult, taislich; salaich; plodanaich, dean plodanachd (no) sugradh air feadh uisge

Dabbler, s Spultair, plodanaiche; fear neo-theòma; fear nach eil domhain an oilean

Dabchick, s. Eun-uisge.

Dace, s. Seorsa èisg aimhne.

Dactyle, s Sioladh fad air a leanachd le dithis ghoirrid mar anns an fhocal *ărdănăch.*

Dactylology, s. Comhradh mheur, balbhanachd.

Dad, Daddy, s Dait, daitidh.

Dædal, a. Eag-samhuil.

Daffodil, s. Lus a chom-chinn.

Dag, s Dag, dagadh, biodag.

Dagger, s Gearra-sgian, sgian-achlais, biodag, greillean.

Daggersdrawing, s Tarruing a bhiodag, a casadh ri chéile, droch-cordadh, aimhreite.

Daggle, v. Slìasbair, eabair, slìasb, slabair, salaich.

Daggletail, a. Salach; salaichte.

Daggletail, s Té shlaodach, stràill.

Daily, a. Lathail, gach lath

Daily, *adv.* Gach la, gu lathail, gu minic, gu tric

Daintily, *adv.* Gu finealta, gu cuanta; gu soghar, gu soghmhor, gu blasda, gu deagh-bhlasda, gu glan, gu greanta, gu muirneach.

Daintiness, s. Finealtachd, cuantachd, sogmhorachd, sogh; blasdachd, millse, greantachd, muirneachd

Dainty, a Finealta, cuanta; soghmhor; blasda, milis, greanta, muirneach, greanta, glan, snàsda, snasmhor, gasda.

Dainty, s. Millsean; earcan.

Dairy, s Tigh bainne; airidh; ruidhe.

Dairymaid, s. Banarach, banaireach.

Daisy, s Buidheag, neonan, buidheag Bhealtuinn, gugan. Great daisy, *easbuig bàn*

Dale, s Dail; gleann, gleannan.

Dalliance, s Beadradh; comh-bheadradh, comh-chaidreamh, briodal, sùgradh, cluich, cluicheag, iomairt; macnus, dàil.

Dallier, s. Beadraiche, briodalair.

Dally, v n Dean beadradh, dean briodal, cluich, caith aimsir; cuir dàil.

Dally, v a. Cuir dheth, cuir dàil.

Dam, s. Màthair; linne, lochan; tuil-dhorus; slob; (*a mill-dam*), linne mhuilinn; (*a dyke*), dìge, banc.

Dam, v. Druid, cuir stigh, linn.

Damage, s. Dochann, dochair, diobhail, urchoid, dolaidh, lochd, ciurradh, ciurram, call, calldach; ath-dhioladh, dioladh.

Damage, v a. Lochd, dochannaich, dean dochann, dean dolaidh, mill, ciurr, cuir dholaidh.

Damageable, a So-dhochannadh, so-dhochanta, so-chiurradh; ciurrail, dochannach.

Damascene, s. Seòrsa plumbais.

Damask, s Anart no siod air fhighcadh le dealbhaibh, anart dealbhach, anart bùird, dearg. Damask-rose, *ròs dearg.*

Dame, s. Ban-tighearna, bain-tighearna; brinneach; bean-tighe gun inbhe.

Damn, v. a. Malluich; sgrios gu siorruidh; dit; cronaich; càin.

Damnable, *a.* Ro-aingidh, fior-olc, diabhluidh; léir-sgrios-ach; malluichte, damanta, fuathasach, oillteil, gràineil, curt

Damnably, *adv.* Gu diabhluidh, gu fuathasach; ga h-oillteil, gu graineil, gu damanta.

Damnation, *s.* Sgriosadh, sgrios, leir-sgrios, damnadh, mallachadh, diteadh, breitheanas.

Damned, *part.* Mallaichte, damanta, gràineil, fu dhìt, ditte; oillteil, fuathasach, gràineil.

† **Damnify**, *v. a.* Ciurr, mill, dochannaich, lochd, cuir dholaidh.

Damp, *a.* Aitidh, fliuch, tais, bog, neo-mhisneachail, mall, tuirseach.

Damp, *s.* Aitidheachd, fliuchadh, taise, buige.

Damp, *v.* Fliuch, taislich, àitich; (*deject*), dubhaich, tilg sios, meataich; (*weaken*), lagaich, fannaich.

Dampish, *a.* Leth-char aitidh, leth-char taise, taiseil.

Dampishness, *s.* Taisealachd, aitidheachd, fliuchadh.

Dampy, *a.* Muladach, dubhach, tuirseach, bronach

Damsel, *s.* Ainnir, nighean, cailinn, oigh, cruinneag; rimh-inn; geirseach, geirseag; caile.

Damson, *s.* Seòrsa plumbais, damh-mheas.

Dance, *v. n.* and *a.* Danns, damhs; rinc; leum, dean danns.

Dance, *s.* Dannsadh, damhsadh, leumartaich.

Dancer, *s.* Dannsair, damhsair, rincear. The merry dancers, *na fir chlis*, a good dancer, *deagh dhamhsair.*

Dancing, *s.* Dannsadh, damhsadh, dannsaireachd. *Part* a dannsadh.

Dancing-master, *s.* Maighstir dannsaidh, maighstir dannsair.

Dancing-school, *s.* Sgoil-dannsaidh, sgoil-damhsaidh.

Dandelion, *s.* Bearnan bride. The dandelion, *am bearnan bride.*

Dandiprat, *s.* Garlach, gircean, ceigean, caifean

Dandle, *v.* Frith-luaisg, saobanaich, siùdain, altrumaich, dean beadradh, breug

Dandriff, *s* Ceann ghalar, ceann-chàrr

Danger, *s.* Cunnart, cuntart, gabhadh, gabhail, baoghal, càs, eigin, crudal, doruinn, teinne, teanntachd; guais, guaiseachd.

Dangerous, *a.* Cunnartach, baoghalach, cruadalach, dor-uinneach; guasach.

Dangle, *v.* Croch.

Dangler, *s.* Suirthiche, suiriche.

Dank, *a.* Aitidh, bog, fliuch.

Dap, *v.* Bog, tum.

Dapper, *a.* Beag, beothail, brogail, broganta, giobach, cuimir, glan, tapaidh, gasda, deas, cunnailteach, cun-bhailteach.

Dapperling, *s.* Duine beag, gircean, ceigean, bodachan

Dapple, *a.* Eag-samhuil, breac, ball-bhreac; ballach, riach, riabhach, peighinneach

Dapple, *v.* Bread, breacaich, eag-samhuilich.

Dare, *v. a.* and *n.* Dùlanaich, thoir dùlan, faod, cuir gu fulang, luis, dùraig, dùirig You dare not, *cha n'eil mhis-neach agad, cha n' fhaod thu, cha duraig thu.*

Dare, *s.* Dùlan; durachdainn, misneach.

Daring, *a.* Dàna, misneachail, danarra, ladurna; beag-narach.

Daringly, *adv.* Gu dana, gu misneachail, gu danarra, gu ladurna, gu beag-narach.

Daringness, *s.* Dànadas, dànachd, misneach, danarrachd, ladurnachd, beagnarachd

Dark, *a.* Dorch, doilleir, ceothar, duibhreach; dubh, gruamach; dall; aineolach, dubhach

Dark, *s.* Dorchadh, doirche, dorchadas, aineolas, duibhre, aineolas

Darken, *v* Dorchaich; duibhrich, salaich.

Darkling, *a.* Dorch, doilleir, dall.

Darkly, *adv.* Gu dorch, gu doilleir, gu dall, gu gru-amach

Darkness, *s.* Dorchadas, doirche, duirche, dubhar, doilleire-achd, duibhre; aineolas, cion-leirsinn, aingidheachd, cumhachd an aibhiseir.

Darksome, *a* Dorcha, dubh, doilleir, gruamach.

Darling, *a* Gaolach, gradhach, ionmhuinn.

Darling, *s* Gaolach, graidhean, mùirnean, annsachd, gaol My darling, *a ghaoil, a ghaolaich.*

Darn, *v. a.* Càirich, cair, dluthaich.

Darnel, *s.* Dithean, breoillean, roille.

Dart, *s.* Gath, saighead, bannsach, guaine

Dart, *v. a.* and *n.* Tilg, saighead, tilg gath Dart forward, *saighead*

Dash, *v* Spealg, sgeilc, spealt, buail, spairt, taom, spult, spliot, measg, coimbeasg, sgrioch, nàraich, cuir gu nàire Dash to the ground, *spairt gu talamh*

Dash, *s* Sgeilc, buille, spealt, spairt; taomadh; sgrioch no lin (—) mar chomhar stad

Dastard, *s.* Cladhair, gealtair, cailleach, tràill.

Dastardly, *a* Cladhaireach, gealtach, cailleachail

Date, *s* La do 'n mhios, am (no) la air an sgriobhar litir; crioch, finid; buanachd.

Date, *v.* Am-chomharaich, comharaich an la air an sgriobhar ni sam bi.

Date, *s* Dait, pailm Date-tree, *crann pailm*

Dative, *a.* Tabhartach.

Daub, *v. a.* Sliob, liobh, salaich, suath.

Dauber, *s.* Sliobair, liobhair, suathair; sodalaiche.

Dauby, *a.* Righinn.

Daughter, *s* Nighean, inghean; té, boirionnach.

Daunt, *v* Mi-mhisnich, taisich, eagalaich, cuir eagal air, thoir mi-mhisneach.

Daunted, *a* Eagalaichte, mi-mhisnichte, fu eagal.

Dauntless, *a* Misneachail, dàna, neo-eagallach, neo-sgathach, neo-ghealtach

Dauntlessness, *s.* Misneach, dànadas.

Daw, *s* Cathag: cnamh-fhitheach

Dawn, *v. n* Soillsich, soillerich, bris, mar ni fàire.

Dawn, *s.* Soilleireachd, camhanaich, brise na fàire, soillse

Day, *s* La, lath, lo; dé, † di, † dia; (*light*), solus. From day to day, *o la gu la;* to-day, *an diugh*, we have lost the day, *chaill sinn an la, chaidh an la nar n' aghaidh*, the day is ours, *is leinn an la, chaidh an la leinn*, at this time of day, *mu 'n tràth so la*, before day, *roimh àithne an la*, by day-break, *mu bhriseadh na fairc*, noon-day, *meadhon latha*, the height of day, *airde an la*, broad day, *airde gheal an la*, vacation-day, *la sollain*, Christmas-day, *La nollaig;* Candlemas-day, *An fheill-bride*, Easter-day, *La caisg*, every day, *gach la, na h-uile la*, every other day, *gach dolach la*, t'other day, *an la roimh*, a day or two ago, *o cheann la no dhà*, day by day, *gach la*, on a set day, *air la sonruichte*, the day before yesterday, *air bhò 'n dé*, this day week, *seachduin o 'n diugh*, a holy day, *la sollain, làth féill*, a day and a half, *la gu leth*, in the days of William the Conqueror, *ri linn Uilleam nam buadh*, I have had my own day, *bha la gun robh*

Day-book, *s* Iris-leabhar

Day-break, *s.* An t-soilleireachd; briseadh na fàire, a chamhanaich, tuaileachd, càmhair, breac-sholus.

Day-labour, *s* Obair là

Day-labourer, *s* Baidsear, fear obair lagha

Daylight, *s* Airde an làtha, solas an latha

Day-spring, *s* Eiridh an la, briseadh an la, càmhair, urmhadainn, tuailleachd, breac-sholus

Day-star, *s* Reul na maidne, maidneag.

Dazzle, *v.* Lannraich, dealraich, dearrsaich

Deacon, *s* Diacon, fairbheach, ministear òg, éildear.

Dead, *a* Marbh, gun deò; fuar, gun chàil, gun mhothuchadh; tiamhaidh, samhach, fàsail. As dead as a herring, *tho mharbh ri sgadan*, better be dead, *b'fhearr bhith marbh*, he is dead, *tha e marbh, theasd e, dh'eug e*, a dead body, *corp, cairbhe*, in the dead of night, *am marbh na h-oidhche, ann am marbh mheadhon na h-oidhche*

Dead, *s* Mairbh The dead, *na mairbh*, the dead of night, *marbhadh na h-oidhche, marbh mheadhon oidhche*, the dead of winter, *dùbhlachd a gheamhraidh*

Deaden, *v a* Marbhaich, marbh, maolaich, funtuinn, lagaich, ciùnaich, dean neo-bhlasta.

Deadly, *a* Marbhtach, mortail, millteach, sgriosail, borb, fuilteach, garg; nimheach, gamhlasach

Deadness, *s* Marbhantachd, funtuinn, méileachadh, laigsinn.

Deaf, *a* Bodhar, odhar

Deaf, Deafen, *v a.* Bodhair, dean bodhar.

Deafness, *s* Buidhre, bodhrad

Deal, *s* Pairt, cuid, roinn, cuibhrionn; mòran, mòrnaich, maoin, dorlach, deile, planc, clàr

Deal, *v a* Roinn, sgap; buin, dean gnothach, dean marsontachd Deal kindly with him, *buin gu caoimhneil ris.*

Dealer, *s* Fear malairt, fear roinn, marsonta

Dealing, *s* Roinn, ceannachadh, ceannachd; gnothach, comunn, caidreamh.

Deambulation, *s* Iomlad.

Dean, *s.* Deadhan

Deanery, *s.* Deadhanachd

Dear, *a* Daor, costail, cosdail, priseil, luachmhor, ainneamh, gann, (*beloved*), ionmhuinn, gradhach, gaolach, caomh

Dear, *s* Cridhe, gaolach, graidhean, ceisdean My dear, *a chridhe, a ghaolaich*, your dear, *do cheisdean.*

Dear-bought, *a* Daor, luachmhor, cosdail

Dearly, *adv.* Gu daor, gu gradhach

Dearness, *s.* Daorad, daoiread, caoimhe, prisealachd, luachmhoireachd.

Dearth, *s* Daorsa, daorsuinn, gainne, gortas

Death, *s* Bas, eug; teim; teimhe, irt, bann, amhailt, meilg, (*slaughter*), marbhadh, mortadh, àr Put to death, *cuir gu bas*, as sure as death, *cho chinnteach ris a bhàs, cho chinnte is am bas*

Death-bed, *s* Leabadh bhàis

Deathful, *a* Marbhtach, fuilteach, millteach, eug-mhor

Deathless, *a.* Neo-bhasmhor, bith-bhuan

Deathlike, *a* Bàsail, eugail, eugmhor; marbh, tosd, tiamhaidh

Death's-door, *s.* Gob an eug.

Deathsman, *s.* Crochadair

Death-watch, *s* Bodach a cheapain, cnaimh fiodha a ni diog mar uaireadair

Deauration, *s* Oradh

Debar, *v a.* Bac, cum air ais, fogair.

† **Debark**, *v. a* and *n* Rach air tir, cuir air tir.

Debase, *v. a.* Islich, ilsich, irioslaich, masluich, tàmailtich; truaill. *Debased*, islichte, irioslaichte, masluichte.

Debasement, *s.* Isleachadh, irioslachadh, insleachadh; maslachadh, tàmailteachadh.

Debaser, *s.* Masluchair.

Debatable, *a* Ion-chonspoideach, fu chonspoid.

Debate, *s* Connsach, connsachadh, arguinn, argumaid; conspoid, deasboireachd.

Debate, *v.* Arguinn, deasboirich, connsaich.

Debateful, *a* Connsachail.

Debatement, *s* Connsach, connsachadh, cur a mach; arguinn

Debater, *s.* Conspoidiche

Debauch, *v* Mill, truaill, truaillich, mi-ghnathaich; thoir gu taobh, cuir air seachran, meall, cuir dholaidh

Debauch, *s.* Craos, geoc, geocaireachd, pòit, baois, meisge.

Debaucher, *s* Craosair, geocair, pòitear, meisgear, fear neo-gheimnidh

Debauchery, *s* Craosaireachd, geocaireachd, poitearachd, baoise, neo-gheimnidheachd, ana measarrachd, grainealachd.

Debenture, *s.* Bann marsontachd

Debile, *a* An-fhann, an-mhunn, fann, lag; marbhanta, neo-sgairteil, meuranda, breoite; truagh

Debilitate, *v. a* Anfhannaich, anmhunnaich, fannaich, lagaich

Debility, *s* Anfhannachd, anmhuinneachd, laigse.

Debonair, *a* Modhail, sibhealta; siobhailt, cùirteil, beusach, suairc; sunntach.

Debt, *s* Fiach, an-fhiach. Debts, *fiachan, an-fhiachan*

Debtor, *s* Féichneach, fiachair, fear-fhiach Debtors, *feichnichean*

Decade, *s.* Deichnear

Decagon, *s.* Deich-shlisneag, deich-shlisneach.

Decalogue, *s* Na deich aitheantan.

Decamp, *v* Muth camp, triall, rach imirich.

Decampment, *s* Triall adh, imirich.

Decant, *v* Taom, taoisg

Decanter, *s* Searrag ghloine; buideal, botal

Decapitate, *v.* Di-cheannaich; di-cheann. Decapitated, *di-cheannaichte.*

Decapitation, *s* Di-cheannachadh, di-cheannachd.

Decay, *s.* Caitheamh, crionadh, seachdadh, seacadh, seargadh, ainneas, lobhadh, grodadh

Decay, *v.* Caith, crion, seac, seachd, searg, meath.

Decayed, *part* and *a.* Caithte, crionta, seachdta, seargta, seargte It has decayed, *tha e air caitheamh (no) air crionadh*

Decease, *v* Faigh bàs, rach eug, teasd, basàich.

Decease, *s.* Bàs, eug

Deceit, *s* Cealg, ceilg, cuilbheart, cuilbheartachd, mealltaireachd, slaoighte, foill, feall, cluain, meantail, eadarnaidh, breaslang.

Deceitful, *a* Cealgach, cuilbheartach, mealltach, fealltach, cluainteach, fallsa; slaoighteil, meabhlach, ceabhachdach, sligheach.

Deceitfully, *adv.* Gu cealgach, gu cuilbheartach, gu meallta, gu fealltach, gu fallsa, gu slaoighteil, gu cluainteach, gu sligheach.

Deceitfulness, *s* Cealgaireachd, cuilbheartachd, mealltaireachd, slaoighteireachd, foill, feall, fealltaireachd; cluaintearachd, fallsachd

Deceivable, *a.* So-mhealladh.

Deceive, *v.* Meall, thoir an car a. Deceived, *meallta;* deceiving, *mealladh, mealltaireachd.*

Deceiver, *s.* Mealltair, cealgair, slaoightear.

December, *s.* Mios mu dheireadh na bliadhna, an dùbhlachd; *mar an ceudna;* an deicheamh mios, do bhrigh gun do thòisich a bhliadhna o shean sa Mhàirt.

Decemvirate, *s.* An deichnear riaghlairean san Roimh; deichnear, riaghladh dheichnear.

Decency, *s.* Modh, beus; stuaim, stuamachd; cneastachd; eireachdas; cliù; onoir, macantas, oirmhidh, maise, soinealachd.

Decent, *a.* Modhail, beusach, stuama, cneasta, moltach; onorach; eireachdail, cliùiteach, macanta, maiseach, ciatach, freagarrach; cubhaidh, iomchuidh.

Decently, *adv.* Gu modhail, gu beusach, gu stuama, gu cneasta, gu macanta, gu moltach, gu cliùiteach, gu h-onorach; gu h-eireachdail, gu ciatach, gu freagarrach, gu cubhaidh.

Deceptible, *a.* So-mhealladh.

Deception, *s.* Cuilbheart; cleas; ceilg, mealltaireachd, cealgaireachd.

Decerpt, *a.* Sgaithte, bearrte, buainte.

Decession, *s.* Imeachd, trialladh, falbh, imirich.

Decide, *v.* Thoir breith; co-dhùin; criochnaich.

Decidedly, *a.* Gun teagamh, gu cinnteach, gu dearbh, gu deimhinn.

Decidence, *s.* Tuiteam, sgiolladh.

Decider, *s.* Breitheamh.

Deciduous, *a.* Seargach, crionach.

Decimal, *a.* Deicheach, deicheamhach.

Decimate, *v.* Deicheamhaich.

Decimation, *s.* Deicheamhachadh; deicheamhachd.

Decipher, *v.* Leugh, foillsich, minich.

Decision, *s.* Breith, breitheanas, crioch-connsaich, sònrachadh.

Decisive, *a.* Criochnach.

Decisively, *adv.* Gu criochnach; gu cinnteach.

Deck, *v. a.* Sgeadaich, sgiamhaich, còmhdaich, eid, sgeimh. Decked, *sgeadaichte.*

Deck, *s.* Urlar luinge, clar luing.

Decker, *s.* Sgeadachair, comhdachair.

Declaim, *v.* Dean òraid; òraidich.

Declaimer, *s.* Oraidiche, brasghaille.

Declamation, *s.* Oraid, brasghalladh.

Declamatory, *a.* Oraideach, ràiteach.

Declarable, *a.* So-dhearbhadh.

Declaration, *s.* Glaodh; gairmeadh; dearbhadh; aidmheil; foillseachadh; innseadh; nochdadh; reuladh.

Declarative, *a.* Aidmheileach, foillseach, foillseachail.

Declaratory, *a.* Aidmheileach, foillseachail, a cur an céill; foillseach, dearbhach.

Declare, *v. a.* Cuir an céill, foillsich, dean aithnichte; glaodh, aidmhich, nochd, innis, dearbh. Declared, *foillsichte, aithnichte.*

Declarer, *s.* Foillseachair, dearbhair, nochdair.

Declension, *s.* Isleachadh, tearnadh; leathad; cromadh, lubadh, claonadh.

Declination, *s.* Leathad; caitheamh, crionadh; cromadh, lubadh, claonadh.

Decline, *v. a.* and *n.* Lub, crom, claon; diùlt, òb, seachain, cuir gu taobh; crion, caith, rach an lughad, rach am miosad.

Decline, *s.* Caitheamh, cromadh, crionadh, meathachadh, tuiteam, air falbh.

Declivity, *s.* Leathad, leacainn, bruach, claonadh, tulchlaonadh, tul-staonachd, claon-bhruthach, leth-bhruthach.

Declivous, *a.* Claon, leacainneach, bruachach, corrach.

Decoct, *v.* Bruith, bruich.

Decoctible, *a.* So-bhruicheadh.

Decoction, *s.* Bruicheadh, sùgh-bhruicheadh.

Decollation, *s.* Di-cheannachadh; †dioghart.

Decompose, *v. a.* Dì-mheasg; dealaich, sgar; ath-mheasg.

Decomposition, *s.* Dì-mheasgadh; dealachadh; athmheasgadh.

Decorate, *v. a.* Sgeadaich, sgiamhaich, naisnich, breaghaich, maisich, *busgainn.* Decorated, *sgeadaichte, sgiamhaichte.*

Decoration, *s.* Sgeadachadh, sgiamhachadh, naisneachadh, breaghachadh, *busgainn*, breaghachd, riomhadh, usgar.

Decorator, *s.* Sgeadachair, sgiamhachair.

Decorous, *a.* Beusach, ciatach, stuama, cubhaidh.

Decorticate, *v.* Cairt, sgrath.

Decortication, *s.* Cartadh, sgrathadh.

Decorum, *s.* Modh, beus, stuaim, stuamachd, ciataichead, soinealachd, cneastachd, eireachdas, macantas, maise, cùbhaidheachd.

Decoy, *v.* Meall, thoir an car a; rib, breug, thoir a thaobh, buan.

Decoy, *s.* Mealladh, ribeadh, breug, buaireadh, ribe, *trap.*

Decrease, *s.* Lughdachadh, beagachadh, traogh.

Decrease, *v. a.* and *n.* Lughdaich, beagaich, traogh, cuir an lughad, rach an lughad.

Decree, *s.* Reachd, aithne, lagh, ordugh; sonrachadh, decreut.

Decree, *v. a.* Orduich, àithn, sonraich.

Decrepit, *a.* Breoite, briste; mall, bacach, crioplaichte, ciorramach, deireasach, clairinneach.

Decrepitate, *v.* Crac, dean cracail.

Decrepitude, *s.* Breosteachd, crioplachd; malltachd.

Decretal, *a.* Orduchail, decreutach, decreutail.

Decretal, *s.* Reachdan, reachdaidh Eaglais na Roimhe.

Decretory, *a.* Breathriachail, orduchail, decreutach.

Decrial, *s.* Cronachadh, coireachadh, binn, trod, sglamhruinn, tarcuis, spid.

Decry, *v.* Cronaich, coirich, tarcuisich, càin, dimheas.

Decumbence, *s.* Luidhe sios, sìneadh.

Decuple, *a.* Deicheach, deich uairean, deich fillte.

Decurion, *s.* Ceannard (no) uachdaran dheichnear.

Decursion, *s.* Ruithe sios (no) ri leathad.

Decurtation, *s.* Giorrachadh, cutachadh.

Dedecorous, *a.* Nàr, maslach, graineil, tàireil.

Dedentition, *s.* Cur fhiacal, call fhiacal.

Dedicate, *v.* Coisrig, naomhaich; cuir leabhar fo thearmunn neach. Dedicated, *coisrigte, naomhaichte; air chur fu thearmunn mar leabhar, tiomnadh.*

Dedication, *s.* Coisreagadh; naomhachadh, tabhartas, tiomnadh.

Dedition, *s.* Striocadh, geilleadh, geilleachduinn, tiomnadh suas.

Deduce, *v. a.* Taruinng; thoir o.

Deducement, *s.* Tuigsinneachd; leanachd, saoilsinneas.

Deducible, *a.* A tighinn an lorg reusoin; saoilsinneach.

Deduct, *v. a.* Thoir o, lughadaich, beagaich, math, lagh; dealaich.

Deduction, *s.* Lughadachadh, beagachadh, giorrachadh, mathadh, mathalachd; comh-reuson.

Deed, *s* Gniomh, tùrn, euchd, obair, treubhantas; sgriobhaidh, bann, cairteacha A good deed, *deadh ghniomh*, a bad deed, *droch thùrn.*

Deedless, *a.* Neo-ghniomhach, neo-euchdail, neo-threubhanta; neo-sgairteil, leasg, neo-bheò, marbhanta.

Deem, *v* Saoil, smuainich, baralaich; co' dhùin, sònraich, sùnraich

Deemster, *s.* Breitheamh.

Deep, *a* Domhainn, doimhne, eagach; (*in temper*), fadsheallach, sicir; cuilbheartach, do thuigsinn; fad-thall, (*in music*), garbh, tormanach; (*in colour*), dorch, dubh; (*sorrowful*), brònach, dubhach

Deep, *s* Doimhneachd, doimhne, aigean, luim-dheirg, dubhaigean.

Deepen, *v a* Doimhnich

Deeply, *adv.* Gu domhainn; gu sicir; gu seolta, gu cuilbheartach; gu dubhach.

Deep-mouthed, *a.* Ròcanach, garbh, tormanach.

Deep-musing, *a.* Smuaireanach, smuainteachail, smaointeachail.

Deepness, *s* Doimhneachd, doimhne.

Deer, *s.* Fiadh; damh feidh, agh feidh, earb, boc, boc earb A number of deer, *fiadhach.*

Deface, *v.* Dubh, dubh a mach, dubh as, duaichnich, mill, sgrios.

Defacement, *s* Dubhadh, duaichneachd, milleadh, dochair.

Defacer, *s* Dubhadair, duaichniche, milltear

Defalcate, *v.* Bearr, sgath; snaith, lughadaich; beagaich; giorraich.

Defalcation, *s.* Bearradh, sgathadh, gearradh, lughdach, beagachadh, giorrachadh.

Defalk See **Defalcate.**

Defamation, *s.* Toibheum, sgainneal, masladh, mi-chliù, càineadh, tuaileas, spid, tair

Defamatory, *a* Toibheumach, sgainnealach, tuaileasach, spideil, tàireil, tarcuiseach.

Defame, *v.* Dean tàir, thoir toibheum, cul-chàin, sgainnealaich, maslaich, tarcuisich, mi-chliùich, mi-chliùthaich, tuaileasaich

Defamer, *s.* Fear cùl-chàin, fear-toibheuma, toibheumaiche, tuaileasaiche, fear tuaileis, maslachair

Defatigate, *v* 'Sgithich, sàruich, fannaich, thoir thairis, claoidh.

Default, *s.* Dearmad, dichuimhneachadh, cron, coire, failinn, faillne, lochd, dìth.

Defaulter, *s.* Failinniche.

Defeasance, *s.* Di-lâghachadh, cur ma làr.

Defeasible, *a* So-chur ma làr.

Defeat, *s.* Saruchadh, buaidh, fairtleachadh, d.ombuaidh; ruaig, cosgairt.

Defeat, *v.* Buaidhich, fairtlich, ruaig, sàruich, ceannsaich, cosgair; cuir air theich; gréidh; thoir buaidh. Defeated, *sàruichte, ceannsaichte.*

Defecate, *v.* Glan, sgùr, nigh, siolaidh, traogh.

Defecate, *a* Glan, siolaidhte, traoghta

Defecation, *s.* Glanadh, sioladh, traoghadh.

Defect, *s.* Easbhuidh cagmhais, eugmhais, dìth, cron, coire, lochd, fabhd, giomh, gaoid, ciurram, fàilinn; meairachd

Defectibility, *s.* Easbhuidheachd, eugmhaiseachd, ciurraimachd; fàilinneachd

Defectible, *a.* Easbhuidheachd, neo-iomlan, deireasach, uireasbhuidheach.

Defection, *s.* Tréigsinn, fàgail, claonadh, dol a thaobh, ceannairc, éiridh, fàilinn, fàillne, mealladh

Defective, *a.* Easbhuidheach, uireasbhach, neo-iomlan, fàillneach.

Defectiveness, *s.* Easbhuidheachd, uireasbhachd, neoiomlanachd, fàillneachd

Defence, *s* Dion, dionadh, dìdean, tearmunn; geard; fasgadh; fireannachadh, leithsgeul, tagradh.

Defenceless, *a.* Lom, ruisgte; neo-armaichte; neo-ullamh; gun dion, gun dìdean, gun tearmunn; lag; faun, anfhann.

Defend, *v. a.* Dion; geard, geardainn, cum taic ri; cuir le; fireannaich; cum suas, toirmisg, bac.

Defendable, *a.* So-dhionadh.

Defendant, *s.* Fear dionaidh; (*in law*), fear tagraidh, dìdneachair; urradh.

Defender, *s.* Fior dionaidh, dionair; fear dìdein, fear tagraidh; tagairtear; curaidh, gaisgeach.

Defensative, *s.* Dion, dìdean, geard; (*in surgery*), plàsd, bann

Defensible, *a* So-dhionaidh, so-dhionta, dionach.

Defensive, *a* Dionach, dìdeanach. Defensive arms, *airm dhìdeanach*

Defensive, *s.* Dion, dionadh, dìdean; tearmunn.

Defer, *v. a* Cuir dheth, cuir dàil, ath-lathaich; fuirich, feith, stad dean moile

Deference, *s* Meas, urram, miadh, miagh, onoir; umhlachd; cead.

Defiance, *s.* Dùlan, dùbhlan, dùlanachadh, dùlanachd.

Deficience, **Deficiency**, *s.* Fàilinn, fàillne, uireasbhuidh, neo-iomlanachd.

Deficient, *a* Failinneach, fàillneach, uireasbhuidheach, neo-iomlan; geàrr.

Defier, *s* Dubhlanaiche.

Defile, *v.* Salaich, truaill, truaillich, mi-ghnathaich; mill, éignich Defiled, *salaichte, truaillte, truaillichte, mi-ghnathaichte, millte, neo-ghlan, eignichte.*

Defile, *s* Bealach, glac, gleannan, caol-ghleann.

Defilement, *s* Sal, truailleachd; truaillidheachd; truaille, neo-ghloine.

Defiler, *s.* Truaillear, fear-truaillidh, éigneachair, fear éigneachaidh

Definable, *a* So-mhìneachadh, so-dhearbhadh; so-bheachdachadh

Define, *v n.* and *a* Mìnich, soilleirich, cuairtich; beachdaich; sonraich, sunraich.

Definer, *s* Fear mìneachaidh, sònrachair

Definite, *a.* Cinnteach, cumait, dearbhte, sonraichte.

Definition, *s.* Ciall, brìgh, breith; mìneachadh.

Definitive, *a.* Sonraichte; pongail; runaichte; dearbhta; socraichte, cinnteach

Deflagrable, *a.* So-losgadh, so-lasadh, lasach.

Deflagration, *s.* Losgadh, lasadh.

Deflect, *v n.* Claon, tionndaidh; rach gu taobh.

Deflection, *s.* Claonadh, cromadh.

Defloration, *s.* Truailleadh, éigneachadh; éigin.

Deflower, *v.* Truaill, truaillich, éignich.

Deflowerer, *s* Truaillear, éigneachair

Deflexion, *s.* Siuthadh, cur mach le casdaich; sioladh; ruithe

Defoedation, *s.* Truaille, truailleachd, grainealachd, mosachd.

Deforcement, *s.* Breith air éigin, foirneart, ainneart.

Deform, *v a.* Duaichnich; dean mi-chiatach (no) gràineil, mi-dhealbh, truaill

Deform, *a.* Gràta, grannd, duaichnidh, neo-aogasach, mi-dbealbhach, truailleadh, neo-dhreachmhor.

Deformation, *s.* Duaichneachd, granndachd.

Deformed, *a.* Gràta, grannd, duaichnidh, neo-aogasach, neo-dhreachmhor, mosach, mi-dhealbhach, neo-sgiamhach; crotach, troicheil; gràineil.

Deformity, *s.* Granndachd, duaichneachd; mosaiche; mi-dhreachmhorachd, crotachd, troicheileachd.

Defraud, *v.* Meall, thoir an car a.

Defraudation, *s.* Mealladh, cealg, ceilg, slaoighte.

Defrauder, *s.* Mealltair, cealgair, slaoightear.

Defray, *v.* Paigh, diol, giùlain cosd.

Defrayment, *s.* Paigheadh, dioladh cosdais.

† **Deft**, *a.* Cuimir, cannach, deas, ullamh, eallamh.

Defunct, *a.* Marbh, fo 'n ùir, fo 'n talamh, air dol eug, nach beò, nach maireann.

Defunct, *s.* Urr mharbh, neach marbh.

Defunction, *s.* Bàs, eug.

Defy, *v.* Thoir dùlan, cuir gu dùlan, dùlanaich, dànaich.

Degeneracy, *s.* Claonadh o'n chòir, ais-ghineadh; droch-bheairt; tamailt; dol gu taobh, tréigsinn; diblidheachd, truaighe.

Degenerate, *a.* Diblidh, neo-chliùiteach, truagh, iriosal.

Degenerate, *v.* Rach am measad; aisghinealaich; tuislich; rach gu donas.

Degeneration, *s.* Dol an olcas, dol gu donas, dol am measad, diblidheachd.

Deglutition, *s.* Slugadh.

Degradation, *s.* Isleachadh, irioslachadh, tàmailteachadh.

Degrade, *v.* Islich, irioslaich, tàmailtich, cuir o inbhe.

Degree, *s.* Inbhe, inmhe; airde; ceum; buaidh, uidhe, glùn; ordugh, rang, breath, sreath. *By degrees*, uidhe air an uidhe, ceum air cheum, chuid is a chuid.

Dehort, *v.* Comhairlich o, thoir misneach, cuir dheth.

Dehortation, *s.* Comhairleachadh o nì (no) an aghaidh nì.

Deicide, *s.* Dia-mharbhadh.

Deification, *s.* Dia-dheanamh, diadhachadh.

Deiform, *a.* Mar dhia, ainglidh, neamhuidh.

Deify, *v.* Dia-dhean; neamhaich.

Deign, *v.* Deonaich, aontaich; leig le, builich.

Deism, *s.* Ana-creideamh, Dia-chreideamh.

Deist, *s.* Ana-creidiche, ana-criosduigh, Dia-chreidmheach.

Deistical, *a.* Ana-creideach.

Deity, *s.* Diadhachd. A Deity, *Dia.*

Deject, *v. a.* Tilg sios (no) bhàn; mi-mhisnich, dubhaich, muladaich.

Deject, *a.* Dubhach, tuirseach, bronach, airsnealach, trom, smuaireanach, trom-inntinneach.

Dejectedly, *adv.* Gu dubhach, gu tuirseach, gu brònach, gu h-airsnealach, gu trom, gu smuaireanach.

Dejection, *s.* Truime-inntinn, tuirse, dubhachas, mulad, smuairean, airsneal; laigsinn, truime.

Delaction, *s.* Cur air diol, cur bhàrr na eiche; casgadh.

Delate, *v.* Giùlain, iomchair, thoir; cronaich, coirich, dean casaid.

Delation, *s.* Giulan, iomchar; cronachadh, coireachadh, casaid.

Delator, *s.* Fear brath, casaidiche.

Delay, *v.* Cuir dheth, cuir dàil, dean moill, ath-lathaich, fuirich, stad.

Delay, *s.* Dàil, moill, mairneal, stad, stadachd, fuireach, fuireachd, fois; iomcheist; fardal.

Delectable, *a.* Taitneach, ciatach, sòlasach, tlachdmhor.

Delectableness, *s.* Taitneachd, ciatachd, sòlas, tlachd.

Delectably, *adv.* Gu taitneach, gu ciatach, gu sòlasach, gu tlachdmhor.

Delectation, *s.* Solas, suaimhneas, sogh, tlachd, saimh.

Delegate, *v.* Cuir air theachdaireachd.

Delegate, *v.* Teachdair; fior ionaid; riochdair; fear gnothuiche.

Delegation, *s.* Teachdaireachd.

Delete, *v.* Dubh a mach, duaichnich.

Deleterious, *a.* Puinsionta, puinsionach, nimhe, nimheach, marbhtach, millteach, sgriosail.

Deletion, *s.* Dubh' a mach, sgriosadh; léir sgriosadh.

Delf, *s.* Gaireal, gairbheal; obair chreadha.

Deliberate, *v.* Smuainich, smaointich, beachd-smuainich, meòraich, gabh comhairle.

Deliberate, *a.* Faicilleach, cùramach; soimeach, socrach; crionna, sicir; mairnealach, athaiseach; màigheanach.

Deliberately, *adv.* Gu faicilleach, gu cùramach; gu soimeach, gu socrach, gu crionna; gu sicir; gu mairnealach, gu h-athaiseach; chuid is a chuid.

Deliberateness, *s.* Faicilleachd, curamachd; crionnachd; smuainteachadh.

Deliberation, *s.* Faicill, smuainteachadh, smaointeachadh; cùram.

Deliberative, *a.* Faicilléach, smuainteil, beachdail.

Delicacy, *s.* (*In taste*), sogh, seimhe; (*in manners*), mùirn, beus, mìneachd, suairceas, modhalachd, greanntas, cinealtas; (*female delicacy*), bandaidheachd, malltachd, banalas, adh-nàire, geimnidheachd; (*in food*), millsean; (*in dress*), grinneas, eireachdas; (*in constitution*), malltachd, maothachd; meurandachd.

Delicate, *a.* (*In taste*), soghmhor, seimh; (*in manners*), mùirneach, beusach, suairc, modhail, greannta, cinealta, mìn; (*as a female*), bandaidh, banail, mallta, geimnidh, glan; (*as food*), milis, blasda, taitneach; (*fine*), finealta, grinn; (*in constitution*), mallta, meuranda, truagh.

Delicately, *adv.* Gu soghmhor, gu seimh; gu mùirneach, gu beusach, gu modhail, gu suairc, gu greannta, gu cinealta, gu mìn; gu bandaidh, gu banail, gu mallta; gu geimnidh, gu glan; gu milis, gu blasda, gu taitneach, gu finealta; gu greinn, gu h-eireachdail.

Delicateness, *s.* Mùirneachd, maothalachd; modhaileachd; bandaidheachd, banalas, geimnidheachd.

Delicious, *a.* Milis blasda, taitneach.

Deliciously, *adv.* Gu milis, gu blasda, gu taitneach.

Deliciousness, *s.* Sogh, seimhe, saimh, millse, taitneachd, sòlas, aoibhneas, éibhneas.

Delight, *s.* Aoibhneas, eibhneas, saimh, tlachd, mor-thlachd, sagharlachd, toil-inntinn, sunnt, sunntan.

Delight, *v. a.* and *n.* Toilich, sàsuich, gabh tlachd, faigh tlachd.

Delighted, *a.* Aoibhinn, eibhinn, toilichte, làn-toilichte.

Delightful, *a.* Grinn, taitneach, sòlasach, tlachdmhor, suaimhneach.

Delightfully, *adv.* Gu grinn, gu taitneach, gu sòlasach, gu tlachdmhor, gu suaimhneach.

Delightfulness, *s.* Grinneas, taitneachd, sòlasachd, tlachdmhorachd, suaimhneachd.

Delineate, *v. a.* Lìnich, dealbh, cuir an céill.

Delineation, *s.* Lìneachadh, dealbhadh, dealbh; uirdhreachadh.

Delinquency, *s.* Fabhd, coir, cron; cionnt, droch-thùrn.

Delinquent, *s.* Ciontach.

Deliquate, *v.* Leagh.

Deliquation, *s.* Leaghadh.

Deliquium, *s.* Paisean.

Delirious, *a.* Breisleachail, breilleiseach, breolaideach; thar chéill; gòrach; eutrom

Deliriousness, *s* Breisleachd, breilleiseachd, breolaidheachd; gòraiche, breothas, bainnidh, cuthach, cearachadh.

Delirium, *s.* Breilleis

Deliver, *v* Thoir suas, tiomnadh, tairbheir, thoir, thabhair, builich; (*save*), saor, liuthair, fuasgail, tuasgail; cuir fa sgaoileadh; leig fu réir, (*as a woman*), beir; (*utter*), cuir dhiot, labhair; innis She is delivered of a child, *tha i air a h-aisead.* (*Saved*), saorta, fuasgailte

Deliverance, *s* Liuthradh, saorsadh, fuasgladh, saorsainn, sgaoileadh; (*of children*), aisead, beirsinn, breith, (*utterance*), labhairt; (*giving up*), tiomnadh, toirt thairis, (no) suas, tuisleadh

Deliverer, *s* Fear saoraidh, òraidiche

Delivery, *s* Tabhairt, tiomnadh; fuasgladh, saorsadh, (*in speech*), labhairt; (*of children*), breith, beirsinn, aisead.

Dell, *s* Lag, lagan, gleannan, ùrlar

Delph See Delf

Deludable, *a.* So-mhealladh

Delude, *v.* Meall, thoir an car a, diobair *Deluded*, meallta

Deluder, *s* Mealltair, cealgair, slaoightear.

Deluge, *s* Tuil, litheadh, dile, dilinn The general deluge, *an tuil ruadh.*

Deluge, *v* Tuiltich, dilich; bàth.

Delusion, *s* Mealladh, mealltaireachd, slaoightearachd, cealg, ceilge; cluaintearachd, cleasachd, mearachd, doillemntinn; breug

Delusive, *a* Mealltach, cealgach, faoin, fallsa, fallsail

Delusory, *a.* Mealltach, faoin, fallsail

Delve, *v* Ruadhair, cladhaich, tochaill, †ceachail *Delved*, ruadhairte.

Delver, *s* Fear ruadharaidh, tochailtiche

Demagogue, *s.* Ceannard-gràisge, ceannard-comuinn, comh-fhlaith, ceann-feadhna

Demain, *s* Oighreachd, tirteagh, saor-sheilbh

Demand, *v.* Iarr, sir; fedraich, foighneach, tathaich

Demand, *s* Iarrtas, sireadh, tathaich; aisgidh, athchuinge, feòrachadh, foighneachd, ceisd.

Demandable, *a* So-iarruidh, so-shireadh, a dh' fhaodar iarruidh

Demandant, *s* Iarradair, iarrtair

Demander, *s* Iarradair, iarrtair, ath-chuingiche.

Demean, *v a* Giùlain, iomchair, ìslich, irioslaich.

Demeanour, *s* Giùlan, iomchar, caith-beatha, dol a mach, gnàthachadh.

Dementation, *s* Boile, cuthach

Demerit, *s.* Droch-thoilltinneas, mi-thoilltinneas.

Demerit, *v a.* Tòill peanas

Demesne, *s* Oighreachd, saor-sheilbh

Demi, *inseparable particle* Leth.

Demidevil, *s* Leth-dhiabhol, leth-dheamhon, droch-ghin; spealg do 'n aibhiseir

Demigod, *s.* Leth-dhia, flath-threun.

Demiman, *s* Leth-mhadadh

Demirep, *s.* Striopach, leth-shiùrsach.

Demise, *s.* Bàs, eug, caochladh, siubhladh

Demise, *v* Fag mar dhìleab

Demission, *s.* Isleachadh; tamailteachadh; tuisleachadh.

Demit, *v* Croch; leig tuiteam le ni.

Democracy, *s.* Comh-fhlaitheachd.

Democrat, *s.* Comh-fhlathaiche; *bus-dubh.*

Democratical, *a.* Comh-fhlaitheach.

Demolish, *v a.* Tilg sios, leig; sgrios, mill.

Demolisher, *s.* Leagadair, milltear, sgriosadair.

Demolition, *s.* Leigeil, tilgeadh sios, milleadh, sgriosadh.

Demon, *s.* Deamhon, diabhol, droch-spiorad.

Demoniac, *s.* Urr sa bheil deamhon.

Demoniacal, *a.* Diabhluidh, deamhanach, aingidh.

Demonstrable, *a.* So-dhearbhadh, so-chomhdachadh, soilleir, dearbh-chinnteach

Demonstrate, *v* Dearbh, dearbhaich; lan-dearbh, comhdaich, soillsich, taisbean

Demonstration, *s* Dearbhadh, lan-dearbhadh, taisbean; cinntealas

Demonstrator, *s.* Dearbhair, taisbeanaiche

Demulcent, *a.* Maoth, bog, moglaidh, bogar

Demur, *v* Cuir dàil, cuir teagamh; stad

Demur, *s* Teagamh, stad, dàil; iomcheist.

Demure, *a.* Stuami, macanta, beusach, bandaidh, suidhichte, socrach; glic, crionna, ciatach

Demureness, *s* Stuaim, macantas, beus; bandaidheachd; geimnidheachd.

Demurrage, *s.* Luathsachadh airson moille a chur air luingeas

Demurrer, *s* Stadachd, ag, bac.

Den, *s* Uamh, uagh, uamhaidh, uaghaidh, sloc, slochd, cós, toll, garaidh, broc-luinn; fuathais.

Deniable, *a* So-àicheadh, so-dhiùltadh

Denial, *s* Diùltadh, euradh, òb, òbadh, àicheadh, àichean, seun, ag

Denier, *s* Diùltair, àicheanaiche.

Denigrate, *v.* Dubh, duaichnich, salaich.

Denigration, *s* Dubhadh, duaichneachd, salachadh

Denizen, *s* Saoranach, saor-dhuine

Denominate, *v.* Ainmich, goir

Denomination, *s* Ainm.

Denominative, *a* Ainmeach, ainmeannach

Denominator, *s* Ainmeanaiche.

Denotation, *s* Comhar, comharradh

Denote, *v* Comharaich, ciallaich.

Denounce, *v* Bagair, fuagair, innis, gairm, glaodh; cronaich, coirich.

Denouncement, *s* Bagairt, fuagradh, gairmeadh; cronachadh, coireachadh.

Dense, *a* Tiugh, dlù; teann, druid; domhail

Density, *s* Tiughad, teannad.

Dent, *s* Feag

Dental, *a.* Fiaclach

Dental, *s* Faochag bheag.

Denticulation, *s* Fiaclachadh, feag

Denticulated, *a* Fiaclach, fiaclaichte

Dentifrice, *s* Fùdar fhiacal

Dentist, *s* Deudaiche, deudair, deud-cheartaiche, leighfhiacall.

Dentition, *s* Gearradh nam fiacall

Denudate, *v a* Rùisg, lomair, dean lomartach.

Denudation, *s* Rùsgadh, lomradh.

Denude, *v.* Rùisg, lomair

Denunciation, *s* Bagradh, bagairt fhollaiseach; cronachadh follaiseach

Denunciator, *s* Bagrair, fear-casaid

Denunciatory, *a.* Bagairteach.

Deny, *v* Aicheadh, diult, eur, òb, seun, cuir as aicheadh.

Deobstruct, *v.* Glan, dean réidh, fosgail, réitich.

Deodand, *s.* Naomh-ghibhte, naomh-thabhartas, naomh-dheirc.

Deoppilate, *v. a.* Glan, reitich, fosgail.

Deoppilation, *s.* Glanadh, reiteachadh, fosgladh.

Deosculation, *s.* Pògadh, pògarsaich, pòg, pògan, pòigean; *provincial*, pàg.

Depart, *v. n.* Falbh, folbh, imich, triall, coisich; siubhail, rach eug; teasd, tréig. He departed, *dh' fhalbh e; shiubhail e; theasd e.*

Department, *s.* Ionad, àite; dreuchd; inmhe; roinn.

Departure, *s.* Falbh, folbh, imeachd, coiseachd, triall, tréigsinn; siubhladh; bàs, eug.

Depauperation, *s.* Bochduinn, truaghas.

Depectible, *a.* Righinn, rithinn, leanailteach, tiugh.

Depend, *v.* Earb ri, cuir earbsa ann, croch ri.

Dependance, Dependancy, *s.* Earbadh, earbsadh; muinghinn, crochadh; eisiomail, eisiomalachd, iochdranachd.

Dependant, Dependent, *s.* Fear an crochadh ri (no) an eisiomail; ceatharnach, iochdaran.

Dependant, Dependent, *a.* Eisiomaileach, earbsadh ri, an crochadh ri.

Depender, *s.* Iochdaran.

Deperdition, *s.* Sgrios, sgriosadh, léir-sgrios.

Depict, *v.* Dealbh, tarruing.

Depilous, *a.* Lom, maol, sgiolta.

Depletion, *s.* Taomadh, taosgadh, falamhachadh.

Deplorable, *a.* Muladach, bronach, dubhach, cumhach, doineach, tuirseach.

Deplorableness, *s.* Muladachd, truaighe, tuirseachd.

Deplorably, *adv.* Gu muladach, gu truagh, gu bronach, gu tuirseach.

Deploration, *s.* Caoineadh, cumhadh, gul, gal, caoidh, tuireadh.

Deplore, *v.* Caoidh, caoin, dean bròn, dean tuireadh, dean cumha.

Deplorer, *s.* Cumhadair, fear tuiridh (no) bròin.

Deplumation, *s.* Spioladh iteagan, spionadh iteagan.

Deplume, *v.* Cloimh, sgoll; beann, spiol (no) spion iteagan.

Depone, *v.* Innis air do mhionnan, thoir fiannis; cuir an geall.

Deponent, *s.* Fianuis, fianuis air a mhionnan.

Depopulate, *v.* Bànaich, sgrios, mill, fàsaich, diothaich, diolàraich.

Depopulation, *s.* Sgriosadh, milleadh, fàsachadh, diothachadh, diolàrachadh, leir-sgrios, deilgionadh.

Depopulator, *s.* Sgriosadair, milltear.

Deport, *v.* Guilain, iomchair, gluais.

Deport, *s.* Giùlan, iomchar, beus, caith-beatha, dol mach, gluasad.

Deportation, *s.* Diobarachadh, fògradh.

Deportment, *s.* Giùlan, iomchar, caith-beatha, beus, dol a mach, gluasad. Good deportment, *deagh iomchar, deagh chaith-beatha.*

Depose, *v. a* and *n.* Cuir gu taobh, leig sios, di-chathairich; ìslich, irioslaich, tàmailtich; (*on oath*), deimhinnich, mionn; thoir fiannis.

Deposit, *s.* Geall, urras, earlas, tasgadh.

Deposit, *v.* Taisg, cuir seachad; cuir an geall; cuir air riadh.

Deposition, *s.* Fianuis, teisteas, teisteanas; cur gu taobh, cur fa làr, di-chathrachadh, irioslachadh.

Depository, *s.* Tigh-stòr, taisg-ionad, tigh-tasgaidh.

Depravation, *s.* Coiripidheachd; coirpteachd; truaillidheachd, aingidheachd, dubhailc.

Deprave, *v.* Truaill, truaillich, mill, thoir a thaobh.

Depravedness, *s.* Coiripidheachd, truaillidheachd, aingidheachd.

Depraver, *s.* Milltear, truaillear.

Depravity, *s.* Coirpidheachd, coirpteachd, aingidheachd, dubhailc.

Deprecate, *v.* Asluich (no) guidh olc a chumail air falbh.

Deprecation, *s.* Asluchadh, guidhe, urnuigh, athchuinge, aoradh.

Deprecator, *s.* Leithsgeulaiche.

Depreciate, *v.* Di-meas, dìmeasaich; lughadaich ann luach; fo-mheas.

Depreciation, *s.* Dìmeas; dimeasachd.

Depredate, *v.* Spùill, spùinn, creach, slad, slaid, *robainn.*

Depredation, *s.* Spùille, spùilleadh, spùillinn, spùinn, spuinneadaireachd, creach, creiche, creachadaireachd, togail, robaireachd, fuadachd, sladadh, slad.

Depredator, *s.* Spuilleadair, spùinneadair, creachadair, robair, sladaiche.

Deprehend, *v. a.* Glac, beir air, faigh a mach.

Deprehension, *s.* Glacadh, beirsinn; faotainn (no) faghail a mach.

Depress, *v.* Cum sios (no) bhàn; leig sios, tilg sios, ìslich, irioslaich, mi-mhisnich.

Depression, *s.* Leigeil sios, tuiteam; ìsleachadh, irioslachadh; truime, truime-inntinn; trumadas; dinneadh, mulad.

Depressor, *s.* Fear sàruchaidh.

Deprivation, *s.* Toirt air falbh; calldach, call, creachadh.

Deprive, *v. a.* Thoir o; caill; bac, amail.

Depth, *s.* Doimhne, doimhneachd; aigean, luimdheirig; (*of winter*), an dùbhlachd.

Depucelate, *v.* Truaill, truaillich, thoir maighdeannas o.

Depulsion, *s.* Sgiùrsadh, ruagadh.

Depurate, *v. a.* Glan, sgùr; sioladh, siothladh.

Depurate, *a.* Glan, siolaidhte; soilleir.

Depure, *v. a.* Glan, sioladh.

Deputation, *s.* Teachdaireachd, cuireadh; gnothuch cudthromach.

Depute, *v.* Cuir air theachdaireachd; thoir comas (no) ùghdarras.

Deputy, *s.* Fear ionaid, riochdair, teachdair.

Dequantitate, *v.* Beagaich, lughadaich.

Deracinate, *v. a.* Spion as a bhun, di-fhreumhaich; sgrios, léir-sgrios.

Deraign, *v. a.* Comhdaich, dearbh, deimhinnich, cuir thar a cheile (no) air aimhreidh; claon.

Deraignment, *s.* Còmhdachadh, dearbhadh, deimhinneachadh; eas-ordugh, mi-riaghailt; claonadh; naomhthréigsinn.

Derange, *v.* Cuir air aimhreidh (no) thar a chéile. *Deranged*, thara chéile; gòrach.

Derangement, *s.* Aimhreite, eas-ordugh mi-riaghailt; (*of mind*), dìth-ceill, gòraiche.

Dereliction, *s.* Fagail, tréigsinn, glan-thréigsinn, turchùl.

Deride, *v.* Mag, dean fochaid, dean fanaid, dean sgeig, fanaidich, fochaidich, sgallasaich.

Derider, *s.* Magair, fochaidiche, sgeigear, cnadair.

Derision, *s.* Fanaid, fanoid, fochaid, magadh, sgeig; sgallais, cnadaireachd, cnaide; tàir, tarcuis; ball fanaid; aobhar-ghàire.

Derisive, *a.* Fanaideach, fochaideach; sgeigeil, magail.

Derivation, *s.* Sruth-chlaonadh; sruthadh; tarruing.

Derivative, *a.* Sruthach; a teachd o.

Derivative, *s.* Sruth, sruthan; sruth-fhocal.

Derive, *v a* and *n.* Sruth-chlaon; sruth, tarruing; thig o

Dernier, *a.* Deireannach, deiridh, mu dheireadh, fa dheireadh

Derogate, *v.* Di-mheas; tarcuisich; dean tàire, lughadaich, beagaich.

Derogation, *s.* Laghdachadh, beagachadh; atharrachadh; dimeas, tarcuis, càin.

Derogatory, *a* Tarcuiseach, tàireil; dimeasail.

Dervis, *s* Sagart Turcach.

Descant, *s.* Òran, fonn; còmhradh; càntaireachd; seanachas; connsachadh.

Descant, *v n* Seinn, dean càntaireachd (no) fonn, connsaich; labhair, cuir dhiot

Descend, *v n* and *a.* Thig nuas (no) bhàn, rach sios (no) bhàn, rach fodha, teirinn, tuirling, tuit, thig o. He descended, *thuirling e, theirinn e*, a race shall descend from thee, *thig sliochd uaite.*

Descendant, **Descendants**, *s* Gineal, sliochd, siol, pòr, clann, iarmad.

Descended, *part* Tuirlingte, teirinnte; air teachd nuas, air teachd o Of whom is he descended, *co uaith a thàinig e*

Descendent, *a.* A tuiteam, a tuirling, a teirinn

Descension, *s* Tuiteam, tuirling, tuirlinn

Descent, *s.* Teirinn, tuirlinn, dol sios (no) bhàn, teachd sios (no) bhàn; (*declivity*), leathad, leth-bhruthach, (*assault*), ionnsuidh; (*offspring*), siol, pòr, gineal, clann, ginealach

Describe, *v.* Sgriobh, innis, thoir cunntas mu, cuir an céill; comharaich, tarruing, meas.

Describer, *s.* Fear meas, fear a chuireas an céill.

Description, *s* Cunntas, mìn-chunntas, sgeul, cur an céill; tarruing, meas.

Descriptive, *a.* Samhlachail.

Descry, *v* Beachdaich, faic, thoir a mach, amais, airmis; gabh brath, gabh sgeul; foillsich, nochd, innis, leig ris.

Desecrate, *v* Mi-naomhaich, truaill, mill.

Desecration, *s.* Mi-naomhachadh, truailleadh

Desert, *s.* Fàsach, dìthreabh, aonach, frithe, uaigneas.

Desert, *s* Toilltinneas; luach, fiachan, luaidheachd, duais, gar. According to his desert, *a réir a thoilltinneis.*

Desert, *a* Fàsail, fàs, dìthreabhach, uaigneach

Desert, *v a.* Fàg, treig, cuir cùl ri, teich.

Deserter, *s* Treigsinneach, *discartair.*

Desertion, *s.* Treigsinn, fagail, teicheadh, teicheachd, cùlachadh, *disheartuinn*, ar a mach.

Desertless, *a* Neo-fhiachail, neo-thoilltinneach, neo-airidh

Deserve, *v* Toill; coisinn; bi airidh air math no olc You deserve punishment, *thoill thu peanas*, you well deserved it, *is math a thoill thu e*

Deservedly, *adv.* Gu toilltinneach, gu fiachail, a reir toilltinneis.

Deserver, *s* Toilltinneach.

Deserving, *a* Toilltinneach, airidh air maith, chùiteach.

Desiccate, *v. a.* Tiormaich, tràigh, crion.

Desiccation, *s* Tioramachadh, tràigheadh, crionadh.

Desiccative, *a.* Tiormalach, tioramach, crionachail

† **Desiderate**, *v. a* Iarr, sanntaich, miannaich, rùnaich

Desideratum, *s.* Easbhuidh, dìth

Design, *v a* Tarruing; linich; rùnaich, cuir romhad; sònraich; teannsgail. I design to stop here, *tha mi' cur romham stadachd an so*, who designed this work? *co theannsgail an obair so?*

Design, *s.* Rùn, miann, inntinn, smuain, comhairle; teannsgal, innleachd; tarruing; dealbh, foir-dhealbh.

Designate, *v. a.* Ainmich, comharraich; ciallaich.

Designation, *s.* Ainmeachadh, comharrachadh, rùn, inntinn; rùnachadh sonrachadh, sunrachadh, orduchadh; àite, inbhe, oifig, dreuchd.

Designedly, *adv.* Gu toileach, gu sonruichte, a dh' aon ghnothach, a dh' aon obair, a dheòin.

Designer, *s.* Foir-dhealbhair; innleachdaiche.

Designing, *a* Sligheach, eòlach, cuilbheartach, cealgach, carach, mealltach.

Designment, *s.* Rùn, miann, foir-dhealbh

Desirable, *a.* Miannach, taitneach; ionmhuinneach, ionmhiannaichte.

Desire, *s.* Miann, sannt, fonn, deidh, dùrachd, toil, rùn, togar; iarrtas; ordugh, anamhiann; duil, àilghios; àill, sireadh; guidhe. He did it at my desire, *rinn e air m' iarrtas e;* what is your desire? *ciod a b' aill leat?* by desire, *a réir ordugh.*

Desire, *v* Miannaich, sanntaich, togair, sir, iarr, guidh, asluich. I desire no more, *cha sir mi tuille;* he desires to see you, *tha e' sireadh d' fhaicinn.* Desired, *miannaichte, sanntaichte, air iarruidh.*

Desirer, *s.* Miannachair, asluchair

Desirous, *a.* Miannach, togarach, sanntach, deònach, deidheil, an geall, an càs He is very desirous to have it, *tha e an geall air, (no) an càs air*

Desirously, *adv.* Gu miannach, gu togarach, gu sanntach, gu dìonach, gu deidheil.

Desist, *v. n.* Sguir, stad, leig dhiot, seas, guait.

Desistance, *s.* Sgur, sgurachd, sgurachdainn, stadachd, seasamh, guaiteal

Desk, *s* (*For writing*), crinnlean, sgriobh-chlar; claonbhord; (*a pulpit*), crannag, cùbait araidean.

Desolate, *a.* Fàs, fàsail, dìthreabhach, neo-aitichte; uaigneach, aonaranach

Desolation, *s* Fàsalachd, fàsachadh, sgrios, léir-sgrios, lom-sgriob, dòlas

Despair, *s* Eu-dòchas, mì-mhisneach, mì-mhuinghinn.

Despair, *v* Cail dochas (no) muinghinn, bi ann eudòchas.

Despairer, *s.* Eu-dochasaiche

Despairingly, *adv.* Gu h-eu-dòchasach

Despatch, *v.* Deifirich, cuir an falbh an cabhaig; (*kill*), marbh, cuir as da.

Despatch, *s.* Cabhag, deifir, tapadh; teachdair.

Despatchful, *a* Cabhagach, deifireach, luath, tapaidh.

Desperado, *s* Fear air bhainidh, fear baoghail; fear ainniseach, fear air bhreathas.

Desperate, *a* Eu-dochasach, brais, cas, dian, neo-smuainteachail, garg; ainniseach, air bhreathas

Desperately, *adv.* Gu eu-dochasach, gu brais, gu dian, gu h-ainniseach.

Desperateness, *s.* Eu-dochasachd, ainniseachd.

Desperation, *s* Eu-dochas, ainneas, breathas, bainnidh.

Despicable, *a* Suarrach, diblidh, neo-fhiachail, gun fhiù; simplidh; truagh, bochd, dorga, tàireil.

Despicableness, *s* Suarraichead, diblidheachd.

Despicably, *adv* Gu suarrach, gu diblidh, gu simplidh.

Despisable, *a.* Neo-mheasail, suarrach, leibideach.

Despise, *v a.* Cuir air dimeas (no) air dearmad, dean tàir, dean tarcuis, cuir an mì-shuim (no) air bheag suim, tarcuisich. I would despise to do it, *cha b' fhiach leam a dheanamh.* Despised, *an a chur air dimeas.*

Despiser, *s.* Fear tarcuiseach, di-measair, sgeigear, tarcuisiche.

Despite, *s.* Mi-run, gamhlas, tnù, tnùth, fuath, spid, tailceas, drochmhein; droch-mheineachd, tàir, tarcuis.

Despite, *v. a.* Buair; masluich; meall.

Despiteful, *a.* Mi-runach, gamhlasach, tnùmhor, fuathach, tailceasach, spideil, droch-mheineach, tàireil, tarcuiseach, naimhdeil, aingidh.

Despitefully, *adv.* Gu mi-runach, gu gamhlasach, gu tnùmhor, gu fuathach, gu tailceasach, gu spideil, gu droch-mheineach, gu taireil, gu tarcuiseach, gu naimhdeil, gu h-aingidh.

Despoil, *v.* Spùill, spùinn, creach, slad, robainn, argainn, spoch.

Despoliation, *s.* Spuilleadh, spuinneadh, creach, spuinneadaireachd, creachadh, creachadaireachd, creiche, sladadh, robainn, argnadh, spochadh.

Despond, *v. n.* Tuit an eu-dòchas, bi an eu-dochas, call misneach.

Despondence, *s.* Eu-dochas, droch-mhuinghinn, truim-inntinn, lag-mhisneach.

Despondent, *a.* Eu-dochasach; muladach, neo-mhisneachail. He became despondent, *thainig eu-dochas air, chinn e eu-dochasach, chaill e 'mhisneach.*

Desponsate, *v. a.* Geall (no) thoir am pòsadh, ceangail.

Desponsation, *s.* Gealltuinn am posadh, ceangladh, cordadh.

Despot, *s.* Ard-thighearn, ain-tighearn, ain-righ, anuachdaran, cruaidh-uachdaran.

Despotic, *a.* Ain-tighearnail; iomlan ann an cumhachd.

Despotism, *s.* Ain-tighearnas; an-uachdaranachd, ard-uachdaranachd.

Despumate, *v. n.* Tog cobhar (no) còp.

Despumation, *s.* Cobhar, còp.

Dessert, *s.* Deir-dhunnan.

Destinate, *v. a.* Sònraich, sùnraich, rùnaich.

Destination, *s.* Crioch; rùn; ordugh, orduchadh. Place of destination, *ceann uidhe.*

Destine, *v. a.* Sùnraich, sònraich, orduich. Destined, *sonraichte, an dàn, air a shònruchadh.*

Destiny, *s.* Dàn; ordugh Dhé; mànadh, ceann radhairc, sul-radharc.

Destitute, *a.* Tréigte, cuitichte, diobairte; feumach, uiresabhuidheach, truagh, folamh, falamh, easbhuidheach; diblidh; aonaranach.

Destitution, *s.* Cuiteachadh, diobaradh, feum, bochduinn uireasbhuidh, truaighe, truaghanachd, easbhuidheachd; diblidheachd.

Destroy, *v. a.* Mill; sgrios, diothaich; donaich, tilg sios; dean fàs; (*kill*), marbh, mort, cuir as do. Destroyed, *millte, air a mhilleadh; marbh.*

Destroyer, *s.* Milltear, sgriosadair; aibhisear, marbhaiche, marbhadair, mortair.

Destructible, *a.* So-mhilleadh, so-sgriosadh; so-mharbh.

Destruction, *s.* Sgrios, milleadh; fàsalachd; fàsachadh; diothachadh; àr, arach, marbhadh, mortadh, plaigh, forran.

Destructive, *a.* Sgriosail, sgriosach; millteach, fàsail, bàsail; marbhtach, nimheach, nimhneach, puinnsionach, puinnsionta.

Destructively, *adv.* Gu sgriosail, gu sgriosach, gu milltεach, gu fàsail; gu marbhtach, gu nimheach.

Destructiveness, *s.* Sgriosalachd, millteachd; fàsalachd; marbhtachd.

Desudation, *s.* Fallas, follas, sruthadh follais.

Desuetude, *s.* Ana-cleachd, ana-cleachduinn.

Desultory, *a.* Luaineach, neo-shuidhichte, defireach; goirrid.

Desume, *v. a.* Thoir o, 'gabh an coingheall.

Detach, *v. a.* Cuir air leth, dealaich, roinn; cuir buidheann a thoirt ionnsuidh, (no) air ghnothach.

Detachment, *s.* Buidheann, cuideachd shaighdear.

Detail, *v. a.* Innis gu poncail, nochd, foillsich.

Detail, *s.* Cunntas, innseadh.

Detain, *v. a.* Cum air ais, bac, grab, cum, cuir moille, amail; cum an laimh, coimhead, gleidh.

Detainer, *s.* Fear gleidhidh; grabair, fear-grabaidh, grabadh.

Detect, *v. a.* Nochd, foillsich, faigh a mach, glac, leig ris, fàisnis, innis.

Detecter, *s.* Nochdair, foillseachair.

Detection, *s.* Dìobhrath; foillseachadh ceilg, brath, cealgbhrath; leigeil ris.

Detention, *s.* Cumail, amaladh, bac, grabadh, priosunachd.

Deter, *v. a.* Mi-mhisnich, cuir eagal air, cum air ais.

Deterge, *v. a.* Siab, sgriob, glan, nigh, rub, ruinnse, ruinnsich; sruthail, sgrab; sgùr.

Detergent, *a.* Siabach; glanadach; ruinnseach, nighteach, ruinnseach, sruthlach, sgrabach; sgùrach.

Deteriorate, *v. a.* Ciùrr, cuir am miosad.

Deterioration, *s.* Dol am miosad.

Determinable, *a.* So-shonrachadh, a ghabhas sònrachadh.

Determinate, *a.* Sònruichte, suidhichte, runaichte, cinnteach, criochnaichte, comharraichte mach.

Determination, *s.* Sonrachadh, miann; breith; comhairle, run suidhichte.

Determine, *v. a.* Sonruich, suidhich; breith, comhairlich; cuir gu taice; criochnaich. Determined, *sonruichte, suidhichte, rùnaichte, criochnaichte; air a shonruchadh.* I am determined upon it, *tha mi sonraichte air.*

Determined, *part.* and *a.* See **Determine**.

Deterration, *s.* Bùrachadh, cladhachadh.

Detersion, *s.* Siabadh, sguabadh, glanadh, nigheadh, sruthladh, sgùradh, ruinnseadh.

Detersive, *a.* Siabach, sguabach, glanail, ruinnseach, sgùrach.

Detest, *v. a.* Oilltich, fùrlaich, fuathaich, gràinich, gabh gràin (no) fuath. I detest him, *dh' oilltich mi ris.*

Detestable, *a.* Oillteil, furlachail, fuathach, fuathasach, gràineil, uamhor, uamharra, sgreamhail.

Detestably, *adv.* Gu h-oillteil, gu fùrlachail, gu fuathach, gu fuathasach, gu gràineil, gu h-uamharra, gu sgreamhail.

Detestation, *s.* Oillt, fùrlachadh, fuath, gràinealachd, gràin, sgreamh.

Dethrone, *v. a.* Di-chathairich, di-chrunaich, di-rioghaich. Dethroned, *dì-chathairichte.*

Dethronement, *s.* Di-chathaireachadh, di-chrùnachadh.

Detonation, *s.* Cracail, braidhe.

Detort, *v. a.* Toinneamh, mi-chiallaich.

Detract, *v. a.* Mi-chliùich; sgainnealaich, cain, tarcuisich; dimeas, lughdaich, beagaich, tuaileasaich, maslaich.

Detracter, *s.* Fear-cul-chàinidh, fear tarcuiseach, tarcuisiche, maslachair; tuaileasaiche.

Detraction, *s.* Càin, cùl-chàin, tàir, tarcuis, tarcuisne, masladh, dimeas, tuaileas, sgainneal; faun-sgeul, miothlachd.

Detractive, *a.* Lughadachail; tàireil, tarcuiseach, culchaineach, tuaileasach, sgainnealach.

Detractory, *a.* Tàireil, tarcuiseach, cùl-chaineach, tuail-easach, sgainnealach.

Detractress, *s* Ban-tuaileasaiche.

Detriment, *s.* Call, calldach, earchall, dochann, dolaidh, diùbhal, urchoid; lochd, cron, ciurradh, ciurram, aimhleas, donas.

Detrimental, *a.* Caillteach, diùbhalach, diùbhaileach, dochannach, cronail, ciùrrail, lochdach, aimhleasach.

Detrude, *v.* Puc sios (no) a mach.

Detruncate, *v. a.* Bearr, gearr, sgath, sgud, giorraich.

Detruncation, *s.* Bearradh, gearradh, sgathadh, sgudadh, giorrachadh.

Detrusion, *s.* Pùcadh sios, pùcadh bhàn

Devastate, *v* Dean fàs, mill, sgrios, di-threabhaich.

Devastation, *s.* Fàsachadh, milleadh, sgriosadh, di-threabhachd

Deuce, *s.* Cairt dha-bhall, (no) le da spot; an diobhal; ditlis Deuce take you, *an diobhal thu, an diobhal leis thu, gu gabhadh a bhochduinn thu.*

Deuteronomy, *s.* Dara leabhar an lagha, (no) cuigeamh leabhar Mhaois.

Develop, *v. a* Nochd, leig ris, innis, foillsich, soilleirich

Development, *s.* Nochdadh, leigeil ris, innseadh, foillseachadh, soillseachadh, soilleireachadh

† **Devergence**, *s.* Leathad, leth-bhruthach.

Dexex, *a* Corrach, aomach, claon.

Dexexity, *s* Corraichead, aomadh, claonadh.

Deviate, *v n.* Rach a thaobh, rach air seacharan, claon; rach am mearrachd, rach air iomrol; peacaich

Deviating, *a.* 'Seachranach, di-shligheach, iomrolach.

Deviation, *s* Seachran, iomrol; claonadh; mearachd, peacadh

Device, *s* Seol, doigh, innleachd, tionnsgnadh, smuaine, comhairle, dealbh; cleas, coslas

Devil, *s* Diabhol, deamhan, donas, aibhisear, aibhistear; an nathair, am buairear, am fear is miosa.

Devil's-bit, *s* Dubhan ceann-chosach.

Devilish, *a.* Diabhluidh, deamhanach, donasach, aingidh, olc, coirpte, nimheil, sgriosail; fuathasach. Devilish pretty, *fuathasach laoghach, diabhluidh laoghach (no) bòidheach.*

Devil's-bit, *s.* Uarach mhullach; odharach mhullach.

Devilship, *s* Diabhlachd.

Devious, *a* Iomralach, luaineach, siùbhlach, seachranach.

Devise, *v. a.* and *n* Tionnsgain, smuainich, beachdaich, dealbh, deilbh; cnuasaich, faigh a mach, fag mar dhileab

Devise, *s* Dileab.

Devised, *part.* Dealbhte, deilbhte, tionnsgainte; cnuasaichte.

Deviser, *s* Dileabaiche.

Deviser, *s* Tionnsgnair, tionnsgnaiche, fear-innleachdach, dealbhadair

Devoid, *a* Falamh, folamh, fàs. Devoid of, *gun*, devoid of shame, *gun nair, air bheag nàire, beagnarach*

Devoir, *s.* Dleasdanas; seirbheis, beannachd, cùirteas.

Devolve, *v a* and *n.* Ròil; ruidhil; cuir (no) tuit air neach eile.

Devolution, *s.* Ròthladh, ruidhleadh.

Devote, *v.* Coisrig, naomhaich; moid, cuir air leth; dìt, malluich, mollaich; thoir suas

Devoted, *a.* Coisrigte; naomhaichte; malluichte.

Devotedness, *s.* Coisrigeachd; cleachd, dùrachd

Devotee, *s* Baoth-chreideamhach.

Devotion, *s.* Diadhuidheachd, diadhachd, crabhadh, aoradh; moideadh, seirbheis; dùrachd, déine.

Devotional, *a.* Diadhuidh, crabhach, naomh.

Devotionalist, *s.* Crabhaiche.

Devour, *v.* Ith suas, mill, marbh, beubanaich, cuir as da; ith gu glamhach, sluig, grab, geòc, † long.

Devourer, *s* Milltear, marbhaiche; struidhear.

Devout, *s* Diadhuidh, diadhaidh, cràbhach, naomh, treibh-dhireach, ionraic.

Devoutly, *adv.* Gu diadhuidh, gu crabhach, gu naomh, gu treibh-dhireach; gu dùrachdach.

Devoutness, *s.* Diadhuidheachd, cràbhadh, treibh-dhireas.

Dew, *s* Drùchd, driùchd, dealt, braon, ceo-braon; cuirneag.

Dew, *v. a.* Dealt, taislich, fliuch.

Dewberry, *s.* Sùgh-chraobh.

Dewclaw, *s.* Spor.

Dewdrop, *s.* Cuirneag; cluigean driùchd, dealt-shileag, braon-drùchd.

Dewlap, *s.* Sprogaill, sprochaill, sparsan.

Dewlapt, *a.* Sprogailleach, sparsanach.

Dew-worm, *s.* Dealt-dhaolag, daolag mhadainn.

Dewy, *a.* Dealtach, braonach, driùchdach, drùchdach, drùchdail.

Dexter, *a.* (*In heraldry*), an deas, deiseal.

Dexterity, *s* Teomachd, seoltachd, lathailteachd, lathailt, tapadh, tapachd, sgil, eolas, treubhachd.

Dexterous, *a* Teoma, seolta, tapaidh, ealanta, sgairteil, deas, treubhach, sgileil.

Dexterously, *adv.* Gu teoma, gu seolta, gu tapaidh, gu h-ealanta, gu sgairteil, gu deas, gu treubhach

Dextral, *a.* Deas, ceart; neo-chli.

Diabetes, *s* Fual-ruithe.

Diabolic, **Diabolical**, *a* Diabhluidh, deamhnaidh, an-diadhaidh, gràineil, aingidh, olc, coirpte; deistinneach, oillteil.

Diacoustics, *s.* Claistinl, claist-eolas.

Diadem, *s* Crùn, coron, fleasg, crùn rìgh, crùn rioghail.

Diademed, *a* Cruinte, coronaichte.

Diadrom, *s* Tiot, tiotag, mionait.

Diæresis, *s.* Siol-roinn

Diagonal, *a.* Tarsuing, trasda, crosgach, bho oisinn gu oisinn.

Diagonally, *adv.* Gu trasda, gu crosgach, trasda, crosgach, bho oisinn gu h-oisinn.

Diagram, *s.* Dealbh.

Dial, *s.* Uaireadair gréine; grian-chlach

Dialect, *s.* Doigh-labhairt, cainnt, cànmhuinn, atharrachadh na cainnt cheudna, mar Ghaidhlig Albannach agus Eireannach

Dialectic, *a.* Arguinneach

Dialogist, *s.* Comh-labhairtiche.

Dialogue, *s.* Còmhradh, bruidhinn, cracaireachd; conaltradh; iomagal, comh-labhairt dheise.

Diameter, *s.* Crosg-lìn, crois-lìn, tarsnean, tarsuan

Diametrical, *a* Crosg-lìneach, crois-lìneach.

Diamond, *s.* Daoimean, leug chruaidh riomhach Diamonds, (*in cards*), daoimean

Diaper, *s* Anart-bùird, greus anart, tuailte.

Diaphaneity, *s.* Trid-shoillse.

Diaphanous, *a* Trid-shoilleir.

Diaphoresis, *s.* Fallus.

Diaphoretic, *a.* Fallusach, fallusail.

Diaphragm, *s.* An sgairt.

DIARRHŒA, s. Buinneach, sgàrd, tualag, gearrach.
DIARY, s. Irisleabhar, meamhranach, dialan, cunntas latháil.
DIATRIBE, s. Ràsanachd; langanachd.
DIBBLE, s. Pleadhan, pleadhag.
DICE, s. pl. Dìstean, dìslean. Dice box, *dìslean*; a gamester will not hide his dice, *cha chéil cearraiche a dhìstean.*
DICER, s. Dìstear, cearraiche.
DICKER, s. Deich seicheannan.
DICTATE, v. a. Orduich, deachd, innis seòl, cuir roimh.
DICTATE, s. Deachdadh, ordugh, focal, riar, comannt.
DICTATOR, s. Deachdair, riaghlair, uachdaran Roimheach.
DICTATORIAL, a. Deachdaireach, smachdail.
DICTATORSHIP, s. Deachdaireachd; ughdarras, uachdaranachd, comannt.
DICTION, s. Cainnt.
DICTIONARY, s. Foclair; deachdannair, abardair.
DID, *pret.* of do; Rinn.
DIDACTIC, a. Teagasgach. A didactic poem, *duan, laoidh.*
DIDDER, v. n. Crith.
DIDST, *pret. sec pers.* of do; Rinn. Thou didst, *rinn thu*, didst thou? *an do rinn thu?* didst thou not? *nach do rinn thu?*
DIDUCTION, s. Dealachadh.
DIE, s. Dath, ligh, lith; dreach, neul; (*in gaming*), dìste.
DIDAPPER, s. Eun fairge, dubh-eun, gairge, gairg-eun, curra-ghalan, dubh-shnamhair.
DIE, v. a. Dath, ligh.
DIE, v. n. Teasd, rach eug, faigh bàs, caochail, siubhail, eug, bàsaich; searg, crion; meath. He died, *theasd e, dh' eug e, shiubhail e.*
DIER, s. Dathadair, lithiche.
DIET, s. Lòn, biadh, cuid, cuid an tràth, beathan, (*a meeting*), mòr-thionail, flath-mhòd.
DIET, v. a. and n. Biath; ith.
DIET-DRINK, s. Deoch leighis.
DIFFER, v. n Eadar-dhealaich; atharraich, cuir eadar, connsaich, cuir a mach They differed, *dh' éirich eatorra, chuir iad a mach air cheile; bha diubhair eatorra.*
DIFFERENCE, s. Eadar-dhealachadh, eadar-dhealach, diubhair, mùth, dealachadh, atharrachadh, caochladh, (*quarrel*), connsach, connspoid, cur a mach.
DIFFERENT, a. Eu-coslach, neo-chosmhal, éile. In a different manner, *air mhùth doigh, air chaochladh sheòl, air dhoigh eile, air sheol eile.*
DIFFERENTLY, *adv.* Air mhùth doigh, air chaochladh sheòl
DIFFICULT, a. Duilich, doilich, cruaidh, do-dheanamh, deacair, docair, docail; (*to please*), crosda, cainnteach, dothoileachadh, do-thaitinn; do-riarach
DIFFICULTY, s Deacaireachd, docaireachd, cruadal, cruaidh-chas, teinne, iom-cheist, airc, càs; trioblaid, spairn, iomairt. With difficulty, *air eigin*
DIFFIDE, v. Cuir amharus, ain-earb.
DIFFIDENCE, s. Amharus, an-amharus, fàitcheas, fàitghios, neo-earbsachd, cion-muinghinn; teagamh.
DIFFIDENT, a. Amharusach, an-amharusach, fàiteach; neo-earbsach, teagamhach, eagallach.
DIFFLUENCE, s. Dortadh, taomadh, taosgadh, sruthadh, sgaoileadh.
DIFFLUENT, a. Dortach, taomach, taosgach, sruthach, sgaoilteadh.
DIFFORM, a. Eu-cosmhuil, eag-samhuil.
DIFFORMITY, s. Eu-cosmhuileachd; eag-samhlachd

DIFFRANCHISEMENT, s. Tabhairt a cheartan o bhaile air bi, dì-cheartachadh, di-chòireachadh.
DIFFUSE, v Taom, sgaoil, craobh-sgaoil; dòirt a mach
DIFFUSE, a. Sgaoilte, sgaoilteach; leudach; neo-shuidhichte; pailt, lionmhor, neo-phoncail, neo-chuimir.
DIFFUSED, a. Sgaoilte, sgapta. Diffusedly, *gù sgaoilte, gu sgapta, gu farsuing, fa sgaoil*
DIFFUSION, s. Sgaoileadh, sgapadh, craobh-sgaoileadh, srabhadh, pailteas
DIFFUSIVE, a. Sgaoilteach, sgapach, farsuing, srabhach; pailt, saibhir.
DIG, v. Buraich, ruadhair, cladhaich, tochail, tochailt, pleaghaich, (*to dig a grave*), bhuraich (no) chladhaich sinn uaigh
DIGAMY, s. Ath-phòsadh.
DIGEST, v. a. Cuir an ordugh; gleus; eagair, cnamh, dilich.
DIGEST, v n Iongaraich.
DIGESTER, s Cnamhair, cnamhaiche; eagarair
DIGESTIBLE, a. So-chnamh, so-chnàmhadh, a ghabhas cnamh.
DIGESTION, s Cnàmh, cnàmhadh, eagaradh, gleusadh; cur an ordugh.
DIGESTIVE, a Cnamhach; eagarach
DIGGER, s Bùrachair, fear ruadharaidh, tochailuche, tochailtear.
DIGHT, v. a. Glan, sgeadaich, nàisnich, uigheamaich, breaghaich
DIGIT, s Tri cheathrannan òirlich, an dara cuid deug do ghnùis na gréine (no) na gealaich; meur, corag, comhar nuimhir sam bi fo dheich.
DIGITATED, a. Meurach, meanglanach, ladhrach, gniomhach.
DIGLADIATION, s. Lannaireachd, feannsaireachd, basbaireachd
DIGNIFICATION, s. Ardachadh
DIGNIFY, v a. Ardaich, urramaich, inbhich; sgeadaich.
DIGNITARY, s Ard-shagart, priomh-shagart.
DIGNITY, s Airde, arduchadh, urram, inbhe, ard-inbhe, onoir, meas; † arrachdas.
DIGRESS, v. Rach gu taobh, claon; rach bharr an rothaid.
DIGRESSION, s. Dol gu taobh, claonadh, iomrol, seachran
DIKE, s. Claise, staing, garadh; balladh, dìge, feadan uisge.
DILACERATE, v a. Reub, beubanaich, spiòn, spiol, srac, strac.
DILACERATION, s. Reubadh, beubanachadh, spionadh, spioladh, sracadh, stracadh.
DILACERATE, v. a. Reub, beubanaich, spion, spiol, srac, strac
DILAPIDATE, v a. and n. Tilg sios, dean na laraich; tuit na nochd-laraich
DILAPIDATION, s. Tuiteam
DILATATION, s Sìneadh, sgaoileadh, at, aithris.
DILATE, v a and n. Sin, sgaoil, at, aithris
DILATORINESS, s Moille, mairnealachd, athaiseachd, maidheanachd, leisge; slaodachd, leisge, lunndaireachd.
DILATORY, a. Mall, mairnealach, athaiseach, maidheanach, leasg, neo-chabhagach, neo-sgairteil, slaodach, cleubach, lunndaireach, leagach
DILECTION, s. Gràdhachadh, gràdh, gaol
DILEMMA, s Iomcheist; teagamh, càs, airc In a dilemma, *eadar dhà chomhairle, an iomcheist.*
DILIGENCE, s. Dìcheall, dìchioll, cùram; beargachd, gnàthdheanadas, oidhirp, cabhag

Diligent, *a* Dìchiollach, curamach, deanadach, oidhirpeach, *luidh*, neo-leasg, coisgludh.

Diligently, *adv.* Gu dìchiollach, gu deanadach, gu h-oidhirpeach

Dilling, *s.* Leanaban; gaolach.

Dilucid, *a.* Soilleir, glan

Dilucidate, *v. a.* Soilleirich, soillsich, glan; mìnich.

Dilucidation, *s* Soilleireachadh, soillseachadh, mìneachadh.

Dilute, *v a.* Tanaich, dean anfhann; baist, (no) measg le uisge.

Dilute, *a* Tan; caol; sreangach.

Dilution, *s* Tanachadh, anfhannachadh, baisteadh, (no) measgadh le uisge.

Diluvian, *a.* Dìlinneach; tuilteach.

Dim, *a* Doilleir, dorch, neo-shoilleir, dall.

Dim, *v a* Doilleirich, dorchaich, dall.

Dimension, *s* Meud, tomad, tomalt, tomhas.

Diminish, *v a.* and *n.* Lughadaich, beagaich; fàs ni 's lugha (no) ni 's crìne.

Diminution, *s.* Lughadachadh, beagachadh.

Diminutive, *a* Beag, crion, gearr, goirrid, cutach, crubta.

Diminutiveness, *s.* Crìne; (*of person*), girceanachd.

Dimish, *a* Leth-dhorch, leth-char dorch (no) doilleir

Dimity, *s.* Seorsa aodaich canaich

Dimly, *adv.* Gu dorch, gu dall.

Dimness, *s.* Doille, dorchadas, cion-leirsinn, ròsblachd; doirche.

Dimple, *s* Laganmeath-ghair, lagan smige.

Dimply, *a* Laganach

Dim-sighted, *a.* Leth-dhall, ròsblach, mall-shùileach.

Din, *s.* Stairn, gaoir, fuaim, glaodh, farum, toirm, torghan, gnà-fhuaim, dararaich, dairearaich, strailidh, straplaich, bloisg

Din, *v. a.* Bodhair. You din me, *tha thu 'g am bhodhradh.*

Dine, *v n* Gabh dinneir (no) biadh nòin; ith, ios; thoir dinneir; dinneirich. Have you dined? *an d' fhuair thu do dhiot mhòr?*

Ding, *v a* Buail, straoighil, spad, splad, smàl, tilg sios, spàirt

Dingle, *s* Lagan, gleannan.

Dining-room, *s.* Proinn-lios

Dinner, *s* Dinneir; diot-mhòr, biadh-nòin

Dinner-time, *s* Trath dinnearach

Dint, *s* Buille, straoidhle, strac; neart; éigin; aile buille

Dint, *v a* Buail, sàth, diong.

Diocesan, *s.* Easbuig

Diocese, *s.* Cuairt easbuig, sgìreachd Easpuig.

Dip, *s.* Bogadh, tumadh, tomadh.

Dip, *v a.* Bog, tum, tom; bogaich, taislich. Dipped, *tomta, tumta, bogta*

Diploma, *s* Cairt, foghraimh, coir-chairteal, (no) sgriobhadh ' bhuilicheas còir.

Dipper, *s.* Bogadair, tomadair, tumadair

Diphthong, *s.* Da-ghuthach, da-fhoghair, da-phong.

Dipsas, *s* Seorsa nathrach.

Dire, *a.* Eagallach, fuathasach, oillteil, uamharra, uamhasach, uamhannach; dianasach, borb, garg, muladach brònach

Direct, *a.* Dìreach; neo-chrom; soilleir, so-thuigsinn; saor

Direct, *v.* Seòl, stiùir, cuir dìreach, treoraich, treoruich, àithn, orduich, teagasg.

Direction, *s.* Seoladh, stiùireadh, treòrachadh; (*of a ship*), gabhail; (*order*), ordugh, àithne; (*guide*), iùl.

Directive, *a.* Seolach, stiùireach, treòrachail.

Directly, *adv.* Gu dìreach, gu caol dìreach; (*instantly*), an ceart uair, air a mhionait, air ball, air an spot, gu grad, gu h-ealamh, gun dàil, gun mhoille, gun stad, gun fhois, gun fhuireach; (*apparently*), gu soilleir, a reir coslais.

Directness, *s.* Dìrichead; gabhail.

Director, *s.* Riaghladair, fear riaghlaidh, stiùradair, fear stiùraidh.

Directory, *a.* Orduchail, riaghlachail.

Directory, *s.* Seoladh, riaghailt; riaghailt urnuigh.

Direful, *a.* Eagallach, fuathasach, oillteill, uamharra, uambasach, uamhannach, dianasach, borb, garg, brònach, muladach

Direness, *s* Oillt, oilltealachd, uamhann, uamhannachd, uamhasachd, uamharrachd, dianasachd, fuathas, fuathasachd.

Direption, *s.* Goid, gaduigheachd, méirle, robaireachd, spùinne, spùille.

Dirge, *s* Caoineadh, tuireadh, cumha, marbh-rann, coranach.

Dirk, *s.* Biodag; durc.

Dirt, *s.* Salachar, sal, aolach inneir, cac, gaor; poll, làthach; clabar, laban, eabar; cant, canaich, ceachar, grib, cladach; broghail, trusdaireachd

Dirtiness, *s.* Salachar, sal, aolach; poll, lathach, seilche, mosaiche, trusdaireachd, diblidheachd; miutharachd.

Dirty, *a* Salach, mosach, cac, bréin, labanach, lathachail, cantach, brothach miùthar; crion; truaillidh, (*in language*), drabhasach, drabasda.

Dirty, *v. a* Salaich; dean tàir; naraich, càin.

Diruption, *s* Sgàineadh, sgagadh, sgoltadh, sracadh.

Disability, *s* Anfhannachd, laigsinn, cion comais, neo-chomasachd.

Disable, *v.* Ciùrr, leon, ciurramaich; bac; lagaich, anfhannaich; mill, cuir a dholaidh

Disabuse, *v a* Cuir ceart

Disaccustom, *v. a.* Mi-chleachd; cuir air dhioladh.

Disacquaintance, *s.* Ain-eolas.

Disadvantage, *s.* Ana-cothrom, mi-chothrom; calldach, dochoir, coire, mi-thairbhe.

Disadvantage, *v. a* Dochainch.

Disadvantageous, *a.* Ana-cothromach, mi-tharbhach, mi-chothromach, neo-chothromach; docharach, olc, diùbhalach Disadvantageously, *gu mi-chothromach, le h-ana-cothrom*

Disadvantageousness, *s* Mi-chothromachd; mi-thairbhe, neo-iomchuidheachd, dochair, diùbhail.

Disadventurous, *a* Mi-fhortanach, mi-shealbhar.

Disaffect, *v. a.* Dean mi-thoilichte (no) diombach.

Disaffected, *a.* Neo-thoilichte, diombach; mi-runach, ann droch rùn, mi-rioghail.

Disaffectedly *adv.* Gu neo-thoilichte, gu diombach.

Disaffection, *s.* Beag-ghradh, diombachd, diombuidheachd, droch rùn, droch mhein, cion-seirce, mi-rioghalachd.

Disaffirmance, *s.* Aicheadh, seunadh

Disagree, *v.* Droch coird, mi-choird, cuir a mach air, connsaich, eadar-dhealaich They have disagreed, *dhroch-coird iad, chuir iad a mach air cheile.*

Disagreeable, *a.* Mi-thaitneach, neo-thlachdmhor; gràd, greannta; neo-iomchuidh, neo-fhreagarrach.

Disagreeableness, *s* Mi-thlachdmhoireachd; greantachd

Disagreement, *s.* Eu-cosmhalachd; mi-fhreagarachd;

droch-cordadh, cur a mach, aimhreite; easaonachd, connsach, tuasaid, tabaid.

Disallow, *v. a.* Bac, toirmisg; diult, ob, mi-cheadaich.

Disallowable, *a.* Toirmisgte; do-cheadachadh, neo-iomchuidh; neo-cheadachail.

Disallowance, *s.* Bac, bacadh, diùltadh.

Disanimate, *a.* Marbh, cuir gu bàs.

Disannul, *v. a.* Cuir air chùl; cuir gu neoni, dean gun bhrigh (no) gun toirt.

Disappear, *v.* Rach as an t-sealladh; rach as an radharc; falbh.

Disappearance, *s.* Dol as an t-sealladh; falbh.

Disappoint, *v.* Meall; teirmeasg, mearalaich. He disappointed me, *mheall e mi;* disappointed, *air a mhealladh, mearalaichte.*

Disappointment, *s.* Mealladh; mearalachadh; mearaladh; mealladh dochais.

Disapprobation, *s.* Achmhasan, cronachadh; dìteadh; neo-thaitneachd; droch-ghean.

Disapproval, *s.* Achmhasan, cronachadh; coireachadh, dìteadh.

Disapprove, *v. a.* Achmhasanaich, cronaich, coirich; dìt; fuathaich; mi-dhearbh. He disapproved of it, *cha d' thàinig e ris.*

Disarm, *v.* Faobhaich; di-armaich.

Disarmed, *a.* Faobhaichte; di-armaichte; gun airm.

Disarrange, *v.* Cuir a ordugh, cuir thar a chéile, cuir air aimhreadh.

Disarray, *s.* Aimhreite, eas-ordugh.

Disarray, *v. a.* Rùisg, lom, neo-eid, neo-sgeaduich.

Disaster, *s.* Calldach, carchall, urchoid, trioblaid, anradh, sgiorradh, truaighe, tubaist, bochduinn, doirbheas.

Disastrous, *a.* Mi-shealbhar; urchoideachd, anradhach, sgiorrail, truagh, tubaisteach, muladach trioblaideach; doirbheasach. Disastrously, *gu mi-shealbhar, gu h-urchoideach.*

Disastrousness, *s.* Mi-shealbharachd, urchoideachd, truaighe.

Disavouch, *v.* Aicheadh, cuir as aicheadh, diult, seun, òb.

Disown, *v.* Aicheadh, diult, seun, òb.

Disavowal, *s.* Aicheadh, diùlt, diultadh, seunadh, òbadh.

Disband, *v. a.* Thoir cead do, cuir fa sgaoil, leig air falbh, fuasgail; sgaoil, sgap.

Disbark, *v. a.* Cuir air tìr.

Disbelief, *s.* Mi-chreidimh.

Disbelieve, *v. a.* Na creid, di-chreid.

Disbeliever, *s.* Mi-chreideach.

Disburden, *v. a.* and *n.* Eutromaich, mi-luchdaich, neo-luchdaich. Disburden your mind, *eutromaich d' inntinn.*

Disburse, *v.* Cosd, cuir mach airgiod, builich airgiod.

Disbursement, *s.* Cosd, cosdas, costas, cur mach airgid.

Discalceation, *s.* Di-chois-bheartachadh.

Discard, *v.* Cuir air falbh, thoir cead do, cuir as aite.

Discern, *v. a.* Faic, beachdaich; faigh a mach; tuig; aithnich, fairich; diubhar, dealaich.

Discerner, *s.* Beachdair, breitheamh.

Discernible, *a.* So-fhaicinn, faicsinneach, ri fhaicinn; so-thuigsinn, mothachail. It is not discernible, *tha e do-fhaicinn, cha ghabh e faicinn.*

Discernibleness, *s.* Faicsinneachd.

Discerning, *a.* Tuigseach, geur, crionna, sicir; fiosrach, eolach, beachdail; furachair.

Discernment, *s.* Tuigse, geire, mothachadh; eòlas.

Discharge, *v. a.* Eutromaich; leig fa sgaoil, leig as, leig air falbh; (*a gun*), leig, tilg; (*a creditor*), paigh, diol, ioc; (*a servant*), cuir air falbh; (*perform*), coimh-lion.

Discharge, *s.* Fuasgladh, sgaoileadh, leigeil as (no) air falbh; (*of a debt*), pàigh, dioladh, iocadh; (*of a soldier*), saoradh, *disearsadh.*

Disciple, *s.* Deisciobul, sgoilear, leanmhuinniche, seirbheiseach.

Discipleship, *s.* Deisciobulachd.

Disciplinable, *a.* So-theagasg, so-ionnsachadh.

Disciplinarian, *s.* Smachdair.

Discipline, *s.* Ionnsachadh, oilean, foghlum, teagasg; smachd, riaghailt; peanas.

Discipline, *v. a.* Ionnsuich, foghlum, teagasg, oileanaich; smachd, riaghail, peanasaich.

Disclaim, *v.* Aicheadh, diùlt, seun, òb; cuir cùl ri.

Disclose, *v.* Leig ris, feuch, nochd, innis, taisbean, foillsich.

Disclosure, *s.* Leigeil ris, nochdadh, innseadh, taisbean, foillseachadh, aideachadh.

Discoloration, *s.* Di-dhathachadh, mùth dath.

Discolour, *v. a.* Dath, dì-dhreach.

Discomfit, *v.* Fairtlich, cuir air theich, sàruich, claoidh, buadhaich air, ruaig.

Discomfit, *s.* Fairtleachadh, saruchadh, claoidh, ruaig; sgrios.

Discomfiture, *s.* Saruchadh, claoidh, ruaig, sgrios, diùbhail, cosgairt.

Discomfort, *s.* Docair, trioblaid, buaireas, an-shocair, mulad, tuirse.

Discomfortable, *a.* Docrach, muladach, bronach, tuirseach.

Discommend, *v. a.* Cronaich, coirich, faigh coire do, di-mhol.

Discommendable, *a.* Coireachail, airidh air cronachadh.

Discommendation, *s.* Di-mholadh, cronachadh, coireachadh.

Discommode, *v. a.* Cuir dragh air, cuir moille air. You discommode me, *tha thu 'cur dragh orm.*

Discommodious, *a.* Neo-iomchuidh; draghail; buaireasach; neo-fhreagarrach.

Discommodity, *s.* Neo-iomchuidheachd, dragh, buaireas.

Discompose, *v. a.* Cuir a ordugh, cuir thar a chéile, cuir air aimhreadh; buair; farranaich. You discompose me, *tha thu 'cur dragh* (*no*) *farran orm, tha thu 'g am bhuaireadh.*

Discomposure, *s.* Eas-ordugh, buaireadh, buaireas.

Disconcert, *v. a.* Buair, farranaich; cuir thar a chéile.

Disconformity, *s.* Neo-fhreagarrachd, neo-iomchuidheachd, neo-chubhaidheachd.

Disconsolate, *a.* Dubhach, bronach, tuirseach, eu-dochasach, fo mhulad, gunsolas, gun chomh-fhurtachd.

Disconsolateness, *s.* Dubhachas, bròn, tuirse, eu-dochas.

Discontent, *a.* Neo-thoilichte, mi-thoilichte, diombach, diombuidheach docrach, mi-shocrach.

Discontent, *s.* Diombachd, docras.

Discontent, *v. a.* Mi-thaitinn, mi-thoilich. It discontented him, *mhì-thaitinn e ris, cha d' thainig e ris.*

Discontented, *a.* Mi-thoilichte, neo-thoilichte, diombach, diomach; mi-fhoisneach do-thoileachadh, do-riarachaidh.

Discontentedness, *s.* Docair, diombachd, diom, mi-fhoisneachd, mi-shuaimhneas.

Discontentment, *s.* Docras, diombachd, diomachd, mi-shuaimhneas.

Discontinuance, *s.* Sgur, sgurachd, teireachduim; sgaradh, sgarachduinn, sgaineadh, dealachadh.

Discontinuation, *s* Sgurachd, teireachduinn.
Discontinue, *v. a.* Sguir, teirig, leig dhiot, cuir stad.
Disconvenience, *s.* Neo-fhreagarrachd, mi-chubhaidheachd, eu-cubhaidheachd.
Discord, *s.* Droch-cordadh, ana-cordadh, aimhreite
Discord, *s* Droch-coird, cuir a mach; mi-fhreagair.
Discordant, *a.* Neo-chordach; aimhreiteach; iom-reusonach
Discover, *v a.* Foillsich, faigh a mach, nochd; leig ris, innis, taisbean; brath.
Discoverable, *a.* So-fhaotainn mach, so-sgrudadh, so-nochdadh, léirsinneach.
Discovered, *part.* Foillsichte, air fhaotainn mach, taisbeanta; air bhrath
Discoverer, *s* Innleachdair; foillseachair; brath, fear brathaidh, fear coimhid
Discovery, *s* Foillseachadh, leigeil ris, nochdadh, taisbeanadh
Discount, *s.* Laghachadh, laghadh, mathadh; meachainn; riadh
Discount, *v. a.* Lagh, math, math beagnaich airson airgiod ullamh
Discountenance, *v. a.* Cuir a misneach, mi-mhisnich, nàraich. Discountenanced, *fomh-mhisneach, nàr.*
Discountenance, *s* Mi-mhisneach; di-fabhair, fionnarachd, fuar-chairdeas
Discourage, *v. a.* Cuir fo mhi-mhisneach, cuir fu cagal.
Discouragement, *s* Mi-mhisneach
Discourse, *s* Comhradh, comh-labhairt, bruidhinn, cainnt; searmoin
Discourse, *v n.* Labhair, bruidhinn, dean cainnt, arguinn.
Discourser, *s* Labhairtear, òraidiche
Discoursive, *a.* Comhradhach, comhraiteach, arguinneach.
Discourteous, *a.* Borb, neo-shiobhailte, dorganta, mi-mhodhail.
Discourtesy, *s.* Buirbe, neo-shiobhailteachd, mi-mhodh
Discous, *a* Leathan, leabagach.
Discredit, *s* Mi-chreideas; tàir, mi-chliù, sgainneal, mi-mheas
Discredit, *v.* Di-chreid, mi-earb, naraich, sgainnilich
Discreet, *a* Glic, crionna; suairc, tuigseach, modhail, siobhailt; faicilleach, faiceallach, geimnidh, stuama.
Discreetly, *adv* Gu glic, gu crionna, gu suairce, gu tuigseach, gu modhail, gu siobhailt, gu faiceallach.
Discreetness, *s* Crionnachd, suairceas, tuigse, modhaileachd, siobhailteachd, faiceallachd.
Discrepancy, *s.* Diubhair, eag-samhuileachd, neo-freagairachd
Discrepant, *a* Eu-cordach, eag-samhail.
Discretion, *s* Crionnachd, eagnadh, stuaim, stuamachd; ailghios, toil. At your discretion, *air d' ailghios.*
Discretionary, *a* Neo-cheangailte, gun bhacadh. Discretionary power, *làn chomds.*
Discriminable, *a.* So-chomharachadh, so-aithneach
Discriminate, *v.* Comharaich, diubharaich, tagh, atharraich, eadar-dhealaich.
Discrimination, *s* Eadar-dhealachadh; comharachadh, atharrachadh, diubhrachadh.
Discriminative, *a* Diubharach, diubhrachail.
Discumbering, *s.* Leth-luidhe.
Discursive, *a.* Seabhaiseach, seabhasach, siùbhlach, luaineach; comhraideach, briathrach, arguinneach
Discursory, *a* Arguinneach
Discus, *s.* Leac-peilisdeir, cloch-neart.

Discuss, *v.* Sgrud, rannsuich, ceasnaich, arguinn; bris; bruan, spealg.
Discusser, *s.* Sgrudair, ceasnachair; arguinnear.
Discussion, *s.* Sgrudadh, ceasnuchadh, rannsachadh; cnuasachadh, arguinn, argumaid; bocadh.
Disdain, *v. a.* Dean tair, tarcuisich, fanaid, cuir cùl; cas. I would disdain to do it, *cha b' fhiach leam a dheanamh.*
Disdain, *s.* Spid, tair, tarcuis, dimeas, fanaid; miothlachd; ardan, stràice, sgailleas.
Disdainful, *a.* Spideil, tàireil, tarcuiseach, dimeasail; sgailleasach; ardanach, straiceil, uaibhreach Disdainfully, *gu spideil, gu tàireil, gu tarcuiseach, gu dimeasail, gu stràiceil, gu h-uaibhreach.*
Disdainfulness, *s.* Spidealachd, tairealachd, tarcuiseachd; ardanachd, stràicealachd, sgailleasachd.
Disease, *s.* Galar, tinneas, eucail; euslainnte, plaigh; macraidh, casadh, tamh; othras.
Disease, *v. a.* Eucailich; saruich, claoidh, cradh.
Diseased, *a* Galarach, eucaileach, tinn, euslan, neo-fhallain
Diseasedness, *s* Galarachd, eucaileachd, tinneas, euslainnteachd.
Disedged, *a* Maol, gun fhaobhar.
Disembark, *v.* Cuir air tìr, tìrich; rach air tìr.
Disembarkation, *s.* Tìreachadh.
Disembarrass, *v.* Fuasgail, tuasgail, saor.
Disembarrassment, *s.* Fuasgladh, tuasgladh
Disembitter, *v* Milsich.
Disembodied, *a.* Neo-chorporra, neo-chorpail, spioradail.
Disembogue, *v* Doirt, taom
Disembowelled, *a* Air a thoirt as a mhionach.
Disembroil, *v. a* Fuasgail, liothair o iomcheist, sgaoil, leig ma réir
Disenable, *v. a.* Ciùrr, leòn; anfhannaich.
Disenchant, *v. a* Bris druidheachd (no) buidseachd.
Disencumber, *v. a.* Eutromaich; fuasgail.
Disencumbrance, *s.* Eutromachadh.
Disengage, *v a.* Fuasgail, cuir ma réir, saor, sgaoil, cuir fa sgaoil Disengaged, *fuasgailte, neo-cheangailte, saorta, fa sgaoil.*
Disengagement, *s.* Fuasgladh; saorsainn; socair
Disentangle, *v a* Réitich, fuasgail, tuasgail, thoir as a chéile, cuir ma reir, cuir fa sgaoil, saor Disentangled, *réitichte, fuasgailte, tuasgailte, saor, fa sgaoil, as a chéile.*
Disentanglement, *s.* Réiteachadh, fuasgladh, tuasgladh.
Disenthral, *v.* Saor, cuir fa sgaoil.
Disenthrone, *v.* Di-chathairich
Disespouse, *v. a.* Eadar-dhealaich.
Disesteem, *v.* Dean dimeas, cuir air mi-shuim (no) air bheag suim
Disesteem, *s.* Di-meas, mi-shuim, beag suim.
Disfavour, *s.* Cion-fabhair, cion-maoidhein.
Disfiguration, *s.* Duaichneachadh, mi-dhreachadh
Disfigure, *v. a.* Duaichnich, mill, salaich, gné-mhill.
Disfigurement, *s* Duaichneachadh, milleadh, salachadh
Disforest, *v* Treabh, thoir sìgh, di-fhrithich.
Disfranchise, *v. a.* Di-chòirich
Disfranchisement, *s.* Di-chòireachadh.
Disglorify, *v.* Di-ghlòirich, cuir air di-meas, mi-chliùich
Disgorge, *v.* Sgeith, tilg, ursluig. Disgorged, *sgeithte, tilgte, air a sgeith, air a thilgeadh*, disgorging, *a sgeith, a tilgeadh.*

Disgrace, *s.* Tàmailt, masladh, nàir; tarcuis, tair sgainneal, droch-ainm. In disgrace, *fu thàmailt, fo mhasladh.*

Disgrace, *v. a.* Tàmailtich, maslaich, naraich, cuir gu nàir, sgainnealaich; cuir air falbh, cuir as inmhe, cuir fu mhi-chliù. He is disgraced, *tha e fu thàmailt*, (*no*) *fu mhi-chliu.*

Disgraceful, *a.* Tàmailteach, maslach, nàr, narach, gràineil. Disgracefully, *gu tàmailteach.*

Disgracefulness, *s.* Tamailteachd, maslachd.

Disgracious, *a.* Neo-thaitneach, neo-chiatach.

Disguise, *v. a.* Céil, folaich, atharraich cruth, cuir am anriochd; duaichnich.

Disguise, *s.* Céileadh, folachadh, aimhriochd, an-riochd, gise, gidhis; feall-chruth.

Disguisement, *s.* Céileachadh.

Disguiser, *s.* Gisear, gidhisear; duaichniche.

Disgust, *s.* Déistinn, sgàth, gràin, sgreamh, fuath, droch-bhlas; droch-ghean.

Disgust, *v. a.* Deistinn, gràinich; oilltich, gabh déistinn, (*no*) fuath; gabh sgreamh, fùrlaich ri, gabh sgàth.

Disgustful, *a.* Deistinneach, gràineil, fuathach; mi-bhlasda.

Dish, *s.* Mias; saothach, soitheach, troinnsear, aigheann; measair; ballan; biadh.

Dish, *v. a.* Riaraich.

Dishabille, *s.* Leth-aodach; leth-uigheam.

Dish-clout, *s.* Clut-soithichean.

Dishearten, *v. a.* Mì-mhisnich, cuir a misneach. Disheartened, *fu mhi-mhisneach.*

Dishevel, *v. a.* Sgaòil folt, sgaoil gruaig.

Dishonest, *a.* Neo-onorach, eas-ionraic, bradach, goideach; cealgach, fealltach.

Dishonesty, *s.* Eas-onoir, méirle, braide, goideachd, gad-uigheachd; mi-mhacantas, mi-gheimnidheachd.

Dishonour, *v. a.* Mi-chliùich, maslaich, nàraich, tàmailtich; eas-urramaich; (*a female*), truaill, truaillich; (*censure*), cronaich, coirich.

Dishonour, *s.* Mi-chliù, masladh, nàir, tamailt, eas-urram; eas-onoir, sgainneal; (*of a female*), truailleadh; (*censure*), cronachadh, coireachadh.

Dishonourable, *a.* Nàr, nàrach, tàmailteach, tàireil, eas onorach, neo-urramach. Dishonourably, *gu nàr, gu tamailteach.*

Dishonourer, *s.* Fear-mi-mhodhail; truailliche.

Dishumour, *s.* Droch-ghean.

Disincarcerate, *v. a.* Saor, cuir fa sgaoil, cuir fa réir.

Disinclination, *s.* Ain-deonachd, mi-thoil, neo-thoirt, cion tograidh; coimheiseachd.

Disinclined, *a.* Ain-deonach, mi-thoileach, coimheis.

Disingenuity, *s.* Ceilge, foill, mi-ionracas.

Disingenuous, *a.* Cealgach, fealltach, neo-fhìreannach, eas-ionraic, sligheach; eolach, ceabhachdach. Disingenuously, *gu cealgach; gu sligheach.*

Disingenuousness, *s.* Ceilge, cealgachd, fealltachd, eas-ionracas; ceabhachdaireachd.

Disinherit, *v. a.* Cuir as a chòir, di-chòirich; fògair, thoir còir-bhreith o. He disinherited him, *thug e' chòir-bhreith uaithe.*

Disinter, *v.* Ais-adhlaic.

Disinterest, *s.* Còir, dochann; coimheiseachd.

Disinterested, *a.* Neo-bhuntuinneach; neo-fhein-chuiseach; fior, ceart, fìreannach, ionraic.

Disinterestedness, *s.* Ceirte, fìrinn, ionracas.

Disjoin, *v. a.* Dealaich, thoir as a chéile, roinn, sgar.

Disjoint, *v. a.* Cuir as an alt, dealaich, thoir as a chéile, fuasgail, bris, bruan, reub na mhìreannan.

Disjointed, *a.* As an alt; dealaichte; as a cheile; briste, bruanta, reubte.

Disjunct, *a.* Dealaichte; as a chéile.

Disjunction, *s.* Dealachadh, sgaradh, sgarachduinn, fuasgladh, briseadh, reubadh, bruanadh, spealgadh; (*disagreement*), eas-aonachd.

Disjunctive, *a.* Eas-aonachail, neo-chordach.

Disk, *s.* Aghaidh na greine, (*no*) na gealaich, gnuis reul sam bi; peil'stear; clach-nairt.

Diskindness, *s.* Mi-shuairceas, mi-chaoimhneas, cion-seirce.

Dislike, *s.* Fuath, mi-thaitneachd; grain, mio-thlachd, cion-graidh. She has a dislike to him, *tha fuath aice dhàth, tha gràin aice roimhe.*

Dislike, *v. a.* Fuathaich, oilltich ri. I dislike it, *cha toigh leam e, dh'oilltich mi ris.*

Dislikeness, *s.* Eu-coslachd, ea-cosmhalachd.

Dislimb, *v. a.* Di-bhallaich, di-bhall; reub as a chéile.

Dislocate, *v. a.* Cuir as an alt; dinaitt. He dislocated his foot, *chuir e 'chas as an alt.*

Dislocation, *s.* Dol as an alt, dinaiteadh.

Dislodge, *v. a.* Cuir as an aite; fògair; cuir air falbh; iomain a mach, cuir air imirich.

Disloyal, *a.* Mi-rioghail, neo-dhìleas do 'n righ, eas-ionraic, neo-dhìleas.

Disloyalty, *s.* Mi-rioghalachd, neo-dhilseachd, eas-ionracas, eas-umhlachd, traoightearachd.

Dismal, *a.* Brònach, muladach, dubhach; neo-shubhach; oillteil, uamhasach, eagallach, dorcha, doilleir, neo-shuilbhear, uaigneach. Dismally, *gu brònach, gu muladach, gu dubhach, gu neo-shubhach, gu h-oillteil, gu h-eagallach, gu dorcha, gu h-uaigneach.*

Dismalness, *s.* Doirche, dorchadas, dubhachas; oillteal-achd, uamhasachd, uaigneachd.

Dismantle, *v. a.* Lom, dean lom; mi-sgeadaich; tilg sios, sgrios.

Dismask, *v.* Leig ris, foillsich, nochd.

Dismast, *v. a.* Di-chrannaich. Dismasted, *di-chrannaichte.*

Dismay, *v. a.* Cuir oillt (*no*) eagal air; creanaich, meataich.

Dismay, *s.* Oillt, eagal, crith-eagal, uamhann; aithmheal; cion-misnich, meatachd, fàitcheas.

Disme, *s.* Deicheamh; càin, cìse.

Dismember, *v. a.* Di-bhall; dì-bhallaich, spion as a cheile; gearr na mhìreannan, bris, bruan, spealg.

Dismiss, *v. a.* Cuir air falbh, cuir fu sgaoil, thoir cead do. He dismissed them, *chuir e air falbh iad, chuir e fa sgaoil iad, thug e 'n cead doibh.*

Dismissed, *part.* Air falbh; fa sgaoil, air a chur fa sgaoil; sgaoilte.

Dismission, *s.* Sgaoileadh; *disearsadh.*

Dismount, *v. a.* and *n.* Cuir (*no*) tilg sios; teirinn bhàrr eich, tuirlinn, tuirling.

† **Dissatured**, *a.* Mi-nadurra.

Disobedience, *s.* Eas-umhlachd, ceannairc.

Disobedient, *a.* Eas-umhal, mi-dhleasnach, ceannairceach; ceann-laidir, neo-striochdail.

Disobey, *v. a.* Bi eas-umhal, bi mi-dhleasnach; na toir umhlachd; bris ordugh, na striochd. Disobey him, *na toir umhlachd dha.*

Disobligation, *s.* Oilbheum; di-chomain.

Disoblige, *v. a.* Diùlt, thoir oilbheum.

Disobliging, *s.* Neo-shiobhailt, oilbheumach, mi-mhodhail. Disobligingly, *gu neo-shiobhailt, gu h-oilbheumach.*

Disobligingness, *s.* Neo-shiobhailteachd, oilbheumachd, mi-mhodhaileachd.

Disorder, *s.* Eas-ordugh, mi-riaghailt, buaireas; comhstri; tuasaid; aimhreite; (*disease*), eucail tinneas, galar. In disorder, *troimh chéile, thar a chéile, air feadh chéile.*

Disorder, *v. a.* Cuir a ordugh, buair, cuir air feadh chéile, cuir thar a chéile, eucailich, galaraich

Disordered, *a* Mi-riaghailteach, buairte; aingidh; druiseach; (*in mind*), thar céill, gòrach.

Disorderly, *a* Mi-riaghailteach, gun riaghailt, mi-laghail; gun doigh, aingidh, drùiseach, gun ordugh

Disordinate, *a* Ana-measarra, aingidh, neo-gheimnidh.

Disown, *v* Diùlt, àicheadh, na gabh ri, seun, cuir cùl ri

† **Dispand**, *v* Sgaoil a mach, spréid

Dispansion, *s* Sgaoileadh, spréideadh

Disparage, *v.* Dean tàir, (no) tarcuis; fanoid, dean spreig, thoir mi chliù, cuir air di-meas, cuir suarrach.

Disparagement, *s* Tàir, tarcuis, mi-chliù, spreig, fanaid, tarcuis, sgainneal

Disparager, *s* Tarcuisiche, di-meusair

Disparity, *s* Diubhar, eag-samhlachd, ea-cosmhalachd, eu-coslas, neo-ionannachd

Dispart, *v* Roinn, dealaich, bris, sgain, sgoilt Disparted, *roinnte, dealaichte*

Dispassion, *s* Soimeachd (no) socair inntinn

Dispassionate, *a* Soimeach, socrach, riaghailteach, cne asta, neo-chlaon Dispassionately, *gu soimeach, gu socrach*

Dispel, *v. a* Sgap, sgaoil, ruaig, sgànraich, iomain, sgiùrs air falbh, fògair, iom-ruaig, iom-sgaoil

Dispensary, *s.* Leigheas-lann

Dispensate, *v* Roinn, riaraich

Dispensation, *s* Riarachadh, roinneadh, fritheal̇adh, cead, comas, saorsainn, comas o 'n Phàp

Dispensator, *s* Riarachair, roinneadair, frithealair

Dispense, *v a* Fritheil, roinn, riaraich, builich, ceadaich, bi as dith Dispensing blessings, *a builеachadh bheannachd*, I cannot dispense with it, *cha 'n urradh dhomh bhith as a dhìth*

† **Dispense**, *s* Cead, comas

Dispenser, *s* Frithealaiche, roinneadair, riarachair, tabhairtear

Dispeople, *v.* Fàsaich, di-threabhaich, sgrios, dean fàs Dispeopled, *fùsaichte, fàs, dithreabhach.*

Dispeopler, *s* Dìthreabhaiche; sgriosadair, milltear

Disperse, *v* Sgap, sgaoil, spreigh; fuadaich, ruaig, iomsgaoil, iom-ruaig, sgànraich, roinn, riaraich Dispersed, *sgapta, sgaoilte, fuadaichte, fa sgaoil*

Disperser, *s* Sgapair, sgaoiltear, fuadachair, ruagair, sgànraiche

Dispersion, *s* Sgaoileadh, sgapadh, ruaig, fuadachadh, sgànradh, iom-sgaoileadh.

Dispirit, *v a* Mi-mhisnich, meataich, cuir cagal air

Dispirited, *a* Neo-bheò, neo-bheothail, meata, neo-smiorail, fu cagal

Dispiritedness, *s* Mi-mhisneach, meatachd, cion-misnich; tuirse

Displace, *v a* Cuir a àite; cuir thar a chéile (no) a lathailt, cuir air falbh

Displacency, *s* Mi-mhòdhaileachd, sgreite

Displant, *s* Ath-shuidhich, ath-phlanndaich, cuir imirich, fuadaich.

Displantation, *s* Ath-shuidhcachadh; atharrachadh sluaigh, fuadachadh, imirich.

Display, *v* Feuch, foillsich, leig ris, nochd, sgaoil a mach; tog san t-sealladh.

Display, *s.* Feuchainn, foillseachadh; sealladh.

Displease, *v. a.* and *n.* Mi-thaitinn, thoir oilbheum; dean diomach, cuir mio-thlachd, cuir diom. It displeased him, *cha d' thainig e ris.*

Displeased, *a* Diomach, diombach, diombuidhcach, neo-thoilichte, mi-thoilichte, neo-bhuidheach.

Displeasure, *s.* Corruich, fearg, feirge, diom; oilbheum.

Displosion, *s* Braidhe.

Disport, *s.* Cluiche, spuirt, iolath, ealuidh, *dibhearsain.*

Disport, *v.* Cluich, dean spuirt, dean ioladh; mir.

Disposable, *a* So-bhuileachadh, so-sheachnadh, so-reiceadh, a dh' fhaodar bhuileachadh, a dh' fhaodar reiceadh.

Disposal, *s.* Riaghailt; riaghladh, sgòd, còir; builеachadh, tabhairt, *comannt* At thy disposal, *fo 'd sgòid.*

Dispose, *v* Orduich, cuir an ordugh; builich, thoir air falbh; aom, rùnaich; (*dispose of*), reic, creic, thoir air falbh, (*disposed*), air a chur an ordugh, aomta; (*disposed of*), reicte.

Dispose, *s.* Ughdarras, urradh, seoladh, riaghailt, sgòd.

Disposer, *s.* Riaghladair, fear-riaghlaidh

Disposition, *s* Nadur, gné, càil, tùr; cridhe, ordugh, riaghailt

Dispossess, *v a* Cuir a seilbh, cuir as àite; dibir, thoir o.

Dispraise, *s.* Di-moladh, coir, cron, dimeas, tarcuis, mi-chliù

Dispraise, *v a.* Di-mhol, coirich, cronaich; dean tàir.

Dispraiser, *s* Di mheasair, di mholadair.

Dispread, *v a* Iom-sgaoil, sgap.

Disprofit, *s* Call, calldach, earchall

Disproportion, *s* Mi-chumadh; eu-cumadh, mi-dhealbhachd; mi-chothromachd, mi-fhreagarrachd, neo-ionannachd

Disproportion, *v a.* Mi-chum, mi-dhealbh, mi-chothromaich.

Disproportional, *a* Eu-cumadail, neo-ionann, neo-chothromach, neo-chuimir, neo-fhreagarrach, a cumadh, thar cumadh

Disproportionate. See **Disproportional**

Disprove, *v* Breugaich, breugnaich, fallsaich, mi-chòmhdaich, mi-dhearbh

Disprover, *s* Breuguachair.

Disputable, *a* Connsachail, comh-strigheach, neo-shonraichte; neo-chinnteach

Disputant, *s* Connspaidiche, connsachair, argumneach, deasboir, conspair

Disputation, *s.* Connsachadh, deasboireachd, connspoid, tagradh, argumn, argumaid

Disputatious, *a* Connsachail, deasboireach, argumneach

Dispute, *s* Connsach, connsachadh, argumn, tabaid, connspoid, tagradh, cur a mach, droch-cordadh

Dispute, *v a.* and *n* Connsaich, deasboirich, argumn, tagair, cuir a mach, cum a mach

Disputer, *s* Connsachair, deasboir, deasboiriche; fear tagraidh.

Disqualification, *s* Eas-urrainn; ea-comas, mi-mhurrachas

Disqualify, *v a* Dean ea-comasach (no) mi-mhurrach.

Disquiet, *s* Mi-shuaimhneas, mi-shuaimhneachd; buaireas; farran, iomaguin, an-shocair, mi-fhoisneachd; cion fois.

Disquiet, *v.* Mi-shuaimhnich, buair, cuir dragh air.

Disquietness, *s* Mi-shuaimhneas, mi-shuaimhneachd, buaireas, farran, iomaguin, an-shocair, mi-fhoisneachd; brion.

Disquietude, *s.* Mi-shuaimhneas, buaireas, iomaguin; mi-fhoisneachd, an-shocair; brion

Disquisition, *s.* Rannsuchadh, ceasnachadh, sgrudadh, deasboireachd.

Disregard, *s.* Mi-sheadh, mi-shuim, dearmad; tarcuis.

Disregard, *v. a.* Cuir air bheag seadh, (no) air mi-shuim, cuir air dearmad, leig air dearmad, tarcuisich.

Disregardful, *a.* Mi-sheadhar, neo-shuimeil, dearmadach; tarcuiseach.

Disrelish, *s.* Deistinn, gràin, sgreamh, droch-bhlas.

Disreputable, *s.* Neo-onorach, tàireil, dearmadach, tarcuiseach, tàmailteach.

Disreputable, *a.* Eas-onorach, sgainnealach, tàmailteach.

Disreputation, *s.* Tàir, mi-chliù, tamailt.

Disrepute, *s.* Droch iomradh, easonoir, di-cliù, easurram.

Disrespect, *s.* Eas-urram, dìmeas, tarcuis, tàir, mi-mhodh, cion-modha.

Disrespectful, *a.* Eas-urramach, di-measach, tarcuiseach, tàireil; mi-mhodhail. Disrespectfully, *gu h-easurramach, gu mi-mhodhail.*

Disrespectfulness, *s.* Easurramachd, tarcuiseachd, mimhodhaileachd.

Disrobe, *v. a.* Lom, dean lom, neo-sgeadaich, rùisg.

Disruption, *s.* Sgàineadh, sgoltadh, briseadh; bearn.

Dissatisfaction, *s.* Mi-thaitneachd; diomachd, diombachd; neo-thoileachas inntinn.

Dissatisfactory, *a.* Neo-thaitneach.

Dissatisfied, *a* Neo-thoilichte, neo-bhuidheach, diomach, diombach

Dissatisfy, *v.* Mi-thaitinn, mi-thoilich, na tig ri It dissatisfied him, *mhi-thaitinn e ris, cha tàinig e ris.*

Dissect, *v.* Gearr as a chéile, snàs; gearr; sgrud.

Dissection, *s.* Gearradh; snàsadh, snasadaireachd, corpshnasadaireachd

Dissector, *s.* Snàsadair, corp-shnasadair

Dissemble, *v. a.* Leig ort, gabh ort, céil, folaich, na leig ris; meall.

Dissembler, *s.* Cealgair, mealltair, fear fuar-chrabhaidh

Dissemblingly, *adv.* Gu cealgach, gu mealltach.

Disseminate, *v. a.* Sgap, siol-chuir, sgaoil, craobh-sgaoil; iom-sgaoil.

Dissemination, *s.* Sgapadh, siol-chur, sgaoileadh; iomsgaoileadh.

Disseminator, *s* Sgaoilear, sgapadair.

Dissension, *s* Eas-aonachd, easontas, droch-cordadh, cur a mach, connsach, connspoid, tabaid, aimhreite.

Dissensious, *a.* Eas-aonach, eas-aontach; tuasaideach, connspoideach, tabaideach, aimhreiteach, taglinneach, iorghuilleach.

Dissent, *v. a.* Dealaich, bi air chaochladh barail; easaontaich, sgar o.

Dissent, *s* Dealachadh, eas-aontachd, eas-aontachadh.

Dissentaneous, *a.* Eas-aontachail; neo-chubhaidh, neofhreagarrach

Dissenter, *s* Fear dealachaidh, eas-aontachair, fear a dhiultas commun ris an Eaglais Shasunnach

Dissertation, *s* Rannsuchadh, sgrudadh.

Disserve, *v. a* Ciùrr, dochainn, dochannaich

Disservice, *s.* Ciurradh, dochann, lochd, cron

Disserviceable, *a.* Dochannach, ciurrail.

Dissilience, *s.* Sgagadh, sgoltadh.

Dissilient, *a.* Sgagach, sgoltach, sgàinteach.

Dissimilar, *a.* Eu-cosmhuil, neo-chosmhuil, neo-choslach, eag-samhuil, neo-ionann.

Dissimilarity, *s.* Eu-cosmhuileachd, eag-samhladh, eagsamhuileachd; neo-ionannachd.

Dissimilitude, *s.* Eu-cosmhuileachd, eag-samhlachd, neoionannachd, diubhair.

Dissimulation, *s.* Crabhadh, fuar-chrabhadh, cealgaireachd, ceilge, mealltaireachd, blanndar, gnùis-mhealladh, beul-ghradh, cluain.

Dissipable, *a* So-sgapaidh.

Dissipate, *v a.* Sgaoil, sgap, caith, dean ana-caitheamh

Dissipated, *a.* Caithteach, struigheil, strodhail, struigheasach, ana-measarra, neo-gheimnidh, mi-chneasta, mistuama.

Dissipation, *s* Ana-caitheamh, caitheamh, struighe, strogha, struighealachd, stroghalachd, sgaoilteachd

Dissociate, *v* Dealaich, eadar-dhealaich

Dissolvable, *a* So-leaghadh, a ghabhas leaghadh

Dissolve, *v a* Leagh; fuasgail, tuasgail; sgaoil, dealaich

Dissolvent, *a* Leaghach, leaghtach

Dissolute, *a.* Neo-shuidhichte, neo-gheimnidh, fuasgailte, fiadhaich, ana-cneasta, ana-measarra; mear, drùiseil, dionasgach. Dissolutely, *gu h-ana cneasta, gu h-ana measarra*

Dissoluteness, *s* Neo-gheimnidheachd; ana-cneastachd, ana-measarrachd, mire, drùis.

Dissolution, *s.* Leaghadh, fuasgladh; (*of an assembly*), sgaoileadh, (*of morals*), mi-gheimnidheachd, (*of the body*), bàs, caochladh, sgrios.

Dissonance, *s* Neo-chordadh; seirbhe-ciùil.

Dissonant, *a* Searbh, neo-fhonnmhor; eu-cordach

Dissuade, *v. a* Ath-chomhairlich Dissuaded, *ath-chomhairlichte.*

Dissuader, *s* Ath-chomhairliche.

Dissuasion, *s.* Ath-chomhairle.

Dissuasive, *a.* Ath-chomhairleach

Dissyllable, *s.* Dà-shioladh

Distaff, *s.* Cuigeil

Distain, *v a* Salaich

Distance, *s* Astar, céin, uighe, eadar-fhonn, urram, meas Keep your distance, *cum agad fhein*

Distance, *v a.* Fag, rach seachad air

Distant, *a* Fad air falbh, an'céin, céin, air astar; (*in a manner*), neo-shulchair, fad thall, coimheach.

Distaste, *s.* Deistinn, sgàth, gràin, sgreamh, coidheiseachd, cion-gradh, mi-chiat.

Distasteful, *a* Déistinneach, sgàthail, gràineil, grada, neo-thaitneach; olc-nadurra

Distemper, *s.* Galar, tinneas, eucail, droch ghean.

Distemper, *v. a.* Galraich, eucailich, buair Distempered, *fo eucail, làn eucail; fu bhuaireas*

Distemperature, *s* Buaireas, mi-riaghailt, boile

Distend, *v. a.* Leudaich, meudaich, sgaoil, boc.

Distension, *s.* Leudachadh, meudachadh, sgaoileadh, bocadh.

Distich, *s.* Caraid rann, ceathramh

Distil, *v. a* and *n* Tarruing, sil, tog, drùidh Distil whisky, *tog (no) tarruing uisge beatha*, he is distilling, *tha e a togail, tha e ris an tarruing;* distilling honey, *a sileadh meala*

Distillation, *s.* Sileadh; druidheadh, tarruing, grudaireachd

Distiller, *s.* Grudair; fear togalach, fear poit.

Distinct, *a* Air leth, leis fein; poncail; osgarra, eugsamhuil; ballach. That is a distinct case, *is cuis air leth sin, is rud leis fein sin.*

Distinction, *s.* Diubhar, diubhair; mùthadh; dealach, dealachadh, eadar-dhealachadh; atharrachadh; onoir, urram, meas; inbhe; eug-samhuileachd; tuigse.

Distinctive, *a.* Diubharach; tuigseach.

Distinctly, *adv.* Gu poncail, gu h-osgarra; gu soilleir. Speak distinctly, *labhair gu poncail.*

Distinguish, *v.* Diubharaich; dealaich; cuir dealach eadar comharraich; sonraich; aithnich; dean follais; dean ainmeil, urramaich.

Distinguishable, *a.* So-chomharrachadh, so-aithneachadh; airidh air cliù.

Distinguished, *a.* Ainmeil, cliùiteach, comharraichte; sònruichte.

Distinguisher, *s.* Breitheamh; diubharaiche.

Distort, *v. a.* Toinneamh, toinn, sniomh, cam, crom, cas.

Distortion, *s.* Toinneamh; sniomhadh; camadh, crom, casadh; (*of the mouth*), braoisg, goill.

Distract, *v.* Buair, claoidh, sàraich; cuir an iom-cheist; cuir air chuthach; cuir thar a cheile; iom-tharruing; dealaich, roinn. Distracted, *buairte, claoidhte, sàruichte; air a chuthach, air bhoile.*

Distractedly, *adv.* Gu mi-chéillidh, gu buaireasach, gu bainnidheach.

Distraction, *s.* Dealachadh, eadar-dhealachadh; iom-cheist; claoidh, saruchadh; cuthach, boile; aimhreite, mi-riaghailt, eas-ordugh.

Distrain, *v.* Glac, dein breith air éigin.

Distrainer, *s.* Glacadair.

Distraint, *s.* Glacadh, breith air éigin.

Distress, *s.* An shocair, amhghar, tinneas; teanntachd, cruaidh-char; claoidheadh, saruchadh, eigin, teinn, airc; trioblaid; bochduinn; deuchainn; cruaidhaig, cruadhail; glacadh.

Distress, *v.* Sàruich, claoidh; buair; cuir gu trioblaid; glac, dean laimh.

Distressed, *a.* An-shocrach, truagh, bochd, fu thrioblaid.

Distressful, *a.* Truagh, anshocrach, trioblaideach; bochd, craiteach.

Distribute, *v.* Roinn; comh-roinn; riaraich, pàirtich; fritheil.

Distribution, *s.* Roinn, comh-roinn; riarachadh, pairteachadh; frithealadh, fritheal.

Distributive, *a.* Roinneadail, riarachail.

District, *s.* Taobh dùcha, earainn, slios, cearn, maorsainneachd; sgìreachd; duthaich.

Distrust, *v. a.* An-earb, cuir amharus, mi-chreid, thoir mi-chreideas.

Distrust, *s.* An-earbsadh; amharus, teagamh, mi-mhuinghinn.

Distrustful, *a.* An-earbsach, amharusach; teagamhach; mi-mhuinghinneach; eagallach, meata, giorragach.

Distrustfulness, *s.* An-earbsachd, amharusachd.

Disturb, *v.* Buair, grab, cuir dragh air, bac, cuir moille, cuir miothlachd, cuir troimh-chéile. You disturb me, *tha thu cur dragh orm.*

Disturbance, *s.* Buaireas, iom-cheist, iom-guin, grabadh, mio-thlachd; tuasaid, tabaid, aimhreit, tuailleas.

Disturber, *s.* Buaireadair, fear aimhreite, aimhreitiche, tuailleasaiche.

Disunion, *s.* Dealachadh, sgaradh; eas-aontachadh, droch-cordadh, mi-chordadh.

Disunite, *v. a.* Dealaich, sgar, cuir eadar.

Disunity, *s.* Easaonachd, sgarachduinn.

Disuse, *s.* Ana-cleachd, ana-cleachdainn.

Disvaluation, *s.* Tàmailt, tàir; mi chliù; droch-iomradh.

Disvouch, *v. a.* Breugnaich, cuir an aghaidh, eu-comhdaich.

Ditch, *s.* Clais, staing, claidh, cladh, dìge; amar, eitridh.

Ditch, *v.* Claisich, cladhaich; staingich. Ditched, *claisichte, staingichte.*

Ditcher, *s.* Claisear, claisiche, dìgear; staingear, tochailtear, tochaillear.

Dithyrambic, *s.* Baoth-rann; oran molaidh do'n fhion.

Dithyrambic, *a.* Baoth, fiadhaich.

Dittany, *s.* Lus a phiobair.

Ditto, *s.* An ni ceudna, an rud roi-ainmichte.

Ditty, *s.* Oran, rann; duanag, luinneag.

Diuretic, *a.* Fual-bhrosdaidh.

Diurnal, *a.* Lathail, gach làtha.

Diurnally, *adv.* Gu lathail, gach là.

Diuturnity, *s.* Maireannachd, maireachdninn.

Divan, *s.* Ard chomhairle an Turcaich.

Divaricate, *v. a.* and *n.* Dealaich mar ni da rathad.

Divarication, *s.* Eadar-dhealachadh bharailean, eadar-dhealachadh rothadan.

Dive, *v.* Tom, tum, rach fo'n uisge, dubh-shnamh.

Diver, *s.* Tomadair, tumadair, dubh-shnamhair; gairgear.

Diverge, *v.* Dealaich mar ni da rathad.

Divers, *a.* Iomadh, iomad, iomadach, tuille is a h-aon; eag-samhuil.

Diverse, *a.* Ioma, iomadh, iomad; eug-samhuil.

Diversification, *s.* Mùghadh, mùthadh, caochladh, atharrachadh; eug-samhuileachd.

Diversify, *v. a.* Mùgh, mùth, atharraich; eug-samhlaich.

Diversion, *s.* Tionndadh gu taobh, cur a thaobh; claonadh; (*sport*), spuirt, spòrsa, ealaidh, ioladh, iolach, aighear, fearas-chuideachd, sùgradh, culiche, cluicheag, mire, mireag, abhachd, *dibhearsan.*

Diversity, *s.* Iolar, iolaras, cumasg, eu-coslas, neo-choslas; eadar-dhealachadh, saineas.

Divert, *v.* Tionndaidh, cuir gu taobh, claon; aom; breug, cum cluich ri.

Divertisement, *s.* Aighear, iolach, ioladh; cluiche.

Divest, *v.* Rùisg, neo-sgeadaich; lom, dean lomartach, thoir o.

+ Dividable, *a.* So-dhealachadh; so-phairteachadh.

Divide, *v. a.* and *n.* Roinn, pairtich, sgar, eadar-sgar; still. Divide it amongst you, *roinnibh eadaruibh e.*

Dividend, *s.* Cuid, roinn, earann, suim ri roinn.

Divider, *s.* Roinneadair, liadh.

Dividers, *s.* Gabhal-roinn.

Dividual, *a.* Roinnte, pàirtichte.

Divination, *s.* Fiosachd, fàisneachd, fàistinn, geasadaireachd, druidheachd; taraghail, fàidheadaireachd.

Divine, *a.* Naomh, neamhuidh, diadhaidh; ainglidh.

Divine, *s.* Diadhair, ministear, sagart, pears' eaglais.

Divine, *v. a.* Roi-innis, fàisnich, deàn faisneachd; baralaich; taraghail.

Diviner, *s.* Faidh, faidhcadair, fiosaiche, fear fiosachd, fàisniche, geasadair, druidh.

Divineness, *s.* Ban-fhaidh, ban-fhiosaiche, ban-gheasadair, ban-druidh.

Divinity, *s.* (*Theology*), diadhaireachd; (*a god*), diadhachd, dia; (*the Divinity*), an t-Ard Bhith, am Fear is fhearr.

Divisible, *a.* So-roinneadh, so-phairteachadh, a ghabhas roinn.

Division, *s.* Roinn, roinneadh, pairteachadh; dealachadh; easaonachd, sgaradh, pairt (no) earann do-shearmoin.

Divisor, *s.* Aireamh roinnidh (no) leis an roinnear; roinneadair.

Divorce, *s.* Dealachadh eadar fear agus a bhean; eadar-dhealachadh; litir-dhealachaidh.

Divorce, *v.* Eadar-dhealaich, dealaich. She divorced him, *dh' eadar-dhealaich i ris.*

Divorcement. See Divorce.

Divulge, *v. a.* Innis, fòillsich, gairm, dean follaiseach, nochd; craobh-sgaoil.

Divulger, *s.* Foillseachair, gairmeadair.

† **Dizzard**, *s.* Umaidh, guraiceach, burraidh, amadan.

Dizziness, *s.* Tuaineal, tuainealach, tuaicheal; clodh-ghalar, uim-chlodh.

Dizzy, *a.* Tuainealach, ann an tuaicheal, eutrom, gaoithe, faoin, neo-smuainteachail.

Do, *v. a.* Dean, gnathaich, cuir an gniomh; criochnaich. This will do, *ni so an gnothach; ni so am put;* how do you do? *cia mar a tha thu?* what had I better do? *ciod is fhearr dhomh dheanamh?* much to do, *mòran ri dheanamh;* what dost thou? *ciod ris a bheil thu? ciod mu bheil thu?*

Docile, *a.* So-theagasg, so-ionnsachadh.

Dock, *s.* Copag, copagach.

Dock, *s.* Bun earbuill, rumpall.

Dock, *s.* (*For ships*), long-phort; nos-luingeis.

Dock, *v.* Gearr, dean cutach, dean dùitseach.

Docked, *a.* Gearrta, cutach, dùitseach. A docked cock, *coileach duitseach.*

Dock-cresses, *s.* Duilleag mhaith.

Doctor, *s.* Ollamh, leigh, damh oid, teallsanach, *dochdair.* Doctor of laws, *ollamh lagh;* doctor of medicine, *ollamh leigheis;* doctor in divinity, *ollamh diadhaireachd.*

Doctor, *v.* Leigheas; *dochdairich.*

Doctorship, *s.* Ollamhachd; *dochdaireachd.*

Doctrinal, *a.* Teagasgail, foghlumail.

Doctrine, *s.* Foghlum, teagasg, aithne, oilean, oileanachd, faoladh, † foircheadal; ealadhan.

Document, *s.* Aithne, riaghailt, ordugh, seòladh; sparradh.

Dodge, *v. a.* Meall, bi ri ceabhacaireachd.

Dodman, *s.* Seorsa faoich.

Doe, *s.* Earb, maoisleach, èilid, agh. Does, *earbaichean.*

Doer, *s.* Deanadair, gniomhair, fear gnàthachaidh.

Doff, *v. a.* Cuir dhiot, cuir a bhàn, cuir dheth; cuir dàil, dàilich.

Dog, *s.* Cu, madadh, mastaidh, cuilean, madradh, gaothar; † gregh. Dogs, *coin, madraidh;* you dog! *a choin! a choin tha thu ann!*

Dog, *v. a.* Faigh a mach, sir, lorgaich, lorg, sròinich.

Dog-berry, *s.* Coinbhil.

Dog-bolt, *s.* Garbhan.

Dog-briar, *s.* Coindreas, coindris, coin-droighionn, preas nam mucag.

Dogcheap, *a.* Saor, neo-luachmhor.

Dog-days, *s.* An t-iuchar, airde an t-shamhraidh.

Doge, *s.* Ard-dhiuchd ann taobh tuath na h-Eadailt.

Dog-fish, *s.* Gobag, murlach.

Dog-fly, *s.* Creadhal, seorsa cuileig.

Dogged, *a.* Doirbh, iargalta, duranta, neo-gheanail, coimheach, gruamach; cainnteach; bodachail. Doggedly, *gu doirbh.*

Doggedness, *s.* Doirbhe, durantachd, iargaltas, coimheachas.

Dogger, *s.* Luing Dhùitseach le aon chrann.

Doggerel, *a.* Neo-chialach, neo-ghrinn, gràd.

Doggess, *s.* Galladh.

Doggish, *a.* Madrail, madachail; dùr; duranta, brùideil, crosda, sgiorrail, doirbh.

Doghearted, *a.* Cruaidh-chridheach, cruadalach.

Dog-hole, *s.* Fail-chon; conbhair; coit.

Dog-louse, *s.* Mial-chon.

Dogma, *s.* Barail-shuidhichte, barail shocraichte.

Dogmatic, *a.* Suidhichte, socraichte; smachdail, diorrasach, ainneanta.

Dogmatist, *s.* Fear fèin-bharaileach.

Dog's-ear, *s.* Gearan.

Dog's-meat, *s.* Fuighleach, fuigheal, spruilleach, spronnan.

Dog-star, *s.* Reul na h-iucharach do'n goirear *Sirius.*

Dog-trick, *s.* Droch-phrat.

Dog-weary, *a.* Sgìth, air toirt thairis, cho sgith ri cù.

Doily, *s.* Seorsa oluinn; tuailte bheag a chuirear fu ghloinichean bùird.

Doings, *s.* Deanadas, deantanas, gniomh, dol a mach, caith-beatha; iomairt, ioladh, ealaidh.

Doit, *s.* Cùin bheag.

Dole, *s.* Cuid, pairt; cuid an tràth.

† **Dole**, *s.* Bròn, dubhachas.

Doleful, *a.* Brònach, dubhach, muladach, dulbhar, tuirseach, deistinneach. Dolefully, *gu brònach, gu muladach.*

Dolesome, *a.* Brònach, dubhach, muladach, tuirseach, trom, trom-inntinneach, neo-shunntach.

Doll, *s.* Gilleagan, luag, leanabh liudhach, leanabh leinibh, culaidh chleasachd leinibh, dealbh, dealbh-chruth.

Dollar, *s.* Dolar.

Dolorific, *a.* Muladach, trioblaideach.

Dolorous, *a.* Brònach, muladach, tuirseach; goirt, piantachail.

Dolour, *s.* Bròn, mulad, tuirse, cumha; pian, cradh.

Dolphin, *s.* Leumadair.

Dolt, *s.* Buraidh, baoghlan, baothair, gu uraiceach, tamhanach, umaidh, corra-cheann.

Doltish, *a.* Buraidheach, baoghlanach, gu uraiceil, tamhanta; neo-thuigseach, biasdail.

Domain, *s.* Rioghachd, seilbhe, oighreachd; tighearnas, uachdranachd.

Dome, *s.* Aitreabh, aros, tigh, teach, ardoch, fardoch; lann, dùn; † dom; pàiliunn; pula-mhullach, cuach-mhullach.

Domestic, *a.* Tigheil; tighe, teaghlaich; aig an tigh, diomhair. Domestic happiness, *sonas teaghlaich.*

Domestic, *s.* Seirbheiseach, oglach, gille, sgalag; banoglach, searbhanta.

Domesticity, *s.* Seirbheis.

Domicile, *s.* Aros, aitreabh, tigh, ardoch, fardoch.

Domify, *v. a.* Cataidh; taiteadh; ceannsaich.

Dominant, *a.* Riaghlach, ceannsach, ceannasach, ceannsalach.

Domination, *s.* Cumhachd, uachdranachd, ceannsal, ceannsaladh; ain-tighearnas, iompaireachd, ùghdarras, smachd, ard-cheannas; tàinisteas.

Dominative, *a.* Smachdail, ceannasach, ceannsalach.

Domineer, *v.* Riaghail; dean stràic, bi stràiceil; saruich.

Dominical, *a.* Dòmhnachail.

Dominion, *s.* Iompaireachd, rioghachd; ard-cheannas, cumhachd, ughdarras, uachdranachd; lamh an uachdar; dùthaich, tìr.

Don, s Duine uasal Spàinnteach.
† Don, v a Cuir ort.
Donary, s. Gibhte, tabhartas, tiodhlac.
Donation, s Gibhte, tabhartas, gean maith, tiodhlac; oirchios, mio-chuimeas, deirc, naomh-dhéirc.
Donative, a Gibhte, tabhartas
Done, part Deanta, deante, deas, ullamh, criochnaichte.
Donor, s Tiodhlacair, tabhartair
Doodle, s. Sgonn; fear gun fhiù.
Doom, s Diteadh, breitheanas, breithe; crioch, deireadh, crannchur, cor; dàn; sgrios, damnadh.
Doom, v a Dìt; thoir mach binn, thoir breith, orduich, sònraich, sùnraich
Doomsday, s. Lath bhreitheanais, an là deireannach, la 'bhràth
Doomsday-book, s An leabhar dubh, leabhar anns am bheil oighreachdan na rioghachd air an àireamh, a sgriobhadh a reir ordugha Righ Uilleam nam buadh
Doomsman, s Breitheamh, breith, fear ditidh.
Door, s. Dorus, còmhladh, geat, fo' dhorus; bealach Doors, *dorsan*, out of doors, *a mach, a muigh*, get out of the door, *thoir an dorus ort*, *gabh mach air an dorus*, at the door, *aig an dorus*, from door to door, *o dhorus gu dorus*, a front door, *dorus beòil*, a back door, *dorus cùil*
Doorkeeper, s. Dorsair, portair.
Doquet, s. Barantas
Dormant, a Codalach, cadalach; an tamh; diomhair, uaigneach, céilte, ag aomadh, neo-dhireach na sheasamh
Dormitory, s. Suain-lann, suain-airm, cladh
Dormouse, s Dallag, dallag-fheòir, feothan
Dorn, s. Dronnag, seorsa éisg.
Dorr, v a Bodhair.
Dorsel, s Croidhle.
Dorture, s. Suain-lann, seòmair codail
Dose, s. Uiread leighis 's as còir a ghabhail air aon uair; sgailc, dram; cuid, pàirt.
Dossil, s. Topag lìn, ribeag lin.
Dot, s Punc, ponc, pong
Dot, v Punc, ponc, pong.
Dotage, s Laanabaidheachd, leanabas, sean-aois; caillcachas, laigse-inntinn, goirgeachd, laigse chàileachd
Dotard, s. Duine o'n tug aois a chiall; neo-dhuine
Dote, v Bi an trom-ghaol; bi an dara uair mar leanabh
Doter, s Sean duine; fear o'n tug sean-aois a chiall
Dotingly, adv. Gu h-ana-ghradhach
Dottard, s. Bun craoibhe.
Dotterel, s Amadan mòintich
Double, a Dùbailt, fillte; da-fhillte, a dha uiread; caraideach, (*in mind*), cealgach, fealltach Double beer, *leann làidir*
Double, v a and n Fill, dùblaich; dean dùbailt, meudaich, dean cleas, cuir car
Double, s Dà uiread; dublainn, dùblachadh, car, cleas, cuilbheart; filleadh, plaigh; lionn-làidir The double of it, *a dha uiread, a dhùblainn*
Double-dealer, s Slaoightear, cealgair, fear carach, (no) slighcach, cuilbheartair.
Double-dealing, s Slaoighte, slaoightearachd, slighcadaireachd, cuilbheartach.
Double-faced, a Cealgach, ceabhacach, carach, deilaodannach.
Double-handed, a. Da-lamhach
Double-headed, a Da-cheannach
Double-minded, a. Cealgach, mealltach, carach, dùbailt, ceabhacach, gabhadach, mangach.
Doubleness, s. Dùblachd, dùblaichead
Doubler, s. Dùblair, filleadair.
Doublet, s. Dublett.
Double-tongued, a Cealgach, mealltach, breugach.
Doublets, s. pl. Paidhir, caraid, dithis, déise
Doublon, s. Cùin Spàinnteach.
Doubly, adv Da uair; gu da-fhillte, gu fillte, gu dùbailte.
Doubt, v a and n. Cuir an teagamh, cuir amharus; anearb, mi-earb; bi an iom-cheist. I doubt that, *tha mi cur sin an teagamh*.
Doubt, s. Teagamh, ag, amharus; an-earbsa, iomcheist; iom-chomhairle; aincheas, † contabhairt, cruaidh-chàs, teinn. Without doubt, *gun teagamh, air chinnte*, I have no doubt, *cha 'n eil teagamh agam*.
Doubtful, a. Teagamhach, amharusach, neo-chinnteach; neo-shonraichte; an-earbsach; fu amharus, eadar dha chomhairle; agail. Doubtfully, *gu teagamhach*.
Doubtfulness, s Teagamhachd, amharusachd, neo-chinntealas, cunnart
Doubtless, a Cinnteach, neo-amharusach, neo-theagamhach
Doubtless, adv Gun teagamh, gun amharus.
Dough, s. Taois. My cake is dough, *cha d'éirich leam*.
Doughty, a. Flathail, euchdail, gaisgeil, treubhanta; curanta, crodha, làidir, calma, foghainteach, ainmeil
Doughy, a. Taoismhor, taoiseil.
Douse, s. Pluinnse, tumadh.
Dove, s. Columan, colman, calaman, colm.
Dovecote, s Tigh choluman, colm-lann, columach.
Dovetailed, a Eagaichte.
Dowager, s Ban-dubhairiche; bantrach uasal.
Dowdy, s. Sgumrag, lamrag; té shlaobach neo-chruinneil.
Dowdy, a Slaobach, neo-chruinneil, leagach
Dower, Dowery, Dowry, s. Dubhairidh, tochar, tochradh, libhearn, càil.
Dowered, a Dubhairichte, air a tochradh
Dowerless, a Gun dubhàiridh; gun tochar, gun airgiod.
Dowlass, s Anart garbh, (no) glas, anart neo-ghealaichte.
Down, s Clòimh, clùimh, clòimhne, cleite, cléiteach; clòiteach mhìn, cluimheach, olann mhìn, mìn-chléite, minite; brothairne.
Down, s. Tulach, tulach fad reidh, raon, raodhair.
Down, prep. Le, leis, sios, a bhàn, le leathad, le bruthach. Down the stream, *leis an sruth*
Down, adv. Air làr, air an làr, a bhàn; shios, iolar; gu h-iosal, (*as the sun*), air luidhe, as an t-sealladh. I am down, *tha mi fodha*, down in the mouth, *trom, neoshunntach*, right down, *direach a bhàn, direach sios*, a down look, *sealladh dubhach*.
Down, interj Sios, a bhan. Down with them! *sios leo!* Down to hell, and say I sent thee!—(*Shak*) *Sios dh' ifrinn is abair gur mise a chuir ann thu!*
Down, v. a Smàl, spad, tilg sios, saraich, claoidh, fairtlich.
Downcast, a. Trom, dubhach, tuirseach, muladach, smuaireanach, fu bhròn, crom.
Downfal, s. Sgrios, tuiteam, truaighe; grad-chaochladh.
Downfallen, part. Air sgriosadh, air tuiteam; truagh; tuirseach, dubhach
Downhill, s. Leathad; leacainn. Going downhill, *a dol ri leathad*
Downhill, a Corrach.

Downlooked, *a.* Tuirseach, trom; gruamach; stùiceanta; gnò.

Downlying, *s.* Luidh-siùbhla, breith-cloinne.

Downright, *a.* and *adv.* Fireannach, fior, dìreach; neo-chealgach; saor; follaiseach; soilleir; as an aghaidh. He is a downright rascal, *is e 'm fior chrochair e*; she is a downright whore, *is i 'm fior-shiursach th' innte, tha i na siùrsach as an aghaidh.*

Downsitting, *s.* Suidhe, suidhe sios, fois, anail.

Downward, *adv.* Sios, a bhan; a nuas; le leathad, le bruthach. He went downward, *chaidh e sios,* (*no*) *le leathad*; come down, *thig a bhàn,* (*no*) *a nuas.*

Downward, *a.* Corrach, aomach.

Downy, *a.* Clòimheach, cluimheach, cloimhteach, clùimhteach; bog, bogar, mìn.

Dowry, *s.* Dubhairidh, gibhte; fortan; maoin; deolaidh.

Doxology, *s.* Gloir do 'n athair, mar bheirear anns na briathraibh *Gu mu beannuichte gu robh an Tigdearna Dia Israel,* no *Is leatsa an riaghachd agus an cumhachd agus a ghlòir, gu siorruidh.*

Doxy, *s.* Striopach.

Doze, *v. a.* and *n.* Bi an leth-chodal (no) san turamanaich, (no) ann an clo-chodal. He is dozing, *tha e na chlo-chodal.*

Dozen, *s.* A dha dheug, deusan.

Doziness, *s.* Turra-chodal, turamanaich, clo-chodal; leisge.

Dozy, *a.* Codalach, turamanach, drùbleach, drùbshuileach; lunndach, leasg, leagach.

Drab, *s.* Siùrsach, striopach, strabaid; stràill.

Drachm, *s.* Cùin Roimheach; an t-ochdamh a dh' ùnnsa.

Draff, *s.* Drabh; treasg, deasgann; fàgail fuigheall.

Draffy, *a.* Deabhach; treasgach.

Draft, *s.* Tarruing, treobhadh. A draft horse, *each cartàch.*

Drag, *v. a.* Tarruing, slaoid; spion, spiol.

Drag, *s.* Tarruing; slaod.

Draggle, *v.* Làbaich, salaich, eabair, slaoid tre pholl.

Draggler, *s.* Slàbair, slaibear.

Dragnet, *s.* Lion iosgaich, breac-lion; lion aigein; lion sgriobaidh.

Dragon, *s.* Dreagan; dric; nathair sgiathach; duine borb; bansgal; comh-shoillsean fagus do 'n rionnag tuathach; seorsa luibh.

Dragonfly, *s.* Seorsa cuileig theumnaiche.

Dragonish, *a.* Fiadhaich; borb.

Dragoon, *s.* Trupair, saighdear marcachd.

Drain, *v.* Traogh, falmhaich, taom, taomaich, tioramaich; tarruing.

Drain, *s.* Guitear, clais; amar, leabaidh uisge.

Drake, *s.* Dreac, coileach lacha.

Dram, *s.* (*A measure*), darcon, an t-ochdamh cuid a dh' unnsa a reir an leigh-thomhais; (*of liquor*), dram; sgailc; *proverbially*, gràinnean.

Drama, *s.* Dealbh-chluiche, cluiche, duan dealbh-chluiche.

Dramatic, *a.* Dealbh-chluicheach.

Dramatist, *s.* Bard dhuan dealbh-chluich.

Drank, *pret.* of drink. Dh' òl.

Draper, *s.* Ceannaiche, fear reic aodaich.

Drapery, *s.* Obair aodaich; figheadaireachd.

Drastic, *a.* Làidir mar phurgaid.

Draught, *s.* Tarruing, tarruinn; dealbh; cairteal; deoch; na h-uiread 's a dh' òlas neach air aon tarruing; guitear, claise; fear feòirn.

Draught-house, *s.* Tigh-aolaich; tigh salachair.

Draughts, *s.* Taileasg, taileasgan.

Draw, *v. a.* Tarruing, slaoid, spion, spiol; linich, dealbh; (*allure*), meall. Draw dry, *traogh, cuir an deabhadh*; draw near, *druid am fogus, thig am fogus, dlùthaich ri*; draw a sword, *tarruing claidheamh, rùisg claidheamh.*

Draw, *v.* Tarruing; crann-chur.

Draw-bridge, *s.* Drochait thogalach.

Draw-well, *s.* Tobar, tobar tairnidh, tiobairt, fuaran.

Drawer, *s.* Fear tarruing, gille buird; tarruingear; cisteag tharruingeach, tairneag.

Drawers, *s.* Fo-bhriogan, fo-bhriogais, drais.

Drawing, *s.* Tarruing; dealbh.

Drawing-room, *s.* Seomar coinneachaidh.

Drawl, *v. n.* Dean bruidhinn shlaodach, dean ràsanachd; slaod; snàg.

Drawling, *a.* Ràsanach, langanach, slaodach.

Drawn, *part.* Tarruingte, tarruinte, tairnte; (*as a sword*), ruisgte; (*equal*), ionann, comh-ionann.

Dray, *s.* Seorsa cartach.

Drayhorse, *s.* Each cartach.

Drayman, *s.* Cairtear.

Drazel, *s.* Stràill, sgliurach, dràichd.

Dread, *s.* Eagal, eagall, oillt, geilt, fiamh; crith-eagal; uamhann, ball-chrith, criothnachadh, geilt-chrithe, aobhar eagail.

Dread, *a.* Eagalach, oillteil, fuathasach; uamhannach, uamhasach.

Dread, *v. a.* Oilltich ri; fuathaich, criothnaich, bi fu eagal. He dreads him, *dh' oilltich e ris, tha eagal air roimhe; tha eagal air as.*

Dreadful, *a.* Oillteil, eagalach, fuathasach, uamhasach déistinneach. Dreadfully, *gu fuathasach, gu h-uamhasach.*

Dreadfulness, *s.* Oillteileachd, eagallachd, uamhasachd.

Dreadless, *a.* Neo-sgathach, neo-eagallach; misneachail.

Dream, *s.* Bruadar; aisling, faoin-smuain, faoin-dhochas, brionglaid; breisleach; faoin-amharus. In my dream, *ann mo bhruadar.*

Dream, *v.* Bruadair, breislich; bi ann am breisleach; faoin-smuainich. I dreamed, *bhruadair mi.*

Dreamer, *s.* Aislingeach, aislingiche, bruadaraiche, breisleachair; lunndair, leisgeau.

Dreaming, *a.* Aislingeach, bruadarach, breisleachail; leasg, lunndach.

Drear, *a.* Dubhach, bronach, muladach; tiomhaidh, tiamhaidh; uaigneach; neo-shuilbhear; gruamach.

Dreariness, *s.* Dubhachas; mulad; tiamhaidheachd; uaigneachd; gruaime.

Dreary, *a.* Dubhach, bronach, muladach; tiamhaidh, uaigneach, neo-shuilbhear.

Dredge, *s.* Lion sgriobaidh, lion eisirein.

Dredger, *s.* Iasgair eiseirein.

Dregginess, *s.* Deasguinneachd, drabhachd, druaipeileachd, druaipe; mosaiche, salachar, seilche.

Dreggy, *a.* Deasguinneach, drabhach, druaipeach, drabhach, drabhagach, salach, driodarach, gruideach.

Dregs, *s.* Deasgainn, deasgunnan, gruid, druaipe, grunnd, grunndas; drabh, fuigheal, trusdaireachd.

Drench, *v.* Fliuch, bog, tum, tom; taislich, uisgich; nigh; glan. Drenched, *fliuchta, nighte, glanta, glainte.*

Drench, *s.* Tarruing, deoch.

Drenching, *s.* Fliuchadh, bogadh, tumadh, tomadh, uisgeachadh, nigheadh, glanadh.

Dress, *v. a.* (*Clothe*), uigheamaich, uidheamaich, sgeadaich, sgiamhaich; eid, aodaich, comhdaich; earr; eudhaich; (*rectify*), càirich, ceartaich, cuir ceart, cuir gu doigh; (*cook*), greidh, greadh, deasaich, còcairich. Dress yourself, *cuir ort d' aodach, cuir d' aodach ort, rach ad uigheam.*

DRESS, *s* Uigheam, uidheam, aodach, eididh, riomhadh, earradh, comhdach, deise, culaidh

DRESSER, *s* Sgeadachair; (*of a kitchen*), clar, corn-chlàr; (*of meat*), còcair.

DRESSING, *s* Sgeadachadh, comhdachadh; (*of meat*), greidh, còcaireachd, (*of a hook*), busgainn; (*of a wound*), plàsd, sabh, cuaran, leigheas

DRESSING-ROOM, *s.* Seomar earraidh.

DRESSY, *a.* Breagh, briagh

DREST, *part* Uidheamaichte, uigheamaichte

DRIB, *v a* Gearr, bearr, sgath

DRIBBLE, *v* Sil; ronnaich.

DRIBBLET, *s* Beagnithe

DRIFT, *s* (*Direction*), cùrsa, gabhail; (*of snow*), cathamh, cuitheamh, (*intention*), rùn, miann, aire, tuaiream; uspag.

DRILL, *v a* Toll, (*as a soldier*), oil chum airm.

DRILL, *s.* Torradh, tolladh, inneal tollaidh; sruthan, alltan beag.

DRINK, *v. a* and *n* Òl, òil, ibh; sùig, sùigh, sluig Drink to, *ol deoch slainnte*, drink off, *ol as, ol suas, sguab as.*

DRINK, *s* Deoch, ibh Take a drink of it, *gabh deoch dheth*, drink-money, *airgiod òl*

DRINK, *s* Òl, geòc, pòit, meisge

DRINKER, *s* Misgear, meisgear, geòcair, pòitear, ruitear.

DRINKING, *s.* Ol; meisge; pòit; dinib

DRIP, *v. a.* Sil, sruth, driùigh

DRIP, *s.* Sileadh, sileag, braon.

DRIPPING, *s* Sileadh, reamhrachd

DRIPPING-PAN, *s.* Aghann silidh

DRIVE, *v* Iomain; iomainich, greas, buail, ruaig Drive cattle, *iomain, saodaich*, what does your speech drive at? *ciod e fath* (*no*) *brìgh do comhraidh?* drive away time, *caith aimsir*, he came as fast as he could drive, *thàinig e cho luath is a b' urradh dha, thàinig e cho luath is a bha na chasaibh, thainig e na dheannaibh*, drive a cart, *greas cairt;* drive off, *ruaig*, drive off or banish, *diobair, fògair*, drive off or delay, *cuir dheth, cuir dail;* let a ship drive, *leig ruithe le luingeas*, driven, *iomainichte; ruaigte, fògairte, air iomain*, clouds driven with a storm, *neoil air an iomain le h-iomaghaoithe.*

DRIVEL, *v* Sil ronnan, ronnaich, seilich

DRIVEL, *s.* Ronnan, seile, smugaideachd, siligeadh; subhlach

DRIVELLER, *s.* Ronnair; amadan, neo-dhuine

DRIVEN, *part* See DRIVE

DRIVER, *s* Greasadair; gille-greasaidh, cairtear, coisdear, carbadair, iomainiche, saodair, fear saodachaidh.

DRIZZLE, *v. a* and *n.* Sil gu mall

DRIZZLY, *a* Driùchdach, druchdach, braonach, baindealach, smuideanach

DROLL, *s* Neònachas, iongantas; sùgair, sgistear, cleasaiche; sgeigear; ioladh; drabh-luinneachd, cleasachd

DROLL, *a* Neònach, aighearrach, iongantach, sunntach, cridheil; baoth.

DROLLERY, *s* Neonachas, aighearrachd, fearas-chuideachd, sgeigearachd.

DROMEDARY, *s* Droman, dromadair.

DRONE, *s* Seillean lunndach, lunndair; rongair; slaod, torman, gaothaiche

DRONISH, *a.* Diamhanach, lunndach, leasg, neo-dheanadach, leagach, rongach

DROOP, *v. n.* Searg, crion, crom, meath; fas lag, caith air falbh; aom.

DROOPING, *a.* Crom-cheannach, meath, mall.

DROOPING, *s.* Seargadh, crionadh, cromadh, meathadh, giùig.

DROP, *s* Sil, sileag, diot, diotag, boinne, boinneag, braon; cluas-fhàil, crochadan cluais

DROP, *v. a.* and *n.* Sil, drùigh, snigh; (*a hint*), thoir sànas; (*cease*), sguir, leig dhiot. Drop down, *tuit*, he dropped down dead, *thuit e' bhàn marbh;* (*speckle*), breac, breacaich

DROPLET, *s* Sileag; diot, diotag.

DROPPING, *s.* Sileadh, snighe.

DROPSICAL, *a.* Meud-bhronnach.

DROPSY, *s* Meud-bhronn.

DROSS, *s.* Smùrach, smùr; smùirne, pronnag; grùid; dùs, dùslach, † teimeal.

DROSSY, *a* Smùirneach; pronn; salach

DROVE, *pret.* of drive; which see.

DROVE, *s.* Dròbh, greigh, iomain, treud, tàin, (*of people*), lòd, bannal, buidheann, cuideachd.

DROVER, *s.* Drobhair

DROUGHT, *s.* Tioramachd, tirime, tart; path; pathadh, iot.

DROUGHTINESS, *s* Tiormachd, tart; tartmhorachd, pathadh, iot

DROUGHTY, *a.* Tioram, tartmhor, pàiteach, iotmhor; air pathadh

DROWN, *v a* Bàth; tachd; mùch

DROWSE, *v n* Codail, bi san turamanaich.

DROWSILY, *adv* Gu codalach, gu trom, gu lunndach, gu slaodach.

DROWSINESS, *s* Codalachd, codaltachd; drùb-shuileachd, lunndaireachd, slaodachd, aimhleisge.

DROWSY, *a.* Codalach, codaltach; drub-shùileach; trom; lunndach, slaodach, aimhleasg, leagach.

DRUB, *v. a* Buail, gréidh, slacuinn, slachduinn, gabh air.

DRUB, *s* Buille, dorn, slachduinn

DRUBBING, *s* Bualadh, dornachadh, slachduinn, greidh; caraiste He gave him a proper drubbing, *thug e 'dheagh shlachduinn da, thug e 'dheagh ghréidh dha.*

DRUDGE, *s.* Tràill

DRUDGE, *v.* Dean obair thràilleil.

DRUDGER, *s* Tràill; làbanaiche.

DRUDGERY, *s.* Traillealachd, obair dhiblidh, saothair.

DRUDGINGLY, *adv.* Gu tràilleil, gu saothaireachail, gu diblidh.

DRUG, *s* Leigheas, cungaidh leigheis, *drog;* ni gun fhiù.'

DRUGGET, *s.* Drògait

DRUGGIST, *s.* Leigh

DRUID, *s.* Drùidh; sagart am measg nan sean Bhreatunnach

DRUIDISM, *s.* Drùidheachd

DRUM, *s* Druma, inneal caismeachd, drumair

DRUM, *v a.* Dean drumaireachd

DRUM-MAJOR, *s* *Drum-maidsear.*

DRUM-MAKER, *s* Drumadair

DRUMSTICK, *s.* Bioran druma.

DRUNK, DRUNKEN, *a.* Air mheisg, air an daoraich, misgeach

DRUNKARD, *s.* Misgear, meisgear, pòitear, ruitear.

DRUNKENNESS, *s* Misge, meisge, pòite, ruitearachd

DRY, *a* Tioram, seac, seacaichte, seargta, crion; air crionadh, gun bhrigh; pàiteach, iotmhor, tartmhor; traighte;

air deabhadh; neo-thorrach; (*as a cow*), an diosgadh; (*severe*), cruaidh, coimheach, fuaraidh.

Dry, *v. a.* and *n.* Tioramaich, seac, seacaich, searg, crion.

Dryad, *s.* Doire-oigh.

Dryly, *adv.* Gu tioram; gu coimheach; gu neo-chàirdeil.

Dryness, *s.* Tiormachd, crainnteachd, crionachd; (*of manner*), coimheachas; (*barrenness*), seisge; neo-thorrachas.

Drynurse, *s.* Banaltrum sheasg, (no) thioram.

Dryshod, *a.* Cas tioram.

Dual, *a.* Dithis, deise.

Dub, *s.* Buille; straoidhle, *dunt.*

Dub, *v.* Ridirich; ardaich chum inbhe.

Dubious, *a.* Teagamhach, neo-chinnteach, agail; eadar dha chomhairle; neo-shoilleir.

Dubiously, *adv.* Gu teagamhach, gu h-agail.

Dubiousness, *s.* Teagamhachd, agaileachd; neo-chinntealas.

Ducal, *a.* Diùchdail.

Ducat, *s.* Dùcait; cùin airgid agus oir air a bhualadh le diùchdaibh.

Duck, *s.* Tunnag. A wild duck, *tunnag fhiadhaich, lach, gaill-chearc; cromadh cinn; clach losg-bhra-teine.*

Duck, *v. a.* and *n.* Tom, tum, bog, cuir fo 'n uisge; rach fo 'n uisge, dubh-shnamh.

Ducker, *s.* Dubh-shnamhair.

Duck-legged, *a.* Clad-chosach, clàr-chosach, gearrachosach.

Duckling, *s.* Isean tunnaig.

Duckmeat, *s.* Seorsa luibh, gran lachain; mac gun athair.

Duct, *s.* Claise, claisean, pioban; cùl, seòladh.

Ductile, *a.* So-lubaidh, so-aomaidh, so-tharruing, maoth, tais.

Dudgeon, *s.* Biodag; droch ghean, dod, spid, tnù. He took it in high dudgeon, *ghabh e gu ro dhon e, ghabh e gu ro shoithich e.*

Due, *a.* Dligheach; ri phàigh, cubhaidh; direach.

Due, *s.* Dlighe; ceartas, ceirte, còir.

Duel, *s.* Comh-lann, comhraig déise.

Dueller, *s.* Comhlannaiche, comhlannair.

Duenna, *s.* Ban-tuitear; sean bhoireannach aig am bi curam bhan òg.

Dug, *s.* Sinne, (no) deala beothaich, ùth.

Dug, *pret.* of dig. Bhùraich, chladhaich.

Duke, *s.* Diùchd.

Dukedom, *s.* Oighreachd Diuchd, inmhe Diùchd.

Dull-brained, *a.* Amaideach, baoghalta, maol, tamhanta.

Dulcet, *a.* Milis; binn, fonnmhor, ceolmhor; tiamhaidh.

Dulcification, *s.* Millseachadh.

Dulcify, *a.* Millsich.

Dulcimer, *s.* Seorsa inneil ciùil,

Dulcorate, *v. a.* Millsich.

Dulcoration, *s.* Millseachadh.

Dullhead, *s.* Corra-cheann, burraidh, umaidh, baoghlan, amharan, amhlair; ceothallan.

Dull, *a.* Baoghalta, neo-gheur, tiugh, plocanta; maol; aineolach; tamhanta, amhasach; trom, muirgineach; mall, smuaireanach, neo-shuilbhear, duilbhear.

Dull, *v. a.* Maolaich; tromaich.

Dullard, *s.* Burraidh, baoghlan, corra-cheann, umaidh, ceothallan, amhlair.

Dully, *adv.* Gu baoghalta; gu mall; gu trom, gu muirgineach.

Dulness, *s.* Aineolachd; baoghaltachd; mi-ghéire; truime; duiseal.

Duly, *adv.* Gu cubhaidh, gu ceart, gu dligheach, gu freagarrach, gu riaghailteach.

Dumb, *a.* Balbh, tosd, tosdach, samhach, seimh; meann, maon. A dumb person, *balbhan.*

Dumfound, *v.* Cuir sàmhach.

Dumbly, *adv.* Gu balbh, gu tosdach, gu samhach.

Dumbness, *s.* Balbhad, bailbhe, balbhanachd, tosdachd.

Dump, *s.* Truime, trumadas, dubhachas, airsneal; dodstùirtealachd.

Dumpish, *a.* Trom, dubhach, tuirseach, airsnealach; dodach.

Dun, *a.* Donn, dubh-dhonn, lachdunn, mudaidh.

Dun, *v.* Tathaich, cruaidh-thathaich, togair. He duns you for money, *tha e 'tathaich airgid ort.*

Dun, *s.* Fear tathaich, tathaichear.

Dunce, *s.* Corra-cheann, burraidh; ceothallan.

Dunderhead, *s.* Corracheann, burraidh, guraiceach.

Dung, *s.* Innear, mathachadh, aolach, gaor, cac, buachar, sal, salachar, giodar.

Dung, *v. a.* Inneirich, aolaich, mathaich, leasaich.

Dungeon, *s.* Toll-buth, gainntir, priosan.

Dunghill, *s.* Otrach, breunan, dùnan, dùn-aolaich; tutair.

Dungy, *a.* Salach, breun; dìblidh.

Dungyard, *s.* Clobhsa innearach.

Dunner, *s.* Fear thagradh fhiach, tathaichear.

Dupe, *s.* Fear neo-ghramail, culaidh mheallaidh.

Dupe, *v. a.* Thoir an car a, meall.

Duplicate, *v. a.* Dùblaich, fill.

Duplicate, *s.* Dùblachadh do ni sam bi; amhladh, lethbhreac.

Duplication, *s.* Dùblachadh, filleadh.

Duplicature, *s.* Dùblainn; filleadh.

Duplicity, *s.* Cealg, ceilge, leam leat.

Durability, *s.* Maireannachd, marsuinneachd, buainead.

Durable, *a.* Mairionn, maireann, maireannach, mairtheannach, buan, daingean; laidir.

Durableness, *s.* Maireannachd, buanachd.

Durably, *adv.* Gu maireann, gu buan, gu laidir.

Durance, *s.* Priosanachadh, priosan; † buanachadh.

Duration, *s.* Maireannachd.

Dure, *v.* Mair, buanaich.

Duresse, *s.* Priosunachd.

During, *prep.* Ré, am feadh.

Durity, *s.* Cruadhas, gramalas, diongaltachd.

Durst. See **Dare.**

Dusk, *a.* Dorch, ciar.

Dusk, *s.* Eadar-sholus, solus nan tràth, dorchadh, feasgar, beul na h-oidhche.

Duskish, *a.* Dorch, ciar.

Duskiness, *s.* Duirche, doirche, ciaire, céire.

Dusky, *a.* Leth-char dorch, doilleir, ciar; tiamhaidh.

Dust, *s.* Dus, duslach, dusladh; stùr, smur, talamh; ùir; an uaigh.

Dust, *v.* Stùr, glan.

Dustman, *s.* Sal-bhodach, làbair.

Dusty, *a.* Salach, stùrach, smùirneach; pronn, mìn.

Dutchess, *s.* Ban-diùchd.

Duteous, *a.* Dleasnach, ùmhal, striochdail; modhail.

Dutiful, *a.* Dleasnach, dleasnachail, ùmhal, striochdail, modhail.

Dutifully, *adv.* Gu dleasnach, gu dleasnachail, gu h-ùmhal, gu striochdail, gu modhail.

Dutifulness, *s.* Umhlachd, striochdaileachd, modhaileachd

Duty, *s.* Dleasdanas, dleasnas; gnothach; dual, dlighe, morlanachd; (*tax*), cìs, càin

Dwarf, *s.* Troich, droich, arrachd, brideach, cruitean, cruiteachan, crotair, luch-armunn; abhach, galoban.

Dwarfish, *a* Troicheanta, arrachdail, crotach, abhachail, iosal, beag, goirrid, stumpach, cutach.

Dwarfishness, *s* Troicheantachd, arrachdas.

Dwell, *v* Comhnuich, fan, fuirich, àitich, gabh comhnuidh, gabh tamh; socraich Where does he dwell? *c' àite am bheil e'fanachd?*

Dweller, *s.* Comhnuiche, fear comhnuidh, fear àiteachaidh.

Dwelling, *s.* Aros, fardoch, aitreabh, tigh, teach, ionad còmhnuidh.

Dwelling-house, *s* Tigh còmhnuidh, aros, aitreabh; fardoch.

Dwelling-place, *s* Aite còmhnuidh, ionad còmhnuidh.

Dwindle, *v* Crion, searg; caith air falbh

Dying, *part* A bàsuchadh, ris a bhàs, a dol eug, a faotainn a bhàis, a siubhal, aig gob an éig, a dathadh.

Dynasty, *s.* Riaghladh, riaghladaireachd, uachdaranachd, ughdarras

Dysentery, *s* Gearrach, buinneach, tualag, siubhal, sgàird, tinneas gearraidh

Dyspnœa, *s.* Cuing-analach.

Dysury, *s.* Eigin fhuail, galar fuail.

E

E, Cuigeamh litir na h-aibidil

Each, *a* Gach, cach, gach aon; a h-aon do 'n dithis Each other, *a chéile, cach a chéile*; each the other, *gach aon a chéile*, on each side, *air gach taobh*, each of us, *gach aon againn, gach neach againn*, love each other, *gradhaichibh a chéile*, take each other by the hand, *gabhaibh a chéile air laimh*

Eager, *a.* (*Earnest*), an càs, dian, brais, cas, togarach, dianthogarach; dealasach, miannach, dùrachdach; (*sharp set*), acrach, ocrach, gionach, cìocrach; (*in taste*), geur, goirt, searbh, teumnach, beumnach, geur, searbh

Eagerly, *adv* Gu dian, gu togarach, gu dealasach, gu ciocrach, gu miannach, gu dàmhaireach.

Eagerness, *s* Déine, déineas, dianad, dian-thogar, miann, dùrachd, braisead, caisead, togar, ciocras; (*in taste*), searbhas, seirbhe, geurad.

Eagle, *s* Iolair, fir-eun, suaicheantas nan Sean Ròimheach.

Eagle-eyed, *a* Geur, geur-shuileach, fad-shuileach, biorach, rosgach

Eagle-speed, *s.* Luathas na h-Iolaire

Eaglet, *s.* Iolair òg, isean iolaire

Ear, *s.* (*Of the body*), cluas, (*of corn*), dias, ceann déise; (*for music*), cluas-chiùil; (*hearing*), claistinn, claisneachd; (*audience*), éisdeachd Give an ear, *eisd, thoir éisdeachd*, set together by the ears, *cuir a chaonnag, cuir an seilbh* (*no*) *an dàil a chéile, cuir an sàs sa chéile, stuig*, over head and ears, *thar a cheann 's a chluasan*, the lap of the ear, *leabag na cluaise*, the ear of a pot, *cluas*

† Ear, *v a* Ar, treabh, crann, ruathar

Ear-ache, *s* Galar cluaise

Eared, *a.* Cluasach.

Earl, *s* Iarla, Iar-fhlath

Earldom, *s* Iarlachd, oighreachd Iarla

Earless, *a* Gun chluasan, gearr-chluasach.

Earliness, *s* Moiche, moichead, moch-eiridh.

Early, *a* Moch, much, tràthail, maidneach. Early in the morning, *moch sa mhadainn*, too early, *tuille is moch, tuille is tràthail.*

Early, *adv.* Gu moch, gu tràthail, gu maidneach

Earn, *v. a* Coisinn, buidhinn; cothaich, faigh. Earned, *coisinnte, buidhinnte, cothaichte*

Earnest, *s.* Dùrachd, (*a pledge*), earlas; iarlas, geall-daighnich, geall-daighneachaidh In earnest, *a rìreadh, do rìreadh*, in real earnest, *a cheart rìreadh*

Earnest, *a* Dùrachdach; dealasach, dian, an càs, fiughach.

Earnestly, *adv.* Gu dùrachdach, le dùrachd, gu dealasach, gu dian, gu fiughach.

Earnestness, *s* Dùrachd; dealasachd, déine, deothasachd; iomaguin

Earring, *s.* Cluas-fhàil, cluas-fhàinne; fainne cluais, aigealan, aileabhag cluaise, cluigean, crochadan-cluaise.

Earth, *s* Talamh; ùir; dùs, duslach; criadh, (*world*), an domhan, an cruinne, an cruinne cé, cé, an saoghal; tlachd, fonn, † tealla, (*county or land*), talamh, tir, fonn, fearann On earth, *air thalamh, air an t-saoghal*, a fox's earth, *toll balgair, brochdluinn*, earth raised up, *bruach, dùn, banc*, commit to the earth, *or* bury, *adhlaic, tiodhlaic*, cast up the earth, *bùraich*

Earth, *v. a.* and *n.* Céil, comhdaich le ùir, cuir fo 'n ùir; rach fo 'n talamh

Earthborn, *s* Talmhaidh, saoghalmhor; diblidh; bochd, truagh

Earthen, *a* Talmhaidh; ùireil; creadha. Earthenware, *soithchean creadha, eathraichean.*

Earthiness, *s* Ùirealachd, truaillidheachd.

Earthliness, *s* Talmhaidheachd; truaillidheachd

Earthly, *a* Talmhaidh, truaillidh, diblidh; corporra, saoghalta. Earthly-minded, *saoghalta*, earthly-mindedness, *cùram an t-saoghail*

Earth-nut, *s.* Braonan, cnò-thalmhainn

Earthquake, *s.* Crith-thalmhainn

Earth-shaking, *a* Fonn-chritheach, cruinne-chritheach.

Earth-worm, *s* Durag, daolag; cnuimh, cnuimheag; cruimh, cruimheag, craimheag, (*in contempt*), truaghan; spiocair

Earthy, *a* Talmhaidh, talmhainneach, saoghalmhor; corporra; diblidh, truaillidh. Cold is the earthy hillock, *is coimheach an tom an ùir.*

Earwax, *s.* Sal-cluaise

Earwig, *s* Gobhlachan.

Ease, *s.* Fois, tamh, socair, athais, anail, soimeachd, lasachadh; (*pleasure*), saimh, seimhe, sogh. At ease, *aig fois*, take your ease, *dean air do shocair, dean air d' athais, leig d' anail*, ill at ease, *an-shocrach, docrach, mi-shuaimhneach*, with ease, *gu furas, gu soimeach, gu socrach*; at heart's ease, *soimeach*, the landed man is at his ease, the tradesman well off, *is soimeach fear fearainn, is sona fear ceirde.*

Ease, *v. a.* Lasaich, thoir lasachadh; eutromaich, lughdaich. Eased, *lasaichte.*

Easeful, *a.* Samhach, ciùin, socarach, athaiseach.

Easement, *s.* Lasachadh; furtachd, coghnadh. A house of easement, *tigh beag, tigh oiche.*

Easily, *adv.* Gu furas, gu socrach, gu soimeach; gun dragh; (*gently*), gu ciùin, gu farasda, gu caoimhneil. Easily pleased, *so-thoileachadh.*

Easiness, *s.* Furasachd; athaiseachd; (*of address*), caoimhne, caoimhnealas; (*of mind*), ciùineas, farasdachd; soimeachas, socair.

East, *s.* 'N ear, an aird an ear, shios, soir; oirthir, oirsceart, éiridh na gréine. From the east, *o 'n ear.*

Easter, *s.* A chàisg. Easter-day, *là càisg.*

Easterly, *a.* O'n ear, near; shios. An easterly wind, *gaoth 'n ear.*

Eastern, *a.* Soir, shios, near, a laimh na h-airde 'n ear.

Eastward, *adv.* Sios, chum na h-airde an ear.

Easy, *a.* Furas, furasd; (*of temper*), soimeach, math-nadurra; (*in circumstances*), soimeach, socrach, cothrom-ach; (*quiet*), samhach, ciùin. Easy to be borne, *so-ghiùlan, so-iomchar, so-fhulang;* (*indifferent*), coma, comadh, coidheis; (*at leisure*), socair, air do shocair, air d' athais. It is easier said than done, *is fhusa a radh no dheanamh;* easy of belief, *baoghalta; maol; simplidh, neo-amharusach.*

Eat, *v. a.* Ith; sluig; ios; caith; (*corrode*), cnàmh; (*nibble*), creim. Eat, drink, and be merry, *ithibh, òlaibh is bithibh subhach;* an appetite to eat, *sannt ithe; sannt bidh.*

Eatable, *a.* Ion-ithe, so-ithe, a ghabhas itheadh; itheach; (*nibble*), creim. Eat together, *comh-ith, gabh com-ithe* (*no*) *comaidh.*

Eatable, *s.* Biadh, ni sam bi a dh' fhaodas itheadh.

Eaten, *part.* Ithte, air itheadh, caithte, sluigte; cnamhta.

Eater, *s.* Geòcair, craosair, fear ithe; bagair, bronnair, gionaiche.

Eating, *s.* Itheadh; (*corroding*), cnàmh; (*nibbling*), creim. Great eating, *craos, craosuireachd.*

Eating, *part.* Ag itheadh, a cnàmh; a creimeadh.

Eaves, *s.* Anuinn.

Eaves-dropper, *s.* Fear far-cluaise.

Ebb, *v. a.* Traogh; rach air ais.

Ebb, *s.* Traoghadh; dol air ais, lughdachadh; caitheamh; aomadh.

Ebon, Ebony, *s.* Dubh-fhiodh.

Ebriety, *s.* Meisge, misge, pòit, òl, daoraich. In a state of ebriety, *air a mheisge, air an daoraich.*

Ebriosity, *s.* Meisgeireachd.

Ebullition, *s.* Goil, goileadh; at.

Eccentric, *a.* Mi-riaghailteach; neònach; seachranach, iomrolach.

Eccentricity, *s.* Teannadh o'n mheadhon, mi-mheadhon-achd; seachranachd; neònachas.

Ecclesiastic, *a.* Eaglaiseach, caglaise, a bhuineas do 'n eaglais (no) do 'n chléir.

Ecclesiastic, *s.* Sagart, ministear; pears 'eaglais; cliar.

Ecclesiastical, *a.* Eaglaiseach, a bhuineas do 'n eaglais, no 'n chléir.

Echo, *s.* Mac-talla; ath-ghairm, ath-ghlaodh, ath-fhuaim, gair-chreag, freagradh.

Echo, *v. a.* and *n.* Ath-ghairm, ath-fhuaim.

Echoing, *a.* Fuaimneach, fuaimearra.

Eclaircissement, *s.* Mìneachadh, foillseachadh.

Eclat, *s.* Onoir, moladh, cliù; urram.

Eclectic, *a.* Roghainneach, roghnachail.

Eclipse, *s.* Dubhradh, dorchadh, sgàil, duibhre; grian-dhubhadh; *clibse.* Tha ghrian air a dubhadh le eadar-theachd na gealaich, agus a ghealach le faileas na cruinne. A solar eclipse, *dubhradh gréine;* a lunar eclipse, *dubhradh gealaich.*

Eclipse, *v. a.* Dubh, dorchaich; cuir air chùl; cuir gu nàir.

Ecliptic, *s.* A ghrian-chrios.

Eclogue, *s.* Oran buachaille, buachoilleag; coilleag.

Economic, Economical, *a.* Caonntach, gléadhtach, gleidh-teach; grunndail.

Economize, *v.* Dean bail, caomhain; gleidh, cuir seachad.

Economist, *s.* Riaghladair, riaghladair tighe; fear tighe, bean tighe.

Economy, *s.* Caonntachd; grunnd, grunndalas, baile; fearachas tighe; beanachas tighe; crìonnachd; gleadh-tachd; riaghailt.

Ecstacy, Ecstasy, *s.* Saimh, mor-ghairdeachas; sàth-shaimh, ard-shodan, ard-aoibhneas; plath.

Ecstatic, *s.* Ard-aoibhinn, aoibhneachail.

Ecurie, *s.* Stàbul.

Edacious, *a.* Lonach, gionach, glamhach, goineach, geòcail, craosach, glutach.

Edacity, *s.* Lon, gion, glamhachd, geòc geocaireachd, cràos, glutaireachd.

Edder, *v. a.* Barranaich, cuir barran air garaidh, daighnich callaid.

Edder, *s.* Barran.

Eddish, *s.* Asbhuain, fasbhuain.

Eddy, *s.* Faochag, cuairt-shruth, cuairteag, taobh-shruth.

Eddy, *a.* Faochagach, cuairteagach.

Edematose, *a.* Atmhor.

Edentated, *a.* Gann-fhiaclach, cabach.

Edge, *s.* (*Of a blade*), faobhar, géire; (*a point*), roinn; (*of a pot*), fraidhe; (*of a garment*), foir, oir; faim; iomall; (*of a river*), bruach, foir. It set my teeth on edge, *chuir e déistinn orm;* fallen by the edge of the sword, *air tuiteam le faobhar a chlaidheimh.*

Edge, *v. a.* Faobhraich, geuraich; iomallaich; faim.

Edged, *a.* Faobhraichte, geuraichte; geur, iomallaichte, faimte. A two-edged sword, *claidheamh dà fhaobhar.*

Edgeless, *a.* Neo-gheur, maol, gun fhaobhar.

Edgetool, *s.* Faobharach, ball-faobhrach.

Edgewise, *s.* Air oir, gu h-oireil, a leth taobh air a chaol.

Edging, *s.* Oir, foir, fabhradh, faim, iomall.

Edible, *a.* A dh' fhaotar itheadh, airson itheadh.

Edict, *s.* Gairm, glaodh, ordugh, aithne, fuagradh, reachd.

Edification, *s.* Togail suas, togail; teagasg; oilean, foghlum, deagh-fhoghlum; tairbhe, leas.

Edifice, *s.* Aitreabh, togail, aros.

Edifier, *s.* Fear teagaisg, teagasgair, fear foghluim.

Edify, *v. a.* Foghlum, teagasg, oileanaich, cuir impidh; tog; leasaich.

Edition, *s.* Cur mach, clo-bhualadh, na chuirear mach do leabhar air aon tarruing.

Editor, *s.* Fear a chuireas leabhar a mach, ceartachair.

Educate, *v.* Ionnsuich, teagasg, oil, oileanaich, foghlum, muin; araich, tog; thoir suas. Educated, *ionnsuichte, teagasgte, foghluimte.*

Education, *s.* Ionnsach, † ionnsuchadh, teagasg, oilean, foghlum, munadh; beus.

Educe, *v. a.* Thoir as; foillsich, nochd.

Eduction, *s.* Foillseachadh, nochdadh.

Edulcorate, *v. a.* Millsich, dean milis.

Edulcoration, *s.* Millseachadh, deanamh milis.

Eel, *s.* Easg, easgann.

E'en. See Even.

Effable, *a.* So-innseadh, so-chur an céill.

Efface, *v. a.* Dubh a mach, mill.

Effect, *s.* Buil, toradh; éifeachd; crioch, deanmhas; ceann thall, deireadh; brìgh; rùn; miann, ciall; maoin, airneas. In effect, *a rireadh;* he brought the matter to effect, *thug e 'n gnothuch gu crìche;* effects (*among merchants*), maoin, bàrr; (*consequences*), toraidh, buil. Of no effect, *faoin, gun fhiù, gun fheum;* to no effect, *gu diumhain.*

Effect, *v.* Thoir gu criche, criochnaich, coimh-lion; faigh, dean.

Effectible, *a.* So-dheanamh.

Effective, *a.* Eifeachdach, éifeachdail, oibreachail, deanadach, feumail, neartmhor, treun, foghainteach, calma, crodha, làidir, comasach, murrach, uidhiseil.

Effectively, *adv.* Gu h-éifeachdach, gu deanadach, gu feumail, gu neartmhor, gu treun, gu foghainteach, gu calma, gu crodha, gu làidir, gu comasach, gu tarbhach.

Effectless, *a.* Gun éifeachd; anfhann, gun stà, gun uidhis, gun fheum.

Effecter, *s.* Deanadair, fear criochnachaidh; dealbhair.

Effectual, *a.* Eifeachdach, cumhachdach, tarbhach, comasach, murrach. Effectual calling, *gairm eifeachdach;* effectually, *gu tur; gu h-éifeachdach.*

Effectuate, *v.* Dean; thoir gu crìche, coimh-lion.

Effeminacy, *s.* Meath-chridheachd, boige, neo-chruadalachd, taise; sogh, seimhe, saimh, meatachd, cailleachantas.

Effeminate, *a.* Meath-chridheach, neo-dhuineil, cailleachanta; bog, neo-chruadalach, tais, fann, maoth, banail; sòghmhor. Effeminately, *gu meath-chridheach, gu tais, gu fann.*

Effeminate, *v. a.* and *n.* Meathaich, bogaich, taislich, fas meath, bog, (no) tais.

Effervesce, *v.* Goil, oibrich.

Effervescence, *s.* Goil, goileadh; teas, oibreachadh.

Effete, *a.* Aimrid, seasg, neo-thorrach; neo-ghineadach.

Efficacious, *a.* Eifeachdach, comasach, cumhachdach, tarbhach, foghainteach, murrach, treun, gniomhach, làidir, fearanta, calma, crodha, tamhasach, deanasach.

Efficaciously, *adv.* Gu h-éifeachdach, gu comasach, gu tarbhach; gu tur.

Efficacy, *s.* Eifeachd, comas, tairbhe, cumhachd, murraiche.

Efficiency, *s.* Eifeachdachd, tairbhe, cumhachd, murraiche, murrachas, deanadas, gniomhachd.

Efficient, *a.* Eifeachdach, tarbhach, comasach, diongmhalta, diongalta, gramail, treun, foghainteach.

Effigiate, *v.* Dealbh.

Effigy, *s.* Dealbh, coslas, eugmhas, aogas, iomhaigh, cruth.

Efflorescence, *s.* Blàithean, fo-bhlàth; (*in physic*), briseadh mach, guirean, bucaid.

Efflorescent, *a.* Blàthach, blàthachail, a teachd fo bhlàth.

Effluence, *s.* Sruthadh, dòrtadh.

Effluent, *a.* A sruthadh, a dòrtadh, a teachd o.

Effluvia, *s.* Fàile, tòthadh.

Effluvium, *s.* Fàile, tòchd, tòthadh, ceò.

Efflux, *s.* Dortadh, taomadh; sruthadh.

Efform, *v.* Dealbh, cruthaich, thoir cumadh, dean cumadail.

Efformation, *s.* Dealbhadh, cruthachadh.

Effort, *s.* Spairn, oidhirp, spraic. Make an effort, *thoir oidhirp (no) deuchainn.*

Effossion, *s.* Cladhachadh, bùrachadh, tochladh, tochailt, tochaill.

Effraiable, *a.* Fuathasach, umhasach, eagallach, umharra.

Effrontery, *s.* Peirtealachd, dànadas, ladurnachd, beagnaire, mio-nàire.

Effulgence, *s.* Boisge, boisgealachd, loinnir, lannair, soillse, soillseachd, dealradh, dealraichead.

Effulgent, *a.* Boisgeil, lonnradh, lannaireach, dealrach, soillseach, soilleir, lomhar.

Effuse, *v. a.* Taom, dòirt, taosg.

Effusion, *s.* Dortadh, taomadh, taosgadh; cur thairis, ana-caitheamh. Effusion of blood, *dòrtadh fola.*

Effusive, *a.* Dortach, taomach, taosgach.

Eft, *adv.* Gu luath, gu h-ealamh.

Eft, *s.* Dearc luachair.

Egg, *s.* Ubh, ugh. Eggs, *uibhean;* lay an egg, *beir ubh;* hatching eggs, *a guradh;* a hatching of eggs, *gur, guradh;* an addle-egg, *ubh gluig;* a rotten egg, *ubh grod;* a pullet's egg, *ubh eireig;* the white of an egg, *gealagan uibh.*

Egg, *v. a.* Brosnaich, prosnaich, stuig.

Eglantine, *s.* Seorsa ròs.

Egotism, *s.* Féineachd, fein-iomradh, fein-luaidh, fein-mholadh, fein-chliù.

Egotist, *s.* Fein-mholadair.

Egregious, *a.* Comharaichte, sonraichte, corr, gast, ard, mòr, ana-barra; fior olc; curt. Egregiously, *gu sònraichte, gu còrr.*

Egress, *s.* Imeachd, trialladh, dol a mach, imrich, gluasad, falbh.

Egression, *s.* Dol a mach, imeachd.

Egypt, *s.* An Eiphit. The land of Egypt, *talamh na h-Eiphit.*

Egyptian, *s.* Eiphiteach.

Egyptian, *a.* Eiphiteach.

Eider, *s.* (*In ornithology*), seorsa geòidh air am bheil clòimh ro-phriseil.

Eigh, *interj.* Aoibh, aoibh!

Eight, *s.* Eilean aimhne.

Eight, *a.* Ochd, ochdnar.

Eighteen, *a.* Ochd-deug. Eighteen men, *ochd fir-dheug;* eighteen women, *ochd mnathan deug.*

Eighteenth, *a.* An t-ochdamh-deug. The eighteenth man, *an ochdamh fear deug.*

Eightfold, *a.* Ochd uairean, ochd fillte, ochd uiread.

Eighth, *a.* An t-ochdamh. The eighth at cards, *an t-ochdamh air chairtean.*

Eighthly, *adv.* San ochdamh aite; gu h-ochdail.

Eightieth, *a.* An ochdmhad, an ceithir ficheadamh.

Eight-score, *a.* Ochd fichead.

Eighty, *a.* Ceithir fichead.

Either, *pron.* An darna h-aon, an darna fear, aon, aon air bith, aon sam bith, gach. If either of us were present, *nam biodh h-aon againn ann (no) an sin;* let either of you come, *thigeadh an darna h-aon agaibh.*

Either, *adv.* An darna cuid, no. Either this or the other, *an darna cuid so no ud eile.*

EJACULATE, *v. a.* Tilg a mach, cuir a mach, labhair

EJACULATION, *s.* Tilgeadh; asluchadh, urnuigh ghoirrid, éigh.

EJACULATORY, *a.* Cabhagach; deannail; goirid mar urnuigh.

EJECT, *v.* Tilg, tilg a mach; diobair, cuir air falbh, fògair. Ejected, *air chur a mach, (no) air falbh, tilgte, diobairte, fògairte, cairt-te, air thilgeadh, air dhiobradh, air fhògradh.*

EJECTMENT, *s.* Cur a mach (no) air falbh, tilgeadh, fògradh, diobradh

EJECTION, *s.* Cur a mach, tilgeadh a mach, diobradh

EJULATION, *s* Gul, gal, caoineadh, caoidh.

EKE, *conj.* Cuideachd, mar an ceudna, fòs, a bharrachd air; a bharras air.

EKE, *v a.* Cuir ri, meudaich, fadaich, ic; ioc, iocainn. Eked out, *air iocainn*

ELABORATE, *v.* Oibrich, saothair, gabh saothair.

ELABORATE, *a.* Saothaireachail; air a dheanamh le moran strigh.

ELABORATELY, *adv* Gu saothaireachail, gu dlchiollach, le moran strigh.

ELANCE, *v. a.* Tilg mar shaighead.

ELAPSE, *v n* Ruith seachad, rach seachad; aom. Elapsed, *air dol seachad*, after two years had elapsed, *air do dhà bhliadhna dol seachad.*

ELASTIC, *a.* Lùbach, géilleach; grad-lubach, ais-leumach.

ELASTICITY, *s.* Lùbachd, geilleachd, grad-lubachd.

ELATE, *a.* Ardanach, uallach, leòmach, stràiceil, uaibhreach; séidte suas, air atadh He is elated with praise, *tha e air a thogail le aoibhneas.*

ELATION, *s.* Uabhar, ardan, uallachd, stràic, mor-uaille, uaille; leoim.

ELBOW, *s.* Uileann; luib, car. Be at the elbow, *bi am fagus, bi aig laimh.*

ELBOW, *v. a* Uileannaich, pùc le uileann

ELBOW-CHAIR, *s.* Cathair da laimh.

ELD, *s.* Aois, sean-aois.

ELDER, *s.* (*In botany*), fearn, droman.

ELDER, *s.* Foirbheach; (*ancestor*), sinnsear, *among the Jews*), naghladair; (*in the New Testament*), seanair, pears' eaglais, (*among the Presbyterians*), eildear.

ELDER, *a* Sine, ni 's sine, ni 's aosmhoire. An elder brother, *brathair mòr.*

ELDERSHIP, *s.* Seanaireachd; sinnsearachd.

ELDEST, *a.* Sine, aosmhoire, is sine, is aosmhoire.

ELECAMPANE, *s* An aillean.

ELECT, *v. a.* Tagh, roghnaich; rùnaich. Elected, *taghta, taghte, roghnaichte*

ELECT, *a.* Taghta, taghte, roghnaichte.

ELECTIC, *a.* Taghach, roghainneach, roghnach

ELECTION, *s.* Taghadh, roghnachadh; runachadh, socrachadh; (*in theology*), roimh-thaghadh, roimh-shonrachadh.

ELECTIVE, *a.* Taghadach, taghach, roghnachail

ELECTOR, *s* Taghadair, roghnachair; Prionnsa aig am bheil guth ann am roghnachaidh Iompair na Gearmailte

ELECTORATE, *s* Oighreachd taghadair, taghadroinn

ELECTRE, *s.* Omar, rud sam bi, air dha bhi, air a shuath, a thairneas ga ionnsuidh ní eutrom, mar iteig

ELECTRIC, ELECTRICAL, *a.* Dlu-thairneach, grad-thairneach; grad.

ELECTRICITY, *s.* Comas a th'aig cuid nithe, air dhoibh bhi air an suath car tacain, air rudan eutroma, mar phaipeir no iteagan, a tharruin ga 'n ionnsuidh.

ELECTUARY, *s.* Seorsa leigheis.

ELEEMOSYNARY, *a.* Déirceach, bleideireach; mar dheirc.

ELEGANCE, ELEGANCY, *s* Eireachdas, maise, maisealachd, tlachd, snàs, boidhche, boidhichead, dreach, àille

ELEGANT, *a.* Eireachdail, maiseach, tlachdmhor, ciatach, snàsmhor, bòidheach, dreachmhor, aillidh.

ELEGANTLY, *adv.* Gu h-eireachdail, gu maiseach, gu tlachdmhor, gu ciatach, gu snàsmhor, gu boidheach, gu dreachmhor, gu h-aillidh

ELEGIAC, *a* Marbh-rannach, brònach, muladach; tuirsdh

ELEGIAST, *s.* Marbh-rannaiche.

ELEGY, *s.* Marbh-rann, tuire, tuireadh, cumhadh, duan.

ELEMENT, *s.* Bunabhas, ceud-aobhar; duil; foroideas, toiseach foghluim, na ceithir dùilean, mar their iad riu; is iad sin talamh, àile, teine is uisge

ELEMENTAL, *a* Dùileachail, priomh; bunabhasach.

ELEMENTARY, *a.* Simplidh, neo-mheasgta; priomh, bunabhasach

ELEPHANT, *s* Oilleabhaint, oillbheint.

ELEPHANTIASIS, *s* Gné luibhre.

ELEVATE, *v a.* Ardaich, tog; dean aoibhinn; dùisg, séid suas. Elevated, *ardaichte, togte, togta, aoibhinn*

ELEVATION, *s.* Togail suas, togail 'n airde, ardachadh, airde; inmhe, ard-inmhe, mòrachd, urram, dùsgadh.

ELEVATOR, *s* Inneal dearg-leigh

ELEVEN, *a.* A h-aon deug, aon deug. Eleven times, *aon uair (no) tarruing deug;* eleven o'clock, *aon uair deug*, eleven men, *aon fhear deug.*

ELF, *s.* Sìthiche; duine sìth; tàcharan; siobhrag; ailmse; àbhach; siochair; taibhse; duine beag; luch-armunn; deamhan.

ELFIN, ELFISH, ELVISH, *a.* Sitheach; ailmseach

ELICIT, *v a.* Buail mach, thoir mach, tarruing.

ELICIT, *a.* Tairnte, air a tharruing a muigh (no) mach; foillsichte; aithnichte

ELIDE, *v. a.* Bris, spealg, bruan.

ELIGIBLE, *a.* So-roghnachaidh, aridh air raoghainn; taitneach; iomchuidh, miannach.

† ELIMINATE, *v a* Cuir a mach, fògair, cuir cùl ri

† ELIMINATION, *s* Fògradh, fuadachadh, diobradh, culachadh

ELINGUID, *a* Balbh, tosdach, gun chainnt.

ELISION, *s* Gearradh, giorrachadh, cutachadh; dealachadh.

ELIXATION, *s* Bruicheadh, bruitheadh; tarruing brigh ni sam bith, le bhruicheadh

ELIXIR, *s.* Brigh, blàth-shugh, ioc-shlainnte, cungaidh leigheis.

ELK, *s* Lon, seorsa feidh le adhaircean mòr

ELL, *s* Cuig càirtean; slat-thomhais, slat.

ELLIPSIS, *s* (*In geometry*), ubh-chearcall; no cearcall aig am bi aon chrois-lìn a theid troimh 'n mheadhon, ni 's fhaide no 'n lìn eile, a theid dìreach tarsuing oirre, a deanamh dà leth dhith

ELM, *s.* Leamhan, sleamhan, slamhan An elm-tree, *craobh leamhain*

ELOCUTION, *s.* Ur-labhradh, uirghioll, deas-chainnt, snàslabhairt

ELOGY, *s.* Moladh, cliù

ELONGATE, *v a* and *n.* Fadaich; tarruing mach, buail a mach, cuir ni 's fhaide air falbh; sìn a mach; rach am fad; rach an céin, rach air astar

ELONGATION, *s.* Fadachadh; sìneadh mach; astar, céin; trialladh, falbh.

ELOPE, *v. a.* Ruith air falbh, rach am fuadach, rach as, teich, fuadaich, rach air theich. She eloped with him, *chaidh i am fuadach leis.*

ELOPEMENT, *s.* Dol am fuadachadh, fuadach, fuadachadh, ruith air falbh gun fhios, teicheachd, dol air theich.

ELOPS, *s.* Iasg; nathair

ELOQUENCE, *s.* Ùr-labhairt, uirghioll, binn-bhriathrachd, deas-chainnt, snàs-labhairt, fileantachd

ELOQUENT, *a.* Ur-labhrach, binn-bhriathrach, deas-bhriathrach, deas-chainnteach, fileanta As eloquent as a bard, *cho fileanta ri bard*

ELSE, *pron* Eile, aon eile, aon a thuillead, aon a bharrachd. Who else? *co eile?* somebody else, *urr-eigin eile*, somewhere else, *an aite eigin eile*

ELSE, *adv* Neo, air neo Or else, *no*, do it, else I will, *dean e, air neo ni mise e*

ELSEWHERE, *adv.* An àite eile, an ionad eile. Go elsewhere, *rach a dh' àite eile.*

ELUCIDATE, *v. a.* Soilleirich, dean soilleir (no) so-thuigsinn, mìnich, soillsich Elucidated, *soilleirichte, mìnichte, soillsichte, air a dheanamh soilleir, air a dheanamh mìn.*

ELUCIDATION, *s.* Soilleireachadh, mìneachadh, soillseachadh

ELUCIDATOR, *s.* Fear mìneachadh, mìneachair

ELUDE, *v. a.* Rach as le car, thoir an car a, meall, seachain

ELUDIBLE, *a* So-mhealladh.

ELUSION, *s* Dol as o cheasnachadh, seachnadh, cuilbheart, ceabhachd, car

ELUSIVE, *a* Carach, cuilbheartach, ceabhachdach, eolach, mealltach

ELUSORY, *a.* Fealltach, mealltach, fallsail.

ELUTE, *v. a* Nigh, glan, sruthail.

ELUTRIATE, *v a.* Siothladh, taomaich

ELUTRIATION, *s* Siothladh, taomachadh

ELYSIAN, *a.* Pàrasail, neamhaidh, sona, taitneach, ro-shòlasach

ELYSIUM, *s* Pàras; flathinnis nan cinneach, aite rothaitneach sam bi

EMACIATE, *v. a* and *n.* Caith, searg, crion, caolaich, fas tana, fàs caol, fas bochd, rach an dolaidh Emaciated, *caithte, caol, truagh, tana, bochd*

EMACIATION, *s* Caitheamh, seargadh, crionadh, caolachadh, tanachadh, caoile

EMACULATION, *s* Glanadh, gloine, fior-ghloine

EMANANT, *a* Sruthach, brùchdach

EMANATE, *v n* Sruth, brùchd, ruith

EMANATION, *s.* Sruth, sruthadh, brùchd, bruchdadh, ruithe

EMANCIPATE, *v. a* Saor, fuasgail; leig fa sgaoileadh.

EMANCIPATION, *s.* Saoradh, saorsainn, saorsadh, fuasgladh

EMASCULATE, *v a.* Spoth, dean tais (no) meath; anfhannaich Emasculated, *spothte, anfhannaichte*

EMASCULATION, *s.* Spothadh, spothadaireachd, taiseachadh, an-fhannachadh, mi-fhearantas, boige

EMBALE, *v* Trus, ceangail suas, pacainn

EMBALM, *v. a.* Spiosraich, lion le spiosradh, gleidh corp marbh le spiosraidh Embalmed, *spiosraichte, air a ghleidh le spiosraidh*

EMBALMER, *s* Spiosraiche; spiosradair.

EMBAR, *v a* Dùin, druid, iom-dhruid, bac, cuir moille (no) bac air.

EMBARCATION, *s.* Barcachadh; dol air bord luing; luchdachadh luing.

EMBARGO, *s* Seòl-bhacadh, bacadh o sheòladh, stad air comh-cheannachd, earghair.

EMBARK, *v. a* and *n.* Barcaich; rach air bord luing; luchdaich luing, cuir air luing.

EMBARRASS, *v. a* Cuir thar a chéile; cuir an iom-cheist, cuir an éigin, cuir an teinne, buair, bac, grab Embarrassed, *thar a chéile, an iomcheist, an teinne.*

EMBARRASSMENT, *s.* Iom-cheiste, teinne, airc, cruaidhchas; grabadh.

EMBASE, *v. a* Truaill, truaillich, mill; dìblich. Embased, *truaillte, truaillichte, millte.*

EMBASSADOR, *s.* Teachdair.

EMBASSAGE, EMBASSY, *s* Teachdaireachd, gnothuch follaiseach, gnothuch rioghachd

EMBATTLE, *v a* Cuir an ordugh catha Embattled, *an ordugh catha*

EMBAY, *v. a* Druid (no) dùin ann an geòtha (no) an òban.

EMBELLISH, *v a.* Sgeadaich, sgiamhuich, maisich, nàisnich, breaghaich, greus, riomhaich Embellished, *sgeadaichte, sgiamhaichte, an a sgeadachadh.*

EMBELLISHMENT, *s* Sgeadachadh, sgiamhachd, maise, nàisneachd, breaghachd, greusadh, riomhadh.

EMBERS, *s* Griosach, beo-luath, beo-luaithre

EMBERWEEK, *s* Seachduin na luaithre

EMBEZZLE, *v a* Mi-ghnathaich, goid, cealaich, ana-caith; caith ort fein airgiod a dh' carbar ruit chum a ghleidh.

EMBEZZLEMENT, *s* Mi-ghnathachadh airgid, cealachadh; braid, mi-bhuil

EMBLAZON, *v a* Lannaich, sgiamhaich le suaicheantais

EMBLAZONRY, *s* Dealbhan air sgiathaibh (no) targaidibh.

EMBLEM, *s.* Samhladh, coslas, ciall-dhealbh, riochd, samhlachadh, mac-samhailt

EMBLEMATIC, EMBLEMATICAL, *a* Samhlachail; cosmhal, ciallachail

EMBLEMATICALLY, *adv.* Gu samhlachail, gu ciallachail; mar shamhladh, mar choslas.

EMBOSS, *v* Grabhal, grean, breac; cuairtich, comhdaich, dùin, ruaig

EMBOSSMENT, *s* Grabhaladh, cnap, ruag, meallan, plucan.

EMBOWEL, *v. a* Thoir ann mionach as

EMBRACE, *v a* Glac gu gaolach, pòg, cuir fàilte air; (*taken in*), gabh, (*comprise*), cum

EMBRACE, *s* Glac, pòg, beadradh, criatachadh, caidreamh, fàilte.

EMBRASURE, *s* Barr-bhalladh

EMBROCATE, *v* Suath le leigheas; earra-bhruich

EMBROCATION, *s* Suathadh le leigheas; foirccan

EMBROIDER, *v. a* Greus, grinnich Embroidered, *greusta, grinnichte*

EMBROIDERER, *s* Greusadair, druinneach, dualadair.

EMBROIDERY, *s.* Greusadh, grinneachadh, obair ghreus, greus-obair; obair shnàthaid, snàthad-obair, druin.

EMBROIL, *v a* Cuir am mi-riaghailt, cuir air aimbreidh, tog aimhreite, tog tuasaid; buair, cuir troimh chéile, cuir thar a chéile, cuir an iomcheist, cuir dragh air, cuir miothlachd air.

EMBRYO, *s* Ceud-fhas; torrachas anabuich; neo-abachd. The business is but in embryo as yet, *cha 'n eil an gnothach ach na thoiseach fhathast.*

EMENDABLE, *a* So-leasachadh, so-cheartachadh

EMENDATION, *s.* Leasachadh, ceartachadh, atharrachadh, mùthadh air taobh an fheobhais

EMENDATOR, *s.* Leasachair, ceartachair.

EMERALD, *s.* Smarag, clach uaine ro luachmhor

EMERGE, *v n* Eirich as, eirich an uachdar, thig a mach; plaoisg

Emergence, Emergency, *s.* Eiridh suas, teachd an uachdar, teachd am follais, plaosgadh; éigin, teanntachd, airc, càs, tubaist.

Emergent, *a.* Ag éiridh, a teachd am follais; tubaisteach.

Emerods, *s.* Neasgaidean fola.

Emersion, *s.* Teachd am follais, plaosgadh, an t-am air an tig rionnag anns an t-sealladh, nach gabhadh faicinn le bhith tuille is fagus do 'n ghrian

Emery, *s* Seorsa mèin iaruinn.

Emetic, Emetical, *a* Sgeathach, sgeitheach, sgeithreach, ur-shlugaidh, diothaireach.

Emetic, *s.* Purgaid beòil; purgaid thilgidh; tilgeadh

Emication, *s.* Sradadh, dealrachd, drillineachd, caoireadh

Emiction, *s* Mùn, fual

Emigrant, *s.* Fear imrich, fear fuadain, iomrolaiche.

Emigrate, *v. n.* Imrich, rach air imrich; rach o aite gu h-aite; fag an duthaich

Emigration, *s.* Imrich, dol air imrich, dol o aite gu h-aite, fagail an dùthaich, iomroladh

Eminence, *s.* Airde; mullach; tom; meas, inbhe, onoir; cliù, urram; ainmeileachd; morachd; oirdheirceas

Eminency, *s.* Airde, inbhe, inmhe

Eminent, *a.* Ard; inbheach, mòr; onorach, measail; cliùiteach, urramach, ainmeil; (*excellent*), oirdheirc, gasd, corr; (*conspicuous*), follaiseach

Eminently, *adv.* Gu h-ainmeil; gu follaiseach; gu corr, gu gasd.

Emissary, *s.* Fear gnothuich, teachdair; fear-brathaidh; spithear; riochd-fhear diomhair.

Emission, *s.* Cur a mach, leigeil a mach, tilgeadh mach, dòrtadh.

Emit, *v a.* Cuir mach, leig a mach, tilg a mach, dòirt

Emmet, *s.* Seangan, sneaghan, moirb.

Emollient, *a.* Bog, bogar; tais, maoth, maothalach

Emollient, *s.* Leigheas mhaothalach, maothalachd.

Emolument, *s.* Tairbhe, coisinn, buidhinn; buannachd, *proidhit;* buaidh

Emotion, *s* Buaireas, buaireadh, grad-chlisgeadh, gluasad inntinn; creathnachadh.

Empale, *v. a.* Daingnich, daighnich; druid, dùin, iomdhruid; troimh-lot; cuir neach gu bàs le 'chur air gath (no) bior.

Empannel, *v a.* Mionnaich agus druid a stigh luchd-deuchainn.

Emperor, *s* Iompair. Emperors, *iompairean*

Emphasis, *s.* Cudthrom sonraichte air a leigeil air focal no air sioladh; osgarrachd; brìgh, blas

Emphatic, Emphatical, *a* Drùighteach, neartmhor, osgarra, brìghmhor, blasda. Emphatically, *gu drùighteach, gu neartmhor, gu h-osgarra, gu brìghmhor, gu blasda, a reir coslais.*

Empierce, *v. a.* Sàth, lot, troimh-lot; bior, bioraich

Empire, *s.* Iompaireachd, cumhachd, uachdaranachd

Empiric, *s* Feall-leigh, *dochdair bi gis.*

Empiricism, *s* Feall-*dhochdaireachd.*

Emplaster, *s.* Plàsd

Emplastic, *a.* Rithinn, leanailteach; bidheanta.

Emplead, *v. a.* Cronaich, coirich, dìt; casaid

Employ, *v. a.* Gnathaich; uidhsinn, thoir obair do

Employ, *s.* Seirbheis, obair, gnothach, dreuchd; àite

Employment, *s* Gnothach, ceairde, obair, dreuchd, aran, àite.

Empoison, *v.* Puinnsionaich, truaill.

Empoisonment, *s* Puinnsionachadh

Emporium, *s* Margadh, margad, baile margaidh.

Empoverish, *v. a.* Cuir gu bochduinn, dean bochd, dean ainnis, dean truagh, fag bochd, fag ainnis (no) truagh

Empoverishment, *s.* Bochduinn, truaighe, baigearachd, uireasbhuidh, uireasbhachd

Empower, *v a.* Thoir barrantas, thoir ughdarras, thoir comas, ceadaich

Empress, *s* Ban-iompair. Empresses, *ban-iompairean*

Emptied, *part.* Taomaichte, falamhaichte, air a thaomadh

Emptier, *s* Falamhachair, taomadair

Emptiness, *s* Falamhachd, folamhachd, fàslachd; faoineas; cion maoin, (*of head*), aineolas; cion eolais.

Empty, *a* (*Void*), falamh, folamh, neo-làn; (*vain*), fàs, faoin, (*needy*), easbhuidheach, ditheach; acrach, ocrach; (*ignorant*), aineolach; (*barren*), neo-thorrach, dì-threabhach.

Empty, *v. a.* Taom, taomaich, falamhaich, traogh; † diolgion Emptied, *taomaichte, falmhaichte.*

Empurple, *v a* Deargaich, dearg, corcaraich. Empurpled, *deargaichte.*

Empuzzle, *v. a* Cuir an iom-cheist, cuir am breislich

Empyema, *s* Iongrachadh.

Empyrean, *a.* Neamhuidh, adhareil.

Empyreuma, *s* Losgadh, dothadh

Empyrosis, *s* Losgadh.

Emulate, *v.* Strìgh, dean strìgh, dean spairn, dean co-fharpuis, lean

Emulation, *s* Strìgh, comh-strìgh, spairn, comh-dheuchainn, comh-fharpuis; eud, tnù, farmad

Emulative, *a* Comh-strìgheach, spairneach, eudmhor, comh-fharpail

Emulator, *s.* Comh-fhear-strìgh, comh-dheuchainniche.

Emulge, *v a.* Bleoghainn, falmhaich.

Emulgent, *s* Bleoghannach, sùigheach, traoghach

Emulous, *a* Comh-strìgheach, comh-fharpuiseach, spairneach, eudmhor. Emulous of renown, *an geall air cliù*

Emulously, *adv* Gu comh-strìgheach, gu spairneil, gu h-eudmhor

Emunctory, *s.* Falmhachair follais no ni sam bi a thig as a choluinn.

Enable, *v a* Dean murrach (no) comasach, neartaich.

Enact, *v. a* Reachdaich, orduich, daighnich, dean, coimhlion. Enacted, *orduichte, daighnichte*

Enactor, *s.* Reachdair

Enambush, *v. n* Dean feall-fholach, dean plaid-luidhe, dean luidheachan

Enamel, *s* Doichinnmheal

Enamel, *v a* Doichinnmhil

Enamour, *v a.* Lion le gaol; gradhaich, miannaich Enamoured, *an gaol*, he is enamoured of her, *tha e 'n gaol oirre.*

Enarration, *s* Innseadh, sgeulachd

Engaoe, *v. a* Druid, duin suas

Encamp, *v. a* Campaich, dean camp, dean foslong-phort He encamped, *champaich e*

Encamped, *part* Campaichte, ann an camp.

Encampment, *s* Campachadh; camp, foslong-phort.

Encave, *v a* Còsaich, folaich ann an toll, uamhaich Encaved, *còsaichte, folaichte, uamhaichte*

Enchafe, *v. a* Cuir air bainni, cuir air bhoile, buair, feargaich, brosnuich.

Enchain, *v a* Cuibhrich, ceangail, cuir ann geimhlibh,

cuir air theathair. Enchained, *cuibhrichte, air chuibhreachadh*

Enchant, *v. a.* Cuir fo' gheasan, cuir fo' dhruidheachd; cuir buidseachd air, thoir ard thoil-inntinn. Enchanted, *fo' gheasan, fo' dhruidheachd, làn aoibhinn.*

Enchanter, *s.* Druidh, draoidh, fiosaiche, fear fiosachd, piseagaiche.

Enchantment, *s.* Druidheachd, draoidheachd, piseag, buitseachd; ard-shòlas, ard-thoil-inntinn.

Enchantress, *s.* Ban-druidh, ban-fhiòsaiche, buitseach; boirionnach ro mhaiseach, rìmhinn.

Enchase, *v a* Druid, dùin, iomallaich, foirich; leig

Enchiridion, *s* Leabhar laimh, leabhran

Encircle, *v a.* Cuairtich, cuartaich, iom-dhruid, uimdhruid. Encircled, *cuairtichte*, encircling, *a cuairteachadh.*

Encirclet, *s* Cearclag; fàinne, fàile.

Enclose, *v. a* Dùin, druid, iom-dhruid, cuairtich Enclosed, *dùinte, cuairtichte*, enclosing, *a dùnadh, a druideadh.*

Enclosure, *s* Dùnadh, iom-dhruidheadh, cuairteachadh; pairc; loinn; iolann, iadhlann

Encomiast, *s.* Moladair; fear moladh.

Encomium, *s.* Moladh, cliù

Encompass, *v* Cuairtich, cuartaich, druid, dùin, iomdhruid, iadh Encompassed, *cuairtichte*, encompassing, *cuartachadh, cuairteacheadh, dùnadh.*

Encompassment, *s.* Cuairteachadh, cuartachadh, cuairteachd, iomdhruideadh

Encore, *adv* A ris, a rithist, a rithistich, uair eile, aon uair eile, fhathast.

Encounter, *s.* Comh-lainn, comhrag-déise, comhrag, cath, baiteal; comhdhail, coinneamh

Encounter, *v. a* Coinnich, thoir coinneamh; thoir ionnsuidh; thoir aghaidh air; cog He encountered him, *thug e aghaidh air.*

Encounterer, *s.* Namhaid, comhragaii

Encourage, *v* Brosnaich, brosnuich, prosnaich, stuig, thoir misneach, do, cuir misneach ann. Encourage him, *cuir misneach ann, stuig e*

Encouragement, *s.* Brosnuchadh, misneachadh; còghnadh; maoidhean, fabhor, taobh

Encourager, *s.* Brosnuchair, prosnachair, misneachair, caraid.

Encroach, *v.* Thig a stigh air crioch, thig gun fhios, thoir ionnsuidh, dinn.

Encroacher, *s* Gabhaltaiche, fear ionnsuidh, fear leamh

Encroachment, *s.* Teachd thar crioch, gabhaltas, gabhail gu neo-laghail; dinneadh.

Encumber, *v.* Bac, cuir bacadh (no) moille, cuir roimh; amail, cuir dragh; eallaich, luchdaich, cumraich, cuir eithre It encumbers me, *'tha e 'cur amail orm, tha e 'g am amaladh.*

Encumbrance, *s* Eithre, luchd, eallach, uallach, moille, amal, bacadh, dragh.

Encyclopædia, *s* Uile fhoghlum, cuairt-fhoghlum.

Encysted, *a* Cisuchte, ann an ciste, ann an soitheach.

End, *s* Crioch, finid, deireadh, dùnadh, comh-dhùnadh, ceann, ceann-thall; iomall, foir-cheann, ceann-uidhe, (*death*), bàs, (*design*), run, miann, (*consequence*), buile On end, *na sheasamh;* from beginning to end, *o thoiseach gu deireadh*, at the end of the street, *aig ceann na sràide*, at the year's end, *aig deireadh na bliadhna*, I fear what will be the end of it, *tha eagal orm ciod gus an d'thig e*, to what end do you say this? *c'arson tha thu ag radh so?* from the ends of the world, *o iomallaibh an t-saoghail;* an ill end, *droch chrioch;* hinder end, *ceann-deiridh;* in the end, *mu dheireadh, air a cheann thall*, to what end? *c'arson?* to the same end, *chum na chriche cheudna;* to the end that, *chum as gu, a chum agus gu*, for which end, *uime sin, air son sin;* near an end, *fagus do chrioch, fagus air bhith ullamh;* to no end, *gu diomhain, gu faoin.*

End, *v. a.* and *n* Criochnaich, thoir gu crioch, cuir crioch air; dùin, comh-dhùin, marbh; cuir gu bàs; thig gu crioch (no) ceann Ended, *criochnuichte, ullamh*

Endamage, *v.* Mill, cuir dholaidh, ciurr, dochannaich, ciurramaich.

Endanger, *v.* Cuir an cunnart, cuir an gàbhadh

Endear, *v a.* Dean ionmhuinn, dean gradhach, iomhuinnich, gradhaich. She is endeared to him, *is ionmhuinn leis i.*

Endearment, *s* Ionmhuinneachd, gradhachd; beadradh, gradh, gaol, tlachd, seirc; miodal

Endeavour, *s.* Oidhearp, oidhirp, dicheall; spairn, strigh, gleac, gleic. The best endeavour in my power, *an oidhearp is fhearr is urrainn mi.*

Endeavour, *v a* and *n* Feuch ri, thoir deuchainn, thoir oidhirp, dean oidhirp, dean strigh.

Endenize, *v a.* Saor, dean saor.

Endict, *v.* Cuir as leth, cronaich, coirich, dit

Endictment, *s* Cur as leth, coireachadh, cronachadh; foillseachadh laghail, dìteadh

Endite, *v. a.* Sgriobh, deachd.

Endive, *s.* Eunaich ghàraidh

Endless, *a.* Siorruidh, neo-chriochnach, neo-chriochnuidheach, gun cheann; do ghnàth; bith-dheanta, bi-dheanta, bi-bhuan, bith-bhuan, maireannach, sior-mhaireannach.

Endlessness, *s.* Siorruidheachd, neo-chriochnachd, bidheantas, maireannachd.

Endlong, *adv.* An comhar a chinn, dìreach air aghaidh

† **Endmost**, *adv.* Air deireadh, air dheireadh

Endorse, *v.* Cùl-sgriobh, cuir lamh ri bann, bann-sgriobh; dean thairis Endorsed, *cul-sgriobhte, deanta thairis, air a dheanamh thairis*

Endorsement, *s.* Cul-sgriobhadh; daingneachadh, bannsgriobhadh

Endow, *v* Thoir cuibhrionn; thoir pòrsan, thoir tochar, thoir gibhte, beartaich.

Endowment, *s* Beartas, saibhreas, maoin; tochar, tochradh, gibhte, tabhartas; (*of mind*), eòlas, fiosrachadh; càil, feart.

Endue, *v a* Builich, sgeadaich, feartaich. Endued, *sgeadaichte, càilichte.* Endued with good qualities, *sgeadaichte le deagh chailibh*

Endurance, *s* Maireachdainn, mairsinn, buanachadh, buanas; fulang, giulan, foighidinn.

Endure, *v. a* and *n* Fulaing, fuluing, fuilig, giùlain, giùlain le, mair, buanaich; leig le He endured many hardships, *dh'fhuluing e iomad teanntachd.*

Endwise, *adv* Air a cheann, an comhair a chinn; na sheasamh

Enecate, *v. a* Marbh, mill, sgrios, cuir gu bàs.

Enemy, *s* Nàmhaid, nàmh, eas-caraid Enemies, *naimhdean, eas-cairdean*, (in theology), *an diabhol, aibhisear, aibhisdear.*

Energetic, *a.* Osgarra, cruaidh, làidir, reachdmhor, neartmhor, eifeachdach, tabhachdach; gniomhach, sgairteil.

Energy, *s* Cumhachd, neart, tréine, tabhachd, eifeachd, osgarrachd, sgairtealachd.

Enervate, *v. a.* Anfhannaich, anmhunnaich, lagaich, taisich, bogaich; dean an-fhann; dean lag; dean tais (no) bog. Enervated, *an-fhannaichte.*

Enervation, *s.* An-fhannachadh, anmhunnachadh, lagachadh, boige, taise, taisealachd, neo-fhearantas.

Enfeeble, *v. a.* and *n.* Anfhannaich, anmhunnaich, lagaich, dean fann, fannaich; thoir thairis. Enfeebled, *anfhannaichte, anmhunnaichte, fannaichte.*

Enfeoff, *v. a.* Thoir seilbh, gabh seilbh.

Enfeoffment, *s.* Seilbheachadh, gabhail seilbh, bannseilbhe.

Enfilade, *s.* Slighe chughann; rathad aimhleathann.

Enforce, *v. a.* Neartaich, cuidich; éignich; thoir sparradh; earalaich; cuir a dh'aindeoin; brosnaich, stuig; còmhdaich. Enforced, *neartaichte, éignichte.*

Enforcedly, *adv.* Air éigin.

Enforcement, *s.* Aindeoin, éigin, éigneachadh, comhéigneachadh.

Enforcer, *s.* Eigneachair.

Enfranchise, *v. a.* Dean saor, saor, thoir saorsadh; builich saorsa baile margaidh air neach; cuir fa sgaoileadh.

Enfranchisement, *s.* Saorsadh, saorsainn; saoradh o ghainntir (no) a dhaorsadh.

Engage, *v. a.* and *n.* Gabh as laimh; thoir geall; cuir geall; freagair airson, bi freagarrach (no) buailteach; gabh; cuir fo gheall (no) fo bhann, ceangail; tionsgainn air ni; cathaich, buail comhrag, gabh sa cheile, thoir aghaidh air. He engaged to do it, *ghabh e as laimh a dheanamh, gheall e a dheanamh;* they engaged in battle, *ghabh iad sa cheile;* engaged (as a servant), *gabhta, gabhte.*

Engagement, *s.* (*Battle*), cath, combrag, baiteal, blàr; (*promise*), gealladh, gealltuinn, bann, ceangal, comhcheangal, gabhail as laimh.

Engaol, *v.* Priosanaich, gainntirich.

Engender, *v.* Gein, gin; torraich, thoir a mach, beir.

Engine, *s.* Inneal; inneal feachd; innleachd; obair uisge; obair-cheardail; fear-gnothuich.

Engineer, *s.* Innleachdair.

Enginery, *s.* Gunnraidh.

Engird, *v. a.* Cuairtich, cearclaich, iomdhruid, iadh.

England, *s.* Sasgunn, Sasunn, Sagsunn.

English, *s.* Beurla, beurla Shasunach.

English, *a.* Sasunnach, Sasgunnach, Sagsunnach.

Englut, *v. a.* Lion, sàthaich, sluig.

Engore, *v. a.* Reub, beubanaich.

Engorge, *v. a.* Sathaich, lion; sluig; glut; ith suas, ith gu glàmhach.

Engrail, *v. a.* Ballaich, breac, breacaich, dean eugsamhuil.

Engrain, *v. a.* Dath gu domhainn.

Engrapple, *v. a.* Glac, teann-ghlac, gramaich, greimich.

Engrasp, *v. a.* Glac, teann-ghlac, gramaich, greimich, dean greim.

Engrave, *v. a.* Grabh, dealbh, cearb, gearr.

Engraver, *s.* Grabhair, grabhadair, dealbhair, gearradair, dualaiche.

Engraving, *s.* Grabhadh, dealbh, gearradh.

Engrieve, *v. a.* Farranaich, cuir farran (no) feirge air, cuir mio-thlachd air.

Engross, *v. a.* Tiughaich; meudaich; domhlaich; reamhraich; gabh roimh laimh; ceannaich an t-iomlan do bhàrr chum a reic ni 's daoire; sglamhaich; leir-ghlac; garbhsgriobh.

Engrosser, *s.* Roimh-stallair, sglamhaiche; cis-mhangair, suil-mhangair, garbh-sgriobhair.

Engrossment, *s.* Sglamhachadh, leir-cheannachadh, leirghlacadh.

Enhance, *v. a.* Arduich luach no prios ni sam bi; arduich, tog, tog suas, meudaich, an-tromaich.

Enhancement, *s.* Arduchadh, togail, éiridh; an-tromachadh.

Enigma, *s.* Toimhseagan, toimhseachan, ceist; dubhcheist; dubh-fhocal.

Enigmatical, *a.* Dorch, do-thuigsinn, teagamhach, doilleir.

Enjoin, *v. a.* Orduich, iarr, thoir ordugh, thoir sparradh. Enjoined, *orduichte, air orduchadh.*

Enjoinment, *s.* Ordugh, iarrtas, comannt, sparradh.

Enjoy, *v. a.* Meall, sealbhaich, gabh seilbh, taitinn, toilich. May you wear and enjoy it! *gu meall is gu 'n caith thu e!* you cannot enjoy them, *cha 'n urrudh dhuit am mealltuinn.*

Enjoyment, *s.* Mealltuinn, sealbhachadh; sonas, suaimhneas.

Enkindle, *v. a.* Las, loisg, fadaidh, beothaich. Enkindled, *laiste, loisgte, beothaichte.*

Enlarge, *v. a.* Meudaich, farsuingich; cuir am meud, rach am meud, fas mòr; cuir am farsuingeachd; cuir fa sgaoil. Enlarged, *meudaichte.*

Enlargement, *s.* Meud, meudachadh, farsuingeachadh; saorsadh.

Enlarger, *v.* Meudachair.

Enlighten, *v. a.* Soillsich; seòl, oileanaich, teagaisg, ionnsuich; beothaich. Enlightened, *soillsichte, oileanaichte, teagasta, ionnsuichte, beothaichte.*

Enlightener, *s.* Soillseachair; fear teagaisg.

Enliven, *v.* Beothaich, thoir misneach do, cuir misneachann; dean beothail (no) misneachail.

Enlivener, *s.* Misneachair, brosnaichair; fear brosnachaidh.

Enmity, *s.* Naimhdeas, naimhdealas, mi-rùn; droch-ghean, farmad, tnù.

Ennoble, *v. a.* Ardaich, uaislich, urramaich, dean cliùiteach. Ennobled, *ardaichte, uaislichte; urramaichte.*

Ennoblement, *s.* Ardachadh, uaisleachadh.

Enodation, *s.* Fuasgladh snaidhm, fuasgladh, tuasgladh, fuasgal, tuasgal.

Enormity, *s.* Mi-riaghailteachd; eucoir; uamhasachd, uamharrachd, aingidheachd; ciont. Enormities, *ciontan, uamharra.*

Enormous, *a.* Mi-riaghailteach; thar a cheile; farranta, uamhasach, fuathasach; olc, aingidh; curt; ro-mhòr; thar tomhas. Enormously, *gu h-uamharra, gu fuathasach.*

Enormousness, *s.* Uamharrachd, ana measarrachd.

Enough, *s.* Pailteas, goireas, leòir. That is enough, *is leòir sin, is leòir e;* it is not enough, *cha leòir e;* I have enough, *tha pailteas agam, tha goireas agam;* enough is as good as a feast, *is fhearr gu leòir na tuille is a chòir, is co math na 's leòir is iomadaidh.*

Enough, *adv.* Gu leòir, ni 's leòir, na leòir. Far enough, *fad gu leòir, fad ni 's leòir;* I am well enough, *tha mi gu làn mhath;* sure enough, *cinnteach gu leòir, air chinnte;* this is quite enough, *foghnaidh so, is leòir so.*

Enow, *pl.* of **Enough**.

En passant, *adv.* San dol seachad; eadar dha sgeul.

Enrage, *v.* Buair, cuir corruich air, brosnuich, broisg, feargaich. Enraged, *buairte, air bhuaireadh, fo bhuaireas.*

Enrank, *v.* Sreath, sreadaich, rangaich, cuir an ordugh.

Enrapture, *v. a.* Dean lan-aoibhinn, dean eibhinn, aoibhnich, éibhnich, suaimhnich.

Enravish, *v.* Dean lan-aoibhinn, aoibhnich, éibhnich, suaimhnich.

Enravishment, *s.* Lan aoibhneas, suaimhneas.

Enrich, *v. a.* Saibhrich, dean beartach, (no) saibhir; (*land*), mathaich, inneirich. Enriched, *saibhrichte.*

Enrichment, *s.* Saibhreachadh; beartas, saibhreas.

Enridge, *v.* Iomairich.

Enripen, *v.* Abuich, abaich, dean abaich; thoir gu h-inmhe.

Enrobe, *v. a.* Sgeadaich, eid, aodaich, breaghaich.

Enrol, *v.* Sgriobh sios, ainmich; ròil; cuir uime.

Enrolment, *s.* Ainm-chlar, ainm-litir.

Enroot, *v.* Freumhaich.

Ens, *s.* Bith.

† **Ensample**, *s.* Eisiomplair, eisimpleir, ball-sampuill, samhladh, samplair, bann-shampuill.

Ensconce, *v.* Daighnich, daingnich.

Enseam, *v. a.* Fuaidheal, fuaigh.

Ensear, *v. a.* Loisg.

Enshield, *v. a.* Dion; còmhdaich.

Enshrine, *v. a.* Gleidh mar nì coisrigte.

Ensiform, *a.* Mar chlaidheamh, cloidheil.

Ensign, *s.* Bratach, suaicheantas, suaitheantas; loman, comhar, sròl, crann-tàir, crois-tair; fear-brataich, luimneach.

Ensign-bearer, *s.* Fear brataich.

Enslave, *v. a.* Thoir am bruid (no) am braighdeanas, tràillich, tràillealaich, finn-reic, thoir fo' dhaorsadh. Enslaved, *am braighdeanas.*

Enslavement, *s.* Bruid, braighdeanas, tràillealachd, daorsadh, daorsainn.

Enslaver, *s.* Finn-reiceadair, sàruchair.

Ensue, *v. a.* and *n.* Lean, tachair, thig an lorg, thig gu criche; rach an tòir, soirbhich. What ensued, *ciod a thainig an lorg air sin;* the ensuing year, *a bhliadhna a leanas.*

Ensurance, *s.* Urras, paineachas.

Ensure, *v.* Dean cinnteach; rach ann urras. I will ensure him, *theid mi ann urras air.*

Ensurer, *s.* Urrasair, urras.

Entail, *a.* Suidhichte, a reir an lagha, sònraichte, nach gabh reiceadh.

Entail, *v. a.* Suidhich oighreachd air achd is nach gabh i reiceadh, cuir fo chòir.

Entailment, *s.* Suidheachadh (no) socrachadh oighreachd.

Entangle, *v. a.* Rib, bac, cuir bac, amail; prab cuir thar a cheile; cnodaich; cuir an iom-cheist. Entangled, *ribte, bacta, air ribeadh.*

Entanglement, *s.* Ribeadh, bacadh, iom-cheist; cuibhreach; buarach.

Entangler, *s.* Ribeadair.

Enter, *v. a.* Rach a stigh, thig a steach (no) a stigh; inntrinn; cuir sios.

Entering, *s.* Inntrinn, dol a stigh (no) steach; trannsa.

Enterparlance, *s.* Comhradh, bruidhinn.

Enterplead, *v.* Eadar-thagair.

Enterpleader, *s.* Eadar-thagradh, eadar-thagairt.

Enterprise, *s.* Gniomh cruaidh, (no) cunnartach, guais, cùis chruaidh, cùis dheacair; deuchainn cunnartach, ard-chuis.

Enterpriser, *s.* Fear a ghabhas as laimh nithibh deacair.

Enterprising, *a.* Misneachail, ard-chuiseach, guaismhor, guais-bheartach.

Entertain, *v. a.* Bruidhinn ri, comh-labhair; cum comhradh ri, thoir feist (no) cuirm; biataich; thoir aoidheachd; taitinn, toilich. Entertain an opinion, *bi am barail.*

Entertainer, *s.* Fear fial, fear cuirm, aoidhear, fear aoidheil.

Entertaining, *part.* and *a.* A riarachadh; a toileachadh; taitneach, sunntach, cridheil; neonach, spuirteil.

Entertainment, *s.* Comhluadar, conaltradh, comhradh; aoidheachd, feisd, fuireas, fleagh, cuirm; bratachd; furan; toileachadh; aighear, spuirt, ealaidh; cluiche.

Enthrone, *v. a.* Cuir air righ-chathair; arduich. Enthroned, *arduichte, na shuidhe air righ-chathair.*

Enthusiasm, *s.* Dian-dhealas; baoth-dhiadhuidheachd, baoth-chreideamh, dian-chreideamh; breug-fhios, ard-inntinneachd; bainnidh.

Enthusiast, *s.* Baoth-chreideach, dian-chreideach; aon a shaoileas e fein anabarra diadhaidh.

Enthusiastic, *a.* Baoth, dian-dhealasach, baoth-dhiadhuidh; ard-inntinneach.

Entice, *v.* Meall, tàlaidh, breug, thoir a thaobh, brosnuich.

Enticement, *s.* Mealladh, tàlaidh, breugadh, buaireadh, culaidh-bhuairidh, saimh-ghriosadh.

Enticer, *s.* Mealltair, breugaiche, buairear; fear tàlaidh.

Enticing, *a.* Mealltach, taladhach, buaireasach, drùighteach, tairngeach. Enticing, *gu mealltach, gu tàladhach, gu buaireasach, gu druighteach, gu tairneach.*

Entire, *a.* Iomlan, slàn, uile; (*uncorrupted*), neo-thruaillichte; (*sincere*), ionraic, treibhdhireach; dìleas; (*firm*), daingean, cinnteach. The entire year, *a bhliadhna iomlan.*

Entirely, *adv.* Gu h-iomlan, gu slàn, gu h-uile, gu léir, gu tur, gu baileach; gu buileach. Take it with you entirely, *thoir leat e gu h-iomlan,* (*no*) *gu baileach,* (*no*) *gu léir; thoir leat an t-iomlan.*

Entireness, *s.* Iomlanachd, sláine; (*sincerity*), ionracas, tréibhdhireas.

Entitle, *v.* Thoir còir; tiodalaich, builich tiodal, ainmich, gairm, goir. Entitling, *a toirt còir.*

Entitled, *part.* Còirichte; còraichte; ainmichte; do 'n goirear, ris an goirear. A book entitled a dictionary, *leabhar do 'n goirear foclair* (*no*) *abartair;* he is entitled to it, *tha còir aig air;* he is well entitled to it, *tha deagh chòir aig air;* the servant is entitled to his hire, *tha còir aig seirbheiseach air a dhuais, is airidh seirbheiseach air a dhuais.*

Entitulation, *s.* Tiodalachadh.

Entity, *s.* Bith.

Entoil, *v. a.* Rib, glac, cuir an sàs, grab.

Entomb, *v. a.* Adhlaic, ollanaich; cuir san ùir, cuir san uaigh, cuir fo 'n talamh. Entombed, *adhlaicte, ollanaichte; san uire, san uaigh, fo 'n talamh.*

Entrails, *s.* Mionach, greallach, caolain innigh ionar.

Entrance, *s.* Inntrinn, dol a steach, dol a stigh; trannsa; stairsneach; toiseach, tòiseachadh.

Entrance, *v. a.* Rach am platha; tuit ann am paisean, rach ann an neul; cuir ann am plath-sheimh.

Entrap, *v.* Rib, glac ann an rib, (no) ann an gaisde; paintirich; meall, gabh cothrom air.

Entreat, *v. a.* Guidh, grios, asluich, athchuing, sir (no) iarr gu dùrachdach. I entreat you, *tha mi 'guidhe ort; tha mi 'grios ort;* entreat gently, *pròis.* Entreated, *guidhte, griosta, asluichte;* easily entreated, *caoimhneil; so-chomhairlichte.*

Entreaty, *s.* Guidhe, griosadh, asluchadh, athchuinge, urnuigh, iarrtas ro dhùrachdach.

Entry, *s.* Trannsa; stairsneach; dol a steach; inntrinn; sgriobhadh (no) cur sios ann an leabhar.

Enumerate, *v.* Cunnt, cunnt suas, àireamh. Enumerated, *air a chunntadh, aireamhte.*

Enumeration, *s.* Cunntadh, cunntas, aireamh, aireamhachadh.

Enunciate, *v. a* Glaodh, gairm, cuir an céill, nochd, innis, foillsich.

Enunciation, *s* Glaodh, gairm, cur an céill, nochdadh, innseadh, foillseachadh, fiosrachadh, fios, labhradh

Envelope, *v.* Còmhdaich; cuairtich; folaich. Enveloped, *comhdaichte.*

Envelope, *s.* Còmhdach; cubhrainn; truaille

Envenom, *v. a.* Puinnsionaich, truaill; feargaich, cuir air bhoile, cuir air a chuthach. Envenomed, *puinnsionaichte.*

Enviable, *a.* Airidh air farmad.

Envier, *s.* Fear tnùth, fear mi-runach.

Envious, *a.* Farmadach, tnuthail, gamhlasach, miosguineach, iomhach.

Enviously, *adv.* Gu farmadach, gu tnùthail, gu gamhlasach, gu miosguineach.

Environ, *v. a.* Cuairtich, iadh, iom-dhruid Environed, *cuairtichte.*

Environs, *s.* Nàbachd, nabuidheachd, coimh-fhearsnachd, iomal; frith-bhailtean, fo-bhailtean.

Envoy, *s.* Teachdair; teachdair dùthcha.

Envy, *s.* Farmad, tnù, tnùth, gamhlas, iomhadh; cud. Envy will split a stone, *sgoiltidh farmad a chlach*

Envy, *v. a.* Gabh farmad ri; maoidh air. He envied me, *ghabh e farmad rium;* I do not envy you it, *cha 'n eil mi 'g a mhaoidh ort.*

Enwomb, *v. a.* Dean torrach (no) leth-tromach, adhlaic, folaich.

Epact, *s.* Uimhir leis am faighear aois na gealaich

Epaulette, *s* Babag air a deiltreadh le h-òr, no le airgiod, riomhadh gualle

Epha, *s.* Tomhas Eabhruidheach

Ephemera, *s.* Teasach (no) fiabhras nach mair ach aon la, cnuimh nach mair ach aon là

Ephemeral, *a.* Làthail, siùbhlach, neo-mhairionn, nach mair ach aon là.

Ephemeris, *s.* Cunntas lathail; reul chunntas, reul-iomradh

Ephemerist, *s.* Reuladair, speuradair.

Epic, *a.* Eachdraidheil, eachdraidheach, gaisgeil, mòrdha, mòr. An epic poem, *dan mòr*

Epicedium, *s.* Marbh-rann, tuireadh, coronach.

Epicure, *s.* Sòghair; geòcair, poitear, craosair; fear mi-gheimnidh na lòn is na mhiannaibh.

Epicurean, *a* Soghmhor, suaimhneach, geòcach, mi-stuam, craosach

Epicurism, *s.* Sogh, geòcaireachd, meisge, saimh, suaimhneas, colla

Epicycle, *s* Oisbheas; cuairteag bheag, cuairteag an taobh stigh cuairteig

Epidemia, *s* Tinneas (no) galar sgaoilteach; plaigh; teasach ghabhaltach, teasach bhuailteach

Epidemic, **Epidemical**, *a.* Sgaoilteach, cumanta, coitchionn. An epidemic distemper, *galar sgaoilteach.*

Epidermis, *s.* 'Craiceann a cholla, far-chraiceann.

Epiglottis, *s.* Sgorn-chailbhe

Epigram, *s.* Gearr-bhardachd, bardachd, ghearr, sgaiteach, osgriobhan.

Epigrammatic, *a.* Gearr-bhardach.

Epigrammatist, *s.* Gearr-bhard.

Epilepsy, *s.* An tuiteamas, an tinneas tuiteamas, guin na ré, tinneas na gealaich, cion mothachaidh, cion càileachd, † guinneire.

Epileptic, *a.* Tuiteamach, cudamaiseach.

Epilogue, *s.* Crioch-rann, crioch-sgéil

Epiphany, *s.* Foillseachadh an Tighearna; féill an righ, cuirm an righ, an dara la deug an deigh Nollaig.

Episcopacy, *s.* Easpuidheachd, easpuigeachd

Episcopal, *a* Easpuigheach, easbuigeach.

Episcopate, *s.* Easpuigheachd, easpachd

Episode, *s.* Taobh-sgeul, sgeul a leth-taobh.

Epispastic, *a.* Tairneach, leusach

Epistle, *s* Litir Epistles, *litrichean*

Epistolary, *a* Litireach.

Epitaph, *s.* Marbh-rann, cumha, sgriobhadh air lic-lighe, feart-ghrabh, marbhuach.

Epithalamium, *s* Oran pòsaidh, oran bainnse.

Epithet, *s* Foir-bhriathar, buaidh-fhocal, foir-ainm

Epitome, *s* Giorrachadh, as-tharruing.

Epitomise, *v a* Giorraich, beagaich, cutaich. Epitomised, *giorraichte, cutaichte.*

Epitomiser, *s* Giorradair

Epoch, *s* Ceann aimsir, am ainmeil o 'n tòisich aireamh aimsir, mar bhreith an t-Slanuigheir bheannaichte; uair ainmeil sam bi mar bhliadhna Phrionnsa, no la Sliabh an t-Siorraidh.

Epopee, *s.* Dàn mor.

Epulary, *a* Cuirmeach, féisdeach, fleadhach, aighearach.

Epulation, *s.* Mor-fhleadh, fleadh, cuirm, feisd, aighear

Equability, *s* Co-ionannas, co-ionannachd, ionannas, coslaichead, cothromaichead, co-choslas

Equable, *a.* Co-ionann, ionann, co-choslach, comhad, direach.

Equal, *a* Ionann, co-ionann, cosmhal, cosmhuil, coimeas, cothromach, comhad, (*adequate*), murrach, comasach; (*in parts*), cuimeir, cumadail, (*impartial*), neo-chlaon, direach, ceart; (*smooth*), comhnard, réidh

Equal, *s* Leth-bhreac, leithid, leithid eile, ionann, neach san aon inbhe, companach, combach, comh-aois I never saw your equal, *cha 'n fhac mi riamh do leithid* (*no*) *do leth-bhreac*

Equal, *v a.* and *n* Dean ionann, ionannaich, bi-ionann, bi co-ionann.

Equalise, *v. a* Dean ionann, (no) co-ionann

Equality, *s* Ionannas, ionannachd, co-ionannachd, combanas, caidreamh, comhadachd

Equally, *adv* Gu h-ionann, gu ceart; gu neo-chlaon

Equangular, *a.* Co-luibeach, co-uileannach, co-oisinneach

Equanimity, *s* Fulangas, soimeachd, socair inntinn.

Equanimous, *a.* Fulangach, soimeach, socrach, soitheamh, sobhdanach.

Equation, *s.* Co-ionannachadh.

Equator, *s* Cearcall a cuairteach' an domhainn near agus niar, ag a roinn na dha leth, tuath agus deas, lìn a chomh fhad-thràth

Equerry, *s* Maighstir nan each; gille stàbuill, stàbul

Equestrian, *a* Marcach, air muin eich.

Equidistant, *a.* Comh-fhad air falbh, comh-astarach, comh-chian

Equiformity, *s* Ionannachd, comh-chruth, comh-chumadh, co-shliosnachd; comh-choslas, comh-eugas

Equilibrate, *v* Comh-chothromaich, ceart-chudthromaich, ceart-chothromaich

Equilibration, *s.* Comh-chothromachadh, ceart-chothromachadh

Equinoctial, *s.* Lìn a chomh-fhad-thrà.

Equinox, *s* Comh-fhad-thrà The vernal equinox, *comh-fhad-thrà 'n earraich*, the autumnal equinox, *comh-fhad-thrà 'n fhogharaidh*

Equinumerant, *a.* Comh-lìonmhor

Equip, *v. a.* Uigheamaich, cuir an uigheam, sgeaduich, deasaich, ullamhaich. Equipped, *uigheamaichte*, fully equipped, *na làn uigheam, na lan deise*

Equipage, *s.* Uigheam, deise; carbad riomhach; fritheal-adh; muinntir, airneis, cungaidh, fasair, fasradh

Equipendency, *s* Comh-chothromachd, comh-chudthrom

Equipment, *s* Uigheamachadh

Equipoise, *s* Comh-thruimead, comh-chothromachd

Equipollence, *s* Comh-éifeachd; comh-thréine, comh-chumhachd

Equipollent, *a* Comh-threun; comh-chumhachdach.

Equitable, *a* Ceart, cothromach, dìreach, neo-chlaon; ionraic; saor, soilleir.

Equitably, *adv.* Gu ceart, gu cothromach, gu dìreach, gu neo-chlaon, gu h-ionraic

Equity, *s.* Ceartas, cothrom; fìrinn, ionracas, treibhdhireas, neo-chlaonad

Equivalence, *s* Comh-ionannas, comh-luach, comh-éifeachd

Equivalent, *a* Ionann, comh-ionann, co-mhath, co-éifeachdach

Equivalent, *s.* Luach, fiach, dìoladh An equivalent for your services, *luach (no) fiach do shaothaireach*

Equivocal, *a* Neo-chinnteach, teagamhach, doilleir.

Equivocally, *adv.* Gu neo-chinnteach, gu teagamhach; gu doilleir.

Equivocalness, *s* Teagamhachd, neo-chinntealas

Equivocate, *v. a* Bi san tumhartaich, (no) ann an teagamh, dean céil-inntinn

Equivocating, *a* Car-bhriathrach, cealgach, céil-inntinneach

Equivocation, *s* Car-bhriathar; doilleireachd cainnte, cealgaireachd, leith-sgeulachd; taisg-inntinn, ceil-inntinn

Equivocator, *s* Fear car-bhriathrach.

Era, *s* Am ainmeil sam bi, linn, aire-thràth See Epoch

Eradiation, *s* Dealradh, loinreadh, dearsachd, boisge, boisgealachd, gathan soluis

Eradicate, *v* Spìon as a bhun, sgrios, buain, lom-sgrios, tur-sgrios

Eradication, *s* Spìonadh, sgriosadh, cladhachadh

Erase, *v a* Sgrios, dubh a mach, mill, sgrìoch as; cuir a bun Erased, *sgriosta, sgrioste, dubhte a mach, millte, sgrìochte as, as a bhun.*

Erasement, *s.* Sgriosadh, dubhadh, milleadh, sgrìochadh as

Ere, *adv* Roimh, mun, man, sol Erenow, *roimh so, roimh an am so*, erelong, *a chlisge, a chlisgeadh, gu goirrid, an ceann ghoirrid, eadai so is ceann ghoirrid*

Erect, *a* Dìreach, na sheasamh; dàna; muinghinneach

Erect, *v a* Tog, cuir suas, ardaich, dìrich

Erection, *s* Togail, éiridh, dùsgadh; socrachadh

Erectness, *s* Dìrichead

Erelong, *adv.* An ceann ghoirrid, a chlisgeadh, an ceann tacain

Eremite, *s.* Dìthreabhach, aonaran

Eremitical, *a* Dìthreabhach, aonaranach, uaigneach

Eristical, *a.* Connspaideach, tagluinneach.

Ergo, *conj.* Uime sin, air an aobhar sin, fa 'n aobhar sin.

Ermine, *s* Fionna geal ro-mhìn, earmhìn

Erode, *v. a* Cnamh, ith; creim.

Erogation, *s.* Buileachadh, tabhairt, toirt seachad.

Erosion, *s* Cnamhadh, ithe, creimeadh

Err, *v n* Rach am mearrachd, dean mearrachd, rach a thaobh, rach air seachran, seabhaid, iomroll, claon, rach air aimhreidh; tuit ann am mearrachd You err, *tha thu am mearrachd.*

Errand, *s* Gnothuch, teachdaireachd. Go on an errand, *rach air ghnothuch*

Errant, *a* Iomrollach, seachranach, seabhaideach, gràineil A knight errant, *ridir nan spleadh*, an errant jade, *dearg bhaobh.*

Errantry, *s.* Seachranachd, seachran, iomrollachd, iomroll; spleadhachas.

Errata, *s.* Mearachdan clo-bhualaidh, clo-mhearachdan

Erratic, *a* Seachranach, siubhlach, luaineach; mùghteach, neo-bhunailteach

Erroneous, *a* Mearachdach, neo-cheart, mi-cheart, cearr, claon, saobh, fordalach; seachranach; air aimhreidh; earraideach.

Erroneously, *adv.* Gu mearachdach, gu mi-cheart, gu cearr, gu claon

Error, *s* Mearachd; seachran, iomroll, fordal, seabhaid, aimhrios, mealladh, coire, cionta, peacadh You are in an error, *tha thu am mearachd.*

Erst, *adv.* Air thùs, air tùs; roimh so; a cheann fhad, o cheann fad, o chian

Erubescence, *s.* Ruithteachd, ruthadh, deirge

Erubescent, *a* Ruithteach, ruiteach, dearg

Eruct, *v* Brùchd, dìoghrog.

Eructation, *s* Bruchd, brùchdadh, brùchdail; dìoghrog.

Erudite, *a* Ionnsuichte, foghluimte, oileanaichte

Erudition, *s* Ionnsach, ionnsuchadh, foghlum, oilean, teagasg, eòlas, muineadh, foircheadal, ealdhain, fios, † guth, † treith

Eruginous, *a* Coparach.

Eruption, *s* Bròth, bròthadh, brùthadh, teas, briseadh mach

Eruptive, *a* A briseadh a mach, brothach, bruthach, guireanach, bucaideach, carrach, teth.

Erysipelas, *s* Teine dé.

Escalade, *s* Balladh-streapaidh.

Escalop, *s.* Màorach, eisirean, creach, creachann, slige-chreachainn.

Escape, *v a* and *n* Rach as, teich, teich o chunnart, grad-theich, seachain, tearuinn They will not escape, *cha téid iad as* Escaped, *air dol as, a cunnart.*

Escape, *s* Dol as o chunnart, teicheachd, grad-theicheadh; ruithe air falbh, comas teicheachd, culag; di-chuimhne, mearachd; leithsgeul; doigh air dol as

Escargatoire, *s* Ionad far an gleidhear seilicheagan.

Eschalot, *s.* Seorsa uinnein, sgalaid

Eschar, *s* Alle, athailte, creim, craonn, carr, sgreub, calunn.

Escharotic, *a.* Losgach, leusach, screubach, ruisgeach.

Escharotic, *s* Losg-leigheas, losgadh, leus-leigheas

Escheat, *s* Dlighe uachdarain; fearann a thig air neach a dhìth oighre.

Eschew, *v. a* and *n* Seachain, teich o.

Escort, *s* Coimheadachd, freiceadan, *geard*

Escort, *v.* Rach maille ri, léidinn, thoir leidig (no) léidinn, coimhead o àite gu h-àite

Escot, *s* Seorsa cise

Escot, *v a.* Paigh lach fir eile; cum suas, biath

Esculent, *a.* Airson itheadh, a dh' fhaodar itheadh, biadhar, biachar.

Esculent, *s.* Biadh.

Escutcheon, *s.* Suaicheantas.

Espalier, *s.* Craobh gàraidh (no) ballaidh; spallair.

Especial, *a.* Sonruichte, araidh, araid, priomh. Especially, *gu sonruichte, gu h-araidh, gu h-araid; air chòrr.*

Especially. See Especial.

Espial, *s.* Fear coimhead.

Espousal, *s.* Ceangladh, gealltuinn pòsaidh, còrdadh.

Espousals, *s. pl.* Ceangladh, cordadh, geall pòsaidh, cumhnant pòsaidh.

Espouse, *v. a.* Geall am pòsadh, geall pòsadh, ceangail; pòs, cuplaich, dion; cum taobh ri.

Espy, *v. a.* Thoir a mach, faic fad as; beachdaich, comharraich; dean faire.

Esquire, *s.* Gille-airm ridir, colann ridir, fear is fhaigse do ridir; duine measail air bi gun tiodal.

Essay, *v. a.* Feuch ri, thoir deuchainn, thoir oidhirp; cuir gu deuchainn, thoir ionnsuidh. He essayed to do it, *dh' fheuch e ri 'dheanamh.*

Essay, *s.* Feuchainn, deuchainn, oidhirp; eall.

Essayist, *s.* Deuchainniche.

Essence, *s.* Brigh, briogh; as-tharruing, bith; blàdh; fàil, deagh bholadh.

Essential, *a.* Feumail, ro-fheumail; nach gabh seachnadh; cudthromach; priomh; glan, fior-ghlan; freagarrach.

Essential, *s.* Bith.

Essentially, *adv.* Gu ro-fheumail; gu freagarrach, gu freagarrach.

Establish, *v. a.* Socraich, sonraich, cuir air chois, daighnich, daingnich; dealbh.

Established, *part.* Socraichte, sonraichte, daighnichte, air chois, air a shocrachadh. The established church, *an Eaglais shocraichte (no) dhaighnichte.*

Establisher, *s.* Sonrachair, sùnrachair, daighneachair, dealbhadair.

Establishment, *s.* Socrachadh, sonrachadh, daighneachadh; comh-dhealbhadh; reachdadh; muinntearas; duais.

Estate, *s.* (*Of life*), staid, inbhe, inmhe, cor; (*honour*), meas, urram; (*land*), oighreachd, fearann; beatha, beartas, saibhreas. He has bettered his estate, *mheudaich e 'oighreachd*; a low estate, *staid dhìblidh (no) bhochd*; man's estate, *inmhe duine*; I am come to a great estate, *dh' fhàs mi mòr, thainig mi gu h-inmhe.*

Esteem, *v. a.* Meas; thoir meas (no) urram do; gabh meas do, gabh seadh do. I esteem him, *tha meas agam dheth.*

Esteem, *s.* Meas, urram, seadh, miagh. Of no esteem, *dìblidh, iriosal, neo-mheasail.*

Esteemer, *s.* Measadair, fear measa.

Estimable, *a.* Airidh air meas, measail, urramach, priseil, luachmhor.

Estimableness, *s.* Measaileachd, urramachd, priseileachd, luachmhoireachd.

Estimate, *v. a.* Meas, prisich; cùnnt, aireamh. Estimated, *air a mheasadh prisichte.*

Estimate, *s.* Measadh, meas, barail; prìs, priseachadh, luach.

Estimated, *part.* See Estimate.

Estimator, *s.* Measadair, fear meas, priseadair; reiceadair; cunntair.

Estival, *a.* Samhrail, samhraidh.

Estivation, *s.* Samhrachadh, caitheamh an t-samhraidh.

Estrange, *v. a.* Cum air falbh, tarruing a thaobh, bi coimheach, dean coimheach; cum air ais. Estranged, *air thionndadh air falbh.*

Estranged. See Estrange.

Estrangement, *s.* Coimheachas; fuath; dol air falbh, falbh.

Estuary, *s.* Caolas, cneas-màra; bagh, camus.

Estuate, *v. a.* Boch, at, goil; lion is traogh.

Estuation, *s.* Bochadh, atadh, lionadh is traoghadh, tulgatuinn.

Esurient, *a.* Ocrach, acrach, ciocrach.

Etc. Mar sin sios e.

Etch, *v.* Dealbh; tarruing. Etched, *tarruingte, dealbhte.*

Etching, *s.* Dealbh.

Eternal, *a.* Bi-bhuan; bith-bhuan; siorruidh; neo-chriochnach; neo-bhasmhor; bith-mhairionn; neo-chaochlaideach; bidheanta, gun sgur.

Eternal, *s.* An t-Aon bith-bhuan, aon dh' ainmean Dhé.

Eternalize, *v. a.* Dean bith-bhuan (no) siorruidh.

Eternally, *adv.* Gu bith-bhuan, gu siorruidh, gu suthain siorruidh, gu bràth, fad shaoghal nan saoghal; gun sgur, gun chàirde, am bidheantas, an comhnuidh.

Eternity, *s.* Bith-bhuantachd, siorruidheachd, neo-bhàsmhorachd.

Eternize, *v. a.* Dean bith-bhuan, dean neo-bhàsmhor, dean siorruidh.

Ether, *s.* Athar, àile, iormailt.

Ethereal, *a.* Atharail, atharach, aileach, iormailteach, neamhuidh, spioradail.

Ethic, *a.* Modhannach, modhannail; saoghalta.

Ethics, *s.* Modhannan.

Ethnic, *a.* Neo-chreideach; ana-criosduigh, *paganta.*

Ethnics, *s.* Ana-creidich; ana-criosduidhean.

Etiquette, *s.* Modhaileachd; modh.

Etymological, *a.* Freumh-fhoclach, bun-fhoclach. An etymological dictionary, *freumh-fhoclair.*

Etymologist, *s.* Freumh-fhoclaiche.

Etymology, *s.* Freumh-fhocal, bunadhas, caismeart, sainfhios, seanasan, foras, foras-fhocal.

Etymon, *s.* Tùs, prìomh, freumh-fhocal, freumh, bunfhoclach.

Eucharist, *s.* Buidheachas, suipeir an tighearna, comanach, sàcramait.

Eucharistical, *a.* A bhuineas do shuipeir an Tighearna.

Eucrasy, *s.* Slainnte, fallaineachd.

Eulogy, *s.* Moladh, cliù, urram.

Eunuch, *s.* Caillteanach, fear spoghte; sput, neo-dhuine; gillean.

Eunuchate, *v. a.* Spogh, spoth.

Euphony, *s.* Deagh fhonn, binn-ghuth, binneas.

Euphrasy, *s.* Soillse nan sùl, seorsa plannda.

Euroclydon, *s.* Gaoth chuairteach as an near thuath, a tha robh ghailbheach air muir na Meadhon-thir.

Europe, *s.* Eorpa.

European, *a.* Eorpach.

European, *s.* Eorpach.

Evacate, *v. a.* Taomaich, falmhaich, tilg a mach.

Evacuate, *v. a.* Dean fas, dean reidh, dean (no) fag falamh; fag, cuitich; taomaich, falmhaich. Evacuated, *fàs, falamh, reidh; cuitichte; taomaichte, falmhaichte.*

Evacuated, *part.* See Evacuate.

Evacuation, *s.* Taomachadh, falmhachadh; cur a mach; fagail, fàsachadh, cuiteachadh.

Evade, *v. a.* Seachain, cuir gu taobh, cuir seachad.

Evagation, *s.* Iomroladh, seachran, seabhaid.

Evanescent, *a.* Siùbhlach, grad-shiùbhlach, do-fhaicinn.

Evangelical, *a.* Soisgeulach.

Evangelism, *s* Soisgeulachd.

Evangelist, *s.* Soisgeulaiche

Evangelize, *v.* Searmonaich an soisgeul, iompaich chum Criosduigheachd.

Evangely, *s.* Soisgeul, sgeul sìth, teachdaireachd neamhuidh, nuaidheachd slainnte.

Evanish, *v n* Rach as an t-sealladh.

Evaporate, *v.* Tioramich, deabh, rach an deò, rach an smuid, rach an deabhadh. It evaporated, *chaidh e na dheò, chaidh e na smùid* (*no*) *na dheathach.*

Evaporation, *s* Tioramachadh, dol an deabhadh, dol an deò, dol an smùid, deatach, deathach, deabhadh

Evasion, *s* Leithsgeul, car, siomaguad, cur seachad (no) gu taobh, ceilge, cur dheth.

Evasive, *a* Leithsgeulach; cealgach, carach.

Eve, Even, *s.* Trà nòin, oidhche; feasgar, beul na h-oidhche, beul an fheasgair, tuaileachd; eadar-sholus, anmoch, trosg roimh fhéill.

Even, *v* Dean comhnard, dean comhad, dean réidh

Even, *a.* Comhnard, comhad, comh-fhad, reidh, réith; ciuin, riaghailteach; dìreach; ionann, comh-ionann; ceart, a ain-fhiach An even piece of ground, *réidhlean*, even motion, *imeachd réidh*

Even, *adv* Eadhon. Even as, *mar, ceart mar*, even so, *ceart mar sin, eadhon mar sin, gu ma h-amhluidh a bhitheas*

Even-handed, *a.* Ceart, cothromach, neo-chlaon, dìreach, neo-chlaon-bhreitheach.

Evening, *s* Feasgar, beul na h-oidhche, beul an fheasgair, oidhche; eadar-sholus

Evenly, *adv.* Gu còmhnard, gu comhad, gu ciùin, gu réidh, gu neo-chlaon, gu ceart, gu cothromach.

Evenness, *s* Comhnardachd, comhadachd, neo-chlaonachd, ceartas, ciùineas. Evenness of temper, *soimeachd inntinn.*

Even-song, *s* Laoidh feasgair, urnuigh nòin, feasgar, beul na h-oidhche

Eventide, *s.* Feasgar; mu 'n anamoch.

Event, *s* Tubaist, cineamhuinn, aobhar, cuis; crioch, buile

Eventful, *a.* Cùiseach; tubaisteach; cudthromach.

Eventilate, *v. a.* Fasgain, glan, sgrud, ceasnuich; fidir.

Eventual, *a.* A teachd an lorg, an lorg, a leanntuinn, tubaisteach

Eventually, *adv.* Mu dheireadh, air cheann thall

Ever, *adv* (*At any time*), aig (no) air am sam bith; idir, riomh, (*always*), daonalt, daonannta, a choidh, a choidhche, an còmhnuidh, an cumaint, a ghnàth, do ghnàth, gu siorruidh, gu brath, gu dilinn, am feasd, gun chàirde, gun sgur, am bidheantas. Ever since, *riomh o, riomh o sin*, ever and anon, *an dras is a ris, an tràths' is a rithist*, for ever, *a choidhche, gu bruth, gu siorruidh*, for ever and ever, *fad shaoghal nan saoghal, gu suthain siorruidh*, ever before, *riomh roimh*. were you here ever before, *an robh thu riomh roimh an so*, or ever, *mun, roimh*, or ever the sun gave light, *mun d' thug a ghrian solus*, be he ever so rich, *air a bheartaichead 's a bheil e*, as soon as ever I can, *cho lom luath 's a dh' fhaodas mi.*

Ever-burning, *a.* Sior-losgadh, bith-losgadh, do-mhùchadh, sior-loisgeach

Everduring, *a.* Maireannach, bith-bhuan.

Evergreen, *a.* and *s.* Sior-uaine.

Everlasting, *a.* Bith-bhuan, siorruidh, mairionn, maireann, neo-bhasmhor.

Everlasting, *s.* Bith-bhuantachd, neo-bhasmhorachd. From everlasting to everlasting, *o bhith-bhuantachd gu bithbhuantachd, gu suthain siorruidh.*

Everlastingly, *adv.* Am bidheantas, gun chrioch, gun sgur, an conuidh.

Everlastingness, *s* Bith-bhuantachd; neo-chriochnuigheach, siorruidheachd, sior-mhaironnachd

Everliving, *a.* Sior-bheò; neo-bhàsmhor, siorruidh, bithbhuan.

Evermore, *adv.* Gu brath, gu dilinn, am feasd, a so suas.

Everpleasing, *a.* Sior thaitneach.

Every, *a.* Gach, uile, h-uile, gach uile. Every day, *gach la, na h-uile là*, every other day, *gach doluch là*, at every word, *aig gach focal*, every man, *na h-uile fear, gach uile dhuine*, every where, *anns na h-uile aite*, every way, *na h-uile rathad; air na h-uile doigh*, every whit, *na h-uile mìr*, every mother's son of you, *na h-uile mac màthar agaibh*, every single one of you, *na h-uile fear riamh agaibh.*

Evesdropper, *s.* Fear farcluaise, sgonn a théid mu 'n cuairt a dh' eisdeachd aig uinneagaibh an deigh dhorch' oidhche.

Eugh, *s* (*In botany*), iuthar

Evict, *v a.* Thoir o, thoir air falbh, dìthich; comhdaich.

Eviction, *s* Dìtheachadh, toirt air falbh; dearbhadh, comhdachadh, fianuis, teisteas, teisteannas

Evidence, *s* Fianuis, teisteas, teisteannas, faicealachd.

Evidence, *v.* Comhdaich, deaibh, feuch.

Evident, *a* Soilleir, dearbhta, follaiseach, cinnteach. Evidently, *gu soilleir, gu dearbhta, gu follaiseach, gu cinnteach, gu fior.*

Evil, *a.* Olc, aingidh, suarrachd, droch; coirbte, peacach, dubhailceach; millteach, sgriosail; urchoideach, carchallach, dochannach, curt

Evil, *s* Olc, aingidheachd, dubhailc, donas; peacadh; truaighe, lochd, cionta; earchall, urchoid; tinneas, galar, eucail. Evil betide the prophet, *gu mu h-ann a ghonar am fiosaiche*, evil comes by talking of it, *thig an donas ri iomradh.*

Evil-affected, *a.* Neo-chaoimhneil, dorganta, mi-runach

Evil-doer, *s.* Peacach, ciontach, fear dheanamh uile.

Evil-favoured, *a* Gràda, granna, grannda

Evil-minded, *a.* Mi-rùnach, gamhlasach, spideil, tnuthar, tnùmhor, droch-mhuineach, droch-mhuinte; aingidh, olc, coirbte

Evil-speaking, *s.* Sgainneal, càin, cùl-chàineadh, tuaileas; droch-iomradh, toibheum, anacainnt.

Evil-speaking, *a* Sgainnealach, tuaileasach

Evil-wishing, *a* Droch-mhuinte, gamhlasach, mi-runach.

Evil-wishing, *s* Droch-ghuidhe, droch-dhùrachd, tnù, gamhlas.

Evil-worker, *s.* Peacair, droch-neach.

Evince, *v.* Feuch, leig ris, leig fhaicinn, nochd, dean soilleir, dearbh, còmhdaich

Evincible, *a* So-fheuchainn, so-dhearbhadh.

Evirate, *v a* Spoth. Evirated, *spothte*

Evirated, *a.* Spothte, spothta.

Eviration, *s* Spothadh

Eviscerate, *v a* Thoir am mionach a

Evitable, *a* So-sheachnadh, so-sheachanta, seachantach.

Evitate, *v. a* Seachain

EVITERNAL, *a.* Maireann, buan.

EVOCATION, *s.* Eigh, eighich, eubh, glaodhaich, glaodh, gairm.

EVOLATION, *s.* Itealachadh, itealaich, itealachd.

EVOLVE, *v. a.* Tuasgail, fuasgail, thoir as a chéile; fosgail.

EVOLUTION, *s.* Fosgladh; lamhachas.

EVULSION, *s.* Spionadh, spioladh as.

EWE, *s.* Caor, othaisg.

EWER, *s.* Soitheach uisge.

EX. Focal Laitin air chur roimh fhocail Beurla a ciallachadh air uairibh *as* (no) *a;* agus air uairibh a toirt an tuillead céill do chuid fhocail.

EXACERBATE, *v.* Searbhaich; feargaich; thoir an tuillead seirbhe.

EXACERBATION, *s.* Searbhachadh, feargachadh; airde thinneis.

EXACT, *a.* Poncail, puncail; greanta, ceart, freagarrach; dìreach; deas, beachdaidh; onorach, ionraic, glan; sicir.

EXACT, *v. a.* Tog; iarr mar chòir (no) mar cheart, iarr gu smachdail; thoir a dh' aindeoin o. Exacted, *togte, air a thogail.*

EXACTOR, *s.* Sracair, fear fòirneirt.

EXACTION, *s.* Sracaireachd, foirneart, sàruchadh, an-togail.

EXACTLY, *adv.* Gu freagarrach, gu glan, gu dìreach, gu snasmhor. Exactly so, *dìreach glan.*

EXACTNESS, *s.* Poncalachd, puncalachd, sicireachd; riaghailteachd; deisead, beachd; freagarraichead.

EXAGGERATE, *v. a.* Cuir am meud, meudaich, cuir ri, cuir am mòid, antromaich, carn, cnuasaich.

EXAGGERATION, *s.* Meudachadh; antromachadh.

EXAGITATE, *v.* Crath, cuir troimh chéile, cuir thar a chéile.

EXALT, *v. a.* Arduich, tog suas, cuir 'n airde; tog gu h-inmhe (no) gu h-urram; crùn; sgeaduich; mol; leasaich. Exalted, *arduichte, air arduchadh, ard, mòr.*

EXALTATION, *s.* Arduchadh, urram, inmhe, airde.

EXAMEN, *s.* Sgrudadh, ceasnachadh, ceasnach, rannsuchadh.

EXAMINATE, *s.* Neach fo sgrudadh; deuchainniche.

EXAMINATION, *s.* Sgrudadh, ceasnachadh, rannsuchadh, deuchainn.

EXAMINATOR, *s.* Sgrudair, ceasnachair, rannsuchair, fear ceasnachaidh.

EXAMINE, *v. a.* Sgrud, ceasnaich, ceistich, rannsuich; cuir ceistean ri; criathraich; cuir air deuchainn; cuir gu deuchainn. Examined, *ceasnaichte, rannsaichte.*

EXAMINER. See EXAMINATOR.

EXAMPLARY, *a.* Eisiomplaireach, eisiomlaireach, mar eisiomlair, mar bhall sampuill.

EXAMPLE, *s.* Eisiomplair, eisiomlair, ball sampuill, samhladh; gniomh-sampuill. Make an example of him, *dean ball sampuill dheth.*

EXANIMATE, *a.* Marbh; marbhanta, neo-bheò, neo-bheothail, trom.

EXANIMATION, *s.* Marbhantachd.

EXANIMOUS, *a.* Marbh; marbhanta; neo-bheò, neo-spioradail.

EXANTHEMATA, *s.* Briseadh mach, broth, càrr, guireanan, bucaidean.

EXANTHEMATOUS, *a.* Carrach, creimeach, guireanach, bucaideach.

EXANTLATE, *v. a.* Tarruing mach, taom, taomaich, falmhaich.

EXASPERATE, *v. a.* Buair, feargaich, brosnuich, prosnuich; farranaich, greannaich. Exasperated, *buairte, feargaichte, brosnuichte, farranaichté.*

EXASPERATION, *s.* Buaireadh, fearg, corruich, farran, farranachd, brosnuchadh.

EXAUCTORATE, *v. a.* Cuir a inmhe, cuir air falbh, maslaich.

EXCANDESCENCE, *s.* Teas, teothachadh; feirg, corruich.

EXCANTATION, *s.* Toirt air falbh druidheachd (no) buitseachd.

EXCAVATE, *v.* Cladhaich, toll, bùraich, tochail, pleadhaich. Excavated, *cladhaichte, bùraichte.*

EXCAVATION, *s.* Cladhachadh, bùrachadh, tolladh, pleadhachadh; toll.

EXCEED, *v. a.* and *n.* Thoir barrachd, faigh barrachd, rach os ceann; rach tuille is fad, rach thar (no) thairis. You exceed him, *tha barrachd agad air; fhuair thu barrachd air, thug thu barrachd air.*

EXCEEDING, *a.* Anabarra, anabarrach, anabharra, ro. Exceeding good, *ro-mhaith.*

EXCEEDINGLY, *adv.* Gu h-anabarra, gu fuathasach, gu ro mhòr.

EXCEL, *v. a.* and *n.* Faigh barrachd, fairtlich; saruich; fag; rach os ceann, bi os ceann, bi sonraichte, bi cliùiteach, bi ainmeil. You excell him, *fhuair thu barrachd air.*

EXCELLENCE, EXCELLENCY, *s.* Airde, ardachd, morachd, oidheirceas; ainmeileachd, cliùiteachd; maitheas, feobhas, luach, fiach.

EXCELLENT, *a.* Luachmhor; oirdheirc; cliùiteach, ainmeil; gasd, barrail, barrasach, ro-mhath, grinn, urramail. Excellently, *gu gasd; gu grinn, gu ro-mhath, gu h-urramail.*

EXCEPT, *v. a.* Fag as.

EXCEPT, EXCEPTING, *prep.* and *adv.* Ach; saor o, mur. All except you, *na h-uile ach thusa;* except that he did this, *saor o gun do rinn e so.*

EXCEPTION, *s.* Fàgail a mach; eisceach, cunnuil; coire, cron. Take an exception at a thing, *faigh cunnuil do ni, gabh gu dona ni, faigh cron (no) coire.*

EXCEPTIONABLE, *a.* Buailteach do chunnuil (no) do choire, ion dhiultaidh.

EXCEPTIOUS, *a.* Crosda, do-thoileachadh; cainnteach, tabaideach.

EXCEPTOR, *s.* Cunnuileach, fear a gheibh coire.

EXCERN, *v.* Siolaidh; traogh; dealaich.

EXCERPTION, *s.* Taghadh, roghnachadh.

EXCESS, *s.* Anabharr; anameasarrachd; iomarcaich, tuille is a chòir; thuille na còrach.

EXCESSIVE, *a.* Anabharrach, anabarrach, anameasarra, anameasarrach, uamharra; fuathasach, ro mhòr.

EXCESSIVELY, *adv.* Gu h-anabarrach, gu h-anameasarra; gu h-uamharra, gu fuathasach; gu ro-mhòr.

EXCHANGE, *v. a.* Malairtich, malairt, thoir am malairt, iomlaidich, suaip, thoir an iomlaid.

EXCHANGE, *v.* Iomlaid, malairt, iomlaideachadh; diubhair eadar luach cuinne gach rioghachd; aite malairt; aite san coinnich ceannaichean chum an ghnothuichean a chur gu doigh.

EXCHANGER, *s.* Malairtiche, iomlaidiche.

EXCHEQUER, *s.* An-t-ionmhas, cuirt anns an gabhar beachd air teachd stigh na rioghachd.

EXCISE, *s.* Cìse, bàrr-chìse, maoin-chìse.

EXCISABLE, *a.* Cìse-bhuailteach.

EXCISEMAN, *a.* Cìsear, cìs-fhear, fear leigeil chìse.

EXCISION, *s.* Gearradh, sgathadh, bearradh; sgrios, sgriosadh.

EXCITATION, *s.* Dùsgadh, brosnachadh, buaireadh; feargachadh, brodadh, brogadh, misneachadh, stuigeadh, greasadh.

EXCITE, v. a. Dùisg, brosnuich, prosnaich, buair; feargaich, brod, brog, stuig, greas, spor. Excited, *duisgte, brosnuichte, buairte, air adh' usgadh, air a bhuaireadh*, she is excited, *tha i air a buaireadh.*

EXCITEMENT, s. Brosnuchadh, prosnachadh, buaireadh, brod, stuigeadh, greasadh, spor.

EXCITER, s Brosnuchair, prosnachair, buaireadair, brodair.

EXCLAIM, v Glaodh, éigh, eubh, gàir, dean gàir He exclaimed, *ghlaodh e*

EXCLAIM, s. Glaodh, éigh, eubh

EXCLAIMER, s Fear a ghlaodhas (no) bhruidhneas gu ladurna

EXCLAMATION, s Glaodh, eigh, eubh, gàir, tuir-ghuth

EXCLAMATORY, a. Eigheach, eubhach.

EXCLUDE, v Druid a mach, cuir a mach, bac, fògair, cùlaich Excluded, *air a dhruidcadh mach.*

EXCLUSION, s. Druideadh mach, fògradh, cùlachadh.

EXCLUSIVE, a A dhruideas a mach, a bhacas; saor o, ach, a bharrachd air, a bharras air An exclusive right, *còir àraidh*, exclusive of that, *a bharras air sin.*

EXCLUSIVELY, adv Ach, saor o, a bharras, gu barrasach Exclusively of that, *saor o sin, a bharras air sin*

EXCOCT, v. Goil, cuir air a ghoil

EXCOGITATE, v. Tionnsgain, dealbh, cruthaich, dean

EXCOGITATION, s. Tionnsgnadh, innleachd, dealbhadh.

EXCOMMUNICATE, v Ascaoinich, cuir ascaoin eaglais air neach, malluich; cuir a comunn, diobair, cuir cùl ri Excommunicated, *ascaoinichte, air uscaoineadh, malluichte, fògairte.*

EXCOMMUNICATION, s Ascaoin eaglais, malluchadh, fogradh

EXCORIATE, v a Rùisg, fionn, thoir an croiceann bhàrr ni no neach.

EXCORIATION, s. Rùsgadh, fionnadh

EXCORTICATION, s Rùsgadh craoibh, cartadh

EXCREATE, v a Tilg a mach as a bheul

EXCREMENT, s. Cac, gaor, aolach, inneir, salachar, mùn.

EXCRESCENCE, s. Meall, plucan, pluc; ain-fheoil, fiodh, foinne

EXCRETION, s Cur mach ni as a chorp, mar mhùn, no gaor; mùn, salachar

EXCRUCIATE, v. a. Cradh, claoidh, pian, ceus, cuir gu pian

EXCRUCIATING, a Craidhteach, claoidheach, piantachail, goirt, piantachail.

EXCUBATION, s. Faire oidhche, faire, faireachadh

EXCULPATE, v. Saor a choire, gabh leithsgeul, di-choirich

EXCULPATION, s Di-choireachadh, fìreannachadh.

EXCURSION, s Sgriob, tùrus (no) cuairt ghoirrid He is gone on an excursion, *chaidh e air sgriob*

EXCURSIVE, a Iomrolach, seabhaideach, siubhlach, luaineach.

EXCUSABLE, a A dh' fhaodar mhathadh, so-mhathadh, ion-mhathadh, ion-leithsgeulach.

EXCUSATION, s Leithsgeul

EXCUSE, v. Gabh leithsgeul, math, lagh

EXCUSE, s. Leithsgeul A good excuse, *deagh leithsgeul*

EXCUSELESS, s Gun leithsgeul, gun aobhar.

EXCUSER, s. Fear leithsgeil, leith-sgeulaiche, tagrair

EXCUSSION, s. Glacadh, cur lamh air.

EXECRABLE, a Fuathach, oillteil, gràineil, uamharra Execrably, *gu h-oillteil, gu gràineil*

EXECRABLENESS, s Fuathachd; oilltealachd, gràinealachd, uamharrachd

EXECRATE, v. Mallaich, mollaich, dean guidhe, guidh mallachd air, fùrlaich. He execrated her, *mhallaich e i; dh' fhurlaich e rithe*, execrated, *malluichte, mollaichte.*

EXECRATION, s. Mallachadh, mollachadh, mallachd, droch-ghuidhe.

EXECUTE, v Coimh-lion, dean, criochnaich; gnàthaich, cuir an gniomh; cuir bas, (*hang*), croch, (*behead*), dìcheannaich. Executed, *comh-lionta, criochnaichte; gnàthaichte, air a chur gu bàs, crochte, dìcheannaichte.*

EXECUTED, part See EXECUTE.

EXECUTER, s. Coimh-lionair, fear coimh-lionaidh

EXECUTION, s Deanamh, coimh-lionadh; criochnachadh; cur gu bàs, (*hanging*), crochadh, (*beheading*), dicheannachd, (*seizure*), glacadh

EXECUTIONER, s. Crochadair, marbhadair, fear-millidh.

EXECUTIVE, a. Gniomhachail, coimh-liontachail, cumhachdail

EXECUTOR, s Cileadair, tuitear

EXECUTRIX, s Ban-chileadair, ban-tuitear

EXECUTORSHIP, s Cileadaireachd, tuitearachd.

EXEGESIS, s Mìneachadh

EXEMPLAR, s Sampull, samhladh, ball sampuill

EXEMPLARY, a. Eisiomlaireach; deagh-bheusach, cliùiteach; airidh air leanachd, ion-mholta.

EXEMPLIFICATION, s. Samhladh.

EXEMPLIFY, v Mìnich le samhladh; ath-sgriobh; sgriobh thairis

EXEMPT, v a Saor, fuasgail, tuasgail, ceadaich

EXEMPT, a Saor, neo-bhuailteach, fuasgailte, dheth Exempt from blame, *saor o choire*, exempt from tax, *neo-bhuailteach do chìs*

EXEMPTION, s Sochair, saorsainn, saoradh, fuasgladh; ceadachadh.

EXENTERATE, v. Thoir am mionach a

EXEQUIAL, a Adhlacaidh.

EXEQUIES, s. Deas-ghnath adhlacaidh, deas-ghnath torraidh

EXERCENT, a Gnathach, gniomhach, a cur an gniomh

EXERCISE, v. Gnàthaich; cuir an gniomh, oibrich, cleachd, dean, oil, tog suas Exercise yourself in piety, *cleachd thu fein chum diadhachd*, exercised in war, *deanta ri cogadh, cleachdta ri cogadh* Exercising, *a gnàthachadh, a cleachdadh.*

EXERCISE, s Saothair, obair, iomairt, gnathachadh; cleachd; (*of soldiers*), làmhachas, *treunadh*, (*task*), obair sgéithte.

EXERCITATION, s Saothair, obair, iomairt, cleachd

EXERT, v Dean spairn, dean dichioll; cuir ris; cuir thuige (no) h-uige. Exert yourself, *feuch thu fein, dean do dhichioll*

EXERTION, s Spairn, dichioll, oidhirp, dean oidhirp. Competition causes exertion, *is e farmad a ni treabhadh.*

EXESION, s Itheadh, cnamhadh, creimeadh.

EXESTUATION, s Goil; gaoir; buaireas

EXFOLIATE, v a. Sgrath, rùisg, dealaich mar ni spealg do chnaimh grod o 'n iomlan.

EXHALABLE, a So-chur an deò.

EXHALATION, s Ceò, smùid, deatach, deathach, grian-deathach; tothadh, sgamal.

EXHALE, v. Smùidich, cuir deathach (no) smùid, tiormaich, cuir an deabhadh

EXHALEMENT, s. Smùid, deatach, deathach, ceò.

EXHAUST, v a Traogh, tràigh, traoghaich; tiormaich,

falmhaich; (*oppress*), cuir gu fulang, sàruich, lagaich, fannaich, thoir thairis. Exhausted, *traoghte, tràighte; air toirt thairis.*

Exhaustion, *s.* Traoghadh, tiormachadh, falmhachadh; fannachadh.

Exhaustless, *a.* Do-thraoghadh, do-thiormachadh.

Exhibit, *v.* Feuch, nochd, leig fhaicinn, taisbein, foillsich, cuir a làthair, leig ris. Exhibited, *nochdta, taisbeinte, foillsichte, air a leigeil ris, air fheuchainn.*

Exhibition, *s.* Sealladh, foillseachadh, nochdadh, taisbean; duais.

Exhilarate, *v.* Dean cridheil, dean sunntach, dean subhach.

Exhort, *v. a.* Thoir misneach, comhairlich, earalaich, earail, greanaich. Exhort him, *earail air;* exhorted, *comhairlichte, earalaichte.*

Exhortation, *s.* Earail, earalachadh, comhairle; greanachadh.

Exhorter, *s.* Earalair, earalaiche, comhairliche; greanachair.

Exigence, *s.* Feum, uireasbhuidh, easbhuidh; gainne; cruadal, teanntachd, cruaidh-chas, teinne, éigin, eiginteas, riachdanas; cungarachd.

Exigent, *s.* Teinne, teanntachd, càs, cruaidh chas; gnothuch cudthromach.

Exiguity, *s.* Meanbhad; crìne.

Exile, *s.* Fògradh, diobairt, deòrachd, deòraidheachd. In exile, *air fogradh.*

Exile, *s.* Fògarach, deòraidh, diobaireach.

Exile, *v.* Fògair, fògaraich, diobair, deòraich, cuir air fògradh, cuir air dheòrachd.

Exilement, *s.* Fògradh, diobaireachd, deòrachd.

Eximious, *a.* Cliùiteach, ainmeil, còrr, follaiseach.

Exist, *v.* Mair, bi beò, bi a lathair, bi ann.

Existence, *s.* Bith; beath.

Existent, *a.* A lathair, beo, ann, maireann.

Exit, *s.* Falbh, triall, imeachd, siubhal, dol a mach, dol as; bàs.

Exodus, *s.* Falbh, triall, imeachd, siubhal; tùrus, dara leabhar Mhaois.

Exonerate, *v. a.* Eutromaich, aotromaich; (*from a charge*), di-choirich. Exonerated, *eutromaichte, aotromaichte.*

Exoneration, *s.* Eutromachadh, aotromachadh; di-choireachadh.

Exorable, *a.* So-lùbadh, so-chomhairleachadh, so-ghuidhe; so-labharra.

Exorbitance, Exorbitancy, *s.* Iomarcas; fuathsachd, uamharrachd; neo-chuimheasachd; mor-aingidheachd, truaillidheachd.

Exorbitant, *a.* Iomarcach, neo-riaghailteach, fuathasach, uamharra; neo-chuimheasach, thar tomhas, thar cuimheis; mi-reusonta; strodhail, struigheil.

Exorbitate, *v.* Rach air seachran (no) a thaobh.

Exorcise, *v. a.* Fuadaich deamhan, geas; dean geasadaireachd.

Exorciser, *s.* Geasadair; druidh.

Exorcism, *s.* Geasadaireachd, druidheachd, draoidheachd, tilge a mach dheomhan.

Exorcist, *s.* Geasadair, druidh, draoidh, fear thilge mach dheamhan, cleasaiche, dubh-chleasaiche.

Exordium, *s.* Toiseach, roimh-radh.

Exotic, *a.* Coimheach, allmharach, cian, deoranta.

Expand, *v. a.* Sgaoil, fosgail, spréid, meudaich; at, bolg. Expounded, *sgaoilte, fosgailte; spreidte, meudaichte.*

Expanse, *s.* Comhnard fad farsuing; foir-leud, farsuingeachd; iormailt.

Expansible, *a.* So-sgaoileadh, so-spreideadh, so-leudachadh.

Expansion, *s.* Sgaoileadh, fosgladh; atadh; bolgadh; leud, farsuingeachd, feadh.

Expansive, *a.* Foir-leathann, sgaoilteach.

Expatiate, *v. a.* Meudaich; sìn; leudaich; rach fa sgaoil.

Expatriate, *v. a.* Fògair, fògraich, diobair, deòraich; ruaig as an dùthaich. Expatriated, *fògraichte, fògairte, diobairte.*

Expatriation, *s.* Fogradh, diobaradh.

Expect, *v. a.* and *n.* Bi 'n dochas, bi an dùil, feith ri, fan, fuirich. When do you expect him? *c'uine tha dùil agad ris?* I expected to have seen him, *bha mi 'n dùil ri 'fhaicinn, bhu dòchas agam ri ' fhaicinn.*

Expectance, *a.* Dùil, dochas, fiughair; fuireach, fanachd.

Expectant, *a.* A fuireach; an dùil ri; fiughaireachd.

Expectation, *s.* Dùil, dòchas, bun dòchais; sùil, feitheamh, fuireach, furachas. I am in expectation of his coming, *tha dùil (no) sùil agam ri ' theachd.*

Expectorate, *v.* Casd a mach, tilg mach le smugaid (no) le casd.

Expectoration, *s.* Smugarsaich; smugaideachd, casdaich; clochar; carrasan.

Expedience, Expediency, *s.* Cubhaidheachd, freagarrachd, iomchuidheachd; feum; cabhag.

Expedient, *a.* Cubhaidh, freagarrach; iomchuidh; feumail; grad; luath, cabhagach.

Expedient, *s.* Seol; doigh; innleachd.

Expediently, *adv.* Gu cubhaidh, gu freagarrach, gu h-iomchuidh, gu feumail.

Expedite, *v. a.* Luathaich, greas, cuir cabhag air.

Expedite, *a.* Grad, luath, cabhagach; ealamh, tapaidh, clis, smiorail.

Expedition, *s.* Luathas, luathailt, ealamhachd, tapachd; (*hostile*), turus naimhdeil, ionnsuidh; sluaigheachd; sgriob, targhraidh.

Expeditious, *a.* Luath, luathailteach, ealamh, grad, ullamh, tapaidh, clis. Expeditiously, *gu luath, gu luathailteach, gu h-ealamh, gu grad.*

Expeditiousness, *s.* Luathas, luathailteachd, ealamhachd; tapachd.

Expel, *v. a.* Fògair, cuir a mach, diobair, ruaig; diùlt; òb; cuir cùl ri, cum a mach, cum air falbh. They expelled him, *dh' fhogair iad e,* he is expelled, *tha e air fhògradh.*

Expend, *v.* Caith, cosd, builich. Expended, *caithte, air chosdadh.*

Expenditure, *s.* Cosd, cosdas, cosgas, caitheamh; cur a mach.

Expense, *s.* Cosd, cosdas, cosgas, cosg.

Expenseless, *a.* Neo-chosdail, saor.

Expensive, *a.* Cosdail, cosgail, daor, prìseil, luachmhor; fiol. Expensive dress, *eudach cosdail.*

Expensiveness, *s.* Cosdaileachd; prìsealachd; luachmhoireachd, struidhe.

Experience, *s.* Féin-fhios, mothuchadh, féin-fhiosrachadh; gnath-eòlas, eòlas, fionnachdainn; deuchainn, dearbhadh. Want of experience, *aineolas;* of no experience, *aineolach, air bheag eòlais;* my own experience, *m' fhiosrachadh féin.*

Experience, *v. a.* Feuch, fainich, fairich, mothuich, faigh mothuchadh, gnàthaich. Experienced, *eolach, eolach tre fhéin-fhiosrachadh;* experienced in war, *deanta ri cogadh, eolach air cogadh.*

Experiment, *s.* Feuchainn, deuchainn, dearbhadh, oidhirp.

EXPERIMENTAL, *a.* Fiosrachail; dearbhachail, aithnichte, deuchainnte.

EXPERIMENTALLY, *adv.* Thaobh deuchainn, thaobh feuchainn, thaobh beachd.

EXPERIMENTER, *s* Deuchainniche, dearbhadair, fear a chuireas gu dearbhadh (no) deuchainn

EXPERT, *a.* Teoma, còlach, sgileil, ealamh, tapaidh, deas; seolta; tuigseach Expertly, *gu teoma, gu deas, gu seolta*

EXPERTNESS, *s.* Teomachd, eolas, sgile, ealamhachd, tapachd, deise, seoltachd

EXPIABLE, *a.* So-dhioladh, so-réiteachadh.

EXPIATE, *v.* Dean réite airson cionta.

EXPIATION, *s.* Réiteachadh, dioladh, sàsuchadh.

EXPIATORY, *a* Réiteachail, diolach; sasuchail.

EXPIRATION, *s* Fosadh, seide-analach; tothadh; crioch, call an deò, bàsuchadh

EXPIRE, *v a* and *n.* Séid, cuir mach anail; thoir suas an deò, faigh bàs, rach eug, siubhail, caochail, criochnaich

EXPLAIN, *v a.* Minich, cuir an céill, soilleirich, soillsich, nochd, fuasgail, tuasgail, dean rèidh (no) so-thuigsinn.

EXPLAINABLE, *a.* So-mhìneachadh, so chur an céill, so nochdadh

EXPLAINER, *s.* Mìneachair, eadar-theangair

EXPLANATION, *s.* Mineachadh, soilleireachadh, nochdadh, soillseachadh, eadar-theangachadh.

EXPLANATORY, *a* Mìneachail, soillseachail, soilleir.

EXPLICABLE, *a* So-mhìneachadh, soilleir, so-thuigsinn, sothuasgal.

EXPLICATE, *v. a* Minich, soillsich, nochd, dean so-thuigsinn, fosgail; fuasgail, tuasgail, dean rèidh; réitich Explicated, *minichte, soillsichte, fosgailte, fuasgailte.*

EXPLICATION, *s* Mineachadh, soillseachadh; soilleireachadh, nochdadh, foillseachadh, fosgladh, fuasgladh, deanamh rèidh, réiteachadh, eadar-theangachadh

EXPLICATIVE, *a.* Mìneachail, soillseachail.

EXPLICIT, *a* Soilleir, so-thuigsinn; poncail, fuasgailte, réitichte, reidh, saor. Explicitly, *gu soilleir, gu poncail, gu follaiseach.*

EXPLICITNESS, *s* Soilleireachd; soillseachd, poncaileachd

EXPLODE, *v* Tilg a mach le tàir, cuir air mi-shuim, leig braidhe, blosg Exploded (as an opinion), *air thilgeadh a mach, air chuir air mi-shuim*

EXPLOIT, *s* Euchd, mor-ghniomh, ard-ghniomh, gaisge, beart, treunas, spleadhachas

EXPLORATE, *v a* Rannsuich, faigh a mach, lorgaich

EXPLORATION, *s* Rannsuchadh, lorgaireachd

EXPLORATOR, *s* Rannsuchair; sgrudair

EXPLORE, *v a* Rannsuich, sir; sgrud, ceasnuich, feuch, cuir gu deuchainn Explored, *rannsuichte*

EXPLOREMENT, *s* Rannsuchadh, sireadh, deuchainn

EXPLOSION, *s* Braidhe, spraidhe, blosgadh, fuaim

EXPLOSIVE, *a* Blosgach, so-lasaidh; braidheach

EXPORT, *v a.* Thoir a mach (no) as an dùthaich

EXPORT, *s* Bàthar a chuirear as an dùthaich.

EXPORTATION, *s* Cur bàthar as an tìr air muir, cur a mach

EXPORTER, *s.* Fear a bheir (no) chuireas bathar as an dùthaich.

EXPOSE, *v* (*Uncover*), leig ris, nochd, rùisg, foillsich, dean follaiseach; (*affront*), nàraich, cuir gu nair, dean ball magaidh, (*to danger*), cuir ann an cunnart *Exposed,* nochdta; ruisgte, foillsichte; (*to danger*), an cunnart, am baoghal, an gàbhadh; (*to laughter*), mar ball abhacais, mar bhall magaidh, mar aobhar ghàir.

EXPOSITION, *s.* Mineachadh; eadar-theangachadh; (*situation*), deisear gréine, luidhe, staid, suidheachadh.

EXPOSITOR, *s.* Mineachair, eadar-theangair.

EXPOSTULATE, *v.* Agair, reusonaich, riasonaich, deasboirich, connsaich, casaid, gearain.

EXPOSTULATION, *s.* Agradh, reusonachadh, co-reusonachadh, deasboireachadh, deasboireachd, connsachadh, casaid, gearain.

EXPOSTULATOR, *s.* Agrair, riasonaiche; deasboiriche, connspuidiche.

EXPOSURE, *s* Leigeil ris, leigeil fhaicinn, nochdadh; foillseachadh, suidheachadh, (*to the sun*), deisear gréine, grianan.

EXPOUND, *v* Minich, eadar-theangaich; innis, leig ris, riochd, sgrud, rannsuich, Expounded, *minichte*

EXPOUNDER, *s.* Mìneachair, fear mìneachaidh; eadar-theangair.

EXPRESS, *v. a* Innis, cuir an céil, nochd; feuch; labhair; abair; aithris, ciallaich; (*squeeze*), samhlaich, fàisg, astharruing, (*express your mind*), innis (no) nochd d' inntinn.

EXPRESS, *a.* Cosmhuil, cosmhal, coslach, soilleir, follaiseach, riachdail, so-fhaicinn; saor; a dh'aon ghnothuch, a dh'aon obair Expressly, *a dh'aon obair, a dh'aon ghnothuch, gu h-araidh, gu follaiseach, gu soilleir, gu riachdail, as an aghaidh.*

EXPRESS, *s* Teachdair, grad-theachdair; teachdaireachd.

EXPRESSIBLE, *a* So-labhairt, so-innseadh, so-aithris, so chur an ceil, so-fhàsgadh, a ghabhas fàsgadh.

EXPRESSION, *s* Briathar, radh; focal, cainnt, seanachas; labhairt, aithris; fàsgadh. Flashy expression, *briathran atmhor, glòr*

EXPRESSIVE, *a.* Drùighteach; freagarrach; a cur an céil. Expressive language, *cainnt dhruighteach*, expressive of his thought, *a cur an céile a smuaintibh*

EXPRESSIVELY, *a* Gu drùighteach; gu soilleir, gu riachdail, gu direach.

EXPRESSIVENESS, *s* Drùighteachd. Expressiveness of language, *drùighteachd cainnte.*

EXPRESSLY, *adv* See EXPRESS

EXPROBRATE, *v a* Cuir as leth, coirich, cronaich, troid, masluich, tarcuisich, sglàmhruinn.

EXPROBRATION, *s* Cur as leth, coireachadh, cronachadh, trod, masluchadh, masladh, sglamhrainn

EXPUGN, *v* Buadhaich air, fairtlich air, gabh

EXPUGNATION, *s.* Buaidh, gabhail

EXPULSE, *v a* Cuir a mach, fogair, diobair.

EXPULSION, *s.* Diobradh, fògradh, fogairt, air a mach a dh' aindeoin.

EXPULSIVE, *a.* Diobrachail, fògrachail.

EXPUNCTION, *s* Dubhadh mach, sgriochadh, milleadh.

EXPUNGE, *v. a* Dubh a mach, sgrioch, glan as. Expunged, *air a dhubh' a mach*

EXPURGATION, *s* Glanadh, sgùradh

EXPURGATOR, *s* Glanadair, sgùradair.

EXQUISITE, *a* Gasd, grinn, còrr, maiseach; riomhach; foirfe coimhlionta; ro-mhath, oirdheirc, taghta, taghte, ro-ghrinn, ro-chorr, ro-mhaiseach, ro-olc, fìor-olc.

EXQUISITELY, *adv* Gu gasd, gu grinn, gu corr, gu maiseach, gu riomhach, gu coimhlionta, gu ro-mhath, gu taghta.

EXQUISITENESS, *s* Grinneas, grinnead, maise, riombachd, oirdheirceas.

EXSCRIPT, *s.* Sgriobhadh, samhladh.

EXSICCANT, *a* Tiormachail

EXSICCATE, *v. a* Tiormaich

EXSICCATION, *s.* Tiormachadh.

EXSUCTION, *s* Sùgadh, sùigheadh.

EXSUDATION, *s.* Fallusachadh; fallus; drùchd.
EXSUFFOLATE, *v.* Cogair, cagair, dean cagar (no) cogar.
EXTANT, *a.* A lathair, beò, maireann, ann, air uachdair talmhainn, san t-saoghal; follaiseach.
EXTEMPORAL, *a.* Grad, ealamh, deas, air an uair, air an spot.
EXTEMPORANEOUS, *a.* Gun smuaine, neo-chnuasaichte.
EXTEMPORARY, *a* Gun smuaine, neo-chnuasaichte; grad, ealamh, air an spot, air an uair.
EXTEMPORE, *adv.* Gun smuaine, gu grad, gu h-ealamh, air ball.
EXTEMPORIZE, *v. n.* Labhair gun roimh-smuaine, (no) air an spot.
EXTEND, *v. a.* and *n* Sìn, leudaich, meudaich, farsuingich, cuir am meud; sgaoil; ruig. Extend your bounds, *leudaich do chriochaibh*, his fame extended far, *ràinig a chliù am fad*; extended, *sìnte, leudaichte, meudaichte, farsuingichte*
EXTENSIBLE, *a.* So-shìneadh, so-leudachadh, so-mheudachadh.
EXTENSION, *s.* Sìneadh, meudachadh, leudachadh, farsuingeachd, leathanachd, leithne
EXTENSIVE, *a.* Farsuing, mòr, leathan, fad farsuing, coitchionn. Extensively, *gu farsuing, gu leathann, gu fad farsuing.*
EXTENSIVENESS, *s.* Farsuingeachd, leathanachd, leithne, leud.
EXTENT, *s* Farsuingeachd, leithne, leathanachd, leud, meud; † fairce, cuairte; feadh.
EXTENUATE, *v. a.* Lughdaich, beagaich; ìslich, ìsich; gabh leithsgeul; (*spin out*), caolaich dean caol (no) truagh, (*thin*), tanaich, dean tana
EXTERIOR, *a.* A muigh, a mach; (*substantively*), an taobh a mach, an taobh a muigh, an leth a muigh.
EXTERMINATE, *v.* Dìthich, sgrios, fogair, cuir air falbh; spion as a bhun, bun sgrios, tur-sgrios. Exterminated, *dìthichte, fogairte.*
EXTERMINATION, *s.* Dìtheachadh, sgrios, fògradh, fògairt
EXTERMINATOR, *s* Sgriosadair, fograir, sàruchair
EXTERNAL, *a* A muigh, a mach.
EXTIL, *v.* Sil, sruth; tuit an diotagan.
EXTILLATION, *s* Sileadh, sruthadh, tuiteam an diotagan
EXTIMULATION, *s.* Brogadh, brosnuchadh, brosnachadh, prosnachadh, greasadh, brodadh, sporadh, stuigeadh; seirbhe.
EXTINCT, *a.* As, air dol as, air chùl; mùchta; marbh
EXTINCTION, *s.* Mùchadh, cur as; dol air chùl; sgriosadh, dìtheachadh Extinction of a family, *dìtheachadh teaghlaich*; (*of fire*), mùchadh.
EXTINGUISH, *v. a.* (*A flame*), cuir as, mùch; (*destroy*), sgrios, dìthich, cuir gu dì; (*obscure*), dorchaich, (*a candle*), cuir as, smàl as, mùch. The fire is extinguished, *tha 'n teine air a mhùchadh* (*no*) *mùchte.*
EXTINGUISHABLE, *a.* So-chur as, so-mhuchadh, so-sgriosadh; a dh' fhaodar chur as, a dh' fhaodar mhùchadh.
EXTINGUISHER, *s.* Mùchadair, smàladair.
EXTINGUISHMENT, *s* Mùchadh, smàladh, sgriosadh
EXTIRPATE, *v a.* Spion as a bhun, gearr as, sgrios, dìthich, cuir gu dì, mill. Extirpated, *as a bhun, sgriosta, dìthichte.*
EXTIRPATION, *s.* Spionadh as a bhun, gearradh as, sgriosadh, dìtheachadh, milleadh.
EXTIRPATOR, *s* Spionadair; sgriosadair; milltear
EXTOL, *v.* Mol, arduich, ard-mhol, cliùthaich, tog suas. Extolled, *molta, arduichte, cliùthaichte.*
EXTOLLER, *s.* Moladair, fear moladh.

EXTORSIVE, *a* Sàruchail, foirneartach, eigneachail, sracach, eucorach.
EXTORT, *v.* Srac, dean fòirneart, thoir a dh' aindeoin o, spion, gabh air éigin
EXTORTION, *s* Sracadh, sracaireachd, foirneart, eucoir, ana-cothrom
EXTORTIONER, *s* Sracair, fear foirneirt, sàruchair, fear sàruchaidh
EXTRA, *a.* A thuille, a thuillead, oscionn
EXTRACT, *v a* Tarruing, as-tharruing, thoir a, sùigh, tagh, roghnaich
EXTRACT, *s* As-tharruing, brìgh, sùgh, leth-bhreac, samhladh, sampull
EXTRACTION, *s m* As-tharruing, tarruing a mach; (*race*), cinneadh, cinneach, sliochd, siol, cinneadas
EXTRACTOR, *s* Urr (no) nì a tharruingeas mach
EXTRAJUDICIAL, *a* Neo-laghail, neo-riaghailteach.
EXTRAMUNDANE, *a* Neo-shaoghalmhor, spioradail.
EXTRANEOUS, *a* Deòranta, gun stà.
EXTRAORDINARILY, *adv.* Gu h-iongantach, gu miorbhuileach.
EXTRAORDINARY, *a.* Iongantach, miorbhuileach, sonruichte, ainmeil, neo-chumanta
EXTRAPAROCHIAL, *a* Neo-sgìreachdail, as an sgìreachd.
EXTRAVAGANCE, *s* Mi-riaghailt, ana-measarrachd, caitheamh, strodha, struidhe, ana-caitheamh
EXTRAVAGANT, *a.* Mi-riaghailteach; ana-measarra; iomarcach; strodhail, struidheil, strodhasach, struidheasach; caithteach. Extravagantly, *gu h-ana-measarra, gu struidheil.*
EXTRAVAGANTNESS, *s.* Mi-riaghailteachd, ana-measarrachd; struidhealachd.
EXTRAVASATED, *a.* Brùite, brùithte, air a bhruthadh. Extravasated blood, *fuil bhrùite.*
EXTREME, *a.* Anabarrach, anabharra; iomallach, ro, air; cruaidh Extreme old age, *ro sheann aois*, extremely, *gu h-anabarra, gu mòr, ro, gu ro.*
EXTREME, *s* Crioch, ceann thall, iomall.
EXTREMITY, *s* Crioch, ceann, ceann thall, iomall, teinn, éigin, càs. In great extremity, *ann an ro theinn, ann an ro chàs*
EXTRICATE, *v* Saor, fuasgail. Extricated, *fuasgailte, fasguoileadh saor.*
EXTRICATION, *s.* Saoradh, fuasgladh.
EXTRINSIC, *a.* A muigh, a bhuineas do nì eile.
EXTRINSICALLY, *adv.* O'n leth muigh.
EXTRUCT, *v.* Tog, tog suas
EXTRUCTOR, *s.* Fear togalach; dealbhair
EXTRUDE, *v. a.* Pùc a mach, tilg a mach, ruaig a mach
EXTRUSION, *s.* Pùcadh mach, tilgeadh mach.
EXUBERANCE, *s.* An-fhàs; tarbhachas, pailteas, mor-phailteas, lionmhoireachd.
EXUBERANT, *a.* Pailt, ro-phailt, ro-lionmhor, tarbhach
EXUBERATE, *v n.* Bi ro phailt, (no) ro lionmhor.
EXUCCOUS, *a* Tioram, neo-bhrìghmhor, mi-shùghar, seac
EXUDATE, *v n* Cuir mach follas, brùchd mach mar fhollas
EXULCERATE, *v n.* Leannaich; feargaich, ith, iongraich
EXULCERATION, *s.* Leannachadh, iongrachadh
EXULT, *v n* Dean gairdeachas (no) aoibhneas, bi aoibhinn, bi éibhinn, dean aighear, dean naill, dean sodan, leum le sodan.
EXULTATION, *s* Gàirdeachas, aoibhneas, éibhneas, sodan, luathghair.
EXUSTION, *s* Itheadh, losgadh, cnàmhadh.

Eyas, *s.* Seabhag òg, garrag seabhaig.

Eye, *s* (*Of the body*), Sùil, rosg; (*eyesight*), radharc, fradharc, rosg, sealladh, leirsinn; (*countenance*), gnùis, beachd; aghaidh; (*a loop*), sùil, lùb, dul; (*of a needle*), crò. Having one eye, *cam, air leth shùil*, your eyes are bigger than your belly, *is mò do shùilean no do bhrù;* he is wise in his own eyes, *tha e glic no shùilean* (*no*) *na bheachd féin*, a little eye, *sùileag, lùbag*, an eye-witness is better than an ear-witness, *is fearr faicinn no cluinntinn*; eyed, *sùileach*; one-eyed, *air leth-shuil, cam*, a leering eye, *sùil mhiog-leach*, a sharp eye, *sùil gheur, sùil bhiorach*, a squint eye, *sùil chlaon*, a blear eye, *sùil ròsblach*, before my eyes, *roimh mo shùilibh*, an evil eye, *droch shùil*, keep an eye upon him, *cum suil air, cum beachd air*, having a cast in the eye, *claon*, far from the eye, far from the heart, *fad o'n t-sùil, fad o'n chridhe*

Eye, *v. a.* Beachdaich, cum sùil air, seall, amhairc

Eyeball, *s.* Ubhall na sùl

Eyebright, *s* Soillse na sul, roinn an roisg.

Eyebrow, *s.* Malaich, malaidh. Having large eyebrows, *mailidheach.*

Eyed, *a.* Sùileach; làn shùilean.

Eyedrop, *s.* Deur

Eyeglance, *s.* Sealladh, platha, gliosg; sméideadh.

Eyelash, *s* Fabhradh, abhra, abhradh.

Eyeless, *a.* Dall.

Eyelet, *s.* Lubag, sùileag; cruchag, toll.

Eyelid, *s.* Rosg.

Eyesight, *s* Fradharc, radharc, leirsinn, sealladh na sùl.

Eyespotted, *a.* Breacaichte, sùileagach.

Eyesore, *s.* Mio-thlachd.

Eyesalve, *s.* Fobhar shùl, sabhal shùl, sùil-leigheas.

Eyewink, *s.* Priobadh, sméideadh.

Eyewitness, *s* Fianuis.

Eyre, *s* Cùirt cheartais.

Eyrie, Eyry, *s* Nead seabhaig.

F.

F, *s* Seathamh litir na h-Aibidil. F R.S, *Ball do 'n Chomunn rioghail.*

Fabaceous, *a* Pònaireach.

Fable, *s.* Sgeul, faoin sgeul, fionn-sgeul, ur-sgeul; breug, do-sgeul, uisgeul

Fabled, *a.* Cliuiteach ann am fionn-sgeulachd

Fabler, *s* Sgeulaiche, ur-sgeulaiche; seanachaidh, uisge-ulaiche

Fabric, *s* Aitreabh, togail, tigh; forgnadh, foirgneadh

Fabric, *v a* Tog, cruthaich, dealbh, deilbh, cruthaich; aithris breugan

Fabricate, *v a.* Tog, comh-thog, dealbh; deilbh, cruthaich.

Fabrication, *s* Fogail; dealbhadh; breug

Fabulist, *s.* Ur-sgeulaiche, breugair

Fabulous, *a* Faoin; ursgeulail; dealbhte; breugach

Face, *s* Aghaidh, gnùis, aodann, eudann, ceann-aghaidh, tuar, gné, aogas, cugas, bathais, lathaireachd, tul; dealbh Face to face, *aghaidh ri h-aghaidh*, before my face, *roimh mo ghnùis*, a wry face, *goill*, in the face of the sun, *an àin gheal an là*

Face, *v a* Thoir aghaidh air, aghaidhich, coinnich, tachair air, cuir aghaidh ri h-aghaidh. Faced, *aghaidhichte*, bare-faced, *beagnarach*

Faced, *a* Aghaidhichte Double-faced, *dùbailt, cealgach.*

Facetious, *a* Mearr, suigeartach, suilbhear, ait, cridheil, sunntach, greannar, greannmhor

Facetiousness, *s* Mire; suigeartachd, suilbhearachd, aiteas, cridhealas, fearas-chuideachd, greannmhorachd

Facile, *a* Furas, so-dheanamh; so-dheanta, neo-dhuilich, reidh; socrach, easgaidh; so-lubaidh, soirbh

Facilitate, *v a* Furasaich, dean furas, luathaich, cuid-ich, dean coghnadh; dean réidh, réitich

Facility, *s* Furasachd, furasdachd, socair, ullamhachd, deise; lathailteachd, teòmachd

Facing, *s* Aghaidh

Facing, *part.* Fa chomhair, fa-chomhar, mu choinhair, mu chomhar. The house facing us, *an tigh mu 'r comhar*

Facinorous, *a.* Olc; Droch-bheartach; ain-ghniomhach aingidh

Fact, *s.* Gniomh, tùrn, beart; firinn In fact, *gu fior;* it is a fact, *tha e fior.*

Faction, *s* Pàirtidh, buidheann, bannal; aimhreite, tuasaid, conghair.

Factious, *a* Pàirtidheach; easardach, easaontach, aimh-reiteach, tuasaideach, buidheannach, ceannairceach, úrch-oideach.

Factiousness, *s* Pàirtidheachd; easardachas, eas-aontas, eas-aontachd, aimhreite

Factitious, *a.* Ealadhanta.

Factor, *s* Fear-gnothuich, fear ionaid; seumarlan.

Factorship, *s* Seumarlanachd.

Factory, *s.* Tigh luchd gnothuich

Factotum, *s* Seirbheiseach a ni h-uile ni, seirbheiseach fior easgaidh.

Faculty, *s.* Comas, comasachd, murrachas, murraichead; cumhach, neart; (*of the mind*), càil, cumhachd inntinn; (*a company*), buidheann, bannal, coinneamh.

Faddle, *v. n.* Breug, cluich ri.

Fade, *v n.* Searg, seac, crion, crup, caith, tiormaich. It faded, *sheaig e*, it has faded, *tha e air seargadh.*

Fæces, *s.* Cac, gaor, aolach; salachar, deasguinn, grunntas, drabhag

Fag, *v. a.* Fannaich, sgithich, sàruich, thoir thairis; saothairich.

Fag-end, *s* Ceann-eididh; fuigheal, fuighleach.

Fagot, Faggot, *s* Cual, brosnadh, creamhachdan; bruthan, achlasan connaidh.

Fail, *v n.* and *a* Fàilinnich, fàilnich, fàilinn; fannaich; bàsaich, rach an cùl, tréig, dearmaid, thig gearr air. His memory has failed, *tha 'chuimhne air fàilinn.*

Fail, *s* Fàilinn, fàilneachadh, dith, tuisleachadh; bàs. Without fail, *gun fhàilinn.*

Failing, *s* Failinn, tuisleadh, tuislinn; (*fault*), lochd; coire, cron; (*disappointment*), mealladh dòchais.

Failure, *s.* Dith, gainne; sgurachd; dearmad, failneach-adh, gainnachadh, briseadh, ciont, coire, tuislinn.

Fain, *a.* Toileach, an geall, an càs, ait, cridheil, sunntach. You will be fain to do it, *bidh tu 'n geall air a dheanamh.*

Fain, *adv.* Gu toileach, le làn toil.

Fain, *v n.* Bi an geall, bi an càs, miannaich.

Faint, *a* An-fhann, an-mhunn, fann, lag, gun lùth, gun chli, tinn, euslan, breòite, gealtach, meath, meath-chridheach, tais; mall, dubhach, tuirseach; neo-smiorail; trom.

Faint, *v. n.* Searg, crion; lagaich, fannaich; tuit (no) rach ann am paisean. He fainted, *chaidh e na phaisean, chaidh e am pladha.*

Fainthearted, *a.* Meath-chridheach, gealtach, tais, bog, cladhaireach, cailleachail, cailleachanta.

Faintheartedness, *s.* Meath-chridheas, geilte.

Fainting, *s.* Fannachadh, lagachadh, dol am pladha, dol an neul, *paisean.*

Faintish, *a.* Leth-char fann, leth-char lag.

Faintling, *a.* Eagallach, gealtach, meath-chridheach.

Faintly, *adv.* Gu fann, gu lag, gu mall, gu gealtach, gu meath-chridheach.

Faintness, *s.* Laigsinn, laige, fainne, an-fhannachd, an-mhunnachd.

Fainty, *a.* Lag, fann, an-fhann, anmhunn; gun lùth, gun chlì.

Fair, *a.* (*Beautiful*), Boidheach, sgiamhach, aillidh, maiseach; briagh, breagh; (*just*), ceart, cothromach; (*in complexion*), bàn; (*pure*), glan, soilleir, geal; (*mild*), suairc, caoimhneil; (*as wind*), soirbheasach. The day is fair, *tha 'n là na thur;* fair and square, *cothromach, ceart;* fair and softly, *socair;* keep fair with him, *cum réidh ris;* a fair face is half a portion, *ni aghaidh bhòidheach maraiste.*

Fair, *s.* Rìmhinn, ban, boirionnach bhoidheach. The fair, *na boirionnaich.*

Fair, *s.* (*Market*), Margadh, margad, féill, faidhir; aonach, tlachd; cleide, eachras, oireachdas.

Fairing, *s.* Faidhrean, faidhir; brontanas; gibhte; tiodhlac.

Fairly, *adv.* Gu boidheach, gu maiseach; gu soilleir; gu ceart; gu direach, gu h-ionruic.

Fairness, *s.* (*Beauty*), boidhchead; maise; àille; (*justice*), ionracas, ceartas.

Fairspoken, *a.* Suairc, caoimhneil; beulchar.

Fairy, *s.* Sìthich, duine sìth, scobhrag, fé, ban-drùidh, ban-fhiosaiche. Fairies, *sìthichean, daoine sìth, daoine beaga.*

Fairy, *a.* Sìtheil, sìth.

Fairy-land, *s.* Sìth-bhrùth, sìth-bhrog.

Fairy-flax, *s.* Lion na ban-sìthe.

Faith, *s.* Creideamh; tairisneachd; muinghinn, dochas; creideas; ionracas, tréibhdhireas, onoir; geall. On my faith, *air m' onoir;* he broke his faith, *bhris e 'gheall.*

Faithful, *a.* Diadhuidh, ionraic, treibhdhireach, creidimheach; dìleas, onorach, fìor, fìreannach, tairiseach. Faithfully, *gu diadhuidh, gu h-ionraic, gu tréibhdhireach, gu dìleas; gu fìreannach, gu tairiseach.*

Faithfully, *adv.* See **Faithful.**

Faithfulness, *s.* Ionracas, treibhdhireas; tréibhdhireachd, fìreantachd, fìrinneachd.

Faithless, *a.* Neo-chreideach, neo-ionruic; eas-ionraic, neo-dhìleas; cealgach, mealltach, traoidhteil.

Faithlessness, *s.* Eas-ionracas; neo-dhìlse; cealgaireachd, traoightearachd.

Fakir, *s.* Ionracan truagh iomrolach do chreideamh Mhathomeit.

Falcated, *a.* Crom, corranach.

Falchion, *s.* Claidheamh crom, cloidhean.

Falcon, *s.* Seabhag, seobhag.

Falconer, *s.* Seabhagan, fear a dh' eunaicheas le seabhagaibh.

Fall, *v. n.* Tuit, tuislich; *fell,* thuit, thuislich; (*happen*), tachair, eirich; (*as price*), tuit; rach an lughaid; (*come down*), teirinn, thig a nuas; (*as water*), traogh; (*as wind*), siolaidh. The wind has fallen, *tha ghaoth air sioladh;* they fell a fighting, *leig iad air caonnag, bhuail iad air caonnag;* fall away, *or* revolt, *dean ceannairc* (*no*) *cùl-mhutaireachd;* fall away from religion, *cùl-sleamhnaich;* fall in one's way, *tachair, thig an caraibh;* fall out *or* disagree, *droch-coird, cuir mach.* They fell out, *dhroch-coird iad, chuir iad a mach;* they fell together by the ears, *chaidh iad an dàil a chéile, chaidh iad an sgornan a chéile;* this fell to my share, *thàinig so ormsa;* fall on *or* attack one, *buail air, leum air, eirich air, thoir ionnsuidh air, sàs air;* fall under, *or* yield, *géill, striochd;* ready to fall, *thua tuiteam;* I almost fell, *theab mi tuiteam;* fall off, *searg, crion, fàs truagh* (*no*) *caol.*

Fall, *s.* Tuiteam, tuisleachadh, tuisleadh; leigeadh, torchar, tearnadh, easgar, tuiteamas; splad; tapag, tapadh, spirlinn, tubaist, teagmhas; sgrios; leathad; dol sios; (*of water*), spùt, eas. The fall, *an leagadh.*

Fallacious, *a.* Mealltach, cealgach; fallsa, fallsail; mearachdach. Fallaciously, *gu mealltach, gu cealgach; gu fallsa, gu fallsail.*

Fallaciousness, *s.* Mealltachd, cealgachd, fallsachd, fallsaileachd.

Fallacy, *s.* Mealltachd, cealgachd, ceilge; car.

Fallen, *part.* Air tuiteam, air sgriosadh; air làr; sgriosta. Fallen out, *or* happened, *air teachd gu crìche;* fallen out, *or* quarrelled, *air cur mach, mach air chéile;* one fallen away from the faith, *cùl-sleamhnachair.*

Fallibility, *s.* Tuiteamachd, neo-chinntealas, tuisleachd.

Fallible, *a.* Tuiteamach, tuisleachail, buailteach do mhearachd; aineolach, ion-mheallta.

Falling, *s.* Tuiteam, tuisleachadh. A falling out with, *cuir a mach, droch cordadh, aimhreite.*

Falling sickness, *s.* An tuiteamas, tinneas na gealaich, guin na ré.

Fallow, *a.* Ruadh, dearg; donn; bàn neo-threabhte.

Fallow ground, *s.* Eilidh; ar-samhruidh, talamh fàs, (no) falamh, talamh air a threabhadh.

Fallow, *v. a.* Dean eilidh (no) ar-samhruidh.

False, *a.* Fallsa, fallsail, meallta, breugach, eithich; cealgach, traoidhteil; mealltach, neo-dhìleas, neo-fhìor, mearachdach, fàs. A false dealer, *cealgair, slaoightear;* a false oath, *mionnan eithich;* a false accusation, *casaid bréige;* a false heart, *cridhe fàs;* a false opinion, *baraíl mheallta;* better be poor than false, *is fearr a bhi bochd no bhi breugach.*

Falsehearted, *a.* Cealgach, mealltach, traoidhteil, fàs-chridheach.

Falsehood, *s.* Breug; neo-fhìrinn; fallsachd, traoidhte.

Falseness, *s.* Ceilge; breùg, traoidhte, cealgaireachd, traoidhtearachd.

Falsifier, *s.* Mealltair, cealgair.

Falsify, *v. a.* and *n.* Breugaich, breugnaich, innis breug; (*corrupt*), truaill.

Falsity, *s.* Breug; mearachd.

Falter, *v.* Dean tiob; dean ag; bi liodach bi gagach (no) manntach.

Faltering, *a.* Tiobach, agach, liodach, gagach, manntach. Falteringly, *gu tiobach, gu h-agach, gu liodach, gu gagach, gu manntach.*

Fame, *s.* Cliù, ainm, deagh iomradh, meas, blàdh, luaidh, luadh-radh, cloth, luadh, alladh; fabhra, fabhunn, iomradh, guth. His fame shall not die, *cha teid a chliù an dìth.*

Famed, *a.* Cliùiteach, ainmeil, iomraiteach, measail, allail.

Fameless, *a.* Neo-chliùiteach, neo-ainmeil, neo-iomraiteach, neo-mheasail, neo-allail.

FAMILIAR, *a.* (*Intimate*), eolach air; (*unceremonious*), cairdeil, faoilidh, caidreamhach, caidreach, ionmhuinn; (*common*), cumaint, cumannt, coitchionn; tric, minic. They are very familiar, *tha iad ro mhòr aig a chéile*, familiar with grief, *air a chleachd ri bròn*.

FAMILIAR, *s.* Companach, combach, guailliche; droch spiorad, leannan sìth.

FAMILIARITY, *s.* Caidreamhas, caidreamhachd, caidreamh, ro-eòlas, co-chaidreamh, eolas, companas, comunn.

FAMILIARIZE, *v. a.* Cleachd, gnàthaich, dean ri. Familiarized, *cleachda, air a chleachd, deanta ri*.

FAMILIARLY, *adv.* Gu caidreach; gu h-ionmhuinn, gu minic, gu tric, gu cumannta; gun mhodhaileachd.

FAMILY, *s.* Teaghlach; sliochd, clann, àl, treubh; tigheadas, gniealach; saintreabh. Of a noble family, *uasal*, death and removings undo a family, *eug agus imrich a chlaoidheas tigheadas*.

FAMINE, *s.* Gorta, gainne, gorta, ocras, acras, cion-lòin, daorsa, daorsadh.

FAMISH, *v. a* and *n.* Marbh le gorta, bàsaich le gorta. He is almost famished, *tha e thun bàsachadh leis an acras*, famished (as cattle), *air an togail, gortach*.

FAMISHMENT, *s.* Gorta, ocras, acras, cion-bìdh.

FAMOUS, *a.* Cliùiteach, ainmeil, iomraiteach, measail, allail. Famously, *gu cliùiteach, gu h-ainmeil, gu h-iomraiteach, gu h-allail*.

FAMOUSNESS, *s.* Cliùiteachd, ainmeileachd, iomraiteachd, allaileachd.

FAN, *s.* (*For women*), fuaragan, gaothran, sgàileagan, (*for winnowing*), guit, beantag, fasgnag, dallan, asnag; caigean.

FAN, *v.* Fuaraich, gaothraich, fionnaraich; fasgain, càth, caignich.

FANATIC, FANATICAL, *a.* Baoth, faoin-dhiadhuidh.

FANATIC, *s.* Baoth-chreideamhach, urr a theid gu h-anabarra le creideamh.

FANATICISM, *s.* Baoth-chreideamh; faoin chreideamh; boile-chreideamh.

FANCIFUL, *a.* Dòchasach, macnasach, faoin-bharaileach, neònach, iongantach; eutrom, gogaideach, binneach; meanmach, faoin. Fancifully, *gu dochasach, gu neònach, gu h-eutrom, gu faoin, gu binneach, gu gogaideach*.

FANCIFULNESS, *s.* Dòchasachd, macnasachd; meanmachd.

FANCY, *s.* Meanmadh, mac meanmadh, inntinn; smuain, dòchas; barail, faoin-bharail, miann, faoin-innleachd. He took a fancy for her, *ghabh e dòchas dith, leig e inntinn oirre*.

FANCY, *v. a.* Smuainich, smuaintich, smaoinich, baralaich, beachdaich; saoil; miannaich. He fancied, *smuainich e, shaoil e, ghabh e na bheachd*.

FANCYMONGER, *s.* Faoin-innleachdair.

FANE, *s.* Teampull, eaglais, cill, lann.

FANFARON, *s.* Bramsdair.

FANG, *s.* Ionga, tosg, crubh; clàr-fhiacall, goinneag. Fanged, *iongaichte, iongach, tosgach*.

FANGLE, *s.* Oidhirp leibideach, innleachd fhaoin, faoin-innleachd.

FANGLED, *a.* Breagh, faoin-mhaiseach; ciadlusach.

FANGLESS, *a.* Neo-fhiaclach, cabach; gun fhiacall, gun ionga, gun tosg.

FANNEL, *s.* Sròl sagairt.

FANTASIED, *a.* Dòchasach, faoin.

FANTASTIC, FANTASTICAL, *a.* Faoin, dòchasach, neònach, faoin-bharaileach; gogaideach, guanach, mi-reusonta; amaideach, gòrach.

FANTASY, *s.* See FANCY.

FAR, *adv.* Fad, fada, am fad, an céin, fad as. Far off, *fad air falbh, fad as, an cian*, by far, *gu mòr, gu ro mhòr*; far be this from me, *gu ma fad so uam*, far and near, *am fad agus am fogus*, as far as, *cho fhad ri*, as far as I can, *cho fad 's is urrainn mi, fhadsa 's urradh dhomh*, how far? *cia cho fad? cia fhad?* so far, *fhad is so*; thus far, *gu ruig so, thun so*.

FAR, *a.* Fad; cian; iomallach, iom-chian. It is a far cry to Loch Awe, *is fhad an eubh o Loch Abh*.

FAR, *s.* Al muic, uirceanan, bròd dh' uirceana; cuain, mucraidh.

FARCE, *v. a.* Starr, sparr, pùc, lion, sath.

FARCE, *s.* Baoth chluiche; ealaidh, abhachd.

FARCICAL, *a.* Iongantach, neònach, abbhachdach.

FARCY, *s.* Cloimh eich.

FARDEL, *s.* Glacag, glaclach, dornag, ceanglach; trusgan; cual, cualan, eallach, prunnan, droinnse, droinnseach.

FARE, *v. n.* Imich, triall, falbh; dean tùrus, dean cuairte; bi slàn, bi gu math dheth, bi gu dona dheth; ionaltair, ith. How fare you? *cia mar a tha thu?* fare thou well, *slainnte leat, slàn leat, soraidh leat*; fare ye well, *slainnte leibh, slàn leibh, sàr (no) soraidh leibh*.

FARE, *s.* Biadh, lòn; duais, diol, paigh.

FAREWELL, *s.* Cead, beannachd. Bid him farewell, *gabh cead dheth, gabh beannachd leis*.

FAREWELL, *adv.* (*To thee*), beannachd leat, slainnte leat, slàn leat, gu robh Dia maille riut, sàr leat, soraidh leat; (*to you*), beannachd leibh, slainnte leibh, slàn leibh, sar leibh, soraidh leibh.

FAR-FETCHED, *a.* Eil-thireach; air a thoirt an céin.

FARINA, *s.* Min, min mhìn.

FARM, *s.* Fearann, fonn; gabhail fearainn; gabhaltas, baile.

FARM, *v. a.* Gabh air màl, leig air màl; treabh, crann, thoir a stigh.

FARMER, *s.* Tuathanach, gabhaltaiche.

FARMING, *s.* Tuathanachas, treabhadh.

FARMOST, *a.* Is fhaide, is iomallaiche.

FARNESS, *s.* Astar, céin.

FARRAGINOUS, *a.* Iol-ghnétheach, ioma-ghnétheach.

FARRAGO, *s.* Brothas.

FARRIER, *s.* Each-leigh; each-lighiche; lighiche each.

FARROW, *s.* Bainbh, cuain.

FARROW, *v. a.* Beir uirceanan, breith cuain.

FART, *s.* Dean braoim, leig braoim, braoim, breim.

FART, *v.* Braoim, breim.

FARTHER, *a.* Faide, ni 's fhaide, air taobh thall.

FARTHER, *adv.* Ni 's fhaide.

FARTHERMORE, *adv.* Tuille fòs, a thuille, a thuille air sin, a thuille air so, a bharras air sin, a bharrachd air sin (no) so.

FARTHERMOST, *a.* Is fhaide, is céin, is iomallaiche.

FARTHING, *s.* Feoirlinn, feoirling, fardan; an ceithreamh cuid do sgillinn. Farthing's worth, *luach fardain*.

FARTHINGALE, *s.* Cearcall.

FASCIA, *s.* Cuaran; bann.

† FASCIATED, *a.* Cuaranaichte, ceangailte le cuaran.

FASCIATION, *s.* Ceangladh suas, cuaran.

FASCINATE, *v. a.* Goin; cuir fo gheasachd, cuir buitseachd, cuir druidheachd.

FASCINATING, *a.* Ro ionmhuinn; drùighteach.

FASCINATION, *s.* Druidheachd, geasachd, buitseachd.

FASHION, *s.* Cumadh, dealbh, samhlachadh, deanamh; fasan, doigh, modh, gnàs, gnàth, cleachda, † mos, nòs, sgiamh, dreach; tul, munadh. In the fashion, *anns an fhasan;* after this fashion, *air an doigh so;* without fashion, *gun chumadh.*

Fashion, *v. a.* Dealbh, cum, sgeith, cruthaich.

Fashionable, *a.* Fasanta, nòsail; gnathaichte, cleachdach. Fashionably, *gu fosanta, gu nòsail, gu cleachdach.*

Fashioned, *a.* Cumta, deilbhte, sgéithte, deanta. Old-fashioned, *sean-aimsireil; sean fhasanta.*

Fashionist, *s.* Spailpear; gaothan, lasgair.

Fast, *v. n.* Troisg, traisg, fuirich o bhiadh, bi àir ocras, claòidh.

Fast, *s.* Trosgadh, trasgadh.

Fast, *a.* Daingeann, teann, diongalta, diongmhalta; gramail; socraichte; suidhichte; laidir; (*in pace*), luath, cabhagach. Fast and loose, *mùghteach, caochlaideach, luaineach, siùbhlach;* faster, *ni's luaithe; ni's daighne;* a hold-fast, *spiocair;* fast and firm, *gu teànn, docrach.*

Fast, *adv.* Gu daingeann, gu teann, gu diongalta, gu gramail, gu socraichte, gu suidhichte; gu luath.

Fast day, *s.* Là troisg, là trosgaidh.

Fasten, *v. a.* and *n.* Teannaich, gramaich, daingnich, tàth, cuir sa chéile, cum sa chéile. He fastened upon me, *shàs e orm; leum e orm.*

Fastened, *part.* Teannaichte, gramaichte, daingnichte, tàdhta, tàdhte, an sàs.

Fastening, *s.* Daighneachadh, ceangladh, ceangal.

Faster, *s.* Trosgair, fear trosgaidh.

Fast-handed, *a.* Cruaidh, cruadalach; gionach; saoghalta, sanntach; luath-lamhach.

Fastidious, *a.* Di-measail, stràiceil; òrraiseach, tàireil, tarcuiseach. Fastidiously, *gu stràiceil; gu tarcuiseach.*

Fastidiousness, *s.* Stràicealachd, orraiseachd, tàirealachd, tarcuiseachd, diombachd.

Fastly, *adv.* Gu luath, an cabhaig, le deifir; gu h-ealamh.

Fastness, *s.* Diongaltachd, diongmhaltachd; neart; aitedaighnichte, daingneach.

Fat, *a.* Reamhar, sultmhor, feòlmhor, feòlar; domhail, dumhail, bronnach; beartach; trom, tiugh, promhaidh, meith.

Fat, *s.* Reamhrachd, sult, saille; smior; grìse, blonag; meitheachd, feòlmhorachd; (*the fat of cattle*), ìth, geire; (*the fat of a sow*), muc-bhlonag; (*of a goose*), blonag gheoidh.

† Fat, *s.* Dabhach.

Fat, *v. a.* and *n.* Reamhraich, dean reamhar (no) sultmhor, fas reamhar. Fatted, *reamhar, biadhta.*

Fatal, *a.* Marbhtach, sgriosail, dochannach, diùbhlach, millteach, teagmhaiseach, cineamhuinneach, bàsmhor; an dàn; do-sheachnadh. Fatally, *gu marbhtach, gu millteach, gu bàsmhor, gu sgriosail.*

Fatality, *s.* Roi-orduchadh, dàn, tuiteamas, cineamhuinn; sul-radharc, ordugh Dhé.

Fatalness, *s.* Bàsmhorachd; sgrios.

Fate, *s.* Dàn; bàs; sgrios; aobhar bàis; crioch, deireadh; mi-shealbharachd. Black was his fate, *bu dubh a dhiol;* none ever prevented his fate, *cha do shaltair neach riamh air a phiseach.*

Fated, *a.* Orduichte; sonraichte; an dàn, dànail. That death was fated him, *bha 'm bàs sin an dan da.*

Father, *s.* Athair; daidean, gintear; sinnsear; sean duine. The Father, *an t-Athair, a cheud pearsa do 'n Trianaid; an Cruith-fhear;* a stepfather, *leth athair oide;* a godfather, *oide-baistidh;* a father-in-law, *athair céile;* by the father's side, *a thaobh athar;* forefathers, *sinnsearan, aithrichean;* that was not like your father, *cha b' e sin cleas d-athar, cha bu dual athar duit sin;* father confessor, *oide aidmheil.*

Father, *v. a.* (*Adopt*), gabh ri, uchd-mhacaich; (*impute*), cuir as leth; cuir urr air fear.

Fatherless, *a.* Gun athair, dilleachdanach, dilleach.

Fatherliness, *s.* Athaireileachd.

Fatherly, *a.* Mar athair, athaireil, caomh, càirdeil, carthannach.

Fathom, *s.* Àitheamh; sea troidhean.

Fathom, *v. a.* Grunndaich; rannsuich.

Fathomless, *a.* Gun grunnd, gun iochdar.

Fatidic, *a.* Fiosachdail, foir-innseach, fàisneach.

Fatidic, *s.* Fiosaiche, fàidh, faidheadair.

Fatigable, *a.* So-sgitheachadh, so-fhannachadh, so-thoirtthairis.

Fatigue, *s.* Sgios, saothair, allaban, treachladh; guais.

Fatigue, *v. a.* Sgìthich, dean sgìth, sàruich. Fatigued, *sgìthichte, sgìth;* quite fatigued, *air toirt thairis.*

Fat-kidneyed, *a.* Reamhar, sultmhor.

Fatling, *s.* Ainmhidh biadhta.

Fatner, *s.* Biadhtach.

Fatness, *s.* Reamhrachd, sult, feolmhorachd; blonag, ìdh; geire; meathlas; meitheachd.

Fatten, *v. a.* and *n.* Reamhraich, dean sultmhor (no) sultmhor; biadh, fàs reamhar. Fattened, *reamhraichte, biadhta.*

Fatty, *a.* Reamhar, sultmhor; blonagach.

Fatuity, *s.* Amaideachd, amaide, gòraiche; baoghaltachd.

Fatuous, *a.* Amaideach, gòrach; faoin.

Fatwitted, *a.* Baoghalta, umaidheach.

Faucet, *s.* Spiocaid, leigeadair; dealg, pinne.

Fault, *s.* Coire, ciont, cron, lochd, giomh, gaoid; criomchaig, mearachd, failinn; iom-chomhairle. Every man has his fault, *tha 'chron fhéin aig na h-uile fear;* find fault, *cronaich, faigh coire;* it is you who are in fault, *is tusa tha sa choire;* full of faults, *lochdach;* at fault, *air dhochair;* what fault has he committed? *ciod an cronn rinn e, ciod rinn e air dhochair.*

Faultily, *adv.* Gu docharach, gu cearr, gu ciontach.

Faultiness, *s.* Coire, olcad, lochd.

Faultless, *a.* Neo-choireach, neo-lochdach, iomlan, foirfe; glan, ionraic, gun choire, gun chiont, gun lochd, gun ghiomh.

Faulty, *a.* Ciontach; coireach; sa choire, ri choireachadh, lochdach, giomhach; cearr, dona, olc.

Favillous, *a.* Luaithreach; griosachail.

Favour, *s.* Fabhor, maoidhean, baigh, gean, deagh-ghean, càirdeas, comain, caoimhneas; taic, cùl-taic, taobh; maitheanas; suaicheantas. By your favour, *le do chead;* as a favour, *mar fhàbhor.*

Favour, *v. a.* Bi fabhorach, bi baigheil (no) cairdeil; nochd fàbhor (no) baigh, nochd cairdeas (no) caoimhneas; cum taobh ri, dean coghnadh le; bi coslach ri. Favour him, *bi cairdeil da, cum taobh ris;* you favour him in the face, *tha thu coslach ris san aghaidh.*

Favourable, *a.* Fabhorach, cairdeil, còir, baigheil, caoimhneil, caomhail, deagh-rùnach; iomchuidh, soirbheasach. A favourable construction, *ciall fabhorach;* a favourable wind, *gaoth shoireasbhach.* Favourably, *gu fàbhorach, gu càirdeil, gu baigheil, gu caoimhneil, gu caomhail.*

Favoured, *part.* and *a.* Fo mhaoidhean, fo-bhaigh; maoidheanach; breagh, briagh, maiseach, deagh-mhaiseach; sultmhor; eireachdail.

Favourer, *s.* Fear coghnaidh; cùl-taic, caraid.

Favourite, *s.* Caomhach; graidhean, ceistean, annsachd, aontlachd.

Favourless, *a.* Neo-fhabhorach; neo-mhaoidheanach; gun charaid, gun chùl-taic.

Fawn, *s.* Laogh feidh, mang, meann earb, earbag; (*flattery*), miodal.

Fawn, *v. n.* Beir mang.

Fawn, *v. a.* Sir maoidhean, dean miodal no blandar; striochd; lùb.

Fawner, *s.* Miodalaiche, fear miodalach, fear sodalach.

Fawning, *a.* Miodalach, sodalach. Fawningly, *gu miodalach, gu sodalach.*

Fay, *s.* Sìthiche, gointe. He has fay blood in his veins, *tha fuil ghointe na cheann.*

Fea-berry, *s.* (*a local word.*) Gròsaid.

Fealty, *s.* Umhlachd; dìllseachd; urram.

Fear, *v. a.* Gabh eagal ro; gabh eagal a; cuir eagal air. You need not fear, *cha ruig leas eagal a ghabhail.*

Fear, *s.* Eagal, sgàth, faitcheas, geilte, gealt, uamhann, oillt; iomaguin, athadh. Great fear, *crith-eagal;* he put him in bodily fear, *chuir e eagal a thòin air;* there is no fear of that, *cha 'n eagal da sin;* there is no fear of him, *cha 'n eagal da, is beag eagal da.*

Fearful, *a.* Gealtach, meath-chridheach; tais, cailleachanta, meata; geatrach; 'sgeanach, fiamhach; (*awful*), eagallach, oillteil, uamharra, uamhasach. Fearfully, *gu h-oillteil, gu h-eagallach.* The eye that is hurt is ever fearful of harms, *is fiamhach an t-sùil a lotar.*

Fearfulness, *s.* Geilte, eagal, oillt, uamhunn.

Fearless, *a.* Nea-eagallach, neo-ghealtach, misneachail; treubhanta, dàn.

Fearlessness, *s.* Neo-eagallachd, misneach, treubhantas.

Feasible, *a.* So-dheanta; coslach.

Feast, *s.* Féisd, féist, cuirm, cuilm, fleadh, féill, fuireas, ròic.

Feast, *v. n.* Thoir cuirm (no) féisd; thoir fleadh; faigh cuirm (no) féisd, gabh ròic, sàsuich.

Feaster, *s.* Fear féill, fear cuirm; geòcair.

Feastful, *a.* Cuirmeach, féilleach, fleadhail.

Feat, *s.* Gniomh, éuchd, cleas, obair, beart, feart; morghniomh, ard-ghniomh; treunas, gaisge, treubhantas.

Feat, *a.* Deas, teòma, ealanta; ullamh, ealamh, snàsmhor, sgilcil; eireachdail.

Feather, *s.* Iteag, ite; clòinne, clòinneag, cléite, cléiteag; cléiteach; clòiteach, cuille, peann; cluimh, cloimh.

Feather-bed, *s.* Leabadh chloimh, leabadh chluimh.

Feathered, *a.* Iteach, iteagach, cléiteach, cluimhteach, cloimheach, cluimhneagach.

Feathery, *a.* Iteagach, iteach, cléiteach, cluimhcach, cloimheach.

† **Featly**, *adv.* Gu deas, gu teoma, gu h-ealanta.

Feature, *s.* Cruthachd, cruitheachd; gné, gnùis, tuar, aogas.

Febrifuge, *s.* Leigheas fiabhruis.

Febrile, *a.* Teasachail.

February, *s.* Dara mios na bliadhna, mios an dubh-chathamh, am faoilteach.

Feces, Fæces, *s.* Cac, gaor, aolach, salachar; deasgainn; grunndas.

Feculence, *s.* Deasgann, grunnd, salachar.

Feculent, *a.* Deasgannach, grunndach, salach.

Fecund, *a.* Torrach, geneil, siolmhor, lionmhor, tarbhach.

Fecundate, *v. a.* Dean torrach (no) siolmhor.

Fecundity, *s.* Torrachas, siolmhorachd, lionmhorachd, tarbhachd, tarbhachas.

Fed, *a.* Biadhta, beathaichte; sàthach, buidheach.

Federal, *a.* Comhnantach, comh-bhannta; bannail.

Federate, *a.* Cumhnantaichte; comh-bhannta, bannail.

Fee, *s.* Duais, tuarasdal; dìol, pàigh; luach-saoithreach.

Fee, *v.* Dìol, tuarasdail, pàigh; ceannaich, briob; gabh. He is feed with me, *tha e gabhte agamsa.*

Feeble, *a.* Lag, fann, an-fhann, anmhunn; neo-chomasach, eiglidh, breoite, meuranta, mall, spreòchanta; † airealach. He is more feeble than you, *is e is laige na thusa.* Feebly, *gu lag, gu fann, gu h-an-fhann.* Feeble is the arm of him who has no brother, *is lag gualainn gun bhrathair.*

Feebleminded, *a.* Lag-chridheach, lag-inntinneach.

Feebleness, *s.* Laigsinn, laigse, fainne, anfhannachd, anmhunnachd, éiglidheachd, breòiteachd.

Feed, *v.* Biath, biadh, beathaich, àraich, tog, cum suas; ionaltair. Put out to feed (as cattle), *tog, feuraich, cuir mach air feurachadh;* feed the fire, *leasaich an teine;* feed voraciously, *dean poit* (*no*) *geòc, craos;* feed, and the world will clothe, *cuir innte is cuiridh 'n saoghal uimpe.*

Feed, *s.* Biath, lòin; boite; feurach, feurachadh, ionaltradh, innlinn, annlann.

Feeder, *s.* Biadhtair, beathachair, fear biathaidh.

Fee-farm, *s.* Gabhail fearainn, gabhaltas sioruidh.

Feel, *v. a.* and *n.* Mothuich, fainich, fairich, bean, buin. I will make you feel it, *bheir mise ort gum fainich thu e;* I did not feel it, *cha d' fhainich mi orm e.*

Feeler, *s.* Mothuchair; faireachair.

Feeling, *s.* Mothuchadh; caomhalachd; faireachadh, faineachadh, càileachd.

Feeling, *a.* Caomh, mothuchail; tiom-chridheach, teochridheach, blàth-chridheach.

Feelingly, *adv.* Gu caomh, gu tiom-chridheach, gu teochridheach.

Feet, *pl.* of foot. Casan, cosan; traidhean, troidhean.

Feetless, *a.* Gun chasan, gun chosan.

Feign, *v.* Gabh ort, leig ort, dealbh; breugaich, innis breug. He feigned to be sick, *gabh e air a bhith tinn.*

Feigned, *a.* Dealbhta, deilbhte, earach, leithsgeulaichte, cealgach, meallta. Feignedly, *gu cealgach, gu meallta.*

Feigner, *s.* Dealbhadair; cealgair, mealltair.

Feint, *s.* Breug-choslas; coslas fallsa; leigeil air, gabhail air; faoin-ionnsuidh.

Feint, *a.* Faoin; fallsa, fallsaidh; mealltach, cealgach.

Felicitate, *v. a.* Fàiltich, cuir fàilt, dean sona, altaich beath.

Felicitation, *s.* Fàilte, fàilteachadh, co-ghàirdeachadh.

† **Felicitous**, *a.* Sona.

Felicity, *s.* Sonas, agh, soirbheas, soirbheachadh, beannachadh, saimh.

Fell, *a.* Borb, garg, fuathasach, eagallach, uamharra, fiadhaich, fuilteach.

Fell, *v. a.* (*As a tree*), gearr sios, gearr bhàn, sgath, buain; (*a person*), spad, smàl, leig, tilg sios. Felled, *gearrta sios, sgathte; buainte; spadte, air leigeil.*

Fell, *s.* Craicionn, croiceann, seic, seiche.

Fell, *pret.* of fall; which see.

Feller, *s.* Gearradair; sgathadair; fear sgathaidh.

Fellmonger, *s.* Fear chroicne, fear sheicean.

Fellness, *s.* Buirbe; gairge, bainnidh; fuathasachd, uamharrachd; fuilteachd.

Felloe, Felly, *s.* Cuairsgean.

Fellow, *v. a.* Freagarraich; carraidich.

Fellow, *s.* Companach, combach, leth-bhreac; gille, balaoch; diùlnach; fear neo-inmheach; (*a member*), ball; (*servant*), comh-sheirbheiseach, comh-oibriche. A sorry fellow, *sgonn-bhalaoch*; a bedfellow, *coimh-leabaiche*; a young fellow, *balachan*; fellow of a society, *ball comuinn*; a naughty fellow, *droch bhalaoch, crochair*; a sorry fellow, *sgroingean*; *bodach*.

FELLOW-CREATURE, *s.* Comh-chreutair. My fellow-creature, *mo chomh-chreutair*.

FELLOW-FEELING, *s.* Comh-mhothuchadh, mothuchadh, truacantas; truas; iochd; comh-iochd; comh-thruas; comh-fhulang.

FELLOW-HEIR, *s.* Comh-oighre.

FELLOW-HELPER, *s.* Fear cuideachaidh, fear còghnaidh, comh-oibriche.

FELLOW-LIKE, *a.* Ionann, comh-chosmhal, comh-ionann.

FELLOW-SERVANT, *s.* Comh-sheirbheiseach.

FELLOWSHIP, *s.* Comunn, co-chomunn, caidreamh, companas, compantas, comh-bhoinn.

FELLOW-SOLDIER, *s.* Comh-shaighdear.

FELLOW-STUDENT, *s.* Comh-sgoilear, comh-stuidear.

FELLOW-SUFFERER, *s.* Comh-fhulangair, comh-fhulangaiche.

FELLOW-SUFFERING, *s.* Comh-fhulangas.

FELO-DE-SE, *s.* Fein-mhortair.

FELON, *s.* *(A criminal)*, ciontach; *(whitlow)*, glacach; ìnras.

FELONIOUS, *a.* Ciontach, olc, aingidh, coirbte, cealgach, fealltach, mì-runach; coireach, airidh air bàs. Feloniously, *gu ciontach, gu h-aingidh, gu cealgach, gu fealltach.*

FELONY, *s.* Crochaireachd; mor-chiont, ard-chionta, mor-choire; ciont airidh, air bas.

FELT, *v.* Luaidh, luthaidh; dluthaich, tiughaich.

FELT, *s.* Peilleag, stuth do 'n deanar adaichean.

FELTRE, *v. n.* Slamaich.

FELUCCA, *s.* Bàt shé-ràmhan, sé-ramhach.

FEMALE, *s.* Boirionnach, bainionnach, bean, té.

FEMALE, *a.* Boirionn, bainionn, banail.

FEME-COVERT, *s.* Te phòsda.

FEME-SOLE, *s.* Nighean, te shingilte.

FEMINATELY, *adv.* Boirionnas, bainionnas, boirionnachd, bainionnachd, banaileachd; bandaidheachd.

FEMININE, *a.* Boirionn, bainionn, banail, bandaidh, malta.

FEMORAL, *a.* Màsach, màsail.

FEN, *s.* Bog, criatharach, boglach, fèith, mòinteach, curach, bogan, talamh iosal fliuch.

FEN-BERRY, *s.* Seorsa dearcaig.

FENCE, *s.* Tiadhlann, iolann, lann, loinn, fàl, gàradh, dìg; ganail; cosnadh, callaid, tuaim, cladh, daighneach.

FENCE, *v. a.* Iadh, cuairtich, cuartaich, druid, iom-dhruid, callaidich. Fenced, *iadhta, cuartichte, druidte, callaidichte.*

FENCE, *v. n.* Dean basbaireachd (no) feannsaireachd.

FENCELESS, *a.* Fosgailte; gun dion; gun dìg.

FENCER, *s.* Basbair, feannsair, lannair, fear cladheimh.

FENCIBLES, *s.* Dion-fheachd; freiceadan.

FENCING, *s.* Basbaireachd, feannsaireachd.

FENCING-MASTER, *s.* Basbair, feannsair, maighstir feannsair.

FENCING-SCHOOL, *s.* Sgoil fheannsaireachd.

FEND, *v. a.* Cum air falbh, dion.

FENDER, *s.* Dionadair; fear dion.

FENERATION, *s.* Ain-riadh.

FENNEL, *s.* Lus an t-saoidh.

FENNY, *a.* Bog, fliuch, fèitheach, criathrachail, càtharach, mòinteachail, làthachail, frogach.

FENUGREEK, *s.* Ionntag Ghreugach.

FEOD, *s.* Gabhail fearainn, cumail fearainn.

FEODARY, *s.* Gabhaltaiche, fear gabhail, òglach, iochdaran.

FEOF, FEOFF, *v. a.* Cuir an seilbh, thoir còir.

FEOFFEE, *s.* Fear seilbhe, sealbhadair.

FEOFFMENT, *s.* Cur an seilbhe, tabhairt seilbhe.

† FERACITY, *s.* Torraichead.

FERIATION, *s.* Féill, sollain.

FERINE, *a.* Fiadhaich, borb, garg; coimheach.

FERITY, *s.* Buirbe, fiadhaichead.

FERMENT, *v. a.* and *n.* Buair; oibrich; bi fo bhuaireas.

FERMENT, *s.* Buaireas; aimhreite, an-riaghailt.

FERMENTABLE, *a.* So-oibreachadh.

FERMENTATION, *s.* Oibreachadh, fiuchadh, comh-ghluasad.

FERN, *s.* Raineach.

FERNY, *a.* Raineachail, làn rainiche.

FEROCIOUS, *a.* Borb, garg, fiadhaich, feargach, cruadalach, ain-iochdmhor.

FEROCIOUSNESS, *s.* Buirbe, gairge, fiadhaichead, ain-iochd, ain-iochdmhoireachd.

FERREOUS, *a.* Iarunnaidh, iarnaidh, iarunnach.

FERRET, *s.* Neas; neas-abhag; baineasag, coinneas; stiom chaol.

FERRET, *v. a.* Sir le neasaibh, ruaig coinean le neas.

FERRETER, *s.* Neasadair.

FERRIAGE, *s.* Fàradh; airgiod aisig.

FERRUGINOUS, *a.* Iarunnaidh, iarnaidh.

FERRULE, *s.* Bairecan.

FERRY, *v. a.* Aisig.

FERRY, *s.* Aiseag; faradh; iomarach; iomchar; port. He who waits at the ferry will get across some time, *am fear a dh' fheitheas aig an aiseag, gheibh e thairis uair 'gin.*

FERRY-BOAT, *s.* Bàt aiseig, bat puirt.

FERRY-MAN, *s.* Fear aiseig, fear bàta, portair.

FERTILE, *a.* Torrach, torrail, tarbhach, siolmhor, pailt, lionmhor. Fertilely, *gu torrach, gu tarbhach, gu pailt.*

FERTILITATE, *v. a.* Dean torrach, mathaich.

FERTILITY, *s.* Torraichead, tarbhachas, siolmhoireachd, pailteas.

FERTILIZE, *v. a.* Dean torrach, mathaich, inneirich, leasaich.

FERULE, *s.* Crios leathair, sgiùrsadh, tàs.

FERVENCY, *s.* Deòthas, dealas, dianas, deine, eudmhorachd, dùrachd, teas.

FERVENT, *a.* Deòthasach, dealasach, dian, cas, eudmhor, dùrachdach, teth, loisgeach, teintidh. Fervent heat, *dian-theas.* Fervently, *gu deothasach, gu dealasach, gu dian, gu h-eudmhor, gu dùrachdach, le deòthas diadhaidh.*

FERVID, *a.* Teth, goileach, losgach, loisgeach; teintidh; dian, deothasach. Fervidly, *gu teth, gu goileach, gu loisgeach, gu teintidh, gu dian, gu deothasach.*

FERVIDNESS, *s.* Teas, deothasachd, dealasachd, eudmhorachd.

FERVOUR, *s.* Deòthas, dùrachd, déine; teas, blàs, eudmhoireachd.

FESTAL, *a.* Féilleach, cuirmeach, cuilmeach, fleadhach, aoibhneach, ait, sollain.

FESTER, *v.* Feargaich, iongaraich, lobh.

† FESTINATION, *s.* Cabhag.

FESTIVAL, *a.* Féilleach, cuirmeach, cuilmeach, fleadhach, aoibhneach, ait, sollain.

FESTIVAL, *s.* Féill, làth féill. An anniversary festival, *féill-bhliadhnail.*

FESTIVE, *a.* Féilleach, cuirmeach, fleadhach; aoibhneach, ait, sugach, subhach, gàirdeach, sollain.

Festivity, *s.* Feilleachd, cuirmeachd, aiteas, gairdeachas, aoibhneas, subhachas.

Festoon, *s.* Crochadan, cluigean.

Festucine, *a.* Odhar, air neul fodair.

Fetch, *v.* Thoir, tabhair, beir, tarruing; dean; ruig. Fetch away, *thoir air falbh;* this will fetch money, *ni so airgiod, bheir so airgiod;* fetch a compass, *thoir cuairt;* fetch down or lessen, *lughdaich;* fetch forth, *thoir a mach; thoir a làthair;* fetch a leap, *thoir leum;* fetch [go for] him, *rach 'g a shireadh.*

Fetch, *s.* Cleas, car, cuilbheart, seòl, innleachd.

Fetid, *a.* Lobhach, loibheach, breun, lobhta; grod, gluig. A fetid smell, *boladh grod.*

Fetidness, *s.* Lobhachas, loibheachas, bréine, breinead, breunad.

Fetlock, *s.* Ruitean.

Fetor, *s.* Droch-thòchd, droch bholadh, breine.

Fetter, *s.* Ceangladh, geimhle, geimhleadh, geimhleach, cuibhreach, cord, ròp. Fetters, *gleimhlean, cuibhrichean, †boltuidh.*

Fetter, *v. a.* Ceangail, cuibhrich, geimhlich.

Fetus, Fœtus, *s.* Torrachas anabuich; ceud-fhas.

Feu, *s.* Gabhail.

Feud, *s.* Fàlachd, comh-stri, comh-strigh, tuasaid, cur a mach, caonnag, connsach, connsachadh, cogadh.

Feudal, *a.* Iochdranach; feodhnach; fàlachdach.

Feudal, *s.* Gabhail fearainn, fearann air ann bi gabhail aig neach.

Feudatory, *s.* Gabhaltaiche.

Fever, *s.* Teasach, fiabhrus. The yellow fever, *an teasach bhuidhe.*

Feverish, *a.* Teasachail, fiabhrusach, teth; neo-chinnteach, mùghteach.

Feverishness, *s.* Fiabhrusachd, teas.

Feverous, *a.* Tinn le fiabhrus, ann an teasach.

Feuillage, *s.* Duille, duilleach.

Few, *a.* Ainmig, tearc, gann; beagan, ainneamh; †gamaineach. They are but few, *cha 'n eil iad ach ainmig,* (*no*) *tearc;* in a few days, *ann am beag làithe;* they are few, *is ainmig iad, is tearc iad;* in a few words, *ann am beag dh' fhocaill;* fewer, *ni's ainmig, ni's teirce.*

Fewness, *s.* Ainmigead, tearcad, teirce, teircead, gainnead.

Fib, *s.* Breug.

Fib, *v. n.* Innis breug, dean breug.

Fibber, *s.* Breugair.

Fibre, *s.* Freumh chaol; sreang, toinntean snàithne.

Fibrous, *a.* Freumhach; sreangach, toinnteanach, snàithneach.

Fibula, *s.* Cnaimh crom na coise.

Fickle, *a.* Mughteach, iomlaideach, iom-luath, neo-bhunailteach, neo-bhuan, neo-sheasmhach; siubhlach, luaineach, luaimneach, guanach, eutrom, gaoithe; so-lùbaidh, so-mhùghadh. Fickly, *gu mughteach, gu iom-luath, gu neo-bhuan, gu siùbhlach, gu luaineach, gu guanach.*

Fickleness, *s.* Mughteachd, iomlaideachd, iom-luathas, neo-bhunailteachd, neo-sheasmhachd; siùbhlachd, luaineachd, luaimneachd, guanachd.

Fictile, *a.* Creuchmhor, creuchaidh, creadha.

Fiction, *s.* Breugnaidh, ruanachd; sgeul, sgeulachd, fionnsgeul, ur-sgeul; nuaidheachd, breige.

Fictitious, *a.* Fallsa, fallsail, breugach, meallta; mealltach; fo' shamhladh, faoin; neo-fhior. Fictitiously, *gu fallsa, gu breugach, gu meallta.*

Fiddle, *s.* Fiodhall.

Fiddle, *v.* Cluich air an fhiodhall.

Fiddle-faddle, *s.* Faoineas, moran iomairt mu neoni, ceigeanachd, striopais.

Fiddle-faddle, *a.* Faoin, iomairteach; rudach, ceigeanach, fagharsach; leanabaidh.

Fiddler, *s.* Fìdhlear; fear ciùil.

Fiddlestick, *s.* Bogh-fìdhle.

Fiddlestring, *s.* Teud, teud fìdhle.

Fidelity, *s.* Tréibh-dhireas, ionracas, tairiseachd, disleachd, dìlseachd.

Fidget, *v.* Dean iomairt (no) striopais. How you do fidget, *is ann ort tha 'n iomairt.*

Fidgetting, *s.* Iomairt, striopais, ceigeanachd; luasgan.

Fidgety, *a.* Iomairteach, rudach, ceigeanach; luasganach; neo-fhoisneach.

Fiducial, *a.* Dòchasach, muinghinneach, cinnteach.

Fiduciary, *s.* Creideasaiche, fear aig am bheil ni sam bi air creideas; fear a chuireas a dhochas an creideamh dh' easbhuidh oibre.

Fie! *interj.* Mo naire!

Fief, *s.* Gabhail.

Field, *s.* Achadh, fàiche, magh, machair; fearann, fonn, gort, pàirc, feart, faoch, grian, bruigh, treann; (*room*), rùm, farsuingeachd; (*of battle*), blàr, blar-catha, àrach, (*space*), rùm.

Fieldfare, *s.* Liathtruis, liathtruisg.

Fieldmarshal, *s.* Feachd-mharasgal.

Field-mouse, *s.* Luchag fàiche, dallag fheòir.

Field-officer, *s.* Ceannard, ard-oichear, milidh.

Fieldpiece, *s.* Gunn-àraich.

Fiend, *s.* Deamhan, deamhon, diabhol, droch spiorad; eascaraid, namhaid.

Fierce, *a.* Fiadhaich, borb, garg, dioganta, ruaineach; dian, feargach; buaireasach, air bhuaireadh, laidir, treun. Fiercely, *gu fiadhaich, gu borb, gu garg, gu dioganta.*

Fierceness, *s.* Buirbe, gairge, feirg, dioganiachd, ruaineachd; déine; buaireasachd, ainneart.

Fieriness, *s.* Teas, teinntidheachd; feirge, fearg; obannachd, crosdachd.

Fiery, *a.* Teth, teinntidh, teinnteach, lasach, leusach, loisgeach; feargach, contuinneach; dian, deothasach, obann, cabhagach, crosda.

Fife, *s.* Feadag, feadan.

Fifer, *s.* Fear feadaig, feadanaiche, fear feadain.

Fifteen, *a.* Cuig-deug, còig-deug. Fifteen men, *cuig fir dheug.*

Fifteenth, *a.* Cuigeamh deug. The fifteenth man, *an cuigeamh fear deug.*

Fifth, *a.* Cùigeamh. The fifth part, *an cùigeamh cuid.*

Fifthly, *adv.* Anns a chùigeamh àite.

Fifty, *a.* Leth-cheud, caogad.

Fig, *s.* Figis, fiogais. A fig-tree, *crann-figis.*

Fight, *v. a.* and *n.* Cog, strìgh, gleac, cuir blàr, cuir cath; dean caonnag, thoir ionnsuidh.

Fight, *s.* Cath, comhrag, blàr, baiteal; cogadh, caonnag, comhrag-déise, tuasaid. A cock-fight, *cogadh choileach.*

Fighter, *s.* Milidh, fear blàir, fear comhraig, gaisgeach, laoch; laochan; fear-feachd.

Fighting, *s.* Cath, còmhrag, cathachadh, caonnag. Set them a fighting, *cuir a chaonnag iad.*

Figment, *s.* Innleachd; breug; sgeul.

Figulate, *a.* Creadha, talmhaidh.

Figurable, *a.* So-dhealbhadh, so-chruthachadh, so-oibreachadh, a ghabhas dealbh no cumadh.

Figurate, *a.* Dealbhaidh, dealbhach, cruthach.

Figuration, *s.* Dealbhadh, dealbhachadh, cruthachadh, cumadh, cumachd, deanamh.

Figurative, *a.* Samhlachail.

Figure, *s.* Dealbh, dreach, cumadh, cumachd; cruth, deanamh; aogas, coslachd, samhladh; iomhaigh; morchuis; (*in arithmetic*), figeir, *a local word.*

Figure, *v. a.* Dealbh, cum cruthaich; eag-samhlaich, dean eag-samhuil; (*in the mind*), beachdaich, smuainich, samhluich. Figured, *dealbhta, cumta, cruthaichte, eag-samhlaichte.*

Fig-wort, *s.* Farach dubh

Figured, *part.* See Figure.

Filaceous, *a.* Sreangach, toinnteanach

Filament, *s.* Sreangan, toinntean, snàithne, snàithnean.

Filbert, *s* Cnù, cnò, faoisgeag.

Filch, *v.* Goid, slaid, slaoight.

Filch, Filcher, *s.* Goidich, gaduiche, mearleach, sladaiche, sladair, sliomair.

Filching, *s.* Goideadh, goideachd, gaduidheachd, meirle, slad, sliomaireachd.

File, *s.* Ròl; (*of soldiers*), sread, sreath, rang; (*for metal*), eighe, eitheadh, liomhan, liobhan.

File, *v. a.* Liobh, liomh, méil le liobhan (no) le eighe; falbh ann an rang

File-cutter, *s.* Liobhanaiche.

Filemot, *s.* Dath donn, crotal.

Filer, *s.* Fear liomhaidh, liobhadair

Filial, *a.* Macail, dleasnach, dleasdanach.

Filigree-work, *s.* Òr-ghreus.

Filings, *s.* Min iaruinn, min stàilinn.

Fill, *v. a.* Lion; foirlion; dean buidheach, dean sàthach, sàsuich.

Fill, *s.* Làn, sàthadh, teannath, teann-shath. He drank his fill, *dh' òl a theannath* (*no*) *theann-sàth.*

Filler, *s* Lionadair.

Fillet, *s.* Stiom, bann, oideag, crios-gruaig, tiugh a mhàis.

Fillip, *s.* Cliudan, sgeafag, sgleafard, pealaid, smiotan.

Filly, *s.* Loth, lothag, loth-bhiorach, biriche, bromach òg, làir, cliobag.

Film, *s.* Sgannan; sgrath, sgailean, seicean.

Filmy, *a.* Sgannanach; sgrathach, sgàileanach, seiceanach.

Filminess, *s.* Sgannanachd, sgàileanachd.

Filter, *v. a* Siolaidh, grunndaich, faisg.

Filter, *s.* Siolachan, siothlachan; siothlag, criathar; criabhar, criathrag.

Filth, *s.* Salachar, sal, aolach, gaor, inneir, cac; gaor; mosaiche, poll, eabar; trusdaireachd, truaillidheachd

Filthily, *adv.* Gu salach, gu mosach, gu gràda; (*in language*), gu drabasta, gu draosda.

Filthiness, *s.* Salachaireachd, salachar, neo-ghloine, truaillidheachd, mosaiche.

Filthy, *a.* Salach, mosach, musach, gràda, cac, neo-ghlan; neo-gheimnidh, drabasta, draosda; gràineil You filthy beast, *a bhéist mhosaich; a thrusdair.*

Filtrate, *v.* Siothlaidh, grunndaich; criathraich.

Filtration, *s.* Siothlachadh, grunndachadh.

Fin, *s.* Ite, sgiath éisg, gaine éisg.

Finable, *a.* Airidh air umhladh, ùmhlachail.

Final, *a.* Deireannach, mu dheireadh; bàsmhor, millteach.

Finale, *s.* Deireadh, crioch.

Finally, *adv.* Mu dheireadh, air cheann thall; fa-dheòidh; gu tur.

Finance, *s.* Tighinn stigh, màl, cìs.

Finances, *s. pl* Tighinn stigh rioghachd.

Financier, *s.* Ionmhasair, fear do 'n aithne airgiod rioghachd a bhuileachadh gu ceart.

Finch, *s.* Lasair choille

Find, *v* Faigh; (*by searching*), airmeis, amais; (*feel*), mothuich, fairich, fairich; (*maintain*), cum suas, tog, beathaich, cum ri, cum ann; (*observe*), beachdaich, cuir an céile, thoir fanear. I have found it, *fhuair mi e, dh' airmeis mi air*, how do you find yourself, *cia mar tha thu 'g ad fhaineach' féin*, he will find him in money, *cumaidh e airgiod ris, cumaidh se ann an airgiod e*, find out or discover, *faigh a mach, fuasgail*, find fault, *coirich, cronaich, faigh coire do.*

Finder, *s.* Fear faghail.

Find-fault, *s* Cronachair, lochdair

Fine, *a.* (*Elegant*), Grinn, maiseach, finealta, gasda, eireachdail, ceanalta, sgeamnaidh, gleusda; caoin, blathmhor; dathail; (*pure*), glan, fior-ghlan, soilleir, tana; (*smooth*), min, (*dexterous*), deas, seòlta, teoma, (*cunning*), eolach, cuilbheartach. Fine in clothes, *eireachdail, briagh, breagh, riomhach*

Fine, *s.* Umhladh, paineachas, càin, plaic, fionail, sraith

Fine, *v a* (*Make fine*), glan, ath-ghlan, dean finealta, grinnich, dean min; dean caol; (*amerce*), cuir umhladh air, leig umhladh air. He fined them, *chuir e ùmhladh orra.*

Fine, *s* Crioch, deireadh, ceann-thall. In fine, *mu dheireadh, anns an aite is deireannaiche.*

Fine-fingered, *a* Ealanta, grinn; snàsmhor, maiseach.

Finely, *adv.* Gu grinn, gu maiseach, gu finealta, gu gasda, h-eireachdail, gu gleusda; gu glan, gu min, gu snàsmhor; gu seòlta, gu h-ealanta. He is finely, *tha e gu grinn, tha e gu gasda, tha e gu gleusda*

Fineness, *s.* Eireachdas, grinneas, grinnead, deise, maise, dathalachd; fior-ghloine, minead, caoilead, ealantachd, riomhadh.

Finer, *s.* Glanadair, fear glanaidh; leaghadair, umhlachair.

Finery, *s.* Riomhadh, breaghachd, briaghachd, dathalachd, deise.

Fine-spoken, *a.* Beulchar, goileamach; modhail

Finesse, *s.* Seoladh, slighe, car, cuilbheart.

Fin-footed, *a* Clar-chosach.

Finger, *s.* Meur, miar, corag; gniomh, smòg A forefinger, *colagag*, middle-finger, *meur fad*, third-finger, *meur an fhàinne, mathair na lùdaig*, little finger, *lùdag, lùdagan, lùidean*, a finger's breadth, *leud meòir.*

Finger, *v. a* Meuraich; cluich air; dean gu finealta.

† **Fingle-fangle**, *s.* Faoineas.

Finical, *a.* Sgòdail, uallach, leòmach, moiteil, spòrsail; gogaideach, gogailleach; ceigeanach, baoth, faoin. Finically, *gu sgodail, gu moiteil, gu h-uallach, gu ceigeanach, gu faoin*

Finis, *s.* Crioch, deireadh, comh-dhunadh.

Finish, *v. a.* Criochnaich, criochnuich, coi-lion, thoir gu criche, dean foirfe Finished, *criochnaichte*, quite finished, *lan chriochnaichte, coi-lionta.*

Finisher, *s.* Criochnachair, fear-criochnachaidh.

Finishing, *s.* Criochnachadh, deasachadh, snàsadh. The finishing stroke, *am buille mu dheireadh*

Finite, *a.* Criochnaidheach, criochnach, criochnaichte, cruthaichte.

Finitude, *s.* Criochnaidheachd.

Finless, *a.* Gun ite, gun iteagan

Finny, *a.* Iteach, iteagach mar éisg, gaineach

Fin-toed, *a.* Clàr-chosach

Fipple, *s.* Stoipeal; àrcan.

Fir, *s.* Giuthas, giubhas. A fir wood, *coille ghiuthais, giuthasach.*

Fire, *s.* Teine, eibhle, lasair, gealbhan, breo, † buite, buitealach; teas; deothas, dealas. Set on fire, *cuir ri theine;* on fire, *ri theine;* with fire and sword, *le teine is claidheamh;* mend the fire, *leasaich an teine;* a bonfire, *teine éibhneis;* St. Anthony's fire, *teine dé; deire.*

Fire, *v. a.* and *n.* Cuir ri theine, loisg; beothaich, fàdaidh; thoir teine; tilg.

Fire-arms, *s.* Airm-theine; acfhuinn theine, gunnachan.

Fire-ball, *s.* Ball teine, ball tairneanaich.

Firebrand, *s.* Aithinne; caoir; fear aimhreite, culaidh bhuairidh, brun.

Fire-cross, *s.* Crann-tàir, crois-tàir, craun-tàra, crois-tàra.

Fire-drake, *s.* Dreag.

Firelock, *s.* Musga, musgaid, gunna, gunna glaic.

Fireman, *s.* Fear-teine; duine crosda cas.

Fire-office, *s.* Losg-lann, teine-bhùth.

Firepan, *s.* Aghann, aghann theine.

Firer, *s.* Losgair, losgadair.

Fireship, *s.* Long-theine.

Fire-shovel, *s.* Sluasaid, sluaisde, croman luatha, croman luaithre.

Fireside, *s.* Taobh an teine, teintean; teallach. One who is fine at a fair, may be dirty at his fire side, *is tric a bha breagh air an fhéill, mosach na thigh féin.*

Fire-stone, *s.* Clach-theine, cloch-theine, sporadh.

Fire-wood, *s.* Connadh, gual, mòin, mòineadh, bradhadair; spruan, crionach.

Fire-work, *s.* Obair theine.

Firing, *s.* (*Fuel*), connadh, gual, mòin, mòineadh, bradhadair; spruan, crionach; (*of arms*), tilgeadh, làmhach, làmhachas, gunnaireachd.

Firk, *v. a.* Buail, gréidh, smachdaich.

Firken, *s.* An ceathramh cuid do bhairill.

Firm, *a.* Daingeann, làidir, teann, neo-ghluasadach, deangalta, diongalta, diongmhalta, docrach; maireann, bunailteach, bunaiteach, cruaidh, duineil; bunach; gramail; foirfe, suidhichte. Firm land, *tìr-mhòr, mòr-thìr.*

Firm, *v. a.* Daighnich, teannaich, suidhich.

Firm, *s.* Buidheann; comh-bhoinn, comunn.

Firmament, *s.* Iormailt, athar, adhar, aidhear, neamh, speuran, failbhe.

Firmamental, *a.* Iormailteach, atharail, neamhuidh, speurail.

Firmly, *adv.* Gu daingeann, gu laidir, gu teann, gu neo-ghluasadach gu diongmhalta, gu docrach; gu maireann, gu bunaiteach, gu cruaidh, gu duineil, gu gramail; gu suidhichte.

Firmness, *s.* Bunailteachd, bunaiteachd, neart, treòir; teanndachd; neo-ghluasadachd; duinealas, gramalas. There is no firmness in the world in him, *cha n' eil gramalas air an t-saoghal ann.*

First, *a.* Ceud, ceudamh; toiseach, priomh, tùsail; sàr, corr. At the first sight, *air a cheud sealladh.*

First, *adv.* An toiseach, air thoiseach, an tùs, air tùs, air thùs, anns a cheud àite. Go first, *rach air thoiseach;* first and foremost, *an ùr is air thoiseach.*

First-begotten, *a.* Ceud-ghin. His first begotten child, *a cheud-ghin cloinne.*

First-born, *a.* Ceud-ghin. My first-born, *mo cheud-ghin.*

First-fruits, *s.* Ceud-thoradh.

Firstling, *s.* Ceud-ghin.

Firstling, *a.* Ceud.

Fisc, *s.* Ionmhas, màl, cios, cìs, tighinn stigh rioghachd.

Fiscal, *a.* Ionmhasach, a bhuineas do 'n ionmhas.

Fish, *s.* Iasg. A little fish, *iasg beag;* a river fish, *breac, iasg aimhne;* the gills of a fish, *giùran;* a fish hook, *dubhan;* a fishing line, *driamlach.*

Fish, *v. a.* Iasgaich; rannsaich.

Fisher, *s.* Iasgair.

Fisher-boat, *s.* Bàt iasgaich.

Fisherman, *s.* Iasgair. Fishermen, *iasgairean.*

Fishery, *s.* Iasgaireachd, iasgachd.

Fishful, *a.* Lan éisg.

Fish-hook, *s.* Dubhan iasgaich, dubhan.

Fishing, *s.* Iasgach, iasgachadh, iasgachd, iasgaireachd. A fishing, *ag iasgachadh, ag iasgachd.*

Fish-kettle, *s.* Coire éisg, aghann éisg.

Fishmonger, *s.* Fear éisg, iasgair, marsonta éisg.

Fishpond, *s.* Poll éisg, poll iasgaich.

Fish-woman, *s.* Bean éisg, cailleach éisg, te reic éisg.

Fishy, *a.* Làn éisg, iasgail.

Fissile, *a.* So-sgoltaidh.

Fissure, *s.* Sgoltadh, sgaradh, gag, sgàineadh, grian-sgoltadh.

Fist, *s.* Dorn; cròg, glac, mul-dhorn. A fistful, *lan dùirn, lan cròig.*

Fist, *v. a.* Dorn, dornaich, buail, straoidhil.

Fisticuffs, *s.* Dornaireachd, dornadh.

Fistula, *s.* Piob, pioban, feadan; seorsa neasgaid.

Fistular, *a.* Piobach, piobanach, feadanach.

Fit, *s.* Neul, platha, paisean, tinneas, greis; an tuiteamas; (*freak*), dochas; *gì.*

Fit, *a.* (*Reasonable*), ceart, cothromach; cubhaidh; (*proper*), oireamhnach; còir; (*convenient*), freagarrach; iomchuidh; (*seasonable*), amail; (*decent*), eireachdail; bòidheach; (*capable*), murrach, comasach; (*ready*), deas, ullamh.

Fit, *v. a.* and *n.* Dean freagarrach; freagair; (*fit out*), uigheamaich, deasaich, cuir an uigheam.

Fitchet, *s.* Neas.

Fitful, *a.* Neulach, plathach, tinn, truagh, neo-shlainnteil.

Fitly, *adv.* Gu ceart, gu còir, gu cubhaidh, gu h-iomchuidh, gu freagarrach.

Fitness, *s.* Cubhaidheachd, iomchuidheachd, freagarrachd.

Fitz, *s.* Mac.

Five, *a.* Cùig, còig, cùignear, còignear. Five years old, *cuig bliadhna dh' aois;* five hundred, *cuig ceud.*

Fivefold, *a.* A chuig uiread, cùig fillte.

Five-foot, *s.* Reult-iasg.

Fives, *s.* Seorsa cluiche.

Fix, *v. a.* and *n.* Suidhich, daighnich, fàstaidh, sonraich, socraich; sath, troimh-lot; gabh tamh, gabh gu fois. Fixed, *orduichte, sonraichte, socraichte, socrach;* fix a day, *sonraich làth;* fix into the earth, *sàth 's talamh;* a fixed time, *am sònruichte,* (*no*) *suidhichte.*

Fixation, *s.* Gramalas, bunailteas; tamh; stadachd.

Fixedness, *s.* Bunailteachd, bunaiteachd; diongmhaltachd gramalachd; socair, socrachd; (*of mind*), suidheachadh inntinn.

Fixture, *s.* Airneis shuidhichte.

Fizgig, *s.* Seorsa muirdheadh.

Flabbiness, *s.* Buige, fleoganachd; bogluinneachd; boglainneachd; neo-theanndachd.

Flabby, *a.* Bog, maoth, fleoganach; boglainneach, neo-rag, neo-ghramail; neo-theann; sleamhuinn.

Flaccid, *a.* Anfhann, maoth, fann, lag; fuasgailte, sùbailt, so-lùbaidh, neo-rithinn, neo-rag.

Flaccidity, *s.* Anfhannachd, fainne, laigsinn.

Flag, *v. n.* Croch gu leabagach; fàs trom (no) tuirseach; fannaich.

Flag, *s.* Seilistear, luachair; bratach, suaicheantas.

Flag, *s.* Leac.

Flag, *v. a.* Leacaich, leig le leacaibh.

Flag-broom, *s.* Sguab, sguabach.

Flagelet, *s.* Seorsa feadaig, feadan.

Flagellated, *a.* Sgiùrstà, cuipinnte.

Flagellation, *s.* Sgiùrsadh, cuipinn.

Flagginess, *s.* Anfhannachd, laigsinn, sùbailteachd.

Flaggy, *a.* Anfhann, lag, neo-rag, subailt, neo-bhlasda.

Flagitious, *a.* Olc, aingidh, coirbte, droch-mhuinte; ciontach, crosda.

Flagitiousness, *s.* Aingidheachd, coirbteachd; droch-mhuine; mi-ghniomh.

Flag-officer, *s.* Ard-mharaiche

Flagon, *s.* Soitheach; plaichead; *flagan*

Flagrancy, *s.* Dian-theas, teas loisgeach.

Flagrant, *a.* Teth, dealasach, deothasach; teth dearg; caoireach; ain-teth; anbharra; fuathasach; comharaichte, sònruichte, foillsichte, aithnichte.

Flagrantness, *s.* Dealasachd; ainteas; anbharrachd; fuathasachd

Flagration, *s.* Losgadh.

Flagship, *s.* Long ard-mharaiche, priomh-luingeas

Flag-staff, *s* Crann brataich, lorg brataich

Flail, *s.* Sùiste, buailtean.

Flake, *s.* Clòimneag, clòimhneag, clùimhneag, clàdan, toipean; sleantach; sp'ang; breath, sreadh, leac. A flake of snow, *cloimhneag sneachdaidh;* a flake of ice, *leac eighe.*

Flaky, *a.* Clòimneagach, clòimhneagach, cluimhneagach, toipeanach; leacach, splangach.

† **Flam**, *s.* Breug, leithsgeul

Flambeau, *s.* Leus, torr-leus; blincean.

Flame, *s.* Lasair, leus; teine; lasadh, losgadh; teas; deine, dealradh. It broke out into a flame, *bhris e mach na lasair;* the flame of love, *teas (no) déine gaoil.*

Flame, *v. a.* Las; leus, lasainnich, loisg, dealraich, gabh.

Flame-coloured, *a.* Buidhe-dhearg, air dhreach teine.

Flamen, *s.* Sagart.

Flaming, *a.* Lasach, leusach, loisgeach, teinntidh, lasarra; caoireach.

Flammable, *a.* Lasach, leusach, so-losgaidh.

Flammation, *s.* Losgadh.

Flammiferous, *a.* Lasach, teinntidh, lasarra

Flammy, *a.* Lasach, leusach, loisgeach.

Flank, *s.* Taobh, slios, loch-bhlein. Flank of an army, *slios feachd.*

Flank, *v. a.* Buail air feachd san t-slios; thoir ionnsuidh air slios; dineartaich

Flannel, *s.* Plaid thana mhìn, clòth bàn mìn, plaid bhàn, cùirtean, aodach bàn.

Flap, *s.* Leabag, libeag, cluas, sgiort; (*blow*), boiseag, buille leis an laimh, sgleafart, gleog; *sgealp*

Flap, *v. a.* Buail leis an laimh; sgleafartaich, *sgealp*, dean fuaim mar ni eun le sgiathaibh; *clapainn*, a local word; croch mar leabag.

Flap-eared, *a.* Spad-chluasach.

Flapped, *a.* Leabagach.

Flare, *v.* Dearrsaich; leus; leagh mar choinneal.

Flash, *s.* Boisge, grad, bhoisge, pladha, lasadh, lannair, drilinn; splang, splangradh.

Flash, *v.* Las, boisg; plath; dealraich.

Flashy, *a.* Faoin, sgòdail, basdalach, loinneach; neo-bhlasda.

Flask, *s.* Adharc fhùdair, creachan, copan, searrag, soitheach.

Flat, *a.* Comhnard, réidh, iosal, comh-iosal, (*as drink*), marbh, domblasda, neo-bhlasda, neo-bhrisg, (*prostrate*), sinte, air spadadh, spàdte; (*dull*), trom, neo-smiorail; (*in sound*), neo-gheur, neo-bhinn. A flat piece of ground, *réidhlean, réidhe, comhnard, ùrlar.*

Flat, *s.* Comhnard, réidhe, ùrlar, dail, lòn, réidhlean

Flat, *v* Dean comhnard, dean réidh; dean mi-bhlasda.

Flatly, *adv* Gu còmhnard, gu réidh, gu h-iosal; gu marbh, gu neo-bhrisg, gu neo-smiorail; as an aghaidh He denied me flatly, *dhiùlt e mi as an aghaidh.*

Flatness, *s.* (*Of ground*), comhnardachd; (*of taste*), neo-bhrisgead.

Flatten, *v a.* and *n* Dean còmhnard, dean réidh, dean min, dean leathan, leathnaich, dean domblasda; cuir a misneach.

Flatter, *v a.* Dean miodal, dean baigh, dean sodal, dean blandar, mealt, breug, tàlaidh. He flatters himself, *tha e 'deanamh baigh (no) miodal ris féin*

Flatterer, *s* Miodalaiche, sodalaiche, soileasaiche, fear miodalach, fear goileamach (no) beulchar.

Flattering, *a.* Miodalach, sodalach, goileamach, beulchar, brionnalach.

Flattery, *s* Miodal, sodal, goileam, blandar, brionnal, brosgal.

Flattish, *a.* Leth-char, marbh.

Flatulency, *s.* Gaoth, gaothanachd, gaoth cuim; bramsag; faoineas, diomhanas

Flatulent, *a* Gaothar; bolgach; faoin, falamh, diomhain

Flatus, *s.* Gaoth cuim, breim.

Flaunt, *v. n.* Imich gu spairiseach, bi uallach a eididh

Flaunting, *a.* Spairiseach, uallach, leòmach.

Flavour, *s.* Blas; fàile cubhraidh, deagh thòchd, deagh bholadh.

Flavorous, *a* Blasda; deagh-bhlasda; cubhraidh.

Flaw, *s.* Crac, sgoltadh, cron, lochd, coire. Without flaw, *gun choire*

Flaw, *v a.* Crac, bris, sgoilt, ciurr.

Flawy, *a.* Lan chracan, lochdach

Flax, *s* Lion. Fairy flax, *lion na ban-sithe*, purging flax, *lion na bann sithe*

Flax-comb, *s.* Seiceal. Flax-combs, *seiclean.*

Flax-dresser, *s.* Seicilear. Flax-dressers, *seicilearean*

Flaxen, *a.* Lin, do lion, bàn

Flay, *v.* Fionn, thoir an croiceann deth

Flea, *s.* Deargann, deargant.

Flea-bite, *s.* Teum (no) pioc deargainn

Flea-bitten, *a.* Teumta le deargann; truagh, diblidh, iriosal, suarrach.

Fleam, *s.* Tuadh fhola, sgian fhola, cuisleag.

Fleck, *v* Breac, breacaich, ballaich, eag-samhluich, dean ballach (no) breac. Flecked, *breac, breacaichte, ballach, ballaichte, eagsamhuil*

Flecker, *v. a.* Breacaich, dean breac, ballaich, dean ballach, dean eag-samhuil.

Fled. See **Flee**

Fledge, *a.* Iteagach, iteach; sgiathach, is urrainn dol ar sgiathaibh.

FLEDGE, *v. a.* Iteagaich, sgiathaich. Fledged, *iteagaichte, seathaichte, sgiathach.*

FLEE, *v. a.* Teich, ruith, rach air theicheadh, ruith air falbh, gabh an teicheadh, ruith (no) teich o chunnart; thoir na casan asad, thoir na buinn asad. He fled, *theich e, ruith e, chaidh e air theicheadh.*

FLEECE, *s* Lomradh, lomairt, rùsg.

FLEECE, *v. a.* Lomair, rùisg, bearr, spùinn, robainn, creach. He fleeced the sheep, *rùisg (no) lomair e iad;* he fleeced (cheated) them, *ruisg (no) spùinn e iad.*

FLEECY, *a.* Ollach, ollainneach

FLEER, *v. n.* Mag, dean fanaid, fochaid. Fleering, *a magadh, a fanoid.*

FLEER, *s.* Magadh, fanaid, fanoid, fochaid, sgeig

FLEERER, *s* Magair, sgeigear, fear fochaid.

FLELT, *s.* Cabhlach

FLEET, *s* Camus, geòth, geò.

FLEET, *a* Luath, siubhlach, luaineach, cas, ealamh, dian; beothail, grad, tapaidh

FLEET, *v. a* and *n.* Itealaich, falbh gu grad, siubhail gu luath, rach as an t-sealladh

FLEETING, *a.* Siùbhlach, grad-shiùblach, nach mair ach re sealladh, sgumach. A fleeting dish, *sguman*

FLEETLY, *adv.* Gu luath, gu siubhlach, gu grad, gu luaineach

FLEETNESS, *s.* Luathas, siùbhlachd; luathailteachd, luaineachd

FLESH, *s.* Feoil; broth; + bruith, searcall; colainn, coluinn, corp

FLESH, *v a* (*A hunting term*), cleachd; sàsuich.

FLESH-BROTH, *s.* Càl feòla

FLESH-COLOUR, *s.* Dath feòla, dath croicne

FLESH-FLY, *s.* Cnuimheag (no) cnaimheag fheòla, feòil chnuimh, feoil-chraimheag

FLESH-HOOK, *s* Cromag feòla, gramaich, greimiche, adhal.

FLESHINESS, *s.* Feolmhorachd, sultmhorachd; reamhrachd.

FLESHLESS, *a.* Truagh, caol; gun fheòil.

FLESHLILY, *adv.* Gu corporra, gu feòlmhor

FLESHLINESS, *s* Corporrachd, feòilmhorachd, macnusachd

FLESHLY, *a.* Corporra, feòilmhor, macnusach, druiseil, mi-gheimnidh, talmhaidh, neo-spioradail.

FLESH-MEAT, *s.* Feòil, annlan, innlean

FLESHMONGER, *s* Feòladair, druisear, drùsdar.

FLESH-POT, *s* Poit, coire, soitheach anns am bruithear feòil.

FLESHY, *a.* Feòlar, feolmhor, sultmhor, reamhar, tiugh, dòmhail, dùmhail.

FLETCHER, *s.* Fleisdear, fear a dheanamh bhoghachan agus shaighead.

FLEW, *pret* of FLY.

FLEW, *s.* Craos masdaidh; seorsa lion-iasgaich.

FLEWED, *a.* Craosach, gnosach, grosach.

FLEXIBILITY, *s* So-lùbachd, so-lùbaidheachd, sùbailteachd, (*of mind*), soimeachd, soimeachas, so-chomhairleachd.

FLEXIBLE, *a.* So-lubta, maoth, s'atanta; so-chlaonadh, so-chamadh; so-lubaidh; subailt; (*in mind*), soimeach; so-chomhairleach.

FLEXILE, *a.* Maoth, so-lùbaidh, lùbach, slatanta, sùbailt; so-chlaonadh, so-thionndadh.

FLEXION, *s.* Lùbadh, luib, filleadh.

FLEXUOUS, *a.* Lùbach, luibeach, neo-dhìreach, cam, camusach; sniomhain; caochlaideach, mughteach

FLEXURE, *s.* Lùbadh, luib, camadh, fiaradh, claonadh; lùth, alt.

FLICKER, *v. n.* Crith-luaisg, frith-luaisg; crithich; itealaich.

FLIER, *s.* Fògaraiche, fear a ruitheas air falbh; (*of a machine*), cothrom, riaghladair.

FLIGHT, *s.* Teicheadh, teicheachd, ruaig, dol as, ruith air falbh, dol air theicheadh; itealach, ealt, ealtuinn; (*of stones*), fras; (*of imagination*), siubhal inntinn. Put to flight, *cuir air theicheadh*

FLIGHTY, *a* Fiadhaich, neo-shuidhichte, luaineach, luaimneach, luath, siùbhlach; caochlaideach, gaoithe; dòchasach.

FLIMSY, *a* Anfhann, neo-ghramail, neo-chruadalach, neo-dhiongalta, lag, breòite; meuranda, mall, truagh, dìblidh.

FLINCH, *v. a* Rach air ais (no) a thaobh, fannaich, fàilinn, fàilnich.

FLING, *v.* Tilg; tilg air falbh, thoir urchair. Fling down, *tilg a sios, tilg a bhàn, sgrios, thoir ionnsuidh air.*

FLING, *s* Tilgeadh, urchair air cloich; fochaid, sgeig, beum, gearradh.

FLINGER, *s* Fear tilgidh, tilgear; fochaidiche, sgeigear, beumadair

FLINT, *s.* Cloch-theine; sporadh, spor gunna, ailbhinn.

FLINTY, *a.* Cruaidh, ailbhinneach; cruadalach; cruaidh mar chloich-theine, cruaidh mar ailbhinn; cruaidh-chridheach, ain-iochdmhor; fiadhaich, borb

FLIP, *s.* Deoch lionn is uisge beatha air feadh 'chéile.

FLIPPANT, *a* Gobach, lonach, bruidhneach; luath-theangach, luaineach, luaimneach, mi-mhodhail, beag-narach.

FLIRT, *s* Gogaid; sgòdag, caileag bheag-narach; goileag; càile-bhalaoch; cleas, cluiche.

FLIRT, *v n* Sgeig, dean fochaid (no) fanoid.

FLIRTATION, *s* Cluicheag, beadradh, bòilich.

FLIT, *v. n.* Teich, rach imirich, rach air imirich, imirc; itealaich.

FLITCH, *s.* Cliathach muic air a sailleadh, leth-taobh.

FLITTERMOUSE, *s* Ialtag, ialtag anmoch.

FLITTING, *s* Cron, lochd, fàilinn, toiltinneas.

FLIX, *s* Fionnadh.

FLIXWEED, *s.* Fineal mhuire.

FLOAT, *v. n* and *a* Snamh, plod, luinneanaich, bi air an t-snamh, bi air luinneanaich. Floating, *a snamh, a plodadh, a luinneanaich*

FLOAT, *s.* Plodadh, rath; arcan driamlaich (no) lion-iasgaich; lionadh mara.

FLOATY, *a* Plodach, snamhach; clàraidh

FLOCK, *s* (*Of cattle*), dròbh, treud; (*of birds*), ealt, ealtuinn, (*of people*), lòd, bannal, cuideachd; (*of wool*), clòimhneag, toipean, topan.

FLOCK, *v.* Tionail, teanail, cruinnich.

FLOG, *v* Sgiùrs, cuipinn, slachduinn, smachdaich.

FLOOD, *s.* Tuile, dilinn, dile; lionadh mara; uisge; muir, abhainn. A land flood, *beum sleibhe.*

FLOOD, *v. a.* Tuilich, tuiltich, comhdaich le uisge; cuir fo'n uisge

FLOOD-GATE, *s* Tuil-dhorus.

FLOOD-MARK, *s.* Comhar lan mara, dubh-chladach

FLOOK, *s.* Fiacal achdair; seorsa eisg, fleogan

FLOOR, *s* Urlar, lar. A deal floor, *urlar bhord*, a stone floor, *ùrlar chloich*

FLOOR, *v. a* Urlaraich. Floored, *urlaraichte, spadte.*

FLOOR-CLOTH, *s* Làr-bhrat, brat ùrlair

FLOORING, *s.* Urlar; clàraich; paibhil.

FLORAL, *a.* Plùrach, plùranach, plùireanach

Florence, *s.* Seorsa aodaich.
Floret, *s.* Plùran.
Florid, *a.* Ruiteach, dearg, gruaidh-dhearg; blàthach, blàthmhor; ceann dearg.
Floridness, *s.* Ruiteachd, deirge, rughadh; grinneas.
Floriferous, *a.* Plùrach, plùranach, ruiteach, dearg.
Florist, *s.* Plùranaich, plùireanaiche; lusragan, luisreagan.
Florulent, *a.* Plùranach, plùrach, blàthmhor.
Flota, Flotilla, *s.* Cabhlach.
Flounce, *s.* Iochdar cota boirionnaich; froinnse, fabhra.
Flounce, *v. a.* and *n.* (*Fringe*), froinnsich; (*in water or snow*), pluinnsich, imich gu sgairteil air feadh uisge no sneachdaidh; tom ann an uisge.
Flounder, *s.* Leabag, fleogan.
Flounder, *v. n.* Spairtich, mar ni each air feadh phuill; faragair, luinneanaich.
Floundering, *s.* Luinneanach, luinneanaich.
Flour, *s.* Min mhìn, min-phlùr.
Flourish, *v. a.* and *n.* Soirbhich, fàs gu h-àluinn; bi fo bhlàth; dean uaill; (no) bòsd; bragainn, sgiamhaich, briaghaich, nàisnich.
Flourish, *s.* Blath; uaill, bòsd; fèin-speis; breaghas, sgiamh. An idle flourish of words, *rabhdadh, glòr, glo-irmeas.*
Flourisher, *s.* Duine soirbheasach.
Flout, *v.* Dean mag; mag, fanoid, fochaid, sgeig.
Flout, *s.* Magadh, fanaid, fanoid, fochaid, sgeig.
Flouter, *s.* Magair, fanaidiche, sgeigear.
Flow, *v. n.* Ruith, sruth; còmhdaich, cuir thairis; (*melt*), leagh; (*abound*), bi làn, bi pailt, cuir thairis; (*flood*), tuiltich; (*flow about*), iom-shruth; (*flow over*), ruith thairis.
Flow, *s.* (*Of water*), ruithe, sruthadh, sruth, tuile; (*sudden plenty*), pailteas, mor-phailteas, lan-phailteas; (*of the sea*), lion mara; (*of language*), deas-chainnt, deas-labhairt.
Flower, *s.* Plùr, pluran, plùirean; (*blossom*), blàth, guc, gucag, barra-guc; (*the best of any thing*), a chuid is fhearr; brod; roghadh, rath; (*in full flower*), fu làn-bhlàth; (*flower-garden*), garadh phlùran. She is in the flower of her age, *tha i am blàth a h-aimsir;* in the flower of his age, *ann trèine a neirt.*
Flower, *v. a.* Pluraich; sgiamhaich, greus, grinnich.
Flower, *v. n.* Cuir a mach blàth, bi fo bhlàth.
Flown, *part.* of fly. Air teicheadh; sèidte; air at, air bolgadh, bolgaichte.
Floweret, *s.* Plùran; gucan.
Floweriness, *s.* Pluranachd, gucanachd, blàthachd; (*of speech*), ùr-labhradh, ur-labhairt, grinneas, cainnte.
Flowery, *a.* Plùrach; blaitheach, blàthmhor, sgiamhaichte le blàth; grinn.
Flowingly, *adv.* Gu deas-chainnteach; gu pailt.
Flowk, *s.* Leabag, fleogan.
Fluctuant, *a.* Iom-luath, luaimneach, luaineach, neo-chinnteach; neo-bhunailteach, siùbhlach, neo-sheasmhach.
Fluctuate, *v. n.* Bi a plodachadh, plodaich; bi ag udal; udalaich, bi an iom-chomhairle, bi neo-chinnteach (no) neo-sheasmhach; bi san turamanaich (no) san tomhartaich.
Fluctuation, *s.* Plodachadh, udal, udaladh, iom-chomh-airle, neo-shuidheachadh, neo-sheasmhachd.
Flue, *s.* Sorn, piob deathaich; cloimh, cloimhneag; gruag, fionnadh; feusag.
Fluency, *s.* Sruthadh; comas cainnte, deas-labhairt, ùr-labhairt; luath-bheulachd.
Fluent, *a.* Sruthach; (*in words*), deas-labhrach, deas-chainnteach, reidh-bhruidhneach.
Fluent, *s.* Sruth, sruthan, srùlag. Fluently, *gu deas-labhrach, gu rèidh-chainnteach.*
Fluid, *a.* Uisgeil, sruthach, tana mar uisge.
Fluid, *s.* Ni tana sam bi, mar athar no uisge; (*in physic*), fuil; sùgh.
Fluidity, *s.* Uisgealachd, tainead.
Fluke, *s.* Fiacal achdair.
Flummery, *s.* Càth-bhrìgh, càth-bhruich; làdhan, làgan.
Flung, *part.* of fling. Tilgte, air thilgeadh. He was flung, *bha e air a thilgeadh;* she was flung, *bhi i air a tilgeadh;* they were flung, *bha iad air an tilgeadh.*
Fluor, *s.* Sruthadh; sruth nam ban, mios-shruth, sileadh cuim. Fluor albus, *sruth Chonain.*
Flurry, *s.* Othail, cabhag, iomairt; osag, oiteag.
Flush, *v. n.* and *a.* Rughaich, dearg, fàs dearg mar ghru-aidh, las; sèid suas, at. Flushed with victory, *air shèide-adh suas le buaidh, air lasadh le buaidh.*
Flush, *a.* Ùr; brighmhor; treun; cloimheach, iteagach; †saibhir, *a cant word.*
Flush, *a.* (*With joiners*), comhad, direach, comhnard, locraichte.
Flush, *s.* Deannadh; gluasad, dian-ghluasad.
Flushed, *part.* Rughaichte, dearg; air atadh, air lasadh. Flushed with victory, *air atadh (no) air lasadh le buaidh.*
Fluster, *v. a.* Deargaich, dean dearg (no) ruiteach; cuir air an daoraich.
Flustered, *part.* Air an daoraich.
Flute, *s.* Feadan ciùil, feadag; clais.
Flute, *v.* Clais, claisich. Fluted, *claisichte; piobanach.*
Flutter, *v. n.* Itealaich; crithich; crith-ghluais; plab-raich; bi air fuadan, iom-luaisg, bi an iomairt, bi ann an cabhaig; (*in speech*), bi manntach, liodach, agach (no) glugach.
Flutter, *v. a.* Sgiùrs air falbh, cuir thar a chéile, cuir troimh a chéile, cuir an cabhaig, deifrich.
Flutter, *s.* Crithe, crith-ghluasad, frith-ghluasad; cabhag; iomairt, buaireas.
Flux, *s.* Sruthadh; lionadh na mara; (*of the body*), siubhal, buinneach, gearrach, ruithe, sgaird; (*concourse*), tional, teanal, cruinneachadh, comh-ruithe.
Flux, *v. a.* Leagh.
Fluxility, *s.* So-leaghachd.
Fluxion, *s.* Sruthadh.
Fly, *v. n.* Rach air iteig, itealaich; siubhail gu grad, ruith ann ad dheannaibh; thoir na casan asad, thoir na buinn asad, teich; (*asunder*), sgag (no) leum as a chéile, bris, bruan, spealg. Fly at him, *leum air, thoir sic air, thoir ionnsuidh air, sàs air;* he flew at his throat, *shàs e air a sgornan;* fly away, *leum air falbh, ruith air falbh;* he who does not fly will be fled from, *am fear nach teich, teichear uaithe.*
Fly, *v. a.* Seachain, teich, cuitich; treig, fàg. Fly evil, *seachain an t-olc.*
Fly, *s.* Cuileag. A Spanish fly, *cuileag Spainnteach;* a horse-fly, *creadhail.*
Fly-blow, *s.* Ubh cuileig.
Fly-boat, *s.* Luath-long, sgoth, geòl.
Flyer, *s.* Leumnaiche, fear air sgiathaibh, fear air iteig.
Foal, *s.* Searrach, lothag, loth, *foilidh,* a local word.
Foal, *v.* Beir searrach, tilg searrach.
Foam, *s.* Cobhar, cop, coip, cothanach, othan, adhan, uthan, carran, sgeim, cuitheach. In foam, *fo chobhar.*
Foam, *v. n.* Bi fo chobhar, (no) fo chòp.

Foamy, *a.* Cobharach, còpach, fo chobhar, fo choip; cobhrachail.
Fob, *s.* Pòc beag, pòc uaireadair.
Fob, *v. a.* (*Cheat*), meall, thoir an car a; (*delay*), cuir dheth, cuir dàil.
Focil, *s.* Lurgainn, cnaimh na lurgainn; cnaimh beag a ghairdein.
Focus, *s.* Ionad (no) pong anns an coinnich gathan na gréin, an deidh dhoibh dol troimh ghloine; pong sonruichte ann an crosg-lìn cearcaill (no) cuairsgein.
Fodder, *s.* Fodar, feur, saoidh, connlach; aunlann, innlean; inilt, glasghart, foirne.
Fodder, *v. a.* Biadh, feuraich.
Fodderer, *s.* Biadhadair, feurachair.
Foddering, *s.* Feurach, feurachadh.
Foe, *s.* Namhaid, eas-caraid, eas-cara; namh. Foes, *namhaidean, naimhdean, eas-cairdean.*
† Foeman, *s.* Namhaid, namh, eas-caraid.
Fœtus, *s.* Torrachas anabuich; ginean.
Fog, *s.* Ceò, ceòth; ceathach, ceòbanach, neul, smùid; còineach, còinneach.
Foggy, *a.* Ceomhor, ceothar; ceathachail, neulach; dorch, gruamach. A foggy person, *urr reamhar, urr bhaoghalta.*
Foh! *interj.* Fuidh! ab! ab! pu!
Foible, *s.* Fàilinn; faoin-chiont; fabhd, meanbh-chiont.
Foil, *v. a.* Fairtlich; claoidh; gabh roimh; maolaich.
Foil, *s.* Fairtleachadh; cothrom; claidheamh gun roinn; diùltadh.
Foin, *s.* Pùc, staradh, sàth, sparadh.
Foist, *s.* Tùt.
Foist, *v. a.* Pùc a steach, dinn a stigh, star; sparr.
Foistiness, *s.* Cloimh liath; liath-chloimh.
Foisty, *a.* Liath le cloimh, mar aran.
Fold, *s.* (*For cattle*), crò, buaile, cròilean, fàl, fang, mainnir; (*plait*), filleadh, lùbadh; pleat; crioch. Two-fold, *da-fhillte.*
Fold, *v. a.* (*Cattle*), fang, fangaich; druid, cuir ann an cro (no) am buaile; crothaich; (*double*), fill, lùb, dùblaich; (*folded, as cattle*), fangaichte; (*as clothes*), fillte.
Foliaceous, *a.* Duilleagach.
Foliage, *s.* Duille, duilleach, ùr-dhuilleach.
Foliate, *v.* Buail mach (no) tanaich mar dhuilleig.
Foliation, *s.* Bualadh mach, tanachadh.
Folio, *s.* Leabhar aig am bheil site clòdha anns gach da dhuilleag.
Folk, *s.* Sluagh, muinntir, feodhainn, pobull, dream, droing, buidheann, bannal; cuideachd; (*in a bad sense*), gràisg, prabar.
† Folkmote, *s.* Coinneamh, mòd.
Follow, *v. a.* and *n.* Lean, rach an tòir, rach an deigh, ruaig; sir.
Follower, *s.* Leanmhuinniche, fear leantuinn. Followers, *luchd-leanmhuinn.*
Folly, *s.* Amaideachd, faoineachd, baoghaireachd.
Foment, *v. a.* Blàthaich; fothraig, foircin; earrabhruich; suath; thoir misneach; cum taobh ri; tog, buair, brosnaich. Foment divisions, *tog aimhreite;* fomented, *blàthaichte, buairte, brosnaichte.*
Fomented, *part.* See Foment.
Fomenter, *s.* Buaireadair, brosnachair.
Fond, *a.* Deidheil, ceisteil, an geall, geanail, gaolach, gradhach, beadarach, caomhail; amaideach; faoin. Fond of her, *deidheil oirre, an gaol oirre, an geall oirre;* a fond girl, *caileag bheadarach;* fond of drinking, *deidheil air an òl;* fondly, *gu deidheil, gu ceisteil, gu geanail, gu beadarach.*

Fondle, *v. a.* Dean beadradh; breug, tàlaidh. Fondle the child, *dean beadradh ris an leanabh, breug an leanabh.*
Fondler, *s.* Urr bheadrach.
Fondling, *s.* Beadragan, breugadh, tàladh.
Fondness, *s.* Amaideachd, gean, cean; baoth-ghradh, faoin-ghradh.
Font, *s.* Tobar (no) amar baistidh.
Fontanel, *s.* Silteach.
Food, *s.* Biadh, lòn, aran, beathachadh, teachd an tìr. Food for cattle, *connlach.*
Foodful, *a.* Biadhar; pailt ann am biadh.
Fool, *s.* Amadan, baothair, baoghlan, burraidh, amblair, gurraiceach; càmar, camaran, gàmairle. Make a fool of him, *dean amadan deth;* no fool like an old fool, *cha 'n eil ann do shean amadan.*
Fool, *v. a.* and *n.* Cluich; caith; cuir air amaideachd, dean amadan do.
Foolery, *s.* Amaideachd, faoineas, baothaireachd.
Fool-happy, *a.* Fortanach.
Fool-hardiness, *s.* An-dànadas, mear-dhànadas.
Fool-hardy, *a.* An-dàn, ro dhàn, ladurna; mear-dhàna.
Foolish, *a.* Amaideach, gòrach, amaideil, faoinealach, neo-ghlic; baoghalta, neo-mhothuchail, mi-reusonta; eu-ceill-idh, neo-thuigseach, eagonach; (*in Scripture*), aingidh, peacach. Foolishly, *gu h-amaideach.*
Foolishness, *s.* Amaideachd, gòraiche, di-céill; baothaire-achd, cion tuir (no) tuigse.
Foot, *s.* Cas, cos, troidhe; dà oirleach dheug air fad; (*of a hill*), bun, cos; (*of a pillar*), bonn; (*infantry*), coisridh. Half a foot, *leth throidhe;* a foot and a half, *troidhe gu leth;* on one foot, *air leth choise;* the sole of the foot, *bonn na coise;* (*state*), còr, staid, inmhe; on foot, *air choise, air coise;* walking on foot, *ga choise, ga coise;* tread under foot, *stramp;* foot to foot, *bonn ri bonn.*
Foot, *v. a.* Breab; imich, coisich; ceum socraich, suidhich.
Football, *s.* Creutag, criatag, ball iomainich; ball.
Footboy, *s.* Gille ruithe, gille coise.
Footcloth, *s.* Sumag.
Foothold, *s.* Rum coise.
Footing, *s.* Seasamh, aite seasamh; bun, bunaite; aite, seilbhe; dannsa; rod, rathad; tùs, toiseach; staid, inbhe.
Footlicker, *s.* Tràill; sodulaiche.
Footman, *s.* Gille coise, gille duine-uasail, gille ruithe; saighdear coise.
Footpad, *s.* Robair, spuinneadair ga chois.
Footpace, *s.* Coiseachd, ceumnachadh, coise-cheum.
Footpath, *s.* Frith rod, frith-rathad, ceum-coise.
Footpost, *s.* Post, teachdair coise, gille ruithe.
Footstall, *s.* Stiorap boirionnaich.
Footstep, *s.* Ceum, aile coise, lorg; eisiomlair. You will never fill your father's footsteps, *cha mhac an aite an athar thu.*
Footstool, *s.* Stòl, stòl-coise, creupan.
Fop, *s.* Lasgair, gaothan, leoimean.
Foppish, *a.* Gaoithe, cutrom, briagh, breagh; laoineach, farumach, faoin, sgòdail, uallach, leòmach.
For, *prep.* Airson, a thaobh; a bhrigh, For that part, *air son sin;* for that part of it, *air son sin deth;* is this for me? *an ann air mo shonsa tha so?* for a while, *car tacain, re sealladh, car tamuil;* for nothing, *gun dad idir, a nasguidh, fàr nasguidh;* for ever, *gu bràth, gu siorruidh;* as for me, *air mo shonsa dheth;* for anger, *a brìgh feirge;* for fear he may see us, *air eagal gu 'm faic e sinn;* for fear that, *air eagal gu, d' eagal gu;* for so much, *air leithid so luach.*

For, after *good*, *fit*, *lawful*, *profitable*, is commonly rendered by *do*, simple or compounded. It is good for you, *tha e math dhuit*; it is a shame for you, *is nàr dhuit e*; for the sake of, *air son*, *air sgàth*, for the most part, *mar is tric*; for what cause? *carson?* for which cause? *uime sin?* for that cause, *air shon sin*, *air son sin*, they are for me, *tha iad air mo shonsa*, *tha iad air mo thaobh-sa*; I would get it but for you, *gheibhinn e mar bhiodh thusa.*

For, *conj.* Oir, a chionn, a bhrigh, do bhrigh.

Forage, *s.* Solar; biadh, lòn, inileann, annlan.

Forage, *v. n.* and *a.* Solair, rach a sholar bidh, creach, robainn, spùinn, spùill.

Forager, *s.* Solaraiche.

Foraminous, *a.* Tolltach, lan tholl.

Forasmuch, *conj.* Air a mheud, do bhrigh, a chionn, on, o. Forasmuch as, *air a mheud is gu*, *do bhrigh gu.*

Forbade, *pret.* of forbid; which see.

Forbear, *v. n.* and *a* Sguir, stad, fuirich; leig dhiot; fulling, fuilig, leig le; giùlain le; nochd baigh, maith, caomhain. He forbore, *sguir e*, *leig e dheth*, *chaomhain e.*

Forbearance, *s.* Sgurachd, stadachd, fulangas, fad-fhulangas; foighidinn, baigh.

Forbid, *v. a.* Toirmisg, bac, † malluich. He forbade, *thoirmisg e*, he forbade him his house, *dhiùlt e' thigh da*, God forbid! *nar leigeadh Dia!* forbidding, *a toirmeasgadh*, *a bacadh.*

Forbiddance, *s* Toirmeasgadh, bac, diùltadh.

Forbidden, *part.* Toirmisgte; neo-laghail, neo-cheadaichte. Forbidden ground, *talamh toirmisgte*, forbidden fruit, *meas toirmisgte.*

Forbiddenly, *adv.* Gu neo-laghail.

Forbidding, *part.* See Forbid.

Forbore. See Forbear.

Force, *s.* Neart, spionn, spionnadh, tréine, cumhachd, riachdanas; (*violence*), ainneart, éigin, foirneart, déine; (*military*), feachd, armailt, slogh, (*virtue*), brìgh, éifeachd With all his force, *le uile neart*; by force, *a dh' aindeoin*, of force, *gun taing*, of great force, *treun*

Force, *v. a.* Eignich, thoir air; gnathaich ainneart, gabh a dh' aindeoin Force him to do it, *thoir air a dheanamh*, he forced her, *dh' éignich e i*; they forced him to do it, *thug iad air a dheanamh*; she was forced, *dh' eignicheadh i*, *chaidh a h-éigneachadh*, lazy is the work that is forced, *is leasg an obair is fheudar.*

Forced, *part.* Eignichte; a dh' aindeoin; air eigin. A forced laugh, *gàir a dh' aindeoin*, a forced cry or weeping, *gul* (*no*) *gal air éigin*; the land which he is forced to leave, *an talamh is eigin* (*no*) *is fheudar dha fhàgail.*

Forcedly, *adv.* Gu h-aindeonach, a dh' aindeoin, air eigin.

Forceful, *a.* Ainneartach, foirneartach, laidir, treun.

Forceless, *a.* Anfhann, lag, fann, mall.

Forceps, *s.* Spioladair.

Forcer, *s.* Fear foirneirt, fear éigneachaidh; bualadair, greasadair, fairche.

Forces, *s. pl.* Feachd, armailt, sluagh, slogh, (*foot*), coisridh.

Forcible, *a.* Neartmhor, laidir, treun, cumhachdach; dian; éifeachdach; cudthromach; (*as language*), brighmhor, sgealparra, cruaidh, drùighteach.

Forcibleness, *s.* Neartmhoireachd, tréine; deine; eifeachd, brìghmhorachd.

Forcibly, *adv.* Le neart, le spionnadh, le h-ainneart, gu h-ainneartach, gu h-aindeonach.

Ford, *s.* Àthan; foras. Cross the ford, *rach thar an àthan.*

Ford, *v. a.* Coisich troimh abhainn, rach thar àthan, sgarbh.

Fordable, *a.* Tana, neo-dhomhainn.

Fore, *adv.* Ro, roi, roimh.

Fore-advise, *v a.* Roi-chomhairlich.

Fore-appoint, *v. a.* Roimh-shonraich.

Fore-arm, *v a.* Roimh-armaich.

Forebode, *v* Innis roimh-laimh, fàisnich, fàistinnich, dean faisneachd, cuir air mhànadh; foir-innis; targhail.

Foreboder, *s* Fàistinnear, fàisnear, fàidh

Forecast, *v. a.* Dealbh, tionnsgain, faic roimh-laimh.

Forecast, *s.* Roimh-fheuchainn; doigh, seòladh, tionnsgnadh

Forecaster, *s* Tionnsgnair.

Forecastle, *s.* Toiseach luinge.

Forechosen, *part.* Roimh-thaghta, roimh-roghnaichte.

Forecited, *a.* Roimh-radhte, air a roimh-radh, roi-ainmichte.

Foreclose, *v a* Dùin, druid, bac.

Foredeck, *s* Bord mu thoiseach.

Foredesign, *s.* Dealbh roimh-laimh; tionnsgain.

Foredoom, *v. a.* Roimh-orduich, orduch (no) sonruich roimh laimh

Fore-end, *s* Ceann toiseach

Forefather, *s* Sinnsear, athair, ginntear. Forefathers, *sinnsearan*, *aithrichean*, *ginntearan*, *sinnsearachd.*

Forefend, *v. a.* Bac, toirmisg; cuir gu taobh.

Forefinger, *s.* Corag, colagag

Forefoot, *s.* Cas toiseach.

Forego, *v a* Fàg, tiomnadh, cuitich, tréig, seachain, caill, deilich, dealaich, rach air thoiseach

Foregoer, *s.* Sinnsear, athair, ginntear

Forehand, *a.* Roimh laimh.

Forehanded, *a.* Much, moch, tràthail, amail

Forehead, *s.* Aodann, eudann, gnùis, aghaidh, clàr an aodainn; ceann-aghaidh, dànadas, beag-narachd

Foreign, *a.* Còigreachail, coimheach, deòranta, allmharach, eil-thireach, cian

Foreigner, *s* Coigreach, deor, gall, all-mharach, eilthireach

Foreknow, *v a.* Roimh-aithnich. Foreknown, *roimh-aithnichte.*

Foreknowledge, *s.* Roimh-aithneachadh, roimh-aithne, roimh-eòlas; roimh-fhios, roimh-fhiosrachadh

Foreland, *s.* Rutharh, ceann, maol, sròin

Forelay, *v. a* Dean plaid-luidhe

Forelock, *s.* Ciabhag

Foreman, *s.* Fear amhairc, griobh.

Foremast, *s* Crann toisich

Forementioned, *part.* Roi-ainmichte.

Foremost, *a.* Is urramaiche, is airde; priomh; air thùs, air thoiseach.

Forenamed, *part* Roi-ainmichte.

Forenoon, *s.* Roi-mheadhon la; roimh meadhon làth; an uine eadar briseadh na fàire agus meadhon là.

Forenotice, *s.* Sànas, rabhadh, roimh-fhios

Fore-ordain, *v. a* Roimh-orduich, roimh-shonruich, orduich, (no) sonruich roimh-laimh.

Forepart, *s.* Taobh beòil, beulaobh, taobh air bheòil.

Forepossessed, *a.* Roimh-shealbhaichte.

Forerank, *s.* Ceud sreath, ceud rang, toiseach, an t-sreath is toisiche

Forerfcited, *a.* Roi-aimnichte.

Forerun, *v. a* Rach air thoiseach.

Forerunner, *s.* Roimh-theachdair, teachdair; comhar.

Foresay, *v. a.* Roimh-innis, roi-innis, fàisnich, faistinnich.

Foresee, *v n.* Faic roimh-laimh.

Foreshew, *v* Feuch roimh-laimh; roimh-innis, faisnich, samhluich

Foreship, *s.* Taobh beoil luing.

Foreshorten, *v. a.* Roimh-ghiorraich.

Foreshortening, *s.* Roimh-ghiorrachadh.

Foresight, *s.* Roi-eolas, roimh-eòlas, roimh-fhiosrachadh, roimh-shealladh, roimh-shealltuinn.

Foresightful, *a* Fad-sheallach.

Foresignify, *v* Samhluich, cialluich.

Foreskin, *s.* Roimh-chroicionn, roimh-chraicionn.

Foreskirt, *s* Sgiort beòil

Foreslack, *v* Cuir air dearmad.

Foreslow, *v a.* Amail, bac, cuir moille air.

Forespent, *a* Sgìth, air fannachadh, air toirt thairis

Forespurrer, *s.* Gille ruithe.

Forest, *s.* Frith, fàsach; coille; fearann fàs.

Forestall, *v a* Gabh (no) glac roimh laimh, ceannaich suas roimh laimh, mill margadh.

Forestaller, *s* Pris-mhangair; suil-mhangair; roimh-stallair

Forestborn, *a.* Fiadhaich, coillteach.

Forester, *s.* Forasair, forsair, fear ghleidh frithe.

Foretaste, *s.* Roimh-fhios, roimh-eolas, roimh-bhlas.

Foretaste, *v. a* Roimh-bhlais, blais roimh-laimh, gabh a cheud bhlas Foretasted, *roimh-bhlasta, air a roimh-bhlasadh*

Foretell, *v a* Roimh-innis, innis roimh laimh, fàisnich, fàistinnich, dean fàisneachd Foretelling *ri fàisneachd, a deanamh faisneachd*, foretold, *fàisnichte, air fhàisneachadh*

Foreteller, *s* Fàidh, faidheadair.

Forethink, *v n* Roi-smuainich, roi-bheachdaich Forethought on, *roi-smuainichte.*

Forethought, *s* Roi-smuainc, roimh-smuaine, roimh-bheachd, roimh-fhios.

Foretooth, *s* Clàrag, clàr-fhiacal, fiacal beòil

Foretop, *s.* Binnean

Foreward, *s* Tùs (no) toiseach feachd.

Forewarn, *v. a.* Thoir sànas, thoir fios (no) fiosrachadh, thoir rabhadh, innis roimh laimh

Forewish, *v. a* Roi-mhiannaich Forewished, *roi-mhiannaichte*

Foreworn, *a* Caithte, air caitheamh

Forfeit, *v* Caill. Forfeit your word, *bris d' fhocal.*

Forfeit, *s* Umhladh, pàineachas; call.

Forfeiture, *s.* Umhladh, pàineachas, call

Forge, *s.* Teallach, ceardach, (*counterfeit*), feall-choslas; feall-chùin

Forge, *v a* Dealbh gu fallsa, feall-chuin, dean ceardachd (no) goibhneachd Forged silver, *airgiod feall-chùinte.*

Forger, *s* Dealbhair, feall-dhealbhair; cùinnear, cùinneadair

Forgery, *s.* Meall-chùinne; meall-chùinneadaireachd, goibhneachd

Forget, *v. a.* Di-chuimhnich, dio-chuimhnich, leig air di-chuimhne; leig air dearmad; dearmadaich; dearmad. I quite forgot it, *dhi-chuimhnich mi e gu tur*, I forgot it, *cha n' eil cuimhne agam air*, forgotten, *air di-chuimhne*

Forgetful, *a.* Dearmadach; di chuimhneach; neo-chùramach; neo-sheadhar; neo-aireachail; dithleach.

Forgetfulness, *s.* Dearmadachd, di-chuimhne; neo-shuim, cion-aire.

Forgetter, *s.* Urr dhi-chuimhneach, neach di-chuimhneach.

Forgive, *v.* Maith, math; laghaich, lagh, thoir maitheanas. Forgive him, *maith dha, thoir maitheanas da*; forgiven, *maithte, air a mhathadh*, he forgave me, *mhaith e dhomh.*

Forgiveness, *s.* Maitheanas, mathanas, laghadh.

Forgot, *pret.* of forget. Dhì-chuimhnich.

Forgotten, *part* Di-chuimhnichte, air di-chuimhne, air dearmad I had forgotten it, *dhi-chuimhnich mi e.*

Fork, *s* Forc; gabhlag, gabhan, gobhlag, gobhlan, glacan. A hay-fork, *forc saidhe*, a dung-fork, *forc (no) gobhlag òtraich*

Fork, *v.* Forc; diasaich

Forked, *a.* Gobhlach, gabhlach; gobhlanach, gabhlagach.

Forkedness, *s.* Gobhlaichead

Forkhead, *s* Roinn saighde.

Forlorn, *a* Tréigte, cuitichte; eudochasach, aonaranach; diblidh, truagh; uireasbhach; guasachdach

Forlornness, *s*, Eu-dochasachd; aonaranachd; diblidheachd, truaighe, uireasbhachd.

Form, *s* (*Shape*), dealbh, deanamh, cumadh, cumachd, cruth, cruthadh, dreach, riochd; aogas, (*manner*), modh, seòl, doigh, fasan, nòs; (*ceremony*), foirm; (*class*), sread, rang; (*of a hare*), leabadh, (*bench*), beinc

Form, *v a.* Dealbh, dean, cum, cruthaich, gleus, dreach

Formal, *a.* Deas-ghnàthach; riaghailteach, nosail; foirmeil; rudach, ceigeannach.

Formality, *s.* Nòsaileachd; foirmeileachd, deas-ghnath; doigh, modh; ceigeanachd

Formally, *adv* Gu nòsail; gu foirmeil, gu riaghailteach.

Formation, *s.* Deanamh, dealbhadh, cruthachadh, cumadh.

Former, *s.* Dealbhair, dealbhadair, cruthachair, cruithear, cumadair, fear dealbhaidh.

Former, *a* Roimh, ceud; air dol seachad, air falbh. The former year, *a bhliadhna roimh*, in former times, *anns na h-amanna air dol seachad.*

Formerly, *adv* Roimh so, a chian, o shean.

Formidable, *a.* Eagallach, oillteil, uamhar, uamhannach, uamhasach; cunnartach, fuathasach.

Formidableness, *s* Eagallachd, oillteachd, uamharrachd,

Formidably, *adv* Gu h-eagallach, gu h-oillteil, gu h-uamharra, gu fuathasach

Formless, *a.* Gun chumadh, gun chruth, gun dreach, neo-chumadail,

Formula, *s*, Riaghailt, riaghailt shonruichte.

Formulary, *s* Leabhar riaghlaidh,

Fornicate, *v. a* Dean siùrsachas

Fornication, *s.* Striòpachas, siursachas, neo-ghloine, druis, baos

Fornicator, *s.* Drustar, druistear, drùisear, fear neo-ghloine, baosair.

Fornicatress, *s.* Siùrsach, siùrsdach, striopach, strumpaid

Forsake, *v a* Fàg, tréig, dearmaid, cuir cùl ri; dealaich ri Forsaken, *tréigte*

Forsaker, *s* Tréigear, fear tréig, tréigsinneach

Forsooth, *adv.* Gu dearbh, air chinnte, gu fìor.

Forswear, *v a.* and *n.* Cuir cùl ri; thoir mionnan eithich.

Forswearer, *s* Fear (no) urr eithich.

Fort, *s.* Daighneach, daingneach, dùn, tùr, dion; fort, dion-charn, sonnach, mur, caisteal, babhunn, long-phort; sgonsa

Forth, *adv.* A mach, a lathair, air aghaidh. And so forth, *agus mar sin sios a;* from this time forth, *a so suas.*

Forthcoming, *a.* Aig laimh, a làthair.

Forthright, *adv.* Gu direach, air adhairt.

Forthright, *a.* Rathad dìreach.

Forthwith, *adv.* Gun mhoille; gu grad, gun dàil, gu h-ealamh; air an uair, air ceart uis, air a mhionaid.

Fortieth, *a.* An da fhicheadamh.

Fortifiable, *a.* So-dhionadh, so-dhaingneachadh.

Fortification, *s.* Daighneach, daingneach, caisteal, dùn, tùr, dion; babhunn; iom-chladhachadh.

Fortify, *v. a.* Daighnich, daingnich, dion; dean laidir. Fortified, *daighnichte, daingnichte, dionta.*

Fortitude, *s.* Cruadal, misneach, treubhantas, gaisge, feartas; neart, trèine.

Fortlet, *s.* Dùncan, babhunn beag.

Fortnight, *s.* Ceithir la deug. This day fortnight, *ceithir là deug o 'n diugh.*

Fortress, *s.* See Fort.

Fortuitous, *a.* Tubaisteach, teagambach, cineamhuinneach. Fortuitously, *a thaobh tubaist.*

Fortuitousness, *s.* Tubaisdeachd, teagamhachd, teagamhas, cineamhuinneachd.

Fortunate, *a.* Adhmhor, aghmhor, fortanach, sona, sealbhar, soirbheasach, seamhsar, seamhsail. Fortunately, *gu fortanach, mar bha 'm fortan, mar tha 'm fortan.*

Fortunateness, *s.* Adhmhorachd, sealbharachd; seamhsalachd.

Fortune, *s.* Agh, seun, fortan, sonas; soirbheas, crannchur; (*riches*), saibhreas, maoin, seilbhe, oighreachd. Fortune be with you, *soirbheas leat;* as fortune would have it, *mar bha 'm fortan;* bad fortune, *droch fhortan, mi-shoirbheas;* as bad fortune would have it, *mar bha 'bhochduinn;* furth, fortune, and fill the fetters, *bi triall, bi soirbheasach, is lion na ceanglaichean;* good fortune attends the liberal, *sonas an lorg na caitheimh.*

Fortune, *v. n.* Tachair, thig gu crìche, éirich.

Fortune-book, *s.* Leabhar an fhortain.

Fortune-teller, *s.* Fiosaiche; cleasaiche; dubh-chleasaiche.

Forty, *a.* Da-fhichead; † ceithreachad.

Forum, *s.* Aite margaidh: crois, crosgadh; cùirt lagha.

Forward, *a.* Dian, deothasach, obann, teth, cabhagach, deifireach; cas; dana, ceann-laidir, ladurna; beag-narach, muinghinneach; deas, ealamh, grad; adhartach.

Forward, Forwards, *adv.* Air adhairt, air aghaidh. Straight forward, *dìreach air adhairt;* go forward, *rach air d' adhairt;* go ye forward, *rachaibh air 'ur n-aghaibh;* coming forward in the world, *tighinn h-uige;* backward and forward, *air ais is air adhairt;* from this time forward, *o so suas.*

Forward, *v. a.* Cuir air aghaidh, cùir air adhairt; luathaich, deifirich.

Forwardly, *adv.* Gu dian, gu deothasach, gu h-obann, gu cabhagach, gu cas, gu deifireach, gu grad, gu h-ealamh, gu h-adhartach.

Forwardness, *s.* Déine, dianas, dianad, deothasachd, obainne, teas; deifireachd, caise; dànadas, muinghinneachd, dùrachd, togarachd; adhartachd.

Fosse, *s.* Staing, clais, dìge, cladhachadh.

Fosse-way, *s.* Aon do roidean mòra nan Roimheach, a chithear an Sasunn.

Fossil, *a.* Tochailte, tochailteach, méineach.

Foster, *v.* Tog, beathaich, biath, banaltraich, altrum, altrumaich; àraich; cum suas.

Fosterage, *s.* Comhaltas, comh-dhaltas; altrumadh, togail, àraich.

Foster-brother, *s.* Comh-dhalta.

Foster-child, *s.* Dalta, leanabh altruim.

Foster-dam, *s.* Banaltradh, banaltrum.

Fostered, *part.* Togta, togte, altruimte, altrumaichte, àraichte.

Foster-father, *s.* Oide. Foster-fathers, *oideachan.*

Foster-mother, *s.* Banaltrum.

Foster-son, *s.* Dalta.

Fought. See Fight.

Foul, *a.* (*Dirty*), salach, mosach, musach, gràda, broghach, neo-ghlan; (*vicious*), aingidh, gràineil, draosta, drabasda; (*ill-favoured*), duaichnidh; (*unfair*), eucorach, neocheart. Foul play, *ana-cothrom;* foul weather, *aimsir shalach.* (*As the sky*), dorcha, grumach, neo-shoilleir.

Foul, *v. a.* Salaich; duaichnich, dubh.

Foul-faced, *a.* Salach, duaichnidh, dubh.

Foully, *adv.* Gu salach, gu mosach, gu mosach salach; gu gràineil, gu nàr.

Foul-mouthed, *a.* Droch-bheulach, droch-chainnteach, tarcuiseach, droch-labhrach.

Foulness, *s.* Sal, salachar, duaichneachd, gràinealachd; neo-ghloine, truaillidheachd; aingidheachd; mosaiche.

Found, *pret.* of Find; which see.

Found, *v. a.* Socraich, suidhich, steidhich, leig bunait, cuir air chois; tog; tilg, leagh.

Foundation, *s.* Bunait, bunailt, bunachur, steigh, steighdhaighnich, bun, iochdar; tùs, toiseach; suidheachadh. Before the foundation of the world, *ro leigeadh bunaitean an domhain;* a foundation stone, *clach bhun;* foundation of hope, *bun dòchais;* from the very foundation, *o 'n fhior bhun.*

Founder, *s.* Fear togalach, fear suidheachaidh, steidhear; (*of metals*), leaghadair.

Founder, *v. a.* and *n.* Bacaich, dean bacach (no) crùpach, mar each; rach fodha, mar luinge.

Foundery, Foundry, *s.* Tigh leaghaidh; leaghadaireachd.

Foundling, *s.* Faotailiche, leanabh tréigte.

Foundress, *s.* Ban-steighear.

Fount, Fountain, *s.* Fuaran, tobar, tiobairt; mathair uisge; spùtan; tùs, aobhar, mathair aobhar, ceann aobhar. The fountain that never dries up, *an tobar nach traogh.*

Fountful, *a.* Fuaranach, tobarach, tiobairteach.

Four, *a.* Ceithir.

Four-cornered, *a.* Ceithir-oisinneach, ceithir chearnach.

Fourfold, *a.* Ceithir fillte; ceithir plaighe.

Four-footed, *a.* Ceithir-chosach.

Four hundred, *a.* Ceithir cheud.

Four-score, *a.* Ceithir fichead.

Fourth, *a.* Ceathramh. The fourth part, *an ceathramh cuid;* King George the Fourth, *Righ Seòrsa ceithir.*

Four-wheeled, *a.* Ceithir-chuibhleach, ceithir-rothach.

Fowl, *s.* Eùn, ian, eunlan, eunlath. Fowls, *eòin, eunlaith.*

Fowl, *v. n.* Eunaich, ianaich. He is gone to fowl, *tha e an falbh a dh' eunachadh.*

Fowler, *s.* Eunadair.

Fowling, *s.* Eunach, eunachadh. A fowling, *ag eunachadh.*

Fowling-piece, *s.* Gunn-eunaich; gunna glaic.

Fox, *s.* Balgair, balagair, sionnach; madadh-ruadh. The fox's watch over the sheep, *gleidheadh 'n t-sionnaich air na caoirich.*

Fox-case, *s.* Craiceann sionnaich

Fox-chase, *s.* Ruaig sionnaich, faoghaid.

Foxglove, *s.* Brog na cuthaig. Lady's-foxglove, *cuineal mhuire.*

Fox-hunter, *s.* Sealgair, brocair, fear shionnach.

Foxship, *s.* Cuilbheart.

Fraction, *s.* Briseadh; biteag; a bheag sam bith do dh' iomlan.

Fractious, *a.* Bruidhneach, crosda, tuasaideach, draghail.

Fracture, *s.* Briseadh, bruthadh, sgaradh; sgoltadh; bearn, dealach.

Fracture, *v. a.* Bris, bruth, sgoilt.

Fragile, *a.* Brisg, so-bhriseadh; anfhann, lag; teagamhach; breòite.

Fragility, *s.* Brisgead, an-fhannachd, laigsinn; breòiteachd.

Fragment, *s.* Mìre, sgealb, spealg, pìos, iarmad, earann, bloigh, bloighde, bruan, roinn, fuigheall, fuighleach, spruilleach. Fragments, *mìrean, spealgan, pronnagan, bloighdean, bruanagan.*

Fragrance, Fragrancy, *s.* Deagh-àile, fàile cùbhraidh, boltrach cubhraidh; deagh bholadh.

Fragrant, *a.* Cùbhraidh, deagh bholtrachail. Fragrantly, *gu cùbhraidh.*

Frail, *a.* Breòite; lag, fann, anfhann, mall; brisg, creabhaidh; brùithte; so-bhriseadh; neo-sheasamhach, so thoirt gu taobh.

Frailty, *s.* Breòiteachd, laigsinn, an-fhannachd, brisgead; neo-sheasamhachd.

Fraise, *s.* Seorsa caraiceig.

Frame, *v. a.* Dealbh, cruthaich, cum, dean; tionnsgain; cuir ceart (no) gu doigh.

Frame, *s.* Aitreabh, togail; foire, fraidhe; dealbh, cumadh, cruth; dreach, snuadh. Frame of mind, *staid inntinn.*

Framer, *s.* Dealbhair, dealbhadair, cumadair.

† Frampold, *a.* Cainnteach, crosda, aithghearr, cas, cabhagach, dian.

Franchise, *s.* Saorsadh, saoirse, còir.

Franchise, *v. a.* Saor, dean saor, ceadaich.

Frank, *a.* Faoilidh, fial, fialuidh, furanach; fosgailte; ionraic; neo-chealgach, saor; soilleir. Frankly, *gu faoilidh, gu furanach, gu saor.*

Frank, *s.* Fail-mhuc; litir shaor, litir air nach cuirear eise, cùin Francach is fhiach deich sgillinn.

Frank, *v.* Biath, dean reamhar; saor litir.

Frankincense, *s.* Tùis.

Frankly. See Frank.

Frankness, *s.* Faoilidheachd, fialachd, furanachd, saorsuinn, saor-inntinneachd.

Frank-tenement, *s.* Gabhail saoghail, oighreachd.

Frantic, *a.* Cuthach, cuthachail, feargach, air bhoile, air bhreathas, air a chuthach. Quite frantic, *air a ghlan chuthach, air an dearg chuthaich.*

Franticness, *s.* Cuthach, boile, bainnidh, buirbe, breathas, dearg a chuthaich.

Fraternal, *a.* Bràthaireil. Fraternal love, *gradh brathaireil.* Fraternally, *gu brathaireil.*

Fraternity, *s.* Brathaireachas; comunn.

Fratricide, *s.* Brathar-mhortadh.

Fraud, *s.* Cealg, ceilge, feall, foill, car, cealgaireachd, meang, mealltaireachd, cuilbheart, lùb, slighe, sloighte.

Fraudful, *a.* Cealgach, fealltach, carach, mealltach, meangach; cuilbheartach; lùbach; dùbailt; sligheach, sloighteil; eucorach; cam, fiar.

Fraudulence, *s.* Cealgaireachd, mealltaireachd; meangachd, sloightearachd.

Fraudulent, *s.* Cealgach, fealltach, carach, cam, fiar; meangach, cuilbheartach, sligheach, lùbach, seolta, eolach sloighteil; neo-onorach, neo-ionraic, neo-cheart; eu-corach.

Fraudulently, *adv.* Gu cealgach, gu fealltach, gu carach, gu cam, gu fiar, gu cuilbheartach, gu sligheach, gu lubach, gu seolta, gu sloighteil; gu h-eucorach.

Fraught, *part.* of freight. Luchdaichte.

† Fraught, *s.* Luchd, làn, faradh, lòd.

† Fraught, *v. a.* Luchdaich, lion.

Fray, *s.* Tuasaid, tabaid; caonnag, cath; duaireachas; comhrag-deise; ruisg.

Fray, *v. a.* Rub, suath.

Freak, *s.* Taom, nual, dochas, faoin-dhòchas.

Freak, *v.* Breac, breacaich, ballaich.

Freakish, *a.* Dòchasach, faoin, luaineach, neònach.

Freakishness, *s.* Dòchasachd, luaineachd.

Fream, *v.* Dean gnòsd mar mha-ghamhuinn.

Freckle, *s.* Breac-sheunan, breac-seunanach; caisreaman.

Freckled, *a.* Breac-seunach, seunanach, ballach, breac.

Free, *a.* Saor; (*open*), fosgailte; cridheil; fiùghantach, ionraic; (*in giving*), fial, fialuidh; (*common*), coitchionn; (*without expense*), saor, gun chosd; (*at leisure*), soimeach; air athais. A free gift, *saor-ghibhte;* a free school, *saor-sgoil;* free from guilt, *saor o chiont.*

Free, *v.* Saor, fuasgail, tuasgail, leig tuasgailte (no) fuasgailte; leig fa sgaòil. Freed, *saor, fuasgailte, ceadaichte, fa sgaoileadh.*

Freebooter, *s.* Fear-reubainn, reubair, spuinneadair, tothair, creachadair, goidiche, gaduiche. Freebooters, *luchd-reubainn.*

Freebooting, *s.* Reubainn, spùinne, spùinneadaireachd; spùille, creachadaireachd, creachadh, togail.

Free-born, *a.* Saor. A free-born man, *saaoranach.*

Free cost, *a.* Saor.

Freed-man, *s.* Fear saor, duine saor, saor-dhuine, saoranach.

Freedom, *s.* Saorsadh, saorsainn, comas, socrachd, cead; còirichean. The freedom of a city, *coirichean baile;* the freedom of my will, *saorsadh mo thoile.*

Freehearted, *a.* Fiùghantach, fosgailte, fialuidh, cridheil, saor-chridheach; uasal.

Freehold, *s.* Fearann saor; oighreachd.

Freeholder, *s.* Fear fearainn, neach aig am bheil fearann saor. Freeholders, *luchd-fearainn.*

Freely, *adv.* Gu saor; gu fiùghantach, gu fialuidh; gun mhoile, gun bhac, gun chosd; a nasguidh, fa 'r nasguidh, do dheòin; gu neo-chuibhrichte. Freely given, *builichte a nasguidh.*

Freeman, *s.* Duine saor, saor-dhuine, saoranach.

Freeminded, *a.* Saor inntinneach, neo-chùramach; mi-fhaicilleach.

Freeness, *s.* Saorsadh; ionracas; fialachd.

Free-school, *s.* Saor-sgoil, sgoil-shaor.

Free-spoken, *a.* Ladurna, neo-fhaicilleach, ann an cainnt.

Free-stone, *s.* Clach-shreathal.

Free-thinker, *s.* Baoth-chreidmheach.

Free-thinking, *s.* Baoth-chreideamh.

Free-will, *s.* Saor-thoil.

Free-woman, *s.* Saor-bhan; ban-saoranach.

Freeze, *v. a.* and *n.* Reoth, marbh le fuachd, bàsaich le fuachd; bi air funntainn le fuachd.

Freight, *v. a.* Luchdaich.

Freight, *s.* Luchd, lòd, callach, uallach, faradh luing, luchd luing.

FREIGHTER, *s.* Luchdair.

FRENCH, *a.* Frangach, Francach.

FRENCH-BEAN, *s.* Ponair Francach.

FRENETIC, *a.* Cuthach, air bhoile, air bhreathas, air bhuaireadh.

FRENZY, *s.* Cuthach, boile, dearg-chuthach, breathas, bainnidh, buaireadh, mire; breilleas.

FREQUENCY, *s.* Tricead, minigead, cumantas, bidheantas.

FREQUENT, *a.* Tric, minic, cumaint, bidheanta; làn. Frequently, *gu tric, gu minic, iomad uair*

FREQUENT, *v* Tathuich, tathaich.

FREQUENTATION, *s.* Tathachadh, tathaich.

FREQUENTER, *s.* Fear tathaich, fear tathachaidh

FREQUENTLY, *adv.* Gu tric, gu minic; tric, minic; am bidheantas, iomad uair.

FRESCO, *s* Fionnarachd; duibhre.

FRESH, *a.* Ùr, ùrar, (*as weather*), fionnar, fionn-fhuar; (*as water*), neo-shaillte, (*new*), nodha, nuadh, og; (*lively*), beò, beothail, cridheil, slainnteil, brisg; blathmhor; (*opposed to stale*), ùr, milis; cubhraidh A fresh, *as ùr, a ris*, fresh water, *bùrn.*

FRESHEN, *v. a.* and *n* Ùraich, dean ùr, dean fionnar, fionnaraich; fàs ùr (no) fionnar. Freshened, *ùraichte, fionnaraichte.*

FRESHET, *s* Bùrn, srùlag bhùirn.

FRESHLY, *adv.* Gu h-ùr, gu h-urar; gu fionnar, gu beò, gu beothail, gu cridheil, gu ruiteach.

FRESHNESS, *s.* Urachd, ùraireachd; ùiread; tréine, slainnte; brigh, òige; fionnarachd, fionn-fhuaireachd; beothalas, cridhealas, ruiteachd.

FRESH-WATER, *a.* (*Sea epithet*), aineolach, neo-theoma.

FRESH-WATER, *s* Bùrn; uisge.

FRET, *s.* (*Frith*), cneas-mara; caolas; (*of temper*), frionas, friotal, oibreachadh, iomart, cnamh, crosanachd

FRET, *v. a.* and *n.* Cuir thar a chéile, buair, feargaich, ith, creim, cnamh; suath, rub, mèil, breac, breacaich, ballaich, dean iomairt, dean frionas Fretted, *buairte, feargaichte, cnamhta, breac, breacaichte, ballach.*

FRETFUL, *a* Frionasach, friotalach, crosda, doirbh, cainnteach, dranndanach, aithghearr, cas. Fretfully, *gu frionasach, gu crosda, gu cainnteach, gu cas.* The fretful temper is like the thorn, *am fear a bhios feurg air a ghnà, is cosmhal a ghne ris an dris.*

FRETFULNESS, *s* Frionasachd, friotalachd.

FRETTY, *a.* Ballach, breac, ballaichte, breacaichte.

FRETWORK, *s.* Obair bhreac, garbh-chlachaireachd

FRIABLE, *a.* So-bhruanadh, so-mhéileadh, so-phronnadh, brisg.

FRIAR, *s.* Brathair bochd, mànach.

FRIARLY, *a.* Mànachail, diadhuidh, naomh.

FRIARY, *s.* Co-thional bhrathaire bochd, co-thional mhànach

FRIBBLE, *v. n* Dean faoineas, bi faghharsach.

FRIBBLER, *s.* Fear faoin; poichean, caifean; gircean; fear faghharsach.

FRICASSEE, *s* Seorsa bidh; air a dheanamh do dh' fheòil phroinnte.

FRICTION, *s.* Rubadh, suathadh, méileadh, méilt

FRIDAY, *s.* Di-h-aoine.

FRIEND, *s.* Caraid, cara, fear rùin; caomh, caomhan. A good friend, *deagh charaid*, a friend in need, *caraid um feum;* try your friend before you trust him, *dearbh do charaid mun earb thu ris.* Friends, *cairdean, luchd-daimh.* A she friend, *ban-charaid*, a back friend, *namhaid;* be friends with him, *bi réidh ris;* every relation is not a friend, *cha bhuidheach gach ro dhìleas.*

FRIENDLESS, *a.* Gun charaid, aonaranach, uireasbhach, dibhidh, truagh, tréigte

FRIENDLILY, *adv.* Gu cairdeil, gu caomh, gu caoimhneil.

FRIENDLINESS, *s.* Cairdealachd, cairdeas, caoimhnealachd, caoimhnealas, caoimhne

FRIENDLY, *a.* Càirdeil, caomh, caomhail; caoimhneil, còir.

FRIENDSHIP, *s.* Cairdeas, caomhalachd, caoimhneas

FRIEZE, *s* Aodach garbh caiteanach

FRIGATE, *s* Luingeas chogaidh, aig am bith eadar fichead is leth-cheud gunna.

FRIGEFACTION, *s* Fuarachadh, fionnarachadh.

FRIGERATORY, *s* Tigh eighe

FRIGHT, *s* Eagall, oillt, clisge, grad-eagal, sgeun, uamhann, faitcheas, faitchios, maoim; sgàth.

FRIGHT, *v. a* Cuir eagall (no) oillt air, cuir air sgeun

FRIGHTEN, *v* Cuir eagal air, cuir clisg air, cuir air sgeun He frightened him out of his wits, *chuir e crithe na chous-bhcart air, chuir e eagal a thòin air.*

FRIGHTFUL, *a.* Eagallach, uamhasach, uamharra, oillteil, fuathasach Frightfully, *gu h-eagallach, gu fuathasach.*

FRIGHTFULNESS, *s* Eagallachd, uamhasachd, uamharrachd, oillteileachd

FRIGID, *a.* Fuar, reothta; lag, neo-bhrisg. Frigidly, *gu fuar, gu reòthta.*

FRIGIDITY, *s.* Fionnarachd, fionn-fhuarachd; reòtachd; laigsinn, neo-shuilbhearachd, cion-mothuchaidh, cion graidh

FRIGORIFIC, *a* Reòta, reòtach

FRILL, *v n* Crith le geilt.

FRILL, *s* Anart finealta, ribeag

FRINGE, *s* Froinnse, iomall, bile, foir, fàim, ribeag, fabhradh

FRINGE, *v a.* Froinnsich, faim, cuir bile (no) foir air

FRINGED, *a* Froinnsichte, froinnseach, faimte, ribeagach.

FRIPPERY, *s.* Sean aodach, luideagan, cearbagan.

FRISEUR, *s.* Bearradair; barbair.

FRISK, *v n* Leum, dean beiceil, danns, ruith-leum, sgàthleum, dean mire

FRISK, *s.* Leumnaich, leumartaich, beiceil, dannsadh, rucas, beadradh; mire, sgath-leumnaich, macnus. Frisking, *ri mire, a chluicheadh, ri cluicheag.*

FRISKY, *a.* Beò, mear, meamnach, beadrach, ait, aighearach, sodanach; macnusach; beiceasach, curaideasach.

FRIT, *s* Salann is luaithre air feadh chéile.

FRITH, *s.* Caolas, caolas mara, cneas-mara; cneasmhuir; muir chumhann, sàilean, sàil-linn

FRITTER, *v.* Pronn, min-phronn, gearr na mhìrean.

FRITTER, *s.* Toitean, colag; seorsa caraiceig; sgealp, spealg, mìre, crioman, criomag

FRIVOLITY, *s* Faoineas, suarrachas.

FRIVOLOUS, *a* Faoin, suarrach, air bheag seadh. Frivolously, *gu faòin, gu suarrach.*

FRIVOLOUSNESS, *s* Faoinead, faoineas, suarraichead.

FRIZZLE, *v a* Cas, cas folt

FRIZZLED, *a.* Casta, air chasadh, greannach. Frizzled hair, *folt casta.*

FRO, *adv.* Air ais, sios, uaith. To and fro, *air ais is air adhairt, sios is suas, h-uige is uaith, null is a nall*

FROCK, *s.* Gun beag; earrasaid.

FROG, *s* Losgann, losgann buidhe, màigean, smàigean; muile-mhàg.

FROG-FISH, *s.* Seorsa éisg.

FROLIC, *s.* Cleas, prat; sùgradh, mire, ealaidh.

FROLICSOME, *a.* Cleasanta, pratach, sugach, sùgrach, mear, cuileagach; ait, sunntach, aobhach

FROLICSOMENESS, *s* Cleasantachd, sugrachd, mìre.

FROM, *prep* O, ua, bho, a, as, mach as, mach o. From my youth up, *o m' òige suas*, from the creation of the world, *o thoiseach an t-saoghail, o leigeadh bunaitean an domhain*, from between her feet, *o eadar a casaibh*; from day to day, *o là gu là*, from my heart, *o mo chridhe*; from that time, *o 'n am sin*, from above, *os àird*; from abroad, *o chéin, o chéin-thir, as na rìoghachdan mach*, from house to house, *o thigh gu tigh*, from man to man, *o fhear gu fear*, from hence, *a so*, from henceforth, *a so suas*, from whence? *co as? c'aite as? cia as?* the place from whence he came, *an t-àite as an d-thàinig e*, from that time, *o sin, o 'n am sin*, from time to time, *o am gu h-am, air uairibh, an tràths' is a rìs*, from without, *o 'n leth a muigh*, from me, *uam*, from thee, *uait*, from him, *uaith*, from her, *uaipe*, from us, *uainn, uaithne*, from you, *uaibh*, from them, *uapa*

FRONT, *s* Aodann, aghaidh, clàr an aodainn, (*of battle*), tùs, toiseach The front of an army, *tùs feachd*, front to front, *aghaidh ri h-aghaidh*, a person with a bold front, *neach dùna (no) beagnarach.*

FRONT, *v a* and *n* Thoir aghaidh; gabh roimh; coinnich, seas mu choinneamh

FRONTIER, *s* Crioch, iomall, eirthir, bruach

FRONTISPIECE, *s* Aghaidh, aodann; clàr-aghaidh

FRONTLESS, *a.* Beag-narach, dàna

FRONTLET, *s.* Stiom, failtean, bann, crochaid, brindealan.

FRONT-ROOM, *s* Seomar beòil

FROST, *s.* Reoth, reothadh, reòta, eithre; cruaidh-reoth, sioc, siocadh, fuachd, cuisne White frost, *liath-reoth.*

FROST-BITTEN, *a* Air funtainn, air marbh-lapadh, seacaichte, air reothadh

FROST-BITE, *s* Beum reotha

FROSTED, *a* Reoithte, air reothadh

FROSTILY, *adv.* Gu fuar, gu reòtaidh.

FROSTY, *a.* Reòtaidh, fuar

FROTH, *s* Cobhar, cobhragach, cothannach, còp, còragaich; othan

FROTH, *v n* Cuir mach cobhar, bi fo chobhar (no) fo chòp

FROTHINESS, *s.* Cobharachd, cothanachd, còpachd

FROTHSTICK, *s* Loinid, slamhach.

FROTHY, *a* Cobharach, cothanach, copach, làn cobhair, fo chobhar; faoin, fàs.

FROUNCE, *v* Cas folt mu 'n aodann

FROUSY, *a* Loibheach, lobhach, breun; duaichnidh, dorcha.

FROWARD, *a* Crosda, cas, obann, dan; feargach, droch-mhuinte, do-cheannsachadh; aingidh; ruaineach, fiochar. Frowardly, *gu crosda, gu cas, gu h-aingidh*

FROWARDNESS, *s.* Crosdachd, obainne, aingidheachd.

FROWN, *s.* Gruaim, graing; gnoimh

FROWN, *v. n* Amhairc le gruaim; cas d' aghaidh; graingich.

FROWNING, *a* Gruamach, graingeach, coimheach; dorch Frowningly, *gu gruamach.*

FROZEN, *part* Air reothadh, reòithte; reotaidh, siocaichte; air funtainn. The frozen ocean, *a mhuir reòtaidh.*

FRUCTIFEROUS, *a.* Tarrach, tarbhach, siolmhor.

FRUCTIFY, *v a.* Dean torrach, dean tarbhach.

FRUCTUOUS, *a* Torrach, tarbhach.

FRUGAL, *a* Caonntach, caomhantach, gleadhtach, crionna, solarach, cùramach; neo-struidheil A frugal woman, *criontag.* Frugally, *gu caonntach, gu caomhantach, gu crionna, gu gàbhuidh.*

FRUGALITY, *s.* Caonntachd, caomhantachd, crionnachd, crionntachd; baile; buileachas; fearachas-tighe, beanachas tighe, deagh fhearachas-tighe, deagh bheanachas-tighe.

FRUIT, *s* Meas, toradh; gineil, tairbhe; math; sochair, piseach; faghaltas, buidhinn, coisinn Ripe fruit, *meas abuich*, the fruit of the womb, *siol, clann*, the first fruits, *ceud thoradh.*

FRUITERER, *s.* Fear meas, fear a reiceadh meas

FRUITERY, *s.* Aite gleidh meas; lobhta meas.

FRUITFUL, *a* Torrach, siolmhor, pailt. Fruitfully, *gu torrach, gu siolmhor.*

FRUITFULNESS, *s.* Torraichead, siolmhoireachd, toraileachd.

FRUITION, *s.* Mealtuinn, sealbhadh, sealbhachadh.

FRUITLESS, *a.* Neo-thorrach, neo-shiolmhor, neo-tharbhach; aimrid, seasg, (*useless*), faoin, diomhain.

FRUMENTY, *s.* Brochan cruithneachd

FRUMP, *v.* Mag, dean fanaid (no) fochaid.

FRUMPER, *s.* Magair, sgeigear.

FRUMPISH, *a* Magail, fanaideach, fochaideach.

FRUSH, *v a* Bris, bruan, bruth, broth.

FRUSTRANEOUS, *a.* Faoin, diomhain; neo-tharbhach.

FRUSTRATE, *v.* Meall, bac, cuir an aghaidh, diobhail.

FRUSTRATE, *a.* Meallta, faoin, diomhain, diobhailte.

FRUSTRATION, *s.* Mealladh; toirt a char a.

FRUSTRATIVE, *a* Mealltach.

FRY, *s* Sgaoth, sgaoth éisg, miniasg; gràisg; sgaoth bhèistean.

FRY, *s.* Seorsa criathar

FRY, *s* Feoil ròiste, ròstadh.

FRY, *v* Ròist, griosaich, sgreig; leagh le teas. Fried, *roiste, griosaichte.*

FRYING, *s.* Ròstadh, griosachadh, sgreigeadh A frying-pan, *aghann griosachaidh, aghann sgreigidh.*

FUB, *s.* Cnap (no) plubair giùllain, cnabanach.

FUCATED, *a* Dathte; dubhta; duaichnichte.

FUDDLE, *v.* Cuir air a mheisge (no) air an daoraich.

FUDDLING, *a.* Meisgeach, misgeach, pòiteil. A fuddling fellow, *misgear.*

FUEL, *s.* Connadh; gual; fiodh, mòine, cùlag. Wet fuel will burn, but stones will not, *gabhaidh am fliuch, ach cha gabh a chlach.*

FUGACIOUS, *a* Luaimneach, luaineach, siùbhlach, luath.

FUGACITY, *a* Luaineachd, siùbhlachd, luathas.

FUGITIVE, *a* Luaineach, siùbhlach, neo-bhunaiteach; fogarrach, diobarach, iomlaideach; seachranach

FUGITIVE, *s* Diobarach, diobaraiche, ruagalaiche, fogarraiche; reubaltach.

FULCRUM, *s* Prop.

FULFIL, *v. a.* Coi-lion, coimh-lion, dean; criochnaich. Fulfil your promise, *coimh-lion do ghealladh*, fulfil his desire, *dean a thoile* Fulfilled, *coimh-lionta.*

FULFILMENT, *s* Coimh-lionadh, criochnachadh.

FULFRAUGHT, *a.* Iomlàn.

FULGENCY, *s* Dealradh, lannair, soillse, glonradh.

FULGENT, *a.* Dealrach, dearrsach, soillseach, glonrach.

FULGID, *a* Dealrach, dearrsach, soillseach, glonrach.

FULGOUR, *s.* Dealradh, dearrsadh, soillse, lannair.

FULGURATION, *s.* Soillseachadh, teine-adhair, dealanach, lasadh

FULIGINOUS, *a.* Dubh, sùidheach, deathachail.

FULIMART, *s.* Fòcullan; breun-fhòcullan.

Full, *a.* (*Filled*), làn, lionta. Quite full, *iom-làn*, *dean làn*. (*Plump*), toiceach, sultmhor, reamhar, cruinn; (*full-fed*), riaraichte, sàthach, sàsaichte, buidheach; (*as clothes*), farsuing, rùmar; (*perfect*), coilionta, foirfe. Full three days, *tri laithean iomlàn;* the moon is at full, *tha ghealach na h-àirde;* I am full glad, *tha mi làn toileach*, (*no*) *ro bhuidheach*, (*no*) *fior bhuidheach;* it is full time, *tha e mithich;* full in the wind, *an aghaidh na gaoithe;* half full, *leth-làn*.

Full, *s.* Laine, lan, iomlan.

Full, *v.* Glan, sgùr, lùth, luaith, fùc; calc, galc.

Fullblown, *a.* Ann an làn bhlàth.

Fullbottomed, *a.* Tònach.

Fulleared, *a.* Diasach, tarbhach.

Fuller, *s.* Fùcadair, muillear luathaidh, luathadair, calcair, galcair.

Fulleyed, *a.* Lan-shuileach, mòr-shuileach.

Full-fed, *a.* Sàthach, sàsaichte, làn, biadhta, riaraichte.

Full-laden, *a.* Luchdaichte.

Fullery, *s.* Fùcaireachd; calcaireachd.

Fulling-mill, *s.* Muileann luathaidh; muileann calcaidh.

Fully, *adv.* Gu làn, gu h-iomlan, gu pailt, gun easbhuidh.

Fulminant, *a.* Fuaimneach, torunnach.

Fulminate, *v. a.* Dean toruun, no tairneanach.

Fulmination, *s.* Fuaim, ard-fhuaim, torunn.

Fulminatory, *a.* Torunnach; eagallach.

Fulness, *s.* Lànachd, pailteas, laine, iomlan, foirfeachd, iomlanachd; sàth, farsuingeachd, meud.

Fulsome, *a.* Grada, gràineil, breun; lobhach, loibheach, mosach, draosda, drabasta, macnusach.

Fulsomeness, *s.* Gràinealachd, bréine; lobhadh; draosdachd, macnus.

† **Fumage**, *s.* Airgiod toit, airgiod teallaich.

Fumble, *v.* Lamhaich, meuraich; lamhaich gu ciotach (no) gu cearr.

Fumbler, *s.* Neach neo-shoineil (no) ciotach.

Fumblingly, *adv.* Gu neo-shoineil, gu ciotach, gu cearr.

Fume, *s.* Deathach, deatach, ceò, tòit, smùid; gal; toth, corruich, fearg.

Fume, *v. a.* Smùid, cuir deathach; bi fo fheirge.

Fumet, *s.* Cac feidh.

Fumid, *a.* Deathachail, smùideil, toiteil.

Fumigate, *v.* Deathaich, toit, fàilich. Fumigated, *deathaichte*.

Fumigation, *s.* Deathachadh, deathach, toit, fàileachadh.

Fumitory, *s.* Lus an deathaich.

Fun, *s.* Ealaidh, spuirt, cluich, mire, sùgradh, aighear, fearas-chuideachd, *dibhearsain*.

Function, *s.* Dreuchd, gnothuch, oifig, ceaird, ealdhain; comas.

Fund, *s.* Stòras; stoc, ionmhas.

Fundament, *s.* Deireadh, ceann-deiridh, tòin, ceòsach, toll tòn; bunamhas.

Fundamental, *a.* Bunaiteach, bunailteach.

Funeral, *s.* Adhlac, adhlacadh, tiodhlac, tiodhlacadh; torradh, ollanachadh.

Funeral, *a.* Adhlacaidh, tiodhlacaidh; dubh, brònach, muladach.

Fungous, *a.* Faisgeanach, cluaranach, spoingeach.

Fungus, *s.* Fàs na h-aon oidhche; bonaid an losgainn; spoing, spuing.

Funicle, *s.* Cord caol, toinntean, sgéinne, sreang.

Funk, *s.* Tòchd, fàil, bréine, stoich.

Funnel, *s.* Lionadair, tunnadair; pioban.

Fur, *s.* Bian ròinneach, fionnadh min, croicionn, giobach.

Fur, *v. a.* and *n.* Comhdaich le fionnadh min; fas ròmach; fas salach mar theaugadh ann an teasach.

† **Furacious**, *a.* Bradach.

Furacity, *s.* Braide, meirle.

Furbelow, *s.* Froinnse; ribeag.

Furbelow, *v.* Froinnsich, ribeagaich.

Furbish, *v. a.* Soilleirich, sgùr, lannairich; glan.

Furbisher, *s.* Sgùradair, glanadair.

Furcated, *a.* Gobhlach, gabhlach.

Furcation, *s.* Gobhlachd, gobbal, dealachadh mar ni dà rathad.

Furfur, *s.* Cochul; garbhan.

Furious, *a.* Cuthachail, cuthaich, garg, borb, air a chuthach, feargach; air bhreathas ain-sgeunach. Furiously, *gu borb, gu feargach, gu cuthaich*.

Furiousness, *s.* Cuthach, buirbe, feirge, breathas, boile, bainnidh.

Furl, *v.* (*As a sail*), fill, gabh seòl.

Furlong, *s.* An t-ochdamh cuid do mhìl, da cheud is fichead slat; staid.

Furlough, *s.* Cead; cead goirrid gheibh saighdear a dhol dhachaidh.

Furnace, *s.* Amhuinn, fuirneas; copar (no) coire mhòr.

Furnish, *v. a.* Uigheamaich, deasaich, dean suas, sgiamhaich; cum ri; builich air. A furnished table, *bord deasaichte;* a furnished house, *tigh uigheamaichte*.

Furnisher, *s.* Fear uigheamachaidh.

Furniture, *s.* Airneis; uigheam; breaghas; gaoirreas. Household furniture, *airneis tighe*.

Furrier, *s.* Fear deasachaidh leathair.

Furrow, *s.* Clais, amar, sloc, slochd, dìge; (*on the face*), preasag; (*a rib*), airbhe.

Furrow, *v. a.* Claisich, clais; (*rib*), airbhich. Furrowed, *claisichte*, (*ribbed*), *airbhichte*, *airbheach*.

Furry, *a.* Ròinneach, molach; ròmach; blanach.

Further, *a.* Ni 's fhaide, ni 's fhaide air falbh, nis fhaide air astar, ni 's fhaide uaith. I will not move a step further, *cha charaich mi ceum ni 's fhaide*.

Further, *adv.* A thuille air sin.

Further, *v.* Cuir air aghaidh, luathaich, cuidich le.

Furtherance, *s.* Coghnadh, cuideachadh.

Furtherer, *s.* Fear-coghnaidh, fear cuideachaidh.

Furthermore, *adv.* Osbarr, tuille fòs, a thuille air so (no) air sin.

Furthermost, *a.* Is iomallaiche, is cein, is fhaide air astar.

Furtive, *a.* Bradach, fealltach.

Furtively, *adv.* Le braide, gu fealltach, le foill.

Furuncle, *s.* Guirean, bucaid, neasgaid, fealan.

Fury, *s.* Cuthach, bainni, breathas, fearg, corruich, ard-chorruich, buaireas; baobh, bansgal. In a fury, *air bhreathas*.

Furze, *s.* Conasg, conas.

Furzy, *a.* Conasgach, conasach.

Fuse, *v. a.* Leagh, cuir gu leaghadh. Fused, *leaghta*.

Fusee, *s.* Gunna glaic; fadadh cluaise na toirm-shlige.

Fusible, *a.* Leaghtach, so-leaghadh.

Fusil, *s.* Gunna glaic; gunna beag grinn, gunna caol dùirn.

Fusileer, *s.* Musgadair; saighdear fo armaibh.

Fusion, *s.* Leaghadh, ruithe.

FUSS, *s* (*A low cant word*), iomairt, othail, ùinich, cabhag; strigh, tailmrich, toirm

FUST, *s*. Tochd trom breun

FUSTIAN, *s*. Aodach canaich, aodach cotain. Fustian language, *glòr, urd-chainnte*.

FUSTIC, *s*. Seorsa fiodha a thig as na h-Innseachan shuas, ro fheumail ann an dathadaireachd.

† FUSTIGATE, *v. a* Buail, greidh, straoidhil.

FUSTINESS, *s* Bréine, liatas, liathanachd, ruadhainneachd.

FUSTY, *s* Liath, ruadhain, breun, salach.

FUTILE, *a*. Faoin, diomhain; neo-thàbhachdach, bruidhneach, lonach, peilpeach.

FUTILITY, *s*. Faoineas, diomhanas, neo-thabhachd; lonais, peilp

FUTURE, *a*. Ri teachd. In future time, *anns an am ri teachd*; in future, *tuille, a so sios*.

FUTURITY, *s*. Am ri teachd.

FUZ-BALL, *s*. Bolgan beiceach, ballan losgainn, fàs na h-aon oidhche.

FY, *interj* Mo naire, mo mhasladh, mo nàire 's mo mhasladh, mo nàire shaoghalta. Fy on you, *mo naire ort, mo nàire ort fhéin*

G.

G, Seachdamh litir na h-Aibidil

GABARDINE, *s* Earrasaid, arrasaid, fearrasaid

GABBLE, *v* Dean gobais (no) lonais

GABBLE, *s*. Gobais, lonais, faoin-chomhradh, faoin chainnt, gob, peilp

GABBLER, *s*. Gobair, gabair; glagair, fear lonach, sgilm.

GABBLING, *a*. Gobach, lonach, peilpeanta.

GABEL, *s*. Cìse, càin

GABION, *s* Cliabh làn gainmheich (no) creadha chum dionadh balla idh air am bi namhaid a toirt ionnsuidh

GABLE, *s* Stuadh, tulachann; ceann tighe; mullach tighe.

GAD, *s* Gàd; geinn stàilinn

GAD, *v. n* Ruith gu lonach o thigh gu tigh; bi ri seabhas.

GADDER, *s* Urr lonach luaineach, sgilm; seabhasaiche, iomrolaiche, céilidhiche

GADDING, *s*. Céilidheach

GADFLY, *s*. Conspeach; gleithear, gleathair; meanbh-chuileag.

GAFF, *s* Gath-dòrain, gath riobhagach, muireadh, dubhan mòr, clic

GAFFLES, *s*. Spuir a chuireas iad air coilich mu 'n cog iad

GAG, *v a* Druid am beul, sparragaich, cabstaraich.

GAG, *s*. Sparrag, cabstar, cabstan.

GAGE, *v a* Geall, cuir geall, cuir an geall, ceangail, gabh; tomhais

GAGE, *s*. Geall, gealladh, earlas, gleus tomhais.

GAIETY, *s* Aiteas, cridhealas, aoibhneas, aigeantas; sunnt, mire; breaghas, briaghas

GAILY, *adv*. Gu h-ait, gu cridheil, gu h-aoibhneach, gu h-eibhinn, gu suilbhcara, gu gleusda, gu sunntach, gu mear; gu breagh.

GAIN, *s*. Coisinn, tairbhe, buidhinn, buannachd, math, proidhit, leas Loss and gain, *call is coisinn*. there is no gain without loss, *cha deanar buannachd gun chall*

GAIN, *v. a*. and *n*. Coisinn, buidhinn, buain, faigh, fàs, cinn. I have gained my point, *rinn mi am put*, you have not gained much by it, *cha mhòr a choisinn thu air*, a penny saved is a penny gained, *is cho math peighinn a chaomhnadh is peighinn choisinn*

GAINER, *s*. Fear buannachd, fear buidhinn, fear proidhit. You will not be a gainer by it, *cha bhuidhinn thu air*.

GAINABLE, *a*. So-choisinn, so-fhaotainn.

GAINFUL, *a*. Tarbhach, tairbheach, buannachdail, buidhneach; proidhiteil, proidhiteach

GAINFULNESS, *s*. Buannachd, coisinn; proidhit.

GAINLESS, *a* Neo-tharbhach, mi-tharbhach, neo-buannachdail, mi-phroidhteil.

GAINSAY, *v*. Cuir an aghaidh; labhair air ais, breugnaich; cuir as àicheadh, àicheadh, àichean.

GAINSAYER, *s*. Breugnachair; àicheanaiche

GAIRISH, *a* Briagh, breagh; uallach, leomach, riomhach, sgòdail

GAIRISHNESS, *s*. Briaghachd, breaghachd, breaghad, uallachd, riomhachd, sgòd.

GAIT, *s*. Rod, rathad; triall, ceum, coiseachd, imeachd; falbh Gang your gait, *gabh do rathad*; an airy gait, *falbh, uallach coiseachd sgòdail*.

GAITERS, *s*. Spad-choisbheart

GALAXY, *s*. A bhainne-shlighe; a bhainne-chrios, crios *no* stiom soillseach a chithear sna speuraibh ri oidhche reultaidh air bi.

GALE, *s*. Gaoth sgairteil, drothan, osag, deanna gaoithe.

GALEATED, *a* Ceann-bheartaichte, clogaideach.

GALIOT, *s*. Sgòth, sgoth-long.

GALL, *s* Domblas, nimhe; bearran; fearg; tnùth, gamhlas, mio-run, farran. The gall of bitterness, *domblas na seirbhe*.

GALL, *v. a*. Feargaich; cradh, saruich, farranaich; rùisg, méil Galled, *ciùrta, rùisgte, cràidhte, sàruichte*.

GALL, *s* Feargachadh; rùsgadh.

GALLANT, *a* (*Brave*), gasda, curanta, misneachail, gaisgeil, treubhanta, cruadalach, treun, làidir; (*foppish*), uallach, spairiseach, breagh, briagh, riomhach; (*polite*), macanta, muinte, modhail, suairc.

GALLANT, *s*. Lasgair, suiriche; leannan, balaoch bhan; adhaltranach.

GALLANTLY, *adv*. Gu gasda, gu curanta, gu misneachail, gu gaisgeil, gu treubhanta, gu cruadalach; gu treun, gu laidir, gu h-uallach, gu spairiseach, gu breagh, gu macanta, gu modhail, gu mòralach, gu mòrdhalach, gu h-uasal

GALLANTRY, *s*. (*Bravery*), curantachd, gaisge, treubhantas, tréine, misneach; (*foppish politeness*), riomhachd, uallachd, spairsiseachd, macantas, modhaileachd; suireadh, suirthcadh; (*criminal*), adhaltranas; drùis, baòis

GALL-BLADDER, *s*. Baigean leasaich.

GALLEASS, *s* Seorsa luingeis.

GALLED, *a*. Feargaichte, faranaichte; sàruichte.

GALLEON, *s*. Luingeas mhòr spàinnteach.

GALLERY, *s* Lobhta; trannsa; gleachas.

GALLEY, *s*. Long-fhada, ramh-long.

GALLEY-SLAVE, *s*. Long-thràill

GALLIARD, *s*. Lasgair.

GALLIC, GALLICAN, *a*. Francach.

Gallican, *a.* Francach.

Gallicism, *s.* Francradh.

Galligaskins, *s.* Mogain; briogais fharsuing; *sumag.*

Gallimatia, Bòilich, glòr, glòrmas, rabhdadh.

Galling, *a.* Farranach; cruaidh; docrach; piantachail.

Gallipot, *s.* Criadh-phoiteag, poiteag chreadha.

Gallon, *s.* Galan, galun, da phiunt Albanach.

Gallop, *s.* Aonaich, cruaidh-ruithe; *galapainn.*

Gallop, *v. a.* and *n.* Aonaich, cruaith-ruith, réis, steud. Spurring a horse when he gallops, *a greas' an eich is e na ruithe.*

Galloway, *s.* Gearran; each beag Gaidhealach.

Gallows, *s.* Croich; crochair. Go to the gallows, *gabh thun na croiche.*

Gallus, *s.* Coileach.

Gamble, *v. n.* Cluich; dean feall-chluich; meall.

Gambler, *s.* Fear iomairt; cluicheadair, mealltair; slaoightear, disnear, cearraiche, baoth-shùgraiche.

Gambling, *s.* Iomairt; mealltaireachd; slaoightearachd.

Gambol, *s.* Leumardaich, dannsadh, mire, ruithe, cleasachd, lùth-chleas, cluicheag, sùgradh.

Gambrel, *s.* Cas deiridh eich.

Game, *v. n.* Cluich, cluich airson airgid.

Game, *s.* Spuirt, cluiche, ealaidh, ioladh; sugradh; fuarsgallais; cleas; (*in hunting*), eoin-ruadh; fiadhachd, sealg. Starting of game, *faoghaid;* almost never killed game, *cha do rinn theab riomh sealg;* make game, *dean ealaidh* (*no*) *ioladh; dean fanoid.*

Game cock, *s.* Coileach dùnain, coileach cogaidh.

Gamekeeper, *s.* Eunadair; forsair fiadhachd.

Gamesome, *a.* Mireagach, sugrach, sugach, mear, àbhaisteach; anamadail, anamanta.

Gamesomeness, *s.* Mire, sugradh; macnus; ealaidh.

Gamester, *s.* Cearraiche, disnear, baoth-shugraiche, mealltair, slaoightear, fear a chluicheas airson airgid. A dexterous gamester will not hide his dice, *cha chéil cearraiche a dhìstean.*

Gaming-house, *s.* Dìs-lann, tigh-sùgraidh; tigh chearraiche.

Gammon, *s.* Taobh muic air a shailleadh, muic-fheoil shaillte; seorsa cluiche le dìsnean.

Gamut, *s.* Gleus ciùil.

Ganch, *v. a.* Croch neach air clicibh mar a nthear an talamh an Turcaich.

Gander, *s.* Gannradh, gànra.

† **Gang**, *v. n.* Rach, falbh; imich.

Gang, *s.* Buidheann, bannal, compailt, cuideachd, bròd, gràisg, lòd.

Gangrene, *s.* Cnàmhuinn, buirbean.

Gangrene, *v. a.* Fàs marbh (no) grod.

Gangrenous, *a.* Marbh; grod, cnàmhtach, cnàimhteach.

Gantelope, **Gantlet**, *s.* Ruithe-sguirsadh, seorsa peanais san arm, far an feum an ciontach ruithe eadar dà shread shaighdeara, o cheann gu ceann, agus buille fhaotainn o gach fear air an teid e seachad.

Ganza, *s.* Geadh fhiadhaich.

Gaol, *s.* Gainntir, priosan, carcar, toll-bùth; mainnir, luchlann.

Gaoler, *s.* Fear gainntir, fear coimhid gainntir.

Gap, *s.* Bearn, bealach; beum; cab; toll; craosaireachd. A gap in the ground, *sgagadh.*

Gape, *v. n.* Dean méanan, meananaich; spleuc, spleuc le beul fosgailte. Gape after, *miannaich, bi 'n geall air, bi 'n càs air.*

Gaper, *s.* Spleucair.

Gap-toothed, *a.* Cabach.

Gaping, *s.* Meananaich.

Garb, *s.* Culadh, culaidh, eide, eididh, eudach, aodach, deise, earradh. The Highland garb, *an eididh Ghaidhealach.*

Garbage, *s.* Mionach, greallach; ionar.

Garble, *v. a.* Criathair; dealaich; tagh.

Garboil, *s.* Tuasaid, buaireas, buaireadh, eas-ordugh; aimhreit; trioblaid.

Gard, *s.* Freiceadan, faire; cùram, dionadh, dìdean.

Garden, *s.* Gàradh, lios. A kitchen garden, *garadh càil.*

Garden, *v. a.* Gàraich, dean gàradaireachd (no) gàraidheachd.

Gardener, *s.* Gàradair, gairnealair, liosadair, fear gàraidh.

Gardening, *s.* Gàradaireachd, gairnealaireachd, liosadaireachd.

Gare, *s.* Olann gharbh, olann a chinneas air cosaibh chaoorach.

Gargarism, *s.* Purgaid beòil, beul phurgaid; beul-ghlanadh.

Gargle, *s.* Purgaid beòil; beul-phurgaid, glugaran.

Gargle, *v. a.* Nigh (no) glan beul le uisge leigheis, glugair.

Garland, *s.* Blàth-fhleasg, blàdh-fhleasgaidh; luschrùn.

Garlic, **Garlick**, *s.* Gairgean gàraidh.

Garlick-eater, *s.* Sgonn-bhalaoch.

Garment, *s.* Trusgan, earradh, còmhdach, culaidh, déise, fàluing.

Garner, *s.* Siol-lann, ionad taisg, ionad tasgaidh, gaoirneal, gearnal, sabhal, tigh stòr.

Garnet, *s.* Seorsa cloich uasail.

Garnish, *v.* Sgeadaich, sgiamhaich, grinnich, deasaich. Garnished, *sgeadaichte, sgiamhaichte.*

Garnish, *s.* Sgeadachadh, grinneas; (*in gaols*), ceanglaichean.

Garnished. See **Garnish.**

Garnishment, *s.* Sgeadachadh, sgiamhachd, grinneas; airneis.

Garniture, *s.* Airneis; grinneas; uigheam.

Garran, *s.* Gearran; each Gaidhealach.

Garret, *s.* Garait, lobhta, seomar mullaich.

Garreteer, *s.* Garaitiche, tamhaiche ann an seomar mullaich; ùghdar bochd.

Garrison, *s.* Daingneach, daighneach, dùn, tur, caisteal, dion-long phort; gearasan, gearasdan.

Garrison, *v. a.* Dion, daighnich, daingnich.

Garrulity, *s.* Sgoilmeiseachd, sgoilmeis, sgeilmearachd; peilpe, sgeilm, lonais, gobais, gob, glagaiseachd; glòr.

Garrulous, *a.* Sgoilmeach, sgoilmearra, lonach, peilpeanta, gobach, glagaiseach, luath-chainnteach, luath-bheulach

Garter, *s.* Gartan, glùinean; crios coise. A knight of the Garter, *Ridir a ghartain.*

Garter, *v.* Gartanaich; ceangail osan le gartan. Gartered, *gartanaichte.*

Garth, *s.* Domhlas, reamhad, tiughad.

Gas, *s.* Seorsa àile nach gabh slamachadh; àile *ghasda.*

Gasconade, *s.* Bòsd, bragainn, bragaireachd; spagluinn, roiseal.

Gash, *v. a.* Gearr, lot, beubanaich; beum, sgoch.

Gash, *s.* Gearradh, lotadh, beubanachadh, cruaidhlot, sgoch.

Gasp, *v.* Ospagaich, plosg, bi a plosgail, (no) a plosgartaich, bi ag àinich.

Gasp, *s.* Ospag, uspag, plosgadh, àinich. In the last gasp, *anns na h-ospagan mu dheireadh.*

GASPING, *s.* Ospagaich, uspagaich, plosgail, àinich.

GASTRIC, *a.* Goileach, a bhuineas do 'n ghoile no do 'n bhrù Gastric juice, sùgh na goile.

GASTRILOQUY, *s* Bronn, labhairt; bruidhinn mar gun tigeadh e as a bhrù

GAT, *pret* of get. Fhuair See GET.

GATE, *s* Geata, dorus mor, cachliath, inntеach, bealach

GATE-KEEPER, *s.* Portair, fear geata.

GATHER, *v. a.* Teanail, tionail, cruinnich, trus; dioghluim; cruach; cnuasaich; cuir ri chéile Gather together, *comh-thionail, coimh-theanail.* Gathered, *teanailte, cruinnichte; cruinn, an ceann a chéile*, (plaited), *preasagach, casta*

GATHER, *s* Preas, preasag, fillеadh, filleag, crupag

GATHERER, *s* Cruinneachair, fear cruinneachaidh

GATHERING, *s* Teanaladh, tionaladh, cruinneachadh, coimhthionaladh, trusadh, dioghlumadh; cnuasachadh The Gathering of the Clans, (a Highland air so called), *ccann na drochaid bige*, the Gathering of the Macdonalds, *craig an fhithich*, of the Grants, *craig eileachaidh; of* the Macphersons, *croit ubh or craig dhubha*, of the Macfarlanes, *loch sloigh*, of the Macgregors, *ard choillich*, of the Mackenzies, *tulaich ard*, of Braemar, *carn na cuimhne.*

GAUD, *s* Rud laoghach; briaghachd

GAUDERY, *s.* Briaghachd, uallachd.

GAUDINESS, *s* Breaghachd; riomhachd; bastalachd.

GAUDY, *a.* Briagh, breagh, riomhach; bastalach, uallach; leòmach, fàicheil

GAUDY, *s* Féisd, fleagh, cuirm, la sollain.

GAVE. See GIVE

GAVEL-KIND, *s.* Gabhail-cine

GAUGE, *v a* Tomhais soitheach.

GAUGER, *s.* Fear-tomhais shoithichean; *gàidsear.*

GAUNT, *a* Tana, caol, cruaidh, seang, gann-fheoileach, bochd, truagh.

GAUNTLET, *s* Lamhuinn iaruinn; bracan

GAUNTLY, *adv.* Gu tana, gu caol, gu cruaidh, gu seang, gu bochd, gu truagh.

GAUZE, *s.* Sròl, pearluinn

GAWK, *s.* Cuthag; (*a stupid person*), umaidh, baoghlan; òinnseach

GAWNTREE, *s.* Sorchan leigidh, stòl.

GAY, *a* Beò, brisg, sunntach, aighearach, suilbhear, mear, eutrom; (*gallant*), uallach, sgiamhach, leomach, spairseach, grinn, barrail

GAZE, *v. n* Spleuc, spleuc, amhairc, seall, sgeann, dilbheachdaich.

GAZE-HOUND, *s.* Spleuc-mhadadh, seorsa miol-choin.

GAZER, *s* Spleucair, sgeannair.

GAZETTE, *s.* Cairteal nuaidheachd.

GAZETTEER, *s* Fear nuaidheachdan.

GAZING-STOCK, *s* Ball amhairc, ball àbhachdais, ball-àbhachd.

GEAR, *s.* Innsridh, airneis, maoin; gaoireas; carradh, breaghas.

GEESE, *s.* Geòidh.

GELABLE, *a.* So-shlamaich, so-shlamachadh.

GELATINOUS, *a.* Slamach, slamanach.

GELD, *v. a.* Spoth neach no ainmhidh, caill. Gelded, *spothta, cail te.*

GELDED, *part.* Spothta A gelded man, *fear spoghta, caillteanach.*

GELDER, *s* Spothadair, cailltear

GELDING, *s.* Each òg, loth.

GELID, *a* Reòtaidh, ro-fhuar.

GELIDITY, *s.* Fuachd, ro-fhuachd.

GELLIED, *a.* Slamaichte, slamanaichte.

GELLY, *s.* Slamag, slaman milis.

GELLY, *v n.* Slamaich.

GEM, *s.* Leug, cloch-buaidh, seud, neamhuin; neamhnaid, neònaid; ceud-bhlàth.

GEM, *v.* Sgiamhaich, sgeadaich.

GEMINATE, *v. a.* Dùblaich Geminated, *dùblaichte.*

GEMINATION, *s.* Dùblachadh.

GEMINI, *s* Na leth-aona, aon do chomharan a ghrianchrios

GEMINOUS, *a* Dùbailt, da-fhillte.

GEMINY, *s* Leth-aona, deise, paidhir, carraid.

GENDER, *s.* Gné, seorsa, gin, cineal

GENDER, *v. a.* Gin, faigh (no) beir clann

GENEALOGICAL, *a.* Sloinnteachail, seanachail

GENEALOGIST, *s.* Sloinntear, seanachaidh.

GENEALOGY, *s.* Sloinntearachd, seanachas; gineal, cineadh, sinnsearachd.

GENERAL, *a* Coitchionn, coitchionnta, cumanta; mòr. In general, *an cumantas, mar is tric.*

GENERAL, *s.* Seanarail, ceann-feadhna, ceannard feachd.

GENERALISSIMO, *s.* Ard-cheann feadhna, ard-cheannard, tuargnach catha.

GENERALITY, *s* Cumantas, coitchiontas; mòr-chuid, gharbhchuid, a chuid is mo.

GENERALLY, *adv.* Gu cumanta, an cumantas, mur as tric.

GENERALTY, *s.* An t-iomlan; a mhòr-chuid, a gharbh chuid.

GENERANT, *a* Gineach, gineadach.

GENERATE, *v a* Gin, gein; cinn; siol-chuir; craobhsgaoil; dean torrach

GENERATION, *s.* Gineal, ginealach, sliochd; siol; àl; glùn, linn.

GENERATIVE, *a.* Gineadail; gineadach; siolmhor, sliochdar, sliochdmhor, torrach, clannmhor.

GENERATOR, *s* Gineadair, fear ginidh, athair.

GENEROSITY, *s* Fuighantachd, féile, féileachd, suairceas, fialachd, suairceas, tabhartachd, fial-mhorachd, toirbheartas; mor-chùis.

GENEROUS, *a.* Fiughanta, fial, fialaidh, faoilidh, arraidh; tabhartach, suairc, fialmhor, toirbheartach, eug-mhaiseach; saoi, uasal; misneachail, suilbhear, mor-chuiseach.

GENEROUSLY, *adv* Gu fiughanta, gu fial, gu fialaidh, gu faoilidh, gu suairc, gu fialmhor, gu toirbheartach, gu h-eugmhaiseach, gu mòr-chuiseach

GENESIS, *s.* Gineal, ginealach, ceud leabhar Mhaois (no) an-t-sean tiomnaidh

GENET, *s.* Gearran Spàinnteach.

GENEVA, *s* Sùgh an aiteil

GENIAL, *a.* Nadurra, gineamhuinneach; gineil, caoimhneil; suilbhear, aighearach. Genial spring, *an t-earrach caoimhneil*

GENICULATED, *a.* Mulpach, meallanach, plucach, plucanach.

GENITAL, *a.* Gineadach.

GENITALS, *s.* Buill dhiomhair; ionairc.

GENITIVE, *s.* Gineamhuinneach.

GENITIVE, *a.* Gineamhuinneach.

GENIUS, *s.* Cumhachd inntinn; càil; nàdur; tùr; càil-eachd. A good genius, *deagh spiorad;* an evil genius, *droch spiorad.*

GENTEEL, *a.* Suairc, modhail; stuama; eireachdail, tlachd-mhor, fiùranta; dàicheil; fàicheil uasal; deas; snàsda, ciatach. Genteelly, *gu suairc, gu modhail; gu h-eire-achdail, gu tlachdmhor, gu fiùranta.* No man is more genteel than his trade, *cha 'n uaillse duine na cheirde.*

GENTEELNESS, *s.* Suairceas, modhaileachd, stuaim; eir-eachdas, tlachdmhoireachd, fiùrantachd; dàichealachd; uaillse.

GENTIAN, *s.* Lus a chubhain, muilceann.

GENTILE, *s.* Gintealach, fear do nach aithne Dia, Pàganach, neo-chreideach, fiadh-chreideach.

GENTILE, *a.* Gintealach, Pàgantach; ana-creideach.

GENTILISM, *s.* Gintealachd, Pagantachd, iodhal-aoradh.

GENTILITIOUS, *a.* Dùchasach, dùthchasach.

GENTILITY, *s.* Suairceas, modhalachd; eireachdas; tlachd-mhoireachd.

GENTLE, *a.* (*In manner*), seimh, ciùin, caomh, mallta, suairc, soirbh, baigheil; samhach; (*as a beast*), soitheamh, soimeach, socrach, ceannsa; (*to the touch*), mìn; (*in birth*), uasal, inmheach, mòr, breth-inmheach; ard. A gentle breeze, *gaoth sheimh, gaoth shoirbheasach, feochan gaoithe.*

† GENTLE, *s.* Uasal, duine uasal.

GENTLEFOLK, *s.* Uaislean, uailsean.

GENTLEMAN, *s.* Duine-uasal. Gentlemen, *daoine uasal.*

GENTLEMANLIKE, *a.* Mar-dhuine uasal, eireachdail, modh-ail, ciatach.

GENTLENESS, *s.* (*In birth*), uaillse, airde, inmheachd; (*in manner*), seimheachd, suairceas; caomhalachd, macantas; socair, soirbhe, ciùineas, ciùineachd.

GENTLEWOMAN, *s.* Bean uasal, bantighearn, baintighearna.

GENTLY, *adv.* Gu seimh, gu caomh, gu ciùin; gu suairc; gu soirbh; gu macanta; gu baigheil; gu socrach, gu soimeach. Go gently, *rach air do shocair, dean air do shocair;* gently, gently, *socair, socair; socair ort.*

GENTRY, *s.* Uaislean, uailsean.

GENUFLECTION, *s.* Glùn lubadh.

GENUINE, *a.* Fior, neo-thruaillte, glan, fireannach, oireamh-nach; nadurrail.

GENUINENESS, *s.* Neo-thruaillteachd, glaine, oireamhnachd.

GENUS, *s.* Seorsa, gné; modh, nòs; fineur, teaghlach, clann, sliochd; toiseach fine.

GEOGRAPHER, *s.* Tlachd-sgriobhair, cruinne-ghrabhair, cé-ghrabhair, fonn-grabhair.

GEOGRAPHICAL, *a.* Tlachdach; cruinneadach, cé-ghrabhail.

GEOGRAPHY, *s.* Cruinne-eòlas, cé-ghrabhadh, tlachd-sgri-obhadh.

GEOLOGY, *s.* Cruinne-eolas.

GEOMANCER, *s.* Fiosaiche, druidh, draoidh; cleasaiche; mealltair.

GEOMANCY, *s.* Fiosachd, druidheachd.

GEOMANTIC, *a.* Fiosachail; druidheach.

GEOMETER, *s.* Cruinne-thomhasair, cé-thomhasair; tlachd-thomhasair.

GEOMETRIC, GEOMETRICAL, *a.* Cruinne-thoimhseach, cé-thoimhseach.

GEOMETRICALLY, *adv.* Gu cé-thoimhseach.

GEOMETRICIAN, *s.* Cruinne-thomhasair, cé-thomhasair.

GEOMETRY, *s.* Cé-thomhas, tlachd-thomhas, cruinne-thomhas.

GEORGE, *s.* Dealbh Dheorsa an naoimh air muin eich.

GEORGIC, *s.* Dàn tuathanachd.

GERM, *s.* Fiùran; fàillean; maothan; gineag; gineamhuinn.

† GERMAN, *a.* Càirdeach, dìleas.

GERMAN, *s.* Caraid. A brother-german, *dearbh-bhrathair;* a sister-german, *dearbh-phiuthar.*

GERMAN, *s.* and *a.* Gearmailteach.

GERMANDER, *s.* Seorsa plannta, darag thalmhainn.

GERMINATE, *v. n.* Gin, fas; thig fo bhlàth.

GERMINATION, *s.* Gineamhuinn, gineadh; fàilleanachadh, fàilleanachd, fàs, cinneas, cur a mach.

GESTATION, *s.* Truime-cuim, leth-tromachd, torraichead.

† GESTS, *s.* Gniomharan gaisgeil.

GESTICULATE, *v. n.* Dean ain-cheart, bi ain-cheartach, bi atharraiseach.

GESTICULATING, *a.* Ain-cheartach, atharraiseach.

GESTICULATION, *s.* An-cheartachd, atharraiseachd, atharr-ais, baoth-chleasachd.

GESTURE, *s.* Giùlan, iomchar, modh, gnùis.

GET, *v. a.* and *n.* Faigh; ((*gain*), coisinn, buidhinn; (*procure*), solair; (*learn*), foghluim; (*reach*), ruig. Get aside, *rach gu taobh;* get off, *bi falbh; thoir an rathad ort;* get acquainted, *faigh eolach;* get *or* beget, *gin;* get with child, *faigh urr ri;* get by heart, *faigh air do chridhe* (*no*) *air do chuimhne;* you cannot get at it, *cha n' urradh dhuit ruigheachd air.*

GETTER, *s.* Fear faotainn; gineadair; gintear.

GETTING, *s.* Faotainn, faghaltas, coisinn, buidhinn; solar; tairbhe.

GEWGAW, *s.* Faoin-rud, aileagan, faoineachd, culaidh-chleasachd.

GHASTLINESS, *s.* Eugaileachd, aogaileachd, taibhsealachd, bàine, glasdachd, do-neulachd; eagallachd.

GHASTLY, *a.* Eugail, aogail, taibhseil, do-neulmhor, uabh-asach, ailmseach; smeileach, tana, truagh.

GHERKIN, *s.* Cularan saillte.

GHOST, *s.* Taibhse, aibhse, tannasg, aog, eug, ailmse, spiorad, bodach, bòcan; an treas pearsa do 'n Trianaid; an Spiorad Naomh; anam, deò. Give up the ghost, *faigh bas, rach eug, thoir suas an deò.*

GHOSTLY, *a.* Spioradail, spioradalta, neo-fheolmhor.

GIANT, *s.* Famhair, fuamhair, fathach, athach, àbhas, † lalach.

GIANTESS, *s.* Ban-fhamhair, ban-athach.

GIANTLIKE, *a.* Famhaireach, athachail, mòr, uamhasach.

GIANTSHIP, *s.* Famhaireachd.

GIBBERISH, *s.* All-ghlòr; glòr, sgleò, giolam; tuath-chainnt; cainnt cheard.

GIBBET, *s.* Croich.

GIBBET, *v. a.* Croch. Gibbetted, crochta, crochte, air a chrochadh.

GIBBOSITY, *s.* Cruit, crotachd, dronnachd.

GIBBOUS, *a.* Crotach, dronnach.

GIBCAT, *s.* Sean chat.

GIBE, *v. a.* and *n.* Fanaid, mag, fochaid, dean fanaid, dean fochaid; cuir air ioladh; beum; gearr; thoir beum air; thoir dheth.

GIBE, *s.* Magadh, fanaid thàireil, sgeige, beum; gearradh, buirte.

GIBER, *s.* Magair, fear fochaid, sgeigear, beumair.

GIBINGLY, *adv.* Gu beumnach, gu fochaideach, gu sgeigeil, gu tarcuiseach.

GIBLET, *s.* Turusgar geoidh, no mheud 's a ghearar dheth mun ròistear e.

GIDDILY, *adv.* Gu neo-bhunailteach, gu h-eutrom, gu gaoithe, gu mi-sheadhail, gu neo-churamach, gu diudan-ach, gu guanach.

GIDDINESS, *s.* Tuaineal, tuainealachd; tuàicheal; diudan, eutromas, eutruime, neo-bhunailteachd, iomluas, guanachd, guanachas; gogailleachd

GIDDY, *a* Diudanach, eutrom, guanach, gaoithe, neo-sheadhail, neo-churamach, (*unsteady*), neo-bhunailteach, neo-sheasmhach, iom-luath, luaineach, mughteach.

GIDDYBRAINED, *a.* Eutrom, gaoithe, guanach, neo-sgoinnear, iollapach.

GIDDYPACED, *a.* Luaineach

GIFT, *s.* Tiodhlac, tabhartas, gibhte; deolchair, brontanas, eirneadh, cumhachd, (*of nature*), feart, càil, tùr Free gift, *saor-thabhartas*, gift of bounty, *oir-chiseachd*

GIFTED, *a* Builichte, càilichte.

GIG, *s* Ruithlean, roithlean; aileagan, srannan, srannachan; carbad beag air dhà chuidhle

GIGANTIC, *a* Famhaireach, athachail; mòr; tomadach

GIGGLE, *v n* Sior-ghair, sitrich

GIGGLET, *s.* Gogaill, gogailt; oinnseach.

GIGGLING, *s* Sitrich

GILD, *v a* Òr, òraich dealtraich, deiltrich Gilded, *òraichte, deiltrichte*

GILD, *s* Càin, cìse; comunn, bratharreachas.

GILDER, *s.* Òradair, deiltriche.

GILDING, *s.* Òradh, dealtradh, deiltreadh.

GILL, *s* Siola, siolag; (*of fish*), giùran.

GILLHOUSE, *s* Tigh-lionna, tigh òsda

GILLYFLOWER, *s* Lus leth an t-samhruidh; pincean

GIM, *a.* Innealta, finealta, sgilmeil, sginmeil, snàsmhor, deas, sgairteil

GIMLET, *s.* Gimleid, tolladair, toradh tairnge.

GIN, *s.* Lion, ribe, gaisde, painntir, brigh an aiteil

GINGER, *s.* Dinnseir, ràcadal.

GINGERBREAD, *s* Aran milis

GINGERLY, *a* Faiceallach, cùramach, sicir.

GINGIVAL, *a.* Càireanach

GINGLE, *s* Gleang, gleangarsaich, gliosgar

GINGLING, *a.* Gleangach, gleangarsach, gliosgarach

GINGLING, *s* Gleangail, gleangarsaich

GIPSY, *s* Ruagalaiche, ceard, ban-cheard; ban-fhiosaiche, giobag

GIRANDOLE, *s* Coinnlear meurach

GIRASOL, *s.* Plùr na gréine; seud uasal

GIRD, *v a* Crioslaich; giortaich, ceangail, druid, cuartaich, cuàirtich

GIRD, *s* Greim, guin.

GIRDED, *part* Crioslaichte, giortaichte, ceangailte, cuartaichte, cuairtichte; sgeadaichte, uigheamaichte, eudaichte

GIRDLE, *s* Crios, giort; cuairteag, cuairtle, bann, iolann My tongue is not under your girdle, *cha n' eil mo theangadh fo d' chrios*

GIRDLE, *v* Crioslaich; druid, dùin, iom-dhruid

GIRDLE-BELT, *s* Crios, crios cuim

GIRL, *s* Caileag, nionag, cailinn, caile A clumsy girl, *gustag, ban caile*

GIRT, GIRTH, *s.* Crios, bronnach, tarrach, giort, cuairte.

GIRTH, *v.* Giortaich

GIVE, *v a.* Thabhair, thoir, tabhair, builich; deonaich, ceadaich; fuiling Give away, *thoir air falbh*, give forth, *leig ris, nochd, foillsich*, give back, *thoir air ais*, give freely, *thoir (no) builich gu deònach, toirbheir, deonaich*, give ear, *thoir éisdeachd, éisd*, give over or desist, *sguir*, *leig dhiot, stad*; give out or distribute, *riaraich, pàirtich*; give way, *géill, rach gu taobh*, give up, *cuitich, tiomnadh, liobhair, thoir suas, sguir*, give in, *thoir stigh; géill.*

GIVEN, *part.* Builichte, air a thoirt. Given to wine, *deidheil air fion*, given over for dead, *a dheth.*

GIVER, *s.* Tabhairtear, tabhairtiche, fear buileachaidh.

GIVES, *s.* Ceanglaichean, geibhlean, cuibhrichean.

GIVING, *s.* Tabhairt, toirt, buileachadh.

GIZZARD, *s* Sgròban, geuban, ciaban, goile.

GLACIAL, *a.* Eigheil, reòta, reòidhte, reotaidh.

GLACIATE, *v.* Reoth.

GLACIATION, *s.* Reothadh, ròtadh, reòtadh.

GLAD, *a.* Aoibhinn, eibhinn, aoibhneach, ait, toileach, sodanach, sugach, subhach, aighearach, sunndach, cridheil.

GLADDEN, *v a.* Dean aoibhinn (no) aoibhneach, dean ait, (no) cridheil, dean sunntach (no) sodanach, tog, thoir sòlas.

GLADDER, *s.* Fear togalach (no) misneachaidh, fear sòlais, furtachair

GLADE, *s.* Leanuinn-coille, reithlean coille, blàran.

GLADIATOR, *s.* Basbair, gleachdair, duais-chathaiche, cearraiche claidheimh; *feannsair.*

GLADLY, *adv* Gu h-aobhinn, gu h-éibhinn, gu h-ait, gu toileach, gu sodanach, gu sugach, gu subhach, gu h-aighearach, gu sunndach, gu cridheil.

GLADNESS, *s* Aoibhneas, éibhneas, aiteas, toil-inntinn, gàirdeachas, suilbhearachd, subhachas.

GLADSOME, *a* Ait, sòlasach, taitneach.

GLAIRE, *s.* Gealagan uibhe.

GLANCE, *s* Plath, soluis, baoisge, platha-bhaoisge, grad-bhaoisge; platha sùl, gliosg. I got a glance of it, *fhuair mi plath dheth*

GLANCE, *v.* Grad-sheall, grad-amhairc; thoir plath; boisg; gliolc, grad-imich

GLAND, *s* Faireag, faithnidh Full of glands, *fàireagach.*

GLANDERS, *s* Gràn aobrainn.

GLANDIFEROUS, *a* Fàireagach

GLARE, *v n.* Baoisg, soillsich, dealraich, dearrsaich; (*with the eyes*), sgeann, spleuc.

GLARE, *s* Dealradh, dealrachd, dearrsa, soillse, baoisge lannair; (*of the eyes*), spleuc, sgeann, sgeannadh.

GLASS, *s.* Gloine. Drink off your glass, *òl (no) sguab as do ghloine*, an hour glass, *uaireadair gainciмh*, a dressing-glass, *sgàthan*

GLASS, *a* Gloinidh, gloineach

GLASS-GRINDER, *s* Gloineadair

GLASS-HOUSE, *s* Tigh ghloineachan; tigh-teth

GLASS-MAKING, *s.* Gloineadaireachd.

GLASS-MAN, *s* Gloineadair

GLASS-WORK, *s* Obair-ghloine

GLASS-WORT, *s.* Seorsa luibh

GLASSY, *a.* Gloinidh, gloineach, sleamhuinn, min, soilleir.

GLAVE, *s* Claidheamh

GLAVER, *v n* Dean miodal (no) sodal.

GLAVERING, *a.* Miodalach, sodalach, goileamach, beulchar.

GLAZE, *v* Gloinich Glazed, *foinichte.*

GLAZIER, *s.* Gloineadair

GLAZING, *s.* Gloineachadh, sliomachadh.

GLEAM, *s.* Baoisge, boillsge, lannair, gath soluis, drilinn.

GLEAM, *v. n.* Baoisg, boillsg, lannair; dearrs; drilinn.

GLEAMING, GLEAMY, *a* Soillseach, baoisgeach, gathach; caoireach; dearsach, drilinneach.

Glean, *v* Dioghluim; teanail seasgan; cruinnich. Gleaning corn, *a dioghlum arbhair.*

Gleaning, *s.* Dioghlum; seasgan; spruilleach.

Glebe, *s.* Gllob, fearann ministeir; fonn, clod; caob.

Glebous, *a.* Clodach, caobach.

Glede, *s.* Clamban, claman, clamhan gobhlach; seabhag.

Glede, Gleid, *s.* Eibhleag.

Glee, *s* Sunnt, aighear, aiteas, toil-inntinn, aoibhneas, mire; sunntan

Gleeful, *a.* Sunntach, aighearrach, ait, aoibhinn, eibhinn, mearr, sugach, cridheil.

Gleek, *s.* Ceòl; fear ciùil.

† **Gleek**, *v. a.* Mag; fanoid, fochaid

Gleen, *v. n* Soillsich, lannair, baoisg.

Gleet, *s* Ruitheadh, sruthadh, sileadh, siol-shruthadh; sruth-chonain, *clap*

Gleet, *v. n.* Ruith, sruth, sil

Gleety, *a.* Ruithteach, silteach, sruthach.

Glen, *s.* Gleann. A little glen, *gleannan*, glens, *glinn.*

Glib, *s.* Min, réidh, sleamhuinn; ruithteach, so-ruithleadh, ruithleach. Glibly, *gu réidh*

Glibness, *s.* Minead, sleamhneachd.

Glide, *v n.* Sleamhnaich; ruith gu seimh.

Glimmer, *v.* Breac-shoillsich, fann-shoillsich.

Glimmer, *s.* Breac-sholus, fann-sholus, gann-sholus.

Glimmering, *a.* Fann, (no) gann ann an solus. A glimmering light, *solus gann.*

Glimpse, *s.* Sealladh, goirrid, plath, solus gann.

Glisten, *v. n.* Soillsich; lonnraich, lannraich.

Glister, *v. n.* Soillsich, lannair; lonnraich, lannraich, dealraich.

Glistering, *a.* Soilleir, lannaireach, lonnaireach, dealrach.

Glitter, *v.* Dealraich, soillsich, dearsaich, lonnraich, lannraich, lannair; boisg.

Glitter, *s.* Dealradh, dearsadh; breaghas.

Glittering, *a.* Soilleir; dealrach, dearsach, lonnaireach, lannaireach, loinreach

Gloar, *v. n.* Seall fiar (no) claon.

Globard, *s.* Cuileag shionnachain.

Globated, *a* Cruinn, cearslaichte.

Globe, *s.* Ball, cearsal; cuairteag; cuach; ni iom-chruinn sam bi. The terrestrial globe, *an cruinn cé, an cruinne*

Globy, *a.* Cruinn, ball-chruinn.

Globular, *a.* Cruinn, ball-chruinn; bas-charnta; cearslach, ceirtleach, ceartlach, cearclach.

Globule, *s.* Bolg, bolgan, builgean.

Glomerate, *v. a.* Cearslaich, ceirslich, dean ball-chruinn, dean iom-chruinn. Glomerated, *cearslaichte, ceartlaichte, cruinn, iom-chruinn.*

Glomeration, *s.* Cearslachadh, ceartlachadh, ceirsleachadh

Glomerose, *a.* Cruinn, ball-chruinn; ceartlaichte.

Gloom, *s.* Duibhre, duirche, doirche, doilleireachd, dorchadas, dubhar, dubhradh, gruamaichead, doirchead gruamaiche, gruaim; (*of sorrow*), dubhachas, truime, bròn, dubh-bhròn, duiseal.

Gloom, *v. n.* Gruamaich, dorchaich; bi gruamach, cuir gruaim ort The day gloomed, *dhorchaich an là.*

Gloomily, *adv.* Gu gruamach, gu dorcha, gu doilleir; gu dubhach, gu tuirseach, gu neo-shunntach.

Gloominess, *s.* Gruamachd, gruaim, gruaimean, duibhre, gruamaichead, doilleireachd; duirche; neo-shuilbhearachd, duilbhire; truim-inntinn, dubhachas.

Gloomy, *a.* Gruamach, dorcha, dubharach, doilleir; (*in mind*), trom, dubhach, muladach; duisealach, duisneulach, dubhar.

Gloria Patri, *s.* Glòir Dhé.

Glorification, *s.* Glòraicheadh, moladh, glòir, iomlanachd glòir.

Glorify, *v. a.* Glòraich; mol, ard-mhol; ardaich; thoir ardurram, thoir gloir, thoir aoradh, dean aoradh Glorified, *glòraichte, naomhaichte, beannuichte, neamhuidh.*

Glorious, *a.* Glòirmhor, mòr, mordha, mòrdhalach, beannuichte, neamhuidh, naomh, flath-mhaiseach, òirdheirc, urramach, uasal, ard, sàr; corr, urramach.

Gloriously, *adv.* Gu gloirmhor, gu mordha; gu beannuichte, gu flath-mhaiseach, gu h-oirdheirc, gu corr

Glory, *s.* Glòir, moladh, ard-mholadh, ard-chliù, urram, caithream; dealradh, dearsadh, soillse.

Glory, *v. n.* Dean uaill, dean ràiteachas, dean bòsd.

Glose, Gloze, *v. a* Dean miodal, meall, breug.

Gloss, *s.* Mineachadh; soillseachadh; sliogadh, sliobadh, liomhadh

Gloss, *v.* Minich, soillsich, sliog, sliob, liomh.

Glossary, *s.* Foclair

Glossator, *s* Mineachair, fear mineachaidh.

Glossed, *a.* Minichte, sliogaichte, sliobta, liomhta.

Glosser, *s.* Mineachair; liomhair

Glossographer, *s* Fear mineachaidh

Glossy, *a.* Sliosmhor, sliobarra, sliogta, liomh, liomharra, min, soillseach, soilleir, lannaireach.

Glottis, *s.* Detiach

Glove, *s*, Lamhuinn; meatag, miotag; bracan

Glover, *s.* Lamhuinnear, lamhuinniche, fear lamhuinn.

Gloveress, *s.* Ban-lamhuinniche

Glout, *v.* Seall le gruaim.

Glouting, *a* Dodach, stodach, gruamach, stodanach, dùr.

Glow, *v. n.* Leus, loisg, teòth, las, feargaich He glowed with anger, *lus e le corruich.*

Glowing, *a.* Leusach, loisgeach, teth, dian-theth, lasanta

Glow, *s.* Teas, dian-theas, gaoir-theas; dian-fhearg, dian-chorruich

Glow-worm, *s.* Cnuimh-shionnachain, cuileag shionnachain

Gloze, *s* Miodal, sodal, goileam, blanndar.

Glozer, *s* Miodalaiche, sodalaiche, goileamair.

Glozing, *s.* Miodal, sodal, goileam blanndar.

Glozing, *a.* Miodalach, sodalach, goileamach

Glue, *v a.* Glaodh; tàth. Glued, *glaoidhte, tàthte*

Glue, *s* Glaodh, bigh

Gluer, *s.* Glaodhair, tàthair

Glum, *a.* Gruamach, dorch, dùr, gnò

Glut, *v. a.* Lion, sàsuich, lion gu sàth, giorr, sluig Glutted, *sasuichte, làn-bhuidheach, làn.*

Glut, *s.* Lan, sàth, teann-shath; iomarcadh, tuille is a chòir.

Glutinous, *a.* Glaodhail, glaodhar, bitheanta, leanailteach, rithinn, sticeach

Glutton, *s.* Craosair, geòcair, glamhair, glamhaiche, glamhsair, slugair, bagair

Gluttony, *s* Craosaireachd, geòcaireachd, glamhaireachd, slugaireachd, bagaireachd, craos, graigeanas

Gluy, *a.* Glaodhar, bitheanta, leanailteach, rithinn, sticeach.

Gnarl, *v* Dean drannd mar ni cù

Gnarled, *a* Meallach, mulpach, mulpanach, plucach, plucanach; gathach; neo-lom

Gnash, *v. a.* Diosgain, giosgain, cas na fiaclan, snag na fiarlan; bi fo chorruich. They gnashed at him, *chas iad am fiaclan ris.*

Gnat, *s.* Meanbh-chuileag.

Gnaw, *v. a.* Cnamh, creim, ith, cagainn; caith. Gnawed, *cnamhta, creimte, cagainnte, caithte;* gnawing, *moibleadh.*

Gnomon, *s.* Snathad (no) pinne uaireadair greine.

Go, *v. n.* Rach, imich, falbh, theirig, gabh, siubhail, gluais, triall, bi 'g coiseachd, bi a triall, bi 'g imeachd. Go hang yourself, *gabh gu do chrochadh;* go about your business, *gabh mu d' ghnothuch;* go after, *lean, rach an tòir;* go backward, *rach air ais, rach an comhar do chùil;* go beyond or cheat, *meall, thoir an car a;* go in, *rach a steach; inntrinn;* go out, as fire, *rach as;* go on, *rach air adhairt;* go up, *rach an airde, rach a suas, dìr;* go aside, *rach gu taobh (no) air seacharan;* go to meet, *rach an coinneamh, rach an còdhail;* go to meet him, *rach na choinneamh;* go forward, *rach air adhairt;* go forward, or thrive, *thig spéid, soirbhich.*

Goad, *s.* Bior, bior greasaidh, brog; ceaan-chunn.

Goad, *v. a.* Bior, greas, brog, stuig, spor, cuir h-uige, brosnuich. Goaded, *greasta, brugta, stuigte.*

Goal, *s.* Ceann-uighe, crioch bàire; crioch, ceann, ceann-thall.

Goat, *s.* Gabhar, gobhar. A year old goat, *miseach;* a goat's hide, *boiceann.* The goat is deaf when she plucks the ripe ear, *bithidh a ghabhar bodhar san fhoghar.*

Goatchaffer, *s.* Seorsa daòil.

Goatherd, *s.* Buachaill ghabhar.

Goatish, *a.* Gobharail; drùiseil; macnusach; slatail.

Gobbet, *s.* Glaim, glamhsa, lan beòil, greim, mìre, smat; durc, plaoic. At one gobbet, *air aon ghlamhsa.*

Gobbet, *v. a.* Sluig, glug.

Gobble, *v.* Sluig, glug, sluig gu lonach.

Gobbler, *s.* Glàmair, glamhsair, slugair, geocair, craosair.

Go-between, *s.* Fear eadargain.

Goblet, *s.* Gòblait, aghann, cuach, copan, sgalan.

Goblin, *s.* Bòcan, taibhse, ùraisg, bodach; sithiche, ailmse.

Go-by, *s.* Car, cuilbheart; seòl.

God, *s.* Dia; ni math; iodhal. For Godsake, *air ghaol Dia, air ghaol ni math;* God be with, *Dia leat;* by God's help, *a dheòin Dia;* God forbid! *nar leigeadh Dia!* God speed you! *Dia leat;* God bless you! *beannachd Dhé leat! beannachd leat!*

Godchild, *s.* Dalta; leanabh baistidh.

God-daughter, *s.* Dalta bainionn, dalta inghinn.

Goddess, *s.* Bandia.

Godfather, *s.* Oide.

Godhead, *s.* Diadhachd.

Godless, *a.* Mi-dhiadhaidh; ain-diadhuidh; baoth; pàganta.

Godlike, *a.* Diadhail, mar Dhia; flath-mhaiseach.

Godliness, *s.* Diadhaidheachd, diadhachd; fior-chràbhadh.

Godly, *a.* Diadhaidh, naomh, cràbhach, math; ionraic fìreannach, saoi.

Godmother, *s.* Muime, mathair baistidh.

Godson, *s.* Dalta, dalta fir, mac baistidh.

Godward, *adv.* Chum De.

Godwit, *s.* Seorsa eoin.

Goer, *s.* Coisiche, siùbhlaiche.

Goff, *s.* Cluiche liathroide.

Goffclub, *s.* Caman.

Gog, *s.* Iomairt, gog. A gog for a thing, *an càs air ni.*

Goggle, *v.* Seall claon, seall fiar, (no) fiar-shuileach.

Goggle-eyed, *a.* Claon, starr-shuileach, fiar shuileach.

Going, *s.* Dol, falbh, coiseachd, imeachd, gluasad, trialladh; (*pregnancy*), leth-tromachd. A going back, *pilltinn, dol air ais;* set him a-going, *cuir air deannanaich e;* a going down, *dol sios; dol a bhàn;* as of the sun, *dol fuidh, luidhe.*

Gold, *s.* Òr. Yellow as gold, *buidhe mar an òr;* gold ore, *méin oir.*

Goldbeater, *s.* Fear dheanamh òr-dhuilleag.

Goldbeater's-leaf, *s.* Sgrath croicne a chuireas iad cadar na h-òr dhuilleagan, aig am dhoibh bhi gam bualadh mach.

Goldbound, *a.* Or-cheangailte, òr-chuairtichte.

Golden, *a.* Òrach, ordha, òrail, mar an òr, buidhe, òr-bhuidhe, dealrach, loinnreach; luachmhòr, priseil, grinn; sona.

Goldfinch, *s.* Lasair choille; buidheag.

Goldfoil, *s.* Òr-dhuilleag.

Goldheaded, *a.* Òr-cheannach.

Goldleaf, *s.* Or-dhuille, òr-dhuilleag.

Goldsmith, *s.* Òr-cheard.

Gome, *s.* An dubh-shal a chruinnicheas eadar rotha agus aisil cartach.

Gondola, *s.* Sgoth Eadailteach, eithear.

Gone, *p. part.* of go. Air falbh; air folbh; air imeachd, caillte; marbhta, marbh; dheth. I am gone, *tha mise dheth;* gone to wreck and ruin, *air dol ghlan dholaidh;* gone to nothing, *air dol gu neoni;* get you gone, *bi falbh, bi triall; thoir an rathad ort, gabh romhad;* gone with child, *leth-tromach;* gone in liquor, *air a mheisge, air an daoraich;* gone in years, *aosmhor, sean; ann an sgrog aois;* gone out, *air dol a mach;* he is quite gone (dead), *tha e riaraichte (no) dheth;* he is a gone man, *tha e dheth.*

+ Gonfalon, *s.* Suaicheantas, bratach, meirghe.

Gonorrhœa, *s.* Clap.

Good, *a.* (*In morals*), math, maith; deagh, diadhaidh, ionraic, còir, onorach, direach, tréibhireach, fior; (*merciful*), tròcaireach; baigheil; (*convenient*), iomchuidh, freagarrach, ceart; uidhiseil; (*wholesome*), math, fallain, slainnteil; (*complete*), làn, iomlan, foirfe, coimhlionta; (*skilful*), sgileil, teoma; (*decent*), beusach, ciatach, eireachdail; (*social*), mear, sunntach, deagh, cridheil, ro. A good man, *duine math, deagh dhuine, ro dhuine;* a good day's work, *deagh obair là;* I have a good mind, *tha mhiann orm, tha mi 'los;* a good deal, *mòran, mar mhòr, dorlach;* a good deal of people, *dorlach sluaigh;* good for nothing, *gun fhiach, gun fhiù;* in good faith, *air mo riar, air mo bhriathar;* in good time, *ann an deagh thràth;* as good as, *cho mhaith ri;* make good, *coimh-lion;* good and quickly seldom meet, *cha bhi luathas agus grinneas;* he is as good a man as lives, *tha e na dhuine cho mhaith 's a tha beò, is e roghadh nan daoine e.*

Good, *s.* Math, maithe, leas, tairbhe; soirbheas; adhas; sgabhaiste; rìreamh; subhailc, deagh-bheus. It will do you good, *ni e maith dhuit;* he who does not see his good, has missed the purpose of being wise, *am fear leis nach léir a leas, is mor do cheill a chailleas e.*

Goodliness, *s.* Maise, maisealachd, eireachdas, sgiamh, dàichealachd, ceanaltas.

Goodly, *a.* Maiseach, sàr-mhaiseach, eireachdail, sgiamhach, ciatach, boidheach, dreachmhor, daicheil, grinn, ceanalta; sultmhor, dòmhail.

Goodman, *s.* Fear tighe. The goodman, *fear an tighe.*

Goodness, *s.* Maitheas; ionracas, treibhdhireas; baigh, fabhor, trocair.

Goods, *s.* Maoin; bàthar; earrdha; airneis, uigheam; codach, cuid.

Goodwife, *s.* Bean tighe. The goodwife, *bean an tighe.*

Goody, *s.* Banag

Goosander, *s.* Sioltaiche.

Goose, *s* Geadh. Geese, *geòidh*; wild geese, *muir-gheoidh*, a tailor's goose, *geadh, iarunn tàileir*; the leader of a flock of wild geese, *feadhan*, where there are geese there are goslings, *far am bi geoidh bithidh iseanan.*

Gooseberry, *s.* Grosaid, groiseid, spiontag.

Goosecap, *s.* Baoghlan, baothair.

Goosegrass, *s.* Garbh-lus.

Gordian-knot, *s.* Dubh-shnaim, snuim nach 'gabh fuasgladh.

Gorbellied, *a.* Bronnach, bagach; gaor-bhronnach, reamhar; dumhail, domhail, garrach.

Gorbelly, *s.* Bag, seileid, bagair, bronnair.

Gore, *s.* Fuil, flann, cru; fuil shlamach, braghadh.

Gore, *v.* Sàth, lot, gon, beubanaich.

Gorge, *s.* Sgornan, sgornach, deiach; goile.

Gorge, *v. a.* Lion, sàsuich, lion gu ruig na sgornan; dean sàthach, sàth; dean sàth, sluig. Gorged, *lionta, sàsuichte.*

Gorgeous, *a.* Bragh, breagh, riomhach; spleadhnach, moralach, gasda; balardach, lonnair. Gorgeously, *gu briagh, gu riomhach, gu mòralach, gu lonnair.*

Gorgeousness, *s.* Briaghachd, riomhachd, spleadhnachas.

Gorget, *s.* Eididh muineil, gòrsaid.

Gormand, *s.* Craosair, geocair, bagair, glutair, glamhair.

Gormandize, *v.* Craos, glutaich, glàmhaich, sluig, lion, sàsuich.

Gormandizing, *s.* Craos, craosaireachd, glutaireachd, glamhaireachd.

Gorse, *s* Conasg, preas deilgneach.

Gory, *a.* Fuilteach.

Goshawk, *s.* Seabhag mhor

Gosling, *s.* Isean, isean geoidh, geadh òg.

Gospel, *s.* Soisgeul.

Gospelled, *part.* Soisgeulaichte.

Goss. See Gorse.

Gossip, *v. n.* Dean lonais, bi a goisdeachd.

Gossip, *s.* Oide, goisdidh, companach, combach; lonag, sgeilm urr lonach, sràcair, goisdidh

Gossiping, *s.* Céilidh; sràcaireachd, goisdeachd. The gossiping stroke, *earrag chéilidh.*

Got, *pret* of get. Fhuair, choisinn, bhuidhinn, bhuain. See Get.

Gotten, *part.* Air fhaotainn; coisinnte, buidhinnte; ginte.

Govern, *v. a.* Riaghail, riaghailtich; riaghlaich, stiùir, smachd, ceannsaich. Governed, *riaghlaichte, ceannsaichte*

Governable, *a.* So-riaghlaidh, umhall, so-smachdaidh, so-stiùraidh

Governance, *s.* Riaghladh, stiùradh, comannt

Governant, Governess, *s* Ban-mhaighstir, ban-tuitear, bean oilein.

Governed, *part.* See Govern.

Government, *s.* Riaghlachadh, riaghladh; riaghailt; flaitheachd; (*of a ship*), sgiobaireachd.

Governor, *s.* Riaghladair; uachdaran; riaghlair, tuitear, oide ionnsuich, maighistir; ollamh; (*of a ship*), stiuradair, sgiobair.

Gouge, *s.* Seorsa gileib.

Gourd, *s.* Seorsa plannta, gùrd.

Gout, *s.* Tinneas nan alt, alt-thinneas; gut.

Gout, *s.* Blas; toile, miann, togar.

Gown, *s* Gùn. A short gown, *gùn goirrid*, a bedgown, *gùn oidhche.*

Gowned, *s.* Gùnaichte

Gownsman, *s* Fear gùin

Grabble, *v. n.* Meuraich, smeuraich, lamhrachdaich, sgmògraich

Grabbling, *s.* Meurachadh, smeurachadh, lamhrachadh smògarsaich.

Grace, *s* (*Favour*), gràs, fàbhor, deagh-ghean, caoimhneas, (*virtue*), subhailc, beus, deagh-bheus; (*pardon*), maitheanas, mathanas, baigh, trocair, truacantas, deolaidh, (*of exterior*), maise, eireachdas, dàichealachd, sgeimhe, breaghas, àille; (*privilege*), còire, ceart; (*at meat*), altach, altachadh, beannachd; tiotal Diùchd agus ard Easbuig With a good grace, *gu cubhaidh, gu h-eireachdail, gu lathailteach*, grace-cup, *deoch slainnte, deoch an doruis*

Grace, *v* Briaghaich, breaghaich, sgeaduich, sgiamhaich, grinnich, naisnich.

Grace-cup, *s* Deoch an doruis, deoch slainnte.

Graceful, *a* Maiseach, boidheach, eireachdail, ciatach, briagh, dàicheil.

Gracefully, *adv.* Gu maiseach, gu boidheach, gu h-eireachdail, gu ciatach.

Gracefulness, *s.* Maise, dàichealachd, ciataichead, eireachdas, grinneas.

Graceless, *a.* Gun ghràs, mi-naomh, aingidh, dubhailceach; tréigte; beag-narach, beadaidh.

Graces, *s* Maoidhean, deagh-thoil, deagh ghean

Gracious, *a* Gràsmhor, tròcaireach, baigheil, suairc, caomh, còir, caoimhneil; deagh-bheusach, taitneach, modhail. Gracious God! *a Dhé ghrasmhoire!*

Graciously, *adv* Gu gràsmhor, gu trocaireach, gu baigheil, gu suairc, gu caomh, gu còir, gu caoimhneil, gu cairdeil, gu taitneach, gu modhail

Graciousness, *s* Gràsmhorachd, tròcair, baighealachd, suairceas; modhaileachd.

Gradation, *s.* Ceumnadh, éiridh; foi-cheumnadh, direadhriaghailteach, ordugh, † gradh.

Gradatory, *s.* Staidhir.

Gradient, *a.* Gluasach, gluasadach, imeachdail.

Gradual, *a* Athaiseach, socrach, chuid is a chuid.

Gradually, *adv.* Ceum air cheum, uidh air uidh, uidh air an uidh, chuid is a chuid

Graduate, *v. a.* Ollamhaich, ardaich, urramaich; gluaiach

Graduate, *s.* Ollamh, ard-sgoilear

Graduation, *s.* Ceumnachd, ceumnaidheachd

Graff, Graft, *s* Nòdachadh; tàthadh. A young graft, *fùillean, gineag.*

Graff, Graft, *v. a* Nòdaich, tath Grafted, *nodaichte*

Graffing, *s* Nódachadh, tàthadh

Grafter, *s.* Nòdachair; fear nòdachaidh mheangan

Grain, *s* Siol, gràn, grainne, grainnean; (*in weight*), gràinne; (*hair*), fionnadh, calg, cuilg, (*of wood*), calg, (*of pease*), citean Against the grain, *an aghaidh 'chuilg, an aghaidh nàduir.*

Grained, *a* Grainneanach; garbh, molach, neo-mhìn

Grains, *s* Treasg; drabh.

Grainy, *a* Grànach, grainneanach, arbharach

† **Gramercy**, *interj* Maitheanas domh.

Gramineous, *a* Feurach

Graminivorous, *a* Feur-itheach; fàicheil.

Grammar, *s* Gràmadair, sgrìobhan; doigh sgrìobhaidh, doigh-labhairt, snàs-labhairt; leabhar doigh-chainnt.

Grammarian, *s.* Sgrìobhantair, gràmadair.

Grammatical, *a.* Sgrìobhanta, snàsda, ceart, gràmadach.

Grample, *s* Crùban.

Granam, *s.* Sean-mhathair

Granary, *s.* Sgiobal, siol-lann, gaoirneal, gairneal, tigh tasgaidh, tigh stòr

Grand, *a.* Mòr, ard, uasal; loghmhor; aillidh, grinn; riomhach, oirdheirc

Grandam, *s.* Sean-mhathair; sean-chailleach, cailleach odhar.

Grand-daughter, *s* Ogha nighne, ogha.

Grandchild, *s.* Ogha

Grandee, *s.* Flath, armunn, duine mòr(no) uasal Grandees, *uaislean, uailsean.*

Grandeur, *s.* Mòrchuis, lòiseam, riomhadh, mòrachd, airde.

Grandevous, *a.* Sean, aosmhor.

Grandfather, *s* Sean-athair Great grandfather, *seann sean-athair.*

Grandiloquence, *s* Glòr; ard-ghlòr; gloiream.

Grandmother, *s* Sean-mhathair.

Grandsire, *s* Sean-athair, sinnsear.

Grandson, *s* Ogha, fear-ogha; mac mic (no) nighinn.

Grange, *s.* Grainnseach, fearann; tigh tuathanaich

Granivorous, *a.* Gran-itheach

Grant, *v a* Ceadaich, deònaich, builich, thabhair, tabhair, thoir; aidich. Grant me this, *deonaich so domh, builich so orm*, grant it be so, *leig gur ann mar sin a tha*, granted, *ceadaichte, deonaichte, builichte*, God grant, *gu deonaicheadh Dia, gu 'n leigeadh Dia, gu tugadh Dia.*

Grant, *s.* Tabhartas, buileachas, buileachadh, tiodhlac, brontas, gealladh, cead, comas.

Grantee, *s.* Faotalaiche.

Granter, *s.* Tabhartair, tabhairtear, tiodhlacair.

Granulary, *a* Gràinneach, grainneanach, làn mar ghràinnein.

Granulate, *v a* Gràinich, gràinnich, pronn

Granulation, *s.* Gràinuchadh, gràinneachadh, pronnadh

Granulous, *a* Gràinach, gràinneach, grainneanach, garbh.

Grape, *s* Torradh an fhion-chroinn, fion-chaor, fion-dhearc.

Grapnel, *s.* Cromag; achdair bheag; creagair, clic, greimeir, greamair.

Grapple, *v a* and *n.* Gramaich, greimich; grab, gleachd; rach an greamachas, rach an dòideachas, glac, beir air.

Grasp, *v* Glac, beir air, gramaich, dean greim, cum san laimh

Grasp, *s.* Glac, glacadh, greim, teannachadh, preach.

Grasper, *s* Glacair, greimeir; teannachair

Grass, *s* Feur After grass, *iar-fheur*, grass grows not on the highway, *cha chinn feur air an rathad mhor*, dogs-grass, *feur choinein.*

Grasshopper, *s.* Diurrasan, dreollan teasbhuidh, fionnan feòir, leumnach uaine.

Grassy, *s* Feurach

Grassplot, *s* Faiche, leanan, lòinean.

Grate, *s* Similear; creadhal theine, gràt; cliath-uinneig, cliath.

Grate, *v.* Cliathraich.

Grate, *v. a.* and *n* Dean fuaim déistinneach, suath, rub, caith; méil; farranaich. A sound that grates me, *fuaim a tha cur déistinn orm.*

Grateful, *a.* (*Thankful*), taingeil; buidheach; (*pleasant*), taitneach, grinn, sòlasach.

Gratefully, *adv.* Gu taingeil, gu buidheach.

Gratefulness, *s.* Taingealachd, taingealas, buidheachas; sòlas, tlachd, taitneas

Grateolent, *a.* Fàileach.

Grater, *s* Sgrìobachan, sgrìobadair, inneal bleith, inneal méilidh, méileadair.

Gratework, *s.* Obair chleith, cliath-obair

Gratification, *s* Toileachadh; sòlas, toileach-inntinn; luidheachd, sàsuchadh

Gratify, *v. a.* Toilich, sasuich, taitinn, thig ri; breug; diol.

Grating, *a.* Déistinneach; sgreadach.

Gratingly, *adv.* Gu déistinneach; gu neo-thaitneach, gu gràda

Gratis, *adv* A nasguidh, far nasguidh, gu saor, gun luach, gun dad idir

Gratitude, *s* Taingealachd.

Gratuitous, *a.* Saor, a nasguidh.

Gratuitously, *adv* Gu saor; a nasguidh

Gratuity, *s.* Gibhte, tabhartas, saor-thabhartas, tiodhlac, luidheachd

Gratulate, *v* Co-fhàiltich, dean co-ghairdeachas.

Gratulation, *s.* Fàilte; co-fhailteachadh, co-fhàilte, co-ghairdeachas, co-luathghàir.

Gratulatory, *a.* Co-ghairdeachail, co-ghairdeach, co-fhailteach, co-fhailteachail,

Grave, *s* Uaigh, tuam, torr, sloc; cladh, † feart, † dearc; iarla, flath.

Grave, *a.* Tiamhaidh; socrach, ciallach, suidhichte, glic, crionna; (*important*), cudthromach; (*in sound*), tormanach.

Grave, *v a.* Gearr, snaidh, grabh, sgrìobh, cearb; corbh; breac; † adhlaic, (*grave a ship*), calc.

Graveclothes, *s.* Aodach mairbh, aodach bàis, marbhphaisg.

Gravel, *s* Grinneal, grothal, gaireal, gairbheal, gaineamh, gaineach; (*a malady*), galar fuail, clach fhuail

Gravel, *v a.* Grinnealaich; gairealaich, comhdaich le gaineamh; grab, cuir an iom-cheist. Gravelled, *gairealaichte, ann an iomcheist*, as a ship, *air.*

Graveless, *a* Neo-adhlaicte.

Gravelly, *a.* Gaineamhach, gaineachaidh; gairealach, garbh

Gravely, *adv* Gu tiamhaidh, gu socrach, gu suidhichte, gu mall; gu crionna

Gravelpit, *s.* Toll gaineimh, toll gaineich, sloc-gaineimh.

Graveolent, *a.* Loibheach, lobhach, breun.

Graven, *part* Gearrta, snaidhte.

Graver, *s.* Snaidhear, gearradair, grabhair, rionnaiche, breacair, grabhalaiche, gileab, inneal grabhaidh.

Gravestone, *s* Clach uaigh, leac lighe, leac.

Graved, *a* Torrach, trom, leth-tromach.

Gravidity, *s.* Torraichead, truime, leth-tromachd.

Graving, *s.* Grabhadh, gearradh, snaidheadh, grabhaladh, obair ghrabhaidh, rionnal, rionnachas; creachaireas

Gravingtool, *s.* Inneal grabhaidh, gileab; breacair.

Gravitate, *v. n.* Cudthromaich, tromaich, aom.

Gravitation, *s.* Tromachadh

Gravity, *s.* Cudthrom, truime; tromad, tromadas; (*of mind*), tiamhaidheachd, crionnachd, suidheachadh inntinn.

Gravy, *s.* Sugh, brìgh, sugh feòl ròiste, sabhsa.

Gray, *a.* Glas, liath; riathach, ciar, gorm; odhar.

Gray, *s.* Broc, taoghan.

Graybeard, *s.* Sean duine, bodach.

Gray-eyed, *a.* Ciar shùileach.

Grayling, *s.* Seorsa éisg.

Grayness, *s.* Leithe, glaise, glaisead, riathaichead, guirme.

Graze, *v. a.* and *n.* Ionaltair; bi 'g ionaltradh, innilt, feuraich; (*rub*), suath, rub.

Grazer, *s.* Ionaltraiche, beothach ionaltraidh.

Grazier, *s.* Àireach, aodhair, tuathanach feòir.

Grazing, *s* Ionaltradh, àireachas, feurach

Grease, *s.* Créis, geire, ìgh, saill, reamhrachd, blonag, smearadh, smioradh. Cart-grease, *créis cartach.*

Greasiness, *s.* Reamhrachd.

Greasy, *a.* Créiseach, créiseil, geireach, ìgheach, sailleach, reamhar, ùillidheach, sleamhuinn.

Great, *a.* (*In bulk*), mòr, domhail; (*important*), cudthromach; (*in extent*), farsuing, leathan, fad, fad farsuing, (*chief*), ard, prìomh; (*wonderful*), iongantach, miorbhuileach; neònach; (*noble*), mòr, ard, uasal, flathail, ainmeil, òirdheirc, urramail; (*in mind*), mor-chuiseach, ard-inntinneach, borr; (*proud*), ardanach, atmhor; (*pregnant*), trom, torrach, leth-tromach; (*difficult*), duilich, doilich, deacair, cruaidh. He is very great with him, *tha e ro mhòr aige*, however great he be, *air a mheud 's a bheil e*, a great deal, *mòran*, a great deal more, *mòran tuille*, a great many, *mòran, iomad*, how great! *cia cho mòr'* how great he was! *cho mòr is a bha e!* greater, *ni 's mo, ni 's airde*, somewhat greater, *beagan ni 's mò;* by a great deal, *mar mhòran.*

Great, *s.* An t-iomlan.

Greatbellied, *a.* Bronnach, bagach, mòr-bhronnach; torrach.

Greathearted, *a* Mòr-chridheach, mor-chuiseach, ard-chinntinneach; misneachail.

Greatly, *adv* Gu mòr, mòran, mar mhòran; gu h-ard, gu flathail, gu gaisgeil.

Greatness, *s.* Meud, meudachd, cumhachd, inbhe, airde; urram, onoir, mòrachd, óirdheirceas; mòr-chuis, mòralachd. Greatness with one, *maoidhean.*

Greaves, *s.* Coisbheart, eididh calpa, lurg-bheairt

Grebe, *s* Spàg ri tòin

Grecian, *s* Greugach.

Greece, *s.* A Ghréig.

Greed, *s.* Sannt, lon, gion; ciocras. Hapless greed ill betides, *sannt gun sonas éiridh 'n donas da.*

Greedily, *adv.* Gu lonach, gu gionach, gu glamhach, gu glutach, gu ciocrach, gu sanntach, gu spiocach.

Greediness, *s* Lon, gion, gionaichead, glamhaireachd, ciocras, sannt, spiocaireachd, spioc.

Greedy, *a* Lonach, gionach, glamhach, glutach, ciocrach; sanntach, spiocach

Greek, *s.* Greugach The Greek language, *Greugais*

Green, *a* Uaine; gorm, glas; (*fresh*), ùr; (*not ripe*), anabuich; tais, amh; (*sickly*), glas, glasdaidh, bàn. Light green, *uaine eutrom;* as green as grass, *cho gorm ris an fheur;* as green as colewort, *cho glas ris a chal.*

Green, *s.* (*Colour*), uaine; gorm; (*plain*), fàiche, lòn, faighean, raon; gorm, réidh, feur, duille

Greenfinch, *s.* Glaisean daraich.

Greengage, *s.* Seorsa plumbais.

Greenhouse, *s.* Tigh teth.

Greenish, *a.* Leth-char uaine, glas, glasdaidh.

Greenly, *adv.* Gu h-uaine, gu glasdaidh; gu h-ùr, gu h-amh, gu h-anabuich.

Greenness, *s.* Uainead, uaine, glaisead, glaise, guirme, ùiread; amhachd, amhad, anabachd

Green-sickness, *s* Galar glasdaidh.

Green-sward, *s.* Ailean, fiadhar, sgrath ghlas

Green-wood, *s.* Ùr-choille, fàs-choille.

Greet, *v. a* Fàiltich, cuir fàilt, cuir furan. He greeted me, *chuir e fàilte orm.*

Greeting, *s* Altuchadh beatha, cùr fàilte, fàilteachadh, beannachd. Send greeting, *cuir beannachd*

Gregarious, *a* Greigheach; treudach, ealtach

Grenade, *s* Toirm-shlige bheag.

Grenadier, *s.* Saighdear ard

Grew, *pret* of grow Chinn, dh' fhàs.

Greyhound, *s.* Miol-chu, gadhar, gaothar.

Grice, *s* Uircean, òg-chullach

Gridelin, *s* Gris-dhearg.

Gridiron, *s* Brandal, brandair; cliath rostaidh; groideal, groidle.

Grief, *s* Bròn, tuirse, mulad, dòlas, doilghios, doilgheas, cumhadh, amhghar, an-shocair, dobhròn, dubhròn, dubhachas, trioblaid.

Grievance, *s* Cuis ghearain, cruaidh-chas, buaireadh, urchoid

Grieve, *v a* Cradh, craidh, claoidh, gortaich, goirtich, pian, ciurr, dochainn, farranaich, dean tuirseach, cuir fo mhulad, buair

Grieve, *v n* Dean bròn, dean cumha.

Grievingly, *adv* Gu craidhteach, gu brònach, gu tuirseach

Grievous, *a* Craidhteach, craiteach, claoidhteach, dochannach, doilghiosach, dòlasach, trioblaideach, buaireasach, trom; do-ghiùlan, anabarra.

Grievously, *adv* Gu craidhteach, gu dochannach, gu doilghiosach, gu trioblaideach, gu dòlasach; gu h-anabarra.

Grievousness, *s.* Bròn, doilghios, amhghar, pian, earchall, urchoid.

Griffin, *s.* Uil-bheist le ceann agus smogan leomhainn, agus le sgiathaibh iolair

Grig, *s* Circean, easgan, nirean

Grill, *v. a.* Ròist; griosaich.

Grillade, *s* Ròstadh; toitean, colag

Grilse, *s* Bànag.

Grim, *a.* Gruamach, dorcha, duaichnidh, grànda, dordha, gnò, neo-aoidheil; eagallach. Grimly, *gu gruamach, gu granda, gu gnò.*

Grimace, *s.* Braoisg, góill, spluig, camadh beòil, cair

Grimalkin, *s.* Sean chat; cat odhar.

Grime, *s.* Salachar, sal

Grime, *v a.* Salaich; dubh; truaill; mill

Grimness, *s.* Gruamaiche, gruamachd, duirche, duaichneachd, dordhachd.

Grin, *v.* Cas beul, cuir braoisg, cas fiacal, dean cair

Grin, *s.* Casadh beòil, braoisg; spluig, gnoimh, cair, draoin; magadh, sgeig, † lion, ribe.

Grind, *v. a* Méil, bleith, pronn; geuraich

Grinder, *s.* Meilear, méileadair, muillear, fear meilt, fear méilidh; (*a tooth*), fiacal cùil

Grindstone, *s* Clach-gheuraich, clach gheurachaidh, clach bhleithe, clach liobhar, clach liobhraidh.

Grinner, *s* Braoisgear.

Grinning, *s* Braoisgeil; gnoimh.

GRIPE, *v* Glac, gramaich, greimich, teannaich, goirtich; fàisg

GRIPE, *s* Greim; goimh, trughaid, guin, bainn fola; coiligin; foirneart; trioblaid, amhghar, teanntachd.

GRIPER, *s* Spiocair, sracair.

GRISKIN, *s*. Grisgean.

GRISLY, *a* Oillteil, uamhasach, eagallach, gràda, granda, duaichnidh

GRIST, *s* Meilltir, lòn, arbhar

GRISTLE, *s* Brisgean, maothan, sgannan

GRISTLY, *a* Brisgeanach, maothanach.

GRIT, *s* Garbhan, corlach; gaineach, gaineamh.

GRITLY, *a* Garbhanach; gaineamhach, gaineachaidh

GRIZZLE, *s* Gris-fhionn

GRIZZLED, *a* Liath, glas-liath, riathach; gris-fhion.

GROAN, *v* Osnaich, acainich, cnead, gnòsd; dean osann, dean acain. Groaning, *ag osnaich, ag acainich*

GROAN, *s* Osann, acain, cnead, gnosd, gnùsd

GROAT, *s* Gròt, ceithir, sgillinn, cota bàn

GROATS, *s* Treasg; sgiolan

GROCE, *s* Da dhusan deug

GROCER, *s* Ceannuiche, marsonta, marsal, grosdair

GROCERY, *s* Bathar ceannuiche, grosdaireachd

GROG, *s* Deoch laidir

GROGGY, *a* Air an daoraich

GROIN, *s* Luch-lèin, blion, blean

GROOM, *s* Gille each, gille-stàbuill, gille, seirbheiseach

GROOVE, *s*. Claise; sloc, feag

GROOVE, *v*. Claisich, dean claise

GROPE, *v. a*. and *n* Màgair smàgaich, smògaich, smeuraich, smògaich san dorcha

GROPER, *s* Màgair, smàgair, smògair.

GROSS, *a* Garbh, tiugh, tomadach, domhail, dumhail, reamhar, neo-thuigseach; sultmhor, (*in speech*), drabasta, draosda, neo-bheusach

GROSS, *s* An t-iomlan, a chuid mhòr, a gharbh-chuid, a chuid is mò, a chuid is pailt, dà dhusan deug In the gross, *gu lèir*

GROSSLY, *adv*. Gu garbh, gu tomadach; gu drabasta, gun ghrinneas, gun mhodh, as an aghaidh

GROSSNESS, *s* Gairbhe, tiughad, tomad, dumhalas, dòmhalas, sultmhorachd, reamhad, (*in speech*), drabasdachd, draosdachd.

GROT, *s* Uamh, uamhaidh, uaghaidh, còs

GROTESQUE, *a*. Neònach, mi-nadurra, mi-dhaicheil

GROTTO, *s* Uamh, uamhaidh, còs, sgàil-thigh

GROUND, *s* Talamh, làr, ùrlar, grunnd; uir, oighreachd, fearann, deasgann, reuson, ciall. Under ground, *fo 'n talamh*, on the ground, *air làr*, above ground, *os cionn talmhain, beò, a làthair*, give ground, *géill*, of the ground, *talmhaidh*, a ground, *air*, gain ground, *coisinn air, fairtlich air, thig spéid*, a plot of ground, *mir fearainn, acair, croit*, the ground of a thing, *bun, bunamhas*

GROUND, *part* Bleithte, méilte.

GROUND, *v a* Steidhich; grunndaich, daighnich, suidhich, dean diongalta, cuir air an talamh

GROUNDED, *part* Steidhichte, grunndaichte, daighnichte, suidhichte Well grounded in any thing, *air a dheagh theagasg*

GROUND-FLOOR, *s* Ùrlar.

GROUND-IVY, *s*. Iadh-shlat, eitheann, athair-lus.

GROUNDLESS, *a* Neo-bhunaiteach; gun bhunait, gun bhunachar, gun reuson, breugach, fallsa.

GROUNDLING, *s* Seorsa èisg; sgonn-bhalaoch

GROUND-PLOT, *s* Làr, ùrlar.

GROUND-ROOM, *s* Seumar làir, seumar iosal, seumar urlair.

GROUNDS, *s pl* Deasgainn, deasgann; grunnd.

GROUNDSEL, *s* Grunnais

GROUNDWORK, *s*. Bun, steigh, bùnachar, bunait, steighdhaighnich; ceud-thùs; priomh-aobhar; mathair-aobhar.

GROUP, *s* Dorlach, cròilean, dròbh, baguid, bagaid; torr.

GROUP, *v. a*. Cruinnich, dlùthaich ri chéile.

GROUT, *s* Treasg; garbhan, seorsa ubhal fiadhain; froileis.

GROUSE, *s* Eoin ruadh, cearc no coileach fraoich.

GROVE, *s*. Doire, badan coille, bad, garan

GROVEL, *v*. Luidir, luarganaich, snàg; bi mio-thur

GROVELLING, *a* Iosal, diblidh; mio-thur, luarganach. A grovelling person, *luargan*.

GROVELLING, *s*. Lamhachas, luarganachd.

GROW, *v n* Cinn, fàs, meudaich, rach am meud, rach am feabhas Grow up in age, *thig gu h-inmhe*, it grows late, *tha e fas anmoch*. Grown, *air fàs, air cinntinn, air teachd gu h-inmhe* (*no*) *gu aois, deanta, iomlan*. We are grown acquainted, *tha sinn air fàs eòlach* He who grows not in his sleep, will not grow when awake, *am fear nach cinn na chodal, cha chinn e na fhaireach*.

GROWER, *s* Fear suidheachaidh.

GROWING, *s* Fàs, meudachadh, cinntinn, cinneas

GROWL, *v n* Dean duarman, gearain, talaich, dean callaid; dean dùrdan, dean nuallan.

GROWLING, *s*. Duarman, nuallan, gearan, talachadh.

GROWN, *part* Air cinntinn, air fàs.

GROWTH, *s*. Fàs, toradh, cinneas, cinntinn, fàs mòr, dol meudachadh, leasachadh, am meud. A growth of nettles, *ionntagach*, a growth of docks, *copagach*.

GRUB, *s* Bùraich, cladhaich, pleadhaich, buain as an fhreumh, thoir as a bhun, (*grub-weeds*), gart-ghlan.

GRUB, *s* Cnuimh mhillteach, cnuimh-fhochainn, brideach.

GRUBBING, *s* Bùrachadh, cladhachadh, pleadhachadh Grubbing axe, *grafan*

GRUBBLE, *v* Smeuraich, smògaich, smògarsaich.

GRUDGE, *s* Faladh, falachd, farmad, gamhlas, tnù, tnùth, miorùn, diom, sean-ghamhlas, miosguinn, maoidh Grudge of conscience, *agartas coguis*.

GRUDGE, *v*. Talaich, maoidh, dean talach, dean gearain, bi gamhlasach I will not grudge it you, *cha mhaoidh mi ort e*, I grudge the price of it, *is mòr leam a phris*; better grudged than not had, *is fhearr a mhaoidh no dhiobhradh*.

GRUDGING, *s*. Talachadh, maoidh, gearan, gamhlas, tnù.

GRUDGINGS, *s pl*. Fuighleall, fuighleach, fàgail.

GRUEL, *s* Plodag, easach; brochan, du-bhrochan, leth-bhrochan

GRUFF, *a*. Doirbh, gnò, gruamach, searbh. Gruffly, *gu doirbh, gu gnò, gu searbh*

GRUFFNESS, *s* Doirbhe, seirbhe, searbhas, gruamaiche, gruaim, gruaimead

GRUM, *a* Doirbh, gnò, searbh

GRUMBLE, *v n* Talaich, gearain, dean monmhor, dean ciarsan, dean callaid (no) ceasachd, dean duarman.

GRUMBLER, *s* Fear talachaidh, talachair, fear gearain; duarmanaiche

GRUMBLING, *s* Talachadh, monmhor, ciarsanachd, ceasad, ceasachd, duarmanaich, duarmanachd.

GRUME, *s* Slaman, ni slamaichte air bi

GRUMOUS, *a*. Tiugh, slamach.

GRUNT, *s*. Gnòsd, gnùsd, gròsd, gronnsal

Grunt, *v.* Dean gnòsd.

Grunter, *s.* Gnòsdair; grosair; seorsa èisg.

Grunting, *s.* Gnòsdail, gnùsdail.

Gruntling, *s.* Uircean.

Gry, *s.* Ni sam bi gun fhiù.

Guarantee, *s.* Urras, urradh.

Guaranty, *v. a.* Rach an urras.

Guard, *v. a.* Dion, coimhead, gleidh; cum faire; *geard-ainn*, cum *geard.*

Guard, *s.* Dionadh, dion, didean, coimhead, faicill, faire, fear faire, *geard*, freiceadan; (*hilt*), dornchur. Set a guard, *cuir faire, suidhich faire;* be on your guard, *bi air d'fhai-cill.*

Guarder, *s.* Fear dionaidh, fear faire, fear coimhead, *geard.*

Guardian, *s.* Fear dionaidh, dion, cileadair; gocaman, fear coimhiad, coimheadair; (*of an orphan*), tuitear.

Guardian, *a.* Dionach, dionaidh. A guardian angel, *aingeal dionaidh.*

Guardianship, *s.* Coimhеadachd, cùram; dreuchd tuiteir; tuitearachd.

Guardless, *a.* Gun dion, neo-dhionta; neo-churamach; neo-omhailleach, neo-umhailleach.

Guardship, *s.* Luingeas dionaidh, dion-long, long-dhìdein.

Gubernation, *s.* Riaghladh; smachd, stiùradh.

Gudgeon, *s.* Bronnag; baoghlan; mealladh.

† **Guerdon**, *s.* Duais, diol, diol-thuarasdal.

Guess, *v. a.* and *n.* Baralaich, meas, thoir barail; thoir tuairmeis; faigh a mach; tomhais.

Guess, *s.* Barail, meas, beachd. As far as I can guess, *a réir mo bharail-se, air mo bheachd-sa;* you did not give a bad guess, *cha bu don' a bharail thug thu;* by guess, *a thaobh tuairmeis*, bi gis.

Guesser, *s.* Baralaiche.

Guessing, *s.* Baralachadh, measadh, tomhasadh.

Guest, *s.* Aoidh, coigreach, fear cuairt, deòr, loisdineach. An entertainer of guests, *fear féill;* he is a bad guest whom the house is the worse for, *is olc an aoidh is meisde an tigh.*

Guggle, *v. n.* Glug; dean glugail (no) glugam.

Guidance, *s.* Treòrachadh, seòladh, stiùradh, riaghladh, riaghailt. Under guidance, *fo stiùraidh.*

Guide, *s.* Fear seòlaidh, fear stiùraidh; riaghladair, fear riaghlaidh, stiùradair.

Guide, *v.* Treòraich, seòl, stiùir, riaghail.

† **Guider**, *s.* Fear seòlaidh, riaghladair, fear stiùraidh.

Guild, *s.* Comunn, buidheann, comh-chorp.

Guile, *s.* Cealg, feall, foill, cluain, cuilbheart, slaoighte, car, mealltaireachd, cluaintearachd.

Guileful, *a.* Cealgach; fealltach, mealltach, cluainteach, cluaineach; slaoighteil, cuilbheartach, eòlach; sligheach, carach.

Guilefully, *adv.* Gu cealgach, gu fealltach, gu mealltach, gu cluainteach, gu cuilbheartach, gu h-eòlach, gu sligheach, gu carach.

Guilefulness, *s.* Cealgachd, cealgaireachd, mealltaireachd, cluaintearachd, slaoightearachd.

Guileless, *a.* Gun chealg, neo-chealgach, neo-charach, ionraic, dìreach, treibhdhireach, simplidh.

Guillotine, *v. a.* Di-cheannaich. Guillotined, *di-cheann-aichte.*

Guilt, *s.* Ciont; coire; cron; lochd.

Guiltily, *adv.* Gu ciontach, gu h-aingidh.

Guiltiness, *s.* Ciont, ciontachd; aingidheachd, truaillidh-eachd.

Guiltless, *a.* Neo-chiontach, neo-choireach, neo-lochdach, glan.

Guiltlessly, *adv.* Gu neo-chiontach, gu neo-choireach.

Guiltlessness, *s.* Neo-chiontas.

Guilty, *a.* Ciontach, coireach; aingidh; truaillidh.

Guinea, *s.* Sgillinn 'ar fhichead Shasunnach.

Guinea-hen, *s.* Cearc Innseanach.

Guinea-pig, *s.* Beathach beag le gros uircein, do nach aithne dhomhsa ainm ni 's fhearr na *muc-radan.*

Guise, *s.* Modh, fasan, nòs, gnàth, cleachd; dreach, aogas; deise, culaidh.

Guitar, *s.* Inneal ciùil Feadailteach.

Gulch, *s.* Bagair (no) craosair beag.

Gulf, *s.* Geòth, geòthadh, camus, bàgh; aigean; cuairteag shluigeach.

Gulfy, *a.* Geòthach, camusach, cuairteagach, sluigeach.

Gull, *v. a.* Meall, thoir an car a.

Gull, *s.* Mealladh; cuilbheart, car; baoghlan; (*in ornithology*), faoileann, aoileann, aoileag, faoileag.

Gull-catcher, *s.* Mealltair, cealgair, cluaintear.

Guller, *s.* Mealltair, cealgair, cluaintear.

Gullet, *s.* Sgornan, sgornach; pioban, detiach, steig-bhràgaid.

Gulosity, *s.* Craosaireachd, glàmhaireachd.

Gully-hole, *s.* Toll guiteir, guitear.

Gulp, *v. a.* Glug thairis, sluig le glug.

Gulp, *s.* Balgam.

Gum, *s.* Bith, bith craoibh, ròsaid; (*of the teeth*), càirean, gailleach.

Gummy, *a.* Mar bhith, làn bithe, ròsaideach; sticeach, rithinn.

Gun, *s.* Gunna, musg, musgaid. Guns, *gunnachan, musg-aidean.*

Gunner, *s.* Gunnair.

Gunnery, *s.* Gunnaireachd.

Gunpowder, *s.* Fùdar, fudar gunna.

Gunshot, *s.* Urchair gunna. About a gunshot, *beul ri urchair gunna;* a gunshot wound, *leòn peileir.*

Gunsmith, *s.* Ceard ghunnachan, gobhainn arm.

Gun-stick, *s.* Slat, slat gunna.

Gun-stock, *s.* Stoc.

Gunwale, *s.* Stoc luinge, beul mòr, luinge.

Gurge, *s.* Cuairt-shlugan, slugan.

Gurgeon, *s.* Garbhan; bràn, min'gharbh.

Gurgle, *v. n.* Dean torman mar shrùlaig, dean glugail.

Gurnet, *s.* Seorsa eisg mara.

Gush, *v. n.* Sruth, brùchd, taom, spùt, sil. The water gushed forth, *bhrùchd an t-uisge a mach.*

Gush, *s.* Sruth, brùchd, spùt; ladar, taom.

Gushing, *s.* Sruthadh, bruchdadh, spùtadh, sileadh.

Gusset, *s.* Gusait, eang.

Gust, *s.* Blas, faireachas; miann; (*of wind*), osag, oiteag.

Gustable, *a.* Blasda; milis, taitneach.

Gustation, *s.* Blasadh, blasdachd, feuchainn.

Gustful, *a.* Blasda, milis, taitneach.

Gusto, *s.* Blas; miann.

Gusty, *a.* Osagach, oiteagach, gaothar, stoirmeil, gre-annach.

Gut, *s.* Caolan; greallach, ionar; (*proverbially*, stomach;) goile, bag, stamac; (*gluttony*), craos.

Gut, *v. a.* Thoir am mionach a, thoir na caolain a.

Gutt, *s.* Boinne, deur, diotag, sileag.

Gutter, *s.* Guitear, clais uisge

Gutter, *v a* Clais, claisich; staingich; cladhaich.

Guttle, *v a.* and *n.* Sluig, craos, glàmh

Guttler, *s* Glutair, glamhair.

Guttulous, *a.* Boinneach, diotagach, sileagach.

Guttural, *a.* Bladach; mùgach, tùchanach.

Guy, *s.* Seorsa ulaig, tarruing.

Guzzle, *v. n.* Òl, pòit; geòc, sluig

Guzzler, *s.* Pòitear, geòcair, craosair, glàmhair.

† Gybe, *s.* Beum.

Gymnastic, *a.* Iomairteach; gleachdach; reachdmhor, comasach.

Gypsum, *s* Seorsa aoil.

Gyration, *s.* Sniomhan, rothladh, ruithleadh.

Gyre, *s* Cuairteag, cearcall.

Gyred, *a.* Sniomhanach.

Gyves, *s.* Geimhlean, cuibhrichean, ceanglaichean; ceap.

H.

H, Ochdamh litir na h-aibidil

Ha! *interj* Ha!

Haberdasher, *s* Ceannaiche aodaichean; marsonta pac, cluthadair, clothadair

Haberdashery, *s* Aodaichean, clothadaireachd.

Haberdine, *s* Bodach ruadh cruaidh, saillte.

Habergeon, *s* Eididh uchd, gòrsaid, luireach mhàillcach

Habiliment, *s.* Aodach, eudach, deise, culaidh, uigheam, eideadh, earradh, trusgan, sgeadachadh

Habilitate, *a* Uigheamaich; freagarraich.

Habit, *s* Cor ni sam bi, staid; dreach; (*dress*), uigheam, deise, culaidh, (*custom*), cleachd, gnàth, nòs, fasan, abhaist A bad habit of body, *droch cor, droch cal, droch staid cuirp*, a bad habit, *droch chleachd, droch fhasan*

Habit, *v* Aodaich, eid, comhdaich, earr.

Habitable, *a* Ion-àiteachadh; àitichte; airson comhnuidh 'ghabhail ann

Habitant, *s* Tamhaiche, fear taimh. An habitant of Edinburgh, *fear mhuinntir Dhun-Eidin.*

Habitation, *s.* Comhnuidh, ionad comhnuidh, àite comhnuidh, ionad taimh, aros, fardach

Habitual, *a* Gnàthaichte, gnàthach, cleachdta, cleachdach, minig, cumannta, coitchionn

Habitually, *adv* Gu gnàthaichte, gu gnàthach, gu minig, gu cumannta, a reir gnàtha, a reir cleachd

Habituate, *v a* Cleachd, gnàthaich, cruaidhich, dean ri Habituated, *cleachdta, gnàthaichte, deanta ri.*

Hack, *v. a.* Pronn gu min, dean na mhìribh, gearr, snaidh, cosgair, beubanaich

Hack, *s* Each reidh, mainnsir; lobht saidh, piocaid

Hacking, *s.* Snaith; gearradh, sneagaireachd.

Hackle, *v.* Seicil, cìr

Hackle, *s* Seiceal Hackles, *seiclean*

Hackney, *s* Each reidh; each iasachd, carbad reidh; siùrsach, striopach.

Hackney, *v a* Cleachd; dean cumannta Hackneyed, *cleachdta.*

Haddock, *s.* Adag.

Haft, *s* Cas, cos, lamh, samhach; cluais.

Hag, *s* Buitseach, bansgal; cailleach, sean bhanaisg bhochd, (*nightmare*), an tromlighe.

Hag, *v a.* Craidh, claoidh; sàruich, buair, pian, ciurr

Haggard, *a* Fiadhaich, fuathsach, eagallach, oillteil, uamharra; duaichnidh, truagh, ailmseach, grànda

Haggard, *s.* Urr (no) beothach fiadhaich sam bi, seorsa seabhaig

Haggess, *s* Taigeis

Haggish, *a.* Gràda, duaichnidh.

Haggle, *v. a.* and *n* Gearr, pronn, min-phronn; gearr gu neo-dhàicheil, beubanaich; (*bargain*), dean plocaireachd (no) priginn; dean tròcainn.

Haggler, *s.* Plocair; fear priginn; greimisgear.

Haggling, *s.* Pronnadh, gearradh neo-dhàicheil; beubanachadh; plocaireachd, priginn, tròcainn.

Hagiographer, *s* Naomh-sgriobhair; diadhair.

Ha ha! *interj.* Ha ha!

Ha ha, *s* Bac sam bi, mar uisge no balladh, air an tig neach gun fhios da

Hail, *s.* Clach shneachd, clach-shneachdaidh, cloch (no) clach meallain, clachan meallain Hail often begins and ends a shower, *toiseach is deireadh na sìne, clachan mìn meallain*

Hail, *v n* Cuir clachan meallain.

Hail, *interj.* Aibhe; slainnte, fàilte; do bheath, bhur beath. Hail, horrors! hail, infernal world! *Uamhasa, 's e bhur beath, do bheathsa 'shaoghail nan oillte.*

Hail, *v a.* Cuir fàilte, fàiltich.

Hailstone, *s* Clach mheallain, clach shneachd, clach shneachdaidh.

Hair, *s.* Folt, falt, gruaig, gaoisd, guaire; fionnadh, ròinne, ròinneag, calg, colg A hair's breadth, *leud ròinneig*, a lock of hair, *dual*, the hair of the eyelids, *fabhradh*, grey hair, *folt liath*, golden hair, *folt òr-bhuidhe;* a single hair, *roinneag*, (of a quadruped), *fionnadh*, (of a horse's mane or tail), *gaoisd*, against the hair, *ana ghaidh a chuilg*

Hair-bell, *s.* Plùran cluigeanach

Hairbrained, *a* See Harebrained

Hairbreadth, *s* Leud ròinneig Hairbreadth escape, *sgiorradh.*

Haircloth, *s.* Aodach ròinne, aodach gaoisd.

Hairiness, *s* Ròmaiche, ròmaichead, molaichead; ròinneachd, giobaichead.

Hair-lace, *s* Cochlach.

Hairless, *a* Maol, lom, gun fholt, gun fhionnadh.

Hair-lip, *s.* Bearn-mhiol

Hairy, *a.* Molach, ròmach, fionnach, giobach, guairsgeach.

Hake, *s.* Seorsa èisg

Halberd, *s* Ailbeard, tailbeard

Halberdier, *s* Ailbeardach, tailbeardach, fear ailbeird.

Halcyon, *a.* Samhach, ciùin, seimh, sona. Halcyon days, *laithe seimh (no) sona*

Halcyon, *s* Eun mara mu 'n dubhradh gum bi an àile na féith ann am dhith bhith 'gur, gobh uisge; iasgair diomhain

Hale, *a* Slainnteil, fallain, slàn; sunntach, tuaireil.

Hale, *v. a.* Tarruing, slaod, slaoid.

Haler, *s.* Tarruingear, fear tairnidh.

Half, *s.* Leth; earann, cuid, pàirt, roinn. Half a year, *leth bhliadhna;* a year and a half, *bliadhna gu leth;* half and half, *leth mar leth;* he is half asleep, *tha e na leth-chodal.*

Half, *adv.* Na dhà leth, gu leth.

Half-blooded, *a.* Diblidh, iosal, bochd, truaillidh, diolan.

Half-brother, *s* Leth-bhrathair.

Half-dead, *a.* Leth mharbh, bloidh marbh.

Half-faced, *a.* Leth-cheannach, leth-aodainneach

Half-heard, *a.* Leth-chluinnte

Half-moon, *s.* Gealach leth-làn, leth-ghealach.

Halfpenny, *s.* Bonn-sea, peighinn. Hap and a half-penny is enough, *is fhearr peighinn an fhortain no 'n ròst is cuig ceud.*

Half-pint, *s.* Leth-phinnt.

Half-round, *a.* Leth-chruinn.

Half-scholar, *s.* Leth-sgoilear.

Half-seas-over, *a.* Air an daoraich.

Half-seen, *a.* Leth-fhaicte, leth-fhaicinnte, doilleir

Half-sighted, *d.* Gearr-sheallach, gann-sheallach

Half-sphere, *s* Leth-chruinne

Half-sword, *s.* Lamh air laimh

Half-verse, *s.* Leth rann.

Half-way, *s* Leth roid, le rathaid, leth-shlighe.

Half-wit, *s* Nòthaist, baoghlan, umaidh, guraiceach, amadan, leth-amadan.

Half-witted, *a.* Gòrach, neo-chrionna, eu-crionna. A half-witted person, *leth-amadan, leth-oinnseach*

Halibut, *s.* Seorsa éisg.

Halidam, *s* Moire.

Halimas, *s.* Féill nan uile-naomh, samhuinn

Halituous, *a* Ceòthar, mùigeach.

Hall, *s.* Talla, talladh: cùirt, tigh mòid, seomar mòr. Hall days, *laithean cùirt.*

Hallelujah, *s* Òran molaidh, focal Eabhruidheach a ciallachadh *thugaibh cliù do 'n Tighearn*

Halloo, *v.* Glaodh, sgairtich, dean gàir.

Hallow, *v.* Naomhaich, coisrig, beannaich.

Hallowed, *part* and *a.* Naomhaichte, coisrigte, naomh

Hallow-day, *s.* Samhuinn, la samhna Hallow-e'en, *oidche shamhna.* When Hallow-day falls on Wednesday, *nur is Ceadnaich 'n t-Samhuinn.*

Hallucination, *s.* Mearachd.

Halm, *s* Fodar, connlach, cnàmharlach; dias, diasad

Halo, *s.* Ré-chearcall, roth gréin (no) gealaich.

Halser, *s* Cord, ròp, todh, ball bàta, taod.

Halt, *v. n.* Stad, bi bacach (no) crùbach; bi an iom-cheist. He halts in his gait, *tha e bacach, tha stac crub-aich aige.*

Halt, *s.* Bac, stac, stac crùbaich, luirceanachd; stad, stadachd They made a halt, *rinn iad stad.*

Halt, *a.* Bacach, crùbach, stacach.

Halter, *s.* Fear bacach, bacach, crùbach, stacach; luir-cean.

Halter, *s.* Aghastar, (aghaidh-stiùir); cord, tàod, cord na croiche.

Halter, *v. a.* Cuir aghastar air.

Halve, *v. a.* Roinn, dean dà leth, lethich.

Ham, *s.* Co aca ann an toiseach no 'n deireadh focaill a ciallachadh tigh, fearann, no baile beag

Ham, *s.* Spàg, iosgaid, feoil chrochta, spàg dubh, an ceith-reamh deiridh, ceithreamh muic-sailte. A smoked ham, *spag dubh.*

Hamated, *a.* Dubhanaichte; corrach; crom

Hame, Hames, *s.* Bràid chluaisean

Hamlet, *s.* Baile beag, clachan, frith-bhaile.

Hammer, *s* Ord, fairche, fairc, geannair, geinnear.

Hammer, *v. a.* and *n.* Buail le ord, geinnich, straoidhil, bi a straoidhlearachd.

Hammerer, *s* Òrdair; fear ùirde, straoidhlear.

Hammock, *s.* Leabadh luinge, leabadh chrochta; spiris.

Hamper, *v.* Cliabh, cliabhan, croidhle, sgùilean

Hamper, *v a.* Cuibhrich; cuir moill air, cuir an iom-cheist.

Hamstring, *s* Féith-lùthaidh, féith iosgaid, spearrach.

Hamstring, *v. a* Gearr iosgaid, gearr féith luthaidh na h-iosgaid, spearraich.

Hanaper, *s* Ionmhas.

Hand, *s.* Lamh; bas; bos, màg, cròg, dòid, glac, dorn, màn, crodh, crubh, gniomh; oibriche; tomhas cheithir, òirleach On all hands, *air gach laimh,* the right hand, *an lamh dheas;* the left hand, *an lamh chlì,* he knows not his right hand from his left, *cha 'n aithne dha 'lamh dheas seach air lamh chlì;* short hand (*writing*), *gearr-sgriobhadh,* having but one hand, *air leth lamh,* take in hand, *gabh os laimh,* a clenched hand, *dorn,* the back of the hand, *cùl an dùirn;* the hollow of the hand, *glaic na laimh,* beforehand, *roimh laimh,* behindhand, *air dheire-adh,* his hands bound behind his back, *a lamhan ceangailte air a chulaobh;* on the mending hand, *a dol am feobhas,* on the other hand, *air an lamh eile,* out of hand, *air an spot, air ball, gun smuaine,* hand in hand, *lamh air laimh,* near at hand, *am fogus, aig laimh,* hand-basket, *croidh-leag, basgaid,* a handbreadth, *leud boise,* a handful, *lan dùirn,* a hand-gun, *gunna glaic,* hand and glove, *a réir chéile, mòr aig a chéile;* the upper hand, *lamh an uachdar,* I have no hand in it, *cha n'eil cuid no pàirt agam dheth,* at hand, *am fogus, an gearr, an gai, aig laimh,* the quickest hand has the best share, *am fear is luaithe lamh, is e 's fhearr cuid,* his hands fell to his side, *thuit a dha lamh ri 'thaobh.*

Hand, *v a.* Thoir, thabhair, tabhair; thoir air laimh, beir air laimh, beir, glac; lamhaich, toirbheir; sin, ruig Hand me my staff, *thoir* (*no*) *sìn dhomh mo lorg*

Hand-barrow, *s.* Barr-laimh, barra da laimh, barra

Hand-basket, *s* Bascaid; croidhleag, croidhleag laimh, cliabh.

Hand-bell, *s.* Clagan dùirn, clag laimh

Handbreadth, *s.* Leud boise; bos, bas

Handcuff, *s.* Glas laimh. A promise is not a handcuff, *cha chuirear gad air gealladh.*

Handed, *a.* Làmhach Left-handed, *ciotach, clì*

Handful, *s.* Lan dùirn, làn cròig, glacaid, lan glaic, màm A handful over and above the sack, *mam air muin an t-saic.*

Hand-gallop, *s.* Aonachadh. He went at a hand-gallop, *dh' fhalbh e 'g aonachadh*

Hand-gun, *s* Gunna glaic, gunna cutach

Handicraft, *s.* Ceaird, caladhain.

Handicraftsman, *s.* Fear ceairde

Handily, *adv* Gu lamhchair, gu teoma, gu h-ealanta, gu lathailteach, gu deas-lamhach

Handiwork, *s* Obair laimh

Handkerchief, *s* Neapaigin pòc, seilcadan, neapaig, neapaigin muineil, neapaigin amhaich

Handle, *v a* Làmhaich, laimhsich, lamhrachdaich, bean,

buin ri; rach an dàil (no) an seilbh, gabh os laimh. He handled him roughly, *thug e grinneach dha.*

HANDLE, *s.* (*Of a knife or axe*), cas, cos, samhach, lamh; (*of a cup*), cluas; (*of an oar*), lunn; (*occasion*), ball, inneal.

HANDLED, *a.* Lamhaichte, laimhsichte, air a lamhachadh.

HANDLESS, *a.* Gun lamh, neo-dheas, neo-ealadhanta.

HANDLING, *s.* Lamhachadh, laimhseachadh, buntuinn. He got a rough handling, *fhuair e buntuinn rìs gu geur.*

HANDMAID, *s.* Ban-oglach; searbhanta.

HANDSAW, *s.* Sabh dùirn.

HANDSEL, *s.* Sainnseal, gibhte, tiodhlac, tabhartas; earlas.

HANDSEL, *v.* Faigh sainnseal.

HANDSOME, *s.* Eireachdail, àluinn, aillidh, boidheach, grinn, maiseach, gasd, dreachmhor, ciatach.

HANDSOMELY, *adv.* Gu h-eireachdail, gu h-àluinn, gu h-aillidh, gu bòidheach, gu grinn, gu maiseach, gu gasd, gu dreachmhor, gu ciatach.

HANDSOMENESS, *s.* Eireachdas, àille, àilne, boidhche, bòidhchead, grinneas, maise.

HANDSPIKE, *s.* Seorsa geimhleig.

HANDVICE, *s.* Gramaich bheag, sgrobha laimh.

HANDWRITING, *s.* Lamh-sgriobhaidh. A good handwriting, *deagh lamh-sgriobhaidh,*

HANDY, *a.* Lamhchair, greanta, iomchuidh; teoma.

HANDY-DANDY, *s.* Seorsa cluiche cloinne, bas an righ.

HANG, *v. a.* and *n.* Croch; tachd. He will be hanged, *theid a chrochadh;* go and be hanged, *gabh 'g ad chrochadh, gabh thun na croiche;* he who is born to be hanged cannot be drowned, *am fear do 'n dàn a chroich, cha téid gu brath a bhathadh.*

HANGER, *s.* Ni sam bi leis an crochar rud, mar bhùlas poite.

HANGER, *s.* Claidheamh cutach crom, cloidhean.

HANGING, *s.* Crochadh, tachdadh.

HANGMAN, *s.* Crochadair.

HANK, *s.* Iornadh, iurnadh, iornan; cearsail.

HANKER, *v.* Croch ri, lean, miannaich, bi deigheil.

HANKERING, *s.* Crochadh ri, leanachd, miannachadh, deigh.

HANSE, *s.* Buidheann mharsonta.

HANSE TOWNS, *s.* Bailtean buidhne.

HAP, *s.* Tubaisd, tuiteamas, teagmhas, cineamhuin, cineamhuineas. Good hap, *deagh rath;* by hap, *a thaobh tubaisd;* by good hap, *mar bha 'm fortan.*

HAP, *v. n.* See HAPPEN.

HAPHAZARD, *s.* Teagmhas, cineamhuin, tubaisd, cunnart.

HAPLESS, *a.* Mi-shealbhar, neo-shona, truagh, bochd, mi-aghmhor; gun sealbh, gun sonas. Hapless greed does poorly speed, *sannt gun sonas, éiridh 'n donas da.*

HAPLY, *adv.* Theagamh, math-dh' fhaoidte, maith dh' fhaoidte, dh' fhaoidte.

HAPPEN, *v. n.* Tachair, tuit, thig gu crìche, éirich. Happen what will, *ciod air bi a dh' éireas;* it happened ill, *is bochd mar a dh' eirich (no) mar thachair;* it happened that he died, *thachair e gun d' fhuair e bàs.*

HAPPILY, *adv.* Gu sealbhar, gu fortanach; gu buadhar, gu sona.

HAPPINESS, *s.* Sonas, agh, sòlas, toil-inntinn, sodan, deagh fhortan, rath. Happiness keeps the tract of the generous, *bithidh sonas an lorg na caitheimh.*

HAPPY, *a.* Sona, aghmhor, sòlasach, sodanach, buadhach, taitneach; beannaichte.

HARANGUE, *s.* Òraid; scrùit, sruith; ruanachd, duan, rannachd; seanachas.

HARANGUE, *v. a.* Dean òraid; cuir dhiot.

HARANGUER, *s.* Òraidiche.

HARASS, *v. a.* Sgìthich, claoidh, sàruich, treachail; buair. Harassed, *claoidhte, sàruichte, treachailte.*

HARBINGER, *s.* Teachdair; gille ruithe, gille coise.

HARBOUR, *s.* Càla, càladh; achdarsaid, port; camus, bàgh, long-phort, cuan.

HARBOUR, *v. a.* and *n.* Dion, tearmunn, thoir tearmunn, gabh steach; gabh comhnuidh.

HARBOURAGE, *s.* Dion, dionadh, tearmunn; fasgadh; aoidheachd.

HARBOURER, *s.* Dionair, fear dionaidh, fear tearmuinn; dion, tearmunn.

HARBOURLESS, *a.* Gun chàla, gun phort; gun dion; gun fhasgadh, gun tearmunn.

HARD, *a.* (*Not soft*), cruaidh; teann, daingeann; docrach; (*in taste*), searbh, goirt; (*difficult*), deacair, doilich, duilich, do-dheanamh; (*cruel*), cruaidh, cruadalach; doirbh; ain-iochdmhor; (*avaricious*), teann, cruadhalta, cruaidh, crion, spiocach, gionach, cruadalach. A hard heart against hard hap, *cridhe cruaidh ri h-uchd feum;* hard to come at, *duilich a ruigheachd, do-ruigsinn, do-fhaotainn;* hard by, *am fogus, fagus air laimh;* hard by us, *fagus duinn; fagus oirnne;* be hard at work, *éirich air obair;* hold a thing hard, *gramaich, greimich, teann-ghlac;* drink hard, *geòc;* make hard, *cruadhaich;* put hard to it, *cuir h-uige, cuir an càs;* hard to learn, *do-ionnsuchadh;* hard to be pleased, *do-thoileachadh; duilich a thoileachadh;* it freezes hard, *tha 'n cruaidh reoth ann.*

HARD, *adv.* Gu cruaidh, gu dùrachdach, gu teann; gu stoirmeil, gu gaillionach.

HARDEN, *v. a.* and *n.* Cruadhaich; cleachd; dean ri, fas (no) cinn cruaidh. Hardened, *cruadhaichte; cleachdta, deante ri.*

HARDENER, *s.* Cruadhachair.

HARDFAVOURED, *a.* Gruamach, doirbh, neo-bhoidheach.

HARDHANDED, *a.* Cruaidh-lamhach.

HARDHEARTED, *a.* Cruaidh-chridheach, ain-iochdmhor, neo-thròcaireach.

HARDHEARTEDNESS, *s.* Ain-iochd.

HARDIHOOD, *s.* Cruadal; tuairealachd.

HARDILY, *adv.* Gu cruadalach, gu tuaireil, gu misneachail.

HARDINESS, *s.* Cruadalachd, cruadal, tuairealachd, treunas, gaisge, dànachd, cruadhas, † sgiothas.

HARDLABOURED, *a.* Saoithreachail; sàruichte.

HARDLY, *adv.* Air éigin, is gann; ach gann; le moran iomairt, gu saoithreachail; (*sharply*), gu doirbh, gu geur, gu cruaidh, gu teann. I hardly arrived when he died, *is gann a thainig mi nur theasd e.*

HARDMOUTHED, *a.* Cruaidh-bheulach; ceann-laidir, ragmhuinealach.

HARDNESS, *s.* (*In opposition to softness*), cruadhas, diongaltas; (*firmness*), teannad; (*scarcity*), gainne, gortadh, bochduinn; (*cruelty*), buirbe; (*bitterness*), seirbhe; (*stinginess*), spiocaireachd; crìne, gion; (*difficulty*), deacaireachd.

HARDOCK, *s.* Cobagach.

HARDS, *s.* Asgart, pab, barrach.

HARDSHIP, *s.* Cruaidh-chas, càs, teanntachd, cruadal, teinne; cruadhaig; cruadhail, foirneart, treachladh, dochann; buadhairt; sgìtheas.

HARDWARE, *s.* Cruaidh-bhathar, bathar cruaidh, mar sgeinichean as an leithidibh sin.

HARDY, *a.* (*Of hardship*), cruadalach, fulangach; tuaireil; (*bold*), dàna, ladurna; (*firm*), teann, daingeann; (*valiant*), misneachail, treubhanta, gaisgeil.

HARE, *s.* Maigheach, moigheach, gearr-fhiadh

Harebrained, *a.* Gogaideach, gaoithe; gorach, eutrom; amaideach; fiadhaich, baoth.

Harehearted, *a.* Gealtach, eagallach.

Harefoot, *s.* Cos maighiche.

Harelip, *s.* Bearnadh mhiol; bearnadh beòil.

Harrier, *s.* Abhag; gaothar, cu-luirg, tollair beag.

Hark, *v. n.* Eisd.

Hark, *interj.* Eisd! caisd! h-isd!

Harl, *s.* Pab.

Harlequin, *s.* Baoth-chleasaiche, cleasaiche.

Harlequinade, *s.* Cleasachd, baoth-chleasachd.

Harlot, *s.* Siùrsach, striopach, dearg-striopach, meirdreach, strapaid, stropaid, bidse; stràill.

Harlotry, *s.* Siùrsachd, striopachas.

Harm, *s.* Coire, dolaidh, dochoir, dochair, cron, dochann; beud; ciurram, ciurradh; lochd, diùbhail; urchoid, earchall; calldach; ciont. There is no harm, *cha n' eil dolaidh ann;* without harm, *gun dolaidh.*

Harm, *v. a.* Ciurr, dochainn.

Harmful, *a.* Lochdach, urchoideach, dochannach, olc.

Harmless, *a.* Neo-choireach, neo-lochdach, neo-chronail, neo-chiontach; (*as a horse*), soimeach, socrach.

Harmlessly, *adv.* Gu neo-choireach, gu neo-lochdach, gu neo-chiontach; gu soimeach.

Harmlessness, *s.* Neo-chiontas.

Harmonic, *a.* Ceolmhor, binn, fonmhor, co-sheirmeach.

Harmonious, *a.* Co-sheirmeach, ceolmhor, fonnmhor.

Harmoniously, *adv.* Gu co-sheirmeach, gu ceòl-mhor, gu fonnmhor.

Harmoniousness, *s.* Ceòlmhorachd, fonnmhorachd.

Harmonize, *v.* Co-fhreagair; dean ceòlmhor.

Harmony, *s.* Co-sheirm; ceòl; càirdeas.

Harness, *s.* Acfhuinn; uigheam, armachd; fasair, fasradh, airneis.

Harness, *v. a.* Uigheamaich.

Harp, *s.* Clàrsach, cruit, cruit-chiùil; ainm reult àraidh.

Harp, *v.* Cluich air cruit (no) clarsaich.

Harper, *s.* Clàrsair, cruitear; filidh. He is a harsh harper who has but one tune, *is searbh clàrsair an aon phuirt.*

Harpoon, *s.* Seorsa gath no muireadh leis am buailear muc mhara.

Harpy, *s.* Eun millteach smògach le aghaidh oigh; (*oppressor*), fear foirneirt, spiocair.

Harridan, *s.* Seann siùrsach.

Harrow, *s.* Cliath, cliath forsaidh.

Harrow, *v. a.* Cliath; reub; spùirm, spùill; buair.

Harrower, *s.* Cliathadair; forsair.

† **Harry**, *v. a.* Creach, mill; buair, saruich.

Harsh, *a.* (*Severe*), borb, doirbh, gràiceach, ainneartach, dalma, reasgach, coimheach, crosda, mi-thlusail, cruaidh, searbh, garg; (*to the taste*), searbh, garg, goirt; (*in sound*), déistinneach, searbh.

Harshly, *adv.* Gu borb, gu doirbh, gu dalma, gu h-ainneartach, gu reasgach, gu coimheach, gu cruaidh, gu searbh, gu garg, gu déistinneach.

Harshness, *s.* Buirbe, doirbhe, coimheachas, cruadhas; (*to the taste*), seirbhe; searbhas, gairge, gairgead; (*in sound*), déistinneachd.

Hart, *s.* Damh feidh, damh, ullaiche.

Hartshorn, *s.* Sugh adhaircean, seorsa leigheis; adharc feidh.

Hartstongue, *s.* Cneamh nam muc fiadhaich.

Harvest, *s.* Foghar, fogharadh; arbhar abaich; toradh gniomh. A harvest day, *la fogharaidh.*

Harvester, *s.* Buainiche.

Harvest-home, *s.* Ceann; deireadh thairnidh; féill an fhogharaidh, arlogh.

Harvest-man, *s.* Buainiche, fear fogharaidh.

Has, *v.* See **Have**.

Hash, *v. a.* Mìn-ghearr, pronn.

Hash, *s.* Biadh pronn.

Hasp, *s.* Crambaid, clasb, bùcal.

Hassock, *s.* Cluasag ghlùin.

Haste, *s.* Cabhag, deifir; griobhag, greasachd, greasdachd; luathas, spéid; déine. Make haste, *dean cabhag, greas ort;* why in such haste? *ciod fàth na cabhaig? carson a tha' chabhag?* the more haste the less speed, *mar is mo 'chabhag is ann lugha an spéid.*

Haste, Hasten, *v. a.* and *n.* Greas, luathaich, luathraich, deifirich, cuir an cabhaig, cuir cabhag air, dean cabhag, greas ort, bi tapaidh. Hasten your pace, *luathaich do cheum, tarruing a chos air deireadh.*

Hastened, *a.* Greasta, deifirichte, luathraichte.

Hastener, *s.* Greasair, greasadair, brogair.

Hastening, *s.* Cabhag, deifreachadh, greasachd, greasdachd.

Hastily, *adv.* Gu cabhagach, gu luath, gu grad; gu feargach, gu cas, gu crosda, gun smuaine; gu dian; ann an cabhaig.

Hastiness, *s.* Cabhag, spéid, luathas, luathailteachd; crosdachd, cainnteachd.

Hastings, *s.* Peasair thràthail; peasair luath.

Hasty, *a.* Cabhagach, luath, grad, obann; (*testy*), cas, dian, ealamh; crosda, doirbh; diorrasach, cainnteach; (*premature*), abaich roimh chéile; tràthail.

Hasty-pudding, *s.* Lite; brochan.

Hat, *s.* Ad, bioraid, comhdach, cinn.

Hatband, *s.* Bann aid.

Hatch, *v. a.* Gur, dean gur; thoir a mach; dealbh, smuainich, cnuasaich, tionnsgain.

Hatch, *s.* Gur, guradh; àlach, àl; nochdadh.

Hatch, *s.* Leth-dhorus, dorus uachdrach, luinge, aistidh.

Hatchel, *s.* Seiceal.

Hatchel, *v. a.* Seicil, cìr.

Hatcheller, *s.* Seicealair.

Hatches, *s. pl.* Sailtichean.

Hatchet, *s.* Tuadh, † biail.

Hatchment, *s.* Euchd.

Hate, *v. a.* Fuathaich, grainich, sgreamhaich, oilltich. I hate him, *dh' oilltich mi ris.*

Hate, *s.* Fuath, gràin, sgreamh; oillt, miorun, mi-run, mi-osguinn.

Hateful, *a.* Fuathmhor, gràineil, sgreamhail, oillteil, mi-runach, miosguinneach. Hatefully, *gu fuathmhor, gu graineil.*

Hatefulness, *s.* Fuathmhorachd, grainealachd, sgreamhaileachd, miosguinneachd.

Hater, *s.* Fear fuatha, fuathachair, fear mio-runach.

Hath, *v.* See **Have**.

Hatred, *s.* Fuath, gràin; mio-run; galltanas, tnù, gamhlas, naimhdeas, fàladh, deistinn.

Hatter, *v. a.* Buair, sàruich; claoidh.

Hatter, *s.* Adair, fear dheanamh adaichean.

Hattock, *s.* Adag.

Hauberk, *s.* Lùireach, eididh uchd.

Haughtily, *adv.* Gu h-ardanach, gu h-uaibhreach, gu h-aillghiosach, gu h-uallach, gu sgòdail, gu leòmach.

Haughtiness, *s.* Ardan, uaibhreas, uaibhreachd, àill-ghiosachd, uaille, sgòd, leoime

Haughty, *a.* Ardanach, uaibhreach, ailghiosach, ard, ard-innuinneach, uallach, sgòdail, leomach, dasachdach, uragh-usach

Haul, *v* Tarruing, slaod.

Haul, *s* Tarruing, slaod.

Haulm, *s* Fodar, srabh, dias, diasad.

Haulyard, *s* Tarruing

Haunch, *s.* Sliasad, cruachann, màs, ceithreamh deiridh, iosgaid.

Haunt, *v.* Tathaich, lean gu minig, bith-lean.

Haunt, *s* Aite tathaich, àite coinneimh; (*den*), uamh-aidh; (*custom*), cleachd, àbhaist, nòs. He returned to his old haunt, *phill e gu 'shean chleachdan*

Haunter, *s* Fear tathaich.

Haunting, *s* Tathaich.

Hautboy, *s* Seorsa inneal ciùil

Haut-gout, *s.* Fàile (no) tochd laidir.

Have, *v. a* Na bi a dhìth, meal, sealbhaich; faigh; gabh, gleidh What have you to do with me, *ciod do ghnothuch riumsa*, he has a fair wind, *tha soirbheas aig*, have a care, *thoir an aire*, you have enough to do, *tha do thoil ri dhe-anamh agad*. I have been, *bha mi, tha mi air bith*, have at you, *h-ugad, chugad.*

Haven, *s* Càla, càladh, port, bagh, geòdh, canais; dion, tearmunn, fasgadh, †conair

Haven, *s* Sealbhair, fear seilbh

Haver, *s* Sealbhadair, fear seilbh.

Having, *s* Sealbhachadh, saibhreas; greim; oighreachd

Havock, *s.* Fàsachadh, sgriosadh, sgrios; lom-sgriosadh, milleadh, àr, beubanachd, marbhadh, dubh-mharbhadh, oirlioch

Haw, *s* (*A berry*), sgeachag; (*a piece of ground*), dail, ach

Hawk, *s* Seabhag, seobhag, meirneal, speireag. Between hawk and buzzard, *san tomhartaich*

Hawk, *v a* Seabhagaich, reic ni le bhi 'g a ghlaodhaich air feadh nan sraidean

Hawk, *s.* Carasan, carasanaich Hawking, *ri carasanaich*

Hawked, *a* Crom

Hawker, *s.* Seabhagair, marsonta màileid, fear paca

Hawthorn, *s* Sgitheach, droighionn, crann sgeachag.

Hawthorn-berry, *s* Sgeachag

Hay, *s* Saoidh, sùidh; feur caoinichte Meadow hay, *saoidh lòin*, clover hay, *saoidh chlòbhair*

Haycock, *s* Cuidhle, cuidhleag, rucan, mulan.

Hayloft, *s.* Lobhta saidh

Haymaker, *s* Fear caoineachaidh, saoidhear The hay-makers, *muinntir na saidh.*

Hayrick, *s* Cruach saidh, cruach shaoidh, mir saidh, mulan feòir, rucan

Hayruff, *s* Garbh-lus.

Haystack, *s* Cruach saidh, mir saidh

Hazard, *s* Tuiteamas, cineamhuinn, tubaisd, baoghal, cunnart, guasachd, sgiorradh

Hazard, *v a* Cuir an cunnart, feuch ri.

Hazardous, *a.* Cunnartach, guasachdach, tubaisdeach, neo-thearuinnte, buailteach do chall.

Hazardousness, *s.* Cunnart, tubaisd, guasachd, cunnart-achd

Haze, *s* Ceò, ceathach, dall-cheo, braon, crith-reotha.

Hazel, *s.* Caltuinn.

Hazel, *a.* Caltuinn A hazel nut, *cnò challtuinn;* hazel rods, *cuilleasg.*

Hazy, *a.* Ceòthar, ceathachail, mùigeach; dorch, braonach, tiugh.

He, *pron.* E, esa, esan, se; fìrionnach; fìrionn.

Head, *s.* (*Of the body*), ceann, †coll; (*in ridicule*), plub, ploc, (*brain*), eanchainn, (*chief*), priomh, comanntair, ceannard, ceann fine, ceann cinnidh, (*understanding*), tuisge, inntinn, ciall; (*resistance*), aghaidh, comhdhail, †gart; (*make head*), thoir aghaidh; (*of a bed*), mullach; (*of a discourse*), ceann, steidh; earann, (*of a ship*), ceann toisich, (*of a stream*), tobar; (*of an army*), tùs, toiseach, ceann; (*power*), cumhachd, neart, (*of land*), ceann, rughadh, maol, muil, sròin. Head and ears, *eadar cheann 's a chasan*, head and shoulders, *a dh' aindeoin*, at the head of an army, *air tùs feachd;* at the head of his army, *aig ceann a shlogh*, they laid their heads together, *chuir iad an cinn ri chèile*, what put that in your head? *ciod a chuir sin ad cheann?* a clear head, *eanchainn shoilleir*, from head to foot, *o mhullach gu bonn*, get a-head, *tionail feachd*, (at sea), *faigh air thoiseach;* an addle-head, *ceann gaoithe, ceann eutrom, ceann àrcain*, give head, (as to a horse), *thoir comas cinn*, the forepart of the head, *aghaidh, aodann, cruaic*, hinder head, *cùl cinn;* at a head, (as a boil), *abaich*, swimming of the head, *tuaineal, tuainealach, tuaicheall*, a large head on the wise man, and a hen's head on a fool, *ceann mòr air duine glic, is ceann circe air amadan.*

Head, *v.* Treòruich, riaghail, rach no imich an tus (no) aig ceann.

Headache, *s* Ceann goirt; goirteas cinn

Headband, *s.* Stiom cinn, fuiltean, failtean

Headborough, *s* Maor baile, constabull

Head-dress, *s* Ceann bheart, deise cinn, uigheam cinn, còmhdach cinn

Headiness, *s* Cabhag, deifir, caise, caisead, obainne; reasg-achd.

Headless, *a* Gun cheann, air dhìth cinn; gun cheannard; dì-cheannaichte, baoghalta, aineolach, neo-thapaidh.

Headland, *s* Ceann, maol, muil, rughadh, ceann-tìre, sròin.

Headlong, *a* Corrach, cas, grad, dian, cabhagach, ceann-laidir, brais, neò-smaointeachail

Headlong, *adv* An comhar a chinn, gu cas, gu grad, gu brais, gun dàil.

Headmost, *a* Air thoiseach, toiseachail, is fhaide air thois-each.

Headpiece, *s* Clogaid, ceann bheart, ceann, inntinn, cath-bharr; dìnìath, †gailia, tuigse

Head-quarters, *s* Fardoch

Headship, *s* Ceannas, ceannardachd, lamh an uachdar, inmhe, ùghdaras

Headstall, *s* Claigeannach; ceannasg

Headstone, *s.* Clach mullaich; clach ann, clach uaigh.

Headstrong, *a* Ceann-laidir, reasgach, rag, dian, cas, brais, rag-mhuinealach, luaimneach

Head-workman, *s* Griobh

Heady, *a.* Brais, ceann-laidir, rag, reasgach; dian, do-cheannsach; luaimneach; (*as liquor*), laidir.

Heal, *v a.* and *n.* Slànuich, leighis, ic, dean gu math; cneasaich, réitich, dean réith. Healed, *slanuichte, leighiste.*

Healer, *s.* Slanuchair, leigh

Healing, *a.* Leigheasach, leigheasail, iceil, ciùin, seimh, bogar.

Healing, *s.* Slanuchadh, leigheasadh, comhdachadh.

Health, *s.* Slainnte, fallaineachd, fallaine. Here is a health to you, *so air do shlainnte.*

Healthful, *a.* Slainnteil, fallain, slàn.

Healthfully, *adv.* Gu slainnteil, gu fallain, gu slàn.

Healthfulness, *s.* Slainnte, fallaineachd; anacal.

Healthiness, *s.* Slainnte, fallaineachd.

Healthless, *a.* Tinn, euslan, neo-fhallain, truagh, mall, breòite.

Healthy, *a.* Slainnteil, fallain, slàn.

Heam, *s.* Deireanach.

Heap, *s.* Carn, cruach, cruachan; crucach; torr; cnoc; dùn, dùnan, mullach, maoil, cnoc; dorlach, mòran; (*crowd*), lòd, bròd, teanaladh, cruinneachadh. Stones in heaps, *clachan na 'n dunaibh, cùirn.*

Heap, *v. a.* Carn, cruach, torr; cruinnich; cuir ri chéile, cnuasaich. Heaped, *carnta, cruachta, cruinnichte.*

Heaping, *s.* Carnadh, cruachadh, cruinneachadh, cur ri chéile.

Hear, *v. a.* and *n.* Cluinn, fairich; éisd, caisd. Hear you? *bheil thu'cluinntinn? an cluinn thu;* hear me a little, *éisd rium beagan;* I have heard, *chual mi;* he was favourably heard, *dh' eisdeadh ris gu fabharach;* what the young hear they repeat, *an ni chluinneas na big 's e chànas na big.*

Hearer, *s.* Fear éisdeachd. Hearers, *luchd éisdeachd.*

Hearing, *s.* Éisdeachd; claisteachd, claistneachd, claisneachd; feuchainn, deuchainn. The hearing of the ear, *claisteachd na cluaise;* in my hearing, *ann am éisdeachd;* obtain a hearing, *faigh éisdeachd.*

Hearken, *v.* Eisd, cluinn, caisd, thoir an aire, thoir aire.

Hearkener, *s.* Fear far-cluaise.

Hearsay, *s.* Iomradh, fabhur, fabhunn, cainnt, sgeul beòil, sgeul.

Hearse, *s.* Dubh-charbad, cro-charbad.

Hearselike, *a.* Dubh, brònach, muladach; eugaidh.

Hearse-cloth, *s.* Dubh-bhrat, brat-dubh, brat bròin.

Heart, *s.* Cridhe; (*courage*), misneach, spiorad; (*desire*), miann, togar, càile; (*memory*), cuimhne; (*good-will*), toil, deadh thoil; (*middle*), meadhon, teis-meadhon, builsgean. His heart fell into his hose, *thuit a chridhe na thòin;* be of good heart, *bi misneachail;* with all my heart, *le m' uile chridhe;* out of heart, *air dhìth misnich,* (as ground), *truagh, bochd;* heart of oak, *darach;* for my heart, *a dh' aindeoin mo chridhe;* get that by heart, *faigh sin air do chridhe;* grief of heart, *truime cridhe;* sweetheart, *ceistean, graidhean, gaolach;* stout of heart, *laidir, treubhanta, crodha.*

Heartache, *s.* Tinneas cridhe, bròn, do-bhron, tuirse, mulad, cumha.

Heartbreak, *s.* Briseadh-cridhe.

Heartbreaking, *a.* Brònach, muladach.

Heartburn, *s.* Losgadh bràghaid.

Heartburning, *s.* Tinneas goile, coiliginn; gamhlas; tnù.

Heartdear, *a.* Gradhach; ionmhuinn.

Heartsease, *s.* Samchair, tamh, fois.

Hearted, *a.* Misneachail, crodha, calma; cridheil. Light-hearted, *suilbhear; sunntach, biolachair.*

Hearten, *v. a.* Thoir misneach, brosnuich, prosnaich, neartaich, tog; (*land*), leasaich, mathaich.

Hearth, *s.* Teallach, teinntean, cagailt, clach an teallaich.

Heartily, *adv.* As a chridhe, le cridhe, gu toileach, le làn toil, a dheòin; gu cridheil; gu sgairteil; gu tréibhdhireach, gu h-ionraic, gu neo-chealgach. Laugh heartily, *gàir gu cridheil.*

Heartiness, *s.* Cridhealas, cridhealachd, ionracas, tréibhdhireas, spiorad, sgairtealas.

Heartless, *a.* Lag-chridheach, neo-mhisneachail, tais; anfhann.

Heartlessly, *adv.* Gu lag-chridheach, gu h-anmhunn.

Heartlessness, *s.* Mi-chridhealachd, cion misnich, tuirse, truime.

Heartrending, *a.* Trioblaideach, brònach, muladach.

Heartsick, *a.* Tinn, an-shocrach.

Heartstring, *s.* Féith a chridhe.

Heartstruck, *a.* Gonta, gointe, air bhualadh le gaol (no) le eagal.

Heart-wounded, *a.* Gonta, cridhe-leòinte.

Hearty, *a.* (*Cheerful*), cridheil; suilbhear; sulchair, sunntach; (*sincere*), treibhdhireach; ionraic; dùrachdach, deònach; (*well*), slàn, fallain, slàinnteil, laidir.

Heat, *s.* Teas, blàs, blàthas, teasaigheachd; (*passion*), fearg, corruich. The heat of the day, *teas (no) àirde an latha;* intense heat, *dian-theas;* a heat, (*in races*), *cùrsa.*

Heat, *v. a.* Blathaich, blàitich, blàtaich, teòth; gar, teòthaich. Heated, *blathaichte, teothta.*

Heath, *s.* Fraoch; frithe; monadh; sliabh.

Heath-cock, *s.* Coileach fraoich, coileach dubh, coilcach ruadh.

Heathen, *s.* and *a.* Gintealach, paganach, cinneach, neo-chreideach, ana-criosduigh.

Heathenish, *a.* Gintealach, paganta, borb, fiadhaich.

Heathenism, *s.* Gintealachd, pagantachd, ana-criosdachd.

Heath-hen, *s.* Cearc fhraoich, liath chearc.

Heathpout, *s.* Pùt.

Heath-pease, *s.* Cairmeal.

Heathy, *a.* Fraochail, fraochach, fraoich, làn fraoich.

Heave, *v. a.* and *n.* (*Raise*), tog, ardaich; (*vomit*), tilg, sgeith; (*swell*), at, boch; éirich. Heave a sigh, *tarruing osunn.*

Heave, *s.* Togail, eallach, uallach; éiridh; at; bochthonn; uspag; tur thilge, sannt sgeithe.

Heaven, *s.* Neamh, flaitheas, flaitheanas, flath-innis, †ceal, †carc.

Heavenborn, *a.* Naomh, neamhaidh, ainglidh.

Heaven-directed, *a.* Air stiùradh; chum neamh; treoraichte le neamh.

Heavenly, *a.* Neamhuidh, ainglidh; ro-aghmhor; flathmhaiseach.

Heavenwards, *adv.* Chum na neamhaibh, chum neamh.

Heave-offering, *s.* Tabhartas ceud thoraidh.

Heavily, *adv.* Gu trom, gu tuirseach, gu dubhach, gu brònach, gu cràiteach, gu doilich, gu dolasach, gu docrach, gu liosta.

Heaviness, *s.* Truime, tromadas, trumadas, (*of mind*), dubhachas, bròn, tuirse, dòlas, doilghios, sprochd, mulad; cradh; sàrachadh; (*drowsiness*), tur-chodail.

Heavy, *a.* (*In weight*), trom, cothromach, cudthromach; (*sad*), dubhach dolasach, duilich, docrach, airsnealach, éisleanach; liosda; (*slow*), leasg, lunndach; slaodach; mairnealach, aimhleasg; (*requiring pains*), saothaireachail.

Heavyhanded, *a.* Trom, neo-dheas, neo-ealanta.

Heavyheeled, *a.* Luidseach.

Hebdomadal, *a.* Seachduineach, gach seachduin.

Hebetate, *v.* Maolaich. Hebetated, *maolaichte.*

Hebetude, *s.* Maolad; baoghlanachd.

Hebraism, *s.* Radh Eabhrach.

Hebraist, *s.* Sgoilear Eabhrach, fear eolach air an Eabhra.

Hebrew, *s.* Eabbra, cainnt nan Eabhrach.

Hebrew, *a.* Eabhrach, Eabhruidheach.

Hecatomb, *s.* Iobairt ceud damh, iobairt ceud ceann cruidh.

Hectic, *a.* Cnaoidhte, caithteach, seargach; éitich. A hectic flush, *rughadh éitich.*

Hector, *s.* Eachann; gaisgeach na Troimh; laochan, buamsdair, blaghair.

Hector, *v. a.* Bòsd, dean bòsd, bragainn; bagair, ràith, dean blaghaireachd.

Hedge, *v. a.* and *n.* Dùin, fàlaich, druid, iom-dhruid, uimdhruid.

Hedge, *s.* Callaid, fàl, gàradh; daighneach, ganal, falgleuta. On the wrong side of the hedge, *ann am mearachd.*

Hedgeborn, *a.* Bochd, iosal, dìblidh.

Hedgehog, *s.* Gràineag.

Hedge-pig, *s.* Graineag òg.

Hedge-sparrow, *s.* Gealbhan, gealbhan gàraidh.

Hedging-bill, *s.* Sgian bearraidh, sgian gairnealair.

Heed, *v. a.* Thoir aire, thoir fanear, gabh beachd, cuimhnich. Do not heed him, *na gabh ort e.*

Heed, *s.* Cùram, aire, faicill; beachd. Take heed, *thoir aire gabh beachd.*

Heedful, *a.* Cùramach, aireachail, faicilleach, beachdail, suidhichte, furachair. Heedfully, *gu cùramach, gu faicilleach.*

Heedfulness, *s.* Cùram, faicill, faicilleachd.

Heedless, *a.* Dearmadach, neo-chùramach, neo-aireachail, neo-omhailleach.

Heedlessness, *s.* Dearmad, dearmadachd, neo-chùram, neo-aire, cion aire, cion omhaill, dìth umhaill.

Heel, *s.* Sàil; (*of a shoe*), sàil bròige, breaban deiridh, ceathramh sàlach. Take to your heels, *thoir do chasan asad, thoir na buinn asad;* lay by the heels, *ceangail, gabh an laimh.*

Heel, *v. n.* and *a.* Danns, damhs; aom, aom gu taobh mar ni luing; sàilich.

Heelpiece, *s.* Ceathramh sàlach.

Heft, *s.* Oidhirp; deuchainn, éiridh.

Hegira, *s.* Focal Arabach, a ciallachadh an t-am air am b' fheudar do Mhathomeid teicheachd o Mhecca, ni a thachair air di h-Aoine, an seathamh la deug do 'n Iul, sa bhliadhna sè ceud, fichead 's a dhà.

Heifer, *s.* Agh, atharla; biorach, colpach; coilt.

Heigh ho, *interj.* Och, och! oich, oich! ochòin, och fhéin, ochòin fhéin, och mise, heich ho.

Height, *s.* Airde; inbhe, meud; mullach; binnean, bàrr, ardan.

Heighten, *v. a.* Arduich; meudaich; leasaich; dùisg, tog. Heightened, *arduichte; meudaichte; air arduchadh.*

Heightening, *s.* Arduchadh, meudachadh; leasachadh.

Heinous, *a.* Uamharra, fuathasach; ro-aingidh, peacach; antrom. Heinously, *gu h-uamharra, gu fuathasach.* A heinous crime, *fiamh-lochd.*

Heinousness, *s.* Uamharrachd, aingidheachd; an-tromaichead.

Heir, *s.* Oighre; dilibeach. A rich man never died without an heir, *cha d' eug duine riamh gun dileabach.*

Heir, *v.* Sealbhaich.

Heiress, *s.* Ban-oighre.

Heirless, *a.* Gun oighre.

Heirloom, *s.* Oighre mhàoin.

Held. See **Hold**.

Heliacal, *a.* A fàgail dealradh na greine.

Helical, *a.* Sniomhaineach, sniomhach, cuairteach, sgrobhail, casda, lùbach.

Heliography, *s.* Grian-chunntas.

Helioscope, *s.* Gloine gréine.

Heliotrope, *s.* Plùr na gréine, grian-luibh, plùr sam bi a thionndas ris a ghrian.

Hell, *s.* Ifrinn; ì-fuar-fhonn, iutharn, ionad comhnuidh dheamhana, an sloc.

Hellbred, *a.* Diabhluidh, deamhnaidh, ifrinneach, aingidh.

Hell-broth, *s.* Puinnsean.

Helldoomed, *a.* Ifrinneach, mallaichte, diabhluidh.

Hellhated, *a.* Fuathaichte mar ifrinn.

Hellhound, *s.* Deamhan; cu ifrinn, diabhol-mhadadh.

Hellish, *a.* Diabhluidh, deamhnaidh, ifrinneach, ifrionta; aingidh. Hellishly, *gu diabhluidh, gu deamhnaidh, gu h-aingidh.*

Hellishness, *s.* Diabhluidheachd, deamhanachd.

Helm, *s.* Stiùir, sdiùir, bioraid, clogaid.

Helmet, *s.* Ceann bheart, clogaid; bioraid, sgaball.

Help, *v.* Coghain, cuidich, cobhair; fuasgail, furtaich, dean còghnadh, dean cobhair. I cannot help it, *cha n' eil comas agam air;* help me, *cuidich mi; cuideach leam;* God help us, *Dhia cuidich sinn, Dhia cuidich leinn;* help! help! *cobhair! cobhair!*

Help, *s.* Còghnadh, cuideachadh, cobhair, cabhair; fuasgladh, furtachd. With God's help, *le còghnadh Dhé;* there is no help for it, *cha 'n eil comas air.*

Helper, *s.* Fear coghnaidh, fear cuideachaidh; cungantair.

Helpful, *a.* Cuideachail, còghnachail.

Helpless, *a.* Truagh, bochd, dìblidh, uireasbhach, gun chòghnadh; do-leigheasadh. A helpless person, *truaghan.*

Helplessness, *s.* Truaghanachd, dìblidheachd, uireasbhachd.

Helter-skelter, *adv.* Thar a cheile, air feadh chéile, gu mi-riaghailteach.

Helve, *s.* Cas, cos, lamh, samhach, lamh tuaidh (no) ùird.

Helve, *a.* Cuir cos (no) lamh ann ni.

Hem, *s.* Faim, foir, oir, iomall, buinne.

Hem, *v. a.* Faim, foir.

Hem, *v. n.* Dean cnead (no) casd, cnead, casd.

Hemi. Leth.

Hemicircular, *a.* Leth-chruinn, leth-chearclach.

Hemicycle, *s.* Leth-chruinne, leth-chearcall.

Hemisphere, *s.* Leth-chruinne.

Hemispherical, *a.* Leth-chruinn.

Hemistic, *a.* Leth-rann.

Hemlock, *s.* Iteodha; minmhear, mongach mhear.

Hemorrhage, *s.* Gearrach fola, flann-bhuinneach.

Hemorrhoids, *s.* Neasgaidean fola.

Hemp, *s.* Còrcach, càrcach; caineab.

Hempen, *a.* Còrcach, càrcach.

Hen, *s.* Cearc. A hen's egg, *ubh circe;* a heath hen, *cearc fhraoich;* a turkey hen, *cearc Fhrangach;* a pea-hen, *peubh-chearc.*

Henbane, *s.* An deodha, gafann, crann gafann.

Hence, *adv.* A so, o so, o so suas; (*begone*), air falbh; bi 'coiseachd.

Henceforth, *adv.* O so suas, a so suas, tuille.

Henceforward, *adv.* O so suas, a so suas, tuille.

Henchman, *s.* Gille, gille coise, seirbheiseach.

† **Hend**, *v. a.* Glac, beir air.

Henhearted, *a.* Meata, gealtach, cailleachanta, tais, bog.

Henpecked, *a.* Fo riaghladh mna.

Henroost, *s.* Sparadh, spiris, fàradh chearc.

Hepatic, *a.* Sgamhanach.

Heptagon, *s.* Seachd-shlisneag.

Heptagonal, *a.* Seachd shlisneach, seachd oisinneach.

Heptangular, *a.* Seachd oisinneach, seachd-uilneach.

Heptarchy, *s.* Seachd-fhlaitheachd; uachdaranachd sheachdnar

Her, *pron.* I, ise. Herself, *i féin;* she herself, *ise féin*, by herself, *le féin, na h-aonrachd, na h-aonar, na h-aonrachdan.*

Her, *pron.* A. Her hand, *a lamh*, her own hand, *a lamh féin.*

Herald, *s.* Bollsgair, fear eighich; gairmear; suaicheantaiche, teachdair; maor gairm, griom-challair.

Heraldry, *s.* Ealadhain suaicheantais; suaicheantachd, seanachas, ginealachd.

Herb, *s* Luibh, lus, luibhean, luisean The herb that cannot be found, will heal no wound, *an luibh nach fhaighear cha 'n i 'chobhaireas.*

Herbaceous, *a.* Luibheach, lusach, luibheanach, luiseanach, feurach.

Herbage, *s.* Feur feurach, ionaltradh.

Herbalist, *s.* Lusragan

Herbed, *a.* Feurach, luibheach.

Herbous, *a.* Luibheach, luiseanach.

Herby, *a.* Luibheanach, luiseanach

Herculean, *a.* Ro dheacair; spairneil; treun

Herd, *s.* Treud, iomain, greigh; buidheann, buachaill.

Herd, *v. n.* Greigh.

Herdman, *s* Buachaill, aodhair, aireach; aoireann.

Here, *adv.* An so, 's an àite so Here's to you, *so dhuit*, (in drinking), *so leat*, here he is, *so e*, here he is for you, *so agad e*, here and there, *an so 's an sud, thàll is bhos, null is a null.*

Hereabout, Hereabouts, *adv.* Mu so, timchioll so, mu 'n àite so.

Hereafter, *adv.* An deigh so, an deigh laimh; a so suas, san ath-bheath Hereafter, for ever, *o suas, a choidh.*

Hereafter, *s* Ath-bheath.

Hereat, *adv* Aig so.

Hereby, *adv.* Le so, leis a so

Hereditament, *s* Seilbhe, sealbhachadh.

Hereditary, *s.* Dùchasach; oighreachdail.

Herein, *adv.* An so.

Hereon, *adv.* Air so.

Heresiarch, *s* Ard-eiriceach.

Heresy, *s.* Eiriceas, eiriceachd, saobh-chreideamh, dobharail.

Heretic, *s.* Eiriceach, saobh-chreideach.

Heretical, *a.* Eiriceach, eiriceil, so-chreideachail. Heretically, gu h-éiriceach.

Hereto, *adv.* Chum so, chuige so, gu ruig so, gu ruig so, ri so.

Heretofore, *adv* Roimh so, o cheann fada, o cheann fhada.

Herewith, *adv.* Le so, leis a so.

Heritage, *s.* Oighreachd, fearann, seilbhe

Hermaphrodite, *s.* Urr firionn boirionn

Hermit, *s.* Dìthreabhach, aonaran, aonaranach

Hermitage, *s* Aros aonarain, uamh, uamh-aros, garaidh, cill-aonarain.

Hermitess, *s.* Ban aonarain

Hermitical, *a.* Aonaranach, uaigneach, dithreabhach.

Hern, *s.* See Heron.

Hernia, *s.* Mam-sloc.

Hero, *s.* Gaisgeach, curaidh, laoch, flath, treunlaoch, diùlnach, diùnlaoch, mìlidh.

Heroic, Heroical, *a* Gaisgeil; treubhanta, conspullach, euchdach, treun, feartach, buadhach, buadhmhor, cruadalach, dàn, misneachail. An heroic poem, *dan mòr.* Heroically, *gu gaisgeil, gu treubhanta, gu h-euchdach.*

Heroine, *s.* Ban-ghaisgeach, ban-churaidh, ban-fhlath.

Heroism, *s.* Gaisge, treubhantas, euchd, feart, connspullachd

Heron, *s* Corr-riabhach, corr-ghribeach, corr-ghlas.

Herpes, *s.* Teine dé.

Herring, *s* Sgadan. No wonder that a herring cask smells of herring, *cha 'n ioghnadh boladh nan sgadan a bhith do 'n t-soitheach sam bi iad*

Hers, *pron poss* Leath-sa; a It is hers, *is leath-sa e*, not my house but hers, *ni h-cadh mo thigh-se, ach a tigh-se*

Herse. See Hearse

Herself, *pro* I féin, si féin She herself, *ise féin.*

Hesitancy, *s* Agaileachd, eu-cinnte; iomcheist, turamanaich, iom-chomhairle, tomhartaich

Hesitate, *v* Bi an iomcheist, bi san turamanaich, bi san tomhartaich, dean moille, stad, cuir an ag, (*in speech*), bi manndach, bi agach, dean ag (no) mannd.

Hesitation, *s* Eu-cinnte, iomcheist, teagamh, moille, amharus, tomhartaich

Hesper, *s.* Feasgar, rionnag feasgair

Hesperia, *s* An eadailt, an Spàin

† **Hest**, *s* Ordugh, iartas, aithne, reachd.

Heteroclite, *s* Neo-riaghailte.

Heterodox, *a* Do-bharaileach, neo-fhallain.

Heterodoxy, *s.* Do-bharail

Heterogeneal, Heterogeneous, *a.* Iol-ghnétheach; iol-ghnéach

Heterogeneity, *s.* Iol-ghneth.

Hew, *v a.* Sgud, sgath, gearr sios, gearr bhàn, snaith, saoithich, buain Hewn, *sgudte, sgathte, gearrte, snaithte, buainte.*

Hewer, *s* Gearradair, sgathair, sgathadair, snaithear.

Hewing, *s* Snaitheadh, gearradh, sgathadh, buaineadh.

Hexagon, *s* Sé-shlisneach, sé-shlisneag.

Hexagonal, *a* Sé-shlisneach.

Hexagony, *s.* Sé-shlisneag

Hexameter, *s* Rann fad; rann shé cos

Hexangular, *a.* Sé-oisinneach.

Hexapod, *s.* Beothach sé-chosach.

Hey, *interj.* Eigh! h-eidh

Heyday, *interj* H-eia, obh! obh! comadh leam!

Heyday, *s* Mire.

Hewn See Hew.

Hiation, *s.* Meanan, meananaich

Hiatus, *s.* Fosgladh beòil; bearn, sgoltadh.

Hibernal, *a.* Geamhrail, geamhradail, gaillionach, geamhraidh

Hiccius doccius, *s.* (*Hic est doctus*), cleasaiche, fear chleasachd, dubh-chleasaiche.

Hiccough, *s.* Aileag.

Hiccup, *s.* Aileag

Hid. See Hide.

Hidden, *a.* Folaichte, falaichte, céilte, comhdaichte, am folach; as an t-sealladh; diomhair; do-fhaicinn, dothuigsinn. Hidden from me, *folaichte orm, folaichte uam*

Hide, *v a.* Folaich, falaich, céil, comhdaich, cuir as an t-sealladh. I hid it, *dh' fholaich mi e.*

Hide, *s.* Seic, seiche; boiceann, croicionn, craiceann, bian

Hide, *s* Crann fearainn.

HIDE-AND-SEEK, *s.* Folach fead.

HIDEBOUND, *a.* Cruaidh-chroicneach; doirbh; dorganta, cruaidh, spiocach.

HIDEOUS, *a.* Uamharraidh, uamharra, uamhasach, oillteil, eagallach, fuathasach, sgréitidh, sgreataidh, granda, gràda; duaichnidh.

HIDEOUSLY, *adv.* Gu h-uamharra, gu h-uamhasach, gu h-oillteil, gu h-eagallach, gu fuathasach, gu sgreitidh, gu sgreataidh, gu granda, gu gràda, gu duaichnidh.

HIDEOUSNESS, *s.* Uamhas, uamhasachd, uamhunn, oillteal-achd, sgreitidheachd.

HIDER, *s.* Fear folachaidh, céileadair.

HIE, *v. n.* Greas, deifirich, dean cabhag (no) deifir.

HIERARCH, *s.* Naomh-cheannard, naomh-phriomh.

HIERARCHY, *s.* Naomh-riaghladh, riaghladh eaglais.

HIEROGLYPHICAL, *a.* Samhlachail; fo shamhladh.

HIEROGLYPHICS, *s.* Samhladh sgriobhaidh, comhar, samhl-ladh dealbh.

HIEROGRAPHER, *s.* Diadhair, naomh-sgriobhair.

HIEROGRAPHY, *s.* Naomh-sgriobhadh.

HIGGLE, *v. n.* Dean priginn, reic o dhorus gu dorus.

HIGGLEDY-PIGGLEDY, *adv.* Thar a chéile, roimh chéile, troimh chéile, feadh chéile, gu mi-riaghailteach.

HIGGLER, *s.* Fear a cheannaicheas agus a reiceas uibhean is cearcan is an leithidibh sin; greimisgear.

HIGGLING, *s.* Greimisgearachd; greimisg.

HIGH, *a.* Ard; (*in rank*), mòr, uasal, inmheach, uaibhreach, moralach; (*in price*), daor; (*in stature*), ard, mòr. On high, *shuas, uthard, a nàird;* (*in heaven*), air neamh, anns na neamhaibh, anns na h-ardaibh.

HIGHBLEST, *a.* Ard-shona, fior-shona.

HIGHBLOWN, *a.* Athte, lionta; bocta, làn, seidte suas.

HIGHBORN, *a.* Uasal, ard, oirdheirc.

HIGHCOLOURED, *a.* Ruiteach; dubh-dhearg, flanndearg.

HIGHDESIGNING, *a.* Ard-inntinneach, mòr-chuiseach.

HIGHEST, *a.* Is airde, is mò; is uailse.

HIGHFED, *a.* Giorrta, làn bidh.

HIGHFLAMING, *a.* Dearg lasach.

HIGHFLIER, *s.* Baoth-chreideach, an-dhiadhair.

HIGHFLOWN, *a.* Uasal, uallach, leòmach, sgòdail; ard.

HIGH-HEAPED, *a.* Cruachta.

HIGH-HEELED, *a.* Ard-shàilteach.

HIGHLAND, *a.* Ard, monadail, sliabhach, sliabhtach, Gaidhcalach, Gaidhealach.

HIGHLAND, *s.* Airde, bràighe; fearann ard.

HIGHLANDER, *s.* Gaidheal, bràigheach.

HIGHLANDS, *s. pl.* Bràighdean, àrdan; Gaidhealtachd na h-Alba, a Ghaidhealtachd.

HIGHLY, *adv.* Gu mòr, gu h-uaibhreach, gu h-ardanach. He highly deserves this, *is math is fhiach e so;* I value him highly, *tha meas mòr agam dheth.*

HIGHMETTLED, *a.* Stuthail, ardanach; spioradail, mear-achdasach; dian, beothail, beò; ruaineach; (*as a horse*), sgeunach.

HIGHMINDED, *a.* Ard-inntinneach, ard-bharaileach, inn-tinneach, ardanach, aigeannach, aigeantach, uallach, uasal.

HIGHMOST, *a.* Is airde, is mò, is iubhiche.

HIGHNESS, *s.* Airde; (*in dignity*), mòrachd, mòralachd.

HIGHPRINCIPLED, *a.* Baoth-bharaileach.

HIGHSEASONED, *a.* Blasda; saillte.

HIGHSIGHTED, *a.* Ard-sheallach.

HIGHSPIRITED, *a.* Spioradail, aigeantach, ard-inntinneach, dàna, ladarna, ruaineach, danarra; cruadalach.

HIGHSTOMACHED, *a.* Dùr, rag, rag-mhuinealach, reasgach; uasal, uallach, ardanach.

HIGHTASTED, *a.* Blasda, milis, deagh-bhlasda.

HIGHWATER, *s.* Lan mara, airde an làin; muir làn.

HIGHWAY, *s.* Rod mòr, rathad mòr, rathad mor an righ.

HIGHWAYMAN, *s.* Fear reubainn, robair; creachadair, spuinneadair.

HIGHWROUGHT, *a.* Ealanta.

HILARITY, *s.* Aighear, ealaidh, mire, cridhealas, ioladh, sugradh, suilbhire.

HILDING, *s.* Sgonn, sgonn bhalaoch; baobh, bidse.

HILL, *s.* Monadh, sliabh, beann, beinn, cruach, cruachan, cnoc, tom, torr, dùn, tolm, meall, aonach, tulach, ard, druim; mam, din, maol, craig, †aisgear, carn, druimear, druman; uchdan, uchdach. Up hill, *ri bruthach, ris a mhonadh;* the side of a hill, *leacainn; slios;* down hill, *ri leathad, le bruthach;* the foot of the hill, *bun mhonaidh; bun an uchdain;* up hill is no longer than down hill, *cha mho uchdaich na leothaid;* a hill on fire is not lasting, *is diombuan tom is teine ris.*

HILLOCK, *s.* Cnoc, cnochdan, beannan, cruachag, cruachan, torran, tolman, tom, toman, tulachan, dùnan, dùcan, droman, sornan, uchdach, uchdan; croit, carn. It is a good hillock that has luck on its top, *is math 'n tom air am bi sealbh.*

HILLY, *a.* Monadail, beanntach, sleibhteach, sliabhach, cnocach, garbh, creagach, creagach; uchdanach, tomanach, cnocanach.

HILT, *s.* Dorn-chur, dorn-chladh, ceann claidheimh.

HIM, *pron.* E, esa, esan. Strike him, *buail e;* his guilt, *a chiont-san.*

HIMSELF, *pron.* E féin. He himself, *esan féin,* by himself, *leis féin, leis fhéin; na aonar.*

HIN, *s.* Tomhas Iudhach a chumadh beul ri deich pinntean Sasunnach.

HIND, *a.* Deireannach, deiridh, culaobh, cùil. Hind legs, *casan deiridh.*

HIND, *s.* Eilid, eild; agh feidh; (*a rustic*), tuathanach, ba-laoch, feamanach.

HINDBERRY, *s.* Suidheag.

HINDER, *v. a.* Bac, grab, coisg, caisg, amail, toirmisg, cuir moille air, cum air ais, cuir stad air, cum air falbh. You hinder me, *tha thu 'g am amal, tha thu a cur moille* (no) *bac orm.*

HINDERED, *part.* Bacta, grabta, coisgte, caisgte, amailte, toirmisgte.

HINDERANCE, *s.* Bacadh, stad, moille, grabadh, amal.

HINDERER, *s.* Bacair, grabair.

HINDERLING, *s.* Sgonn, sgonn-bhalaoch.

HINDERMOST, HINDMOST, *a.* Deireannach, is deireannaiche; air dheireadh, air deireadh.

HINGE, *s.* Lùdach, lùdanan, bann, ceangal, cùl-cheangal, slaodrach; bacan, lùth. Hinges, *ceanglaichean, lùdaichean.*

HINGE, *v. a.* Lùdaich.

HINT, *v. a.* Thoir sànas, thoir tuaiream, cuir an cuimhne.

HINT, *s.* Sanas, tuaiream, tomhas; sméid, fios.

HIP, *s.* Mucag.

HIP, *s.* Sliasad, léis, iosgaid, màs, cruachann, croman, tòin.

HIPPISH, *a.* Dubhach, tuirseach, trom.

HIPPOGRIFF, *s.* Each sgiathach.

HIPPOPOTAMUS, *s.* Each uisge.

HIPSHOT, *a.* As an tòin; as na meidhinnean.

HIRE, *s.* Duais, tuarasdal, diol, luach, luach saoithreach, pàigh.

Hire, *v. a.* Gabh; fasdaich, gabh air thuarasdal, tuarasdalaich. Hired, *gabhte.*

Hireling, *s.* Fear air thuarasdal, seirbheiseach; siùrsach.

Hirsute, *a.* Ròmach, molach, garbh.

His, *pron. poss.* A. His sword, *a chlaidheamh;* himself and his, *e fèin is na bhuineas da, e fein is a theaghlach*

Hispid, *a.* Garbh, molach, friogbanach; giobach, ròinneach, roibeanach.

Hiss, *v.* Séid (no) fead mar ni nathair.

Hiss, *s.* Séid, séideil, fead, feadail; cronachadh.

Hist, *interj.* Caisd, eisd, cluinn, bi 'd thosd, bi samhach

Historian, *s.* Eachdair, eachdraiche, fear sgriobhadh eachdraidh, seanachaidh, starrair, sgeulaiche; aoisdana.

Historical. Eachdaireach, eachdrachail.

Historify, *v. a.* Cuir sios ann eachdraidh

Historiographer, *s.* Eachdair, eachdraiche.

History, *s.* Eachdraidh, eachdruidh, seanachas, sgeul

Hit, *v. a.* Buail, cuimsich, straoidhil, ruig; amais, airmeis. Hit or agree about a thing, *coird*

Hit, *s.* Buille; steur; straoidhle; urchair thuiteamais; breab; amas; tubaisd, bualadh.

Hitch, *v. a.* and *n.* (*Catch*), glac, grab; cuir an sàs; (*move further*), caruich, gluich; (*hop*), leum air aon chois

Hithe, *s* Port, geòth, bàdh; camus beag, àite sam bith far an cleachd earra chur a luing.

Hither, *adv.* Gu so, gus a so, an so, am fogus Come hither, *thig an so*, hither and thither, *nùll is a nall, h-uige is uaith, sios is suas.*

Hither, *a.* Is fhoigse, ni 's fhaigse. Hither Spain, *an Spàinn is fhoigse.*

Hithermost, *a.* Is fhoigse, is fhaigse, is fhoigse do laimh.

Hitherto, *adv.* Gu so, gus an am so; gus a nis, fathast, fhathast; a fhathast; gus an am so.

Hitherward, *adv.* An rod so, an rathad so, an car so, mar so; thun so.

Hive, *s* Sgeap, sgeap sheillean; beach-lann; coirceag, corcag, coisridh, cuideachd, conaltradh.

Hive, *v. a.* and *n.* Sgeap cuir ann an seap, dion, cuir am fasgadh; gabh fasgadh

Hiver, *s* Sgeapair.

Ho, *interj.* H-aobh, h-aoibh.

Hoar, *a.* Liath.

Hoar-frost, *s* Liath-reòtha, sioc liath.

Hoard, *v. a.* Carn suas, cnuasaich, dean ulaidh

Hoard, *s.* Cnuasach, cnuasachadh, cnuasachd, ulaidh, ionmhas; falachan. Hoarded, *cnuasaichte, tionailte*

Hoarder, *s.* Cnuasair.

Hoariness, *s* Leithe; liathanachd.

Hoarse, *a.* Tùchta, tùchte, fromhaidh; ròcanach, tlochanach, garbh-ghuthach, garbh.

Hoarsely, *adv.* Gu tùchta; gu fromhaidh, gu ròcanach; gu garbh.

Hoarseness, *s* Tùchan, tùchadh, tlochan, rùsgadh cleibh.

Hoary, *a.* Liath; arsda, geal

Hoay, *interj* H-aoibh.

Hobble, *v.* Imich gu stacach, imich gu luirceanach (no) san luirceanachd.

Hobble, *s.* Ceum bacach, bac, stac, stacanaich, stacarsaich, luirceanachd.

Hobbler, *s.* Neach bacach, (no) stacach, luircean, crioplach.

Hobbler, *s.* Marcair Eireannach, saighdear Eireannach air muin eich.

Hobblingly, *adv.* Gu bacach, gu crùbach, gu stacach.

Hobby, *s.* Gearan Gaidhealach, gearan Eireannach, *seallaidh*, maide air am marcaich balachan, umaidh, baoghlan; seorsa seabhaig.

Hobby-horse, *s.* Each maide; culaidh-shugraidh, ni gradhaichte sam bi

Hobgoblin, *s.* Bòcan, bodach, taibhse, tannasg, ùruisg, umhruisg.

Hobnail, *s.* Tarrag crudha; tacaid; balaoch.

Hobnailed, *a.* Tacaideach

Hock, *s.* Seorsa fiona; fion na Réin.

Hock, *s.* Cuid do chùl cois eich; ceann caol ceithreamh, deiridh muic, spàg mhuic-fheolach

Hock, Hockle, *v. a* Gearr iosgaid; spearraich, cuir spearrach air.

Hocus-pocus, *s.* Cleasaiche; mealltair; cleasachd

Hod, *s.* Amar aòil; soitheach a ghiùlan aoil, capull.

Hodge-podge, *s.* Càl coimeasgta

Hodman, *s.* Aoladair, fear oibreach aòil, fear iomchar creadha

Hodmandod, *s.* Seorsa éisg

Hoe, *s.* Tobh, sgrioban gart-ghlanaidh, croman uir; croman garaidh.

Hoe, *v. a.* Tobh, tobhainn

Hog, *s.* Muc, gullach spothte; ruig og; sgonn bhalach. The fat hog is basted, *is ann air a mhuic reamhar theid an t-ìm*, a young hog, *uircean*, hog's-grease, *muc-bhlonag.*

Hog-cote, *s* Fail mhuc.

Hoggerel, *s.* Othaisg, dionag

Hoggish, *a.* Mucail; mosach; (*cross*), dorganta, gnò, doirbh, brùideil; (*covetous*), spiocach, cruadalach, crion, teann, cruaidh. Hoggishly, *gu mucail, gu mosach, gu brùideil*

Hoggishness, *s.* Mucalachd; mosaiche, brùidealachd.

Hog-herd, *s.* Buachaill mhuc

Hogshead, *s.* Togsaid, tosgaid.

Hogsty, *s.* Fail mhuc

Hogwash, *s* Drabh

Hoiden, *s.* Caile, caile bhalaoch; dubh-chaile, caile gun oilean.

Hoist, *v a.* Tog, tarruing (no) slaoid suas.

Hold, *v a* and *n.* Cum, glac, gramaich, greimich, teannaich, fàstaich; gleidh; beir air, grab, cuir moille; (*hold* or *affirm*), cum a mach; (*last*), mair. Hold close together, *teannaich*, hold out, *cum a much; mair, buanaich*, hold forth, *labhair, cuir dhiot*, how he did hold forth, *is e 'chuir dheth*, hold off, *fan agad fein, cum air falbh*, hold in, *cum a stigh, cum a steach, ceannsuich*, hold on, *cum air, buanaich, rach air adhairt*, hold out, *sin a mach, mair, buanaich*, hold up, *tog, tog nùird, cum suas;* hold together, *cum sa chéile, coird*, hold or stop, *seas, stad, fuirich ort, socair, air do shocair*, hold your peace, *cum do theangadh, bi ad thosd, bi bìth, bi samhach*, he held it, *chum se e*, he who holds his tongue holds his friend, *am fear a ghleidheas a theangadh, gleidhidh e 'charaid*

Hold, *s* Greim; glac, glacadh, beirsinn, (*prison*), gainntir, tollbuth; carcar; (*den or hiding-place*), brocluinn, aite folaich, toll, sloc, slochd, daighneach, (*authority*), smachd, comas. A strong hold, *daighneach*, the hold of a ship, *grunnd luing*, let go your hold, *leig as do ghreim*, lose your hold, *caill do ghreim*, there is no hold of water or of fire, *cha n' eil greim ri ghabhail a dh' uisge no do theine.*

Holden, *part.* Air a chumail, glacte, gramaichte, greimichte, teannaichte, gleidhte

Holder, *s.* (*Of land*), tuathanach, gabhaltaiche, greimeir, A holder forth, *fear bruidhneach*

Holdfast, *s* Gramaiche, clic, crambaid, greimeir; spiocair.

Holding, *s.* (*Tenure*), gabhail; (*a keeping*), cumail, glacadh; (*of a song*), luinneag. There was no holding of him, *cha ghabhadh e cumail;* a holding up, *cumail suas, taic.*

Hole, *s.* Toll, sloc, slochd, fròg. The arm-hole, *lag na h-achlais;* a badger's hole, *brocluinn;* full of holes, *làn thuill, tolltach, frògach;* you shall not bore a hole that I will not find a nail to it, *cha chuir thusa toll, nach cuir mise tarrag;* an eye-hole, *sùil, sùileag.*

Holidam, *s.* A bhan-naomh.

Holily, *adv.* Gu naomh, gu diadhaidh.

Holiness, *s.* Naomhachd, diadhaidheachd, diadhachd; ainm urraim do 'n Phàp.

Holla, *interj.* H-oilò! A thief's whistle is worse than his holla, *is miosa 'n fhead no 'n éigh.*

Holla, *v.* Gairm (no) glaodh air neach; sgairtich, éigh.

Holland, *s.* An Òlaint; anart Òlainteach.

Hollow, *a.* Fàs; falamh; domhain; glacach; (*deceitful*), cealgach, fealltach, carach, mealltach; (*sounding*), fuaimneach.

Hollow, *s.* Lag, glacag; toll, uamha; sloc; pìoban. Full of hollows, *glacagach.* (*Of the hand*), crodhan.

Hollow, *v. a.* Cladhaich; doimhnich, dean fàs. Hollowed, *cladhaichte, fàs.*

Hollow-hearted, *a.* Cealgach, fealltach, mealltach, ceabhachdach, slaoighteil.

Hollowly, *adv.* Gu tolltach, gu fàs; gu cealgach.

Hollowness, *s.* Fàsachd, folamhachd, failbhe; (*cunning*), ceilge, slaoighte.

Holly, *s.* Cuileann, crann cuilinn. Sea holly, *cuileann tràgha.*

Hollyhock, *s.* Ros mall.

Holm, *s.* Crann tuilm, darach sior uaine; eilean aimhne.

Holpen, *part.* Cuidichte.

Holocaust, *s.* Iobairt loisgte.

Holster, *s.* Olasdair, còmhdach airson dag marcaich.

Holt, *s.* Doire, coille bheag, badan.

Holy, *a.* Naomh; diadhaidh; math; coisrigte, seunta; neo-lochdach; glan.

Holyday, *s.* Lath féill, làth fleadha, làth sollain, am subhachais.

Holy ghost, *s.* An Spiorad naomh, an Comh-fhurtair, an treas pearsa do 'n Trianaid.

Holyrood, *s.* Crois naomh, crann ceusaidh, an crann naomh.

Holy Thursday, *s.* Di 'r daoine na deas-ghabhail.

Holy water, *s.* Uisge coisrigte.

Homage, *s.* Umhlachd, urram, striochd, géill; seirbheis, dleasnas, dleasdanas. Do homage, *thoir umhlachd, dean striochd.*

Homage, *v. a.* Thoir urram (no) ùmhlachd; striochd, géill.

Homager, *s.* Striochdair, fear a ni géill do dhuine mòr.

Home, *s.* Dachaidh, tigh, aite tàimh, aros, aitreabh, loisdin, dùthaich. Without country or home, *gun dùthaich, gun dachaidh;* at home, *aig an tigh;* from home, *bho 'n tigh, o 'n tigh;* long home, *uaigh;* a home blow, *buille thaothaill, buille foghnaidh;* the old man's haste from home, *triall' o bhodaich o 'thigh féin.*

Home, *adv.* Dhachaidh, a dhachaidh. Come home, *tiucainn a dhachaidh.*

Homeborn, *a.* Nadurra; dùchasach; dùthcha; neo-bhallsgail, aineolach.

Homebred, *a.* Duchasach; dùthcha; aineolach; neo-fhiosrach; neo-bhallsgail, neo-fhoghlumta.

Homeless, *a.* Gun dachaidh, gun tigh.

Homeliness, *s.* Neo-ghrinneas, neo-riomhachas.

Homely, *a.* Neo-ghrinn, neo-riomhach, neo-eireachdail; *cursa.*

Homely, *adv.* Gu neo-ghrinn, gu neo-eireachdail, neo-shnàsmhor.

Homemade, *a.* Cumaint, *cursa*, neo-ghrinn; dùthcha, dùcha. Homemade cloth, *aodach dùcha.*

Homer, *s.* Tomhas Iudhach a chumadh trì pinntean.

Homespun, *a.* Neo-ghrinn, neo-eireachdail; garbh, *cursa;* aineolach. Homespun cloth, *aodach dùcha.*

Homespun, *s.* Umaidh, balaoch, bodach.

Homeward, *adv.* Dh'achaidh, dachaidh.

Homicidal, *a.* Mortach, fuilteach, fuileach.

Homicide, *s.* Mortadh, murtadh, sgriosadh; mortair.

Homilitical, *a.* Cridheil, suilbhear, mear, sunntach, aighearach.

Homily, *s.* Searmoin, òraid naomh.

Homocentric, *a.* Co-chruinn, ion-chruinn.

Homogeneal, *a.* Ion-ghnetheach, aon-ghnetheach.

Homologous, *a.* Ionann.

Homonymous, *a.* Dùbailt; iol-ainmeach; doilleir.

Hone, *s.* Clach gheurachaidh, clach fhaobhair; airneamh.

Honest, *a.* Onorach, ionraic, treibhdhireach, ceart, fior, simplidh, direach, fireannach, cothromach; (*chaste*), geamnaidh, geimnidh, gast, glan, cneasta. Honestly, *gu h-onorach, gu h-ionraic, gu treibhdhireach, gu cneasta.*

Honesty, *s.* Onoir, ionracas, ceartas, tréibhdhireas, geimnidheachd, fìrinn, subhailc, cneastachd. Honesty is better than gold, *is cliùitiche 'n onoir na 'n t-òr.*

Honey, *s.* Mil, meil; earc; millse. My honey, *a ghaolaich;* sweet as honey, *cho mhilis ri mil;* there is honey in the prattle of the rich, *is mil o 'n bheartach an gabhann.*

Honeycomb, *s.* Cìr-mheal.

Honeydew, *s.* Drùchd meal; earc.

Honeymoon, *s.* Mios mheal, mios an deigh pòsaidh.

Honeysuckle, *s.* Deolag, deolagan, bainne-ghamhnach, lus a mheal, lus a chrois; féith.

Honeyed, *a.* Milis, fior-mhilis, blasda, milseanta.

Honorary, *a.* Onorach, urramach. An honorary member, *ball onorach.*

Honour, Honor, *s.* Onoir, urram, meas, cliù, iomradh, moladh; (*chastity*), subhailc, onoir, geimneachd. On my honour, *air m' onoir;* keep up your honour, *cum suas d' onoir;* honour is delicate, *is beadarach an ni 'n onoir.*

Honour, *v.* Onoirich, urramaich, ardaich; thoir onoir, thoir urram (no) meas, thoir ùmhlachd.

Honourable, *a.* Onorach, urramach, uasal; ard; ceart, cothromach, fìreannach, cliùiteach. Honourably, *gu h-onorach, gu h-urramach, gu h-uasal, gu ceart, gu cothromach.*

Honours, *s. pl.* Onoirean; inmhean; dreuchdan; oifigean; dleasnasan; coirichean. The honours of the table, *dleasdanasan a bhùird* (no) *na cuilm.*

Hood, *s.* Curachd, comhdach cinn, bréide, sùbag. A little hood, *curaiceag.*

Hood, *v. a.* Dall; cur curachd air, curacaich. Hooded, *curacaichte.*

Hoodman blind, *s.* Dallan dàite.

Hoodwink, *v. a.* Dall, meall, rosg-dhall, sùil-dhall.

Hoof, *s.* Ionga, crubh, bròg, crodhan; speir. Hoofs, *iongan.*

Hoofed, *a.* Iongach, brogach; speireach.

Hook, *s.* Dubhan, cromag, clic, † cruca; bacan; (*a reaper's hook*), corran; (*snare*), dùl; (*a pot-hook*), bùlas. By hook or by crook, *a dheòin no dh' aindeoin;* sharp is the point of a hook, *is corrach gob an dubhain.*

Hook, *v. a.* Glac le dubhan, clic, cuir an sàs.

Hooked, *a.* Crom, cam; lùbta; air dubhan, an sàs.

Hookland, *s.* Talamh treabhaidh, talamh theid a threabhadh gach bliadhna.

Hooknosed, *a.* Crom-shroineach, cam-shroineach.

Hoop, *s.* Cearcall.

Hoop, *v. a.* Cearcaill, cearclaich; cuairtich, iom-dhruid.

Hoop, *v. a.* and *n.* Glaodh, sgairtich; sgread, eigh, eubh.

Hooper, *s.* Cùpair, cearclair, cearclaiche, rongair.

Hooping-cough, *s.* An t-sriuth-chasd; an t-sriuth.

Hoot, *v. a.* and *n.* Glaodh, dean ulfhart, ulfhartaich; eigh; sgannraich.

Hoot, *s.* Glaodhaich, sgairtich, éighich; sgannraich; torghan.

Hop, *v. n.* Leum, damhs, danns, dean beiceis, rinc.

Hop, *s.* Leum, leum beag, frith-leum.

Hop, *s.* Searbh-luibh àraidh a chuireas blas air lionn, op, top.

Hope, *s.* Dòchas, dùil, muinghinn. Were it not for hope, the heart would break, *mur bhiodh an dòchas, bhriseadh an cridhe;* he is past hope, *tha e dheth;* there is hope from the wars, but none from the grave, *bithidh dùil ri fear feachd, ach cha bhi dùil ri fear lic.*

Hope, *v. a.* and *n.* Cuir dochas, cuir muinghinn; bi an dòchas, bi 'n dùil. I hope, *tha mi 'n dùil, tha mi 'n dòchas, tha dochas* (*no*) *dùil agam;* hoped for, *ris am bhéil dòchas* (*no*) *dùil.*

Hope, *s.* Raon; raodhair.

Hopeful, *a.* Ciatach, creideasach; coltach, coslach, dochasach, muinghinneach. Hopefully, *gu ciatach, gu creideasach, gu coslach.*

Hopeless, *a.* Eu-dòchasach, gun dòchas, gun mhuinghinn.

Hopper, *s.* Dannsair, damhsair; (*of a mill*), treabhailt; crannag; croidhleag, binn.

Horal, *a.* Uaireil.

Hordaceous, *a.* Eorna, air a dheanamh do dh'eorna.

Horde, *s.* Bròd, munntir; clann, fine, cinneach; buidheann luaineach.

Horehound, *s.* Grafan bàn. Stinking horehound, *grafan dubh.*

Horizon, *s.* Iomall seallaidh; cuairt nan speur.

Horizontal, *a.* Direach, còmhnard, reidh.

Horn, *s.* Adharc; sludhagan; cabar; beann, cròc. A drinking-horn, *corn;* the far cow has long horns, *adhaircean fad air a chrodh tha fad uainn.*

Hornbook, *s.* Brod; ceud leabhar cloinne; sludhach.

Horned, *a.* Adhairceach, cabrach; beannach, cròcach.

Horner, *s.* Ceard, ceard spàineachan; adharcair.

Hornet, *s.* Connspeach; speach, creadhal; beach each.

Horn-mad, *a.* Eudmhor; eudach, amharusach.

Horn-owl, *s.* Cailleach oidhche; coileach oidhche; cumhachag, comhachag; mulchan, ullchabhagan.

Hornpipe, *s.* Seorsa dannsaidh.

Hornwork, *s.* Obair daighnich, seòrsa obair dionaidh.

Horny, *a.* Adhairceach, cruaidh mar adhairc.

Horologe, *s.* Uaireadair; uaireadair gréine; clog, clag.

Horometer, *s.* Uaireadair.

Horoscope, *s.* Suidheachadh nan reult air uair breith neach.

† **Horrent**, *a.* Uamharra, umhasach, fuathasach, oillteil.

Horrible, *a.* Oillteil, uamharra, uamhasach, fuathasach. Horribly, *gu h-uamharra, gu h-uamhasach, gu fuathasach, gu h-oillteil.*

Horribleness, *s.* Uamharrachd, uamhasachd, oillteal achd.

Horrid, *a.* Oillteil, uamharra, eagallach, uamhannach, fuathasach, sgréitidh, goirisneach. Horridly, *gu h-oillteil, gu h-uamharra, gu fuathasach.*

Horridness, *s.* Oillteal achd, uamharrachd, eagallachd, uamhann.

Horrific, *a.* Eagalach, oillteil, uamhasach.

Horripilation, *s.* Greannachadh.

Horrour, Horror, *s.* Oillt, fuathas, eagal, crith-oillt, uamhann, goirisinn.

Horse, *s.* Each, gearan, marc, steud; (*of an army*), eachraidh, marc-shluagh. Take horse, *marcaich, gabh each;* an ambling horse, *each falaireachd;* a sorry horse, *drèug;* a cart-horse, *each cartach;* a hack, *each reidh;* a stone-horse, *àigeach, aigheach;* a wild horse, *each sgeunach;* a race-horse, *each steud;* a saddle-horse, *each diolaid, each marcaich;* a sea-horse, *each mara, each uisge;* a war-horse, *each milidh;* put a horse to full speed, *cuir each na steudaibh;* if a horse be good, his colour is good, *ma 's math each is math 'dhreach.*

Horse, *v. a.* Cuir air muin eich, marcaich.

Horseback, *s.* Marcach, marcachadh, marcachd, muin eich. On horseback, *air muin eich.*

Horse-bean, *s.* Ponair eich. Horse-dung, *inneir* (*no*) *cac eich.*

Horse-boat, *s.* Bat each, bat mòr aiseig.

Horse-boy, *s.* Gille stàbuill.

Horse-breaker, *s.* Fear bhriseadh each.

Horse-collar, *s.* Bràide, bràghaid.

Horse-courser, *s.* Gille each, gille marcaich.

Horse-dung, *s.* Inneir eich, cac eich.

Horse-dealer, *s.* Copair.

Horse-flesh, *s.* Feòil each.

Horse-fly, *s.* Beach each, creadhal.

Horse-hair, *s.* Gaoisd.

Horse-leech, *s.* Deal nan each, deal tholl, each-leigh.

Horse-laugh, *s.* Craos-ghaire.

Horse-litter, *s.* Carbad.

Horseman, *s.* Marcair; marcaiche; deagh mharcair.

Horsemanship, *s.* Marcaireachd, marcachd, falaras.

Horsemeat, *s.* Biadh eich, connlach, fodar.

Horse-pond, *s.* Lochan each.

Horse-race, *s.* Réis, réis each, reim each, steud.

Horse-radish, *s.* Ràcadal, meacan each.

Horse-shoe, *s.* Crudh, crudh eich. Horse-shoes, *cruidhean.*

Horse-way, *s.* Rod each.

Hortation, *s.* Earalas, earalachadh, misneachadh, comhairleachadh; rabhadh, sànas, comhairle.

Hortative, *a.* Comhairleach, earaileach.

Hortative, *s.* Earail, earalas, comhairle.

Hortatory, *a.* Prosnachail, brosnachail, a tabhairt misnich; rabhachail; comhairleach, sànusach.

Horticulture, *s.* Gàraidheachd, garadaireachd, gairnealaireachd.

Hortulan, *a.* Gàraidh, gàrachail.

Hosanna, *s.* Moladh do Dhia, buidheachas do Dhia.

Hose, *s.* Osan, *pl.* osain. Tartan hose, *osain chadath.*

Hosier, *s.* Fear reic osan no stocnais.

Hosiery, *s.* Osanachd.

Hospitable, *a.* Fial, faoilidh, fialuidh, fiùghanta, fiùghantach, daonnach, arraidh; aoidheil, daonnachdach, còir, càirdeil, earailteach, furanach.

Hospitably, *adv.* Gu fial, gu fialuidh, gu faoilidh, gu daonnach, gu h-aoidheil, gu còir, gu cairdeil, gu furanach.

Hospital, *s.* Spideal; tigh eiridinn, tigh euslain, tigh nam bochd.

HOSPITALITY, *s.* Fiaile, féile, féill, aoidheachd, aoidhealachd; faoilidheachd, fialachd, cairdealachd, biatachd.

HOSPITALLER, *s.* Fear tigh-eiridinn; fear féill, fear fialuidh

HOSPITATE, *v. n.* Gabh aoidheachd; faigh aoidheachd.

HOST, *s* Fear tighe, osdair, fear a bheir fardoch (no) aoidheachd.

HOST, *s* Feachd, armailt, slogh, sluagh, cuideachd, buidheann, bannal

HOST, *s.* An t-abhlan beannuichte.

HOSTAGE, *s.* Braighde gill. Hostages, *braighdean gill, braighdean tairis*

HOSTELRY, *s* Tigh òsd.

HOSTESS, *s* Bean tighe, osdag, bean-osdair, bean tigh-òsda

HOSTICIDE, *s* Fear a mharbhas namhaid.

HOSTILE, *a* Naimhdeil; feargach, feachdail, an aghaidh

HOSTILITY, *s.* Naimhdeas, cogadh

HOSTLER, *s* Gille stàbuill, gille each

HOT, *a* Teth, garg, dian, brais, obann; timeach, greadanta, teinntidh, goileach; anamiannach, macnusach Scalding hot, *goileach teth*, red hot, *teth dearg*, hot on the tongue, *garg, searbh, goirt*, make hot again, *ath-bhlathaich, ath-bhlàiteach*

HOTBED, *s* Leabaidh theth, geadadh teth

HOTBRAINED, *a.* Dian, brais.

HOTCH-POTCH, *s.* Càl coimeasgta

HOT-COCKLES, *s.* Dallan dàite

HOTEL, *s* Tigh òsda, tigh mòr.

HOTHEADED, *a* Dàn, dian, brais.

HOTHOUSE, *s* Tigh teth.

HOTLY, *adv.* Gu teth, gu dian, gu brais

HOTMOUTHED, *a* Reasgach, rag-mhuinealach, do-cheannsachadh

HOTNESS, *s.* Teas; déine, braise; cuthach.

HOTSPUR, *s* Fear dian brais.

HOTSPURRED, *a* Dian, brais, cas.

HOUGH, *s.* Easgaid, iosgaid, bac na h-iosgaid

HOUGH, *v.* Gearr féith luthaidh, toch, spearraich, cuir spearrach.

HOUND, *s* Gaothar, gadhar, tollair, tobhlair, cù luirg, miol-chu

HOUND, *v a* Ruaig

HOUR, *s* Uair, an ceathramh cuid fichead do là; am, ùine, aimsir. The last hour, *an uair dheireannach, am a bhais*; half an hour, *leth uair*, an hour and a half, *uair gu leth*

HOURGLASS, *s.* Uaireadair gaineimh, uaireadair gaineich.

HOURLY, *adv* Gach uair, na h-uile uair, uaireil, tric, minig

HOURPLATE, *s.* Clàr uairean, brod uairean

HOUSE, *s* Tigh, teach, fardoch, aros, tigh-comhnuidh, aitreabh, saintreabh, †bruigheas, †eachras, lann, lios, †dom; (*family*), teaghlach, sliochd, siol, fine House-eves, *ànuinn*, House of Lords, *tigh na flath-chomhairle*, House of Commons, *tigh na tuath-chomhairle*, a storehouse, *tigh stòr*, an alehouse, *tigh lionna, tigh òsda*, a bakehouse, *tigh fuinidh*, a brewhouse, *tigh togalach*, a milkhouse, *tigh bainne*

HOUSE, *v. a* and *n* Cuir a steach (no) stigh, cuir an tigh; cuir fo dhion, gabh fasgadh, rach fo dhion, gabh tamh, dean comhnuidh.

HOUSEBREAKER, *s* Tigh-chreachadair, meirleach; spuinneadair, robair

HOUSEBREAKING, *s* Tigh-chreachadh, tigh-spùinneadh, tigh-reubainn, robaireachd.

HOUSE-DOG, *s* Mastaidh, cu mòr tighe

HOUSEHOLD, *s.* Teaghlach; muinntir, tigheadas

HOUSEHOLDER, *s.* Fear tighe, fear a ghabhas tigh arson màil.

HOUSEHOLD-STUFF, *s* Airneis, innsridh 's airneis, airneis tighe.

HOUSEKEEPER, *s.* Fear tighe; bean tighe; ban-stiùbhart.

HOUSEKEEPING, *s.* Beanachas tighe, ban-stiùbhardachd; féile.

HOUSEL, *s.* Suipeir an Tighearna.

HOUSELEEK, *s* Creamh gàraidh.

HOUSELESS, *a.* Gun tigh, gun aros, gun dachaidh.

HOUSEMAID, *s.* Searbhanta, caile shearbhanta, searbhanta tighe, ban-òglach.

HOUSEROOM, *s* Rùm tighe

HOUSE-WARMING, *s* Teasachadh tighe; feisd air tùs tighcadais, feisd imrich.

HOUSEWIFE, *s.* Bean tighe, té ghrunndail.

HOUSEWIFERY, *s* Beanachas tighe, deagh bheanachas tighe, grunndalas

HOUSING, *s.* Cur a steach, cròdhadh, cur fo dhionadh; arosan, tighean, aitreabhan.

HOVE See HEAVE.

HOVEL, *s* Bothan.

HOVEN, *part.* Togta, air atadh, air bolgadh, air éiridh.

HOVER, *v* Croch os-cionn, iadh os-cionn; bi ann iomchomhairle. Hovering about the fire, *crochadh mu'n teine.*

HOVERING, *s.* Bruachaireachd; crochadh, iadhadh.

HOW, *adv* Cia mar, cionnas, c'arson How long? *cia fhad?* how great? *cia mor? cia cho mòr?* how many? *cia meud?* how many times? *cia meud uair?* how then? *cia mar mata? ciod mar sin?* how is it? *cia mar so?* how little? *cia beag? cia crion?*

† HOWBEIT, *adv* Gidheadh, ach, fhathast

HOW-D'YE, *s* Cia mar a tha thu, cionnas a tha thu.

HOWEVER, *adv* Ciod air bith an doigh, ciamar air bith, gidheadh; co dhuibh; fathast, fhathast However great, *cia mor air bith*, however great it will be, *cia mor air bith bhitheas e, air meud sam bi e.*

HOWL, *s* Ulfhart, dualart, gulfhart, donnal, donnalaich, burral, burralaich.

HOWL, *v* Dean ulfhart (no) gulfhart, dean donnal, sgal. A dog will howl when struck with a bone, *ni 'n cù sgal rò chnaimh.*

HOWLING, *s* Ulfhurtaich, gulfhurtaich, donnal, donnalaich, burralaich, comhartaich

HOWSOEVER, *s* Cia mar air bi, cia doigh air bi, ciod air bi an doigh, ge b' e air bi an doigh.

HOX, *v a* Toch. Hoxed, *tochte, tochta*

HOY, *s* Bàt mòr; long bheag.

HUBBUB, *s.* Tabaid, aimhreite, othail, buaireas, mi-riaghailt.

HUCKLEBACKED, *s* Crom-shlinneanach; crotach, crom.

HUCKLEBONE, *s.* Cnaimh ua sléise, ruitin.

HUCKSTER, *s* Fear pac, neach a reiceas nithe beag, marsonta faighreach, ceannaiche iomralach

HUDDLE, *v.* Cuir air feadh chéile, cuir a ordugh (no) thar a chéile, coimeasg, ciurtaich, comhdaich ann an cabhaig, dùmhlaich.

HUDDLE, *s.* Dròbh sluaigh, mob; buaireas, aimhreite.

HUE, *s* Dath, ligh, dreach, neul, aogas

HUE AND CRY, *s* Ruaig, rabhadh

HUFF, *s* Atadh; dod, sdod, stùrt.

HUFF, *v. a* and *n.* Séid suas, at; thoir achmhasan sgaiteach, bagair, bosdainn, bi dodach, gabh dod

HUFFER, *s* Buamasdair, bragair, fear bragach, bagarair, bagairtear, blaghair

Huffish, *a* Ardanach; peirteil, lonach; peilpeanta; beagnarach; dodach, sdodach, stùrtail, bagarach. A huffish person, *sdodan, sdodanach.*

Huffishly, *adv.* Gu h-ardanach, gu peirteil, gu lonach, gu beagnarach; gu dodach, gu sdodach, gu sturtail, gu bagarach.

Huffishness, *s* Ardanachd, peirtealachd, lonais, stodanachd, stùrtalachd, bagarachd, buamsdaireachd

Hug, *v. a.* Glac (no) teannaich gu gaolach, gabh gu caidreamhach, cum teann, teann-ghlac.

Hug, *s.* Glac; caidreadh, greim.

Huge, *a.* Mor, anmhor, aibhseach, aibheil, anabharrach, gailbheach; athachail; ard

Hugely, *adv.* Gu mòr, gu h-anmhor, gu h-aibhseach, gu h-aibheil, gu h-anabharra, gu gailbheach

Hugeness, *s.* Aibhseachd, aibheileachd.

Hugger-mugger, *s* Aite diomhair, aite uaigneach, uaigneachd. In hugger-mugger, *gu diomhair, os-iosal.*

Huke, *s* Clòc, cleòc.

Hulk, *s.* Slige luing; long gun chroinn, ni sam bi trom, neo-chumadail, caile dhomhail, neo-chearmanta, bun caile

Hulk, *v a.* Thoir am mionach a beothaich, gu h-àraidh a maigheach

Hull, *s.* Cochall, rusg, plaosg; slige luing

Hully, *a* Cochallach, rùsgach, plaosgach.

Hulver, *s.* Cuileann

Hum, *v* Srann, dean srann, dean crònan, dean dranndan.

Hum, *s* Dranndan, srann, crònan, siansan, durdan, torman

Human, *a.* Saoghalmhor, saoghalta, talmhaidh.

Humane, *a* Daonna, daonnach, baigheil, seirceil, caomh, caomhail, còir, sèimh, siobhailt.

Humanely, *adv* Gu daonna, gu daonnach, gu baigheil, gu seirceil, gu caomh, gu caomhail, gu còir, gu siobhailt.

Humanist, *s.* Fear fòghlumaidh, foghlumaiche.

Humanity, *s.* Daonnachd, daonachdas, baighealachd, seirce, caoimhneas, truacantas, deagh thoil, fiùghantachd, mathasachd, nadur an duine, oilean, foghlum, ionnsachadh

Humanize, *v* Dean soirbh, dean daonna, dean muinte, oileanaich, ciùinich.

Humankind, *s* An cinneadh daoine

Humanly, *adv.* Gu talmhaidh; gu corporra; a rèir barail dhaoine.

Humbird, *s.* Drannd-eun.

Humble, *a.* Iosal, iriosal; neo-uasal, umhall, mallta. Humbly, *gu h-iosal, gu h-iriosal*

Humble, *v a* Islich, illsich, irioslaich; cuir gu làr, cuir fo'; saruich, claoidh, ceannsuich, smachduich, aontaich He shall be humbled, *islichear e*

Humble-bee, *s.* Seillean, seillean dranndanach.

Humbler, *s* Isleachair; ceannsair, smachdair, fear smachdaidh.

Humble-mouthed, *a* Macanta, ciùin, bith

Humbles, *s.* Mionach feidh, greallach feidh

Humdrum, *a.* Baoghalta, baothaireach.

Humdrum, *s.* Baothair, baoghlan, tuafair

Humect, *v a* Fliuch, bogaich.

Humect, *a* Fliuch, bog, tais, àitidh.

Humectation, *s* Fliuchadh, bogachadh

Humeral, *a* Gairdeanach, guailneach

Humid, *a.* Fliuch, àitidh, bog, uisgidh, tais.

Humidity, *s* Fliuchnachd, fliuchlachd, àitidheachd, uisgidheachd.

Humiliation, *s.* Isleachadh, illseachadh, irioslachadh; irioslachd, illse, isle

Humility, *s.* Irioslachd, malltachd, macantas.

Humourist, *s.* Fear macnusach, fear dòchasach; fear aigheir.

Humorous, *a.* Luaineach; dòchasach, mi-riaghailteach, mear, aighearach, cridheil, neònach, ain-cheartach

Humorously, *adv* Gu mear, gu cridheil, gu luaineach, gu neònach.

Humorousness, *s* Luaineachas; dòchasachd, aighear, ealaidh, cridhealas

Humorsome, *a.* Crosda, cainnteach, doirbh, neònach, dòchasach, crinceanach, mi-nosach, ainbheasach, do-riarachadh

Humour, *s.* (*Temper*), nàdur, càileachd inntinn, (*good humour*), gean math, caoimhne, (*bad humour*), droch-ghean, (*mirth*), aighear, sunnt, cridhealas, macnus, mire, fearas-chuideachd, (*caprice*), faoineas, miann, dòchas, gith; (*of the body*), fliceachd; (*of a sore*), iongar That is his humour, *is e sin a nadur*, I am not in the humour of eating, *cha n' eil sannt bidh orm*, of good humour, *math nadurrach*, of bad humour, *olc nadurrach*, be in good humour, *caoimhne ort*, put him in good humour, *cuir a ghean math air.*

Humour, *v a* Toilich, breug.

Hump, *s* Croit, meall, mulp

Hump-back, *s* Croit, (*a person*), croitean, crotair

Humpbacked, *a* Crotach

Hunch, *v. a.* Puc, mulc.

Hunch-back, *s.* Troich, cruitean, cruiteachan; crotair.

Hunchbacked, *a.* Crotach; cruiteanach

Hundred, *a* Ceud, ciad, cuig fichead.

Hundred, *s* Earann dùthcha

Hundredth, *a.* Ceudamh.

Hundred-weight, *s* Cothrom ceud punnt is a dha dheug

Hung, *pret* and *part* of hang Chroch; crochta See Hang.

Hunger, *s* Acras, ocras, ciocras, gort, gortas, †ampal, sannt bidh, cion bidh Dying with hunger, *a bàsuchadh leis an acros*, hunger is a good cook, *as math an còcair an t-ocras*

Hunger, *v n.* Bith air ocras, bi acrach (no) ocrach, mothuich ocras, fairich ocras, bi an càs ni.

Hungerbit, *a* Ocrach, acrach, air ocras

Hungerly, *a* Acrach, ocrach

Hungerstarved, *a* Ciocrach, (*as cattle*), air an togail

Hungred, *a.* Acrach, ocrach, ciocrach, air ocras, acrasach

Hungry See Hungred

Hunks, *s.* Spiocair, fear spiocach, fear sanntach

Hunt, *v a* Fiadhaich; eunaich, sealgaich, ruaig, lean, cruaidh-lean; rach an tòir.

Hunt, *s* Sealg, faoghaid, sealgaireachd, fiadhachd, eunachadh; (*a hunt of dogs*), lothainn chon

Hunter, *s.* Sealgair; eunadair; cù eunaich

Hunting, *s* Sealg, sealgaireachd, eunachadh

Hunting-horn, *s* Tùtach, dùdach, dùdag; adharc fiadhachd, adharc seilg

Huntress, *s.* Ban-sealgair

Huntsman, *s* Sealgair, fear deidheil air sealgaireachd

Hurdle, *s* Cliath, cliath-shlat

Hurds, *s* Pab, barrach, ascard.

Hurl, *v* Ruithil, ruidhil, tilg sios, cuir car air char

Hurl, *s* Tuasaid, tabaid, aimhreite

Hurlbat, *s.* Slachdan

Hurler, *s* Ruithlear, ròthlair, tuasaid.

HURLY, HURLY-BURLY, s. Buaireas, tabaid, aimhreite, eadarluas, eas-ordugh. When the hurly-burly's o'er, *nur bhios an tuasaid thairis*.

HURRICANE, s. An-uair, doinionn, stoirm, gaillionn.

HURRIER, s Fear deifreachaidh (no) greasaidh; fear buaireis

HURRY, v. a and n. Greas, luathaich, luathraich, cuir cabhag, deifirich, dean deifir

HURRY, s. Greasdachd, cabhag, luathas, deifir, buaireadh, cathais, tuasaid I am in a hurry, *tha cabhag orm, tha mi 'mo chabhaig*; you are in a hurry, *tha thu ad chabhaig*.

HURST, s. Doire, coille, badan coille.

HURST, v a Ciùrr, dochainn, dochannaich; goirtich, leòn, lot, bruth, docharaich, mill; truaill.

HURT, s Ciurram, ciurradh, diobhail, urchoid, dochann, dochair, lot, cron; naitheas, dosgann, olc.

HURT, part Air chiurradh; ciùrrta; (*spoiled*), truaillte, millte, (*wounded*), leònta, leòinte, (*bruised*), brùthte, brùite

HURTFUL, a Ciurrail, diobhalach, urchoideach, dochannach; docharrach; dosgannach, millteach, naitheasach, neo-fhallain

HURTFULNESS, s. Diobhalachd, urchoid, docharrachd, dosgannachd; neo-fhallaineachd

HURTLE, v Stroidhil, buail; stear; thoir ruathar

HURTLEBERRY, s Dearcag choille.

HURTLESS, a Neo-chiontach, gun chron; (*as a beast*), soitheamh

HURTS, s Dearcag choille.

HUSBAND, s Fear, duine, céil, cia; fear pòsda; fear caonntach (no) spiocach, tuathanach. Such a husband as I have, I get children by, *am fear a bhios ann, nithear clann ris*

HUSBAND, v Gnathaich; caomhain; treabh

HUSBANDLESS, a Gun fhear, gun duine, neo-phosda; bantrachail

HUSBANDLY, a Caonntach, cùramach, grunndail.

HUSBANDMAN, s. Tuathanach, treabhaiche, fear croinn, fear treabhaidh Husbandmen, *tuathanaich, tuath*

HUSBANDRY, s Tuathanachas, treabhachas, treabhadh, treabhachd, tuathanachd, àiteachadh, fearachas tighe Good husbandry, *deagh thuathanachas, deagh threabhachas*

HUSH! interj Caisd, éisd, bi ad thosd, bi samhach (no) bìth

HUSH, v. a. Cuir samhach, caisg, coisg, gabh gu clos, tàlaidh Hush up, *cum samhach*

HUSH, a. Samhach, tosdach, bìth; balbh.

HUSHMONEY, s. Brib airson a bhith samhach, airgiod tosd

HUSK, s Plaosg, cochull, spalag, crotal, càithlean, (*of peas*), meiligeag

HUSK, v a Plaoisg, sgioll, sgil, fosgail

HUSKED, a. Cochullach.

HUSKY, a Plaosgach, cochullach; caithleanach; (*in voice*), ròcanach.

HUSSAR, s Trupair Ongthireach.

HUSSY, s Baobh, dubh-chaile, té air bheag meas

HUSTINGS, s Mòd, coinneamh; cùirt; comhairle

HUSTLE, v. a Crath sa cheile, pùc, put, mulc.

HUSWIFE, s. (*Corrupted from housewife*), bean-tighe, stràille

HUSWIFERY, s Beanachas tighe

HUT, s. Bothan, bùth, croth; bothag; caban.

HUTCH, s Ciste coirce; binne.

HUZZ, v Dean torman (no) dranndan, dean dùrdan.

HUZZA, interj. Aoibh

HUZZA, s. Gàir aoibhneis, comh-ghàir.

HUZZA, v a. Furanaich; dean comhghair, glaodh, dean ard-iolach

HYACINTH, s. Seorsa neoinein; cloch uasal.

HYACINTHINE, a. Neònanach, plùranach

HYADES, s. Griglean; grigleachan, na seachd rionnagan.

HYALINE, a. Gloineach, gloinidh, criostalach.

HYDATIDES, s. Bolgan uisge a chithear an com luchd meud-bhroinn

HYDRA, s Uile-bhéist ioma-cheannach; nathair nimhe uamhasach.

HYDRAULICS, s Ealadhain phiob-uisge, eolas mu uisge tharruing troimh phioban.

HYDROGRAPHER, s. Muir-dhealbhair.

HYDROGRAPHY, s. Muir-eolas, muir dhealbhadh.

HYDROMEL, s Mil-dheoch.

HYDROMETER, s Inneal a thomhas uisge

HYDROMETRY, s Tomhas uisge, uisge-thomhas

HYDROPHOBIA, s Galar cuthaich, galar o theum coin chuthaich, uisge-oillt

HYDROPIC, HYDROPICAL, a. Meud-bhronnach.

HYDROSCOPE, s Uaireadair uisge.

HYDROSTATICS, s Ealadhain uisge-thomhas

HYDRUS, s Nathair uisge

HYEMAL, a. Geamhrail.

HYENA, s. Fiadh bheist fuilteach cosmhuil ri madadh allaidh.

HYGROMETER, s Fliche-inneal

† HYM, s Seorsa coin

HYMEN, s. Posadh, maighdeannas; dia phòsaidh

HYMENEAL, a. Òran posaidh, òran bainnse.

HYMENEAL, a. Pòsachail, pòsaidh, maraisteach.

HYMN, s Laoidh, oran naomh (no) diadhuidh; caireall, dàn spioradail

HIP, v Mi-mhisnich, cuir fu mhi-mhisnich, cuir fo lionn-dubh

HYPERBOLE, s Oisbhreug; spleadhachas, spleadh-bhriathar, sgleò mar ni neach nur their e nì fo no thar a chòir, mar *tha e cho luath ris an dealanach, cho sean ris na cragaibh, cho dubh ris an aibhisear.*

HYPERBOLICAL, a Spleadhach.

HYPERBOLIZE, v Dean spleadhachas (no) glòir.

HYPERBOREAN, a. Boirdheach, tuath, tuathach

HYPERCRITIC, s. Rannsuchair sgaiteach, neach ro ullamh gu coire fhaotainn.

HYPERMETER, s Ni sam bi os cionn tomhas

HYPHEN, s Comhar ceanglaidh mar (-) ann an geurleanmhuinn

HYPNOTIC, s. Ioc-shlainnt chodalach

HYPOCHONDRIA, s Lionn-dubh; tuirse, truime-inntinn

HYPOCHONDRIAC, a Tuirseach, trom, neo-mhisneachail, dubhachail

HYPOCHONDRIAC, s Neach air am bheil an lionn-dubh.

HYPOCRISY, s. Cealgaireachd, mealltaireachd; fuar-chrabhadh, ceilg, gò, saobh-chrabhadh.

HYPOCRITE, s. Cealgair, mealltair.

HYPOCRITIC, HYPOCRITICAL, a Fallsa, cealgach, neo-fhior, mealltach, fuar-chrabhach, saobh-chrabhach.

HYPOCRITICALLY, adv. Gu fallsa, gu cealgach, gu neo-fhior, gu fuar-chrabhach, gu saobh-chrabhach

HYPOSTASIS, s. Bith, pearsa

Hypothesis, *s.* Barail, saoilsinn, smuaine.

Hypothetic, Hypothetical, *a.* Baraileach, baralach, cumhnantach.

Hypothetically, *adv.* Gu baralach, a réir barail; air chumhnant.

Hyrst, Hurst, *s* Doire, coille, badan coille, coille bheag

Hyssop, *s.* Seorsa luibh, isop.

Hysterical, *a.* Leth-taobhail, leth-taobhach.

Hysterics, *s* An leth-taobh, eiridh leth-taobh, greis, tinneas builg, tinneas mhnathan, tinneas cuim.

I.

I, *s.* An naothamh litir do 'n aibideal

I, *pron* Mi. I myself, *mi féin, mise féin, mi fhéin*, it is I, *is mise th' ann.*

Iambic, *s.* Cam-dhàn.

Ice, *s.* Eigh, eidhre, eithre, deidh, cuisne, reothadh

Ice-house, *s.* Tigh reòtaidh, tigh eighe

Ichneumon, *s.* Beist beag a bhriseas uibhean nan croghall

Ichor, *s.* Iongar tana, siltcach.

Ichorous, *a.* Iongarach; uisgidh

Ichthyology, *s.* Eolas mu iasg, cunntas mu nadur agus gné nan iasg.

Ichthyophagist, *s.* Urr a thug beò air iasg

Icicle, *s.* Biodag eighe, bior eighe, dealg eighe, cluigean eighe, eigheanach.

Iciness, *s.* Reòtachd, reòtadh.

Icon, *s.* Dealbh, coslas; eugmhas, aogas

Iconoclast, *s* Fear brisidh iomhaigh, drong eirceach.

Iconolater, *s.* Fear iodhal-aoraidh.

Iconology, *s.* Cunntas ma dhealbhan no iomhaighean, dealbhadaireachd.

Icteric, Icterical, *a.* Tinn leis a ghriuthach, math air-son na griuthaich.

Icy, *a.* Eigheach, eithreach, eighe, fuar, reòtaidh, reòtach, fionnar.

Idea, *s* Beachd na h-inntinn, barail, smuain; smuaintidh

Ideal, *a* Beachdail, dòchasach, faoin

Identic, Identical, *a.* Ceudna; ceudnach, ionann. The identical man, *a cheart duine.*

Identify, *v.* Ceudnaich, dean dà ni ionann, ionannaich

Identity, *s* Ceudnachd, ionannachd.

Ides, *s.* An cuigeamh là deug a réir aireamh nan Ròimh-each do, Mhios Bhealtuin, (*May*), do 'n Mhios bhuidhe; (*July*), agus do 'n lùnasd, (*August*), ach an treas la deug do gach mios eile.

Idiocy, *s.* Amaideachd nadurra, oinnsealachd, amhlaireachd, dith céill; gòraiche

Idiom, *s.* Doigh-labhairt, doigh sgrìobhaidh.

Idiot, *s.* Amadan, baothair, baoghlan, neo-dhuine; oinn-seach, nothaist, amhlair, càmar, càmaran

Idiotism, *s.* Amaideachd, nòthaistealachd, oinnsealachd; faoineachd; baoth-bhriathar, baoth-radh, doigh labhairt.

Idle, *a.* Diomhanach, leasg, leagach, lunndach, (*vain*), diomhain, faoin; gun stà, gun tairbhe.

Idle, *v. a.* Caith uine gu diomhanach, spaisdeirich.

Idleheaded, *a.* Amaideach, mi-reusonta, gòrach

Idleness, *s.* Diomhanas, leisge, lunndaireachd, tamh; faoine, faoineas

Idler, *s.* Leisgean, leisgeir, lunndair, diomhanaiche; rong, droll; spaidsear, spaisdear, leagair.

Idly, *adv.* Gu diomhanach, gu leasg, gu lunndach, gu faoin.

Idol, *s.* Iodhal, iomhaigh, dealbh, dia bréig

Idolater, *s.* Iodhladair, fear iodhal-aoraidh.

Idolatress, *s* Ban-iodhladair, bean (no) té iodhal aoraidh

Idolatrous, *a* Iodhladaireach, iodhal-aorach

Idolatry, *s* Iodhal-aoraidh, iodhladaireachd

Idolist, *s* Iodhladair; fear iodhal-aoraidh

Idolize, *v.* Gradhaich gu mòr, dean iodhal do ni (no) neach

Idoneous, *a* Cubhaidh, iom-chuidh, freagarrach, ceart

Idyl, *s.* Dan beag

If, *conj.* Ma If he be willing, *ma 's toille leis, ma 's deòn-ach leis*, if not, *mur*, but if not, *ach mur*, he may come, but if not, *faotaidh e teachd, ach mur tig*, as if, *mar*, *mar gu b' e*, *mar gu b' ann, mur gu b' eadh*, if so be that, *ma 's e agus gu*, if so be that not, *ma 's e 's nach*, as if one should say, *mar gun abradh neach*, see if he be at home, *seall (no) faic bheil e aig an tigh*

Igneous, *a* Teinntidh, teinnteach, lasach, loisgeach

Ignifluous, *a* Sruthadh le teine

Ignipotence, *s* Smachd air teine.

Ignipotent, *a* Aig am bheil smachd air teine.

Ignis-fatuus, *s.* Teine sionnachain

Ignite, *v.* Cuir ri theine, las, fadaich, cuir an gabhail, beothaich.

Ignitible, *a* Lasach, so-lasadh, so-chur an gabhail, so-chur r' a theine.

Ignition, *s* Lasadh, gabhail, fàdadh

Ignoble, *a* Iosal; neo-inbheach, an-uasal, diblidh, bochd, truagh; gun fhiach, gun fhiù, iriosal, neo-urramach, ùranach, suarrach, neo-fhiachail.

Ignobly, *adv* Gu h-iosal, gu h-an-uasal, gu diblidh, gu bochd, gu neo-urramach, gu suarrach, gu maslach, gu tàireil, gu h-iriosal.

Ignominious, *a* Truaillidh, maslach, tàireil, suarrach, nàr, nàrach, sgainnealach, mi-chliùiteach.

Ignominiously, *adv* Gu truaillidh, gu maslach, gu tàir-eil, gu suarrach, gu nàr.

Ignominy, *s.* Masladh, tàir, mi-chliù, sgainneal, nàir, tru-aillidheachd, dìblidheachd

Ignoramus, *s.* Baoghlan; burraidh

Ignorance, *s.* Aineolas, cion eòlais, cion fiosrachaidh, dith ionnsuich, dìth oilein, ain-fhios Ignorance is a heavy load, *is trom an eire an t-aineolas*

Ignorant, *a.* Aineolach, neo-fhiosrach, ain-fhiosach, ain-easach, borb, gun colas, gun oilean, gun ionnsach

Ignorant, *s* Urr aineolach, aineol

Ignorantly, *adv.* Gu h-aineolach, gu neo-fhiosrach, gu h-ain-fhiosrach, gu h-aineasach

Ile, *s* (*Of a church*), oilean, (*of corn*), dias, diasad

Ilex, *s* Darach sìor-uaine

Iliac, *a.* Caolain, cuim, a bhuineas do na caolain Iliac passion, tinneas caolain.

† **Ilk**, *s* and *a.* Ceudna, gach.

Ill, *a.* (*Bad*), olc, dona, droch, (*sick*), tinn, euslan, soith-ich. He is not an ill man, *cha n eil e na dhroch dhuine.*

Ill, *s* Olc, aingidheachd, truaighe, dochair, mi-shealbh, cron, dolas, dochann, donas.

Ill, *adv* Gu h-olc, gu dona, gu tinn, gu soithich, gu h-euslan He is very ill, *tha e gu ro thinn, tha e gu ro shoithich*, ill of a cold, *gu dona leis a chrutan*, one time well, another time ill, *an darn' uair gu math, is an uair eile gu tinn*

Illaborate, *a.* Neo-shaoithreachail, air bheag dragha.

Illacerable, *a* Do-reubadh, do-phàirteachadh.

Illachrymable, *a* Cruaidh, duincil, cruadalach, nach gabh cur a ghal

Illapse, *s* Ionnsuidh, teachd, tighinn, inntrinn

Illaqueate, *v* Glac le dul, cuir an sàs

Illaqueation, *s.* Dul, lùb, gainntir.

Illation, *s* Deireadh, comh-dhùnadh, ceann-thall

Illaudable, *a.* Neo-chliùiteach, neo-airidh

Illaudably, *adv* Gu neo-chliùiteach, gu neo-airidh.

Illegal, *a* Neo-laghail, mi-laghail, neo-cheart, neo-chothromach, toirmisgte, mi-reachdail, an aghaidh an lagha

Illegality, *s* Mi-laghaileachd, neo-laghaileachd.

Illegible, *a* Do-leughadh, duilich leughadh, nach gabh leughadh, neo-shoillcir

Illegitimacy, *s.* Diolanas

Illegitimate, *a* Diolain, dìblidh An illegitimate child, *leanabh diolain, urr dhiolain*

Illeviable, *a* Do-thogail mar chàin, duilich a thogail, nach gabh togail

Illfavoured, *a* Duaichnidh, granda, gràda, neo-bhoidheach, neo-laoghach.

Illfavouredness, *s* Duaichneachd, duaichnidheachd, grandachd, gràinead

Illiberal, *a* Neo-uasal, mio-thur, crion; truaillidh, cruaidh, cruadalach, sgroingeanach; neo-thabhartach, gortach An illiberal mind, *inntinn chrion*

Illiberality, *s* Mio-thurachd, crìne, sgroingeanachd, gortachas

Illiberally, *adv* Gu mio-thur, gu crion, gu truaillidh, gu cruaidh, gu cruadalach.

Illicit, *a* Neo-laghail, toirmisgte, neo-cheadaichte, mi-fhreagarrach

Illimitable, *a* Neo-chriochnaidh, gun chrioch, gun cheann

Illimited, *a.* Neo-chriochnachadh

Illimitedness, *s* Neo-chriochnachd

Illiterate, *a* Neo-ionnsuichte, ain-fhiosach, aineolach, neo-fhoghluimte, borb, gun ionnsach, gun oilean.

Illiterateness, *s* Aineolas, cion ionnsuich, ain-fhios, cion foghluim, cion oilein

Illnature, *s* Droch nàdur, droch ghné, mi-rùn, mio-sguinn, cion seirc, droch rùn

Illnatured, *a* Olc nadurrach, droch nadurrach, miosguinneach, mi-rùnach, droch-ghnetheach, crosda, doirbh, cainnteach, mi-ghnétheil, drranndanach

Illnaturedly, *adv.* Gu droch nadurrach, gu miosguinneach, gu mi-runach, gu crosda, gu cainnteach

Illness, *s* Tinneas, euslainnte, galar, eucail, laigsinn, olcas.

Illogical, *a* Neo-reusontach, neo-argumaideach

Illude, *v a* Meall, thoir an car a, mag, dean fochaid, dean fanoid.

Illume, *v a.* Soillsich, soilleirich; loinnrich. Illumed, *soillsichte*

Illuminate, *v a.* Soillsich; thoir solus, soilleirich; dean soilleir, dearrs, dearrsaich, dealraich, dean soillseach; sgiamhaich le lochranaibh soluis; mìnich, dean so-thuigsinn. Illuminated, *soillsichte; soilleirichte, mìnichte.*

Illumination, *s* Soillseachadh; dearrsadh; solus eibhneis; léirsinn spioradail.

Illuminative, *a* Soillseachail, soillseach, dealrach, dearrsach.

Illuminator, *s* Soillseachair, dealbhair, (no) fear do 'n gnothuch dealbhan a chur air toiseach chaibdeilean.

Illumine, *v.* Soillsich, sgiamhaich, nàisnich.

Illusion, *s.* Mealladh; mearachd; fanoid; mealladh shùl; faileas, faoineas.

Illusive, *a.* Mealltach; fanaideach; faoin

Illusory, *a.* Mealltach, fallsa, fallsail, faileasach, faoin.

Illustrate, *v a.* Soillsich; mìnich, soilleirich, dean soilleir (no) so-thuigsinn. Illustrated, *soillsichte, mìnichte, soilleirichte*

Illustration, *s* Soillseachadh, mìneachadh, soilleíreachadh, deanamh so-thuigsinn.

Illustrative, *a.* Soillseachail, a tilg soluis, mìneachail.

Illustrious, *a.* (*Famous*), cliùiteach, ainmeil, measail; (*in rank*), ard, uasal, oirdheirc, urramach, mor; corr.

Illustriously, *adv* Gu cliùiteach, gu h-ainmeil, gu measail, gu h-ard, gu h-uasal, gu h-oirdheirc, gu corr.

Illustriousness, *s* Ainmealachd, oirdheirceas, mòrachd; uaillse; àirde

Ill-will, *s* Mi-run, gamhlas, droch-rùn, tnù, tnùth.

I'm, (*for* I am) Tha mi, a ta mi, taim.

Image, *s.* Iomhaigh, dealbh, aogas, eugas, coslas; cruth, riochd; (*of idolatry*), dealbh, iodhal A painted image, *dealbh dathte*, a graven image, *dealbh snaithte.*

Image, *v. a* Smuainich, beachdaich.

Imagery, *s.* Dealbhaidh; cruthachd, cruthachadh, caslachdan.

Imaginable, *a* Smuainteachail, ion-smuaineachadh, so-bheachdachadh

Imaginant, *a.* Beachdail, smuainteachail, tùrail

Imaginary, *a.* Faoin, beachdaidh, neo-fhior. An imaginary ailment, *tinneas dòchais,*

Imagination, *s.* Breithneachadh; (*fancy*), meamnadh, meamna, (*thought*), smuain, inntinn, reusonachadh, dòchas, rùn, (*contrivance*), innleachd.

Imaginative, *a* Beachdachail, dòchasach, inntinneach.

Imagine, *v* Smuainich, smuaintich, smaointich, meas; (*contrive*), dealbh, deilbh, tùr, tionnsgain.

Imaginer, *s* Smuaintear, smuaineachair

Imbecile, *a* Anfhann, fann, lag, mall, breoite, spreòchanta, truagh.

Imbecility, *s* Anfhannachd, anfhainne, ainmhainneachd, anmhannachd, fainne, laigsinn, malltachd, spreòchantachd.

Imbibe, *v a.* Òl; sùig; sugh; gabh, gabh steach; deoghail.

Imbiber, *s* Olair, sughair, suigear, deoghlair.

Imbibition, *s* Oladh, sughadh, sùgadh, deoghladh.

Imbitter, *v a.* Dean searbh, dean goirt, dean geur; searbhaich, goirtich, cradh; cuir fu bhuaireas, feargaich, cuir air bhoile (no) air bhuair.

Imbody, *v. a.* and *n.* Co-chorpaich, corpaich; dùmhlaich (no) teannaich sa cheile; fàs sa chéile.

Imbolden, *v a.* Dean dàna (no) misneachail, dean fearail, cuir misneach ann; misnich.

Imbosom, *v.* Gabh (no) glac an ad uchd, caidir, teannaich ri d' uchd, comhdaich, dion

Imbound, *v. a* Druid, dùin a stigh, iom-dhruid; cuairtich, cuartaich.

Imbower, *v.* Fasgaich; cuir fo dhùbhradh, comhdaich; dion; sgàilich. Imbowered, *fasgaichte, sgàilichte.*

Imbowment, *s.* Boghadh, druim-bhoghta.

Imbricated, *a.* Claisichte; feagaichte.

Imbrown, *v. a.* Donnaich, dean donn; doilleirich.

Imbrue, *v. a.* Bog, tom, tum; fliuch, salaich; measgaich. Imbrued, *tomta, fliuch; salaichte.* He imbrued his hands in blood, *thum e 'lamhan am fuil;* hands imbrued in blood, *lamhan fliuch le fuil.*

Imbrute, *v. a.* Brùidich; truaillich, salaich.

Imbued, *a.* Dathta, daithte; salaichte.

Imbue, *v. a.* Dath, dathaich; salaich; neulaich.

Imitable, *a.* So-leanachd, so-leantuinn, so-leanmhuinn; airidh air leanachd.

Imitate, *v. a.* Lean, lean eisiomlair; lorgairich, dean do rèir; aithris, dean coslach. Imitated, *an a leantuinn; aithriste, lorgairaichte.*

Imitation, *s.* Leanachd; leanadachd; lorgaireachd; aithris; dublachadh, coslachadh, samhlachadh.

Imitative, *a.* Leanadach, leantuinneach, lorgaireach, aithriseach.

Imitator, *s.* Leanmhuinniche, lorgair, leanadachd, samhlachair; fear abhachais; aithrisear.

Immaculate, *a.* Glan, fior-ghlan, gun smàl, gun chron, neo-shalach, neo-thruaillidh.

Immanacle, *v. a.* Cuibhrich; ceangail, dòmhlaich.

Immane, *a.* Mòr, fuathasach, borb, garg, uamharra.

Immanity, *s.* Buirbe, gairge.

Immanuel, *s.* Criosd.

Immarcessible, *a.* Neo-sheargach.

† **Immartial**, *a.* Neo-chruadalach, neo-ghaisgeil, neo-churanta.

Immaterial, *a.* Neo-chorporra, neo-thalmhaidh, spioradail; aibhseil; (*of no moment*), air bheag seadh, air bheag luach, air bheag suim; fadharsach; neo-thabhachdach; faoin.

Immateriality, *s.* Neo-chorporrachd; spioradailteachd, neo-thabhachd.

Immaterialized, *a.* Neo-chorporra, spioradail.

Immaterialness, *s.* Neo-chorporrachd, spioradailteachd.

Immateriate, *a.* Neo-chorporra, neo-thalmhaidh, spioradail.

Immature, *a.* Anabuich, anabuidh, neo-abuich; neo-iomlan, obann; grad; cabhagach, luath; tuille is luath, tuille is tràthail.

Immaturely, *adv.* Tuille is tràth, tuille is tràthail, tuille is luath.

Immatureness, *s.* Anabachd; anabuichead, neo-iomlanachd.

Immeasurable, *a.* Do-thomhas, nach gabh tomhas; nach fheudar thomhas, neo-chriochnach.

Immeasurably, *adv.* Thar tomhas.

Immediate, *a.* Grad, ealamh; fogus, neo-mheadhonach; aig laimh.

Immediately, *adv.* Gu grad, gu luath, air a mhionait, an ceart uair, air an uair, air ball, air an spot, gun mhoil, gun dàil, gun stad, gun fhuireach.

Immediateness, *s.* Graide, ealamhachd; lathaireachd.

Immedicable, *a.* Do-leigheas, nach gabh leigheas.

Immemorial, *a.* A cuimhne, thar cuimhne, cian, o chian. From time immemorial, *o amanna cian.*

Immense, *a.* Neo-chriochta; neo-chriochnach; gun chrioch, aibhseach; do-thomhas, ro mhòr, fuathasach mòr, mòr thar tomhas.

Immensity, *s.* Anabharra meudachd, do-thomhas, eu-criochnachd.

Immensurable, *a.* Do-thomhas, duilich thomhas, nach gabh tomhas, thar tomhas.

Immerge, *v. a.* Tom, tum, bog, cuir fo 'n uisge, baist.

Immerit, *s.* Mi-thoiltinneas.

Immerse, *v.* Tom, tum, bog, cuir fo 'n uisge, baist. Immersed, *tomta, tumta, fo 'n uisge, air chur fo 'n uisge, air bhaisteadh.*

Immersion, *s.* Tomadh, tumadh, bogadh, cur fo 'n uisge, baisteadh.

Immethodical, *a.* Neo-riaghailteach, mi-riaghailteach, gun ordugh, gun doigh, gun riaghal, gun lathailt

Immethodically, *adv.* Gun neo-riaghailteach, gun ordugh, gun doigh, gun riaghal, gun lathailt, troimh chéile.

Imminent, *a.* Bagarach, cunnartach; am fogus, aig laimh; an crochadh.

Immingle, *v. a.* Measg, measgnaich, co-mheasg; coi-mheasg. Immingled, *measgta, coimheasgta.*

Immiscible, *a.* Do-mheasgadh.

Immission, *s.* Cur a stigh (no) steach; leigeil stigh (no) steach.

Immit, *v. a.* Cuir a stigh (no) steach, leig a stigh, leig a steach.

Immix, *v. a.* Measg, coi-mheasg. Immixed, *measgta, coi-mheasgta.*

Immixable, *a.* Do-mheasgadh, do-choi-mheasgadh.

Immobility, *a.* Do-charuidheachd, do-ghlideachd.

Immoderate, *a.* Neo-mheasarra, ana-measarra, ana-measarrach; ana-barra, ana-barrach, ana-bharrach, mi-stuama, neo-cheannsa, ana-cuimseach.

Immoderately, *adv.* Gu neo-mheasarra, gu ana-measarrach, gu anabarrach.

Immoderation, *s.* Neo-mheasarrachd, ana-measarrachd, mi-stuaim, ana-cuimse.

Immodest, *a.* (*In manner*), mi-gheimnidh, mi-gheamnuidh, neo-gheimnidh, mi-stuama; neo-bheusach, neo-ghlan, beagnarach; (*in language*), draosta, drabasta, drùiseil. An immodest person, *drusdar, trustar.*

Immodestly, *adv.* Gu-mi-gheimnidh, gu mi-gheamnuidh, gu mi-stuama, gu mi-bheusach, gu neo-ghlan, gu beagnarach; (*in language*), gu draosta, gu drabasta, gu drùiseil.

Immodesty, *s.* Mi-gheimnidheachd, mi-stuaim, mi-bheus, draostachd, drùis.

Immolate, *v.* Iobair, thoir suas mar iobairt.

Immolation, *s.* Iobairt.

Immoment, *a.* Fadharsach, faoin.

Immoral, *a.* Mi-bheusach; neo-bheusach, drùiseil; eas-ionraic; mi-dhiadhuidh; dubhailceach, mi-mhodhail.

Immorality, *s.* Mi-bheus, drùis, eas-ionracas, dubhailc, mi-mhodh.

Immorally, *adv.* Gu mi-bheusach; gu drùiseil; gu dubhailceach.

Immortal, *a.* Neo-bhàsmhor, bith-bhuan, siorruidh.

Immortality, *s.* Neo-bhasmhorachd, neo-bhasmhoireachd; bith-bhuantachd, siorruidheachd.

Immortalize, *v.* Dean neo-bhasmhor, (no) bith-bhuan.

Immoveable, *a.* Do-charuchadh, do-ghlideachadh, do-ghluasadach; daingean; bunaiteach, bunailteach.

Immunity, *s.* Sochair; saorsadh; còir.

Immure, *v.* Druid eadar dha bhalla, mùch.

Immusical, *a.* Neo-bhinn, neo-cheolmhor.

Immutability, *s.* Neo-chaochlaideachd, seasmhachd, maireannachd, bunaiteachd, bunailteach.

Immutable, *a.* Neo-chaochlaideach, neo-chaochlach, seasmhach, do-atharrachadh, do-chaochladh; maireannach.

Immutably, *adv.* Gun chaochladh, gu seasmhach.
+ **Imp**, *s.* Mac, clann, sliochd
Imp, *s.* Deamhan beag; ablach; (*in gardening*), nòd, nòdachadh
Imp, *v.* Leudaich, fadaich, meudaich, cuir ri, ic
Impact, *v. a* Dluthaich, stramp; pacaich.
Impair, *v a* and *n* Mill, cuir dholaidh, dean ni 's miosa, dochannaich, lughdaich, cuir an lughaid, rach a dholaidh, fàs ni 's miosa
Impairment, *s.* Lughdachadh, dol a dholaidh, fàs ni 's miosa
Impalpable, *a.* Do-mhothuchadh, do-fhaineachadh, do-fhaireachadh, do-fharachduinn.
Imparity, *s.* Neo-ionannachd, neo-choslachd
Impark, *v a* Cuir am pàirc, druid, dùin, fàl.
Impart, *v a* Tabhair, thabhair, thoir, builich, bairig, deònaich, pàirtich
Impartial, *a* Ceart, cothromach, dìreach, fior, fireannach, neo-chlaon.
Impartiality, *s* Ceartas, cothromachd, fireannachd, firinn
Impartially, *adv* Gu ceart, gu cothromach, gu direach, gu fireannach, gu neo-chlaon
Impartible, *a.* Do-phàirteachadh, do-bhuileachadh
Impassable, *a.* Do-shiubhal, do-choiseachadh, do-imeachd.
Impassibleness, *s* Do-choiseachd, do-imeachd.
Impassioned, *a.* Fo bhuaireas, buairte.
Impatience, *s* Mi-fhoighidinn, cion-foighidinn, deothasachd, déine, cabhag, mio-fhurasachd
Impatient, *a.* Mi-fhoighidinneach, mi-fhaighdinneach, neo-fhulangach, dian, cabhagach, deothasach, cas
Impatiently, *adv.* Gu mi-fhoighidinneach, gu dian, gu cabhagach, gun fhoighidinn.
Impawn, *v. a* Cuir an geall; thoir an geall
Impeach, *v a* Cronaich, coirich, eilich, dit, cuir as leth, † bac
Impeachable, *a* Airidh air cronachadh; so-chronachadh
Impeacher, *s.* Cronachair, coireachair, eileachair
Impeachment, *s* Cronachadh, coireachadh; cùis dhìtidh; cùis-bhacaidh
Impearl, *v a* Neamhnuich, sgeadaich le neonaidibh
Impeccability, *s* Fior-ghlaine, neo-chiontas.
Impeccable, *a* Fior-ghlan, neo-chiontach
Impede, *v a.* Bac, stad, amail, cuir stad, cuir amal, cuir moille
Impeded, *part* Bacta, amailte, air bhacadh, air amaladh
Impediment, *s* Bac, bacadh, amal, stadaich, moille, aghaidh, (*in speech*), ag.
Impel, *v a* Greas air aghaidh, cuir air adhairt, puc; starr, iomain air aghaidh, saodaich Impelled, *greasta, air a ghreasadh, air chur air aghaidh*
Impellent, *a.* Greasadach, iomaineach
Impend, *v* Croch, bi an crochadh, bi osciono.
Impendence, *s.* Crochadh, foigse, fogsachd
Impendent, *a* An crochadh, fogus, fagus, aig laimh, os-cionn
Impenetrability, *s* Do-dhrùigheachd, ro-chruadhas. Impenetrability of heart, *ro chruadhas cridhe*
Impenetrable, *a* Do-dhrùigheadh, ro chruaidh, air nach gabh druigheadh; do-tholladh
Impenetrableness, *s.* Do-dhrùigheachd; ro-chruadhas.
Impenitence, *s.* Neo-aithreachas, cruadhas cridhe.
Impenitent, *a.* Neo-aithreach, neo-aithreachail; cruaidh-chridheach.
Impenitently, *adv.* Gu neo-aithreachail.
Impennous, *a* Gun sgiathan.
Imperative, *a.* Àithneach, aitheantach, ordughach, iarrtachail, smachdail.
Imperatively, *adv.* Gu smachdail.
Imperceptibility, *s* Do-fhaineachduinn, do-fhaicinn, do-fharachduinn, do-mhothuchadh.
Imperceptible, *a* Do-fhaicinn, do-fhaicsinn; neo-fhaicsinneach, do-fhaineachadh, do-mhothuchadh, do-fharachduinn, nach faicear, nach fainichear, nach mothuichear.
Imperceptibleness, *s.* Neo-fhaicsinneachd.
Imperceptibly, *adv* Gu neo-fhaicsinneach, gun fhios.
Imperfect, *a.* Neo-iomlan, neo-fhoirfe, neo-choimhlionta; neo-chriochnuichte; fàilneach
Imperfection, *s* Neo-iomlaine, gaoid, ciurram, fàilne, fàilneadh, neo-fhoirfeachd
Imperfectly, *adv* Gu neo-iomlan, gu neo-fhoirfe.
Imperfectness, *s.* Neo-iomlanachd; neo-fhoirfeachd, neo-choimhliontachd
Imperforable, *a.* Do-tholladh, nach gabh tolladh, do-thollta.
Imperforate, *a* Neo-thollta.
Imperial, *a* Rioghail, iompaireach, iompaireil
Imperialist, *s* Saighdear rìgh, saighdear rioghail.
Imperious, *a.* Smachdach, smachdail, stràiceil, ceannasach, forail, ardanach, uasal, uallach, cumhachdach, cruaidh
Imperiously, *adv* Gu smachdail, gu stràiceil, gu ceannasach, gu forail; gu h-àrdanach, gu h-uasal, le smachd, leis an lamh làidir.
Imperiousness, *s.* Smachd, stràic, ceannasachd; cumhachd, foraileachd.
Imperishable, *a* Do-sgriosadh, do-mharbhadh, nach gabh sgrios (no) marbhadh; maireann, maireannach
Impersonal, *a* Neo-phearsonta.
Imperspicuous, *a.* Dorcha, doilleir, do-thuigsinn, do-fhaicinn, neo-shoilleir.
Impersuasible, *a* Do-chomhairleach, nach gabh comhairle, do-thionndadh.
Impertinence, *s* Beadaidheachd, beagnarachd, danadas, meachranachd, amaideachd.
Impertinent, *a* Beadaidh, beagnarach, dàna, meachranach, leamh, amaideach, faoin The compliments of the impertinent to the troublesome, *urram a bhleìdire do'n strucair*
Impertinently, *adv.* Gu beadaidh, gu beagnarach, gu dàna, gu meachranach, gu leamh, gu h-amaideach; gu faoin.
Imperturbable, *a.* Socrach, do-chur thar a chéile.
Imperturbed, *a.* Socrach, ciùin, sàmhach
Impervious, *a.* Do-shiubhal, do-imeachd
Impetible, *a* Do-ruigheachd, do-ruigsinn, do-fhaghail, do-fhaotainn.
Impetigines, *s.* Teine dé
Impetrable, *a* So-fhaghail, so-fhaotainn; a ghabhas faotainn.
Impetrate, *v.* Faigh an cois urnuigh.
Impetuosity, *s.* Deine, déinead, buirbe, gairge, gairgead; toirceannachd, bruilsgeantachd, raigealachd, spionnadh.
Impetuous, *a* Dian, borb, garg, deannmhor, fuathasach; obann, laidir, treun, neartmhor.
Impetuously, *adv.* Gu dian, gu borb, gu garg, gu làidir.

Impetuousness, *s.* Déine, dèinead, dianad, spionnadh, obainne.

Impetus, *s.* Déine; deann, oidhirp; sìth.

Impierceable, *a.* Do-thòlladh.

Impiety, *s.* Mi-naomhachd, mi-dhiadhachd, aingidheachd.

Impignorate, *v.* Cuir an geall.

Impignoration, *s.* Geall.

Impinge, *v. a.* Buail, sgeilc.

Impinguate, *v. a.* Reamhraich.

Impious, *a.* Mi-naomh, mi-dhiadhaidh, aingidh, malluichte, olc.

Impiously, *adv.* Gu mi-naomha, gu mi-dheadhaidh, gu h-aingidh.

Impiousness, *s.* Mi-naomhachd, mi-dhiadhachd, aingidheachd.

Implacability, *s.* Do-chiosnachd, do-choisgeachd, gamhlasachd, buirbe.

Implacable, *a.* Do-chiosnach, do-chiosnachaidh, do-chasgadh, gamhlasach.

Implacableness, *s.* Do-chiosnachd, do-choisgeachd, gamhlasachd, buirbe.

Implacably, *adv.* Gu do-chiosnach, gu do-chiosnachaidh, gu gamhlasach, gu borb.

Implant, *v. a.* Planntaich, suidhich, socraich; cuir; nòdaich. Implanted, *planntaichte, suidhichte, socraichte.*

Implantation, *s.* Planntachadh, suidheachadh, socrachadh.

Implausible, *a.* Neò-bheulchar.

Implement, *s.* Inneal, ball acfhuinn; airneis, tursgan, colìonadh.

Impletion, *s.* Lìonadh, làn.

Implex, *a.* Do-fhuasgladh; deacair, duilich.

Implicate, *v. a.* Rib, bac; cronaich, coirich; fill, paisg.

Implication, *s.* Ribeadh, bacadh; cronachadh, coireachadh; filleadh, pasgadh; ciallachadh.

Implicit, *a.* Ciallaichte; soilleir; saor; neo-ribte, fuasgailte; earbsach, umhal, iomlan, lan. Implicit confidence, *earbsadh, iomlan, lan earbsadh.* Implicitly, *gu h-umhal, gu h-iomlan;* (in words), *gu doilleir, gu neo-chiallachail.*

Implore, *v.* Guidh, grìos, iarr, athchuing, asluich. I implore you, *guidheam ort, tha mi grios ort.*

Implorer, *s.* Griosair.

Implumed, *a.* Gun chloimh, gun iteach, lom mar gharraig.

Imply, *v. a.* Ciallaich; fill.

Impoison, *v. a.* Puinsionaich, puinnseanaich.

Impolite, *a.* Mi-mhodhail, neo-shiobhailt, neo-shuairc, neo-shìbhealta, neo-eireachdail; borb.

Impoliteness, *s.* Mi-mhodhaileachd, mi-shuairceas.

Impolitic, *a.* Eu-crionna, neo-ghlic.

Imponderous, *a.* Eutrom.

Import, *v. a.* Thoir a steach, thoir a stigh; thoir nì steach do 'n rioghachd; ciallaich, ciall. This imports me, *buinidh so dhomhsa, is e so mo ghnothuch-sa.*

Import, *s.* Ni sam bi air a thoirt a steach do 'n rioghachd; toirt a stigh; bathar eil-thireach; ciall. The import and export of the country, *toirt a steach is toirt a mach na dùcha.*

Importance, *s.* Cudthrom; feum; tabhachd, meud, mòrachd; leas, buntuinneas. Of little importance, *suarrach;* of great importance, *cudthromach.*

Important, *a.* Cudthromach; tabhachdach; feumail, seadhail; mòr. The important day came at last, *thainig an la mòr mu dheireadh.*

Importation, *s.* Toirt a steach, toirt a stigh, tabhairt a steach do rioghachd; earras (no) bathar coimheach.

Importer, *s.* Fear thoirt a stigh bhàthar.

Importless, *a.* Air bheag suim, air bheag luach, suarrach.

Importunate, *a.* Leamh, liosda, iarrtachail, nach gabh diùltadh; beadaidh; draghail; lonach, sior-iarrtach.

Importunately, *adv.* Gu leamh, gu liosda; gu lonach, gu beadaidh.

Importunateness, *s.* Leamhachas, liosdachd, sior-iarruidh.

Importune, *v. a.* Sior-iarr, guidh, grios, asluich, iarr gu leamh (no) gu dùrachdach.

Importunity, *s.* Leamhachas, liosdachd, dian-liosdachd, sior-iarruidh; lon.

Imposable, *a.* So-leigeadh.

Impose, *v. a.* Leig, leig cìs, cuir dh' fhiachaibh air; cuir as leth. Impose on, *meall, thoir an car a.*

Imposed, *part.* (*As a tax*), Leigte, air a leigeadh. Imposed on, *air a mhealladh;* (*enjoined*), orduichte, air a sparradh.

Imposer, *s.* Leigear, fear leigeil; (*of a tax*), cìs-leigear.

Imposition, *s.* Leigeadh, cur air; cìs-leigeadh; càin, cìs; (*cheating*), mealladh, foill; (*burden*), eallach, uallach; (*injunction*), ordugh.

Impossibility, *s.* Do-dheantas; neo-chomasachd.

Impossible, *a.* Do-dheanamh, do-dheanta, nach gabh deanamh; neo-chomasach.

Impost, *s.* Cìs, càin; gnàthadh.

Imposthumate, *v. n.* Iongraich, leannaich, teanail.

Imposthume, *s.* Iongrachadh, leannach, leannachadh, neasgaid, othras.

Impostor, *s.* Cealgair, mealltair, ceabhachdair, slaoightear, sgonn.

Imposture, *s.* Cealg, mealladh, ceilge, cealgaireachd, mealltaireachd; ceabhachdaireachd, slaoightireachd.

Impotence, *s.* Laigse, laigsinn, cion treoir, neo-chomas, cion neirt, cion comais, fainne, anfhannachd.

Impotent, *a.* Lag, fann, anfhann, anmhunn, neo-chomasach, mall, gun spionna gun treòir, gun neart.

Impotently, *adv.* Gu lag, gu fann, gu h-anfhann, gu mall.

Impoverish, *v. a.* Dean bochd (no) truagh, thoir gu bochduinn. Impoverished, *bochd, truagh, uireasbhach.*

Impoverishment, *s.* Bochduinn, truaghanachd, uireasbhachd.

Impound, *v.* Druid, dùin, cuir a stigh.

Impracticability, *s.* Do-dheantas.

Impracticable, *a.* Do-dheanamh, do-dheanta, do-chur an gniomh, do-ghnàthachadh, neo-chomasach; duilich dheanamh; nach gabh deanamh; do-cheannsachadh reasgach, rag.

Impracticableness, *s.* Do-dheantas; deacaireachd; do-cheannsachd, reasgachd.

Imprecate, *v.* Guidh; mallachd, mollachd, guidh mallachd, dean droch ghuidhe.

Imprecation, *s.* Guidhe, guidheachan, mallachd, droch ghuidhe malluchadh, contrachd.

Impregn, *v. a.* Dean torrach.

Impregnable, *a.* Do-ghlacaidh, do-ghabhail, do-shàruchadh; do-charuchadh; daingean, daighnichte. An impregnable fortress, *daighneach do-ghlacaidh.* Impregnably, *gu daingean.*

Impregnate, *v. a.* Dean torrach; lìon. Impregnated, *torrach, trom, leth-tromach.*

Impregnation, *s.* Torrachas, siolmhorachd; lìonadh làn, teann-shàth.

Imprejudicate, *a.* Neo-chlaon, direach, ceart.

Impress, *v. a.* Clo-bhuail, cuir ann an clò; glac chum airm; stramp; sparr.

Impress, *s.* Lorg, athail, athailte; glacadh chum airm.

Impressible, *a.* So-ghlacadh, buailteach do ghlacadh.

Impression, *s.* Clo-bhualadh; dealbh; comhar, comharradh, athail, lorg, strampadh; (*of an attack*), drùghadh, drùghachdainn. It made an impression on him, *dhrùigh e air.*

Impressure, *s.* Comhar (no) lorg, feag, athail.

Imprimis, *adv.* Anns a cheud àite.

Imprint, *v.* Clò-bhuail, cuir an clò; (*on the memory*), suidhich sa chuimhne.

Imprison, *v. a.* Cuir an laimh, cuir am priosun, cuir an gainntir, cuir an carcar, cuir an toll-buth; cuir a stigh, druid a stigh, gainntirich, priosunaich.

Imprisonment, *s.* Priosunachadh, priosunachd, gainntireachd.

Improbability, *s.* Neo-chosmhalachd, neo-choslachd, eucoslachd, neo-dhaichealachd, neo-aogasachd.

Improbable, *a.* Neo-choslach, mi-aogasach, do-chreidsinn, baoth. Improbably, *gu neo-choslach.*

Improbity, *s.* Cealg, foill, slaoighte, eas-ionracas.

Improper, *a.* Neo-cheart, mi-cheart, cearr; neo-iomchuidh, neo-fhreagarrach, neo-oireamhnach.

Impropriate, *v.* Gabh, (no) glac chugad fein; builich fearann eaglais.

Impropriation, *s.* Buileachadh fearann eaglais.

Impropriety, *s.* Neo-cheartachd, mi-fhreagarrachd, neo-oireamhnachd.

Improsperous, *a.* Neo-fhortanach, mi-shealbhar, truagh.

Improvable, *a.* So-leasachadh, a ghabhas leasachadh.

Improve, *v. a.* Leasaich, builich, dean ni 's fear; thoir h-uige; (*ground*), thoir a stigh, mathaich.

Improve, *v. n.* Rach am feabhas, fàs ni 's fhearr, brotaich, thig h-uige.

Improvement, *s.* Leas, leasachadh; buannachd, feabhas, tairbhe; math, maithe; fàs; brotachadh, builcachadh.

Improver, *s.* Leasachair, buileachair.

Improvidence, *s.* Neo-fhreasdalachd; cion freasdail, mi-fhaicill, cion-smuaine.

Improvident, *a.* Neo-fhreasdalach, neo-fhaiceallach, neo-sholarach, neo-chrionna, neo-smuainteachail, neo-churamach.

Improvidently, *adv.* Gu neo-fhreasdalach, gu neo-fhaiceallach, gun fhreasdal, gun fhaicill.

Improvision, *s.* Cion smuaine, cion faicill.

Imprudence, *s.* Gòraiche, amaideachd, mi-chiall, mi-ghliocas.

Imprudent, *a.* Gòrach, amaideach, neo-chrionna, eucrionna; neo-ghlic, neo-churamach, neo-smuainteachail; cas, brais. Imprudently, *gu gòrach, gu h-amaideach.*

Impudence, *s.* Beag-narachd, dànadas, neo-stuamachd, peirtealachd.

Impudent, *a.* Beag-nàrach, mi-narach, dàn, beadaidh, dalma, mi-bheusach, peirteil, gobach, lonach, ladarna.

Impudently, *adv.* Gu beag-narach, gu dàn, gu beadaidh, gu dalma, gu peirteil, gu gobach, gu lonach, gu ladarna.

Impugn, *v.* Thoir ionnsuidh, thoir aghaidh, cuir an aghaidh; cronaich, coirich, faigh coir (no) cron; troid.

Impugner, *s.* Fear ionnsuidh; fear cronachaidh.

Impulse, *s.* Gluasad; dian-ghluasad; greasdachd, pùc; prosnachadh, brosnachadh.

Impulsive, *a.* Gluasadach, carachail; brosnachail.

Impunity, *s.* Saorsadh a pheanas.

Impure, *a.* Neo-ghlan, mi-naomh; mi-dhiadhaidh, salach; ciontach; truaillidh; neo-gheimnidh, draosda, drabasta, drùiseil; deasgannach.

Impurely, *adv.* Gu neo-ghlan, gu mi-naomh, gu mi-dhiadhuidh, gu ciontach, gu salach; gu drabasta.

Impurity, *s.* Neo-ghlaine; mi-dhiadhachd; sal; deasguinneachd, draostachd, draosdaireachd, drabasdachd, drùis, mi-gheimneachd.

Impurple, *v. a.* Dearg, dean dearg-mar chorcur.

Imputable, *a.* A ghabhas cur as leth, so chur as leth.

Impute, *v. a.* Cuir as leth, coirich.

Imputation, *s.* Cur as leth; casaid, cuis dhìtidh.

Imputrescible, *a.* Do-ghrodadh, do-mhilleadh, nach gabh grodadh.

In, *prep.* Ann, an, am anns, 'sa, a stigh, a steach. Come in, *thig a stigh;* in town, *anns a bhaile, sa bhaile;* in me, *annam;* in thee, *annad;* in him, *ann;* in her, *innte;* in us, *annainn;* in you, *annaibh;* in them, *annta;* in short, *gu h-aithghearr;* in ease, *am fois, an tamh;* in the dark, *san dorchadh;* in that, *a chionn;* in as much, *a chionn;* in existence, *beò, làthair;* in very deed, *gu dearbh; gu deimhin;* in comparison of, *an aite, seach;* in a manner, *air sheòl, air mhodh;* in a trice, *ann am briosg, gu h-ealamh, an am platha, ann am priob na sùl;* in as much as, *air a mheud is gu, a chionn gu;* in all, *uile, gu léir;* in common, *ann an còmharnaich;* in comparison of, *seach, laimh ri;* in the mean time, *an tràths, an dràsdaich, air an uair;* in sight, *anns an t-sealladh;* in presence of, *an lathair; roimh;* in sight of all, *gu follaiseach, an lathair nan uile.*

Inability, *s.* Neo-chomas, neo-chomasachd, neo-mhurrachas, cion comais, laige, laigsinn, laigse, fainne, anmhunnachd.

Inabstinence, *s.* Mi-stuaim, neo-gheimneachd.

Inaccessible, *a.* Do-ruigheachd, do-ruigsinn, duilich a ruigheachd, nach gabh ruigsinn (no) ruigheachd.

Inaccuracy, *s.* Mearachd; coire, neo-phongaileachd, dochair.

Inaccurate, *a.* Neo-phongail, mearachdach, dochararach; air aimhreidh, neo-cheart.

Inaction, *s.* Tamh, fois; diomhanas; neo-dheanadachd.

Inactive, *a.* Leasg, lunndach, ann an tamh, neo-dheanadach, diomhanach, neo-shùrdail, mall, athaiseach, neo-bhisidh. An inactive fellow, *fear lunndach, fear leasg (no) diomhanach; lunndair, leagair, leisgean.* Inactively, *gu leasg, gu lunndach, gu diomhanach.*

Inactivity, *s.* Leisge, lunndaireachd; diomhanachd, diomhainichead; tamh, fois.

Inadequate, *a.* Neo-fhreagarrach, mi-fhreagarrach, neo-oireamhnach, neo-iomchuidh. Inadequately, *gu mi-fhreagarrach.*

Inadvertence, *s.* Dearmad, neo-aire, cion-aire, mi-sheadh, mi-shuim, mi-omhail.

Inadvertent, *a.* Neo-churamach, neo-omhaileach, dearmadach; neo-aireachail, gun chùram, gun omhail.

Inadvertently, *adv.* Gu neo-chùramach, gu neo-omhaileach, gu dearmadach, gu neo-aireachail.

Inaffable, *a.* Doirbh, coimheach.

Inalienable, *a.* Do-bhuileachadh, do-dhealachadh, nach gabh buileachadh air neach.

Inalimental, *a.* Neo-fhallain.

Inamissible, *a.* Do chall.

Inamorato, *s.* Leannan, ceistean, graidhean, gaol, fear an gaol, gaolach.

Inane, *a.* Falamh, folamh, fàs, faòin.

Inanimate, **Inanimated**, *a.* Marbh, marbhanta, neo-bheò, neo-bheothail, neo-spioradail, neo-smiorail; neo-ghluasadach, gun bheath.

Inanition, *s.* Failbhe, faoine, falmhachd, an-fhannachd cuim.

Inanity, *s.* Faoine, faoineas, fàsalachd, failbhe.

Inappetency, *s.* Diocras; dìthstamaic; neo-mhiann.

Inapplicability, *s.* Neo-fhreagarrachd.

Inapplicable, *a.* Neo-fhreagarrach.

Inapplicableness, *s.* Neo-fhreagarrachd.

Inapplication, *s.* Lundaireachd, leisg.

Inaptitude, *s.* Neo-fhreagarrachd, neo-chubhaidheachd.

Inarable, *a.* Do-threabhadh, do-thabhairt stigh, do ruatharadh, nach gabh treabhadh.

Inargentation, *s.* Greus, grinneachadh, sgeadachadh le airgiod.

Inarticulate, *a.* Neo-phongail; neo-shoilleir, do-thuigsinn, cabhagach an cainnt.

Inarticulately, *adv.* Gu neo-phongail, gu neo-shoilleir.

Inarticulateness, *s.* Neo-phongaileachd.

Inartificial, *a.* Neo-ealanta.

Inattention, *s.* Neo-aire, cion aire, neo-chùram, mi-chùram, dearmad.

Inattentive, *a.* Neo-chùramach, mi-churamach, dearmadach, neo-omhaileach, mi-sheadhail.

Inattentively, *adv.* Gu neo-churamach, gu mi-churamach, gu dearmadach, gu neo-omhaileach, gu mi-sheadhail.

Inaudible, *a.* Do-chluinntinn; samhach.

Inaugurate, *v.* Coisrig, cuir an seilbh.

Inauguration, *s.* Coisreagadh.

Inaurate, *v. a.* Òr, òraich.

Inauration, *s.* Òradh, òrachadh.

Inauspicious, *a.* Mi-shealbhar, neo-shonadh, mi-fhortanach, duasach, dosguinneach, dosgannach, mi-aghmhor.

Inauspiciously, *adv.* Gu mi-shealbhar, gu mi-fhortanach, gu duasach, gu dosgannach.

Inauspiciousness, *s.* Mi-shealbharachd, duasachd.

Inborn, *a.* Nadurra, nadurrach, nadurrail.

Inbreathed, *a.* Tarruingte, sùighte.

Inbred, *a.* Nadurra, nadurrail.

Inca, *s.* (*In Peru*), righ, prionnsa.

Incage, *v. a.* Dùin, druid, cuir stigh.

Incalculable, *a.* Do-chunntadh, do-àireamh.

Incalescence, Incalescency, *s.* Blàthas, blàs.

Incalescent, *a.* Blàth; a fas teth (no) blàth.

Incantation, *s.* Piseag, ubag, seun, orchan, eas-arluidheachd; druidheachd, draoidheachd; eolas.

Incantator, *s.* Seunadair, druidh, draoidh.

Incapability, *s.* Mi-mhurrachas, neo-chomas, eu-comas, neo-chomasachd; aineolas.

Incapable, *a.* Mi-mhurrach, neo-chomasach; aineolach.

Incapacious, *a.* Cumhann, cumhang, aimhleathan, neo-luchdmhor; neo-rumar.

Incapaciousness, *s.* Cumhainne; cumhainge, cumhannachd, aimhleathanachd.

Incapacitate, *v. a.* Dean mi-mhurrach, (no) neo-chomasach; thoir comas o. Incapacitated, *mi-mhurrach, neo-chomasach, eu-comasach.*

Incapacity, *s.* Cion comais, cion cumhachd, eu-comas, neo-mhurraichead, neo-mhurrachas.

Incarcerate, *v.* Priosunaich, gainntirich, cuir an laimh, cuir am priosun.

Incarcerated, *part.* Priosunaichte, gainntirichte.

Incarceration, *s.* Priosunachd.

Incarn, *v.* Thoir feòil (no) craicionn air.

Incarnadine, *v. a.* Dearg, dean dearg.

Incarnate, *a.* Feòlmhor; san fheòil; daonna, talmhaidh.

Incarnation, *s.* Feòl-ghabhail; teachd san fheòil.

† **Incase**, *v. a.* Comhdaich, cuibhrig.

Incautious, *a.* Mi-fhaicilleach, neo-churamach, neo-aireachail; brais, neo-smuainteachail, amaideach.

Incautiously, *adv.* Gu mi-fhaicilleach, gu neo-chùramach.

Incautiousness, *s.* Mi-fhaicill, mi-fhaicilleachd, mi-chùram; cion-aire, obainne, cion-smuaine.

Incendiary, *s.* Losgadair; buaireadair, brosnachair; aithinne.

Incense, *s.* Tùis.

Incense, *v. a.* Boltraich; dean cubhraidh.

Incense, *v. a.* Brosnuich, buair, feargaich, tog, cuir fearg air.

Incensed, *part.* Brosnuichte, buairte, feargaichte, feargach, air bhoile, air bhainnidh.

Incensed, *part.* Boltraichte.

Incensement, *s.* Fraoch, corruich; lasadh, losgadh.

Incension, *s.* Losgadh, lasadh.

Incensor, *s.* Brosnuchair; buaireadair.

Incentive, *s.* Prosnuchadh, brosnachadh, buaireadh.

Inception, *s.* Toiseach, toiseachadh, tùs.

Inceration, *s.* Cèireachadh.

Incertitude, *s.* Eu-cinntealas, teagamhachd.

Incessant, *a.* Daonann, bitheanta, bidheanta; leanailteach, sior-dheananaich.

Incessantly, *adv.* Daonann, daonannta, daonalta, am bidheantas, an comhnuidh, gun sgur, gun chàird, gun stad, do ghnàth, a ghnàth.

Incest, *s.* Col.

Incestuous, *a.* Collaidh, collach. Incestuously, gu collaidh.

Inch, *s.* Òirleach, an dara cuid deug do throidh.

Inchoate, *v. a.* Toisich.

Inchoation, *s.* Toiseach, tòiseachadh.

Incide, *v. a.* Gearr, peasg.

Incidence, *s.* Tuiteam; tuiteamas, tubaist, toirt, teagmhas.

Incident, *s.* Buailteach; a dh' fheudas tachairt, tubaisdeach, teagmhaiseach.

Incidentally, *adv.* A thaobh tubaisd.

Incinerate, *v.* Loisg, crion-loisg, luaithrich. Incinerated, *loisgte na luaithre.*

Incineration, *s.* Losgadh, luaithreachadh.

Incircumspect, *a.* Neo-sheadhail, mi-churamach, neo-fhaicilleach.

Incised, *part.* Gearrte, air a ghearradh, air a sgochadh.

Incision, *s.* Gearradh, peasg, peasgadh, sgoch.

Incisive, *a.* Geur.

Incisor, *s.* Gearradair; sgochadair, inneal sgochaidh, inneal gearraidh; (*a tooth*), clàrag, clar-fhiacal.

Incisory, *a.* Geur.

Incisure, *s.* Gearradh, fosgladh, peasgadh, peasg.

Incitation, *s.* Brosnachadh, prosnachadh; buaireadh, bragadh, stuigeadh; beothachadh.

Incite, *v. a.* Brosnaich, prosnaich, buair, stuig, brog, spor, cuir h-uige; beothaich. Incited, *brosnaichte, prosnaichte, buairte.*

Incitement, *s.* Brosnachadh, prosnachadh, buaireadh, stuigeadh, spor, brogadh; beothachadh.

Incivil, *a.* Mi-mhodhail; mi-bheusach, neo-shiobhailte; mi-shuairce, borb, dorganta, doirbh.

Incivility, *s.* Mi-mhodhaileachd, mi-bheus, mi-shuairceas, cion-modh; buirbe, doirbhe.

Inclemency, *s.* Neo-iochdmhorachd, aiu-iochd, mi-thruacantas, buirbe, gairbhead, mi-thròcair.

Inclement, *a.* Neo-iochdmhor, ain-iochdmhor, neo-thruacanta, borb, garbh, stoirmeil; beumnach. Inclement weather, *aimsir stoirmeil, an-uair.*

Inclinable, *a.* Toileach; claon; so-chlaonadh.

Inclination, *s.* Toil, rùn, miann, togar, togradh, gradh; aomadh, claonadh, lùbadh. Against my inclination, *an aghaidh mo rùin;* of my own inclination, *do m' dheòin.*

Inclinatory, *a.* Aomach, claon; so-chlaonadh.

Incline, *v. a.* and *n.* Aom, claon, lùb, feachd; crom, bi toileach. Inclined, *aomta, claon, lubta, crom.*

Inclined, *a.* Claon; crom; lubta, aomta; (*willing*). Inclined to mercy, *ealamh chum trocair.*

Incloister, *v.* Druid, dùin, cuir fu riaghail eaglais (no) abaite.

Inclose, *v.* Duin, druid, iom-dhruid.

Inclosure, *s.* Iadhlann, beo-fhàl; pàirc.

† **Incloud**, *v. a.* Dorchaich, doilleirich, duibhrich. Inclouded, *dorchaichte, doilleirichte, dorch, doilleir.*

Include, *v.* Druid (no) dùin a stigh, gabh, cum; gabh a steach.

Inclusion, *s.* Druideadh, dùnadh, gabhail steach.

Inclusive, *a.* A gabhail a steach, a druideadh; maille ris, leis.

Incoagulable, *a.* Do-shlamachadh, do-thiughachadh.

Incog, *adv.* Am folachadh, gu diomhair; gun fhios, gun aithne.

Incogitancy, *s.* Dì-smuaine.

Incogitant, *a.* Neo-bheachdail, neo-smuainteachail, neo-aireachail.

Incognito, *adv.* Am folach, gu diomhair, gun fhios, gun aithne, os iosal, gu neo-fhallaiseach, gu folaichte.

Incognoscible, *a.* Do-aithneachadh, nach gabh faineachadh.

Incoherence, Incoherency, *s.* Neo-aontachas, neo-aontachd, neo-fhreagarrachd; neo-leanailteachd, baoth-aireachd; neo-lathailteachd.

Incoherent, *a.* Neo-aontach, neo-aontachail, neo-fhreagarrach, neo-leanailteach; baoth, neo-lathailteach.

Incombustibility, *s.* Do-losgaidheachd.

Incombustible, *a.* Do-losgaidh, neo-losgach, neo-lasanta, nach gabh ri teine, do-chur ri theine.

Income, *s.* Tighinn stigh, teachd a stigh, tighinn a steach, màl, beathain, buannachd.

Incommensurable, *a.* Do-thomhas.

Incommodated, *part.* Ciurrta, dochannaichte.

Incommode, *v. a.* Cuir dragh (no) moille air neach, amail; buair; cuir mio-thlachd; cuir gu dragh.

Incommodious, *a.* Neo-iomchuidh; neo-gharail; draghail; neo-fhreagarrach; farranach; neo-choidheas, neo-lathailteach.

Incommodiously, *adv.* Gu neo-iomchuidh, gu draghail, gu neo-fhreagarrach, gu farranach; gu neo-lathailteach.

Incommodiousness, *s.* Neo-iomchuidhead, draghaileachd, farranachd.

Incommodity, *s.* Neo-chridheasachd, dragh, moille, farran amal.

Incommunicableness, *s.* Neo-bhairigeachd, neo-phairtealachd.

Incommunicable, *a.* Neo-bhairigeach, do-bhuileachadh, neo-phairteachail; do-labhairt, do-innseadh, do-chur an céile.

Incommunicably, *adv.* Gu neo-bhairigeach, gu neo-phàirteachail, gu do-innseadh, thar iomradh.

Incommunicative, *a.* Doirbh; coimheach; fiat, fad thall.

Incommutable, *a.* Do-mhùthadh, do-mhalairteach.

Incompact, *a.* Neo-dhiongalta, lasach, neo-chruinn, neo-sgiobalt; luidseach, neo-chearamanta.

Incomparable, *a.* Neo-choimeasach, neo-choimeasta; oirdheirc; gun choimeas; barrach.

Incomparably, *adv.* Gun choimeas, gu h-oirdheirc.

Incompassionate, *a.* Neo-thruacanta; ain-iochdmhor, cruaidh, cruadalach, neo-throcaireach, cruaidh-chridheach.

Incompatibility, *s.* Neo-fhreagarrachd; neo-lathailteachd.

Incompatible, *a.* Neo-fhreagarrach, neo-lathailteach, neo-oireamhnach.

Incompatibly, *adv.* Gu neo-fhreagarrach, gu neo-lathailteach; gu neo-aogasach.

Incompetency, *s.* Neo-mhurraichead, cion comais.

Incompetent, *a.* Neo-fhreagarrach, neo-iomchuidh; neo-mhurrach, neo-chomasach.

Incompetently, *adv.* Gu neo-fhreagarrach, gu neo-iomchuidh, gu neo-lathailteach.

Incomplete, *a.* Neo-chriochnaichte; neo-iomlan, neo-fhoirfe.

Incompletely, *adv.* Gu neo-iomlan, gu neo-chriochnaichte.

Incompleteness, *s.* Neo-iomlanachd.

Incompliance, *s.* Diùltadh, obadh, seun; raige, reasgachd.

Incomposed, *a.* Neo-shocrach, docrach, luaineach, iomaguineach, neo-fhoisneach, an-shocrach, neo-shuidhichte; troimh chéile.

Incomprehensibility, *s.* Do-thuigsinneachd.

Incomprehensible, *a.* Do-thuigsinn, do-smuaineachadh, do-smaoineachadh, do-bheachdachadh, os cionn tuigse, os cionn beachd.

Incomprehensibly, *adv.* Thar tuigse, thar beachd, os cionn smuaine.

Incompressible, *a.* Do-theannachadh, do-fhàsgadh.

Inconcealable, *a.* Do-fholach, do-fholachadh, do-chéileadh.

Inconceivable, *a.* Do-thuigsinn, do-bheachdachadh, do-smuaineachadh, do-smaoineachadh, do-bharalachadh.

Inconclusive, *a.* Neo-chinnteach, fallsail.

Inconclusiveness, *s.* Neo-chinnte, fallsaileachd.

Inconcoct, *a.* Neo-abaidh, neo-abuich, an-abuich; tràthail.

Inconcoction, *s.* Anabachd.

Incondite, *a.* Neo-riaghailteach; neo-ghrinn.

Inconditional, *a.* Gun chumhnant; neo-chumhnantach; Inconditionally, *gun chumhnant.*

Inconformity, *s.* Eu-coslas; mi-aontachadh.

Incongruence, *s.* Neo-fhreagarrachd; mi-oireamhnachd; neo-lathailteachd; an-riaghailt; baothaireachd.

Incongruity, *s.* Neo-fhreagarrachd; mi-oireamhnachd; neo-lathailteachd; an-rioghailt; neonachas, baothaireachd.

Incongruous, *a.* Neo-fhreagarrach, neo-iomchuidh, neo-aireamhnach; neo-lathailteach; neo-cheart, neo-chubhaidh.

Incongruously, *adv.* Gu neo-fhreagarrach, gu neo-iomchuidh, gu neo-lathailteach, gu neo-chubhaidh.

Inconscionable, *a.* Gun choguis; cruaidh.

Inconsiderable, *a.* Suarrach, neo-luachmhor, neo-fhiachail; gun fhiù; neo-airidh; diblidh, beag, suail.

Inconsiderableness, *s.* Suarraichead; neo-luachmhorachd, suailead.

Inconsiderate, *a.* Neo-chùramach, neo-fhaicealllach, dearmadach; mi-sheadhail; brais, cas, mi-ombailleach, obann, amaideach.

Inconsiderately, *adv.* Gu neo-chùramach, gu neo-fhaiceallach, gu dearmadach, gu mi-sheadhail, gu mi-omhaille-ach, gu brais, gu cas, gu h-obann.

Inconsiderateness, *s.* Mi-chùram, mi-fhaicill; dearmad; braise, caise, obainne, neo-aire.

Inconsistence, Inconsistency, *s.* Neo-fhreagarrachd; neo-aontachas; neònachas; mi-chubhaidheachd; neo-lathailteachd, luaineachd, luaineachas.

Inconsistent, *a.* Neo-fhreagarrach, neo-chubhaidh, neo-aontachail, neo-lathailteach, neònach, luaineach; mùiteach

Inconsistently, *adv.* Gu neo-fhreagarrach, gu neo-chubhaidh, gu neo-aontachail, gu neo-lathailteach; gu luaineach, gu neo-chubhaidh

Inconsolable, *a* Dubhach, dubhrònach, dobhronach, tuirseach, ro bhronach, ro dhubhach, nach gabh comhfhurtachd.

Inconsonancy, *s* Neo-fhreagarrachd; neo-lathailteachd

Inconspicuous, *a.* Do-fhaic nn, do-fhaicsinn, doilleir, neo-fhaicinneach, nach gabh faicinn

Inconstancy, *s* Luaineachd, luaimneachd, neo-sheasmhachd, caochlaideachd, neo-bhunailteachd, eutruime

Inconstant, *a.* Luaineach, luaimneach, neo-sheasmhach, caochlaideach, neo-bhunailteach, eutrom, gaoithe.

Inconsumable, *a* Do-chaitheamh, nach gabh caitheamh, do-losgadh.

Inconsumptible, *a* Do-chaitheamh, do-losgadh, do-mhilleadh.

Incontestable, *a.* Do-àicheadh, do-chur an aghaidh, nach gabh àicheadh, nach gabh cur an aghaidh

Incontestably, *adv.* Gu cinnteach, gun teagamh, gun cheist.

Incontiguous, *a* Neo-cheangailte; neo-dhlùth

Incontinence, Incontinency, *s.* Mi-gheimnidheachd, neo-gheimnidheachd, mi-stuaim, mi-stuamachd, neo-ghloine, drùis.

Incontinent, *a* Mi-gheimnidh, neo-gheimnidh, mi-stuama, neo-bheusach, neo-ghlan, drùiseil

Incontinently, *adv* Gu mi-gheimnidh, gu mi-stuama, gu mi-bheusach, gu neo-ghlan, gu drùiseil.

Incontrovertible, *a.* Do-chur as àicheadh, do-àicheadh, cinnteach, neo-chonnsachail, dearbhta, gun teagamh, gun cheist.

Incontrovertibly, *adv.* Gu cinnteach, gu neo-chonnsachail, gu dearbhta, gun cheist, gu dearbh-chinnteach

Inconvenience, *v. a.* Amail, cuir dragh.

Inconvenience, *s* Neo-iomchuidheachd, mi-ghoireasachd, neo-fhreagarrachd; dragh, amaladh, moille.

Inconvenient, *a* Neo-iomchuidh, mi-ghoireasach; neo-fhreagarrach.

Inconveniently, *adv.* Gu neo-iomchuidh, gu mi-ghoireasach, gu neo-fhreagarrach; gu draghail.

Inconversable, *a* Coimheach; neo-chomhraiteach, neo-bhruidhneach; neo-chonaltrach, dùr, doirbh; dorganta.

Inconvertible, *a.* Do-mhùthadh, do-iompaichte, do-iompachaidh, neo-mhùiteach

Incorporal, *a* Neo-chorporra, spioradail, spioradailt, atharail; faoin

Incorporally, *adv* Gu neo-chorporra, gu spioradail.

Incorporate, *v. a* and *n.* Aontaich, cuir sa chéile, comh-dhealbh, comh-chorpaich, dean mar aon, fas sa chéile.

Incorporated, *part* Aontaichte, comh-dhealbhta, comh-chorpaichte, ann an aon chorp

Incorporation, *s.* Aontachadh, comh-dhealbh, buidheann, bannal, communn.

Incorporeal, *a* Neo-chorporra; spioradail, spioradailt; atharail; faoin.

Incorrect, *a.* Neo-cheart; cearr, air-aimhreidh, mearrachdach, ann am mearrachd, meallta, cu-ceart, docharach, neo-phongail

Incorrectly, *adv.* Gu neo-cheart, gu cearr, gu mearachdach, gu meallta, gu docharach.

Incorrectness, *s.* Mearachd.

Incorrigible, *a.* Do-smachdadh, do-cheannsachadh, do-chur gu doigh; do-chomhairleachadh, olc thar tomhas, ro-aingidh, coirbte.

Incorrigibleness, *s* Aingidheachd, ro-aingidheachd.

Incorrigibly, *adv* Gu do-smachdadh, gu do-cheannsachadh, gu h-aingidh.

Incorrupt, *a* Ionraic, onorach, direach, treibhdhireach, neo-thruaillidh, fior, foirfe

Incorruptibility, *s.* Neo-thruaillidheachd.

Incorruptible, *a* Neo-thruaillidh, neo-chaithteach, fiorghlan, nach gabh truailleadh.

Incorruptibleness, *s* Neo-thruaillidheachd.

Incorruption, *s* Neo-thruaillidheachd, fior-ghloine, fiorghloinead

Incorruptness, *s.* Treibhdhireas; onoir

Incrassate, *v a* Tiughaich, dean tiugh; slamaich. Incrassated, *tiughaichte*, *tiugh*, *slamaichte*.

Incrassation, *s* Tiughachadh.

Increase, *v. a.* and *n* Meudaich, cuir am meud, cuir ri, cinn fàs, rach am meud, rach an lionmhorachd Increased, *meudaichte*, *air a chur am meud*, *air fàs*, *air cinntinn*, increasing, *a fas*, *a dol am meud*, *a cinntinn*

Increase, *s.* Fàs, cinntinn, cinneas, cinneachdainn, cinneachadh, meudachadh, torradh, gineamhuinn

Increate, *a.* Neo-chruthaichte.

Incredibility, *s.* Neo-choslachd

Incredible, *a.* Do-chreidsinn, eu-coslach, neo-chreideasach, nach fhaodar a chreidsinn, thar creidimh.

Incredibly, *adv.* Thar creidimh.

Incredulity, *s* Mi-chreideas, di-chreideamh; amharus

Incredulous, *a* Neo-chreideasach, do-chreideamhach, mall-chreideamhach, amharusach

Incredulousness, *s* Mi-chreideas, di-chreideamhach

Incremable, *a* Do-losgadh, do-lasadh.

Increment, *s.* Fàs, cinntinn, cinneas, cinneachdainn, torradh

Increpate, *v* Troid, cronaich, coirich; sglamhrainn

Increpation, *s* Trod, trodadh, sglamhrainn, cronachadh, coireachadh; tachairt

Incrust, Incrustate, *v a.* Comhdaich, còtaich; creim

Incrustation, *s* Comhdachadh; còt, creim, càrr

Incubate, *v n.* Gur, luidh air uibhean, luidh air ghur, rach air ghur, bi air ghur.

Incubation, *s.* Guradh

Incubus, *s.* Trom-lighe

Inculcate, *v. a* Sparr, thoir sparr, thoir teann-sparr, caralaich, earail-teagaisg

Inculcated, *a.* Sparrta, air a sparradh

Inculcation, *s* Sparradh, teann-sparradh, earail, teagasg, comhairleachadh

Inculpable, *a.* Neo-chiontach, neo-choireach, neo-lochdach; cothromach, ionraic, tréibhdhireach, direach, fior, onorach, ceart.

Inculpably, *adv* Gu neo-chiontach, gu neo-choireach, gu neo-lochdach, gu h-ionraic, gu treibhdhireach, gu direach, gu fior, gu h-onorach; gu ceart.

Incult, *a.* Neo-threabhta, fàs, fiadhaich

Incumbency, *s* Luidhe, taic, leigeil taic

INCUMBENT, *a.* A luidh, a leigeil taic; air; mar fhiachaibh. It is incumbent on me to do it, *tha e mar fhiachaibh orm a dheanamh, tha e orm a dheanamh.*

INCUMBENT, *s.* Neach aig am bheil beathachadh san eaglais, sealbhadair, ministear

INCUR, *v.* Toill, bi toilltinneach; bi buailteach; tarruing ort fein. The close mouth incurs no scores, *cha bhi fiach an beul dùinte*

INCURABILITY, *s* Do-leigheasadh

INCURABLE, *a.* Do-leigheas, do-shlànachadh, nach gabh leigheas

INCURABLY, *adv* Thar doigh leigheis

INCURIOUS, *a* Dearmadach, neo-omhailleach, mi-sheadhail, coimheis, comadh.

INCURSION, *s* Ionnsuidh; oidhirp, ruaig; sgiorradh

INCURVATE, *a.* Crom, lùb, cam. Incurvated, *cromta, crom, lubta, lubte, cam*

INCURVATION, *s.* Cromadh, lùb, lùbadh, cam, caime.

INCURVITY, *s* Cromadh, lùb, caime.

INDAGATE, *v a* Lorg, lorgaich, lean, sir; sgrud, ceasnaich

INDAGATION, *s* Lorgachadh, lorgaireachd, dian-lorg, aireachd; sgrudadh, ceasnachadh.

INDAGATOR, *s* Sgrudair, lorgair.

INDART, *v* Buail a stigh, tilg a stigh

INDEBT, *v. a* Cuir an ain-fhiach; cuir an comain, cuir fo chomainibh.

INDEBTED, *a.* (*In debt*), an ain-fhiach, am fiachaibh, (*obliged to*), an comain. I am much indebted to you, *tha mi moran ad chomain*

INDECENCY, *s* Mi-bheus; mi-chiatachd, draosdachd, draosdaireachd, neo-ghloine; neo-chiatachd; neo-bhanalachd, drùis. neo-gheimneachd

INDECENT, *a* Mi-bheusach, mi-theisteal, mi-chiatach, draosda, drabasta, mi-mhodhail, neo-ghlan, nàr, drùiseil, mi-bhandaidh, mi-bhanail, neo-bhandaidh, neo-bhanail, neo-gheimnidh, macnusach

INDECENTLY, *adv* Gu mi-bheusach, gu draosda, gu drabasta, gu mi-mhodhail, gu neo-ghlan, gu nàr, gu neo-bhanail, gu neo-bhandaidh, gu macnusach

INDECIDUOUS, *a* Neo-thuiteamach, sior-uaine

INDECISION, *s* Dith gramalas; dith sònrachaidh.

INDECOROUS, *a* Mi-bheusach, mi-chiatach, neo-eireachdail, neo-aogasach

INDECORUM, *s.* Mi-bheus, mi-mhodh.

INDEED, *adv.* Gu dearbh, gu deimhin, gun amharus, a rireamh, gu fior. Indeed? *'n ann rireamh?*

INDEFATIGABLE, *a.* Do-sgìtheachadh, neo-sgìth, do-fhannachadh, do-chlaoidh, bidheanta, sìr, sior

INDEFATIGABLY, *adv.* Gu bidheanta, gu sior, gun sgur, gun sgìtheachadh, gun fhàillneachadh

INDEFEASIBLE, *a* Do-leasachadh, do-sgriosadh, do-mhilleadh.

INDEFECTIBILITY, *s* Neo-fhàilneachd, bi-bhuantachd.

INDEFECTIBLE, *a* Neo-fhàilneach; buan, bi-bhuan

INDEFENSIBLE, *a.* Do-dhionadh

INDEFINITE, *a* Neo-shònruichte, neo-chriochnach.

INDEFINITELY, *adv* Gu neo-chriochnach, gu neo-shonruichte

INDEFLAGRABLE, *a* Do-lasadh, do-losgadh, do-chur ri theine, do-chaitheamh.

INDELIBLE, *a* Do-dhubhadh as, do-dhubhadh, nach gabh dubhadh, do-mhilleadh; do-sgriosadh

INDELICACY, *s.* Mi-mhodh, beag-nàire, macnus, mi-gheimnidheachd; mi-stuaim.

INDELICATE, *a.* Mi-mhodhail, beag-narach, neo-cheanalta, neo-ghlan, mi-gheimnidh, macnusach.

INDEMNIFICATION, *s.* Deanamh suas, dioladh, deanamh suas airson calldaich

INDEMNIFY, *v. a.* Dion (no) saor o dhiobhail.

INDEMNITY, *s.* Saorsadh o pheanas

INDEMONSTRABLE, *a.* Do-chòmhdachadh; do-dhearbhadh.

INDENT, *v. a.* and *n.* Feargaich, fiaclaich, grob, gearr cosmhal ri fiaclan; cùmhnantaich.

INDENTATION, *s* Fiaclachadh, grobadh, gearradh; luib.

INDENTURE, *s.* Cumhnant; bann eadar maighistir ceairde agus foghlumaiche.

INDEPENDENCE, *s.* Saorsadh, saorsadh o chomant, neo-eisiomalachd.

INDEPENDENT, *a.* Saor; neo-chuibhrichte; neo-cheangailte, neo-eisiomaileachd

INDEPENDENTLY, *adv* Gu neo-eisiomaileach, gu saor, saor o Independently of that, *saor o sin.*

INDETERMINED, *a.* Neo-shonruichte, neo-shuidhichte, neo-shocrach.

INDESERT, *s* Mi-thoilltinneas

INDESIROUS, *a* Neo-thogarrach; coimheis, cion-shuarrach, comadh.

INDESTRUCTIBLE, *a* Do-sgriosadh; do-mhilleadh.

INDETERMINABLE, *a.* Neo-shuidhichte, neo-shocraichte, do-shuidheachadh, do-shocrachadh.

INDETERMINATE, *a* Neo-shuidhichte, neo-shocraichte, neo-bheachdaidh.

INDETERMINED, *a* Neo-shuidhichte, neo-shocraichte.

INDEVOTION, *s.* Mi-dhiadhaidheachd, mi-chrabhadh

INDEVOUT, *a* Mi-dhiadhuidh, neo-chrabhach, mi-naomh; olc, peacach.

INDEX, *s.* Feuchadair, lamh uaireadair, clar-innsidh.

INDEXTERITY, *s* Neo-lamhachaireachd; neo-lathailteachd.

INDICANT, *a.* A feuchainn.

INDICATE, *v. a.* Feuch, cuir an céil, innis, foillsich.

INDICATION, *s.* Feuchainn, comhar, comharradh, coslas; innseadh; mìneachadh, foillseachadh.

INDICATIVE, *a.* A feuchainn; ag innseadh, a soillseachadh

INDICT, *v.* Coirich; cronaich; dìt; cuir as leth.

INDICTABLE, *a* So-dhiteadh, buailteach do dhiteadh, airidh air dìteadh.

INDICTION, *s* Gairm, glaodh; (*in the Romish church*), cruinneachadh eaglais

INDIFFERENCE, *s.* Dearmad, coimheiseachd, coimheasachd; neo-aire, caoin-shuarachd; neo-chlaon-bhreith

INDIFFERENT, *a* Suarach, caoin-shuarach; coimheis, comadh, dearmadach, an iarruidh; eadar an da chuid; neo-chlaon, cothromach.

INDIFFERENTLY, *adv.* Gun leth-bhreith, gu cothromach; gu coimheis, an iarruidh; eadar an da chuid.

INDIGENCE, *s* Bochduinn, easbhuidh, uireasbhuidh, daibhreas, aimbeairt, aimbeartas, riachdanas, truaghanachd, feum, gainne

INDIGENOUS, *a* Dùchasach, dùthcha

INDIGENT, *a.* Bochd, truagh, uireasbhach, easbhuidheach, aimbeartach, aimbeairteach, feumach, fàs, falamh

INDIGESTED, *a* Neo-chnamhta, neo-chnamhte, gun dileachadh, neo-riaghailteach

INDIGESTION, *s.* Dith-cnamhaidh, ana-cnamhadh

INDIGITATE, *v.* Tomh ri, comharaich a mach le meur.

INDIGITATION, *s.* Tomhadh.

INDIGNANT, *a* Feargach, diomach, diombach, *angrach*, air boile Take a thing indignantly, *gabh ni gu dona.*

Indignation, *s.* Feirg, fearg, diom, corruich; *angar.*

Indignity, *s.* Tàir, masladh, easonoir.

Indigo, *s.* Guirmean, cloch ghorm.

Indirect, *a.* Neo-dhireach, claon, fiar, cam; neo-chothromach, eu-ceart; cealgach, cearr; neo-cheart, air aimhreidh.

Indirectly, *adv.* Gu neo-dhireach, gu claon, gu fiar, gu neo chothromach, gu cealgach, gu neo-cheart, gu cearr, gu docharach.

Indirectness, *s.* Claonad, claonadh, fiaire, fiarad; cealg, foill.

Indiscernible, *a.* Do-fhaicinn, do-fhaicsinn, do-fharachdainn, do-mhothachadh, do-chomharrachadh, dorcha.

Indiscernibleness, *s.* Do-fhaicsinneachd.

Indiscernibly, *adv.* Gu do-fhaicinn, gu do-fharachdainn, gu dorcha, gu doilleir.

Indiscerptible, *a.* Do-sgaradh, nach gabh toirt as a chéile.

Indiscovery, *s.* Uaigneas, uaigneachd, diùbhras.

Indiscreet, *a.* Eu-crionna, neo-ghlic, amaideach, gòrach; neo-thuigseach, mi-fhaicilleach, neo-smuainteachail, neo-sheolta.

Indiscretion, *s.* Eu-crionnachd, neo-chrionnachd, mi-ghliocas, neo-sheoltachd; amaideachd; gòraiche; obainne.

Indiscriminate, *a.* Feadh a chéile, gun diubhair.

Indiscriminately, *adv.* Feadh chéile, gun diubhair.

Indispensable, *a.* Do-sheachnaidh, ro-fheumail; nach gabh seachnadh, nach gabh a bhi as eugmhais.

Indispensableness, *s.* Do-sheachnachd, feumalachd.

Indispensably, *adv.* Gu do-sheachnadh, gu ro-fheumail.

Indispose, *v. a.* Cuir a riaghailt, cuir a doigh, cuir a fonn, cuir a gleus.

Indisposed, *a.* Ann an mi-riaghailt; a fonn, a gleus, a gearainn, tinn, soithich.

Indisposition, *s.* Tinneas, galar, aicidh, trealamh, eus-lainnte; mi-thoile; diombachd, cion toile.

Indisputable, *a.* Cinnteach, do-chur as aicheadh, gun teagamh, gun cheist; soilleir, riachdail; do-aighneasadh.

Indisputably, *adv.* Gu cinnteach, gun teagamh, gun cheist, gu soilleir, gu riachdail.

Indissolvable, *a.* Do-leaghadh, do-sgaoileadh, nach gabh leaghadh.

Indissolubility, *s.* Diongaltachd, maireannachd.

Indissoluble, *a.* Diongalta, daingeann, maireann, maireannach, teann; do-sgaoileadh, do-leaghadh.

Indissolubleness, *s.* Diongaltachd; maireannachd, daingeannachd.

Indistinct, *a.* Doilleir, neo-shoilleir, do-fhaicinn; do-thuigsinn, neo-phongail, mi-riaghailteach.

Indistinction, *s.* Eu-cinnteas; aimhreite, tuaireap.

Indistinctly, *adv.* Gu doilleir, gu neo-shoilleir, gu do-thuigsinn, gu neo-phongail; gu neo-chinnteach, gu mi-riaghailteach.

Indistinctness, *s.* Doilleireachd; aimhreite, eu-cinnte, neo-phongaileachd.

Indisturbance, *s.* Ciùineas; samhachair.

Indite, *v.* Sgriobh; deachd; dìt.

Individual, *s.* Aon, aon fa leth, fear, urr, neach. Every individual, *gach aon, gach neach.*

Individually, *adv.* Fa leth; gach aon, gach fear, gach aon.

Individuate, *v. a.* Sonruich fa leth, sunraich fa leth, comharaich a mach.

Individuation, *s.* Sonrachadh fa leth, sunrachadh fa leth.

Indivisibility, *s.* Do-phàirteachd; do-sgarachduinn.

Indivisible, *a.* Do-roinneadh, do-phàirteachadh, nach gabh roinneadh (no) pàirteachadh, do-roinnte; do-bhriseadh.

Indocile, *a.* Do-theagasg, do-ionnsachadh, nach gabh teagasg, nach gabh ionnsachadh; dùr.

Indocility, *s.* Dùiread, dubh-aineolas.

Indoctrinate, *v.* Teagasg, ionnsuich, oil, oid.

Indoctrination, *s.* Teagasg, ionnsuchadh, ionnsach, oileau, oideas.

Indolence, *s.* Leisg, lunndaireachd; cion aire, mi-chùram.

Indolent, *a.* Leasg, lunndach; mi-sheadhar; aolaisdeach, neo-churamach, neo-chraiteach, neo-ghoirt; neo-phiantachail, neo-mhothachail.

Indolently, *adv.* Gu leasg, gu lunndach; gu mi-sheadhar, gu neo-churamach.

Indow, *v. a.* Beairtich, saibhrich, dean beairteach; tochair, tocharaich.

Indowed, *part.* Beairtichte, saibhrichte; tocharaichte; sgeadaichte.

Indowment, *s.* See **Endowment**.

Indraught, *s.* Loch; linne; camus.

Indrench, *v.* Bog, fliuch, lobanach. Indrenched, *lobanaichte.*

Indubious, *a.* Cinnteach, neo-amharusach, neo-theagamhach.

Indubitable, *a.* Cinnteach, riachdail, follaiseach, neo-theagamhach, neo-amharusach.

Indubitably, *adv.* Gu cinnteach, gu riachdail, gu follaiseach, gun cheiste, gun teagamh.

Indubitate, *a.* Cinnteach, riachdail, follaiseach.

Induce, *v. a.* Thoir air, aom, claon, sdiùir, seòl; (*by entreaty*), guidh, grios, earalaich; (*allure*), meall, brosnaich. What induced you to do this? *ciod a thug ort so dheanamh?*

Induced, *part.* Brosnaichte; earalaichte, aomta.

Inducement, *s.* Brosnachadh, earail, cuireadh, mealladh.

Inducer, *s.* Fear earail, brosnachair; earalaiche.

Induct, *v. a.* Thoir a stigh, thoir a steach; cuir an seilbh, thoir seilbh.

Induction, *s.* Toirt a stigh; toirt seilbh, sealbhachadh, gabhail seilbh air eaglais.

Inductive, *a.* Earaileach; brosnachail.

Indue, *v.* Éid, eudaich, aodaich, sgeadaich. Indued, *eudaichte, sgeadaichte.*

Indulge, *v. a.* Beadraich; breug; tàlaidh; toilich; ceadaich, fulaing; thoir comas; leig le. He indulges him too much, *tha e 'g a bheadrachadh tuille is a chòir;* he indulges himself, *tha e a gabhail a thoil, tha e 'g a thoileachadh féin.*

Indulgence, *s.* Beadradh; leigeil le; cead, ceadachadh, comas; caoimhneas, caomhalachd; (*in the Romish church*), laghadh, maitheanas.

Indulgent, *a.* Caoimhneil, ciùin, suairc; ceadachail; gràsmhor, caomh.

Indulgently, *adv.* Gu caomh, gu caoimhneil, gu suairc.

Indult, *s.* Còir, ceart.

Indurate, *v. a.* and *n.* Cruadhaich, dean cruaidh; fàs cruaidh. Indurated, *cruadhaichte, cruaidh.*

Induration, *s.* Cruadhachadh; reasgachd, raige, cruadhas cridhe.

Industrious, *a.* Gniomhach, saoithreachail, dìcheallach, deanadach, sùrdail, griongalach; grunndail, oidhirpeach; easguidh; *bisidh*, iomartach. The industrious man's morsel is on every man's table, *bithidh mìre a ghille easgaidh air gach méis.*

Industriously, *adv.* Gu gniomhach, gu saoithreachail,

gu dichealIach, gu deanadach, gu surdail, gu grunndail, gu h-oidhirpeach; a dh' aon obair, a dh' aon ghnothuch.

INDUSTRY, s. Saothair; dicheall, grunndalas, grunnd surd, sùrdalachd, iomartas; deanadas.

INEBRIATE, v. a. Cuir air a mheisge (no) air an daoraich. Inebriated, *air a mheisge, air an daoraich.*

INEBRIATION, s. Meisge, misge, daoraich, pòit.

INEFFABLE, a. Do-labhairt, do-chur an céill, do-labhradh, do-innseadh, thar comhraidh.

INEFFABLY, adv. Gu do-labhairt, gu do-labhradh, gu do-innseadh.

INEFFECTIVE, a. Neo-éifeachdach, gun stà, neo-uidhiseil; neo-dheanadach.

INEFFECTUAL, a. Neo-éifeachdach, neo-chomasach, neo-mhurrach, neo-tharbhach, neo-threun.

INEFFECTUALLY, adv. Gu neo-éifeachdach, gu neo-mhurrach, gu neo-tharbhach, gu neo-chomasach, gun éifeachd, gun chomas.

INEFFECTUALNESS, s. Mi-éifeachd, eu-comas, mi-mhurrachas.

INEFFICACIOUS, a. Neo-tharbhach, neo-éifeachdach, lag, fann.

INEFFICACIOUSLY, adv. Gu neo-tharbhach, gu neo-éifeachdach; gu lag, gu fann, gun tairbhe, gun éifeachd.

INEFFICACY, s. Mi-éifeachd, eu-treoire, neo-éifeachd, cion-éifeachd.

INEFFICIENT, a. Neo-éifeachdach, neo-chomasach, neo-mhurrach.

INELEGANCE, s. Mi-eireachdas, mi-bhoidhchead, mi-shnàsmhorachd.

INELEGANT, a. Neo-chiatach, mi-chiatach, neo-shnasmhor, neo-eireachdail, neo-bhoidheach, neo-àluinn; neo-fhinealta; molach, ròmach, garbh.

INELOQUENT, a. Neo-labhradh, neo-bhriathrach, neo-dheaschainnteach, neo-ùr-labhrach.

INEPT, a. Faoin, faoineasach, amaideach; neo-fhreagarrach, gun uidhis, gun stà.

INEPTLY, adv. Gu faoin, gu amaideach, gu faoineasach, gu neo-fhreagarrach.

INEPTITUDE, s. Faoineas; neo-fhreagarrachd.

INEQUALITY, s. Neo-ionannachd; neo-chothromaichead; gairbhe; eadar-dhealachadh.

INERRABILITY, s. Neo-mhearachdas, neo-mhearachd.

INERRABLE, a. Neo-mhearrachdach; do-chur air aimhreidh.

INERRABLY, adv. Gu neo-mhearachdach, gun mhearachd.

INERRINGLY, adv. Gun mhearachd.

INERT, a. Marbh, marbhanta; neo-ghluasadach; dùr; leasg; leagach.

INERTION, s. Neo-ghluasadachd, neo-ghluasad; cion caruchaidh; leisge, lunndaireachd; leagaireachd.

INESTIMABLE, a. Do-mheas, luachmhor, do-bharalachaidh, luachmhor thar cunntas.

INEVIDENT, a. Neo-shoilleir, dorch, neo-riachdail, neo-dhearbhta.

INEVITABILITY, s. Do-sheachnachd, do-sheachantachd; cinnteas.

INEVITABLE, a. Do-sheachnadh, do-sheachanta, do-chur gu taobh; cinnteach.

INEXACT, a. Neo-phongail, neo-cheart.

INEXACTNESS, s. Neo-phongaileachd.

INEXCUSABLE, a. Gun-leithsgeul; neo-leith-sgeulach, do-laghadh, do-mhathadh.

INEXCUSABLENESS, s. Do-laghachd, neo-leithsgeulachd.

INEXCUSABLY, adv. Gun leithsgeul; gu neo-leithsgeulach.

INEXHALABLE, a. Do-dheabhadh.

INEXHAUSTED, a. Neo-thraghta, neo-thraighte, neo-thaomaichte, gun traghadh, gun ruithe a mach.

INEXHAUSTIBLE, a. Do-thraghadh, do-chaitheamh, nach tragh; nach tràigh; nach tràighear.

INEXISTENCE, s. Cion bith, neo-bhith.

INEXISTENT, a. Neo-lathair.

INEXORABLE, a. Do-aomadh, do-ghriosadh, do-lubadh, do-chiosachadh, nach gabh aomadh, nach gabh lùbadh.

INEXPEDIENCE, s. Neo-iomchuidhead, neo-ghoireas, neo-fheumalachd, neo-fhreagarrachd.

INEXPEDIENT, a. Neo-iomchuidh, neo-ghoireasach, neo-fheumail, neo-fhreagarrach.

INEXPERIENCE, s. Ana-cleachd, aineolas, cion cleachdaidh, cion eòlais, cion fiosrachaidh.

INEXPERIENCED, a. Neo-eolach, gun fhéin-fhiosrachadh.

INEXPERT, a. Neo-eolach, neo-theoma, neo-thapaidh, neo-dheas, neo-ealamh, neo-lamhchair; neo-sgìleil.

INEXPIABLE, a. Do-shàsuchadh, do-réiteachaidh.

INEXPLICABLE, a. Do-mhìneachadh, do-thuigsinn, do-shoillseachadh; do-léirsinn, do-réiteachadh; nach gabh mìneachadh.

INEXPLICABLY, adv. Gu do-mhìneachadh, gu do-thuigsinn.

INEXPRESSIBLE, a. Do-làbhairt, do-innseadh, do-chur an céil.

INEXPRESSIBLY, adv. Gu do-labhairt, gu do-innseadh, thar cunntas, thar iomradh.

INEXPUGNABLE, a. Do-chlaoidh, do-shàruchadh.

INEXTINGUISHABLE, a. Do-mhùchadh, do-chosgadh, do-chosgaidh, do-chur as.

INEXTRICABLE, a. Do-réiteachadh, do-liobhradh, do-fhuasgladh.

INFALLIBILITY, s. Neo-mhearrachd, neo-fhailneachd.

INFALLIBLE, a. Neo-mhearrachdach, neo-fhàilneach, nach gabh cur am mearrachd, cinnteach.

INFALLIBLY, adv. Gu cinnteach, gun teagamh.

INFAMOUS, a. Mì-chliùiteach, maslach, narach, nar, beagnarach, olc. An infamous woman, *striopach.*

INFAMOUSLY, adv. Gu mi-chliùiteach, gu maslach, gu nàr.

INFAMOUSNESS, s. Mi-chliù, masladh, naire, sgainneal.

INFANCY, s. Òige, naoidheanachd; tùs (no) toiseach ni sam bi.

INFANT, s. Naoidhean, naoidh, leanabh, urr òg, urrag; leanaban, pàisd, garlach. An infant beginning to walk, *caodachan*; imeachdan; the hands of an infant, but the stomach of a man, *lamhan leinibh, ach goile seann duine.*

INFANT, a. Og; anabuich.

INFANTA, s. Ban-phrionnsa Spàinnteach.

INFANTICIDE, s. Mortadh leinibh.

INFANTILE, INFANTINE, a. Leanabanta, leanabail; naoidheanach.

INFANTRY, s. Coisridh, saighdearan coise, arm coise.

INFATUATE, v. a. Buair, saobh; cuir thar a cheile, cuir gòrach, gon. Infatuated, *buairte, gointe.*

INFATUATION, s. Buaireadh, amaideachd, draoidheachd, gonadh; gòraiche.

INFEASIBLE, a. Do-dheanamh, do-chur an gniomh, do-ghnàthachadh.

INFECT, v. Thoir galar, puinnseanaich, truaill.

INFECTION, s. Gabhaltas galair; gabhaltachd, puinnsean.

INFECTIOUS, a. Gabhaltach, sgaoilteach. An infectious disease, *tinneas sgaoilteach.*

INFECTIOUSNESS, s. Gabhaltachd, sgaoilteachd.

Infective, *a.* Gabhaltach, sgaoilteach

Infecund, *a.* Neo-thorrach, neo-shìolmhor, neo-shìolar, neo-chlannail, seasg, aimrid

Infecundity, *s.* Neo-thorrachas, neo-shìolmhoireachd, aimrideachd

Infelicity, *s.* Mi-shealbharachd, mi-shealbh, earchall, droch-fhortan, mi-fhortan, truaighe, mi-agh.

Infer, *v.* Tuig; ciallaich; comh-dhùin

Inference, *s* Ciall; comhdhùnadh; barail.

Inferior, Inferiour, *a.* Iochdarach, iochdrach, is iochdaraiche, ni 's iochdaraiche. is neo-inmhiche, is ìsle, is ìlse, is lugha, ni 's neo-inmhiche, ni 's ìlse, ni 's lugha, ni 's suarraiche, ni 's crìne.

Inferior, *s* Iochdaran, iochdran.

Inferiority, *s.* Isle, ìlseachd, iochdaranachd.

Infernal, *a* Ifrinneach, deamhanach, diabhlaidh, olc, fìor olc, ro olc; gràineil, oillteil

Infertile, *a* Neo-thorrach, neo-shìolmhor, neo-shìolar, truagh.

Infertility, *adv.* Neo-thorraichead, neo-shìolmhoireachd

Infest, *v.* Buair, sàruich, claoidh, trioblòidich, cuir dragh

Infestered, *a.* Feargach; dùr, rag

Infestively, *s* Dubhachas, bròn, mulad, tuirse, cumhadh

Infidel, *s.* Anacreideach, ana-criosduidh, pàganach, gintealach.

Infidel, *a* Ana-creideach, gun cheidcamh.

Infidelity, *s.* Ana-creideamh, ana-creidsinn; neo-dhìllseachd, traoidhtearachd.

In-field, *s.* Baile geamhraidh.

Infinite, *a.* Neo-chrìochnach, neo-chrìochnuidheach, anabarrach, gun chrìoch, gun cheann, gun toiseach, no deireadh, do-thomhas, do-mheas

Infinitely, *adv.* Gu h-anabarra, gu h-anabharra, gu ro-mhor.

Infiniteness, *s.* Neo-chrìochnachd, neo-chrìochnuidheachd

Infinitude, *s.* Neo-chrìochnachd, neo-chrìochnuidheachd, anbharrachd

Infirm, *a* Lag, fann, anfhann, anmhunn, breòite, tuisleach, mall, truagh, tinn, eu-slainnteach, eu-slan; neo-ghramail, neo-bhunaiteach.

Infirmary, *s.* Tigh eiridinn, tigh-leigheis.

Infirmity, *s* Laige, laigse, laigsinn, fainne, anfhannachd, anfhainneachd, anmhunnachd, breòiteachd, fàilinn, euslainnte eucail, tinneas. Many infirmities attend old age, *thig gach uile ri h-aois, thig baoth, thig boil, thig bàs*

Infix, *v.* Sàs; sàth; gramaich; fastaich.

Inflame, *v. a* Cuir ri theine, cuir r' a theine, loisg, fadaidh, las, feargaich; buair. Inflamed, *ri theine, loisgte, air lasadh, feargaichte, buairte.* Inflamed with anger, *air lasadh le feirge.*

Inflammability, *s.* So-fhadaidheachd.

Inflammable, *a* So-chur r' a theine, so-losgadh, so-lasadh, so-fhadadh, lasaireach, lasanta

Inflammableness, *s.* So-fhadaidheachd, lasantachd.

Inflammatory, *a.* Buaireasach, feargach.

Inflate, *v a.* Sèid, seid suas, bolg, at, boch

Inflation, *s.* Seideadh, bolgadh, at, bochadh.

Inflect, *v.* Lùb, claon, crom, cam, fiar.

Inflection, *s* Lùbadh, cromadh, fiaradh.

Inflexibility, *s* Raigead, raige, raigsinn, dùiread; ceannlaidireachd; rag-mhuinealachd, danarachd; do-lubaidheachd.

Inflexible, *a.* Rag, do-lùbadh, do-lùbaidh; dùr; ceannlaidir; rag-mhuinealach, do-ghluasad; nach gabh lùbadh, rithinn.

Inflexibly, *adv.* Gu rag, gu dùr; gu ceann-laidir, gu rag-mhuinealach, gu rithinn, gun sgur, gun sgurachd, gun chàirde.

Inflict, *v. a* Leig mar pheanas (no) mar umhladh, dean peanas; peanasaich.

Inflicter, *s* Peanasair, umhladair; fear ni peanas, fear a leigeas umhladh.

Infliction, *s* Peanasachadh, peanas.

Inflictive, *a* Peanasach

Influence, *s.* Cumhachd, *pùdhair*, creideas, smachd, dìon, maoidhean He has no influence in the world over him, *cha n' eil smachd air an t-saoghal aige air*

Influence, *v* Aom, treòraich; comhairlich.

Influent, *a* A sruthadh stigh

Influential, *a* Smachdail, cumhachdach, éifeachdach

Influx, *s.* Sruth; lìonadh, comar, †cumhachd

Infold, *v a* Fill, paisg Infolded, *fillte, paisgte*

Inform, *v* Innis; teagaisg; oid, thoir fios, seòl, cuir an céil, dean aithnichte Inform on him, *innis air, dean brath air*

† **Informal**, *a* Mi-riaghailteach, mi-laghail, neo-fhreagarrach

Informality, *s.* Mi-riaghailt

Informant, *s* Brathadair, fear brathaidh

Information, *s.* Fios; eolas, oilean, oideas, ionnsachadh, seoladh, fiosrachadh, beachd-sgeul, sgeul, brathadh; diteadh.

Informer, *s* Brathadair, fear brathaidh, fear innsidh.

Informity, *s.* Mi-chumadh.

Infortunate, *a* Mi-fhortanach, mi-shealbhar, mi-aghmhor.

Infract, *v a.* Bris

Infraction, *s* Briseadh Infraction of a condition, *briseadh cumhnaint*

Infrangible, *a* Do-bhriseadh, nach gabh briseadh, nach còrr a bhriseadh

Infrequency, *s* Teirce, tearcad, ainmigead; neo-chumantachd, neo-bhitheantachd, ainneamhachd

Infrequent, *a* Tearc, ainmig, ainneamh, neo-bhìdheanta, neo-thric, neo-chumanta, neo-lìonmhor

Infrigidate, *v a.* Dean fuar, fionnaraich, fuaraich.

Infringe, *v a* Bris, mill; amail. Infringed, *briste*

Infringement, *s* Briseadh.

Infringer, *s* Fear brisidh, briseadair

Infuriate, *a.* Air a chuthach, air bhoile, air bainnidh, air bhreathas; cuthaich.

Infuscate, *v. a* Dubh, dorchaich, salaich, duibhrich.

Infuscation, *s* Dubhadh, duibhreachadh; dorchadas, duirche, duibhre.

Infuse, *v.* Doirt stigh; taosg, sil, bog; teagaisg, muin

Infusible, *a.* So-dhòrtadh steach, so-thaosgadh, so-bhogadh, do-leaghadh.

Infusion, *s* Taosgadh, dòrtadh, bogachadh, sileadh

Ingathering, *s* Tarradh, tarragh, trodhadh, tionaladh, teanaladh, cruinneachadh

Ingeminate, *v* Dùblaich, aithris

Ingemination, *s* Aithris, aithriseadh

Ingenerate, *a* Nadurra

Ingenious, *a* Innleachdach, teannsgalach, tapaidh, eanchainneach, seòlta, eolach, ceillidh; ealanta, ioraillteach

Ingeniously, *adv* Gu h-innleachdach, gu teannsgalach, gu h-eanchainneach, gu seolta, gu ceillidh.

Ingeniousness, *s* Innleachd, teannsgalachd, tapadh, eanchainneachd, seoltachd; ealantachd, ioraillteachd.

INGENITE, *a.* Nadurra, nadurrail

INGENUITY, *s* Innleachd, teannsgal, eanchainn.

INGENUOUS, *a* Fireannach, fior; fosgailte, fial, suairc, soilleir, saor, flathail, oirdheirc.

INGENUOUSLY, *adv* Gu fireannach, gu fior, gu fuasgailte, gu fial, gu suairc, gu soilleir, gu flathail, gu h-òirdheirc.

INGENUOUSNESS, *s.* Fireannachd, fiaile, fialachd.

INGEST, *v a* Sluig

INGESTION, *s* Slugadh

INGLORIOUS, *a* Mi-chliùiteach, neo-onorach, neo-uasal, neo-urramach.

INGOT, *s.* Geinn (no) gàd òir, geinn (no) gàd airgid; unga

INGRAFF, INGRAFT, *v a* Suidhich; cuir domhain, comhghlrabh, nòdaich Ingrafted, *nòduichte*

INGRAFTMENT, *s* Nòdachadh.

INGRATE, *a* Neo-thaingeil, mi-thaingeil; neo-chiatach.

INGRATEFUL, *a* Neo-thaingeil, mi-thaingeil.

INGRATIATE, *v a* Faigh maoidhean neach, faigh stigh air neach· cuir stigh maoidhean

INGRATIATING, *a* Furanach, mio-chuiseach, maoidheanach.

INGRATITUDE, *s* Mi-thaingealachd, neo-thaingealachd.

INGRAVITATED, *a* Torrach, leth-tromach.

INGREDIENT, *s* Cungaidh

INGRESS, *s* Inntrinn, dol a steach, dol a stigh.

INGROSS, *v. a* Sglamhaich; gabh dhuit féin; garbh-sgriobh

INGUINAL, *a.* Bleinneach, blionach, loch-bhleineach.

INGULF, *v a* Sluig, sluig suas

INGURGITATE, *v a* Sluig gu gionach, glug thairis

INGURGITATION, *s.* Slugadh, glugadh, glugam.

INGUSTABLE, *a* Do-bhlasadh

INHABILE, *a* Neo-thapaidh, neo-sgileil, neo-dheas, neo-theoma

INHABIT, *v a* and *n.* Sealbhaich, àitich, comhnuich, tamhaich, tamh, fuirich, fan Inhabited, *sealbhaichte, àitichte*

INHABITABLE, *a* A dh' fhaodar àiteachadh, aiteachail, ion-aiteachadh

INHABITANT, *s* Fear àiteachaidh, fear àitich, fear comhnuidh, tamhaich Inhabitants, *luchd aiteachaidh*

INHABITATION, *s* Aros, fardoch, aite tamh, aitreabh

INHABITER, *s.* Fear aiteachaidh, fear àitich, fear comhnuidh

INHALE, *v a* Tarruing stigh leis an anail

INHARMONIOUS, *a* Neo-cheolmhor, neo-fhonnmhor, neo-bhinn, mi-bhlasda.

INHERE, *v* Stic ri, lean ri, dlù-lean

INHERENT, *a* Nadurra, nadurrail; dual

INHERIT, *v a* Sealbhaich, sealbhaich mar oighreachd; faigh. Inherited, *sealbhaichte*

INHERITABLE, *a.* Seilbheil, sealbhail, sealbhachail

INHERITANCE, *s* Oighreachd, sealbhachadh, duchas; seilbh.

INHERITOR, *s.* Oighre

INHERITRESS, *s* Ban-oighre.

INHESION, *s.* Dlù-leanachd, dlù-leantuinn, sticeadh.

INHIBIT, *v* Bac, stad, cuir stad, cuir moille, amail; cum air ais, cuir na thamh; toirmisg. Inhibited, *toirmisgte.*

INHIBITION, *s* Bacadh, amaladh, toirmeasgadh

INHOSPITABLE, *a* Iargalta, neo-fhial, neo-fhialaidh, uipearach, coimheach, borb, doichiollach, doirbh, dorganta, cruaidh, cruadalach, neo-dhaonna.

INHOSPITABLY, *adv* Gu h-iargalta, gu neo-fhialaidh, gu h-uipearach, gu coimheach, gu doichiollach.

INHOSPITALITY, *s.* Iargaltas, neo-fhialachd, neo-fhéille, uipearachd, buirbe, droch-bhiatachd.

INHUMAN, *a.* Borb, ain-iochdmhor, neo-iochdmhor, mi-chneasta, all-mharra, cruaidh-chridheach, cruadalach, bruideil, aingidh, neo-dhaonna

INHUMANITY, *s.* Buirbe, ain-iochd, ain-iochdmhor, achd, all-mharrachd, cruadhas cridhe, mi-chneastachd, mi-dhaonnachd.

INHUMANLY, *adv.* Gu borb, gu h-ain-iochdmhor, gu neo-iochdmhor, gu mi-chneasta, gu cruadalach, gu brùideil, gu h-aingidh, gu neo-dhaonna

INHUMATION, *s.* Adhlacadh, tiodhlacadh; torradh; cur fo 'n ùir.

INHUME, *v a.* Adhlaic, cuir san ùir, cuir san uaigh, cuir fo 'n talamh, tiodhlaic.

INIMICAL, *a* Naimhdeil; neo-chairdeil; mi-runach, ciurrail; dochannach

INIMITABLE, *a* Do-leanachd, do-leanmhuinn, nach gabh leanachd, do-aithriseadh.

INIMITABLY, *adv.* Gu do-leanmhuinn.

INIQUITOUS, *a.* Olc, aingidh, peacach; cearr, neo-cheart, eu-corach, ciontach

INIQUITOUSLY, *adv* Gu h-olc, gu h-aingidh, gu peacach; gu cearr, gu h-eucorach

INIQUITY, *s* Aingidheachd; eu-ceart; ana-ceartas; peacadh, droch-bheairt, eucoir, olc, ciont, lochd

INITIAL, *a.* Ceud, air thoiseach.

INITIATE, *a.* Tionsgain, seòl, tòisich, ionnsuich; gabh a stigh

INITIAMENT, *s.* Tùs, toiseachadh

INITIATION, *s* Gabhail a steach, gabhail a stigh, tionnsgnadh; toiseachadh; inntrinn

INJECT, *v.* Tilg stigh, tilg a steach, tilg suas, tilg

INJECTION, *s.* Tilg stigh, tilgeadh; sgiortadh.

INJOIN, *v a.* See ENJOIN.

INJUDICABLE, *a* Do-bhreithneachadh.

INJUDICIAL, *a* Neo-laghail

INJUDICIOUS, *a.* Neo-thuigseach, neo-theòma, neo-thoinisgeil; neo-sheòlta; neo-chrionna, gun tuigse, gun toinisg.

INJUDICIOUSLY, *adv.* Gun toinisg.

INJUDICIOUSNESS, *s* Mi-thoinisg, eu-crionnachd

INJUNCTION, *s.* Sparradh, ordugh, aithne, iarrtas, carail, *comannt*

INJURE, *v. a* Ciùrr, dochoirich, dochannaich, dochainn; dean cron, diobhailich; eucoirich; mill, cuir dholaidh; dean dochoir, dean diobhail, dean eucoir, dean urchoid; cuir air aimhreidh, dean coire

INJURED, *part.* Ciùrrta; dochoirichte; dochannaichte.

INJURER, *s* Fear eucoir; dochannaiche, fear dochainn.

INJURIOUS, *a* Ciurrail, dochannach, docharach, cronail, eucorach, millteach, olc, diobhaileach Injuriously, *gu dochannuch, gu ciurrail, gu cronail, gu diobhaileach.*

INJURY, *s.* Dochann, ciurradh, cron, dochoir, dochair, diobhail, eucoir, lochd, urchoid, beud, calldach; earchall. Do one an injury, *dean coire do neach*

INJUSTICE, *s.* Eu-ceartas, eu-ceirte, eucoir, ana-cothrom, mi-chothrom.

INK, *s* Dubhadh, dubhadan, dubhagan, dubh sgriobhaidh

INK, *v a.* Dubh, sliob no spairt le dubhadan.

INKHORN, *s.* Dubhach, searrag dubhadain; dubhagan

INKLE, *s.* Stiom aimh-leathan.

INKLING, *s* Faireachadh, sànas, rabhadh, cogar, cagar, fios

INKMAKER, *s.* Dubhadair.

INKY, *a.* Dubh, dubhadanach.

INLAND, *a.* Stigh san tìr, stigh san duthaich; meadhonach.

Inlapidate, *v.* Dean mar chloich; dean garbh (no) clochach.

Inlay, *v. a.* Breacaich; eag-samhlaich; leig. Inlaid, *breacaichte, eag-samhail.*

Inlet, *s.* Steach-shlighe; slighe, rod, bealach, cosan, giolaid; caolas.

Inmate, *s.* Co-thamhaiche, co-aitreamhaiche.

Inmost, *a.* Ion-mheadhonach, is fhaide a stigh.

Inn, *s.* Tigh mòr, tigh òsd, tigh lionna; ceann uidhe, greasailt, greas-lann.

Innate, *a.* Nadurra, nadurrail.

Innavigable, *a.* Do-sheòladh, nach gabh seòladh air.

Inner, *a.* Stigh, steach, is fhaide a stigh.

Innermost, *a.* Ion-mheadhonach.

Innholder, *s.* Osdair, fear tigh òsda, mangair, fear tigh mòra.

Innkeeper, *s.* Osdair, fear tigh òsda, mangair, fear tigh mòra.

Innocence, Innocency, *s.* Neo-chiontas, fìor-ghloine, sochaireachd, neo-urchoid; fìreannachd, tréibhdhireas, ionracas; simplidheachd, aon-fhillteachd.

Innocent, *a.* Neo-chiontach, glan, neo-lochdach, neochronail, fìor-ghlan, neo-urchoideach; tréibhdhireach, ionraic, simplidh, aon-fhillteach, aon-fhillte.

Innocent, *s.* Neach neo-chionntach, ionracain; (*idiot*), baothair, umaidh, oinseach.

Innocently, *adv.* Gu neo-chiontach, gu neo-lochdach, gu neo-chronail, gu fìor-ghlan, gu neo-urchoideach, gu h-ionraic.

Innocuous, *a.* Neo-chiurrail; neo-chronail.

Innocuously, *adv.* Gu neo-chiurrail, gu neo-chronail, gun chron.

Innominable, *a.* Nach còrr ainmeachadh.

Innominate, *a.* Gun ainm.

Innovate, *v. a.* Ath-nuadhaich, nuadhaich, mùgh, atharraich.

Innovation, *s.* Nuadhachadh, ath-nuadhachadh, anagnath, mùghadh, caochladh, atharrachadh.

Innovator, *s.* Nuadhadair, atharrachair, caochladair.

Innoxious, *a.* Neo-lochdach, neo-choireach; neo-chiontach.

Innoxiously, *adv.* Gu neo-lochdach, gu neo-choireach; gu neo-chiontach.

Innoxiousness, *s.* Neo-chiontas.

Innuendo, *s.* Sànas, sméid.

Innumerable, *a.* Do-àireamh, do-chunntadh, nach gabh àireamh, nach gabh cunntadh, thar cunntas.

Innumerably, *adv.* Thar cunntas.

Innumerous, *a.* Do-àireamh, do-chunntadh, thar cunntas.

Inoculate, *v.* Nòdaich, tàth, suidhich; cuir breac air. Inoculate him, *cuir a bhreac air.*

Inoculation, *s.* Nòdachadh, tàthadh, suidheachadh; cur breac air neach.

Inoculator, *s.* Nòdair, tàthair; fear a chuireas breac air neach.

Inodorate, *a.* Neo-chubhraidh, gun tòchd, gun fhaile.

Inoffensive, *a.* Neo-chiontach, neo-lochdach, neo-choireach; soitheamh, soimeach; gun bhac, gun mhoille.

Inoffensively, *adv.* Gu neo-chiontach, gu neo-lochdach, gu soitheamh, gu soimeach.

Inofficious, *a.* Mi-mhodhail, neo-shiobhailt.

Inopinate, *a.* Obann, grad.

Inopportune, *a.* Neo-iomchuidh, neo-fhreagarrach.

Inordinacy, *s.* Mi-riaghailt, ana-cuimse, ana-goireas.

Inordinate, *a.* Mi-riaghailteach; ana-cneasta, ana-measarra, ana-miannach, ana-cuimseach, ana-goireasach.

Inordinately, *adv.* Gu neo-iomchuidh, gu neo-fhreagarrach, gu h-ana-cneasta.

Inordinateness, *s.* Mi-riaghailteachd, ana-cneastachd, ana-measarrachd.

Inorganic, *a.* Gun bhuill, gun riaghailt.

Inosculate, *v. n.* Dlùthaich, tàth ri chéile. Inosculated, *dlùthaichte.*

Inosculation, *s.* Dlùthachadh, tàthadh.

Inprocino, *adv.* Deas, ullamh, aig laimh.

Inprospicience, *s.* Eu-crionnachd, cion-smuaine, eu-cùram.

Inquest, *s.* Sgrudadh, rannsuchadh, mìn-rannsuchadh, ceasnach, ceasnachadh.

Inquietude, *s.* Mi-shuaimhneas, an-shocair, neo-fhaisneachd.

Inquinate, *v. a.* Truaill, salaich, mill.

Inquination, *s.* Truailleadh, salachadh, milleadh.

Inquirable, *a.* So-rannsuchadh, so-fhiosrachadh.

Inquire, *v. a.* Foighnich, foighneachd, fiosraich, feoruich, farraid, rannsuich, sir; lorgaich, cuir ceist ri; iarr; fiafraich. Inquire of him, *foighnich (no) foighneachd dheth;* I would have you inquire, *b' àille leam thu fhoighneachd.*

Inquired, *part.* Fiosraichte, feoruichte, rannsuichte; lorgaichte.

Inquirer, *s.* Fiosrachair, feòrachair, rannsuchair, lorgair.

Inquiry, *s.* Foighneachd, foighneachadh, feòrach, feorachadh, garraid; fiosrachadh, rannsach, rannsuchadh, sireadh, lorgachadh, ceasnachadh, ceasnach, ceisd, ceist.

Inquisition, *s.* Mìn-rannsuchadh, ceasnachadh; dian-sgrudadh, dian-lorgaireachd, cruaidh-cheasnachadh.

Inquisitive, *a.* Sireadach, iarradach, foighneachdail, fiosrachail, rannsuchail.

Inquisitiveness, *s.* Sireadachd; foighneachd, fiafrach; lorgaireachd, ceasnachd.

Inquisitor, *s.* Sgrudair, rannsuchair, ceasnachair, rannsuchair Ròimheach, fear dreuchd ann an cuirt sgrudaidh eaglais na Ròimh.

Inrail, *v. a.* Druid, dùin, iom-dhruid.

Inroad, *s.* Ionnsuidh, foghail; ruaig; ruathar.

Insalubrious, *a.* Neo-shlainnteil, neo-fhallain.

Insalubrity, *s.* Neo-shlainntealachd, neo-fhallaineachd.

Insalutary, *a.* Neo-shlainnteil, neo-fhallain; olc.

Insalutariness, *s.* Neo-shlainntealachd, neo-fhallaineachd.

Insanable, *a.* Do-shlanuchadh, do-leigheas, nach gabh slànuchadh (no) leigheas.

Insane, *a.* Cuthaich, gòrach, thar chéill, air mhearaichinn, baoghal.

Insaneness, Insanity, *s.* Cuthach, gòraiche, mearaichinn, mire, breathas.

Insatiable, *a.* Do-shàsuchadh, do-shàsuchaidh, do-lionadh, do-thoileachadh, nach gabh sàsuchadh (no) toileachadh; gionach, craosach, ciocrach; lonach.

Insatiably, *adv.* Gu do-shàsuchadh, gu craosach, gu ciocrach.

Insatiate, *a.* Do-shàsuchadh, do-shàsuchaidh, do-thoileachadh, do-lionadh.

Insaturable, *a.* Do-lionadh, do-shàsuchadh.

Inscribe, *v.* Sgriobh, grabh; cuir leabhair fo thearmun duine ainmeil.

Inscription, *s.* Sgriobh, sgriobhadh, grabhadh; tiodal; (*epitaph*), mnigh, feart-ghrabh, marbhuach.

Inscrutable, *a.* Do-rannsuchadh, do-rannsuchaidh, dofhaotainn a mach; folaichte.

Inscrutableness, *s.* Do-rannsuidheachd.

Insculp, *v. a.* Grabh; gearr; snaith.

Insculpture, *s.* Grabhadh, gearradh.

Insect, *s.* Cuileag, beach, speach, no an leithidean sin; biasdag, beisteag.

Insectator, *s.* Fear-leanmhuinn, dian-leanmhuinneach, bith-leanmhuinniche.

Insecure, *a.* Neo-thearuinte; neo-dhiongalta, neo-dhiongmhalta.

Insecurity, *s.* Neo-thearuinteachd, neo-dhiongaltachd, cunnart.

Insemination, *s.* Siol-chur, cur sìle.

Insensate, *a.* Baoth, neo-smuainteachail, neo-thuigseach, neo-thoinisgeil.

Insensibility, *s.* Neo-mhothachadh, cion-mothachaidh, mi-thuigse, funntainn.

Insensible, *a.* Neo-mhothachail, neo-thuigseach, baoth; gun chàil; air funntuinn.

Insensibly, *adv.* Gun aire, gun mhothachadh; a chuid is a chuid.

Inseparable, *a.* Do-sgaradh, do-dhealachadh, neo-sgarail, nach sgar, nach dealaich, nach gabh sgaradh, nach gabh dealachadh, dlu-cheangailte, do thoirt as a chéile.

Inseparably, *adv.* Gu do-sgaradh, gu do-dhealachadh, gu dlù-cheangailte.

Insert, *v. a.* Cuir sios, sgriobh, cuir a stigh.

Insertion, *s.* Cur sios; cur a stigh; sgriobhadh.

Inside, *s.* Leth a stigh, taobh a stigh.

† **Insidiator**, *s.* Fear plaid-luidhe.

Insidious, *a.* Fealltach, foilleil, cealgach, cuilbheartach, ceabhachdach, sligheach, eòlach, meallta, mealltach, traoidhteil.

Insidiously, *adv.* Gu fealltach, gu foilleil, gu cealgach, gu cuilbheartach, gu ceabhachdach, gu sligheach, gu meallta.

Insidiousness, *s.* Foille, ceilge, cealgaireachd, cuilbheart, cuilbheartachd, mealltaireachd, mealltachd, traoidhtearachd.

Insight, *s.* Sealladh, eòlas, fiosrachadh, rannsuchadh, tuigse.

Insignia, *s.* Suaicheantas, buill airm.

Insignificance, *s.* Neo-fhiach, mi-thàbhachd, suaraichead, faoinead; fagharsachd.

Insignificant, *a.* Suarach, neo-thabhachdach, faoin, air bheag seadh, neo-fhiachail, neo-luachmhor, fagharsach, air bheag luach.

Insignificantly, *adv.* Gu suarach, gu neo-thabhachdach, gu faoin, gu fagharsach.

Insincere, *a.* Neo-fhior, neo-fhireannach, neo-ionraic, neo-dhìleas; neo-thairis; neo-dhùrachdach, cealgach.

Insincerity, *s.* Mi-dhillseachd, mi-thairiseachd, mi-dhùrachd, ceilge.

Insinuant, *a.* Maoidheanach.

Insinuate, *v. a.* and *n.* Sàth steach, cuir (no) pùc a stigh; starr, sparr, thoir tuair, thoir sànas; ciallaich, dean miodal, dean blanndar; faigh maoidhean (no) fabhor, faigh stigh air neach.

Insinuation, *s.* Blanndar, miodal, goileam; sodal; sànas.

Insinuative, *a.* Blanndarach, miodalach, sodalach.

Insinuator, *s.* Miodalair, miodalaiche, sodalaiche.

Insipid, *a.* Domblasda, neo-bhlasda, gun bhlas; neo-sheadhar; marbh; mall; neo-spioradail.

Insipidity, *s.* Domblasdachd, neo-bhlasdachd.

Insipidly, *adv.* Gun bhlas, gu domblasda, gu neo-bhlasda.

Insipidness, *s.* Neo-bhlasdachd, domblasdachd.

Insipience, *s.* Amaideachd; baoghaltachd.

Insist, *v. n.* Seas air, seas ri, lean ri, lean air, cum air, cum a mach, buanaich ann; càir air.

Insnare, *v. a.* Rib, glac, cuir an sàs, meall. Insnared, *ribte, glacta, an sàs.*

Insnarer, *s.* Ribeadair; mealltair.

Insobriety, *s.* Meisg, misg, daoraich, neo-stuamachd, geòcaireachd, pòitearachd, ruite.

Insociable, *a.* Coimheach, neo-chompanta, udlaidh, ùmadail; doirbh, gnò.

Insolate, *v.* Grianaich, caoinich. Insolated, *grianaichte, tiormaichte sa ghrian, caoinichte.*

Insolated, *part.* Grianaichte, caoinichte.

Insolence, *s.* Stràichd, peirtealachd, mi-mhodh; peilp, ardan, uaill, mi-naire, droch-mhunadh, mortas, beadaidheachd.

Insolent, *a.* Stràiceil, miobhail, mi-mhodhail; peilpeanta, beadaidh, beagnarach, peirteil, uaibhreach, ardanach, minarach, drochmhuinte.

Insolently, *adv.* Gu stràiceil, gu h-uaibhreach, gu mimhodhail, gu beadaidh, gu beagnarach, gu peirteil.

Insolvable, *a.* Do-fhuasgladh, do rèiteachadh, do-phàigh, nach gabh fuasgladh, réiteachadh (no) paigh.

Insolvent, *a.* Briste, an ain-fhiach. He is insolvent, *tha e briste.*

Insolvency, *s.* Briseadh, ain-fhiach.

Insoluble, *a.* Do-sgaradh; do-leaghadh.

Insomuch, *conj.* Ionnas, a mheud; air achd, air a chor.

Inspect, *v.* Amhairc, seall air, cum sùil air, beachdaich, gabh beachd, rannsuich, ceasnaich.

Inspection, *s.* Geur amharc; beachdachadh; dearcadh; mion-rannsuchadh.

Inspector, *s.* Fear coimhid; fear amhairc, griobh.

Insperse, *v. a.* Spairt, spult, dòirt.

Inspersion, *s.* Spairteadh, spultadh, dòrtadh.

Inspirable, *a.* So-tharuinn steach, so-shùgadh.

Inspiration, *s.* Tarruing analach, analachadh, anail; teagasg neamhuidh, deachdadh.

Inspire, *v. a.* Séid, séid a steach, cuir san inntinn; beothaich, brosnaich, prosnaich; cuir misneach ann, thoir aigne.

Inspired, *part.* Brosnaichte; deachdta le neamh.

Inspirit, *v. a.* Beothaich; brosnaich; prosnaich. Inspirited, *beothaichte, brosnaichte.*

Inspissate, *v. a.* Tiughaich; dean tiugh; slamaich. Inspissated, *tiughaichte; tiugh, slamaichte.*

Inspissation, *s.* Tiughachadh.

Instability, *s.* Diombuanas, diombuanachd, neo-sheasmhachd, neo-bhunailteachd, caochlaideachd, luaineachd.

Instable, *a.* Diombuan, neo-sheasmhach, neo-bhunailteach, caochlaideach, luaineach, mùiteach, mughteach, siùbhlach, neo-mhaireann.

Install, *v. a.* Cuir an seilbh; cuir an dreuchd. He is installed, *tha e air a chur an seilbh.*

Installation, *s.* Cur an seilbh, cur an dreuchd, suidheachadh.

Instalment, *s.* Cuir an seilbh; pàigh.

Instance, *s.* Iarrtas, liosdachd, athchuinge; (*example*), eisiomlair, sampull.

Instance, *v. a.* Thoir mar eisiomlair, thoir sampull.

Instant, *a.* Dùrachdach, dian, bitheanta, bidheanta, grad, cabhagach, ealamh.

Instant, *s.* Mionaid, tiota, plath; briosg, priob sùl, gradag, mamuin, tamul; am, uair. At this instant, *air a mhionaid* so; in an instant, *ann an tiota, ann an gradaig;* I will come this instant, *thig mi air a mhionaid, thig mi an ceart uair.*

INSTANTANEOUS, *a.* Grad, obann, ann am mionaid, an am priob na sùl, ann an tiota, air a mhamuin, ann an gradaig.

INSTANTLY, *adv.* Gu grad, gu h-ealamh, ann an tiota, ann am priobadh na sùl, ann an gradaig, an ceart uair, air a mhionaid; gu dian, gu dùrachdach.

INSTATE, *v.* Cuir an dreuchd.

INSTAURATION, *s.* Nuadhachadh; aisigeadh; dealachadh.

INSTEAD *of, prep.* Ann aite, 'n aite, an ionad, an riochd, airson. Instead of me, *ann am àite, ann m' àite, air mo shòn;* instead of her, *na h-aite;* instead of them, *nan àite.*

INSTEEP, *v. a.* Bog, bogaich, cuir am bog.

INSTEP, *s.* Uchdan na coise, uchdan na troidhe, uchdar na coise.

INSTIGATE, *v. a.* Brosnuich, brosnaich, prosnaich; brog, stuig; earalaich; cuir h-uige, buair. Instigated, *brosnaichte, brosnuichte, prosnaichte, stuigte.*

INSTIGATION, *s.* Brosnachadh, brosnuchadh, prosnachadh, bragadh, earalachadh, stuigeadh, cur h-uige, beothachadh, toirt misneach, buaireadh.

INSTIGATOR, *s.* Brosnachair, fear brosnachaidh, buaireadair,

INSTIL, *v. a.* Dòirt a steach, sil a stigh, teagaisg. Instilled, *air a dhòrtadh a steach.*

INSTILLATION, *s.* Dòrtadh steach; teagasg; sileadh.

INSTINCT, *s.* Claonadh nadurra, miann nadurra, nàdur.

INSTINCTIVE, *a.* Nàdurra, nàdurrail. Instinctively, *gu nadurra, a thaobh nàduir.*

INSTITUTE, *v. a.* Socraich, cuir air chois, suidhich, orduich, sònruich, reachdaich, àithn, daighnich, daingnich, toisich, eagair, deasaich; teagaisg, oid.

INSTITUTE, *s.* Reachd, lagh, àithne, ordugh.

INSTITUTED, *part.* Socraichte, air chois, suidhichte, orduichte, sonruichte, reachdaichte, daingnichte.

INSTITUTION, *s.* Ordugh, reachd, aithne, lagh; suidheachadh, socrachadh, bunadhas; teagasg; foghlum, oilean.

INSTITUTIONARY, *a.* Tùsail; prìomh, bunadhasach.

INSTITUTOR, *s.* Suidheachair, sonrachair, socrachair; oid, fear teagaisg.

INSTRUCT, *v.* Teagaisg, oid, ionnsuich, foghluim, oileanaich; seol. Instructed, *teagaisgte, ionnsuichte, foghluimte, oileanaichte.*

INSTRUCTER, *s.* Fear teagaisg, oid-ionnsuich, maighstir sgoile.

INSTRUCTION, *s.* Teagasgadh, ionnsuchadh; teagasg, ionnsach, oilean, oideas, foghlum; eòlas, seòladh; ordugh, iarrtas, rabhadh. According to the king's instructions, *a réir ordugh an righ.*

INSTRUCTIVE, *a.* Teagasgach, a buileach' eolais.

INSTRUMENT, *s.* Inneal, acfhuinn, ball, ìnsrumaid airneas; sgrìobhadh; gnìomh; cùmhnant, bann, gleus, bun, comhghar. Instruments of war, *innealan cogaidh;* a musical instrument, *inneal ciùil.*

INSTRUMENTAL, *a.* Cuideachail, uidhiseil, freagarrach; na impidh, na mheadon air.

INSUFFERABLE, *a.* Do-ghiùlan, do-iomchar, do-fhulang, do-fhulachdainn, gràineil, oillteil, déistinneach.

INSUFFICIENCY, *s.* Neo-chomasachd, mi-mhurraichead, cion neo-fhoghainteachd, comais; neo-dhiongaltachd; cion sgile.

INSUFFICIENT, *a.* Neo-chomasach, mi-mhurrach, eu-comasach, neo-fhoghainteach; neo-sgileil, neo-sheolta, aineolach.

INSUFFICIENTLY, *adv.* Gu neo-chomasach, gu neo-mhurrach, gu h-eu-comasach, gu mi-fhreagarrach; gu neo-sgileil, gu neo-sheòlta.

INSUFFLATION, *s.* Séideadh analach, tothadh analach.

INSULAR, INSULARY, *a.* Eileanach, oileanach, na aonar.

INSULATED, *a.* Aonaranach, singilte, leis féin.

INSULT, *s.* (*Leap*), leum, leumadh, saltairt.

INSULT, *s.* Masladh, tàir, tarcuis, tàmailt, beum, toi-bheum. Add insult to injury, *cuir tàmailt ri dochann.*

INSULT, *v. a.* and *n.* Dean tàmailt (no) tàir air, maslaich, tarcuisich, cuir gu nàir, saltair.

INSULTER, *s.* Fear tàireil, fear tarcuiseach, toibheumaiche.

INSULTING, *a.* Tarcuiseach, tàireil, beumnach. Insultingly, *gu tarcuiseach, gu tàireil, gu beumnach.*

INSUPERABLE, *a.* Do-chlaoidheadh, do-cheannsuchadh, do-shàruchadh, buadhmhor, nach gabh claoidheadh, nach gabh fairtleach' air, do chur gu taic.

INSUPERABLENESS, *s.* Do-chlaoidheachd, buadhmhorachd, do-chlaoidhteachd.

INSUPERABLY, *adv.* Gu do-chlaoidh, gu do-cheannsuchadh.

INSUPPORTABLE, *a.* Do-ghiùlan, do-iomchar, do-fhulang, nach gabh giùlan, nach gabh iomchar, nach fhaodar ghiùlan.

INSURANCE, *s.* Arachas, airgiod arachais; urras.

INSURE, *v. a.* Dean arachas, dean cinnteach.

INSURER, *s.* Fear arachais, urras, arachair.

INSURMOUNTABLE, *a.* Do-cheannsachadh, do-sharuchadh, do-chlaoidh; do-dheanamh.

INSURRECTION, *s.* Ceannairc, ar a mach, culmhùtaireachd, éiridh.

INSUSCEPTIBLE, *a.* Nach gabh mothuchadh.

INSUSURRATION, *s.* Dranndan, cogar, cagar, cogarsaich, cagarsaich; torman, borbhan.

INTACTIBLE, *a.* Do-mhothuchadh, do-fharachdainn, do-fhaineachadh.

INTAGLIO, *s.* Seud, leug.

INTEGER, *s.* Aireamh iomlan, iomlan, an t-iomlan.

INTEGRAL, *a.* Iomlan.

INTEGRAL, *s.* An t-iomlan.

INTEGRATION, *s.* Slànuchadh; ath-nuadhachadh.

INTEGRITY, *s.* Ionracas, treibhdhireas, fìreannachd, fìreantachd, macantas, macantachd; gloine, neo-chiontas; iomlanachd.

INTEGUMENT, *s.* Comhdach, comhdachadh, croicneag.

INTELLECT, *s.* Inntinn, tuigse, ciall, mothuchadh; eanchainn; ceann, ceudfaidh. A sound intellect, *inntinn fhallain.*

INTELLECTION, *s.* Tuigsinn.

INTELLECTIVE, *a.* Inntinneach, ean-chainneach, tuigseach, mothachail, ciallachail.

INTELLECTUAL, *a.* Inntinneach, ceudfathach.

INTELLIGENCE, *s.* Fios, eolas; tuigse, toinisg, inntinn, sgile; spiorad, aingeal. Get intelligence, *faigh fios.*

INTELLIGENCER, *s.* Teachdair, gille ruithe.

INTELLIGENT, *a.* Tuigseach, toinisgeil; ionnsuichte, foghluimte, oileanaichte, fiosrach, eòlach.

INTELLIGENTIAL, *a.* Spioradail, spioradailte, inntinneach.

INTELLIGIBILITY, *s.* So-thuigsinneachd, soilleireachd.

INTELLIGIBLE, *a.* So-thuigsinn, soilleir, riachdail furas a thuigsinn.

INTELLIGIBLY, *adv.* Gu so-thuigsinn, gu soilleir, gu riachdail.

INTEMERATE, *a.* Neo-thruaillte, glan, neo-thruaillichte.

INTEMPERAMENT, *s.* Droch chàile, euslainnte.

INTEMPERANCE, *s.* Ana-cneastachd, ana-bharrachd, anameasarrachd, mi-stuaim, neo-mheasarrachd, mi-gheimnidheachd, meisge, pòit, geòc, geòcaireachd, poitearachd, ana-goireas, ana-cuimse.

Intemperate, *a.* Ana-cneasta, ana-bharr, ana-measarra, ana-measarrach, mi-stuama, mi-gheimnidh, geòcach, ana-goireasach, ana-cuimseach.

Intemperately, *adv.* Gu h-ana-cneasta, gu h-anabharra, gu h-ana-measarra; gu mi-stuama, gu geòcach.

Intemperateness, *s.* Ana-cneastachd, ana-bharr, ana-bharrachd, ana-measarrachd, geocaireachd, pòitearachd; ana-goireasachd.

Intenable, *a.* Do-chumail, do-dhìonadh.

Intend, *v. a.* Miannaich, rùnaich, cuir romhad, bi los; ciallaich. I intend, *tha mi a cur romham, tha mi los, tha mhiann orm.*

Intendant, *s.* Griobh, fear coimhid, riaghladair.

Intendency, *s.* Griobhachd, riaghladaireachd.

Intense, *a.* Dian, làidir, aibhseach; teann. Intense heat, *dian-theas.*

Intensely, *adv.* Gu dian; gu làidir; gu teann; gu fuathasach.

Intenseness, *s.* Déine, déinead, teinnead; teannad.

Intent, *a.* Ro-dhìcheallach, dian; sonruichte, suidhichte, dùrachdach.

Intent, *s.* Miann, sannt, rùn, togar; beachd; aire; (*meaning*), ciall. With a good intent, *le deagh rùn;* a bad intent, *droch rùn.*

Intention, *s.* Miann, sannt, rùn, togar, beachd; aire; ciall. I had no intention to hurt you, *cha robh mhiann* (*no*) *shannt orm do chiurradh.*

Intentional, *a.* A dh' aon obair, a dheòin, miannaichte, rùnaichte.

Intentionally, *adv.* A dh' aon obair, a dheòin, a dh' aon ghnothuch.

Intentive, *a.* Dùrachdach, dìchiollach.

Intentively, *adv.* Gu dùrachdach, gu dìchiollach, le dùrachd, le dìchioll.

Intently, *adv.* Gu geur, gu beachdail, gu h-aireachail, le dian-thogar, le geur-bheachd.

Intentness, *s.* Geur-bheachd, geur-aire.

Inter, *v. a.* Adhlaic, tiodhlaic, ollanaich, cuir san ùir (no) san uaigh; cuir fo 'n talamh, torr.

Intercalary, *a.* Barrachd. Intercalary day, *là barrachd.*

Intercalate, *v. a.* Eadar-chuir.

Intercalation, *s.* Eadar-chur.

Intercede, *v. a.* Eadar-ghuidh, dean eadar-ghuidhe, dean air son, dean réite airson.

Interceder, *s.* Eadar-ghuidhear, eadar-mheadhonair.

Intercept, *v. a.* Stad, bac, glac, cuir stad air, cuir bac air, gabh roimh, còmhlaich.

Interception, *s.* Stadachd, bacadh, glacadh, gabhail roimh, còmhlachadh.

Intercession, *s.* Eadar-ghuidhe, eadar-mheadhon, eadar-mheadhonaireachd; réiteachadh, réite.

Intercessor, *s.* Eadar-ghuidhear, eadar-mheadhonair, fear réiteachaidh.

Interchain, *v. a.* Ceangail ri chéile; co-cheangail.

Interchange, *v. a.* Malairt, malairtich, co-mhalairt, iomlaid, iomlaidich, thoir (no) gabh am malairt, comh-iomlaidich.

Interchange, *s.* Malairt, comh-mhalairt, iomlaid, comh-iomlaid, suaip.

Interchangeable, *a.* So-mhùthadh airson a chéile; (*of colours*), eag-samhuil.

Interchangement, *s.* Comh-mhalairt, comh-iomlaid.

Intercipient, *a.* A ghabhas roimh, a bhacas, amalach, grabach.

Intercision, *s.* Bacadh, bac, amal, amaladh, stad.

Interclude, *v. a.* Gabh roimh, bac, dùin a mach, gabh eadar; grab.

Interclusion, *s.* Gabhail roimh; bac; bacadh, dunadh mach, gabhail eadar; grabadh.

Intercolumniation, *s.* Eadar dha cholmhuinn, eadar dha stùc.

Intercommon, *v.* Gabh comaidh (no) comith, comh-ith, ith an comharnaich; comh-ionaltair, comh-roinn.

Intercommunity, *s.* Comunn, caidreamh, cuideachd.

Intercostal, *a.* Eadar-aisneach, eadar dha aisinn.

Intercourse, *s.* Comunn, co-chomunn, geilios, comh-roinn, malairt, iomlaid; caidreamh, caigleachd; conaltradh, co-luadar; eòlas.

Intercurrence, *s.* Comh-ruithe; eadar-rod, eadar-slighe.

Intercurrent, *a.* A ruitheas eadar, a ruith eadar.

Interdict, *v.* Bac, grab, toirmisg; (*in Romish ecclesiastical matters*), malluich, molluich. Interdicted, *toirmisgte; malluichte.*

Interdict, *s.* Toirmeasg; (*papal*), mallachd, mollachd.

Interdiction, *s.* Toirmeasg, toirmeasgadh; (*papal*), dubh-malluchadh, mallachd, molluchadh, mollachd, dubh-mhallachd.

Interdictory, *a.* Toirmeasgach.

Interest, *v. a.* and *n.* Taitinn, taitnich, toilich, gabh tlachd do, gluais, mar chàil na h-inntinn; gabh pàirt ann, gabh cùram do, gabh gnothuch ri, cuir air. You do not interest yourself in this matter, *cha n' eil thu a gabhail cùram* (*no*) *tlachd do 'n chuis so.*

Interest, *s.* (*Advantage*), leas, math, maith, tairbhe, buannachd, proidhit, buintinn, buntainn, coisinn; (*influence*), creideas, maoidhean; (*right*), còir; (*of money*), riadh; (*share*), cuid, pairt; (*concern*), cùram, tlachd, toil. Compound interest, *riadh air riadh, riadh reidh;* put money at interest, *cuir airgiod air riadh;* make interest for me, *dean maoidhean air mo shon* (*no*) *as mo leth.*

Interested, *a.* Féin-chuiseach.

Interesting, *a.* Cudthromach; ciatach; cail-ghluasadach.

Interfere, *v. a.* Buin ri, gabh gnothuch ri; cuir eadar; meachranaich, rub sàil ri sàil (no) bonn ri bonn, suath ionga ri bonn, rub cas ri cas, mar ni each.

Interference, *s.* Buntuinn ri; beanachd ri; cur eadar.

Interfluent, *a.* A ruitheas eadar, ruith eadar, sruth eadar.

Interfused, *a.* Eadar-sgapte, eadar-sgaoilte.

Interim, *s.* An t-am, an uair, eadar-ùine. In the interim, *san am, air an am, air an uair, an tràths' an dràsda, an dràsdaich.*

Interior, *a.* A stigh, a steach, is fhaide a steach.

Interior, *s.* An leth a stigh, an leth a steach, an t-ùite a steach.

Interjacency, *s.* Eadar-luidhe.

Interjacent, *a.* Luidh eadar.

Interjection, *s.* Grad-ghlaodh, mar, *O! och! mo chreach!*

Interjoin, *v. a.* Tàth, comh-thàth; comh-cheangail.

Interknowledge, *s.* Comh-eòlas, eadar-eòlas, comh-aithne.

Interlace, *v. a.* Comh-fhigh, coimeasg.

Interlapse, *s.* Eadar-aimsir, eadar-ùine. In the interlapse, *san eadar-ùine.*

Interlard, *v. a.* Coimeasg; eadar-chuir. Interlarded, *coimeasgta.*

Interleave, *v. a.* Eadar-dhuillich. Interleaved, *eadar-dhuillichte.*

Interline, *v. a.* Eadar-llnich, sgriobh eadar sreathaibh (no) llnibh. Interlined, *eadar-llnichte.*

Interlineary, *a.* Eadar-lìneach, eadar-llnichte.

Interlink, *v. a.* Eadar-thinn, eadar-cheangail, comh-cheangail. Interlinked, *eadar-cheangailte.*

Interlocution, *s.* Comhradh déise, comhradh, seanachas.

Interlocutor, *s.* Fear a labhras ri neach eile. Interlocutors, *luchd-comhraidh.*

Interlocutory, *a.* Comhraideach, briathrach, seanachasach.

Interlope, *v. a.* Leum eadar dhaoine, leum eadar, ceannaich gun chòir (no) gun chomas.

Interloper, *s.* Fear a leumas air ni nach buin da, fear a ghabhas gnothuch ri ni nach còir dha.

Interlude, *s.* Eadar-chluiche.

Intermarriage, *s.* Eadar phòsadh, eadar mharaiste, posadh eadar dà theaghlach.

Intermarry, *v. n.* Eadar-phòs, pòs air feadh chéile.

Intermeddle, *v. a.* Meachranaich, buin ri, gabh gnothuch gun chòir.

Intermeddler, *s.* Fear meachranach, fear ghabhas gnothuch ri ni nach buin da.

Intermeddling, *s.* Meachranachd.

Intermediacy, *s.* Eadar-theachd, eadar-thighinn.

Intermedial, *a.* Meadhonach, san eadar-mheadhon.

Intermediate, *a.* Meadhonach, eadar-mheadhonach, san eadar-meadhon.

Interment, *s.* Adhlac, adhlacadh, tiodhlac, tiodhlacadh, † clannadh.

Intermigration, *s.* Imirich, dol air imirich.

Interminable, *a.* Neo-chriochnach, neo-iomallach, gun chrioch, gun cheann, gun teòr, gun iomall.

Interminate, *a.* Neo-chriochnach, gun chrioch, gun cheann, gun teòr.

Intermingle, *v.* Coimeasg. Intermingled, *coimeasgta.*

Intermission, *s.* Stad, stadachd, sgur, sgurachd, tamh, lasachadh. Without intermission, *gun sgur, gun stadachd, gun sgurachd, am comhnuidh, am bitheantas, gun lasachadh.*

Intermissive, *a.* A thig an traths' is a ris, a thig air uairibh, neo-bhitheanta.

Intermit, *v. a.* and *n.* Sguir, car tamuil, sguir beagan.

Intermittent, *a.* A sguireas car ùine, neo-bhitheanta. An intermittent fever, *teasach nan tràth.*

Intermix, *v. a.* Coimeasg, measg, measgnaich, cuir air feadh chéile. Intermixed, *coimeasgta.*

Intermixture, *s.* Coimeasg, coimeasgadh.

Intermural, *a.* Eadar-bhallaibh; eadar-bhallach.

Internal, *a.* A stigh, a steach; fior, nàdurail.

Internally, *adv.* A stigh, a steach; air an taobh stigh; san taobh stigh.

Internecine, *a.* Marbhtach, millteach, mortach, sgriosail.

Internecion, *s.* Marbhadh, àr, milleadh, mortadh, murtadh.

Internuncio, *s.* Teachdair, teachdair eadar da bhuidheann.

Interpellation, *s.* Gairm; iarrtas; † suman.

Interpolate, *v. a.* Cuir ni far nach còir dha bhith, eadar-sparr.

Interpolation, *s.* Cur ri, eadar-sgriobhadh; eadar-sparradh.

Interpolator, *s.* Eadar-sgriobhair, eadar-sparradair, fear a chuireas sgriobhadh, far nach còir dha bhith.

Interposal, *s.* Eadraiginn; cur eadar; eadar-mheadhon.

Interpose, *v. a.* Dean eadraiginn, cuir eadar, dean eadar-mheadhon.

Interposer, *s.* Fear eadraiginn.

Interposition, *s.* Eadraiginn; eadar-mheadhon; eadar-ghnothuch.

Interpret, *v. a.* Mìnich, eadar-theangaich, tarruing, tarruing o aon chainnte gu cainnte eile; soilleirich, eadar-mhìnich. Interpreted, *mìnichte; eadar-theangaichte.*

Interpretable, *a.* So-mhìneachadh.

Interpretation, *s.* Mìneachadh, eadar-theangachadh, eadar-mhìneachadh.

Interpreter, *s.* Mìneachair, eadar-theangair, eadar-mhìneachair.

Interpunction, *s.* Eadar-phongadh.

Interreign, *s.* Eadar-thriath.

Interrogate, *v.* Ceasnaich, ceasnuich, feoraich, fiosraich, farraid, foighneachd, ceisdich, cuir ceist ri.

Interrogation, *s.* Ceasnach, ceasnuchadh, sgrudadh, rannsuchadh, feorachadh, fiosrachadh, farraid, foighneachd, ceist. A point of interrogation, *comhar ceiste.*

Interrogator, *s.* Ceasnachair, sgrudair, rannsuchair, fear ceasnachaidh, fear sgrudaidh.

Interrogatory, *s.* Ceiste, ceasnach, rannsuchadh, ceasnachadh, sgrudadh, feorachadh, foighneachd, farraid.

Interrogatory, *a.* Ceasnachail, ceisteil, farraideach, sgrudail, rannsuchail.

Interrupt, *v.* Bac, grab, gabh roimh, cuir bac, cuir moille air; amail; comhlaich; toirmisg, cuir stad air. He interrupted me, *chuir e bac orm.*

Interruption, *s.* Bac, bacadh, grab, grabadh, moille, amaladh; toirmeasg; eadar-theachd, eadar-thighinn.

Interscapular, *a.* Eadar an da shlinnean.

Interscend, *v. a.* Gearr dheth.

Interscribe, *v. a.* Eadar-sgriobh. Interscribed, *eadar-sgriobhta.*

Intersect, *v. a.* and *n.* Eadar-ghearr, co-ghearr, gearr crosgach.

Intersection, *s.* Eadar-ghearradh, comh-ghearradh.

Intersert, *v.* Cuir eadar, eadar-chuir.

Intersertion, *s.* Eadar-chur.

Intershock, *v. a.* Comh-bhuail.

Intershock, *s.* Comh-bhualadh.

Intersperse, *v. a.* Sgaoil (no) sgap air feadh chéile, eadar-sgap, eadar-sgaoil. Interspersed, *eadar-sgaoilte, eadar-sgapte.*

Interspersion, *s.* Eadar-sgaoileadh, eadar-sgapadh.

Interstellar, *a.* Eadar-reultach.

Interstice, *s.* Sgagadh, fosgladh; eadarsgaradh.

Interstitial, *a.* Sgagach; eadar-sgarach.

Intertexture, *s.* Eadar, fhigheadh, eadar, pleatadh, figheadh, toinneamh.

Intertwine, *v. a.* Eadar-fhigh; eadar-phleat, figh (no) pleat air feadh chéile, toinneamh, figh, pleat.

Interval, *s.* Eadar-astar; eadar-uine, eadar-am.

Intervene, *v. a.* Eadar-thig, thig eadar, dean eadar-mheadhon.

Intervenient, *a.* A thig eadar, tighinn eadar, eadar-mheadhonach.

Intervention, *s.* Eadar-theachd; eadar-mheadhòn; eadar-mheadhonaireachd.

Intervert, *v.* Cuir gu feum eile.

Interview, *s.* Comhdhail, codhail, coinneamh.

Interweave, *v. a.* Figh, pleat, toinn, toinneamh, eadar-fhigh, eadar-phleat, eadar-thoinneamh. Interwoven, *fighte, toinnte, eadar-fhighte, eadar thoinnte.*

Intestate, *a.* Gun teismeid, gun tiomnadh.

Intestinal, *a.* A bhuineas do na caolain.

Intestine, *a.* A steach, a stigh; dùchasach.

Intestine, *s.* Caolan. Intestines, *caolain, greallach mion-ach, innigh.*

Inthral, *v.* Tràillich, cuir an daorsadh, cuir an bruid, cuir am braighdeanas; cuibhrich. Inthralled, *tràillichte, an daorsadh, ann am bruid, ann am braighdeanas, cuibh-richte.*

Inthralment, *s.* Tràilleachd, tràillealachd, bruid, braigh-deanas, cruaidh-chàs; teanndachd.

Inthrone, *v. a.* Cuir air cathair righ, cuir air cathair rioghail.

Intimacy, *s.* Caidreamh, eòlas, companas, dlù-eolas, ro-eolas, ionmhuinneachd; muinntireas.

Intimate, *a.* Eòlach air, ro eolach air, mion-eolach, mor aig, ionmhuinneach; muinntireach, a steach, a stigh; fog-us. An intimate friend, *caidreamh, dlù-charaid*; they are very intimate, *tha iad ro mhor aig a chéile.*

Intimate, *s.* Caidreamh, dlù-charaid, ro-charaid, compan-ach.

Intimate, *v. a.* Thoir fios, innis, cuir fios; thoir sanas.

Intimately, *adv.* Gu h-eolach, gu ro-eòlach, gu dlù; ro dhlu, gu h-ionmhuinn. Intimately connected with him, *ro dhlù an daimh dha.*

Intimation, *s.* Fios, guth, sànas, innseadh; seoladh.

Intimidate, *v. a.* Cuir fo eagal, cuir eagal (no) fiamh air, cuir fo mhi-mhisnich, dean meata. Intimidated, *fo gheilt, fo eagal, fo-fhiamh.*

Intimidation, *s.* Eagal, geilt, fiamh, uamhas, mi-mhis-neach.

Intire, *a.* Slan, iomlan.

Intireness, *s.* Slaine, iomlaine, iomlanachd, slànachd.

Into, *prep.* Do, a dh' ionnsuidh, a steach do, a stigh do.

Intolerable, *a.* Do-fhulang, do-ghiùlan, do-iomchar, ro-olc, nach gabh fulang, nach gabh giùlan, nach gabh iomchar.

Intolerableness, *s.* Do-fhulangachd.

Intolerably, *adv.* Gu do-fhulang, gu do-ghiùlan, gu do iomchar.

Intolerant, *a.* Nach urrainn fulang; mi-fhoighidinneach, reasgach.

Intomb, *v.* Adhlaic, tiodhlaic, cuir san uaigh (no) san torr.

Intonation, *s.* Torunn; stairn, toirm, fuaim; braidhe, stairearaich.

Intone, *v. a.* Dean torunn, dean toirm; dean dranndan.

Intort, *v. a.* Toinneamh, toinn, figh, pleat, dual, dualaich.

Intoxicate, *v. a.* Cuir air a mhisg, cuir air an daoraich. Intoxicated, *air a mhisge, air an daoraich.*

Intoxication, *s.* Misg, meisg, daoraich, meisgearachd, misgeireachd; asarlachd. In a state of intoxication, *air a mhisg.*

Intractable, *a.* Do-cheannsach, do cheannsachaidh, do-smachdaidh, mi-riaghailteach; rag, ceann-laidir, ragmhuin-ealach; reasgach; do-chur gu doigh, do chur gu taic; do riaghladh, do-stiùradh.

Intractableness, *s.* Do-cheannsachd, rag-mhuinealachd reasgachd.

Intractably, *adv.* Gu do-cheannsach, gu ceann-laidir, gu rag, gu reasgach.

Intranquillity, *s.* Docair; buaireas, dìth fois, mi-fhois-neachd.

Intransmutable, *a.* Do-mughadh, do-chaochladh.

Intrap, *v. a.* Cuir an sàs, glac, rib. Intrapped, *an sàs, ribte, glacta.*

Intreasure, *v. a.* Carn suas ionmhas; taisg, cuir mu 'n seach.

Intreat, *v.* See Entreat.

Intreaty, *s.* See Entreat.

Intrench, *v. a.* and *n.* Thoir ionnsuidh, bris a steach air; cladhaich, claisich, daighnich (no) dìon le clais. In-trenched, *claisichte, daighnichte le clais.*

Intrenchment, *s.* Clais, cladh, clais daighneachaidh.

Intrepid, *a.* Misneachail, treun, gaisgeil, flathail, misneach-ail, dàn, neo-eagalach, cruadalach, neo-sgàthach.

Intrepidity, *s.* Misneach, gaisge, gaisgealachd, tréine, flathaileachd, treunad, treunadas, dànadas, cruadalachd.

Intrepidly, *adv.* Gu misneachail, gu gaisgeil, gu treun, gu flathail, gu dàn, gu neo-sgàthach.

Intricacy, *s.* Ribleach, ribeachd, prablach; achran; deacaireachd; airc; duirche; do-sgaoilteachd, cruaidh-cheangladh.

Intricate, *a.* Achranach, ribte, prabta; neo-réidh, mi-riaghailteach, do-sgaoileadh, do-réiteachadh, do-thoirt as a chéile, cruaidh-cheangailte; docail, deacair, dorch, do-thuigsinn.

Intricately, *adv.* Gu h-achranach, gu prabta, gu mi-riaghailteach, gu do-sgaoileadh, gu do-reiteachadh.

Intrigue, *s.* Co-bhoinn; cuis dhiomhair; cuis gaoil, cuis leanannachd, leanannachd.

Intrigue, *v. n.* Cuir cuis dhiomhair air adhairt; dean le-anannachd dhiomhair.

Intriguer, *s.* Fear cuis dhiomhair; fear gaol-chùiseach.

Intriguingly, *adv.* Gu diomhair; gu cuilbheartach, gu carach, gu h-innleachdach.

Intrinsic, **Intrinsical**, *a.* Ion-mheadhonach, fior, na-durrail; a stigh.

Intrinsically, *adv.* Gu fior.

Introduce, *v. a.* Thoir a steach, thoir a làthair, cuir eolas eadar.

Introducer, *s.* Treorachair, fear a bheir neach steach a dh' aite aineolach, no chum lathaireachd urr eile.

Introduction, *s.* Tabhairt a stigh; roi'-radh; tùs eòlais, toiseach, toiseachadh.

Introductory, *a.* Roi'-radhach, deasachail, toisich.

Introgression, *s.* Inntrinn, dol a steach, teachd a steach.

Intromission, *s.* Cur a steach; leigeil a steach dol a stigh.

Intromit, *v. a.* Cuir a steach, leig a stigh (no) a steach.

Introspect, *v.* Seall a steach, seall a stigh.

Introvenient, *a.* Teachd a steach, tighinn a steach.

Introspection, *s.* Sealladh a stigh.

Intrude, *v.* Inntrinn gun chuireadh, rach gun iarruidh; sath a steach, puc a steach, dinn a stigh.

Intruder, *s.* Sgimilear, neach a theid dh' aite sam bi gun sireadh, gun iarruidh.

Intrusion, *s.* Sàthadh steach; dìnneadh; sgimilearachd, inntrinn gun chuireadh, fein-iarruidh, foirneadh.

Intrusive, *a.* Leamh, dan, ladurna, beagnarach.

Intrust, *v.* Earb; cuir earbsa ann.

Intuition, *s.* Grad-eòlas, geur-eòlas, còlas gun oilcan, eòlas nadurra.

Intuitive, *a.* So-aithnichte; geur-inntinneach, nadurra, grad-fhaicinneach.

Intumescence, *s.* At, bolgadh.

Intunable, *a.* Do-ghleusadh, nach gabh ghleusadh.

Inturgescence, *s.* At, bolgadh, bochadh.

Intwine, *v. a.* Figh, pleat, toinn, toinneamh, dualaich. In-twined, *fighte, toinnte, dualaichte.*

† **Inumbrate**, *v. a.* Sgàilich, còmhdaich, duibhrich. In-umbrated, *sgailichte, comhdaichte, duibhrichte.*

Inunction, *s.* Ungadh.

Inundate, *v. a.* Bath le tuil, comhdaich le h-uisge.

Inundation, *s.* Tuil, dilinn, lighe; comh-shruth, comar.

Inurbanity, *s.* Mio-mhodhaileachd.

Inure, *v.* Cleachd, dean ri, cruadhaich. He is inured to it, *tha e air a chleachd ris*, (*no*) *deante ris.*

Inurement, *s.* Cleachdadh, cleachduinn, cruadhachadh; àbhaist.

Inurn, *v. a.* Adhlaic.

Inustion, *s.* Losgadh.

Inutility, *s.* Neo-fheumalachd, neo-thairbhe.

Invade, *v. a.* Thoir ionnsuidh, bris a steach, thoir ruathar; sàruich, claoidh; ding.

Invader, *s.* Namhaid, fear foghail, fobhair, sgriosadair, milltear.

† **Invalescence**, *s.* Slainnte, neart.

Invalid, *a.* Anfhann, anmhunn, lag, fann, breòite; euslan.

Invalid, *s.* Urr euslan, urrthinn, saighdear leòinte; ciurramach, euslan.

Invalidate, *v. a.* Anfhannaich, anmhunnaich; dean faoin.

Invalidity, *s.* Anfhannachd, anfhainneachd, anmhunnachd, laigse, laigsinn, tinneas, euslainnte.

Invaluable, *a.* Luachmhor, ro luachmhor, ro phrìseil, os cionn luach, os cionn prìs, ana-bharra luachmhor, sàr, còrr.

Invariable, *a.* Neo-chaochlaideach, neo-mhùiteach, bunaiteach, neo-atharrachail, seasmhach, bitheanta.

Invariableness, *s.* Neo-chaochlaideachd, bunaiteachd, bunailteachd, seasmhachd; bitheantas.

Invariably, *adv.* Gu neo-chaochlaideach, gu bunaiteach, gu seasmhach; am bitheantas, an comhnuidh.

Invasion, *s.* Ionnsuidh; ruathar.

Invective, *s.* Tàir, tarcuis, cainnt thàireil, trod, sglamhradh, sglamhruinn; criomchaig.

Invective, *a.* Taireil, tarcuiseach, sglamhrach, beumach, sgaiteach.

Invectively, *adv.* Gu tàireil, gu tarcuiseach, gu sglamhrach, gu beumnach.

Inveigh, *v. a.* Dean tair, tarcuisich, càin, masluich, coirich, cronaich, trod, tachair ri.

Inveigher, *s.* Fear tàireil, fear tarcuiseach.

Inveigle, *v. a.* Meall, thoir a thaobh; tàlaidh, rib. Inveigled, *meallta, ribte.*

Inveigler, *s.* Mealltair, ribeadair.

Invent, *v. a.* Faigh a mach, tionnsgain, cnuasaich; dealbh, deilbh, smaoinich, smuainich, tùir.

Invention, *s.* Innleachd, inntleachd; tùradh, faotainn a mach; tionnsgnadh, tapachd.

Inventor, *s.* Fear innleachd, dealbhadair, innleachd air; cùinneadair, fear deilbh.

Inventive, *a.* Innleachdach, tionnsgalach, tùrail.

Inventory, *s.* Clàr amais, cunntas maoin.

Inventress, *s.* Ban-innleachdair, ban-dealbhadair.

Inverse, *a.* Tionndaidhte, air mhùgh doigh, air chaochladh doigh.

Inversion, *s.* Tionndadh, mùgh.

Invert, *v. a.* Cuir bun os cionn, tionndadh, cuir air chaochladh doigh.

Invest, *v. a.* Sgeaduich, uigheamaich; cid; cuir an seilbh; (*as an enemy*), iomdhruid, cuairtich, cuir séisd ri.

Invested, *p. part.* Sgeaduichte, uigheamaichte; cuairtichte, iomdhruidte.

Investient, *a.* Sgeadachadh, uigheamachadh, comhdachadh.

Investigable, *a.* So-rannsuchadh, so-sgrudadh, so fhaotainn mach.

Investigate, *v. a.* Rannsuich, sgrud, ceasnaich, lorgaich, faigh a mach. Investigated, *rannsuichte lorgaichte, air fhaotainn a mach.*

Investigation, *s.* Rannsuchadh, sgrudadh, ceasnachadh, lorgachadh, sireadh 'mach.

Investiture, *s.* Toirt seilbh, cur an seilbh.

Investment, *s.* Earradh, aodach, eudach, eididh, deise, culaidh, sgeadachadh, uigheam.

Inveteracy, *s.* Cruadhas; buanas, buanachd; déine; ceann-laidireachd; danarrachd.

Inveterate, *a.* Buan; sean; dian; guineach; danarra; rag; feargach; ceann-laidir, crosda; dùr. An inveterate foe, *namhaid dian;* an inveterate disease, *tinneas buan.*

Inveterateness, *s.* Buanachd; déine, cruadhas.

Inveteration, *s.* Cruadhachadh le buanachd (no) le haois.

Invidious, *a.* Farmadach, gamhlasach, tnùmhor, tnuthmhor, mi-runach, eudmhor.

Invidiously, *adv.* Gu farmadach, gu gamhlasach, gu tnùmhor, gu mi-runach, gu h-eudmhor.

Invidiousness, *s.* Farmad, farmadachd, gamhlas, gamhlasachd, eudmhorachd; galltanas.

Invigorate, *v. a.* Neartuich, beothaich. Invigorated, *neartuichte, beothaichte.*

Invigoration, *s.* Neartachadh, beothachadh.

Invincible, *a.* Do-shàruchadh, do-chlaoidh, do-cheannsuchadh, nach gabh sàruchadh (no) claoidh, nach gabh fairtleachd air; buadhach, buadhmhor, uile-bhuadhach.

Invincibleness, *s.* Buadhmhorachd.

Invincibly, *adv.* Gu do-chlaoidh, gu do-cheannsuchaidh, gu buadhmhor.

Inviolable, *a.* Seunda, coisrigte; do-bhriseadh, neothruaillte, do-thruailleadh; do-bhriseadh; do-chiurradh, nach còir a bhriseadh.

Inviolate, *a.* Gun chiurradh, gun chron, gun dochair; neo-thruaillte, neo-bhriste, gun bhriseadh, slàn.

Invious, *a.* Neo-choisichte, gun slighe, gun rod.

Invisibility, *s.* Neo-fhaicsinneachd, do-fhaicsinneachd.

Invisible, *a.* Do-fhaicinn, neo-fhaicinneach, neo-fhaicsinneach; as an t-sealladh; neo-léirsinneach.

Invisibly, *adv.* Gu do-fhaicinn, as an t-sealladh.

Invitation, *s.* Cuireadh, gairm, iarrtas, iarruidh, sireadh. He got an invitation, *fhuair e cuireadh.*

Invite, *v. a.* Cuir, thoir cuireadh, iarr, gairm, sir; (*allure*), meall. Invite him, *thoir cuireadh dha;* invited, *air chuireadh.*

Inviter, *s.* Fear cuiridh.

Inviting, *a.* Tàladhach; mealltach.

Invitingly, *adv.* Gu tàladhach, gu mealltach.

Invocate, *v. a.* Gairm air, guidh air, asluich.

Invocation, *s.* Gairmeadh, glaodh, guidhe, aslachadh, urnuigh, griosadh.

Invoice, *s.* Clàr (no) cunntas maoin; cunntas lòd luing.

Invoke, *v. a.* Gairm air, glaodh air, guidh air, asluich.

Involuntary, *a.* Neo-thoileach, neo-dheònach, a dh' aindeoin. Involuntarily, *a dh' aindeoin.*

Involution, *s.* Fillcadh; ribeadh, toinneamh, ribleach, prablach.

Involve, *v. a.* Comhdaich; fill; rib, glac; toinneamh, coimeasg; cuir gu dragh.

Invulnerable, *a.* Do-leònadh, do-chiurradh, nach gabh leònadh, nach gabh ciurradh, do-dhochann.

Inwall, *v. a.* Druid a stigh le balladh; pàirc.

Inward, **Inwards**, *adv.* An taobh stigh, a stigh, a steach.

Inward, *a.* A stigh, a steach, ion-mheadhonach.

Inwards, *s.* An taobh stigh, mionach, innigh, greallach.

Inweave, *v. a.* Figh, pleat (no) cas a steach.

Iota, *s.* An naothamh litir do 'n Aibideal ghreugach; pong.

Ipecacuanha, *s.* Seorsa purgaid Innseanaich.

Irascible, *a.* Feargach, cas, crosda, cainnteach diorrasanach; dodach.

Ire, *s.* Fearg, corruich, lasan feirge, miothlachd.

Ireful, *a.* Feargach; crosda; cas.

Irefully, *adv.* Gu feargach, gu crosda; gu cas.

Iris, *s.* Bogha frois, bogha frais, bogha braoin, bogha uisge; bir-bhogha.

Irish, *a.* Eireannach.

Irk, *v. a.* Cuir mio-thlachd, farranaich, brod. It irks me, *tha e a cur mio-thlachd orm; tha e 'cur farrain orm.*

Irksome, *a.* Farranach, mio-thlachdach, neo-thaitneach draghail, maidheanach, fadalach.

Irksomely, *adv.* Gu farranach, gu mio-thlachdmhor, gu draghail; gu màidheanach.

Irksomeness, *s.* Farran, farranachd, mio-thlachd, dragh, draghaileachd, màidheanachd, fadalachd.

Iron, *s.* Iarunn; (*chain*), ceangladh, cuibhreach.

Iron, *a.* Iaruinn, iarnach, iarnaidh, cruaidh mar iarunn, cruaidh; do-bhriseadh.

Iron, *v. a.* Iarnaich, iarunnaich.

Ironical, *a.* Geur-bhriathrach; fanoideach, fochaideach, sgeigeil.

Ironmonger, *s.* Marsant iaruinn.

Iron-mould, *s.* Spot; sgàm, sgàm iaruinn.

Ironwood, *s.* Seorsa fiodha ruaidh a fàs an *America.*

Irony, *a.* Iarunnach, iarnaidh.

Irony, *s.* Sgeig, fanaid, fochaid; ag radh aon ni is callachadh ni eile, cruaidh-fhochaid.

Irradiation, *s.* Dealradh, dearrsadh; drilinn, soillse, soillseachadh.

Irradiate, *v. a.* Dealraich, deàrsaich, soillsich, lannair.

Irrational, *a.* Mi-reusonta; neo-thuigseach, mi-thoinisgeil; mi-iomchuidh; baoth.

Irrationality, *s.* Cion reusoin, cion tuigse, dìth toinisg.

Irrationally, *adv.* Gu mi-reusonta, gu neo-thuigseach, gu mi-thoinisgeil; gu baoth.

Irreclaimable, *a.* Do-leasachadh, do-iompachadh, do-cheannsuchadh, do-smachdachadh.

Irreconcilable, *a.* Do-réiteachadh, do-réiteachaidh, do-chiosnachadh; do-lùbadh; cruaidh-chridheach; neo-fhreagarrach.

Irreconciled, *a.* Neo-chiosnaichte.

Irrecoverable, *a.* Do-aiseag, do-fhaotainn air ais, nach gabh faotainn air ais; do leasachadh, do-leigheasadh.

Irrecoverably, *adv.* Caillte gun dòchas (no) gu tur, tur-chaillte. It is lost irrecoverably, *tha e caillte gu tur.*

Irreducible, *a.* Do-aiseag; do thoirt air ais.

Irrefragable, *a.* Do-dhiùltadh, do-sheunadh, do-chur as àicheadh, nach gabh diùltadh, nach gabh àicheadh; do-fhreagairt. An irrefragable proof, *dearbh do-sheunadh.*

Irrefutable, *a.* Do-chur a mach; nach gabh feagairt.

Irregular, *a.* Mi-riaghailteach, gun riaghailt, gun ordugh; baoth; anameasarra, anabarrach, anabarra.

Irregularity, *s.* Mi-riaghailt, mi-riaghailteachd; eas-ordugh; ana-cneastachd; ana-measarrachd.

Irregularly, *adv.* Gu mi-riaghailteach, thar e cheile, gun riaghailt, gun ordugh, gu h-anacneasta.

Irregulate, *v. a.* Mi-riaghailtich, cuir a ordugh, cuir thar a chèile (no) air aimhreidh.

Irreligion, *s.* Ana-creidimh, ana-creideamh, mi-dhiadhachd, aingidheachd, mi-naomhachd, ain-diadhachd.

Irreligious, *a.* Mi-dhiadhuidh, mi-naomh, neo-naomh, aingidh, anacreideach, baoth; an-diadhuidh.

Irreligiously, *adv.* Gu mi-naomh, gu mi-dhiadhaidh, gu h-aingidh, gu baoth.

Irremeable, *a.* Nach gabh pilltinn air.

Irremediable, *a.* Do-leigheasadh, do-leigheas, do-leasachadh, do-leasachaidh.

Irremissible, *a.* Do-mhathadh, do-laghadh, nach gabh mathadh (no) laghadh, thar maitheanais.

Irremoveable, *a.* Do-charuchadh, do-charuchaidh, do-ghlideachadh.

Irreparable, *a.* Do-fhaotainn air ais; do-leasachadh, do-leasachaidh.

Irreparably, *adv.* Gun leasachadh; gu tur.

Irreprehensible, *a.* Neo-choireach, neo-lochdach.

Irreproachable, *a.* Neo-choireach, neo-chiontach, neo-sgainnealach; gun choire, gun chiont; ionraic.

Irreproachably, *adv.* Gu neo-choireach; gu neo-chiontach; gu h-ionraic.

Irreproveable, *a.* Neo-choireach, neo-lochdach.

Irreproveably, *adv.* Gu neo-choireach, gun choire, gun lochd.

Irresistible, *a.* Do-sheasamh, do-ghabhail roimh, do chur na aghaidh, nach gabh cur na aghaidh, nach fhaodar gabhail roimh.

Irresoluble, *a.* Do-bhriseadh, do-bhruanadh, do-sgealpadh.

Irresolute, *a.* Neo-sheasmhach, neo-shuidhichte, neo-bhunailteach, neo-ghramail, neo-chinnteach, neo-shònruichte, teagmhach, mùiteach; gaoithe, luaineach; luaimneach.

Irresolutely, *adv.* Gu neo-sheasmhach, gu neo-ghramail, gu teagmhach, san turamanaich, san tomhartaich.

Irresolution, *s.* Neo-sheasmhachd; neo-ghramalas, teagmhachd, turamanaich, tomhartaich, iomcheist, iomchomhairle.

Irretrievable, *a.* Do-fhaotainn air ais; do-leasachadh, tur-chaillte. An irretrievable loss, *tur-chall, dubh-challdach.*

Irreverence, *s.* Mi-mhodh, eas-umhlachd, cion urraim, neo-urramachd; mi-naomhachadh.

Irreverent, *a.* Mi-mhodhail, eas-umhal, neo-urramach; mi-naomh.

Irreversible, *a.* Do-atharrachadh, neo-chaochlaideach, nach gabh atharrachadh, do-mhùghadh.

Irrevocable, *a.* Do-thoirt air ais; do atharrachadh, neo-chaochlaideach. An irrevocable doom, *dìt nach gabh atharrachadh (no) caochladh.*

Irrigate, *v. a.* Fliuch, taislich, uisgich, maoth.

Irrigated, *a.* Taislichte, uisgichte.

Irrigation, *s.* Fliuchadh, taisleachadh, uisgeachadh.

Irriguous, *a.* Fliuch, bog, àitidh, uisgidh, uisgichte, braonach, sruthanach.

Irrision, *s.* Gair fanaid, sgeig, fochaid.

Irritable, *a.* Feargach, cas, cainnteach, crosda, drranndanach, aithghearr, goirrid.

Irritate, *v.* Feargaich, brosnaich, brosnuich, buair; stuig, cuir h-uige, graoineagaich. Irritated, *feargaichte, brosnaichte, buairte.*

Irritation, *s.* Feargachadh, brosnach, brosnachadh, buaireadh; graoineag; stuigeadh, cur h-uige.

Irruption, *s.* Briseadh steach, maom, brùchdadh; ionnsuidh.

Is, *v.* Is, tha, ta. It is he who did it, *is esan a rinn e;* he is going, *tha e' falbh;* is it so? *'n ann mar sin a tha e?* it is just so, *is ann ceart (no) direach mar sin tha e;* it is well, *is math e.*

Ischury, *s.* Eigin-fhuail.

Island, *s.* Eilean, oilean, innis, l.

Islander, *s.* Eileanach; innseanach.

Isle, *s.* Eilean, oilean, innis, l.

Issue, *s.* Dòrtadh, sruthadh; (*end*), crioch, buil, ceannthall; (*a seton*), silteach; (*offspring*), siol, sliochd, clann, teaghlach.

Issue, *v. a.* and *n.* Cuir a mach; thig a mach, sruth a mach, dòirt, thig o, thig uaith.

Issueless, *a.* Gun chlann, gun siol.

Isthmus, *s.* Doirlinn, tairbeart, tairbeirt; ceann tìre.

It, *pron.* E, se; i, esa, esan, ise, isan. It struck me, *bhuail e mi;* it struck him, *bhuail se e;* it was it that struck me, *b' esan a bhuail mi;* it is I, *is mise th' ann;* shame on it, *mo nàir air;* from it, *uaithe;* off it, *dheth;* with it, *leis.*

Itch, *s.* Cloimh, sgriobach; tachas; (*desire*), dian-chiocras, ana-miann.

Itch, *v. n.* Bi tachasach; bi 'n càs; gabh fadal; bi 'n geall.

Itching, *s.* Tachas, tachasadh; (*in the sole*), meill-chartan.

Itchy, *a.* Tachasach; carrach, creimeach, guireanach, clomhach.

Item, *conj.* Mar an ceudna, a ris, cuideachd, agus.

Item, *s.* Rud eile; sànas, sméid.

Iterant, *a.* Aithriseach.

Iterate, *v. a.* Aithris, abair a ris.

Iteration, *s.* Aithris, aithriseadh.

Itinerant, *a.* Luaimneach, luaineach, siubhlach, iomrolach, neo-shuidhichte; taisdealach.

Itinerary, *a.* Siùbhlach, taisdealach, tùrusach, falbhanach.

Itinerary, *s.* Leabhar thùrusan.

Its, *a.* A. Its strength, *a neart.*

Itself, *pron.* E féin, e fhein, i féin, i fhéin, esan féin. The thing itself will show, *feuchaidh a chùis e féin e.*

Ivory, *s.* Deud-chnaimh, fiacal (no) tosg oileaphaint.

Ivory, *a.* Deud-chnaimheach, deud-gheal.

Ivy, *s.* Iadh-shlat, eadh-shlat, eitheann.

J.

J. An deicheamh litir do 'n Aibideal.

Jabber, *v. n.* Dean goileam, dean gobais; bi luath-chainnteach.

Jabber, *s.* Goileam, gobais, giolam, faoin-chainnt, glag, glòr, clab.

Jabberer, *s.* Fear goileamach, fear gòbach, glagair, glugair, gobair, clabair.

Jacent, *a.* Sìnte; na shìneadh, na luidhe; na sìneadh.

Jacinth, *s.* Leug buidhe dhearg; seorsa neòinein dheirg.

Jack, *s.* (*A name*), Ian, Eoin; Seoc; (*for boots*), spiolbhot; (*culinary*), inneal a ghluaiseas bior ròstaidh; (*a fish*), geadasg òg; (*cup*), copan leathair, màille. Jack of all trades, *uile-cheardach;* Jack with a lantern, *poidean mearbhail.*

Jackal, *s.* Béist crion a sholaireas airson leomhainn.

Jackalent, *s.* Baoghlan, baothair, burraidh, guraiceach.

Jackanapes, *s.* Sgeigeir, sgiogair, baothan; baoth-chleasaiche, ap.

Jack-boots, *s.* Cois-bheart.

Jackdaw, *s.* Cathag; cnaimh-fhitheach.

Jacket, *s.* Deacait, peiteag, còt goirrid; peiteag mhuilichinneach.

Jack-ketch, *s.* Crochadair; crochdair.

Jack-pudding, *s.* Baoth-chleasaiche, umaidh, amadan.

Jacobine, *s.* Mànach a dh' ordugh àraidh, (*in ornithology*), columan cireanach, seorsa columain aig am bheil top (no) dos air mullach a chinn.

Jacob's-staff, *s.* Crois-lorg; lorg biodaig.

Jacobite, *s.* Leanmhuinneach air na Righribh Stiùbhartach; *Seumasach.*

Jactitation, *s.* Iomairt; udal, saobanachd, siùdanachd.

Jaculation, *s.* Tilgeadh, tilgeil; caitheamh.

Jade, *s.* Drèug, cuileasg, each leasg; each gun aigne, bannsgal, baobh, bidse.

Jade, *v. a.* Sàruich, cuir h-uige, fannaich.

Jadish, *a.* Olc; bidseach; baobhail, siùrsachail; neogheamnaidh.

Jag, Jagg, *v.* Gearr, beairn, bearn, feagaich, neagaich, fiaclaich, grob; bior.

Jag, Jagg, *s.* Feag, neag, gròb; bearn, bior.

Jaggy, *a.* Feagach, neagach, gròbach, bearnach, stobach, biorach; neo-chomhnard, claiseach.

Jail, *s.* Priosun, priosan, gainntir, toll-buth, carcar.

Jail-bird, *s.* Priosunach, fear a bha 'm priosun.

Jailer, *s.* Fear priosuin, fear gainntir; maor.

Jakes, *s.* Tigh oich, tigh beag, tigh cac.

Jalap, *s.* Seorsa purgaid.

Jam, *s.* Millsean, meas air a bhruicheadh le siucar agus uisge.

Jam, *v. a.* Pùc, stailc, teannaich, geinn, sàth, put.

Jamb, *s.* Ursann; peirceall doruis.

Jangle, *v. a.* and *n.* Troid; dean lad, connsaich, conspoid; gleang, gliong.

Jangler, *s.* Fear tapaideach, fear conspoideach; glagair.

Janizary, *s.* Freiceadan an Turcaich.

Janty, *a.* Uallach, riomhach, eireachdail, gasd, deas.

January, *s.* Ceud mhios na bliadhna.

Japan, *s.* (*Eilean ann an* Asia *far an do dhealbhadh obair sgiamh-bhreac an toiseach*). Obair sgiamh-bhreac bhallach.

Japan, *v.* Sgiamhaich; sliob; sgiamh-bhreac.

Japanner, *s.* Sgiamh-bhreacadair, sliobair.

Jar, *v. n.* Gliong, gleang; straoidhil; troid, connsuich, cuir a mach; bi a fonn (no) a gleus.

Jar, *s.* Fuaim neo-bhinn; neo-fhonnmhorachd; fuaim dhéistinneach, droch cordadh, eu-cordadh; tabaid.

Jar, *s.* Soitheach creadha, pigidh.

Jargon, *s.* Cainnt neo-dheas; cainnt bhriste; goileam, lonais; gobais; clab.

Jasmine, *s.* Blàth-làir le fàil cubhraidh.

Jasper, *s.* Clach uasal bhuidhe
Jaundice, *s* A bhuidheach
Jaundiced, *a.* Gu soithich leis a bhuidheach.
Jaunt, *v* Imich (no) rach air chuairt, gabh cuairt, rach air turus bheag
Jaunt, *s.* Tùrus goirrid, gearr-thùrus, cuairt bheag, iomrol
Javelin, *s* Gath, sleagh, craosnach
Jaw, *s.* Peirceall, gial Jawbone, *cnaimh* (*no*) *craimh peirall, cnaimh* (*no*) *craimh géil*, jaw-tooth, *fiacail cùil*
Jealous, *a* Eudmhor, amharusach; tnùthmhor; farmadach, gioragach, eudach, an-amharusach.
Jealously, *adv* Gu eudmhor, gu h-amharusach, gu tnùthmhor, eudach, gu h-araidh an cuis gaoil
Jealousy, *s* Eud, eudmhorachd, amharus; tnùth, tnù, farmad
Jeer, *v a* Fanoid, fanaid, fochaid, mag, sgeig
Jeer, *s* Fanoid, fanaid, fochaid, magadh, sgeig.
Jeerer, *s* Sgeigear, fear fanaid, fear fochaid.
Jeeringly, *adv* Gu sgeigeil, gu fochaideach, gu fanaideach
Jehovah, *s* Dia, ainm Dhé 'sa chainnt Eabhrach.
Jejune, *a* (*Poor*), uireasbhuidheach, uireasbhach, bochd, truagh, (*fasting*), ocrach, acrach, air ocras, air acras; (*empty, barren*), iolamh, falamh, leamh, tiorram, lom, fàs; neo-thorrach, aimrid
Jejuneness, *s* Uireasbhachd, bochduinn, ocras, acras, luime, tioramachd
Jellied, *a.* Slamaichte
Jelly, *s* Millsean air dheanamh do shùgh nan dearcan Frangach; slaman, milis
Jenneting, *s* Seorsa ubhall thràthail
Jeopardous, *a* Tubaisdeach, cunnartach, iomcheisteach, baoghlach
Jeopardy, *s* Iomcheist, cunnart, gabhail, gabhadh, baoghal
Jerk, *v a* and *n* Grad-bhuail, buail gu h-ealamh, buail gu brisg, thoir utag
Jerk, *s* Buille brisg, grad-bhuille, utag, putag, purradh, uladh, grad-thulgadh; tughadh; spraidhe
Jerkin, *s* Deacait, peiteag, cot-goirrid, gearra-chot
Jersey, *s* Dears-I, eilean fogus do 'n Fhrainc, sonruichte airson snàth grinn olainn, snath olainn finealta.
Jerusalem, *s* Plùr na gréine
Jessamine, *s* Lus làir le blàth cubhraidh, seasamain.
Jest, *s* Sùgradh, feal dhà, mire, ealaidh, spuirt, fearas chuideachd, aisdigheachd; spòrs, àbhachas, ball magaidh, + dibhearsain Between jest and earnest, *eadar fheal dhà 's rìreadh*
Jester, *s* Sgeigear, fear spòrsa, baoth-chleasaiche, baoth-shugraiche, umaidh, amadan, baothair
Jestingly, *adv* Ri feal-dhà, ri baothaireachd.
Jesuit, *s* Iosuid, cealgair.
Jesuitical, *a.* Iosuideach; breugach, cealgach
Jesus, *s* Iosa, aon dh' ainmeanna ar slanuighir
Jet, *s* Finichd; (*a spout*), sput, spùtan
Jet, *v a* and *n.* Tilg (no) spùt uisge san adhar, sin a mach, mar rughadh
Jet d'eau, *s* Spùtan uisge.
Jetsam, *s* Faodail gaillinn; maoin a ghiùlaineas tuinn gu tràigh ri h-am anrath cuain.
Jetty, *a* Dubh mar fhinichd
Jew, *s* Iùdhach; Eabhrach Jews, *Iudhaich, Eabhraich*
Jewel, *s* Seud, leug, cloch buaidh; neonaid; graidhean, gaolach A jewel is no better than its worth, *cha 'n fhearr seud na luach.*
Jeweller, *s.* Seudair.
Jewellery, *s* Seudaireachd; seudraidh
Jewess, *s.* Ban-Iudhach, ban-Eabhrach.
Jewish, *a.* Iudhach, Eabhrach
Jewry, *s.* Iudhachd, Eabhrachd
Jews-ear, *s* Scorsa spuinc
Jew's-harp, *s.* Tromp.
Jib, *s* Seòl toisich
Jig, *s* Damhsadh deise, srath-spé; fonn sunntach.
Jig, *v n* Damhs, danns.
Jigmaker, *s* Damhsair sunntach; fidhlear
Jigambob, *s.* Faoineag, gilleagan.
Jilt, *s* Ban-mhealltair, té a mheallas a leannan, fuachaid; bidse.
Jilt, *v. a.* Meall, cuir cùl ri.
Jingle, *v n* Gliong, gleang, gleangraich, ghongraich, dean gleaug, dean gliong (no) gliongarsaich.
Jingle, *s* Gliong, gleang, gleangarsaich, ghongarsaich, ghongraich, gleadhran, gleadhraich
Job, *s* Obair, tùrn, gniomh; ceartach; obair là, obair neo-chiatach, gon, sàth
Job, *v a* and *n* Goin, sàth, dean gnohtuch; reic is ceannaich
Jobber, *s* Ceannaiche, reiceadair; fear gnothuich, oibriche.
Jobbernowl, *s* Umaidh, burraidh, baoghlan, baothair, amadan, amhlair, guraiceach, ceothallan, gobhallan
Jobe, *v. a.* (*In the universities*), troid, tachair ri, cronaich.
Jockey, *s* Gille each, drobhair each, cobair, fear a mharcaicheas each-réise; cealgair, mealltair
Jockey, *v. a* Meall, thoir an car a.
Jocose, *a* Cridheil, sunntach, mear, sugach, suigeartach, ait, sodanach, suilbhear, aighearach, sulchar.
Jocosely, *adv.* Gu cridheil, gu sugach, gu suilbhear
Jocoseness, *s.* Cridhealas, sunnt, mire, aighear, oiteas.
Jocular, *a* Cridheil, sunntach, mear, sugach, suilbhear, suigeartach, aighearach, ait, aobhach, mireagach, sulchar.
Jocularity, *s* Cridhealas, sunnt, mire, suilbhearachd, aighearachd, aiteas, sulchaire.
Jocund, *a* Cridheil, aobhach, aoibhinn, éibhinn, ait, sunntach, suilbhear, sodanach, beothail, biolagach, sulchar.
Jocundly, *adv* Gu cridheil, gu h-aobhach, gu h-aoibhinn, gu h-ait, gu sunntach, gu biolagach.
Jog, *v. a* and *n.* Crath, seògain; bog, dean bogadanaich, dean gog, pùc, put, purr, thoir utag.
Jogger, *s.* Fear aithiseach, leagair
Jogging, *s* Bogadh, bogadanaich, seòganaich.
Joggle, *v a.* and *n.* Crath, bog, dean bogadanaich.
Join, *v a* and *n.* Tàth, cuir ri, cuir sa chéile, altuich, ceangail, snaim, snuim, dlùthaich; cuplaich; ioc, carraidich; dean co-bhoinn Joined, *ceangailte, tàthte, snaimte, snuimte, dlùthaichte, iocta.* They joined in battle, *chaith iad an dàil a chéile*
Joiner, *s* Saor
Joinery, *s* Saorsainneachd.
Joining, *s.* Aoradh, tàth, lùthadh, ceangal
Joint, *s* Lùth, comhladh, alt, ceangal; (*in wood*), gàth; (*of an animal*), ceithreamh ainmhidh Out of joint, *as an alt, air aimhreidh*, a joint of veal, *spolla laoigh.*
Joint, *a* Roinnte, ann comh-roinn; an comh-bhoinn, co-rannaich, coitchionn, ceangailte ri chéile. A joint-heir, *comh-oighre.*

Joint, *v.* Altuich; lùthaich, tàth. Jointed, *altuichte, lùthaichte, tàthte.*

Jointed, *a.* Altuichte, luthaichte, tàthte, ceangailte ri chéile, dlùthaichte; làn ghath; gearrte; snàsta.

Jointer, *s.* Locar tàthaidh.

Joint-heir, *s.* Comh-oighre.

Joint-heiress, *s.* Comh-bhan-oighre.

Jointly, *adv.* An comh-roinn, an comh-bhoinn, cuideachd, maraon, le chéile, combluath, comhlath.

Jointress, *s.* Dubhairiche.

Joint-stool, *s.* Creupan lùthaidh.

Jointure, *s.* Dubhairidh; tochar.

Joist, *s.* Sail; suidhe; spàrr; dìst.

Joist, *v. a.* Sailich, sail.

Joke, *s.* Sùgradh, fal-dhà, feal-dhà, cridhealas, †dibhearsain; abhacas. Between joke and earnest, *eadar fhal-dha is rìreamh.*

Joke, *v.* Dean ealaidh, dean fal-dhà (no) àbhacas. Joking, *ri fal-dha, ri baothaireachd.*

Joker, *s.* Fear ealaidh, fear mear, fear sùgraidh.

Jole, *s.* Gruaidh, gial, pluic; ceann éisg.

Joll, *s.* Straoidhle, buille, bruthadh.

Jollily, *adv.* Gu sùgrach, gu suilbhear, gu subhach, gu h-aighearach.

Jolliness, Jollity, *s.* Sùgradh, mire, subhachas, aighear, ealaidh, sunnt, cridhealas.

Jolly, *a.* Sugrach, sùgach, mear, subhach, aighearach, sunntach, cridheil, suigeartach, sulchar, éibhinn, aoibhinn, ait; (*in person*), reamhar, làn, sultmhor; moigeanach.

Jollyboat, *s.* Sgoth le ceithir ràmhaibh.

Jolt, *v. a.* and *n.* Breab, crath, mar ni cairt air feadh chlocha.

Jolt, *s.* Breab, crathadh.

Jolthead, *s.* Ceann mòr, ceann-pluic; umaidh, guraiceach.

Joltheaded, *a.* Polla-cheannach.

Jonquille, *s.* Lus a chrom-chinn.

Jorden, *s.* Poit mùin, poit fhuail, pigidh mùin, poit leapach.

Jostle, *v. a.* Put, pùc, utagaich, thoir utag, purr; thoir purrag leis an uileann.

Jot, *s.* Dad, smad; dadum; pong; a bheag, an rud is lugha.

Jovial, *a.* Aighearach, subhach, sùgrach, sugach, cridheil, ait, mear, sunndach, aoibhneach, aoibhinn, eibhinn; greannmhor, greannar, sulchar.

Jovially, *adv.* Gu h-aighearach, gu subhach, gu cridheil, gu h-ait, gu mear, gu sunndach, gu h-aoibhinn, gu greannar, gu sulchar.

Jovialness, *s.* Aighearachd, subhachas, sùgradh, mire, cridhealas, aiteas, luathghair, sunnt, aoibhneas, éibhneas, sulchaire.

Journal, *s.* Cunntas làthail; paipeir nuaidheachd lathail.

Journey, *s.* Tùrus, taisdeal, slighe, siubhal, astar, cuairt.

Journey, *v. n.* Rach air tùrus, rach air chuairt.

Journeyman, *s.* Tuarasdalaiche; fear oibre fastaichte.

Journey-work, *s.* Obair latha.

Joust, *s.* Samhladh catha.

Joy, *s.* Aiteas, gàirdeachas, aoibhneas, éibhneas sunnt, fonn, luathghair, sòlas, gairdeas, cridhealas, suilmhire, suilbhire, mire; meaghairn, aighear, saimh, laichneas. I wish you joy, *gu ma subhach a robh thu, gu ma h-aoibhinn a robh thu;* I wish you joy of it, *gu meal thu e;* there is no joy without annoy, *cha n' eil sòlas gun dòlas;* there is seldom much joy, without some grief at hand, *cha n' fhacas riomh meaghairn mhòr, nach robh na deigh dubh-bhròn.*

Joy, *v. a.* and *n.* Dean aoibhneas, bi gairdeach; comhghairdich.

Joyful, *a.* Ait, aoibhneach, aoibhinn, éibhinn sunntach, fonnmhor, sòlasach, cridheil, suilbhear, subhach, toileach, meaghrach, aighearach, sulchar.

Joyfully, *adv.* Gu h-ait, gu h-aoibhinn, gu h-éibhinn, gu sunntach, gu fonnmhor, gu cridheil, gu suilbhear, gu subhach, gu toileach.

Joyfulness, *s.* Aiteas, aoibhneas, eibhneas, sunnt, fonnmhorachd, sòlas, cridhealas, suilbhearachd, subhachas, toileachas, aighearachd.

Joyless, *a.* Neo-ait, neo-aoibhinn, dòlasach, dubhach, trom, tuirseach, muladach.

Joyous, *a.* Ait, aoibhinn, eibhinn, mear, sunntach, cridheil, subhach, inntinneach, togarrach.

Jubilant, *a.* Caithreamach, caithreimeach, buadhmhor.

Jubilation, *s.* Caithream.

Jubilee, *s.* Féill, ard-fhéill, am sollain; bliadhna saorsaidh.

Jucundity, *s.* Taitneas, sòlas, greannarachd, ciataichead, grinnead.

Judaism, *s.* Iudhachd, creideamh nan Iudhach.

Judge, *s.* Breith, breth, breitheamh; †brith. A good judge, *deagh bhreith.*

Judge, *v.* Thoir breith, breithnich; breathnaich; thoir binn; baralaich, thoir barail, brath. Judge me, *thoir breith orm;* as I judge, *a reir mo bharail-se.*

Judgment, *s.* Breathanas, breitheamhnas; breith; (*opinion*), barail, brath, beachd; (*sense*), tuigse, ciall, toinisg, tonaisg. The day of judgment, *là bhreathnais;* in my jndgment, *a réir mo bharail-se, a reir mo bheachd-sa.*

Judicatory, *a.* Buileachadh ceartais, cuirt-lagha.

Judicature, *s.* Coir ceartas a bhuileachadh; lagh; cuirt ceartais. Court of judicature, *reachd-lann, reachd-airm, reachd-mhod.*

Judicial, *a.* Laghail, riaghailteach.

Judicially, *adv.* Gu riaghailteach, gu laghail, a réir ceartais, a réir lagha.

Judiciary, *a.* Breathnach.

Judicious, *a.* Glic, crionna, eagnaidh, eagnuidh, tuigseach, toinisgeil, ciallach, sicir, seòlta.

Judiciously, *adv.* Gu glic, gu crionna, gu h-eagnaidh, gu tuigseach, gu toinisgeil; gu sicir, gu seòlta.

Judiciousness, *s.* Gliòcas, eagnachd, tuigse, toinisg, ciall.

Jug, *s.* Soitheach dibhe, soitheach beag bronnach, *mog, mug,* cluaisean; crùisgean; fiaradh ciùil na spìdeig.

Juggle, *s.* Cleas, cleasachd; cealg, foill, mealltaireachd.

Juggle, *v. n.* Dean cleasachd; meall.

Juggler, *s.* Cleasaiche, dubh-chleasaiche, cealgair, mealltair. A she-juggler, *ban-chleasaiche.*

Jugglingly, *adv.* Gu cealgach, gu mealltach.

Jugular, *a.* Bràghadach, sgornach, muinealach. The jugular vein, *an fhéith bhràghadach.*

Juice, *s.* Sùgh, sùth, brìgh, bith; bogarachd.

Juiceless, *a.* Tiorram, neo-bhrighar, gun sùgh, gun bhrìgh.

Juiciness, *s.* Sùghmhorachd, sùgharachd, bogarachd.

Juicy, *a.* Sughmhor, sughar, brìghmhor, suthanach, maoth, bogar.

Juke, *v.* Teirinn mar eun; crom an ceann.

Julap, *s.* Deoch leigheis, uisge milis.

Julus, *s.* Lus leth 'n t-samhraidh.

July, *s.* Iùl, mios buidhe, an seachdamh mios do 'n bhliadhna; mios deire' an t-samhruidh.

Jumble, *v. a.* Coimeasg, cuir air, feadh chéile, measgnaich, cuir thar a cheile, crath air feadh chéile.

JUMBLE, *s* Coimeasg, cumasg.
JUMENT, *s.* Ainmhidh cartach, beothach oibre
JUMP, *v.* Leum, surdagaich, thoir surdag, frengair.
JUMP, *s* Leum, leumadh, leumardaich, sùrdag.
JUNCATE, *s* Millsean.
JUNCOUS, *a* Luachrach, làn luachair.
JUNCTION, *s* Coinneachadh; aonachd, cairdeas, comar
JUNCTURE, *s* Tàth, lùth, alt, ceangal; cairdeas, (*of affairs*), cruaidh-chas, càs, teinne, gàbhadh.
JUNE, *s* Og-mhios, mios meadhon an t-samhraidh
JUNIOR, *a* Is òige, a b' oige, iochdrach.
JUNIPER, *s* Aitinn, aiteal, iubhar beinne Juniper-berry, *dearcag aitinn*
JUNK, *s* Focal Innseanach a ciallachadh, bàt beag; mireanna còrcaich
JUNKET, *s* Millsean, bradh (no) aran milis, féisd gun fhios, cuirm dhiomhair, bleid-chuirm, féisd bhleideil.
JUNKET, *v n* Feisd gu bleideil.
JUNTO, *s* Bannal, buidheann, comunn, bann, cruinneachadh
JURAT, *s* Dligheanair, riaghladair.
JURIDICAL, *a.* Abhuineas do chùirt lagha
JURISCONSULT, *s.* Fear comhairle, fear lagha
JURISDICTION, *s* Ranntachd, dligh-chomas, comas laghail
JURISPRUDENCE, *s* Dligh-eòlas, eolas dlighe, eolas lagha.
JURIST, *s* Fear lagha
JUROR, *s.* Fear deuchainn
JURY, *s* Luchd deuchainn, dream a chuirear fo mhiannaibh chum ceartas a bhuileachadh a réir fiannis
JURYMAN, *s* Fear deuchainn
JUST, *a.* Ceart, ionraic, math, deagh, direach, fior, fireannach, cothromach, neo-chiontach, glan, foirfe, dligheach, laghail; riaghailteach. A just cause, *deagh aobhar;* a just reward, *diol dligheach.*
JUST, *adv.* Ceart, direach. Just so, *ceart mar sin, dìreach mar sin;* just as if I were going, *ceart mar gu bithinn a falbh*
† JUST, *s* Samhladh cath.
JUSTICE, *s.* Ceartas, ceirte, còir, cothrom, cothromachd, breathanas. Give me justice, *thoir ceartas dhomh;* justice melts in the mouth of the feeble, *leaghaidh 'chòir am beul an anfhainn*
JUSTICE, *s.* Breith, sith-bhreith.
JUSTICES, *s.* Breitheanna.
JUSTICESHIP, *s* Dreuchd breith.
JUSTIFIABLE, *a.* So-dhionadh, a ghabhas dionadh, sofhireannachadh; a réir ceartais.
JUSTIFIABLENESS, *s.* Ceirte
JUSTIFIABLY, *adv.* A réir ceartais.
JUSTIFICATION, *s* Fireannachadh, dionadh, dion.
JUSTIFICATOR, *s.* Fear fireannachaidh, fear dionaidh.
JUSTIFIER, *s.* Fear fireannachaidh, fear dionaidh.
JUSTLE, *v a* Pùc, purr, put, utagaich, purragaich Justle with your elbow, *thoir utag (no) purrag le d' uileann.*
JUSTLY, *adv.* Gu ceart, gu h-ionraic, gu fireannach, a réir dlighe, a réir ceartais, gu toilltinneach.
JUSTNESS, *s.* Ceartas; ceirte, reusontachd; pongaileachd, cubhaidheachd
JUT, *v n.* Sin a mach, buail a mach; stùc.
JUVENILE, *a.* Og, ògail, balachail, òganta.
JUVENILITY, *s* Òige; ògaileachd, ògantachd.
JUXTAPOSITION, *s* Fogusachd. In juxtaposition, *ann am fogusachd.*

K.

K, *s* An t-aon litir deug do 'n Aibideal.
KALENDER, *s.* Miosachan; feilire.
KALI, *s.* Feamuinn; roc, lus mara.
KAM, *a* Cam, crotach, fiar, claon, neo-dhìreach.
KAW, *v. n* Ròc, dean ròcail mar ni fitheach (no) ròcas
KAW, *s* Ròc, ròcail, gàcail
KAYLE, *s* Cailise, cluich nan naoth tholl
KECK, *v n* Bi ri tur thilgc.
KECKSY, *s.* Iteodha
KEDGE, *v* Slaod luing air amhainn
KEDGER, *s* Achdair beag; greimeir, clic
KEEL, *s* Druim luing (no) bàta, druim direach luing; clach dhath, cill
KEELAGE, *s* Càin no cls puirt; paigh, puirt
KEELSON, *s* Planng iochdair luing
KEEL-HALE, *s* Tum bàthaidh, peanas maraiche, nur bheirear tumadh bàthaidh dha.
KEEN, *a* (*Eager*), dian, dùrachdach; damhaireach, gionach, dealaidh; (*sharp*), geur; guineach; goineach, beumnach, sgaiteach; (*pungent*), searbh; doirbh, goirt, geur, urloisgeach A keen wind, *gaoth choimheach*
KEENLY, *adv* Gu dian, gu dùrachdach; gu dealaidh, gu geur, gu guineach; gu searbh, gu doirbh
KEENNESS, *s* Déine; dianad, déinead, géire; geiread, faobhar, searbhas, doirbheas. Keenness of appetite, *ocras, ciocras*
KEEP, *v. a.* and *n* Gleidh, coimhead, cum; tog, àl, cum suas; bac. Keep on your way, *cum air d' adhairt;* keep or last, *mair, gleidh,* keep back, *cum air ais,* keep your bed, *cum do leabaidh,* keep close (*conceal*), *cèil, cum samhach,* keep company, *cum conaltradh;* keep (*defend*), dion, † geard, geardainn, keep (*dwell*), *fuirich, fan, tamhaich; stad,* keep an eye on him, *cum sùil air,* keep, *or* hinder from, *bac, cum o,* keep fair with, *cum beul breagh ri;* keep in repair, *cum suas,* keep him employed, *cum obair ris;* keep (*nourish*), *tog, cum suas, cum tòin ri,* keep out of sight, *cum as an t-sealladh,* keep to yourself, *cum agad fhéinn, cum ort,* keep in prison, *cum an laimh;* keep under, *cum fodh, cum an iochdar, ceannsuich,* he kept hold of me, *ghreamaich e rium, chum e greim dhiom,* keep the fair on the fair-day, *cum an fheill air an là.*
† KEEP, *s* Gleidh, gleadh; † geard; dion.
KEEPER, *s.* Fear coimhid; † geard, dion; fear gleidhidh, coimheadaiche. A keeper of woods, *maor coille,* of game, *eunadair.*
KEEPERSHIP, *s.* Coimheadachd, coimhead, gléidheadh, gleadha, dionadh.
KEEPING, *s* Gleidh, gleidheadh, dion, dionadh, coimhead.
KEG, *s* Buideal, bairill beag; gothan, cingean; tunna.
KELL, *s.* (*In cookery*), càl, (*in anatomy*), sgairt, sgamhan, sgannan saille.
KELP, *s* Feamainn loisgte (no) leaghta, seòrsa luibh mara.
KEN, *s.* Aithne, fios, eòlas.

† KEN, *v. a.* Fainich, fairich, aithnich, faic; thoir a mach.
KENNEL, *s.* Fail chon, con-bhar, tigh chon; brochdluinn.
KENNEL, *s.* Guitear, amar uisge, claise; clabar.
KEPT, *pret.* of keep. Ghleidh, chum; bhac, dion
KEPT, *p. part.* of keep. Gleidhte; dionta
KERCHIEF, *s* Bréid; curachd, sùbag.
KERCHIEFED, *a.* Breidte, curacaichte.
KERF, *s.* Sgoltadh, sgagadh, crion-sgolt; sgoch, sgath
KERN, *s.* Ceatharn, ceatharnach, oglach; saighdear
KERN, *s* (*Handmill*), Bràdh, bràth, braghainn; muileann laimh; (*freebooter*), ceatharn; (*bumpkin*), balaoch, bromanach.
KERN, *v. a.* Cruadhaich; tioramaich; gràinaich, pronn.
KERNEL, *s.* Eitean; eitneach, biadh; (*in anatomy*), fàireag
KERNEL, *v. n.* Abuich; fàireagaich.
KERNELLY, *a* Fàireagach; eiteanach.
KERSEY, *s.* Eudach giobach.
KERSEYMERE, *s.* Eudach finealta air figheadh nam plaideachan.
KESTREL, *s.* Seorsa seobhaig.
KETCH, *s.* Long lòdail
KETTLE, *s.* Aghann, *ceatal*, coire, tulan. Out of the kettle into the fire, *as a choire anns an teine.*
KETTLEDRUM, *s.* Drum, gall-drum
KEX, KECKSY, *s.* Iteodha.
KEX, *s.* Pioban; ribheid, feadan.
KEY, *s.* Iuchair; (*landing-place*), port; laibhrig, clachran. Keys, *iuchraichean*
KEYAGE, *s.* Càin puirt.
KEYHOLE, *s.* Toll iuchrach.
KEYSTONE, *s.* Clach cheangail, clach ghlasaidh, clach mheadhon, iuchair.
KIBE, *s.* Cusb; guirean; meallan tachais. A little kibe, *cusban*
KIBED, *a.* Cusbach, cusbanach, guireanach, tachasach
KICK, *v. a.* and *n* Breab, stramp. You kicked him, *bhreab thu e.* Kicked, *breabta, breabte.*
KICK, *s.* Breab; buille; spraidhe, spreth.
KICKER, *s.* Breabair; breabadair.
KICKING, *s* Breabail.
KICKSHAW, *s* Faoineas, obair amaideach.
KICKSY-WICKSEY, *s.* Bansgal, ainm tàireil airson mna
KID, *s.* Meann, minnean, minigean; (*burden*), cual, druinnse; (*child*), urr air ghoideadh.
KID, *v. n.* Breith meann, beir meann.
KIDDER, *s.* Drùinnsear, fear a cheanglas connadh na chualaibh, fear a cheannaicheas bàrr chum a reic gu daor.
KIDNAP, *v.* Goid, goid leanabh.
KIDNAPPER, *s.* Goidiche (no) meirleach cloinne.
KIDNAPPING, *s.* Goideadh (no) meirle cloinne.
KIDNEY, *s* Àr, àra, arainn; dubhan; luain, (*disposition*), gné, seòrsa, gineal
KIDNEY-BEAN, *s* Pònair Fhrangach.
KILDERKIN, *s.* Leth-bhairill, buideal.
KILL, *v. a* Marbh, cuir gu bàs, mort, murt; mill, cuir gu dìth, cuir an t-anam a, cuir as do. I killed him, *mharbh mi e, chuir mi as da.*
KILLER, *s.* Marbhaiche; mortair, murtair; milltear.
KILLING, *s.* Marbhadh, mortadh, murtadh; cuir gu bàs, milleadh; (*of cattle*), casgradh.
KILN, *s.* Àth A lime-kiln, *àth aoil*, a malt-kiln, *ath bhrachaidh*, a drying-kiln, *ath chruadhachaidh*; a brick-kiln, *àth chriadh-chlach, ath chreadh*, kiln straw, *streathainn, streathainn.*
KILNDRY, *v. a.* Cruadhaich, tioramaich air àth.
KIMBO, *a.* Crom, cam, crosgach; lubta, feachdta. With arms a-kimbo, *le lamhan crosgach.*
KIMNEL, *s.* Ballan; measair.
KIN, AKIN, *s.* Seòrsa, gineadh, cinneadh, cinne, cinneach; daimh, caidreamh, cairdean. Near akin, *dlù an daimh*, kin by blood, *cairdeach.*
KIND, *s* Seòrsa, seòrsda, gné What kind of men are they? *ciod an seorsa* (*no*) *ciod a ghné dhaoine th' annta?* of this kind, *do 'n seorsa so, a leithid so*, of all kinds, *do na h-uile seòrsa.*
KIND, *a.* Còir, suairc, caoimhneil, cairdeil, baigheil, tlùsail, cinneadail; muinntireach, baigheil, fiùghantach, math, carrthanach; (*favourable*), fàbhorach.
KINDLE, *v a* and *n.* Las, fàdaidh, loisg, cuir ri theine, cuir an gabhail, beothaich, gabh, gabh teine Does the fire kindle? *bheil an teine 'beothachadh* (*no*) *'gabhail?* did the fire kindle? *an do ghabh* (*no*) *an do bheothaich an teine?*
KINDLE, *v a.* Beir (no) breith mar ni coinean.
KINDLER, *s* Beothachair, fear fadaidh; brosnuchair, fear beothachaidh, fear fadaidh, fear brosnuchaidh; buairear.
KINDLING, *s.* Beothachadh; lasadh; gabhail; bradhadair
KINDLY, *a* Caomh, caomhail, caoimhneil, fiùghantach, cardeil, cinneadail, suairc, maoth, blàth, carthanach.
KINDLY, *adv* Gu caomh, gu caomhail, gu caoimhneil, gu fiùghantach, gu cairdeil, gu cinneadail, gu suairc, gu maoth, gu blàth, gu còir, gu carthanach, gu fàbhorach.
KINDNESS, *s* Caoimhneas, caoimhne, caoimhnealas, fiughantas, cairdealas, suairceas, baigh, carrthanachd, oirchios, (*goodwill*), gradh, deagh-thoil, deagh-rùn, run cridhe, (*favour*), fàbhor, deagh thurn.
KINDRED, KIN, *s.* Daimh, càirdeas, caidreamh; cairdean, dillsean, dislean, cinneach, cinne, cinneadh. I am next akin to myself, *Is mi 's cairdiche dhomh féin.*
KINDRED, *a.* Cairdeach, dlù an daimh, comh-ghineadach.
KINE, *s.* Crodh, buar, mairt, feudail, spreidh; bà, crodh bainne.
KING, *s* Rìgh; triath, flath, prionnsa, † breas, seaghlan King at arms, *righ shuaicheantas, bollsgair mòr, gairmeadair cogaidh*
KING-APPLE, *s* Seorsa ubhaill.
KINGCRAFT, *s.* Riaghlaireachd, uachdaranachd.
KINGDOM, *s* Rioghachd, iompaireachd; dùthaich, talamh, mòr-roinn.
KINGFISHER, *s.* Gobh-uisge; biorra 'n iasgair, iasgair diomhain; cruitean.
KINGLIKE, KINGLY, *a.* Rioghail, righeil, flathail, oirdheirc, mòr-chuiseach.
KINGLY, *adv.* Gu rioghail; gu flathail; gu mor-chuiseach.
KING'S BENCH, *s* Cùirt (no) beinc an Righ
KING'S EVIL, *s.* Tinneas an righ
KINGSHIP, *s.* Rioghalachd; flathachd; mòrachd
KINSFOLK, *s.* Luchd, daimh, cairdean, caidreamh, luchd gaoil, luchd cinnidh.
KINSMAN, *s* Fear daimh, caraid, fear gaoil, fear cinnidh A kinsman is dear, but a foster-brother is dearer, *is caomh le fear a charaid, ach is e smior a chridhe a chomhalt.*
KINSWOMAN, *s.* Ban-charaid, bana-charaid, bean-chinnidh
KIRK, *s.* Eaglais, *gu h-àraidh*, an Eaglais Albannach
KIRTLE, *s* Gùn uachdair; fàluing uachdrach, earrasaid, fearrasaid; seorsa cosaig
KISS, *v. a* Pòg, thoir pog, thoir pòigean
KISS, *s.* Pòg, pogadh; pògan, pòigean, † ceas.
KISSER, *s.* Pògair.

Kissing, *s* Pògadh, pogarsaich.

Kit, *s* Gogan, cingean, botal mòr, buideal, miosgan, curasan, (*fiddle*), fidheall bheag; buis

Kitchen, *s* Cearn, cearnadh, biadh-chluan, † citsinn, (in Scotland, *food*,) annlan, innlean.

Kitchen-garden, *s*. Gàraidh càil, lios chàil, gàraidh mòr, lios chearn.

Kitchen-maid, *s* Searbhant, ban-oglach, caile shearbhaint.

Kitchen-stuff, *s* Meithreas

Kitchen-wench, *s* Caile shoithichean, dubh-chaile

Kitchen-work, *s* Obair chearn; obair stigh

Kite, *s* Clamhan, claman, clamhan gobhlach, preachan, parra riabhach nan cearc

Kitten, *s* Piscan, piseag, fiseag, piscan cait

Kitten, *v n* Beir piscanan. The cat has kittened, *rug an cat piscanan*

Klick, *v n* Gliog

Klicker, *s* Cliccar, gille greasaiche, fear sgéith leathair.

Knab, *v* Teum, creim, cnuas, cruas

Knabble, *v a*. Creim, cream, teum, tiolam

Knack, *s* Seòl, lathailt, rod, rathad, eòlas, car, teòmachd, luath-lamhachd, faoineas; cleas You have the knack of it, *tha 'n lathailt (no) an car agad air*

Knack, *v n* Cnac, crac, braidhe, sgeilc

Knacking, *s* Cracail, sgeilceil

Knag, *s* Gath; snaim, snuim, snaidhm, snuidhm, meall, mulpan, cnap, crap.

Knaggy, *a* Gathach, snuimeach, meallanach, mulpanach, cnapach

Knap, *s* Meall, meallan, cnap; dùnan; caitean; (*of a hill*), tom; binnean, meall

Knap, *v a* and *n* Creim, cream, teum, tiolam, cnap, cnac, crap, crac, sgeilc

Knapple, *v n* Cnac, crac, bris, sgeilc.

Knapsack, *s* Màileid, mailios, balg; cnap-saic, cuarag

Knar, *s* Cnap, crap, meall, cnot, gath.

Knave, *s* Sgonn, sgonn-bhalaoch, ceabhachdair, crochair, cealgair, sloightear, mealltair, rogair, cluaintear; (*at cards*), balach, (*a servant*), gille, òglach, sgalag Let the knave be kept under, *fear na foille an iochdar*

Knavery, *s* Crochaireachd; slaoightearachd, cluaintearachd, cluain, ceilge, cealgaireachd, foille, feall, cleasachd

Knavish, *a*. Fealltach, cealgach, mealltach, cluainteach, olc, aingidh, slaoighteil, foilleil

Knavishly, *adv*. Gu fealltach, gu cealgach, gu mealltach, gu cluainteach

Knead, *v* Gréidh, greadh, taoisinn, fuin, deasaich

Kneading-trough, *s*. Sgàl, losaid, clar fuinidh

Knee, *s*. Glùn Knees, *glùintean, glùinean, glùnan*, on his knees, *air a ghlùnaibh*, a little knee, *glunan*, a bowing of the knee, *glùn-lùbadh, lubadh glùin, beic.*

Kneed, *a* Glùnach Knock-kneed, *bleith-ghlùnach*

Knee-deep, *a* Airde a ghluin, gu ruig an glùn

Kneel, *v n*. Striochd; dean striochd, lub glùn, rach air do ghlùnaibh, glùn-lub, feachd

Knee-pan, *s* Falaman, falman; sgalan, failcean, falaman a ghluin

Knee-tribute, *s* Striochd, striochdadh, glùn-lubadh; modh

Knell, *s* Beum cluig, creidhil bàis; clag adhlaic

Knew, *pret* of know Dh' fhairnich, dh' aithnich, dh' fhairich I knew you, *dh' aithnich mi thu*, I knew not, *cha robh fios agam*

Knick, *s*. Cnac, crac leis na coragaibh; (*with the teeth*), giosgan.

Knick-knack, *s*. Faoineas; rud fagharsach.

Knife, *s* Sgian; corc, lann, golaidh; † meadach, † meadag, biodag A chopping-knife, *goilibhear, sgian pronnaidh, sgian fcòla*, a two-edged knife, *sgian da fhaobhar;* a pruning-knife, *sgian bearraidh, sgian gairnealair*, a pocket-knife, *sgian phòc*, a pen-knife, *sgian pheann*, a peasant's hacking-knife, commonly worn in a sheath, *sgian dubh*, a pocket-dagger, *sgian achlais*, the handle of a knife, *dorn sgein.*

Knight, *s*. Ridir, righidir, marcair, marcaiche; cùraidh A knight-errant, *ridir seabhaiseach, baoth-ridir, ridir iomralach*, Knight of the Thistle, *Ridir a Chluarain*, a Knight of the Mountain Eagle, *Ridir iolair nam beann*,—the name of an order of knighthood which the Chevalier de St George intended to have conferred on the adherents of his family and fortunes, had he been placed on the Scottish throne, See also Ridir.

Knight, *v a* Ridirich. Knighted, *ridirichte.*

Knighthood, *s* Ridireachd

Knightly, *adv* Gu flathail; gu modhail, gu ridireil.

Knightly, *a* Ridireil, flathail, modhail; sàr, corr

Knit, *v* Figh, figh de dealgaibh; dlùth, dlùthaich, tarruing sa chéile, nòd, cnòd Knitted, *fighte, dlùthaichte, cnòdaichte.*

Knit, *s* Figheadh, dealg-fhigheadh.

Knitter, *s* Dealg-fhigheadair, figheadair dhealg

Knitting, *s*. Figheadh, figheadaireachd; dlùthadh, cnòdadh.

Knitting-needle, *s*. Dealg, dealgan, deilgean

Knob, *s* Cnap, cnapan, meall, meallan, mulp, mulpan, moilp, moilpean; (*of a buckler*), còp, còpan

Knobbed, *a* Cnapach, meallanach, mulpanach

Knobbiness, *s*. Cnapanachd, meallanachd, mulpanachd.

Knobby, *a* Cnapach; cnaparra; meallach, meallanach; cruaidh

Knock, *v a* Buail, straoidhil, stear, spairt, spad, smàil. Knock down, *spairt gu làr, spad gu talamh*, knock off, *sgud*, knock under, *géill*, knock the clown on the ear and the dog on the nose, *buail am balach air a charbad, is am madadh air t-sròin*

Knock, *s* Buille, straoidhle, stear, gnog, gleadhar; sgleafart What a knock you got, *is tu fhuair an gleadhar.*

Knocked, *part.* Buailte, spadte, air a spairt, smàilte, smàlta, air a spadadh, air a smàladh.

Knocker, *s* Bualadair, buailtear, glagan; casur A door-knocker, *glagan doruis*

Knoll, *v* Buail (no) seinn clag adhlaic (no) bàis

Knoll, *s* Tom, toman, cnoc, dùn, dùnan, tuam, torr.

Knop, *s*. (*corruption of* nap) Bad, badan, dos, goisean.

Knot, *s* (*Of a cord*), cnòt, cnòd, snaim, snuim, snaidhm, snuidhm, ceangal, ceangladh; (*cockade*), dos, cocàd, (*in wood*), gath, meall, meallan, cnap; (*confederacy*), bann, bannal, (*a cluster*), baguid, bagaid, bagaist, (*difficulty*), cruadhas, doruinn.

Knot, *v a*. Cnòd, snuim, snaim, cuir snaim, cuir cnòd He who will not knot his thread will lose his first stitch, *am fear nach cuir snaim caillidh e 'cheud ghreim.*

Knot-grass, *s*. Gluineach dhearg Climbing knot-grass, *gluineach dhubh*, spotted knot-grass, *gluineach mhor*, water knot-grass, *gluineach teth*

Knotted, *a* Cnòdaichte, snuimte, snaimte, snuimeach; snaimeach, cruaidh, cnapach; altaichte.

Knottiness, *s* Cruadhas; deacaireachd, ribleachd, rioblachd

Knotty, *a.* Snaimeach, snuimeach; duilich; doilich, deacair, do-fhuasgladh.

Know, *v. a.* and *n.* Aithnich, fainich, tuig, bi fiosrach, bi eolach air. I know well, *tha sàr-fhios agam, tha seall-fhios agam;* I know, *tha fhios agam, a fios agam;* do you know him? *an aithn dhuit e? bheil thu eolach air? am bheil eolas agad air?* will you know him? *am fainich thu e?* I know him by sight, *is aithne dhomh e thaobh faicinn;* as you well know, *mar a tha sàr fhios agad;* know by inquiry, *faigh a mach;* let him know, *innis dha, thoir fios dha;* when he knew their thoughts, *air aithneachadh dha an smuaintean.*

Knowable, *a.* Ion-aithneachadh, so-aithneachadh.

Knowing, *a.* Eòlach, seolta, fiosrach; glic, sgileil.

Knowing, *s.* Faineachadh, farachdainn.

Knowingly, *adv.* Gu h-eòlach, gu fiosrach, a dheòin, le deòin.

Knowledge, *s.* Eòlas, fiosrachadh, tuigse, toinisg, gliocas, fios, sgile; (*learning*), foghlum, ionnsach, ionnsuchadh, oilean, sgoil. He was not there, to my knowledge, *cha robh e 'n sin fhad 's a fhiosrach mi* (*no*) *a réir mo bheachd;* without my knowledge, *gun fhios domh;* a sure knowledge, *sàr-bheachd.*

Known, *p. part.* of know. Aithnichte, air aithneachadh, comharaichte, iomraiteach. He is well known, *tha e air a dheagh aithneachadh;* known for a rogue, *comharaichte air son crochair;* made known, *foillsichte; air innseadh;* known before, *roimh-aithnichte;* notoriously known, *sòn-ruichte, ainmeil.*

Knubble, *v. a.* Buail, straoidhil, stear.

Knuckle, *s.* Rùdan; alt; udan.

Knuckle, *v. n.* Striochd, géill, feachd. He will not knuckle, *cha striochd* (*no*) *cha ghéill e.*

Knuckled, *a.* Rùdanach; altach, altaichte.

Knuff, *s.* Umaidh, baoghlan, ceothallan, gobhallan, burraidh, sgleamhraidh.

Knur, *s.* Cnòd, snuim, snaim, meall, mulp.

Koran, *s.* Leabhar lagha Mhathomeid.

L.

L, *s.* An dara litir deug do 'n Aibideal; mar *nuimhir*, is co-ionann i ri (50) leth cheud; ann an cothrom tha i a seasamh airson *punnt;* agus ann cunntas airgid, airson punnt Sasunnach. LL.D., *Ollamh lagha.*

La! *interj.* (*for* lo!) Feuch! faic! seall! faicibh! fhaicibh!

Label, *s.* Sgriob; criomàn paipeir air am bheil ainm ni.

Labent, *a.* Sleamhnachadh.

Labial, *a.* Bileil; bil-fhorlach, liobach, lipeil.

Labiated, *a.* Bileach; fraidheach, liobach.

Laboratory, *s.* Tigh ligheis, bùth lighe.

Laborious, *a.* Saoithreachail, deanadach, gniomhach, seabhasach, cùramach, dìchiollach, easguidh; (*difficult*), duilich, doilich, deacair, cruaidh, duadhmhor, fannachail, cruadalach.

Laboriously, *adv.* Gu saoithreachail, gu deanadach, gu gniomhach; gu cùramach, gu dìchiollach, gu h-easguidh.

Laboriousness, *s.* Saothair, saoithreachas, dìchioll, doghruinn, doruinn, dòruinneachd, seabhasachd, deacaireachd.

Labour, *v.* Saoithrich, oibrich, gabh saothair, cuir ris, éirich air; dean dìchioll, dean spairn; (*endeavour*), dean oidhirp, thoir oidhirp. Labour with child, *bi ri saothair chloinne;* labour in vain, *thoir saothair an diomhain;* labour at thy work, *éirich air d' obair.*

Labour, *s.* Obair, saothair, duadh; gniomh; cruadal, spairn, oidhirp; tràillealachd; (*in childbed*), saothair chloinne, breith cloinne.

Laboured, *a.* Saoithrichte; duilich; le strigh.

Labourer, *s.* Saothairiche, fear obair, oibriche. A fellow-labourer, *comh-oibriche.* Labourers, *luchd-oibre.*

Labouring, *a.* A saoithreachadh, ag oibreachadh. A labouring man, *fear oibre.*

Labouring, *s.* Saothair, saoithreachadh, obair, oibreachadh.

Labyrinth, *s.* Cuairtean, iom-chuairtean.

Lac, *s.* Seòrsa céir.

Lace, *s.*[1] Sreang, stiom, seòrsa ruibein; aigealan; iall, gais, trap; (*fringe*), froinnse; (*for the hair*), fuiltean, failtean.

Lace, *v. a.* (*Tighten*), sreangaich, iallaich, iall, teannaich, ceangail; (*ornament*), sgeadaich, froinnsich, grinnich, greus, riomhaich. Laced, *or* tightened, *sreangaichte, iallaichte, teannaichte;* ornamented, *sgeadaichte, froinnsichte, grinnichte, greusta.*

Lace, *v. a.* (*Strike*), buail, slachduinn, straoidhil.

† **Laced-mutton**, *s.* (*a cant word.*) Siùrsach, striopach, strabaid.

Laceman, *s.* Fear reic sreang, fear iall, sreangair, ialladair.

Lacerable, *a.* So-shracadh, so-reubadh.

Lacerate, *v. a.* Srac, strac, reub, stròic, stroichd; beubanaich.

Laceration, *s.* Sracadh, stracadh, reubadh, stròichd, beubanachd.

Lachrymary, *a.* Deurach.

Lachrymation, *s.* Sileadh dheur, gul, gal.

Lacinated, *a.* Froinnsichte.

Lack, *v. a.* Bi a dh' easbhuidh, bi a dhith, bi am feum, bi an uireasbhuidh. He lacks wit, *tha e dhith tuigse* (*no*) *céill.*

Lack, *s.* Dìth, uireasbhuidh, easbhuidh, gainne, feum, bochduinn. Lack of judgment, *dìth toinisg;* lack of food, *dìth bidh; ocras, acras, gortas;* of custom, *ana-cleachd, dìth cleachd.*

Lackbrain, *s.* Amadan, baoghlan, baothair, amhlair, gobhallan, ceothallan, guraiceach.

Lacker, *s.* Sgrath bhuidhe, falaid bhuidhe.

Lacker, *v. a.* Sliob le falaid bhuidhe, dean buidhe.

Lacking, *a.* Easbhuidheach; uireasbhach, bochd, truagh; a dhìth, ann an dìth. Lacking but little, *ach beag.*

Lackey, *s.* Gille coise, gille ruithe, gille, feamanach.

Lack-lustre, *a.* Dorch, doilleir, dubh; salach, neo-shoilleir.

Laconic, *a.* Gearr, goirrid, aithghearr, cas, cutach; gearrbhriathrach, gearr-chainnteach.

Laconicism, *s.* Gearr-bhriathar, gearr-bhriathrachas, casbhriathar, gearr-chainnt.

Laconically, *adv.* Gu gearr, gu goirrid, gu cas, gu gearrbhriathrach, gu gearr-chainnteach.

Lactary, *a.* Bainnear, bainneach.

Lactary, *s.* Tigh bainne.

Lactation, *s.* Deoghladh, a tabhairt deoghladh, a tabhairt cìche.

Lacteal, **Lacteous**, *a.* Bainneach, bainnear.

Lactescent, *a.* A toirt bainne; bainneach, bainnear.

Lactiferous, *a.* Bainnear, bainneach.

Lad, *s* Balaoch, gille, giullan; òganach, òg, ògan, òigear A young lad, *balachan, giullan*, a stout young lad, *cnapanach gille.*

Ladder, *s.* Àr, àradh; fàr, fàradh; dreamair.

Lade, *s* Beul aimhne.

Lade, *v a* Luchdaich, lion; lòd, cuir lod air, cuir eallach air; (*as water*), taom, taomaich, falmhaich, tilg mach

Lading, *s.* Luchd, làn, lòd, callach, eithre, last, lionadh A ship's lading, *lòd luing.*

Laden, *part* Luchdaichte, lionte, làn, fo' eallaich. Laden with honour, *luchdaichte le h-onoir.*

Ladle, *s* Liadh, ladar; taoman The fill of a ladle, *làn leidh.*

Ladleful, *s* Làn leidh, taomadh.

Lady, *s* Bain-tighearn, ban-tighearna, bean uasal, bean ridir, ban-mhorair; nighean diùchd, nighean marcuis, nighean morair. A young lady, *rìmhinn, oigh*

Lady-bird, Lady-cow, Lady-fly, *s* Daolog bheag dhearg; daolag bhreac; clòc-dearg

Ladyday, *s.* Là Mhuir.

Ladylike, *a* Mallta, banail, bandaidh, bain-tighearnail

Ladyship, *s.* Ban-tighearneas, bain-tighearnas, ban-tighearnachd

Lady's-mantle, *s* Crubh-leomhainn, falluing mhuire, còt preasach, nighean an righ.

Lag, *a.* Deireanach; mall, mairnealach, fadalach, leasg; anmhunn, anfhann; a tuiteam air dheireadh.

Lag, *s* Ceann deiridh, deireadh, rumpall; deireanach

Lag, *v n* Bi air dheireadh, tuit air dheireadh; dean mairneal; fannaich; thoir thairis He begins to lag, *tha e teann ri fannachadh (no) toirt thairis*

Lagger, *s* Deireanach; fear athaiseach (no) leasg, lunndair, leisgein, leagair.

Lagging, *s.* Tuiteam air dheireadh, fannachadh; leagaireachd

Laid, *pret.* and *part pass* of lay, which see.

Lain, *p part* of lie Air luidh.

Lair, *s* Fail (no) foil tuirc; sid, leabaidh fhiadh-bheathaich, brocluinn

Laird, *s* Tighearn, fear fearainn

Laity, *s* Sluagh, tuath The laity, *an sluagh, an tuath*

Lake, *s.* See Loch

Lama, *s* Ard-shagart na Tart-thir

Lamb, *s* Uan, luan, lubhan A little lamb, *uanan*, the Lamb, *am Fear-Saoraidh beannuichte*

Lambent, *a.* Sgìobach, sglobanta, mireagach; lighte, iomlaichte

Lambkin, *s* Uanan, uan òg

Lamblike, *a.* Seimh, ciùin, macanta, soitheamh.

Lamb's-wool, *s* Olann uain; lionn air a mheasgadh le suth ubhlan ròiste

Lame, *a.* Crùbach, bacach, crioplach, ciùrramach, deireasach, luirceanach; crioplaichte; suarrach, neo-sgileil, neo-thapaidh. A lame piece of work, *obair shuarrach, obair mu'n laimh*, lame of a leg, *crùbach, bacach*, a lame hand or foot, *lùg*, lame of an arm, *air leth laimh*, lame with age, *breòite*, lame-handed, *lùgach*

Lame, *v a* Dean crùbach, dean bacach, bacaich

Lamellæ, *s.* Sgrathan, leacan tana.

Lamellated, *s* Comhdaichte le sgrathaibh; leacanta, leacaichte

Lamely, *adv.* Gu bacach, gu crùbach, gu crioplach; gu luirceanach, gu suarrach, mu 'n laimh, gu neo-sgileil, gu neo-sheòlta; gu breòite

Lameness, *s.* Bacaichead, crioplachd, suarraichead, breòiteachd

Lament, *v.* Caoidh, caoin, guil, dean bròn, dean cumhadh, dean tuireadh, dean caoidh; sgread, gul-chaoin.

Lament, *s.* Caoidh, caoin, tuireadh, cumhadh, bròn, gulchaoin.

Lamentable, *a.* Brònach, muladach; caointeach, dubhach, cumhach, tuirseach, deurach.

Lamentably, *adv.* Gu brònach, gu muladach, gu dubhach.

Lamentation, *s.* Tuireadh, cumha, cumhadh, caoidh, caoin, caoineadh, bròn; gul-chaoin; triamhuinn, treanadh, ulfhart.

Lamenter, *s.* Cumhadair, caointear, fear bròin, fear monmhorrach.

Lamina, *s* Sgrath, leac than, slige than.

Laminated, *a* Leacarra, leacanta.

† **Lamm**, *v. a.* Sachduinn, buail. Lammed, *slachduinnte, buailte*

Lammas, *s* Liùnasd, lùnasd, lunasdal

Lamp, *s.* Lòchran, buaid, crùisgean, crùisdean, lanndair, coinneal, solus, leus, trillsean, inolis, stapal.

Lamp-black, *s* Seorsa dubhagain airson nam bròga, dubh bhròg

Lampoon, *s.* Aoir, aoireadh; bardachd, rannachd, càineadh, baoth-bhardachd

Lampoon, *v a* Dean aoireadh air, dean bardachd (no) rannachd air, càin

Lampooner, *s.* Aoireadair; fear rannachd, bard, baothbhard, fear càinidh

Lamprey, *s* Buarach na baoidhe; rochnaid, langar lleach.

Lance, *s* Gath, sleagh, gais, geis, bior.

Lance, *v. a.* Gath; gearr; tilg; gon, gath.

Lancer, *s.* Ruibhneach, sleaghair, sleaghadair.

Lancet, *s* Cuisleag, sgian fhola.

Lanch, *v. a.* Tilg, mar ghath

Lancinate, *v a.* Reub, beubanaich, srac; gon, guin, goimh, gath

Lancinating, *a.* Reubach; guineach, goirt, geur; beugach, goimh.

Lancination, *s.* Srac, strac, sracadh, reubadh; gonadh, goimh

Land, *s.* Tir, dùthaich, fearann, fonn, talamh By land and by sea, *air muir is air tìr;* what land on the face of the world? *ciod an dùthaich air druim an t-saoghail?* on land, *air tìr*, main land, *mor-thìr*, lay land, *talamh fàs, talamh bàn*, cared land, *talamh treabhte (no) treabhaidh;* a land between two furrows, *banc, bailc*, an inland country, *meadhon-thìr*, a land cape, *sròin, rughadh, ros, maol;* land forces, *feachd tìr.*

Land, *v a* and *n.* Cuir air tìr, rach air tìr, thig air tìr. We landed them, *chuir sinn air tìr iad*, we landed, *chaidh sinn air tìr*, as soon as we landed, *cho luath 's a chaidh sinn air tìr*, an earing of land, *treabhadh, ar, crann*

Landau, *s* Carbad aigheir.

Landed, *a* Aig am bheil fearann saor (no) oighreachd. Landed property, *oighreachd*, landed, *or* on shore, *air tìr.*

Landfall, *s* Builcachas fearainn, dìleab fearainn

Landflood, *s.* Tuile, lighe, dilinn. Landfloods, *tuiltean.*

Landholder, *s* Fear fearainn; tighearna. Landholders, *luchd fearainn*

Landing, *s.* Dol air tir; tìr; (*landing-place*), clachran, port, càla, (*of a stair*), mullach staidhreach

Landing-place, *s* Clachran, laibhrig; mullach staidhreach.

Landjobber, *s.* Fear a reic (no) cheannach fearainn.

Landlady, *s.* Bean tighe; bean osda. The landlady, *bean an tighe.*

Landless, *a.* Gun fhearann, gun fhonn.

Landlord, *s.* Fear tighe; maighstir; fear tigh-osda, fear tigh mòra. The landlord, *fear an tighe, fear an tigh mhòir;* a good landlord was never laid in the dirt, *cha deach ceann fir math tighe riamh air an òtrach.*

Landmark, *s.* Clach chriche, comhar tìre.

Landscape, *s.* Duthaich, sealladh dùthcha; dealbh.

Landtax, *s.* Cis-fuinn, fonn-chìs.

Landwaiter, *s.* Fear a chumas sùil ciod am bàthar a chuireas luingeas air tìr.

Landward, *adv.* Gu tìr.

Lane, *s.* Sràid chumhann; loininn, lonaig.

Language, *s.* Cainnt, cànain, canmhuin, teangadh, labhairt, uirghioll, uirgheall; comhradh, seanachas. Good language, *deagh-chainnt;* bad language, *droch sheanachas, droch-chainnt;* fair language, *goileam;* speaking many languages, *ioma-chainnteach.*

Languaged, *a.* Iom-chainnteach.

Language-master, *s.* Oid chainntean.

Languid, *a.* Fann, anfhann, anmhunn, lag, teiglidh, tais, gun chlì, tlà, mall; marbh, marbhanta; spaideil, spaideanta, trom, neo-shunntach. A languid look, *sealladh tlà.*

Languidly, *adv.* Gu fann, gu h-anfhann, gu lag, gu teiglidh, gu tais, gun chlì, gu mall, gu trom, gu neo-shunntach.

Languidness, *s.* Fainne, fannachadh, anfhannachd, anfhainneachd, anmhunnachd; laigse, laige, laigsinn.

Languish, *v. n.* Fannaich, searg, crion, caith air falbh, lagaich, fannaich le gaol (no) le tinneas.

Languishing, *a.* Fann, anfhann. A languishing look, *sealladh fann; (in love)*, sealladh gaol-bhlàth, (no) gradhach.

Languishingly, *adv.* Gu fann, gu h-anfhann, gu lag, gu mall, gu mallta, gu seimh.

Languishment, *s.* Fannachadh, anfhainneachd, malltachd, seimhe.

Languor, *s.* Laigse, laigsinn, anfhannachd, an-fhainneachd, anmhunnachd; taise, cion clì, neo-shunntachd, cion sunnt, cion aire.

Laniate, *v.* Reub, srac, beubanaich.

Lanifice, *s.* Obair olainn.

Lanigerous, *a.* Olannach, olainneach.

Lank, *a.* Lasach, neo-làn, neo-theann, seang, sliom, tlà, tlàth; bochd, truagh; tana; falamh.

Lankness, *s.* Truaghas, seangachd.

Lansquenet, *s.* Saighdear coise; seorsa cluich air chairtean.

Lantern, *s.* Lòchran, buaid, trillsean; tigh soluis.

Lantern-jaws, *s.* Aghaidh fhad pheirceallach.

Lanuginous, *a.* Clòimheach; ollach, olainneach.

Lap, *s.* Filleadh, filleag; leabag sgiurt, sgiort; (*when sitting*), glùn; (*of the ear*), leabag.

Lap, *v. a.* Imlich; fill; paisg. Lapped, *imlichte, fillte, paisgte.*

Lapdog, *s.* Measan, crann-chù.

Lapful, *s.* Làn uchd, làn sgiort, làn sgiurt.

Lapidary, *s.* Cloch-ghearradair, cloch-mhìneachair, leug ghearradair, liomhadair.

Lapidate, *v. a.* Marbh (no) cuir gu bàs le clochaibh, clach gu bàs.

Lapideous, *a.* Garbh, clachach, clochach; cragach.

Lapidification, *s.* Clach ghineadh.

Lapidific, *a.* Clach ghineadach.

Lapis, (*In natural history*), clach, cloch.

Lapis-lazuli, *s.* A chlach ghorm.

Lapped, *part.* Fillte, paisgte.

Lappet, *s.* Filleag, leabag.

Lapse, *s.* Aomadh, aom, sruth, sruthadh, ruithe, dol sios, dol seachad; tuisleadh, tuiteam, sleamhnachadh, mearrachd, tapag. The lapse of time, *aom* (*no*) *sruth na h-aimsir.*

Lapse, *v. n.* Aom, tuit chuid is a chuid, sleamhnaich, tuislich.

Lapwing, *s.* Adharcan luachrach; adhaircean, curacag, pibhinn.

Lapwork, *s.* Obair fhillte, obair sam bheil aon chuid air fhilleadh thar cuid eile.

Larboard, *s.* Bord cùlach, taobh clì luing. Starboard and larboard, *bord deas as clì.*

Larceny, *s.* Meirle, bleide, gaduigheachd, goide, goideachd. Petty larceny, *meanbh-bhleide.*

Larch, *s.* Learag.

Lard, *s.* Blonag, muc-bhlonag.

Lard, *v. a.* Reamhraich, blonagaich. Larded, *reamhraichte.*

Larder, *s.* Tigh feòla, feòil thaisgeach.

Lardon, *s.* Sliseag mhuic-fheoil.

Large, *a.* Mòr, tomadach, tomaldach, meudmhor, leathann, leudach, farsuing, farsuinn; pailt; fial. He is at large, *tha e fa sgaoileadh;* make large, *dean mor, dean tomadach, meudaich, leudaich.*

Largely, *adv.* Gu mor, gu tomadach, gu tomaldach, gu leathann, gu leudach, gu farsuing; gu pailt, gu fial.

Largeness, *s.* Meud, meudachd, meudmhorachd, tomad, leud, farsuinneachd, farsuingeachd, pailteachd.

Largess, *s.* Tabhartas, tiodhlac, tiodhlacadh, briob, gibhte; òirchiseachd.

Largition, *s.* Tabhairt, buileachadh.

Lark, *s.* Reubhag, riobhag, uiseag. There is no smoke in the lark's house, *cha 'n eil deathach an tigh na-h-uiseig.*

Larkspur, *s.* Seorsa plùir.

Larum, *s.* Caismeachd, sànas, maoidhm.

Larynx, *s.* Detiach, steic bhràghaid.

Lascivient, *a.* Mear, sunntach, mireagach.

Lascivious, *a.* Drùiseil, macnusach, baoiseach, ana-miannach; neo-gheimnidh; slatail.

Lasciviously, *adv.* Gu drùiseil, gu macnusach, gu baoiseach, gu h-anamannach, gu neo-gheimnidh.

Lasciviousness, *s.* Drùis, drùisealachd, macnusachd, baois, anamhiann, mi-gheimnidheachd.

Lash, *s.* Sgiùrsadh; sgiùrsair; cuip; iall, cracair; slat; tàs; beum, gearradh. Under his lash, *fu' smachd.*

Lash, *v. a.* Sgiùrs, cuipinn, buail le slait; gearr; (*bind*), ceangail, dlù-cheangail; fastaich.

Lashed, *part.* Sgiùrsta, cuipinnte; air a sgiùrsadh; ceangailte, fastaichte. Lashed to the helm, *ceangailte ris an stiùir.*

Lasher, *s.* Sgiùrsair; fear sgiùrsaidh.

Lashing, *s.* Sgiùrsadh, cuipinn; cord sgiùrsaidh, iall, ceangladh.

Lask, *s.* Buinneach, sgaird.

Lass, *s.* Caile, cailinn, cailin, oigh, cruinneag, caileag, nighean, rìmhinn, geirseach, geirseag; † toth bhachain.

Lassitude, *s.* Sgìtheas, sgios, fannachd, treachladh; neo-shunnt.

Lass-lorn, *a.* Trèigte le leannan.

Last, *a.* Deireannach, deigheanach; mu dheireadh, a 's deireannaiche. The last hour, *an uair dheireannach;* the last year, *an uiridh;* the year before the last, *air bhò 'n uiridh;* the last man, *am fear mo dheireadh;* the last day, *an là deireannach, la ' bhreathanais;* the last, *an deireadh, an ceann mo dheireadh;* last night, *an reidhir, an raoir;*

the night before last, *air bho 'n raoir;* the last week, *an seachdain so a chaidh;* he breathed his last, *thug e suas an deò, dh' eug e, theasd e.*

Last, *adv.* Air dheireadh, air deireadh, mu dheireadh, air a cheann thall, fa dheireadh, fa dheòidh.

Last, *s.* Ceap, ceap-bròige.

Last, *v. n.* Mair, buanaich, fan.

Last, Lastage, *s.* Luchd, lòd; lòd luing; eìs luing; (*of herrings*), deich mìle sgadan; (*of hides*), dà sheic dheug.

Lasting, *a.* Buan, maireann, maireannach, bith-bhuan, bi-bhuan, seasmhach, sìorruidh, bhuan-mhaireann. A hill on fire is not lasting, *is diombuan an tom is teine ris.*

Lasting, *s.* Buanachadh, marsuinn.

Lastingness, *s.* Buanachd, maireannachd, marsuinneachd.

Lastly, *adv.* Mu dheireadh, fa dheòidh, fa dheireadh, san àite as deireannaiche.

Latch, *s.* Iall, iall-chathadh; dealan doruis; stiolan doruis.

Latchet, *s.* Iall, barr-iall.

Late, *a.* Anmoch, anamach, fadalach, mairnealach, maidheanach. The late king, *an rìgh a dh' eug, an rìgh a dh' fhalbh, an sean rìgh.*

Late, *adv.* Gu h-anmoch; a chianamh.

Lated, *a.* Anmoch, anamoch.

Lately, *adv.* Gu h-anamoch; a chianamh, o cheann ghoirrid.

Lateness, *s.* Anamoichead, anamoiche.

Latent, *a.* Uaigneach, céilte, folaichte, falaichte, am folach, uaigneach, diomhair.

Latent, *a.* Is deireannaiche, is anamoiche.

Lateral, *a.* Leth-taobhach, an comhair leth-taobh, taobhach.

Laterally, *adv.* An comhair a thaobh, an comhair a leth-taobh.

Lateran, *s.* Mur a Phàpa san Roimh.

Lateward, *a.* A leth-char anamoch.

Lath, *s.* Spealt thana, sgoiltean maide.

Lathe, *s.* Beairt thuairneir.

Lather, *s.* Cobhar siapuinn; cobhar, còp, siabunn oibrichte.

Lather, *v. a.* Tog cobhar, dean cobhar, oibrich.

Latin, *s.* Laitinn, cainnt nan sean Romhanach.

Latinist, *s.* Laitinnear.

Latinize, *v. a.* Tionndaidh gu Laitinn.

Latish, *a.* A leth-char anmoch.

Latitant, *a.* Folaichte, falaichte, céilte.

Latitude, *s.* Leud, lead, farsuingeachd; (*in geography*), leudad; (*liberty*), comas, rùm.

Latitudinarian, *a.* Neo-chuibhrichte; gun chrioch.

Latitudinarian, *s.* Fear a thréigeas o'n chreidimh cheart.

Latrant, *a.* A tathunnaich, a comhartaich, tathunnach.

Latria, *s.* Ard-aoradh a measg nam Pàpanach.

Latrocination, *s.* Reubainn, reubainneachd, reubaireachd, robainn, robaireachd, spuinne; togail, gaduigheachd; foghluidheachd.

Latten, *s.* Prais, umha; pleòdar.

Latter, *a.* Mu dheireadh, is deireannaiche; is deireannaiche do dhithis; a chianamh, ùr. The latter half, *an leth mu dheireadh.*

† Latterly, *adv.* (*A low word*), a chianamh, o cheann ghoirrid.

Latter-math, *s.* An dara bàrr.

Lattice, *s.* Cliath uinneig; far-uinneag; cliath iarruinn.

Lattice, *v. a.* Cliathraich.

Laud, *s.* Moladh, cliù, urram; iomradh; ainm.

Laud, *v. a.* Mol; glòirich. I lauded him, *mhol mi e.*

Laudable, *a.* Cliù-thoilltinneach, ionmholta; slainnteil.

Laudableness, *s.* Ionmholtachd.

Laudably, *adv.* Gu h-ionmholta.

Laudanum, *s.* Suain-leigheas.

Laugh, *s.* Gàir, golach, fiodadh. A hearty laugh, *gàir cridheil, geal gàir;* a laugh of derision, *gàir fanoid;* a forced laugh, *gàir dh' aindeoin.*

Laugh, *v. a.* Gàir, dean gàir; † fiod, tibh. Laugh at, *dean gàir fanaid;* he began to laugh, *thoisich e air gàrachdaich.*

Laughable, *a.* Neònach, a bhrosnaicheas gàir. It is quite laughable, *is aobhar ghàir e.*

Laugher, *s.* Fear cridheil, fear ealaidh; fear fanaid.

Laughing, *s.* Gàir, gàireachdaich, gàrachdaich, iolach. A laughing from the teeth outwards, *gàir dh' aindeoin.*

Laughing, *a.* Cridheil, sunntach, mear.

Laughingstock, *s.* Ball magaidh, aobhair ghàire, ball abhacais.

Laughter, *s.* Gàireachdaich, gàrachdaich, iolach; gàir-fanaid.

Launch, *v. a.* Cuir air fairge; tarruing, tarruinn; leudaich.

Launch, *s.* Bàt mòr.

Laund, *s.* Reidhlean.

Laundress, *s.* Bean nigheachain, bean nigheadaireachd.

Laundry, *s.* Tigh nigheachain.

Laureate, *a.* Laibhrichte. A poet-laureate, *filidh, ard-fhilidh.*

Laurel, *s.* Laibhreas; laibhreal; luaidhreal; taibhreal. A laurel-tree, *crann laibhreil.*

Lavation, *s.* Nigheadh, ionnlaid, sruthladh, glanadh.

Lavender, *s.* Lothair.

Lave, *v. a.* Nigh, ionnlaid, sruthail; taom.

Laver, *s.* Soitheach nigheachain, measair; soitheach ionlaid, taoman.

Lavish, *a.* Struidheil, strodhail, strodhach, caithteach, sgaoilteach, sgapteach, sgapach, struidheasach.

Lavish, *v. a.* Caith, sgaoil, sgap, cuir a shean, dean droch-bhail, dean struidh, dean ana-caitheamh.

Lavisher, *s.* Fear caithteach, fear struidheil, fear strodhail, fear struidheasach; struidhear.

Lavishment, Lavishness, *s.* Stròdh, struidh, caitheamh, sgabadh, sgaoileadh, ana-caitheamh; droblas, sgaireap.

Law, *s.* Lagh, àithne, ordugh, riaghailt, reachd, foras, achd, dlighe, ceart, còir. The statute law, *lagh nan reachd, an lagh reachdail;* the ceremonial law, *lagh nan gnàthanna;* the common law, *lagh nan chleachdna, lagh nan nòs;* moral law, *lagh nan modhanna;* military law, *lagh airm, feachd lagh;* game laws, *lagh na fiadhachd, dleachd;* a doctor of law, *ollamh lagha;* at law, *aig an lagh.*

Lawful, *a.* Laghail, dligheach; dligheil, ceart, ceadaichte. Not lawful, *neo-laghail, mi-dhligheil.*

Lawfully, *adv.* Gu laghail, gu dligheach, a reir an lagha.

Lawfulness, *s.* Laghaileachd; dligheachd, ceirte.

Lawgiver, *s.* Reachdair, reachdadair; reachd-thabhartair.

Lawless, *a.* Neo-laghail, neo-dhligheach, mi-dhligheach, diobarrach.

Lawlessly, *adv.* Gu neo-laghail, gu mi-dhligheach.

Lawn, *s.* Magh (no) raon eadar dha choille; réidhlean; achadh; anart finealta; anart cléir.

Lawsuit, *s.* Càis lagha.

Lawyer, *s.* Fear lagha; fear tagraidh.

Lax, *a.* Lasach, tuasgailte, fuasgailte; neo-dhiongalta, tuasglach, faoin; (*careless*), coimheis, comadh, neo-shuimeil.

Lax, *s.* Fuasgladh, tuasgladh, buinneach, sgaird, ruithe, ceinn.

Laxation, *s.* Fuasgladh, tuasgladh, lasuchadh.

Laxative, *a.* Fuasglach, fuasgailteach, tuasglach, purgaideach, gluasadach

Laxative, *s* Purgaid.

Laxativeness, *s.* Fuasglachd cuim, gluasad cuim, fuasgladh, tuasgladh, tualag.

Laxity, *s.* Fuasgailteachd, fuasglachd, fosgailteachd.

Lay, *pret.* of lie. Luidh As much as lay in me, *fhad 's a bha e mo chomas*, he is lain, *tha e na luidhe*, they are lain, *tha iad nan luidhe.*

Lay, *v. a.* Leig; cuir; taisg. Lay a foundation, *leig bunaite, suidhich;* lay apart, *cuir gu taobh;* lay by, *cuir seachad, taisg;* lay down, *leig sios, leig a bhàn;* lay in, *taisg, cuir sios, cuir a stigh*, lay hold of, *glac, beir air, cuir an laimh;* lay open, *leig ris, nochd, foillsich, innis, cuir an céill;* lay on, *éirich air, buail;* lay waste, *fàsaich*, lay an egg, *beir ubh*, lay a wager, *cuir geall.* Laid, *leigte*

Lay, *s.* Sreath, breath; leabaidh; (*a bet*), geall

Lay, *s.* Dàn, duan; fonn, òran, ceòl, duanag, luinneag.

Lay, *a.* (land.) Bàn, fiadhair.

Lay, *a.* Neo-chleireach, tuathanach, tuatha, nach buin do 'n chléir.

Layer, *s.* Sread, sreath, breath; leabaidh; cearc a bheireas uibhean.

Layman, *s.* Neo-chléireach; tuathanach.

Laystall, *s.* Otrach, dùcan innearach.

Lazar, *s.* Clamhdair; fear air a mhilleadh le h-eucail.

Lazaretto, *s.* Tigh-eiridinn

Lazily, *adv.* Gu leasg, gu lunndach, gu diomhanach, gu h-athaiseach, gu leagach

Laziness, *s.* Leisge, lunnd, lunndaireachd, leagaireachd, diomhanachd, malltachd; coimhiseachd; athaiseachd; mairnealachd; failliche. Laziness will never permit a man to do a good turn, *cha leig an leisge, da deòin, duine air slighe chòir am feasd.*

Lazy, *a.* Leasg, lunndach, diomhanach, mallta; mairnealach, athaiseach, diomhanach, neo-dheanadach, leagach, neo-ghniomhach, diomhain.

Lea, Ley, *s.* Fiadhair, glas-thalamh, talamh bàn.

Lead, *s.* Luaidh. Lead drops, *luaidh chaol* Leads, *mullach tighe.*

Lead, *v. a.* Treòruich, treòraich, stiùir, sdiùir, seòl, iomain; saodaich, meall, tàlaidh; caith. Lead forth, *thoir a mach, thoir a làthair;* lead the way, *feuch an rathad;* lead a good life, *caith deagh bheath.*

Lead, *s.* Toiseach, tus. He took the lead, *ghabh e an toiseach.*

Leaden, *a* Luaidhe; luaidheach; trom, marbh.

Leader, *s.* Treòrachair; ceann-feadhna; ceannair; ceannard; stiùradair; iùl, ceann iùil; caiptean, comanndair.

Leading, *part. a.* Prìomh; ard, uasal; a treòrachadh. A leading man, *prìomh-fhear;* leading the way, *air thoiseach, a feuchainn an rathaid*

Leading, *s.* Treòrachadh; tarruing; tarragh; tàthadh.

Leaf, *s.* Duille, duilleag; bileag. Leaves (*of trees*), *duilleagan, duilleach;* (of a book), *duilleagan.*

Leafless, *a.* Gun duille.

Leafy, *a.* Duilleach, duilleagach Leafy trees, *craobhan duilleagach*

League, *s.* Comh-bhann, co-bhann, comh-bhoinn, co-bhoinn; bann, bannal, (*in distance*), trì mile, léig.

League, *v. n.* Dean comh-bhoinn, dean comh-bhann Leagued, *ann an comh-bhann.*

Leaguer, *s.* Leigeart, séisd, iom-dhruideadh, saruchadh.

Leak, *s.* Toll a leigeas uisge a stigh; eu-dion.

Leak, *v. n.* Bi eu-dionach, bi neo-dhionach.

Leaky, *a.* Ao-dionach, eu-dionach, neo-dhionach, tolltach, † gnuach; (*talkative*), bruidhneach, gobach, goileamach, lonach.

Lean, *v. a.* Leig taic, leig cothrom, aom, crom, claon Lean upon this, *leig do thaic (no) d' uilinn air so*

Lean, *a* Caol, bochd, truagh, tana, contruagh; neo-reamhar, lom, tiorram. Lean flesh, *feòil thruagh, bliònach*

Leanly, *adv* Gu caol, gu bochd, gu truagh, gu tana.

Leanness, *s* Caoile, caoilead; bochduinn, truaighead, truaghas

Leap, *s.* Leum, sùrdag, cruinn leum.

Leap, *v n* Leum, thoir leum, thoir sùrdag, thoir cruinn leum.

Leaper, *s* Leumadair.

Leap-frog, *s* Seorsa cluich cloinne.

Leaping, *s* Leumnaich, leumartaich

Leap year, *s.* Bliadhna bhisidh, bliadhna-leum.

Learn, *v. a.* and *n.* Ionnsuich, oilein, teagaisg, fòghluim, oileanaich You are not to learn, *cha n' eil thu gun fhios, cha 'n 'eil thu ri ionnsach*

Learned, *a* Ionnsaichte, fòghluimte; oileanaichte, sgileil Learnedly, *gu h-ionnsuichte, gu foghluimte.*

Learner, *s.* Sgoilear.

Learning, *s* Ionnsach, ionnsuchadh, foghlum, oilean, sgoil, eòlas

Lease, *s* Gabhail, aonda, aontainn

Lease, *v a.* Thoir gabhail; thoir aonda.

Lease, *v. a.* Dioghluim, glan, trus, tionail, teanail, cruinnich, tog.

Leash, *s* Bann, iall, ceangal, treas; trì; triùir.

Leash, *v. a.* Ceangail, fastaich. I leashed him, *cheangail mi e.*

Leasing, *s.* Breugan, mealltaireachd

Least, *a* Is lugha, is crìne. The least difference, *an diubhair is lugha*

Least, *adv* Air a chuid is lugha; air a lughaid.

Leather, *s.* Leathar, learach.

Leather-dresser, *s.* Fear dheasachadh leathair, fear chartadh leathair

Leathern, *a.* Leathair, learaich A leathern belt, *crios leathair*, a leathern thong, *iall; crios*, a leathern bag, *bag, maileid, mailios.*

Leave, *s* Cead; comas; aontachadh With your leave, *le d' chead*, take your leave of him, *gabh do chead dheth*, *gabh slàn leis*, absent without leave, *air fulbh gun chomas*, give me leave, *thoir cead domh, leig leam*, without leave, *gun chead, gun chomas*

Leave, *v. a.* Fàg, tréig, cuitich; dealaich ri, cuir cùl ri, leig dhiot. Leave your country, *fàg do dhùthaich*, leave your folly, *leig dhiot d' amaideachd*, leave off, *leig dhiot, sguir.*

Leaved, *a* Duillichte, duilleagaichte; duilleagach.

Leaven, *s* Taois, laibhinn

Leaven, *v a* Taoisinn, laibhinnich Leavened, *taoisinnte*, leavened bread, *aran taoisinnte.*

Leavening, *s* Toisneadh.

Leavings, *s pl.* Fuigheal, fuighleach, spruilleach, iarmad.

Lecher, *s* Fear drùiseil, drusdar, trusdar, slatair An old lecher, *drusdar bodaich.*

Lecherous, *a.* Drùiseil, macnusach, neo-gheimnidh, anamiannach, baoiseil.

Lecherously, *adv* Gu drùiseil, gu macnusach, gu neò-gheimnidh.

Lecherousness, *s* Drùisealachd, macnusachd, baoisealachd.

Lechery, *s* Drùis, neo-gheimnidheachd; baois, ana-miann

Lecture, *s.* Leughadh, leughdachd, mineachadh, searmoin, † ceachd.

Lecture, *v.* Leugh; minich, thoir teagasg am follais

Lecturer, *s.* Leughadair, mìneachair; searmonaiche, ceachadair.

Led, *pret.* and *p part.* of lead. Threòruich; treoraichte A led horse, *each aice*

Ledge, *s* Oir foir, fraigh, iomall; tadhach, trasnan, sread, breath, leabaidh

Ledger, *s.* Leabhar cunntais

Led horse, *s.* Each aice.

Lee, Lees, *s* Grùid, grunnd, deasgainn, deasgannan, drabhag, drabh, druaip.

Lee, *s* (*On sea*), leis The lee side, *an taobh leis, taobh an fhasgaidh*, he came off by the lee, *thainig e as le is chuid is dorra*

Leech, *s* Leigh: deal, dealan, dallag.

Leech, *v. a* Cuir deal ri, deal.

Leechcraft, *s.* Leigheasadh, slànuchadh.

Leek, *s.* Léigis, creamh gàraidh, lios-chreamh

Leer, *s* Scalladh taobh, fiar-shealladh.

Leer, *v n* Thoir fias-shealladh, thoir scalladh taobh

Leering, *a.* Fiar-shuileach, fiar sheallach

Lees See **Lee**

Leet, *s* Là mòid, là cùirt, mòd

Leeward, *a* Leis. The leeward side, *an taobh a leis, taobh an fhasgaidh*

Left, *pret* and *p. part* of leave Thréig, dh' fhàg, tréigte, cuitichte; (*remaining*), air fhàgail

Left, *a* Cearr clì. The left hand, *an lamh chearr, an lamh chlì, a chiotag*, the left wing of the army, *sgiath chlì na feachd.*

Left-handed, *a* Ciotach, cearr-lamhach, clì

Leg, *s* Cos, cas, lurgann, luirigeann, calpa. Leg harness, *cois-bheart*

Legacy, *s.* Dileab.

Legal, *a.* Laghail, dligheil, dligheach, ceart, ceadaichte

Legality, *s.* Laghaileachd, laghalachd, dlighealachd, ceartas, ceirte.

Legally, *adv.* Gu laghail, gu dligheil, a réir an lagha.

Legalize, *v a* Ceadaich, dean laghail Legalized, *ceadaichte.*

Legate, *s* Teachdair; teachdair on Phàp

Legatee, *s* Dìleabaiche.

Legation, *s* Teachdaireachd, cuireadh

Legator, *s* Dìleabach, tionnachair, tiomnaidhear.

Legend, *s.* Faoin-sgeul, fionn-sgeul, ur-sgeul, sgeulachd, seanachas, eachdruidh, aithris.

Legendary, *a.* Ur-sgeulach, seanachail, spleadhach, aithriseil.

Leger, *s.* Leubhair cunntais marsanta.

Legerdemain, *s* Cleasachd, dubh-chleasachd, lamh-chleasachd, caisreabhachd, mealladh

Legged, *a* Cosach, casach

Legible, *a.* So-leughadh, a ghabhas leughadh; soilleir Legibly, *gu soilleir.*

Legion, *s.* Feachd Roimheach mu thuairmeis chùig mìle; feachd, sluagh

Legionary, *a* Feachdail, feachdach.

Legislate, *v. a* Reachdaich, dean lagh.

Legislation, *s.* Reachdadh, reachdaireachd.

Legislative, *a* Reachdail

Legislator, *s* Reachdair, reachdadair; reachd-thabhartair, reachd-dhealbhadair.

Legislature, *s.* Lagh chumhachd, reachd-chomas; dlighe.

Legitimacy, *s* Dligheachd, dlighealachd, laghaileachd, dlisteanas.

Legitimate, *a* Laghail, dligheil, pòsda, pòiste, neo-dhiolan.

Legitimate, *v a* Dean dligheil, dean laghail.

Legitimately, *adv.* Gu dligheil, gu laghail.

Legitimation, *s.* Breith laghail

Legume, *s.* Peasair; gall pheasair, eiteanan peasrach.

Leisurable, *a* Athaiseach, air athais, air socair, socrach.

Leisure, *s* Athais, socair, fois; sobhdan; neo-charraidcachd. Are you at leisure? *bheil thu air d' athais* (*no*) *air do shocair?* she is at leisure, *tha i air a socair*, come at leisure, *thig air do shocair* (*no*) *air d' athais*, at leisure, *socair, socair ort, air do shocair*

Leisurely, *adv* Gu h-athaiseach, gu socrach, gu fòill, gu réidh

† **Leman**, *s* Leannan, graidhean, ceisdean

Lemon, *s.* Lioman, liomaid.

Lemonade, *s* Deoch air a dheanamh suas le h-uisge, siucar, agus liomaid

Lend, *v a.* Thoir an coingheall, thoir an iasad. Lending the devil a mill, *b'e iasad an deomhain do'n mhuilionn e.*

Lender, *s* Fear iasachd.

Length, *s* Fad, astar. In length and breadth, *air fhad 's air leud*, at length, *mu dheireadh, air a cheann thall, fadheoidh.*

Lengthen, *v a.* and *n.* Fadaich, dean ni 's faide; sin a mach, rach am faide, cuir dàil Lengthened, *fadaichte, sìnte*

Lengthwise, *adv.* Air fhad.

Lenient, *a* Maoth, socharach; baigheil, suairc, caoimhneil, maothar, bogar.

Lenify, *v. a.* Dean maoth, dean bogar, ciùinich.

Lenitive, *a* Maoth, socharach, baigheil

Lenitive, *s.* Nì sam bith a choisgeas pian.

Lenity, *s* Baigh, iochd, caomhalachd, suairceas, ciùineas, seimhe

Lens, *s.* Gloine losgaidh, gloine speuclair, gloine amhairc.

Lent, *part.* An coingheall, an iasachd, air choingheall, air iasad.

Lent, *s* Carbhas, carghus, aimsir troisg.

Lentil, *s.* Gall-pheasair, peasair nan luch.

Lentor, *s.* Righneachd; mairnealachd, slamachas.

Lentous, *a.* Righinn, slamachail.

Leonine, *a.* Leòmhannach, leòmhainn

Leopard, *s.* Liopard, liobard.

Leper, *s* Lobhar Lepers, *lobhair, lobhran*

Lepid, *a* Gearr, beumnach

Leprosy, *a.* Loibhre, luibhre, lobharachd, mùire, ballghalar.

Leprous, *a.* Lobhrach, luibhreach.

Lerry, *s* Trod

Less, Lesser, *a* Is lugha, is crìne; ni 's lugha, ni 's crìnè. Much less, *mòran ni 's lugha*, growing less and less, *a dol an lughaid*, you are less than he is, *is tu is lugha na esa.*

Lessee, *s.* Gabhaltaiche, fear aig am bheil gabhail, fear gabhail

Lessen, *v. a.* and *n* Lughdaich, dean ni 's lugha, beagaich, cuir an lughaid, rach an lughaid; irioslaich, leig sios He lessened my allowance, *lughadaich e mo chuibhrionn*, he lessened himself, *dh' irioslaich se e fein*.

LESSON, *s.* Teagasg, leigheann; † leasan; aithne, ordugh · Read a lesson to (chide) one, *troid ri, tachair ri*.

LEST, *conj* An d' eagal, d' eagal, air eagal; gun fhios, san teagamh. Lest he hurt you, *air eagal gun ciùrr e thu*, lest he come not, *air eagal* (or) *d' eagal nach tig e*.

LET, *v. a.* Leig le, ceadaich, ludhaig, fuluing, thoir cead (no) comas, leig air riadh. Let go, *leig air falbh, leig ruithe le*, let in, *leig stigh*; let out on hire, *leig a mach air riadh*; let pass, *leig air dio-chuimhne*, let him past, *leig seachad e*, let him begone, *leig leis a bhith trialladh*; let blood, *thoir fuil o, leig fuil a*; let down, *leig sios* (no) *bhàn*, he let himself to a master, *tha e 'g a chosnn*.

LET, *v. a.* Bac, grab, toirmisg, gabh roimh, stad.

LET, *s.* Bac, bacadh, grabadh, toirmeasg, gabhail roimh, stad.

LETHARGIC, *s.* Codalach, suaineach, turra-chodalach; trom-inntinneach; trom, marbhanta.

LETHARGY, *s.* Clo-chodal, suain-ghalar, turra-chodal, spad-thinneas.

LETHIFEROUS, *a.* Marbhtach, millteach; bàsmhor.

LETTER, *s.* Fear a bheir cead (no) comas; fear a bhacas

LETTER, *s.* Litir. *Letters*, litrichean; (*learning*), ionnsach, foghlum, oilean, sgoil A man of letters, *fear foghluimte*

LETTER, *v a.* Litrich.

LETTERED, *a.* Ionnsuichte, foghluimte, oileanaichte, litrichte, air a litreachadh.

LETTING, *s.* (*Hindering*), bacadh, grabadh A letting of blood, *leigeil fola*; a letting down, *leigeil sios* (no) *a bhàn*; a letting pass, *leigeil seachad*; (*permission*), ceadachadh.

LETTUCE, *s.* Liatus, luibh inite

LEVANT, *s.* Ceann shios Muir na Meadhon-thir

LEVEE, *s.* Éiridh, am éiridh; cuideachd maidne, cuideachd mhoch-thrath; a chuideachd a dh' fheitheas air duine mòr sa mhadainn

LEVEL, *a.* Comhnard, réidh, mìn. A level country, *magh, machair*; a level plot of ground, *reidhlean, réidh, lón*.

LEVEL, *v. a.* Dean comhnard, dean réidh, minich.

LEVEL, *v. n.* Gabh beachd (no) fradharc, comharaich, gabh cuimeis.

LEVEL, *s* (*In surface*), réidhlean, comhnard; réidh, (*of a gun*), amharc; (*equality*), ionannachd, coimeas; (*in masonry*), riaghladh, riaghailt. A carpenter's level, *loman locraidh*, put yourself on a level with him, *cuir thu fèin ann an coimeas ris* (no) *comhad ris*

LEVELLED, *a.* Comhnard, réidh, dìreach, a reir riaghailte

LEVELLER, *s.* Fear a ni comhnard; comh-fhlaitheach.

LEVELLING, *s.* Deanamh comhnard, deanamh réidh

LEVELNESS, *s.* Comhnardachd; comhnard, réidh, ionannachd.

LEVEN. See LEAVEN.

LEVER, *s* Geimbleag, lùdan

LEVERET, *s.* Cuilean maighiche, maigheach òg, gearr-fhiadh.

LEVIABLE, *a* A dh' fhaodar thogail, so-thogail, mar chìs (no) càin, so-chruinneachadh, ion-thogta.

LEVIATHAN, *s.* Croghall mòr; muc-mhara.

LEVIGATE, *v. a.* Pronn, méil; suath; minich

LEVITE, *s.* Léibhitheach, Léibheach.

LEVITICAL, *a.* Léibhitheachail, Léibheachail.

LEVITY, *s.* Eutruime, eutromachd, eutruimeachd, eutruimead, gòrraichead, amaideachd; luaineachd, luaimneachd; guanachd, gogaideachd, gogailleachd; faoineas, gigearsaich.

LEVY, *v. a.* Tog; cruinnich. Levy soldiers, *tog saighdearan*

LEVY, *s.* Togail shaighdearan, togail cìse (no) càin.

LEWD, *a.* Drùiseil, baoiseach, baoiseil; mi-gheimnidh; drabasta, draosda, ana-miannach, neoghlan, siùrsachail, slatail, feòlmhor, teth

LEWDLY, *adv* Gu drùiseil, gu baoiseil, gu drabasta; gu draosda, gu h-ana-miannach, gu neoghlan, gu mi-gheimnidh, gu feòlmhor.

LEWDNESS, *s.* Ana-miannachd, drùis, drùisealachd, mi-gheimnidheachd, neo-gheimnidheachd, neo-ghloine, feòlmhoireachd.

LEWDSTER, *s.* Drùisear, drusdar, trusdar, trudar.

LEXICOGRAPHER, *s* Foclairiche, sgriobhair leabhair-fhocal

LEXICOGRAPHY, *s* Foclaireachd

LEXICON, *s* Foclair, focloir, leabhar fhocal, deachdadair; deachdainnear.

LEY, *s* Talamh bàn, talamh fas, glas-thalamh, fàiche, lón.

LIABLE, *a* Buailteach; coireach, cionntach; freagarrach. Liable to tax, *buailteach do chìs, cìs-bhuailteach*

LIAR, *s.* Breugair; breugag, eithear. Ask the thief if I be a liar, *ceisd bradaig air breugaig*.

LIARD, *a.* Gris-dhearg.

LIBATION, *s.* Iobairt fhiona, iobairt dhibh; iobairt òil.

LIBBARD, *s.* Liobard.

LIBEL, *s* Aoireadh; bardachd; breug-mhasladh; càineadh; saobh-sgriobhadh, tàir chainnt, casaid.

LIBELLER, *s.* Aoireadair, fear dheanamh aoireannan, maslachair, burdanaich, fear-càinidh.

LIBELLOUS, *a.* Maslachail, tàireil, tàir-chainnteach.

LIBERAL, *a* Fial, fialaidh, faoilidh, toir-bheartach, fiùghanta, fiùghantach, tabhartach, daonachdach, uasal The liberal arts, *na h-ealadhain uasal* (no) *ard*; a liberal giver, *fear toir-bheirteach, fear fial* (no) *fiùghanta*

LIBERALITY, *s* Fialachd, fialaidheachd, faoilidheachd, toirbheartas, fiùghantas, féile; gart; eanghnamh, oineach.

LIBERATE, *v a* Cuir fa sgaoil, leig fa sgaoil; saor, thoir saorsadh.

LIBERATION, *s* Saorsadh; saoradh, leigeil (no) cur saor, leigeil fa sgaoil (no) fa réir.

LIBERTINE, *s* Ana-creideach; fear neo-mheasarradh, fear ana-cneasta, fear mi-dhiadhaidh; fear saor, saoranach

LIBERTINE, *a.* Ana-creideach, ana-cneasta, baoth

LIBERTINISM, *s* Ana-creidsinn, ana-cneastachd, ana-mhiann.

LIBERTY, *s.* Saorsadh, saorsa, saorsainn, saorsachd; cead comas; dànadas; an-toil, ana-mhiann At liberty, *saor, fa sgaoileadh*; set at liberty, *saor*; a setting at liberty, *cur fa sgaoileadh, saoradh*, a setter at liberty, *fear-saoraidh*, liberty and equality, *saorsadh is co-ionannachd*, give him his liberty, *thoir a chead dha*; you are at liberty, *tha do chead agad*, you are at full liberty to do it, *tha làn chead agad a dheanamh*

LIBIDINOUS, *a.* Ana-miannach, an-toileach, drùiseil, neoghlan; baoiseil, macnusach, drabasta, draosda

LIBIDINOUSLY, *adv.* Gu h-ana-miannach, gu h-an-toileach, gu druiseil.

LIBRARIAN, *s* Fear-leabhar-lann.

LIBRARY, *s.* Leabhar-lann, leabhradan

LIBRATE, *v n* Co-chothromaich, cothromaich

LIBRATION, *s* Cothromachadh

LICE, *s. pl.* Mialan.

LICENSE, *s* (*Liberty*), comas, cead, saorsadh, ughdarras, antoil: (*permit*), còir; cead, comas

LICENSE, *v a.* Ceadaich, thoir cead do, thoir comas do, ughdarraich.

LICENSED, *a.* Ceadaichte, reachd-shaor.

Licenser, *s.* Ceadachair, fear ceadachaidh.

Licentiate, *s.* Fear a gheibh ainm urraim o cholaisde air bith; ard-sgoilear; fear lagha.

Licentious, *a.* An-toileach, ana-cneasta, neo-mheasarra, mi-riaghailteach; baoth; do-cheannsachadh, ansrianta.

Licentiously, *adv.* Gu h-antoileach, gu h-anacneasta, gu h-anameasarra.

Licentiousness, *s.* Antoil, ana-cneastachd, ana-measarrachd; ain-sriontachd.

Lick, *v.* Imlich. Lick up, *imlich suas.*

Lick, *s.* (*A low word*), buille, stear, gleadhar.

Lickerish, *a.* Lonach, geòcach, ciocrach; samh.

Licorice, *s.* Crann mheal, bioran milis, carr meal, cairmeal.

Lictor, *s.* Beadal a measg nan sean Roimheach.

Lid, *s.* Faircill, brod, clàr, comhdach, failceann, stoipeal. A pot lid, *brod poit;* an eyelid, *fabhradh.*

Lie, *s.* Breug, brionn; fionn-sgeul; sgleò, gò, fabhal; (*of soap and water*), sgùrainn. An arrant lie, *tul-bhreug, dearg-bhreug.*

Lie, *v. n.* Innis breug. You lie, *tha thu'g innseadh* (*no*) *ag radh nam breug, tha thu ris na breugan, tha thu breugach* (*no*) *mealltu;* you lie as much as the dog steals, *tha thu cho bhreugach is a tha 'n cù cho bhradach.*

Lie, *v.* Luidh; sln. Lie by, *gabh fois, fuirich sàmhach;* lie down, *luidh a bhàn, luidh sios;* she lies in, *tha i na luidh-siùbhladh;* lie with, *luidh le;* what lieth in you, *na dh' fhaodas tu, na's urrainn duit;* he is lien down, *tha e air luidh;* lie supine, *leth-luidh, oisìn.*

† **Lief**, *adv.* Gu toileach. I had as lief, *b' àille leam, b' fhearr leam, bu cho mhaith leam;* I had just as lief, *bu cheart cho mhath leam.*

Liege, *a.* Iochdranach.

Liege, *s.* Uachdaran, righ, triath. My liege lord, *m' uachdaran dìlis.*

Lien, *p. part.* of lie; which see.

Lientery, *s.* Seorsa buinnich.

Lieve, *adv.* Gu toileach, a dheòin.

Lieu, *s.* Àite. In lieu, *an àite, airson.*

Lieutenancy, *s.* Fo-uachdranachd.

Lieutenant, *s.* Fo-uachdran; ceannard leth-cheud, fear ionaid.

Life, *s.* Beath; (*soul*), anam; (*breath*), anail; deò; (*world*), saoghal; (*conduct*), caith-beatha, giùlan, iomchar, dol a mach; (*spirit*), spiorad, beothalas, smior, smioralas. In all my life, *re mo làithe, ri ma bheò, fhad 's is beò mi;* put life in him, *cuir spiorad ann;* everlasting life, *beath shìorruidh;* a giving of life, *beothachadh;* long life, *saoghal fad;* to the life, *cruthach;* if you value your life, do it not, *air d' anam na dean e.*

Lifeguard, *s.* Freiceadan, freiceadan righ.

Lifeless, *a.* (*Dead*), marbh, gun deò; (*spiritless*), marbhanta, gun spiorad, trom, neo-bheothail.

Life-rent, *s.* Tuarasdal beò-shlainnte, màl beo-shlainnte.

Lifetime, *s.* Saoghal, beath, là, lò, fad saoghail.

Lift, *v. a.* Tog, tog suas, ardaich. Lifted up, *air a thogail suas.*

Lift, *s.* Togail; eallach, eollach, oidhirp; còghnadh.

Lifter, *s.* Fear togail, fear togalach.

Ligament, *s.* Ceangal, ceangal nan cnaimh.

Ligation, *s.* Ceangladh, fastachadh.

Ligature, *s.* Ceangal.

Light, *s.* Solus, solas, soillse, soilleireachd, leus, sorchadh, glum, soillseachd, deàrsadh; glus; (*candle*), coinneal, coillinn, lòchran. Day-light, *solus an là, àin an la, soilleireachd;* before day-light, *roimh an t-soilleireachd;* bring to light, *thoir am follais, thoir chum soluis;* candle-light, *solus coinnle, solus coille.*

Light, *a.* (*In weight*), eutrom, aotrom; (*in judgment*), guanach, gaoithe, gòrach, gogach, gog-cheannach, gogaill-each; pigheideach; (*not dark*), soilleir; boisgeanta; (*active*), grad, clis, tapaidh, smiorail, smearail, bearraideach; (*merry*), mear, mireagach; (*empty*), falamh, folamh, faoin, fàs; (*in value*), suarrach, faoin. Make light of, *cuir air ioladh.*

Light, *v. a.* Fàdaidh, fàdaich, cuir an gabhail; cuir ri theine, las, beothaich; soillsich; eutromaich.

Light, *v. n.* Teirinn, thig a bhàn, thig a nuas; tuit, tuit air, amais, airmeis. I lighted on (found) it, *dh' airmeis mi air.*

Lighten, *v. a.* and *n.* (*As the clouds*), dealanaich; las; soillsich; (*make light*), eutromaich, dean suilbhear. The clouds lightened, *las na neòil.*

Lighter, *s.* Seorsa bàt; bat eutromachaidh.

Light-fingered, *a.* Bleideil, bradach, deas-lamhach, fadlamhach.

Light-footed, *a.* Luath, luath-chosach, eutrom; clis; beothail, sgairteil.

Light-headed, *a.* Gaoithe, guanach, luaimneach, luaineach, gòrrach, eutrom, gibheasach, gogaideach, gogailleach, gog-cheannach; (*delirious*), ann am breilleas, breilleasach.

Light-headedness, *s.* Guanachd, luainneachd, luaineachd, gogailleachd; breilleas, mire.

Light-hearted, *a.* Sunntach, mear, suigeartach, sodanach.

Lighthouse, *s.* Tigh soluis.

Light-legged, *a.* Eutrom, luath.

Lightless, *a.* Dorch, doilleir; neo-shoillseach; tiomhaidh, uaigneach.

Lightly, *adv.* Gu h-eutrom, gu h-aotrom; (*easily*), gu furas, gu furasda; (*nimbly*), gu luath, gu grad; (*merrily*), gu suuntach, gu sodanach, gu suigeartach.

Lightness, *s.* Eutruime, eatruime, eutromachd, eutruimead, eutromas; (*fickleness*), luaimneachd, luaineachd; (*wantonness*), mire, macnus.

Lightning, *s.* Dealan, dealanach, tein-adhair, teintreach.

Lights, *s.* An sgamhan.

Lightsome, *s.* Soilleir; suilbhear; eutrom aighearach; solasta glan.

Lightsomeness, *s.* Soilleireachd, soillse; suilbhire, aighearachd.

Ligneous, *a.* Fiodha, fiodhach.

Lignum-vitæ, *s.* Seorsa fiodha chruaidh.

Like, *a.* Coslach, cosmhuil, cosmhal, amhuil, ionann, ionsamhuil; mar; (*provincial*), colsach, coldach. He is like me, *tha e cosmhuil riumsa;* like to die, *ris a bhàs;* he is like to die, *tha e thun bàsachadh, tha e ris a bhàs;* he was like to die, *theab e teasd;* like enough, *glè choslach;* not like, *eu-coslach, neo-chosmhuil;* somewhat like, *leth-char coslach;* like a friend, *mar charaid;* in like manner, *air a mhodh cheudna, air a mhodh chiadna; air an lagh cheudna, air an lagh chiadna;* like a man, *gu fearail, gu duineil;* like to be, *thun a bhith, theab a bhith;* there was like to be peace, *theab siochath 'bhith ann.*

Like, *s.* Leithid, samhladh; mac samhuil, leth-bhreac, eugas, aogas, coimeas. I never saw your like, *cha n' fhac mi riamh do leithid;* such like, *a lethid sin, an leithidean sin.*

Like, *v. a.* Togar, gabh ciat do, tagh; bi toigheach. I like her, *is toigh leam i, is toigh leam fhéin i;* he likes her very much, *is ro thoigh leis i, ghabh i ciat mhòr dhith.*

Likelihood, *s.* Coslas, coslachd, cosmhalachd. In all likelihood, *a reir coslais; a rèir na h-uile coslais.*

Likely, *adv.* Coslach, cosmhal, cosmhuil, a réir coslais. It is very likely, *tha e glé choslach.*

Likely, *a.* Coslach, cosmhuil, cosmhalach; eugasach, dàicheil.

Liken, *v. a.* Samhlaich, samhluich, coimeas. Likened, *samhlaichte.*

Likeness, *s.* Samhladh, eugas, aogas, coslas, riochd; samhlachadh; dreach, sunnailt, tiunnal.

Likening, *s.* Samhlachadh, coimeas.

Likewise, *adv.* Mar an ceudna, air a mhodh cheudna, air a mhodh chiadna, air an lagh cheudna, fòs, cuideachd; os barr, a thuille, a thuille air sin (no) so, a bharras air sin (no) so, a bharrachd air sin (no) agus rud eile dheth.

Liking, *s.* Togar, togradh, tlachd, ciat, toil, miann, rùn; deagh chal. According to your liking, *a réir do thoil, a rèir do mhiann;* good liking, *deagh thoil, deagh rùn;* in good liking, *ann an deagh chal.*

Lilach, *s.* Seorsa ràs-chroinn phlùranaich.

Lilied, *a.* Neònanaichte, comhdaichte le neonainibh, neònanach, buidheagach, lilidheach.

Lily, *s.* Neònan, buidheag, lili. Lily, daffodil, *lus a chrom-chinn.*

Lily-livered, *a.* Gealtach, cailleachanta, meat, eagallach.

Limature, *s.* Sgrìoilleach a thig bhàrr iarunn loisgte.

Limb, *s.* (*Of the body*), ball; (*of a tree*), meur, geug, meanglan; (*an edge*), oir, foir, fraighe, iomall. A limb of the law, *fear lagha.*

Limb, *v. a.* Tarruing as a chéile, thoir na mhìreannan, leub.

Limbeck, *s.* Poit thogalach.

Limbed, *a.* Cumta. Well-limbed, *cumadail, glan; cuimir.*

Limber, *a.* Sùbailt, tais, so-lùbaidh, maoth; maothanach, bog. A limber twig, *maothan.*

Limbo, *s.* Àite gun sòlas gun dòlas; gainntir, priosun, toll-buth.

Lime, *s.* Aol; seorsa glaodha. Slacked-lime, *aol bàithte;* bird-lime, *seorsa glaodha a ghlac eoin, bith eoin.*

Lime, *v. a.* Glac; rib; plàsd le aol; math le aol.

Lime, *s.* Teile, crann teile.

Lime, *s.* Seorsa liomaid.

Limeburner, *s.* Aoladair, fear àth aoil.

Limekiln, *s.* Àth aòil.

Limestone, *s.* Clach aoil, cloch aoil. Limestones, *cluchan (no) clochan aoil.*

Lime-water, *s.* Uisge aoil.

Limit, *s.* Crioch, iomall, foir, foir iomallach; teoradh, teoran, †breach.

Limit, *v. a.* Criochnaich, cuairtich, iomallaich; bac, cuibhrich; ceagail. Limited, *iomallaichte, ceangailte;* the limits of a country, *criochan dùthcha.*

Limitary, *s.* Fear crioch-choimhead; criochadair.

Limitation, *s.* Bac, bacadh; crioch; cur crioch (no) iomall ri ni; ceangladh.

Limn, *v. a.* Tarruing, dealbh. Limned, *dealbhta, dealbhte, tarruingte.*

Limner, *s.* Dealbhair, fear tharruing dhealbh.

Limous, *a.* Làthachail, salach, aolar; sleamhuin; sticeach.

Limp, *v. n.* Imich san luirceanachd, bi bacach, bi crùbach.

Limpet, *s.* Cairneach; seorsa faoich.

Limpid, *a.* Glan, soilleir, trid-shoilleir, deàlrach, brisgdheal.

Limpidness, *s.* Glaine, soilleireachd.

Limping, *s.* Luirceanachd; stac crùbaich.

Limpingly, *adv.* Gu bacach, gu crùbach, gu luirceanach.

Limy, *a.* Aolar; salach; lathachail.

Linchpin, *s.* Pinn aisil, tarrag aisil.

Linctus, *s.* Leigheas a theid imlich leis an teangadh.

Linden, *s.* Teile, crann teile.

Line, *s.* (*A line drawn*), lìn, sgrioch, stròc. A little line, *lìnean;* a fishing line, *driamlach, driomlach, drogha;* (*a cord*), sreang, sreangan, toinntean, ruaim, sgéin, cord; (*a plumbline*), sreang riaghailt; (*ancestry*), sliochd, siol, clann, seorsa, cinne, cinneadh; ginealach; (*of battle*), ordugh cath; (*a row*), sread, sreath, breath; (*in fortification*), staing, cladh, clais; (*flax*), lion, lian. They forced the enemy's lines, *bhrùchd iad steach do champ an nàmhaid;* a line in breadth, *an deicheamh cuid do dh' oirleach.*

Line, *v.* Lìnich, lìnig; daighnich.

Lineage, *s.* Siol, sliochd, cinne, cinneadh, ginealach, gineal.

Lineal, *a.* Lìneach, lìnteach; dìreach; dligheach. Lineally, *gu direach.*

Lineament, *s.* Aile; gné; gnuis.

Linear, *a.* Lineach, dìreach.

Lineation, *s.* Lìneachadh.

Linen, *s.* Anart; anrad, lion-eudach. A linen shirt, *léin anairt;* twilled linen, *tùilinn.*

Linen-draper, *s.* Fear reic anairt.

Ling, *s.* Langach; seorsa fraoich; gné éisg.

Linger, *v. n.* Dean maidheàn, dean moille, dean dàil, bi mairnealach; bi an iomchomhairle. Linger out, *cuir dàil, cuir dheth.*

Lingerer, *s.* Fear athaiseach, fear mairnealach.

Lingering, *s.* Moill, mairneal, mairnealachd.

Lingeringly, *adv.* Gu mall, gu h-athaiseach, gu mairnealach.

Lingo, *s.* Cainnt, cànain, cànmhuin, teangadh, seanachas; comhradh.

Linguacious, *a.* Bruidhneach; còmhraiteach, lonach.

Linguist, *s.* Teangair, cànainiche; fear ionnsuichte anns na cainntean.

Liniment, *s.* Cungaidh leigheis, oladh leigheis, sàbh.

Lining, *s.* Lìnig, lìninn, linigeadh. The lining of a horn, *slabhag, slodhag.*

Link, *s.* Tinne; dul; (*torch*), leus, torr-leus; blincean. Links, *tinneachan; leusan.*

Link, *v. a.* Ceangail; tàth; dlùthaich; cuplaich; dlucheangail. Linked together, *dlù-cheangailte ri chéile;* (in affinity), *dlù an daimh.*

Linkboy, *s.* Giullan leòis.

Linking, *s.* Ceangladh, tathadh, dlù-cheangladh, cuplachadh.

Linnet, *s.* Bricean beithe, gealbhan lìn.

Linseed, *s.* Ros, ros lìn, fras lìn.

Linsey-woolsey, *s.* Drògaid; ciolar; aodach lìn is olla.

Linstock, *s.* Fadadh cluaise.

Lint, *s.* Lion; catas.

Lint dam, *s.* Linn lìn.

Lintel, *s.* Ardorus, far-dhorus.

Lion, *s.* Leòmhann, leòghann. A sea-lion, *leomhann mara.*

Lioness, *s.* Leomhann boirionn, ban-leòmhann.

Lionish, *a.* Leomhannta; borb.

Lip, *s.* Lip, liop, bile; (*of a pot*), fraighe; (*of a beast*), gial, bus. Lips, *lipean, bilean.*

Lip-labour, *s.* Briathran gun bhrìgh.

Lipped, *a.* Bileach, lipeach, liopach; fraigheach. Thick-lipped, *clabach.*

Lippitude, *s.* Brach, shuileachd.

Lip-wisdom, *s.* Gliocas beòil.

Liquable, *a.* So-leaghadh.

Liquate, *v. a.* Leagh.

Liquation, *s.* Leaghadh.

Liquefaction, *s.* Leaghadh, leaghachadh.

Liquefiable, *a.* So-leaghadh, so-leaghta, a ghabhas, leaghadh.

Liquefy, *v. a.* and *n.* Leagh. Liquefied, *leaghta, leaghte.*

Liqueur, *s.* Dram cùbhraidh.

Liquid, *a.* Uisgeil, tan; (*in sound*), seimh. The liquid letters, *is iad sin, l, m, n, r.*

Liquid, *s.* Uisge; subhlach, brac.

Liquidate, *v. a.* Glan air falbh, cuir an lughaid, beagaich.

Liquidity, *s.* Uisgealachd, sùbhlachd.

Liquor, *s.* Subhlach; leaghan; deoch; deoch làidir, uisge laidir.

Lisp, *v. n.* Bi liodach (no) manndach, dean briot.

Lisp, *s.* Ag, mannt, liod, briot, mab, mabadh.

Lisper, *s.* Fear agach, fear manndach, fear briotach, fear liodach.

List, *s.* Aireamh, cunntas; ròl, clàr innsidh, ainm-chlàr; (*of cloth*), stiom, ciumhas, stiall, foir; (*in fighting*), aite caonnaig.

List, *s.* Toil, miann, deigh, rùn, togar, àille, taghadh, roghainn. I have no list to go with you, *cha n' eil deigh agam air dol maille riut.*

List, *v. n.* Togair, toilich; miannaich; iarr. Let him go whither he lists, *rachadh e far an togair e.*

List, *v. a.* Gabh; tog; fuaigh. List soldiers, *gabh saighdearan, tog saighdearan;* he listed into the army, *ghabh e sna saighdearan.*

Listed, *a.* Stiollaichte, stiomaichte, stiallach, stiomach, eagsamhuil.

Listen, *v. n.* Eisd, caisd, cluinn, thoir aire. Listening, *ag eisdeachd;* listen to me, *eisd rium, thoir aire dhomh.*

Listener, *s.* Fear far-cluaise; fear èisdeachd; claistear.

Listening, *s.* Eisdeachd, caisdeachd, cluinntinn, claistinn.

Listless, *a.* Neo-omhailleach, neo-umhailleach, mi-sheadhar, neo-chùramach, neo-aireachail; coimheis, coma.

Listlessly, *adv.* Gu neo-omhailleach, gu mi-sheadhar, gu neo-chùramach, gu neo-aireachail.

Listlessness, *s.* Cion omhaile, dìth omhaile, dìth umhaile, cion cùraim, cion aire.

Lit, *pret.* of light. Las.

Litany, *s.* Liotan.

Literal, Literally, *a.* A reir na litreach.

Literary, *a.* Ionnsuichte, oileanaichte, foghluimte, oileanach.

Literati, *s.* Daoine foghluimte; feallsanaich.

Literature, *s.* Ionnsach, ionnsuchadh, oilean, foghlum, feallsanachd.

Litharge, *s.* Luaidh gheal; cac an airgid.

Lithe, Lither, Lithsome, *a.* Sùbailt, maoth, maothanach, so-lùbaidh.

Lithographer, *s.* Cloch-ghrabhair.

Lithography, *s.* Cloch-ghrabhadh.

Lithotomist, *s.* Dearg-leigh a 's urraiun clach thoirt as an aotroman.

Litigant, *s.* Tagartair, tagairtear.

Litigant, *a.* Tagrach; tagluinneach.

Litigation, *s.* Tagairt, tagradh, cùis-lagha, tagairt lagha.

Litigious, *a.* Tagluinneach, tagrach, conn-spoideach.

Litigiously, *adv.* Gu tagluinneach, gu tagrach.

Litigiousness, *s.* Tagluinneachd.

Litter, *s.* Leabadh thogalach, cra-leabadh, leabadh làir; uirigh; leabadh chonnlaich; (*brood*), àl, àlach, bròd; (*for cattle*), fortas; leabadh. The litter of a fox in the den, *saobhaidh.*

Litter, *v. n.* Beir, thoir a mach àl; cuir leabadh fo chrodh.

Little, *a.* Beag, crion, crian, meanbh, cutach, stumpach, iosal. A little while, *tacain bheag, uine bheag, grathuinn bheag;* in a little, *an ceann tacain, eadar so is ceann tacain;* by little and little, *a chuid is a chuid, na bheaganaibh;* very little, *ro bheag, ro chrion;* how little soever it be, *air lughaid sa bheil e;* little finger, *lùdag, cuisdeag;* a little one, *pàisd, leanabh, urrag;* (of a bitch, and of most wild quadrupeds), *cuilean;* (of a bird), *garrag;* (of a cat), *pisean, piseag.*

Little, *adv.* Beagan; ach beag; air bheag; leth-char. A little too much, *beagan tuille's a chòir;* a little fatigued, *leth-char sgìth;* little worth, *suarrach, air bheag luach.*

Little, *s.* Beagan, cuid bheag, beagnaiche, beagnithe.

Littleness, *s.* Crionachd, crionad, crìne, lughad, meanbhad.

Littoral, *a.* Tìreach, cladaich.

Liturgy, *s.* Urnuigh choitchionn.

Live, *v. n.* Bi beò, mair; fan, fuirich. Long live the king, *gu mu fad beò an Righ;* as long as I live, *fhads is beò mi;* as good a man as lives, *duine cho mhath 's a tha beò;* he lives by alms, *tha e tighinn beo air dhéircibh;* where does he live? *c'aite bheil e fanachd?* live on fish, *thig beo air iasg;* does he live? *am beo e? am mair e? am bheil e lathair?* likely to live, *beothail.*

Live, *a.* Beò, maireann, a làthair. Live and well, *beò slàn.*

Livelihood, *s.* (*Maintenance*), beathachadh, aran, teachd an tìr; beathain, tighinn beò; (*estate*), oighreachd, seilbhe, maoin; (*business*), ceaird.

Liveliness, *s.* Beothalachd, beathalachd, smioralachd, tapadh, spiorad, smior, smiodam, anamantachd.

Livelong, *a.* Buan, buan-mhaireann, maireannach. The livelong day, *ré fad an làtha.*

Lively, *a.* Beò, beothail; bochail, brisg, meòghrach, tapaidh, anamanta; smiorail, smearail; biogail, sunntach, togarrach, cridheil; mear, suilbhear. A lively hope, *beò-dhochas.*

Liver, *s.* Grùan, grùbhan, àinean.

Liver-coloured, *a.* Ruadh, dubh-dhearg.

Livery, *s.* Sealbhachadh, gabhail seilbhe; eudach seirbheisich; saoranach bhaile Lunuinn.

Liveryman, *s.* Gille duine uasail; Saoranach bhaile Lunuinn.

Lives, *pl.* of life. Sluagh beò.

Livid, *a.* Dubh-ghorm, gorm.

Lividity, *s.* Guirme.

Living, *a.* Beo, maireann, ann; làthair; (*active*), smiorail, tapaidh, anamanta. To all the living, *do na h-uile bheòthaibh;* is he living? *bheil e beò? bheil e làthair, am beò e?* he is not living, *cha bheò e, cha bheò dha;* a living creature, *ainbhith; anaman.*

Living, *s.* (*Maintenance*), beathachadh, beathain, teachd an tìr, tighinn beò; aran; (*estate*), maoin. How does he gain his living? *cia mar tha e 'coisinn arain?*

Livre, *s.* Cuinne Frangach is fhiach deich sgillinn.

Lixivium, *s.* Uisge sam bheil a theannath salainn.

Lizard, *s.* Dearc luachrach.

Lo! *interj.* Feuch! faic! seall! amhairc! fhaicibh! faicibh!

Loach, *s.* Seorsa éisg aimhne; breac beididh.

Load, *s.* Luchd, lòd; eallach, uallach, eithre, eire; cual, cualag; druinnse, druinnseach; ultach; muirin, maois, maoiseag, † airbhinn; cothrom, truime, truimead. He has a load on his spirits, *tha truime air inntinn*; a cart load, *lòd cartach.*

Load, *v. a.* Luchdaich; truimich; tromaich, lòdaich; cuir eallach air; (*a gun*), lion gunna, *searsuinn.*

Loaded, *a.* Luchdaichte; fo luchd, fo eallaich, fu eithre. as a gun, làn, *searsuinnte.*

Loader, *s.* Luchdair; lòdair, fear luchdachaidh.

Loading, *s.* Luchdachadh.

Loadsman, *s.* Stiùradair, fear stiùir, fear stiùraidh, sgiobair.

Loadstar, *s.* Reannag maraiche, reannag iùil.

Loadstone, *s.* Clach iùil.

Loaf, *s.* Builionn, buileann. A sugar-loaf, *buileann siucair.* Loaves, *builinnean.*

Loam, *s.* Criadh, creuch, talamh reamhar.

Loamy, *a.* Criadhach, creuchaidh; creadha, créich.

Loan, *s.* Coingheall, iasad, iasachd. Give in loan, *thoir an coingheall, thoir an iasad;* out on loan, *a mach air choingheall.*

Loath, *a.* Neo-thoileach, neo-thogarach, ain-deonach; duilich; deacair; gràineil. I am loath to leave you, *is duilich leam d' fhàgail;* it makes me loath, *tha e cur sgreamh* (*no*) *déistinn orm.*

Loathe, *v. a.* Fuathaich, gràinich, oilltich ri, fùrlaich ri; gabh gràin, gabh déistinn, gabh sgreamh (no) sgàth.

Loather, *s.* Fear fuathachaidh.

Loathful, *a.* Fuathach, gràineil, oillteil, deistinneach, sgreamhail.

Loathing, *s.* Fuath, gràin, oillt, déistinn, sgreamh, sgreatas, sgàth.

Loathing, *a.* Fuathach; gràineil, oillteil, deistinneach, sgreamhail.

Loathly, *adv.* Gu h-ain-deonach, gu neo-thoileach.

Loathness, *s.* Ain-deoin, ain-deonachd, mi-thoile.

Loathsome, *a.* Gràineil, oillteil, gràd, sgreamhail, sgreatail, fuathach, fuathmhor.

Loathsomeness, *s.* Gràinealachd, oilltealachd, sgreamhalachd, fuathmhorachd.

Loaves. See **Loaf**.

Lob, *s.* Ni luidseach sam bi; slaodair; leagair; bodach; seorsa duraig; (*lobs-pound*), toll-buth, tigh eiridinn.

Lob, *v. n.* Leig le splad.

Lobby, *s.* Seòmar fosgailte.

Lobe, *s.* Roinn; pàirt, earann; cuibhrionn.

Lobster, *s.* Giomach, gliomach.

Local, *a.* Àiteil; dùthcha, ionadach.

Locality, *s.* Ionadachd; àite, ionad.

Location, *s.* Àiteachadh.

Loch, *s.* Loch, lochan, linn. Loch Tay, *Loch Tatha;* Loch Erochd, *Loch Eireachd;* Loch Earn, *Loch Eire;* Lochness, *Loch Nìos;* Loch Fyne, *Loch Fìne;* Loch Chatterinn, *Loch Chatrian;* Loch Awe, *Loch Abh.*

Lock, *s.* (*Of a door*), glas; crann; (*of wool*), topan, toipean, tutag, tutan; (*of hair*), dual, ciabh, ciabhag; (*in wrestling*), greim, gramachadh; (*of a canal*), glas linn. Under lock and key, *fo ghlas is iuchair; fo mheuran a ghobhainn;* bushy locks, *ciabhagan bachlach.*

Lock, *v. a.* Glais, glas, dùin, druid; (*in the arms*), glac, teannaich. Locked, *glaiste, air a ghlasadh.*

Locker, *s.* Ciste, cisteag; corn-chlar.

Locket, *s.* Crios muineil, coilear; bann.

Lockram, *s.* Seòrsa anairt.

Locomotion, *s.* Gluasad; glideachadh, carachadh.

Locomotive, *a.* Gluasadach.

Locust, *s.* Dreollan teasbhuidh, dreollan.

Lodge, *v. a.* Aitich; suidhich, socraich; taisg; dìon, thoir aoidheachd, thoir ceithreannan oidhche; leig mar arbhar. I lodged him, *thug mi fàrdoch dha, thug mi rum tighe dhà.*

Lodge, *v. n.* Fuirich, fan, tamh, tamhaich, gabh tamh, gabh còmhnuidh; (*as corn*), tuit; laoim.

Lodged, *a.* Aitichte, suidhichte, socraichte; (*as corn*), air tuiteam, leigte, laoimte.

Lodge, *s.* Tigh beag, bothan; tigh samhruidh; teach; tigh geat, tigh portair.

Lodgement, *s.* Àite, àiteachadh; cruinneachadh iongair.

Lodger, *s.* Aoidh, àrosaiche, loisdineach, tùiniche.

Lodging, *s.* Aros, ionad-còmhnuidh, fardoch, fardachd, aoidheachd, fasgadh, dionadh. A night's lodging, *cuid oidhche, ceathrannan oidhche;* I would give him a night's lodging though he had a man's head under his arm, *bheirinn cuid oidhche dha ged bhiodh ceann fir fo achlais.*

Loft, *s.* Lobhta, lobhtadh, faradh; garait.

Loftily, *adv.* Gu h-ard; gu h-uaibhreach, gu h-uallach, gu stàideil, gu h-stràiceil.

Loftiness, *s.* Airde; uaille; uabhar; uaibhreas stràic.

Lofty, *a.* Ard; (*in mind*), uallach, uaibhreach, stràiceil, ard-inntinneach.

Log, *s.* Creamhachdan, creamhchd, smutan, eallag, oirdefhiodh.

Logarithms, *s.* Seòl goirrid air cunntas a dheanamh.

Logbook, *s.* Cunntas mu ghabhail luing.

Loggerhead, *s.* Ceann-maide; baothair, baoghlan, umaidh; umarlan, ceothallan, gobhallan, guraiceach. They went to loggerheads, *chaidh iad an dàil a chéile, shàs iad sa chéile, chaidh iad ann sgornan chéile.*

Logic, *s.* Ealadhain reusonachaidh (no) deisboireachd.

Logical, *a.* Reusonach, riasonach, reusonachail, argumaideach, arguinneach; toinisgeil.

Logician, *s.* Fear deaspoireachd, fear reusonachaidh, arguinniche.

Lohock, *s.* Seorsa leighis.

Logline, *s.* Sreang a thomhaiseas siubhal luing.

Logwood, *s.* Dearg-fhiodh.

Loin, *s.* Blian, leasradh, léis. Loins, *luain, airnean, leasraidh.*

Loiter, *v. n.* Dean maille, dean maidhean, bi mairnealach.

Loiterer, *s.* Leisgean, slaod, slaodair, leagair, lunndair, droll, mairnealaiche; rong; loigear, snàgair.

Loitering, *s.* Slaodaireachd, lunndaireachd, rongaireachd, leagaireachd, loigearachd, snàgaireachd.

Loll, *v. n.* and *a.* Leig taic ri; claon; lethluidh. Loll the tongue, *cuir mach an teangadh;* he is lolling, *tha e na leth-luidhe.*

Lone, *a.* Aonaranach, uaigneach, tiamhaidh; diomhair; singilte.

Loneliness, *s.* Aonaranachd, aonracanachd, uaigneachd; tiamhaidheachd, diomhaireachd.

Lonely, *a.* Aonaranach, aonracanach, uaigneach, tiamhaidh, diomhair, leis fein; *fem.* leatha féin; *pl.* leo féin.

Loneness, *s.* Aonaranachd, uaigneas, tiamhaidheachd, diomhaireachd.

Lonesome, *a.* Aonaranach, uaigneach, tiamhaidh, diomhair, leis féin.

LONG, *a.* Fad; neo-ghearr. A long day, *làth fad;* I think the day long, *is fhad leam an làtha;* how long? *cia fhad? cia cho fad?* as long, *cho fhad;* as long as, *cho fhad ri, fhad is, am feadh;* as long as this, *cho fhad* (*no*) *co fad ri so;* as long as you stay, *fhads a dh' fhuireas tu;* it will not be long ere he come, *cha n' fhad gus an tig e;* long ago, *o chian, o cheann fad;* long enough, *fad gu leòir, fad ni 's leòir;* it is long of you, *is tusa is coireach;* ere long, *a chlisgeadh;* longer, *ni 's fhaide, is fhaide, a 's fhaide;* all my life long, *ré fad mo bheath.*

LONG, *v. n.* Gabh fadail, miannuich, guidh, iarr. He longs for you, *tha e' gabhail fadail asad* (*no*) *air do shon;* longed after, *miannuichte.*

LONGANIMITY, *s.* Fad-fhulangas, fulangas, foighidinn.

LONG-BOAT, *s.* Bat fad.

LONGE, *s.* Sathadh, purradh, putadh, stobadh.

LONGEVITY, *s.* Aosmhorachd, aoismhorachd.

LONGEVOUS, *a.* Aosmhor, aoismhor, sean, fad-shaoghlach, maireann, buan.

LONGIMETRY, *s.* Céin-thomhas.

LONGING, *s.* Ciocras, fadal, dùrachd; (*in pregnancy*), lios.

LONGISH, *a.* Leth-char fad.

LONGITUDE, *s.* Faidead, faideachd, leth-chuairte cruinne; leth chuairte na cruinne air a tomhas o ionad sam bi, an t-astar a tha aite sam bi, an ear no 'n iar, a Lunuinn, no o ard-bhaile dùthcha air bi.

LONGITUDINAL, *a.* Air fad.

LONGITUDINALLY, *adv.* Air fad, air fhad, a thaobh fad.

LONGSOME, *a.* Fadalach, tiortalach.

LONG-SUFFERING, *a.* Fad-fhulangach, foighidneach, foighidinneach; baigheil, caomh.

LONG-WINDED, *a.* (*Tedious*), fadalach; ràsanach; aig am bheil deagh anail.

LONGWISE, *adv.* Air fhad.

LOOBILY, *a.* Leibideach, luidseach, lunndach.

LOOBY, *s.* Sgonn-bhalach; sgonn, baothan, baoghlan, umaidh, burraidh.

LOOF, *v. n.* Rach ri gaoth; fan ri gaoth.

LOOFED, *a.* Air astar.

LOOK, *v. a.* and *n.* Amhairc, seall, faic. Look this way, *seall mar so;* look after or search, *sir;* look after or watch, *cum suil air;* look into, *rannsuich, ceasnuich, sgrud;* look like, *bi coslach* (*no*) *cosmhal ri;* look to, *thoir aire, thoir an aire;* let him look to it, *thugadh e aire;* look before you leap, *amhairc romhad mun toir thu do leum.*

LOOK, *interj.* Seall! faic! fhaicibh! faicibh! feuch! thoir an aire.

LOOK, *s.* Sealladh, aogas, eugas, tuar, coslas, fiamh, amharc, gnùis, aghaidh. A cheerful look, *sealladh sunntach;* a side look, *sealladh cùil;* a lofty look, *sealladh ard;* a down look, *sealladh dùr;* a sour look, *sealladh searbh.*

LOOKER, *s.* Fearr seallaidh, sealladair; spleucair.

LOOKING-GLASS, *s.* Sgàthan.

LOOM, *s.* Beairt, beairt figheadair.

† LOON, *s.* Sgonn, sgonn bhalaoch; crochair; seorsa eòin.

LOOP, *s.* Sùil, sùileag, dul, lùb, lùbag.

LOOPED, *a.* Sùileach, lùbach.

LOOP-HOLE, *s.* Sùil, dul, lùb, toll; port gunna; (*a shift*), seòl, doigh, modh, rathad, slighe.

LOOP-HOLED, *a.* Lùbach, sùileach.

LOOSE, *v. a.* Fuasgail, tuasgail, tulaig, lasaich; thoir lasachadh, leig fa sgaoil, leig ma réir.

LOOSE, *v. n.* Seòl, tog acarsaid.

LOOSE, *a.* (*Slack*), lasach, fuasgailte, tuasgailte, tualaigte, neo-cheangailte; (*hanging down*), leabagach, luidseach, leabhar; fleoganach; (*wanton*), drùiseil, mi-gheimnidh, neo-macnusach; (*dissolute*), neo-riaghailteach, neo-stuama, neo-cheannsuichte; (*in body*), tuasgailte. Break loose, *bris a mach;* set loose, *cuir fa sgaoil, leig tuasgailte.*

LOOSE, *s.* Saorsa, saorsadh, saorsainn, comas, cead.

LOOSELY, *adv.* Gu lasach, gu fuasgailte, as a chéile; (*in morals*), gu neo-stuama, gu mi-riaghailteach.

LOOSEN, *v. a.* Fuasgail, tuasgail, tualaig, sgaoil, thoir as a chéile. Loosened, *fuasgailte, taasgailte, tualaigte, sgaoilte, as a chéile.*

LOOSENESS, *s.* (*Of bowels*), siubhladh, siubhal, buinneach, tualag, ruithe, sgaird; (*of morals*), mi-stuaim, mi-gheimnidheachd, macnus, mi-riaghailt, mi-bheus, dubhailc; (*slackness*), fuasgailteachd, lasachd.

LOP, *v. a.* Gearr, bearr; sgath.

LOP, *s.* Barrach, barralach.

LOP, *s.* Deargann, dearganta.

LOPPER, *s.* Bearradair, gearradair, sgathadair, fear sgathaidh.

LOQUACIOUS, *a.* Bruidhneach, gobach; lonach, gob-easguidh, cainnteach, arraghloireach. A loquacious person, *gobair.*

LOQUACITY, *s.* Bruidhneachd, bruidhinn, gob, gab, cab, gobais, gobaireachd, lonais; siorchainnt; arraghloir.

LORD, *s.* Tighearn; uachdaran, triath; flath, morair, iarla, iar-fhlath; maighistir; fear. My lord, *a mhorair; a thighearna.*

LORD, *v.* Smachdaich, riaghail, dean smachd.

LORDLIKE, *a.* Uallach, stràiceil, mor-chuiseach.

LORDLINESS, *s.* Urram, ard-inbhe; stràic, stràichd, uaille; làdas, uaibhreas; làsdalachd.

LORDLING, *s.* Tighearnan, tighearn beag.

LORDLY, *a.* Stràiceil, spràiceil, uallach, uaibhreach, ardanach, leòmach; ard-inntinneach, ard, mòr; sgòdail, làdasach, làsdach. In a lordly manner, *gu stràiceil, gu h-uallach, gu h-uaibhreach, gu làdasach, gu lasdach.*

LORDSHIP, *s.* Moraireachd; tighearnas; oighreachd. Your lordship, *do mhòrachd.*

LORE, *s.* Oilean, oideas, foghlum, ionnsach, teagasg.

LORICATE, *v.* Comhdaich, màillich, lùirich.

LORIMER, *s.* Srianadair, diaghladair, dioladair.

LORN, *a.* Cuitichte, tréigte, caillte.

LOSE, *v. a.* and *n.* Caill; diobhail; na coisinn; na buidhinn. He will lose himself, *theid e air seacharan;* he will not lose the droppings of his nose, *cha chaill e sileag a shròin;* he gathers in straws and loses in handfuls, *tha e a teanal' nan srabh is call nam boiteal;* lose your way, *rach air seacharan;* he lost the use of his limbs, *chaill e lùth nam ball.*

LOSEABLE, *a.* So-chall.

LOSER, *s.* Fear calldaich, neach a chailleas.

LOSS, *s.* Call, calldach; dochann, earchall; dìth, sgriosadh. You have gained a loss, *choisinn thu call;* I am at a loss, *tha mi an iom-chomhairle;* repair a loss, *dean suas calldach;* causing loss, *dochannach, millteach.*

LOST, *part.* Caillte, air chall; (*beyond recovery*), tur-chaillte. Lost to all decency, *mi bheusach;* lost to all sense of goodness, *fioraingidh.*

LOST, *pret.* of lose. Chaill. I have lost my labour, *chaill mi mo shaothair, thug mi mo shaothair an diomhanas.*

LOT, *s.* Cor, staid, inbhe; crannchur; crann; roinn, cuibhrionn, carann. Cast lots, *cuir croinn, tarruing croinn;* I pity your lot, *is truagh leam do chor.*

LOTION, *s.* Ionnlaid; ionnladh, nigheadh.

LOTTERY, *s.* Crannchur; tuiteamas.

Loud, *a.* Labhar, labharra, àrd, gleadhrach, cruaidh, sgealparra, bruidhneach, tuaireapach. A loud voice, *guth ard.*

Loudly, *adv.* Gu labhar, gu h-àrd, gu gleadhrach, gu sgealparra, gu bruidhneach, gu tuaireapach.

Loudness, *s.* Ard-fhuaim; bruidhneachd; cruadhas, airde; brionglaid.

Lough, *s.* See Loch.

Lounge, *v. n.* Bi lunndach; dean spaisdearachd dhiomhanach, bi diomhanach.

Lounger, *s.* Lunndair; rong, rongair, spaisdear, fear diomhanach.

Lounging, *s.* Lunndaireachd; spaisdearachd.

Louse, *s.* Mial, miol. A crab-louse, *mial iongnach;* a wood-louse, *reudan.*

Lousily, *adv.* Gu mialach, gu miolach; gu mosach, gu salach.

Lousiness, *s.* Mialachd; mosaiche.

Lousy, *a.* Mialach, miolach, mosach, salach; dìblidh.

Lout, *s.* Umaidh, burraidh, tuaifear; balaoch.

Loutish, *a.* Umaidheach; balachail; luidseach.

Lovage, *s.* Siùnas, lus an liogair.

Love, *s.* Gaol, gradh, deigh, miann, rùn, gean, deagh-ghean, cion, seirc, ceisd, tocha. A beloved person, *gaol, gaolach, graidhean, ceisdean;* esteem, *speis, meas, ciat;* for the love of God, *air ghaol nì math;* my love, *a rùin, a ghaoil, a ghaolaich, a ghradh;* in love, *an gaol;* a love affair, *leannanachd, cùis graidh;* what kind of love? *ciod a ghnè graidh?* fall in love, *tuit an gaol;* a love-fit, *tinneas gaoil.*

Love, *v. a.* Gradhaich, bi an gaol. She loves him, *tha i an gaol air, is ro thoigh leath e, is ionmhuinn leath e;* he loves drinking, *is toigh leis an t-òl, tha e trom air an òl.*

Love-knot, *s.* Snaidhm gaoil, snuim pòsaidh.

Love-letter, *s.* Litir gaoil, litir leannanachd.

Loveliness, *s.* Gradhalachd, ionmhuinneachd, seirc, àille.

Lovely, *a.* Aillidh, gaolach, ionmhuinneach, maiseach, ciatach, lurach, greannar.

Lover, *s.* Suiriche, leannan; ceisdean, fear gaoil; cèile.

Lovesick, *a.* Tinn le gaol, an gaol, an trom-ghaol.

Lovesickness, *s.* Tinneas gaoil.

Lovesong, *s.* Òran gaoil.

Lovesuit, *s.* Suireadh.

Lovetoy, *s.* Gibhte gaoil, gibhte leannain.

Loving, *a.* Gaolach, gradhach, caomh, caoimhneil, seirceil, carthanach.

Loving-kindness, *s.* Caoimhneas gradhach, caoimhneas graidh; fàbhar, baigh, tròcair, truacantas.

Lovingly, *adv.* Gu caoimhneil, gu gradhach, gu caomh, gu seirceil.

Lovingness, *s.* Caoimhnealas, seirc, seircealachd.

Low, *a.* (*Not high*), iosal; iochdarach; (*in stature*), beag, crion, goirrid; (*humble*), iriosal, dìblidh, bochd; (*in spirits*), trom, trom-inntinneach, tuirseach; (*brought low*), ìslichte. Low in value, *saor, suarach;* shallow, *tana.*

Low, *adv.* Gu h-iosal, shios; iolar, gu h-iogaradh.

Low, *v.* Geum, dean geum, langanaich, dean langan.

Lower, *v. a.* and *n.* Islich, illsich, irioslaich, cuir fodha, lughdaich; cuir sios, cuir a bhàn, leig sios, leig a bhàn, tuit. Lower the value of a thing, *lughdaich prìs ni.*

Lower, *a.* Ni 's illse, ni 's ìsle; ni 's doimhne, ni 's fhaide shios, ni 's fhaide iolar. The lower places, *na h-àiteachan is illse.*

Lower, *s.* Gruaim, gruamaiche, gruamaichead; (*darkness*), duirche, doirchead, dubhlachd, stoirm; (*heaviness*), truime.

Lowering, *a.* Gruamach; dorch, trom.

Lowermost, *a.* Is iochdaraiche, is illse, is ìsle, is doimhne, is fhaide shios (no) iolar.

Lowing, *s.* Geumnaich, bàirich; langanaich, geum, langan.

Lowland, *s.* Machair, fearann iosal.

Lowland, *a.* (*Scotch*), Gallda; (*in general*), iosal.

Lowlander, *s.* Gàll; dubh-Ghall.

Lowliness, *s.* Irioslachd, ìllseachd, ìsleachd; dìblidheachd.

Lowly, *a.* Iriosal, iosal, dìblidh; ciùin; neo-uallach, macanta.

† **Lown**, *s.* Umaidh, burraidh, guraiceach.

Lowness, *s.* (*Of condition*), isleachd, illseachd; irioslachd, dìblidheachd, neo-inbheachd; (*of spirits*), tuirse, mulad, truime inntinn; (*of stature*), ìsleachd, crìne, meanbhad. Opposed to height, *illse, ìsle, ìsleachd.*

Low-spirited, *a.* Trom, trom-inntinneach, tuirseach, dubhach, muladach.

Low-thoughted, *a.* Neo-aingeantach.

Loyal, *a.* Dìleas; rioghail; tairis; seasmhach. Loyal to the king, *dìleas do 'n rìgh.*

Loyally, *adv.* Gu dìleas, gu seasmhach.

Loyalist, *s.* Fear rioghail (no) dìleas do 'n rìgh.

Loyalty, *s.* Rioghaileachd; rìgh-dhilseachd, leanmhuinneachd, fìrinn.

Lozenge, *s.* Seòrsa cearnaig.

Lubbard, *s.* Slaodair, cleaob, lunndair.

Lubber, *s.* Rong, rongair, slaodair, slaod, lunndair, umaidh.

Lubberliness, *s.* Rongaireachd, slaodaireachd, lundaireachd.

Lubberly, *a.* Slaodach, lunndach, leasg.

Lubberly, *adv.* Gu slaodach, gu lunndach, gu leasg.

Lubric, *a.* Sliom, sleamhuinn; neo-chinnteach, macnusach, drùiseil.

Lubricate, *v. a.* Sliom, sliomaich, liomh, dean sleamhuinn, maothaich. Lubricated, *sliomaichte, liomhta.*

Lubricity, *s.* Sliomachd; sleamhnad; (*lewedness*), macnus, drùis, baois.

Lubrifaction, **Lubrification**, *s.* Sliomachadh, maothachadh.

Luce, *s.* Geadasg, gead-iasg.

Lucent, *a.* Dealrach, soilleir, loinnreach, lonnrach, glan, dearrsach.

Lucerne, *s.* Seorsa feòir.

Lucid, *a.* Soilleir, dealrach, glan, lonnrach, loinnreach, desarsach, oillseach.

Lucidity, *s.* Soilleireachd, lannaireachd, lannair, loinnreadh, dealraichead, soillseachd; soillse, glainead.

Lucifer, *s.* Reult na maidne, a mhaidneag; an diabhol.

Luciferous, *a.* Soillseach.

Luck, *s.* Tuiteamas, amhartan, fortan, rath, soirbheas, seun, sonas, agh, seamhas, sealbh. Good luck, *deagh rath, deagh fhortan;* bad luck, *bochduinn, doirbheas, truaighe;* as good luck would have it, *mar bha 'm fortan;* good luck to you, *soirbheas leat.*

Luckily, *adv.* Gu fortanach, gu h-aghmhor, mar bha 'm fortan.

Luckiness, *s.* Deagh fhortan, deagh rath, soirbheas.

Luckless, *a.* Mi-shealbhar, mi-aghmhor, neo-shonadh, mi-fhortanach.

Luck-penny, *s.* Meachainn.

Lucky, *a.* Sealbhar, fortanach, amhartanach, aghmhor, soirbheasach.

Lucrative, *a.* Buannachdail, proidhiteach, tarbhach.

Lucre, *s.* Buannachd, proidhit, coisinn, buidhinn, tairbhe.

Luctation, *s.* Spairn, gleachdadh.

Lucubration, *s.* Sgriobhadh le solus coinnle.

Luculent, *a* Soilleir; cinnteach.

Ludicrous, *a* Neònach, cleasail; cleasanta; sugach, aighearrach, drabhlainneach, àbhachdach.

Ludicrously, *adv.* Gu neònach, gu cleasail, gu sugach, gu h-aighearrach

Ludicrousness, *s.* Neònachas, cleasantachd, cleasaileachd, aighearrachd, drabhlainneachd

Luff, *v n* Fuirich air fuaradh, fan ri gaoth

Luff, *s* Bas, bos.

Lug, *v* Slaod, tarruing

Luggage, *s* Bagaisd; goireas air astar, imrich, airneis, cungaidh, trailich.

Lugubrious, *a* Brònach, muladach, doilgheasach, duilgheasach, tuirseach; trom, tiamhaidh - Lugubriously, *gu brònach, gu muladach, gu doilgheasach, gu tuirseach, gu trom, gu tiamhaidh*

Lukewarm, *a* Meath-bhlàth, maoth-bhlàth, blàth, caoin-shuarrach, coidheis, comhdh.

Lukewarmly, *adv.* Gu caoin-shuarrach, gu coidheis

Lukewarmness, *s* Meath-bhlàithead, blàthas, (*of heart*), caoin-shuarraichead, coimhsead

Lull, *v. a* Cuir a chodal, cuir gu fois, cuir a luidhe, cuir a laidhe, tàlaidh, coisg, cuir samhach

Lullaby, *s* Oran codail; fonn codail, crònan.

Lumbago, *s.* Tinneas leasraidh, tinneas caol na droma

Lumber, *s* Cungaidh, airneis, tràillich, trealaich

Luminary, *s* Solus, soillse, soillseachd.

Luminous, *a* Soillseach, deàlrach, deàrsach, drilinneach

Luminousness, *s.* Soillseachd, dealraichead

Lump, *s* Meall, meallan, mulp, mulpan, cnap, faob, fàidse In the lump, *an t-iomlan, ann aon mheall*, a shapeless, large lump, *maosganach, uspan*, a round lump of stone, *pulbhag.*

Lumping, *a* Mòr, trom, tomadach

Lumpish, *a.* Trom, cnapach, meallach, cnaparra, cnapanta, mulpach, mulpanach, faobach, trom, tomadach.

Lumpy, *a* Faobach, caobach, cnapach, cnapanach, crapach, meallach

Lunacy, *s* Tinneas na gealaich, caothach, cuthach, bainidh, boile, breathas

Lunar, *a.* Gealachail, gealaich Lunar rainbow, *bogh-gealaich*

Lunated, *a* Leth-chruinn, air cuma na leth-ghealaich.

Lunatic, *a.* Gòrach, air a chuthach, baoth, cuthaich

Lunatic, *s.* Urr ghòrach, neach air am bheil tinneas na gealaich

Lunation, *s* Cuairte na gealaich.

Lunch, *s* Biadh noin, greim bidh

Lunch, *v n* Gabh biadh nòin, gabh greim bidh.

Lune, *s.* Nì sam bi air cumadh na leth-ghealaich; leth-chruinne; cuthach, boile

Lunette, *s* Leth-ghealach.

Lunged, *a.* Sgamhanach

Lungs, *s.* Sgamhan

Lungwort, *s* Crotal-coille.

Lunt, *s.* Fàdadh cluais

Lupine, *s* Gall-pheasair.

Lurch, *s* Teinne, teanntachd, càs, cruaidh-chas, iom-cheist, amhghar; cleas. I left him in the lurch, *dh' fhag mi e san fhéith*

Lurch, *v. n.* and *a.* Meall; dean plaid-luidhe; mill, sgrios, sluig, ith; goid.

Lurcher, *s.* Cù eunaich; glamhair, slaoightear, mealltair.

Lure, *s.* Mealladh, buaireadh; ni mealltach; boit.

Lure, *v* Meall, thoir gu taobh, glac le foill, rib

† **Lurid**, *a* Dorch, gruamach.

Lurk, *v n.* Luidh am folach, luidh gu h-uaigneach, fath-fheith, fà-fheitheamh; giolc.

Lurker, *s.* Méirleach, mearlach; fear fà-fheitheimh; giolc, air.

Lurking-place, *s.* Aite folaich; ionad diomhair.

Luscious, *a* Milis, meilis, blasda, soghmhor; taitneach.

Lusciousness, *s.* Milseachd, blasdachd, millse, millsead.

Lush, *a.* Dorch, dubh, dubh-dhorch.

Luskish, *a.* Leasg, lunndach, leagach

Lusorious, *a.* Aighearach, cridheil, sunndach, ait.

Lust, *s* Ana-miann, ana-mhiann, fonn, drùis, sannt, macnus, baois.

Lustful, *a.* Ana-mhiannach, ana-miannach, sanntach, drùiseil, baoiseil.

Lustfully, *adv.* Gu h-ana-mhiannach, gu sanntach, gu drùiseil.

Lustfulness, *s.* Ana-mhiann, sannt, drùisealachd, sannt, baoisealachd.

Lustily, *adv* Gu laidir, gu treun, gu neartmhor

Lustiness, *s* Sultmhoireachd, dòmhaileachd, neart, treuntas.

Lustration, *s.* Glanadh (no) nigheadh le uisge

Lustre, *s* Dealradh, deàrsadh, lannair, soillse, drilinn; ùine chùig bliadhna.

Lustrous, *a* Dealrach, dearsach, soillseach, drilinneach

Lustrum, *s.* Lusga

Lusty, *a.* Sultmhor, reamhar, cnaparra, calma, neartmhor, laidir, treun, slainnteil, steillcach. A lusty, lazy fellow, *steillear.*

Lutarious, *a* Làbachail, làbanta, lobanach.

Lute, *s* Inneal ciùil; clàrsach; taois creadha, criadh-ghlaodh

Lute, *v. a.* Glaodh (no) tàth le criadh.

Lutulent, *a* Salach, mosach, musach, thar a chéile, troimh chéile mar uisge.

Luxate, *v a* Cuir as an alt.

Luxuriance, *s.* Cinneas anabarrach; pailteas

Luxuriant, *a* Pailt, lionmhor; tarbhach A luxuriant crop, *barr tarbhach.*

Luxurious, *a* Stroghail, soghmhor, sòghail, soghar, ana-caithteach, drùiseil, samh. A luxurious poor man can never be happy, *cha bhith 'm bochd sòghar sona*

Luxuriously, *adv.* Gu drùiseil, gu soghmhor, gu soghail, gu drùiseil

Luxury, *s.* Sogh, saimh; ana-caitheamh; macnus, drùis, baois

Lye, *s* See Lie.

Lying, *s.* Deanamh bhreug, breugan, breugaireachd.

Lying, *s* Luidhe, sineadh. Lying down, *luidhe bhàn (no) sios*, a lying-in of a female, *luidhe siùbhal.*

Lymph, *s.* Uisge.

Lymphatic, *a.* Uisgeil

Lynx, *s.* Fiadh-bheist sònruichte airson luathais agus léirsinn.

Lyre, *s.* Cruit, clàrsach.

Lyric, *a* Crùitidh, clàrsaich A lyric poet, *cruit-fhilidh.*

Lyrist, *s.* Clàrsair, cruitear.

M.

M, *s.* An treasamh litir deug do 'n aibideal; a ciallachadh air uairibh, mile, (1000) agus air uairibh, maigbistir. MS, *sgriobhadh;* MSS., *sgriobhaichean*

Mac, *s.* Mac; nighinn; ni 'n. Macintyre, *Mac an t-saoir; (a female of the said name)*, nighinn 't-saoir, ni 'n t-saoir.

Macaroni, *s.* Lasgair, gasganach.

Macaroon, *s.* Sgonn, burraidh, ceothallan, gobhallan.

Macaw, *s.* Scorsa piorraid.

Mace, *s.* Seorsa spiosraidh; slat shuaicheantais; caman iarainn.

Mace-bearer, *s.* Fear giùlain slat-shuaicheantais.

Macerate, *v. a.* Bog, bogaich, tum ann uisge; dean bochd (no) truagh; sàruich, claoidh; fannaich.

Maceration, *s.* Leaghadh ann uisge teth, claoidheadh; sàruchadh, fannachadh; caitheamh.

Machinal, *a.* Innleachdach, ealanta; inntinneach.

Machinate, *v.* Dealbh, tionnsgain.

Machination, *s.* Innleachd; dealbhadh; tionnsgnadh.

Machine, *s.* Inneal; inntinn, obair inntinneach; oirneis.

Machinery, *s.* Obair chuidhleachan; obair inntinneach mar a chithear ann am muillnibh.

Machinist, *s.* Innleachdair, oirneisear, fear innleachdach.

† **Macilency**, *s.* Caoile, truaghas.

Macilent, *a.* Caol, tana, bochd, truagh.

Mackarel, *s.* Rionnach.

Mackarel-gale, *s.* Buath gaoithe.

Macrocosm, *s.* An cruinne cé.

Mactation, *s* Marbhadh, àr; beubanachd, cosgradh

Macula, *s.* Ball, spot; sal, gò, coire.

Maculate, *v a* Ballaich, breacaich, salaich, dean ballach (no) breac, spot.

Maculated, *a* and *part* Ballach, breac; ballaichte, breacta, spotach, spotagach

Maculation, *s* Ball, spot, sal, salachar

Macule, *s.* Ball, spot, sal, gò, coire.

Mad, *a.* Cuthaich, gòrach, thar a chéill, air a chuthach, air bhoil, air bhreas, air bhreathas, air bhaoghal, baobhail, air mhire, air bainnidh. Are you mad? *bheil thu air a chuthach?* he is stark mad, *tha e air ghlan chuthach, tha 'n dearg chuthach air;* he is raving mad, *tha e air dearg a chuthaich*, a mad dog, *cu cuthaich.*

Mad, *v. a.* and *n.* Cuir gòrach, buair, cuir thar chéill, cuir air chuthach (no) air bhreathas; bi air chuthach, rach gòrach (no) air a chuthach.

Madam, *s.* Tiodal a bheirear do bhoirionnaich; a bhan, a bhaintighearna, a bhan-tighearn; ban

Madbrained, *a.* Cuthaich, gòrach, thar a chéil, gaoithe, eutrom.

Madcap, *s* Fear fiadhaich ceannlaidir.

Madden, *v. a.* Cuir gòrach, cuir air chuthach, cuir air bhreathas; buair.

Madder, *s* Seorsa plannt.

Made, *pret.* and *p. part.* of make. Rinn; deanta, deante. See Make. Well made, *cumadail*

Madefaction, *s.* Bogachadh, fliuchadh, taisleachadh.

Madefy, *v. a.* Bogaich, fliuch, taislich.

Madhouse, *s.* Tigh cuthaich.

Madly, *adv.* Gu cuthaich, gu borb, gu garg.

Madman, *s.* Fear gòrach, fear cuthaich, amhas.

Madness, *s.* Cuthach, boil, breathas, breas, gòraiche, mearachinn, dith céill, cion céill, bainidh, buaireadh; mire chuthaich.

Madrigal, *s.* Coilleag, luinneag

Maffle, *s.* Bi liodach (no) manntach, labhair gu liodach.

Maffler, *s* Fear liodach (no) manntach

Magazine, *s* Tigh stòir, tigh stòrais, tigh-tasgaidh; òirchiste; gairneal, gaoirneal, seorsa leabhair a thig mach air amaibh

† **Mage**, *s.* Druidh.

Maggot, *s* Cnaimheag, cnuimheag, craimheag, cnamhag, cnuimh, craimh, beisteag, durrag; daolag; *(whim)*, dòchas; gìth, smuain

Maggoty, *a.* Cnaimheagach, cnuimheagach, daolagach, durragach, *(whimsical)*, dochasach, neonach; luaineach

Magi, *s.* Oir-dhruidhean; speuradairean a bha san airde an ear o chian.

Magic, *s.* Druidheachd, draoidheachd; dubh-chleasachd, cleasachd, easarluidheachd; piseag.

Magic, *a.* Druidheach, draoidheach, easarluidheach, druidheachail, druidheil Magic art, *dubh-chleasachd.*

Magician, *s* Druidh, draoidh, cleasaiche, dubh-chleasaiche.

Magisterial, *a.* Uaibhreach, straiceil, smachdail, ceannasach; ardanach; maighistireil. Magisterially, *gu h-uaibhreach, gu stràiceil, gu smachdail.*

Magistracy, *s* Riaghlaireachd, riaghladaireachd

Magistrate, *s.* Riaghlair, riaghladair

Magnanimity, *s* Mòr-inntinneachd, mòr-aigne, mòr-aigeantachd, mòr-chridhe, mòr-chridheachd, gaisge, mor-chuis.

Magnanimous, *a.* Mor-inntinneach, mòr-aigneach, aigneach, mòr-chridheach, gaisgeil, mòralach, mòr-chuiseach Magnanimously, *gu mòr-inntinneach, gu mòr-chuiseach.*

Magnesia, *s.* Leigheas tuasglach.

Magnet, *s.* Cloch iùil; cloch tharruing, clach tairnidh

Magnetic, Magnetical, *a.* Tarruingeach, dlù-thairneach

Magnetism, *s.* Dlù-tharruingeachd.

Magnific, *a.* Greannda, grinn; glonnmhor; mor, ard, urramach, cliùiteach, mor-chuiseach; uasal, mor-ghniomhach.

Magnificence, *s.* Greanndachd, grinneas, glonn, mòrghlonn, mòralachd, mòr-chuis, mòr-chuiseachd, airdreim

Magnificent, *a.* Greannda, grinn, glonnmhor; mòr, ard, urramach, cliùiteach, mòr-chuiseach, uasal, mor-ghniomhach, mòralach, riomhach.

Magnificently, *adv.* Gu greannda, gu grinn, gu glonnmhor, gu h-urramach, gu mòr-chuiseach, gu mòralach, gu riomhach.

Magnifico, *s.* Morair Eadailteach

Magnifier, *s.* Arduchair, ardachair; fear ardachaidh, fear molaidh

Magnify, *v. a.* Arduich, ardaich, mòraich, mol, tog suas, meudaich

Magnifying, *s* Arduchadh, moladh, mòrachadh, meudachadh. A magnifying-glass, *gloine meudachaidh.*

Magnitude, *s.* Meudachd, meud; tomad, co-mheudachd.

Magpie, *s.* Pigheid

Mahomet, *s.* Mathomait

Mahometan, *a.* Mathomaiteach.

Mahometanism, *s.* Creideamh Mhathomeid

Maid, *s* Maighdeann, maighdinn, oigh; cailinn, caile, nighean, ighean, *(servant)*, ban-òglach, searbhanta. An old maid, *sean chaile*, a little maid, *caileag, rionag*, a fatherless maid is soon wooed, *is fhuras fear fhaotainn d' inghinn gun athair.*

MAIDEN, *s.* Seorsa éisg.

MAIDEN, *a.* Oigheil, maighidinneil, ùr; neo-ghnathaichte, neo-thruaillte; bandaidh.

MAIDENHAIR, *s.* Seorsa plannt ris an goirear dubh-chosach (no) failtean fionn.

MAIDENHEAD, MAIDENHOOD, *s.* Maighideannas, maighidinneas.

MAIDENLY, *a.* Oigheil, banail, beusach, mallta, gasda.

MAIDHOOD, *s.* Maighdeannas.

MAIDSERVANT, *s.* Ban-òglach, searbhanta, nighean.

MAIL, *s.* Màile, màill, lùireach, lùireach mhàilleach, armachd; balg litir; balg teachdair, poc pùist, pasgan litreach.

MAIL, *v.* Lùirich, armaich, màillich.

MAIM, *s.* Ciurradh, *ciurram*, dochann, coir, *cron*, bruthadh, gaoid, leòn, lotadh.

MAIM, *v. a.* Ciùrr, ciurramaich, dochannaich, dochainn, leòn; lot, mill, bruth; breoth.

MAIMED, *part.* Ciurrta, ciurramach, brùite, leòinte, leonta, millte; breòite.

MAIN, *a.* Prìomh, ard, mòr; neartmhor; araid, sonruichte; cinn; toisich. The main land, *an tìr-mhòr;* a mainmast, *crann meadhonach, crann mòr.*

MAIN, *s.* A chuid mhor; an t-iomlan, a gharbh-chuid, a mhuir, a mhuir mhòr; neart, spionnadh, foirneart; (*a hamper*), cliabh; sgùilean, croidhle. With might and main, *le uile spionnadh.*

MAINLAND, *s.* Tìr-mhor, mòr-thir.

MAINLY, *adv.* Gu àraidh, gu h-àraid.

MAINPERNOR, *s.* (*In law*), urras, fear a theid an urras.

MAINPRISE, *v. a.* Gabh an urras.

MAINSAIL, *s.* Seol meadhonach, seol meadhoin.

MAINSHEET, *s.* Sgod an siùil mhòir.

MAINTAIN, *v. a.* (*Affirm*), cum a mach, abair, càir; (*support*), cum suas, dion, cum taic ri, àl, tog, coimhead, gleidh. Maintain a family, *cum suas* (*no*) *tog teaghlach.*

MAINTAINABLE, *a.* So-dhionadh; ceart.

MAINTAINER, *s.* Fear togalach, dionair, fear dionaidh.

MAINTENANCE, *s.* Cumail suas; teachd an tìr; tighinn beo, dion; dionadh.

MAINTOP, *s.* Barr a chroinn mhòir, crannag a chroinn mhòir.

MAINYARD, *s.* Slat shiùil a chroinn mhòir.

MAIZE, *s.* Coirc Innseanach, cruineach Innseanach.

MAJESTIC, MAJESTICAL, *a.* Mòralach, lòghmhor, flathail, gasta, ard, rioghail, riomhach, stàideil.

MAJESTY, *s.* Mòrachd, mòrdhachd.

MAJOR, *a.* A's mò, is mo; a 's sine. The major part, *a chuid is mò, a gharbh chuid.*

MAJOR, *s.* (*In the army*), fo-cheannard air mile, màidsear; (*in law*), neach air teachd gu h-aois. Major domo, *fear tighe; bean tighe, urr a chuireas gnothuichibh tighe gu doigh airson neach eile.*

MAJORATION, *s.* Meudachadh.

MAJORITY, *s.* A chuid is mò, a gharbh chuid, barrachd; (*in law*), làn aois, aois lagha; (*in the army*), màidsearachd.

MAKE, *v. a.* Dean, cruthaich, dealbh; (*settle*), socraich, suidhich, daighnich; (*compel*), éignich, thoir air; (*reach*), ruig. Make away, *marbh, cuir as do;* make account, *creid, saoil;* make free with, *cuir air bheag suim;* make good, *coimhlion;* make light of, *cuir air ioladh;* make love, *dean suireadh, dean suas ri;* make merry, *bi subhach, dean sùgradh;* make out, *dearbh; comhdaich; mìnich;* make over, *thoir thairis, toirbheir;* make up, *dean suas; càirich; coimhlion;* make known, *dean aithnichte, nochd;* I make no doubt, *cha n' eil teagamh agam, cha n' eil omhail agam, cha n' eil mi 'cur omhail;* what make you here? *ciod a tha thu 'deanamh an so? ciod an gnothuch th' agad an so?* make a virtue of necessity, *fuilig an rud nach gabh seachnadh;* make away with your money, *cuir a shean* (*no*) *caith d' airgiod;* make for the shore, *stiùir thun tìr;* make as if, *gabh ort, gabh ort féin;* make off, *thoir na casan asad, thoir na buinn asad, bi triall, gabh romhad, ruith air falbh.* Made, *deanta, deante, criochnuichte; ullamh, deas;* well made, *cumadail;* he made much exertion, *rinn e mòran strìgh;* what made you rise so early? *ciod a thug ort éiridh cho moch?*

MAKE, *s.* Deanamh, dianamh, cumadh, cumachd, dealbhadh, cruthachadh; cruth, gné.

MAKE-BATE, *s.* Fear aimhreite, fear buaireis.

MAKE-PEACE, *s.* Fear réiteachaidh; fear réite.

MAKER, *s.* Cruthai'ear, cruthadair, dealbhadair, cumadair.

MAKING, *s.* Deanamh, cumadh, dealbhadh. That was the making of him, *b' e sin a rinn duine dheth, b' e sin a rinn suas e.*

MALACHITE, *s.* Clach uasal.

MALADY, *s.* Galar, tinneas, eucail, euslainnte; aicidh.

MALADMINISTRATION, *s.* Mi-riaghladh, mi-stiùradh, droch riaghladh, droch stiùradh.

MALAPERT, *a.* Sgeilmeach, lonach, beag-narach; peilpeanta.

MALAPERTLY, *adv.* Gu sgeilmeach, gu lonach, gu beagnarach, gu peilpeanta.

MALAPERTNESS, *s.* Sgeilmeachd, lonais, beag-nàrachd; peilp.

MALAXATE, *v. a.* Bogaich; taoisinn.

MALAXATION, *s.* Bogachadh; taoisinn.

MALCONTENT, MALCONTENTED, *a.* Mi-thoilichte, miumhall, diombach, diomach, diombuidheach; mi-rioghail, ceannairceach.

MALCONTENTEDNESS, *s.* Mi-thoileachas, diombachd.

MALE, *a.* Firionn.

MALE, *s.* Firionnach.

MALEADMINISTRATION, *s.* Mi-riaghladh, mi-stiùradh, droch riaghladh, droch stiùradh.

MALEDICTION, *s.* Mallachd, malluchadh, mollachd, guidhe, droch ghuidhe.

MALEFACTION, *s.* Droch thùrn, droch ghniomh, drochbheart, ciont, coire.

MALEFACTOR, *s.* Cioptach; fear droch bheairt; crochair.

MALEVOLENCE, *s.* Gamhlas, mi-run, mio-rùn, tnù, tnùth, miosguinn, fuath, droch-rùn, olc, nàduir, droch-mheineachd, galltanas.

MALEVOLENT, *a.* Gamhlasach, mi-runach, mio-rùnach, tnùmhor, miosguinneach.

MALICE, *s.* Gamhlas, mi-run, mio-run, droch-rùn, farmad, tnù; miosguinn, droch mheineachd, olc nàduir, galltanas.

MALICIOUS, *a.* Gamhlasach, mi-rùnach, farmadach, acaiseach, miosguinneach.

MALICIOUSLY, *adv.* Gu gamhlasach, gu mi-runach, gu farmadach, gu miosguinneach, gu droch-rùnach, gu drochmheineach.

MALICIOUSNESS, *s.* Gamhlasachd; droch-rùnachd, drochmhéineachd.

MALIGN, *a.* Gamhlasach, farmadach; millteach, claoidhteach; gabhaltach.

MALIGNANCY, *s.* Gamhlas, farmad, spìd, mi-run, mio-run, droch rùn; millteachd, droch-mhéin.

MALIGNANT, *a.* Gamhlasach, mi-runach, farmadach, spìdeil, millteach, garg, droch-bheairteach, droch-mhuinte, aingidh.

Malignant, *s.* Urr mhi-runach.

Malignantly, *adv.* Gu gamhlasach, gu mi-runach, gu farmadach, gu h-aingidh.

Malignity, *s.* Mi-rùn, mio-run, gamhlas, farmad, spid tnù; droch-mhéin, droch-mheineachd, droch-mhuine.

Malignly, *adv.* Gu mi-runach, gu gamhlasach, gu farmadach.

Malkin, *s.* Mob air a dheanamh do chlùtaibh; bòchdan; stràill, strabaid.

Malpractice, *s.* Droch chleachd, droch àbhaist.

Mall, *s.* Fairche, fairc, ord, geinnear, geinneir; buille.

Mall, *s.* Sràid sam b' abhaist doibh a bhith cluich air bhall.

Mall, *v. a.* Buail le ord no le fairc, straoidhil, slachduinn.

Mallard, *s.* Lach a chinn uaine; dreac, tunnag fhiadhaich.

Malleable, *a.* So-thanachadh, ion-thanachadh; ion-oibrichte; a thanaicheas le ord.

Malleate, *v. a.* Tanaich, buail le ord.

Mallet, *s.* Fairc, farachan, geinnear.

Mallows, *s.* Maloimh; gropais, fochas.

Malmsy, *s.* Mailmheas.

Malt, *s.* Braich. A malt kiln, *àth bhracha, àth bhrachaidh.*

Malt-floor, *s.* Urlar-bracha, urlar brachaidh.

Maltman, Maltster, *s.* Brachadair.

Malversation, *s.* Droch-ghnàthachadh, tual-bheart, droch-bheart.

Mam, Mamma, *s.* Mathair; *in the vocative*, a bhean; a mhathair.

Mammiform, *a.* Air cumadh cìche; copach.

Mammock, *s.* Bloidh, mìre, spealg, sgealb. Mammocks, *bloidhdean, mìreannan, spealgan.*

Mammon, *s.* Maoin, saibhreas, beartas.

Man, *s.* Duine, fear, † cia, † ce, aon; (*servant*), gille, òglach, seirbheiseach, sgalag; † cearn, ceatharn. Man, (*mankind*), *an duine, an cinneadh daoine;* a man, (*not a woman*), *firionnach;* a grown-up man, *duine deanta;* what do you say, man? *ciod a tha thu 'g radh, dhuine?* every man, *na h-uile fear;* every man has his day, *tha làth féin aig na h-uile fear;* I am my own man, *tha am aig mo thoil féin;* man by man, *fear an deigh fir, fear an deigh chéile;* a footman, *gille coise, gille ruithe;* man's estate, *inbhe duine;* an honest man, *duine còir;* you are the wale of men, *is tu rogha nam fear;* a young man, *òg, òganach;* a man of war, *luingeas cogaidh; mìlidh, cùraidh;* a man of no account, *duine gun fhiù;* a man-child, *duine cloinne.*

Man, *v. a.* Cuir lamhan ann; gabh aig ni le daoinibh; daighnich; daingnich; dion.

Manacles, *s.* Cuibhrich; ceanglaichean; glas laimh.

Manacle, *v.* Cuibhrich, ceangail.

Manage, *s.* Riaghailt, sgòd, comannt.

Manage, *v. a.* Stiùir, riaghail, orduich; ceannsaich; cuir gu doigh, cuir air adhairt.

Manageable, *a.* So-stiùradh, so-riaghladh, so-riaghlaidh, so-cheannsachaidh, a ghabhas stiùradh (no) riaghladh; (*as a horse*), soitheamh, socrach, soimeach.

Management, *s.* Riaghladh, orduchadh, stiùradh, riaghlachadh, fearachas tighe; comannt; sgòd; deagh bhuileachas.

Manager, *s.* Fear riaghlaidh, riaghladair, riaghlair.

Managery, *s.* Riaghladh, riaghailt, riaghlachadh, fearachas tighe, beanachas tighe; grunndalas.

Manchet, *s.* Buileann beag.

Mancipate, *v.* Traill, traillich, cuir fo dhaorsadh, cuibhrich, ceangail, teannaich.

Mancipation, *s.* Tràill, traillealachd, daorsadh, bruid, braighdeanas, teannachadh.

Mandamus, *s.* Ordugh breith; ordugh rioghail.

Mandarin, *s.* Uachdaran ann an *Tìna*, uachdaran Tìneach.

Mandate, *s.* Ordugh, iarrtas, àithne, reachd, comannt.

Mandator, *s.* Reachdadair.

Mandible, *s.* Peirceall, craos, gial.

Mandibular, *a.* Peirceallach, craosach, gialach.

Mandilion, *s.* Fàluing (no) clòc saighdeir; earrasaid, fearrasaid.

Mandrake, *s.* Codalian; seorsa plannt; ubhlan beag a bha cinntinn ann an Iudea.

Manducable, *a.* So-chagnadh, ion-ithe, so-chnamh.

Manducate, *s.* Cagain, cagainn; cnamh; ith.

Manducation, *s.* Cagnadh; cnamhadh; ith.

Mane, *s.* Muing, mùidh; muinnidh.

Maned, *a.* Muingichte.

Manes, *s.* Taibhse, aog, eug, tannasg, spiorad, taibhsean, spioradan.

Manful, *a.* Duineil, fearail, gaisgeil, treubhanta, dàn; smiorail, smearail, misneachail; stoirmeil.

Manfully, *adv.* Gu duineil, gu fearail, gu gaisgeil, gu treubhanta, gu dàn, gu smiorail, gu misneachail.

Manfulness, *s.* Duinealas, fearalas, gaisge, treubhantas, dànad.

Mange, *s.* Cloimh spreidhe, cloimh chon, cloimh.

Manger, *s.* Prasach, praiseach, mainnsear, amar.

Manginess, *s.* Cloimh, cream, carr.

Mangle, *v. a.* Beubanaich, srac, strac, reub as a chéile, gearr, sgòr. Mangled, *beubanaichte, reubte.*

Mangle, *s.* Inneal chum anart a mhìneachadh, mìneachan.

Mangle, *v. a.* Mìnich anart.

Mangler, *s.* Reubair, sracair; reubadair.

Mango, *s.* Meas saillte a thig as na h-Innseachan shios.

Mangy, *a.* Clomhach, creamach, carrach; sgabach, claimheach, guireanach.

Manhood, *s.* Fearachas, fearachd; cinneadh daoine, ball fir; misneach, gaisge, treubhantas, cruadal, tiomachd.

Maniac, *s.* Urr ghòrach; òinseach; fear cuthaich.

Maniac, *a.* Gòrach, cuthaich.

Manicle, *s.* Glas laimh, glas dùirn; dornasg; ceangal, ruitheach.

Manifest, *a.* Soilleir, follaiseach, riachdail, dearbhta, dearbhte. It is manifest, *tha e soilleir.*

Manifest, *v. a.* Soilleirich, soillsich, foillsich, nochd, taisbein, dean soilleir, sorcaich; feuch. Manifested, *foillsichte, nochdta.*

Manifestable, *a.* So-fheuchainn, so-shoillseachadh, so-dhearbhadh, so-nochdadh.

Manifestation, *s.* Foillseachadh, foillseach, nochdadh, feuchainn; làn-dearbhadh.

Manifestly, *adv.* Gu soilleir, gu dearbhta, gu riachdail.

Manifestness, *s.* Soilleireachd, follais, riachdaileachd.

Manifesto, *s.* Gairm fhollaiseach.

Manifold, *a.* Iomad, iomadh, iomadach, lionmhor, iomadaidh, iom-ghnetheach, eag-samhuil.

Mankind, *s.* An cinneadh daoine.

Manless, *a.* Gun duine.

Manlike, *a.* Duineil, fearail, misneachail, smiorail, smearail; stràiceil; stoirmeil.

Manliness, *s.* Duinealas, fearalas, fearalachd, misneach, smioralas, smearalas, tapadh, tapachd; daoineas.

Manly, *a.* Duineil, fearail, misneachail, smiorail, stràiceil tapaidh; arrachdach. If you be manly, gloom not, *ma 's fearail thu, na biodh gruaim ort.*

MANNA, *s.* Aran neamhuidh, bith craoibh.

MANNER, *s.* Modh, seòl, nòs, gnàth, gné, fasan, cleachd, àbhaist; rod, rathad, slighe, doigh, achd; cor. According to this manner, *air a mhodh so, air an t-seòl so;* after his manner, *a reir a chleachd, a reir 'àbhaist;* what manner of men are they? *ciod a ghné dhaoine th' annta?* in a manner, *air sheòl, air achd, air dhoigh;* after another manner, *air sheòl eile;* in some manner, *air chor eigin;* in what manner soever, *ciod air bith an doigh;* in divers manners, *ioma-ghnetheach, air iomad seòl;* in like manner, *air an doigh cheudna, air an lagh cheudna, air a mhodh cheudna;* in such a manner, *air achd, air chor;* in such a manner as, *air achd is (no) agus, air chor is (no) agus;* good manners, *deagh bheusan;* ill manners, *droch bheusan, mi-mhodh; droch ghiùlan;* the manners which a man has in the house, he will have abroad, *an cleachd a bhitheas aig duine aig an tigh, bithidh so aig air chéilidh.*

MANNERLY, *a.* Modhail, beusach, tuigseach; iùlmhor.

MANNERS, *s.* Beusan, deagh ghiùlan, modhalachd; cleachdanna, àbhaistean.

MANNIKIN, *s.* Fearagan, bodachan, abhach, arrachd.

MANNISH, *a.* Duineil, dàn, fearail.

MANŒUVRE, *s.* Teabhadh; cleas, cleasachd; gniomh; car.

MANOR, *s.* Fearann, oighreachd.

MANSE, *s.* Tigh ministeir.

MANSION, *s.* Teach, tigh, àros, àite comhnuidh.

MANSLAUGHTER, *s.* Mortadh gun droch rùn.

MANSUETE, *a.* Soimeach, socrach, ciùin, soitheamh, sìolaidhte.

MANTELET, *s.* Ciotag, clòc beag, tonnag.

MANTLE, *s.* Earradh uachdair, fàluing, faluinn, clòc, earrasaid, † glo, † clo, cleòc, brat, còmhdach, comhdachadh. Lady's mantle, *falluing mhuire, crubh leomhainn.*

MANTLE, *v. a.* and *n.* Comhdaich, éid, eudaich, folaich; brat; (*froth*), oibrich, cuir cobhar.

MANTUA, *s.* Gùn bain-tighearna; gùn.

MANTUA-MAKER, *s.* Tàilear; ban-tàilear, banalaiche.

MANUAL, *a.* Laimh; lamhach.

MANUAL, *s.* Leabhran, leabhar beag.

MANUALIST, *s.* Fear ceaird, fear ealadhain.

MANUBIAL, *a.* Fomhach, faobhach.

MANUBRIUM, *s.* Lamh, cluas.

MANUDUCTION, *s.* Toirt air laimh, treòrachadh, seòladh air laimh.

MANUFACTURE, *s.* Obair, obair laimh, lamh-obair, ni sam bi air a dhealbh, gu h-ealanta.

MANUFACTURE, *v.* Oibrich, dean, dealbh, dean suas.

MANUFACTURER, *s.* Fear oibre, fear ceairde, dealbhadair.

MANUMISE, *v.* Saor, cuir fa sgaoil, cuir fa réir, fuasgail.

MANUMISSION, *s.* Saoradh, saorsadh, sgaoileadh, cuir fa réir, fuasgladh, saorsainn.

MANUMIT, *v.* Saor, cuir fa sgaoil, fuasgail, thoir saorsadh, thoir cead, thoir comas.

MANURABLE, *a.* A ghabhas mathachadh, so-mhathachadh, so-thoirt a stigh, so-leasachadh.

MANURE, *v. a.* Mathaich, leasaich, inneirich, thoir a stigh.

MANURED, *a.* Mathaichte, leasaichte, inneirichte.

MANUREMENT, *s.* Mathachadh, leasachadh.

MANURER, *s.* Tuathanach, fear mathachaidh.

MANUSCRIPT, *s.* Sgriobhadh, lamh-sgriobhadh. Manuscripts, *sgriobhaichean.*

MANY, *a.* Iomad, iomadh, mòran, iomadach, iomadaidh, lionmhor, pailt; eag-samhuil. Many a man, *iomad fear;* too many, *tuille is a chòir, tuile is lionmhoire;* many a time, *iomad uair, tric, minic;* a great many, *mòran;* how many? *cia meud?* how many years are you? *cia meud bhliadhna tha thu?* a good many, *dorlach;* as many as, *na h-uibhir is;* as many as you, *na h-uibhir riutsa;* how many times soever, *cia co tric air bith; air a thricead;* so many, *na h-uibhir, na h-uibhir ri so; an uibhir so;* many ways, *iomad rod, iomad seòl; iomad doigh.*

MANY, *s.* Mòran; cuideachd; dorlach, buidheann, bannal, lòd.

MANY-COLOURED, *a.* Ioma-dathach, eag-samhuil, ioldhathach.

MANY-CORNERED, *a.* Ioma-chearnach.

MANY-HEADED, *a.* Ioma-cheannach.

MANY-LANGUAGED, *a.* Ioma-chainnteach.

MANY-PEOPLED, *a.* Ioma-shluaghach, sluaghmhor.

MANY-TIMES, *adv.* Tric, iomad uair, minig.

MAP, *s.* Cairteal, cairt, dealbh baile (no) dùthcha, dealbh rioghachd. A map of the world, *dealbh na cruinne.*

MAP, *v.* Dealbh, linich, dealbhaich.

MAPLE, *s.* Seorsa craoibh.

MAPPERY, *s.* Dealbhachadh, lìneachadh, dealbhadaireachd.

MAR, *v.* Ciurr, mill, cuir dholaidh, dochainn, docharaich, cuir air dhochair; truaillich; grab.

MARASMUS, *s.* Caitheamh, éiteach.

MARAUDER, *s.* Reubair, robair, fear reubainn, spùinneadair, saigheadair creachaidh, spùinn-shaighidear.

MARAUDING, *s.* Creachadh, spùinneadh, spùilleadh, reubainn, robaireachd, togail, cobhartach.

MARBLE, *s.* Marmhor, marmor.

MARBLE, *v. a.* Breac, breacaich, dean eag-samhuil.

MARBLE-HEARTED, *a.* Cruaidh-chridheach, cruadalach.

MARCASITE, *s.* Seòrsa méin.

MARCH, *s.* Màirt; màrt; treas mios na bliadhna.

MARCH, *v. a.* Triall, siubhail, imich, coisich, ceum, ceumnaich.

MARCH, *s.* Triall, trialladh, triall feachd, imeachd, spaidsearachd, spaisdearachd, mearsal; (*tune*), mearsa; caismeachd, piobaireachd; (*boundary*), crioch, iomall, teoradh.

MARCHER, *s.* Fear chriochnan.

MARCHES, *s.* Criochnan, criochan, iomallan, teoraidh.

MARCHIONESS, *s.* Ban-mharcuis, ban-mharcais.

MARCH-PANE, *s.* Seorsa arain milis.

MARCID, *a.* Caol, truagh, tana, seac, seargte, crion.

MARCOUR, *s.* Caoile, truaghas, taine, seargadh, crìne, caitheamh, éiteach.

MARE, *s.* Capull, làir. A mare filly, *lothag;* the nightmare, *an trom-laighe.*

MARESCHAL, *s.* Ceann feadhna, marasgal, ard-cheannard.

MARGARITE, *s.* Neònaid.

MARGIN, *s.* Foir, oir, bruach; leth oir duilleig; iomall, iomarach, marghan, iomag. The margin of a river, *bruach aimhne.*

MARGINAL, *a.* Foireannach.

MARGRAVE, *s.* Tiodal Gearmailteach; fear gleidh chriochan.

MARIGOLD, *s.* Lus mhàiri, a bhile bhuidhe. Common marigold, *liathan.*

MARINATE, *v. a.* Saill iasg.

MARINE, *a.* Mara, margha, muireil.

MARINE, *s.* Saighdear luing, saighdear mara, saighdear fairge; gnothuichean mara.

MARINER, *s.* Maraiche, seòladair.

† Marish, *s.* Féith, cathar, bog.

Maritated, *a.* Pòsda, pòisde.

Maritime, *a.* Muireil, mara, ri taobh na mara, tràgha.

Marjoram, *s.* Lus Mharsali.

Mark, *s.* Comhar, comharadh, dearbhadh, còmhdach, teoran talmhainn; (*in money*), marg; trì sgillinn deug Sasunnach is ceithir sgillinn; dà mharg dheug Albannach; (*footstep*), aile, lorg. An ear-mark, *comhar cluaise;* a landmark, *comhar crìche, clach crìche;* a watermark, *comhar tràigh, comhar uisge.*

Mark, *v. a.* Comharraich, comharaich; (*observe*), beachdaich, gabh beachd, thoir an aire, cum sùil air. Mark out, *comharaich a mach.*

Marked, *a.* Comharaichte; sònruichte.

Marker, *s.* Fear comharachaidh, beachdair.

Market, *s.* Margadh, margad; féill, faighir; aonach, ceannachadh; prls. A market day, *là faighreach;* a market place, *creanait, ait faighreach;* a market town, *baile margaidh;* a market cross, *crosg, crois;* market folks, *muinntir margaidh, muinntir faighreach.*

Market, *v. n.* Ceannaich no reic, dean margad.

Marketable, *a.* Margadail, margail, airson a mhargaidh a ghabhas reic no ceannuchadh.

Marl, *s.* Criadh reamhar, mathachadh, màrla.

Marl, *v. a.* Màrla, mathaich le màrla.

Marlpit, *s.* Toll màrla.

Marly, *a.* Marlach.

Marmalade, *s.* Seorsa millsein.

Marmoset, *s.* Ap.

Marmorean, *a.* Marmharach, marmorach.

Marmot, *s.* Radan mòr.

Marque, *s.* Comas glacaidh.

Marquee, *s.* Bùth, bothan caineib; sgàilean.

Marquesate, *s.* Marcuiseachd, marcaiseachd.

Marquess, *s.* Marcuis, marcais, an t-inmhe is fhaigse do dhiuchd.

Marrer, *s.* Fear millidh, fear grabaidh, grabair.

Marriage, *s.* Pòsadh; maraiste. A forced marriage, *pòsadh air éigin, pòsadh a dh' aindeoin;* a marriage song, *oran pòsaidh;* promise in marriage, *geall ann am posadh;* promise marriage, *geall pòsadh, thoir geall pòsaidh;* going to the marriage, *a dol thun a phòsaidh;* marriage at hand and gossipping afar, *cleamhnas am fogus is goisdeachd am fad.*

Marriageable, *a.* Ion-phòsda.

Married, *a.* Pòsda, pòisde. A married woman, *breideach.*

Marring, *s.* Milleadh, grabadh.

Marrow, *s.* Smior, smear; (*of the back-bone*), smior cnuimh na droma.

Marrow-bone, *s.* Cnaimh smior; (*in burlesque language*), glùn.

Marrow-fat, *s.* Seorsa peasrach.

Marrowless, *a.* Gun smior; aogail, aogaidh; gun lethbhreac.

Marry, *v.* Pòs; (*as a priest*), pòs, ceangail ann am pòsadh. She married him, *phòs i e;* he married her, *phòs e i.*

Marry, (*a sort of oath.*) Nàile, air nàile; air Moire, Moire, Muir, air Muir; moramas, moireamas.

Marsh, *s.* Bog, boglach, boglachd, cathar, criathrach, lod, féith, rumach, fròg; beo-ghaineach, corcach, curach, corrach; seasgann.

Marshal, *s.* Marasgal; ceannard freiceadain; ceann-feadhna; teachdair. A field-marshal, *feachd-mharasgal.*

Marshal, *v. a.* Cuir an ordugh, tarruing suas, cuir air riaghailt, marasgail, marasglaich.

Marshaller, *s.* Marasglair.

Marshalling, *s.* Cuir an ordugh; tarruing suas, marasgladh.

Marshalsea, *s.* Gainntir th' ann an Lunnuinn.

Marshalship, *s.* Marasglachd.

Marshmallow, *s.* Malomh, grobais; leamhadh, fochas.

Marshy, *a.* Bog, féitheach; criathrachail; catharach; frògach. Marshy ground, *criathrach, féithe, curach.*

Mart, *s.* Margadh, margad; bargan, ceannach.

Marten, *s.* Seorsa neas; taoghan; (*a bird*), gobhlan gaoithe, ainleag mhara.

Martial, *a.* Cogail, crodha, curanta, gaisgeil, treun. A martial air, *fonn cogaidh.*

Martialist, *s.* Cùraidh, gaisgeach.

Martingal, *s.* Iall chasaidh.

Martinmas, *s.* Féill Martuinn, féill Mhartuinn an Naoimh.

Martinet, Martlet, *s.* Gobhlan gaoithe, gobhlachan gaoithe.

Martyr, *s.* Naomh-fhianuis; fianuis a chuirear gu bàs airson creidimh.

Martyr, *v. a.* Marbh airson creidimh.

Martyrdom, *s.* Bàs airson creidimh.

Martyrology, *s.* Seanachas na droing a dh' fhuilingeas bàs airson creidimh.

Marvel, *s.* Miorbhuil, miarbhail, iongantas, iongnadh, uamhann, neònachas. No marvel, *cha 'n eil iongantas ann.*

Marvel, *v.* Gabh miorbhuil, gabh iongantas, gabh neònachas.

Marvellous, *a.* Miorbhuileach, miarbhaileach, iongantach, neònach.

Marvellously, *adv.* Gu miorbhuileach, gu miarbhaileach, gu h-iongantach, gu neònach.

Marvellousness, *s.* Miorbhuileachd, iongantachd, iongantas, neonachas.

Masculine, *a.* Firionn; mar dhuine; duineil, fearail.

Mash, *s.* Biadh proinnte; mogal, masg, cumasg.

Mash, *v.* Pronn, bruth, coimeasg, measg. Mashed meat, *biadh proinnte, biadh pronn.*

Mashing-tub, *s.* Dabhach.

Mask, *s.* Cìdhis, gidhis; sgàile, culaidh-shùgraidh; duaichneachd, céil.

Mask, *v. a.* Sgàil, cuir cìdhis air, folaich, céil. Masked, *sgàilte, céilte, fo chidhis.*

Masker, *s.* Cìdhisear, gìdhisear.

Mason, *s.* Clachair, clochair. A drystone mason, *comhair.*

Masonry, *s.* Clachaireachd, clochaireachd.

Masquerade, *s.* Cìdhisearachd, gìdhisearachd.

Masquerader, *s.* Cìdhisear, gìdhisear.

Mass, *s.* (*Lump*), meall, torr, dùn; tomad, cruinneachan; cruinneagan; (*in the Romish church*), aifrionn.

Massacre, *s.* Mort, murt, mortadh, murtadh, àr, beubanachd, marbhadh, cosgair, cosgradh, casgradh, du-mharbhadh. Bloodshed and massacre, *mortadh is marbhadh, léir-mhortadh, sàs-mhortadh.*

Massacre, *v. a.* Mort, murt, àr, marbh; cosgair, casgair; beubanaich, léir-sgrios, dubh-mharbh.

Massiness, *s.* Truime, tomad, meud, truimead, domhaileachd.

Massive, *a.* Trom, tomadach, dàmhail, dòmhail.

Mast, *s.* Cnù dharaich, cnù fhaibhill.

Mast, *s.* Crann, crann luing. Mainmast, *crann mòr, crann meadhon;* foremast, *crann toisich.*

Masted, *a.* Crainnte, crannaichte, crannach. A masted boat, *bàt crainnte, bat croinn.*

Master, *s.* (*Teacher*), maighistir; oid ionnsuich, fear teagaisg; (*ruler*), fear riaghlaidh, riaghlair; (*chief*), priomh, ceann; (*overseer*), griobh. Master of arts, *maighistir ealadhna;* a master mason, *priomh-chlachair;* a master thief, *righ nam méirleach;* a dancing-master, *maighistir dannsaidh;* he who has a master has found his match, *am fear aig am bheil maighistir bithidh seise aig.*

Master, *v.* Smachdaich, ceannsuich, cum air ordugh, cum fo; rioghaich, riaghlaich; sàruich, claoidh, fairtlich air.

Master, *s.* Priomh-iuchair, iuchair a dh' fhosgaileas gach glas.

Master-builder, *s.* Ard-chlachair, priomh-chlachair.

† **Masterdom**, *s.* Lamh an uachdar; riaghailt, smachd.

Masterhand, *s.* Fear ealadhanta; lamh ghrinneil.

Masterless, *a.* Gun mhaighstir; neo-cheannsuichte.

Masterliness, *s.* Ard-sgil, ro sgile.

Masterly, *a.* Ealadhanta, sgileil, teoma, eòlach, seòlta, smachdail.

Masterpiece, *s.* Mor-ghniomh, ard-ghniomh.

Mastership, *s.* Maighistireachd, ceannas, riaghailt, barrachd, lamh an uachdar; sgile, eòlas.

Masterwort, *s.* Mòr fhliogh.

Mastery, *s.* Maighistireas, ceannas, barrachd, lamh an uachdar, smachd, eolas, sgil.

Masticate, *v. a.* Cagain, cagainn, cnàmh, cràmh. Masticated, *cagainte.*

Mastication, *s.* Cagnadh, cnamhadh, cramhadh.

Mastich, *s.* Maisteag, seorsa bith craoibh a thig as na h-eileanan Greugach. Mastich tree, *maisteag.*

Mastiff, *s.* Mastuidh, madadh, cu feòladair. A fool is like a mastiff, *ceann coin air madadh balaich* (*no*) *air mac na caillich.*

Mastless, *a.* Gun chrann.

Mastlin, *s.* Maislinn.

Mat, *s.* Stràille, brat luachair.

Mat, *v. a.* Brat, comhdaich, cùrainnich; figh, pleat, dual.

Match, *s.* Fadadh cluaise.

Match, *s.* (*At play*), bair, cluich, strìgh, comh-strìgh.

Match, *s.* (*Couple*), seise, coimeas, leithid, leth-bhreac; tiunnal; pòsadh, maraiste, cupall.

Match, *v. a.* Coimeas, diong, cuplaich; ionannaich, pòs; dean fragarrach, freagair.

Match, *v. n.* Freagair; bi freagarrach, coird; bi cubhaidh.

Matchable, *a.* Cubhaidh, freagarrach, ionann, co-ionann, so-dhiongadh.

Matched, *a.* Cuplaichte; freagaraichte; coimeasta; pòsda.

Matchless, *a.* Gun choimeas.

Matchlessness, *s.* Neo-choimeasachd, barrachd; barrghrinneas; bàrr-mhaise.

Matchmaker, *s.* Fàdair.

Mate, *s.* Céile; fear no bean, companach; fear comith; an dara fear ann an inbhe air bord luing. A surgeon's mate, *iar-léigh;* a master's mate, *iar-mhaighstir, iar-chaiptean.*

Mate, *v.* Diong; pòs; cuplaich; cuir cuideachd.

Material, *a.* Corporra, brighmhor, stuthail, talmhaidh, corporail; cudthromach; feumail; àraidh, àirid.

Materialist, *s.* Fear àichein nitheanna spioradail.

Materiality, *s.* Corporrachd, brìghmhorachd.

Materially, *adv.* Gu corporra; gu feumail; gu cudthromach, gu h-araidh, gu h-araid.

Materials, *s. pl.* Cungaidh; cungaidhean.

Materiate, *a.* Talmhaidh.

Maternal, *a.* Màthaireil; màthar.

Maternity, *s.* Màthaireileachd, màthairealachd.

Math, *s.* Spagh, spaghadh, uibhir is a ghearras iarunn fàladair air aon tarruing.

Mathematician, *s.* Fear tomhais-iùl.

Mathematics, *s.* Ealadhain a thig air tomhas is àireamh, tomhas-iùl; àireamh iùl, iùl tomhais is àireimh.

Matin, *s.* Madainn, maduinn.

Matin, *a.* Madainn, maidneach.

Matins, *s.* Urnuigh mhadainn, aoradh maidne.

Matrass, *s.* Seorsa buideil, buideal bronnach; leabaidh iochdrach; seide.

Matrice, *s.* Bolg, balg, machlag, brù; soire na cloinne, molltair.

Matricide, *s.* Màthar-mhort, mathar-mhortadh, màtharorn.

Matricide, *s.* Màthar-mhortair, mortair mathar.

Matriculate, *v.* Gabh a steach mar bhall colaiste, cuir ainm sgoileir ann an leabhar colaiste; gabh stigh, gabh.

Matriculation, *s.* Gabhail a steach mar bhall colaiste; inntrinn.

Matrimonial, *a.* Pòsach, pòsail, pòsaidh, maraisteach, maraisteil.

Matrimony, *s.* Pòsadh, maraiste.

Matrix, *s.* Machlag, bolg, balg, brù, soire na cloinne.

Matron, *s.* Banaisg, beanaisg, bean phosda, mathair teaghlaich; bean chiallach; cailleach.

Matronal, *a.* Banaisgeach, banaisgeil.

Matter, *s.* (*Corruption*), iongar, silteach; (*substance*), stuth; ni; rud; brìgh; (*business*), gnothuch, cùis, aobhar; gniomh; (*moment*), omhail, umhail. Full of matter, *làn iongair, làn brìgh;* there is no matter, *cha n' eil omhail, cha n' omhail ann;* what is the matter with you? *ciod a tha cur ort? ciod a dh' fhairich thu?*

Matter, *v. n.* and *a.* Gabh suim, thoir an aire; bi cudthromach, iongaraich. What matters it? *ciod an omhail? ciod an omhail th' ann?* the pimple mattered, *dh' iongaraich an guirean.*

Mattery, *a.* Iongarach, lan iongair.

Mattock, *s.* Piocaid; gràip, greap, buraiche, caib, spaid, tobha; croman inuearach; pleadhan.

Mattress, *s.* Matrais; leabadh fhlocais, fo-leabadh.

Maturate, *v. a.* and *n.* Abaich, dean abaich, fàs abaich (no) abuidh.

Maturation, *s.* Abuchadh, abachudh.

Mature, *a.* Abaich, abuich, foirfe, ullamh, deas, iomlan.

Mature, *v. a.* Dean abuich, thoir gu h-abachd; thoir gu ceann, dean iomlan.

Maturely, *adv.* Gu h-abaich, gu foirfe, gu h-ullamh, tràthail, moch, much.

Maturity, *s.* Abachd, abuidheachd, abuichead, foirfeachd, iomlanachd.

Maudlin, *a.* (*perhaps a corruption of* Magdalen, *whom painters draw with swollen eyes and a disordered look. The face of an intoxicated person may have been so named, from a fancied resemblance to Magdalen's picture.*) Misgeach, froganach, air a mheisge, air a mhisge, air an daoraich.

Maudlin, *s.* Seorsa luibh.

Maugre, *prep.* A dh' aindeoin, ge b' oil le.

Maul, *v. a.* Bruth, mill, beubanaich, dornaich, pronn, buail, ciùrr. Mauled, *brùite, beubanaichte, pronnta, proinnte, dornaichte, buailte.* He got himself terribly mauled, *fhuair e 'dhroch chiurradh;* she got herself mauled, *fhuair i a ciurradh.*

Maul, *s.* Fairche, fairc, geannair, geinneir, ord da lamh.

Maund, *s.* Clabhag; sgùlean, croidhle, croidhleag, basgaid.

Maunder, *v. n.* Dean borbhan (no) durdan, dean monmhor, talaich, dean talachadh; dean ciarsan.

Maunderer, *s.* Borbhanaiche, fear talachaidh, fear ciarsanach, ciarsanaiche.

Maundering, *a.* Borbhanach, durdanach, dranndanach, ciarsanach; tormanach, ciùrlanach.

Maundering, *s* Borbhanaiche, dùrdanaiche, dranndan, ciarsanachd, tormanaich, ciùrlan.

Maundy-Thursday, *s.* (*from* mande, *a basket, according to Spelman, in which the king was wont to give alms to the poor*) Di 'r daoine a bhrochain mhòir.

Mausoleum, *s.* Tuam riomhach: an tuam chùiteach a thogadh do Mhasolus rìgh Charia le 'bhanrighinn Artemisia.

Mavis, *s.* Smeorach.

Maw, *s.* Goile; *stamac;* sgròban.

Mawkish, *a.* Trom, droch bhlasda.

Mawkishness, *s.* Tur-thilge.

Mawks, *s.* Caile bhalaoch.

Maw-worm, *s* Cnuimh ghoile; durrag

Maxillar, *a.* Gialach peirceallach, a bhuineas do 'n ghial (no) do 'n pheirceall.

Maxim, *s.* Radh fior, suidhichte; bun-radh; radh suidhichte, gnath-bhriathar, fior-radh.

Maximum, *s.* A mhòr chuid, a chuid is mo.

May, *s.* Bealtuinn, mios bhealtuinn, maidh, an céitean; an cùigeamh mios May-day, *la bealtuinn, la buidhe bealtuinn.*

May, *v. aux.* Feudaidh, faodaidh; feud, bi comasach, ceadaich. I may, *feudaidh mi*, I may not do it, *cha n' fheud mi a deanamh;* as soon as may be, *cho luath 's a ghabhas, cho lom luath is a ghabhas*, you may for me, *faodaidh tu air mo shonsa dheth;* whilst you may, *fhads is urrainn thu*, as great as may be, *air a mheud*, as little as may be, *air a lughaid*, may be (perhaps), *math dh' fhaoidte, maith dh' fhaoidte, theagamh*, it may be, *faodaidh e 'bhith*, may it please you, *gum b' e do thoil e*

May-bug, *s.* Daol feasgair

May-day, *s.* Là bealtuinn, là buidhe bealtuinn.

May-flower, *s.* Seorsa luibh

May-fly, *s.* Cuileag chéitein, cuileag Mhàidh.

May-game, *s.* Cluich bhealtuinn, cluich a bhlàtha.

Mayor, *s.* Maor baile, priomh-mhaor, ard-mhaor, maor mòr, riaghlair baile margaidh

Mayoralty, *s.* Ard-mhaorsainneachd, ard-mhaorachd.

Mayoress, *s* Ard bhan-mhaor, ban-phriomh-mhaor

Maypole, *s.* Crann céitein, crann ard mu 'n danns òigridh air là bealtuinn.

Mayweed, *s.* Seorsa cambhile.

Mazard, *s* Gial, craos, peirceall.

Maze, *s.* Cuairt, cuairtean; aimlisg; ioma-cheist; briong-laid, seacharan.

Maze, *v a* Cuir thar a chéile, cuir troimh a chéile; cuir air seacharan; seachranaich.

Mazer, *s.* Cuach, cuachan, corn, copan; sgàl

Mazy, *a.* Cuairteach, iom-chuairteach, cuairteanach; aimlisgeach; deacair.

Me, *pron.* Mi, mise.

Meacock, *s.* Fear slatail; cladhair, cailleach; gealtair.

Meacock, *a.* Meat, cladhaireach, bog, cailleachanta, cailleachail; gealtach.

Mead, *s.* Mildheoch; clabhair.

Mead, Meadow, *s* Lòn, dail, ailean, miadan, fàiche, ach, mìn-fheur. Meadow-hay, *saoidh lòin*

Meagre, *a.* Caol, bochd, tana, truagh; lom, seannachail

Meagre, *v. a.* Dean caol, dean tana, (no) bochd.

Meagreness, *s* Caoile, taine, tainead, truaghas, bochdainn, luime.

Meal, *s* Min Fine meal, *min mhìn*, oatmeal, *min choirce*, barleymeal, *min eorna*, wheatmeal, *min chruithneachd*, ryemeal, *min sheogail*, peasemeal, *min pheasrach*, beanmeal, *min phònair*, mealtub, *ciste mhin, stannd*, a mealsieve, *criathar min*, a mealtrough, *sgàl;* coarsely-ground meal, *corrlach*

Meal, *s* (*Diet*), cuid, cuid an tràth, lòn, biadh Two meals a day, *da lòin san làtha*

Mealman, *s.* Fear min, marsonta min, mineadair, muillear

Mealtime, *s* Tràth bidh, tràth lòin. After mealtime, *an deigh thràth bidh.*

Mealtub, *s* Stann, stannd, stannd min

Mealy, *a* Mincar; mar mhin

Mealy-mouthed, *a.* Narach; tlà-bhileach, beulchar.

Mean, *a* (*Poor*), iosal, neo-uasal, neo-inbheach, suarrach, diblidh, bochd, truagh; truaghanta; (*in spirit*), crion, goirt, gortach, suarrach, gun fhiu, mosach, musach, neo-eireachdail. A mean soul, *cridhe crion*, a mean man, *duine diblidh;* mean conduct, *iomchar neo-eireachdail.*

Mean, *a* (*Middle*), meadhonach; eadar-mheadhonach; stuam, measarra.

Mean, *s* Meadhonachd; meadhon; (*method*), inneal, achd, seòl, doigh, modh, cor. By all means, *air na h-uile doigh, air na h-uile cor*, by your means, *trid-san, troimhibh-se, leat-san, leibh-se*, by what means? *ciod an doigh, ciamar?* by foul means, *le foill*, by some means, *air sheòl éigin*, by any means, *air aon chor*, by outward means, *le meadhona o'n leth muigh*

Mean, *v a* and *n* Ciallaich, rùnaich, cuir romhad; saoil, bi a los. What do you mean? *ciod tha thu 'ciallachadh? ciod th' air d' aire? ciod tha uait?* I mean to go, *tha mi los falbh, tha mi 'cur romham falbh*, you know whom I mean, *tha fhios agad co tha mi a ciallachadh.*

Meander, *v n.* Lùb, mar ni amhuinn; fiar

Meander, *s* Lùb, lùban, car, tionndadh, cuir.

Meandering, *a.* Lùbach, luibeach, carach; cuairteanach

Meaning, *s* Ciall, brìgh, rùn, tuigse. With a bad meaning, *le droch rùn*, what is the meaning of it? *ciod is ciall da?*

Meanly, *adv.* Gu meadhonach, gu h-iosal; gu mi-chuiseach, gu truagh, gu goirt, gu truaghanta, gu neo-urramach, gu neo-uasal, gu mosach, gu musach, gu crion, gu neo-eireachdail

Meanness, *s* (*Of birth*), bochduinn, truaighe, truaghanachd, (*of mind*), crìne, mi-chuis, mi-chuiseachd, diblidheachd, truaillidheachd, cladhaireachd, geilte.

Means, *s.* Còghnadh, fear còghnaidh, (*substance*), maoin, inbhe, beartas, saibhreas, taic, toic. Having great means, *beartach, saibhir, toiceil*

Mean-spirited, *a* Crion, crian; mi-chuiseach

Meant, *pret* and *p. part* of mean. Ciallaichte. See Mean

Meantime, *s.* Meadhon uair, meadhon am In the meantime, *anns a mheadhon uair, air an am, air an uair, an tràths.*

Mease, *s* Maois; cuig ceud sgadan.

Measled, *a* Anns a ghriuthach, gu h-olc leis a ghriuthach, bruiceanach.

Measles, *s* Griuthach. The measles, *a ghriuthach.*

Measurable, *a.* So-thomhas, a ghabhas tomhas, furas thomhas, iom-thomhas.

Measurably, *adv.* Gu so-thomhas, gu meadhonach, gu stuaim, gu cneasta.

Measure, *s* Tomhas; meidh; (*moderation*), meadhon, cuimheas; (*purpose*), seòl, doigh, rùn; (*of a gun*), miosar Beyond measure, *thar tomhas*, take measures, *gabh seol;* take my measure, *gabh mo thomhas.*

Measure, *v.* Tomhais; cothromaich, gabh tomhas. Measure out, *sgéith*

Measured, *a* Tomhaiste; sgéithte; cothromaichte A measured pace, *ceum socrach*

Measurer, *s* Fear tomhais, tomhasair

Measuring, *s* Tomhasadh; cothromachadh, sgéith

Measureless, *a* Do-thomhas, thar tomhas, nach gabh tomhas.

Measurement, *s.* Tomhas, tomhasadh.

Meat, *s* Biadh, lòn, teachd an tir, cuid; (*flesh*), feòil. Meat and drink, *biadh is deoch*, roast meat, *feòil ròiste, rost*, boiled meat, *biadh bruich*, sweet meat, *biadh milis, mealannan*, minced meat, *biadh pronn, biadh proinnte*, broken meat, *spruilleach;* dress meat, *greadh biadh;* provide meat, *solair lòn, solair biadh*, meat for cattle, *connlach.*

Meated, *a* Biadhta, biadhte

Meathe, *s* Deoch mhilis, mil-dheoch

Meat-offering, *s* Tabhartas bidh

Meatus, *s* Rod, slighe, eileach; amar, fosgal

Mechanic, *s* Fear ceairde Mechanics, *luchd ceairde*

Mechanic, Mechanical, *a* Ceardail, iosal, innleachdach. Mechanical arts, *ceairde.*

Mechanics, *s* (*The science*), ceardachd; dealbhachd, innleachd, ceaird

Mechanician, *s* Fear innleachdach, fear dealbhaidh, dealbhadair, fear ceaird

Mechanism, *s* Dealbhadh, cruth, dealbh.

Meconium, *s* Suain leigheas, cac leinibh

Medal, *s* Meideal; sean chùinn; bonn commuinn, bonn a bhuailear an onoir neach (no) ni; dealbh.

Medalist, *s* Meidealaiche

Medallion, *s* Sean mheideal

Meddle, *v* Bean do, bean ri, buin ri, meachranaich, gabh gnothuch ri, gabh eadar Do not meddle with him, *na bean da*, I shall neither meddle nor make with it, *cha bhi cuid no pàirt agam dheth*

Meddler, *s* Fear meachranach, fear meachranaiche; fear rudach, fear leam leat, fear a ghabhas gnothuch ri rud nach buin dà.

Meddlesome, *a.* Meachranach, rudach

Meddling, *s* Buntuinn ri, beanachd.

Mediate, *v n* Dean réith, dean sìth, cuir réith, dean réite, cuir eadar, dean eadar-mheadhon

Mediate, *a.* Eadar-mheadhonach, eadar-mheadhonail

Mediation, *s.* Eadar-mheadhon, eadar-mheadhonachd, tagradh

Mediator, *s* Eadar-mheadhonair; fear réite; tagrair, fear tagraidh; comhairliche, an Slànuighear

Mediatorial, *a* Eadar-mheadhonach, eadar-mheadonaireach; réiteachail

Mediatorship, *s.* Eadar-mheadhonaireachd, eadar-mheadhonachd.

Mediatrix, *s* Ban-eadar mheadhonair.

Medical, *a.* Leigheasach, leigheach, ioc-shlainnteach. A medical man, *leigh, dearg-leigh*, dochtair

Medicament, *s* Leigheas, cungaidh leigheis, ioc-shlainnte.

Medicamental, *a* Leigheasach, leigheasail, ioc-shlainnteach.

Medicate, *v.* Measg le leigheas. Medicated, *measgta le leigheas.*

Medication, *s* Measgadh le leigheas.

Medicinable, *a.* Leigheasach, ioc-shlainnteach.

Medicinal, *a.* Leigheasach, leigheasail, ioc-shlainnteach.

Medicine, *s.* Leigheas, cungaidh leigheis, ioc-shlainnt; ealadhain leigheis. A doctor of medicine, *ollamh leaghas;* a purging medicine, *purgaid, leigheas tualaig;* binding medicine, *leigheas daingneachaidh*

Mediety, *s.* Meadhonachd; leth, bloidh.

Mediocrity, *s.* Meadhonachd, eatorras; cneastachd, cuimeis

Meditate, *v* Smuainich, smaoinich, smuaintich, beachdsmuainich, beachdaich; dealbh.

Meditation, *s* Smuaineachadh, smaoineachadh, breathnachadh, breithneachadh; beachd-smuaineachadh.

Meditative, *a.* Smuaineachail, smaoineachail, smaointeachail

Mediterranean, *a.* Meadhon-thireach, eadar-thireach. Mediterranean sea, *muir na meadhon thìr.*

Medium, *s* Meadhon, eadar dha chuid, eadar da anabharradh; measarrachd.

Medlar, *s.* Meidil A medlar tree, *crann meidil, craobh mheidil*

Medley, *s.* Coimeasg, cumasg

Medley, *a.* Coimeasgta, coimeasgte, air feadh chéile, troimh chéile

Medullar, Medullary, *a* Smiorach, smiora.

Meed, *s.* Duais, tuarasdal, luach-saothaireach, luaidheachd, gibhte, tabhartas, buileachas

Meek, *a* Macanta, ciùin, seamh, mìn, stuama; tlà, soitheamh, neo-uallach, iriosal.

Meekly, *adv* Gu macanta, gu ciùin, gu seamh, gu mìn, gu stuama, gu tlà, gu soitheamh, gu h-iriosal.

Meekness, *s* Macantas, ciùineas, seimhe, seimheachd, stuaim, tlàthas, irioslachd, ceannsachd.

Meer, *s.* Loch, lochan, linne; (*bound*), crioch, teoradh, iomall.

Meet, *a.* Cubhaidh, ceart, freagarrach; iomchuidh, eugasach As it was meet, *mar bu chubhaidh.*

Meet, *v. a* and *n.* Coinnich, thoir coinneamh, rach an codhail, thoir còdhail, rach an dàil, thoir aghaidh air; cruinnich, thig ann ceann a chéile; tachair, faigh I met him, *choinnich mi e*, they meet, *thachair iad*, meet half way, *coinnich le rathaid*, go to meet him, *rach na chodhail;* go to meet her, *rach na codhail*

Meeting, *s* Coinneamh, coinneachadh, cruinneach, cruinneachadh, co-chruinneach, co-chruinneachadh, mòd; tional, teanal, co-thional; còdhail. Give him a meeting, *thoir coinneamh dha*, the meeting of two streams, *comar, ionar, co-shruth, roinn*, the meeting of two roads, *coinneachadh dà rathaid*

Meeting-house, *s* Tigh coinneamh, tigh cruinneachaidh.

Meetly, *adv* Gu ceart, gu cubhaidh, gu freagarrach, gu h-iomchuidh

Meetness, *s.* Ceartas, cubhaidheachd, freagarrachd, iomchuidhead, iomchuidheachd.

Megrim, *s.* Cinnidh; tuaineal, tuainealach

Meine, *v. a.* Measg, coimeasg

Melancholic, *a* Dubhach, muladach, tuirseach, brònach, trom, dubh-leanntach, dubh-lionntach, dubhronach.

Melancholy, *s* Lionn-dubh, liunn-dubh, dubh-lionn; mulad, dubhachas, bròn, tuirse, sprochd, truime-inntinn, doilghios, do-bròn

Melancholy, *a.* Dubhach, muladach, brònach, doilgh-iosach, trom, trom-inntinneach, neo-shunntach, tuirseach.

Melancholy-thistle, *s.* Cluas an fheidh.

Meles, *s.* Broc, brochd, taghan.

Melilot, *s.* Seorsa luibh.

Meliorate, *v. a.* Leasaich; càirich; cuir am feairrd; dean ni 's fhearr, cuir am feabhas. Meliorated, *leasaichte*.

Melioration, *s.* Leasachadh, cur am feairrd (no) am feabhas, càramh.

Meliority, *s.* Feairrd.

Mell, *v. a.* Measg; measgnaich; suath, cuir troimh chéile.

Mellifluent, **Mellifluous**, *a.* Mileach; mileil; meile-ach; milis, meilis.

Mellow, *a.* (*In sound*), tiomhaidh, tiamhaidh, tlà; seimh; (*ripe*), abuich, làn abuich, bog, bogar; (*with liquor*), meisg-each, air an daoraich, froganach, sunntach. Mellow apples, *ubhlan abuich* (*no*) *bogar*; not mellow, *searbh, neo-abuich*.

Mellow, *v. a.* Abaich, abuich, dean abuich; bogaich, seimhich, mìnich, millsich. Mellowed, *abuich, bogaichte, seimh, millsichte, milis*.

Mellowness, *s.* Abachd, abuidheachd; làn-abachd, làn aois.

Melodious, *a.* Ceòlmhor, fonnmhor, binn; bochthuinn. co-sheirmeach; biolagach. Melodiously, *gu ceòlmhor, gu binn*.

Melodiousness, *s.* Ceòlmhorachd, ceolmhoireachd, oir-fideachd.

Melody, *s.* Ceol, fonn, co-sheirm, airfideadh, binn-cheòl; binneas, òran, luinneag; coilleag.

Melon, *s.* Mileag, mil-ubhal, mil-mhucag, mil-mhuc.

Melt, *v. a.* Leagh; taislich; bogaich. Melted, *leaghta, air a leaghadh, taislichte, bogaichte*.

Melter, *s.* Leaghadair.

Melting, *a.* Drùighteach; leaghach.

Melting, *s.* Leaghadh, leaghadaireachd.

Melting-house, *s.* Tigh leaghadaireachd.

Member, *s.* Ball; aon; earann, roinn. Member of a so-ciety, *ball comuinn*; member of the house of peers, *ball tigh na flath-chomhairle*; member of the house of com-mons, *ball tigh na tuath-chomhairle*; a privy member, *ball diomhair, cungaidh, rud, cuid*.

Membranaceous, *a.* Sgannanach, meamrach.

Membrane, *s.* Sgannan, foir-chraiceann, meamradh.

Membranous, *a.* Sgannanach, meamrach, meamranach.

Memento, *s.* Cuimhneachan; sànas, fios, fathunn.

Memoir, *s.* Meanbh-eachdruidh; cunntas; fios, bann.

Memorable, *a.* Ion-chuimhneachail; cliùiteach.

Memorandum, *s.* Cuimhneachan.

Memorial, *s.* Cuimhneachan; cuimhne; ath-chuimhne.

Memorialist, *s.* Ath-chuingiche.

Memorize, *v.* Sgriobh, cuir sios.

Memory, *s.* Cuimhne; meoghair, meomhair, meamhair. A good memory, *deagh chuimhne*; a bad memory, *droch chuimhne*; keep in memory, *cum air chuimhne*; commit to memory, *ionnsuich air do chridhe* (*no*) *air do theangaidh*; out of memory, *a cuimhne*.

Men, *pl.* of man. Daoine, fir, droing; gaisgich, laoich.

Menace, *v. a.* Bagair, ràith. I threatened him, *bhagair mi air, ràith mi air*.

Menace, *s.* Bagar, bagradh, bagairt, ràithe.

Menacer, *s.* Bagrair, bagairtear, fear bagraidh, fear bagairt.

Menacing, *a.* Bagrach, bagairteach.

Menacing, *s.* Bagradh, bagairt, ràithe.

Menagerie, *s.* Aite san gleidhear eoin agus fiadh-bhéist-ean, lann fhiadh-bheistean.

Mend, *v. a.* and *n.* Càirich, càir, leasaich, ceartaich; slà-nuich; rach am feobhas, rach am feairrd. Mend my shoes, *càirich mo bhrògan*; he mends in health, *thu e 'dol am feobhas*.

Mendable, *a.* So-chàramh; a ghabhas càramh, so-leas-achadh.

Mendacity, *s.* Breug, fallsachd.

Mended, *pret.* Càirichte, leasaichte, ceartaichte, slànuichte, air dol am feobhas.

Mender, *s.* Neach a chàiricheas (no) a leasaicheas, fear càramh; (*of shoes*), brògair.

Mendicancy, *s.* Bochduinn, baigearachd, baigeireachd.

Mendicant, *s.* Urr bhochd; duine bochd, déirceach; baigear, baigeir; brathair bochd; bleidear.

Mendicant, *a.* Bochd, truagh, uireasbhach, uireasbhuidh-each.

Mendicity, *s.* Bochduinn, uireasbhuidheachd, easbhuidh, uireasbhuidh; baigearachd, baigeireachd.

Mending, *s.* Càramh; dol am feobhas, brotachadh. On the mending hand, *air taobh an fheabhais*.

Menial, *a.* Tighe, muinntearach.

Menial, *s.* Seirbheiseach, feamanach, gille.

Menses, *s.* Mios-shruth; ruithe nam ban, fuil mios, ban-luasgadh.

Menstrual, **Menstruous**, *a.* Miosail; lamanta, ban-luasgach.

Mensurable, *a.* So-thomhas, a ghabhas tomhasadh.

Mensurate, *v. a.* Tomhais. Mensurated, *tomhaiste*.

Mensuration, *s.* Tomhas; tomhas-iùl.

Mental, *a.* Inntinneach; inntinn, san inntinn. Mental powers, *buaidh inntinn, feartan inntinn, càilean*.

Mentally, *adv.* San inntinn, sa bheachd, sa chridhe.

Mention, *s.* Iomradh, ainm. Make mention, *dean iomradh*; make mention of me, *dean iomradh orm, labhair umam*.

Mention, *v.* Dean iomradh, ainmich, innis, aithris. Men-tioned, *ainmichte*; forementioned, *roimh-ainmichte, air a roimh-radh*.

Mentioning, *s.* Ainmeachadh, innseadh, aithriseadh, labh-airt, bruidhinn.

Mephitic, **Mephitical**, *a.* Puinnsionta, puinnseanach, breun, breunta, loibheach.

Meracious, *a.* Glan, soilleir, neo-mheasgta.

Mercantile, *a.* Malairteach, marsontach.

† **Mercat**, *s.* Margad, margadh.

Mercature, *s.* Ceannachadh, ceannachd, coigleadh.

Mercenary, *a.* A ghabhas briob; gionach, cruaidh, air paigh, air thuarasdal.

Mercenary, *s.* Aon a ghabhas briob; urr air thuarasdal.

Mercer, *s.* Marsonta sioda.

Merchandize, *s.* Marsontachd, ceannachd, bàthar, earradh.

Merchandize, *v. a.* Ceannuich, malairt, dean ceannachd, dean co-mhalairt.

Merchant, *s.* Ceannuiche, marsonta, marsal, malartaiche.

Merchantable, *a.* Arson a mhargaidh; a ghabhas reic.

Merchantman, *s.* Loingeas mharsonta, loingeas (no) luing bhathar.

Merciful, *a.* Baigheil, iochdmhor, tròcaireach, truacanta, daonach, còir, gràsmhor, caomh.

Mercifully, *adv.* Gu baigheil, gu h-iochdmhor, gu tròc-aireach, gu truacanta, gu daonach, gu còir, gu gràsmhor.

Mercifulness, *s.* Trocaireachd, baighealachd, iochd-mhoireachd, daonachd, truas.

Merciless, *a.* An-iochdmhor, ain-iochdmhor, neo-thruacanta, cruaidh, cruaidh-chridheach, cruadalach, borb.

Mercilessly, *adv.* Gu h-an-iochdmhor, gu neo-thruacanta, gu cruadalach, gu borb.

Mercilessness, *s.* Ain-iochdmhorachd, neo-thruacantachd, neo-thròcaireachd.

Mercurial, *a.* Beò, beothail; luath, luaimneach; do bheò-airgiod, beo-airgiodach.

Mercury, *s.* Beo-airgiod, airgiod beò; suilbhire, beòthalachd, paipear nuaidheachd; teachdair; seorsa luibh.

Mercy, *s.* Tròcair, baigh, iochd, truas, maitheanas, mathanas, gràs, caoimhneas.

Mercy-seat, *s.* Cathair breathanais, cathair tròcair.

Mere, *a.* Fior. A mere fool, *fior amadan.*

Mere, *s.* (*Lake*), loch, lochan, linne; (*bound*), crioch, teoradh, iomall.

Merely, *adv.* Amhàin; ach gann; direach. Merely this, *amhàin so.*

Mere-stone, *s.* Clach crìche.

Meretricious, *a.* Macnusach, siùrsachail, striopachail, mi-gheimnidh, mi-gheamnaidh, neo-ghlan, drùiseil, drabasta; faoin-bhriagh.

Meretriciously, *adv.* Gu macnusach, gu striopachail, gu mi-gheamnaidh, gu drùiseil.

Meretriciousness, *s.* Macnusachd, siùrsachd, mi-gheimneachd; drùisealachd, striopachas.

Meridiation, *s.* Codal nòin.

Meridian, *s.* Meadhon làtha àirde an làtha. A meridian line, *lìn mheadhon làtha, an deas-lìn;* the sun is on the meridian, *tha ghrian na h-airde.*

Meridian, *a.* Deas.

Meridional, *a.* Deas, deisearach.

Meridionality, *s.* Deisearachd.

Merit, *s.* Toillteanas, toilltinneas; còir; ceart; gar, garaidheachd, leas, luach, luaidheachd, òirdheirceas, fiundas, fiunas. According to your merit, *a réir do thoillteannais;* a man of merit, *ro-dhuine.*

Merit, *v. a.* Toill; bi airidh air. You well deserve it, *is math thoill thu e; is math is fhiach thu e.*

Meritorious, *a.* Toilltinneach, cliù-thoilltinneach, aithrigh, airidh.

Meritoriously, *adv.* Gu toilltinneach, gu h-airidh.

Meritoriousness, *s.* Toilltinneachd.

† Merk, *s.* Marg.

Merlin, *s.* Seorsa seabhaig; meirneal.

Mermaid, *s.* Maighdeann mhara.

Merrily, *adv.* Gu mear, gu suilbhear, gu subhach, gu suigeartach, gu sugach, gu sunntach, gu cridheil, gu mear.

Merrimaking, *s.* Ealaidh, sùgradh, spuirt, aighear; fleagh, cuirm.

Merrimaking, *a.* Sugach, sunntach, aighearach, ri sugradh, ri h-aighear.

Merriment, *s.* Ealaidh, sùgradh, cridhealas, aighear, subhachas, spuirt, ioladh, fearas chuideachd, gàrachdaich, gàireachdaich.

Merriness, *s.* Mire, sunnt, cridhealas, sùgradh, aighear.

Merry, *a.* Mear, cridheil, sunntach, ait, aighearach, subhach, aobhach, suigeartach, suilbhear. You have a merry time of it, *is ann agad tha 'n uair chridheil dheth;* a merry-andrew, *baothair.*

Merry-andrew, *s.* Baothair; sgeigeir; baoth-chleasaiche.

Merry-thought, *s.* Cnaimh gobhlach ann an uchd circ.

Mersion, *s.* Tumadh, tomadh, bogadh.

Meseems, *v. imper.* Their leam, their leam fhéin; tha mi a saoilsinn.

Mesh, *s.* Mogal, mogal lìn. A mesh vat, *dabhach.*

Mesh, *v.* Glac (no) rib le lion.

Meshy, *a.* Mogulach, liontaichte, liontaidh, mar obair lìn, ribeach.

Meslin, *s.* Maslaim, maislean.

Mess, *s.* Mias bhidh; biadh; comaidh, comithe, comithe cheathrar. A mess of pottage, *mias bhrochain, mias easaich.*

Mess, *v.* Ith, gabh comith, ith an còmhroinn, dean comaidh (no) comith, ith cuideachd.

Message, *s.* Gnothuch, gnothach; teachdaireachd, fios. Go on a message, *rach air ghnothuch.*

Messenger, *s.* Teachdair; fear gnothuich; gille ruithe; post. A messenger at arms, *tearraid.*

Messiah, *s.* Slànuighear an t-saoghail, Criosd, Prionnsa na sìth.

Messieurs, *s.* Sàir, daoine uailse; daoine uasal.

Messmate, *s.* Fear comaidh, fear com-ithe.

Messuage, *s.* Tigh comhnuidh agus fearann leis.

Met, *pret.* and *p. part.* of meet. Choinnich, thachair; coinnichte, air tachairt.

Metacarpus, *s.* Caol an-dùirn.

Metachronism, *s.* Ùine-mhearachd.

Metage, *s.* Tomhas guail.

Metal, *s.* Miodailt, meatailt, meiteal; òr; airgiod, prais, umha, peòtar, pleòtar, luaidh; stuth, misneach; spiorad.

Metalist, *s.* Miodailtiche, meitealair.

Metallic, Metalline, *a.* Miodailteach, meiteal.

Metallurgy, *s.* Obair mhiodailt.

Metamorphose, *v. a.* Cruth-chaochail, cruth-atharraich.

Metamorphosis, *s.* Cruth-chaochladh, cruth-atharrachadh.

Metaphor, *s.* Coslachd, cosmhalachd, coslas, samhladh, fo-shamhladh.

Metaphorical, *a.* Coslachail, samhlachail. Metaphorically, *fo-shamhladh.*

Metaphrase, *s.* Eadar-theangadh.

Metaphrast, *s.* Eadar-theangair.

Metaphysician, *s.* Teallsanach, feallsanach.

Metaphysics, *s.* Seorsa teallsanachd.

Metatarsus, *s.* Troidhe.

Metathesis, *s.* Cur gu taobh; mùth aite.

Mete, *v. a.* Tomhais; meidh, cothromaich. Meted, *tomhaiste.*

Metempsychosis, *s.* Siubhladh anam o aon chorp gu corp eile.

Meteor, *s.* Dreug, dreag; nì sam bi air ghin san adhar; grian, deathach.

Meteorology, *s.* Adhar-eòlas, aile-eòlas, adhar (no) aileiùl.

Meteorous, *a.* Dreugach, dreuganta.

Meter, *s.* Tomhasair, fear tomhais; fear meidh.

Metewand, Meteyard, *s.* Slat thomhais.

Metheglin, *s.* Mildheoch.

Methinks, *v. impers.* Their leam; tha mi 'saòilsinn.

Method, *s.* Seòl, doigh, achd, rod, rathad, lathailt; slighe, modh; riaghailt, ordugh.

Methodical, *a.* Riaghailteach; ordughail, lathailteach. Methodically, *gu riaghailteach, gu lathailteach, a réir riaghailt.*

Methodicalness, *s.* Riaghailteachd, riaghailt, lathailteachd, ordugh.

Methodize, *v. a.* Cuir an ordugh, riaghail, cuir an lathailt.

Methodist, *s.* Leigh eòlach; baoth-shearmonaiche; cràbhach.

Methodistical, *a.* Cràbhach, ain-diadhuidh, ana-crabhach.

Methought, *pret.* of methinks. Shaoil mi, their leam.

Metoposcopy, *s.* Gnùis-fhiosachd.

Metre, *s* Dàn; rannachd; bardachd

Metropolis, *s.* Priomh-bhaile, priomh-chathair; ard-bhaile, ard-chathair, ard-bheirbhe, mathair-bhaile; baile mòr

Mettle, *s* Stuth; (*spirit*), duinealas, smior, smioralas, fearalas; feartas; tapadh, misneach, cruadal spiorad. Good mettle, *deag stuth.*

Mettled, *a.* Stuthail; duineil, smiorail, fearail, tapaidh, misneachail, spioradail, (*as a horse*), beò, stuthail, sgeunach.

Mettlesome, *a.* (*As a horse*), stuthail, beothail; beò, sgeunach, fiadhaich; (*in mind*), stuthail, misneachail, smiorail, beò, tapaidh.

Mew, *s.* Fàl, lann, fang, cup, crò; (*stable*), cachlann, stabull; (*a sea-fowl*), aòileann, faòileann

Mew, *v. a.* Druid, dùin suas; fangaich, cuir an crò, tilg (no) cuir ite.

Mew, *v. n.* Sgiamh, miamh, sgiamhuil, miamhuil mar a ni cat, sgiamhlaich.

Mewing, *s.* Miamhuil, miagail, sgiamhuil.

Mewl, *v. n.* Sgreach mar leanaban.

Mezereon, *s.* Seorsa laibhreil.

Mezzotinto, *s.* Seorsa dealbh sgriobhaidh; leth-ghrabhaladh.

Miasm, *s.* Toth (no) fàil neo-fhallainn, toth euslainnte

Mice, *pl* of mouse. Luchaidh, luchagan.

Michaelmas, *s.* Féill-mhìcheil, fèill an ard Aingil Mhìcheil air a cumail, air an naothamh mios do 'n bhliadhna

† **Micher**, *s.* Giolcair.

† **Mickle**, *a.* Mòr, mòran

Microcosm, *s* Saoghal beag; an duine

Micrography, *s.* Meanbh-sgriobhadh

Microscope, *s* Gloine meudachadh, gloine meanbh-sheall-adh.

Mid, *a.* Meadhonach, meadhon.

Midcourse, *s.* Leth rathaid, meadhon rathaid

Mid-day, *s.* Meadhon là, airde an là, nòin

† **Midding**, *s.* Òtrach

Middle, *a.* Meadhonach, meadhanach, meadhon, meadhan

Middle, *s.* Meadhon; meadhan, teis-meadhon, teis air meadhon. In the middle, *anns an teis-mheadhon*, in the middle of them, *nan teis meadhon*, the middle of winter, *an teis meadhon a gheamhraidh*, (the waist), *cneas*, the middle finger, *am meur fad.*

Middlemost, *a* Meadhonach, sa mheadhon, anns teis-mheadhon.

Middling, *a* Meadhonach, eatorra; an eatorras, eadar an da chuid; an iarruidh He is but middling, *cha n' eil e ach an eatorras*, he is middling well; *tha e 'n iarruidh ghleusda.*

Midge, *s.* Meanbh-chuileag

Midland, *a.* Eadar thìreach, eadar da thalamh

Midleg, *s.* Leth na lurgainn; calpa

Midnight, *s.* Meadhon oidhche, marbh' na h-oidhche.

Midriff, *s.* Sgairt.

Mid-sea, *s.* Muir na meadhon-thìr

Midshipman, *s.* Oifigiche air luing

Midst, *a.* Meadhon, meadhan, meadhonach, meadhanach.

Midst, *s.* Meadhon; eadar-mheadhon, teis meadhon, teis air mheadhon. In the midst, *anns an eadar-mheadhon*, *anns an teis air mheadhon*, *anns an teis meadhon.*

Midsummer, *s* Airde an t-samhraidh, leth 'n t-samhraidh, an t-aon la 'ar fhichead do 'n Òg-mhios

Midway, *s* Leth rathaid, bloigh rathaid

Midwife, *s* Bean ghlùine; bean choganta, bean leona, cnaimhseach, bean fhrithealaidh. Midwives, *mnathan glùin*

Midwiffry, *s* Ealadhain mna ghlùin, aisead.

Midwinter, *s.* Dùbhlachd, an dubhlachd; marbh' a gheamhraidh, meadhon a gheamhraidh, teis meadhon a gheamhraidh

Mien, *s* Gnùis, aghaidh, gné, fiamh, coslas, eugas, cruth

Might, *pret* of may Dh' fhaotadh, dh' fheudadh I might, *dh' fhaodainn*; they might, *dh' fheudadh iad*

Might, *s* Neart, spionnadh, treòir, cumhachd, tréine With all my might, *le m' uile neart*, want of might, *dìth neart*, *cu-comas*, *eu-treoir.*

Mightily, *adv.* Gu neartmhor, gu làidir, gu treun, gu cumhachdach, gu mòr, gu ro mhòr.

Mightiness, *s.* Neart, spionnadh, tréine, cumhachd, airde, mòrachd, mòralachd, treunadas. Your High Mightiness, *d'Ard Threunadas.*

Mighty, *a.* Cumhachdach, mòr; (*strong*), làidir, neartmhor; foghainteach, calma, treun; uamhasach; (*impetuous*), dian, brais

Mighty, *adv.* Gu mòr, gu ro mhòr. *Cha 'n fhaicear is cha chluinnear am focal so, ach ann an cainnte nach mòr is fhiach*

Migration, *s.* Imrich, dol air imrich, dol o àite gu h-àite

Milch, *a.* Bainne, bhainne. A milch cow, *bo bhainne*, *mart bainne.*

Milching, *s.* Bleoghann, bleothann, leigeil A milching fetter, *buarach.*

Mild, *a.* Seimh, ciùin, maoth, malta, tlà, mall, mìn, macanta; còir, caoimhneil; (*to the taste*), blasda, maoth, seimh.

Mildew, *s* Mill-cheo, fuar-dhealt, liatas.

Mildly, *adv.* Gu seimh, gu ciùin, gu maoth, gu mall, gu mìn, gu macanta, gu caoimhneil, gu blasda, gu maoth.

Mildness, *s.* Ciùineas, ciùineachd, malltachd, seimhe, tlàs, blasdachd

Mile, *s* Mìl; mìl shlighe; seachd ceud deug is tri fichead slat Twenty miles of road, *fichead mìl shlighe*

Milestone, *s.* Clach mhìle

Milfoil, *s.* Cathair thalmhainn.

Miliary fever, *s.* Teasach griseach

Militant, *a.* Mìlidheach, comhragach, cathach, saighdearail, ciapalach, seasmhach

Military, *a.* Saighdearail, comhragach, comhragail, cogail

Military, *s* Arm, saighdearachd, feachd tìr.

Militia, *s* Feachd dùthcha, feinne, feinneachas, finnidh-eachd. Militia-man, *fear feinneachais (no) feinne.*

Milk, *s.* Bainne, bliochd, blighe, † lachd, † lac, † finne, † as, luim, † aisnig. A cow's milk comes from her chops, *is ann a cheann a bhlighear o bho*

Milk, *v. a* Bleoghainn, bleothainn; bligh, leig Milked, *bleoghainnte*

Milker, *s* Bleoghainnear, fear bleoghainn; banarach

Milkiness, *s* Bainnearachd; bliochdarachd; (*of complexion*), bàine, gile

Milklivered, *a* Gealtach, eagalach, tais, meat, caill-eachanta

Milkmaid, *s* Banarach, banaireach.

Milkpail, *s.* Gogan bleoghainn, gogan, cuman, cuman bleoghainn; curasan

Milkpan, *s.* Soitheach bhainne

Milk-pottage, *s.* Easach bhainne, brochan bainne, lite bhainne.

Milk-score, *s.* Fiachan bainne,

Milksop, *s* Fear cailleachanta, cailleach, boganach, taiseanach

Milk-weed, *s.* Spuirse

Milk-white, *a.* Bainne-gheal, còp-gheal

Milk-woman, *s* Bean a bhainne, té reic bhainne

Milky, *a* Bainnear, bainneach, bliochdach, bliochdar; bainne-gheal. *(smooth)*, tla, seimh, ciùin.

Milky-way, *s.* A bhainne-shlighe.

Mill, *s.* Muilionn, muileann A corn-mill, *muileann min*, a flax-mill, *muileann lìn*, a fulling-mill, *muilionn luathaidh*, a malt-mill, *muilionn brachaidh*, a wind-mill, *muilionn gaoithe*, make a church or a mill of it, *dean dìh no muilionn deth*, lending the devil a mill, *b' e iasud an deamhain do 'n mhuilionn e*

Mill, *v a* Méil, méill, bleith, pronn, mìn-phronn.

Mill-clack, *s* Clabar muilinn, glagair muilinn.

Mill-cog, *s.* Fiacail cuidhle mhuilinn; clar-fhiaclan.

Mill-dam, *s.* Linne mhuilinn.

Mill-dust, *s.* Stùr min

Millenarian, *s.* Mìleanach, no fear a tha 'n dùil, gun rioghaich Criosd an domhainn, maille ris na naoimh, car mìl bliadhna an deigh na h-aiseiridh.

Millenary, *a* Mìl.

Millenium, *s.* Mìl bliadhna, an uine a their cuid dhiadhairean, a rioghaicheas Criosd air thalamh maille ris na naoimh.

Millepedes, *s* Corr-chòsag; sgleatair, mial fiodha

Miller, *s* Muillear The miller sleeping when the water runs past, *codal a mhuilleir is an t-uisge dol seachad.*

Millesimal, *a* Mìleamh.

Millet, *s* Mileid

Mill-horse, *s* Each muilinn.

Milliner, *s* Gréis-bhan, ban-ghreusair.

Millinery, *s.* Greùsadaireachd, greusadh

Million, *s.* Muilean, deich ceud mìl

Mill-mountain, *s.* Minneach.

Millpond, *s* Linne-mhuilinn

Millstone, *s.* Cloch mhuilinn, clach mhuilinn.

Milt, *s* *(In fish)*, mealag, bealag; iuchair eisg.

Milt, *s* *(Spleen)*, an dubh-liath.

Milter, *s.* Iasg fironn.

Mime, *s.* Sgeigear; fear sgeig

Mime, *v.* Fanaid, fochaid, dean sgeig

Mimer, *s.* Baoth chleasaichè, amadan, fear fanaid

Mimic, *s.* Sgeigear, fochaidiche.

Mimic, *a* Fochaideach, fanaideach, magail, aisdeach, abhachdach

Mimicry, *s* Fochaid, fanoid, fanaid, magadh, abhachdas, sgeige, aithriseachd, sgeigeireachd, atharrais.

Minacious, *a* Bagrach, bagairteach.

Minaciousness, *s* Bagairteachd.

Mince, *v a.* Pronn, mìn-phronn.

Mince, *v. n* Imich sa ghirceanachd, coisich, gu h-iullagach.

Mincing, *s* Pronnadh, gearradh, mìn-phronnadh; *(in gait)*, iullagadh.

Mincing, *a* Pronntach; *(in gait)*, iullagach

Mincingly, *adv.* Am beaganaibh; *(in gait)*, gu h-iullagach, gu seimh, gu ciùin.

Mind, *s.* *(Thinking faculty)*, inntinn; aigne, tuigse, smuain, meamnadh, aigne, innleachd; *(desire)*, rùn, miann, toil, togar, aille; *(memory)*, meamhair, cuimhne, aire; *(opinion)*, barail, beachd. The faculties of the mind, *feartan na h-inntinn*, they are to my mind, *tha iad gu (no) réir mo thoil;* an evil mind, *droch aigne, droch rùn*, of the same mind, *do 'n aon bharail, dh' aon inntinn;* it darted into my mind, *ghrad-bhuail e mi*, I have a mind, *tha mhiann orm, tha mi los*, I have half a mind, *tha mi leth los;* set your mind on, *leig d' inntinn air*, keep in mind, *cum an cuimhne*, put him in mind, *cuir na chuimhne*, out of mind, *a cuimhne;* of one mind, *dh' aon inntinn, dh' aon rùn;* a putting in mind, *cur an cuimhne;* mind yourself, *thoir an aire ort fhéin.*

Mind, *v. a.* Cuimhnich; gabh beachd; thoir aire; thoir an aire Mind what you are about, *cuimhnich ciod mu bheil thu*, never mind him, *na gabh ort e.*

Minded, *a.* Toileach, deònach; cuimhnichte. High-minded, *ard-inntinneach;* ill-minded, *mi-runach;* fully-minded, *làn sònruichte*, envious-minded, *farmadach.*

Mindful, *a.* Cuimhneachail, cùramach, suimeil; fritheilteach, furachail, fuireachail, fuirearach, furachair, omhaileach, umhaileach, aireachail Mindfully, *gu cuimhneachail, gu h-aireachail*

Mindfulness, *s.* Cuimhne; cùram, aire, fuirearachd, furachras, suim

Mindless, *a.* Neo-chuimhneachail, neo-chùramach, neo-shuimeil, neo-fhritheilteach, neo-fhurachail, neo-omhaileach, neo-aireachail, neo-aireach.

Mine, *a.* Mo, m', am; leam, leamsa. My mother, *mo mhathair*, my father, *m' athair*, this is mine, *is leamsa so.*

Mine, *s.* Méin, meun, méinn; sloc, toll; *(in a siege)*, tochail.

Mine, *v.* Cladhaich, tochail, bùraich.

Miner, *s.* Méinnear; tochailtiche

Mineral, *s.* Méinn, méin, clach mhéin.

Mineral, *a.* Méinnear, méinear.

Mineralogist, *s.* Méinearach, méinnearach

Mineralogy, *s* Méinn-eòlas, méinearachd.

Mingle, *v.* Measg, co-mheasg, coi-mbeasg, coimeasg, measgnaich Mingled, *measgte, co-measgta, measgnaichte.*

Mingle, *s.* Measgadh, co-mheasgadh, cumasg

Mingler, *s.* Measgadair.

Mingling, *s* Measgadh, co-mheasgadh.

Miniature, *s* Dealbh beag, meanbh-chruth, mìn-dhealbh.

Minikin, *s.* Prìn beag, prìn baintighearna.

Minikin, *a* Beag, crion, meanbh, girceanach, mineanach

Minim, *s.* Arrach; urr bheag; comhar ciùil.

Minion, *s* Mùirnean; graidhean.

Minish, *v a.* Beagaich, lughdaich, cuir an lughaid.

Minister, *s.* Ministear, minisdear, sagart; pears' eaglais, fear ionaid; seirbheiseach, òglach, fear frithealaidh. A parish minister, *ministear sgìreachd.*

Minister, *v a.* and *n* Fritheil, dean fritheal, frithealaich; thoir, thabhair, builich.

Ministerial, *a.* Ministeireil, minisdeireil, sagairteil, sagartach.

Ministrant, *a* Fuireachail, frithealach, furachair.

Ministration, *s.* Frithealadh, fritheal, feitheamh; ministeirealachd.

Ministry, *s.* Minisdeireachd, seirbheis, frithealadh, minisdeirealachd.

Minium, *s.* Luaidh dhearg

Minnow, *s.* Breac beag, sgildaimhne, doirbeag.

Minor, *a.* Beag, crion, is lugha, is crine.

Minor, *s.* Òganach, neach fo bhliadhna 'ar fhichead; neach òg fu thuitearachd.

Minority, *s.* Mìn aois; òige; fo' bhliadhna 'ar fhichead, a mheanbh chuid, a chuid is lugha.

Minster, *s.* Mànaistear, màinistear.

Minstrel, *s.* Clàrsair, cruitear; fear ciùil.

Minstrelsy, *s.* Clàrsaireachd, ceòl, comh-sheirm.

Mint, *s.* (*A plant*), mionnt; cartal. Wild-mint, *mionnt fiadhaich.*

Mint, *s.* Tigh cùinnidh.

Mint, *v. a.* Cùin, cùinn.

Mintage, *s.* Cùineadh, cùinneadh.

Minter, *s.* Cùinnear, cùinneadair.

Mintmaster, *s.* Maighstir cùinnidh.

Minuet, *s.* Seorsa damhsaidh.

Minum, *s.* Aon bhuille ciùil, a chuid as lugha do dh' fhonn, socair.

Minute, *a.* Crion, beag, meanbh, caol; mìn, faoin, poncail; mionaiteach. A minute detail, *aithris phoncail, mìnchunntas;* minutes of hours or of records, *mionaitean.*

Minute, *s.* Mionaid, mionait; tiot; cùnntas.

Minute, *v. a.* Sgrìobh sios, gabh cunntas.

Minute-book, *s.* Leabhar mhionaite.

Minute-hand, *s.* Lamh mhionaite.

Minutely, *adv.* Gu pongail, gu mìn, gu caol.

Minuteness, *s.* Crionachd, crìne, meanbhad, lughad, poncaileachd, pongaileachd.

Minx, *s.* Geirseach, caile bheag narach; baobh, bidse.

Miracle, *s.* Miorbhuil; iongantas.

Miraculous, *a.* Miorbhuileach, iongantach; uamhasach.

Miraculously, *adv.* Gu morbhuileach, gu h-iongantach.

Miraculousness, *s.* Miorbhuileachd.

Mire, *s.* Salachar, poll, làthach, clabar, munloch, eabar, aolach, mosaiche, inneir.

Mire, *v.* Salaich.

Mire, *s.* Seangan, sneadhan.

Miriness, *s.* Sal, salachar, seilche, salaichead.

Mirksome, *a.* Dorch, doilleir, duaichnidh, dubh.

Mirror, *s.* Sgàthan; (*pattern*), eisiomlair, ball sampuill. The eye of a friend is a good mirror, *is math an sgàthan sùil caraid.*

Mirth, *s.* Aighear, ealaidh, gàirdeachas, sùgradh, mire, ioladh, aoibhneas, aiteas, cridhealas, sodan, sunnt.

Mirthful, *a.* Aighearach, mear, subhach, sugach, suigeartach, aoibhneach, ait, cridheil, sunntach, suilbhear; sulchair. Mirthfully, *gu h-aighearach, gu mear, gu subhach, gu sugach, gu suigeartach, gu h-ait, gu cridheil, gu sunntach, gu suilbhear, gu sulchair.*

Mirthless, *a.* Duilbhear, gun aighear; trom, tuirseach, tiamhaidh.

Miry, *a.* Salach, eabrach, mosach, musach, aolach, clabarach.

Misadventure, *s.* Mi-shealbh, mi-chineamhuin, drochfhortan, tubaisd, sgiorradh, doirbheas.

Misadventured, *a.* Mi-shealbhar, neo-fhortanach, tubaisdeach.

Misadvise, *v. a.* Thoir droch chomhairle (no) comhairle chearr.

Misadvised, *a.* Droch comhairlichte, air dhroch comhairleachadh.

Misanthrope, *s.* Fuathadair dhaoine.

Misanthropy, *s.* Fuath-dhaoine.

Misapplication, *s.* Mi-bhuileachadh, mi-bhuileachas, mighnàthachadh.

Misapply, *v. a.* Mi-bhuilich, mi-ghnàthaich.

Misapprehend, *v. a.* Tog am mearachd, mi-thuig, mearachdaich, tog gu cearr (no) air aimhreidh.

Misapprehension, *s.* Mi-thuigsinn, mearachd, togail am mearachd.

Misassign, *v. a.* Thoir reuson cearr.

Misbecome, *v.* Bi neo-oireamhnach, (no) neo-chiatach, na tig do. It misbecomes you, *is olc thig e dhuit, cha tig e dhuit.*

Misbecoming, *a.* Neo-eireachdail, neo-chiatach.

Misbehave, *v. n.* Rach am mearachd, dean gniomh nàr, imich gu maslach.

Misbehaved, *a.* Mi-nòsail, mi-mhodhail; beag-narach; mi-bheusach.

Misbehaviour, *s.* Mi-nòs, droch ghiùlan, droch dhol mach, dol mach nàr, mi-ghnàthachadh; mi-bheus.

Misbelief, *s.* Ana-creideamh, mi-chreideas, mi-chreideamh, ana-creideas, mi-chreidsinn.

Misbelieve, *v. a.* Mi-chreid, cuir an teagamh; cuir an amharus.

Misbeliever, *s.* Ana-creideach, ana-creidiche, neo-chreideach.

Misbelieving, *a.* Ana-creideach, amharusach, an-earbsach.

Miscal, *v. a.* Thoir frith-ainm, tog frith-ainm, thoir farainm, frith-ainmich.

Miscalculate, *v.* Cunnt am mearachd, cùnnt air aimhreidh.

Miscalculation, *s.* Cunntas ceàrr.

Miscalled, *part.* Frith-ainmichte.

Miscarriage, *s.* Fàilinn, fàilneachadh, mi-shealbh; tuisleadh, aisead (no) breith roimh 'n mhithich, sgarachdainn ri clann.

Miscarry, *v. a.* Fàilinn, fàilnich; breith roi 'mhithich, sgar ri leanabh.

Miscast, *v.* Mi-chùnnt, cunnt air aimhreidh.

Miscellaneous, *a.* Measgta, measgte, coimeasgta, iolchoimeasgta.

Miscellany, *s.* Measgadh, coi-measgadh, cumasg, iolchumasg.

Mischance, *s.* Mi-shealbh; droch thuiteamas, tubaisd, breamas, doirbheas, rosad.

Mischief, *s.* Cron, coire, duaidh, dochair, ciurradh, dochoir, dochann, bochduinn, tubaisd, sgiorradh, earchall; aimsgith, aimhleas, droch-bheairt, miostadh. What a mischief is this, *ciod a bhochduinn a th' air so;* a mischiefmaker, *fear droch-bheairt.*

Mischief, *v. a.* Ciùrr, dochainn, dochannaich.

Mischief-maker, *s.* Fear droch-bheairt, crochair.

Mischievous, *a.* Olc, cronail, dochannach, aingidh, mithleanach, droch bheairteach; sgriosail, millteach, lochdach; (*spiteful*), mi-runach, duaidheach, gamhlasach. A mischievous deed, *droch bheairt, droch ghniomh, droch thùrn.*

Mischievously, *adv.* Gu h-olc, gu cronail, gu dochannach, gu h-aingidh; gu gamhlasach.

Miscible, *a.* So-mheasgadh, ion-mheasgadh.

Miscomputation, *s.* Cunntas cearr (no) mearachdach.

Misconception, *s.* Barail chearr, mearachd, barail fhallsail, barail mhearachdach.

Misconduct, *s.* Droch iomchar, droch-ghiùlan, mi-riaghailt.

Misconduct, *v. a.* Mi-riaghail, mi-riaghailtich.

Misconjecture, *s.* Barail cheàrr.

Misconjecture, *v. a.* Thoir barail cheàrr.

Misconstruction, *s.* Seadh mearachdach, barail mhearachdach, barail cheárr.

Misconstrue, *v.* Eadar theangaich gu cearr, mìnich am mearachd, tog am mearachd, tog air aimhreidh.

Miscontinuance, *s.* Sgurachd, stad, stadach.

Miscount, *v.* Cùnnt gu ceàrr, cunnt am mearachd, mi-chùnnt, mi-àireamh.

Miscreance, *s.* Ana-creideamh, ana-creidimh; baoth-chreideamh.

Miscreant, *s.* Crochair; diù duine; ana-creideach, mi-chreideach.

Misdeed, *s.* Droch thùrn, droch ghniomh; eucoir.

Misdeem, *v. a.* Gabh am mearachd, tog am mearachd.

Misdemean, *v.* Imich gu neo-chiatach.

Misdemeanour, *s.* Ciont, coire, coireadh, droch-iomchar, droch-ghiùlan, droch dhol mach.

Misdevotion, *s.* Baoth-chrabhadh.

Misdo, *v. a.* Dean cron, dean coire, ciontaich, dean droch-thùrn.

Misdoer, *s.* Ciontach.

Misdoing, *s.* Droch ghniomh, ciont, coire, cron, droch thùrn, fabhta.

Misdoubt, *v. a.* Cuir an amharus, cuir an teagamh.

Misdoubt, *s.* An amharus, an-earbsadh; iomcheist, teagamh.

Misemploy, *v. a.* Mi-ghnàthaich, mi-bhuilich.

Misemployment, *s.* Mi-ghnàthachadh, mi-bhuileachadh.

Miser, *s.* Spiocair, truaghan, duine gortach (no) sanntach.

Miserable, *a.* (*Wretched*), truagh, truaghanta, dìblidh, neo-shona; miothur, bronach; ainis, ainnis, bochd, amhgharach, bearranach; trioblaideach; truigeanta; (*narrow*), gortach, spiocach, teann, cruaidh, cruadalach, crion, miothur, mìughar.

Miserableness, *s.* Truaghanachd, truaghantachd, mi-shonas, ainniseachd, bochduinn, trioblaid; (*niggardliness*), spiocaireachd, crìne, miughaireachd.

Miserably, *adv.* Gu truagh, gu dìblidh, gu neo-shona, gu mìothur, gu brònach, gu bochd; gu spìocach, gu miothur.

Miserly, *a.* Gortach, truagh, spiocach, cruaidh, cruadalach, sanntach, gionach.

Misery, *s.* Truaighe, amhghar, bochduinn, mor-thruaighe, donas; leth-trom, droch agh, riachdanas, gionachd, gion, gean, sannt.

Misfashion, *v. a.* Mi-dhealbh, mi-shum. Misfashioned, *mi-dhealbhta, mi-chumta.*

Misform, *v. a.* Mi-dhealbh, mi-chum. Misformed, *mi-dhealbhta, mi-chumta.*

Misfortune, *s.* Mi-shealbh, mi-adh, mi-agh, earchall, mi-fhortan, droch-fhortan, mi-shoirbheas, tubaist, donas, aimhleas, annrath. He who is doomed to misfortune will find no relief in summer, *am fear air am bi 'n anrath, cha 'n ann 's t-samhradh is fhusa leis.*

Misgive, *v. a.* Fàilnich, lion le amharus (no) le teagamh.

Misgiving, *s.* Amharus, teagamh.

Misgovern, *v.* Mi-riaghail, mi-riaghlaidh, mi-stiùir. Misgoverned, *mi-riaghlaichte.*

Misgovernment, *s.* Mi-riaghladh, mi-stiùradh, mi-riaghlachadh; mi-riaghailt; droch-riaghladh, droch-riaghlachadh.

Misgoverned, *a.* Borb, neo-cheannsaichte.

Misguidance, *s.* Droch stiùradh, mi-stiùradh.

Misguide, *v. a.* Mi-stiùir, mi-threòraich; cuir air aimhreidh, cuir am mearachd; mi-chomhairlich. Misguided, *mi-threòraichte, air seacharan.*

Mishap, *s.* Tubaist, sgiorradh, mi-shealbh, earchall, mi-agh, mi-thapadh; mi-fhortan.

Mishmash, *s.* Subas; cumasg; masg; driùlagain, druibhleagan.

Misinform, *v. a.* Thoir fios meallta, thoir droch thuairisg. Misinformed, *meallta.*

Misinformation, *s.* Fios meallta, fios mearachdach, faoin-sgeul, faoin-thuairisgeul.

Misinterpret, *v.* Mi-mhìnich. Misinterpreted, *mi-mhìnichte.*

Misinterpretation, *s.* Mi-mhìneachadh.

Misjoin, *v. a.* Cuir ri chéile gu cearr, tath gu neo-chuimeir.

Misjudge, *v. a.* Thoir breith chearr; tog am mearachd.

Mislaid, *pret. pass.* of mislay. San àite chearr; air a chall.

Mislay, *v.* Cuir san àite chearr.

Misle, *v. n.* Sìl mar bhraon, ceòbanaich.

Mislead, *v. a.* Mi-threoraich, mi-stiùir, mi-sheòl; thoir a thaobh, cuir air aimhreidh, cuir am mearachd. You misled him, *chuir thu am mearachd e.*

Misled, *part.* Mi-threòraichte; air aimhreadh, am mearachd.

Mislen, *s.* Maislean, mislean, arbhar cumasg, dà na trì sheorsan arbhair a cinntinn am measg a chéile.

Misletoe, *s.* Uile-ice.

Mislike, *v. a.* Mi-rùnaich, mi-mhiannaich, gabh mi-chiat.

Mislike, *s.* Mi-rùn, mi-mhiann, mi-chiat, tnù.

Mismanage, *v. a.* Mi-riaghail; mi-bhuilich; mi-stiùir. Mismanaged, *mi-riaghlaichte, mi-bhuilichte.*

Mismanagement, *s.* Mi-riaghladh, droch-riaghladh; droch bheanachas tighe, droch-stiùradh.

Misname, *s.* Thoir ainm cearr, thoir frith-ainm, thoir far-ainm.

Misogamy, *s.* Fuath pòsaidh.

Misogyny, *s.* Fuath bhan.

Misorder, *s.* Eas-ordugh, mi-ordugh, mi-riaghailt.

Misorderly, *a.* Mi-riaghailteach.

Mispersuasion, *s.* Barail chearr, barail mheallta.

Misplace, *v.* Cuir as àite, cuir san àite chearr.

Mispoint, *v. a.* Mi-phong, mi-phongaich. Mispointed, *mi-phongaichte.*

Misprint, *s.* Clo-mhearachd.

Misprision, *s.* Dìmeas, tamailt; mearachd; (*in law*), ceilltinn, ceannairc.

Misrecite, *v. a.* Mi-aithris. Misrecited, *mi-aithriste.*

Misreckon, *v.* Cunnt am mearachd, cunnt air dhochair, mi-aireamh. Misreckoned, *mi-aireamhta.*

Misrelate, *v. a.* Mi-aithris, aithris gu meallta. Misrelated, *mi-aithriste.*

Misrelation, *s.* Mi-aithris, droch aithris, aithris mheallta, cunntas docharach.

Misreport, *v. a.* Thoir cunntas docharach, mi-aithris.

Misreport, *s.* Cunntas docharach; faoin-sgeul.

Misrepresent, *s.* Cuir an céill gu docharach; thoir sgeul chearr; thoir cunntas docharach.

Misrepresentation, *s.* Cunntas docharach; aithris mheallta; faoin-aithris.

Misrule, *s.* Eas-ordugh, mi-riaghailt; tabaid; buaireas; ceannairc.

Miss, *s.* Té uasal òg gun phòsadh; oigh, nighean; (*a kept miss*), striopach; leannan.

Miss, *v. a.* and *n.* Thig gearr air; mearachdaich; bi am

mearachd; na cuimsich; ionndrainn, ionntruinn; caill; (*miss fire*), diùlt teine. I missed you sorely, *dh' ionndrainn mi thu gu goirt.*

Miss, *s.* Call, calldach; dochann, dìth; mearachd.

Missal, *s.* Leabhar aifrionn.

Missay, *v. a.* Abair air aimhreidh (no) gu docharach.

Misshape, *v.* Mi-chum, mi-dhealbh; duaichnich.

Missile, *a.* So-thilgeadh; tilgidh, siùbhlach.

Missing, *a.* Air a chall, air iontrainn; gun bhi air sgeul, air dol a leth-taobh. He was missing, *bha e air ionntruinn.*

Mission, *s.* Cuireadh; cur air thùrus, teachdaireachd.

Missionary, *s.* Fear teagaisg; ministear a theagasgas na daoine fiadhaich, searmonaiche; neach a chuireadh a shearmonachadh.

Missive, *a.* Air a chur air falbh; tilgidh, tilgte. A missive letter, *litir laimh.*

Misspeak, *v.* Labhair (no) bruidhinn air aimhreadh.

Misspend, *v.* Caith; struidh, sgap; caith gu struidheil; ana-caith; dean ana-caitheamh, mi-bhuilich. Misspent, *ana-caithte.*

Misspender, *s.* Ana-caithtiche; ana-caithiche; strùidhear.

Misspending, *s.* Caitheamh, ana-caitheamh, struidhe.

Misstate, *v. a.* Thoir cunntas cearr.

Mist, *s.* Ceò, ceathach; ceòban, braon, duibhre. It vanished into mist, *chath e na cheò, ghabh e a ghaoth;* a blasting mist, *mill-cheò.*

Mist, *v.* Dorchaich, duibhrich.

Mistake, *v. a.* and *n.* Gabh am mearachd, tog am mearachd; rach am mearachd, rach air aimhreidh; mearachdaich. If I mistake not, *mar meallta mise, mur 'eil mi air mo mhealladh;* I mistook your meaning, *thog mi am mearachd thu.*

Mistake, *s.* Mearachd; seachran, mearbhal; ailmse. You are in a gross mistake, *tha thu fad am mearachd.*

Mistaken, *a.* Meallta, ann am mearachd, am mearachd. You are mistaken, *tha thu meallta.*

Mistakingly, *adv.* Gu mearachdach, gu meallta.

Misteach, *v. a.* Mi-theagasg, mi-oileanaich, teagasg air aimhreadh (no) air dhochair.

Mistell, *v. a.* Mi-aithris, innis gu docharach. Mistold, *mi-aithriste.*

Misthought, *s.* Droch bharail.

Mistily, *adv.* Gu ceòmhor, gu ceòthar, gu ceòbanach, gu braonach, gu mùigeach, gu mùigeanach.

Mistiness, *s.* Ceòmhorachd, ceòtharachd, ceòbanachd, mùige, mùigeanachd.

Mistion, *s.* Cumasg, coimeasg.

Mistletoe, *s.* Uile-ice, lus nan druidhean, druidh-lus; lus sior uaine a tharuingeas a bhith o phlannt eile.

Mistook. See **Mistake.**

Mistress, *s.* Ban-mhaighistir; (*of a house*), bean tighe; (*in love*), leannan, rùnach, graidhean, coimh-leabaiche; siùrsach. The mistress of a starving family is soonest lost, *bean-tighe ghanntair is i 's luaithe 'chailltear.*

Mistrust, *s.* An-earbsa, an-earbsadh, amharus, an-amharus; mi-chreideas.

Mistrust, *v.* An-earb, cuir amharus air, mi-chreid.

Mistrustful, *a.* An-earbsach, an-amharusach, amharusach.

Mistrustfully, *adv.* Gu h-an-earbsach, gu an-amharusach, gu h-amharusach.

Mistrustfulness, *s.* An-amharus, an-earbsadh, teagamh.

Misty, *a.* Ceòmhor, ceòthar, ceòbanach, braonach, mùigeach, mùigeanach, dorch, neulach, doilleir, duaichnidh.

Misunderstand, *v.* Mi-thuig, tog am mearachd, gabh am mearachd. You misunderstand me, *cha 'n eil thu 'g am thuigsinn;* you misunderstood me, *thog thu am mearachd mi, cha do thuig thu mi.*

Misunderstanding, *s.* Mi-thuigsinn; mearachd; droch-còrdadh; cur a mach.

Misusage, *s.* Mi-ghnàthachadh, droch-càramh; mi-bhuileachas; droch uidhisinn; mi-mhodh; masladh.

Misuse, *v. a.* Mi-ghnàthaich; droch càirich, mi-bhuilich, droch-uidhisinn; buin gu maslach ri, cuir gu mi-bhuile. Misused, *mi-ghnathaichte, droch càirichte.*

Misuse, *s.* Droch càramh, mi-ghnàth, droch uidhisinn.

Miswend, *v. n.* Rach air seacharan (no) am mearachd.

Misy, *s.* Seòrsa méinn.

Mite, *s.* Fionnag, flannag, fineag; ni meanbh sam bi; smad; bonn beag, peighinn.

Mithridate, *s.* Seòrsa leigheis math an aghaidh nimhe.

Mitigant, *a.* Caisgeach; bogar; seimh, seimhidh; traoighteach, maoth, maothar.

Mitigate, *v. a.* Coisg, ciùinich, siothchaich; tragh, traoigh, ìslich; fuaraich.

Mitigated, *part.* Coisgte, ciùinichte, traoighte, islichte.

Mitigation, *s.* Ciùineachadh, traoghadh; ìsleachadh.

Mitre, *s.* Coron sagairt.

Mitred, *a.* Coronaichte mar shagairt.

Mittens, *s.* Meatagan, miotagan, lamhainnean; meanaigean.

Mittimus, *s.* Ordugh a bheir breitheamh chum neach a chur am priosun.

Mity, *a.* Fionnagach, flannagach; fineagach.

Mix, *v. a.* Measg, coimeasg, measgnaich; masg, cuir air feadh chéile; tàth; ceangail. Mixed, *measgta, measgte, coimeasgta, measgnaichte, air feadh chéile.* Wine mixed with water, *fion air a mheasg le h-uisge.*

Mixen, *s.* Otrach.

Mixtion, *s.* Cumasg, coimeasgadh, masgadh.

Mixture, *s.* Cumasg, coimeasg, coimeasgadh, masgadh. Pure without mixture, *fior-ghlan.*

Mizen (mast), *s.* Crann deiridh.

Miz-maze, *s.* Iom-chuairtean.

Mizzy, *s.* Bog, boglach, féithe, cathar.

† **Mo**, *a.* and *adv.* Tuille, nis mo, ni 's fhaide.

Moan, *s.* Caoidh, caoin, dean caoidh, gearain, dean gearan, dean bròn; dean cumhadh, dean tuireadh.

Moan, *s.* Caoidh, caoin, caoineadh, gearan; cumhadh, tuireadh, bròn.

Moanful, *a.* Caointeach; tuirseach; brònach, gearanach. Moanfully, *gu caointeach, gu tuirseach, gu brònach.*

Moat, *s.* Cladh, staing, clais, dìge.

Moat, *v. a.* Cladhaich, cuairtich le clais (no) staing.

Mob, *s.* Prabar, gràisg; cruinneachadh sluaigh; conaghair, tuasaid, mob, daosgar sluaigh.

Mob, *v.* Dean tuasaid, tog buaireas; buair, sàruich; cuir stùr ri; *mobainn.*

Mobbish, *a.* Prabarach; tuasaideach; daosgarach.

Mobile, *s.* Am prabar, a ghràisg.

Mobility, *s.* Luaineachd, luaimneachd, luathas, caochlaideachd.

Mock, *v. a.* Fanaid air, dean fanaid, dean fanoid; mag, dean magadh, fochaid air; dean fochaid (no) sgeig; meall; aithris; thoir beum; thoir an car a. Mocked, *or* deceived, *meallta.*

Mock, *s.* Fanaid, fanoid, magadh, fochaid, sgeig, beum, gearradh.

Mock, *a.* Fallsa, fallsail, faoin, breugach, bréig, meallta.

MOCKER, *s* Fear fanaid, fear magaidh, fear fochaid, sgeigear, mealltair.

MOCKERY, *s* Fanaid, magadh, fochaid, sgeig, abhacas; abhachdas, spuirt, ioladh, sgallais.

MOCKING, *s.* Fanaid, fochaid, sgeig.

MOCKING, *a* Fanaideach, fochaideach, sgeigeil.

MOCKINGLY, *adv.* Gu fanaideach, gu fochaideach, gu sgeigeil, gu h-àbhacach.

MOCKING-STOCK, *s.* Ball abhacais, ball magaidh

MODE, *s.* Doigh, seòl, modh, achd, ròd, rathad, slighe, riaghailt; nòs, fasan, scorsa; gleus, dealbh, fuirm

MODEL, *s* Dealbh, samhladh, coslas, eisiomlair, samplair.

MODEL, *v* Dealbh, cum, samhlaich, sgéith Modelled, *dealbhta, cumta, samhlaichte.*

MODELLER, *s* Dealbhadair, cumadair, fear cumaidh

MODERATE, *a.* Measarra, measarradh, cuimheasach, stuama; meadhonach

MODERATE, *v n.* Ciùinich, ceannsaich, smachd, smachdaich, riaghlaich, dean measarra, coisg

MODERATELY, *adv* Gu measarra, gu measarradh, gu stuama, gu ciùin; meadhonach, an iarruidh; eadar an da chuid.

MODERATENESS, *s.* Measarrachd, cuimeis, stuamachd, stuaim

MODERATION, *s* Measarrachd, cuimeis, stuamachd, stuaim.

MODERATOR, *s* Riaghlair, riaghladair, fear riaghlaidh

MODERN, *a.* (*New*), ùr, nuadh, nodha; (*not ancient or antique*), nco-shean-aimsireil, freacnarach The moderns, *na freacnaraich.*

MODEST, *a* Mallta, nàrach; macanta, athach, seimh; tuigseach; banail, bandaidh, geimnidh, geamnuidh, beusach; measarra, stuama; ceannsa A modest woman, *boirionnach bheusach*

MODESTLY, *adv.* Gu mallta, gu nàrach, gu macanta, gu seimh, gu tuigseach, gu banail, gu geimnidh, gu beusach, gu measarra, gu stuama.

MODESTY, *s.* Malltachd, macantas, seimh; banalas, geimnidheachd, geimneachd, beus, beusaichead, stuaim

MODICUM, *s.* Cuibhrionn, mìr beag, cuimhseach.

MODIFICATION, *s* Atharrachadh, mùth, caochladh

MODIFY, *v a.* Atharraich, mùth, caochail, ciùnaich, ciùinich, minich. Modified, *atharraichte*

MODISH, *a.* Modhail, fasanta, nòsmhor.

MODISHNESS, *s.* Modhaileachd, fasantachd; nosmhorachd

MODULATE, *v* Gleus, cuir air ghleus, dean ceòl Modulated, *gleusda*

MODULATION, *s.* Gleusadh; ceòl, fonn.

MODULE, *s* Dealbh; foirm; samhladh.

MOHAIR, *s.* Snàth gaoisid, snàth ròinne, snàth air a dheanamh do ròinne a chamhail.

MOGUL, *s* Iompair Innseanach, treubh Thartarach

MOHOC, *s* Innseanach boib, duine fiadhaich

MOIDORE, *s.* Cùinn a 's fhiach seachd sgillinn fichead Sasunnach

MOIETY, *s* Leth; earrann; roinn

MOIL, *v. a* Làbanaich, lobanaich, loibeanaich, salaich, buail (no) spairt le poll, treachaill, bi 'g oibreachadh san làthach Moiled, *làbanaichte, lobanaichte*

MOILING, *s* Làbanaich, lobanaich, loibeanachd.

MOIST, *a.* Aitidh, fliuch, tais, bog.

MOISTEN, *v a* Taislich, fliuch, bogaich Moistened, *taislichte.*

MOISTURE, *s.* Taisleachadh, fliuchadh, fliuchras, taisealdachd, fliuchneachd, àiteachd, àitidheachd, buige Moisture oozing through the roof of a house, *snithe, fraighshnithe.*

MOLASSES, *s.* *Treicеal*, deasgann an t-siucair, uachdar (no) sgum brìgh slait an t-siucair

MOLE, *s.* (*On the skin*), ball dòrain, ball dobhrain; miann; (*an animal*), famh, ùir-fhamh; caochan; dubh-reabh,— *a corruption of* ùir-fhamh; (*in fortification*), bruach, banc; cladh daighnich.

MOLECAST, MOLEHILL, *s.* Dùcan uir-fhamh, dùcan faimh, dùn faimh, carnan caochain.

MOLE-CATCHER, *s.* Fàmhair, fear ghlacadh fhamh; fear uir-fhamh.

MOLEST, *v.* Cuir moil, cuir dragh, buair; farranaich, cradh. Do not molest him, *na cuir moil air; na toir farraid air;* you molest me, *tha thu cur dragh orm.*

MOLESTATION, *s.* Moil, dragh, buaireas, farran, trioblaid, buaireadh, utrais.

MOLESTER, *s* Moileadair; buaireadair, draghair, fear draghail, fear draghalach

MOLLIENT, *a* Bogar, maoth, maothar, maothach; seimh, seimhidh.

MOLLIFIABLE, *a* A ghabhas bogachadh.

MOLLIFICATION, *s.* Bogachadh, maothachadh, traoghadh, ciùineachadh

MOLLIFIER, *s.* Cosgadair, fear cosgaidh

MOLTEN, *p part.* of melt Leaghta, leaghte, air leaghadh.

MOME, *s* Burraidh, baoghlan, umaidh, amadan, baothair, ceothallan, gobhallan, amhlair; guraiceach.

MOMENT, *s* (*Of time*), tiot, tiotag; sealladh, gliosg, platha, briosg; mamuin; mionaid; (*importance*), cudthrom, cudthrom, cudthromachd; luach. For a moment, *car tiota;* in a moment, *ann an tiot, ann am briosg, ann am platha, ann a priob na sùl*

MOMENTARY, *a* Gearr, grad; goirrid, siùbhlach, plathail.

MOMENTOUS, *a.* Feumail, cudthromach.

MONACHAL, *a.* Mànachail.

MONACHISM, *s.* Mànachd.

MONAD, *s.* Dadmun, smad

MONARCH, *s* Righ, uachdaran, aon-fhlath, ard-fhlath.

MONARCHAL, *a* Rioghail, flathail.

MONARCHIC, *a* Aon-fhlathach, rioghail.

MONARCHY, *s* Aon-fhlaitheachd; ard-rioghachd, iompaireachd.

MONASTERY, *s* Mànaistear, mainistear; abaid, abait.

MONASTIC, *a.* Mànachail; aonaranach.

MONASTICAL, *a.* Mànachail, aonaranach

MONDAY, *s.* De luain, Di luain Monday next, *Di luain so 'tighinn;* last Monday, *Di luain so 'chaidh*, on a Monday, *air la luain*

MONEY, *s.* Airgiod; † cearb; † monadh. Ready money, *airgiod ullamh, airgiod laimh*, interest money, *riadh, airgiod reidh.* want of money, *gainne airgid*, entrance money, *gearsom*

MONEY-BAG, *s.* Sporan leathair.

MONEY-BOX, *s.* Cisteag airgid

MONEYED, *a* Beartach, beairteach, saibhir, toiceil.

MONEYLESS, *a.* Daibhir; bochd, truagh; gun airgiod, aimbeartach.

MONEY-MATTER, *s* Cùis airgid.

MONEY'S-WORTH, *s* Luach peighinn; nì luachmhor sam bi, nì a bheir airgiod.

MONGCORN, *s.* Maslaim, maislim, maislean

MONGER, *s* Fear lamhrachaidh; fear reic (no) ceannachaidh.

MONGREL, *s.* Beothach o dha sheorsa.

MONGREL, *a* Tarsuing; dìblidh, iosal; suarrach, truaillidh Mongrel breed, *siol tarsuing, gin tarsuing.*

† Monish, *v. a.* Comhairlich.
† Monisher, *s.* Comhairliche.
Monition, *s.* Sànas, comhairle; fios, rabhadh.
Monitor, *s.* Comhairliche; fear comhairleachaidh, rabhadair.
Monitory, *a.* Sànusach, rabhach.
Monitory, *s.* Sànus, sànas, rabhadh, comhairle.
Monk, *s.* Mànach; brathair bochd.
Monkery, *s.* Mànachas.
Monkey, *s.* Ap, apa, apag; ainm tàireil; biasd.
Monkhood, *s.* Mànachd, mànachas; seorsa luibh, curachd mànaich.
Monkish, *a.* Mànachail, a bhuineas do mhanach, aonaranach.
Monk's-hood, *s.* Seòrsa luibh, curachd mànaich
Monocular, Monoculous, *a.* Aon-shuileach, leth-shuileach; air leth-shùil.
Monody, *s.* Rann aonarain, rann aon neach, aon-rann.
Monogamist, *s.* Fear nach ceadaich pòsadh da uair.
Monogamy, *s.* Pòsadh aon mhna
Monologue, *s* Bruidhinn aonaranach
Monomachy, *s.* Comhrag déise.
Monopetalous, *a.* Aon-duilleach, aon-duilleagach.
Monopolist, *s.* Léir-reiceadair; fear milleadh margaidh.
Monopolize, *v* Faigh còir reic dhuit féin amhain; léircheannaich, mill margadh.
Monopoly, *s.* Còir reic aig aon neach.
Monosyllable, *s.* Siol-fhocal, aon-sioladh, focal air aon sioladh.
Monotony, *s.* Aon-fhonn, ràsanachd.
Monsoon, *s.* Gaoth nan tràth; gaoth a shéideas sa mhuir mhòr gu deas.
Monster, *s.* Uilebheist; ainmhidh an-chunnta; torthair, béist.
Monstrosity, *s.* Aibheileachd, fuathasachd, oilltealachd.
Monstrous, *a* Aibheileach, torthaireach, fuathasach, uamhasach, oillteil, duaichnidh, mi-dhaicheil, neo dhealbhach, an-chumta; iongantach, miorbhuileach.
Monstrously, *adv* Gu fuathasach, gu h-uamhasach, gu h-oillteil, gu duaichnidh.
Monstrousness, *s.* Aibheileachd, torthaireachd, uamhasachd; oilltealachd; gràinealachd.
Montero, *s.* Curachd marcaiche
Month, *s.* Mios, ceithir seachduinean; † mi Every month, *gach mios, na h-uile mios*, every other month, *gach dolach mios*; this day month, *mios bho 'n diugh*, once a month, *uair sa mhios*
Month's-mind, *s* Miann, fadal, durachd.
Monthly, *a.* Miosail, gach mios.
Monticle, *s.* Monadh beag, dùnan, beannan, binnean.
Monticulous, *a.* Dùnanach, beannanach, binneanach.
Monument, *s.* Carn cuimhne, cuspair cuimhne, comhar cuimhne; tuam, clach uaigh, cuimhneachan, clach cuimhne
Monumental, *a* Cuimhneachail; tuamail
Mood, *s.* (*Of a verb*), modh, riaghail, mùth, foirn
Mood, *s* (*Humour*), gleus, doigh, modh, seòl, gean, gné; (*anger*), fearg, frogan, gith; (*in music*), siubhladh, meas. He is in an ill mood, *tha droch ghean air*, what mood are you in? *ciod an gleus th' ort?*
Moody, *a.* Feargach; neònach; luaineach; muthteach.
Moon, *s.* Gealach, luan, ré, † easga, teasgon; (*month*), mios. Half moon, *leth-ghealach*; the new moon, *a ghealach ùr*, full moon, *gealach làn*; the moon is at full, *tha ghealach na làn*, Michaelmas moon, *gealach bhuidhe na feill Mìcheil*, eclipse of the moon, *dubhradh na gealaich, clibse*, the body or globe of the moon, *cruinne na gealaich.*
Moonbeam, *s* Gath gealaich.
Mooncalf, *s.* (*In the womb*), torraicheas bréig; torthair; (*simpleton*), umaidh, amhlair, gobhallan
Mooneyed, *a.* Bràch-shùileach, ròsblach; ròsb-shuileach.
Moonlight, *s.* Solus na gealaich, dealradh na gealaich.
Moonshine, *s.* Solus na gealaich, dearsadh na gealaich
Moonstruck, *a.* Gòrach
Moor, *s.* (*Hill*), làirich, làirichd, mon, monadh, sliabh, aonach; (*marsh*), boglach, riasg, cathar.
Moor, *s.* Fear dubh.
Moor, *v. a* and *n.* Acairich, cuir air acair, marcuich mar luing air acair. Moored, *acairichte*
Moorcock, *s.* Coileach fraoich
Moorhen, *s* Cearc fhraoich, liath-chearc.
Mooring, *s* Acair-pholl
Moorish, *a.* Riasgail, sliabhach, fraochail, mointidh, monadail; (*marshy*), bog, féithear
Moorland, *s.* Boglach, curach, mointeach, sliabh.
Moory, *a.* See Moorish.
Moose, *s* Fiadh mor a th' ann America.
Moot, *s.* Aidhneas dlighe; mòd; còdhail.
Moot, *v* Tagair, arguinn, dean aidhneas.
Mooted, *a.* As an fhreumh, as a bhun.
Mooter, *s* Adhnaiche; fear lagha.
Mop, *s* Moipeal, mob, moipean.
Mop, *v. a* Rub le moipeal, moipeanaich.
Mope, *v. a.* Bi neo-smiorail, bi san turamanaich, bi tuirseach, (no) neo-shunntach.
Mope, *s.* Lunndair, slaod, rong, rongair, leagair, droll.
Mope-eyed, *a.* Cam, air leth-shùil.
Mopsical, *a.* Cam, air leth-shùil
Mopus, *s.* Lunndair, slaod, rong, rongair, leagair; droll.
Moral, *a.* Beusach, subhailceach; modhail, modhannail, moralta. The moral law, *lagh nam modhanna.*
Moral, *s.* Modh, bun-chiall, bun-bhrigh Morals, *beusan, modhannan*
Moralist, *s* Modhannair; moraltair
Morality, *s* Modhanna, beus, béusalachd, moraltachd.
Moralize, *v.* Labhair (no) sgriobh mu mhodhanna, (no) mo dheadh bheusan.
Moralizer, *s.* Moraltaiche
Morally, *adv.* Gu subhailceach, gu beusach, gu modhail, gu modhannach; a réir coslais
Morals, *s. pl.* Beusan, modhannan; àbhaistean, cleasan, cleachdnan, nòsan, gnàth, subhailc; caitheamh, beatha, iomchar, giùlan. Good morals, *deagh bheusan*, bad morals, *droch bheusan.*
Morass, *s.* Féith, feath, bog, boglach, càthar, suil-chrithEach; easgaidh, mointeach, monadh
Morbid, *a* Euslainnteach, truaillidh, neo-fhallain, eucailEach, tinn.
Morbidness, *s* Euslainnteachd, euslainnte, truailleachd, eucail, tinneas
Morbific, *a* Euslainnteach, eucaileach, galarach, neo-fhallain, aicideach, acaideach
Morbose, *a.* Euslainnteach, tinn, neo-fhallain.
Morbulent, *a.* Euslainnteach, tinn, neo-fhallain
Mordacious, *a* Cnàmhtach, cnàimhteach, creimeach.
More, *a* Tuille, tuilleadh, tuillead; còr Take more care, *thoir tuille aire*, I will take the more care, *bheir mi an tuillead aire*, seven years or more, *seachd bliadhna is còr.*

MORE, *adv.* Tuille; os cionn, nis mò; a ris, ni 's fhaide; (*the particle that forms the comparative*), a 's, is, ni 's. More than two years, *tuille na dà bhliadhna, oscionn da bhliadhna*, any more, *tuille*; he will not come any more, *cha tig e tuille, cha tig e ni 's mò*; I will not go any more than you, *cha téid mi ann ni 's mò na thusa, cha d' théid mi ann ni 's mò na theid thusa*, more and more, *ni 's mò agus ni 's mò*; what more have I to do? *ciod tuille th' agam ri dheanamh?* a little more, *beagan tuille*; a little more willingly, *beagan ni 's toiliche*, as much more again, *na h-uibhir eile, na h-uircead eile*, I got as much more again as you, *fhuair mi na h-uibhir eile riutsa*, and more than all this, *agus a thuille air so, agus a thuillead air so, a bharras air so*, what more have you to say? *ciod tuille th' agad ri radh?* more than enough, *tuille is a chòir*, more than usual, *tuille na 's àbhaist, tuille na b' àbhaist*.

MORE, *s.* Tuille, tuillead, barrachd.

MOREL, *s* Siris shearg.

MORELAND, *s* Ard, bràighe, dùthaich ard

MOREOVER, *adv.* Os barr, tuille fòs, cuideachd, a thuille air so, a thuille air sin, a bhàrr air so, a bhàrr air sin; a thuillead air so (no) sin, a bharrachd air (so) no sin, a bharras air so (no) sin, os cionn so (no) sin.

MORIGEROUS, *a.* Umhal, so-chomhairleach, easgaidh.

MORION, *s.* Ceann-bheart, clogaid, curac, bioraid, bonaid

MORKIN, *s* Cairbh, beothach fiadhaich a gheibh bàs le h-cucail no thaobh tubaist

MORLING, *s.* Olann caorach a gheibh bàs.

MORMO, *s.* Bòcan, bodach, taibhse, tannasg.

MORN See MORNING.

MORNING, *s* Maduinn, madainn; roimh-mheadhon là; moch-thràth, much-thràth; moch, much. In the morning, *anns a mhadainn, mochthràth*, to-morrow morning, *much (no) moch am màireach*, Monday morning, *moch Di luain, moch-thrath Di luain*, from morning till night, *o mhuch gu dubh*, a spring morning is piercing, *ceann goimh air madainn carraich*.

MORNING-DAWN, *s.* Glocnid, gloicnid.

MORNING-GOWN, *s.* Gùn maidne, earrasaid, fearrasaid.

MORNING-STAR, *s.* Reult na maidne; maidneag.

MOROSE, *a.* Gruamach, doirbh, crosda, dùr, cainnteach, friotalach, doimhe, aithghearr, frionasach, ciapalach, crin-geanach, neo-aoidheil. A morose fellow, *dùran*.

MOROSENESS, *s.* Cringean, crosdachd, doirbheas, doirbhe, frionasachd.

MORPHIN, *s.* Lobhradh, sgròile aodainn; sgròilleag chraicne a thig air uairibh a bhàrr an aodainn

MORRIS, *s* Seorsa dannsaidh.

MORROW, *s.* Màireach To-morrow, *am màireach*, to-morrow morning, *moch am màireach*, to-morrow se'nnight, *seachduin bho 'm màireach*; on the morrow, *air an là 'r na mhàireach, air an là màireach*

MORSE, *s.* Each mara.

MORSEL, *s.* Crioman, criomag, mir, greim, làn beòil A morsel of bread, *crioman (no) greim arain*, the industrious man's morsel is on every man's table, *bithidh mìr a ghille easguidh air gach mìas*

MORSURE, *s.* Teum, teumadh, creim.

MORT, *s* Marbh-rann; tuireadh. Mort cloth, *brat dubh*

MORT, *s.* Mòran.

MORTAL, *a* (*Subject to death*), bàsmhor; (*deadly*), marbh-tach, sgriosail, sgriosar, garg, guasachadh; (*human*), daonna, talmhaidh. Every man is mortal, *tha gach duine bàsmhor*, a mortal wound, *leon bàis, leòn marbhtach*; he was in a mortal fright, *bha eagal' anam air*.

MORTAL, *s.* Duine; creutair.

MORTALITY, *s.* Bàsmhorachd, bàsmhoireachd; bàs; marbh-achd, plaigh.

MORTALLY, *adv.* Gu bàsmhor, gu millteach; gu sgriosail, gu bàs. He was mortally wounded, *bha e air a leònadh gu bàs, fhuair e leòn bàis*.

MORTAR, *s.* Aol, mort-aol, criadh-aol. A pounding mortar, *moirteal*; (*in gunnery*), gunna toirm-shlige.

MORTGAGE, *s.* Gealladh; tigh no fearainn air thoirt an geall.

MORTGAGE, *v a.* Thoir an geall, geall. Mortgaged, *air a ghealltuinn, gealtuinnte*.

MORTGAGEE, *s.* Neach a gheibh gealladh.

MORTGAGER, *s.* Neach a bheir gealladh.

MORTIFEROUS, *a.* Bàsail, bàsmhor, marbhtach, sgriosail, mortach.

MORTIFICATION, *s.* (*Self-denial*), claoidh; smachdachadh, irioslachadh, féin-irioslachadh; (*trouble*), farran, docair, mi-shuaimhneas; (*gangrene*), cnàmhuinn; grodadh.

MORTIFY, *v a.* Claoidh, farranaich; islich, smachdaich, truaillich; fàs grod. Mortify your members, *claoidhibh 'ur buill*, mortified, *claoidhte, farranaichte, smachdaichte, truaillichte, air fas grod*

MORTIFYING, *a* Claoidheach; farranach; docrach.

MORTISE, *s* Toll tàthaidh; toll ann an ceann maide.

MORTISE, *v.* Tàth; tàth maide an ceann maide eile.

MORTMAIN, *s.* Seilbh shocrach; seilbh nach gabh reic.

MORTUARY, *s.* Naomh-dhéirc, dìleab dh' eaglais.

MOSAIC, *a.* Maoiseach, spairneagach; ioma-dathach.

MOSQUE, *s.* Teampull Turcach.

MOSQUETO, *s.* Cuileag Innseanach.

MOSS, *s.* Còinneach; còineach, mòinteach, cathar.

MOSS, *v.* Còinnich; comhdaich le còinneach.

MOSSY, *a* Còinneachail, còinneach, mòinteachail. Mossy ground, *càthar*

MOST, *a.* Is mò, mò. The most learned man of them, *am fear is ionnsuichte dhiubh*, the most part, *a chuid is mò, a chuid is fearr*; for the most part, *mar is tric*; most frequently, *mar is tric*.

MOST, *adv.* Ro; sàr. Most excellent, *ro-òirdheirc, sàr-mhaith*.

MOST, *s.* A chuid is mo, a mhòr-chuid, a gharbh-chuid.

MOSTLY, *adv.* Mar is tric; mar is cumaint; air a chuid is mò, gu h-imbhe bhig, ach beag.

MOTE, *s.* Leoman, leomann, reudan; (*in the eye*), caimean, smùirne, smùirnean; (*meeting*), mòd, coinneamh.

MOTHER, *s.* Màthair; †naing, †brinneach, muime. A mother-in-law, *mathair céile*, a stepmother, *muime*; a grandmother, *sean-mhathair*; a great grandmother, *seann sean-mhathair*; godmother, *muime*, mother of liquors, *deasgann, grunnd*; mother-of-pearl, *neamhuin, neamhnan*; like mother like daughter, *theid dubhag ri dualchas*; the turf is a good mother-in-law, *is math mhathair céile an fhòid*.

MOTHERLESS, *a.* Gun mhathair.

MOTHERLINESS, *s.* Mathairealachd.

MOTHERLY, *a.* Màthaireil, mar mhathar.

MOTHERY, *a.* Deasgannach, grunndach.

MOTHY, *a* Leomannach, lan, leomann, reudanach.

MOTION, *s* Gluasad, gluasachd, gluasadh, siubladh, siubhal, carachadh, gluideachadh; (*for a bill*), athchuinge; gluasad; tairgse. At my own motion, *do mo dheòin*, the motions of an enemy, *sligheachan namhaid*, a motion of the mind, *gluasad inntinn*.

Motionless, *a.* Neo-ghluasadach; gun chomas carachaidh, gun charachadh, gun ghlideachadh; gun lùth.

Motive, *s.* Aobhar; reuson; brosnachadh.

Motive, *a.* Carachail, gluasadach.

Motley, *a.* Ioma-dathach; iol-dathach; ioma-ghnetheach; iol-ghnetheach; eag-samhuil.

Motor, *s.* Fear carachaidh, carachair.

Motto, *s.* Focal suaicheantais.

Mould, *s.* (*Soil*), talamh, ùir; criadh; (*for casting*), molltair, mulladh; (*of bread*), cloimh liath, liatus.

Mould, *v. a.* Dealbh, tilg, cum; cruth; comhdaich le ùir; (*bake*), fuin; (*as bread*), liathaich mar aran le aois. Moulded, *dealbhta, tilgte, fuinte, liath.*

Mouldable, *a.* So-dhealbhadh, so-thilgeadh, so-chumadh.

Mould-board, *s.* (*Of a plough*), bord ùrchroinn.

Moulder, *s.* Mòltair, molltair, cumadair, dealbhadair, criathadair.

Moulder, *v. a.* Crion, luaithrich, tionndaidh gu luaithre, rach an smùr. Mouldered, *air dol na luaithre.*

Mouldily, *adv.* Gu liath, gu liatusach.

Mouldiness, *s.* Liathanachd, liatus, léithe, leithead.

Moulding, *s.* Clais.

Mouldwarp, *s.* See **Mole**.

Mouldy, *a.* Liath, sean, musgach, mutach, ascaoin, grod; air liathadh.

Moult, *v. n.* Caill (no) cuir iteagan, tilg iteagan, tilg cloimh.

Moulting, *s.* Call (no) cur iteag (no) clòimh.

† **Mounch**, *v. a.* Cagain, cnuas, cruas, cruasb.

Mound, *s.* Bruach, dùn; cladh, daighneach, dion-bhruach.

Mound, *v. a.* Daighnich le cladh, dion le bruach.

Mount, *s.* Dùn, dùnan; tom, toman, cnoc, cnocan; (*hill*), aonach, sliabh, beinn.

Mount, *v. a.* and *n.* Eirich, éir, dir, dìrich, rach suas, rach a nairde, rach ri bruthach; leum air muin eich: ardaich, sgeadaich; gleus. He mounted his horse, *leum e air 'each;* mounted with silver, *sgeadaichte le h-airgiod.*

Mountain, *s.* Sliabh, beinn, monadh, meall, cruach, dùn, ard mhonadh. Mountains, *sleibhtean, beanntan, beanntaidh, monaidh, monachan.*

Mountaineer, *s.* Sliabhair. A Scotch mountaineer, *Gaidheal.*

Mountainous, *a.* Sliabhach, beanntach, monadail, cnocach; ard; mor. A mountainous country, *bràid.*

Mountebank, *s.* Feall leighiche, dochdair bi gis, cleasaiche, baoth-leighiche.

Mounter, *s.* Fear a dhìreas, fear dìridh.

Mourn, *v. a.* Dean bròn, dean caoidh, dean tuireadh caoin, caoidh. Mourning her husband, *a caoidh a céile* (*no*) *a fir.*

Mourner, *s.* Fear bròin. Mourners, *luchd bròin.*

Mournful, *a.* Muladach, brònach, doilghiosach, duileasach, dòlasach, dubhach, tuirseach, duilich, doilich, bearranach; duilbhear, gleodhach, deurach, deoranta, ciamhaireach. A mournful tale, *sgeul bròin, sgeul muladach.*

Mournfully, *adv.* Gu muladach, gu bronach, gu doilgheasach, gu dolasach, gu tuirseach.

Mournfulness, *s.* Mulad, bron, doilghios, duilgheas, dòlas, dubhachas, tuireadh, tuirse, tuirseachd.

Mourning, *s.* Mulad, bròn, doilghios, tuireadh, caoinead, gul, cumhadh; (*clothes*), eideadh bròin.

Mouse, *s.* Luch, luchag. Mice, *luchaidh, luchagan;* a dormouse, *dallag.*

Mouser, *s.* Urr a ghlacas luchaidh.

Mouse-hole, *s.* Toll luchaig.

Mouse-trap, *s.* Crann-chat; cat-luch; gaisde luch.

Mousing, *a.* Seolta, eòlach, sligheach, seabach.

Mouth, *s.* Beul; craos, gros, cab, bile; blad, braoisg. The mouth of a beast, *craos, gros;* a toothless mouth, *cab;* a wry mouth, *goill, gaill;* (of the stomach), *goile;* make a mouth, *cuir braoisg ort;* a talkative, impertinent mouth, *beilean;* a gaping mouth, *clab;* it is the mouth that refuses at last, *is e 'm beula dh' obas mu dheireadh.*

Mouth, *v. a.* and *n.* Glaodh; ith, glàm, craos, cruas, cagain, cagainn.

Mouthed, *a.* Beulach, gnosach, gobach, cabach. Foul-mouthed, *droch-chainnteach, ana-cainnteach, mi-mhodhail;* mealy-mouthed, *nàrach, mallta, ciùin, seimh;* wide-mouthed, *craosach.*

Mouth-friend, *s.* Caraid beòil.

Mouthful, *s.* Làn beòil; srùbag; greim; mìr; crioman.

Mouthless, *a.* Gun bheul.

Movable, *s.* Innsridh, airneis.

Movable, *a.* So-ghluasad, so-charachadh, so-ghlideachadh. A movable feast, *féill thràthail, féill nan tràth.*

Move, *v. a.* and *n.* Gluais, caraich, caruich, altuich, glidich, atharruich; luaisg; (*affect*), buair; drùigh air; (*persuade*), dean furail, earail; (*go*), siubhail, falbh, folbh; triall; (*propose*), iarr, sir, guidh; athchuing; (*remove*), rach imirich, rach air imirich; (*shake*), crath, luaisg. It moves the heart of a stone, *bheireadh sniosnach air cridhe na cloich.*

Moved, *a.* (*Angered*), buairte, feargaichte; (*shaken*), luaisgte, gluaiste, crathta; (*affected*), duilich, fo mhulad. Moved up and down, *saobanaichte, air udal;* easily moved, *so-bhuaireadh, so-luasgadh, so-ghluasad.*

Moveless, *a.* Do-charachadh, do-ghluasad, do-ghlideachadh.

Movement, *s.* Gluasad, gluasachd, glideachadh, carachadh; modh gluasad.

Mover, *s.* Carachair; athchuingiche.

Moving, *a.* Drùighteach, brìoghar, brònach, muladach.

Movingly, *adv.* Gu drùighteach, gu brìoghar, gu bronach, gu muladach.

Mow, *s.* Mìr; cruach, daise, mìr connlaich. Hay in a mow, *saoidh sa mhir;* a hay-mow, *mìr saidh.*

Mow, *v. a.* Cuir stigh saoidh; dean mìr (no) daise; gearr saoidh; gearr le fàladair, speal, buain, gearr sios, sgud.

Mow, *v. n.* Cruinnich, tarradh; dean goill.

Mowburn, *v. n.* Loisg (no) gabh teas sa mhir (no) sa chruaich.

Mower, *s.* Spealadair, buainiche, fear fàladair, gearradair.

Mowing, *s.* Gearradh, buaineadh; spealadh, spealadaireachd, fàladaireachd.

Mown, *part.* Buainte, gearrta.

Moyle, *s.* Muileid.

Much, *a.* Mòr, mòran, ioma, iomad. Much good may it do you, *gu deanadh e mòran maith dhuit;* much ado about nothing, *mòran iomairt mu bheag nithe.*

Much, *s.* Mòran, mòrnaich, mor-nithe. Much more, *mòran tuille;* much ado, *iomairt;* with much ado, *air éigin;* too much, *tuille is a chòir, thuille na còrach;* how much? *cia meud?* as much, *na h-uibhir;* as much again, *na h-uibhir eile;* just as much as this, *a cheart uibhir ri so;* this much, *a mheud so, na h-uibhir so;* much like, *gli choslach;* much the same, *mu 'n am tuairmeis;* twice as much, *na h-uibhir eile;* he who has much will get more, *am fear aig am bheil im, gheibh e im.*

Mucid, *a.* Sleamhainn, slambanach, sliobach.

Mucilage, *s.* Deoch slambanach.

Mucilaginous, *a.* Sleamhuinn, slamach, slamanach.

MUCK, *s.* Inneir, aolach, sal, salchar, cac, òtrach; buachar, mathach, màthachadh.
† MUCK, *a.* Àitidh, fliuch.
MUCK, *v. a.* Cairt; leasaich, mathaich, inneirich, aolaich.
MUCKENDER, *s.* Neapaicinn pòc.
MUCKER, *v. a.* Cnuasaich, tionail, carn suas, cuir ri chéile.
MUCKHILL, *s.* Dùn aolaich, dùn innearach, òtrach, dùnan.
MUCKINESS, *s.* Sal, salachar.
† MUCKLE, *a.* Mòr, mòran.
MUCKWORM, *s.* Durag aolaich; spiocair.
MUCKY, *a.* Salach, mosach, musach, bréin.
MUCOUS, *a.* Sglongach, smugach, smuigeach, seileach, slamach.
MUCOUSNESS, *s.* Sglongachd, slamanachd, sleamhnachd.
MUCRO, *s.* Roinn; bior.
MUCRONATED, *a.* Roinnte, biorach.
MUCULENT, *a.* Sliobach, smugach, sglongach.
MUCUS, *s.* Sglong, smuig, seil, sal na sròn.
MUD, *s.* Poll, làthach, salachar, eabar, clabar, munloch.
MUDDED. See MUDDY.
MUDDILY, *adv.* Gu salach, gu druaipeach.
MUDDINESS, *s.* Sal, salachar, druaip, eabar.
MUDDLE, *v. a.* Salaich; cuir air an daoraich.
MUDDY, *a.* Salach, druaipeach, làthachail, eabrachail, drabhagach, dorch.
MUDWALL, *s.* Balladh creadha, balladh talmhainn.
MUE, *v.* Tilg (no) cuir iteagan.
MUFF, *s.* Ròmag; mutan.
MUFFLE, *v. a.* and *n.* Còmhdaich, céil; ròl suas, labhair gu briotach (no) gu mùgach.
MUFFLER, *s.* Aodach bràghaid.
MUFTI, *s.* Ard Shagart Turcach.
MUG, *s.* Mog; mugan.
MUGHOUSE, *s.* Tigh lionna, tigh òsda.
MUGGISH, MUGGY, *a.* Tais, fliuch, àitidh.
MUGWORT, *s.* Liath-lus.
MULATTO, *s.* Urr eadar bhi dubh is geal, urr aig am bheil aon phàrant dubh, agus aon eile geal.
MULBERRY, *s.* Maol-dhearc. A mulberry-tree, *craobh mhaol-dhearc.*
MULCT, *s.* Ùmhlah, fional.
MULCT, *v. a.* Cuir umhladh air, leig umhladh.
MULE, *s.* Muileid, muilead, maolainn, ainmhidh eadar each agus asail.
MULETEER, *s.* Gille mhuileid; gille each; cairtear.
MULIEBRITY, *s.* Boirionnas, bainionnas, banalas, banaileas, bandachd, bandaidheachd.
MULL, *v. a.* Millsich, millid, millsichte.
MULLEN, [great white mullen], *s.* Cuineal mhuire.
MULLER, *s.* Cloch méillidh.
MULLET, *s.* Muilead, scorsa éisg mara.
MULLIGRUBS, *s.* Bru ghoirt; doirbheas, dod.
MULLOCK, *s.* Salachar, prabar, trusdaireachd.
MULSE, *s.* Fion air a mheasg le mil.
MULTANGULAR, *a.* Ioma-chearnach, iol-chearnach, iom-oisinneach, iom-uilinneach.
MULTICAPSULAR, *a.* Ioma-chòsach, iol-chòsach.
MULTIFARIOUS, *a.* Iomadach, iomad, iomadaidh, ioma-ghnetheach.
MULTIFARIOUSNESS, *s.* Iomadachd.
MULTIFORM, *a.* Ioma-chruthach, iol-chruthach.

MULTILATERAL, *a.* Ioma-shliosnach.
MULTILOQUOUS, *a.* Cainnteach, gobach, bruidhneach.
MULTIPAROUS, *a.* Siolmhor.
MULTIPEDE, *s.* Ioma-chosach, iol-chosach, marr chorr-chòsaig.
MULTIPLE, *a.* Iom-fhillte; iomad uair, iomadach.
MULTIPLIABLE, *a.* So-mheudachadh, so-chur am meud.
MULTIPLICAND, *s.* Aireamh a bhios ri mheudachadh.
MULTIPLICATION, *s.* Meudachadh, iomadachadh.
MULTIPLICATOR, *s.* Meudachair, iomadachan.
MULTIPLICITY, *s.* Iomadachd, lionmhorachd, iomadaidh.
MULTIPLIER, *s.* Meudachair, iomadachan.
MULTIPLY, *v. a.* and *n.* Meudaich, iomadaich; rach am meud, rach an lionmhoireachd.
MULTIPRESENCE, *s.* Ioma-lathaireachd.
MULTISONOUS, *a.* Ioma-ghuthach, iol-ghuthach.
MULTITUDE, *s.* Sluagh, pobull; mòran sluaigh, slogh, bannal, cuideachd, mòr-chuideachd; lòd, drobh; aireamh mhor, tachdar, lionmhoireachd, iomadalachd.
MULTITUDINOUS, *a.* Iomadach, lionmhor, sluaghmhor.
MULTIVAGOUS, *a.* Iomrollach, luaineach, siùbhlach.
MULTOCULAR, *a.* Ioma shuileach.
MULTURE, *s.* Molltair; ullag.
MUM! *interj.* Caisd! eisd!
MUM, *s.* Lionn cruithneachd.
MUMBLE, *v. a.* and *n.* Dean briot; dean gearain, dean durdan; cagain; creim.
MUMBLER, *s.* Fear dùrdanach, duine briotach.
MUMM, *v.* Rach air ghìdhisearachd.
MUMMER, *s.* Cìdhisear, gìdhisear.
MUMMERY, *s.* Cìdhisearachd, bréig riochd; amaideachd; baoth-chleasachd.
MUMMY, *s.* Corp spiosraichte.
MUMP, *v.* Cneim, creim, cagain, glàm, cnuas, cruas.
MUMPER, *s.* Baigear, urr bhochd, déircear.
MUMPS, *s.* Dod, stùrd, ardan; tinneas plocach. He is in the mumps, *tha e san dod.*
MUMPISH, *a.* Dodach, stodach, ardanach, coimheach, ceann-laidir.
MUNCH, *v.* Cneim, cnuas, cruasb, glàm; cagain.
MUNCHER, *s.* Glàmsair.
MUNCHING, *s.* Glàmadh, glàmsaireachd, cagnadh, dian-chagnadh, cruasbail.
MUNDANE, *a.* Saoghalmhor, saoghalta, talmhaidh.
MUNDATION, *s.* Glanadh, glanadaireachd.
MUNDATORY, *a.* Glanta; sgùrach, glanadail.
MUNDIC, *s.* Seorsa meiteil.
MUNDIFICATION, *s.* Glanadh, sgùradh.
MUNDIFY, *v. a.* Glan, sgùr, ionnlaid.
MUNDIVAGANT, *a.* Siùbhlach, iomrollach.
MUNDUNGUS, *s.* Breunan, ni breun sam bi, tumbac grod.
MUNICIPAL, *a.* Comunnach, comunnail, cuideachail, a bhuineas do bhaile mòr.
MUNICIPALITY, *s.* Taobh duthcha, carann, roinn.
MUNIFICENCE, *s.* Fiùghantas, mor-chùis, toir-bheartas, fial-mhorachd, féile, tabhartachd.
MUNIFICENT, *a.* Fiùghanta, mòr-chuiseachd, toir-bheartach, fialuidh, fialmhor, fial; mathasach.
MUNIFICENTLY, *adv.* Gu fiùghanta, gu mor-chuiseach, gu toir bheartach, gu fialuidh, gu fial.
MUNITION, *s.* Dionadh, dion, daighneachadh, daighneach, daingneach.
MUNIMENT, *s.* Dion, dionadh, daighneach, daighneachadh.

Murage, *s.* Airgiod (no) cìs a chumail suas balladh cathrach.

Mural, *a.* Ballach, ballaidh.

Murder, *s.* Mort, murt, mortadh, murtadh, marbhadh, àr.

Murder, *v. a.* Mort, murt, marbh, mill, cuir gu bàs, cuir as do.

Murderer, *s.* Mortair, murtair, milltear, marbhaiche, marbhadair, sgriosadair. Murderers, *luchd mortaidh.*

Murderess, *s.* Bana-mhortair.

Murderous, *a.* Mortach; sgriosail, marbhtach, fuilteach, fuileach, fealltail.

Mure, *v. a.* Iom-dhruid.

Muriatic, *a.* Saillte.

Murk, *s.* Dorchadas, doirche, duirche, duibhre, doilleireachd, mùige.

Murky, *a.* Dorch, doilleir, dubh, mùigeach.

Murmur, *s.* Monmhor; torman, borbhan, mothar, torghan, dùrdan; diurrasan, darsan, canran, monaghair, siùsan, ciùlan, glamhsan, gearan, talachadh; ciùrlan, ciùrachdan.

Murmur, *v. n.* Dean monmhor, dean torman, dean borbhan, dean dùrdan; dùrdanaich, borbhanaich; (*complain*), talaich, gearain.

Murmurer, *s.* Glamhsair, fear gearanach, fear talachaidh, cànranaiche, gearanaiche. Murmurers, *luchd cànrain.*

Murmuring, *s.* Monmhor, tormanaich, borbhanaich, durdanaich, monaghair, talach, talachadh, gearan.

Murrain, *s.* Earnach; eucail, galar, plaigh, conach.

Murrey, *a.* Dubh ruadh, donn, dubh-dhonn.

† **Murth**, *s.* Pailteas arbhair.

Muscadel, Muscadine, *s.* Seorsa fion, seorsa peur.

Muscle, *s.* Féith, féith chaol, féith lùthaidh; (*a fish*), faoch, maorach, iasgan.

Muscular, *a.* Làidir, feitheach, gramail, calma, luthmhor.

Muse, *v. a.* Smuainich, beachd-smuainich; cnuaisich.

Muse, *s.* Smuaine, beachd-smuaine; comas (no) lathailt air filidheachd (no) air ceòl; aoisdana; (*in heathen mythology*), cliar-oigh. The muses, *an ceòlraidh;* the muse of a hare, *leabadh maighiche.*

Museful, *a.* Smuaineachail, smuainteachail.

Muser, *s.* Fear smuaine, smuainteachair.

Museum, *s.* Tigh neònachais, seud-lann.

Mushroom, *s.* Ballag losgainn; fàs na h-aon oidhche; (*in contempt*), gircean, ablach, caifean.

Music, *s.* Ceol, fonn, co-sheirm; oirfid, caireall; airfideadh, céilleir. Music without luck, *ealaidh gun rath.*

Musical, *a.* Ceòlmhor, ceòlar, céillearach, binn; binnghuthach; leadanach. Musically, *gu ceòlar, gu binn.*

Musicalness, *s.* Ceòlmhorachd.

Musician, *s.* Fear ciùil, filidh.

Music-master, *s.* Maighistir ciùil, oide ciùil.

Music-school, *s.* Sgoil ciùil.

Musk, *s.* Seorsa boltraich, musg.

Musk-apple, *s.* Seorsa ubhail.

Musket, *s.* Musg, musgait, gunna saighdeir. A musket-ball, *peilear gunna.*

Musketeer, *s.* Fear musgaid.

Musketoon, *s.* Gearra-ghunna, gunna glaic.

Muskiness, *s.* Boladh musg.

Musky, *a.* Cubhraidh, boltrachail, fàileach.

Muslin, *a.* Aodach finealta canaich, pearluinn.

Musrol, *s.* Sroin-iall sréin.

Mussulman, *s.* Creideach Turcach.

Must, *s.* Fion ùr, (no) milis.

Must, *v. imperfect.* Feumaidh, is éigin, is fheudar, feudaidh, faodaidh. I must be gone, *feumaidh mi a bhi falbh, is éigin do coiseachd;* what must be done? *ciod is fheudar a dhianamh?*

Mustaches, Mustachios, *s.* Ciabhagan; roibean, feusag a bhile uachdair.

Mustard, *s.* Sgeallan; mustard.

Muster, *v. a.* Cruinnich, cnuasaich, cuir ri chéile, solair, tionail, teanail; beachdaich, gabh beachd.

Muster-roll, *s.* Ainm-lite, ainm-chlàr; aireamh feachd, ròl.

Mustiness, *s.* Leithe, liatus, liathradh.

Musty, *a.* Liath, rudhain; musgach, mutach; air cur thairis le cloimh; liath; air liathradh; marbh, trom.

Mutability, *s.* Caochlaideachd, neo-bhunaiteachd, neo-bhunailteachd; mùiteachd; luaineachd.

Mutable, *a.* Caochlaideach, neo-bhunaiteach, mùiteach, luaineach, luaimneach, neo-sheasmhach, neo-steidheil.

Mutableness, *s.* Caochlaideachd, neo-bhunaiteachd.

Mutation, *s.* Caochladh, mùth, atharrach, atharrachadh.

Mutchkin, *s.* Bodach, muisginn.

Mute, *a.* Balbh, bìth, samhach, tosd, tosdach; amhlabhair. As mute as a mouse, *cho bìth ri luchaig.*

Mute, *s.* Balbhan. Mutes, *balbhain.*

Mute, *s.* (*Of a bird*), cac eoin.

Mutely, *adv.* Gu balbh, gu bìth, gu tosdach, gu sàmhach.

Muteness, *s.* Bailbhe; balbhanachd, tosd, tosdachd, samhchair.

Mutilate, *v.* Ciùrr, ciurramaich, leòn, gearr, beubanaich, spoth.

Mutilated, *part.* Ciurramach, ciurramaichte, leònta, gearrta, gearrte, beubanaichte, spothta, spothte.

Mutilation, *s.* Gearradh; beubanachadh; spothadh.

Mutineer, *s.* Cùl-mhutair, fear ceannairc.

Mutinous, *a.* Ceannairceach, buaireasach.

Mutinously, *adv.* Gu ceannairceach, gu buaireasach.

Muting, *s.* Ceannairc, àr a mach, cul-mhutaireachd, éiridh.

Muting, *v. n.* Eirich; dean ceannairc (no) àr a mach, dean cùl-mhutaireachd.

Mutter, *v. n.* Dean dranndan, dean borbhan, dean dùrdan; gearain, talaich.

Mutter, *s.* Dranndan, borbhan, dùrdan, siùsan, torman; gearan, talach, talachadh, ceasachd.

Mutterer, *s.* Fear dranndanach, fear talaich.

Muttering, *s.* Borbhanaich, dranndanaich, diurrasanaich; gearan, talachadh.

Muttering, *a.* Borbhanach, dranndanach, dùrdanach, siùsanach, tormanach; gearanach.

Mutton, *s.* Muilt-fheòil; caor.

Mutual, *a.* Mu 'n seach, do chèile; aisreamnach, còmhlath; aontachail.

Mutually, *adv.* Mu 'n seach, do chéile, a cheile, gach aon a chéile, gu h-aontachail. They mutually loved each other, *ghradhaich iad a chéile, bha gradh aca do chéile.*

Muzzle, *v. a.* and *n.* Cabstaraich, cabstanaich, spearraich, cuir busiall air; cuir sàmhach; dùin beul; grosaich.

Muzzle, *s.* Beul, craos, gros, cab, bus; (*for the mouth*), bus-iall, glomhar, spearrach.

My, *a. pron.* Mo. My book, *mo leabhar,* or, emphatically, *mo leabhar-sa;* my horse, *m' each,* or, emphatically, *m' each-sa.*

Myopy, *s.* Doille, cion-léirsinn.

Myriad, *s.* Deich mile, aireamh mhor air bith.

Myrmidon, *s.* Buamasdair, constabull, uipear gun toinisg.

Myrrh, *s.* Mir, bith cubhraidh.

Myrrhine, *a.* Do mhir, mir.

Myrtle, *s.* Miortal, cannach. A myrtle grove, *doire miortail.*

Myrtle, *a.* Miortalach, miortail.

Myself, *pron.* Mi fèin, mi fhèin. I myself, *mise fèin*

Mystagogue, *s.* Fear mìneachaidh rùn diomhair.

Mysterious, *a.* Dorch, doilleir, do-thuigsinn, diomhair, diomhaireach, folaichte

Mysteriously, *adv* Gu dorch, gu doilleir, gu do-thuigsinn.

Mystery, *s* Rùn-diomhair, diomhaireachd, ceaird.

Mystic, **Mystical**, *a.* Dorch, doilleir, do-thuigsinn, diomhair, folaichte, céilte.

Mystically, *adv.* Gu dorch, gu doilleir, gu do-thuigsinn, gu diomhair.

Mythological, *a* Faoin-sgeulach.

Mythologist, *s.* Faoin-sgeulaiche.

Mythology, *s.* Faoin-eachdraidh Dhé nam Pàganach; faoin-sgeulachd.

N.

N, *s.* An ceathramh litir deug do 'n aibideal.

Nab, *v a* Glac, beir air, dean greim, cuir an lamh

Nacker, *s.* Slige neamhnuid

Nadir, *s.* Am ponc a tha dìreach fo 'n casaibh air taobh eile na cruinne

Nag, *s* Gearan, each beag, *scaltaidh*, leannan

Naiad, *s.* Oigh mara.

Nail, *s* Tarrag, tarrang, tarrung, tarruinn, tacaid, (*in measure*), iongna, an seathamh cuid deug do shlait: (*of the body*), iongna On the nail, *gu h-ealamh, air ball, air an spot*, scratch with the nail, *sgriob, sgròb*

Nail, *v a.* Tarraig, tarraing, tairn, sparr Nail to the cross, *sparr ris a chrann*, nailed, *taraigte, tairnte, sparrta, air a sparradh*, nailed to the cross, *air a sparradh ris a chrann*

Nailer, *s.* Tarrangair, fear tharaigean, fear thairigean, fear thairnean.

Naked, *a* Lom, rùisgte, lomnochd, lomardach, lomraisteach, nochd, maol, soilleir, simplidh Naked is the eye that wants the eye-lashes, *is lom an t-sùil gun an rosg*, poor is the want that is naked, *is bochd an ainnis an lomardach*

Nakedly, *adv* Gu lom, gu rùisgte, gu lomnochd, gu lomraisteach, gu maol; gu soilleir

Nakedness, *s* Nochd, lomnochdadh, nochduigheachd.

Name, *s* Ainm; (*renown*), cliù; onoir, alladh, iomradh. A nickname, *frith ainm*, a surname, *sloinne*, a bad name, *droch cliù, droch iomradh*, a proper name, *ainm dìleas*, what is your name? *c' ainm th' ort?* a namesake, *fear cinnidh*, (a female), *bean chinnidh*, the name without the thing, *an t-ainm gun an tairbhe*

Name, *v.* Ainmich; sonruich, gairm; abair, goir, labhair, innis, aithris A man named John, *fear do 'n goirear Eoin.*

Namely, *adv* Gu sònruichte, gu h-àraidh, is e sin ri radh, eadhon, i. e

Nameless, *a* Gun ainm; neo-chliùiteach, neo-ainmeil, gun chliù, gun iomradh, neo-ainmichte, iosal, nach còr ainmeachadh.

Namer, *s.* Ainmeachair.

Namesake, *s* (*Male*), fear cinnidh, (*female*), bean chinnidh

Nap, *s* Codal, cadal, pramh; lochdan, lochd; teanail chadail, (*of cloth*), caitean, ròinneach aodaich, calg

Nap, *v* Codail, cadail, gabh pramh.

Nape, *s.* Cùl na h-amhaich, cùl a mhuineil

Napkin, *s* Neapaicinn, neapaigin, neapaig; brat laimh; (*for the neck*), neapaicinn amhaich; (*for the pocket*), neapaicinn pòc

Nappiness, *s.* Caiteanachd, calg, colg.

Napless, *a.* Lom, gun chaitean, gun roinne, gun chalg.

Nappy, *a.* Cobharach, còpach

Narcissus, *s* Lus a chrom-chinn.

Narcotic, *a* Codalach, cadalach, suainear.

Narcotic, *s.* Pramh-leigheas, leigheas codail.

Narrable, *a.* So-innseadh

Narrate, *v. a.* Innis, aithris.

Narration, *s.* Aithris, eachdraidh, eachdruidh, nuaidheachd, naigheachd, sgeul, seanachas, sriut, sriutach.

Narrative, *a.* Aithriseach; sgeulach; sriutaiche.

Narrative, *s* Aithris, eachdraidh, sgeul, sgeulachd.

Narrator, *s* Sgeulaiche, seanachaidh.

Narrow, *a.* Aimhleathan, aithleathann, cughann, cumhang, caol, teann, (*niggard*), crion; spìocach; (*sharp*), dlù, geur, faiceallach A narrow arm of the sea, *caolas; caslas mara, cneas mara*, a narrow heart, *cridhe crion*, a narrow pass, *bealach.*

Narrow, *v a* Cughannaich, dean aimhleathan, dean aithleathan, dean cughann, dean caol, beagaich

Narrowly, *a.* Gu h-aimhleathan, gu cughann; air éigin; gu faiceallach, gu geur.

Narrowness, *s* Aimhleathanachd, cughannachd; crìne, spiocaireachd, spioc

Narwhale, *s* Seorsa muic-mara.

Nasal, *a* Sròineach, sròinail, mùgach.

Nastily, *adv.* Gu mosach, gu musach, gu salach, gu grannda, gu gràda, gu breun, gu loibheach, gu neo-ghlan.

Nastiness, *s* Salachar, sal, neo-ghloine, trusdaireachd, cac, mosaiche, musaiche.

Nasty, *a* Mosach, musach, salach, grannd, gràda, neoghlan, breun, (*in language*), draosda, drabasta, macnusach.

Natal, *a.* Dùthchasach, dùchasach, breith A natal hour, *uair breithe*

Natation, *s* Snamhadh, snàmh, snamhaireachd, plodadh; eadar dha liunn.

Nation, *s* Sluagh, cinneach, pobull; muinntir, dùthaich, rìoghachd, talamh.

National, *a.* Dùthchasach, dùchasach, dùchail, rìoghachdail, cinneadail

Nationally, *adv.* Gu dùchasach, gu dùchail, gu cinneadail

Native, *a.* Dùthchasach, dùchasach, dùthcha, dùcha; nadurra, nadurrail.

Native, *s.* Fear àiteachaidh, fear mhuinntir. A native of the Lowlands, *fear mhuinntir na machrach, dubh-Ghall*, women and priests are natives nowhere, *cha bhi dùchas aig mnai no sagairt*

Nativity, *s* Breith; tuismeadh, dùchasachd

Natural, *a.* Nàdurra, nàdurrail; a réir nàduir; thaobh nàduir; (*as a child*), diolain.

Natural, *s.* Amadan, leth-amadan, neo-dhuine, amhlair.

Naturalist, *s.* Fear a tha eòlach air oibribh nàduir agus na cruitheachd.

Naturalization, *s.* Gabhail steach do dhùthaich (no) do chomunn, buileachadh còir dùcha.

Naturalize, *v. a.* Thoir ceart bhreith; gabh steach; dean nàdurra; builich còir baile (no) dùcha air neach, gabh mar fhear dùcha; cleachdaich.

Naturally, *adv.* Gu nàdurra, gu nàdurrail, gu gnétheil, a réir nàduir, a thaobh naduir, gu neo-chealgach.

Nature, *s.* Nàdur, an domhan, an cruinne; an cruthachadh; cùrsa, nàduir; (*disposition*), nàdur, aigne, cail; gné; (*sort*), seòrsa, gné. According to nature, *a réir nàduir;* it is his nature, *is e sin a nàdur;* this is our nature, *is e so ar nàdur, is ann mar so a chruthaicheadh sinn;* good nature, *deagh nàdur;* bad nature, *droch nàdur;* against nature, *air aghaidh nàduir, ann aghaidh chuilg;* by nature, *a thaobh nàduir.*

Natured, *a.* Nadurrach, nadurra. Good-natured, *math nàdurrach, soitheamh, soimeach;* bad-natured, *olc nadurrach, doirbh, crosda, cainnteach.*

Naught, *a.* Olc, aingidh, coirpte, coirpidh, truaillidh, dona.

Naughtily, *adv.* Gu h-olc, gu h-aingidh, gu coirpte, gu truaillidh, gu coirpidh, gu dona.

Naughtiness, *s.* Olcas, olc, aingidheachd, coirpidheachd, droch-bheus, droch-bheairt, donas.

Naughty, *a.* Olc, aingidh, truaillidh, coirpidh, coirpte, dona.

Naulage, *s.* Faradh.

Naumachy, *s.* Long-throid, muirghrim.

Nausea, *s.* Déistinn, déisdinn, sgreamh, tur thilge, tliochd, togar gu diobhairt.

Nauseate, *v. n.* Gabh sgreamh, gabh déistinn.

Nauseous, *a.* Déistinneach, déisdinneach, sgreamhail; gràineil, mosach.

Nauseously, *adv.* Gu déistinneach, gu déisdinneach, gu sgreamhail, gu gràineil.

Nauseousness, *s.* Déistinn, déisdinn, sgreamh, gràin, mosaiche.

Nautical, *a.* Mara, marach, longach.

Nautilus, *s.* Faochag sgiobach.

Naval, *a.* Cabhlaich, mara, muireil. A naval fight, *blàr (no) cath mara.*

Nave, *s.* (*Of a wheel*), cioch, ceap cartach, cairt-cheap, ceap, ceap rotha, crub; (*of a church*), meadhon eaglais.

Navel, *s.* Imleag, iomlag.

Navelwort, *s.* Lamhan cat leacainn.

Navigable, *a.* So-sheòladh, so-sheòlta, domhainn, a ghabhas seòladh, a dh' fheudar a sheòladh.

Navigate, *v. a.* Seòl.

Navigation, *s.* Seoladh, seòladaireachd.

Navigator, *s.* Seòladair, mairiche, maraiche.

Navy, *s.* Cabhlach, feachd mara, plod.

Nay, *adv.* Ni h-eadh; ni bheil, cha n' eil, nach eil. He that will not when he may, when he would he shall have nay, *am fear nach gabh nur a gheibh, cha n' fhaigh nur is àille;* a nay word, *diùltadh.*

† **Neaf**, *s.* Dorn.

Neal, *v. a.* Mi-fhaobhraich, thoir faobhar o.

Neap, *a.* Iosal. Neap-tide, *contraigh.*

Near, *a.* and *adv.* Fagus, fagus, dlù, an cois, aig lamh, am fogus, am fagus, an gàr; laimh ri; (*parsimonious*), cruadalach, gann, spiocach, crion. Come near me, *thig laimh rium;* (almost), *ach beag, thun bhith;* far and near, *am fad is am fogus;* near now, *a chianamh;* though near me be near, upon me is nearer, *ged is fhogus domh, is fhoigse orm;* near in blood, *càirdeach, dlù an daimh.*

Nearer, *a.* Is fhoigse, ni 's fhoigse, is fhoisge, is fhaigse, ni 's fhaigse. A nearer way, *rathad is giorra, rathad is fhaigse; ni 's gainne, is gainne.*

Nearest, *a.* Is fhoigse, ni 's fhoigse, is fhaisge, ni 's fhaisge; is giorra, ni 's giorra; is gainne, ni 's gainne. This is the nearest way by far, *is e so 'n rod is fhaigse gu mòr.*

Nearly, *adv.* Cha mhòr, air bheag, ach beag, thun, a thun. He is nearly dead, *tha e thun bhith marbh;* nearly or parsimoniously, *gu gann, gu spiocach, gu crion.*

Nearness, *s.* Fogasachd, dlùthas; (*by blood*), cairdeas; (*by marriage*), daimh; (*niggardliness*), crìne, spiocaireachd, gion.

Nearsighted, *a.* Gearr-sheallach.

Neat, *s.* Feudail, faodail, crò, crodh; bo, mart, meudail.

Neat, *a.* Cuimeir, cuimear, deàs, finealta, innealta, snàsmhor, sgeinmeil, sgilmeil, urlaimh; (*unadulterated*), glan, gasda, neo-thruaillte.

Neatherd, *s.* Buachaill bhò, aodhair.

Neatly, *adv.* Gu cuimeir, gu deas, gu finealta, gu innealta, gu snàsmhor, gu sgeinmeil.

Neatness, *s.* Deisead, innealtachd, finealtachd, innealtas, finealtas, snàsmhorachd; sgeilmeachd, gloinead.

Neb, *s.* Gob, gros, beul, sròin.

Nebula, *s.* Ceò, neul, nial, mùig.

Nebulous, *a.* Ceòthar, neulach, nialach, mùigeach, dorcha, doilleir, dubh.

Necessaries, *s.* Nithe feumail, nitheannan feumail, riachdanas.

Necessarily, *adv.* Gu do-sheachanta; a thaobh dàn.

Necessary, *a.* Feumail; riachdanach; do-sheachadh; an dàn. A necessary-house, *tigh beag, tigh oich, tigh cac.*

Necessary, *s.* Tigh beag, tigh oich, tigh cac.

Necessariness, *s.* Feumalachd, riachdanas, do-sheachantachd.

Necessitude, *v. a.* Eignich, foireignich, thoir air. Necessitated, *éignichte, fo dh' easbhuidh; foiréignichte.*

Necessitation, *s.* Eigneachadh.

Necessitous, *a.* Bochd uireasbhach, uireasbhuidheach, truagh, diblidh, gann. The necessitous spoil credit, *millidh airc iasad.*

Necessity, *s.* Éigin, foireigin, uireasbhuidh, eiginneachd; (*fate*), dàn. I am under the necessity, *is éigin domh;* there is a necessity for this, *tha feum air so;* there is no fence against necessity, *cha 'n eil beart an aghaidh na h-éigin;* necessity will make a shift, *gleidhidh airc innleachd.*

Neck, *s.* Amhach, muineal, bràghad, coilear; (*in ridicule*), sgroig, sgroigean; (*of a bottle*), sgeòc, sgeòcan. In spite of your neck, *ge b' oil le d' amhaich e;* a wry neck, *amhach gheocach, geoic;* a neck of land, *doirlinn, tairbeirt;* on the neck, *dlù an deigh.*

Neckatee, *s.* Neapaicinn amhaich boirionnaich; sgoiltean.

Neckcloth, *s.* Neapaicinn amhaich; eididh muineil, brat bràghaid.

Necklace, *s.* Truis-bhràghad, ursgar bhràghad, muinsheud.

Neckweed, *s.* Còrcach, càrcach; cord na croiche.

Necromancer, *s.* Fiosaiche, druidh, eug-dhruidh, eòlasair; cleasaiche, dubh-chleasaiche, mànaran.

Necromancy, *s.* Fiosachd, druidheachd, eòlas, dubhchleasachd, eug-dhruidheachd; marbh-dhruidheachd, geas, manaranachd.

Necromantic, *a.* Fiosachdail, druidheil, druidheach, manaranach.

Nectar, *s.* Deoch mhilis; deoch nan dée.

Nectareous, *a.* Milis, fior mhilis.

Need, *s.* Feum; uireasbhuidh, easbhuidh, feumalachd, dìth; gainne, bochduinn, daibhreas, riachdanas; éigin, càs. I have need of it, *tha feum agam air.*

Need, *v. a* and *n* Feum; bi a dhìth. I will need it, *feumaidh mi e*, you need not, *cha ruig thu leas;* I must needs, *feumaidh mi, is éigin domh;* you need not fear, *cha ruig thu leas eagal 'ghabhail.*

Needful, *a.* Feumail; feumach, riachdanach, iomchuidh, do-sheachanta Very needful, *ro-fheumail.*

Needfulness, *s.* Feum, feumalachd

Needle, *s.* Snàthad; (*of a mariner*), taruing art. The eye of a needle, *crò snàthaid*, a needleful, *làn snathaid.*

Needler, *s.* Snathadair; fear shnàthadan

Needless, *a* Neo-fheumail, uaireach

Needlessly, *adv.* Gu neo-fheumail, gu h-uaireach.

Needle-work, *s.* Obair shnàthaid, greus, greus-obair.

Needs, *adv* Gu feumail I must needs go, *is éigin do falbh, is fheudar dhomh bhith coiseachd*

Needy, *a* Bochd, uireasbhach, uireasbhuidheach, feumach, truagh, daibhir, daibhreach; (*hungry*), ocrach, acrach, gortach The needy must not be bashful, *cha bhith nàir aig caol gortach*, long is the hand of the needy, *is fad lamh an fheumaich*

Ne'er, *adv.* See **Never**

Nef, *s.* Meadhon eaglais

Nefarious, *a* Olc, aingidh, dona; coirpidh, coirpte, graineil, mallùichte, fuathasach, curt.

Negation, *s.* Diùltadh, seunadh, àicheadh, òb

Negative, *a* Diùltach, seunach, àicheanach.

Negative, *s.* Aichean, diùltadh It was carried in the negative, *fhuair e'n diùltadh, chaidh dhiùltadh.*

Negatively, *adv.* Le diùltadh, le h-àicheadh.

Neglect, *v. a* Dearmaid, dearmadaich, dichuimhnich, diochuimhnich, dean dearmad; cuir air dearmad, dean dimeas, cuir air mi-shuim; cuir dheth, cuir dàil; faillich, aillsich.

Neglect, *s* Dearmad, dichuimhne, diachuimhne, neo-chùram, cion cùraim, neo-aire, mi-shuim, dimeas.

Neglecter, *s* Fear dearmaid, fear neo-churamach, urr dhearmadach

Neglectful, *a.* Dearmadach, dichuimhneach, mi-sheadhar, mi-shuimeil, neo-churamach, mi-churamach, neo-aireach, neo-spéiseil, maineachdach, fàillidheach, aillseach.

Neglection, *s* Dearmad, mi-shuim.

Neglective, *a.* Dearmadach, dichuimhneach, mi-sheadhar, mi-shuimeil, neo-shuimeil, neo-chùramach, neo-aireachail, mi-fhaiceallach.

Negligence, *s* Dearmadachd, di-chuimhne; dio-chuimhne, mi-sheadh, mul-snéamh, neo-chùram, neo-aire, cion aire, mi-shuim

Negligently, *adv* Gu dearmadach, gu di-chuimhneach, gu mi-sheadhar, gu mi-shuimeil, gu neo-churamach, gu neo-shuimeil, gu mul-sneamhail

Negligent, *a.* Dearmadach, di-chuimhneach, dio-chuimhneach, mi-sheadhar, mul-sneamhail, mi-shuimeil, neo-chùramach, leasg, aillseach.

Negotiate, *v n* Dean gnothuch; cuir gnothaichean air an aghaidh, tròchd, tràchd, cuir gnothuch gu doigh, roinn, coird ri, ceannaich, dean ceannach is reic, marasglaich Negotiating, *a roinn, a marasglachadh, a tròchd, a ceannachadh*

Negotiation, *s.* Riaghailteachadh, socrachadh, cur ghnothuichean gu doigh, comh-ghnothuch.

Negotiator, *s.* Fear gnothuich.

Negro, *s.* Duine dubh, urr dhubh, Aifriceach. Negroes, *daoine dubh, sluagh dubh.*

Neif, *s.* Dorn.

Neigh, *v.* Sitrich, dean sitrich. He began to neigh, *thòisich e air sitrich.*

Neigh, *s.* Sitir, sitrich

Neighbour, *s.* Coimhearsnach, coifhearsnach, nàbuidh, companach. A next neighbour, *ath-choimhearsnach;* the neighbours, *na coimhearsnach.*

Neighbourhood, *s.* Coimhearsnachd, coifhearsnachd, nàbachd, nàbuidheachd. In the neighbourhood, *anns a choifhearsnachd, anns an nàbachd.*

Neighbouring, *a.* Fogus, fagus, coimhearsnachaidh, nabaidh. Neighbouring people, *sluagh coimhearsnachaidh.*

Neighbourly, *a.* Coimhearsnachail, nàbachail, còir, slobhailt

Neither, *adv* and *conj* Ni mo, ni 's mo, no; fòs; ni h-aon diubh, cha 'n e h-aon chuid. Neither your word, *ní mo thusa no mise*, she will take neither you nor him, *cha ghabh i aon chuid thusa no esan.*

Neophyte, *s.* Iompachan, urr iompaichte.

Neoteric, *a.* Ùr, nodha, nuadh.

Nephew, *s* Mac bràthar no peathar.

Nephritic, *a.* Àirneach, àirneasach.

Nereides, *s. pl* Ban deé na mara; oighean mara.

Nerve, *s.* Féith; lùth.

Nervous, *a.* Féitheach, féithear, lùthmhor, lùthar, grainail, làidir; euslainnteach, fann, neo-ghramail.

† **Nervy**, *a* Laidir, féithear, lùthar, gramail.

Nescience, *s* Aineolas

† **Nesh**, *a* Maoth, fann, mallta, so-chiurradh.

Ness, *s* Sròin, ceann, maol, muil, rutha, teangadh; innis.

Nest, *s.* Nead, aite clùmhar, còs. Nest-egg, *ubh nid.*

Nest, **Nestle**, *v.* Neadaich, tog nead. Nestling, *a neadachadh, a togail nid.*

Nestling, *s.* Garrag; gearcan, eun air a thoirt as an nead.

Net, *s.* Lion, lian, eangach, gaisd. A fishing-net, *lion iasgaich*, catch in a net, *rib, glac, le lion.*

Nether, *a.* Iochdrach, iochdarach. The nether world, *an saoghal iochdrach, ifrinn.*

Nethermost, *a* Is iochdaraiche, is ìsle, is ìsle.

Netting, *s.* Lion, obair lin.

Nettle, *s* Eanndag, feanndag, eanntag, ionntag, loitcag, iunntag A crop of nettles, *eanntagach*, the stinging of a nettle, *gath (no) losg eanntaig.*

Nettle, *v.* Gion, loisg, cradh, sgar, farranaich, buair, brosnuich, feargaich. Nettled, *farranaichte.*

Neuter, *a.* Neachdar; nach buin do thaobh sam bi; meadhonach, sa mheadhon eadar an da thaobh

Neutral, *a.* Neachdarach.

Neutrality, *s.* Neachdarachd

Neutrally, *adv.* Gu neachdarach.

Never, *adv.* Riamh, a riamh, gu bràth, am feasd. It never happened before, *cha do thachair e 'riamh*, never deny it, *na àicheadh am feasd e*, were I never so rich, *air a bheartaichead 's gu bithinn*, be it never so little, *air a lughaid 's gum bi e*

Never-blushing, *a* Beagnarach, dàn; ladurna, peilpeanta.

Never-ceasing, *a.* Bidheanta; maireann, an comhnuidh, gun chaird, gun stad, gun sgur.

Never-erring, *a.* Neo-mhearachdach.

Never-fading, *a.* Bibhuan, sior-bhuan, buan, maireann, maireannach; sior-uaine.

Nevertheless, *adv.* Gidheadh, air shon sin, air son sin.

New, *a.* Nodh, nuadh, ùr. Quite new, *ùr nodh;* the new year, *a bhliadhna ùr;* new-year's-day, *là na bliadhna ùr;* the new moon, *a ghealach ùr;* new coat, *còt nodh;* a coat quite new, *coat ùr nodh;* new-year's-gift, *sainnseal;* new obedience, *nuadh-ùmhlachd;* the feast of the new year, *calluinn;* somewhat new, *leth-char ùr, leth-char nodha.*

New-born, *a.* Air ùr bheirsinn.

New-built, *a.* Air ùr thogail.

New-come, *a.* Air ùr thighinn, air ùr theachd.

New-comer, *s.* Coigreach.

New-fangled, *a.* Nodh, ciadlusach.

New-fangledness, *s.* Ciadlus.

New-fashioned, *a.* Ann am fasan ùr, air ùr a dheanamh; ùr, nòdh.

New-formed, *a.* Air ùr dheanamh, deanta as ùr.

Newing, *s.* Beirm, deasgann; grunndas, grunnd.

Newly, *adv.* Gu h-ùr. Newly come, *air ùr theachd.*

Newness, *s.* Nuadhachd, nuadhachadh, ùiread, ùrad; mùthadh, atharrachadh. Newness of life, *nuadhachadh beatha.*

News, *s.* Nuaidheachd, naigheachd, sgeul ùr; sgeul. Good news, *nuaidheachd mhath, deagh nuaidheachd;* what news? *ciod an nuaidheachd?* what is the best of your news? *ciod an nuaidheachd is fhearr th' agad?* I have no news, *cha n' eil sgeul ùr agam.*

Newsmonger, *s.* Fear nuaidheachd.

Newspaper, *s.* Paipear nuaidheachd.

Newt, *s.* Seorsa dearc-luachrach.

New-year's-gift, *s.* Sainnseal, iarsmadh, gibhte.

Next, *a.* and *adv.* Is fhoigse, is fhaigse, is fhoisge, is gàr, is dlù; ath; a ris, a rithist, a rithistich, an deigh sin. The man next you, *am fear is fhaigse duit;* the next man, *an ath fhear;* the next year, *an ath bhliadhna;* this time next year, *an tràth so'n ath bhliadhna;* the next in kin, *is dlùithe an daimh;* who comes next, *co a thig a ris;* he next told me, *dh' innis e dhomh an deigh sin (no) a rithist.*

Nias, *a.* Baoghalta, amaid, amaideach, neo-sheolta.

Nias, *s.* Seobhag òg.

Nib, *s.* Gob; roinn; bàrr. The nib of a pen, *bàrr (no) roinn peann.*

Nibbed, *a.* Biorach, roinneach, gobach.

Nibble, *v. a.* and *n.* Creim, teum, pioc, ith chuid is a chuid, faigh coire (no) cron, cronaich. Nibbling, *creimeadh, piocadh, piocail, piocarsaich.*

Nibbler, *s.* Piocadair, creimeadair, teumadair.

Nice, *a.* (*Dainty*), milis, blasda, sogh; (*accurate*), pungail, poncail, pongail, sicir; (*scrupulous*), ceigeanach; rudach, amharusach; (*fine*), grinn, eireachdail, speisealta, finealta, innealta, ciatach; (*dangerous*), cunnartach; sleamhuinn; deacair.

Nicely, *adv.* Gu poncail, gu pungail; gu grinn, gu h-eireachdail; gu speisealta, gu finealta, gu h-innealta.

Niceness, *s.* Pongalachd, pongaileachd, pungaileachd.

Nicety, *s.* Pongalachd, pungaileachd; (*of work*), grinneas; innealtachd; (*scrupulousness*), ceigeanachd.

Niche, *s.* Niùc, oisinn, buailt, cùil. Niches, *niùcan, oisinnean, buailtean, cùiltean.*

Nick, *s.* Sneag; gearradh, bearn, sgoch, sgòr, sgrioch; neag; mionaid.

Nick, *v. a.* Buail; sneagaich, neagaich; freagaraich; claoidh, sàruich, meall, thoir an car a.

Nickname, *s.* Frith-ainm, leas-ainm, leth-ainm, far-ainm.

Nickname, *v. a.* Thoir frith-ainm, frith-ainmich. Nicknamed, *frith-ainmichte.*

Nictate, *v.* Caog, priob, prib.

Nictation, *s.* Caog, caogadh, priob, priobadh.

Nide, *s.* Al, àlach, bròd.

Nidification, *s.* Neadachadh.

Nidulate, *v. a.* Neadaich, tog nead.

Niece, *s.* Nighean bràthar (no) peathar; gairghean, gairingean.

Niggard, *s.* Spìocair, duine gionach, duine sanntach (no) cruadalach, sgroingean, loman. Misery follows the niggard, *gheibh loman an donas.*

Niggard, *a.* Spìocach, spongach, gionach, sanntach, miothur, crion, cruaidh, cruadalach; biastail; gann; sgroingeanach, ceapanta.

Niggardish, *a.* Leth-char spìocach.

Niggardliness, *s.* Spioc, spiocaireachd, spongalachd, spongaireachd, sannt, crìne, cruadhas, sgroingeanachd.

Niggardly, *a.* Spìocach, gionach, geanach, sanntach, miothur, crion, cruaidh, cruadalach, biastail, gann.

Niggardly, *adv.* Gu spiocach, gu gionach, gu sanntach, gu miothur, gu crion, gu cruaidh; gu cruadalach, ceapanta.

Nigh, *adv.* and *prep.* Fogus, fagus, am fogus, am fagus, aig laimh, am fogasg, an cois, an gàr. Well nigh, *air bheag, thun a bhith;* the corn is well nigh cut up, *tha 'n t' arbhar thun a bhith buainte;* he is nigh dead, *tha e thun a bhith marbh;* he was nigh dead, *theab e teasd;* come nigh, *thig am fogus.*

Nigh, *a.* Fogus, fagus, dlù, dlùth, cairdeach, càr, dìleas. Nigher, *ni 's fhoigse; ni 's dlùithe.*

Nighness, *s.* Fogusachd, foigseachd, fagusachd, faisge, faigse, dlùthas.

Night, *s.* Oiche, oidhche; duibhre, dorchadas. Tonight, *an nochd; an oidhche an nochd;* before night, *roimh dhorch' oidhche;* every other night, *gach dolach oidhche;* last night, *an raòir, an reidhir;* the night before last, *air bho 'n raoir;* late at night, *anmoch;* good night to you, *oidhche mhath dhuit;* all night, *ré na h-oidhche;* night-lodgings, *cuid oidhche, ceathrannan oidhche;* the dead of night, *marbh na h-oidhche, marbh mheadhon na h-oidhche;* by night and by day, *dh' oidhche 's do là, dh' oidhche 's a là;* a pitch dark night, *oidhche dhubh dhorch;* during night, *air feadh na h-oidhche.*

Nightbird, *s.* Eun oidhche.

Nightcap, *s.* Currachad oidhche.

Nightcrow, *s.* Eun oidhche, eun a sgreadas san oidhche; coileach oidhche.

Nightdew, *s.* Dealt (no) drùchd feasgair.

Nightdress, *s.* Culaidh oidhche, aodach oidhche, gùn oidhche.

Nighted, *a.* Dorch, air dorchadh; (*ignorant*), aineolach; borb.

Nightfire, *s.* Teine sionnachain, coillinn mairbh.

Nightfly, *s.* Cuileag fheasgair.

Night-foundered, *a.* Annrach, air seachran san oidhche.

Nightgown, *s.* Gùn oidhche, gùn leapach.

Nighthag, *s.* Dubh-bhuidseach. Night-hags, *dubh-bhuidsichean; trom-lighe.*

Nightingale, *s.* Spìdeag, eosag, smileach, smiol, smileag; binn-bheul.

Nightly, *a.* Oidhcheil, gach oidhche, gach dolach oidhche.

Nightman, *s.* Sal-bhalach.

Nightmare, *s.* Trom-lighe.

Night-raven, *s.* Cailleach oidhche.

Night-rule, *s.* Tabaid oidhche.

Nightshade, *s.* Lus na h-oidhche.

NIGHT-SHRIEK, *s.* Sgairt (no) ulfhart oidhche.

NIGHT-WALK, *s.* Sràid oidhche, sràid fheasgàir.

NIGHT-WATCH, *s.* Faire oidhche, faire, faireachadh.

NIGHT-WALKER, *s.* Fear a dh' imicheas na chodal.

NIHILITY, *s.* Nionitheachd, neo-bhith.

NILL, *v. a.* Diùlt, àicheadh, seun, òb.

NILL, *s.* Luath ceardaich, splangach.

NIMBLE, *a.* Luath, beò, beothail, clis, deas, bearraideach, grad, ealamh, ullamh, easgaidh, sgairteil, tapaidh, luthar. Nimble motion, *deannadh; stilleadh;* nimble is he who has taken fright, *is luath am fear san tàr an t-cagal.*

NIMBLE-FOOTED, *a.* Luath-chosach; luath.

NIMBLENESS, *s.* Luathas; graide; sgairteileachd, tapadh, deannadh.

NIMBLY, *adv.* Gu luath, gu beothail, gu clis, gu deas, gu grad, gu h-ealamh.

NINCOMPOOP, *s.* Amadan, umaidh, baoghlan, amhlair, ceothallan, gobhallan, burraidh, guraiceach.

NINE, *a.* Naoi; nao; naoinear. Nine men, *naoinear dhaoine;* nine o'clock, *naoi uairean;* the nine at cards, *an naothamh.*

NINEFOLD, *a.* Naoi fillte, a naoi uiread.

NINE-SCORE, *s.* Naoi fichead.

NINETEEN, *a.* Naoi deug, naoth deug. Nineteen men, *naoi fir dheug;* the nineteenth, *an naothamh deug.*

NINETY, *a.* Naogad, deich is ceithir fichead, ceithir fichead 's a deich, naochad.

NINNY, *s.* Baoghlan, baothair, leth-amadan, caifean, ablaoch.

NINNYHAMMER, *s.* Baoghlan, baothair, caifean.

NINTH, *a.* An naothamh.

NIP, *v.* Pioc, gòmagaich, thoir pioc, thoir greim; teum; beum, searg, crion, sàruich, claoidh; (*nipped as a plant*), seargta, seargte, air crionadh.

NIP, *s.* Pioc, gomag, teum.

NIPPERS, *s.* Turcais, gramaiche, greimiche.

NIPPINGLY, *adv.* Beumnach, teumnach.

NIPPLE, *s.* Sinne, sinneadh; dealadh, ceann cìhe.

NIPPLE-WORT, *s.* Duilleag mhaith; duilleag mhìn.

NIT, *s.* Sneamh, sneadh.

NITENCY, *s.* Gloine, loinnir.

NITED, *a.* Glan, soilleir, lonnrach, deàlrach.

NITRE, *s.* Creag-shalann; natar.

NITROUS, *a.* Salannach.

NITTILY, *adv.* Sneamhach, sneadhach.

NIVAL, *a.* Sneachdaidh, sneachdach, sneachdail.

NIZY, *s.* Baoghlan, baoghair, umaidh, gurraiceach.

NO, *a.* and *adv.* Ni h-eadh, ni; cha 'n ann, cha 'n eil, cha 'n e. I make no doubt, *cha 'n eil mi cur an teagamh;* I have no time, *cha 'n 'eil ùine agam;* no pains, no gains, *gùn tùrn, gun tuarasdal;* no one is here, *cha 'n eil neach an so;* I will ask no more, *cha sir mi tuille;* to no purpose, *faoin, gun fheum;* no matter, *cha 'n eil omhail.* The rendering of *no* varies according to the question, as, will you come? no; *an tig thu? cha tig;* will you strike? no; *am buail thu? cha bhuail;* will you be there? no; *am bi thu an sin? cha bhi.*

NOBILITATE, *v. a.* Uaislich, uaillsich, àrduich. Nobilitated, *uaislichte, uaillsichte, arduichte.*

NOBILITY, *s.* Maithean, maitheamh, uaislean, uaillsean; mòr-uaislean; airde, inbhe, onoir, mòrachd.

NOBLE, *a.* (*In rank*), uasal, ard, prìomh; mòr; mòralach; (*illustrious*), ainmeil, cliuiteach, iomraiteach; (*generous*), fial, fialuidh, oirdheirc, mordha; (*excellent*), grinn, maiseach, sàrmhaiseach, bàrrail, gorm, allonta, allail, eireachdail. A noble act, *gniomh corr; gaisge, euchd.*

NOBLE, *s.* Flath, maith; sé sgillinn sasunnach is ochd sgilinn.

NOBLEMAN, *s.* Flath, maith, duine uasal.

NOBLENESS, *s.* Mòrachd, mòralachd, airde, inbhe, urram.

NOBLY, *adv.* Gu flathail, gu mòr, gu moralach; gu h-ainmeil, gu h-iomraiteach; gu fial, gu fialaidh, gu h-oirdheirc; gu h-allonta; gu h-alloil.

NOBODY, *s.* Neo-neach, neo-dhuine.

NOCENT, *a.* Ciurrail, dochannach, olc; ciontach, coireach.

NOCTAMBULO, *s.* Neach a dh' imicheas na chodal.

NOCTUARY, *s.* Cunntas oidhche.

NOCTURNAL, *a.* Oidhcheil, oidhche.

NOD, *v.* Sméid; crom; carruich, crath; gog, bi san turramanaich.

NOD, *s.* Sméid, sméideadh, cromadh cinn, gog, turam, turaman, turadan; modh.

NODATION, *s.* Nòdachadh, cnòdachadh.

NODDING, *s.* Turaman, turadan, turamanaich, gogadh, gog. Nodding of heads does not make the boat row, *cha 'n e gogadh nan ceann a ni 'n t-iomram.*

NODDLE, *s.* Ceann, plub, ploc, cnuàc.

NODDY, *s.* Baoghlan, gurraiceach.

NODE, *s.* Nòd, cnòd; cròd; cnap, at, meall, meallan, snaim, snuim.

NODOSITY, *s.* Snaim, snuim, cnodàchd, cnapantachd.

NODOUS, *a.* Snuimeach, cnòdach, cnapach, làn shnuim.

NOGGIN, *s.* Mog, noigean, gogan.

NOISE, *s.* (*Loud sound*), fuaim, toirm, farum, stararaich, stairirich, mòthar, fuaimrich, torran, torunn, callaid, toirneas; ballart, straoidhlearachd, gleadhraich; (*of voices*), gàir, gaoir, bruidhinn, clagarnach, lad, glag, glaodh, glaodhaich, clambar, glaothar, sgairtich; (*a murmuring noise*), torman, diurrasan, monar, monmhur, monaghair; (*a report*), fabhunn, fabhur, iomradh; (*of a gun*), braidhe, sgeile, fuaim; (*of a bee*), dranndan, dranndanaich; (*a gnashing noise*), diosgan, diosgadh, giosgan; (*a crashing noise*), géisg, géisgeil, ràn; (*of dancing*), rant, rantaireachd.

NOISE, *v. a.* Dean fuaim (no) farum. Noised, *iomraiteach;* noised abroad, *fa sgaoil, am beul an t-sluaigh.*

NOISEFUL, *a.* Fuaimearra, fuaimneach, farumach, gleadhrachail, gleadhrach, clambarach, bruidhneach, torranach; bruidhneach, clagarnach; tormanach; monaghaireach.

NOISELESS, *a.* Samhach, tosd, seimh, ciùin, tiamhaidh, bìth, balbh.

NOISEMAKER, *s.* Rantair.

NOISESOME, *a.* Sgreitidh, sgreataidh, loibheach, olc, déistinneach, gràd, grannda; mi-chiatach, urchoideach, lochdach.

NOISY, *a.* Fuaimneach, fuaimearra; farumach, gleadhrachail, ballartach, bruidhneachail, clambrach; ràpach, clagarnach, tormanach, monaghaireach.

NOLENS VOLENS, *adv.* A dheòin no dh' aindeoin; olc ar mhath. Whether you be willing or not, *olc ar mhath leat e, co aca is math no olc leat e;* take him with you nolens volens, *thoir leat, a dheòin no dh' aindeoin, e.*

NOLI ME TANGERE, *s.* Guirean feargach; cluaran, aigheannach.

NOLITION, *s.* Ain-deoineachd, diombuidheachd, diombachd, neo-thoil, neo-thogar.

NOLL, *s.* Ceann, plub, ploc.

NOMBLES, *s.* Greallach feidh.

NOMBRIL, *s.* Iochdar, suaicheantais.

NOMENCLATURE, *s.* Foclair, abardair; ainmeachadh.

Nominal, *a.* A thaobh ainm; ainmeach. Nominally, *a thaobh ainm.*

Nominate, *v. a.* Ainmich, sònruich, sùnruich, orduich. Nominated, *ainmichte, sonruichte.*

Nominating, *s.* Ainmeachadh, sònruchadh, sonrachadh, orduchadh.

Nomination, *s.* Ainmeachadh, sònruchadh, òrduchadh.

Nominative, *s.* Ainmeanach.

Non, *adv.* Neo, cha n' fhaicear am focal so idir leis fein, ach ceangailte ri focal eile, mar, *neoni*, nothing; *neonitheachd*, nonentity

Nonage, *s.* Oige, leanabalachd, neo-aois; neo-inmhe, neo-iomlanachd.

Nonconformist, *s.* Neo-aontachair, fear nach aontaich leis an Eaglais shasunnach.

Nonconformity, *s.* Neo-aontachd; neo-fhreagarrachd, neo-aontachadh leis an Eaglais shasunnach.

None, *a.* Ni-aon. None will see you, *cha n' fhaic neach (no) gin thu;* I love none but you, *cha toigh leam neach ach thusa;* there is none but knows, *cha 'n eil gin nach aithne,* there is none without faults, *cha n' eil a h-aon gun choire.*

Nonentity, *s.* Neo-nitheachd; neo-bhith, neo-ni.

Non-existence, *s* Neo-bhith, neo-nitheachd.

Non-juring, *a.* Nach mionnaich ùmhlachd do 'n righ; *Seumasach.*

Non-juror, *s.* *Seumasach;* fear a tha sa bharail, gum b' ann le h-eucoir a chaidh Righ Seumas a dhà 'chur bhàir na cathrach; fear nach mionnaich umhlachd do righ a mheasas e mi dhligheach.

Non-naturals, *s.* Is ead sin, adhar, biadh agus deoch, codal agus faireach, fois agus gluasachd, maille ri càil na h-inntinn.

Nonpareil, *s.* Barrachd, barrachas, bar-mhais; neo-shamhladh; seorsa ubhal; (*in printing*), meanbh-phrionnt.

Non-payment, *s.* Fàilinn diolaidh

Non-performance, *s.* Fàilinn coimhlionaidh.

Nonplus, *v a.* Cuir an iomcheist, cuir thar a chéile, cuir gu stad.

Non-residence, *s.* Neo-thàmeachadh; neo-thamhachd, neo-àiteachadh.

Non-resident, *s.* Neo-thàmeachair, neo-thamhaiche, fear nach fhuirich aig an tigh.

Non-resistance, *s.* Géill, ùmhlachd, làn-striochd.

Nonsense, *s.* Amaideachd, baothaireachd; faoineachd; cainnt gun chiall, glòrmas, gleòrmas, bòilich

Nonsensical, *a.* Amaideach, neo-thuigseach, neo-sheadhar, mi-thuigseach, faoin.

Nonsensicalness, *s.* Amaideachd, baothaireachd.

Non-solvent, *s.* Fear briste, urr bhriste.

Non-sparing, *a.* Neo-thruacanta, neo-bhaigheil, millteach, cruadalach.

Nonsuit, *v.* Cuir a mach

Noodle, *s.* Burraidh, baoghlan, àmadan, ceothallan, gobhallan, guraiceach, amhlair.

Nook, *s.* Cùil, mùc, oisinn. Nooks, *cùiltean, mùcan.*

Noon, *s* Meadhon là, nòin Noon-day, *airde an la.*

Nooning, *s.* Codal nòin.

Noon-tide, *s.* Tràth, nòin.

Noose, *s.* Lùb, lùb ruithe, dul, sùil, sùileag.

Noose, *v. a.* Glac; snaim, snuim, ceangail, cuir an sàs.

Nope, *s.* Earr-dhearg.

Nor, *conj.* Ni, no, na, ni mo, ni 's mo. Neither you nor I, *ni mo thusa no mise.*

Normal, *a.* A reir riaghailt; direach, riaghailteach.

North, *s.* Tuath, an taobh tuath, an airde tuath; tuaisgeart From the north, *a tuath, as an taobh tuath,* the north-east, *an ear thuath,* the north-west, *an iar thuath;* a north wind, *gaoth thuath, gaoth a tuath.*

North, *a* Tuath, tuathach, gus an airde tuath, o laimh na h-airde tuath. The north-star, *an rionnag tuatha,* a north-country man, *tuathach*

Northward, *adv.* Gu tuath, gus an airde tuath

Nose, *s.* Sròin; comar. Follow your nose, *lean do shròin, rach dìreach air d' aghaidh;* the tip of the nose, *bàrr na sròna,* the gristle of the nose, *cnaimh na sròine,* (scent), *fàil; tòchd.*

Nose, *v. a.* Srònagaich, sròineagaich, sròinaisich; thoir aghaidh; cuir roimh, bòsd

Nosegay, *s* Blath-fhleasg, plùr, plùirean.

Nose-smart, *s.* Biolair.

Nosle, *s* Sròin, gros, gnos, *strub,* beul.

Noseless, *a.* Gun sròin

Nostril, *s.* Pollair, polt, cuinnean.

Not, *adv.* Ni, ni h-eadh, ni h-ann; cha 'n e, cha 'n ann; no, na I will not say, *cha 'n abair mi,* I did not say, *cha dubhairt mi;* do not, I pray, *na dean, guidheam ort;* not so, *ni h-eadh, ni h-ann mar sin, cha 'n ann mar sin,* not at all, *cha 'n ann idir, ni h-ann idir, ni h-eadh air dhoigh sam bi,* will you not be quiet yet, *nach bi thu samhach fhathast.*

Notable, *a.* Ainmeil, chùiteach; comharaichte, sònruichte, ion-chomharadh; oirdheirc, allaill, nuall.

Notableness, *s.* Ainmealachd, òirdheirceas, ion-chomharachd, alladh.

Notably, *adv.* Gu h-ainmeil, gu chùiteach, gu comharaichte, gu sonruichte.

Notary, *s.* Nòtair, sgriobhair.

Notation, *s.* Sgriobhadh; ciall.

Notch, *s.* Feag, neag, sneag, beairn, peasg, sgoch

Notch, *v.* Feag, sneag, bearnaich, sneagaich. Notched, *feagaichte, bearnach, beairneach.*

Note, *s.* Comhar, comharadh; (*notice*), fios, aire, guth, sànas, (*tune*), fonn; (*a letter*), bileit; (*fame*), chù, ainm, iomradh, (*promissory*), bann, (*of explanation*), mìneachan, mìneachadh

Note, *v.* Comharaich, beachdaich, thoir an aire, gabh beachd, thoir fanear, sgriobh.

Note-book, *s* Leabhar pòc; leabhar cunntais, meamhranach, meòmhranach; leabhar meabhrain.

Noted, *a.* Ainmeil, chùiteach, iomraiteach, comharaichte, sonruichte, allonta, allail.

Noter, *s* Beachdair; sgriobhair, cléireach

Nothing, *s.* Neoni. The world was formed out of nothing, *dhealbhadh an saoghal a neoni,* there is nothing here, *cha 'n eil dad an so,* for nothing, *a nasguidh, far nasguidh, gun dad idir,* what ails you? nothing, *ciod tha cur ort? cha 'n eil dad, ciod a dh' fhairich thu? cha d' fhairich dad,* it came to nothing, *thàinig e gu neoni,* good for nothing, *suarrach, gun fhiù,* little is better than nothing, *is fearr beagan no bhith gun ni;* it is a bad thing to have nothing, *is olc an ni bhith falamh.*

Nothingness, *s.* Neonitheachd, neoni, neobhith.

Notice, *s.* Fios, guth, eòlas, sànas, rabhadh, faireachadh, fanear, aire, aithne, beachd; omhail. Give him notice, *thoir fios da;* take notice, *thoir an aire, gabh beachd,* I took notice of him, *thug mi an aire dha,* take no notice of him, *na gabh ort e.*

Notification, *s.* Fiosrachadh, toirt fios, aithneachadh deanamh aithnichte; fios, guth, sànas, tuairisg.

NOTIFY, *v.* Innis, nochd, foillsich, dean aithnichte, thoir fios.

NOTION, *s.* Barail, smuain, smuaineach, dòchas, beachd; breathnachadh.

NOTIONAL, *a.* Baraileach, dòchasach, smuaineachail, smuainteachail; faoin.

NOTORIETY, *s.* Ainmealachd, follaiseachd, follaiseachadh, fiosrachadh; fios.

NOTORIOUS, *a.* Ainmeil, sonruichte, comharaichte, follaiseach, soilleir.

NOTWITHSTANDING, *conj.* Gidheadh, fathast, fhathast, air son sin; thar a cheann sin.

NOTUS, *s.* Gaoth dheas, a ghaoth a deas.

NOUGHT, *s.* Neoni. It came to nought, *thàinig e gu neoni;* set at nought, *cuir air bheag suim;* he will sink into nought whose word cannot be depended on, *am fear nach guth a ghuth, cha rath a rath.*

NOUN, *s.* Ainm.

NOURISH, *v.* Tog, àraich, beathaich, biath, altruim cum suas, oileamhuin, oid, ionnsuich, teagaisg. I nourished him, *thog mi e.*

NOURISHABLE, *a.* So thogail, beathachail.

NOURISHED, *a.* Togta, togte, àraichte, beathaichte, biathta.

NOURISHMENT, *s.* Biadh, beath, beathachadh, lòn.

NOUSLE, *v. a.* Tog, àraich, beathaich, biath, altrum, cum suas; glac, cuir an sàs, glac air shròin.

NOVATION, *s.* Nuadhachadh; mùthadh, atharrachadh.

NOVEL, *a.* Nuadh, nodha, ùr, neo-chumanta, annasach.

NOVEL, *s.* Faoin-sgeul, ùr-sgeul, faoin-sgeulachd, ur-sgeulachd, sgeulachd; ruanachd, ròiseal.

NOVEL, *s.* Sgeulaiche, faoin sgeulaiche, ùr-sgeulaiche.

NOVELTY, *s.* Nuadhachd, iongantas, annas; ùrad.

NOVEMBER, *s.* Naoimhios; ceud mios a gheamhraidh, mios dubh.

NOVERCAL, *a.* Muimeach, muimeil.

NOVICE, *s.* Urr neo-eòlach, sgoilear òg; (*in religion*), nuadhchreideach, ùranach.

NOVICIATE, *s.* Ur-thoiseach.

NOW, *adv.* A nis, a nois, nis, nois, an tràths, an dràsda, an dràsdaich, an ceart uair, air an am so; air an uair. Just now, *an ceart uair, a chianamh;* now and then, *an tràths is a ris, còrr uairean;* now and for ever, *a nis agus gu siorruidh;* now-a-days, *anns na lathaibh so, anns na h-amanna so;* well now, *seadh mata;* now then, *so mata, so a nis;* now at length, *mu dheireadh, mu dheireadh thall, mu dheireadh is mu dhiù.*

NOWHERE, *a.* Ni 'n àite sam bi.

NOWISE, *adv.* Ni h-eadh (no) ni h-ann air aon doigh, idir.

NOXIOUS, *a.* Millteach, olc, dochannach, graineil, puinnseanta, urchoideach, neo-fhallain, lochdach.

NOXIOUSLY, *adv.* Gu millteach, gu h-olc, gu dochannach, gu gràineil, gu puinnseanta, gu h-urchoideach.

NOXIOUSNESS, *s.* Dochannachd, puinnseantachd, urchoideachd, neo-fhallaineachd.

NOZLE, *s.* Sròin, gros, gnos.

NUBIFEROUS, *a.* Neulach, nialach.

NUBILATE, *v.* Dorchaich; neulaich.

NUBILE, *a.* Arson pòsaidh, ion-phòsta; pòsail.

NUBILOUS, *a.* Neulach, dorch, dubh, dubharach, doilleir, dùbhlaidh.

NUCIFEROUS, *a.* Cnòthach, cnòthar.

NUCLEUS, *s.* Eitean; cridhe.

NUDATION, *s.* Rùsgadh, nochdadh, leigeil ris.

NUDE, *a.* Lomnochd, rùisgte, lomardach, lomraisdeach.

NUDITY, *s.* Lomnochdaidh, nochd; ionair; buill diomhair.

NUGACITY, *s.* Faoineas.

NUGATION, *s.* Faoineachd, faoineas, cluithe.

NUGATORY, *a.* Faoin, suarrach, neo-tharbhach, gun fhiù.

NUISANCE, *s.* Gràin, déistinn; mosaiche; urchoid; salachar.

NUKE, *s.* Cùl na h-amhaich.

NULL, *a.* Faoin, gun bhrigh, gun stà, gun éifeachd, neonitheach, neo-sheasmhach, falamh.

NULL, *v. a.* Thoir gu neoni, dean faoin.

NULLIFICATION, *s.* Toirt gu neoni, milleadh, sgriosadh; cur air chùl, dìtheachadh.

NULLIFY, *v. a.* Thoir gu neoni; mill, sgrios.

NULLITY, *s.* Neonitheachd, neoni, neo-bhith.

NUMB, *v. a.* Funntainn, dean marbh le fuachd, meillich.

NUMB, *a.* Marbh, fuar-mharbh, marbh-lapach, air funntainn, balbh, neo-mhothachail, éileachanaichte.

NUMBEDNESS, *s.* Marbhlapachd, marbhlopadh, funntainn, méilleachadh.

NUMBER, *v.* Cunnt, àireamh, àireamhaich, dean suas, meas, tionas. Numbers, *aireamhta, aireamhaichte;* it cannot be numbered, *cha ghabh e cunntadh.*

NUMBER, *s.* Mòran, iomad, iomadaidh, àireamh, uibhir, nuimhir; (*music*), fonn, ceòl, seirm; (*of people*), lòd, dròbh, bannal. Without number, *gun àireamh, gun chunntas, thar cunntas.*

NUMBERER, *s.* Aireamhair, cunntair.

NUMBERLESS, *a.* Gun àireamh, do-àireamh, do chunntadh, nach gabh cunntadh, thar cunntas. Numberless as the stars, *do-àireamh mar na rionnagan.*

NUMBLES, *s.* Greallach feidh.

NUMBNESS, *s.* Funntainn, funndainn, meilleachadh, marbhlapadh.

NUMERABLE, *a.* So-àireamh, so-chunntadh a ghabhas àireamh, a ghabhas cunntadh, a dh' fhaotas aireamh.

NUMERAL, *a.* Aireamhach, àireamhail, nuimhireil.

NUMERALLY, *adv.* A réir àireimh.

NUMERATION, *s.* Àireamh, cunntadh, cunntas, àireamhachadh.

NUMERATOR, *s.* Aireamhair, cunntair.

NUMERICAL, *a.* Aimhreach, nuimhreach.

NUMERIST, *s.* Aireamhair, cunntair.

NUMEROSITY, *s.* Lionmhorachd, iomadachd.

NUMEROUS, *a.* Lionmhor, iomad, iomadh, iomadach, iomadaidh, àireamhach, iomadail.

NUMEROUSLY, *adv.* Gu lionmhor.

NUMEROUSNESS, *s.* Lionmhorachd, lionmhoireachd, iomadachd.

NUMSKULL, *s.* Burraidh, siadair, umaidh, sgleamhruidh; ceann, plub.

NUN, *s.* Cailleach dhubh, ban-naomh.

NUN, *s.* Seorsa eòin.

NUNCHEON, *s.* See LUNCHEON.

NUNCIATURE, *s.* Teachdaireachd.

NUNCIO, *s.* Teachdair a Phapa; fear nuaidheachd.

NUNCUPATIVE, *a.* Le focal beòil.

NUNNERY, *s.* Tigh bhan-naomh, tigh chailleacha dubh.

NUPTIAL, *a.* Pòsaidh, maraisteach, bainnse. A nuptial song, *òran bainnse, òran pòsaidh.*

NUPTIALS, *s.* Pòsadh, maraiste, banais.

NURSE, *s.* Banaltradh, banaltrum; beanaltrum. A wet nurse, *banaltradh cìche.*

NURSE, *v.* Banaltruim, banaltraich, banaltrumaich, àraich, tog, tog suas, beathaich; cum suas.

Nurser, *s.* Altrumaiche, fear altruim. A nurser of quarrels, *fear altruim chonnspoid.*

Nursery, *s.* Seomar cloinne, seomar altruim, seomar àraich.

Nursing, *s.* Banaltrachd, banaltrumachd.

Nursle, *v.* Siùdan, siùdanaich.

Nursling, *s.* Leanabh, leanaban; dalta, bandalta.

Nurture, *s.* Biadh, beath, lòn, beathachadh; togail, cumail suas, àrachadh; (*teaching*), foghlum, oilean, ionnsuchadh.

Nurture, *v. a.* Tog, tog suas, cum suas; oileanaich, àraich, ionnsuich, oid.

Nustle, *v.* Àraich, altruim; siùdain, siùdanaich.

Nustling, *s.* Arachadh, altrum, siùdan, siùdanachd, siùdanaich.

Nut, *s.* Cnò, cnù, cnòth, cnùth, crò. A hazle-nut, *cnò challtuinn;* a rotten nut, *cnò fhàs;* a chesnut, *gall-chnò;* take a nut from the top of the cluster, *cno o uachdar a mhogail.*

Nutbrown, *a.* Donn.

Nutcrackers, *s.* Cracair, cracairean.

Nutgall, *s.* Creutag dharaich.

Nuthook, *s.* Cromag chnò.

Nutmeg, *s.* Cno spiosraidh.

Nutshell, *s.* Sgrath chnò, cochall chnò, plaosg chnò.

Nutrication, *s.* Biathadh, beathachadh.

Nutriment, *s.* Biadh, lòn, teachd an tìr; beathachadh.

Nutrimental, *a.* Beathachail.

Nutrition, *s.* Biadh, lòn, teachd an tìr, beathachadh.

Nutritious, Nutritive, *a.* Biadhar, biadhmhor, fallain, susbuinneach.

Nut-tree, *s.* Craobh-chnò, preas-chnò.

Nuzzle, *v. a.* Altrum, banaltraich, tog suas, cum suas, gleidh.

Nymph, s. Ban dia choilltean is uisgeacha; oigh, maighdeann, cailinn, ainnir.

Nymphal, *a.* Oigheil, banail.

O.

O. An cuigeamh litir deug do 'n aibideal.

O, *interj.* O! a! O Lord! *O Thighearn! A Thighearn!* O that I had been there! *Is truagh nach robh mi 'n sin!*

Oaf, *s.* Baoghlan, guraiceach, burraidh, baothair, amhlan.

Oafish, *a.* Baoghlanach, amhlanach, amaideach.

Oafishness, *s.* Baoghlanachd, amhlanachd.

Oak, *s.* Darach, darag, dar, dairbhre.

Oakapple, *s.* Cnò dharaich.

Oaken, *a.* Daraich.

Oakum, *s.* Calc, calcadh; ascard; còrcach, barrach; pab.

Oar, *s.* Ràmh. Pull the nighest oar, *an ramh is faisge iomair.*

Oar, *v.* Iomair, iomramh.

Oarweed, *s.* Trusgar.

Oary, *a.* Ràmhach.

Oatcake, *s.* Bonnach coirce, breacag coirce, breacag.

Oaten, *a.* Coirce; coirceach.

Oath, *s.* Mionn, mionnan, mòid. A false oath, *mionnan eitheach, boid, sgrogag;* put him on his oath, *cuir air a mhionnan e;* he rapt out an oath, *thàinig e mach le mionnan;* give your oath, *thoir do mhionnan.*

Oath-breaking, *a.* Eithich, eitheach, fallsa.

Oatmalt, *s.* Braich coirce.

Oatmeal, *s.* Min choirce.

Oats, *s.* Coirc; siol. Oat-seeds, *càth, pronn.*

Obambulation, *s.* Folbhan, falbhan, spaisdearachd, spaidsearachd, sràidear, sraid-imeachd, imeachd, ceumadh.

Obduce, *v.* Comhdaich, tarruing thairis.

Obduction, *s.* Comhdachadh.

Obduracy, *s.* Cruadhas cridhe; ain-iochd; cion-mothuchaidh.

Obdurate, *a.* Cruaidh-chridheach, ain-iochdmhor; cruadalach, neo-aithreachail; rag, rag-mhuinealach.

Obdurately, *adv.* Gu cruaidh-chridheach, gu cruadalach, gu h-ain-iochdmhor.

Obdurateness, *s.* Cruadhas cridhe, ain-iochd, ain-iochdmhorachd.

Obduration, *s.* Cruadhas, cruadhas cridhe, ain-iochd.

Obdured, *a.* Cruadhaichte, rag, cruadalach; neo-aithreachail.

Obedience, *s.* Ùmhlachd, géile, striochd; †fomas. Bring under obedience, *thoir fo smachd, ceannsaich.*

Obedient, *a.* Umhal, striochdail; dìleas; easguidh; freagarrach.

Obediential, *a.* Umhlachdail.

Obediently, *adv.* Gu h-umhal, gu striochdail, gu h-easguidh.

Obeisance, *s.* Umhlachd, urram, striochd.

Obelisk, *s.* Liagan.

Obequitation, *s.* Marcachd mu 'n cuairt.

Oberration, s. Iomroladh, seachran, athamanaich, siubhal mu 'n cuairt.

Obese, *a.* Reamhar, sultmhor.

Obeseness, Obesity, *s.* Reamhrachd, sult, sultmhorachd.

Obey, *v. a.* Thoir géill, bi umhal, striochd, dean striochd; feachd, freagair. Obey him, *géill dha, freagair e.*

Obit, *s.* Tiodhlac, adhlac, adhlacadh.

Obituary, *s.* Clàr ìnnse nam marbh.

Object, *s.* Cusbair, cuspair; ball, aobhar; comhar, nì, rud; cuis, rùn. An object of hope, *cusbair dòchais;* a beautiful object, *rud maiseach;* what is your object in this? *ciod e do rùn san nì so?*

Object, *v. a.* Cuir an aghaidh; tilg suas; dean tàir.

Objection, *s.* Cunnuil; coire; fath gearain; frith-bheirt. He found an objection, *fhuair e cunnuil (no) coire.*

Objectionable, *a.* Cunnuileach; coireach.

Objective, *a.* Cuspaireach.

Objector, *s.* Cunnuiliche, cunnuileach, fear cur na aghaidh.

Objuration, *s.* Mionnachadh.

Objurgate, *v.* Cronaich, achmhasanaich, troid, tachair ri, smachdaich.

Objurgation, *s.* Cronachadh, achmhasan, trod, tachairt ri, smachdachadh.

Oblation, *s.* Tabhartas, iobairt.

Oblectation, *s.* Aiteas, gàirdeachas, aighear, eòlas, culaidh shùgraidh, toileach-inntinn.

Obligate, *v. a.* Ceangail le bann, ceangail le comain, ceangail, cuibhrich.

Obligation, *s.* Ceangladh, ceangal, comain, bann, cumhnant, urras, dleasdanas. I am under great obligations to you, *tha mi nìoran ad chomain*, bind by obligation, *ceangail le comainibh.*

Obligatory, *a.* Ceanglach, ceangalach.

Oblige, *v.* Cuir fo chomain, ceangail le comainibh; (*force*), thoir air, cuir thuige, èignich; (*please*), toilich, taitinn. I am obliged to you, *tha mi ad chomain*, oblige him to do it, *thoir air a dheanamh.*

Obliged, *a* Ceangailte; fo chomain; èignichte. I am obliged to do it, *tha e ceangailte orm a dheanamh, tha e orm a dheanamh, is èigin domh a dheanamh.*

Obliging, *a* Comh-stadhach, socharach; siobhailt, sibhealta, còir, suairc, soilcasach; modhail, easguidh.

Obligingly, *adv.* Gu socharach, gu siobhailt, gu còir, gu suairc, gu modhail, gu h-easguidh.

Obligingness, *s.* Suairceas, siobhailteachd, modhaileachd, easguidheachd.

Obliquation, *s.* Claonadh, aomadh, cromadh

Oblique, *a* Claon, fiar, crom, aomta, cam, neo-dhìreach, an comhar a thaobh, a leth-taobh

Obliquely, *adv* Gu claon, gu fiar, gu crom, gu cam, gu neo dhìreach, a leth taobh

Obliquity, *s* Claonadh, fiaradh, aomadh, leathad

Obliterate, *v a* Dubh a mach, dubh as, mill, sgrios Obliterated, *dubhta a mach*

Obliteration, *s* Dubhadh mach, milleadh, sgrios.

Oblivion, *s* Dìchuimhne, dìo-chuimhne, dìchuimhneachadh, tur-dhìchuimhne, dearmad; laghadh, mathadh. The land of oblivion, *tìr na dìchuimhne*

Oblivious, *a* Dìchuimhneach, dearmadach, seachmhallach

Oblong, *a.* Fad, leth-fhad.

Oblongness, *s.* Leth-fhad.

Obloquy, *s* Masladh, toibheum, tàir, càineadh, cùl-chàineadh, sgainneal, tuaileas; coire-iomchair.

Obmutescence, *s.* Bailbhe, balbhachd

Obnoxious, *a* Buailteach; coireach, ciontach, lochdach, fosgailte; damanta.

Obnubilate, *v* Dorchaich; duibhrich; dubh-neulaich; sgàilich. Obnubilated, *dorchaichte, duibhrichte.*

Obreption, *s.* Scapadh, ealadh, snàgadh.

Obscene, *a.* Draosda, draosta, drabasta; macnusach; neo-stuama, drùiseil; neo-ghlan, mi-gheimnidh, beag-narach. Obscenely, *gu draosta, gu drabasta, gu macnusach, gu drùiseil*

Obscenity, *s.* Draosdachd, draostachd, draosdaireachd, drabastachd, mi-mhacantas, mìo-naire, graoltas, mi-gheimnidheachd, macnus, drùis, mi-shealbharachd

Obscuration, *s.* Dorchadh, dorchadas, duibhir, doilleireachd.

Obscure, *a* Dorch, doilleir, dubh, duaichnidh, dubh-neulach, gruamach; folaichte, uaigneach; (*unintelligible*), deacair, do-thuigsinn, diomhair

Obscure, *a* Dorchaich, folaich, céil, comhdaich. Obscured, *dorchaichte*

Obscurely, *adv.* Gu dorch, gu doilleir, gu dubh, gu duaichnidh, gu h-uaigneach; gu deacair, gu do-thuigsinn

Obscureness, Obscurity, *s.* Dorchadas, doirche, doilleireachd, diomhaireachd. Full of obscurity, *do-thuigsinn, teagamhach.*

Obscuring, *s.* Dorchadh, duibhreachadh; folachadh, céileadh

Obsecrate, *v. a.* Guidh, grios, athchuing, asluich.

Obsecration, *s* Guidhe, grios, griosadh, athchuing, urnuigh, ùirnigh, aslach, aslachadh, dian-athchuinge.

Obsequies, *s.* Onoir adhlacaidh, riomhadh tiodhlaic; tuireadh, marbh-rann.

Obsequious, *a* Easguidh, umhal, freagarrach.

Obsequiously, *adv.* Gu h-easguidh, gu h-umhal, gu freagarrach.

Obsequiousness, *s.* Umhlachd, easguidheachd; freagarrachd.

Obsequy, *s.* Tiodhlac, adhlac, adhlacadh, torradh.

Observable, *a.* So-fhaicinn, so-fhaicsinn; so-chomharrachadh, comharaichte, sonraichte.

Observance, *s.* Meas, urram, modh; gnàth, àbhaist, aire, beachd, ùmhlachd.

Observant, *a.* Aireachail, dìchiollach, frithealach; furachair.

Observation, *s* Aire, beachd; ordugh; toirt fanear; cumail; géill

Observator, *s.* Beachdair, beachdadair.

Observatory, *s.* Àite amhairc, àite seallaidh; beachdionad.

Observe, *v a* Thoir fanear, thoir aire, thoir an aire, beachdaich, gabh beachd; (*keep*), cum, gleidh; (*see*), faic, seall, amhairc, coimhid, coimhead; (*remark*), abair. Observe what I say, *thoir an aire ciod a tha mi 'g radh*, do you observe me? *bheil thu toirt an aire dhomh?* observe the sabbath, *cum an t-sàbaid*

Observer, *s* Fear faire, beachdair; fear gleidh.

Observing, *a.* Aireachail, faireachail, furachair, faiceallach

Obsession, *s* Séisdeadh, iom-dhruideadh.

Obsolete, *a* Sean, neo-chleachdach, sean-aimsireil, neo-fhasanta, as an fhasan.

Obstacle, *s.* Bac, bacadh, moil, grabadh, amal, easbhacaig, ball toirmisg.

Obstetric, *a.* Aiseadach.

Obstinacy, *s.* Ceann-laidireachd, raigse, reasgachd, reasgaichead, an-toile, crosantachd, dùiread.

Obstinate, *a.* Rag, ceann-laidir, reasgach, dalma, antoileach, rag, rag-mhuinealach, ceannairceach, an-srianta; casumhal; dùr, crosd.

Obstinately, *adv* Gu rag, gu ceann-laidir, gu reasgach, gu h-antoileach, gu ceannairceach, gu h-an-srianta, gu h-casumhal.

Obstipate, *v. a.* Duin suas, calc, teannaich Obstipated, *duinte suas, calcta, teannaichte.*

Obstipation, *s* Dùnadh; calcadh, teannachadh

Obstreperous, *a.* Callaideach, fuaimneach, fuaimearra, labhrach, tabaideach, stairneil, gleadhrach, buaireasach.

Obstreperously, *adv.* Gu callaideach, gu fuaimneach, gu fuaimearra, gu stairneil

Obstruction, *s.* Bann, ceangladh, ceangal

Obstruct, *v. a* Bac; dùin suas, druid, comhlaich, stad, grab, cuir moil, cuir an aghaidh; toirmisg, eagair, amail. Obstruct his progress, *cuir bac air gabh roimh.*

Obstructer, *s.* Bacair, fear grabaidh, fear comhlaich, fear toirmisg, fear amalaidh.

Obstructing, *s.* Bacadh, grabadh, amaladh, gabhail roimh, amaladh.

Obstruction, *s* Bac, bacadh, grab, grabadh, amal; cnabstarradh, stad, eagar, dùnadh

Obstructive, *a.* Amalach, grabach.

Obstruent, *a* Amalach, grabach.

Obstupefaction, *s.* Marbhantachd, nothaistealachd.

Obtain, *v. a.* Faigh, buannaich, buidhinn, coisinn; buadhaich, fairtlich, faigh lamh an uachdar.

Obtainable, *a.* So-choisinn, so-fhaotainn.
Obtemperate, *v. a.* Géill.
Obtend, *v.* Cuir an aghaidh; cum a mach; gabh ort.
Obtenebrate, *v.* Dorchaich, duibhrich, sgàilich.
Obtenebration, *s.* Dorchadas, duibhre, dubhar, duirche, sgàil.
Obtest, *v.* Guidh, asluich, athchuing, grios
Obtestation, *s* Guidhe, guidheadh, asluchadh, athchuinge, grios, griosadh, ùrnuigh, ùirnigh.
Obtrectation, *s* Càineadh, cul-chàineadh, toibheum.
Obtrude, *v. a.* Cuir a dh' aindeoin, cuir a steach, pùc, sàth; diong, foisg; rach gun chuireadh (no) gun chead.
Obtruder, *s.* Sgimlear, sràcair; goistidh.
Obtrusion, *s* Sàthadh, pùcadh; starradh, beagnarachd, beadaidheachd, leamhachas, leamhad.
Obtund, *v. a.* Maolaich, dean maol.
Obtuse, *a* Maol, neo-gheur; gun roinn; tamhach, spaideanta, màll, neo-sgairteil.
Obtusely, *adv.* Gu maol, gu neo-gheur, gu tamhach, gu spaideanta, gu mall, gu neo-ghuineach
Obtuseness, *s.* Maoile, maolad, maoilead; maolachd; spaideantachd, neo-sgairtealachd
Obumbrate, *v. a.* Dorchaich, duibhrich.
Obumbration, *s.* Duirche, doirchead, dorchadas, duibhre, sgàil.
Obvallation, *s.* Cladhachadh; claiseachadh, dionadh.
Obviate, *v. a.* Bac, coinnich, amail, cuir an aghaidh, grab, tachair ri.
Obvious, *a.* So-fhaicinn, so-fhaicsinn, soilleir, teagmhaiseach. Obviously, *gu soilleir, a réir coslais.*
Obviousness, *s.* So-fhaicinneachd, soilleireachd, teagmhaiseachd.
Occasion, *s.* (*Opportunity*), fàth, cion-fath, ceann-fath, cothrom; (*reason*), ceann-aobhair, aobhar, reuson; (*time*), uair, ùine, am; (*want*), feum, siocair; ocaid; gleus. Take hold of the occasion, *glac an cothrom;* on occasion, *air uairibh;* I have no occasion for you, *cha 'n eil feum agam ort;* on that occasion, *an sin, air an am sin*, I will give you occasion to weep, *bheir mise aobhair ghuil dhuit*, occasions, *gnothuichean, amanna.*
Occasion, *v. a.* Tog; dean; faigh. Occasion joy, *tog aoibhneas.*
Occasional, *a.* Air uairibh, an tràths is a ris, còrr uairean.
Occasionally, *adv.* Air uairibh, an tràths is a ris, còrr uairean.
Occecation, *s.* Dalladh.
Occidental, *a.* Shuas, iarail, niarach, shiar, iar, a lamh na h-airde 'n iar.
Occiput, *s.* Cùl a chinn.
Occision, *s.* Marbhadh, mortadh, sgriosadh, milleadh.
Occlude, *v. a.* Dùin suas, druid.
Occluse, *a* Dùinte; druidte; uaigneach, aonaranach.
Occlusion, *s.* Dùnadh, drùideadh.
Occult, *a.* Folaichte, falaichte, céilte, diomhair, doilleir, dorch, do-thuigsinn; deacair.
Occultation, *s.* Folach réil.
Occultness, *s* Diomhaireachd, dorchadas, deacaireachd.
Occupancy, *s.* Sealbhachadh, gabhail seilbhe.
Occupant, *s.* Sealbhadair.
Occipate, *v. a.* Sealbhaich.
Occupation, *s.* Sealbhachadh; ceaird; ealadhain.
Occupier, *s.* Sealbhadair, sealbhachair, fear seilbh.

Occupy, *v a.* and *n.* Sealbhaich, gabh seilbh; cum, gleidh, gnàthaich; caith, lean ceaird; oibrich, saoithrich.
Occupying, *s.* Sealbhachadh, gnàthachadh; oibreachadh
Occur, *v. n.* Tachair, tuit, éirich, thig an cuimhne, buail, cuimhnich; thig a làthair; bac; coinnich A bad business has occurred, *thachair droch thuiteamas*, it occurred to me, *bhuail e mi*
Occurrence, Occurrent, *s* Tuiteamas, tubaisd, teagmhail, cineamhuinn
Occursion, *s.* Coinneach, coinneachadh, straoidhleadh, aireis, ireas, tachairt, teagmhail.
Ocean, *s.* Cuan, fairg, muir, aibhis, taimh, aigean. The ocean, *a mhuir mhòr.*
Oceanic, *a* Cuantach, fairgeach, aibhiseach.
Ocellated, *a* Sùileach, coslach ri sùil.
Ochre, *s.* Ruadh chill, ruadh chailc, talamh dearg.
Ochrey, *a.* Ruadh, ruadh-chailceach, ruadh thalamhach.
Octagon, *s* Ochd-chearnag, ochd-shlisneag.
Octagonal, *a* Ochd-chearnach, ochd-oisneach, ochd-shliosnach.
Octangular, *a.* Ochd-chearnach, ochd-oisinneach, ochd-shliosnachail.
Octave, *s.* Ochdamh là an deigh feill; ochdach.
Octavo, *s* Site anns a bheil ochd duilleagan; ochdamh.
Octennial, *a.* Ochd-bhliadhnach, ochd-bhliadhnail.
October, *s.* Mios mu dheireadh an fhogharaidh, an deicheamh mios.
Octogenary, *a.* Ceithir fichead bliadhna dh' aois
Octonary, *a.* Ochdamhach
Octonocular, *a* Ochd-shuileach.
Octopetalous, *a.* Ochd dhuilleach, ochd dhuilleagach, ochd-bhileagach.
Octuple, *a* Ochd fillte.
Ocular, *a* Sùl, sùileach. Ocular proof, *dearbh sùl.*
Ocularly, *adv* Gu beachd.
Oculate, *a.* Sùileach, aig am bheil sùilean
Oculist, *s* Sùil-leigh, léigh shùl, lighiche shùl
Odd, *a.* Neònach, iongantach, ioghantach, aighearrach, neo-eireachdail, corr, àirid, (*fantastical*), luaimneach, luaineach
Oddly, *adv.* Gu neònach, gu h-iongantach, gu h-ioghantach
Oddness, *s.* Neo-chothrom; neònachas; ioghnadh, iongantas
Odds, *s* Corr, corrlach; tuasaid.
Ode, *s.* Duan, duanag, luinneag, dàn, rann, òran.
Odible, *a.* Fuathmhor, gràineil
Odious, *a.* Fuathmhor, gràineil, oillteil, fuathach, fuathasach.
Odiously, *adv.* Gu fuathmhor, gu gràineil, gu h-oillteil, gu fuathach.
Odiousness, *s.* Fuathmhorachd, gràinealachd, oilltealachd
Odium, *s* Fuath; coire; tnùth
Odontalgic, *a* Cnaimh fhiaclach.
Odorate, *a* Fàileach, cùbhraidh, boltrachail.
Odoriferous, *a.* Deagh-fhàileach, cubhraidh, deagh-bholtrachail
Odorous, *a.* Cùbbraidh, deagh bholtrachail
Odour, Odor, *s.* Fàile, àile, tòchd, deagh fhàile, deagh bholadh, deagh thòchd.
Œconomy See **Economy**.
Œconumenical, *a.* Coitchionn.
Œiliad, *s.* Priobadh, plathadh, caogadh, sméid.

Œsophagus, *s.* Goile, detiach, sgornach, sgornan, steic bhraghad.

Of, *prep.* Do, de, dhe, dheth, d', dh'; o, bho, ua. The elder of you, *am fear is sine dhibh*, the eldest of the three, *am fear a 's sine dhe 'n triùir (no) do 'n triùir*, the love of money, *gaol airgid*, this stick of yours, *air lorg so th' agad*, this poet of ours, *am bard so th' againn*, I have heard it of many, *chual mi e o mhòran*, of set purpose, *a dh' aon obair*, of my own accord, *do mo dheòin*, I am of the same opinion with you, *tha mi do 'n aon bharail riutsa, tha mi do 'n bharail cheudna riutsa*, what kind of man is he? *ciod an seorsa fir th' ann?* of late, *a chianamh*, of a certainty, *air chinnte*, of old, *o chian, o shean*, of whom were you talking? *cia uime an ro sibh labhairt?*

Off, *adv.* Air falbh, air astar, fad as; an céin; dhe, o, bho. He got off, *thuair e as (no) dheth*, a mile off, *mile air falbh*, a good way off, *greis air astar*, from off, *q dheth, a bharr*, off and on, *san tomhartaich*, a great way off, *fad air falbh, fad air astar*, be off, *bi triall*, well off, *gu math dheth*, ill off, *gu h-olc dheth*

Offal, *s.* Spruilleach, fuigheall, fuighleach; ollag, cairbh, greallach, mionach, meanach

Offence, *s.* Ciont, coire, olc, lochd; dochair, dochoir, diòbhal, dolaidh, urchoid, dochann, fearg, masladh, oilbheum, sgainneal; ionnsuidh Take offence, *gabh gu dona*.

Offenceful, *a.* Dochannach; urchoideach; oilbheumach

Offenceless, *a.* Neo-choireach, neo-chiontach.

Offend, *v. a* and *n* Feargaich, cuir fearg air; buair, brosnuich, peacaich; dean cron; gabh gu dona Be not offended at what I shall say, *na gabh gu dona na their mi.*

Offended, *a.* Diomach, diombach, ciurrta.

Offender, *s* Ciontach, peacair, peacach

Offensive, *a* Urchoideach, millteach, lochdach; gràineil, mosach, breun, loibheach, mio-thlachdmhor, mi-thaitneach On the offensive, *air taobh na h-ionnsuidh*, an offensive weapon, *inneal ciurruidh (no) leònaidh*

Offensively, *adv* Gu gràineil, gu mio-thlachdmhor, gu dochannach.

Offensiveness, *s* Urchoideachd, urchoid, coire, dochann, mi-thaitneachd, mio-thlachd, gràinealachd

Offer, *v a* Tairg, cuir an tairgse, furail, iobair, ofrail; thoir suas, oidhirpich, dean oidhirp, thoir oidhirp Offer up a request, *cuir suas athchuinge*, offer thy gift, *thoir uait do thiodhlac;* he who offers praise, *esan a dh' iobras moladh*, he offered himself, *thairg se e féin, thug se e fein suas*

Offer, *s* Oidhirp, tairgse. Make an offer, *thoir tairgse*, put in his offer, *cuir na thairgse*

Offerer, *s* Tairgseach, fear iobairt; fear ofrail.

Offering, *s.* Tabhartas, ofrail, iobairt

Offertory, *s* Tabhairteadh, builea chadh, tairgseadh.

Office, *s.* Dreuchd, oifig, oich, gairm, cùram, inmhe, inbhe, post, gnothuch An office or good turn, *deagh thùrn.*

Officer, *s* Oichear, oifigeach, dreuchdair, ceannard; (*bailiff*), maor righ. The great officers of state, *ard-mhaoir na rioghachd.*

Official, *a.* Dreuchdail, oifigeach

Officiate, *v n* Gnàthaich, dean gnothuch; coimhlion, dean

Officious, *a* Meachranach, soileasach, còir, caoimhneil, casgaidh, feamantach, dùrachdach, frithealach, frithealteach

Officiously, *adv* Gu meachranach, gu coir, gu caoimhneil

Officiousness, *s* Meachranachd; soileas; casgaidheachd; fritheilteachd

Offing, *s.* Suùradh o chladach; seòladh o thir, doimhneachd, fagus do thir.

Offscouring, *s.* Sàlachar, sal, anabas, trusdaireachd.

Offset, *s.* Fiùran; fàilean; gineag.

Offspring, *s.* Siol, sliochd, gineal, clann

Offuscate, *v.* Dorchaich, doilleirich, duibhrich.

Offusation, *s.* Dorchadas; doilleireachadh, duibhreachadh.

Offward, *adv.* Mach, a mach.

Oft, Often, *adv.* Tric, minig, gu tric, gu minig, iomad uair, lion uair. Very often, *ro thric*, too often, *tuille is tric, mùth 's tric*, how often? *cia tric? cia cho tric?* ever so often, *air a thricead*, many a time and oft, *is iomad uair 's is tric.*

Oftentimes, Oft-times, *adv* Tric, minig, gu tric, gu minig, iomad uair.

Ogle, *v.* Sméid, caog, seall gu miag-shuileach.

Ogler, *s* Urr mhiag-shuileach.

Ogling, *a* Miag-shuileach; fiar-shuileach.

Ogling, *s* Miag-shuileachd, sealladh gaolach

Oglio, *s* Cumasg

Oh! *interj* O! och! mo thruaighe!

Oil, *s* Oladh, ùillidh, ùille. Linseed oil, *uille an rosaidh*, wheel oil, *ùille chuidhleachan*, holy oil, *oladh naomh.*

Oil, *v.* Uill, ùillich

Oiliness, *s.* Uillidheachd, ùillearachd; reamhrachd.

Oily, *a* Uilleach, reamhar, grlseach, oladhar.

Oint, *v a* Ung; sliob; ùill.

Ointment, *s.* Oladh, oladh ungaidh, unamaid, oladh leighis; acfhuinn shuaite; (*ointment made of fresh butter and herbs*), sailm uchd.

Old, *a* Sean, aosar, aosmhor, aosda; arsadh, fion, seanda, arsanta, † fionach, † bro Of old, *o chian, o shean*, an old man, *sean duine, duine aosmhor*, as the old saying is, *mar a thar 'n sean fhocal*, you are in your old wont, *tha thu san sean chal (no) fhasan*, older, *is sine*, somewhat old, *leth char sean*, an old carle, *bodach*, the oldest of them, *an neach a 's sine dhiubh*, old age, *sean aois*, many infirmities attend old age, *thig gach uile ni re h-aois, thig baoth, thig boile, thig bàs.*

Olden, *a.* See Old.

Old-fashioned, *a* Sean-fhasanta, sean-aimsireil; neo-chumanta

Oldish, *a* Leth char sean.

Oldness, *s* Aois, seanachd, aosmhorachd, arsaidheachd, seandachd

Oleaginous, *a* Oladhar, ùilleach, reamhar; sùghar, brighmhor

Olfactory, *a.* Fàileach, àileach, boltrach.

Olid, Olidous, *a* Breun, loibheach, grod.

Oligarchical, *a* Iar-fhlaitheach, iar-fhlathach

Oligarchy, *s.* Iar-fhlaitheachd, iar-fhlathachd, iar-lachd.

Olivaster, *a.* Dubh-dhonn

Olive, *s.* Crann olaidh, ol-mheas; ol-dhearcag.

Olympiad, *s.* Ùine cheithir bliadhna, a reir aireimh nan Greugach

Ombre, *s* Cluiche air chairtean.

Omega, *s* An litir mu dheireadh san aibideal Ghreugach; deireadh

Omelet, *s* Scorsa caraiceig, breacag.

Omen, *s.* Tuar, comhar, taragradh, mànadh; fàisneachd, targhail. A good omen, *deagh thuar, deagh chòmhar.*

Omentum, *s.* Sgairt.

Ominate, *v. a.* Tuar, targhail, galraich.

Omination, *s.* Tuar, targhal, fòisneachd.

Ominous, *a.* Mi-aghmhor, aghmhor, mi-fhortanach, droch-tharagrach, fàistinneach, tubaisteach, cineamhuinneach.

Ominousness, *s.* Mi-aghmhorachd, droch tharagrachd.

Omission, *s.* Dichuimhne, dio-chuimhne, dearmad, fàgail; fàilinn.

Omit, *v. a.* Dichuimhnich, dio-chuimhnich, dearmaid, fàillich, fag as (no) a mach.

Omnifarious, *a.* Iom-ghnetheach, iol-ghnéthach.

Omniferous, *a.* Uile-bheirteach, uile-thabhartach.

Omniform, *a.* Uile-chruthach.

Omnigenous, *a.* Uile-ghnethach, ioma-ghnethach.

Omnipotence, Omnipotency, *s.* Uile-chumhachd.

Omnipotent, *a.* Uile-chumhachdach.

Omnipresence, *s.* Uile làthaireachd.

Omnipresent, *a.* Uile làthaireach.

Omniscience, *s.* Uile-fhiosrachd, uile léirsinneachd, uile-léirsinn.

Omniscient, *a.* Uile-fhiosrach, uile-eolach, uile-léirsinneach.

Omnivorous, *a.* Uile-itheach.

On, *adv.* Air adhairt, air aghaidh. On, thou hero! *air d' adhairt, a laoich!*

On, *prep.* Air. On me, *orm;* on thee, *ort;* on him, *air;* on her, *oirre, orra;* on us, *oirnne;* on you, *oirbhe;* on them, *orra;* on what ground? *carson?* on his side, *air a thaobh-sa, leis-san;* on a sudden, *ann an ealamhachd, gu h-obann;* on both sides, *air gach taobh;* on horseback, *air muin eich;* on the ground, *air an làr, air làr, air an talamh;* he lives on little, *tha e tighinn beò air bheag-nithe;* he came on foot, *thainig e d' a chois;* on these terms, *air na teirmean sin;* on this side, *air an taobh;* on the other side, *air an taobh eile; thall.*

Once, *adv.* Aon uair, uair, roimh so, aon tarruing. At once, *air a cheud tarruing;* (*together*), maraon; a dh' aon tarruing, mu chòmhladh. Once on a time, *roimh so;* you cannot do two things at once, *cha 'n urradh dhuit dà ni 'dheanamh mu chòmhlath.*

One, *a.* Aon, h-aon. It is all one, *tha e uile ionann;* one o'clock, *aon uair, an uair;* it is all one to me, *tha e uile ionann domhsa, tha e 'n t-aon chuid domhsa;* one is better than none, *is fhearr h-aon na bhith falamh;* one with another, *réir a chéile;* one another, *a chéile;* one day as I was on the hill, *làth dhomh a bhith sa bheinn.*

One, *s.* Fear; urr; neach; té; aon; uair an deigh mheadhon là. One of them, *fear dhiubh, h-aon dhiubh.*

One-eyed, *a.* Cam; aon-shuileach, leth-shuileach, air aon sùil, air leth shùil.

Oneirocritic, *s.* Fear mìneachaidh bhruadar.

Oneness, *s.* Aonachd; ionannachd.

Onerate, *v. a.* Luchdaich, eallaich, uallaich.

Oneration, *s.* Luchdachadh; eallachadh, uallachadh.

Onerous, *a.* Luchdmhor, luchdar, trom, cothromach.

Onion, *s.* Unnean.

Only, *adv.* A mhàin; mhàin. Only thou, *thusa 'mhàin.*

Only, *a.* Aon, singilte, aonaranach. An only child, *aon urr cloinne, aon-ghin cloinne;* only man-child, *aon fhear cloinne.*

Onset, *s.* Ionnsuidh, oidhirp, ruathar, dian-ionnsuidh. Make an onset, *thoir ionnsuidh.*

Onslaught, *s.* Ionnsuidh, ruathar.

Onward, *adv.* Air adhairt, air adhart, air aghaidh; a chuid is a chuid.

Onyx, *s.* Seorsa cloich phrìseil.

Ooze, *s.* Làthach, eabar, poll; sal; snith, snitheadh.

Ooze, *v. n.* Sil, snith; drùidh.

Oozy, *a.* Làthachail, salach, eabarach, pollar; snitheach; fliuch, neo-dhion.

Opacate, *v.* Dorchaich, doilleirich, duibhrich.

Opacity, *s.* Dorchadas, doirche, doirchead, doilleireachd, duibhre.

Opacous, *a.* Dorch, doilleir, neo-shoillseach.

Opal, *s.* Seorsa cloich phrìseil.

Opaque, *a.* Dorch, neulmhor, doilleir.

Opaqueness, *s.* Dorchadas, doirche, doirchead, neulmhorachd, doilleireachd.

Ope, *v.* See Open.

Open, *v. a.* Fosgail, sgaoil, fuasgail; (*explain*), soilleirich; minich; feuch; cuir an céill; (*as a flower*), plaoisg; (*disclose*), nochd, innis; (*as a dog*), tathuin. Open the door, *fosgail an dorus;* (*as the body*), tuasgail, tualaig.

Open, *a.* Fosgailte; soilleir; sgaoilte, follaiseach; (*in heart*), fial, suairc, fialuidh, fosgailte, faoilidh; (*sincere*), simplidh, tréibhdhireach, dìreach; (*uncovered*), neo-chomhdaichte, lom. Open to danger, *buailteach do chunnart;* an open heart, *cridhe fosgailte* (*no*) *fial.*

Opener, *s.* Fosglair; fuasglair; mìneachair.

Open-eyed, *a.* Sùileach, faiceallach; fuireachail.

Open-handed, *a.* Fialaidh, fialuidh, fial, toirbheartach, fiùghantach, suairc.

Open-hearted, *a.* Fial, fialuidh; teo-chridheach; dìreach, simplidh, tréibhdhireach.

Open-heartedness, *s.* Fialuidhcachd; tréibhdhireas; simplidheachd; fiùghantas.

Opening, *s.* Fosgladh; bearn; briseadh; sgoltadh, sgàgadh; bealach; sànus; ceud shealladh; (*of dogs*), tathunnaich.

Openly, *adv.* Gu fosgailte, gu follaiseach, gu soilleir, os àirde; ann san t-sealladh.

Open-mouthed, *a.* Craosach, le beul fosgailte, spleucach, gionach, geanach, glamhach; glagaireach, lonach.

Openness, *s.* Follaiseachd, soilleireachd, fialachd, fialuidheachd; fosgailteachd; athais; (*of the bowels*), tualag.

Opera, *s.* Cluich ciùil.

Operate, *v.* Oibrich, dean, gnàthaich, cuir an gniomh.

Operation, *s.* Oibreachadh, obair, tùrn, gnathachadh, gniomh, gniomhachadh.

Operative, *a.* Deanadach; gnàthachail, oibreachail, éifeachdach.

Operator, *s.* Oibriche, deanadair.

Operose, *a.* Saothaireachail, draghail; dìchiollach; duilich, deacair, do-dheanamh.

Ophthalmy, *s.* Galar sùl, sùil-ghalar.

Opiate, *s.* Suain-leigheas, pramh-leigheas, culaidh chodail.

Opine, *v. a.* Smuainich, smaoinich, smaointich; saoil; baralaich.

Opiniative, *a.* Dòchasach, danarra, rag-bharaileach, féin-bharaileach.

Opinion, *s.* Barail, beachd; meas, dòchas, inntinn, smuain, breith, breitheanas. In my opinion, *ann mo bheachd-sa, ann mo bharail-se;* according to my opinion, *a réir mo bharail-se;* they are of one opinion, *tha iad dh' aon bharail.*

Opinionative, *a.* Dòchasach; danarra; rag-bharaileach; féin-fhoghainteach, féin-bharaileach, dian, dur.

Opinionatively, *adv.* Gu dòchasach, gu danarra, gu rag-bharaileach.

Opinionativeness, *s.* Dòchasachd, danarrachd

Opinionist, *s.* Fear féin-bharaileach, fear a tha glic na bharail fein.

Opium, *s* Sugh codalian; suain leigheas

Oppidan, *s.* Fear mhuinntir baile.

Oppignerate, *v a.* Fàg (no) cuir an geall.

Oppilate, *v a* Carn suas.

Oppilation, *s.* Carnadh suas.

Oppleted, *a.* Lionta, lan, dearr-làn, domhlaichte.

Opponent, *s.* Namhaid; eascar, eascaraid; co' sheise

Opportune, *a.* Iomchuidh; cubhaidh, tràthail, amail; deas, freagarrach, ceart.

Opportunely, *adv.* Gu h-iomchuidh, gu cubhaidh, gu tràthail, ann an deagh thràth.

Opportunity, *s.* Cothrom, fàth, cion fàth, tràth, am, ùine, iomchuidhead; athais. At my first opportunity, *air mo cheud cothrom.*

Oppose, *v.* Cuir an aghaidh, bac, grab, gabh roimh, thoir aghaidh, coinnich, thoir coinneamh, tachair ri. Oppose an enemy, *thoir aghaidh air nàmhaid.*

Opposeless, *a.* Do-chur an aghaidh, do-shàruchadh, do-chlaoidh.

Opposer, *s* Namhaid, eascaraid; fear cònspoid

Opposite, *a.* Mu chomhar, mu choinneamh, fa chomhar; an aghaidh; naimhdeil. Opposite to you, *mu do chomhar*, opposite to him, *fa 'chomhur*, opposite to us, *fa 'r comhar*, opposite to them, *fa 'n comhar, na 'n aghaidh.*

Opposition, *s.* Aghaidh, cur an aghaidh, naimhdeas, amal, grabadh, bac, strìgh, comh-strìgh; contraill. In opposition to nature, *an aghaidh nàduir.*

Oppress, *v a* Saruich, claoidh, ceannsaich, antromaich, dean fòirneart. He oppressed them, *shàruich (no) chlaoidh e iad.*

Oppression, *s* Sàruchadh, claoidh, ceannsachadh, antromachadh, antruime, foirneart, foireigin, breith air éigin; cruaidh-chas, teinne, teanntachd, sracaireachd.

Oppressive, *a.* Ain-iochdmhor, fòirneartach, sàruchail, antrom, neo-chneasta, sracanta, cruaidh, cruadalach.

Oppressor, *s* Fear fòirneirt, fear foireigin, foireigniche, fear sàruchaidh; sracair.

Opprobrious, *a.* Sgainnealach, maslach, tàireil, nàr, mi-chliùiteach

Opprobriously, *adv* Gu sgainnealach, gu maslach, gu tàireil

Opprobriousness, *s* Sgainnealachd, tairealachd

Oppugn, *v* Cuir an aghaidh.

Oppugner, *s* Fear a chuireas an aghaidh, eascaraid.

Opsonation, *s.* Solar bidh.

Opsonator, *s.* Solaraiche.

Optable, *a.* Taitneach, roghnachail

Optic, *a* Fradhrac, seallaidh.

Optic, *s.* Inneal fradhairc, inneal amhairc.

Optics, *s.* Iùl fradhairc.

Optimacy, *s.* Maithean, uaislean

Option, *s.* Rogha, roghainn, taghadh, roghnachadh.

Optional, *a* A reir toil.

Opulence, *s* Beartas, beairteas, saibhreas, maoin, taic, toic, pailteas.

Opulent, *a* Beartach, beairteach, saibhir, cothromach, maoineach, toiceil.

Or, *conj* No, na. Or else, *neo, air neo*, peace or war, *cogadh na sith*, whether you come or not, *co aca thig thu no nach tig*, you or they, *thusa no iadsan*; or ever, *mun*

Or, *s.* (*In heraldry*), òr.

Oracle, *s* Guth-àite; aireacal; teampull 's am faighear fàisneachd; fear glic seòlta.

Oracular, *a.* Aireacalach; dorch, do-thuigsinn.

Oraison, **Orison**, *s.* Ùrnuigh, ùrnigh, athchuinge, guidhe, grios, aoradh

Oral, *a.* Beoil; beulach; labhairteach. Oral tradition, *aithris;* orally, *le focal beòil.*

Orange, *s.* Òraisd, òr-ubhal, òr-mheas. Orange-wife, *cailleach òraisd.*

Oration, *s* Òraid, seanachas; duan.

Orator, *s.* Òraidiche, deas chainntear, ur-labhairtear, cainntear.

Oratorical, *a* Òraideach, deas-bhriathrach, deas-chainnteach, uirghiollach.

Oratory, *s.* Ùr-labhradh, ùrlabhairt, cainntearachd, seanachas, deas-labhairt, uirghioll; ionad ùrnuigh.

Orb, *s.* Cruinne, cearcall; cuairt, roth, cuidhle; an cruinne cé; reann, reannag, reult, ré; (*of the eye*), sùil, ubhal na sùl.

Orbed, *a.* Cruinn, cearcallach, cearclaichte.

Orbicular, *a* Cearclach, cearcallach.

Orbiculated, *a.* Cruinn, cearclaichte.

Orbit, *s.* Cruinn-lin, cuairt-lin, cearcall, cuairte; cuairteag. The earth's orbit, *cuairte na cruinne.*

Orc, *s* Ròn; muc mhara

Orchal, *s* Seorsa guirmein, clach gadhair.

Orchard, *s.* Gàraidh ùbhlan, garaidh meas, lios meas.

Orchestra, *s.* Aite ciùil, tigh cluiche.

Ordain, *v* Orduich, sonraich, sunraich, socraich; ainmich, eagaraich; roimh-orduich; cuir air chois; suidhich.

Ordained, *part.* Orduichte, sonraichte, sunraichte, socraichte, eagaraichte; roimh-orduichte; suidhichte.

Ordainer, *s.* Orduchair, sonrachair.

Ordaining, *s.* Orduchadh, sonrachadh; sunrachadh; socrachadh, suidheachadh.

Ordeal, *s* Gàbhail; seorsa deuchainn le teine agus uisge a chuireadh air chùl ri linn Righ Iain, an Sasunnach; bha e air an neach a chuireadh gu deuchainn air an doigh so, imeachd caslom agus le 'shùilean dùinte; air feadh ghadaibh teth dearg iaruinn; agus nan tigeadh e as gun dochann, bu chomhar cinnteach neo-chiontais e.

Order, *s.* (*Command*), ordugh, aithne, iarrtas, reachd, comannta; sparradh; (*method*), riaghailt, lathailt, seòl; (*rank*), rang, sread, sreadh, breath; (*custom*), àbhaist, nòs, cleachd In order, *ann an ordugh*, put in order, *cuir an ordugh*, according to his orders, *a réir ordugh*, in order to, *chum, a chum*, out of order, *thar chéile, a riaghailt*, under orders, *fo smachd*

Order, *v. a.* Orduich, àithn, thoir ordugh, riaghail, riaghlaich, riaghailtich, cuir an ordugh. Order him, *àithn dha, thoir ordugh dha.*

Orderer, *s.* Orduchair; riaghladair.

Ordering, *s.* Orduchadh, aithne, riaghladh; sgòd

Orderless, *a.* Eas-ordughach, aimhreiteach, mi-riaghailteach, a ordugh, thar a cheile, air aimhreidh.

Orderly, *a.* Riaghailteach, deas; réidh, (*obedient*), ùmhal, soitheamh, (*sober*), cneasta, measarra, stuama.

Orderly, *adv.* Gu riaghailteach, a reir ordugh, ann an ordugh, gu réidh, a réir riaghailt.

Orderliness, *s.* Riaghailteachd; ordugh; seòl, lathailt.

Ordinal, *a.* Riaghailteach; ordugh.

Ordinance, *s* Ordugh, riaghailt, reachd, lagh; seol; orduchadh; ainmeachadh, sonrachadh.

Orders, *s.* Cléir, ministearachd.

Ordinarily, *adv.* An cumantas, mar is tric, gu coitchionn.

Ordinary, *a.* Cumaint, cumanta, trie, coitchionn; gnathach, gnathaichte, iosal, dìblidh; meadhonach; eadar an dà chuid; neo-bhoidheach.

Ordinary, *s* Breith, breitheamh, bord coitchionn; ait comh-ithe.

Ordinate, *v a.* Orduich; sonruich; socraich, ainmich Ordinated, *orduichte, sonruichte, socraichte.*

Ordination, *s.* Sonruchadh, orduchadh, ainmeachadh, socrachadh; cléir-shonruchadh (no) cur fir air leth chum a bhith na shagart.

Ordnance, *s* Gunnraidh, gunnaidh mòr.

Ordure, *s.* Cac, sal, salachar, salchar, inneir, aolach, gaorr.

Ore, *s.* Méin, meun, meinn Lead ore, *méin luaidhi;* gold ore, *méin oir.*

Organ, *s.* Ball; (*in music*), orgaid. Organ of speech, *ball labhairt*, organ of hearing, *ball claistinn.*

Organic, Organical, *a.* Innealach; buill.

Organism, *s.* Dealbhadh, deanamh, cruth.

Organist, *s.* Orgaidiche.

Organization, *s.* Dealbhadh, comh-dhealbhadh, suidheachadh, riaghailteachadh.

Organize, *v. a.* Dealbh, comh-dhealbh, deilbh, suidhich, riaghailtich

Organ-loft, *s.* Lobht orgaid.

Organ-pipe, *s* Piob orgaid.

Organy, *s.* Oragan.

Orgasm, *s.* Dian-oidhirp.

Orgies, *s.* Ruitearachd, ruite, pòite.

Orient, *a.* Shios, a laimh na h-airde an ear; near; soilleir, glan, dealrach.

Orient, *s* Lamh na h-airde an ear, an taobh shios.

Orientalism, *s.* Soir bhriathrachas.

Orifice, *s.* Toll, beul, sgolt, sgoltadh, fosgal, fosgladh, sùileag.

Oriflamb, *s.* Bratach sean rìghre na Fraine do 'n goirteadh bratach an Naoimh Dhionis.

Origin, Original, *s.* Bun, bunachas, bunachar, toiseach, tùs, aobhar, mathair aobhar; ceud-thùs, ceud aobhar; sinnsir; freumh; samplair, sampull. That was the origin of it, *b' e sin bu toiseach dha*, the origin of the world, *toiseach an t-saoghail.*

Original, *a.* Bunadhasach, tùsail; toiseachail, priomh, ceud, sean, gin, gineadh, gineamhuinn. Original sin, *peacadh gin.*

Originally, *adv.* O thoiseach, a tùs, air tùs, air thùs, an toiseach.

Originate, *v. a.* and *n.* Tòisich, thoir gu bith How did it originate? *ciamar a thòisich e?*

Origination, *s* Toiseachadh, toiseach; freumhachd, bunadhas.

Orison, Oraison, *s.* Urnuigh, ùirnigh, athchuing, guidhe.

Ork, *s.* See Orc.

Orlop, *s.* Crannag, bord iochdair luing.

Ornament, *s.* Sgiamh, sgeimh, breaghachd, briaghachd, greus, sgiamhachd, grinneas, seud; arraichd; oir-ghreus, maise, snàs; onoir.

Ornament, *v. a.* Sgiamhaich, breaghaich, sgeadaich, grinnich, uigheamaich, snàsaich. Ornamented, *sgeadaichte, sgiamhaichte; finealta.*

Ornamental, *a.* Sgiamhach, sgiamhachail, briagh, breagh, dreachail, snàsmhor, grinn.

Ornate, *v.* Grinn, sgiamhach, briagh, greusda, breagh, dreachail, snàsmhor, grinn.

Ornateness, *s* Grinneas, sgiamhachd, sgeimh, breaghas, eireachdas, dreach, snàsmhorachd.

Ornature, *s.* Briaghas, breaghas; sgeadachadh, eideadh

Orphan, *s.* Dilleachdan, dìlleachd.

Orphanage, *s* Dilleachdanachd

Orpiment, *s.* Seòrsa méinn.

Orpine, *s.* Laogh-lus.

Orrery, *s* Reultradh.

Orris, *s.* Seorsa luibh.

Orthodox, *a.* Fallain am beachd no 'n creideamh, ceartchreideach

Orthodoxy, *s* Ceart-chreideamh

Orthographer, *s* Ceart-sgriobhair.

Orthographical, *a* Ceart-sgriobhach.

Orthography, *s.* Ceart-sgriobhadh, litreachadh.

Orthological, *a.* Ceart-labhairteach.

Orthology, *s.* Ceart-labhairt.

Ortolan, *s* Gne eòin ro bhlasda ri itheadh.

† **Orts**, *s.* Fuigheal, fuighleach, fortus, fortas; spruilleach, faladair

Oscillation, *s* Seòganaich, saobanaich, siùdanaich.

Oscillatory, *a.* Seoganach, saobanach, siùdanach

Oscitant, *a.* Meananach, meunanach; codalach, trom, drùb-shuileach

Oscitation, *s.* Meunan, meanan, meananaich.

Osier, *s.* Seileach do 'n deanar bascaidean; bùnsach.

Ossifrage, *s.* Iolair mhòr na mara, iolair mara, cnaimheach.

Osprey, *s.* Iolair uisge, iolair mara.

Osseous, *a.* Cnaimheach, craimheach.

Ossicle, *s.* Cnaimh beag

Ossification, *s* Cnaimheachadh.

Ossify, *v. n.* Cnaimhich, tionndaidh chum cnaimh

Ossivorous, *a* Cnaimh-itheach

Ossuary, *s.* Cnaimh-ionad, tigh chnaimhean, tigh chairbh, tigh mairbh, meambra.

Ostensible, *a.* Faicinneach, coslach, soilleir; a reir beachd, a réir coslais

Ostensive, *a.* A feuchainn; a ciallachadh.

Ostent, *s.* Tuar, comhar; droch comhar, aogas, sealladh; gné.

Ostentation, *s.* Spleadhachas, blomas, spleadh, spagluinn; sgleup, bòsd; bragainn; fearas-mhòr; *spagadaglig*

Ostentatious, *a* Spleadhach, blomasach, spagluinneach, bòsdail, uallach, faoin.

Osteology, *s.* Eachdraidh (no) tràchd mu chnamhan.

Ostiary, *s.* Inbhear, comar, beul aimhne

Ostler, *s.* Gille stàbuill; gille each.

Ostracism, *s* Slige-dhìteadh, seorsa ditidh a bha cumainnt a measg nan Greugach, diobaradh.

Ostrich, *s.* Struth; struth-chamhal.

Other, *a* Eile Another man, *fear eile;* the other day, *an là roimh*, some time or other, *uair h-éigin, uair no uair eigin*, each other, *a chéile*, one another, *a chéile*, every other day, *gach dolach là.*

Othergates, *adv* Air dhoigh eile, air sheòl eile; air mhùth doigh, air atharrach; ni 's fhearr.

Otherguise, *adv.* Do sheòrsa eile.

Otherwise, *adv.* Air sheòl eile; air mhùth doigh, air dheo, air neo, neo.

Otter, *s.* Dobhran, doran, biast dubh; dobhar-chu, madadh donn.

Ottoman, *s.* Turcach.

Ottoman, *a.* Turcach.

Ouch, *s.* Unga, muin-sheud.

Ought, *s.* Dad, ni. Have you ought, *bheil dad agad.*

Ought, *v. imperf.* Is còir, bu chòir, is cubhaidh, bu chubhaidh, is fheudar; feumaidh. Ought not Christ to have died? *nach bu chòir do Chriosd bàsuchadh?* I ought to go, *is còir dhomh falbh;* I ought to have gone, *bu chòir dhomh falbh.*

Ounce, *s.* Unnsa, unnsadh; seòrsa fiadh-bhéist. Three ounces, *tri unnsan, tri unnsachan;* two ounces, *da unnsa.*

Ouphe, *s.* Sithiche, tannasg, ailmse, bòchdan; bodach.

Ouphen, *a.* Sithicheil, ailmseach.

Our, *a. pron.* Ar, againne, *for* a th' againne. Our father, *ar n-athair;* our mother, *ar màthair;* our house, *an tigh againne;* ours, *leinn; air an taobh againn;* whose is it? ours or yours, *co leis e? leinn no leibhse.*

Ourself, *pron., (used by majesty.)* Sinn-féin, mi-féin.

Ourselves, *pron.* Sinn-féin. Between ourselves, *eadarainn féin.*

Ouse, *s.* Sgrath dharaich, cairt an daraig; cairt an daraich.

Ousel, *s.* Lon dubh.

Oust, *v. a.* Falmhaich; cuir air falbh, cuir a mach; tilg a mach, cuir as àite.

Out, *adv.* Mach, a mach, muigh, a muigh, as, mach as; falamh, folamh. I was out, *bha mi a mach;* the bottle is out *or* empty, *tha 'n searrag falamh;* out of my sight, *a (no) as mo shealladh;* out of love, *a thaobh gaoil, trid gaol (no) gradh, a bhrìgh gaoil;* out of favour, *a maoidhean, a fàbhor;* out of the way, *as an rathad;* out of order, *thar a chéile;* the fire is out, *tha 'n teine as (no) a mach;* hold out, *cum a mach;* out of me, *asam;* out of thee, *asad;* out of him, *as;* out of her, *aisde;* out of us, *asainne;* out of you, *asaibh;* out of them, *asda;* out of breath, *as an anail.*

Out, *interj.* Ut.

Out, *v. a.* Cuir a mach, diobair.

Outbalance, *v.* Cothromaich, thoir cothrom a. Outbalanced, *coth-thromaichte.*

Outbar, *v. a.* Dùin a mach, druid a mach.

Outbid, *v.* Tairg thairis air, tairg barrachd luach.

Outborn, *a.* Eil-thìreach, all-mharach, coigreach.

Outbound, *a.* Dol o 'n tigh, dol an cian; a seòladh mach.

Outbreak, *s.* Briseadh mach, bris' a mach, bruth, broth, brothadh; teas-bhruth.

Outcast, *a.* Tilgte a mach, diobairte, fògaraichte, air fogairt.

Outcast, *s.* Dìobarach, dìbearach, dìbhireach, fogarach; fear-fuadain.

Outcry, *s.* Glaodh, glaodhaich, sgairt, gàir; buaireadh; *(sale),* reic; ropainn.

Outdo, *v. a.* Rach thairis, faigh barrachd (no) lamh an uachdar, fairtlich air.

Outer, *a.* A mach, mach, a muigh, muigh, is fhaide mach, is iomallaiche.

Outermost, *a.* Is-fhaide a mach, is iomallaiche.

Outface, *v. a.* Aghaidhich; nàraich; cuir a mach.

Outfit, *s.* Uigheamachadh, deasachadh.

Outform, *s.* Aogas, dealbh, coslas, riochd.

Outgate, *s.* Fosgladh, bealach, bearn, dorus iomallach.

Outgo, *v. a.* Rach thairis, rach an uachdar, faigh farrachd air; fairtlich air; fàg; thoir an car a meall.

Outgrow, *v. a.* Fas (no) cinn thairis; fas (no) cinn gu h-anabarra.

Outhouse, *s.* Tigh mach, tigh beag, coit.

Outknave, *v. a.* Thoir barrachd air mealltair, thoir an car a mealltair.

Outlandish, *a.* Eil-thireach, allmharach.

Outlast, *v. a.* Mair (no) buanaich ni 's fhaide.

Outlaw, *s.* Fògarach, diobarach, fear nach fhaotar dhion. An outlaw, *fear air charn, robair, spùinneadair, creachadair.*

Outlaw, *v. a.* Fògaraich, diobaraich; cuir air carn.

Outlawry, *s.* Dìbhreachadh, dìobrachadh.

Outleap, *v. a.* Leum thairis, leum ni 's fhaide.

Outlearn, *v. a.* Ionnsuich ni 's luaithe.

Outlet, *s.* Fosgladh; bealach, caolas, bearn; rod mach; leigeil mach.

Outline, *s.* Crioch; dealbh; teòradh, iomall; sgrioch.

Outlive, *v.* Mair (no) fan beo ni 's fhaide, iar-mhair.

Outlying, *a.* Cian, air asdar, am fad; a mach.

Outlook, *v. a.* Cuir a h-aghaidh.

Outmarch, *v. a.* Imich ni 's luaithe, fàg, fàg air dheireadh.

Outmeasure, *v. a.* Rach thar tomhas.

Outmost, *a.* Is iomallaiche, is fhaide a mach; iomallach.

Outnumber, *v.* Rach thairis an lionmhoireachd, bi ni 's lìonmhoire, bi ni 's pailte.

Outpace, *v. a.* Fàg, fàg air dheireadh.

Outparish, *s.* Sgireachd mach.

Outpart, *s.* Aite a mach, aite iomallach. Outparts, *aitean iomalluch, aitean a mach.*

Outport, *s.* Cian-chàla, port air astar o phriomh-chathair sam bi, gu h-àraidh o bhaile Lunnuinn.

Outpour, *v. a.* Doirt a mach, cuir a mach.

Outrage, *v. a.* Eucoirich, buin gu h-eucorach ri; buin gu nàr (no) tàireil ri.

Outrage, *s.* Ainneart, fòirneart, eucoir, spid, boile, tarcuis, tair, tamailt, buaireas.

Outrageous, *a.* Ainnearteach, foirneartach, eucorach, tarcuiseach, tàireil, tamailteach; borb, feargach, fiadhaich, air boile, air chuthach, buaireasach; fuathasach. Outrageous conduct, *iomchar borb;* he is quite outrageous, *tha e air a ghlan chuthach.*

Outrageously, *adv.* Gu h-ainneartach, gu fòirneartach, gu h-eucorach, gu tarcuiseach, gu tàireil, gu tamailteach, gu borb, gu fiadhaich.

Outreach, *v. a.* Rach ni 's fhaide, rach thar, rach thairis air.

Outride, *v. a.* Marcaich seachad air, marcaich ni 's luaithe.

Outrider, *s.* Maor; marcair; fear ghnothuichean.

Outright, *adv.* Gu h-ealamh, as laimh, gun dàil, air ball, air an spot; gu tur.

Outroot, *v.* Freumhaich, spion as an fhreumh, spion as a bhun.

Outrun, *v. a.* Ruith ni 's luaithe, ruith seachad air, fàg, fàg air dheireadh.

Outsail, *v.* Seòl seachad air, seòl ni 's luaithe.

Outsell, *v. a.* Reic air pris ni 's airde; faigh luach (no) pris ni 's airde.

Outshoot, *v. a.* Tilg ni 's fhaide.

Outside, *s.* An taobh a mach, an taobh a muigh; an leth a mach; dreach. On the outside, *air an taobh mach, air an leth muigh.*

Outsit, *v. a.* Suidh ni 's fhaide, suidh tuille is fad, suidh mach. He outsat me, *shuidh e mach mi.*

Outsleep, *v. a.* Codail tuille is fad.

Outspread, *v. a.* Sgaoil a mach sgaoil, spréid.

Outstand, *v. a.* and *n.* Cuir an aghaidh, gabh roimh; seas a mach; aom.

Outstretch, *v.* Sìn, sgaoil tuille is fad.

Outstreet, *s.* Sràid mach, sràid iomallach.

Outstrip, *v. a.* Fairtlich air, faigh lamh an uachdar air, faigh barrachd; fàg air dheireadh.

Out-talk, *v. a.* Cuir a mach le comhradh.

Outvalue, *v.* Rach thairis am prìs; bi ni 's luachmhoire.

Outvie, *v. a.* Fairtlich, faigh barrachd. He outvied him, *dh' fhairtlich e air, fhuair e barrachd air.*

Outvote, *v.* Fairtlich le tagh-ghuth.

Outwalk, *v. a.* Fairtlich le coiseachd, imich ni 's luaithe, fàg air dheireadh.

Outwall, *s.* Balladh mach.

Outward, *a.* O 'n leth muigh, o 'n taobh a mach; eilthireach, an céin; a mach, mach; gu rioghachdan céin; corporra; feòlmhor. The ship is outward bound, *tha 'n luing a seoladh mach.*

Outwardly, *adv.* A muigh, a mach, o 'n leth muigh, o 'n taobh mach; a réir coslais.

Outwatch, *s.* Faire iomallach; faire a mach.

Outwatch, *v. a.* Fair tuille is fad.

Outwear, *v.* Caith a mach; mair ni 's fhaide no ni eile.

Outweed, *v. a.* Gart-ghlan.

Outweigh, *v.* Cothromaich, thoir an cothrom a. He will outweigh you, *bheir e 'n cothrom asad.*

Outweighed, *part.* Cothromaichte.

Outwit, *v. a.* Meall, thoir an car a. I outwitted him, *mheall mi e, thug mi 'n car as.*

Outwork, *s.* Obair a mach; obair iomallach.

Outworn, *part.* Caithte, air fannachadh, air toirt thairis.

Outwrought, *part.* Sàruichte, air fannachadh.

Oval, *a.* Ubhail, leth-chruinn, air chumadh uibhe.

Ovary, *s.* Machlag, bolg, balg.

Ovation, *s.* Caithream; leth-chaithream ro chumannta, am measg nan seans Roimheach.

Oven, *s.* Àmhuinn, uamhainn, sorn, greadag.

Over, *prep.* Os-cionn, os-ceann, thar, thair, thairis; tarsuing, trasda, traisd. Over the river, *thar an abhainn;* all the world over, *air fad an t-saoghail;* over me, *tharam;* over thee, *tharad;* over her, *thairte;* over us, *tharuinn;* over you, *tharuibh;* over them, *tharta.*

Over, *adv.* Os-cionn, thar a cheann; gu léir, o thaobh, gu taobh, ro, troimh. Over and above that, *a thuille air sin;* over what is just, *thuille na còrach;* over happy, *tuille is sona;* over and over, *thairis is thairis, iomad uair;* over much, *tuille is mo, tuille is a chòir;* over against, *mu choinneamh;* over against me, *mu m' choinneamh;* over against us, *mu 'r coinneamh;* it is all over, *tha e thairis;* it is all over with him, *tha e dheth;* the rain is over, *tha 'n t-uisge air teireachduinn;* the business is all over, *tha 'n gnothuch criochnuichte;* you are all over dirt, *tha thu air cur thairis le salchar;* over wise, *ro ghlic;* over heavy, *an-trom, tuille is trom;* give over, *leig dhiot, sguir, stad.*

Overabound, *v.* Cuir thairis, bi cur thairis.

Overact, *v.* Dean tuille is a chòir, dean iomarcach.

Overanxious, *a.* Ro-chùramach, tuille is cùramach.

Overawe, *v. a.* Cum fo, cum fo gheilt (no) fo smachd, cuir eagal air.

Overbalance, *v. a.* Cothromaich, thoir an cothrom a, an-tromaich.

Overbalancer, *s.* Cothrom; antruime.

Overbear, *v. a.* Foir-eignich, sàruich, claoidh, antromaich.

Overbearing, *a.* Foir-eigneach, fòirneartach, ainneartach; cruaidh.

Overbid, *v. a.* Tairg os-cionn, tairg tuille is a chòir, tairg thar neach eile.

Overblow, *v. a.* Séid air falbh.

Overboard, *adv.* Thar bord, thar luing.

Overbold, *a.* Beagnarach; ladurna, dàn, danarra.

Overburden, *v. a.* Luchdaich thar a chòir, an-tromaich, sàruich, an-luchdaich.

Overburden, *s.* An-luchd.

Overbuy, *v. a.* Ceannaich tuille is daor.

Overcast, *v.* Dorchaich, dubharaich.

Overcharge, *v.* (*Oppress*), sàruich, claoidh; (*fill*), sàsuich, lion gu sàth; (*load*), luchdaich; dean dearr làn; (*in price*), dean tuille is daor. Overcharged, *sàruichte; claoidhte; sasuichte; luchdaichte; dearr làn; tuille is daor.*

Overcloud, *v. a.* Dorchaich, dubharaich. Overclouded, *dorchaichte, dorch.*

Overcloy, *v. a.* Sàth, sàsuich, lion gu sàth. Overcloyed, *sàsuichte.*

Overcome, *v.* Sàruich, claoidh faigh lamh an uachdar, foireignich, fairtlich air, ceannsuich, thoir buaidh. He shall overcome, *bheir e buaidh.*

Overcome, *part.* Sàruichte, claoidhte, ceannsaichte, fo cheannsal, fo smachd, foireignichte.

Overcomer, *s.* Sàruchair, claoidhear, ceannsachair, ceannsair, smachdair.

Overcover, *v.* Còmhdaich.

Overdo, *v. a.* Dean tuille 's a chòir.

Overdress, *v.* Sgiamhaich, sgeadaich, breaghaich.

Overdrive, *v.* Cuir h-uige; iomain (no) greas tuille is luath, cuir thar a luathas.

Overeye, *v. a.* Amhairc, cum sùil air, beachdaich, gabh beachd, sgall air, coimhead.

Overfal, *s.* Spùt; eas.

Overfeed, *v. n.* Ith dunaidh, sàsuich, sàth, ith tuille is a chòir.

Overfloat, *v.* Snamh; bi plodanaich.

Overflow, *v. a.* Cuir thairis; sruth thairis; cuir fo le h-uisge.

Overflow, *s.* Cur thairis; lan-phailteas; tuil.

Overflowing, *s.* Làn-phailteas; cur thairis.

Overforward, *a.* Tuille is luath, tuille is grad; tuille is dàn.

Overforwardness, *s.* An-luathas, an dànadas.

Overfreight, *v. a.* An-luchdaich, an-tromaich.

Overfreight, *s.* An-luchd, an-eallach, an-truime.

Overget, *v. a.* Faigh, ruig, beir air.

Overglance, *v. a.* Thoir plath thairis, grad-sheall thar.

Overgo, *v. a.* Rach thairis, fàg, fairtlich, faigh barrachd.

Overgreat, *a.* Tuille is mòr.

Overgrow, *v.* Cinn (no) fàs gu h-anabarra; cinn thairis.

Overgrown, *a.* Mòr, tuille is mòr, domhail, dumhail: bairteach, saibhir.

Overgrowth, *s.* An-fhas.

Overhale, *v.* Feuch, sgrud, ceasnaich, ath-cheasnuich.

Overhang, *v. a.* and *n.* Croch thairis.

Overharden, *v.* Cruadhaich, dean tuille is cruaidh.

Overhead, *adv.* Gu h-ard, as airde, os-cionn.

Overhear, *v.* Cluinn, farcluaisich. I overheard him, *chual mi e.*

Overheat, *v. a.* Dean tuille is teth; fallasaich, cuir fo fhallus.
Overjoy, *v. a.* Lion le éibhneas. Overjoyed, *aobhinn, éibhinn.*
Overjoy, *s.* Aiteas, éibhneas, aoibhneas, mor-eibhneas.
Overlabour, *v. a.* Sàruich; saoithrich, oibrich gu h-anabharra. Over-laboured, *sàruichte.*
Overlade, *v. a.* Luchdaich, sàruich, an-luchdaich, antromaich. Overladen, *luchdaichte, antromaichte.*
Overlarge, *a.* Ro mhòr, tuille is mòr.
Overlay, *v. a.* Mùch; comhdaich, antromaich, luchdaich; dorchaich.
Overleap, *v. a.* Leum thairis; leum ni 's fhaide.
Overleather, *s.* Leathar nachdar, leathrach uachdar.
Overlive, *v. a.* Iar-mhair, mair beò ni 's fhaide.
Overload, *v. a.* An-luchdaich, an-tromaich.
Overlong, *a.* Tuille is fad.
Overlook, *v. a.* (*Inspect*), seall thairis; seall os airde; rannsuich, beachdaich, seall, amhairc thairis; cum sùil air; (*neglect*), dichuimhnich; na toir fanear, dearmad; (*pardon*), lagh, laghaich, math.
Overlooker, *s.* Fear coimheid, rannsuchair; griobh.
Overlooking, *s.* Sealladh thairis, coimhead; cùram; (*neglecting*), dearmad, dichuimhne, dio-chuimhne; (*pardoning*), mathadh, laghadh.
Overmaster, *v.* Fairtlich air, faigh lamh an uachdar, buadhaich, sàruich, claoidh.
Overmatch, *v.* Sàruich, claoidh, fairtlich air. Overmatched, *sàruichte, claoidhte.*
Overmost, *a.* Uachdrach, is uachdraiche.
Overmuch, *a.* Tuille is a chòir, anabarra, thuille na còrach.
Overname, *v. a.* Ainmich lion fear is fear.
Overnight, *s.* An deigh dhorchadh oidhche, san oidhche, feadh na h-oidhche, an deigh thuiteam oidhche.
Overofficious, *a.* Tuille is fritheilteach, ro-easgaidh, tuille is easgaidh, ro dheidheil.
Overpass, *v. a.* Rach thar, rach thairis, theirig thairis (no) seachad; dearmaid.
Overpast, *a.* Air dol seachad.
Overpay, *v. a.* Pàigh thuille na còrach, pàigh tuille is a chòir.
Overplus, *s.* Barrachd, corrlach, còrr, tuille is a chòir, barrachd; fuighleach, fuigheall, iarmad.
Overpoise, *v. a.* Cothromaich, thoir an cothrom a.
Overpower, *v.* Sàruich, claoidh, fairtlich air; éignich, fòireignich, foirneartaich.
Overpress, *v.* Saruich; bruth.
Overprize, *v. a.* Ana-meas, thoir an-luach, meas thar a luach.
Overreach, *v. a.* Meall, thoir an car a; éirich gu h-ard.
Overreacher, *s.* Slaoightear, mealltair.
Overread, *v.* Leugh.
Overripe, *a.* Tuille is abuich, an-abuich.
Overripen, *v. n.* Fàs anabuich (no) tuille is abuich.
Overrule, *v. a.* Riaghail, riaghlaich, cum fo smachd (no) fo riaghail, orduich.
Overrun, *v. a.* Sàruich, mill, dean fàs; sgaoil, comhdaich.
Oversee, *v. a.* Coimhead; cum sùil, gabh beachd.
Overseen, *part.* Meallta, ann am mearachd.
Overseer, *s.* Griobh, fear amhairc, fear coimheid, riaghlair, fear riaghlaidh, grainnsear.
Overseeing, *s.* Griobhachd; grainnsearachd.
Overset, *v. a.* and *n.* Tilg bun os-cionn, rach bun os-cionn, cuir thairis.
Overshade, *v. a.* Duibhrich, sgàilich, dorchaich.
Overshadow, *v. a.* Duibhrich, sgàilich, dorchaich, tilg dubhar (no) sgàile.
Overshoot, *v.* Tilg thairis, tilg ni 's fhaide.
Oversight, *s.* Amharc; cùram; (*neglect*), dearmad, dichuimhne, mearachd, cion omhaill.
Overskip, *v.* Leum thairis.
Oversleep, *v. n.* Codail tuille is fad.
Overslip, *v. a.* Dearmaid, dichuimhnich, dean dichuimhne, leig air dearmad (no) air dichuimhne.
Oversoon, *a.* Tuille is luath, ro luath, tuille is moch, tuille is tràthail.
Overspent, *part.* Sgìth, fannaichte, air fannachadh, air toirt thairis, sàruichte.
Overspread, *v. a.* Sgaoil, comhdaich, spréid.
Overstock, *v. a.* Lion tuille is lan, sàth; an-lion, domhlaich, dumhlaich.
Oversway, *v. a.* Ceannsaich, cum fo smachd, cum an ordugh.
Overt, *a.* Fosgailte, follais, follaiseach.
Overtake, *v. a.* Beir air, thig suas ri. I overtook them, *bheir mi orra.*
Overtask, *v.* Claoidh, tràillich, sàruich.
Overthrow, *v. a.* Fairtlich air, sgrios, mill, thoir buaidh, sàruich.
Overthrow, *s.* Léireadh, sgrios, milleadh ruaig; teicheadh; teicheachd.
Overthwart, *prep.* Tarsuing, trasd, crosgach air.
Overtly, *adv.* Gu follais, gu follaiseach.
Overtop, *v. a.* Éirich os-cionn; faigh barrachd.
Overture, *s.* Fosgladh; tairgse, tairgsinn.
Overturn, *v.* Tilg sios, leig sios, tilg bun os-cionn; mill, léir-sgrios, ruaig.
Overvalue, *v.* Ana-meas, meas thar a luach.
Overweak, *a.* An-fhann, an-mhunn, ro lag.
Overween, *v. a.* Bi dòchasach (no) ard-bharaileach.
Overweening, *a.* Dochasach, baraileach, ard-bharaileach, faoin-dhochasach.
Overweigh, *v. a.* Cothromaich, thoir an cothrom a.
Overwhelm, *v. a.* Sàruich, claoidh; comhdaich.
Overwise, *a.* Ro-ghlic, tuille is glic, muth 's glic.
Overworn, *part.* Caithte; ana-caithte, glan-chaithte, tur-chaithte.
Overwrought, *a.* Sàruichte, tràillichte.
Overzealous, *a.* Tuille is dian.
Oviform, *a.* Ubhail, leth-chruinn.
Oviparous, *a.* Ubh-bhreitheach.
Owe, *v. a.* Bi 'm fiachaibh, bi 'n comain. He owes me money, *tha airgiod agam air;* I owe him money, *tha airgiod aig orm;* I have paid what I owed you, *phàigh mi na bh' agad orm;* do I owe any thing, *bheil dad agad orm.*
Owing, *a.* Ann am fiachaibh; coireach. This mischief is owing to you, *is tusa is coireach airson an uile so.*
Owl, Owlet, *s.* Cailleach oidhche, coileach oidhche, comhachag, sgreachag oidhche, sgreachag reilge; corra-sgreachag.
Owler, *s.* Ciot charuiche, cùl mhutair; *smuglair.*
Own, *s.* Féin, fhéin, *and* sa, se, san, na, *we put after the substantive.* Thy own hand, *do lamh-sa féin;* their own hands, *an lamhan-san féin;* our own house, *air tigh-ne féin;* their ownselves, *iadsan féin; leo féin;* one's own goods, *cuid neach féin;* it is she her own self, *is ise féin a th' ann;* of my own accord, *do mo dheòin.*

Own, *v a* (*Confess*), aidich, aidmhich; (*possess*), sealbhaich; (*acknowledge*), gabh ri. Owned, *aidichte*, *ardmhichte*; *sealbhaichte*.

Owner, *s*. Sealbhadair, fear seilbhe.

Ownership, *s* Sealbhachadh, seilbhe, còire.

Owning, *s*. Sealbhachadh, aideachadh; gabhail ri.

Owre, *s*. Seorsa beothaich.

Ox, *s* Damh, tarbh spoghte; crodh; mart; fearb, bò. Oxen, *daimh*

Ox-fly, *s*. Creadhail Ox-flies, *creadhlaichean*

Oxgang (of land), *s*. Fichead achdair

Ox-stale, *s*. Mainnir dhamh, bothigh, bàthaich.

Ox-tongue, *s*. Bog lus

Oxygen, *s* Aile bheathail, beath-àile

Oxymel, *s* Deoch mhil is fhiongheur

Oyer, *s* Seorsa cùirt lagha

Oyes! *interj* Thugaibh an aire! èisdibh!

Oyster, *s* Eisirean, faoch, faochag

Oyster-wench, **Oyster-woman**, *s*. Caile eisirean, bean eisirean, bansgal.

Ozæna, *s* Polla-ghuirean, guirean breun a chinneas ann an cuinneanaibh na sròn.

P.

P. An seathamh litir deug do 'n aibideal

Pabular, *a*. Biathar, biadhar, biathmhor, biadhchar, biathachail, feurach

Pabulation, *s* Biathadh, beathachadh, feurachadh

Pabulum, *s*. Biadh, lòn, teachd an tìr

Pace, *s*. Ceum, sinteag, cois-cheum; trosdan, tri troidhean, imeachd; (*of asses*), drobh

Pace, *v. n.* Ceum, ceumnaich, gluais gu socrach (no) ceum air cheum, tomhais le sinteagan; sinteagaich, (*as a horse*), falairich. Slow-paced, *mall-cheumnach*, *socrach*, *athaiseach*, *càileanta*

Pacer, *s*. Falair, each a bheir ceum goirrid.

Pacific, *a*. Siochail, ciùin, seimh, samhach, siothchaintеach.

Pacification, *s*. Ciùnachadh.

Pacificator, *s*. Ciùnadair, fear dheanamh sìth

Pacifier, *s*. Sìothchaiche; ciùnadair, fear ciùnachaidh, fear siothchath

Pacify, *v. a* Ciùnaich, ciùinich, siochaich, socraich, coisg. Pacified, *ciùinichte*, *samhach*, *tosd*, *sìth*, *coisgte*

Pack, *s* Pac, pacaid, trusachan, trusgan, paisgean, ulltach, eallach; màileid, ceanglachan, buindeal; (*of dogs*), lomhainn chon A pack of cards, *pac no stoc chairtean*, (*a pack or crew*), bannal, cuideachd, lòd, gràisg

Pack, *v a*. Pacainn, trus, ceangail suas, paisg Pack off, *bi falbh*, *trus ort*, *tog ort*, packed up, *pacainnte*, *ceangailte suas*, *trusta*, *paisgte*.

Packcloth, *s*. Aodach pacainn, aodach pasgaidh

Packer, *s* Fear trusaidh, pacair, paisgear.

Packet, *s*. Pacaid; trusag, trusgan, cuairsgean, post-long, long litreach, bàt-aisig.

Packhorse, *s*. Each eallaich, each màileid

Packing, *s*. Pacainn, trusadh, pasgadh, ceangladh suas

Packsaddle, *s*. Srathair; pillean, sumag

Packthread, *s*. Sgéinnidh, snathainn ceanglaidh, snáth pacainn.

Pact, *s*. Bargan, cùmhnant, cumhadh, cunradh, cordadh

Paction, *s* Bargan, cùmhnant, cunradh, cumhadh, cordadh.

Pactitious, *a* Cumhnantaichte, barganaichte, sonraichte

Pad, *s* (*Road*), rad, rathad, rod, slighe, frith-rod, casan, (*soft saddle*), pillean, sumag; (*pillows*), boghsdair, cluasag, (*horse*), falair, gearran, gearran socrach, (*footpad*), robair, reubair, slighe-robair, spùinneadair, creachadair

Pad, *v*. Falbh (no) imich gu socrach; spùinn, spùill, robainn, creach.

Padder, *s*. Spùinneadair, robair, creachadair.

Paddle, *v. a* Luinneanaich, luinnearaich, plodanaich, dean plubais (no) pluisrich, iomair

Paddle, *s* Seorsa raimh Innseanaich; ramh beag, pleadhan

Paddling, *s* Plodanachd, pluisrich.

Paddock, *s* Màigean, smàigean, losgan, muile-mhàg, pairc fhiadh

Paddock-stool, *s* Bonaid an losgainn

Padlock, *s*. Glas-chrochaidh

Pad-nag, *s* Fàlair

Pæan, *s* Oran buaidh, buaidh-chaithream

Pagan, *s*. Ana-criosduigh, ana-creideach, neo-chreideach, pàganach, geintileach, gintealach

Paganism, *s* Ana-criosdachd

Page, *s* Taobh duilleig, duil-thaobh, gille frithealaidh.

Pageant, *s* Sgiamh; breaghachd, briaghachd; scalladh riomhach

Pageant, *a* Sgiamhach, breagh, fàicheil, mòralach, spagluinneach.

Pageantry, *s* Riomhachd, breaghachd, gloiream, sgòideas, grinneas, riomhadh, mòr-chuiseachd

Pagod, *s* Iodhal Innseanach; teampull Innseanach; teampull iodhalach

Paid, *pret* and *p part* of pay Phàigh; dhiol; pàighte

Pail, *s* Cuinneag, measair, ciotadh, tuban A milk-pail, *cuinneag bhleoghainn*, *gogan*, *curusan*.

Pailful, *s* Làn cuinneig; làn gogain

Pailmail, *s* Dian

Pain, *s*. Pian, goimh; gum, beug, biogadh, goirteas, treathaid, dòlas, cradh; craon, amhghar, peanas; (*in the plural*), piantan; saothair, dragh; (*of childbed*), saothair chloinne: tinneas cloinne The pain has abated, *tha 'm pian air traghadh*, full of pain, *làn péin*, great pains, *mòran saothair*, take pains on it, *gabh saothair air*, you take pains to no purpose, *tha thu 'toirt do shaothair an diomhanas*, did you get the value of your pains? *an d' fhuair thu fiach do shaothaireach?*

Pain, *v a* Pian, cradh, craidh, claoidh, cuir gu pian, ciurr, goirtich; craon, guin

Painful, *a*. Goirt, piantachail, cràiteach, claoidhteach, dòlasach, treathaideach, beugach; craonach; (*difficult*), deacair, duilich, draghail, (*laborious*), saothaireachail, dicholllach, oidhirpeach

Painfully, *adv* Gu goirt, gu piantachail, gu cràiteach, gu claoidhteach, gu dòlasach.

Painfulness, *s* (*Of mind*), sprochd, dòlas, bròn, (*exertion*), saothair, dichioll, oidhirpeachd

Painim, *s* Anacreideach, pàganach.

PAINSTAKER, s Fear-saothaireachail.

PAINSTAKING, a. Saoithreachail, saothaireachail, saothaireach, a gabhail saothair, dichiollach, oidhirpeach.

PAINT, v Dath; ligh, dealbh, dathaich, neulaich; cinnmhiol; croinic, (*beautify*), nàisnich, grinnich, sgiamhaich; (*a picture*), tarruing. Painted, *dathta, dathte.*

PAINT, s. Dath, ligh, neul, tuar, deann, cinnmhiol.

PAINTER, s Dathadair; dealbhair, fear tarruing

PAINTING, s (*The action of*), dealbhadh; tarruing, cinnmhiolladh, croiniceachd, (*a picture*), dealbh

PAIR, s. Paidhir, càraid, deise, dithis, cupall; coingir A pair of gloves, *paidhir lamhuinnean*, a faithful pair, *caraid dhìleas*, a pair of pistols, *paidhir dhagaichean*, they came in pairs, *thainig iad nam paidhrichean*

PAIR, v a Paidhrich, caraidich, cuplaich, cuir an càraidibh, cuir cuideachd; diong

PALACE, s Pailiunn, luth-chuirt, luth-chairt, mùr, dùnlios, righ-lann, breas-lann

PALACIOUS, a Rìaghail, riomhach

PALANQUIN, s Cathair iomchar Innseanach air a giùlan le traillibh

PALATABLE, a Blasda, taitneach, milis

PALATE, s Uachdar beoil, càirean; blas

PALATINATE, s Duthaich rioghail

PALATINE, s Fear aig am bheil coirichean rioghail

PALATINE, a Rioghail

PALE, a Bàn, glàs, glasdaidh, odhar, gorm, uaine, smeileach, do-neoil; neo-shoilleir. A pale face, *aghaidh bhan* (no) *ghlas*

PALE, s Cliath, post; dion-phost; speac; fàl, fàl-gleuta, duthaich

PALE, v Duin steach, druid, callaid, callaidich, iomdhruid, cuairtich, dùin le cleathaibh

PALEFACED, a Bàn, glas, glasdaidh

PALELY, adv Gu bàn, gu glas, gu glasdaidh

PALENESS, s. Bàine, bàinead, glaise, glasdachd, glasdaidheachd, cion-rughadh Increasing in paleness, *a dol am bàinead*

PALFREY, s Each beag bain-tighearna, fàlair, gearran

PALINDROME, s Focal a tha ionnan co aca a leughar e air ais no air adhairt, mar am focall beurla *madam*

PALINODE, s Atharrachadh, iompachadh.

PALING, s Callaid, fàl

PALISADE, PALISADO, s Dion-phuist, callaid

PALISH, a Glasdaidh, leth char bàn.

PALL, s Dubh-bhrat, brat dubh, brat mairbh, righ-fhaluing; fàluing (no) gùn easbuig; clòc, cleoc; suanach; peall, peallag

PALL, v a. and n. Cleòc, comhdaich, fàluingich, fàluinnich, fas mi-bhlasda (no) domblasda; anfhannaich, sàsaich

PALLED, a (*Dead*), marbh, domblasda

PALLET, s Leabaidh bheag shuarach, uiridh, uirigh; leabaidh sheistear, seid

PALLIAMENT, s Fàluing, eididh, brat, comhdach

PALLIATE, v a Ciùranaich; dion, gabh leith-sgeul, leithsgeulaich, folaich, falaich, ceil; comhdaich; lughdaich, leigheis; eutromaich

PALLIATION, s Dionadh, lughadachadh (mar choire), leithsgeul, leigheasadh, eutromachadh

PALLIATIVE, a Dionach, leithsgeulach, lughadachail; leigheasach, lasuchail.

PALLIATIVE, s. Leigheas, nì sam bith a bheir lasuchadh, leigheas lasuchaidh.

PALLID, a Bàn, glas, glasdaidh; do-neulach, odhar

PALLMALL, s. Àite airson cluich air bhall.

PALM, s. (*Of the hand*), bos, bois, bas, dearn, dearnadh; (*tree*), pailm, crann pailm; (*breadth of the hand*), leud bois, tri oirlich; (*victory*), buaidh.

PALM, v. a. Folaich sa bhois, meall, thoir an car a; cniataich

PALMER, s. Pailmear; taisdealaiche a philleadh a tìr Chanàin a giùlan meanglain pailm

PALMETTO, s Seorsa pailm.

PALMIFEROUS, a. Pailmeach, pailmidh.

PALMIPEDE, a Cas-leathann, spleagh-chosach mar thunnaig

PALMISTER, s Dearnadair, lamh-dhruidh.

PALMISTRY, s Dearnadaireachd

PALMY, a Pailmidh, pailmeach

PALPABLE, a Ion-mhothachaidh; ion-mhothuchail, garbh, so-fhaineach, soilleir, riachdail. A palpable proof, *dearbh soilleir.*

PALPABLY, adv. Gu h-ion-mhothuchaidh; gu soilleir, gu riachdail

PALPITATE, v n Plosg, frithbhuail, plosgartaich My heart palpitates, *tha mo chridhe sa phlosgail* (no) *sa phlosgartaich*

PALPITATION, s Plosgadh, plosgail, plosgartaich; bualadh, frith-bhualadh Palpitation of the heart, *plosgail cridhe, biogadh*

PALSGRAVE, s. Flath aig am bheil curam pailiuinn righ.

PALSIED, a. Parailiseach.

PALSY, s. Crith-ghalar, parailis.

† PALTER, v a. and n Dean slaoighte (no) cealg; caith, ana-caith, struidh

† PALTERER, s Mealltair, slaoightear.

PALTRINESS, s Suarraichead, suarrachas, truaillidheachd, diblidheachd, crìne, sgroingeanachd; fadharsachd.

PALTRY, a Suarrach, dìblidh, truagh, truaillidh, crion, sgroingeanach, gun diù, fadharsach

PALY, a. Ban, glas, glasdaidh, odhar.

PAMPER, v Lion, sàth, sàsuich; sathaich, giorr; lion le biadh 's le deoch Pampered, *sàsuichte, sathach, buidheach bidh, beadarach*

PAMPHLET, s Leabharan, leabhar fuaidhte, paimhleid; duilleachan.

PAMPHLETEER, s Paimhleidiche.

PAN, s Aghann; panna; Dia bréig nan coilltean The knee-pan, *falman a ghlùin*, a warming-pan, *greadair*, a frying-pan, *griosair*

PANACEA, s Uile ice

PANADA, PANADO, s Aran air a bhruich ann uisge, easach.

PANCAKE, s. Caraiceag, breacag, bonnag, bannag, bannagan, pannag

PANCREAS, s. Brisgean milis

PANCY, s Seorsa plùraın

PANDECT, s. Tur-oilean, tur-oideas; leabhar anns am bheil air an cur sios baraılean agus breathnasan nan sean luchdlagha.

PANDEMIC, a. Coitchionn, cumanta, cumaint.

PANDER, s. Drùisear, trusdar, druith-bhlosgair, druith-mhangair, druis-bhalaoch.

PANDERISM, s Drùisearachd, drùith-mhangaireachd.

PANDERLY, a. Drùisear, drùiseach, druith-mhangach

PANE, s Cearnag ghloine; gloine uinneig.

PANEGYRIC, s. Moladh, cliù; duan molaidh, brasailt, direadh

Panegyrical, *a.* Moladach, moltainneach.

Panegyrist, *s.* Moladair, fear molaidh.

Pang, *s.* Goimh, cradh, pian, craon, doruinn, uspag, ospag, peilghuin. The pangs of death, *ospagan a bhàis.*

Pang, *v. a.* Pian, craidh, cradh; craon, goimh, goin

Panic, *s.* Grad-eagal, grad-mhaoidhm, eagal gun chionfath.

Pannel, *s* Pillean, sumag, braiceam

Pannier, *s.* Cliabh, curran, croidhle, bascaid, sgùlean, pasgart.

Panoply, *s* Armachd.

Pant, *v n.* Plosg, sèitrich, àinich, gabh ro-fhadail, bi an ro-dheigh, bi an càs airson ni

Pant, *s.* Plosgadh, plosgail, plosgartaich.

Pantaloon, *s.* Triubhas, brigis fhad; baoth-chleasaiche

Pantheon, *s.* Teampull nan uile-Dhé

Panther, *s* Uilbheist bhallach mhillteach

Panting, *s* Plosgail, plosgartaich

Pantler, *s.* Fear pantraidh (no) air am bheil cùram arain teaghlaich.

Pantofle, *s* Cuaran, bròg gun iall.

Pantomime, *s* Balbh-chluiche

Pantry, *s* Pantair, pantraidh; lanntair, biadh-lann, biadh-thaisg, seileir bidh; ioslann They have struck her head against the pantry, *bhuail iad a ceann air an amraidh*

Pap, *s.* Cioch, sinne; biadh leinibh.

Papa, *s* Athair, ainm leinibh airson 'athar; boban; am Pàp.

Papacy, *s.* Pàpanachd.

Papal, *a* Pàpail; pàpanach.

Paper, *s.* Paipeir. Writing-paper, *paipeir sgriobhaidh, paipeir geal*, brown paper, *paipeir donn*, a newspaper, *paipeir nuaidheachd.*

Paper, *a.* Tan; faoin.

Paper, *v* Paipeirich, comhdaich le paipeir

Paper-maker, *s.* Fear dheanamh paipeir.

Paper-mill, *s* Muileann paipeir.

Papilio, *s.* Dealman dé, dealbh an dé

Papist, *s* Pàpanach.

Papistical, *a.* Pàpanach.

Papistry, *s* Pàpanachd, a chreidimh Roimheach

Pappy, *a.* Bog, bogar, sùghar, sùghmhor, brighmhor

Par, *s* Ionannachd, co-ionannachd

Parable, *s* Samhladh, coslas, co-samhlachd, comhadadh.

Parabolic, **Parabolical**, *a* Samhlachail, co-shamhlachail, comhadail

Parabolically, *adv* Gu samhlachail

Paracentric, *a* Neo-chruinn.

Parachronism, *s.* Mearrachd ann an cunntas aimsir

Paraclete, *s* An Comh-fhurtair.

Parade, *s* Lòiseam airm; fearas-mhòr; bòsd, spagluinn, riomhadh, mor-chuis, breaghachd, aite spaisdearachd, fàiche, raon

Paradigm, *s.* Samplair, samhladh, cosamhlachd, eiseimpleir.

Paradise, *s* Pàras, flaitheas, flaitheanas.

Paradox, *s.* Baoth-bharail, baoth-bheachd, frith-bharail, barail an aghaidh coslais

Paradoxical, *a.* Baoth-bharaileach.

Paragon, *s.* Sampull, samplair, eiseimpleir, samhladh; dearbh-chompanach; leth-bhreac.

Paragraph, *s.* Earann, earann air leth, roinn

Parallel, *s.* Lìn direach, sgrioch dhìreach, easbanach; lìn air druim na cruinne a comharrachadh mach an leudad, samhladh, eugas, coslas, coimeas, cosamhlachd Run a parallel, *samhlaich*, he is without parallel, *tha e gun choimeas.*

Parallel, *a* Co-dhìreach, co-ionann, easbanach.

Parallel, *v. a* Cum co-dhìreach, dean comhad, samhluich, coimeas.

Parallelogram, *s.* Cearnag aig am bheil a taobhan a tha mu chomhar chéile, co-dhìreach, agus co-ionann

Paralogism, *s* Barail bhreugach, barail chearr

Paralysis, *s* Crith-ghalar, parailis

Paralytic, **Paralytical**, *a* Crith-ghalarach, parailiseach.

Paralyse, *v. a* Marbh, funntainn, dean gun chlì

Paramount, *a* Priomh, os cionn, ni 's cudthromaiche

Paramour, *s* Leannan, ceistean, graidhean, gaol, gaolach, co-chéilidh, céile, coi' leabaich

Paranymph, *s.* Fleasgach bean bainnse.

Parapet, *s* Obair uchd, barra-bhalladh.

Paraphernalia, *s.* Maoin (no) codach inna

Paraphimosis, *s* Breall

Paraphrase, *s.* Mìneacheadh, soilleireachadh.

Paraphrase, *v.* Mìnich, soilleirich, soillsich.

Paraphrast, *s.* Mìneachair, fear mìneachaidh

Parapluie, *s* Fasgadan

Parasite, *s* Sodalaiche, fear miodal, miodalaiche, beadaidhean, goilean, miolcair.

Parasitic, **Parasitical**, *a* Sodalach, miodalach.

Parasol, *s* Sgàilean, sgàilean gréin, grian-sgàile, grian sgàilean

Parboil, *v a.* Leth bhruich Parboiled, *leth-bhruich, leth-bhruith*

Parcel, *s.* Trusachan, trusgan, aslachan, achlas, achlasan; trusag; dorlach, ceanglachan, paisgean.

Parcel, *v a* Trus, ceangail, paisg; roinn; earannaich

Parch, *v a* and *n* Gread, searg, doth, tiormaich; cruaidhich Parched, *searg te, dothte, tiormaichte, tioram, cruadhaichte*, parched corn, *greadan, gradan, grùn gradan*

Parchedness, *s* Tiormachd, tirime, pathadh

Parchment, *s* Croiceann sgriobhaidh, meamhran, meamran

Pard, **Pardale**, *s* Liobard, uile bheist ballach sam bi. Bearded like the pard, *ròmach mar an liobard*

Pardon, *v. a* Math, maith, lagh, laghaich, thoir maitheanas Pardon me, *maith dhomh, gabh mo leithsgeul*

Pardon, *s.* Mathanas, maitheanas, laghadh Ask pardon, *iarr maitheanas*, I beg your pardon, *tha mi 'g iarruidh maitheanais ort*, delay to the wicked is not a pardon, *ge dàil do fhear an uile cha dearmad*

Pardonable, *a* Ion-mhathadh, ion-laghadh, so-mhathadh; so-laghadh

Pardoner, *s* Fear a bheir maitheanas do neach eile

Pare, *v a.* Sgath, sgrath, lom, snaidh, bearr, beagaich, gearr, sgròillich, sgriob. Pared, *sgathta, snaidhte, bearrta*

Parent, *s* Ginitear, pàrant, athair (no) màthair

Parentage, *s* Cinneadh, gineadh, ginealach, muinntir

Parental, *a.* Ginitearach, pàrantach, parantail.

Parget, *s.* Aol-phlàsd, plàsd aoil

Pargeter, *s* Aol-phlasdair, aol-phlasdaiche, plàsdair

Parhelion, *s* Sgàil-ghrian

Parietal, *a* Ballach, ballaidh, ballail; leth-cheannach The parietal bone, *cnaimh an leth-cheann*

PARING, *s* Rùsg, rùsgadh, sgrath, sgathach, plaosg. (*of wood*), sliseagan; sliseag, slisneach, cairt

PARISH, *s.* Sgìreachd, paraisd

PARISH, *a* Sgìreachdail, paraisdeach

PARISHIONER, *s* Fear sgìreachd. Parishioners, *luchd* (*no*) *muinntir sgìreachd*

PARITOR, *s* Beadal

PARITY, *s* Ionannachd, cosmhalachd, coslas, eugas

PARK, *s* Pàirc; garaidh, lann-gleuta, seachlag, cluain, fearann cuairtichte, cròidhlean chaorach

PARK, *v a* Dùin, drùid, fàl, pàircich

PARKER, *s* Pàircear, fear pàirc

PARLEY, *s* Comhradh, conbharsaid, fosadh airm, eineach

PARLIAMENT, *s* Ard-chomhairle, comhdhail, seanait, parlamaid Is i parlamaid Bhreatuinn, co-chruinneachadh *thrì inbhean* na rìoghachd, is iad sin, an iar-fhlathachd, a chléir, agus luchd ionad na tuath, chum gnothuichibh na rìoghachd a chur gu doigh, agus chum reachdan a dheanamh.

PARLIAMENTARY, *a* Seanaiteach, parlamaideach

PARLOUR, *s* Pronn-lios, seomar na drotha, paralus

PARLOUS, *a* Geur, guasachdach, cealgach, carach, cuilcagach

PARLOUSNESS, *s* Geire, geurad, cealg; car

PAROCHIAL, *a* Sgìreachd; sgìreachdail, paraisteach, pairisteach

PAROLE, *s* Focal

PAROXYSM, *s* Tinneannas, airde tinneis, brais, taom, athphilleadh, greis

PARODY, *s.* Baoth-dhuan

PAROLE, *s.* Focall, briathar, onoir, gealladh

PARONYCHIA, *s* Gath tearradh

PARONYMOUS, *a.* Aon-chiallach, ionann ann an ciall

PAROQUET, *s* Piorraid. Paroquets, *piorraidean*

PAROTID, *a* Seileach, smugaideach

PARRICIDE, *s* Mortair athar (no) mathar, dubh-mhortair, mortadh pàranta; fionnghail.

PARROT, *s* Piorraid

PARRY, *v a* Cuir gu taobh, seachain, cum o, cuni air falbh; basbairich

PARSE, *v a* Pairtich Parsed, *pairtichte*

PARSIMONIOUS, *a* Crion, crionnta, caonntach, cruaidh, cruadalach, spìocach, sanntach, gleatach A parsimonious female, *crìontag*.

PARSIMONIOUSLY, *adv* Gu crion, gu crionnta, gu caonntach, gu cruaidh, gu cruadalach, gu spìocach, gu sanntach, gu gleatach, gu grunndail

PARSIMONIOUSNESS, *s* Crìne crìontachd, caonntachd, spìocaireachd

PARSIMONY, *s.* Crìne, caonntach, caomhnadh, cruadhas, cruadal, spìoc, spìocaireachd, sannt, sanntachd, gìon, grunndalas, fearachas tighe, bèanachas tighe

PARSLEY, *s* Pearsal, peirseal

PARSNIP, *s* Curran geal, meacan

PARSON, *s.* Sagart, ministear, minisdear, pears' eaglais

PARSONAGE, *s* Tigh sagairt, tigh minisdeir

PART, *s*, Pàirt, roinn, cuibhrionn, cuid, earann; mìr, taobh, (*duty*), dleasdanas, gnothuch Take his part, *cum taobh ris*, take in good part, *gabh gu math*, take in bad part, *gabh gu dona*, *gabh gu h-olc*, *gabh gu soitheach*, for the most part, *mar is tric*, *un cumantas*, the fore part of the house, *beulaobh* (*no*) *taobh a' bheoil an tighe*, back part, *culaobh* (*no*) *taobh ar chuil*, as for my part, *air mo shonsa*, *air mo shonsa dheth*, on the other part, *air an lamh eile*, in part, *an cuid*, parts, *càilean*, *feartan*, the parts, *na bhuill dhiomhair*, in some parts, *ann an cuid dh' àitean*

PART, *v* Roinn; riaraich; dealaich; pàirtich; sgar, eadarsgar, cuir as a chéile. They parted it amongst them, *roinn* (*no*) *riaraich iad eatorra e*, part it in two, *dean dà leth dheth*, part with him, *dealaich ris*, part from, *fàg*, *cuir cùl ri tréig*.

PORTABLE, *a* So-roinn, so-riarachadh, so-dhealachadh.

† PARTAGE, *s* Roinn, cuibhrionn, pàirt, cuid.

PARTAKE, *v a* and *n*. Faigh cuid, faigh pairt, gabh (no) faigh comaidh; co-phairtich; roinn; roinn-phairtich. He partook of it, *fhuair sinn comaidh dheth.*

PARTAKER, *s* Fear co-phairt, fear-roinn; fear comaidh rann phairtiche, roinn-phairtiche; fear comh-roinn, companach.

PARTER, *s* Fear dealachaidh, fear eadargainn.

PARTERRE, *s.* Gàraidh phlùran.

PARTIAL, *a.* Leth-bhreitheach, claon bhreitheach, neochothromach, neo-cheart, fiar, fallsa, fallsaidh; neo-iomlan, neo-choitchionn

PARTIALITY, *s.* Leth-bhreith, claon-bhreith; claonaiseachd.

PARTIALLY, *adv* Gu leth-bhreitheach, gu claon-bhreitheach, gu neo-chothromach, gu neo-cheart, gu fiar, gu fallsa.

PARTIBLE, *a* So-phairteachadh, so-dhealachadh, so-roinn, so-riarachadh, a ghabhas pàirteachadh, a ghabhas dealachadh, a ghabhas riarachadh, a dh' fhaotar pàirteachadh (no) dealachadh, a dh' fhaotar riarachadh.

PARTICIPABLE, *a.* So-phàirteachadh, so-roinn, a ghabhas pàirteachadh (no) roinn

PARTICIPATE, *v a* and *n* Co-phàirtich, bairig, gabh pairt, faigh cuid (no) pàirt, faigh (no) gabh comaidh He participated in the praise, *fhuair e' chuid do 'n mhol;* participated, *co-phairtichte*

PARTICIPATION, *s.* Gabhail (no) faotainn cuid (no) pàirt, co-phairteachadh, bairigeadh, rann-phairt, comh-roinn, comaidh, cuibhrionn.

PARTICIPLE, *s.* Rann-phairt, comh-roinn.

PARTICOLOURED, *a* Breac, ballach, cadath, iol-dhathach, ioma-dathach

PARTICLE, *s* Ponc; earann bheag; smad, smùirnean, dadum.

PARTICULAR, *a* Araid, àraid, àraidh, sonruichte, aonda; pongail, sicir, neonach, iongantach; rudach A particular person, *urr àraidh*, *neach àraidh*, in particular, *gu h-àraidh*, *gu h-araid.*

PARTICULAR, *s* Ni, rud, cùis

PARTICULARITY, *s* Sònrachas; neonachas

PARTICULARIZE, *v. a* Ainmich, innis gu poncail, sonraich, feuch gu poncail

PARTICULARLY, *adv* Gu sonruichte, gu h-àraidh, gu h-araid, gu h-iongantach

PARTING, *s* Dealach, dealachadh, eadar-dhealach, sgaradh. The parting cup, *deoch an doruis*

PARTISAN, *s* Ailbeart, fear còghnaidh, taobhaiche, randach, ceann-feadhna

PARTITION, *s.* Dealach, dealachadh, balladh; dealachaidh; speinnse, clàraidh, callaid; sgioth, roinn, lantair. A partition wall, *fraigh*, *lan'air.*

PARTITION, *v a.* Dealaich, eadar-dhealaich, cuir eadar, sgar.

PARTLET, *s* Ainm airson circe

PARTLY, *adv* Ann an cuid; ann am pàirt.

PARTNER, *s* Companach, fear pàirt, caidreamh, (*in dancing*), co-dhamhsair; ban-chompanach.

PARTNERSHIP, *s.* Companas, compantas, comh-roinn, comhrannaich, cuideachd, co-chuideachd, bannal In partnership, *ann an comh-roinn*

Partook. See **Partake.**

Parturient, *a.* Làn leth-tromach.

Partridge, *s.* Cearc thomain, peirleag. Partridges, *cearcan tomain.*

Parturition, *s.* Breith cloinne, beirsinn cloinne, aisead.

Party, *s.* Cuideachd, coisridh, pàirtidh, buidheann, bannal; (*faction*), taobh; aimhreit. A party of pleasure, *cuideachd aigheir;* I am of the same party with you, *tha mi do 'n aon taobh riutsa;* a party of soldiers, *buidheann* (*no*) *bannal shaighdeara;* (*at law*), tagrair, no neach aig lagh ri neach eile; (*a party or person*), urr, neach.

Partyman, *s.* Fear aimhreiteach, fear pàirtidh.

Partywall, *s.* Balladh dealachaidh, balladh eadargain.

Parvis, *s.* Eaglais, ailear eaglais.

Pas, *s.* Còir toiseachaidh, ceum toisich, toiseach.

Paschal, *a.* Càisg, càisgeil. The paschal lamb, *uan na càisg.*

Pash, *s.* Aghaidh, eudann, aodann.

Pash, *v. a.* Buail, straoidhil, slachduinn, stear, bruith.

Pasquin, **Pasquinade**, *s*, Baoth-rann, baoth-rannachd.

Pass, *s.* (*Road*), bealach; caol-ghleann, slighe agus craig air a da thaobh; (*condition*), inmhe, inbhe, staid, cor; (*passport*), comas, cead, triall-chomas; (*in fencing*), sàthadh, ionnsuidh. Are you come to that pass? *bheil thu air teachd chum na h-inbhe sin?*

Pass, *v. a.* and *n.* Rach seach, rach seachad, gabh seachad, rach air adhairt, gabh air adhairt; rach thairis; rach thar, folbh, falbh; imich; teirig, thig gu crìch; bi thairis; sàth, thoir ionnsuidh. He passed the river, *chaidh e thar* (*no*) *chroisg e 'n amhuinn;* he passed [forded] the river, *chaidh e troimh 'n amhainn;* pass *or* filter, *sioladh;* pass *or* neglect, *dearmaid, dearmadaich, dichuimhnich;* pass *or* excel, *thoir barrachd, fairtlich air;* pass away, *caith, teirig, sguir, rach thairis;* send from place to place, *cuir o aite, gu h-àite;* pass by *or* excuse, *gabh leithsgeul, leith-sgeulaich;* pass your time, *caith d' aimsir, caith d' ùine;* pass a month, *cuir seachad* (*no*) *caith mios;* the beauty of the world passeth away, *falbhaidh sgiamh air t-saoghail, theid sgiamh an t-saoghail thairis;* pass under examination, *rach fo sgrudadh;* let pass, *leig seachad.*

Passable, *a.* So-thrialladh, so-choiseachadh, so-imeachd a ghabhas trialladh, a ghabhas coiseachd (no) imeachd; so-fhulang; (*tolerable*), an eatorras, an iarruidh, eadar an dà chuid.

Passado, *s.* Sath, sàthadh, starradh, puc, stobadh, gonadh.

Passage, *s.* (*Road*), tùrus, rod, rathad, slighe; dorus; (*of a river*), aiseag; (*of a book*), roinn, earann.

Passed. See **Pass.**

Passenger, *s.* Fear tùrais, fear triall, tùrasaiche, fear gabhail rathaid, taisdealaiche; (*by a boat*), fear aisig; luchd aisig.

Passer, *s.* Fear triall, fear tùrais, tùrusaiche, taisdealaiche, fear gabhail an rathaid.

Passible, *a.* Cuimheasach, ion-fhulang.

Passing, *a.* (*Excellent*), barrachdail; sàr, corr; ro, fior, mòr, òirdheirc. Passing wonder, *sàr iongantach, ro iongantach;* (*transitory*), siùbhlach, neo-mhaireann, diombuan, gearr. Passing well, *gu sar-mhath, ro mhath.*

Passing, *s.* Dol seachad, trialladh. In passing, *san dol seachad.*

Passing-bell, *s.* Clag tiodhlaic (no) adhlaic.

Passion, *s.* (*Anger*), taom, fearg, aineas, buath, corruich; (*of the mind*), càil, aigne, mothuchadh, inntinn; (*love*), gradh; gaol, dian-ghradh; (*jealousy*), eud, deothas; (*suffering*), fulangas, fulang, an-fhulangas; (*desire*), miann, togar, ana-miann; (*impetuosity*), deine, dianad. The Passion, *a Phais, an Ceusadh;* put into a passion, *cuir fearg air;* a fit of passion, *lasan.*

Passionate, *a.* Feargach, aineasach; cas, crosda, dorganta, lasanta, cainnteach; aith-ghearr, gearr, obann, dian, cabhagach; teinntidh, dàn, borb.

Passionately, *adv.* Gu feargach, gu dian-ghradhach, am feirg, an corruich, le feirge, le corruich, le mor-ghradh.

Passionateness, *s.* Feargachd, cainnteachd, teinnteachd, buirbe.

Passion-week, *s.* Seachduin a cheusaidh, seachduin na paise.

Passive, *a.* Fulangach, striochdail, géilleachdail, soitheamh, soimeach.

Passively, *adv.* Gu fulangach, gu striochdail.

Passiveness, *s.* Fulangas, ciùineas, géill.

Passover, *s.* Càisg. The passover, *a chàisg.*

Passport, *s.* Cead siubhail; triall-chomas; slàn-imeachd.

Past, *part.* Thairis, air dol thairis, seachad, air dol seachad. The storm is past, *tha 'n doinionn seachad* (*no*) *thairis;* in times past, *an céin, anns na h-amanna chaidh seachad, roimh so;* a quarter past ten, *ceithreamh an deigh dheich;* last part, *a chaidh.*

Past, *prep.* Thar, thair, thairis, seach, seachad, oscionn. Past computation, *thar cunntas;* past me, *seachum, tharrum.*

Paste, *s.* Glaodh; taois-ghlaodh, fuidreadh.

Paste, *v. a.* Stic, tàth, glaodh.

Pasteboard, *s.* Paipear tiugh, paipear glaodhta.

Pastern, *s.* Rùdan eich, ruitean, an earann sin do chos eich a tha eadar an alt iochdarach is a bhròg; leabhar chlàr.

Pastime, *s.* Cluiche; cluithe, cluicheag, ealaidh, fearaschuideachd, caitheamh aimsir, ioladh, spuirt. In pastime, *ri feal dhà.*

Pastor, *s.* Aodhar, buachaill, *ciobair*, ministeir, pears'-eaglais.

Pastoral, *a.* Aodhaireil, buachailleach, buachailleill. Pastoral life, *aireachas, buachailleachd, aodhaireachd.*

Pastoral, *s.* Coilleag, oran buachaill.

Pastry, *s.* Pitheann, pitheannan.

Pastrycook, *s.* Fuineadair, phitheannair.

Pasturage, *s.* Feurach, feurachadh, ionaltradh, fearann ionaltraidh.

Pasture, *s.* Feur; talamh feurachaidh, feurach; feurachadh, ionaltradh. Pasture ground, *talamh ionaltraidh, feurachadh, talamh feurachaidh.*

Pasture, *v. a.* and *n.* Feuraich, biath, ionaltair. Pastured, *feuraichte, biathta.*

Pasty, *s.* Pitheann.

Pat, *a.* Iomchuidh, cubhaidh; freagarrach; deas; ceart.

Pat, *s.* Boiseag, buille beag, goilleag, *sgealp.*

Pat, *v. a.* Criataich, creutaich, buail gu h-eutrom.

Patch, *v. a.* Càir, càr, càirich; cnòdaich; (*as cloth*), clùd, cludaich; cearb; sgeamh. Patched, *càirichte, clùdaichte, cearbach, luideagach.*

Patch, *s.* (*Of cloth*), clùd, cearb, luideag, caramh; (*of a shoe*), preaban; breuban; (*of ground*), croit; (*a low fellow*), sgonn, sgonn-bhalach.

Patched, *part.* Càirichte, clùdaichte; cnòdaichte; cearbach. A patched garment, *lùireach.*

Patcher, *s.* Clùdair; (*of shoes*), brògair, preabanaiche, breubair.

Patchery, *s.* Clùdaireachd, brògaireachd, càramh, cnòdachadh.

Patching, *s.* Càramh, clùdaireachd; brògaireachd; cnòdachadh Honour will not bear patching, *cha 'n fhuiling an onoir clùd*

Patchwork, *s.* Obair chàirichte.

Pate, *s* Ceann, plub, claigeann, eanchainn

Pated, *a* Carach, cuilbheartach, sligheach, còlach, seòlta, amaideach Long-pated, *seòlta, innleachduch, sicir*, shallow-pated, *baoghalta, maol*

Patefaction, *s* Nochdadh, leigeil ris, fosgladh

Patent, *a* Fosgailte A letter-patent, *litir fhosgailte, litir ceadachaidh*

Patent, *s* Còir, cead o'n rìgh

Patentee, *s* Aon aig am bheil còir (no) cead

Paternal, *a* Athaireil, athaireach, dùchasach, duthchasach

Pater-noster, *s.* Urnuigh an Tighearna, a phaidir.

Path, *s* Rod, rathad, rathad mor, slighe, frith-rod, aisridh chos, aisridh, caisleach

Pathetic, **Pathetical**, *a* Drùiteach, drùighteach, muladach, gluaisdeach

Pathetically, *adv* Gu drùiteach, gu drùighteach, gu muladach

Pathless, *a* Do-choiseachd, gun slighe

Pathology, *s* Cunntas ghalar

Pathway, *s* Aisridh, frith-rod, casan

Patible, *a* So-fhulang, so-ghiùlan, so-iomchar

Patience, *s* Foighidinn, faighidinn, fulangas, fad-fhulangas Have a little patience, *gluc beagan foighidinn;* out of patience, *a faighidinn*, victory is got by patience, *buinigear buaidh le foighidinn*

Patience, *s* Seorsa cobagaich

Patient, *a* Foighidinneach, foighdneach, faighdinneach, fulangach, (*of labour*), saothaireachail

Patient, *s* Euslan, urr thinn

Patiently, *adv* Gu faighdinneach, gu faighidinneach, gu fulangach, gu soimeach, gu foighdneach

Patin, *s* Mulag

Patly, *adv* Gu freagarrach, gu h-iomchuidh

Patriarch, *s* Priomh-athair, ard-athair, sinnsear, priomh-easbuig

Patriarchal, *a* Priomh-athaireachail, sinnsearail

Patriarchate, *s* Priomh-athaireachd, sinnsearachd.

Patrician, *a* Ard, uasal, flathail

Patrician, *s* Duine uasal, fear dh' uaislean na Romh

Patrimonial, *a* Dùchasach, dùthchasach

Patrimony, *s* Dùchas, oighreachd; domhghnas, athairinhaoin

Patriot, *s.* Tir-ghradhaiche, duine dìleas do 'dhùthaich, duine dùchasach

Patrocinate, *v* Dìon, cum taobh ri, cum suas, cum taic ri

Patrocination, *s.* Dìonadh, cumail suas, tearmunn, taic

Patrol, *s* Fear chuairt, fear faire, freiceadan, dìonadair, cuairteachadh

Patrol, *v. a* Cuairtich, dìon, cum faire

Patron, *s* Fear dionaidh, dionair, dionadair, tearmunnaiche, tearmunnair, tagrair, fear aig am bheil còir air eaglais a bhuileachadh.

Patronage, *s* Dìon, dionadh, tearmunn

Patroness, *s.* Ban-dionadair, ban-tearmunnaiche

Patronimic, *s* Sloinne, sloinneadh, cinne, cinneadh

Patronise, *v a* Dìon, cum suas, cum taobh ri, cum leis.

Patten, *s* Clabaran, bròg iaruinn (no) fhiodh a chithear air boirionnaich ri uair fhliuch, (*of a pillar*), iochdar, bun

Patter, *v* Dean stairn, dean stairearaich. Pattering, *ri staircaraich.*

Pattern, *s* Samhladh, cumadh, cumachd, dealbh, coslas, cosamhlas, samplair, ball sampuill, eisiomlair.

Pauciloquent, *a* Gearr-bhriathrach, tosdach.

Paucity, *s.* Gainne, gainnead, teirce, tearcad

Paunch, *s.* Maodal, goile, brù, bag.

Pauper, *s* Bochd, urr bhochd, truaghan, déirceach, bleideear, baigear.

Pause, *s* Stad, stadadh, stadachd, sgurachd, seasamh, fuireachadh, fosadh; briseadh; teagamh; iom-cheist; iomchomhairle I stand in pause, *taim seasamh an iom-cheist.*

Pause, *v n.* Stad, seas, fuirich Pause upon, *smuainich, beachd-smuainich, thoir faneur*

Pave, *v a* Leig le leacaibh, leacaich, cabhsairich, ùrlaraich Paved, *leacaichte, cabhsairichte*

Pavement, *s* Cabhsair, ùrlar-leac, ùrlar cloich

Paver, **Pavier**, *s* Cabhsairiche.

Pavilion, *s* Pailliun, bùth

Pavilion, *a* Pailliunaich, buthaich

Paving, *s* Leacachadh Paving-stones, *pail-chlochan.*

Paw, *s* Cruidhean, mòg, màg, smòg, smàg, spàg, cròg, cràg, crudh, lapadh

Paw, *v a* Mògaich, smàgaich, smògaich; crògaich; lamhsaich, buail mar 'ni each le chois toisich, sgrob, dean miodal

Pawed, *a* Mògach, smògach, smàgach, crògach, cruidhcanach

Pawn, *s.* Geall, gealladh, earlas

Pawnbroker, *s* Geall-mharsonta, fear a bheir airson geall, marson gill; fear earlais.

Pay, *v a.* Pàigh, dìol, dean suas; (*beat*), buail, gréidh, luinnsich. I will make you pay for it, *bheir mise ort a phàigh, bheir mise ort gum paigh thu e*, I will make you pay (suffer) for it, *bheir mise ort gu creun thu air;* I have paid my debt, *phàigh mi m' ain-fhiach*

Pay, *s* Pàigh, pàigheadh, dìol, dìoladh, dìol-thuarasdal, tuarasdal, duais, luach-saoithreach, luaidheachd, dualchas; peanas

Payable, *a* Ri phàigh, ri dhìol

Payday, *s* La pàigh, la dìolaidh

Payer, *s* Pàighear, dìoladair, dìolair, fear dìolaidh

Paymaster, *s.* Fear pàigh freiceadain

Payment, *s* Pàigh, pàigheadh, dìol, dìoladh, dìol thuarasdal, duais, tuarasdal; peanas

Pea, *s* Eitean peasrach, peasair, speilgean

Peace, *s* Sìth, sìothchath, sìochainnt, pais, tosd, tosdachd, tamh, samhchair, ciùineas, seimhe, socair, balbhachd Peace of mind, *ciùineas inntinn*, a peace-officer, *maor, maor na sith*, hold your peace, *bi samhach, bi tosd, cum do theangaidh*, bringing peace, *sìothchainnteach, sìth-bheirteach*

Peace, *interj* Samhach, bi sambach (no) tosd, bithibh samhach, tosd (no) bìth

Peaceable, *a.* Sàmhach, sìochail, sìothchail, sìochainnteach, tosdach, soitheamh, soimeach, socrach, neo-bhuaireasach, neo-thuasaideach

Peaceableness, *s* Samhchair, sìothchainnt, tosdachd, seimhe, ciùineas

Peaceably, *adv* Gu samhach, gu tosdach, gu bìth; gu soitheamh, gu seimh, gu socrach; gu tiamhaidh.

Peaceful, *a* Samhach, sìochail, tosd, tosdach, bìth, ciùin, sìochainnteach, soitheamh, soimeach, socrach, neo-bhuaireasach, neo-thuasaideach.

Peacefully, *adv* Gu sàmhach, gu sìochail, gu tosd, gu

...bìth; gu soimeach, gu soitheamh, gu socrach, gun chogadh, gun strìgh.

Peacefulness, *s.* Samchair, tosdachd, seimhe, socair, ciùineas.

Peacemaker, *s.* Fear-réite, fear réiteachaidh; siochainntiche.

Peace-offering, *s.* Tabhartas sìth; sìth-thabhartas; ofrail naomh a measg nan Iudhach mar dhìol airson ciont.

Peace-officer, *s.* Maor rìgh.

Peach, *s.* Peitse, peitseag.

Peachick, *s.* Peubh-eireag.

Peacock, *s.* Peubh-choileach, peucag.

Peahen, *s.* Peubh-chearc, peucag.

Peak, *s.* Beann, binnean; mullach, bàrr; roinn; fiormhullach: curachd bheannach, bioraid.

Peal, *s.* Fuaim, farum; gàir, gaoir; beum cluig; toirm, toran, torunn, fuaim tairneanaich; gunnaireachd; braighe; cith. A peal of bells, *seirm.*

Peal, *v.* Dean fuaim, dean farum, dean gàir, dean torunn, fuaimnich; cuir air feadh chéile.

Pear, *s.* Peur, seorsa meas do 'm bheil ceithir fichead agus a ceithir seòrsa ann.

Pearl, *s.* Neamhnaid, neamhnuid, neamhuinn, neònaid. A pearl in the eye, *leus;* mother-of-pearl, *slige neamhuinn.*

Pearl-eyed, *a.* Leus-shuileach.

Pearly, *a.* Neamhnaideach, neonaideach.

Pear-main, *s.* Ubhal.

Pear-tree, *s.* Craobh-pheuran.

Peasant, *s.* Tuathanach; bodach, balaoch; ceatharnach.

Peasantry, *s.* Tuath, tuath-cheathairne; cumantraidh.

Peascod, *s.* Meilgeag, meiligeag; meiligeag pheasrach, moinigeag, meinigeag, cochall, cochull.

Pease, *s.* Peasair. White pease, *peasair gheal;* pease straw, *fodar peasrach:* pease pottage, *brochan peasrach;* husk of pease, *spàlag, meiligeag.*

Peat, *s.* Mòin, fòid mhòin, fòid.

Peatmoss, *s.* Mòinteach, aite mòin, poll mòin, bachdmòin.

Pebble, *s.* Grigeag; sgilleag; clachag, seud, leug.

Pebbled, **Pebbly**, *a.* Grigeach, grigeagach, garbh, gaineamhach.

Peccable, *a.* Buailteach do pheacadh.

Peccadillo, *s.* Peacadh beag.

Peccant, *a.* Ciontach, peacach, coireach, truaillidh, olc, coirpte, coirpidh.

Peck, *s.* Peic, peichd, an ceithreamh cuid do dh' fheorlan; mòran.

Peck, *v. a.* Pìoc, spiol, piol mar ni eun le ghob. Peck at, *faigh coir.*

Pecker, *s.* Piocair, spioladair. A woodpecker, *cnag.*

Peckled, *a.* Breac, breacta, ballach.

Pectinal, *s.* Clreach, fiaclach, mar chìre.

Pectoral, *a.* Maodhanach, maothanach, uchdach.

Pectoral, *s.* Leigheas maodhain; eididh uchd.

Peculate, *v.* Goid on mhòr chuideachd.

Peculation, *s.* Meirle, fogluidheachd air airgiod coitchionn, goideachd, gaduidheachd.

Peculator, *s.* Meirleach, gaduiche, goidiche, sloightir.

Peculiar, *s.* Còir.

Peculiar, *a.* Àraidh, àraid, sonruichte, dual, dlleas, iongantach, neonach. Peculiarly, *gu h-àraidh, gu sonruichte.*

Peculiarity, *s.* Araideachd; neònachas.

Pecuniary, *a.* Airgid.

Pedagogue, *s.* Maighstir sgoil, fear teagaisg.

Pedagogy, *s.* Oideas, oilean, ionnsach, ionnsuchadh, foghlum, teagasg.

Pedant, *s.* Maighstir sgoil; aon a ni uaill a foghlum, spadfhoghlumaiche; sgòd-fhoghlumaiche, brod-fhoghlumaiche; brumair.

Pedantic, *a.* Sgòdasach, uallach a oilean.

Pedantry, *s.* Spad-fhòghlum, sgod-fhoghlum, brod-fhoghlum.

Peddle, *v. n.* Bi rudach, gabh gnothuch ri, bean ri.

Pedestal, *s.* Bun cholamh, bun-cholmhuinn, bun stùc.

Pedestrial, *a.* Air chois, da chois, a coiseachd.

Pedestrian, *s.* Coisiche, fear siubhail.

Pedestrian, *a.* Coiseach, coiseachaidh.

Pedicular, *a.* Mialach.

Pedigree, *s.* Gineal, ginealach, sliochd, sinnsearachd, glùn ginealaich.

Pedler, *s.* Fear pac, pacair, ceannaiche, ceannuiche; greimeisgear, ceannuiche iomrolach, cois-cheannuiche, ceannuiche seachrain, grimisgear.

Pedling, *s.* Pacaireachd.

Pedobaptism, *s.* Naoidh-bhaisteadh.

Pedobaptist, *s.* Naoidh-bhaistiche.

Pedometer, *s.* Cuidhil thomhasaidh, cuairt mheasair.

Peel, *v. a.* Plaoisg, rùisg, cairt, sgrath; (*spoil*), spùinn, spùill. Peeled, *plaoisgte; ruisgte; spuinnte, spùillte.*

Peel, *s.* Plaosg, plaosgadh, rusg, sgrath, craiceann, sgròill, sgroilleag, cairt; sliseag, snaidh, snuidh.

Peel, *s.* Spàin àmhuinn, no inneal leis an cuir fuineadar aran san àmhuinn; inneal leis an croch clodh-bhualadair paipeir suas chum tiormachadh; bord tana chum pitheannan iomchar mar a chithear air ceann fuineadair.

Peeler, *s.* Rùsgair, rùsgadair, fear rùsgaidh, plaosgair, sgrathadair; spùinneadair.

Peep, *v. n.* Plaoisg; gabh sealladh bradach; dìdeagaich.

Peep, *s.* Plaosgadh; sealladh bradach, dìdeag, brad-shealladh.

Peeper, *s.* Eun circe, eun a teachd as an ubh, bìdean.

Peer, *s.* Leth-bhreac; samhladh, companach; (*nobleman*), maitheamh-flath; iarla, iarfhlath, morair.

Peerage, *s.* Moraireachd.

Peeress, *s.* Ban-mhorair.

Peerless, *a.* Gun choimeas, neo-choimeasta, gun lethbhreac; barr-mhaiseach.

Peerlessness, *s.* Barrachd, barr-mhaise.

Peevish, *a.* Crosda, cainnteach, frionasach, catail, frithearach; duairc, duairceach, saonasach, aithghearr, friotalach, crosanta, speacharra, speachanta; do-riarach; dothoileach, gearanach, draingeach, ciùrlanach, adriuchalach. A peevish look, *driuch.*

Peevishly, *adv.* Gu crosda, gu cainnteach, gu frionasach, gu frithearach, gu duairc, gu duairceach, gu saonasach, gu speachanta, gu speacharra, gu draingeach.

Peevishness, *s.* Crosdachd, cainnteachd, frionasachd, frithearachd, saonasachd, friotalachd, draing, draingealachd.

Peg, *s.* Pinne, geinne, faraiche; alachag; crann tarruing; dul.

Peg, *v.* Pinn; faraich.

Pelf, *s.* Airgiod, beartas, maoin, earras, toic.

Pelican, *s.* Eun air fhasaich.

Pell, *s.* Croiceann, craiceann, seiche, seichd.

Pellet, *s.* Peileir; peilear; cnap; meall beag cruinn.

Pelleted, *a.* Peilearach; cnapanach.

Pellicle, *s.* Croicneag, sgrath, sgannan.

Pellitory, *s.* Seorsa luibh. Pellitory of Spain, *lus na Spainne;* pellitory of the wall, *lus a bhallaidh.*

Pell-mell, *adv.* Air feadh chéile; troimh chéile, thar a chéile; trom tric; buille air bhuille.

Pellucid, *a.* Soilleir, glan.

Pellucidity, *s.* Soilleireachd, gloine.

Pelt, *s.* Croicionn, craiceann, seiche, seichd; peileag.

Pelt, *v.* Buail; tilg air, spairt. Pelting him with stones, *a tilg chlochan air.*

Pelting, *a.* Suarrach.

Pelting, *s.* Bualadh; spairteadh.

Peltmonger, *s.* Seicheadair, seiceadair.

Pelvis, *s.* Machlag, iochdar na bronn.

Pen, *s.* (*For writing*), peann, ite, cuille, cléite, cléite sgriobhaidh bearan.

Pen, *v. a.* Sgriobh; deachd. Penned, *sgriobhta, deachta.*

Pen, *s.* (*Fold*), mainnir, crodh, cròilean; banrach, lanngleuta, fàl, buail, fang.

Pen, *s.* Cròdhaich, cuir a stigh, dùin, druid, cuir am fàl, fang.

Penal, *a.* Peanasail, peanasach, peanasda.

Penalty, *s.* Peanas; pàineachas; geall, ùmhladh. Impose a penalty, *cuir ùmhladh air, leig ùmhladh.*

Penance, *s.* Peanas, dioladh, réite.

Pencase, *s.* Peannair, peannar, peannagan.

Pence, *s.* Sgillinnean, peighinnean.

Pencil, *s.* Peannsal; peann dubh-luaidhe; dealbh-bhruis, cléitean.

Pencil, *v. a.* Dealbh.

Pendant, *s.* Crochadan; cluas-fhàile, cluas-fhàinn, cluigean cluaise; sròl, suaicheantas.

Pendence, *s.* Claonadh, claonad.

Pendency, *s.* Crochadh; iom-cheiste, iom-chomhairle, teagamh, tomhartaich, turamanaich.

Pendent, *a.* An crochadh, crochta, crochte.

Pending, *a.* An crochadh.

Pendulous, *a.* Crochta, crochadach, seòganach, an crochadh.

Pendulum, *s.* Crochadan; uaireadair.

Penetrable, *a.* So-dhruigheadh, so-thＯlladh, neo-dhionach.

Penetrant, *a.* Drùighteach; geur, guineach, lotach.

Penetrate, *a.* Toll, troimh-tholl, lot, troimh-lot; gearr, drùigh air, bris; tuig. He penetrated into my meaning, *thuig e mi.*

Penetration, *s.* Tolladh, troimh-tholladh, lot; sàr-bheachd, geur-bheachd, geur-thuigse, geur-thoinisg.

Penetrative, *a.* Drùiteach, drùighteach; goineach, guineach, aithneachail, geur, toinisgeil, tuigseach.

Penguin, *s.* Scorsa geòidh.

Peninsula, *s.* Doirlinn; cean tìre, tairbeart.

Peninsulated, *a.* Doirlinneach.

Penis, *s.* Bod, bodan, slat, ball, stoilean.

Penitence, *s.* Aithreachas, bròn airson, peacaidh, aithmhealadh, doilghios, duilgheas.

Penitent, *a.* Aithreach, aithreachail, làn aithreachais, doilghiosach, duilghiosach, doilgheasach.

Penitent, *s.* Aithreachan, aithreachag; iompachan, iompachag. The fair penitent, *an aithreachag àillidh.*

Penitential, *a.* Aithreachail.

Penitentiary, *s.* Aite aithreachais; aithreachan, iompachan.

Penitently, *adv.* Gu h-aithreachail.

Penknife, *s.* Sgian pheann.

Penman, *s.* Sgriobhair, maighistir sgriobhaidh; ughdar. A good penman, *deadh sgriobhair.*

Penmanship, *s.* Sgriobhadh, sgriobhaireachd.

Pennant, *s.* Sròl, bratach, suaicheantas.

Pennated, *a.* Sgiathach.

Penner, *s.* Sgriobhair; sgriobhadair; ùghdar; peannagan.

Penniless, *a.* Truagh, bochd, uireasbhach, gun airgiod, gun sgilinn, gun pheighinn.

Penny, *s.* Sgilinn, peighinn; airgiod. Luck-penny, *meachainn;* a pennyworth, *luach peighinn;* a penny saved is a penny gained, *is cho maith peighinn chaomhnadh is a choisinn.*

Penny-grass, *s.* Muilcionn, muilceann.

Pennywise, *a.* Caonntach.

Pennyworth, *s.* Luach peighinn; deagh bhargan, deagh chùnradh.

Pensile, *a.* Crochadach, an crochadh.

Pension, *s.* Na h-urrad sa bhliadhna; bun-chios.

Pensionary, *a.* Bun-chiseach.

Pensioner, *s.* Bun-chisear, fear aig am bheil na h-urrad sa bhliadhna.

Pensive, *a.* Brònach, dubhach, trom, tiamhaidh; tuirseach, muladach; smuaireanach, smuainteachail.

Pensively, *adv.* Gu bronach, gu dubhach, gu trom, gu tiamhaidh, gu tuirseach, gu muladach, gu smuaireanach.

Pensiveness, *s.* Bron, truime, tiamhaidheachd, mulad, smuaireanachd.

Pent, *part.* of pen. Dùinte suas, druidte, glaiste.

Pentagon, *s.* Cuig-oisneag, cuig-shlisneag.

Pentagonal, *a.* Cuig-oisinneach, cuig-shlisneach.

Pentangular, *a.* Cuig-oisinneach, cùig dhuilleach.

Pentapetalous, *a.* Cùig dhuilleagach.

Pentateuch, *s.* Cuig leabhraichean Mhaois.

Pentecost, *s.* Cuingels, caingeis.

Penthouse, *s.* Sgimheal, sgàilean, sgàil-thigh; tigh mach.

Pentile, *s.* Sgleut mullaich.

Penultima, *s.* An sioladh is deireannaiche ach h-aon.

Penumbra, *s.* Leth-sgail, leth-fhaileas, leth-dhuibhne.

Penurious, *a.* Crion, spiocach, spongach; ganntarach, gann; gionach, sanntach, gortach, truagh, miothur, bochd; cruaidh, cruadalach.

Penuriously, *adv.* Gu crion, gu spiocach, gu spongach, gu gionach; gu sanntach, gu gortach, gu truagh, gu miothur, gu cruaidh, gu cruadalach.

Penuriousness, *s.* Crìne, criontachd, sploc, splocaireachd, peintealachd, bochduinn; gainne, miothur, cruadhas, cruadalas.

Penury, *s.* Bochduinn, uireasbhuidh, aimbeart, gort; gortachd; ainniseachd.

Peony, *s.* Seorsa plùir.

People, *s.* Sluagh, aitim, slogh, cinneach, muinntir, feodhainn, pobull, daoine. Much people, *moran sluaigh;* the rascally sort of people, *prabar, gràisg.*

People, *v. a.* Lion le sluagh, planntaich.

Pepper, *s.* Spios, spiosradh, peabar, peubar.

Pepper, *v. a.* Spios, spiosraich, peubaraich.

Pepper-box, *s.* Bocsa peubair.

Pepper-corn, *s.* Eitean peubair.

Pepper-grass, *s.* Glas-leun.

Peppermint, *s.* Mionnt, miunnt, miontuinn, miunntinn.

Peradventure, *adv.* Maith dh' fhaoidte, a theagamh, theagamh, faodaidh e bhith.

Perambulate, *v. n.* Spaisdeirich; cuairtich, imich, timchioll.

Perambulation, *s.* Imeachd, timchioll; cuairteachadh, cuair; spaisdearachd, spaidsearachd; beachdachadh

Perambulator, *s.* Cuidhle thomhais; fear cuairt; spaisdear, spaidsear.

Perceivable, *a.* So-fhaicinn, so-mhothachadh, ion-mhothachadh, ion-mhothaichte; faicinneach.

Perceive, *v. a.* Faic, fairich, beachdaich, mothuich, fainich, aithnich, tuig, thoir fanear, thoir aire, cuir omhaill If he perceives it I am undone, *ma dh' aithnicheas e so, tha mise dheth.*

Perceptibility, *s* So-fhaiceannachd, ion-fhaicsinneachd

Perceptible, *a.* So-fhaicinn, so-fhaireachadh, so-mhothuchadh, so-fhaineachadh, so-fhaireachdainn, ion-mhothuchadh.

Perception, *s.* Mothuchadh, beachd, faineachas, farachdainn; faicinn, toirt fanear

Perch, *s.* (*A fish*), creagag, creagag uisge; (*in measure*), cuig slat is leth shlat; (*for hens*), spàr, iris, spiris

Perch, *v.* Suidh mar eun.

Perchance, *adv.* A theagamh, theagamh, maith dh' fhaoidte; faodaidh e bhith; gu cineamhuinneach, thaobh tubaisd.

Percolate, *v a.* Siolaidh, siolaich, traogh.

Percolation, *s.* Sioladh.

Percolator, *s.* Siolachan.

Percussion, *s.* Bualadh, buille, dlù-bhualadh.

Percutient, *a.* Bualadach.

Perdition, *s.* Sgrios, léir-sgrios; truaighe, milleadh, lànmhilleadh; † call; bàs siorruidh.

Perduration, *s.* Buanachd, maireannachd

Peregrinate, *v.* Rach air thùrus, rach air chuairt

Peregrination, *s.* Tùrus, taisdeal, tùrusachd, taisdealachd

Peregrine, *a.* Coimheach, allmharach; eil-thireach, deòrach, deoraidh, tùrusach, taisdealach, eachdranach

Peremptorily, *adv.* Gu smachdail; gu teann, gu h-iomlan; gu sparrail.

Peremptory, *a.* Smachdail, teann, iomlan, sparrail.

Perennial, *a* Bliadhnail; a mhaireas ré na bliadhna; maireann, bidheanta, maireannach.

Perfect, *a.* (*Complete*), iomlan, foirfe, foirfidh, coimhlionta, gun mhearachd, neo-lochdach, glan; neo-chiontach; (*skilful*), sgileil, eòlach, seòlta, teòma. A perfect fool, *fior amadan;* a perfect hero, *sàr ghaisgeach.*

Perfect, *v. a.* Criochnaich, coimhlion, dean iomlan, iomlainich. Perfected, *criochnaichte, coimhlionta, ullamh*

Perfection, *s.* Iomlanachd, iomlaineachd, iomlaine, foirfeachd, foirfidheachd. Practice makes perfection, *ni cleachd teòmadh.*

Perfectly, *adv.* Gu h-iomlan, gu foirfe, gu coimhlionta, gu tur, gu pongail. Perfectly well, *gu làn mhath.*

Perfectness, *s.* Iomlaine, iomlaineachd, iomlanachd; coimhliontachd, sgile; foirfeachd.

Perfidious, *a.* Fealltach, mealltach, fallsail, fallsa, cealgach; slaoighteil, traoidhteil, meanntalach, fealltanach; breugach; neo-fhior, neo-dhìleas, carrach

Perfidiously, *adv.* Gu fealltach, gu mealltach, gu fallsail, gu fallsa, gu cealgach, gu slaoighteil, gu meanntalach, gu fealltanach; gu breugach; gu neo-fhior, gu carrach.

Perfidiousness, *s.* Fealltachd, mealltachd, mealltaireachd, fallsachd, ceilge, cealgaireachd.

Perfidy, *s.* Foille, feall, feill, cealg; ceilge, meabhal, easionracas, neo-fhirinn, slaoighte, traoidhte.

Perflate, *v. a.* Séid troimh.

Perflation, *s.* Séideadh; gaotharachd

Perforable, *a.* So-tholladh.

Perforate, *v. a.* Toll, troimh-tholl. Perforated, *air a tholladh, tollta*

Perforation, *s* Tolladh, toll.

Perforator, *s* Torradh; tolladair

Perforce, *adv.* A dh' aindeoin; air éigin

Perform, *v a* Dean, gnàthaich, cuir an gniomh, coimhlion, criochnaich, thoir gu crich, thoir a bhuile. Perform your promise, *coimhlion do ghealladh.*

Performance, *s* Euchd, gnothuch, gniomh, obair; deanadas, tùrn; coimh-lionadh, co-lionadh.

Performer, *s* Deanadaiche, deanadair, fear gniomh, gniomhaiche; fear cluiche.

Performing, *s* Deanamh, oibreachadh, coimh-lionadh

Perfricate, *v a* Rub, suath

Perfrication, *s* Rubadh, suathadh

Perfume, *s.* Fàile, boladh, deagh-bholadh, boltrach cubhraidh, tòchd griun

Perfumer, *s* Lusragan; boltrachan

Perfumitorily, *adv* Gu neo-sheadhail, gu neo-shuimeil

Perfuse, *v a* Sgaoil, iom-sgaoil; dath Perfused, *sgaoilte*

Perhaps, *adv.* Theagamh, a theagamh, theag, maith dh' fhaoidhte, feudaidh e bhith

Pericardium, *s.* Cochall (no) sgannan a chridhe

Periclitation, *s* Gàbhadh, gàbhail, cunnart, teanntachd, teinne, iomacheist; deuchainn.

Pericranium, *s.* Cochull (no) sgannan an eanchainn.

Perigee, *s.* An t-ionad sin sna neamhaibh anns am faigse am bi reul do 'n chruinne.

Perihelium, *s.* An t-ionad do chuairt reul is fhaigse do 'n ghrian.

Peril, *s.* Cunnart, baoghal, gàbhadh, gàbhail, guasachd, teinne He is in peril of his life, *tha e 'n cunnart 'anam,* at your peril do it not, *air d' anam na dean e,* without peril, *gun chunnart, tearuinnte*

Perilous, *a* Cunnartach, baoghalach, gàbhaidh, guasachdach. Perilously, *gu cunnartach.*

Perilousness, *s* Cunnart, guasachd; teanntachd.

Perimeter, *s.* Cuairt, iom-chuairt; cuairt-lin, cuairteag.

Perineum, *s.* Ceòsach

Period, *s* (*End*), crioch, ceann, ceann thall, finid, (*of time*), tùn-chuairt, (*season*), am, ùine, uair, aimsir; (*a point*), pong, pung, lan-phong

Periodic, **Periodical**, *a.* Tràthach, amach, tim-chuairteach, amail, air amaibh sònruichte A periodical wind, *gaoth nan tràth.*

Periodically, *adv.* Air amaibh sònruichte, air uairibh

Periosteum, *s* Sgannan cnaimh.

Peripatetic, *s.* Feallsanach Aithneach a b' abhaist deaspoireachd agus coiseachd air aon am.

Periphery, *s* Cuairt, cuairteag, cuairtean, cuairt-lin.

Periphrasis, *s.* Cuairt-bhriathar, leud-bhriathar.

Periphrastical, *a.* Cuairt-bhriathrach

Peripneumony, *s* Caitheamh; tinneas sgamhan

Perish, *v. n* Bàsuich, sgrios, rach chum sgrios, bi caillte; bàsuich gu siorruidh, thig gu neoni.

Perishable, *a* Bàsmhor; so-sgriosadh, so-chur as, somhilleadh

Perishableness, *s.* Bàsmhorachd.

Peristaltic, *a.* Gluasadach, uim-ghluasadach. Peristaltic motion, *uim-ghluasad mionaich, gluasad cuim.*

Peritoneum, *s.* Sgannan a mhionaich iochdaraich.

Periwig, *s.* Piorbhuic; gobhàrr, gruaig fhighte; breugfholt, breug-chiabh.

Periwinkle, *s.* Faochag, faoch, gille fuinbrinn, seorsa luibh.

Perjure, *v. a.* Thoir mionnan eithich. He perjured himself, *thug e mionnan eithich.*

Perjured, *a.* Eithich, fallsa, fallsail, breugach, dearg-bhreugach. Perjured people, *luchd eithich.*

Perjurer, *s.* Fear eithich; dearg-bhreugair.

Perjury, *s.* Mionnan eithich; dearg-bhreug, brasluidhe.

Perk, *v. a.* and *n.* Bi gog-cheannach (no) eutrom; bi uallach, sgeadaich, sgiamhaich, breaghaich. Perked, *gog-cheannach; uallach, iallagach, sgiamhaichte, sgeadaichte; breaghaichte.*

Perk, *a.* Gog-cheannach; eutrom, uallach, iollapach, iullagach.

Permanence, Permanency, *s.* Buannachd, buanachd, buanas, maireannachd, maireachduinn.

Permanent, *a.* Buan, maireann, maireannach, mairionnach, buan-mhaireann; neo-chaochlaideach.

Permanently, *adv.* Gu buan, gu maireann, gu maireannach.

Permeable, *a.* So-shiùbhladh; so-tholladh.

Permeate, *v. a.* Rach troimh (no) thairis, siubhail troimh (no) thairis, drùigh.

Permeation, *s.* Siubhladh troimh, siubhladh thairis; iom-sgaoileadh.

Permiscible, *a.* So-mheasgadh.

Permissible, *a.* Ceadachail, a ghabhas ceadachadh, ceadaichte.

Permission, *s.* Cead, comas; aontachadh. With your permission, *le do chead;* with God's permission, *a dheoin Dia;* without permission, *gun chomas.*

Permissive, *a.* A tabhairt cead (no) comas; ceadachail.

Permissively, *adv.* Le cead, le comas, gun bhac.

Permistion, *s.* Measgadh, coimeasgadh, cumasg.

Permit, *v. a.* Ceadaich, laghaich, lughaig; luathsaich; thoir cead (no) comas, fulaing, leig le, aontaich. Permit me to go, *ceadaich dhomh falbh, leig leam falbh.*

Permit, *s.* Barandas; cead; comas.

Permittance, *s.* Cead, comas.

Permixtion, *s.* Coimeasg, cumasg, measgadh.

Permutation, *s.* Mùthadh, atharrachadh; malairt.

Permute, *v.* Mùth; malairt; thoir am malairt.

Permuter, *s.* Malairtiche, fear malairt.

Pernicious, *a.* Sgriosail, millteach, marbhtach, urchoideach, cronail, sgriosadach, olc, dochannach.

Perniciously, *adv.* Gu sgriosail, gu millteach, gu h-urchoideach, gu sgriosadach.

Perniciousness, *s.* Sgriosaileachd; sgriosalachd, urchoideachd, millteachd, urchoideachd.

Pernicity, *s.* Luathas, luas.

Peroration, *s.* Ceann òraid, crioch òraid.

Perpend, *v.* Beachd-smuainich; beachdaich, làn-sgrud.

Perpender, *s.* Cloch mullaich, cloch oisinn.

Perpendicular, *a.* Dìreach na sheasamh, dìreach a n'airde, dìreach a bhàn, dìreach ri bruthach, ingearach.

Perpendicular, *s.* Ingear.

Perpendicularly, *adv.* Gu h-ingearach.

Perpetrate, *v. a.* Cuir an gniomh, dean; gnàthaich, ciontaich.

Perpetration, *s.* Ciontachadh, coireachadh; gnàthachadh, gniomhachadh, deanamh, cur an gniomh.

Perpetual, *a.* Buan, bi-bhuan, bith-bhuan, maireann, mairionn, maireannach, mairionnach; siorruidh, suthain; bunaiteach, bunailteach, buan-mhaireann, seasamhach.

Perpetually, *adv.* Gu bith-bhuan; gu siorruidh, gu suthain, gu suthain siorruidh; an còmhnuidh, am bidheantas; an cumaint is an comhnuidh; daonann, daonalta.

Perpetuate, *v. a.* Siorruich, dean buan (no) bith-bhuan, gnàth-chuimhnich, cum an gnath-chuimhne; dean mairionn.

Perpetuity, *s.* Siorrachd, siorruidheachd, buanas, buantachd, bi-bhuantachd, bith-bhuantachd; maireannachd; bidheantas.

Perplex, *v. a.* Buair, cuir thar a chéile, cuir an iom-cheist, cuir an iom-chomhairle; rib, grab; trioblaidich; (*vex*), farranaich, cuir farran air.

Perplexed, *a.* (*As a question*), duilich, doilich, deacair, cruaidh, docail, do-thuigsinn, do-fhuasgladh; (*doubtful*), an iom-cheist, an iom-chomhairle; (*confounded*), thar a chéile, prabta, prabte, ribte; (*troublesome*), iom-cheisteach, buaireasach, trioblaideach, farranach.

Perplexedly, *adv.* Gu doilich, gu duilich, gu deacair, gu cruaidh, gu docail, gu do-fhuasgladh; an iom-cheist; an iom-chomhairle; thar a cheile.

Perplexedness, *s.* Iom-cheist, iom-chomhairle, ioma-chomhairle; doilghios, duilgheas, buaireadh, trioblaid.

Perplexity, *s.* Iom-cheist, ioma-cheist, iom-chomhairle, ioma-chomhairle, buaireadh; trioblaid, ro-churam; teanntachd, teinne, càs, cruaidh-chas.

Perpotation, *s.* Òl, pòit, ruite, ruitearachd.

Perquisite, *s.* Còir, buannachd, cuid, luach-saoithreach, ni a bhuineas do neach a thuille air pàigh.

Perquisition, *s.* Sgrud, sgrudadh, làn-sgrudadh, cruaidh-sgrudadh, ceasnachadh.

Perry, *s.* Peur-shùgh, lionn pheuran.

Persecute, *v. a.* Geur-lean, cruaidh-lean, cràidh, claoidh, sàruich, ruaig, dean geur-leanmhuinn; buair. He persecuted them, *gheur-lean e iad, rinn e geur-leanmhuinn orra.*

Persecuted, *a.* and *p.* Sàruichte, cràidhte, claoidhte; ruaigte. They are persecuted, *tha iad sàruichte (no) air an saruchadh, tha iad air an geur leanmhuinn.*

Persecuting, *s.* Geur-leanmhuinn, geur-leantuinn, geur-leanachd, sàruchadh, claoidh, ruaig.

Persecution, *s.* Geur-leanmhuinn, geur-leantuinn, geur-leanachd, sàruchadh, claoidh, ruaig.

Persecutor, *s.* Fear-geur-leanmhuinn; geur-leantair, fear-sàruchaidh. Persecutors, *luchd geur-leanmhuinn, luchd sàruchaidh.*

Perseverance, *s.* Buanachadh, buanachd, buantachd, tabhuanachd; seasmhachd, bun-sheasamhachd, tùl-chuis, tul-chuiseachd, dìchioll, seasamh a mach.

Persevere, *v. n.* Buanaich, seas a mach, buan-sheas, bi seasamhach.

Persevering, *a.* Buan, seasamhach, buan-sheasamhach, bun-sheasamhach, dìchiollach, oidhirpeach; tul-chuiseach. Perseveringly, *gu buan, gu seasamhach, gu dìchiollach; gu tulchuiseach.*

Persist, *v. n.* Cum a mach seas a mach, buanaich; buan-sheas, bi diongalta. Persist in your opinion, *buanaich ann ad bharail.*

Persistance, *s.* Cumail a mach, buanachadh; buan-sheasamh; rag-mhuinealas, rag-mhuinealachd, danarachd.

Persistive, *a.* Buan; buan-sheasamhach, rag, rag-mhuinealach.

Person, *s.* Neach, pearsa, urr; gin, duine; aogas, riochd. Many persons think so, *tha iomad neach (no) urr sa bharail sin;* is there any person there? *bheil gin an sin?* a certain person, *neach àraidh;* any person, *neach sam bith, urr air bith;* an elegant person, *pearsa dluinn;* I hate not the person but his sins, *cha 'n fhuath leam an duine ach a* *pheacanna;* he came in person, *thàinig se e féin;* in his own person, *na phearsa féin;* persons, *pearsan, sluagh, feodhainn, aiteam.*

PERSONABLE, *a.* Tlachdar, tlachdmhor, ceanalta, eireachdail, tàbhachdach, maiseach, aluinn, pearsonta.

PERSONAGE, *s.* Pearsa, pearsadh; aogas; dreach; urr inmheach.

PERSONAL, *a.* Pearsail; corporra; a bhuineas do phearsa; àraidh. A personal insult, *tamailt pearsa;* with the personal consent of each person, *le cead àraidh gach pearsa;* personal acquaintance, *eòlas pearsaidh.*

PERSONALLY, *adv.* Gu pearsail; gu corporra; a lathair. He came personally, *thainig se e féin;* I am personally acquainted with him.

PERSONATE, *v.* Pearsaich, samhluich. Personated, *pearsaichte, samhluichte.*

PERSONATION, *s.* Pearsachadh, samhluchadh, riochdadh.

PERSONIFICATION, *s.* Pearsachadh; samhlachadh.

PERSONIFY, *v. a.* Pearsaich, samhluich.

PERSPECTIVE, *s.* Gloine amhairc; sealladh; dealbh, caladhain leis an dealbhar sealladh nithe air paipeir.

PERSPECTIVE, *a.* Fradharcach.

PERSPICACIOUS, *a.* Geur, grad-shuileach, geur-shuileach, sùileach, grad-sheallach, geur-sheallach; iolair-shùileach; furachair.

PERSPICACITY, *s.* Geur-shealladh, grad-shealladh; grad-leirsinneachd, géire; furachaireachd.

PERSPICIENCE, *s.* Geur-shealltuinn; geur-amharc.

PERSPICUITY, *s.* Soilleireachd; riachdaileachd; trid-shoilleireachd.

PERSPICUOUS, *a.* Soilleir; riachdail, so-thuigsinn; glan.

PERSPICUOUSLY, *adv.* Gu soilleir, gu riachdail, gu so-thuigsinn; gu glan.

PERSPICUOUSNESS, *s.* Soilleireachd, riachdaileachd; trid-shoilleireachd.

PERSPIRABLE, *a.* Fallusach, fallusail.

PERSPIRATION, *s.* Fallus.

PERSPIRATIVE, *a.* Fallusach, faillseach.

PERSPIRE, *v. a.* Cuir fallus, fallusaich. He pêrspired, *chuir e fallus deth.*

PERSTRINGE, *v. a.* Rub, suath, sgiob.

PERSUASABLE, *a.* So-earalachadh, so-chomhairleachadh.

PERSUADE, *v. a.* Cuir impidh, comhairlich, thoir air; thoir comhairle, dean deònach, earalaich, sparr; comh-éignich, thoir chreidsinn. Would you persuade me to that? *an comhairlicheadh tu dhomh sin? an tugadh tu chomhairle orm sin a dheanamh?* they persuaded me to do it, *thug iad orm a dheanamh.*

PERSUADED, *part.* Comhairlichte, earalaichte, earailichte; comh-éignichte, cinnteach. I am quite persuaded of it, *tha mi làn chinnteach as.*

PERSUADER, *s.* Fear earalachaidh; fear comhairleachaidh; earalaiche.

PERSUASIBLE, *a.* So-earalachadh, so-chomhairleachadh.

PERSUASION, *s.* Comhairleachadh, sparradh; comh-eigneachadh, earalachadh, earail; (*opinion*), barail, dochas, creideamh, creidimh.

PERSUASIVE, *a.* Comhairleachail, drùiteach, drùighteach, impidheach.

PERSUASIVELY, *adv.* Gu h-impidheach.

PERSUASIVENESS, *s.* Impidheachd.

PERSUASORY, *a.* Earalach, impidheach, drùighteach.

PERT, *a.* Beag-narach, peasanta, peasanach; danarra, brisg, beò, beothail, tapaidh; ladurna; làdasach; gobach, beadaidh. A song from the pert hen, *òran na circe beadaidh.*

PERTAIN, *v. n.* Buin.

PERTINACIOUS, *a.* Rag, ceann-làidir, ceann-dàn, rag-mhuinealach, danarra; beagnarach, peasanta, beadaidh; buan, rag, dùr seasamhach.

PERTINACIOUSLY, *adv.* Gu ceann-làidir, gu rag, gu danarra, gu beag-narach, gu peasanta, gu dùr.

PERTINACITY, PERTINACY, *s.* Danarrachd, rag-mhuinealachd, ceann-dànadas; peasantachd, beadaidheachd, eas-umhlachd; seasamhachd, bunailteachd.

PERTINENCE, *s.* Freagarrachd, cubhaidheachd, iomchuidheachd, iom-chuidhead, oireamhuin.

PERTINENT, *a.* Freagarrach, cubhaidh, iomchuidh, oireamhuineach.

PERTINENTLY, *adv.* Gu freagarrach, gu cubhaidh, gu h-iomchuidh.

PERTLY, *adv.* Gu danarra, gu peasanach, gu peasanta, gu mì-mhodhail, gu beag-narach, gu lonach, gu gobach.

PERTNESS, *s.* Danarrachd, peasanachd, peasantachd, mi-mhodh, mi-mhodhaileachd; cainnt; beathalachd, lonais, gobais, gob; glaodhar.

PERTURB, PERTURBATE, *v. a.* Buair, cuir a ordugh, cuir a riaghailt, cuir air aimhreidh, cuir thar a chéile. Perturbed, *buairte, air aimhreidh, thar a chéile; a riaghailt.*

PERTURBATION, *s.* Buaireas, buaireas inntinn, buaireadh, aimhreite; triobloid.

PERTURBATOR, *s.* Buaireadair, fear-aimhreite.

PERUKE, *s.* Piorbhuic, gruag; breug-chiabh, gobhàrr.

PERUKEMAKER, *s.* Gruagadair, fear phiorbhuicean.

PERUSAL, *s.* Leughadh, sgrudadh.

PERUSE, *v. a.* Leugh; beachdaich, sgrud, thoir fanear.

PERUSER, *s.* Leughair, leughadair.

PERVADE, *v. a.* Sgaoil thar, rach thar (no) air feadh.

PERVERSE, *a.* Dalma, crosda, cainnteach, eithich, reasgach, rag-bheartach, ceann-laidir, coirbte, strangalach, aingidh; crosanta, droch-mhuinte, tarsuing; aimhleasach; claon.

PERVERSELY, *adv.* Gu dalma, gu crosda, gu cainnteach, gu h-eithich, gu reasgach, gu ceann-laidir, gu coirbte, gu h-aingidh, gu crosanta, gu droch-mhuinte; gu h-aimhleasach.

PERVERSENESS, *s.* Dalmachd, crosdachd, crosantachd, aimhleas, peasanachd, peasantachd.

PERVERSION, *s.* Mùthadh; mi-sheadhachd, fiaradh, claonadh.

PERVERSITY, *s.* Dalmachd, crosdachd, crosantachd.

PERVERT, *v. a.* Thoir a thaobh, cuir dholaidh, claon, truaill, fiar, mill. He perverted her mind, *thruaill e a h-inntinn.*

PERVERTED, *a.* Truaillte, claon, air fiaradh, air claonadh.

PERVERTER, *s.* Fear millidh, milltear.

PERVERTIBLE, *a.* So-chlaonadh, so-fhiaradh, so-thoirt a thaobh, so-mhilleadh.

PERVICACIOUS, *a.* Rag, reasgach, dùr, ceann-laidir, danarra, rag-mhuinealach.

PERVICACIOUSLY, *adv.* Gu rag, gu reasgach, gu dùr, gu ceannlaidir, gu danarra.

PERVICACITY, *s.* Raige, raigsinn, reasgachd, dùrad, danarrachd, rag-mhuinealachd.

PERVIOUS, *a.* So-dhrùigh, so-imeachd troimh, a ghabhas imeachd troimh, neo-dhionach.

PEST, *s.* Plàigh; breamas, dragh, moille; càs, teinne.

PESTER, *v. a.* Cuir dragh; farranaich, buair, cuir moille.

PESTERER, *s* Draghair, draghadair; fear draghalach, buaireadair.

PESTEROUS, *a.* Draghail, buaireasach.

PESTHOUSE, *s.* Tigh leigheis na plaigh

PESTIFEROUS, *a.* Plàigheil, millteach, marbhtach, sgriosail; gabhaltach; olc.

PESTILENCE, *s* Plàigh, galar millteach, galar mòr, galar sgaoilteach; càs, teinne.

PESTILENT, PESTILENTIAL, *a.* Plàigheil, plàigheil, gabhaltach, sgaoilteach; marbhtach, millteach, olc.

PESTILLATION, *s.* Bruthadh, pronnadh bruanadh.

PESTLE, *s.* Meile, bruthadair, pronnadair; piostal.

PET, *s* Dod, frogan, gnog, sdod, sraoin, sdoid, spuaic; mighean, droch-ghean, peat, peatadh; graidhean, gaolach; urr dhodach; dodag, dodan, sdodag sdodan.

PETAL, *s.* Blath lubh, duilleag, bile, bileag.

PETALOUS, *a* Blathmhor

PETAR, PETARD, *s* Cracair.

PETER'S-PENCE, *s.* Peighinn a Phàp.

PETIT, *a.* Beag, crion.

PETITION, *s* Urnuigh, ùirnigh, athchuinge, guidhe, griosadh, iarrtas

PETITION, *v. a.* Guidh, grios; athchuing, ath-chuingich, iarr.

PETITIONER, *s.* Guidhear, griosair, ath-chuingiche, iarrtasaiche.

PETITIONARY, *a.* Ath-chuingeach, griosach, griosail.

PETRE, *s.* Clach shalainn, creag-shalann.

PETRIFACTION, *s.* Creugachadh

PETRIFY, *v. a.* Creugaich, dean cruaidh, fàs mar chloich. Petrified, *creugaichte, cruadhaichte.*

PETROLEUM, *s* Craig-ùillidh.

† PETRONEL, *s.* Seorsa daig, gunna marcaiche.

PETTICOAT, *s.* Còt boirionnaich, còt mna

PETTIFOGGER, *s.* Fear làgh suarrach, sgriobhair gun fhiù.

PETTIFOGGING, *a.* Suarrach, neo-inmheach, neo-mheasail.

PETTINESS, *s.* Crìne, suarrachd, crionachd, neo-mheasaileachd.

PETTISH, *a* Dodach, gnogach, grogach, sdodach, cainnteach, gnoigeasach, spuacach, spruacach, sornach A pettish female, *gnogag.*

PETTISHNESS, *a.* Sdodachd, gnogachd, gnogaiseachd

PETTITOES, *s* Cosan uircein, ladhran uircein.

PETTO, *s.* Broilleach, uchd

PETTY, *a* Crion, crian, beag, suarrach, neo-luachmhor, air bheag fiach

PETULANCE, *s.* Peasanachd, lonais, gobais, beag-narachd, beileanachd, leamhadas, iasan, droch-mhunadh, leamhadas.

PETULANT, *a.* Peasanach, beadaidh, lonach, beileanach; gobach, beagnarach, brais, dàn, ladurna, mi-mhodhail, droch-mhuinte, leamh; peilpeanta A petulant fellow, *peasan, beadagan, beadan, peilpean*, a petulant female, *lonag, beadag*

PETULANTLY, *adv.* Gu peasanach, gu lonach, gu gobach, gu beagnarach, gu brais, gu dàn, gu ladurna, gu mi-mhodhail, gu droch-mhuinte, gu peilpeanta

PEW, *s.* Suidheagan eaglais, caithir.

PEWET, *s* Dilit, adhaircean luachrach; curcag.

PEWTER, *s.* Peòdar, pleòdar, staòin.

PEWTERER, *s.* Peòdarair, pleodarair

PHAGEDENA, *s* Neasgaid chnamhtach.

PHAGEDENIC, *a.* Cnamhtach.

PHALANX, *s.* Dlù-chuideachd, dlù-bhuidheann

PHANTASM, PHANTASMA, *s.* Faoin-dhòchas, faoin-smuaine, faoin-bharail; taisbean, tannas; teadhbhais.

PHANTOM, *s.* Taisbean, tannas, tannasg; taibhse; faoinbheachd.

PHARE, *s* Tigh soluis.

PHARISAICAL, *a.* Fuar-chrabhach; phairiseach, cealgach.

PHARMACEUTIC, PHARMACEUTICAL, *a.* Leighiseach.

PHARMACOLOGY, *s.* Leigh-eolas, leigheas-eòl.

PHARMACOPŒIA, *s.* Leabhar leigheasan.

PHARMACOPOLIST, *s.* Leigh; leigheadair; fear reiceadh leigheasan

PHARMACY, *s* Leigheadaireachd.

PHASIS, *s.* Scalladh, aogas, dreach; cruth.

PHASM, *s.* Tannas, tannasg, taibhse, sealladh, taisbean.

PHEASANT, *s.* Easag.

† PHEESE, *v a.* Cir, réitich.

PHENIX, *s.* Tearc-eun; eun aonaranach mu 'n abair iad, air basuchadh dha, gun cinn eun eile as a luaithre.

PHENOMENON, *s.* Iongantas, neònachas; sealladh iongantach.

PHIAL, *s* Searrag bheag, gloine, botal, buideal; cop, cup, copan, cupan, cuib, cuirteag

PHILANTHROPY, *s.* Daonnachd, seirce, gradh dhaoine, caomhalachd

PHILANTHROPIST, *s.* Urr dhaonnach, seircean.

PHILIBEG, *s* Féile, féile bheag.

PHILIPPIC, *s* Sglamhradh; òraid, briathrachas, seanachas.

PHILOLOGER, PHILOLOGIST, *s.* Cainmhuiniche; cànainiche, deas-chainntear, gramadach.

PHILOLOGICAL, *a.* Càineanach, càinmbuineach; deaschainnteach, deas-labhairteach; gramadach.

PHILOLOGY, *s.* Cainnt-eòlas; càinmhuineachd; oilean, ionnsuchadh

PHILOMATH, *s* Sgoilear.

PHILOMEL, PHILOMELA, *s.* Spideag, smileach, smiolach.

PHILOMOT, *s.* Dath crotail, crotal.

PHILOSOPHER, *s.* Teallsanach, feallsanach; duine ionnsuichte (no) eagnaidheach.

PHILOSOPHER'S-STONE, *s.* Clach an teallsanaiche; clach a thionndas gu h-òr gach nì ris am bean e.

PHILOSOPHIC, PHILOSOPHICAL, *a.* Teallsanta, feallsanta, teallsanach, feallsanach, eagnaidheach, teallsanachail, feallsanachail, ionnsuichte, foghluimte; caonntach, stuama, measarra

PHILOSOPHICALLY, *adv.* Gu teallsanta, gu feallsanta, gu h-eagnaidheach.

PHILOSOPHIZE, *v a.* Teallsanaich, feallsanaich, be ri teallsanachd

PHILOSOPHY, *s* Teallsanachd, feallsanachd, eagnaidh; ionnsachadh, foghlum

PHILTER, *s* Gradh-ghliseag, deoch gaoil.

PHILTER, *v a.* Easarlaich; thoir deoch gaoil

PHIZ, *s* Aodann, eudann, aghaidh, gnùis, gné.

PHLEBOTOMIST, *s* Féith-ghearradair, fear-leigeil fola.

PHLEBOTOMIZE, *v. a.* Leig fuil, thoir fuil a, tarruing fuil.

PHLEBOTOMY, *s.* Féith-ghearradh, féith-fhosgladh, tarruing fola, fuil-tharruing; sgaoileadh fola.

PHLEGM, *s.* Cailidear, uisge colla, ronnan; musgan; cailidear.

PHLEGMATIC, *a* Uisgidh; ronnach; trom, marbh, fuar.

PHLEGMON, *s* At, atadh, neasgaid.

† PHLEME, *s.* Tuadh fola, tuadbana.

PHLOGISTON, *s.* Uisge theinntidh, uisge lasarach.

Phosphor, Phosphorus, *s.* A mhaidneag, reul na maidne, rionnag maidne; stuth a loisgeas le blàthas an àile.

Phrase, *s.* Doigh-labhairt, doigh-bhriathar, gnàth-fhocal, gnàth-bhriathar; radh, labhairt.

Phrase, *v. a.* Goir, ainmich.

Phraseological, *a.* Doigh-bhriathrach, gnàth-fhoclach, gnàth-bhriathrach.

Phraseology, *s.* Cainnt, gnath-chainnt, gnàth-bhriathar, doigh-sgriobhadh, doigh-labhairt.

Phrenetic, *a.* Cuthach, air chuthach, air bhòile, bainnidh, gòrach, eutrom.

Phrenitis, *s.* Cuthach, boile, bainnidh, breathas, gòraiche; baois.

Phrensy, *s.* Cuthach, boile, breathas, bainnidh, gòraiche, baois, dìobhail, céill, mear-chinn.

Phthisic, *s.* Caitheamh, tinneas caitheimh, éiteach.

Phthisical, *a.* Caithteach; éiteachail.

Phthisis, *s.* Caitheamh, tinneas caitheimh, éiteach, sgamh-chnuimh; meath-thinneas.

Phylactery, *s.* Foir; stiom (no) faim leathann a measg nan Iudhach air an robh sgriobhadh sonruichte.

Phymosis, *s.* Breall.

Physic, *s.* Leigheas, cungaidh leigheis; purgaid; ealadhain leigheis; leigheadaireachd.

Physic, *v.* Leighis; purgaidich.

Physical, *a.* Nàdurra, a réir nàduir; (*medicinal*), leigheasail, leigheasach, fallain.

Physically, *adv.* A réir nàduir; a réir na leigheadaireachd.

Physician, *s.* Leigh, lighiche; olladh, ollamh, ollamh re leigheas.

Physico-theology, *s.* Diadhachd air a foillseachadh trid oibribh nàdair.

Physics, *s.* Teallsanachd; ealadhain nàduir.

Physiognomer, *s.* Gnùis-fhiosaiche, gnùis-bhreitheamh.

Physiognomy, *s.* Gnùis-fhiosachd; aghaidh, gnùis.

Philologist, *s.* Teallsanach nàdurra.

Physiology, *s.* Eòlas nadurra, eolas mu oibribh nàduir; teallsanachd nadurra.

Phytivorous, *a.* Gràintheach.

Phytology, *s.* Luibh-eolas.

Piacular, Piaculous, *a.* Réiteachail; coire-shàsuchail; ciontach.

Pia mater, *s.* Sgannan a tha comhdachadh na h-eanchainn.

Pianet, *s.* Pigheid.

Piazza, *s.* Sraid cholmhuinneach, sràid fo dhion, sràid chomhdaichte.

Picaroon, *s.* Robair, reubair, fear reubainn, spùinneadair.

Pick, *v. a.* (*Choose*), tagh; (*gather*), tionail, dioghluim, trus; (*rob*), goid; (*a lock*), fosgail, fosgail glas a dh' aind eoin; (*pluck*), pioc, piol, spiol; (*a bone*), creim, pioc.

Pick, *s.* Piocaid.

Pickaxe, *s.* Piocaid.

Picked, *a.* Taghta, taghte; biorach, geur.

Picker, *v. a.* Goid, reubainn, robainn.

Picker, *s.* Piocair; piocaid; piocadair.

Pickerel, *s.* Geadasg òg.

Pickle, *s.* Sàil, piceal; staid, cor, inbhe, càs.

Pickle, *v. a.* Saill, picill, dean saillte.

Pickle-herring, *s.* Baoghlan, amadan.

Picklock, *s.* Glas-phiocair, glas-phiocadair, meirleach, spùinneadair.

Pickpocket, *s.* Meirleach, gaduiche, goidiche, gearrasporran.

Pickthank, *s.* Sgilm, lonag, lonan.

Picktooth, *s.* Bior-fhiacal.

Picts, *s.* Cruinnich, Piocaich; daoine dathte.

Picture, *s.* Dealbh, iomhaigh, samhladh, aogas. Draw a picture, *tarruing dealbh.*

Picture, *v. a.* Dealbh, dealbhaich; samhlaich. Pictured, *dealbhta, dealbhaichte; samhlaichte.*

Piddle, *v. n.* Creim; iom-chreim, pioc, ith crioman an sud is an so.

Piddler, *s.* Ioma-chreimiche; fear faoin, fear gun fhiù.

Piddling, *a.* Faoin, fadharsach.

Pie, *s.* Pithean.

Pie, *s.* Pigheid; eun breac air bith.

Piebald, *a.* Ballach, breac, breachd, brocach, ball-bhreac.

Piece, *s.* Mìr, bloidh, bloighid, pìos, crioman, biteag, cuid, earann, pàirt, cuibhrionn; iarmad; fuigheall, fuighleach; (*a gun*), gunna, gunna mòr, gunna glaic; (*in money*), cùinn; (*a whore*), striopach; (*instrument*), cungaidh, inneal. A piece, *gach aon, gach urr, an urr, gach fear, gach té; fa leth;* a broken piece, *bloighid, bloighde, sgealb, spealg; sgcireag;* all of a piece, *uile ionann;* cut it in pieces, *gearr e na mhìreannan;* the men got five shillings a-piece, *fhuair na daoine crùn am fear.*

Piece, *v. a.* Ceangail, tàth; cuir ri chéile; ic; clùd, càirich.

Pieceless, *a.* Iomlan, slàn.

Piecemeal, *adv.* Ann am mìreannan, ann am biteagan, uidh air an uidh, crioman air chrioman.

Pied, *a.* Breac, ballach, ball-bhreac, brocach, eug-samhuil.

Piedness, *s.* Breac, brice, bricead, breacachd, ballachd; eag-samhuileachd.

Pieled, *a.* Maol, gun fholt.

Pier, *s.* Stuc, colmhuinn, colbh, carradh; clachran, laimhrig.

Pierce, *v. a.* Lot, toll, troimh-lot, drùigh, gon, sàth. He pierced his foe, *lot e (no) throimh-lot e 'nàmhaid;* it pierced me to the soul, *ghon e mi thun a chridhe.*

Piercer, *s.* Tolladair, torradh, boireal, gimleid.

Piercing, *a.* Lotach, tollach, geur, guineach, drùighteach, neimhneach. A piercing cry, *sgairt gheur (no) chruaidh, sian, sgread, an-sgairt, an-ghlaodh.*

Piercingly, *adv.* Gu guineach, gu geur, gu drùighteach, gu neimhneach; (*as a cry*), gu sgreadach.

Pierglass, *s.* Sgathan mòr.

Piety, *s.* Diadhachd, diadhaidheachd, cràbhadh, naomhachd.

Pig, *s.* Uircean, uircein, bainbh, muc; torc; morc, lupait. The pig's delight, pluck and eat, *cnuasach an uircein, buain is ith.*

Pig, *v. a.* Bainbh, beir uircean, thoir mach àl mar mhuc.

Pigeon, *s.* Colaman, calaman, colman, colm, colum.

Pigeon-livered, *a.* Meath, tais, bog.

Piggin, *s.* Pigean; soitheach beag fiodha; gogan; coindean.

Pigment, *s.* Dath; lìth.

Pigmy, *s.* Arrachd, tacharadh; slochair, garrach, brideachabhach, luch-armunn, girceau, tamhasg.

Pignoration, *s.* Gealladh, gealltuinn.

Pignut, *s.* Cnò thalmhainn, cnò làir.

Pike, *s.* Geadas, geadasag, gead, pioc uisge, gaill-iasg.

Pike, *s.* Gath, sleagh; forc.

Piked, *a.* Biorach, geur.

Pikeman, *s.* Sleaghair, sleaghadair. Pikemen, *sleaghairean.*

Pikestaff, *s.* Crann sleagh, crann gatha.

PILCH, s. Brad, giobal.

PILCHARD, s. Seorsa sgadain, seorsa éisg a tha ro lionmhor air tràigh Chorn-bhall.

PILE, s. Maide air a shàth anns an talamh, callaid, post, bacan; (*heap*), cruach, dùn, meall; carn, cnuasachd; (*of building*), togail, aitreabh; (*hair or grain*), colg, calg, folt, ròinne; (*of money*), aon taobh cùinne. Against the pile, *an aghaidh chuilg;* a funeral pile, *oll-dreug.*

PILE, v. a. Carn, cruach. Piled, *carnte, cruachta, cruachte.*

PILEATED, a. Biorach; stobach.

PILER, s. Carnair, cruachair, fear carnaidh, cnuasair.

PILES, s. (*In medicine*), ruithe fola anns na màsaibh.

PILEWORT, s. Searraiche.

PILFER, v. a. Goid.

PILFERER, s. Meirleach, gaduiche, goidiche, urr bhradach, meanbh-mheirleach.

PILFERING, s. Goid, goideadh, gaduidheachd, meirleadh, mìn-ghoid, meanbh-ghoid, mìn-mheirleadh.

PILFERY, s. Meirleadh, goid, goideadh, bleid.

PILGRIM, s. Oilthireach, eilthireach, fear-tùruis, tùrusaiche, deòradh, taisdealaiche, eachdranach.

PILGRIMAGE, s. Oilthireachd, naomh-thùras, deòrachd, deòraidheachd, taisdealachd.

PILING, s. Cruachadh, carnadh, cruinneachadh, cnuasachd.

PILL, s. Peil; peileir.

PILL, v. a. Robainn, spùinn, spùill, creach; càirt, ruisg, sgrath, plaoisg.

PILLAGE, s. Robaireachd, reubainn, spùinneadh, spùilleadh, creachadh, creich, ruathar, cobhartach, slad, togail.

PILLAGE, v. a. Robainn, spùinn, spùill, creach.

PILLAGER, s. Robair, fear reubainn, spuinneadair; spùilleadair, sladaiche.

PILLAR, s. Stùc, carradh, colbh, colmhuinn, post; dion, dionair, cùl-taic.

PILLARED, a. Stùcach, colbhach, colmhuinneach.

PILLED-GARLICK, s. Fear maol; sgonn-bhalach, cladhair.

PILLION, s. Pillean, sumag, diolaid boirionnaich.

PILLORY, s. Ballan stiallach, stol nam meirleach; brangas, cabhag, guin-cheap.

PILLOW, s. Cluasag, adhartan.

PILLOW, v. a. Cluasagaich. Pillowed, *cluasagaichte.*

PILOSITY, s. Ròmachas, ròinneachd.

PILOT, s. Fear stiùraidh, sgiobair, stiùradair, fear iùil, piolaid.

PILOT, v. Stiùir, sdiùir; riaghail, treoruich, seòl.

PILOTAGE, s. Stiùradaireachd, duais stiùradair.

PIMP, s. Solaraiche, maor striopaich, drùisear, drusdar; fualan.

PIMP, v. Drùis-sholair.

PIMPERNEL, s. Seorsa plannt, loisgean.

PIMPING, a. Crion, beag, suarach, fadharsach.

PIMPLE, s. Guirean, plucan, leus, bucaid; broth, brachag.

PIMPLED, a. Guireanach, plucanach, bucaideach, clomhach, brothach, creamach, sgabach, carrach, brachach.

PIN, s. Prìn; pinne, pinneadh; dul; dealg, dealgair, binnear. I do not value him a pin, *cha tugainn prìn* (*no*) *srabh air.*

PIN, v. a. Prìn; prìnich; ceangail, trus; dealg; pinn; pinnich; druid, duin; geinn, fang, *pinnid*, prìnte; pinnte; pinnichte.

PINCASE, s. Prìneachan.

PINCERS, s. Turcais; gramaiche, greimiche, teannachair, spioladair.

PINCH, v. a. Pioc, teannaich, gòmagaich, fàisg; mùch, sàruich, claoidh; teum. Pinched, *teannaichte, sàruichte, claoidhte; ann an càs;* pinch the stranger, *pioc an coimheach.*

PINCH, s. (*With the fingers*), pioc, gòmag; (*with the teeth*), teum, tiolam; (*strait*), cruadal, càs, teinne, feum, riachdanas; (*a small quantity*), deann, deannan, deannag; (*of snuff*), snuisean. In a pinch, *ann gàbhaidh, ann an cruadal, ann an càs, ann an teinne.*

PINCHFIST, s. Splocair, spongair; sgroingean.

PINCUSHION, s. Prìneachan; cluasag.

PINE, s. Giuthas, crann giuthais, gall-ghiuthas; pion.

PINE, v. a. and n. Searg, crion, caith, méith; caoidh; bi doilich.

PINED, a. Seargta, seargte, crion; caithte.

PINE-APPLE, s. Pion ubhall.

PINEAL, a. Pionail, pionach, pionamhuil. The pineal gland, *an fhaireag phionail.*

PINFOLD, s. Eachdtarra, buaile-phùind; mainnir; fang.

PINGLE, s. Clobhsa; loinn.

PINGUID, a. Reamhar; gréiseach.

PINION, s. Sgiath eoin; cuibhrichean, ceangal, ceanglaichean.

PINION, v. a. Cuibhrich, ceangail. Pinioned, *cuibhrichte, ceangailte.*

PINIONING, s. Cuibhreachadh, ceangladh.

PINK, s. Seorsa plùrain àluinn do sheorsa lus leth 'n t-samhruidh; dath gorm; seorsa luing le earr chughann, sgòth-long; breac; gobhlachan. Sea-pink, *millsean mara.*

PINK, v. a. Caog, priob; toll.

PINMAKER, s. Prìneadair, bioranachan, bioranaiche.

PINMAKING, s. Prìneadaireachd; bioranachd.

PINMONEY, s. Airgiod pòc mna.

PINNACE, s. Bat aigheir sgoth; bad fad.

PINNACLE, s. Binnean, sturrag, mullach, goicean mullaich, ard-bheann, turaite, stuaic, forbhruach; spiric, spiricean.

PINNACLED, a. Beannach, binneanach.

PINNER, s. Brat cinn mna; prìneadair, bréid.

PINT, s. Pinnt, leth-chàrt, an ceithreamh cuid do phinnt Albannach.

PIONEER, s. Tochailtiche, saighdear tochailte.

PIOUS, a. Diadhaidh, diadhuidh, cràbhach, math, naomh, saoi, deagh bheusach.

PIOUSLY, adv. Gu diadhaidh, gu diadhuidh, gu cràbhach, gu math, gu naomh; gu saoi.

PIONY, s. Lus phoinc, lus a phion.

PIP, s. Guirean fo bhàrr teangaidh circe; duilleag, bileag.

PIP, v. Biog, dean biog, dean biogail.

PIPE, s. Piob, pioban, feadan; feadag; cuislean, claise; (*a flute*), feadan. A bagpipe, *piob mhal;* (of a conduit), *pioban, feadan, claise;* a reedpipe, *ribheid;* windpipe, *goile;* a pipe or faucet, *buagair.*

PIPE, v. a. Cluich air piob (no) feadan.

PIPER, s. Piobair; fear feadain.

PIPING, a. Lag, anfhann, anmhunn, meuranda; spreòchanta, sgreadach; goileach, teth.

PIPKIN, s. Soitheach beag creadha; goileadair, poit bheag.

PIPPIN, s. Ubhal beag goirt.

PIQUANCY, s. Géire, geurad.

PIQUANT, a. Geur, garg, goirt; gobach, goileamach, beumnach, sgaiteach, sgeilmeach; biorach. Piquantly, *gu geur, gu garg, gu beumnach, gu sgaiteach; gu biorach.*

PIQUE, s. Mi-run, farmad, gamhlas, galltanas, droch-rùn,

farran, fàlachd, miosguinn. He has a pique at him, *tha farmad aig ris.*

Pique, *v. a.* Farranaich, feargaich, gon, buair.

Piquet, *s.* Seorsa cluithe air chairtean.

Piracy, *s.* Muir-reubainn, creachadh mara, fogluidheachd fairge.

Pirate, *s.* Muir-spùinnear, creachadair mara, creachadair, fairge; fogh-mharaiche.

Piratical, *a.* Fògluidheach.

Piscation, *s.* Iasgachadh, iasgachd, iasgaireachd.

Piscivorous, *a.* Iasg-itheach.

Pish, *interj.* Fuidh! ab, ab!

Pismire, *s.* Sneaghan, seangân.

Piss, *v. a.* Mùin, mùn, dean uisge.

Piss, *s.* Mùn, fual; maistir.

Piss-a-bed, *s.* Blath a bheamain bhride.

Piss-pot, *s.* Poit mhùin, amar fuail.

Pistol, *s.* Dag; dagadh; piostal.

Pistol, *v. a.* Tilg le dag, piostalaich.

Pistolet, *s.* Dag bheag.

Piston, *s.* Steallair; slat taomadair, slat piob-thaosgaidh.

Pit, *s.* Sloc, slochd, toll; clais, staing; lag, uaigh, poll. The bottomless pit, *sloc an dubh-aigean;* a sand-pit, *toll gaineich;* a sawpit, *sloc-shàbhaidh;* the armpit, *lag na h-achlais.*

Pit, *v. a.* Tochaill, cladhaich, toll; breac.

Pit-a-pat, *s.* Frith-bhualadh; plosgartaich.

Pitch, *s.* Pic, pichd, tearr; (*stature*), inbhe, inmhe, meud, àirde.

Pitch, *v. a.* Pic, tearr, comhdaich le teàrr no pic; suidhich, tilg an comhar chinn, tilg thar cheann. Pitch a tent, *suidhich bùth, leig bùth;* (descend), *teirinn, luidh, tuit;* he pitched upon his head, *thuit e air a cheann.*

Pitcher, *s.* Cuinneag, soitheach uisge, crogan.

Pitched, *a.* Picichte; gearrte.

Pitchfork, *s.* Forc no gobhlan saidh, gobhlan arbhair.

Pitchiness, *s.* Doirche, dubh-dhorchadas.

Pitchy, *a.* Piceach, dorch, dubh-dhorch, duaichnidh, dubh. Pitchy darkness, *dubh-dhorchadas;* pitch dark, *dubh dhorch.*

Pitcoal, *s.* Gual sluic, gual tochailte.

Piteous, *a.* Muladach, brònach; truagh, diblidh; suarrach; (*compassionate*), truacanta; baigheil. A piteous voice, *ciùrlan, ciùrachdan.*

Piteously, *adv.* Gu muladach, gu bronach, gu truagh, gu diblidh, gu suarrach, gu truacanta, gu baigheil, gu ciùrlanach.

Piteousness, *s.* Brònachd, truacantachd; diblidheachd; suarraichead; ciùrlanachd.

Pitfall, *s.* Sloc, slochd, toll, frog; féith, feall-tholl.

Pith, *s.* Neart, treoir, stuth; spionnadh; (*of wood*), glaodhan, laodhan; (*substance*), bith, brigh, smior, smear, tàbhachd.

Pithily, *adv.* Gu neartmhor, gu treun, gu làidir, gu foghainnteach, gu stuthail, gu smiorail, gu tabhachdach.

Pithiness, *s.* Neart, neartmhoireachd, treòir, spionnadh, stuth, brigh, smior, tàbhachd.

Pithless, *a.* Eu-treòrach, fann, lag, anfhann, meuranta, meuranda, gun chll, gun treòir, gun bhrigh, breòite; seochlanach.

Pithy, *a.* Neartar, neartmhor, treun, laidir, foghainnteach; brioghar, brighmhor; smiorail, smearail. Pithy language, *cainnt bhrioghar.*

Pitiable, *a.* Truagh, bochd, diblidh; truaillidh, iontrocair.

Pitiful, *a.* (*Lamentable*), muladach, bochd brònach; (*compassionate*), truacanta, tiom-chridheach, teo-chridheach, maoth-chridheach; baigheil, iochdmhor; (*worthless*), suarrach, diblidh; leibideach; crion. A pitiful case, *cor truagh;* a pitiful fellow, *sgonn;* he is a pitiful fellow who would invite me to a feast and make me pay for it, *is duine dona gun fheum a chuireadh cuir orm féin is caitheamh.*

Pitifully, *a.* Gu muladach, gu bronach; gu truacanta, gu tiom-chridheach, gu h-iochdmhor, gu baigheil; gu suarrach, gu diblidh; gu leibideach.

Pitifulness, *s.* Iochdmhorachd, iochdmhoireachd, iochd; baigh, bàighealachd, truacantas; suarraichead, suarraiche.

Pitiless, *a.* Neo-iochdmhor, ain-iochdmhor, neo-bhaigheil, neo-thruacanta, cruaidh, cruadalach, borb; cruaidh-chridheach.

Pitilessness, *s.* Neo-iochdmhorachd, ain-iochd, ain-iochdmhorachd, neo-bhaighealachd, cruadhas cridhe, cruadal, buirbe.

Pitman, *s.* Sàbhair iochdrach; sloc-shàbhair.

Pitsaw, *s.* Sloc-shàbhaidh, slochd-shàbh.

Pittance, *s.* Lòn (no) cuid mànaich; beagan, deannan, luathsachadh.

Pitted, *a.* (*With the small-pox*), breac.

Pituitous, *a.* Ronnach; uisgidh.

Pity, *s.* Truas, truaghas, truacantas, iochd, baigh, tròcair; comh-mhothuchadh. Take pity on him, *gabh truas ris;* it is a pity that he has not come, *is duilich nach d' thàinig e;* it would be a pity, *b' olc an airidh e.*

Pity, *v. a.* and *n.* Gabh truas ri; bi duilich, bi baigheil. I pity you, *tha mi gabhail truas riut, tha mi duilich air do shon, is truagh leam thu;* I pity your case, *is truagh leam do chor;* I pity not the sigh of my stepmother, *cha 'n oil leam cneud mo leas mhathair.*

Pix, *s.* Naomh-chisteag.

Pizzle, *s.* Slat tairbhe.

Placability, *s.* Ciosnachd, ciùineachd, ceannsachd, sìthaigeantachd, baigh.

Placable, *a.* Ciosnachail, so-chiosnachadh, so-chiùnachadh, baigheil.

Placard, *s.* Ordugh, àithne, fuagradh; iarrtas follaiseach; sànas.

Placate, *v.* Ciùinich, socraich, ceannsaich.

Place, *s.* Àite, ionad; spot, †loc; (*office*), dreuchd, oifig, oich; (*dignity*), inbhe, inmhe, staid, airde; (*room*), àite, rum. A fortified place, *dùn, caisteal, daighneach;* a mansion-place, *aitreabh, àiteas;* in place of, *an àite, 'n àite, airson;* in another place, *ann àite eile;* in any place, *an àite air bith;* in some place, *an àite eigin;* in that place, *san àite sin, san ionad sin, an sin;* in this place, *san àite so, an so;* in this very place, *anns a cheart àite so;* in what place? *c' àite, ciod an t-aite?* by what place? *ciod an rathad?* from what place? *co as?* to some place, *dh' àite eigin;* to what place? *c' àite, cin?* from place to place, *o àite gu h-àite;* give place, *géill, rach gu taobh,* (*no*) *as an rathad.*

Place, *v.* Àitich, socraich, suidhich; cuir, sonraich; cuir air riadh. Place behind, *cuir air chùl;* placed, *àitichte, socraichte, suidhichte.*

Placed, *a.* Ciùin, seimh, samhach, mallta, siochail, siochainnteach, soitheamh, socrach, baigheil.

Placidity, *s.* Ciùineas, seimhe, samhchair.

Placidly, *adv.* Gu ciùin, gu seimh, gu samhach, gu mallta, gu siochail, gu siochainnteach, gu soitheamh, gu baigheil.

Placidness, *s.* Ciùineas, seimhe, samhchair; socair ciùineachd, socraichead.

Placit, *s.* Ordugh, reachd, rùn.

Placket, *s.* Spaidhir; cota.

Plagiarism, *s* Braid-fhòghluim, bleid-fhoghluim.

Plagiary, *s* Braid-fhoghlumaiche; bleid-fhoghlumaiche

Plague, *s.* Plaigh; galar mòr; càs, truaighe; teinne, bochduinn, dragh; mìothlachd; buaireadh Plague take you! *gu gabhadh a bhochduinn thu!*

Plague, *v. a* Buail le plaigh; cuir dragh air, buair, cuir moile air, trioblòidich, farranaich, pian, claoidh. You plague me, *tha thu 'cur dragh orm*

Plagued, *a.* Air buaireadh, buairte, farranaichte, pianta I am plagued with it, *tha mi air mo phianadh leis.*

Plaguy, *a.* Plaigheil; draghail, draghalach, farranach, buaireasach, trioblaideach

Plaice, *s.* Leathag, seorsa éisg

Plaid, *s* Breacan, breachdan, cadath, plaid; gibeal; giobal. A belted plaid, *féile bhreacain.*

Plain, *a* (*Even*), réidh, réith, còmhnard, mìn; socrach; neo-chorrach; (*evident*), soilleir, riachdail, so-thuigsinn; (*honest*), còir, onorach, treibhdhireach; neo-charach, simplidh; (*without ornament*), neo-sgiamhach, neo-bhriagh, neo-ghrinn, gun ghrinneas A plain country, *machair, magh-thìr*, a plain field, *lòn, réidh, réidhlean*, to be plain with you, *leis an fhìrinn innseadh;* that is quite plain, or not doubted, *tha fhios air sin*, tell him the plain truth, *innis an fhìrinn da, innis a cheart fhìrinn da.*

Plain, *s* Réidh, réith, lòn, comhnard, machair, learg, faiche, raon, réidhlean, blàr, blàran, ach, achadh.

Plain, *v a* Dean còmhnard, dean réidh, mìnich dean mìn, dean socrach, locair, locraich.

Plain-dealing, *s* Ionracas, tréibhdhireas

Plain-dealing, *a* Ionraic, treibhdhireach, onorach, neo-charach.

Plaining, *s.* Caoidh, gul, tuireadh

Plainly, *adv* Gu comhnard, gu réith, gu follaiseach, gu riachdail, gu soilleir, a rìreadh.

Plainness, *s.* Comhnardachd, simplidheachd; ionracas; riachdalas, soilleireachd, fosgailteachd, neo-ghrinneas

Plaint, *s* Caoidh, gearan, bròn, cumha, tuirse; acain, tuireadh, casaid, gearan, ciùrlan, ciùrachdan

Plaintful, *a* Tuirseach, brònach, muladach; ciurlanach, ciùrachdanach

Plaintiff, *s* Fear casaid, casaidiche.

Plaintive, *a.* Brònach, muladach, tuirseach, acaineach; gearanach, caointeach, ciùrlanach

Plaister, *s* See **Plaster**.

Plait, *s* Fille, filleadh, filleag; dual, pleat; cas, preasag, rocan Full of plaits, *preasagach*

Plait, *v a.* Fill, preas, preasagaich, cas, (*as hair*), dual, dualaichte, pleat, fìgh Plaited, *fillte, preasta, casta*, plaited hair, *falt dualaichte*

Plaiter, *s.* Filleadair; dualaiche, dualadair

Plan, *s* Seòl, doigh, modh, achd, rathad, lathailt, rod, innleachd, déalbh The proper plan, *an seòl ceart, an doigh cheart*

Plan, *v.* Dealbh Planned, *dealbhta*

Planched, *a.* Plangaichte, clàrach.

Plane, *s* Locar, lochdar A hand-plane, *lochdar dùirn*, a plow-plane, *locar gròbaidh*, a jack-plane, *locar sguitsidh*, a jointer-plane, *locar dluthaidh.*

Plane, *v.* Locair, lochdair, locraich, mìnich. Planed, *locraichte.*

Plane, *s.* (*In geometry*), réidh.

Planet, *s* Reul sheachranach, reul sheabhaideach.

Planetarium, *s.* Reul-dhealbh

Planetary, *a.* Reulach, reultach

Planet-struck, *a* Seargta; fo uamhann.

Plane-tree, *s.* Pleandruinn.

Planish, *v. a.* Locair, mìnich, dean réidh; soillsich, dean glan (no) soilleir

Plank, *s* Planc, plang, bord, clàr, deile. A floor of planks, *urlar bhord.*

Plank, *v a.* Plancaich, dèilich. Planked, *plancaichte.*

Plant, *s.* Plannt; luibh; meacan, meachdan; maothan, fiùran; (*of the foot*), bonn

Plant, *v. a.* Planntaich; suidhich, cuir; socraich; cuir air chois. Plant a colony, *suidhich bruidheachd*, plant a tree, *suidhich craobh.*

Plantage, *s.* Luibh, lus.

Plantain, *s* Cuach phadruig; seorsa craoibh Innseanaich.

Plantation, *s.* Planntachadh, suidheachadh; lios, gàradh; ùr-aiteachadh, bruidheachd

Planted, *part.* Planntaichte, suidhichte; socraichte.

Planter, *s.* Fear suidheachaidh, planntair.

Plash, *s* Slob, lochan; geòt; uisge, aite fliuch slobach.

Plash, *a* Meanglan tàthta.

Plash, *v a.* Figh, dual, dualaich, pleat

Plashy, *a* Fliuch, aitidh, slobach, geòtach, uisgidh, bog. A plashy place, *slob, geòt, boglach.*

Plasm, *s* Molltair.

Plaster, *s.* Plasd aoil, aol-phlàsd, dòb, (*in medicine*), plàsd, plàsd dubh, trait. No plaster is applied to a threat, *cha téid plàsd air bagairt*

Plaster, *v. a.* Plàst, plàsd, dòb, plasdaich. Plastered, *plasdaichte.*

Plaster, *s* Aoladair, plàsdair

Plastering, *s* Plàsdadh, dòbadh.

Plastic, *a* Dealbhach.

Plastron, *s.* Sumag basbair, mìr leathair air uchd fir teagaisg fheannsaireachd

Plat, *v. a.* Figh, dual, dualaich, pleat.

Plat, *s.* Mìr beag fearainn, goirtean, innseag.

Plat, *s.* Figheadh, dual.

Platane, *s* Pleandruinn.

Plate, *s* (*Of metal*), lann; mìr tana meiteal; mias, aisead, troinnsear, trainnsear, soithichean airgid, airgiod bùird, airgiod grabhailte; tachdar airson an ruith eich réis

Plate, *v. a.* Lannaich, buail tana mar iarunn.

Platform, *s* Réidh, àite comhnard; seòl, dealbh.

Plato, *s* Ainm feallsanaich a bha san Aithne. Platonic love, *gradh aigne, càil-ghradh, fior-ghradh.*

Platoon, *s* Buidheann beag shaighdearan.

Platter, *s* Mias, aisead, troinnsear, aine

Plaudit, *s* Moladh, cliù

Plauditory, *a* Moladach, moltainneach; cliùiteachail.

Plausibility, *s.* Dàichealachd; coslas, coslachd, cosamhlachd.

Plausible, *a.* Dà'cheil, dathail, coslach, beulchar, sgeimheil, ceabhachdach.

Play, *v. a* Cluith, cluich, iomairt; dean mire, dean sùgradh. Play at cards, *cluich air chairtean*, it has no room to play, *cha 'n eil rum cluiche aige*, what shall we play at? *ciod air an cluich sinn?* play on or mock, *fanaid, fochaid.*

Play, *s* Cluithe, cluiche, cluicheag, sùgradh, mire, ealaidh; iomairt, rum (no) comas cluiche (no) carruchaidh. Boy's play, *cluiche cloinne*; a play-house, *tigh cluiche*, a stage-play, *cluiche, sgearach.*

Playbook, *s* Leabhar cluiche.

Playday, *s.* Là cluiche, la sollain.

Player, *s.* Fear cluiche; cleasaiche

Playfellow, *s.* Comh-shùgraiche, co-shùgraiche, comh-chearrach.

Playful, *s.* Mear, sugach, mireagach; sunntach; mac-nusach. Playfully, *gu mear, gu sugach.*

Playgame, *s.* Cluiche cloinne.

Playhouse, *s.* Tigh cluiche, tigh cluithe.

Playsome, *a.* Mear, mireagach, sugach.

Playsomeness, *s.* Mire; sùgradh.

Plea, *s.* Cùis lagha, cùis; leithsgeul; eillimh, dion.

Plead, *v. a.* Tagair; agair, reusonaich; thoir mar leithsgeul; dean aighneas, dion, cuir a mach.

Plaything, *s.* Culaidh shùgraidh, culaidh chleasachd, deideag; ailleagan.

Pleadable, *a.* A dh' fhaotas agradh, so-thagradh.

Pleader, *s.* Tagrair, fear lagha, aghnaiche, agairtear; agartair; † aighne.

Pleading, *s.* Tagradh, agradh, tagairt, agairt.

Pleasant, *a.* Taitneach, grinn, ciatach, sòlasach; (*sweet*), milis; blasda, taitneach; (*merry*), suilbhear, sunntach, greannar; lurach, cridheil. A pleasant day, *là grinn*, a pleasant girl, *caileag ghreannar*, somewhat pleasant, *leth-char taitneach;* pleasant abroad and surly at home, *eife-achdach a muigh, is brèineach aig an tigh;* pleasant is the bet that is shared, *is sona gach cuid an comaidh.*

Pleasantly, *adv.* Gu taitneach, gu grinn, gu ciatach; gu suilbhear, gu sunntach.

Pleasantness, *s* Taitneachd, ciataichead, ciatachd; sòlas; sunnt; cridhealas, greannarachd.

Pleasantry, *s* Conn; subhachas.

Please, *v. a.* and *n.* Taitinn, toilich, taitnich; togair; thig ri. Please him, *toilich e, thig ris, taitinn ris;* (*humour*), breug. If you please, *ma 's e do thoil e, mu thogras tu*, pleased, *toilichte, toileach;* easy to be pleased, *so-thoileach-adh*, hard to be pleased, *do-thoileachadh, do-riarachadh, doirbh.*

Pleasing, *a.* Taitneach, ciatach, sòlasach, greannar.

Pleasurable, *a* Taitneach, ciatach, sòlasach.

Pleasure, *v.* See **Please**.

Pleasure, *s.* Tlachd, toileach-inntinn, toil-inntinn, toile-achadh, sògh, saimh, samhain, subhachas, suaimhneas; (*choice*), roghainn; (*will*), toil; ailghios; àille, (*service*), seirbheis, deagh thùrn. It gave me much pleasure, *thug e mòran toil-inntinn dhomh*, if it be your pleasure, *ma 's e do thoil e;* a man of pleasure, *fear saimhe*, take your plea-sure, *gabh do thoil.*

Pleasure, *v. a* See **Please**.

Plebeian, *s.* Iochdaran, urr chumanta, ceatharnach, bodach, tuathanach.

Plebeian, *a.* Iochdarach, cumanta, cumaint.

Pledge, *s* Geall, gealladh, earlas; iarlas; urradh; paine-achas, urras.

Pledge, *v.* Cuir an geall; thoir an urras, rach an geall; rach an paineachas.

Pledget, *s.* Cadas; catas, giobag, ascairt

Pleiades, *s.* Comh-shoillse mu thuath, an grioglean.

Plenariness, *s.* Iomlanachd, foirfeachd

Plenary, *a* Iomlan, foirfe; làn.

Plenipotence, *s.* Làn-chumhachd, iomlanachd, cumhachd.

Plenipotent, *a.* Làn-chumhachdach.

Plenipotentiary, *s.* Làn-chumhachdair; teachdair; ard-fhear gnothuich; sith-fhear-ionaid

Plenist, *s.* Lànadair, fear chumas a mach nach 'eil ni air bith fòlamh

Plenitude, *s.* Làine, iomlanachd, lànachd.

Plenteous, *a.* Pailt, lionmhor; torrach, saibhir.

Plenteously, *adv.* Gu pailt, gu lionmhor, gu saibhir

Plenteousness, *s.* Pailteas, lionmhorachd, lionmhoireachd, torrachas; saibhreas.

Plentiful, *a.* Pailt, lionmhor, saibhir, torrach.

Plentifully, *adv.* Gu pailt, gu lionmhor, gu saibhir.

Plentifulness, *s.* Pailteas, lionmhoireachd, saibhreas, torrachas, torraichead, saibhireachd.

Plenty, *s* Pailteas, lionmhoireachd, saibhreas, saibhireachd, torraichead, toic. Great plenty, *làn-phailteas*, I have plenty, *tha 'm pailteas agam, tha pailteas agam*, the crumbs of plenty are better than the middle dish of want, *is fhearr iomall a phailteis, no teis meadhon na gainne.*

Pleonasm, *s* Làn-bhriathar

Plethora, *s* Iomadaich lionnta agus fola; domhaileachd

Plethoric, *a.* Domhail, dumhail, làn.

Plethory, *s.* Dòmhaileachd, dùmhaileachd.

Plevin, *s* Barandas, urras

Pleurisy, *s.* Greim fola, boinn fola, treathaid, greim san taobh.

Pleuritic, *a* Greimeannach.

Pliable, *a.* Sùbailt, so-lùbadh, so-lùbaidh, maoth, maoth-anach, so-fhilleadh, so-fhillte; so-chomhairleachadh, umhal, soitheamh, soimeach.

Pliableness, *s.* Sùbailteachd, maothanachd, maothalachd, soimeachd.

Pliancy, *s.* Subailteachd, sùblachd; maothalachd

Pliant, *a.* Sùbailt; maoth, maothanach, maothalach, slat-anta, so-lùbaidh; rithinn; so-chomhairleachadh; ùmhal, easgaidh, soirbh

Pliantness, *s.* Sùblachd, sùbailteachd, so-lùbachd, maoth-alachd, soimeachd.

Plication, Plicature, *s.* Filleadh.

Pliers, *s.* Gramaiche.

Plight, *v. a.* Geall, thoir an geall, thoir an urras

Plight, *s.* (*State*), cor, staid, inbhe, inmhe, cal, (*fold*), filleadh, preasag; (*pledge*), geall, coingheall A good plight, *deagh chal*

Plinth, *s.* Bun stùic.

Plod, *v. a* Saothraich, saoithrich, allabanaich.

Plodder, *s.* Fear saoithreachail, allaban, fear trom baogh-alta.

Plodding, *s* Saoithreach, saothaireach, allabanaich, obair, iomairt, sior dheananaich

Plot, *s.* (*Of ground*), goirtean, innseag, croit; (*stratagem*), innleachd, seòl; (*conspiracy*), comh-bhoinn, ceannairc dhiomhair, comh-rùn; (*of a building*), dealbh; (*a sea chart*), cairt iùil.

Plot, *v. a.* Dean ceannairc dhiomhair, dean comh-bhoinn; cnuasaich; dealbh, sonraich

Plotter, *s.* Fear ceannairc, fear comh-bhoinn

Plover, *s.* Feadag, triollachan; faideag.

Plough, *s.* Crann, crann araidh; (*tillage*), ar, aradh, tuath-anachas, treabhachas.

Ploughboy, *s.* Gille iomain, gille greasaidh; baoghlan, gu-raiceach.

Plough, *v a* Treabh, crann, thoir a stigh, dean dearg, dean ar. Ploughed, *treabhta, treabhte.*

Ploughing, *s* Treabhadh, ar, treabhachas, tuathnachas

Ploughland, *s* Talamh treabhaidh; talamh treabhta, crann fearainn.

Ploughman, *s.* Fear croinn, airean, tuathanach, fear araidh, crannair.

Ploughshare, *s.* Coltar.

Pluck, *v. a.* Spiol, spian, spion, piol, buain, tarruing, lomair. Pluck up your spirits, *tog do mhisneach;* pluck from the root, *spion as a bhun;* the pig's pleasure, pluck and eat, *cnuasach an vircein, buain is ith.*

Pluck, *s.* Spioladh, spiol, spian; tarruing; pluchd; an sgamhan is an cridhe, abach; (*courage*), misneach, smior; (*effort*), oidhirp, deuchainn.

Plucker, *s.* Spioladair, spianadair.

Plucking, *s.* Spioladh, spianadh.

Plug, *s.* Stoipeal; ploc, tarrang.

Plug, *v.* Stoipealaich, ploc.

Plum, *s.* Plumbais; deich ceud mìle punnt Sasunnach. A plum-tree, *craobh phlumbais.*

Plumage, *s.* Ite, iteach, iteagan, clòiteach, clòimh, clòimhteach, cléite, cléiteach.

Plumb, *s.* Luaidh-shreang, ingear; luaidh sreing.

Plumb, *adv.* Dìreach na sheasamh.

Plumb, *v. a.* Tomhais, grunndaich; grunnaich.

Plumber, *s.* Luaidhear.

Plumcake, *s.* Aran milis.

Plume, *s.* Ite, iteach, iteagan; clòimh, clòimhteach, cléite, dos; (*pride*), ardan, leoim, sgòd. A plume of feathers, *dos iteagan;* (*of a helmet*), seoc, seocan. A little plume, *dosan.*

Plume, *v.* Sgiamhaich, breaghaich, briaghaich, sgeadaich, ardaich; spion, spiol; dean leoim (no) sgòd (no) uaille.

Plumigerous, *a.* Iteagach, clòimheach, clùimheach, clùimhneagach.

Plumiped, *a.* Cloimh-chosach, clùimh-chasach.

Plummet, *s.* Sreang thomhais, sreang riaghailt; ingear, meas-chaor.

Plumosity, *s.* Cluimheachd, clòimheachd.

Plumous, *a.* Cloimheach, clùimheach, iteagach.

Plump, *s.* Bad; dos, cluigean; baguid.

Plump, *a.* Sultmhor, sultar, reamhar; sliogta, sliosmhor, feòlar; dòmhail, dùmhail, tiugh.

Plump, *v. a.* and *n.* At; séid suas, domhlaich, fàs reamhar; dean plub mar ni cloch san uisge.

Plump, *adv.* Le plub, n'a phlub.

Plumpness, *s.* Sultmhorachd, sultmhoireachd, sult, tiughead, ramhad, reamhad.

Plumporridge, *s.* Brochan plumbais, lite phlumbais.

Plumpudding, *s.* Putag phlumbais, argnadh.

Plumpy, *a.* Sultmhor, reamhar, tiugh, domhail.

Plumy, *a.* Iteagach, clòimheach.

Plunder, *v. a.* Spùinn, spùill, creach, tog creach; robainn, reubainn, plundrainn, fasaich. Plundered, *spuinnte, spuillte, creachta, robainte, reubainnte;* he will not plunder a country, *cha chreach e dùthaich.*

Plunder, *s.* Spùinn, spùinneadh, creach, creachadh, creich, cobhartach, *plundrainn.*

Plunderer, *s.* Spuinneadair, fear spùinne, creachadair, robair, fear reubainn, méirleach, gaduiche.

Plundering, *s.* Creachadh, creach, spùinn, spùilleadh *plundrainn.*

Plunge, *v. a.* and *n.* Pluinns; tum, tom; tilg sios; rach fo 'n uisge.

Plunge, *s.* Pluinnse, tumadh, tomadh; tilgeadh; càs, teanntachd; teinne.

Plungeon, *s.* Sgarbh.

Plunger, *s.* Pluinnsear; tumadair, tomadair.

Plunging, *s.* Plubraich, pluiunsinn.

Plunket, *s.* Seorsa guirme.

Plural, *a.* Tuille is a h-aon, iomad, iomadh; iolar.

Pluralist, *s.* Iom-bheathaiche; minisdear aig am bheil tuille is aon eaglais.

Plurality, *s.* Iomadachd, iomadaidh, mòran.

Plush, *s.* Eudach giobagach.

Pluvial, *a.* Uisgeach, uisgidh; frasach, fliuch.

Ply, *v. a.* Figh gu teann; toinneamh, iomair, iomramh; oibrich, cuir ri; lùb; géill, striochd, asluich, guidh.

Ply, *s.* Dual, lùb, lùbadh; pleat; car, toinneamh.

Pneumatic, Pneumatical, *a.* Àilear; gaoithe.

Pneumatics, *s.* Aile-eolas, àile-theagasg; (*in the schools*), eolas mu bhith spioradail.

Pneumatology, *s.* Teagasg (no) foghlum mu bhith-spioradail.

Poach, *v. a.* Earr-bhruich, leth-bhruich; faoin-bhruich sgaillt; goid sitheann goid.

Poached, *a.* Earra-bhruich, leth bhruich.

Poacher, *s.* Fàiche-mheirleach; fògluiche, fiadhachd.

Poachiness, *s.* Àitidheachd.

Poaching, *s.* Fiadh-mheirle, fàiche-mheirle.

Pock, *s.* Poc, pochd; pocan, balg, pùidse, màl, maileid; bolg do 'n bhreac.

Pocket, *s.* Pòc, pochd, pòcaid, pùidse; mealbh.

Pocket, *v. a.* Pòcaich, pùidseach, cuir ann am pòc; fulaing (no) giùlain tàmailt; cuir suas le tàmailt.

Pocketbook, *s.* Leabhar pòc.

Pocketglass, *s.* Gloine pòc.

Pockhole, *s.* Bolg bric, aile bric.

Pockiness, *s.* Breac, brice.

Pocky, *a.* Breac.

Poculent, *a.* Airson òl.

Pod, *s.* Cochull, (no) rùsg peasrach, meiligeag, moinigeag, plaosg, sgrath, spalag.

Podagrical, *a.* Alt-ghalarach.

Podge, *s.* Clabar, eabar, poll, slob, làthach; cumasg.

Poem, *s.* Dàn, duan, rann, bardachd, rannachd, laoidh.

Poesy, *s.* Bardachd, filidheachd, dànachd, dàntachd.

Poet, *s.* Bard, filidh, fear dàn, †mal, †lamais; †bol. A poet-laureate, *priomh-bhard.*

Poetaster, *s.* Sgonn-bhard.

Poetess, *s.* Ban-bhard.

Poetic, Poetical, *a.* Bardail, filidheach, duantach.

Poetry, *s.* Bàrdachd, ranntachd, duantachd, duantaireachd; dantachd, filidheachd.

Poignancy, *s.* Géire, géiread, gonadh; (*of taste*), seirbhe, searbhas.

Poignant, *a.* Geur, searbh, trioblaideach, gonach; beumnach, faobharach, amhgharach.

Point, *s.* (*Of a sharp instrument*), roinn, bior; (*in reading*), pong, stad; (*case*), cùis, rud, gnothach; (*of land*), rutha, rugha, sròin, maol; innis, ceann eang; (*tip*), bàrr, mullach; (*of the compass*), airde; (*object*), cuspair, cusbair; (*to tie with*), iall, sreang; ceangal; (*of a discourse*), ceann teagaisg. In point of, *a thaobh;* point blank, *as an aghaidh, calg dhìreach;* at the point of death, *thun a bhàis, ris a bhàs;* the point of a needle, *roinn snàthaid;* armed at all points, *còmhdaichte gu h-iomlan le armachd.*

Point, *v.* Rann; roinn, pongaich; geuraich, bioraich; comharraich, seòl; stiùir; tomh, feuch. Point the way, *feuch an rathad;* point at him, *tomh ris.*

Pointed, *a.* and *part.* Geur; biorach; pongail, geuraichte, bioraichte, roinnichte.

Pointedly, *adv.* Gu pongail, gu pungail.

Pointedness, *s.* Géire, geurad, geiread; pongaileachd.

Pointer, *s.* Cù eunaich.

Pointingstock, *s.* Ball àbhachd, ball magaidh, ball fochaid.

Pointless, *a.* Maol, neo-bhiorach, neo-gheur.

Poison, *s.* Puinnsean, nimh, dùigh.

Poison, *v. a.* Puinnseanaich, truaill. Poisoned, *puinnseanaichte;* he is poisoned, *tha e air a phuinnseanachadh, tha e puinnseanaichte.*

Poisonous, *a.* Puinnseanta, puinnseanach; nimheach, nimhneach, nimheil.

Poisonously, *adv.* Gu puinnseanta, gu nimheil, gu neimhneach.

Poisonousness, *s.* Puinnseantachd, nimhneachd.

Poitrel, *s.* Beart uchd, uchd-bheairt, uchdach, uchdeididh.

Poize, Poise, *s.* Cothromaich, cudthromaich, tromaich; tomhais. Poized, *comhthromaichte, tomhaiste.*

Poize, *s.* Cothrom, cudthrom; co-chothrom.

Poke, *s.* Pòc; balg, màileid.

Poke, *v. a.* Smeuraich, meuraich, bi ri meuragaich; ruathar, bùraich; caruich, sir, rannsuich; (*as fire*), bruillich.

Poker, *s.* Bior caruchaidh; brod iaruinn.

Polar, *a.* Mul-cheannach.

Pole, *s.* Cabar; lorg mhòr; lonn, lunn, cuaille, geadh; tomhas chuig slat gu leth air fad; (*of the earth*), mulcheann, mul-ghart, mul-chuth.

Poleaxe, *s.* Tuadh da fhaobhar, tuadh catha.

Polecat, *s.* Fòcallan, fòclan.

Polemic, Polemical, *a.* Connspuideach, connspaideach, connsachail, deasboireach.

Polemic, *s.* Connspuidiche, deasboiriche.

Polestar, *s.* An rionnag thuathach.

Police, *s.* Riaghladh bhaile mòir; riaghailt dùcha.

Policed, *a.* Riaghlaichte, riaghailtichte.

Policy, *s.* Riaghladh; crionnachd; seòl, cuilbheart, car; seòltachd.

Polish, *v. a.* Soillèirich, soillsich, mìnich; locair; glan, dean glan, sliog, lonnairich, sgùr, caislich.

Polish, *s.* Sgùr, sgùradh, mìneachadh, lannair, lonnair.

Polishable, *a.* So-sgùradh, so-mhìneachadh.

Polished, *a.* Glan, soilleir, loinreach; funndruinn; caislichte.

Polisher, *s.* Sgùradair, mìneachair, bearradair; deasachair.

Polite, *a.* Modhail, beusach, iulmhor, siobhailt, sibhealta, suairc. Politely, *gu modhail, gu beusach.*

Politeness, *s.* Modhaileachd, modhalachd, beus, beusaichead, iùlarachd, suairceas.

Politic, *a.* Seolta, crionna, glic, sìcir, carach, cealgach, domhainn.

Political, *a.* Rioghachdail; riaghlachail. Politically, *gu carach, gu seòlta.*

Politician, *s.* Fear eòlach air riaghladh; cuilbheartair.

Politics, *s.* Iùl riaghlaidh, seòltachd riaghlaidh, riaghladh, riaghladaireachd.

Politure, *s.* Sliobadh, loinnreachd.

Polity, *s.* Riaghladh; modh riaghlaidh.

Poll, *s.* Ceann, cunntas cheann. Poll-money, *airgiod cinn.*

Poll, *v. a.* Bearr; sgath; gearr; sgud; lom, spùinn, spùill, creach; tog.

Pollard, *s.* Garbhan, bràn; seorsa éisg; craobh sgathte.

Pollavering, *a.* Rabhdach, bruidhreach; bòileiseach. A pollavering fellow, *rabhdair.*

Pollen, *s.* Plùr mìn.

Pollenger, *s.* Crionach, creathach.

Poller, *s.* Robair, creachadair, spùinneadair; taghadair; fear roghnachaidh, roghnachair.

Polling, *s.* Bearradh, sgathadh, gearradh, sgudadh; lomairt.

Pollock, *s.* Tulag, pulbhag; seorsa éisg.

Pollute, *v. a.* Mill, salaich, truaill, truaillich, mi-naomhaich. He polluted her, *thruaill e i.*

Polluted, *a.* Millte, salaichte, truaillte, truaillichte.

Polluter, *s.* Truailleadair; milltear; trualliche; truaill-each; fear truaillidh.

Pollution, *s.* Truailleachd, truailleadh, truaillidheachd, neo-ghloine, salachadh, mi-naomhachadh.

Poltroon, *s.* Cladhair, gealtair.

Polyanthus, *s.* Seorsa blàth (no) plùrain; an iomadhuilleag.

Polyedrical, Polyedrous, *a.* Ioma-shlisneach, iomshliosach, ioma-thaobhach.

Polygamy, *s.* Iol-phòsadh; iomnuachadh.

Polyglot, *a.* Ioma-chainnteach, ioma-chànuineach, iolchainnteach.

Polygon, *s.* Ioma-chearnag, iol-chearnag.

Polygonal, *a.* Ioma-chearnach, iol-chearnach, iom-oisinneach.

Polygraphy, *s.* Ogham, ioma-sgriobhadh, iol-sgriobhadh.

Polymathy, *s.* Iol-oilean.

Polylogy, *s.* Bruidhneachd, gobais.

Polypody, *s.* Cloch-reathnach; ceis-chrann.

Polypous, *a.* Ioma-chosach.

Polypus, *s.* Ainmhidh iom-chosach; an iom-chosag.

Polysyllabical, *a.* Iom-shiolach.

Polysyllable, *s.* Iom-shioladh.

Polytheism, *s.* Ioma-dhia-chreideamh.

Polytheist, *s.* Ioma-dhia-chreideach.

Pomaceous, *a.* Ubhlach.

Pomade, *s.* Gruaig-ungadh, ungadh cubhraidh.

Pomander, *s.* Ball cùbhraidh.

Pomatum, *s.* Gruaig-ungadh.

Pome, *v. n.* Fàs cruinne, cinn cruinn mar ubhal, ceartlaich, cearslaich.

Pomegranate, *s.* Gràn ubhall.

Pommel, *s.* Cnap; ploc; meallan; ceann.

Pommel, *v. a.* Gréidh, buail, straoidhle; bruth, dornaich. Pommelled, *buailte, dornaichte.*

Pomp, *s.* Greadhnachas, mòr-chuis, spagluinn; fearas mhòr, uaill, gloiream.

Pompion, *s.* Seorsa mil-ubhall, peapoc.

Pompous, *a.* Greadhnach, mòr-chuiseach, greadhnachail, mòralach, stràiceil, uallach, atmhor, spagluinneach, glòireiseach, staideil, gloireamach; mileanta.

Pompously, *adv.* Gu greadhnach, gu mòr-chuiseach, gu moralach, gu stràiceil, gu h-uallach, gu h-atmhor, gu spagluinneach.

Pompousness, *s.* Greadhnachas, mor-chuis, mòralachd, stràic, uaille, atmhorachd, spagluinneachd.

Pond, *s.* Lochan, loch, poll, linne; slob.

Ponder, *v. a.* Cnuasaich, beachdaich, cothromaich, beachdsmuainich, smuainich.

Ponderable, *a.* So-chothromachadh, so-thomhasadh.

Ponderation, *s.* Cothromachadh, tomhasadh.

Ponderer, *s.* Cnuasair, fear smuainteachail.

Ponderosity, *s.* Cothrom, truime.

Ponderous, *a* Trom, cudthromach, cothromach

Ponderously, *adv.* Gu trom, gu cudthromach, gu cothromach.

Ponderousness, *s* Cudthrom, cothrom, truime.

Pondweed, *s.* Linne-lus. Broad-leaved pondweed, *duilleasg na h-aibhne*

Poniard, *s* Biodag; durc; sgian fhada; sgian achlais.

Ponk, *s.* Tannas, tannasg, taibhse, bòchdan

Pontage, *s* Cìs drochaide.

Pontiff, *s.* Ard-shagart, am Pàpa

Pontifical, *a* Ard-shagartail, sagartail

Pontificate, *s.* Ard-shagartachd; pàpachd.

Pontifice, *s.* Obair drochaide.

Ponton, *s* Drochaid shnamhaidh; drochaid mhaide

Pony, *s* Gearran, each beag; *sealtaidh*, *pònaidh*

Pool, *s* Poll, lochan, linne. A deep pool, *glumagan*, having deep pools, *glumagach*

Poop, *s* Ceann deiridh luing, earradh luing.

Poor, *a* Bochd, truagh, aimbeartach, uireasbhach, uireasbhuidheach, daibhir, docrach; ainniseach, ainnis; iosal, neo-inbheach, diblidh, neo-shona, (*as land*), lom, tana; (*in body*), trungh, caol; meuranda; glas A poor man, *duine bochd;* a poor creature, *truaghan*, the poor man's money does not take cold, *cha ruig fuachd air airgiod aimbeirt* (*iomairt*).

Poor, *s.* Bochd

Poorhouse, *s.* Tigh eiridinn.

Poorly, *adv.* Gu truagh, gu bochd, gu h-uireasbhach; (*in health*), gu soithich. Poorly off, *gu bochd dheth, gu h-olc dheth.*

Poorness, *s* Bochduinn, uireasbhuidh, aimbeartas, truaghas, truaghanachd, daibhreas, ainniseachd

Poorspirited, *a.* Suarrach, crion, truaillidh, bochd, neo-mhisneachail, cailleachail, cailleachanta, gealtach

Pop, *s* Braidhe, urchair bheag, sgeilc

Pop, *v. a* and *n* Giolc, leum, ruith, grad-imich He popped in upon us, *ghiolc e stigh oirnn.*

Pope, *s* Seorsa éisg.

Pope, *s* Am Pàpa

Popery, *s.* Pàpanach.

Pope's-eye, *s.* Fàireag mhàis

Pop-gun, *s.* Gunna gailc, gunna cailc

Popinjay, *s* Piorraid; cnag, (*puppy*), uaillean, leoimean

Popish, *a.* Pàpanach

Poplar, *s* Critheann, critheach. A poplar tree, *crann critheann, craobh chritheann, craobh phobhuill, crann pobhuill.*

Poppy, *s.* Crom-lus, codalian; beilbheag.

Populace, *s* Pobull, sluagh, an cumantas, an cumanta, an tuath, an sluagh cumaint; a mhor-mhuinntir, gràisg, prabar.

Popular, *a* Furanach, earailteach, measail aig an t-sluagh, ionmhuinn

Popularity, *s* Meas an t-sluaigh.

Populate, *v. n* Sluaghaich, fàs sluaghmhor (no) lionmhor.

Population, *s* Aireamh sluaigh; sluaigh, sluaigheachd, cinneachduinn dhaoine, àiteachadh.

Populous, *a.* Sluaghmhor, lionmhor, daoineach, pobullach

Populousness, *s.* Sluaghmhoireachd.

Porcelain, *s.* Earraichean creadha, creadh finealta, seorsa luibh.

Porch, *s.* Ailear, foir-dhorus, for-dhorus, poirse.

Porcupine, *s.* Gràineàs

Pore, *s* Tucha, tiuchan, sùileag; tollan ro bheag sa chraiceann trid an tig fallus

Pore, *v. n.* Amhairc, geur-amhairc, dearc, seall.

Poring, *s.* Amharc, geur-amharc, dearcadh, sealltuinn

Pork, *s.* Muic-fheoil

Porker, *s.* Muc, uircean.

Porket, *s* Uircean

Porkling, *s.* Uircean òg

Porous, *a.* Tolltach.

Porousness, *s.* Tolltachd.

Porphyry, *s.* Seorsa marmhoir ghrainneanaich.

Porpoise, *s.* Peileag, muc-bhiorach.

Porraceous, *a.* Uaine.

Porrection, *s* Sìneadh.

Porret, *s.* Léigis.

Porridge, *s.* Brochan, lite, easach, praiseach. A porridge pot, *poit bhrochain.*

Porringer, *s* Trainnsear, troinnsear, mias, aisead

Port, *s* Port, càla, càladh, achdarsaid; dorus, geat.

Port, *s* Giùlan, imeachd, iomchar, dol a mach; méinn.

Port, *s* Fion dearg, (*on board of ship*), taobh cli luing.

Portable, *a.* So-ghiulan, so-iomchar, a ghabhas giùlan; so-fhulang

Portal, *s.* Geat, port, dorus.

Portance, *s.* Giulan, iomchar; dol a mach, caitheamh beatha.

Portcullis, *s.* Drochaid thogalach; cliath thogalach.

Porte, *s.* Cùirt an Turcaich

Ported, *a* Air iomchar gu riaghailteach

Portend, *v. a.* Fàisnich, fàistinnich, roimh-innis, cuir air mhànadh, roimh-fheuch, feuch (no) innis roimh laimh.

Portent, *s* Droch chomhar, droch shànas, tuar.

Portentous, *a.* Tuarach, mi-aghmhor; tubaisdeach.

Porter, *s* Portair, fear geat, dorsair; (*of burden*), portair, fear iomchar, malcair; (*in brewery*), portair.

Porterage, *s* Airgiod, caraiste, malcaireachd, duais fear iomchair

Porthole, *s.* Gunna-tholl, toll gunna

Portico, *s* Sraid chomhdaichte; sgàilean, ailear.

Portion, *s.* Pàirt, cuibhrionn, cuid, earann, mir, roinn, crannchur; (*in marriage*), tochar, pòrsan, crodh, dubhairidh. The fool's portion is at the mouth of the sack, *tha cuid an amaduin am beul a bhuilg.*

Portion, *v a.* Roinn, pàirtich, riaruich; (*in marriage*), pòrsanaich. Portioned, *roinnte, pairtichte, pòrsanaichte.*

Portioner, *s.* Riarachair

Portliness, *s* Stàidealachd, maise, uallachd; spairiseachd, sultmhoireachd

Portly, *a.* Stàideil, maiseach, uallach, flathail, tabhachdach, spairiseach; làn, domhail, dumhail, sultmhor.

Portman, *s.* Bùirdeasach, fear mhuinntir h-aon do na cuig càlaidh.

Portmanteau, *s.* Maileid, mailios, bag, sacaid

Portrait, *s.* Dealbh, eugas, riochd, samhladh.

Portraiture, *s.* Dealbh, aogas, samhladh, coslas, riochd.

Portray, *v. a.* Dealbh, tarruing, sgiamhaich. Portrayed, *dealbhta, tarruingte*

Portress, *s* Ban-phortair, bean iomchair, ban-dorsair.

Porwiggle, *s.* Ceann-phulag; adag bulgach.

Pory, *a* Tolltach, làn tholl.

Pose, *v. a.* Cuir an iomcheist; sgrud, ceasnaich, ceistich.

Poser, *s* Sgrudair, ceasnachair.

Posited, *a.* Àitichte, suidhichte, socraichte

Position, *s.* Àite, staid; seasamh, suidheachadh.

Positive, *a.* Cinnteach, dearbh-chinnteach, deimhinn, seasmhach, beachdail, beachdaidh; dòchasach, fèin-bharaileach, rag-bharaileach.

Positively, *adv.* Gu fior, gu cinnteach, gu deimhinn; gu beachdail, gu dòchasach, gu fèin-bharaileach, gu fèin-bharaileachd.

Positiveness, *s.* Deimhinneachd, beachdalachd, dòchasachd, fein-bharaileachd.

Posnet, *s.* Beasan; sgeileit, aghann; soitheach.

Posse, *s.* Buidheann; bannal; dròbh, lòd.

Possess, *v. a.* Sealbhaich, faigh, gabh seilbh, faigh seilbh. Possessed, *sealbhaichte.*

Possession, *s.* Sealbhachadh, seilbh, tùinidh; toic; urlamh, urlamhas, forlamhas. Take possession, *gabh seilbh; in full possession, ann an làn sheilbhe;* put out of possession, *cuir a seilbh;* in my possession, *ann mo sheilbhe, orm, agam.*

Possessive, *a.* Sealbhach, seilbheach.

Possessor, *s.* Sealbhadair, sealbhaiche; urlamhaiche; fear seilbhe.

Posset, *s.* Easach bhainne; barrag.

Possibility, *s.* Coslas, coslachd, comas.

Possible, *a.* Coslas, colsach, comasach, comasail, a dh' fhaotas bhith, a dh' fhaotas tachairt. Is it possible? *bheil sin comasach? an urrainn sin tachairt?*

Possibly, *adv.* Gu coslach; theagamh, dh' fhaoidte.

Post, *s.* Post; teachdair cabhagach; (*in the army*), post, oich; (*a stake*), post, cabar, cuaille, colbh, stac; (*office*), oifig, dreuchd, aite; (*of a door*), ursann.

Post, *v. a.* Aitich, suidhich; tar-sgriobh; dean astar gu luath, grad-shiùbhail, dean luath-thùrus; dean deifir.

Postage, *s.* Paigh litreach.

Postboy, *s.* Gille litrichean; gille ruithe, teachdair.

Postdiluvian, *a.* Deigh-dhilinneach.

Poster, *s.* Teachdair, fear (no) gille ruithe.

Posterior, *a.* An deigh, deireannach, deireannaiche, iar; an deigh laimh.

Posteriors, *s.* Ceann deiridh, tòin, màsan.

Posterity, *s.* Siol, sliochd, clann, gineal; iarmad; fuil, linntean ri teachd.

Postern, *s.* Geat beag, dorus beag, for-dhorus.

Post-hackney, *s.* Eich reidh.

Post-haste, *s.* Siubhal, cabhagach, deifir, cabhag. In post-haste, *an cabhaig; ann an deifir.*

Post-house, *s.* Tigh litrichean.

Posthumous, *a.* An deigh bàis.

Postil, *s.* Mìneachadh, soilleireachadh.

Postil, *v. a.* Mìnich, soilleirich, soillsich.

Postillion, *s.* Gille greasaidh; carbadair, gille carbaid.

Postman, *s.* Post, gille ruithe, fear litrichean, teachdair.

Postmaster, *s.* Ard-phost; post.

Postmeridian, *s.* An deigh mheadhon là.

Post-office, *s.* Tigh litrichean.

Postpone, *v. a.* Cuir dheth, cuir dàil, dàilich, dean moille.

Postscript, *s.* Fà-sgriobhadh, fos-sgriobhadh, deigh-sgriobhadh.

Postulate, *s.* Iarruidh, sireadh, iarrtas.

Postulate, *v. a.* Iarr, sir, iarr gu smachdail.

Postulation, *s.* Smuaineachadh.

Posture, *s.* Suidheachadh; staid, àite, seòl; seasamh.

Posy, *s.* Blàth-dhos; sgriobhadh air fàinne.

Pot, *s.* Poit, coire, aghann, prais; corcan; cop, cup, copan. A small pot, *corcran, caiteag;* a chamber-pot, *poit mhùin, poit leabach;* an earthen pot, *poit chreadha, suacan, pigidh;* the brim of a pot, *fraidhe* (*no*) *foir poit;* he has gone to pot, *chaidh e dholaidh, chaidh e thun an diabhoil.*

Pot, *v. a.* Poit, poitich, cuir ann am poit.

Potable, *a.* Ion-òltadh, so-òladh, a dh' fhaodas (no) a ghabhas òl.

Potargo, *s.* Saillean Innseanach.

Potash, *s.* Luaithre feamuinn (no) rainich. A lye of potash, *fileadh.*

Potation, *s.* Òl, deoch, tarruing.

Potatoe, *s.* Buntàt; bun taghta.

For the latter ingenious and happy rendering (meaning *choice root*) of the word *potatoe*, the Gaelic language is indebted to the late Sir John M'Gregor Murray, Bart. of Lendrick.

Potbellied, *a.* Bronnach, bagach, gaor-bhronnach, poitbhronnach.

Potbelly, *s.* Bru mhòr, bag, seileid.

Potch, *s.* Sàth, puc, starr.

Pot-companion, *s.* Companach, goisdidh.

Potency, *s.* Cumhachd, neart, tréine, treòir; tairbhe; comas, éifeachd.

Potent, *a.* Cumhachdach, neartmhor, treun; laidir; tarbhach, éifeachdach.

Potentate, *s.* Cumhachdach, uachdran, flath, righ.

Potential, *a.* Coslach; neartmhor, comasach, murrach, treun, éifeachdach, tarbhach.

Potently, *adv.* Gu cumhachdach, gu treun, gu làidir, gu neartmhor, gu h-éifeachdach.

Pothanger, *s.* Bùthlas, bùlas, bùthal, slabhruidh, drolla.

Pother, *s.* Iomairt, obair; buaireas, tuasaid; stairn.

Pother, *v. a.* and *n.* Dean oidhirp dhiomhain; cuir an iomcheist.

Pot-herb, *s.* Luibh poit; poit-luibh.

Pot-hook, *s.* Bùlus, bùthlas, bùthal, drolla.

Potion, *s.* Deoch, deoch leigheis.

Pot-lid, *s.* Brod poit; clàr poit, failceann, fairceall.

Potsherd, *s.* Slige chreadha.

Pottage, *s.* Brochan, lite, easach, praiseach, crocad.

Potter, *s.* Criadhadair, criadhair, criadh-fhear; pigeadair.

Pottery, *s.* Criadhadaireachd; obair chreadha.

Potting, *s.* Òl, pòit, geòc, ruite, ruitearachd.

Pottle, *s.* Pinnt Albannach, leth ghalan; ceithir pinntean Sasunnach; poiteal.

Potulent, *a.* Air an daoraich; a ghabhas òl.

Pouch, *s.* Pòc, pòchd, pùitse; sporran; màl, màileid.

Pouch, *v. a.* and *n.* Pòc, pòcaich, pùitsich; sluig; dean spluig, dean goill.

Pouch-mouthed, *a.* Grosach, gnosach, goilleach, meillmeach.

Poult, *s.* Eireag, isean, pùt, eun òg; (*a blow*), buille, straoidhle, stear, gleadhar.

Poulterer, *s.* Fear reic eun, eun-reiceadair.

Poultice, *s.* Plàsd; tràit; ceirean.

Poultry, *s.* Eunlaith challta; tigh cheare; eun mhargadh.

Pounce, *s.* Iongna, ìne, cràg eoin; fudar sgriobhaidh.

Pounce, *v. a.* Toll, troimh-tholl; greimich le ionga.

Pounced, *a.* Iongnach, ìneach; crògach. Pounced box, *bocsan tolltach.*

Pound, *s.* Punnd, punnd cothroim; (*in money*), punnd Sasunnach. Half a pound, *leth-phunnd;* a pound and a half, *punnd gu leth;* ten pound weight, *deich puinnd cothroim;* ten pounds sterling, *deich puinnd Shasunnach;* (*enclosure*), fàl; mainnir, fang.

Pound, *v. a.* Pronn, bruth, méil; bruan, bris; (*as cattle*), cuir stigh. He will pound it to ashes, *pronnaidh se e gu luaithre.* Pounded, *pronnta, proinnte, méilte;* (as cattle), *dùinte stigh, air an cur stigh.*

Poundage, *s.* Na h-uibhir as a phunnt; cìs air son crodh a theid a chur stigh.

Pounder, *s.* Pronnadair, bruthadair, méileadair

Pour, *v. a* and *n* Taom, dòirt, taosg, sruth, bras-bhrùchd, brùchd, dian-ruith.

Pourer, *s* Taomair, taomadair, dòrtair

Pouring, *s* Taomadh, dòrtadh, taosgadh, sruthadh; brùchd, dian-ruithe. A pouring forth, *dòrtadh mach.*

Pout, *s.* Seorsa éisg, eun, pùt.

Pout, *v n.* Bi gnoigeach, dean stoid. One who pouts, *méillicean, méillear.*

Pouting, *a* Méilleach, meilleagach, meillиceach. One with pouting lips, *meillicean*

Poverty, *s* Bochduinn, aimbeart, aimbeairt, aimbeartas, uireasbhuidh, daibhreas, gainne, baigearachd, dealbhas, glaise, billeachd, intreadh No poverty like entire want, *cha 'n eil airc ann gu airc na h-ainnis*

Powder, *s* Fùdar; dùs, duslach, luaithre, ceal Sneezing powder, *snaoisean*

Powder, *v a* Mìn-phronn, pronn, méil; fùdaraich; saill Powdered, *pronn, proinnte, fùdaraichte, saillte.*

Powder-box, *s* Bocsa fùdair

Powder-horn, *s.* Adharc fhudair.

Powder-mill, *s* Muileann fudair

Powder-room, *s.* Ionad fùdair, aite fùdair.

Powdering-tub, *s* Saillear, sailleir; stannd feòl.

Powdery, *a* Mìn, pronnta, pronn, so-phronnadh

Power, *s* (*Ability*), comas, neart, cumhachd, tréine, treise, spionnadh, urrainn, treòir, pùghair, (*authority*), ughdarras, ceannas, ceannsal, smàichd, smachd, inbhe, (*plenty*), pailteas, moran, lòd, (*of the mind*), càil, buaidh, feart; (*sovereign*), righ-flath; (*army*), feachd, sluagh, slogh. As far as lies in my power, *fhads a tha e ann mo chomas, fhads is urrainn mi, fhads a dh' fhaotas mi*, it was not in my power, *cha robh e ann mo chomas*, if it be in your power, *ma 's urrainn thu*, the powers of the mind, *feartan* (*no*) *buaidhean na h-inntinn*, a power of people, *lòd sluaigh*, the powers of Europe, *rìghrean na h-Eòrpa*, give power, *thoir cead, builich cead* (*no*) *comas*

Powerful, *a* Làidir, treun, cumhachdach, neartmhor, comasach, inbheach, crodha, calma, murrach, tarbhach; (*effectual*), éifeachdach.

Powerfully, *adv.* Gu làidir, gu treun, gu cumhachdach, gu neartmhor, gu comasach, gu crodh, gu calma, gu h-éifeachdach

Powerfulness, *s.* Cumhachd, neart, comas, tréine, treise, spionna, treòir, urrainn

Powerless, *a* Anfhann, anmhunn, fann, lag, neo-threun, neo-chomasach, truagh, meirranta, breòite, spreòchanta.

Pox, *s* Breac, breachd The small-pox, *a bhreachd*, the cow-pox, *breac a chruidh*, the chicken-pox, *a bhreac òtraich*, the French pox, *an galar Frangach, a ghall-bholgach*

Practicable, *a.* So-dheanamh, so-dheanta, a ghabhas deanamh; comasach

Practicability, *s.* Comasachd

Practical, *a* Deantach, gnàthach

Practically, *adv* A thaobh gnàth, a réir gnàth

Practice, *s* Gnàth, gnàthachadh, cleachd, cleachduinn, cleachdadh; nòs, àbhaist It was my practice, *bu chleachd leam, bu ghnàth leam, b' àbhaist domh*, the practice of medicine, *gnàthachadh leigheis*, put in practice, *gnathaich, cuir an gniomh;* practice makes perfection, *cleachd a ni teòmadh.*

Practise, *v. a* Cleachd; gnàthaich; dean ri Practise upon one, *meall neach, thoir an car a neach.* Practiced, *cleachdte, cleachdta, deanta ri.* Practiced in war, *deanta ri cogadh.*

Practiser, *s.* Gnàthachair, cleachdair.

Practitioner, *s* Gnàthachair, fear gnathachaidh A medical practitioner, *fear gnàthachaidh leigheis.*

Precognita, *s.* Roimh-eòlas, roimh-bheachd, roimh-fhios, fios (no) eolas roimh-laimh.

Pragmatic, Pragmatical, *a.* Rudach; meachranach; ceigeanach; beadaidh.

Pragmatically, *adv.* Gu rudach, gu meachranach; gu beadaidh, gu ceigeanach.

Praise, *s* Mol, moladh, cliù, iomradh, alladh, luaidh; onoir, urram. He got great praise, *fhuair e mòran cliù;* praise from the worthless, *moladh na daoidheachd.*

Praise, *v.* Mol, cliùthaich, ard-mhol, ardaich, arduich, glòirich, càn moladh; (*prize*), meas Praise the good day in the evening, *mol a là math mu oidhche.*

Praiser, *s.* Moladair; fear molaidh

Praising, *s* Mol, moladh, cliùthachadh, ardachadh; (*of goods*), measadh.

Praiseworthy, *a* Ionmholta, airidh air cliù, airidh air moladh; cliù-thoilltinneach

Praiseworthiness, *s* Ionmholtachd.

Prance, *s.* Bàt comhnard

Prance, *v n.* Leum, sùrdagaich, meamnaich, gluais gu meamnach.

Prancing, *a.* Leumnach, sùrdagach; beiceasach; meamnach.

Prank, *v. a.* Sgeadaich, sgiamhaich, breaghaich, briaghaich, uigheamaich, nàisnich, grinnich.

Prank, *s* Prat, aincheart; cleas; cluithe; droch ghniomh, droch thùrn

Prate, *s* Goileam, lonais, gob, gobais, gobaireachd, faoin-chòmhradh, sior-chainnt, glagais, glag, sgistearachd. Leave off your prate, *leig dhiot do lonais.*

Prate, *v* Dean goileam, dean lonais, dean gobais, labhair gu faoin

Prater, *s* Gobair, glagair, sgilm, roithre, sgistear.

Prating, *s* See Prate

Prating, *a* Goileamach, gobach, lonach A prating girl, *caireag*

Prattle, *v. n.* Dean goileam (no) lonais, dean gobais, labhair gu faoin. How you do prattle! *is ann ort a tha 'n lonais!*

Prattle, *s.* Goileam, lonais, beulais, gob, gobais, gobaireachd, faoin-chainnt, faoin-chomhradh, glag, glagais, arraghloir, clab, beilean, peilp, biolasg

Prattler, *s.* Gobair, ràcair, glagair, sgilm-clabair, beilean, peilpean.

Prattling, *s* Goileam, gobais, gob, lonais, ràcaireachd, gobaireachd, clabaireachd, peilpeanachd, beileanachd.

Prattling, *a.* Goileamach, lonach, gobach, beileanach, peilpeanta, biolasgach

Pravity, *s* Truailleachd, aingidheachd, coirpteachd, dubhailc, olcas.

Prawn, *s* Carthan; cloidheag

Pray, *v a* and *n.* Guidh, athchuing, grios, dean ùrnuigh, asluich, iarr, sir. I pray you, *guidheam ort, griosam ort.*

Prayer, *s* Ùrnuigh, ùirnigh, athchuinge, guidhe, grios, asluchadh, iarrtas, dubaist, fighil. At prayer, *ri ùrnuigh, ag ùrnuigh, aig an ùrnuigh.*

Prayer-book, *s.* Leabhar ùrnuigh.

Preach, *v. n.* and *a.* Searmonaich, dean searmoin; sgaoil, craobh-sgaoil. He preached well, *is maith a shearmoinich e.*

Preacher, *s.* Searmoiniche, ministear; minisdear.

Preaching, *s.* Searmonachadh.

Preamble, *s.* Roi-radh.

Preapprehension, *s.* Roimh-bheachd.

Prebend, *s.* Stìpean mhinisteara Sasunnach.

Prebendary, *s.* Priomhlaid.

Precarious, *a.* Neo-chinnteach, neo-chinnte, teagamhach.

Precariously, *adv.* Gu neo-chinnteach, gu teagamhach.

Precariousness, *s.* Neo-chinntealas, teagamhachd.

Precaution, *s.* Aire, furfhogradh, rabhadh, faicill.

Precede, *v. a.* Rach roimh, thig roimh, rach air thoiseach, roimh-imich, roimh-ruith, foir-imich, foir-cheumnaich; faigh barrachd.

Precedence, *s.* Toiseach, tùs; onoir, inbhe; barrachd.

Precedent, *s.* Eisiomlair, eisiomplair.

Precedent, *a.* Air thoiseach, toiseachail, a gabhail roimh, roimh.

Precedently, *a.* A roimh, a roimh laimh.

Precentor, *s.* Clèireach, fear a chur mach shalm, fear shalm.

Precept, *s.* Àithne, ordugh, reachd, riaghail; riaghailt. According to your precept, *a rèir d' àithne.*

Preceptive, *a.* Teagasgach; riaghailteachail.

Preceptor, *s.* Oid-ionnsuich, teagasgair, fear teagaisg, maighistir, maighstir sgoil, tuitear, fath-oid.

Precession, *s.* Gabhail roimh, dol roimh, imeachd roimh, tùs-imeachd.

Precinct, *s.* Crioch, foir, oir, iomall, foir-iomall.

Precious, *a.* Prìseil, luachmhor, measail, daor, cosdail; riomhach.

Preciously, *adv.* Gu prìseil, gu luachmhor, gu measail; gu daor.

Preciousness, *s.* Prìsealachd, luachmhoireachd, meas.

Precipice, *s.* Cas-chreag, bruach; cas-bhruthach, oill-bhinn.

Precipitance, Precipitancy, *s.* Cabhag, deifir, luathas, braise, braisead, dèine.

Precipitant, *a.* Cabhagach, brais, deifireach, ruith an comhar a chinn, tuiteam an comhair a chinn.

Precipitantly, *adv.* Gu cabhagach, gu brais, gu deifireach, an comhair a chinn, gu dian.

Precipitate, *v. a.* and *n.* Tilg sios, tilg an comhair a chinn; tilg cas thar a cheann.

Precipitate, *a.* Corrach; an comhair a chinn, cas thar cheann; (*rash*), cabhagach, obann, dian, brais.

Precipitately, *adv.* An comhair a chinn, cas thar a cheann; (*rashly*), gu cabhagach, gu h-obann, gu dian, gu brais.

Precipitation, *s.* Tilgeadh an comhair a chinn, tuiteam an comhair a chinn; dian-ruithe, dian-chabhag, toireannachd.

Precipitous, *a.* (*Steep*), cas, corrach; (*rash*), brais, obann, deifireach, dian.

Precise, *a.* Pongail, riaghailteach; foirmeil, cuimeir, deas, freagarrach; sicir; goirrid, aithghearr; (*finical*), rudach; ceigeanach, meachranach.

Precisely, *adv.* Gu poncail, gu riaghailteach, gu dìreach, gu foirmeil, gu freagarrach, gu cuimeir, gu deas, gu sicir; (*finically*), gu rudach, gu ceigeanach, gu meachranach. Precisely so, *dìreach mar sin.*

Preciseness, *s.* Pongaileachd, pungaileachd, foirmealachd.

Precision, *s.* Pongaileachd, pungaileachd; cuimeireachd; freagarrachd; ceigeanachd.

Preclude, *v.* Dùin a mach, druid a mach; bac. Precluded, *dùinte a mach.*

Precocious, *a.* Abaich tuille is tràthail, abuich roi 'n mhithich, dian-abaich.

Precociousness, *s.* Abuidheachd, dian-abachd.

Precocity, *s.* Abachd roimh an am, dian-abachd.

Precogitate, *v. a.* Roimh-smuainich, roimh-bheachdaich.

Precognition, *s.* Roimh-eòlas, eòlas roimh-laimh, roimh-fhiosrachadh.

Preconceit, *s.* Roimh-bharail, roimh-smuaine, roimh-bheachd.

Preconceive, *v.* Roimh-bharalaich, roimh-smuainich, baralaich (no) smuainich roimh-laimh.

Preconception, *s.* Roimh-bharail; roimh-bheachd, barail roimh-laimh.

Precontract, *s.* Roimh-cheangal, ceangal (no) bargan roimh-laimh.

Precontract, *v. a.* Roimh-cheangail, ceangail (no) barganaich roimh-laimh.

Precursor, *s.* Roimh-theachdair; teachdair; fear (no) gille ruithe.

Predaceous, *a.* Creachadach, creachach; foirneartach; spùinneach; bradach.

Predation, *s.* Reubainn, creach, creachadh, creich, spuinneadh.

Predatory, *a.* Reubainneach, foirneartach, creachadach, spùinneadach; ciocrach, cion-acrach.

Predecessor, *s.* Fear a bha roimh (no) air thoiseach air fear eile; sinnsear.

Predestinarian, *s.* Fear a tha creidsinn ann an roimh-orduchadh (no) ann dàn.

Predestinate, *v. a.* Roimh-thagh, roimh-orduich, cuir an dàn.

Predestination, *s.* Roimh-orduchadh, roimh-thagh.

Predestine, *v. a.* Roimh orduich, roimh-thagh.

Predetermination, *s.* Roimh-shònruchadh; roimh-òrduchadh, dàn.

Predetermine, *v. a.* Roimh-shonruich, roimh-orduich, sonruich (no) orduich roimh-laimh. Predetermined, *roimh-shonruichte, roimh-orduichte.*

Predicament, *s.* Ordugh; àireamh; gné, seòrsa.

Predicant, *s.* Dearbhair; foillseachair, fear a chuireas an cèil.

Predicate, *v.* Dearbh, abair, labhair, cuir an cèil, cuir as leth.

Predicate, *s.* For-bhriathar; ni sam bi a theid radh, aicheadh mu neach sam bi, mar tha 'n duine ciallach, cha n-eil an duine neo-bhàsmhor.

Predication, *s.* Dearbhadh, foillseachadh.

Predict, *v. a.* Fàisnich, fàistinnich; roimh-innis, fàistinn, nochd roimh-laimh.

Prediction, *s.* Faistinn, faistinneachd; faisneachd, fàidhdearachd; sànas; tuar.

Predictive, *a.* Fàistinneach, faisneachail.

Predictor, *s.* Fàidh, faidheadair, fiosaich.

Predigestion, *s.* Ana-cnamh.

Predispose, *v. a.* Freagarraich, ullamhaich roimh-laimh; aom roimh-laimh.

Predominance, Predominancy, *s.* Barrachd, lamh an uachdar.

PREDOMINANT, *a.* Uachdrach; buadhach; cumant, cumaint, riaghlach.

PREDOMINATE, *v. n.* Riaghlaich, buadhaich, bith an uachdar.

PRE-ELECT, *v. a.* Roimh-thagh, tagh roimh-laimh; roghanaich a roimh-laimh.

PRE-EMINENCE, *s.* Barrachd, toiseach, inbhe, uachdranachd, àirde.

PRE-EMINENT, *a.* Barrachdail, gun choimeas, sàr.

PREEN, *v. a.* Deasaich iteagan mar ni na h-eòin chum itealachadh ni 's luaithe sna speuraibh.

PRE-ENGAGE, *v.* Gabh roimh-laimh, geall roimh-laimh, fàstaidh roimh-laimh.

PRE-ENGAGEMENT, *s.* Gabhail roimh-laimh, gealladh roimh-laimh.

PRE-ESTABLISH, *v. a.* Socraich (no) sònruich roimh-laimh, roimh-shocraich, roimh-shònruich.

PRE-EXIST, *v.* Bi beò roimh.

PRE-EXISTENCE, *s.* Roimh-bhith, roimh-bheath, ceud-bhith, ceud-bheath.

PREFACE, *s.* Roimh-radh, roi' radh; tionsgnadh, toiseach, roimh-bhriathar.

PREFATORY, *a.* Tòisich, tòiseachaidh, roimh-radhach. Prefatory words, *briathran tòiseachaidh.*

PREFECT, *s.* Uachdaran, uachdran, ceannard, comanntair.

PREFECTURE, *s.* Uachdranachd; maorsainneachd.

PREFER, *v. a.* Roghnaich, arduich, tog, thoir gu h-inmhe; thoir air adhairt. I prefer that to this, *is àille leam so no sin;* which do you prefer? *co dhiùbh is docha leat?*

PREFERABLE, *a.* Roghnaiche, fearr, ion-roghnachadh. Which of them do you think preferable? *co dhiubh is roghnaiche leat?*

PREFERENCE, *s.* Roghainn, taghadh.

PREFERMENT, *s.* Arduchadh, inbhe, inmhe, staid, urram.

PREFERRED, *part.* Roghnaichte, taghte, taghta; (*in dignity*), ardaichte, arduichte, urramaichte.

PREFERRING, *s.* Roghnachadh, taghadh.

PREFIGURATION, *s.* Roimh-dhealbhadh, roimh-shamhlachadh.

PREFIGURE, *v. a.* Roimh-dhealbh, roimh-shamhlaich. Prefigured, *roimh-shamhlaichte, roimh-dhealbhta.*

PREFIX, *v. a.* Roimh-shonruich, socraich (no) sonruich a roimh-laimh; suidhich, socraich, sonruich; cuir roimh. Prefixed, *air a chur roimh, roimh-shonruichte, roimh-shocraichte.*

PREFORM, *v. a.* Roimh-dhealbh. Preformed, *roimh-dhealbhta.*

PREGNANCY, *s.* Leth-tromachd, torrachas, torraichead.

PREGNANT, *a.* Leth-tromach, torrach; làn, trom, mòr. She became pregnant, *dh' fhas i torrach, chinn i leth-tromach, thorraicheadh i.*

PREGNANTLY, *adv.* Gu torrach, gu làn, gu trom, gu riachdail.

PREGUSTATION, *s.* Roimh-bhlasdachd.

PREJUDGE, *v.* Thoir breith roimh-laimh; roimh-bhreith; roimh-dhìt, dìt roimh-laimh.

PREJUDICATE, *v. a.* Thoir breith roimh-laimh, roimh-bhreith.

PREJUDICATION, *s.* Roimh-bhreith; breith roimh-laimh.

PREJUDICE, *s.* Foir-bhreith; droch-bharail, claon-bhreith; fuath; cron, dochair, dochoir, dochann. Hear without prejudice, *éisd gun chlaon-bhreith;* I have a prejudice against him, *tha droch bharail agam dheth;* without prejudice to me, *gun dochoir dhomhsa.*

PREJUDICE, *v. a.* Dochoirich, dochairich; lughdaich; thoir droch-bharail.

PREJUDICIAL, *a.* Dochannach; cronail; olc, ciurrail; leth-tromach.

PRELACY, *s.* Easbuigeachd, easbuidheachd; priomhlaideachd.

PRELATE, *s.* Easbuig; priomhlaid.

PRELATION, *s.* Cur a roimh; roghnachadh, arduchadh, taghadh.

PRELECTION, *s.* Leughadh; òraid; searmoin.

PRELIBATION, *s.* Roimh-bhlas, roimh-bhlasdachd.

PRELIMINARY, *a.* Roimh, roimh-laimh; deasachail. Preliminary arrangements, *roimh-cheartaichean.*

PRELUDE, *s.* Roimh-chluiche; ceòl toisich, tùs-cheòl.

PRELUSIVE, *a.* Roimh, roimh-laimh.

PREMATURE, *a.* Tuille is luath, tuille is tràthail; roimh an mhithich, roimh an am, an-abuich, for-abuich; tuille is cabhagach.

PREMATURELY, *adv.* Tuille is luath, tuille is tràthail; roimh an mhithich, roimh 'n àm.

PREMATURENESS, PREMATURELY, *s.* Anabachd, for-abachd, ana-cabhag; luathas.

PREMEDITATE, *v.* Roimh-bheachdaich, roimh-smuainich, roimh-smuaintich.

PREMEDITATION, *s.* Roimh-bheachdachadh, roimh-smuaineachadh, roimh-smuainteachadh.

PREMICES, *s.* Ceud-thorradh; ceud-mheas.

PREMIER, *a.* Toiseach; priomh, ard, ceud.

PREMISE, *v. a.* Mìnich (no) soilleirich roimh-laimh; abair roimh-laimh; socraich air tùs.

PREMISES, *s.* Tighean; talamh.

PREMIUM, *s.* Duais airson barrachd, diol, tuarasdal, duilgne.

PREMONISH, *v.* Roimh-chomhairlich, comhairlich a roimh laimh, roimh-fhiosraich.

PREMONISHMENT, *s.* Roimh-chomhairleachadh, roimh-chomhairle, roimh-fhios, roimh-fhiosrachadh, roimh-shànas, rabhadh.

PREMONITION, *s.* Roimh-chomhairle, roimh-fhios, roimh-chomhairleachadh, roimh-fhiosrachadh, roimh-shànas.

PREMONITORY, *a.* Sànasach, roimh-shànasach, roimh-chomhairleachail.

PRENOMINATE, *v. a.* Roi-ainmich; roimh-ainmich; roimh-shonruich. Prenominated, *roimh-ainmichte.*

PRENOTION, *s.* Roimh-fhios, roimh-bheachd.

PRENUNCIATION, *s.* Roimh-innseadh; roi'-innseadh.

PREOCCUPANCY, *s.* Roimh-shealbhachadh, roimh-sheilbh.

PREOCCUPATE, *v.* Roi-shealbhaich, roimh-shealbhaich.

PREOCCUPATION, *s.* Roimh-sheilbh, roimh-shealbhachadh.

PREOCCUPY, *v. a.* Roimh-shealbhaich, gabh seilbh an toiseach. Preoccupied, *roimh-shealbhaichte.*

PREOMINATE, *v.* Fàisnich, fàistinnich.

PREOPINION, *s.* Roimh-bharail, roimh-bheachd.

PREORDAIN, *v. a.* Roi-orduich, roimh-orduich. Preordained, *roimh-orduichte.*

PREPARATION, *s.* Deasachadh, deasach, ullamhachadh, ullachadh, deanamh deas.

PREPARATIVE, *a.* Deasachail, ullachail; mar dheasachadh, mar ullachadh; roimh.

PREPARE, *v. a.* Deasaich, dean deas, ulluich, ullamhaich, dean ullamh, dean réidh; uigheamaich. Prepared, *deasaichte; deas, ullamh, uigheamaichte, air ullachadh;* (appointed), *sonruichte, ainmichte.*

PREPAREDNESS, *s.* Ullamhachd.

PREPARER, *s.* Deasachair, fear deasachaidh.

PREPENSE, PREPENSED, *a.* Roimh-rùnaichte, roimh-thograichte, roimh-smuainichte, roimh-chnuasaichte, a dheòin. Malice prepense, *droch rùn roimh-laimh, droch rùn cridhe; galltanas.*

Preponderance, *s.* Cothromachadh, cothrom.

Preponderate, *v.* Cothromaich, thoir an cothrom a; dean ni 's truime; fairtlich le cothrom. Preponderated, *cothromaichte.*

Preponderation, *s.* Cothromachadh.

Preposition, *s.* Roimh-bhriathar.

Prepossess, *v. a.* Roimh-shealbhaich; sealbhaich roimh-laimh; thoir deagh bharail. I am prepossessed in its favour, *tha deagh bharail agam dheth.*

Prepossession, *s.* Roimh-sheilbh, roimh-shealbhachadh; roimh-bheachd, roimh-bharail.

Preposterous, *a.* Docharach, tuathaisteach, cearr, amaideach, baoth, neònach; cearbach; fo-riarach. Preposterously, *gu tuathaisteach, gu cearr, gu h-amaideach, gu baoth, gu neònach, gu cearbach.*

Preposterousness, *s.* Docharachd, cearbachd, amaideachd.

Prepotency, *s.* Barrachd, lamh an uachdar, ceannas.

Prepuce, *s.* Roimh-chroiceann, roimh-chroicionn; oirchneis.

Prerequire, *v. a.* Iarr (no) sir roimh-laimh.

Prerogative, *s.* Còir, ceart-choir, ceart.

Presage, *v.* Faisneachd, faistinn, fàisneachd, fiosachd; comhar, sànas, tuar.

Presage, *v.* Faisnich, fàistinnich, dean fiosachd (no) faidheadaireachd, dean fàistinneachd.

Presagement, *s.* Fàistinn, fàistinneachd; fiosachd, tuar, faidheadaireachd.

Presbyter, *s.* Sagart, ministear, pearsa eaglais, seanair, foirfeach.

Presbyterian, *s.* and *a.* Seanaireach.

Presbytery, *s.* Seanaireachd; seanadh.

Prescience, *s.* Roimh-eòlas, roimh-bheachd, fiosachd, taibhsdearachd.

Prescient, *a.* Fiosrachail, fiosachdail, roimh-fhaicinneach, fàistinneach; fàisneach, fàisneachail.

Prescind, *v.* Sgath, sgud, bearr. Prescinded, *sgathte.*

Prescribe, *v.* Riaghail, seòl, orduich, àithn, iarr. What did the physician prescribe? *ciod dh' orduich an leigh?* Prescribed, *orduichte.*

Prescript, *s.* Riaghladh, seòl, ordugh, àithne, iarrtas; ordugh leigh.

Prescription, *s.* Cleachd; àbhaist; ordugh leigh.

Presence, *s.* Làthaireachd, làthair; dàil, còir; (*port*), méin, iomchar; (*person*), pearsa; (*look*), sealladh, gne, tuar. In my presence, *ann mo làthair;* out of my presence, *a mo làthair, a mo shealladh;* in presence of, *an làthair;* To her the sovereign presence thus replied, *Dhise, mar so, thug am pearsa rioghail freagairt;* the presence chamber, *seomar a chonaltraidh, seòmar na h-èisdeachd, seòmar na làthaireachd;* presence of mind, *tapachd (no) graide inntinn.*

Presension, *s.* Roimh-aithneachadh; fàisneachd.

Present, *s.* Tabhartas, gibhte, buileachas, gibhteamas, tiodhlac, gean maith; litir, ordugh sgriobhte. As a present, *mar ghibhtè;* be it known to all by these our presents, *biodh e aithnichte do na h-uile, le sin ar orduighean sgriobhte;* a wedding present, *preasan.*

Present, *a.* Làthair, a làthair, aig lamh, san am; fabhorach. He is present, *tha e 'làthair;* the present, *an tràthsa;* at present, *an tràthsa, an dràsda, an dràsdaich, a nis, air an uair, air an am.*

Present, *v.* Thabhair, thoir, tabhair, builich, barraig, tiodhlaic, thoir mar ghibhte; thoir làthair, feuch, foillsich, nochd, taisbein. Present battle, *brosnuich chum cath;* present arms, *gabh beachd, gabh fradharc, gabh cuimse, cuimsich.*

Presentable, *a.* So-thabhairt, so-bhuileachadh, a dh' fhaotas bhuileachadh, a ghabhas buileachadh.

Presentation, *s.* Buileachadh; còir buileachaidh, còir eaglais a bhuileachadh; sealladh; feuchainn.

Presentee, *s.* Fear beathachaidh, neach air am builichear eaglais.

Presenter, *s.* Tabhairtear, buileachair.

Presenting, *s.* Tabhairt, toirt, buileachadh.

Presently, *adv.* An ceart uair, air an uair, air a mhionaid, san spot; gu luath, gu grad; gu h-ealamh, gu goirrid; ann an gradaig, ann an briosg, ann am platha.

Presentment, *s.* Tabhairt, toirt, buileachadh, tabhartas, foillseachas; breith.

Presentness, *s.* Graide inntinn.

Preservable, *a.* So-ghleidh, so-choimhead; a ghabhas gleidh, so-thearnadh.

Preservation, *s.* Saorsadh, saorsuinn, teasairgeadh, teasairginn; tearnadh, sabhaladh, dìonadh, gleidh, gleidheadh; coimhead. In preservation, *tearuinnte;* in a state of preservation, *ann an staid thearuinnte;* in high preservation, *gu làn tearuinnte.*

Preservative, *s.* Leigheas.

Preservative, *a.* Coimheadail, gleidhteach, teasairgeach, sàbhalach; a coimhead, a gleidh; a bacadh.

Preserve, *v. a.* Gleidh, saor, tearuinn, sabhail, teasairgin, liobhair, dion. Preserve us! *gléidh sinn!* preserve us from evil, *dion (no) gleidh sinn o olc.* Preserved, *gleidhte, tearuinnte.*

Preserve, *s.* Meas gleidhte.

Preserver, *s.* Fear coimhid, sàbhalaiche, sàbhalair, dionair, fear tearnaidh, fear liobhraidh.

Preside, *v.* For-shuidh; riaghail, bi os ceann; seòl.

Presidency, *s.* Riaghladaireachd.

President, *s.* Ceann suidhe; fear riaghluidh, riaghladair.

Presidentship, *s.* Riaghladaireachd.

Press, *v. a.* (*Squeeze*), teannaich, mùch, dòmhlaich, diong; (*wring*), fàisg; (*bruise*), brùth; (*oppress*), sàruich, claoidh, cuir h-uige; (*urge*), earalaich, sparr, thoir sparradh; (*press forward*), pùc air adhairt, gabh air adhairt; (*seize*), glac.

Press, *s.* Inneal fàsgaidh; clodh, clodh-chlar; (*crowd*), sluagh; dòmhlas; mùch, mùchadh, pùchd; (*for cheese*), fiodhan, faisgean.

Press-bed, *s.* Leabadh lùbaidh; leabadh thogalach.

Pressed, *part.* Fàisgte, sàruichte, claoidhte, teannaichte, mùchta, domhlaichte.

Presser, *s.* Teannachair, mùchadair, bruthadair, clodhbhualadair.

Press-gang, *s.* Bannal glacaidh, connlain-glacaireachd, comunn glacaidh.

Pressman, *s.* Clodh-bhualadair.

Pressmoney, *s.* Airgiod glacaidh, airgiod a bheirear do neach a theid a ghlac airson seirbheis an rìgh.

Pressure, *s.* Bruthadh, cudthrom, cothrom; truime; mùchadh; teannachadh; aile, comhar; amhghar, dòlas, claoidh, earchall.

† **Prest**, *s.* Coingheall.

Prester, *s.* Deathach teinnteach.

Prestiges, *s.* Cleasan, cleasachd.

Prestigiation, *s.* Mealladh, cleasachd.

Presumable, *a.* A dh' fhaotas saoilsinn.

Presume, *v. n.* Saoil, baralaich, bi ann am barail smuainich, beachdaich; gabh do dhànadas.

Presuming, *pret.* and *a.* A saoilsinn, a' smuaineachadh, dàn, ladurna.

Presumption, *s.* (*Conjecture*), beachd, barail; (*confidence*), dànadas, muinghinn; an-dànadas, tòsdal. Have you the presumption? *bheil a dhànadas agad?*

Presumptive, *a.* Smuaintichte; a réir barail; dàn, ladurna.

Presumptuous, *a.* Dàn, an-dàn, ladurna, beadaidh; tòsdalach, neo-dhiadhaidh.

Presumptuously, *adv.* Gu dàn, gu h-andàn, gu ladurna, gu neo-dhiadhuidh

Presupposal, *s.* Roimh-bharail, roimh-bheachd

Presuppose, *v.* Roimh-smuainich, saoil roimh-laimh, roimh-shaoil.

Presupposition, *s.* Roimh-bharail, roimh-bheachd, roimh-shaoilsinn.

Pretence, *s* Leithsgeul; sgàth; sgàil. As a pretence, *mar leithsgeil*

Pretend, *v a* and *n* Leig ort, gabh ort; cuir am fiachaibh; tagair, baralaich, cuir stigh. Pretend sickness, *leig ort a bhith tinn*, pretend to it, *cuir stigh air a shon*

Pretender, *s* Agrair, tagrair neo-dhligheach, fear agairt

Pretendingly, *adv.* Gu dàn, gu ladurna, gu làdasach, gu beadaidh

Pretension, *s* Agradh; agartas, còir, ceart.

Preterit, *a.* Air dol seachad, a chaidh seachad, air aomadh

Pretérition, *s* Dol seachad

Preterlapsed, *a.* Air dol seachad, air aomadh.

Preterlegal, *a.* Neo-laghail

Pretermission, *s* Di-chuimhne, diochuimhne.

Pretermit, *v a.* Di-chuimhnich, leig seachad

Preternatural, *a* Thar nàduir, mi-nadurail, mi-nadurra; neo-riaghailteach

Pretext, *s* Leithsgeul; sgàth, sgàil

Pretor, *s.* Breitheamh Roimheach

Prettily, *adv* Gu laoghach, gu boidheach, gu lurach, gu h-eireachdail, gu grinn, gu snàsmhor, gu finealta

Prettiness, *s* Grinneas, eireachdas, bòidhche, bòidhchead, deasad, maise, finealtas.

Pretty, *a.* Laoghach, bòidheach, lurach, ciatach, grinn, snàsmhor, eireachdail, tlachdmhor, maiseach, greannar. A pretty girl, *caileag laoghach* (*no*) *bhòidheach*, pretty well, *an eatorras, ann iarruidh ghleusda, leth-char*, pretty rich, *ann iarruidh bheairtach*, pretty favourable, *leth-char soirbheasach;* more pretty than handsome, *is ann boidheach is cha 'n ann dàicheil.*

Prevail, *v n* Buadhaich, fairtlich, thoir buaidh, thoir barrachd; thoir air, cuir impidh, drùigh air, earalaich, carail I prevailed upon him, *dh' earail mi air*, I prevailed over him, *bhuadhaich mi air, dh' fhairtlich mi air*, I prevailed upon him to do it, *thug mi air a dheanamh.*

Prevailing, *a.* Comasach, cumhachdach, buadhach; cumanta. A prevailing opinion, *baruil chumaint.*

Prevalence, *s* Barrachd; comas; cumhachd; ceannas, neart, éifeachd.

Prevalent, *a.* Buadhach; neartmhor; an uachdar; faotainn, barrachd, cumanta, cumaint A prevalent report, *iomradh cumanta.*

Prevalently, *adv.* Gu cumanta; gu neartmhor, gu h-éifeachdach.

Prevaricate, *v n.* Dean breug, bi leam is leat; meall, foir-mheang

Prevarication, *s.* Breugadh, breug, leam leat, mealltaireachd; breugaireachd, ceabhachdaireachd

Prevaricator, *s.* Breugair, fear leam leat, mealltair, ceabhachdair.

Prevent, *v. a.* Bac, bachd, amail, gabh roimh, coisg, caisg, grab, toirmisg, cuir bac air, cum air ais. He prevented me, *dh' amail e mi*, do not prevent me, *na bac mi, na cuir bac orm.*

Prevented, *part.* Bacta, bachdta, air a bhacadh, grabta; toirmisgte. She is prevented from coming, *tha i air a bacadh o thighinn.*

Preventer, *s.* Bacair, bacadair, grabair, fear grabaidh.

Prevention, *s.* Bac, bacadh, amal, amaladh, moille, grabadh, toirmeasg.

Preventive, *a.* Bacail, amalach, grabach, toirmeasgach.

Preventive, *s.* Cosg-leigheas, leigheas grabaidh; tearnadh

Previous, *a.* Roimh, air thoiseach.

Previously, *adv.* Roimh, mun, roimh-laimh, air tùs, air thùs. Previously to his arrival, *roimh a theachd, mun tig e.*

Prey, *s.* Creach, creich, cobhartach, spùinne, spùinneadh, spùille, spùilleadh, spùilinn, togail, foghluidheachd, argnadh, bothaireachd; feudail, eudail.

Prey, *v. n.* Creach, spùinn, dean foghluidheachd, tog cobhartach, cnamh, ith suas He preys upon them, *tha e 'g an creachadh*, it preys upon my vitals, *tha e 'g am ith suas.*

Preyer, *s* Creachadair, spùinneadair, foghluiche, fear reubainn, robair.

Priapism, *s.* Slat-sheasamh.

Price, *s.* Prìs, luach, fiach, meas, duais, diol. What is the price of it? *ciod is fhiach e?* of high price, *daor*, at a little price, *air bheag luach*, at such a price, *air leithid so luach;* at so little a price, *air cho bheag luach.*

Prick, *v. a.* and *n.* Brod, bior, stob, toll; spor, starr; stuig; cuir h-uige; dean searbh; breaghaich, uigheamaich. You prick me, *tha thu 'g am mo bhioradh.*

Prick, *s.* Piocair, bior; stob, spor; (*in the mind*), agartas coguis; (*a mark*), comhar.

Pricker, *s* Stob, bior, piocair, brod

Pricket, *s.* Boc-earb, boc da-bhliadhnach

Pricking, *s* Brodadh, bioradh, stobadh, tolladh, sporadh, starradh; stuigeadh.

Prickle, *s.* Stob, bior, sgolb

Prickliness, *s* Biorachas, guineachd, droighneachd.

Prickly, *a.* Biorach, stobach, guineach, goineach, droighneach.

Pricklouse, *s.* Ainm tàir airson tàilleir

Pride, *s.* Uaille, uabhar, uamhar, uaibhreachas, ardan, leoim, stràic, stràichd; spagluinn; sgòd, gò; borr, borralachd; cuidealachd, ard-inntinn, spaglainn; ràiteachas, brod, greadhnachas, mòr-chuis; *spagadagliog.* Pride spurns not profit, *cha bhi uaille 'n aghaidh na tairbhe.*

Pride, *v a.* Arduich, uallaich, dean uaille, dean briodal; bi leòmach, bi sgòdail He prides himself in his doings, *tha e 'deanamh uaille a 'dheanadas, is briagh leis a dheanadas.*

Prier, *s.* Sgilm, sgilmean; urr lonach; sgimilear.

Priest, *s.* Sagart, cairneach, ministear, pears' eaglais. It is not a priest's first word you are to believe, *cha 'n e ceud sgeul an t-sagairt bu choir a chreidsinn.*

Priestcraft, *s.* Cléir-chuilbheart, car cairnich.

Priestess, *s* Ban-sagart.

Priesthood, *s.* Sagartachd, sagairteachd.

Priestly, *a.* Sagartail, sagairteil.

Priest-ridden, *a.* Fo chléir; fo shagairtean.

Prig, *s.* Gircean; ceigean, duine beag sgeacharra.

Prill, *s.* Turbait, seorsa éisg.

Prim, *a.* Deas, rudach, foirmeil, sgilmeil, sgìnmeil, sgeinmeil, cuimir.
Prim, *v.* Deasaich, uigheamaich, breaghaich, briaghaich
Primacy, *s.* Prìomhachd, cléir-phrìomhachd, ard-easbuidheachd.
Primal, *a.* Ceud, tùsail.
Primarily, *adv.* An tùs, air tùs, air thùs, an toiseach, air thoiseach, sa cheud àite.
Primary, *a.* Ceud, prìomh.
Primate, *s.* Ard-easbuig, ard-shagart
Prime, *s.* Mochrath, mochthrath, muchradh, a chàmhanaich, a mhadainn; toiseach; a chuid is fhearr, brod, airde; blath. She is in her prime, *tha i am blàth a h-aimsir*, the prime or best of any thing, *brod, sgoitheun.*
Prime, *a.* Prìomh, ceud, ard; sar-mhath, gasda; corr.
Prime, *v.* Fùdar cluaisich
Primely, *adv.* Air thùs, an tùs, anns a cheud àite.
Primer, *s* Leabhar cloinne.
Primero, *s.* Seorsa cluiche air chairtean.
Primeval, Primevous, *a.* Ceud linneil; sean-aimsireil; seantaidh.
Primigenial, *a.* Ceud-ghinte; ceud-ghineil, tùsail, prìomh; bunamhasach.
Primitive, *a.* Aosda, sean, aosmhor, seantaidh, seanaimsireil; foirmeil, seantaidh.
Primitively, *adv.* Air thùs, air tùs; gu h-aosda, gu seantaidh, gu sean-aimsireil.
Primitiveness, *s.* Aosmhorachd, seantachd, seantaidheachd, sean-aimsireileachd
Primness, *s* Foirmeileachd, sgilmeileachd, sgìnmeileachd
Primogeniture, *s.* Prìomh-ghin, ceud-ghin; ceart-bhreith.
Primordial, *a.* Ceud; tùsail.
Primordial, *s.* Tùs, ceud-thus, toiseach; bunamhas
Primrose, *s.* Sobhrach, sobhrag, soraidh, soirigh, muisean, sambaircean.
Prince, *s.* Prionnsa; triath, flath, uachdran; armunn, triath; righ, mac righ, ceannfine. Princes, *prionnsan* or *prionnsachan.*
Princedom, *s.* Prionnsachd.
Princelike, *a.* Prionnsail, flathail, rìoghail.
Princeliness, *s.* Prionnsalachd, flathaileachd.
Princely, *a.* Prionnsail, flathail, rìoghail; breasail
Princess, *s.* Ban-phrionnsa; nighean rìgh.
Principal, *a.* Prìomh, ceud, ard, feumail, àraidh. A principal city, *ard-bheirbhe*
Principal, *s* Prìomh, ceann, tùs; riaghladair; ceann cinnidh, ceannard; (*in money*), calpa. Principal and interest, *riadh is calpa.*
Principality, *s.* Prionnsachd; oighreachd prionnsa, uachdaranachd; prionnsa; barrachd.
Principally, *adv.* Gu h-àraidh; gu sònraichte, gu h-àraid; os cionn na h-uile.
Principle, *s.* Ceud-thùs; bunamhas, bunachur, mathair aobhair, aobhar; rùn, barail, tionsgnadh.
Principle, *v a.* Suidhich, socraich; steighich; teagaisg
† **Princock**, *s.* Uaillean; leoimean
Prink, *v.* Sgeadaich, uigheamaich, sgiamhaich.
Print, *v. a.* Prionnt; cuir am prionnt; prionntaich, clodhbhuail; comharaich, cuir am prionnt; stramp, grabh, gearr.
Print, *s* Comhar, aile, lorg, sliochd, dealbh; prionnt. Set a print on him, *cuir comhar air*
Printed, *a.* Prionntaichte; clodh-bhuailte; comharraichte, grabhta, gearrta.
Printer, *s.* Prionntair, clodhair, clodh-bhualadair.

Printing, *s.* Prionntadh, prionntachadh, clodh-bhualadh; grabhadh, gearradh; strampadh. A printing-house, *tigh clodh-bhualaidh*, a printing-press, *crann teannta, clodh*
Printless, *a.* Gun aile, gun chomhar
Prior, *a.* Air thoiseach, roimh, air thùs.
Prior, *s.* Prìomh-mhànach, aba, mànach
Prioress, *s.* Ban-aba, ard bhan-naomh.
Priority, *s.* Toiseach; tùs, barrachd.
Prisage, *s* Fìon-chìs, buaidh-chìs, cìs-chreich; chuid a bhuineas do 'n rìgh do gach luingeas, a spùillear gu laghail air a mhuir.
Prism, *s.* Gloine sgar-sholuis, gloine a sgaras dathan soluis.
Prison, *s* Prìosan, gainntir, carcar, carcur, toll-buth; tigh braighde, caobhan.
Prison, *v* Prìosunaich, gainntirich, cuir an laimh; cuir am prìosan; ceangail, cuibhrich; druid, dùin. Prisoned, *prìosunaichte, gainntirichte; ceangailte, cuibhrichte.*
Prisoner, *s.* Prìosonach, cìomach, braighde; daor.
Prison-house, *s.* Prìosun, carcar, gainntir, tigh braighde, tigh daorsa
Prisonment, *s.* Prìosunachadh, prìosunachd, gainntireachd, braighdeanas; daorsadh.
Pristine, *a* Sean, seantaidh, arsaidh, seanta; ceud.
Prithee. Guidheam ort
Prittle-prattle, *s.* Goileam, lonais, gob
Privacy, *s.* Dìomhaireachd, tosdachd, uaigneas, rùn, céilt.
Privado, *s* Caraid cridhe
Private, *a.* Dìomhair, uaigneach, céilte, aonaranach, diubhrasach; (*in life*), iosal, diblidh, cumaint. A private man, *duine cumaint*, in private, *an uaigneas*
Private, *s.* Gnothuch dìomhair
Privateer, *s.* Long-creich, long spùinnidh
Privately, *adv* Gu dìomhair, gu h-uaigneach, gu h-aonaranach, gu céilte, os iosal
Privateness, *s.* Dìomhaireachd, uaigneas, diùbhrasachd; (*in life*), ìlse, cumantas
Privation, *s.* Dìobhail, dìobhaileachd, easbhuidheachd, uireasbhuidh, dìth.
Privative, *a* Dìobhaileach; easbhuidheach, dìtheach.
Privet, *s* Ràs-chrann sìor-uaine.
Privilege, *s.* Còir; comas; ceart-chòir, sochair.
Privilege, *v* Builich còir.
Privily, *adv.* Gu dìomhair; os iosal, gu sàmhach, gu tosdach.
Privities, *s.* Ionaire; ceòsach; lomnochd, buill dhiomhair.
Privity, *s* Dìomhaireachd, fiosrachd; rùn, fios, aithne, eòlas Without my privity, *gun fhios domh, gun aithne dhomh.*
Privy, *a* Dìomhair, uaigneach, céilte, folaichte; fiosrach; fianuiseach I am privy to it, *tha mi fiosrach air.*
Privy, *s* Tigh beag, tigh oich, tigh cac
Prize, *s.* Dìol thuarasdal, duais; geall; cobhartach, creach; feudail, tachdar.
Prize, *v.* Meas Prized, *measta; measail.*
Prizer, *s* Measadair
Prize-fighter, *s* Duais-chùraidh.
Pro. Le, leis, airson
Probability, *s.* Coslas, coslachd; dàchaileachd.
Probable, *a* Coslach, colsach; coltach, a dh' fhaodas bhith, dàchail, dàcha, dàchadh. It is very probable, *tha e glé choslach*, I think it probable, *is dàcha leam.*
Probably, *adv.* A réir coslais; a theagamh, maith dh' fhaoidte.

PROBATION, *s.* Dearbhadh, deuchainn, feuchainn, teisteas, ceasnuchadh, sgrudadh.

PROBATIONARY, *a.* Dearbhach, deuchainneach.

PROBATIONER, *s.* Deuchainniche, fear fo cheasnuchadh (no) fo dheuchainn.

PROBATIONERSHIP, *s.* Deuchainneachd.

PROBATORY, *a.* Deuchainneach.

PROBATUM EST. *Laitinn, a ciallachadh*, deuchainnte, dearbhta.

PROBE, *s.* Iarradair, sireadair, iarradan, sireadan, rannsuchair.

PROBE, *v. a.* Iarr, sir, brod, rannsuich, bruillich.

PROBITY, *s.* Ionracas, tréibhdhireas, fìrinn, fìreanntachd, còiread, simplidheachd.

PROBLEM, *s.* Ceisd, ceist.

PROBLEMATICAL, *a.* Teagamhach; neo-chinnteach; ceisdeil; connspuideach, neo-chinnteach.

PROBOSCIS, *s.* Soc elephaint.

PROCACIOUS, *a.* Beadaidh, ladurna, beagnarach, peasanach, làdasach, peilpeanta.

PROCACITY, *s.* Beadaidheachd; beadamanachd, peasanachd.

PROCEDURE, *s.* Dol air adhairt, dol a mach, deanaich, deananaich; iomchar; gniomh, cùis.

PROCEED, *v. n.* Rach air adhairt; triall, gluais; thig o, cinn a; thig spéid. Proceed a little further, *rach air adhairt beagan ni's fhaide: rach air d' adhairt beagan fhathast;* proceed against one, *cuir neach h-uige.*

PROCEED, *s.* Cinneas, torradh, fàs; barr; coisinn, buannachd.

PROCEEDING, *s.* (*Business*), gnothach, gnothuch; (*doings*), iomchar; giùlan, deananaich, tùrn, dol a mach.

PROCERITY, *s.* Airde, inbhe, uaillse.

PROCESS, *s.* Imeachd, trialladh, siubhladh, cùrsa, inneal, modh; (*at law*), cùis, cuis lagha. Bring a process against, *cuir h-uige.*

PROCESSION, *s.* Mearsa solaimte; dubh-mhearsa, dubhthriall.

PROCLAIM, *v. a.* Gairm, glaodh, nochd, ballardaich, foillsich, dean aithnichte, sgaoil, innis gu soilleir. Proclaim peace, *gairm sìth;* he was proclaimed, *chaidh 'ghlaodhachadh.* Proclaimed, *gairmte, foillsichte, air a dheanamh aithnichte, sgaoilte.*

PROCLAIMER, *s.* Gairmear, gairmeadair, fear gairm, eighcadair, bollsair.

PROCLAMATION, *s.* Gairm; glaodh, gairm fhollaiseach, for-fhuagradh; abach.

PROCLIVITY, *s.* Aomadh, togradh, togar, miann; calamhachd, lethad, lethfhad, claonad, tul-chlaonad; bruthach.

PROCLIVOUS, *a.* Aomta, cas, corrach, claon, uchdach.

PROCRASTINATE, *v. a.* and *n.* Cuir dàil, dàilich, ath-lathaich, bi mairnealach, cuir seachad, cuir dheth, dean moille.

PROCRASTINATING, *a.* Mairnealach; masanach; leagach.

PROCRASTINATION, *s.* Dàil, mairneal, mairnealachd, athlathachadh, mul-sneamh, fàrdal; masanachd, leagaireachd.

PROCRASTINATOR, *s.* Fear mairnealach, masan, leagair.

PROCREANT, *a.* Gineadach, ginteach, torrach, siolmhor; clanmhor, clannar.

PROCREATE, *v. a.* Gin, siolaich, ginealaich; torraich, faigh clann; beir, thoir a mach.

PROCREATION, *s.* Gineadh, ginealachadh, siolachadh, clannachadh.

PROCREATIVE, *a.* Ginteach, gineadach, siolmhor, clannmhor.

PROCREATOR, *s.* Gineadair, gintear. Procreators, *ginteirean.*

PROCTOR, *s.* Procdair, prochdair, fear tagraidh.

PROCTORSHIP, *s.* Prochdaireachd.

PROCUMBENT, *a.* Na luidhe sios, sìnte; sìnteach.

PROCURABLE, *a.* So-fhaotainn, so-fhaghail, a ghabhas faotainn, so-ghlacadh, so-choisinn.

PROCURACY, *s.* Riaghladh, riaghlachadh, riaghailt.

PROCURATION, *s.* Solar, solaradh, fritheäladh, faotainn, faghail.

PROCURATOR, *s.* Fear riaghlaidh, fear gnothuich, fear tagraidh, prochdair; riaghladair.

PROCURE, *v.* Faigh, fuigh, solair; fritheil, riaghailtich, coisinn, buannaich; dealbh, cnuasaich. He procured many friends, *fhuair e mòran chairdean;* to procure, *a dh' faotainn; a choisinn.*

PROCUREMENT, *s.* Solar, solaradh; faotainn, faghail, frithealadh.

PROCURER, *s.* Solaraiche; (*in a bad sense*), drustar, trusdar.

PROCURESS, *s.* Striopach, stràille.

PRODIGAL, *a.* Struidheil, stròghail, stroghasach, struidheasach, domailteach, diobhalach; caithteach, neo-ghrunndail.

PRODIGAL, *s.* Struidhear, stroghair, ana-caithtiche.

PRODIGALITY, *s.* Struidhe, strògh, struidheas, struidheasachd, stroghalachd, domail, diobhalachd.

PRODIGALLY, *adv.* Gu struidheil, gu stroghail, gu caithteach, gu diobhalach.

PRODIGIOUS, *a.* Iongantach, uamhasach, ana-barrach, fuathasach, miorbhuileach, neònach, oillteil, foir-iongantach.

PRODIGIOUSLY, *adv.* Gu h-iongantach, gu h-uamhasach, gu h-anabarra, gu fuathasach.

PRODIGIOUSNESS, *s.* Iongantachd, uamhasachd, anabarrachd, fuathasachd, miorbhuileachd; diobhalachd.

PRODIGY, *s.* Iongantas; miorbhuil; miorbhailt; uamhas, foir-iongantas.

PRODITION, *s.* Traoidhtearachd, brath.

† PRODITOR, *s.* Traoidhtear, brathadair.

PRODUCE, *v.* Thoir a mach, gin; beir; thoir seachad, thoir làthair, taisbein. Produce fruit, *thoir a mach meas;* produce your evidence, *thoir a lathair d' fhianuisean;* produced, *ginte; air bheirsinn; air thoirt a mach.*

PRODUCE, *s.* Toradh, bàrr, buannachd; meud, fàs, gineadas, cinneas.

PRODUCER, *s.* Gineadair, gintear.

PRODUCT, *s.* Toradh; cinneas, fàs; bàrr; aireamh.

PRODUCTILE, *a.* So-fhadachadh, a ghabhas fadachadh, a ghabhas tarruing.

PRODUCTION, *s.* Fàs, toradh, cinneas, bàrr, gineadas; cruthachadh; leabhar, sgriobhadh.

PRODUCTIVE, *a.* Tarbhach, torrach, siolmhor, lionmhor, pailt; gineadach.

PRODUCTIVENESS, *s.* Torrachas, torraichead, siolmhorachd.

PROEM, *s.* Roimh-radh, roimh-bhriathar.

PROFANATION, *s.* Mi-naomhachadh, truailleadh; midhiadhuidheachd. Profanation of the Sabbath, *mi-naomhachadh na Sàbaid.*

PROFANE, *v. a.* Mi-naomhaich, mi-urramaich, truaill, mighnàthaich. Profaned, *mi-naomhaichte.*

PROFANE, *a.* Mi-naomh; an-diadhuidh, mi-dhiadhuidh, aingidh, olc, baoth; neo-ghlan, peacach; aimsgith. A profane expression, *baoth-bhriathar;* a profane saying, *baoth-radh.*

PROFANELY, *adv.* Gu mi-naomh, gu mi-dhiadhuidh, gu h-aingidh, gu baoth, gu neo-ghlan, gu peacach, gu h-aimsgith.

PROFANENESS, s. Mi-naomhachd; an-diadhachd, aingidheachd, aimsgith, aimsgitheachd.

PROFANER, s. Mi-naomhachair, truaillear, truailleadair.

PROFANING, s. Mi-naomhachadh, truailleadh.

PROFECTION, s. Dol air adhairt, imeachd, siùbhladh.

PROFESS, v. a. and n. Aidich, aidmheil, cuir an céill, dearbh; nochd; innis gu riachdail.

PROFESSEDLY, adv. A réir aidmheil; gu follaiseach, gu soilleir, gu riachdail; as an aghaidh.

PROFESSION, s. Aidmheil; aideachadh; gairm; ceaird, ealadhain.

PROFESSOR, s. Aidmheilear; aidmheiliche, fear teagaisg; teagasgair, ard-theagasgair.

PROFFER, v. Tairg; thoir tairgeas; oidhirpich, dean oidhirp. Proffered, *air thairgsinn.*

PROFFER, s. Tairgse; oidhirp. He made a proffer of his services, *thairg e 'sheirbheis.*

PROFFERER, s. Tairgseach, tairgsiche.

PROFICIENCY, s. Buannachd, coisinn; foghnadh, spéid, leas, leasachadh, piseach; adhartachd; tairbhe.

PROFICIENT, s. Fear ionnsuichte; adhartaiche.

PROFICUOUS, a. Buannachail, tarbhach, feumail.

PROFILE, s. Leth-aghaidh, leth-aodainn, leth-ghnùis.

PROFIT, s. Tairbhe, buannachd, proidhit, leas, leasachadh, math, maith, buidhinn; feum, stà. Pride spurns not profit, *cha bhi uaill an aghaidh na tairbhe.*

PROFIT, v. Buannaich, leasaich; buing, dean maith; buidhinn, faigh tairbh, faigh buannachd. I did not profit much by it, *cha mhòr a bhuidhinn mi air.*

PROFITABLE, a. Tarbhach, buidhneach; proidhiteach; maith; uiseil, feumail.

PROFITABLENESS, s. Tairbhe, tarbhaichead, buannachd, feumaileachd, feumalachd.

PROFITABLY, adv. Gu tarbhach, gu buidhneach, gu proidhideach, le tairbhe, le buannachd.

PROFITLESS, a. Neo-tharbhach, neo-bhuidhneach, neo-bhuannachail.

PROFLIGACY, s. Mi-gheimnidheachd, mi-stuamachd; struidhe, strogh, stroghalachd, struidheas, an-sriantachd, an-srianachd.

PROFLIGATE, a. Mi-gheimnidh, mi-stuama; mi-bheusach; an-srianta, neo-cheannsaichte, mio-narach, struidheil, stroghail, struidheasach.

PROFLIGATE, s. Fear ana-cneasta, fear mi-stuama, struidhear, stroghair.

PROFLIGATENESS, s. Struidh, strògh; struidheas, struidhealachd, struidheasachd.

PROFLUENCE, s. Sruth, sruthadh, ruithe, siubhal.

PROFLUENT, a. A sruth, a ruithe, siùbhlach; ruithteach.

PROFOUND, a. Domhainn, domhain; iosal, iriosal, umhal; do-thuigsinn; (*learned*), ionnsuichte, oileanaichte, foghluimte.

PROFOUND, s. Doimhne, doimhneachd, aigean, muir, cuan.

PROFOUNDLY, adv. Gu domhain; gu h-ionnsuichte.

PROFOUNDNESS, s. Doimhne, doimhneachd.

PROFUNDITY, s. Doimhne, doimhneachd.

PROFUSE, a. Bàibleach, sgaoilteach, sgapach, sgaireapach, caithteach, stroghail, struidheil, neo-ghrunndail; (*plenteous*), pailt, ro phailt, lionmhor.

PROFUSELY, adv. Gu bàibleach, gu sgaoilteach, gu sgapach, gu caithteach, gu stroghail, gu struigheil, gu pailt.

PROFUSENESS, s. Bàibleachd, strògh, struidhe, struidheas, stroghalachd, struidhealachd, caitheamh, ana-caitheamh.

PROFUSION, s. Strògh, struidhe, struidheas, sgaireap, caitheamh, ana-caitheamh, sgapadh; (*plenty*), pailt, pailteas, ro-phailteas, làn-phailteas.

PROG, v. n. Goid, creach, spùinn, spùill; dean reubainn (no) meirle.

PROG, s. Biadh, lòn.

PROGENERATION, s. Gineadh; siolachadh.

PROGENITOR, s. Gintear; sinnsear; athair.

PROGENITORSHIP, s. Sinnsearachd.

PROGENY, s. Sliochd, siol, gineal, clann; fuil; iarmad.

PROGNOSTIC, a. A feuchainn.

PROGNOSTIC, s. Fàisneachd; fiosachd, comhar.

PROGNOSTICATE, v. a. Dean fàisneachd, innis roimh-laimh; feuch.

PROGNOSTICATION, s. Fàisneachd, fàistinneachd, faidheadaireachd; comhar; fiosachd.

PROGNOSTICATOR, s. Fàidh; fiosaiche, fàisniche, speuradair.

PROGRESS, s. Cùrsa, siubhladh, imeachd; trialladh; fòghnadh, piseach; cinneachdainn; spéid; leasachadh; cuairt; tùrus. Make progress, *thig spéid.*

PROGRESSION, s. Teachd air aghaidh, dol air adhairt, adhartachd; trialladh, siubhladh; leas, spéid.

PROGRESSIVE, a. Adhartach; reimeil; gluasadach. Progressive motion, *siùbhladh (no) gluasad adhartach.*

PROGRESSIVELY, adv. Gu h-adhartach; air adhairt, air aghaidh, uidh air uidhe, uidh air 'n uidhe; chuid is a chuid, ceum air cheum.

PROHIBIT, v. a. Bac, toirmisg, grab, amail, cum air, air ais, cuir bac air; stad, cuir stad air.

PROHIBITER, s. Bacair, grabair, fear grabaidh, fear toirmisg.

PROHIBITION, s. Bac, bachd, bacadh, toirmeasg, toirmeasgadh, amal, amaladh, grabadh, stad.

PROHIBITORY, a. Bacail, toirmeasgach, amalach, grabach.

† PROIN, v. a. Gearr, bearr, sgath.

PROJECT, v. n. Sin a mach, buail a mach, stic a mach; croch thar; tilg thar; seas a mach mar ni creag; far-bhuail, far-sheas.

PROJECT, v. a. Lamhaich, tionnsgain; cnuasaich, dealbh; smuainich, meamhraich. Projected, *tionnsgainte, cnuasaichte, dealbhta.*

PROJECT, s. Tionnsgnadh; cnuasachd; innleachd, seòl, doigh, modh.

PROJECTILE, a. Gluasadach, gluasadail, adhartach.

PROJECTILE, s. Gluas-rud.

PROJECTING, a. (*As a rock*), stùcach; sroineach. A projecting rock, *stuc, sròin, sròineag.*

PROJECTION, s. Far-bhualadh; barra-bhailc; doigh; modh; stùc; sròin, sròineag; cumadh, dealbh.

PROJECTOR, s. Tionnsgnair, tionnsgnaiche; caislear.

PROJECTURE, s. Far-bhualadh; stuc, sròin; rutha.

PROLATE, v. Abair, innis, labhair, cuir an céill.

PROLATION, s. Innseadh, labhairt.

PROLEGOMENA, s. Roimh-radh.

† PROLETARIAN, a. Truagh, iosal, diblidh.

PROLIFIC, PROLIFICAL, a. Torrach, siolmhor, clannmhor leth-tromach.

PROLIFICALLY, adv. Gu siolmhor, gu clannmhor.

PROLIFICATION, s. Gineadh; beirsinn (no) breith cloinne.

PROLIFICNESS, s. Siolmhorachd, torraichead.

PROLIX, *a* Fad, fadalach, mall, mairnealach; maidhcaneach; leudach, briathrach, ràsanach, neo-ghearr, neo-chuimir.

PROLIXITY, *s.* Fadalachd, fadal, mairnealachd, maidheanachd, moille, ràsanachd, briathrachd.

PROLIXLY, *adv.* Gu fadalach, gu mairnealach, gu maidheanach, gu leudach, gu briathrach, gu ràsanach.

PROLIXNESS, *s.* Fadalachd, mairnealachd, maidheanachd, moille, maille, ràsanachd

PROLOCUTOR, *s.* Fear labhairt.

PROLOGUE, *s* Roimh-dhuan, roimh-rann, duan roimh bhard-chluiche; roimh radh

PROLONG, *v. a* Fadaich, cuir dàil, dàilich; ath-lathaich, cuir dheth, cuir seachad, buanaich; leudaich Prolong from day to day, *cuir dheth o là gu là*, he prolonged his departure, *chuir e dàil na imeachd.*

PROLONGATION, *s* Fadachadh, dàil, dàileachadh; buanachadh, cur dheth (no) seachd o am gu h-am

PROLUSION, *s* Cluithe, cluiche, ealaidh, ioladh, *dibhearsain.*

PROMENADE, *s* Sràid, àite spaisdearachd; sràideas, sràidimeachd, spaisdearachd, spaidsearachd.

PROMINENCE, PROMINENCY, *s.* Meall, fara-bhailc, stùc, beannan

PROMINENT, *a.* Fara-bhailceach, far-bhualach; corrach, stùcach; so-fhaicinn

PROMISCUOUS, *a* Coimeasgta, measgta, air feadh chéile; feadh chéile

PROMISCUOUSLY, *adv* Air feadh cheile, gun diubhair.

PROMISCUOUSNESS, *s.* Cumasg, coimeasgadh

PROMISE, *s.* Gealladh, coimhlionadh geallaidh, dùil, dòchas Give me your promise, *thoir dhomh do ghealladh*, I think him a youth of great promise, *tha dochas mòr agam as an òganach;* a promise-breach, *briseadh geallaidh*, a promise-breaker, *fear briseadh fhocaill*, perform your promise, *coimhlion do ghealladh*, keep your promise, *cum ri do ghealladh;* a promise is not a handcuff, *cha chuirear gad air gealladh*, a promise is a debt of honour, *is fiach air duine na gheallas e*

PROMISE, *v a* Geall, thoir gealladh, thoir cinnte. Promise again, *ath-gheall*, I promised (to) him, *gheall mi dha*, I promised him *or* it, *gheall mi e*, promise in marriage, *geall am pòsadh*, promise mutually, *comh-gheall*, vow, *bòidich, thoir bòid, mionn*, promising, *a gealltuinn;* a promise without performing, *gealladh gun cho-ghealladh*

PROMISED, *part* Geallta, gealtuinnte He is promised, *tha e air a ghealladh (no) air a ghealltuinn*, she is promised, *tha i air a gealladh (no) air a gealltuinn*, they are promised, *tha iad air an gealltuinn (no) air an gealladh*

PROMISSORILY, *adv.* Mar ghealladh.

PROMISSORY, *a.* Gealltuinneach

PROMONTORY, *s* Rughadh, ruthadh, maol, muil, ceann, ceann-tire; sròin, innis, ros.

PROMOTE, *v a* Cuir an adhairt, luathailtich; arduich; tog gu h-inmhe; urramaich; inbhich; leasaich. Promoted, *luathailtichte, arduichte, air 'thogail gu h-inmhe*

PROMOTER, *s.* Fear còghnaidh, fear misneachaidh, brosnuchair; (*of discord*), fear aimhreite

PROMOTION, *s.* Arduchadh, togail, urramachadh, togail gu h-inmhe, inbhe, urram

PROMPT, *a* Deas, ealamh, ullamh, aig lamh, grad, tapaidh; luath, geur; brosglach, smiorail; (*easy*), furas, furasd Prompt payment, *airgiod ullumh.*

PROMPT, *v. a.* (*Aid*), còghain, dean coghnadh le, cuir roimh, innis as iosal, fo' theagaisg, fo' innis; (*incite*), stuig, brosnuich, brosnaich; (*remind*), cuir an cuimhne He prompted him to do it, *bhrosnuich se e chum a dheanamh.*

PROMPTER, *s.* Sànusair; brosnuchair; cuimhneachair; cuimhneadair

PROMPTING, *part.* A brosnuchadh, a stuigeadh, a cur an cuimhne.

PROMPTITUDE, *s.* Ealamhachd, tapachd, graide; brosglachd, smioralas.

PROMPTLY, *adv.* Gu h-ealamh, gu tapaidh, gu deas, gu teoma, gu smiorail, gu deas.

PROMPTNESS, *s* Ealamhachd; tapachd; graide.

PROMPTUARY, *s.* Tigh tasgaidh, tigh stòr.

PROMULGATE, *v* Foillsich, dean follais, craobh-sgaoil. Promulgated, *foillsichte.*

PROMULGATION, *s.* Foillseachadh, nochdadh, craobh-sgaoileadh.

PROMULGER, *s.* Foillseachair, nochdair.

PRONE, *a.* Crom; striochta; air bhrù; corrach, cas; ag aomadh, aomta, aomte, claon, cam, neo-dhireach; dian; an comhar chinn, deas, trom, ealamh, dioltach. Prone to drink, *ealamh chum òl, dioltach air an òl*

PRONENESS, *s.* Cromadh, aomadh, lùbadh, claonadh, claonad, calamhachd, leathad, miann; taobh. A proneness to drinking, *taobh ris an òl*

PRONG, *s.* Gobhal, gabhal, forc, gobhlan, gobhlag, meur, ladhar

PRONOMINAL, *a* Riochd-fhoclach, iar-fhoclach.

PRONOUN, *s.* Riochd-fhocal, iar-fhocal

PRONOUNCE, *v a* Labhair, abair; aithris, thoir breith. Pronounce distinctly, *labhair gu pongail.*

PRONUNCIATION, *s* Doigh-labhairt, labhairt

PROOF, *s.* (*Testimony*), fianuis, teisteas, (*test*), deuchainn; (*demonstration*), dearbhadh, dearbh, comhdach; (*armour*), cruaidhe; armachd; (*in printing*), ceud chlodh-bhualadh. Put to the proof, *cuir gu deuchainn*, I will give you a proof of it, *bheir mi dhuit dearbh air*, armed all in proof, *comhdaichte gu léir le cruaidhe.*

PROOF, *a.* Daingeann, diongalta, dionach; do-tholladh; do-dhrùigh, dùinte Water-proof, *dionach;* proof against temptation, *dùinte an aghaidh bhuairibh.*

PROOFLESS, *a* Neo-dhearbhta, neo-chòmhdaichte

PROOF, *v a* Cum suas, cum taic, cuir taic ri, *prop* Prop it up, *cum taic ris, cuir taic ris*, a lie needs to be propped, *imiridh breug gobhal.*

PROP, *s.* Taic, cul-taic, cuaille, *prop*, leth-thaic, aice, gobhal.

PROPAGABLE, *a* So-sgaoileadh, a ghabhas sgaoileadh, sgaoilteach.

PROPAGATE, *v a.* and *n.* Siolaich, craobh-sgaoil, sgaoil, iom-sgaoil, gin; leudaich, meudaich, fàs, cinn, siol-chuir, foir-shiol. Propagated, *siolaichte, sgaoilte, iom-sgaoilte, meudaichte, leudaichte.*

PROPAGATION, *s* Siolachadh, siol-chur; sgaoileadh, craobh-sgaoileadh, foir-shioladh; meudachadh, leudachadh.

PROPAGATOR, *s.* Fear sgaoilidh; gineadair; brosnuchair.

PROPEL, *v.* Put, pùc, pùchd, fùchd; dinn, sparr, starr.

PROPELLING, *s* Putadh, pùcadh, fùcadh; dinneadh, sparradh, starradh.

PROPEND, *v. n.* Aom chum taobh sam bi.

PROPENDENCY, *s.* Aomadh, claonadh; smuaineachadh, beachd-smuaine

PROPENSE, *a.* Aomta, claon, toileach, deigheil.

PROPENSION, PROPENSITY, *s.* Aomadh, claonadh; toil, deigh, taobh, miann, togar He has a propensity to drunkenness, *tha taobh aig ris an òl.*

PROPER, *a* (*Fit*), ceart, cubhaidh, iomchuidh, freagarrach, oireamhnach; (*peculiar*), sònruichte, àraidh; (*handsome*), calma, maiseach, eireachdail, deas, speisealta.

Properly, *adv.* Gu ceart, le ceartas, gu cubhaidh; gu freagarrach. This properly belongs to me, *buinidh so dhomhsa le ceartas.*

Properness, *s.* Cubhaidheachd, freagarrachd, ceirte; maise, eireachdas.

Property, *s.* (*Possession*), cuid, seilbh, còir, ceart, maoin, airneas; (*disposition*), feart, buaidh, càil, nàdur, gné. Invade another's property, *leum air cuid duine eile;* the properties of the mind, *feartan na h-inntinn.*

Prophecy, *s.* Fàisneachd, faidheadaireachd, fàistinn, targhail; fiosachd.

Prophesier, *s.* Fàidh.

Prophesy, *v. a.* Fàisnich, dean faisneachd, dean faidheadaireachd, dean fiosachd, targhail; innis roimh-laimh.

Prophet, *s.* Fàidh, fàistinnear, fiosaiche. Prophets, *fàidhean.* Evil betide the prophet, *gu ma th' ann a ghonar am fiosaiche.*

Prophetess, *s.* Ban-fhàidh; ban-fhiosaiche.

Prophetic, Prophetical, *a.* Fàisneachail, fàistinneach; fiosachdail.

Prophylactic, *a.* Tearnach.

Propinquity, *s.* Foisge, fogusachd; coimbearsnachd; (*kindred*), càirdeas, caidreamh, daimh.

Propitiable, *a.* So-shàsachadh, so-réiteachadh, so-chosgadh, so-chiùnachadh.

Propitiate, *v.* Réitich, ciùinich, coisg, caisg, dean réidh, toilich, diol, sàsuich, dean fàbhorach. Propitiated, *réitichte, ciùinichte, coisgte, sàsuichte, toilichte.*

Propitiation, *s.* Réiteachadh, réite, diol, dioladh, sàsuchadh, toileachadh, ciùineachadh, ciùnachadh, cosgadh.

Propitiator, *s.* Fear sàsuchaidh; fear diolaidh.

Propitiatory, *a.* Ciùineadach, réiteachail.

Propitious, *a.* Ciùin, baigheil, caomh, caomhail, fabhorach, tròcaireach; seunmhor, aghmhor, soirbh.

Propitiously, *adv.* Gu ciùin, gu caomh, gu caomhail, gu fabhorach, gu tròcaireach, gu seunmhor, gu h-aghmhor, gu soirbh.

Propitiousness, *s.* Baighealachd, caomhalachd, fabhorachd, seunmhorachd, soirbheas.

Proplasm, *s.* Cumadh, molltair.

Proportion, *s.* Roinn; dealbh; co-chudthrom; cumadh, cumachd, snàs. In proportion to my ability, *a réir m' urrainn;* if he be tall, he is thick in proportion, *ma tha e ard, tha e garbh a réir sin;* without proportion, *d' a réir.*

Proportion, *v. a.* Comh-fhreagaraich, cum, dean a réir a chéile. Proportioned, *a reir a chéile, freagarrach, cumadail;* ill-proportioned, *neo-shnàsmhor, mi-chumadail.*

Proportionable, *a.* Dealbhach, cumadail; comh-fhreagarrach, cothromach.

Proportionably, *adv.* A réir; gu cumadail, gu freagarrach.

Proportional, *a.* Cudthromach; cumadail; comh-fhreagarrach, comh-cheart, a reir chéile.

Proportionally, *adv.* Gu cudthromach, gu cumadail, gu comh-fhreagarrach, gu cubhaidh, gu comh-cheart.

Proportionate, *v. a.* Dean comh-cheart, comh-cheartaich.

Proportionate, *a.* Comh-cheart, comh-fhreagarrach; cumadail.

Proportionately, *adv.* Gu comh-cheart; gu comh-fhreagarrach; a réir.

Proposal, *s.* Gluasadh; gluasad; tairgse; ural; cialtradh.

Propose, *v. a.* and *n.* Tairg, sònruich, gluais, dean gluasad, cuir an tairgse; ainmich, cuir an ainmeachadh; cuir roimh; bi ag ural. I propose to myself, *tha mi 'cur am romham;* propose a member, *cuir ball an tairgse,* (*no*) *an ainmeachadh;* proposed, *tairgste, sònruichte, ainmichte.*

Proposer, *s.* Gluasadair, tairgear, fear gluasaid, fear a chuireas an tairgse.

Proposition, *s.* Cialtradh; tairgse, tairgsinn.

Propound, *v.* Gluais; tairg, cuir an tairgse.

Propounder, *s.* Gluasadair, fear gluasaid; fear a chuireas an tairgse.

Proprietary, *s.* Sealbhadair, sealbhachair, fear seilbhe.

Proprietor, *s.* Sealbhadair, sealbhachair, fear seilbhe, maighstir. Proprietors, *sealbhadairean, luchd seilbhe.*

Proprietress, *s.* Ban-mhaighstir.

Propriety, *s.* Ceart, ceartas; cubhaidheachd; còir.

Propt, *a.* Propainnte; air a chumail sùas.

Propugn, *v. a.* Dion, gabh leithsgeul, gabh taobh, cuir le. He propugned me, *ghabh e mo leithsgeul, chuir e leam.*

Propugnation, *s.* Dionadh; leithsgeul.

Propugner, *s.* Dionair, dionadair.

Propulsion, *s.* Sparradh; starradh, stailceadh, putadh, pùcadh, fùcadh.

Prorogation, *s.* Dàileachadh, cur dheth. Prorogation of parliament, *cur dheth na parlamaid.*

Prorogue, *v. a.* Dàilich, cuir dàil, cuir dheth; athlathaich.

Proruption, *s.* Briseadh mach.

Prosaic, *a.* Rosgach.

Proscribe, *v. a.* Diobraich, diobair, fògair, deòraich, arfhuntaich, fuadaich, dit; sgrios, mill. Proscribed, *diobraichte, diobairte, deòraichte, arfhunntaichte, fuadaichte.*

Proscriber, *s.* Diobrair; deòradair; fuadachair, fear ditidh, sgriosadair.

Proscription, *s.* Diteadh, arbfuntachadh, arfuntachd, fògradh, sgrios, sgriosadh.

Prose, *s.* Rosg.

Prosecute, *v. a.* Cuir h-uige; cuir gu lagh; tagair; ruaig; buanaich, mair, lean. I prosecuted him, *chuir mi h-uige* (*no*) *gu lagh e.*

Prosecution, *s.* Tagradh, tagairt, leanachd, cur h-uige cùis lugha; ruaig.

Prosecutor, *s.* Fear agairt, fear tagraidh, tagrair.

Proselyte, *s.* Iompachan.

Prosemination, *s.* Siolchur; craobh-sgaoileadh.

Prosodian, *s.* Toinneolaiche.

Prosody, *s.* Toinneolas; rann eòlas.

Prosopopœia, *s.* Pearsachadh.

Prospect, *s.* Seall, sealladh; beachd, shealladh; dòchas, dùil, sealltuinn, dearcadh, amharc.

Prospective, *a.* Roimh-bheachdach; crionna, sicir, seanacar, beachdail, fad-sheallach. A prospective glass, *gloine amhairc;* a prospective view, *sealladh roimh, sealladh beòil.*

Prosper, *v. a.* and *n.* Soirbhich; fàs, cinn; beannuich, dean soirbheas, buitich soirbheas. He prospered, *shoirbhich e, dh' éirich soirbheas leis, thainig rath air.* Prosper us, *soirbhich leinn.*

Prosperity, *s.* Soirbheas, rath, soirbheachadh, sonas, seun, agh, maith, deagh fhortan, buadhalachd. Prosperity attend you, *soirbheas leat, soirbheas math leat.*

Prosperous, *a.* Soirbheasach, sealbhar, aghmhor, rathail, rathmhòr, sona, seunmhor.

Prosperously, *adv.* Gu soirbheasach, le soirbheas, gu rathail, le rath, gu h-aghmhor.

Prospicience, *s.* Roimh-amharc; crionnadh.

Prosternation, *s.* Luidhe sios, tilgeadh sios.

Prostitute, *s.* Siùrsach, siùrtach, striopach, oinigh, strapaid, meirdreach, strumpaid, beasg, bidse; baobh, stràille, drùthanag.

PROSTITUTE, *v.* Siùrsaich; truaill, truaillich. She prostituted herself, *thruaill si i fèin.*

PROSTITUTE, *a.* Cumaint, cumanta.

PROSTITUTION, *s* Meirdreachas, siùrsachas, siùrsachd, striopachas, striopachd, truailleadh, truailleachd.

PROSTRATE, *a.* Sìnte, na luidhe, air smàl, spadte, tilgte sios, striochdta; sleuchdta

PROSTRATE, *v a* Tilg sios; spad, striochd, glùn-lub; sleuchd

PROSTRATION, *s.* Tilgeadh sios, spadadh, striochdadh, glùn-lubadh, sleuchdadh

PROTECT, *v a* Dion, gleidh, tearuinn, tearmuinn, saor, cum tearuinnte, cum slàn Protected, *dionta, tearuinnte.*

PROTECTION, *s.* Dionadh, tearnadh, tearmunn, dìdean, dion; culaidh-dhion, fasgadh, coghnadh, cuideachadh

PROTECTIVE, *a.* Dionach, tearnach, tearmunnach, dìdeanach, fasgadhach

PROTECTOR, *s.* Dionadair, fear dion; dìdean, tearmunnair, dionair, fear coghnaidh, fear cuideachaidh, aodhair.

PROTECTRESS, *s.* Ban-dionair, ban-dìdean

PROTEND, *v a.* Cum a mach, sìn a mach

PROTERVITY, *s.* Cainnteachas; beadaidheachd

PROTEST, *v a* Thoir briathar, earail, earailich, foillsich, cuir an aghaidh, gairm fianuis; dearbh, còmhdaich

PROTEST, *s* Earail, rùn-fhoillseachadh

PROTESTANT, *a.* Ath-leasaichte, *protastanach*

PROTESTANT, *s* Protastanach, neach a tha do 'n aon chreideamh riusan a sgar o eaglais na Roimh

PROTESTANTISM, *s* Protastanachd

PROTESTATION, *s* Foillseachadh, earail, bòid fhollaiseach

PROTESTER, *s* Earalaiche

PROTHONOTARY, *s.* Ard-notair, priomh-chléireach

PROTHONOTARYSHIP, *s.* Ard-notaireachd, priomh-chléir-sinneachd

PROTOCOL, *s* Ceud sgriobhadh

PROTOLOGY, *s* Roimh-radh

PROTOTYPE, *s* Priomh-sgriobhadh, samhladh, eisiomlair

PROTRACT, *v.* Cuir dàil, cuir dheth, dàilich, sìn a mach, fadaich.

PROTRACT, *s* Mairneal, dàil, màidhean

PROTRACTER, *s* Sìneadair, fadachair, maidheanaiche, seorsa inneil tomhais

PROTRACTION, *s.* Dàileachadh, fadachadh, cur dheth, sìneadh

PROTRACTIVE, *a.* Dàileach, mairnealach, màidheanach; mall, aolaisteach

PROTRUDE, *v a* and *n* Sparr, pùc, puchd, starr, sath; bolg (no) balg a mach, brùchd.

PROTRUSION, *s* Sparradh, pùc, starradh, sàthadh

PROTUBERANCE, *s* Meall, meallan, mulp, mulpan, cnap, crap, toman, at, bolg, balg, brùchd Full of protuberances, *meallanach, mulpach, mulpanach, cnapach, tomanach.*

PROTUBERANT, *a* Meallach, meallanach, cnapach, tomanach; bolgach, bolganta

PROTUBERATE, *v a* Bolg a mach; at.

PROUD, *a* (*Foppish*), uallach, leòmach, sgòdail, stràiceil, stàideil, (*haughty*), uaibhreach, ardanach, ard-inntinneach, mòralach, ailghiosach, ceannasach, mòr, mòr-chuiseach, spagluinneach; barracaideach A proud man, *fear uaibhreach,* a proud bitch, *galladh air ghasair,* proud flesh, *feòil ghrod,* proud speaking, *gloiream, bòilich,* the proud despise to seem cold on the coldest day, *cha bhi fuachd air uallach air fhuaraid an là.*

PROUDLY, *adv.* Gu h-uallach, gu leòmach, gu sgòdail, gu stràiceil, gu stàideil; (*haughtily*), gu h-ardanach, gu h-uaibhreach, gu h-ailghiosach, gu ceannasach.

PROVE, *v a.* and *n* Dearbh, còmhdaich; feuch, cuir gu deuchainn, fiosraich; (*become*), fàs, cinn, tionndaidh mach. He proved a rascal, *thionndaidh e na chrochair,* prove your words, *dearbh do bhriathran.*

PROVABLE, *a.* So-dhearbh, so-dhearbhadh, so-chòmhdachadh, a ghabhas còmhdachadh, a ghabhas dearbhadh

PROVENDER, *s* Connlach, innlinn, biadh, spreidh, fodar, saoidh, feur.

PROVERB, *s.* Gnàth-fhocal, sean-fhocal, sean radh, gnath-labhairt, leth-fhocal, sean ràite. Make true the old proverb, *firinnich an sean-fhocal,* according to the proverb, *a rèir an sean-fhocail*

PROVERBIAL, *a* Gnàth-fhoclach, sean-fhoclach, leth-fhoclach, coitchionn, cumaint. A proverbial saying, *radh cumaint*

PROVIDE, *v a* Ullaich, ullamhaich, deasaich, solair, freasdail, solaraich; tionail, (*stipulate*), cumhnantaich, dean bann (no) cùmhnant Provide food, *solair biadh,* they are well provided for, *is maith tha iad air faicinn aca;* provided, *ullaichte, ullamhaichte, deasaichte, solaraichte,* provided for, *air gabhail aig, air fhaicinn aige,* not provided, *neo-ullamh, neo-dheasaichte,* provided (yet), *fhathast, fathast, ach,* provided that, *mu 's e agus gu, mu 's e as gu, air chùmhnant is gu*

PROVIDENCE, *s* Freasdal; crionnachd; faicill, faiceallachd, caonntachd The providence of God, *freasdal Dé.*

PROVIDENT, *a* Solarach, cùramach, faiceallach, freasdalach, crionna, fad-sheallach, caomhnach, caonntach, sul-radharcach, tul-radharcach

PROVIDENTIAL, *a* Freasdalach

PROVIDENTIALLY, *adv* Gu freasdalach; a réir freasdail, gu fortanach, mar bha 'm fortan.

PROVIDENTLY, *adv* Gu crionna, gu faiceallach, gu glic, gu tul-radharcach.

PROVIDER, *s* Solaraiche, freasdalaiche, cnuasair, fear solair, fear solaraidh

PROVIDING, *s* Solaradh, deasachadh, tionaladh, cnuasachadh.

PROVINCE, *s* Mòr-roinn, roinn, dùthaich, tìr, talamh, fonn, cuntaidh; siorrachd; (*office*), gnothuch, oich, dreuchd, àite This is not my province, *cha n' e so mo ghnothuch-sa,* the United Provinces, *na Comh-Roinnean*

PROVINCIAL, *a* Mòr-roinneach, dùchail, tìreil

PROVING, *part.* A dearbhadh, a comhdachadh

PROVINGLY, *adv* Gu farranach.

PROVISION, *s* (*Preparation*), deasachadh, uallachadh, uighcam, solar, cnuasachadh, (*food*), biadh, lòn, connlach; (*term*), teirm, cumhnant, bann. Make provision, *dean deasachadh,* provision for a journey, *biatsadh*

PROVISIONAL, *a* Air chois car ùine, cumhnantach, a réir cùmhnaint

PROVISO, *s* Cùmhnant, teirm, bann, cumha.

PROVISOR, *s* Fear solair, fear solaraidh, solaraiche.

PROVOCATION, *s* Brosnuchadh, brosnachadh, buair, buaireadh, graoineag, farran. None gives provocation but gets with a return, *cha tug sàr nach d' fhuiling sàr.*

PROVOCATIVE, *a.* Brosnachail, brosnuchail, dùsgach.

PROVOKE, *v a* Buair, brosnuich, brosnaich, prosnaich, feargaich, cuir fearg air; cuir corruich air, farranaich, cuir farran air, goil, meall, thoir a thaobh Provoked, *buairte, brosnuichte, brosnaichte, feargaichte, farrandch, farranaichte, meallta*

PROVOKER, *s.* Buairear, buaireadair; brosnachair, brosnuchair, fear brosnuchaidh.

PROVOKING, *a.* Farranach, buaireasach.

PROVOST, *s.* Prothaist, riaghladair cathrach.

PROW, *s.* Toiseach luing, saidh; siola, siol, braineach

† PROW, *a.* Gaisgeil, treun, curanta.

PROWESS, *s* Gaisge, cùrantachd, neart, treunas, tréine, spionnadh, calmachd. Having prowess, *gaisgeil, curanta, neartmhor, treun, calma, garbh.*

PROWL, *v. n.* Ealaidh mun cuairt, ealaidh airson cobhartaich, seap.

PROWLER, *s.* Ealadair; seapair, siapair.

PROXIMATE, *a.* Fagus, fogus, dlùth, gàr, am fogus, is fhoigse, is dlùithe.

PROXIMITY, *s.* Fogsachd, fogusachd, foigse, foisge, foigseachd, neasachd, nàbachd, nabuidheachd, coimh-fhearsnachd, coimhearsnachd

PROXY, *s.* Riochdair, riochd-fhear, fear ionaid fir eile.

PRUDE, *s.* Uailleag; boirionnach mhòiteil, gogaill.

PRUDENCE, *s* Gliocas, crionnachd, tuigse, eagnachd, toinisg, faicill; tiarmalachd.

PRUDENT, *a* Glic, crionna, tuigseach, eagnach; eagnuidh, sicir, cnuachdach, toinisgeil, seanacar. It is not prudent in a man to tell all his grief, *cha cheòl do dhuine a bhròn uile aithris.*

PRUDENTIAL, *a.* Faiceallach, cùramach; toinisgeil.

PRUDENTIALLY, *adv.* Gu faiceallach, a réir gliocais.

PRUDENTLY, *adv.* Gu glic, gu crionna, gu tuigseach, gu h-eagnaidh, gu sicir, gu toinisgeil.

PRUDERY, *s.* Mòitealachd, pròisealachd, susdalachd, gogcheannachd, gogailleachd.

PRUDISH, *a.* Mòitealach, pròisealach, susdalach, gogcheannach.

PRUNE, *v a* Sgath, bearr, gearr; snaith; cuir an ordugh.

PRUNE, *s.* Airneag fhrangach, plumbais, seargta, bulos

PRUNELLO, *s.* Seorsa side do 'n deanar gùintean mhinisteara; plumbais.

PRUNER, *s.* Sgathadair, bearradair; fear sgathaidh, fear bearraidh.

PRUNING-HOOK, *s* Sgian bearraidh, sgian sgathaidh, sgian gairmealair, corran sgathaidh.

PRURIENCE, PRURIENCY, *s.* Tachas; mòr-dheidhe

PRURIENT, *a.* Tachasach.

PRURIGINOUS, *a* Clombach, tachasach

PRY, *v. n.* Geur amhairc; dearc, dìdeagaich. Prying eyes, *sùilean geur.*

PSALM, *s.* Salm, laoidh naomh.

PSALM-BOOK, *s.* Salmadair.

PSALMIST, *s.* Salmair; salmadair.

PSALMODY, *s.* Salmadaireachd; seinn shalm

PSALTER, *s.* Salmadair.

PSALTERY, *s.* Saltair, cruit, cruit chiùil, clàrsach

PSEUDO, *s.* and *a* Fallsa, fallsaidh, baoth, faoin, bréig.

PSHAW, *interj.* Fuigh! ab! ab!

PTISAN, *s* Seorsa dibh.

PTYALISM, *s.* Seile, smugaideachd, ronnaireachd.

PUBERTY, *s.* Ur-ghreannachd; an t-am air am fàs roinne air na buill dhiomhair.

PUBESCENCE, *s.* Ur-ghreannachd.

PUBLIC, *a.* Follaiseach, coitchionn, cumanta, cumaint; fosgailte; aithnichte; sgaoilte A public-house, *tigh mòr, tigh òsda;* a public disgrace, *tàmailt fhollaiseach*

PUBLIC, *s.* Sluagh, mor-shluagh. The public, *an sluagh, an saoghal,* the good of the public, *math an t-sluaigh,* in public, *am follais, an sealladh, an t-sluaigh*

PUBLICAN, *s.* Cis-mhaor; fear tigh osda; publicanach

PUBLICATION, *s.* Foillseachadh, sgaoileadh, gairmeadh, craobh-sgaoileadh, cur a mach.

PUBLICITY, *s* Follaiseachd.

PUBLICLY, *adv.* Gu follaiseach, am follais; gun chéiltinn.

PUBLICNESS, *s* Fosgailteachd; follaiseachd, coitchionntas

PUBLIC-SPIRITED, *a* Mòr-chuiseach; meamnach, fial, flathail.

PUBLISH, *v. a.* Foillsich, dean aithnichte; dean follaiseach; gairm, glaodh; cuir an céill, innis, cuir a mach. Publish a book, *cuir mach leabhar,* published, *foillsichte, air a dheanamh aithnichte,* (as a book), *air a chur mach*

PUBLISHER, *s.* Foillseachair, fear chur mach leabbraichean

PUCELAGE, *s.* Maighdeannas

PUCK, *s* Bòcan; ailmse

PUCKER, *v. a.* Liurc, liurcaich, cas, preas. Puckered, *liurcta, liurcaichte.*

† PUDDER, *v.* Buair, dean cullaid, dean tuasaid.

PUDDER, *s.* Buaireas, callaid, tuasaid, tabaid, aimhreite.

PUDDING, *s* Marag, putag. A white pudding, *marag gheal,* a black pudding, *marag dhubh,* hasty pudding, *mealcair,* a pudding made of calf's entrails, *creachan.*

PUDDING-TIME, *s.* Tràth dinnearach, trath bidh.

PUDDLE, *s.* Poll, eabar, lathach, laib, rumach, slob, munloch, lod There is no door without a puddle, and some have two, *cha 'n eil dorus gun laib, is cuid aig am bheil dhà.*

PUDDLE, *v. a.* Làbanaich, luinneanaich, salaich, eabaraich, eabair.

PUDDLING, *s.* Làbanachd, luinneanach.

PUDDLY, *a.* Làbanach, salach, eabarach, laibeach.

PUDENCY, *s.* Malltachd, nàrachd, geimnidheachd; teistealachd, stuamachd, macantas

PUERILE, *a.* Leanabaidh, leanabail, leanabanta, faoin, balachail

PUERILITY, *s* Leanabachd, leanabaidheachd, leanabantas, leanabalachd, balachanachd

PUET, *s* Dilit

PUFF, *s.* Osag, oiteag, séide; feochan; soighnean; tothadh, (*mushroom*), bolgan beiceach, caochag; (*for the hair*), toipean, moibean

PUFF, *v a.* Séid suas, at; bi 'g àinich

PUFFIN, *s.* Seorsa eòin uisge; seorsa éisg; bolgan beiceach

PUFFINESS, *s* Gaotharachd; atmhorachd

PUFFY, *a.* Gaothar, osagach, oiteagach, atmhor, falamh, faoin, bolgach.

PUFFING, *s* Séideadh, séideil, séidrich.

PUG, *s.* Ap, apag, ainm muirneach, airson neach sam bi

PUGH, *interj.* Ab! ab! fuigh

PUGIL, *s.* Ullag, cruidhean

PUGILISM, *s.* Dornaireachd.

PUGILIST, *s* Dornair; dorn-churaidh, dorn-laoch.

PUGNACIOUS, *a* Tuasaideach; buaireasach, aimhreiteach

PUGNACITY, *s.* Tuasaideachd; aimhreite

PUISNE, *a.* Òg, beag; crion; meanbh, iochdarach, suarrach

PUISSANCE, *s.* Cumhachd, neart; comas, tréine, treunas

PUISSANT, *a* Cumhachdach, neartmhor, foghainteach, treun, gaisgeil, mòr, aigeannach.

PUKE, *s* Sgeithe, sgeathrach, cliabh-sgeathrach; tilgeadh, diobhairt, cur a mach.

Puke, *v. n.* Sgeith, tilg, cuir a mach; fosgail. He began to puke, *thòisich e air sgeith* (*no*) *tilgeadh.*

Pulchritude, *s.* Bòidhche, maise, eireachdas, àille.

Pule, *v. n.* Biog, dean biog mar eireig; dean sgiuganaich, guil, caoin.

Pull, *v. a.* Tarruing, slaoid, spion, dragh, spiol. Pull asunder, *sgar;* pull from the root, *spion as a bhun;* pull up your spirits, *tog do mhisneach;* pulled, *tarruingte, spionta, spiolta;* pull the nighest oar, *an ramh is fhaigse iomair.*

Pull, *s.* Tarruing, spioladh, slaod; oidhirp; draoth; strìgh, comhstrigh.

Puller, *s.* Tarruingear; spioladair, draghair.

Pullet, *s.* Eireag.

Pulley, *s.* Ulag.

Pulling, *s.* Tarruing, spioladh, slaod, spionadh, draghair, draothadh.

Pulmonary, **Pulmonic**, *a.* Sgamhanach. A pulmonary affection, *tinneas sgamhan.*

Pulp, *s.* Laoghan, laodhan; taois.

Pulpit, *s.* Cùbaid, crannag, pulpaid.

Pulpous, *a.* Bogar, sùghar, sùghmhor, laodhanach, brìoghmhor, brìoghar, feòlar, feòlmhor.

Pulpousness, *s.* Bogarachd, sugharachd; laodhanachd.

Pulpy, *a.* Bog, bogar, sùghmhor, sùghar, brìoghmhor.

Pulsation, *s.* Frith-bhualadh, gluasad na fola, cuisleadh.

Pulsator, *s.* Bualadair, frith-bhualadair.

Pulse, *s.* Cuisle, gluasad na fola; (*vegetable*), peasair; ponair, pòr moinigeach sam bi. May your pulse beat as your heart may wish, *rùn do chridhe air do chuisle.*

Pulsion, *s.* Bualadh, sparradh, starradh, stailceadh, pùcadh.

Pulverizable, *a.* So-phronnadh, so-bhruanadh, fùdarach, brisg.

Pulverization, *s.* Pronnadh, mìn-phronnadh.

Pulverize, *v. a.* Pronn, bruan, mìn-phronn, méil. Pulverized, *pronn, mìn-phronn, mìn, méilte.*

Pulvil, *s.* Fàil cubhraidh.

Pumice, *s.* Sligeart; mìn-chlach.

Pump, *s.* Piob thaosgaidh, taosgair, caideal; taomadair, taoman; (*a shoe*), brog dannsaidh, pumpais.

Pump, *v.* Taoisg; tarruing; taom; tarruing sgeul. Pumped, *taoisgte, tarruingte, taomta.*

Pumper, *s.* Taosgair, taomair, fear taosgaidh.

Pumping, *s.* Taosgadh, taomadh, tarruing.

Pun, *s.* Gearr-fhocal, dubh-fhocal, toimhseachan, beum, gearradh.

Pun, *v. n.* Beum, gearr.

Punch, *s.* Tolladair; boireal, tor, toradh.

Punch, *v. a.* Toll.

Punch, *s.* Puinnse, deoch làidir; (*puppet*), gilleagan, cleasaiche, amadan; (*a stout fellow*), fear beag, staigean; bun; cnapanach.

Puncheon, *s.* Togsaid gu leth.

Puncher, *s.* Tolladair, boireal toradh.

Punctilio, *s.* Modh, modhaileachd.

Punctilious, *a.* Modhail; ceigeanach, rudach.

Punctilious, *s.* Modhaileachd; ceigeanachd.

Punctual, *a.* Pongail; pungail, seasmhach, cinnteach, riaghailteach.

Punctuality, *s.* Pongaileachd, pungaileachd, seasmhachd, sicireachd.

Punctually, *adv.* Gu pongail, gu pungail, gu seasmhach, gu cinnteach, gu sicir.

Punctuation, *s.* Pongadh, pungadh.

Puncture, *s.* Stob, bior, peasg, peasgadh.

Pundle, *s.* Geinneag; tònag; beanag, bun.

Pungency, *s.* Geurad, geiread; goirteas, gairgead, gairge.

Pungent, *a.* Geur, goirt, garg; guineach, biorach, dealgach, deilgneach; teumnach, beumnach.

Punic, *a.* Meallta; cealgach; breugach, fallsa.

Puniness, *s.* Crìne, suarraichead.

Punish, *v. a.* Peanasaich; pian, craidh, smachdaich; sgiùrs, cuipinn, dean peanas air; sàoth; gréidh. Punished, *peanasaichte, pianta, craidhte, smachdaichte; sgiùrsta, cuipinnte.*

Punishable, *a.* So-pheanasadh, so-phianadh, so-chradh, so-smachdachadh, airidh air peanas, a ghabhas peanasachadh, ion-pheanasda.

Punisher, *s.* Dioladair, peanasaiche; fear-smachdaidh.

Punishment, *s.* Peanas, dioladh, dioghaltas, smachdachadh, sgiùrsadh; greidh, caraiste.

Punition, *s.* Peanas, dioghaltas.

Punitive, *a.* Peanasach; smachdach; sgiùrsach.

Punk, *s.* Siùrsach, striopach. Punks, *siùrsaichean, striopaichean.*

Punning, *a.* Beumach; beumannach.

Punster, *s.* Beumadair, beumannair, fear beumnach, fear bheumanna; fear gearranachd.

Puny, *a.* Crion, beag, suarrach; anfhann; fann, lag, truagh, meuranda; leibideach; òg. Oft has the puny thriven, while the vigorous drop, *is tric chinn an cneadach is a dh' fhalbh an sodach.*

Puny, *s.* Siochair, ablach, rag, biast, garrach.

Pup, *v. n.* Beir cuileanan.

Pupil, *s.* (*Of the eye*), ubhall na sùl; clach na sùl; (*scholar*), sgoilear, deisciobal, foghlumaiche; neach òg fo chùram tuiteir.

Pupilage, *s.* Leanabantachd, oige.

Puppet, *s.* Gilleagan, mearagan; dealbh, fear bréige; ablach.

Puppy, *s.* Cuilean; ablach, rag, balach gun iùil, gun mhodh. The play of the puppy with the greyhound, *cluich a chuilein ris a mhial-chu.*

Puppy, *v. n.* Beir cuileanan.

Purblind, *a.* Gear-sheallach, leth-sheallach, gann-sheallach, spid-shuileach, ròsb-shuileach, leth-rosgach.

Purblindness, *s.* Gearr-shealladh, leth-shealladh, dalladh eun.

Purchasable, *a.* So-cheannachadh, a ghabhas ceannachadh, a dh' fhaotas ceannachadh.

Purchase, *v. a.* Ceannuich, ceannaich; faigh, buidhinn. Purchased, *ceannaichte.*

Purchase, *s.* Ceannach, ceannachadh, cunnarach.

Purchaser, *s.* Ceannuiche, fear ceannachaidh, ceannachadair.

Pure, *a.* (*Clean*), glan, fior-ghlan; (*clear*), soilleir, glan; (*mere*), fior. A pure rascal, *fior chrochair.* (*Incorrupt*), neo-thruaillichte, teisteil, gasda, slàn, fallain; (*chaste*), geamnaidh, geimnidh, mallta, gasda, fìreannach, bandaidh, macanta; (*unmixed*), fior, neo-mheasguaichte, neo-thruaillichte; (*innocent*), neo-chiontach, neo-choireach. Pure as unsunned snow, *cho glan ri sneachd nan cös.*

Purely, *adv.* Gu glan, gu fior ghlan; gu soilleir; gu fior; gu teisteil, gu gasda; gu geimnidh, gu macanta, gu neo-chiontach.

Pureness, *s.* Glaine, fior-ghloine, soilleireachd, firinn; teistealachd, geimnidheachd; neo-chiontas.

Purfile, *s.* Froinnse greusta; riobag.

Purfle, *v. a.* Greus; riobagaich, grinnich.

Purgation, *s.* Glanadh, sgùradh.

Purgative, *s.* Glanadach, sgùrach; fosglach, purgaideach, tualagach.

Purgative, *s.* Purgaid, sgùr-leigheas, leigheas fosglaidh, leigheas tualaig.

Purgatory, *s.* Purgadair, ionad glanaidh, ionad ionlaid; aite (a réir nam pàpanach) far an glanar anamana dhaoine mun teid iad a steach do fhlaitheanas.

Purge, *v.* Glan, sgùr, purgaidich; nigh, ionnlaid; cairt; soilleirich. Purge the body, *sgùr an com.* Purged, *glanta, glante, sgùrta, purgaidichte; nighte.*

Purge, *s.* Purgaid; sgùradh cuim, glanadh cuim.

Purging, *s.* Glanadh, sgùradh; ionnlaid; siubhal.

Purging-flax, *s.* Minneach, miosach.

Purification, *s.* Glanadh, sgùradh, ionnlaid, nigh; sioladh.

Purificative, *a.* Glanadach, glanta, sgùrtach.

Purifier, *s.* Glanadair, sguradair; glantair; fear glanaidh, fear leaghaidh.

Purify, *v. a.* Glan; ath-ghlan, tur-ghlan; soilleirich; siolaidh, sgùr, nigh, ionnlaid; leagh. Purified, *glanta, soilleirichte, siolaidhte, sgùrta, nighte, ionnlaidte.*

Puritan, *s.* Cràbhair, urr chrabhach; neach a ghabhas air a bhith ro dhiadhuidh, cealgair.

Puritanical, *a.* Cràbhach; ana-cràbhach; cealgach.

Puritanism, *s.* Ana-crabhadh; cealgaireachd.

Purity, *s.* Glaine, gloine, gloinead; fìor-ghloine, neochiontas; geimnidheachd, macantas, teistealachd; ionndras.

Purl, *s.* Lionn luibheanach, lionn lusanach.

Purl, *v. a.* Froinnsich; giobagaich; greus.

Purl, *v. n.* Dean torman, dean monar; dean crònan mar ni caochan.

Purlieu, *s.* Iomall, fàl.

Purling, *s.* Torman, crònan, tormanaich, crònanaich.

Purloin, *v. a.* Goid. He purloined the money and ran off, *ghoid e 'n t-airgiod agus thug e na buinn as.*

Purloiner, *s.* Meirleach, goidiche, gaduiche.

Purple, *s.* Corcar, corcur, purpur.

Purple, *a.* Corcar, corcarach, cro-dhearg, flann-dearg.

Purple-melic-grass, *s.* Bun glas.

Purplish, *a.* Flann-dearg, cro-dhearg, leth-char dearg.

Purport, *s.* Ciall, brìgh, rùn, seadh. I know not the purport of your language, *cha 'n aithne dhomh brìgh do sheanachais.*

Purport, *v. n.* Bi los, cuir romhad, bi 'brath, smuainich, rùnaich, ciallaich.

Purpose, *v. a.* and *n.* Rùnaich, miannaich, cuir romhad, sonruich, bi brath, bi los. I purpose to be off to-morrow, *tha mi a brath bhith falbh a maireach.*

Purpose, *s.* Rùn, miann, togar, smuain; gnothuch; cuis; deòin; brath. I had a purpose to meet you, *bha mhiann orm do choinneachadh, bha mi 'brath do choinneachadh;* a full purpose, *rùn suidhichte;* on purpose, *a dh' aon obair, a dh' aon ghnothuch, a dh' aon deòin;* to what purpose is all this? *carson a tha so? ciod is ciall do so?* to no purpose, *diomhain, faoin, gun fhiù, gun tairbhe;* your labour is to no purpose, *is diomhain do shaothair.*

Purposely, *adv.* A dh' aon obair, a dh' aon ghnothuch; le deòin. He did it purposely, *rinn e dh' aon obair e.*

Purr, *v. n.* Dean crònan, dean dùrdan. When the cat has hold she purrs, *nur bhios ni aig a chat ni i dùrdan.*

Purring, *s.* Crònan; dùrdan.

Purse, *s.* Sporan, màl, malaidh, ionmhas; tiachag; peasan; bag, balg, spiochan. A Highland purse, *sporran molach;* draw your purse, *tarruing do sporran;* a cutpurse, *gearra-sporan.*

Purser, *s.* Gille sporrain; ionmhasair, fear coimhead airgid.

Purse, *v. a.* Cùir an sporran; liurcaich; cuir gruaim ort.

Pursiness, *s.* Gainne analach; sultmhorachd, reamhad, reamhrachd, pocanachd.

Purslain, *s.* Purpaidh, puirpidh. Purslain tree, *lus a phuirpidh.*

Pursuable, *a.* A ghabhas leanachd, a dh' fhaotas leanachd.

Pursuance, *s.* Leanachd, leantuinn.

Pursuant, *a.* A réir, do réir. Pursuant to orders, *a réir orduigh.*

Pursue, *v.* Lean, ruaig, tòraich; rach an tòir; buanaich, mair. Pursue him, *rach an tòir air, lean e, rach na thòir;* he pursued them hotly, *lean e iad gu cruaidh;* pursue at law, *cuir h-uige; tagair.*

Pursuer, *s.* Fear tòir, ruagair, fear geur-leanmhuinn.

Pursuing, *s.* See **Pursuit**.

Pursuit, *s.* Ruaig, ruagadh, tòir; tòireachd; leanachd, leantuinn, geur-leanmhuinn, geur leanachd; buanachadh.

Pursuivant, *s.* Maor; teachdair.

Pursy, *a.* Pocanach, reamhar, cutach, bagach, bronnach. A pursy fellow, *pocan.*

Purtenance, *s.* Greallach, mionach, meanach.

Purvey, *v. a.* and *n.* Solair, freasdail, cnuasaich, cruinnich; faigh.

Purveyance, *s.* Solar, solaradh, freasdaladh, cnuasachd.

Purveyor, *s.* Solaraiche, fear solaraidh, cnuasair; trusdar, drùisear.

Purulence, **Purulency**, *s.* Iongar, ioghar, braghadh.

Purulent, *a.* Lan iongair, iongarach, braghachail.

Pus, *s.* Iongar, ioghar, braghadh.

Push, *v. a.* Pùc, pùchd, pùrr, starr, sàth, staile; ding, put, putagaich, utagaich. Push him *or* it back, *pùc air ais e;* push with a sword, *sàth:* push on, *or* make haste, *buail air adhairt;* push, *or* put to a strait, *cuir gu deuchainn, teannaich.*

Push, *s.* Pùc, pùcadh, purr, purradh, purrag, utag, putadh, starr, starradh, sàth, sàthadh, stailc, stailceadh; urchair, dingeadh; (*a strait*), càs, deuchainn, teanntachd; (*attack*), ionnsuidh; (*pimple*), guirean, bucaid. He is put to the push, *tha e an càs, tha e 'g a shàruchadh;* I will have another push for it, *bheir mi aon deuchainn eile dha.*

Pusher, *s.* Pùcair, pùcadair.

Pushing, *a.* Adhartach, teoma, beothail; dichiollach, oidhirpeach, deuchainneach.

Push-pin, *s.* Cluich phrìneachan.

Pusillanimity, *s.* Cladhaireachd, geilte, gealtaireachd, crìne; leanabaidheachd.

Pusillanimous, *a.* Gealtach, cladhaireach, crion, crìan, lag-chridheach, neo-chuiseach. Thou pusillanimous fellow! *fhir an anaim chrìne! a ghealtair! a chladhair! a chrionaiche!*

Pusillanimousness, *s.* Gealtaireachd, geilte, cladhaireachd.

Puss, *s.* Cat, busaidh; maigheach, gearr-fhiadh.

Pustule, *s.* Guirean, bucaid; at, briseadh mach, plucan, bolg, bolgan, builgean.

Pustulous, *a.* Guireanach, bucaideach, plucanach, bolgach, builgeanach.

Put, *v. a.* and *n.* Cuir. Put by, *cuir seach, cuir seachad; cuir gu taobh, taisg;* put off, *cuir dheth; cuir dail;* put off thee, *cuir dhiot;* put down, *cuir sios, cuir bhàn;* put up, *cuir suas, cuir 'n airde;* put up thy sword, *cuir suas do chlaidheamh;* put on, *cuir air;* put on thee, *cuir ort;* put on them, *cuir orra;* (incite), *brosnuich, stuig;* put to or add, *cuir ri;* put to it, *cuir ris;* put on or impute, *cuir as leth;* put to them, *cuir as an leth;* put out, *cuir mach;* (extinguish), *cuir as, mùch;* put to death, *marbh, cuir gu bàs, cuir as do;* put to it, *sàruich;* put up with, *fulaing, giulan le, fulaing le, fuilig le, cuir suas le;* put on, *cuir air adhairt, stuig, brog;* put upon trial, *cuir gu deuchainn;* put together, *cuir ri chéile;* put in for, *cuir stigh airson;* put to sea, *cuir gu sàil;* put to usury, *cuir air riadh;* put the case to be so, *leig gur ann mar sin a tha chùis;* a put-off, *leithsgeul;* put aside, *cuir gu taobh; cuir a leth taobh.*

PUTATIVE, *a.* Smuainichte.

PUTID, *a.* Crion, iosal, diblidh, suarrach, gun fhiach, faoin, gun fhiù, fagharsach.

PUTIDNESS, *s.* Crìne, diblidheachd, suarraichead.

PUTREDINOUS, *a.* Breun, lobhach, grod.

PUTREFACTION, *s.* Bréine, breuntas, lobhadh.

PUTRID, *a.* Breun, grod, lobhach, loibheach, malcta.

PUTRIDNESS, *s.* Breuntas, grodadh, groide, lobhadh.

PUTRIFY, *v. a.* and *n.* Grod, lobh, malc, breun; fas grod. Putrified, *grod, lobhta, malcta.*

PUTTER, *s.* Purradair; fear stuig, brosnuchair.

PUTTING-STONE, *s.* Clach-neart.

PUTTOCK, *s.* Beilbhean ruadh.

PUTTY, *s.* *Potaidh,* tàth-thaois, taois tàthaidh.

PUZZLE, *v. a.* and *n.* Cuir an iomcheist; sàruich, pian, buair.

PUZZLE, *s.* Iomcheist, toimhseachan; buaireadh, cruadal, gàbhaidh; teinne; breislich.

PUZZLER, *s.* Buaireadair.

PYGARG, *s.* Earra-gheal.

PYGMEAN, *a.* Crion, crian, meanbh, beag, girceanach.

PYGMY, *s.* Luch-armunn, bideach, garrlach, arrachd, troich, ablach, gircean, rag; duine beag.

PYLORUS, *s.* Ioghoile.

PYRAMID, *s.* Bior-charradh, bior-stùc, carradh barr-chaol, bioramaid.

PYRAMIDAL, PYRAMIDICAL, *a.* Barra-chaol, biorach, binneanach; bioramaideach.

PYRAMIS, *s.* See PYRAMID.

PYRE, *s.* Cairbh-theine, connadh cairbh-theine.

PYRITES, *s.* Breoth-chlach, chlach theine.

PYROMANCY, *s.* Teine-fhiosachd, breoth-dhruidheachd.

PYROTECHNICS, *s.* Obair theine; eòlas mu obair theine.

PYRRHONISM, *s.* Teagamhachd.

PYX, *s.* Bocsa.

Q.

Q. An seachdamh litir deug do 'n Aibideal Shasunnach.

QUAB, *s.* Seorsa éisg.

QUACK, *v. n.* Sgreach mar ni tunnag; glag, gloc, dean gagail, dean gobais.

QUACK, *s.* Feall-leigh; scoitiche; *dochdair bi gise;* cleasaiche, carach.

QUACK, *a.* Scoiteach.

QUACKERY, QUACKISM, *s.* Scoiteachd, scoitidheachd.

QUACKSALVER, *s.* Scoitiche, feall-leigh, faoin-leigh; *dochdair bi gise.*

QUADRAGESIMA, *s.* A cheud domhnach do 'n Charbhas.

QUADRAGESIMAL, *a.* Carbhasach, carbhas.

QUADRANGLE, *s.* Ceithir-chearnag, ceithir oisinneag, ceithir-shlisneag; fioghait.

QUADRANGULAR, *a.* Ceithir chearnach, ceithir oisinneach.

QUADRANT, *s.* Ceithreamh, càirt, ceithreamhan, seorsa inneal tomhais, càirt cearcaill.

QUADRATE, *s.* Ceithir shlisneag, ceithir-chearnag.

QUADRATE, *a.* Ceithir-chearnach, ceithir shliosach.

QUADRATURE, *s.* Ceithir-chearnag; ceithreamh na gealaich.

QUADRENNIAL, *a.* Ceithir bhliadhnach, ceithir bhliadhnail.

QUADRIBLE, *a.* Cearnachail.

QUADRILATERAL, *a.* Ceithir-shlisneach.

QUADRILLE, *s.* Seorsa cluiche air chairtean; seorsa dannsaidh.

QUADRIPARTITE, *a.* Ann an ceithir phàirtean; ceithreannaichte.

QUADRIPARTITION, *s.* Ceithreannachadh.

QUADRISYLLABLE, *s.* Ceithir siolach.

QUADRUPED, *s.* Ceithir-chosach, beothach ceithir-chosach.

QUADRUPLE, *a.* Ceithir fillte.

QUÆRE, QUERY, *s.* Ceist; teagamh, ag.

QUÆRE, *v.* Foighnich, foighneachd, feòraich.

QUAFF, *v. a.* Òl, sluig, gabh teann-shath dibh.

QUAFFER, *s.* Òladair; pòitear, meisgear, ruitear.

QUAFFING, *s.* Òl, pòit, meisge, ruite, ruitearachd.

QUAGGY, *a.* Bog, boglach, rumach, féithear.

QUAGMIRE, *s.* Bog, boglach, suil-chritheach, cathar, lod, feith; curach.

QUAIL, *s.* Gearra-goirt.

QUAINT, *a.* Rudach, ceigeanach; cuimir; snàsmhor, greanta, finealta, freagarrach, lathailteach, fior lathailteach.

QUAINTLY, *adv.* Gu rudach; gu cuimir; gu greanta, gu finealta, gu lathailteach.

QUAINTNESS, *s.* Finealtachd; cuimireachd; lathailteachd.

QUAKE, *v. n.* Crith, criothanaich, bi air chrith, crath.

QUAKE, *s.* Critheadh, crath; crith, criothnachadh.

QUAKING, *s.* Critheadh; crith, criothnachadh. Quaking with terror, *crith-eagal, crith-oillt.*

QUALIFICATION, *s.* Deasachadh, uigheamachadh, deasachd; taiseachadh; lughadachadh; (*of mind*), feart, buaidh, càil, gné. Qualified, *deasaichte, ullamhaichte; murrach.*

QUALIFY, *v. a.* Deasaich, ullamhaich; dean freagarrach; taisich; lasuich; riaghail.

QUALITY, *s.* (*State*), inmhe, uaillse, airde; (*of mind*) gné, buaidh, càil, feart; (*persons of rank*), uaillsean. Good qualities, *deagh bhuaidhean, deagh chàilean, deagh mhodhannan.*

QUALM, *s.* Gaise, tur-thilge, sleogadh, ornais.

QUALMISH, *a.* Sleogach.

QUALMISHNESS, *s.* Gaiseachd; tur-thilge.

QUANDARY, *s.* Teagamh; ag.

QUANTITY, *s.* Meud, uibhir, uimhir, tomad; tomald, cudthrom; na h-urrad; †diorna. A great quantity, *mòran, dorlach.*

QUANTUM, *s.* Meud, uibhir, an t-iomlan.

Quarantine, *s.* Ùine dha fhichead la is éigin do luingeas a thig as na talmhainnean a mach fànachd, mu 'm faod i seòladh steach do chàla.

Quarrel, *s.* Comh-strì, comh-strigh, connsach, trogbhail, droch cordadh, iorghuil, tuasaid, tabaid, aimhreite, cur a mach; trod, trodan; cuis ghèarain; dróch rùn; seorsa saighde.

Quarrel, *v. a.* Cuir a mach, troid, connsaich, strigh, droch-coird. They quarrelled, *chuir iad a mach air chéile;* you would quarrel with your shins, *dheanamh tu caonnag ri do dha lurgainn.*

Quarreller, *s.* Fear tuasaid, fear aimhreite, ciaplaiche.

Quarrelous, **Quarrelsome**, *a.* Tuasaideach, brionglaideach, aimhreiteach, crosda, carraideach, connspaideach, trodach, ciaplach, bruidhneach, strangalach, streapaideach.

Quarrelsomeness, *s.* Tuasaideachd, brionglaideachd, strangalachd; sheapaideachd.

Quarry, *s.* Cearnag ghloine; seorsa saighde.

Quarry, *s.* Gairbheal. A quarry-man, *clachadair, fear gairbheal.*

Quarry, *v.* Tochail, tochailtich, cladhaich; bùraich.

Quart, *s.* Càirt, an ceathramh cuid do ghalan.

Quartan, *s.* Seorsa fiabhruis.

Quarter, *s.* (*Fourth part*), càirt, ceithreamh, ceathramh; (*coast*), aite, cearn, ionad, tìr, dùthaich, earainn do bhaile no dhùthcha, airde; (*of a year*), ràidhe, ràithe; (*of an hour*), ceithreamh uair, ceithreamh na h-uair; (*lodgings*), cairteal, cairtealan, ceithreannan; (*mercy*), baigh, tròcair, iochd. From all quarters, *as gach àite, as gach àirde;* the winter quarter, *ràithe a gheamhraidh;* the spring quarter, *ràithe an earraich;* the summer quarter, *ràithe an t-samhraidh;* the harvest quarter, *ràithe an fhogharaidh;* winter quarters, *ceithreannan geamhraidh;* a quarter's good nursing is better than a whole year, *is fhearr altrum ràithe no altrum bliadhna.*

Quarter, *v. a.* Càirtich; roinn na cheithir earrannan, cairteal, aitich; gabh comhnuidh, cùir suas, fan, fuirich.

Quarterage, *s.* Cuid ràithe, luathsachadh ràithe.

Quarter-day, *s.* La màil, lath riadh.

Quarter-deck, *s.* Caisteal deiridh; ceann deiridh.

Quarterly, *a.* and *adv.* Gach ràithe; ràitheil; raidheil, ràidheachail, uair san ràithe.

Quartermaster, *s.* Maighstir cheithreannan.

Quartern, *s.* Siol, siolag, ceithreamh phinnt; noigean; ceithreamh. A quartern loaf, *builionn cheithreimh.*

Quarters, *s.* Ceithreannan; cairtealan. Night's quarters, *ceithreannan oidhche.*

Quarter-session, *s.* Cùirt ràithe.

Quarter-staff, *s.* Cuaille dion.

Quarto, *a.* Ceathramh, ceithreamh.

Quash, *v. a.* Mùch, bruth, fàisg; coisg, cum sios, cum samhach; sàruich; cuir air chùl, ceannsuich, grad cheannsaich. Quashed, *mùchta; coisgte, caisgte; ceannsuichte.*

Quashing, *s.* Mùchadh, cosgadh, casgadh, cumail fo (no) samhach.

Quaternary, *s.* Ceithir.

Quaternion, *s.* Ceithir, cearthar, buidheann cheathrar.

Quaternity, *s.* Ceithir.

Quatrain, *s.* Rann cheithir-lìneach anns am bheil am focal is deireannaiche anns gach sread a freagairt ma seach; mar,

> " A Shnlobhain, a 's glaise ciabh,
> Thubhairt Starno nan sgiath donn
> Siubhail gu Ardbheinn nan sliabh
> Gu Selma mu 'n iadh an tonn."—*Oss.*

Quaver, *v. n.* Crith, crath; bog, céileirich.

Quaverer, *s.* Ceileiriche.

Quay, *s.* Ceatha; clachran, laibhrig.

Quean, *s.* Caile, dubh-chaile, droll; sraoilleag, striopach.

Queasiness, *s.* Tur thilge, gais, sleogadh, sgreatas.

Queasy, *a.* Tinn, sleogach.

Queen, *s.* Ban rìgh, ban-righinn.

Queer, *a.* Neònach, iongantach, aighreach, dràbhlainneach; sònruichte.

Queerly, *adv.* Gu neònach, gu h-iongantach; gu drabhlainneach.

Queerness, *s.* Neònachas, iongantas.

Queest, *s.* Smudan, colaman coille.

Quell, *v. a.* Mùch, cum fo; smachdaich, coisg, caisg, ciùinich; ceannsaich; ceannsuich, saruich. Quelled, *mùchta; smachdaichte, ceannsuichte, coisgte, ciùinichte, sàruichte.*

Queller, *s.* Muchadair; smachdair, cosgadair, fear smachdaidh, fear sàruchaidh.

Quench, *v. a.* Cuir as, mùch, bàth, traoigh, coisg, fionnaraich. Quenched, *muchta, traoighte, coisgte;* quench the fire, *mùch* (*no*) *cuir as an teine;* quench your thirst, *coisg do phath;* hot water quenches fire, *bàthaidh uisge teth teine.*

Quenchable, *a.* So-mhùchadh, so-chur as, a ghabhas cur as, a dh' fhaotar mhùchadh.

Quencher, *s.* Mùchadair, coisgear.

Quenchless, *a.* Do-chur as, do-mhùchadh, do-chosgadh; do-bhàth, sior-losgadh, nach gabh cur as (no) muchadh.

Querent, *s.* Gearanaiche; fear casaid, casaidiche.

Querimonious, *a.* Gearanach, gearaineach, casaideach; sraonaiseach, ciùrlanach, ciurachdanach.

Querimoniously, *adv.* Gu gearaineach, gu gearanach, gu casaideach, gu sraonaiseach.

Querimoniousness, *s.* Sraonaiseachd, gearanachd, casaideachd, ciùrlanachd, ciurachdanachd.

Querist, *s.* Iarradair, ceasnachair, sgrudair.

Quern, *s.* Bràdh, braghain, brà, muileann laimh, bronn.

Querpo, *s.* Deacaid.

Querulous, *a.* Gearaineach, casaideach, dranndanach, sraonaiseach; ciùrlanach, ciùrachdanach. A querulous person, *ciùrlan; brònean, brònag.*

Querulously, *adv.* Gu gearaineach, gu casaideach, gu dranndanach, gu sraonaiseach.

Querulousness, *s.* Gearaineachd, casaideachd, dranndanachd; ciùrlanachd, ciurachdanachd.

Query, *s.* Ceisd, ceist, foighneachd.

Query, *v.* Feòraich, foighneach, fiosraich.

Quest, *s.* Sireadh, rannsuchadh, foighneachd, sgrudadh, tòir, iarrtas, iarruidh, àille, ailne; deigh.

Quest, *v. n.* Sir, rach a shireadh, rach an tòir.

Questant, *s.* Sireadair.

Question, *s.* Ceisd, ceist; teagamh; amharus, anamharus; deuchainn; connspoid, deasboireachd; fiafraidh, foighneachd. Without question, *gun cheist; gun teagamh;* put the question to him, *cuir a cheist ris;* a dark question, *dubh-cheist, toimhseachan.*

Question, *v. a.* Feòruich, feòraich, ceasnaich, ceistich, sgrud, farraid, foighneachd, foighnich; cuir an teagamh, cuir omhaill, cuir amharas.

Questionable, *a.* Amharusach, teagamhach, neo-chinnteach.

Questionableness, *s.* Amharusachd, teagamhachd.

QUESTIONARY, *a.* Febrachail, ceasnachail, sgrudach, rannsuchail

QUESTIONLESS, *a* Cinnteach, gun teagamh, gun ag, gun amharus

QUESTUARY, *a.* Gionach, sanntach.

QUIB, *s.* Beum, geur-fhocal, car-fhocal, earra-ghloir.

QUIBBLE, *s* Beum, geur-fhocal, car-fhocal, beulais

QUIBBLE, *v. n.* Beum, thoir beum, labhair le beum.

QUIBBLER, *s* Beumadair, car-fhoclaiche, deasboiriche.

QUIBBLING, *s.* Beumadh, beumnachadh, beumnaich.

QUICK, *a,* Grad, ealamh; beò, beothail, smiorail, tapaidh, ullamh, deas, luath, easgaidh; cabhagach Quick, quick, *bi tapaidh*, quick of wit, *beumnach*, quick with child, *beò-thorrach*

QUICK, *s* Beò, an-fheòil, àite mothuchail do 'n chorp I cut him to the quick, *ghearr mi thun a bheò e, ghon mi e*

QUICK, *adv* Gu grad, gu h-ealamh, gu beò, gu cabhagach, gu tapaidh

QUICKBEAM, *s* Seorsa uinnsinn

QUICKEN, *v a.* Beothaich, ath-bheothaich, brosnaich, brosnuich, greas, deifirich; geuraich. Quickened, *beothaichte, ath-bheothaichte.*

QUICKENER, *s.* Brosnachair, fear brosnachaidh, beothachair, fear beothachaidh, greasadair.

QUICK-GRASS, *s* Conan

QUICK-LIME, *s.* Aol-beò, aol gun bhàth.

QUICKLY, *adv* Gu grad, gu h-ealamh, gu luath, gu smiorail, gu tapaidh, gu beothail, ann am platha, ann am mionaid, air a mhionaid, air an spot, air ball, ann an gradaig

QUICKNESS, *s* Luathas, graide, luathailt; beothalachd, deifir, cabhag, tapadh, tapachd, smioralas; géire; seirbhe.

QUICKSAND, *s* Beò-ghaineamh, beò-ghaineach, slugàite

QUICKSET, *s* Planntan sgithiche, sgitheach òg

QUICKSIGHTED, *a* Geur-shuileach, geur-sheallach, geur, biorach, bior-shuileach, grad-sheallach, grad-shuileach.

QUICKSIGHTEDNESS, *s.* Geur-shealladh, geurad, biorachas

QUICKSILVER, *s.* Beò-airgiod.

QUIDDIT, *s.* Car-bhriathar, car-fhocal

QUIDDITY, *s* Car-cheist, ceist chuilbheartach

QUIESCENCE, *s* Samhchair, suaimhneas, fois, tamh, seimhe, socair, bailbhe, féithe, fé

QUIESCENT, *a.* Samhach, feitheil, socarach, balbh, tosdach, foisneach, féitheil, ciùin, os iosal, bìth.

QUIET, *a* (*Silent*), samhach, tosdach, bìth, ciùin; (*mild*), mallta, macanta, suaire, socarach, suaimhneach, soitheamh, soimeach; (*at peace*), aig fois, siothchainnteach, feitheil Be quiet, *bi sàmhach, gabh gu fois, caisd*, will not you be quiet? *nach bi thu samhach, nach caisd thu?*

QUIET, *s* Fois, samhchair, seimhe, ciùineas, tamh, sìth, siothchainnt, siothchath, suaimhneas, tosdachd, tosd

QUIET, *v. a* Coisg, caisg, cuir samhach, ciùinich, siochaich, foisnich, socraich Quieted, *coisgte, ciuinichte, foisnichte, socraichte, air chur samhach*

QUIETER, *s.* Cosgair, ciùnachair.

QUIETISM, *s* Socair, samhachair, tosd, bailbhe, seimhe.

QUIETLY, *adv.* Gu samhach, gu ciùin, gu bìth, gu siochail, gu balbh, gu soitheamh, os iosal

QUIETNESS, *s.* Samhchair, ciùineachd, ciùineas, samhchaireachd, sìth; seimhe, fois, féith, anacail.

QUIETUDE, *s.* Sìth, fois, socair, tamh

QUILL, *s* Peann, ite, iteag, cléite, fitean.

QUILLET, *s.* Cuilbheart; car, cleas

QUILT, *s* Cubhrainn, cùirinn, cùirig, brat leapach, cuailt; cuillsean.

QUINARY, *a.* Cuignear.

QUINCE, *s* Cuinnse, crann cuinnse, craobh chuinnse.

QUINCUNX, *s.* Planndachadh ioma-shreadach; ioma-shreadachan

QUINQUAGESIMA, *s.* Di-dòmhnaich innd.

QUINQUANGULAR, *s.* Cuig-oisinneach, coig-oisinneach, cuig-chearnach.

QUINQUEFOLIATED, *a* Cùig-bhileach, còig-bhileach.

QUINQUENNIAL, *a.* Cuig-bliadhnach; coig-bliadhnach.

QUINSEY, *s* Galar plocach; amhach ghoirt, at bhràgaid.

QUINT, *s.* Cùignear, còignear, cùig, còig.

QUINTAIN, *s.* Post le barr cuairteanach.

QUINTAL, *a* Ceud punnt cothroim.

QUINTESSENCE, *s.* Brìgh, blàdh, feart; cuigeamh bith.

QUINTUPLE, *a* Cùig-fillte, còig-fillte; a chùig uiread, a chòig uiread, cuig uairean.

QUIP, *s.* Mag, magadh, fochaid, sgeig, beum, abhachd.

QUIRE, *s.* (*Choir*), co-sheirm, co-seinn, co-cheòl; ceòlraidh

QUIRE, *v. n* Co-sheinn, seinn co-luath.

QUIRE, *s.* (*Of paper*), ceithir site fichead paipeir; deighlean.

QUIRISTER, *s.* Fear ciùil, fear co-sheirm.

QUIRK, *s.* Car, cuilbheart; slighe, cleas, ain-cheart. Full of quirks, *carrach, cuilbheartach.*

QUIT, *v a.* Fag; tréig, cuitich, cuir cùl ri; sgar, dealaich; seachuinn, seachain; pàigh, diol; ath-dhiol. He quitted the country, *dh' fhàg e 'n dùthaich*, quitting hold as the old woman did of the wanton calf, *cead na cailliche do 'n laogh mhear.*

QUIT, *a.* Saor, ionnan, cuit, gu saor, gu co-ionnan; uile ionnan. I got quit of him, *fhuair mi cuit dheth.*

QUITCHGRASS, *s.* Conan, feur nan con.

QUITE, *adv.* Gu tur, gu buileach, gu baileach, gu h-iomlan, gu léir.

QUITTANCE, *s.* Cuiteachadh; saorsadh, saorsainn

QUITTER, *s* Saoradair, fear saoraidh.

QUIVER, *s.* Dorlach, bolg, bolg (no) balg shaighead, bolgan saighde.

QUIVER, *v. n.* Crith, crath, ball-chrith

QUIVERED, *a* Bolgach, balgach.

QUOB, *v* (Plosg, dean plosgartaich; carraich mar a ni urr bheag sa bholg

QUODLIBET, *s* Car, carachd, cealgaireachd, car-bhriathar.

QUODLIBETARIAN, *s.* Deasboiriche; cealgair.

QUOIF, *s.* Fuiltean, failtean, gruaig, curachd, sùbag.

QUOIF, *v a.* Curaichdich

QUOIN, *s* Oisinn, cùil, buailt, cearn, geinn.

QUOIT, *s* Peilistear, leac peilisteir Play at quoits, *cluich air peilistearan.*

QUONDAM, *a.* Roimh so, a bha, a bh' ann roimh.

QUORUM, *s* Àireamh àraidh do bhreitheana; beinc bhreitheanna; àireamh bhall a ni comunn, aireamh iomchuidh

QUOTER, *s* Cuid, pàirt, roinn, earann.

QUOTATION, *s.* Còmhdachadh, earann o leabhar no sgriobhadh neach eile, mar chomhdachadh.

QUOTE, *v a* Ainmich ùghdar, thoir mar ùghdar, thoir mar ùghdarras, comhdaich

QUOTH, *v imperf* Ars' arsa, ol Quoth he, *ars' esan;* quoth I, *arsa mise.*

QUOTIDIAN, *a.* Lathail, gach lath

QUOTIDIAN, *s.* Fiabhras critheannach, crith-theasach

QUOTIENT, *s.* A choilion uair, cuibhrionn.

QUOTING, *s.* Còmhdach, comhdachadh, a toirt mar ùghdar.

R.

R, An t-ochdamh litir deug do 'n Aibideal.

† Rabato, s Bann muineil, crios bràghaid.

Rabbet, v. a. Sliseagaich, snaith.

Rabbet, s. Tàth, gleus.

Rabbi, Rabbin, s. Ollamh (no) olladh Iùdhach

Rabbinical, a. Olladhachail, ollamhanach

Rabbit, s. Conan, coinean, rabait Rabbits, *conanan, rabaitean.*

Rabbit-hole, s Toll conain, toll coinein, toll rabait.

Rabble, s. Graisg, prabar; raidheann, cuire; bannal, buidheann, bròd.

† Rabblement, s. Lòd sluaigh; prabar; trusdaireachd.

Rabid, a. Cuthaich, aineasach, borb, garg.

Race, s. (*Running*), réis, ruithe, steud, comh-ruithe; coimhleang; cùrsa, blàr réis; (*progeny*), gineal, ginealach, cineal, cineadh; sliochd, siol, sileadh, clann, fineadh, teaghlach; àl. Run a race, *cuir réis, cuir steud;* (ginger), *dinsear;* a race before a leap, *rotach, ceum ruithe*

Race-horse, s. Each réis, each steud, steud-each

Racemation, s. Baguid, dos

Racemiferous, a. Baguideach, dosach.

Racer, s. Réisear; fear réis; fear-ruithe, steudair; each réis, steud-each.

Raciness, s. Searbhas, gairge, gairgead, goirteas

Rack, s. Inneal pianaidh, cuidhle sgaraidh, (*for hay*), mainnsear, mainnseir, prasach, praiseach; (*distaff*), cuigeal; (*in commerce*), seorsa dibhe làidir, (*a kitchen rack*), rag, clàr; (*a bottle rack*), clàr bhuideal; (*in meteorology*), neoil a ruithe ro ghaoth. Put to the rack, *claoidh, craidh*, a rack pin, *pinne teannachaidh*, at rack and manger, *gu soimeach sàthach.*

Rack, v. a. (*Pain*), sàruich, claoidh, cradh, pian; craon, (*stretch*), sin, tarruing, sgaoil; (*clean*), glan Why do you rack me? *c'arson a tha thu 'g um chlaoidh?* racked with pains, *claoidhte le piantaibh.*

Racket, s. (*At tennis*), glagair; buailtear; bachall, (*noise*), cullaid, glaodhar, gleadhraich, straoidhlich, straoidhlearachd, tuasaid, tabaid; (*confused talk*), gaoir, gaire, glag, clab.

Racking, a. Claoidheil, cradhach, piantach, piantachail, craonach.

Racking, s. Claoidheadh, cradhadh, craonachadh, sàruchadh; sineadh, tarruing.

Rack-rent, s. Màl-mor; an-mhàl, màl-sàruchaidh, ardmhàl, màl air éigin.

Racoon, s. Ainmhidh eilthireach cosmhuil ri broc.

Racy, a. Laidir, deagh-bholtrach.

Raddock, Ruddock, s Bric-dhearg, bronn-dearg.

Radiance, Radiancy, s Lannair, soillse, boisge, boisgealachd, lonnrachas; lonnraichead, dealradh, dearrsadh; glòir.

Radiant, a. Lannaireach, soillseach, boisgeil, boisgeach, dealrach, dearrsach; glan, soilleir

Radiate, v. Dealraidh, dealraich, soillsich, lannair, boisg, caoir, caoirich; gathaich, cuir mach (no) tilg gath-soluis

Radiation, s. Dealrachadh; dealrachd, dearrsachadh, lannaireachd, gathachadh, boisge, boisgealachd

Radical, a. Bunadhásach, bunamhasach; gnétheil, nadurra, suidhichte.

Radical, s. Bun-sgriosadair, fear a tha cumail a mach na tù nithe so (1) Gu bheil còir aig gach Breatunnach air buill a thaghadh chum suidhe sa Phailamaid (2) Gu 'm bu leas do na buill sin a bhi air an roghnachadh le crannchur. (3) Nach bu chòr do 'n Pharlamaid cheudna suidhe dà bhliadhna an deigh chéile.

Radicality, s. Bunamhasachd

Radically, adv Gu bunamhasach; aig bun; gu gnétheil, gu nàdurra, gu suidhichte

Radicate, v. a. Freumhaich, gabh freumh, suidhich gu domhain. Radicated, *freumhaichte.*

Radish, s. Meacan, curran dearg

Radius, s. Roth; spoc, spòchd, leosach, leosmhang.

Raff, s. Diù, prabar.

Raff, v. a. Sguab, tionail ri chéil air chor eigin.

Raffle, v n Dìslich, cluich air dhìslean.

Raffle, s. Crannchur, dìslean; deuchainn airson gill.

Raft, s Ramhach, slaod, slaod uisge.

Rafter, s Taobhan, sail

Raftered, a. Taobhanaichte.

Rag, s. Luideag, clùd, cearb, giobag, gibeag, ciabhrog, dudag, giobal, broineag. Full of rags, *luideagach*, a little ragged female, *ciabhrag.*

Ragamuffin, s. Sgonn, sgonn-bhalach, slaoightear.

Rage, s. Buath, boile, bainni, bainnidh, feirge, cuthach, fraoch, corruich, condasachd; buair, buaireadh, breas, dian-thogar, anamhiann, an-togar He is in a rage, *tha e air a bhoile*, what a rage he is in, *nach ann air a tha 'm boile*, a rage for money, *an-togar airson airgid*, the rage of the sea, *unradh na mara.*

Rage, v n. Bi fu fheirg, bi air a bhoile, bi air bhuair, bi fu bhuaireas

Rageful, a Dian, feargach, cuthach, air bhuaireadh, air bhreas.

Ragged, a. Luideagach, clùdach; broineagach; ciuirteach, giobagach, dudach, giobalach, garbh. A ragged fellow, *sgraitean*, a ragged female, *sgraiteag.*

Raggedness, s. Ciuirteachd; gairbhe.

Raging, a. Buaireasach, feargach, fraochail, air chuthach, air bhoile. The raging main, *an cuan anrach*, he is raging mad, *tha buath 'chuthaich air, tha e air a ghlan chuthach.*

Ragingly, adv. Gu buaireasach, gu feargach, gu fraochail.

Ragman, s. Fear luideag, bodach luideag

Ragout, s. Feòil air a stobhadh agus air a deasachadh, a réir seòl nam Frangach.

Rag-stone, s. Clach ghrod; clach gheurachaidh

Ragwort, s Buaghallan, am buaghallan buidhe

Rail, s. Cliath, cleth is casan, crosaid, iadh-lann, fàl, callaid, (*a bird*), treun ri treun.

Rail, v. a and n. Druid, fàl, cuir fàl suas; callaidich, troid; sglamhruinn, sglamhraich, thoir ana-cainnt, càin. He railed at him, *thug e ana-cainnt da*, how he railed at him, *is e thug an sglamhradh dha*, a place railed in, *iadhlann.*

Railer, s. Fear ana-cainnt; fear càinidh.

Railing, s. Iadh-lann; fàl; callaid, ana-cainnt, caineadh

Raillery, s Sgallais, fuar-sgallais, sglamhradh, anacainnt, ioladh

Raiment, *s.* Eudach, aodach, eide, eididh, earradh, comhdach, faluing.

Rain, *v.* Sil; fras; dòirt; dean uisge. The day is going to rain, *tha 'n la dol a dheanamh an uisge;* it rains, *tha e ris an uisge.*

Rain, *s.* Uisge, fras, fros, feur-thuinn; tuile; fliuchadh. Gentle rains, *frasan;* drizzling rain, *braon, cebban, smuideanaich, smodan, baindealaich;* what comes by the wind, goes by the rain, *an rud thig leis a ghaoth, falbhaidh e leis an uisge.*

Rainbow, *s.* Bogha frois, bogha frais, bogha uisge, bogha braoin, bior-bhogha.

Rain-deer, *s.* Fiadh.

Rain-goose, *s.* Learg.

Rain-water, *s.* Uisge nan neul.

Rainy, *a.* Fliuch, frasach, frosach; bailceach, uisgidh, silteach. A rainy day, là fliuch.

Raise, *v. a.* Tog, tog suas; ardaich, arduich; dùisg; cuir suas; meudaich; brosnuich, corruich. Raise scandal, *tog sgainneal;* raise a shout, *sgairt; glaodh;* incite, *buair.*

Raiser, *s.* Fear togalach; togadair; arduchair.

Raisin, *s.* Fion-dhearc chaoinichte; reiseid.

Rake, *s.* Ràsdal, ràc, ràcan; (*debauchee*), ràcair, trusdar, drùsair, drùisear.

Rake, *v.* Ràsdail, ràc, ràsdalaich, cruinnich, trus, tionail ri chéile; sir; bruillich. Rake the ashes of the dead, *càin na mairbh.*

Rake-hell, *s.* Sgonn-bhalach, fear neo-mheasarra, ràcair, druisear, trusdar.

Rakehelly, *a.* Fiadhaich, ana-cneasta, ana-measarra.

Rakish, *a.* Ana-cneasta, ana-measarra, mi-bheusach, neo-gheimnidh.

Rally, *s.* Ath-bhrosnachadh; ath-chruinneachadh. Rallying-point, *ceap.*

Rally, *v. a.* Ath-bhrosnuich, ath-chruinnich; bearradairich, gearr, beum.

Ram, *s.* Reithe, mult reithe; (*in war*), inneal cogaidh, slachdran. Rams, *reitheachan.*

Ram, *v. a.* Sparr, starr, stailc.

Ramble, *v. a.* Iomrolaich, iomralaich, seabhaid; bi rasuidheachd, rach air iomrol.

Ramble, *s.* Iomral, seabhaid, rasuidheachd, spaidsearachd; cuairt aigheir.

Rambler, *s.* Iomrolaiche; spaidsear; fear luaineach, neo-shuidhichte.

Rambling, *s.* Iomroladh, seabhaid, rasuidheachd.

Rambling, *a.* Iomrolach, seabhaideach, rasuidheach, luaineach, neo-shuidhichte.

Ramification, *s.* Craobh-sgaoileadh; sgaoileadh, meurachadh, ioma-sgaoileadh.

Ramify, *v. a.* Craobh-sgaoil, sgaoil, meuraich. Ramified, *sgaoilte.*

Rammer, *s.* Fairc, farachan, faraiche; slat gunna; calcair.

Rammish, *a.* Làidir, fàileach; drùiseil, slatail.

Ramous, *a.* Meanglanach, meurach; gobhlach, gobhlanach.

Ramp, *v. n.* Leum, surdagaich; reim, dian-leum.

Ramp, *s.* Leum, leumadh, surdag.

† Rampallion, *s.* Sgonn, sgonn-bhalaoch.

Rampancy, *s.* Pailteas, lionmhoireachd.

Rampant, *a.* Ruith-leumnach, mearachdasach, macnusach, surdagach, ard-leumnach; seasamh air na cosan deiridh; pailt, lionmhor.

Rampart, *s.* Balladh, dionaidh, dìdean, balladh dìdein, babhunn, baideal.

Rampion, *s.* Seorsa luibh.

Ran, *pret.* of run; which see.

Rancid, *a.* Fàileach, trom-fhàileach, breun.

Rancidness, *s.* Breunas, bréine.

Rancor, Rancour, *s.* Mi-rùn, mio-rùn, gamhlas, fuath, miosguin, tnù, tnùth, galtanas.

Rancorous, *a.* Mi-runach, gamhlasach, fuathach, miosguineach, tnuthar.

Rand, *s.* Foir, oir, iomall, fraidhe.

Random, *s.* Tubaist, cineamhuinn. At random, *a thaobh tubaist, a thaobh tuairmeis.*

Random, *a.* Tubaisteach, cineamhuinneach, tuairmeasach. A random shot, *urchair tubaist.*

Rang, *pret.* of ring. Sheinn.

Range, *s.* Ordugh, sread, sreud, sreath; breath; cuairt, seabhaid; creadhal-theine mhòr; criathar.

Range, *v.* Cuir an ordugh, marasglaich; sreadaich, cuir am breathan, riaghailtich; cuairtich; siubhail, rach sios is suas.

Ranger, *s.* (*Searcher*), siceadair, rannsuchair; (*robber*), robair, spùinneadair; (*dog*), abhag; (*of woods*), forsair, forsair coille, maor coille.

Rank, *a.* Brais, laidir, ard, garbh mar fheur; torrach; (*in smell*), breun, fàileach, boltrach, boltanach; (*in taste*), blasta, geur.

Rank, *v. a.* and *n.* Rangaich, sreadaich, sreathaich, cuir an sreath, cuir an ordugh, cuir taobh ri taobh, inbhich; àitich, gabh aite (no) inmhe.

Rank, *s.* Sreath, sreud; rang; ordugh; inbhe; staid.

Rankle, *v. n.* Feargaich, at; iongraich.

Rankly, *adv.* Gu geur; gu breun, gu làidir, gu pailt.

Rankness, *s.* (*Smell*), fàil, breunas, bréine; (*in growth*), pailteas; lionmhorachd.

Ranny, *s.* Dallag.

Ransack, *v. a.* Creach, spùinn, spùill, sgrios, lom-sgrios; rannsuich; arguin; truaillich, truaill. Her house was ransacked, *chaidh a tigh chreachadh.* Ransacked, *creachta, creachte, spùinnte, spùillte.*

Ransom, *s.* Eiric, diol, pàigh, fuasgladh; saorsadh.

Ransom, *v. a.* Ceannaich, fuasgail, saor, leig, fo shaorsadh.

Ransomer, *s.* Ceannaiche, fear saoraidh.

Rant, *v. n.* Dean stairn, dean staircaraich, glaodh mar ni cuid mhinisteara sa chùbaid.

Rant, *s.* Gleadhraich, beucail; ard-bhruidhinn, ard-reim.

Ranter, *s.* Fear ard-reimeach; rantair.

Rantipole, *a.* Fiadhaich, baoth, mi-gheamnaidh.

Ranunculus, *s.* Lus an ròcais.

Rap, *v. a.* and *n.* Buail, grad-bhuail; dean eibhinn; spiol air falbh; malairtich.

Rap, *s.* Buille, straoidhle, sgailleag, sgleafart, pailleart, peileid, gleog, cnap, crap, sgeilc, cnagaid.

Rapacious, *a.* Fòirneartach, glàmhach, gionach, sanntach, fogluidheach.

Rapaciously, *adv.* Gu foirneartach, gu glàmhach, gu gionach, gu sanntach.

Rapacity, *s.* An-shannt, foghluidheachd; glamhachd, gion, sannt, creachadaireachd.

Rape, *s.* Eigneachadh, éigin, truailleadh; fuadachadh; (*of a county*), siorrachd, roinn; maorsainneachd.

Rapid, *a.* Cas, brais, dian, grad, luath, ealamh, clis. A rapid stream, *dian-shruth, sruth brais, buinne-shruth.*

Rapidity, *s.* Braise, déine, graide, luas, luathas, luathailt, casad.

Rapidly, *adv.* Gu cas, gu brais, gu grad, gu luath, gu dian, gu h-ealamh, gu clis

Rapier, *s.* Gearr-chlaidheamh; roipear, ropair; seorsa eisg.

Rapine, *s.* Creachadh, spùinne, spùinneadh, spùille, spùilleadh, fogluidheachd, foirneart, ainneart.

Rapper, *s.* Buailtear; glagan.

Rapt, *a.* Air thogail. She is rapt, *tha i air a togail.*

Rapt, *s.* Paisean, neul; platha.

Rapture, *s.* Eibhneas, ard-eibhneas, mor-aoibhneas; neul, saimh, ard-thoileachadh.

Raptured, *a.* Eibhinn, aobhinn, air thogail.

Rapturous, *a.* Aoibhneach, eibhneach, gàirdeachail, soaimhneach, aoibhneachail.

Rare, *a* (*Seldom*), ainmig, tearc, gann; annasach; (*excellent*), ainneamh, sar-mhath, oirdheirc; (*thin*), tana.

Raree-show, *s.* Scalladh, faoin-shealladh; neònachas.

Rarefaction, *s.* Tanachadh; meudachadh.

Rarify, *v. a.* and *n.* Tanaich; leudaich, dean tana, fàs (no) cinn tana.

Rarely, *adv.* Ainmig, ainmic; gu h-ainmic, gu tearc, gu gann, an tràths is a ris; gu h-ainneamh.

Rareness, *s.* Ainmigead, neo-chumantachd, teirce, tearcad; (*thinness*), tainead, tanad Rareness of the atmosphere, *tainead na h-àile.*

Rarity, *s.* Neo-chumantachd; ainmigead, tainead; ainmheag, annas; ainmheid

Rascal, *s* Crochair, sgonn, sloightear; ablach, dailtean, rogair. An arrant rascal, *fior chrochair, dearg chrochair.*

Rascallion, *s.* Sgonn, sgonn bhalach, fear gun fhiù.

Rascality, *s.* Prabar, gràisge, sluagh cumaint; slaoightearachd, crochaireachd

Rascally, *a.* Diblidh, iosal, suarrach; foilleil.

Rase, *v.* See Raze.

Rase, *s.* Sgriob, sgriobadh, leòn beag.

Rash, *a.* Dàn, brais, cas, grad, obann, dian, dasachdach, diorusgach; ceann-laidir, an-dana, ruiseil, neo-smuainteachail, cabhagach.

Rash, *s.* Briseadh mach, bruthadh.

Rasher, *s* Sliseag mhuic-fheoil

Rashly, *adv.* Gu dàna, gu brais, gu cas, gu grad, gu dian, gu dasachdach, gu diorusgach, gu ceann-laidir, gu h-andana, gu cabhagach; gun smuaine.

Rashness, *s.* Dànadas, braisead, déine, obainneachd

Rasp, *s.* Suidheag, sùghag; (*a file*), eighe.

Rasp, *v.* Méil le h-eighe.

Raspberry, *s* Suidheag, sughag. A raspberry-tree, *preas shuidheag, sùbh chraobh.*

Rasure, **Razure**, *s.* Sgriobadh, gearradh, tomadh, bearradh.

Rat, *s.* Radan. A water-rat, *radan uisge;* smell a rat, *cuir amharus.*

Ratable, *a.* Luachail, fiachail, priseach.

Ratafia, *s.* Seorsa dibhe làidir.

Ratch, *s.* (*In clock-work*), cuidhle nan uairean

Rate, *s.* Pris, luach, fiach; cis, càin; modh, doigh, seòl. I know your rate, *is aithne dhomh do phris*, at a high rate, *daor;* at that rate, *air an doigh sin, air an t-seòl sin*, do that at any rate, *dean sin co dhiùbh.*

Rate, *v. a.* and *n.* Meas; pris, prìsich; leig cis, leig càin; (*chide*), troid, tachair ri. He rates it highly, *tha e 'g a mheasadh tuille is daor;* I will rate him for this, *tachair mise ris air son so.*

Rater, *s.* Measadair, fear meas

† **Rath**, *a.* Moch, much, tràthail, luath

Rather, *adv.* Docha, fearr, càr, an àite, an àite sin, ni 's ro thoiliche. I rather you than him, *is docha leam thusa no esan*, I rather go than stay, *is àille leam falbh, na fanachd;* I had rather, *b' àille leam, bu docha leam*, nay, rather, *air àite sin.*

Ratification, *s* Daingneachadh, co-dhaighneachadh, socrachadh

Ratify, *v. a.* Daingnich, daighnich, socraich; deimhinnich, réitich

Ratiocinate, *v. a.* Arguinn, reusonaich, riasonaich, deasboirich.

Ratiocination, *s.* Arguinn, reusonachadh, deasboireachd, co-reusonachadh

Rational, *a* Reusonta, reusonach, riasanta; glic, crionna, toinisgeil, tuigseach.

Rationality, *s* Reusonachd, riasanachd.

Rationally, *adv* Gu reusonta, gu riasonta; gu glic, gu crionna, gu toinisgeil.

Ratsbane, *s.* Fuath radan, nimh radan, puinnsion.

Ratfen, *s* Seorsa eudaich.

Rattle, *v n* Dean torghan, dean braoilich, (no) stairn, dean gleadhraich. Rattle off, *troid ri, tachair ri.*

Rattle, *s.* Faoin-chainnt, glag, clach-bhalg; gleadhraich, torghan; staireamaich, stairn, braoilich A child's rattle, *glaodhran, glaodhrachan.*

Rattle-headed, *a.* Gog cheannach, guanach, luaineach, eutrom, gaoithe

Rattling, *s* Torghanaich, braoilich, stairn, stairnich, gleadhraich, straoidhlearachd; (*chiding*), trod, sglàmhruinn.

Rattling, *a.* Torghanach, braoileach, gleadhrach

Rattlesnake, *s.* Nathair ghleadhrach.

Raucity, *s.* Tùchadh, tùchan, toirm; borbhan.

† **Rought**, *pret.* of reach. Ruig, ràinig.

Ravage, *v. a.* Sgrios, lom-sgrios, dean fàs, fàsaich, creach, spùill, spùinn, léir-sgrios, robainn.

Ravage, *s* Sgriosadh, lom-sgrios, fàsachadh, creachadh, spùille, spùillinn, spùinne, leir-sgrios, robainn.

Ravager, *s.* Sgriosadair, creachadair, spùilleadair, spuinneadair

Ravaging, *s.* Sgriosadh, fàsachadh, creachadh, spuilteadh

Rave, *v n.* Bi 'm breilleis, bi 'm breislich, bi air bhoile, bi air mhire, bi air bhuaireadh. He raves in sickness, *tha e na bhreilleis* (*no*) *na bhreislich*, he raves in madness, *tha e air bhoile.*

Ravel, *v.* Rib; rioblaich, cuir air aimhreidh, buair; cuir an iomcheist, fuasgail, tuasgail, tualaig, thoir as a chéile. Ravelled, *ribte, rioblaichte; fuasgailte, tuasgailte.*

Ravelin, *s* Dion-obair an chumadh na leth-ghealaich.

Raven, *s.* Fitheach, preachan, cnaimh-fhitheach, bran The raven's lot befall thee, *bàs an fhithich ort*, the boding of the raven, *fios fithich.*

Raven, *v. a.* and *n* Reub gu fuileachdach, ith gu ciocrach, sluig gu gionach.

Ravenous, *a* Fuileachdach, fuilteach, fuileach, ciocrach, slugach, glamhach, beuchdach, geòcach, ocrach, acrach, craosach.

Ravenously, *adv.* Gu fuileachdach, gu fuilteach, gu ciocrach, gu slugach, gu geòcach, gu h-ocrach

Ravenousness, *s.* Fuileachdas; cioeras, ocras, acras, miann creich

Raven, *s.* Creach, fiadhach, cobhartach, spùinn, spùill; bealach.

Raving, *a.* Air bhoile, air chuthach, air bhuaireadh, air bhreathas, breisleachail, ann am breislich. He is raving mad, *tha e air ghlan chuthach, tha 'n dearg chuthach air.*

RAVISH, *v. a.* Éignich, truaill, truaillich, mill; fuadaich; thoir a dh' aindeoin o; toilich, dean aoibhinn. Ravished, *eignichte; truaillte; aoibhinn.*

RAVISHER, *s.* Eigneachair; fear fòirneirt.

RAVISHING, *s.* Eigin, éigneachadh, truailleadh, truailleachadh; fuadachadh; deanamh aoibhinn.

RAVISHMENT, *s.* Éigneachadh, éigin, truailleadh, truailleachadh, eibhneas; làn-eibhneas; mòr-aoibhneas, saimh.

RAW, *a.* Amh, amhaidh; glas, ùr; anabuich; fuar; neobhruich; neo-dheasaichte; neo-theoma.

RAWBONED, *a.* Cnamhach.

RAWHEAD, *s.* Bòchdan, bodach.

RAWLY, *adv.* Gu h-amh; gu h-ùr; gu glas; gu neosgileil, gu neo-theòma.

RAWNESS, *s.* Amhad, amhachd; anabachd; (*ignorance*), aineolas; mi-chleachd.

RAY, *s.* Gath soluis, gath gréin; dealradh; dearrsadh, leosach; seorsa luibh; seorsa éisg.

RAY, *v. n.* Sgrioch.

RAZE, *v. a.* Tilg sios, leig; sgrios, lom-sgrios, léir-sgrios, fàsaich; dubh a mach.

RAZOR, *s.* Ealadhain, sgian bearradair; bearra-sgian; ràsar.

RAZURE, *s.* Dubhadh mach, sgriobadh, sgriochadh.

RE, *inseparable prep.* Ath; (*as re-vive*), ath-bheothaich.

REACH, *v. a.* and *n.* Ruig; sìn; faigh, fuigh. They reached the haven, *ràinig iad an càla;* reaching to the sea, *a ruigheachd thun na mara;* I cannot reach to it, *cha n' urradh dhomh ruigheachd air;* reach me my staff, *sìn dhomh mo lorg.*

REACH, *s.* Ruigsinn, ruigheachd; comas, comas ruigsinn, comas ruigheachd; cumhachd; urrainn, urradh; sìneadh; (*fetch*), car, cuilbheart, cleas, seòl. It is out of my reach, *cha 'n 'eil e mar fhad ruigheachd orm, cha n' urrainn mi ruigheachd air;* a man of deep reach, *fear geur, fear eòlach;* a reach *or* vomiting, *tur thilge.*

REACHING, *s.* Ruigsinn, ruigheachd.

REACT, *v. a.* Ath-bhuail; ath-ghluais.

REACTION, *s.* Ath-bhualadh, ath-ghluasad, ath-ghluasadh.

READ, *v. a.* and *n.* Leugh, leubh, leabh; foghluim; faigh mach; tuig; rannsuich. I read it carefully, *leugh mi gu cùramach e;* read *or* guess, *baralaich, thoir barail;* who is't can read woman? *co th' ann is urrainn boirionnach a rannsuchadh?*

READ, *part.* Leughta, leughte; foghluimte, ionnsuichte. A well-read man, *duine ionnsuichte.*

READEPTION, *s.* Ath-fhaotainn; ath-choisneadh.

READER, *s.* Leughair, leubhair, leughadair, pearsa eaglais.

READERSHIP, *s.* Leughaireachd, leughadaireachd.

READILY, *adv.* Gu deas, gu h-ullamh, gu toileach, gu tapaidh, gu h-ealamh, gu furas, gu soimeach.

READINESS, *s.* Ullamhachd, eallamhachd, luathailteachd, furasachd, furasdachd, deise, teòmachd. Be in readiness, *bi deas;* (in readiness), *aig lamh.*

READING, *s.* Leughadh, leubhadh, leabhadh. A reading-desk, *crannag.*

READMISSION, *s.* Ath-ghabhail; ath-leigeil steach. On our readmission, *air ar n-ath-leigeil steach.*

READMIT, *v. a.* Ath-ghabh; ath-leig stigh.

READORN, *v. a.* Ath-sgeadaich, ath-sgiomhaich, sgeaduich (no) sgiamhuich an dara uair.

READY, *a.* Ullamh, deas, deasaichte; ealamh, toileach; furas. Be ready, *be deas;* are you ready? *bheil thu ullamh (no) deas?* ready at hand, *deas aig laimh;* ready money, *airgiod ullamh, airgiod laimh, airgiod dùirn;* make ready, *deasaich;* made ready, *deasaichte;* of a ready wit, *geur, sgaiteach, beumnach;* make yourself ready, *cuir an uigheam thu féin.*

READY, *adv.* Gu deas, gun dàil; a cheana.

REAFFIRM, *v. a.* Ath-dheimhinnich, ath-dhearbh, ath-dhaighnich. Reaffirmed, *ath-dheimhinnichte, ath-dhearbhta;* he reaffirmed it, *dh' ath-dhearbh se e.*

REAFFIRMANCE, *s.* Ath-dheimhneachadh, ath-dhearbhadh, ath-dhaighneachadh.

REAL, *a.* Fior; fìreannach, cinnteach; dìreach.

REALITY, *s.* Fìrinn, cinnteachd, cinntealas. In reality, *gu fior.*

REALIZE, *v. a.* Thoir gu brìgh, thoir gu buil.

REALLY, *adv.* Gu fior, gu fìreannach; a rìreadh, a rìreamh, gu dearbh, gu deimhinn.

REAM, *s.* Buinseal paipeir; fichead cuair.

REALM, *s.* Rioghachd, dùthaich, talamh, tìr, fonn.

† REALTY, *s.* Fìreanntachd; fìrinn.

REANIMATE, *v. a.* Ath-bheothaich, ath-bheathaich. Reanimated, *ath-bheothaichte.*

REANNEX, *v. a.* Ath-chuir ris; ath-dhlùthaich.

REAP, *v. a.* Buain, gearr sios, gearr bhàn; buannaich, buidhinn, coisinn, faigh, cruinnich, teanal, tionail, cnuasaich. Reaped, *buainte.*

REAPER, *s.* Buainiche, buanaiche. Reapers, *buainichean.*

REAPING-HOOK, *s.* Corran.

REAR, *s.* Deireadh, deireadh feachd, deireadh cabhlaich, ceann deiridh. Attack the rear, *thoir ionnsuidh air a cheann deiridh.*

REAR, *v. a.* Tog, àraich; àl; brosnuich, mosgail; éirich; éirich mar each air a chosan deiridh. Rear a building, *tog aitreamh;* reared, *air thogail, àraichte.*

REAR-ADMIRAL, *s.* Ceannard mara, ard-mharaiche.

REARING, *s.* Togail, àrachadh, brosnachadh, éiridh.

REARMOUSE, *s.* Ialtag.

REARWARD, *s.* Deireadh, ceann deiridh.

REASCEND, *v. a.* and *n.* Ath-dhìr, ath-dhìrich, ath-éirich.

REASON, *s.* (*Faculty*), ciall, inntinn; (*cause*), aobhar, reuson, riasan, fàth, cionfàth; (*understanding*), toinisg, tuigse; (*right*), ceartas, ceirte; (*moderation*), cuimeis; (*argument*), argumaid. Void of reason, *gun chiall;* he lost his reason, *chaill e 'chiall, chaidh e thar a chéill;* what is the reason of this? *ciod is riason do so?* for this reason, *air son so;* a good reason, *deagh reuson;* you have no reason *or* moderation, *cha n' eil cuimeis ort;* by reason of, *a chionn, thaobh, a thaobh;* by reason of her youth, *thaobh a h-òige.*

REASON, *v. a.* Reusonaich, riasonaich, co-riasonaich, deasboirich, tagair. He reasoned with me, *reusonaich e rium.*

REASONABLE, *s.* Reusonta, riasanta, reusonach, ciallach; (*moderate*), measarra, measarrach, meadhonach, cuimeiseach; (*just*), ceart, cothromach; còir, coguiseach. A reasonable soul, *anam reusonta.*

REASONABLENESS, *s.* Reusontachd, riasantachd; ciall; cothromachd, measarrachd, cuimeis.

REASONABLY, *adv.* Gu reusonta, gu riasonta, gu reusonach, gu cothromach, gu ceart, gu coguiseach, le reuson, le ceartas.

REASONER, *s.* Deasboir, deasboiriche, reusonaiche, arguinniche.

REASONING, *s.* Deasboireachd, reusonachd, reusonachadh, tagradh, argumaid, connsachadh, achmhasan.

Reasonless, *a.* Gun reuson, neo-reusonta; mi-reusonta.

Reassemble, *v. a.* Ath-chruinnich, ath-theanail. Reassembled, *ath-chruinnichte, ath-theanailte.*

Reassert, *v. a.* Ath-dhearbh, ath-dheimhnich, ath-chàirich Reasserted, *ath-dhearbhta, ath-dheimhnichte.*

Reassume, *v. a.* Ath-ghabh; ath-dhean.

Reassure, *v. a.* Thoir ath-chinnte, dean ath-chinnteach

Rebaptize, *v. a.* Ath-bhaist. He rebaptized him, *dh' ath-bhaist se e;* he was rebaptized, *dh' ath-bhaisteadh e.*

Rebate, *v. a* and *n.* Maolaich; maith, lughdaich

Rebate, *s.* Lughdachadh, beagachadh, mathadh.

Rebatement, *s.* Mathadh, lughadachadh.

Rebec, *s.* Seorsa fìdhle le trì teudan

Rebel, *s.* Ceannairceach, fear ceannairc, fear àr a mach, reubaltach.

Rebel, *v. a.* Eirich; dean ceannairc, dean àr a mach. They rebelled against him, *dh' éirich iad na aghaidh, rinn iad ceannairc na aghaidh.*

Rebeller, *s.* Ceannairceach, fear ceannairc, reubaltach.

Rebellion, *s.* Éiridh, ceannairc, ar a mach.

Rebellious, *a.* Ceannairceach, eas-umhall.

Rebelliously, *adv.* Gu ceannairceach, gu h-eas-umhall.

Rebellow, *v. a.* Ath-gheum, ath-bheuc, ath-sgal, ath-sgairt, ath-ghlaodh.

Reboation, *s.* Ath-ghlaodh, ath-bheuc, ath-sgal.

Rebound, *v.* Ath-bhuail, ath-leum, ais-leum, leum air ais.

Rebound, *s.* Ath-leum, ais-leum, ath-bhualadh.

Rebounding, *s.* Ath-bhualadh, ath-leumadh, ais-leum.

Rebuff, *s.* Ath-bhualadh; diùltadh

Rebuff, *v a.* Buail air ais, diùlt, mi-mhisnich

Rebuild, *v. a.* Ath-thog, tog a ris, tog an dara uair Rebuilt, *ath-thogta, ath-thogte, air 'ath-thogail.*

Rebukable, *a.* Airidh air achmhasan.

Rebuke, *v. a.* Thoir achmhasan, achmhasanaich, trod ri, cronaich. He was rebuked, *fhuair e achmhasan, fhuair e' chronachadh.*

Rebuke, *s.* Achmhasan, trod, cronachadh, glamhruinn, cramban

Rebuker, *s.* Achmhasanaiche, fear achmhasain, cronachair, fear cronachaidh; fear comhairle; caralaiche.

Rebus, *s.* Dubh-dhuan.

Rebut, *v. a* Cuir air ais, buail air ais, cuir an aghaidh

Rebutter, *s.* Freagairt.

Recall, *v. a.* Ath-ghairm, ais-ghairm, gairm air ais, glaodh air ais, thoir air as. Recalled, *ath-ghairmte, air thoirt air ais.*

Recall, *s* Ath-ghairm, ais-ghairm.

Recant, *v. a.* Seun, àichean, cuir as àicheadh, ath-dhean, thoir air ais. Recant your opinion, *mùth do bharail*, I will not recant my word, *cha toir mi air ais m' fhocall.*

Recantation, *s* Seunadh, àicheadh, àichean, àicheanadh, cur an aghaidh aidmheil a rinneadh roimh; tarruing air ais.

Recanter, *s* Seunair, seunadair, fear a bheir air ais 'fhocall.

Recapitulate, *v. a.* Aithris; ath-ainmich; ath-innis; rach thairis a ris; ath-cheumnaich.

Recapitulation, *s.* Aithris; ath-innseadh.

Recaption, *s.* Ath-ghlacadh, ath-ghabhail.

Recapitulatory, *a.* Aithriseach.

Recarry, *v.* Ath-ghiùlan, giùlain a ris, giùlain air ais; ath-iomchair.

Recede, *v. n.* Rach air ais, teann air ais, teich, sguir, pill.

Receipt, *s.* Gabhail; gabhail ri; laghadh; bann cuitich, bann cuiteachaidh, bann dealachaidh, bann-saorsuinn; fàilte; comhairle (no) ordugh leigh sgrìobhte.

Receivable, *a.* Gabhaileach, a ghabhas faotainn, a dh' fhaotar a ghabhail.

Receive, *v a.* Gabh, gabh ri, ceadaich, glac, faigh You will receive no refusal, *cha 'n fhaigh thu 'n diùltadh*, receive guests, *thoir aoidheachd.*

Receiver, *s.* Gabhaltaiche, glacadair, fear gabhail; fear togail, fear faotainn. A receiver of taxes, *fear thogail chisean, cìsear*, (in the church), *fear comanaich.*

Recency, *s.* Ùiread, ùrad, nuadhachd.

Recension, *s* Cunntadh, àireamh; beachdachadh.

Recent, *a.* Ùr, nuadh, o cheann ghoirid, a chianamh.

Recently, *adv.* Gu h-ùr, a chianamh, o cheann ghoirid.

Recentness, *s.* Ùiread, nuadhachd

Receptacle, *s.* Ionad taisg, ionad tasgaidh; gabhadan, eidean, fasgadh; meiligeag, meinigeag

Reception, *s.* Gabhail, faotainn; failte, gabhail ri, furan; beathachadh, altachadh, comhdhail.

Receptive, *a.* Gabhaileach; a ghabhas

Recess, *s.* Uaigneas, diomhaireachd, diuibheal, falbh; aonaranachd, samhchair, sgaoileadh, dealachadh, fàgail, sgur, sguradh

Recession, *s* Pilltinn, dol air ais

Rechange, *v. a.* Ath-mhuth, mùth a ris, atharruich.

Recharge, *v* Ath-chasaid, ath-ghearain, ath-chronaich; ath-lion, thoir ath-ionnsuidh, leum a ris air

Recidivation, *s.* Cùl-sleamhnachadh, ath-thuiteam, tuiteam air ais.

Recipe, *s.* Ordugh (no) comhairle sgrìobhta leigh.

Recipient, *s.* Gabhadair.

Reciprocal, *a.* Malairteach, aonachdail, co-mhùiteachail, air gach taobh, o gach taobh, a réir a chéile, ma seach.

Reciprocally, *adv* Air gach taobh, o gach taobh, a reir chéile, ma seach, mu 'n seach

Reciprocate, *v. a.* Malairt, dean mu 'n seach, dean réir chéile.

Reciprocation, *s.* Co-mhùthadh, co-mhùth, co-ghniomhachd, comh-chéileachd

Recision, *s.* Gearradh, sgathadh, bearradh.

Recital, Recitation, *s* Aithris; aithriseadh, ath-aireamh, innseadh, sgeulachd

Recitative, *s.* Fonn, fonn duain, càntaireachd.

Recite, *v a.* Aithris, ath-aithris, ath-àireamh; innis, athinnis. Recited, *aithriste.*

Reciter, *s* Aithrisear; fear labhairt

† **Reck**, *v. a.* and *n* Thoir aire, thoir an aire, gabh beachd, gabh cùram, cuimhnich.

Reckless, *a.* Neo-chùramach, neo-umhailleach, neo-omhailleach, comadh, coidheis, dà choma

Recklessness, *s* Neo-chùramachd, cion-omhaill, coidheiseachd.

Reckon, *v. a.* (*Count*), cùnnt, àireamh, àireamhaich; (*esteem*), meas, smuainich, saoil; (*design*), sònruich, sùnruich. I will reckon that gain, *measam sin mar thairbhe;* I reckon it an honour, *is onoir leam e;* reckon little of, *cuir air bheag suim*, he is reckoned an honest man, *tha e air a mheas na dhuine còir;* reckoned, *aireamhte, àireamhaichte, measta*

Reckoner, *s.* Cunntair, àireamhair.

Reckoning, *s.* Meas, cunntas, cunntadh, àireamh; (*at an inn*), lach.

RECLAIM, v. a. Leasaich, ath-leasaich, iompaich, ais-ghairm, ceannsuich, smachdaich.

RECLAIMING, s. Leasachadh, ath-leasachadh, iompachadh; ceannsachadh.

RECLINE, v. n. Sìn, leth-luidh, luidh air leth taobh; claon sios, crom sios, leig taic.

RECLINING, s. Sineadh, leth-luidhe, luidhe air leth-taobh; claonadh (no) cromadh.

RECLOSE, v. Ath-dhùin, ath-dhruid, dùin (no) druid an dara uair.

RECLUDE, v. a. Fosgail. Recluded, *fosgailte.*

RECLUSE, s. Aonaranach, aonaran, diomharan, mànach; ban-naomh.

RECLUSE, a. Aonaranach, uaigneach; mànachail, druidte; diomhair.

RECLUSENESS, s. Aonaranachd, uaigneas; diomhaireachd.

RECOAGULATION, s. Ath-ghruthachadh, ath-shlamachadh.

RECOGNIZANCE, s. Gealladh, gabhail ri, aideachadh, bann, comhar, breith, barail, ceasnachadh, lorgaireachd.

RECOGNIZE, v. a. Aidich; cuimhnich; aithnich; fainich. He recognized me at once, *dh' fhainich e mi air a cheud tarruing*

RECOGNITION, s. Aideachadh, cuimhneachadh; aithneachadh, faineachadh, cur aithne.

RECOIL, v. n. Brùchd air ais, leum (no) clisg air ais, teann air ais, ath-leum.

RECOIL, s. Ath-leum, clisgeadh air ais, leum air ais.

RECOIN, v. a. Ath-chùin, cùin a ris (no) an dara uair. Recoined, *ath-chùinte.*

RECOINAGE, s. Ath-chùineadh.

RECOLLECT, v. a. Cuimhnich, ath-chuimhnich; ath-chruinnich, ath-thionail. Do you recollect? *bheil cuimhne agad?* I recollected, *chuimhnich mi, chuimhnich mi orm.*

RECOLLECTION, s. Cuimhne; cuimhneachadh, ath-chuimhneachadh. I have no recollection at all of it, *cha 'n 'eil cuimhne sam bi agam air.* I have no recollection in the world of it, *cha 'n 'eil cuimhne air an t-saoghal agam air.*

RECOMMENCE, v. a. Ath-thòisich, ath-thionnsgain, toisich as ùr.

RECOMMEND, v. a. Mol, cliùthaich. I would recommend it to you to begone, *mhollainn duit a bhith falbh.* I would recommend that to you, *mholainn sin duit*

RECOMMENDING, s. Moladh, mol, cliùthachadh.

RECOMMENDATION, s. Moladh, deadh-mholadh; cliù, teisteannas, cliùthachadh

RECOMMENDATORY, a. Moladach, moltainneach, cliùthachail. A recommendatory letter, *litir mholadh, litir eòlais.*

RECOMMENDER, s. Fear molaidh

RECOMPACT, v. a. Tàth a ris, ath-cheangail, tàth (no) ceangail as ùr.

RECOMPENSE, v. Pàigh, diol, ath-dhiol, ath-phàigh, ath-fhuasgail, cuitich, dean suas. I cannot recompense you fully, *cha n' urrainn mi do làn-dhioladh.* I will recompense your loss, *ni mi suas do challdach.*

RECOMPENSE, s. Pàigh, diol, dioladh, ath-dhioladh, luach saoithreach, luach saothair, luigheachd, diol-thuarasdal, tuarasdal. Without recompense, *a nasguidh, far nasguidh, gun dad idir.*

RECOMPOSE, v. Ath-choisg, ath-chiùinich, ath-shocraich, ath-shiothchaich; coisg as ùr, ciùinich a ris, socraich an dara uair; ath-dhean, ath-dhealbh, cuir ri chéile a ris.

RECOMPOSITION, s. Ath-chur ri chéile

RECONCILE, v. a. Dean réidh, réitich, ciùinich, coisg, coird. Reconciled, *réith, réidh, ciùinichte, coisgte, a réir chéile.* he is reconciled to me, *tha e réidh rium.*

RECONCILABLE, a. So-réiteachadh; a ghabhas réiteachadh, so-chosgaidh.

RECONCILEMENT, s. Réite, réiteachadh, ath-réiteachadh, cordadh, sith.

RECONCILER, s. Fear réiteachaidh.

RECONCILIATION, s. Réite, réiteachadh, ath-réite, cordadh, sìth

RECONCILIATORY, a. Ath-réiteachail, réiteachail.

RECONDITE, a. Diomhair, dorch, doilleir, domhain, do-thuigsinn, céilte.

RECONDUCT, v. a. Ath-threòraich, ath-threòirich, ath-sdiùir.

RECONNOITRE, v. Beachdaich, gabh beachd, gabh fiadhairc.

RECONQUER, v. a. Ath-cheannsuich, ath-bhuadhaich, ath-shàruich, ath-cheannsaich, ceannsuich (no) sàruich an dara uair; cuir fo a ris. Reconquered, *ath-cheannsaichte.*

RECONSECRATE, v. a. Ath-choisrig, ath-naomhaich, coisrig an dara uair, coisrig (no) naomhaich a ris. Reconsecrated, *ath-choisrigte, ath-naomhaichte.*

RECONVENE, v. n. Ath-choinnich, ath-chruinnich; ath-thionail. Reconvened, *ath-choinnichte, ath-chruinnichte*

RECOVERY, v. a. Ath-threòruich; thoir air ais, thoir a ris; ath-bhuilich.

RECORD, v. a. Sgriobh, cuir dios, cuir an cuimhne, cum air chuimhne, meamhraich. Record in your mind, *taisg ann ad inntinn, cum ann do chuimhne.* recorded, *sgriobhte, sgriobhta, air a chur sios.* it is recorded of her, *tha e air sgriobhadh uimpe, tha e air a chur sios uimpe.*

RECORD, s. Leabhar cuimhne, sgriobhadh, meamhrach, meamhran, eachdruidh, cuimhneachan, taibhle cuimhne; fianuis. Bear record, *thoir fianuis.*

RECORDER, s. Meamhraiche; eachdruiche; seanachaidh; cuimhnachair; fear coimhid na taibhle chuimhne.

RECOUCH, v. n. Luidh a ris.

RECOUNT, v. a. Innis, aithris, cuir an céill. Recorded, *air innseadh, aithriste*

RECOUNTMENT, s. Innseadh, aithriseadh, aithris.

RECOURSE, s. Ath-philleadh, ath-philltinn; coileasachadh; cuideachadh; dìdean; tathaich; còmhdhail. He had recourse to us for aid, *thàinig e gar n-ionnsuidh airson còghnaidh, dh' iarr e còghnadh uaithne, thathaich e còghnadh oirnne*

RECOVER, v. a. and n. Coisinn, buidhinn, saor; faigh air ais, thig o; fàs gu math. He recovered what he lost, *choisinn e na chaill e.* he recovered the people's favour, *fhuair e air ais deagh-run an t-sluaigh.* he is sick, but he shall recover, *tha e gu tinn, ach thig e uaithe.*

RECOVERABLE, a. So-choisinn, so-chosnadh; so-leigheas; a ghabhas coisinn, a ghabhas leigheas; a dh' fhaotar 'choisinn, a dh' fhaodar leigheas.

RECOVERED, part. and a. Coisinnte; buidhinnte, buidhnte; saorta, air fhaotainn air ais; (*from sickness*), leighiste, air teachd uaithe.

RECOVERY, s. Aiseag, faotainn (no) faghail air ais; (*from sickness*), dol am feabhas, leigheas, fàs gu math, slànuchadh. He is past recovery, *tha e dheth, tha e caillte.*

RECREANT, a. Gealtach, meata, crion, bog, tais, gun spiorad, neo-smiorail, neo-dhuineil; fallsa, fallsail.

RECREATE, v. a. Ath-bheothaich, ath-ùraich, ùraich; toilich, taitinn ri, sòlasaich, eutromaich. Recreated, *ath-bheothaichte, ùraichte, toilichte*

RECREATION, s. Caitheamh aimsir; culaidh shùgraidh, sùgradh, ioladh, ealaidh, spuirt, cluiche, lasachadh.

RECREATIVE, a. Ùrachail; a toirt ealaidh (no) cridhealais, eutromach; lasachail, a toirt lasachaidh.

Recrement, *s.* Deasgainn, drabhag; smùrach, smùr, luaithre, trusdaireachd.

Recremental, *a.* Deasgannach, drabhagach.

Recriminate, *v. a.* Ath-chronaich, ath-choirich, cuir (no) tilg coire air ais air neach eile.

Recrimination, *s.* Ath-chronachadh, ath-choireachadh, ath-chasaid.

Recruit, *v. a.* and *n.* Leasaich, ath-neartuich, ath-leasaich, ath-lion, tog saighdearan. He is recruiting his strength, *tha e a faotainn air ais a shlàinnte.*

Recruit, *s.* (*Supply*), leasachadh; saighdear òg (no) air ùr thogail, ùranach.

Rectangle, *s.* Ceart-chearnag, dron-uille.

Rectangular, *a.* Ceart-chearnach, dron uilinneach.

Rectifiable, *a.* Ceartachail, leasachail, so-cheartachadh, so-leasachadh, a ghabhas ceartachadh.

Rectification, *s.* Ceartachadh, leasachadh, cur gu doigh.

Rectifier, *s.* Ceartachair, fear ceartachaidh.

Rectify, *v. a.* Ceartaich, leasaich, cuir gu doigh, ath-leasaich; seòl; cuir ceart; (*in chemistry*), ath-tharruing. Rectified, *ceartaichte, leasaichte, ath-leasaichte*; (as spirits), *ath-tharruingte.*

Rectilinear, *a.* Dìreach; lìnear.

Rectitude, *s.* Dìrichead; (*uprightness*), ionracas, tréibh-dhireas, fìreantachd.

Rector, *s.* Riaghlair, riaghladair; ministear sgìreachd sasunnach.

Rectory, *s.* Tigh minisdeir, sgìreachd easbuigeach.

Recubation, *s.* Luidhe, leth-luidhe; sìneadh.

Recumbency, *s.* Luidhe, leth-luidh; aomadh; socraichead.

Recumbent, *a.* Na luidhe, na leth-luidhe, air aomadh, aomta, aomachail.

Recuperation, *s.* Faotainn air ais, coisinn, ath-buidhinn.

Recur, *v. a.* Thig an aire, thig am beachd, thig an cuimhne, ath-chuimhnich; pill, ath-phill. It recurred to me, *thàinig e 'm aire.*

Recurrence, *s.* Pilltinn, pilleadh, aith-philltinn, tachairt.

Recurrent, *a.* Pilltinneach, ath-philtinneach, ath-phille-achail; a philleas air uairibh.

Recursion, *s.* Pilltinn, pilleadh.

Recurvation, *s.* Cromadh, cùl-chromadh, cromadh an comhair a chùil, cùl-lùbadh, cùl-aomadh.

Recurved, **Recurvous**, *a.* Lùbta air ais, crom, aomta.

Recusant, *s.* Dorganach, fear a dhiùltas caidreamh ris a mhòr-chomunn.

Recuse, *v. a.* Diùlt.

Red, *a.* Dearg, ruadh, cruan, scàrlaid. A red colour, *dearg, dath dearg*; red-hot, *bruithneach*; it is red-hòt, *tha e teth dearg*; dark red, *ruiteach*; somewhat red, *leth-char dearg*; red-haired, *ruadh.*

Redbreast, *s.* Am bru-dhearg, brònn-dearg.

Redcoat, *s.* Dearganach; saighdear dearg.

Redden, *v. a.* and *n.* Deargaich; dean dearg, fàs dearg, cinn dearg, rugh.

Reddishness, *s.* Ruadhan, fiamh-dhearg, rughadh.

Reddition, *s.* Toirt air ais; aiseag.

Reddle, *s.* Cìll, cear-dhearg, ruadhan, clach dhath dhearg.

† **Rede**, *s.* Comhairle, sànus.

Redeem, *v. a.* Saor; fuasgail; ath-cheannaich. He redeemed them, *shaor e iad.*

Redeemable, *a.* So-shaoradh, so-fhuasgladh, a ghabhas saoradh no fuasgladh, a dh' fhaotar shaoradh no fhuasgladh.

Redeemer, *s.* Fuasglair, fear saoraidh; slànuighear. The Redeemer, *am fear-Saoraidh, an Slànuighear.*

Redeliver, *v.* Ath-shaor, ath-fhuasgail; thoir air ais.

Redelivery, *s.* Toirt air ais, ath-thoirt air ais.

Redemand, *v. a.* Iarr air ais, sir air ais.

Redeeming, **Redemption**, *s.* Saorsadh, saorsainn, saorsuinn, sàbhaladh, fuasgladh, ath-fhuasgladh; éirig. There is no redeeming from death, *cha 'n eil fuasgladh ann o'n bhàs.*

Redemptory, *a.* Saorsachail, éiriceil.

Red-hot, *a.* Teth-dearg, caòireach, bruithneach.

Redintegrate, *v. a.* Nuadhaich, ath-nuadhaich, ùraich. Redintegrated, *nuadhaichte, ath-nuadhaichte, ùraichte.*

Redintegration, *s.* Nuadhachadh, ath-nuadhachadh, ùrachadh.

Red-lead, *s.* Basg-luaidhe, basg chriadh; luaidhe dhearg, basguir.

Redness, *s.* Dearg, deirge, deirgead, ruaidhead, ruaidhe.

Redolence, *s.* Cùbhraidheachd, boltrachas, boltrach.

Redolent, *a.* Cùbhraidh, boltrachail, deagh-bholtrachail.

Redouble, *v. a.* Dùblaich, ath-dhùblaich. Redoubled, *dùblaichte.*

Redoubling, *s.* Dùblachadh, ath-dhùblachadh.

Redoubt, *s.* Dùn beag, dùn catha.

Redoubtable, *a.* Eagallach, fuathasach, uamhasach; buadhach.

Redound, *v. n.* Pill air, thig air ais air, tuit air; cuir ri. That will redound to your credit, *cuiridh sin ri do chliù*; that will redound to me, *thig sin ormsa.*

Redress, *v. a.* Cuir ceart, ceartaich, leasaich; fuasgail; furtaich; diol; dean suas.

Redress, *s.* Leasachadh, dìoladh, dìol, fuasgladh, furtachd; pàigh; deanamh suas; leigheas.

Redstart, **Redtail**, *s.* Earr-dhearg, cam-ghlas, gob-labhradh.

Redstreak, *s.* Seorsa ubhal.

Reduce, *v. a.* (*Lessen*), laghdaich, lughdaich, dean ni 's lugha; cuir an lughaid; (*lower*), ìllsich, ìslich, irioslaich; (*distress*), cuir fo, thoir gu bochduinn, sàruich, claoidh, ceannsaich, buadhaich; smachdaich, ceannsalaich, cuir fo cheannsal. Reduce to nothing, *thoir gu neoni*; reduced, *laghdaichte, illsichte, ceannsaichte, smachdaichte.*

Reducement, *s.* Laghdachadh, lughdachadh, ceannsach-adh.

Reducer, *s.* Laghdachair, lughdachair, ceannsachair.

Reducible, *a.* Laghdachail; lughdachail, so-lughdachadh.

Reduction, *s.* Laghdachadh, lughdachadh, cur an lughaid.

Reduction, *s.* Laghadachadh, lughdachadh, beagachadh; sàruchadh, claoidh.

Redundance, **Redundancy**, *s.* Anabharradh, lionmhorachd, làine.

Redundant, *a.* Iomarcach, anabharr, làn, barrachdail, anabarrach, làn-phailt.

Reduplicate, *v. a.* Dùblaich, ath-dhùblaich.

Reduplication, *s.* Dùblachadh, ath-dhùblachadh.

Reduplicative, *a.* Dùbailte.

Reduvia, *s.* Craiceann bun nan ionga, craiceann nathrach.

Ree, *v. a.* Criathair, criathraich, ruidil.

Re-echo, *v. n.* Ath-fhuaim; ath-fhuaimnich, ath-sgal, ath-ghlaodh, ath-thoirm.

Reedmace, *s.* Bodan.

Reed, *s.* Cuilc; gainne, giolc, giolcach; feadan, rìbhid, reudan. The common reed, *lachan*; a weaver's reed, *slinn.*

Reeden, *a.* Cuilceach, gainneach, giolcach, ribhideach.
Reedy, *a.* Cuilceach, giolcach, gainneach; ribhideach.
Reek, *s.* Deathach, deatach, smùid, tòit.
Reek, *v n.* Cuir deathach, cuir smùid
Reeky, *a* Deathachail, deatachail, smùideach, toiteach.
Reel, *s.* Crois, crois thachrais, cuidhle thachrais; (*in dancing*), ruidhle.
Reel, *v n* Crois, tachrais, tochrais; (*in walking*), seòganaich, siùganaich.
Re-election, *s.* Ath-thaghadh, ath-roghnachadh
Re-embark, *v a* Ath-chuir air bord, ath-imich air bord
Re-embarkation, *s* Ath-dhol air bord
Re-enforce, *v. a.* Ath-neartuich, ath-lion.
Re-enforcement, *s* Ath-neartachadh, ath-lionadh, ath-choghnadh, foirlionadh airm.
Re-engage, *v a.* Ath-ghabh, gabh a ris.
Re-enjoy, *v. a.* Ath-mheal, ath-shealbhaich.
Re-enter, *v a* Rach steach a ris, ath-inntrinn
Re-entrance, *s* Ath-inntrinn, ath-dhol steach
Re-enthrone, *v. a* Ath-chathairich. Re-enthroned, *ath-chathairichte.*
Re-establish, *v. a* Ath-shocraich, ath-dhaighnich. Re-established, *ath-shocraichte.*
Re-establishment, *s* Ath-shocrachadh, ath-dhaighneachadh, ath-dhaingneachadh
† Reeve, *s* Griobh, stiùbhard
Re-examination, *s.* Ath-cheasnuchadh, ath-sgrudadh, ath-rannsuchadh
Re-examine, *v a.* Ath-cheasnuich, ath-sgrud, ath-rannsuich. Re-examined, *ath-cheasnuichte.*
Refectory, *s* Proinnlios, biadh-lann.
Refel, *v a* Cuir an aghaidh.
Refer, *v a.* and *n.* Leig gu ràidhe, buin.
Referee, *s.* Ràidhe, breithe
Reference, *s* Ràidhe, leigeil gu ràidhe; comharadh. In reference to these things, *a thaobh na nithe sin*
Referendary, *s* Ràidhe, breith.
Refine, *v a* Ath-ghlan, tur-ghlan. Refined, *ath-ghlanta, tur-ghlanta*, refined manners, *beusan uasal.*
Refined, *a.* Ath-ghlanta, glan, uasal, grinn
Refinement, *s* Ath-ghlanadh; snàs, glaine; grinneas, finealtachd, eireachdas
Refiner, *s.* Glanadair, ath-ghlanadair, leaghadair, ath-leaghadair.
Refit, *v. a.* Ath-chàirich, ath-chuir suas, tog a ris
Reflect, *v. a.* Tilg air ais, ais-thilg, ath-bhuail, iomcharaich, smuainich, smuaintich
Reflection, *s* (*Thought*), smuain, ath-smuainteachadh; beachd; seadh, suim; (*reprehension*), mi-mheas, cronachadh, coire, (*reverberating*), ais-thilgeadh; ath-shoillse, ath-bhualadh. Without reflection, *gun smuain.*
Reflective, *a.* Smuainteachail, smuainteachail, smuaireanach, a thilgeas faileas; sgàthanach, sgàthanta.
Reflector, *s.* Smuainteachair; beachdair, beachdadair.
Reflex, *a* Ath-bhuailte, ais-bhuailte, buailte air ais.
Reflexible, *a* So-thilg air ais, so-lùbadh, so-aomadh.
Refloat, *s* Traoghadh, traghadh.
Reflourish, *v* Tilg blàth as ùr, cuir mach blath as ùr, ath-chinn, ath-fhàs.
Reflow, *v n.* Ath-lion; ath-shruth
Refluent, *a* Traghadh, traoghach, a dol air ais
Reflux, *s.* Traghadh, traoghadh, dol air ais.

Refocillation, *s.* Urachadh, ath-urachadh, ath-neartachadh.
Reform, *v.* Leasaich, ath-leasaich; ath-dhealbh, ath-chruth, ceartaich, iompaich. Reformed, *leasaichte, ath-dhealbhta, ceartaichte, iompaichte.*
Reform, *s.* Leasachadh; ath-leasachadh; ath-dhealbhadh; ceartachadh, iompachadh, ath-chruthachadh.
Reformation, *s.* Ath-leasachadh, leasachadh; atharrachadh, ath-chruthachadh, ceartachadh, feabhas; (*of manners*), iompachadh.
Reformer, *s* Leasachair, fear leasachaidh, ath-leasachair; ath-chruthachair.
Refract, *v. a* Tionndadh, cuir gu taobh; claon, aom. Refracted, *tionndaidhte, air chur gu taobh*, a refracted ray, *gath claon*
Refraction, *s.* Tionndadh; claonadh. Refraction of a ray of light, *claonadh gath soluis.*
Refractive, *a.* So-thionndadh, so-chlaonadh, a ghabhas tionndadh no claonadh
Refractor, *s.* Gloine meudachaidh.
Refractoriness, *s.* Ceann-laidireas, ceann-laidireachd, crosdachd, reasgachd, dùiread, fèin-thoil.
Refractory, *a* Ceann-laidir, crosda, reasgach, dùr, ragmhuinealach, fèin-thoileil, coirbte.
Refragable, *a.* So-chur an aghaidh, a ghabhas cur an aghaidh.
Refrain, *v a* and *n* Cum air ais, smachdaich, ceannsuich; cum o, cum ort, guait, treig, caisg, coisg; na dean; caomhain. Refrain from sin, *cum o pheacadh*
Refrangible, *a.* So-chlaonadh, mar ghath soluis; sosgaradh.
Refrangibility, *s* Claonadh; sgaradh, sgarachduinn.
Refrenation, *s* Ceannsachadh; cumail sìos, cumail air ais.
Refresh, *v a* Ùraich, ath-ùraich, ath-neartaich, beothaich, ath-bheothaich, fuaraich, fionnaraich; furtaich; eutromaich; gabh fois, gabh lasuchadh. Refreshed, *ùraichte, ath-ùraichte, ath-neartaichte, beothaichte, ath-bheothaichte*; give over working, and refresh yourself a little, *leig dhiot d' obair agus gabh beagan lasuchaidh*
Refreshing, *s.* Ùrachadh, ath-urachadh, ath-neartachadh, beothachadh, ath-bheothachadh.
Refreshment, *s.* Ùraireachd, fois, taimh, lasuchadh; lòn, biadh. Take some refreshment, *gabh beagan uraireachd (no) biadh.*
Refret, *s.* Luinneag
Refrigerant, *a.* Fionnar, fionn-fhuar, fuaraidh; slainnteachail, iallain.
Refrigerate, *v a.* Fionnaraich; fuaraich. Refrigerated, *fionnaraichte, fuaraichte.*
Refrigeration, *s.* Fionnarachadh, fuarachadh.
Refrigerative, *a* Fionnar.
Refrigeratory, *s.* Leigheas fionnar air bith.
Refuge, *s.* Dion, dìdean, fasgadh, tearmunn; dion-aite, dion-airm. Take refuge, *gabh fasgadh, gabh tearmunn, rach fu dhion, gabh comaraich*
Refuge, *v. a.* Dion, tearmunn, thoir tearmunn.
Refugee, *s.* Neach a theicheas chum tearmunn, fògarach.
Refulgence, *s.* Lannaireachd, dealradh, dealraichead, dearrsa, dearrsadh, boisge, baoisge.
Refulgent, *a.* Lannaireach, dealrach, dearrsach, boisgeil.
Refulgently, *adv.* Gu dealrach, gu dearrsach, gu boisgeil.
Refund, *v. a.* Dòirt air ais; pàigh, diol, dean suas, aisig, ath-dhiol

Refusal, *s.* Diùlt, diùltadh, àicheadh; earadh, cùlachadh; eitheadh; òb, òbadh, seunadh. He got a refusal, *fhuair e 'n diùltadh;* a flat refusal, *rogha dhiult, diùltadh as an aghaidh.*

Refuse, *v. a.* and *n.* Diùlt, àicheadh; òb, seun; cùlaich. They refused to obey, *dhiùlt iad a bhith ùmhal;* I will refuse you nothing, *cha dhiùlt mi nì dhuit.*

Refuse, *s.* Fuigheall, fuighleach, spruilleach, deireadh, diù, diùbhadh; fortas, anabas, trusdaireachd; deasgann, drabh; mosan, daosgar; diùireas. Refuse of grain, *fàsan, siolman;* refuse of malt, *braicheas, drabh.*

Refused, *a.* Air dhiùltadh, air àicheadh; seunta.

Refuser, *s.* Diùltair; cùlachair.

Refusing, *s.* Diultadh, àicheadh, òbadh, seunadh.

Refutal, *s.* Cur a mach, tosdadh.

Refutable, *a.* So chur a mach, so chur samhach.

Refutation, *s.* Cur a mach, tosdadh; dìteadh, breugnachadh.

Refute, *v. a.* Cuir a mach, cuir samhach, cuir an aghaidh; dìt, breugnaich. He is refuted completely, *thu e air a chur mach gu tur.*

Regain, *v. a.* Faigh air ais, coisinn, ath-bhuidhinn, ath-bhuannaich, ath-choisinn. Regained, *ath-choisinnte, ath-bhuannaichte.*

Regaining, *s.* Faotainn air ais, coisinn, ath-bhuannachadh.

Regal, *a.* Rioghail.

Regal, *s.* Scorsa inneal-ciùil.

Regale, *v. a.* Ath-bheothaich, ath-uraich; ùraich; thoir cuirm.

Regale, **Regalement**, *s.* Cuirm, cuilm, féisd, féist, fleagh.

Regalier, *s.* Suaicheantais rioghail, ard-shuaicheantas.

Regality, *s.* Rioghalachd, uachdranachd.

Regard, *v. a.* Gabh suim, gabh beachd, thoir suim, thoir fa near, thoir an aire; gabh seadh, gabh cùram, gabh meas, thoir urram (no) meas. I do not regard him, *cha 'n' eil mi 'gabhail suim (no) seadh dheth.*

Regard, *s.* Suim, beachd, seadh, aire, cùram, meas, urram; ciat, deigh, conall, sealladh. He will pay no regard to it, *cha ghabh e suim dheth, tha e com' air;* have you no regard for yourself, *nach eil meas agad ort féin;* he has a great regard for him, *tha meas (no) ciat mhor aig dheth;* with regard to those things, *a thaobh na nithe sin;* he has a great regard for her, *tha ciat mhor aig dh' i.*

Regardable, *a.* Airidh air meas, ion-mheasta.

Regardful, *a.* Furachair, faicilleach, faiceallach, cùramach, suimeil, seadhail, aireachail. Regardfully, *gu furachair, gu faicilleach, gu cùramach, gu suimeil, gu seadhail.*

Regardless, *a.* Neo-fhurachair, neo-fhaicilleach, neo-chùramach, dearmadach.

Regardlessness, *s.* Neo-fhurachras, neo-fhaicilleachd, neo-chùramachd.

Regency, *s.* Riaghlaireachd, riaghlachadh; tàinistearachd, ùghdarras; crioch-smachd rioghachd am min-aois an righ.

Regenerate, *v. a.* Ath-ghin, ath-bhreith, ath-nuadhaich. Regenerated, *ath-ghinte, ath-bhreithte, ath-nuadhaichte.*

Regenerate, *a.* Ath-ghinte, ath-bhreithte, ath-nuadhaichte.

Regeneration, *s.* Ath-ghineamhuinn, ath-bhreith, ath-nuadhachadh.

Regent, *s.* Tàinistear; riaghlair, riaghlachair.

Regentship, *s.* Tainistearachd, riaghlaireachd.

Regerminate, *v. a.* Ath-ghin.

Regerminating, *s.* Ath-ghin, ath-ghineadh.

Regicide, *s.* Righ-mhortadh, righ-mharbhadh; righ-mhortair.

Regimen, *s.* (*In food*), lòn-riaghladh, lòn-riaghailt, biadh riaghailt; (*government*), riaghladh, riaghladaireachd, riaghlachadh.

Regiment, *s.* Cath-bhuidheann; mìle saighdear, *réismeid.*

Regimental, *a.* Cath-bhuidhneach, réismeideach.

Region, *s.* Tìr, duthaich, fearann, fonn, cearn, airde talamh, roinn, ceithreamh.

Register, *s.* Clàr cuimhne; leabhar cuimhne; meamhranach.

Register, *v. a.* Sgriobh, cuir sios. Registered, *sgriobhte, air a chur sios.*

Registrar, *s.* Fear cumail clàr-cuimhne; meamhranaiche.

Registry, *s.* Sgriobhadh sios, cur sios; àite clàr-chuimhne.

Regnant, *a.* A rioghachadh; air a chathair; barrachdail.

Regorge, *v.* Tilg; sgeith; ath-shluig.

Regrant, *v. a.* Ath-bhuilich, thoir air ais, aisig.

Regrate, *v. a.* Thoir déistinn, cuir gràin air.

Regrate, *v. n.* See Forestall.

Regrater, *s.* See Forestaller.

Regreet, *v. a.* Cuir fàilte a ris, cuir ath-fhàilte.

Regress, *s.* Pilltinn, ath-theachd, dol a mach, dol air ais. Egress and regress, *dol agus teachd.*

Regression, *s.* Pilltinn, pilleadh, tilleadh, teachd air ais.

Regret, *s.* Duilichinn, doilghios, duilgheas, farran, mio-thlachd. It gave me much regret, *chuir e mòran duilichinn orm.*

Regret, *v. a.* Gabh duilichinn, bi doilich, bi farranach. I regret having come, *tha mi duilich gun tàinig mi.*

† **Reguerdon**, *s.* Duais, tuarasdal, diol, pàigh.

Regular, *a.* Riaghailteach; a réir riaghailt; lathailteach, sonruichte, suidhichte. A regular or temperate man, *duine cneasta (no) measarra;* regularly, *gu riaghailteach, gu lathailteach.*

Regular, *s.* Sagart.

Regularity, *s.* Riaghailt, lathailt.

Regulate, *v.* Riaghail, riaghlaich, riaghailtich; seòl, cuir ceart, cuir gu doigh, cuir an ordugh, cuir fu riaghladh. Regulated, *riaghlaichte, air a chur gu doigh.*

Regulating, *s.* Riaghladh, riaghlachadh; seòladh; cur ceart, ceartachadh, cur gu doigh.

Regulation, *s.* Riaghailt; reachd, ordugh; riaghlachadh, lathailt.

Regulator, *s.* Riaghladair; reachdadair; fear iùl, fear seòlaidh.

Regurgitate, *v. n.* Dòirt air ais, tilg air ais; ath-shluig.

Regurgitation, *s.* Dòrtadh air ais; ath-shlugadh.

Rehear, *v. a.* Ath-chluinn, ath-éisd ri.

Rehearsal, *s.* Aithris; ath-innseadh, meamhrachadh. A quick rehearsal, *sriut, sriutach.*

Rehearse, *v. a.* Aithris; meamhraich. Rehearsed, *aithriste.*

Rehearser, *s.* Réisiche. A rapid rehearser, *sriutaiche.*

† **Reigle**, *s.* Clais.

Reign, *v. n.* Rioghaich, riaghlaich; buadhaich. He who reigns, *esan a tha rioghachadh, esan aig am bheil uachdranachd.*

Reign, *s.* Rioghachadh, riaghlachadh; uachdranachd; rioghachd; cumhachd.

Reimburse, *v. a.* Pàigh, diol, ath-dhiol, diol (no) pàigh a ris.

Reimbursement, *s.* Pàigh, dioladh, ath-dhioladh.

Rein, *s.* (*Of a bridle*), iall sreine, arannach sréin; srian, rian. Reins of the body, *airnean, dubhan, caol na droma.*

Rein, *v. a.* Ceannsuich, ceannsaich, smachdaich, cum stigh.

Reinforce, *v. a.* Ath-neartuich, foirlion. Reinforced, *ath-neartaichte.*

Reinforcement, *s.* Ath-neartachadh, foirlionadh airm.

Reinsert, *v. a.* Ath-chuir sios.

Reinspire, *v. a.* Ath-bheothaich. Reinspired, *ath-bheothaichte.*

Reinstate, *v. a.* Cuir an seilbh a ris.

Reintegrate, *v. a.* Ath-ùraich, ath-bheothaich; nuadhaich. Reintegrated, *ath-ùraichte, ath-bheothaichte, nuadhaichte.*

Reintegration, *s.* Ath-ùrachadh, ath-bheothachadh, nuadhachadh.

Reinvest, *v. a.* Cuir an seilbh a ris; cuir ath-shéisd ri baile.

Reit, *s.* Seorsa feamuinn.

Reiterate, *v. a.* Aithris, ath-dhean, dean a ris, dean uair is uair. Reiterated, *aithriste.*

Reject, *v. a.* Diùlt, òb, seun, cuir cùl ri, cùlaich; tilg air falbh, cuir air dùireas. He is rejected, *tha e air a dhiùltadh;* she is rejected, *tha i air a diùltadh;* neither eat nor reject the child's bit, *na ith is na òb cuid an leinibh bhig.*

Rejection, *s.* Diùltadh, cur cùl ri, cùlachadh; dìmeas.

Rejoice, *v. a.* and *n.* Dean gairdeachas, dean aoibhneas, dean luath-ghàir, dean mire, bi ait, bi sunndach, bi aoibhinn, bi sugach; dean ait, dean sunndach, dean aoibhinn. Rejoice with another, *dean comh-ghairdeachas.*

Rejoiced, *a.* Aoibhinn, ait, sunndach.

Rejoicing, *s.* Aoibhneas, eibhneas, aiteas, gairdeachas; mealasg.

Rejoin, *v. a.* Cuir ri; ath-choinnich; ath-fhreagair.

Rejoinder, *s.* Ath-fhreagairt; ath-fhreagradh.

Rejudge, *v. a.* Ath-sgrud, ath-cheasnuich, ath-raunsuich; ath-bheachdaich.

Rekindle, *v. a.* Ath-bheothaich, ath-las, beothaich a ris, las a ris.

Relapse, *v. n.* Tuislich (no) tuit air ais, sleamhnaich a air ais, ath-thuislich, ath-thuit, ath-shleamhnaich.

Relapse, *s.* Ath-thuisleachadh, ath-thuiteam, tuiteam air ais.

Relate, *v. a.* and *n.* Innis, aithris, cuir an céill; buin do, buin ri. Relate the tale of your woes, *innis sgeul do thruaighe;* this relates to you, *buinidh so dhuitse.*

Related, *part.* and *a.* Inniste, air innseadh, aithriste, air aithris; (*akin*), càirdeach, an daimh. He is nearly related to me, *tha e ro chàirdeach domh, tha e dlù 'n daimh dhomh.*

Relater, *s.* Aithrisear; fear aithris, eachdruiche; seanachaidh.

Relation, *s.* Innseadh, aithris, aithriseadh, cunntas, cur an ceill; (*tale*), aithris, sgeul, sgeulachd, nuaidheachd; (*kindred*), caraid. A female relation, *bana-charaid;* in relation to me, *da mo thaobh sa;* it is so by relation, *their iad sin;* in relation to us, *da 'r taobh-ne;* relations, *càirdean, dillsean, luchd daimh.*

Relative, *s.* Caraid; fear cinnidh; daimh; (*female*), bancharaid. Relatives, *càirdean, dillsean, luchd daimh.*

Relative, *a.* Daimheil; a bhuineas do; mu thimchioll, a thaobh.

Relax, *v. a.* and *n.* Lasaich, dean lasach; fuasgail, tuasgail, tualaig; dearmadaich, cuir air dìchuimhne; dean socair.

Relaxation, *s.* Lasachadh, fuasgladh, tuasgladh; tualagadh, socair, athais, fois; dearmadachd.

Relay, *s.* Muth each.

Release, *v. a.* Fuasgail, saor, cuir fa sgaoil, leig fa sgaoil, leig saor.

Relegate, *v. a.* Diobair, fuadaich, fògair. Relegated, *diobairte, fuadaichte, fògairte.*

Relegation, *s.* Diobradh, fuadachadh, fògradh.

Relent, *v.* Maothaich; taisich, bogaich, ciùinich, gabh truas.

Relentless, *a.* Neo-thruacanta, neo-iochdmhor, cruaidh, cruadalach.

Relevation, *s.* Togail, ardachadh.

Reliance, *s.* Earbsa, muinghinn, dochas, bun. I have no reliance on him, *cha n' eil earbsa agam as.*

Relic, *s.* Fuigheall, fuighleach, fàgail, iarmad; cuimhneachan. A holy relic, *guimean.*

Relict, *s.* Bantrach, baintreach, bantrach mhna.

Relief, *s.* Lasach, lasachadh, còghnachadh, coghnadh, furtachd, cobhair, cuideachadh; (*of mind*), sòlas. He got some relief, *fhuair e beagan lasachaidh.*

Relievable, *a.* So-lasuchadh, so-chòghnadh, so-chuideachadh.

Relieve, *v. a.* Lasaich, cobhair, cuidich; dean còghnadh; thoir còghnadh; mùth, atharraich. Relieve a sentinel, *atharraich freiceadan.*

Reliever, *s.* Fear còghnaidh, fear cuideachaidh, fear cobhair; furtachair.

Relieving, *s.* Còghnadh, cuideachadh, cobhair, lasachadh, furtachadh.

Relievo, *s.* Dealbh grabhta a seasamh mach o bhord no lic.

Relight, *v. a.* and *n.* Ath-las, ath-shoillsich, ath-ghabh.

Religion, *s.* Diadhachd, diadhaidheachd, crabhadh, creidimh, aidmheil. The Christian religion, *a chreidimh Chriosduigh.*

Religionist, *s.* Baoth-chreideach.

Religious, *a.* Diadhaidh, diadhuidh, cràbhach, naomh, creidmheach. Religiously, *gu diadhaidh, gu crabhach.*

Religiousness, *s.* Diadhaidheachd, crabhachd.

Relinquish, *v.* Tréig, fàg, cuir cùl ri, dealaich ri, diobair, dibir. Relinquished, *tréigte, dealaichte ri.*

Relinquishing, *s.* Tréigeadh, tréigsinn, fàgail, dealachadh ri; diobradh.

Relish, *s.* Blas taitneach; taitinn, deigh, sòlas, miann, toil, tlachd. Of good relish, *deagh bhlasda;* of a bad relish, *domblasda, searbh, goirt, garg, geur.*

Relish, *v. a.* and *n.* Fàilich; thoir blas do ni, dean blasda, blasdaich, gabh tlachd do ni; bi blasda.

Relishable, *a.* Blasda, deagh-bhlasda.

Reluct, *v. a.* Gleachd, dean strìgh, dean spairn.

Relucent, *a.* Trid-shoilleir, soilleir, deàrsach.

Reluctance, **Reluctancy**, *s.* Aindeoin, aindeonachd, neo-thoil, cion toile, neo-thoilichead, diombachd.

Reluctant, *a.* Aindeonach, neo-thoileach, diombach, diombuidheach, diomach. Reluctantly, *gu h-aindeonach, dh' aindeoin, gu neo-thoileach, an aghaidh toile.*

Reluctation, *s.* Strìgh, spairn, comhstri, comhstrìgh, gleac, gleachd, gleic, iomairt.

Relume, *v. a.* Ath-las, ath-ghabh; ath-shoillsich.

Relumine, *v. a.* Ath-shoillsich, soillsich a ris.

Rely, *v. a.* Earb, cuir dòchas, cuir muinghin, dean bun. I rely on him, *earbam asad, tha mi cur earbsa asad.*

Remain, *v. n.* Fuirich, fan; mair, buanaich. Remain where you are, *fuirich far am bheil thu;* remain as you are, *fuirich* (*no*) *fan mar a tha thu;* this remains over and above, *tha so ann thuille na còrach* (*no*) *an deigh laimh;* remaining, *a fanachd; a làthair.*

Remainder, *s.* Fuigheal, fàgail, fuighleach; spruilleach; an corr.

Remains, *s. pl.* (*Of the dead*), duslach; dùs; (*remainder*), fuigheal, fuighleach, fàgail.

Remake, *v. a.* Ath-dhean, dean a ris.

Remand, *v. a.* Cuir air ais, cuir fios air ais, gairm air ais.

Remark, *s.* Beachd, beachdachadh, tearrachd, focal, radh.

Remark, *v. a.* Beachdaich, thoir fanear; thoir os near, comharraich a mach; tomh. He remarked, *thug e fanear, thug e os near, thubhairt e.*

Remarkable, *a.* Comharraichte, ion-chomharruichte, sònruichte; suaicheanta; iongantach, neònach. Remarkably, *gu sonruichte, gu h-iongantach, gu neònach.*

Remedied, *part.* Leighiste, slànuichte, slàn.

Remedy, *s.* Leigheas, ic, ioc-shlainte, cungaidh leigheis; (*help*), comas, còghnadh. There is no remedy (help) for you, *cha 'n 'eil comas ort;* I have no remedy for you, *cha 'n 'eil comas agam ort.*

Remedy, *v. a.* Leigheas, leighis, slànuich, leasaich. Remedied, *leighiste, slànuichte, leasaichte.*

Remember, *v. a.* and *n.* Cuimhnich, meamhraich, cum an cuimhne; cuir an cuimhne. Now I remember, *a nis tha cuimhne agam;* I do not remember it, *cha 'n 'eil cuimhne agam air, cha 'n 'eil cuimhne am air, cha chuimhne leam e;* remember me to her, *thoir mo bheannachd dh' i, thoir mo bheannachd ga h-ionnsuidh.*

Rememberance, *s.* Cuimhne; cuimhneachan. In remembrance, *air chuimhne;* in remembrance of me, *mar chuimhneachan ormsa;* perpetual remembrance, *gnàth-chuimhne.*

Remembrancer, *s.* Seanachaidh, eachdruiche; cuimhneachan.

Remigration, *s.* Pilltinn, pilleadh, ath-imirich.

Remind, *v. a.* Cuir an cuimhne, thoir an cuimhne, cuimhnich. It reminded me, *chuir e am chuimhne.*

Reminiscence, *s.* Cuimhne, cuimhneachadh.

Remiss, *a.* Tais, mi thapaidh; neo-chùramach, dearmadach, leasg, neo-aireachail, neo-shuimeil, mall, mairnealach.

Remissible, *a.* So-mhathadh, a dh' fhaodar mhathadh.

Remission, *s.* Mathanas, maitheanas, maitheamhnas, fuasgladh; saorsadh, lasachadh.

Remissly, *adv.* Gu tais, gu neo-chùramach, gu dearmadach, gu leasg, gu mall, gu mairnealach.

Remissness, *s.* Mairneal, neo-aire, dearmad, neo-chùram, neo-shuim.

Remit, *v. a.* and *n.* Lasaich; maith, math; laghaich, thoir suas; dàilich, cuir dàil; cuir air ais.

Remitment, *s.* Cur air ais.

Remittance, *s.* Suim airgid, pàigh.

Remnant, *s.* Fuigheal, fuighleach, iarmad, an corr, † brath.

Remitter, *s.* Pàighear, fear pàigh.

Remolten, *part.* Ath-leaghta, ath-leaghte.

Remonstrance, *s.* Arguinn; cur an aghaidh, earail.

Remonstrate, *v. a.* Arguinn, cuir an aghaidh, reusonaich, thoir reuson, earail.

Remora, *s.* Bac, amal, moille.

Remorse, *s.* Agartas coguis, cnàmh coguis; iochdmhorachd; truacantachd.

Remorseful, *a.* Iochdmhor, maoth, truacanta.

Remorseless, *a.* Ain-iochdmhor, cruaidh, cruadalach, borb, alluidh, garg.

Remote, *a.* Iomallach, cian, an cian, an céin, air astar, fad as, fad air falbh, iomchian; eil-thireach, allmharach. Remotely, *gu h-iomallach, an cian, an céin, air astar, fad as, fad air falbh.*

Remoteness, *s.* Céin, iomallachd, astar, neo-fhagusachd.

Remotion, *s.* Gluasad, gluasadh, glideachadh, carachadh.

Removable, *a.* Gluasadach, so-ghluasad, so-ghlideachadh, a dh' fhaodar ghluasadh.

Removal, *s.* Gluasad, gluasachd, imrich, imirich; glideachadh, carachadh, atharrachadh, atharrach. A summon of removal, *bardainn, barnaigeudh, barnag.*

Remove, *v. a.* and *n.* Cuir as àite, cuir air falbh, cuir air imirich; falbh, gluais, rach air imrich, imrich.

Remove, *s.* Falbh; imeachd, gluasad, gluasachd, carachadh, mùth; ceum, astar beag.

Removed, *part.* and *a.* Gluaiste; air chur air falbh, air a chur as àite.

Removedness, *s.* Céine, ioma-chéine, astar.

Remover, *s.* Gluasadair.

Remount, *v. a.* Ath-dhìrich.

Remunerable, *a.* Luigheachdail, diolachail; so-dhioladh, a ghabhas dioladh.

Remunerate, *v* Pàigh, diol, ath-dhiol, ath-iochd; cuitich.

Remuneration, *s.* Pàigh, diol, dioladh, ath-dhioladh, luigheachd; meacan.

Remurmur, *v. a.* Ath-dhuarmanaich, dean ath-dhuarman.

Renard, *s.* Seannach, balgair.

Renascent, *a.* Ath-ghineach.

Renavigate, *v. a.* Ath-sheòl, seòl a ris.

Rencounter, *s.* Còmhrag, còrag, strì, strìgh, comhstrìgh, teagmhail; coinneamh.

Rencounter, *v. n.* Coinnich, buail, teagmhail; rach an dàil, thoir ionnsuidh, dean comhrag, thoir coinneamh; comhlaich.

Rend, *v. a.* Srac, srachd, strac, strachd, reub; beubanaich. Rend in pieces, *srachd na mhireannan.*

Render, *s.* Sracair, srachdair, strachdair.

Render, *v. a.* Ioc, diol, ath-dhiol; builich, thoir, tabhair, eadar-theangaich, mìnich; thoir suas (no) thairis, liobhair; tiomnadh. Rendered, *iocta, builichte; eadar-theangaichte, mìnichte, liobhairte.*

Rendezvous, *s.* Àite-coinneimh, àite comh-dhail, aite comhlachaidh.

Rendezvous, *v. n.* Coinnich; comhlaich.

Rendition, *s.* Liobhradh, liobhairt, toirt suas, tiomnadh.

Renegade, Renegado, *s.* Naomh-threigeach; fear ceannairceach.

Renew, *v. a.* Ath-nuadhaich, ath-ùraich, ùraich, nuadhaich, ath-thòisich, tòisich as ùr. They renewed the fight, *dh' ath-ùraich iad am blàr;* renewed, *ath-nuadhaichte, ath-ùraichte, ùraichte, nuadhaichte.*

Renewal, *s.* Ùrachadh, nuadhachadh, ath-ùrachadh, ath-nuadhachadh; ath-thoiseachadh.

Renewing, *s.* See **Renewal**.

Renitency, *s.* Cur an aghaidh, gabhail an aghaidh.

Rennet, *s.* Binid, leasach; deasgainn.

Renovate, *v. a.* Ath-nuadhaich, ùraich, nuadhaich. Renovated, *ath-nuadhaichte, ùraichte, nuadhaichte.*

Renovation, *s.* Ath-nuadhachadh, ùrachadh, nuadhachadh.

Renounce, *v. a.* Diùlt, àicheadh, tréig, cuir cùl ri, seun, òb, cùlaich, dealaich ri. Renounce vice, *dealaich (no) cuir cùl ri dubhailc;* renounce your companions, *tréig (no) cuir cùl ri do chompanaich.*

Renouncement, *s.* Diùltadh, aicheadh, seunadh, tréigsinn, culachadh, òbadh, dealachadh ri.

Renown, *s.* Cliù, alladh, luadh, iomradh, ainm, mor-chliù, luadhradh. Of great renown, *allail, cliùiteach;* of no renown, *mi-chliùiteach.*

Renowned, *a.* Cliùiteach, allail, ainmeil, iomraiteach.

Rent, *s.* Srac, srachd, strachd, reub; bearn; gearradh; (*revenue*), màl, tighinn stigh; cls. Raise rent, *ardaich màl.*

Rent, *v. a.* Gabh (no) thoir airson màil, leig a mach air màl; srachd, reub; leub.

Rent, *part.* Srachdte, srachdta, reubta, reubte.

Rental, *s.* Màl, màl oighreachd, ròl màil; cls.

Renter, *s.* Màladair; tuathanach.

Renting, *s.* Gabhaltas.

Renumerate, *v. a.* Ath-chunnt, cunnt a ris; ath-dhiol, aithris.

Renunciation, *s.* Cùlachadh, diùltadh, àicheadh.

Reobtain, *v. a.* Faigh a ris.

Reordain, *v. a.* Ath-orduich, ath-shuidhich, ath-shocraich. Reordained, *ath-orduichte, ath-shuidhichte, ath-shocraichte.*

Reordination, *s.* Ath-orduchadh, diùltadh, aicheadh.

Repacify, *v. a.* Ath-chiùinich, ath-choisg.

Repaid, *part.* Paighte, ath-dhiolta.

Repair, *v. a.* and *n.* Càirich, ath-chàirich, leasaich, ath-thog; gabh, imich falbh, siubhail; tog ort. Repair clothes, *càirich* (*no*) *clùd eudach.*

Repair, *s.* Càramh; ath-nuadhachadh; leasachadh; àros, àite comhnuidh, tigh.

Repairer, *s.* Fear càramh; (*of shoes*), brògair; (*of clothes*), tàillear; clùdair.

Reparable, *a.* So-leasachadh, a ghabhas leasachadh.

Reparation, *s.* Càramh, togail, leasachadh, dioladh, deanamh suas, ceartachadh.

Repartee, *s.* Freagairt gheur, beum.

Repass, *v. n.* Ath-choisich, ath-shiubhail, ath-thriall; pill.

Repassing, *s.* Ath-choiseachd, ath-shiubhal, ath-thrialladh, ath-philltinn.

Repast, *s.* Biadh, lòn, teachd an tìr.

Repay, *v. a.* Pàigh, diol, ath-dhiol, ioc, iochd.

Repayment, *s.* Pàigh, diol, dioladh, ath-dhioladh.

Repeal, *v. a.* Gairm air ais; neo-dhean; cuir sios, thoir gu neoni.

Repeal, *s.* Cur air chùl, cur sios.

Repeat, *v. a.* Aithris; abair a ris; abair air do theangaidh, abair air do chridhe; innis a ris; ath-dhean; dean a ris; thoir deuchainn eile. Repeating, *ag aithris.*

Repeatedly, *adv.* Gu minic, gu minig, gu tric, uair is uair, thairis is thairis.

Repeater, *s.* Aithrisear; uaireadear a bhuaileas na h-uairean, uaireadair bualaidh.

Repel, *v. a.* Tilg air ais, buail air ais, cuir air ais, diùlt. She repelled him, *dhiùlt i e;* repelled, *buailte air ais.*

Repelling, *s.* Tilgeadh air ais, bualadh air ais, cur air ais, diùltadh.

Repent, *v. n.* and *a.* Gabh aithreachas, dean aithreachas, bi aithreachail. Repent of your deeds, *gabh aithreachas do* (*no*) *a 'd ghniomharaibh;* I repent, *is aithreach leam, tha mi 'gabhail aithreachais.*

Repentance, *s.* Aithreachas; agartas coguis.

Repentant, *a.* Aithreachail, làn aithreachais; brònach, duilich.

Repeople, *v. a.* Ath-lion le sluagh.

Repercussion, *s.* Cur air ais, bualadh air ais.

Repertory, *s.* Ionnas, tigh stòr, taisg ionad.

Repetition, *s.* Aithris; ath-dheanamh; ath-iarrtas.

Repine, *v. a.* Dean talach, dean frionas, dean monmhur (no) gearan, gearain, talaich; bi frionasach, bi mi-thoilichte. Repine not, *na dean talach.*

Repiner, *s.* Fear talachaidh, fear frionasach.

Replace, *v. a.* Cuir na àite a ris; cuir air ais; cuir an aite.

Replait, *v.* Ath-phleat; ath-fhill, fill a ris, dual (no) dualaich a ris.

Replant, *v. a.* Ath-phlanntaich, ath-shuidhich. Replanted, *ath-phlanntaichte, ath-shuidhichte.*

Replantation, *s.* Ath-phlanntachadh, ath-shuidheachadh.

Replenish, *v. a.* Lion; stoc; ath-lion; airneisich. Replenished, *lionta, ath-lionta; airneisichte; air a stocadh.*

Replete, *v.* Làn, iomlàn, dearr-làn.

Repletion, *s.* Làine, sàth, làn.

Replication, *s.* Freagairt, freagradh, ath-fhreagradh.

Reply, *v. n.* Freagair, thoir freagairt. Reply to him, *thoir freagairt air.*

Reply, *s.* Freagairt, freagradh. I did not think him worthy of reply, *cha tug mi meas freagairt air.*

Repolish, *v. a.* Ath-liobharaich, ath-mhìnich, ath-ghlan, ath-sgùr.

Report, *v. a.* Innis, aithris; abair, sgaoil, craobh-sgaoil; thoir fios. It is reported, *tha air a radh, tha iad ag radh;* reported, *aithriste, air innseadh, air iomradh.*

Report, *s.* Fathunn, fathur, biùthas, nuaidheachd; iomradh, sgeul, guth, tuairisgeul; (*of a gun*), fuaim, toirm, braidhe. There is a report, *tha iomradh ann;* a bad report, *droch sgeul, droch iomradh.*

Reporter, *s.* Aithrisear; fear nuaidheachd.

Reposal, *s.* Gabhail tamh (no) fois, foisneachadh.

Repose, *v. a.* and *n.* Foisnich, gabh fois, gabh tamh; codail, cadail. Repose yourself, *gabh gu fois;* repose trust, *cuir earbsa;* I reposed great confidence in him, *chuir mi mòran creideis ann.*

Repose, *s.* Fois, tamh, socair; codal, suain. At repose, *aig fois;* he has no repose night or day, *cha 'n 'eil fois aig dh' oidhche no là;* he is taking repose, *tha e 'gabhail pramh.*

Reposedness, *s.* Foisneachd, fois, tamh.

Reposit, *v.* Taisg, cuir suas; cuir seachad.

Reposition, *s.* Tasgadh, cur suas.

Repository, *s.* Ionad tasgaidh, taisg-ionad; tigh stòir; lonailt, gleasan, gleadhadan; cillean, taisg-lann. Repository for small things, *taplach.*

Repossess, *v. a.* Ath-shealbhaich. Repossessed, *ath-shealbhaichte.*

Repossession, *s.* Ath-shealbhachadh.

Reprehend, *v.* Cronaich, coirich, troid ri, achmhasanaich, smachdaich. I reprehended him, *chronaich mi e;* reprehended, *cronaichte, coirichte, achmhasanaichte.*

Reprehender, *s.* Fear cronachaidh.

Reprehensible, *a.* Ion-chronachadh, ion-choireachadh, achmhasanach.

Reprehension, *s.* Achmhasan, cronachadh, trodadh, coireachadh.

Reprehensive, *a.* Achmhasanach; cronachail.

Reprehensory, *a.* Achmhasanach, sglamhrach.

Represent, *v. a.* Feuch; nochd; foillsich, taisbein, cuir an cèill; dealbh; riochdaich.

Representation, *s.* Nochdadh, foillseachadh, taisbean, taisbeanadh, coslas; riochd, dealbh, iomhaigh, eugas, aogas.

Representative, *s.* Riochdair, fear ionaid, fear a ni gnothuch air son neach eile.

Representer, *s.* Foillseachair, nochdair, fear taisbein.

Repress, *v. a.* Coisg, caisg; cum fo, sàruich; ceannsaich, ciosnaich, smachdaich; mùch. Repressed, *coisgte, sàruichte, ceannsaichte, ciosnaichte; mùchta.*

Repression, *s.* Cosgadh, sàruchadh, ceannsachadh, ciosnachadh, smachdachadh, mùchadh, cumail fo.

Repressive, *a.* Ceannsachail, ciosnachail, smachdail.

Reprieve, *v. a.* Maith, math, saor; cuir dàil am peanas.

Reprieve, *s.* Maitheadh, mathadh; maitheanas; saorsa; dàil peanais.

Reprimand, *v. a.* Achmhasanaich, cronaich, troid ri, tachair ri. He reprimanded him sharply, *chronaich se e gu geur, dheadh throid e ris.*

Reprimand, *s.* Achmhasan, spràic, cronachadh, trodadh, trod, sglamhradh.

Reprint, *v. a.* Ath-phrionnt, ath-chlo-bhuail, prionnt (no) clodh-bhuail a ris.

Reprisal, *s.* Éiric; ath-ghabhail, diol.

Reproach, *v. a.* Cronaich; masluich; cuir as leth, tilg suas ri. He reproached him with crimes which he committed not, *chuir e as a leth ciontaibh nach do chuir e 'n gniomh.*

Reproach, *s.* Cronachadh, maslachadh; mi-chliù, masladh, sgainneal, tàmailt, tasart; athais; tailceas, beud. A man without reproach, *fear gun bheud;* you have not put the reproach far from your own doors, *cha 'n fhad uait chuir thu 'n athais.*

Reproachable, *a.* Ion-chronachadh, ion-mhaslachadh, maslachail, mi-chliùiteach, sgainnealach.

Reproachful, *a.* Maslach, sgainnealach, nàrach, gràineil, tàmailteach; tailceasach, toibheumach. Reproachfully, *gu maslach, gu sgainnealach, gu tàmailteach.*

Reproachfully, *adv.* Gu maslach, gu sgainnealach; gu tàmailteach; gu tailceasach, gu toibheumach.

Reprobate, *s.* Droch dhuine, crochair, rogair.

Reprobate, *a.* Olc, aingidh, baoth.

Reprobate, *v. a.* Mi-cheadaich; cuir cùl ri, dìt.

Reprobateness, *s.* Aingidheachd.

Reprobation, *s.* Dìteadh; di-mheas.

Reproduce, *v. a.* Thoir mach a ris; cuir làthair a ris.

Reproduction, *s.* Ath-thoirt a mach.

Reproof, *s.* Achmhasan, trod, sglamhradh, cronachadh, armaradh.

Reprovable, *a.* Airidh air achmhasan, ion-chronachadh.

Reprove, *v. a.* Troid ri, sglamhruich; cronaich, coirich, faigh coir (no) cron. He reproved her, *chronaich e i, fhuair e coire dh' i;* reproved, *cronaichte, coirichte.*

Reprover, *s.* Fear cronachaidh.

Reprune, *v. a.* Ath-sgath, ath-bhearr, sgath a ris.

Reptile, *s.* Snàgair, snàigean; biasd; ablach.

Reptile, *a.* Snàgach, snàigeach.

Republic, *s.* Co-fhlaitheachd.

Republican, *a.* Co-fhlaitheachdach; nach geill do righ, aimhreiteach.

Republican, *s.* Co-fhlaitheach, fear comh-fhlaitheachd.

Repudiate, *v. a.* Dealaich ri, cuir air falbh.

Repudiation, *s.* Dealachadh, eadar-dhealachadh, eadar-sgaradh.

Repugnant, *a.* An aghaidh, contrardha, eas-umhal, diomach, diombach, mi-thoileach. Repugnantly, *gu contrardha, gu diomach, gu diombach, gu mi-thoileach.*

Repulse, *v.* Cuir air ais, cuir air falbh, buail air ais, sgiùrs air falbh.

Repulse, *s.* Pilleadh, pilltinn; diùltadh.

Repulsive, *a.* Gruamach, doirbh, dorganta; oillteil.

Repurchase, *v. a.* Ath-cheannaich, ceannuich a ris. Repurchased, *ath-cheannuichte.*

Reputable, *a.* Urramach, cliùiteach, creideasach. Reputably, *gu creideasach.*

Reputableness, *s.* Urramachd, cliùiteach, cliù, creideasachd, creideas.

Reputation, *s.* Cliù, meas, alladh, luadh, iomradh, ainm, onoir, deagh-ainm. In the height of his reputation, *an àirde a chliù;* he gained reputation, *choisinn e cliù;* a bad reputation, *droch cliù, droch iomradh.*

Repute, *v. a.* Meas; creid; saoil.

Repute, *s.* Cliù, meas, iomradh, ainm. In low repute, *air bheag meas; nach fiù, nach fhiach.*

Reputeless, *a.* Neo-chliùiteach; mi-chliùiteach.

Request, *s.* Iarrtas, guidhe, asluchadh, iarruidh, athchuinge, meas. At my request, *air m' iarrtas;* present a request, *cuir suas athchuinge;* request requires no blame, *cha toill iarrtas achmhasan.*

Request, *v. a.* Iarr, sir, guidh, athchuing, asluich, grios.

Requester, *s.* Iarradair, asluchair, ath-chuingiche.

Requicken, *v. n.* Ath-bheothaich, beothaich a ris. Requickened, *ath-bheothaichte.*

Requickening, *s.* Ath-bheothachadh.

Requiem, *s.* Marbh-rann, marbh-dhàn, tuireadh.

Require, *v. a.* and *n.* Iarr; sir; iarr mar chòir, feum, gabh. Require of him, *iarr air;* it will require ten yards, *gabhaidh (no) feumaidh e deich slatan.*

Requisite, *a.* Feumail, iomchuidh, freagarrach. Requisitely, *gu feumail, gu h-iomchuidh.*

Requisite, *s.* Ni feumail.

Requisiteness *s.* Feum, feumalachd, iomchuidhead.

Requital, *s.* Luigheachd, luidheachd, diol, pàigh, éiric, diol-thuarasdal. In requital, *an éiric.*

Requite, *v. a.* Diol, ath-dhiol, pàigh. I will requite you, *diolaidh mise dhuit.*

Reremouse, *s.* Ialltag, ialltag anmoch.

Rereward, *s.* Deireadh, ceann deiridh.

Resale, *s.* Ath-reic.

Resalute, *v. a.* Ath-fhailtich, cuir fàilte a ris.

Rescind, *v.* Sgath, gearr sios, cuir siòs lagh. Rescinded, *sgathta.*

Rescission, *s.* Sgathadh, gearradh sios.

Rescribe, *v. a.* Ath-sgriobh, sgriobh air ais, sgriobh a ris. Rescribed, *ath-sgriobhte.*

Rescript, *s.* Reachd righ (no) iompair.

Rescue, *s.* Saoradh, fuasgladh, liobhradh.

Rescue, *v. a.* Saor, fuasgail, cuir fa sgaoil; liobhair, tearuinn. He rescued them from destruction, *shaor e iad o sgrios;* rescued, *saorta, fuasgailte; liobhairte, tearuinnte.*

Rescuer, *s.* Fear saoraidh, fuasglair.

Research, *s.* Rannsuchadh, rannsachadh, ceasnachadh, sgrudadh, ath-shiorrachas; ath-shireadh, ath-iarruidh, fiafraidh, eisreadh.

Research, *v. a.* Rannsuich, ceasnaich, sgrud.

Reseize, *v. a.* Ath-ghlac. Reseized, *ath-ghlacta.*

Reseizure, *s.* Ath-ghlacadh.

Resemblance, *s.* Samhladh, coslas, eugas, aogas, cosamhlachd, coslachd; iomhaigh; suaip. Some vices have the resemblance of virtue, *tha cuid dhubhailcean ann aig am bheil eugas subhailce;* he bears you a great resemblance, *tha suaip mhòr aig riut.*

Resemble, *v. n.* Samhluich, coimeas; bi cosmhuil. He resembles him, *tha e cosmhuil ris.*

Resembling, *a.* Coslach, cosmhuil.

Resent, *v. a.* Gabh gu dona, gabh gu h-olc, gabh gu soithich, gabh mar thàmailt; tàmailtich.

Resentful, *a.* Dioghaltach; mio-rùnach; feargach, gamhlasach.

Resentment, *s.* Fearg, feirg, corruich, dioghaltas. Stifle your resentment, *mùch do chorruich.*

Reservation, *s.* Folach, falach, cùl-caralas, céileadh, ceiltinn.

RESERVATORY, *s.* Taisg lann, taisg ionad, tigh stòir.

RESERVE, *v. a.* Gleidh, taisg, cuir gu taobh, coimhid, coimhead, folaich, caomhain.

RESERVE, *s.* Tasgadh, tasgadan, folachan; (*of soldiers*), cùl-earalas, buidheann còghnaidh; (*modesty*), stuaim, nàir, macantas, ogluidheachd.

RESERVED, *a.* Mallta, stuama, macanta; dùinte; fad thall, mùigeach; fiata; neo-shaor; caomhanta, caomhainnte, taisgte. Reservedly, *gu mallta, gu dùinte, gu fiata, gu mùigeach.*

RESERVEDNESS, *s.* Mùig, mùigealachad, fiatachd, ogluidheachd, macantas, nàire.

RESERVOIR, *s.* Lochan, linneag; tiobar; tobar; †cann.

RESET, *v. a.* Gabh ri meirle.

RESETTLE, *v. a.* Ath-shocraich; ath-shuidhich. Resettled, *ath-shocraichte, ath-shuidhichte.*

RESETTLEMENT, *s.* Ath-shocrachadh, ath-shuidheachadh.

RESIDE, *v. n.* Traogh, sìolaidh; fuirich, gabh còmhnuidh, còmhnuich, fan, cuir suas. Where does he reside, *c' àite am bheil e fanachd.*

RESIDENCE, *s.* Àros, teach, fardoch, àrdoch, tigh, àite còmhnuidh, ionad còmhnuidh.

RESIDENCE, *s.* Deasgann, drabhag.

RESIDENT, *a.* A fanachd, a fuireachadh.

RESIDENT, *s.* Teachdair rìgh; tamhaiche, fear àiteachaidh.

RESIDUE, *s.* Fuigheal, fuighleach, iarmad, iarsma.

RESIGN, *v.* Thoir suas; thoir sìos, tiomnadh, géill, cuitich. Resign your office, *thoir suas do dhreuchd;* resign yourself to his will, *géill do 'thoil.*

RESIGNATION, *s.* Toirt suas, toirt seachad; géilleachdainn, umhlachd, strìochdadh, tiomnadh, géilleadh.

RESIGNMENT, *s.* Toirt suas, toirt seachd, tiomnadh.

RESILIENCE, RESILIENCY, *s.* Leum air ais.

RESIN, *s.* Bith craoibh, teàrr, ròsaid.

RESINOUS, *a.* Tearrach, ròsaideach.

RESIPISCENCE, *s.* Aithreachas.

RESIST, *v. a.* Cuir an aghaidh, seas an aghaidh. They resist one another, *tha iad a cur an aghaidh 'chéile.*

RESISTANCE, *s.* Strìgh, strì, aghaidh; cur an aghaidh, cosnamh, bacadh, grabadh.

RESISTIBLE, *a.* A ghabhas cur an aghaidh, a ghabhas bacadh, so-bhacadh, so-chomhlachadh.

RESISTLESS, *a.* Dian, do-chòmhlachadh, do chur an aghaidh.

RESOLVE, *v. a.* and *n.* Sonruich, sùnruich; cuir romhad; (*resolve doubts*), fuasgail, tuasgail; (*into powder*), pronn, mìn-phronn; (*melt*), leagh. I am resolved on it, *tha mi sonraichte air.*

RESOLVE, *s.* Rùn, rùn suidhichte.

RESOLVED, *a.* Sonruichte, sùnruichte, suidhichte. Fully resolved, *làn sonruichte;* I am resolved on it, *tha mi sonruichte air.*

RESOLVEDNESS, *s.* Danarachd; bunailteachd, diongaltachd.

RESOLVENT, *a.* Leaghach; leaghadach.

RESOLUTE, *a.* Suidhichte, sònruichte, sùnruichte, dàn, danarra, misneachail, diongalta, gramail, bunailteach, seasmhach.

RESOLUTELY, *adv.* Gu sònruichte, gu dàn, gu danarra, gu misneachail, gu diongalta, gu gramail, gu bunailteach.

RESOLUTENESS, *s.* Danarrachd, misneach, bunailteachd.

RESOLUTION, *s.* Rùn, inntinn, rùn suidhichte; rùn sonruichte; sonrachadh; bunailteachd, bunaiteachd; (*of difficulties*), fuasgladh, mìneachadh. Nothing can make him alter his resolution, *cha toir ni air 'inntinn a mhuth;* this is my resolution, *is e so mo rùn;* resolution of a question, *fuasgladh ceist;* resolution of an assembly, *riaghailt, ordugh, sonrachadh, reachd;* (of the nerves), *parailis, pairilis.*

RESOLUTIVE, *a.* Leaghtach.

RESONANCE, *s.* Fuaim, toirm, ath-fhuaim, ath-fhuaimnich.

RESONANT, *a.* Ath-fhuaimearra, ath-fhuaimneach.

RESORPTION, *s.* Ath-shlugadh.

RESORT, *v.* Tathaich; gabh (no) rach gu follaiseach.

RESORT, *s.* Tional, teanal, coimh-thional, cruinneach, cruinneachadh; coinneamh, comhdhail; (*refuge*), fasgadh, dìonadh, tearmunn. A place of resort, *aite comhdhail, àite tathaich.*

RESORTER, *s.* Fear tathaich.

RESOUND, *v. a.* Ath-fhuaimnich, ath-thoirm.

RESOURCE, *s.* Culaidh chobhair, cùl earalais, tearmunn; seòl, doigh.

RESPECT, *v. a.* Urramaich, meas, thoir meas (no) urram. Respected, *urramaichte, measail.*

RESPECT, *s.* Urram, meas, spéis, onoir. Worthy of respect, *airidh air urram;* respect of persons, *leth-bhreith;* in this respect, *anns a bheachd so, air an doigh so;* in what respect, *cia mar;* in respect of, *do thaobh, a thaobh;* send my respects, *cuir mo bheannachd;* arms procure respect, *dleasaidh arm urram.*

RESPECTABLE, *a.* Measail, urramach.

RESPECTER, *s.* Fear leth-bheith.

RESPECTFUL, *a.* Modhail, cùirteil, beusach. Respectfully, *gu modhail, gu beusach.*

RESPECTFULNESS, *s.* Modhaileachd; cùirtealachd.

RESPECTIVE, *a.* Sonruichte, sonraichte; àraid.

RESPECTIVELY, *adv.* Fa leth.

RESPERSION, *s.* Spultadh, spairteadh.

RESPIRATION, *s.* Tarruing analach; analachadh, fois, socair. Difficult respiration, *gainne analach.*

RESPIRE, *v. a.* Tarruing anail, gabh anail, séid.

RESPITE, *s.* Fois, anail, tamh; fosadh, dàil, càird. Respite of punishment, *dàil peanais;* (of a disease), *lasachadh, eutromachadh;* after some respite, *an deigh tacain bheag;* without respite, *gun dàil, gun chàird.*

RESPITE, *v. a.* Thoir fois; cuir dàil, dàilich; cuir dheth; allsaich.

RESPLENDENCE, RESPLENDENCY, *s.* Dealrachd, dealraidheachd, dealradh, lonnaireachd, dearrsadh, soillse, boisge.

RESPLENDENT, *a.* Dealrach, lonnarra, lonnrach, dearrsach, boisgeil.

RESPOND, *v. a.* Freagair, ath-fhreagair, thoir freagairt.

RESPONDENT, *s.* Fear freagairt.

RESPONSE, *s.* Freagairt, freagradh; iriall.

RESPONSIBLE, *a.* Freagarrach. I will be responsible for that, *bithidh mise freagarrach air son sin.*

RESPONSIBLENESS, *s.* Freagarrachd.

RESPONSION, *s.* Freagairt, freagradh.

RESPONSIVE, *a.* Freagarrach; ath-fhuaimneach, fuaimearra.

REST, *s.* Fois, tamh, codal, sìth, samhchair, sìothchath, socair, suaimhneas, ciùineas, clos; sgur; féith; (*prop*), taic, prop; (*in music*), stad. At rest, *aig fois.*

REST, *v. n.* Codail, cadail, dean codal, gabh fois; leig d' anail, sguir, dean tamh, gabh gu clos; (*remain*), fuirich, fan; (*rely*), earb ri, earb a; cuir doigh ann. Rest on, *leig taic;* rest or light upon, *tuirling, suidh.*

REST, *s.* (*Remainder*), fuigheal, fuighleach, chuid eile; an còrr; càch. I will do the rest myself, *ni mi a chuid eile leam féin;* I will go as well as the rest, *théid mi ann cho mhath ri càch.*

Restauration, *s.* Urachadh, nuadhachadh.

Rested, *a.* Aomta; an taic.

Restful, *a.* Samhach, ciùin.

Restiff, *a.* Ceann-laidir, reasgach, miolasgach, stodach, rag-mhuinealach.

Restifness, *s.* Ceann-laidireachd, reasgachd, miolasgachd; stoid.

Restinction, *s.* Cur as, mùchadh.

Resting-place, *s.* Ionad taimh; ceann uighe.

Restitution, *s.* Dioladh, ath-dhioladh, aiseag; co-leasachadh, toirt air ais.

Restive, *a.* See **Restiff**.

Restless, *a.* (*Having no rest*), mi-fhoisneach, an-shocrach, mi-fhoighdneach; mi-shuaimhneach; (*in continual motion*), luaimneach, luaineach, neo-shuidhichte, iomairteach, ciomach; (*turbulent*), aimhreiteach, buaireasach. Restlessly, *gu mi-fhoisneach, gu h-an-shocrach, gu mi-fhoighdneach, gu mi-shuaimhneach; gu luaimneach, gu luaineach, gu buaireasach.*

Restlessness, *s.* Mi-fhoisneachd, an-shocair, mi-fhoighdinn, neo-fhoisneachd, mi-shuaimhneas, dìth fois, dìth codail, luaireasg.

Restorable, *a.* A ghabhas toirt air ais, so-aiseag.

Restoration, *s.* Aiseag, aiseagadh; ath-nuadhachadh. Restoration-day, *là aisig Righ Tearlach a dhà.*

Restorative, *a.* Leigheasail, beothachail, ath-bheothachail.

Restorative, *s.* Leigheas beothachaidh.

Restore, *v. a.* Thoir air ais; ath-dhiol; leighis, ath-bheothaich. Restored, *aisigte; ath-bheothaichte, leighiste;* restored to its place, *air a chur na àite féin.*

Restorer, *s.* Ath-bheothachair; aiseagair, fear a bheir air ais.

Restrain, *v. a.* Bac; bachd; coisg; cum air ais, toirmisg, ceannsaich, cum stigh, cum fo, smachdaich, cum fo smachd (no) fo cheannsal. Restrained, *coisgte, toirmisgte, ceannsuichte, smachdaichte.*

Restraint, *s.* Bac, bacadh, moile, toirmeasgadh, grabadh, ceannsachd; amal.

Restrict, *v. a.* Bac, ceannsuich, grab, amail, cum stigh; ceangail.

Restriction, *s.* Bacadh; grabadh, cuibhreachadh, ceangladh.

Restrictive, *a.* Ceanglach.

Restringe, *v.* Ceangail; crup, teannaich.

Restringent, *s.* Ceanglach, crupach.

Resty, *a.* Reasgach; dùr, ceannlaidir.

Result, *v. n.* Tachair, thig gu buile, thig gu crich; leum air ais.

Result, *s.* Buile, crioch; ceann deiridh, deireadh, codhùnadh. That will be the result of it, *is e sin as deireadh dha;* what will be the result of it, God knows, *ciod gus an tig e, is an aig Dia tha brath.*

Resume, *v. a.* Ath-thòisich, tòisich a ris, ath-thionnsgain; gabh air ais, gabh a ris.

Resuming, *s.* Ath-thòiseachadh, ath-thionnsgnadh.

Resumption, *s.* Ath-ghabhail; ath-thòiseachadh, ath-thionnsgnadh.

Resupination, *s.* Luidhe air an druim.

Resurvey, *v. a.* Ath-bheachdaich; gabh ath-bheachd; ath-thomhais.

Resurrection, *s.* Ais-éirigh, ath-éiridh.

Resuscitate, *v.* Ath-dhùisg; dùisg a ris; ath-bheothaich. Resuscitated, *ath-dhùisgte, dùisgte a ris, ath-bheothaichte.*

Resuscitation, *s.* Ath-dhùsgadh, ath-bheothachadh.

Retail. See **Retale**.

Retain, *v. a.* Cum, gleadh, gleidh, coimhid, coimhead, gabh, bac.

Retainer, *s.* Fear leanmhuinn, leanmhuinniche.

Retake, *v. a.* Ath-ghabh, gabh a ris, ath-ghlac. He retook the town, *dh' ath-ghabh e 'm baile, dh' ath-ghlac e 'm baile;* retaken, *ath-ghabhta, ath-ghlacta.*

Retale, *v. a.* Reic chuid is a chuid, reic am beaganaibh (no) uigh air an uigh; roinn; mìn-reic, meanbh-reic.

Retale, *s.* Meanbh-reic.

Retaler, *s.* Meanbh reiceadair, mìn-reiceadair.

Retaliate, *v. a.* Ath-dhiol, diol air ais; thoir buille airson buille.

Retaliation, *s.* Dioladh, ath-dhioladh, dioghaltas.

Retard, *v. a.* and *n.* Amail, bac, cum air ais, cuir amal air, cum, grab, cuir moille air, cum air ais. You retard me, *tha thu 'g am amaladh.*

Retardation, *s.* Amal, bac, grab, grabadh, moille.

Retarder, *s.* Bacair, grabair.

Retch, *v.* Sgeith, sgeath, tilg.

Retching, *s.* Sgeith, tur-thilge.

Retection, *s.* Nochdadh, foillseachadh.

Retention, *s.* Cumail; cuimhneachadh; meamhair, cuimhne; druideadh, dùnadh.

Retentive, *a.* Dionach; cuimhneachail.

Reticence, *s.* Céiltinn; sàmhchair.

Reticle, *s.* Mìn-lìon, meanbh-lìon, sgannan.

Reticular, *a.* Mar lìon; lìontaidh; sùileagach, sgannanach.

Retinue, *s.* Lùghaird, lùchairt; luchd-leanmhuinn, coisridh, coigleachd.

Retire, *v. n.* Rach air ais, rach gu taobh; falbh, teich. He retired into the house, *ghabh e stigh.*

Retired, *a.* Diomhair, uaigneach; aonranach; as an rod.

Retiredly, *adv.* Gu diomhair, gu h-uaigneach.

Retiredness, *s.* Diomhaireachd, uaigneas.

Retirement, *s.* Diomhaireachd, uaigneas, aonranachd.

Retort, *v. a.* Ais-thilg; tilg air ais, leum air ais; lùb air ais.

Retort, *s.* Geur fhreagairt; cas-fhreagairt; seorsa buideil.

Retouch, *v. a.* Ath-bhean ri; leasaich; dean ni 's fhearr.

Retrace, *v. a.* Ath-lorgaich.

Retract, *v. a.* Tarruing air ais, thoir air ais.

Retractation, *s.* Tarruing air ais, toirt air ais.

Retraction, *s.* Tarruing air ais.

Retreat, *s.* Diomhaireachd, uaigneas, ionad diomhair; tearmunn, didean, dion, àite teichidh, fasgadh; (*of an army*), teicheachd, teicheadh, cùl-tharruing, *ratreut.*

Retreat, *v. a.* Teich; rach an diomhaireachd. Make to retreat, *cuir air theich.*

Retrench, *v. a.* Gearr dheth, sgath; lughdaich, laghdaich; caomhain.

Retrenchment, *s.* Lughdachadh, laghdachadh; sgathadh; bearradh.

Retribute, *v. a.* Ath-dhiol, ath-phàigh, diol (no) pàigh a ris.

Retribution, *s.* Ath-dhioladh, dioladh, pàigh.

Retributive, *a.* Diolach, dioghaltach, a bheir dioladh.

Retrievable, *a.* So-bhuidhinn, a ghabhas buidhinn (no) faotainn air ais.

Retrieve, *v. a.* Faigh air ais, aisig, ath-bhuidhinn; athghairm.

Retrocede, *v.* Rach air ais, rach an comhair do chùil.

RETROCESSION, *s.* Dol air ais.

RETROGRADATION, *s.* Dol air ais.

RETROSPECT, *s.* Sealladh cùil, sealladh air ais; ath-sheall-adh.

RETROSPECTION, *s.* Sealladh air ais, sealltuinn air ais, amharc air ais.

RETURN, *v. n.* and *a.* Thig air ais, pill, till; diol, pàigh, ioc; thoir air ais, cuir air ais.

RETURN, *s.* Pilltinn, pilleadh, tilleadh; teachd air ais; dioladh, pàigh, freagairt; tairbhe; buannachd. A grateful return, *dioladh comain;* after my return, *an deigh dhomh pilltinn.*

RETURNER, *s.* Diolair, fear diolaidh.

REUNION, *s.* Ath-aontachd; ath-cheangladh, ath-chordadh.

REUNITE, *v. a.* Cuir ri chéile a ris; dean réidh a ris, ath-cheangail, ath-dhluthaich, ath-reitich.

REVEAL, *v.* Nochd, foillsich, taisbein, leig ris; innis, aithris, dean follaiseach, sgaoil.

REVEALER, *s.* Foillseachair, fear foillseachaidh, taisbean-aiche.

REVEL, *s.* Féisd, cuirm; ruite, ruitearachd, craos, meisge.

REVEL, *v. a.* Tarruing air ais, thoir air ais.

REVEL, *v. n.* Dean geòc, dean pòit, dean ruitearachd, bach.

REVELATION, *s.* Foillseachadh, nochdadh, taisbean, taisbe-anadh.

REVELER, *s.* Ruitear, pòitear, meisgear, bachair, geòcair, craosair.

REVELRY, *s.* Ruitearachd, pòit, poitearachd, bàch, baois-leachd. The noise of revelry, *bach-thorman, bach-thoirm;* sickness occasioned by revelry, *bach-thinneas;* a house of revelry, *baoisleach.*

REVENGE, *v. a.* Gabh dioghaltas, diol, thoir aichbheil, àichbheilich. Revenge me, *diol mi.*

REVENGE, *s.* Dioghaltas, dioghalt, dioladh; peanas; agart. Take revenge, *gabh dioghaltas.*

REVENGEFUL, *a.* Dioghaltach; dogaltach. Revengefully, *gu dioghaltach.*

REVENGEMENT, *s.* Dioghaltas, peanas.

REVENGER, *s.* Fear dioghaltais; peanasair.

REVENUE, *s.* Tighinn stigh, teachd stigh, màl; cis. The revenue of the kingdom, *tighinn stigh rioghachd.*

REVERBERANT, *a.* Ath-fhuaimneach; fuaimearra.

REVERBERATE, *v. a.* Ath-fhuaim, dean ath-fhuaim, ath-ghairm.

REVERBERATION, *s.* Ath-fhuaimnich, ath-ghairm.

REVERBERATING, *a.* Ath-fhuaimneach.

REVERE, *v. a.* Urramaich, thoir urram, thoir meas, onoirich.

REVERENCE, *s.* Meas, mòr-mheas, urram, ard-urram, miagh; ùmhlachd, onoir, modh, striochd. Want of reverence, *dìth modh, mi-mhodh.*

REVERENCE, *v. a.* Urramaich, thoir urram.

REVEREND, *a.* Measail, urramach, oirdheirc, ionmheasta.

REVEREND, *s.* Ministear.

REVERENT, REVERENTIAL, *a.* Iriosal, umhal, umhlachd-ail, striochdail.

REVERENTLY, *adv.* Gu modhail, gu striochdail.

REVERER, *s.* Fear a bheir urram, fear a ni striochd.

REVERSAL, *s.* Atharrachadh breitheanais.

REVERSE, *v. a.* Cuir bun os cionn; atharraich, mùth, tiond-aidh, caochail.

REVERSE, *s.* Caochladh, atharrach, mùth; taobh cùin air nach 'eil an ceann. It is the very reverse, *is e cheart chaochladh th' ann.*

REVERSIBLE, *a.* Atharrachail.

REVERSION, *s.* Ath-shealbhachadh; còir sealbhachaidh.

REVERT, *v. a.* and *n.* Mùth, atharruich; tiondaidh, pill.

REVERY, REVERIE, *s.* Smuaine, trom-smuaine; beachd-smuaine.

REVEST, *v. a.* Ath-chòmhdaich; ath-chuir an seilbh, cuir an seilbh a ris.

REVESTIARY, *s.* Seomar éide.

REVICTION, *s.* Ath-bheothachadh; ath-theachd gu beath.

REVIEW, *v. a.* Rannsaich; sgrud; ath-sgrud, beachdaich, ath-bheachdaich, gabh beachd; ath-sheall.

REVIEW, *s.* Rannsuchadh; ath-sgrudadh, beachdachadh, ath-bheachdachadh; ath-shealltuinn.

REVIEWER, *s.* Rannsuchair.

REVILE, *v. a.* Càin, maslaich, tarcuisich, dean tàir (no) tarcuis. Reviled, *maslaichte, tarcuisichte.*

REVILER, *s.* Fear càinidh, fear tarcuis, maslachair.

REVILINGLY, *adv.* Gu tàireil, gu tarcuiseach, gu spìdeil.

REVISAL, *s.* Ath-bheachdachadh, ath-leughadh; ath-sgrud-adh, ath-cheasnachadh.

REVISE, *v. a.* Ath-leugh, leugh a ris; ath-bheachdaich, ath-sgrud, ath-cheasnuich.

REVISE, *s.* Ath-leughadh; ath-bheachdachadh, ath-sgrud-adh.

REVISER, *s.* Sgrudair, ceasnachair, fear sgrudaidh, fear ceasnachaidh.

REVISION, *s.* Ath-leughadh, ath-bheachdachadh.

REVISIT, *v.* Rach a dh' fhaicinn a ris.

REVIVAL, *s.* Ath-bheothachadh.

REVIVE, *v. a.* and *n.* (*Bring to life again*), ath-bheothaich; (*renew*), ùraich; (*come to life again*), thig beò a ris; thig h-uige; (*encourage*), dùisg, brosnuich; (*take courage*), glac misneach.

REVIVED, *part.* and *a.* (*Brought to life again*), ath-bheoth-aichte; (*renewed*), ùraichte; (*encouraged*), brosnuichte, air teachd h-uige, air tighinn h-uige.

REVIVER, *s.* Ath-bheothachair, brosnuchair, fear brosnuch-aidh.

REVIVIFICATION, *s.* Ath-bheothachadh.

REVIVING, *a.* Beothail, beathail, beothachail.

REVOCABLE, *a.* Atharrachail, a ghabhas atharrachadh, a dh' fhaotar atharrachadh.

REVOCATE, *v. a.* Gairm air ais, ais-ghairm.

REVOCATION, *s.* Ais-ghairm; atharrachadh.

REVOKE, *v. a.* Ais-ghairm, ath-ghairm; gairm air ais, atharraich.

REVOLT, *v. n.* Dean ceannairc, dean àr a mach, ceannair-cich; éirich. They revolted, *rinn iad ceannairc* (*no*) *àr a mach; dh' éirich iad.*

REVOLT, *s.* Ceannairc, àr a mach; éirigh.

REVOLTER, *s.* Ceannairceach, fear àr a mach.

REVOLVE, *v. a.* and *n.* Uim-ròl; (*in the mind*), cnuasaich, beachd-smuainich.

REVOLUTION, *s.* Cuairt; uim-ròladh; atharrachadh; ceann-airc; teachd Righ Uilleam 's Mhàiri.

REVOLUTIONARY, *a.* Ceannairceach.

REVOMIT, *v. a.* Sgeith; ath-sgeith.

REVULSION, *s.* Tarruing air ais, ath-tharruing.

REVULSIVE, *a.* Ath-thairneach, as-thairneach.

REWARD, *v.* Ath-dhiol, diol, pàigh; thoir luidheachd. Rewarded, *pàighte, diolta;* he is rewarded, *tha e paighte, fhuair e 'dhuais;* he is well rewarded, *tha e air a dheagh phàigh.*

Reward, *s.* Diol, dioladh, pàigh, duais, tuarasdal, diol-thuarasdal, luach-saoithreach, luaigheachd, meacan.
Rewardable, *a.* Ion-dhioladh, ion-dhiolta.
Rewarder, *s.* Fear diolaidh, diolair, dioladair.
Rhapsodist, *s.* Ard-ghlòraiche.
Rhapsody, *s.* Glòr, ard-ghlòr, cainnt ard-ghlòrach.
Rhetoric, *s.* Ùr-labhradh, snàs-labhairt; briathrachas, uirighioll.
Rhetorical, *a.* Ùr-labbradh, briathrach; deas-bhriathrach, deas-chainnteach, uirighiollach.
Rhetorically, *adv.* Gu h-ùrlabhradh, gu deas-bhriathrach, gu deas-chainnteach.
Rhetorician, *s.* Snàs-labhairtiche; òraideach, òraidear.
Rheum, *s.* Tias, mùsgan, cailidear.
Rheuminess, *s.* Musganachd.
Rheumatism, *s.* Lòinidh; alt-ghalar, alt-thinneas, nimhneachan.
Rheumy, *a.* Loinidheach; mùsgach, mùsganach.
Rhinoceros, *s.* Uile-bhéist a chithear sna h-Innseachan shios, le adharc air a shròin; treun-adhairceach, sròin-adhairceach.
Rhodomontade, *s.* Bòsd, spagluinn; baoth-sheanachas.
Rhodomontade, *v. a.* Bòsdainn, dean bòsd (no) spagluinn.
Rhomb, *s.* Nì sam bi ceithir shliosnach aig am bheil a cheithir oisnean biorach is co-ionnan, agus a shliosnan comhfhad; ni sam bi air an dealbh cheudna.
Rhomboid, *s.* Turbaid.
Rhomboidal, *a.* Turbaideach, mar thurbaid.
Rhombus, *s.* See Rhomb.
Rhubarb, *s.* Purgaid, luibh phurgaideach, rurgaid.
Rhyme, *s.* Rann; dàn; dràn, dràmag, reimeas, ramas; rannachd, ranndachd; bardachd. Extemporaneous rhyme, *rith-learg.*
Rhyme, *v. a.* and *n.* Rannaich, dean rannachd, dean rann.
Rhymer, *s.* Bard, rannair, fear rannachd, duanair; duanaiche; sriutaiche.
Rhyming, *s.* Bardachd; duanaireachd.
Rib, *s.* Aisinn; aisne, cliath; stiom; (*a wife*), bean; (*of a boat*), tarsuinnean, tarsnan.
Ribald, *s.* Baobh, bansgul; trusdar; *adjectively*, drabasda.
Ribaldry, *s.* Cainnt ana-cneasta; draosdachd; draosdaireachd.
Ribbed, *a.* Aisneach, cleathach, cliathach; airbheach, stiomach.
Riband, **Ribbon**, *s.* Riobain, ribean; bann, stiom, sròl.
Ribs, *s. pl.* Aisnean; (*of a vessel*), fiughrach luinge no bàta, tarsuingean, tarsuinnean.
Ribwort, *s.* Slàn-lus.
Rice, *s.* Rìs, seorsa gràin.
Rich, *a.* Beartach, beairteach, saibhir, toiceil, toiceach; (*valuable*), costail, luachmhor, prìseil, ainneamh; (*fruitful*), pailt, torrach; tarbhach, lionmhor, reamhar. Make rich, *dean beartach;* grow rich, *fàs (no) cinn beartach;* rich ground, *talamh torrach (no) tarbhach;* as rich as he is, *air bheartaichead sa bheil e.*
Riches, *s.* Beartas, beairteas, saibhreas, maoin, stòras, earras, pailteas, toic.
Richly, *adv.* Gu beartach, gu beairteach, gu saibhir; gu pailt, gu prìseil; gu h-ainneamh. Richly ornamented, *sgeadaichte, gu h-ainneamh;* he richly deserved punishment, *is maith a thoill e peanas, a dheagh thoill e peanas.*
Richness, *s.* Beartas, beairteas, saibhreas, maoin, stòras, toic, earras; (*of land*), torraichead.

Rick, *s.* Ruchd, ruchdan, rucan, cruach; cuidhleag, còil, mulan feòir (no) arbhair, currachdag.
Rickets, *s.* Teannadh, seòrsa tinneis leinibh.
Ricture, *s.* Meanan; fosgladh; sgath, sgag, sgolt.
Rid. See **Ride**.
Rid, *v. a.* Saor, cuir saor, fuasgail; cuir air falbh; dìobair, fuadaich. Your innocence will rid you, *saoraidh do neochiontas thu;* rid from, *fuasgailte;* get rid of him, *faigh cuit dheth; cuir air falbh e; cuir as an rathad e, marbh e;* ridding, *a fuasgladh, a reiteachadh.*
Riddance, *s.* Fuasgladh; saoradh, cuiteachadh; réiteachadh.
Ridding, *s.* Fuasgladh, saoradh; cuiteachadh; réiteachadh.
Riddle, *s.* Toimhseachan, dubh-cheisd, cruaidh-cheisd.
Riddle, *s.* Ruideal; criathar, gàbaidh, rillean.
Riddle, *v. a.* Ruidealich, ruidie, rill; (*solve*), fuasgail.
Ride, *v. a.* Marcaich, marcuich, rach cas gobhlach air ni; (*domineer*), smachdaich. Ride hard, *cruaidh-mharcaich;* he rid, *mharcaich e;* he rode past, *mharcaich e seachad, chaidh e seachad air muin eich.*
Rider, *s.* Marcair, marcaiche. Riders, *marcairean, marcaichean;* a good rider, *deagh mharcair.*
Ridgel, **Ridgeling**, *s.* Ruige, ruigleachan, rigleachan, reithe spoghta, reithe spoighte.
Ridge, *s.* Druim, croit, cruit, mullach; creachann, aonach; gead; (*in plowing*), iomaire, sgriob. The ridge-bone, *cnaimh na droma;* a ridge or flute, *clais.*
Ridge, *v. a.* Dean iomair, dean sgriob; dean clais.
Ridgy, *a.* Dromanach, druimeanach, binneanach.
Ridgeband, *s.* Dromach.
Ridicule, *s.* Fanaid, fanoid, fochaid, magadh, sgeig; dìmeas, spòrsa; fearas chuideachd.
Ridicule, *v. a.* Mag air, fanaid air; dean fòchaid, dean sgeig, dean ealaidh. He ridiculed him, *rinn e fochaid air, rinn e baothair dheth, rinn e ball magaidh dheth.*
Ridiculous, *a.* Aithreach, aighearach, neònach; amaid.
Ridiculously, *adv.* Gu h-aithreach, gu h-aighearach, gu neònach.
Riding, *s.* Marcachd, marcachadh; earann dùthcha. Tired with riding, *sgìth marcachd.*
Riding, *part.* A màrcachd. Riding astraddle, *a marcachd cas gobhlach.*
Riding-habit, *s.* Culaidh mharcachd, culaidh mharcaich, eudach marcaiche.
Riding-coat, *s.* Còt marcaich.
Riding-hood, *s.* Seorsa curaic.
Rife, *a.* Pailt, lionmhor, cumanta, coitchionn; barachdail.
Rifeness, *s.* Pailteas; lionmhorachd.
Riff-raff, *s.* Prabar; trusdaireachd.
Riffle, *v. a.* Spùinn, spùill, creach, slad; goid; glac, robainn.
Rifler, *s.* Spùinneadair; creachadair, goidiche, mearleach, robair, fear reubainn.
Rift, *s.* (*Split*), sgolt, sgoltadh, sgagadh, gag; (*belch*), brùchd, brùchdadh, roichd.
Rift, *v. a.* and *n.* (*Split*), sgoilt, sgag, sgàin; (*belch*), brùchd, roichd.
Rig, *s.* Striopach, siùrsach, meirdreach, bidse; gogaill.
Rig, *v. a.* Uigheamaich; sgeadaich, éid, deasaich. Rigged, *uigheamaichte; deasaichte.*
Rigadoon, *s.* Seorsa dannsaidh.
Rigation, *s.* Fliuchadh, uisgeachadh.
Rigging, *s.* Achduinn luing; siùil agus acfhuinn luing.

RIGGISH, *a.* Siùrsachail; striopachail, drùiseil, neo-gheimnidh, mi-bhandaidh, macnusach; eutrom, gaoithe, gogailleach.

RIGHT, *a.* Ceart; cubhaidh; freagarrach; (*straight*), dìreach; (*honest*), onorach, treibhdhireach, còir; (*in health*), slàn; (*true*), fior, fìreannach. The right hand, *an lamh cheart;* right forward, *dìreach air adhairt;* right well, *sàr mhath; làn mhath, ro cheart;* I know him right well, *is aithne dhomh e gu làn mhath;* to the right hand, *chum na laimh deise;* right against the wind, *dìreach (no) calg dhìreach an aghaidh na gaoithe;* not right, *ceàrr, docharach, air aimhreidh, cli;* right or wrong, *ceart no docharach, ceart no cearr;* make right, *cuir ceart.*

RIGHT, *s.* Ceartas, ceirte; còir, dlighe; firinn; comas, ughdarras. You have no right to it, *cha 'n 'eil còir agad air;* by rights, *le ceartas;* better speak than lose right, *is fhearr guth no méithe.*

RIGHT, *adv.* Gu ceart, gu freagarrach, gu fior, gu h-onorach. You did quite right, *rinn thu gu ro cheart, rinn thu gu ro mhath.*

RIGHT, *v. a.* Ceartaich, cuir ceart, cuir gu doigh, thoir ceartas.

RIGHTEOUS, *a.* Fìreannach, fìrinneach, fior, tréibhdhireach, còir, math, ionraic, cothromach; subhailceach. Righteously, *gu fìrinneach, gu fìreannach, gu tréibhdhireach, gu còir, gu h-ionraic, gu cothromach.*

RIGHTEOUSNESS, *s.* Fìreanntachd, fìrinn, treibhdhireas, ionracas.

RIGHTFUL, *a.* Dligheach, dligheil, dlisteanach, ceart, laghail; còir, ionraic. Rightfully, *gu dligheach, a réir dlighe, a réir ceartais.*

RIGHTFULNESS, *s.* Ceirte, dligheachas; laghaileachd.

RIGHTLY, *adv.* Gu ceart, a réir ceartais, gu freagarrach, gu h-iomchuidh; gu h-ionraic; gu dìreach.

RIGHTNESS, *s.* Ceirte; fìrinn.

RIGID, *a.* Rag, do-lùbaidh; forganta, doirbh; dùr, duranta, cruaidh, fuar, leacanta; teann, geur, geur-theann.

RIGIDITY, *s.* Raige, raigsinn; do-lùbachd; dorgantas; dùiread, durantachd, cruas.

RIGIDLY, *adv.* Gu rag, gu do-lubaidh, gu dorganta, gu dùr, gu dùranta; gu cruaidh; gu fuar, gu leacanta; gu teann, gu geur.

† RIGOL, *s.* Cearcall, cuairteag.

RIGOROUS, *a.* Cruaidh, ain-iochdmhor, cruadalach, gàbhaidh; pongail.

RIGOROUSLY, *adv.* Gu cruaidh, gu h-ain-iochdmhor, gu cruadalach, gu gabhaidh, gu pongail.

RIGOUR, *s.* Fuachd; crith-fhuachd; cruas, ain-iochd, déine.

RILL, RILLET, *s.* Sruthan, caochan, allt, alltan, srùlag.

RIM, *s.* Foir, oir, iomall, bile.

RIME, *s.* Liath, reoth, crith-reotha.

RIME, *v. a.* Reòt, ròt, reoth.

RIMPLE, *v. a.* Preas, preasaich, preasagaich, liurc, cas.

RIMY, *a.* Ceòthar; ceo-bhraonach, ceòbhranach; tais, liath le reotha.

RIND, *s.* Rùsg, plaosg, sgrath, cochull, cairt.

RIND, *v. a.* Rùisg, plaoisg, cairt.

RING, *s.* Fàinne, fàil; foir; ailbheag, failbheag, cearcall, cuairteag; naisg, cruinneag; gleang. An ear-ring, *fàinne cluais, cluigean cluais;* a ring of people, *croilean sluaigh.*

RING, *v. a.* and *n.* Seinn, buail, beum, fuaim. Ring the bell, *seinn an clag, buail an clag;* the sky rung again with the shouts, *dh' ath-fhuaim na speuran leis a chaithream.*

RINGDOVE, *s.* Smùdan; fearan, columan coille.

RINGER, *s.* (*Of bells*), fear cluig.

RINGING, *s.* Seinneadh (no) bualadh chlag, † aothachd.

RINGLEADER, *s.* Ceann; ceann feudhna; ceann gràisge.

RINGLET, *s.* Dual, dualan, dualag, bachlag, ciabh, ciabhag, fàineag, cearclag. Full of ringlets, *dualach, bachlagach.*

RINGSTREAKED, *a.* Stiallach, srianach, riabhach, ballach, tàr-gheal.

RINGTAIL, *s.* Bréid air tòin, seorsa clamhain.

RINGWORM, *s.* Durag chuairteach, cuairt-dhurag.

RINSE, *v. a.* Sruthail, nigh, ruinnse, ruinnsich. Rinsed, *sruthailte, nighte, ruinnsichte.*

RINSER, *s.* Sruthlair, nigheadair.

RIOT, *s.* (*Tumult*), tuasaid, tabaid, caonnag, mi-riaghailt, aimhreite, buaireas; (*debauch*), neo-mheasarrachd, ruitearachd. Make a riot, *tog buaireas (no) aimhreite.*

RIOT, *v. n.* Dean ruit (no) ruitearachd; tog buaireas, tog aimhreite.

RIOTER, *s.* Fear aimhreite.

RIOTOUS, *a.* Tuaiseadeach, tuasaideach, buaireasach, ruitearach, neo-mheasarra, ceannasach.

RIOTOUSLY, *adv.* Gu tuasaideach, gu neo-mheasarra, gu buaireasach.

RIOTOUSNESS, *s.* Tuasaideachd, buaireasachd, ruitearachd, neo-mheasarrachd.

RIP, *v.* Srac, sracbd, strachd, reub, strachd suas, srachd as a chéile, sgàin; sgoilt; nochd, innis, foillsich, leig ris. He ripped up its belly, *shrachd e suas a bhrù;* he ripped up all their doings, *leig e ris an gniomharan gu h-iomlan.*

RIPE, *a.* Abaich, abuich, abuidh, foirfe; foirfidh; ionbhuainte; inmheach; iomlàn. Ripely, *gu h-abaich.*

RIPEN, *v. a.* and *n.* Abuich, fàs abuich.

RIPENESS, *s.* Abachd, abaidheachd, abuichead; iomlanachd, foirfeachd.

RIPPER, *s.* Reubair, srachdair.

RIPPLE, *v. n.* Faochanaich; fraochanaich.

RIPPLING, *a.* Faochanach, faochagach; cuairteagach.

RISE, *v. n.* Éirich; dìrich; bris a mach, dean ceannairc, dean àr a mach. What made you rise so soon? *ciod a thug ort éiridh cho moch?* rise up, *eirich suas, eirich 'n airde.*

RISE, *s.* (*Ascending*), éiridh, éirigh; dìreadh; (*origin*), toiseach, tùs; aobhar; ceann, tobar, bun. Sunrise, *éirigh na gréine.*

RISEN, *part.* Air éiridh.

RISER, *s.* Fear éirigh; fear ceannairc. An early riser, *fear moch-éiridh.*

RISIBLE, *a.* Gàireachail, gàireachdaich, gàir.

RISK, *s.* Cunnart, cuntart, sgiorradh, guasachd.

RISK, *v. a.* Cuir an cunnart.

RITE, *s.* Deas-ghnàth.

RITUAL, *a.* Deas-ghnàthach.

RITUAL, *s.* Leabhar dheas-ghnàth.

RITUALIST, *s.* Deas-ghnàthaiche, fear deas-ghnàth.

RIVAL, *s.* (*Competition*), co-dheuchainniche, co-shaoithriche; † riobhlach. In love, *co-shuiriche, co-ghraidhean, co-leannan.*

RIVAL, *a.* Comh-strigheach; spairneach, spairneil, cospairneach, eudmhor.

RIVALRY, *s.* Comh-dheuchainn, co-dheuchainneachd, comh-eud, naimhdeas, spairn.

RIVALSHIP, *s.* Comh-eud, spairn.

RIVE, *v. a.* and *n.* Reub, sracbd, strac, strachd; sgàin, sgoilt, sgag.

RIVEL, *v. a.* Cas, preas, preasagaich, liurc. Rivelled, *preasagaichte.*

RIVEN, *part.* Reubta, srachdta, sgàinte.

RIVER, *s.* Amhainn, abhainn, sruth, cuisge; allt, †dothar, †dobhar, †snuadh. The river's side, *taobh na aibhne.*

RIVER-DRAGON, *s.* Croghall mòr.

RIVERET, *s.* Alltan, amhainn bheag.

RIVER-HORSE, *s.* Each uisge.

RIVET, *s.* Sparrag teannachain, drithlean.

RIVET, *v. a.* Sparr, teannaich, gramaich.

RIVULET, *s.* Sruthan, allt, alltan, caochan, srùlag.

RIXDOLLAR, *s.* Cùinn as fhiach ceithir agus sé sgillinn.

ROACH, *s.* Breac mara, roisteach.

ROAD, *s.* Rod, rathad, slighe, aisridh, aisrith; innteach; ionnsuidh, turus; (*for ships*), poll marcaich, bàdh, bàdhan, òban. The high road, *an rathad mòr;* the great military road, *rathad mòr an righ;* a bad road, *droch rathad;* a level road, *rathad còmhnard.*

ROAM, *v. n.* Seabhaid; rach air seachran, rach gu taobh, bi san athmanaich.

ROAMER, *s.* Seabhaidiche, seachranaiche; fògaraiche, fear cùirn.

ROAN, *a.* Gris-fhionn, riabhach, odhar, glas.

ROAR, *v. n.* Beuc, geum, eubh, éigh, glaodh, sgairt; bùir, bùirich, langanaich, roichd; gàir, burral, ulfhart.

ROAR, *s.* Beuc, beucadh, geum, roichd, eubh, éigh glaodh, sgairt, bùireadh, tailmrich, burralaich, ulfhartaich.

ROARER, *s.* Beucair, geumair, roichdear.

ROARING, *s.* Beucail, beucaich, geumnaich, roichdil, bùbail, eighich, glaodhaich, bùirich, tailmrich, basraich.

ROAST, *s.* Ròst, ròstadh, feòil ròiste. Rule the roast, *smachdaich.*

ROAST, *v. a.* Ròist.

ROASTING, *s.* Ròstadh. He got a roasting, *fhuair e 'ròstadh.*

ROB, *v. a.* Spùinn, spùill, robainn, creach, slad, goid. Robbed, *spùinnte, creachte, robainnte.*

ROBBER, *s.* Spùinneadair, spùilleadair, creachadair, reubainnear, robair, goidiche, foghluiche.

ROBBERY, *s.* Reubainn, robaireachd, spuinneadh, spùille, creach; foirneart. What harm in the robbery if we are not the poorer? *ciod is misde duine a chreach, mar lughaid a phòr e?*

ROBBING, *s.* Spùinneadh, robainneadh, spùilleadh, creachadh, goideadh.

ROBE, *v. a.* Éid, sgeadaich, còmhdaich.

ROBE, *s.* Earradh, trusgan, sgeadachadh, fàluing, falluing, gùn.

ROBIN, *s.* Bru-dhearg; broinn dearg, broinn-deargachan.

ROBUST, †ROBUSTIOUS, *a.* Garbh, làidir, calma, neartmhor, comasach, ruaimneach, riongach, blosgach, bunanta, lùthar, féitheach. A robust fellow, *seirsealach.*

ROBUSTNESS, *s.* Neart, tréine, spionnadh, ruaimneachd.

ROCHET, *s.* Gùn uachdrach sagairt; léine aifrionn; seorsa éisg.

ROCK, *s.* Carraig, carruig, creag, craig; roc; sgòr-bheann; (*distaff*), cuigeal. A rock of offence, *carruig oilbheum.*

ROCKY, *a.* Creagach, cragach, carraigeach, garbh; clochach, cruaidh, rocach. Hard rocky ground, *sgreagan, crachann.*

ROCK, *v. a.* Luaisg, siùd, siùdanaich; seòg, seòganaich; cuir chodal, tàlaidh. Rock the cradle, *luaisg a chreadhal.*

ROCKET, *s.* Seorsa obair theine.

ROCKWORK, *s.* Obair gharbh; obair chreagach.

ROD, *s.* Slat, slatag; barrag; sgiùrsadh, cuip, colbh, eachlasg; cleath, cliath.

RODE, *pret.* of ride. Mharcaich. See RIDE.

ROE, *s.* Earb; maoisleach; seorsa feidh a tha ro lionmhor anns a Ghaidhealtachd; iùchair éisg. What made the roe take to the water? *ciod chuir an earb san loch?* roes (deer), *earbaichean;* (of fish), *iuchraichean éisg.*

ROEBUCK, *s.* Boc-earb.

ROGATION, *s.* Asluchadh, athchuinge, grios, ùrnuigh. Rogation-week, *seachduin na h-ath-chuinge.*

ROGUE, *s.* Crochair, cluainear, daighear, rogair, slaoightear, sloightir, mealltair, cealgair, gaduiche, goidiche, bleidear, calma, neallair. A rogue in grain, *dearg chrochair, crochair as an aghaidh;* the rogue thinks every one a thief, *saoilidh bradaich nam bruach gur goidich uile càch.*

ROGUERY, *s.* Crochaireachd, cluainearachd, sloightearachd, cealgaireachd, bleideireachd, mealltaireachd, rogaireachd.

ROGUISH, *a.* Cealgach, sloighteil, bleideach, bleideil, ceabhachdach.

ROIST, ROISTER, *v. n.* Dean gleadhraich.

ROISTER, *s.* Rantair, straoidhlear, buamsdair.

ROLL, *v. a.* Ruidhil, ròl, caruich; fill; robhainn; cuir car air char; tonn-luaisg.

ROLL, *s.* Ròladh, ròl, ruidhleadh, carachadh, filleadh, rodhainn, ròlag, rodha, sgròl, ròl sgriobhaidh. A roll of carded wool, *rolag;* a roll *or* volume, *ròl, ròlan, rolag.*

ROLLER, *s.* Ruidhlear, ròlair; rodhair; crios, stiom, bann, foirneachan.

ROLLING, *s.* Ròladh, ruidhleadh, caruchadh; (*at sea*), tonnluasgach.

ROLLING, *part.* and *a.* A ròladh, a ruidhleadh, a caruchadh, tonn-luasgach, luasganach. A rolling wave, *bàir-linn.*

ROMAGE, *s.* Rannsuchadh, sireadh.

ROMANCE, *s.* Faoin-sgeul, fionn-sgeul, ur-sgeul, baoth-sgeul, sgeulachd, do-sgeul, brasgeul; ràcaireachd, ruanachd; riseach.

ROMAN-CATHOLIC, *s.* Pàpanach.

ROMANCE, *v.* Innis sgeul, abair breug.

ROMANTIC, *a.* Fiadhaidh; faoin, faoin-sgeulach, neo-choslach, neo-fhior, fiadhaich.

ROME, *s.* An Roimh.

ROMISH, *a.* Pàpanach, Ròmanach, Roimheach.

ROMP, *s.* Caile bhalach; cluiche, ioladh, ealaidh.

ROMP, *v.* Cluich le stairn.

RONDEAU, *s.* Ranndadh.

RONION, *s.* Brounag, té bheag reamhar, tòmag, tònag.

RONT, *s.* Meanbhlach spreidh.

ROOD, *s.* Ròd, an ceithreamh cuid dh' acair; sé troidh deug air fad; (*cross*), crois, crann ceusaidh.

ROODLOFT, *s.* Lobhta na crois, lobhta air an cuirear a chrois agus iomhaighean nan naomh.

ROOF, *s.* Mullach, mullach tighe, druim tighe, cleith; (*of the mouth*), uachdar a chàirein, carbad uachdrach. Under my roof, *fo mo chleith.*

ROOF, *v. a.* Cuir mullach (no) druim air; cuir ann an tigh.

ROOK, *s.* Cnaimheach; ròcas; (*cheat*), cealgair, mealltair, rogair.

ROOK, *v. a.* Thoir an car a; meall.

ROOKERY, *s.* Ionad ròcais; aite sam bith ròcais a neadachadh, nid ròcais.

ROOKERY, *a.* Ròcasach; làn ròcais.

ROOM, *s.* (*Chamber*), seòmar, seumar; (*space*), rum; farsuingeachd; (*place*), aite; ionad. A back room, *seòmar cùil;* a front room, *seòmar beòil;* a drawing room, *seòmar conaltradh;*

he will come in my room, *thig e ann am àite;* I have no room, *cha 'n 'eil rum agam;* I have no room to turn, *cha 'n 'eil comas carachaidh agam;* make room, *rach gu taobh.*

ROOMAGE, *s.* Farsuingeachd, aite, rum.

ROOMINESS, *s.* Farsuingeachd, àite, rum.

ROOMY, *a.* Farsuing, mòr, leathan, rùmar.

ROOST, *s.* Spàr, spàr chearc, spàrdan, iris, iris chearc, fàradh; codal.

ROOST, *v. n.* Rach air spàr, codail mar eunlaith.

ROOT, *s.* Freumh; stoc, bun; tùs, mathair aobhair, aobhar; meacan. From the root, *as an fhreumh, as a bhun;* root and branch, *eadar bhun is bhàrr.*

ROOT, *v. a.* and *n.* Freumhaich, gabh freumh; suidhich, daingnich, daighnich; spìon as a bhun; bùraich.

ROOTED, *a.* Freumhaichte; teann, daingean, suidhichte, domhain, bunaiteach. A rooted evil, *olc suidhichte;* rootedly, *gu teann, gu daingean, gu suidhichte, gu domhain.*

ROOTING, *s.* Freumhachadh; spìonadh as a bhun.

ROOTY, *a.* Freumhach; rithinn.

ROPE, *s.* Cord, taod, ròp, teud; sreang, tobha, sugan, cabal, ball. Ropes, *cùird, taodan, ròpaichean, teudan;* (of onions), *dos, buinnse, cordaidh.* A rope of straw, *sìomun;* a hempen rope, *cord còrcach.*

ROPE, *v. n.* Rithnich, fàs rithinn (no) sreangach.

ROPEDANCER, *s.* Cord-chleasaiche, ur a dhannsas air cord.

ROPEDANCING, *s.* Cord-chleasachd.

ROPEMAKER, *s.* Cordair, cord-fhigheadair.

ROPEMAKING, *s.* Obair chord, cord-fhigheadaireachd, cordaireachd.

ROPERY, *s.* Crochaireachd, droch bheairt.

ROPINESS, *s.* Rithineachd, rithinneachd, ridhinneachd.

ROPY, *a.* Rithinn.

ROQUELAURE, *s.* Cleòc (no) clòc fir; cloc mòr, carrasaid.

RORID, *a.* Drùchdach, driùchdach, dealtach.

RORIFEROUS, *a.* Drùchdach, driùchdach, driùchdar, dealtach.

RORIFLUENT, *a.* Ruith le dealt.

ROSARY, *s.* Paidearan, paidirean Pàpanaich.

ROSA SOLIS, *s.* Ròs soluis.

ROSCID, *a.* Driùchdach, drùchdach.

ROSE, *s.* Ròs; plùran, plùirean, blàth. A red rose, *ròs dearg;* a white rose, *ròs geall;* a place where roses grow, *ròsarnach.*

ROSE, *pret.* of rise. Dh' éirich. See RISE.

ROSED, *a.* Dearg, ruiteach.

ROSEATE, *a.* Ròsach, blàthmhor, dearg, ruiteach, dathta, dathte.

ROSE-GARDEN, *s.* Ròsarnach.

ROSEMARY, *s.* Ròs-mhàiri; ròs sìor-gheal.

ROSE-NOBLE, *s.* Cùin Sasunnach a b' fhiach sé sgillinn deug Sasunnach.

ROSE-TREE, *s.* Preas ròs, ròs chrann.

ROSE-WATER, *s.* Uisge ròs.

ROSIN, RESIN, *s.* Ròsaid, ròiseid; ice.

ROSIN, RESIN, *v. a.* Rub le ròsaid.

ROSSEL, *s.* Seorsa talmhainn.

ROSSELY, *a.* Eutrom mar chuid sheòrsan talmhainn.

ROSTRUM, *s.* Gob; toiseach luing; crannag, cùbait, pùbait.

ROSY, *a.* Ròsail, dearg, ruiteach, dearg mar an ròs.

ROT, *v. a.* and *n.* Grod, lobh, breun; malc; fàs grod, fàs lobhach. Lie there till you rot, *luidh an sin gus an grod thu.*

ROT, *s.* (*Disease*), galar teth, galar chaorach; (*in wood*), malcadh tiorram.

ROTARY, *a.* Cuairteach, ruithteach, cuidhleach, saiothanach.

ROTATION, *s.* Ròladh, ruithleadh, car. You shall have it by rotation, *gheibh sibh e car mu 'n cuairt.*

ROTE, *v.* Faigh air chuimhne, faigh (no) ionnsuich air do theangadh.

ROTE, *s.* Focaill air an teangaidh, focaill air an ionnsach air an teanga (no) air a chridhe. He has it by rote, *tha e aig air a chridhe* (*no*) *air a theangaidh.*

ROTTEN, *a.* Grod, lobhta, lobhach, loibheach, malcta, lobh, breun. A rotten sore, *guirean breun, lot breun.*

ROTTENNESS, *s.* Groide, grodlachd, lobhadh.

ROTUND, *a.* Cruinn.

ROTUNDITY, *s.* Cruinnead; cruinne; cruinnealachd.

ROUGE, *s.* Dearg, dath dearg.

ROUGH, *a.* Garbh; (*hairy*), molach, ròmach, ròinneach; ròbach, catanach; (*grim*), gruamach, gnò; (*boisterous*), dobhaidh, gailbheach, garbh, gàbhaidh, doinionnach, stuadh-ghreannach; (*in temper*), sgaiteach, sgaithteach, coimheach, gailbheach, doirbh; (*in taste*), garg, searbh, geur, goirt; (*prickly*), dealgach, biorach; (*rocky*), garbh, creagach, clachach. The rough bounds, *na garbh-chriochan;* rough-hewn or unmannerly, *balachail, neo-sgilmeil, mi-mhodhail, baoghalta;* rough weather, *aimsir ghailbheach;* rough or proud, *uaibhreach, ardanach, sgòdail;* rough places lying untilled, *garbhlach.*

ROUGHCAST, *v. a.* Tilg (no) dealbh air chor eigin.

ROUGHCAST, *s.* Ceud thilgeadh, dealbh gun snàs.

ROUGH-DRAUGHT, *s.* Ceud-tharruing.

ROUGHEN, *v. a.* and *n.* Dean garbh, fàs garbh; fàs gruamach, sgaithteach no coimheach; fàs gailbheach. The weather roughened upon us, *dh' fhàs an aimsir gailbheach oirnne.*

ROUGHLY, *adv.* Gu garbh, gu molach, gu ròmach; gu gruamach, gu gnò; gu sgaithteach, gu coimheach, gu gailbheach, gu doirbh; gu garg, gu searbh, gu geur.

ROUGHNESS, *s.* Gairbhe, gairbhead, molaichead, gairge, coimheachas; seirbhe; gailbheachad.

ROUND, *a.* Cruinn; cearclach, slàn; glan, cuimeir, riachdail; pongail, luath; sgairteil. As round as a ball, *cho chruinn ri ball;* a round, unvarnished tale, *sgeul phongail gun snàs;* round about, *mu 'n cuairt;* a round pace, *ceum sgairteil.*

ROUND, *s.* Cuairt; cuairteag, cearcall; car. Take a round, *gabh cuairt.*

ROUND, *adv.* Mu 'n cuairt; air gach taobh; tiomchioll, timchioll. All the year round, *ré na bliadhna.*

ROUND, *v. a.* Dean cruinn; cuairtich; tionndaidh. Rounded, *cruinn;* when I rounded the corner, *nur thionndadh mi 'n oisinn.*

ROUNDELAY, *s.* Dan, duan, luinneag, coilleag.

ROUNDHEAD, *s.* Bearra-phlub, fear leanmhuinn Chrombheil.

ROUNDHOUSE, *s.* Toll-buth, gainntir.

ROUNDISH, *a.* Leth-char cruinn.

ROUNDLY, *adv.* (*In form*), gu cruinn; (*in speech*), gu riachdail, gu pongail; (*in pace*), gu sgairteil, gu luath, gu brisg; (*freely, honestly*), gu h-iomlan; as an aghaidh; a rreamh; (*sharply*), gu geur. Roundly told, *air innseadh gu pongail.*

ROUNDNESS, *s.* Cruinnead; mìnead.

ROUSE, *v. a.* and *n.* Dùisg; caraich; brosnuich; mosgail, brosgail; brod. I roused from myself, *dhùisg mi, mhosgail mi;* he began to rouse, *theann e ri dùsgadh;* roused, *dùisgte, mosgailte, brosnuichte.*

ROUSER, *s.* Dùsgair, mosglair, brosnuchair, brosglair.

ROUSING, *s.* Dùsgadh, carachadh, brosnuchadh, mosgladh, brosgladh, brodadh.

Rousing, *a.* Brosnuchail, mosglach, brosglach.

Rout, *s.* Gangarais, prabar, cumasg sluaigh; (*of an army*), ruaig; (*noise*), tuasaid, gaoir.

Rout, *v. a.* Ruaig, cuir air theich, cuir fo ruaig, sgab, sgiùrs.

Route, *s.* Rathad, rod, slighe.

Rove, *v. a.* and *n.* Seabhaid, rach air iomrol, siubhail gu luaineach. Your mind is always roving, *tha d' inntinn an comhnuidh air iomrol.*

Rover, *s.* Seabhaidiche; fear luaineach; creachadair, creachadair mara, foghluiche mara. At rovers, *gu seabhaideach, gu h-iomrolach, gu luaineach, gun tuairmeis.*

Roving, *a.* Seabhaideach, seachranach; luaineach, neo-shuidhichte, iomrolach.

Row, *s.* Sread, sreath, breath, rang, eang.

Row, *v. a.* Iomair. Rowing, *iomram, iomramh;* rowed, *iomairte, air iomramh.*

Rowel, *s.* Spor, silteach eich.

Rowel, *v. a.* Lot; spor, starr, sparr, stob; cum leòn o leigheas.

Rower, *s.* Iomaraiche, ràmhair, ràmhaiche. A rower's bench, *searbaid, tota.*

Royal, *a.* Rioghail, riogha.

Royalist, *s.* Fear dìleas do 'n rìgh, rìgh-leanmhuinniche.

Royally, *adv.* Gu rioghail.

Royalty, *s.* Rioghalachd.

Roynish, *a.* Crion; balachail, bodachail.

Rub, *v. a.* Rub, suath; tachais; sgriob; teannaich; glan, sgùr. Rub up, *sgùr, mosgail, dùisg, brosnaich;* rubbed, *rubta, suathta, tachaiste, sgriobta, sgùrta.*

Rub, *s.* Rub, rubadh, suath, suathadh; bac, moille; (*in speech*), beum, teum.

Rubber, *s.* Sgriobadair, rubadair, rubair; seorsa eighe; clach gheuraich, clach niaradh.

Rubbish, *s.* Salachar, trusdaireachd, luaithre, mosan, sguilleach.

Rubicund, *a.* Dearg, ruiteach, ruadh.

Rubied, *a.* Dearg.

Rubiform, *a.* Dearg, air dhath dearg.

Rubify, *v. a.* Dearg, deargaich. Rubified, *deargaichte.*

Rubric, *s.* Sgriobhadh dearg, leabhar dearg.

Rubric, *v. a.* Deargaich, dean dearg.

Rubric, *a.* Dearg.

Rubricated, *a.* Dearg, deargaichte.

Ruby, *s.* Ruiteachan, ruban; dearg-sheud; deirge; guirean (no) plucan dearg.

Ruby, *a.* Dearg.

Ructation, *s.* Brùchd, brùchdail, brùchdadh, rùchdail.

Rudder, *s.* Stiùir, sdiùir, falmadair, bior dubh luing.

Ruddiness, *s.* Deirge, ruthadh, ruiteachd.

Ruddle, *s.* Céir dhearg, cill, clach dhath dhearg.

Ruddock, *s.* Am brù-dhearg.

Ruddy, *a.* Dearg, ruiteach, gruaigh-dhearg, ruadh.

Rude, *a.* Borb; balachail, doirbh, mi-mhodhail; brùideil, aineolach, neo-fhoghluimte, neo-shnàsmhor; neo-ghrinn, neo-ealanta; neo-sgileil, neo-theoma, tomanta. A rude wind, *gaoth bhorb.*

Rudely, *adv.* Gu borb, gu balachail, gu doirbh, gu mi-mhodhail, gu neo-fhoghluimte, gu neo-ealanta, gu neo-sgileil, gu tomanta.

Rudeness, *s.* Buirbe; mi-mhodh; brùidealachd; aineolas; deine.

† **Rudesby**, *s.* Buamsdair.

Rudiment, *s.* Ceud thoiseach, toiseach, ceud-fhoghlum, tionnsgnadh, foir-theagasg.

Rudimental, *a.* Ceud-thoiseachail, toiseachail, tionnsgnach, tionnsgnaidh.

Rue, *v. a.* Crean, gabh aithreachas, bi duilich. You will rue it, *gabhaidh tu an t-aithreachas dheth;* I will make you rue it, *bheir mise ort gun crean thu air.*

Rue, *s.* Rugh, ruibh.

Rueful, *a.* Muladach, brònach, dubhach. A rueful look, *sealladh muladach.*

Ruefully, *adv.* Gu muladach, gu bronach.

Ruefulness, *s.* Mulad, bròn, doilghios.

Ruel-bone, *s.* Falman.

Ruff, *s.* Gibeag muineil, frilleag amhaich; seorsa èisg aimhne.

Ruffian, *s.* Crochair; rogair, gearra-choilear, droch-dhuine, mortair.

Ruffian, *a.* Olc, aingidh.

Ruffle, *v. a.* Cuir a ordugh; buair; tog greann mar a ni gaoth air uisge; pleat, cas, fill. Ruffled, *thar a chéile a ordugh, buairte, lan phleata.*

Ruffle, *s.* Frille, frilleag, gibeag; buair, tabaid, aimhreite. Ruffles, *frilleagan.*

Rug, *s.* Brat, stràille, brat teallaich.

Rugged, *a.* Garbh, creagach, cragach, sturrach, neo-chomhnard; bacach, bacanach, stacach, stacanach, molach; (*in manner*), droch-mhuinte, doirbh, borb, brùideil; mi-mhodhail; gailbheach.

Ruggedly, *adv.* Gu garbh, gu creagach, gu cragach, gu bacach, gu bacanach, gu stacach, gu doirbh, gu borb, gu brùideil; gu gailbheach.

Ruggedness, *s.* Gairbhe, gairbhead; buirbe; molaichead, gailbheachad.

Rugine, *s.* Eighe dearg-leigh.

Rugose, *a.* Preasagach, làn phreasag, caisreagach.

Ruin, *s.* Sgrios, leir-sgrios; lom-sgrios; dìth; dioth; mi-shealbh; (*of a house*), làrach. An old ruin, *sean làrach, aois-larach;* it lies in ruins, *tha e na làrach;* silent is the process of ruin, *is samhach an obair dol dholaidh.*

Ruin, *v. a.* Sgrios, léir-sgrios; mill, dean truagh, truaill, tilg sios, leig; (*ruined*), sgriosta, aomta, air sgriosadh, millte, truaillte, caillte, na làrach. Unless you wish to be ruined, *mar àille leat bhith caillte.*

† **Ruinate**, *v. a.* Tilg bun osceionn, tilg sios, sgrios.

Ruination, *s.* Sgrios, sgriosadh, dioth, lom sgrios, léireadh.

Ruiner, *s.* Sgriosadair, milltear, fear sgriosaidh.

Ruinous, *a.* Sgriosail, millteach, sgriosadail; fàsachail, neo-dhluigheil.

Ruinously, *adv.* Gu sgriosail, gu millteach.

Rule, *s.* Riaghailt; aithne; ordugh; riaghladh; smachd, ceannas; (*custom*), nòs, cleachd, gnàth, abhaist; (*example*), eisiomlair, sampull; (*law*), lagh, reachd. The rule of a kingdom, *riaghladh duthcha;* without rule, *gun riaghailt, gun ordugh;* under rule, *fo smachd;* according to rule, *a réir riaghailt.*

Rule, *v. a.* Riaghail; stiùir; riaghailtich; smachdaich; cuir gu doigh. Ruled, *riaghlaichte, smachdaichte;* a well-ruled country, *dùthaich air a deagh riaghladh.*

Ruler, *s.* Uachdaran, ceannard, riaghlair, riaghladair, riaghlachair; (*for lines*), riaghailt; ròlair, rodhair. Rulers, *uachdaranan, ceannardan, flaithean, maithean.*

Rum, *s.* Seorsa dubh làidir air a tharruing o shiucar.

Rum, *s.* Ministear duthcha.

Rumble, *v. n.* Dean torman, druidhil, ruidhil.

Rumbler, *s.* Ramlair, druidhlear.

RUMBLING, *s.* Tormanaiche, torrunn; gleadhraich, straoidhlearachd, rùbail

RUMINANT, *a.* A chnàmhas cìr.

RUMINATE, *v n.* and *a.* Cnàmh cìr; cnuasaich; ath-chagainn, smuaintich.

RUMINATION, *s.* Cnamhadh cìr, cagnadh cìr, ath-chagnadh, cnuasach, cnuasachadh; smuaineachadh.

RUMMAGE, *v. a.* Rannsuich, ruathair; sir.

RUMMAGE, *s.* Rannsach, rannsachadh, ruathar; sir, sireachas; (*confusion*), buaireas, aimhreite.

RUMMAGER, *s.* Rannsachair; fear rannsachaidh.

RUMMER, *s* Gloine; cuach.

RUMOUR, *s.* Fathunn, fathur, iomradh, sgeul. There is a rumour, *tha fathunn ann, tha iad agradh.*

RUMOUR, *v. a* Sgaoil, innis, aithris, abair.

RUMOUR-BEARER, *s.* Fear nuaidheachd.

RUMP, *s* Rumpall, rumball, feaman, bun an earbaill, màs; tòin

RUMPLE, *s.* Preas; preasag; cas, liurc.

RUMPLE, *v.* Preas, preasagaich, liurc, cas; bruth

RUN, *v n* Ruith, greas, steud; teich, (*as a stream*), ruith, sruth; (*melt*), leagh Run quickly, *ruith gu luath;* the river runs past, *tha 'n amhainn a ruith* (*no*) *sruthadh, seachad;* run after, *rach an tòir, sir, lean*, run away with, *ruith air falbh, ruith am fuadach le*, he ran away (eloped) with, *dh' fhalbh e am fuadach leatha*, run out, *ruith a mach*, (as water), *ruith as, teirig, thig gu crìch;* run in with *or* comply, *aontaich le*, run *or* drop, *sil*, run a race, *cuir steud*, run as fast as your feet can carry you, *ruith cho luath is bheir do chasan thu, ruith cho luath 's a tha ann ad chosan, thoir na casan asad*, the boat ran aground, *chaith am bàt air*, they ran away from the field, *theich iad o 'n bhlàr*, run out *or* spend, *caith, cuir a shean, sgap*, run for it, *thoir na buinn* (*no*) *na casan asad*, he ran headlong, *ruith e 'n comhair a chinn*, run mad, *rach gòrrach* (*no*) *air chuthach*, run *or* boil over, *cuir thairis.*

RUN, *v a.* (*Run through* or *stab*), troimh-lot, sàth; (*into danger*), rach an cunnart, (*melt*), leagh Run down *or* pursue, *geur-lean, sàruich, claoidh, ruaig;* run down *or* traduce, *càin;* run upon, *leum air, thoir ionnsuidh air.*

RUN, *s.* Ruithe, réis, steud; gluasad, gluasadh, cùrsa, rod At the long run, *air cheann thall, air a cheann mo dheireadh*, a run before a leap, *rotach, ceum ruithe.*

RUNAGATE, *s.* Dìobarach, fear fuadain

RUNAWAY, *s.* Dìobarach; dìobaireach, fear fuadain, cladhair, gealtair

RUNDLET, *s* Buideal, bairill bheag.

RUNG, *s.* Rong, rongas, cabar.

RUNG See RING.

RUNNEL, *s* Sruthan, srùlag

RUNNER, *s.* Steudair; fear ruithe, gille ruithe; teachdair; (*of a mill*), cloch mhuilinn.

RUNNET, *s.* Leasach, binid, minid; deasgainnean

RUNNING, *s* Ruithe, steudadh; réisearachd. A running together, *comh-ruithe*, a running together of streams, *comar.*

RUNNING, *a* Ruithe; réis, steudach; siùbhlach, luath. A running horse, *each réis.*

RUNNION, *s.* Sgonn, sgonn-bhalach, umaidh.

RUNT, *s.* Mart beag; arrach. Runts, *meanbh-spreidhe.*

RUPTION, *s.* Briseadh, bearnadh, bearn.

RUPTURE, *s.* Briseadh mach; sgàineadh; mam-sioc, siocsgàineadh.

RUPTURE, *v. a.* Bris, sgàin.

RURAL, *a.* Dùchail, dùthcha, tìreil; aodhaireach.

RURICOLIST, *s.* Tuathanach.

RUSH, *s* Luachar, buigneach; ni suarrach sam bi. A rushbed, *leabadh luachair.*

RUSH, *v. a.* Bruchd, ruith, pùc, pùchd, buail air adhairt; sginn, stiall. He rushed upon them, *leum e orra.*

RUSHING, *s* Brùchdadh, ruithe, pùcadh.

RUSK, *s.* Briosgaid chruaidh; briseadh mach

RUSHY, *a.* Luachrach.

RUSSET, *a.* Donn, ruadh, dubh-ruadh.

RUSSET, *s.* Drogaid, eididh dùthcha.

RUSSETING, *s.* Seorsa ubhail, ròs-ubhal.

RUST, *s.* Meirge, meirgeadh.

RUST, *v. a.* and *n.* Meirg. It will rust, *meirgidh e.*

RUSTIC, *a.* Dùthchail; borb, mi-mhodhail, neo-shnàsmhor, aineolach, brùideil; neo-chealgach, simplidh.

RUSTIC, *s* Balach, bodach, buamsdair, baoghlan; tuathanach.

RUSTICAL, *a* Balachail, borb, mi-mhodhail, neo-shnasmhor; aineolach, tuathail.

RUSTICALNESS, *s.* Balachaileachd, buirbe, mi-mhodhaileachd, neo-shnàsmhorachd.

RUSTICATE, *v. n.* Tàinich san duthaich

RUSTICITY, *s.* Simplidheachd, neo-sheòltachd, neo-chealgachd, buamsdaireachd.

RUSTINESS, *s.* Meirge, meirgeadh, meirgead. Rustiness has destroyed it, *chaidh e dholaidh le meirge*, I never saw such a sword for rustiness, *cha 'n fhac mi riamh leithid so chlaidheamh air mheirgead.*

RUSTLE, *v. n* Dean starbhanaich (no) starbhan, dean farum beag, fuaimich, farumaich.

RUSTLING, *s* Starbhan, starbhanaich, farum beag; (*of arms*), gleang, fuaim. The rustling of the leaves, *starbhan* (*no*) *farum nan duilleag.*

RUSTLING, *a* Starbhanach; farumach; (*as arms*), gleangach, fuaimearra.

RUSTY, *a.* Meirgte, meirgeach, làn meirge.

RUT, *v. n.* Langanaich, raoichd, raoichdich, bùirich, bùir.

RUT, *s.* Damhair; dàradh feidh, dàradh tomain; aile cartach; slaodan, sgriob, lorg.

RUTH, *s.* Truas, truacantas, baigh, bròn, dubhachas.

RUTHFUL, *a.* Muladach, truagh, brònach, dubhach.

RUTHFULLY, *adv.* Gu muladach, gu truagh, gu brònach, gu dubhach, gu trom, gu tuirseach.

RUTHLESS, *a.* Cruaidh, borb, cruadalach, neo-thruacanta, ain-iochdar, ain-iochdmhor

RUTHLESSNESS, *s.* Cruadhas cridhe, buirbe, cruadal, neothruacantas, ain-iochd.

RUTTING, *s.* Dàmhair; dàradh.

RUTTISH, *a.* Macnùsach; drùiseil; teth, slatail

RYE, *s.* Seagal, seogal

RYEGRASS, *s.* Seorsa feòir.

S.

S. An naothamh litir deug do 'n Aibideal. F. R. S., *Ball do 'n Chomunn Rioghail;* R. S. A., *Comunn rioghail nan Arsaidheara.*

Sabaoth, *s.* Feachd, armailt, armailtean, sloigh.

Sabbath, *s.* Sàbaid; dòmhnach; fois, tamh. The Sabbath-day, *là na Sàbaid, di-domhnaich, là 'n Tighearna, an t-Sàbaid, an dòmhnach.*

Sabbatarian, *s.* Sàbaideach; fear a ghleidheas naomh an seachdamh là do 'n seachduin, an àite a cheud là.

Sabbath-breaker, *s.* Fear briseadh na sàbaid.

Sabbatical, *a.* Sàbaideach.

Sabbatism, *s.* Sàbaideachd, crabhadh domhnach.

Sabine, *s.* Seorsa luibh, saibhin.

Sable, *s.* Dubh-radan, bian an dubh-radain; fionnadh dubh-dhonn.

Sable, *a.* Dubh, dorch, ciar. The sable mantle of night, *falluing dhorch na h-oidhche, brat ciar na h-oidhche.*

Sabre, *s.* Claidheamh crom, cloidhean.

Sabulosity, *s.* Gaineamhachd, gaineamhuinneachd; grainneanachd.

Sabulous, *a.* Gaineamhach, gaineamhuinneach, làn gàineamhaich, grainneanach, garbh.

Saccharine, *a.* Siucarach, milis.

Sacerdotal, *a.* Sagairteach, sagartach, sagairteil, sagartail.

Sachel, *s.* Pochd, poc; màileid, mailios, sacan, sacaid, pocan, bag, balg, bolg.

Sack, *s.* Sac, poc; bolg, balg, soire. The fool's portion is at the mouth of the sack, *tha cuid an amadain am beul a bhuilg.*

Sack, *v. a.* Sacaich, cuir an sac. Sacked, *sacaichte.*

Sack, *v. a.* Creach, sgrios, gabh baile a dh' aindeoin. Sacked, *creachta, sgriosta.*

Sack, *s.* Creach, creachadh, reubainn, creach baile, spùinn; (*wine*), seic, fion a chuan iar-i.

Sackbut, *s.* Seorsa pioba.

Sackcloth, *s.* Eudach saic, sac-eudach.

Sacker, *s.* Creachadair, milltear, sgriosadair, séisdear, spùinneadair.

Sackful, *s.* Làn saic, làn poc.

Sacking, *s.* Creachadh, sgriosadh, reubainn, milleadh; spùinneadh.

Sack-posset, *s.* Brochan bainne is fiona.

Sacrament, *s.* Sàcramaid, comanach, comanachadh, combar faicsionnach air gràs spioradail cuirp Chriosd; ordugh, mionn.

Sacramental, *a.* Comanachail, sacramaideach.

Sacred, *a.* Naomh, seunta, coisrigte; diadhaidh.

Sacredly, *adv.* Gu naomh, gu seunta, gu coisrigte.

Sacredness, *s.* Naomhachd, seuntachd.

Sacrific, *a.* Iobairteach, ofraileach.

Sacrificable, *a.* Ion-iobradh.

Sacrificator, *s.* Iobrair, iobairtear, iobradair.

Sacrifice, *s.* Iobairt, ofrail, tabhartas; doibhre. A sacrifice for sin, *iobairt pheacaidh, iobairt réitich.*

Sacrifice, *v. a.* Iobair, ofrail, thoir suas, ioc, marbh; (*consecrate*), coisrig; (*quit*), tréig, fàg, cuitich, cuir cul ri. Sacrificed, *iobairte, ofrailte.*

Sacrificial, *a.* Iobairteach, ofraileach.

Sacrilege, *s.* Ceal-shlad, ceal-ghoid, ceaslaid, goid nithe naomha, robainn eaglais; Dia-mhasladh.

Sacrilegious, *a.* Ceal-shladach; mi-dheadhaidh, mi-naomh.

Sacrilegiously, *adv.* Gu ceal-shladach, gu mi-dhiadhuidh.

Sacring, *part.* A coisreagadh.

Sacrist, *s.* Fear creacair.

Sacristy, *s.* Creacan, naomh-ionad.

Sad, *a.* Brònach, dubhach, muladach, dosgach, tuirseach, trom, dimnidheach, dòlasach, doilghiosach, neo-aoibhinn, neo-eibhinn; duilbhear, dubh, dorch; (*shameful*), nàr, maslach; (*evil*), olc, aingidh, fuathasach, curt; (*foul*), duaichnidh, salach, déistinneach. It is a sad thing, *is brònach* (*no*) *is bochd am nì e;* a sad heart, *cridhe trom;* a sad fellow, *fear curt;* sad-coloured clothes, *eudach dubh.*

Sadden, *v.* Dean brònach, dean dubhach, dean muladach, dean tuirseach (no) trom; dean doilghiosach.

Saddle, *s.* Diollaid, diollad, pillean, sadhal.

Saddle, *v. a.* Diollaidich, cuir diollaid air.

Saddle-backed, *a.* Cam-dhromach.

Saddlemaking, *s.* Diolladaireachd.

Saddler, *s.* Diolladair.

Sadly, *adv.* Gu brònach, gu muladach, gu dubhach, gu tuirseach, gu trom, gu dòlasach; gu nàr; gu h-olc, gu fuathasach, gu bochd.

Sadness, *s.* Bròn, dubhachas, mulad, tuirse, truime, dòlas, sprochd, doilgheas, doilghios, duilbhire.

Safe, *a.* Tearuinnte, slàn, sàbhailte. Safe and sound, *gu beò slàn, gu slàn fallain;* safe may you be, *gu mu slàn an robh thu.*

Safe, *s.* Lanntair, biadh-chisteag, aite gleidhteach.

Safeguard, *s.* Dìon, dìdean, tearmunn, tearuinnteachd, comraich. Under safeguard, *fo dhion, fo thearmunn.*

Safely, *adv.* Gu tearuinnte, gu slàn.

Safety, *s.* Tearuinnteachd; siochalachd; slainnte; gainntearas.

Saffron, *s.* Cròch.

Saffron, *a.* Croch, buidhe; uaine.

Sag, *v. a.* and *n.* Luchdaich, tromaich; cròch gu leibideach.

Sagacious, *a.* Gear, glic, tuigseach, toinisgeil, fad-sheallach, geur-chuiseach, sicir, crionna, cùl-radharcach; tiarmail, innleachdach, toimhseal.

Sagaciously, *adv.* Gu geur, gu glic, gu tuigseach, gu toinisgeil, gu geur-chuiseach, gu crionna, gu sicir.

Sagacity, *s.* Géire, tuigse, toinisg, gliocas, crionnachd, tiarmalachd.

Sage, *s.* Sàisde; slàn-lus. Mountain-sage, *athair liath.* Bha barail ro mhòr aig na sean Eadailtich do 'n lus so, mar a chithear o 'n rann a leanas.

Cur moriatur homo cui salvia crescit in horto?
C'arson a gheibheadh duine bàs,
Aig am bheil sàisde fàs na gharaidh?

Sage, *a.* Glic, crionna, eagnaidh, foghluimte; sicir.

Sage, *s.* Duine glic, feallsair, teallsair, teallsanach, feallsanach; ro-dhuine.

Sagely, *adv.* Gu glic, gu crionna, gu h-eagraidh, gu foghluimte, gu sicir.

Sageness, *s.* Gliocas, crionnachd, toinisge, tuigse, eagnachd, foghlum, teallsanachd, feallsanachd.

Saginate, *v. a.* Lion, sàth, dean reamhar, sasuich, lion gu sàth.

Sagittal, *a.* Saigheadail, saigheadach; guineach.

Sagittary, *s.* An saighead, an do chomhara na greinchrios.

Sago, *s.* Seorsa gràin a thig as na h-Innseachan.

Said, *pret.* and *part.* of say. Thubhairt; mar a thubhradh, mar a thubhairt, a thubhradh. As I said, *mar thubhairt mi*; as has been said, *mar a thubhradh*; it is said, *tha e air a radh, tha iad ag radh*; the said person, *an neach ceudna*; as aforesaid, *mar a thubhradh*.

Sail, *s.* Seòl; brat siùil, bréid siùil, long, luingeas. Sails, *siùil*; ten sail of the line, *deich luingeasan cogaidh*; a sail of the line, *luingeas cogaidh*; mainsail, *seòl mòr*; topsail, *seòl uachdrach*; mizzensail, *seòl deiridh*.

Sail, *v. a.* and *n.* Seòl, stiùir.

Sailfish, *s.* Cairbean.

Sailor, *s.* Maraiche, mairiche, seòladair.

Sailyard, *s.* Slat-shiùil.

Saim, *s.* Muc-bhlonag.

Sainfoin, *s.* Seòrsa saoidh le blàth fìor dhearg, saoidh dhearg.

Saint, *s.* Naomh. Saint John, *Eoin an Naomh*; Saint John's wort, *caod, aslachan Cholum chille, ealabhuidh*; a she-saint, *ban naomh*.

Saint, *v. a.* Naomh, naomhaich, aireamh am measg nan naomh. Sainted, *naomhaichte, naomh, diadhuidh, math, coisrigte*.

Saintlike, *a.* Naomh, crabhach, diadhuidh.

Saintship, *s.* Naomhachd.

Sake, *s.* Son, sgàth. For my sake, *air mo shon, air mo sgàth*; for his sake, *air a sgàthsa, air a shonsa*; for God's sake, *air sgàth Dhé, air ghaol ni math*.

Saker, *s.* Seorsa gunna mor.

Sal, *s.* Salann.

Salacious, *a.* Macnusach, drùiseil, neo-gheimnidh, mi-bhanail.

Salaciously, *adv.* Gu macnusach, gu drùiseil, gu neo-gheimnidh, gu mi-bhanail.

Salacity, *s.* Macnus, druis, drùisealachd, macnusachd.

Salad, *s.* Biadh lus, salaid.

Salamander, *s.* Seorsa creutair nimhe mu 'n abrar gum mair e beò san teine, far an gin e.

Salary, *s.* Tuarasdal, duais, pàigh, diol; luach saoithreach; (*income*), tighinn stigh; (*stipend*), stiopain.

Sale, *s.* Reic, creic, robainn, reiceadh.

Saleable, *a.* Margail, a ghabhas reic, a dh' fhaotar reic.

Saleableness, *s.* Margaileachd.

Salebrous, *a.* Cragach, creagach, garbh, clochach.

Salesman, *s.* Reiceadair, fear reicidh, fear reic, marsonta.

Salient, *a.* Leumnach, sùrdagach, stinleagach.

Saline, *a.* Saillt.

Salique (law), *s.* Lagh Francach trid am bheil boirionnaich air an druideadh mach o 'n chrùn.

Saliva, *s.* Smugaid, seile, ronnan, ronn.

Salival, *a.* Smugaideach, ronnach.

Salivate, *v.* Ronnaich.

Salivation, *s.* Ronnach, ronnachadh, ronn-ghalar.

Salivous, *a.* Ronnach, smugaideach.

Sallow, *s.* Geal-sheileach, seileach.

Sallow, *a.* Buidhe, bàn, glas, uaine, glasdaidh.

Sallowness, *s.* Bàine, bànad, glaise, uainead.

Sally, *s.* Brùchd, ionnsuidh, briseadh mach; siurtag, ruaig.

Sally, *v. n.* Brùchd bris a mach.

Salmagundi, *s.* Ioma-chumasg air a dheanamh suas le feoil phronn sgadan, ùille, fion-geur, peubar is uinneinibh.

Salmon, *s.* Bradan, glas-bhreac, colgan, toineamh, eigne. Salmon-trout, *breac geal, bricean, glas-bhreac, colgan, colagan*.

Salsuginous, *a.* Saillte.

Salt, *s.* Salann, salainn; blas.

Salt, *a.* Saillte; goirt; macnusach; drùiseil. Salt fish, *iasg saillte*.

Salt, *v. a.* Saill, salannaich, cuir salann air.

Saltant, *a.* Leumnach, surdagach, leumartach, leumardach.

Saltation, *s.* Leumnaich, leumardaich, leumadaireachd, dannsadh, bualadh, plosgartaich.

Saltcellar, *s.* Saillear.

Salter, *s.* Sailleadair; fear reic shalainn.

Saltern, *s.* Obair shalainn.

Saltinbanco, *s.* Cleasaiche, baoth-chleasaiche.

Saltish, *a.* Leth-char saillte, goirt, garg, leth-char goirt (no) garg, rud eigin goirt (no) garg.

Saltless, *a.* Domblasda, neo-bhlasda, neo-shaillte, ùr.

Saltness, *s.* Saillteachd, goirteachd.

Saltpetre, *s.* Seorsa salainn.

Salubrious, *a.* Slainnteil, fallain, slainnteach, slainnteachail.

Salubrity, *s.* Slainntealachd, slainnte, fallaineachd.

Salutary, *a.* Slàinnteil, slàinnteach, slàn, tearuinte.

Salutation, *s.* Fàilte; altachadh beatha furan.

Salute, *v. a.* Cuir fàilte, cuir furan, dean beath, fàiltich, beannaich, furanaich, pòg. Salute him, *cuir fàilte air*.

Salute, *s.* Fàilte, furan, pòg, beannachadh, beannachd.

Salutiferous, *a.* Slàinnteil, fallain.

Salvable, *a.* Ion-shàbhaladh, ion-shaoradh.

Salvation, *s.* Saoradh, saorsadh, saorsain, sabhaladh; slàinnte; dionadh, slànuchadh.

Salvatory, *s.* Ionad tasgaidh, ionad dionaidh.

Salve, *s.* Cungaidh leigheas, ioc, ungadh, sàbh, unamaid, coghnadh.

Salve, *v. a.* Leigheas, leighis, dean gu math, slanuich, coghain.

Salver, *s.* Trainnsear, troinnsear, mias, aisead.

Salvo, *s.* Leithsgeul.

Same, *a.* Ionann, ceudna; ceart. On the same day, *air an là cheudna*; on the very same day, *air a cheart là sin*; at the same time, *air an aon am*; it is quite the same thing, *tha e 'n t-aon chuid*; the very same thing, *a cheart ni cheudna*; it is all the same thing to me, *tha e uile ionann domhsa*.

Sameness, *s.* Ionannachd.

Samlet, *s.* Bradan òg, òg-bhradan, glas-bhreac.

Samphire, *s.* Saimbhir.

Sample, *s.* Sampull, samhladh, siomplair, samplair.

Samplar, Sampler, *s.* Samplair, siomplair; ban-shampall, eisiomlair.

Sanable, *a.* So-leigheas, leigheasail, a dh' fhaotar leigheas, a ghabhas leigheas.

Sanation, *s.* Leigheasadh, slànuchadh.

Sanative, *a.* Leigheasach, slànach, slàinteach; slainnteil, fallain.

† **Sance**, *prep.* for *sans*. Gun, do dhìth, a dhìth, dh' easbhuidh, as easbhuidh, as eugais.

Sanctification, *s.* Naomhachadh; coisreagadh.

Sanctifier, *s.* Naomhachair; fear naomhachaidh; fear coisreagaidh.

Sanctify, *v. a.* Naomhaich; coisrig; dean naomh. Sanctified, *naomhaichte, air a naomhachadh*; sanctified men, *daoine coisrigte*.

Sanctifying, *s.* Naomhachadh, coisreagadh.

Sanctimonious, *a.* Cràbhach, diadhuidh, naomh.

Sanctimony, *s.* Naomhachd, cràbhachd.

Sanction, *s.* Aontachadh; daighneachadh; ughdarras; rùn; toil; comas, cead; reachd; ordugh; decreut.

Sanctitude, *s.* Naomhachd; cràbhadh, cràbhachd.

Sanctity, *s.* Naomhachd; mathas, diadhachd, diadhuidheachd, glaine, neo-ghloine.

Sanctuary, *s.* Ionad naomh; tearmunn, ionad dionaidh, dìdean, comaraich. Take sanctuary, *guidh comaraich, gabh comaraich.*

Sand, *s.* Gaineamh, gaineamhach, grothal, gairbheal. Sand-pit, *toll gaineamhaich, slochd gaineamhaich;* shelves of sand, *bruachan gaineimh.*

Sandal, *s.* Cuaran; bonn-bhròg, bròg fhuasgailte.

Sandarach, *s.* Seorsa méin; bith aiteil.

Sand-blind, *a.* Leth-dhall, gearr-sheallach; ròsblach.

Sand-blindness, *s.* Dalladh eun.

Sanded, *a.* Gaineichte, gaineamhaichte; gaineachaidh, gaineamhuinneach; neo-thorrach; ballach; spotagach, breac, ball-bhreac.

Sanders, *s.* Seorsa fiodha Innseanaich.

Sandiness, *s.* Gaineamhachd, gaineamhuinneachd.

Sandish, *a.* Gaineamhach, gaineamhuinneach, garbh.

Sandstone, *s.* Clach ghainmheach.

Sandy, *a.* Gaineamhach, gaineachaidh, gainmheachar, gaineamhuinneach, garbh.

Sane, *a.* Crionna; glic, ciallach, suidhichte; cruinn; slàn; slainnteil; fallain.

Sang, *pret.* of sing. Sheinn.

Sanguiferous, *a.* Fuil-bheirteach.

Sanguification, *s.* Tionndadh gu fuil.

Sanguinary, *a.* Fuilteach, fuileach, fuileachdach, garg, borb, mortach, marbhtach, àrail, àr-meineach, ain-iochdmhor, mi-thlusar.

Sanguine, *a.* Dearg; flann-dearg; teth, blath, dian, deothasach, earbsach, dian-dhòchasach, toileil; suilbhear.

Sanguineness, *s.* Dòchasachd, mor-dhòchas; dian-earbsa, dian-chinnte.

Sanguineous, *a.* Fuilteach, fuileach, làn fola.

Sanhedrim, *s.* Ard-chomhairle nan Iudhach.

Sanicle, *s.* Seorsa luibh. Yorkshire sanicle, *bodan dubh.*

Sanies, *s.* Iongar, iongħar, fuil, flann.

Sanious, *a.* Iongarach, iongharach.

Sanity, *s.* Gliocas, ciall, céill, slàinnte.

Sank, *pret.* of sink. It sank, *chaidh e fodh.*

† **Sans**, *prep.* Gun, a dhìth.

Sap, *s.* Brìgh, sùgh, sùth, snothach, ùraireachd.

Sap, *v. a.* Fo-thochaill, fo-chladhaich.

Sapid, *a.* Blasda, deagh-bhlasda, milis.

Sapidity, *s.* Blasdachd, millse, milseachd.

Sapience, *s.* Gliocas, toinisg, crionnachd, tuigse.

Sapient, *a.* Glic, toinisgeil, crionna, tuigseach.

Sapless, *a.* Gun sùgh, gun sùth, gun bhrigh, neo-bhogar; tiorram, neo-bhrìghmhor.

Sapling, *s.* Fàillean, fàilean, fiùran, maothan; òg-mheangan, gineag.

Saponaceous, *a.* Siabunnach, siapunnach, siapunnaidh.

Sapor, *s.* Blas.

Sapphire, *a.* Sàpir, cloch uasal ghorm.

Sapphirine, *a.* Sàpireach.

Sappiness, *s.* Sùgharachd, bogarachd, brighmhorachd; ùraireachd.

Sappy, *a.* Sùghar, sùghmhor, sùthar, sùthmhor, brìghmhor; ùrar, bogar; maothanach; òg, fann.

Saraband, *s.* Dannsadh Spàinnteach.

Sarcasm, *s.* Gearradh, beum, burdan; tearrachd, geuranachd.

Sarcastic, **Sarcastical**, *a.* Beumnach, geur, eisgeil, burdanach, tearrachdail, geuranach.

Sarcastically, *adv.* Gu beumnach, gu geur, gu h-éisgeil, gu burdanach, gu tearrachdail.

Sarcenet, *s.* Seorsa sioda, sarsnaid.

Sarcle, *v. a.* Gart-ghlan.

Sarcophagous, *a.* Feòil-itheach, feòil-chnamhach.

Sarcophagy, *s.* Feol-itheadh.

Sarculation, *s.* Gart-ghlanadh.

Sardel, **Sardine**, **Sardius**, *s.* Seorsa cloich phrìseil.

Sardonyx, *s.* Seorsa cloich phrìseil.

Sarsaparilla, *s.* Seorsa freumha a bheirear as na h-Innseachan shuas.

Sarse, *v. a.* Criathar.

Sarse, *s.* Seorsa criathar fhinealta; min-chriathar.

Sart, *s.* Goirtean.

Sash, *s.* Crios; bann; sròl; uinneag a thogas agus a leigeas le h-ulagaibh.

Sasafras, *s.* Seorsa freumh a thig a America.

Sasse, *s.* Tuil-dhorus.

Sat, *pret.* of sit. Shuidh. See **Sit**.

Satan, *s.* An diabhol, an t-aibhisear, an t-aibhisdear am buairear, am buaireadair, am fear is miosa.

Satanic, *a.* Diabhluidh, deamhnach, deamhnaidh, aingidh, ifrinneach.

Satchel, *s.* Pocan, màileid, maillos, mala beag, gearrphocan.

Sate, *v. a.* Sàth, lion gu sàth, sàsuich. Sated, *sàthach, sàsuichte.*

Satellite, *s.* Cuairt-reul, cuairt-rionnag.

Satiate, *v. a.* Sàth, lion gu sàth, sàsuich, sàthaich; toilich, làn-toilich.

Satiate, *a.* Sàthach, sàsuichte, slàn, toileach, toilichte.

Satiated, *a.* Sàthach, sàsuichte, lionta, lan, toileach, toilichte, buidheach. Satiated with vengeance, *sàthach le dioghaltas, buidheach dioghaltais.*

Satiety, *s.* Làn, sàth, teannadh, teann-shath.

Satin, *s.* Seòrsa sioda, sròl.

Satire, *s.* Aoireadh; tearrachd, càineadh; bardachd, dàn eisgeil.

Satirical, *a.* Bardail, càinteach, sgath-bhardail, beumnach, sgaiteach.

Satirist, *s.* Bard, sgath-bhard, aoir, bard beumnach.

Satirize, *v.* Deàn aoireadh; càin, bardaich, gearr.

Satisfaction, *s.* Taitneas, sàsuchadh, toileachadh; reiteachadh, làn-toileachadh; (*reparation*), diol, dioladh, éiric, sagharlachd. Make satisfaction, *dean suas, diol.*

Satisfactorily, *adv.* Gu taitneach.

Satisfactory, *a.* Taitneach.

Satisfied, *a.* Toilichte; sàsuichte; sàthach; buidheach. I am fully satisfied, *tha mi làn toilichte, tha mo thoil agam.*

Satisfy, *v. a.* and *n.* Toilich, sàsuich, sàth; diol; dean cinnteach; (*please*), thoir toileachas inntinn, taitinn ri, thig ri, dean buidheach, dean toileach. Satisfy your ambition, *sàsuich do mhiann;* satisfy a creditor, *diol fear creideis;* he did not satisfy me, *cha do thaitinn e rium, cha tàinig e rium.*

Saturable, *a.* So-shàsachachadh, so-lionadh.

Saturant, *a.* Sàsachail, liontach.

Saturday, *s.* Di sathuirne, de sathuirne. A Saturday, *là sathuirne.*

Saturate, *v.* Sàsuich, lìon. Saturated, *sàsuichte, lìonta.*

Saturity, *s.* Sath, sàith, sàithead, làn.

Saturn, *s.* Sathuirn; aon do na reultan iomrollach; agus a ghabhas deich bliadhna fichead a dol a cuairt; (*in chemistry*), luaidh.

Saturnian, *a.* Sona, aghmhor; òrdha.

Saturnine, *a.* Dorch, gruamach; dubhach, brònach, trom, tiamhaidh.

Satyr, *s.* Seorsa apa; Dia coille am measg nan sean Ghintealach; fiadh-dhuine.

Sauce, *s.* Leannra, leannradh; sùgh; sabhsa.

Sauce, *v. a.* Sabhsaich.

Saucebox, *s.* Sgeilm; fear lonach, ablach, gobair, peasan, peilpean.

Saucepan, *s.* Sgeileid, aghann.

Saucer, *s.* Fo-chopan, sabhsar.

Saucily, *adv.* Gu beagnarach, gu gobach, gu lonach, gu beadaidh, gu peasanach, gu peilpeanta.

Sauciness, *s.* Beag-narachd, beadaidheachd, peasanachd, gobaireachd, mi-mhodh.

Saucy, *a.* Gobach, lonach, mi-mhodhail, miobhail, làsdach, stràiceil, beadaidh; peasanach, barracaideach, peilpeanta.

Saunter, *v. n.* Spaisdeirich, spaidseirich; cealaich.

Sauntering, *s.* Spaisdearachd, spaidsearachd, sràideas.

Sausage, *s.* Isbean, ìspean.

Savage, *a.* Fiadhaich, borb, borbarra, alluidh, allmharra, allmharrach; brùideil; ain-iochdmhor; cruadalach; neo-thruacanta, cruaidh-chridheach; coillteil.

Savage, *s.* Duine fiadhaich, urr fhiadhaich, fiadh-dhuine, fear allaidh.

Savagely, *adv.* Gu fiadhaich, gu borb, gu h-alluidh, gu brùideal; gu h-ain-iochdmhor, gu cruadalach, gu h-allaidh.

Savageness, *s.* Buirbe, borbarrachd, fiadhaichead, an-iochdmhorachd, ain-iochdmhoireachd, brùidealachd, allmharrachd.

Savagery, *s.* Buirbe, ain-iochd.

Savanna, *s.* Magh fad réidh; feurach ann *America.*

Save, *v. a.* Saor, teasairg, sabhail, anacail, tearuinn, dion, gleidh, coimhid; (*not spend*), caomhain, dean baile. Save him from destruction, *saor o sgrios 'e*; God save you (at parting), *Dia leat, gu gleidheadh Dia thu*; (at meeting), *fàilte ort*; saved, *saorta, sàbhailte, tearuinnte, dionta, gleidhte*; (reserved), *caomhainte*; God save us, *gu gleidheadh Dia sinn, a Dhia gléidh sinn*; save harmless, *cum (no) gleidh tearuinnte, cum gun dochann.*

Save, *adv.* Ach; saor o. All save you, *na h-uile ach thusa*; save this alone, *saor o so amhain*; the last save one, *am fear mu dheireadh ach a h-aon.*

Saved, *part.* (*From danger*), saorta, saor, sàbhailte, tearuinnte, dionta, gleidhte; (*reserved*), caomhainte.

Saver, *s.* Fear saoraidh, fear caonntach.

Savin, *s.* Seorsa luibh; saibhin, samhan.

Saving, *a.* Caonntach, grunndail, gléidhteach, gleadhtach, spiocach, spiocaireach, crion.

Saving, *s.* (*Reserving*), caomhnadh; gleidheadh; (*preserving*), tearnadh, saoradh, teasairgin.

Saving, *adv.* Ach, saor o. Saving that, *ach sin, saor o sin.*

Savingly, *adv.* Gu caonntach, gu grunndail, gu gleidhteach, gu caonntachail, gu sàbhailteach.

Savingness, *s.* Caonntachd, grunnd, grunndalas; grunndalachd, spiocaireachd.

Saviour, *s.* Fear saoraidh, Slànuighear.

Savory, *a.* Garbhag ghàraidh.

Savour, *s.* Fàil, tòchd, boltrach, bol, boladh; blas.

Savour, *v.* Cuir fàil (no) tòchd. It savours of smoke, *tha tòchd na deathaich dheth.*

Savourily, *adv.* Gu boltrachail, gu blasda, gu milis.

Savouriness, *s.* Boltrachd, blasdachd; millse.

Savoury, *a.* Boltrachail, cubhraidh, fàileach milis; blasda.

Savoy, *s.* Seorsa càil.

Saw, *pret.* of see. Chunna, chunnaic, bheachdaich, dhearc.

Saw, *s.* Sàbhadh, sàbh, tuireasg. A handsaw, *sabh dùirn*; (*old saying*), sean-fhocal, gnàth-fhocal.

Saw, *v. a.* Sàbh. Sawn, *sàbhta*; serrated, *fiaclaichte, gròbach.*

Sawdust, *s.* Min shàbhaidh, meanan saibh; sgamhar, sadadh, pronnan.

Sawfish, *s.* Iasg adhairceach.

Sawing, *s.* Sàbhadh; sàbhaireachd, sàbhadaireachd.

Sawmill, *s.* Muileann sàbhaidh.

Sawn, *part.* Sabhta, sàbhte, air a shàbhadh, air a sàbhadh.

Sawpit, *s.* Sloc-shàbhaidh.

Sawyer, *s.* Sàbhair, sàbhadair.

Saxifrage, *s.* Lus nan cluas.

Saxifragous, *a.* Cloch-bhriseach, cloch-bhruanach.

Say, *v. a.* Abair, innis, labhair, aithris. Say not so, *na h-abair sin*; say you so? *bheil thu 'g radh sin?* what have you to say? *ciod th' agad ri radh?* what will people say? *ciod their an sluagh?* as I may say, *mar gun abairinn*; to say the truth, *a dh' innseadh na firinn*; they say, *tha iad ag radh, their iad*; say to him, *abair ris*; says he, *ars' esan*; that is to say, *is e sin ri radh*; say not a word, *na h-abair focal (no) diog*; say on, *abair air d' adhairt*; he said, *thubhairt e*; say by heart, *abair air do chridhe, abair air do theangadh.*

† **Say**, *s.* Labhairt, comhradh, radh; (*sample*), sampull.

Saying, *s.* Radh, focal, briathar, gnàth-fhocal. An old saying, *sean radh, sean-fhocal*; as the saying is, *mar a their iad, mar a tha 'n sean fhocal.*

Scab, *s.* Creim, cream, sgreab, sgab, càrr; cloimh, broth, tachas, sgriobach, stinle, gearbh, guirean.

Scabbard, *s.* Truaille, duille; faighean, dùbla.

Scabbed, Scabby, *a.* Creimeach, creamach, sgreubach, sgabach, carrach, guireanach, clomhach, brothach; cearbach, crion, truagh, diblidh, mosach. A scabbed sheep, *caor chlothach*; every man has a blow at the scabbed man's head, *buille gach aon fhir an ceann an fhir charraich.*

Scabbedness, *s.* Creim, sgreub, carr, sgriobach.

Scabious, *a.* Creimeach, creamach, sgreubach, sgabach, carrach, clodhach.

Scabrous, *a.* Garbh, neo-mhìn, molach.

Scabrousness, *s.* Gairbhe, gairbhead.

Scad, *s.* Sgad, seorsa éisg.

Scaffold, *s.* Sgàilean; lobhta; *sgafald.*

Scaffoldage, *s.* Lobhtachan, *scafaladan.*

Scaffolding, *s.* Lobhtachan, lobhtachadh, *sgafaldan.*

Scalade, Scalado, *s.* Streapaid; fàrachadh, streapadh, dreimireachd.

Scald, *v. a.* Sgallt, loisg, plod.

Scald, *s.* Càrr, creim, ceann-chàrr, càrr cinn, sgreab; (*with hot water*), losgadh, sgalltadh, plodadh.

Scaldhead, *s.* Ceann-chàrr, gné luibhre.

Scale, *s.* Lann; sgol, meidhe; slige thomhais, laithe; gainne éisg; (*ladder*), fàradh, àradh, dreimire; (*of the head*), sgreab, sgrath, sgròilleag; aon do chomharan na gréin-chrios.

Scale, *v. a.* (*Climb*), streap, streap le fàradh, fàraich, dreap; (*weigh*), cothromaich, tomhais; (*strip off*), lannaich, sgrath, sgròillich.

Scaled, *part.* and *a.* Streapta, lannach, gainneach, iteach; sligeach.

Scalene, *a.* Tri-oisneag aig nach 'eil dithis d' a slisnean comh-fhad.

Scall, *s.* Luibbre, lobhrachd; marbh-mhaoile; càrr, sgreab.

Scallion, *s.* Creamh gàraidh, léigis.

Scallop, *s.* (*Fish*), Seorsa éisg; sgolap; mac muirigheach; (*shell*), slige chreachainn.

Scalp, *s.* Comhdach a chlaiginn, sgrath chlaiginn.

Scalpel, *s.* Sgian leigh.

Scaly, *a.* Lannach; iteach, sligeach; sgroilleagach; sgrath-ach.

Scamble, *v. n.* and *a.* Sgròbaich, iongnaich; bi tuasaideach, mill, beubanaich, reub.

Scamble, *s.* Tuasaid; streapaid, topainn.

Scambler, *s.* Sgimlear, sgeimlear.

Scammony, *s.* Seorsa purgaid, sùgh purgaideach.

Scamper, *v.* Teich, bi triall, thoir no buinn asad, thoir na casan asad. He scampered off, *thig e na buinn as, thug e 'n rathad air.*

Scamper, *s.* Teich, teichcachd, ruaig, ruithe, steud.

Scan, *v.* Tomhais; ceasnuich, sgrud.

Scandal, *s.* Sgainneal, masladh, tàmailt, tuaileas, toibheum, oilbheum, càin, cùl-chàineadh, oilbheumachd, dimeas.

Scandal, *v. a.* Sgainnealaich, maslaich, tuaileasaich, dean, tàir, nàraich.

Scandalize, *v. a.* Sgainnealaich, maslaich, masluich, dean tàir (no) dimeas. Scandalized, *sgainnealaichte, maslaichte.*

Scandalous, *a.* Maslach, maslachail, tàmailteach, sgainn-ealach, nàr, tàireil. A scandalous action, *gniomh nàr.*

Scandalously, *adv.* Gu nàr, gu maslach, gu tàmailteach.

Scandalum-magnatum, *s.* Toibheum.

Scant, *v. a.* Cughannaich; druid (no) dùin a stigh.

Scant, *a.* Gann, tearc, ainmig; gortach, crion; gearr, spiocach, caonntach.

Scantily, *adv.* Gu gann, gu h-ainmig, gu gortach.

Scantiness, *s.* Gainne, gainnead, crine, cumhangachd.

Scantlet, *s.* (*Small quantity*), beagan, beagnithe, crioman, criomag; (*proportion*), cuid, cuibhrionn; tomhas, roinn.

Scantly, *adv.* Gu gann, gu cumhann, gu caonntach, gu spiocach; gun fhad, gun leud.

Scantiness, *s.* Gainne, gainnead; aimhleathanachd.

Scanty, *a.* Gann, cughann, crion; gearr, beag, bochd, spiocach. My portion is but scanty, *cha 'n 'eil mo chuibh-rionn ach gann.*

Scape, *v. n.* Teich; rach as, seachain.

Scape, *s.* Teich, teicheachd, dol as, tearnadh, seachnadh; saoradh; sgiorradh.

Scapula, *s.* Slinnean, cnaimh slinnein; leithe; † iomdha.

Scapular, *a.* Slinneanach.

Scar, *s.* Aile, athailte; comhar; cream, creim; càrr; sliochd.

Scar, *v. a.* Comharaich, leòn.

Scarab, *s.* Daol, daol dubh.

Scaramouch, *s.* Baoth-chleasaiche, amadan.

Scarce, *a.* Gann; tearc; ainmig; ainneamh. Growing scarce, *a cinntinn (no) fàs gann;* money is scarce, *tha 'n t-airgiod gann.*

Scarce, Scarcely, *adv.* Air éigin, ach gann, is gann. He could scarcely do it, *b' ann air éigin a rinn se e;* there were scarcely a hundred men, *is gann a bha ceud fear ann.*

Scarceness, Scarcity, *s.* Gainnead, gainne, teirce, tearcad, ainmigead; daorsadh. Scarcity of money, *gainne airgid.*

Scarcity, *s.* See **Scarceness**.

Scare, *v. a.* Fuadaich, fògair, cuir eagal air, sgiùrs, creathnaich.

Scarecrow, *s.* Fuath; bodach ròcais; bòchdan; clach-bhalg.

Scarefire, *s.* Eagal teine.

Scarf, *s.* Mantal; fàlluinn; sgioball; guaillean, tonnag.

Scarfskin, *s.* Croiceann, craiceann; sgannan.

Scarification, *s.* Sgòradh, sgròilleachadh; sgoch.

Scarificator, *s.* Sgòradair, sgriobadair, sgochadair.

Scarify, *v. a.* Sgòr; sgriob, sgoch. Scarified, *sgòrta, sgriobta, sgochta.*

Scarlet, *s.* Scarlaid.

Scarlet, *a.* Scarlaid. Scarlet clothes, *eudach scarlaid.*

Scatches, *s.* Casan corrach.

Scate, Skate, *s.* Sgat, scat, sornan, bròg speidhil.

Scate, Skate, *v. n.* Spéil, speidhil.

Scatebrous, *a.* Fuaranach, tobarach, tiobarach, sruthanach.

Scath, *s.* Sgath, milleadh, caitheamh, cron, sgad.

Scathe, *v.* Sgath, mill, caith.

† **Scathful**, *a.* Millteach, cronail; dochannach.

Scating, Skating, *s.* Spéileadh, speidhleadh, spéile-arachd.

Scatter, *v. a.* and *n.* Sgap, sgaoil, sgainnir; spréid. Scattered, *sgapta, sgaoilte.*

Scatteredness, *s.* Sgaoilteachd; taincad.

Scattering, *s.* Sgapadh, sgaoileadh; crath.

Scatteringly, *adv.* Gu sgapach, gu sgaoilteach.

Scavenger, *s.* Clabarach, clabaraiche, labanaiche; loib-eanaiche; sguabadair sràide.

Scene, *s.* Coslas; sealladh; taisbean, roinn do bhard-chluiche; brat crochaidh tigh cluiche; both.

Scenery, *s.* Sealladh; coslas àite; fionn-bhoth; dealbh-choslas.

Scent, *s.* Fàil, tòchd, boladh, àile; sròin, sròineiseach.

Scent, *v. n.* Cuir mach fàil (no) tòchd.

Scented, *a.* Boltrach. Sweet-scented, *deagh-bholtrach;* ill-scented, *breun.*

Scentless, *a.* Neo-bholtrach, gun tòchd, gun àile, gun bholadh.

Sceptic, *s.* Neo-chreideach, neo-chreidiche.

Sceptical, *a.* Neo-chreideach; amharusach, teagamhach, neo-chreidsinn.

Scepticism, *s.* Mi-chreidimh, mi-chreideamh.

Sceptre, *s.* Righ-cholbh, slat rioghail, breas-cholbh.

Schedule, *s.* Sgriobhadh, sgròl, ròl paipeir.

Scheme, *s.* Seòl, doigh, modh, innleachd; dealbh, foir-dhealbh; gleus, fuirm.

Schemer, *s.* Innleachdair, dealbhair, dealbhadair, foir-dhealbhair, foir dhealbhadair; tionsgnair.

Schism, *s.* Sgaradh, sgarachduinn, dealachadh, eas-aonachd, eas-aontachd, siosma.

Schismatic, *s.* Sgaradair; neach a dhealaicheas ris an eaglais, siosmach.

Schismatical, *a.* Eas-aonach, eas-aontach, eas-aonachail.

Schismatically, *adv.* Gu h-eas-aontach.

Schismatizing, *s.* Sgaradaireachd, siosmaireachd.

Scholar, *s.* Sgoilear, fòghlumach, fòghlumaiche; deisciobul, fear ionnsuichte. A good scholar, *deagh sgoilear;* a bad scholar, *droch sgoilear.*

Scholarship, *s.* Sgoilearachd; ionnsach, ionnsachadh, foghlum, oilean.

Scholastic, *a.* Damhdha, sgoildha.

Scholastical, *a.* Sgoileisdeach, sgolaisteach; ionnsuichte.

Scholiast, *s.* Fear mìneachaidh.

Scholion, **Scholium**, *s.* Mìneachadh.

Scholy, *s.* Mìneachadh.

School, *s.* Sgoil; tigh sgoil, tigh foghluim, oil-thigh; sgoil-aite, sgolaisd. A dancing school, *sgoil dannsaidh;* a fencing school, *sgoil fheannsaireachd, sgoil bhasbaireachd;* a sewing school, *sgoil fhuaghail;* a reading school, *sgoil leughaidh;* a riding school, *sgoil mharcachd.*

School, *v. a.* Teagaisg, ionnsuich, foghluim, oileanaich, oil, tog.

Schoolboy, *s.* Sgoilear; balachan sgoil.

Schoolday, *s.* Là sgoil.

Schoolfellow, *s.* Comh-sgoilear.

Schoolhouse, *s.* Tigh sgoil, tigh foghluim, sgolaisd.

Schoolmaster, *s.* Maighstir, maighstir sgoil, oide-ionnsuich, fear teagaisg, teagasgair, damh-oide, fath-oide.

Schoolmistress, *s.* Ban-mhaighstir sgoil, ban-mhaighstir.

Sciatic, **Sciatica**, *s.* Loini, loinidh, greim loini.

Sciatical, *a.* Loinidheach.

Science, *s.* Treartha, trearach, ealdhain; eagnaidheachd, foghlum; eolas, sànas; fios; nard; fadh.

Scientific, *a.* Ealdhaineach, ealdhanta; eòlach; ionnsuichte.

Scientifically, *adv.* Gu h-ealdhaineach, gu h-ealdhanta.

Scimitar, *s.* Claidheamh crom, cloidhean; greidlean.

Scink, *s.* Laogh anabuich air a chur.

Scintillate, *v. n.* Srad, caoir, sradagaich.

Scintillating, *a.* Sradach, caoireach, sradagach.

Scintillation, *s.* Sradadh, caoireadh.

Sciolist, *s.* Faoin-sgoilear, fear air bheag eòlais.

Scion, *s.* Fàillean, maothan, fiùran, fiùirean, meangan òg, òg-mheangan, ùr-fhàs, gineag.

Scirrhosity, *s.* Cruadhachadh fàireig, at fàireig, plocadh, plucadh.

Scirrhous, *a.* Cruaidh (no) plocach mar fhàireig, plocach.

Scirrhus, *s.* Fàireag phlocach.

Scissible, *a.* So-sgoltadh, so-sgoltaidh, so-ghearraidh, so-sgaraidh.

Scission, *s.* Sgoltadh, sgaradh, gearradh.

Scissors, *s.* Siosar; deimheas, deamhais.

Scissure, *s.* Sgolt, sgoltadh, sgàin, sgàineadh, gag, gagadh, sgag, sgagadh, peasg, peasgadh; crac, crachd.

Sclerotic, *a.* Cruaidh. The sclerotic coat, *aon do chomhdaichean na sùl.*

Scoat, **Scotch**, *v.* Gabh roimh cuidhil le cloch (no) rud sam bi.

Scoff, *v. n.* Fanaid, fanoid, fochaid, mag, fanaidich, sgallaisich. He began to scoff at him, *thòisich e air fanoid air.*

Scoff, *s.* Sgeig, fochaid, fanaid, mag, magadh, beum.

Scoffer, *s.* Sgeigear, magair; beumair, fear fochaid, fear fanoid. Scoffers, *luchd fanoid.*

Scoffingly, *adv.* Gu sgeigeil, gu fanoideach, gu fochaideach.

Scold, *v.* Troid; cronaich; càin; connsaich, cuir a mach. Scold him, *troid ris;* they began to scold, *thòisich iad air trod.*

Scold, *s.* Trod, trodadh; sglàmhruinn, armaradh; cramhan; té chainnteach, sglamhruinn bhoirionnaich, tuaileasag.

Scolding, *a.* Sglamhrach, eallsgail.

Scollop, *s.* Slige, slige chreachainn, creach.

Scolopendra, *s.* Nathair nimhe; seorsa luibh.

Sconce, *s.* Dùn, dùn catha; dion; coinnlear crochaidh, umhladh, càin.

Scoop, *s.* Liadh, ladar, sluasaid, pleadhan; taoman; buille, sgiap. At one scoop, *air aon sgiap.*

Scoop, *v. a.* Sluasaid, sluaisdich, toll, pleadhaich, cladhaich.

Scooper, *s.* Sluaisdear, tolladair.

Scope, *s.* Rùn, ciall, miann; rum, àite, comas; saorsainn.

Scopulous, *a.* Creagach, cragach, garbh.

Scorbutic, *a.* Carrach, tachasach. Scorbutically, *gu carrach, gu tachasach;* a scorbutic affection, *tachas tiorram.*

Scorch, *v. a.* Loisg, doth; (*as grain*), tiormaich, gread, cruadhaich. Scorched, *loisgte, dòthta, dòthte, tiormaichte, cruadhaichte.*

Scorching, *s.* Losgadh, dothadh; (*grain*), tiormachadh, tiormach, cruadhachadh, greadadh. Scorching heat, *greàdan.*

Scorching, *a.* Teth, bruich, losgach.

Scordium, *s.* Seorsa luibh.

Score, *s.* Sgrioch; sgriob; lìn; sreath; feag, peasg; sgàth, cunntas. Draw a score, *tarruing sgrioch;* (in number), *fichead;* an old score, *sean ainmheach, sean fhiach;* on the score of friendship, *air sgàth cairdeis a thaobh cairdeis, airson cairdeis;* a close mouth incurs no scores, *cha teid feich air beul dùinte.*

Score, *v. a.* Sgrioch, sgriob; sgròb, comharaich.

Scoria, *s.* Smùrach, smùr, smùirne.

Scoring, *s.* Sgriochadh, sgriobhadh, sgròbadh, comharachadh.

Scorious, *a.* Smùrachail, smùirneach.

Scorn, *v. a.* and *n.* Dìmeas, cuir air dìmeas, tarcuisich, dean tàir, fanoid, tamailtich. He scorned him, *rinn e tarcuis (no) tàir air;* I would scorn it, *cha b' fhiach leam e;* I would scorn to do it, *cha b' fhiach leam a dheanamh.*

Scorn, *s.* Dìmeas, tàir, tarcuis, tarcuisne, fanaid, spìd; spòrsa.

Scorner, *s.* Dimeasair, fear fanoid, fochaidiche, spìdear, fear spìde, fear spòrsa, sgeigear.

Scornful, *a.* Dìmeasach, di-measail, fanoideach, fochaideach, spìdeil, sgeigeil, tàireil, tarcuiseach, tarcuisneach, leagarra.

Scornfully, *adv.* Gu dimeasach, gu fanoideach, gu fochaideach, gu spìdeil, gu sgeigeil, gu taireil, gu tarcuiseach.

Scornfulness, *s.* Dìmeas, dìmeasachd, fanoid, fanaid, fanaideachd, spìde, spìdealachd, tàirealachd, tarcuis, tarcuiseachd.

Scorpion, *s.* Sgairp, seorsa béisteig nimhe nach eil eu-cosmhal ri giomach og, ach gu bheil 'earball biorach; aon do chomharran na grein-chrios; sgiùrsa; sgiùrsadh.

Scot, *s.* Albannach; dubh Ghall.

Scot, *s.* Pàigh, roinn, cuibhrionn, cuid, pàirt. Scot and lot, *cìs sgìreachd.*

Scotch, *v. a.* Gearr, mìn-phronn, peasg, sgoch.

Scotch, *s.* Gearradh, pronnadh, peasg, sgoch.

Scotch, *v.* Albannach.

Scotch-collops, **Scotched-collops**, *s.* Biadh pronn, feòil phronn, laoigh-fheoil air a pronnadh.

Scotchman, *s* Albannach.

Scotch mist, *s.* Braon, ceòthrach.

Scot-free, *a.* Saor; gun phàigh, gun chìs, tearuinnte; gun chiurram, gun pheanas.

Scotomy, *s.* Tuaineal, tuainealach, tuaicheal

Scoundrel, *s.* Crochair; sgonn-bhalach, slaoightire.

Scour, *v a.* Sgùr, sgurainn; glan, soilleirich, dean soilleir; nigh. Scour *or* drive away, *cuir stùr ri, sgannraich*, scoured, *sgùrta, sgùirte, glanta, nighte*

Scourer, *s.* Sguradair, glanadair; nigheadair.

Scourge, *s.* Sgiursadh, cuipe, slat, tàs; peanas; fear-fòirneirt, fear sgiùrsaidh.

Scourge, *v. a.* Sgiùrs, sgiùrsaich, cuipinn; peanasaich Scourged, *sgiùrsta, sgiùrsaichte, cuipinnte.*

Scourger, *s.* Fear sgiùrsaidh, sgiùrsair

Scourging, *s.* Sgiùrsadh, cuipinn.

Scourging, *a.* Sgiùrsach; peanasach; fòirneartach.

Scout, *s.* Fear coimhid, beachdair, spithear.

Scout, *v. n.* Beachdaich, coimhead, dean spithearachd, cum sùil air.

Scowl, *v. a.* Bi fo ghuaim, gruaimich.

Scowl, *s.* Gruaim, gruamaiche, gruaimean; groig, gnoig, graing, gnoimh.

Scowlingly, *adv.* Gu gruamach

Scrabble, *v. n.* Smeuraich, sgròb, sgriob

Scrag, *s.* Feòil bhochd, sgrag.

Scragged, *a.* Garbh, creagach, cragach; molach.

Scraggedness, *s.* Caoile; tainead, garbhlach.

Scraggy, *a.* Caol, tana, bochd truagh; garbh, creagach, cragach

Scramble, *v.* Smeuraich, smògaich, sgròbaich, iongnaich; streap, sgràmail.

Scramble, *s.* Sgrobachadh, smògachadh, smògarsaich, streapadh, streapais, sgràmalanaich.

Scrambler, *s.* Sgròbair, smògair, streapair.

Scrambling, *s.* Smeurachadh, sgròbachadh, streapadh

Scranch, *v.* Cruasb, cnabair, cnuas, dean giosgan

Scranching, *s.* Cruasbadh, cruasbail, cnabaireachd, giosgan

Scrap, *s.* Crioman, criomag, spronnan, mìr, pioc, fuigheal, bruanag.

Scrape, *s.* Cruaidh-chas, iom-cheiste, càs, teanntachd, dragh; sgriobadh, sgròbadh; dul; paintear

Scrape, *v. a.* Sgriob; sgròb; sgrath; rub, lom, faigh, cnuasaich, teanail. Scraped, *sgriobhta, sgriobte, sgròbta, rubta, cnuasaichte, teanailte.*

Scraper, *s.* Sgriobachan, sgriobadair; droch-fhidhlear; spiocair.

Scraping, *s.* Sgriob, sgriobadh, sgròb, sgròbadh, rub, rubadh, lomadh, cnuasachadh.

Scrat, *s* Neach fìrionn boirionn; odharag, fitheach fairge

Scratch, *v. a.* Sgriob, sgròb; sgrioch, tachais; rub, suath. Scratched, *sgriobta, air a sgriobadh, sgròbta, sgròbte, air a sgròbadh.*

Scratch, *s* Sgriob, sgròb; sgoch, sgrioch, leòn

Scratcher, *s.* Sgriobadair, sgròbadair; sgriochair, sgriochadair.

Scraw, *s.* Sgrath, fàl, uachdar.

Scrawl, *s.* Sgròb, sgròbaireachd, droch-sgriobhadh.

Scrawl, *v. n.* Sgròb.

Scrawler, *s.* Sgròbair, sgròban, sgròbadair, droch sgriobhair.

Screak, *s.* Sgread, sgreuch; sgriach, éigh, eubh, sgairt

Screak, *v. n.* Sgread, sgreuch, sgriach, éigh, sgairtich.

Scream, *s* Sgread, sgreach, sgriach, eigh, eubh, sgairt, glaodh, sgiamh, ràn, sian.

Scream, *v. n* Sgread, sgreach, sgreuch, éigh, eubh, sgairt, glaodh, ràn, sian

Screamer, *s* Sgreadair, sgreachair, sgreuchair, sgreachag

Screaming, *s.* Sgreadail, sgreachail, sgreuchail, éighich, sgairtich, sianail

Screech, *v n* Sgreach, sgread, éigh, eubh, sgairt, glaodh

Screech, *s.* Sgreach; sgread; éibh, sgairt, glaodh, sgiamh.

Screeching, *s* Sgreachail, sgreadail, éibhich, éighich, sgairtiche

Screechowl, *s* Comhachag, cailleach, oidhche

Screen, *v. a.* Dion, sgàil, sgàilich, falaich, céil, fasgnadh, fasgnaich, criathar, criathraich, rideal

Screen, *s.* Dion, sgàilean, fasgadh; fasgnadh, fasgan, criathar, rideal

Screw, *s.* Bithis, bidhis, sgrobha.

Scribble, *v a* Sgriobh gu suarrach, sgròb, dean sgròbail (no) droch sgriobhadh.

Scribble, *s.* Sgròbail, droch sgriobhadh, dribheanachd

Scribbler, *s.* Droch sgriobhair, ughdar gun fhiach.

Scribe, *s.* Sgriobhair, sgriobhaiche; fear teagaisg Iudhach.

† **Scrimer**, *s* Basbair, feannsair.

Scrip, *s* Màla, màileid, mailios, poc, pocan, balg, sporran, sgriobhadh.

Scriptory, *a* Sgriobhta, sgriobhte

Scriptural, *a.* Sgriobturach, sgriobtarach, sgriobturail.

Scripture, *s* Sgriobtuir, sgriobtur, sgriobtar, sgriobh naomh

Scrivener, *s.* Sgriobhair; sgriobhainnear.

Scrofula, *s.* Tinneas an righ, silticheen

Scrofulous, *a.* Silteach.

Scroll, *s* Sgròl, scròl, ròl

† **Scroyle**, *s* Sgonn-bhalach

Scrub, *v a.* Rub; glan, nigh, sgur, suath, sgrob

Scrub, *s* Spiocair; biosgair, sgrubair, sgruimbean, duine sanntach, sgoun, siochair, sean sguab

Scrubbed, Scrubby, *a.* Suarrach, crion, gun fhiù, gun fhiach, sgruimbeanach

Scruff See **Scurf**.

Scruple, *s* Amharus, teagamh, ag, iom-cheist, iom-chomhairle; tomhas leigh, fichead gràinn air cothrom, sgreapal A scruple of conscience, *agartas coguis, beum coguis*

Scruple, *v n* Cuir amharus, òb, stad, sòr, bi an teagamh, bi an iomchomhairle He will not scruple to kill thee, *cha shòr e do mharbh.*

Scrupler, *s* Teagamhaiche, amharusaiche

Scrupulosity, *s.* Amharus, ag, teagamh, amharusachd, teagamhachd, coguiseachd

Scrupulous, *a* Agail, teagamhach; faicilleach, amharusach

Scrupulously, *adv* Gu h-agail, gu teagamhach, gu faicilleach, gu h-amharusach.

Scrupulousness, *s.* Agaileachd, teagamhachd, faicilleachd.

Scrutable, *a* So-sgrudaidh, so-rannsuchaidh.

Scrutation, *s* Sgrudadh, ceasnachadh, rannsach; rannsachadh, sireadh.

Scrutator, *s.* Sgrudair, rannsachair, ceasnachair, fear sgrudaidh, fear ceasnachaidh.

Scrutineer, *s.* Sgrudair, rannsachair, ceasnachair

Scrutinize, *v a.* Sgrud, rannsaich, ceasnaich, mìn-cheasnaich, geur-rannsuich

SCRUTINY, *s.* Sgrud, sgrudadh, rannsachadh, ceasnachadh.

SCRUTOIRE, *s.* Clàr sgriobhaidh.

SCUD, *v. n.* Ruith, rach an deannaibh, teich.

SCUFFLE, *s.* Brionglaid, tuasaid, caonnag, tabaid, streapaid, boilisg, buaireadh, bruidhinn.

SCULK, *v. n.* Folaich, rach am folach, teich, dean cùilt-earachd.

SCULKER, *s.* Fògaraiche, cùiltear, fear cùirn; giolcair.

SCULKING, *s.* Folachadh, cuiltearachd; giolcadh.

SCULL, *s.* Claigionn; croidhleag; sgoth, eithear.

SCULLER, *s.* Eithear; sgòth, curach, bàt beag; ramhair.

SCULLING, *s.* Pleadhanachd.

SCULLION, *s.* Sguidlear, stràilleag, caile shoithchean; dubh-chaile, sraoilleanach, sraoilleag.

SCULPTOR, *s.* Grabhair, grabhadair, dealbhadair, dualaiche.

SCULPTURE, *s.* Grabhadh, grabhadaireachd, rionachas, dualaidheas, creachaireas.

SCULPTURE, *v. a.* Gearr, grabh, dealbh.

SCUM, *v.* Sgum.

SCUM, *s.* Bàrrag, uachdar, sgum, cobhar.

SCUMMER, *s.* Sguman, sgumadair.

SCURF, *s.* Sgrath; creim, càrr, sgreab, sgròill.

SCURFY, *a.* Sgrathach, creimeach, carrach, sgreabach, sgròill.

SCURRILITY, *s.* Sglamhruinn, ana-cainnt; draosd, draosd-achd.

SCURRILOUS, *a.* Sglàmhruinneach, sgainnealach, ana-cainnteach, sglamhach, sglamhrach; ana-cainnteach; dra-basta.

SCURRILOUSLY, *adv.* Gu sglàmhruinneach, gu sgainneal-ach, gu sglamhach, gu sglamhrach, gu drabasta.

SCURRILOUSNESS, *s.* Sglàmhruinn, sglamhruinneachd, sgainneal; drabastachd.

SCURVILY, *adv.* Gu miothur, gu neo-fhiachail, gu suarrach, gu mosach.

SCURVY, *s.* Tachas tioram.

SCURVY, *a.* Sgabach, creamach, creimeach, carrach, suarr-ach, neo-fhiachail, truagh, crion.

SCURVY-GRASS, *s.* Amaraich.

SCUTCHEON, *s.* Suaicheantas, suaitheantas.

SCUTTLE, *s.* Sguiteal; cliabh, cliabhan, ceis; ruith, dian-ruith, dian-choiseachd; ioma-cheumnachd.

SCYTHE, *s.* Speal, fàladair, iarunn faladair.

SEA, *s.* Muir, cuan, fairge, lear, tàif, aigean, linne; †rian, †bagh, uisge, uisgeachan. A calm sea, *muir chiùin;* a rough sea, *muir mholach, muir gharbh* (*no*) *ghaillionach;* the Black sea, *a mhuir Dhubha;* the Yellow sea, *a mhuir bhuidhe;* the White sea, *a mhuir bhàn;* the Red sea, *a mhuire Dhearg;* the Dead sea, *a mhuir Mharbh;* the Mediterranean sea, *muir na Meadhon-thìr;* on the high seas, *air ard a chuain;* half seas over, *air an daoraich;* a high sea, *boch-thonn, sumain, sumaid, garbh-thonn, bàirlinn;* powerful at sea, *treun air muir.*

SEA-BEACH, *s.* Taobh na mara, tràigh, cladach.

SEA-BEATEN, *s.* Tonn-bhuailte.

SEA-BOAT, *s.* Bàt dionach (*no*) diongalta.

SEA-BOY, *s.* Giullan luing, maraiche òg, giullan maraiche.

SEA-BREACH, *s.* Briseadh mara.

SEA-BREEZE, *s.* Gaoth (*no*) drothan fairge, lear-ghaoth.

SEA-CALF, *s.* Ròn, mulach.

SEA-CAP, *s.* Sgrogan luing.

SEA-CHART, *s.* Cairt-iùil.

SEA-COAL, *s.* Gual mara (*no*) gual a bheirear air mhuir dh' aite sam bith.

SEA-COAST, *s.* Tràigh, eirthir, cladach, còrsa, taobh mara.

SEA-COMPASS, *s.* Compais, iùl.

SEA-FARER, *s.* Maraiche, seòladair; taisdealaiche mara.

SEA-FIGHT, *s.* Muir-ghrim, blàr mara.

SEA-FOWL, *s.* Eunlath mara, eun mara.

SEA-GIRT, *a.* Lear-chuairtichte.

SEA-GREEN, *a.* Gorm, uaine, liath-ghorm.

SEA-GULL, *s.* Aoileann, faoileann.

SEA-HOG, *s.* Peileag.

SEA-HOLM, *s.* Eilean diomhair (*no*) faoin; feamain.

SEA-HORSE, *s.* Each uisge; tarbh uisge.

SEAL, *s.* Ròn.

SEAL, *s.* Seul, naisg, comhar.

SEAL, *v. a.* Seulaich; seul; daighnich, naisg; dùin. Sealed, *seulaichte, seulta;* a sealed letter, *litir sheulaichte.*

SEALER, *s.* Seuladair, seulair.

SEALING, *s.* Seulachadh, seuladh. Sealing-wax, *ceir lit-reach, ceir ghlasaidh.*

SEAM, *s.* Faim; fuaigheal, fuaghal; tàth; creim; (*tallow*), geir, reamhrachd, muc-bhlonag; (*a measure*), ceithreamh, ochd buisealan gràin. A seam of glass, *sé fichead puinnt cothroim do ghloine.*

SEAM, *v. a.* Tàth; fuaigh, faim. Seamed, *tàthta, fuaighte, faimte.*

SEAMAID, *s.* Maighdeann mhara.

SEAMAN, *s.* Seòladair, seòldair, maraiche.

SEA-MARK, *s.* Comhar làn mara; cuspair amhairc air muir.

SEA-MEW, *s.* Aoileann, faoileann.

SEAMLESS, *a.* Gun tàth, gun fhaim.

SEA-MONSTER, *s.* Uile-bhéist mara.

SEA-MOSS, *s.* Coireall, còinneach mara.

SEAM-RENT, *s.* Sgaradh, fosgladh, sgag.

SEAMSTER, *s.* Tàillear.

SEAMSTRESS, *s.* Ban-fhuaghlaiche, banalaiche.

SEAMY, *a.* Làn thàth, làn fhaimean.

SEAN, *s.* Eangach, eang, lìon, lion iasgaich.

SEA-NYMPH, *s.* Oigh mara; ban-dia mara.

SEA-ONION, *s.* Lear-uinnean, uinnean mara.

SEA-PIECE, *s.* Dealbh mara; cinnmhiol mara.

SEA-PINK, *s.* Milsean mara.

SEA-POOL, *s.* Linne mara; linne sàil; poll sàil.

SEA-PORT, *s.* Càla, caladh, port, long phort. A sea-port town, *baile puirt.*

SEAR, *v. a.* Loisg; sgaillt. Seared, *loisgte, air a losgadh.*

SEARCE, *s.* Criathar; siolachan; piobhar.

SEARCE, *v. a.* Criathair; dràbh. I have searced it, *chria-thar mi e.*

SEARCER, *s.* Criathradair.

SEARCING, *s.* Dràbhadh, siothladh.

SEARCH, *v. a.* Sir, rannsuich; sgrud, iarr, feuch. Search after, *sir, rach an tòir air;* search out, *rannsuich faigh a mach;* search or trace, *lorgaich.*

SEARCH, *s.* Sireadh, rannsuchadh; sgrudadh; iarruidh; tòir. They are in search of him, *tha iad an tòir air.*

SEARCHER, *s.* Rannsuchair, sireadair, sgrudair.

SEARCHING, *s.* Sireadh, rannsuchadh, sgrudadh.

SEARCLOTH, *s.* Eudach céirte; céir-bhrat, plàst.

SEA-RISK, *s.* Cunnart mara; sgiorradh luing.

SEA-ROBBER, *s.* Muir-reubair, foghluiche mara.

SEA-ROOM, *s.* Farsuingeachd cuain.

SEA-SERPENT, *s.* Nathair mara.

SEA-SERVICE, *s.* Seòladaireachd.

SEA-SHELL, *s.* Spairneag, slige mara, faochag.

Sea-shore, *s.* Tràigh, eirthir, cladach, tìr, taobh na mara.

Sea-sickness, *s.* Tinneas mara.

Season, *s.* Am, aimsir, tràth; cothrom, am iomchuidh. At this season of the year, *mu 'n tràth so bhliadhna;* in season, *na thràth;* in good season, *ann an deagh thràth;* in season and out of season, *ann am is ann an-am.*

Season, *v. a.* Blasdaich, dean blasda; cuir blas air, saill; dean ri, cleachd ri; (*season a cask*), toirnich. Seasoned, *air a dheanamh blàsda; deanta ri, cleachda ri;* not seasoned to work, *neo-chleachda ri h-obair.*

Seasonable, *a.* Amail, ann an deagh am; ann an deagh thràth, iomchuidh, freagarrach. Seasonably, *ann an deagh am.*

Seasoning, *s.* Blasdachadh, blasdachd.

Seat, *s.* Cathair, seithir, suidheagan, suidheachan, beinc, stòl, creuban, saide, aite suidhe, àros, àite comhnuidh, aite suidhe; àite; tirteag; tòin. A country seat, *tigh dùthcha, tigh samhraidh;* a seat of war, *ionad cogaidh;* take a seat, *gabh cathair, dean suidh.*

Seat, *v. a.* Suidh; dean suidh, socraich, daighnich. He is seated, *tha e na shuidhe;* she is seated, *tha e na suidhe;* he seated himself, *shuidh e, rinn e suidhe.*

Sea-term, *s.* Focal maraiche.

Sea-water, *s.* Sàil.

Seaward, *adv.* Chum na mara.

Sea-weed, *s.* Feaman, turasgar, lus mara, barra-rochd, rod.

Sea-wreck, *s.* Fithreach.

Secede, *v. n.* Dealaich, sgar, rach a thaobh. He seceded from the church, *dhealaich e ris an eaglais.*

Seceder, *s.* Sgaradair, neo-aontachair.

Secern, *v. a.* Sgar; siolaidh, criathar.

Secession, *s.* Sgaradh; eas-aonachd, eas-aontachd, siosmaireachd.

Seclude, *v. a.* Druid, druid a mach, dealaich.

Seclusion, *s.* Druideadh, dealachadh; uaigneas, aonaranachd.

Second, *s.* Tiota; (*in a duel*), dionair, fear-coghnaidh.

Second, *a.* Dara; faisge, faigse. The second man, *an dara fear;* a second coming, *ath-theachd;* a second time, *uair eile, ath-uair, a ris;* the second time, *an dara uair.*

Second, *v. a.* Coghain, cuidich; dion, tearmunn; cum taobh ri, cum taic ri. Seconded, *cuidichte.*

Secondary, *a.* Iochdarach, dara.

Secondary, *s.* Riochdair, fear ionaid, teachdair.

Second-hand, *s.* Dara-shealbhachadh; roimh-ghnathachadh, ath-ghnàthachadh.

Secondly, *adv.* San dara àite, a ris; san ath-aite, san aite is faisge.

Second-rate, *s.* Dara inbhe. A second-rate ship, *loingeas do 'n dara inbhe.*

Second-sight, *s.* Da-shealladh, taibhsdearachd; fàisneachd, fiosachd.

Secrecy, *s.* Diomhaireachd, diùbhras, uaigneas, uaigneachd; rùn, cleith.

Secret, *a.* Diomhair, uaigneach; folaichte; céilte, dorcha; do-thuigsinn. A secret place, aite uaigneach. Keep secret, *cum ceilte.*

Secret, *s.* Ni uaigneach, sgeul rùin; rùn, rùn diomhair, cogar, cagar, sanas, coigle. I will make no secret of it, *cha chéil mi e.*

† **Secret**, *v. a.* Folaich, céil, cleith. Secreted, *folaichte, ceilte.*

Secretaryship, *s.* Rùn-chleirsinneachd.

Secretary, *s.* Rùn-chléireach, rùn-sgriobhair.

Secrete, *v. a.* Folaich, céil, cleith; dealaich, sgar; siothlaidh, fàisg.

Secreting, *s.* Folachadh, céileadh.

Secretion, *s.* Fàsgadh, siothladh; dealachadh.

Secretly, *adv.* Gu diomhair, gu h-uaigneach, os iosal, gun fhios do, gun aire do, an uaigneas.

Secretness, *s.* Diomhaireachd, uaigneas.

Sect, *s.* Droing, pairt, roinn, muinntir, luchd co-bharail, saindrean.

Sectary, *s.* Fear leanmhuinn, deisciobul.

Section, *s.* Rann, roinn; earann, pairt, gearradh.

Sector, *s.* Roinneadair.

Secular, *a.* Saoghalta, talmhaidh; neo-chleireach, a thachaireas uair sa cheud bliadhna. Secular affairs, *gnothuichean saoghalta.*

Secularity, *s.* Saoghaltachd, talmhaidheachd.

Secularize, *v. a.* Dean saoghalta (no) talmhaidh.

Secularly, *adv.* Gu saoghalta, gu talmhaidh.

Secundine, *s.* Iar-bhreith.

Secure, *a.* Tearuinnte; neo-churamach, gun chùram, cinnteach.

Secure, *v.* Tearuinn; dean cinnteach; gabh aig; dion, dean diongalta; glac, cuir lamh air. Secured, *tearuinnte air gabhail aig; an lamh.*

Securely, *adv.* Gu tearuinnte; gu neo-chùramach, gun chùram, gun smuairean; gu gramail.

Security, *s.* Dion, dionadh, fasgadh; tearuinnteachd, cinnte, urras; mi-chùram, cion aire, mi-sheadh.

Securement, *s.* Dion, dionadh, fasgadh.

Sedan, *s.* Carbad laimh, cathair (no) seithir iomchair.

Sedate, *a.* Ciùin, samhach, bìth, socrach, soimeach, mallta, trosdail, suidhichte, steigheil, stolda.

Sedately, *adv.* Gu ciùin, gu sàmhach, gu suidhichte, gu socrach, gu stolda.

Sedateness, *s.* Ciùineachd, ciùineas, socair; stoldachd; steighealachd; trosdalachd.

Sedentary, *a.* Suidheach.

Sedge, *s.* Seilisdear.

Sedgy, *s.* Seilisdearach.

Sediment, *s.* Grunnd, grùid, dràbh, dràbhag, deasgann, deasgannan, druaip.

Sedition, *s.* Ceannairc, àr a mach, éirigh, bruidheann, buaireas, iom-reuson, saine; creanair. Stir up to sedition, *brosnuich chum ceannairc.*

Seditious, *a.* Ceannairceach, buaireasach. Seditiously, *gu ceannairceach, gu buaireasach.*

Seditiousness, *s.* Ceannairc, buaireas, buaireasachd.

Seduce, *v. a.* Thoir a thaobh; buair; meall; truaill. He seduced her, *thruaill e i;* seduced, *buairte, meallta, truaillte.*

Seducement, *s.* Buaireadh, mealladh.

Seducer, *s.* Mealltair, buairear, buaircadair, fear meallaidh, truaillear.

Seducible, *a.* So-mhealladh, so-bhuaireadh, so-thruailleadh.

Seducing, *s.* Mealladh, buaireadh, truailleadh, mealltaireachd.

Seduction, *s.* Mealladh, buaireadh, truailleadh, mealltaireachd.

Sedulity, *s.* Dìchioll, dìcheall, dìchiollachd, dùrachd, tulchuiseachd.

Sedulous, *a.* Gu dìchiollach, gu dìcheallach, gu dùrachdach, gu h-adhartach, gu saoithreachail, gu tul-chuiseach.

Sedulousness, *s.* Dìchiollachd, dìcheallachd, dìcheall.

See, *s.* Cathair easpuig.

See, *v. a.* and *n.* Faic, seall, amhairc; dearc; feuch. See to, *thoir aire, thoir an aire;* see to him, *thoir an aire air, cum sùil air;* see where he is, *seall c'àite am bheil e;* as far as I can see, *fhads is léir dhomh;* let me see your hand, *faiceam do lamh;* methinks I see him, *their leam gu bheil mi 'g a fhaicinn; their leam gur léir dhomh e;* nothing to see to, *gun fhiach, gun fhiù;* they were seen, *bha iad air am faicinn, chunnacas iad;* he was seen, *bha e air 'fhaicinn, chunnacas e;* well seen, *sgileil, teoma;* he is well seen to, *tha deagh aire air a thoirt air; tha e air gabhail aig gu math.*

See, *interj.* Faic, seall, feuch.

Seed, *s.* Siol, fras; ros, pòr; (*race*), cineal, gineal, clann, sliochd; (*of ground corn*), càth, càithlean.

Seed, *v. n.* Siolaich; cuir ros.

Seedcake, *s.* Aran milis.

Seeding, *s.* Gineadh.

Seediness, *s.* Càithleanachd.

Seedling, *s.* Fàillean, ògan.

Seedsman, *s.* Fear curaidh.

Seedtime, *s.* Am curaidh, am cur an t-sìl; earrach, céitein.

Seedy, *a.* Càthar, càithleanach; siolach, pòrach.

Seeing, *s.* Fradharc; léirsinn; faicinn, sealltuinn.

Seeing, *adv.* Achionn, chionn, on.

Seek, *v. a.* Sir, iarr, rannsuich; feuch ri, thoir oidhirp; feòraich, fiosraich. I seek your good, *tha mi 'g iarruidh do leas;* he sought for her, *shir e i;* I sought your good, *dh' iarr mi do leas.*

Seeker, *s.* Iarradair; rannsuchair, ruinnsear, sgrudair; fear siridh, fear rannsuchaidh.

Seel, *v. n.* Aom gu taobh, aom a leth taobh mar luing; (*the eyes*), priob; (*a hawk*), dall.

Seel, *s.* Luasgadh luing, tulgadh tuinn.

Seem, *v. a.* Bi mar, bi cosmhuil; gabh ort, leig ort. Seem to be sorry, *gabh ort a bhi duilich;* it seems to me, *is e mo bheachd-sa; their leam;* it seems, *is coslach.*

Seeming, *a.* Aogasach, coslach, a réir coslais; neo-fhior, o'n leth muigh.

Seeming, *s.* Aogas, coslas; beachd.

Seemingly, *adv.* A réir coslais.

Seemliness, *s.* Éireachdas, bòidhchead, maise.

Seemly, *a.* Eireachdail, ceanalta, bòidheach, eugasach, maiseach, grinn, ciatach; freagarrach, iomchuidh, cubhaidh.

Seemly, *adv.* Gu h-eireachdail, gu bòidheach, gu maiseach, gu freagarrach, gu h-iomchuidh, gu cubhaidh.

Seen, *p. part.* of see.

Seer, *s.* Fear seallaidh, fear da-shealladh; feuchadair, taibhsdear; fiosaiche, fàidh, fear fàisneachd, fear fiosachd.

Seerwood, *s.* Connadh seaç, spruan.

See-saw, *s.* Udlanachd.

Seeth, *v. a.* and *n.* Bruich, carra-bhruich; bearbh, cuir air ghoil; goil, bi air ghoil.

Seether, *s.* Coire, poit; aghann, gòblaid.

Segment, *s.* Gearradh cuairteig, bearradh.

Segregate, *v. a.* Dealaich; sgar, cuir a thaobh. Segregated, *dealaichte.*

Segregating, *s.* Dealachadh, sgaradh, sgarachduinn.

Segregation, *s.* Dealachadh, sgaradh, sgarachduinn.

Seignurial, *a.* Cumhachdach, flathail.

Seignior, *s.* Morair, flath, triath; morair Eadailteach; Iompair Turcach.

Seigniorage, *s.* Cumhachd.

Seigniory, *s.* Tighearnas; dùthaich.

Seine, *s.* Seorsa lion-iosgaich.

Seiner, *s.* Iasgair lìn.

Seize, *v. a.* Glac, greimich, dean greim air, cuir lamh air, gabh; beir air. Seize him, *glac e, beir air.*

Seizin, *s.* Sealbhachadh.

Seizure, *s.* Glacadh; glac; greim; fàsd. Under seizure, *am fàsd.*

Seldom, *adv.* Ainmig, tearc; gu h-ainmig, gu tearc. Very seldom, *ro ainmig; fìor ainmig;* he is seldom to be seen, *is ainmig a chithear e, tha e ainmig ri 'fhaicinn.*

Select, *v. a.* Tagh, roghnaich; sònruich. Selected, *taghta, taghte, roghnaichte.*

Select, *a.* Taghta, roghnaichte, sònruichte. Select men, *daoine taghta.*

Selection, *s.* Taghadh, roghnachadh.

Selector, *s.* Taghair, taghadair, fear taghaidh.

Selenography, *s.* Cunntas mu 'n ghealaich.

Self, *pron.* and *a.* Aon e féin, neach e féin, a cheart ni, féin. Myself, *mi féin, mi fhéin, mise féin:* thyself, *thu féin, thu fhéin, thusa féin;* I will pay it myself, *pàighidh mi féin e;* self do, self have, *mar a chuireas tu, buainidh tu;* of himself, *dheth féin;* of themselves, *dhiubh féin;* he is beside himself, *tha e gòrach, tha e thar a chéill.*

Self-begotten, *a.* Féin-ghinte.

Self-conceit, *s.* Féin-spéis, dòchasachd, leoim, sgòd.

Self-conceited, *a.* Fein-spéiseil; dòchasach, leòmach, sgòdail.

Self-denial, *s.* Féin-dhiùltadh.

Self-evident, *a.* Féin-shoilleir; leòir-shoilleir; làn-shoilleir; riachdail.

Self-existence, *s.* Féin-bhith.

Self-existing, *a.* Féin-bheò.

Self-interest, *s.* Féin-bhuannachd, féin-chuis, spìoc.

Self-interested, *a.* Féin-chuiseach, spiocach, crion; teann.

Selfish, *a.* Féin-chuiseach; féin-spéiseil.

Selfishly, *adv.* Gu féin-chuiseach, gu féin-spéiseil.

Selfishness, *s.* Féin-chuiseachd, féin-spéisealachd.

Self-love, *s.* Féin-ghradh; féin-spéis.

Self-moved, *a.* Féin-ghluasadach.

Self-murder, *s.* Féin-mhort, féin-mhortadh.

Self-murderer, *s.* Féin-mhortair.

Self-opinioned, *a.* Dòchasach, féin-bharaileach; féin-spéiseil.

Self-preservation, *s.* Féin-dhionadh.

Self-same, *a.* Ionann; ceudna; ceart-ionann, ceart cheudna. On the self-same day, *air a cheart la cheudna;* the self-same thing, *a cheart ni cheudna.*

Self-slaughter, *s.* Féin-mhortadh.

Self-sufficiency, *s.* Féin-fhoghainteachd; dòchasachd.

Self-sufficient, *a.* Féin-fhoghainteach; féin-bharaileach, dòchasach.

Self-will, *s.* Féin-thoil; reasgachd.

Self-willed, *a.* Féin-thoileil, rag, reasgach, ceannlaidir; rag-bheartach, strangalach.

Sell, *v. a.* Reic; creic. Sold, *reicte, air a reiceadh.*

Seller, *s.* Reiceadair, fear reic.

Selling, *s.* Reic, reiceadh, creiceadh.

Selvage, *s.* Foir (no) faim eudaich, balt, cumhais.

Selves, *pro. plural* of self. Féin. Ourselves, *sinn féin;* themselves, *iad féin;* they themselves, *iadsa féin;* yourselves, *sibh féin;* you yourselves, *sibhse féin;* he and I, by ourselves, *esa agus mise, leinn féin.*

Semblance, *s.* Samhladh, coslas, coslachd, aogas, dreach, riochd.

† **Semblant**, *a.* Cosmhuil, coslach.

† **Semblative**, *a.* Freagarrach.

Semen, *s.* Siol, pòr.

Semi, *a.* Leth.

Semi-annular, *a.* Leth-chruinn; leth-chearclach.

Semibref, **Semibreve**, *s.* Comhar ciùil.

Semicircle, *s.* Leth-chuairt, leth-chuairteag, leth-chearcall, leth-chruinneag.

Semicircular, *a.* Leth-chruinn, leth-chearclach.

Semicolon, *s.* Pong (no) stad mar so (;).

Semicupium, *s.* Bat a ruigeas an imleag.

Semi-diameter, *s.* Leth-tharsnan, roth.

Semilunar, *a.* Mar leth-ghealaich; leth-chearclach, leth-chruinn.

Semi-metal, *s.* Leth-mhiotal, leth-mheiteal.

Seminal, *a.* Siolach, pòrach. Seminal weakness, *ruithe sìl.*

Seminary, *s.* Aite sìl; sgoil.

Semination, *s.* Siolachadh, cur, siol-chur.

Seminific, *a.* Siolmhor; pòrach.

Semiopacous, *a.* Leth-dhorcha.

Semipellucid, *a.* Leth-shoilleir.

Semiquaver, *s.* Seorsa comhar ciùil.

Semispherical, *a.* Leth-chruinn.

Semivowel, *s.* Leth-ghuth; leth-fhoghair.

Sempiternal, *a.* Siorruidh, bith-bhuan.

Sempiternity, *s.* Siorruidheachd, bith-bhuantachd.

Senary, *a.* Seanar, sianar.

Senate, *s.* Seanait, seanadh, ard-sheanadh, ard-chomhairle. Senate-house, *seanait, tigh ard-chomhairle;* a full senate, *seanait dhomhail (no) làn.*

Senator, *s.* Seanair; combairleach, † duanartach.

Senatus consultum, *s.* Reachd seanaite, achd parlamaid.

Send, *v.* Cuir; cuir fios. God send he live, *gu tugadh Dia gur beò e;* send for him, *cuir fios air;* send away, *cuir air falbh;* send into banishment, *fògair, fògaraich, fuadaich;* send on an errand, *cuir air ghnothuch;* send forth, *cuir a mach.*

Senescence, *s.* Dol an aois.

Seneschal, *a.* Seanaschal; stiùbhard.

Senile, *a.* Sean; aosmhor, aosda; bodachail.

Senior, *s.* Seanair; fear a 's sine.

Senior, *a.* Is sine, ni 's sine.

Seniority, *s.* Barrachd aois, aois, sinead.

Senna, *s.* Seorsa purgaid.

Sennight, *s.* Seachduin. This day sennight, *seachduin o 'n diugh;* to-morrow sennight, *seachduin o 'm maireach.*

Senocular, *a.* Sé-shuileach, sla-shuileach.

Sensation, *s.* Mothach, mothuchadh; càil, beachd, faineachadh; farachduinn.

Sense, *s.* (*Feeling*), mothach, mothuchadh; càil, beachd; (*meaning*), brìgh; ceadfaidh, barail, seadh; ciall; (*judgment*), tuigse, toinisg. The sense of seeing, *fradharc, radharc, seall na sùl;* (of hearing), *claistinn;* a quick sense, *geur-mhothuchadh;* you have no sense, *cha 'n eil toinisg agad;* what sense did you take it in? *ciod an seadh san do ghabh thu e?*

Senseless, *a.* (*Without feeling*), neo-mhothuchail, gun mhothuchadh; gun chàil; (*foolish*), neo-thuigseach; baoghalta, amaideach, baoth, gun tuigse, gun toinisg; gun chiall. A senseless fellow, *umaidh, baothair, gobhallan.*

Senselessly, *adv.* Gu neo-mhothuchail, gu neo-thuigseach, gu baoghalta.

Senselessness, *s.* Amaideachd, baoghaireachd.

Sensibility, *s.* Mothuchadh, mothachalachd; càil.

Sensible, *a.* Mothachail; so-fhaineach, so-fharachduinn; (in Scotland, *intelligent*), tuigseach, toinisgeil; glic, crionna.

Sensitive, *a.* Mothuchail. Sensitively, *gu mothuchail;* a sensitive soul, *anam mothuchail.*

Sensual, *a.* Feòlmhor, collaidh; soghmhor, nàdurra; migheimnidh, macnusach. Sensually, *gu feòlmhor, gu collaidh; gu nadurra; gu macnusach.*

Sensualist, *s.* Fear mi-gheimnidh; fear macnusach; drùisear, trusdar, soghair, saimhear.

Sensuality, *s.* Feòlmhorachd, collaidheachd, saimhe; macnus, macnusachd, mi-gheimnidheachd.

Sensualize, *v. a.* Dean feòlmhor, dean macnusach; truaill.

Sent, *p. part.* of send.

Sent, *pret.* of send. Chuir.

Sentence, *s.* Ciallradh, cialtradh; earann; (*of a judge*), breith, breitheanas, binn, roisceal. Sentence of condemnation, *dìt, binn.*

Sentence, *v. a.* Binn, dìt, thoir breith, thoir binn, thoir a mach binn. He was sentenced to die, *chaidh 'dhìt gu bàs.*

Sententious, *a.* Brìghmhor; drùighteach, goirrid.

Sententiousness, *s.* Brìghmhorachd, brìgh, giorrad, cainnte.

Sentient, *a.* Mothachail, faineach.

Sentiment, *s.* Smuain, barail, beachd, rùn, miann, durachd.

Sentinel, *s.* Fear faire; foireach; freiceadanaiche; *geard.*

Sentry, *s.* Faire; fear faire, foir-fhear; freiceadan, freiceadanaiche.

Sentry-box, *s.* Bothan aire, bothan faire, bothan foirich.

Separable, *a.* So-sgaraidh, so-dhealachadh, dealachail, a dh' fhaodar dhealachadh.

Separate, *v. a.* and *n.* Dealaich, sgar, tearbaidh, tearb, roinn, cuir as a chéile; cuir air leth sgaoil.

Separate, *a.* Dealaichte, roinnte, as a chéile, o chéile, air leth; leis féin. That is a separate question, *is ceist air leth sin.*

Separately, *adv.* Gu dealaichte; lion fear is fear.

Separation, *s.* Dealachadh, sgaradh, tearbadh; sgaoileadh; eadar dhealachadh, eadar dhealach. Though separation be hard, there never were two who were not separated, *ga cruaidh sgarachduinn, cha robh dithis riomh gun dealachadh.*

Separator, *s.* Sgaradair, dealachair; fear sgaraidh, fear dealachaidh.

Seposite, *v. a.* Cuir air leth, cuir gu taobh.

Seposition, *s.* Cur air leth, cur gu taobh; sgaradh.

Sept, *s.* Cinneach, gineal, clann, sliochd, treubh, fine, droing.

Septangular, *a.* Seachd oisinneach.

September, *s.* An seachdamh mios, mios meadhonach an fhogharaidh.

Septenary, *a.* Seachdnar.

Septennial, *a.* Uair sna seachd bliadhnan.

Septentrion, *s.* An taobh tuath, an airde tuath.

Septentrion, **Septentrional**, *a.* Tuath.

Septentrionally, *adv.* Gu tuath, gus an airde tuath.

Septical, *a.* Lobhach, loibheach, breun.

Septilateral, *a.* Seachd-shlisneach, seachd-shliosnach.

SEPTUAGESIMA, *s.* An treas dòmhnach ro' n charbhas.

SEPTUAGINT, *s.* Am piobull Greugach a chaidh eadar-theangachadh le tri fichead fear is a dhà.

SEPTUPLE, *a.* Seachd fillte; a sheachd ùiread.

SEPULCHRAL, *a.* Tuamail; muladach.

SEPULCHRE, *s.* Aite adhlaic; torr, tuam, uaigh, feart, seipeil.

SEPULCHRE, *v. a.* Adhlaic, cuir fo 'n ùir, torr, tiodhlaic.

SEPULTURE, *s.* Adhlac, adhlacadh, tòrradh, tiodhlacadh, ollanachadh.

SEQUACIOUS, *a.* Leanailteach; sùbailt, rithinn.

SEQUEL, *s.* Ath-carrann, an ni a leanas, crioch, deireadh, ceann thall.

SEQUENCE, *s.* Leanmhuinn, leanachd, leantuinn.

SEQUENT, *a.* Leanmhuinneach, leanailteach.

SEQUESTER, *v. a.* Cuir gu taobh, cuir air leth, dealaich; thoir air falbh, reic, creic.

SEQUESTERED, *a.* Air leth, diomhair, uaigneach.

SEQUESTRATE, *v. a.* Cuir gu taobh; dealaich, reic.

SEQUESTRATION, *s.* Dealachadh; tabhairt air falbh buannachd seilbhe.

SERAGLIO, *s.* Tigh mhnathan; tigh bhan-òg.

SERAPH, *s.* Ard aingeal, aingeal, bith ainglidh.

SERAPHIC, *a.* Ainglidh, neamhaidh, naomh.

SERE, *a.* Tioram, seac, crion, seargta.

SERENADE, *s.* Ceòl leannanachd, caismeachd oiche, ceòl oidhche.

SERENADE, *v. a.* Cluich, dean ceòl (no) caismeachd oiche.

SERENE, *a.* Soilleir, soineanta; glan; samhach, féitheil, ciùin, foisneach; maiseach, farasda. A serene visage, *gnùis fharasda, suilbhear.*

SERENE, *v. a.* Soilleirich, ciùinich, coisg, cuir samhach.

SERENELY, *adv.* Gu soilleir, gu samhach, gu féitheil, gu ciùin.

SERENENESS, *s.* See SERENITY.

SERENITY, *s.* Ciùineas, ciùnas, soilleireachd, féith, samhchair, fois, farasdachd.

SERGE, *s.* Seorsa clo, cùrainn thana; stuth.

SERGEANT, *s.* Ceannard air da shaighdear dheug; *searsan;* maor.

SERIES, *s.* Sreath, sread, òrdugh; lìn; cùrsa.

SERIOUS, *a.* Stolda, smuaireanach, crionna; glic, suidhichte, trosdail, farasda; dùrachdach; foisneach; diadhaidh; cudthromach, trom. I am quite serious, *tha mi 'cheart rireamh.*

SERIOUSLY, *adv.* Gu stolda, gu farasda; (*in earnest*), a rìreamh.

SERIOUSNESS, *s.* Stoldachd; farasdachd; aire dhùrachdach.

SERMONICATE, *v. n.* Searmoinich, bruidhinn, cum comhradh.

SERMON, *s.* Searmoin, searmaid; teagasg.

SERMONIZE, *v. a.* Searmoinich, dean searmoin.

SEROSITY, *s.* Uisgealachd.

SEROUS, *a.* Uisgidh, uisgeil, meugar, tana, bùrnach.

SERPENT, *s.* Nathair, buafan. A poisonous serpent, *nathair nimhe;* a water-serpent, *biorbhuasach;* a serpent's sting, *gath nathrach;* serpents, *nathraichean.*

SERPENTINE, *a.* Lùbach, carach; cuairteanach.

SERPIGO, *s.* Teine dé.

SERRATE, SERRATED, *a.* Gròbach, fiaclach.

SERRATION, *s.* Gròbachadh, fiaclachadh.

SERRATIM, *s.* Gròbachadh, gròbachas.

SERUM, *s.* Meug, miog.

SERVANT, *s.* Seirbheiseach, gille, òglach, sgalag, maodlach, feamanach, feadhmanach; (*a female*), searbhanta, innilt, nighean, ban-oglach, caile-shearbhaint, dubh-chaile. A humble servant or suitor, *suiriche.*

SERVE, *v.* Dean seirbheis; thoir ùmhlachd; (*aid*), cuidich, coghain; (*suffice*), foghain; (*satisfy*), toilich, taitinn; (*as dinner*), riaraichte. I will serve you, *ni mi seirbheis dhuit;* I will serve your turn, *ni mise do ghnothuch; fòghnaidh mise dhuit;* this will serve, *ni so an gnothuch, fòghnaidh so, is leòir so;* served up, *riaraichte.*

SERVICE, *s.* (*To a master*), seirbheis; òglachas; muinntireas, dreuchd, obair; (*duty*), dleasnas, dleasdanas, gnothuch; (*aid*), còghnadh, feum, stà, uidhis, deagh thurn; (*at church*), aoradh; (*at table*), cùrsa, riarachadh. In the service of a certain person, *ann an seirbhis neach àraidh;* hard service, *obair chruaidh, obair ghoirt;* can I do you any service? *'n urrainn mi feum dheanamh dhuit?* you are of no service, *cha 'n eil stà annad;* he put him out to service, *chuir e mach g' a choisinn e;* I did him a good service, *rinn mi deagh thurn da.*

SERVICE, *s.* Seorsa craoibh; craobh chaoran.

SERVICEABLE, *a.* (*Useful*), feumail; uidhisell; iomchuidh, stàdhar; (*officious*), easguidh, dichiollach.

SERVICEABLY, *adv.* (*Usefully*), gu feumail; gu h-uidhiseil; gu h-iomchuidh; gu stàdhar; (*officiously*), gu h-easguidh, gu feumail.

SERVICEABLENESS, *s.* Feumalachd, uidhisealachd, iomchuidhead, easguidheachd; stà, feum.

SERVILE, *a.* Tràilleil; dìblidh, suarrach; truaillidh, dimeasail, eisiomaileach, eismeileach.

SERVILELY, *adv.* Gu tràilleil, gu dìblidh, gu suarrach, gu dìmeasail.

SERVILENESS, SERVILITY, *s.* Dìblidheachd, tràillealachd; suarrachas.

SERVING-MAN, *s.* Gille, seirbheiseach, òglach, sgalag.

SERVITOR, *s.* Stuidear suarrach; gille, sgalag.

SERVITUDE, *s.* Daorsa, tràillealachd; seirbheis; muinntearas; muinntir.

SESS, *s.* Cìs, càin.

SESSION, *s.* Seisean; suidhe; mòd; an uine a bhios mòd na shuidhe, suidhe mòid, suidhe cùirt.

SESSOR, *s.* Cìsear.

SESTERCE, *s.* Cùin Roimheach a b' fhiach beul ri 8*l.* 1*s.* 5½*d.*

SET, *v. a.* and *n.* Cuir; suidhich, socraich, àitich, planntaich; (*appoint*), sonruich, orduich. Set down, *leig, leig bhàn, leig sios;* be set against one, *gabh fuath ri neach, cuir an aghaidh neach;* set agog, *cuir thar a chéile,* (*no*) *air a ghaoithe;* set apart, *cuir gu taobh, cuir air leth;* set a bone, *cuir ceart cnaimh;* set a dog on one, *stuig cù ri neach;* set on, *stuig, brosnuich, buair, brog;* set forth or publish, *cum a mach, cuir a mach, leig ris;* set forth or adorn, *sgeadaich, sgiamhaich;* set at liberty, *leig as, thoir saorsa, saor;* set hands on one, *glac, beir* (*no*) *cuir lamh air neach;* set a hen, *cuir cearc air ghur;* set about a thing, *gabh mu ni;* set about your work, *gabh mu d' obair;* set in order, *dean réidh, cuir an ordugh;* set off, *mol, ardaich;* set out as on a journey, *tog ort, triall;* set as the sun, *luidh, laidh, rach fo;* set up, *tog;* set up for a place, *iarr, sir, cuir stigh;* set up, as a shop, *cuir suas;* set on or attack, *thoir ionnsuidh, leum air, gabh air;* set a crying, *cuir a ghal;* I set not much by him, *cha 'n 'eil mòran meas agam air;* set down in writing, *cuir sios, sgriobh;* set down your burden, *leig sios* (*no*) *bhàn d' eallach;* set on foot, *cuir air chois;* set out of the way, *cuir as an rathad;* set to rights, *cuir ceart, ceartaich;* he set his teeth at me, *chas e fhiacail rium;* set up, as at an aim, *cuir suas;* set up laughter, *tog iolach;* set to, *cuir ris.*

Set, *part.* Suidhichte, socraichte, sònruichte; riaghailteach; àitichte. Set open, *fosgailte;* I am set upon it, *tha mi sonruichte air;* set, as a bone, *air chur;* set, as the sun, *air luidhe;* on a set day, *air là sònruichte, air là àraidh;* set on evil, *suidhichte air olc;* on set purpose, *a dh' aon ghnothuch, a dh' aon obair;* he is hard set, *tha e na chàs, tha e air a shàruchadh;* sharp-set, *ocrach, acrach, ciocrach;* a set speech, *òraid dheanta;* a man well set, *fear cumadail;* set awry, *fiar, claon, cam;* set forth, *foillsichte, sgaoilte, nochdta;* set open, *fosgailte.*

Set, *s.* Sread, dorlach do ni sam bi; (*of clothes*), culaidh, trusgan; (*pair*), paidhir, carraid, leth-bhreacan; (*of cards*), pachd; (*of trees*), sread, breath, rang; (*of horses*), greigh, dròbh; (*of men*), bannal, buidheann, cuideachd; (*of a tree*), plannt. Sunset, *luidhe na grèin, dol fo na grèin.*

Setaceous, *a.* Frioghanach.

Seton, *s.* Silteach.

Settee, *s.* Langasaid; suidheagan.

Setter, *s.* Cù eunaich; planntair. A setter forth, *foillseachair;* (a pimp), *maor striopaich.*

Setting, *s.* Socrachadh, suidheachadh; leigeadh, leigeil. Setting forward, *trialladh;* setting off, *trialladh, moladh;* setting up, *togail;* setting of the sun, *luidhe na grèine;* a setting on, or assault, *ionnsuidh, leumadh air.*

Setting-dog, *a.* Cù eunaich.

Settle, *s.* Cathair, beinc, suidheagan; leabadh.

Settle, *v. a.* and *n.* Socraich, suidhich; àitich; tùinich; siolaidh; traogh, ciùinich, coisg. Settle an estate, *suidhich oighreachd;* settle or light upon, *tuirlinn.*

Settled, *a.* Socraichte, suidhichte, àitichte; siolaidhte, traoghta, ciùinichte, coisgte.

Settledness, *s.* Socraichead, socairead, socair; daingne; seimhe, samhchair.

Settlement, *s.* (*Establishing*), socrachadh, suidheachadh; (*agreement*), cordadh, sonrachadh, bann; (*dowry*), dubhairidh; (*dregs*), grùid, grunnd, deasgann; (*colony*), aiteachas; tuineachas, sluaigheachd.

Seven, *a.* Seachd. Seven times, *seachd uairean;* seven o'clock, *seachd uairean;* the seven stars, *an griglean, an crann arain;* seven years old, *seachd bliadhna dh' aois.*

Sevenfold, *a.* Seachd fillte, a sheachd uiread, a sheachd uimhir.

Sevennight, *s.* Seachduin.

Sevenscore, *a.* Seachd fichead.

Seventeen, *a.* Seachd deug.

Seventh, *a.* Seachdamh.

Seventhly, *adv.* San seachdamh àite.

Seventy, *a.* Deich is tri fichead, tri fichead 's a deich.

Sever, *v. a.* Sgar, thoir as a chéile, dealaich; truth. Severed, *sgarta dealaichte.*

Several, *a.* Iomad, iomadh, iomadaidh, mòran; àraidh. Several times, *iomad uair.*

Several, *s.* Dealachadh, dealach; lann.

Severally, *adv.* Gach aon, fa leth, lion fear is fear, gu dealaichte.

Severance, *s.* Dealachadh, sgaradh.

Severe, *a.* Geur, cruaidh, teann, doirbh; gruamach; ain-iochdmhor, borb, neo-thruacannta, docrach, garg, goirt, dioganta, baoghlach; geur-theann; gabhaidh, gaillionnach. He is severe on you, *tha e geur ort, tha e goirt* (*no*) *trom ort;* a severe winter, *geamhradh gaillionnach* (*no*) *cruaidh;* severe sickness, *tinneas geur* (*no*) *goirt.*

Severely, *adv.* Gu geur, gu cruaidh, gu doirbh; gu gruamach; gu borb, gu docrach, gu garg, gu goirt; gu dioganta. He dealt severely with him, *bhuin e ris gu geur.*

Severity, *s.* Cruadhas, cruas, géire; teinne, teinnead; doirbhe, ain-iochd, buirbe; neo-thruacanntas; docair, gairge, diogantas; baoghlachd, gàbhaidh; truime.

Sew, *v. a.* Fuaigh, fuaidh, fuaighil, fuaidhil; stic. Sewed, *fuaighte, fuaighlte.*

Sewer, *s.* (*One who sews*), fuaghlaiche; fuaghladair, tàithlear; (*of a feast*), gille cuirm; (*a drain*), guitear; clais uisge, piob uisge.

Sewing, *s.* Fuaidheal, fuadhladh.

Sex, *s.* Gineal, cineal, insge, †moth. The male sex, *an cineal firionn;* the female sex, *an cineal boirionn.*

Sexagenary, *a.* Tri fichead bliadhna dh' aois.

Sexagesima, *s.* An dara dòmhnach roimh 'n Charbhas.

Sexagonal, *a.* Sé chearnach, sé oisinneach, sé shlisneach.

Sexagesimal, *a.* Tri ficheadamh.

Sexangled, *a.* Sé oisinneach, sé chearnach.

Sexennial, *a.* Sé bhliadhnach.

Sextain, *s.* Rann shé lìn.

Sextant, *s.* An seathamh cuid do chearcal.

Sexton, *s.* Beadal, fear cluig; maor eaglais.

Sextuple, *a.* Sé fillte; a shé uiread.

Shab, *s.* Sgonn.

Shabbily, *adv.* Gu suarach; gu crionn, gu leibideach, gu sgaiteach. He is shabbily dressed, *tha e air a dhroch chluthachadh.*

Shabbiness, *s.* Suaraichead, crìne, leibideachd.

Shabby, *a.* Suarach, crion, leibideach, neo-fhiachail, broineagach. A shabby fellow, *fear suarach, clàmhan oglaich, sgonn, ablach, rag lugan;* shabby clothes, *eudach suarrach.*

Shackle, *v.* Ceangail, geimhlich, cuibhrich; slabhruich; slabhruidhich. Shackled, *ceangailte, geimhlichte, cuibhrichte, slabhruichte.*

Shackles, *s.* Ceanglaichean, geimhlean, cuibhrichean, slabhruidhean. In shackles, *fo cheanglaichean.*

Shad, *s.* Seorsa éisg.

Shade, *s.* Sgàil, dubhar, dubhradh, duibhre, doirche, duirche; dion, fasgadh; (*for the face*), sgàil, sgàilean; (*ghost*), taibhse, tannasg, aog, eug, taisbean, sealladh, ailmse. Under a shade, *fo sgàil, fo dhubhradh.*

Shade, *v. a.* Sgàil, duibhrich, dorchaich; dion, cuir sgàil air. Shade from harm, *dion o dhochann.*

Shadiness, *s.* Duibhre, duirche, dubhradh.

Shadow, *s.* (*Shade*), faileas, aileas; dubhar, dubhradh; falcas; (*favour*), dion, fasgadh, fàbhor, tearmunn; (*sign, trace*), comhar, lorg; (*type*), samhladh. A mere shadow, *ailmse, samhladh;* (ghost), *taibhse, tannasg, taisbean, sealladh, samhladh, ailmse;* cast a shadow, *tilg faileas.*

Shadow, *v. a.* Duibhrich, dorchaich, dubhraich, sgàil; dion, cuir faileas, cuir sgail. Shadowed, *duibhrichte, dorchaichte, dubhraichte.*

Shadowy, *a.* Faileasach, aileasach, sgàileach; dubharach, dubhrach, dorch; (*typical*), samhlachail.

Shady, *a.* Dubhrach, dubharach, sgàileach, dorch.

Shaft, *s.* Gath, saighead; (*of a church*), spiric, spiricean, stiopall. The shaft of a knife, *lamh, lamhragan, cas, cos, samhach.*

Shaft, *a.* Cumhann, cughànn, aimhleathan, domhainn.

Shag, *s.* Fionnadh, colg, calg; seorsa eudaich.

Shag, *s.* Seorsa eòin mara.

Shaggy, *a.* Molach, ròmach, ròinneach, ròbach, catanach, roinneachail, gibeach, giobach, mogach; peallagach. Despise not a ragged boy, nor a shaggy colt, *na dean tàir air mac luideagach no air loth pheallagach.*

Shagreen, *s.* Croicionn murlaich.

Shake, *v. a.* and *n.* Crath; cuir air chrith, luaisg, crith, criothnaich; (*in music*), tri-bhuail. Shake hands, *crath an lamh*, shake hands with him, *gabh crath an laimh dheth*; the earth shook, *chriothnaich am fonn*, shake with fear, *crith le h-eagal*.

Shake, Shaking, *s.* Crath, crathadh; bogadh, luasgadh; critheadh; (*in music*), tri-bhualadh, trileann, trileanta Give it a shake, *thoir crath dha*

Shaker, *s.* Crathadair; bogadair.

Shale, *s corruption* of shell Sgrath

Shall, *v def.* sign of the future, and not translatable. I shall strike, *buailidh*, he shall be struck, *buailear e*

Shalloon, *s.* Seorsa clo

Shallop, *s* Eithear, sgoth, curach

Shallow, *a* (*As water*), tana, ea-domhain; (*in art*), fàs, faoin, baoghalta; lag. Shallowly, *gu tana, gu faoin*; shallow water, *tanalach*.

Shallow, *s.* Tanalach; àthan

Shallowbrained, *a* Faoin; amaideach, simplidh, baoghalta; neo-dhanarra

Shallowness, *s* Tainead; tanalachd, (*of mind*), baoghaltachd.

Shalm, *s* Seorsa pioba.

Sham, *v a* Meall, thoir an car a He shammed him, *mheall se e, thug e 'n caras*.

Sham, *s* Mealladh, leith-sgeul, cur dheth; cur seachad; cleas, car

Sham, *a* Fallsail, mealltach, neo-fhior

Shambles, *s.* Bro-thigh, bro-ionad; margadh feòla. One who sells at the shambles, *feòladair*

Shambling, *a.* Luidseach, neo-chuimeir A shambling fellow, *ludragan, loigear*.

Shamade, *s.* Caismeachd trompaid (no) druma.

Shame, *s.* (*Disgrace*), nàire, masladh; mi-chliù, tàir, tàmailt, eas-onair, (*modesty*), nàisneachd If you have any shame, *ma tha nàire agad*, having little shame, *air bheag nàire*, put to shame, *cuir gu nàire*, shame upon you, *mo nàire ort*

Shame, *v a* and *n.* Nàraich, cuir gu nàire, masluich, gabh nàire. She shamed him, *nàraich i e*, shamed, *nàraichte, masluichte, fu nàire*.

Shamefaced, *a* Nàrach, gnùis-nàrach, nàisneach, òglaidh

Shamefacedly, *adv* Gu nàrach, gu nàisneach, gu h-òglaidh

Shamefacedness, *s* Nàisneachd, òglaidheachd

Shameful, *a.* Nàr, nàrach, maslach, tàmailteach, tàireil, sgainnealach. It is a shameful business, *is nàr an gnothuich e*, a shameful death, *bàs tàmailteach*

Shamefully, *adv.* Gu nar, gu maslach, gu tamailteach.

Shamefulness, *s* Masladh, tamailteachd, sgainnealachd.

Shameless, *a* Beag-narach, mi-narach, dàn, beadaidh, ladurna Shamelessly, *gu beag-narach, amhnarach*

Shamelessness, *s* Beag-nàire, beag-narachd, beadaidheachd, amhnas.

Shammer, *s* Mealltair, cealgair; breugair.

Shamrock, *s* Seamrag, seamhrag

Shank, *s.* Luirgeann, lurgann; lurg; cas, samhach. The shankbone, *cnaimh na luirginn*

Shanked, Shanky, *a* Luirgneach, lurgach; lurgainneach; (*in contempt*), seireanach.

Shape, *v a* Cum, dealbh, cruth; (*clothes*), sgéith Shaped, *cumta, dealbhta, sgéithte*

Shape, *s.* Cum, cumadh, cumachd, dealbh, cruth, deanamh, aogas, coslas, riochd; (*of clothes*), deanamh, sgéithe A good shape, *deagh chumadh*; having a good shape, *cumadail*.

Shaped, *a.* Cumta, dealbhta; sgéithte. It is well-shapen, *tha e air a dheagh chumadh*; well-shaped, *cumadail*, ill-shaped, *neo-chumadail*.

Shapeless, *a.* Neo-chumadail, mi-dhealbhach, neo-eireachdail, gun chumadh, gun dealbhadh, gun dreach, a cumadh

Shapelessness, *s.* Mi-chumadh, mi-dhealbhadh.

Shapeliness, *s.* Cumadaileachd, deagh chumadh, eireachdas.

Shapely, *a* Cumadail, cumachdail, dealbhach, eireachdail, dreachmhor, cuimir.

Shard, *s.* Bloigh, bloighde, sgealp do phoit creadha, clàr, slige, leac

Share, *v a* Roinn, pàirtich, riaraich; gabh cuibhrionn (no) pairt, faigh cuibhrionn. Shared, *roinnte, pàirtichte, riaraichte*.

Share, *s* Roinn, earann, cuid, pàirt, cuibhrionn, crannchur; comaidh, comithe You got your own share of it, *fhuair thu do chuid fhéin deth*, take a share of the food, *gabh comaidh*, for my share, *air mo shonsa dheth*.

Share, *v a.* Gearr, bearr, lom.

Sharebone, *s.* Cnaimh gobhail, cnaimh na tòn.

Sharer, *s* Fear roinn, roinneadair, fear pàirt, fear comaidh (no) comith

Shark, *s.* Iasg fuilteach craosach; fear cuilbheartach, gionach; cuilbheart, car, cleas.

Shark, *v a.* and *n.* Goid; meall, thoir an car a

Sharp, *a.* (*Inactive*), Geur; smiorail, sgairteil, titheach, tapaidh, ealamh, dealasach, deas; (*in edge*), geur, faobhrach; (*in the point*), biorach, beurtha; guineach, lotar, (*in taste*), geur, goirt, garg; (*in wit*), geur, beumnach; (*cruel*), borb, garg, cruaidh, (*in sound*), sgreadach, cruaidh; (*rough*), garbh, (*sharp-set*), ocrach, acrach, ciocrach; (*lean*), tàna, truagh. It has grown sharp or sour, *tha e air fàs goirt*, sharper than you, *ni 's géire no thusa*.

Sharp, *s* Geur-ghuth; geur-fhonn, biodag; cealgair.

Sharp, *v. n* Goid; meall, thoir an car a.

Sharpen, *v a* Geuraich, roinnich, bioraich, faobhraich; thoir roinn, thoir faobhar. Sharpened, *geuraichte, bioraichte, biorach*

Sharpening, *s* Geurachadh, roinneachadh, biorachadh, faobhrachadh

Sharper, *a. com.* of sharp.

Sharper, *s.* Cealgair, mealltair, cuilbheartair, cuilbheartaiche, caraiche; gaduiche, meirleach.

Sharply, *adv.* Gu geur, gu cruaidh, gu sgairteil, gu guineach, gu biorach.

Sharpness, *s.* Géire, géiread, guineachas; faobhar.

Sharp-set, *a.* Ocrach, acrach, ciocrach

Sharpsighted, *a.* Geur, geur-shuileach, geur-sheallach, bior-shuileach, biorach, geur

Sharpwitted, *a.* Geur, beumnach.

Shatter, *v. a.* Bris, bruan, bloighd, pronn, dean na mhìreannan. Shattered to pieces, *bruanta na mhìreannan*

Shatter-brain, *s* Amadan, baoghalan

Shattery, *a.* Brisg, bruanach.

Shave, *v a* Bearr, lom, rùisg, lomair He shaved himself, *bhearr se e fein*, shaven, *bearrta, rùisgte*.

Shaveling, *s* Bràthair bochd; fear bearrta.

Shave-grass, *s.* Biorag

Shaven, *part.* Bearrta, bearrte.

Shaver, *s.* Bearradair, barbair; spiocair; fear reubainn.

Shaving, *s.* Bearradh, bearradaireachd; (*of wood*), sliseag, spealg.

† **Shaw**, *s.* Doire, bad (no) badan coille; tom.

Shawl, *s.* Filleag.

Shawm, *s.* Seorsa piob.

She, *a.* Boirionn; boirionnach, ban. A she-friend, *bancharaid.*

She, *pron.* I, ise, si. He married her, *phòs e i;* who did it? she, *co rinn e? ise;* she struck her, *bhuail si i.*

Sheaf, *s.* (*Of corn*), sguab; (*sheaves*), sguabaichean; (*of arrows*), dorlach; (*a bundle*), trusgan, ceanglachan, glacan; buindeal, buinnseal.

Shear, *v. a.* Buain; (*as sheep*), bearr, lom, lomair; (*as a ship*), fiar, claon. Shorn, *buainte; bearrta, lomairte.*

Sheard, *s.* Sgealb, sgolb, mìr, clàr.

Shearer, *s.* Buainiche; bearradair, lomadair.

Shearing, *s.* (*Of corn*), buaineadh; (*of sheep*), lomairt, lomaradh.

Shearman, *s.* Bearradair, lomadair.

Shears, *s.* Siosar, deimheas.

Sheath, *s.* Truaill, duille.

Sheath, Sheathe, *v. a.* Truaill, cuir an truaill. He sheathed his sword, *thruaill e 'chlaidheamh;* sheathed, *truaillte.*

Sheathy, *a.* Truailleach.

Shed, *v. a.* Dòirt, taom, sil; cuir; sgaoil, sgap; caill. He sheds tears, *tha e 'sileadh dheur;* shed blood, *dòirt fuil;* shed the hairs, as a quadruped, *cuir fionnadh.*

Shed, *s.* Bùth, sgàil; bothan fosgailte.

Shedder, *s.* Doirtear, dòrtair, fear dortaidh.

† **Sheen**, *a.* Loinnreach; glan, soilleir.

Sheep, *s. sing.* and *plur.* Caor; othaisg; *pl.* caoraich; (*in ridicule*), baoghlan. A sheep without horns, *caor mhaol;* a sheep's eye, *sealladh tlà;* a flock of sheep, *dròbh chaorach.*

Sheepcot, *s.* Crò-chaorach, fang, mainnir; banrach.

Sheepfold, *s.* Fang, crò chaorach, banrach; buaile.

Sheephook, *s.* Cromag, cromag chiobair, bachall buachaille.

Sheepish, *a.* Baoghalta, nàr.

Sheepishness, *s.* Baoghaltachd, nàire, gnuis-nàire.

Sheepshearing, *s.* Lomairt, rùsgadh chaorach.

Sheep-pen, *s.* Crò chàorach, fang.

Sheep-walk, *s.* Ionaltradh chaorach.

Sheer, *a.* Glan, fior.

Sheer, *adv.* Gu glan, gu h-ealamh, air a cheud tarruing.

Sheer off, *v. n.* Tionndaidh, goid air falbh; teich.

Sheet, *s.* Site, ròl paipeir; (*of linen*), brath lìn, brat-lìn, leth-eudach, lion-eudach, pìll; (*a sail*), seòl, brèid, sgod siùil; (*of ice*), leac.

Sheet, *v. a.* Comhdaich; paisg.

Sheet-anchor, *s.* Achdair-éigin.

Shekel, *s.* Cùin Iudhach a b' fhiach beul ri leth-chrun.

Shelf, *s.* Sgeilp; (*in a kitchen*), corn-chlar, clàr; beiseil; (*rock*), sgeir, sgòr; (*sand*), beo-ghaineach.

Shelfy, *a.* Sgòrach, sgeireach, creagach, cragach, beo-ghaineachaidh.

Shell, *s.* Plaosg, sgrath; slige, spairneag, sparnag. The shell of an egg, *cairnean uibh, ballag;* a little shell, *moir-eag.*

Shell, *v. a.* Plaoisg, sgrath, fosgail, sgiol. Shelled, *plaoisgte; sgiolta.*

Shelling, *s.* (*Of nuts*), plaosgadh; (*of grain*), sgioladh.

Shellfish, *s.* Maorach, faoch.

Shelly, *a.* Sligeach; faochagach, spairneagach.

Shelter, *s.* Fasgadh, dion, dionadh, tearmunn, dìdean, sgàil, càladh, port; fear dionaidh. Under shelter, *ann am fasgadh, fo dhion.*

Shelter, *v. a.* Dion, tearmuinn, thoir tearmunn.

Sheltered, *a.* Ann am fasgadh, tiorail, fo dhion.

Shelterer, *s.* Dionair, fear dionaidh.

Shelterless, *a.* Gun dion, gun fhasgadh.

Shelving, *a.* Claon, aomta, corrach, cas, leacainneach. The shelving side of a hill, *leacainn.*

Shelvingness, *s.* Claonad, corraichead, leacainn.

Shelvy, *a.* Tan, ea-domhainn, creagach, sgeireach.

Shepherd, *s.* Buachaill, aodhair, adhair, cìobair; *ministear.*

Shepherdess, *s.* Ban-bhuachaill, ban-aodhair, ban-chiobair.

Sherbet, *s.* Deoch air dheanamh suas le siucar uisge agus sùgh nan lìmaide; searbhaid.

Sherd, *s.* Slige-chreadha.

Sheriff, *s.* Siorradh, siorram.

Sheriffalty, *s.* Siorrachd, siorramachd.

Sherry, *s.* Seorsa fion Spàinntich.

Shew, *v. a.* and *n.* Feuch, nochd, foillsich, dearbh; cuir an céill, minich, leig ris, taisbein, dean aithnichte; innis, gairm. Shew that you are clever men, *feuchaibh gur daoine tapaidh sibh;* shew mercy, *nochd truacantas;* shew me, *feuch dhomh, leig fhaicinn domh;* shew cause, *thoir reuson, feuch aobhar.*

Shew, *s.* Seall, sealladh, ball amhairc, coslas, aogas. Make a shew or pretend, *gabh ort;* they make a shew of one thing, and do another, *tha iad a gabhail orra aon ni, is a deanamh ni eile.*

Shewing, *s.* Feuchainn, nochdadh, foillseachadh, taisbean, leigeil ris.

Shewed, Shewn, *pret.* of shew. Air fheuchainn, feuchainnte, nochdta, foillsichte, aithnichte.

Shield, *s.* Sgiath, targaid; dion, didean, tearmunn.

Shield, *v. a.* Dion, tearmunn, gleidh, tearuinn, coimhead, coimhid, còmhdaich.

Shield-bearer, *s.* Sgiathadair; fear sgeith.

Shift, *v. a.* and *n.* Caraich, glidich, mùgh, muth, rach a aite; tionndaidh, solair, rach as. Shift off, *cuir gu taobh;* shift or remove from a house, *rach air imirich.*

Shift, *s.* (*Expedient*), seòl, modh, doigh; (*device*), innleachd; tùr, cleas; car, ceabhachd, cuilbheart; (*shirt*), léine boirionnaich. Is there no shift by which we can escape? *nach 'eil doigh air bith dol as againn?*

Shifter, *s.* Cealgair, cuilbheartair.

Shifting, *a.* Cealgach, carach, cuilbheartach. A shifting fellow, *fear carach.*

Shifting, *s.* Carachadh, glideachadh, gluasad, mùgh; imirich.

Shiftless, *a.* Gun innleachd, neo-innleachdach; neo-sholarach, neo-thùrail.

Shilling, *s.* Sgillin Shasunnach.

Shily, *adv.* Gu fiat, gu coimheach, gu brocanta.

Shin, *s.* Lurgainn, faobhar na lurgainn.

Shine, *v.* Dealraich, dearrs, soillsich, loinnir. Shine out, fair sun, *dearrs a mach, a ghrian àillidh.*

Shine, *s.* Aimsir ghrianach; dealradh, soillse, lannair.

Shiness, *s.* Fiatachd, coimheachas, brocantas.

Shingles, *s. pl.* Deire, seorsa theine dé.

Shining, *a.* Dealrach, dearrsach, soillear, soillseach, glan, loinnreach, gliosgardach.

Shiny, *a.* Dealrach, dearrsach, soilleir, soillseach, glan, loinnreach.

Ship, *s.* Long, loingeas, luingeas; barc, sgiob, eathar, bat, curach, libhearn. The bow of a ship, *ceann caol;* a ship of war, *luingeas chogaidh.*

Ship, *v. a.* Cuir air bord luing.

Shipboard, *s.* Bord luing. On shipboard, *cuir bord luinge.*

Shipboy, *s.* Gille luing, seòladair òg.

Shipbuilder, *s.* Saor luing.

Shipman, *s.* Maraiche, seòladair.

Shipmaster, *s.* Maighstir luing; sgiobair; long-mhaighstir.

Shipping, *s.* Cabhlach; seòladh.

Shipwreck, *s.* Long-bhriseadh.

Shipwright, *s.* Saor-luing, saor luingeis.

Shire, *s.* Siorrachd, siorramachd.

Shire-mote, *s.* Mòd siorraidh.

Shirt, *s.* Léine, † caimis. Shirts, *léintean.*

Shirt, *v. a.* Léintich.

Shirting, *s.* Leintean.

Shirtless, *a.* Gun léine; lom, rùisgte, lomardach.

Shit, *pret.* of shite. Chac.

Shite, *v. n.* Cac, dean cac.

Shitten, *part.* Cac; mosach, salach.

Shittim, *s.* Seorsa fiodha Arabaich.

Shive, *s.* Sliseag; sgealb, bloigh; mìr, bruanag, mìr arain, sliseag buileinn.

Shiver, *v. n.* Crith; bruan; bris. Shivered, *arr a bhruanadh, briste;* shivering with cold, *a crith leis an fhuachd.*

Shiver, *v. a.* Bruan, bris, spealg, sgealb.

Shiver, *s.* Sgealb, spealg, bruan, bloighde, mìr. Break into shivers, *bris na spealgan (no) na bloighdean e;* in shivers, *na spealgaibh, na bloighdibh, na mhìreannan.*

Shivering, *s.* Crith, crith-fhuachd; ball-chrith; (*in pieces*), briseadh, bruanadh, sgealbadh, spealgadh.

Shivery, *a.* Breòite; truagh, neo-thuaireil.

Shoal, *s.* Oitir; tanalach; sgeir; (*of fish*), sgaoth, lòd, sgann.

Shoal, *a.* Tan, neo-dhomhainn.

Shoaly, *a.* Tan, neo-dhomhainn.

Shock, *s.* Crith, criothnachadh; oilbheum; oillt; gràine, allsga, déistinn; (*of a foe*), ionnsuidh; ruathar. A shock of an earthquake, *crith-thalmhainn;* it gave a shock to my feelings, *chuir a déistinn (no) gràine orm, chuir e oillt orm;* the first shock is the worst, *is i cheud ionnsuidh is miosa;* (*of corn*), adag, rucan, mulan.

Shock, *s.* Cù molach.

Shock, *v. a.* Adagaich; rucanaich. Shocked, *adagaichte, rucanaichte.*

Shock, *v. a.* Crith, crath, criothnaich; thoir oilbheum, thoir déistinn; cuir déistinn, cuir gràine (no) oillt air, cuir fuath air, cuir goirisinn air.

Shock, *v. n.* Thoir ionnsuidh; rach an dàil; leum air.

Shocking, *a.* Oillteil, eagallach, gràineil; goirisneach, critheach, fuathasach.

Shod, *part.* Crudhta, air a chrudh; brògach.

Shoe, *s.* (*Of a person*), brog, cuarag; (*of a horse*), crudh, crubh. A shoe-sole, *bonn bròig;* my shoe-sole, *bonn mo bhròig.*

Shoe, *v. a.* Brògaich; (*as a horse*), crudh, crubh.

Shoeboy, *s.* Gille bhròga.

Shoeing-horn, *s.* Adharc bhròga.

Shoemaker, *s.* Greasaiche, greusaiche; brògair; asair.

Shoetie, *s.* Iall bròig, barr-iall.

Shog, *s.* Utag; putag, crath.

Shog, *v. a.* Put, thoir utag, crath.

Shone, *pret.* of shine. Shoillsich, dealraich.

Shoot, *v. a.* and *n.* Tilg; cuir a mach, fàs, cinn. Shoot him, *tilg e;* shoot a burden, *leig sios (no) bhàn eallach;* shoot corn, *taomaich gràin;* shoot *or* push, *pùc, purr, put;* the trees begin to shoot, *tha na craobhan ag ùrachadh (no) cur a mach, tha na craobhan a cinntinn;* shoot at, *tilg air;* shoot off the gun, *leig dheth (no) cuir dheth an gunna.*

Shoot, *s.* Tilgeadh, urchair; (*of a tree*), meangan, meanglan, beangan, meur, fàilean, maothan, ùr-fhas, fiùran, fiùirean, gineag.

Shooter, *s.* Tilgear, fear tilgidh; fear taomachaidh, sàighdear, gunnair.

Shooting, *s.* Gunnaireachd, lamhach; tilgeadh; pùc. Shooting of a star, *sgeith ronnaig;* (*growing*), fàs, cinntinn, gineadh; (*emptying*), taomachadh, dortadh.

Shop, *s.* Bùth; bùth bathair, bùth-oibre.

Shopboard, *s.* Bord bùtha, clàr bùtha.

Shopbook, *s.* Leabhar cunntais.

Shopkeeper, *s.* Marsonta, ceannuiche, marsal.

Shore, *s.* (*Of the sea*), tràigh, cladach, tìr, taobh mara, oirthir, eirthir; (*sewer*), guitear, claise uisge; (*prop*), taic, prop. Wrecks are most frequent near the shore, *bath mòr aig oirthir;* by the shore, *ri taobh tìre.*

Shore, *v. a.* Cum suas, cum taic ri; cuir air tìr.

Shoreless, *a.* Gun tràigh, gun chladach.

Shoreling, *s.* Croicionn caorach lomairte; pealaid.

Shorn, *part.* Lomairte, lom, lomta, bearrta, buainte.

Short, *a.* Goirrid; gearr; beag; crion; cutach; gann; ath-ghearr, cainnteach, crosda; (*compendious*), cuimeir. Short in speech, *gearr-bhriathrach;* short and blunt, *mutach;* to be short, *ann am beag bhriathraibh, ann am beag dh' fhocaill;* a short while, *tacain bheag, ùine bheag, ùine ghoirrid;* in a short time, *ann ùine bheag;* short of, *gearr air, air an taobh so;* he came short of it, *thàinig e gearr air;* short of twelve years, *gearr air dà bhliadhna dheug, air an taobh so dha bhliadhna deug;* run short, *ruith goirrid, ruith as;* short of money, *gann dh' airgiod.*

Short-breathed, *a.* Gearr-analach.

Short-cut, *s.* Rathad aithghearr; ath-ghearradh.

Shorten, *v. a.* Giorraich; fearr, cuir an giorrad, gearr, bearr. Shortened, *giorraichte, bearrta.*

Shortening, *s.* Giorrachadh.

Short-hand, *s.* Sgriobhadh goirrid.

Short-lived, *a.* Gearr-shaoghlach, diombuan.

Shortly, *adv.* Gu goirrid, gu grad, gu h-aithghearr, a chlisgeadh. Shortly after that, *goirrid an deigh sin.*

Shortness, *s.* Giorrad, giorradas, giorrachd, diombuanachd. Shortness of breath, *gainne analach, cuinge analach.*

Short-sighted, *a.* Gearr-sheallach, gearr-shuileach.

Short-sightedness, *s.* Gearr-shealladh.

Short-waisted, *a.* Gearr-chneasach; gearr-chorpach, cutach.

Short-winded, *a.* Gearr-analach; bagach, bronnach.

Short-winged, *a.* Gearr-sgiathach.

Shory, *a.* Tràghach, air traigh, air taobh na mara.

Shot, *pret.* and *p. part.* of shoot. Thilg; chinn; tilgte.

Shot, *s.* Urchair, urchuir; braidhe, spraidhe, làmhach (*for guns*), peilearan. Small shot, *luaidh chaol;* a volle of small shot, *fras luaidhe chaol;* about a gun-shot off, *beul ri urchair gunn as.*

Shot, *s.* Pàigh, cuid do lacha. Shot-free, *saor, gun pheanas.*

Shote, *s.* Seorsa éisg.

Shot-free, *a.* (*Invulnerable*), do-leònadh; (*from a reckoning*), saor.

Shough, *s.* Cù molach.

Shoulder, *s.* Gualainn, slinnean; druim, droman. The shoulder of a beast, *slinnean;* having great shoulders, *slinneanach;* broad-shouldered, *slinneanach;* out of the shoulder, *as a ghualainn.*

Shoulder-belt, *s.* Crios guaille, airm-chrios.

Shoulder-blade, *s.* Cnamh slinnein.

Shoulder-clapper, *s.* Companach.

Shout, *s.* Glaodh, iolach, gàir, sgairt, caithream; comhghair, claor. Raise a shout, *tog iolach;* a shout of triumph, *caithream;* (of joy), *iolach.*

Shout, *v. a.* Glaodh, dean glaodh, tog iolach.

Shouting, *s.* Glaodhaich, iolach, gàirich; caithream.

Shove, *v.* Pùc, fùc, put, thoir utag, ding. He shoved me, *phut e mi, thug e utag dhomh.*

Shove, *s.* Pùc, pùcadh, pùt, putadh, utag, putag, airleag.

Shovel, *s.* Sluasaid. A fire-shovel, *croman luatha.*

Shovel, *v. a.* Sluasaid, sluaisd.

Shoveller, *s.* Sluaisdear, sluaisdiche.

Show, *s.* Sealladh, iongantas; ball-amhairc; greadhnachas, mòr-chuis; spagluinn.

Show, *v. a.* Feuchd, nochd, leig ris, foillsich, taisbean.

Showbread, *s.* Aran taisbein, aran coisrigte.

Shower, *s.* Fras, fros; sileadh, sion, sian, casair, caoth, braon, ceothran. When the wind is low the shower is blunt, *nur luidheas a ghaoth is maol gach sian.*

Shower, *v. a.* Fras, dòirt, sil, taom.

Showery, *a.* Frasach, fliuch, feur-thuinneach, uisgeil, silteach, dòrtach. A showery day, *la fliuch.*

Showering, *s.* Frasadh, dòrtadh, sileadh, taomadh.

Shown, *part.* Feuchainnte, nochdta, foillsichte.

Showy, *a.* Breagh, briagh, grinn; greadhnach; spleaghach. riombach, basdalach, spairiseach.

Shrank, *pret.* of shrink. Chrup.

Shred, *s.* Mìr, leub, srac. He cut it in shreds, *shrac e na leuban e.*

Shred, *v. a.* Srac, leub, srac na mhìreannan.

Shrew, *s.* Té ladurna; ban-cheard; bansgal, biride.

Shrewd, *a.* Crionna, seanacar, sicir, glic, ciallach, toinisgeil; dùbailt, cealgach, seòlta; geur, olc, dona; guineach, goirt; cunnartach.

Shrewdly, *adv.* Gu crionna, gu sicir, gu glic, gu ciallach, gu toinisgeil.

Shrewdness, *s.* Crionnachd, sicireachd; ceilge, cuilbheart; seòltachd.

Shrewish, *a.* Ladurna, sglamhrach, beadaidh; bansgalach.

Shrewishly, *adv.* Gu ladurna, gu sglamhach, gu beadaidh.

Shrewishness, *s.* Ladurnachd, sglamhachas, beadaidheachd.

Shrewmouse, *s.* Neas, easag.

Shriek, *v. n.* Sgread, sgreach, sgairt, glaodh, éigh, eubh, ràn, sgal, sian.

Shriek, *s.* Sgread, sgreach, sgairt, glaodh, eigh, eubh, ràn, iolach, sian.

Shrieking, *s.* Sgreadail, sgreachail, sgairtich, glaodhaich, eighich, rànaich, sianail.

† **Shrift**, *s.* Aideachadh.

Shrill, *a.* Sgreadach, cruaidh, sgalach, binn, geur, sgalanta.

Shrilly, *adv.* Gu sgreadach, gu cruaidh, gu binn, gu geur.

Shrimp, *s.* Carran; cloidheag; duine beag, gircean, ablach.

Shrine, *s.* Creacar; naomh-chobhan.

Shrink, *v. n.* Crup; preasaich; criopagaich; cas; fàs gealtach; crion, searg. Shrunk, *crupta, air crupadh, air crionadh;* his heart is shrunk with grief, *tha 'chridhe air crionadh le bròn.*

Shrink, *s.* Crup, crupadh, preasag, cas, criopag, cripeag, crionadh.

Shrinker, *s.* Gealtair.

Shrive, *v. a.* Eisd ri (no) gabh aideach.

Shrivel, *v. n.* Crup, preas, preasagaich, criopagaich, cas, searg, liurc; sgreag. Shrivelled, *crupta, preasagach, preasta, preasagaichte, seargta.*

Shrivelled, *a.* Preasach, preasagach, criopagach, seargta, sgreagta. A thin, shrivelled person, *seirgeal.*

Shroud, *s.* Comhdach, brat, fasgadh; marbh-phaisg, corpleine, ais-leine, lionnsag, aodach mairbh. I wish your shroud were on you, *marbh phaisg ort.*

Shroud, *v. a.* and *n.* Comhdaich, dion, folaich, paisg, céil; marbh-phaisg; gabh fasgadh, rach fo dhion.

Shrove-tide, Shrove-Tuesday, *s.* Oinid, Inid, di màirt Inid.

Shrub, *s.* Preas, ras-chrann; deoch bhlasda làidir. Any sweet-scented shrub, *cannach.*

Shrubbery, *s.* Preasarnach, preasach, caillteamach.

Shrubby, *a.* Preasach, preasarnach; dosach, badach.

† **Shruff**, *s.* Smùr, smùrach.

Shrug, *v. a.* (*The shoulders*), clamhar. He shrugs with cold, *tha giùig air leis an fhuachd.*

Shrug, *s.* Clamhradh; clòimhteachadh; (*with cold*), giùig, croit, cruit.

Shrunk, *part.* Crupta, air crupadh, crionta, air crionadh.

Shudder, *v. n.* Crith, oilltich. I shudder to think of it, *dh' oilltich mi ri smuaineach' air.*

Shudder, *s.* Crith, oillt, crith-oillt, ball-chrith, allsga.

Shuffle, *v. a.* Cuir thar a chéile, cuir troimh chéile; dean iomairt; mùgh; coimeasg, measg. Shuffle off, *faigh cuit, cuir gu taobh.*

Shuffle, *s.* Measgadh, coimeasg; (*trick*), cleas, cuilbheart, siomaguad.

Shuffler, *s.* Fear measgaidh, cleasaiche, cuilbheartair.

Shufflingly, *adv.* Gu h-iomairteach.

Shun, *v. a.* Seachain; teich; siach. That can be shunned, *so-sheachnaidh;* do not seek and shun it, *na bi 'g a shireadh is 'g a sheachnadh.*

Shunless, *a.* Do-sheachnadh.

Shut, *v. a.* Dùin, druid; crann; bac; iadh; stop. Shut out, *dùin a mach, druid a mach;* shut up, *druid* (*no*) *dùin suas;* he shut them out, *dhùin e mach iad.*

Shut, *a.* Dùinte, druidte.

Shutter, *s.* Brod uinneig.

Shuttle, *s.* Spàl.

Shuttlecock, *s.* Gleicean; cal-chearcain, cail-chircein.

Shy, *a.* Fiata, coimheach, brocanta, taoghanta, pùtanta; fiadhaich, ogluidh; mòitealach.

Shyness, *s.* Coimheachas, brocantas, pùtantachd, mòitealachd.

Sibilation, *s.* Feadail, fead.

Sicamore, *s.* Crann sice.

Siccate, *v. a.* Tiormaich.

Siccation, *s.* Tiormachadh.

Siccity, *s.* Tirime, tiormachd, tioramachd, tart.

Sice, *s.* An seathamh air dhisdean.

SICK, *a.* Tinn, euslan, euslainnteach, fann, breòite. Sick and feverish, *tinn, teth.*

SICKEN, *v. n.* Fàs tinn; fannaich; gabh (no) glac tinneas.

SICKISH, *a.* Tinn, euslan, euslainnteach, fann, leth-char tinn

SICKLE, *s.* Corran, corran buainidh.

SICKLEMAN, *s* Buainiche, fear corrain.

SICKLINESS, *s* Euslainnte, tinneas, galar, eucail

SICKLY, *adv.* Gu tinn, gu h-euslan.

SICKLY, *a.* Tinn, euslan, euslainnteach, fann, breoite, meur-anda, neo-fhallain, driachanach

SICKNESS, *s* Tinneas, euslainnte, eucail, galar. The falling sickness, *an tinneas tuiteamais, an tuiteamas.*

SIDE, *s* Taobh, slios, (*party*), taobh, pàirtidh, pàirt, cuid-eachd, muinntir, (*brim*), oir, foir, fraidhe; (*of the body*), cliathaich, leth-taobh The side of a country, *taobh dùth-cha*, a pain in his side, *goimh na chliathaich*, a side-face, *leth-aghaidh*, by the side of, *ri taobh, laimh ri*, by the way-side, *ri taobh an rathaid*, a relation by my mother's side, *caraid thaobh mo mhathar*, of the same side, *a dh' aon taobh*, on all sides, *air gach taobh*, on the inside, *air an taobh stigh*, on the east side, *air an taobh shios*, the side of a river, *taobh aimhne*, on this side, *air an taobh so, bhos.*

SIDE, *v n* Aom; cum taobh, còghain, cuidich, cuir le Side with him, *cum taobh ris, cuir leis*

SIDEBOARD, *s.* Bord cùil

SIDELONG, *adv* An comhair thaobh, an comhair a leth-taobh, air leth-taobh

SIDELONG, *a.* Leth-taobhach, aomta, an comhair a thaobh A sidelong glance, *sealladh leth-taobh*

SIDERAL, *a.* Steornail, reultach, reannagach.

SIDERATED, *a* Seargta, seargte, grod

SIDERATION, *s.* Seargadh; grodadh.

SIDESADDLE, *s.* Diolaid (no) pillean boirionnaich.

SIDEWISE, *adv.* An comhair a thaobh.

SIDING, *s* Coghnadh, cumail taobh ri

SIEGE, *s* Sèisd, iom-dhruideadh, baile-chuairteachadh Lay siege, *cuir sèisd*

SIEVE, *s* Criathar, rideal, ruideal, rillean, robhar, piobhar. A meal-sieve, *criathar min.*

SIFT, *v a* Criathair, criathraich, ridill, rill; (*search*), rann-suich, sgrud, ceasnuich, min-cheasnuich, feòraich, dearbh Sift me as much as you please, *sgrud mi fhadsa thogras tu*, sifted, *criathraichte*

SIFTER, *s.* Criathradair.

SIFTING, *s.* Criathradh, rilleadh, (*searching*), rannsuchadh, sgrudadh, ceasnuchadh, feòrachadh

SIGH, *s.* Osunn, osann, acain, osnadh. A deep sigh, *osann throm*, fetch a sigh, *tarruing osann*

SIGH, *v. a* Osnaich, dean osann (no) acain

SIGHING, *s* Osnaich, acainich.

SIGHT, *s.* (*View*), sealladh, (*eyesight*), sealladh sùl, fradh-arc, radharc, rosg, amharc, léirsinn, (*presence*), làthair, làthaireachd. A fine sight, *sealladh grinn*, he lost his sight, *chaill e 'léirsinn, chaill e 'shealladh*, out of my sight, *a mo shealladh, as mo làthair, a làthair mo shùl*, out of sight, *as an t-sealladh*, keep sight of him, *cum sùil air, cum san t-sealladh e*, I know him by sight, *is aithne dhomh e thaobh faicinn*. at first sight, *air a cheud sealladh*, vanish out of sight, *rach as an t-sealladh*, dimness of sight, *doille, dalladh léirsinn*

SIGHTED, *a* Sùileach. Quick-sighted, *geur biorach, geur shuileach*

SIGHTLESS, *a.* Dall, gun sealladh, gun radharc, gun léirsinn.

SIGHTLY, *a.* Taitneach, eireachdail, speisealta, ciatach.

† SIGIL, *s.* Seul

SIGN, *s.* Comhar, comharradh; iongantas, ioghnadh; mior-bhuil; neonachas; (*footstep*), aile, lorg; (*standard*), brat-ach, meirghe; (*symbol*), samhladh; (*a nod*), sméid; (*of a house*), dealbh, sop-reic This is a sign, *is comhar so;* a good sign, *deagh chomhar, comhar math.*

SIGN, *v. a.* Cuir lamh ri, cuir ainm ri; comharraich; ciallaich

SIGNAL, *s* Sànus, fios.

SIGNAL, *a.* Sònruichte, sùnruichte, ion-chomharraichte, mòr.

SIGNALIZE, *v. a* Dean ainmeil.

SIGNALLY, *adv* Gu sònruichte, gu h-ainmeil, gu h-allaidh.

SIGNATURE, *s* Ainm, comhar, comharradh, fo-sgriobhadh.

SIGNET, *s* Seul, comhar, seul righ.

SIGNIFICANCE, SIGNIFICANCY, *s.* Ciall; seadh, suim, meas, urram, cothrom, cudthrom.

SIGNIFICANT, *a.* Ciallachail, ciallaidheach.

SIGNIFICATION, *s* Ciall, brìgh; blàdh, blàth, seadh, suim.

SIGNIFICATIVE, *a.* Ciallachail, ciallaidheach, brìgheil.

SIGNIFY, *v a* Feuch, innis, dean aithnichte, cuir an céill, thoir sànus, thoir fios; ciallaich. He signified to me, *thug e fios domh.*

SIGNIORY, *s* Morairreachd, cumhachd.

SIGNPOST, *s.* Post.

SILENCE, *s* Tosd, samhchair, ciùineas, seimhe, féith, tamh, fois Keep silence, *bi samhach, bi ad thosd, cum samhach;* silence is confession, *is ionann tosd is aideach*

SILENCE, *v a.* Cuir samhach, dean bìth, dean tosd. Silence them, *cuir samhach iad.*

SILENT, *a.* Samhach, tosdach, balbh, ciùin, bìth.

SILENTLY, *adv.* Gu samhach, gu ciùin, gu tosdach, gu bìth, os iosal.

SILICULOSE, *a* Plaosgach, sgrathach, cochullach

SILIQUA, *s.* Cochall, cochull, meiligeag, moinigeag

SILIQUOSE, *a.* Cochullach, càithleanach

SILK, *s* Siod, sìde, sròl

SILKEN, *a* Sioda, sìdear; mìn, siodachail.

SILKMERCER, *s* Marsun sìde.

SILKWEAVER, *s* Figheadair sìde (no) sioda

SILKWORM, *s.* Cnuimh shioda.

SILKY, *a* Siodach, sìdeach, sidear, siodachail, mìn, bogar, sliogta

SILL, *s* Clach an doruis.

SILLABUB, *s* Cobhar, oghan; fuarag, ceath oibrichte.

SILLILY, *adv* Gu faoin, gu baoghalta, gu h-amaideach.

SILLINESS, *s* Faoineachd, baoghaltachd; amaideachd, mi-thoinisg, feamachas.

SILLY, *a* Faoin, baoghalta, fachunnta, neo-thoinisgeil, amaideach, ea-crionna, simplidh, seochlanach, meirbh. A silly fellow, *baothair, baoghlan, guraiceach, dreollan, seochlan, dirlean.*

† SILT, *s.* Poll, eabar, clabar, làthach.

SILVAN, *a* Coillteach, coilltidh

SILVER, *s* Airgiod Quicksilver, *beò-airgiod.*

SILVER, *a* Airgiodach, airgid, bàn (no) geal mar airgiod. The silver moon, *a ghealach bhàn*

SILVER, *v a* Comhdaich (no) sgeaduich le airgiod.

SILVERLING, *s* Cùinn airgid

SILVERY, *a* Airgiodach

SILVERSMITH, *s.* Ceard airgid.

SILVERY, *a.* Airgiodach.

SIMAR, *s* Gùn boirionnaich.

Similar, *a.* Coslach, cosmhuil, cosmhal, ionann, co-ionann. Similar to, *coslach ri.*

Similarity, *s.* Coslas, coslachd, co-shamhlachd, ionann-achd, co-ionannachd.

Similarly, *adv.* Gu coslach, gu cosmhal.

Simile, *s.* Samhladh, cosmhalachd, coslachd, coimeas.

Similitude, *s.* Samhladh, coslas, coslachd, cosmhalachd, coimeas.

Similitudinary, *a.* Samhlachail, coslachail.

Simmer, *v. n.* Bruich, earrabhruich, earr-bhruich.

Simnel, *s.* Seorsa arain milis, millsean.

Simoniac, *a.* Sìmonach, sìmonaiche.

Simoniacal, *a.* Sìmonach.

Simony, *s.* Sìmonachd, goid (no) reic nithe naomha, ceal-shlàd.

Simper, *s.* Feith ghàire, faoin-ghàir, gàir, fo-ghàir, snodh-ghàire.

Simper, *v. n.* Gàir, dean snodh-ghàire.

Simple, *a.* (*Pure*), glan, neo-thruaillte; (*not two*), singilte, aon-fhillte; (*harmless*), simplidh, neo-chiontach, neo-chronail; (*sincere*), socharach, còir, onorach; (*plain*), neo-sgiamhach, iriosal; (*foolish*), amaideach, baoghalta, ea-crionna; aineolach, neo-theoma. A simple fellow, *baoghlan, baothair.*

Simple, *s.* Luibh.

Simpleness, *s.* Aon-fhillteachd, simplidheachd, tréibh-dhireachd, socharachd; neo-dhanarrachd.

Simpler, *s.* Lusragan, lusranaiche.

Simpleton, *s.* Baoghlan, baothair, gobhallan.

Simplicity, *s.* Simplidheachd, aon-fhillteachd, treibh-dhireas; socharachd; baoghaltachd.

Simplify, *v. a.* Simplich, dean simplidh. Simplified, *simplichte.*

Simplist, *s.* Lusragan, lusranaiche.

Simply, *adv.* Gu simplidh; gu neo-theòma; gu baoghalta; gun cheilg, gun sgleò, gu fior.

Simulate, *v. a.* Gabh ort, leig ort.

Simulation, *s.* Cealg, ceilg, cealgaireachd, mealltaireachd, blandar.

Simultaneous, *a.* Mu chomh-luath, maraon, a dh' aon tarruing, cuideachd, cuideachail.

Sin, *s.* Peacadh; ciont, lochd, coire; † adhall, † andagh. Original sin, *peacadh gin;* it is a sin to you, *is peacadh dhuit e;* a sin-offering, *iobairt pheacaidh.*

Sin, *v. n.* Peacaich; ciontaich. Sin against God, *peacaich an aghaidh Dhé;* I am more sinned against than sinning, *Is mò mo dhroch-caramh no mo chiont.*

Sinapism, *s.* Seorsa plàsda.

Since, *adv.* Cheann, chionn, a chionn, on. Since that is the case, *on is ann mar sin a tha 'chùis, a chionn gur ann mar sin a tha 'chùis, chionn gu bheil a chùis mar sin.*

Since, *prep.* O, bho, on; o cheann. Since that time, *o 'n am sin;* this is the third day since I heard, *is e so 'n treas là on chual mi;* since the world began, *o thoiseach an t-saoghail;* two months since, *o cheann da mhios;* ever since, *riamh o;* ever since that, *riamh o sin;* long since, *o cheann fad, o chéin;* a little while since, *a chianamh;* how long since? *cia fhad o?* how long is it since? *cia fhad a tha uaith?* is it long since he came? *bheil fad on thàinig e.*

Sincere, *a.* Tréibhdhireach, ionraic, onorach, còir, direach, fior, fìreannach, iomlan, coimhlionta, cridheil, glan. A sincere Christian, *fior Chriosduigh;* a sincere friend, *fior charaid.*

Sincerely, *adv.* Gu tréibhdhireach, gu h-ionraic, gu h-onorach, gu fior; do' rìreamh, a rìreamh.

Sincereness. See **Sincerity**.

Sincerity, *s.* Tréibhdhireas, ionracas, fìrinn.

Sindon, *s.* Paisgean.

Sinecure, *s.* Dreuchd gun dragh.

Sinew, *s.* Féith; feith lùthaidh; taic. Having strong sinews, *féitheach, cuisleach;* sinews, *féithean.*

Sinewed, *a.* Féitheach, lùthmhor; laidir, treun.

Sinewy, *a.* Féitheach; lùthmhor, cuisleach, laidir, treun.

Sinful, *a.* Peacach, aingidh, olc, mi-naomh, cionntach, coireach, truaillidh.

Sinfully, *adv.* Gu peacach, gu h-aingidh, gu mi-naomh, gu ciontach.

Sinfulness, *s.* Peacadh, aingidheachd, ciont, truaillidh-eachd.

Sing, *v. a.* and *n.* Seinn, sinn, càn, gabh ceòl, mol. Sing a song, *gabh òran, seinn òran;* (*as a nurse to a child*), tàlaidh, breug. He sang, *sheinn e.*

Singe, *v. a.* Doth, loisg. He singed his clothes, *dhoth e 'eudach;* singed, *dòithte, dòthta, loisgte.*

Singeing, *s.* Dothadh, losgadh.

Singer, *s.* Càntair, oranaiche; seinneir.

Singing, *s.* Seinneadh, cànadh, cantaireachd.

Singing, *a.* Càntach.

Singingmaster, *s.* Maighistir cànaidh, oide seinn.

Single, *a.* Singilte; aon-fhillte; àraidh; aonaranach; (*in a Scriptural sense*), glan, iomlan, foirfe, simplidh. A single man, *gille;* a single state, *staid shingilte.*

Single, *v. a.* Dealaich, sonruich, tagh; singil. He singled him out, *thagh e mach e;* singled out, *dealaichte, sonruichte, taghta.*

Singleness, *s.* Singilteachd; aon-fhillteachd; (*of mind*), simplidheachd, foirfeachd, ionracas.

Singly, *adv.* Na aonar, leis fein, fa leth; gu simplidh, gu h-ionraic.

Sing-song, *s.* Bùrdan; langan, ròsan.

Singular, *a.* Singilte; àraid, àraidh, sonruichte, neònach, aithreach, iongantach; òirdheirc, sàr, còrr. The singular number, *an nuìmhir shingilte.*

Singularity, *s.* Sonruichead, àraideachd.

Singularize, *v. a.* Dean sonruichte.

Singularly, *adv.* Gu sònruichte, gu h-àraidh.

Sinister, *a.* (*Left*), cearr, clì; (*bad*), olc, cas-ionraic; neo-cheart, neo-chothromach; (*unlucky*), mi-shealbhar, mi-shona.

Sinistrous, *a.* Eithich, baoth.

Sinistrously, *adv.* Gu clì; gu baoth.

Sink, *v. a.* and *n.* Cuir fodha; bàth, tom, tum, cuir fodha, céil, sàruich, illsich; rach fodha; rach fo; rach air chùl, rach gu neoni; traogh, drùigh. The earth sunk prodigiously, *dh' illsich an talamh gu fuathsach;* the boat sank, *chaidh am bàt fodha;* sink through, as liquor, *drùigh;* sink, as paper, *òl, sùgh.*

Sink, *s.* Guitear; clais; taigh cac.

Sinking, *s.* Dol fodha; traoghadh; ìllseachadh, isleachadh.

Sinless, *a.* Neo-lochdach, neo-chiontach, neo-thruaillidh, glan, fior ghlan.

Sinlessness, *s.* Neo-chiontas.

Sinner, *s.* Peacair, peacach, ciontach, ciontaiche.

Sin-offering, *s.* Tabhartas peacaidh, iobairt pheacaidh.

Sinoper, **Sinople**, *s.* Çìll, criadh dhearg.

Sinuate, *a.* Lùbach, luibeach, carach.

Sinuation, *s.* Lùb, lùbadh; sniomhadh.

Sinuous, *a* Lùbach, carach.

Sinus, *s*. Camas, geo, geòth, bàdh; filleadh

Sip, *v. a.* Ol, òl.

Sip, *s* Balgam, bolgam, làn beòil, diod, diodag, diotag.

Siphon, *s*. Pioban uisge

Sippet, *s* Diotag, diodag, deuran, deannan.

Sir, *s*. A shàir; a ridir, a righdir; a thighearna; fhir uasail, dhuine uasail, a thriath, a mhaigstir. Sir Ewen Mac Gregor, *an ridir Eòghann Mac Ghriogair*.

Sire, *v. a* Gin, beir

Sire, *s*. Athair; gintear; (*in addressing a king*), a righ, a thriath, a shàir, (*in addressing an aged man*), a dhuine; (*of beasts*), fìrionn A grandsire, *sean-athair*, great grandsire, *seann sean-athair*.

Siren, *s* Maighdeann mhara; muradhach Siren-song, *ceòl na muradhaich*

Siriasis, *s* Beum soluis, beum gréine.

Sirius, *s* Reul a choin

Sirname, *s* See **Surname**.

Sirocco, *s*. Gaoth as an ear dheas.

Sirrah, *s* Ainm dìmeas, a dhuine, a sgleamhsadh, a sgleamhraidh

Sirup, *s* Millsean

Siruped, *a* Milis.

Sirupy, *a*. Milis

Sister, *s*. Piuthair. A full sister, *dearbh-phiuthair, làn-phiuthair*, half-sister, *leth-phiuthair*, of a sister, *peathair*, sisters, *peathraichean*, dear sister, *a phiuthair ghaolaich, mo phiuthair gaoil*.

Sisterhood, *s*. Peathrachas

Sisterly, *a* Piutharail, mar pheathar, mar pheathraichean.

Sit, *v n*. Suidh, dean suidhe Sit down, *suidh bhàn, dean suidhe*, sit astraddle, *suidh cas gobhlach*, sit cross-legged. *suidh cas crosgach*, sit, as a hen, *gur, dean gur*, sit up or watch, *suidh nàirde, dean faire*, which way does the wind sit? *co as a tha 'ghaoth?* he sat, *shuidh e*

Site, *s*. Suidheachadh, aite, làrach.

Sith, *conj*. On, a chionn

Sithe, *s*. Fàladair, iarunn fàladair.

Sitter, *s* Suidhear, eun air a ghuradh

Sitting, *s* Suidhe, gur, guradh. At two sittings, *air dà shuidhe*, a short sitting is better than a long standing, *is fhearr suidhe beag, na seasamh fad*

Situate, Situated, *a* Suidhichte.

Situation, *s*. Aite, inmhe, inbhe, cor; staid, suidheachadh

Six, *a*. Sé, sia Six men, *seanar dhaoine, sé fir*, six days, *sé lathan*, six hundred, *sé ceud*, six thousand, *sé mil*

Sixfold, *a*. Sé fillte, sia fillte; a shé uiread.

Sixpence, *s*. Sé sgillinn, sia sgillinn, leth-thasdan

Sixscore, *s*. Se fichead, sia fichead

Sixteen, *s*. Sé deug, sia deug

Sixteenth, *a*. Seathamh deug. The sixteenth man, *an seathamh fear deug*.

Sixth, *a*. Seathadh, seathamh

Sixth, *s*. An seathamh, an seathamh cuid.

Sixthly, *adv* Anns an t-seathamh àite

Sixtieth, *a* Tri ficheadamh.

Sixty, *a* Tri fichead, seasgad.

Sizable, *a* Meudar, tomadach, dealbhach, mòr, iomchuidh

Sizableness, *s*. Meud, tomad, buc

Size, *s* Meud, meudachd, tomad, tomald, uimhir

Size, *v a*. Tomhais, sonruich.

Siziness, *s*. Rithneachd.

Sizy, *a*. Rithinn, glaodhar.

Skate, *s* (*Fish*), scad; leabag, sornan; (*for sliding*), brog speilidh

Skate, *v. n*. Speil, speidhil.

Skean, *s*. Sgian, scian, golaidh.

Skeg, *s* Earnag, fearnag.

Skein, *s* Sgéinn, sgéin, sgéinnidh; iornadh

Skeleton, *s* Aog, eug; cnaimhean creutair sam bi air an ceangladh ri cheile.

† **Skellum**, *s*. Sgonn-bhalach, crochair.

Skep, *s* Sgeap, sgeap sheillean; guite; cliabh

Skeptic, *s*. Fear teagamhach, teagamhaiche.

Skeptical, *a* Teagamhach, amharusach.

Skepticism, *s*. Teagamhachd, amharusachd.

Sketch, *s* Dealbh cabhagach, tarruing; ceud dhealbh, ceud tharruing; lìneachadh

Sketch, *v*. Dealbh, tarruing

Skewer, *s* Dealg; pinne; † breathnas.

Skewer, *v. a* Dealgaich, pinn.

Skiff, *s* Sgoth, eathar, geòl, geòladh, curach, sgaf.

Skilful, *a* Sgileil, eòlach, seòlta, teòma; toinisgeil, tuigseach; tapaidh, deas. A skilful physician, *leigh sgileil*.

Skilfully, *adv* Gu sgileil, gu h-eòlach, gu seòlta, gu teòma, gu toinisgeil, gu tuigseach.

Skilfulness, *s*. Sgile, eòlas, seòltachd, teòmachd, tapachd.

Skill, *s* Sgile, eòlas, fiosrachd; teòmachd, tapachd. Try your skill, *feuch do sgile*.

Skilled, *a* Sgileil, seòlta, eòlach, fiosrach, toinisgeil, teòma, tapaidh, deas

Skillet, *s* Aghann, sgeileid.

Skim, *v a* and *n* Sgiob, sgiap, sgùm. Skimmed milk, *bainne lom*

Skim, *s*. Sgùm, cobhar, anabas.

Skimmer, *s* Sguman, sgumadair, spàin ceatha

Skim-milk, *s* Bainne lom.

Skin, *s* Croicionn, craiceann, bodhag; (*of a beast*), bian, seic, seiche. A bare sheepskin, *pealaid*, peel, *rùsg, plaosg, sgrath*, a kid's skin, *minniceag, minnicean*, in spite of your skin, *ge b'oil le do chroicionn e*; a skinful, *làn seic*; as full as his skin could hold, *cho làn 's a chumadh a chroicionn*; a sheepskin, *croicionn caor*, take off the skin, *fionn*.

Skin, *v a*. and *n*. Fionn, thoir an croicionn do, rùisg, comhdaich le croicionn Skinned, *comhdaichte, cruaidh, cruicneach*

Skinflint, *s* Spìocair

Skinker, *s* Gille copain.

Skinned, *a*. Croicnichte, bianach; cruaidh, caiteanach

Skinner, *s*. Fear chroicne, marsonta chraicionn, fear deasachaidh chroicne, seathadair

Skinniness, *s*. Taine, caoile, lapachas; seirge.

Skinny, *a*. Tana, caol, sgàileanta, lapach, glogach, searg.

Skip, *v. n*. Leum, rach thairis, rach seach.

Skip, *s* Leum, sùrdag, frith-leum

Skip-kennel, *s* Gille coise.

Skipper, *s* Sgiobair; maighstir luing, luingeas Dùitseach.

Skipping, *s*. Leumnaich, leumardaich, beiceasaich, beiceil, beiceis

Skipping, *s* Leumnach, sùrdagach, beiceasach

Skirmish, *s* Comhrag, teugmhail, cath, tuasaid, tabaid, rùsg, sgolb, strìgh, deabhaidh, baiteal, pleithe, deannal.

Skirmish, *v. n*. Cuir cath.

Skirmisher, *s.* Fear teugmhail.

Skirr, *v. a.* and *n.* Sgùr; siùbhail le cabhaig.

Skirrets, *s. pl.* Crumagan. Skirret *or* wild tansy, *brislean, briosglan, brisgean.*

Skirt, *s.* Sgiort, sgioball; sgòid; oir, foir; balt, bailt; easball, iomall, fraidhe, taobh, faobbar. The skirts of a country, *iomall (no) criochan dùthcha.*

Skirt, *v. a.* Sgiortaich; baltaich.

Skirting, *s.* Sgiortadh; baltachadh, sgiort, iomall, oir, foir.

Skit, *s.* Faoin dhòchas; beum, sgath-rannachd.

Skittish, *a.* Fiat, gealtach, sgeunach; luaineach, luaimneach, eutrom, miolasgach, guanach, mear.

Skittishly, *adv.* Gu fiat, gu gealtach, gu sgeunach, gu luaineach, gu luaimneach, gu h-eutrom, gu guanach, gu mear.

Skittishness, *s.* Geilte, luaineachd, luaimneachd, luaineachas; guanaiche, mire.

† **Skue, Skew**, *a.* Claon; fiar.

Skulk, *v. a.* Folaich, falaich, di-fholaich, céil; giolc.

Skull, *s.* Claigeann, claigionn, † sgol.

Skullcap, *s.* Clogaid, ceann-bheart.

Sky, *s.* Speur, athar, adhar, iarmaillt. The skies, *na speuran.*

Sky-coloured, Sky-dyed, *a.* Gorm, gorm eutrom, liathghorm.

Skyish, *a.* Gorm, mar na speuran, iarmailteach.

Skylark, *s.* Riabhag, reubhag, uiseag.

Skylight, *s.* Fàir-leus, far-uinneag, bàrr-uinneag.

Skyrocket, *s.* Seorsa obair theine.

Slab, *s.* Clabar, eabar, poll, làthach; (*of stone*), leac.

Slabber, *v. n.* Sil ronn; smugaich, ronnaich, fliuch, salaich.

Slabbered, *a.* Fliuch, smugaideach, ronnach.

Slabberer, *s.* Ronnair, slabair, smugair; leth-amadan.

Slabbering, *a.* Ronnach, smugach.

Slabbery, *a.* Drabasta, draosda.

Slably, *a.* Fliuch; rithinn, tiugh.

Slack, *a.* Lasach, fuasgailte, tuasgailte, tualaigte, neodhaingeann, neo-dhiongalta; (*remiss*), tais, mall, maidheanach, mairnealach, athaiseach; neo-chùramach; fann, lag, neo-spioradail.

Slack, Slacken, *v. a.* and *n.* Lasaich, dean lasach, fuasgail, tuasgail; tualaig; failinn, faillinn, fannaich; dean maidhean, dean moille; furtaich.

Slack, *s.* Gual mìn, gual pronn.

Slackly, *adv.* Gu lasach; gu mall, gu mairnealach, gu maidheanach, gu neo-chùramach.

Slackness, *a.* Lasaiche, lasaichead; fuasgailteachd; maille, moille, maidheanachd, mairnealachd, athaiseachd, cionomhail, mi-chùram.

Slag, *s.* Luaithre (no) smùr iaruinn.

Slaie, *s.* Slinn.

Slain, *part.* See **Slay**.

Slake, *v. a.* Mùch, caisg, bàth. Slaked lime, *aol bàthta.*

Slake, *s.* (*Of a loom*), slinne; (*of snow*), clòinneag, clòimhneag.

Slam, *v. a.* Bruth, marbh; splad, dùin dorus le splad.

Slander, *s.* Tuaileas, masladh, sgainneal, càineadh, cùlchaineadh, tàir, tarcuis, tarcuisne, mi-chliù; droch ainm.

Slander, *v. a.* Càin, masluich, tarcuisich, dean tàir, cùlchàin.

Slanderer, *s.* Fear tuaileis, fear cul-chàinidh. Slanders, *luchd tuaileis, luchd cùl-chainidh.*

Slanderous, *a.* Tuaileasach, gabhannach, tàireil, tarcuiseach.

Slanderously, *adv.* Gu tuaileasach, gu gabhannach, gu tàireil, gu tarcuiseach.

Slang, *pret.* of sling. Thilg.

Slant, Slanting, *a.* Claon, fiar, aomta, ag aomadh, neodhireach.

Slantly, Slantwise, *a.* Gu fiar, gu claon.

Slap, *s.* Boiseag, sgleafard, sgealp, buille, deisealan, deillseag; peileid, cleabhaid, pailleart, cliobhag, cliudan, gleog; (*on the breech*), deillseag. A slap given by children to one another at play, *sgibid.*

Slap, *v. a.* Boiseagaich, sgleafardaich, thoir boiseag, thoir pealaid (no) gleog, cliobhagaich.

Slapdash, *adv.* A dh' aon bheum, a dh' aon bhuille, gu grad, le dararaich.

Slash, *v. a.* Gearr, sgath; beum; leoin, beubanaich, peasg; sgiùrs, cuipinn. Slashed, *gearrta, sgathte, leòinte.*

Slash, *s.* Gearradh, leòn, beum.

Slashing, *s.* Gearradh, leònadh, beubanachadh, beumadh; sgathadh, sgudadh.

Slate, *s.* Sgleat, sgliat, leac, leachd.

Slate, *v. a.* Sgleat, sgleataich. Slated, *sgleataichte;* a slated house, *tigh sgleat.*

Slater, *s.* Sgleatair, sgliatair.

Slating, *s.* Sgleatadh, sgliatadh, sgleataireachd.

Slattern, *s.* Stràille, dràichd, sgliùrach, slabag, trusdar caile, drabag, doimeag, straoileag, straoileid.

Slaty, *a.* Sgleatach, leacach.

Slaughter, *s.* Marbhadh, marbh, àr, mort, mortadh, murtadh, beubanachd, milleadh, casgradh, cosgradh, casgairt, casrach, rochar.

Slaughter, *v.* Marbh, àr, mort, murt, beubanaich, casgair, cosgair, rochair.

Slaughterer, *s.* Cosgrair, fear cosgraidh, àrair, mortair.

Slaughterhouse, *s.* Tigh casgraidh, tigh marbhaidh, broththigh, broth-lann.

Slaughterman, *s.* Feòladair, fear cosgraidh.

Slaughterous, *a.* Millteach, marbhtach, fuilteach, àrail, àr-meineach, àr-mhiannach.

Slave, *s.* Tràill, mar a chithear sna h-Innseachan shuas, agus anns a Ghaidhealtachd; daor-oglach, ciomach, daoranach, sglàbh, sglabhaiche; sgalag. A female slave, *bàntràill;* slaves, *tràillean.*

Slaver, *v. n.* Sil ronnan.

Slaver, *s.* Ronn, ronnan, smugaid, smugaidean, seile.

Slaverer, *s.* Ronnair, leth-amadan.

Slavery, *s.* Traillealachd, tràilleachd, tràillidheachd, daorsa, daorsadh; sglàbhaidheachd, ciomachas, magh-suinne; seirbheis thràilleil.

Slavish, *a.* Tràilleil, tràilleach. Slavishly, *gu tràilleil;* slavish work, *obair thràilleil.*

Slavishness, *s.* Tràillealachd; daorsa; sgalagachd; eisiomaileachd; umhlachd.

Slay, *v. a.* Marbh, cuir as do, cuir gu bàs, cosgair, casgair; mort, murt; beubanaich. He slew them, *mharbh e iad, chuir e as doibh;* slain, *marbhta, cosgairte, marbh;* he was slain, *mharbhadh e, chaidh a mharbhadh.*

Slay, *s.* Slinn.

Slayer, *s.* Milltear, mortair, murtair.

Sled, Sledge, *s.* Carn, carn slaòid, losgann.

Sledge, *s.* (*Hammer*), ord mòr; (*sledge*), carn slaòid; losgann.

Sleek, *a.* Mìn, sliogach, sliogta, sliom, slìobach, sleamhuinn.

Sleek, *v. a.* Mìnich, dean mìn, sliom, sliobaich; cìr.

Sleekly, *adv.* Gu mìn, gu sliogta, gu sliom, gu sleamhuinn.

Sleekness, *s.* Mìnead, slìobachd, sliomachd.

Sleekstone, *s.* Clach-mhìneachaidh.

Sleep, *v. n.* Codail, cadail, dean codal, rach a chodal, gabh pramh, sùain. Whether we sleep or wake, *co aca is codal no faireach dhuinne.*

Sleep, *s.* Codal, cadal, pramh, suain; fois. Take a sleep, *gabh pramh;* a dead sleep, *trom-chodal, trom-shuain;* a wink of sleep, *drùb chodail;* causing sleep, *codalach, pramhach, suaineach.*

Sleeper, *s.* Codalaiche, leisgean, lundair, leagair; droll.

Sleepily, *a.* Gu codalach, gu trom, gu drùb-shuileach, gu leasg, gu lundach.

Sleepiness, *s.* Codal, codalachd; truime; drùb-shuileachd.

Sleeping, *s.* Codal, codaladh.

Sleepless, *a.* Gun chodal.

Sleepy, *a.* Codalach, codaltach; drùb-shuileach; trom, airsnealach. I am sleepy, *tha 'n codal orm;* a sleepy draught, *pramh-leigheas.*

Sleet, *s.* Clàmhainn, gliob, flichneach, flichneachd, flichne.

Sleet, *v. n.* Cuir clàmhainn. The day sleets, *tha 'n là ris a chlàmhainn.*

Sleety, *a.* Clàmhainneach, gliobach, flichneach.

Sleeve, *s.* Muinicheall, muilicheann, muinicheann, muinle. Sleeves, *muinlean.*

Sleeved, *a.* Muinicheallach, muilicheannach, muinleach.

Sleeveless, *a.* Gun mhuinicheall, gun mhuinlean; mi-reusonta.

Sleight, *s.* Cleas, cleasachd, dubh-chleasachd; lathailt, seòl, car.

Slender, *a.* Tana, caol, fanlanta, seang, bochd, truagh, lag, fann; meuranta; beag, crion, gann; brisg; breoite.

Slenderly, *adv.* Gu caol, gu seang, gu bochd, gu truagh, gun tomad, gu crion, gu gann, gu brisg, gu breoite.

Slenderness, *s.* Caoile, caoilead, tainead; dìth tomaid; gainne.

Slept, *pret.* of sleep. Chodail.

Slew, *pret.* of slay. Marbh. See **Slay**.

Sley, *v. a.* Figh, dual, dualaich, toinn, toinneamh, pleat, cas.

Slice, *s.* Slis, sliseag; snaithe; (*an instrument*), spaideal; pleadhan, sleantach. In slices, *na shliseagan;* a slice of cheese, *sliseag chàise.*

Slice, *v. a.* Sliseagaich, snaith. Sliced, *sliseagaichte, snaithte.*

Slid, *pret.* of slide. Shleamhnaich.

Slide, *v. n.* Sleamhnuich, speidhil, spéil; tuislich; sruth gu seimh mar aimhne.

Slide, *s.* Spéileadh, spéilean, speidhlean; sleamhnachadh; sruth.

Slider, *s.* Spéilear.

Sliding, *s.* Spéileadh, spéilearachd; sleamhnachadh; (*on the breech*), tònlagan.

Slight, *s.* Dearmad, tàmailt, dìmeas, tàir.

Slight, *a.* (*Thin*), tana; neo-ghramail; (*trifling*), faoin, beag, suarrach, eutrom, fadharsach. Slight clothes, *eudach tana;* a slight mistake, *mearachd bheag.*

Slight, *v. a.* Dearmaid, dearmadaich, cuir air dearmad, cuir air dìmeas (no) air bheag suim; tàmailtich.

Slighter, *a.* Dìmeasair.

Slightingly, *adv.* Gu dìmeasach, gu dearmadach.

Slightly, *a.* Gu neo-ghramail, gu faoin, gu suarrach, gu fadharsach; gun treòir; gu dìmeasach; gun fhiach, gun fhiù.

Slightness, *s.* Anmhainne, anfhainne, anfhannachd; eu-treoir.

Slily, *adv.* Gu cuilbheartach, gu sligheach, gu h-eòlach, gu seòlta.

Slim, *a.* Seang, caol, maoth, fann, lag.

Slime, *s.* Làthach; pic-thalmhainn, smug.

Slim-gutted, *a.* Seang, seang-chorpach, caol.

Sliminess, *s.* Rithneachd; bitheantachd.

Slimy, *a.* Rithinn, tiugh, bitheanta, sticeach, sleamhuinn.

Sliness, *s.* Cuilbheart, cuilbheartachd, ceabhachdaireachd, sligheadaireachd; innleachd.

Sling, *s.* Crann-tabhuill, glochdan, glocan, tailbh; tilgeadh, urchair; (*for the arm*), bann, ceangal, crios.

Sling, *v. a.* Tilg le crann tabhuill; croch. He slung, *thilg e, chroch e.*

Slinger, *s.* Fear crann tabhuill; tailbhear.

Slinging, *s.* Tilgeadh.

Slink, *v. n.* Seap, siap, giolc; snàg air falbh, goid air falbh (no) as an ròd.

Slink, *v. a.* Beir ro 'n mhithich.

Slinker, *s.* Seapair, siapair.

Slinking, *s.* Seapadh, goideadh air falbh, snàgadh as an ròd.

Slip, *s.* Speidhleadh, speileadh, tuisleadh; mearachd, car; (*of yarn*), ceirsle; (*a small bit*), crioman, stiall; (*of a plant*), maothan. He gave him the slip, *thug e 'n car as.*

Slip, *v. n.* Sleamhnuich, spéil, spéidhil, tuislich; tuit; seap, snàg; dean mearachd, rach as; (*crop*), bearr, gearr, sgath. If I slip, put me right, *ma ni mi mearachd, cuir ceart mi;* slip aside, *snàg gu taobh, giolc gu taobh.*

Slipboard, *s.* Bord sleamhnachaidh.

Slipknot, *s.* Lùb-ruithe.

Slipper, *s.* Cuaran, pliathroid.

Slipperiness, *s.* Sleamhnachd; ceilge; eu-cinntealas; mi-gheimnidheachd.

Slippery, *a.* Sleamhuinn; cunnartach; mùghteach. A slippery tongue, *teangadh ladurna;* a slippery trick, *cuilbheart;* slippery is the stone at the great man's door, *is sleamhuinn leac an tigh mhòir.*

Slip-slop, *s.* Spùidreach, spùt, spùdarsaich.

Slit, *v. a.* Sgoilt, gearr, peasg, sgoch.

Slit, *s.* Sgolt, sgoltadh, gearradh, peasgadh, peasg, sgoch.

Slive, Sliver, *v. a.* Sgoilt, sgath; srac, srachd.

Sliver, *s.* Sgoiltean; meanglan gearrta; meangan briste; mìr.

Sloe, *s.* Airneag; fearnag, airne, bulaistear.

Sloop, *s.* Soitheach aon chroinn.

Slop, *v. a.* Ol gu gionach; glug; spult.

Slop, *s.* Spùt, spùidreach.

Slop, *s.* Triubhas fharsuing.

Slope, *s.* Leathad, claon-bhruthach; fiaradh, claonadh.

Slope, *v.* Claon, aom, fiar.

Slope, Slopewise, *adv.* Gu claon, gu fiar, claon, fiar, aomta, gu taobh.

Sloppy, *a.* Fliuch, salach, eabarach, lathachail; drabasta.

Slot, *v. a.* Splad, duin le splad.

Slot, *s.* Lorg feidh; (*of the breast*), beul màothain.

Sloth, *s.* Leisg; lunndaireachd; diomhanas; neo-churam.

Sloth, *s.* Béist crithir-chosach snàigeach a ghabhas là iomlan dol leth cheud slat.

Slothful, *a.* Leasg, lunndach, diomhanach, slaodach, aolaisdeach, neo-churamach. Grow slothful, *fàs leasg;* a slothful person, *leisgean, slaod, lunndair; droll.*

Slothfully, *adv.* Gu leasg, gu lunndach, gu diomhanach, gu slaodach, gu neo-chùramach, gu h-aolaisdeach.

Slothfulness, *s.* Leisge, lunndaireachd, diomhanas, slaodaireachd.

Slouch, *s.* Cromadh, cruit.

Slouch, *v. n.* Imich, gu cruiteach.

Slouching, *a.* Crom, cruiteach, crotach.

Slough, *s.* Rumach, slob, làthach; cathar; eusgaidh; cochall; (*skin*), sean chraiceann, craiceann air a chur.

Sloughy, *a.* Rumachail, slobach, làthachail, bog; cochullach.

Sloven, *s.* Stràille, dràichd; tàsan, urr liobasda; slaod; droll, slàbair, leisgean, drabair, gliomach.

Slovenliness, *s.* Stràilleachd, dràichdealachd, liobasdachd, neo-chruinnealas; leisge, slàbach.

Slovenly, *a.* Dràichdeil, slaodach, liobasda, neo-chearmanta, salach, lunndach, ràpach, gliomach.

Slovenly, *adv.* Gu dràichdeil, gu slaodach, gu liobasda, gu neo-chearmanta, gu lunndach, gu salach.

Slow, *a.* Mall, mairnealach, maidheanach, athaiseach, tàsanach, aolaisteach, slaodach; màsanach; leasg, lunndach, leagach, neo-dheas, neo-thapaidh; mall-cheumach, mallthriallach. Slow of heart, *mall-chridheach;* in judgment, *maol, baoghalta;* a slow discourse, *tàsan, ràsan.*

Slowly, *adv.* Gu mall, gu mairnealach, gu maidheanach, gu h-athaiseach; gu slaodach. Walk slowly, *imich air d' athais.*

Slowness, *s.* Moille, maille; mairnealachd, maidheanachd, athaiseachd, slaodachd; leisge, lunndaireachd.

Slow-worm, *s.* Daol dall; nathair chaltuinn.

Slubber, *v. a.* Dean gu mi-sheadhar, dean air chor eigin.

Slubberdegullion, *s.* Sgonn-bhalach, sgonn.

Sludge, *s.* Poll, eabar, làthach.

Slug, *s.* Leisgean, lunndair; slaod; droll, rong; (*hinderance*), bac, moille, grabadh, amal; (*snail*), seilicheag; (*for a gun*), ruagair.

Slug-a-bed, *s.* See **Sluggard**.

Sluggard, *s.* Leisgean, lunndair, slaod, slaodair, leagair, rong. Slow is the sluggard going to bed, and seven times slower to rise, *is leasg le leisgean dol a luidh, is seachd leisge leis èiridh.*

Sluggish, *a.* Leasg, lunndach slaodach, leagach, aolaisdeach, dearmadach, codalach; trom, marbhanta, athaiseach, mall.

Sluggishly, *adv.* Gu leasg, gu lunndach, gu slaodach, gu leagach, gu h-aolaisdeach, gu dearmadach; gu trom, gu marbhanta, gu h-athaiseach, gu mall.

Sluggishness, *s.* Leisge, 'lunndaireachd, slaodaireachd, dearmadachd; truime, marbhantachd.

Sluice, *s.* Tuil-dhorus; guitear. Sluices, *tuil-dhorsan.*

Sluicy, *a.* Tuil-dhorusach, dòrtach, taomach.

Slumber, *v. n.* Codail, aom gu codal, gabh pramh.

Slumber, *s.* Codal, cadal, clo-chodal, pramh, suain.

Slumberous, **Slumbery**, *a.* Codalach, cadalach, trom, suaineach.

Slung. See **Sling**.

Slunk. See **Slink**.

Slur, *v. a.* Salaich, mill, truaill; meall. Slurred, *salaichte.*

Slur, *s.* Ball, spot, sal; tàir.

Slut, *s.* Breunag, bréineag, botrumaid, gliomach, drabag, dràichd, doimeag, trusdar caile, slabag. A slut's husband is known in the sheets, *aithnichear fear doimeig air na sràidibh.*

Sluttery, *s.* Breunachas, mosaiche, sal.

Sluttish, *a.* Salach, breun, mosach, musach, brothach, gliomach.

Sluttishly, *adv.* Gu salach, gu breun, gu mosach.

Sluttishness, *s.* Salachar, seilche, mosaiche, drabaireachd.

Sly, *a.* Carach, cuilbheartach, seòlta, eòlach, ceabhachdach, sligheach, daighearra; cuileagach, lùrdanach.

Smack, *v. a.* Blais; pòg; (*as a whip*), crac.

Smack, *s.* Blas, blaisean, deagh bhlas; pòg, pògan, pòigean.

Smack, *s.* Long aon chrannach, mar a tha seoladh gach seachduin eadar Lunnuinn is Lite.

Small, *a.* (*Short*), beag, crion, crìan; gearr, cutach; (*slender*), caol; (*as powder*), meanbh; mìn, pronn. Small cattle, *meanbh chrodha;* of small account, *suarrach;* small beer, *lionn caol;* however small, *air a lughaid;* of small price, *air bheag luach, suarrach, saor.*

Small, *s.* Caol. The small of the hand, *caol an dùirn;* of the leg, *caol na cois, caol a chalpa;* of the back, *caol na droma.*

Smallage, *s.* Peirseal.

Small-beer, *s.* Lionn caol.

Small coal, *s.* Gual pronn.

Small craft, *s.* Long bheag.

Smallness, *s.* Bigead, crìne, lughad, caoile, caoilead; taine; laigead, di-neart.

Small-pox, *s.* A bhreac; a ghall bholgach; a bheanmhath.

Smalt, *s.* Gorm, dath gorm, guirmean.

Smart, *a.* Sgairteil, tapaidh, beothail; sgealparra, smearail, smiorail, sgeilmeil, geur, guineach; beumnach. Not smart, *lùigeanach, neo-sgairteil, neo-thapaidh, neo-bheothail.*

Smart, *s.* Pian, guin, goimh, craon.

Smart, *v.* Fainich, pian, goirtich, geur-mhothaich, crean. You will smart for that, *creanaidh tu air sin;* I will make you smart for it, *bheir mise ort gu crean thu air* (*no*) *gum fainich thu e.*

Smartly, *adv.* Gu sgairteil, gu tapaidh, gu beothail, gu sgealparra, gu smiorail, gu sgeilmeil; gu geur, gu guineach; gu beumnach.

Smartness, *s.* Sgairtealachd, tapadh, tapachd, beothalachd, smioralas, sgeilmealachd; gèire; gèiread.

Smatch, *s.* Blas; fuigheal, fuighleach.

Smatter, *s.* Leth-eòlas, faoin-eòlas.

Smatterer, *s.* Fear leth-ionnsuichte; fear gun oilean.

Smear, *v. a.* Luath, sliob; smiùr, sleadsaich, spairt.

Smeary, *a.* Sliobach; sleasdach.

Smell, *v. a.* and *n.* Gabh tòchd, fainich tòchd, srònagaich, srònaisich.

Smell, *s.* Tòchd, fàile, àile, boladh. A grateful smell, *deagh bholadh, tochd grinn;* a bad smell, *boladh breun.*

Smell-feast, *s.* Geòcair; craosair; sgimilear.

Smelt, *s.* Dubh-bhreac; mealag.

Smelt, *v. a.* Leagh. Smelted, *leaghta, leaghte.*

Smelter, *s.* Leaghadair.

Smelting, *s.* Leaghadh.

Smerk, **Smirk**, *v. n.* Gàir gu mear; amhairc gu tlà.

Smerky, **Smirky**, *a.* Breagh, briagh, greadhnach; sgeilmeil.

Smicker, *v. n.* Seall gu tlà (no) gu gaolach, seall gu macnusach.

Smicket, *s.* Léine bheag; léine boirionnaich, smigead.

Smile, *v. n.* Dean min-ghàir; dean snodh gàire; bi fu' fhiamh-ghàire, seall le gean maith, seall gu caomh.

Smile, *s.* Féith-ghàire, snodh gàire, fiamh-ghàire; miog, sealladh gaoil. Smiles are not companions of pain, *cha 'n ann do 'n ghuin an gàir.*

SMILING, *a.* Ri gàir, fu fhiamh-ghaire.

SMILINGLY, *adv.* Fo' ghàir, fo' fhéith-ghàire, le fiamh-ghàire.

SMIRCH, *v. a.* Salaich; truaill, dubh.

SMIRK, SMERK, *v. n.* Seall gu tlà, seall gu macnusach, thoir sealbhadh graidh.

SMIRKING, *a.* Guamagach. A smirking female, *guamag.*

SMITE, *v. a.* Buail, marbh, mill, cuir gu bàs, cuir as do, claoidh, sàruich. I smote him, *bhuail mi e.* Smitten, *buailte, marbhta.*

SMITER, *s.* Bualadair, buailtear, fear bualaidh.

SMITH, *s.* Gobhainn, gobhadh; ceard. Smiths, *goibhnean.*

SMITH-CRAFT, *s.* Goibhneachd.

SMITHY, *s.* Ceardach. The ashes of a smithy, *splangach.*

SMITT, *s.* Seorsa creadha.

SMITTEN, *part.* See SMITE.

SMOCK, *s.* Smigead, léine boirionnaich.

SMOCK-FACED, *a.* Bàn, glas, glasdaidh.

SMOKE, *s.* Smùid, deathach, deatach, gal, ceò, toit, mùig. No fire no smoke, *far am bi deathach bithidh teas;* it vanished into smoke, *dh' fhalbh e na cheò.*

SMOKE, *v. n.* Cuir smùid, tilg smùid, cuir deathach, toit; gabh piob.

SMOKE, *v. a.* Fàilich, toit; tiormaich (no) croch san deathach; mag, dean fanaid.

SMOKER, *s.* Fear a ghabhas piob tombac.

SMOKE-JACK, *s.* Cuidhle deathaich.

SMOKELESS, *a.* Gun deathach, gun smùid, gun toit.

SMOKY, *a.* Deathachail, làn deathaich, deatachail, smùideach, toitcach, mùigeach.

SMOKING, *s.* Smùidrich.

SMOOTH, *a.* Mìn, liomha, maoth, sleamhuinn, réidh, còmhnard; (*in language*), tlà, ciùin; (*as a stream*), seimh; (*without hair*), lom.

SMOOTH, *v. a.* Mìnich; dean réidh; dean comhnard, sliob, sliogaich; sleamhnuich, criataich; breug, ciùinich.

SMOOTH-FACED, *a.* Mall-ghnùiseach, farasda.

SMOOTHLY, *adv.* Gu mìn, gu réidh, gu ciùin, gu seimh, gu comhnard, gu furas.

SMOOTHNESS, *s.* Mìnead; liomhachas; sleamhnad, ciùinead.

SMOOTH-TONGUED, *a.* Miodalach, beulchar, goileamach; tlà.

SMOTE, *pret.* of smite. Bhuail; mharbh.

SMOTHER, *v. a.* Mùch, tachd, marbh; (*conceal*), coisg, caisg, cuir as, céil, cum samhach. Smothered, *mùchta, coisgte; céilte.*

SMOTHER, *s.* Smùid, mùig, deathach, deatach; toit; mùchan, muchdadh, smùchdan.

SMOTHERING, *s.* Mùchadh, tachd, marbhadh, cosgadh.

SMUG, *a.* Deas, sginmeil, sgilmeil, spailpeanta; cuimir.

SMUGGLE, *v. a.* Thoir steach (no) mach bathar gun chìs, ciotcharaich.

SMUGGLER, *s.* Ciot charuiche; cìs-sheachnaiche, *smuglair,* culmhutair.

SMUGGLING, *s.* Ciot-charachd, cis-sheachnadh, culmhutaireachd, *smuglaireachd.*

SMUGLY, *adv.* Gu cuimir, gu sgilmeil.

SMUGNESS, *s.* Sgilmeileachd, sgeinmeileachd.

SMUT, *s.* Salachar, ball, spot; smoigleadh; smad; (*in language*), draostachd, drabasdachd.

SMUTTILY, *adv.* Gu salach, gu dubh; gu draosta.

SMUTTINESS, *s.* Salachar, drabhas, drabasdachd, draosdachd.

SMUTTY, *a.* Salach; dubh; draosta, drabasta; drabhasda; (*as corn*), buailte le milcheo, seargta.

SNACK, *s.* Roinn, pàirt, cuid, cuibhrionn, rann, earann. Go snacks, *rach an comhrannaich.*

SNAFFLE, *s.* Cabstar, srian.

SNAFFLE, *v.* Srian; cum stigh, smachdaich.

SNAG, *s.* Fiacail; cnap, biorag; snaim, snuim, pluc, meallan.

SNAGGED, SNAGGY, *a.* Fiaclach, cnapach, snuimeach, plucach, plucanach, meallanach.

SNAIL, *s.* Seilcheag, seilicheag.

SNAKE, *s.* Gné nathrach neo-nimheach; nathair challtuinn.

SNAKEROOT, *s.* Seorsa luibh a tha sònruichte airson gath nathrach a leigheas.

SNAKEWOOD, *s.* Seorsa fiodha sniomhanaich.

SNAKY, *a.* Nathaireil; lùbach, toinnte.

SNAP, *v. a.* and *n.* Crac, bris, teum, beum, tiolam, thoir sithe; glac; cronaich, troid.

SNAP, *s.* Cnac, bris, teum, beum, tiolam, sithe; mìr, bideag, crioman, creim, greim; lonan; meirle.

SNAPPER, *s.* Tiolamair, beumadair; glacadair.

SNAPPISH, *a.* Tiolamach; beumnach; geur, cainnteach, dranndanach, crosda.

SNARE, *s.* Rib, ribeadh, riob, gaisde, gaisdeag, dul, painntir, lion; ceap-tuislidh.

SNARE, *v. a.* Rib, riob, glac.

SNARL, *v. n.* Dean draing (no) dranndan, grònaich; thoir tiolam.

SNARLER, *s.* Fear dranndanach; diorrasan; cainntean.

SNARLING, *a.* Draingeach, drangach, dranndanach, crosda; cainnteach.

SNARY, *a.* Ribeachail; cealgach, mealltach; sligheach.

† SNAST, *s.* Smàl coinnle.

SNATCH, *v. a.* and *n.* Glac, beir air; tiolp, teum, thoir tiolam (no) glamhsa, thoir sichd, thoir sithe. Snatched, *glacta.*

SNATCH, *s.* Greis, speal; mìr, crioman; tiolp, tiolpan, greim bidh; lan beoil, boite.

SNATCHING, *s.* Glacadh, glacail; tiolpadh; teumadh.

SNATCHINGLY, *adv.* Gu cabhagach, gu tiolpach.

SNEAK, *v. n.* Snàg, crùb, crùbain, giolc, sleag; ealaidh; seap, di-fholaich. He sneaked off, *shnàg (no) sheap e air falbh.*

SNEAKER, *s.* Snàgair, seapair; giolcair, spiocair, sleagair.

SNEAKING, *a.* Snàgach, seapach, giolcach; sleagach, truagh, iosal, dìblidh, sanntach, gionach, spiocach.

SNEAKING, *s.* Snàgadh, seapadh, giolcadh; sleagadh.

SNEAKINGLY, *adv.* Gu snàgach, gu seapach, gu sanntach, gu spiocach.

SNEAKINGNESS, *s.* Snàgaireachd, seapaireachd; spiocaireachd.

† SNEAKUP, *s.* Snàgair, seapair, ceabhachdair, cladhair.

SNEAP, *v.* Trod, tachair ri.

SNEAP, *s.* Trodadh.

SNECK, *s.* Snaig, crann, dealan, leasgar.

SNEER, *v. n.* Seall gu tarcuiseach, dean gair, tarcuiseach, dean fanoid, fochaid, mag.

SNEER, *s.* Sealladh magaidh, sealladh fanoid, focal tàireil; beum, gearradh.

SNEERER, *s.* Fear fanoid, fear fochaid; beumadair.

SNEERING, *a.* Fanaideach, fochaideach, tàireil; beumach, beumannach.

Sneeze, *v. n.* Sreoth, dean sreothart. He began to sneeze, *thòisich e air sreothartaich.*

Sneeze, *s.* Sreoth, sreothart.

Sneezing, *s.* Sreothartaich.

Sneezewort, *s.* Ragaim, meacan ragaim.

Snib, *v. a.* Bac, grab; cronaich.

Snicker, Snigger, *v. n.* Dean gàir macnusach.

Sniff, Snift, *v. n.* Smot; srub.

Snip, *s.* (*A small bit*), bideag, crioman; (*a mark*), ball, spot.

Snip, *v. a.* Sgud (no) gearr le deamhas; stiom. Snipped, *sgudte.*

Snipe, *s.* Butagochd, meannan adhair, cubhag, naosg; gabhar adhair; (*in ridicule*), baothair, amadan.

Snippet, *s.* Cuid, earann, cuibhrionn bheag; bideag, crioman, deannan.

Snip-snap, *s.* Comhradh sgaiteach; giolam.

Snite, *v. a.* Séid (no) glan sròin.

Snivel, *s.* Sglong, sglongaid, sgloingean, smuig.

Snivel, *v. n.* Dean smùchanaich.

Sniveller, *s.* Gulurtair, gulfhurtair; boigean, bleomhnach.

Snivelling, *a.* Smùchanach, mùgach; bog.

Snivelling, *s.* Smuchanaiche.

Snore, *s.* Srann, srannaich, srann codail.

Snore, *v.* Dean srann; dean srannartaich mar ni neach na chodal. How you do snore, *is ann agad tha'n srann.*

Snorer, *s.* Srannair.

Snoring, *s.* Srannail, srannartaich.

Snort, *s.* Srannartaich, séidrich, srannail; smotail.

Snort, *v. n.* Séid (no) smot mar ni each, bi srannail.

Snorting, *part.* A smotail, a séidrich, a srannartaich.

Snot, *s.* Smug, smuig, slong, sglongaid, sglongas, sgloingean, suigleadh; cailidear.

Snotty, *a.* Smugach, sglongach, salach.

Snout, *s.* Sròin, soc; bus, gnos, gros; beul; sorn.

Snouted, Snouty, *a.* Socach; busach, gnosach, grosach; smeatach.

Snow, *s.* Sneachd; sneachdadh; † lachd. White as the snow, *geal mar an t-sneachd;* a wreath of snow, *cuitheamh;* a ball of snow, *caob shneachd, caob shneachdaidh;* a large ball of snow, *muc shneachdaidh;* as white as the snow of one night, *cho gheal ri sneachd na h-aon oidhche.*

Snow, *v. n.* and *a.* Cuir sneachd; tuit mar shneachd. It snows, *tha e ris an t-sneachd, tha e 'cur an t-sneachdaidh.*

Snowball, *s.* Caob shneachd, caob shneachdaidh; meall sneachd. A large snowball, *muc shneachdaidh.*

Snowdrop, *s.* Blàth shneachdaidh, gealag làir.

Snow-white, *a.* Sneachdaidh, geal mar shneachd.

Snowy, *a.* Sneachdach; sneachdaidh. A snowy day, *là sneachdaidh.*

Snub, *s.* (*In wood*), meall, cnap; gath.

Snub, *v. a.* Troid ri, tachair ri, cronaich; smachdaich.

Snub, *v. n.* Dean sgiuganaich.

Snubbing, *s.* Trod, trodadh, tachairt, cronachadh; sgiuganaich.

Snudge, *v. n.* Luidh gu lunndach, bi soimeach.

Snudge, *s.* Spiòcair; fear sanntach.

Snuff, *s.* (*Of a candle*), smàl, smàl coinnle; (*pounded tobacco*), snaoisean, snuisean.

Snuff, *v. a.* and *n.* Smot, sròineisich; (*a candle*), smàil, smàl, diosmuig; (*take snuff*), gabh snaoisean, gabh tombac. He snuffs a great deal, *tha e trom air an tombac;* snuff with disdain, *peich.*

Snuffbox, *s.* Bocsa tombaca, muileann snaoisein.

Snuffer, *s.* Fear smotach (no) mùgach; snaoiseanaiche.

Snuffers, *s.* Smàladair, smàladairean.

Snuffle, *v. n.* Labhair gu mùgach.

Snuffler, *s.* Mùgair, fear mùgach.

Snuffling, *a.* Mùgach; snaoiseanach.

Snug, *a.* Clùmhar, clùmhor; còsagach; tiorail, caitneach; blàth; goireil; cothromach, soimeach. He is snug in bed, *tha e gu bog blàth na leabadh.*

Snuggle, *v.* Luidh gu clùmhor.

So, *adv.* Mar sin, mar so, mar sud, air an doigh so, air an doigh sin, air an doigh ud, air an t-seòl so, air an seòl sin, air an seòl ud; air an achd so, air an achd sin, air an achd ud. It is so, *tha e mar sin;* they say so, *tha iad ag radh sin;* be it so, *mar sin bitheadh e;* if so be that, *ma 's e agus gu;* grant it be so, *leig gur ann mar sin tha* (*no*) *bhitheas e;* it is even so, *tha e ceart mar sin;* why so? *c'arson so? c'arson sin?* as the matter stands so, *on is ann mar sin tha 'chùis;* so as that, *air chor is gu, chum agus gu;* so much, *cho, co;* I am not so bad as you, *cha n'eil mi cho olc riutsa;* I am not so void of sense, *cha n'eil mi air cho bheag toinisg;* so far, *cho fhad, fhad so;* so far as I know, *fhads' is aithne dhomh;* so far from, *an àite;* so far from doing that, *an àite sin a dheanamh;* so far as, *fhadsa;* so great, *cho mor, co mhòr;* so little, *cho bheag;* so far off, *cho fad as* (*no*) *air falbh;* so long as, *fhads' a;* so oft, *cho tric;* so, so, *seadh, seadh;* (indifferently), *mar sin fhéin; mu 'n laimh;* and so forth, *agus mar sin sios e;* so (*so that*), *saor o; air chumhnant is gu;* I will do what I can, so I be not undutiful to my father, *ni mi na fhaodas mi, saor o nach bi mi mi-dhleasnach do m' athair;* so much, *na h-uimhir, na h-uiread, liuthad;* he did not so much as move, *cha d' rinn e na h-uimhir is glideachadh;* so and so, (*pretty well*), *an iarruidh ghleusda.*

Soak, *v. n.* and *a.* Sùig, òl; sùgh; fliuch, luisgich, bog.

Soaker, *s.* Geòcair.

Soam, *s.* Langair.

Soap, *s.* Siabunn. A soap-ball, *ball siabuinn.*

Soar, *v.* Itealaich gu h-ard; éirich.

Soar, *s.* Ard-itealaich; éiridh.

Sob, *s.* Osunn, osnadh, osmagail, osmag, ospag, plosgail, sgiuganaich.

Sob, *v.* Dean osunn, dean osnaich; tarruing osunn, bi ri sgiuganaich.

Sobbing, *s.* Osnaich, osmagaich; sgiuganaich; macras.

Sober, *a.* Measarra, measarradh, neo-mhisgeach; stuama, cneasda, geimnidh, ciùin; riaghailteach; suidhichte; tiamhaidh. As sober as a judge, *cho suidhichte ri breitheamh.*

Sober, *v. a.* Dean measarra; thoir gu céill.

Soberly, *adv.* Gu measarra, gu neo-mhisgeach, gu stuama, gu geimnidh, gu ciùin.

Soberness, *s.* Measarrachd; socair; ciùineas; stuaim, stuamachd, geimnidheachd.

Sobriety, *s.* Measarrachd; stuaim; stuamachd, cneasdachd, ciùineas; socair; geimnidheachd.

Soccage, *s.* Socach.

Sociable, *a.* Caidreamhach, cuideachail, céilidheach, càirdeil; comunnta, companta, conaltrach.

Sociableness, *s.* Caidreamhachd; compantachd.

Sociably, *adv.* Gu caidreamhach; gu companta.

Social, *a.* Caidreamhach, comunnach, daonnach.

Society, *s.* Comunn, cuideachd; aonachd; cinneadh daoine; comhluadar.

Socinian, *s.* Fear a chumas mach nach co-ionann Criosd ri Dia.

Sock, *s.* Soc; cuaran, bròg bhréide, triachan.

Socket, *s* Soc, socaid, bonn, slocan na sùl, lag na sùl.

Sod, *s* Caob, fòid; clod, sod, sgroth; tobhtag. He is now on the sod of truth, *tha e nis air fòid na firinn*

Sod, *pret.* of seethe. Bhruich

Sodality, *s* Bràthaireachas, compantas.

Sodden, *part.* Bruich; leth-bhruich

Soder, *v a.* Tàth, sodar.

Soe, *s* Meadar

Sodomite, *s* Bugair

Soever, *adv* Air bith, sam bith

Sofa, *s* Suidheagan riomhach, suidheagan seomair

Soft, *a* Bog, bogar; tais, (*gentle*), maoth, tlà; mìn, ciùin seimh; bánail, bandaidh, mallta, farasda, faoil, fòil, caomh, caoimhneil; (*silly*), baoghalta

Soft, *interj* Socair, air do shocair

Soften, *v a* and *n.* Bogaich, taislich, maothaich, ciùinich. Softened, *bogaichte, taislichte, maothaichte, ciùinichte.*

Softener, *s* Ice; rud a ni bogar, furtachd.

Softening, *s* Bogachadh, maothach, taisleachadh.

Softening, *a.* Bogar, iceach, maoth, leigheasail.

Softly, *adv.* Gu tais, gu maoth, gu tlà; gu mìn, gu ciùin, gu samhach, gu seimh, gu farasda, gu faoil; (*leisurely*), gu h-athaiseach, gu socrach

Softness, *s* Buige, taise, caoimhneas, ciùineas, banalas, banndaidheachd, maothalachd, bogarachd.

Soho' *interj.* H-aoibh'

Soil, *v. a* Salaich, dubh; mill, truaill; (*manure*), math, mathaich, innearaich Soiled, *salaichte*

Soil, *s* Ùir, talamh, ire, earraghalt, fearann, tìr, innear, aolach, salachar, sal, spot

Soiliness, *s* Salachar, dubhadh.

Sojourn, *v. n.* Comhnuich, dean (no) gabh comhnuidh; tùinich, fan, fuirich.

Sojourn, *s.* Comhnuidh, cuairt; tùineachadh, tùinidh.

Sojourner, *s* Fear cuairt, aoidh, tùiniche, aithnichinn, eil-thireach, taisdealach

Sojourning, *s* and *part* Cuairt, tùineachadh, air chuairt.

Solace, *s* Sòlas, furtachd, comh-fhurtachd, co-ghairdeachas, toileach-inntinn, cluiche

Solace, *v. a.* Thoir solas, sòlasaich, thoir furtachd (no) comh-fhurtachd, comfhurtaich, furtaich

Solan-goose, *s* Sulair

Solar, *a* Greine; grianar; grianach, soilleir A solar halo, *cearcall* (*no*) *roth gréine*

Sold, *pret* and *p part.* of sell. Reic, chreic, reicte; creicte.

† **Sold**, *s* Pàigh saighdeir.

Soldan, *s.* An Turcach.

Solder, *v a* Tàth, sòdair, lunn-tàth.

Solder, *s* Sodar, liunn-tàth, llunn-tàthaidh

Soldier, *s.* Saighdear, milidh, cathan, laoch, gaisgeach, ceatharn, fionn; fear misneachail A good soldier, *deagh shaighdear*, an old soldier, *seann saighdear*, a trained soldier, *saighdear deante*, a foot soldier, *saighdear cois*, enlist as a soldier, *gabh sna saighdearaibh*. a raising of soldiers, *togail shaighdeara*, a brave soldier, *laochan, gaisgeach, risgeanach*

Soldierlike, Soldierly, *a.* Misneachail, gaisgeil

Soldiership, *s.* Saighdearas; milidheachd

Soldiery, *s* Saighdearachd

Sole, *s* (*Of the foot*), bonn na coise, (*of a shoe*), bonn bròig, iochdar bròig; (*a fish*), leabag

Sole, *v a* Cuir bonn air

Sole, *a.* Singilte, aon; amhàin.

Solecism, *s* Baich-labhradh, baoth-labhradh, eadalabhradh.

Solely, *adv.* Amhàin; gu sònruichte.

Solemn, *a* (*Awful*), sòlaimte, solamanta; greadhnach; (*ritual*), foirmeil; (*as an air*), tiamhaidh, trom, muladach; (*affectedly serious*), suidhichte, glic; (*yearly*), bliadhnail. A solemn oath, *mionnan sòlaimte.*

Solemnity, *s.* Sòlaimteachd; deas-ghnath bliadhnail; greadhnachas, ard-fhéill, féill naomh

Solemnization, *s.* Sòlaimnachadh.

Solemnize, *v* Cum (mar fhéill) gach bliadhna, urramaich, sòlamnaich.

Solemnly, *adv.* Gu sòlaimte; gu greadhnach, (*ritually*), gu foirmeil; (*as an air*), gu tiamhaidh, gu suidhichte, gu durachdach, gu glic.

Solicit, *v. a* Asluich, guidh, grios, sir, creabh; mosgail, dùisg, brosnuich.

Solicitation, Soliciting, *s* Asluchadh, guidhe, griosadh, greiseachd; sireadh, creabhadh, mosgladh, dùsgadh, brosnuchadh

Solicitor, *s* Tagrair, fear tagairt, fear lagha

Solicitous, *a* Iomaguineach, cùramach; deigheil.

Solicitously, *adv.* Gu h-iomaguineach, gu cùramach.

Solicitress, *s.* Ban-athchuingiche; ban-tagrair.

Solicitude, *s.* Iomaguin, cùram; ro-chùram, iomluasg.

Solid, *a.* Teann, daingeann, diongalta, gramail; tiugh, trom, tarbhach; neò-fhas, laidir; fior; glic, suidhichte, crionna, ciallach, sicir, céillidh A solid foundation, *bun diongalta*, a solid judgment, *inntinn shuidhichte*

Solid, *s.* Trom-ni, tiugh-ni; ni sam bi aig am bheil fad, leud agus tiughad

Solidity, *s* Tairbhe, tiughad, diongaltas, gramalas; (*of mind*), ciall, toinisg.

Solidly, *adv.* Gu teann, gu daingeann, gu diongalta, gu gramail, gu neo-fhàs; gu fior; gu glic, gu suidhichte, gu crionna, gu ciallach, gu sicir, gu céillidh

Solidness, *s.* Tiughad, gramalas, ciall, toinisg.

Solids, *s* (*In physic*), tarbhach-chuid na colla

Solidungulous, *a.* Slàn-iongach.

Solifidian, *s.* Neach a tha sa bharail nach 'eil ni ach creideamh feumail chum fireannachaidh.

Soliloquist, *s.* Féin-labhairtiche, uath-labhairtiche, fear a bhruidhneas leis féin

Soliloquize, *v.* Dean comhradh aonarain, labhair riut féin. He soliloquizes, *tha e 'labhairt ris féin.*

Soliloquy, *s.* Comhradh aonarain, féin-labhairt, féin-bhruidhinn, uath-labhairt, uath-comhradh

Solipede, *s* Ainmhidh slàn-iongach.

Solitaire, *s* Aonaran; seud muineil

Solitarily, *adv* Gu h-aonaranach, gu h-uaigneach, gu fàs

Solitariness, *s* Uaigneas, aonaranachd, dìthreabh.

Solitary, *a.* Aonaranach; uaigneach, fàs, faoin; tiamhaidh, fàsail, cianail, cianalach A solitary place, *àite uaigneach, leis féin*, a solitary valley, *gleannan fàs* (*no*) *uaigneach*, a solitary person, *urr aonaranach, aonaran, caonaran*

Solitary, *s* Aonaran, dìthreabhach, dìthreamhach

Solitude, *s* Uaigneas, aonaranachd, dìthreamh. A lonely place, *fàsach*, in solitude, *ann uaigneas.*

Sollar, *s* Garait.

Solo, *s* Port aon inneil, fonn aonarain

Solstice, *s* Grian-stad. Summer solstice, *grian-stad shamhraidh, airde an t-samhraidh*, winter solstice, *grian-stad gheamhraidh, dùbhlachd.*

Soluble, *a.* So-leaghaidh, so-leaghadh, a ghabhas leaghadh, furas a leaghadh; (*in physic*), purgaideach, fuasgalach, tuasgalach.

Solution, *s.* Dealachadh, sgaradh; leaghadh; (*of a question*), fuasgladh, tuasgladh, mìneachadh.

Solutive, *a.* Fuasglach, tuasglach, purgaideach, tualagach.

Solve, *v. a.* Fuasgail, tuasgail, mìnich. He solved the question, *fhuasgail e 'cheist.* Solved, *fuasgailte, tuasgailte, mìnichte.*

Solvency, *s.* Murrachas air dioladh (no) air pàigh.

Solvent, *a.* Murrach air dioladh (no) air pàigh.

Solvible, *a.* So-fhuasgladh, so-mhìneachadh.

Some, *a.* Cuid, pàirt, roinn, beagan, eigin, ceud éigin, ni h-eigin, ni 'gin; feodhainn, muinntir. Some of us, *cuid againn;* some do not like it, *cha toil le cuid e;* some people, *cuid shluagh, cuid dh' fheodhainn;* some people say, *thoir ceud dh' fheodhainn;* some one, *urr eigin;* some one or other, *urr no urr eigin.*

Somebody, *s.* Aon, urr éigin, neach éigin, urr h-éigin.

Somehow, *adv.* Air chor éigin, air sheòl éigin, air achd éigin, air mhodh éigin. Somehow or other, *air chor éigin, air chor no chor éigin.*

Somerset, *s.* Car a phocain ollaidh.

Something, *s.* Rud eigin, ni h-eigin, ni 'gin; càileigin. Something or another, *ni no ni 'gin.*

Something, *adv.* Beagan, air bheag, leth-char. Something taller than you, *beagan ni 's airde na thusa.*

Sometime, *adv.* Aon uair, roimh so; uair eigin. Sometime or other, *uair no uair eigin.*

Sometimes, *adv.* Air uairibh, air uairean, corr uair, corr uairean, n' uairean, na uairean; an tràths' is a ris. Sometimes he comes and sometimes not, *air uairibh thig e, 's air uairibh nach tig.*

Somewhat, *s.* Beagan, ni h-éigin; cail-eigin.

Somewhat, *adv.* Leth-char, beagan. Somewhat hungry, *leth-chur acrach;* somewhat less, *beagan ni 's lugha.*

Somewhere, *adv.* An àite eigin, an àite 'gin. Somewhere else, *an àite eigin eile;* somewhere thereabouts, *an àite eigin mu sin.*

Somniferous, **Somnific**, *a.* Codalach, cadalach, codaltach; suaineach; suainidh, suainear.

Somnolency, *s.* Codalachd; turra-chodal.

Son, *s.* Mac; †luan, †bar, †orc. Sons, *mic.* The sons of men, *clann nan daoine;* **the Son**, *am Mac, no 'n dara pearsa do 'n Trianaid.*

Son-in-law, *s.* Cliamhuinn, mac an dlighe.

Sonata, *s.* Port; fonn.

Song, *s.* Òran; luinneag, dàn, duan, rann, balanta, fonn, bardachd. Sing a song, *seinn òran, gabh òran;* buy for a song, *ceannuich air bheag luach* (*no*) *air neo-ni.*

Songster, *s.* Òranaiche; bàrd.

Songstress, *s.* Ban òranaiche; ban bhàrd.

Soniferous, *a.* Fuaimear, fuaimneach.

Sonnet, *s.* Luinneag, duan, duanag; gearr-òran, gearr-dhàn.

Sonnetteer, *s.* Bard gun fhiù.

Sonorific, *a.* Fuaimear, fuaimneach.

Sonorous, *a.* Fuaimear, ard, ard-ghuthach, cruaidh, sgalanta, sgealparra; tiamhaidh.

Sonorously, *adv.* Gu fuaimear, gu h-ard, gu sgalanta.

Sonorousness, *s.* Fuaimneachd, sgalantachd; tiamhachd.

Soon, *adv.* A chlisge, gu luath, ann ùine ghoirrid, tràth, tràthail, moch, luath, grad. He will come soon, *thig e 'chlisge;* too soon, *tuille is tràthail; tuille is moch;* as soon as, *cho luath agus, cho luath as, cho luath 's;* as soon as ever, *cho lom luath agus;* at the soonest, *air a chuid is luaithe.*

Sooner, *adv.* Ni 's luaithe, ni 's moiche, ni 's tràthail. I would sooner die, *bu luaithe gheibhinn bas;* no sooner did he come than—, *cha bu luaithe thàinig e na—.*

Soot, *s.* Sùidhe; dubhagan, dubhdan.

Sooted, *a.* Sùidhte; mathaichte no comhdaichte le sùidhe.

Sooterkin, *s.* Faoin-ghin; rud, a rèir comhraidh, a bheireadh na ban Dhùitsich le bhith suidh air na h-àmhuinnean aca.

† **Sooth**, *s.* Firinn. In good sooth, *gu dearbh, gu fìor, a dh' innseadh na fìrinn.*

† **Sooth**, *a.* Taitneach, sòlasach.

Soothe, *v. a.* (*A child*), breug, tàlaidh; (*please*), toilich, dean blandar; ciùinich, coisg. Soothed, *breugta, tàlaidhte; toilichte; ciùinichte.*

Soother, *s.* Talaidhear; fear tàlaidh; fear breugaidh; fear cosgaidh.

Soothsay, *v. a.* Innis roimh-laimh, fàisnich.

Soothsayer, *s.* Fiosaiche, fàidh, fear fiosachd, fàisniche, druidh, fear fàisneachd. Soothsayers, *fiosaichean, fàidhean; luchd fiosachd; druidhean.*

Soothsaying, *s.* Fiosachd, fàisneachd, fàidheadaireachd; druidheachd.

Sootiness, *s.* Dubh; duibhe, sùidhe; duaichneachd.

Sooty, *a.* Sùidheach, dubh mar an t-sùidhe, dorch, duaichnidh.

Sop, *s.* Aran tumta am fion no ann an deoch laidir sam bi.

Sop, *v. a.* Tum, tom, bog.

Soph, *s.* Stuidear òg Sasunnach.

Sophi, *s.* Iompair *Phersia.*

Sophism, *s.* Breug-arguinn, breug-radh, cealg-radh, briosarguinn, aighneas breugach.

Sophist, **Sophister**, *s.* Breug-arguinniche.

Sophistical, *a.* Fallsa, neo-fhior, breugach, cealgach, meallta.

Sophistically, *adv.* Gu fallsail, gu neo-fhior, gu breugach, gu cealgach.

Sophisticate, *v.* Truaill, mill.

Sophisticated, *a.* Truaillidh, millte.

Sophistication, *s.* Truailleadh, milleadh.

Sophistry, *s.* Breug-arguinn, briosagnaidheachd, reusonachd mheallta.

Soporiferous, **Soporific**, *a.* Codalach, cadalach, codaltach, suaineach.

Sopper, *s.* Bogair, bogadair, tumadair.

Sorbile, *a.* So-òlaidh, a ghabhas òl, furas òl.

Sorbition, *s.* Òl; sùgadh, sùigheadh.

Sorbs, *s. pl.* Caoran, craobh chaoran.

Sorcerer, *s.* Dubh-chleasaiche, fiosaiche, druidh.

Sorceress, *s.* Ban-fhiosaiche, ban-druidh, buitseach, briosag.

Sorcery, *s.* Dubh-chleasachd, fiosachd, druidheachd, buitseachd, buitseachas, buisdreachd, dolbh.

Sord, *s.* Gorm, fòid ghorm, fàl.

Sordes, *s.* Salachar; seilche, deasgann, trusdaireachd.

Sordet, *s.* Pioban beag.

Sordid, *a.* Salach, gràda, grannda, mosach, musach; crion, miothur, biastail, spiocach, cruaidh, gàbhaidh; dìblidh, truagh, ìriosal; dulchanach; sorb.

Sordidly, *adv.* Gu salach, gu gràda, gu mosach, gu miothur, gu biastail, gu spiocach; gu dìblidh, gu truagh.

Sordidness, *s.* Graundachd, mosaiche; miothurachd, crìne, biastaileachd, biastalachd, spiocaireachd.

SORE, *s.* Creuchd, lot, neasgaid, cneadh, guirean, aite goirt, rud goirt, udhar.

SORE, *a.* Goirt, cràiteach, goimheil, guineach, craonach, piantail, nimheil. A sore heart, *cridhe goirt.*

SORE, *s.* Boc cheithir bhliadhna aois.

SOREL, *s.* Boc tri bhliadhnach.

SORELY, *adv.* Gu goirt; gu dona.

SORENESS, *s.* Goirteas, goirtead, guin, goimh, goimhealachd, piau.

SORORICIDE, *s.* Peathar-mhortadh.

SORRAGE, *s.* Fochann; foichlean; gineadh, fàs.

SORREL, *s.* Sabhadh, sealbhag, puinneag, puinneagan. Wild sorrel, *sealbhag nam fiadh; feada coille.*

SORRILY, *adv.* Gu truagh, gu bochd, gu dìblidh, gu suarrach.

SORRINESS, *s.* Truaighe, bochduinn, suarraichead, crìne, truaghanachd.

SORROW, *s.* Mulad, bròn, dubhachas, duilgheas, doilghios, cradh, sprochd, reachd, tuirse, do-bhron, do-bron, cumha; leanndubh; snithe. In sorrow, *fo mhulaid;* sorrow come take thee, *droch comhdhail ort, droch bhàs ort, mar phaisg ort.*

SORROWFUL, *a.* Muladach, brònach, dubhach, duilich, airsnealach; tuirseach, trom, caointeach, doilghiosach, dulchaointeach; pramhail, murcach. Sorrowful news, *nuaidheachd bhrònach; sgeul broin; droch nuaidheachd; sgeul dunaich.*

SORROWFULLY, *adv.* Gu muladach, gu brònach, gu dubhach, gu duilich, gu tuirseach, gu doilghiosach.

SORRY, *a.* Duilich, muladach, brònach; deacair; droch; (*vile*), suarrach. I am sorry for you, *is truagh leam thu, tha mi duilich air do shon;* he who hears not well, gives but a sorry answer, *am fear nach cluinn gu math, cha toir e ach droch fhreagairt;* in a sorry way, *mu 'n laimh.*

SORRY, *a.* Crion, truagh, dìblidh, neo-luachmhor, neofhiachmhor, gun fhiù.

SORT, *s.* (*Kind*), seòrsa, sòrt, gné; inmhe; gineal, cineal, buidheann, bannal; (*manner*), modh, seòl, doigh, achd, rod, rathad; (*a pair*), paidhir, carraid. What sort of a man is he? *ciod an seorsa fir th' ann?* after this sort, *air an doigh so;* in like sort, *air an doigh cheudna;* of all sorts, *iol-ghnétheach;* of what sort? *ciod an seorsa?* of the same sort, *do 'n aon seorsa;* of one sort, *dh' aon seorsa.*

SORT, *v. a.* Cuir gu doigh, cuir an ordugh; seòrsaich; roinn; (*come together*), tionail. Well sorted, *ann an deagh ordugh.*

SORTANCE, *s.* Freagarrachd, cubhaidheachd.

SORTILEGE, *s.* Tilgeadh chrann, crann-thilgeadh, crannchur.

SORTING, *s.* Cur gu doigh, orduchadh.

SORTMENT, *s.* Cur gu doigh, cur an ordugh.

SOT, *s.* Buraidh, umaidh, baothair; tamhanach, misgear, poitear.

SOTTISH, *a.* Umadail, neo-thuigseach; misgeach, meisgeach, òlar, geòcach, poiteach, poitear.

SOTTISHLY, *adv.* Gu h-umadail, gu neo-thuigseach; gu misgeach.

SOTTISHNESS, *s.* Umaidheachd; meisge; geòc, pòit; ruitearachd.

SOUGH, *s.* Guitear.

SOUGHT, *pret.* and *p. part.* of seek; which see.

SOUL, *s.* Anam; spiorad; (*a person*), urr, ceann. Upon my soul, *air m' anam;* do it not for your soul, *air d' anam na dean e;* thirty thousand souls, *deich mil fichead ceann;* poor little soul, *an t-anaman truagh,* voc. *anamain thruaighe;* a reasonable soul, *anam reusonta;* a vegetative soul, *anam fàis;* a sensitive soul, *anam mothuchail.*

SOULLESS, *a.* Crian; gealtach, neo-mhisneachail, tais; meath, cailleachail, cailleachanta, neo-spioradail.

SOUND, *a.* Slàn, fallain; calma; (*of mind*), crionna, glic; céillidh. A sound mind, *inntinn fhallain;* safe and sound, *gu slàn fallain;* he is in a sound sleep, *tha e na thurram suaine.*

SOUND, *s.* (*At sea*), caolas; tanalach mara.

SOUND, *s.* (*In surgery*), sireadan.

SOUND, *v. a.* Tomhais; doimhnich; sgrud, rannsaich. Sounded, *tomhaiste; doimhnichte; sgrudta; rannsuichte.*

SOUND, *s.* (*Loud sound*), fuaim, toirm, farum, stairn; torman, torunn; (*voice*), guth; (*a tinkling sound*), gleang, gliong; (*continued tinkling sound*), gleangail, gliongail, gleangarsaich, gliongarsaich; (*a soft sound*), borbhan; torman.

SOUND, *v. n.* Dean fuaim, dean toirm, dean gleang; sgal.

SOUND, *v. a.* Gleang. Sound an alarm, *séid (no) buail caismeachd.*

SOUNDABLE, *a.* So-thomhas, furas thomhas.

SOUNDING, *a.* Fuaimearra, fuaimneach; sgalanta. Sounding back, *ath-fhuaimneach;* sounding shrill, *binn, sgalanta, cruaidh, sgreadach.*

SOUNDLY, *adv.* Gu slàn, gu fallain; gu làidir, gu neartmhor, gu diongalta.

SOUNDNESS, *s.* Fallaineachd, slàinnte; slàine; neart; fìrinn, treibhdhireas, neo-thruaillidheachd.

SOUP, *s.* Eunbhrigh, eanaraich; leannra.

SOUR, *a.* Goirt, geur, garg, searbh; (*in temper*), doirbh, crosda, dùr, nuadarra, gruamach. Sour wine, *fion geur, fion goirt;* a sour look, *sealladh gruamach, gruaim;* it is somewhat sour, *tha e leth-char goirt, tha car goirt aige.*

SOUR, *v.* Goirtich, searbhaich, dean geur (no) garg; (*in temper*), feargaich, dean mi-thoilichte, mi-thoilich. Soured, *goirtichte; searbhaichte.*

SOUR, *v. n.* Fas geur, cinn searbh (no) goirt.

SOURCE, *s.* Tobarr; aobhar, ceud aobhar, mathair-aobhar, bun, freumh.

SOURED, *part.* Goirtichte, searbhta, searbhaichte; (*vexed*), feargaichte; farranaichte.

SOURING, *s.* Goirteachadh, searbhachadh; (*for milk*), leasach.

SOURISH, *a.* Leth char goirt, leth char geur, leth char garg, leth char searbh.

SOURLY, *adv.* Gu goirt, gu geur, gu garg, gu searbh.

SOURNESS, *s.* Géire, géiread, gairge, gairgead; seirbhe, searbhas, searbhad.

SOUS, *s.* Sgillinn Fhrangach.

SOUSE, *v. a.* and *n.* Buail gu trom, tuit le splad; suidh le splad; pluinns.

SOUSE, *adv.* Le splad; le sic, le pluinnse.

SOUTH, *s.* An àirde deas, deas. The south, *an taobh deas, an àirde deas;* to the south, *gu deas;* from the south, *a deas, as an taobh deas, as an airde deas.*

SOUTH, *a.* Deas. A south wind, *gaoth dheas, gaoth a deas.*

SOUTH-EAST, *s.* An ear-dheas, àirde an ear-dheas.

SOUTHERLY, *a.* A laimh na h-airde deas, as an taobh deas, deiseil, deasail.

SOUTHERN, *a.* Deas, deasail.

SOUTHERNWOOD, *s.* Meath-challtuinn.

SOUTHWARDLY, *adv.* Gu deas, thun na h-airde deas.

SOUTHWEST, *s.* An iar dheas.

SOVEREIGN, *s.* Righ; ard-uachdaran, ard-thriath, ardfhlath.

Sovereign, *a.* Rioghail; flathail, corr. Sovereign power, *cumhachd rioghail.*

Sovereignty, *s.* Uachdaranachd; ard-chumhachd.

Sow, *s.* Muc; meall luaidhe.

Sow, *v. a.* Cuir, siol-chuir. He sowed, *chuir e;* sown, *cuirte; air churadh;* as you sow you will reap, *mar a chuireas tu, buainidh tu;* sow *or* spread, *sgaoil, sgap.*

Sower, *s.* Sioladair, fear cuiridh.

Sowing, *s.* Cur, siol-chur.

Sowens, *s.* Làgan, làghan, càbhruich.

Sowe, *v.* Tarruing air na cluasan.

Sown, *part.* of sow. Cuirte, air chur.

Sow-thistle, *s.* Bog a ghiogain.

Space, *s.* (*Room*), uidhe, rùm; farsuingeachd; (*time*), uine; (*time* or *distance*), astar, grathuinn, greis; (*a space between two periods of time*), eadar-ùine; (*a short space of time*), sealan; treall, tachdain.

Spacious, *a.* Farsuing, mòr, rùmar; leud-mhor, leudach.

Spaciously, *adv.* Gu farsuing, gu mòr, gu rùmar.

Spaciousness, *s.* Farsuingeachd, meudachd, airdead, rum.

Spaddle, *s.* Pleadhan, pleadhag, spaideal.

Spade, *s.* Caibe, laige; spaide; fiadh tri bhliadhnach; cailltcanach.

Spadille, *s.* Eus an spaide.

Spake, *pret.* of speak. Thubhairt.

Spalt, Spelt, *s.* Seorsa cloich leacaiche.

Span, *s.* Reis; *spang,* naoi òirlich. Spic and span new, *ùr nomha.*

Span, *v. a.* Tomhais le reis, reisich, spangaich.

Spane, *v. a.* Cuir air dioghail, dioghail.

Spangle, *s.* Lannair, aiglean dealrach.

Spangle, *v. n.* Lannair, loinrich.

Spaniel, *s.* Cu eunaich; seapair.

Spanish, *a.* Spàinnteach, Spàinneach.

Spank, *v. a.* Boiseagaich, buail, gleog.

Spanner, *s.* Acduinn gunna.

Spar, *s.* Tarsnan, tarsuinnean; crann, glas. Of a gate, *speac.*

Spar, *v. a.* Dùin, druid, crann, glas.

Spar, *v. n.* Dornaich; *bogsainn.* A sparring match, *bogsainn.*

Sparable, *s.* Tarrag, tarang bheag; tacaid sàlach.

Spare, *v. a.* and *n.* Caomhain, coigil, sàbhail, bi baigheil ri; maith; (*be without*), seachain, seachainn, bi a dhìth, bi caonntach, dean baile, bi a dhìth, bi as dìth. Spare yourself, *caomhain thu féin;* I cannot spare it, *cha 'n urrainn mi 'sheachnadh, cha 'n urrainn mi bhith as a dhìth.*

Spare, *a.* Tana, caol, truagh; gann, caonntach.

Sparer, *s.* Fear caonntach, spiocair.

Sparerib, *s.* Aisinn air bheag feòla.

Spargefaction, *s.* Spultadh.

Sparing, *a.* Gann, neo-phailt; spìocach, caonndach, gleadhtach, grunndail.

Sparingly, *adv.* Gu gann; gu spìocach, gu caonndach, gu gleadhtach, gu grunndail.

Sparingness, *s.* Spiocaireachd, spìoc, caonndachas, caonndachd.

Spark, *s.* Srad, sradag; drillinn; (*fop*), lasgair, gasganach, òganach spairiseach, leoimean. Often has a small spark kindled a great fire, *is tric a bheothaich srad bheag teine mòr.*

Sparkful, *a.* Smiorail, smearail, spioradail, cridheil.

Sparkish, *a.* Uallach, leomach, breagh, briagh, sgiamhach, spairiseach, spairisdeach.

Sparkle, *s.* Srad, sradag; lannair, dealradh; (*from an anvil*), tuireann.

Sparkle, *v. n.* Lannair, dealradh; srad, sradagaich, drillinnich; cuir craobh.

Sparkling, *a.* Loinreach, deàlrach; sradach, sradagach; drillinneach, caoireach.

Sparklingly, *adv.* Gu soillseach, gu dealrach, gu drillinneach, gu caoireach, gu craobhach.

Sparrow, *s.* Glas-eun, gealbhonn, gealbhan.

Sparrow-grass, *s.* Creamh mac feidh.

Sparrow-hawk, *s.* Speireag, speir-sheabhag; bain-speireag.

Spasm, *s.* Iodha, orc, féith-chrup.

Spasmodic, *a.* Iodhach, féith-chrupach.

Spat, *pret.* of spit. He spat, *thilg e smugaid.*

Spatter, *v. a.* Spult, salaich; càin; tilg smugaid. Spattered, *air a spultadh, salaichte.*

Spatterdashes, *s.* Eididh calpa, spad-choisbheart.

Spatula, *s.* Spaideal, maide poit.

Spaw, *s.* Àite sonruichte airson uisge leigheis.

Spawl, *v. n.* Tilg smugaid, sliob.

Spawl, *s.* Smug, smugaid.

Spawn, *v. a.* and *n.* Claidh; beir, gin.

Spawn, *s.* Iuchraichean éisg; siol. Frog-spawn, *glothagach.*

Spawner, *s.* Iuchrag.

Spawning, *s.* Cladh, cladhadh.

Spay, *v. a.* Spoth. Spayed, *spothta, spothte.*

Speak, *v. n.* Labhair, bruidhinn, abair, càn, dean bruidhinn, dean comhradh; innis, luaidh, aithris. I cannot speak a word, *cha 'n urrainn domh focal a radh;* speak ill, *labhair gu toibheumach; càin;* he spoke, *labhair e;* I will speak, *labhraidh mi;* speak but little, and speak well, *na abair ach beagan is abair gu math.*

Speakable, *a.* So labhairt, so-chànadh, so-innseadh, sochur an céill.

Speaker, *s.* Fear labhairt, labhairtiche.

Speaking, *s.* Comhradh, labhairt, bruidhinn, càntuinn.

Speaking-trumpet, *s.* Gall tromp.

Spear, *s.* Sleagh, lann, gath, craosach, craosnach, géis, figheis, muirgheadh, morghath, duileann.

Spear, *v. a.* Sàth, lot, troimh lot.

Spearman, *s.* Fear sleagha, sleaghadair.

Spearmint, *s.* Mionnt, mionntuinn.

Spear-wort, *s.* Glais-leun.

Special, *a.* Àraidh, àraid, àirid, sonruichte; sunruichte; gasta, oirdheirc.

Specially, *adv.* Gu h-àraidh, gu h-àraid, gu h-àirid, gu sònruichte.

Specialty, *s.* Àraideachd, sonruichead; lamh-sgriobhadh.

Species, *s.* Gné, seòrsa, sòrt; ordugh; gineal; cùin.

Specific, Specifical, *a.* Araid, àraidh, sònruichte.

Specifically, *adv.* A réir seorsa, a réir gné.

Specificate, *v. a.* Comharaich, sònruich; ainmich.

Specification, *s.* Comharachadh, sonruchadh.

Specify, *v.* Comharaich, sònruich, sùnruich, ainmich. Specified, *comharaichte, sonruichte, ainmichte.*

Specimen, *s.* Samhladh; sampull.

Specious, *a.* Greadhnach; dealthach; aogasach; a réir coslais; (*in language*), beulchar.

Speciously, *adv.* Gu greadhnach, gu aogasach, gu beulchar.

Speciousness, *s.* Greadhnachas; aogasachd.

Speck, *s* Smàl; sal; gaoid, spot, ball.

Speck, *v. a.* Smàl, salaich, spot.

Speckle, *s.* Spotag, ball.

Speckle, *v. a.* Spot, spotagaich, ballaich, breac, breacaich.

Speckled, *a.* Breac, ballach, spotagach.

Spectacle, *s* Sealladh, taisbeanadh, taisbean, ball amhairc. Spectacles, *speuclairean.*

Spectacled, *a.* Speuclairichte

Spectator, *s.* Fear amhairc, fear coimhid, spiothair.

Spectre, *s.* Aog, eug, tannasg, taibhse.

Spectrum, *s* Faileas, iomhaigh, eugas.

Specular, *a.* Faileasach.

Speculate, *v n.* and *a.* Smuaintich, beachdaich, dealbhaich, dealbh, cnuasaich; cunnartaich, cuir air chunnart.

Speculation, *s* Beachdachadh, smuainteachadh, smuaineachadh, rannsuchadh, dealbhadh.

Speculative, *a.* Beachdail, smuaineachail.

Speculator, *s.* Dealbhadair, tionnsgnaiche; (*a spy*), spiothair, fear coimhid.

Speculum, *s.* Sgàthan.

Sped, *pret* of speed. Ghreas, luathaich.

Speech, *s* Cainnt, bruidhinn; labhairt, seanachas, comhradh; oraid, uirghioll.

Speechless, *a* Balbh, gun chainnt, tosdach, gun diog, bìth, sàmhach

Speed, *v. a* and *n.* Greas, luathaich, deifirich, cuir ann cabhaig, coghain; marbh, cuir as do, sgrios; bi soirbheasach.

Speed, *s* Luathailt; luathas, deifir, cabhag, spéid, soirbheachadh, soirbheas Good speed to you, *soirbheas mhath leat*, make speed, *dean deifir, dean cabhag, greas*, come speed, *thig spéid*, done with speed, *air dheanamh an cabhaig* (no) *roimh chéile.*

Speedily, *adv.* Gu luath, gu cabhagach, gu deifireach, gu grad, gu h-obann

Speediness, *s.* Luathailt, luathas, deifireachd.

Speedy, *a* Luath, cabhagach, deifireach, grad, ullamh; astarach

Spell, *s* Giseag, gisreag; sian, seun; greis (no) grathuinn air obair

Spell, *v n.* Litirich, ceart-sgrìobh

Spelter, *s.* Seorsa miotailt

Spence, *s.* Pantraidh

Spend, *v a* Caith, cuir a shean; cosd, sgaoil, sgap; saruich, claoidh, fannaich, thoir thairis He spent all he had, *chaith na bh' aig*, spent, *caithte.*

Spender, *s* Struidhear, stroghair, caithtiche

Spending, *s* Caithe, caitheamh, struidhe, strogh, shuidheas, stroghas. It is but one man gathering, and another spending, *cha n'eil ann ach fear ri caomhnadh's fear ri caithe.*

Spendthrift, *s* Struidhear, stroghair, dràig, glaimhean, caithtiche, fear struidheil, (no) ana-caithleach. It would be well with a spendthrift if he got as he spent, *bhiodh sonas aig an dràig nam faigheadh e mar dhòrtadh e.*

Spent, *part.* Caithte, air caitheamh; fannaichte, air toirt thairis, air teireachdainn.

Sperm, *s* Siol urr bheò.

Spermaceti, *s* Blonag muic mhara.

Spermatic, *a* Siolach.

Spermatize, *v. a.* Cuir siol, siolaich.

Spet, *v. a.* Dòirt gu pailt, taom.

Spew, *v. a.* and *n.* Tilg, sgeith, sgeath, diubhair; cuir a mach. I am ready to spew, *tha mi thun tilgeadh*

Spewing, *s.* Tilgeadh, sgeith, sgeath, diubhradh.

Sphacelate, *v.* Grod, fàs grod, truaillich.

Sphacelus, *s.* Truailleachadh, grodadh.

Sphere, *s.* Cuairt cruinne, cruinne cé, domhan, cruinneag; ball.

Sphere, *v. a.* Dean cruinn, cruinnich.

Spheric, Spherical, *a.* Cruinn.

Sphericalness, *s* Cruinnead.

Spheroid, *s.* Cruinneag caol fad.

Spherule, *s.* Cruinneag.

Sphinx, *s.* Uilbhéist Eiphiteach aig an robh aghaidh oighe agus coluinn leomhainn.

Spice, *s* Spios Spices, *spiosan*, (a small quantity), *deannan.*

Spice, *v. a.* Spios, spiosraich. Spiced, *spiosraichte.*

Spicer, *s.* Spiosair, spiosadair; spiosraiche, spiosradair, fear spiosraidh.

Spicery, *s* Spiosraidh.

Spicy, *a.* Spiosach, spiosadach, spiosrach; cubhraidh.

Spider, *s.* Damhan, damhan alluidh, figheadair fodair; cuideag. A spider's web, *lion damhain alluidh.*

Spigot, *s.* Pinne; leigeadair, spiocaid.

Spike, *s.* Dias, diasad; tarrag mhòr, bior fad iaruinn.

Spike, *v a.* Tairn, taraig; bioraich; sparr tarrag ann an toll cluaisein gunna mor.

Spikenard, *s.* Bòltrachan.

Spill, *s.* Sliseag; gàd tana iaruinn.

Spill, *s* Beagan airgid

Spill, *v a* and *n.* Dòirt; taom, caill, mill, cuir dholaidh; caith. He spilled his blood, *dhoirt e 'fhuil*

Spiller, *s.* Doirtear, dortair; milltear

Spilling, *s.* Dortadh, milleadh, call, taomadh

Spilt, *part* Dòirte, taomta, taomaichte

Spilth, *s.* Ni taomta sam bith, taomlach.

Spin, *v. a.* Sniomh, toinn, toinneamh; ruith (no) ruidhil mu 'n cuairt, dàilich, cuir dheth, cuir dàil; (*issue out*), sruth, sil. Spin out, *fadaich;* spun, *shniomh;* spun, *sniomhta, sniomhte.*

Spinage, *s.* Bloinigean gàraidh.

Spindle, *s.* Dealgan, fearsaid. Spindle legs, *casan dealgain.*

Spindle-shanked, *a.* Dealg-chasach, dealg-chosach; speireach, luirgneach

Spindle-tree, *s.* Feoras

Spine, *s* Cnaimh na droma

Spinel, *s* Seorsa cìll.

Spinet, *s.* Seorsa cruit; spionaid

Spiniferous, *a.* Biorach, deilgneach, stobach, dreasach, droighionnach.

Spink, *s* Buidheag, lasair choille.

Spinner, *s.* Sniomhair, sniomhadair, sniomhaiche; damhan alluidh

Spinning, *s.* Sniomhadh.

Spinning-wheel, *s* Cuidheal, cuidhil, cuidheal shniomhaidh.

Spinosity, *s.* Deilgneachd.

Spinous, *a.* Biorach, deilgneach, stobach, dreasach, droighionnach, colgach.

Spinster, *s* Ban-sniomhaiche, ban-sniomhair, (*in law*), boirionnach singilte (no) neo-phòsda

Spinstry, *s.* Sniomhadh; sniomhaireachd

Spiny, *a.* Biorach, dreasach, deilgneach, stobach; droighionnach; deacair, duilich.

Spiracle, *s* Toll gaoithe.

Spiral, *a.* Sniomhach, sniomhanach; bidhiseach. A spiral line, *lìn sniomhanach.*

Spirally, *adv.* Gu sniomhanach, mar sgrobha.

Spire, *s.* Troraid, spirichd, spiricean; fior bhàrr; stiopull; toinneamh.

Spirit, *s.* Spiorad; (*the Holy Spirit*), an Spiorad Naomh; (*a goblin*), taibhse, tannasg, aog, eug; spiorad; (*soul*), anam; (*courage*), misneach, anam, spiorad, smior, smioralas, smearalas, beothalas, smiodam, anam; (*temper*), nadur, gné, càil; (*genius*), inntinn; (*eagerness*), sannt, deigh, miann; (*breath*), deo, beath, anam; (*liquor*), uisge beathail; (*an evil spirit, or goblin*), droch spiorad; (*a familiar spirit*), leannan sìth; (*give up the spirit*), leig suas an deò; (*a broken spirit*), spiorad brùite. Pluck up your spirit, *tog do mhisneach;* you have not the spirit to do it, *cha 'n 'eil dh' anam* (*no*) *mhisneach agad a dheanamh;* full of spirit, *spioradail, misneachail, smiorail, meamnach, aigneach, aigeantach.*

Spirit, *v. a.* Misnich, brosnuich, prosnaich; meall, tàlaidh, goid air falbh. Spirited, *misnichte, brosnuichte.*

Spirited, *a.* Misneachail, smiorail, smearail, duineil, beo, beothail, anamadail, sgairteil.

Spiritedness, *s.* Misneach, smioralas, duinealas; beothalas, sgairtealas.

Spiritless, *a.* Neo-mhisneachail, neo-smiorail, neo-dhuineil, neo-bheò, neo-sgairteil; cailleachanta; gealltach, meat; trom, marbh, meirbh, neo-shunntach, neo-sgrideil.

Spiritual, *a.* Spioradail, neo-chorporra, neamhuidh; naomh, diadhuidh, inntinneach. Spiritually, *gu spioradail, gu neo-chorporra.*

Spirituality, *s.* Spioradaileachd, neo-chorporrachd; gluasad inntinn.

Spiritualization, *s.* Spioradachadh; fior-ghloine.

Spiritualize, *v.* Spioradaich, naomhaich, glan.

Spiritous, *a.* Laidir, beathail; beò, misneachail, brisg. Spiritous liquor, *uisge làidir* (*no*) *beathail.*

Spirt, Spurt, *v. a.* Sgiurd, sgiurt; spùt, spult, steall.

Spirt, Spurt, *s.* Sgiurd, sgiurt, spùt, clisgeadh; cabhag.

Spiry, *a.* Spiriceach; barra-chaol, biorach.

Spiss, *a.* Tiugh.

Spissitude, *s.* Tiughad, tiuighead.

Spit, *s.* Bior, bior feòl, bior ròstaidh. Though it has escaped the spit, it has not escaped the pot, *ged is ann o 'n bhior cha 'n ann o 'n choire.*

Spit, *v. a.* Cuir air bior; sàth.

Spit, *v. a.* and *n.* Tilg smugaid, sgiort; cuir mach seile. He spat, *thilg e smugaid.*

Spitchcock, *v. a.* Pronn easg chum a ròstadh.

Spite, *s.* Mi-run, mio-run, farmad, miosguinn, gamhlas, tnu, tnùth, spìd; galltanas. In spite of you, *a dh' aindeoin ort;* in spite of your teeth, *ged b' oil le d' fhiaclan e.*

Spite, *v. a.* Docharaich, dochannaich.

Spiteful, *a.* Mi-runach, mio-runach, farmadach, miosguinneach, gamhlasach, tnùmhor, spìdeil.

Spitefully, *adv.* Gu mi-runach, gu fannadach, gu miosguinneach, gu gamhlasach.

Spitefulness, *s.* Mi-run, mi-runachd, miosguinneachd, gamhlasachd.

Spittal, Spital, *s.* Spiteal; tigh eiridinn.

Spitter, *s.* Gille bior; smugair, smugaidear; (*deer*), fiadh òg, damh òg feidh, agh feidh.

Spittle, *s.* Smugaid, seile, smug; blimh, blinn.

Spit-venom, *s.* Nimhe beòil.

Splash, *v. a.* Spult, spairt, salaich.

Splash, *s.* Spult, spultadh, spairt, spairteadh; sput; slob, làthach.

Splashing, *s.* Spultadh, spairteadh.

Splashy, *a.* Spultach, slobach, salach, lathachail.

Splay, *v. a.* Cuir as an alt, cuir as a ghualainn, cuir a cnaimh na droma, cuir as na meidhinnean.

Splay-footed, *a.* Brod-chasach, brad-chosach, sgabhrach, spad-chosach; cràgach.

Splay-mouth, *s.* Braoisg, goille.

Spleen, *s.* Dubh liath; sealg, tamhan; trealais; fearg; tnù, farmad, gamhlas; mire.

Spleenful, *a.* Farmadach, gamhlasach, miosguineach, feargach, tamhanach.

Spleeny, *a.* Crosda, cainnteach.

Splendent, *a.* Loinreach, dearsach, dealrach, boisgeil, soillseach, glan.

Splendid, *a.* Dealrach, loinreach, lonnrach, boisgeil, faicheal; ro ghrinn; greadhnach, mòr-chuiseach.

Splendidly, *adv.* Gu dealrach, gu loinreach, gu boisgeil, gu faicheil, gu greadhnach, gu mòr-chuiseach.

Splendour, *s.* Dealradh, dearrsadh, soillse, lannair, boisgeadh, lòiseam, glaine, greadhnachas, loghmhorachd.

Splenetic, *a.* Friothnasach, cainnteach, crosda; coimhis.

Splenetive, *a.* Teth, teinntidh, dian.

Splice, *v. a.* Tath.

Splint, *s.* Bloigh, bloighid, sgealb, sgoiltean.

Splint, *v. a.* Pinn, geinn.

Splinter, *s.* Bloighid, sgealb, sgoltadh, spealg, sgeireag, bruan. Break it in splinters, *bris na bhloighdibh e;* it broke into splinters, *chaidh e na spealgaibh;* the splinter of a bone, *sgeireag chnaimh.*

Splinter, *v. a.* and *n.* Bris, bruan, sgoilt, sgealb.

Split, *v. a.* and *n.* Sgoilt, sgealb; bris, bruan; crac; sleasg, srac, sgàin. He almost split with vexation, *theab e sgàin le farran.*

Split, *pret.* and *p. part.* of split. Briste, sgealbta, sgealbte, air sgoltadh.

Splitter, *s.* Sgoltair, sgoiltear, fear sgoltaidh.

Splitting, *s.* Sgoltadh; sgealbadh, briseadh, bruanadh; crac, cracail, sleasgadh.

Splutter, *s.* Tuasaid, tabaid, caonnag, aimhreite, miriaghailt, connsachadh.

Spoil, *v. a.* and *n.* Spùinn, spùill, creach, argainn, spearl; reubainn, robainn; mill, truaill, truaillich, cuir dholaidh. They spoiled the town, *spuinn iad am baile;* why do you spoil the boy on me? *c'arson a tha thu 'cur a ghuillain dholaidh orm?* you have spilt it, *mhill thu e.*

Spoil, *s.* Cobhartach, faobh, creich, creach; reubainn; togail; feudail, meirle, goid; sean chraiceann.

Spoiler, *s.* Creachadair, fear creiche, faobhair, spuinneadair, robair, fear reubainn, reubair; milltear; (*of chastity*), fear truaillidh, truaillear.

† **Spoilful**, *a.* Millteach; caithteach.

Spoke, *s.* Spòc, speac, tarsnan, tarsnan rotha.

Spoke, *pret.* of speak. Thubhairt, labhair.

Spokesman, *s.* Fear labhairt.

Spoliate, *v. a.* Spùill, spùinn, creach, mill, dean fàs.

Spoliation, *s.* Spùilleadh, spùinneadh, creachadh, reubainn; togail, spearladh, foghluidheachd.

Sponge, *s.* Spoing, spuing, spong, caisleach spuing; faisgean, cluaran.

Sponge, *v.* Suath le spuing; faigh le foill; mill, dubh, salaich.

Sponginess, *s.* Spuingealachd.

Sponging, *s.* Suathadh le spuing, siabadh; mealltaireachd, ceilg.

Sponging-house, *s.* Toll bùth, gainntir.

Spongious, *a.* Spuingeach; fliuch; àitidh, bog.

Spongy, *a.* Spoingeach, spongach, spuingeil; fàs, còsagach.

Sponk, *s.* Caisleach spuing, spuing.

Sponsal, *a.* Maraisteach, pòsaidh.

Sponsion, *s.* Gabhail ri; dol an urras.

Sponsor, *s.* Oide, oide baistidh; urras, urradh.

Spontaneity, *s.* Deòin, saor-thoil.

Spontaneous, *a.* Saor, toileach, neo-aindeonach.

Spontaneously, *adv.* A dheoin, d' a dheoin, gu saor, d'a thoil féin.

Spontaneousness, *s.* Deònachd.

Spool, *s.* Spàl.

Spoom, *v.* Seol gu luath mar luing, sgiob.

Spoon, *s.* Spàin; liadh, liach.

Spoon, *v. n.* Seòl ro 'n ghaoth.

Spoonbill, *s.* Gob spàineach.

Spoonful, *s.* Làn spàine. Two spoonfuls, *dà làn spàine.*

Spoon-meat, *s.* Biadh spàine.

Sport, *s.* Cluiche, cluithe, spuirt, spòrsa, ioladh, ealaidh; fal dhà, fearas chuideachd; *dibhearsain;* fanaid, àbhachdas; (*of sportsmen*), faoghaid, fiadhachd, sealg; iasgachd, eunachadh; (*in sport*), ri fal dhà. Every man likes his own sport, *a chluiche féin do na h-uile fear;* make sport of him, *dean ball abhachdais dheth;* sport has often turned to earnest, *is tric chaidh fal-dhà, gu fal-rìreadh.*

Sport, *v. a.* Cluich, mir, dean mireadh, dean sùgradh, dean spòrs, dean iomairt; mag; cuir air ioladh. You sport away your time and money, *tha thu 'caitheamh d' aimsir is d' airgiod gu faoin.*

Sportful, *a.* Cridheil, sunndach, aighearach, mear, sugach, suigeartach.

Sportfully, *adv.* Gu cridheil, gu sunndach, gu h-aighearach, gu mear, gu sugach, gu suigeartach.

Sportfulness, *s.* Cridhealas, sunnd, mire, aighearachd, suigeartachd.

Sporting, *s.* Mire, cluiche, sunnd.

Sportive, *a.* Mear, cridheil, sunndach, aighearach, sugach, beadrach, mearganta.

Sportiveness, *s.* Mire, cridhealas, sunnd, aighear, beadradh, meargantas.

Sportsman, *s.* Sealgair; eunadair, casgair.

Spot, *s.* Smal, ball, spot; gaoid; sal; aite ionad; tàmailt. A spot of arable ground, *goirtean; innseag, acair;* on the spot, *air ball, air an spot;* a beauty-spot, *ball seirce.*

Spot, *v. a.* Salaich, spot; ballaich, breac; truaill, mill.

Spotless, *a.* Gun smàl, gun ghaoid, gun bhall, gun spot; gun choire, glan, fior-ghlan, neo-thruaillichte.

Spotted, Spotty, *a.* Ballach, breachd, breac, spotach; bailgeann, neo-ghlan; truaillidh. It is but the comparison of the spotted goose and its mother, *cha 'n 'eil ann ach comhad a gheoigh bhric is a màthar.*

Spousal, *s.* Pòsadh, maraiste.

Spousal, *a.* Maraisteach, pòsaidh.

Spouse, *s.* Céile, fear pòsda, bean phòsda, dear, bean.

Spoused, *a.* Posda, pòisde; naisgte, ceangailte.

Spouseless, *a.* Gun chéile.

Spout, *s.* Piob, pioban; feadan, spùt, srùlag, sdeall, steall. A water spout, *spùt uisge; maom (no) maoim sleibh;* (*a cock*), goc.

Spout, *v. a.* Sput, steall, sdeall.

Spoutfish, *s.* Muirsgian.

Sprain, *s.* Sniomh, leun; siach. He sprained his foot, *shniomh e 'chos;* sprained, *sniomhta, sriomhte, leunta.*

Spraints, *s.* Cac dobhrain.

Sprang, *pret.* of spring. Leum; chinn; dh' fhàs.

Sprat, *s.* Sprodh, sairdeal, sardail.

Sprawl, *v. a.* Sàmgaich, smògarsaich.

Sprawler, *s.* Smògair, smàgair; sgràmlair.

Sprawling, *s.* Smògail, smàgarsaich, sgràmlanaich.

Sprawling, *a.* Smògail, smàgail, sgràmlanach.

Spray, *s.* (*Of the sea*), cathamh mara; (*of a branch*), bàrr géig, meangan, meanglan; fiùran, fàillean, maothan.

Spread, *v. a.* Sgaoil; spréid; sgap; comhdaich; nochd, foillsich, dean follais. Spread out, *fosgail; sgaoil mach;* spread a report, *tog iomradh;* the report has spread, *tha 'n t-iomradh air sgaoileadh;* spread the sails, *sgaoil (no) spréid na siùil;* having a tendency to spread, *sgaoilteach.*

Spread, *part.* Sgaoilte, spréidte; sgapta; fosgailte. Spread sails, *siùil spréidte;* spread far and near, *sgaoilte am fad is am fagas;* a table spread out, *bord sgaoilte.*

Spread, *s.* Sgaoileadh; spréideadh; leud; farsuingeachd.

Spreader, *s.* Fear sgaoilidh; fear foillseachaidh, sgapair.

Spreading, *s.* Sgaoileadh, spreideadh, sgapadh; fosgladh. The spreading of a plague, *sgaoileadh plaigh.*

Spreading, *a.* Sgaoilteach. A spreading distemper, *galar sgaoilteach.*

Sprig, *s.* Fàillean; meanglan òg, fiùran, maothan.

Spriggy, *a.* Fàilleanach; meanglanach, meanganach, fiùranach, fiùranta.

Spright, *s.* Spiorad, tannasg, ailmse, taibhse, taillse, aog; (*courage*), misneach.

Sprightful, *a.* Beò, beothail, cridheil, anamanta, suilbhear, sulchair, sunndach, mear; cuileagach, smiorail, eutrom.

Sprightfully, *adv.* Gu beò, gu beothail, gu cridheil, gu suilbhear, gu sunndach, gu mear, gu cuileagach, gu smiorail, gu h-eutrom.

Sprightfulness, *s.* Beothalas, beothalachd, cridhealas, suilbhire, sunnd, mire, smioralas.

Sprightless, *a.* Trom, marbh, neo-sunndach.

Sprightliness, *s.* Beothalas, beothalachd, cridhealas, suilbhire, suilbhireachd; sunnd, sunndaichead, smioralas, smearalas.

Sprightly, *a.* Beo, beothail, anamanta, mear, cridheil, smiorail, smearail, sunndach, sulchair, suilbhear; eutrom, meamnach. Sprightly is the early riser, *is meamnach gach moch-thrathach.*

Spring, *v. n.* and *a.* (*Grow*), fàs, cinn; (*as water*), sruth a mach; spùt; (*appear*), thig san t-sealladh; (*leap*), leum, thoir leum, thoir cruinn-leum. Spring a leak, *sgag, leig stigh uisge, mar bhàta;* he sprang upon me, *leum e orm;* springing game, *ri faoghaid;* sprung, *air fàs; air a ghintinn.*

Spring, *s.* (*Of the year*), earrach, céitean; céite; (*a leap*), leum, grad-leum, cruinn-leum, sùrdag; bonnag; (*fountain*), tobar, fuaran, tiobairt; fior thobar; (*a leak*), sgag, sgàineadh; (*beginning*), toiseach, tùs, aobhar, ceann-aobhar, mathair aobhar; (*an elastic body*), earraid. In the spring, *anns t-earrach, san earrach, sa chéitean;* the spring of the day, *càmhanaich, briseadh na fàire;* on the spring, *air earraid, air eige;* the spring has many an excuse for being cold, *is ioma leithsgeul th' aig an earrach air bhith fuar.*

Springe, *s.* Dul, ribe.

Springer, *s.* Fear faoghaid, sealgair.

Springiness, *s.* Critheanachd.

Springing, *s.* Fàs, cinntinn, leumadh; leumardaich, leumnaich; spùtadh.

Springle, *s.* Dul, ribe.

Spring-tide, *s.* Reothairt; aislear.

Springy, *a.* Critheanach, lùbach; so-lùbaidh, sùbailt, earraideach.

Sprinkle, *v. a.* Spult; crath; sgap; sgaoil; fliuch. Sprinkle it with water, *spult le uisge e.*

Sprinkling, *s.* Spultadh, crathadh, sgapadh, sgaoileadh, fliuchadh, maoth-fhliuchadh.

Sprit, *v.* Fàs, cinn, cuir mach fàillean.

Sprite, *s.* Spiorad, tannasg, ailmse, taibhse, aog.

Sprit-sail, *s.* Seòl spreòid.

Sprout, *v.* Cinn, fàs, cuir a mach fàillean.

Sprout, *s.* Faillean, fiùran, maothan, buinneag, bunsag, ur-fhas, gineag, bailleag. Sprouts, *càl òg;* having sprouts, *fàilleanach, fiùranach, maothanach, bunsagach, bailleagach.*

Sprouting, *s.* Fàs, cinntinn, ùr-fhàs, gineadh, ascairt, boineadh, borcadh.

Spruce, *a.* Sgilmeil, sgeinmeil; greanta, sgiolta; briagh, breagh, snàsmhor; finealta; gasda, spailpeanta; deas, biolar. A spruce youth, *òganach sgilmeil.*

Spruce, *v. n.* Sgeaduich, rach an uigheam.

Spruce, *s.* Seorsa giuthais.

Sprucely, *adv.* Gu sgilmeil, gu sgeinmeil, gu greanta, gu breagh, gu finealta, gu spailpeanta.

Spruceness, *s.* Sgilmeileachd, sgeinme, finealtas.

Sprunt, *s.* Maide garbh cutach, rong; guitseal; bun; (*stump*), stulc, cibean.

Spud, *s.* Golaidh, sgian cutach, sgian dubh; sgian achlais; (*in derision*), duine beag, staigean, brogach.

Spume, *s.* Cobhar, còp; cobhragach, othan.

Spumy, *a.* Cobharach, còpach.

Spun, *pret.* and *p. part* of spin. Shniomh; sniomhta, sniomhte.

† **Spunge.** See **Sponge.**

Spur, *s.* Spor; brog; bior stuigeadh, brosnuchadh. A cock's spur, *spor coilich.*

Spur, *v. a.* Spor, brog; greas, deifirich; stuig, brosnuich; cuir h-uige, brod.

Spurge, *s.* Spuirse.

Spurious, *a.* Fallsa, fallsail; meallta, mealltach, truaillidh, truaillichte, diolain. A spurious child, *urr dhiolain;* spuriously, *gu fallsa, gu mealltach, gu truaillidh.*

Spuriousness, *s.* Fallsachd, fallsaileachd; diolanas.

Spurn, *v. a.* Breab, stramp; cuir air dimeas; diùlt le h-ardan.

Spurn, *s.* Breab, stramp ardanach, dimeas, tàir.

Spurning, *s.* Breabadh (no) strampadh le h-ardan; ardanachd, uaibhrichead.

Spurrer, *s.* Brogair, fear stuige, brosnachair; fear brosnachaidh, fear brogaidh.

Spurrier, *s.* Sporadair.

Spurring, *s.* Sporadh; greasadh, cur h-uige, stuigeadh, brosnuchadh.

Spurt. See **Spirt.**

Spurway, *s.* Rod marcachd.

Sputter, *v. n.* Bi bladach (no) gagach an cainnt, labhair le cabhaig.

Sputter, *s.* Braon, ronn; sileadh, spultadh; (*bustle*), tuasaid, tabaid, iomairt.

Sputterer, *s.* Ronnair; bladair, fear gagach (no) liodach.

Sputtering, *a.* Braonach; ronnach; spultach; (*in speech*), gagach, liodach.

Spy, *s.* Fear coimhid, spioth; fear brathaidh, fear rannsuchaidh, beachdair.

Spy, *v. a.* Beachdaich, faic, fairich, thoir a mach, faigh mach; brath, cum sùil air; rannsuich.

Spy-boat, *s.* Bàt brathaidh.

Spy-fault, *s.* Rinneadair; creamadair; fear cronachaidh.

Spy-glass, *s.* Gloine amhairc.

Squab, *a.* Neo-chloimhichte mar gharraig; goirrid, cutach, bunach, domhail; tiugh; reamhar, pocanach, pocanta.

Squab, *s.* Seorsa seithir, uiridh; pillean.

Squab, *s.* Calman, colman.

Squab, *v. n.* Suidh (no) tuit le splad.

Squabbish, *a.* Reamhar, sultmhor, tiugh, domhail, feòlar; pocanach, cutach.

Squabble, *v. n.* Cuir a mach, connsaich, dean comhstri, dean tuasaid. They began to squabble, *thòisich iad air connsach* (*no*) *air cur a mach;* they squabbled among themselves, *chuir a mach air chèile.*

Squabble, *s.* Tuasaid, tabaid, connsach, brionglaid, buaireas, braoilich, aimhreite, duaireachas, cur mach.

Squabbler, *s.* Fear aimhreite, fear tuasaideach, fear tuasaid, buaireadair.

Squabbling, *a.* Tuasaideach, tabaideach, brionglaideach.

Squabbling, *s.* See **Squabble.**

Squadron, *s.* Earrann cabhlaich (no) feachd, trup, bragàd.

Squalid, *a.* Salach; mosach, musach, granda, gràda, déisneach, déistinneach.

Squall, *v. n.* Sgal, sgread, sgiamh, sgreach, éigh, eubh.

Squall, *s.* Sgal, sgread, sgiamh, sgreach, éigh, eubh; (*of wind*), osag, osunn, oiteag, piorradh gaoithe, sgal gaoithe.

Squaller, *s.* Sgalair, sgreachair.

Squally, *a.* Osagach, oiteagach, gaothar.

Squalor, *s.* Seilche, sal, mosaiche.

Squamose, **Squamous**, *a.* Lannach; sligeach; sgrathach.

Squander, *v. a.* Caith, struigh, sgap; cosd.

Squanderer, *s.* Struighear, stroghair, fear stroghail; fear stroghasach.

Square, *a.* Ceithir chearnach; cothrom; comhad; laidir, bunanta; ceart, ionraic.

Square, *s.* Ceithirc-hearnag; riaghail; riaghailt, usgar; cearnag. A square of glass, *cearnag ghloine;* out of square, *gun* (*no*) *a riaghailt.*

Square, *v. a.* and *n.* Socraich, riaghail; dean ceithirchearnach, dean cothromach; tomhais, riaghailtich; dealbh.

Squash, *s.* Splad, splaitseadh, plaitseadh; ni bog sam bi; seorsa luibh, peapag.

Squash, *v. a.* Bruth, pronn.

Squash, *v. n.* Tuit (no) suidh le splad.

Squat, *v. n.* Crùb, crùbain, dean crùban, curaidh, dean curaidh, luidh sios, sìn, suidh air làr.

Squat, *s.* Crùban, curaidh.

Squat, *a.* Saigeanach, saigeanta, cutach, bunach, bunanta, crùbanach, na chrùban, na churaidh, na luidhe.

Squat, *s.* Seorsa méin.

Squeak, *v. n.* Sgiamh; bìd, sgread, sgreach, iach, éigh, sian, dean sgiamh, dean bìd, dean sgread, leig sgread (no) sgiamh asad.

Squeak, *s.* Sgiamh, bìd, sgread, sgreach, iach, éigh, sian.

Squeaking, *s.* Sgiamhail, bìdil, sgreadail, sianail, sianaich.

Squeal, *s.* Sgal, sgiamhail, sgreachail, sianail, sianaich.

Squeamish, *a.* Sgleatail, orraiseach, sgreamhail, déistinneach, gràineil. Squeamishly, *gu sgleatail, gu sgreamhail.*

Squeamishness, *s.* Sgleatadh, sgleatas, orrais, orraiseachd, sgàth; sgreamh, sgreamhalachd, gràin, deistinn.

Squeeze, *v. a.* Teannaich, mùch; domhlaich, bruth, fàisg; sàruich, claoidh. Squeezed, *teannaichte, mùchta, faisgte; sàruichte, claoidhte.*

Squeeze, *s.* Teannach, mùchadh, domhlachadh; fàsgadh; sàruchadh.

Squeezer, *s.* Teannachair, mùchadair; fasgear; fear sàruchaidh.

Squeezing, *s.* Teannachadh, mùchadh, domhlachadh, bruthadh, fasgadh, sàruchadh.

Squelch, *s* Splad, spladse, pladse, pladseadh.

Squib, *s.* Cracair; teine sionnachain.

Squill, *s.* Lear-uinnean

Squinancy, *s* Galar plocach, amhach ghoirt

Squint, *a* Claon, fiar-shuileach, caog-shuileach.

Squint, *v. a.* Seall claon (no) fiar, thoir sealladh taobh; fiaraich, claon, claonaich

Squint-eyed, *a* Claon, fiar, fiar-shuileach, caog-shuileach.

Squire, *s* Sguair; fear is fhaigse do ridir; còlainn

Squire, *v. a.* Feith (no) fritheil air; comhaidich, treòraich.

Squirrel, *s.* Feòrag, easag.

Squirt, *v. a* Sgiort, sgiurt, sgiurd, steall, taosg.

Squirt, *s* Sgiort, sgiurt, sgiurd, sgiùrdan, steall; sput; steallair, stealladair, sgiùrdan, sgiordan; spùtachan; gunna sputachain

Stab, *v a* Sàth, lot, leòn, troimh-lot, dochannaich, leon gu bàs.

Stab, *s* Sàth, lot, leòn, creuchd, dochann, buille.

Stabber, *s.* Fear lotaidh, leònadair.

Stabbing, *s.* Sàth, sàthadh, lotadh, leònadh, dochannadh.

Stabiliment, *s* Diongaltas, gramalas, daighneachadh

Stability, *s* Buan-sheasamh, buanachd, buanad, bunaiteachd, bunailteachd, maireannachd, cinnteachd.

Stable, *s.* Daingean, buan, bunaiteach, bunailteach, seasmhach, maireann, maireannach, làidir.

Stable, *s* Stàbull, each-lann.

Stable, *v. a* Cuir an stàbull.

Stable-boy, *s* Gille stàbuill, gille each.

Stableness, *s.* Daighneachd, buanas, bunaiteachd, bunailteachd, seasmhachd.

Stablish, *v. a.* Daighnich, socraich, cuir air chois Stablished, *daighnichte, socraichte*

Stack, *s* Cruach, mulan, rucan, ruc. A stack of hay, *cruach shaidh*, (of corn), *rucan.*

Stack, *v. a* Cruach, cruachaich, cruinnich, carn. Stacked, *cruachta, cruachaichte, cruinnichte*

Stadle, *s* Prop; taic, gobhal; craobh òg, maothan.

Stadle, *v.* Prop, cum suas, cum taic ri

Stadtholder, *s.* Riaghladair na h-Olaint.

Staff, *s.* Bat, lorg; bachull; cuaille; droll, urlann, (*of a spear*), samhach, cos; (*of a ladder*), ceum (no) stap, (*ensign*), suaicheantas, (*power*), cumhachd, (*support*), taic, cùl taic, (*in verse*), rann, earann, ceathramh, ceithreamh

Stag, *s* Damh feidh, damh

Stage, *s.* Sgafall, sgafald; fionn-bhùth; ionad cluiche, tigh cluiche, ceann uidhe, uidhe Stage by stage, *uidhe air uidhe*

Stage-coach, *s.* Coisde ruithe

Stage-play, *s.* Cluiche, cluithe, dealbh-chluiche, sgearadh.

Stage-player, *s.* Fear cluiche

Stager, *s* Fear cluiche; cuilbheartair.

Staggard, *s* Damh feidh ceithir-bhliadhnach

Stagger, *v. n.* and *a.* Breathlaich, tuainealaich, tuislich, bi thun tuiteam, ruidhil, tiob; bi san tomhartaich (no) an iomcheist; oilltich, cuir am breathal

Staggers, *s* Seorsa galair a measg each.

Stagnancy, *s.* Neo-ghluasad, tamh, seasamh.

Stagnant, *a* Neo-ghluasadach, seasamhach, tamhach, marbh, seimh Stagnant water, *marbh-uisge.*

Stagnate, *v. n.* Lodaich, stad mar ni uisge.

Stagnation, *s.* Lodachadh, stadachd, cion gluasaid, seasmhachd

Staid, *a.* Crionna, suidhichte, glic, siochainnteach.

Staid, *pret* of stay. Dh' fhan, dh' fhuirich, dh' fheith.

Stain, *s* Ball, sal, spot, coire, truailleadh; lochd, gaoid; (*colour*), dath, ligh; (*shame*), tàmailt, nàire, mi-chliù.

Stain, *v a.* Salaich, spot; truaillich; tàmailtich; nàraich; (*dye*), dath. Stained, *salaichte, truaillichte, nàraichte, dathta.*

Stainer, *s.* Fear salachaidh; dathadair.

Staining, *s* Salachadh, spotadh, truailleadh, nàrachadh; dathadh

Stainless, *a.* Neo-lochdach, neo-choireach, neo-chionntach, glan, gun bhall, gun sal, gun spot, gun choire.

Stair, *s.* Staidhir. Stairs, *staidhrichean*, go up stairs, *rach suas (no) nàirde an staidhir*; he is up stairs, *tha e uthard (no) shuas an staidhir*, winding stairs, *staidhir sniomhain.*

Staircase, *s* Staidhir

Stake, *s.* Post, cuaillé, maolanach; carradh, colbh; (*wager*), geall; (*for cattle*), bacan. At stake, *ann an cunnart.*

Stake, *v. a* Gramaich, daighnich, gabh aig; (*wager*), cuir an geall

Stalactites, *s* Seorsa miodailt air chumadh bior eidhe.

Stalactical, *a.* Mar bhior eighe, biorach.

Stalder, *s* Sorchan leigidh.

Stale, *a.* Sean; goirt, searbh; stolda; domblasda; grod; (*as bread*), liath. Stale beer, *lionn goirt.*

Stale, *s.* (*Beer*), lionn goirt; (*urine*), fual goirt, mùn; (*wench*), striopach; (*allurement*), taiteadh, mealladh; (*handle*), lamh, cas, samhach

Stale, *v n.* Mùin, dean uisge

Staleness, *s* Stoldachd, seandachd, goirteas, (*of bread*), leithe; liathad; (*triteness*), cumantas.

Stalk, *v. n.* Ceumnaich; spaisdeirich, meùrs, ath-cheumnaich; imich ceum air cheum, imich gu stàideil.

Stalk, *s* Ceum uallach, (no) staideil, proiseal; (*of grass*), cos cuiseig, lorg, lurg, feòirnean.

Stalky, *a* Cuiseagach, lorgach.

Stall, *s.* Mainnir, prasach, buail, buaitheal, ionad biathaidh; bàich.

Stall, *v. a.* Biath Stalled, *biathta*; a stalled ox, *damh biathta (no) air a bhiath*

Stall-fed, *a.* Biathta

Stallion, *s* Àigeach, àigheach, greidheach; (*a gallant*), fear slatail

Stamina, *s.* Brigh, brìogh, stuth, smior, smiodam; susbuin.

Stamineous, *a* Toinnteanach, sreangach, sreangunach.

Stammel, *s.* Dath dearg àraidh

Stammer, *v n.* Bi manndach (no) liodach, glugairich, labhair le mannd; labhair (no) leugh air éigin.

Stammer, *s.* Mannt, liod, briot, ag, gag.

Stammerer, *s.* Fear manndach, fear liodach, glugair

Stammering, *s* Manntaichead, glugaireachd, ag.

Stammering, *a* Manntach, glugach, liodach, briolach, agach, gagach.

Stamp, *v. a.* Stramp, pronn, bruth; comharaich. He stamped upon it, *stramp e air, stramp e fo 'chosaibh e.*

Stamp, *s.* Stramp, aile; dealbh, comhar; comharadh; seorsa, sliochd. Men of that stamp, *daoine do 'n seorsa sin.*

Stamper, *s.* Strampair; pronnadair, bruthadair

Stanch, Staunch, *v. a* and *n.* Stad (no) coisg fuil, sguir, stad.

STANCH, *a.* Dian; diongalta, daingean, làidir, bunaiteach, bunailteach, fireannach, fior. A stanch friend, *fior charaid;* a stanch hound, *cù luirg.*

STANCHER, *s.* Fear (no) ni chuireas stad air fuil.

STANCHION, *s.* Prop; gàd.

STAND, *s.* Seasamh, àite seasamh; stad, stàdachd; ag, teagamh; iomcheiste; bùth; (*a spinning-wheel*), stanar, stanard. He is at a stand, *tha e 'n teagamh;* make a stand, *thoir aghaidh.*

STAND, *v. n.* and *a.* Seas, seasamh; dean seasamh, fuirich, fan, stad; éirich. Stand up, *seas nàirde;* (endure), *fuilig, fulaing, giùlain;* stand aside, *seas gu taobh;* stand against, *cuir an aghaidh, gabh roimh;* stand away (at sea), *tionndaidh, stiùir air falbh;* stand out, *cum mach;* stand to, *cum ris;* stand by, *cum taobh ri;* stand in, *cosd;* stand one in stead, *dean feum (no) stà do neach;* stand to, *cum ri;* stand upright, *seas dìreach.*

STANDARD, *s.* Suaicheantas, bratach, meirghe; stanard; craobh, saclan.

STANDARD-BEARER, *s.* Fear brataich, fear suaicheantais.

STANDEL, *s.* Sean chraobh.

STANDER, *s.* Fear seasamh; sean chraobh. A stander by, *fear amhairc.*

STANDING, *s.* Seasamh; buanachadh; cor; inbhe. A standing place, *aite seasamh;* he is standing, *tha e na sheasamh;* she is standing, *tha i na seasamh;* you are standing, *tha sibh na 'r seasamh;* they are standing, *tha iad nan seasamh.*

STANDISH, *s.* Seas dubh.

STANG, *s.* Còig slat gu leth.

STANK, *pret.* of stink. Lobh.

STANNARY, *s.* Méin peòdair.

STANNARY, *a.* Peòdarach, peodarra.

STANZA, *s.* Rann, earann, ceithreamh, ceathramh.

STAPLE, *s.* Marg, margadh; (*a loop of iron*), stìnleag, stapull.

STAPLE, *a.* Socraichte, sonruichte, sunruichte, suidhichte.

STAR, *s.* Rannag, reannag, rionnag, reannan, reul, reult; steorn, reulag. A wandering star, *reul seachranach.*

STARBOARD, *s.* Taobh deas luing o 'n stiùir; bord beuladh.

STARBRIGHT, *a.* Reul-ghlan.

STARCH, *s.* Stalcair, stalcadair, *staofainn.*

STARCH, *v. a.* Stalc, stalcaich, *staofainn.* Starched, *stalcaichte.*

STARCHED, *a.* Stalcaichte; foirmeil.

STARCHLY, *adv.* Gu foirmeil; gu rudach; gu ceigeanach.

STARCHNESS, *s.* Foirmealachd, foirmeileachd.

STARE, *v. n.* Spleuc, spleuchd, spleachd; sgeann, geurbheachdaich. He stared me in the face, *spleuc e san aghaidh orm.*

STARE, *s.* Spleuc, spleac; geur-amharc, stalc.

STARE, *s.* Truid, truideag.

STARER, *s.* Spleuchdair, spleachdair, stalacair.

STARGAZER, *s.* Reuladair, speuradair, reul-dhruidh, reannair.

STARGAZING, *s.* Reuladaireachd, speuradaireachd.

STARHAWK, *s.* Seorsa seabhaig.

STARING, *s.* Spleuchdadh, spleachdadh, sgeannadh. His eyes staring in his head, *a shùilean a sgeannadh na cheann.*

STARK, *a.* Fior, iomlan, rag, làidir; garbh; diomhain, seimh.

STARK, *adv.* Gu fior, gu tur, gu h-iomlan. Stark naked, *dearg ruisgte;* stark mad, *air an dearg chuthach, air a ghlan chuthach.*

STARLESS, *a.* Gun reul-sholus, gun rionnag.

STARLET, *s.* Reilteag, reulag, reannan.

STARLIGHT, *s.* Reul-sholus.

STARLIKE, *a.* Reannagach, rionnagach, loinnreach, dealrach, soillseach, drilinneach.

STARLING, *s.* Truid, truideag.

STARPANED, *a.* Rionnagaichte, air cur thairis le rionnagaibh.

STARRED, *a.* Rionnagach, reultach, reulagach.

STARRING, *a.* Rionnagach, reultach.

STARRY, *a.* Rionnagach, reannagach, reultach.

STARSHOOT, *s.* Sgeith-rionnaig.

START, *v. n.* and *a.* Clisg, grad-leum, crith, criothnaich, falbh, siubhail; cuir clisg air; cuir as an alt; cuir as àite; cuir an céill, foillsich, cuir san rod, thig san rod. I started, *chlisg mi;* you started me, *chuir thu clisge orm.*

START, *s.* Clisge, clisgeadh; briosg, grad-leum; teannadh air falbh; toiseach. Get the start of him, *faigh air thoiseach air.*

STARTER, *s.* Fear gealtach; cù eunaich.

STARTING, *s.* Clisgeadh, briosgadh, criothnachadh; biogadh.

STARTING-POST, *s.* Post réis.

STARTLE, *v. a.* and *n.* Clisg, cuir clisge air; crith, criothnaich, grad-leum; oilltich, cuir eagal air.

STARTLE, *s.* Clisge, clisgeadh, crithe, oillt, crithe oillt.

STARTLISH, *a.* Gealtach, eagallach.

STARVE, *v. a.* and *n.* Cuir gu bàs le gort (no) fuachd marbh le ocras; basaich le ghort (no) fuachd.

STARVELING, *s.* Urr bhochd, creutair truagh, ocrach, ciocran.

STARVELING, *a.* Ocrach, acrach, truagh, caol.

STARVING, *s.* Bàsachadh le gort (no) fuachd.

STATARY, *a.* Suidhichte, àitichte, socraichte; daingeann.

STATE, *s.* (*Condition*), staid, inbhe, inmhe, àite, cor, gné; (*government*), riaghladh, rioghachd, dùthaich; (*office*), àite, dreuchd; (*pomp*), mòr-chuis, greadhnachas. What state is he in? *ciod an staid sa bheil e?* if you were in my state, *nam biodh tu 'm àite se, nam bu tu mise;* state affairs, *gnothuichean rioghachd;* I pity your state, *is truagh leam do chor;* a bed of state, *leabaidh riomhach.*

STATE, *v. a.* Suidhich, socraich; rùnaich; cuir an céil.

STATELINESS, *s.* Stàidealachd, mòr-chuis, mòr-chuiseachd, greadhnachas, loghmhorachd, riomhadh, maise; uaille.

STATELY, *a.* Stàideil, àluinn; foinneamh, flathail, mòrchuiseach, mileanta; greadhnach; riomhach, maiseach, spairisdeach, uallach. A stately step, *ceum stàideil.*

STATELY, *adv.* Gu stàideil; gu h-aluinn; gu flathail, gu mor-chuiseach, gu greadhnach, gu riomhach, gu h-uallach, gu spairiseach.

STATE-ROOM, *s.* Seomar riomhach.

STATES, *s.* Uaillsean, maithean.

STATESMAN, *s.* Riaghladair duthcha.

STATICS, *s.* Ealadhain thoimhsean.

STATION, *s.* Seasamh; àite, ionad; dreuchd, post, oifig, inbhe.

STATION, *v. a.* Socraich; suidhich; àitich. Stationed, *socraichte, suidhichte.*

STATIONARY, *a.* Socraichte, suidhichte, àitichte, anns an aon àite.

STATIONER, *s.* Fear reic leabhraichean, leabhar-reiceadair, fear reic paipeir.

STATUARY, *s.* Dealbhadh, grabhadh, snaitheadh; dealbhadair, dealbhair cloich, grabhair; dualaiche.

STATUE, *s.* Iomhaigh; riochd, dealbh.

STATURE, *s.* Airde, meud, meudachd, inmhe.

STATUTABLE, *a.* Laghail, reachdail, dligheil, a reir lagh.

STATUTABLY, *adv.* A réir lagh.

Statute, *s.* Lagh, reachd, òrdugh, dlighe, achd; statuis.

Stave, *v. a.* and *n.* Cuir na chlàraibh, bris (no) thoir as a chéile. Stave off, *pùc air falbh*, the vessel is staved, *tha 'n soitheach na chlàraibh*

Staves, *s. pl.* Bataichean; lorgaichean; (*of a barrel*), clàran

Stay, *v. a.* and *n.* Fuirich, fan, feith, stad, seas; buanaich; (*dwell*), comhnuich, tàmh, cum bac, coisg, gabh roimh, (*prop*), prop, cum suas; cum taic ri. Stay here a little, *fuirich* (*no*) *fan an so beagan;* stay your hand, *cum air do laimh*, whom do you stay for? *co ris tha thu fanachd?* shall we stay for you? *am fuirich sinn riut?* where do you stay? *c' àite bheil thu 'fanachd?* stay away, *fan air falbh.*

Stay, *s.* Fanachd, fantuinn, fuireach, fuireachd, fuireachadh, feitheamh, buanachd, stadachd, stad; dàil; bac; crionnachd; (*prop*), taic, gobhal, cul taic; prop, dion, tearmunn; (*stays of a ship*), stàdh, (*of a female*), cliabh, staidhinnean, staidhsa You made a long stay, *is fhad an fhuireach a rinn thu*

Stayed, *p.* and *a.* Suidhichte, socraichte, stolda, socrach, crionna, bacta, grabta; ciùin, ciùinichte. A stayed man, *fear suidhichte* (*no*) *stolda*

Stayedly, *adv.* Gu suidhichte, gu socraichte, gu socrach, gu crionna, gu glic

Stayedness, *s.* Suidhichead, socair, crionnachd, ghocas.

Stayer, *s* Taic, cùl-taic, prop, dion.

Staying, *s* Fanachd, fuireach, fuireachd, fantuinn, feitheamh, buanachd, stad, stadachd, (*curbing*), grabadh, cosgadh.

Staylace, *s.* Iall cleibh.

Stays, *s.* Cliabh mna, staidhinnean; gorsaid; (*of a ship*), stàdh; (*support*), prop, taic, gobhal, gabhal

Stead, *s* Aite, ionad; son; (*use*), stà, feum, còghnadh. In your stead, *ann ad àite, air do shon*, stand in stead, *dean feum* (*no*) *stà*.

† **Stead**, *v. a.* Dean feum, còghain, cobhair, cuidich le, foir air.

Steadfast, *a* See Stedfast

Steadfastly, *adv* See Stedfastly.

Steadfastness, *s* See Stedfastness.

Steadily, *adv* Gu bunaiteach, gu bunailteach, gu gramail, gu seasmhach, gu daingeann, gu dìleas, gun chrath, gu réith.

Steadiness, *s* Bunaiteachd, bunailteachd, gramalas, diongaltacnd; socair, sònruichead.

Steady, *a.* Bunaiteach, bunailteach, gramail; diongalta, daingeann, réidh, socrach, suidhichte. As steady as a rock, *cho diongalta ri craig;* a steady resolution, *rùn suidhichte*, a steady light, *solus réidh*, steady motion, *imeachd shocrach.*

Steady, *v a.* Socraich, dean diongalta, daighnich, cum suas

Steak, *s.* Stiog, staoig, toitean; colag, fill.

Steal, *v a.* Goid; reubainn, robainn Steal away, *goid* (*no*) *seap air falbh*, he stole upon me, *ghoid e orm*, *sheap* (*no*) *shnàg e orm.*

Stealer, *s* Goidiche, gaduiche, méirleach Stealers, *goidicheann, meirlich, luchd braide.*

Stealing, *s.* Goid, goideadh, gaduidheachd, meirleadh; braid

Stealingly, *adv* Gu goideach, gu bradach; gu scapach.

Stealth, *s.* Goid, meirleadh, meirle, gaduigheachd, braid; reubainn By stealth, *os iosal, gu diomhair, gun fhios, gun aithne*

Stealthy, *a.* Bradach, seapach, siapach.

Steam, *s* Toit, toth, deathach, smùid, gal.

Stedfast, *a.* Bunaiteach, bunailteach, seasmhach, buan, danara, daingean, dìlis.

Stedfastly, *adv.* Gu bunaiteach, gu bunailteach, gu seasmhach, gu buan, gu daingeann, gu dìleas.

Stedfastness, *s.* Bunaiteachd, bunailteachd, seasmhachd, danarachd.

Steed, *s* Each, steud; steud-each; marc.

Steel, *s.* Stàilinn, cruaidhe. Hard as steel, *cho chruaidh ri stàilinn*, a steel knife, *sgian stàilinn.*

Steel, *v. a.* Cruadhaich, stàilinnich, stàilnich. Steel your heart, *cruadhaich do chridhe;* steeled, *cruadhaichte.*

Steeling, *s.* Cruadhachadh, stàilneachadh.

Steely, *a.* Cruaidh mar stàilinn, stàilneach, stàilinneach.

Steelyard, *s* . Meidh, toimhsean, meidh-thomhais.

Steen, *s.* Soitheach creadha (no) cloich.

Steep, *a* Corrach, cas. A steep bank, *bruach chorrach;* a steep place, *bruthach, uchdan.*

Steep, *s.* Bruach, uchdan, uchdach, bruthach; lethad.

Steep, *v.* Bog, bogaich, cuir am bog, tom, tum, fliuch. Steeped, *bogaichte, tomta, am bogadh.*

Steeping, *s* Bogadh, bogachadh, cur am bog, tomadh, tumadh.

Steeple, *s* Stiopall, spiric, spiricean, tùr, turaid; claigeach.

Steeply, *a.* Gu cas, gu corrach

Steepness, *s.* Caisead, casad, corraichead, bruthach, uchdan.

Steepy, *a* Corrach, cas, creagach.

Steer, *s.* Damh òg.

Steer, *v. a* Sdiùir, stiùr, seòl; riaghail, treòruich. He steered homewards, *sheòl e dhachaidh.*

Steerage, *s.* Sdiùradh, stiùradh, seòladh, riaghladh, riaghailt; taobh deiridh luing.

Steersman, *s* Sdiùradair, fear sdiùraidh, fear sdiùir; seòladair, sgiobair.

Steganography, *s* Sgriobhadh diomhair

Stellar, *a.* Steornail, steornach, rionnagach, reannagach.

Stellate, *a.* Rionnagach, reannagach.

Stellation, *s* Dealradh, soillseadh, drillinn

Stellion, *s* Dearc (no) earc luachair, dearc luachrach.

Stem, *s.* (*Of an herb*), lorg, cas, cuiseag; (*of a tree*), bun, stoc; (*race*), sliochd, clann, gineal, teaghlach; (*of a ship*), toiseach luing Stock and stem, *eadar bhun is bhàrr*, from stem to stern, *o thoisich gu deireadh luing, o thulchainn gu stiùir.*

Stem, *v. a* Gabh roimh, cum roimh, bac, coisg, stad; thoir aghaidh do.

Stench, *s* Boladh, droch thòchd, droch fhàil, bréine, tòchd loibheach.

Stenography, *s.* Gearr-sgriobhadh.

Stentorophonic, *a.* Osgarra, labhra

Step, *v. n.* Ceum, thoir ceum, imich, ceumnaich, coisich, gluais, rach, falbh. Step aside, *imich gu taobh, rach gu taobh, thoir ceum gu taobh* (*no*) *leth taobh.*

Step, *s.* Ceum; glùn, stap; lorg, rod. Step by step, *ceum air cheum*, steps, *ceumanna, stapan, stapaichean;* the step of a door, *cloch* (*no*) *leac stairsnich.*

Stepchild, *s.* Dalta, leas-urr, leas-leanabh.

Stepdame, *s* Muime; mathair chéile.

Stepfather, *s* Oide, athair céile; leas-athair, leth-athair.

Stepping, *s.* Ceumnachadh, imeachd ceum air cheum.

Steppingstone, *s.* Clach, clachran, ceum.

Stepmother, *s.* Leas mhathair, leth-mhathair, muim.

Stercoraceous, *a.* Innearach.

Stercoration, *s.* Mathadh, mathachadh, leasachadh.

Sterile, *a.* Seasg, neo-thorrach, aimrid; (*as land*), tiorram, fàs, fochd, lom, cruaidh.

Sterility, *s.* Fasalachd, seasgad, seisge, neo-thorraichead, tiormachd.

Sterilize, *v. a.* Dean fàs, dean seasg, dean neo-thorrach.

Sterling, *a.* Sasunnach mar chùin, fior, fireannach.

Sterling, *s.* Cùin no airgiod Sasunnach.

Stern, *a.* Gruamach, duairc, duairceach, gnò, gnù; dorch, cruaidh; neo-thruacanta; doirbh; bodachail. A stern look, *sealladh gruamach;* a stern command, *ordugh cruaidh.*

Stern, *s.* Sdiùir, stiùir, falmadair, bior dubh luing; deireadh luing, ceann deiridh; tòin, tulchann.

Sternly, *adv.* Gu gruamach, gu gnò, gu gnù, gu dorch, gu cruaidh, gu cruadalach, gu doirbh, gu danarra.

Sternness, *s.* Gruaim, gruamaiche, gruamaichead; cruadhas, duairceas; doirche.

Sternutation, *s.* Sreothartaich, sreortaich, sreathartaich

Sternutative, *a.* Sreothartach, sreathartach.

Sternutatory, *s.* Snaoisean.

Stew, *v. a.* Stobh: earr-bhruich

Stew, *s.* Stobh; tigh teth; tum-aite; drùthlann; (*for fish*), lochan, linneag.

Steward, *s.* Stiùbhard; griobh; maor, riaghlair.

Stewardship, *s.* Stiùbhardachd, griobhachd, maorsainneachd; riaghlaireachd, feadhmantas.

Stewing, *s.* Stobhadh.

Stewpan, *s.* Aghann stobh.

Stick, *s.* Bioran, maide, bat, lorg. A clumsy stick, *droll, rong, guitseal,* a stick for turning a quern, *méile,* a curse falls not on stones nor on sticks, *cha luidh guidh air clach no air crann.*

Stick, *v. a.* and *n.* Sàth; lot, stic; stic ri; dluthaich ri; lean ri, stad, cum ri Stick in the ground, *sàth anns talamh;* stick between, *cuir eadar,* stick by one, *cum taobh ri neach,* stick by, *lean ri, stic ri,* stick to your word, *cum ri d' fhocal*

Stickiness, *s.* Leanailteachd, rithneachd, rithne.

Stickle, *v.* Connsaich, seas ri, cum taobh ri

Stickleback, *s.* Breac beag, gobhlachan

Stickler, *s* Breith, fear a chumas taobh ri neach; fear a chumas mach gu dian.

Sticky, *a.* Sticeach, rithinn, leanailteach.

Stiff, *a.* (*Not pliable*), rag, rithinn, do-lùbaidh; (*obstinate*), reasgach, aimneanda, rag, dùr; teann, cruaidh, deacair; (*affected*), foirmeil; *staof,* provincial; (*with cold*), marbh, air funtainn, air marbhlabadh.

Stiffen, *v a.* and *n* Dean rag (no) rithinn, rithnich, fàs rag, cruaidh (no) rithinn.

Stiff-hearted, *a.* Dùr, cruaidh, cruadalach, rag-mhuinealach, reasgach, cruaidh-chridheach.

Stiffly, *adv.* Gu rag, gu rithinn, gu do-lùbaidh, gu reasgach, gu dùr, gu cruaidh, gu deacair, gu foirmeil.

Stiff-necked, *a.* Rag, dùr, rag-mhuinealach, reasgach

Stiffness, *s.* Raige, raigead, raigsinn, ragaichead; dùiread; (*with cold*), funntainn; (*formality*), foirmealachd; (*rigour*), cruadhas.

Stifle, *v.* Mùch, tachd; cum fodha, coisg, folaich, céil; cuir as. Stifle your anger, *coisg do chorruich;* stifled, *mùchta, tachdta, céilte.*

Stifler, *s* Mùchadair.

Stifling, *s.* Mùchadh, tachdadh, cosgadh, folachadh, céiladh.

Stigma, *s.* Comhar, comharadh; lorg, sliochd; tàmailt, sgainneal, mì-chliù.

Stigmatic, Stigmatical, *a.* Comharaichte; fo thàmailt; tàmailteach, sgainnealach, tàireil.

Stigmatize, *v. a.* Comharaich; cuir fu thàmailt. Stigmatized, *comharaichte, fu thàmailt (no) thàir*

Stile, *s.* Staidhir, stapan; ceum bealaich; (*of a dial*), meur uaireadair gréine; clagmheur. A turnstile, *geat cuairtein, geat ruidhleanach.*

Stiletto, *s.* Biodag chaol

Still, *adv.* Fhathast, a fhathast, fathast, fòs; a ghnàth, gu so, gus a nios Are you here still? *bheil thu 'n so fhathast?*

Still, *a* Sàmhach, ciùin, seimh, bìth, tosdach, socrach; féitheil. Be still, *bi samhach, gabh gu fois*

Still, *s* Poit dubh, poit thogalach, coire thogalach; breiseachan; (*silence*), samhchair, tosd.

Still, *v a.* and *n* Ciùinich, ciùnaich, cuir samhach, coisg, siothchaich; (*drop*), sil, sruth

Stillatitious, *a.* Braonach, silteach, snitheach

Stillatory, *s.* Poit thogalach

Stillborn, *a.* Marbh.

Stillicide, *s.* Sileadh, snithe, sil air shil; silteachd, braonadh

Stillicidious, *a.* Silteach, braonach; sileagach, ceòbanach, ceòthranach.

Stillness, *s.* Samhchair, ciùineas, tosd, féith; fé

Stilly, *adv.* Gu samhach, gu ciùin, gu bìth

Stilt, *s.* Trosnair, tròsdan; (*of a plough*), uaidne.

Stilts, *s* Trosnan, tròsdan, casan corrach, clabhdain, luirg The stilt of a plough, *uaidne.*

Stimulate, *v. a* Spor, brod, stuig, brosnuich, earalaich, cuir h-uige, buair. Stimulated, *brosnuichte, buairte, earalaichte*

Stimulating, *s.* Sporadh, brodadh, stuigeadh, brosnachadh, earalachadh.

Stimulus, *s* Spor, brod, brog, brosnach, brosnachadh, buaireadh

Sting, *s.* Gath; lot; guin, goimh. A serpent's sting, *gath nathrach,* (of conscience), *agartas (no) beum coguis;* there are few smooth tongues without a sting behind, *is tearc teangaidh mhìn gun ghath air a cùl*

Sting, *v. a* Gath, cuir gath, gathaich, lot It stung me, *chuir e gath unnam.*

Stingily, *adv* Gu sanntach, gu gionach, gu crion, gu teann, gu spiocach, gu miothur, gu reotanach

Stinginess, *s.* Sanntachd, gion, crìne, spioc, spiocaireachd reotanachd.

Stingless, *a.* Gun ghath, neo-ghuineach.

Stingo, *s.* Sean lionn.

Stingy, *a.* Sanntach, gionach, crion, teann, cruaidh, spiocach, reotanach, reotanda

Stink, *v. n.* Dean fàil, dean droch bholadh, cuir droch thòchd, tog boladh breun.

Stink, *s* Boladh breun, tòchd loibheach, droch fhàil.

Stinkard, *s.* Spiocair; tùtair; fear loibheach, miothur.

Stinker, Stinkpot, *s.* Ni breun sam bi.

Stint, *v. a* Criochnaich, socraich; cum stigh bac.

Stint, *s.* Crioch, teòradh, ceann, bac, earann.

Stipend, *s.* Stiopain; duais, tuarasdal, pàigh, luach saoithreach

Stipendiary, *s.* Fear tuarasdail, tuarasdalaiche.

Stipendiary, *a.* Tuarasdalach

Stipulate, *v. a.* Cùmhnantaich, socraich, sonruich, dean cùmhnant; dean bargan. Stipulated, *cùmhnantaichte.*

STIPULATION, *s.* Cùmhnantachd, cùmhnant, socrachadh; bann, cor; bargan; ceangladh.

STIPULATIVE, *a.* Cùmhnantach.

STIPULATOR, *s.* Cùmhnantaiche, fear cùmhnaint.

STIR, *v. a.* and *n.* Gluais, carruich, glidich; brosnuich; beothaich; stuig, cuir h-uige; tog. Stir not from thence, *na carruich a sin;* stir not a foot, *na glidich cas;* stir up to anger, *brosnuich chum feirge;* raise a tumult, *tog aimhreite (no) buaireas;* stir up yourself, *cuir car dhiot;* stir up and down, *crath;* stir any inspissated fluid, *suath;* stir a fire, *bruillich;* stirred, *gluaiste, carruichte, glidichte, brosnuichte, beothaichte;* stir up your stumps, *tarruing a chas a th' air deireadh, cuir car dhiot.*

STIR, *s.* Buaireas, othail, ùinich, tuasaid, aimhreite, strìgh, iomairt. Much stir about nothing, *mòran iomairt mu neoni;* raise a stir, *tog buaireas (no) aimhreite.*

† STIRP, *s.* Siol, sliochd.

STIRRER, *s.* Buaireadair, brosnuchair; carrachair, fear buaireis, fear aimhreite; fear moch-eiridh,

STIRRING, *s.* Buaireadh, brosnuchadh, carrachadh; togail, suathadh. What news are stirring? *ciod an nuaidheachd a tha dol?*

STIRRUP, *s.* Stiorap. Stirrup-cup, *deoch an doruis.*

STITCH, *v. a.* Fuaigh; fuaighil, tàth; càirich. Stitched, *fuaighte, càirichte.*

STITCH, *s.* Stic, greim snàthaid, greim, fuaigheal; *(furrow),* clais; *(pain),* guin, goimh, treathaid.

STITCHING, *s.* Obair shnàthaid, fuaghal, fuaigheal.

STITHY, *s.* Innean.

STIVE, *v. a.* Mùch, domhlaich, bruich, dean teth.

STIVER, *s.* Bonn sé Dùitseach.

STOAT, *s.* Neas, easag.

STOCCADO, *s.* Sàthadh.

STOCK, *s.* Stoc; ploc, creamhachdan, post, bun; *(fool),* baothair, guraiceach, umaidh; *(for the neck),* stoc; *(race),* siol, sliochd, clann, gineal, pòr, teaghlach, tigh; *(store),* stòr, stoc, stòras, maoin; *(of cards),* stoc, pac, pachd. The stock of a tree, *bun (no) stoc craoibh;* stocks, *ceap.*

STOCKS, *pl.* of stock. Stuic.

STOCK, *v. a.* Lion, stoc; cruach, cnuasaich, cruinnich. Stock up, *thoir as a bhun;* stocked, *lionta, làn.*

STOCKDOVE, *s.* Smùdan.

STOCKFISH, *s.* Bodach ruadh air a thiormachadh.

STOCKING, *s.* Stocainn, stocaidh, osan, cas-bheart. Stocking-hose, *osain Ghaidhealach.*

STOCKJOBBER, *s.* Fear ocair.

STOCKISH, *a.* Baoth, umaidheach, amhasach.

STOCKLOCK, *s.* Glas-chip.

STOCKS, *s.* Ceap.

STOIC, *s.* Teallsanach, feallsanach, feallsair, teallsair; fear leanmhuinn Séno; fear a tha coidhis ciod 'thig air.

STOLE, *s.* Mantal, sgiobal, éide, eudach, earradh, còta fada; earrasaid, earradh rioghail; gun sagairt.

STOLE, *pret.* of steal. Ghoid.

STOLEN, *part.* of steal. Air ghoideadh, goidte; diomhair. A stolen glance, *sealladh diomhair.*

STOLIDITY, *s.* Baothaireachd, umaidheachd, amaidheachd.

STOMACH, *s.* Goile, stamac, maodal; *(appetite),* sannt bidh ocras; *(passion),* feirge, ardan, misneach. It turns my stomach, *thà e 'cur deistinn orm;* the stomach of a calf or sheep, *minid.*

STOMACH, *v. a.* and *n.* Gabh gu dona, gabh corruich; cùimhnich le feirge.

STOMACHED, *a.* Feargach, làn corruich (no) feirg.

STOMACHER, *s.* Cliabh boirionnaich, crios uchd.

STOMACHFUL, *a.* Dùr, reasgach, rag, rag-mhuinealach.

STOMACHFULNESS, *s.* Dùiread, reasgachd, raigsinn.

STOMACHIC, STOMACHICAL, *a.* Goileach, maodalach, math air son na stamaic.

STOMACHIC, *s.* Leigheas goile.

STOMACHLESS, *a.* Neo-ocrach, gun ocras, gun stamac.

STONE, *s.* Cloch, clach; art, leac; liagan, doirneag; tiadhan, pulbhag; ceithir puint deug chothroim, ochd clachan cothroim. A large round stone, *pulbhag;* a stone-weight, *clach cothroim;* blood-stone, *clach dhearg;* chalk-stone, *caile, clach chailce;* a mill-stone, *clach mhuilinn;* a precious stone, *leug, liag, seud;* a whetstone, *clach gheurachaidh, clach niaradh;* a hewn stone, *clach shnaithte;* a stone of wool, *clach olainn;* stones or testicles, *clachan, magairlean;* *(calculus),* galar fuail.

STONE, *a.* Cloich, cruaidh mar chloich. A stone floor, *urlar chloich.*

STONE, *v. a.* Clach, cloch, tilg clachan, clach gu bàs.

STONEBLIND, *a.* Dall.

STONECAST, *s.* Urchair cloich. About a stonecast off, *beul ri urchair cloich as.*

STONECHATTER, *s.* Cloichrean; clachlain.

STONECUTTER, *s.* Snaithear, snaitheadair, fear snaithe, clach-ghearradair.

STONEFRUIT, *s.* Meas anns am bheil clach.

STONEHORSE, *s.* Aigeach, òigeach, greidheach.

STONEPIT, *s.* Gairbheal.

STONEPITCH, *s.* Pic chruaidh.

STONEPLOVER, *s.* Feadag; cloichrean.

STONEWALL, *s.* Balla cloich.

STONEWORK, *s.* Obair chloich.

STONINESS, *s.* Cruathas; cruaidhe.

STONY, *a.* Garbh, clachach, clochach, làn chlach, cruaidh, cragach; sgairneach; *(in heart),* cruaidh; cruadalach, neo-iochdmhor.

STOOD, *pret.* of stand. Sheas.

STOOL, *s.* Stòl, creupan; sorchan, suidheagan; ionad suidhe, falachadh. A footstool, *stol cois;* go to stool, *rach dheanamh do ghnothuich.*

STOOP, *v. n.* Crom, lùb, aom, géill, striochd.

STOOP, *s.* Cromadh, lùb, lùbadh, aom, aomadh, tuiteam.

STOOP, *s.* Soitheach da phinnt.

STOP, *v. a.* and *n.* Stad, cuir stad, gabh roimh, bac, toirmisg, cum o, grab, coisg, caisg, cuir dheth, cuir dàil; sguir, leig dhiot, fan, fuirich. Stop up, *duin no druid suas, lion.*

STOP, *s.* Stad, stadachd, grabadh, toirmeasg; cosgadh; sgurachd; fanachd, fuireach; dàil. Put a stop to it, *cuir stad air.*

STOPCOCK, *s.* Goc.

STOPPAGE, *s.* Aobhar stad, bac; stadachd, sgurachd; dàil, moille, toirmeasg.

STOPPLE, *s.* Stoipeal; staipeal arcan.

STORE, *s.* Maoin, stòr, stòras, beartas, pailteas, stoc, ionmhas; feudail; tigh tasgaidh.

STORE, *v. a.* Uigheamaich, airneasaich, stòr, cuir suas, stocaich, taisg, carn suas, cnuasaich, tionail, cuir seachad. Stored, *stocaichte, cnuasaichte, tionailte.*

STOREHOUSE, *s.* Tigh stòr, tigh tasgaidh, ionmhas, gleasan, deasadan, gairneal, lonailt.

STOREKEEPER, *s.* Fear tigh tasgaidh.

STORER, *s.* Fear tasgaidh, cnuasair; fear cnuasachd; fear tionalaidh.

STORK, *s.* Corra bhàn.

STORK'S-BILL, *s.* Seorsa luibh.

STORM, *s.* Anradh, anfhath, gailionn, doinionn, stoirm an

uair; iunnras, garbhuaic, † dardal; (*distress*), teinne, càs, amhghar; (*a sea-storm*), anradh cuain; (*of a town*), ionnsuidh, an-fhorlan.

Storm, *v. a.* and *n.* Thoir ionnsuidh, glac le an-fhorlan, tog gailionn (no) doinionn; bi fu chorruich.

Stormy, *a.* Anradhach, anfhathach, gailionnach, doinionnach, stoirmeil, doimheal; gaothar, eachanach, crosda.

Story, *s.* (*Tale*), nuaidheachd, sgeul, sgeulachd; eachdraidh, ursgeul; (*falsehood*), breug, *stòiridh*, (*in height*), urlar, staidhir, *stòiridh*. Tell a story, *innis sgeulachd*.

Story-teller, *s.* Sgeulaiche, seanachaidh; breugair.

Stote, *s.* Each òg; damh òg, seorsa easaig.

† **Stound**, *v. n.* Bi fu phéin; craon, cradh.

Stound, *s.* Ioghnadh; iongantas, uamhann, bròn; pian, goimh, craon.

Stout, *a.* Làidir, treun, foghainteach, neartail, comasach, toirteil, calma, balcanta, gramail, garbh, tiugh; tuarail, dàn, danarra, misneachail. Stout *or* jolly, *seamanach, sultmhor.*

Stout, *s.* Lionn làidir, portair dùbailt.

Stoutly, *adv.* Gu làidir, gu treun, gu comasach, gu calma, gu gramail, gu garbh; gu dàn, gu dànarra

Stoutness, *s* Treise, spionnadh, tréine, gramalas, dànadas; reasgachd, misneach.

Stove, *s.* Tigh teth; amhuinn, seorsa fùirneis.

Stove, *v. a.* Blàthaich.

Stow, *v a.* Taisg, cuir suas, carn suas, sùmhlaich, dais

Stowage, *s* Àite (no) rum tasgaidh; ionad tasgaidh, taisgeadh.

Strabism, *s.* Sealltuinn claon, sealladh claon.

Straddle, *v n.* Seas (no) imich cas gobhlach Ride astraddle, *marcaich cas gobhlach.*

Straddling, *a* Gobhlach, cas gobhlach

Stragle, *v n.* Rach air iomrol, rach air seacharan, seabhaid, rach air fhaontradh

Straggler, *s.* Iomrolaiche, seachranaiche, seabhaidiche, fear fuadain.

Straggling, *s* Iomrol, iomroladh, seacharan, seabhaid, seabhaideachd

Straggling, *a.* Iomrolach, seachranach, seabhaideach

Straight, *a.* Dìreach, neo-cham, ard; deas Stand straight, *seas dìreach*, straight on, *dìreach air adhairt;* straight against the wind, *calg dhìreach an aghaidh na gaoithe*, straight *or* stretched, *sìnte*, *sìnteach.*

Straight, *adv.* Gu grad, gu h-ealamh, air ball, gu luath, gun stad, gun dàil.

Straighten, *v. a.* Dìrich, dean dìreach; ceartaich Straightened, *dirichte.*

Straightening, *s.* Direachadh; ceartachadh

Straightly, *adv.* Gu dìreach.

Straightness, *s* Dìrichead.

Straightway, *adv* Air ball, gun dàil, gu h-ealamh, gu luath.

Strain, *v. a.* and *n* (*Squeeze*), fàisg, (*filter*), siolaidh; dlochd, dlochair, (*in embrace*), teannaich, dlùthaich; (*sprain*), siach, sniomh, leun; (*straiten*), cughannaich, teannaich; (*force*), éignich; (*exert*), dean spairn, feuch le spairn, thoir dian-oidhirp

Strain, *s.* (*Air*), fonn; (*sprain*), siachadh, sniomh, leun, (*effort*), spairn, dian-oidhirp, cruaidh-dheuchainn; (*disposition*), nàdur.

Strainer, *s.* Siolachan, siolag, dlochd.

Strait, *a.* (*Narrow*), cughann, cumhann, aimhleathan; (*intimate*), dlùth, (*strict*), geur, cruaidh; (*difficult*), cruaidh, duilich, deacair.

Strait, *s.* (*Frith*), caolas, cneas mara, creas mara, cunglach, airleag; (*distress*), càs, teinne, teanntachd; bochduinn, saruchadh, uireasbhuidh He is in a strait, *tha e na chàs, tha e 'g a shàruchadh*

Strait, *v. a.* Teannaich, sàruich, claoidh.

Straiten, *v. a.* (*Tighten*), teann, teannaich, cughannaich, dean cughann (no) aimhleathan; (*distress*), sàruich, teannaich, claoidh.

Straitening, *s.* (*Tightening*), teannadh, teannachadh, cughannachadh; (*distressing*), sàruchadh, claoidheadh.

Straithanded, *a* Cruaidh, crion, teann, spiocach, caonntach, cruadalach.

Straitlaced, *a* Teann, teannaichte; rag, neo-aontachail, diadhuidh ma 's fhior

Straitly, *adv.* Gu teann, gu cughann; gu geur, gu cruaidh; gu dlùth.

Straitness, *s* Aimhleathanachd, cughannachd; géire, geurad, cruadhas, teanntachd, teinne, càs

Strand, *s* Tràigh, cladach, srath; dual (no) pleat cùird.

Strand, *v. a* and *n* Cuir air, rach air; cuir (no) rach air cladach. The boat stranded, *chaidh am bàt air.*

Strange, *a* (*Wonderful*), iongantach, neonach, miorbhuileach; (*foreign*), coimheach, coigreach, allmharach, eil-thireach, eachdranach, gallda, (*shy*), coimheach, pùtanta, brocanta, fiadhaich A strange thing, *iongantas, neònachas, miorbhuil*, I think it strange, *is iongantach leam*

Strange, *interj.* Aoibh! obh!

Strangely, *adv.* Gu h-iongantach, gu neònach; gu miorbhuileach

Strangeness, *s* Iongantas, neònachas; coimhichead, coimhEachas; uamhunnachd.

Stranger, *s* Coigreach, eil-thireach, allmharach, gall Strangers, *coigrich* You are a stranger to me, *tha thu ad choigreach dhomh.*

Strangle, *v a* Tachd, mùch, croch, marbh She strangled him, *thachd i e*, strangle to death, *tachd gu bàs.*

Strangled, *part.* and *a.* Tachdta, mùchta, crochta

Strangler, *s* Crochadair.

Strangles, *s* Galar greidh.

Strangling, *s* Tachdadh, mùchadh.

Strangulation, *s* Tachdadh, mùchadh, crochadh

Strangury, *s.* Galar fuail, gabhail fhuail, cuing-fhuail

Strap, *s* Crios, iall, stiom, strap

Strap, *v* Buail le crios, gréidh, sgiùrs, cuipinn

Strappade, *s* Caraiste, gréidh.

Strapper, *s.* Caile dheas.

Strapping, *a* Mòr, calma, deas, foghainteach, tlachdmhor, tlachdar

Strata, *s.* Leapaichean; sreathan

Stratagem, *s.* Car, cuilbheart, innleachd, seòl, modh, cleas

Stratified, *a.* Ann an leapaichean

Stratify, *v a* Cuir ann an leapaichean, luidh ann am breithibh

Stratum, *s.* Leabaidh; breath; sreath.

Straw, *s* Fodar; connlach, tubh, (*straw spread beneath grain on a kiln*), sreathainn, streathainn A straw, *srabh, feòirnean*, it is not worth a straw, *chu n' fhiach e srabh*, a straw-bed, *leabaidh fhodair, leabaidh chonnlaich*, every straw is a stake at night, *is bior gach srabh san oidhche.*

Strawberry, *s.* Suidheag làir, sùbh làir

Strawbuilt, *a* Deanta le fodar (no) sràbhan

Strawy, *a* Connlachail, fodarach, sràbhach

Stray, *v. n.* Rach air seacharan; rach air iomrol, seabhaid; rach am mearachd, (*as a horse*), rach air eòlas

STRAY, *s* Ainmhidh air seachran.

STREAK, *s* Stiall, strioc, stiom, srian.

STREAK, *v. a.* Stiall, stiallaich, stiom, dean ballach, dean gris-fhionn.

STREAKED, STREAKY, *a* Stiallach, stiomach, srianach, gris-fhionn, ballach, riabhach.

STREAM, *s* Sruth; buinne, buinne-shruth, caisleac, abhainn. Down the stream, *leis an t-sruth;* a little stream, *sruthan,* a rapid raging stream, *buinne-shruth, mire-shruth*

STREAM, *v. n* Sruth, ruith (no) siubhail mar uisge; aom; dòirt .

STREAM-ANCHOR, *s.* Achdair srutha.

STREAMER, *s.* Suaicheantas, sròl, bratach.

STREAMING, *s* Sruth, sruthadh, ruithe, siubhal; dortadh.

STREAMLET, *s.* Sruthan, srùlag

STREAMY, *a.* Sruthach, siùbhlach, luath.

STREET, *s.* Sràid, stràid. On the street, *air an t-sràid;* streety, *sràideachean;* a place where two streets meet, *coinneach da shràid*

STREETWALKER, *s.* Siùrsach, siùrtach, striopach

STRENGTH, *s* Neart, spionn, spionnadh, trèine, treise; mearsuinn, arrachdas, laidreachd, lùth, treoir, cumhachd; gramalas, forlan; diongaltas; dion; tearmunn; càile na h-inntinn, dùn, daighneach; armailt With all my strength, *le m' uile neart,* every man in his strength, *gach fear na ghreim,* the strength of the fire, the strength of the sea, and the strength of a foolish fellow, *neart teine, neart mara is neart balaich.*

STRENGTHEN, *v. a* Neartaich; beothaich; (*as a city*), daighnich; dean làidir; socraich, suidhich. Strengthened, *neartaichte,* (as a city), *daighnichte*

STRENGTHENER, *s* Neartachair, beothachair; leigheas neartachaidh.

STRENGTHENING, *s.* Neartachadh, beothachadh, leigheasadh.

STRENGTHLESS, *a* Fann, anfhann, lag, gun treòir, breòite.

STRENUOUS, *a* Dàna; gaisgeil, misneachail, dùrachdach, oidhirpeach; curanta, crodha; dian, dealasach.

STRENUOUSLY, *adv* Gu dàna, gu gaisgeil, gu misneachail, gu dùrachdach, gu h-oidhirpeach

STREPEROUS, *a.* Ladurna, glagach, ard, fuaimneach. Streperously, *gu ladurna, gu glagach, gu h-ard*

STRESS, *s* Cudthrom, cothrom, strìgh; spairn; ainneart, foirneart; eallach; èigin Stress of weather, *an-uair*

STRETCH, *v. a.* Sin, sgaoil, ragaich; sin a mach; leudaich. Stretched, *sìnte, sgaoilte, ragaichte, sìnte a mach, leudaichte*

STRETCH, *s* Sìneadh; oidhirp The whole year is a long stretch, *is fad slios na bhliadhna.*

STRETCHER, *s* Ragadair; sineadair; bord cois mar th' aig fear iomraimh .

STREW, STROW, *v. a.* Sgaoil, sgap, crath, tilg sios is suas air chor eigin. Strewed, *sgaoilte, sgapta, crathta, craithte*

STREWER, *s* Fear sgaoilidh, sgapair, crathadair

STREWING, *s.* Sgaoileadh, sgapadh, crathadh.

STREWMENT, *s.* Sgaoileadh, sgapadh, crathadh.

STRIÆ, *s.* Claisean spairneig.

STRIATE, STRIATED, *a.* Claiseach mar spairneig.

STRICK, *s* Comhachag, cailleach oiche; (*of lint*), cuigealach

STRICKEN, *part.* and *a.* Buailte. Stricken again, *athbhuailte,* stricken in age, *sean, aosmhor, aosar,* stricken through, *troimh-shathta*

STRICKLE, *s* Stràc, stràchd.

STRICT, *a* Teann, cruaidh, geur; doirbh; leacanta; gabhaidh, deacair; poncail, dìreach. Have a strict eye on him, *cum sùil gheur air;* a strict master, *maighstir cruaidh.*

STRICTLY, *adv.* Gu teann, gu cruaidh, gu geur, gu doirbh, gu diongalta; gu pongail.

STRICTNESS, *s.* Teanntachd; cruadhas; cruas; gèire; teinnead, pongaileachd.

STRICTURE, *s.* Crupadh, teannachadh; buille; beanachd, beantuinn.

STRIDE, *v. n.* Thoir slnteag, thoir sùrdag, rach gobhlach, thoir ceum fada.

STRIDE, *s.* Slnteag, sùrdag, ceum, fad-cheum. What strides you take, *is tu ghabhas na sìnteagan.*

STRIDULOUS, *a* Diorrasanach; dranndanach, sgreadach.

STRIFE, *s* Strìgh, còmhstri, co-strìgh, connsach, connsuchadh, buaireas, utag, tabaid, aisith, tuasaid, aimhreite, bàir; droch còrd, cur a mach. Fall at strife, *cuir mach.*

STRIFEFUL, *a* Buaireasach, tabaideach, tuasaideach, aimhreiteach

STRIKE, *v. a.* and *n* Buail, dornaich. Strike, as a horse, *breab,* strike *or* afflict, *drùigh,* strike in pieces, *bruan;* strike, as a measure of corn, *stràc;* strike out, *dubh a mach,* strike off, *sgud;* strike through, *sàth, troimh-lot;* strike to the ground, *smal (no) spairt gu talamh;* strike up, *tog, tog suas; submit,* striochd, gèill Strike in with, *aontaich le,* strike as you feed, *na buail ach mar bhiathas tu.*

STRIKE, *s.* Ceathramh, ceithreamh, feorlan, buiseal.

STRIKER, *s.* Buaileadair, buailtear.

STRIKING, *a* Druighteach, muladach; iongantach.

STRIKING, *s.* Bualadh, dornachadh; builleachas; caraiste; greidh, slachduinn; lundrainn; striochd; gèilleadh.

STRING, *s* Sreang, sreangan, toinntean, tainntean; stiolan, cord, teud. Of pearls, *car neamhuin.*

STRING, *v. a* Sreang, teudaich; teud; toinnteanaich; cnòd ri chèile Stringed, *teudaichte.*

STRINGED, *part.* and *a.* Teudaichte; sreangach, toinnteanach.

STRINGY, *a.* Sreangach, toinnteanach, tainnteanach, stiolanach, teudach, rithinn.

STRIP, *v a* Rùisg, lom, nochd, sgath, faobhaich; cairt; robainn, reubainn; sgrath, plaoisg Stripped, *rùisgte,* stripped *or* naked, *lomardach.*

STRIP, *s* Stiall, striall, stiom In strips, *na stiallan, na striallan*

STRIPE, *v. a.* Stiall, stiallaich, striall, leub; buail; sgiùrs, sguitse, cuipinn. Striped, *stiallaichte; stiallach, air a sgiùrsadh, cuipinnte.* Cut into stripes, *striall.*

STRIPLING, *s.* Og, òganach, fleasgach, balachan, fiùran gille, riabhan, dailtean.

STRIVE, *v.* Dean spairn, cuir strìgh, dean cruaidh-oidhirp, gleachd Strive hard, *dean spairn chruaidh, connsaich,* he strove with them, *ghleachd e riu*

STRIVER, *s.* Fear comh-strìgh, fear strìgh, spairniche.

STRIVING, *s.* Comh-strìgh, strìgh, comh-spairn, gleachd, gleachdadh.

STROKE, *s.* Buille, gleadhar, cnap, straoidhle, stear, earrag, gleog, stràc, sgleafart; sgrioch, stròc, beartar. A stroke on the ear, *gleog san leth-cheann.*

STROKE, *v. a.* Suath, mìnich, ciùinich, sliog, sliob, criataich. Stroke a sorry fellow and he will scratch you, *sliob am bodach is sgròbaidh e thu.*

STROKING, *s* Suathadh, mìneachadh, ciùineachadh, criatachadh.

STROLL, *v.* Sràid-imich, sràideisich, seabhaid, gabh sràid.

STROLL, *s* Sràidimeachd, sràideas, sandaireachd, spaisdearachd, spaidsearachd, seabhaid, seabhas, ramlaireachd.

Stroller, *s.* Spaidsear, spaisdear, seabhasaiche; fògaraiche, sabhdair.

Strolling, *s.* Sràideas; spaisdearachd, seabhasachd, sabhdaireachd; cnocaireachd, faicheachd.

Strong, *a.* Làidir, neartar, neartmhor, treun, cumhachdach; calma, ruaimneach, foghainteach, bairgeanta, crodha, gramail; murrach; bunnsaidh, fallain, slainnteil; dian, deothasach; diongalta; daingeann; seirsealach. A strong man, *duine laidir (no) treun;* very strong by land and sea, *ro mhurrach air muir is air tìr.*

Strongfisted, *a.* Cruaidh-dhornach, rùdanach.

Strong-hand, *s.* Lamh làidir, éigin, fòirneart.

Strongly, *adv.* Gu làidir, gu neartmhor, gu treun, gu cumhachdach; gu h-éifeachdach; gu diongalta.

Strophe, *s.* Rann, ceithreamh, earann.

Strove, *pret.* of strive; which see.

Strow, *v. a.* Sgaoil, sgap; spréid; spult, crath. Strowed, *sgaoilte, sgapta.* If you think it little, throw luck upon it, *ma 's beag leat e, crath sonas air.*

Struck, *pret.* and *p. part.* of strike. Bhuail; buailte.

Structure, *s.* Togail; aitreabh, aros; dealbh.

Strude, Strode, *s.* Greigh chapull.

Struggle, *v.* Gleachd; dean spairn, dean strìgh; streap, dean iomairt. Struggle together, *dean comh-strìgh;* struggling with difficulties, *a gleachd (no) streapadh ri cruadal;* success will follow those who bravely struggle, *cha do chuir a bhun ris nach do chinnich leis.*

Struggle, *s.* Gleachd, gleic, spairn, strìgh, streapadh, tagluinn; cruaidh-oidhirp, connsach, iomairt, uspairn, utag.

Struggling, *s.* Gleachd, gleachdadh, spairn, strìgh, comhstrìgh, streapadh, uspairn, utag.

Strumous, *a.* Silteach.

Strumpet, *s.* Siùrsach, siùrtach, oinigh, striopach, strabaid, meirdreach, strumpaid, gairsleag, gastag, gliathrach.

Strut, *v. n.* Imich gu stràiceil (no) gu h-uallach; at; boch.

Strut, *s.* Lasdalachd, coiseachd uallach (no) stràiceil, ceum uallach (no) stàideil.

Stub, *s.* Bun, stump; stulc, stulcan, creamhachd, creamhachdan.

Stub, *v.* Spion as a bhun, thoir as an fhreumh.

Stubbed, *a.* Bunach, stumpach, stulcach, stulcanach, creamhachdach; goirrid, cutach.

Stubble, *s.* Fas-bhuain, asbhuain, asbhain, bunain, stailcneach, fasach.

Stubborn, *a.* Dùr, rag, ceann-laidir, rag-mhuinealach, reasgach, eas-umhal; rithinn, danarra, † cadranta.

Stubbornly, *adv.* Gu dùr, gu rag, gu ceann-laidir, gu reasgach, gu rag-mhuinealach, gu h-easumhal; gu rithinn.

Stubbornness, *s.* Dùiread, ceann-laidireachd, reasgachd, rag-mhuinealachd, eas-umhlachd; danarrachd.

Stubby, *a.* Bunach, bunanta, creamhachdanta; goirrid, cutach, stumpach. A stubby fellow, *bun balaich.*

Stubnail, *s.* Tacaid, tarrag; bun tarraig.

Stucco, *s.* Seòrsa plàst.

Stuck, *pret.* and *p. part.* of stick. Stic; shàth; sticte; sàthta.

Stuckle, *s.* Adag.

Stud, *s.* Tarrag, tarrang, tarruing, tacaid; reultag; dual; còp; putan muinichill; (*of horses*), greigh.

Student, *s.* Sgoilear, stuidear, foghlumaiche, oileanaiche.

Studied, *a.* Ionnsuichte, foghluimte.

Studier, *s.* Stuidear.

Studious, *a.* Dìchiollach, cùramach, deigheil air foghlum; smuainteachail; meòrach. Studiously, *gu dichiollach, gu curamach.*

Study, *s.* Smuaineachadh, smuainteachadh; cnuasachd, meòrachd, meorachadh; foghlum; eisgeach, seòmar foghluim.

Study, *v.* Smuainich, smuaintich, smaointich; cnuasaich, meòraich.

Stuff, *s.* Stuth; airneis; uigheam; eudach; seorsa clo; cungaidh; bagaisd.

Stuff, *v. a.* Lion, dinn, teannaich; lion gu sàth; sparr, giorr. Stuff up, *tachd, teannaich.* Stuffed, *lionta, dinnte, teannaichte.*

Stuffing, *s.* Lionadh, dinneadh, teannachadh; sparradh.

Stultiloquence, *s.* Glòireamas, ràite; faoin-chomhradh.

Stum, *s.* Fion ur; braileis.

Stum, *v. a.* Ùraich fion.

Stumble, *v. n.* Tuislich, sleamhnaich, sgrios, speidhil; rach am mearachd, dean mearachd.

Stumble, *s.* Tuisleadh, sleamhnachadh, sgriosadh, speidhle, mearachd, failinn.

Stumbler, *s.* Tuislear, sleamhnachair, fear nach cum a chosan.

Stumbling, *s.* Tuisleadh, tuisleachadh, sleamhnachadh, sgriosadh, spéidhlidh, clibeadh.

Stumbling-block, *s.* Ceap tuislidh.

Stumbling-stone, *s.* Clach tuislidh.

Stump, *s.* Bun; stulc; stump; ceapan.

Stumpy, *a.* Bunach, bunanta; stulcach, stumpach; cruaidh; rag.

Stun, *v. a.* Cuir an tuaineal, cuir am breislich, cuir am paisean.

Stung, *pret.* and *p. part.* of sting. Ghath.

Stunt, *v. a.* Cum o fhàs (no) o chinntinn.

Stupe, *s.* Foircinn.

Stupefaction, *s.* Cion-mothuchaidh; breilleas; tamhantachd.

Stupefactive, *a.* Breilleasach; tamhanta.

Stupendous, *a.* Mòr, anabarrach, iongantach, uamhasach, fuathasach.

Stupendousness, *s.* Uamhasachd, fuathasachd.

Stupid, *a.* Neo-mhothachail; neo-thoinisgeil, baoghalta; tamhanta; amaideach; trom. A stupid fellow, *bumlair, buimlear, baothair, gurraiceach, amhlair, amadair, amhas, amhasan, gleogair.*

Stupidity, *s.* Neo-mhothuchadh; cion-toinisg, baoghaltachd, amaideachd.

Stupidly, *adv.* Gu neo-thoinisgeil, gu baoghalta, gu h-amaideach.

Stupify, *v. a.* Cuir am breislich; cuir thar a chéill; cuir paisean air.

Stupor, *s.* Paisean, breislich, tamhantachd.

Stuprate, *v. a.* Éignich; truaill, truaillich.

Stupration, *s.* Eigneachadh, truailleadh, truailleachadh.

Sturdily, *adv.* Gu làidir, gu neartmhor, gu gramail, gu duineil, gu calma, gu brogail, gu rithinn, gu rag.

Sturdiness, *s.* Làidireachd, neart, gramalas, duinealas, brogalas, rithneachd; bunantas, bunantachd, talcantas.

Sturdy, *a.* Làidir, neartmhor, bunanta, balcanta, talcanta, talcarra, gramail, calma, foghainteach, duineil, bairgeanta, rithinn, rag, buan.

Sturgeon, *s.* Stirean.

Sturk, *s.* Gamhuinn; gamhnach; bliadhnach.

Stut, Stutter, *v. n.* Bi manntach (no) liodach, bi agach (no) glugach. He stutters, *tha e manntach (no) liodach.*

Stutter, *s.* Mannt, liod, ag, briot; mab, mabadh.

Stutterer, *s.* Manntair, fear manntach, fear liodach.

Sty, *s.* Fail, fail mhuc; crò; (*on the eyelid*), leamhracan, leamhragan

Sty, *v a* Cuir am fail, duin stigh mar mhuc.

Stygian, *a.* Ifrinneach; deamhnaidh, diabhluidh; dorch; doilleir.

Style, *s* Modh labhairt; doigh labhairt, modh sgriobhaidh; doigh sgriobhaidh; tiodal, ainm, urram dligheach; seòl, modh, doigh; peann iaruinn, pinne uaireadair gréine

Style, *v a.* Ainmich, goir.

Styling, *s.* Ainmeachadh.

Styptic, Stypticál, *a* Leigheasach; cosgach, math airson fuil chosgadh.

Styptic, *s* Leigheas a chuireas stad air fuil

Suasible, *a* So-caraladh, so-chomhairleachaidh, so-aomaidh

Suasory, *a.* Earailcach

Suavity, *s* Millse, millsead, taitneachd; caoimhne.

Sub, *in composition* Fo, fu, fuidh, fodh; rud eigin; lethchar

Subacid, *a* Leth-char goirt, leth-char geur, leth-chàr searbh, rud eigin goirt (no) geur, rud eigin searbh.

Subacrid, *a* Leth-char goirt (no) geur, leth-char searbh, rud eigin goirt

Subact, *v a* Ceannsuich; cuir fo.

Subaction, *s* Lughdachadh, pronnadh.

Subaltern, *s.* Iochdaran, iochdran

Subaltern, *a.* Iochdarach, iochdrach.

Subastringent, *a* Leth-char goirt no searbh.

Sub-beadle, *s* Fo-bheadal

Subcelestial, *a* Saoghalmhor, talmhaidh.

Subconstellation, *s* Co-shoillsean

Subcutaneous, *a.* Fu 'n chroiciono

Subdivide, *v a* Ath-roinn, ath-phairtich

Subdivision, *s* Ath-roinn, ath-phàirt

Subdolous, *a.* Cuilbheartach, eòlach, slighcach, cealgach, innleachdach

Subduce, Subduct, *v. a.* Thoir o, thoir air falbh, lughdaich, beagaich.

Subduction, *s* Toirt o, toirt air falbh, lughdachadh.

Subdue, *v. a.* Ceannsaich, ciùinich, sàruich, cuir fo, ciosnaich, bris. Subdued, *ceannsaichte, ciosnaichte.*

Subduer, *s* Ceannsachair, fear ceannsachaidh, fear sàruchaidh.

Subduing, *s* Sàruchadh, ceannsachadh, smachdachadh.

Subjacent, *a.* Fo, fodha

Subject, *v. a.* Cuir fo smachd, smachdaich, ceannsaich, sàruich, cuir fo cheannsal, tràillich, dean buailteach, dean freagarrach

Subject, *a.* Umhal; fo smachd, ceannsaichte, fo chis; buailteach Subject to us, *buailteach do chìs*

Subject, *s* Iochdaran, iochdran, (*text*), ceann teagaisg, stéigh, teagaisg

Subjected, *part.* Ceannsaichte; claoidhte, buailteach

Subjection, *s.* Ceannsachd, ceannsachadh, ceannsal, saruchadh, riaghlachadh, smachd, marasglachd In subjection, *fo cheannsal, fo mharasglachd, fo chìs.*

Subingression, *s* Inntrinn dhiomhair.

Subitaneous, *a* Grad, cabhagach, obann

Subjoin, *v. a.* Cuir ri; fath-sgriobh; fo-sgriobh

Subjugate, *v a.* Sàruich, claoidh, ceannsaich, ciosnaich, cuir fo Subjugated, *sàruichte, claoidhte, ceannsaichte, ciosnaichte.*

Subjugation, *s.* Sàruchadh, claoidheadh, ceannsuchadh, irioslachadh

Subjunction, *s.* Cur ri; leasachadh.

Subjunctive, *a.* Fàth-sgriobhta.

Sublapsarian, *a.* An deigh an leagaidh.

Sublation, *s* Goid, tabhairt air falbh os iosal, goidnich.

Sublevation, *s.* Togail, arduchadh, leasachadh.

Sublimate, *v a* Tog le spionn teine; àrdaich, leasaich.

Sublimation, *s.* Togail le spionn teine; àrdachadh.

Sublime, *a.* Ard; oirdheirc; mòr, mòralach; uaibhreach, greadhnach; mòr-chuiseach.

Sublime, *v. a* Tog le spionnadh teine, ardaich; leasaich.

Sublimely, *adv.* Gu h-ard; gu h-oirdheirc, gu mòr, gu mòralach

Sublimity, *s* Airde; oirdheirceas; mòralachd.

Sublingual, *a* Fo 'n teangadh

Sublunar, Sublunary, *a.* Talmhaidh, saoghalmhor.

Submarine, *a.* Fo 'n mhuir.

Submerge, *v a.* Cuir fo 'n uisge; bàth, bog, tum, tom.

Submersion, *s* Cuir fo 'n uisge, bàthadh, bogadh, tomadh.

Subminister, Subministrate, *v a.* Builich, thabhair; cum ri

Submiss, *a.* Ùmhal, iosal, iriosal.

Submission, *s.* Ùmhlachd, géill, striochd, striochdadh, fomas, aidmheil; meas, urram With submission, *le d' chead, le 'r cead.*

Submissive, *a* Umhal, iriosal, striochdail; freagarrach.

Submissively, *adv.* Gu h-umhal, gu h-iriosal, gu striochdail.

Submissiveness, *s.* Umhlachd, striochd, geilleachduinn.

Submissly, *adv.* Gu h-umhal, gu h-iosal, gu h-iriosal.

Submit, *v a* and *n.* Géill, striochd, thoir géill, dean striochd, lùb, feachd, irioslaich. Submit to him, *géill dha.*

Submitting, *s.* Géilleadh, striochdadh, lùbadh.

Subordinacy, *s.* Iochdranachd.

Subordinate, *a.* Iochdarach, fo', fu', fodh, fuidh.

Subordinate, *v. a.* Cuir ann an ordugh fo chéile

Subordination, *s* Iochdaranachd

Suborn, *v a* Solair os iosal, briob, ceannuich fianuis.

Subornation, *s* Feall-sholar, foill-cheannachadh, briobadh.

Suborner, *s.* Fear foill

Subpœna, *s.* Rabhadh, *suman.*

Subrector, *s.* Fo-reachdair, iar-reachdair, iar-riaghlair.

Subreption, *s.* Gabhdadh, goideachd, ceabhachdaireachd.

Subreptitious, *a.* Gabhdach, gabhdail, fallsa, breugach, bréige.

Subrision, *s* Fiamh-ghàire, fé ghaire, niamh ghaire, snodh ghaire

Subscribe, *v. a.* Cuir ainm ri, sgriobh; fàth-sgriobh; aontaich ri, aidich.

Subscriber, *s.* Fo-sgriobhair, fear a chuireas ainm ri, aontachair.

Subscribing, *s* Fo-sgriobhadh, aontachadh.

Subscription, *s* Fo-sgriobhadh, coghnadh, cuideachadh, aontachadh.

Subsecutive, *a.* Leantuinneach, leantuinn, a teachd; a teachd an lorg.

Subsequence, *s* Leantuinn, leanachd.

Subsequently, *adv.* An deigh laimh.

Subserve, *v a.* Fritheil; cuidich.

Subservience, Subserviency, *s* Frithealadh, cuideachadh, coghnadh, stà, uidhis

Subservient, *a.* Fritheilteach, frithealtach, cuideachail, coghnachail, co-ghnathach, uidhiseil, feumail.

Subsextuple, *a.* Seathamh cuid.

Subside, *v. n.* Traogh, traoigh, tuit sios; ciùinich, islich, illsich, tuit thun a ghrunnd, sioladh.

Subsidence, Subsidency, *s.* Traoghadh, sioladh, tuiteam sios.

Subsidiary, *a.* Cuideachail; co-ghnathach.

Subsidise, *v. a.* Cuidich, dean coghnadh le.

Subsidy, *s.* Cuideach, cuideachadh, coingheall, cobhair, cabhair, tarrail.

Subsign, *v. n.* Fo-sgriobh, sgriobh fo, 's.

Subsist, *v.* Buanaich, thig beo, thig suas

Subsistence, *s.* Bith; beath; buanachadh, tighinn beò, teachd beò, beathachadh, teachd an tìr, lòn, biadh, aran.

Subsistent, *a.* Beò

Substance, *s.* Bith; corp; (*pith*), brigh, briogh, stuth, tairbhe; tabhachd; (*riches*), maoin, toic, saibhreas, beartas; oighreachd; susbuinn, bunaite

Substantial, *a.* Fior, beò, corporra; laidir; gramail; socarach, tarbhach; toiceil, taileil, saibhir; brioghmhor; biadhchar, stuthail; susbuineach.

Substantiality, *s.* Corporrachd.

Substantially, *adv* Gu fior; gu laidir, gu gramail, gu tarbhach, gu toiceil, gu saibhir, gu susbuineach.

Substantialness, *s* Tarbhaichead; toic; gramalas; buanachd, taileileachd.

Substantiate, *v. a.* Firinnich.

Substantive, *s.* Ainm

Substitute, *v a* Cuir an aite ni (no) neach-eile

Substitute, *s.* Riochdair, fear ionaid

Substituted, *part.* Air chur air aite ni (no) neach

Substitution, *s.* Riochdachadh, cur an aite, cur an riochd.

Substruction, *s.* Fo-thogail.

Subsultive, *a.* Leumnach, clisgeach.

Subtend, *v. n.* Sìn mu chomhar; bi mu chomhar

Subtense, *s.* Cord; sreang.

Subter, *Latin, in composition, means* fo, fu, fodh, fuidh.

Subterfluent, *a.* Ruithe fo, ruithe an iochdar.

Subterfuge, *s.* Leithsgeul, car, cleas, cur seachad; sibht.

Subterraneal, Subterraneous, *a* Fo 'n talamh.

Subterrany, *a.* Fo 'n talamh.

Subtile, *a.* Tana; caol; seang; finealta, seimhidh; geur, carach, cealgach, cuilbheartach, geur-chuiseach, colach, seolta, innleachdach.

Subtilely, *adv.* Gu tana; gu caol, gu finealta; gu seang; gu geur, gu carach, gu h-innleachdach, gu seòlta

Subtileness, *s.* Taine, tainead, caoile, caoilead, finealtachd; géire, geurad, innleachd, cuilbheartachd.

Subtiliate, *v a.* Tanaich, dean tan, dean finealta, sreangaich.

Subtiliating, *s* Tanach, caolachadh, sreangachadh.

Subtilise, *v. a.* and *n.* Tanaich, dean tana, dean finealta; glan; labhair gu géur-chuiseach.

Subtilty, *s.* Taine, tanad, finealtachd; geur-chuis; geurchuiseachd; car, cuilbheart, cealgaireachd, innleachd.

Subtle, *a.* Carach, cuilbheartach, seòlta, eòlach, sligheach.

Subtly, *adv.* Gu carach, gu cuilbheartach, gu seòlta, gu h-eolach, gu sligheach.

Subtract, *v. a.* Thoir air falbh, thoir o; lughdaich: Subtracted, *air thabhairt o; lughdaichte.*

Subtraction, *s* Tabhairt o, tabhairt air falbh, lughdachadh.

Subtuple, *a.* Treasadh.

Suburb, *s.* Fo' bhaile, mach-bhaile, dlu-bhàile, frith-bhaile, iomall baile (no) cathrach. Suburbs, *fo-bhailtean, iomall-bhailtean, mach-bhailtean, dlù-bhailtean.*

Subventaneous, *a* Gluig; gaothar.

Subvention, *s* Cuideachadh, coghnath.

Subverse, *v. a.* Tilg sios, tilg bun os cionn, sgrios, mill

Subversion, *s.* Tilg sios, cur bun os cionn, milleadh

Subversive, *a.* A tilg sios, a milleadh, a cur bun os cionn, a cur air aimhreidh

Subvert, *v. a* Tilg sios, cuir bun os cionn, sgrios, mill, truaill

Subverter, *s.* Sgriosadair, milltear.

Subworker, *s.* Fear oibre, fear oibre iochdrach.

Succedaneous, *a* An àite ni eile.

Succedaneum, *s.* Ni 'theid chur an àite rud eile

Succeed, *v. a.* and *n* Lean, thig an deigh, thig an lorg, thig an àite; foir-chéimnich; soirbhich, thig speid Who succeeded him? *co thàinig na àite?* he succeeded well, *chaidh leis, shoirbhich e, dh' éirich leis*, he did not succeed well, *cha do shoirbhich leis, cha d' éirich leis*

Succeeder, *s.* Fear a leanas, fear a thig an àite fir eile.

Success, *s.* Soirbheas, soirbheachadh, adh, agh; buaidh; rath, fortan. Success to you! *soirbheas leat! buaidh leat!*

Successful, *a.* Soirbheasach, adhmhor, buadhach, sealbhar, fortanach

Successfully, *adv.* Gu soirbheasach, gu h-aghmhor, gu fortanach, gu sealbhar.

Successfulness, *s* Soirbheas, soirbheasachd, agh, aghmhorachd, fortan, sealbharachd

Succession, *s* Leanachd, leantuinn, comharbas; foraimh; foi-cheumnachadh.

Successive, *a* Leantuinneach; a leanas; an ordugh, an riaghailt.

Successively, *adv* Ann an ordugh, an deigh chéile, fear an deigh chéile

Successless, *a.* Mi-fhortanach, mi-aghmhor, mi-shealbhar, neo-rathail.

Successor, *s* Comharba, fear a leanas, fear a thig an àite fir eile.

Succinct, *a.* Cuimir, cearmanta; truiste; deas, criosta, criosruichte, gearr, aith-ghearr, cutach.

Succinctly, *adv.* Gu cuimir, gu cearmanta; gu truiste; gu deas, gu criosta, gu gearr, gu h-aithghearr, gu cutach

Succinctness, *s.* Cuimireachd, cearmantachd, ath-ghearrad, cutaichead.

Succory, *s* Lus an t-siucair; castearbhan, castearbhan nam muc.

Succour, *v. a.* Coghain, dean coghnath, cuidich, cobhair, furtaich, dean cobhair, thoir furtachd; thoir co-fhurtachd, thoir sòlas. Succour him, *dean coghnath leis, cuidich e, cuidich leis, dean cobhair air.* Succoured, *coghainte, cuidichte, furtaichte.*

Succour, *s* Coghnath, coghnadh, cuideachadh, cobhair, furtachd.

Succoured, *part* See Succour.

Succourer, *s.* Fear coghnaith.

Succourless, *a.* Gun chò-ghnath; dìblidh.

Succulence, *s.* Brigh, briogh, brioghmhorachd, brioghar-achd, sùgharachd, sùghmhorachd, bogarachd

Succulent, *a* Brioghar, brioghmhor, sughar, sughmhor, bogar, sultmhor.

Succumb, *v. n* Géill, striochd, lùb, feachd, aontaich, dean géille (no) striochd He succumbed, *ghéill e.*

Succussation, *s.* Trot, trotail, bogadanaich.

Succussion, *s.* Crathadh, bogadanaich.

SUCH, *a. pron.* A leithid; a shamhuil; mar. Such a lie! *leithid sin bhreug!* such things, *leithid sin do nithe;* I am such as I ought to be, *tha mi mar bu chòrr dhomh 'bhith.*

SUCK, *v. a.* Sùig, sùigh, deoghail; srùb.

SUCK, *s.* Sùgadh, sùghadh, deoghal, deoghladh, srùbadh, bainne cìche.

SUCKER, *s.* Sùgair, sùghair, sùchan, deoghlan, deoghladair; (*a twig*), fàillean, fiùran, maothan, bunsag, bailleag.

SUCKET, *s.* Millsean.

SUCKING-BOTTLE, *s.* Mulan beòil, cnag beòil, ni sam bi a chuirear am beul leinibh, chum a dheoghladh ann aite na cìche.

SUCKLE, *v. a.* Àraich, banaltraich, tog, thoir cioch.

SUCKLING, *s.* Ciochran, naoidhean.

SUCKSPIGOT, *s.* Meisgear, poitear, ruitear.

SUCTION, *s.* Sùgadh, sùghadh; sùigheadh, deoghal, deoghladh.

SUD, SUDS, *s.* Tutag, tudagan.

SUDATION, *s.* Follas, fallus.

SUDATORY, *s.* Bat falluis; tigh teth.

SUDDEN, *a.* Grad, obann, cas, ealamh, cabhagach; disgir. On a sudden, *gu grad, gu h-obann, gun fhios, a dh' aon bheum.*

SUDDENLY, *adv.* Gu grad, gu h-obann, gu cas, gu h-ealamh, a dh' aon bheum.

SUDDENNESS, *s.* Obainne, obainnead; graide, graidead.

SUDORIFIC, *a.* Fallusach.

SUDS, *s.* Cobhar siabuinn, tud, tudan.

SUE, *v. a.* and *n.* (*At law*), cuir h-uige, lean, tagair, agair; (*seek*), guidh, asluich, aslaich, sir, iarr. He sued him, *chuir e h-uige e;* they sued for peace, *ghuidh iad sìth;* sue for a place, *iar maoidhean airr son àite.*

SUET, *s.* Geire, ìgh, blonag, reamhrachd.

SUETY, *a.* Reamhar, blonagach.

SUFFER, *v. a.* Fuluing, fuiling, fulaing, fuilig, giùlain, iomchair; leig le; luathsaich; thoir cead, ceadaich. Suffer punishment, *failing peanas;* suffer me, *leig dhomh, leig leam, ceadaich dhomh.*

SUFFERABLE, *a.* So-fhulang, so-fhulangadh, so-ghiùlan, so-iomchar.

SUFFERABLY, *adv.* Gu so-fhulang, gu so-ghiùlan, gu so-iomchar.

SUFFERANCE, *s.* (*Of pain*), fulang, fulangas; (*toleration*), foighidinn, faighidinn, giùlan; (*liberty*), cead, comas. Long-sufferance, *fad-fhulangas.*

SUFFERER, *s.* Fulangair, fulangaiche.

SUFFERING, *s.* Fulangas, foighidinn, pian, cradh, earchall.

SUFFICE, *v. n.* and *a.* Fògham; sàsuich. That suffices me, *is leòir sin domh, fòghnaidh sin domh.*

SUFFICIENCY, *s.* Pailteas; foghainteas; foghnadh, daothain; leòir, na 's leòir; sàsuchadh; foghainteachd; éifeachd. I got a sufficiency, *fhuair mi mo dhaothain, fhuair mi na 's leòir;* self-sufficiency, *fein-fhoghainteach.*

SUFFICIENT, *a.* Leòir, na 's leoir; iomchuidh, goireasach, freagarrach; cubhaidh; murrach, comasach. It is sufficient, *is leòir e;* I got what is sufficient for me, *fhuair mi na 's leòir, fhuair mi mo dhaothain;* self-sufficient, *féin-fhoghainteach.*

SUFFICIENTLY, *adv.* Gu leòir, na leòir, na 's leòir, ni 's leòir.

SUFFOCATE, *v. a.* Tachd, mùch. He suffocated him, *mhùch* (*no*) *thachd iad e.*

SUFFOCATED, *part.* Mùchta, tachdta, air tachdadh.

SUFFOCATION, *s.* Tachdadh, tachd, mùch, mùchadh.

SUFFOCATIVE, *a.* Tachdach, mùchach.

SUFFRAGAN, *s.* Easbuig.

SUFFRAGATE, *v. a.* Aontaich le; tagh le.

SUFFRAGE, *s.* Tagh ghuth; foc; fogha; aontachadh.

SUFFUMIGATION, *s.* Smùideachadh, toiteachadh.

SUFFUSE, *v. a.* Sliob, spréid, comhdaich. Suffused with a blush, *comhdaichte le ruthadh gruaidh.*

SUFFUSION, *s.* Sliobadh, spréideadh, comhdachadh, sgaoileadh.

SUG, *s.* Seorsa cuileig.

SUGAR, *s.* Sucar, siucar, millsean.

SUGAR, *v. a.* Millsich, siucaraich, dean milis. Sweetened, *millsichte.*

SUGARY, *a.* Siucarach, milis.

SUGGEST, *v. a.* Thoir sanus; cuir an ceann, cuir an cuimhne, cuir an aire; cogair, cagair. I suggested to him, *chuir mi na cheann.*

SUGGESTER, *s.* Sanusair.

SUGGESTION, *s.* Sanus, rabhadh, cogar, brodadh, diomhair.

SUGGILLATE, *v.* Buail neach gus am bi e dubh ghorm.

SUICIDE, *s.* Féin-mhortadh, féin-mhort, féin-mhurtadh, féin-mhortair; féin-mhurt.

SUILLAGE, *s.* Guitear, clais.

SUIT, *s.* (*Request*), iarrtas, iarruidh; sireadh; (*at law*), cùis, cùis lagha, cuis tagairt, cuis tagraidh; (*of clothes*), culaidh, deise, trusgan; (*for a wife*), suireadh, suir-thagh; (*series*), ordugh, riaghailt, sread. A suit of cards, *pachd chairtean.*

SUIT, *v. a.* and *n.* Freagarraich, freagair; uigheamaich; deasaich; éid; còird. This will not suit, *cha fhreagair so.*

SUITABLE, *a.* Freagarrach, iomchuidh; eugasach, lathailteach; toilltinneach; airidh.

SUITABLENESS, *s.* Freagarrachd, iomchuidhead; eugasachd, lathailteachd.

SUITABLY, *adv.* Gu freagarrach, gu h-iomchuidh, gu h-eugasach, gu lathailteach, gu toilltinneach, gu h-airidh.

SUITOR, *s.* Suiriche; graidhean, leannan; iarrtair. Suitors, *suirichean.*

SUITRESS, *s.* Ban-athchuingiche.

SULCATED, *a.* Claiste, claisichte.

SULKINESS, *s.* Gruaime, gruaimean; moit, moitealachd, dod, sdod, mùige, dùiread, reasgachd.

SULKY, *a.* Grùamach, dodach, busach, sdodach, moiteil, iargalta, muigeach, doirbh, coimheach, nuadarra, dùr, reasgach. A sulky female, *gnòigeag, moiteag.*

SULL, *s.* Crann.

SULLEN, *a.* Doirbh, doireanta, dodach, sdodach, gruamach, mùigeil, coimheach, neo-aoidheil, doichiollach; gnò; dùr, reasgach, ceann laidir; trom; tuirseach.

SULLENLY, *adv.* Gu doirbh, gu doireanta, gu dodach, gu sdodach, gu gruamach, gu mùigeil, gu neo-aoidheil, gu gnò, gu dùr, gu reasgach, gu ceannlaidir; gu trom; gu tuirseach.

SULLENNESS, *s.* Doirbhe, doirbheas, doireantachd, gruamaichead; mùigealachd, dùiread, reasgachd.

SULLENS, *s.* Dod, sdod, doirbhe, sdùrd.

SULLIED, *a.* and *part.* Salach, dubh; salaichte, dubhta, truaillte; millte.

SULLY, *v. a.* Salaich, dubh, truaill; spot, cuir smal air, mill. He sullied his character, *mhill e 'chliù.*

SULLY, *s.* Sal, dubh, smùr, gaoid.

SULPHUR, *s.* Pronnusg, proinistear, gronnustal.

SULPHUREOUS, SULPHUROUS, *a.* Pronnusgach, riubh.

SULPHURY, *a.* Pronnusgach.

SULTAN, *s.* An Turcach, an t-Iompair Turcach.

SULTANA, *s.* A Bhan-Turcach, Ban-Iompair nan Turcach.

Sultanry, *s.* Turcaidh; talamh an Turcaich.

Sultriness, *s.* Teas, blàthas, blàs, bruthainneachd.

Sultry, *a.* Teth, blàth, bruich, bruthainneach. A sultry day, *làth bruich.*

Sum, *s.* Àireamh, suim, uimhir; an t-iomlan. A sum of money, *suim airgiod;* the sum total, *an t-iomlan.*

Sum, *v. a.* Àireamh, suim, cunnt, cuir ri chéile, sumhlaich. To sum up all, *ann am bheag bhriathraibh.*

Sumless, *a.* Do-àireamh, do-chunntadh, nach gabh àireamh, nach fhaodar àireamh, nach gabh cunnt, nach fhaodar chunnt.

Summarily, *adv.* Gu h-aithghearr, gu gearr, gu goirid.

Summary, *a.* Aith-ghearr, gearr, goirrid.

Summary, *s.* Gearr-fhoirm, ath-chumair, giorrachadh, sùmhlachadh, sùmhlach, beagachadh.

Summed, *part.* Air chunntadh suas, àireamhte.

Summer, *s.* Samhradh, samh, aimsir (no) am an t-samhraidh; *(in architecture)*, sail ùrlair. The beginning of summer, *toiseach an t-samhraidh;* middle of summer, *meadhon (no) teis meadhon an t-samhraidh;* a fine summer's day, *la Geal samhraidh.*

Summer, *v. n.* and *a.* Samhraich, caith an samhradh, cuir seach an samhradh; blàthaich, cum blàth.

Summer-house, *s.* Tigh-samhraidh.

Summersault, *s.* Leum thar cheann is chosaibh, car a phocain olla.

Summit, *s.* Mullach, binnean, fior mhullach, bàrr. The summit of a mountain, *mullach monaidh.*

Summon, *v. a.* Gairm, òrduich; gairm chum làthaireachd; suman, tionail, cruinnich, tog suas.

Summoned, *part.* Gairmte, orduichte; tionailte, cruinnichte.

Summoner, *s.* Gairmear, fear gairm, fear rabhaidh, barnaigear.

Summoning, *s.* Gairmeadh; tionaladh, cruinneachadh.

Summons, *s.* Gairm, ordugh, rabhadh; iarrtas. A summons of removal, *bairlinn, bardainn, barnaigeadh.*

Sumpter, *s.* Each trusairnis.

Sumptuary, *a.* A riaghladh cosdais.

Sumptuous, *a.* Cosdail; sòghail; riomhach, greadhnach; stroghail, struidheil, struidheasach. A sumptuous banquet, *cuirm riomhach.*

Sumptuously, *adv.* Gu cosdail; gu soghail, gu riomhach, gu greadhnach; gu stroghail, gu struidheil.

Sumptuousness, *s.* Cosd, cosdaileachd, sogh, soghaileachd; riomhachas, greadhnachas, strogh, struidhe, stroghalachd, struidhealachd.

Sun, *s.* Grian; †gre, †gri, †grioth, †titan. The heat of the sun, *teas na gréine;* bask in the sun, *grianaich; aonagaich sa ghrian;* the light of the sun, *solus na gréine;* the beams of the sun, *dealradh (no) dearrsadh na gréine; gath gréine;* an eclipse of the sun, *dubhradh gréine;* under the sun, *fo 'n ghréine, anns an t-saoghal, air fad an t-saoghail.*

Sun, *v. a.* Cuir sa ghrian, cuir an teas na gréine, grianaich, caoinich.

Sunbeam, *s.* Gath gréine, dearrsadh gréine, gath soluis.

Sunbright, *a.* Dealrach, dearrsach.

Sun-burning, *s.* Losgadh na gréine, dubhadh na gréine.

Sunburnt, *a.* Loisgte (no) odhar leis a ghrian.

Sunclad, *a.* Dealrach, glòirmhor.

Sunday, *s.* Di dòmhnuich, là na sàbaid, an t-sàbaid, là 'n Tighearna, a cheud là do 'n seachduin. Sunday-letter, *an litir dòmhnach.*

Sunder, *v. a.* Dealaich, sgar, cuir eadar, cuir as a chéile.

Sunder, *s.* Dà chuid, dà phàirt.

Sundew, *s.* Ròs an t-soluis.

Sundew, (round-leaved), *s.* Gealdruidh.

Sun-dial, *s.* Uaireadair greine.

Sundry, *a.* Iomadh; iomad, iomadaidh, mòran; eagsamhuil.

Sundries, *s. pl.* Ioma nithe.

Sun-flower, *s.* Plùr na gréine.

Sung, *pret.* and *p. part.* of sing. Sheinn; seinnte.

Sunk, *part.* of sink. Air dol fodh.

Sunless, *a.* Gun ghrian, gun bhlàthas.

Sunlike, *a.* Dealrach, dearrsach.

Sunny, *a.* Grianach; dealrach, ialach, dearrsach.

Sunrise, **Sunrising**, *s.* Éiridh na gréine.

Sunset, *s.* Luidhe na gréine, dol fo na gréine.

Sunshine, *s.* Solus, na gréine, dealradh na gréine.

Sunshine, **Sunshiny**, *a.* Grianach; dealrach, dearrsach. A fine sunshine day, *là geal grianach.*

Sup, *v. a.* and *n.* Òl; gabh suipeir. Sup it up, *òl as a;* have you supped, *an d' fhuair thu do shuipeir.*

Sup, *s.* Balagam, balgam, bolgam; lan beòil, diot, diòtag; deur, deuran.

Superable, *a.* So-shàruchaidh, so-cheannsachaidh.

Superabound, *v. n.* Bi lionmhor, bi anabarra pailt, cuir thairis.

Superabundance, *s.* Tuille is a chòir; anabarr pailteis, mòr-phailteas, làn-phailteas.

Superabundant, *a.* Anabarra, pailt, anabarrach, lionmhor; cur thairis.

Superabundantly, *adv.* Gu h-anabarra; gu h-anabarrach, thuille na còrach.

Superadd, *v. a.* Cuir ri; superadded, air a chur ri.

Superaddition, *s.* Cur ri.

Superadvenient, *a.* Teachd air; teachd gun fhios.

Superannuate, *v. a.* Dean eu-comasach trid aois.

Superannuated, *a.* Sean, aosmhor.

Superannuation, *s.* Aois, aosmhorachd.

Superb, *a.* Riomhach, greadhnach; mòrchuiseach; oirdheirc, mòralach, flathail.

Superbly, *adv.* Gu riomhach, gu greadhnach, gu mòrchuiseach; gu h-òirdheirc.

Supercargo, *s.* Cléireach luing.

Supercelestial, *a.* Neamhuidh.

Supercilious, *a.* Ardanach, uallach, ard, uaibhreach, smachdail, dio-measail.

Superciliously, *adv.* Gu h-ardanach, gu uallach, gu h-uaibhreach, gu smachdail, gu dio-measail.

Superciliousness, *s.* Ardan, ardanachd, uaibhreachas, uallachd, uaille.

Superconception, *s.* Ath-bhronn-ghabhail.

Supercrescence, *s.* Ath-fhàs, ath-chinneas.

Supereminence, *s.* Barrachd, barr-mhaise.

Supereminent, *a.* Barrachdach, neo-choimeasta, oirdheirc, barr-mhaiseach.

Supererogation, *s.* Bàrr-obair, barr-ghniomh, obair a 's anabarra; obair bhàrrachd; barrachd.

Superexaltation, *s.* Ardachadh.

Superexcellence, *s.* Barrachd; neo-choimeas, fior-mhaise, barr-mhaise.

Superexcellent, *a.* Barrach; neo-choimeasta; anabharra grinn; fior mhaiseach, barr-mhaiseach.

Superfetation, *s.* Ath-bhronn-ghabhail; ath-thorraichead.

Superfice, *s.* Uachdar, foir-iomall; aghaidh.

Superficial, *a.* Uachdarach; foir iomallach; suarrach,

caoin-shuarrach, gun fhiù; faoin; neo-dhiongalta, neo-ghramail; neo-ionnsuichte; neo-dhomhain

Superficially, *adv.* Gu suarrach, gu caoin-shuarrach, gu faoin; gu neo-dhiongalta, gu h-aineolach, gu neo-ionnsuichte, gu neo-dhomhain

Superficialness, *s* Suarraichead; eu-doimhneachd, aineolas, faoin-chiosdas

Superficies, *s* An taobh a muigh, an taobh a mach, uachdar; aghaidh, aodann, gnùis.

Superfine, *a.* Ro-fhinealta, ro-ghrinn; barr-mhaiseach.

Superfluitance, *s* Snamhadh.

Superfluitant, *a* Snamhach, air druim an uisge

Superfluity, *s.* Anabarra, anabharr, tuille is a chòir; sogh

Superfluous, *a.* Anabarrach; neo-fheumail, thuille na còrach, gun stà, gun fheum.

Superfluously, *adv.* Gu h-anabarrach; gu neo-fheumail.

Superfluousness, *s.* Anabarrachd, neo-fheumaileachd.

Superflux, *s* Anabharr

Superhuman, *a* Os cionn nàduir.

Superimpregnation, *s* Ath-bhronn-ghabhail.

Superincumbent, *a.* Air muin, luidhe air muin, an uachdar

Superintend, *v a* Riaghail, amhairc (no) seall thairis, seòl, orduich

Superintendence, *s.* Riaghladh, riaghailt; cùram, feadhmantas, griobhachd.

Superintendent, *s.* Riaghladair; riaghlair; griobh, ceann

Superior, *a.* A's airde, is airde, a's inbhiche, is fearr, os cionn, toirt barrachd

Superior, *s* Uachdaran; uachdran, riaghlair, riaghladair

Superiority, *s* Uachdaranachd, uachdranachd, ceannas, barrachd; lamh an uachdar

Superlative, *a.* Sàr, còrr, barr-mhaiseach; is fearr, is airde.

Superlatively, *adv* Gu còrr, gu barrachdail, gu h-anabarrach

Superlativeness, *s* Barrachdas, anabarrachd

Superlunar, *a.* Os cionn na gealaich.

Supernal, *a* Neamhuidh, naomh, flaitheasach.

Supernatant, *a.* Snàmhach, a snàmh, plodanach.

Supernatation, *s* Snàmh, snàmhadh

Supernatural, *a.* Os cionn nàduir, mìorbhuileach

Supernaturally, *adv* Os cionn nàduir, gu mìorbhuileach

Supernumerary, *a* Còrr, thuille na còrach

Supernumerary, *s.* Fear còrr

Superplant, *s.* Luibh gun mhathair gun athair, plannt a chinneas air plannt eile cosmhal ris an uile ice

Superreflection, *s.* Ath-fhaileas

Superscribe, *v. a* Sgriobh air an taobh muigh

Superscription, *s* Sgriobhadh air an taobh muigh, tiodal.

Supersede, *v n* Cuir gu taobh, cuir air chùl

Superserviceable, *a.* Tuille is easguidh.

Superstition, *s* Saobh-chrabhadh; giseag.

Superstitious, *a.* Saobh-chrabhach, giseagach, gisreagach

Superstruct, *v* Tog, tog suas

Superstruction, **Superstructure**, *s* Togail, aitreabh

Supervacaneous, *a* Neo-fheumail, faoin

Supervacaneously, *ad* Gu neo-fheumail, gu faoin

Supervenient, *a.* Air chur ri; a thuillead

Supervise, *v. a.* Rannsuich; riaghail; seall thairis; seòl; dean griobhachd.

Supervisor, *s* Fear coimhid; griobh; riaghlair, rannsuchair.

Supervising, *s.* Riaghladh, seòladh, griobhachd.

Supervive, *v. n.* Mair (no) fan beò ni 's fhaide.

Supination, *s.* Luidhe air an druim.

Supine, *a.* Air an druim; neo-chùramach, leasg, lunndach, mairnealach, maidheanach, coidheis, comadh, dà chomadh.

Supinely, *adv* Air an druim, beul suas, gu leasg, gu neo-chùramach, gu mairnealach, gu maidheanach, gu coidheis.

Supineness, *s* Leisge, neo-chùram, lunndachd; mairnealachd, maidheanachd.

Suppedaneous, *a.* Fo na cosaibh.

Supper, *s.* Suipeir. Supper-time, *tràth suipearach.*

Supper, *v a.* Suipeirich.

Supperless, *a* Gun suipeir; neo-shuipeirichte.

Supplant, *v a* Cuir a aite; cuir air falbh, cuir gu taobh, cuir as an rod, tilg sios le camacag.

Supple, *a* Sùbailt, lùbach, so-lùbaidh, maoth, maothanach, (*crafty*), carach, miodalach, goileamach, beulchar.

Supple, *v. a* and *n* Sùblaich, dean sùbailt, dean maoth; fàs sùbailt

Supplement, *s* Leasachadh, tuillead, cur ri; fo-sgrobhadh.

Supplemental, **Supplementary**, *a.* Ath-leasachail; a thuillead.

Suppleness, *s.* Sùblachd, sùbailteachd

Suppletory, *a.* A ni suas, a deanamh suas.

Suppliant, *a* Asluchail, guidheach, griosach, athchuingeach.

Suppliant, **Supplicant**, *s* Asluchair, griosair, athchuingiche

Supplicate, *v a.* Asluich, guidh, grios, athchuingich, sir gu dùrachdach

Supplication, *s* Asluchadh, guidhe, griosadh, ùrnuigh, ùrnigh, athchuinge.

Supplicatory, *a* Asluchail, guidheach, griosail.

Supply, *v a* Dean suas; thabhair, builich; cum ri, frithealll, riaraich, furtaich Supply his loss, *dean suas a challdach*, supply him with money, *cum airgiod ris*

Supply, *s* Còghnadh, còghnath, cobhair, cabhair, furtachd, deanamh suas

Support, *v a* Cum suas, prop, cum taic ri, dean cùl-taic, cum taobh ri, còghain, dean còghnadh le, cuidich, dean cobhair, beathaich, cum biadh ri, dion

Support, *s* Taic, cùl-taic, prop, sorchan, trostan, (*help*), coghnadh, cobhair, cuidеachadh

Supportable, *a* So-ghiùlan, so-iomchar, so-fhulang.

Supporter, *s.* Fior dion, fear cumail suas, dionadair; prop, taic, cul-taic.

Supposable, *a.* So-shaoilsinn, a ghabhas (no) a dh' fhaodas saoilsinn, so-bharalachadh

Supposal, *s.* Saoilsinn, barail, beachd, creidsinn

Suppose, *v a.* Saoil, smuainich, smaoinich, smuaintich, baralaich, beachdaich, abair As you suppose, *mar tha thu 'saoilsinn*, sooner than you suppose, *ni 's luaithe na shaoileas tu;* suppose the case to be so, *abair gur ann mar sin tha chùis.*

Supposer, *s* Fear a shaoileas

Supposition, *s* Saoilsinn, barail, smuain, smaoin, smuainte, beachd

Supposititious, *a* Fallsa, fallsail; breugach; neo-fhior

Supposititiousness, *s.* Fallsachd, fallsaileachd.

Suppress, *v a* Ceannsaich, lùb, cum fodh, sàruich,

claoidh; (*as a report*), folaich, céil, mùch, cum samhach; (*the voice*), cum stigh.

Suppressed, *part.* Ceannsaichte, lùbta, saruichte, claoidhte; (*as a report*), folaichte, falaichte, céilte, mùchta.

Suppression, *s.* Ceannsachadh, cumail fodh, lubadh, saruchadh; (*of a report*), folachadh, céileadh, muchadh.

Suppressor, *s.* Ceannsachair, saruchair, céileadair, mùchadair.

Suppurate, *v. a.* Iongraich, iongaraich, leannaich.

Suppuration, *s.* Iongrachadh, leannachadh.

Suppurative, *a.* Iongarach, iongrachail, leannachail.

Supputation, *s.* Àireamh, cunntadh; cunntas.

Suppute, *v. a.* Àireamh, cunnt.

Supra, (*Latin*), *in composition*, os cionn; roimh.

Supralapsary, *a.* Roimh an leagaidh.

Supravulgar, *a.* Os cionn a chumanta.

Supremacy, *s.* Uachdranachd, ard-uachdranachd, ceannasachd.

Supreme, *a.* Ard, is airde; priomh; ceann uachdranach.

Supreme, *s.* Dia, an Ti 's àirde.

Supremely, *adv.* Gu ro ard, gu ro mhòr.

Suraddition, *s.* Sloinne.

Sural, *a.* Calpach; luirgneach.

Surance, *s.* Barrantas; urras; cinntealas.

Surbate, *v. a.* Bruth na cosan le coiseachd.

Surcease, *v. n.* Sguir, stad. Surceased, *air sgur, air sgurachd, air stad, air stadachd.*

Surcease, *s.* Sgur, sgurachd, sgurachdainn; stad, stadachd, fois, fosadh.

Surcharge, *v. a.* Luchdaich, an-luchdaich, an-tromaich.

Surcharge, *s.* An-luchd, an-eallach, an-truime.

Surcharger, *s.* An-luchdair.

Surcingle, *s.* Tarrach, giort, bronnach, crios, uachdair.

Surcle, *s.* Fàillean, fiùran, maothan.

Surcoat, *s.* Còt uachdair, earrasaid, fearrasaid.

Surd, *a.* Bodhar.

Surdily, *adv.* Gu bodhar.

Surdity, *s.* Buidhre.

Sure, *a.* (*Certain*), cinnteach, fior, fiosrach; lan-chinnteach; daingeann, deangalta; tearuinte; (*faithful, firm*), dìleas, fior. I am sure of it, *tha mi cinnteach as;* to be sure, *air a chinnte;* as sure as death, *cho chinnteach ris a bhàs;* be sure that you do it, *bi cinnteach gun dean thu e; faic* (*no*) *feuch gun dean thu e;* as sure as you are alive, *cho chinnteach is a tha thu beo, cho fior is a tha thu beò;* sure bind, sure find, *fàg tearuinnte, is faigh tearuinnte;* are you sure, *bheil thu cinnteach.*

Sure, *adv.* Air chinnte, gun teagamh.

Surefooted, *a.* Grama-chosach, treasdach.

Surely, *adv.* Gu cinnteach, air chinnte, gu dearbh, gun teagamh; gu diongalta; gu fior.

Sureness, *s.* (*Certainty*), cinntealas; (*faithfulness*), firinn; fireanntachd; (*safety*), tearuinnteachd; (*firmness*), gramalas; (*stability*), buanachd, maireannachd.

Suretiship, *s.* Urrasachd.

Surety, *s.* (*Against loss*), urras, urradh; (*safety*), tearuinnteachd, nasgar; (*evidence*), fianuis, teisteannas; (*ratification*), daighneachadh. Go surety, *rach an urras.*

Surface, *s.* Uachdar, aghaidh, aodann; druim; taobh a muigh.

Surfeit, *v. a.* and *n.* Sàsuich, lion gu sàth; ith gu sàth. Surfeited, *sàsuichte, sàthach, làn.*

Surfeit, *s.* Sàsuchadh; sàth; tarbhas, teann-shàth, seat, gràin, gais. Surfeit from drunkenness, *buch-thinneas.*

Surfeiter, *s.* Sàsuchair, geòcair.

Surfeiting, *s.* Sàsuchadh; sàth.

Surge, *s.* Sumain, tonn, boch-thonn.

Surge, *v. n.* At; éirich mar ni tonn, boch, bolg.

Surgeon, *s.* Dearg-leigh, lamh-leigh; lighiche, taith-leigh, ollamh, olladh.

Surgery, *s.* Lighicheachd, lamh-leigheachd.

Surgical, *a.* Ligheach, lamh-leigheasach, lamh-leigheach, dearg-leigheasach, dearg-leigheach.

Surgy, *a.* Sumaineach, sumaideach, tonnach, marannach, atmhor.

Surlily, *adv.* Gu doirbh, gu sdùrdail, gu gruamach, gu h-iargaltach, gu doimh, gu dorrach.

Surliness, *s.* Doirbhe, sdùrdalachd, gruamachd, gruamaiche.

Surly, *a.* Doirbh, dolma, dolum, sdùrdail, gruamach, iargalta, dorrach, dortha, nuarranta, nuadharra, mi-mhodhail; neo-shiobhailt, bréineach, duairc, duairceach, gnò. A surly obstinate fellow, *dùran, dur-bhalaoch, sdùrdan.*

Surmise, *v. a.* Cuir omhail, cuir amharus; saoil, baralaich, bi am beachd, bi am barail. As I surmise, *a réir mo bheachd, a réir mo bharail.*

Surmise, *s.* Beachd; barail, dòchas, saoilsinn, fios, neo-chinnteach; an-amharus; sànas, fabhunn, fabhur, forgradh, fargradh.

Surmount, *v. a.* Rach os cionn, rach thairis, faigh, farrachd; fairtlich, buadhaich, faigh lamh an uachdar, ceannsaich.

Surmountable, *a.* So-cheannsachaidh; a ghabhas fairtleach air.

Surmounter, *s.* Ceannsachair; fear a dh' fhairtlicheas.

Surmounting, *s.* Dol os cionn, dol thairis; fairtleachadh, buadhachadh faotainn barrachd, (no) lamh an uachdar.

Surname, *s.* Sloinne, sloinneadh; cinneadh; ainm cinnidh. What is your surname? *ciod is sloinne dhuit?*

Surname, *v. a.* Sloinn. They surnamed him, *shloinn iad e;* a man surnamed Grant, *fear do 'n sloinne Granntach.*

Surpass, *v. a.* Thoir bàrr, thoir barrachd, fairtlich, buaidhich; bi os cionn. It surpasses my comprehension, *tha e os cionn mo bheachd;* I have surpassed them all, *thug mi barrachd orra uile.*

Surpassing, *a.* Oirdheirc; barrachdail, barraichte, a toirt barrachd; barr-mhaiseach, anabarrach.

Surpassingly, *adv.* Gu h-òirdheirc, gu barrachdail, gu h-anabarrach.

Surplice, *s.* Léine aifrionn.

Surplus, **Surplusage**, *s.* Còrr, corrlach, fuigheall, fuighleach; iarmad.

Surprisal, *s.* See **Surprise**.

Surprise, *s.* Ioghnadh, iongantas; fuathas; neònachas; clisge, eagal, uamhas; amhluadh. By surprise, *gun fhios, gun aire, gun aithne.*

Surprise, *v. a.* Gabh gun fhios, thig gun fhios, cuir coghnadh (no) iongantas air; cuir gu h-amhluadh. You surprised me, *thainig thu orm gun fhios domh;* you surprise me, *tha thu 'cur iongantais orm;* I was surprised, *ghabh mi iongantas, ghabh mi neònachas;* surprised, *fo ioghnadh; fo amhluadh.*

Surprising, *a.* Iongantach, neònach, miorbhuileach, grad, obann.

Surprisingly, *adv.* Gu h-iongantach, gu neònach, gu miorbhuileach.

Surrender, *v. a.* and *n.* Striochd, géill; thoir suas; thoir air ais. Surrender on condition, *géill air chumhnant;* surrendered, *striochdta; air ghéilleadh.*

SURRENDER, *s.* Striochd, striochdadh, géill, géilleadh, geilleachduinn; thoirt thairis dìteadh.

SURREPTION, *s.* Giolcadh; snàgadh; seapadh, gabhdadh.

SURREPTITIOUS, *a.* Gabhdach, fealltach, fallsa.

SURREPTITIOUSLY, *adv.* Gu gabhdach, gu fealltach; gu fallsa.

SURROGATE, *v. a.* Cuir an àite ni (no) neach eile.

SURROGATION, *s.* Cur an àite neach eile.

SURROUND, *v. a.* Cuairtich, cuartaich, ioma-dhruid, timchioll. Surrounded, *cuairtichte, cuartaichte, ioma-dhruidte, séisdte.*

SURROUNDING, *s.* Cuairteachadh, cuartachadh, ioma-dhruideadh; séisdeadh.

SURTOUT, *s.* Còt uachdair, còt uachdrach, rocan, earrasaid.

SURVEY, *v. a.* Gabh beachd, beachdaich, amhairc, gabh, fradharc, gabh seall.

SURVEY, *s.* Sealladh, fradharc, beachd. Take a survey, *gabh beachd, gabh sealladh.*

SURVEYING, *s.* Beachdachadh, sealltuinn, gabhail fradhairc.

SURVEYOR, *s.* (*Measurer*), fear tomhais; (*overseer*), fear riaghlaidh; griobh; (*architect*), ard-chlachair.

SURVEYORSHIP, *s.* Riaghlaireachd, griobhachd.

SURVIVE, *v. a.* and *n.* Mair, fan beò, bi lathair, mair an deigh, bi beo an deigh.

SURVIVOR, *s.* Urr a bhitheas lathair an deigh neach eile; beò. To the survivors, *do na beòthaibh.*

SUSCEPTIBILITY, *s.* Mothuchaileachd.

SUSCEPTIBLE, *a.* Mothuchail, comasach air ni thuigsinn (no) mhothuchadh.

SUSCEPTION, *s.* Gabhail.

SUSCIPIENCY, *s.* Gabhail, gabhail ri.

SUSCITATE, *v. a.* Dùisg, brosnaich, mosgail.

SUSCITATION, *s.* Dùsgadh, brosnuchadh, mosgladh.

SUSPECT, *v.* Cuir amharus, cuir omhaill; bi amharusach, cum an teagamh; baralaich; saoil. I suspect you, *tha mi cur omhaill ort;* how came you to suspect? him *cia mar a chuir thu amharus air?*

SUSPECT, *a.* Amharusach, omhailleach, neo-chinnteach.

SUSPECTED, *a.* Fo amharus.

SUSPEND, *v. a.* Croch, croch 'n àirde, croch suas; bac; dàilich, cuir dàil; cuir a dreuchd (no) oifig.

SUSPENDED, *a.* Crochta, crochte; an chrochadh; air chur a àite.

SUSPENSE, *s.* Eu-cinnte, teagamh, iom-chomhairle, ag, ioma-cheist; tomhartaich, turamanaich. In suspence, *ann an teagamh, an iom-cheist, san turamanaich.*

SUSPENSE, *a.* Bacta, grabta; ann an teagamh.

SUSPENSION, *s.* Crochadh; bacadh, cur dheth, dàileachadh, grabadh; sgurachd.

SUSPICION, *s.* Amharus, omhaill; dùileachd. Fall under suspicion, *tuit fo amharus.*

SUSPICIOUS, *a.* Amharusach, an-amharusach; eu-cinnteach; fo amharus.

SUSPICIOUSLY, *adv.* Gu h-amharusach, gu h-anamharusach.

SUSPICIOUSNESS, *s.* Amharus, anamharus, amharusachd.

SUSPIRATION, *s.* Osunn, tarruing analach.

SUSPIRE, *v. n.* Tarruing anail; tarruing osunn.

SUSTAIN, *v. a.* Cum suas, giùlain; prop, cum taic ri; tog, araich, beathaich; cum an aghaidh, cuidich, coghain; fuiling, fuilig, fulaing. Sustain a family, cum suas (no) beathaich teaghlach.

SUSTAINABLE, *a.* So-chumail suas, so-ghiùlan; so bheathachaidh; so choghnath, so fhulang.

SUSTAINER, *s.* Fear a chumas suas, fear togalach, beathachair.

SUSTENANCE, *s.* Biadh, biatachd, lòn, beathachadh, teachd an tìr.

SUSURRATE, *v. n.* Cogair, cagair; dean cogar; dean diurrasan.

SUSURRATION, *s.* Cogar, cagar, cogarsaich, cagarsaich.

SUTLER, *s.* Samhasaiche, fear a reiceas biadh agus deoch ann an camp.

SUTTLE, *s.* Fìor-thomhas.

SUTURE, *s.* Tàthadh, ceangal, fuaigheal.

SWAB, *s.* Mob, moibean, toipean.

SWAB, *v. a.* Glan le moibean.

SWADDLE, *v. a.* Paisg, spaoil, spéil. Swaddler, *paisgte, spaoilte, spéilte.*

SWADDLE, *s.* Faicean, faichdean; crios pasgaidh.

SWADDLING-CLOTH, *s.* Crios pasgaidh, aodach pasgaidh, brat spéilidh, faicean, faichdean; streachdan, striolla.

SWADDLNG, *s.* Pasgadh, spéilleadh.

SWAG, *v. n.* Croch gu trom; bi trom (no) cothromach.

SWAGE, *v. a.* Ciùinich, furtaich, thoir lasuchadh.

SWAGGER, *v. n.* Dean spagluinn; dean buamsdaireachd, bi spagluinneach, bi spaillichdeil, dean bòsd, bragainn.

SWAGGER, *s.* Buamsdair, fear spagluinneach, fear spaillichdeil; fear bòsdail.

SWAGGY, *a.* Trom, an crochadh, leibideach, leobhar.

SWAIN, *s.* Òg, òganach, fleasgach, gille; tuathanach, buachaille, treudaiche, aodhair.

SWALE, SWEAL, *v. n.* Caith air falbh, leagh; las, boisg, dealraich.

SWALLOW, *s.* Gobhlan, gobhlachan, gobhlan gaoithe, gobhlachan gaoithe; (*throat*), slugan, sgornan; gion. One swallow will not make a summer, *cha dean aon smeòrach samhradh.*

SWALLOW, *v. a.* Sluig, cuir thairis, òl; gabh. Swallowed, *sluigte.*

SWALLOW-TAIL, *s.* Seorsa seilich.

SWAM, *pret.* of swim. Shnamh.

SWAMP, *s.* Bog, boglach, féith, cathar, curach.

SWAMPY, *a.* Bog, boglach, criathrach.

SWAN, *s.* Eala, ealadh; geis; geill.

SWAP, *adv.* Gu grad, gu cabhagach, gu dian.

SWARD, *s.* Uachdar, sgrath, sod, clod; feur, gorm, fòid, fóid ghorm.

SWARDED, *a.* Gorm, comhdaichte le feur.

SWARE, *pret. a.* of swear. Mhionn.

SWARM, *s.* Sgaoth, sgann, bròd, sgiùnach.

SWARM, *v. n.* Tionail (no) cruinnich mar sgaoth.

SWART, SWARTH, *a.* Dubh, dorch, donn, ciar, do-neoil, riabhach; gruamach.

SWART, *v. a.* Dùbh, dorchaich, dean dubh, ciar (no) donn.

SWARTHILY, *adv.* Gu dubh, gu dorcha, gu ciar.

SWARTHINESS, *s.* Dubhadh, duibhe, doirche, ciarad.

SWARTHY, *a.* Dubh, ciar, donn, dubh-dhonn, dorcha, do-neòil.

SWASH, *s.* Pluinnse, plubartaich.

† SWASHER, *s.* Buamsdair.

SWATH, *s.* Spagh, ròlag feoir; (*tie*), bann, crios, stiom brat.

SWATHE, *v. a.* Paisg, spéill, spaoil. Swathed, *paisgte speillte, spaoilte.*

SWATHING, *s.* Pasgadh, spéilleadh.

Sway, *v. a.* and *n.* Iomairt; riaghail, riaghailtich, smachdaich, orduich, comannt; seòl, sdiùir, bi cothromach.

Sway, *s.* Iomairt lainn; cothrom, truime; comas; cumhachd; seoladh, riaghladh, smachd, comannt, ordugh.

Sweal, *v. n.* Leagh (no) las air falbh mar ni coinneal.

Swear, *v. n.* and *a.* Mionn, mionnaich, dean mionn, dean mionnan; lughaich; thoir mionnan; cuir gu mionnan, cuir air mhionnaibh, gabh mionnan. Swear falsely, *thoir mionnan eithich;* swear one, *gabh mionnan neach, mionnaich neach.*

Swearer, *s.* Mionnachair; fear mhionnan.

Swearing, *s.* Mionnan; mionnachadh, lughachadh; lughadh, lughachan

Sweat, *s.* Follas, fallus, obair ghoirt; greis air obair; smùidrich

Sweat, *v. n* and *a.* Cuir fallas, fallasaich; cuir am fallas; cuir smùid.

Sweater, *s.* Fear a chuireas fallas; ni sam bi a thogas fallas.

Sweaty, *a* Fallasach; follasach, tràilleach, goirt.

Swede, *s.* Suaineach.

Swedish, *a.* Suaineach

Sweep, *v. a* and *n.* Sguab, glan; sglob; rub, suath, gradshiubhail. Sweep it off, *sguab as e*, he swept past me, *sguab e seachad orm.*

Sweep, *s* Sguabadh; deannadh; sglobadh; sguabair.

Sweeper, *s.* Sguabair.

Sweepings, *s.* Sguab, sguabadh, trusdaireachd. The house-sweepings, *sguabadh 'n tighe.*

Sweepnet, *s.* Lion iadhaidh

Sweepstakes, *s.* Lom-sgriob, sgriob lom.

Sweepy, *a.* Sguabach, sgiobach, grad-shiùbhlach, seannail.

Sweet, *a.* (*To the taste*), milis, meilis, blasda, deaghbhlasda; (*to the smell*), cubhraidh, (*affable*), caoimhneil, caoin, caomh, beulchar, tlà; (*pleasant*), taitneach, sòlasach, seimh; (*as music*), binn, ceòlmhor, (*pretty*), ciatach, laoghach, boidheach, lurach, grinn, greannar, mallta. A sweet look, *sealladh tlà*, a sweet face, *aghaidh mhallta*, sweet music, *ceol binn*, a sweet smell, *fàil cubhraidh.*

Sweet, *s.* Millse, millseachd, millsead, focal tlà; boltrachas.

Sweetbread, *s.* Brisgean milis.

Sweetbrier, *s.* Ròs-phreas fiadhaich

Sweeten, *v. a.* and *n.* Millsich; dean mallta, dean tlà; ciùinich. Sweetened, *millsichte, ciùinichte.*

Sweetener, *s* Millseachair, millseadair; millsean.

Sweetheart, *s* Ceisdean, ceistean, leannan, graidhean, seircean, annsachd, cèile.

Sweetish, *a.* Leth-char milis, leth-char blasda.

Sweetly, *adv.* Gu milis, gu blasda; gu cubhraidh, gu caoimhneil; gu caomh; gu beulchar; gu tlàth, gu min, gu seimh.

Sweetmeat, *s.* Mealannan; milseanan; aran milis, biadh milis.

Sweetness, *s.* Millse, millseachd, millsead; (*of smell*), cubhraidheachd; (*of temper*), malltachd, caoimhne, caomhalachd, (*of words*), goileam, sgleò, glòr; (*of aspect*), tlàthas, tlàs, ciùineas.

Sweetwilliam, *s.* Lus leth 'n t-samhraidh.

Swell, *v. a.* and *n.* At, séid, boc, boch, bolg; † siat, † beac, séid suas, bolg a mach, rach am meud, meudaich. He swelled with pride, *dh' at e le h-ardan;* swelled, *air atadh, air séideadh, air bolgadh.*

Swelling, *s.* At, atadh, séideadh, bochdadh, bocadh, bolgadh, borcadh.

Swelling, *a.* Atmhor, bocach; bòsdail. Swelling words, *briathran atmhor, ràite.*

Swelter, *v. a.* and *n.* Tiormaich, crion, searg.

Sweltry, *a.* Bruich, ro theth.

Swept, *p. part.* of sweep. Sguabta

Swerve, *v.* Claon, fiar, rach a thaobh, aom; lùb.

Swerving, *s.* Claonadh, fiaradh, dol a thaobh, aomadh, lùbadh

Swift, *a.* Luath, siùbhlach, lùthar, lùthmhor, grad, discir, deifireach; cliste, eutrom; ullamh, deas, easgaidh.

Swift, *s.* Sruth; (*in ornithology*), gobhlan dubh, gobhlan gaineimh.

Swiftly, *adv.* Gu luath, gu siubhlach, gu lùthmhor, gu grad, gu discir, gu deifireach, gu cliste, gu h-eutrom, gu h-ullamh, gu deas, gu h-easgaidh.

Swiftness, *s.* Luathas, luas, deifir, cabhag. The swiftness of the eagle, *luathas na h-iolair.*

Swig, *v. n.* Sluig, òl gu lonach, gabh balgam mòr.

Swig, *s.* Balgam, bolgam, làn beòil

Swill, *v. a* Òl gu lonach, pòit, ruit; nigh; cuir air mheisge

Swill, *s.* Biadh mhuc.

Swiller, *s* Misgear, meisgear, pòitear, ruitear.

Swilling, *s.* Òl, pòit, meisge, ruite, pòit.

Swim, *v. a* Snamh, bi air luinneanaich, bi air 'n t-snamh, bi eutrom (no) tuainealach.

Swim, *s.* Bealag, mealag.

Swimmer, *s.* Snamhair. A good swimmer, *deagh shnamhair, snamhaiche.*

Swimming, *s.* Snamh, snamhadh Between sinking and swimming, *eadar dha liunn*

Swimmingly, *adv.* Gu ciùin, gu socrach, gu réidh, gun bhac, gun mhoille.

Swindle, *v.* Meall, dean feall (no) foille, thoir an car a.

Swindler, *s.* Meålltair, cealgair, fealltair.

Swindling, *s.* Mealltaireachd, cealgaireachd, fealltaireachd

Swine, *s.* Muc; mucan

Swinebread, *s* Seorsa luibh

Swineherd, *s.* Buachaill mhuc, mucair; caoiseachan.

Swinepipe, *s.* Seorsa lon-duibh.

Swing, *v. a.* and *n* Saobain, saobanaich, seògain, seòganaich, luaisg, siùdain, siùdanaich, siùd.

Swing, *s* Greallag, greollag; saoban, siùdan, seògan, luasgan; luasgadh, comas

Swinge, *v a* Sgiùrs, cuipinn, singil, slachdainn, buail, peanasaich.

Swingebuckler, *s.* Dorn-churaidh

Swingeing, *a.* Mor; sultmhor; cnaparra

Swinger, *s.* Luasgair, luasgadair.

Swinging, *s.* Saobanachd, seòganachd, luasgadh, siùdanachd.

Swinging, *a.* Saobanach, seòganach, luasganach, siudanach.

Swingle, *v. n* Saobanaich; seòganaich, luaisg.

Swingle-tree, *s.* (*Scotch*). Amall.

Swinish, *a.* Mucail; brùideil.

Switch, *s.* Slat, slatag, barrag, cuipe, sgiùrsadh.

Switch, *v a.* Slàits, buail le slait, cuipinn.

Swive, *v. n.* Rach air boirionnach.

Swivel, *s* Udalan, udlan; gunna mòr.

Swollen, **Swoln**, *part. pass* of swell. Air atadh, air séideadh suas, atmhor.

Swoon, *s.* Tuit ann am plath, tuit ann am paisean, tuit ann an neul, rach am plath (no) am paisean, rach an neul.
Swoon, *s.* Plath, neul, paisean, suain, taimh-neul, neul.
Swoop, *v. a.* Glac le sic, glac gu h-iongach.
Swoop, *s.* Sic, sichd, sglòb, ionnsuidh mar bheir seabhag air cun, no fiadh-bheist air cobhartach.
Sword, *s.* Claidheamh, lann; slaighre, cliaranach. A short sword, *duibheagan;* a two-edged sword, *claidheamh da fhaobhair;* a two-handed sword, *claidheamh da laimh;* put up or sheath thy sword, *cuir suas do chlaidheamh, cuir do chlaidheamh san truaille;* a sword in the hand of a fool, and a staff in a foolish woman's, *claidheamh an lamh amadain, is slacan an laimh òinnsich;* a rusty old sword, *greillean.*
Sworder, *s.* Mortair; saighdear.
Swordfish, *s.* Iasg biorach.
Swordgrass, *s.* Luachar.
Swordlaw, *s.* Eigin; lamh ard, fòirneart.
Swordplayer, *s.* Basbair, feannsair.
Swore, *pret.* of swear. Mhionn.
Swum, *pret.* and *p. part.* of swim. Shnàmh; shnamhta, shnamhte.
Swung, *pret.* and *p. part.* of swing. Luaisg, luaisgte.
Syb, *a.* Cairdeach, daimheil.
Sybow, *s.* Siobard, siobann.
Sycamore, *s.* Sice.
Sycophancy, *s.* Miodal, briondal, sodal, blandar, miolasg.
Sycophant, *s.* Sodalaiche, bladair, miodalaiche, breugair, brasair.
Sycophantic, *a.* Sodalach, miodalach, breugach, lonach, goileamach, miolasgach.
Syllabic, Syllabical, *a.* Sioladhach.
Syllabically, *adv.* A lion siol' is sioladh.
Syllable, *s.* Siol, sioladh, focal; pong, earann.
Syllabus, *s.* Giorrachadh, sùmhlachadh.
Syllogism, *s.* Co-arguinn, argumaid chuairteanach mar a leanas, *Gheibh gach duine bàs; is duine an Rìgh; uime sin, gheibh an Rìgh bàs.*
Sylph, *s.* Sithiche.
Syllogistical, *a.* Co-arguinneach.
Sylvan, *a.* Coillteach, coillteil; dubharach.
Sylvan, *s.* Duine fiadhaich; dia coille.
Symbol, *s.* Samhladh, coslas, comharradh, tuaireasg, tuairisg, samhlachadh; giorrachadh.
Symbolical, *a.* Samhlachail.
Symbolically, *adv.* Gu samhlachail.
Symbolization, *s.* Samhlachadh, coslas, eugas, aogas.
Symbolize, *v. a.* and *n.* Samhlaich. Symbolized, *samhluichte.*
Symmetrical, *a.* Co-fhreagarrach, freagarrach, cumadail.
Symmetry, *s.* Co-fhreagarrachd; cumadh, cumachd.
Sympathetic, *a.* Co-mhothuchail; truacannta.
Sympathize, *v. a.* Gabh truas ri; co-mhothuich, cofhulaing.
Sympathy, *s.* Truas, co-mhothuchadh, co-fhulangas, truacantas.
Symphonious, *a.* Co-sheirmeach.
Symphony, *s.* Comh-sheirm.
Symptom, *s.* Comhar, comharadh, coslas.
Symptomic, *a.* A tachairt air uairibh.
Synagogue, *s.* Sinagog, eaglais Iùdhach, co-chruinneachadh Iùdhach.
Synchronical, *a.* Comh-amail, aon amail, a tachairt aig an aon am.
Synchronism, *s.* Co-thachair, nithe.
Synchronous, *a.* Comh-amail, a tachairt aig an aon am.
Syncope, *s.* Neul, plath, paisean, suain.
Synod, *s.* Seanadh, seanaid.
Synodal, *a.* Seanaideach.
Synodic, Synodical, *a.* Seanaideach.
Synodically, *adv.* A réir seanaid, le ordugh seanaid.
Synonymous, *a.* Co-chiallach; còslach.
Synopsis, *s.* Giorrachadh; cinn teagaisg.
Syntactical, *a.* Tàthta, comh-thàthta.
Syntax, *s.* Co-thàth, cur ri chéile.
Synthesis, *s.* Co-thàth, cuir ri chéile.
Syption, Siption, *s.* Pioban, pioban taosgaidh.
Syringe, *s.* Sgiort, sguirt, sgiùrdan, gunna spùtachain, sdeallair.
Syringe, *v.* Sgiort, sgiurt, nigh le sgiort.
Syrtis, *s.* Beò-ghaineamh, beò-ghaineach, boglach.
System, *s.* Riaghailt; doigh; seòl; innleachd, lathailt.
Systematical, *a.* Riaghailteach, a reir riaghailt; lathailteach.
Systematically, *adv.* A réir riaghailt, gu riaghailteach, gu lathailteach.
Systematize, *v. a.* Riaghail, thoir gu riaghailt.
Systole, *s.* Crion cridhe.

T.

T. Am ficheadamh litir do 'n Aibideal.
Tabby, *s.* Seorsa sìde.
Tabby, *a.* Slatach, riabhach; eug-samhuil. A tabby cat, *cat riabhach.*
Tabefaction, *s.* Caitheamh, éiteach.
Tabefy, *v. n.* Caith, caith air falbh.
Taberd, Tabard, *s.* Earradh-righ-theachdair; gùn leobhar.
Tabernacle, *s.* Pàilliun, bùth, pubull, fionn bhuth, bothùn; caban; ionad aoraidh.
Tabernacle, *v. n.* Pàilliunaich.
Tabid, *a.* Galarach, gaoideil, caol, tana, éiteachail.
Tabidness, *s.* Caoile; caitheamh; tainead.
Table, *s.* Bord; clàr; clàr innseadh; brod, taibhle, bois; (*picture*), dealbh. A sacrament table, *bord comanaich;* serve a table, *riaruich bord;* lay the table, *comhdaich am bord, leig am bord.*
Table, *v. n.* and *a.* Cuir air bhord; bord; biath, beathaich cuir sios an ordugh, dean clàr-innseadh.
Table-beer, *s.* Lionn caol, lionn bùird.
Tablecloth, *s.* Anart bùird, aodach bùird; tubhailt, tuailte, searadair.
Tableman, *s.* (*At draughts*), fear feoirne. A robber, *spuinneadair.*
Tabler, *s.* Bordair, fear air bhord.
Tablespoon, *s.* Spàin bùird.
Tabletalk, *s.* Comhradh conaltraidh, seanachas bùird.
Tablet, *s.* Bordan, brod, clàr; (*in medicine*), cearnag leigh.
Tabour, *s.* Drum beag, drum laimh.

Tabourer, *s.* Drumair.

Tabouret, Tabourine, *s.* Guit-dhrum; drum meoir.

Tabular, *a.* Clàrach; cearnach, ceithir chearnach; leacach.

Tabulate, *v. a.* Leig na chlàraibh; dean réidh; cearnaich.

Tabulated, *a.* Réidh, comhnard, leacach.

Tach, Tache, *s.* Cromag, lùb, lùbach, lùbag, dul, sùil; cluas crambaid; putan.

Tachygraphy, *s.* Sgriobhadh luath.

Tacit, *a.* Sàmhach, tosdach, tosd, bìth; balbh; ceilte. A tacit assent is an acknowledgment, *is ionann tosd is aiteachadh.*

Tacitly, *adv.* Gu sàmhach, gu tosdach, gu tosd, gu bìth; os iosal.

Taciturnity, *s.* Tosd, sàmhchair, bailbhe.

Tack, *v. a.* Tàth, fuaigh, fuaidhil, cnòd, diong, ic; (*at sea*), tionndadh, fiar.

Tack, *s.* Tacaid, tac, tarrag bheag, pinne; (*at sea*), aonda, fiaradh luing, gabhail, gabhail luing, siubhal luing an aghaidh na gaoithe.

Tackle, *s.* Acfuinn, acfhuinn, cungaidh, uigheam; cordraidh.

Tackling, *s.* Acfhuinn, acfhuinn luing, droineap, cungaidh, trealaich.

Tactic, Tactical, *a.* Rangachail; a bhuineas dh' ordugh catha.

Tactics, *s.* Rangachadh, cur an ordugh catha, rang-oilean, rang-eòlas.

Tactile, *a.* A ghabhas beanachd ri.

Taction, *s.* Beanachd, leantuinn.

Tadpole, *s.* Ceann simid; ceann-phulag; adag bulgach.

Taffeta, *s.* Taifeid, seorsa sìde.

Tag, *s.* Aigilean; othaisg; ni suarrach sam bi. The tag-rag people, *am prabar, a ghràisg.*

Tag, *v. a.* Tàth, ceangail, fuaigh.

Tagtail, *s.* Seorsa durraig aig am bheil corp is earbull air mhùth datha.

Tail, *s.* Earbull, earr, feaman, breaman, rumpall; los; ceann deiridh. Turn tail, *ruith air falbh, gabh an teich;* the tail of a garment, *sgiort, sgioball;* cat's-tail, *bodan;* great cat's-tail, *bodan dubh.*

Tailed, *a.* Earbullach, feamanach, breamanach.

Taillage. See Tallage.

Tailor, *s.* Tàithlear, tàillear.

Taint, *v. a.* and *n.* Salaich, truaill, mill; bi salach (no) truaillidh. Tainted, *salaichte, truaillte.*

Taint, *s.* Sal, salachar; gaoid; galar; coire, ball, spot.

Taintless, *a.* Gun sal, gun ghaoid, gun bhall, gun choire, gun spot.

Tainture, *s.* Sal; gaoid; ball; spot; coire.

Take, *v. a.* and *n.* Gabh, glac, beir air, cuir lamh air; cuir an sàs. Take care, *thoir aire, thoir an aire;* take down, *thoir sios, thoir a bhàn;* take down or swallow, *sluig, leig sios, leig thairis;* take down or subdue, *ceannsuich, smachdaich;* take an oath, *mionn, mionnaich, gabh mionnan;* take in or cultivate, *thoir a stigh, ruathar, ar, crann;* take in or cheat, *meall, thoir an car a;* take away, *thoir* (*no*) *thabhair air falbh;* take or seize, *glac beir air, cuir an laimh;* take or understand, *tuig;* do you take me? *bheil thu 'g am thuigsinn?* take after, *lean;* take asunder, *thoir as a chéile, sgar;* take for, *gabh airson, saoil, smuainich;* what do you take me for? *ciod tha thu 'saoilsinn a th' annam?* or, *ciod a tha thu smuaineach gur mi?* as I take it, *a réir mo bheachd-sa;* take ill, *gabh gu dona, gabh gu soithich;* take on thee, *gabh ort, leig ort, gabh ort fhéin;* take on thee to be deranged, *gabh ort* (*no*) *ort fhéin, a bhith gòrach;* take to, *gabh gu, rach gu, tog ort dh' ionnsuidh;* it will not take to him, *cha tig e ris;* take up or lodge, *cuir suas, cuir 'n àirde;* take notice, *thoir an aire;* take off, *mag, sgeig, thoir dheth, sluig, sguab as;* take a share, *gabh cuibhrionn, gabh comith;* take place, *tachair;* take or succeed, *eirich le, rach le, soirbhich;* it did not take, *cha d' eirich leis, cha deach leis, cha do shoirbhich e;* whether you take it well or ill, *olc air mhath leat e;* you took me up wrong, *thog thu mi gu docharrach;* take in a bad sense, *gabh ann an droch sheadh.*

Taken, *p. part.* of take. Glacta, glacte, air a ghabhail, air a ghlacadh. Taken, as a female, *air a gabhail, air a glacadh;* he is greatly taken with her, *tha e air a thogail leatha;* taken off (he), *air 'thoirt air falbh;* (she), *air a toirt air falbh;* (they), *air an toirt air falbh.*

Taker, *s.* Glacair, glacadair.

Taking, *s.* Glacadh, gabhail, glacail; triobloid.

Talbot, *s.* Gadhar, gaothar.

Tale, *s.* Sgeul, sgeulachd, naidheachd, nuaidheachd; sgeul ùr, ùr-sgeul; aithris, doisgeul, fionnsgeul, faoin-sgeul, breug, sgleò; spleadh. Tell a tale, *innis sgeul;* a tale to be told, *sgeul ri innseadh, sgeul ri aithris;* a tale not vouched is not heeded, *cha 'n fhiach sgeul gun urrainn.*

Tale, *s.* Aireamh; suim; cunntas.

Talebearer, *s.* Fear tuaileis, fear gabhannach; breugair, urr lonach, sgeulaiche. Talebearers, *luchd tuaileis.*

Talebearing, *s.* Tuaileas; lonais.

Talent, *s.* Tàlann, tàlaint, suim àraidh airgid; (*of mind*), càile; ceud fath, comas, cumhachd, feart.

Talisman, *s.* Dealbh cleasachd, giseag, gisreag, seun.

Talismanical, *a.* Dubh chleasachdail, giseagach, gisreagach, diomhair, druidheach.

Talk, *v. a.* Labhair, bruidhinn, dean comhradh, càn. Talk idly, *dean glòirmeas:* of whom are you talking? *co mu dheimhinn* (*no*) *c' uime tha thu 'labhairt?* you must speak to him, *feumaidh tu bruidhinn ris;* much talked of, *iomraiteach, ro iomraiteach.*

Talk, *s.* Labhairt, bruidhinn, comhradh, cainnt, brosgal, seanachas; (*in a contemptuous sense*), gob, gobais, goileam, cabaireachd, glòr, glòirmeas; (*chat*), cracaireachd; (*report*), fabhunn, fabhur, iomradh. Keep talk to him, *cum comhradh ris;* there is a talk, *tha iomradh ann, tha iad ag radh.*

Talk, *s.* (*In mineralogy*), talc, tailc, seorsa cloich.

Talkative, *a.* Bruidhneach, cabach, gobach, goileamach, comhraiteach, lonach, cainnteach, gabhannach, beulchar; beulanach, beileanach, brosgulach, beulach, beolach.

Talkativeness, *s.* Bruidhneachd, cabaireachd, gob, gobaireachd, gobais, goileam, lonais, beilean, beileanachd, rabhdadh, ràite.

Talker, *s.* Gobair; urr bhruidhneach. An idle talker, *glòirmeas, rabhdair.*

Talking, *s.* Labhairt, bruidhinn, comhradh, cainnt, deanachas.

Talky, *a.* Talcach, tailceach.

Tall, *a.* Ard, mòr, fad. A tall tree, *craobh ard.*

Tallage, *s.* Càin, cìs.

Tallow, *s.* Geire, ìgh; blonag, reamhrachd, gris, gréis.

Tallow, *v. a.* Geir, sliob le geire (no) ìgh.

Tallowchandler, *s.* Fear dheanamh choinnlean, coinnleadair.

Tally, *v. a.* and *n.* Dean freagarrach; freagair.

Talmud, *s.* Leabhar beul-aithris nan Iùdhach.

Talness, *s.* Airde.

Talon, *s.* Ionga, crudh, smòg, smàg; spor, cròg.

Tamarind, *s.* Seorsa meas.

Tambour, *s.* Drum laimh; greus-obair, obair shnathaid; criathar ro mhin.

Tambourin, *s.* Drum meòir.

Tame, *a.* Ciùin, soimeach; soirbh; soitheamh; socrach; (*broken*), briste, callta, (*spiritless*), neo-spioradail, meata, tais, cailleachanta.

Tame, *v. a* Ciùinich, ciùnaich, smachdaich; thoir stigh, dean soirbh, dean soimeach, càtaich, dean socrach; bris; claoidh, sàruich, fairtlich air. Tamed, *ciùinichte, smachdaichte, cataichte, briste.*

Tameable, *a.* So-chiùineachadh, so-smachdachadh, so-bhriseadh; a ghabhas briseadh (no) smachdachadh.

Tamely, *adv* Gu ciùin, gu soimeach, gu soirbh, gu socrach, gu soitheamh, gu briste; gu neo-spioradail, gu meata, gu tais, gu cailleachanta, gu strìochdach.

Tameness, *s* Ciùineas; ciùnas, socair; soimeachd; ceannsachd

Tamer, *s* Fear smachdaidh; ceannsuchair.

Taminy, **Tammy**, *s.* Seorsa olainn.

Tamkin, *s.* Ploc gunna

Tamper, *v.* Bean ri, bean do, buair.

Tan, *v. a.* Cairt, buail; dean odhar leis a ghrian.

Tang, *s* Blas làidir, droch bhlas.

Tang, *v a.* Tarruing mach, fadaich.

Tangible, *a.* So-lamhachadh, so-laimhseachadh, a dh' fhaodar lamhachadh.

Tangle, *v. a.* Rib, cuir an sàs, cuir air aimhreidh, prab, buair Tangled, *ribte, prabta*

Tangle, *s.* Prablach, rioblach; (*sea-weed*), slat-mhara, stamh, feaman, roc.

Tanistry, *s*, Tànaisteachd, tàinistearachd.

Tank, *s* Amar.

Tankard, *s* Tancair; pigidh.

Tanner, *s.* Fear cartaidh; fear deasachaidh leathair, sutair

Tanpit, *s* Slochd-cartaidh.

Tansy, *s* Seorsa luibh chubhraidh. White tansy, *brislean, briosglan*

Tantalize, *v* Thoir lon a You tantalize him, *tha thu 'toirt an lon as.*

Tantamount, *a.* Co-ionann.

Tantivy, *adv.* Gu cabhagach, le cabhag, le deifir.

Tantling, *s.* Faoin-bheachdair.

Tanyard, *s* Lios cartaidh, tionas.

Tap, *v a.* (*Strike softly*), maoth-bhuail, bean; (*a hogshead*), bris air, fosgail, leig, bungair.

Tap, *s* Maoth-bhuille, buille beag; (*of a hogshead*), goc, pioban taosgaidh, piob leigidh.

Tapp, *s.* Stiom chaol, crios caol, bann.

Taper, *a* Clogaideach, biorrach, barra-chaol, spiriceach

Taper, *v a* and *n.* Dean barra-chaol, fas barra-chaol.

Taper, *s.* Lòchran, leus, coinneal, solus, dreòs, soillsean.

Tapestry, *s* Greus-obair, obair-ghréis, greus

Taphouse, *s.* Tigh lionna, tigh òsda

Tapster, *s* Buidealair.

Tar, *s* Teàrr; pic; bith craoibh.

Tar, *v a.* Teàrr, (*excite*), brosnuich, buair, brog, stuig, cuir h-uige, farranaich

Tar, *s.* Seòladair, maraiche, mairiche.

Tarantula, *s.* Seorsa damhain alluidh nimhe a tha fàs san Eadailt, cha ghabh a theum slànachadh ach le ceòl.

Tardation, *s* Bacadh, grabadh, amaladh, moille.

Tardigrade, *a* Athaiseach, mall-cheumach, mairnealach, slaodach, socrach.

Tardiloquent, *a.* Athaiseach ann an comhradh mall-bhruidhneach; socrach, slaodach.

Tardily, *adv.* Gu h-athaiseach, gu mall, gu maidheanach, gu mairnealach, gu slaodach, gu leagach.

Tardiness, *s.* Athais, athaiseachd, mairnealachd, slaodachd, maidheanachd, moille, leagaireachd.

Tardy, *a.* Athaiseach, mall, mairnealach, moineasach, aolaisdeach, slaodach, fadalach, socrach, eimhilt; ionsanach, leibideach, leasg, lunndach, leagach.

Tare, *s.* Cogall, cagull; roille, dìthean, peasair each; (*in commerce*), cothrom soithche.

Target, *s.* Targaid, sgiath.

Targeteer, *s* Targaidear, targaidiche, fear targaid.

Tariff, *s.* Cairteal co-cheannachd.

† **Tarn**, *s.* Bog, boglach, féith, cathar, curach, poll, slob, criathrach.

Tarnish, *v a.* Salaich, dubh, truaill; mill. Tarnished, *salaichte, dubhta, truaillte, millte.*

Tarpauling, *s.* Aodach siùil air a thearradh; seòladair, maraiche.

† **Tarriance**, *s.* Stadachd, fanachd, fuireach.

Tarrier, *s* Abhag.

Tarry, *v. n* Fan, stad, fuirich, feith, dean moille. Tarry all night, *fan* (*no*) *fuirich ré na h-oidhche;* I tarried for him, *dh' fheith mi ris*

Tart, *s.* Garg, searbh, goirt, geur; (*biting*), beumnach, teumnach.

Tart, *s* Pithean meas.

Tartan, *s* Cadath; breacan, clò breac.

Tartane, *s.* Long a chithear gu minig air muir na Meadhon-thir le aon chrann agus le seòl tri-oisinneach.

† **Tartar**, *s.* Ifrinn

Tartar, *s.* Tartair, fear mhuinntir na Tart-thir.

Tartar, *s.* Sgràill, sgròill, sgrath cruaidh, sgrisleach, deasgann, sgrath cruaidh a leanas ris na fiaclan (no) ri taobh stigh togsaid fiona.

Tartarean, **Tartareous**, *a.* Ifrinneach, diabhluidh, deamhnaidh.

Tartary, *s.* An Tart-thir.

Tartly, *adv* Gu garg, gu geur, gu goirt, gu searbh, gu doirbh, gu beumnach, gu teumnach.

Tartness, *s.* Gairgead, geurad, géire, seirbhe, searbhas.

Task, *s* Obair sgéithte; tasg; eallach; cuigealach.

Task, *v* Sgéith obair, cuir obair roimh.

Taskmaster, *s* Maighistir cruaidh

Tassel, *s* Aigealan, dos, dosal, cluigean, babhaid, babag, baban

Tasselled, *a.* Aigealach, dosach, dosalach, babagach, babhaideach, babanach

Taste, *v. a.* and *n.* Blais, gabh blas; feuch, fainich, fairich, mothaich.

Taste, *s.* Blas; blasdachd; feuchainn, deuchainn, faineach; sgeinn, sgeilm. Take a taste, *blais, gabh blas*, having a good taste, *blasda, deagh-bhlasda*, without taste *or* insipid, *domblasda, leamh*

Tasteable, *a* Blasda, deagh-bhlasda.

Tasted, *a* Blasda, blaiste. Tasted beforehand, *roimh-bhlaiste.*

Tasteful, *a.* Blasda, deagh-bhlasta; finealta, eireachdail

Tastefulness, *s* Blasdachd; finealtachd

Tasteless, *a.* Neo-bhlasda, domblasda, leamh.

Tastelessness, *s* Domblasdachd, neo-bhlasdachd.

Taster, *s* Blasdair; copan; cuach, cuachag.

Tasting, *s.* Blasdachd, blasadh.

Tatch, *s.* Lùb, crampaid, putan.

Tatter, *v. a.* Reub, srac, strac; streab, leub; roic, stroic, dean na luideagan; ciuirt.

Tatter, *s.* Luideag, clùd, stroic, cearb.

Tatterdemallion, *s.* Luinnsear; fear luideagach.

Tattle, *v. n.* Dean gobais (no) goileam, labhair gu gobach; innis gu lonach.

Tattle, *s.* Gob, gobais, goileam, cabais, lonais, briot, brisg-ghloir, faoin-chainnt, ràite, giorrag.

Tattler, *s.* Gobair; briotair, lonair; ràite.

Tattling, *a.* Biodanach,

Tattling, *s.* See **Tattle**

Tattoo, *s.* Drumaireachd chum saighdearan a chur do 'n cairtealaibh, caismeachd oidhche, caismeachd fheasgair.

Taught, *pret.* and *p part* of teach. Theagaisg, dh' ionn-suich; teagaisgte, ionnsuichte, oileanaichte

Taunt, *v. a.* Beum, thoir beum air, gearr; sgeig, mag, fochaid air, masluich, cuir air dimeas.

Taunt, *s.* Beum, beumadh, teum, gearradh, geur-bhriathar, an-fhocal, magadh, sgeig, fanaid, buirte

Taunter, *s.* Beumair, beumadair, bearradair.

Taunting, *a* Beumnach, sgeigeach, sgeigeil.

Tauntingly, *adv.* Gu beumnach, gu fochaideach, gu sgeigeil.

Tauricornous, *a.* Adhairceach

Tautological, *a.* Cuairt-bhriathrach, aithriseach, ath-bhriathrach, ràsanach,

Tautologically, *adv.* Gu cuairt-bhriathrach, gu h-ath-bhriathrach, gu leudach, gu ràsanach.

Tautology, *s.* Cuairt-bhriathar, aithris, ath-aithris, ràs-anachd.

Tautologist, *s.* Ràsanaiche; fear cuairt-bhriathrach, ath-bhriathraiche.

Tavern, *s.* Tigh mòr, tigh osda; + tabhairn; tigh mhuirn

Taverner, *s.* Fear tigh òsda, òsdair, tabhairnear

Taw, *v.* Gealaich leathar, falmaich, falm. Tawed leather, *leathar falmta.*

Taw, *s.* Bulag; cluich air bhulagan.

Tawdriness, *s.* Leibideachd, slaodachd, faoin-bhreaghas

Tawdry, *a* Leibideach, slaodach, faoin-bhreagh, neo-ghrinn, neo-sgeilmeil A tawdry girl, *ceirteag, stràilleag*

Tawed, *a.* Falmaichte, falmta.

Tawer, *s.* Fear cartaidh, fear deasachaidh leathar.

Tawny, *a.* Odhar, donn, lachdunn, ciar.

Tax, *s.* Cìs, càin, màl, millean; ùmhladh, gabhail.

Tax, *v. a.* Cìs, càin, leig cìs, leig càin; (*lay to one's charge*), cronaich, coirich, cuir as leth; cuir air. They taxed him with murder, *chuir iad mortadh as a leth.*

Taxable, *a.* Buailteach do chìs.

Taxation, *s.* Cìs, càin; cìs-leagadh, umhlachd; coireachadh, cur as leth.

Taxer, *s* Fear a leigeas cìs.

Tax-gatherer, *s.* Cìs-mhaor.

Tea, *s* Lus oirthireach ainmeil, air nach urrainn mise Gaidhlig eile a chur ach an *sùgh-luibh, an sùgh-lus, brìgh an t-sugh luibh*

Teach, *v. a.* Teagaisg, ionnsuich, oileanaich, oid, foghluim, muin; innis, thoir fios.

Teachable, *a.* So-theagasg, so-ionnsuchadh, so-fhoghlum; furas a theagasg, furas ionnsuchadh.

Teacher, *s.* Oid-ionnsuich, fear teagaisg, teagasgair, maigh-stir sgoil.

Teaching, *s.* Teagasg, teagasgadh, ionnsach, ionnsuchadh, fòghlum.

Teague, *s.* Eireannach.

Teal, *s.* Siolta, darcan, dubh-lacha.

Team, *s.* Seisreach. One nail will lame a horse, one horse will break a team, *millidh aon tarrag each, is brisidh aon each seisreach.*

Tear, *s.* Deur, boinne; (*rent*), srac, sracd, strachd, reub, reubadh Shedding tears, *a sileadh dheur*

Tear, *v. a.* Reub, srac, strac, ring; beubanaich; leub, spion; spiol; thoir as a chéile, thoir na mhìreannan, bris, bruan.

Tear, *v. n.* Dean giosgan, bi air bhoile.

Tearful, *a.* Deurach; snitheach, caointeach.

Tearing, *a.* Sracach, reubach, spionach, ringeach.

Tearing, *a* (*A local word*), briagh, breagh, grinn.

Tease, *v.* Cìr, spiol, sgriob; buair, farranaich, cuir dragh air, cuir farran air, caig air. He teases me, *tha e 'caig orm*

Teasel, *s* Lus an fhùcadair

Teaser, *s.* Fear draghalach, fear caige

Teasing, *s* Cìreadh, spioladh; buaireadh, caige

Teat, *s* Sìthne; deala, cioch.

Techily, *adv.* Gu frionasach, gu friothaireach, gu friothar-ach, gu cainnteach, gu crosda, gu sdodach.

Techiness, *s* Frionasachd, friothaireachd, friotharachd, sdodachd, diorrasachd

Technical, *a.* Ealadhanta, ealanta.

Techy, *a.* Frionasach, friothaireach, friotharach, sdodach, dodach, crosda, diorrasach, cainnteach, doirbh, gearr, cas, cabhagach, goirrid.

Ted, *v.* Ròil feur.

Tedder, *s* Teathair, taod, cord, ròp. A tedder's length, *fad teathrach.*

Te Deum, *s.* Laoidh naomh.

Tedious, *a* (*Slow*), mall, mairnealach, maidheanach, aolais-deach, mothar, fadalach, rithinn; (*as a discourse*), fad, ràsanach, (*as a road*), buan; (*irksome*), draghalach

Tediously, *adv* Gu mall, gu mairnealach, gu maidhean-ach, gu h-aolaisdeach, gu mothar; gu buan; gu dragh-alach.

Tediousness, *s* Moille, maille, mairneal, mairnealachd, maidhean, maidheanachd, draghalachd

Teel-tree, *s.* Crann teile

Teem, *v.* Beir, thoir mach, bi torrach, bi lan, bi iom-làn, cuir thairis. Teeming with riches, *a cur thairis le beartas*

Teemful, *a.* Torrach, tarbhach, siòlmhor, làn, iom-làn, dearr-làn.

Teemless, *a.* Neo-thorrach, aimrisg, reasg, neo-tharbhach

† **Teen**, *s.* Mulad, bròn, sprochd, doilghios, tuirse.

Teens, *s.* Deugan; eadar da bhliadhna dheug agus fichead

Teeth, *pl* of tooth Fiaclan See **Tooth**.

Tegument, *s.* Comhdach, rùsg, sgrath, cochull

Teint, *s.* Dath, lith, neul.

Telegraph, *s.* Cian-shanusair; inneal araidh trid an cuirear fios o dhùthaich gu duthaich, ann am beag mhionaidibh

Telegraphic, *a.* Cian-shanusach, cian-ghrabhach.

Telescope, *s.* Gloine amhairc.

Telescopical, *a* Cian-amharcach.

Tell, *v a* Innis, aithris, nochd, cuir an cèill, foillsich, abair, cunnt, aireamh; thoir fios, cuir fios Tell me, *innis dhomh*, I cannot tell, *cha 'n urrainn mi 'innseadh*, (*no*) *'radh*, tell again, *aithris*, tell on, *innis air adhairt.*

Teller, *s.* Fear brathàidh; cunntair.

Tell-tale, *s.* Lonag, urr lonach.

Temerarious, *a.* Brais, dàna, ceann-laidir; obann, cas.

Temerity, *s.* Braise, dànadas, obainne.

Temper, *v. a.* (*Moderate*), ciùinich; measarraich; (*mingle*), measg, measgnaich, coimeasg; (*as steel*), faobhairt, fadhairt.

Temper, *s.* (*Disposition*), nàdur, gné, càile; gean; (*moderation*), measarrachd, stuaim; (*of steel*), faobhar. A man of a good temper, *fear còir, fear caoimhneil;* of an easy temper, *soimeach, soitheamh;* of a generous temper, *fial, mor-chuiseach;* of a surly temper, *doirbh, crosda, cainnteach, gnò;* of an even temper, *mallta, seimh, mìn, ciùin;* a good temper, *deagh nàdur;* a bad temper, *droch nàdur;* bring to a good temper, *cuir gean maith air;* be of good temper, *caoimhne ort.*

Temperament, *s.* (*Of body*), cal, càile, staid colna; (*expedient*), seòl, modh, doigh.

Temperance, *s.* Measarrachd, macantachd, macantas, stuaim, stuamachd, deagh nòs; foighidinn, ciùineas.

Temperate, *a.* Measarra, measarradh, stuama, macanta, cneasta.

Temperately, *adv.* Gu measarra, gu stuama, gu macanta, gu cneasta.

Temperateness, *s.* Measarrachd, stuamachd, cneastachd.

Temperature, *s.* Staid, càile nàduir; meadhonachd.

Tempered, *a.* Fadhairte, faobhairte; nadurrach. Bad-tempered, *droch nadurrach;* good-tempered, *math nadurrach.*

Tempest, *s.* Gaillionn, doinionn, stoirm, anfhadh, anradh, an-uair. A storm at sea, *anfhadh cuain.*

Tempest-tossed, *a.* Tonn bhuailte.

Tempestuous, *a.* Gaillionnach, anfhadhach, anrach, stoirmeil, gailbheach, doinionnach, gaothar.

Templar, *s.* Teampullaiche; stuidear san lagha.

Temple, *s.* Teampull, eaglais; (*of the head*), leth-cheann; camag.

Temporal, *a.* Aimsireach, aimsireil, saoghalta; talmhaidh; leth-cheannach.

Temporality, *s.* Seilbh thalmhaidh, nithe saoghalta.

Temporally, *adv.* Gu h-aimsireil, gu talmhaidh, gu saoghalta.

Temporals, *s.* Nithe saoghalta.

Temporalty, *s.* An tuath; seilbh shaoghalta, nithe saoghalta.

Temporaneous, *a.* Aimsireil, neo-mhaireann, goirrid, neo-sheasmhach, caochlaideach, siùbhlach, ré sealladh, ré aimsir.

Temporariness, *s.* Aimsirealachd; neo-mhaireannachd, neo-sheasmhachd, neo-bhuanachd.

Temporary, *a.* Aimsireil, neo-mhaireann, neo-bhuan, neo-sheasmhach, caochlaideach, siùbhlach.

Temporise, *v. a.* Cuir dàil, dàilich; aontaich; géill do na h-amannaibh, imich a réir na h-aimsir.

Temporiser, *s.* Fear a dh' imicheas a réir na h-aimsir.

Temporising, *s.* Aontachadh, imeachd a réir na h-aimsir.

Tempt, *v. a.* Buair, meall; cathaich; brosnuich, feuch ri, thoir oidhirp. Tempt me not, *na buair mi.*

Temptable, *a.* So-bhuaireadh, so-mhealladh, furas a bhuaireadh (no) bhrosnuchadh.

Temptation, *s.* Buaireadh, mealladh; cathachadh; brosnuchadh.

Tempter, *s.* Buaireadair; brosnuchair, mealltair; an t-aibhisear, an t-aibhisdear, an diabhol.

Temulency, *s.* Meisge, misge, daoraiche.

Temulent, *a.* Meisgeach, misgeach, air a mheisge, air an daoraiche.

Ten, *a.* Deich, deichnear. Ten men, *deich fir, deichnear dhaoine;* ten o'clock, *deich uairean;* ten times, *deich uairean, deich cuairte, deich tarruingean;* tenfold, *deich fillte;* ten years of age, *deich bliadhna dh' aois;* ten thousand men, *deich mìle fear;* the ten at cards, *an deicheamh.*

Tenable, *a.* So-ghleidh, so-choimhead, so-chumail, furas ghleidh, furas choimhead (no) chumail, a ghabhas gleidh, a ghabhas coimhead (no) cumail.

Tenacious, *a.* (*Obstinate*), féin-bharaileach, dòchasach; cumailteach, leanailteach, greimeilteach; rithinn; (*niggardly*), gabhaltach; spiocach, iongach, sporach, crion, gann.

Tenaciously, *adv.* Gu cumailteach, gu leanailteach, gu gabhaltach; gu spiocach, gu h-iongach; gu rithinn.

Tenaciousness, *s.* Cumailteachd, leanailteachd, gabhaltachd; spiocaireachd.

Tenacity, *s.* Leanailteachd, rìthneachd.

Tenancy, *s.* Cumail; seabhachadh.

Tenant, *s.* Tuathanach; màladair; rudhrach, fear aontaidh, fear gabhail. Tenants are stronger than their lord, *is treise tuath na tighearn.*

Tenant, *v. a.* Àitich; gabh airson màil.

Tenantless, *a.* Neo-aitichte, falamh, fàs, uaigneach; gun aitreabh.

Tenantry, *s.* Tuath.

Tench, *s.* Seorsa éisg.

Tend, *v. a.* and *n.* Gleidh, thoir an aire air, cum sùil air, fair, foir; lean, treòruich; fritheil; aom.

Tendance, *s.* Gleidheadh, gleidh, frithealadh; fritheal, fair, foir, cumail.

Tendence, Tendency, *s.* (*Inclination*), aomadh; gabhail; aire; (*drift*), rùn, miann.

Tender, *a.* Maoth, ùr, anfhann, mall, lag, fann, tais, bog; (*in heart*), caomh, suairc, còir, caoimhneil, tlusail, truacanta; (*young*), og, fiùranta, fann; (*scrupulous*), agach, teagamhach. Make tender, *maothaich.*

Tender, *v.* (*Offer*), tairg, cuir an tairgse, nochd; (*regard*), gabh cùram do; (*value* or *respect*), meas; gradhaich.

Tender, *s.* (*Offer*), tairgse; (*watch*), fear faire, faire; (*ship*), long bheag.

Tenderhearted, *a.* Teò-chridheach, tiom-chridheach, blath-chridheach, tlusail, maoth-chridheach, truacanta, caoimhneil, seirceil.

Tendering, *s.* Tairgseadh, tairgse, cur an tairgse.

Tenderling, *s.* Ceud adharc feidh, slabhag.

Tenderly, *adv.* Gu teò-chridheach, gu gradhach, gu h-ionmhuinn, gu gaolach.

Tenderness, *s.* (*Softness*), maothalachd; maoithe, ùiread; anfhainneachd; (*of heart*), caomhalachd, caoimhnealachd; tlùs, tlùsaireachd, caoimhneas, truacantas; (*love*), gradh, gaol; (*care*), cùram; (*scrupulousness*), agaileachd.

Tending, *s.* (*Of cattle*), buachailleachd, cuallach, gleidh spreidhe.

Tendinous, *a.* Féitheach, féithear, rùdanach.

Tendon, *s.* Féith, rùdan, féith lùthaidh.

Tendril, *s.* Maothran, fàillean, fiùran, gineag.

Tenebricose, *a.* Dorch, doilleir.

Tenebrose, *a.* Dorch, dubh, doilleir, gruamach.

Tenebrosity, *s.* Doirche, duirche, dorchadas, doillearachd.

Tenement, *s.* Aitreabh, àros, fardach, tigh; cumail, gabhail fearainn.

Tenerity, *s.* Maothalachd.

Tenet, *s.* Barail, barail shuidhichte, beachd; teagasg; aobhar.
Tenfold, *a.* Deich fillte.
Tennis, *s.* Seorsa cluiche air creutaig.
Tenon, *s.* Tionur.
Tenor, Tenour, *s.* (*Meaning*), brigh, blàdh, ciall, seadh; (*intent*), rùn; (*mode*), staid, inbhe; modh, (*course*), aomadh, claonadh, cùrsa, gabhail; (*in music*), fonn meadhonach.
Tense, *a.* Teann, rag, tarruingte.
Tenseness, *s.* Tinnead, raigead.
Tension, *s.* Teannachadh, teinnead, tinnead
Tensure, *s.* Sineadh, ragachadh, teannachadh, tarruing
Tent, *s.* Bùth, pubull, pailliun; fion-bhuth. Medical tent, *gath cuip;* tent wine, *fionn teinnteach.*
Tentation, *s.* Deuchainn, feuchainn; oidhirp, buaireadh
Tentative, *a.* Feuchainneach, deuchainneach, oidhirpeach.
Tented, *a.* Bùthach, pubullach. The tented field, *magh nam bùth.*
Tenter, *s.* Cromag, clic, dubhan, lùbag; caman, bac, corran; angair.
Tenth, *a.* Deicheamh. The tenth part, *an deicheamh cuid.*
Tenth, *s.* Deicheamh.
Tenthly, *adv.* 'San deicheamh àite.
Tentiginous, *a.* Sìnte, rag.
Tenuity, *s.* Tainead; caoile; mìnead.
Tenuous, *a.* Tana, caol, mìn, meanbh; seang.
Tenure, *s.* Còir fearainn, ceart fearainn
Tepefaction, *s.* Blàthachadh, blàiteachadh.
Tepid, *a.* Blàth, maoth-bhlàth; meath-bhlàth.
Tepidity, *s.* Blàthas, maoth-bhlàthas.
Tepor, *s.* Meath-bhlàithead, maoth-bhlàthas.
Teratology, *s.* Glòr, baoth-chainnt.
Terebinth, *s.* Crann pìon; oladh 'chroinn pìona, ùillidh 'n tairbhint.
Terebrate, *v. a* Toll. Terebrated, *tollta.*
Terebration, *s* Tolladh.
Tergeminous, *a.* Tri-fillte.
Tergiversate, *v. a* Muth taobh, rach air ais, cuir gu taobh, cuir dheth.
Tergiversation, *s.* Dol air ais; cùl-cheumnachadh, dol air ais, cur dheth; car; caochlaideachd.
Term, *s* (*Bound*), crìoch, iomall, teòradh, ceann, (*word*), focal, briathar; ainm; (*condition*), teirm, cumhnant, (*of time*), teirm.
Term, *v. a.* Ainmich, gairm, goir, abair ri.
Termagancy, *s.* Buaireas, aimhreite, droch cordadh.
Termagant, *a.* Buaireasach, aimhreiteach, tuasaideach
Termagant, *s.* Sglamhruinn boirionnaich, bansgal, baobh, bidse.
Terminable, *a.* So-chrìochnachaidh.
Terminate, *v. a.* and *n.* Crìochnaich, thig gu crìche. Terminated, *crìochnaichte.*
Termination, *s.* Crìoch; deireadh, ceann.
Termless, *s.* Neo-chrìochnaichte, neo-chrìochnach, gun chrìoch, gun iomall.
Termly, *adv.* O àm gu h-àm, o theirm gu teirm.
Ternary, *a.* A lìon triùir is triùir
Ternary, *s.* An àireamh tri; aireamh thri
Terrace, *s.* Cloidh, barr-bhaladh; purt; mullach, comhnard tighe.
Terraqueous, *s.* Talmhaidh.
Terrene, *a.* Talmhaidh, saoghalmhor

Terrestrial, Terrestrious, *a.* Talmhaidh, saoghalmhor.
Terrible, *a.* Eagallach, uamhasach, uamharra, fuathasach, oillteil, fuasnach, allsgach.
Terribleness, *s.* Eagallachd, uamhasachd, uamharrachd, fuathasachd, oillteileachd
Terribly, *adv* Gu h-eagallach, gu h-uamhasach, gu h-uamharra, gu fuathasach, gu h-oillteil
Terrier, *s.* Abhag
Terrific, *a.* Eagallach, uamhasach, uamharra, fuathasach, oillteil, gu fuasnach.
Terrify, *v a* Cuir eagal (no) oillt air, clisg, buail, le h-eagal. You terrified him, *chuir thu oillt* (*no*) *eagal air* Terrified, *fo eagal, fo oillt.*
Terrifying, *a* Eagallach, oillteil, fuathasach.
Territory, *s* Tìr, fearann, fonn, dùthaich, talamh; ranntachd; tàinisteachd rìgh no prionnsa.
Terror, *s* Eagal, oillt, crith-oillt, maoim, uamhann, sgaoim; allsga; goirtsinn. Strike them with terror, *buail le h-uamhann iad.*
Terse, *a.* Glan, cuimir, grinn, finealta, speisealta, eireachdail
Tertian, *s.* Fiabhrus critheannach, crith-fhiabhrus.
Tertiate, *v. a.* Dean an treas' uair.
Tesselated, *a.* Daoimeanach.
Test, *s* Deuchainn; ceasnachadh; breith. Put to the test, *cuir gu deuchainn.*
Testacious, *a.* Sligeach, spairneagach, faochagach, plaosgach.
Testament, *s.* Tiomnadh; teismeid.
Testamentary, *a.* Tiomnach, tiomnachail, teismeideach.
Testator, *s.* Fear a dh' fhàgas teismeid, fear ni a theismeid, tiomnachair.
Testatrix, *s.* Ban tiomnachair
Tested, *a.* Deuchainnte; air fheuchainn, air a chur gu deuchainn.
Tester, *s* Sè sgillinn; brat, cùbhrainn.
Testicle, *s.* Clach; magairle, tiarpan, tiadhan
Testification, *s* Toirt fianuis
Testificator, *s.* Fianuis, teisteannas, teistinneas.
Testifier, *s* Fianuis.
Testify, *v. a.* Thoir fianuis, dean fianuis, dearbh, thoir teisteas.
Testily, *adv.* Gu frionasach, gu doirbh, gu crosda, gu cainnteach.
Testimonial, *s* Teisteanas, teisteas.
Testimony, *s* Fianuis, teisteas, dearbhadh; foirgheall, taisbean, aidmheil.
Testiness, *s* Frionasachd, cainnteachd, crosdachd.
Testudinated, *a.* Boghach, boghta
Testy, *a* Frionasach, crosda, cainnteach, dranndanach.
Tetchy, *a.* See Techy.
Tête-a-tête, *s.* Ceann ri ceann; an ceann a chèile, comhradh dèise.
Tether, *s.* Teathair, cord, taod, ròp, tobha
Tether, *v a* Teathair; cuir air theathair
Tetrarch, *s.* Uachdaran Roimheach; uachdaran ceathramh cuid do mhòr-roinn.
Tetrarchate, Tetrarchy, *s* Uachdranachd air a cheathramh cuid do mhòr-roinn.
Tetrical, *a.* Dàn; rag; ceann-laidir, doirbh, crosda, gruamach, gnò.
Tetter, *s.* Teine dé; frìd, frìdeag, guirean, bucaid.
Tew, *v. a.* Buail, gréidh, singil; bogaich

TEW, *s.* Cord, rop, taod, tobha.
TEWTAW, *v. a.* Buail, gréidh, singil.
TEXT, *s.* Ceann teagaisg, steidh teagaisg.
TEXTILE, *a.* So-fhigheadh, so-phleatadh.
TEXTUARY, *s.* Fear eolach air a phiobull.
TEXTUARY, *a.* A réir teagaisg.
TEXTURE, *s.* Figheadh, pleatadh, dualadh, figheadaireachd.
THAN, *adv.* Na, is. Nothing is surer than death, *cha 'n 'eil nì 's cinntiche no 'm bàs;* I love her better than myself, *is docha leam i na mi féin.*
THANE, *s.* Tòiseach, tàiniste.
THANK, THANKS, *s.* Taing, buidheachas. Thanks to God, *buidheachas do Dhia;* thanks to you, *tapadh leat;* many thanks to you, *mòran taing dhuit;* little thanks to you, *beag taing dhuit;* without thanks to you, in spite of you, *gun taing dhuit.*
THANK, *v.* Thoir taing, thoir buidheachas. Thank you, *buidheachas (no) taing dhuit, tapadh leat;* thank God, God be thanked, *buidheachas do Dhia, buidheachas do Ni Math.*
THANKFUL, *a.* Taingeil; buidheach.
THANKFULLY, *adv.* Gu taingeil, gu buidheach.
THANKFULNESS, *s.* Taingealachd, buidheachas.
THANKLESS, *a.* Mi-thaingeil, neo-thaingeil, diombach.
THANKLESSNESS, *s.* Mi-thaingealachd.
THANKOFFERING, *s.* Tabhartas buidheachais, iobairt bhuidheachais.
THANKS. See THANK.
THANKSGIVING, *s.* Breith-buidheachais, buidheachas.
THANKWORTHY, *a.* Airidh air taing.
THARM, *s.* Mionach, greallach, caolain.
THAT, *demon. pro.* Sin, ud, od. That man, *an duine sin, an duine ud;* that way, *an rathad sin, an car sin.*
THAT, *rel. pro.* A. The man that struck me, *an duine a bhuail mi.*
The same that or *as.* Mar, ceart mar, co-ionann. He is the same that he was, *tha e ceart mar bha e:* God is the same that Christ is, *is co-ionann Dia ri Criosd.*
THAT, *conj.* Gu, gum, gun, gur, chum, chum as gu, chum as gum, chum agus gu. I say that he will die, *tha mi 'g radh gum faigh e bàs;* they say that he is a bad man, *tha iad ag radh gur olc an duine e;* to the end that, *chum na crìche gu.*
That—not. Nach, chum as nach, chum agus nach. That you may not die, *chum agus nach bàsaich thu.*
So—that. Chum agus nach; cho—as, cho—agus. Are you *so* ignorant *that* you know not this? *bheil thu cho aineolach* as *nach aithne dhuit so.*
THAT, *adv.* (*Because*), gu, gun, gum; a chionn gu, chionn gu, do bhrigh. I am glad that you are come back safe, *tha mi aoibhinn gu bheil thu air pilltinn slàn;* so that, *ionnas gu.*
THATCH, *s.* Tubha; tugha; dion.
THATCH, *v. a.* Tugh, comhdaich le tugha, dean tughadaireachd. Thatched, *tughta, tughte.*
THATCHER, *s.* Tughadair.
THATCHING, *s.* Tughadh, tughadaireachd.
THAW, *s.* Aiteamh; leaghadh.
THAW, *v. a.* and *n.* Leagh; dean aiteamh. The day thaws, *tha 'n là ris an aiteamh.*
THE, (*the definite article.*) An, am, a, 'n. The man, *an duine, am fear;* the woman, *a bhean;* the Mac Donell, *an Dònullach, Gleanngarradh;* the Mac Gregor, *an Griogarach;* the self-same man, *a cheart duine cheudna;* the one man, the other man, *an t-aon fhear, am fear eile;* from the one end to the other, *o cheann gu ceann, o 'n t-aon cheann gu ruig an ceann eile, o 'n darna ceann thun a cheann eile;* the more you drink, the worse you will be, *mar is mò dh' olas tu, is ann is misd a bhitheas tu;* the more we have, the more we desire, *mar is mò 'bhitheas againn,is mòid a dh' iarras sinn.*
THEATRE, *s.* Tighe cluiche; tigh cruinneachaidh.
THEATRICALLY, *adv.* Mar fhear-cluiche.
THEE, *s. pro.* Thu, thusa. To thee, *dhuit, dhuitse, dhut;* of thee, *dhiot;* on thee, *ort;* from thee, *uait;* in thee, *annad;* out of thee, *asad;* under thee, *fodhad;* with thee, *leat;* about thee, *umad;* before thee, *romhad;* over thee, *tharad;* through thee, *tromhad.*
THEFT, *s.* Meirle, meirleadh, gaduidheachd, goide, goideachd, braid; searb.
THEIR, *a. pron.* An, am. Their business, *an gnothuichean;* their towns, *am bailtean.*
THEIRS, *a. pron.* Leo, leo-sa, leo-san; aca, aca-san. This is theirs, *is leo-sa so;* it is not my house but theirs, *cha n' e mo thigh-se th' ann, ach an tigh aca-san;* it is not my business but theirs, *cha n' e mo gnothach-sa e, ach an gnothuch-sa.*
THEISM, *s.* Dia-chreidsinn, Dia-chreidimh.
THEIST, *s.* Dia-chreideach, Dia-chreidimhich.
THEM, *pron.* Iad, iadsan. To them, *dhoibh;* of them, *dhiu, dhiusan;* on them, *orra, orra-san;* in them, *annta, annta-san;* out of them, *asda, asda-san;* at them, *aca, aca-san;* between them, *eatorra;* beneath them, *fodhpa, fodhpa-san;* towards them, *h-uca, h-ucasan;* with them, *leo, leo-san;* about them, *umpa, umpa-san;* from them, *uapa, uapa-san;* with them, *riu, riu-san;* before them, *rompa, rompa-san;* over them, *tharta, thairis orra;* through them, *trompa, trompa-san.*
THEME, *s.* Steigh, cùis, aobhar, grunnd.
THEMSELVES, *pron.* Iad féin. They themselves, *iadsa féin.*
THEN, *adv.* Air sin, air an àm sin, an deigh sin; (*therefore*), uime sin, mata, ma seadh. What shall I do then? *ciod a nì mi mata;* now and then, *an traths' is a ris; corr uair, corr uairean.*
THENCE, *adv.* As sin, as an àite sin, o'n am sin; o sin; airson sin.
THENCEFORTH, *adv.* O sin a mach, o 'n am sin, o sin suas.
THENCEFORWARD, *adv.* O sin a mach, o sin suas.
THEOCRACY, *s.* Dia-riaghladh.
THEOCRATICAL, *a.* Dia-riaghlach.
THEODOLITE, *s.* Inneal tomhasaidh.
THEOLOGER, THEOLOGIAN, *s.* Diadhair.
THEOLOGICAL, *a.* Diadhach, diadhaireach.
THEOLOGICALLY, *adv.* A réir diadhachd (no) diadhaireachd, gu diadhuidh.
THEOLOGIST, THEOLOGUE, *s.* Diadhair.
THEOLOGY, *s.* Diadhachd, diadhaireachd.
THEORBO, *s.* Inneal ciùil Eadailteach.
THEOREM, *s.* Barail; radh fior.
THEORETIC, *a.* Smuainteachail, beachdail, inntinneach.
THEORETICALLY, *adv.* A réir smuaine, a réir beachd.
THEORIC, *a.* Smuainteachail, beachdail, inntinneach.
THEORIST, *s.* Beachdair.
THEORY, *s.* Smuainteachadh, beachd; dealbh inntinn, obair inntinn.
THERAPEUTIC, *a.* Leigheasach, leigheasail.
THERE, *adv.* An sin, an sud, san àite sin; (*thither*), do 'n àite sin, an sin. What are you doing there? *ciod tha thu 'deanamh an sin?* here and there, *an so 's an sin, thall 's a bhos.*

Thereabout, *adv.* Feadh sin, air feadh sin, mu 'n àite sin, mu sin; mu 'n tuairmeis sin.

Thereafter, *adv.* An deigh sin, na dhéigh sin.

Thereat, *adv.* An sin, aig sin; air son sin; san àite sin.

Thereby, *adv.* Le sin, air son sin.

Therefore, *adv.* Uime sin, air an aobhar sin, le sin, air-son sin

Therefrom, *adv.* O sin, o sud, o so, uaith sin, uaith so.

Therein, *adv.* Ann sin, ann, stigh an sin.

Thereinto, *adv.* A steach an sin, a stigh an sin.

Thereof, *adv.* Do sin, do so, dheth sin.

Thereon, *adv.* Air sin, air so, so air.

Thereout, *adv.* A sin, mach a sin, as.

Thereto, Thereunto, *adv.* Thuige sin, a chum sin, chuig sin.

Thereunder, *adv.* Fo' sin, fu 'sin.

Thereupon, *adv.* Air sin; air ball, an lorg sin.

Therewith, *adv.* Le sin, leis sin, air ball.

Theriacal, *a.* Leigheasach, leigheachail.

Thermometer, Thermoscope, *s.* Teas-thoimhsean, teas-mheidh.

These, *pron* Sin, iad sin, iad so, iad san. These men, *na daoine sin;* not those but these, *ni h-eadh iad sin ach iad-so;* these and those, *iad so is iad sin* (*no*) *iad sud.*

Thesis, *s.* Argumaid, iom-chomhradh.

Thews, *s. pl.* Modhannan, àbhaistean.

They, *pron.* Iad, iadsan; ad, *provincial.* They who cannot do as they will, will do as they can, *iadsan nach dean mar is àille, ni iad mar dh' fhaotas.*

Thick, *a.* Tiugh, garbh; dòmhail, dumhail; reamhar. Thick and short, *goirid garbh*, thick of hearing, *leth-char bodhar*, thick *or* clumsy, *peilliceach*, thick *or* muddy, *làbach, salach.*

Thick, *s* (*Of the leg*), calpa; (*thickness*), tiughad, tiugh-alachd; (*thicket*), preas, preasarnach.

Thick, *adv* Gu tric, gu minic, gu dlù, gu luath; gu teann.

Thicken, *v. a.* and *n.* Tiughaich; dumhlaich, domhlaich; neartaich, fàs tiugh, fàs domhail Thickened, *tiughaichte, dumhlaichte*

Thicket, *s.* Doire tiugh, tom-drise, preasarnach, cabarach; preas; dlù-phreas, dos, † ansgairt, † rochdan

Thickly, *adv.* Gu tiugh, gu dlù.

Thickness, *s* Tiughad, tiughead, dùmhlas, domhlas, gairbhe; (*of edge*), maolad; (*of hearing*), buidhre.

Thickset, *a.* Tiugh, dlù (no) teann air chéile.

Thickset, *s.* Seorsa aodaich.

Thickskin, *s.* Umaidh, burraidh, guraiceach.

Thickskull, *s.* Umaidh, burraidh, guraiceach.

Thickskulled, *a* Tiugh; neo-thuigseach; baoghalta.

Thief, *s.* Meirleach, gaduiche, goidiche, bradach; bradaiche, ladran, robair, creachadair, fear reubainn, spuinnead-air, sliomair, sladair, sladuiche, bradaiche Thieves, *meirlich, gaduichean.* The rogue thinks every man a thief, *saoilidh bradaiche nam bruach gur gaduichean uile càch.*

Thief-catcher, *s.* Fear glachdaidh mheirleach, fear glac-aidh, maor righ Thief-catchers, *luchd glacaidh.*

Thieve, *v. n.* Goid, dean méirleadh.

Thievery, *s.* Méirleadh, braid, slad, sladachd, slaide, goid, gaduigheachd, sliomaireachd, sloighte, reubainn, robair-eachd, togail, creachadh.

Thievish, *a.* Bradach, sladach, goideach; bleideil, sloigh-teil.

Thievishly, *adv.* Gu bradach, gu sladach; gu bleideil, gu sloighteil.

Thievishness, *s.* Meirleadh, bradaichead, braide, sladachd, sladuigheachd, slaide; sloighte.

Thigh, *s.* Sliasaid, leis. Thigh-bone, *cruachann.*

Thilk, *a.* Sin féin, sin fhéin

Thill, *s.* Tramp cartach.

Thillhorse, Thiller, *s* Each deiridh, cas dearg

Thimble, *s.* Meuran.

Thin, *a.* (*Not thick*), caol, neo-thiugh, finealta; (*few*), gann, tearc, ainmig, (*lean*), tana, truagh, caol, bochd.

Thin, *v a* Caolaich, dean caol, tanaich, lughdaich. Thinned, *caolaichte, tanaichte.*

Thin, *adv.* Gu caol, gu tana; gu gann

Thine, *pron.* Do, d', agad-sa, leat-sa Thine arm, *do ghairdean*, this is not mine but thine, *cha leam-sa so ach leat-sa.*

Thing, *s.* Ni, rud, cùis; gnothuch. It is a bad thing, *is olc an rud e*, *is don' an nì e*, that is another thing, *is rud eile sin*, it is a usual thing with me, *is nòs leam, is cleachd leam;* thou nasty thing, *a rud mhosaiche*, above all things, *os cionn gach uile ni*, any thing, *rud sam bi, rud air bi, ni sam bi, ni air bi*, something, *ni 'gin, rud eigin;* some little thing, *beag nithe.* Things, *nithe, nitheannan, rudan, cuimgaidh, buill, codach, cuid;* these things, *na nithe so, na rudan so, na nithe-se* The name without the thing, *an t-ainm gun an tairbhe.*

Think, *v* Smuainich, smaoinich, smuaintich, smaointich; saoil, baralaich, meòraich. I think, *tha mi 'saoilsinn, is i mo bharail*, what think you? *ciod their leat?* what think you of this man? *ciod do bharail do 'n duine so?* when I was thinking on these things, *a smuaineachadh dhomh air na nithe sin*

Thinker, *s.* Smuaintear.

Thinking, *s.* Smuaineachadh, smaoineachadh, smuainte-achadh; baralachadh; beachdachadh, saoilsinn

Thinly, *adv.* Gu tana; gu tearc, gu h-ainmig; gu caol, gu bochd, gu truagh.

Thinness, *s* Tainead, tearcad, teirce, teircead, ainmigead, caoilead.

Third, *a.* Treas, triamh. A third part, *trian, treas cuid*

Third, *s.* Trian, an treas cuid.

Thirdly, *adv* 'San treas àite

Thirl, *v a* Toll

Thirst, *s* Pathadh, tart; iot, iotadh, tiormachd, tiormal-achd; (*eagerness*), ro-mhiann, càs.

Thirst, *v. n.* Bi pàiteach (no) air pathadh. I thirst, *tha mi pàiteach, tha pathadh orm.*

Thirstiness, *s.* Pathadh, tart, tartmhorachd, iot, iotmhor-achd; tiormachd

Thirsty, *a.* Pàiteach; tartmhor, iotmhor, tioram.

Thirteen, *a.* Trideug. Thirteen men, *tri fir dheug.*

Thirteenth, *a.* An triamh deug, an treas deug The thirteenth man, *an treas fear deug.*

Thirty, *a.* Deich thar fhichead.

This, *a.* So This man, *an duine so*, this very man, *a cheart duine so*, to this place, *air so, thun so, do 'n àite so*, from this place, *a so, as an àite so.*

Thistle, *s* Cluaran, foghnan, foghannan, aigheanach, oigh-eanach, giogan Sow-thistle, *bliochd fochadain*

Thistly, *a* Cluaranach, aigheannach, foghnanach.

Thither, *adv.* Thun sin, an sin, gu ruig sin, gu nuig sin, do 'n àite sin. Hither and thither, *sios is suas, nunn is a nall, chuig is uaith*

Thitherto, *adv.* Thun sin, gu ruig sin, chum na crìche sin.

Thitherward, *adv.* Gu sin, gu ruig sin; gus a sin

Tho' See Though.

THONG, *s.* Iall, iallag. Thongs, *iallan;* a quantity or assortment of things, *iallach;* a thong for leading a dog, *lomhainn.*

THORACIC, *a.* Uchdach; maothanach.

THORAL, *a.* A bhuineas do 'n leabaidh; uiridheach.

THORN, *s.* Droighionn, droigheann, dreas, dris, sgitheach, sgeach, stob. Black thorn, *droighionn dubh.* If one pass through the thorn for me, I will pass through the briar for him, *am fear a theid san droighionn domh, theid mi san dris da.*

THORNY, *a.* Droighneach, droigheannach, dreasach, sgitheachail; stobach; deacair.

THOROUGH, *a.* Iomlan, foirfe, glan, fior. A thorough rogue, *fior* (*no*) *tur chrochair.*

THOROUGH, *prep.* See THROUGH.

THOROUGHFARE, *s.* Rod, slighe, casan, aisridh.

THOROUGHLY, *adv.* Gu h-iomlan, gu tur, gu foirfe.

THOROUGH-PACED, *a.* Iomlan, foirfe, fior.

THOROUGH-STITCHED, *adv.* Gu h-iomlan, gu tur.

THORP, *s.* Baile beag.

THOSE, *pron.* Iad sud, iad sin; sud, sin, ud. Not these but those, *ni h-eadh iad so, ach iad sud;* those men, *na daoine ud.*

THOU, *s. pron.* Thu, tu. Thou thyself, *thusa féin.*

THOUGH, *conj.* Ged; giodh, gidheadh, ged tha. Though he come, *ged thig e;* as though, *mar gum b'ann; mar gum b'eadh.*

THOUGHT, *pret.* and *p. part.* of think. Shaoil; smuainichte. I thought I would have died, *shaoil mi gum faighinn bàs.*

THOUGHT, *s.* Smuain, smaoin, aire, beachd, barail, smuairean; seadh, suim, cùram; dùil, dochas. This was his thought, *b' e so 'inntinn* (*no*) *àire;* I will speak my thoughts, *labhraidh mi m' inntinn;* idle thoughts, *faoin-smuaintean, faoin-dhòchasan.*

THOUGHTFUL, *a.* Smuaineachail, smuainteachail, smaointeachail, smuaireanach, iomaguineach, curamach, faicilleach, suidhichte, sicir, crionna, eagnaidheach.

THOUGHTFULLY, *adv.* Gu smuaineachail, gu smuainteachail, gu h-iomaguineach.

THOUGHTFULNESS, *s.* Iomaguin, cùram, smuairean, tromsmuaineachadh, ana-cùram, ro-churam.

THOUGHTLESS, *a.* Neo-smuainteachail, mi-sheadhar, misheadhail, neo-chùramach, mi-chùramach, mi-shuimeil. A thoughtless person, *diudan.*

THOUGHTLESSLY, *adv.* Gu neo-smuainteachail, gu misheadar, gu neo-chùramach.

THOUGHTLESSNESS, *s.* Mi-sheadh, mi-sheadharachd, michùram, mi-shuim, diudan.

THOUSAND, *a.* Mìl. A thousand men, *mìl fear;* two thousand, *dà mhìl;* a thousand times, *mìl uair, iomad uair;* thousands, *mìltean.*

THOUSANDTH, *a.* Mìleamh. The thousandth man, *am mìleamh fear.*

THOWL, *s.* Putag, urrachdag, bac, bacal.

THRALL, *s.* Tràill; tràilleachd, tràillealachd, daorsa, braighdeanas, bruid.

THRALDOM, *s.* Tràillealachd, daorsadh, braighdeanas, bruid. In thraldom, *fu dhaorsadh, fu bhraighdeanas.*

THRASH, *a.* Buail; slachduinn; (*drub*), gréidh; boiceannaich, boicnich, puinneanaich, dornaich. Thresh the corn, *buail an t-arbhar;* she thrashed him, *ghréidh i e;* he got himself properly thrashed, *fhuair e 'dheagh ghréidh* (*no*) *charaiste.*

THRASHER, *s.* Fear bualaidh, buailtear, bualadair.

THRASHING, *s.* Bualadh, slachduinn; gréidh, boiceannach, caraiste, lundrainn, puinneanach; (*with a flail*), bualadh, sùisteachd.

THRASHING-FLOOR, *s.* Urlar bualaidh.

THRASONICAL, *a.* Bòsdail, spagluinneach, làdasach.

THRAVE, *s.* Treabh; dà adag, ceithir sguab fhichead arbhair.

THREAD, *s.* Toinntean, tainntean, snàthainn, snàth, stiolan, lìn, sreang, sreangan.

THREAD, *v. a.* Sreang, sreangaich, snàith.

THREADBARE, *a.* Lom.

THREADEN, *a.* Toinnteanach, sreangach.

THREAT, *s.* Bagairt, bagradh, maoitheadh, maoidheadh, muiseag. A threat requires not a plaster, *cha luidh plàsd air bagairt.*

THREAT, THREATEN, *v. a.* Bagair, maoidh. Threaten him, *bagair air;* he began to threaten me, *thòisich e air bagairt orm;* threaten, but strike not, *bagair is na buail.*

THREATENER, *s.* Bagarair, bagrair, bagairtear; fear bagairt.

THREATENING, *s.* Bagaradh, bagradh; bagairt; maoidheadh; muiseagadh.

THREATENING, *a.* Bagarach, bagairteach; maoidheach, smàdail, muiseagach.

THREATENINGLY, *adv.* Gu bagarach, gu bagairteach.

THREATFUL, *a.* Bagrach, bagairteach, smàdail.

THREE, *a.* Trì, triùir. Three men, *tri fir; triùir dhaoine;* the three or trey point at cards or dice, *an triamh.*

THREEFOLD, *a.* Tri fillte, tri dualach.

THREEPENCE, *s.* Trì sgillinn. Threepence halfpenny, *trì sgillinn is bonnsè.*

THREEPENNY, *a.* Suarrach; dìblidh.

THREESCORE, *a.* Tri-fichead.

THRENODY, *s.* Cumha, tuireadh, coranach.

THRESHOLD, *s.* Stairsneach.

THREW, *pret.* of throw. Thilg.

THRICE, *adv.* Tri uairean, tri chuairt, tri tarruingean.

THRIFT, *s.* Sùrd, deagh bheanachas tighe, grunndalas. An herb so called, *tonn a chladaich.*

THRIFTILY, *adv.* Gu grunndail, gu sùrdail; gu gniomhach, gu deanadach.

THRIFTINESS, *s.* Grunndalas, sùrdalachd.

THRIFTLESS, *a.* Neo-ghrunndail, neo-shùrdail, neo-ghniomhach, neo-dheanadach, struidheil, stroghail.

THRIFTY, *a.* Grunndail, sùrdail; cùramach, gniomhach, deanadach.

THRILL, *v. a.* and *n.* Toll; guin; cuir gaoir ann. Thrilled, *tollta;* it thrilled through me, *chuir e gaoir annam.*

THRIVE, *v. n.* Soirbhich; cinn, fàs. He will not thrive, *cha shoirbhich e, cha soirbhich leis, cha n' éirich leis; cha téid leis.*

THRIVER, *s.* Fear soirbheasach; mac ratha.

THRIVING, *a.* Soirbheasach; rathail, cinneasach, fortanach.

THRIVINGLY, *adv.* Gu soirbheasach, gu cinneasach.

THROAT, *s.* Sgernan, sgornach, goile, culair. He cut his throat, *ghearr e 'sgornaibh.*

THROATPIPE, *s.* Detiach, steig bhràgad, steic bhràgad.

THROB, *s.* Plosg, plosgaidh, plosgail, plosgartaich, osmag, ospag; osunn.

THROB, *v.* Dean plosg (*no*) plosgail, bi sa phlosgartaich, frith-bhuail.

THROBBING, *s.* Plosgadh; plosgail, osmag, ospag, ospagaich, osunn.

THROBBING, *a.* Goirt, guineach, goimheach, craonach.

THROE, *s.* Uspag, éigin, greim; tarruing.

THROE, *v. a.* Cradh; claoidh.

THRONE, *s.* Rìgh-chathair, cathair rioghail.

Throne, *v. a.* Cuir air righ-chathair.
Throng, *s.* Domhladas, buidheann, lòd, sluagh, cruinneach.
Throng, *v. a.* Domhlaich, teannaich; mùch, bruth, pùc, cruinnich. They thronged him, *dhomhlaich iad e.*
Thronged, *a.* and *part.* Domhail; *trang;* làn, domhlaichte, teannaichte, mùchta.
Throstle, *s.* Smeòrach; truid, truideag; liatruisg.
Throttle, *s.* Detiach, steic-bhràgad, sgornach, sgornan, amhach.
Throttle, *v. a.* Tachd, mùch.
Throve, *pret.* of thrive. Shoirbhich.
Through, *prep.* Troimh, tre, trid; roi. Through me, *tromham, tromham-sa, -san;* through thee, *tromhad, tromhad-sa, -san;* through him, *troimhe, troimhse;* through her, *troimpe, troimpse;* through us, *tromhainn, tromhainne;* through you, *tromhaibh, tromhaibh-se;* through them, *trompa, trompasa, -san;* through my means, *da m' thridsa;* through thy means, *da do thridsa;* through his means, *tridsan, da 'thridsan;* through her means, *da tridsan;* through their means, *da 'n tridsan;* through and through, *troimh is troimh, glan troimh.*
Through, *adv.* Troimh; thun na crìche.
Through-bred, *a.* Ionnsuichte, làn ionnsuichte.
Throughly, *adv.* Gu tur, gu h-iomlan, gu h-uile.
Throughout, *prep.* Tre, troimh, air feadh, trid a mach.
Throughout, *adv.* Gu h-iomlan, anns gach àite.
Throughpaced, *a.* Iomlan, foirfe.
Throw, *v. a.* and *n.* Tilg; thoir urchair. Throw up *or* vomit, *tilg, sgeith;* throw all about, *sgap, sgaoil;* throw away, *tilg air falbh; caith;* thrown, *tilgte; air 'thilgeadh.*
Throw, *s.* Urchair; tilgeadh, buille; dian-oidhirp; cor, staid.
Thrower, *s.* Tilgear; fear tilge; bonnsair.
Throwing, *s.* Tilgeadh, tilgeil.
Thrum, *s.* Fuidheag, faochag. Thrums, *fuidheagan.*
Thrum, *v. a.* Dreang, dean dreangail, srann.
Thrush, *s.* Smeòrach, truid, truideag, liatrosg.
Thrush, *s.* Briseadh mach air croicionn naoidhein.
Thrust, *v. a.* and *n.* Sàth; sparr; put, pùc, purr, ding, fuadaich, thoir ionnsuidh.
Thrust, *s.* Sàth, sàthadh, sparradh, put, pùcadh, purradh, foirneadh, ionnsuidh ghuineach. What a thrust he made at him! *is e thug an ionnsuidh air!*
Thrust, *part.* Sàithte, sàthta.
Thruster, *s.* Sàthair; fear sàthaidh, sparradair; purradair.
Thrusting, *s.* Sàthadh; sparradh, putadh, pùcadh, purradh.
Thustle. See Throstle.
Thumb, *s.* Òrdag. The thumb at strife with the palm, *an òrdag an aghaidh na glaic.*
Thumb, *v. a.* Meuraich, smeuraich, smògaich.
Thumbband, *s.* Siaman ordaig.
Thumbstall, *s.* Meuran ordaig.
Thump, *s.* Buille, gleadhar, straoidhle, gleog, stear; stràchd, trom-bhuille, dunt.
Thump, *v. a.* Buail; slachduinn, dornaich.
Thumper, *s.* Buailtear; cnap (no) bun balaich, cnapanach, bun caile.
Thumping, *a.* Bunanta, bunach, làidir, cnaparra.
Thunder, *s.* Tairneanach, torunn; toirneas; stairn.
Thunder, *v. a.* and *n.* Tairneanaich; dean tairneanach (no) torunn.
Thunderbolt, *s.* Dealan, dealanach, teine athair; peilear tairneanaich, caor teinntidh.
Thunderclap, *s.* Braidhe toirneanaich.
Thunderer, *s.* Torunnair.
Thunderous, *a.* Torunnach.
Thunder-shower, *s.* Fras tairneanaich; beum sleibh.
Thunderstrike, *v.* Buail le tairneanach; buail, le h-eagal (no) uamhunn.
Thursday, *s.* Dir-daoine. Next Thursday, *dir-daoine so 'tighinn;* Maundy Thursday, *dir-daoine a bhrochain mhòir.*
Thus, *adv.* Mar so, air an doigh so; *provincial,* mur so. The matter is thus, *is ann mar so tha 'chùis;* thus far, *fhad so;* thus much, *a mheud so.*
Thwack, *v. a.* Buail, slachduinn, slachdanaich, slachdair; gréidh; lunndrainn.
Thwack, *s.* Buille, straoidhle, gleog, steur; garbh-bhuille.
Thwart, *s.* Trasd.
Thwart, *a.* Crosgach; neo-iomchuidh; neo-fhreagarrach, crosda, reasgach, eithich, aingidh.
Thwart, *v. a.* Cuir an aghaidh.
Thwarting, *a.* Eithich; crosda; neo-aontachail.
Thy, *pron.* Do, d', t'. Thy mother, *do mhàthair;* thy father, *d' athair.*
Thyme, *s.* Mionnt; lus mhic righ Bhreatuinn.
Thyself, *pron. reciprocal.* Thu féin, thu fhein, thusa féin.
Tiar, Tiara, *s.* Ceann-eididh, crùn (no) coron a Phàpa.
† Tice, *v. a.* Meall.
Tick, *s.* Creideas; earbsadh; mial chruidh; mial chaorach.
Tick, *s.* (*Of a bed*), toichd.
Ticken, Ticking, *s.* Toichd.
Ticket, *s.* Ticeid; comhar, comharradh.
Tickle, *v. a.* Cigeall, gigeall, giogall.
Tickle, *a.* Neo-ghramail, neo-sheasmhach.
Ticklish, *a.* Neo-sheasmhach, neo-chinnteach, teagamhach; deacair; giogallach, ciogailteach.
Ticklishness, *s.* Neo-sheasmhachd, teagamhachd; deacaireachd; giogallachd.
Tid, *a.* Milis, blasda, taitneach.
Tid-bit, *s.* Crioman milis, millsean.
Tidder, Tiddle, *v. a.* Dean mùirn, dean beadradh; mùirnich, breug, pròis.
Tide, *s.* Am, uine, aimsir; seol mara, lan-mara, tragh-mara; sruth, buinne-shruth. A spring-tide, *reothairt;* the rage of a spring-tide, *mire reothairt;* neap-tide, *contraigh.*
Tide, *v. a.* Aom mar shruth.
Tidegate, *s.* Tuil-dhorus.
Tidewaiter, *s.* Oifigeach cusmuin.
Tidily, *adv.* Gu sgiolta, gu sgiobalta, gu cruinn, gu cearmanta, gu cuimir, gu sgeilmeil, gu grinn, gu deas.
Tidiness, *s.* Sgioltachd, sgiobaltachd, cearmantachd, sgeilmealachd; freagarrachd, deise, deiseachd, gasdachd.
Tidiness, *s.* Nuaidheachd; sgeul; sgeul ùr.
Tidy, *a.* Sgiolta, sgiobalta, sùmhail, cruinn, cearmanta, cuimir, sgeilmeil, freagarrach, deas; glan; gasda, piollach.
Tie, *v. a.* Ceangail, snaim, snuim, fastaich, fastaidh; trus; bac, grab. Tie hand and foot, *ceangail eadar lamhan is chosan;* tied, *ceangailte, fastaichte; snaimte, snuimte.*
Tie, *s.* Ceangal, ceangladh, snaim, snuim; cnòd.
Tier, *s.* Sreath, breath, sread; rang.
Tierce, *s.* Bairill gu thrian.
Tiff, *s.* Deoch; (*a pet*), dod, sdod.
Tiff, *v. n.* Droch còird, cuir mach.
Tiffany, *s.* Seorsa sìde.

TIGER, *s.* Tiogair.

TIGHT, *a.* Teann, daingeann; gramail, cuanta; cuimir; sùmhail, diongalta. Air tight, or water tight, *dionach;* a tight young man, *smaidseart, gasganach.*

TIGHTENING, *s.* Teannachadh, daighneachadh, gramachadh; sùmhlachadh.

TIGHTEN, *v. a.* Teannaich, gramaich; sùmhlaich, dionaich, cneasnaich. Tightened, *teannaichte; sùmhlaichte, cneasnaichte.*

TIGHTLY, *adv.* Gu teann, gu gramail, gu diongalta, gu dionach.

TIGHTNESS, *s.* Teinnead, gramalas, diongaltas, dionachas.

TIGHTENING, *s.* Teannachadh, gramachadh, sùmhlachadh, cneasnachadh.

TIGRESS, *s.* Tiogair bhoireann.

TIKE, *s.* Mial chon.

TILE, *s.* Leac shuaine, criadh-leac, teile. Tiles, *slinnteach.*

TILE, *v. a.* Leacaich, criadh-leacaich, tugh le leacaibh. A tiled house, *tigh leacaichte.*

TILER, *s.* Leacadair, criadh-leacadair, tughadair.

TILING, *s.* Leacachadh, tughadh; tughadaireachd.

TILL, *s.* Cobhan; taisgean, cisteag.

TILL, *prep.* Gu, gus, gu ruig. Till now, *gu so;* till then, *gu sin;* till a while ago, *gus a chianamh, gus o cheann ghrathuinn.*

TILL, *v. a.* Ar, treabh, crann, ruathar, ruadhar, dean treabhadh, dearg, saothraich, saothairich.

TILLABLE, *a.* So-threabh, a ghabhas ar (no) treabh.

TILLAGE, *s.* Treabhadh, ar, treabhachas, saoithreachadh, tuathanachas.

TILLER, *s.* Treabhaiche, airean, fear croinn, tuathanach.

TILMAN, *s.* Treabhaiche, fear croinn; airean, tuathanach.

TILT, *s.* Sleaghadaireachd; traochluiche; bùth, sgàilean; comhdach; (*of a vessel*), aomadh.

TILT, *v. n.* Rach an dàil, ruith an aghaidh; aom.

TILTER, *s.* Sleaghadair.

TILTH, *s.* Treabhadh, treabhachas, ar, tuathanachas.

TILTH, *a.* Treabhaidh, a ghabhas ar.

TIMBER, *s.* Fiodh; connadh; maide. Timber for a boat, *fiodhrach;* (for a ship), *reingean;* side timbers for a house, *baireinn.*

TIMBERED, *a.* Togta, dealbhta.

TIMBERSOW, *s.* Riodan, reudan.

TIMBREL, *s.* Tiompan, buabhall.

TIME, *s.* Uine, àm, aimsir, uair, tràth, tìm, tamul. For a time, *car ùine, re sealladh, re tamuil;* you came in good time, *thàinig thu ann deagh thràth;* it is high time to be gone, *is mithich a bhith falbh;* seasonable time, *àm iomchuidh;* I have no time, *cha 'n 'eil ùine agam, cha 'n 'eil mi air mo shocair;* how have you been this long time? *cia mar tha thu o cheann fada?* in due time, *ann an deagh thràth;* about that time, *mu 'n àm sin;* at this present time, *an tràths* (*an tràth so*) *an dràsd, an dràsdaich, air an uair;* at that time, *an sin, air an uair sin, aig an àm sin, san am sin;* from this time forth, *a so suas;* at what time, *c'uine;* in a little time, *ann ùine ghoirrid, ann an gradaig; a chlisgeadh; ach tamul beag;* in a year's time, *ann an ceann bliadhna;* of late, *a chianamh, o cheann ghoirrid;* one time more, *aon tarruing eile, aon uair eile;* in the day-time, *ann ùine an làtha;* times, *amanna;* in the times of old, *sna h-amanna cèin; an am o aois.*

TIME, *v.* Cum tìm.

TIMEFUL, *a.* Àmail; tràthail.

TIMELESS, *a.* Neo-àmail; neo-thìmeil.

TIMELINESS, *s.* Àmaileachd; tràthaileachd, deagh àm.

TIMELY, *a.* Àmail, ann an deagh thràth, ann an deagh àm.

TIMELY, *adv.* Gu h-àmail, gu tràthail; gu h-ullamh, ann an deagh àm, ann an deagh thràth.

TIME-PLEASER, *s.* Fear lùbach; cuilbheartair, ceabhachdair; fear leam leat.

TIMID, *a.* Eagallach, gealtach, cailleachanta, meath, meathchridheach, clisgeach; fiat; diùide.

TIMIDITY, *s.* Eagallachd, geallachd, geilte, sgàth, sgàthachd, cladhaireachd.

TIMOROUS, *a.* Eagallach, gealtach, sgàthach.

TIMOROUSLY, *adv.* Gu h-eagallach, gu gealtach, gu sgàthach.

TIMOROUSNESS, *s.* Gealtachd, eagall, sgàth.

TIN, *s.* Iarunn geal, staoin.

TINCAL, *s.* Seorsa méinn.

TINCT, *v. a.* Dath.

TINCTURE, *s.* Dath; lìth; tarruing, as-tharruing, boistcadh.

TINCTURE, *v. a.* Dath; tom, tum.

† TIND, *v. a.* Fàdaidh, las; cuir an gabhail; cuir ri theine.

TINDER, *s.* Fàdadh spuinge.

TINE, *s.* Fiacal cleith; forc; trioblaid, amhghar.

TINE, *v. a.* Fàdaidh, las, cuir an gabhail; cuir ri theine.

TINFOIL, *s.* Sgragall.

TING, *s.* Diong, diongail, gleang, gleangarsaich.

TINGE, *v. a.* Dath, lith; salaich.

TINGLE, *v.* Gleang, dean gleang, dean gleangarsaich. Like a tinkling cymbal, *mar thiombuail a ni gleangarsaich;* the pain tingled to my elbow, *chaidh gaoir gu ruig m' uileann.*

TINGLING, *s.* Gleangarsaich, tiong, diong, tiongail, diongail, gleangail; (*in the ear*), gaoir, glaoim.

TINK, *v.* Gleang, tiong, diong, gliog.

TINKER, *s.* Ceard. Tinkers, *ceairde.*

TINKLING, *a.* Gleangach, tiongach, diongach; gaoir, glaoim.

TINMAN, TINNER, *s.* Ceard iaruinn ghil, staoinear, staonair.

TINNY, *a.* Staoineach, staonach.

TINSEL, *s.* Soillsean; faoin-bhreaghas, faoineas.

TINSEL, *a.* Soillseach, faoin-bhriagh, drillinneach.

TINSEL, *v.* Soillsich, faoin-shoillsich, dean drillinneach.

TINT, *s.* Dath, lith, ligh.

TINWORM, *s.* Cnuimheag bheag dhearg.

TINY, *a.* Crion, crian, meanbh; meuranda, truagh.

TIP, *a.* Bàrr, fior bhàrr, mullach, binnean, bior, ceann. The tip of the nose, *bàrr na sròin;* a silver tip, *ceann airgid.*

TIP, *v. a.* Barraich; cuir barr no mullach air; bean ri, buail. A rock tipped with a wreath, *craig barraichte le cuitheamh.*

TIPPET, *s.* Eididh muineil; tubait.

TIPPLE, *v. n.* and *a.* Òl gu tric, bi trom (no) deigheil air an òl.

TIPPLE, *s.* Òl; deoch.

TIPPLED, *a.* Air an daoraich, air a mheisge.

TIPPLER, *s.* Misgear, pòitear, druaipear.

TIPPLING, *s.* Òl, meisge, druaip, meisge, pòite.

TIPSTAFF, *s.* Fear luirg, fear bachuil; lorg a chinn airgid.

TIPSY, *a.* Meisgeach, misgeach; air an daoraich, air a mheisge, air a mhisge.

TIPTOE, *s.* Bàrr ladhair, bàrr ordaig; corpag. He is on his tiptoes, *tha e air a chorpaguibh.*

TIRE, *s.* Sread, sreath, breath, rang; (*head-dress*), curachd, aodach cinn, fuiltean, failtean; (*furniture*), airneas; (*of a wheel*), roth cuidhle.

Tire, *v. a.* Sgìthich, sgìothaich, dean sgìth, fàs sgìth; fannaich, thoir thairis; (*clothe*), éid, eudaich, còmhdaich

Tired, *a.* Sgìth, sgìthichte, air toirt thairis. I am quite tired of it, *tha mi seachd sgìth dheth.*

Tiredness, *s* Sgìtheas, sgìothas.

Tiresome, *a.* Sgìth; draghalach, fadalach, mairnealach.

Tiresomeness, *s.* Sgìtheas; draghalachd, fadalachd, mairnealachd.

Tirewoman, *s.* Ban-fhuaidhealaich, *pron* banalaiche.

Tiring-house, *s.* Tigh éide.

Tir-wit, *s.* Seorsa eoin, dilit; adharcan luachair. 'Tis, *for* it is, *is e, 'se, is i, 's i; seadh; is ann*, 'tis so, *tha e mar sin;* 'tis to me you are obliged, *is ann domhsa tha thu 'n comain, is ann am chomain-se 'tha thu.*

Tissue, *s* Greus-obair, obair ghréis; grinneas, greus

Tissue, *v. a* Greus, grinnich. Tissued, *greusta*

Tit, *s* Each beag, gearran; té, seorsa eoin, ciochan

Titbit, *s*, *for* tidbit.

Tithe, *s.* Deicheamh, deachamh; càin chléir.

Tithe, *v. a.* and *n.* Deicheamhaich, deichmhich; leig deicheamh, cuir deicheamh. Tithed, *deicheamhaichte.*

Tither, *s.* Deicheamhaiche.

Tithing, *s.* Deicheamh, deichmheachadh.

Titillation, *s.* Giogal, gigeal.

Titillate, *v. a* Giogail, ciogail, giogall, ciogall

Titillation, *s.* Giogal, ciogal, giogailt.

Titlark, *s.* Gabhagan.

Title, *s.* Tiodal, buaidh, ainnm, feart; ceann-ghrabhadh; còir, dlighe. Title of honour, *buaidh-ainm*

Title, *v. a.* Ainmich, goir, tiodalaich

† **Titleless**, *a.* Gun ainm, gun bhuaidh, gun tiodal

Title-page, *s.* Clàr ainmeachaidh.

Titling, *s.* Gabhagan.

Titmouse, *s*. Ciochan, miondan, miontan

Titter, *v. a.* Dean sitir, sitrich

Titter, *s.* Fo-ghàire, snodh gaire, sitrich

Tittle, *s.* Pong, pung; iota; smad, dad, a bheag, a chuid is lugha. He will not part with a tittle of his right, *cha dhealaich e ri bheag do chòir.*

Tittle-Tattle, *s.* Goileam; lonais, bòilich, faoin-chomhradh.

Tittle-tattle, *v. a.* Dean goileam, dean bòilich (no) lonais

Titubate, *v.* Tuit; sleamhnuich; tuislich.

Titubation, *s.* Tuiteam, sleamhnachadh; tuisleachadh, tuisleadh

Titular, *a.* Tiodalach.

Titularity, *s.* Tiodalachd.

Titulary, *a.* Tiodalach.

Titulary, *s.* Fear aig am bheil tiodal; tiodalaiche.

Tivy, *adv.* Gu luath, gu h-ealamh, gu grad, ann an cabhaig, ann an ealamhachd.

To, *prep.* Do, dh' ionnsuidh; ri, ris; gu, gus; chum, thun; le. He went to the Indies, *chaidh e do na h-Innseachan*, he went to the man, *chaidh e dh' ionnsuidh 'n duine*, it was acceptable to me, thee, her, them, *thainig e, (no) thaitinn e, rium, riut, rithe, riu, bha e taitneach dhomh, dhuit, dh'i, dhoibh*, to the best of my power, *mar is fhearr a dh' fhaotas mi*, what kind of woman have you to wife? *ciod an seorsa té is bean dhuit?* I am resolved to go, *tha mi sonruichte air dol (no) falbh;* to-day, *an diugh*, to-morrow, *am màireach*, to-night, *an nochd;* to and fro, *h-uige agus uaith; null agus a nall, sios is suas, thall's a bhos*, to no purpose, *gu diomhain;* to this end, *chum na crìche so; thun a cheann so*, to wit, *is e sin ri radh;* to what end, *cuige, c' arson, cuime*, to be, *gu bhith, a bhith*, he is not worthy to be free, *cha 'n 'eil e àiridh (no) toilltinneach air bhith saor*, it is to be sold, *tha e gu bhith air a reic*, according to, *a réir*, to me, *dhomh, a m' ionnsuidh, ga m' ionnsuidh*, to thee, *dhuit, a d' ionnsuidh, gu d' ionnsuidh*, to him, *dha, ga ionnsuidh*, to her, *dh'i, ga h-ionnsuidh, da h-ionnsuidh;* to us, *dhuinn; g' ar n-ionnsuidh, d' ar n-ionnsuidh*, to you, *dhuibh, g' ur ionnsuidh, d' ur ionnsuidh*, to them, *dhoibh, g' an ionnsuidh*, set to, *cuir a ris.*

To, *sign of the infinitive*, A To strike, *a bhualadh*, to break, *a bhriseadh*, to fill, *a lionadh*

Toad, *s* Losgunn nimhe; losgunn, smàigean, màigean When the toad is staked it screams, *nur théid bior san losgunn ni e sgreach*

Toadstool, *s* Balg losguinn, boineid an losguinn; fàs na h-aon oidhche Great toadstool, *trioman*

Toadstone, *s* Clach, a their iad, a gheibhear ann an ceann, losguinn nimhe

Toast, *s* (*In drinking*), deoch slàinnte; (*at fire*), ròst, ròstadh, (*a female*), rìmhinn, àilneag, àilleag

Toast, *v.* Òl deoch slàinnte, slàinntich, (*at the fire*), ròist, cruadhaich, sgreag, caoinich

Tobacco, *s.* Tombac, tombac cagnaidh, tombac *seabh.*

Tobacconist, *s.* Fear reic tombac.

Tobacco-pipe, *s.* Piob tombac.

Tobacco-stopper, *s.* Spliùcan, spliùcan tombac

Tod, *s* Ochd puinnt fhichead olla

Toe, *s* Meur cois, ordag cois, ladhar

Toga, *s.* Gùn gun mhuilichean am measg nan sean Roimhneach; fearrasaid, earrasaid

Toged, *a* Gùnaichte

Together, *adv.* Le chéile, comhlath, comhluath, mar chomhluath, ri chéile, cuideachd, maraon, gu léir They went both of them together, *dh' imich iad cuideachd le chéile*, gather together, *tionail ri chéile*, they consulted together, *chuir iad an cinn ri chéile*, when shall we be together, *c'uine a bhitheas sinn cuideachd (no) cuid ri chéile;* together with, *maille ri, mar ri, cuid ri*

Toil, *v n* and *a* Saothraich, saoithrich, oibrich; gabh saothair; sgìthich, fannaich.

Toil, *s.* (*Labour*), saothair, obair ghoirt, obair, sàruchadh, (*snare*), ribe, ribeadh; gais

Toilsome, *a* Saoithreachail, goirt; sgìth. Toilsome work, *obair ghoirt*

Toilsomeness, *s.* Saoithreachas, sgìtheas

Token, *s.* Comhar, comharadh; gibhte, tabhartas. A love token, *seadh suiridh.*

Told, *pret* and *p part* of tell. Dh' innis, thubhairt, dh 'aithris; chunnt; air innseadh; aithriste, air a chunntadh As I told you, *mar dh' innis mi dhuit, mar a thubhairt mi riut;* a thing that may be told, *ni a dh' fhaotar innseadh*, easy to be told, *furas innseadh, so-innseadh; so-chunntadh*, not to be told, *nach fhaodai (no) nach gabh innseadh (no) cunntadh, do-innseadh, do-chunntadh, do-labhairt, do-chur an céill*

Toledo, *s* Baile Spàinnteach sònruichte airson chloidhean

Toledo, *s.* Claidheamh do 'n seorsa is fhearr, claidheamh Spàinnteach.

Tolerable, *a* (*That may be borne*), so-fhulang, ion-fhulang, a dh' fhaotar fhulang, a ghabhas fulang, ceaduichte, (*indifferent*), meadhonach, an eatorras; an iarruidh, mar sin is mar sin, mar sin fhéin, mu 'n laimh.

Tolerably, *adv.* An eatorras; an iarruidh; gu meadhonach, mar sin is mar sin, mar sin fhéin. Tolerably well, *an iarruidh ghleusda, an iarruidh mhath*, tolerably pretty, *an iarruidh bhòidheach*

TOLERANCE, *s.* Fulangas, foighidinn, faighidinn

TOLERATE, *v a* Fulaing, fuilig, leig le, giùlain le, ceadaich, ludhaig, luathaich Tolerated, *fulaingte, ceadaichte*

TOLERATION, *s.* Fulang, ceadachadh, cead, comas.

TOLL, *s.* Càin, cìs; gearradh.

TOLL, *v n* Buail (no) seinn clag.

TOLL-BOOTH, *s* Toll-bùth, carcar, gainntir, priosun

TOLL-BOOTH, *v a* Priosunaich, gainntirich, cuir am priosun.

TOLL-GATHERER, *s* Cìsear, cìseadair.

TOLUTATION, *s* Fàlaireachd

TOMB, *s.* Uaigh, uamh, tuam, torr, aite adhlaic, rath adhlacaidh, cladach

TOMBLESS, *a.* Gun uaigh; neo-thorrta, neo-adhlaicte

TOMBOY, *s* Caile bhalach.

TOM-CAT, *s* Moth-chat, cat firionn.

TOME, *s* Ròl, ill-eabhar, mac-leabhar.

TOMTIT, *s* Gabhagan

TON, *s* Tunna Tons, *tunnaichean*

TON, *s* Nòs, fasan, cleachd, àbhaist. Haut ton, *airde an fhasain*

TONE, *s* Fonn, guth; gleus; caoin A sorrowful tone, *ciùrlan, ciùrachdan, acain*

TONG, *s* Crambaid, teanga

TONGS, *s.* Clobh, clodh, clobhachan, gramaiche, maide briste

TONGUE, *s* Teanga, teangadh, (*language*), cainnt, cànain, cànmhuinn Her tongue runs before her wit, *is luaithe a teanga na 'ciall*, hold your tongue, *cum do theanga, bi sàmhach, bi tosd*, a tongue of land, *rugha, sròin*, he who holds his tongue will hold his friend, *am fear a chumas a theangadh cumaidh e 'charaid*

TONGUE, *v a* and *n* Troid, tachair ri

TONGUED, *a* Teangach teangaidheach Double tongued, *dùbailt, fallsa, cealgach, breugach*, smooth-tongued, *miodalach, goileamach, beulchar, tlà*.

TONGUELESS, *a* Gun teanga, balbh

TONGUEPAD, *s* Gobair, gabair, clabair, glagair

TONGUETIED, *a* Manntach, gagach, glugach, liotach

TONIC, *a* Gleusach

TONNAGE, *s* Luchd no (lòd) luing, tunn-chìs

TONSIL, *s.* Glugan.

TONSOR, *s* Bearradair, fear bearraidh, barbair

TONSURE, *s* Bearradh, lomadh, lomairt, luime

TOO, *adv* Cuideachd, fòs, mar an ceudna; thuille na còrach, tuille is, tuille is a chòir, mù 's. And I too, *agus mise cuideachd*, too full, *tuille is làn, mù 's làn*, too much, *tuille 's a chòir.*

TOOK, *pret* of take Ghabh See TAKE

TOOL, *s* Inneal, ball, ball acfhuinn, innsrimaid, tailm, cungaidh A graving tool, *sgrìobair;* a tool, or convenient person, *feumannach*

TOOT, *v n* Rannsuich, gabh geur-bheachd

TOOTH, *s* Fiacail, fiacal. The fore tooth of a horse, *biorag*, gag-tooth, *criochdair*, tooth and nail, *le uile neart*, to the teeth, *as an aghaidh*, in spite of your teeth, *ge b' oil le d' fhiaclan e*, shew the teeth, *bagair*, wisdom tooth, *fiacal forais*, the tongue may cast a knot which the teeth cannot untie, *cuiridh an teangadh snaim nach fuasgail an fhiacal*

TOOTH, *v n* Fiaclaich; gròbaich. Toothed, *fiaclaichte, fiacluch, gròbach.*

TOOTHACH, *s.* Cnaimh fhiacail, cnuimh, déide, deud-ith

TOOTHLESS, *a* Gun fhiacal, cabach.

TOOTHPICK, *s.* Bior fhiacal, dealgan fhiacal.

TOOTHSOME, *a* Blasda, deagh-bhlasda, milis.

TOOTHSOMENESS, *s.* Blasdachd.

TOP, *s* Mullach, bàrr, binnean, uachdar, druim, bràighe; roinn, top; (*a boy's toy*), piridh, dòtaman. The top of the hill, *mullach (no) druim a mhonaidh*, from top to bottom, *o mhullach gu bonn, o mhullach gu bun;* the very top, *fìor mhullach.*

TOP, *v. a* Barraich; thoir barrachd, bearraich. Top the candle, *smàl a choinneal*

TOPARCH, *s.* Prionnsa beag, uachdaran.

TOPAZ, *s* Cloch bhuidhe phriseil

TOPE, *v n.* Òl, òil, pòit, bi trom air an òl.

TOPER, *s* Pòitear, meisgear, misgear, druaipear.

TOP-FULL, *a* Iom-làn, lom làn, dearr làn

TOP-GALLANT, *s.* Seòl mullaich

TOPHEAVY, *a* Ceann-throm

TOPHET, *s.* Ifrinn.

TOPIC, *s* Cùis; steidh, ceann còmhraidh.

TOPICAL, *a* Ionadach

TOP-KNOT, *s* Bad mullaich, dos-cinn, barr-dhos.

TOPLESS, *a.* Gun bhàrr, gun mhullach.

TOPMOST, *a* Uachdaraiche, is àirde

TOPPING, *a* (*A low word*), uallach; grinn.

TOPPLE, *v n* Tuit, tuislich

TOP-PROUD, *a.* Uaibhreach, sgòdail.

TOPSAIL, *s.* Seòl mullaich, seòl uachdrach

TOPSTONE, *s.* Clach mhullaich.

TOPSY-TURVY, *s* Bun os cionn, thar cheann

† TOR, *s* Torr, tùr

TORCH, *s* Leus, dreos, lòchran, soillsean, blincean, trillsean.

TORCHBEARER, *s* Leusair, leusadair, dreòsair

TORCHER, *s* Leusair, leusadair, dreòsair.

TORCH-LIGHT, *s* Solus leòis.

TORE, *pret* of tear. Shrac, reub.

TORMENT, *v a.* Craidh pian, claoidh, sàruich. Tormented, *craidhte, pianta, claoidhte, sàruichte.*

TORMENT, *s* Cradh, pian, pianadh, claoidh, claoidheadh; amhghar, dòghruinn; peilghuin.

TORMENTER, TORMENTOR, *s.* Claoidhear, ceusadair, fear sàruchaidh.

TORMENTIL, *s.* Leanartach, bàrr braonan nan con.

TORN, *p part* of tear Sracta, reubta.

TORNADO, *s* Srann-ghaoth, iom-ghaoth.

TORPEDO, *s.* Craimpiasg, orc-iasg

TORPENT, *a* Marbh, marbh-lapach, funtuinneach.

TORPID, *a.* Marbh, marbh-lapach, neo-mhothuchail, gun chil, gun chàil

TORPIDNESS, TORPITUDE, *s* Mairbhe, funntuinn, marbhlapachd.

TORPOR, *s.* Marbh-lapadh

TORREFACTION, *s.* Cruadhachadh, tiormachadh, sgreagachadh

TORREFY, *v.* Tiormaich, cruaidh-thiormaich, sgreagaich. Torrefied, *tiormaichte, sgreagaichte*

TORRENT, *s* Buinne-shruth, bras-shruth, maoim sleibhe, beum sleibhe

TORRID, *a* Teth, bruich, tioram, dearg-theth, teth dearg.

TORSEL, *s.* Sniomhan, toinntean

TORSION, *s* Sniomhadh, toinneamh.

TORTILE, *a* Sniomhanach, sniomhte, toinnte.

Tortoise, *s.* Sligeanach.

Tortuous, *a.* Sniomhach, sniomhanach, toinneamhach, cuairteanach, lùbach.

Torture, *s.* (*Extreme pain*), cradh, pian, craon, claoidh; (*wheel*), rag-roth, cuidhle, cràidh; (*distress*), amhghar, doghruinn.

Torture, *v. a.* Craidh, pian, claoidh, ceus, cuir gu cradh, gallruich; cuir gu pian; cuir air an rag-roth.

Torturer, *s.* Pianadair, claoidhear, fear claoidh, fear sàruchaidh.

Tory, *s.* Fear a chumas taobh ris an Eaglais Shasunnach; Eireannach fiadhaich; roisg-mhéirleach.

Tose, *v. n.* Cìr (no) spion olainn.

Toss, *v. a.* Luaisg, gluais, tilg, tilg sios agus suas, tilg null is a nall; siùdain, seòganaich; crath; buair.

Toss, *s.* Tilge, tilgeadh; luasgadh; urchair.

Tossed, *part.* Luaisgte, gluaiste, tilgte. Tossed by the waves, *tonn-luaisgte.*

Tossing, *s.* Luasgadh, gluasad, siùdanachd, siùdanaich; seòganaich. Tossing or floundering in water, *luinneanaich*, plubraich.

Toss-pot, *s.* Meisgear, misgear.

Tost, *pret.* and *p. part.* of toss. Luaisg; luaisgte.

Total, *a.* Iomlan, uile; làn, slàn. The sum total, *an t-iomlan.*

Totally, *adv.* Gu h-iomlain, gu h-uile, gu léir, gu tur.

Totality, *s.* Iomlanachd.

Totter, *v. n.* Crithich, crith, turamanaich, bi thun tuiteam. The tree totters, *tha 'chraobh san turamanaich.*

Tottering, *a.* Critheach, turamanach, air chrith, gluganach, seòganach, sleamhuinn.

Touch, *s.* (*Touching*), beanachd, beantuinn; buntuinn; (*the feel*), mothach; mothachadh, faineach; (*of a disease*), car; (*essay*), feuchainn, deuchainn; car; speal, greadan; (*feature*), suaip; (*stroke*), buille; (*hint*), sànas; (*taste*), blas; (*of conscience*), agartas coguis; cronachadh coguis; (*a small quantity*), deannan, beagan, cailigin, beag nithe, rud eigin; (*of the hand on a musical instrument*), làmhachadh, laimhseachadh. Have a touch at it, *thoir deuchainn da, thoir car air, thoir speal* (*no*) *greadan air;* the beer has a touch of acid, *tha car goirt aig an leann;* I have a touch of your condition that cannot bear the accent of reproof, *tha rud eigin do d' uaillse annam fhéin, nach fhuilig an guth a chronaicheas mi.*

Touch, *v. a.* and *n.* Bean do, buin do, buin ri, cuir meur air, cuir corag air, lamhaich, laimhsich; (*affect*), drùigh air. Touch me not, *na bean domh, na bean rium;* as far as touches me, *air mo shonsa dheth;* this affair touches you, *buinidh an gnothuch so dhuitse;* he is touched or deranged, *tha e gòrach* (*no*) *thar a chéill;* touched with liquor, *air an daoraich;* we touched at that place, *chaidh sinn air tìr aig an àite sin;* touch up or repair, *càirich, leasaich;* I will touch or affect him, *drùighidh mi air.*

Touchable, *a.* A ghabhas beanachd ri.

Touch-hole, *s.* Toll cluais, toll cluaisein.

Touchiness, *s.* Foithearachd, cainnteachas, crosdachd, aith-ghearrachd,

Touching, *a.* Drùighteach; muladach.

Touching, *prep.* Mu, mu thimchioll, a thaobh, mu dhéimhinn.

Touchingly, *adv.* Gu drùighteach; gu mothachail.

Touch-stone, *s.* Dearbh-chlach, dearbhag; doigh-leug; doilig, dearbhadh, deuchainn. Now do I play the touchstone, *is ann a nis a tha mi'g ad chur gu deuchainn* (*no*) *gu dearbhadh.*

Touchwood, *s.* Caisleach spuing.

Touchy, *a.* Cainnteach, crosda, aith-ghearr, fritheanach, cas, cabhagach.

Tough, *a.* Rithinn, righinn; buan, rag; (*viscid*), sticeach, leanailteach; (*hard*), cruaidh; (*difficult*), duilich, deacair.

Toughen, *v. a.* and *n.* Rithnich; dean rithinn, fàs rithinn.

Toughness, *s.* Rithneachd, rithnead, righneachd, righnead; (*hardness*), cruathas.

Toupet, *s.* Ciabh, ciabhag, dual, bachlag.

Tour, *s.* Cuairt, tùrus. On a tour, *air chuairt;* the tour of the continent, *cuairt na mòr-thìr.*

Tournament, *s.* Faoin-chomhrag, spleadh-chomhrag; ionnsuidh; traochluiche, sleaghadaireachd.

Tourniquet, *s.* Inneal a chosgadh fola.

Touse, *v. a.* Slaoid, tarruing; reub.

Tow, *s.* Pab; ciob, barrach, asgart; (*rope*), taod, tobha. The cardings of tow, *beard, beardan.*

Tow, *v. a.* Slaoid, tarruing, tobh.

Toward, Towards, *prep.* and *adv.* Do, chum, thun, dh' ionnsuidh; a thaobh; mu thimchioll, fagus do, fogus air; an car, an caraibh. Towards the top, *fogus do 'n mhullach* (*no*) *do 'n bhàrr;* look towards me, *amhairc am char-sa* (*no*) *am rathad-sa;* love towards you, *gradh dhuit* (*no*) *do d' thaobh;* towards the end, *fagus do 'n chrioch;* towards the right hand, *chum na laimh deise.*

Toward, Towardly, *a.* So-theagasg, so-fhoghlum; so-ionnsuchaidh; aontachail.

Towardness, *s.* Ealamhachd chum teagaisg.

Towel, *s.* Searadair, tubhailt, lamh-anart.

Tower, *s.* Tùr, tor, dùn, turait; caisteal; baideal; daighneach.

Tower, *v. n.* Itealaich gu h-ard.

Towered, Towery, *a.* Tùrach, turaiteach; baidealach; sgiamhaichte.

Towering, *a.* Ard; tùrach; baidealach; binneanach; spiriceach. A towering spirit, *inntinn ard.*

Town, *s.* Cathair, baile, baile mòr; †brugh, †taim, †poit. From town to town, *o bhaile gu baile;* towns, *bailtean;* a chief town or metropolis, *ard-chathair, ard-bheirbhe;* *baile mòr.*

Town-clerk, *s.* Cléireach sgriobhaidh baile.

Town-house, *s.* Tigh mòr baile, tigh mòid.

Townsman, *s.* Comh-bhailiche. Towns-people, *muinntir baile.*

Township, *s.* Buidheann baile.

Town-talk, *s.* Comhradh 'n t-sluaigh.

Toxica, *s.* Nimhe Innseanach; seorsa nimhe anns an cleachd do na Innseanaich an saighdean a thumadh.

Toxical, *a.* Nimheach, nimheil, puinnsionta.

Toy, *s.* Ailleagan, deideag; rud laoghach; faoin-dhòchas.

Toy, *v. n.* Cluich; mir; dean mire. Toying with, *a cluicheadh ri, a mireadh ri.*

Toying, *s.* Cluiche, cluithe, cluicheag, mire.

Toyish, *a.* Mear; faoin.

Toyishness, *s.* Mire.

† **Toze**. See **Touse**.

Trace, *s.* (*Mark*), lorg, aile, comhar; sgriob; sliochd; (*harness*), acfhuinn, beart.

Trace, *v. a.* Lorgaich; rach an tòir; comharraich a mach, linich. Traced, *lorgaichte.*

Tracer, *s.* Lorgair.

Track, *s.* Lorg, aile, comhar; slaodan; rod, rathad.

Trackless, *a.* Do-shiùbhladh, nach gabh coiseachd.

Tract, *s.* Àirde; ceann; dùthaich; cùrsa; tràchd.

TRACTABLE, *a.* Soitheamh, soimeach; so-theagasg, aont-achail, ciùin, socrach, oidheamach

TRACTABLENESS, *s.* Soimeachas, ciùineas; socair.

TRACTABLY, *adv.* Gu soitheamh, gu soimeach, gu ciùin, gu socrach

TRACTILE, *a.* A ghabhas bualadh mach, a ghabhas fa-duchadh

TRACTION, *s.* Tarruing, slaodadh.

TRADE, *s.* Ceaird; ealadhain; (*commerce*), co-cheannachd, co-chaidreamh, malairt, muinntireas; (*custom or way of life*), cleachd, gnàth; àbhaist Let every one follow his own trade, *leanadh gach fear a cheaird fhéin*, he has turned to his old trade, *tha e air pilltinn gu sheann àbhaist-ean*

TRADE, *v.* Dean co-cheannachd; malairtich

TRADED, *a.* Eòlach, cleachdta

TRADER, *s.* Fear malairt, marsonta

TRADESFOLK, *s.* Luchd ceirde.

TRADESMAN, *s.* Fear ceirde, fear ealadhain

TRADITION, *s.* Aithris, beul-aithris, iomradh, beuladas, beul-oideas, seann sgeul, fionn-sgeul.

TRADITIONAL, *a.* Aithriseach, beul-aithriseach

TRADITIONALLY, *adv.* A réir beul-aithris

TRADITIONARY, TRADITIVE, *a.* Aithriseach, beul-aithris-each

TRADUCE, *v. a.* Cronaich, càin, cul-chàin, dean tàir (no) tarcuis, achmhas sanaich. He traduced me, *chàin e mi, rinn e tàir orm*

TRADUCEMENT, *s.* Cronachadh, càineadh, cùl-chaineadh, tàir, toibheum, tarcuis

TRADUCER, *s.* Fear càinidh, fear cul-chàinidh Traducers, *luchd càinidh, luchd tàir.*

TRADUCTION, *s.* Càineadh, cul-chàineadh, tàir, tarcuis, toibheum

TRAFFIC, *s.* Ceannachd, ceannachadh, malairt.

TRAFFIC, *v.* Malairtich, ceannaich, comh-cheannaich

TRAFFICKER, *s.* Fear malairt, ceannaiche Traffickers, luchd malairt; ceannaichean.

TRAGACANTH, *s.* Seorsa plannt

TRAGEDIAN, *s.* Tràighiche; slaonasair, bròn-bhard.

TRAGEDY, *s.* Slaonasadh, traighidheachd; bròn-chluiche; dealbh-chluiche bròin

TRAGIC, TRAGICAL, *a.* Brònach, muladach.

TRAGICALLY, *adv.* Gu brònach, gu muladach

TRAGI-COMEDY, *s.* Cluiche sam faicear aobhar bròin is aoibhneis.

TRAIL, *v. a.* Slaoid, tarruing; lorgaich

TRAIL, *s.* Lorg; sguain, slaod

TRAIN, *v. a.* (*Entice*), tarruing; taiteadh, thoir a thaobh; meall, (*rear*), tog, àraich; (*teach*), oid, teagaisg, ionn-suich, oileanaich, (*enure*), cleachd, dean ri.

TRAIN, *s.* (*Artifice*), mealladh; (*retinue*), cuideachd, buidh-eann, (*of a gown*), earbull, ean, sguain, sgiort, iomall, (*a train or order of things*), ordugh, cùrsa; (*train of ar-tillery*), gunnraidh

TRAIN-BANDS, *s.* Dion-fheachd

TRAIN-BEARER, *s* Sguaimear, sguainiche

TRAINED, *a.* Ionnsuichte, àraichte, oileanaichte, cleachdta; deanta

TRAIN-OIL, *s.* Uille muc-mhara

TRAIPSE, *v. n.* Stràille, draip

TRAIT, *s.* Buille; beanachd; tuar, suaip.

TRAITOR, *s.* Fear brathaidh, brathadair, traoightear, arra-bhalaoch, arra-dhuine.

TRAITOROUS, *a.* Brathach; cealgach, fealltach, traoidhteil.

TRAITOROUSLY, *adv.* Gu cealgach, gu fealltach, gu traoidhteil.

TRAITRESS, *s.* Ban-bhrathadair, ban-traoidhtear

TRAJECT, *v. a.* Tilg troimh, troimh-thilg.

TRAJECT, *s.* Aiseag.

TRAJECTION, *s.* Tilgeadh troimh.

TRAMMEL, *s.* Lion; geise, ribe, riob; grab; cuibhreach

TRAMMEL, *v. a.* Glac, cuir an sàs, rib; grab, stad.

TRAMPLE, *v. a.* Saltair, stramp Trampled, *saltairte.*

TRAMPLER, *s.* Strampair, fear a shaltaireas (no) strampas le chosaibh

TRAMPLING, *s.* Saltairt; strampail, leumnaich. Trampling of cloth in a tub, *postadh.*

TRANATION, *s.* Snàmhadh thairis.

TRANCE, TRANSE, *s* Neul, platha, paisean He fell into a trance, *thuit e ann am platha, chaidh e na phaisean.*

TRANCED, *a* Ann an neul, ann am platha, ann am paisean.

TRANGRAM, *s.* Neònachas, rud neònach

TRANNEL, *s* Pinne geur.

TRANQUIL, *a* Sàmhach, siochail, ciùin, féitheil, seimh, tosdach, tosd.

TRANQUILLITY, *s* Samhchair, siothchath, siothchainnt, ciùineas, féith, féithealachd, seimhe.

TRANSACT, *v. a.* Dean gnothuch; cuir air adhairt (no) gu doigh.

TRANSACTION, *s* Gnothuch, gniomh, cùis, ni, tùrn.

TRANSCEND, *v. a* Rach thairis, thoir barrachd.

TRANSCENDENCE, TRANSCENDENCY, *s* Barrachd, barrach-as, barr-mhaise.

TRANSCENDENT, *a.* Barrachdail, bàrrail, bàrr-mhaiseach.

TRANSCOLATE, *v. a.* Sìolaidh. Transcolated, *siolaidhte.*

TRANSCOLATION, *s.* Sìoladh.

TRANSCRIBE, *v. a.* Ath-sgriobh Transcribed, *ath-sgriobhta.*

TRANSCRIBER, *s.* Ath-sgriobhair.

TRANSCRIPT, *s.* Ath-sgriobhadh; mac-sgriobhadh.

TRANSCRIPTION, *s* Ath-sgriobhadh

TRANSCUR, *v. n.* Ruith sios is suas.

TRANSCURSION, *s.* Ruithe sios is suas; seabhaid

TRANSE See TRANCE.

TRANSFER, *v. a.* Thoir thairis; dean suas; reic

TRANSFER, *s* Malairt, toirt thairis, buileachadh.

TRANSFERABLE, *a* So-thoirt thairis, so-bhuileachadh.

TRANSFERENCE, *s* Toirt thairis, tabhairt thairis

TRANSFIGURATION, *s* Cruth-chaochladh, cruth-atharrach-adh

TRANSFIGURE, *v. a* Cruth-atharruich Transfigured, *cruth-atharruichte.*

TRANSFIX, *v. a.* Sàth, lot, troimh-lot; toll troimh.

TRANSFORM, *v.* Cruth-atharruich, caochail cruth (no) dealbh, mùth

TRANSFORMATION, *s.* Cruth-atharruchadh, cruth-chaoch-ladh, caochladh cruth, snàs-mhùthadh, atharruchadh, caochladh

TRANSFUSE, *v.* Dòirt (no) taomaich o shoitheach gu soith-each, tar-dhòirt, tar-thaomaich, coimeasg, measg.

TRANSFUSION, *s.* Dòrtadh, taomachadh, tar-dhòrtadh, tar-thaomachadh, coimeasgadh

TRANSGRESS, *v. a* and *n.* Rach thairis, bris, peacaich, cionntaich.

TRANSGRESSION, *s* Coire, cionnt, peacadh, eusontas

TRANSGRESSIVE, *a.* Coireach, cionntach, eusontach.

TRANSGRESSOR, *s* Cionntach, peacach, peacair.

TRANSIENT, *a.* Siùbhlach, diombuan, grad-shiùbhlach, gearr, neo-mhaireann, caochlaideach.

TRANSIENTLY, *adv.* Gu siùbhlach, gu diombuan, gu grad-shiùbhlach, gu gearr, gu neo-mhaireann.

TRANSIENTNESS, *s.* Siubhlachd, diombuainead, diombuanas.

TRANSILIENCE, TRANSILIENCY, *s.* Leumardaich o ni gu ni; luaineachas.

TRANSIT, *s.* Imeachd reult sam bi eadar an talamh is rionnag; eadar-dhol, seach-imeachd. The transit of Venus, *eadar-dhol Bhénuis;* the transit of Mercury, *eadar-dhol Mhercuir.*

TRANSITION, *s.* Siùbhladh, imeachd, grad-imeachd, caochladh, mùth, atharrachadh.

TRANSITORILY, *adv.* Gu siùbhlach, gu diombuan, gu caochlaideach.

TRANSITORINESS, *s.* Siùbhlachd, diombuanas.

TRANSITORY, *a.* Siùbhlach, diombuan, grad-shiùbhlach, caochlaideach, neo-mhaireann, gearr-shaoghlach.

TRANSLATE, *v. a.* Eadar-theangaich; cuir ann am mùth cainnt, cuir gu aite eile, atharruich.

TRANSLATION, *s.* Eadar-theangachadh; aisdridh; atharruchadh easbuig.

TRANSLATOR, *s.* Eadar-theangair.

TRANSLOCATION, *s.* Atharruchadh; mùthadh.

TRANSLUCENCY, *s.* Trid-shoillseachd.

TRANSLUCID, *s.* Trid-shoilleir, glan.

TRANSMARINE, *a.* Allmharach; eil-thìreach; thall thar muir.

TRANSMIGRANT, *a.* Tùrusach, taisdealach, siùbhlach, seabhaideach.

TRANSMIGRATE, *v. a.* Rach air imrich an céin.

TRANSMIGRATION, *s.* Cian-imrich; sior-imrich.

TRANSMISSION, *s.* Cur, cur o àite gu h-àite.

TRANSMISSIVE, *a.* Air a chur sios.

TRANSMIT, *v. a.* Cuir thairis, thoir thairis, thoir suas, liobhair; cuir o àite gu h-àite.

TRANSMITTAL, *s.* Cur, cur o àite gu h-àite.

TRANSMUTABLE, *a.* Mùthteach, mùiteach, a ghabhas mùth (no) atharruchadh, tur-mhùiteach.

TRANSMUTATION, *s.* Tur-mhùth, tar-mhùth; tur-chaochladh.

TRANSMUTE, *v.* Tur-mhùth, tur-chaochail; mùth, caochail.

TRANSOM, *s.* Tarsuinnean, tarsnan.

TRANSPARENCY, *s.* Trid-shoillse, glaine, soilleireachd.

TRANSPARENT, *a.* Trid-shoilleir, soilleir, glan, lannaireach; tar-shoillseach, lomhar.

TRANSPICUOUS, *a.* Trid-shoilleir; a ghabhas faicinn troimh.

TRANSPIERCE, *v. a.* Troimh-shàth, troimh-lot, toll.

TRANSPIRATION, *s.* Cur smùid; cur follais; dol an ceò.

TRANSPIRE, *v. a.* and *n.* Rach an smùid; rach an ceò; bris a mach. The business transpired among the people, *bhris an gnothuch mach am measg an t-sluaigh.*

TRANSPLACE, *v. a.* Atharruich, cuir as àite, cuir dh' àite eile.

TRANSPLANT, *v. a.* Atharruich, cuir as àite.

TRANSPLANTATION, *s.* Atharruchadh, cur a àite.

TRANSPORT, *v. a.* Atharruich, thoir o àite gu h-àite, fògair, cuir air fògradh; cuir air chuthach, cuir air mhire. Transported with anger, *air a bhuair, air a bhreathas.*

TRANSPORT, *s.* (*Vessel*), long aisig; (*carriage*), giùlan, iomchar, caraiste; (*of passion*), boile; breathas, buaireadh; (*joy*), aoibhneas, eibhneas; (*exile*), fograiche.

TRANSPORTATION, *s.* Fògradh, cur air fògairt; atharrachadh.

TRANSPORTER, *s.* Fògarair, fògairtear.

TRANSPOSAL, *s.* Atharruchadh, cur a àite.

TRANSPOSE, *v. a.* Atharruich, cuir a àite.

TRANSPOSITION, *s.* Atharruchadh, comh-atharruchadh.

TRANSUBSTANTIATE, *v. a.* Cuir gu mùth deilbh, brigh-atharruich.

TRANSUBSTANTIATION, *s.* Brìgh-atharrachadh.

TRANSUDATION, *s.* Dol an ceò, cur smùid, fallas, follas.

TRANSUDE, *v. n.* Rach am fallas, rach an ceò.

TRANSUMPTION, *s.* Atharruchadh, toirt o àite gu h-àite.

TRANSVECTION, *s.* Aiseag, aiseagadh, giùlan thairis, toirt thairis.

TRANSVERSAL, *a.* Crosgach, tarsuing.

TRANSVERSE, *v. a.* Mùth; cuir air mhùth doigh, atharruich.

TRANSVERSE, *a.* Crosgach, tarsuing.

TRANSVERSELY, *adv.* Crosgach, tarsuing.

TRAP, *s.* Ribe, riob, inneal glacaidh, geise, dul, goisinn, painntear, trap; plaid-luidhe; seorsa cluiche.

TRAP, *v. a.* Rib, glac; cuir an sàs; (*dress*), sgiamhaich; uigheamaich. Trapped, *ribte, glacta, uigheamaichte.*

TRAP-DOOR, *s.* Dorus diomhair.

TRAPPERY, *s.* Uigheam; riomhadh; briaghas, breaghas.

TRAPSTICK, *s.* Seorsa camain.

TRASH, *s.* Ni gun fhiù; trealaich, treallais, prabar, trusdaireachd, mosan.

TRASH, *v. a.* Bearr, gearr, sgath.

TRASHY, *a.* Suarach, diblidh, gun fhiach, gun fhiù.

TRAUMATIC, *a.* Leòntach.

TRAVAIL, *v. n.* and *a.* Bi ri saothair chloinne, bi an luidhe siùbhladh (no) siùl; sàruich, claoidh, pian, sgithich.

TRAVAIL, *s.* Saothair, éigin; saothair cloinne, tinneas cloinne, luidhe siùbhladh; (*in ridicule*), coiliginn adhairceach.

TRAVEL, *v. n.* Dean tùrus, rach air thùrus, triall, siubhail. Travel on foot, *coisich.*

TRAVEL, *s.* Tùrus, taisdeal, siubhal, astar, cuairt.

TRAVELLER, *s.* Fear tùruis, fear astair, fear siubhail, coisiche, tùrusaiche, tùrusan, taisdealaiche, triallan, triallair, fear gabhail an rathaid.

TRAVELLING, *s.* Siubhal, coiseachd, taisdeal, tùrus, imeachd.

TRAVELLING, *a.* Siùbhlach, taisdealach, tùrusach.

TRAVEL-TAINTED, *a.* Sgìth, air toirt thairis, fannaichte.

TRAVERSE, *adv.* Crosgach, tarsuing.

TRAVERSE, *s.* Bac, moille, grabadh; ni na 'luidhe crosgach (no) tarsuing.

TRAVERSE, *v. a.* Siubhail, triall; coisich, imich; cuir moille, grab, bac; cuir crosgach, leig tarsuing.

TRAVERSE, *s.* (*At sea*), car-sheòladh.

TRAVERSING, *s.* Siubladh, trialladh, coiseachd; spaisdearachd, spaidsearachd.

TRAVESTY, *a.* Neònach; baoth, aighearrach.

TRAY, *s.* Sgàl.

TREACHEROUS, *a.* Cealgach, fealltach, fallsa, mealltach, traoighteil; brathach, cuilbheartach, carach. A treacherous fellow, *cealgair, traoightear, fear brathaidh, arra-bhalaoch.*

TREACHEROUSLY, *adv.* Gu cealgach, gu fealltach, gu fallsa, gu mealltach, gu traoidhteil, gu foilleil.

TREACHEROUSNESS, *s.* Ceilge, cealgaireachd, mealltaireachd, foille, traoidhtearachd.

TREACHERY, *s.* Ceilge, traoidhte, traoidhtearachd, brathadh, tangnadh.

TREACLE, *s.* Drabhag siucair, tréigeal.

TREAD, *v. n.* and *a.* Stramp; ceum, ceumnaich, saltair; (*as a male bird*), cliath.

TREAD, *s.* Ceum; slighe, rod, rathad, aisridh; lorg.

TREADLE, s. Crann coise; cliath. Treadles, croinn chas.

TREASON, s. Foill an aghaidh an rìgh, ceannairc, ar a mach, traoidhtearachd. Petit treason, meanbh-thraoidhte.

TREASONABLE, a. Foilleil, feulltach, traoidhteil.

TREASURE, s. Ionmhas, maoin, stòr, stòras, beartas, saibhreas.

TREASURE, v. a. Taisg, cuir seachad, cnuasaich, carn, crumnich.

TREASURE-HOUSE, s. Tigh stòir (no) stòrais, tigh tasgaidh.

TREASURER, s. Ionmhasair, fear coimhead, ionmhais, oirchistear. Lord treasurer, ard-ionmhasair fleasgan.

TREASURESHIP, s. Ionmhasachd.

TREASURING, s. Carnadh, teanaladh, cnuasachadh.

TREASURY, s. Ionmhas, òir-chiste; taisgeach, tigh ionmhais, aite an ionmhais, aite coimhead ionmhais, saidh. Treasury board, bord ionmhais.

TREAT, v. Socraich, cuir gu doigh, gnàthaich; cùmhnantaich, gabh ri, thoir cuirin, trachd. He was ill-treated, chaidh a dhroch càramh, you treat me like a friend, tha thu 'gabhail rium mar charaid.

TREAT, s. Fleagh, féisd, cuirm, bancait.

TREATABLE, a. Measarra, cuidhseach.

TREATISE, s. Tràchd, tràchdadh; leabhar, seanachas.

TREATMENT, s. Càramh; gnàthachadh, uidhisinn. Good treatment, deagh chàramh.

TREATY, s. Bann, cumhnant; cordadh.

TREBLE, a. Trì fillte, (in sound), binn, cruaidh, sgalanta, sgreadach, caol.

TREBLE, v. a. Dean tri-fillte. Trebled, tri-fillte.

TREBLENESS, s. Tri-fhillteachd.

TREBLY, adv. Tri fillte, trì uairean.

TREE, s. Craobh, crann. A fruit tree, craobh mheas, a tree whose fruit withers, craobh shearg-mheasach, a cotton-tree, craobh chanaich, an aspen-tree, craobh chritheann, a fig-tree, craobh fhigis, crann figis, a beech-tree, crann faibhile, craobh fhaibhile, a cherry-tree, crann siris, craobh shiris, a rose-tree, preas ròs, a vine, crann fion, an olive-tree, crann ola, a fir-tree, craobh ghiuthais, crann giuthais, a walnut-tree, craobh ghall-chuo, an alder, crann feurna, preas fhearna, a mulberry-tree, crann maol-dhearc, a nectarine-tree, crann neachdair, a palm-tree, crann pailm, craobh phailm, an elm-tree, leamhan, an ash-tree, craobh uinnseann, an oak-tree, craobh dharaich, a holly-tree, craobh (no) preas chuilinn, a laurel-tree, craan laibhreal, crann luaidhreal, a lime-tree, crann teile, a medlar-tree, crann meidil, a wild ash-tree, craobh chaoran; an apple-tree, craobh ubhlan, a crab-apple-tree, craobh ubhlan fiadhain, a pear-tree, craobh pheuran.

TREFOIL, s. Seamrag, seamhrag.

TRELLIS, s. Cliatan, cliathrach.

TREMBLE, v. a. Crith, crithich, criothnaich, creathnaich. I will make you tremble to your heels, cuiridh mi crith ad choisbheart ort.

TREMBLING, a. Critheanach; air chrith.

TREMBLING, s. Crith, critheadh, criothnachadh, crathadh.

TREMEFACTION, s. Critheadh, criothnachadh.

TREMENDOUS, a. Uamhasach, fuathasach, eagallach, uamharra, oillteil, gailbheach.

TREMENDOUSLY, adv. Gu h-uamhasach, gu fuathsach, gu h-eagallach, gu h-uamharra, gu h-oillteil, gu gailbheach.

TREMENDOUSNESS, s. Uamhasachd, uamhanachd, oillteileachd.

TREMOUR, s. Crith, criothnachadh, ball-chrith.

TREMULOUS, a. Critheanach, critheach.

TREMULOUSLY, adv. Air a chrith.

TREN, s. Moradh, muireadh.

TRENCH, v. a. Cladhaich, claisich, tochaill, bùraich. Trenched, cladhaichte, claisichte.

TRENCH, s. Clais, staing, claidh, slochd, dìg; clais-bhlàir.

TRENCHANT, a. Geur, beumnach.

TRENCHER, s. Truinnsear, mias, aisead.

TRENCHERFLY, TRENCHERMAN, s. Craosair, pòitear, sgimlear.

TRENCHERMATE, s. Fear comithe, craosair.

TRENDLE, s. Tuairneal.

TREPAN, v. a. Rib, glac, meall; grab; cuir an sàs; toll.

TREPAN, s. Boireal dearg-leighe, ribe, gais, painntear.

TREPANNER, s. Mealltair, cealgair, fear a ghlacas le cuilbheart.

TREPANNINGLY, adv. Gu mealltach, gu cuilbheartach.

TREPIDATION, s. Crith, geilt-chrith, crith-eagal; cabhag.

TRESPASS, v. n. Ciontaich, bris, peacaich.

TRESPASS, s. Ciont, peacadh, dìobhail, coire, eusontas, briseadh.

TRESSED, a. Cnòdaichte; bachlagach, dualach, caisreagach.

TRESSES, s. Bachlag, amlag, dual, dualan, caisreag, ciabhag.

TRESSY, a. Bachlagach, amlagach, dualach, caisreagach, ciabhagach.

TRESTLE, s. Sorchan, sorchan leigidh.

TRET, s. Lughachadh (no) luathsachadh airson call is caitheimh.

TREVET, s. Trì chosach.

TREY, s. An triamh air chairtean (no) air dhìstean.

TRIAD, s. Trianaid.

TRIAL, s. Deuchainn; dearbhadh; (examination), ceasnachadh, ceasnach; (attempt), oidhirp; (search), rannsuchadh, (of skill), spairn, strìgh, (temptation), buaireadh, (at law), cùis lagha. It was a terrible trial, b' fhuathsach an deuchainn e, make trial of it, thoir oidhirp air, thoir deuchainn da, feuch ris, he was put to trial, chaidh 'chur gu deuchainn; I have a trial coming on next week, tha cùis lagha agam a teachd air a h-aghaidh thun na h-ath-sheachduin.

TRIANGLE, s. Trì-oisneag, trì-chearnag, trì-shlisneag, triantan.

TRIANGULAR, a. Trì-oisneach, trì-chearnach.

TRIBE, s. Treubh, fine, fineadh, cinne, cinneadh, clann, teaghlach, sliochd, sìol, pòr, seòrsa; caslach.

TRIBULATION, s. Trioblaid, amhghar, teinne, teanntachd, an-shocair, gàbhadh, éigin, càs; farran.

TRIBUNAL, s. Cathair breitheanais, cùirt lagha.

TRIBUNE, s. Treubhan.

TRIBUNITIAL, TRIBUNITIOUS, a. Treubhanach.

TRIBUTARY, a. Fo chìs, fo cheannsal, ceannsaichte.

TRIBUTARY, s. Iochdaran, fear a phàigheas cìs.

TRIBUTE, s. Cìs, càin, gearradh; ùmhlachd, ceannsal.

TRICE, s. Tiot; sealladh, sealan; gradag. In a trice, ann an tiot, gu h-ealamh, gu grad.

TRICK, s. Car, cleas, cuilbheart, prat, seòl. Trick upon trick, cleas air chleas, a false trick, foill, full of tricks, carach, eòlach, cuilbheartach.

TRICK, v. a. and n. Meall, thoir an car a; dean prat; (dress), sgeadaich, uigheamaich. He tricked me completely, thug e 'n glan char asam.

TRICKER, s. Iarunn leigidh; glacag.

TRICKING, s. Uigheam, sgeadachadh.

TRICKISH, a. Carach, pratach, cuireadach, cleasach, cuilbheartach, eòlach, seòlta.

TRICKLE, v. n. Sil, tuit an sileagan, sruth.

TRICKLING, *a* Sileagach, diotagach.
† TRICKSY, *a.* Bòidheach, laoghach.
TRICKY, *a.* See TRICKISH.
TRICORPORAL, *a* Trì-chorpach, trì-chorporra.
TRIDENT, *s.* Muireadh; *perhaps* muir-ghath.
TRIDENT, *a.* Trì-fhiaclach
TRIDING, *s. corrupted into* RIDING An treas cuid do shiorrachd.
TRIDUAN, *a.* Gach treas làth
TRIENNIAL, *a.* Gach treas bhadhna, tri-bhliadhnach.
TRIER, *s.* Deuchainnear, ceasnuchair, dearbhair, dearbhadh.
TRIFALLOW, *v. a.* Ar an treas uair ro 'n chur.
TRIFID, *a.* Ann an trì earannaibh, trì-roinnte
TRIFISTULARY, *a.* Tri-phiobanach
TRIFLE, *v. n.* Cluich, dean cluich; dean baothaireachd She trifled with him, *chuir i air bhaothaireachd e*, trifle or spend idly, *caith gu faoin.*
TRIFLE, *s* Faoineas; faoin-rud; beag-ni. I got it for a trifle, *fhuair mi air bheag-ni e.*
TRIFLER, *s.* Urr dhiomhanach; baothair.
TRIFLING, *a.* Faoin, suarrach, gun fhiù; diomhanach; beag crion; munaran; fàs, eutrom; neo-chudthromach A trifling fellow, *fear faoin, fear gun fhiù*
TRIFLINGLY, *adv.* Gu faoin, gu suarrach, gun fhiù, gu diomhanach.
TRIFLINGNESS, *s* Faoineas, suarrachas, diomhanachd
TRIFOLIATE, *a.* Trì-dhuilleach, tri dhuilleagach.
TRIFORM, *a.* Trì-dhealbhach.
TRIG, *v. a.* Grab, gramaich, stad
TRIGGER, *s.* Iarunn leigidh, glacag; (*of a wheel*), gramaiche.
TRIGENTALS, *s.* Trigeadan, àireamh dheich 'ar fhichead dh' Aifrionna a chuireadh air an cois, san Eaglais Roimheach, le Griogair an naomh.
TRIGON, *s.* Trì oisneag, trì shlisneag.
TRIGONAL, *a.* Trì-oisneach, trì-chearnach, trì-shlisneach
TRIGONOMETRY, *s.* Tomhas nan triantan, triantanachd
TRILATERAL, *a* Trì-shlisneach, trì-shliosnach
TRILL, *s.* Crith, crath, caireall
TRILL, *v. a* and *n.* Caireall, crith; (*drop*), sil; sruth; snith.
TRILLING, *s.* (*In music*), caireall, crithe; (*dropping*), sileadh, sruth
TRILLION, *s* Muillean mhuillean do mhuilleana, is e sin ri radh, 1 000,000,000,000,000,000
TRILUMINAR, *a* Trì-shoillseach, trì-dhealrach.
TRIM, *v. a.* Uigheamaich, gleus, cuir gu doigh, cuir sùrd, deasaich, cuir an ordugh; càirich, bearr, snàs, ceartaich Trimmed, *uigheamaichte, deasaichte, cairichte, bearrta, snàsta, ceartaichte.* I trimmed him, *chuir mi gu doigh* (*no*) *gu taic e*
TRIM, *v n.* Bi an iomchomhairle (no) eadar dha chomhairle.
TRIM, *s* Uigheam, gleus, ordugh; deise, sgeadachadh, aodach, eideadh; deasachadh. A bow in trim, *bogha air ghleus, bogha air lagh*, in good trim, *ann an deagh ordugh, ann an deagh chal;* keep him in trim, *cum gu taic e.*
TRIM, *a.* Glan, sgiobalta, giobach, speisealta, sgeinmeil, sgilmeil; cuimir, cuanta, piollach.
TRIMLY, *adv.* Gu glan, gu sgiobalta, gu giobach, gu speisealta, gu sgeinmeil, gu sgilmeil, gu cuimir.
TRIMMED See TRIM.
TRIMMER, *s* Bearradair; fear leam-leat; spealg, geinn
TRIMMING, *s.* Sgiamh, breaghas, briaghas.
TRIMNESS, *s.* Sgiobaltachd, giobachas, sgeinm, sgilmealachd.
TRINAL, *a.* Trì fillte.
TRINE, *a.* Trì fillte.
TRINE, *v. a.* Trianaich Trined, *trianaichte.*
TRINITARIAN, *s* Trianaidear, trianaidiche
TRINITY, *s.* An Trianaid, Trionaid, (tri-aon-aid)
TRINKET, *s* Faoin-rud, rud laoghach; cungaidh.
TRIO, *s.* Ceòl thrè phàirt.
† TRIOBOLAR, *a.* Suarrach, dìblidh, gun fhiù.
TRIP, *v a* and *n* Cuir camacag; cuir bacag; glac; tuislich, tuit, sleamhnaich; gabh ceum; gabh cuairt (no) tùrus bheag, rach am mearrachd.
TRIP, *s.* Bacag, camacag; tuisleadh, sleamhnachadh, mearrachd; fàilinn, tùrus bheag He fell by a trip, *thuit e le camacag;* he is going to take a trip, *tha e 'dol 'ghabhail cuairt bheag.*
TRIPARTITE, *a.* Ann an trì earannaibh.
TRIPE, *s.* Maodal, abhsporag, greallach, mionach; brù.
TRIPEDAL, *a.* Tri chosach, tri chasach
TRIPETALOUS, *a* Tri-dhuilleach, tri-dhuilleagach
TRIPHTHONG, *s* Trì fhoghair.
TRIPLE, *a* Trì fillte, triobailt.
TRIPLE, *v. a.* Trioblaich, dean tri fillte. Tripled, *trioblaichte*
TRIPLE-CROWN, *s* Coron a phàp
TRIPLET, *s* Tri dh' aon seorsa.
TRIPLICATE, *a.* Trioblaichte, tri fillte
TRIPLICATION, *s.* Trioblachadh
TRIPLICITY, *s* Trioblachd
TRIPOD, *s.* Stòl thrì-chosach.
TRIPOLY, *s.* Gaineamh gheur.
TRIPOS, *s* Stòl thrì-chosach.
TRIPPER, *s* Gleachdair, fear a leigeas le camacag.
TRIPPING, *a* Luath, deas, tapaidh, eutrom, sgairteil, sgealparra, iullagach.
TRIPPING, *s* Dannsadh; beiceis.
TRIPPINGLY, *adv* Gu luath, gu deas, gu tapaidh, gu heutrom, gu sgairteil, gu sgealparra, gu iullagach. Trippingly, and on your tongue, *gu sgairteil, is air ur teangadh*
TRIREME, *s.* Trì ramhach.
TRISECTION, *s.* Gearradh ann an trì phàirtibh; trì phàirteachadh.
TRISTFUL, *a.* Dubhach, muladach, brònach, tuirseach, trom
TRISYLLABICAL, *a.* Trì-shiolach.
TRISYLLABLE, *s* Trì-shiolaidh.
TRITE, *a.* Cumanta, cumainte, sean, as an fhasan; caithte.
TRITENESS, *s* Cumantas
TRITHEISM, *s.* Tri-Dhiadhachd, an teagamh a tha cumail mach gu bheil gach pearsa anns an Trionaid na Dhia
TRITURABLE, *a* So-bhruanadh, so-phronnadh.
TRITURATE, *v. a.* Pronn, bruan, dean mìn.
TRITURATED, *a* Pronn, mìn
TRIUMPH, *s* Buaidh, caithream, buaidh-chaithream; gloiream.
TRIUMPH, *v. n* Buadhaich, faigh buaidh, dean buaidhchaithream He triumphed over them, *bhuadhaich e orra* (*no*) *os an ceann*
TRIUMPHAL, *a* Buadhach, buadhmhor, caithreamach. A triumphal song, *oran buaidh, caithream*
TRIUMPHANT, *a* Buadhach, buadhmhor, caithreamach.
TRIUMPHANTLY, *adv* Gu buadhach, gu buadhmhor, gu caithreamach; le buaidh, le caithream.

TRIUMPHER, *s.* Fear buadhmhor, buadhair, fear buaidh.

TRIUMVIRATE, *s.* Bann thriùir.

TRIUNE, *a.* Tri-aon, mar an trianaid, a tha na tri 's na h-aon gu siorruidh.

TRIVET, *s.* Trì-chosag, trì-chosach, trì-chasach.

TRIVIAL, *a.* Faoin; suarrach; *gun fhiù, gun seadh, gun* suim, cumanta, cumaint.

TRIVIALLY, *adv.* Gu faoin, gu suarrach, gun fhiu, gun seadh, gun suim, nach fhiach.

TRIVIALNESS, *s.* Suarrachas, suarraichead, faoineas, cumantas.

TROAT, *v. a.* Roichd mar ni am broc.

TROCAR, *s.* Inneal dhearg-leigh.

TROCHEE, *s.* Sioladh fad is tè ghoirrid, mar a leanas, băch-lăg, călă.

TRODDEN, *p. part.* of tread. Saltairte, air shaltradh, fo chosaibh; strampta.

TRODE, *pret.* of tread. Shaltair; (*as poultry*), chliath.

TROGLODYTE, *s.* Aonaran; dithreabhach.

TROLL, *v. a.* Druighil, druil, ruidhil; ruith mu 'n cuairt; gead-iasgaich.

TROLLOP, *s.* Draip, sraoileag, dubh-chaile, stràille.

TRONAGE, *s.* Airgiod tomhsaidh.

TROOP, *v. n.* Triall le cabhaig; ruith.

TROOP, *s.* Buidheann, bannal, cuideachd, lòd, bròd; trup, cuideachd each; marc-shluagh; marcraidh, feachd; mal-shluagh, † diorm.

TROOPER, *s.* Trupair, saighdear marcachd.

TROPE, *s.* Atharrachadh seadh focaill.

TROPHIED, *a.* Sgeaduichte le comharan buaidh.

TROPHY, *s.* Craobh chosgair, comhar buaidh, cearn-chomhar, triathach.

TROPIC, *s.* An t-àite sin do na speuran far an tionndadh a ghrian gu deas no gu tuath.

TROPICAL, *a.* Cruinne-mheadhonach.

TROPOLOGICAL, *a.* Ùr-labhrach.

TROPOLOGY, *s.* Ùr-labhradh, ùr-labhairt.

TROPERS, *s.* Triubhas, briogan, osain.

TROT, *v. a.* and *n.* Trot, cuir na throt, ruith.

TROT, *s.* Trot, trotail; cailleach.

TROTH, *s.* Creideas, firinn, focal, briathar. By my troth, *air m' fhocal, air mo bhriathar, air nàile, nàile, air Moire, gu dearbh, gu fior.*

TROTHLESS, *a.* Breugach, fallsa, neo-fhior.

TROTHPLIGHT, *a.* Gealltuinte.

TROTTER, *s.* Trotair; drùis-chailleach. Sheep's trotters, *cosan caorach.*

TROUBLE, *s.* (*Disturbance*), buaireas, aimhreite; (*pains* or *labour*), dragh, saothair; (*molestation*), dragh, moille, farran, miothlachd; (*perplexity*), iomacheist, iom-chomhairle, gàbhaidh, éigin, airc, cruaidh-chas, teanntachd, teinne, amhluath; (*distress*), anshocair, amhghar, truaighe, trioblaid, dosgach, dosgaidh. He gave him much trouble, *chuir e mòran dragh air;* he came through much trouble, *thàinig troimh mhòran anshocair;* you little know her troubles, *is beag tha fhios air a trioblaidean, is beag is aithn dhuit a trioblaidean.*

TROUBLE, *v. a.* Buair; cuir dragh air, farranaich, cuir moille air, cuir gu dragh, trioblaidich, cuir gu trioblaid, cuir air aimhreidh; cuir thar a chéile. Do not trouble me, *na cuir dragh orm;* do not trouble yourself, *na cuir dragh ort fein;* trouble not yourself about him, *na gabh ort e.*

TROUBLED, *a.* and *part.* Buairte; fo bhuaireadh, fo amhluath, fo thrioblaid, air chur gu dragh; thar a chéile.

TROUBLER, *s.* Buaireadair.

TROUBLESTATE, *s.* Fear aimhreiteach, fear aimhreite.

TROUBLESOME, *a.* Draghail, draghalach; buaireasach, trioblaideach, aimhreiteach, utraiseach. A troublesome fellow, *fear buaireasach;* troublesome times, *amanna trioblaideach* (*no*) *aimhreiteach.*

TROUBLESOMELY, *adv.* Gu draghail, gu draghalach; gu buaireasach, gu trioblaideach, gu h-aimhreiteach.

TROUBLESOMENESS, *s.* Draghalachd, buaireasachd, trioblaideachd.

TROUBLOUS, *a.* Buaireasach; trioblaideach.

TROUGH, *s.* (*For water*), amar; (*for kneading*), sgàl, losaid; (*at sea*), tulg-tuinn, udlanachd.

TROUL, *v. a.* Druidhil, ruidhil.

TROUNCE, *v.* Cuir gu taic; peanasaich; druinnsich, lunndraich, lunndrainn, buail, greidh, puinneanaich, dornaich.

TROUNCING, *s.* Peanas, lunndrainn, druimnseadh, gréidh.

TROWSERS, *s.* Triubhas.

TROUT, *s.* Breac, breachd, bricean. Trouts, *bric;* a salmon-trout, *glas bhreac, bradan.*

TROVER, *s.* Cuis lagha an aghaidh duine a chumas air ais maoin neach eile.

TROW, *v. n.* Saoil, smuainich, baralaich. I trow, *is e mo bharail;* what does the fool mean I trow? *ciod th' air aire an amadain, an saoil mi?*

TROWEL, *s.* Spàin-aoil, trùghan, lioghan, sitheal.

TROYWEIGHT, *s.* Tomhas anns am bheil dà unnsa dheug sa phunnt.

TRUANT, *s.* Leisgean; lunndair, lùrdan.

TRUANT, *a.* Leasg, lunndach, diomhanach; mairnealach.

TRUANTSHIP, *s.* Leisge, lunndaireachd, diomhanachd, mairnealachd.

TRUCE, *s.* Fòsadh, eineach, fosadh comhraig; seasachas; sgurachd.

TRUCIDATION, *s.* Mortadh, marbhadh, milleadh, àr, beubanachd.

TRUCK, *v. n.* and *a.* Dean malairt, thoir am malairt, malairtich.

TRUCK, *s.* Malairt, malairteachd.

TRUCK, *s.* Ruithlean beag làidir.

TRUCKLE, *s.* Ruithlean beag.

TRUCKLE, *v. n.* Striochd, feachd, lùb, géill.

TRUCKLEBED, *s.* Leabadh ròithlein.

TRUCULENCE, *s.* Buirbe, ain-iochd.

TRUCULENT, *a.* Borb, garg, fiadhaich, gruamach; gnò, fuilteach, fuileach, millteach.

TRUDGE, *v. n.* Triall air éigin.

TRUE, *a.* Fior, fireannach, dìleas, treibhdhireach; ceart, dligheach, còir; deimhinn, cinnteach, dearbh; math; tarbhach. He is a true hero, *is fior ghaisgeach e;* true to the king, *dìleas do 'n righ;* a true heir, *oighre dligheach;* as true as death, *cho fior ris a bhàs, cho chinnteach ris a bhàs.*

TRUEBRED, *a.* Fior do 'n seorsa cheart.

TRUEHEARTED, *a.* Fior, ionruic, dìleas, tréibhdhireach, còir, glan,

TRUENESS, *s.* Firinn, ionracas, tréibhdhireas.

TRUEPENNY, *s.* Deagh bhalaoch.

TRUFFLE, *s.* Balg losgainn.

TRUG, *s.* (*For mortar*), capull.

TRULL, *s.* Siùrsach, strapaid.

TRULY, *adv.* Gu fior, gu fireannach, gu dearbh, gu deimhinn.

TRUMP, *s.* Tromp, trompaid, stoc, buabhall; (*at cards*), buaidh-chairt, cairt nam buadh.

TRUMP, *v.* Coisinn le buaidh-chairt. Trumped up, *cnuasaich, dean suas.*

Trumpery, *s.* Faoineachd, treallaich, treallachd; (*in language*), faoin-chomhradh, glòr, glòirmeas; breug; sgleò.

Trumpet, *s.* Tromp, trompaid, stoc, buabhall; dùtach.

Trumpet, *v. a.* Gairm, foillsich, dean aithnichte, dean iomraiteach.

Trumpeter, *s.* Trompaidear, stocair, fear trompaid; seorsa éisg.

Truncate, *v. a.* Ciùrr, gearr, bearr, dean cutach.

Truncation, *s.* Bearradh; deanamh cutach.

Truncheon, *s.* Bat cutach; stràicean.

Trundle, *s.* Ruithlean, ròilean.

Trundle, *v. n.* Ruithil, ròil.

Trundling, *s.* Ruithleadh, ròladh.

Trunk, *s.* (*Of a tree*), stoc, bun craoibh; (*box*), cobhan, ciste, cisteag; (*of an elephant*), gnos oileaphaint.

Trunked, *a.* Stocach.

Trunkhose, *s.* Seorsa briogais.

Trunnion, *s.* Cnap gunna mhòir.

Trusion, *s.* Pùcadh, sàthadh.

Truss, *s.* Trus, trusgan, glacan, buinnseal; beairt; braghairt.

Truss, *v. a.* Trus, ceangail, tog suas. Truss up, *trus suas.*

Trust, *s.* Earbsa, earbsadh, dòchas, muinighinn, creideas. I have trust in him, *tha earbsa agam as.*

Trust, *v. a.* and *n.* Earb a, cuir dòchas ann, cuir muinighinn ann, thoir creideas do, bi earbsach, bi cinnteach, bi an dòchas, bi an dùil. I trust you, *tha mi 'g earbsadh asad, tha mi 'cur dòchas annad;* I will not trust him for a penny, *cha toir mi creideas da airson sgillinn;* they trusted to their own valour, *dh' earb iad ri 'n gaisge, féin;* trust in God, *earb ri Dia, cuir do dhòchas an Dia;* he ought not to be trusted, *cha bu chòir dòchas chur ann.*

Trustee, *s.* Oide; fear earbsaidh. Trustees, *luchd earbsaidh.*

Trusting, *a.* Earbsach; muinighinneach.

Trusting, *s.* Earbsadh, earbsa, muinighinn.

Trustiness, *s.* Fìreanntachd, ionracas.

Trustless, *a.* Neo-fhior, neo-dhìleas; neo-bhunaiteach.

Trusty, *a.* Dìleas, tréibhdhireach, ionraic, fìreannach, fior, earbsach, diongmhalta, diongalta. The trusty man, though passionate, is better than a deceitful tongue, though mild, *is fearr fear foghainteach feargach, na fear mìn cealgach is e ciùin.*

Truth, *s.* Fìrinn, tréibhdhireas; ionracas There is not a word of truth in it, *cha 'n 'eil focal fior dheth;* you say the the truth, *tha thu 'g radh na fìrinn;* to speak the truth, *dh' innseadh na fìrinn;* in truth, *gu fior;* speaking the truth, *fior, fìreannach;* of a truth, *gu fior;* truth is pleasing to God, *is buidheach Dia do 'n fhìrinn;* truth will out with a vengeance, *thig an fhìrinn a mach le tubaisd.*

Trutination, *s.* Tomhasadh, cothromachadh.

Try, *v. a.* Feuch, feuch ri; thoir oidhirp, dean oidhirp, thoir deuchainn; dearbh, cuir gu deuchainn, ceasnaich, rannsuich, sgrud. Try *or* refine, *glan;* try yourself, *feuch thu fhéin;* try it, *feuch ris;* try another method, *feuch seòl eile;* I will try you, *feuchaidh mise riut;* try gold with a touchstone, *dearbh òr le dearbhag.*

Trying, *s.* Deuchainn, feuchainn, oidhirp.

Tub, *s.* Measair, ballan, dabhach, cutainn. As the blind man struck the tub, or as the blind threw his club, *buille an doill mu 'n dabhaich, no mar thilg an dall a phloc.*

Tube, *s.* Piob, pioban, feadan.

Tubercle, *s.* Plucan, guirean, fride.

Tuberosity, *s.* Plucanachd, guireanachd.

Tuberous, *a.* Plucanach, plucach.

Tubular, *a.* Piobach, piobanach, piobanta, feadanach.

Tubulated, **Tubulous**, *a.* Piobach, piobanach, piobanta, feadanach.

Tubule, *s.* Pioban, feadan.

Tuck, *s.* Claidheamh caol, lann chaol; seorsa lìn.

Tuck, *v. a.* Trus, sguiblich, ceangail suas, crios, criosraich.

Tucked, *a.* Trusta.

Tucking, *s.* Trusadh, sguibleachadh, ceangladh suas, criosrachadh.

† **Tuel**, *s.* Toll na tòn.

Tuesday, *s.* Di Màirt. Shrove-Tuesday, *Di Màirt Inid.*

Tuft, *s.* (*Of feathers or ribands*), dos, dosan, dosrach; (*of wool*), toipean, cruinnean; (*of grass*), tolman, toman, bad, badan, millteach; (*as of heath*), gasan, goisean; (*of trees*), bad, doire.

Tufted, **Tufty**, *a.* Dosach, dosanach, dosrach; toipeanach; topanach, badach, badanach; gasanach, goiseanach; tolmanach, tomanach.

Tug, *v. a.* Spiol, spion, tarruing, dragh, slaoid.

Tug, *s.* Spiol, spioladh, spion, spionadh, dragh, draghadh.

Tugger, *s.* Spioladair; draghair.

Tugging, *s.* Spioladh, spionadh, draghadh, draothadh, tarruing.

Tuition, *s.* Ionnsuchadh, oilean, oideas, tuitearachd, cùram foghluim.

Tulip, *s.* Tuiliop.

Tumble, *v. n.* and *a.* Tuit, tuislich; leig, tilg sios cuir, car, ruithil. He tumbled headlong, *thuit e 'n comhar a chinn;* tumbled, *car air char, tilgte sios.*

Tumble, *s.* Tuiteam, splad; leig. What a tumble he got, *is e fhuair an splad.*

Tumbler, *s.* Cleasaiche, car-chleasaiche, fear urlataidh; (*a glass*), copan, gloine-chop, gloine.

Tumbrel, *s.* Cairt innearach.

Tumefaction, *s.* At, atadh, bochadh.

Tumefy, *v. n.* At, boch, séid suas.

Tumid, *a.* Atmhor, air at; làn, lionta; bòsdail, mòr chuiseach, spagluinneach.

Tumorous, *a.* Atmhor, meallanach; spagluinneach.

Tumour, *s.* At; meall; spagluinn; mòr-chuis, fearas mhòr.

Tump, *v. a.* Cuir ùir mu chraobhan.

Tumulose, *a.* Cnocach, dùnach, dùnanach.

Tumult, *s.* Conghair, tabaid, aimhreite, buaireas, mi-riaghailt, bruaillean, cullaid, garbhuaic, iorgail.

Tumultuarily, *adv.* Gu tabaideach, gu h-aimhreiteach, gu buaireasach, gu mi-riaghailteach, gu bruailleanach.

Tumultuariness, *s.* Tabaideachd, buaireasachd, bruailleanachd.

Tumultuary, *a.* Conghaireach, tabaideach, aimhreiteach, buaireasach, mi-riaghailteach, bruailleanach, troimh-cheile, thar a chéile.

Tumultuate, *v. n.* Tog aimhreite, tog buaireas.

Tumultuation, *s.* Tabaid, conghair, aimhreite, buaireas, mi-riaghailt, bruaillean.

Tumultuous, *a.* Conghaireach, tabaideach, aimhreiteach, buaireasach, mi-riaghailteach, iorgaileach, borb.

Tumultuously, *adv.* Gu conghaireach, gu tabaideach, gu h-aimhreiteach, gu buaireasach, gu mi-riaghailteach.

Tumultuousness, *s.* Conghaireachd, tabaideachd, aimhreiteachd, buaireasachd, mi-riaghailteachd.

Tun, *s.* Tunna.

Tun, *v. a.* Tunn, bairill, bairillich.

Tunable, *a.* Binn, ceòlmhor, fonnmhor, fonnar.

Tunableness, *s.* Binnead, ceòlmhorachd, fonnmhorachd.

Tunably, *adv.* Gu binn, gu ceòlmhor, gu fonnmhor.

Tunbellied, *a.* Bronnach, garrach, bagach.

Tundish, *s.* Lionadair, tunnadair.

Tune, *v.* Fonn, séisd; ceòl; co-sheirm. In tune, *air ghleus, gleusda;* out of tune, *a fonn, a gleus.*

Tune, *v. a.* and *n.* Gleus, cuir am fonn, cuir air ghleus, cuir an gleus. Tuned, *gleusda, an gleus, air ghleus.*

Tuneful, *a.* Binn, ceòlmhor, ceòlar, fonnmhor, co-sheirm-each.

Tuneless, *a.* Neo-bhinn, neo-cheòlmhor, neo-fhonnmhor.

Tuner, *s.* Gleusair, gleusadair, fear gleusaidh.

Tunic, *s.* Còta, fearrasaid; deacaid Roimheach.

Tunicle, *s.* Còta, comhdach, sgàilean, sgrath.

Tunnage, *s.* Tunu-chìs.

Tunnel, *s.* Simealair; toll simealair, luidheir; lionadair, tunnadair; piob taosgaidh; pocan lin.

Tup, *s.* Mult reithe, reithe.

Tup, *v. a.* Purr (no) put mar ni reithe.

Turban, *s.* Ceann eididh Turcach, curachd (no) boineid Thurcach.

Turbaned, *a.* Curachdach, curachdaichte mar Thurcach.

Turbary, *s.* Còir mòin a dheanamh, còir cùlaig a bhuain-eadh.

Turbid, *a.* Tiugh, salach, ruaimleach, neo-shoilleir, troimh chéile, thar chéile.

Turbidness, *s.* Ruaimleachd.

Turbinated, *a.* Toinnte, sniomhta.

Turbination, *s.* Toinneamh, sniomhadh, ruidhleadh mun cuairt.

Turbot, *s.* Turbaid.

Turbulence, **Turbulency**, *s.* Buaireas; mi-riaghailt, aimhreite.

Turbulent, *a.* Buaireasach, mi-riaghailteach, ballartach, aimhreiteach; draghail.

Turbulently, *adv.* Gu buaireasach, gu mi-riaghailteach, gu h-aimhreiteach.

Turd, *s.* Tudan cac; cac, inneir, aolach, salachar.

Turf, *s.* Fòid, clod; sgroth; culag; (*for a housetop*), fàl, duibheid.

Turfy, *a.* Fòideach, sgrothach, cùlagach; gorm.

Turgent, *a.* Atmhor, bochanta, séidte; làn; gaothar.

Turgescence, **Turgescency**, *s.* Atmhorachd, atmhoir-eachd, at; làn, séide.

Turgid, *a.* Atmhor; séidte, gaothar; làn, lionta, spag-luinneach. Turgid words, *briathran atmhor.*

Turgidity, **Turgidness**, *s.* Atmhorachd, atmhoireachd, gaotharachd, spagluinn.

Turkey, *s.* Eun francach. A turkey-cock, *coileach fran-cach;* a turkey-hen, *cearc fhrancach.*

Turkois, *s.* Seorsa cloich luachmhoire.

Turmeric, *s.* Dath buidhe a thig as na h-Innsean.

Turmoil, *s.* Buaireas, aimhreite, mi-riaghailt, brionglaid, bruaillean.

Turmoil, *v. a.* Buair, cuir thar chéile; sgìthich.

Turn, *s.* (*Act of turning*), tionndadh; (*winding*), lùb, luib, car; (*circuit*), cuairt; (*change*), mùth, atharrachadh; (*turn-ing back*), tionndadh, pilleadh, tilleadh, pilltinn; (*chance*), teagmhas, tubaist; (*course*), cùrsa; (*while*), grathuinn, tachdain; (*use*), stà, uidhis; gnothuch; (*form*), dealbh, cruth; (*action*), tùrn, gniomh; (*of a disease*), faochadh. Take a turn (walk) round, *gabh car mu 'n cuairt, gabh ceum mu 'n cuairt;* it is my turn now, *is e mo ghrathuinn-se th' ann a nis;* take your own turn of it, *gabh do ghrathuinn fhéin deth;* it will serve my turn, *ni e mo ghnothuch;* he did me a good turn, *rinn e deagh thùrn domh;* the turn of the river, *lùb na h-aibhne;* by turns, *ma seach, mun seach, tarruing mun seach, uair mun seach.*

Turn, *v. a.* and *n.* Pill, till, tionndaidh; (*become*), fàs, cinn; (*shape*), dealbh, cum; (*change*), mùth, atharruich; carraich; (*bend*), lùb; (*from vice*), iompaich. Turn him back, *pill e, tionndaidh e;* he will turn good, *fàsaidh e math;* it will turn to mischief, *thig e gu h-olc;* turn a mill, *cuir mu 'n cuairt muileann;* turn upside down, *cuir bun oscionn;* turn your back on him, *cuir cùl ris, fàg e;* turn the edge, *maol-aich;* turn out or get out, *thoir mach ort;* turn up the ground, *ruathair, bùraich.*

Turncoat, *s.* Fear leam leat, toin chlomhach.

Turned, *a.* Pillte, air philltinn, tionndaidhte, mùthta, atharruichte, lùbta. Well turned, *cumadail.*

Turner, *s.* Tuairnear.

Turning, *s.* Tionndadh, car, lùb.

Turnip, *s.* Neup, neupas, meacàn.

Turnpike, *s.* Cis-chachliath.

Turnsol, *s.* Plùr na gréin, grian-ròs.

Turnsick, *a.* Eutrom.

Turnspite, *s.* Cù bior.

Turnstile, *s.* Bealach gàraidh; geat ruithleanach.

Turpentine, *s.* Tairbhint, bith craobh ghiuthais.

Turpitude, *s.* Gràinealachd.

Turret, *s.* Turait; binnean; baideal; similear, luidheir.

Turreted, *a.* Turaiteach; binneanach, baidealach.

Turtle, *s.* Seorsa éisg luachmhoir; (*dove*), fearan, caidhean.

Tush, *interj.* Bi ad thosd, bi samhach, caisd, éisd.

Tusk, *s.* Tosg, fiacal, fiacal cullaich.

Tusked, **Tusky**, *a.* Tosgach, fiaclach.

Tussilago, *s.* Gallan greannchair.

Tussuck, *s.* Tolman feoir, badan.

Tut, *interj.* Tut, h-ut.

Tutelage, *s.* Oideas; fo-aois, gleidheadaireachd, tuitear-achd.

Tutelar, **Tutelary**, *a.* Dionach. A tutelary angel, *ain-geal dionaidh.*

Tutor, *s.* Oide-ionnsuich, tuitear, maighistir, cileadair.

Tutor, *v. a.* Ionnsuich, teagaisg, foghlum, tog. The child whom you will not tutor at your knee, you will not tutor when he comes to your ear, *an leanabh nach foghlum thu ri do ghlùn, cha 'n fhoghlum thu ri do chluais.*

Tutorage, *s.* Oideas, tuitearachd.

Tutoress, *s.* Ban-mhaighstir.

Tuz, *s.* Ciabhag, badan fuilt.

Twain, *a.* Dithis, dà, dhà, càraid, deise.

Twang, *s.* Srann; langan. The arrow flew with a twang, *shiubhail an t-saighead le srann.*

Twang, *v. n.* Srann, dean srann.

Twank, *v. n.* Srann.

'Twas, [it was]. B' e.

Twattle, *v. n.* Dean goileam, (no) glòrmas.

Twattle, *s.* Goileam, gobais, gob; glòrmas, rabhd, ràiteachas.

Tweak, *v. a.* Pioc, gòmagaich, teannaich.

Tweak, *s.* Pioc, gòmag; càs, cabhag, iom-chomhairle.

Tweedle, *v. a.* Meuraich gu h-eutrom.

Tweedle-dee, **Tweedle-dum**, *s.* Fidhlear, fear ciùil.

Tweezers, *s.* Piocaid; spioladair; spioladairean; gramaiche.

Twelfth, *a.* An dara deug. The Twelfth-day, *an dara là deug.*

Twelve, *a.* Dhà dheug. Twelve men, *dà fhear dheug;* twelve o'clock, *an dà uair dheug, meadhon làtha;* twelve hundred, *da cheud deug;* twelve thousand, *da mhìl dheug;*

twelve miles, *da mhìl dheug;* a twelvemonth, *bliadhna,* this time twelvemonth (past), *an tràth so 'n uiridh,* (future), *an tràth so 'n ath-bhliadhna.*

TWELVEPENCE, *s.* Sgillinn shasunnach.

TWELVESCORE, *a.* Da cheud is da fhichead.

TWENTIETH, *a.* Am ficheadamh. The one-and-twentieth, *an t-aon fhear fichead,* the two-and-twentieth, *an dara fear fichead.*

TWENTY, *a.* Fichead. Twenty-one, *h-aon 'ar fhichead,* two-and-twenty, *dhà 'r fhichead,* three-and-twenty, *tri 'ar fhichead;* two-and-twenty men, *dà fhear thar fhichead,* three-and-twenty men, *tri fir fhichead;* twenty times, *fichead uair.*

TWICE, *adv.* Dà uair; da chuairt; dà tharruing; gu dùbailt.

TWIG, *s.* Fàillean, maothan, maothran, slatag, fiùran, bunsag, caomhan, bailleag, gineag

TWIGGER, *s.* Air a dheanamh le slataibh.

TWIGGY, *a.* Fàilleanach, maothanach, maothranach, slatagach, bunsagach, bailleagach, gineagach.

TWILIGHT, *s.* Eadar-sholus, càmhanaich, dubh-thrath, breacsholus, † tuaileachd, † clab-sholus.

TWILIGHT, *a.* Doilleir, dorch.

TWIN, *s.* Leth-aon; caraid; toirbeart. Twins, *leth-aonan.*

TWIN, *v. n.* Beir dithis, thoir mach dithis air aon bhreith; caraidich.

TWINE, *v. a.* and *n.* Toinn, pleat, dual, cas, figh. Twined, *toinnte, fighte*

TWINE, *s.* Snàth garbh, sgéinnidh, toinntean; toinneamh, car; glac.

TWINGE, *v. a* Faisg, toinn, pian, craon, craidh

TWINGE, *s.* Guin, goimh, pian, cradh; craon, pioc, gòmag

† TWINK, *s.* Prìob; tiot, briosg, sealan.

TWINKLE, *v.* Boisg; prìob.

TWINKLE, *s.* Crith-bhoisge, ghiosgardaich; priobadh; plath

TWINKLING, *s.* Crith-bhoisge, priobadh; plath.

TWINLING, *s.* Uan leth-aon.

TWIRL, *v. a.* and *n* Ruidhil mun cuairt, ruith mun cuairt, druidhil.

TWIRL, *s.* Ruidhle, ròthladh.

TWIST, *v. a.* Toinn, toinneamh, sniomh, figh, dualaich, pleat, cas. Twisted, *toinnte, sniomhta, fighte, cas*

TWIST, *s.* Toinneamh, car; sgéinne, toinntean, sreang, snàthainn, caircheas.

TWISTER, *s.* Toinntear, sniomhair, sniomhadair.

TWISTING, *s.* Toinneamh, sniomhadh.

TWIT, *v a* Beum; sgeig, mag.

TWITCH, *s.* Spiol, spioladh; draothadh.

TWITCH, *v. a.* Spiol, spion, pioc.

TWITCHGRASS, *s.* Seorsa feòir

TWITTER, *v* Dean diorrasan, sitrich, truitrich, crith; bi san tomhartaich; sgeig, mag

TWITTER, *s.* Diorrasan; truitreach, sitrich; sgeigear, fear sgeigeil

TWITTERING, *s.* Truitreach, truitrich

'TWIXT, *prep* Eadar See BETWIXT and BETWEEN.

TWO, *a.* A dhà, dà, dithis; paidhir, carraid. Two by two, *lion dithis is dithis,* one of the two men, *an darna fear dhiubh,* one of the two women, *an darna té dhiubh,* two tied together, *caigeann,* two years old, *da bhliadhna dh' aois, dà bhliadhnach,* every two days, *gach dolach là.*

TWO-EDGED, *a.* Dà fhaobhrach; dà fhaobhar

TWO-FOLD, *a.* Dùbailt, dà fhillte.

TWO-HANDED, *a.* Dà lamhach; da laimh A two-handed sword, *claidheamh da laimh.*

TWOPENCE, *s.* Dà sgillinn.

TYE. See TIE.

TYMBAL, *s* Tim-buail, tiombal

TYMPANUM, *s.* Drum.

† TYNY, *a* Crion, beag, meanbh; girceanta, girceanach.

TYPE, *s.* Samhladh, comhar, comharradh, sgàil; litir clodh.

TYPE, *v. a.* Samhluich.

TYPICAL, Samhlachail.

TYPICALLY, *a.* Le samhladh, mar shamhladh.

TYPIFY, *v. a.* Samhlaich. Typified, *samhlaichte.*

TYPOGRAPHER, *s.* Clodh bhualadair.

TYPOGRAPHICAL, *a.* Samhlachail; clodh-bhualaidh. A typographical error, *mearachd clodh bhualaidh*

TYPOGRAPHY, *s.* Dealbhadh, samhlachadh; clodh-bhualadh

TYRANNIC, TYRANNICAL, *a* An-tighearnail, ain-tighearnail; ain-tighearnach, borb; smachdail, tioranach.

TYRANNICALLY, *adv* Gu h-ain-tighearnail, gu smachdail

TYRANNICIDE, *s.* Mortadh ain-tighearna.

TYRANNY, *s.* Antighearnas, ain-tighearnas; tioranas, tioranachd; ana-cruathas.

TYRO, *s.* Sgoilear; foghlumaiche.

U.

U. An t-aon litir 'ar fhichead do 'n Aibideal

UBERTY, *s* Pailteas, tairbhichead, tairbhe, torraichead.

UBIQUITARY, *s.* Ti uile làthaireach.

UBIQUITARY, *a* Uile ionadach, uile-lathaireach, anns na h-uile àite.

UBIQUITY, *s.* Uile-ionadachd, uile-lathaireachd

UDDER, *s.* Ùth, ùgh, sinne. Udders, *sinneachan.*

UDDERED, *a.* Ùthach, ùthar, sinneach.

UGLILY, *adv* Gu gràda, gu grannda, gu duaichnidh, gu mosach, gu salach.

UGLINESS, *s.* Granndachd, duaichneachd, mosaiche.

UGLY, *a.* Gràda, grannda, duaichnidh, mosach, salach, neo-bhoidheach, neo-laoghach. The ugly beast, *am béist mosach.*

ULCER, *s.* Neasgaid, neasg, othras, leannach, leannachadh; iongrachadh, bolg, leus, bucaid, guirean, buinne, brachaid, gearb. A scrofulous ulcer, *silteach*

ULCERATE, *a.* Iongaraich, iongraich, leannaich Ulcerated, *iongaraichte, leannaichte*

ULCERATION, *s.* Iongrachadh, leannach, leannachadh, othras.

ULCEROUS, *a* Neasgaideach; leannachail, othrasach, silteach

ULIGINOUS, *a* Féitheach, fliuch, bog, làthachail, làbanach, slobach, slobanach, geòtach

ULTIMATE, *a.* Deireannach, is deireannaiche.

ULTIMATELY, *adv.* Mo dheireadh, air a cheann mo dheireadh, air a cheann thall

ULTRAMARINE, *a.* All-mharach; eile-thireach.

ULTRAMARINE, s. Seorsa guirm.
ULTRAMUNDANE, a. Neo-shaoghalta, neo-thalmhaidh, spioradail
ULTRONEOUS, a Toileach; buidheach, a dheòin
UMBELLATED, a. Cluigeanach.
UMBER, s Seorsa lith dhorch, seorsa éisg.
UMBERED, a Dorch, doilleir, dubhrach.
UMBILICAL, a Imleagach
UMBLES, s Mionach (no) greallach feidh.
UMBO, s Cop, còpan, cnap sgeith
UMBRAGE, s (*Shade*), sgàile, dubhar, dubhradh, duibhre, (*pretext*), leithsgeul; (*suspicion*), amharus, omhaill, (*resentment*), corruich, feirge, diom; (*affront*), tàir, masladh, oilbheum He took umbrage at it, *ghabh e gu dona (no) gu soithich e.*
UMBRAGEOUS, a Sgàileach, dubhrach, dorch, duibhreach.
UMBRELLA, s Sgàilean, sgàileag, fasgadan, dion-sgath.
UMBROSITY, s. Duibhre, doirche, duirche, dorchadas, sgàile.
UMPIRE, s Breitheamh, breith; ràithe; (*provincial*), brith.
UMPIRAGE, s Ràithe
UN Neo, mi, eu, as, an, ana; *mar*, unjust, *neo-cheart;* uncivil, *mi-shuairc*
UNABASHED, a Neo-nàraichte
UNABATED, a Gun sgur, gun sgurachd, gun chàirde, bidhcanta, neo-lughaichte, neo-bheagaichte
UNABETTED, a. Neo-chuidichte, gun chò-ghnath
UNABRIDGED, a. Neo-ghiorraichte; neo-lughdaichte, neo-chuingichte.
UNABLE, a. Neo-chomasach, eu-comasach, mi-mhurrach, anfhann; gun chomas
UNACCELERATED, a Neo-luathaichte, neo-dheifrichte.
UNACCEPTABLE, a. Neo-thaitneach, neo-chiatach; neo-fhreagarrach.
UNACCEPTED, a Air a dhiùltadh; diùlte, air obadh, òbta.
UNACCOMMODATED, a Neo-riaruichte, neo-ghoireasaichte
UNACCOMPANIED, a Aonarach, aonaranach, na aonar, leis fein, gun chompanach She was unaccompanied, *bha i na h-aonar, bha i le féin (no) leatha féin*, they were unaccompanied, *bha iad na 'n aonar (no) leo féin*
UNACCOMPLISHED, a Neo-chriochnaichte, neo-choimhleanta, neo-fhoirfe, (*in mind*), neo-oileanaichte, neo-ionnsuichte; gun chàil, gun eireachdas inntinn, gun bhuaidh, gun fheart, neo-fheartaichte.
UNACCOUNTABLE, a. (*Inexplicable*), do-mhìneachadh, do-innseadh, do-chur an céill, do-nochdadh, (*strange*), iongantach, neònach, miorbhuileach, mìorbhuilteach, (*not subject to account*), neo-bhuailteach, saor o chunntas, neo-fhreagarrach
UNACCOUNTABLY, adv Gu do-innseadh, (*strangely*), gu h-iongantach, gu neònach, gu'miorbhuileach
UNACCURATE, a. (*Little used*), neo-phongail, neo-phurpail, neo-chinnteach; neo-cheart, neo-shoilleir
UNACCUSTOMED, a Neo-chleachdta; neo-chleachdach, neo-ghnathaichte; neo-dheanta ri, ùr, neo-chumanta
UNACKNOWLEDGED, a Neo-aidichte, gun ghabhail ri, neo-dheònaichte Unacknowledged guilt, *ciont neo-aidichte*, an unacknowledged book, *leabhar gun ghabhail ris*
UNACQUAINTANCE, s. Aineolas, cion còlais, cion cleachd.
UNACQUAINTED, a. Neo-eòlach, aineolach, gun eòlas, gun aithne Unacquainted with the world, *neo-eolach (no) aineolach air an t-saoghal*
UNACTIVE, a. Neo-thapaidh, mi-thapaidh, mi-bheothail; neo-ruaimneach; mi-bheothail, neo-bheò, neo-calamh, neo-ghrad, neo-ghniomhach, neo-dheanadach; neo-shurdail, neo-theòma; leasg, lunndach, leagach; marbh, marbhanta; neo-smiorail; (*inefficient*), neo-éifeachdach, neo-thabhachdach.
UNACTUATED, a Neo-bhrosnuichte, neo-bheothaichte.
UNADDICTED, a Neo-chleachdta. Unaddicted to vice, *neo-chleachdta ri olc.*
UNADJURED, a. Neo-earalaichte.
UNADMIRED, a Neo-urramaichte, neo-mheasail; air bheag suim, air bheag seadh, air bheag meas (no) spéis.
UNADMONISHED, a. Neo-chomhairlichte, neo-earalaichte.
UNADORED, a. Neo-aorta, neo-aoraichte.
UNADORNED, a Neo-sgeadaichte, neo-sgiamhaichte, neo-ghrinnichte; neo-ghreusta; gun sgeadachadh, gun sgiamh, gun ghrinneas, gun bhreaghas, gun ghreus
UNADULTERATED, a. Neo-mheasgta, glan, fior-ghlan; neo-thruaillichte
UNADVENTUROUS, a. Mi-chuiseach; neo-mhisneachail; gealtach, meat, neo-dhàn.
UNADVISED, a Neo-chomhairlichte; neo-earalaichte; (*rash*), brais, obann, dàn, dian, eu-crionna, gòrach.
UNADVISEDLY, adv Gu brais, gu h-obann, gu dàn, gu dian, gu h-eu-crionna, gu gòrach
UNADVISEDNESS, s Eu-crionnachd, braisead, déine, gòraiche.
UNAFFECTED, a (*Candid*), fior, fireannach, neo-chealgach; còir; (*not moved*), neo-ghluaiste; (*not laboured*), neo-shaothairichte, simplidh.
UNAFFECTEDLY, adv Gu fior, gu fìreannach, gu neo-chealgach, gu simplidh.
UNAFFECTING, a Neo-dhrùighteach, neo-ghluasdach; neo-mhuladach
UNAFFIRMED, a Neo-dhearbhta, neo-dhaighnichte, neo-fhoillsichte, neo-aidichte.
UNAFFLICTED, a Neo-chraidhte, neo-chlaoidhte, neo-shàruichte; neo-ghonta, gun airc, gun truaighe, gun amhghar, gun an-shocair, gun trioblaid.
† UNAGREEABLE, a. Neo-fhreagarrach, neo-iomchuidh, neo-chubhaidh.
UNAIDABLE, a Do-chòghnath, do-chuideachadh, nach gabh còghnath (no) cuideachadh
UNAIDED, a Neo-chuidichte, gun chòghnath, gun chuideachadh
UNALIENABLE, a Neo-bhuileachail, nach gabh buileachadh.
UNALLAYED, a Neo-mheasgta, neo-thruaillte, glan, gun choimeasg.
UNALLIED, a Neo-chairdeach, neo-dhaimheil, gun daimh ri.
UNALLURING, a. Neo-mhealltach, neo-thairneach
UNALTERABLE, a. Neo-chaochlaideach; do-thionndadh; do-chaochladh, do-atharrachadh, do-mhuthadh, diongalta, maireann
UNALTERABLENESS, s Neo-chaochlaideachd.
UNALTERABLY, adv Gu neo-chaochlaideach; gun chaochladh, gun tionndadh, gun mhùth, gun atharrachadh; gu daingeann, gu maireann.
UNALTERED, a Neo-atharraichte, gun chaochladh, gun mhùth
UNAMAZED, a. Neo-bhuailte le h-iongantas; gun iongantas, gun uamhann
UNAMBITIOUS, a Neo-mhiannach, neo-thogarach: neo-uallach, mi-chuiseach, mi-aigneach, mi-aigeantach.
UNAMENDABLE, a. Do-leasachadh, do-chàramh, nach gabh leasachadh (no) càramh
UNAMELIORATED, a. Neo-leasaichte
UNAMENDED, a Neo-leasaichte, neo-chàirichte.
UNAMIABLE, a. Neo-chiatach, neo-lurach, neo-ghreannar, neo-ionmhuinn; neo-ghradhach.

Unanalyzed, *a.* Neo-rannsuichte, neo-bhun-rannsuichte.

Unanimated, *a.* Neo-bhrisg, neo-bheò, neo-bheothail, neo-smiorail, marbh, trom, gun spiorad, gun smiodam.

Unanimating, *a.* Marbh, marbhanta.

Unanimity, *s.* Aon-inntinn, aon-inntinneachd, aon-run, aonachd, aonachd inntinn.

Unanimous, *a* Aon inntinneach; aon-runach, aon-bharail-each; aon-sgeulach.

Unanimously, *adv* Gu h-aon-inntinneach, gu h-aon-sgeulach; a dh' aon inntinn, a dh' aon rùn.

Unanimousness, *s.* Aon-inntinneachd, aonachd.

Unannulled, *a.* Air chois, na sheasamh The law is still unannulled, *tha 'n lagh fhathast na sheasamh* (*no*) *air chois.*

Unanointed, *a* Neo-ungta, neo-choisrigte.

Unanswerable, *a* Do-fhreagairt, do-fhreagarradh, nach gabh freagairt.

Unappalled, *a.* Neo-allsgaichte; neo-sgàthach, gun eagal, gun uamhann, gun allsga, treubhanta.

Unappareled, *a* Neo-eudaichte; neo-chomhdaichte, lom-nochd, ruisgte, lomardach; gun eudach.

Unapparent, *a.* Doilleir, dorch, neo-shoilleir, do-thuigsinn, neo-fhaicsinneach.

Unappeasable, *a.* Do-chiosnachadh, do-chiùnachadh, do-chosgadh; do-chosgaidh

Unappeased, *a.* Neo-chiosnaichte, neo-choisgte, neo-thraoghta.

Unapplicable, *a.* Neo-fhreagarrach; neo-lathailteach.

Unappraised, *a,* Neo-mheasta

Unapprehensive, *a.* Aineolach, neo-fhiosrach, neo-thap-aidh; baoth, baoghalta; àmhasanach, gun smuain, gun omhaill, gun amharus Unapprehensive of danger, *gun smuain mu chunnart.*

Unapproached, *a* Do-ruigheachd, nach gabh ruigheachd

Unapt, *a.* Baoghalta, maol; àmhasanach, neo-eanchainn-each, tiugh; (*unsuitable*), neo-fhreagarrach; neo-iomchuidh, neo-lathailteach.

Unaptly, *adv.* Gu neo-fhreagarrach, gu neo-iomchuidh, gu neo-lathailteach

Unaptness, *s* Neo-fhreagarrachd, mi-lathailt; amhas-anachd.

Unargued, *a.* Neo-arguinnte

Unarmed, *a.* Neo-armaichte; gun airm.

Unarraigned, *a* Neo-chronaichte, neo-choirichte; neo-dhite.

Unarranged, *a* Neo-réitichte; thar a chéile, a ordugh, gun ordugh.

Unarrayed, *a* Neo-sgeaduichte, neo-uigheamaichte.

Unartful, *a* (*Unskilful*), baoghalta, neo-theòma, neo-sgileil, neo-ealadhanta, neo-ealanta, neo-sheòlta, (*not cunning*), neo-chuilbheartach, simplidh

Unartfully, *adv.* Gu baoghalta, gu neo-theoma, gu neo-sgileil, gu neo-ealanta, gu neo-sheòlta; (*not cunning*), gu neo-chuilbheartach, gu simplidh.

Unarticled, *a.* Neo-chumhnantaichte, neo-cheangailte; neo-bhanntaichte.

Unasked, *a* Gun sireadh, gun iarruidh, gun chuireadh He came unasked, *thàinig e gun iarruidh* (*no*) *gun chuir-eadh*

Unaspiring, *a.* Neo-mhiannach, mi-chuiseach.

Unassailable, *a* Do-bhualadh, do-shàruchadh, air nach gabh ionnsuidh thoirt, dionta.

Unassailed, *a.* Neo-bhuailte, neo-shàruichte

Unassayed, *a* Neo-fheuchainnte

Unassionable, *a.* Do-bhuileachadh, neo-bhuileachail

Unassisted, *a.* Gun chòghnath, neo-chuidichte.

Unassuming, *a.* Neo-stràiceil.

Unassured, *a* Neo-chinnteach

Unattainable, *a* Do-ruigheachd, do-ruigsinn, do-fhaot-ainn, do-fhaghail

Unattempted, *a* Neo-fheuchainnte, neo-oidhirpichte, gun deuchainn, gun oidhirp

Unattended, *a* Gun chuideachd, gun chonaltradh, aon-arach, aonaranach, na aonar, leis féin He went away un-attended, *dh' fhalbh e na aonar* (*no*) *leis féin*, pleasure unat-tended with pain, *subhachas gun dubhachas*

Unattending, *a.* Neo-aireachail, neo-shuimeil

Unattentive, *a.* Neo-aireachail, neo-shuimeil, neo-chur-amach, neo-fhuireach, neo-sheadhar, mi-sheadhair.

Unauthorized, *a* Gun ughdarras

Unavailable, *a.* Faoin, neo-éifeachdach, gun stà, gun fheum

Unavailing, *a* Faoin, gun stà, gun fheum, gun fhiù

Unavoidable, *a* Do-sheachnaidh, do-sheachanta; nach gabh seachnadh.

Unavoidableness, *s.* Do-sheachantach

Unavoided, *a.* Neo-sheachainte.

Unaware, **Unawares**, *adv.* Gun fhios, gun aire, gun aithne; gu h-obann. He came upon me unawares, *thainig e orm gun fhios domh.*

Unawed, *a.* Gun agh, gun fhiamh, gun eagal.

Unbacked, *a* Neo-cheannsaichte; neo-chuidichte.

Unbalanced, *a* Neo-chothromaichte.

Unbanded, *a* Gun bhann, neo-bhannta, neo-iallaichte, gun iall

Unbar, *v a* Di-chrannaich, thoir crann bhàrr; fosgail Unbar the door, *thoir an crann bhàrr an doruis.*

Unbashful, *a.* Beag-narach, dàna, ladurna, beadaidh

Unbashfully, *adv.* Gu beag-narach, gu dàna, gu ladurna, gu beadaidh.

Unbaste, *v.* Thoir as a cheile

Unbathed, *a* Neo-nighte, neo-fhliuch Unbathed with tears, *neo-fhliuch le deuraibh.*

Unbattered, *a.* Neo-bhuailte; neo-ghréidhte.

Unbay, *v. a.* Fosgail, leig ris.

Unbeaten, *a.* Neo-bhuailte; neo-ghreidhte, neo-sharuichte; neo-strampta.

Unbecoming, *a* Neo-chiatach, mi-chiatach, mi-bheusach, neo-aogasach, neo-lathailteach, neo-eireachdail.

Unbecomingness, *s* Mi-bheusachd, mi-aogasachd, mi-lathailteachd

Unbed, *v. a.* Tog a leabaidh

Unbefitting, *a* Neo-fhreagarrach, neo-lathailteach

Unbeheld, *a.* Neo-fhaicinnte, nach deach' fhaicinn.

Unbegotten, *a.* Neo-ghinte, neo-chruthaichte, siorruidh

Unbelief, *s* Ana-creidimh, mi-chreidimh, mi-dhiadhachd, eas-cairdeas

Unbeliever, *s* Ana-creideach, ana-creidiche, eas-caraid

Unbeloved, *a* Neo-ghradhaichte, neo-ionmhuinn

Unbend, *v a* Fuasgail, dirich

Unbending, *a* Rag, dian, rithinn, do-lùbadh, ailghiosach, diongalta

Unbenevolent, *a* Neo-sheirceil, mi-sheirceil, neo-chòir

Unbenighted, *a* Bith-shoilleir, mar a tha mulcheann deas na cruinne anns a gheamhradh, is am mul-cheann tuath anns t-samhradh

Unbenign, *a.* Neo-chaoimhneil, neo-chòir, spideil, mi-runach.

Unbent, *a.* Neo-lùbta; dìreach; neo-cheannsaichte; neo-shàruichte.

Unbequeathed, *a.* Neo-thiomnaichte

Unbeseeming, *a.* Neo-chiatach, mi-chiatach, neo-bhoidheach; mi-aogasach, mi-bheusach, mi-eireachdail

Unbesought, *a* Gun sireadh, gun iarruidh, gun chuireadh, neo-chuirte. He did this unbesought, *rinn e so gun iarruidh*, he came unbesought, *thàinig e gun chuireadh*

Unbestowed, *a* Neo-bhuilichte

Unbetrayed, *a.* Neo-bhrathta.

Unbewailed, *a* Neo-chaoidhte; gun chaoidh.

Unbiassed, *a.* Neo-aonta; gun leth-bhreith

Unbiassedly, *adv* Gun chlaon-bhreith, gun leth-bhreith.

Unbid, Unbidden, *a* Gun iarruidh, gun sireadh, gun chuireadh, neo-chuirte; (*he*), d'a dheòin; (*she*), d'a deoin; (*they*), d'an deòin.

Unbind, *v. a.* Fuasgail, tuasgail, tualaig; sgaoil Unbound, *fuasgailte, tuasgailte, tualaigte, sgaoilte.*

Unbitted, *a* Neo-shrianaichte; neo-cheannsaichte; neo-bhriste.

Unblamable, *a* Neo-chiontach, neo-lochdach, neo-choireach, glan, gun chiont, gun choire, gun lochd, neo-airidh air achmhasan

Unblamed, *a* Neo-choirichte, neo-chiontach, neo-lochdach, gun choire, gun chiont.

Unblemished, *a.* Neo-chiurramach, gun lochd, gun chionnt, gun ghaoid.

Unblenched, *a.* Glan, gun smàl, gun lochd

Unblended, *a.* Neo-mheasgta, glan

Unblest, *a.* Neo-bheannuichte, malluichte, dona, truagh.

Unbloody, *a* Neo-bhorb; neo-fhuileach, neo-fhuilteach

Unblown, *a.* Gun bhlàth.

Unblunted, *a.* Neo-mhaol, neo-mhaolaichte.

Unbodied, *a.* Neo-chorporra, neo-chorpach, neo-chorpaichte, spioradail

Unboiled, *a.* Neo-bhruichte, neo-bhruich, amh

Unbolt, *v.* Fosgail, thoir an crann dhe Unbolt the door, *thoir an crann bhàrr an doruis*

Unbolted, *a* Fosgailte; di-chrannaichte, (*as corn*), garbh.

Unbonneted, *a* Gun bhoineid, ceann-lom.

Unbookish, *a.* Aineolach, neo-ionnsuichte, neo-oileanaichte.

Unbooted, *a* Gun bhòt, gun bhòtan, neo-bhòtaichte.

Unborn, *a.* Gun bhreith, neo-ghinte, neo-bheirte.

Unbosom, *v.* Leig ris; fosgail; innis, nochd.

Unbottomed, *a.* Gun ghrunnd.

Unbought, *a.* Neo-cheannuichte

Unbound, *a.* Tuasgailte, fuasgailte, neo-cheangailte, lasach.

Unbounded, *a.* Neo-chriochnach, neo-iomallach o gun chrioch

Unboundedly, *adv* Gun chrioch, gu neo-chriochnach

Unboundedness, *s.* Neo-chriochnaidheachd, *contracted*, neo-chriochnachd.

Unbowed, *a* Neo-lùbta, direach.

Unbowel, *v a.* Thoir am mionach a

Unbrace, *a* Fuasgail, lasaich. Unbraced, *fuasgailte*

Unbraid, *v.* Fuasgail, thoir as a chéile, tualaig

Unbred, *a.* Neo-chleachdta; *neo-ionnsuichte.*

Unbreeched, *a* Gun bhriogan, gun bhriogais

Unbribed, *a* Neo-bhriobta, neo-bhribte, gun bhriob

Unbridle, *v.* Thoir srian de (no) bhàrr Unbridle my horse, *thoir an t-srin bhàrr m' each*

Unbridled, *a.* An-srianta; neo-cheannsuichte, neo-chiosnaichte

Unbroken, *a.* Slàn; neo-bhriste; (*untamed*), neo-cheannsuichte; neo-chiosnaichte.

Unbrotherly, *a.* Neo-bhràthaireil.

Unbruised, *a.* Neo-bhrùthte, neo-chiurrta, gun bhruth, gun chiurram.

Unbuckle, *v.* Fuasgail, tuasgail, tualaig.

Unbuild, *v a.* Tilg sios, leig

Unburden, *v.* Aotramaich, eutromaich, di-luchdaich; tilg bhàrr

Unburdened, *a.* Aotromaichte, eutromaichte

Unburied, *a.* Neo-adhlaicte; gun uaigh.

Unburned, Unburnt, *a* Neo-loisgte; neo-sheargte.

Unburning, *a.* Neo-loisgeach.

Unbutton, *v.* Fosgail, fuasgail, tuasgail, tualaig

Uncalcined, *a.* Neo-loisgte.

Uncalled, *a.* Gun chuireadh, gun sireadh, gun iarruidh, neo-ghairmte, neo-chuirte He came uncalled, *thàinig e gun chuireadh.*

Uncalm, *v a* Buair.

Uncandid, *a* Neo-fhìreannach, dùinte.

Uncandied, *a.* Neo-channdaichte.

Uncared (for), *v.* Gun spéis, gun suim, neo-mheasail

Uncase, *v* Rùisg, leig ris, plaoisg, sgrath.

Uncaught, *a* Neo-ghlacta.

Uncautious, *a* Neo-aireachail, neo-smuainteachail, mi-fhaiceallach, gun omhaill, gun seadh, eu-crionna.

Unceasing, *a.* Gun sgur, bith-bhuan, daonalt, daonann, bitheanta, siorruidh.

Uncensured, *a.* Neo-achmhasanaichte; gun-achmhasan, neo-chronaichte.

Uncertain, *a.* Neo-chinnteach; teagamhach; amharusach, neo-fhiosrach, neo-shuidhichte. I am uncertain what to do, *cha 'n 'eil fhios a gam ciod a ni mi.*

Uncertainty, *s.* Neo-chinnteachd, neo-chinntealas; teagamhachd; neo-fhiosrachd.

Unchain, *v* Fuasgail, tuasgail, di-chuibhrich. Unchained, *fuasgailte.*

Unchangeable, *a.* Neo-chaochlaideach, maireannach, bunaiteach

Unchangeableness, *s.* Neo-chaochlaideachd, maireannachd, bunaiteachd

Unchangeably, *adv* Gu neo-chaochlaideach; gu bunaiteach

Uncharitable, *a.* Neo-sheirceil, mi-sheirceil, neo-thruacanta, neo-charthanach.

Uncharitableness, *s.* Mi-sheircealachd, mi-charthanach.

Uncharitably, *adv.* Gu mi-sheirceil, gu neo-charthanach.

Unchaste, *a.* Neo-gheamnuidh, neo-gheimnidh, neo-ghlan, drùiseil, feòlmhor, siùrsachail, mi-theisteil, mi-bhandaidh, mi-bheusach.

Unchastity, *s.* Mi-gheimnidheachd, drùisealachd, drùs.

Unchecked, *a.* Neo-cheannsuichte, gun bhac, neo-ghrabta, neo-bhacta.

Uncheerfulness, *s* Mi-shuilbhire, dubhachas; bròn

Unchewed, *a* Neo-chagainnte, neo-chnamhta

Unchristian, *a.* Mi-chriosdail, mi-chriosduigh; neo-iompuichte, borb

Unchristianness, *s.* Mi-chriosduigheachd.

Uncircumcised, *a.* Neo-thimchioll-ghearrta

Uncircumcision, *s* Neo-thimchioll-ghearradh

Uncircumscribed, *a* Neo-chriochnach.

Uncircumspect, *a* Neo-fhaiceallach, eu-crionna.

Uncivil, *a.* Mi-shuairc, mi-mhodhail, borb, mi-shiobhailte, balachail, bodachail

Uncivilized, *a.* Borb, fiadhaich; mi-bheusach.

Uncivilly, *adv.* Gu mi-mhodhail, gu mi-shuairc.

Uncle, *s.* Brathair athar (no) mathar.

Unclean, **Uncleanly**, *a.* Salach, mosach, musach, neo-ghlan, gràda, drùiseil.

Uncleanliness, **Uncleanness**, *s.* Neo-ghloine, salachar; drùis.

Uncleansed, *a.* Neo-nighte; salach, mosach, neo-ghlan.

Unclerical, *a.* Neo-chléireachail; neo-chliarach.

Unclinch, *v. a.* Fosgail dorn.

Unclipped, *a.* Neo-bhearrta; slàn.

Unclog, *v. a.* Eutromaich; fuasgail, leig fa sgaoil.

Unclose, *v.* Fosgail. Unclosed, *fosgailte.*

Unclothe, *v.* Rùisg, dean lomardach.

Unclouded, *a.* Neo-ghruamach; soilleir.

Uncloudy, *a.* Soilleir, gun neul.

Uncloudedness, *s.* Soilleireachd.

Uncoagulated, *a.* Neo-shlamaichte.

Uncock, *v.* (*As a gun*), cuir bharr a chocainn.

Uncoil, *v. a.* Thoir a còil, sgap.

Uncoined, *a.* Neo-chùinte.

Uncollected, *a.* Neo-chruinnichte, neo-thionailte; neo-chnuasaichte, neo-shicir.

Uncoloured, *a.* Neo-dhathta; neo-lighte.

Uncombed, *a.* Neo-chirte, gun chìreadh.

Uncomeliness, *s.* Mi-eireachdas; mi-bheus.

Uncomely, *a.* Mi-chiatach; neo-bheusach, mi-bheusach, neo-eireachdail.

Uncomfortable, *a.* Mi-shuaimhneach, docrach, duaichnidh; neo-chothromach, neo-chomhnard, dubhach.

Uncomfortableness, *s.* Mi-shuaimhneas, docair, dubhachas.

Uncomfortably, *adv.* Gun suaimhneas, gu mi-shuaimhneach.

Uncommanded, *a.* Neo-aithnichte; gun àithne.

Uncommon, *a.* Neo-chumanta; neo-ghnàthach, ainneamh; neònach, tearc, gann.

Uncommonness, *s.* Neo-chumantachd, teirce, ainmigead.

Uncommunicated, *a.* Neo-bhuilichte.

Uncompact, *a.* Neo-chuimir; neo-dhiongmhalta.

Uncompassionate, *a.* Mi-thruacanta; borb, cruaidh, cruadalach.

Uncomplaisance, *s.* Mi-shuairceas, mi-mhodhaileachd, mi-mhodh.

Uncomplaisant, *a.* Mi-shuairc; neo-chùirteil, mi-mhodhail.

Uncomplete, *a.* Neo-chriochnaichte, neo-fhoirfe, neo-ullamh.

Uncompounded, *a.* Neo-mheasgta, neo-choimeasgta, singilte.

Uncomprehensible, *a.* Do-thuigsinn.

Uncomprehensive, *a.* Mi-thuigseach, neo-thuigseach.

Uncompressed, *a.* Neo-theannaichte; neo-dhomhlaichte.

Unconcealed, *a.* Neo-fholaichte; neo-cheilte, nochdta; air a leigeil ris.

Unconceivable, *a.* Do-thuigsinn, do-smuaineachadh; nach gabh tuigsinn (no) beachdachadh.

Unconceived, *a.* Neo-smuainichte; neo-bheachdaichte.

Unconcern, *s.* Neo-aire, neo-chùram.

Unconcerned, *a.* Neo-chùramach; neo-aireachail, air bheag seadh, air bheag omhaill, gun omhaill, gun chùram; comadh, coidhis.

Unconcernedly, *adv.* Gu neo-churamach, gu neo-aireachail, gu coidhis.

Unconcernedness, *s.* Neo-chùram, neo-chùramachd, coidhiseachd.

Unconcluded, *a.* Neo-chriochnaichte.

Unconcocted, *a.* Neo-chnamhta, neo-chnamhte.

Uncondemned, *a.* Neo-dhìte, gun dhìteadh.

Unconditional, *a.* Gun chùmhnant, neo-chùmhnantach.

Unconfinable, *a.* Gun chrioch, neo-chriochnach, gun iomall.

Unconfined, *a.* Saor; gun bhac; neo-theann; neo-chriochnach; gun iomall.

Unconfirmed, *a.* Neo-dhaingnichte, neo-dhaighnichte; neo-dhearbhta.

Unconform, *a.* Neo-choslach, eu-coslach, eu-cosmhal; neo-chubhaidh.

Unconformable, *a.* Neo-fhreagarrach; mi-chubhaidh, neo-iomchuidh.

Unconformity, *s.* Neo-fhreagarrachd, neo-iomchuidhead.

Unconfused, *a.* Riachdail; follaiseach; riaghailteach, pongail.

Unconfusedly, *adv.* Gu riachdail; gu follaiseach, gu riaghailteach, gu pongail.

Unconfutable, *a.* Do-fhreagairt, do chur as àicheadh, do chur mach.

Uncongealed, *a.* Neo-reòthta.

Unconjugal, *a.* Mi-mharaisteach; neo-mharaisteach, mi-chéilidh.

Unconnected, *a.* Lasach; tuasgailte, fuasgailte; neo-cheangailte; neo-chairdeach.

Unconquerable, *a.* Do-cheannsachadh, do-shàruchaidh, nach gabh ceannsachadh.

Unconquered, *a.* Neo-cheannsaichte, neo-shàruichte.

Unconscionable, *a.* Gun choguis, mi-reusonta, mi-choguiseach.

Unconscionably, *adv.* Gu mi-reusonta, gu mi-choguiseach.

Unconscious, *a.* Neo-fhiosrach; aineolach.

Unconsecrated, *a.* Neo-choisrigte, neo-naomhaichte.

Unconsidered, *a.* Neo-smuaintichte, neo-bheachdaichte.

Unconsonant, *a.* Neo-fhreagarach; neo-iomchuidh.

Unconstant, *a.* Neo-sheasamhach, neo-bhunailteach; mùghteach, siùbhlach, luaineach, neo-shuidhichte.

Unconstitutional, *a.* Neo-laghail.

Unconstrainable, *a.* Do-caralachadh, do-chomhairleachadh; do-smachdaidh.

Unconstrainedly, *adv.* Gu deònach, a dheòin, gu saor.

Unconstraint, *s.* Saorsa-toil, socair, athais.

Unconsulting, *a.* Bràis, dàn, obann.

Unconsumed, *a.* Neo-chaithte; neo-mhillte; gun chaitheamh.

Uncontemned, *a.* Neo-tharcuisichte.

Uncontented, *a.* Neo-thoilichte, diombach, diomach, neo-bhuidheach.

Uncontestable, **Uncontested**, *a.* Soilleir, so-thuigsinn, neo-chonnsachail, nach gabh cur as aicheadh.

Uncontrite, *a.* Neo-aithreachail; neo-chrabhach.

Uncontrollable, *a.* Do-smachdachadh, do-cheannsachadh.

Uncontrolled, *a.* Neo-smachdaichte; gun bhac.

Uncontrolledly, *adv.* Gu neo-smachdaichte.

Uncontroverted, *a.* Neo-thagairte.

Unconvertible, *a.* Nach gabh cur as àicheadh (no) an aghaidh.

Unconversible, *a.* Neo-chaidreamhach, neo-bhruidhreachail, fiata coimheach; fad thall, dùinte.

Unconverted, *a.* Mi-dhiadhaidh; neo-iompaichte.

Uncooked, *a.* Neo-dheasaichte, neo-ghreadhta, neo-ghreidhte.

Uncord, *v.* Fuasgail, tuasgail, fosgail.

Uncork, *v.* Thoir àrcan a, tarruing àrcan.

Uncorrected, *a.* Neo-leasaichte; neo-cheartaichte; neo-smachdaichte.

Uncorrupt, *a.* Ionrac; dìreach, treibhdhireach, neo-thruaillte, onorach.

Uncorrupted, *a.* Neo-thruaillte.

Uncorruptible, *a.* Neo-thruaillidh, nach gabh truailleadh.

Uncorruptness, *s.* Ionracas; treibhdhireas.

Uncover, *v.* Rùisg, lom; sgrath, plaoisg, leig ris.

Uncovered, *a.* Rùisgte; lom; plaoisgte.

Uncountable, *a.* Do-chunntadh, do-aireamh.

Uncourteous, *a.* Mi-shuairc, mi-mhodhail, mi-chuirteil.

Uncouth, *a.* Iongantach; neònach, aighearach; neo-chearmanta.

Uncouthly, *adv.* Gu h-iongantach, gu neònach, gu neo-chuimir.

Uncouthness, *s.* Neònachd, neo-chearmantachd.

Uncreate, *v. a.* Cuir gu neo-bhith.

Uncreated, *a.* Neo-chruthaichte.

Uncreditable, *a.* Mi-chreideasach.

Uncreditably, *adv.* Gu mi-chreideasach.

Uncropped, *a.* Neo-bhearrta; neo-ghearrta; neo-bhuainte.

Uncrowded, *a.* Neo-dhomhail.

Uncrown, *v.* Di-chrùnaich.

Uncrumple, *v. a.* Thoir cas, preas (no) liurc a aodach.

Unction, *s.* Ungadh.

Unctuous, *a.* Reamhar, sailleil, sleamhuinn, geireach; gréiseach.

Unctuousness, *s.* Reamharachd, saille.

Unculled, *a.* Neo-thionailte, neo-theanailte.

Unculpable, *a.* Neo-choireach, neo-chiontach, glan, neo-lochdach.

Uncultivated, *a.* Neo-threabhta; gun treabhadh, fàs; fàsail, fiadhaich; neo-fhoghluimte, neo-aitichte.

Uncumbered, *a.* Neo-luchdaichte.

Uncurable, *a.* Do-leigheasadh.

Uncurbed, *a.* Neo-cheannsaichte, fuasgailte; ana-cneasta, ain-srianta.

Uncured, *a.* Neo-leighiste, neo-leagheasta.

Uncurled, *a.* Neo-chasta; neo-chlearcach; neo-dhualach, neo-thoinnte.

Uncursed, *a.* Neo-mhalluichte.

Uncustomary, *a.* Neo-chumanta, mi-nòsar.

Uncut, *a.* Neo-ghearrta; neo-bhuainte.

Undamaged, *a.* Neo-dhochairichte; neo-dhochannaichte, gun choir, gun dochann.

Undaunted, *a.* Neo-ghealtach; misneachail, dàn, spreigeil.

Undauntedly, *adv.* Gu neo-ghealtach, gu misneachail, gu dàna, gu spreigeil.

Undauntedness, *s.* Misneach; dànadas, treubhantas, treuthantas, spreigealachd.

Undebauched, *a.* Neo-thruaillte; neo-thruaillichte.

Undecayed, *a.* Neo-sheargte, neo-sheacta, slàn, fallain.

Undeceive, *v.* Cuir ceart, mi-mheall.

Undeceived, *a.* Neo-mheallta, air chur ceart.

Undecided, *a.* Neo-chinnteach; neo-shonruichte; teagmhach, san turamanaich, san tomhartaich.

Undecisive, *a.* Neo-chinnteach, neo-shonruichte.

Undecked, *a.* Neo-sgiamhaichte, neo-sgeadaichte, neo-sgiamhach, neo-bhriaghaichte.

Undedicated, *a.* Neo-choisrigte, neo-naomhaichte.

Undefaced, *a.* Neo-mhillte; neo-shalach, glan, neo-thruaillte.

Undefeasible, *a.* Seasmhach; nach gabh cur air chùl.

Undefied, *a.* Neo-dhùlanaichte.

Undefiled, *a.* Neo-thruaillidh, neo-shalach, glan, neo-thruaillichte.

Undefined, *a.* Neo-mhìnichte; gun iomall (no) crioch.

Undeformed, *a.* Ceart-chruthaichte; gun ghaoid, gun chiurr.

Undeliberated, *a.* Neo-bheachdaichte.

Undelighted, *a.* Neo-aoibhneach, neo-aoibhinn, neo-thoileach.

Undelightful, *a.* Neo-shòlasach, neo-thaitneach.

Undemolished, *a.* Neo-sgriosta; neo-leigte; a lathair.

Undemonstrable, *a.* Do-dhearbhadh, do-chomhdachadh; nach gabh dearbhadh, nach gabh comhdachadh.

Undeniable, *a.* Do-àicheadh, nach gabh àicheadh; soilleir, riachdail.

Undeniably, *adv.* Cho soilleir is nach gabh' àicheadh.

Undeplored, *a.* Neo-chaoidhte.

Undepraved, *a.* Neo-thruaillichte.

Under, *prep.* Fo, fodha, fuidh, fa; an iochdar. Under me, *fodham;* under thee, *fodhad;* under her, *fuidhpe;* under him, *fodha;* under us, *fodhainn;* under you, *fodhaibh;* under them, *fodhpa;* be under, *bi fodha;* bring under, *ceannsaich, faigh lamh an uachdar;* brought under, *ceannsaichte, ciosnaichte;* under ground, *fo 'n talamh.*

Underbear, *v.* Giùlain, fulaing; cum suas, iomchair.

Under-bearer, *s.* Fear-iomchair.

Underbid, *v.* Tairg fodha.

Undercited, *a.* Fo-radhte, fo-sgriobhta.

Underclerk, *s.* Cléireach iochdarach.

Under-fellow, *s.* Sgonn-bhalaoch, sgleamhsa, ablach.

Undergo, *v.* Fulaing, fuiling, fuilig, giùlain, iomchair. Underwent, *dh' fhulaing, dh' fhuilig.*

Underground, *s.* Fo 'n talamh.

Undergrowth, *s.* Frith-choille; preasarnach, crionach.

Underhand, *a.* Diomhair, uaigneach; cealgach, fealltach. Underhand dealing, *foill, sloighte.*

Underhand, *adv.* Gu diomhair; os iosal, gu cealgach, gu fealltach.

Under-labourer, *s.* Fear oibre; traill, sgalag.

Underlay, *v. a.* Cuir fodha.

Underleather, *s.* Leathar buinn, leathrach buinn.

Underling, *s.* Iochdaran; siochair; fear gun fhiù.

Undermine, *v.* Fo-tholl, fo' bhùraich, cladhaich, fo' chladhaich; tochail, cuir neach as àite gun fhios. Undermined, *cladhaichte, bùraichte, tochailte.*

Underminer, *s.* Tochailtear, cladhaiche, nàmhaid diomhair.

Undermost, *a.* Is ìlse, is ìsle, iochdarach, is iochdaraiche, an iochdar.

Underneath, *prep.* Fo, fodha, fuidh, fa.

Under-officer, *s.* Iochdaran.

Under-petticoat, *s.* Còt iochdair, còt iochdrach.

Underpin, *v.* Prop, geinn; cum roimh, cum suas.

Underplot, *s.* Fo-chluiche; cluiche a leth-taobh.

Underpraise, *s.* Di-mhol; fo' mhol.

Underprize, *v.* Di-mheas.

Underprop, *v.* Cum taic, cum suas.

Underrate, *v.* Di-mheas. Underrated, *di-mheasta.*

Under-secretary, *s.* Fo-sgriobhair, cleireach iochdrach.
Undersell, *v.* Reic ni 's saoire (no) tuille is saor.
Underset, *v. a.* Prop, cum taic ri, cum suas.
Under-setter, *s.* Prop, taic, cùl-taic.
Under-sheriff, *s.* Fo-shiorradh, siorradh iochdarach.
Under-song, *s.* Luinneag.
Understand, *v. a.* and *n.* Tuig; mothuich, rosg, foghluim. I understand, *tha mi 'tuigsinn;* understand amiss, *tog am mearachd;* give him to understand, *leig dha aithneachadh;* I understood you, *thuig mi thu.*
Understanding, *s.* Tuigse, toinisg: ciall, inntinn; cordadh, deadh rùn, tuigsinn, tuigeil, mothuchadh. Of quick understanding, *geur mhothuchail;* a man of little understanding, *fear air bheag toinisg.*
Understanding, *a.* Seòlta, sgileil, tuigseach, toinisgeil.
Understandingly, *adv.* Gu seòlta, gu sgileil, gu tuigseach, gu toinisgeil, le sgile, le tuigse, le toinisge.
Understrapper, *s.* Fo' sheirbheiseach; iochdaran.
Undertake, *v. a.* and *n.* Gabh os laimh; gabh ort, dean oidhirp. I will undertake this business, *gabhaidh mi an gnothuch so os laimh;* I have undertaken it, *ghabh mi os laimh e.*
Undertaker, *s.* Fear-ghnothuich; fear adhlacaidh; adhlacachan, fear ghabhas adhlac os laimh.
Undertaking, *s.* Oidhirp; cùis, gnothuch, obair.
Under-treasurer, *s.* Fo-ionmhasair.
Undervalue, *v.* Dimheas; cuir air mi-shuim.
Undervaluer, *s.* Di-mheasair.
Underwent, *pret.* of undergo. Dh' fhulaing.
Underwood, *s.* Preasarnach, frith-choille, crionach, meanbh-choille.
Underwork, *s.* Ceartaichean.
Under-workman, *s.* Fear oibre.
Under-writer, *s.* Cinnteadair; urrasair, neach a theid an geall air ni 'an cunnart.
Underwritten, *a.* Fo-sgriobhta, fo-sgriobhte.
Undescried, *a.* Neo-fhaicinnte, neo-chomharraichte.
Underwrite, *v. a.* Fo-sgriobh, sgriobh.
Undeserved, *a.* Neo-thoilltinneach, mi-thoilltinneach, neo-airidh.
Undeservedly, *adv.* Gu neo-thoilltinneach, gu neo-airidh.
Undeserving, *a.* Neo-thoilltinneach, mi-thoilltinneach, neo-airidh.
Undesignedly, *adv.* Gun fhios, gun rùn. He hurt me undesignedly, *chiùrr e mi gun fhios da.*
Undesigning, *a.* Neo-chealgach; neo-chuilbheartach, ionraic, tréibhdhireach, onorach.
Undesirable, *a.* Neo-thaitneach; nach còrr iarruidh.
Undesired, *a.* Gun iarruidh, gun sireadh. He came undesired, *thainig e gun iarruidh.*
Undesiring, *a.* Coidhis, comadh, neo-thogarach.
Undestroyed, *a.* Neo-mhillte, neo-sgriosta.
Undeterminable, *a.* Do-shònrachadh.
Undetermined, *a.* Neo-shònraichte; neo-shuidhichte; neo-riaghailtichte.
Undiaphonous, *a.* Dorcha, doilleir.
Undigested, *a.* Neo-chnamhta.
Undiminished, *a.* Neo-bheagaichte, neo-laghdaichte.
Undipped, *a.* Neo-thumta, neo-thomta, neo-bhogta.
Undirected, *a.* Neo-threòraichte; gun seòl; gun iarruidh.
Undiscerned, *a.* Neo-fhaicinnte, neo-chomharaichte.
Undiscernible, *a.* Neo-fhaicsinneach, do-fhaicinn, do-chomharachadh.

Undiscerning, *a.* Baoghalta, neo-thuigseach.
Undisciplined, *a.* Neo-cheannsaichte; neo-smachdaichte; neo-oileanaichte, neo-ionnsuichte, aineolach.
Undiscording, *a.* Neo-fhreagarrach, eu-cordadh.
Undiscoverable, *a.* Do-rannsuchadh, do-fhaotainn a mach.
Undiscovered, *a.* Neo-fhaicinnte, neo-aithnichte; neo-rannsaichte.
Undiscreet, *a.* Gòrrach, neo-ghlic, eu-crionna, mi-chiallach, neo-shuairc, mi-shuairc.
Undisguised, *a.* Fosgailte; nochdta; simplidh; fior neo-chealgach. My undisguised thoughts, *m' fhìor dhòchasan.*
Undismayed, *a.* Dàn, misneachail; treubhanta, treuthanta.
Undisobliging, *a.* Neo-choireach.
Undispersed, *a.* Neo-sgapta, neo-sgaoilte.
Undisposed, *a.* Neo-bhuilichte.
Undisputable, *a.* Soilleir; neo-chonnsachail, cinnteach, sàr-chinnteach.
Undissembled, *a.* Neo-chéilte; fior; neo-chealgach; neo-mhealltach.
Undissembling, *a.* Fior; neo-mhealltach.
Undissipated, *a.* Neo-sgapta, neo-sgaoilte.
Undissolvable, *a.* Do-leaghadh, nach gabh leaghadh.
Undistempered, *a.* Slàn, fallain, slàinnteil, gun eucail.
Undistinguishable, *a.* Do-fhaicinn, do-fhaicsinn, do-chomharrachadh, do-bheachdachadh, do-aithneachadh.
Undistinguished, *a.* Neo-aithnichte; neo-iomraiteach, neo-chliùiteach.
Undistracted, *a.* Socrach, siochainnteach, soimeach, neo-bhuairte; neo-ghluaiste.
Undisturbed, *a.* Neo-bhuairte; socrach; seimh, ciùin, samhach, tosdach, siochainnteach.
Undisturbedly, *adv.* Gu socrach, gu seimh, gu ciùin, gu samhach, gu tosdach.
Undividable, *a.* Do-phàirteachadh, do-sgaradh.
Undivided, *a.* Neo-phàirtichte, neo-sgarta, slàn, neo-bhriste.
Undivulged, *a.* Diomhair, céilte.
Undo, *v.* Mill; sgrios; fuasgail, tuasgail, ath-dhean. Undo this knot, *fuasgail an snaim so.*
Undoing, *a.* Sgriosail, millteach.
Undoing, *s.* Sgrios, sgriosadh, milleadh, beud.
Undone, *a.* Neo-ullamh, neo-chriochnuichte; sgriosta, caillte. He is undone, *tha e caillte, tha e dheth.*
Undoubted, *a.* Cinnteach; fior.
Undoubtedly, *adv.* Gu cinnteach, air chinnte, gun teagamh, gun amharus, gun ag.
Undoubting, *a.* Neo-amharusach; cinnteach.
Undress, *v. a.* Neo-sgeadaich; lom; rùisg.
Undress, *s.* Aodach madainn.
Undressed, *a.* Neo-riaghailtichte; neo-sgeadaichte, neo-uigheamaichte; neo-dheasaichte; neo-ghréidhte.
Undried, *a.* Neo-thiormaichte; neo-thioram.
Undrossy, *a.* Gun smùrach, neo-smùirneach.
Undubitable, *a.* Neo-theagamhach, cinnteach.
Undue, *a.* Mi-cheart, neo-cheart, neo-dhligheach, eucorach, mi-laghail.
Undulate, *v.* *Tonn,* éirich *mar thonn;* udail.
Undulation, *s.* Tonn-luasgadh, tulg-tuinn.
Undulatory, *a.* Tonn-luasgach; udalach.
Unduly, *adv.* Gu mi-cheart, gu mi-laghail, gu mi-dhleasdanach, gu mi-dhligheach.
Unduteous, **Undutiful**, *a.* Mi-dhleasdanach; neo-dhleasdanach, eas-umhal, eas-urramach, mi-mhodhail.

Undutifulness, *s.* Mi-dhleasdanas, easumhlachd
Undutifully, *adv.* Gu mi-dhleasdanach, gu h-eas-ùmhal
Undying, *a.* Neo-bhàsmhor, nach bàsaich.
Unearned, *a.* Neo-choisinnte, neo-bhuidhinte, neo-bhuinigte.
Unearthly, *a* Mi-thalmhainneach, neo-chorporra, neo-thalmhaidh, neo-shaoghalmhor, spioradail, aogaidh
Uneasiness, *s* An-shocair, docair; mi-shuaimhnear, iom-cheist, pian; mi-thaitneas, aimheal, utrais
Uneasy, *a* An-shocrach, frithearach, mi-shuaimhneach; neo-shocrach, docrach, deacair, mi-thoilichte, dubhach; neo-shoimeach, iomairteach, aimhealach, utraiseach
Uneaten, *a.* Neo-ithte; neo-chaithte, neo-chnamhta.
Unedifying, *a* Neo-leasachail, neo-tharbhach chum oilein.
Unelected, *a* Neo-thaghta, neo-roghnaichte.
Uneligible, *a.* Neo-roghnachail; neo-àiridh air roghnachadh
Unemployed, *a.* Soimeach, gun obair. Are you unemployed? *bheil thu air do shocair, bheil thu air d' athais?*
Unengaged, *a* Neo-ghabhta, saor
Unenjoyed, *a* Neo-shealbhaichte, neo-mhealta, gun mhealtuinn.
Unenlarged, *a.* Neo-mheudaichte, neo-fharsuingichte, cumhang, aimhleathan.
Unenlightened, *a* Neo-shoillsichte; aineolach; dorch
Unenslaved, *a* Saor, neo-thràillichte, neo-dhaor.
Unentertaining, *a* Neo-aighearrach, neo-shunntach, neo-thaitneach
Unentombed, *a.* Neo-adhlaicte, neo-thiodhlaicte, neo-theorrta.
Unequal, *a.* Neo-ionann; neo-cho-fhad; neo-fhreagarrach
Unequalled, *a* Neo-ionannaichte, gun choimeas, gun leth-bhreac, neo-choimeasta, barrach, barr-mhaiseach.
Unequally, *adv.* Gu neo-ionann
Unequitably, *adv.* Gu neo-cheart; gu neo-chothromach, gu leth-bhreitheach
Unequitable, *a* Neo-cheart, neo-chothromach; neo-dhireach, leth-bhreitheach
Unequivocal, *a* Riachdail, soilleir.
Unerrable, *a* Neo-mhearachdach; direach, cinnteach, neo-sheachranach
Unerring, *a* Neo-mhearachdach, cuimseach, direach, cinnteach; neo-chlaon
Unerringly, *adv* Gu neo-mhearachdach, gu direach, gu cinnteach, gu neo-chlaon.
Unespied, *a* Neo-aithnichte, neo-chomharaichte, neo-fhaicinnte
Unessential, *a.* Suarrach, neo-fheumail; faoin
Unestablished, *a* Neo-shocraichte
Uneven, *a* Neo-chòmhnard; garbh, neo-réidh; neo-chomh-fhad, neo-fhreagarrach. Uneven ground, *talamh garbh*
Unevenness, *s.* Neo-chomhnardachd.
Unevitable, *a.* Do-sheachnadh, do-sheachanta, nach gabh seachnadh, nach fhaodar sheachnadh
Unexamined, *a.* Neo-cheasnuichte, neo-sgrudte, neo-rannsuichte; gun cheasnachadh, gun sgrudadh
Unexampled, *a* Neo-shamhlachail, neo-choimeasail
Unexceptionable, *a.* Do nach fhaighear coire.
Unexcised, *a* Neo-chìs-bhuailteach
Unexcogitable, *a.* Do-rannsuchadh.
Unexecuted, *a.* Neo-choimh lionta, neo-chrìochnuichte.
Unexempt, *a.* Neo-shaor.

Unexercised, *a.* Neo-chleachdta, neo-eolach, neo-dheanta ri
Unexhausted, *a.* Neo-thraighte, neo-thraoghta; neo-fhannaichte, neo-chaithte.
Unexhaustible, *a.* Do-thraghachadh, do-chaith.
Unexpanded, *a.* Neo-sgaoilte, neo-spréidte.
Unexpected, *a.* Gun fhios, obann, gun dùil ri.
Unexpectedly, *adv.* Gun fhios, gun dùil ri, gu h-obann. He came on me unexpectedly, *thainig e orm gun fhios domh (no) gu h-obann.*
Unexpectedness, *s.* Obainne.
† **Unexpedient**, *a.* Neo-fheumail; neo-iomchuidh, neo-fhreagarrach.
Unexperienced, *a.* Neo-chleachdta, neo-eòlach, neo-dheanta ri.
† **Unexpert**, *a* Neo-theoma, neo-sgileil, neo-ionnsuichte; neo-thuigseach
Unexplored, *a* Neo-rannsuichte, neo-aithnichte.
Unexpressible, *a.* Do labhairt, do-chur an ceill, do-innseadh.
Unextinguishable, *a.* Do-mhùchadh, do-chur as; nach gabh cur as, nach gabh mùchadh, nach fhaodar mhùchadh (no) chur as Unextinguishable fire, *teine nach gabh mùchadh (no) cur as*
Unextinguished, *a* Neo-mhùchta, gun mhùchadh, gun chur as, do-mhùchadh
Unfaded, *a* Neo-sheargte, neo-chrionta; ùr
Unfading, *a* Maireannach, bunaiteach, bith-bhuan, buan.
Unfailing, *a.* Cinnteach, neo-mhearachdach, neo-fhailinneach
Unfailingness, *s.* Cinnteas, mi-fhàilinn.
Unfairness, *s* Cuilbheart, ceabhcaireachd, foille, ceilge.
Unfair, *a* Mi-cheart, eucorach, claon, neo-onorach; cuilbheartach, cealgach, foilleil
Unfairly, *adv.* Gu mi-cheart, gu h-eucorach, gu cuilbheartach, gu claon, gu foilleil.
Unfaithful, *a.* Neo-dhileas, mealltach, cealgach; mi-dhiadhuidh, aingidh.
Unfaithfully, *adv.* Gu neo-dhìleas, gu mealltach, gu cealgach; gu mi-dhiadhuidh,
Unfaithfulness, *s* Cealgaireachd, mealtaireachd.
Unfamiliar, *a* Fiat, pùtanta; coimheach, neo-chleachdta, neo-eòlach, neo-dheanta ri, mi-nòsar.
Unfashionable, *a* Neo-fhasanta, neo-chleachdach, sean, sean-fhasanta, as an fhasan, mi-dhealbhaidh.
Unfashionably, *adv* Gu neo-fhasanta; gu neo-theòma; gu neo-chumta, gu mi-dhealbhadh
Unfashioned, *a.* Neo-chumta; leibideach, gun dreach, gun chumadh, gun chumachd
Unfasten, *v* Lasaich, fuasgail, tuasgail, tualaig.
Unfathered, *a.* Gun athair, dilleachdach
Unfathomable, *a.* Gun grunnd, gun iochdar; neo-ghrunndachadh; do-thomhas, thàr toinhas
Unfathomably, *adv* Gun ghrunnd, thar tomhas
Unfathomed, *a.* Neo-ghrunndaichte
Unfatigued, *a* Neo-sgìth; neo-sglthichte, neo-fhannaichte
Unfavourable, *a.* Mi-fhreasdalach, neo-ghoireasach; mi-shealbhar, neo-fhabhorach, neo-chaoimhneil
Unfavourably, *adv.* Gu mi-fhreasdalach, gu mi-shealbhar, gu neo-fhabhorach.
Unfavourableness, *s.* Neo-fhabhorachd, mi-chaoimhneas.

Unfeathered, *a.* Gun chlòimh.
Unfeatured, *a.* Gnò; duaichnidh.
Unfed, *a.* Neo-bhiathta.
Unfeed, *a.* Neo-thuarasdalaichte, neo-phàighte, gun phàigh.
Unfeeling, *a.* Neo-mhothuchail, cruaidh-chridheach, neo-thruacanta, neo-bhaigheil, cruadalach, mi-thlusail.
Unfeelingly, *adv.* Gu neo-mhothuchail, gu cruaidh-chridheach, gu cruadalach, gu mi-thlusail.
Unfeelingness, *s.* Neo-thruacantachd, cruadhas cridhe.
Unfeigned, *a.* Fìor, fireannach, neo-chealgach, ionraic.
Unfeignedly, *adv.* Gu fireannach, gu neo-chealgach, gu h-ionraic.
Unfelled, *a.* Neo-ghearrta, neo-bhuainte.
Unfelt, *a.* Neo-mhothuichte, neo-fhainichte.
Unfenced, *a.* Neo-dhionta, gun dion, gun fhàl.
Unfermented, *a.* Neo-oibrichte.
Unfertile, *a.* Neo-thorrach; fàs, neo-shiolmhor.
Unfetter, *v.* Fuasgail; tuasgail; saor, leig fa sgaoil.
Unfettered, *a.* Neo-chuibhrichte, neo-cheangailte, tuasgailte, saor.
Unfilial, *a.* Neo-mhacail.
Unfilled, *a.* Neo-lìonta, neo-làn.
Unfinished, *a.* Neo-chrìochnuichte, neo-choi-lìonta; neo-ullamh.
Unfirm, *a.* Anfhann, breòit, mall, neo-dhaingeann.
Unfit, *a.* Neo-iomchuidh, neo-mhurrach; neo-airidh; neo-fhreagarrach.
Unfit, *v.* Dean neo-mhurrach (no) neo-iomchuidh.
Unfitly, *a.* Gu neo-mhurrach, gu neo-airidh.
Unfitness, *s.* Neo-iomchuidhead; neo-fhreagarrachd.
Unfitting, *a.* Neo-iomchuidh; neo-fhreagarach, neo-lathailteach, neo-cheart.
Unfix, *v.* Lasaich, fuasgail, tuasgail.
Unfixed, *a.* Lasach; fuasgailte, tuasgailte; neo-shuidhichte; luaineach, siùbhlach, iomrolach.
Unfledged, *a.* Gun chloimh.
Unfleshed, *a.* Neo-threìnte; neo-dheanta ri fuil (no) àr.
Unfóiled, *a.* Neo-shàruichte.
Unfold, *v.* Fosgail, leig ris; nochd, innis, cuir an céill, foillsich. Unfolded, *fosgailte; nochdta, foillsichte.*
Unforbidden, *a.* Neo-thoirmisgte, neo-bhacta.
Unforced, *a.* Neo-éignichte; furas.
Unforeseen, *a.* Neo-fhairichte; obann; gun aire, gun fhios.
Unforeskinned, *a.* Tiomchioll-ghearrta.
Unforfeited, *a.* Neo-chaillte, neo-dhiobairte.
Unforgiving, *a.* Neo-laghach; nach math; borb; cruadalach.
Unforgotten, *a.* Neo-dhi-chuimhnichte.
Unformed, *a.* Neo-chruthaichte; neo-dhealbhta, neo-chumadail, gun chruth, gun chumadh.
Unforsaken, *a.* Neo-dhiobairte, neo-thréigte.
Unfortified, *a.* Neo-dhaingnichte; neo-dhionta; anfhann; gun urras.
Unfortunate, *a.* Mi-shealbhar; mi-fhortanach; mi-shoirbheasach; tubaisteach; diblidh; truagh, dona.
Unfortunately, *adv.* Gu mi-shealbhar, gu mi-fhortanach; gu mi-shoirbheasach.
Unfouled, *a.* Neo-shalaichte; neo-thruaillichte, glan, gun smàl.
Unfound, *a.* Gun fhaotainn, gun fhaghail, neo-airmeiste, neo-amaiste.
Unframed, *a.* Neo-chumta; neo-dhealbhta; gun fhoir.
Unfrequent, *a.* Ainmig, neo-thric, tearc, gann; ainneamh, neo-chumannta.

Unfrequented, *a.* Neo-àitichte; fàsail, fàs, dìthreabhach, uaigneach.
Unfrequently, *adv.* Gu h-ainmig; gu tearc, gu neo-chumanta.
Unfriended, *a.* Gun charaid, gun chairdean, neo-chuidichte, gun chòghnath.
Unfriendliness, *s.* Mi-sheirc, neo-chairdealas, mi-chaoimhneas, mi-chaoimhnealas.
Unfriendly, *a.* Neo-chaoimhneil, neo-chairdeil, neo-chair.
Unfriendly, *adv.* Gu neo-chairdeil; gu neo-sheirceil, gu neo-chaoimhneil.
Unfrozen, *a.* Neo-reòthta.
Unfrugal, *a.* Neo-ghrunndail; neo-chùramach, caithteach, stroghail, struigheasach.
Unfruitful, *a.* Neo-tharbhach; neo-thorrach; seasg, neo-shiolmhor, aimrid.
Unfruitfulness, *s.* Neo-tharbhachd; neo-thorraichead, neo-tharbhaichead.
Unfulfilled, *a.* Neo-choimhlionta. A promise unfulfilled, *gealladh neo-choimhlionta.*
Unfurl, *v.* Sgaoil, fosgail, spréid. Unfurl the banner, *leig am bratach fa sgaoil.*
Unfurnish, *v.* Fàg gun airneis; lom, rùisg.
Unfurnished, *a.* Gun airneis; neo-uigheamaichte, gun uigheam, neo-dheasaichte; falamh.
Ungainful, *a.* Neo-tharbhach, neo-phroidhteach.
Ungainliness, *a.* Neo-chiatachd.
Ungainly, *a.* Neo-chiatach; mi-eireachdail.
Ungalled, *a.* Neo-leònta, neo-chiurta.
Ungarnish, *a.* Mi-sgiamhaich, mi-sgeadaich.
Ungarrisoned, *a.* Neo-dhaingnichte; neo-dhionta, gun ghearasdan.
Ungartered, *a.* Neo-ghartanaichte, gun ghartan.
Ungathered, *a.* Neo-thionailte; neo-charnta, neo-chruinnichte; neo-chnuasaichte.
Ungenerated, *a.* Neo-ghinte.
Ungenerative, *a.* Neo-thorrach, neo-ghineadail, neo-shiolmhor.
Ungenerous, *a.* Mi-shuairc, neo-fhial, neo-fhialuidh; spiocach, crion, neo-uasal.
Ungenial, *a.* Neo-ghineadach, neo-ghineadail, neo-fhabhorach.
Ungenteel, *a.* Neo-eireachdail; neo-bheusach, neo-mhodhail, mi-mhodhail.
Ungentle, *a.* Neo-shuairc; borb, gnò, cruaidh.
Ungentlemanlike, Ungentlemanly, *a.* Neo-uasal; neo-mhodhail; neo-eireachdail.
Ungentleness, *s.* Mi-shuairceas; cruadhas, buirbe; mi-chaoimhneas.
Ungently, *adv.* Gu borb, gu neo-shuairc, gu cruadalach, gu mi-chaoimhneil.
Ungilded, *a.* Neo-òraichte, neo-dheiltrichte.
Ungird, *v.* Fuasgail, tuasgail; fuasgail giort.
Ungirt, *a.* Neo-ghiortaichte, neo-chriosraichte, neo-chrioslaichte; tuasgailte, fuasgailte.
Ungiving, *a.* Neo-thabhartach; neo-fhial.
Unglorified, *a.* Neo-ghlòirichte.
Ungloved, *a.* Gun mheatag, gun làmhuinn.
Unglue, *v.* Thoir as a ghlaodh, thoir as a chéile.
Ungodlily, *adv.* Gu mi-dhiadhuidh, gu h-aingidh, gu h-olc.
Ungodliness, *s.* Mi-dhiadhachd; aingidheachd ain-diadhachd.

Ungodly, *a.* Mi-dhiadhuidh, aingidh, ain-diadhuidh, olc; ana-creideach, daoi; baoth.

Ungored, *a.* Neo-leonta, neo-chiurta.

Ungorged, *a.* Neo-lionta, neo-shathta, neo-bhuidheach, neo-làn.

Ungot, *a.* Neo-bhuidhinnte; neo-choisinnte, gun fhaotainn, gun fhaghail; neo-ghinte, neo-bheirsinnte.

Ungovernable, *a.* Do-cheannsachadh, do-smachdachadh; do-riaghladh; fiadhaich, ain-srianta, borb; duaireasach.

Ungovernableness, *s.* Do-cheannsachd; ain-sriantas, fiadhaichead; duaireas, duaireasachd.

Ungoverned, *a.* Neo-cheannsuichte, neo-smachduichte; neo-riaghlaichte; ain-srianta; gun smachd.

Ungraceful, *a.* Neo-eireachdail; neo-chiatach, neo-ghrinn, neo-speisealta.

Ungracefulness, *s.* Neo-eireachdas, neo-chiatachd, neo-speisealtachd.

Ungracious, *a.* Neo-thaitneach; grainell, neo-chiatach; olc, oilltcil; fuathach.

Ungrammatical, *a.* Neo-ghramadach.

Ungranted, *a.* Neo-bhuilichte.

Ungrateful, *a.* Mì-thaingeil; neo-thaingeil; neo-bhuidheach; neo-thaitneach.

Ungratefully, *adv.* Gu mi-thaingeil; gu neo-thaingeil; gu neo-thaitneach.

Ungratefulness, *s.* Mi-thaingealachd.

Ungrounded, *a.* Gun bhun, gun aobhar, faoin. An ungrounded report, *fabhunn faoin.*

Ungrudgingly, *adv.* Gu suilbhear, gu toileach, gu neo-dhiombach.

Unguarded, *a.* Neo-dhionta; gun dhion; neo-churamach, neo-sheadhail; neo-omhailleach, mi-omhailleach.

Unguent, *s.* Ungadh; oladh.

Unguessed, *a.* Neo-bharalaichte.

Unguided, *a.* Neo-threoruichte; neo-riaghlaichte, neo-stiùrta.

Unhabitable, *a.* Fàs; neo-àitichte, di-threabhta.

Unhabituated, *a.* Neo-chleachta.

Unhacked, *a.* Neo-shneagaichte; neo-ghearrta, neo-shnaithte.

Unhallow, *v.* Mi-naomhaich.

Unhallowed, *a.* Mi-naomh, neo-naomh.

Unhand, *v. a.* Leig as, leig fa sgaoil.

Unhandled, *a.* Neo-lamhaichte.

Unhandsome, *a.* Neo-eireachdail, neo-cheanalta, neo-bhòidheach, neo-ghrinn, neo-chiatach, neo-thlachdmhor; crion.

Unhandsomely, *adv.* Gu neo-eireachdail, gu neo-bhoidheach; gu neo-chiatach, gu neo-thlachdmhor.

Unhandsomeness, *s.* Neo-eireachdas, neo-bhoidhichead, neo-speisealtachd.

Unhandy, *a.* Neo-iomchuidh; neo-lamhachair, leibideach.

Unhanged, *a.* Neo-chrochta.

Unhap, *s.* Tubaiste, teagmhas, earchall, bochduinn.

Unhappily, *adv.* Gu mi-fortanach; gu tubaist, mar bha 'bhochduinn; gu bochd, gu truagh, gu mi-shona.

Unhappiness, *s.* Mi-fhortan, truaighe, bochduinn, earchall, mi-shonas, donas.

Unhappy, *a.* Mì-fhortanach, truagh, bochd, mi-shona, diblidh.

Unharboured, *a.* Gun chàla; gun fhasgadh, gun dion.

Unhardened, *a.* Neo-chruadhaichte; neo-chleachdta.

Unhardy, *a.* Neo-thuaireil, tais; meath, mall, anfhann, meuranda; gealtach.

Unharmed, *a.* Neo-chiurta, neo-dhochannaichte; gun chiurradh, gun dochann, gun lochd, gun dolaidh.

Unharmful, *a.* Neo-chronail.

Unharmonious, *a.* Neo-sheirmeach, neo-cheolmhor, neo-fhonnmhor.

Unharness, *v.* Neo-achduinnich, thoir acfuinn de (no) bhàrr. Unharness the horse, *thoir an acfuinn bhàrr an eich.*

Unhatched, *a.* Neo-bheirsinnte.

Unhealthful, *a.* Neo-shlainnteil; tinn, euslainteach, eucaileach.

Unhealthiness, *s.* Neo-shlainntealachd, euslainnteachd.

Unhealthy, *a.* Neo-shlainnteil; euslan, tinn, truagh, anfhann, meuranda, breòite.

Unheard, *a.* Gun fhios; neo-iomraitcach, samhach. Unheard of, *neo-iomraiteach.*

Unheated, *a.* Neo-theòite, neo-bhlathaichte.

Unheeded, *a.* Gun mheas, gun suim, di-mheasta.

Unheedful, *a.* Neo-aireachail, neo-smuainteachail, neo-churamach.

Unheeding, *a.* Neo-aireachail, brais, neo-churamach, dàn, neo-omhailleach.

Unheedy, *a.* Brais, cabhagach, obann, dàn.

Unhelped, *a.* Neo-chuidichte, gun cho-ghnath.

Unhelved, *a.* Gun samhach, gun lamh, gun chas.

Unhewn, *a.* Neo-shnaidhte, neo-ghearrta.

Unhinge, *v.* Cuir bharr nan lùdan; cuir thair chéile; cuir am breislich, cuir gu h-amhluadh. I unhinged him, *chuir mi 'm breislich e.*

Unholiness, *s.* Mì-naomhachd, aingidheachd.

Unholy, *a.* Mì-naomh; aingidh; truaillidh, olc; daor; baoth.

Unhonoured, *a.* Neo-onoirichte, neo-mheasta, gun onoir, gun mheas; di mheasta.

Unhoop, *v.* Neo-chearclaich; thoir cearcall bhàrr soithche.

Unhoped-for, *a.* Gun dùil ri, gun dochas ri. He came unhoped-for, *thainig e gun dùil ris.*

Unhorse, *v.* Tilg bharr eich.

Unhospitable, *a.* Neo-aoidheil, neo-fhial; coimheach; borb, garg.

Unhospitably, *adv.* Gu neo-aoidheil, gu neo-fhial, gu neo-dhaonnachdach; gu coimheach, gu borb.

Unhostile, *a.* Neo-naimhdeil, càirdeil.

Unhouse, *v.* Fògaraich, fògair; diobraich.

Unhoused, *a.* Fògairte; diobraichte, gun dachaidh, gun tigh.

Unhumbled, *a.* Neo-irioslaichte; neo-cheannsaichte.

Unhurt, *a.* Neo-chiurta; neo-dhochannaichte, gun chron, gun dochann, gun dolaidh, gun chiuram, gun chiurr; slàn. Much may be said by the head that is unhurt, *is mòr a their ceann slàn.*

Unhurtful, *a.* Neo-chronail, neo-mhillteach, neo-dhochannach.

Unhusk, *v.* Plaoisg, faoisg; sgrath. Unhusked, *plaoisgte, faoisgte.*

Unicorn, *s.* Aon-adharcach, buabhall.

Uniform, *a.* Riaghailteach; comh-ionann, aon-chruthach, comh-fhad, aon-dealbhach.

Uniformity, *s.* Riaghailteachd, comh-ionannachd; aon-fhuirm; comh-fhadachd, ionannachd, aondachd.

Unimaginable, *a.* Do-smuainteachadh, do-bheachdachadh, do-bharalachadh.

Unimmortal, *a.* Bàsmhor.

Unimpairable, *a.* Do-dhochannadh; do-caitheamh, do-mhilleadh.

Unimpaired, *a.* Neo-dhochannaichte, neo-chaithte, neo-mhillte; gun dochann, gun dolaidh, gun chaitheamh.

Unimplored, *a.* Neo-ghuidhte; neo-ghriosta.

Unimportance, *s.* Suarraichead; faoineas.

Unimportant, *a.* Suarrach, fadharsach, faothairseach, gun diù, gun fhiach.

Unimportuned, *s.* Neo-earalaichte.

Unimprovable, *a.* Do-leasachadh, nach gabh leasachadh (no) cur am feairrd.

Unimproved, *a.* Neo-leasaichte; neo-ionnsuichte; neo-oileanaichte.

Uninclosed, *a.* Neo-dhionta; gun dion; gun challaid; fosgailte.

Unincreasable, *a.* Do-mheudachadh, nach gabh meudachadh, nach gabh deanamh ni 's mo.

Unindifferent, *a.* Neo-choidhis, deigheil. He is not unindifferent to her, *tha e deigheil oirre, tha taobh aig ri.*

Unindustrious, *a.* Neo-easguidh, neo-chùramach; neo-dhi-chiollach; leasg, lunndach; leagach; neo-dheanadach, neo-shùrdail.

Uninflamed, *a.* Neo-loisgeach; neo-theinnteach; neo-loisgte, neo-lasda.

Uninflammable, *a.* Do-chur ri theine, neo-theinnteach, do-losgaidh, do-lasadh.

Uninformed, *a.* Aineolach; ain-fhiosach; neo-ionnsuichte, neo-oileanaichte, borb.

Uningenuous, *a.* Neo-ionruic, neo-shimplidh, dùbailte.

Uninhabitable, *a.* Do-àiteachadh, nach gabh àiteachadh, fàsail.

Uninhabited, *a.* Neo-àitichte; fàs, uaigneach.

Uninjured, *a.* Neo-chiurrta, neo-dhochannaichte, gun chiurram, gun dochann, gun dolaidh. He is uninjured, *tha e gun dochann.*

Uninspired, *a.* Neo-neamh-ionnsuichte; neo-dheachdta leis an spiorad; neo-bheothaichte, neo-bhrosnuichte.

Uninstructed, *a.* Neo-oileanaichte, neo-ionnsuichte, aineolach, ain-fhiosach.

Uninstructive, *a.* Neo-leasachail, neo-ionnsuchail, neo-tharbhach; neo-theagasgail.

Unintelligent, *a.* Aineolach, neo-ionnsuichte, neo-thoinisgeil.

Unintelligible, *a.* Do-thuigsinn, nach gabh tuigsinn, dointe.

Unintentional, *a.* Neo-rùnaichte; gun rùn, gun sannt.

Uninterested, *a.* Gun seadh, gun suim, comadh; diombach. I am uninterested about him, *cha n' eil suim agam dheth.*

Uninteresting, *a.* Neo-chiatach; neo-chudthromach.

Unintermixed, *a.* Neo-choimh-mheasgta, neo-mheasgta.

Uninterred, *a.* Neo-adhlaicte, neo-thiodhlaicte, neo-thorrta.

Uninterrogated, *a.* Neo-cheasnuichte, neo-sgrudta.

Uninterrupted, *a.* Gun sgur; neo-amailte, neo-bhacta.

Uninterruptedly, *adv.* Gun sgur, gun chàird, gun bhac.

Uninvestigable, *a.* Do-sgrudadh; do-rannsuchadh; do-lorgachadh.

Uninvited, *a.* Neo-chuirte, gun chuireadh, gun sireadh, gun iarruidh.

Union, *s.* Aonachd; co' chòrdadh, co' bhann, caidreamh, daimh, ceangall, bann.

Uniparous, *a.* Aon-bhreitheach.

Unison, *a.* Aon-ghuthach, aon-fhonnach, co-sheirmeach.

Unison, *s.* Aon-ghuth; co-sheirm; gleus.

Unit, *s.* Aonad; aon, h-aon, a h-aon.

Unitable, *a.* So-cheangladh, so-thàth.

Unitarian, *s.* An-thrianaidiche, fear nach eil creidsinn san Trianaid.

Unite, *v.* Ceangal; dlùthaich, aontaich, tàth, cuir ri chéile, diong. United, *ceangailte, dluthaichte, tathta.*

Unition, *s.* Aontachas; diongadh, aontachadh.

Unity, *s.* Aonachd, cordadh, co-chordadh.

Universal, *a.* Coitchionn; uileach.

Universally, *adv.* Gu coitchionn, gu h-uile.

Universe, *s.* An domhan, an cruinne cé.

University, *s.* Ard thigh-sgoil; ard-sgoil, colaist.

Univocal, *a.* Aon-ghuthach, cinnteach; riaghailteach.

Univocally, *adv.* Gu h-aon-ghuthach, gu cinnteach.

Unjointed, *a.* Neo-alltaichte, neo-lùdaichte; as a chéile.

Unjoyous, *a.* Tuirseach, trom, neo-aoibhinn.

Unjust, *a.* Eucorach, mi-cheart, neo-chothromach, mi-chothromach; aingidh, olc.

Unjustifiable, *a.* Do-fhireannachadh, do-dhionadh. He is unjustifiable in my eyes, *cha 'n urrainn mi a leithsgeul a ghabhail.*

Unjustly, *adv.* Gu h-eucorach, gu mi cheart, gu h-aingidh.

Unkennel, *v.* Dùisg; fuadaich.

Unkept, *a.* Neo-ghléidhte; neo-chumta, gun ghleidheadh, gun chumail. His house is unkept, *tha thigh gun chumail;* his commandments are unkept, *tha 'aitheantan gun an gleidheadh (no) gun an cumàil.*

Unkind, *a.* Neo-chaoimhneil, neo-chàirdeil, neo-chòir, neo-sheirceil; neo-fhabhorach, neo-thruacanta, mi-shuairc; neo-bhaigheil.

Unkindly, *adv.* Gu mi-chaoimhneil; gu neo-chòir, gu mi-nadurra, gu neo-sheirceil, gu neo-thruacanta.

Unkindness, *s.* Neo-chaoimhneas; mi-run, tnù, farmad, mi-shuairceas.

Unkissed, *a.* Neo-phògta, neo-phògte.

Unknightly, *a.* Neo-mhodhail, mi-mhodhail, neo-chùirteil.

Unknit, *v.* Thoir as a chéile; sgar, sgaoil, fosgail.

Unknot, *v.* Fuasgail, tuasgail, fosgail, thoir as a chéile. Unknotted, *fuasgailte, tuasgailte.*

Unknowing, *a.* Aineolach; neo-chleachta.

Unknowingly, *adv.* Gu h-aineolach.

Unknown, *a.* Neo-aithnichte; diomhair, folaichte; gun fhios, gun aithne. I am unknown to him, *cha 'n' eil aithne aig orm;* unknown to me, *gun fhios domh.*

Unlaboured, *a.* Neo-threabhaichte; neo-shaothairichte; a dheòin, da dheòin. The earth produced unlaboured, *thug an talamh uaith da dheòin.*

Unlace, *v.* Fuasgail, tuasgail.

Unlade, *v.* Eutromaich, taomaich.

Unladen, *a.* Neo-luchdaichte.

Unlaid, *a.* Neo-leigte; neo-chiùinichte, neo-choisgte. An unlaid egg, *bugan.*

Unlamented, *a.* Neo-chaoidhte.

Unlap, *v.* Fosgail, tuasgail, fuasgail.

Unlash, *v.* Fuasgail, tuasgail. Unlashed, *fuasgailte, tuasgailte.*

Unlawful, *a.* Neo-laghail, mi-laghail, an aghaidh 'n lagh, mi-dhligheach, neo-dhligheach; neo-cheart; eucorach; diolain. An unlawful child, *urr dhiolain.*

Unlawfully, *adv.* Gu mi-laghail, an aghaidh 'n lagh, gu h-eucorach.

Unlawfulness, *s.* Neo-laghaileachd, euceart; diolanas.

Unlearn, *v.* Dichuimhnich; *neo-ionnsuich.*

Unlearned, *a.* Neo-fhoghluimte, neo-ionnsuichte; aineolach, borb, ainiosach.

Unlearnedly, *adv.* Gu neo-fhoghluimte, gu h-aineolach, gu h-ainiosach.

Unleash, *v.* Leig as, leig air falbh, leig fa sgaoil, leig fuasgailte.

Unleavened, *a.* Neo-thaoisinnte, neo-ghoirtichte.

Unless, *conj.* Saor o, mur. Unless he come, *mur tig e.*

Unlessoned, *a.* Neo-ionnsuichte; aineolach.

Unlettered, *a.* Neo-ionnsuichte, neo-fhoghluimte, aineolach, borb; neo-litrichte.

Unlevelled, *a.* Neo-chomhnard; neo-réidh.

Unlibidinous, *a.* Neo-dhrùiseil; geamnuidh; neo-fheòlmhor.

Unlicensed, *a.* Neo-cheaduichte.

Unlicked, *a.* Neo-imlichte; *neo-chumta*, do bhrigh gun abair cuid shluagh, gun imlich ma-ghamhuinn a cuileanaibh chum cumadh thoirt dhoibh.

Unlighted, *a.* Neo-lasda.

Unlightsome, *a.* Dorch, doilleir, uaigneach, neo-shuilbhear, duilbhear.

Unlike, *a.* Eu-cosmhal, eu-coslach, neo-chosmhalach, neo-choslach.

Unlikelihood, *s.* Eu-cosmhalachd; eucosmhalas, eucoslas.

Unlikely, *a.* Eu-cosmhal, neo-chosmhalach, neo-choslach.

Unlikeness, *s.* Eu-coslas.

Unlimitable, *a.* Neo-chriochnachaidh, neo-chriochnuidheach, gun chrioch, gun iomall.

Unlimited, *a.* Neo-chriochnach, gun chrioch.

Unlimitedness, *s.* Neo-chriochnachd, neo-chriochnuidheachd.

Unload, *v.* Eutromaich; taomaich. Unload the cart, *taomaich a chairt.*

Unlock, *v. a.* Fosgail. Unlocked, *fosgailte.*

Unlooked, **Unlooked-for**, *a.* Gun dùil bhi ri. He came unlooked-for, *thainig e gun dùil bhi ris.*

Unloose, *v. a.* Fuasgail, tuasgail, thoir as a chéile.

Unloved, *a.* Neo-ghradhaichte, neo-ionmhuinn.

Unloveliness, *s.* Granndachd, neo-chiatachd.

Unlovely, *a.* Mi-chiatach, mi-chiatach, neo-lurach, neo-ionmhuinn, neo-ghradhaichte, neo-ghreannar.

Unloving, *a.* Neo-ghradhach, neo-chaoimhneil, neo-ghaolach.

Unluckily, *adv.* Gu mi-shealbhar; gu mi-fhortanach.

Unluckiness, *s.* Mi-shealbharachd; droch-fhortan, donas, doirbheas, truaighe.

Unlucky, *a.* Mi-shealbhar, mi-shona, neo-fhortanach, mi-fhortanach.

Unlustrous, *a.* Dorch, neo-loinnreach.

Unmade, *a.* Neo-dheanta; neo-chruthaichte, neo-ullamh.

Unmaimed, *a.* Neo-chiurrta, neo-chiurramach.

Unman, *v.* Spoth; dean tais, dean bog, dean mi-fhearail, mi-mhisnich.

Unmanageable, *a.* Do-smachdachaidh, do-cheannsachadh, do-chur gu taic; trom.

Unmanaged, *a.* Neo-smachdaichte, neo-cheannsaichte, neo-thréinte.

Unmanly, *a.* Neo-fhearail, neo-dhuineil, bog, tais, cailleachanta, meath.

Unmannered, *a.* Mi-mhodhail; air bheag oilein; borb.

Unmannerliness, *s.* Mi-mhodhaileachd, neo-shiobhaltachd, buirbe.

Unmannerly, *a.* Mi-mhodhail, neo-shiobhailte, borb.

Unmanuered, *a.* Neo-innearaichte, neo-mhathaichte.

Unmarked, *a.* Neo-chomharaichte, neo-bheachdaichte, neo-fhaicinnte.

Unmarried, *a.* Neo-phòsda; singilte.

Unmarry, *v. a.* Sgar.

Unmask, *v. a.* Leig ris; nochd, rùisg.

Unmasked, *a.* Leigte ris, nochta; ruisgte.

Unmasterable, *a.* Do-cheannsachadh, do-smachdachadh, nach gabh ceannsachadh, nach gabh smachdachadh.

Unmastered, *a.* Neo-cheannsaichte, neo-smachdaichte.

Unmatchable, *a.* Neo-choimeasta; gun choimeas.

Unmatched, *a.* Gun leth-bhreac, gun choimeas; aiunnamh.

Unmeaning, *a.* Gun seadh, gun chiall, mi-chiallachail; gun bhrigh.

Unmeant, *a.* Neo-rùnaichte.

Unmeasurable, *a.* Do-thomhas, neo-chriochnachadh, nach gabh tomhas; aibhseach.

Unmeasured, *a.* Neo-thomhaiste; pàilt thar tomhas, anbharr.

Unmedicable, *a.* Do-leigheas, nach gabh leigheas.

Unmedicated, *a.* Neo-leighichte.

Unmeditated, *a.* Neo-bheachdaichte roimh laimh.

Unmeet, *a.* Neo-chubhaidh, neo-iomchuidh, neo-fheagarach; neo-airidh, mi-thoilltinneach.

Unmellowed, *a.* Neo-abuich; anabuich.

Unmelted, *a.* Neo-leaghta.

Unmentioned, *a.* Neo-ainmichte.

Unmerchantable, *a.* Nach gabh reic.

Unmerciful, *a.* Eu-trocaireach, borb, cruaidh-chridheach, neo-bhaigheil, ain-iochdmhor, cruadalach.

Unmercifully, *adv.* Gu h-ea-trocaireach, gu borb, gu cruaidh-chridheach, gu neo-bhaigheil, gu h-ain-iochdmhor.

Unmercifulness, *s.* Eu-trocaireachd, buirbe, ain-iochdmhoireachd, ain-iochd.

Unmerited, *a.* Neo-thoilltinnte; neo-airidh.

Unmilked, *a.* Neo-bhleothainte, neo-leigte.

Unminded, *a.* Neo-chuimhnichte; di-mheasta.

Unmindful, *a.* Di-chuimhneach, dearmadach, neo-chùramach, neo-omhaileach, neo-shuimeil.

Unmindfulness, *s.* Di-chuimhneachd, dearmadachd, neo-omhail.

Unmingled, *a.* Neo-choimeasgta; glan, fior.

Unmiry, *a.* Neo-shalach, neo-làbanta.

Unmitigated, *a.* Neo-chiùinichte; neo-choisgte.

Unmixed, *a.* Neo-choimeasgta, neo-mheasgta, glan, fior, neo-thruaillichte.

Unmoaned, *a.* Neo-chaoidhte.

Unmoist, *a.* Neo-fhliuch, neo-àitidh, tioram.

Unmoistened, *a.* Neo-thaislichte.

Unmolested, *a.* Gun dragh; samhach, soimeach; co-thromach, neo-bhuairte.

Unmortgaged, *s.* Neo-ghealltuinte.

Unmortified, *a.* Neo-chradhaichte; neo-fharranaichte; neo-chlaoidhte; neo-thruaillte.

Unmotherly, *a.* Neo-mhathaireil, mi-mhathaireil.

Unmoveable, *a.* Do-charrachadh; do-ghlideachadh, nach gabh carrachadh, do-ghluasad.

Unmoved, *a.* Neo-charraichte; neo-ghluaiste, gun mhothuchadh.

Unmoving, *a.* Seasmhach; neo-ghluasadach; gramail; neo-dhrùiteach.
Unmould, *v.* Cruth-atharraich; cuir a dealbh.
Unmourned, *a.* Neo-chaoidhte.
Unmowed, *a.* Neo-ghearrte, neo-bhuainte.
Unmusical, *a.* Neo-bhinn, neo-cheòlmhor, searbh, déistinneach.
Unmusted, *a.* Neo-liath, fallain.
Unnamed, *a.* Neo-ainmichte; gun ainm.
Unnatural, *a.* Mi-nàdurrail, mi-nàdurra; mi-ghnétheil, éignichte, eithich.
Unnaturally, *adv.* Gu mi-nàdurrail, gu mi-nàdurra; gu h-eithich, gu mi-ghéntheil.
Unnavigable, *a.* Do-sheòladh.
Unnavigated, *a.* Neo-sheòlta.
Unnecessarily, *adv.* Gu neo-fheumail.
Unnecessariness, *s.* Neo-fheumalachd
Unnecessary, *a.* Neo-fheumail.
Unneighbourly, *a.* Neo-chòir, neo-choimhearsnachail, gu mio-runach.
Unnervate, *v.* An-fhannaich; anmhunnaich, meathaich.
Unnervated, *a.* An-fhannaichte.
Unnerve, *v.* An-fhannaich; meathaich.
Unnerved, *a.* An-fhann; an-fhannaichte, tais, bog.
Unnoble, *a.* Dìblidh, suarrach, iosal, truagh, bochd, uireasbhach.
Unnoted, *a.* Neo-chomharaichte; neo-bheachdaichte, neo-urramaichte, neo-mheasail.
Unnoticed, *a.* Neo-chomharaichte; neo-bheachdaichte; di-mheasta; gun fhios, gun aire. He went away unnoticed by them, *dh' fhalbh e gun aire dhoibh.*
Unnumbered, *a.* Neo-àireamhta; do-àireamh, do-chunntadh, thar cunntas.
Unnutritious, *a.* Neo-bhiadhar; neo-tharbhach.
Unobnoxious, *a.* Neo-bhuailteach.
Unobsequious, *a.* Eas-umhal; dùr, neo-easguidh.
Unobsequiousness, *s.* Easumhlachd; dùrad.
Unobservable, *a.* Do-fhaicinn, do-chomharrachadh, do-bheachdachadh.
Unobservant, *a* Neo-shuimeil, neo-aireachail, mi-chùramach, baoghalta.
Unobserved, *a.* Neo-bheachdaichte; neo-fhaicinnte, gun aire, os iosal.
Unobserving, *a.* Neo-shuimeil; mi-churamach, baoghalta.
Unobstructed, *a.* Neo-bhacta, neo-amailte, neo-ghrabta.
Unobtainable, *a* Do-fhaotainn, do-fhaghail, do-ghlacadh, nach gabh faotainn, nach gabh faghail
Unobtained, *a.* Neo-bhuidhinnte, neo-choisinnte.
Unoccupied, *a.* Neo-shealbhaichte; falamh; neo-ghnathaichte
Unoffending, *a.* Neo-choireach, neo-chronail; neo-chiontach; neo-dhochannach, neo-chiurrail; soitheamh; soimeach.
Unoffered, *a.* Neo-thairgsinnte, neo-thairgte, gun tairgse.
Unoperative, *a.* Neo-éifeachdach; neo-thabhachdach.
Unopposed, *a.* Neo-bhacta; neo-aghaidhichte, gun ghabhail roimh, neo-amailte.
Unorderly, *a* Mi-riaghailteach, eas-ordughach, mi-lathailteach.
Unoriginal, Unoriginated, *a.* Neo-ghinte, gun toiseach.
Unorthodox, *a.* Neo-fhallain; baoth
Unowned, *a.* Gun ghabhail ris; neo-aidichte, neo-aidmhichte.

Unpack, *v.* Fuasgail, fosgail; eutromaich.
Unpacked, *a.* Fuasgailte, eutromaichte, neo-phacainnte
Unpaid, *a.* Neo-phàighte; neo-dhiolta, gun dioladh, gun phàigh.
Unpained, *a.* Neo-chradhte, gun chradh, gun phian
Unpainful, *a.* Neo-phiantachail, neo-chraidhteach.
Unpair, *v.* Sgar, cuir o chéile, dealaich. Unpaired, *sgarta; dealaichte*
Unpalatable, *a.* Domblasda, neo-bhlasda, grannd, sgreamhail, mi-thaitneach, sgleatail
Unparalleled, *a.* Neo-choimeasta, gun choimeas; gun leithid, gun lethbhreac.
Unpardonable, *a.* Gun leithsgeul, do-laghadh, nach mathar; nach gabh mathadh (no) laghadh.
Unpardonably, *adv* Thar maitheanas
Unpardoned, *a.* Neo-mhathta, neo-laghta.
Unparliamentary, *a.* An aghaidh nòs na parlamaid
Unparted, *a.* Neo-sgarta, neo-dhealaichte.
Unpartial, *a.* Dìreach, neo-chlaon, cothromach, neo-leth-bhreitheach.
Unpassable, *a.* Do-shiùbhladh, do-imeachadh, nach gabh siubhladh, nach gabh imeachd (no) coiseachd
Unpassionate, *a.* Soitheamh, seimh, ciùin, neo-leth-bhreitheach.
Unpathed, *a.* Gun slighe, gun ròd, gun rathad, gun aisridh, neo-aisrichte, do-shiubhladh.
Unpawned, *a.* Neo-ghealltuinnte.
Unpeaceable, *a* Buaireasach, tabaideach, aimhreiteach, tuaiseideach, brionglaideach, carraideach.
Unpensioned, *a.* Neo-thuarasdalaichte.
Unpeople, *v.* Dean fàs; dithreabhaich; sgrios.
Unperceivable, *a* Do-fhaineachadh, do-fharachduinn, do-mhothuchadh.
Unperceived, *a.* Gun fhios; neo-chomharaichte, neo-aithnichte; gun aire.
Unperfect, *a* Neo-iomlan, neo-fhoirfe, neo-chiochnaichte.
Unperfectness, *s.* Neo-iomlanachd, neo-fhoirfeachd
Unperformed, *a.* Neo-ghnàthaichte, neo-ullamh, neo-choilionta; neo-dheanta.
Unperishable, *a.* Maireannach, bithbhuan, siorruidh, do-sgriosadh
Unperplexed, *a.* Gun amhluadh, fuasgailte, tuasgailte; gun iomcheist
Unpersuadable, *a.* Do-thionndadh, do-aomadh, do-earalachadh, do-chomhairleachadh.
Unpetrified, *a* Neo-cruadhaichte.
Unphilosophical, *a.* Neo-fheallsanta
Unpierced, *a.* Neo-shàthta, neo-thollta
Unpillared, *a.* Gun stùc, gun cholmhuinn.
Unpillowed, *a.* Gun chluasag, neo-chluasagaichte
Unpin, *v* Fuasgail, tuasgail.
Unpitied, *a.* Gun truas bhith air ghabhail ri, neo-airidh air truas
Unpitifully, *adv* Gu neo-thruacannta
Unpitying, *a.* Neo-thruacanta, ain-iochdmhor
Unplaced, *a.* Neo-àitichte, neo-shuidhichte
Unplagued, *a* Neo-bhuairte, neo-chradhta; gun dragh, soimeach, socrach.
Unplanched, *a.* Neo-ùrlaraichte, neo-phlangaichte, gun phlang, gun ùrlar.
Unplanted, *a.* Neo-shuidhichte, neo-phlanndaichte.
Unplausible, *a.* Mi-ghnétheil, neo-bheulchar.

Unpleasant, *a.* Mi-thaitneach, neo-ghreannar, doirbh, mi-chiatach; draghail; deacair.

Unpleasantly, *adv.* Gu mi-thaitneach, gu mi-chiatach.

Unpleasantness, *s.* Mi-chiatachd; doirbheas.

Unpleased, *a.* Mi-thoilichte, neo-tholieach, diombuidheach, diombach.

Unpleasing, *a.* Neo-thaitneach; mi-thaitneach; gràineil, sgréitidh.

Unpliant, *a.* Do-lùbadh, rag; do-aomadh; do-chombairleachadh, dùr.

Unplowed, *a.* Neo-arta; neo-threabhta.

Unpoetical, *a.* Neo-bhardail; neo-fhileanta.

Unpoliced, *a.* Neo-riaghailtichte.

Unpolished, *a.* Neo-mhlnichte; neo-shoilleirichte; neo-shnaidhte, mi-mhodhail; borb.

Unpolite, *a.* Mi-mhodhail; borb; neo-shiobhailte, mi-shuairc.

Unpolluted, *a.* Neo-thruaillichte, neo-thruaillte, neo-shalaichte, glan.

Unpopular, *a.* Neo-ghradhaichte leis an t-sluagh, neo-ionmhuinn.

Unportable, *a.* Do-ghiùlan, do-iomchar.

Unpossessed, *a.* Neo-shealbhaichte.

Unpracticable, *a.* Do-dheanamh, do chur an gniomh.

Unpractised, *a.* Neo-chleachdta, neo-eòlach, neo-dheanta ri; neo-thrèinte; neo-theoma.

Unpraised, *a.* Neo-mholta, gun mhol, gun chliù, mi-chliuiteach, gun iomradh.

Unprecarious, *a.* Cinnteach; cothromach, neo-theagamhach.

Unprecedented, *a.* Gun choimeas.

Unpreferred, *a.* Neo-arduichte.

Unpregnant, *a.* Neo-thorrach; neo-gheur.

Unprejudicate, *a.* Neo-leth-bhreitheach, neo-chlaon.

Unprejudiced, *a.* Neo-leth-bhreitheach, gun leth-bhreith; neo-chlaon; gun taobh ri.

Unpremeditated, *a.* Neo-smuaintichte roi' laimh.

Unprepared, *a.* Neo-ullamh, neo-dheas.

Unprepossessed, *a.* Neo-chlaon, direach, gun leith-bhreith, gun taobh ri.

Unpressed, *a.* Neo-bhruthta; neo-dhumhlaichte, neo-strampta, neo-éignichte.

Unpretending, *a.* Iriosal; neo-uallach, neo-dhàn.

Unprevailing, *a.* Neo-éifeachdach.

Unprevented, *a.* Neo-bhacta; neo-amailte.

Unprincely, *a.* Neo-phrionnsail, mi-fhlathail.

Unprincipled, *a.* Gun choguis; olc, aingidh.

Unprinted, *a.* Neo-chlodh-bhuailte, neo-phriontaichte.

Unprisoned, *a.* Neo-phriosunaichte.

Unprized, *a.* Neo-mheasta, di-mheasta.

Unproclaimed, *a.* Neo-ghairmte, neo-fhoillsichte.

Unprofaned, *a.* Neo-thruaillte.

Unprofitable, *a.* Neo-tharbhach, gun stà, neo-eifeachdach, mi-phroiteach.

Unprofitableness, *s.* Neo-tharbhachd, neo-tharbhaichead.

Unprolific, *a.* Neo-tharbhach; seasg, aimrid; neo-shiolmhor.

Unpromising, *a.* Eu-cosmhal, mi-chosmhal, neo-cugasach.

Unproper, *a.* Neo-iomchuidh, neo-cheart, neo-chubhaidh.

Unpropitious, *a.* Neo-shoirbheasail; neo-fhortanach, droch-mhànach; mi-shealbhar, dubhasach.

Unproportioned, *a.* Neo-chumadail.

Unpropped, *a.* Gun taic, gun chùl-taic; gun *phrop*, neo-*phropainnte*.

Unprosperous, *a.* Mi-shoirbheasach, mi-fhortanach, mi-shealbhar, mi-shoirbheachail.

Unprosperously, *adv.* Gu mi-shoirbheasch, gu mi-fhortanach.

Unprotected, *a.* Gun dion; neo-dhionta.

Unproved, *a.* Gun chomhdach, gun dearbh, neo-dhearbhte, neò-chomhdaichte.

Unprovided, *a.* Neo-sholaraichte; neo-riaraichte.

Unprovoked, *a.* Neo-bhuairte, neo-bhrosnuichte.

Unpruned, *a.* Neo-ghearrta, neo-sholaraichte.

Unpublic, *a.* Diomhair; neo-aithnichte, neo-fhollaiseach, céilte.

Unpublished, *a.* Neo-aithnichte, neo-iomraiteach, céilte.

Unpucker, *v. a.* Thoir preasag (no) liurc a aodach.

Unpulverable, *a.* Do-phronnadh.

Unpulverized, *a.* Neo-phroinnte, neo-phronn.

Unpunished, *a.* Gun pheanas, neo-pheanasaichte.

Unpurchased, *a.* Neo-cheannaichte.

Unpurged, *a.* Neo-sgùrta, neo-nighte.

Unpurified, *a.* Neo-ghlan; neo-nighte, neo-sgùrta.

Unpursued, *a.* Neo-leantuinnte.

Unputrified, *a.* Neo-ghrod, fallain.

Unqualified, *a.* Neo-fhreagarrach, neo-mhurrach.

Unqualify, *v. a.* Dean neo-fhreagarrach (no) mi-mhurach.

Unquenchable, *a.* Do-mhùchadh, do-chur as.

Unquenched, *a.* Neo-mhùchta.

Unquestionable, *a.* Cinnteach; dearbhta, gun teagamh, gun cheist.

Unquestionably, *adv.* Gu cinnteach, gun teagamh, air a chinnte.

Unquestioned, *a.* Neo-cheasnaichte; gun cheist, gun sgrud.

Unquick, *a.* Mall, athaiseach, mairnealach, leagach, lunndach.

Unquickened, *a.* Neo-bheothaichte, neo-bheò.

Unquiet, *a.* Neo-shocrach, neo-fhoisneach, mi-fhoighidneach; docrach, air bhuaireadh; thar a chéile, mi-shuaimhneach.

Unquietness, *s.* Mi-shocair, an-shocair, mi-fhoighidinn, buaireadh, mi-shuaimhneas.

Unracked, *a.* Neo-ghrunndaichte, neo-shiolaidhte.

Unraked, *a.* Neo-ràsdalaichte, neo-chruinnichte, neo-thionailte.

Unransacked, *a.* Neo-spùinnte, neo-spuillte, neo-chreachta.

Unransomed, *a.* Neo-cheannaichte.

Unravel, *v.* Fuasgail, tuasgail, thoir as a chéile, réitich; faigh a mach.

Unrazored, *a.* Neo-bhearrta.

Unread, *a.* Neo-leughta; neo-ionnsuichte, neo-fhoghluimte.

Unreadiness, *s.* Mi-luathailteachd.

Unready, *a.* Neo-dheas, neo-ullamh; mall; neo-gheur, neo-thapaidh, baoghalta.

Unreal, *a.* Neo-fhior, faoin, breugach.

Unreasonable, *a.* Mi-reusonta, ain-reusonta, thar cuimeis, ana-goireasach, ana-barrach. An unreasonable desire, *ain-iarrtas; ana-miann.*

Unreasonableness, *s.* Mi-reusontachd, ana-goireasachd.

Unreclaimed, *a.* Neo-iompuichte; neo-chiosnuichte.

Unreconcileable, *a.* Do-ghuidheadh; nach gabh ciosnachadh, do-dheanamh réidh.

UNRECONCILED, a. Neo-chiosnaichte; neo-réidh, mach air.
UNRECORDED, a. Neo-sgriobhte.
UNRECOUNTED, a. Neo-aithriste, neo-innste
UNREDUCED, a. Neo-laghdaichte.
UNREFORMABLE, a. Do-leasachadh, do-iompachadh
UNREFORMED, a. Neo-leasaichte, neo-ath-leasaichte, neo-iompaichte.
UNREFRESHED, a. Neo-ùraichte; neo-bheotheachte.
UNREGARDED, a. Gun suim, gun seadh, gun mheas, di-mheaste.
UNREGENERATE, a. Neo-ath-ghinte.
UNREGISTERED, a. Neo-sgriobhte.
UNREINED, a. Neo-shrianta; neo-smachdaichte; neo-cheannsaichte.
UNRELENTING, a Cruaidh-chridheach, borb, ain-iochd-mhor; neo-thruacanta.
UNRELIEVABLE, a. Do-chuideachadh, do-choghnath.
UNRELIEVED, a. Neo-chuidichte, gun cho-ghnath.
UNREMARKABLE, a. Neo-iongantach, neo-shonruichte, neo-àiridh air beachd (no) air iomradh
UNREMEDIABLE, a. Do-leigheasadh, do-leasachadh.
UNREMEMBERED, a. Neo-chuimhnichte, di-chuimhnichte
UNREMEMBERING, a Dearmadach, di-chuimhneach
UNREMEMBRANCE, s. Dearmad, dearmadachd, di-chuimhne.
UNREMITTINGLY, adv. Am bidheantas, gun sgurachd, gun chàirde, gun sgur, an comhnuidh, daonann
UNREMOVABLE, a. Do-charruchadh, do-ghlideachadh, do-ghluasad, do-ghluasadh
UNREMOVED, a. Neo-charruichte; neo-ghlidichte, anns an aon aite.
UNREPAID, a. Neo-dhiolta, neo-phàighte
UNREPEALED, a. Air chois
UNREPENTANT, a. Neo-aithreachail, neo-bhrònach
UNREPINING, a. Neo-ghearanach; foighidinneach, neo-fhrionasach
UNREPLENISHED, a. Neo-lionta; gun airneas
UNREPROACHED, a. Neo-chronaichte; neo-mhaslaichte; gun chronachadh, gun mhasladh
UNREPROVEABLE, a. Neo-chronachail, neo-choireachail
UNREPROVED, a. Neo-chronaichte, neo-choirichte, neo-achmhasanaichte; neo-chomhairlichte
UNREPUGNANT, a. Neo-chontrardha, freagarrach
UNREPUTABLE, a Mi-chreideasach
UNREQUESTED, a. Neo-iarrta; neo-chuirte, gun iarruidh, gun chuireadh.
UNREQUITED, a Neo-dhiolta, neo-phaighte.
UNRESENTED, a. Neo-dhiolta
UNRESERVED, a. Saor, fosgailte, suilmhear, cridheil, faoilidh.
UNRESERVEDLY, adv Gu saor, gu fosgailte, gu suilmhear, gu faoilidh.
UNRESERVEDNESS, s Fosgailteachd, suilmhearachd, faoilidheachd
UNRESISTED, a. Gun bhac, gun mhoille, neo-bhacta, gun ghabhail roimh.
UNRESOLVABLE, a Do-fhuasgladh; do-leaghadh.
UNRESOLVED, a. Neo-shonruichte, neo-rùnaichte; neo-shuidhichte
UNRESOLVING, a. Neo-shonruichte; neo-shuidhichte
UNRESPECTIVE, a. Neo-aireachail, mi-sheadhar
UNRESTORED, a Neo-dhiolte; neo-aisigte.
UNRESTRAINED, a Neo-smachdaichte; an-srianta, saor; fuasgailte.
UNRESTRAINT, s. An-sriantas, saorsainn, saorsadh.
UNRETRACTED, a Neo-ghairmte air ais; gun bhith air 'thoirt air ais.
UNREVEALED, a. Neo-fhoillsichte; céilte.
UNREVENGED, a. Neo-dhiolta.
UNREVENGING, a. Neo-dhioltach, neo-dhioghaltach
UNREVERENT, a Mi-mhodhail
UNREVOKED, a Seasmhach, gun mhùth
UNREWARDED, a Neo-dhiolta, neo-phàighte, neo-thuarasdalaichte, gun diol, gun phàigh, gun tuarasdal
UNRIDDLE, v a Fuasgail, tomhais, faigh mach.
UNRIG, v a. Thoir acfhuinn bhàrr ni, lom, rùisg
UNRIGHTEOUS, a. Eas-ionraic, neo-fhireannach, neo-cheart, neo-thréibhdhireach, mi-dhiadhuidh, eucorach, eu-ceart, ain-diadhuidh, aingidh, olc.
UNRIGHTEOUSLY, adv Gu h-eas-ionraic; gu neo-fhireannach, gu h-eucorach, gu h-aingidh, gu h-olc
UNRIGHTEOUSNESS, s. Neo-fhireanntachd, aingidheachd, eas-ionracas, eucoir, eu-ceartas, ain-diadhachd.
UNRIGHTFUL, a Neo-dhligheach, neo-dhligheil, neo-cheart, neo-laghail, mi-dhligheach, mi-cheart, mi-laghail
UNRIP, v a. Fosgail, gearr suas
UNRIPE, a. Anabuich, neo-abuich, amh, uaine, ùr, gorm, neo-thràthail, neo-amail.
UNRIPENED, a. Neo-abuich, anabuich
UNRIPENESS, s Anabachd, anabuichead, amhad, ùiread
UNRIVALLED, a. Gun choimeas, gun leth-bhreac, neo-choimeasta.
UNROL, v Fosgail, fuasgail, thoir, as chéile Unrolled, *fosgailte, as a chéile*
UNROOF, v a. Thoir tugha (no) mullach bhàrr tighe.
UNROOST, v. a Cuir bharr spàradh
UNROOT, v. Spion, bun-spion, buain as a bhun.
UNROUGH, a. Neo-mholach, neo-ghiobach; mìn.
UNROUNDED, a Neo-chruinn
UNRUFFLED, a. Samhach, ciùin, seimh.
UNRULED, a. Neo-riaghlaichte, neo-smachdaichte, gun riaghailt, gun smachd
UNRULINESS, s. Mi-riaghailteachd, an-sriantas
UNRULY, a Mi-riaghailteach; aimhreiteach, tabaideach, tuasaideach, buaireasach.
UNSAFE, a Neo-thearuinnte; cunnartach
UNSAFELY, adv Gu neo-thearuinnte, gu cunnartach
UNSAID, a Neo-ainmichte, gun radh
UNSALEABLE, a. Do-reiceadh, nach gabh reiceadh
UNSALTED, a Neo-shaillte.
UNSALUTED, a. Neo-fhailtichte, neo-fhuranaichte
UNSANCTIFIED, a. Mi-naomh, mi-naomhaichte, neo-choisrigte, neo-dhiadhuidh
UNSATIABLE, a. Do-shàsuchadh, do-shasuchaidh, ciocrach
UNSATISFACTORY, a Neo-thaitneach; neo-thoileachail
UNSATISFIED, a Neo-thoilichte, mi-thoilichte, diombach
UNSAVOURINESS, s Bréine; boladh; domblas, seirbhe
UNSAVOURY, a. Domblasda; mi-bhlasda, breun, loimheach, neo-thaitneach; sgreamhail
UNSAY, v. a. Thoir air ais focall, rach air ais
UNSCALY, a. Neo-lannach, neo-shligeach.
UNSCANNED, a Neo-thomhaiste; gun chunntadh.
UNSCARRED, a Neo-leòinte, neo-leònta
UNSCHOLASTIC, a Neo-ionnsuichte; neo-fhoghluimte
UNSCHOOLED, a. Neo-ionnsuichte; neo-oileanaichte, gun sgoil, gun oilean, gun ionnsuchadh

Unscorched, *a.* Neo-dhòthta, neo-dhòite, neo-sheargta.
Unscoured, *a.* Neo-sgùrta; neo-sgùirte; neo-nighte, salach.
Unscratched, *a.* Neo-sgriobte, neo-sgròbta, neo-sgriochta.
Unscreened, *a.* Neo-dhìonta; neo-sgailichte, neo-chomhdaichte.
Unscriptural, *a.* Mi-sgriobturail.
Unseal, *v.* Fosgail, fuasgail, tuasgail.
Unsealed, *a.* Fosgailte, neo-sheulaichte.
Unsearchable, *a.* Do-rannsuchadh, do-rannsuchaidh, do-sgrudadh
Unsearchableness, *s* Do-rannsachd.
Unsearched, *a.* Neo-rannsuichte
Unseasonable, *a.* Neo-àmail, neo-thràthail, neo-iomchuidh.
Unseasonableness, *s.* Mi-thràth; neo-iomchuidhead.
Unseasonably, *adv.* Gu neo-àmail, gu neo-thràthail.
Unseasoned, *a.* (*With salt*), neo-shaillte; (*out of time*), neo-àmail, neo-thràthail; (*undried*), neo-thioramaichte.
Unseconded, *a* Neo-chuidichte, gun chòghnath, gun chuideachadh.
Unsecret, *a.* Neo-dhiomhair, neo-fholaichte, follaiseach
Unsecure, *a* Neo-thearuinnte.
Unseduced, *a.* Neo-mheallta; neo-thruaillte.
Unseeing, *a* Dall, neo-leirsinneach
Unseemliness, *s.* Mi-chiatachd, mi-chiataichead, mi-eireachdas, mi-bheus
Unseemly, *a* Mi-chiatach; mi-bheusach
Unseemly, *adv* Gu mi-chiatach, gu mi-bheusach
Unseen, *a* Neo-fhaicinnte, am folach, gun fhaicinn, do-fhaicinn, neo-chleachdta.
Unselfish, *a* Neo-fhéin-chuiseach, neo-fhéin-speiseil.
Unseparable, *a* Do-sgaradh, do-sgaraidh, do-sgarachduinn, do-dhealachadh, do-chur as a chéile.
Unseparated, *a* Neo-sgarta, neo-dhealaichte
Unserviceable, *a* Gun stà, neo-fheumail, gun fheum, neo-uidhiseil.
Unserviceableness, *s.* Neo-fheumalachd
Unserviceably, *adv* Gun fheum, gun stà, gu neo-fheumail
Unset, *a* Neo-shuidhichte, neo-àidichte
Unsettle, *v.* Atharraich, cuir thar chéile.
Unsettled, *a* Neo-shocrach, neo-shuidhichte, neo-shonruichte; luaineach, siùbhlach, caochlaideach; neo-àitichte; neo-shocraichte, eutrom, gaoithe.
Unsettledness, *s* Teagamhachd, caochlaideachd, luaineachd
Unsevered, *a.* Neo-sgarta, neo-dhealaichte
Unsew, *v. a* Thoir fuaigheal air ais, sgaoil
Unsex, *v* Mi-ghinealaich
Unshackle, *v* Mi-chuibhrich, mi-gheimhlich, fuasgail.
Unshadowed, *a.* Neo-sgàilichte, neo-dhuibhrichte; soilleir; neo-dhorch
Unshaken, *a* Neo-chrathte; daingeann, diongmhalta, neo-ghluasadach; gun charrachadh, neo-charraichte, neo-ghluaiste.
Unshamed, *a.* Neo-nàraichte.
Unshapen, *a.* Neo-chumadail, duaichnidh, mi-dhreachail, gun chumadh, gun dreach.
Unsharded, *a.* Neo-phàirtichte, neo-riaraichte
Unsheath, *v* Rùisg, tarruing.
Unshed, *a.* Gun dòrtadh, neo-dhòirte
Unsheltered, *a* Neo-dhionta, gun dìon, gun fhasgadh, gun sgàil

Unshielded, *a.* Neo-dhionta, gun dìon, gun sgàil, gun sgiath.
Unship, *v. a.* Thoir a luingeas.
Unshocked, *a.* Neo-oilltichte; gun oillt; gun sgreamh, gun déistinn.
Unshod, *a.* Gun bhrògan, gun chruidhean, gun choisbheart.
Unshoe, *v. a.* Thoir brògan (no) caisbheart dhe.
Unshorn, *a.* Neo-bhuainte; neo-bhearrta, neo-sgathte neo-ghearrta.
Unshot, *a* Neo-thilgte.
Unshowered, *a.* Neo-uisgichte, neo-fhliuchte.
Unshrinking, *a* Neo-ghealtach; neo-eagallach, seasamhach
Unsifted, *a.* Neo-chriathairte, neo-chriathraichte, neo-fhaichainnte.
Unsighted, *a.* Neo-fhaicinnte, do-fhaicinn, as an t-sealladh.
Unsightliness, *s.* Duaichnidheachd; duaichneachd; déistinneachd.
Unsightly, *a.* Duaichnidh; neo-chiatach, neo-laoghach, neo-aogasach, neo-eireachdail, déistinneach.
Unsincere, *a.* Eas-ionrac; neo-dhìleas, cealgach, fealltach; slaoidhteil, neo-fhallain, neo-ghlan.
Unsincerity, *s.* Eas-ionracas, ceilge, foille.
Unsinew, *v. a* Anfhannaich, fannaich.
Unsinewed, *a.* Anfhann, fann, gun treòir, gun lùth.
Unsinged, *a.* Neo-dhothta; gun dothadh, gun losgadh; neo-loisgte
Unsinking, *a.* (*As sand*), neo-ghéilteach, neo-shlugach.
Unsinning, *a.* Neo-pheacach, neo-chiontach.
Unskilful, *a* Neo-sgileil; aineolach, mi-theoma, neo-sheolta.
Unskilfully, *adv.* Gu neo-sgileil, gu h-aineolach, gu neo-sheolta.
Unskilfulness, *s.* Aineolas.
Unskilled, *a.* Aineolach; neo-oileanaichte, neo-eolach; neo-chleachdta
Unslain, *a.* Neo-mharbhta; beò, a làthair.
Unslaked, *a* Neo-mhùchta, neo-bhàthta
Unslate, *v.* Thoir sgleadan dhe.
Unslated, *a.* Neo-sgleadaichte.
Unsleeping, *a.* Gun chodal, am faireach.
Unslipping, *a.* Daingeann, seasmhach, neo-thuisleach.
Unsmirched, *a.* Neo-shalaichte, neo-thruaillichte, neo-shalach, glan
Unsmoked, *a* Gun deatach, gun deathach.
Unsmooth, *a.* Garbh; neo-chomhnard.
Unsociable, *a* Neo-chuideachdail, neo-chaidreamhach; neo-chéilidheach, neo-chairdeil, coimheach; doirbh, dùinte, fad thall
Unsociableness, *s* Mi-chaidreamhachd, mi-chairdeas, coimheachas.
Unsociably, *adv* Gu neo-chaidreamhach, gu doirbh, gu neo-chéilidheach.
Unsoiled, *a.* Neo-shalaichte, neo-thruaillichte.
Unsold, *a.* Neo-chreicte, neo-reicte.
Unsoldier-like, *a* Cailleachanta; crion, gealtach.
Unsolid, *a.* Fàs, neo-ghramail, neo-dhiongmhalta.
Unsolved, *a* Neo-mhìnichte, neo-fhuasgailte.
Unsophisticated, *a.* Ionraic; glan; fior, fior-ghlan.
Unsorted, *a.* Neo-riaghailtichte, gun chur gu doigh.
Unsought, *a* Neo-shirte; neo-chuirte, gun sireadh.

Unsound, *a.* Mi-fhallain, neo-fhallain, euslan, euslainnteach; fàs; grod; eas-ionrac; neo-dhiongmhalta.

Unsounded, *a.* Neo-ghrunndaichte; neo-ghrunnaichte; neo-thomhaiste.

Unsoured, *a.* Neo-ghoirtichte, neo-ghoirt

Unsown, *a.* Neo-chuirte, gun chur.

Unspared, *a.* Neo-chaomhainte

Unsparing, *a.* Neo-chaomhantach, fial, neo-bhaigheil, neo-thruacanta.

Unspeak, *v. a.* Thoir focal air ais; cuir as àicheadh.

Unspeakable, *a.* Do-labhairt, do-innseadh, do-chur an céill; thar iomradh.

Unspeakably, *adv.* Thar iomradh; gu do labhairt.

Unspecified, *a.* Neo-ainmichte; neo-shonruichte.

Unsped, *a.* Neo-ghreasda; neo-choimhlionta.

Unspent, *a.* Neo-chaithte, neo-lughdaichte, neo-thraghta, neo-anfhannaichte.

Unspied, *a.* Neo-chomharaichte; neo-fhaicinnte.

Unspilt, *a* Gun dòrtadh, neo-thaomaichte.

Unspirit, *a.* Mi-mhisnich, taisich.

Unspoiled, *a.* Neo-spùinnichte; neo-chreachta, neo-mhillte; neo-thruaillichte, gun mhilleadh, gun chiurradh; gun dochann, gun dolaidh.

Unspotted, *a.* Neo-shalaichte, neo-thruaillichte; glan, fior-ghlan, neo-chiontach; gun smàl, gun smùr, gun choire, gun ghaoid.

Unsprightly, *a.* Neo-shuilbhear; neo-bheò, marbh, marbhanta, neo-smiorail, trom, tuirseach.

Unsquared, *a.* Neo-chumta.

Unstable, *a.* Neo-sheasamhach, neo-dhaingeann, neo-bhunaiteach, caochlaideach, neo-shuidhichte, mùghteach, luaineach, gaoithe.

Unstaid, *a* Neo-chrionna; eu-crionna, neo-shuidhichte, neo-shicir, muthteach, caochlaideach, luaineach.

Unstained, *a.* Neo-shalaichte, neo-dhathte, neo-lithte, neo-thruaillichte, gun sal, gun lith, gun dath, gun choire

Unstaunched, *a.* Neo-choisgte

Unsteadfast, *a.* Neo-dhaingeann; neo-sheasmhach, neo-bhunaiteach, neo-shuidhichte, neo-shonruichte, mi-steidheil

Unsteadily, *adv* Gu neo-sheasmhach, gu neo-bhunaiteach, gu luaineach, gu siùbhlach, gu muthteach.

Unsteadiness, *s.* Neo-sheasmhachd, luaineachd, caochlaideachd; siùbhlachd; muthteachd.

Unsteady, *a.* Neo-sheasmhach, luaineach, caochlaideach, siùbhlach, muthteach, neo-shuidhichte; mi-steidheil, gaoithe.

Unsteeped, *a.* Neo-bhogaichte, neo-bhogta, neo-thumta.

Unstinted, *a* Neo-ghann, neo-chrìon, fial, pailt.

Unstirred, *a* Neo-charruichte; neo-ghluasda, neo-shuathta.

Unstitch, *v. a.* Sgaoil, thoir as a chéile

Unstooping, *a.* Rag, do-lùbadh, nach lùb, nach géill, nach feachd

Unstop, *v. a.* Fosgail.

Unstopped, *a* Neo-bhacta, gun bhac, gun stad, gun mhoille.

Unstrained, *a.* Neo-fhàsgte; neo-éignichte; furas.

Unstraitened, *a.* Neo-chumhann, neo-chughann, neo-aimhleathan, neo-ghann, neo-éignichte; neo-theannaichte.

Unstrengthened, *a.* Neo-chuidichte; neo-neartaichte; gun choghnath, gun chuideachadh.

Unstring, *v.* Lasaich, fuasgail

Unstruck, *a.* Neo-bhuailte; neo-dhruighte; neo-ghluaisde

Unstuffed, *a.* Neo-lionta, neo-làn, neo-dhòmhail.

Unsubstantial, *a.* Faoin; gun diù, gun bhrìgh, gun neart. Thou unsubstantial air that I embrace, *thusa, àile fhaoin, a tha mi 'glacadh.*

Unsuccessful, *a* Neo-shoirbheasach, mi-shoirbheasach, mi-fhortanach, mi-shealbhar, neo-shoirbheachail.

Unsuccessfully, *adv* Gu neo-shoirbheasach, gu mi-shoirbheasach, gu neo-shoirbheachail, gu mi-fhortanach.

Unsuccessfulness, *s.* Mi-shoirbheas, droch fhortan; tubaist, earchall.

Unsucked, *a.* Neo-shùghta, neo-shùigte.

Unsufferable, *a* Do-ghiùlan; do-fhulang, do-iomchar.

Unsufferably, *adv.* Gu do-ghiùlan, gu do-fhulang, gu do-iomchar.

Unsufficiency, *s* Ea-comas; mi-phailteas, mi-mhurraichead.

Unsufficient, *a* Ea-comasach, neo-chomasach; neo-fhoghainteach.

Unsugared, *a.* Neo-mhillsichte; neo-mhilis; neo-shucaraichte, gun siucar

Unsuiting, *a.* Neo-fhreagarrach, neo-lathailteach

Unsuitable, *a.* Neo-fhreagarrach, neo-iomchuidh, neo-fheumail, neo-lathailteach

Unsuitableness, *s.* Neo-fhreagarrachd, neo-iomchuidhead

Unsuitably, *adv.* Gu neo-fhreagarrach, gu neo-iomchuidh.

Unsullied, *a.* Neò-shalaichte, gun sal, gun truaill, glan

Unsung, *a.* Gun bhi air a sheinn; neo-iomraiteach, neo-chliùiteach, neo-luaidhte.

Unsunned, *a* Neo-ghrianaichte. Pure as unsunned snow, *glan mar an t-sneachd nach fhac a ghrian.*

Unsuperfluous, *a.* Goireasach; gun bhi thuille na còrach.

Unsupplied, *a.* Neo-lionta; gun bhi air cumail ris.

Unsupportable, *a.* Do-ghiùlan, do-iomchar, do-fhulang, nach gabh giulan, gu do-iomchar

Unsupported, *a.* Neo-chuidichte; gun chò-ghnath, gun chuideachadh; gun taic.

Unsure, *a* Neo-chinnteach; teagmhach, neo-sheasmhach, neo-shonruichte.

Unsurmountable, *a* Nach gabh faotainn thairis air, do-smachdachadh, do-cheannsachadh, nach gabh smachdachadh (no) fairtleachd air.

Unsusceptible, *a.* Neo-ghabhaltach, neo-dhrùideach, neo-dhrùighteach.

Unsuspected, *a* Saor o amharus.

Unsuspecting, **Unsuspicious**, *a.* Neo-amharusach, gun amharus, gun omhaill

Unsustained, *a.* Neo-chumta suas, neo-chuidichte, neo-phropainnte.

Unswathe, *v a.* Fuasgail, tuasgail, lasaich

Unswayable, *a.* Do-smachdachadh, do-riaghladh.

Unswayed, *a.* Neo-cheannsaichte, neo-lamhaichte Is the chair empty? is the sword unswayed? *bheil a chathair falamh? bheil an claidheamh gun lamh unn?*

Unswear, *v a* Thoir (no) gairm air ais mionnan.

Unsweat, *v.* Fuaraich, fionnaraich, fionn-fhuaraich

Unsweet, *a.* Neo-mhilis, domblasda, neo-bhlasda, garg; searbh, neo-thaitneach, mi-thaitneach

Unswept, *a.* Neo-sguabta.

Unsworn, *a.* Neo-mhionnuichte.

Unsymmetrical, *a.* Neo-chumadail.

Untainted, *a* Neo-thruaillichte; neo-shalaichte; gun truaill, gun sal, gun spot, gun smùr, glan, gun ghaoid, gun choire, gun chron, neo-chiontach.

Untaken, *a.* Nach 'eil air ghabhail, neo-ghabhta

Untalked-of, *a.* Neo-iomraiteach, neo-ainmichte

Untameable, *a* Do-chiosnachadh, do-smachdachadh, do-cheannsachadh.

Untameableness, *a.* Do-chiosnachd.

Untamed, *a.* Neo-chiosnaichte, neo-cheannsaichte, neo-smachdaichte.

Untangle, *v.* Fuasgail, tuasgail, tualaig, thoir as a chéile. Time, thou must untangle this, not I,—Shakes. *Is tusa, aimsir, a dh' fheumas so fhuasgladh, 's cha mhise*

Untasted, *a.* Neo-bhlasta; neo-fheuchainnte

Untaught, *a* Neo-ionnsuichte, neo-fhoghlumte, gun ionnsuchadh, gun oilean; neo-sgileil, neo-oileanaichte, neo-chleachdta

Unteachable, *a.* Do-theagasgadh, do-ionnsuchadh, dùr.

Untempered, *a* Neo-oibrichte; neo-chruadhaichte, neo-fhaobhairte

Untempted, *a* Neo-bhuairte, neo-bhrosnaichte.

Untenable, *a* Nach gabh cumail; nach gabh dionadh, do-chumail, do-dhionadh

Untenanted, *a* Neo-àitichte, fàs, falamh

Untended, *a* Neo-fhritheilte, gun fhrithealadh

Untender, *a* Neo-shuairc, neo-chaoimhneil, neo-chaomh. So young and so untender?—Shakes *Cho òg is cho neo-shuairc?*

Unterrified, *a* Neo-ghealtach, gun eagall, gun sgàth, gun oillt.

Untether, *v* Cuir bharr na teathrach.

Unthanked, *a* Gun taing, gun bhuidheachas.

Unthankful, *a* Mi-thaingeil, neo-thaingeil, neo-bhuidheach, diombuidheach, *contr.* diombach, neo-thoileach, talachail.

Unthankfully, *adv* Gu mi-thaingeil, gu diombach

Unthankfulness, *s.* Mi-thaingealachd, diombachd.

Unthawed, *a.* Neo-leaghte; gun aiteamh.

Unthink, *v.* Dichuimhnich, na creid Unthink your speaking, and say so no more,—Shakes. *Dichuimhnich do chomhradh, 's na abair sin ni 's mo*

Unthinking, *a* Neo-smuainteachail, mi-sheadhail, neo-chùramach, gun omhaill, gun smuain, gun suim, gun seadh.

Unthorny, *a.* Neo-bhiorach, neo-stobach, gun bhior, gun stob, gun droighionn

Unthought-of, *a* Gun suim, neo-mheasail; gun mheas, gun speis

Unthread, *v* Fuasgail; cuir as chéile He can unthread thy joints,—Milton *Is urradh dha d'altan fhuasgladh.*

Unthreatened, *a* Neo-bhagairte, neo-ràithte.

Unthrift, *s* Struidhear, caithtiche

Unthriftily, *adv.* Gu struigheasach, gu stroghail, gu struigheil, gu caithteach, gu sgapach

Unthriftiness, *s.* Struighe, struigheasachd, stroghalachd, caithcamh.

Unthrifty, *a.* Struigheasach, stroghasach, struigheil, stroghail, caithteach, neo-chaomhntach, sgapach, neo-chaonndach, neo-ghrunndail. An unthrifty person, *dràig*

Unthriving, *a.* Neo-shoirbheasach, mi-shoirbheasach, mi-fhortanach

Unthrone, *v* Di-chathairich, cuir bhàrr na righ-chathrach.

Untidily, *adv* Gu slaodach, neo-ghibeach, neo-chearmanta, neo-chuimir, neo-sgilmeil, neo-ghlan.

Untidiness, *s* Slaodachd, mi-chearmantas.

Untidy, *a* Slaodach, neo-ghibeach, neo-ghiobach, neo-chearmanta, neo-chuimir, neo-sgilmeil. An untidy person, *fleogan, slaod.*

Untie, *v* Fuasgail, tuasgail, fosgail, lasaich, tualaig.

Untied, *a.* Fuasgailte, tuasgailte; fosgailte, lasaichte, tualaigte.

Until, *prep* Gu ruig, gu nuig, gu, gus, fa chomhar. Until this time, *gus an am so, gu ruig an am so;* until then, *gu sin*, until now, *gu so*, until when? *cia fhad, c'uine?*

Untilled, *a.* Neo-threabhta, neo-arta, fàs, falamh.

Untimbered, *a* Neo-phlancaichte; breòite, anfhann.

Untimely, *a.* Tràthail, anabuich, moch. An untimely death, *bàs tràthail*, he died an untimely death, *is moch fhuair e bàs*, an untimely birth, *luath-bhreith, breith roi 'n mhithich*

Untimely, *adv* Ro 'n am, roimh 'n am, roimh 'n mhithich, tuille is tràthail

Untinged, *a* Neo-dhathta.

Untired, *a* Neo-sgìth.

Untitled, *a* Neo-thiodalaichte.

Unto, *prep.* Do, gu, chum, thun, dh' ionnsuidh. See To.

Untold, *a* Neo-fhoillsichte, neo-aithriste, neo-aireamhta, gun innseadh.

Untolled, *a* (*As a bell*), neo-bhuailte. Without a toll, *neo-chàinichte.*

Untouched, *a* Neo-lamhaichte; slàn, neo-dhòthte.

Untoward, **Untowardly**, *a* Rag, reasgach, fiàr, eithich, olc; lùdarra, draghail; do-theagasg

Untowardliness, *s* Reasgachd; raigead, ludarrachd, draghalachd.

Untraceable, *a* Do-lorgachadh; do-leanachd, do-leantuinn.

Untraced, *a* Neo-lorgaichte, neo-leantuinnte.

Untracked, *a* Neo-lorgaichte; gun rod, gun slighe, gun aisridh; neo-choisichte.

Untractable, *a.* Rag, reasgach, ceannlaidir, doirbh, do-smachdachadh, garbh, deacair. The untractable abyss, *an linn dheacair.*

Untractableness, *s.* Reasgachd, raigead, ceannlaidireachd, dairbhe, deacaireachd.

Untrained, *a.* Neo-ionnsuichte, neo-oileanaichte; neo-chleachdta, neo-thréinte, neo-dheanta ri. My wit untrained in any kind of art, *m' aigne neo-chleachdta, do-riaghladh, do-smachdachadh, neo-smachdaichte, ri gné sam bi do chuilbheart*, untrained passion, *anamhiann neo-smachdaichte.*

Untransferable, *a.* Neo-bhuileachail, nach gabh buileachadh

Untransparent, *a* Dorch, doilleir.

Untravelled, *a* Neo-choisichte, fàs, falamh

Untread, *v* Ath-lorgaich, ais-cheumnaich, ais-imich.

Untreasured, *a.* Neo-thaisgte; neo-charnta.

Untreatable, *a.* Reasgach, eithich, doirbh

Untried, *a* Neo-dheuchainnte

Untrod, **Untrodden**, *a* Neo-choisichte, do-imeachd.

Untrolled, *a.* Neo-ruidhlte, neo-ròlta.

Untroubled, *a.* Neo-bhuairte, gun dragh, gun bhuaireas, gun mhoille; samhach, ciùin, seimh, socrach, soimeach.

Untrue, *a.* Fallsa, breugach; cealgach, mealltach; neo-dhileas, neo-fhior.

Untruly, *adv.* Gu fallsa, gu breugach, gu mealtach, gu neo-dhileas.

Untruth, *s* Breug; sgleò; traoidhte.

Untunable, *a.* Neo-cheòlmhor, do-ghleusadh.

Untune, *v* Cuir a gleus

Unturned, *a.* Neo-thiondaidhte; gun tionndadh.

Untutored, *a* Neo-ionnsuichte, neo-oileanaichte; aineolach

Untwine, **Untwist**, *v* Thoir as chéile, thoir as an fhigheadh.

Unurged, *a.* Neo-earalaichte, neo-asluichte, neo-ghuidhte; neo-ghriosta; gun earaladh, gun asluchadh, gun ghuidh.

Unused, *a.* Neo-chleachdta.

Unuseful, *a.* Neo-fheumail; gun stà, gun fheum; faoin, suarrach.

Unusual, *a.* Ainmig; tearc; neo-chumanta; ainneamh.

Unusually, *adv.* Gu h-ainmig, gu tearc, ro chorr uair.

Unusualness, *s.* Ainmigead; teircead.

Unutterable, *a.* Do-labhairt, do-innseadh, do-chur an céill, nach fhaodar labhairt (no) innseadh.

Unvaluable, *a.* Priseil, luachmhor; os cionn pris.

Unvalued, *a.* Di-measta, air dimeas, neo-mheasta; luachmhor, ro-phriseil.

Unvanquished, *a.* Neo-shàruichte, neo-cheannsuichte, neo-chlaoidhte.

Unvariable, *a.* Bunaiteach, seasmhach, maireannach; neo-chaochlaideach, cinnteach; do-atharrachadh, gun mhùth.

Unvariably, *adv.* Gu bunaiteach, gu seasmhach, gu maireannach; gun chaochladh, gun mhùth.

Unvaried, *a.* Gun mhuth, gun atharrachadh.

Unvarnished, *a.* Neo-sgiamhaichte, neo-bhreagh, gun sgiamh, gun eireachdas.

Unvarying, *a.* Neo-chaochlaideach, seasmhach.

Unveil, *v.* Leig ris, foillsich, feuch, nochd.

Unveiled, *a.* Foillsichte; nochdta, air leigeil ris.

Unvenial, *a.* Nach gabh mathadh.

Unveritable, *a.* Fallsa, breugach, neo-fhior.

Unversed, *a.* Neo-eòlach; neo-sgileil; ain-eolach.

Unvexed, *a.* Neo-fharanaichte; gun bhuaireadh; gun mhoille.

Unviolated, *a.* Neo-thruaillichte; neo-thruaillte; neo-bhriste.

Unvirtuous, *a.* Dubhailceach, mi-bheusach.

Unvisited, *a.* Neo-thathaichte.

Unvoyageable, *a.* Do-sheòladh.

Unvulnerable, *a.* Do-leònadh, nach gabh leònadh.

Unwakened, *a.* Neo-dhùisgte; neo-mhosgailte; gun dùsgadh, gun mhosgladh.

Unwalled, *a.* Gun bhalladh; neo-dhionta.

Unwarily, *adv.* Gu neo-fhaiceallach, gu neo-chùramach, gu mi-sheadhail.

Unwariness, *s.* Mi-fhaiceallachd, mi-shuim, cion-aire.

Unwarlike, *a.* Neo-ghaisgeil, neo-churanta.

Unwarned, *a.* Gun rabhadh, gun bhardainn, gun sànas.

Unwarrantable, *a.* Mi-laghail, neo-laghail, neo-bharrandach; neo-cheadaichte.

Unwarranted, *a.* Neo-cheadaichte; neo-bharrandaichte; neo-chinnteach.

Unwary, *a.* Neo-fhaiceallach, mi-chùramach, mi-sheadhail, neo-aireachail, gun seadh, gun suim, gun aire; obann, cabhagach, brais.

Unwashed, *a.* Neo-nighte; neo-ionnlaidhte, salach.

Unwasted, *a.* Neo-chaithte, neo-laghdaichte, slàn.

Unwatched, *a.* Neo-bheachdaichte.

Unwayed, *a.* Neo-chleachdta ri coiseachd.

Unweakened, *a.* Neo-anfhannaichte; neo-fhannaichte.

Unweaponed, *a.* Gun bhall airm.

Unweariable, *a.* Do-sgìtheachadh, do-thoirt, thairis, nach gabh sgìtheachadh (no) fannuchadh.

Unwearied, *a.* Neo-sgìth; do-sgìtheachaidh.

Unwed, *a.* Neo-phòsda, singilte.

Unwedgeable, *a.* Do-gheinneadh; cruaidh, do-sgoltaidh, nach gabh sgoltadh.

Unweeded, *a.* Neo-ghart-ghlante.

Unweeped, *a.* Neo-chaoidhte.

Unweeting, *a.* Aineolach, neo-fhiosrach; gun fhios, gun aire.

Unweighed, *a.* Neo-chothromaichte, neo-thomhaiste.

Unweighing, *a.* Neo-aireachail; obann, cabhagach, brais; neo-smuainteachail, baoghalta. Without question he was an unweighing fellow, *gun teagamh cha robh ann ach balaoch baoghalta.*

Unwelcome, *a.* Neo-thaitneach. You are unwelcome here, *cha 'n e do bheath an so.*

Unwelcomeness, *s.* Mi-thaitneachd.

Unwell, *a.* Tinn, euslan. I am not well, *tha mi tinn, tha mi gu tinn, cha 'n 'eil mi gu math.*

Unwept, *a.* Neo-chaoidhte.

Unwet, *a.* Neo-fhliuch; neo-àitidh; tiorram.

Unwhipt, *a.* Neo-sgiùrsta, neo-chuipinnte.

Unwholesome, *a.* Neo-shlainnteil, neo-fhallain, olc, deireasach, dochannach.

Unwholesomeness, *s.* Neo-fhallaineachd, deireasachd, dochannachd.

Unwieldily, *adv.* Gu trom, gu liobasda, gu ludarra.

Unwieldiness, *s.* Truime, liobasdachd.

Unwieldy, *a.* Trom, liobasda, ludarra, neo-ghrad, neo-ealamh; luidseach.

Unwilling, *a.* Neo-thoileach; ain-deonach; an aghaidh, leasg; neo-thogarach. Make him do it whether he be willing or unwilling, *thoir air a dheanamh a dheoin no dh' aindeoin.*

Unwillingly, *adv.* Gu neo-thoileach, gu diombach, a dh' aindeoin.

Unwillingness, *s.* Mi-thoil, diombachd, aindeonachd, leisge.

Unwind, *v.* Thoir as a chéile, thoir as an fhigheadh.

Unwiped, *a.* Neo-shiabta; neo-ghlan; salach.

Unwise, *a.* Neo-ghlic, neo-chrionna, eu-crionna, gòrach, amaideach.

Unwisely, *adv.* Gu neo-ghlic, gu neo-chrionna, gu h-eucrionna, gu gòrach.

Unwished, *a.* Neo-iarrta, neo-thogairte.

Unwishful, *a.* Neo-thogarach; neo-shanntach.

Unwitnessed, *a.* Gun fhianuis.

Unwittingly, *adv.* Gun fhios.

Unwonted, *a.* Tearc; neo-chumanta, neo-chleachdta.

Unworking, *a.* Soimeach, gun obair; neo-shaothaireachail.

Unworshipped, *a.* Gun aoradh, neo-aorta.

Unworthily, *adv.* Gu neo-àiridh; gu mi-thoilltinneach.

Unworthiness, *s.* Mi-thoillteanneas.

Unworthy, *a.* Mi-thoilltinneach; neo-airidh; suarrach; gun fhiù, gun fhiach.

Unwoven, *a.* Neo-fhighte, neo-dhualaichte.

Unwound, *pret.* and *pass.* of unwind. Neo-thoinnte, neo-thoinneamhte; neo-thacharaiste.

Unwounded, *a.* Neo-leònta; gun dochann, gun chiurram; slàn.

Unwrap, *a.* Fuasgail, fosgail, thoir as a chéile.

Unwreathed, *v. a.* Thoir as an fhighe (no) as an dual.

Unwriting, *a.* Nach sgriobh, nach cuir mach, nach bi na ughdar. The peace of the unwriting subject, *sìth 'n iochdarain leis nach àille bhì na ùghdar.—Arbuthnot.*

UNWRITTEN, *a.* Neo-sgrìobhte, neo-aithriste

UNWROUGHT, *a.* Neo-oibrichte.

UNWRUNG, *a* Neo-fhàisgte, neo-theannaichte.

UNYIELDED, *a.* Gun thabhairt suas, neo-strìochdta, nach 'eil air a thiomnadh, nach 'eil air a thabhairt suas.

UNYOKE, *v.* Neo-bheartaich, fuasgail.

UNYOKED, *a.* Neo-bheartaichte; neo-chiosnaichte; an-srianta; neo-bhriste

UNZONED, *a.* Neo-chriosraichte, neo-chrioslaichte, neo-chearclaichte, gun chrios.

UP, *prep* 'Nairde, suas, ri bruthach, ris an uchdan. I will drive my horse up hill, *cuiridh mi m' each ri bruthach*, he drew up his army, *tharruing e suas 'fheachd*

UP, *adv* Shuas, uthard; gu h-ard; suas; air éiridh, 'nàird, mach uthard, eirich, dirich, mosgail. Up (go up), *mach uthard, 'naird, dìrich*, I am up (risen), *tha mi air éiridh;* up by the roots, *as an fhreumh*, up betimes, *moch-éiridh*, up on end, *dìreach, na sheusamh*, up to, *gu ruig*, he ran his sword into him up to the hilt, *shàth e 'chlaidheamh ann gu ruig an dorn-chur*, up and down, *sios is suas, 'naird is bhàn*, up hill, *ri bruthach*, from my youth up, *o m' òige suas, o m' òige gu so*, up (awaken), *mosgail, mosglaibh*; he is knocked up, *tha e air toirt thairis*, the sun is up, *tha ghrian air éiridh*

UPBEAR, *v a* Tog suas, ardaich, cum suas, cum taic, giùlain

UPBRAID, *v a* Maoidh, cronaich; maslaich, troid, sglamh-raich, tarcuisich

UPBRAIDER, *s* Fear tarcuiseach; trodair.

UPBRAIDINGLY, *adv* Gu tarcuiseach, gu sglamhrach

UPCAST, *a.* Togta, togta suas, air a thogail suas

UPCAST, *s.* Urchair, tilgeadh.

UPHELD, *a* Air chumail suas, togta, propta.

UPHILL, *s.* Uchdach, bruthach.

UPHILL, *a* Ri bruthach, duilich, deacair, cruaidh, carrach.

UPHOARD, *v* Cnuasaich, carn suas, tionail ri chéile

UPHOLD, *v* Cum suas, tog, cum taic ri, prop, propainn; cum ri, mair beò

UPHOLDER, UPHOLSTERER, *s* Taic; fear-chumail suas, fear togalach, airneisiche

UPLAND, *s.* Ard, àirde, bràighe; mullach, raon, aonach, cnochd, cnoc, tulach.

UPLAND, *a* Ard, bràigheach, aonachail, monadhail, borb

UPLANDISH, *a* Ard, monadhail, monadail, garbh, cnochd-ach, cnocach

UPLAY, *v* Carn suas, cnuasaich; tionail ri chéile

UPLIFT, *v* Tog suas, urdaich

UPMOST, *a* Is airde, is uachdraiche, an uachdar, uachdrach

UPON, *prep.* Air, air muin Upon the right hand, *air an lamh dheas*, upon a horse, *air each, air muin eich*; upon record, *air scrìobhadh, scrìobhte*, upon my honour, *air m' onoir.*

UPPER, *a.* Uachdrach. He has got the upper hand of him, *fhuair e lamh 'n uachdar air.*

UPPERMOST, *a.* Is uachdraiche, is airde, uachdrach

UPPISH, *a.* Sgòdail, uallach, leòmach, stràiceil, uaimhreach, ardanach, brodail.

UPPISHNESS, *s* Sgòd, uaille, leoime, stràic, ardan, brod.

UPRAISE, *v* Tog suas, ardaich

UPREAR, *v.* Tog suas, ardaich, tog gu h-ard

UPRIGHT, *a* Dìreach, ionraic, dìreach na sheusamh, treibh-dhireach, onorach, simplidh, ceart, cothromach, fior, fire-annach

UPRIGHTLY, *adv* Gu direach; gu h-ionraic, gu treibhdhir-each, gu fìreannach.

UPRIGHTNESS, *s.* Tréibhdhireas, ionracas, fìreantachd.

UPRISE, *v.* Éirich.

UPRISE, *s* Éiridh. A lark that gives tidings of the sun's uprise, *uiseag a bheir nuaidheachd mu éiridh na gréine.*

UPRISE, *s* Éiridh.

UPROAR, *s.* Conghair; buaireas; gàire, gàrthaich, aimh-reite, mi-riaghailt.

UPROOT, *v.* Spìon as an fhreumh, buain.

UPROUSE, *v* Dùisg, mosgail; buair.

UPSHOT, *s.* Crìoch, fìnid; deireadh, ceann mu dheireadh, co-dhùnadh, ceann thall.

UPSIDE, *adv* An t-uachdar. Upside-down, *bun os cionn, thar a chéile.*

UPSTAND, *v. n.* Seas dìreach.

UPSTART, *s.* Ùr-dhuine, gearra-dhuine; ùranach.

UPSTAY, *v a* Cum suas, cum taic ri, propainn.

UPTAKE, *v. a.* Gabh suas; glac.

UPTURN, *v a* Tilg suas, tionndadh, cuir an taobh tha 'n iochdar an uachdar.

UPWARD, UPWARDS, *adv.* Suas, gu h-ard, ribruthach 'nairde, mach uthard, oscionn. Upward of twenty years, *oscionn fhichead bliadhna;* twenty years and upwards, *fichead bliadhna is tuille, fichead bliadhna is còrr.*

URBANE, *a.* Suairc; modhail.

URBANITY, *s.* Suairceas; modhaileachd; modhalachd; mire, cridhealas, ealaidh

URCHIN, *s.* Gràineag, urrag.

URETER, *s.* Fual-fheadan, feadan fuail.

URETHRA, *s.* Fual-fheadan.

URGE, *v* Earalaich; sparr; asluich; stuig; cuir h-uige; teannaich; fàisg, pùchd, pùc.

URGENCY, *s.* Cabhag; earailteachd, feumalachd, feum.

URGENT, *a.* Dian, earailteach, cabhagach, feumail.

URGENTLY, *adv.* Gu dian; gu h-earailteach.

URGER, *s.* Fear earailteach; earalaiche.

URGEWONDER, *s.* Seorsa eorna.

URINAL, *s.* Buideal fuail, buideal mùin

URINARY, *a.* Fualach, fuailidh. The urinary canal, *am feadan fuailidh, éigin fuail.*

URINE, *s.* Fual, mùn, maistir, uisge. Difficulty of urine, *galar fuail.*

URINE, *v.* Mùin; dean uisge, dean mùn.

URN, *s* Bior-chann, bior-phoit; poit uisge.

URRY, *s* Seorsa creadha.

US, *pron.* Sinn, sinne. With us, *leinne.*

USAGE, *s.* Cleachda, nòs, gnà, gnàth; càramh, uidhisinn. Bad usage, *droch caramh*, good usage, *deadh charamh.*

USANCE, *s.* Riadh, ocar; ocar-am.

USE, *s* Stà, uidhis, math, feum, diol, gnàthachadh, co' ghnath, (*habit*), cleachd, 'nòs, àbhaist, nàth; (*usury*), 'riadh. There is no use in him, *cha 'n 'eil stà ann, cha 'n 'eil math* (*no*) *feum ann*, he will make a bad use of it, *ni e droch uidhis dheth*, use makes perfection, *ni cleachd foirfeachd;* the memory will fail for want of use, *failliniichidh a chuimhne le dìth cleachda*, as was his use, *mar bu nòs da, mar b' àbhaist da*, use of the limbs, *cli nam ball, lùth nam ball;* make use of it, *gnathaich e, uidhisinn e;* bring into use, *thoir san fhasan;* out of use, *a cleachd, as an fhasan.*

USE, *v* Gnàthaich; buin ri, dean feum; caramh, cleachd; giùlain, iomchair, uidhisinn. Use every means, *gnathaich gach meadhon*, why do you use me so? *c'arson tha thu 'g am chàramh mar so?* as I used to do, *mar a chleachd mi* (*no*) *mar b' abhaist domh 'dheanamh*, he is used to it, *tha e air a chleachd ris*, they who use you despitefully, *iadsan tha buntuinn ruibh gu nàimhdeil;* you muse as you use, *is ann reir mar chaitheas duine a bheath, bheir e breith air a choimhearsnach.*

Used, *a.* Gnàthaichte, cleachdta, uidhisinnte. I am used to it, *tha mi cleachdta ris, tha mi air mo chleachd ris*, I am well used to it, *tha mi air mo dheagh chleachd ris*

Useful, *a.* Uidhiseil, feumail, iomchuidh, iomchubhaidh, freagarrach, stàdhar.

Usefully, *adv.* Gu feumail, gu h-uidhiseil, gu h-iomchuidh

Usefulness, *s.* Feum, feumalachd, stà

Useless, *a.* Gun fheum, gun stà, neo-uidhiseil, neo-fheumail, faoin, neo-tharbhach

User, *s* Gnathachair.

Usher, *s.* Fo' mhaighistir, fa' mhaighistir, fath-oide, gille doruis; treoraichair

Usher, *v.* Thoir steach, thoir stigh, feuch steach, feuch stigh.

Usquebaugh, *s* Uisge na beath, uisge beatha

Ustion, *s.* Losgadh

Ustorious, *a.* Losgach, loisgeach, teinnteach, teinntidh

Usual, *a* Cumannta, tric, minic, gnàthach, gnàthaichte As usual, *mar a b' àbhaist, mar is àbhaist*, at the usual time, *air an am is abhaist*

Usually, *adv.* Gu cumannta, an cumanntas, gu minic, a reir abhaist, mar is tric

Usualness, *s.* Cumantas, cleachd, cleachduinn

Usucaption, *s* Cleachd-sheilbh.

Usurer, *s* Ocarair; riadhair, riadhadair, uidhisear, ioncair; an-riadhair; ard riadhair

Usurious, *a* Ocarach, an-riadhach

Usurp, *v.* Glac, gleidh gun chòir; gabh seilbh a dh' aindeoin, mi-shealbhaich.

Usurpation, *s.* Glacadh eucorach, an-sheilbh

Usurper, *s* An-shealbhadair, righ a dh' aindeoin, righ air éigin

Usurpingly, *adv.* Gun chòir; gu h-eucorach.

Usury, *s* Ocar, an-riadh, an-dlighe Lend on usury, *cuir air riadh.*

Utensil, *s.* Ball, acfhuinn, cungaidh, ball-acfhuinn; insrumaid, gaoireas

Uterine, *a* Bolgach, machlagach.

Uterus, *s.* Bolg, balg, machlag, soire chloinne.

Utility, *s* Feum; iomchuidheachd, tairbhe, math, maith. This was written for the utility of scholars, *sgriobhadh so air son maith sgoileirean.*

Utmost, *a* Iomallach, iomallaiche, deireannach, deireannaiche. The utmost bounds of the earth, *foir iomallach na talmhainn*

Utmost, *s.* Meud I will do my utmost, *ni mi a mheud 's a 's urrainn mi, ni mi na dh' fhaotas mi*, he did his utmost, *rinn e na bh' aig, chaidh e fhads a bh' aig.*

Utter, *a* Iomallach; ana goireasach, anabharrach, fior Utter darknesss, *dorchadas iomallach*, he is an utter foe to me, *tha e na fhior namhaid dhomh*

Utter, *v* Labhair, innis, nochd, cuir an céill; reic, sgaoil; cuir a mach

Utterable, *a.* So-labhairt, so-innseadh, so-chur an céill; labhairteach.

Utterance, *s.* Labhairt; guth, uirighioll.

Utterer, *s.* Fear-labhairt, labhairtear; reiceadair; creiceadair.

Utterly, *adv.* Gu tur, gu h-iomlan, gu léir.

Uttermost, *s* A chuid is mò

Uttermost, *a* Is iomallaiche, is fhaide mach, is deireannaiche

Uvula, *s*, Glugan; cioch a mhuineil, cioch-shlugain.

Uxorious, *a.* Deidheil air mnaoi; céil-ghradhach

Uxoriousness, *s.* Céil-ghradh

V.

V. An dara litir fichead do 'n Aibideal.

Vacancy, *s.* Fàslach; aite fàs, aite falamh, failbhe; fois, taimh.

Vacant, *a.* Fàs, falamh; air athais, saor The chair is vacant, *tha 'chathair falamh.*

Vacate, *v.* Falamhaich, falmhaich; fàg; dean faoin, cuir air chùl

Vacation, *s.* Uine shaor; sgaoileadh, tamh Vacation of school, *sgaoileadh sgoil.*

Vaccary, *s* Bàich (i e. bà-theach), bo-lann, buaile, bà-thigh.

Vaccine, *a* Cruidh. Vaccine inoculation, *breac a chruidh*

Vacillancy, *s.* Seòganaich, turamanaich, luainealach, caochlaideachd; tomhartaich.

Vacillate, *v* Bi 's an turamanaich, bi san tomhartaich

Vacuation, *s.* Falamhachadh, falmhachadh, taomachadh.

Vacuism, *s* Faoinead, failbhe

Vacuity, *s* Falamhachd; fàsachd, failbhe

Vacuous, *a.* Falamh, fàs, faoin

Vade-mecum, *s* Leabhar pòchd

Vagabond, *s.* Fear-fuadain, iomrolaiche, seachranaiche, duine seabhaideach, luaidreanaiche, bathalaiche, allaban

Vagabond, *a.* Seachrànach, siùbhlach, iomrolach, seabhaideach, neo-shuidhichte, neo-sheasmhach, luaineach

Vagary, *s.* Faoin-dhòchas, dòchas, faoin-smuain.

Vagous, *a.* Siùbhlach, iomrolach, luaineach, faontrach

Vagrancy, *s* Iomrolachd, seachranachd, faontradh

Vagrant, *a* Siùbhlach, seachranach, iomrolach, seabhaideach, neo-shuidhichte, faontradhach, faontrach.

Vagrant, *s.* Baigeir; fear-fuadain

Vague, *a* Sgaoilte, sgaoilteach, faontrach

Vail, *v* Leig sios, islich, géill, striochd

Vails, *s.* Airgiod doruis

Vain, *a* Faoin, neo-éifeachdach, neo-tharbhach, falamh, fàs, diomhain; uallach, suarrach, fallsa, neo-fhior; sgàileanta; bòsdail, spagluinneach My labour is vain, *is diomhain mo shaothair*, in vain, *diomhain, an diomhanas*, take not the name of God in vain, *na gabh ainm Dhe an diomhanas*

Vain-glorious, *a* Earra-ghloireach, bòsdail, gloir-ghaileach; spailliceil, uallach; faoin rabhdach, rabhdail, ràiteach A vain-glorious person, *rabhdair.*

Vain-glory, *s* Earra-ghloir; arra-ghlòir, gloir dhiomhain, faoin-uaille, ràite, raiteachas, rabhdadh, spaillicealachd

Vainly, *adv* Gu faoin, gu diomhain, gu neo-éifeachdach

Vainness, *s* Faoineachd, diomhanachd, uaille, falamhachd

Valance, *s* Fabhradh; ribeag

Vale, *s*, Gleann, gleannan, srath, srathan

Valediction, *s.* Beannachd, cead, slainnte le, soraidh.

Valedictory, *a* Beannachdail

Valentine, *s.* Leannan, ceisdean, graidhean.
Valerian, *s.* Seorsa luibh.
Valet, *s* Gille-frithealaidh, gille-seomair, gille-cois
Valetudinarian, *a* Eu-slainnteach, tinn, euslan, anfhann, breòite, truagh, meuranda
Valetudinarian, *s* Urr-thinn, urr-euslainteach, euslan
Valetudinary, *a.* Eu-slainnteach, tinn
Valiant, *a* Gaisgeil, treun, foghainteach, treubhanta, breuthanta, curannta, calma, laochanta, laidir, treun, treun, neartmhor, misneachail, cridheil, cumhachdach
Valiantly, *adv* Gu gaisgeil, gu treun, gu foghainnteach, gu treubhanta, gu curanta, gu laochanta, gu laidir, gu neartmhor
Valiantness, *s* Gaisge, tréine, treuthantas, treubhantas, misneach.
Valid, *a* Làidir, tàbhachdach, eifeachdach, comasach, cumhachdach, foghainteach, murrach, tarbhach
Validity, *s* Tàbhachd, eifeachd
Vallancy, *s* Piorbhuic mhòr
Valley, *s* Gleann, gleannan, srath, glacan, lag
Valorous, *a.* Gaisgeil, laochanta, treun, calma, treubhanta, treuthanta
Valorously, *adv* Gu gaisgeil, gu calma, gu treun
Valour, *s* Gaisge, treubhantas, tréine, misneach, cruadal, ceatharnachd
Valuable, *a* Prìseil, luachmhor, costail, daor, ro-mheasail, ion-mheasta
Valuably, *adv* Gu priseil, gu luachmhor, gu costail, gu daor.
Valuation, *s* Meas, measadh, luach; fiach
Valuator, *s* Measadair, fear meas, fear measaidh
Value, *s* Pris, luach, meas, fiach, ciat It is of great value, *is mor a luach*, I have a great value for him, *tha meas mor agam dheth*, of little value, *fuoin, suarach, air bheag luach*, it is of no value, *cha n' fhiach e*
Value, *v* Meas, prìsich I will value your goods, *meas-aidh mi do mhaoin*, I do not value you a straw, *cha 'n 'eil meas sraibh agam ort, cha d' thugainn srabh ort*
Valueless, *a* Suarrach, gun fhiach, air bheag luach
Valuer, *s* Measadair, fear measaidh
Valve, *s* Comhladh, duilleag doruis, dor-dhuilleag
Vamp, *s* Leathar (no) learach uachdair.
Vamp, *v* Càramh, càirich, clùd, clùdaich Vamped, *càir-ichte, cludaichte*
Vamper, *s* Clùdair; brògair.
Van, *s* Toiseach, tùs, toiseach feachd; (*fan*), fuaragan; gaothran
Van-courier, *s* Gille-ruithe, teachdair
Vane, *s* Coileach-gaoithe
Vanguard, *s* Tùs-feachd, toiseach armailt.
Vanilla, *s* Faoineag, seorsa luibh
Vanish, *v* Rach as an t-sealladh, deinmhich, gabh a ghaoth He vanished into air, *ghabh e dha fein a ghaoth* —*Ossian*
Vanished, *a.* As an t-sealladh
Vanishing, *a.* Siubhlach, caochlaideach, re seall, neo-mhaireann
Vanity, *s* Diomhanas, faoinead, deinmheas, teagamhachd, bòsd, spagluinn What is necessary cannot be said to proceed from vanity, *cha b' uaill gun fheum e*
Vanquish, *v* Buadhaich, ceannsaich, ciosnaich, thoir buaidh, sàruich; claoidh; faigh lamh an uachdar, cuir fo smachd, fairtlich air. Vanquished, *ceannsaichte, sàruichte, claoidhte.*
Vanquisher, *s* Buadhair, sàruchair.
Vantage, *s.* Tairbhe, lamh an uachdar, coisinn; cothrom
† **Vantbrass**, *s* Guaill-bheart.
Vapid, *a* Domblasda, neo-bhrigheil, marbh, air dol eug, air bàsachadh, (*mar leann*), air dol dh' aog, droch-bhlasda, leamh.
Vapidness, *s* Domblasdachd, mairbhe, leamhad.
Vaporation, *s.* Smuideachadh, ceò.
Vaporer, *s* Rabhdair, ràite, buamasdair.
Vaporish, *a* Cainnteach, fritheanach, tamhanach
Vaporous, *a* Smùideach, ceòthar, ceòmhor.
Vapour, *s* Deatach, deathach, smùid, ceò, gal; ceo-gréine
Vapour, *v.* Cuir smùid; dean bòsd
Vapours, *s* Leanntras, liunntras.
Variable, *a* Caochlaideach, mughteach, neo-sheasmhach, neo-bhunaiteach, eutrom, luaineach, teagamhach
Variableness, *s* Caochlaideachd; eutromachd.
Variably, *adv* Gu caochlaideach, gu mùthteach; gu siubhlach, gu neo-sheasmhach, gu h-eutrom, gu luaineach
Variance, *s* Droch-cordadh, aimhreite, cur mach. They are at variance, *tha iad mach air chéile*
Variation, *s* Caochladh, mùgh, atharrachadh; difir, diubhair Variation of the compass, *caochladh na cairtiùil.*
Variegate, *v.* Breachd, breacaich, ballaich, eugsamhlaich; ioma-dhath
Variegated, *a.* Breachd, ballach, eugsamhuil, iol-ghneth-each
Variety, *s* Caochladh, atharrachadh, mùth, iomadaidh; caochladh; iolar, breacadh, iolardhas, diubhair.
Various, *a* Ioma, iomad, mòran, eugsamhuil, iomadach, ioma-ghnetheach, mùthteach, breachd, breac; sain, iolar-ach (*i e.* iol-thuarach), iol-ghnetheach
Variously, *adv* Gu h-eugsamhuil, gu h-ioma-ghnetheach, air ioma doigh
Varix, *s* At-féith
Varlet, *s* Sgonn-bhalaoch, crochair; rag, garlach
Varletry, *s* Prabar, gràisg
Varnish, *s.* Sliob-oladh, falaid.
Varnish, *v* Sgiamhaich, sliobaich, sliob.
Varnisher, *s* Sgiamhadair, falaidiche
Vary, *v a* and *n* Muth; mùgh, caochlaidh, caochail, eugsamhlaich, atharraich, breacaich.
Vary, *s* Mùgh, caochladh.
† **Vascular**, *a* Seomrach, cósagach
Vase, *s* Soire, soitheach, ciolarn, stamh
Vassal, *s.* Iochdran, òglach, tuathanach.
Vassalage, *s* Iochdranachd; traillealachd, seirbheis
Vast, *s.* Fàsach.
Vast, *a* Mòr, ro-mhor, anabharrach, anameasarra, fuath-asach, an-mhor, aibhseach
Vastation, *s.* Sgrios, creach
Vastly, *adv* Gu mòr, gu h-an-mhor, gu h-anabarrach.
Vastness, *s.* Ana-cuimseachd, an-mhorachd, anabharrachd.
Vasty, *a* Mòr, an-mhòr, anabharrach, fuathasach, aibhseach.
Vat, *s* Tubag, stannd, measair; soitheach-togalach, soith-each masgaidh
Vaticide, *s* Fàidh-mhortair
Vaticinate, *v.* Dean fàidheadaireachd, dean fàistinneachd; fàisnich
Vault, *s* Bògha, airse, seileir; uamhaidh, tuam, uaghaidh.
Vault, *v* Cuir suas bogha, tog bogha; leum.
Vault, *s* Leum; cruinn-leum.
Vaulted, *a.* Boghta. A vaulted roof, *druim bhoghta.*

Vaulter, *s.* Leumadair.
† **Vaulty**, *a.* See Vaulted.
Vaunt, *s.* Bòsd; earraghloir; brag, uaille rabhdadh, spagluinn.
Vaunt, *v.* Bòsd, dean bòsd, bragainn, dean uaille.
Vaunter, *s* Bragair; rabhdair.
Vauntful, *a.* Bòsdail, uallach, rabhdach, spaglumneach.
Vauntingly, *adv* Gu bòsdail, gu h-uallach, gu rabhdach, gu spaglumneach.
Veal, *s.* Laoigh-fheoil
Vection, **Vecitation**, *s.* Giùlan, iomchar, caraiste
Vecture, *s.* Giùlan, iomchar, caraiste.
Veer, *v. a* and *n* Tionndadh; cuir mu 'n cuairt; cuir tiomchioll, leig a mach.
Veer, *s.* Car-sheòladh.
Vegetability, *s.* Cinneadachd.
Vegetable, *a.* Luibheach, luiseanach
Vegetable, *s.* Luibh, lus; luiseanachd, luibheanachd
Vegetate, *v* Fàs, cinn, beothaich.
Vegetation, *s* Fàs, cinneas
Vegetative, *a.* Fàsanta, cinneadach, cinneasach, so-fhàs A vegetative soul, *unam fuis.*
Vegete, *a* Làidir, treun, lùthar, beò, smiorail, smearail.
Vehemence, *s.* Déineas, déine, buirbe, gairgead, foirneart, deothas.
Vehement, *a.* Dian, deineachdach, borb, garg, deothasach, dibhireach, loisgeanta, greadanta
Vehemently, *adv* Gu dian, gu borb, gu garg, gu deothasach.
Vehicle, *s.* Cairt, feun, carbad, càr, inneal-iomchair
Veil, *s.* Gnùis-bhrat, sgàile; comhdach, brat A necromantic veil which makes the wearer invisible, *dichealtair*
Veil, *v.* Comhdaich, folaich, falaich céil
Vein, *s* Cuisle, féith, gné; cal, stiall, sannt In a pleasant vein, *cridheil, sunntach*, in the usual vein, *anns an sean chal*
Veined, **Veiny**, *a* Cuisleach, feitheach; stiallach
Vellicate, *v.* Spion, spiòl, stang, slam, card
Vellication, *s.* Spionadh, spioladh, cordadh
Vellum, *s* Sreathan, meamram, craicionn min, croicionn sgriobhaidh, croicionn laoigh air a dheasachadh airson sgriobhadh
Velocity, *s.* Luathas, luas, tapachd
Velvet, *s.* Beilbheid.
Venal, *a.* Cuisleach.
Venal, *a.* So-reiceadh, ion-reic, briobach
Venality, *s* Briobachd.
Venatic, *a* Faoghaideach; sealgach
Venation, *s* Faoghaid, faoghailt, sealg
Vend, *v* Reic, creic, tairg
Vender, *s* Reiceadair, creiceadair
Vendible, *a.* Reiceadach, so-reiceadh a ghabhas reiceadh.
Vendition, *s.* Reiceadh, creiceadh; ropainn
Venefic, *a* Nimhneach, puinnsionta, nimhe, nimheil
Venefice, *s* Puinnseanachadh; buidseachas, druidheachd
Veneficial, *a* Puinnsionta, nimhneach, nimhe, buidseachail, druidheach, druidheil.
Venenate, *v* Puinnsionaich
Venenation, *s.* Puinnsion, nimhe
Venene, **Venenose**, *a* Puinnsionta, nimhe
Venerable, *a.* Urramach, measail, oirdheirc, ion-mheasta
Venerableness, *s.* Urramachd, measalachd.

Venerably, *adv.* Gu h-urramach, gu measail.
Venerate, *v* Urramaich; thoir onoir
Venerated, *a* Urramaichte, onoirichte
Veneration, *s.* Urram, ard-urram; mòr-mheas, meas, onoir.
Venereal, *a* Drùiseil; clapach
Venereous, *a.* Drùiseil, macnusach, neo-gheimnidh, sanntach, slatail.
Venery, *s.* Drùis, macnusachd, slataireachd, bodaireachd
Venery, *s* Sealg, sealgachd, faoghaid, faoghailt
Venesection, *s* Leigeil fola, gearradh chuislean.
Vengeable, *a* Dioghaltach, mio-runach, gamhlasach.
Vengeance, *s* Dioghaltas, peanas Taking vengeance, *a deanamh dioghultais*, I will take vengeance on him, *ni mi dioghaltas air*
Vengeful, *a* Dioghaltach, mio-runach, gamhlasach
Veniable, **Venial**, *a* So-mhathaidh, so-laghadh, ceaduichte
Venison, *s* Sitheann; fiadhach.
Venom, *s.* Nimhe, puinnsion
Venomously, *adv* Gu nimheil, gu puinnsionta, gu nimhneach, gu mio-runach, gu gamhlasach
Venomous, *a* Nimheil, puinnsionta, nimhneach, mi-runach, gamhlasach, aingidh, millteach
Venomousness, *s* Nimhealachd; aingidheachd
Vent, *s* Simealair; fosgladh; àile-tholl, leigeil mach, àite dol mach.
Vent, *v* Leig mach; abair, labhair, dòirt mach, thoir gaoth, foillsich
Vent, *s.* Ropainn, reiceadh
Vent, *v* Reic, creic.
Ventage, *s* Toll-coraig, *mar ann am feadan*
† **Ventana**, *s* Uinneag, fuinneog
Venter, *s* Brù, bolg, machlag, mathair
Ventiduct, *s* Toll-gaoithe
Ventilate, *v.* Fuaraich, fionnaraich, glan, fasgain; (*examine*), ceasnuich, rannsuich.
Ventilation, *s.* Fuarachadh, fionnarachadh, fasgnadh
Ventilator, *s* Fuaragan.
Ventose, *a* Gaothar.
Ventosity, *s* Gaotharachd.
Ventricle, *s* Bronnag, bolgan.
Ventriloquist, *s* Bronn-chainntear
Ventriloquy, *s.* Bronn-bhruidhinn
Venture, *s* Tuairmeas; tuaiream; sgiorradh, cunnart, teagamhas, cineamhuinn. At a venture, *thaobh tuairmeis, thaobh tubaist*
Venture, *v* Cuir an cunnart, rach an cunnart, dùraig, dùirig Never venture never win, *mar dùraig thu, cha bhuidhinn thu*
Venturesome, *a* Misneachail, dàn
Venturously, *adv.* Gu misneachail, gu dàn
Venus, *s* Bhénus, ban dia na h-Ailne, drùis, baois
Veracious, *a* Fior, fìreannach
Veracity, *s.* Fìreantachd, fìrinn
Verb, *s* † Fearb
Verbal, *a* Foclach, briathrail, beulach
Verbally, *adv* Focal air fhocal; ann am focail
Verberate, *v.* Fri-bhuail; buail, bruth, straoidhil
Verberation, *s* Fri-bhualadh; bualadh, straoidhlearachd
Verbose, *a* Briathrach, bruidhneach, glòraiseach, rabhdach, ràiteach.

Verbosity, *s.* Briathrachas; bruidhneachd, rabhdadh, ràite.
Verdant, *a.* Gorm; feurach.
Verdantness, *s.* Guirme, gorm.
Verdict, *s.* Breith; roisceal, binn; barail. Pass a verdict, *thoir binn.*
Verdigris, *s.* Meirg prais.
Verdure, *s.* Gorm, guirme; feur.
Verdurous, *a.* Gorm, feurach.
Verecund, *a.* Nàrach, banail, bandaidh, beanail, mallta.
Verge, *s.* Slat; slat-shuaicheantais.
Verge, *s.* Foir, oir, iomall, bruach, fraidhe.
Verge, *v.* Aom; teann. It verges towards night, *tha e teannadh f gus air an oidhche.*
Verger, *s.* Fear slat-shuaicheantais, suaicheantaiche.
Veridical, *a.* Fior, fireannach.
Verification, *s.* Fireannachadh.
Verifier, *s.* Dearbhair.
Verify, *v.* Dearbh; firinnich; daighnich, comhdaich.
Verily, *adv.* Gu fior, gu deimhinn, gu fireannach, gu cinnteach, gun teagamh, gu dearbh. Yea verily, *seadh gu dearbh.*
Verisimilar, *a.* Cosmhalach, coslach.
Verisimilitude, *s.* Cosmhalachd.
Veritable, *a.* Fior, fireannach; cinnteach.
Veritably, *adv.* Gu fior, gu fireannach.
Verity, *s.* Firinn; dearbhradh.
Verjuice, *s.* Sùgh nan ubhlan fiadhain.
Vermicular, *a.* Cuairteagach; daolagach, sniomhanach.
Vermiculation, *s.* Sniomhanachd.
Vermicule, *s.* Durag, cnuimh, cnuimheag, cnaimheag, daolag, doirb, dathag.
Vermiculous, *a.* Duragach, daolagach, cnuimheagach.
Vermifuge, *s.* Fùdar dhurag, leigh airson dhathagaibh.
Vermilion, *s.* Corcur; luaidh dhearg; seorsa deirge.
Vermin, *s.* Meanbh-bhéistean, mar luchaidh radain, mhialan is an leithidibh s'n.
Verminous, *a.* Beisteagach, mialach.
Vermiparous, *a.* Dur-bheirteach, cnuimheagach.
Vernacular, *a.* Dùchasach, dùthchasach, tìreach, ducha. The vernacular language of a country, *beargnadh.*
Vernal, *a.* Earrachail, céiteineach; earraich, ceitein.
Vernant, *a.* Blàthmhor.
Vernility, *s.* Tràillealachd.
Versatile, *a.* So-thionndadh; mùiteach, caochlaideach, luaineach; iol-bheusach.
Versatileness, Versatility, *s.* Caochlaideachd, luaineachd.
Verse, *s.* Rann; rann-ghabhail; ceithreamh bardachd; earrann.
Versed, *a.* Teòma, sgileil, eolach, fiosrach, foghluimte, ionnsuichte.
Verseman, *s.* Bard, ranndair.
Versification, *s.* Ranntachd, duanaireachd.
Versifier, *s.* Bard, ranndair.
Versify, *v.* Cuir am bardachd; dean bardachd.
Version, *s.* Atharrachadh; eadar-theangachadh; tionndadh.
Vert, *s.* Uaine; gorm.
Vertebral, *a.* A bhuineas dh' alt na droma.
Vertebra, Vertebre, *s.* Alt na droma.
Vertex, *s.* Mullach; bior; binnean.
Vertical, *a.* Dìreach osceionn.
Verticity, *s.* Tionndadh; carrachadh.
Vertiginous, *a.* Cuairteanach, tuainealach, eutrom.
Vertigo, *s.* Tuainealach, tuaineal; tuaicheal, clò-ghalar; suathran; buaireadh.
Vervain, *s.* Trombhod; seorsa luibh. Common vervain, crubh leomhainn.
Very, *a.* Fior, fìreannach; ceart. O that in very deed we may behold it! *O gu faiceamaid e gu fior!* that very hour, *a cheart uair sinn.*
Very, *adv.* Ro, sàr, fior. Very good, *ro mhath, sàr mhath, fior mhath.*
Vesicate, *v.* Leusaich, leus, bolgaich, bolg. Vesicated, *leusaichte.*
Vesication, *s.* Leus; leusachadh; bolgadh.
Vesicle, *s.* Leus, bolg, builgean, guirean.
Vesicular, *a.* Fàs, tolltach.
Vesper, *s.* Reannag feasgair; an fheasgrag; a Bhénus nur luidheas i 'n deigh na gréine, neoin-reult, trath nòin.
Vespers, *s.* Urnuigh fheasgair, ùrnuigh nòin.
Vespertine, *a.* Feasgarach.
Vessel, *s.* Soitheach; (*ship*), long, luingeas. A leaky vessel, *bruchog.*
Vest, *s.* Peiteag, deacaid, aodach cuirp.
Vest, *v. a.* Sgeadaich, comhdaich; éid; (*install*), cuir an seilbh, builich.
Vestal, *s.* Maighdeann, oigh.
Vestal, *a.* Maighdinneil, oigheil.
Vestibule, *s.* Ailear, for-dhorus.
Vestige, *s.* Lorg; aile; comhar; iarmad.
Vestment, *s.* Aodach, eudach, éideadh, earradh, trusgan; culaidh, comhdach.
Vestry, *s.* Seomar chulaidh; naomh-thaisg; creacar.
Vestry-keeper, *s.* Beadal.
Vesture, *s.* Aodach, earradh, éideadh, trusgan, falluing, deise, comhdach.
Vetch, *s.* Peasair each, peasair chapull, peasair luch, gall-pheasair.
Veteran, *s.* Seann saighdear.
Veteran, *a.* Deanta ri cogadh.
Veterinarian, *s.* Each-leigh.
Vex, *v. a.* Buair, craidh, claoidh, sàruich, cuir dragh air, cuir moile (no) farran air, farranaich. Vexed, *buairte, craidhte, farranaichte, farranach, fo champar, smalanach.*
Vexation, *s.* Buaireadh, doltrum, cùradh, campar, ciapall, farran, utrais, dragh, moile, aimheal, amhghar, smalan, sprochd, bioran, *angar.* It gave me great vexation, *chuir e mòran farrain orm.*
Vexatious, *a.* Buaireasach, doltrumach, ciapallach, farranach, camparach, utraiseach, draghalach, aimhealach, amhgharrach, smalanach, trioblaideach. A most vexatious thing, *ni ro fharranach.*
Vexatiously, *adv.* Gu buaireasach, gu ciapallach, gu farranach, gu camparach, gu h-utraiseach, gu draghalach.
Vexatiousness, *s.* Buaireasachd, doltrumachd, ciapallachd, farranachd, trioblaideachd.
Vexer, *s.* Buaireadair, fear buairidh.
Vexing, *a.* See Vexatious.
Vial, *s.* Searrag, gloine bheag.
Viand, *s.* Biadh, lòn.
Viaticum, *s.* Lòn-siùbhail; tachdar.
Vibrate, *v.* Crath, cas, luaisg; crith.
Vibrating, *a.* and *part.* A crathadh, a critheadh, seòganach.
Vibration, *s.* Crathadh, critheadh, luasgadh, seòganaich.

Vibratory, *a.* Fri-luasgach; seòganach.

Vicar, *s.* Comh-arba; pearsa eaglais, fear ionaid.

Vicarage, *s.* Comharbachd, beathachadh.

Vicarious, *a.* Ionadach.

Vice, *s.* Dubhailc: aingidheachd; lochd, cron, donas, coire, olc, olcas; arraid. A blacksmith's vice, *gramaich.*

Vice-admiral, *s.* Riochd-ard-mharaich.

Vicegerent, *s.* Riochd-fhear, fear ionaid.

Vice-president, *s.* Iar-cheann-suidhe.

Viceroy, *s.* Fear ionad-righ; iar-righ, iar-fhlath.

Viceroyalty, *s.* Riochd-rioghalachd, iar-rioghalachd.

Vicinage, Vicinity, *s.* Nàbachd, nàbuidheachd, coimhearsnachd, coi' fhearsnachd; dlùthas.

Vicinal, *a.* Fogus, fagus, dlùth air.

Vicious, *a.* Olc, aingidh, dubhailceach, lochdach, droch-mhuinte, guineach, miosguineach.

Vicissitude, *s.* Mùgh, caochladh, atharrachadh, tionndadh.

Victim, *s.* Tabhartas, iobairt.

Victor, *s.* Buadhair, fear buaidh, gaisgeach.

Victorious, *a.* Buadhach, buadhmhor, all-bhuadhach, gaisgeil. Victorious Fingal, *Fionnghal nam buadh;* he was victorious over them, *bhuadhaich e orra, dh' fhairtlich e orra.*

Victoriously, *adv.* Gu buadhach, gu buadhmhor.

Victoriousness, *s.* Buadhachd, buadhmhorachd.

Victory, *s.* Buaidh; athas; lamh 'n uachdar; maighistireachd; caithream. A shout of victory, *buaidh ghàir;* a complete victory, *buaidh làrach.*

Victual, Victuals, *s.* Lòn, biadh, biodailt; teachd an tìr, biathachadh, biath.

Victual, *v. a.* Biath, biadh, beathaich, tog, cum suas. Victualled, *biathta, beathaichte.*

Victualler, *s.* Beathachair; fear tigh osda.

Victualling-office, *s.* Buth beathachaidh.

Videlicet, *adv.* Is e sin ri radh; eadhon.

Viduity, *s.* Bantrachas.

Vie, *v. n.* Strigh, cuir strigh, dean spairn.

View, *v. a.* Beachdaich, seall, amhairc air, feuch, gabh fradharc, gabh beachd, gabh sealladh.

View, *s.* Beachd, seall, fradharc; rùn, aogas. In the view of the world, *an sealladh an t-saoghail;* I have it in view, *tha e ann mo bheachd, tha e ann am aire;* the view of a deer, *lorg feidh.*

Viewer, *s.* Beachdair, fear beachdaidh.

Viewing, *s.* Beachdachadh, amharc.

Viewless, *s.* Dorch, neo-fhaicinnte; neo-leirsneach.

Vigesimal, *a.* Ficheadamh.

Vigesimation, *s.* Cur gach fichead fear, gu bàs.

Vigil, *s.* Faire; trasg, trosg, ùrnuigh fheasgair, féill, beirbheis.

Vigilance, *s.* Faicill, faiceallachd, furachras; faire, beachdalachd, mosgaltachd.

Vigilant, *a.* Faiceallach, furachair, aireach, aireachail, cùramach; airneach.

Vigilantly, *adv.* Gu faiceallach, gu furachar, gu h-aireachail.

Vigorous, *a.* Treun, làidir, neartmhor, gramail, lùthmhor, lùthar, beothanta; beò; sracanta, beochanta.

Vigorously, *adv.* Gu treun, gu laidir, gu neartmhor, gu gramail, gu luthmhor, gu sracanta.

Vigour, *s.* Tréine, spionnadh, treoir, neart, lùth, eifeachd.

Vile, *a.* Suarrach, graineil; truaillidh, diblidh, dimeasda; salach, grannda, gràda, mosach; olc, aingidh, dubhailceach.

Viled, *a.* Tàireil, tarcuiseach.

Vilely, *adv.* Gu suarrach, gu gràineil, gu truaillidh, gu dìblidh; gu dimeasta, gu mosach, gu gràda; gu h-olc.

Vileness, *s.* Suarraichead, gràineileachd, truaillidheachd, dìblidheachd.

Vilifier, *s.* Fear tàireil.

Vilify, *v.* Maslaich; ìslich, dean tair air, di-mheas, truaillich. Vilified, *maslaichte, di-mhéasta.*

Villa, *s.* Tigh dùcha, tigh samhruidh.

Village, *s.* Baile, baile beag, frith-bhaile, clachan. The villagers, *muinntir bhaile.*

Villager, *s.* Fear mhuinntir baile.

Villain, *s.* Slaoightir, cealgair, crochair, daoighear; òglach, iochdran.

Villainage, *s.* Ogluidheachd, tràillealachd.

Villainize, *v.* Maslaich; ìslich. Villanized, *maslaichte, ìslichte.*

Villainous, *a.* Olc, aingidh; dìblidh, suarrach, slaoighteil.

Villainously, *adv.* Gu h-olc, gu h-aingidh, gu suarrach, gu tàireil.

Villainy, *s.* Olc, aingidheachd; ciont, droch thùrn, coire, truaillidheachd; urchoid, diobhail.

Villatic, *a.* Fri-bhailteach.

Villi, *s.* Ròinne.

Villose, *a.* Molach, ròmach, roinneach, giobach, cléiteagach.

Vimineous, *a.* Maothranach, slatagach.

Vincible, *s.* So-shàruchadh, so-chlaoidh.

Vindicate, *v. a.* Fìreannaich, diol; dearbh, dion, cum suas, gabh leithsgeul.

Vindication, *s.* Fìreannachadh, dioladh, dionadh.

Vindicative, *a.* Dioghaltach.

Vindicator, *s.* Dionair; fìreannachair.

Vindicatory, *a.* Peanasach, dioghaltach.

Vindictive, *a.* Dioghaltach.

Vine, *s.* Fionan, fineamhuin, crannfiona.

Vine-fretter, *s.* Cnuimh fionain.

Vinegar, *s.* Fion-geur.

Vineyard, *s.* Garadh-fion, fion-gharadh, fion-lios.

Vine-press, *s.* Fion-amar.

Vinous, *a.* Fionach, fionar.

Vintage, *s.* Fion-fhoghar.

Vintager, *s.* Fear fion fhogharaidh.

Vintner, *s.* Fion-mharson; fear tigh-osda, osdair fiona.

Vintry, *s.* Fion-mhargad.

Viol, *s.* Fidheall.

Violable, *a.* So-chiurradh; so-thruailleadh, so-mhilleadh.

Violate, *v. a.* (*Hurt*), ciùrr, mill, bris; docharaich, dochannaich, dochainn; (*deflower*), truaill, éignich, truaillich. He violated her, *thruaillich e i, dh' éignich e i;* he violated the law, *bhris e 'n lagh.*

Violated, *a.* Ciùrrta, docharaichte, briste; (*as chastity*), truaillichte, éignichte.

Violation, *s.* Ciurram; milleadh, truailleadh, briseadh, do-charachadh; (*of chastity*), éigneachadh; truailleadh.

Violator, *s.* Fear brisidh; (*of chastity*), truaillear, éigneachair.

Violence, *s.* Ain-neart, foirneart, éigin, breth-air-éigin, ionnsuidh; déineas; déine; deothas, ciurram; cron, éigneachadh.

Violent, *a.* Dian; ain-neartach; ceann-laidir; garg, fòirneartach, borb, deothasach.

Violently, *adv.* Le-h-ain-neart, gu h-ain-neartach, gu dion; a dh' aindeoin, gu borb, gu deothasach.

Violet, *s.* Fail-chuach, sail-chuach.

Violin, *s.* Fidheall.

Violist, *s.* Fidhlear.

Viper, *s.* Nathair nimhe.

Viperine, *a.* Nathaireil.

Viperous, *a.* Nimheach, nimhneach, puinnseanta.

Virago, *s.* Ban-ghaisgeach, ban-chùraidh; ban-tuaireap-aiche; té thagluinneach.

Virent, *a.* Uain, gorm.

Virgin, *s.* Oigh, maighdinn; gruagach, nighean; h-aon do chomharan na grein-chrios.

Virgin, *a.* Maighdeannach, maighdinneal, oigheil; òg.

Virginal, *s.* Oigh-cheol.

Virginal, *a.* Oigheil, maighdinneil, bandaidh, banail, mallta, gasda, geimnidh.

Virginity, *s.* Maighdeannas, maighdinneas.

Virgo, *s.* An oigh, aon do chomharan na gréine-chrios.

Virid, *a.* Gorm, uaine.

Viridity, *s.* Guirme, uaine.

Virile, *a.* Fearail; duineil.

Virility, *s.* Fearas; fearalas, duinealas, duineachas, fearachas, fearachd, ciadhas.

Viripotent, *a.* Ion-phosda.

Virtual, *a.* Nadurrail.

Virtuality, *s.* Eifeachd.

Virtue, *s.* Subhailc; deagh-bheus, beus; cruadal, feart; brìgh; buaidh; misneach, neart, comas; éifeachd. By virtue of his power, *a thaobh a chumhachd.*

Virtueless, *a.* Neo-shubhailceach; gun bhrìgh, neo-bhrìghmhor, neo-éifeachdach, gun éifeachd.

Virtuous, *a.* Subhailceach; math, deagh-bheusach; éif-eachdach, comasach, cumhachdach, slainnteil; (*chaste*), † cast, gasd, geimnidh.

Virtuoso, *s.* Fear-ionnsuichte.

Virtuously, *adv.* Gu subhailceach, gu beusach, gu feartail, gu gasda, gu geimnidh.

Virulence, *s.* Nimhe; géire, gairge, gamhlas, mi-run.

Virulent, *a.* Nimhneach; puinnseanta; cnamhtach, garg, geur, gamhlasach, mi-runach.

Virulently, *adv.* Gu nimhneach; gu garg, gu geur, gu gamhlash; gu mi-runach.

Visage, *s.* Aghaidh, eudan, aodann, gnùis, dealbh; seall-adh, dreach. What sort of visage has he? *ciod an seorsa aodainn th' aig?* sour-visaged, *gruamach, dorch.*

Viscerate, *v. a.* Thoir mionach a.

Viscid, *a.* Righinn, rithinn; leanailteach, sticeach, glaod-har, glaodhanta.

Viscidity, *s.* Righneachd, rithneachd; leanailteachd.

Viscosity, *s.* Righneachd, rithneachd, leanailteachd.

Viscount, *s.* Biocas.

Viscountess, *s.* Ban-bhiocas.

Viscous, *a.* Righinn, rithinn; leanailteach, sticeach; gla-odhar, glaodhanta.

Visibility, *s.* Faicsinneachd, soilleireachd.

Visible, *a.* So-fhaicsinn, faicinneach, faicsinneach; soilleir.

Visibly, *adv.* Gu soilleir, gu faicsinneach.

Vision, *s.* Fradharc; radharc, seall, sealladh, taisbean, foill-seachadh; (*ghost*), taibhse, tannasg; (*dream*), bruadar, aisling.

Visional, *a.* Fradharcail.

Visionary, *a.* Faoin, neo-fhior; taisbeanach, baralach, dòchasach.

Visionary, *s.* Taibhsdear; fear da shealladh, bruadaraiche, aislingiche.

Visit, *s.* Céilidh; fiosrachadh. On a visit, *air chéilidh, air aoidheachd.*

Visit, *v. a.* Fiosraich; faic, amhairc air, tadhail, thoir céilidh. He visited me, *thug e céilidh dhomh; dh' fhiosraich e mi, thainig e 'g am fhaicinn.*

Visitant, *s.* Aoidhe, fear céilidh; rochdair.

Visitation, *s.* Fiosrachadh; amharc.

Visor, *s.* Sgàil; cìdhis, gìdhis.

Visored, *a.* Sgàilte, cidhiste, céilte.

Vista, *s.* Sealladh.

Visual, *a.* Seallaidh, radhairc, fradhairc.

Vital, *a.* Beathach, beathail, beothail. Vital air, *beathàile.*

Vitality, *s.* Beathalachd, beothalachd.

Vitals, *s. pl.* Beatha; beothachadh; beathraidh.

Vitiate, *v. a.* Mill; truaill, truaillich; ciùrr, dochannaich; salaich. Vitiated, *millte, truaillte, dochannaichte.*

Vitiation, *s.* Truailleadh; coirbteachd, dochann.

Vitious, *a.* Coirbte; olc, aingidh; truaillidh, coirpidh, miosguineach.

Vitreous, *s.* Gloineach, gloinidh.

Vitrify, *v. a.* and *n.* Gloinich; dean na ghloine, fàs mar ghloine.

Vitriol, *s.* Cnamh-uisge, uisge loisgeach.

Vituline, *a.* Laoghach.

Vituperable, *a.* Coireach, ciontach, ion-chronachadh.

Vituperate, *v. a.* Coirich, cronaich, troid.

Vituperation, *s.* Cronachadh, trod, sglàmhradh, coire.

Vivacious, *a.* Maireann, buan, beò, sean, aosar, beothail, mear, suilmhear, sgairteil, smiorail.

Vivaciousness, *s.* Maireannachd, buanachd, beothalachd, mire, smioralas, suilmhearachd; aosmhoireachd; sgairteil-eachd.

Vivary, *s.* Seachlag, coinicear, broclach.

Vivacity, *s.* Beothalas, suilbhearachd, aosmhorachd, mair-eannachd.

Vive, *a.* Beo.

Vivid, *a.* Beò; boisgeanta; soilleir.

Vividly, *adv.* Gu beò; gu boisgeanta, gu soilleir.

Vividness, *s.* Boisge; smioralas.

Vivify, *v. a.* Thoir beò; beathaich, beothaich.

Vivific, *a.* Beothail, beathail.

Vivificate, *v. a.* Beothaich, dean beò, thoir chum beatha.

Viviparous, *a.* Beothachach; beo-bhreitheach.

Vixen, *s.* Sionnach boirionn; baobh, bidse.

Viz, *adv.* Is e sin ri radh, eadhon.

Vizard, *s.* Sgàil, cìdhis.

Vizard, *v. a.* Sgàilich, folaich, céil.

Vizier, *s.* Ard fhear-comhairle an Turcaich, Priomh-chomhairleach Turcach.

Vocabulary, *s.* Foclair; abardair.

Vocal, *a.* Guthach, foclach, fonnar, fonnmhor.

Vocality, *s.* Labhaireachd.

Vocally, *adv.* Ann am focaill; gu labhradh.

Vocation, *s.* Gairm, gairmeadh; (*trade*), ceaird; (*warning*), rabhadh.

Vocature, *s.* Gairm.

Vociferate, *s.* Glaodh, sgairt; beuc, ràn.

Vociferation, *s.* Glaodhaich, sgairt, beucail, sgairteachd; gàire, gàrthaich; comhaire.

Vociferous, *a.* Beucach, sgairteach; stairneach.

Vogue, *s.* Fasan, cleachd, nòs, àbhaist. When this was in fashion, *nur bha so san fhasan.*

Voice, *s.* Guth, glaodh; focal, fuaim, sgairt, èigh, eubh, radh, labhairt, cainnt. A voice *or* vote, *tagh-ghuth, guth;* a gentle voice, *guth caoin;* raise your voice, *tog do ghuth;* a loud voice, *guth ard, glaodh, sgairt.*

Voiced, *a.* Guthach.

Void, *a.* Falamh, folamh, fàs, faoin, neo-thabhachdach, neo-éifeachdach, diomhain. A void space, *fànas, failbhe.*

Void, *s.* Failbhe, fàsalachd, fànas.

Void, *v. a.* Tilg mach; falmhaich. By urine, *mùin;* by stool, *cac;* by spitting, *or* by vomiting, *sgeith;* make void, *neo-dhean, cur air chùl;* I will make void the law, *neo-ni mi an lath.*

Voidable, *a.* So chur air chùl.

Voidance, *s.* Falamhachadh.

Voider, *s.* Cliabhag.

Voidness, *a.* Falamhachd, folamhachd, fàsalalachd.

Volatile, *s.* Caochlaideach; mùiteach, muthteach, luaineach, luaimneach, itealach, leumnach, grad-shiubhlach; beò, beothail, spioradail, mear; grad-thioram.

Volatility, *s.* Grad-thioramachd; luaimneachd, caochlaideachd; itealachd; luaimnachd, beothalachd.

Volation, *s.* Leumadh, leumnachadh, itealachd.

Volcano, *s.* Monadh-loisgeach, monadh losgaidh, beinn teinntidh.

Vole, *s.* Buaidh-ghearradh.

Volery, *s.* Sgaoth.

Volitation, *s.* Itealachd.

Volition, *s.* Toil, rùn.

Volitive, *a.* Is urrainn roghainn (no) taghadh.

Volley, *v. a.* Tilg a mach.

Volley, *s.* Lòd; làmhach; tilgeadh, gunnaireachd, gàir, gaoir, gàrthaich.

Volleyed, *a.* Tilgte, leigte.

Volubility, *s.* Luaineachd, glagaireachd, mùghteachd, mùiteachd, caochlaideachd; luath-bheulachd; deas-labhairteachd, lonais.

Voluble, *a.* Luaimneach, luaineach, caochlaideach, luath-bheulach, deas-chainnteach; so-ròthladh; lùthar.

Volume, *s.* Ròl; mac-leabhar; leabhar.

Voluminous, *a.* Iomadach; ioma-ròlach.

Voluntarily, *adv.* A dheòin, gu toileach.

Voluntary, *a.* Saor, toileach, a dheoin.

Volunteer, *s.* Saighdear saor-thoil.

Volunteer, *v. a.* Gabh 's na saighdearan, tairg. He volunteered his services, *thairg e a sheirbheis.*

Voluptuary, *s.* Sòghair; drùisear.

Voluptuous, *a.* Mi-stuama; drùiseil, mi-gheimnidh, sòghmhor, soghail.

Voluptuousness, *s.* Mi-stuamachd, drùiseileachd, sogh, suaimhneas, seiseachd.

Volutation, *s.* Ròladh, aornagaich; luidreadh.

Vomica, *s.* Guirean sgamhain.

Vomit, *v. a.* Tilg, sgeith, diubhair.

Vomit, *s.* Tilgeadh, sgeitheamh; sgeith-leigheas; diùbhairt.

Vomition, *s.* Sgeitheamh, sgeithe, tilgeadh.

Vomitory, *a.* Tilgeadach, sgeitheach.

Voracious, *a.* Ciocrach, gionach; craosach, glamhaireach, glutach, lonach, amblach.

Voraciously, *adv.* Gu ciocrach, gu gionach, gu craosach, gu glutach, gu lonach.

Voraciousness, **Voracity**, *s.* Ciocras, gion, craosaireachd, glamhaireachd, gionaichead, lon, †ambladh.

Vortex, *s.* Cuairt-shlugan; faochag.

Vortical, *a.* Tuaicheallach, cuairteagach, faochagach.

Votaress, *s.* Ban-bhòidiche, ban-mhòidiche.

Votary, *s.* Bòidich; bòidear, mòidear.

Votary, *a.* Bòideil, mòideil.

Vote, *s.* Guth, tagh-ghuth.

Vote, *v. n.* Roghnaich, tagh.

Voter, *s.* Taghadair, roghnachair.

Votive, *a.* Bòideach, mòideach, mionnanach, bòide, mòide.

Vouch, *v.* Dearbh, deimhinnich; aidich, thoir fianuis.

Vouch, *s.* Fianuis; dearbhadh; teisteanas.

Voucher, *s.* Dearbhadair, teisteanas.

Vouchsafe, *v. a.* Aontaich, deònaich.

Vouchsafement, *s.* Aontachadh, deònachadh, buileachadh, tabhartas.

Vow, *s.* Bòid, mòid, mionn, mionnan; gealladh, geall, guidhe.

Vow, *v. a.* and *n.* Bòidich, mòidich, mionn, thoir mionnan. He vowed to be faithful, *mhionn e a bhith dìleas.*

Vowel, *s.* Foghair, guth.

Vow-fellow, *s.* Comh-mhionnaiche.

Voyage, *s.* Seòladh; triall, cuan-thuras, astar cuain; taisdeal.

Voyage, *v.* Seòl; triall.

Voyager, *s.* Maraiche, seòladair.

Vulgar, *a.* Cumanta, neo-luachmhor, coitchionn, graisgeil; suarach, iosal, suarrach; tuathail, balachail; neo-shuairc, mi-mhodhail.

Vulgar, *s.* Gràisg, prabar. The vulgar, *a ghràisg, am pràbar, a cheathearnu, an tuath.*

Vulgarism, *s.* Suarraichead, suarrachas; isleachd.

Vulgarity, *s.* Suarraichead; granndachd, irioslachd, uirioslachd, gràisgealachd.

Vulgarly, *adv.* Gu cumannta; gu suarrach, gu ceathearnach; gu neo-shuairc, gu mi-mhodhail.

Vulnerable, *a.* So-leònta; so-leòn, so-dhochannaichte, so-dhochann.

Vulnerate, *v.* Leòn; dochainn, dochannaich, ciùrr.

Vulpine, *a.* Sionnachail.

Vulture, *s.* Preachan; preachan criosach, preachan iongnach; sgreachan criosach, sgreachan iongnach; fang, seobhag, seabhag, confuadach, trodhain; lachar.

Vulturine, *a.* Preachanach.

W.

W. An treas litir fichead do 'n Aibideal.

Wabble, *v. n.* (*A low word*), imich san turamanaich (no) san seòganaich.

Wad, *s.* Trusag. A wad of hay, *cuidhleag.*

Wad, *v. a.* Tionail; cruinnich, cuidhil.

Wadd, *s.* Luaidh dhubh.

Wadding, *s.* (*As hay*), cuidhleadh; (*of a gun*), cuifean.

Waddle, *v. n.* Imich 's an turamanaich, imich gu tònagach.

Waddlingly, *adv.* Gu turamanach, gu tònagach.

Wade, *v. n.* Rach troimh uisge (no) amhainn.

WAFER, *s* Abhlan, dearnagan, breacag, gearragan

WAFER, *v. a.* Abhlanaich. Wafered, *abhlanaichte*

WAFT, *v. a.* Giùlain; iomchair ro 'n athar, snamh

WAFT, *s* Crathadh brataich ri gaoithe

WAFTAGE, *s.* Iomchar, caraiste

WAG, *v. a.* Crath, gluais

WAG, *s.* Cleasaiche, sgeigear, fear cuileagach

WAGE, *v a.* Feuch ri, thoir oidhirp Wage, or take to hire, *gabh*, wage war, *dean cogadh, feuch ri cogadh*

WAGER, *s* Geall I laid a wager, *chuir mi geall*

WAGER, *v a* Cuir geall, cuir an geall

WAGES, *s* Duais, tuarasdal, pàigh, luach-saoithreach; foicheall. One day's wages, *air pàigh latha*

WAGGERY, *s.* Cleasachd, sgeigearcachd, bearradaireachd

WAGGING, *s.* Crathadh, turamanaich.

WAGGISH, *a.* Cleasanta, cuileagach, sgeigeil, sgeigeach, bearradaireach, ain-cheartach

WAGGISHLY, *adv* Gu cleasanta, gu sgeigeil

WAGGLE, *v n.* Imich san seoganaich

WAGGON, *s* Feun, cairt-mhòr, †corb The beam of a waggon, *sglaigean.*

WAGGONER, *s* Feunair, cairtear

WAGTAIL, *s* Breachd an t-sìl

WAIF, *s* Faotail

WAIL, *s* Caoidh, bròn, tuireadh, caoirean, gul, gal, caoineadh

WAIL, *v* Caoidh, caoin, guil, dean tuireadh, dean bròn, gearain

WAILFUL, *a.* Tuirseach, brònach, muladach, dubhach, deurach

WAILING, *s* Tuireadh, bròn, caoine, caoidh, dul-chaoin, cumhadh, gul, gal, caoirean

WAIN, *s* Feun, cairt Charles's wain, †*an ceat-cam —Shaw*, the beam of a wain, *sglaigean*

WAIN-ROPE, *s* Cord cartach, taod cartach

WAINSCOT, *s* Linig; linidh; obair clàraich air taobh stigh ballaidh

WAINSCOT, *v a* Linig, linich

WAIST, *s.* Cneas, maothan, corp.

WAISTCOAT, *s.* Deacaid, peiteag.

WAIT, *v a* and *n* Fan, feith, fuirich, stad Wait for, *fan ri*, wait upon, *fritheil air*

WAIT, *s* Luidhe, plaid-luidh, luidheachan

WAITER, *s.* Gille-frithealaidh, fear-frithealaidh, gille-bùird

WAITING-MAID, WAITING-WOMAN, *s* Ban-fhrithealaiche, ban-òglach, bean-òglach, searbhanta, nighean

WAIVE, *v a* Cuir dhe, cuir gu taobh, trèig, fàg

WAKE, *v a.* and *n.* Dùisg, mosgail, fairich

WAKE, *s.* Feill coisrig eaglais, urnuigh oiche, féill bhliadhnail

WAKEFUL, *a* Furachair, faicilleach, aireachail, gun chodal, tha e 'na fhaireach, *masc.* na faireach, *fem*

WAKEFULNESS, *s* Furachaireachd, dìth codail

WAKEN, *v* Dùisg, mosgail, fairich. Waken him, *dùisg e.*

WAKENED, *part* Duisgte, mosgailte Is he wakened? *bheil e na fhaireach?*

WAKEROBIN, *s* Seorsa luibh

WALK, *s* Sràid; rod, rathad, imeachd, ceum sràid, coiseamachd, *i e* cois-imeachd I am going to take a walk, *tha mi dol a spaisdearachd, tha mi dol ghabhall sràid* (*no*) *ceum sraid*

WALK, *v. a.* and *n.* Coisich, imich, ceum, sraideasaich, sraid-imich, falbh, siubhail.

WALKER, *s.* Coisiche.

WALKING, *s* Imeachd, coiseachd, spaisdearachd, spaidsearachd, sraid-imeachd, ceumnaich Quick walking, *sgutach*

WALKING-STICK, *s.* Lorg, bat; cuaille.

WALK-MILL, *s* Muileann calcaidh, muileann luathaidh.

WALL, *v. a* Cuairtich le balladh; dion; druid, callaidich, iomadhruid

WALL, *s* Balladh; callaid, stuagh Mud wall, *balladh criadha*, stone wall, *balladh, cloich.*

WALLET, *s* Màileid, mailios, mal, balg; brù; bag, pasgan.

WALL-EYE, *s* Suil-leusach.

WALL-EYED, *a.* Leus-shuileach, leusach.

WALL-FLOWER, *s.* Lus-leth 'n t-samhraidh

WALLOP, *v. n.* Luinneanaich, goil

WALLOP, *s* Meall

WALL-LOUSE, *s* Corr-chòsach, corr-chosag

WALLOPPING, *s.* Luinneach, luidreadh.

WALLOW, *v n* Luidir, aornagaich, aornagain; aonairt, aoineagaich He wallows in money, *tha e thar a cheann an airgiod.*

WALNUT, *s* Geinm-chnò, craobh nan geinm chnò.

WALTRON, *s.* Each-uisge

WAMBLE, *v. n.* Goil, ruidhil, ruaimlich, fiuch

WAN, *a* Glas, glasdaidh; glas-neulach, bàn, odhar.

WAND, *s* Slat, slatag

WANDER, *v n* Seachranaich, iomrolaich, seabhaid, rach air seachran, rach air iomrol; rach am mearachd, rach air aimhreidh, rach air faontradh; (*from pasture*), rach air còlas

WANDERER, *s* Seachranaiche, iomrolaiche, fògaraiche; derò, deòraich, fear fògairt

WANDERING, *a* Seachranach, iomrolach, iomralach, fògarach, faontrach, air seachran, am mearrachd, siùbhlach, luaineach

WANDERING, *s* Seachran, iomroladh, iomrol, faontradh; seabhaid, allaban, cearachadh

WANE, *v n* Beagaich, lughdaich, searg, rach air ais, caith air falbh

WANE, (of the moon), *s* Earradhubh; lughdachadh. The church is on its wane, *tha 'n eaglais dol an lughaid.*

WANG, *s* Fiacall peircill, fiacall cuil

WANNED, *a* Bànaichte.

WANNESS, *s* Bàine, glasdaidheachd

WANT, *s* Uireasbhuidh, dìth, dì, gainne, bochduinn, easbhuidh, inneadh, intreabh, riachdanas, feum, cinnseach. There is no want of sense in him, *cha 'n 'eil aon dìth tuigse air*, want of provision, *gainne bidh, gortas*, in want, *an uireasbhuidh, an dì*

WANT, *v n* and *a* Bi am feum, bi an dì, bi an uireasbhuidh, bi dh' easbhuidh; (*seek*), sir, iarr, what do you want? *ciod tha thu a sireadh?* I want rest, *tha feum agam air fois*, he wants sense, *tha dìth toinisg air*, if you will not take it want it, *mar gabh thu e, bi as a dhìth.*

WANT, *s* Ùr-fhamh

WANTING, *a* A dh' easbhuidh, an dìth Wanting courage, *a dh' easbhuidh misnich*

WANTON, *s* Druisear, trusdar, siùrsach, strumpaid, striopach, meirdreach

WANTON, *a* Drùiseil, mi-gheimnidh, neo-bhanail, macnusach, mear, sògach; meamnach; ana-miannach, slatail, stoileanach, eutrom.

Wanton, *v. n.* Dean mire, bi ri mire; cluich ri.

Wantonness, *s.* Drùis, drùiseileachd, macnus; macnusachd, mi-gheimnidheachd, stoileanachd.

Want-wit, *s.* Amadan, baoghlan, baothair, òinnseach.

Wanty, *s.* Giort; tarrach, bronnach.

† **Waped**, *a.* Craidhte, tuirseach, dubhach.

Wapentake, *s.* Earainn (no) taobh dùcha.

War, *s.* Cogadh; còmas, comhbhuaireadh; cath; (*poetically*), feachd, armailt. A man-of-war, *luingeas chogaidh; gaisgeach.*

War, *v. n.* Cog; cathaich; dean cogadh.

Warble, *v.* Cantairich; céileirich; seinn.

Warbler, *s.* Céileiriche; òranaich, céileir.

Warbling, *s.* Càntaireachd, céileir, ceileireachd, bururus; guileag.

Ward, *s.* (*Watch*), faire; (*fort*), dion-ait, daingneach, gearrasdan, dùn; (*prison*), gainntir, priosun; (*pupil*), leanabh fo' thuitearachd, leanabh fo' oide; (*division*), earann, roinn.

Ward, *v. a.* and *n.* Dion; cum gearrd; cum air falbh.

Warden, *s.* Coimheadaiche, fear coimheid. Warden of the Cinque Ports, *coimheadaiche nan cuig càladh.*

Warder, *s.* Fear-faire; beachdair fear coimhid.

Wardmote, *s.* Roinn-mhòd.

Wardrobe, *s.* Seomar-aodaich.

Wardship, *s.* Tuitearachd.

Ware, *a.* Faiceallach; furachair.

Ware, *v. n.* Thoir an aire.

Ware, *s.* Bàthar, earradh; marsontachd.

Wareful, *a.* Sicir; furachair, faicilleach, faireachail.

Warehouse, *s.* Tigh-stòr, tigh-tasgaidh.

Warehouseman, *s.* Fear tigh stòir.

Wareless, *a.* Neo-smuainteachail, neo-chùramach.

Warfare, *s.* Cogadh, comhrag.

Warily, *adv.* Gu faiceallach, gu cùramach.

Wariness, *s.* Faiceallachd, curamachd.

Warlike, *a.* Gaisgeil, cùranta, treubhanta, treuthanta, cogach; comhragach; cathaiseach, naimhdeil.

Warlock, *s.* Druidh, draoidh; dubh-chleasaiche.

Warm, *a.* Blàth; teth; teinnteach; feargach; dian; teochridheach; caoimhneil. Lukewarm, *meadh-bhlàth;* warm and comfortable, *seasgair, clùmhor.*

Warm, *v.* Blàthaich, blàthtaich, teò, teothaich, dean blàth, teasaich.

Warmed, *a.* Blathaichte, teothaichte, blàth, teth.

Warming-pan, *s.* Aghann-theasachaidh.

Warmly, *adv.* Gu blàth, gu teth, gu dian.

Warmness, Warmth, *s.* Blàthas, blàs, teas, déine. Warmth of the sun, *blàs na gréine, grianachd.*

Warn, *v.* Thoir sànus, thoir rabhadh, thoir fur-fhogradh, thoir bardainn (no) bàirlinn.

Warning, *s.* Sànus, rabhadh, comhairle, fur-fhogradh, faireachadh, seamadh, bairlinn, bardainn, fios. A fortnight's warning, *fios cheithir lath deug;* take warning, *gabh sanus (no) comhairle.*

Warp, *v. a.* Tionndadh; rach gu taobh; crup; lùb; dlùth; trus.

Warp, *s.* Dlùth.

Warrant, *s.* Barrandas; urras, comas.

Warrant, *v. a.* Urrasaich, barrandaich, dean cinnteach, deimhinnich. I'll warrant you, *theid mise an urras ort;* I'll warrant (*in an ironical sense*), *theid mise an urras, bheir mise mo gheall.*

Warrantable, *a.* Barrandach; laghail; dligheach. Warrantably, *gu barrandach, gu laghail.*

Warranter, *s.* Urras.

Warranty, *s.* Urras, gealladh.

Warren, *s.* Broclach; seachlag, seachlan.

Warrior, *s.* Milidh, curaidh, gaisgeach, laoch; fear feachd; caimpear, fionn-laoch; † àrg, † luan, † galgadh.

Wart, *s.* Foinneamh.

Warty, *a.* Foinneamhach.

Wart-wort, *s.* Seorsa luibh, foinneamh-lus.

Wary, *a.* Faicilleach, faiceallach, fuirearach, furachair, curamach, crionna, sicir; grunndail.

Was, *v.* Bu, b', bha, bh'. He was a good man, *bha e na dheagh dhuine, bu mhath an duine e;* all that I had, *na h-uile ni bh' agam;* was he there? *an robh e an sin?* thou wast here, *bha thusa 'n so.*

Wash, *v.* Nigh, glan, ionnlaid, sgùr, sruthail, fliuch. What will not wash will not wring, *an nì nach gabh nigheadh, cha ghabh e fàsgadh.*

Wash, *s.* Bog, boglach, féith; uisge siabuinn; spùt; biadhmhuc; sluisrich, nigheachan.

Wash-ball, *s.* Ball-siapuinn.

Washed, *a.* Nighte, sruthailte, glan.

Washer, *s.* Nigheadair; sgùradair.

Washerwoman, *s.* Bean-nigheachain.

Wash-house, *s.* Tigh-nigheachain.

Washing, *s.* Nigheadh, nigheadaireachd, nigheachan, ionnlaid.

Wash-pot, *s.* Soitheach nigheachain, measair.

Washy, *a.* Fliuch, àitidh, uisgidh; bog, tais, lag, spùtach; sluisreach.

Wasp, *s.* Speach, connspeach.

Waspish, *a.* Speachanta; speacharra, catail; camnteach, crosd; nimheil; garg, aingidh, olc.

Wassail, *s.* Seorsa dibhe dh' ùbhlan, shiucar, agus lionn, luinneag; pòit, meisge.

Wassailer, *s.* Pòitear, meisgear.

Wast, *2d person* of was; which see.

Waste, *v. a.* and *n.* Caith, sgrios, struigh, mill; caith air falbh, lughdaich, rach an lughaid.

Waste, *a.* Fàs; sgriosta, uaigneach, dithreabhach; suarrach, gun stà.

Waste, *s.* Caitheamh, ana-caitheamh, struidh, strogh, diombuil; sgrios; lughdachadh, dithreabh. A waste place or common, *dithreabh.*

Wasteful, *a.* Caithteach; sgriosail; millteach; struigheil, struigheasach, stroghail; uaigneach, dithreabhach.

Wastefully, *adv.* Gu caithteach, gu sgriosail, gu struigheil, gu stroghail.

Wasteness, *s.* Di-threabhachd, uaignidheachd.

Waster, *s.* Struighear, stroghair; ana-caithiche, millear; sgriosadair.

Watch, *s.* Faire, faireachadh; (*sentinel*), fear-faire; freiceadan, faire; (*attention*), caithris; beachd, sùil; suidhe; (*timepiece*), uaireadair; tràthadair, àmadair. Keep watch over him, *cum faire air, cum sùil air;* shew me your watch, *feuch d' uaireadair;* watching all night, *suidhe ré na h-oidhche, ri faire ré na h-oidhche.*

Watch, *v.* Dean faire, cum faire; cum ad fhaireach; suidh, suidh n' airde; cum sùil, cum gearrd, dean freiceadan. Watch him, *cum sùil air, gabh beachd dheth;* watch, that you may not be robbed, but treat no man as a thief, *biodh earalas meirlich agad air gach neach, ach na dean meirleach do neach idir.*

Watcher, *s.* Beachdair; fear faire, fear faireachaidh.

Watchet, *a.* Gorm eutrom.

Watchful, *a.* Furachair, faicilleach, faireil, aireach; cùramach, aireachail, cairiseach.

Watchfully, *adv.* Gu furachair, gu faicilleach, gu faireil, gu cùramach, gu h-aireachail.

Watchfulness, *s.* Furachaireachd, faicilleachd, furachras, faicill, cairiseachd.

Watch-glass, *s.* Uaireadair gaineimh; gloine uaireadair.

Watch-house, *s.* Bothan-aire, bothan-airidh; tor faire; (*prison*), gainntir, toll-buth.

Watching, *s.* Faire; di-codail; faireachadh, caithris, furachras.

Watchmaker, *s.* Uaireadairiche.

Watchman, *s.* Fear-faire, fear freiceadain.

Watch-tower, *s.* Tor-faire.

Watchword, *s.* Ciall-chogar; diubhras an airm, focal an airm; sànas.

Water, *s.* Uisge; bùrn; †an, †dobhar, †ean, †lo, †bir. Waters, *uisgeachan.* A water, *amhainn, allt;* a little water or stream, *alltan;* a fall of water, *spùt, eas;* water, *or* urine, *mùn, fual, uisge;* make water, *dean do mhùn;* water is a waster, *tha fiacal aig an uisge;* medicinal waters, *bùrn leigheis;* rain water, *uisge;* running water, *fior uisge, amhainn;* salt water, *sàile;* spring water, *uisge fuarain;* a drink of water, *deoch bhùrn, deoch 'n bhùrn, deoch do 'n bhùrn;* snow water, *uisge an t-sneachdaidh;* standing water, *marbh-uisge;* high water, *làn-mara;* water-tight, *dionach;* holy water, *uisge coisrigte;* water thickened with oatmeal, *tiorman;* a place where water lodges in winter, *turloch.*

Water, *v. a.* Uisgich, fliuch, cuir fras, cuir deur. Water the shirts, *fliuch na léintean;* your eyes water, *tha do shuilean a cur nan deur* (*no*) *sileadh.*

Waterage, *s.* Airgiod (no) pàigh aisig.

Water-bank, *s.* Bruach; banc.

Water-bubble, *s.* Bolgan (no) balgan uisge.

Water-carriage, *s.* Giùlan air uisge.

Water-cresses, *s.* Biolair; dobhar-lus.

Water-dog, *s.* Cu uisge.

Watered, *a.* Uisgichte.

Waterfall, *s.* Spùt, eas, leum uisge, buinne-shruth.

Waterfowl, *s.* Eun-uisge.

Watergood, *s.* Ùraisg.

Watergruel, *s.* Plodag; deoch bhrochain, easach.

Waterhen, *s.* Cearc uisge.

Wateriness, *s.* Aitidheachd, uisgidheachd.

Waterish, *a.* Aitidh, fliuch; uisgidh.

Water-lily, *s.* Duilleag bhàite, bioras.

Waterman, *s.* Fear bàta, portair; fear-aiseig.

Watermark, *s.* Bràigh 'n làin, bràigh an dubh-chladaich; rodh.

Watermill, *s.* Muileann uisge.

Watermint, *s.* Mionnt uisge; mionnt fiadhaich.

Water-rat, *s.* Luchag uisge, radan uisge.

Water-snake, *s.* Nathair uisge; easg.

Water-spaniel, *s.* Cù uisge; *pl.* coin uisge.

Water-spider, *s.* Dannsair dubh 'n uisge.

Waterspout, *s.* Spùt; leum uisge; buinne-shruth.

Water-spring, *s.* Fuaran, tobar; *pl.* tobraichean.

Water-willow, *s.* Seileach uisge.

Waterwork, *s.* Obair uisge.

Watery, *a.* Fliuch, uisgidh, uisgeach, bog, àitidh.

Wattle, *s.* Cliath-shlat; (*of a cock*), cluigean; (*for thatch*), sgolb.

Wattle, *v. a.* Slat-fhigh; figh, dualaich, dual.

Wattled, *a.* Fighte.

Wave, *s.* Tonn, sumain, sumaid, stuadh, lunn. A great or raging wave, *fiadh-thonn, garbh-thonn.*

Wave, *v. a.* and *n.* Tonn; crath, luaisg; cuir dhe, fàg, treig, cuir gu taobh, seachainn. He waved his hat, *chrath e 'ada;* he waved the argument, *chuir e 'n argumaid gu taobh.*

Waved, *a.* Luaisgte; air chur gu taobh, seachainnte.

Waver, *v. n.* Bi san turamanaich, bi an ioma-chomhairle, bi air udal, bi eadar da chomhairle, bi ann an teagamh.

Waverer, *s.* Ioma-chomhairliche, fear luaineach, neo-shocrach.

Wavering, *a.* Ioma-cheisteach; neo-chinnteach; caochlaideach, mughteach; giosgach, san turamanaich. A wavering fellow, *giosgach, giosgair.*

Wavering, *s.* Critheadh, crathadh, caochladh.

Wavy, *a.* Tonnach, sumaideach, sumaineach, stuadhach, garbh, anfhadhach.

Wawl, *v.* Beuc, glaodh, roic, éigh, eubh, sgairt.

Wax, *s.* Céir. Bee's-wax, *céir sheillean;* letter-wax, *céir litreach;* ear-wax, *céir cluaise.*

Wax, *v. a.* Céirich; céir, dùin le céir, *mar litir*, seul, comharaich.

Wax, *v. n.* Fas, cinn. He waxes old, *tha e fàs sean.*

Waxed, *a.* Ceirte, ceirichte.

Waxed, *a.* Air fàs, air cinn, air cinntinn. He is waxed fat, *tha e air fàs reamhar;* he is waxed tall, *tha e air fàs ard, tha e air cinn* (*no*) *air cinntinn, ard.*

Waxen, *a.* Ceireach.

Waxing, *a.* A fàs, a cinntinn.

Way, *s.* Rod, rad, rathad, slighe; car, bealach; aisridh; (*method*), modh, seòl, lathailt, doigh; meadhon. This way, *an rathad so;* come this way, *thig an car so;* go your way, *gabh do rathad;* by the way, *air an rathad;* by the way, or by the by, *le so;* in the way, *anns an rathad;* a beaten way, *aisridh chas;* a by-way, *frith-rathad;* you have not the way of it, *cha 'n 'eil an seòl agad air; cha 'n 'eil an lathailt agad air;* a highway, *rathad mor;* the king's highway, *rathad mòr an righ;* a cart-way, *rathad cartach;* it is but a short way off, *cha 'n 'eil e ach goirrid air astar;* a great way, *fad, am fad;* a great way off, *fad air astar, fad air falbh;* a direct way, *rathad direach;* a deep way, *rathad salach;* by way of sport, *thaobh spuirt;* both ways, *gach rathad; gach doigh;* which way shall I go? *ciod an car théid mi? ciod an rathad théid mi? ciod an taobh théid mi?* this is by a deal the nearest way, *is e so an rod mar mhoran is fhaigse;* every way, *h-uile rathad, h-uile seòl, h-uile doigh;* I tried every way, *dh' fheuch mi ri h-uile seòl;* which way soever, *ciod air bith an rathad;* a long way about, *fad mu 'n cuairt;* out of the way, *as an rathad;* out of the way, [wrong] *air dhochair;* he is on his way home, *tha e air an rathad dhachaidh, tha e air a thùrus dhachaidh;* he went off the way, *chaidh e bhàrr an rathaid;* I lost my way, *chaidh mi air seachran;* go your way, *bi falbh, bi trialladh;* give way, *as an rathad, rach gu taobh, géill;* give way to the times, *geill do na h-amanna;* make way for me, *dean rathad dhomh;* shew the way, *feuch an rod;* set in the way, *cuir san rathad;* set on the way, *cuir air an rod;* he comes straightway, *tha e tighinn caol direach;* lead the way, *feuch an rathad, treoruich.*

Wayfarer, *s.* Fear-tùruis, fear siubhail, taisdealaich, fear astair, coisiche, fear gabhail an rathaid.

Wayfaring, *a.* Tùrusach, triallach, siubhlach.

Wayfaring-tree, *s.* Craobh-fiadhain.

Waylay, *v.* Dean plaid-luidhe, dean feall-fholach, dean fàth-fheitheamh.

Waylayer, *s.* Fear fàth-fheitheamh, fath-fheitheamhaiche; fear plaid-luidhe.

Wayless, *a.* Gun slighe, gun rod; neo-choisichte.

Waymark, *s.* Post roid.

Wayward, *a.* Brais, cabhagach, frithearach, dian, obann, reasgach.

Waywardness, *s.* Braisead, frithearachd, dianad, obainne.

We, *pron.* Sinn, sinne. We ourselves, *sinn-fèin.*

Weak, *a.* Anfhann; anmhunn, lag, fann; aimhneartmhor; eiglidh, meuranda, breoite; mall, tinn, truagh; brisg; trom, tuirseach; gun chlith.

Weaken, *v.* Lagaich, anfhannaich; fannaich; dean lag, dean anfhann, dean fann. Weakened, *anfhannaichte.*

Weakliness, *s.* Anfhannachd, anmhuinneachd, eu-slainnte.

Weakling, *s.* Spreòchan.

Weakly, *adv.* Gu h-anfhann, gu fann; gu lag, gu breoite.

Weakness, *s.* Anfhannachd, laigse, laigsinn, fàilneachadh.

Weak side, *s.* Fàilinn; taobh cheart. Get the weak side of him, *faigh an taobh cheart dhe.*

Weal, *s.* Maith; sonas, soirbheas. Commonweal, *comh-fhlaitheachd.*

† **Weald**, *s.* Doire, coille.

Wealth, *s.* Beartas, beairteas, saibhreas, maoin, ionmhas, earras, pailteas; airgiod; stòr, stòras; airneis; toic, cuid. Boast not of another man's wealth, *na dean uaille a cuid duine eile.*

Wealthy, *a.* Beairteach, saibhir; pailt.

Wean, *v. a.* Cuir air dioghladh [*i. e.* di-dheoghal] cuir bhàrr na ciche, caisg; mi-chleachd.

Weaned, *a.* Bharr na ciche air dioghladh.

Weanel, *s.* Leanabh bharr na ciche (no) air dioghladh.

Weanel, *s.* Dioghlagan; urr air chur bharr na ciche.

Weapon, *s.* Ball airm.

Weaponed, *a.* Armaichte, armte.

Weaponless, *a.* Gun arm, gun bhall airm, neo-armaichte.

Wear, *s.* Tuil-dhorus.

Wear, *v. a.* and *n.* Caith; lughadaich, cuir an lùghaid; saruich; cosd. May you wear your clothes and enjoy them, *gun meal 's gun caith thu d' aodach;* wear out, *thoir thairis, fannaich.*

Wear, *s.* Caitheamh.

Wearer, *s.* Caithtiche, fear caitheamh.

Wearied, *a.* Sgìth; air fannachadh, air toirt thairis.

Weariness, *s.* Sgìtheas, sgìos, fannachadh; fadal; curachd, tuirse.

Wearing, *s.* Caitheamh, cosd.

Wearing, *part.* A caitheamh, a cosd.

Wearish, *a.* Bog; fliuch, fèithear; tana, spùtanta, anfhann, domblasda; doirbh.

Wearisome, *a.* Sgìth; fadalach; seabhasach, draghail; farranach, tuirseach.

Wearisomeness, *s.* Sgìtheas; fadal; seabhas; draghalachd, farranachd.

Weary, *a.* Sgìth; curach; leadairte. I am tired of him or it, *tha mi sgìth dheth;* grow weary, *cinn sgìth, fàs sgìth;* somewhat weary, *leth-char sgìth;* quite weary, *seachd sgìth.*

Weary, *v.* Sgìthich; fannaich; thoir thairis; saruich; oibrich; caith, cuir dragh air.

Wearying, *s.* Sgìtheachadh.

Weasand, *s.* Detlach, steic-bhràgad, sgornan, sgornach, làngan bràghad.

Weasel, *s.* Neas, nios; nas, easag.

Weather, *s.* Aimsir, àm, uair; sìon. Fine weather, *aimsir ghrinn;* bad weather, *aimsir olc;* rainy weather, *aimsir fhliuch.*

Weather, *v.* Seas ri; rach air fuaradh; cuir fodha; cuir ri gaoth. Weather a storm, *seas ri anradh;* I weathered the headland, *chuir mi fodham an rughadh.*

Weatherbeaten, *a.* Sàruichte; breoite; cruadhaichte, cleachdte.

Weatherboard, *s.* Bord-uisge.

Weathercock, *s.* Coileach gaoithe.

Weathergage, *s.* Aile-mheidh.

Weathergaw, *s.* Sionnachla.

Weatherglass, *s.* Athar-mheidh, àile-mheidh.

Weather-wise, *a.* Sgileil mu 'n aimsir.

Weave, *v. a.* Figh, dual, dlùthaich, pleat, cas.

Weaved, *part.* Fighte; dlùthaichte.

Weaver, *s.* Figheadair; breabadair. A silk-weaver, *figheadair sìde;* a weaver's trade, *figheadaireachd;* a weaver's shop, *bùth figheadair;* a weaver's beam, *gairmain;* a weaver's shuttle, *spàl;* a female weaver, *ban-fhigheach, ban-fhigheadair.*

Weaving, *s.* Figheadh; figheadaireachd.

Weaving-loom, *s.* Beairt-figheadair, beairt.

Web, *s.* Eige; eididh. A linen web, *eididh anairt;* a cobweb, *eididh (no) lion an damhain-alluidh;* plaids of the same web, *is ann do 'n aon chlò an cadath.*

Webfooted, *a.* Clàr-chosach.

Webster, *s.* Figheadair, breabadair.

Wed, *v. a.* and *n.* Pòs.

Wedded, *a.* Pòsta, pòsda. Newly wedded, *nuadh-phòsda;* wedded to one's will, *rag, ceann-laidir, dòchasach.*

Wedding, *s.* Pòsadh; banais; † nuadhar. Wedding suit, *cùl bainnse, culaidh bainnse;* a wedding day, *là bainnse.*

Wedge, *s.* Geinn; spile; spalla.

Wedge, *v. a.* Geinn, geinnich.

Wedlock, *s.* Pòsadh, maraiste.

Wednesday, *s.* De-ciadain, Di-ceadain. Next Wednesday, *De-ciadain so 'tighinn;* when Hallow-day comes on Wednesday, *nur is Ciadnaich an t-Samhuinn.*

† **Wee**, *a.* Beag, crion; cutach.

Weed, *s.* Luibh, lus, luibhneach, salachar. Sea-weed, *rod, feamain;* (*dress*), aodach bròin; cul adhlaic. Weeds on the surface of water, *barrag.*

Weed, *v.* Glan, gart-ghlan.

Weeded, *a.* Gart-ghlante.

Weeder, *s.* Gart-ghlanaiche, glanadair.

Weed-hook, *s.* Corran gart-ghlan; clobh-arbhair.

Weedless, *a.* Gun luibh, gun lus.

Weedy, *a.* Lusach, lusanach, salach; luibheanach; fiadhain.

Week, *s.* Seachduin. This day week, *seachduin o 'n diugh;* a week-day, *lath seachduin;* against next week, *air cheann (no) thun na h-ath-sheachduin;* Whitsun-week, *treanadh;* Friday is contrary, be the week foul or fair, *bithidh de h-aoin an aghaidh na seachduin.*

Weekly, *a.* Gach seachduin, seachduineach.

† **Weel**, *s.* Faochag, cuairt-shlugan, coire tuaicheall.

† **Ween**, *v.* Saoil, smuainich.

Weep, *v.* Dean gul, dean caoidh, guil, caoin, dean gal, sil. You made me weep, *thug thu orm gul;* the amber weeps, *silidh an t-omar.*

Weeper, *s.* Caointiche; fear-bròin, fear-guil; riobag muinichill.

Weeping, *s.* Caoidh, gul, caoineadh, càntal.

WEEPING, *a.* Deurach, fliuch; snitheach; sil dheur. He is weeping, *tha e 'sil dheur;* weeping amber, *omar snitheach.*

WEERISH, *a.* See WEARISH.

WEEVIL, *s.* Fionnag; leoman, reudan.

WEFT, *s.* Inneach.

WEFTAGE, *s.* Figheadh, pleatadh.

WEIGH, *v. a.* Cothromaich, tomhais, cudthromaich, meidhich, tog; beachd-smuaintich, smuaintich. Weigh this burden, *tomhais an eallach so;* weigh the matter, *smuaintich air a chùis;* how many stones do you weigh without your clothes? *cia meud clach a chothromaicheas tu gun t' aodach?* weigh down, *cothromaich, thoir an cothrom a.*

WEIGHED, *a.* Tomhaiste, cothromaichte; cleachda, sgileil.

WEIGHER, *s.* Fear-tomhais, tomhasair.

WEIGHING, *s.* Tomhasadh; cothromachadh, beachdachadh, smuainteachadh.

WEIGHT, *s.* Cothrom; tombas, cudthrom; uallach, eallach. A matter of weight, *gnothuch cudthromach.*

WEIGHTILY, *adv.* Gu trom; gu cudthromach.

WEIGHTINESS, *s.* Truime, truimead, cudthromachd.

WEIGHTLESS, *a.* Eutrom; faoin, gun chothrom.

WEIGHTY, *a.* Trom, cothromach, cudthromach.

WELCHMAN, *s.* Caimbreach; Gallach.

WELCOME, *a.* Taitneach; failteach. Welcome news, *nuaidheachd taitneach;* you are welcome, *is e do bheath;* you are welcome home, *is e do bheath dhachaidh;* I was made very welcome, *b' e mo ro bheath.*

WELCOME, *interj.* Fàilte; is e do bheath; is e bhur beath; do bheath, bhur beath.

WELCOME, *v. a.* Fàiltich; altaich beatha, cuir fàilte, furain.

WELCOMER, *s.* Fear fàillte.

WELCOMING, *s.* Fàilteachadh, altachadh.

WELCOME-TO-OUR-HOUSE, *s.* Lus a chomain.

WELD, *v. a.* Tàth.

WELDING, *s.* Tàth, tàthadh.

WELFARE, *s.* Sonas, maith; slainnte; soirbheas.

WELK, *v. n.* Dorchaich, doilleirich.

† WELKIN, *s.* Speuran; gorm.

WELL, *s.* Tobar, fuaran, tiobairt, † sopar, † bior, † curr. Wells, *tobraichean.* Let the wettest go to the well, *am fear is fliuiche rachadh e do'n alld.*

WELL, *a.* Math, maith; ceart, slàn, fallain. He is quite well, *tha e slàn fallain.*

WELL, *adv.* Gu math, gu ceart; gu slàn, gu fallain. It will go well with me, *éiridh gu maith dhomh;* you said well, *is maith thubhairt thu, is ceart thubhairt thu;* you may well wonder, *is maith dh' fhaodas tu iongantas ghabhail;* the business goes on well, *tha 'n gnothuch a soirbheachadh;* all is well that ends well, *is math an ni do 'n éirich gu math;* very well, *ro mhath;* well then, *seadh mata;* well well, *seadh seadh;* well well then, *seadh seadh mata;* you very well know, *is maith is aithne dhuit;* as well as you, *cho mhath riutsa;* as well as I can, *cho mhath 's a dh' fhaotas mi; mar is fhearr as urrainn mi;* you do well, *is math gheibhear thu;* whether you take it well or ill, *olc air mhath leat e.*

WELLADAY, *interj.* Mo chreach! mo thruaigh! mo sgar!

WELL-AIMED, *a.* Air dheagh-chuimeiseachadh.

WELLBEING, *s.* Soirbheas; sonas, slainnte, maith.

WELL-BORN, *a.* Uasal, inbheach, ard.

WELL-BRED, *a.* Modhail; beusach, deagh-bheusach.

WELL-FAVOURED, *a.* Sgiamhach, ciatach, maiseach, eireachdail, buaidheach, bòidheach.

WELL-NATURED, *a.* Math-nadurrach, soimeach, soitheamh, deagh-ghnétheach, ciùin.

WELL-NIGH, *adv.* Am fogus; ach beag, air bheag.

WELL-SPRING, *s.* Tobar, fuaran, tiobairt.

WELL-WISH, *s.* Deagh-rùn, gean maith, deagh thogar.

WELL-WISHER, *s.* Deagh-rùnair, deagh-thogarair.

WELT, *s.* Faim, foir, oir, iomall.

WELT, *v. a.* Faim. He welted, *dh' fhaim e.*

WELTED, *a.* Faimte.

WELTER, *v. n.* Aornagaich; aonagraich, luidir, aornagain, faragair.

WELTERING, *s.* Aornagan, aonragaich, luidreadh, faragradh.

WEM, *s.* Sal, spot; cream; brù, maodal.

WEN, *s.* Foinneamh, flioghan.

WENCH, *s.* Siùrsach, striopach; caile, dubh-chaile.

WENCH, *v. n.* Rach air shiùrsachd, siùrsaich.

WENCHER, *s.* Druisdear, drusdar.

WEND, *v. n.* Rach, imich, siubhail, coisich.

WENNY, *a.* Foinneamhach, flioghanach.

WENT, *pret.* of go. Chaidh, dh' imich. He went away, *dh' fhalbh e;* he went on his way, *dh' imich e air a thùrus.* See GO.

WEPT, *pret.* and *p. part.* of weep. Ghuil, chaoin; caointe. He wept bitterly, *ghuil e gu goirt.*

WERE, *v.* Bha, bu, b'. Who were those people? *co b' iad an sluagh ud?* you were there, *bha thusa an sin;* as it were, *mar gum biodh;* were it not, *mar bhiodh;* were it not for me, *mar bhiodh mise.*

WEST, *s.* An iar, an airde 'n iar, niar, luidhe na greine, an taobh siar. From the west, *o 'n iar, as an taobh shuas.*

WEST, *a.* Suas, shuas, siar. I am going west, *tha mi dol suas;* he is west, *tha e shuas.*

WEST, *adv.* Air an taobh shuas. West of me, *air an taobh shuas dhiom.*

WESTERING, *a.* Siar; gus an airde an iar.

WESTERLY, WESTERN, *a.* As an airde 'n iar, o 'n iar; chum na h-airde an iar; shuas. The westerly wind, *a ghaoth shuas.*

WESTWARD, *a.* Gu 's an airde 'n iar, gu siar; suas.

WET, *s.* Uisge, àitidheachd, fliuiche.

WET, *a.* Fliuch, àitidh; bog, tais. A wet day, *lath fliuch;* wet weather, *aimsir fhliuch;* let the wettest go to the well, *rachadh am fear is fliuiche do 'n ald.*

WET, *v.* Fliuch, uisgich; bogaich.

WETHER, *s.* Mult, mult-reith.

WETNESS, *s.* Fliuichead, àitidheachd.

WETTED, *a.* Uisgichte, fliuch.

WETTISH, *a.* Leth-char fliuch, àitidh.

WHALE, *s.* Muc-mhar; miol-mhòr, † parn.

WHARF, *s.* Céithe.

WHARFAGE, *s.* Céith-chis.

WHARFINGER, *s.* Céithear.

WHAT, *pro.* Ciod; creud. What say you? *ciod tha thu ag radh?* what a great man he is! *nach mòr an duine e!* that [that which], *na;* do what you can, *dean na dh' fhaotas tu;* mind what you are about, *cuimhnich ciod mu bheil thu;* what is that? *ciod sin?* what with one thing, and what with another, *le h-aon rud, 's le rud eile;* what kind? *ciod an seorsa? ciod a ghne?* what countryman is he? *ciod an duthaich da 'm buin e?* to what place? *c'aite?* i. e. *cia aite?* from what place? *co as?* from what place do you come? *co as a thainig thu?* in what place? *c'àite? ciod an t-àite?* in what place soever, *ciod air bith an t-àite;* at what time? *c'uine?* i. e. *cia uine? ciod an t-am air?* at what time did he die? *c'uine fhuair e bàs? ciod an t-am airan d' fhuair e bàs?* for what cause? *c'arson?* i. e. co *airson?* what though, *ciod ged;* what although? *ciod uime? ciod mu dheimhinn?* *Ciod e* is often pronounced as if it were *gu dé.*

Whatever, Whatsoever, *pron.* Ciod air bith, ciod sam bith, ge b'è air bith. Whatever thing you do, *ge b'e air bith ni a ni sibh.*

Wheal, *s.* Guirein, bucaid.

Wheat, *s.* Cruithneachd, cruineachd. Indian wheat, *cruithneachd Innseanach;* wheat flower, *min phlùr.*

Wheaten, *a.* Cruineachda, cruithneachda, cruineachdach. Wheaten bread, *aran cruineachd.*

Wheedle, *a.* Meall; meal le briodal, dean blandar; taladh, taiteadh.

Wheedler, *s.* Blandaraiche; briodalair.

Wheedling, *s.* Blandar, briodal, goileam, bleid.

Wheedling, *a.* Blandach, beulchar, briodalach, goileamach, bleideil.

Wheel, *s.* Cuidhil, cuidheal, roithlean, roth, ruidhlean. A cart-wheel, *cuidhil cartach;* a spinning-wheel, *cuidhil;* a winding-wheel, *cuidhil thachrais;* a fishing-wheel, *cuidhil iasgaich;* a turning-wheel, *beairt thuairneir;* a little wheel, *roithlean, ruidhlean;* wheels, *cuidhleachan.*

Wheel, *v.* Cuidhil, ruidhil, ròil. Wheel about, *cuir cuidhil dhiot, cuir car dhiot.*

Wheelbarrow, *s.* Cuidhil-bharr, cuidhil-bàrr, barr-rotha.

Wheelwright, *s.* Saor-chuidhleachan. The wheelwright, *saor nan cuidhleachan.*

Wheeling, *s.* Cuidhleadh, ruidhleadh.

Wheely, *a.* Cruinn; ròithleach; ruidhleanach, cearclach, cuairteanach.

Wheeze, *s.* Rùcanaich, carrasanaich, piochanaich.

Wheezing, *a.* Rùcanach, carrasanach, piochanach.

Wheezing, *s.* Carrasan, rūcan, piochanaich.

Whelk, *s.* Guirean, pucaid, bucaid, bocaid; *perhaps* bocaite, *a swelled part.*

Whelm, *v.* Comhdaich, cuibhrig, mùch, folaich; adhlaic.

Whelp, *s.* Cuilean, measan.

When, *adv.* Cuin, c'uine, (*i. e.*) cia uine; cia 'n uair, ciod an t-àm. When will that be? *cuin bhitheas sin?*

When, [*at the time when.*] Nur, 'n uair. When they heard that, *nur chual iad sin;* just when you came, *direach nur thàinig thu.*

Whence, *adv.* Cia as, co as, ciod as. Whence came you? *co as a thainig thu?*

Whencesoever, *adv.* Ciod air bith an t-aite as, cia as sam bith, cia as air bith. Whencesoever he comes, *ciod air bith an t-aite as an d' thig e; cia as air bith thig e.*

Whenever, Whensoever, *adv.* Nur, nuair, co luath agus, co luath 's, ceart cho luath 's, ge b' e uair. As soon as he comes, *co luath 's a thig e;* as soon as ever he came, *ceart cho luath 's a thainig e.*

Where, *adv.* C'aite? ciod an t-aite? Where in the world is he? *c'aite air an t-saoghal bheil e?*

Where, [*the place in which*], *adv.* Far. Put it where I can find it, *cuir far am faigh mi e;* any where, *ann aite sam bith.*

Whereabout, *adv.* C' àite, c'aite mu. Whereabout is it? *c'aite mu bheil e?*

Whereas, *adv.* A chionn gu, air a mheud 's gu, air a mheud 's gum, a chionn gum, a chionn gu, on tharladh, do bhrìgh gun, do bhrìgh gum, do bhrìgh gur; a chionn, a chionn gur; ach.

Whereat, *adv.* Far; c' àite.

Whereby, *adv.* Leis; co leis. The knife whereby he cut me, *an sgian leis an do ghearr e mi;* whereby did he do it? *co leis rinn se e?*

Wherever, *adv.* Cia b' e air bith àite, c'aite air bith, c'aite sam bith. Wherever I go, *c' àite air bith an d' thèid mi, c'aite air bith theid mi.*

Wherefore, *adv.* C'arson? ciod arson? air an aobhar sin, uime sin.

Wherein, *adv.* Far, anns an; c'aite? ciod an t-àite anns? Wherein did he put it? *ciod an t-àite anns an do chuir se e?* the place wherein I put it, *an t-àite far an do chuir mi e.*

Whereof, *adv.* Co dheth, co leis. Whereof is the house built? *co dheth thogadh an tigh? co dheth tha an tigh air a thogail?*

Whereof, *adv.* Do; leis, as. The water whereof I drank, *an t-uisge do 'n d' òl mi.*

Whereon, *adv.* Ciod air.

Wheresoever, *adv.* C' àite air bith.

Whereto, *adv.* Ciod fath; ciod do? ciod chrìche do? ciod is crioch do? Whereto serves mercy? *ciod is crioch do throcair?*

Whereupon, *adv.* Ciod air.

Wherewith, *adv.* Co leis, ciod leis.

Wherret, *v. a.* Cuir dragh, farranaich, thoir gleog.

Wherret, *s.* Peileid; sgailleag, gleog, gleadhar, sgleafart.

Wherry, *s.* Atrach, arthrach, bàd da chrainn.

Whet, *v.* Geuraich; faobhraich; feargaich. Whetted, *geuraichte, faobhraichte.*

Whet, *s.* Geurachadh; faobhrachadh; feargachadh.

Whether, *pron.* Co aca? co dhiubh? Whether is that your fault or mine? *co aca is tusa na mise is coireach?*

Whetstone, *s.* Clach-fhaobhair, clach-gheurachaidh; clach niaraidh.

Whetter, *s.* Geuradair.

Whetting, *s.* Geurachadh; creanadas; creanas; sneagaireachd.

Whey, *s.* Meug, meog.

Wheyey, Wheyish, *a.* Meugach, meugar, meugaidh.

Which, *pron. inter.* Co, cia, ciod. Which of these would you have? *co dhiubh sin a b' aille leat?* which way? *ciod an rathad?*

Which, *rel. pron.* A; nach. The house which I bought, *an tigh a cheannaich mi;* the horse which I did not buy, *an t-each nach do cheannaich mi.*

Whichsoever, *pron.* Co air bith, ciod air bith. Which way soever, *ciod air bith an rod, cia b' e air bith an rod, cia b' e air bith rod.*

Whiff, *s.* Tŏth; oiteag, séideag, siobag.

Whiffle, *v. n.* Bi ann iomchomhairle; crath.

Whiffler, *s.* Piobair airm; fear truimp.

Whiffling, *a.* Mùghteach; oiteagach.

Whig, *s.* Meog; blathach; sgathach, cuigse.

Whiggish, *a.* Cuigseach.

Whiggism, *s.* Cuigseachd.

While, *v. a.* Cuir dheth aimsir.

While, *s.* Grathuinn, tachdan; greis; seal; treis, sealan; uine. A while ago, *o cheann ghrathuinn, o cheann tamuil;* a little while ago, *a chianamh;* for a while, *car grathuinn;* it is not worth while, *cha 'n fhiach an gnothuch an dragh;* a long while ago, *o cheann fada.*

While, Whilst, *adv.* Nuair, nur, am feadh, 'n am, fhad 's, am fad 's. While there is life there is hope, *am fad 's a tha beath tha dòchas;* while he thought on the vision, *am feadh a bha e smuaineachadh air an t-sealladh;* while I am doing this, *'n am dhomh bhith deanamh so.*

Whim, *s.* Faoineachd; amaid; faoin-dhòchas, gì, dòchas, amaideachd; neònachas, faoineas, airleag.

Whimper, *v. n.* Sgiuganaich.

Whimpering, *s* Sgiuganaich.

Whimsey, *s* Amaid, faoin-dhochas, neònachas.

Whimsical, *a.* Faoin, neònach, iongantach, amaideach, airleagach, iusanach

Whin, *s.* Conasg

Whine, *v. n* Caoin, gearain, duarmanaich, gul, gal

Whine, *s* Gearain, caoin, duarmanachd, gul, gal.

Whining, *a* Gearanach, caointeach, deurach

Whinny, *v. n* Sitrich

Whip, *s* Sgiùrsadh, cuip, slat

Whip, *v. a* Sgiùrs, cuipinn Whipped, *sgiùrsta, cuipinnte.*

Whip, *v* (*move quickly*) Sguab She whipped past me, *sguab i seachad orm.*

Whip-cord, *s* Cord cuip, cord sgiùrsaidh.

Whip-hand, *s.* Ceannas; lamh 'n uachdar

Whipper, *s* Sgiursair.

Whipping-post, *s.* Carradh-sgiùrsaidh, ceap-sgiùrsaidh.

Whip-saw, *s* Sabhadh-dùirn.

Whirl, *v a* and *n* Cuairtich, cuibhlich, ruidhil

Whirl, *s* Cuairt, cuibhle, ruidhil; rothladh.

Whirlbone (of the knee), *s* Failcean a ghlùin, falaman a ghlùin

Whirligig, *s* Gillemirean, pinidh, dòtaman

Whirlpool, *s* Cuairt-shlugan, faochan, faochag, cuairt-shruth; coire-tuaicheall

Whirlwind, *s.* Ioma-ghaoth, cuairt-ghaoth

Whirring, *s* Srann

Whisk, *s* Sguab, sguabag, sguab aodaich

Whisk, *v* Sguab She whisked past me, *sguab i seachad orm.*

Whisker, *s* Ciabhag, roibean

Whisky, *s* Uisge-beatha, uisge na beath.

Whisper, *v. a* and *n* Cogair, cagair; dean cogar

Whisper, *s* Cogar, cagar, cogarsaich, cagarsaich

Whisperer, *s* Fear-cogarsaich.

Whist! *interj* Caisd! bi 'd thosd! eisd! bi sàmhach, st!

Whist, *s* Seorsa cluiche air chairtean

Whistle, *v* Fead, dean fead, dean fendailich, dean feadaireachd

Whistle, *s* Feadag; feadan

Whistling, *s* Feadailich, feadaireachd

Whistler, *s m.* Fear feadaireachd

Whit, *s.* Mir, dad; tiot, iota, smad He is every whit as bad as I am, *tha e na h-uile mir cho olc riumsa*, it did not trouble me a whit, *cha do chuir e smad orm*, I will not wait a whit, *cha n' fhuirich mi tiot*

White, *a* Geal, bàn, fionn; liath, glan, fior-ghlan, † alain. As white as snow, *cho geal ris an t-sneachd*, pure as unsunned snow, *glan mar shneachd nan còs*, somewhat white, *leth-char geal.*

White, *s.* Gile, geal White of an egg, *gealagan*, white of an eye, *gealan* or *gealagan*, white is not the most lovely, nor yellow the most victorious, *cha ghile a ghradhaichcas, is cha bhuidhe 'bhuadhichcas*

White-lead, *s* Luaidhe gheal.

White-livered, *a.* Gealtach; mi-runach

Whiten, *v a* and *n.* Gealaich, bànaich, fàs geal, fàs bàn Whiten the linen, *gealaich an t-anart*, he whitened when he heard it, *bhànaich e nur chual se e*

Whitener, *s.* Gealachair; fear gealachaidh.

Whiteness, *s* Gile, bàinead, bàine, glaine, glainead.

Whitening, *s.* Gealachan, gealadan; gealachadh.

White-wash, *s* Plàsd-aoil, ionnlaid.

Whitewashed, *a* Fionn aolta

White-wine, *s.* Fion-geal

Whither, *adv* C'aite? c'ionadh, cia 'n taobh, ciod au car, ciod an rathad; far. Whither did he go? *c'ionadh chaidh e? c'aite an deach e?* any whither, *dh' aite 'gin, dh' aite eigin.*

Whithersoever, *adv.* C'aite air bith.

Whiting, *s* (*In ichthyology*), gealag

Whiting, *s.* (*White*), cailc bhog

Whitish, *a* Leth-char geal; leth-char bàn, liath.

White-leather, *s* Leathar falmta.

Whitlow, *s* Gath-tearra.

Whitster, *s.* Fear gealachaidh.

Whitsuntide, *s* Cuingis, Bealtuin. Whitsun-week, *Treanadh*, forever is longer than Whitsuntide, *is fhaide gu bràth no Bealtuin*

Whittle, *s* Sgian, corc; golaidh, sgian-dubh.

Whiz, *v n* Srann He whizzed past me, *shrann e seachad orm*

Whizzing, *s.* Srann, srannail, (*in the throat*), spiochan.

Who, *pron. interrog* Co. Who is this? *co so?* who is he? *co e?*

Who, *rel pron.* A; nach The man who struck him, *an duine a bhuail e*, the man who did not strike him, *an duine nach do bhuail e.*

Whoever, *a.* Co air bith, co sam bith.

Whole, *a* Slàn, fallain; iomlan; uile, gu leir, uile gu léir He swallowed it whole, *shluig e slàn e*, a whole day, *lath iomlan*, as whole as a trout, *cho fallain ri breachd;* made whole, *slànaichte*, make whole, *slànuich*, he is whole and well, *tha e gu beò slàn*, the whole, *an t-iomlan*, the half yesterday would have been better than the whole to-day, *b' fhearr a leth 'n dé na gu leir an diugh.*

Wholeness, *s* Iomlanachd, slànachd.

Wholesale, *s* Mòr-earann, an t-iomlan.

Wholesome, *a.* Slàn, fallain, slainnteil; gun choir, gun ghaoid

Wholesomeness, *s* Fallaineachd.

Wholly, *adv* Gu slàn; gu tùr, gu h-iomlan, gu léir, gu baileach, gu tur

Whom, *pron. rel.* A, nach. The man whom I struck, *an duine a bhuail mi*

Whom, *pron interrog.* Co, cia. Whom did you see? *co chunnaic thu?*

Whomsoever, *pron* Co air bith; aon air bith, aon sam bith.

Whoobub, *s.* Othail

Whoop, *s* Coileach oidhche, fàirleag; columan caidheach; glaodh, gàir, iolach; gàir chatha; glaodhaich, sgairt.

Whoop, *v* Glaodh, dean gàir, dean glaodh

Whore, *s.* Siùrsach, siùrtach, striopach, oinigh, stràbaid, struinpaid, meirdreach, bidse, beasg, gastag. She is nothing but an arrant whore, *cha 'n 'eil innte ach an dearg shiùrtach*

Whore, *v* Siùrsaich, truaill, truaillich He is gone to whore, *dh' fhalbh e shiùrsachadh*, he whored her, *thruaillich e i*

Whoredom, *s* Striopachas, drùis, meirdreachas, neo-ghloine

Whoring, *s* Siùrsachadh; slataireachd.

Whoremonger, *s.* Drùisear, fear-striopachais. Whoremongers, *luchd-striopachais.*

Whoreson, *s.* Mac siùrsaich, mac diolain.

Whorish, *a.* Siùrsachail, striopachail, drùiseil, mi-gheimnidh, macnusach, bidseach, bidseanta.

Whortleberry, *s.* Braoileag, fraochan.

Whose, *pron. interrog.* Co, co leis. Whose is this? *co leis so?* whose cattle are these? *co leis an crodh sin?*

Whose, *pron. rel.* Aig am bheil. He whose heart is hard, *esan aig am bheil cridhe cruaidh.*

Whoso, *pron.* Co air bith.

Whosoever, *pron.* Co leis air bith.

Whosoever, *pron.* Co air bith, co sam bith.

Why, *adv.* C'arson; ciod uime, ceud fàth, c'uige, c'uime. Why did you it? *c'arson a rinn thu e?* why so? *c'arson sin? c'arson so?*

Wick, *s.* Buaic, buaichd, buacais.

Wicked, *a.* Olc, aingidh, daoi; coirbte; coirpidh; malluichte, ciontach, peacach, dubhailceach. Delay to the wicked is not pardon, *ge dàil do 'n daoi, cha dearmad.*

Wickedly, *adv.* Gu h-olc, gu h-aingidh, gu coirbte, gu ciontach, gu peacach.

Wickedness, *s.* Aingidheachd, uilce; olc, drochbheart, peacadh, ciont; olcas, dubhailc.

Wicker, *a.* Slatach, gadach.

Wicket, *s.* Fath-dhorus, fairleus; foir-dhorus, bruchag.

Wide, *a.* Farsuing, leathann, mòr, lachdmhor, leobhar.

Widely, *adv.* Gu farsuing, gu leathann.

Widen, *v.* Leudaich, farsuingich; leathannaich; leudaich.

Widgeon, *s.* Amadan mòintich.

Wideness, *s.* Farsuingeachd, leud, leithne.

Widow, *s.* Bantrach, ban-treabhach, baintreach. The bagpipe is a sorry widow, *is olc a bhantrach a phiob.*

Widower, *s.* Aonrachdan, bantrach fhir.

Widowhood, *s.* Bantrachas; *contr. for* ban-treabhachas, ban-treabhachd.

Width, *s.* Farsuingeachd; leud, leithne.

Wield, *v.* Lamhaich, lamhsaich, laimhsich; stiùir.

Wieldy, *a.* So-laimhseachadh, so-lamhachadh.

Wife, *s.* Bean; bean-phòsda, céil. A little wife, *beanag, cailleachag;* a new-married wife, *bean nuadh-phosda;* an old wife, *cailleach, sean bhean;* marry a wife, *pòs.*

Wig, *s.* Pior-bhuic; gruaig; callaid; *mar an ceudna*, seorsa breacaig no caraiceig.

Wight, *s.* Neach; bith, urr.

Wightly, *adv.* Luath.

Wild, *a.* Fiadhaich; borb; alluidh; allta; allmharach; (*rough* or *rocky*), fiadhain; fàs, garbh, neo-aitichte; creagach. A wild man, *duine fiadhaich;* lead a wild goose chace, *cuir ruith na cuthaig, cuir air firidh fairidh;* a wild apple, *ubhal fiadhain;* wild beast, *fiadh-bheist, uile-bheist.*

Wild, *s.* Fàsach, dithreabh.

Wilder, *v. a.* Cuir air seachran.

Wilderness, *s.* Fasach, di-threabh.

Wildfire, *s.* Fiadh-theine.

Wild-goose, *s.* Cadhan.

Wild-goose-chase, *s.* Ruithe na cuthaig.

Wilding, *s.* Ubhal fiadhain.

Wildly, *adv.* Gu fiadhaich; gu h-alluidh, gu borb.

Wildness, *s.* Fiadhaichead; buirbe; alltas; allmharachd.

Wile, *s.* Car, cleas, cealg, cuilbheart; seòl, sligheadaireachd, ceabhachd.

Wilful, *a.* Rag, reasgach, ceann-laidir; dùr, doirbh, antoileil, ain-srianta.

Wilily, *adv.* Gu cealgach, gu seolta, gu carach, gu cuilbheartach, gu ceabhchdach, gu h-eòlach.

Wiliness, *s.* Ceilge; cealgachd, seoltachd, cuilbheartachd, ceabhchdaireachd.

Will, *s.* Toile, rùn, àille, gean, miann, togar, réir; deoin. Free-will, *saor-thoile;* I wanted no will, *cho robh dìth toile orm;* what is your will? *ciod b' àille leat?* she must have her own will, *feumaidh si toile fhéin bhi aice;* good-will, *deadh-thoile, gean-maith;* ill-will, *droch rùn;* against my will, *an aghaidh mo thoile, a dh' aindeoin orm;* a last will, *teismeid.*

Will, *v.* Iarr; toilich; miannuich; rùnaich, sanntaich; togair. Do what you will, *dean na thogaireas tu;* be it how it will, *bitheadh e mar thogair e;* it will be whether you will or not, *tachraidh se olc no math leat e;* whether you will or not, *olc ar mhath leat e, ge b' oil leat e.*

Willing, *a.* Toileach, deònach. I am willing, *tha mi toileach.*

Willingly, *adv.* Gu toileach, gu deònach, le deadh thoile.

Willingness, *s.* Toilichead, toil, deòntas.

Willow, *s.* Seileach. Sweet willow, *cannach.*

Wily, *a.* Eòlach, seolta, cealgach, cuilbheartach, sligheach, ceabhchdach, innleachdach.

Wimble, *s.* Boireal, gimleid, toradh.

Win, *v. a.* Coisinn; buidhinn, buadhaich. I will win the horse or lose the saddle, *coisnidh mi 'n t-each no caillidh mi 'n t-srathair;* to be given to a woman is one-third of the way to win her, *is trian suiridh samhladh.*

Wince, *v. n.* Breab; tilg.

Winch, *s.* Undais.

Winch, *v. n.* Breab, tilg.

Wind, *s.* Gaoth; soirbheas; anail; feochan, gaotharachd; bramsag. As the wind stands, *mar tha ghaoth;* the ship lieth wind-bound, *tha 'n luingeas ri port;* the wind favours us, *tha 'n ghaoth leinn;* a boisterous wind, *gaoth anradhach, eascair;* a gentle wind, *gaoth chiùin, aiteal, faiteal, feochan;* a slack wind, *gaoth sheimh;* the west wind, *a ghaoth shuas;* the east wind, *a ghaoth shios, a ghaoth a near;* south-west wind, *gaoth niar dheas;* south-east wind, *gaoth near dheas;* the north wind, *a ghaoth a tuath;* the north-east wind, *gaoth near-thuath;* the north-west wind, *gaoth niar thuath;* a whistling wind, *gaoth shrannach:* an eddying wind, *doilean;* take wind, *sgaoil;* what comes by wind, goes by rain, *a ni a thig leis a ghaoithe, falbhaidh e leis an uisge;* when the wind is still, the shower is blunt, *nur luidheas a ghaoth is maol gach sian.*

Wind, *v.* Tionndaidh, toinn, toinneamh, lùb, trus, tachrais; sniomh; rothainn; fàilich. Wind, as a river, *lùb;* wind into bottoms, *ceartlaich.*

Wind-bound, *a.* Ri port.

Winded, *a.* Tachraiste; ceartlaiche. Short-winded, *gearranalach.*

Wind-egg, *s.* Ubh gluig, ubh fàs.

Winded, (blown), *a.* Seidte.

Winder, *s.* Toinneadair, tointear, fear toinneimh, cuidhil thachrais.

Windflower, *s.* Lus na gaoithe.

Windgun, *s.* Gunn-gaoithe.

Windiness, *s.* Gaotharachd.

Winding, *a.* Lùbach; carach.

Winding, *s.* Lùbadh; car, iadhadh.

Windingsheet, *s.* Aodach mairbh; leine mairbh; leinebhàis, marbh-phaisg, taibhse-eudach, eudach aoig.

Windlass, *s.* Undais.

Windle, *s.* Dealg, dealgan.

Windmill, *s.* Muileann gaoithe.

Window, *v. a.* Uinneagaich. Windowed, *uinneagaichte.*

Window, *s.* Uinneag; baideal, fuinneag, feinistear. A glass window, *uinneag ghloine*; a window-shutter, *brod uinneig.*

Windpipe, *s.* Detiach; sgornach.

Windward, *adv.* Fuaradh; an aghaidh na gaoithe. Windward side, *fiogha.*

Windy, *a.* Gaothar; anradhach; anfhadhach; (*giddy*), gaothaidh, eutrom, amaideach.

Wine, *s.* Fion. When the wine is in, the wit is gone, *nur thig fion a stigh, bheir an ciall an dorus air*; I have had a bellyful of wine, *fhuair mi làn mo bhronn dh' fhion*; new wine, *fion ùr*; Port wine, *fion dearg*; white wine, *fion geal*; Rhenish wine, *fion na* (*Réin*) *Réidh-amhainn*; dead wine, *fion marbh, fion domblasda*; muddy wine, *fion-druaimleach*; tart wine, *fion garg.*

Winebibber, *s.* Geòcair, meisgear, ruitear.

Winebibbing, *a.* Geòcach, deidheil air fion, ceisteil air fion.

Winebibbing, *s.* Geòcadh, meisge, ruitearachd.

Winepress, *s.* Fion-amar, amar-fiona.

Wing, *s.* Sgiath. A bird on the wing, *eun air sgiathaibh, no eun ag itealaich.*

Winged, *a.* Sgiathach.

Wink, *s.* Priobadh, caogadh, smèid; drùb. I did not get a wink of sleep, *cha d' fhuair mi drùb chodail.*

Wink, *v.* Caog; piob, sméid; ceadaich, aontaich le. He winked at her, *chaog e ri*; he tipped me the wink, *chaog e shùil rium.*

Winker, *s.* Fear caog-shuileach; caogair, priobair.

Winking, *a.* Caogach, priobach; seamach, caog-shuileach.

Winking, *s.* Caogadh, priobadh, seamadh.

Winner, *s.* Fear na buidhne.

Winning, *a.* Tairngeach, dlù-thairngeach, mealltach, ionmhuinn; maiseach.

Winning, *s.* Cosnadh; buidhinn.

Winnow, *s.* Guite; sgaighnean, rillean.

Winnow, *v. a.* Fasgain; glan, gréidh. Winnowed, *fasgainte.*

Winnower, *s.* Fasgnadair, fear fasguaidh.

Winnowing, *s.* Fasgnadh. A winnowing fan, *dallanach.*

Winnowings, *s. pl.* Muillean, moll; càth, calg.

Winter, *s.* Geamhradh; dùbhlachd. Next winter, *an athgheamhradh*; in the winter-time, *an am a gheamhraidh*; depth of winter, *an dubhlachd a gheamhraidh*; a hard winter, *geamhradh cruadalach.*

Winter, *v. n.* Geamhraich, cuir thairis (no) caith an geamhradh.

Winterly, *a.* Geamhradail, geamhrail.

Wintry, *a.* Geamhrail.

Wipe, *v. a.* Glan, cairt, siab; suath, sgùr.

Wipe, *s.* Siabadh, suath; glanadh; (*blow*), buille, gleadhar.

Wiper, *s.* Siabair, glanadair.

Wire, *s.* Toinntean-iarruinn; teud-mhiodailte, cruaidhtheud.

† Wis, *v. a.* Saoil, smuainich.

Wisdom, *s.* Gliocas, eòlas, ciall, eagnaidh; crionnachd, foghlum, feallsanachd. Bought wisdom is best, *is i chiall a cheannaich is fhearr.*

Wise, *a.* Glic, eòlach, sicir, crionna, ciallach, foghluimte, sgileil, fiosrach. What are you the wiser for it? *ciod is glicid thu e?*

Wiseacre, *s.* Baothair, baoghlan.

Wisely, *adv.* Gu glic, gu crionna, gu sicir.

Wish, *v. a.* Miannuich, guidh, togair; sanntaich, iarr. I could wish, *b' àille leam*; they wish me dead, *is àille leo marbh mi*; he wishes for power, *tha e miannachadh cumhachd*; I wish you well with all my heart, *is aille leam gu math thu le m' uile chridhe*; he wishes me ill, *tha e guidh olc dhomh*; I wish you a good match, *piseach mhath ort.*

Wish, *s.* Miann, àille, togar, togradh; guidh; toile, durachd. I got my wish of it, *fhuair mi mo thoile dheth*; I have a wish to go to Italy, *tha mhiann orm dol do 'n Eadailt*; a bad wish, *droch ghuidh.*

Wisher, *s.* Miannair, togarair; guidh'ear.

Wishful, *a.* Togarach, miannach, sanntach, deigheil, cionach.

Wishfully, *adv.* Gu togarach, gu miannach, gu deigheil.

Wisp, *s.* Sop, boitean. A wisp of straw, *sop fodair*; a wisp from every truss, *sop as gach seide.*

Wist, *pret.* of wis.

Wistful, *a.* Dùrachdach, smuainteach, aireach.

Wistfully, *adv.* Gu dùrachdach, gu smuainteachail.

Wistfulness, *s.* Dùrachd, geur-aire.

Wit (to). Is e sin ri radh.

Wit, *s.* Aigne, ciall, inntinn, tuigse, toinisg, meamnadh. Are you in your wits? *bheil thu ad chiall?*

Witch, *s.* Buidseach; ban-bhuidseach.

Witchcraft, *s.* Buidseachd, rosachd, druidheachd; dolbh, buisdreachd. You are bewitched, *tha buidseachd ort.*

Witchery, *s.* Buidseachd, buidseachas, druidheachd.

† Wite, *v. a.* Coirich, cronaich.

† Wite, *s.* Coire, cron.

With, *prep.* Le, leis, ri, maille ri; mar ri, am fochair. With me, thee, her, him, *leam, leat, leth, leis*; with us, you, them, *leinn, leibh, leo*; he killed him with his own hand, *mharbh se e le lamh féin*; you will come with me, *thig thu mar riumse*; with God's help, *le coghnadh Dhé*; with a good will, *le deagh thoil*; with a bad will, *le droch run*; this is quite the same with that, *is co-ionann so ri sin*; with one-another, *le chéile*; with much ado, *air éigin*; together with, *comh-luath ri, maille ri*; with child, *torrach, lethtromach.*

Withal, *adv.* Osbarr; leis.

Withdraw, *v. a.* and *n.* Falbh, rach an ais, thoir air ais, thoir air falbh, rach a thaobh.

Withdrawing, *s.* Ais-imeachd, falbh, dol air ais; tabhairt air ais.

Withdrawment, *s.* Àite diomhair, diomhaireachd, uaigneas; dol a thaobh; tabhairt a thaobh.

Withe, *s.* Gad; réidh.

Wither, *v.* Searg, seac, crion, caith air falbh; sgreag.

Withered, *a.* Seargta, seacta, seac, crionta, crion, sgreagach, air seargadh, air seacadh, air crionadh.

Withering, *s.* Seargadh, seacadh, crionadh, sgreagadh.

Withers, *s.* Slinneanan.

Withhold, *v.* Cum air ais, cum o, cum uaith.

Within, *adv.* Stigh, steach, an taobh stigh. Is your father within? *bheil d' athair stigh?*

Within, *prep.* An taobh stigh, stigh. Within these few days, *an taobh stigh thrì laithean*; within a little, *an ceann-ghoirrid.*

Without, *prep.* Mach, a muigh; gun; as eugmhais. He is without, *tha e a mach*; without friends, *gun chairdean*; without cause, *gun aobhar*; without consideration, *gun smuaine*; without danger, *tearruinte, gun chunnart*; without doors, *a mach*; without knowing it, *gun fhios*; without much ado, *gu furas*; without noise, *samhach*; without life, *marbh.*

Without, *conj.* Mur, saor o. Without you do it, *mur dean thu e, saor o gun dean thu e.*

Withstand, *v.* Cum ris, cum an aghaidh, cum roimh, seas ri, seas an aghaidh.

Withy, *s.* Gad; seileach.

Witless, *a.* Gòrrach; amaideach, eu-céillidh.

Witling, *s.* Beumadair; leth-amadan.

Witness, *s.* Fianuis. You are witness to this, *tha thusa fianuiseach air so.*

Witness, *v.* Thoir fianuis, dean fianuis, bi fianuiseach.

Witsnapper, *s.* Beumair, fear beumnach.

Witted, *a.* Geur, aigneach, taspullach.

Witticism, *s.* Taspullachd; beumadaireachd, bearradaireachd; geur-chuis, geur-fhocal.

Wittily, *adv.* Gu geur, gu beumnach, gu taspullach.

Witty, *a.* Geur, beumnach, aigneach, taspullach, bearradach.

Wive, *v. a.* Pòs, gabh am pòsadh.

Wives, *s. pl.* Mnathan.

Wizard, *s.* Fiosaiche; buidseach; druidh; baobh.

Woad, *s.* Guirmean.

Woe, †Wo, *s.* Truaighe; anaoibhneas, anaoibhinn, sprochd. Woe to them! *is anaoibhinn doimh! is truagh dhoibh!* woe be to him who makes mirth of another man's woe! *is mairge a dheanadh subhachas ri dubhachas fir eile!*

Woful, *a.* Truagh, dubhach, brònach, muladach, tuirseach, cumhach.

Wofully, *adv.* Gu truagh, gu dubhach, gu brònach, gu muladach.

Wolf, *s.* Madadh alluidh; mac-tire; faol.

Wolfdog, *s.* Faol-chu.

Wolfsbane, *s.* Fuath mhadaidh.

Woman, *s.* Bean; boirionnach, bainnionnach; té, gruagach, †gean, †coinnt. Woman-servant, *searbhanta;* a little woman, *banag, brideag;* a tattling woman, *lonag;* a married woman, *breideach;* let every man have his fill, and every woman have her will, *an toile do na h-uile duine, is an toil uile do na mnathaibh;* women and priests are natives no where, *cha 'n 'eil dùchas aig mnaoi no sagart.*

Womanish, *a.* Banail; bandaidh; mallta.

Womankind, *s.* An cinneadh boirionn.

Womanly, *a.* Banail, bandaidh, mallta.

Womb, *s.* Brù; bolg; machlag, soire na cloinne. A womb with young, *bruighseach.*

Womb, *v. a.* Dùin; gin an uaigneas.

Women, *s. pl.* Mnài, mnathan, boirionnaich.

Wonder, *s.* Iongantas, amhluadh, neònachas, miorbhuil, ainmheid. It struck me with wonder, *chuir e iongantas orm.*

Wonder, *v.* Gabh iongantas, gabh neònachas.

Wonderful, *a.* Iongantach, neònach, miorbhuileach.

Wonderfully, *adv.* Gu h-iongantach, gu neònach, gu miorbhuileach.

Wonderstruck, *a.* Air uamhann, fo amhluadh, fo' iongantas.

Wondrous, *a.* Iongantach; neònach, miorbhuileach.

Wondrously, *adv.* Gu h-iongantach, gu neònach, gu miorbhuileach.

Wont, *s.* Cleachd, nòs, gnàth, gnàs, àbhaist. He returned to his old wont, *phill e dh' ionnsuidh a shean chleachdna.*

Wont, *v.* Gnàthaich, cleachd; is àbhaist, is gnath, is nòs. I was wont to do this, *chleachd mi so dheanamh,* or *b' abhaist domh so 'dheanamh.*

Wonted, *a.* Gnàthaichte; cumannta, cleachda.

Woo, *v.* Suireadhà, dean suireadh; iarr, sir, dean mire (no) beadradh.

Wood, *s.* (*Timber*), fiodh; connadh; maide.

Wood, *s.* Coille; doire. A thick wood, *coille thiugh;* a fir-wood, *coille ghiumhais; giumhasach;* an oak-wood, *coille dharaich;* split-wood, *casnaid.*

Woodbine, *s.* Iadh-shlat; deothlag.

Woodcock, *s.* Coileach coille; crom nan duilleag, udagoc, budagoc.

Wooden, *a.* Fiodha, maide. A wooden house, *tigh fiodha.*

Woodfretter, *s.* Cnuimh-fiodha; reudan.

Woodhole, *s.* Toll-chonnaidh.

Woodland, *s.* Coille, coillteach.

Woodlark, *s.* Riabhag choillteach, uiseag choille.

Woodlouse, *s.* Reudan.

Woodman, *s.* Giomanach; eunadair, sealgair; maor-coille.

Woodmonger, *s.* Fear-reic-fiodha, ceannaiche fiodha.

Woodpecker, *s.* Snag, lasair choille.

Woodpidgeon, *s.* Smudan, colaman coille, colman fiadhaich.

Woodsare, *s.* Smugaid na cuthaig.

Woodsorrel, *s.* Glaodhran, biadh-eunain, biadh eòinein.

Woodward, *s.* Forsair coille, maor-coille.

Woodworm, *s.* Cnuimh fiodha.

Woody, *a.* Coillteach.

Wooer, *s.* Suiriche, suirthiche, graidhean.

Woof, *s.* Inneach.

Wooingly, *adv.* Gu taitneach.

Wool, *s.* Olainn, oluinn, olladh. Frizzled wool, *casladh, cloimh;* the trouble of spinning it makes the slattern think her wool too bulky, *is mòr le donnag a cuid abhras, is cha 'n e 'mhòid ach a dhorrad.*

Woolcard, *s.* Card, carla.

Wool-comber, *s.* Cardair, carlachan, seiclear.

Woollen, Woolly, *a.* Ollach, olladh. Woollen cloth, *eudach olladh.*

Woolpack, *s.* Pac olainn.

Word, *s.* Focal, facal, brathar; †fearb, †duan, †bagh, gealladh, fios, cunntas; an scriobtuir. Upon my word, *air m' fhocal;* keep your word, *cum do ghealladh;* he sent word, *chuir e fios;* a word or two, *focal no dha;* word for word, *focal air fhocal;* I will take you on your word, *gabhaidh mi air d' fhocal thu;* a smart word, *geur-bhriathar;* fair words, *blanndar;* upon my word, *air mo fhocal, air mo* (*bhriathar*) *riar;* full of words, *gobach, lonach;* he whose word is not a word, will find his lot sunk to nought, *am fear nach guth a ghuth, cha rath a rath.*

Word, *v.* Foclaich, deachd; cuir am focaill, sgriobh.

Wordy, *a.* Briathrach; foclach; cainnteach.

Wore, *pret.* of wear. Chaith.

Work, *s.* Obair, saothair, gniomh, gnothuch; cùis, dragh, †monar, †modh, †baoth. I will go another way to work, *feuchaidh mi seòl eile;* you made a good day's work of it, *is math an obair latha rinn thu dheth;* he who does work in season will be half idle, *am fear a ni obair na am, bithidh e na leth thamh.*

Work, *v.* Oibrich, saothraich. Work him hard, *oibrich gu cruaidh e;* the beer works, *tha 'n lionn ag oibreachadh;* he wrought hard, *dh' oibrich e gu goirt;* he who works not at sea will not work by land, *am fear nach treabh air muir, cha treabh e air tir.*

Worker, *s.* Fear-oibre, oibriche. Workers, *luchd-oibre.*

Workfellow, *s.* Comh-oibriche.

Workhouse, *s.* Tigh oibre, tigh eiridinn, tigh nam bochd.

Workingday, *s.* Làth-seachduin.

Workman, *s.* Fear-ceairde; fear-oibre. Workmen, *luchd-oibre.*

Workmanlike, *a.* Teoma, ealadhanta, sgileil.

Workmanship, *s.* Obair.

Workmaster, *s.* Fear ealadhanta, fear oibre.

Workshop, *s.* Tigh oibre, buth oibre.

Workwoman, *s.* Ban-fhuaighealaich, banalaich, searbhant.

World, *s.* Saoghal, domhain, an cruinne, an talamh; † liun, budh. A world of people, *lòd sluaighe;* (mankind), *an cinneadh daoine;* in the whole world, *air fad an t-saoghail;* since the world began, *o thoiseach an t-saoghail, o leigeadh bunaitean an domhain;* there is no use in the world in him, *cha 'n 'eil stà air an t-saoghal ann;* he has the world in a string, *is ann dha chaith an saoghal dheanamh.*

Worldliness, *s.* Saoghaltachd; spìocaireachd.

Worldling, *s.* Spìocair; duine saoghalta.

Worldly, *a.* Saoghalmhor; talmhaidh; saoghaltach, saoghalta, sanntach, spìocach, teann, cruaidh.

Worm, *v. a.* Toinn, sniomh.

Worm, *s.* Cnuimh, cnuimheag, cnaimheag, daolag, durag; biasdag, beisteag, doirb, doirbeag. Glow-worm, *cnuimhshionnachain;* a worm or screw, *scrobha, bidhis.*

Wormeaten, *a.* Cnuimheach, duragach; crion, sean, seac.

Wormwood, *s.* Burmaid; roit; † mormanta; searbhas.

Wormy, *a.* Cnuimheach, cnuimheagach, daolagach.

Worn, *a.* Caithte; cumannta.

Worried, *a.* Reubte, reubta; sàruichte.

Worry, *v.* Reub; tachd; sàruich. Worried, *reubta, tachdta.*

† **Worse**, *v. a.* Dochannaich, ciurr, mill.

Worse, *comp.* Miosa, measa. He is worse than nothing, *is miosa e na neoni;* it can be no worse than it is, *cha 'n urrainn e bhi ni's miosa na tha e;* he is the worse for that, *is misd e sin;* how much worse than that is he? *cia mòr is meas na sin esan?* sometimes better and sometimes worse, *na uairean ni 's fhearr, is air uairibh ni 's miosa.*

Worship, *s.* Urram, onoir, spéis. Your worship, *d' onoir.*

Worship (Divine), *s.* Aoradh, adhradh; urram, airmid.

Worship, *v.* Dean aoradh, dean adhradh.

Worshipful, *a.* Urramach.

Worshipfully, *adv.* Gu h-urramach.

Worshipper, *s.* Adhradair, aoradair, fear aoraidh.

Worst, *a.* Is miosa. You are the worst of all, *is miosa thusa na iad uile;* you got the worst of it, *fhuair thu 'chuid is miosa dheth;* the worst part of any thing, *diù, diùireas.*

Worst, *v.* Sàruich, fairtlich, claoidh.

Worsted, *s.* Bursaid.

Wort, *s.* Seorsa càil.

Wort, *s.* (*Of beer*), brathleis, braithlis. St. John's wort, *caod, allas Muire, caod Cholum chille, eala bhuidhe.*

Worth, *s.* Fiach, diol, luach, pris; oirdheirceas. Of little worth, *air bheag luach, neo-luachmhor;* a jewel is no better than its worth, *cha 'n fhearr seud no 'luach.*

Worth, *a.* Fiù, airidh, fiach. It is not worth, *cha 'n fhiach e;* I would not think it worth my while, *cha b' fhiach leam e;* he is little worth who has no force nor art, *cha 'n fhiach fear gun neart, gun innleachd.*

Worthily, *adv.* Gu h-iomchuidh, gu toiltinneach, gu h-airidh.

Worthiness, *s.* Toilltinneachd; oirdheirceas; subhailc; àiridheachd.

Worthless, *a.* Suarrach, gun fhiù, neo-fhiachail, neoàiridh daoi. Praise from the worthless, *moladh na daoidheachd.*

Worthlessness, *s.* Suarrachas, suarraichead, neo-fhiachalachd, daoidheachd.

Worthy, *a.* Fiachail, airidh, fiù, cubhaidh, toilltinneach, cliù-thoilltinneach. A worthy man, *duine còir;* he is worthy of this, *is fhiach e so, thoill e so;* he is well worthy of reward, *is math 's fhiach e duais.*

† **Wot**, *v. n.* Bi fiosrach. Wot you? *an aithne dhuit? bheil fhios agad?*

Wove, *pret.* of weave. Dh' fhigh.

Woven, *part.* Fighte.

Would, (of will). B' aille. What would you have? *ciod b' aille leat?* he is as I would have him, *tha e mar b' aille leam e;* would to God! *gun d' thoir Dia! gun d' thugadh Dia! gun d' thugadh Ni Math, gun leigeadh Dia.*

Woulding, *s.* Sannt, miann, rùn.

Wound, *s.* Lot, cneadh, creuchd, dochann, leòn, guin; gearradh, udhar.

Wound, *v.* Leon, creuchd, reub.

Wound, *pret.* and *past. part.* of wind. Tachraiste.

Wounded, *part.* Leònta, dochannaichte, reubte.

Wounder, *s.* Leònair, leòntair.

Woundless, *a.* Gun leòn, neo-leointe, slàn.

Wrack, *s.* Briseadh, call, long-bhriseadh.

Wrangle, *v.* Connsuich, deasboirich; cuir a mach.

Wrangler, *s.* Fear connsuchaidh; fear aimhreite, deasboiriche, rabair, connspair, connsachair.

Wrangle, Wrangling, *s.* Connsuchadh, tabaid; deasboireachd; bruidhinn.

Wrap, *v.* Paisg, trus; fill, ceangail suas, cuairsg.

Wrapped, *part.* Paisgte, truste, fillte, ceangailte suas.

Wrapper, *s.* Filleag, paisgeag, comhdach.

Wrath, *s.* Corruich; fearg, feirg, cuthach. Stir up wrath, *brosnuich fearg;* a smooth tongue breaks wrath, *brisidh teangadh bhog an cneadh.*

Wrathful, *a.* Feargach, cuthaich.

Wreak, *v.* Doirt mach dioghltas, dean dioghaltas.

† **Wreak**, *s.* Dioghaltas.

† **Wreakful**, *a.* Dioghaltach, feargach.

Wreakless, *a.* Coidheis, mi-sheadhar, comadh, dà chomadh.

Wreath, *s.* Lion-obair.

Wreath, (chaplet), *s.* Bladh-fhleasg, coron, fleasg, figheachan.

Wreath, (of snow), *s.* Cuitheamh, cuidhe.

Wreathe, *v. n.* Toinn, pleat, dual, cas.

Wreathy, *a.* Sniomhach, sniomhanach, casta.

Wreck, *s.* Call, calldach, earchall, briseadh, longbhriseadh; sgriosadh, léir-sgriosadh, bàthadh. Wrecks are most frequent near the shore, *bàthadh mòr aig oir-thir.*

Wreck, *v.* Bris, bruan, mill, sgrios le anradh cuain.

Wrecked, *a.* Briste (no) sgriosta le anradh cuain.

Wren, *s.* Dreaghan, dreaghan donn.

Wrench, *v.* Toinn, toinneamh, sniòmh; spion; spiol; leun, leòn.

Wrench, *s.* Toinneamh; sniòmhadh, leunadh; casadh.

Wrest, *v.* Spion, toinn, toinneamh.

Wrest, *s.* Toinneamh, sniomhadh, car.

Wrestle, *v.* Gleachd, spairnich.

Wrestler, *s.* Gleacadair, gleachd air, caruiche, spairniche.

Wrestling, *s.* Gleachd, gleachdadh, car gleachdaidh.

Wretch, *s.* Truaghan; trù; truaillean; crochair. Poor wretch thou art, *thruaghain bhochd tha thu ann.*

Wretched, *a.* Truagh; dona, mi-shealbhar, doruinneach, truaillidh, gun diù, crion, suarrach; sgrèitidh, dearral. A wretched condition, *cor truagh.*

Wretchedly, *adv.* Gu truagh; gu dona, gu mi-shealbhar, gu suarrach.

Wretchedness, *s.* Truaighe, donas, bochduinn, doruinn, truaillidheachd

Wriggle, *v.* Fri-oibrich; dean iomairt.

Wriggling, *s.* Crathardaich, crathail, iomairt.

Wright, *s.* Saor. A wheel-wright, *saor chuidhlean*, a cart-wright, *saor chairtean.*

Wring, *v.* Fàisg; toinn, toinneamh; sniomh, (*distress*), sàruich; claoidh, gabh a dh' aindeoin

Wringer, *s.* Faisgeadear, fàsgadair.

Wrinkle, *s.* Preas, preasag, crupag, criopag, liurc, cas, rocan.

Wrinkle, *v.* Preas, Preasagaich, crup, cas, liurcaich, liurc

Wrinkled, *a.* Preasagach; preasagaichte, casach, casta, liurcaichte, liurcach. A wrinkled face, *aghaidh phreasagach, roc-eudann.*

Wrist, *s.* Caol an dùirn.

Wristband, *s.* Bann-dùirn.

Writ, *s.* Sgriobhadh. Holy-writ, *scriobtuir.*

Write, *v.* Sgriobh; grabh. Write to me, *sgriobh am ionnsuidh;* write a bad hand, *sgròb.*

Writer, *s.* Sgriobhair, sgriobhadair, cléireach; (*author*), ughdar.

Written, *part.* Sgriobhte, sgriobhta, air a sgriobhadh Written over, *sgriobhte thairis*

Writhe, *v.* Toinn, toinneamh, sniomh; cas

Writing, *s.* Sgriobhadh, sgriobhaireachd A writing-master, *maighstir-sgriobhaidh*, a hand-writing, *lamh-sgriobhaidh;* writings, *sgriobhaichean*, bad writing, *droch-sgriobhadh, sgròbail.*

Wrong, *s.* Eucoir, euceart, mearachd; dochair, coire. He repented of the wrong he did me, *ghabh e aithreachas as an eucòir a rinn e orm;* he is in the wrong, *tha e air a dhochair; tha e san eucoir.*

Wrong, *adv.* Air aimhreidh, air dhochair.

Wrong, *a.* Eucorach, docharach, mearachdach, olc; coireach, cearr; air aimhreadh. I have taken the wrong sow by the ears, *is ann air an each chearr a tha mi 'cur na srathrach*, right or wrong, *ceart no cearr;* you are wrong, *tha thu air aimhreadh, tha thu air a dhochair.*

Wrong, *v* Dean eucoir, dochannaich, diùbhalaich, ciùrr

Wronger, *s.* Fear eucoir.

Wrongful, *a.* Eu-corach, eu-ceart, mearachdach

Wrongfully, *adv.* Gu h-eucorach, gu h-euceart, gu mearachdach.

Wrongheaded, *a.* Gòrach, amaideach, baoghalta, eucéillidh, thar chéile.

Wrongly, *adv.* Gu neo-cheart, gu h-eucorach, air aimhreidh.

Wrote, *pret.* of write. Sgriobh.

Wroth, *a.* Feargach, ann an corruich; *angrach*

Wrought, *part* Oibrichte; deante, criochnuichte, gnàthaichte.

Wrought, *pret.* of work Dh' oibrich, rinn, ghnathaich.

Wrung, *part.* of wring. Fàisgte; toinnte; sàruichte

Wrung, *pret.* of wring. Dh' fhàisg, thoinn. See Wring

Wry, *a.* Cam, fiàr, claon Wry-necked, *geocach;* wry-legged, *cam-chosach*, wry-mouthed, *cam-bheulach, braoisgeach*, a wry-mouth, *goille, braoisg.*

Wry, *v. a.* and *n.* Crom, dean fiar; fiar, claon, cuir car ann. Wry the neck, *cuir car san amhaich.*

Wry-legged, *a.* Cam-chasach, cam-chosach, cam-luirgneach

Wry-mouthed, *a.* Cam-bheulach, braoisgeach.

Wry-necked, *a* Geocach.

X.

X, Is ionann an litir so is deich, agus bu cheart mar sin i am measg nan Roimheach, mar chithear o 'n rann a leanas.

X *Supra denos numero tibi dat retinendos.*

X, Co-ionann ri (10,000) deich mìl.

X. An ceathramh litir fichead do 'n aibideal Shasunnach Cha 'n fhaicear an litir so air toiseach focal Beurla sambi.

Xiphoides, *s.* Maothan.

Y.

Y, An cuigeamh litir fichead do 'n Aibideal Shasunnach. Am measg nan Roimheach bi' onann y is 150 no 159. *Y dat centenos, et quinquaginta novenos.*

A reir an teallsanaich *Pythagoras* b' i 'n litir so dealbh beath 'n duine. Is i lorg na litreach samhladh neach na naoidhean, nuair bhitheas e dìreach, tréibhdhireach Ach is e 's ciall do ghobhal na litreach an taobh ghabhas duine nur thig e gu h-inbhe, an darna cuid chum maith no chum droch-bheairt.

> Litera Pythagoræ discrimine secta bicorni,
> Humanæ vitæ specimen præferre videtur

Y, Am measg nan Roimheach co-ionann ri 150,000, ceud agus leth-cheud mìle

Yacht, *s.* Sgòth, sgoth-long

Yard, *s.* Gàradh; iadh-lann, lios, loinn, cùirt, clobhsa. A church-yard, *cladh, cladach.*

Yard, *s.* Slat; slat thomhais, tri troidhean air fad; (*of a ship*), slatshiùil.

Yardwand, *s* Slat-thomhais, slat, stannart.

† **Yare**, *a.* Deas, ullamh, geur-chuiseach, dian; ealamh, beò.

Yarely, *adv.* Gu deas, gu h-ullamh, gu geur-chuiseach, gu h-ealamh, gu beò

Yarn, *s* Snàth olladh; snàth, calanas

Yarr, *v. n* Dìorrasanaich, dranndanaich

Yarrow, *s* Cathair-thalmhainn

Yawl, *s* Geòl, geòladh, bàt cheithir ramh; còite.

Yawn, *s* Meunan, meunanaich

Yawn, *v* Dean meunan, dean meunanaich

Yawning, *s* Meunanaich.

Yawning, *a.* Meunanach, codalach.

Yclad, *part.* Sgeadaichte; clùthaichte, combdaichte, eudaichte.

Yclepfd, *part* Ainmichte, ris an goirear, do 'n ainm

Ye, *pron.* Sibh, sibhse.

Yea, *adv.* Seadh. Yea, and more than that, *seadh agus tuille na sin;* yea, marry, *or,* yea, truly, *seadh gu dearbh.*

Yean, *v. n.* Beir uan.

Yeaning, *s.* Uanachd.

Yeanling, *s.* Uanag, uan og, uanan.

Year, *s.* Bliadhna. Once a year, *uair 's a bhliadhna;* he is above thirty years, *tha e os cionn dheich bliadhna fichead;* he is growing in years, *tha e fas ann mbhe (no) ann am bliadhnan;* in the beginning of the year, *ann toiseach na bliadhna;* last year, *a bhliadhna so chaidh, an uiridh;* a year and a-half, *bliadhna gu leth;* every other year, *gach dolach bliadhna;* this time two years, *dha bhliadhna o'n am so;* a two year old, *da-bhliadhnach;* up in years, *aosda, sean, aosmhor;* feast of the new year, *calluinn.*

Yearling, *s.* Bliadhnach, gamhuinn. Yearlings, *gamhnan.*

Yearly, *a.* Bliadhnail, gach bliadhna, na h-uile bliadhna.

Yearn, *v. n.* Gabh truas, mothuich truas; fàisg.

Yearning, *s.* Truacantas, truas.

Yeast, *s.* Beirm.

Yelk, *s.* Buidheagan uibhe.

Yell, *v. n.* Sgreach, sgriach, sgal, dean sgal, glaodh, sgairt, sgread.

Yell, *s.* Sgreach, sgriach, sgal, glaodh, sgairt, ulfhart.

Yelling, *s.* Sgreachail; sgalartaich; ulfhartaich, glaodhaich, éighich, eubh.

Yellow, *a.* Buidhe. As yellow as gold, *cho bhuidhe ris an òr;* grow yellow, *fàs buidhe, cinn buidhe.*

Yellow-haired, *a.* Buidhe, òr-bhuidhe.

Yellow-hammer, *s.* Buidheag bhealuidh, buidheag bhuachair.

Yellowish, *a.* Leth-char buidhe; odhar.

Yellowness, *s.* Buidhead, buidhe.

Yelp, *s.* Tathun, tathunn, tathunnaich, comhartaich.

Yelp, *v. n.* Tathun, tathunn, tathunnaich, comhartaich.

Yeoman, *s.* Tuathanach, ceatharnach; fear gabhail.

Yeomanry, *s.* Tuathanaich; tuath mheasail, tuath-cheatharna.

Yerk, *s.* Sgailleag, fri-bhuille, gleog, gleadhar.

Yerk, *v. n.* Buail gu grad, fri-bhuail.

Yerking, *s.* Breabardaich.

Yes, *adv.* Seadh 'se, tha. The Gael, like the Romans, have no fixed vocable for affirmation as the English have, but they use, both in assertions and in negations, the principal verb of the question.—Did I not say that this would happen? yes, *nach d' thubhairt mi gun tachradh so? thubhairt;* will you go with me? yes, *an d' théid thu maille-rium? théid;* is this your brother? yes, *'n e so do bhrathair? is e;* will you come? no, *an d' thig thu? cha d' thig.*

Yest, *s.* Beirm, deasgann; cobhar, còp.

Yesterday, *adv.* An dé. The day before yesterday, *an làth roimh an dé, air bhò'n de;* this time yesterday, *mu'n tràth so'n dé;* the half would have been better yesterday, than the whole to-day, *b' fhearr a leth an dé no gu léir an diugh.*

Yesternight, *adv.* An raoir, an reidhr.

Yesty, *a.* Beirmeach, deasgannach.

Yet, *conj.* Gidheadh, fòs, fathast, fhathast. Though you deny it yet I know it, *ged tha thu 'g a chur as aicheadh, fathast tha fios agam air.*

Yet, *adv.* Fathast, fhathast; osbàrr, fòs. He has not come yet, *cha d' thainig e fhathast;* not yet, *fathast;* yet again, *fòs a ris;* yet? *'n ann fhathast?* yet again, *sud a ris, uair eile.*

Yew, *s.* Iubhar, iuthar. A place where yews grow, *iuthrach.*

† Yewen, *a.* Iubhrach, iuthrach, iuthair.

Yex, *s.* Aileag.

Yield, *v.* Géill; striochd; lùb, feachd; (*produce*), thoir mach; (*give up*), thoir suas. He forced them to yield, *thug e arra géilleadh;* the earth will yield fruit, *bheir an talamh mach torradh;* yield [consent] *aontaich, ceadaich.*

Yielded, *part.* Striochdta, aontaichte.

Yielder, *s.* Striochdair.

Yielding, *s.* Striochd, géilleadh, géilleachdainn; lùbadh, feachdadh; tiomnadh, tabhairt suas.

Yoke, *s.* Cuinge, ceangal, slabhruidh, caraid; dithis; daorsa, tràilleachd.

Yoke, *v.* Beartaich; sàruich, claoidh, ceannsuich, tràillich.

Yoked, *a.* Beartaichte; sàruichte, ceannsuichte.

Yoke-fellow, *s.* Céile; comh-oibriche, co-sheirbheiseach.

Yolk, *s.* Buidheagan uibhe.

Yon, Yonder, *adv.* Ud, od, sid, sud, *i. e. is sud,* an sud. Yon man, *an duine ud;* yonder he comes, *sud,* [*i. e. is ud*] *e tighinn;* yonder he is, *'s ud e;* he is yonder, *tha e an sud.*

† Yond, *a.* Cuthaich, gòrach; feargach.

Yore, *adv.* O shean, o chian, o aois; roimh so.

You, *pron. sing.* Thu, thusa, tu. You must do it, *feumaidh tu 'dheanamh;* yourself, *thu-féin;* you yourself, *thusa fein.*

You, *pron. pl.* Sibh, sibhse. Yourselves, *sibh féin;* you yourselves, *sibhse féin.*

Young, *a.* Òg. A young man, *òganach;* a young woman, *nighean, oigh;* a young bird, *garrag;* a young horse, *searrach;* a young mare, *loth, lothag.*

Young, *s.* Òigridh; macraidh; big. The young of any creature, *àl;* (of a bird), *àl, garrag, isean;* what the young see, they do, *an rud a chì na big ni na big;* though the raven be black, it thinks its young fair, *ged is dubh am fitheach is geal leis 'isean.*

Younger, *a.* Is òige. The younger of the two, *am fear is òige dhe 'n triùir.*

Youngest, *a.* Is òige.

Youngish, *a.* Leth-char òg.

Youngling, *s.* Creutair òg.

Youngly, *adv.* Gu òg; gu òg h-anfhann, gu h-aineolach.

Youngster, Younker, *s.* Òganach; fleasgach.

Your, *pron. sing.* Do, d'. Your book, *do leabhar;* your horse, *d' each;* what put that in your head, *ciod chuir sin ann ad cheann.*

Your, *pron. pl.* Bhur, ur 'r. This is your part, *is e so bhur gnothuch-sa.*

Yours, *pron. sing.* Leat, leatsa. This book is yours, *is leatsa an leabhar so;* is this yours? *an leat so?* this is not yours, *cha leatsa so.*

Yours, *pron. pl.* Leibh, leibhse.

Yourself, *pron.* Thu-féin. You yourself, *thusa féin.*

Yourselves, *pron.* Sibh féin. You yourselves, *sibhse féin.*

Youth, *s.* Òganach, gille, gille òg, fleasgach. A manly youth, *abarach.*

Youth, *s.* Oige; òigeachd; oigridh.

Youthful, *a.* Òg, ògail, fiùranta.

Youthfulness, *s* Ògalachd.

Youthy, *a.* Òg.

Yule, *s.* Nollaig.

Z.

Z. An seathamh litir fichead, agus an litir is deireannaiche, do 'n Aibideal Shasunnach. Cha 'n eil fior-fhocal Sasunnach sam bi a tòiseachadh leis an litir so.

Zany, *s.* Sgeigear, cleasaiche; baoth-chleasaiche, amadan.

Zeal, *s.* Miann, eud; dian-dheothas; blàth-mhiann; dealas, dùrachd, tnùth.

Zealot, *s.* Tnùthair, eudair; dealasair.

Zealous, *a.* Miannmhor, eudmhor, dealasach, deothasach, dùrachdach, dian; teth.

Zealously, *adv.* Gu miannmhor, gu h-eudmhor, gu dealasach, gu h-eudmhor, gu durachdach, gu dian, gu teth.

Zealousness, *s.* Dealasachd, deothasachd, déine.

Zechin, *s.* Cùinn Eadailteach is fhiach naoi Sgillinn sasunnach.

Zed, *s.* An litir is deireannaiche do 'n Aibideal shasunnach.

Zenith, *s.* Focal Arabach, a ciallachadh, an ionad do na speuran a tha dìreach os cionn neach sam bi.

Zephyr, *s.* Seimh-ghaoth, seimh-ghaoth 'n iar.

Zest, *s.* Blas; pramh 'n deigh mheadhon làtha; sgrath oraisde.

Zest, *v. a.* Dean blasda.

Zig-zag, *a.* Carach; lùbanach.

Zinc, *s.* Speilteir, tutanag.

Zodiac, *s.* Grian-chrios; is e sin, cuairt mhòr sna speuraibh anns an triall an cruinne-ce agus na reultan mu 'n cuairt do 'n ghrian.

Zone, *s.* Crios; cearcal, cuairt; bann.

Zoographer, *s.* Fear a sgriobhas mu ainmhidhean.

Zoography, *s.* Cunntas mu thimchioll deanamh agus naduir ainmhidhean.

Zoology, *s.* Cunntas mu ainmhidhibh.

Zoophyte, *s.* Beo-luibh.

Zootomist, *s.* Cairbh-sgathaiche, snàsadair, corp-shnàsadair.

Zootomy, *s.* Cairbh-sgathadh, corp-shnàsadh.

A SHORT ACCOUNT

OF THE

PRINCIPAL PERSONAGES MENTIONED IN THE POEMS OF OSSIAN.

AGHAIDH-AN-T-SNEACHD, (AGANDECCA), the daughter of Starno, king of Lochlin, whom her father barbarously slew, for having informed Fingal of a plot which had been laid against his life.

AINNIR, (ain-fhear), the father of Erragon, Trothar, and Starno.

ALLAID, (all-àite), a Druid, or, as Ossian terms him, a son of the rock, in allusion to his dwelling among rocks and caverns.

ALENECMA, an ancient name for Connaught in Ireland.

ALTHAN, the son of Conachar, was the chief bard or laureate of Arth, or Art, king of Ireland. On the death of Arth, he attended his son and successor as chief bard.

ALTHOS, one of the sons of Usnoth, chief of Etha, by Slissama, the sister of Cuchullin.

AMUN, an Irish chieftain, was the father of Feard, who was slain in single combat by Cuchullin.

AOIBHIR-ALUINN, the daughter of Branno, king of Lego in Ireland, and wife of Ossian. Her beauty is celebrated in the fourth book of Fingal, and in other poems of Ossian.

AOIBHIR-CHAOMHA, (Evircoma), the wife of Gaul, and daughter of Casduconglas, Tem. B. III. Written also Emhirchaoin.

ARDAR, the son of Usnoth, chief of Etha, and Slissama, the sister of Cuchullin. He was slain in battle at an early age, by Swaran, king of Scandinavia.—*Fing.* book i.

ARTHO, king of Ireland, was the father of that Cormac who was deposed and murdered by Cairbre the son of Borbarduthul.

ATHA. The name of Cairbre's palace in Connaught.

B.

BAILE CLUTHA, signifies the town of the Clyde, and is supposed to be the *Alcluth* of Bede.

BELTANNO, the wife of Cairbre the son of Cormac.

BOLG. The southern parts of Ireland were so called from the Bolg, or British Belgæ, who settled a colony there.

BORBAR, (borb-fhear), the father of Cathmor the generous, and of Cairbre the usurper. He was brother of that Colcullamh, (Colgulla) who rebelled against Cormac, king of Ireland.

BORBARDUTHUL, a name given to the father of Cathmor. See BORBAR.

BOSGEAL, (fair-hand), was daughter of Colgar, a Connaught chief. She was wife of Cairbre, the son of Cormac, king of Ireland, who was dethroned by Cairbre, the son of Borbarduthul.

BOSMIN, (smooth-hand), the only daughter of Fingal, by Clatha, the daughter of Cathula, king of Innistore.

BRAIGH-GHEAL, (fair-neck), the wife of Cuchullin.

BRAIGH-SOLUIS, the sister of Cairbre, who slew Cridhmor in single combat. Braigh-soluis was secretly in love with Cridhmòr: the fatal issue of this contest broke her heart, and hastened her death.

BRAN, the name of Fingal's favourite dog. Bran is a common name given to hounds and shepherd's dogs among the Gaidheal of Scotland.

BRAN, BRANO. A river in Caledonia, probably a brawling stream of that name, which tumbles into the Tay, near Dunkeld, a village in the county of Perth.

BRUMO. A place of worship in Craca, one of the Shetland isles.

C.

CAIRBRE, lord of Atha, in Connaught, and chief of the Firbolg. He was the son of Borbar, or Borbar-duthul. After the violent death of Cormac, king of Ireland, he usurped the government. He was a man of great bravery, but of an insidious and sanguinary disposition; and would make any sacrifice for power. He bore a lurking hatred to Oscar the son of Ossian. At Gabhra, in Ulster, these rival heroes engaged in single combat, and fell by mutual wounds.—*Tem.*

CAIRBRE, the son of Cormac, king of Ireland. He assumed the government after his father, and reigned but a short while. He was succeeded by his son Artho, the father of that Cormac who was dethroned and murdered by Cairbre the son of Borbarduthul.

CAITHBAID, the son of Armin. He was the rival of Dubhchomar, by whom he was slain.—*Fing.* book i.

CAITHBAID, or CATHBAIT, was the grandfather of the renowned Cuchullin.

CALTHONN, the son of that Rathmor who was murdered by Dunthalmo, a prince residing on the Tweed. Calthonn and his brother Colmar were kept in confinement by Dunthalmo, but were liberated by Caolmhal, his daughter.

CAOILTE, a Scandinavian chief, who was slain by Cairbre.

CAOL-ABHAINN, (a narrow river), was the name of the residence of Carrul, and was situated to the south of Agricola's Wall.

CAOLMHAL, (a woman with small eyebrows), was the daughter of Dunthalmo, a cruel and ambitious prince, residing on the Tweed. She rescued from her father's captivity Calthonn and Colmar, the sons of the chief whom he murdered, and afterwards became the wife of the former.

CAOMH-MHAL, the daughter of Saruo, king of the Orkneys.

CARRAIG-THURA, (carraig nan tùr), the seat of Cathulla, king of Innistore.

Carruil, one of the bravest of the sons of Fingal. He was slain in single combat by Gaul, in a dispute of precedence. The bards poured their lamentation over him in the beautiful poem called Bàs Charruil. Another person of the same name was the son of Ceanfeadhna, Cuchullins' bard.

Carthonn, the son of Clessamor and Maona. He was slain by his own father in single combat, in which each had engaged, without knowing his opponent.

Carunn, *i. e.* (Car-amhainn), a stream in Scotland, now called Carron: it falls into the Forth near Falkirk.

Cathbaid, or Cathbait, was grandfather of Cuchullin; another of the same name, was the son of Armin, and the rival of Dubh-chomar, by whom he was slain.

Cathlinn, or, Gath-linn. The name given to a certain star by the Fingalian mariners. Some apply that name to the north polar-star.

Cathmor, the son of Borbarduthul. Unlike his barbarous brother Cairbre, the usurper, his bravery was of the noblest description. He was not more brave than hospitable and generous. His modesty was such, that he could not bear to hear mention made of his own atchievements. He was much attached to his brother, but affection towards such an object was liker a crime than a virtue.

Cathuil, Cathul, the son of Maronnan, or Moran, was the friend and companion of Oscar, the son of Ossian. He was murdered by Cairbre, the Irish usurper, in consequence of his attachment to the family of the dethroned Cormac.

Cathulla, was king of Innistore, and father of Clatho, the second wife of Fingal.

Ceann-nan-daoine, (the head of the people), the son of Duthmaruno, or Dubh-mhic-Roinne.

Claon-mhal, an aged bard or druid.

Claon-rath, a district on the shore of Lego, in Ireland.

Clatho, the daughter of Cathulla, king of Innistore. She was the second wife of Fingal, to whom she bore Reyno, Fillean, and Bosmin.

Clonar, the son of Conglas, of Imòr, one of the Hebrides.

Clono, the son of Sithmhal, of Lora. He became the victim of a jealous Irish chief.

Cluan-fhear, (man of the field), was killed in battle by Cormac Mac Cona, king of Ireland, the father of Roscrana, the first wife of Fingal.

Cluath, Clutha. The river Clyde.

Clun-gheal, the wife of Conmor, king of Inishuna, and mother of the beauteous Suilmhall.

Colc-ullamh, was the brother of Borbarduthul.

Colgach. One of the ancestors of the tribe of Morni.

Colgar, the oldest of the sons of Trathal, the grandfather of Fingal. Another Colgar was the son of Cathmul, and principal bard to Cormac, king of Ireland. The only part of his poems which has come down to posterity, is a tender dialogue on the loves of Fingal, and his first wife Roscrana.

Comal, a Fingalian Chief. He was the unwitting cause of the death of his mistress Gealmhin. Brooding over his calamity, he became weary of life, and in battle he threw himself, unarmed, into the midst of the enemy, and was slain.

Comhal, or, Cumhal, the father of the illustrious Fingal. The accounts of his achievements which have come down to us are but scanty: his life was unfortunate, and his death untimely. He fell in early youth, in an engagement with the tribe of Morni.

Conan, was the Thersites of the Fingalians. Ossian and Ullin never make mention of him but with contempt.

Conar. One of the kings of Ireland: he was the father of that Cormac who was dethroned by Cairbre. Conar was the son of Treunmor, the great grandfather of Fingal. It was owing to this connexion that the great Caledonian hero was involved in so many Irish wars.

Con-ban-carglas, the daughter of Torcuil-torno, king of Crathlun, in Sweden. Her father was defeated by Stairn, and slain: she was carried off by the conqueror, and was driven to distraction by his brutal treatment of her.

Congal, a petty king of Ulster.

Conmor, king of Inishuna, was killed in an invasion of his kingdom. His son Cathmor succeeded him.

Connal, the son of Duth-carron. Another of the same name was a renowned Fingalian, who was slain in battle against Dargo, the Druid. Some say that he fell by the hands of his mistress Cridhmòr.

Cormac, the son of Arth, king of Ireland. He was dethroned and murdered by Cairbre, who usurped the government.

Cormar, one of the warriors who attended Cumhal, the father of Fingal, in his last battle with the sons of Morni.

Craca. One of the Shetland isles.

Cridh-mìn, the second spouse of Dargo. Her premature and sudden death was occasioned by a rash experiment which her husband and his comrades made use of to put her conjugal affection to the test. The catastrophe is related by Ullin, in his pathetic poem, entitled, Dàn an Deirg.

Cridhmòr, the mistress of Connal, the son of Diaran.

Chomghlas, one of the warriors who attended Cumhal, the father of Fingal, in his last battle with the sons of Morni.

Cromla, a mountain in Ulster.

Cromthormod, one of the Orkney, or of the Shetland isles.

Cronan. A stream which emptied itself into the Carron, near Stirling.

Crothar, was the ancestor of Cathmor, and the first of his family who settled in Atha.

Crumthormod, one of the Orkney, or of the Shetland isles.

Cruth-gheal, the son of Grugal, was one of Cuchullin's chiefs. He was slain by Swaran, king of Scandinavia.

Cuchullin. This hero was the son of Seuma, and grandson of Cathbaid, a wise and warlike Druid. In early youth he married Braigh-gheal, the daughter of Sorglan. His wisdom and bravery procured him the guardianship of Cormac, the young king of Ireland, as well as the management of the war against Swaran, king of Scandinavia. His amazing strength is still proverbial among the Gael. Some say that one of his palaces was in the isle of Skye; the remains of which are still shewn. Campbell asserts that he was slain on the banks of the Legon, in battle with Torlath, a chief of Connaught.

D.

Daorghlas. One of Cuchullin's followers: also a name given to Dermid, the primogenitor of the Campbells.

Dardulena, the daughter of Foldath.

Dearg, the son of Collath. He was slain by Ubar. Dearg is also the name of a warlike Druid, who vainly attempted to restore the fallen dignity of his order.

Deo-ghréine, the daughter of Cairbre, and the wife of that Cruthgheal who was slain in battle by Swaran, king of Scandinavia.

Deo-gréine. One of the names of Fingal's standard.

Derd-gheal, the adulterous wife of Cairbre. On separating from her first husband she received the one half of his goods, of which, at Cairbre's request, a fair division had been made by Cuchullin. She became afterwards the wife of Feaird, the son of Amun: but being incensed against

Cuchullin, on account of an imagined unfairness in the division of Cairbre's property, she instigated her husband to a single combat with him, in which he (Feaird) was slain.

Diarmad, the son of Duibhne, a young Fingalian warrior, from whom the Campbells derive their pedigree. His encounter with a wild boar, and his death consequent thereon, are celebrated in a poem by Ossian, in Smith's collection.

Dora, a mountain near Temora.

Dubh-chomar, one of Cuchullin's chiefs. He was Cathbaid's rival for the affections of Morna, and slew him in single combat. He brought intelligence of his fate to the lady; and renewed his addresses, in the hope that his bravery might win her heart. She begged to get his sword still covered with Cathbaid's blood, and plunged into Dubh-chomar's breast. In the agonies of death, he prayed her to extract the weapon. She no sooner did so, than, with a dying effort, he buried it in her bosom.—*Fing.* b. i.

Dubh-mhic-Roinne, the son of Stairnmor. He was a brave warrior; but the poems which give a detail of his exploits are extinct. He was one of the heroes who attended Cumhal, the father of Fingal, in his last battle against the sons of Morni. He lived in the north-e[...]t of Caithness.

Dubh-sron-gheal, one of Cuchullin's horses.

Dubhmor, Dumor, the father of that M[...]shuil who was forcibly taken off by Lamha, one of the le[...]ers of Dumor's army. Minshuil's affections were placed [...] Ronan, who, on hearing of the deforcement, went in pu[...]it of Lamha, whom he worsted and slew.

E.

Eirin (Iar-inn, the Western Isle), Ireland.

Emhir-aluinn. See Aoibhir-aluinn.

Emhir-chaomh. See Aoibhir-chaomh.

Eragon, the son of Annir.

Etha. A tract of country in the west of Scotla[...]

F.

Fàil, a name for Ireland.—*Fing.* book i.

Feaird, the son of Amun, an Irish chief. He fe[...] single combat with Cuchullin, against whom he had [...] instigated by his wife, the infamous Deudgheal.

Feargus was the second son of Fingal. From [...]n descended Fergus, the son of Erc or Arcath, who is [...]d, in Scottish annals, Fergus the Second. This Fergus [...]e to the throne about 100 after the death of Ossian, [...] is, about the beginning of the fourth century. His ge[...]gy is thus recorded by the Gaelic Seanachaies:—" F[...]us mac Arcaith, mhic Chongail, mhic Fhearguis, mhic F[...]ghail nam buadh;" Fergus the son of Arcath, the [...]f Congal, the son of Fergus, the son of Fingal the Victo[...]

Ferait-artho, the son of Cairbre Mac Cormac, kin[...] Ireland, by Baltanno, daughter of Conachar of Ullin.

Fingal, king of the Caledonians, the hero of one of [...] most splendid epic poems in any language. He was [...] son of Cumhal and Morna the daughter of Thaddu. [...] was the father of Ossian. His grandfather was Trathu[...] the son of Treunmòr.

Fideallan, the first king of Innistore.

Fillean, the son of Fingal and Clatho. He lost his life in the cause of the family of Conar, king of Ireland. Ossian often calls him the son of Clatho, to distinguish him from the sons which Fingal had by Roscrana.

Firbolg, supposed to have been a colony of British Belgæ, who, according to Irish antiquarians, settled in the south of Ireland.

Flathal, the wife of Learthonn, chief of the Firbolg.

Foldath, a conspicuous personage in Ossian's Temora. He was of the race of the Firbolg. He was fierce and fearless; but also generous. He was the friend of the usurper Cairbre, and assisted him in dethroning Cormac, king of Ireland.

G.

Gabhra, a narrow vale in Ulster, where Cairbre, king of Ireland, and Oscar, the son of Ossian, fought and fell by mutual wounds.

Gealmhìn, the daughter of Conlaoch, and the mistress of Comal. She was accidentally slain by an arrow shot by her lover.

Goll, Gaul, the son of Morni. He headed his clan for some time, and disputed the superiority with Fingal himself. He was at length worsted and brought to submission. After this he became the most faithful friend and ally of Fingal. He was ardently fond of a warrior's reputation; and sometimes, in the absence of the Caledonian chief, he was intrusted with the command of the Fingalian forces; but his valour was too impetuous for conducting an army. He owed his death to the following circumstance:—A party of Fingalians, having gone to plunder the hostile isle of *Ifreòine*, were followed, some short time after, by Gaul, without any attendants. He landed on the island after his friends had pillaged and quitted it. He was surrounded by the exasperated inhabitants, against whom, with his back to a tree, he maintained a desperate conflict; until, amazed at his valour and afraid of his strength, they rolled down upon him a mass of rock which broke his thigh. The hero thus became incapable of further resistance, and fell a sacrifice to his enemies.

Gorlo, king of the Orkneys.

Gruamhal, the lord of Ardven.

I.

Idalla, Hidalla, the chief of Claonrath, on the shores of Lego in Ireland. In Temora, Ossian speaks in praise of his personal beauty and poetical genius.

Innis-fàil, one of the ancient names of Ireland.

Innis-thoirne, an island in Scandinavia.

Innistore, the Orkneys.

Ithonn, (the Isle of Waves), one of the Hebrides, perhaps Iona.

L.

Lamha, one of the leaders of Dumor's forces. He was an admirer of Dumor's daughter Minshuil, to whom, with her father's consent, he paid his addresses, which were slighted. He carried her off by force; but, being pursued, he slew her. He was slain by Ronan, his rival.

Lamhath, a small stream running behind the mountain Crommal, (Crom-mheall,) in the West Highlands. The rocky banks of this river afforded a hiding-place to Cairbre, the only remnant of the race of Conar, during the usurpation of Cairbre the son of Borbar-duthul.

[...]no, a lake in Scandinavia, the mist of which was said to [...]e pestilential.

[...]hmon, supposed to have been a Pictish prince.

[...]rthonn, was chief of the Firbolg, and ancestor of [...]irbre and Cathmor.

[...] a lake in Ulster.

[...]ann, Lochlinn, Scandinavia.

[...]n, Loda, a place in Scandinavia. Ossian makes

frequent mention of the spirit of Loda; meaning thereby Odin, the divinity of the northern nations.

Lora, a precipitous stream in Argyllshire, near Selma; also the hill where the stream has its source, and which is remarkable for being the place where Cathmor posted himself previously to his engagement with Fingal.

Lorma, king of Innishuna. He succeeded his father Conmor, and was slain in an invasion of his kingdom.

Lotha, a river in the north of Scotland; perhaps the Lochy.

Luath, (Swift). The favourite dog of Cuchullin.

Lubar, a stream rising in Crom-mheal, a hill in the West Highlands. Near it was fought the first battle in which Gaul, the brave son of Morni, commanded the forces of Fingal. Also a river in Ulster.

Lulan, a river in Sweden, now *Lula*.

Lumar, a hill in Inishuna.

M.

Mac-an-Luinn, (the son of Luno), the sword of Fingal; so called from Luno its maker, a Scandinavian armourer. A traditionary account of it says, that every stroke of it was mortal, and that Fingal made use of it only in cases of very pressing danger.

Malmhìn, Malvina, the daughter of Toscar. She was the mistress of Oscar, the son of Ossian.

Manos, king of Scandinavia. He invaded the dominions of Fingal, and, in a personal encounter with that hero, was worsted, disarmed, and bound. He regained his liberty on condition that he would either renew the general engagement, or leave the land as a vanquished foe. He embraced the latter condition with gratitude, and embarked, after swearing that he would never re-invade the country of his conqueror. After setting sail, his men, stung with disappointment and defeat, prevailed on him to return and renew the combat. He yielded to their request, and landed on Fingal's territory. A bloody battle ensued, in which Manos and his bravest chiefs were slain.

Maronnan, the brother of Toscar.

Mingheal, the mistress of Dearg, or Dargo, the son of Collath. Her lament over her husband, who was slain by a boar, is still extant, and is full of pathos and affection.

Moilena, a plain lying between the hills Mora and Lena, through which flowed the stream Lubar.

Momad, a name given to Gaul, the son of Morni.

Mòra, a hill in the West Highlands; also a hill in Ireland.

Mòrbheinn, Morven. All the north-west coast of Scotland was so called; yet some learned antiquarians confine the name to the Isle of Mull.

Morna, the wife of Combàl or Cumhal, and the mother of Fingal. Another female, of the same name, was the mistress of Cathbaid, who was slain by Dubhchomar. — *Fing*. book i.

Morna, a district in the south of Connaught, once famou[s] for being the residence of an archdruid. Here was [a] cavern, supposed to have been haunted by the spirits [of] the Firbolg chiefs.

Morni, the father of Gaul. On his death-bed he direc[ted] his son to lay his sword (the sword of Strumon) by [his] side, with injunctions not to take it away but on occa[sion]s of imminent danger.

N.

Nathos, the son of Usnoth and Slisama the sister [of] Cuchullin.

O.

Og-gholl, or Oguill, the son of Gaul, one of Fingal's allies.

Ossian (a celebrated Caledonian warrior and poet of the third century, was the son of Fingal, the Caledonian king, and Roscrana. He attended his father in most of his wars in Ireland, and succeeded him in the command of the army. At an advanced age he lost his sight, and became of course unfit for the business of the field. He cheered his misfortune and his solitude by celebrating the exploits of other warriors, — the subject of which his poems principally treat. The companion of his loneliness was Malvina, the amiable widow of his son Oscar. It is probable that it is to this female, who committed these poems to memory, that we ought to attribute their dissemination amongst the bards of her time, and their transmission, for fourteen centuries, from one race to another, of appointed rehearsers. They were ultimately collected, arranged, and translated, about the middle of the eighteenth century, partly by James Macpherson, and partly by Dr. J. Smith of Campbelton. The works of Ossian, speedily after their publication, excited the astonishment of every cultivated mind in Europe; and the most enlightened critics placed the bard of Caledonia among the first poets of any age. Ossian has been translated into Italian by Cesarotti; into French by Mons. Le Torneur; and the greater part of them into French verse by Baour-Lormian. The Germans have three different translations of them. Fingal has been translated into Latin hexameters, with very great success, by a Bishop Macdonald, a native of Scotland. The best of Ossian's poems are, of those in Macpherson's collection, Fionnghal and Tighòr; — of those in Dr. Smith's, Dàn an Deirg, Tiomna Ghuill, Diarmad, Trathuil, and Losga Teamhra.

R.

Ronan, the lover of Minshùil, the daughter of Dumor. His mistress was forcibly taken away by his rival Lamha. He went in pursuit, and a bloody engagement ensued, in which Lamha was slain by Ronan; but Lamha, anticipating his fate, [pu]t Minshùil to death. The circumstances of this deforment are recorded in the beautiful poem by Orran, entitled, Cath-lamha.

Roscrana, the wife of Fingal, and the mother of the immortal Ossian. She was the daughter of Cormac Mac Conar, king of Scotland.

Rumar, the father of Lambor.

Runo, Ryno, the son of Fingal and Clatho.

S.

Sellama, Selma, the name of a Fingalian palace, of [w]hich the ruins are still seen in Argyllshire. There was [a]nother Selma in Ulster.

[Si]th-aluinn, (stately pace,) one of Cuchullin's chiefs, who was slain in battle by Swaran, king of Scandinavia. — *Fing*. book i.

[S]ith-fada, (long pace), one of Cuchullin's horses.

Sonmor was the father of Borbar-duthul, chief of Atha, and grandfather of Cairbre the usurper.

Starn, king of Lochlin, was the son of the barbarous Ainnir. He was the avowed foe of Fingal. Revenge, cunning, and cruelty, were the prominent features of his character.

Starnmor, the father of Dubhmaruno.

Strumon, a place in the neighbourhood of Selma. It was the residence of Gaul, the son of Morni.

Struthmor, one of those warriors who accompanied Cumhal, the father of Fingal, in his last battle against the sons of Morni.

SÙILMHALL was the daughter of Conmor, king of Inisthuna. She fell in love with Cathmor, the brother of Cairbre, king of Ireland, who had sent him to the aid of her father, whose territories had been invaded On his departure from Inisthuna, she accompanied him in the disguise of a young warrior; but on the death of her lover, which happened a short time after, she returned to her native country

T.

TI-FOIRMAL, TIGH-FOIRMEIL, the only one of Fingal's palaces that was built of wood Here the bards met yearly to recite their compositions, previously to their being submitted to the judgment of Fingal and of other chiefs

TIGHMÒR, TEMORA, was the residence of the supreme kings of Ireland, and the name of one of Ossian's poems.

TLATHMÌN, the mistress of Clonar the son of Conglass, chief of Imòr.

TONN-THEINE, a star, so called by the Fingalian mariners

TORCUIL-TORNO, king of Crathlun, a district of Sweden He was slain by Starno, king of Scandinavia, in an engagement which took place in consequence of a misunderstanding at a boar-hunt, to which he had invited Starno

TRATHAL, the son of Treunmor and grandfather of Fingal

TREUN-PHEAR, brother to the king of Inniscon, supposed to have been one of the Orkneys.

TREUNMOR, the great-grandfather of Fingal. Though the poems be extinct which recorded the achievements of Treunmor, he was, without question, one of the first warriors of his time He collected and joined the warlike Caledonian clans, and opposed their united strength to the Roman invaders, thus forming a barrier, which defeated all the strength and discipline of the legions of Rome

TÙRA, a castle in Ulster. It was one of Cuchullin's places of residence, hence he is called the Lord of Tura

U.

ÙLEIRIN (iul-Eirin), a star known by that name in Ossian's time, meaning the Guide to Eirin.

USNOTH, the chief of Etha, a district on the west coast of Scotland.

UTHORNO, a bay in Scandinavia.

EXPLANATION

OF THE

ABBREVIATIONS AND MARKS

USED THROUGHOUT THIS WORK.

Box. Lex.	Boxhorn's Lexicon of Old British Words.
Carricth.	Carricthura.
Chron.	Chronicles.
Col.	Colossians.
Com.	Comala, one of Ossian's Poems.
Cor.	Corinthians.
Dan.	Daniel.
Derm.	Dermid, one of Ossian's Poems.
Deut.	Deuteronomy.
Ecc.	Ecclesiastes.
Eph.	Ephesians.
Etym. Mag.	Etymologicon Magnum.
Ex.	Exodus.
Ez.	Ezekiel.
Fin. and Lor.	Finan and Lorma, one of Ossian's Poems.
Fing.	Fingal.
G. B.	Stewart's Gaelic Bible.
G. P.	M'Intosh's Gaelic Proverbs.
Gen.	Genesis.
Gal.	Galatians.
Heb.	Hebrews.
Hos.	Hosea.
Is.	Isaiah.
Jer.	Jeremiah.
Lev.	Leviticus.
Mac Co.	Mac Codrum.
Macd.	Macdonald's Gaelic Vocabulary.
Macdon.	Macdonald, the Author of Alt an t-siucair, &c.
Macfar.	Macfarlane's Collection of Gaelic Poems.
Macfar. Voc.	Macfarlane's Gaelic Vocabulary.
Macint.	Macintyre, the Poet.
Mac K.	Mac Kay, a Gaelic Poet.
Mac Lach.	Mr. Mac Lachlan, of Aberdeen.
Mal.	Malachi.
Matt.	Matthew.
Mic.	Micah.
N. T.	New Testament.
Nah.	Nahum.
Num.	Numbers.
Obad.	Obadiah.
Oinam.	Oigh nam mòr-shùl, one of Ossian's Poems.
Orr.	Orran, a Fingalian Bard.
O. T.	Old Testament.
Ps.	Psalms.
Q. B. ref.	References to the Edinburgh Quarto Edition of the Gaelic Bible.
R.	Ross, the Poet.
R. S.	John Roy Stewart.
Sm.	Smith's Metrical Version of the Psalms.
Statist. Acc.	Sinclair's Statistical Accounts.
Stew.	Stewart's Gaelic Bible.
Tem.	Temora.
Trath.	Trathal.
Turn.	Turner's Collection of Gaelic Songs.
Ull.	Ullin, a Fingalian Bard.
Zech.	Zechariah.

Æol.	Æolic dialect of the Greek.
Alb.	Albanian.
Anglo-Sax.	Anglo-Saxon.
Arab.	Arabic.
Arm.	Armoric dialect of the Celtic.
Armen.	Armenian.
Att.	Attic dialect of the Greek.
Basq. and *Bisc.*	Biscayan dialect of the Celtic.
Boh.	Bohemian dialect of the Sclavonic.
Braz.	Brazilian.
Calm. Tart.	Calmuc Tartar.
Carinth.	Carinthian dialect of the Sclavonic.
Carn.	Carniolese dialect of the Sclavonic.
Chald.	Chaldaic.
Chin.	Chinese.
Cimb.	Cimbric.
Copt.	Coptic, or old Egyptian.
Corn.	Cornish.
Cro.	Croatian dialect of the Sclavonic.
Dal.	Dalmatian dialect of the Sclavonic.
Dan.	Danish.
Dor.	Doric dialect of the Greek.
Du.	Dutch.
Ethiop.	Ethiopic.
Fr.	French.
Germ.	German.
Georg.	Georgian.
Goth.	Gothic.
Gr.	Greek.
Heb.	Hebrew.
Hind.	Hindoostanee.
Hung.	Hungarian.
Ion.	Ionic dialect of the Greek.
Ir.	Irish dialect of the Celtic.
Isl.	Islandic dialect of the Teutonic.
It.	Italian.
Jap.	Japanese.
Lat.	Latin.
Lith.	Lithuanian.
Lus.	Lusatian dialect of the Sclavonic.
Madag.	Madagascar, a language spoken in.
Mal.	Malay.
Mol.	The language of the Molucca isles.
Manks.	Manks dialect of the Celtic.
Mor.	Moravian dialect of the Sclavonic.
Nor.	Norwegian.
Pah.	Pahlavi.
Peg.	Peguinote.

Pers. - - -	Persic.
Phœn. - - -	Phœnician.
Pol. - - - -	Polish dialect of the Sclavonic.
Port. - - -	Portuguese.
Pruss. - - -	Prussian dialect of the Sclavonic.
Pun. - - - -	Punic.
Run. - - - -	Runic.
Russ. - - -	Russian dialect of the Sclavonic.
Sam. - - - -	Samaritan.
Sax. - - - -	Saxon.
Sclav. - - -	Sclavonic.
Sco. - - - -	Scotch.
Shans. - - -	Shanscrit.
Stir. - - - -	Stirian dialect of the Sclavonic.
Swed. - - -	Swedish.
Syr. - - - -	Syriac.
Tart. - - -	Tartar.
Teut. - - -	Teutonic.
Tonq. - - -	Tonquinese.
Turk. - - -	Turkish.
Van. - - - -	Vandal.
W. - - - -	Welch dialect of the Celtic.

a. - - - -	Adjective noun.
adv. - - - -	Adverb.
aff. - - - -	Affirmative.
art. - - - -	Article.
com. - - - -	Comparative degree.
comp. and *compd.*	Compounded.
conj. - - - -	Conjunction.
contr. - - -	Contraction.
d. or *dat.* - -	Dative case.
dim. - - - -	Diminutive.
fem. - - - -	Feminine.
fut. - - - -	Future.
g. or *gen.* - -	Genitive case.
id. - - - -	Idem.
i. e. - - - -	Id est.
imp. - - - -	Imperative.
infin. - - -	Infinitive.
intens. - - -	Intensative.
inter. - - -	Interrogative.
interj. - - -	Interjection.
m. - - - -	Masculine gender.
n. - - - -	Nominative case.
neg. - - - -	Negative.
p. - - - -	Passive voice.
pl. - - - -	Plural.
poss. - - - -	Possessive.
prep. - - - -	Preposition.
pret. - - - -	Preterite.
priv. - - - -	Privative.
pron. - - - -	Pronoun.
ref. - - - -	Marginal References in Stewart's Gaelic Bible.
rel. - - - -	Relative.
s. f. - - - -	Substantive feminine.
s. m. - - - -	Substantive masculine.
sing. - - - -	Singular number.
sub. - - - -	Subjunctive mood.
v. a. - - - -	Verb active.
v. irr. - - -	Verb irregular.
v. n. - - - -	Verb neuter.
† - - - - -	Obsolete.
\` - - - - -	Grave accent.
´ - - - - -	Acute accent.
' - - - - -	Apostrophe.

A LIST OF PROPER NAMES,

IN ENGLISH AND GAELIC.

NAMES OF MEN.

ADAM. *Adhamh.*
ALBERT. *Ailbeart*
ALEXANDER *Alasdair.*
ALLAN. *Ailean.*
ALPIN. *Ailpean.*
ANDREW *Aindrea, Gilliondras.*
ANGUS *Aonghas.*
ARCHIBALD. *Gilleasbuig.*
ARTHUR. *Art, Artair.*
BARTHOLOMEW. *Parlan, Partolan.*
BERNARD. *Bearnard.*
CHARLES. *Tearlach.*
CHRISTOPHER. *Gillecriosd.*
COLIN. *Cailean.*
COLL. *Colla.*
DAVID. *Daibhidh, Dàidh*
DONALD. *Donull.*
DRUMMOND. *Drumad.*
DUGALD. *Dùghall.*
DUNCAN. *Donncha, Donnach.*
EDWARD. *Imhear, Eideard.*
EUGENE. *Uisdean.*
EWEN. *Eòghann.*
FARQUHAR. *Fearchar.*
FERGUS. *Fearghas.*
FILLAN. *Fillean.*
FINGAL. *Fionnghal.*
FINLAY. *Fionnla.*
FRANCIS. *Fraing.*
GEORGE. *Seorus, Seòrus, Deòras*
GILBERT. *Gileabart, Gillebride*
GILLES. *Gille Iosa.*
GODFREY. *Guaidhre.*
GREGOR. *Griogair.*
HENRY. *Eanraic.*
HECTOR. *Eachann.*
HUGH. *Aoidh, Uisdean.*
JAMES. *Seumas.*
JOHN. *Iain*, (in Scripture), *Eoin.*
JOSEPH. *Seòsaidh, Ioseph*
KENNETH. *Coinneach.*
LACHLAN. *Lachlann.*
LAWRENCE. *Labhrainn*
LEWIS. *Luthais.*
LUDOVICK *Maoldòmhnuich.*
MAGNUS. *Manus*
MALCOLM. *Calum, Gille calum*
MARK. *Marcus.*
MARTIN. *Mairtean, Martuin.*
MAXWEL. *Magsal*
MATTHEW. *Mata*
MAURICE. *Gille Moire, Moiris.*
MICHAEL. *Mìcheil*
MOSES. *Maois.*
MUNGO. *Mungan, Mungo*
MURDOCH. *Murcha, Muirdheach.*
NICHOL. *Neacal*
NIEL. *Niall.*
NINIAN. *Ringean*
NIVEN. *Gille Naomh.*
NORMAN. *Tormad*
O'KEAN. *Ocain*
OLIVER. *Oilibhreis*
OWEN. *Aoghann*
PARLAN. *Parlan.*
PAUL. *Pòl.*
PATRICK, PETER. *Padruig, Pàirig, Peadar.*
PHILIP. *Philip*
QUINTIN. *Cuintean, Caointean.*
RICHARD. *Ruiseard.*
ROBERT. *Roibeart, Raibeart, Rob.*
RODERICK, RORY. *Ruaridh.*
RONALD. *Raonull, Raonald.*
SAMUEL. *Samuel*
SOMERLED. *Somhairle.*
SIMON. *Sim, Simon*
SOLOMON. *Solamh.*
STEPHEN. *Steaphan.*
THOMAS. *Tòmas, Tamhus*
WALTER. *Bhaltair.*
WEDDERBURN. *Eadarbhuirn.*
WILLIAM. *Uilleam.*
ZACHARY. *Sachair.*

NAMES OF WOMEN.

AMELIA. *Aimil.*
ANABELLA. *Anabal, Anabladh.*
ANGELICA. *Aingealag.*
ANN. *Anna.*
BARBARA. *Barabarra.*
BEATRICE. *Beitiris.*
CATHARINE. *Caitrine, Ceit, Caitir.*
CHRISTIAN. *Ciorsdan, Cairistine.*
CICELY. *Silis.*
CLARA. *Sorcha.*
DIANA. *Dianna.*
DOROTHY. *Diorbhail, Diormhorguil.*
ELGIN. *Eiliginn.*
ELIZABETH, BETSY. *Ealasaid, Beitidh.*
FLORA. *Fionnghal.*
FRANCES. *Frangag.*
GRACE. *Giorsal.*
HELEN. *Eilidh.*
ISABEL. *Iseabal.*
JANET. *Deònaid, Seònaid.*
JEAN. *Sìn.*
JUDITH. *Siubhan.*
LOUISA. *Liùsaidh.*
LUCRETIA. *Lucreis.*
MARGARET. *Mairearad.*
MARGERY. *Marsali.*
MARION. *Muireal.*
MARY. *Màiri*; (in Scripture), *Moire* or *Muire.*
MAY. *Maoïsidh.*
MILDRED. *Malreud.*
RACHEL. *Rachall, Raonald.*
REBECCA. *Rebeca.*
SARAH. *Mòr, Mòrag.*
SOPHIA. *Beathag.*
SUSAN. *Siùsan.*
VERE. *Eamhair.*
WILHELMINA. *Uilemhin.*
WINIFRED. *Una.*

THE END.

LONDON:
PRINTED BY J. MOYES, BOUVERIE STREET.

Ingram Content Group UK Ltd.
Milton Keynes UK
UKHW020349300523
422541UK00005B/87

9 781016 451062